Whitaker's Almanack

2003

A & C BLACK
LONDON

AN

Almanack

For the Year of Our Lord

2003

ESTABLISHED 1868

BY

JOSEPH WHITAKER, FSA

CONTAINING AN ACCOUNT OF THE

ASTRONOMICAL AND OTHER PHENOMENA

AND

A vast Amount of INFORMATION respecting the
GOVERNMENT, FINANCES, POPULATION,
COMMERCE, and GENERAL STATISTICS of
the various Nations of the WORLD
with an INDEX containing
nearly 10,000
References

LONDON

OFFICE: 37 SOHO SQUARE
LONDON W1D 3QZ

8061849

The traditional design of the title page for Whitaker's Almanack which has appeared in each edition since 1868

Foreword by Sir Trevor McDonald, OBE

It's no coincidence that people in my profession are so drawn to the virtues of *Whitaker's Almanack*. The man who first compiled it way back in 1868 was himself a journalist. He had in mind a book which would commend itself to colleagues in the business and to any serious writers whose work required careful and accurate research. If what Whitaker saw then was a sound and viable proposition, it is even more so today at the dawn of the twenty-first century, when the need for information in an easily accessible form has become greater than ever.

A publication like *Whitaker's Almanack* is a crucial asset to all our lives because, without question, all of us are now inhabitants of that much heralded global village. The diversity of our age demands of us a greater understanding and appreciation of how other people think and why they act as they do. Examples come rushing to mind. In the aftermath of the attacks on New York and Washington in September 2001, we were all sent scurrying to our research books to try to find out more about Islam and Islamic cultures and about why some organisations might claim to act in the name of religion. The Almanack would not have answered all the things which perturbed us, indeed government ministries in many parts of the world are striving to find those very answers. But it would undoubtedly have been an obvious starting point. Turn to the section on International Organisations. In the current international controversy about whether or not the United States and its allies should go to war with President Saddam Hussein's Iraq, the UN Security Council will play a crucial role. The Almanack is very informative about the way the latter works and with uncanny prescience sounds a cautionary warning about what happens if there is not a wide level of consensus among Security Council members. For a long time after 1948, we are reminded, the Council's Military Staff Committee was effectively suspended. Not till 1990 did the Gulf Crisis prompt the convening of an important meeting on the formation and control of UN supervised armed forces.

For many years I have used the Almanack for its detailed chronology of events of previous years. Programmes framed on that basis have become the stuff of many a television schedule. We journalists are accustomed to flitting from one national or international event to another and frequently need to be reminded of all that we have forgotten or simply missed for a variety of reasons in the course of a busy year. This book is an invaluable aid in this department. On a more personal level, I have on many a 'school homework weekend' found myself leafing through the pages of the Almanack on the urging of my young son, anxious to learn a fact or statistic on some far away country about which I once thought I knew a great deal, but in reality turned out to remember very little. It's all there under the heading Countries of the World: A-Z, from Afghanistan's history and culture to the education and political system in Kyrgyzstan and all the way through to general facts and figures you may need to know about the British Antarctic Territory and Tristan Da Cunha. No self-respecting school library can afford to be without such a mighty work of reference.

Looking at my own profession, I would recommend the Almanack as a good authority on last year's broadcasting. Perusing the 2002 edition I found that again it's all there from succinct description of Greg Dyke's first full year as Director General of the BBC to the ratings battles with ITV, to what the book calls 'Panorama Marginalised' and even – would you believe it – the Big Brother phenomenon. This is to be heartily commended not so much as a point of reference, but as a jolly good read and a reminder of the year's most poignant moments both on and off screen. Joseph Whitaker would surely never have thought it. His Almanack is today quite capable of keeping its finger on the global pulse. This book is full of surprises and I eagerly await them in the new edition.

A & C BLACK (PUBLISHERS) LIMITED

37 Soho Square, London WID 3QZ

Whitaker's Almanack published annually since 1868

©135th edition A & C Black (Publishers) Limited

STANDARD EDITION
Cloth covers 0-7136-6497-5
Leather binding 0-7136-6501-7

CONCISE EDITION
Paperback 0-7136-6498-3

Designed by Douglas Martin
Jacket photographs: PA Photos Ltd, Camera Press Ltd
Typeset in Great Britain by TSO, Parliamentary Press, London.
Printed and bound in Great Britain by William Clowes Ltd., Beccles, Suffolk.

Whitaker's Almanack is a registered trade mark of J. Whitaker and Sons Ltd. Registered Trade Mark Nos: (UK) 1322125/09; 1322126/16 and 1322127/41; (EC) 19960401/09, 16, 41, licensed for use by A & C Black (Publishers) Limited

Whitaker's Almanack was compiled with the assistance of: the Audit Bureau of Circulations Ltd; Christian Research; Flagmaster, the quarterly publication of the Flag Institute; Military Balance 2001–2 published by Oxford University Press; People in Power © Cambridge International Reference on Current Affairs (CIRCA) Ltd; The Diplomatic List © Crown Copyright; World Bank Atlas © International Bank for Reconstruction and Development/World Bank; UN Demographic Year Book © United Nations; UN Statistical Year Book 1999/2000 © United Nations; World Mineral Statistics (British Geological Survey) © NERC; International Financial Statistics Year Book 2001 © International Monetary Fund; UK Hydrographic Office; Met Office; Oxford Cartographers

EDITORIAL STAFF
Editor: Lauren Hill
Deputy Editor: Inna Ward
Assistant Editors: Sharon Taylor, Ruth Northey, Lindsay Brown

CONTRIBUTORS: Gordon Taylor (Astronomy); Hemant Kanitkar (Hindu calendar); Norris McWhirter (World Geographical Statistics); Diana Clayton (Education); Klaus Boehm and Jenny Lees-Spalding (Independent Schools); Connie Lyle (Mobile Communications); Karen Harries-Rees (Environment); Martin Miller (Information Technology); Roger Merrick (Mutual Societies); Clive Longhurst (Insurance); Olivia Murphy (Stamp Duty and Legal Notes); Duncan Murray (Scottish Legal Notes); Kenneth Tingley (Taxation); Prof Ewan Anderson (September 11 2001 and Aftermath); Ian Robertson (Archaeology); John Hitchman (Architecture); Ossian Ward (Art); Steve Clarke (Broadcasting); Peter Marren and Matthew Saunders (Conservation); Bridie MacMahon (Dance); Tom Charity (Film); Nicolette Jones (Literature); Peter Nelson (Music); Elizabeth Forbes (Opera); Patrick Robathan (Parliament); Erica Stary (Acts of Parliament); Neil Bone (Science); Jane Edwardes (Theatre); Stan Greenberg (Sports Records); Vanessa White (Sports Results; Weather); Hilary Marsden, Jo Pearce (Editorial).

EDITORIAL CONTACT DETAILS
Tel: 020-7287 5385
Fax: 020-7734 6856 or 020-7439 4599
Email: whitakers@acblack.com
Web: www.acblack.com

A & C BLACK
LONDON

Contents

FOREWORD	3
PREFACE	7

Time and Space

The Year 2003	11
Bank Holidays	12
Forthcoming Events	14
Astronomy	17
Time Measurement and Calendars	83
Calendar for Any Year 1780-2040	92
Tidal Tables	99

The United Kingdom

Area and population	109
National Flag	113
ROYAL FAMILY	**115**
Private Secretaries	117
Finance	120
Military Titles	121
Kings and Queens	126
PRECEDENCE	**131**
FORMS OF ADDRESS	**133**
PEERAGE	**134**
ORDERS OF CHIVALRY	**170**
BARONETAGE AND KNIGHTAGE	**173**
DAMES	**205**
DECORATIONS AND MEDALS	**208**
CHIEFS OF CLANS	**211**
PRIVY COUNCIL	**213**
PARLIAMENT	**216**
Houses of Parliament	217
List of Members	227
General Election Results	236
By-elections	271
THE GOVERNMENT	**272**
Cabinet	272
Law Officers	272
Ministers of State	272
Under-Secretaries of State	273
Government Whips	273
GOVERNMENT DEPARTMENTS AND PUBLIC OFFICES	**274**
Civil Service Statistics	274
Government Departments	275
Public Offices	301
REGIONAL GOVERNMENT	**346**
Greater London Authority	346
National Assembly for Wales	348
Scottish Parliament	352
Northern Ireland Assembly	361
LOCAL GOVERNMENT	**365**
Finance	365
Political Compositions of Councils	371

England	376
London	394
Wales	400
Scotland	403
Northern Ireland	408
Isle of Man	411
Channel Islands	412
THE EUROPEAN PARLIAMENT	**413**
LAW COURTS AND OFFICES	**416**
TRIBUNALS	**433**
POLICE SERVICE	**438**
PRISON SERVICE	**442**
DEFENCE	**447**
Ministry of Defence	448
Royal Navy	451
The Army	453
Royal Air Force	455
Salaries and Pensions	457
EDUCATION	**461**
Overview	461
Local Education Authorities	476
Advisory Bodies, Curriculum Councils, Funding Councils	481
Universities	483
Colleges	491
Professional Education	493
Independent Schools	504
HEALTH STATISTICS	**512**
SOCIAL WELFARE	**513**
National Health Service	513
Personal Social Services	519
WATER	**532**
ENERGY	**535**
TRANSPORT	**540**
Civil Aviation	540
Rail	541
Road	543
Shipping and Ports	546
RELIGION IN THE UK	**548**
Christianity	548
Bahá'í	549
Buddhism	550
Hinduism	550
Islam	551
Jainism	552
Judaism	552
Sikhism	553
Zoroastrianism	553
THE CHURCHES	**554**
Church of England	554
Anglican Communion	554
Church of Scotland	567
Roman Catholic Church	568
Other Churches	571
COMMUNICATIONS	**578**
Postal Services	578
International Dialling codes	580

6

Mobile Communications	582
Information Technology and Computer Science	585

THE ENVIRONMENT — 589

CONSERVATION AND HERITAGE — 592
Countryside Conservation	592
Nature Conservation Areas	595
Wildlife and Habitats Conservation	598
Historic Buildings and Monuments	602
Museums and Galleries	608
Sights of London	616
Hallmarks	621

ECONOMIC STATISTICS — 623

LOTTERIES AND GAMING — 629

FINANCE — 630
British Currency	630
Banking	632
Stamp Duties	633
Mutual Societies	634
National Savings and Investments	639
Insurance	641
Stock Exchange	646
Financial Services Regulation	647
Taxation	650

LEGAL NOTES — 664
Adoption	664
Births	664
Citizenship	665
Consumer Law	666
Deaths	668
Divorce	669
Employment	672
Human Rights	673
Jury Service	674
Landlord and Tenant	674
Legal Aid	676
Marriage	677
Town and Country Planning	680
Voting Qualifications	680
Wills	681

INTELLECTUAL PROPERTY — 684

MEDIA — 686
Broadcasting	686
The Press	698
Book Publishers	711
Annual Reference Books	716

ORGANISATIONS — 720
Employers' and Trade Associations	720
Trade Unions	722
National Academies of Scholarship	725
Research Councils and Associations	727
Sports Bodies	733
Clubs	738
Societies and Institutions	741

The World
World Geographical Statistics	775
Air Distances from the UK	782
The Antarctic	783
Area and Population	784
Currencies and Exchange Rates	789
Time Zones	793
European Union	795
International Organisations	807
Countries of the World A-Z	834
UK Overseas Territories	1119

The Year 2001–2002
Events of the Year	1129
Obituaries	1167
September 11 2001 and the Aftermath	1172
Archaeology	1177
Architecture	1182
Art	1187
Broadcasting	1191
Conservation and Heritage	1196
Dance	1202
Film	1207
Literature	1210
Music	1214
Opera	1219
Parliament	1222
Public Acts of Parliament and White Papers	1232
Science and Discovery	1236
Theatre	1244
Weather	1253
Sports Results and Records	1262

WEIGHTS AND MEASURES — 1290

ABBREVIATIONS — 1296

INDEX — 1303

STOP PRESS — 1341

Preface

To the 135th Annual Volume

Welcome to the 135th edition of *Whitaker's Almanack*. Since the last edition was published in October 2001, much has happened both in the UK and across the globe. The world continues to witness the ramifications of the terrorist attacks in the United States on 11 September 2001; there were triumphs and tears at the World Cup and the Commonwealth Games; Her Majesty the Queen celebrated her Golden Jubilee; property prices in the UK, fuelled by low interest rates, rose rapidly and Europe came to grips with a new currency.

Whitaker's Almanack has also experienced a number of changes. In May 2002, A&C Black Publishers Ltd (a subsidiary of Bloomsbury Publishing) purchased *Whitaker's Almanack* from The Stationery Office. After a summer spent moving offices and dealing with all that new ownership entails, the *Whitaker's Almanack* team has settled comfortably into its new home and we are all delighted to be part of a company whose prestigious stable of reference publications includes *Who's Who* and *The Writers' and Artists' Year Book*. Our new address and other details can be found below.

Following the departure of Vanessa White to start a family, this edition sees a change in editorship. Some readers may remember that I was editor of the 2000 and 2001 editions and in May 2002 I adopted the mantle once again. I am very proud to be back at the helm of such a diverse and factually rich publication, and both myself and the team are looking forward to strengthening and developing the content over the coming weeks, months and years.

As ever, this edition has been fully updated to reflect the numerous changes that have taken place within the social, political and economic infrastructure of the UK and the rest of the world. Inside you will find an assortment of new material including:

● An overview of the events surrounding the September 11 terrorist attacks on the US, and the global aftermath
● Reviews of art and music
● A revised listing of independent schools
● Complete listings of District Judges and Recorders

In addition, we have changed the order of contents so that it is easier for readers to find their way through the book. We have also included a selection of sub-contents pages so that the contents of a particular section (for example, Time and Space, The United Kingdom) can be seen at a glance. Lastly, our index has undergone some restructuring which will make finding exactly what you want to read easier and faster.

In updating *Whitaker's Almanack* we rely on thousands of organisations and individuals in order to get the latest information at the time of going to press. I would like to thank both the editorial team and everyone involved in assisting us with our research, compilation and editing processes. I hope that you find this edition informative and useful. If you have any comments or suggestions about the content of this or future editions, do not hesitate to write to me at the address below.

LAUREN HILL
Editor

Whitaker's Almanack
A & C Black (Publishers) Limited
37 Soho Square, London W1D 3QZ
Tel: 020-7287 5385
Fax: 020-7734 6856 or 020-7439 4599
Email: whitakers@acblack.co.uk
Web: www.acblack.com

Why not take part in the Whitaker's Almanack quiz, which can be found as a loose insert within Whitaker's Almanack 2003 hardback editions, or by visiting www.acblack.com/whitakers? There are £2,000 worth of prizes to be won!

Time and Space

The Year 2003

Calendars, Public Holidays

Forthcoming Events

Centenaries

Astronomy

Time Measurement and Calendars

Calendar for Any Year 1780–2040

Geological Time

Tidal Tables

The Year 2003

CHRONOLOGICAL CYCLES AND ERAS

Dominical Letter	E
Golden Number (Lunar Cycle)	IX
Julian Period	6716
Roman Indiction	11
Solar Cycle	24

	Beginning
Japanese year Heisei 15	1 January
Chinese year of the Goat or Sheep	1 February
Regnal year 52	6 February
Hindu new year	2 April
Indian (Saka) year 1925	22 March
Muslim year AH 1423	4 March
Sikh new year	13 April
Jewish year AM 5764	27 September
Roman year 2756 AUC	

RELIGIOUS CALENDARS

CHRISTIAN

Epiphany	6 January
Presentation of Christ in the Temple	2 February
Ash Wednesday	5 March
The Annunciation	25 March
Maundy Thursday	17 April
Good Friday	18 April
Easter Day (western churches)	20 April
Easter Day (Eastern Orthodox)	27 April
Rogation Sunday	25 May
Ascension Day	29 May
Pentecost (Whit Sunday)	8 June
Trinity Sunday	15 June
Corpus Christi	19 June
All Saints' Day	1 November
Advent Sunday	30 November
Christmas Day	25 December

HINDU

Makara Sankranti	14 January
Vasant Panchami (Sarasvati-puja)	6 February
Mahashivaratri	1 March
Holi	17 March
Chaitra (Hindu new year)	2 April
Ramanavami	11 April
Raksha-bandhan	12 August
Janmashtami	19 August
Ganesh Chaturthi, first day	31 August
Ganesh festival, last day	9 September
Durga-puja	26 September
Navaratri festival, first day	26 September
Sarasvati-puja	3 October
Dasara	4 October
Diwali, first day	23 October
Diwali, last day	26 October

JEWISH

Purim,	18 March
Passover, first day	17 April
Feast of Weeks, first day	6 June
Jewish new year, first day	27 September
Yom Kippur (Day of Atonement)	6 October
Feast of Tabernacles, first day	11 October
Chanucah, first day	20 December

MUSLIM

Muslim new year	4 March
Ramadan, first day	27 October

SIKH

Birthday of Guru Gobind Singh Ji	5 January
Baisakhi Mela (Sikh new year)	13 April
Martyrdom of Guru Arjan Dev Ji	16 June
Birthday of Guru Nanak Dev Ji	8 November
Martyrdom of Guru Tegh Bahadur Ji	24 November

CIVIL CALENDAR

Accession of Queen Elizabeth II	6 February
Duke of York's birthday	19 February
St David's Day	1 March
Earl of Wessex birthday	10 March
Commonwealth Day	10 March
St Patrick's Day	17 March
Birthday of Queen Elizabeth II	21 April
St George's Day	23 April
Europe Day	9 May
Coronation of Queen Elizabeth II	2 June
Duke of Edinburgh's birthday	10 June
The Queen's official birthday	14 June
Princess Royal's birthday	15 August
Lord Mayor's Day	8 November
Remembrance Sunday	9 November
Prince of Wales's birthday	14 November
Wedding Day of Queen Elizabeth II	20 November
St Andrew's Day	30 November

LEGAL CALENDAR

LAW TERMS

Hilary Term	11 January to 16 April
Easter Term	29 April to 23 May
Trinity Term	3 June to 31 July
Michaelmas Term	1 October to 20 December

QUARTER DAYS

England, Wales and Northern Ireland

Lady	25 March
Midsummer	24 June
Michaelmas	29 September
Christmas	25 December

TERM DAYS

Scotland

Candlemas	28 February
Whitsunday	28 May
Lammas	28 August
Martinmas	28 November
Removal Terms	28 May, 28 November

2003

JANUARY					
Sunday		5	12	19	26
Monday		6	13	20	27
Tuesday		7	14	21	28
Wednesday	1	8	15	22	29
Thursday	2	9	16	23	30
Friday	3	10	17	24	31
Saturday	4	11	18	25	

FEBRUARY					
Sunday		2	9	16	23
Monday		3	10	17	24
Tuesday		4	11	18	25
Wednesday		5	12	19	26
Thursday		6	13	20	27
Friday		7	14	21	28
Saturday	1	8	15	22	

MARCH					
Sunday		2	9	16	23	30
Monday		3	10	17	24	31
Tuesday		4	11	18	25
Wednesday		5	12	19	26
Thursday		6	13	20	27
Friday		7	14	21	28
Saturday	1	8	15	22	29

APRIL					
Sunday		6	13	20	27
Monday		7	14	21	28
Tuesday	1	8	15	22	29
Wednesday	2	9	16	23	30
Thursday	3	10	17	24	
Friday	4	11	18	25	
Saturday	5	12	19	26	

MAY					
Sunday		4	11	18	25
Monday		5	12	19	26
Tuesday		6	13	20	27
Wednesday		7	14	21	28
Thursday	1	8	15	22	29
Friday	2	9	16	23	30
Saturday	3	10	17	24	31

JUNE					
Sunday	1	8	15	22	29
Monday	2	9	16	23	30
Tuesday	3	10	17	24	
Wednesday	4	11	18	25	
Thursday	5	12	19	26	
Friday	6	13	20	27	
Saturday	7	14	21	28	

JULY					
Sunday		6	13	20	27
Monday		7	14	21	28
Tuesday	1	8	15	22	29
Wednesday	2	9	16	23	30
Thursday	3	10	17	24	31
Friday	4	11	18	25	
Saturday	5	12	19	26	

AUGUST					
Sunday		3	10	17	24	31
Monday		4	11	18	25
Tuesday		5	12	19	26
Wednesday		6	13	20	27
Thursday		7	14	21	28
Friday	1	8	15	22	29
Saturday	2	9	16	23	30

SEPTEMBER					
Sunday		7	14	21	28
Monday	1	8	15	22	29
Tuesday	2	9	16	23	30
Wednesday	3	10	17	24	
Thursday	4	11	18	25	
Friday	5	12	19	26	
Saturday	6	13	20	27	

OCTOBER					
Sunday		5	12	19	26
Monday		6	13	20	27
Tuesday		7	14	21	28
Wednesday	1	8	15	22	29
Thursday	2	9	16	23	30
Friday	3	10	17	24	31
Saturday	4	11	18	25	

NOVEMBER					
Sunday		2	9	16	23	30
Monday		3	10	17	24
Tuesday		4	11	18	25
Wednesday		5	12	19	26
Thursday		6	13	20	27
Friday		7	14	21	28
Saturday	1	8	15	22	29

DECEMBER					
Sunday		7	14	21	28
Monday	1	8	15	22	29
Tuesday	2	9	16	23	30
Wednesday	3	10	17	24	31
Thursday	4	11	18	25	
Friday	5	12	19	26	
Saturday	6	13	20	27	

PUBLIC HOLIDAYS	England and Wales	Scotland	Northern Ireland
New Year	† 1 January	1, †2 January	† 1 January
St Patrick's Day	–	–	‡ 17 March
*Good Friday	18 April	18 April	18 April
Easter Monday	21 April	–	21 April
Early May	† 5 May	5 May	† 5 May
Spring	26 May	† 26 May	26 May
Battle of the Boyne	–	–	‡ 14 July
Summer	25 August	4 August	25 August
*Christmas	25, 26 December	25, †26 December	25, 26 December

*In England, Wales and Northern Ireland, Christmas Day and Good Friday are common law holidays
In the Channel Islands, Liberation Day is a bank and public holiday
† Subject to royal proclamation
‡ Subject to proclamation by the Secretary of State for Northern Ireland

2004

JANUARY					
Sunday		4	11	18	25
Monday		5	12	19	26
Tuesday		6	13	20	27
Wednesday		7	14	21	28
Thursday	1	8	15	22	29
Friday	2	9	16	23	30
Saturday	3	10	17	24	31

FEBRUARY					
Sunday	1	8	15	22	29
Monday	2	9	16	23	
Tuesday	3	10	17	24	
Wednesday	4	11	18	25	
Thursday	5	12	19	26	
Friday	6	13	20	27	
Saturday	7	14	21	28	

MARCH					
Sunday		7	14	21	28
Monday	1	8	15	22	29
Tuesday	2	9	16	23	30
Wednesday	3	10	17	24	31
Thursday	4	11	18	25	
Friday	5	12	19	26	
Saturday	6	13	20	27	

APRIL					
Sunday		4	11	18	25
Monday		5	12	19	26
Tuesday		6	13	20	27
Wednesday		7	14	21	28
Thursday	1	8	15	22	29
Friday	2	9	16	23	30
Saturday	3	10	17	24	

MAY					
Sunday		2	9	16	23	30
Monday		3	10	17	24	31
Tuesday		4	11	18	25	
Wednesday		5	12	19	26	
Thursday		6	13	20	27	
Friday		7	14	21	28	
Saturday	1	8	15	22	29	

JUNE					
Sunday		6	13	20	27
Monday		7	14	21	28
Tuesday	1	8	15	22	29
Wednesday	2	9	16	23	30
Thursday	3	10	17	24	
Friday	4	11	18	25	
Saturday	5	12	19	26	

JULY					
Sunday		4	11	18	25
Monday		5	12	19	26
Tuesday		6	13	20	27
Wednesday		7	14	21	28
Thursday	1	8	15	22	29
Friday	2	9	16	23	30
Saturday	3	10	17	24	31

AUGUST					
Sunday	1	8	15	22	29
Monday	2	9	16	23	30
Tuesday	3	10	17	24	31
Wednesday	4	11	18	25	
Thursday	5	12	19	26	
Friday	6	13	20	27	
Saturday	7	14	21	28	

SEPTEMBER					
Sunday		5	12	19	26
Monday		6	13	20	27
Tuesday		7	14	21	28
Wednesday	1	8	15	22	29
Thursday	2	9	16	23	30
Friday	3	10	17	24	
Saturday	4	11	18	25	

OCTOBER					
Sunday		3	10	17	24	31
Monday		4	11	18	25	
Tuesday		5	12	19	26	
Wednesday		6	13	20	27	
Thursday		7	14	21	28	
Friday	1	8	15	22	29	
Saturday	2	9	16	23	30	

NOVEMBER					
Sunday		7	14	21	28
Monday	1	8	15	22	29
Tuesday	2	9	16	23	30
Wednesday	3	10	17	24	
Thursday	4	11	18	25	
Friday	5	12	19	26	
Saturday	6	13	20	27	

DECEMBER					
Sunday		5	12	19	26
Monday		6	13	20	27
Tuesday		7	14	21	28
Wednesday	1	8	15	22	29
Thursday	2	9	16	23	30
Friday	3	10	17	24	31
Saturday	4	11	18	25	

PUBLIC HOLIDAYS	England and Wales	Scotland	Northern Ireland
New Year	† 1 January	1, †2 January	† 1 January
St Patrick's Day	–	–	‡ 17 March
*Good Friday	9 April	9 April	9 April
Easter Monday	12 April	–	12 April
Early May	† 3 May	3 May	† 3 May
Spring	31 May	† 31 May	31 May
Battle of the Boyne	–	–	‡ 12 July
Summer	30 August	2 August	30 August
*Christmas	25, 26 December	25, †26 December	25, 26 December
	27, 28 taken in lieu	27, 28 taken in lieu	27, 28 taken in lieu

*In England, Wales and Northern Ireland, Christmas Day and Good Friday are common law holidays
In the Channel Islands, Liberation Day is a bank and public holiday
† Subject to royal proclamation
‡ Subject to proclamation by the Secretary of State for Northern Ireland

FORTHCOMING EVENTS 2003

* provisional dates
† venue not confirmed

JANUARY

2–12	London International Boat Show, Earls Court, London
10–26	London International Mime Festival
15–19	Art 2003, Business Design Centre, London

FEBRUARY

1–3	Chinese New Year Celebrations, London
20–2 March	Sotheby's Contemporary Decorative Art Exhibition
28–5 March	London International Wine Show, Kensington Olympia

MARCH

1–9	Bath Literature Festival
6	World Book Day
6–9	Crufts Dog Show, NEC, Birmingham
7–16	National Science Week
12–6 April	Ideal Home Exhibition, Earls Court, London
16–18	London Book Fair

APRIL

1	Chelsea Art Fair, London
4–6	Cheltenham Festival of Literature Spring Events
April–September	Chichester Festival Theatre season, Tayside

MAY

1	Scottish Parliament, National Assembly for Wales, Northern Ireland Assembly and UK local government elections
*2–18 October	Pitlochry Festival Theatre season
16–1 June	Bath International Music Festival
19–31 August	Glyndebourne Festival Opera season
20–23	Chelsea Flower Show, Royal Hospital, Chelsea
23–1 June	The Hay Festival, Hay-on-Wye, Hereford

JUNE

*3–11 August	Royal Academy Summer Exhibition
12–21	Hampton Court Palace Music Festival
*6–22	The Aldeburgh Festival
15	Trooping the Colour, Horseguards Parade, London
*24–26	Wisley Flower Show, RHS Garden, Wisley
30–3 July	The Royal Show, National Agricultural Centre, Stoneleigh Park

JULY

4–13	York Early Music Festival
4–20	Cheltenham International Festival of Music
5–20	Buxton Festival, Derbyshire
10–13	Hampton Court Palace Flower Show

| 18–13 September | BBC Promenade Concerts, Royal Albert Hall, London |
| *17–26 | The Welsh Proms, St David's Hall, Cardiff |

AUGUST

1–23	Edinburgh Military Tattoo, Edinburgh Castle
2–9	Royal National Eisteddfod of Wales, Meifod, Powys
10–30	Edinburgh International Festival
14–15	Battle of the Flowers, Jersey
17–22	Three Choirs Festival, Hereford
*19–21	Wisley Flower Show, RHS Garden, Wisley
24–25	Notting Hill Carnival, Notting Hill, London
23–25	Town and Country Festival, National Agricultural Centre, Stoneleigh Park
29–2 November	Blackpool Illuminations

SEPTEMBER

6	Braemar Royal Highland Gathering, Aberdeenshire
8–12	TUC Annual Congress, Brighton
21–25	Liberal Democrat Party Autumn Conference, Brighton
12–21	Southampton International Boat Show
28–2 October	Labour Party Conference

OCTOBER

6–9	Conservative Party Conference, Blackpool
*9–13	The LAPADA Show, London
*10	National Poetry Day
30–6 January	The Turner Prize Exhibition

NOVEMBER

*3	London to Brighton Veteran Car Run
8	Lord Mayor's Procession and Show, City of London
16–18	CBI National Conference, International Convention Centre, Birmingham
19–30	Huddersfield Contemporary Music Festival
	London Film Festival, NFT and other venues

SPORTS EVENTS

FEBRUARY

2–9	Snooker: Benson and Hedges Masters, Wembley Conference Centre
15	Rugby Union: Italy v. Wales, Rome
15	Rugby Union: England v. France, Twickenham
16	Rugby Union: Scotland v. Ireland, Murrayfield
22	Rugby Union: Italy v. Ireland, Rome
22	Rugby Union: Wales v. England, Cardiff
23	Rugby Union: France v. Scotland, Paris

MARCH

8	Rugby Union: Ireland v. France, Lansdowne Road
8	Rugby Union: Scotland v. Wales, Murrayfield
9	Rugby Union: England v. Italy, Twickenham
22	Rugby Union: Wales v. Ireland, Cardiff
22	Rugby Union: England v. Scotland, Twickenham
23	Rugby Union: Italy v. France, Rome
29	Rugby Union: France v. Wales, Paris
29	Rugby Union: Scotland v. Italy, Murrayfield
30	Rugby Union: Ireland v. England, Lansdowne Road

APRIL

6	Oxford and Cambridge Boat Race, Putney to Mortlake, London
13	Flora London Marathon
19–5 May	Snooker: Embassy World Championship, Crucible Theatre, Sheffield
26	Rugby League: Challenge Cup final, Millennium Stadium, Cardiff

MAY

1–4	Badminton Horse Trials, Badminton
11	Welsh FA Cup final †
14–18	Royal Windsor Horse Show, Home Park, Windsor
17	The FA Cup final, Millennium Stadium, Cardiff
31	Scottish FA Cup final, Hampden Park, Glasgow
31–6 June	TT Motorcycle Races, Isle of Man

JUNE

2–7	British Amateur Golf Championship, Royal Troon Golf Club
23–6 July	Tennis: Wimbledon Championship, All England Lawn Tennis Club, Wimbledon
30–19 July	Shooting: NRA Imperial Meeting, Bisley Camp, Surrey

JULY

2–6	Rowing: Henley Royal Regatta, Henley-on-Thames
12–26	Sailing: Admiral's Cup, Dun Laoghaire, Ireland
17–20	Golf: The Open, Royal St George's, Sandwich
*20	British Formula 1 Grand Prix, Silverstone, Northants

AUGUST

2–9	Sailing: Cowes Week, Isle of Wight
10	Sailing: Fastnet Race starts, Cowes, Isle of Wight

SEPTEMBER

4–7	Burghley Horse Trials, Burghley Park, Lincs
12–21	Southampton Boat Show
17–21	Horse of the Year Show, NEC, Birmingham

HORSE-RACING

13 March	Cheltenham Gold Cup
22 March	Lincoln Handicap
5 April	Grand National, Aintree, Liverpool
3 May	Two Thousand Guineas, Newmarket
4 May	One Thousand Guineas, Newmarket
6 June	The Oaks, Epsom
6 June	Coronation Cup, Epsom
7 June	The Derby, Epsom
17–20 June	Royal Ascot
26 July	King George VI and Queen Elizabeth Diamond Stakes
13 September	St Leger, Doncaster
4 October	Cambridgeshire Handicap, Newmarket
18 October	Cesarewitch, Newmarket

CRICKET

npower Test Match Series

22–26 May	England v Zimbabwe, 1st, Lord's†
5–9 June	England v Zimbabwe, 2nd, Chester--le-Street†
24–28 July	England v South Africa, 1st, Birmingham†
31 July–4 August	England v South Africa, 2nd, Lord's†
14–18 August	England v South Africa, 3rd, Nottingham†
21–25 August	England v South Africa, 4th, Leeds†
4–8 September	England v South Africa, 5th, Oval†

NatWest Challenge

17 June	England v Pakistan, Manchester†
20 June	England v Pakistan, Oval†
22 June	England v Pakistan, Lord's†

Natwest Series

26 June	England v Zimbabwe, Trent Bridge†
28 June	England v South Africa, Oval†
29 June	South Africa v Zimbabwe, Canterbury†
1 July	England v Zimbabwe, Headingley†
3 July	England v South Africa, Manchester†
5 July	South Africa v Zimbabwe, Cardiff†
6 July	England v Zimbabwe, Bristol†
8 July	England v South Africa, Birmingham†
10 July	South Africa v Zimbabwe, Southampton†
12 July	The Final, Lord's†
4–5 October	Britain v Rest of the World, Millennium Stadium

CENTENARIES OF 2003

1503	
14 December	Nostradamus, astrologer, physician and seer, born
11 January	Girolamo Mazzola, painter, born
1603	
24 March	Elizabeth I, Tudor Queen of England 1558-1603, died
1703	
15/16 May	Charles Perrault, poet, prose writer and storyteller; wrote 'Tales of Mother Goose', died
26 May	Samuel Pepys, diarist, died
17 June	John Wesley, co-founder of the Methodist movement, born
5 October	Jonathan Edwards, theologian and metaphysician, born
1803	
3 March	Alexandre Gabriel Decamps, painter, of the Romantic school, born
25 May	Edward Bulwer Lytton, novelist, playwright, poet, essayist and politician, born
25 May	Ralph Waldo, Emerson, lecturer, poet and essayist, born
5 July	George Borrow, writer and traveller, born
16 October	Robert Stephenson, engineer, born
29 November	Christian Doppler, physicist, developed 'Doppler's Principle', born
11 December	Hector Berlioz, composer, born
21 December	Sir Joseph Whitworth, engineer, born
1903	
10 January	Dame Barbara Hepworth, sculptor, born
11 January	Alan Paton, novelist, born
19 January	Sir Alfred Beit, financier and philanthropist, born

13 February	Georges Simenon, novelist, born
22 February	Hugo Wolf, composer, died
26 February	Major General Orde Wingate, soldier, born
24 March	Malcolm Muggeridge, television broadcaster, born
2 May	Dr Benjamin Spock, paediatrician and child psychologist, born
8 May	Paul Gauguin, post-Impressionist painter, died
12 May	Sir Lennox Berkeley, composer, born
29 May	Bob Hope, actor, born
6 June	Aram Ilich Khachaturian, composer, born
19 June	Walter Hammond, cricketer, born
25 June	George Orwell, author, born
1 July	Amy Johnson, aviator, born
2 July	Lord Home of the Hirsel, Alec Douglas-Home, Prime Minister 1963-4, born
13 July	Baron Kenneth Clark, art historian, born
17 July	James M. Whistler, painter, died
18 August	Marcel Carne, film director, born
22 August	3rd Marquess of Salisbury, Robert Gascoyne-Cecil, Prime Minister 1885-February 1886, July 1886-92, 1895-1902, died
24 August	Graham Sutherland, painter, born
13 September	Claudette Colbert, stage and film actress, born
25 September	Mark Rothko, painter, born
1 October	Vladimir Horowitz, pianist, born
28 October	Evelyn Waugh, novelist, born
13 November	Camille Pissarro, painter, died
4 December	Alfred Leslie Rowse, historian, born
13 December	John Piper, painter, born
28 December	George Gissing, novelist, died

CENTENARIES OF 2004

1204	
13 December	Moses Maimonides, philosopher, jurist and physician, died
1304	
18/19 July	Francesco Petrarch, scholar and poet, born
1604	
29 February	John Whitgift, Archbishop of Canterbury, died
1704	
28 October	John Locke, philosopher and founder of philosophical Liberalism, died
1804	
6 February	Joseph Priestley, physicist, political theorist and clergyman, died
12 February	Immanuel Kant, philosopher, died
14 March,	Johann Strauss, composer, born
1 June	Mikhail Glinka, composer, born
3 June	Richard Cobden, economist and politician, born
1 July	George Sand, novelist, born
4 July	Nathaniel Hawthorne, novelist and short story writer, born
21 December	Earl of Beaconsfield, Benjamin Disraeli, Prime Minister February-December 1868, 1874-80, born
1904	
14 January	Sir Cecil Beaton, photographer; designer for theatre and film, born
18 January	Cary Grant, actor, born
22 January	George Balanchine, choreographer, born
14 April	Sir John Gielgud, actor, born
16 April	Samuel Smiles, Scottish social reformer and author, died
22 April	Robert Oppenheimer, nuclear physicist, born
24 April	Willem de Kooning, painter, born
27 April	Cecil Day-Lewis, poet laureate from 1968-72, born

1 May	Antonin Dvorák, composer, died
2 May	Bing Crosby, singer and actor, born
10 May	Sir Henry Stanley, explorer of Africa; rescued missionary and explorer David Livingstone, died
11 May	Salvador Dalí, painter, principle artist of the Surrealist movement, born
26 May	George Formby, comedian and actor, born
10 June	Frederick Loewe, composer, teacher and singer, born
2 July	René Lacoste, tennis player, born
3 July	Theodor Herzl, Zionist leader, died
5 July	Sir Harold Acton, aesthete, born
12 July	Pablo Neruda, poet and diplomat; won Nobel prize for Literature in 1971, born
14 July	Isaac Bashevis, singer, author, born
14 July	(Stephen J.) Paul Kruger, president of the South African Republic 1883–1902, died
15 July	Anton Chekhov, playwright, died
27 July	Sir Anton Dolin, dancer, choreographer and director, born
21 August	William Basie, pianist, band-leader and composer, born
22 August	Xiaoping Deng, statesman and politician, born
25 August	Henri Fantin-Latour, painter and lithographer, died
26 August	Christopher Isherwood, novelist and playwright, born
17 September	Sir Frederick Ashton, choreographer, born
2 October	Graham Greene, novelist, born
20 October	Dame Anna Neagle, actress and dancer, born
14 November	Harold Larwood, cricketer, bowler at the centre of 'Bodyline' controversy, born
14 November	Baron Ramsey, Archbishop of Canterbury, 1961-74, born

Astronomy

The following pages give astronomical data for each month of the year 2003. There are four pages of data for each month. All data are given for 0h Greenwich Mean Time (GMT), i.e. at the midnight at the beginning of the day named. This applies also to data for the months when British Summer Time is in operation (for dates, see below).

The astronomical data are given in a form suitable for observation with the naked eye or with a small telescope. These data do not attempt to replace the *Astronomical Almanac* for professional astronomers.

A fuller explanation of how to use the astronomical data is given on pages 73–5.

CALENDAR FOR EACH MONTH

The calendar for each month shows dates of religious, civil and legal significance for the year 2003.

The days in bold type are the principal holy days and the festivals and greater holy days of the Church of England as set out in the calendar authorised for use from 1997. Observance of certain festivals and greater holy days is transferred if the day falls on a principal holy day. The calendar shows the date on which holy days and festivals are to be observed in 2003.

The days in small capitals are dates of significance in the calendars of non-Anglican denominations and non-Christian religions.

The days in italic type are dates of civil and legal significance. The royal anniversaries shown in italic type are the days on which the Union flag is to be flown.

The rest of the calendar comprises days of general interest and the dates of birth or death of well-known people.

Fuller explanations of the various calendars can be found under Time Measurement and Calendars (pages 83–91).

The zodiacal signs through which the Sun is passing during each month are illustrated. The date of transition from one sign to the next, to the nearest hour, is given under Astronomical Phenomena.

JULIAN DATE

The Julian date on 2003 January 0.0 is 2452639.5. To find the Julian date for any other date in 2003 (at 0h GMT), add the day-of-the-year number on the extreme right of the calendar for each month to the Julian date for January 0.0.

SEASONS

The seasons are defined astronomically as follows:

Spring from the vernal equinox to the summer solstice
Summer from the summer solstice to the autumnal equinox
Autumn from the autumnal equinox to the winter solstice
Winter from the winter solstice to the vernal equinox

The seasons in 2003 are:

Northern hemisphere

Vernal equinox	March 21d 01h GMT
Summer solstice	June 21d 19h GMT
Autumnal equinox	September 23d 11h GMT
Winter solstice	December 22d 07h GMT

Southern hemisphere

Autumnal equinox	March 21d 01h GMT
Winter solstice	June 21d 19h GMT
Vernal equinox	September 23d 11h GMT
Summer solstice	December 22d 07h GMT

The longest day of the year, measured from sunrise to sunset, is at the summer solstice. The longest day in the United Kingdom will fall on 21 June in 2003. See also page 83.

The shortest day of the year is at the winter solstice. The shortest day in the United Kingdom will fall on 22 December in 2003. See also page 83.

The equinox is the point at which day and night are of equal length all over the world. See also page 83.

In popular parlance, the seasons in the northern hemisphere comprise the following months:

Spring	March, April, May
Summer	June, July, August
Autumn	September, October, November
Winter	December, January, February

BRITISH SUMMER TIME

British Summer Time is the legal time for general purposes during the period in which it is in operation (see also page 77). During this period, clocks are kept one hour ahead of Greenwich Mean Time. The hour of changeover is 01h Greenwich Mean Time. The duration of Summer Time in 2003 is from March 30 01h GMT to October 26 01h GMT.

January 2003

FIRST MONTH, 31 DAYS. *Janus,* god of the portal, facing two ways, past and future

1	*Wednesday*	**Naming and Circumcision of Jesus.** *Bank Holiday in UK*	1
2	*Thursday*	*Bank Holiday in Scotland.* General James Wolfe b. 1727	2
3	*Friday*	J. R. R. Tolkien b. 1892. Josiah Wedgwood d. 1795	3
4	*Saturday*	Sir Isaac Pitman b. 1813. T. S. Eliot d. 1965	4
5	*Sunday*	**2nd S. of Christmas.** Sonny Bono d. 1998	5
6	*Monday*	**The Epiphany.** Rudolf Nureyev d. 1993	*week 1 day* 6
7	*Tuesday*	Gerald Durrell b. 1925. Trevor Howard d. 1988	7
8	*Wednesday*	Elvis Presley b. 1935. François Mitterrand d. 1996	8
9	*Thursday*	Dame Gracie Fields b. 1898. Ruskin Spear d. 1990	9
10	*Friday*	Dame Barbara Hepworth b. 1903. William Frederick Cody d. 1917	10
11	*Saturday*	*Hilary Law Sittings begin.* Thomas Hardy d. 1928	11
12	*Sunday*	**Baptism of Christ. 1st S. of Epiphany**	12
13	*Monday*	James Joyce d. 1941. Stephen Collins Foster d. 1864	*week 2 day* 13
14	*Tuesday*	Sir Cecil Beaton b. 1904. Humphrey Bogart d. 1957	14
15	*Wednesday*	Aristotle Onassis b. 1906. Emma Lady Hamilton d. 1893	15
16	*Thursday*	Anton Chekhov b. 1860. General Sir John Moore d. 1809	16
17	*Friday*	Shari Lewis b. 1934. Allied forces launched "Operation Desert Storm" against Iraq 1991	17
18	*Saturday*	Arthur Ransome b. 1884. Rudyard Kipling d. 1936	18
19	*Sunday*	**2nd S. of Epiphany.** Paul Cézanne b. 1839	19
20	*Monday*	Federico Fellini b. 1920	*week 3 day* 20
21	*Tuesday*	Christian Dior b. 1905. Vladimir Ilyich Ulyanov (Lenin) d. 1924	21
22	*Wednesday*	Francis Bacon b. 1561. Lyndon B. Johnson d. 1973	22
23	*Thursday*	Edouard Manet b. 1832. Anna Pavlova d. 1931	23
24	*Friday*	Dr Charles James Fox b. 1749. Winston Churchill d. 1965	24
25	*Saturday*	**Conversion of St Paul.** Edward III acceded to the throne 1327	25
26	*Sunday*	**3rd S. of Epiphany.** Jacqueline Du Pré b. 1945	26
27	*Monday*	Wolfgang Amadeus Mozart b. 1756. Giuseppe Verdi d. 1901	*week 4 day* 27
28	*Tuesday*	Ronnie Scott b. 1927. William Butler Yeats d. 1939	28
29	*Wednesday*	W. C. Fields b. 1880. Douglas Haig d. 1928	29
30	*Thursday*	Franklin D. Roosevelt b. 1882. Mahatma Gandhi d. 1948	30
31	*Friday*	Tallulah Bankhead b. 1903. A. A. Milne d. 1956	31

ASTRONOMICAL PHENOMENA

d	h	
2	18	Mercury at stationary point
4	01	Mercury in conjunction with Moon. Mercury 5° N.
4	05	Earth at perihelion (147 million km.)
11	02	Venus at greatest elongation W. 47°
11	20	Mercury in inferior conjunction
15	19	Saturn in conjunction with Moon. Saturn 3° S.
19	17	Jupiter in conjunction with Moon. Jupiter 4° S.
20	12	Sun's longitude 300° ≈≈
23	01	Mercury at stationary point
27	15	Mars in conjunction with Moon. Mars 0°.4 N.
28	18	Venus in conjunction with Moon. Venus 4° N.
30	11	Mercury in conjunction with Moon. Mercury 5° N.
31	00	Neptune in conjunction

MINIMA OF ALGOL

d	h	d	h	d	h
1	03.2	12	14.5	24	01.8
4	00.0	15	11.3	26	22.6
6	20.9	18	08.1	29	19.4
9	17.7	21	05.0		

CONSTELLATIONS

The following constellations are near the meridian at

	d	h		d	h
December	1	24	January	16	21
December	16	23	February	1	20
January	1	22	February	15	19

Draco (below the Pole), Ursa Minor (below the Pole), Camelopardus, Perseus, Auriga, Taurus, Orion, Eridanus and Lepdus

THE MOON

Phases, Apsides and Node	d	h	m
● New Moon	2	20	23
☽ First Quarter	10	13	15
○ Full Moon	18	10	48
☾ Last Quarter	25	08	33
Apogee (404,343 km)	11	00	43
Perigee (369,898 km)	23	22	29

Mean longitude of ascending node on January 1, 67°

THE SUN   s.d. 16'.3

Day	Right Ascension h m s	Dec. ° '	Equation of Time m s	Rise 52° h m	Rise 56° h m	Transit h m	Set 52° h m	Set 56° h m	Sidereal time h m s	Transit of First Point of Aries h m s
1	18 44 06	23 03	− 3 10	8 08	8 31	12 03	15 59	15 36	6 40 56	17 16 14
2	18 48 31	22 58	− 3 39	8 08	8 31	12 04	16 00	15 37	6 44 53	17 12 18
3	18 52 56	22 53	− 4 07	8 08	8 31	12 04	16 01	15 38	6 48 49	17 08 22
4	18 57 20	22 47	− 4 35	8 08	8 30	12 05	16 02	15 40	6 52 46	17 04 26
5	19 01 44	22 41	− 5 02	8 07	8 30	12 05	16 03	15 41	6 56 42	17 00 30
6	19 06 08	22 34	− 5 29	8 07	8 29	12 06	16 05	15 42	7 00 39	16 56 34
7	19 10 31	22 27	− 5 56	8 07	8 29	12 06	16 06	15 44	7 04 35	16 52 38
8	19 14 53	22 19	− 6 22	8 06	8 28	12 07	16 07	15 45	7 08 32	16 48 42
9	19 19 16	22 11	− 6 47	8 06	8 27	12 07	16 09	15 47	7 12 28	16 44 47
10	19 23 37	22 03	− 7 12	8 05	8 27	12 07	16 10	15 49	7 16 25	16 40 51
11	19 27 58	21 54	− 7 36	8 05	8 26	12 08	16 11	15 50	7 20 22	16 36 55
12	19 32 18	21 45	− 8 00	8 04	8 25	12 08	16 13	15 52	7 24 18	16 32 59
13	19 36 38	21 35	− 8 23	8 03	8 24	12 09	16 14	15 54	7 28 15	16 29 03
14	19 40 57	21 25	− 8 46	8 02	8 23	12 09	16 16	15 56	7 32 11	16 25 07
15	19 45 16	21 14	− 9 08	8 02	8 22	12 09	16 18	15 57	7 36 08	16 21 11
16	19 49 33	21 03	− 9 29	8 01	8 21	12 10	16 19	15 59	7 40 04	16 17 15
17	19 53 50	20 52	− 9 50	8 00	8 19	12 10	16 21	16 01	7 44 01	16 13 19
18	19 58 07	20 40	−10 09	7 59	8 18	12 10	16 22	16 03	7 47 57	16 09 23
19	20 02 22	20 28	−10 28	7 58	8 17	12 11	16 24	16 05	7 51 54	16 05 27
20	20 06 37	20 15	−10 47	7 57	8 15	12 11	16 26	16 07	7 55 51	16 01 31
21	20 10 52	20 02	−11 05	7 56	8 14	12 11	16 27	16 09	7 59 47	15 57 36
22	20 15 05	19 49	−11 21	7 54	8 13	12 11	16 29	16 11	8 03 44	15 53 40
23	20 19 18	19 35	−11 38	7 53	8 11	12 12	16 31	16 13	8 07 40	15 49 44
24	20 23 30	19 21	−11 53	7 52	8 10	12 12	16 33	16 15	8 11 37	15 45 48
25	20 27 41	19 07	−12 08	7 51	8 08	12 12	16 34	16 17	8 15 33	15 41 52
26	20 31 51	18 52	−12 22	7 49	8 06	12 12	16 36	16 19	8 19 30	15 37 56
27	20 36 01	18 37	−12 35	7 48	8 05	12 13	16 38	16 21	8 23 26	15 34 00
28	20 40 10	18 22	−12 47	7 47	8 03	12 13	16 40	16 23	8 27 23	15 30 04
29	20 44 18	18 06	−12 59	7 45	8 01	12 13	16 42	16 26	8 31 20	15 26 08
30	20 48 25	17 50	−13 09	7 44	7 59	12 13	16 43	16 28	8 35 16	15 22 12
31	20 52 32	17 33	−13 19	7 42	7 58	12 13	16 45	16 30	8 39 13	15 18 16

DURATION OF TWILIGHT (in minutes)

Latitude	52°	56°	52°	56°	52°	56°	52°	56°
	1 January		11 January		21 January		31 January	
Civil	41	47	40	45	38	43	37	41
Nautical	84	96	82	93	80	90	78	87
Astronomical	125	141	123	138	120	134	117	130

THE NIGHT SKY

Mercury is unsuitably placed for observation at first, inferior conjunction occurring on the 11th. For the last few days of the month Mercury may possibly be glimpsed as a difficult morning object, magnitude +0.2, very low above the south-eastern horizon at about the time of beginning of morning civil twilight, though only for observers in southern England. Despite the fact that it is at greatest western elongation early next month it is not well placed for observation since its declination is -20 degrees.

Venus is a magnificent morning object, magnitude -4.4, dominating the south-eastern sky for several hours before sunrise, despite its low altitude above the horizon. The old crescent Moon is in the vicinity of Venus on the mornings of the 28th and 29th. Around the middle of January Venus passes north of Antares. Both Venus and Mars are moving steadily eastwards, Venus being further east by 5 degrees on the 1st; the separation increasing to 17 degrees by the 31st.

Mars, magnitude +1.4, is visible low in the south-eastern quadrant of the sky in the early mornings. At the beginning of January Mars is in Libra but its direct motion carries it through Scorpius, passing north of Antares on the 31st. The old crescent Moon is in the vicinity of the planet on the mornings of the 27th and 28th, giving a pleasant spectacle with Venus (around 200 times brighter than Mars) farther round to the east.

Jupiter is a brilliant object in the night sky. At the beginning of the month it is visible low in the eastern sky by about 20h. By the end of January it is visible for the greater part of the hours of darkness since it comes to opposition early in February. Its magnitude is -2.5. Jupiter is retrograding slowly in Cancer. On the evening of the 19th the Moon, 1 day after Full, passes 3 degrees north of the planet.

Saturn, magnitude -0.3, is an evening object, retrograding very slowly in Taurus. On the evening of the 15th the gibbous Moon passes 2 degrees north of Saturn.

THE MOON

Day	RA (h m)	Dec. (°)	Hor. par. (′)	Semi-diam. (′)	Sun's co-long. (°)	PA of Bright Limb (°)	Phase (%)	Age (d)	Rise 52° (h m)	Rise 56° (h m)	Transit (h m)	Set 52° (h m)	Set 56° (h m)
1	16 59	−23.4	59.3	16.2	243	94	4	27.7	6 56	7 24	10 44	14 27	13 58
2	18 01	−25.4	58.9	16.0	255	80	1	28.7	8 09	8 41	11 44	15 19	14 47
3	19 03	−25.7	58.4	15.9	267	321	0	0.2	9 07	9 37	12 44	16 25	15 55
4	20 03	−24.5	57.7	15.7	279	273	2	1.2	9 49	10 15	13 41	17 39	17 14
5	21 00	−21.9	57.0	15.5	292	263	6	2.2	10 19	10 40	14 33	18 56	18 37
6	21 53	−18.2	56.3	15.3	304	256	11	3.2	10 42	10 57	15 22	20 12	19 59
7	22 42	−13.8	55.6	15.1	316	252	18	4.2	10 59	11 09	16 06	21 26	21 17
8	23 28	− 8.9	55.0	15.0	328	249	27	5.2	11 13	11 19	16 48	22 36	22 32
9	0 13	− 3.8	54.6	14.9	340	248	36	6.2	11 26	11 27	17 29	23 45	23 46
10	0 56	+ 1.4	54.3	14.8	352	248	45	7.2	11 39	11 36	18 09	—	—
11	1 38	+ 6.5	54.2	14.8	5	248	54	8.2	11 52	11 44	18 49	0 53	0 59
12	2 22	+11.3	54.3	14.8	17	250	64	9.2	12 07	11 55	19 32	2 02	2 13
13	3 08	+15.8	54.6	14.9	29	253	72	10.2	12 25	12 08	20 17	3 13	3 29
14	3 56	+19.7	55.0	15.0	41	258	81	11.2	12 48	12 26	21 05	4 25	4 46
15	4 47	+22.9	55.5	15.1	53	263	88	12.2	13 19	12 52	21 57	5 36	6 03
16	5 41	+25.0	56.1	15.3	65	271	93	13.2	14 02	13 31	22 52	6 44	7 14
17	6 38	+25.8	56.7	15.5	77	282	98	14.2	14 58	14 28	23 49	7 43	8 14
18	7 37	+25.2	57.4	15.6	90	312	100	15.2	16 09	15 41	—	8 31	8 59
19	8 36	+23.1	58.0	15.8	102	73	99	16.2	17 28	17 06	0 45	9 07	9 30
20	9 33	+19.7	58.4	15.9	114	95	97	17.2	18 52	18 36	1 41	9 35	9 52
21	10 28	+15.1	58.8	16.0	126	104	92	18.2	20 16	20 07	2 34	9 56	10 07
22	11 21	+ 9.6	59.1	16.1	138	108	85	19.2	21 40	21 36	3 24	10 14	10 20
23	12 13	+ 3.6	59.2	16.1	150	111	76	20.2	23 03	23 05	4 14	10 30	10 31
24	13 04	− 2.5	59.3	16.2	162	111	65	21.2	—	—	5 02	10 46	10 41
25	13 56	− 8.6	59.2	16.1	175	110	54	22.2	0 27	0 35	5 52	11 03	10 53
26	14 49	−14.1	59.1	16.1	187	107	43	23.2	1 52	2 05	6 43	11 23	11 07
27	15 44	−18.9	58.9	16.1	199	103	32	24.2	3 17	3 37	7 37	11 48	11 27
28	16 41	−22.7	58.7	16.0	211	97	22	25.2	4 39	5 06	8 34	12 22	11 55
29	17 41	−25.0	58.3	15.9	223	90	13	26.2	5 54	6 25	9 32	13 08	12 37
30	18 42	−25.8	57.9	15.8	235	81	7	27.2	6 57	7 28	10 31	14 07	13 36
31	19 42	−25.1	57.5	15.7	248	69	2	28.2	7 44	8 12	11 28	15 18	14 50

MERCURY

Day	RA (h m)	Dec. (°)	Diam. (″)	Phase (%)	Transit (h m)	5° high 52° (h m)	5° high 56° (h m)
1	20 01	−20.7	8	36	13 19	16 42	16 14
3	20 02	−20.1	8	27	13 11	16 38	16 11
7	19 54	−19.2	9	10	12 45	16 18	15 53
5	19 59	−19.6	9	18	12 59	16 30	16 04
9	19 45	−19.0	10	4	12 28	16 02	15 37
11	19 34	−18.9	10	1	12 09	15 44	15 19
13	19 23	−18.9	10	1	11 50	8 16	8 40
15	19 12	−19.0	10	5	11 32	7 58	8 23
17	19 04	−19.2	10	10	11 16	7 44	8 09
19	18 57	−19.4	9	17	11 02	7 32	7 58
21	18 53	−19.7	9	24	10 51	7 23	7 49
23	18 52	−20.0	9	31	10 43	7 16	7 43
25	18 53	−20.3	8	37	10 37	7 12	7 40
27	18 57	−20.6	8	43	10 32	7 10	7 38
29	19 02	−20.8	8	49	10 30	7 09	7 38
31	19 08	−21.0	7	54	10 28	7 09	7 38

VENUS

Day	RA (h m)	Dec. (°)	Diam. (″)	Phase (%)	Transit (h m)	5° high 52° (h m)	5° high 56° (h m)
1	15 29	−15.2	28	45	8 48	4 47	5 06
6	15 48	−16.3	26	47	8 48	4 54	5 15
11	16 09	−17.4	25	50	8 48	5 02	5 24
16	16 30	−18.4	23	53	8 50	5 10	5 34
21	16 52	−19.2	22	55	8 52	5 19	5 45
26	17 15	−20.0	21	57	8 56	5 28	5 55
31	17 38	−20.5	20	60	8 59	5 36	6 04

MARS

Day	RA (h m)	Dec. (°)	Diam. (″)	Phase (%)	Transit (h m)	5° high 52° (h m)	5° high 56° (h m)
1	15 09	−17.0	5	94	8 28	4 39	5 00
6	15 22	−17.8	5	94	8 21	4 38	5 01
11	15 35	−18.7	5	93	8 15	4 37	5 02
16	15 49	−19.4	5	93	8 08	4 37	5 03
21	16 02	−20.2	5	93	8 02	4 36	5 03
26	16 15	−20.8	5	92	7 56	4 34	5 04
31	16 29	−21.4	5	92	7 49	4 33	5 04

SUNRISE AND SUNSET

	London 0°05' 51°30'		Bristol 2°35' 51°28'		Birmingham 1°55' 52°28'		Manchester 2°15' 53°28'		Newcastle 1°37' 54°59'		Glasgow 4°14' 55°52'		Belfast 5°56' 54°35'	
	h m	h m	h m	h m	h m	h m	h m	h m	h m	h m	h m	h m	h m	h m
1	8 06	16 02	8 16	16 12	8 18	16 04	8 25	16 00	8 31	15 49	8 47	15 54	8 46	16 08
2	8 06	16 03	8 16	16 13	8 18	16 05	8 25	16 01	8 31	15 50	8 47	15 55	8 46	16 09
3	8 06	16 04	8 16	16 14	8 18	16 06	8 25	16 02	8 31	15 51	8 47	15 56	8 46	16 11
4	8 06	16 05	8 15	16 15	8 18	16 07	8 24	16 04	8 30	15 52	8 46	15 57	8 45	16 12
5	8 05	16 06	8 15	16 16	8 17	16 09	8 24	16 05	8 30	15 54	8 46	15 59	8 45	16 13
6	8 05	16 07	8 15	16 18	8 17	16 10	8 24	16 06	8 30	15 55	8 45	16 00	8 45	16 15
7	8 05	16 09	8 14	16 19	8 17	16 11	8 23	16 07	8 29	15 56	8 45	16 02	8 44	16 16
8	8 04	16 10	8 14	16 20	8 16	16 13	8 23	16 09	8 28	15 58	8 44	16 03	8 43	16 18
9	8 04	16 11	8 14	16 21	8 16	16 14	8 22	16 10	8 28	15 59	8 43	16 05	8 43	16 19
10	8 03	16 13	8 13	16 23	8 15	16 15	8 21	16 12	8 27	16 01	8 43	16 06	8 42	16 21
11	8 03	16 14	8 12	16 24	8 14	16 17	8 21	16 13	8 26	16 03	8 42	16 08	8 41	16 22
12	8 02	16 16	8 12	16 26	8 14	16 18	8 20	16 15	8 25	16 04	8 41	16 10	8 40	16 24
13	8 01	16 17	8 11	16 27	8 13	16 20	8 19	16 16	8 25	16 06	8 40	16 11	8 40	16 25
14	8 00	16 19	8 10	16 29	8 12	16 21	8 18	16 18	8 24	16 08	8 39	16 13	8 39	16 27
15	8 00	16 20	8 09	16 30	8 11	16 23	8 17	16 20	8 23	16 09	8 38	16 15	8 38	16 29
16	7 59	16 22	8 09	16 32	8 10	16 25	8 16	16 21	8 22	16 11	8 37	16 17	8 37	16 31
17	7 58	16 23	8 08	16 33	8 09	16 26	8 15	16 23	8 20	16 13	8 36	16 19	8 36	16 32
18	7 57	16 25	8 07	16 35	8 08	16 28	8 14	16 25	8 19	16 15	8 34	16 21	8 34	16 34
19	7 56	16 26	8 06	16 37	8 07	16 30	8 13	16 27	8 18	16 17	8 33	16 23	8 33	16 36
20	7 55	16 28	8 05	16 38	8 06	16 31	8 12	16 28	8 17	16 19	8 32	16 25	8 32	16 38
21	7 54	16 30	8 04	16 40	8 05	16 33	8 11	16 30	8 15	16 21	8 30	16 27	8 31	16 40
22	7 53	16 31	8 03	16 42	8 04	16 35	8 10	16 32	8 14	16 22	8 29	16 29	8 29	16 42
23	7 52	16 33	8 01	16 43	8 03	16 37	8 08	16 34	8 13	16 24	8 27	16 31	8 28	16 44
24	7 50	16 35	8 00	16 45	8 01	16 38	8 07	16 36	8 11	16 26	8 26	16 33	8 27	16 45
25	7 49	16 37	7 59	16 47	8 00	16 40	8 06	16 37	8 10	16 28	8 24	16 35	8 25	16 47
26	7 48	16 38	7 58	16 48	7 59	16 42	8 04	16 39	8 08	16 30	8 23	16 37	8 24	16 49
27	7 47	16 40	7 56	16 50	7 57	16 44	8 03	16 41	8 07	16 32	8 21	16 39	8 22	16 51
28	7 45	16 42	7 55	16 52	7 56	16 46	8 01	16 43	8 05	16 34	8 19	16 41	8 20	16 53
29	7 44	16 44	7 54	16 54	7 55	16 48	8 00	16 45	8 03	16 36	8 18	16 43	8 19	16 55
30	7 42	16 45	7 52	16 56	7 53	16 49	7 58	16 47	8 02	16 39	8 16	16 45	8 17	16 57
31	7 41	16 47	7 51	16 57	7 51	16 51	7 56	16 49	8 00	16 41	8 14	16 47	8 15	17 00

JUPITER

Day	RA		Dec.		Transit		5° high	
							52°	56°
	h	m	°	'	h	m	h m	h m
1	9	18.3	+16	31	2	37	19 40	19 29
11	9	14.5	+16	50	1	54	18 55	18 44
21	9	09.8	+17	13	1	10	18 09	17 58
31	9	04.6	+17	37	0	25	17 22	17 10

Diameters - equatorial 45" polar 42"

SATURN

Day	RA		Dec.		Transit		5° high	
							52°	56°
	h	m	°	'	h	m	h m	h m
1	5	36.0	+22	02	22	51	6 20	6 36
11	5	32.9	+22	02	22	09	5 37	5 54
21	5	30.1	+22	02	21	27	4 55	5 12
31	5	28.0	+22	02	20	45	4 14	4 30

Diameters - equatorial 20" polar 18"
Rings - major axis 46" minor axis 21"

URANUS

Day	RA		Dec.		Transit		10° high	
							52°	56°
	h	m	°	'	h	m	h m	h m
1	21	55.0	−13	26	15	12	18 45	18 22
11	21	56.8	−13	17	14	34	18 09	17 46
21	21	58.8	−13	06	13	57	17 32	17 10
31	22	00.9	−12	55	13	20	16 57	16 34

Diameter 4"

NEPTUNE

Day	RA		Dec.		Transit		10° high	
							52°	56°
	h	m	°	'	h	m	h m	h m
1	20	48.0	−17	49	14	05	17 04	16 31
11	20	49.4	−17	44	13	27	16 27	15 54
21	20	50.9	−17	38	12	49	15 50	15 17
31	20	52.4	−17	32	12	11	15 13	14 41

Diameter 2"

 **February 2003**

SECOND MONTH, 28 or 29 DAYS. *Februa*, Roman festival of Purification

1	*Saturday*	*Chinese Year of the Goat or Sheep.* Piet Mondrian d. 1944	32
2	*Sunday*	**Presentation of Christ in the Temple (Candlemas). 4th S. after Epiphany.**	33
3	*Monday*	Felix Mendelssohn-Bartholdy b. 1809. George Crabbe d. 1832	*week 5 day* 34
4	*Tuesday*	Charles Lindbergh b. 1902. Patricia Highsmith d. 1995	35
5	*Wednesday*	William S. Burroughs b. 1914. George Arliss d. 1946	36
6	*Thursday*	*Queen's Accession 1952.* Votes for women introduced 1918	37
7	*Friday*	Charles Dickens b. 1812. Ann Radcliffe d. 1823	38
8	*Saturday*	Lana Turner b. 1920. Giles Gilbert Scott d. 1960	39
9	*Sunday*	**5th S. after Epiphany.** Alban Berg b. 1885	40
10	*Monday*	Larry Adler b. 1914. Edgar Wallace d. 1932	*week 6 day* 41
11	*Tuesday*	Thomas Alva Edison b. 1847. John Buchan d. 1940	42
12	*Wednesday*	Charles Darwin b. 1809. Charles M. Schultz d. 2000	43
13	*Thursday*	Léon Jean Goossens d. 1988. Massacre of Glencoe 1692	44
14	*Friday*	St Valentine's Day. Roger de Grey d. 1995	45
15	*Saturday*	Graham Hill b. 1929. Norman Parkinson d. 1990	46
16	*Sunday*	**3rd S. before Lent.** Angela Carter d. 1992	47
17	*Monday*	Edward German b. 1862. Graham Sutherland d. 1980	*week 7 day* 48
18	*Tuesday*	Michelangelo Buonarroti d. 1564. Balthus d. 2001	49
19	*Wednesday*	*Duke of York b. 1960.* Bertolt Brecht b. 1898	50
20	*Thursday*	Marie Rambert b. 1888. Ferruccio Lamborghini d. 1993	51
21	*Friday*	W. H. Auden b. 1907. Margot Fonteyn d. 1991	52
22	*Saturday*	Eric Gill b. 1882. Andy Warhol d. 1987	53
23	*Sunday*	**2nd S. before Lent.** L. S. Lowry d. 1976	54
24	*Monday*	Wilhelm Grimm b. 1786. Bobby Moore d. 1993	*week 8 day* 55
25	*Tuesday*	George Harrison b. 1943. Tennessee Williams d. 1983	56
26	*Wednesday*	Victor Hugo b. 1802. Harry Lauder d. 1950	57
27	*Thursday*	John Steinbeck b. 1902. Spike Milligan d. 2002	58
28	*Friday*	Edward IV (York) b. 1442. Linus Pauling b. 1901	59

ASTRONOMICAL PHENOMENA

d	h	
2	09	Jupiter at opposition
4	01	Mercury at greatest elongation W.25°
12	02	Saturn in conjunction with Moon. Saturn 3° S.
15	20	Jupiter in conjunction with Moon. Jupiter 4° S.
17	22	Uranus in conjunction
19	02	Sun's longitude 330° ♓
22	08	Saturn at stationary point
25	04	Mars in conjunction with Moon. Mars 2° N.
27	13	Venus in conjunction with Moon. Venus 5° N.

MINIMA OF ALGOL

d	h				
1	16.3	13	03.5	24	14.8
4	13.1	16	00.4	27	11.7
7	09.9	18	21.2		
10	06.7	21	18.0		

CONSTELLATIONS

The following constellations are near the meridian at

	d	h		d	h
January	1	24	February	15	21
January	16	23	March	1	20
February	1	22	March	16	19

Draco (below the Pole), Camelopardus, Auriga, Taurus, Gemini, Orion, Canis Minor, Monoceros, Lepus, Canis Major and Puppis

THE MOON

Phases, Apsides and Node

		d	h	m
●	New Moon	1	10	48
☽	First Quarter	9	11	11
○	Full Moon	16	23	51
☾	Last Quarter	23	16	46
	Apogee (404,552 km)	7	21	58
	Perigee (364,845 km)	19	16	15

Mean longitude of ascending node on February 1, 65°

THE SUN   s.d. 16'.2

Day	Right Ascension h m s	Dec. ° '	Equation of Time m s	Rise 52° h m	Rise 56° h m	Transit h m	Set 52° h m	Set 56° h m	Sidereal time h m s	Transit of First Point of Aries h m s
1	20 56 38	17 17	−13 28	7 41	7 56	12 14	16 47	16 32	8 43 09	15 14 21
2	21 00 42	17 00	−13 37	7 39	7 54	12 14	16 49	16 34	8 47 06	15 10 5
3	21 04 46	16 42	−13 44	7 37	7 52	12 14	16 51	16 36	8 51 02	15 06 29
4	21 08 50	16 25	−13 51	7 36	7 50	12 14	16 53	16 39	8 54 59	15 02 33
5	21 12 52	16 07	−13 57	7 34	7 48	12 14	16 54	16 41	8 58 55	14 58 37
6	21 16 54	15 49	−14 02	7 32	7 46	12 14	16 56	16 43	9 02 52	14 54 41
7	21 20 54	15 30	−14 06	7 31	7 44	12 14	16 58	16 45	9 06 49	14 50 45
8	21 24 54	15 11	−14 09	7 29	7 42	12 14	17 00	16 47	9 10 45	14 46 49
9	21 28 53	14 52	−14 12	7 27	7 40	12 14	17 02	16 50	9 14 42	14 42 53
10	21 32 52	14 33	−14 13	7 25	7 37	12 14	17 04	16 52	9 18 38	14 38 57
11	21 36 49	14 14	−14 14	7 24	7 35	12 14	17 06	16 54	9 22 35	14 35 01
12	21 40 46	13 54	−14 15	7 22	7 33	12 14	17 08	16 56	9 26 31	14 31 06
13	21 44 42	13 34	−14 14	7 20	7 31	12 14	17 09	16 58	9 30 28	14 27 10
14	21 48 37	13 14	−14 13	7 18	7 29	12 14	17 11	17 01	9 34 24	14 23 14
15	21 52 32	12 54	−14 11	7 16	7 26	12 14	17 13	17 03	9 38 21	14 19 18
16	21 56 25	12 33	−14 08	7 14	7 24	12 14	17 15	17 05	9 42 18	14 15 22
17	22 00 18	12 12	−14 04	7 12	7 22	12 14	17 17	17 07	9 46 14	14 11 26
18	22 04 10	11 51	−14 00	7 10	7 19	12 14	17 19	17 09	9 50 11	14 07 30
19	22 08 02	11 30	−13 55	7 08	7 17	12 14	17 21	17 12	9 54 07	14 03 34
20	22 11 53	11 09	−13 49	7 06	7 15	12 14	17 22	17 14	9 58 04	13 59 38
21	22 15 43	10 47	−13 43	7 04	7 12	12 14	17 24	17 16	10 02 00	13 55 42
22	22 19 33	10 26	−13 36	7 02	7 10	12 14	17 26	17 18	10 05 57	13 51 46
23	22 23 22	10 04	−13 28	7 00	7 08	12 13	17 28	17 20	10 09 53	13 47 51
24	22 27 10	9 42	−13 20	6 58	7 05	12 13	17 30	17 22	10 13 50	13 43 55
25	22 30 58	9 20	−13 11	6 56	7 03	12 13	17 32	17 25	10 17 47	13 39 59
26	22 34 45	8 57	−13 02	6 53	7 00	12 13	17 33	17 27	10 21 43	13 36 03
27	22 38 32	8 35	−12 52	6 51	6 58	12 13	17 35	17 29	10 25 40	13 32 07
28	22 42 18	8 12	−12 42	6 49	6 55	12 13	17 37	17 31	10 29 36	13 28 11

DURATION OF TWILIGHT (in minutes)

Latitude	52°	56°	52°	56°	52°	56°	52°	56°
	1 February		11 February		21 February		28 February	
Civil	37	41	35	39	34	38	34	37
Nautical	77	86	75	83	74	81	73	80
Astronomical	117	130	114	126	113	124	112	124

THE NIGHT SKY

Mercury is unsuitably placed for observation throughout the month, despite the fact that it is at greatest western elongation on the 4th.

Venus continues to be visible as a magnificent object, magnitude -4.4, low in the south-eastern sky before dawn. The old crescent Moon is near the planet on the mornings of the 27th and 28th, creating favourable opportunities for locating it after the Sun has risen, although both objects are low in the south-south-east. On the first occasion Venus will be about 6 degrees above and to the left of the Moon, while on the second occasion it will be about 10 degrees to the right and above the Moon.

Mars, magnitude +1.1, continues to be visible as a morning object low in the south-eastern sky. Mars enters the constellation of Ophiuchus early in the month and moves into Sagittarius during the last week of February. The crescent Moon is near the planet on the morning of the 25th.

Jupiter, magnitude -2.6, is at opposition on the 2nd and therefore visible throughout the hours of darkness. By the end of the month it is visible low in the eastern sky shortly after sunset. On the early evening of the 15th the Full Moon passes 3 degrees north of the planet. Jupiter is retrograding slowly in the constellation of Cancer.

Saturn, magnitude -0.1, continues to be visible in the south-western quadrant of the sky in the evenings. It is retrograding slowly in Taurus but reaches its second stationary point on the 22nd, and then resumes its direct motion. The waxing gibbous Moon passes 2 degrees north of the planet during the early hours of the 12th.

Zodiacal Light. The evening cone may be observed stretching up from the western horizon, along the ecliptic, after the end of twilight, from the 18th onwards. This faint phenomenon is only visible under good conditions and in the absence of both moonlight and artificial lighting.

THE MOON

Day	RA h m	Dec. °	Hor. par. ′	Semi-diam. ′	Sun's co-long. °	PA of Bright Limb °	Phase %	Age d	Rise 52° h m	Rise 56° h m	Transit h m	Set 52° h m	Set 56° h m
1	20 39	−22.9	57.0	15.5	260	37	0	29.2	8 19	8 42	12 22	16 34	16 12
2	21 33	−19.6	56.4	15.4	272	287	1	0.6	8 44	9 01	13 12	17 51	17 35
3	22 24	−15.4	55.8	15.2	284	263	3	1.5	9 03	9 15	13 59	19 06	18 56
4	23 12	−10.6	55.3	15.1	296	256	7	2.5	9 18	9 26	14 42	20 19	20 13
5	23 57	− 5.5	54.9	14.9	309	252	13	3.5	9 32	9 35	15 23	21 29	21 28
6	0 40	− 0.2	54.5	14.8	321	250	20	4.6	9 44	9 43	16 04	22 38	22 42
7	1 23	+ 5.0	54.3	14.8	333	250	28	5.6	9 57	9 51	16 44	23 47	23 55
8	2 07	+ 9.9	54.2	14.8	345	251	36	6.6	10 11	10 00	17 25	—	—
9	2 51	+14.5	54.3	14.8	357	253	46	7.6	10 27	10 12	18 09	0 56	1 10
10	3 38	+18.6	54.6	14.9	9	257	55	8.6	10 47	10 27	18 55	2 07	2 26
11	4 28	+22.0	55.0	15.0	22	261	65	9.6	11 14	10 49	19 45	3 18	3 43
12	5 20	+24.5	55.6	15.2	34	267	74	10.6	11 51	11 22	20 38	4 27	4 56
13	6 16	+25.8	56.3	15.4	46	274	82	11.6	12 41	12 09	21 34	5 30	6 01
14	7 14	+25.7	57.1	15.6	58	281	89	12.6	13 45	13 16	22 31	6 23	6 53
15	8 12	+24.2	57.9	15.8	70	291	95	13.6	15 02	14 37	23 27	7 04	7 29
16	9 11	+21.2	58.7	16.0	82	306	99	14.6	16 26	16 08	—	7 35	7 54
17	10 08	+16.8	59.3	16.2	94	21	100	15.6	17 53	17 41	0 22	7 59	8 12
18	11 03	+11.5	59.8	16.3	107	93	98	16.5	19 20	19 14	1 15	8 18	8 26
19	11 57	+ 5.4	60.0	16.4	119	105	94	17.5	20 46	20 46	2 07	8 35	8 37
20	12 49	− 1.0	60.1	16.4	131	108	88	18.5	22 13	22 19	2 57	8 51	8 48
21	13 42	− 7.3	59.9	16.3	143	109	79	19.5	23 39	23 51	3 48	9 08	9 00
22	14 36	−13.1	59.6	16.2	155	107	69	20.5	—	—	4 39	9 27	9 13
23	15 31	−18.2	59.2	16.1	167	104	58	21.5	1 05	1 24	5 33	9 51	9 31
24	16 28	−22.2	58.7	16.0	179	99	47	22.5	2 29	2 55	6 29	10 21	9 55
25	17 27	−24.8	58.2	15.9	192	93	36	23.5	3 47	4 17	7 27	11 03	10 32
26	18 27	−26.0	57.7	15.7	204	86	26	24.5	4 52	5 25	8 25	11 58	11 25
27	19 26	−25.6	57.2	15.6	216	78	17	25.5	5 43	6 13	9 22	13 04	12 34
28	20 23	−23.8	56.7	15.4	228	71	10	26.5	6 21	6 46	10 16	14 18	13 54

MERCURY

Day	RA h m	Dec. °	Diam. ″	Phase %	Transit h m	5° high 52° h m	5° high 56° h m
1	19 11	−21.1	7	56	10 28	7 09	7 39
3	19 19	−21.2	7	60	10 28	7 10	7 40
5	19 28	−21.3	7	64	10 29	7 11	7 42
7	19 37	−21.2	6	67	10 31	7 13	7 43
9	19 48	−21.1	6	70	10 33	7 14	7 44
11	19 58	−21.0	6	72	10 36	7 15	7 45
13	20 09	−20.7	6	75	10 39	7 16	7 45
15	20 20	−20.4	6	77	10 43	7 17	7 45
17	20 32	−20.0	6	79	10 46	7 18	7 45
19	20 44	−19.5	6	81	10 50	7 18	7 44
21	20 56	−18.9	5	83	10 55	7 17	7 42
23	21 08	−18.2	5	84	10 59	7 17	7 40
25	21 20	−17.4	5	86	11 03	7 16	7 38
27	21 33	−16.6	5	87	11 08	7 15	7 35
29	21 45	−15.7	5	89	11 13	7 13	7 32
31	21 58	−14.6	5	90	11 18	7 11	7 29

VENUS

Day	RA h m	Dec. °	Diam. ″	Phase %	Transit h m	5° high 52° h m	5° high 56° h m
1	17 43	−20.6	20	60	9 00	5 37	6 06
6	18 07	−21.0	19	62	9 04	5 44	6 14
11	18 31	−21.1	18	64	9 09	5 50	6 19
16	18 56	−21.0	18	66	9 14	5 54	6 23
21	19 21	−20.6	17	68	9 19	5 56	6 24
26	19 46	−20.0	16	70	9 24	5 56	6 23
31	20 10	−19.2	16	71	9 29	5 55	6 20

MARS

Day	RA h m	Dec. °	Diam. ″	Phase %	Transit h m	5° high 52° h m	5° high 56° h m
1	16 32	−21.5	5	92	7 48	4 33	5 04
6	16 45	−22.0	5	91	7 42	4 31	5 03
11	16 59	−22.4	6	91	7 36	4 29	5 02
16	17 13	−22.8	6	91	7 30	4 26	5 00
21	17 27	−23.1	6	90	7 25	4 23	4 58
26	17 41	−23.3	6	90	7 19	4 19	4 55
31	17 55	−23.5	6	90	7 13	4 14	4 51

SUNRISE AND SUNSET

	London 0°05' 51°30'		Bristol 2°35' 51°28'		Birmingham 1°55' 52°28'		Manchester 2°15' 53°28'		Newcastle 1°37' 54°59'		Glasgow 4°14' 55°52'		Belfast 5°56' 54°35'	
	h m	h m	h m	h m	h m	h m	h m	h m	h m	h m	h m	h m	h m	h m
1	7 39	16 49	7 49	16 59	7 50	16 53	7 55	16 51	7 58	16 43	8 12	16 50	8 14	17 02
2	7 38	16 51	7 48	17 01	7 48	16 55	7 53	16 53	7 56	16 45	8 10	16 52	8 12	17 04
3	7 36	16 53	7 46	17 03	7 47	16 57	7 51	16 55	7 54	16 47	8 08	16 54	8 10	17 06
4	7 35	16 55	7 45	17 05	7 45	16 59	7 50	16 57	7 52	16 49	8 06	16 56	8 08	17 08
5	7 33	16 56	7 43	17 06	7 43	17 01	7 48	16 59	7 51	16 51	8 04	16 58	8 06	17 10
6	7 31	16 58	7 41	17 08	7 42	17 03	7 46	17 01	7 49	16 53	8 02	17 00	8 04	17 12
7	7 30	17 00	7 40	17 10	7 40	17 05	7 44	17 03	7 47	16 55	8 00	17 03	8 03	17 14
8	7 28	17 02	7 38	17 12	7 38	17 06	7 42	17 05	7 45	16 57	7 58	17 05	8 01	17 16
9	7 26	17 04	7 36	17 14	7 36	17 08	7 40	17 07	7 43	17 00	7 56	17 07	7 59	17 18
10	7 24	17 05	7 34	17 16	7 34	17 10	7 39	17 09	7 41	17 02	7 54	17 09	7 57	17 20
11	7 23	17 07	7 32	17 17	7 32	17 12	7 37	17 11	7 39	17 04	7 52	17 11	7 55	17 22
12	7 21	17 09	7 31	17 19	7 31	17 14	7 35	17 13	7 36	17 06	7 50	17 14	7 52	17 24
13	7 19	17 11	7 29	17 21	7 29	17 16	7 33	17 15	7 34	17 08	7 47	17 16	7 50	17 26
14	7 17	17 13	7 27	17 23	7 27	17 18	7 31	17 17	7 32	17 10	7 45	17 18	7 48	17 28
15	7 15	17 15	7 25	17 25	7 25	17 20	7 29	17 19	7 30	17 12	7 43	17 20	7 46	17 31
16	7 13	17 16	7 23	17 27	7 23	17 22	7 26	17 21	7 28	17 14	7 41	17 22	7 44	17 33
17	7 11	17 18	7 21	17 28	7 21	17 24	7 24	17 23	7 26	17 16	7 38	17 25	7 42	17 35
18	7 09	17 20	7 19	17 30	7 19	17 25	7 22	17 25	7 23	17 18	7 36	17 27	7 40	17 37
19	7 07	17 22	7 17	17 32	7 17	17 27	7 20	17 26	7 21	17 21	7 34	17 29	7 37	17 39
20	7 05	17 24	7 15	17 34	7 15	17 29	7 18	17 28	7 19	17 23	7 31	17 31	7 35	17 41
21	7 03	17 26	7 13	17 36	7 12	17 31	7 16	17 30	7 16	17 25	7 29	17 33	7 33	17 43
22	7 01	17 27	7 11	17 37	7 10	17 33	7 14	17 32	7 14	17 27	7 27	17 35	7 31	17 45
23	6 59	17 29	7 09	17 39	7 08	17 35	7 11	17 34	7 12	17 29	7 24	17 38	7 28	17 47
24	6 57	17 31	7 07	17 41	7 06	17 37	7 09	17 36	7 09	17 31	7 22	17 40	7 26	17 49
25	6 55	17 33	7 05	17 43	7 04	17 39	7 07	17 38	7 07	17 33	7 19	17 42	7 24	17 51
26	6 53	17 34	7 03	17 45	7 02	17 40	7 05	17 40	7 05	17 35	7 17	17 44	7 21	17 53
27	6 51	17 36	7 01	17 46	7 00	17 42	7 02	17 42	7 02	17 37	7 14	17 46	7 19	17 55
28	6 49	17 38	6 59	17 48	6 57	17 44	7 00	17 44	7 00	17 39	7 12	17 48	7 17	17 57

JUPITER

Day	RA	Dec.		Transit		5° high 52°		56°	
	h m	°	'	h m		h m		h m	
1	9 04.0	+17	39	0 21		7 20		7 31	
11	8 58.7	+18	03	23 32		6 37		6 49	
21	8 53.7	+18	24	22 48		5 55		6 07	
31	8 49.4	+18	41	22 04		5 13		5 26	

Diameters - equatorial 45" polar 42"

SATURN

Day	RA	Dec.		Transit		5° high 52°		56°	
	h m	°	'	h m		h m		h m	
1	5 27.9	+22	02	20 41		4 10		4 26	
11	5 26.6	+22	03	20 01		3 29		3 46	
21	5 26.0	+22	05	19 21		2 50		3 06	
31	5 26.3	+22	07	18 42		2 11		2 28	

Diameters - equatorial 19" polar 18"
Rings - major axis 44" minor axis 20"

URANUS

Day	RA	Dec.		Transit		10° high 52°		56°	
	h m	°	'	h m		h m		h m	
1	22 01.1	−12	53	13 16		16 53		16 31	
11	22 03.3	−12	42	12 39		16 17		15 55	
21	22 05.5	−12	30	12 02		15 41		15 20	
31	22 07.7	−12	18	11 24		15 06		14 45	

Diameter 4"

NEPTUNE

Day	RA	Dec.		Transit		10° high 52°		56°	
	h m	°	'	h m		h m		h m	
1	20 52.6	−17	31	12 07		9 06		9 38	
11	20 54.1	−17	25	11 30		8 27		8 59	
21	20 55.6	−17	19	10 52		7 48		8 20	
31	20 57.0	−17	13	10 14		7 10		7 41	

Diameter 2"

March 2003

THIRD MONTH, 31 DAYS. *Mars*, Roman god of battle

1	*Saturday*	St. David's Day. Yitzhak Rabin b. 1922	60
2	*Sunday*	**S. next before Lent**. Karen Carpenter b. 1950.	61
3	*Monday*	Alexander Graham Bell b. 1847. Robert Adam d. 1792,	*week* 9 *day* 62
4	*Tuesday*	Muslim New Year. Shrove Tuesday	63
5	*Wednesday*	**Ash Wednesday.** Josef Stalin d. 1953	64
6	*Thursday*	Sir Edwin Henry Landseer b. 1802. Davy Crockett d. 1836	65
7	*Friday*	Florence Margaret Smith d. 1971. Stanley Kubrik d. 2000	66
8	*Saturday*	Carl Philipp Emanuel Bach b. 1714. Joe DiMaggio d. 1999	67
9	*Sunday*	**1st S. in Lent.** Yuri Gagarin b. 1934	68
10	*Monday*	*Earl of Wessex b. 1964.* Commonwealth Day.	*week* 10 *day* 69
11	*Tuesday*	Douglas Adams b. 1952. Henry Walford Davies d. 1941	70
12	*Wednesday*	Gabriele d'Annunzio b. 1864. The Girl Guides movement started in the US 1912	71
13	*Thursday*	Sir Hugh Walpole b. 1884. Uranus discovered 1781	72
14	*Friday*	Albert Einstein b. 1879. Karl Marx d. 1883	73
15	*Saturday*	3rd Viscount Melbourne William Lamb b. 1779. Aristotle Onassis d. 1975	74
16	*Sunday*	**2nd S. in Lent.** All 20 European Commissioners resigned following allegations of fraud 1999	75
17	*Monday*	St Patrick's Day. Bank *Holiday in Northern Ireland.*	*week* 11 *day* 76
18	*Tuesday*	Neville Chamberlain b. 1869. The Commune Rising began in Paris 1871	77
19	*Wednesday*	**St Joseph of Nazareth.** Edgar Rice Burroughs d. 1950	78
20	*Thursday*	Sir Isaac Newton d. 1727. Brendan Behan d. 1964	79
21	*Friday*	Ayrton Senna b. 1960. Archbishop Thomas Cranmer d. 1556	80
22	*Saturday*	Sir Anthony van Dyck b. 1599. Johann Wolfgang von Goethe d. 1832	81
23	*Sunday*	**3rd S. in Lent.** Princess Eugenie of York b. 1990	82
24	*Monday*	Steve McQueen b. 1930. Elizabeth I d. 1603	*week* 12 *day* 83
25	*Tuesday*	**The Annunciation.** Treaty of Rome 1957	84
26	*Wednesday*	Tennessee Williams b. 1911. Cecil Rhodes d. 1902	85
27	*Thursday*	Sir Henry Royce b. 1863. Yuri Gagarin d. 1968	86
28	*Friday*	Saint Teresa of Avila b. 1515. General Dwight Eisenhower d. 1969	87
29	*Saturday*	Sir William Walton b. 1902. Carl Orff d. 1982	88
30	*Sunday*	**4th S. in Lent.** Mothering Sunday.	89
31	*Monday*	Professor Charles Best d. 1978. Eiffel Tower completed 1889	*week* 13 *day* 90

ASTRONOMICAL PHENOMENA

d	h	
1	17	Mercury in conjunction with Moon. Mercury 3° N.
11	11	Saturn in conjunction with Moon. Saturn 3° S.
15	02	Jupiter in conjunction with Moon. Jupiter 4° S.
21	01	Sun's longitude 0°♈
22	00	Mercury in superior conjunction
23	05	Pluto at stationary point
25	18	Mars in conjunction with Moon. Mars 3° N.
29	14	Venus in conjunction with Moon. Venus 4° N.

MINIMA OF ALGOL

d	h	d	h	d	h
2	08.5	13	19.8	25	07.0
5	05.3	16	16.6	28	03.9
8	02.1	19	13.4	31	00.7
10	22.9	22	10.2		

CONSTELLATIONS

The following constellations are near the meridian at

	d	h		d	h
February	1	24	March	16	21
February	15	23	April	1	20
March	1	22	April	15	19

Cepheus (below the Pole), Camelopardus, Lynx, Gemini, Cancer, Leo, Canis Minor, Hydra, Monoceros, Canis Major and Puppis

THE MOON

Phases, Apsides and Node	d	h	m
● New Moon	3	02	35
☽ First Quarter	11	07	15
○ Full Moon	18	10	35
☾ Last Quarter	25	01	51
Apogee (405,382 km)	7	16	32
Perigee (359,816 km)	19	19	01

Mean longitude of ascending node on March 1, 64°

THE SUN   s.d. 16'.0

Day	Right Ascension h m s	Dec. ° '	Equation of Time m s	Rise 52° h m	Rise 56° h m	Transit h m	Set 52° h m	Set 56° h m	Sidereal time h m s	Transit of First Point of Aries h m s
1	22 46 04	− 7 50	−12 31	6 47	6 53	12 12	17 39	17 33	10 33 33	13 24 15
2	22 49 49	− 7 27	−12 19	6 45	6 50	12 12	17 41	17 35	10 37 29	13 20 19
3	22 53 33	− 7 04	−12 07	6 43	6 48	12 12	17 42	17 37	10 41 26	13 16 23
4	22 57 17	− 6 41	−11 55	6 40	6 45	12 12	17 44	17 40	10 45 22	13 12 27
5	23 01 01	− 6 18	−11 42	6 38	6 43	12 12	17 46	17 42	10 49 19	13 08 31
6	23 04 44	− 5 55	−11 29	6 36	6 40	12 11	17 48	17 44	10 53 16	13 04 36
7	23 08 27	− 5 31	−11 15	6 34	6 37	12 11	17 50	17 46	10 57 12	13 00 40
8	23 12 09	− 5 08	−11 01	6 31	6 35	12 11	17 51	17 48	11 01 09	12 56 44
9	23 15 51	− 4 45	−10 46	6 29	6 32	12 11	17 53	17 50	11 05 05	12 52 48
10	23 19 33	− 4 21	−10 31	6 27	6 30	12 10	17 55	17 52	11 09 02	12 48 52
11	23 23 14	− 3 58	−10 16	6 25	6 27	12 10	17 57	17 54	11 12 58	12 44 56
12	23 26 55	− 3 34	−10 00	6 22	6 25	12 10	17 58	17 56	11 16 55	12 41 00
13	23 30 36	− 3 11	− 9 44	6 20	6 22	12 10	18 00	17 58	11 20 51	12 37 04
14	23 34 16	− 2 47	− 9 28	6 18	6 19	12 09	18 02	18 00	11 24 48	12 33 08
15	23 37 56	− 2 23	− 9 11	6 15	6 17	12 09	18 04	18 03	11 28 45	12 29 12
16	23 41 35	− 2 00	− 8 54	6 13	6 14	12 09	18 05	18 05	11 32 41	12 25 17
17	23 45 15	− 1 36	− 8 37	6 11	6 11	12 08	18 07	18 07	11 36 38	12 21 21
18	23 48 54	− 1 12	− 8 20	6 08	6 09	12 08	18 09	18 09	11 40 34	12 17 25
19	23 52 33	− 0 48	− 8 02	6 06	6 06	12 08	18 11	18 11	11 44 31	12 13 29
20	23 56 12	− 0 25	− 7 45	6 04	6 04	12 08	18 12	18 13	11 48 27	12 09 33
21	23 59 51	− 0 01	− 7 27	6 02	6 01	12 07	18 14	18 15	11 52 24	12 05 37
22	0 03 29	+ 0 23	− 7 09	5 59	5 58	12 07	18 16	18 17	11 56 20	12 01 41
23	0 07 08	+ 0 46	− 6 51	5 57	5 56	12 07	18 18	18 19	12 00 17	11 57 45
24	0 10 46	+ 1 10	− 6 33	5 55	5 53	12 06	18 19	18 21	12 04 13	11 53 49
25	0 14 25	+ 1 34	− 6 15	5 52	5 50	12 06	18 21	18 23	12 08 10	11 49 53
26	0 18 03	+ 1 57	− 5 57	5 50	5 48	12 06	18 23	18 25	12 12 07	11 45 57
27	0 21 42	+ 2 21	− 5 39	5 48	5 45	12 05	18 24	18 27	12 16 03	11 42 02
28	0 25 20	+ 2 44	− 5 20	5 45	5 42	12 05	18 26	18 29	12 20 00	11 38 06
29	0 28 59	+ 3 08	− 5 02	5 43	5 40	12 05	18 28	18 31	12 23 56	11 34 10
30	0 32 37	+ 3 31	− 4 44	5 41	5 37	12 05	18 30	18 33	12 27 53	11 30 14
31	0 36 16	+ 3 54	− 4 26	5 38	5 35	12 04	18 31	18 35	12 31 49	11 26 18

DURATION OF TWILIGHT (in minutes)

Latitude	52°	56°	52°	56°	52°	56°	52°	56°
	1 March		11 March		21 March		31 March	
Civil	34	37	34	37	34	37	34	38
Nautical	73	80	73	80	74	81	75	84
Astronomical	112	124	113	125	115	128	120	135

THE NIGHT SKY

Mercury remains too close to the Sun for observation throughout the month, superior conjunction occurring on the 21st.

Venus, magnitude −4.2, is a brilliant object in the mornings, low in the south–eastern sky, but by the end of the month it is only visible for a very short time before dawn. On the morning of the 29th the old crescent Moon will be seen approaching the planet.

Mars is a morning object, low above the south–eastern horizon for some time before dawn. Its magnitude is +0.8. It is moving steadily eastwards in Sagittarius. The Moon, at Last Quarter, is near the planet on the mornings of the 25th and 26th.

Jupiter, magnitude −2.4, is a conspicuous object in the eastern sky in the early evenings, and visible in the southern skies for several hours after midnight. The gibbous Moon passes 3 degrees north of the planet on the night of the 14–15th. Jupiter is moving very slowly retrograde in Cancer and observers with binoculars will get a pleasant surprise during March and April as Jupiter will be seen only a couple of degrees south–east of the open cluster Praesepe (the Beehive) – which is just visible to the naked–eye as a misty patch of light.

Saturn is still an evening object in the western sky but by the end of the month is lost to view over the west–north–western horizon by midnight. Its magnitude is 0.0. The Moon, at First Quarter, is near the planet on the evenings of the 10th and 11th.

Zodiacal Light. The evening cone may be observed, stretching up from the western horizon, along the ecliptic, after the end of twilight, from the beginning of the month to the 4th, and again after the 19th.

THE MOON

Day	RA h m	Dec °	Hor. par.	Semi-diam. ′	Sun's co-long. °	PA of Bright Limb °	Phase %	Age d	Rise 52° h m	Rise 56° h m	Transit h m	Set 52° h m	Set 56° h m
1	21 18	−20.7	56.2	15.3	240	62	5	27.5	6 48	7 07	11 06	15 34	15 16
2	22 09	−16.8	55.7	15.2	253	48	1	28.5	7 08	7 22	11 53	16 50	16 37
3	22 57	−12.1	55.3	15.1	265	351	0	29.5	7 24	7 33	12 37	18 03	17 55
4	23 42	− 7.0	54.9	14.9	277	271	1	0.9	7 38	7 42	13 19	19 14	19 11
5	0 26	− 1.8	54.5	14.9	289	257	4	1.9	7 50	7 51	14 00	20 23	20 26
6	1 09	+ 3.5	54.3	14.8	301	253	8	2.9	8 03	7 59	14 40	21 33	21 40
7	1 53	+ 8.6	54.1	14.7	314	252	14	3.9	8 16	8 07	15 21	22 42	22 54
8	2 37	+13.4	54.1	14.7	326	253	21	4.9	8 31	8 17	16 03	23 52	—
9	3 22	+17.7	54.2	14.8	338	256	29	5.9	8 49	8 31	16 48	—	0 10
10	4 11	+21.3	54.5	14.8	350	259	38	6.9	9 12	8 49	17 36	1 03	1 26
11	5 01	+24.0	54.9	15.0	2	264	47	7.9	9 44	9 15	18 26	2 13	2 40
12	5 55	+25.7	55.6	15.1	15	270	57	8.9	10 27	9 55	19 20	3 17	3 49
13	6 51	+26.1	56.3	15.3	27	276	67	9.9	11 23	10 52	20 15	4 13	4 45
14	7 48	+25.2	57.2	15.6	39	283	76	10.9	12 33	12 06	21 11	4 59	5 27
15	8 46	+22.8	58.1	15.8	51	290	85	11.9	13 54	13 32	22 06	5 33	5 56
16	9 43	+19.0	59.0	16.1	63	297	92	12.9	15 20	15 04	23 00	6 00	6 16
17	10 39	+14.0	59.8	16.3	75	306	97	13.9	16 48	16 39	23 53	6 21	6 31
18	11 34	+ 8.0	60.5	16.5	87	331	100	14.9	18 17	18 14	—	6 38	6 43
19	12 28	+ 1.5	60.8	16.6	100	85	99	15.9	19 46	19 49	0 45	6 55	6 54
20	13 22	− 5.1	60.9	16.6	112	104	96	16.9	21 16	21 26	1 37	7 11	7 05
21	14 17	−11.4	60.7	16.5	124	106	91	17.9	22 46	23 03	2 30	7 30	7 18
22	15 14	−17.0	60.3	16.4	136	105	82	18.9	—	—	3 25	7 52	7 34
23	16 12	−21.5	59.7	16.3	148	101	73	19.9	0 15	0 38	4 22	8 20	7 56
24	17 12	−24.6	58.9	16.1	160	95	62	20.9	1 38	2 07	5 21	8 59	8 29
25	18 13	−26.1	58.2	15.9	173	89	51	21.9	2 49	3 22	6 20	9 50	9 17
26	19 13	−26.0	57.4	15.7	185	82	40	22.9	3 44	4 16	7 18	10 54	10 23
27	20 11	−24.5	56.7	15.5	197	76	30	23.9	4 25	4 52	8 12	12 06	11 40
28	21 05	−21.7	56.1	15.3	209	70	21	24.9	4 54	5 15	9 04	13 22	13 02
29	21 57	−17.9	55.6	15.1	221	65	14	25.9	5 15	5 31	9 51	14 37	14 23
30	22 45	−13.4	55.1	15.0	234	60	7	26.9	5 32	5 43	10 35	15 51	15 41
31	23 30	− 8.5	54.7	14.9	246	54	3	27.9	5 46	5 52	11 17	17 02	16 58

MERCURY

Day	RA h m	Dec °	Diam. ″	Phase %	Transit h m	5° high 52° h m	5° high 56° h m
1	21 45	−15.7	5	89	11 13	7 13	7 32
3	21 58	−14.6	5	90	11 18	7 11	7 29
5	22 11	−13.5	5	92	11 23	7 09	7 26
7	22 24	−12.4	5	93	11 28	7 07	7 22
9	22 37	−11.1	5	94	11 33	7 05	7 18
11	22 50	− 9.7	5	96	11 39	7 02	7 14
13	23 04	− 8.3	5	97	11 44	6 59	7 10
15	23 17	− 6.8	5	98	11 50	6 56	7 05
17	23 31	− 5.2	5	99	11 56	6 53	7 01
19	23 45	− 3.5	5	99	12 02	17 15	17 09
21	23 59	− 1.7	5	100	12 08	17 30	17 26
23	0 13	− 0.1	5	100	12 14	17 46	17 43
25	0 27	+ 1.9	5	99	12 21	18 02	18 01
27	0 42	+ 3.8	5	98	12 27	18 19	18 19
29	0 56	+ 5.7	5	96	12 34	18 35	18 37
31	1 11	+ 7.6	5	93	12 41	18 51	18 55

VENUS

Day	RA h m	Dec °	Diam. ″	Phase %	Transit h m	5° high 52° h m	5° high 56° h m
1	20 00	−19.6	16	71	9 27	5 56	6 22
6	20 25	−18.6	16	72	9 32	5 53	6 18
11	20 49	−17.4	15	74	9 37	5 50	6 12
16	21 14	−16.0	15	75	9 41	5 45	6 05
21	21 37	−14.5	14	77	9 45	5 39	5 56
26	22 01	−12.7	14	78	9 49	5 31	5 47
31	22 24	−10.8	13	80	9 53	5 24	5 37

MARS

Day	RA h m	Dec °	Diam. ″	Phase %	Transit h m	5° high 52° h m	5° high 56° h m
1	17 49	−23.4	6	90	7 15	4 16	4 53
6	18 03	−23.5	6	89	7 09	4 11	4 48
11	18 17	−23.6	7	89	7 04	4 06	4 43
16	18 31	−23.5	7	89	6 58	3 59	4 37
21	18 45	−23.4	7	88	6 52	3 53	4 29
26	18 58	−23.3	7	88	6 46	3 45	4 21
31	19 12	−23.0	7	88	6 40	3 37	4 12

SUNRISE AND SUNSET

	London 0°05' 51°30'		Bristol 2°35' 51°28'		Birmingham 1°55' 52°28'		Manchester 2°15' 53°28'		Newcastle 1°37' 54°59'		Glasgow 4°14' 55°52'		Belfast 5°56' 54°35'	
	h m	h m	h m	h m	h m	h m	h m	h m	h m	h m	h m	h m	h m	h m
1	6 47	17 40	6 57	17 50	6 55	17 46	6 58	17 46	6 58	17 41	7 09	17 50	7 14	17 59
2	6 44	17 42	6 54	17 52	6 53	17 48	6 56	17 48	6 55	17 43	7 07	17 52	7 12	18 01
3	6 42	17 43	6 52	17 53	6 51	17 50	6 53	17 50	6 53	17 45	7 04	17 55	7 09	18 03
4	6 40	17 45	6 50	17 55	6 48	17 51	6 51	17 52	6 50	17 47	7 02	17 57	7 07	18 05
5	6 38	17 47	6 48	17 57	6 46	17 53	6 49	17 54	6 48	17 49	6 59	17 59	7 05	18 07
6	6 36	17 49	6 46	17 59	6 44	17 55	6 46	17 55	6 45	17 51	6 57	18 01	7 02	18 09
7	6 33	17 50	6 43	18 00	6 42	17 57	6 44	17 57	6 43	17 53	6 54	18 03	7 00	18 11
8	6 31	17 52	6 41	18 02	6 39	17 59	6 42	17 59	6 40	17 55	6 52	18 05	6 57	18 13
9	6 29	17 54	6 39	18 04	6 37	18 00	6 39	18 01	6 38	17 57	6 49	18 07	6 55	18 15
10	6 27	17 56	6 37	18 06	6 35	18 02	6 37	18 03	6 35	17 59	6 47	18 09	6 52	18 17
11	6 25	17 57	6 35	18 07	6 32	18 04	6 34	18 05	6 33	18 01	6 44	18 11	6 50	18 19
12	6 22	17 59	6 32	18 09	6 30	18 06	6 32	18 07	6 30	18 03	6 41	18 13	6 47	18 21
13	6 20	18 01	6 30	18 11	6 28	18 08	6 30	18 09	6 28	18 05	6 39	18 15	6 45	18 23
14	6 18	18 02	6 28	18 12	6 26	18 09	6 27	18 10	6 25	18 07	6 36	18 17	6 42	18 25
15	6 16	18 04	6 26	18 14	6 23	18 11	6 25	18 12	6 23	18 09	6 34	18 20	6 40	18 27
16	6 13	18 06	6 23	18 16	6 21	18 13	6 22	18 14	6 20	18 11	6 31	18 22	6 37	18 29
17	6 11	18 08	6 21	18 18	6 19	18 15	6 20	18 16	6 18	18 13	6 28	18 24	6 35	18 31
18	6 09	18 09	6 19	18 19	6 16	18 17	6 18	18 18	6 15	18 15	6 26	18 26	6 32	18 33
19	6 06	18 11	6 16	18 21	6 14	18 18	6 15	18 20	6 13	18 17	6 23	18 28	6 30	18 34
20	6 04	18 13	6 14	18 23	6 11	18 20	6 13	18 22	6 10	18 19	6 20	18 30	6 27	18 36
21	6 02	18 14	6 12	18 24	6 09	18 22	6 10	18 23	6 08	18 21	6 18	18 32	6 25	18 38
22	6 00	18 16	6 10	18 26	6 07	18 24	6 08	18 25	6 05	18 23	6 15	18 34	6 22	18 40
23	5 57	18 18	6 07	18 28	6 04	18 25	6 05	18 27	6 02	18 25	6 13	18 36	6 20	18 42
24	5 55	18 19	6 05	18 29	6 02	18 27	6 03	18 29	5 59	18 27	6 10	18 38	6 17	18 44
25	5 53	18 21	6 03	18 31	6 00	18 29	6 01	18 31	5 57	18 29	6 07	18 40	6 15	18 46
26	5 51	18 23	6 01	18 33	5 57	18 31	5 58	18 33	5 55	18 31	6 05	18 42	6 12	18 48
27	5 48	18 24	5 58	18 34	5 55	18 32	5 56	18 34	5 52	18 33	6 02	18 44	6 10	18 50
28	5 46	18 26	5 56	18 36	5 53	18 34	5 53	18 36	5 50	18 35	5 59	18 46	6 07	18 52
29	5 44	18 28	5 54	18 38	5 50	18 36	5 51	18 38	5 47	18 37	5 57	18 48	6 05	18 54
30	5 41	18 29	5 51	18 39	5 48	18 38	5 48	18 40	5 45	18 39	5 54	18 50	6 02	18 56
31	5 39	18 31	5 49	18 41	5 46	18 39	5 46	18 42	5 42	18 41	5 52	18 52	6 00	18 58

JUPITER

Day	RA	Dec.	Transit	5° high 52°	5° high 56°
	h m	° '	h m	h m	h m
1	8 50.2	+18 38	22 13	5 21	5 34
11	8 46.6	+18 52	21 30	4 40	4 53
21	8 44.2	+19 01	20 48	3 59	4 12
31	8 43.0	+19 05	20 08	3 19	3 32

Diameters - equatorial 43" polar 40"

SATURN

Day	RA	Dec.	Transit	5° high 52°	5° high 56°
	h m	° '	h m	h m	h m
1	5 26.2	+22 07	18 50	2 18	2 35
11	5 27.1	+22 10	18 11	1 40	1 57
21	5 28.9	+22 13	17 34	1 03	1 20
31	5 31.3	+22 17	16 57	0 27	0 44

Diameters - equatorial 18" polar 17"
Rings - major axis 42" minor axis 19"

URANUS

Day	RA	Dec.	Transit	10° high 52°	10° high 56°
	h m	° '	h m	h m	h m
1	22 07.3	-12 20	11 32	7 51	8 12
11	22 09.4	-12 08	10 55	7 13	7 33
21	22 11.5	-11 57	10 17	6 34	6 54
31	22 13.4	-11 47	9 40	5 55	6 16

Diameter 4"

NEPTUNE

Day	RA	Dec.	Transit	10° high 52°	10° high 56°
	h m	° '	h m	h m	h m
1	20 56.7	-17 14	10 22	7 17	7 49
11	20 58.1	-17 09	9 44	6 39	7 10
21	20 59.3	-17 04	9 05	6 00	6 31
31	21 00.3	-17 00	8 27	5 21	5 52

Diameter 2"

April 2003

FOURTH MONTH, 30 DAYS. *Aperire*, to open; Earth opens to receive seed

1	*Tuesday*	Prince Otto von Bismarck b. 1815. Jean Anderson d. 2001	91
2	*Wednesday*	HINDU NEW YEAR. Hans Christian Andersen b. 1805	92
3	*Thursday*	Graham Greene d. 1991. Jesse James d. 1882	93
4	*Friday*	Edgar Wallace b. 1875. Martin Luther King d. 1968	94
5	*Saturday*	Sir Nigel Hawthorne b. 1929. Georges Danton d. 1794	95
6	*Sunday*	**5th Sunday in Lent.** Sir John Betjeman b. 1906	96
7	*Monday*	William Wordsworth b. 1770. Henry Ford d. 1947	*week 14 day* 97
8	*Tuesday*	Sonja Henie b. 1912. Kurt Cobain d. 1994	98
9	*Wednesday*	Ian Duncan Smith b. 1954. Sir Robert Helpmann b. 1909	99
10	*Thursday*	General William Booth b. 1829. Evelyn Waugh d. 1966	100
11	*Friday*	George Canning b. 1770. Sir Harry Secombe d. 2001	101
12	*Saturday*	Franklin D. Roosevelt d. 1945. Sugar Ray Robinson d. 1989	102
13	*Sunday*	**Palm Sunday.** Sikh New Year.	103
14	*Monday*	Arnold Toynbee b. 1889. Ernest Bevin d. 1951	*week 15 day* 104
15	*Tuesday*	Benjamin Franklin d. 1790. John Singer Sargent d. 1925	105
16	*Wednesday*	*Hilary Law Sittings end.* Henry Mancini b. 1924	106
17	*Thursday*	**Maundy Thursday.** PASSOVER begins	107
18	*Friday*	**Good Friday.** *Bank Holiday in UK*	108
19	*Saturday*	Easter Eve. Battle of Lexington 1775	109
20	*Sunday*	**Easter Day.** (Western Churches). Odilon Redon b. 1840	110
21	*Monday*	*Bank Holiday in England, Wales and Northern Ireland.*	
		Queen Elizabeth II b. 1926	*week 16 day* 111
22	*Tuesday*	Kathleen Ferrier b. 1912. William Wordsworth d. 1850	112
23	*Wednesday*	**St George.** Roy Orbison b. 1936	113
24	*Thursday*	Stafford Cripps b. 1889. William Cowper d. 1800	114
25	*Friday*	**St Mark.** Michele Alboreto d. 2001	115
26	*Saturday*	Syngman Rhee b. 1875. Kwame Nkrumah d. 1972	116
27	*Sunday*	**1st S. after Easter.** EASTER DAY (Eastern Orthodox)	117
28	*Monday*	Anthony Ashley Cooper b. 1801. Ferruccio Lamborghini b. 1916	*week 17 day* 118
29	*Tuesday*	*Easter Law Sittings begin.* Adolf Hitler d. 1945	119
30	*Wednesday*	Mary II (Stuart) b. 1662. Edouard Manet d. 1883	120

ASTRONOMICAL PHENOMENA

d h
2 22 Mercury in conjunction with Moon. Mercury 4° N.
4 03 Jupiter at stationary point
7 22 Saturn in conjunction with Moon. Saturn 3° S.
11 10 Jupiter in conjunction with Moon. Jupiter 4° S.
16 15 Mercury at greatest elongation E.20°
20 12 Sun's longitude 30° ♉
23 08 Mars in conjunction with Moon. Mars 3° N.
26 12 Mercury at stationary point
28 19 Venus in conjunction with Moon. Venus 2° N.

MINIMA OF ALGOL

d	h	d	h	d	h
2	21.5	14	08.8	25	20.1
5	18.3	17	05.6	28	16.9
8	15.1	20	02.4		
11	12.0	22	23.2		

CONSTELLATIONS

The following constellations are near the meridian at

	d	h		d	h
March	1	24	April	15	21
March	16	23	May	1	20
April	1	22	May	16	19

Cepheus (below the Pole), Cassiopeia (below the Pole),
Ursa Major, Leo Minor, Leo, Sextans, Hydra and Crater

THE MOON

Phases, Apsides and Node	d	h	m
● New Moon	1	19	19
☽ First Quarter	9	23	40
○ Full Moon	16	19	36
☾ Last Quarter	23	12	18
Apogee (406,209 km)	4	04	30
Perigee (357,157 km)	17	04	56

Mean longitude of ascending node on April 1, 62°

THE SUN

s.d. 16'.0

Day	Right Ascension h m s	Dec. + ° '	Equation of Time m s	Rise 52° h m	Rise 56° h m	Transit h m	Set 52° h m	Set 56° h m	Sidereal time h m s	Transit of First Point of Aries h m s
1	0 39 54	4 18	− 4 08	5 36	5 32	12 04	18 33	18 37	12 35 46	11 22 22
2	0 43 33	4 41	− 3 51	5 34	5 29	12 04	18 35	18 39	12 39 42	11 18 26
3	0 47 12	5 04	− 3 33	5 31	5 27	12 03	18 36	18 41	12 43 39	11 14 30
4	0 50 51	5 27	− 3 15	5 29	5 24	12 03	18 38	18 43	12 47 36	11 10 34
5	0 54 30	5 50	− 2 58	5 27	5 21	12 03	18 40	18 45	12 51 32	11 06 38
6	0 58 09	6 13	− 2 41	5 25	5 19	12 03	18 42	18 47	12 55 29	11 02 42
7	1 01 49	6 35	− 2 24	5 22	5 16	12 02	18 43	18 50	12 59 25	10 58 47
8	1 05 29	6 58	− 2 07	5 20	5 14	12 02	18 45	18 52	13 03 22	10 54 51
9	1 09 08	7 20	− 1 50	5 18	5 11	12 02	18 47	18 54	13 07 18	10 50 55
10	1 12 49	7 43	− 1 34	5 16	5 09	12 01	18 48	18 56	13 11 15	10 46 59
11	1 16 29	8 05	− 1 17	5 13	5 06	12 01	18 50	18 58	13 15 11	10 43 03
12	1 20 10	8 27	− 1 02	5 11	5 03	12 01	18 52	19 00	13 19 08	10 39 07
13	1 23 50	8 49	− 0 46	5 09	5 01	12 01	18 54	19 02	13 23 05	10 35 11
14	1 27 32	9 11	− 0 31	5 07	4 58	12 00	18 55	19 04	13 27 01	10 31 15
15	1 31 13	9 32	− 0 15	5 04	4 56	12 00	18 57	19 06	13 30 58	10 27 19
16	1 34 55	9 54	− 0 01	5 02	4 53	12 00	18 59	19 08	13 34 54	10 23 23
17	1 38 37	10 15	+ 0 14	5 00	4 51	12 00	19 00	19 10	13 38 51	10 19 27
18	1 42 20	10 36	+ 0 28	4 58	4 48	11 59	19 02	19 12	13 42 47	10 15 32
19	1 46 03	10 57	+ 0 41	4 56	4 46	11 59	19 04	19 14	13 46 44	10 11 36
20	1 49 46	11 18	+ 0 54	4 54	4 43	11 59	19 05	19 16	13 50 40	10 07 40
21	1 53 30	11 39	+ 1 07	4 52	4 41	11 59	19 07	19 18	13 54 37	10 03 44
22	1 57 14	11 59	+ 1 19	4 49	4 38	11 59	19 09	19 20	13 58 34	9 59 48
23	2 00 59	12 19	+ 1 31	4 47	4 36	11 58	19 11	19 22	14 02 30	9 55 52
24	2 04 44	12 39	+ 1 43	4 45	4 34	11 58	19 12	19 24	14 06 27	9 51 56
25	2 08 30	12 59	+ 1 54	4 43	4 31	11 58	19 14	19 26	14 10 23	9 48 00
26	2 12 16	13 19	+ 2 04	4 41	4 29	11 58	19 16	19 28	14 14 20	9 44 04
27	2 16 02	13 38	+ 2 14	4 39	4 26	11 58	19 17	19 30	14 18 16	9 40 08
28	2 19 50	13 57	+ 2 23	4 37	4 24	11 58	19 19	19 32	14 22 13	9 36 12
29	2 23 37	14 16	+ 2 32	4 35	4 22	11 57	19 21	19 34	14 26 09	9 32 17
30	2 27 26	14 35	+ 2 40	4 33	4 19	11 57	19 22	19 36	14 30 06	9 28 21

DURATION OF TWILIGHT (in minutes)

Latitude	52°	56°	52°	56°	52°	56°	52°	56°
	1 April		11 April		21 April		30 April	
Civil	34	38	35	39	37	42	39	44
Nautical	76	84	79	89	83	96	89	106
Astronomical	120	136	127	147	137	165	152	204

THE NIGHT SKY

Mercury is at greatest eastern elongation (20°) on the 16th and this is the most favourable evening apparition of the planet in 2003. After the first couple of days in April it will be visible low in the western sky about the time of end of civil twilight for almost three weeks, magnitude −1.2 to +1.0.

Venus continues to be visible as a very bright object, magnitude −3.9. However, it can only be seen at a very low altitude above the east-south-east horizon for a very short while before dawn. Venus is near the old crescent Moon on the mornings of the 28th and 29th.

Mars, magnitude +0.3, is visible as a morning object, though it is still poorly placed for observation in the south-eastern quadrant of the sky because of its southerly declination. During the month Mars moves steadily eastwards from Sagittarius into Capricornus. On the morning of the 23rd the Moon, at Last Quarter, will be seen approaching the planet.

Jupiter continues to be visible as a bright object in the evening sky, magnitude −2.2, and can still be seen after midnight. Jupiter reaches its second stationary point on the 4th and then resumes its direct motion: it is in the constellation of Cancer. The gibbous Moon is near the planet on the 11th and 12th.

Saturn, magnitude +0.1, remains visible as an evening object in the western sky. Saturn is in the constellation of Taurus. On the evening of the 7th the waxing crescent Moon passes 2 degrees north of the planet. The rings of Saturn present a beautiful spectacle to the observer with a small telescope, particularly now that they are open to nearly their maximum extent.

THE MOON

Day	RA h m	Dec. °	Hor. par. '	Semi-diam. '	Sun's co-long. °	PA of Bright Limb °	Phase %	Age d	Rise 52° h m	Rise 56° h m	Transit h m	Set 52° h m	Set 56° h m
1	0 14	− 3.2	54.4	14.8	258	41	1	28.9	5 58	6 00	11 58	18 12	18 12
2	0 57	+ 2.1	54.2	14.8	270	307	0	0.2	6 10	6 08	12 38	19 21	19 26
3	1 40	+ 7.3	54.0	14.7	282	261	1	1.2	6 23	6 16	13 19	20 30	20 41
4	2 24	+12.2	54.0	14.7	295	256	4	2.2	6 37	6 25	14 00	21 41	21 56
5	3 09	+16.7	54.0	14.7	307	256	9	3.2	6 53	6 36	14 44	22 52	23 13
6	3 56	+20.5	54.2	14.8	319	258	15	4.2	7 14	6 52	15 30	—	—
7	4 46	+23.5	54.4	14.8	331	262	22	5.2	7 42	7 14	16 19	0 02	0 28
8	5 38	+25.5	54.9	15.0	344	267	31	6.2	8 19	7 48	17 11	1 08	1 39
9	6 33	+26.4	55.4	15.1	356	273	40	7.2	9 09	8 36	18 04	2 07	2 39
10	7 29	+25.9	56.2	15.3	8	279	50	8.2	10 12	9 42	18 59	2 55	3 26
11	8 25	+24.0	57.0	15.5	20	285	61	9.2	11 26	11 01	19 53	3 33	3 58
12	9 21	+20.8	57.9	15.8	32	290	71	10.2	12 48	12 30	20 46	4 01	4 21
13	10 16	+16.3	58.9	16.1	44	295	80	11.2	14 14	14 01	21 38	4 23	4 37
14	11 10	+10.8	59.8	16.3	57	299	89	12.2	15 41	15 35	22 29	4 42	4 50
15	12 03	+ 4.6	60.6	16.5	69	303	95	13.2	17 10	17 10	23 21	4 58	5 01
16	12 57	− 2.1	61.1	16.7	81	310	99	14.2	18 41	18 47	—	5 14	5 11
17	13 52	− 8.7	61.4	16.7	93	65	100	15.2	20 13	20 27	0 14	5 31	5 22
18	14 49	−14.8	61.3	16.7	105	103	98	16.2	21 47	22 07	1 09	5 51	5 36
19	15 49	−20.0	60.9	16.6	118	102	93	17.2	23 17	23 44	2 07	6 17	5 55
20	16 51	−23.8	60.2	16.4	130	98	86	18.2	—	—	3 08	6 52	6 24
21	17 54	−26.0	59.4	16.2	142	92	76	19.2	0 37	1 09	4 09	7 40	7 07
22	18 56	−26.4	58.5	15.9	154	86	66	20.2	1 40	2 14	5 10	8 41	8 08
23	19 56	−25.2	57.6	15.7	166	79	56	21.2	2 27	2 56	6 07	9 53	9 25
24	20 53	−22.7	56.7	15.5	178	74	45	22.2	3 00	3 23	7 01	11 10	10 47
25	21 45	−19.0	56.0	15.2	191	69	35	23.2	3 23	3 41	7 50	12 26	12 10
26	22 34	−14.7	55.3	15.1	203	65	26	24.2	3 41	3 53	8 35	13 40	13 29
27	23 20	− 9.8	54.8	14.9	215	63	18	25.2	3 55	4 03	9 17	14 52	14 46
28	0 04	− 4.6	54.5	14.8	227	61	11	26.2	4 08	4 11	9 58	16 02	16 01
29	0 47	+ 0.7	54.2	14.8	240	59	6	27.2	4 19	4 18	10 38	17 11	17 15
30	1 29	+ 6.0	54.0	14.7	252	58	2	28.2	4 31	4 25	11 18	18 20	18 29

MERCURY

Day	RA h m	Dec. °	Diam. "	Phase %	Transit h m	5° high 52° h m	5° high 56° h m
1	1 18	+ 8.5	5	91	12 44	18 59	19 04
3	1 32	+10.3	6	86	12 50	19 15	19 21
5	1 46	+12.0	6	81	12 56	19 30	19 37
7	1 59	+13.6	6	74	13 01	19 43	19 52
9	2 12	+15.1	6	67	13 06	19 55	20 05
11	2 23	+16.4	7	59	13 09	20 05	20 17
13	2 34	+17.6	7	52	13 11	20 14	20 26
15	2 43	+18.6	7	45	13 12	20 20	20 33
17	2 51	+19.3	8	38	13 12	20 23	20 37
19	2 58	+19.9	8	31	13 11	20 24	20 39
21	3 03	+20.3	9	25	13 08	20 23	20 38
23	3 07	+20.5	9	20	13 03	20 19	20 33
25	3 09	+20.5	10	15	12 57	20 12	20 26
27	3 10	+20.3	10	11	12 49	20 02	20 17
29	3 09	+20.0	11	7	12 40	19 51	20 05
31	3 07	+19.4	11	4	12 30	19 37	19 50

VENUS

Day	RA h m	Dec. °	Diam. "	Phase %	Transit h m	5° high 52° h m	5° high 56° h m
1	22 29	−10.4	13	80	9 53	5 22	5 35
6	22 52	− 8.4	13	81	9 57	5 13	5 24
11	23 15	− 6.2	13	82	10 00	5 04	5 13
16	23 37	− 4.0	12	84	10 02	4 55	5 02
21	23 59	− 1.7	12	85	10 05	4 46	4 51
26	0 22	+ 0.6	12	86	10 08	4 36	4 39
31	0 44	+ 2.9	12	87	10 10	4 27	4 28

MARS

Day	RA h m	Dec. °	Diam. "	Phase %	Transit h m	5° high 52° h m	5° high 56° h m
1	19 15	−23.0	8	88	6 38	3 35	4 10
6	19 28	−22.7	8	87	6 32	3 26	4 00
11	19 41	−22.3	8	87	6 26	3 17	3 49
16	19 54	−21.9	8	87	6 19	3 06	3 38
21	20 07	−21.4	9	87	6 12	2 56	3 26
26	20 20	−20.9	9	87	6 05	2 45	3 14
31	20 32	−20.4	9	87	5 58	2 33	3 01

SUNRISE AND SUNSET

Day	London 0°05' 51°30'		Bristol 2°35' 51°28'		Birmingham 1°55' 52°28'		Manchester 2°15' 53°28'		Newcastle 1°37' 54°59'		Glasgow 4°14' 55°52'		Belfast 5°56' 54°35'	
	h m	h m	h m	h m	h m	h m	h m	h m	h m	h m	h m	h m	h m	h m
1	5 37	18 33	5 47	18 43	5 43	18 41	5 44	18 43	5 40	18 43	5 49	18 54	5 57	18 59
2	5 35	18 35	5 45	18 44	5 41	18 43	5 41	18 45	5 37	18 45	5 46	18 56	5 55	19 01
3	5 32	18 36	5 42	18 46	5 39	18 45	5 39	18 47	5 34	18 47	5 44	18 58	5 52	19 03
4	5 30	18 38	5 40	18 48	5 36	18 46	5 36	18 49	5 32	18 48	5 41	19 00	5 50	19 05
5	5 28	18 40	5 38	18 50	5 34	18 48	5 34	18 51	5 29	18 50	5 39	19 02	5 47	19 07
6	5 26	18 41	5 36	18 51	5 32	18 50	5 32	18 53	5 27	18 52	5 36	19 04	5 45	19 09
7	5 23	18 43	5 33	18 53	5 29	18 52	5 29	18 54	5 24	18 54	5 33	19 06	5 42	19 11
8	5 21	18 45	5 31	18 55	5 27	18 53	5 27	18 56	5 22	18 56	5 31	19 08	5 40	19 13
9	5 19	18 46	5 29	18 56	5 25	18 55	5 24	18 58	5 19	18 58	5 28	19 10	5 37	19 15
10	5 17	18 48	5 27	18 58	5 22	18 57	5 22	19 00	5 17	19 00	5 26	19 12	5 35	19 17
11	5 14	18 50	5 25	19 00	5 20	18 59	5 20	19 02	5 14	19 02	5 23	19 14	5 32	19 19
12	5 12	18 51	5 22	19 01	5 18	19 00	5 17	19 04	5 12	19 04	5 21	19 16	5 30	19 20
13	5 10	18 53	5 20	19 03	5 16	19 02	5 15	19 05	5 09	19 06	5 18	19 18	5 28	19 22
14	5 08	18 55	5 18	19 05	5 13	19 04	5 13	19 07	5 07	19 08	5 16	19 20	5 25	19 24
15	5 06	18 56	5 16	19 06	5 11	19 06	5 10	19 09	5 05	19 10	5 13	19 22	5 23	19 26
16	5 04	18 58	5 14	19 08	5 09	19 07	5 08	19 11	5 02	19 12	5 10	19 25	5 20	19 28
17	5 01	19 00	5 12	19 10	5 07	19 09	5 06	19 13	5 00	19 14	5 08	19 27	5 18	19 30
18	4 59	19 01	5 09	19 11	5 05	19 11	5 04	19 14	4 57	19 16	5 06	19 29	5 16	19 32
19	4 57	19 03	5 07	19 13	5 02	19 13	5 01	19 16	4 55	19 18	5 03	19 31	5 13	19 34
20	4 55	19 05	5 05	19 15	5 00	19 14	4 59	19 18	4 53	19 20	5 01	19 33	5 11	19 36
21	4 53	19 06	5 03	19 16	4 58	19 16	4 57	19 20	4 50	19 22	4 58	19 35	5 09	19 38
22	4 51	19 08	5 01	19 18	4 56	19 18	4 55	19 22	4 48	19 23	4 56	19 37	5 06	19 40
23	4 49	19 10	4 59	19 20	4 54	19 19	4 52	19 24	4 46	19 25	4 53	19 39	5 04	19 42
24	4 47	19 11	4 57	19 21	4 52	19 21	4 50	19 25	4 43	19 27	4 51	19 41	5 02	19 43
25	4 45	19 13	4 55	19 23	4 50	19 23	4 48	19 27	4 41	19 29	4 49	19 43	4 59	19 45
26	4 43	19 15	4 53	19 25	4 48	19 25	4 46	19 29	4 39	19 31	4 46	19 45	4 57	19 47
27	4 41	19 16	4 51	19 26	4 45	19 26	4 44	19 31	4 36	19 33	4 44	19 47	4 55	19 49
28	4 39	19 18	4 49	19 28	4 43	19 28	4 42	19 33	4 34	19 35	4 41	19 49	4 53	19 51
29	4 37	19 20	4 47	19 29	4 41	19 30	4 40	19 34	4 32	19 37	4 39	19 51	4 51	19 53
30	4 35	19 21	4 45	19 31	4 39	19 32	4 38	19 36	4 30	19 39	4 37	19 53	4 48	19 55

JUPITER

Day	RA		Dec.		Transit		5° high 52°		56°	
	h	m	°	'	h	m	h	m	h	m
1	8	42.9	+19	06	20	04	3	15	3	28
11	8	43.2	+19	04	19	25	2	36	2	49
21	8	44.7	+18	58	18	47	1	57	2	10
31	8	47.3	+18	47	18	11	1	19	1	32

Diameters - equatorial 39" polar 37"

SATURN

Day	RA		Dec.		Transit		5° high 52°		56°	
	h	m	°	'	h	m	h	m	h	m
1	5	31.6	+22	17	16	53	0	23	0	40
11	5	34.8	+22	21	16	17	23	44	0	04
21	5	38.5	+22	25	15	42	23	09	23	26
31	5	42.8	+22	28	15	07	22	34	22	51

Diameters - equatorial 17" polar 16"
Rings - major axis 39" minor axis 18"

URANUS

Day	RA		Dec.		Transit		10° high 52°		56°	
	h	m	°	'	h	m	h	m	h	m
1	22	13.6	-11	46	9	36	5	52	6	12
11	22	15.3	-11	36	8	59	5	13	5	33
21	22	16.8	-11	28	8	21	4	34	4	54
31	22	18.0	-11	21	7	43	3	55	4	15

Diameter 4"

NEPTUNE

Day	RA		Dec.		Transit		10° high 52°		56°	
	h	m	°	'	h	m	h	m	h	m
1	21	00.4	-16	59	8	23	5	17	5	48
11	21	01.3	-16	56	7	45	4	38	5	09
21	21	01.9	-16	53	7	06	3	59	4	30
31	21	02.3	-16	52	6	27	3	20	3	50

Diameter 2"

May 2003

FIFTH MONTH, 31 DAYS. *Maia,* goddess of growth and increase

1	*Thursday*	**SS Philip and James.** Ayrton Senna d. 1994	121
2	*Friday*	Alessandro Scarlatti b. 1660. J. Edgar Hoover d. 1972	122
3	*Saturday*	Golda Meir b. 1898. Sugar Ray Robinson b. 1921	123
4	*Sunday*	**2nd S. of Easter.** Audrey Hepburn b. 1929	124
5	*Monday*	*Bank Holiday in UK.* Karl Marx b. 1818	*week* 18 *day* 125
6	*Tuesday*	Tony Blair b. 1953. Rudolph Valentino b. 1895	126
7	*Wednesday*	Johannes Brahms b. 1833. Robert Browning b. 1812	127
8	*Thursday*	Friedrich von Hayek b. 1899. John Stuart Mill d. 1873	128
9	*Friday*	Europe Day. Joan Sims b. 1930.	129
10	*Saturday*	Fred Astaire b. 1899. Joan Crawford d. 1977	130
11	*Sunday*	**3rd S. of Easter.** Douglas Adams d. 2001	131
12	*Monday*	Florence Nightingale b. 1820. John Masefield d. 1967	*week* 19 *day* 132
13	*Tuesday*	Joe Louis b. 1914. United Presbyterian Church of Scotland formed 1847	133
14	*Wednesday*	St Matthias. Eric Morecambe b. 1926	134
15	*Thursday*	Orson Welles b. 1915. Sir Robert Menzies d. 1978	135
16	*Friday*	Liberace b. 1919. Jim Henson d. 1990	136
17	*Saturday*	Edward Jenner b. 1749. Dennis Potter b. 1935	137
18	*Sunday*	**4th S. of Easter.** Pope John Paul II b. 1920	138
19	*Monday*	William Gladstone b. 1898. Sir John Betjeman d. 1994	*week* 20 *day* 139
20	*Tuesday*	Dame Barbara Hepworth d. 1975. First Chelsea Flower Show 1913	140
21	*Wednesday*	Elizabeth Fry b. 1780. Rajiv Gandhi d. 1983	141
22	*Thursday*	Victor Hugo d. 1885. Ceylon proclaimed itself a republic and changed name to Sri Lanka 1972	142
23	*Friday*	*Easter sittings end.* John D. Rockefeller d. 1937	143
24	*Saturday*	Victoria Hanover b. 1819. Samuel Palmer d. 1881	144
25	*Sunday*	**5th S. of Easter.** Miles Davis b. 1926	145
26	*Monday*	*Bank Holiday in UK.* Samuel Pepys d. 1703	*week* 21 *day* 146
27	*Tuesday*	Isadora Duncan b. 1878	147
28	*Wednesday*	Ian Fleming b. 1908. Sir Stephen Spender b. 1909	148
29	*Thursday*	**Ascension Day.** Mount Everest conquered 1953	149
30	*Friday*	Henry Addington b. 1757 Joan of Arc d.1431	150
31	*Saturday*	**Visit of the Virgin Mary to Elizabeth.** Sir Angus Wilson d. 1991	151

ASTRONOMICAL PHENOMENA

d h
2 05 Mercury in conjunction with Moon. Mercury 2° N.
5 09 Saturn in conjunction with Moon. Saturn 3° S.
7 07 Mercury in inferior conjunction (transit)
8 20 Jupiter in conjunction with Moon. Jupiter 4° S.
16 01 Neptune at stationary point
16 04 Total eclipse of Moon
20 08 Mercury at stationary point
21 11 Sun's longitude 60° Ⅱ
21 22 Mars in conjunction with Moon. Mars 3° N.
27 00 Venus in conjunction with Mercury. Venus 2° N.
29 01 Mercury in conjunction with Moon. Mercury 2° S.
29 04 Venus in conjunction with Moon. Venus 0°.1 S.
31 04 Annular eclipse of Sun

MINIMA OF ALGOL

Algol is inconveniently situated for observation during May

CONSTELLATIONS

The following constellations are near the meridian at

	d	h		d	h
April	1	24	May	16	21
April	15	23	June	1	20
May	1	22	June	15	19

Cepheus (below the Pole), Cassiopeia (below the Pole), Ursa Minor, Ursa Major, Canes Venatici, Coma Berenices, Bootes, Leo, Virgo, Crater, Corvus and Hydra

THE MOON

Phases, Apsides and Node	d	h	m
● New Moon	1	12	15
☽ First Quarter	9	11	53
○ Full Moon	16	03	36
☾ Last Quarter	23	00	31
● New Moon	31	04	20
Apogee (406,529 km)	1	07	38
Perigee (357,449 km)	15	15	38
Apogee (406,168 km)	28	13	05

Mean longitude of ascending node on May 1, 61°

THE SUN   s.d. 16'.0

Day	Right Ascension h m s	Dec. + ° '	Equation of Time m s	Rise 52° h m	Rise 56° h m	Transit h m	Set 52° h m	Set 56° h m	Sidereal time h m s	Transit of First Point of Aries h m s
1	2 31 14	14 53	+ 2 48	4 31	4 17	11 57	19 24	19 38	14 34 03	9 24 25
2	2 35 03	15 11	+ 2 56	4 29	4 15	11 57	19 26	19 40	14 37 59	9 20 29
3	2 38 53	15 29	+ 3 02	4 27	4 13	11 57	19 27	19 42	14 41 56	9 16 33
4	2 42 44	15 47	+ 3 09	4 26	4 11	11 57	19 29	19 44	14 45 52	9 04 45
5	2 46 35	16 04	+ 3 14	4 24	4 08	11 57	19 31	19 46	14 49 49	9 08 41
6	2 50 26	16 21	+ 3 19	4 22	4 06	11 57	19 32	19 48	14 53 45	9 04 45
7	2 54 18	16 38	+ 3 24	4 20	4 04	11 57	19 34	19 50	14 57 42	9 00 53
8	2 58 11	16 55	+ 3 28	4 18	4 02	11 57	19 36	19 52	15 01 38	8 56 53
9	3 02 04	17 11	+ 3 31	4 17	4 00	11 56	19 37	19 54	15 05 35	8 52 57
10	3 05 57	17 27	+ 3 34	4 15	3 52	11 56	19 44	20 02	15 21 21	8 37 14
11	3 09 51	17 43	+ 3 37	4 13	3 56	11 56	19 41	19 58	15 13 28	8 45 06
12	3 13 46	17 59	+ 3 38	4 12	3 54	11 56	19 42	20 00	15 17 25	8 41 10
13	3 17 41	18 14	+ 3 40	4 10	3 52	11 56	19 44	20 02	15 21 21	8 37 14
14	3 21 37	18 28	+ 3 41	4 07	3 48	11 56	19 47	20 06	15 29 14	8 29 22
15	3 25 34	18 43	+ 3 41	4 07	3 48	11 56	19 47	20 06	15 29 14	8 29 22
16	3 29 31	18 57	+ 3 40	4 05	3 46	11 56	19 48	20 08	15 33 11	8 25 26
17	3 33 28	19 11	+ 3 39	4 04	3 44	11 56	19 50	20 10	15 37 07	8 21 30
18	3 37 26	19 25	+ 3 38	4 02	3 43	11 56	19 51	20 11	15 41 04	8 17 34
19	3 41 25	19 38	+ 3 35	4 01	3 41	11 56	19 53	20 13	15 45 01	8 13 38
20	3 45 24	19 51	+ 3 33	4 00	3 39	11 56	19 54	20 15	15 48 57	8 09 42
21	3 49 24	20 03	+ 3 30	3 58	3 38	11 57	19 56	20 17	15 52 54	8 05 47
22	3 53 24	20 16	+ 3 26	3 57	3 36	11 57	19 57	20 18	15 56 50	8 01 51
23	3 57 25	20 27	+ 3 21	3 56	3 34	11 57	19 58	20 20	16 00 47	7 57 55
24	4 01 27	20 39	+ 3 17	3 55	3 33	11 57	20 00	20 22	16 04 43	7 53 59
25	4 05 29	20 50	+ 3 11	3 53	3 31	11 57	20 01	20 23	16 08 40	7 50 03
26	4 09 31	21 01	+ 3 05	3 52	3 30	11 57	20 03	20 25	16 12 36	7 46 07
27	4 13 34	21 11	+ 2 59	3 51	3 29	11 57	20 04	20 27	16 16 33	7 42 11
28	4 17 38	21 21	+ 2 52	3 50	3 27	11 57	20 05	20 28	16 20 30	7 38 15
29	4 21 42	21 31	+ 2 44	3 49	3 26	11 57	20 06	20 30	16 24 26	7 34 19
30	4 25 46	21 40	+ 2 37	3 48	3 25	11 57	20 08	20 31	16 28 23	7 30 23
31	4 29 51	21 49	+ 2 28	3 47	3 24	11 58	20 09	20 33	16 32 19	7 26 27

DURATION OF TWILIGHT (in minutes)

Latitude	52°	56°	52°	56°	52°	56°	52°	56°
	1 May		11 May		21 May		31 May	
Civil	39	44	41	48	44	53	46	57
Nautical	89	106	97	120	106	141	115	187
Astronomical	152	204	176	TAN	TAN	TAN	TAN	TAN

THE NIGHT SKY

Mercury is too close to the Sun to be visible in either the early evenings or early mornings during the month. However a transit of the planet across the face of the Sun occurs on the 7th, visible from the British Isles.

Venus, magnitude –3.9, continues to be visible as a bright object, visible at a very low altitude above the eastern horizon for a very short time before dawn. Conditions for detecting the planet are quite critical and observers in northern parts of the British Isles are unlikely to see it at all. On the morning of the 29th Venus will be seen close to the upper edge of the Moon. At sunrise Venus will actually be only 0.5 degrees from the upper edge of the Moon.

Mars is beginning to brighten noticeably during the month, its magnitude changing from 0.0 to –0.7. It continues to be visible in the south-eastern sky in the mornings. The gibbous Moon is near the planet on the mornings of the 21st and 22nd. Mars is in the constellation of Capricornus.

Jupiter, magnitude –2.0, continues to be visible as a brilliant object in the western sky in the evenings. By the end of the month it is lost to view over the western horizon before midnight. On the evening of the 8th the Moon, near First Quarter, passes about 3 degrees north of the planet.

Saturn is now coming towards the end of its evening apparition, only being visible for a short time low in the western sky. Its magnitude is +0.1. It is unlikely to be seen after the middle of the month.

THE MOON

Day	RA h	RA m	Dec. °	Hor. par.	Semi-diam. ′	Sun's co-long. °	PA of Bright Limb °	Phase %	Age d	Rise 52° h	Rise 52° m	Rise 56° h	Rise 56° m	Transit h	Transit m	Set 52° h	Set 52° m	Set 56° h	Set 56° m
1	2	13	+11.0	53.9	14.7	264	49	0	29.2	4	44	4	34	11	59	19	30	19	44
2	2	57	+15.6	54.0	14.7	276	266	0	0.5	5	00	4	44	12	42	20	41	21	01
3	3	44	+19.7	54.1	14.7	288	258	2	1.5	5	19	4	58	13	27	21	52	22	17
4	4	33	+22.9	54.3	14.8	301	260	5	2.5	5	44	5	18	14	16	23	00	23	30
5	5	25	+25.2	54.6	14.9	313	264	11	3.5	6	17	5	47	15	06	—		—	
6	6	19	+26.4	55.0	15.0	325	269	17	4.5	7	02	6	29	15	59	0	02	0	35
7	7	14	+26.3	55.5	15.1	337	275	25	5.5	8	00	7	28	16	52	0	53	1	25
8	8	09	+24.8	56.1	15.3	350	281	35	6.5	9	10	8	42	17	45	1	34	2	02
9	9	04	+22.1	56.9	15.5	2	286	45	7.5	10	27	10	05	18	37	2	04	2	27
10	9	57	+18.1	57.7	15.7	14	291	56	8.5	11	48	11	33	19	27	2	28	2	44
11	10	50	+13.1	58.6	16.0	26	294	66	9.5	13	12	13	03	20	17	2	47	2	57
12	11	42	+ 7.2	59.5	16.2	38	296	77	10.5	14	37	14	34	21	07	3	03	3	08
13	12	34	+ 0.9	60.3	16.4	51	297	86	11.5	16	05	16	08	21	58	3	18	3	18
14	13	27	− 5.7	60.9	16.6	63	297	93	12.5	17	35	17	45	22	51	3	34	3	28
15	14	23	−12.1	61.3	16.7	75	296	98	13.5	19	09	19	25	23	48	3	52	3	40
16	15	21	−17.8	61.3	16.7	87	301	100	14.5	20	43	21	07	—		4	14	3	56
17	16	23	−22.3	61.0	16.6	99	103	99	15.5	22	11	22	42	0	48	4	44	4	19
18	17	27	−25.3	60.5	16.5	112	98	95	16.5	23	26	23	59	1	51	5	26	4	55
19	18	32	−26.5	59.7	16.3	124	91	89	17.5	—		—		2	54	6	23	5	49
20	19	35	−25.9	58.8	16.0	136	84	80	18.5	0	22	0	53	3	56	7	34	7	03
21	20	35	−23.7	57.8	15.7	148	78	71	19.5	1	01	1	27	4	53	8	52	8	27
22	21	30	−20.3	56.9	15.5	160	73	61	20.5	1	28	1	48	5	45	10	11	9	52
23	22	21	−16.0	56.0	15.3	172	69	50	21.5	1	48	2	02	6	32	11	27	11	15
24	23	08	−11.1	55.3	15.1	185	66	40	22.5	2	04	2	13	7	16	12	41	12	33
25	23	53	− 6.0	54.8	14.9	197	65	31	23.5	2	17	2	21	7	57	13	51	13	49
26	0	36	− 0.6	54.4	14.8	209	64	22	24.5	2	28	2	28	8	37	15	01	15	03
27	1	19	+ 4.6	54.1	14.7	221	65	15	25.5	2	40	2	36	9	17	16	10	16	17
28	2	02	+ 9.7	54.0	14.7	234	66	9	26.5	2	52	2	44	9	58	17	19	17	31
29	2	46	+14.5	54.0	14.7	246	69	4	27.5	3	07	2	53	10	40	18	30	18	48
30	3	32	+18.7	54.1	14.7	258	74	1	28.5	3	24	3	06	11	25	19	42	20	05
31	4	21	+22.2	54.3	14.8	270	100	0	29.5	3	47	3	23	12	12	20	52	21	20

MERCURY

Day	RA h	RA m	Dec. °	Diam. ″	Phase %	Transit h	Transit m	52° high h	52° high m	56° high h	56° high m
1	3	07	+19.4	11	4	12	30	19	37	19	50
3	3	04	+18.7	12	2	12	19	19	22	19	34
5	3	00	+17.9	12	1	12	07	19	05	19	17
7	2	56	+17.1	12	0	11	55	5	01	4	50
9	2	52	+16.1	12	0	11	43	4	54	4	44
11	2	48	+15.2	12	1	11	31	4	47	4	37
13	2	44	+14.4	12	3	11	20	4	40	4	31
15	2	41	+13.6	12	5	11	10	4	33	4	25
17	2	39	+13.0	11	8	11	00	4	27	4	20
19	2	39	+12.5	11	11	10	52	4	21	4	14
21	2	39	+12.2	11	14	10	44	4	15	4	08
23	2	40	+12.1	10	18	10	38	4	09	4	03
25	2	42	+12.1	10	21	10	33	4	04	3	57
27	2	46	+12.2	10	25	10	29	3	59	3	52
29	2	50	+12.5	9	28	10	25	3	54	3	47
31	2	56	+12.9	9	32	10	23	3	49	3	42

VENUS

Day	RA h	RA m	Dec. °	Diam. ″	Phase %	Transit h	Transit m	52° high h	52° high m	56° high h	56° high m
1	0	44	+ 2.9	12	87	10	10	4	27	4	28
6	1	06	+ 5.2	12	88	10	13	4	18	4	17
11	1	29	+ 7.5	11	89	10	16	4	09	4	06
16	1	52	+ 9.7	11	90	10	19	4	01	3	56
21	2	15	+11.9	11	91	10	22	3	53	3	47
26	2	38	+13.9	11	92	10	26	3	46	3	38
31	3	02	+15.8	11	93	10	30	3	40	3	30

MARS

Day	RA h	RA m	Dec. °	Diam. ″	Phase %	Transit h	Transit m	52° high h	52° high m	56° high h	56° high m
1	20	32	−20.4	9	87	5	58	2	33	3	01
6	20	45	−19.8	10	87	5	51	2	21	2	48
11	20	57	−19.2	10	87	5	43	2	09	2	35
16	21	08	−18.6	11	87	5	35	1	57	2	21
21	21	19	−18.0	11	87	5	26	1	44	2	07
26	21	30	−17.3	12	87	5	17	1	31	1	53
31	21	41	−16.7	12	87	5	08	1	17	1	38

SUNRISE AND SUNSET

	London 0°05′ 51°30′		Bristol 2°35′ 51°28′		Birmingham 1°55′ 52°28′		Manchester 2°15′ 53°28′		Newcastle 1°37′ 54°59′		Glasgow 4°14′ 55°52′		Belfast 5°56′ 54°35′	
	h m	h m	h m	h m	h m	h m	h m	h m	h m	h m	h m	h m	h m	h m
1	4 33	19 23	4 43	19 33	4 37	19 33	4 35	19 38	4 28	19 41	4 35	19 55	4 46	19 57
2	4 31	19 24	4 41	19 34	4 35	19 35	4 33	19 40	4 25	19 43	4 32	19 57	4 44	19 59
3	4 29	19 26	4 40	19 36	4 34	19 37	4 31	19 42	4 23	19 45	4 30	19 59	4 42	20 01
4	4 28	19 28	4 38	19 38	4 32	19 38	4 29	19 43	4 21	19 47	4 28	20 01	4 40	20 02
5	4 26	19 29	4 36	19 39	4 30	19 40	4 27	19 45	4 19	19 49	4 26	20 03	4 38	20 04
6	4 24	19 31	4 34	19 41	4 28	19 42	4 26	19 47	4 17	19 50	4 24	20 05	4 36	20 06
7	4 22	19 33	4 32	19 42	4 26	19 43	4 24	19 49	4 15	19 52	4 22	20 07	4 34	20 08
8	4 21	19 34	4 31	19 44	4 24	19 45	4 22	19 50	4 13	19 54	4 19	20 09	4 32	20 10
9	4 19	19 36	4 29	19 46	4 23	19 47	4 20	19 52	4 11	19 56	4 17	20 11	4 30	20 12
10	4 17	19 37	4 27	19 47	4 21	19 48	4 18	19 54	4 09	19 58	4 15	20 13	4 28	20 13
11	4 16	19 39	4 26	19 49	4 19	19 50	4 16	19 56	4 07	20 00	4 13	20 15	4 26	20 15
12	4 14	19 40	4 24	19 50	4 17	19 52	4 15	19 57	4 05	20 02	4 11	20 16	4 24	20 17
13	4 12	19 42	4 22	19 52	4 16	19 53	4 13	19 59	4 03	20 03	4 09	20 18	4 23	20 19
14	4 11	19 44	4 21	19 53	4 14	19 55	4 11	20 01	4 02	20 05	4 08	20 20	4 21	20 21
15	4 09	19 45	4 19	19 55	4 13	19 56	4 09	20 02	4 00	20 07	4 06	20 22	4 19	20 22
16	4 08	19 47	4 18	19 56	4 11	19 58	4 08	20 04	3 58	20 09	4 04	20 24	4 17	20 24
17	4 06	19 48	4 16	19 58	4 09	20 00	4 06	20 06	3 56	20 11	4 02	20 26	4 16	20 26
18	4 05	19 49	4 15	19 59	4 08	20 01	4 05	20 07	3 55	20 12	4 00	20 28	4 14	20 27
19	4 04	19 51	4 14	20 01	4 07	20 03	4 03	20 09	3 53	20 14	3 59	20 29	4 12	20 29
20	4 02	19 52	4 12	20 02	4 05	20 04	4 02	20 10	3 51	20 16	3 57	20 31	4 11	20 31
21	4 01	19 54	4 11	20 04	4 04	20 06	4 00	20 12	3 50	20 17	3 55	20 33	4 09	20 32
22	4 00	19 55	4 10	20 05	4 02	20 07	3 59	20 13	3 48	20 19	3 54	20 35	4 08	20 34
23	3 58	19 56	4 09	20 06	4 01	20 08	3 58	20 15	3 47	20 21	3 52	20 36	4 06	20 36
24	3 57	19 58	4 07	20 08	4 00	20 10	3 56	20 16	3 45	20 22	3 51	20 38	4 05	20 37
25	3 56	19 59	4 06	20 09	3 59	20 11	3 55	20 18	3 44	20 24	3 49	20 40	4 04	20 39
26	3 55	20 00	4 05	20 10	3 58	20 13	3 54	20 19	3 43	20 25	3 48	20 41	4 02	20 40
27	3 54	20 02	4 04	20 12	3 56	20 14	3 53	20 20	3 41	20 27	3 46	20 43	4 01	20 42
28	3 53	20 03	4 03	20 33	3 55	20 15	3 51	20 22	3 40	20 28	3 45	20 44	4 00	20 43
29	3 52	20 04	4 02	20 14	3 54	20 16	3 50	20 23	3 39	20 30	3 44	20 46	3 59	20 44
30	3 51	20 05	4 01	20 15	3 53	20 18	3 49	20 24	3 38	20 31	3 43	20 47	3 57	20 46
31	3 50	20 06	4 00	20 16	3 52	20 19	3 48	20 26	3 37	20 32	3 41	20 49	3 56	20 47

JUPITER

Day	RA	Dec.	Transit	5° high 52°	5° high 56°
	h m	° ′	h m	h m	h m
1	8 47.3	+18 47	18 11	1 19	1 32
11	8 51.1	+18 31	17 35	0 42	0 55
21	8 55.8	+18 11	17 00	0 06	0 18
31	9 01.3	+17 48	16 27	23 26	23 38

Diameters - equatorial 36″ polar 33″

SATURN

Day	RA	Dec.	Transit	5° high 52°	5° high 56°
	h m	° ′	h m	h m	h m
1	5 42.8	+22 28	15 07	22 34	22 51
11	5 47.5	+22 32	14 32	22 00	22 17
21	5 52.5	+22 34	13 58	21 26	21 43
31	5 57.8	+22 36	13 24	20 52	21 09

Diameters - equatorial 17″ polar 15″
Rings - major axis 38″ minor axis 17″

URANUS

Day	RA	Dec.	Transit	10° high 52°	10° high 56°
	h m	° ′	h m	h m	h m
1	22 18.0	−11 21	7 43	3 55	4 15
11	22 19.0	−11 16	7 04	3 16	3 36
21	22 19.7	−11 13	6 26	2 37	2 57
31	22 20.1	−11 11	5 47	1 58	2 18

Diameter 4″

NEPTUNE

Day	RA	Dec.	Transit	10° high 52°	10° high 56°
	h m	° ′	h m	h m	h m
1	21 02.3	−16 52	6 27	3 20	3 50
11	21 02.6	−16 51	5 48	2 41	3 11
21	21 02.6	−16 51	5 09	2 01	2 32
31	21 02.4	−16 52	4 29	1 22	1 53

Diameter 2″

June 2003

SIXTH MONTH, 30 DAYS. *Junius*, Roman *gens* (family)

1	*Sunday*	S. after Ascension (6th S. of Easter). Marilyn Monroe b. 1926	152
2	*Monday*	Coronation Day 1953. Sir Edward Elgar b. 1857	*week* 22 *day* 153
3	*Tuesday*	Trinity Law Sittings begin. Arthur Ransome d. 1967	154
4	*Wednesday*	First trooping the Colour ceremony took place on Horse Guards Parade, London 1805	155
5	*Thursday*	Igor Stravinsky b. 1882. Paul Gauguin b. 1848	156
6	*Friday*	FEAST OF WEEKS begins. George Orwell's Nineteen Eighty-Four published 1949	157
7	*Saturday*	Sir John Millais b. 1829. Dennis Potter d. 1994	158
8	*Sunday*	Pentecost (Whit Sunday). Sir Joseph Paxton d. 1865	159
9	*Monday*	Judy Garland b. 1922. Charles Dickens d. 1870	*week* 23 *day* 160
10	*Tuesday*	Duke of Edinburgh b. 1921. Spencer Tracy d. 1967	161
11	*Wednesday*	St Barnabas. Dame Catherine Cookson d. 1998	162
12	*Thursday*	Dr Thomas Arnold d. 1842	163
13	*Friday*	Harriet Beecher Stowe b. 1811. Benny Goodman d. 1986	164
14	*Saturday*	Rt. Revd Trevor Huddleston b. 1913. Henry Mancini d. 1994	165
15	*Sunday*	Trinity Sunday. Stan Laurel b. 1890	166
16	*Monday*	Wallis Simpson b. 1896. Earl Alexander of Tunis d. 1969	*week* 24 *day* 167
17	*Tuesday*	Beryl Reid b. 1920. Battle of Bunker Hill 1775	168
18	*Wednesday*	Roald Amundsen b. 1928. Battle of Waterloo 1815	169
19	*Thursday*	Field Marshal Haig b. 1861. Sir William Golding d. 1993	170
20	*Friday*	Errol Flynn b. 1909. Sir Charles Groves d. 1992	171
21	*Saturday*	Prince William of Wales b. 1982. German fleet scuttled at Scapa Flow 1919	172
22	*Sunday*	1st S. after Trinity. Anna Akhmatova b. 1889	173
23	*Monday*	Gustave Charpentier b. 1860. Sir Leonard Hutton d. 1916	*week* 25 *day* 174
24	*Tuesday*	John the Baptist. George Orwell b. 1903	175
25	*Wednesday*	Robert Erskine Childers b. 1870. Earl Mountbatten of Burma b. 1900	176
26	*Thursday*	Salvador Allende b. 1908. Samuel Crompton d. 1827	177
27	*Friday*	Helen Keller b. 1880. Harriet Martineau d. 1876	178
28	*Saturday*	Ruskin Spear b. 1911. Coronation of Queen Victoria 1838	179
29	*Sunday*	2nd S. after Trinity. SS Peter and Paul.	180
30	*Monday*	Stanley Spencer b. 1891. Night of the Long Knives 1934	*week* 26 *day* 181

ASTRONOMICAL PHENOMENA

d h
1 21 Saturn in conjunction with Moon. Saturn 4° S.
3 06 Mercury at greatest elongation W.24°
5 09 Jupiter in conjunction with Moon. Jupiter 4° S.
7 07 Uranus at stationary point
9 21 Pluto at opposition
19 08 Mars in conjunction with Moon. Mars 2° N.
21 04 Venus in conjunction with Mercury. Venus 0°.4 N.
21 19 Sun's longitude 90° ♋
24 14 Saturn in conjunction
28 13 Venus in conjunction with Moon. Venus 2° S.
29 03 Mercury in conjunction with Moon. Mercury 2° S.
29 10 Saturn in conjunction with Moon. Saturn 4° S.

MINIMA OF ALGOL

Algol is inconveniently situated for observation during June

CONSTELLATIONS

The following constellations are near the meridian at

d	h		d	h
May	1	24	June	15	21
May	16	23	July	1	20
June	1	22	July	16	19

Cassiopeia (below the Pole), Ursa Minor, Draco, Ursa Major, Canes Venatici, Bootes, Corona, Serpens, Virgo and Libra

THE MOON

Phases, Apsides and Node	d	h	m
☽ First Quarter	7	20	28
○ Full Moon	14	11	16
☾ Last Quarter	21	14	45
● New Moon	29	18	39
Perigee (360,425 km)	12	23	17
Apogee (405,232 km)	25	02	24

Mean longitude of ascending node on June 1, 59°

THE SUN s.d. 15′.8

Day	Right Ascension h m s	Dec. + ° ′	Equation of Time m s	Rise 52° h m	Rise 56° h m	Transit h m	Set 52° h m	Set 56° h m	Sidereal time h m s	Transit of First Point of Aries h m s
1	4 33 56	21 58	+2 19	3 46	3 22	11 58	20 10	20 34	16 36 16	7 22 32
2	4 38 02	22 06	+2 10	3 46	3 21	11 58	20 11	20 35	16 40 12	7 18 36
3	4 42 08	22 14	+2 01	3 45	3 20	11 58	20 12	20 37	16 44 09	7 14 40
4	4 46 15	22 21	+1 51	3 44	3 19	11 58	20 13	20 38	16 48 05	7 10 44
5	4 50 21	22 29	+1 41	3 43	3 19	11 58	20 14	20 39	16 52 02	7 06 48
6	4 54 29	22 35	+1 30	3 43	3 18	11 59	20 15	20 40	16 55 59	7 02 52
7	4 58 36	22 41	+1 19	3 42	3 17	11 59	20 16	20 41	16 59 55	6 58 56
8	5 02 44	22 47	+1 08	3 42	3 16	11 59	20 17	20 42	17 03 52	6 55 00
9	5 06 52	22 53	+0 57	3 41	3 16	11 59	20 18	20 43	17 07 48	6 51 04
10	5 11 00	22 58	+0 45	3 41	3 15	11 59	20 18	20 44	17 11 45	6 47 08
11	5 15 08	23 02	+0 33	3 40	3 15	12 00	20 19	20 45	17 15 41	6 43 12
12	5 19 17	23 07	+0 21	3 40	3 14	12 00	20 20	20 46	17 19 38	6 39 16
13	5 23 26	23 10	+0 09	3 40	3 14	12 00	20 20	20 47	17 23 34	6 35 21
14	5 27 35	23 14	−0 03	3 40	3 13	12 00	20 21	20 47	17 27 31	6 31 25
15	5 31 44	23 17	−0 16	3 39	3 13	12 00	20 22	20 48	17 31 28	6 27 29
16	5 35 53	23 19	−0 29	3 39	3 13	12 01	20 22	20 48	17 35 24	6 23 33
17	5 40 02	23 22	−0 42	3 39	3 13	12 01	20 22	20 49	17 39 21	6 19 37
18	5 44 12	23 23	−0 54	3 39	3 13	12 01	20 23	20 49	17 43 17	6 15 41
19	5 48 21	23 25	−1 07	3 39	3 13	12 01	20 23	20 50	17 47 14	6 11 45
20	5 52 31	23 26	−1 20	3 39	3 13	12 01	20 23	20 50	17 51 10	6 07 49
21	5 56 40	23 26	−1 33	3 40	3 13	12 02	20 24	20 50	17 55 07	6 03 53
22	6 00 50	23 26	−1 46	3 40	3 13	12 02	20 24	20 51	17 59 04	5 59 57
23	6 05 00	23 26	−2 00	3 40	3 13	12 02	20 24	20 51	18 03 00	5 56 01
24	6 09 09	23 25	−2 13	3 40	3 14	12 02	20 24	20 51	18 06 57	5 52 06
25	6 13 19	23 24	−2 25	3 41	3 14	12 03	20 24	20 51	18 10 53	5 48 10
26	6 17 28	23 23	−2 38	3 41	3 15	12 03	20 24	20 51	18 14 50	5 44 14
27	6 21 37	23 21	−2 51	3 42	3 15	12 03	20 24	20 50	18 18 46	5 40 18
28	6 25 46	23 18	−3 04	3 42	3 16	12 03	20 24	20 50	18 22 43	5 36 22
29	6 29 55	23 16	−3 16	3 43	3 16	12 03	20 24	20 50	18 26 39	5 32 26
30	6 34 04	23 13	−3 28	3 43	3 17	12 04	20 24	20 50	18 30 36	5 28 30

DURATION OF TWILIGHT (in minutes)

Latitude	52°	56°	52°	56°	52°	56°	52°	56°
	1 June		11 June		21 June		30 June	
Civil	46	58	48	61	49	63	48	61
Nautical	116	TAN	124	TAN	127	TAN	124	TAN
Astronomical	TAN	TAN	TAN	TAN	TAN	TAN	TAN	TAN

THE NIGHT SKY

Mercury, despite the fact that it is at western elongation on the 3rd, remains too close to the Sun for observation throughout June.

Venus continues to be a bright object though only visible to observers in southern England for a few minutes before dawn, very low above the east-north-east horizon. Its magnitude is −3.9.

Mars is still a morning object, its magnitude brightening from −0.7 to −1.4 during the month. By the end of June Mars can be seen as early as midnight low in the south-eastern sky. Mars moves from Capricornus into Aquarius during the month. On the morning of the 19th the gibbous Moon will be seen approaching the planet. The slight reddish tinge in its colour is an aid to its identification.

Jupiter, magnitude −1.8, is still a brilliant object in the western sky in the evenings. Jupiter is in the constellation of

Cancer. The crescent Moon is near the planet on the 4th-5th.

Saturn remains unsuitably placed for observation throughout the month, as it passes through conjunction on the 24th. However it is of interest to note that between mid-May and mid-July Saturn passes through three constellations: it passes from Taurus, through the extreme northern part of Orion and then into Gemini.

Twilight. Reference to the section above shows that astronomical twilight lasts all night for a period around the summer solstice (i.e. in June and July), even in southern England. Under these conditions the sky never gets completely dark as the Sun is always less than 18 degrees below the horizon.

THE MOON

Day	RA h m	Dec. °	Hor. par. ′	Semi-diam. ′	Sun's co-long. °	PA of Bright Limb °	Phase %	Age d	Rise 52° h m	Rise 56° h m	Transit h m	Set 52° h m	Set 56° h m
1	5 12	+24.8	54.5	14.9	283	254	1	0.8	4 18	3 49	13 03	21 56	22 28
2	6 06	+26.2	54.9	15.0	295	263	3	1.8	5 00	4 27	13 55	22 51	23 24
3	7 01	+26.4	55.3	15.1	307	270	8	2.8	5 54	5 21	14 48	23 35	—
4	7 56	+25.3	55.8	15.2	319	276	14	3.8	7 00	6 31	15 41	—	0 04
5	8 51	+22.8	56.3	15.3	332	282	21	4.8	8 14	7 51	16 33	0 08	0 32
6	9 44	+19.2	57.0	15.5	344	287	31	5.8	9 33	9 16	17 23	0 33	0 51
7	10 36	+14.5	57.6	15.7	356	291	41	6.8	10 54	10 43	18 11	0 53	1 05
8	11 26	+ 9.0	58.4	15.9	8	293	52	7.8	12 16	12 11	18 59	1 09	1 16
9	12 17	+ 3.0	59.1	16.1	20	295	63	8.8	13 39	13 40	19 48	1 24	1 26
10	13 08	− 3.3	59.8	16.3	33	294	74	9.8	15 05	15 12	20 38	1 39	1 36
11	14 01	− 9.6	60.3	16.4	45	292	83	10.8	16 35	16 48	21 31	1 55	1 46
12	14 56	−15.5	60.7	16.5	57	288	91	11.8	18 07	18 27	22 29	2 14	1 59
13	15 56	−20.5	60.8	16.6	69	281	97	12.8	19 38	20 06	23 30	2 39	2 18
14	16 59	−24.2	60.7	16.5	81	263	100	13.8	21 01	21 34	—	3 15	2 46
15	18 04	−26.2	60.3	16.4	94	110	100	14.8	22 08	22 41	0 34	4 04	3 31
16	19 09	−26.3	59.6	16.2	106	93	97	15.8	22 56	23 24	1 37	5 10	4 37
17	20 11	−24.7	58.8	16.0	118	84	91	16.8	23 29	23 51	2 38	6 27	5 59
18	21 10	−21.6	57.9	15.8	130	78	84	17.8	23 52	—	3 34	7 48	7 27
19	22 03	−17.5	57.0	15.5	142	73	75	18.8	—	0 09	4 25	9 08	8 53
20	22 53	−12.7	56.1	15.3	155	69	66	19.8	0 10	0 21	5 11	10 25	10 15
21	23 39	− 7.5	55.4	15.1	167	67	56	20.8	0 24	0 30	5 54	11 38	11 34
22	0 23	− 2.1	54.9	14.9	179	66	46	21.8	0 36	0 38	6 35	12 48	12 49
23	1 06	+ 3.2	54.4	14.8	191	67	37	22.8	0 48	0 45	7 15	13 58	14 03
24	1 49	+ 8.4	54.2	14.8	204	68	28	23.8	1 00	0 53	7 55	15 07	15 18
25	2 33	+13.3	54.1	14.7	216	71	20	24.8	1 13	1 02	8 37	16 18	16 33
26	3 19	+17.6	54.2	14.8	228	74	13	25.8	1 30	1 13	9 21	17 29	17 50
27	4 07	+21.3	54.3	14.8	240	80	7	26.8	1 51	1 29	10 08	18 40	19 07
28	4 58	+24.2	54.6	14.9	252	88	3	27.8	2 19	1 51	10 57	19 47	20 18
29	5 51	+25.9	55.0	15.0	265	105	1	28.8	2 57	2 25	11 50	20 46	21 19
30	6 46	+26.4	55.4	15.1	277	221	0	0.2	3 47	3 14	12 43	21 34	22 05

MERCURY

Day	RA h m	Dec. °	Diam. ″	Phase %	Transit h m	5° high 52° h m	5° high 56° h m
1	2 59	+13.1	9	34	10 22	3 47	3 39
3	3 06	+13.7	8	37	10 21	3 43	3 35
5	3 13	+14.4	8	41	10 21	3 39	3 30
7	3 22	+15.1	8	45	10 22	3 36	3 26
9	3 31	+15.9	7	49	10 24	3 33	3 23
11	3 42	+16.8	7	54	10 27	3 31	3 20
13	3 53	+17.7	7	58	10 30	3 29	3 17
15	4 05	+18.6	6	63	10 35	3 28	3 15
17	4 18	+19.5	6	67	10 40	3 28	3 14
19	4 32	+20.4	6	72	10 47	3 29	3 14
21	4 47	+21.3	6	77	10 54	3 31	3 15
23	5 03	+22.1	6	82	11 02	3 35	3 18
25	5 20	+22.8	5	87	11 11	3 39	3 21
27	5 38	+23.4	5	91	11 21	3 45	3 27
29	5 56	+23.9	5	95	11 32	3 53	3 34
31	6 15	+24.1	5	98	11 43	4 02	3 43

VENUS

Day	RA h m	Dec. °	Diam. ″	Phase %	Transit h m	5° high 52° h m	5° high 56° h m
1	3 07	+16.2	11	93	10 31	3 39	3 29
6	3 32	+17.8	11	94	10 36	3 34	3 22
11	3 56	+19.4	10	95	10 41	3 31	3 17
16	4 22	+20.7	10	95	10 47	3 29	3 14
21	4 48	+21.7	10	96	10 53	3 29	3 12
26	5 14	+22.5	10	97	10 59	3 30	3 13
31	5 40	+23.1	10	97	11 06	3 33	3 15

MARS

Day	RA h m	Dec. °	Diam. ″	Phase %	Transit h m	5° high 52° h m	5° high 56° h m
1	21 43	−16.6	12	87	5 06	1 14	1 35
6	21 53	−16.0	13	87	4 57	1 01	1 21
11	22 03	−15.4	14	88	4 46	0 47	1 06
16	22 12	−14.9	14	88	4 36	0 33	0 51
21	22 20	−14.4	15	89	4 24	0 18	0 36
26	22 28	−14.0	16	89	4 12	0 04	0 21
31	22 35	−13.6	17	90	4 00	23 46	0 05

SUNRISE AND SUNSET

	London 0°05' 51°30'		Bristol 2°35' 51°28'		Birmingham 1°55' 52°28'		Manchester 2°15' 53°28'		Newcastle 1°37' 54°59'		Glasgow 4°14' 55°52'		Belfast 5°56' 54°35'	
	h m	h m	h m	h m	h m	h m	h m	h m	h m	h m	h m	h m	h m	h m
1	3 49	20 08	3 59	20 17	3 52	20 20	3 47	20 27	3 36	20 34	3 40	20 50	3 55	20 48
2	3 48	20 09	3 59	20 18	3 51	20 21	3 46	20 28	3 35	20 35	3 39	20 51	3 54	20 50
3	3 48	20 10	3 58	20 20	3 50	20 22	3 46	20 29	3 34	20 36	3 38	20 53	3 54	20 51
4	3 47	20 11	3 57	20 21	3 49	20 23	3 45	20 30	3 33	20 37	3 37	20 54	3 53	20 52
5	3 46	20 12	3 57	20 22	3 48	20 24	3 44	20 31	3 32	20 38	3 36	20 55	3 52	20 53
6	3 46	20 13	3 56	20 22	3 48	20 25	3 43	20 32	3 31	20 39	3 36	20 56	3 51	20 54
7	3 45	20 13	3 55	20 23	3 47	20 26	3 43	20 33	3 31	20 41	3 35	20 57	3 50	20 55
8	3 45	20 14	3 55	20 24	3 47	20 27	3 42	20 34	3 30	20 42	3 34	20 58	3 50	20 56
9	3 44	20 15	3 54	20 25	3 46	20 28	3 42	20 35	3 29	20 42	3 34	20 59	3 49	20 57
10	3 44	20 16	3 54	20 26	3 46	20 29	3 41	20 36	3 29	20 43	3 33	21 00	3 49	20 58
11	3 43	20 17	3 54	20 26	3 45	20 29	3 41	20 37	3 28	20 44	3 32	21 01	3 48	20 59
12	3 43	20 17	3 53	20 27	3 45	20 30	3 40	20 37	3 28	20 45	3 32	21 02	3 48	20 59
13	3 43	20 18	3 53	20 28	3 45	20 31	3 40	20 38	3 28	20 46	3 32	21 03	3 48	21 00
14	3 43	20 18	3 53	20 28	3 45	20 31	3 40	20 39	3 27	20 46	3 31	21 03	3 47	21 01
15	3 43	20 19	3 53	20 29	3 44	20 32	3 40	20 39	3 27	20 47	3 31	21 04	3 47	21 01
16	3 43	20 20	3 53	20 29	3 44	20 32	3 40	20 40	3 27	20 47	3 31	21 04	3 47	21 02
17	3 42	20 20	3 53	20 30	3 44	20 33	3 39	20 40	3 27	20 48	3 31	21 05	3 47	21 02
18	3 42	20 20	3 53	20 30	3 44	20 33	3 39	20 41	3 27	20 48	3 31	21 05	3 47	21 03
19	3 43	20 21	3 53	20 31	3 44	20 34	3 39	20 41	3 27	20 49	3 31	21 06	3 47	21 03
20	3 43	20 21	3 53	20 31	3 44	20 34	3 40	20 41	3 27	20 49	3 31	21 06	3 47	21 04
21	3 43	20 21	3 53	20 31	3 45	20 34	3 40	20 42	3 27	20 49	3 31	21 06	3 47	21 04
22	3 43	20 21	3 53	20 31	3 45	20 34	3 40	20 42	3 27	20 49	3 31	21 06	3 47	21 04
23	3 43	20 22	3 53	20 31	3 45	20 34	3 40	20 42	3 27	20 50	3 31	21 07	3 48	21 04
24	3 44	20 22	3 54	20 31	3 45	20 35	3 40	20 42	3 28	20 50	3 32	21 07	3 48	21 04
25	3 44	20 22	3 54	20 31	3 46	20 35	3 41	20 42	3 28	20 50	3 32	21 07	3 48	21 04
26	3 44	20 22	3 55	20 31	3 46	20 35	3 41	20 42	3 29	20 50	3 33	21 07	3 49	21 04
27	3 45	20 22	3 55	20 31	3 47	20 34	3 42	20 42	3 29	20 49	3 33	21 06	3 49	21 04
28	3 45	20 21	3 55	20 31	3 47	20 34	3 42	20 42	3 30	20 49	3 34	21 06	3 50	21 04
29	3 46	20 21	3 56	20 31	3 48	20 34	3 43	20 42	3 30	20 49	3 34	21 06	3 50	21 04
30	3 46	20 21	3 57	20 31	3 48	20 34	3 44	20 41	3 31	20 49	3 35	21 05	3 51	21 03

JUPITER

Day	RA		Dec.		Transit		5° high			
							52°		56°	
	h	m	°	'	h	m	h	m	h	m
1	9	01.9	+17	45	16	23	23	23	23	35
11	9	08.3	+17	18	15	50	22	47	22	59
21	9	15.2	+16	47	15	18	22	12	22	23
31	9	22.5	+16	13	14	46	21	37	21	47

Diameters - equatorial 33" polar 31"

SATURN

Day	RA		Dec.		Transit		5° high			
							52°		56°	
	h	m	°	'	h	m	h	m	h	m
1	5	58.3	+22	36	13	20	20	48	21	06
11	6	03.8	+22	37	12	46	20	15	20	32
21	6	09.4	+22	37	12	13	19	41	19	58
31	6	15.1	+22	36	11	39	19	07	19	24

Diameters - equatorial 16" polar 15"
Rings - major axis 37" minor axis 17"

URANUS

Day	RA		Dec.		Transit		10° high			
							52°		56°	
	h	m	°	'	h	m	h	m	h	m
1	22	20.1	−11	11	5	43	1	54	2	14
11	22	20.2	−11	11	5	04	1	15	1	34
21	22	19.9	−11	13	4	24	0	36	0	55
31	22	19.4	−11	16	3	44	23	52	0	16

Diameter 4"

NEPTUNE

Day	RA		Dec.		Transit		10° high			
							52°		56°	
	h	m	°	'	h	m	h	m	h	m
1	21	02.3	−16	52	4	25	1	18	1	49
11	21	01.9	−16	54	3	46	0	39	1	09
21	21	01.3	−16	57	3	06	23	55	0	30
31	21	00.5	−17	00	2	26	23	15	23	46

Diameter 2"

July 2003

SEVENTH MONTH, 31 DAYS. *Julius* Caesar, formerly *Quintilis*, fifth month of Roman pre-Julian calendar

1	*Tuesday*	Juan Perón d. 1974. Battle of Gettysburg began 1863	182
2	*Wednesday*	Sir Tyrone Guthrie b. 1900. Betty Grable d. 1973	183
3	*Thursday*	**St Thomas.** Israeli commandoes freed hostages at Entebbe Airport, Uganda 1976	184
4	*Friday*	Dr Thomas Barnardo b. 1845. Marie Curie d. 1934	185
5	*Saturday*	Georges Pompidou b. 1911. Salvation Army founded 1865	186
6	*Sunday*	**3rd S. after Trinity.** George W. Bush b. 1946	187
7	*Monday*	Marc Chagall b. 1887. Ernest Newman d. 1959	*week 27 day* 188
8	*Tuesday*	Percy Grainger b. 1882. Edmund Burke d. 1797	189
9	*Wednesday*	Ann Radcliffe b. 1764. First Wimbledon lawn tennis Championship held 1877	190
10	*Thursday*	Evelyn Laye b. 1900. Louis-Jacques Daguerre d. 1851	191
11	*Friday*	George Gershwin d. 1937. China's "Terracotta Army" discovered 1975	192
12	*Saturday*	Julius Caesar b. 102BC. Alfred Dreyfus d. 1935	193
13	*Sunday*	**4th S. after Trinity.** Paavo Nurmi b. 1897	194
14	*Monday*	Leon Garfield b. 1921. Storming of the Bastille 1789	*week 28 day* 195
15	*Tuesday*	St Swithin's Day. Inigo Jones b. 1573	196
16	*Wednesday*	Sir Joshua Reynolds b. 1723. Ginger Rogers b. 1911	197
17	*Thursday*	Isaac Watts b. 1674. Geoffrey Jellicoe d. 1996	198
18	*Friday*	Dr W. G. Grace b. 1848. Jane Austen d. 1817	199
19	*Saturday*	Edgar Degas b. 1834. Syngman Rhee d. 1965	200
20	*Sunday*	**5th S. after Trinity.** Bruce Lee d. 1973	201
21	*Monday*	Ernest Hemingway b. 1898. Paul Julius von Reuter b. 1816	*week 29 day* 202
22	*Tuesday*	**Mary Magdalene.** Tate Gallery opened 1897	203
23	*Wednesday*	Haile Selassie b. 1892. Jessica Mitford d. 1996	204
24	*Thursday*	Alexandre Dumas b. 1802. Treaty of Lausanne 1923	205
25	*Friday*	**St James.** Start of Sino-Japanese war 1894	206
26	*Saturday*	Aldous Huxley b. 1894. Francesco Cilea b. 1866	207
27	*Sunday*	**6th S. after Trinity.** Korean War ended 1953	208
28	*Monday*	Cyrano de Bergerac d. 1655. Antonio Vivaldi d. 1741	*week 30 day* 209
29	*Tuesday*	David Niven d. 1983. Defeat of Spanish Armada 1588	210
30	*Wednesday*	Henry Moore b. 1898. Prince Otto von Bismarck d. 1898	211
31	*Thursday*	*Trinity Law Sittings end.* Franz Liszt d. 1886	212

ASTRONOMICAL PHENOMENA

d h
1 01 Saturn in conjunction with Mercury. Saturn 2° S.
2 23 Jupiter in conjunction with Moon. Jupiter 4° S.
4 06 Earth at aphelion (152 million km.)
5 10 Mercury in superior conjunction
8 09 Saturn in conjunction with Venus. Saturn 0°.8 S.
17 08 Mars in conjunction with Moon. Mars 0°.3 S.
23 06 Sun's longitude 120° ♌
26 03 Jupiter in conjunction with Mercury. Jupiter 0°.4 S.
27 00 Saturn in conjunction with Moon. Saturn 4° S.
28 19 Venus in conjunction with Moon. Venus 4° S.
29 08 Mars at stationary point
30 16 Jupiter in conjunction with Moon. Jupiter 4° S.
31 04 Mercury in conjunction with Moon. Mercury 4° S.

MINIMA OF ALGOL

d	h	d	h	d	h
3	15.6	15	02.8	26	14.1
6	12.4	17	23.7	29	10.9
9	09.2	20	20.5		
12	06.0	23	17.3		

CONSTELLATIONS

The following constellations are near the meridian at

d	h		d	h
June	1	24	July	16	21
June	15	23	August	1	20
July	1	22	August	16	19

Ursa Minor, Draco, Corona, Hercules, Lyra, Serpens, Ophiuchus, Libra, Scorpius and Sagittarius

THE MOON

Phases, Apsides and Node

		d	h	m
☽	First Quarter	7	02	32
○	Full Moon	13	19	21
☾	Last Quarter	21	07	01
●	New Moon	29	06	53

	d	h	m
Perigee (365,145 km)	10	22	01
Apogee (404,328 km)	22	19	37

Mean longitude of ascending node on April 1, 57°

THE SUN   s.d. 15'.8

Day	Right Ascension h m s	Dec. + ° '	Equation of Time m s	Rise 52° h m	Rise 56° h m	Transit h m	Set 52° h m	Set 56° h m	Sidereal time h m s	Transit of First Point of Aries h m s
1	6 38 13	23 09	− 3 40	3 44	3 18	12 04	20 23	20 49	18 34 33	5 24 34
2	6 42 21	23 05	− 3 52	3 45	3 19	12 04	20 23	20 49	18 38 29	5 20 38
3	6 46 29	23 01	− 4 03	3 45	3 20	12 04	20 22	20 48	18 42 26	5 16 42
4	6 50 37	22 56	− 4 15	3 46	3 21	12 04	20 22	20 48	18 46 22	5 12 46
5	6 54 44	22 51	− 4 25	3 47	3 22	12 05	20 22	20 47	18 50 19	5 08 50
6	6 58 51	22 45	− 4 36	3 48	3 23	12 05	20 21	20 46	18 54 15	5 04 55
7	7 02 58	22 39	− 4 46	3 49	3 24	12 05	20 20	20 45	18 58 12	5 00 59
8	7 07 04	22 33	− 4 56	3 50	3 25	12 05	20 20	20 44	19 02 08	4 57 03
9	7 11 10	22 26	− 5 05	3 51	3 26	12 05	20 19	20 43	19 06 05	4 53 07
10	7 15 15	22 19	− 5 14	3 52	3 27	12 05	20 18	20 43	19 10 02	4 49 11
11	7 19 21	22 11	− 5 22	3 53	3 29	12 05	20 17	20 41	19 13 58	4 45 15
12	7 23 25	22 03	− 5 30	3 54	3 30	12 06	20 17	20 40	19 17 55	4 41 19
13	7 27 29	21 55	− 5 38	3 55	3 31	12 06	20 16	20 39	19 21 51	4 37 23
14	7 31 33	21 46	− 5 45	3 56	3 33	12 06	20 15	20 38	19 25 48	4 33 27
15	7 35 36	21 37	− 5 52	3 57	3 34	12 06	20 14	20 37	19 29 44	4 29 31
16	7 39 39	21 28	− 5 58	3 59	3 36	12 06	20 13	20 35	19 33 41	4 25 35
17	7 43 41	21 18	− 6 04	4 00	3 37	12 06	20 12	20 34	19 37 37	4 21 40
18	7 47 43	21 08	− 6 09	4 01	3 39	12 06	20 11	20 33	19 41 34	4 17 44
19	7 51 44	20 58	− 6 13	4 02	3 40	12 06	20 09	20 31	19 45 31	4 13 48
20	7 55 44	20 47	− 6 17	4 04	3 42	12 06	20 08	20 30	19 49 27	4 09 52
21	7 59 44	20 36	− 6 21	4 05	3 43	12 06	20 07	20 28	19 53 24	4 05 56
22	8 03 44	20 24	− 6 24	4 06	3 45	12 06	20 06	20 27	19 57 20	4 02 00
23	8 07 43	20 12	− 6 26	4 08	3 47	12 06	20 04	20 25	20 01 17	3 58 04
24	8 11 41	20 00	− 6 28	4 09	3 49	12 06	20 03	20 23	20 05 13	3 54 08
25	8 15 39	19 47	− 6 29	4 11	3 50	12 07	20 02	20 22	20 09 10	3 50 12
26	8 19 37	19 34	− 6 30	4 12	3 52	12 07	20 00	20 20	20 13 06	3 46 16
27	8 23 33	19 21	− 6 30	4 13	3 54	12 07	19 59	20 18	20 17 03	3 42 20
28	8 27 30	19 08	− 6 30	4 15	3 56	12 06	19 57	20 16	20 21 00	3 38 25
29	8 31 25	18 54	− 6 29	4 16	3 57	12 06	19 56	20 14	20 24 56	3 34 29
30	8 35 20	18 40	− 6 27	4 18	3 59	12 06	19 54	20 12	20 28 53	3 30 33
31	8 39 14	18 25	− 6 25	4 19	4 01	12 06	19 52	20 10	20 32 49	3 26 37

DURATION OF TWILIGHT (in minutes)

Latitude	52°	56°	52°	56°	52°	56°	52°	56°
	1 July		11 July		21 July		31 July	
Civil	48	61	47	58	44	53	42	49
Nautical	124	TAN	117	TAN	107	146	98	123
Astronomical	TAN	TAN	TAN	TAN	TAN	TAN	182	TAN

THE NIGHT SKY

Mercury passes through superior conjunction on the 5th but remains too close to the Sun for observation throughout the month.

Venus, magnitude −3.9, although a bright object, can only be observed from southern England and then only with difficulty, low above the east-north-eastern horizon just before sunrise. It is unlikely to be detected after the middle of the month as it gets closer to the Sun.

Mars is a bright morning object, its magnitude brightening during the month from −1.4 to −2.3, as it approaches opposition towards the end of next month. Mars, in the constellation of Aquarius, reaches its first stationary point on the 29th, and thereafter its motion is retrograde. A close approach by the gibbous Moon to the planet occurs on the morning of the 17th, the separation being only about 3 degrees before twilight inhibits observation.

Jupiter, magnitude −1.8, is an evening object but only visible for a short while low above the western horizon. By the middle of the month it is lost to view in the gathering twilight. On the evening of the 3rd the crescent Moon will be seen passing about 4 degrees north of the planet.

Saturn is too close to the Sun for observation for most of July but gradually becomes a morning object, during the last few days of the month. It will be difficult to observe at first, because of the long duration of twilight, but keen-sighted observers may be able to locate it low above the east-north-eastern horizon before the sky gets too bright. The magnitude of Saturn is +0.1.

THE MOON

Day	RA h m	Dec. °	Hor. par. ′	Semi- diam. ′	Sun's co- long. °	PA of Bright Limb °	Phase %	Age d	Rise 52° h m	Rise 56° h m	Transit h m	Set 52° h m	Set 56° h m
1	7 42	+25.6	55.9	15.2	289	264	2	1.2	4 51	4 20	13 37	22 11	22 36
2	8 38	+23.4	56.4	15.4	302	275	5	2.2	6 04	5 39	14 30	22 38	22 58
3	9 32	+20.0	56.9	15.5	314	282	11	3.2	7 22	7 04	15 20	22 59	23 13
4	10 24	+15.5	57.4	15.6	326	287	18	4.2	8 43	8 30	16 09	23 16	23 25
5	11 15	+10.2	57.9	15.8	338	291	27	5.2	10 04	9 57	16 57	23 31	23 35
6	12 04	+ 4.4	58.4	15.9	350	292	38	6.2	11 25	11 24	17 44	23 45	23 44
7	12 54	− 1.8	58.9	16.1	3	293	49	7.2	12 48	12 52	18 32	—	23 54
8	13 45	− 8.0	59.4	16.2	15	291	60	8.2	14 13	14 24	19 22	0 00	—
9	14 38	−13.8	59.7	16.3	27	289	71	9.2	15 41	15 58	20 16	0 18	0 05
10	15 34	−19.0	60.0	16.3	39	284	81	10.2	17 10	17 35	21 14	0 39	0 21
11	16 34	−23.1	60.0	16.4	52	277	89	11.2	18 36	19 07	22 15	1 09	0 43
12	17 38	−25.6	59.9	16.3	64	267	96	12.2	19 49	20 23	23 18	1 50	1 19
13	18 42	−26.5	59.6	16.2	76	249	99	13.2	20 46	21 17	—	2 48	2 14
14	19 46	−25.5	59.1	16.1	88	138	100	14.2	21 25	21 51	0 21	4 00	3 30
15	20 46	−22.9	58.4	15.9	100	91	98	15.2	21 53	22 12	1 19	5 21	4 57
16	21 42	−19.1	57.7	15.7	113	80	94	16.2	22 13	22 27	2 13	6 44	6 26
17	22 34	−14.4	56.9	15.5	125	74	88	17.2	22 29	22 37	3 02	8 04	7 52
18	23 23	− 9.2	56.1	15.3	137	70	80	18.2	22 42	22 46	3 48	9 20	9 13
19	0 08	− 3.8	55.4	15.1	149	69	72	19.2	22 54	22 53	4 30	10 32	10 31
20	0 52	+ 1.7	54.9	15.0	161	68	62	20.2	23 06	23 01	5 11	11 43	11 47
21	1 35	+ 7.0	54.5	14.9	174	69	53	21.2	23 19	23 09	5 52	12 53	13 02
22	2 19	+12.0	54.3	14.8	186	71	43	22.2	23 34	23 19	6 33	14 03	14 17
23	3 04	+16.5	54.2	14.8	198	74	34	23.2	23 53	23 33	7 16	15 15	15 34
24	3 52	+20.4	54.3	14.8	210	78	26	24.2	—	23 53	8 01	16 26	16 51
25	4 42	+23.5	54.6	14.9	222	83	18	25.2	0 18	—	8 50	17 35	18 05
26	5 34	+25.6	55.0	15.0	235	90	11	26.2	0 52	0 22	9 41	18 37	19 10
27	6 29	+26.5	55.5	15.1	247	99	6	27.2	1 38	1 05	10 35	19 30	20 02
28	7 25	+26.0	56.0	15.3	259	112	2	28.2	2 38	2 06	11 29	20 10	20 38
29	8 22	+24.2	56.6	15.4	271	156	0	29.2	3 49	3 22	12 23	20 41	21 03
30	9 17	+21.0	57.1	15.6	284	258	1	0.7	5 08	4 47	13 16	21 04	21 20
31	10 10	+16.7	57.6	15.7	296	278	4	1.7	6 29	6 15	14 06	21 23	21 33

MERCURY

Day	RA h m	Dec. °	Diam. ″	Phase %	Transit h m	5° high 52° h m	5° high 56° h m
1	6 15	+24.1	5	98	11 43	4 02	3 43
3	6 34	+24.3	5	99	11 54	4 13	3 53
5	6 53	+24.2	5	100	12 05	19 46 20 05	
7	7 12	+23.9	5	100	12 17	19 55 20 14	
9	7 31	+23.5	5	98	12 27	20 02 20 20	
11	7 49	+22.9	5	97	12 37	20 08 20 25	
13	8 06	+22.1	5	94	12 47	20 12 20 29	
15	8 23	+21.3	5	92	12 55	20 15 20 31	
17	8 39	+20.3	5	89	13 03	20 17 20 31	
19	8 54	+19.2	5	87	13 11	20 18 20 31	
21	9 09	+18.1	5	84	13 17	20 18 20 29	
23	9 23	+16.9	6	81	13 23	20 17 20 27	
25	9 36	+15.7	6	78	13 28	20 15 20 24	
27	9 48	+14.4	6	76	13 33	20 12 20 20	
29	10 00	+13.1	6	73	13 36	20 09 20 16	
31	10 12	+11.8	6	71	13 40	20 05 20 11	

VENUS

Day	RA h m	Dec. °	Diam. ″	Phase %	Transit h m	5° high 52° h m	5° high 56° h m
1	5 40	+23.1	10	97	11 06	3 33	3 15
6	6 07	+23.4	10	98	11 13	3 39	3 20
11	6 33	+23.4	10	98	11 20	3 46	3 27
16	7 00	+23.1	10	99	11 27	3 55	3 37
21	7 27	+22.5	10	99	11 34	4 05	3 48
26	7 53	+21.6	10	99	11 40	4 17	4 01
31	8 19	+20.5	10	100	11 47	4 30	4 15

MARS

Day	RA h m	Dec. °	Diam. ″	Phase %	Transit h m	5° high 52° h m	5° high 56° h m
1	22 35	−13.6	17	90	4 00	23 46	0 05
6	22 41	−13.3	18	91	3 46	23 30	23 47
11	22 46	−13.1	18	92	3 32	23 15	23 31
16	22 50	−13.0	19	93	3 16	22 58	23 14
21	22 53	−13.1	20	94	3 00	22 42	22 58
26	22 55	−13.2	21	95	2 42	22 25	22 41
31	22 56	−13.4	22	96	2 23	22 07	22 23

SUNRISE AND SUNSET

	London 0°05′ 51°30′		Bristol 2°35′ 51°28′		Birmingham 1°55′ 52°28′		Manchester 2°15′ 53°28′		Newcastle 1°37′ 54°59′		Glasgow 4°14′ 55°52′		Belfast 5°56′ 54°35′	
	h m	h m	h m	h m	h m	h m	h m	h m	h m	h m	h m	h m	h m	h m
1	3 47	20 21	3 57	20 31	3 49	20 34	3 44	20 41	3 32	20 48	3 36	21 05	3 52	21 03
2	3 48	20 20	3 58	20 30	3 50	20 33	3 45	20 41	3 33	20 48	3 37	21 05	3 53	21 02
3	3 48	20 20	3 59	20 30	3 50	20 33	3 46	20 40	3 33	20 47	3 38	21 04	3 53	21 02
4	3 49	20 20	3 59	20 29	3 51	20 32	3 47	20 40	3 34	20 47	3 38	21 03	3 54	21 01
5	3 50	20 19	4 00	20 29	3 52	20 32	3 47	20 39	3 35	20 46	3 39	21 03	3 55	21 01
6	3 51	20 19	4 01	20 28	3 53	20 31	3 48	20 38	3 36	20 45	3 41	21 02	3 56	21 00
7	3 52	20 18	4 02	20 28	3 54	20 31	3 49	20 38	3 37	20 45	3 42	21 01	3 57	20 59
8	3 53	20 17	4 03	20 27	3 55	20 30	3 50	20 37	3 38	20 44	3 43	21 00	3 58	20 59
9	3 54	20 17	4 04	20 27	3 56	20 29	3 51	20 36	3 39	20 43	3 44	20 59	3 59	20 58
10	3 55	20 16	4 05	20 26	3 57	20 28	3 52	20 35	3 41	20 42	3 45	20 59	4 00	20 57
11	3 56	20 15	4 06	20 25	3 58	20 28	3 54	20 35	3 42	20 41	3 46	20 57	4 02	20 56
12	3 57	20 14	4 07	20 24	3 59	20 27	3 55	20 34	3 43	20 40	3 48	20 56	4 03	20 55
13	3 58	20 14	4 08	20 23	4 00	20 26	3 56	20 33	3 44	20 39	3 49	20 55	4 04	20 54
14	3 59	20 13	4 09	20 22	4 01	20 25	3 57	20 32	3 46	20 38	3 50	20 54	4 05	20 53
15	4 00	20 12	4 10	20 21	4 03	20 24	3 58	20 31	3 47	20 37	3 52	20 53	4 07	20 52
16	4 01	20 11	4 11	20 20	4 04	20 23	4 00	20 29	3 48	20 36	3 53	20 52	4 08	20 50
17	4 03	20 10	4 13	20 19	4 05	20 22	4 01	20 28	3 50	20 34	3 55	20 50	4 10	20 49
18	4 04	20 08	4 14	20 18	4 06	20 21	4 02	20 27	3 51	20 33	3 56	20 49	4 11	20 48
19	4 05	20 07	4 15	20 17	4 08	20 19	4 04	20 26	3 53	20 32	3 58	20 47	4 12	20 47
20	4 06	20 06	4 16	20 16	4 09	20 18	4 05	20 24	3 54	20 30	4 00	20 46	4 14	20 45
21	4 08	20 05	4 18	20 15	4 10	20 17	4 07	20 23	3 56	20 29	4 01	20 44	4 15	20 44
22	4 09	20 04	4 19	20 14	4 12	20 15	4 08	20 22	3 57	20 27	4 03	20 43	4 17	20 42
23	4 10	20 02	4 20	20 12	4 13	20 14	4 10	20 20	3 59	20 26	4 05	20 41	4 19	20 41
24	4 12	20 01	4 22	20 11	4 15	20 13	4 11	20 19	4 01	20 24	4 06	20 39	4 20	20 39
25	4 13	20 00	4 23	20 10	4 16	20 11	4 13	20 17	4 02	20 22	4 08	20 38	4 22	20 38
26	4 14	19 58	4 25	20 08	4 18	20 10	4 14	20 16	4 04	20 21	4 10	20 36	4 23	20 36
27	4 16	19 57	4 26	20 07	4 19	20 08	4 16	20 14	4 06	20 19	4 11	20 34	4 25	20 34
28	4 17	19 55	4 27	20 05	4 21	20 07	4 17	20 13	4 07	20 17	4 13	20 32	4 27	20 33
29	4 19	19 54	4 29	20 04	4 22	20 05	4 19	20 11	4 09	20 16	4 15	20 30	4 28	20 31
30	4 20	19 52	4 30	20 02	4 24	20 04	4 21	20 09	4 11	20 14	4 17	20 29	4 30	20 29
31	4 22	19 51	4 32	20 01	4 25	20 02	4 22	20 07	4 13	20 12	4 19	20 27	4 32	20 27

JUPITER

Day	RA		Dec.		Transit		5° high			
							52°		56°	
	h	m	°	′	h	m	h	m	h	m
1	9	22.5	+16	13	14	46	21	37	21	47
11	9	30.3	+15	36	14	14	21	02	21	12
21	9	38.3	+14	57	13	43	20	27	20	36
31	9	46.6	+14	16	13	12	19	52	20	01

Diameters - equatorial 32″ polar 30″

SATURN

Day	RA		Dec.		Transit		5° high			
							52°		56°	
	h	m	°	′	h	m	h	m	h	m
1	6	15.1	+22	36	11	39	4	11	3	53
11	6	20.7	+22	34	11	05	3	37	3	20
21	6	26.1	+22	32	10	31	3	04	2	46
31	6	31.4	+22	29	9	57	2	30	2	13

Diameters - equatorial 17″ polar 15″
Rings - major axis 38″ minor axis 17″

URANUS

Day	RA		Dec.		Transit		10° high			
							52°		56°	
	h	m	°	′	h	m	h	m	h	m
1	22	19.4	−11	16	3	44	23	56	0	16
11	22	18.6	−11	21	3	04	23	13	23	32
21	22	17.5	−11	27	2	24	22	33	22	53
31	22	16.3	−11	35	1	43	21	53	22	13

Diameter 4″

NEPTUNE

Day	RA		Dec.		Transit		10° high			
							52°		56°	
	h	m	°	′	h	m	h	m	h	m
1	21	00.5	−17	00	2	26	23	15	23	46
11	20	59.6	−17	04	1	45	22	36	23	07
21	20	58.6	−17	08	1	05	21	56	22	27
31	20	57.5	−17	13	0	25	21	16	21	48

Diameter 2″

 **August 2003**

EIGHTH MONTH, 31 DAYS. *Augustus,* formerly *Sextilis,* sixth month of Roman pre-Julian calendar

1	*Friday*	Herman Melville b. 1819. Swiss Confederation founded 1291	213
2	*Saturday*	Alexander Graham Bell d. 1922. Iraq invaded Kuwait 1990	214
3	*Sunday*	**7th S. after Trinity.** Columbus set sail from Spain in the 'Santa Maria' 1492	215
4	*Monday*	*Bank Holiday in Scotland.* Knut Hamsun b. 1859	*week 31 day* 216
5	*Tuesday*	Marilyn Monroe d. 1962. Richard Burton d. 1984	217
6	*Wednesday*	**The Transfiguration.** Ben Jonson d. 1637	218
7	*Thursday*	John D. Rockefeller b. 1839. Larry Adler d. 2001	219
8	*Friday*	*Princess Beatrice of York b. 1988.* English Poor Law passed 1834	220
9	*Saturday*	Thomas Telford b. 1757. Singapore became an independent sovereign state 1965	221
10	*Sunday*	**8th S. after Trinity.** Greenwich Observatory founded 1675	222
11	*Monday*	Enid Blyton b. 1897. Henry James Pye d. 1813	*week 32 day* 223
12	*Tuesday*	Cecil B. de Mille b. 1881. William Blake d. 1827	224
13	*Wednesday*	Sir Alfred Hitchcock b. 1899. Sir John Millais d. 1896	225
14	*Thursday*	Samuel Wesley b. 1810. Elias Canetti d. 1994	226
15	*Friday*	**Blessed Virgin Mary.** *Princess Royal b. 1950*	227
16	*Saturday*	Georgette Heyer b. 1902. Elvis Presley d. 1977	228
17	*Sunday*	**9th S. after Trinity.** Construction of Berlin Wall began 1961	229
18	*Monday*	Willie Rushton b. 1937. Sir Frederick Ashton d. 1988	*week 33 day* 230
19	*Tuesday*	Coco Chanel b. 1883. Sir Henry Wood d. 1944	231
20	*Wednesday*	Rajiv Gandhi b. 1944. Federico García Lorca d. 1936	232
21	*Thursday*	Donald Dewar b. 1937. Elie Halévy d. 1937	233
22	*Friday*	Xiaoping Deng b. 1904. Dr Jacob Bronowski d. 1974	234
23	*Saturday*	Gene Kelly b. 1912. Rudolph Valentino d. 1926	235
24	*Sunday*	**10th S. after Trinity.** St Bartholomew. Cardinal Cormac Murphy O'Connor b. 1932	236
25	*Monday*	*Bank Holiday in England Wales and Northern Ireland.*	*week 34 day* 237
26	*Tuesday*	Mother Teresa of Calcutta b. 1910. Charles Lindbergh d. 1974	238
27	*Wednesday*	Samuel Goldwyn b. 1882. Sir Rowland Hill d. 1879	239
28	*Thursday*	Johann Wolfgang von Goethe b. 1749. James Henry Leigh Hunt d. 1859	240
29	*Friday*	Ingrid Bergman b. 1915. Sir Charles Napier d. 1853	241
30	*Saturday*	Maria Montessori b. 1870. Mary Wollstonecraft Shelley b. 1797	242
31	*Sunday*	Théophile Gautier b. 1811. Rocky Marciano d. 1969	243

ASTRONOMICAL PHENOMENA

d h
4 14 Neptune at opposition
13 16 Mars in conjunction with Moon. Mars 2° S.
14 21 Mercury at greatest elongation E.27°
18 18 Venus in superior conjunction
21 10 Jupiter in conjunction with Venus. Jupiter 0°.5 S.
22 10 Jupiter in conjunction
23 13 Sun's longitude 150° ♍
23 15 Saturn in conjunction with Moon. Saturn 4° S.
24 10 Uranus at opposition
27 10 Jupiter in conjunction with Moon. Jupiter 4° S.
27 22 Venus in conjunction with Moon. Venus 3° S.
28 14 Mercury at stationary point
28 18 Mars at opposition
29 03 Pluto at stationary point
29 07 Mercury in conjunction with Moon. Mercury 8° S.

MINIMA OF ALGOL

d	h	d	h	d	h
1	07.7	12	18.9	24	06.2
4	04.5	15	15.8	27	03.0
7	01.3	18	12.6	29	23.8
9	22.1	21	09.4		

CONSTELLATIONS

The following constellations are near the meridian at

	d	h		d	h
July	1	24	August	16	21
July	16	23	September	1	20
August	1	22	March	15	19

Draco, Hercules, Lyra, Cygnus, Sagitta, Ophiuchus, Serpens, Aquila and Sagittarius

THE MOON

Phases, Apsides and Node	d	h	m
☽ First Quarter	5	07	28
○ Full Moon	12	04	48
☾ Last Quarter	20	00	48
● New Moon	27	17	26
Perigee (369,433 km)	6	14	03
Apogee (404,102 km)	19	14	22
Perigee (367,926 km)	31	18	48

Mean longitude of ascending node on August 1, 56°

THE SUN   s.d. 16′.1

Day	Right Ascension h m s	Dec. + ° ′	Equation of Time m s	Rise 52° h m	Rise 56° h m	Transit h m	Set 52° h m	Set 56° h m	Sidereal time h m s	Transit of First Point of Aries h m s
1	8 43 08	18 10	− 6 22	4 21	4 03	12 06	19 51	20 08	20 36 46	3 22 41
2	8 47 01	17 55	− 6 19	4 22	4 05	12 06	19 49	20 06	20 40 42	3 18 45
3	8 50 54	17 40	− 6 15	4 24	4 07	12 06	19 47	20 04	20 44 39	3 14 49
4	8 54 45	17 24	− 6 10	4 26	4 09	12 06	19 46	20 02	20 48 36	3 10 53
5	8 58 37	17 09	− 6 05	4 27	4 10	12 06	19 44	20 00	20 52 32	3 06 57
6	9 02 27	16 52	− 5 59	4 29	4 12	12 06	19 42	19 58	20 56 29	3 03 01
7	9 06 17	16 36	− 5 52	4 30	4 14	12 06	19 40	19 56	21 00 25	2 59 05
8	9 10 06	16 19	− 5 45	4 32	4 16	12 06	19 38	19 54	21 04 22	2 55 10
9	9 13 55	16 02	− 5 37	4 33	4 18	12 06	19 36	19 52	21 08 18	2 51 14
10	9 17 43	15 45	− 5 29	4 35	4 20	12 05	19 35	19 49	21 12 15	2 47 18
11	9 21 31	15 27	− 5 20	4 37	4 22	12 05	19 33	19 47	21 16 11	2 43 22
12	9 25 18	15 10	− 5 10	4 38	4 24	12 05	19 31	19 45	21 20 08	2 39 26
13	9 29 04	14 52	− 5 00	4 40	4 26	12 05	19 29	19 42	21 24 05	2 35 30
14	9 32 50	14 33	− 4 49	4 42	4 28	12 05	19 27	19 40	21 28 01	2 31 34
15	9 36 36	14 15	− 4 38	4 43	4 30	12 05	19 25	19 38	21 31 58	2 27 38
16	9 40 20	13 56	− 4 26	4 45	4 32	12 04	19 23	19 35	21 35 54	2 23 42
17	9 44 05	13 37	− 4 14	4 46	4 34	12 04	19 21	19 33	21 39 51	2 19 46
18	9 47 48	13 18	− 4 01	4 48	4 36	12 04	19 19	19 31	21 43 47	2 15 50
19	9 51 32	12 59	− 3 48	4 50	4 38	12 04	19 17	19 28	21 47 44	2 11 54
20	9 55 15	12 39	− 3 34	4 51	4 40	12 03	19 14	19 26	21 51 40	2 07 59
21	9 58 57	12 20	− 3 20	4 53	4 42	12 03	19 12	19 23	21 55 37	2 04 03
22	10 02 39	12 00	− 3 05	4 55	4 44	12 03	19 10	19 21	21 59 34	2 00 07
23	10 06 20	11 39	− 2 50	4 56	4 46	12 03	19 08	19 18	22 03 30	1 56 11
24	10 10 01	11 19	− 2 35	4 58	4 48	12 02	19 06	19 16	22 07 27	1 52 15
25	10 13 42	10 59	− 2 19	4 59	4 49	12 02	19 04	19 14	22 11 23	1 48 19
26	10 17 22	10 38	− 2 02	5 01	4 51	12 02	19 02	19 11	22 15 20	1 44 23
27	10 21 02	10 17	− 1 46	5 03	4 53	12 02	18 59	19 08	22 19 16	1 40 27
28	10 24 41	9 56	− 1 29	5 04	4 55	12 01	18 57	19 06	22 23 13	1 36 31
29	10 28 20	9 35	− 1 11	5 06	4 57	12 01	18 55	19 03	22 27 09	1 32 35
30	10 31 59	9 14	− 0 53	5 08	4 59	12 01	18 53	19 01	22 31 06	1 28 39
31	10 35 37	8 52	− 0 35	5 09	5 01	12 00	18 50	18 58	22 35 02	1 24 44

DURATION OF TWILIGHT (in minutes)

Latitude	52°	56°	52°	56°	52°	56°	52°	56°
	1 August		11 August		21 August		31 August	
Civil	41	49	39	45	37	42	35	40
Nautical	97	121	90	107	84	97	79	90
Astronomical	179	TAN	154	210	139	168	128	148

THE NIGHT SKY

Mercury is unsuitably placed for observation throughout August.

Venus is too close to the Sun for observation, superior conjunction occurring on the 18th.

Mars, magnitude −2.9, reaches opposition on the 28th, and is therefore visible throughout the hours of darkness. It is a conspicuous object in the southern skies as it retrogrades slowly in the constellation of Aquarius.

Jupiter passes through conjunction on the 22nd and therefore remains too close to the Sun for observation throughout the month.

Saturn, magnitude +0.1, is visible as a morning object, in the south-eastern quadrant of the sky. The waning crescent Moon is in the vicinity of the planet on the mornings of the 23rd and 24th. Saturn is in the constellation of Gemini.

Uranus is at opposition on the 24th, in the constellation of Aquarius. Uranus is barely visible to the naked eye as its magnitude is +5.7, but it is readily located with only small optical aid.

Neptune is at opposition on the 4th, in the constellation of Capricornus. It is not visible to the naked eye since its magnitude is +7.8.

Meteors. The maximum of the famous Perseid meteor shower occurs on the morning of the 13th. Unfortunately the brilliance of the Full Moon will severely hamper observation as it is above the horizon all night.

THE MOON

Day	RA h m	Dec. °	Hor. par. '	Semi-diam. '	Sun's co-long. °	PA of Bright Limb °	Phase %	Age d	Rise 52° h m	Rise 56° h m	Transit h m	Set 52° h m	Set 56° h m
1	11 02	+ 11.4	58.1	15.8	308	286	9	2.7	7 52	7 43	14 54	21 38	21 4
2	11 53	+ 5.6	58.5	15.9	320	289	16	3.7	9 14	9 11	15 42	21 52	21 52
3	12 42	− 0.6	58.8	16.0	333	291	25	4.7	10 36	10 39	16 30	22 07	22 02
4	13 33	− 6.8	59.1	16.1	345	291	35	5.7	12 00	12 09	17 19	22 23	22 12
5	14 25	− 12.7	59.2	16.1	357	289	47	6.7	13 26	13 42	18 11	22 43	22 26
6	15 20	− 18.0	59.3	16.2	9	285	58	7.7	14 54	15 16	19 06	23 08	22 45
7	16 17	− 22.3	59.3	16.2	22	280	69	8.7	16 19	16 48	20 04	23 44	23 14
8	17 18	− 25.2	59.3	16.1	34	273	79	9.7	17 35	18 09	21 05	—	—
9	18 21	− 26.5	59.0	16.1	46	264	88	10.7	18 37	19 10	22 07	0 34	0 00
10	19 24	− 26.1	58.7	16.0	58	254	94	11.7	19 22	19 50	23 06	1 40	1 07
11	20 24	− 24.1	58.3	15.9	70	240	98	12.7	19 53	20 16	—	2 57	2 30
12	21 22	− 20.6	57.7	15.7	83	189	100	13.7	20 16	20 32	0 02	4 19	3 58
13	22 15	− 16.2	57.1	15.6	95	95	99	14.7	20 33	20 44	0 53	5 41	5 26
14	23 05	− 11.1	56.5	15.4	107	79	96	15.7	20 47	20 53	1 40	6 59	6 50
15	23 51	− 5.6	55.9	15.2	119	73	91	16.7	21 00	21 01	2 24	8 14	8 10
16	0 36	− 0.1	55.3	15.1	131	70	85	17.7	21 12	21 08	3 06	9 26	9 28
17	1 20	+ 5.4	54.8	14.9	143	70	77	18.7	21 24	21 16	3 47	10 37	10 44
18	2 04	+ 10.6	54.5	14.8	156	71	69	19.7	21 38	21 25	4 28	11 48	12 00
19	2 49	+ 15.3	54.3	14.8	168	73	60	20.7	21 55	21 37	5 10	12 59	13 16
20	3 35	+ 19.4	54.3	14.8	180	76	50	21.7	22 18	21 54	5 55	14 11	14 33
21	4 24	+ 22.8	54.4	14.8	192	81	41	22.7	22 47	22 18	6 42	15 20	15 49
22	5 16	+ 25.2	54.8	14.9	205	86	32	23.7	23 28	22 55	7 32	16 26	16 58
23	6 10	+ 26.5	55.2	15.0	217	93	23	24.7	—	23 48	8 24	17 22	17 55
24	7 05	+ 26.5	55.8	15.2	229	100	15	25.7	0 21	—	9 18	18 07	18 37
25	8 02	+ 25.1	56.5	15.4	241	108	9	26.7	1 29	0 59	10 13	18 42	19 06
26	8 58	+ 22.3	57.2	15.6	253	118	4	27.7	2 46	2 22	11 06	19 07	19 26
27	9 52	+ 18.2	57.9	15.8	266	138	1	28.7	4 08	3 51	11 58	19 27	19 40
28	10 45	+ 13.1	58.5	15.9	278	238	0	0.3	5 32	5 21	12 48	19 44	19 51
29	11 37	+ 7.3	59.0	16.1	290	279	2	1.3	6 56	6 52	13 37	19 59	20 00
30	12 28	+ 1.0	59.4	16.2	302	287	7	2.3	8 21	8 22	14 26	20 13	20 10
31	13 20	− 5.4	59.6	16.2	315	289	14	3.3	9 47	9 54	15 15	20 29	20 20

MERCURY

Day	RA h m	Dec. °	Diam. "	Phase %	Transit h m	5° high 52° h m	5° high 56° h m
1	10 17	+11.1	6	69	13 41	20 03	20 09
3	10 27	+ 9.8	6	67	13 43	19 59	20 03
5	10 37	+ 8.5	6	64	13 45	19 54	19 57
7	10 46	+ 7.3	7	61	13 46	19 48	19 51
9	10 55	+ 6.0	7	59	13 47	19 43	19 44
11	11 03	+ 4.8	7	56	13 47	19 37	19 37
13	11 10	+ 3.7	7	53	13 46	19 30	19 29
15	11 17	+ 2.6	7	50	13 45	19 23	19 22
17	11 23	+ 1.5	8	47	13 43	19 16	19 13
19	11 28	+ 0.6	8	44	13 40	19 08	19 05
21	11 33	− 0.3	8	40	13 36	19 00	18 56
23	11 36	− 1.0	9	36	13 31	18 52	18 47
25	11 39	− 1.6	9	32	13 26	18 43	18 38
27	11 40	− 2.0	9	28	13 19	18 34	18 29
29	11 40	− 2.3	10	23	13 10	18 25	18 19
31	11 39	− 2.4	10	19	13 01	18 15	18 10

VENUS

Day	RA h m	Dec. °	Diam. "	Phase %	Transit h m	5° high 52° h m	5° high 56° h m
1	8 24	+20.3	10	100	11 48	19 02	19 16
6	8 49	+18.9	10	100	11 54	18 59	19 12
11	9 15	+17.2	10	100	11 59	18 55	19 06
16	9 39	+15.4	10	100	12 04	18 50	18 59
21	10 03	+13.4	10	100	12 08	18 43	18 51
26	10 27	+11.2	10	100	12 12	18 36	18 41
31	10 50	+ 8.9	10	100	12 16	18 27	18 31

MARS

Day	RA h m	Dec. °	Diam. "	Phase %	Transit h m	5° high 52° h m	5° high 56° h m
1	22 56	−13.5	22	96	2 19	22 03	22 20
6	22 55	−13.8	23	97	1 58	21 45	22 02
11	22 53	−14.2	24	98	1 36	21 25	21 43
16	22 50	−14.7	25	99	1 13	21 05	21 23
21	22 45	−15.1	25	100	0 50	20 44	21 03
26	22 40	−15.6	25	100	0 25	20 22	20 42
31	22 35	−16.0	25	100	0 00	20 00	20 20

SUNRISE AND SUNSET

	London 0°05′ 51°30′		Bristol 2°35′ 51°28′		Birmingham 1°55′ 52°28′		Manchester 2°15′ 53°28′		Newcastle 1°37′ 54°59′		Glasgow 4°14′ 55°52′		Belfast 5°56′ 54°35′	
	h m	h m	h m	h m	h m	h m	h m	h m	h m	h m	h m	h m	h m	h m
1	4 23	19 49	4 33	19 59	4 27	20 00	4 24	20 06	4 14	20 10	4 21	20 25	4 34	20 25
2	4 25	19 47	4 35	19 57	4 28	19 59	4 25	20 04	4 16	20 08	4 22	20 23	4 35	20 24
3	4 26	19 46	4 36	19 56	4 30	19 57	4 27	20 02	4 18	20 06	4 24	20 21	4 37	20 22
4	4 28	19 44	4 38	19 54	4 31	19 55	4 29	20 00	4 20	20 04	4 26	20 19	4 39	20 20
5	4 29	19 42	4 39	19 52	4 33	19 53	4 30	19 58	4 22	20 02	4 28	20 17	4 41	20 18
6	4 31	19 41	4 41	19 50	4 35	19 51	4 32	19 57	4 23	20 00	4 30	20 14	4 42	20 16
7	4 32	19 39	4 43	19 49	4 36	19 50	4 34	19 55	4 25	19 58	4 32	20 12	4 44	20 14
8	4 34	19 37	4 44	19 47	4 38	19 48	4 36	19 53	4 27	19 56	4 34	20 10	4 46	20 12
9	4 36	19 35	4 46	19 45	4 40	19 46	4 37	19 51	4 29	19 54	4 36	20 08	4 48	20 10
10	4 37	19 33	4 47	19 43	4 41	19 44	4 39	19 49	4 31	19 52	4 38	20 06	4 50	20 07
11	4 39	19 31	4 49	19 41	4 43	19 42	4 41	19 47	4 33	19 50	4 40	20 03	4 51	20 05
12	4 40	19 30	4 50	19 39	4 44	19 40	4 42	19 45	4 34	19 47	4 41	20 01	4 53	20 03
13	4 42	19 28	4 52	19 37	4 46	19 38	4 44	19 42	4 36	19 45	4 43	19 59	4 55	20 01
14	4 43	19 26	4 53	19 36	4 48	19 36	4 46	19 40	4 38	19 43	4 45	19 57	4 57	19 59
15	4 45	19 24	4 55	19 34	4 49	19 34	4 48	19 38	4 40	19 41	4 47	19 54	4 59	19 57
16	4 47	19 22	4 57	19 32	4 51	19 32	4 49	19 36	4 42	19 38	4 49	19 52	5 00	19 54
17	4 48	19 20	4 58	19 30	4 53	19 30	4 51	19 34	4 44	19 36	4 51	19 50	5 02	19 52
18	4 50	19 18	5 00	19 28	4 54	19 28	4 53	19 32	4 46	19 34	4 53	19 47	5 04	19 50
19	4 51	19 16	5 01	19 26	4 56	19 26	4 55	19 30	4 47	19 32	4 55	19 45	5 06	19 48
20	4 53	19 14	5 03	19 23	4 58	19 23	4 56	19 27	4 49	19 29	4 57	19 42	5 08	19 45
21	4 54	19 11	5 05	19 21	4 59	19 21	4 58	19 25	4 51	19 27	4 59	19 40	5 10	19 43
22	4 56	19 09	5 06	19 19	5 01	19 19	5 00	19 23	4 53	19 24	5 01	19 37	5 12	19 41
23	4 58	19 07	5 08	19 17	5 03	19 17	5 02	19 21	4 55	19 22	5 03	19 35	5 13	19 38
24	4 59	19 05	5 09	19 15	5 04	19 15	5 03	19 18	4 57	19 20	5 05	19 33	5 15	19 36
25	5 01	19 03	5 11	19 13	5 06	19 12	5 05	19 16	4 59	19 17	5 07	19 30	5 17	19 34
26	5 02	19 01	5 13	19 11	5 08	19 10	5 07	19 14	5 01	19 15	5 09	19 28	5 19	19 31
27	5 04	18 59	5 14	19 09	5 09	19 08	5 09	19 12	5 02	19 12	5 11	19 25	5 21	19 29
28	5 06	18 57	5 16	19 06	5 11	19 06	5 10	19 09	5 04	19 10	5 13	19 23	5 23	19 26
29	5 07	18 54	5 17	19 04	5 13	19 04	5 12	19 07	5 06	19 08	5 15	19 20	5 24	19 24
30	5 09	18 52	5 19	19 02	5 14	19 01	5 14	19 05	5 08	19 05	5 17	19 17	5 26	19 21
31	5 10	18 50	5 21	19 00	5 16	18 59	5 16	19 02	5 10	19 03	5 19	19 15	5 28	19 19

JUPITER

Day	RA	Dec.		Transit		5° high			
						52°		56°	
	h m	°	′	h m		h m		h m	
1	9 47.4	+14	11	13	09	19	49	19	57
11	9 55.8	+13	28	12	38	19	14	19	22
21	10 04.2	+12	44	12	07	18	39	18	46
31	10 12.6	+11	58	11	36	18	04	18	10

Diameters - equatorial 31″ polar 29″

SATURN

Day	RA	Dec.		Transit		5° high			
						52°		56°	
	h m	°	′	h m		h m		h m	
1	6 31.9	+22	28	9	54	2	26	2	09
11	6 36.8	+22	25	9	19	1	52	1	35
21	6 41.4	+22	21	8	45	1	18	1	01
31	6 45.5	+22	17	8	09	0	43	0	26

Diameters - equatorial 17″ polar 16″
Rings - major axis 39″ minor axis 17″

URANUS

Day	RA	Dec.		Transit		10° high			
						52°		56°	
	h m	°	′	h m		h m		h m	
1	22 16.1	−11	36	1	39	21	49	22	09
11	22 14.7	−11	44	0	58	21	10	21	30
21	22 13.2	−11	52	0	18	20	30	20	50
31	22 11.7	−12	01	23	33	19	50	20	10

Diameter 4″

NEPTUNE

Day	RA	Dec.		Transit		10° high			
						52°		56°	
	h m	°	′	h m		h m		h m	
1	20 57.4	−17	13	0	21	3	25	2	53
11	20 56.3	−17	18	23	36	2	44	2	12
21	20 55.2	−17	23	22	56	2	03	1	31
31	20 54.2	−17	27	22	15	1	22	0	50

Diameter 2″

 # September 2003

NINTH MONTH, 30 DAYS. *Septem* (seven), seventh month of Roman pre-Julian calendar

1	*Monday*	Edgar Rice Burroughs d. 1875. Germany invades Poland 1939	*week 35 day* 244
2	*Tuesday*	J. R. R. Tolkien d. 1973. Fire of London 1666	245
3	*Wednesday*	Ferdinand Porsche b. 1875. Oliver Cromwell d. 1658	246
4	*Thursday*	Anton Bruckner b. 1824. Third French Republic proclaimed 1870	247
5	*Friday*	Jesse James b. 1847. Mother Teresa of Calcutta d. 1997	248
6	*Saturday*	Elie Halévy b. 1870. Hendrik Verwoerd d. 1966	249
7	*Sunday*	**12th S. after Trinity.** Elizabeth I b. 1533	250
8	*Monday*	Peter Sellers b. 1925. Richard I (Plantagenet) b. 1157	*week 36 day* 251
9	*Tuesday*	Captain William Bligh b. 1754. Otis Redding b. 1941	252
10	*Wednesday*	Sir John Sloane b. 1753. Wilfred Scawen Blunt d. 1922	253
11	*Thursday*	President Ferdinand Marcos b. 1917. Nikita Khrushchev d. 1971	254
12	*Friday*	Herbert Asquith b. 1852. Marshal von Blücher d. 1819	255
13	*Saturday*	Roald Dahl b. 1916. Leopold Stokowski d. 1977	256
14	*Sunday*	**13th S. after Trinity. Holy Cross Day.**	257
15	*Monday*	*Prince Henry of Wales b. 1984.* Battle of Britain Day	*week 37 day* 258
16	*Tuesday*	Sir Gordon Newton b. 1907. Maria Callas d. 1977	259
17	*Wednesday*	Sir Frederick Ashton b. 1904. William Henry Fox Talbot d. 1877	260
18	*Thursday*	Dr. Samuel Johnson b. 1709. Sean O'Casey d. 1964	261
19	*Friday*	George Cadbury b. 1834. Dr. Thomas Barnardo d. 1905	262
20	*Saturday*	Florence Margaret Smith b. 1902. Jean Sibelius d. 1957	263
21	*Sunday*	**14th S. after Trinity. St Matthew**	264
22	*Monday*	Michael Faraday b. 1791. Coronation of George III 1761	*week 38 day* 265
23	*Tuesday*	Jim Morrison b. 1952. Sigmund Freud d. 1939	266
24	*Wednesday*	F. Scott Fitzgerald b. 1896. Sir Ian MacGregor b. 1912	267
25	*Thursday*	Mark Rothko b. 1903. Trans-atlantic telephone service began 1956	268
26	*Friday*	T. S. Eliot b. 1888. Daniel Boone d. 1820	269
27	*Saturday*	JEWISH NEW YEAR. Edgar Degas d. 1917	270
28	*Sunday*	**15th S. after Trinity.** Louis Pasteur d. 1895	271
29	*Monday*	**St Michael and All Angels.** Lord Horatio Nelson b. 1758	*week 39 day* 272
30	*Tuesday*	Truman Capote b. 1924. Rudolph Diesel d. 1913	273

ASTRONOMICAL PHENOMENA

d	h	
8	06	Venus in conjunction with Mercury. Venus 5° N.
9	12	Mars in conjunction with Moon. Mars 1° S.
11	02	Mercury in inferior conjunction
20	04	Saturn in conjunction with Moon. Saturn 5° S.
20	09	Mercury at stationary point
23	11	Sun's longitude 180° ♎
24	06	Jupiter in conjunction with Moon. Jupiter 4° S.
24	20	Mercury in conjunction with Moon. Mercury 4° S.
26	22	Venus in conjunction with Moon. Venus 2° S.
27	00	Mercury at greatest elongation W. 18°
27	08	Mars at stationary point

MINIMA OF ALGOL

d	h	d	h	d	h
1	20.6	13	07.8	24	19.1
4	17.4	16	04.7	27	15.9
7	14.2	19	01.5	30	12.7
10	11.0	21	22.3		

CONSTELLATIONS

The following constellations are near the meridian at

d	h	d	h
August	1	24	September	15	21
August	16	23	October	1	20
September	1	22	October	16	19

Draco, Cepheus, Lyra, Cygnus, Vulpecula, Sagitta, Delphinus, Equuleus, Aquila, Aquarius and Capricornus

THE MOON

Phases, Apsides and Node	d	h	m
☽ First Quarter	3	12	34
○ Full Moon	10	16	36
☾ Last Quarter	18	19	03
● New Moon	26	03	09
Apogee (404,714 km)	16	09	22
Perigee (362,835 km)	28	05	59

Mean longitude of ascending node on September 1, 54°

THE SUN   s.d. 15′.9

Day	Right Ascension h m s	Dec. ° ′	Equation of Time m s	Rise 52° h m	Rise 56° h m	Transit h m	Set 52° h m	Set 56° h m	Sidereal time h m s	Transit of First Point of Aries h m s
1	10 39 15	+ 8 31	− 0 16	5 11	5 03	12 00	18 48	18 56	22 38 59	1 20 48
2	10 42 53	+ 8 09	+ 0 03	5 13	5 05	12 00	18 46	18 53	22 42 56	1 16 52
3	10 46 30	+ 7 47	+ 0 22	5 14	5 07	11 59	18 44	18 51	22 46 52	1 12 56
4	10 50 07	+ 7 25	+ 0 41	5 16	5 09	11 59	18 41	18 48	22 50 49	1 09 00
5	10 53 44	+ 7 03	+ 1 01	5 17	5 11	11 59	18 39	18 45	22 54 45	1 05 04
6	10 57 21	+ 6 41	+ 1 21	5 19	5 13	11 58	18 37	18 43	22 58 42	1 01 08
7	11 00 57	+ 6 18	+ 1 41	5 21	5 15	11 58	18 35	18 40	23 02 38	0 57 12
8	11 04 33	+ 5 56	+ 2 02	5 22	5 17	11 58	18 32	18 37	23 06 35	0 53 16
9	11 08 09	+ 5 33	+ 2 23	5 24	5 19	11 57	18 30	18 35	23 10 31	0 49 20
10	11 11 45	+ 5 11	+ 2 43	5 26	5 21	11 57	18 28	18 32	23 14 28	0 45 25
11	11 15 20	+ 4 48	+ 3 04	5 27	5 23	11 57	18 25	18 30	23 18 25	0 41 29
12	11 18 56	+ 4 25	+ 3 26	5 29	5 25	11 56	18 23	18 27	23 22 21	0 37 33
13	11 22 31	+ 4 02	+ 3 47	5 30	5 27	11 56	18 21	18 24	23 26 18	0 33 37
14	11 26 06	+ 3 39	+ 4 08	5 32	5 29	11 56	18 18	18 22	23 30 14	0 29 41
15	11 29 41	+ 3 16	+ 4 30	5 34	5 31	11 55	18 16	18 19	23 34 11	0 25 45
16	11 33 16	+ 2 53	+ 4 51	5 35	5 32	11 55	18 14	18 16	23 38 07	0 21 49
17	11 36 51	+ 2 30	+ 5 12	5 37	5 34	11 55	18 11	18 14	23 42 04	0 17 53
18	11 40 27	+ 2 07	+ 5 34	5 39	5 36	11 54	18 09	18 11	23 46 00	0 13 57
19	11 44 02	+ 1 44	+ 5 55	5 40	5 38	11 54	18 07	18 08	23 49 57	0 10 01
20	11 47 37	+ 1 20	+ 6 17	5 42	5 40	11 54	18 04	18 06	23 53 54	0 06 05
21	11 51 12	+ 0 57	+ 6 38	5 43	5 42	11 53	18 02	18 03	23 57 50	{ 0 02 10 / 23 58 14
22	11 54 48	+ 0 34	+ 6 59	5 45	5 44	11 53	18 00	18 00	0 01 47	23 54 18
23	11 58 23	+ 0 11	+ 7 20	5 47	5 46	11 52	17 57	17 58	0 05 43	23 50 22
24	12 01 59	− 0 13	+ 7 41	5 48	5 48	11 52	17 55	17 55	0 09 40	23 46 26
25	12 05 34	− 0 36	+ 8 02	5 50	5 50	11 52	17 53	17 52	0 13 36	23 42 30
26	12 09 10	− 1 00	+ 8 23	5 52	5 52	11 51	17 50	17 50	0 17 33	23 38 34
27	12 12 46	− 1 23	+ 8 43	5 53	5 54	11 51	17 48	17 47	0 21 29	23 34 38
28	12 16 22	− 1 46	+ 9 04	5 55	5 56	11 51	17 46	17 44	0 25 26	23 30 42
29	12 19 59	− 2 10	+ 9 24	5 57	5 58	11 50	17 43	17 42	0 29 23	23 26 46
30	12 23 36	− 2 33	+ 9 44	5 58	6 00	11 50	17 41	17 39	0 33 19	23 22 50

DURATION OF TWILIGHT (in minutes)

Latitude	52°	56°	52°	56°	52°	56°	52°	56°
	1 September		11 September		21 September		30 September	
Civil	35	39	34	38	34	37	34	37
Nautical	79	89	76	85	74	82	73	80
Astronomical	127	147	120	136	116	129	113	125

THE NIGHT SKY

Mercury passes through inferior conjunction on the 11th and reaches greatest western elongation (18°) on the 27th. It is therefore visible as a morning object after the first three weeks of the month and this is the most favourable morning apparition of the year for observers in the British Isles. It may then be seen low above the eastern horizon around the time of beginning of morning civil twilight. During this period its magnitude brightens from +1.2 to −0.8. On the morning of the 24th the old crescent Moon, only 2 days before New, could be a useful guide to the planet which will be 9 degrees almost vertically below it. Observers should also note that Mercury and Jupiter are fairly close together at this time, both being almost due east with Mercury gradually moving away from Jupiter, eastwards. Mercury is at a much lower altitude than Jupiter.

Venus is unsuitably placed for observation.

Mars is a conspicuous object, magnitude −2.6. It is only just past opposition so it continues to be visible for the greater part of the night. Even by the end of the month it is still visible after midnight, low in the south-western sky. Mars is moving slowly in the constellation of Aquarius, reaching its second stationary point on the 27th, when it resumes its direct motion. The Moon, near Full, is in the vicinity of the planet on the 9th.

Jupiter, magnitude −1.7, emerges from the morning twilight after the first week of the month, becoming visible above the eastern horizon before dawn.

Saturn, magnitude +0.1, continues to be visible as a morning object in the south-eastern quadrant of the sky. By the end of the month it can be seen rising above the east-north-east horizon before midnight. On the morning of the 20th the waning crescent Moon passes 4 degrees north of the planet.

Zodiacal Light. The morning cone may be seen reaching up from the eastern horizon along the ecliptic, before the beginning of morning twilight, from the beginning of the month to the 9th and again after the 24th.

THE MOON

Day	RA	Dec.	Hor. par.	Semi-diam.	Sun's co-long.	PA of Bright Limb	Phase	Age	Rise 52°	Rise 56°	Transit	Set 52°	Set 56°
	h m	°	'	'	°	°	%	d	h m	h m	h m	h m	h m
1	14 12	−11.6	59.6	16.2	327	288	23	4.3	11 14	11 27	16 07	20 47	20 32
2	15 07	−17.1	59.5	16.2	339	286	33	5.3	12 42	13 02	17 01	21 11	20 49
3	16 04	−21.6	59.3	16.2	351	281	44	6.3	14 08	14 36	17 59	21 43	21 14
4	17 04	−24.9	59.0	16.1	4	275	56	7.3	15 27	16 00	18 59	22 27	21 54
5	18 06	−26.5	58.7	16.0	16	268	67	8.3	16 33	17 07	19 59	23 27	22 53
6	19 07	−26.5	58.3	15.9	28	261	77	9.3	17 21	17 52	20 58	—	—
7	20 08	−24.9	57.9	15.8	40	253	85	10.3	17 56	18 21	21 54	0 40	0 10
8	21 05	−21.9	57.4	15.6	52	246	92	11.3	18 21	18 39	22 45	2 00	1 36
9	21 58	−17.7	56.9	15.5	64	237	97	12.3	18 39	18 52	23 33	3 21	3 04
10	22 48	−12.8	56.4	15.4	77	217	99	13.3	18 54	19 01	—	4 40	4 29
11	23 36	−7.4	55.9	15.2	89	117	100	14.3	19 06	19 09	0 18	5 56	5 50
12	0 21	−1.8	55.4	15.1	101	80	98	15.3	19 18	19 16	1 00	7 09	7 09
13	1 05	+3.7	55.0	15.0	113	73	95	16.3	19 30	19 23	1 42	8 21	8 26
14	1 49	+9.1	54.6	14.9	125	72	90	17.3	19 43	19 32	2 23	9 32	9 42
15	2 34	+14.0	54.3	14.8	138	73	83	18.3	19 59	19 42	3 05	10 44	10 59
16	3 20	+18.4	54.2	14.8	150	75	75	19.3	20 18	19 56	3 49	11 56	12 17
17	4 08	+22.0	54.2	14.8	162	79	67	20.3	20 44	20 17	4 34	13 06	13 33
18	4 58	+24.8	54.4	14.8	174	84	58	21.3	21 19	20 47	5 23	14 14	14 45
19	5 51	+26.4	54.7	14.9	186	89	48	22.3	22 07	21 33	6 14	15 13	15 47
20	6 45	+26.9	55.3	15.1	199	95	39	23.3	23 07	22 35	7 06	16 02	16 35
21	7 41	+26.0	55.9	15.2	211	102	29	24.3	—	23 53	8 00	16 41	17 08
22	8 36	+23.7	56.7	15.5	223	108	20	25.3	0 20	—	8 53	17 09	17 31
23	9 31	+20.1	57.6	15.7	235	114	12	26.3	1 40	1 19	9 45	17 31	17 46
24	10 24	+15.4	58.4	15.9	247	121	6	27.3	3 04	2 50	10 36	17 49	17 58
25	11 17	+9.7	59.2	16.1	260	130	2	28.3	4 29	4 22	11 26	18 04	18 08
26	12 09	+3.4	59.8	16.3	272	179	0	29.3	5 55	5 54	12 16	18 18	18 17
27	13 01	−3.2	60.2	16.4	284	278	1	0.9	7 23	7 28	13 06	18 34	18 26
28	13 55	−9.7	60.4	16.5	296	287	5	1.9	8 52	9 04	13 59	18 51	18 38
29	14 50	−15.7	60.4	16.4	309	286	11	2.9	10 24	10 42	14 54	19 13	18 53
30	15 48	−20.7	60.1	16.4	321	283	20	3.9	11 54	12 20	15 52	19 42	19 15

MERCURY

Day	RA	Dec.	Diam.	Phase	Transit	5° high 52°	5° high 56°
	h m	°	"	%	h m	h m	h m
1	11 37	−2.3	10	16	12 56	18 10	18 05
3	11 34	−2.0	10	12	12 44	18 01	17 56
5	11 29	−1.5	10	8	12 31	17 51	17 47
7	11 24	−0.7	11	4	12 17	17 41	17 38
9	11 17	+0.3	11	2	12 03	17 32	17 30
11	11 10	+1.5	11	1	11 48	6 14	6 16
13	11 04	+2.7	10	1	11 34	5 54	5 55
15	10 59	+3.9	10	4	11 22	5 35	5 35
17	10 55	+5.0	10	8	11 10	5 18	5 17
19	10 53	+5.9	9	15	11 01	5 04	5 03
21	10 54	+6.5	9	22	10 55	4 54	4 52
23	10 57	+6.9	8	31	10 50	4 48	4 46
25	11 02	+6.9	8	40	10 48	4 45	4 43
27	11 09	+6.6	7	50	10 47	4 46	4 44
29	11 17	+6.1	7	59	10 49	4 50	4 49
31	11 28	+5.3	6	67	10 51	4 57	4 56

VENUS

Day	RA	Dec.	Diam.	Phase	Transit	5° high 52°	5° high 56°
	h m	°	"	%	h m	h m	h m
1	10 55	+8.4	10	100	12 16	18 25	18 29
6	11 18	+6.0	10	100	12 20	18 16	18 18
11	11 41	+3.6	10	99	12 23	18 07	18 06
16	12 04	+1.0	10	99	12 26	17 57	17 54
21	12 26	−1.5	10	99	12 29	17 46	17 42
26	12 49	−4.1	10	98	12 32	17 36	17 29
31	13 12	−6.6	10	98	12 35	17 26	17 16

MARS

Day	RA	Dec.	Diam.	Phase	Transit	5° high 52°	5° high 56°
1	22 34	−16.1	25	100	23 50	3 50	3 30
6	22 29	−16.3	25	99	23 25	3 24	3 03
11	22 24	−16.5	24	99	23 01	2 58	2 38
16	22 20	−16.5	23	98	22 38	2 35	2 14
21	22 18	−16.3	23	97	22 16	2 13	1 53
26	22 16	−16.1	22	96	21 55	1 54	1 34
31	22 16	−15.7	21	95	21 35	1 37	1 17

SUNRISE AND SUNSET

	London 0°05' 51°30'		Bristol 2°35' 51°28'		Birmingham 1°55' 52°28'		Manchester 2°15' 53°28'		Newcastle 1°37' 54°59'		Glasgow 4°14' 55°52'		Belfast 5°56' 54°35'	
	h m	h m	h m	h m	h m	h m	h m	h m	h m	h m	h m	h m	h m	h m
1	5 12	18 48	5 22	18 58	5 18	18 57	5 17	19 00	5 12	19 00	5 20	19 12	5 30	19 17
2	5 14	18 46	5 24	18 55	5 19	18 54	5 19	18 57	5 14	18 58	5 22	19 10	5 32	19 14
3	5 15	18 43	5 25	18 53	5 21	18 52	5 21	18 55	5 16	18 55	5 24	19 07	5 34	19 12
4	5 17	18 41	5 27	18 51	5 23	18 50	5 22	18 53	5 17	18 53	5 26	19 05	5 35	19 09
5	5 18	18 39	5 28	18 49	5 24	18 47	5 24	18 50	5 19	18 50	5 28	19 02	5 37	19 07
6	5 20	18 37	5 30	18 46	5 26	18 45	5 26	18 48	5 21	18 48	5 30	18 59	5 39	19 04
7	5 22	18 34	5 32	18 44	5 28	18 43	5 28	18 45	5 23	18 45	5 32	18 57	5 41	19 02
8	5 23	18 32	5 33	18 42	5 29	18 40	5 29	18 43	5 25	18 42	5 34	18 54	5 43	18 59
9	5 25	18 30	5 35	18 40	5 31	18 38	5 31	18 41	5 27	18 40	5 36	18 52	5 45	18 57
10	5 26	18 27	5 36	18 37	5 33	18 36	5 33	18 38	5 29	18 37	5 38	18 49	5 46	18 54
11	5 28	18 25	5 38	18 35	5 34	18 33	5 35	18 36	5 30	18 35	5 40	18 46	5 48	18 52
12	5 30	18 23	5 40	18 33	5 36	18 31	5 36	18 33	5 32	18 32	5 42	18 44	5 50	18 49
13	5 31	18 21	5 41	18 31	5 38	18 29	5 38	18 31	5 34	18 30	5 44	18 41	5 52	18 47
14	5 33	18 18	5 43	18 28	5 39	18 26	5 40	18 28	5 36	18 27	5 46	18 38	5 54	18 44
15	5 34	18 16	5 44	18 26	5 41	18 24	5 42	18 26	5 38	18 25	5 48	18 36	5 55	18 42
16	5 36	18 14	5 46	18 24	5 43	18 22	5 43	18 24	5 40	18 22	5 50	18 33	5 57	18 39
17	5 38	18 11	5 48	18 21	5 44	18 19	5 45	18 21	5 42	18 19	5 51	18 30	5 59	18 36
18	5 39	18 09	5 49	18 19	5 46	18 17	5 47	18 19	5 43	18 17	5 53	18 28	6 01	18 34
19	5 41	18 07	5 51	18 17	5 48	18 14	5 49	18 16	5 45	18 14	5 55	18 25	6 03	18 31
20	5 42	18 04	5 52	18 14	5 49	18 12	5 50	18 14	5 47	18 12	5 57	18 22	6 05	18 29
21	5 44	18 02	5 54	18 12	5 51	18 10	5 52	18 11	5 49	18 09	5 59	18 20	6 06	18 26
22	5 46	18 00	5 56	18 10	5 53	18 07	5 54	18 09	5 51	18 07	6 01	18 17	6 08	18 24
23	5 47	17 57	5 57	18 07	5 54	18 05	5 56	18 06	5 53	18 04	6 03	18 15	6 10	18 21
24	5 49	17 55	5 59	18 05	5 56	18 03	5 57	18 04	5 55	18 01	6 05	18 12	6 12	18 19
25	5 50	17 53	6 00	18 03	5 58	18 00	5 59	18 01	5 57	17 59	6 07	18 09	6 14	18 16
26	5 52	17 51	6 02	18 01	5 59	17 58	6 01	17 59	5 58	17 56	6 09	18 07	6 16	18 14
27	5 54	17 48	6 04	17 58	6 01	17 55	6 03	17 57	6 00	17 54	6 11	18 04	6 18	18 11
28	5 55	17 46	6 05	17 56	6 03	17 53	6 04	17 54	6 02	17 51	6 13	18 01	6 19	18 09
29	5 57	17 44	6 07	17 54	6 04	17 51	6 06	17 52	6 04	17 49	6 15	17 59	6 21	18 06
30	5 58	17 41	6 08	17 51	6 06	17 48	6 08	17 49	6 06	17 46	6 17	17 56	6 23	18 04

JUPITER

Day	RA	Dec.		Transit		5° high 52°		56°	
	h m	°	'	h m		h m		h m	
1	10 13.4	+11	54	11	33	5 05		4 59	
11	10 21.6	+11	08	11	02	4 38		4 32	
21	10 29.7	+10	23	10	30	4 11		4 05	
31	10 37.5	+ 9	38	9	59	3 43		3 38	

Diameters - equatorial 31″ polar 29″

SATURN

Day	RA	Dec.		Transit		5° high 52°		56°	
	h m	°	'	h m		h m		h m	
1	6 45.9	+22	16	8	06	0 40		0 23	
11	6 49.5	+22	12	7	30	0 04		23 44	
21	6 52.5	+22	09	6	54	23 25		23 08	
31	6 54.8	+22	06	6	17	22 48		22 31	

Diameters - equatorial 18″ polar 16″
Rings - major axis 40″ minor axis 17″

URANUS

Day	RA	Dec.		Transit		10° high 52°		56°	
	h m	°	'	h m		h m		h m	
1	22 11.6	−12	01	23	29	3 16		2 55	
11	22 10.1	−12	10	22	48	2 34		2 13	
21	22 08.7	−12	17	22	07	1 52		1 31	
31	22 07.5	−12	23	21	27	1 11		0 50	

Diameter 4″

NEPTUNE

Day	RA	Dec.		Transit		10° high 52°		56°	
	h m	°	'	h m		h m		h m	
1	20 54.1	−17	27	22	11	1 18		0 46	
11	20 53.2	−17	31	21	31	0 37		0 05	
21	20 52.5	−17	34	20	51	23 53		23 20	
31	20 51.9	−17	36	20	11	23 12		22 40	

Diameter 2″

October 2003

TENTH MONTH, 31 DAYS. *Octo* (eighth), eighth month of Roman pre-Julian calendar

1	*Wednesday*	*Michaelmas Law Sittings begin.* Stanley Holloway b. 1890.	274
2	*Thursday*	Mahatma Gandhi b. 1869. Graham Greene b. 1904	275
3	*Friday*	William Morris d. 1896. Reunification of Germany 1990	276
4	*Saturday*	Buster Keaton b. 1895. Janis Joplin d. 1970	277
5	*Sunday*	**16th S. after Trinity.** Oxfam founded 1942	278
6	*Monday*	YOM KIPPUR. Charles Stewart Parnell d. 1891	*week 40 day* 279
7	*Tuesday*	Archbishop William Laud b. 1573. Edgar Allen Poe d. 1849	280
8	*Wednesday*	Juan Perón b. 1895. Kathleen Ferrier d. 1953	281
9	*Thursday*	Alfred Dreyfus b. 1859. John Lennon b. 1940	282
10	*Friday*	Sir Ralph Richardson d. 1983. Fiji declared independence 1970	283
11	*Saturday*	FEAST OF THE TABERNACLES begins. Donald Dewar d. 2000	284
12	*Sunday*	**17th S. after Trinity.** Five killed in IRA bombing of Grand Hotel, Brighton 1984	285
13	*Monday*	Arnold Shoenberg b. 1874. Sidney Webb d. 1947	*week 41 day* 286
14	*Tuesday*	General Dwight Eisenhower b. 1890. Errol Flynn d. 1959	287
15	*Wednesday*	Friedrich Nietzsche b. 1844. Cole Porter d. 1964	288
16	*Thursday*	Oscar Wilde b. 1854. Houses of Parliament destroyed by fire 1834	289
17	*Friday*	Rita Hayworth b. 1918. Sir Philip Sidney d. 1586	290
18	*Saturday*	**St Luke.** 3rd Viscount Palmerston d. 1865	291
19	*Sunday*	**18th S. after Trinity.** Kenneth Wood d. 1997	292
20	*Monday*	Sir Christopher Wren b. 1632. Jack Buchanan d. 1957	*week 42 day* 293
21	*Tuesday*	Lord Horatio Nelson d. 1805. Battle of Trafalgar 1805	294
22	*Wednesday*	Ivan Bunin b. 1870. Paul Cézanne d. 1906	295
23	*Thursday*	Diana Dors b. 1931. The Parliament of Great Britain met for the first time 1707	296
24	*Friday*	Dame Sybil Thorndike b. 1882. Pyotr Ilyich Tchaikovsky d. 1893	297
25	*Saturday*	Pablo Picasso b. 1881. Vincent Price d. 1993	298
26	*Sunday*	**Last S. after Trinity.** William Hogarth d. 1974	299
27	*Monday*	RAMADAN begins. Colonel Theodore Roosevelt b. 1858	*week 43 day* 300
28	*Tuesday*	**SS Simon and Jude.** Captain James Cook b. 1728	301
29	*Wednesday*	James Boswell b. 1740. Frances Hodgson Burnett d. 1924	302
30	*Thursday*	Angelica Kauffmann b. 1741. Sir Barnes Wallis d. 1979	303
31	*Friday*	Hallowmass Eve. John Keats b. 1795	304

ASTRONOMICAL PHENOMENA

d h
6　16 Mars in conjunction with Moon. Mars 1°N.
17　14 Saturn in conjunction with Moon. Saturn 5° S.
22　02 Jupiter in conjunction with Moon. Jupiter 4° S.
23　02 Neptune at stationary point
23　20 Sun's longitude 210° ♏
25　10 Mercury in superior conjunction
25　13 Mercury in conjunction with Moon. Mercury 1° S.
26　00 Saturn at stationary point
26　20 Venus in conjunction with Moon. Venus 0°.09 N.

MINIMA OF ALGOL

d	h	d	h	d	h
3	09.5	14	20.8	26	08.0
6	06.3	17	17.6	29	04.8
9	03.1	20	14.4		
12	00.0	23	11.2		

CONSTELLATIONS
The following constellations are near the meridian at

d	h		d	h
September	1	24	October	16	21
September	15	23	November	1	20
October	1	22	November	15	19

Ursa Major (below the Pole), Cepheus, Cassiopeia, Cygnus, Lacerta, Andromeda, Pegasus, Capricornus, Aquarius and Piscis Austrinus

THE MOON

Phases, Apsides and Node	d	h	m
☽ First Quarter	2	19	09
○ Full Moon	10	07	27
☾ Last Quarter	18	12	31
● New Moon	25	12	50
Apogee (405,692 km)	14	02	25
Perigee (358,547 km)	26	11	30

Mean longitude of ascending node on October 1, 53°

THE SUN   s.d. 16'.1

Day	Right Ascension h m s	Dec. – ° ′	Equation of Time m s	Rise 52° h m	Rise 56° h m	Transit h m	Set 52° h m	Set 56° h m	Sidereal time h m s	Transit of First Point of Aries h m s
1	12 27 12	2 56	+10 03	6 00	6 02	11 50	17 39	17 37	0 37 16	23 18 55
2	12 30 50	3 20	+10 23	6 02	6 04	11 49	17 36	17 34	0 41 12	23 14 59
3	12 34 27	3 43	+10 42	6 03	6 06	11 49	17 34	17 31	0 45 09	23 11 03
4	12 38 05	4 06	+11 01	6 05	6 08	11 49	17 32	17 29	0 49 05	23 07 07
5	12 41 43	4 29	+11 19	6 07	6 10	11 49	17 29	17 26	0 53 02	23 03 11
6	12 45 21	4 52	+11 37	6 08	6 12	11 48	17 27	17 23	0 56 58	22 59 15
7	12 49 00	5 15	+11 55	6 10	6 14	11 48	17 25	17 21	1 00 55	22 55 19
8	12 52 39	5 38	+12 12	6 12	6 16	11 48	17 23	17 18	1 04 52	22 51 23
9	12 56 19	6 01	+12 30	6 14	6 18	11 47	17 20	17 16	1 08 48	22 47 27
10	12 59 59	6 24	+12 46	6 15	6 20	11 47	17 18	17 13	1 12 45	22 43 31
11	13 03 39	6 47	+13 02	6 17	6 22	11 47	17 16	17 11	1 16 41	22 39 35
12	13 07 20	7 09	+13 18	6 19	6 24	11 47	17 14	17 08	1 20 38	22 35 40
13	13 11 01	7 32	+13 33	6 20	6 26	11 46	17 11	17 06	1 24 34	22 31 44
14	13 14 43	7 54	+13 48	6 22	6 28	11 46	17 09	17 03	1 28 31	22 27 48
15	13 18 26	8 17	+14 02	6 24	6 30	11 46	17 07	17 01	1 32 27	22 23 52
16	13 22 09	8 39	+14 15	6 26	6 32	11 46	17 05	16 58	1 36 24	22 19 56
17	13 25 52	9 01	+14 28	6 27	6 34	11 45	17 03	16 56	1 40 21	22 16 00
18	13 29 36	9 23	+14 41	6 29	6 36	11 45	17 01	16 53	1 44 17	22 12 04
19	13 33 21	9 45	+14 52	6 31	6 38	11 45	16 58	16 51	1 48 14	22 08 08
20	13 37 07	10 06	+15 04	6 33	6 41	11 45	16 56	16 48	1 52 10	22 04 12
21	13 40 53	10 28	+15 14	6 34	6 43	11 45	16 54	16 46	1 56 07	22 00 16
22	13 44 40	10 49	+15 24	6 36	6 45	11 45	16 52	16 43	2 00 03	21 56 20
23	13 48 27	11 11	+15 33	6 38	6 47	11 44	16 50	16 41	2 04 00	21 52 25
24	13 52 15	11 32	+15 41	6 40	6 49	11 44	16 48	16 39	2 07 56	21 48 29
25	13 56 04	11 53	+15 49	6 41	6 51	11 44	16 46	16 36	2 11 53	21 44 33
26	13 59 53	12 13	+15 56	6 43	6 53	11 44	16 44	16 34	2 15 49	21 40 37
27	14 03 44	12 34	+16 02	6 45	6 55	11 44	16 42	16 32	2 19 46	21 36 41
28	14 07 35	12 54	+16 07	6 47	6 57	11 44	16 40	16 29	2 23 43	21 32 45
29	14 11 26	13 14	+16 13	6 49	7 00	11 44	16 38	16 27	2 27 39	21 28 49
30	14 15 19	13 34	+16 17	6 50	7 02	11 44	16 36	16 25	2 31 36	21 24 53
31	14 19 12	13 54	+16 20	6 52	7 04	11 44	16 34	16 23	2 35 32	21 20 57

DURATION OF TWILIGHT (in minutes)

Latitude	52°	56°	52°	56°	52°	56°	52°	56°
	1 October		11 October		21 October		31 October	
Civil	34	37	34	37	34	38	35	39
Nautical	73	80	73	80	74	81	75	83
Astronomical	113	125	112	124	113	124	114	126

THE NIGHT SKY

Mercury continues to be favourably placed for observation as a morning object for the first 10 days of the month, low above the eastern horizon around the time of beginning of morning civil twilight. During this period its magnitude brightens from –0.8 to –1.2. Mercury passes through superior conjunction on the 25th.

Venus is unsuitably placed for observation during October.

Mars, its magnitude fading from –2.1 to –1.2, continues to be visible in the evenings, low in the south-western quadrant of the sky. By the end of the month it is no longer visible after midnight. The gibbous Moon is near the planet on the evening of the 6th. Mars is in the constellation of Aquarius.

Jupiter, magnitude –1.8, continues to be visible as a brilliant morning object in the eastern sky. By the end of the month it may be seen low in the east shortly after 02h.

On the morning of the 22nd the old crescent Moon passes 3 degrees north of the Moon. The four Galilean satellites are readily observable with a small telescope or even a good pair of binoculars provided that they are held rigidly.

Saturn, although technically a morning object, is now visible in the eastern sky in the late evenings and by the end of October is visible low above the east-north-east horizon by about 21h. Its magnitude is 0.0. The gibbous Moon is near the planet on the nights of the 16–17th and 17th–18th. Saturn is moving slowly direct in Gemini until the 25th when it reaches its first stationary point and moves retrograde. The rings of Saturn present a beautiful spectacle to the observer with a small telescope. The Earth passed through the ring plane in 1995 and since then the rings have been slowly opening up: the diameter of the minor axis is now 18 arcseconds, slightly greater than the polar diameter of the planet itself.

THE MOON

Day	RA h m	Dec. °	Hor. par. ′	Semi- diam. ′	Sun's co- long. °	PA of Bright Limb °	Phase %	Age d	Rise 52° h m	Rise 56° h m	Transit h m	Set 52° h m	Set 56° h m
1	16 49	−24.4	59.7	16.3	333	278	30	4.9	13 18	13 51	16 53	20 23	19 50
2	17 51	−26.5	59.1	16.1	345	271	41	5.9	14 29	15 04	17 54	21 18	20 43
3	18 54	−26.9	58.5	15.9	357	265	52	6.9	15 23	15 56	18 53	22 28	21 56
4	19 54	−25.6	57.9	15.8	10	258	63	7.9	16 01	16 27	19 50	23 46	23 20
5	20 52	−22.9	57.3	15.6	22	252	73	8.9	16 27	16 48	20 42	—	—
6	21 45	−19.0	56.7	15.5	34	246	82	9.9	16 47	17 01	21 30	1 06	0 47
7	22 36	−14.3	56.2	15.3	46	242	89	10.9	17 02	17 11	22 15	2 25	2 12
8	23 23	− 9.0	55.7	15.2	58	238	95	11.9	17 14	17 19	22 57	3 41	3 34
9	0 08	− 3.5	55.3	15.1	70	232	98	12.9	17 26	17 26	23 39	4 55	4 53
10	0 52	+ 2.1	54.9	15.0	83	205	100	13.9	17 37	17 32	—	6 07	6 10
11	1 36	+ 7.5	54.6	14.9	95	85	100	14.9	17 50	17 40	0 20	7 18	7 26
12	2 20	+12.7	54.3	14.8	107	75	97	15.9	18 04	17 49	1 01	8 30	8 43
13	3 06	+17.3	54.1	14.7	119	74	94	16.9	18 22	18 01	1 44	9 42	10 01
14	3 53	+21.2	54.0	14.7	131	77	88	17.9	18 44	18 19	2 29	10 53	11 18
15	4 43	+24.2	54.1	14.7	143	81	81	18.9	19 15	18 44	3 16	12 02	12 33
16	5 34	+26.2	54.3	14.8	156	86	74	19.9	19 57	19 23	4 06	13 05	13 39
17	6 28	+27.0	54.6	14.9	168	92	65	20.9	20 51	20 18	4 58	13 58	14 32
18	7 22	+26.6	55.2	15.0	180	98	55	21.9	21 58	21 28	5 50	14 39	15 10
19	8 16	+24.8	55.8	15.2	192	103	45	22.9	23 13	22 50	6 42	15 11	15 35
20	9 10	+21.8	56.6	15.4	204	109	35	23.9	—	—	7 33	15 34	15 53
21	10 03	+17.5	57.5	15.7	216	113	26	24.9	0 34	0 17	8 24	15 53	16 05
22	10 55	+12.3	58.5	15.9	229	117	17	25.9	1 57	1 47	9 13	16 09	16 15
23	11 46	+ 6.3	59.4	16.2	241	120	9	26.9	3 22	3 18	10 02	16 23	16 24
24	12 38	− 0.3	60.2	16.4	253	122	4	27.9	4 49	4 51	10 52	16 37	16 33
25	13 31	− 7.0	60.8	16.6	265	129	0	28.9	6 19	6 27	11 44	16 53	16 43
26	14 27	−13.4	61.1	16.7	278	279	0	0.5	7 52	8 07	12 39	17 13	16 56
27	15 25	−19.0	61.1	16.7	290	285	3	1.5	9 26	9 49	13 38	17 39	17 15
28	16 27	−23.4	60.8	16.6	302	281	9	2.5	10 58	11 28	14 40	18 16	17 45
29	17 31	−26.2	60.2	16.4	314	275	17	3.5	12 18	12 53	15 44	19 07	18 32
30	18 36	−27.1	59.5	16.2	326	269	27	4.5	13 20	13 55	16 46	20 15	19 41
31	19 39	−26.2	58.7	16.0	339	262	37	5.5	14 04	14 33	17 45	21 33	21 04

MERCURY

Day	RA h m	Dec. °	Diam. ″	Phase %	Transit h m	5° high 52° h m	5° high 56° h m
1	11 28	+ 5.3	6	67	10 51	4 57	4 56
3	11 39	+ 4.3	6	75	10 54	5 05	5 05
5	11 50	+ 3.1	6	81	10 58	5 15	5 16
7	12 03	+ 1.8	6	86	11 03	5 26	5 28
9	12 15	+ 0.4	5	90	11 08	5 38	5 41
11	12 28	− 1.0	5	93	11 12	5 50	5 55
13	12 41	− 2.5	5	95	11 17	6 03	6 09
15	12 53	− 4.0	5	97	11 22	6 16	6 23
17	13 06	− 5.4	5	98	11 27	6 29	6 37
19	13 18	− 6.9	5	99	11 31	6 41	6 51
21	13 31	− 8.4	5	100	11 36	6 54	7 05
23	13 44	− 9.8	5	100	11 41	7 07	7 19
25	13 56	−11.2	5	100	11 45	7 19	7 34
27	14 08	−12.5	5	100	11 50	7 32	7 48
29	14 21	−13.8	5	100	11 54	7 45	8 02
31	14 33	−15.0	5	100	11 59	7 57	8 16

VENUS

Day	RA h m	Dec. °	Diam. ″	Phase %	Transit h m	5° high 52° h m	5° high 56° h m
1	13 12	− 6.6	10	98	12 35	17 26	17 16
6	13 35	− 9.0	10	98	12 38	17 15	17 04
11	13 58	−11.4	10	97	12 42	17 05	16 51
16	14 22	−13.7	10	97	12 46	16 56	16 38
21	14 46	−15.8	10	96	12 51	16 47	16 26
26	15 11	−17.7	10	95	12 56	16 38	16 15
31	15 36	−19.5	11	95	13 01	16 31	16 04

MARS

Day	RA h m	Dec. °	Diam. ″	Phase %	Transit h m	5° high 52° h m	5° high 56° h m
1	22 16	−15.7	21	95	21 35	1 37	1 17
6	22 17	−15.1	20	94	21 17	1 22	1 03
11	22 19	−14.5	19	93	20 59	1 08	0 50
16	22 22	−13.8	18	92	20 43	0 56	0 39
21	22 27	−13.0	17	91	20 28	0 46	0 30
26	22 32	−12.1	16	90	20 14	0 37	0 22
31	22 38	−11.2	15	90	20 01	0 29	0 15

SUNRISE AND SUNSET

	London 0°05' 51°30' h m h m	Bristol 2°35' 51°28' h m h m	Birmingham 1°55' 52°28' h m h m	Manchester 2°15' 53°28' h m h m	Newcastle 1°37' 54°59' h m h m	Glasgow 4°14' 55°52' h m h m	Belfast 5°56' 54°35' h m h m
1	6 00 17 39	6 10 17 49	6 08 17 46	6 10 17 47	6 08 17 44	6 19 17 54	6 25 18 01
2	6 02 17 37	6 12 17 47	6 10 17 44	6 11 17 44	6 10 17 41	6 21 17 51	6 27 17 58
3	6 03 17 35	6 13 17 45	6 11 17 41	6 13 17 42	6 12 17 38	6 23 17 48	6 29 17 56
4	6 05 17 32	6 15 17 42	6 13 17 39	6 15 17 40	6 14 17 36	6 25 17 46	6 31 17 54
5	6 07 17 30	6 17 17 40	6 15 17 37	6 17 17 37	6 16 17 33	6 27 17 43	6 32 17 51
6	6 08 17 28	6 18 17 38	6 16 17 34	6 19 17 35	6 17 17 31	6 29 17 41	6 34 17 49
7	6 10 17 26	6 20 17 36	6 18 17 32	6 20 17 32	6 19 17 28	6 31 17 38	6 36 17 46
8	6 12 17 23	6 22 17 33	6 20 17 30	6 22 17 30	6 21 17 26	6 33 17 35	6 38 17 44
9	6 13 17 21	6 23 17 31	6 22 17 27	6 24 17 28	6 23 17 23	6 35 17 33	6 40 17 41
10	6 15 17 19	6 25 17 29	6 23 17 25	6 26 17 25	6 25 17 21	6 37 17 30	6 42 17 39
11	6 17 17 17	6 27 17 27	6 25 17 23	6 28 17 23	6 27 17 18	6 39 17 28	6 44 17 36
12	6 18 17 15	6 28 17 25	6 27 17 21	6 30 17 21	6 29 17 16	6 41 17 25	6 46 17 34
13	6 20 17 12	6 30 17 22	6 29 17 18	6 31 17 18	6 31 17 14	6 43 17 23	6 48 17 31
14	6 22 17 10	6 32 17 20	6 30 17 16	6 33 17 16	6 33 17 11	6 45 17 20	6 50 17 29
15	6 23 17 08	6 33 17 18	6 32 17 14	6 35 17 14	6 35 17 09	6 47 17 18	6 52 17 27
16	6 25 17 06	6 35 17 16	6 34 17 12	6 37 17 11	6 37 17 06	6 49 17 15	6 53 17 24
17	6 27 17 04	6 37 17 14	6 36 17 10	6 39 17 09	6 39 17 04	6 51 17 13	6 55 17 22
18	6 29 17 02	6 39 17 12	6 38 17 07	6 41 17 07	6 41 17 02	6 53 17 10	6 57 17 20
19	6 30 17 00	6 40 17 10	6 39 17 05	6 42 17 05	6 43 16 59	6 55 17 08	6 59 17 17
20	6 32 16 58	6 42 17 08	6 41 17 03	6 44 17 03	6 45 16 57	6 57 17 05	7 01 17 15
21	6 34 16 56	6 44 17 06	6 43 17 01	6 46 17 00	6 47 16 55	6 59 17 03	7 03 17 13
22	6 35 16 53	6 45 17 04	6 45 16 59	6 48 16 58	6 49 16 52	7 01 17 01	7 05 17 10
23	6 37 16 51	6 47 17 02	6 47 16 57	6 50 16 56	6 51 16 50	7 03 16 58	7 07 17 08
24	6 39 16 49	6 49 17 00	6 48 16 55	6 52 16 54	6 53 16 48	7 06 16 56	7 09 17 06
25	6 41 16 47	6 51 16 58	6 50 16 53	6 54 16 52	6 55 16 45	7 08 16 54	7 11 17 04
26	6 42 16 45	6 52 16 56	6 52 16 51	6 56 16 50	6 57 16 43	7 10 16 51	7 13 17 01
27	6 44 16 44	6 54 16 54	6 54 16 49	6 58 16 47	6 59 16 41	7 12 16 49	7 15 16 59
28	6 46 16 42	6 56 16 52	6 56 16 47	6 59 16 45	7 01 16 39	7 14 16 47	7 17 16 57
29	6 48 16 40	6 58 16 50	6 57 16 45	7 01 16 43	7 03 16 37	7 16 16 44	7 19 16 55
30	6 49 16 38	6 59 16 48	6 59 16 43	7 03 16 41	7 05 16 34	7 18 16 42	7 21 16 53
31	6 51 16 36	7 01 16 46	7 01 16 41	7 05 16 39	7 07 16 32	7 20 16 40	7 23 16 51

JUPITER

Day	RA h m	Dec. ° '	Transit h m	5° high 52° h m	5° high 56° h m
1	10 37.5	+9 38	9 59	3 43	3 38
11	10 45.0	+8 55	9 27	3 15	3 11
21	10 52.0	+8 14	8 55	2 46	2 42
31	10 58.5	+7 36	8 22	2 16	2 13

Diameters - equatorial 32″ polar 30″

SATURN

Day	RA h m	Dec. ° '	Transit h m	5° high 52° h m	5° high 56° h m
1	6 54.8	+22 06	6 17	22 48	22 31
11	6 56.3	+22 04	5 39	22 10	21 54
21	6 57.1	+22 03	5 00	21 32	21 15
31	6 57.1	+22 03	4 21	20 52	20 36

Diameters - equatorial 19″ polar 17″
Rings - major axis 43″ minor axis 18″

URANUS

Day	RA h m	Dec. ° '	Transit h m	10° high 52° h m	10° high 56° h m
1	22 07.5	−12 23	21 27	1 11	0 50
11	22 06.5	−12 28	20 46	0 30	0 09
21	22 05.8	−12 32	20 06	23 46	23 24
31	22 05.3	−12 34	19 27	23 06	22 44

Diameter 4″

NEPTUNE

Day	RA h m	Dec. ° '	Transit h m	10° high 52° h m	10° high 56° h m
1	20 51.9	−17 36	20 11	23 12	22 40
11	20 51.6	−17 38	19 32	22 33	22 00
21	20 51.4	−17 39	18 52	21 53	21 20
31	20 51.5	−17 39	18 13	21 14	20 41

Diameter 2″

November 2003

ELEVENTH MONTH, 30 DAYS. *Novem* (nine), ninth month of Roman Pre-Julian calendar

1	*Saturday*	**All Saints' Day.** First hydrogen bomb exploded by the United States 1952	305
2	*Sunday*	**4th S. before Advent.** All Souls.	306
3	*Monday*	Karl Baedeker b. 1801. Henri Matisse d. 1954	*week 44 day* 307
4	*Tuesday*	William of Orange b. 1650. Yitzhak Rabin d. 1995	308
5	*Wednesday*	Angelica Kauffmann d. 1807. Gunpowder Plot - Guy Fawkes Night 1605	309
6	*Thursday*	John Philip Sousa b. 1854. Colley Cibber b. 1671	310
7	*Friday*	Steve McQueen d. 1980. October Revolution in Russia 1917	311
8	*Saturday*	John Milton d. 1674. 11 people killed by an IRA bomb in Enniskillen 1987	312
9	*Sunday*	**3rd S. before Advent.** Remembrance Sunday.	313
10	*Monday*	Giuseppe Verdi b. 1813. Richard Burton b. 1925	*week 45 day* 314
11	*Tuesday*	Søren Kierkegaard d. 1855. Sir Edward German d. 1936	315
12	*Wednesday*	Auguste Rodin b. 1840. Sinking of the Tirpitz 1944	316
13	*Thursday*	Dr George Carey b. 1953. Gioacchino Rossini d. 1868	317
14	*Friday*	*Prince of Wales b. 1948.* Claude Monet b. 1840	318
15	*Saturday*	Richmal Crompton Lamburn b. 1890. Brazil declared itself a Republic 1889	319
16	*Sunday*	**2nd S. before Advent.** Sir Oswald Mosley b. 1896	320
17	*Monday*	Eric Gill d. 1940. Heitor Villa-Lobos d. 1959	*week 46 day* 321
18	*Tuesday*	Sir William Gilbert b. 1836. Louis-Jacques Daguerre b. 1789	322
19	*Wednesday*	Franz Schubert d. 1828. Sir Basil Spence d. 1976	323
20	*Thursday*	*Queen's Wedding Day 1947.* Francisco Franco d. 1975	324
21	*Friday*	François-Marie Voltaire b. 1694. René Magritte b. 1898	325
22	*Saturday*	Sir Peter Hall b. 1930. C. S. Lewis d. 1963	326
23	*Sunday*	**Christ the King. S. next before Advent.**	327
24	*Monday*	Baruch Spinoza b. 1632. Freddie Mercury d. 1991	*week 47 day* 328
25	*Tuesday*	Karl Friedrich Benz b. 1844. Isaac Watts d. 1748	329
26	*Wednesday*	Charles M. Schultz b. 1922. John McAdam d. 1836	330
27	*Thursday*	Jimi Hendrix b. 1942. Alexandre Dumas d. 1895	331
28	*Friday*	William Blake b. 1757. Enid Blyton d. 1968	332
29	*Saturday*	Gaetano Donizetti b. 1798. George Harrison d. 2001	333
30	*Sunday*	**Advent Sunday. St Andrew.**	334

ASTRONOMICAL PHENOMENA

d	h	
3	11	Mars in conjunction with Moon. Mars 3° N.
8	13	Uranus at stationary point
9	01	Total eclipse of Moon
13	20	Saturn in conjunction with Moon. Saturn 5° S.
18	19	Jupiter in conjunction with Moon. Jupiter 4° S.
22	18	Sun's longitude 240° ♐
23	23	Total eclipse of Sun
25	03	Mercury in conjunction with Moon. Mercury 0°.3 N.
25	18	Venus in conjunction with Moon. Venus 2° N.

MINIMA OF ALGOL

d	h	d	h	d	h
1	01.6	12	12.9	24	00.2
3	22.5	15	09.7	26	21.0
6	19.3	18	06.5	29	17.8
9	16.1	21	03.3		

CONSTELLATIONS

The following constellations are near the meridian at

	d	h		d	h
October	1	24	November	15	21
October	16	23	December	1	20
November	1	22	December	16	19

Ursa Major (below the Pole), Cepheus, Cassiopeia, Andromeda, Pegasus, Pisces, Aquarius and Cetus

THE MOON

Phases, Apsides and Node		d	h	m
☽	First Quarter	1	04	25
○	Full Moon	9	01	13
☾	Last Quarter	17	04	15
●	New Moon	23	22	59
☽	First Quarter	30	17	16

	d	h	m
Apogee (406,301 km)	10	12	04
Perigee (356,811 km)	23	23	16

Mean longitude of ascending node on November 1, 51°

THE SUN   s.d. 16′.2

Day	Right Ascension h m s	Dec. – ° ′	Equation of Time m s	Rise 52° h m	Rise 56° h m	Transit h m	Set 52° h m	Set 56° h m	Sidereal time h m s	Transit of First Point of Aries h m s
1	14 23 06	14 13	+16 23	6 54	7 06	11 44	16 32	16 20	2 39 29	21 17 01
2	14 27 01	14 33	+16 25	6 56	7 08	11 44	16 31	16 18	2 43 25	21 13 05
3	14 30 56	14 52	+16 26	6 58	7 10	11 44	16 29	16 16	2 47 22	21 09 10
4	14 34 53	15 10	+16 26	6 59	7 12	11 44	16 27	16 14	2 51 18	21 05 14
5	14 38 50	15 29	+16 25	7 01	7 14	11 44	16 25	16 12	2 55 15	21 01 18
6	14 42 48	15 47	+16 24	7 03	7 17	11 44	16 24	16 10	2 59 12	20 57 22
7	14 46 47	16 05	+16 22	7 05	7 19	11 44	16 22	16 08	3 03 08	20 53 26
8	14 50 46	16 23	+16 19	7 07	7 21	11 44	16 20	16 06	3 07 05	20 49 30
9	14 54 47	16 40	+16 15	7 08	7 23	11 44	16 19	16 04	3 11 01	20 45 34
10	14 58 48	16 58	+16 10	7 10	7 25	11 44	16 17	16 02	3 14 58	20 41 38
11	15 02 50	17 15	+16 04	7 12	7 27	11 44	16 15	16 00	3 18 54	20 37 42
12	15 06 53	17 31	+15 58	7 14	7 29	11 44	16 14	15 58	3 22 51	20 33 46
13	15 10 57	17 47	+15 51	7 15	7 31	11 44	16 12	15 56	3 26 47	20 29 50
14	15 15 02	18 03	+15 43	7 17	7 33	11 44	16 11	15 55	3 30 44	20 25 55
15	15 19 07	18 19	+15 33	7 19	7 36	11 45	16 09	15 53	3 34 41	20 21 59
16	15 23 14	18 34	+15 24	7 21	7 38	11 45	16 08	15 51	3 38 37	20 18 03
17	15 27 21	18 49	+15 13	7 22	7 40	11 45	16 07	15 49	3 42 34	20 14 07
18	15 31 29	19 04	+15 01	7 24	7 42	11 45	16 05	15 48	3 46 30	20 10 11
19	15 35 38	19 19	+14 49	7 26	7 44	11 45	16 04	15 46	3 50 27	20 06 15
20	15 39 48	19 33	+14 36	7 28	7 46	11 46	16 03	15 45	3 54 23	20 02 19
21	15 43 59	19 46	+14 21	7 29	7 48	11 46	16 02	15 43	3 58 20	19 58 23
22	15 48 10	19 59	+14 06	7 31	7 50	11 46	16 01	15 42	4 02 17	19 54 27
23	15 52 22	20 12	+13 51	7 33	7 52	11 46	15 59	15 40	4 06 13	19 50 31
24	15 56 35	20 25	+13 34	7 34	7 53	11 47	15 58	15 39	4 10 10	19 46 35
25	16 00 49	20 37	+13 17	7 36	7 55	11 47	15 57	15 38	4 14 06	19 42 40
26	16 05 04	20 49	+12 59	7 37	7 57	11 47	15 56	15 37	4 18 03	19 38 44
27	16 09 19	21 00	+12 40	7 39	7 59	11 47	15 56	15 35	4 21 59	19 34 48
28	16 13 36	21 11	+12 20	7 41	8 01	11 48	15 55	15 34	4 25 56	19 30 52
29	16 17 52	21 22	+12 00	7 42	8 03	11 48	15 54	15 33	4 29 52	19 26 56
30	16 22 10	21 32	+11 39	7 44	8 04	11 49	15 53	15 32	4 33 49	19 23 00

DURATION OF TWILIGHT (in minutes)

Latitude	52°	56°	52°	56°	52°	56°	52°	56°
	1 November		11 November		21 November		30 November	
Civil	36	40	37	41	38	43	40	45
Nautical	75	84	78	87	80	90	82	93
Astronomical	115	127	117	130	120	134	123	138

THE NIGHT SKY

Mercury is unsuitably placed for observation during the month.

Venus, magnitude –3.9, emerges gradually from the evening twilight, becoming visible as a bright evening object, very low in the south-western sky after sunset. Because of its southerly declination observers in Scotland are unlikely to be able detect the planet before the last week of the month.

Mars is still visible in the evenings, though no longer such a conspicuous object that it was at opposition, as its magnitude fades from –1.2 to –0.4 during November. Its northward movement in declination is now more pronounced, making it visible at a higher altitude in the south-western sky than it was at opposition. The gibbous Moon is near the planet on the 3rd. Mars is in the constellation of Aquarius.

Jupiter, magnitude –1.9, continues to be visible in the eastern sky as a brilliant morning object. By the end of the month it should be visible very low in the east shortly after midnight. The old crescent Moon is in the vicinity of the planet on the mornings of the 18th and 19th.

Saturn, magnitude –0.2, is now visible for the greater part of the night as it approaches opposition on the last day of the year. On the evening of the 13th the waning gibbous Moon passes 4 degrees north of the planet. Saturn is in the constellation of Gemini.

Meteors. Although the Leonids do not usually produce a brilliant display there has been considerable activity during the last few years. Analysis of the observations thus obtained has led to predictions of considerable activity in the early hours of the 17th. From the British Isles it might be worthwhile looking out after the radiant rises, say, after 22h 30m on the 16th. There will be some interference from moonlight (Moon at Last Quarter).

THE MOON

Day	RA h m	Dec. °	Hor. par. '	Semi- diam. '	Sun's co- long. °	PA of Bright Limb °	Phase %	Age d	Rise 52° h m	Rise 56° h m	Transit h m	Set 52° h m	Set 56° h m
1	20 38	−23.8	57.9	15.8	351	255	48	6.5	14 34	14 56	18 39	22 54	22 33
2	21 33	−20.1	57.1	15.6	3	250	59	7.5	14 55	15 11	19 29	—	23 59
3	22 24	−15.5	56.4	15.4	15	246	69	8.5	15 11	15 21	20 14	0 14	—
4	23 12	−10.4	55.8	15.2	27	244	78	9.5	15 24	15 29	20 57	1 30	1 21
5	23 57	− 4.9	55.2	15.1	39	242	85	10.5	15 35	15 36	21 38	2 44	2 40
6	0 41	+ 0.6	54.8	14.9	52	242	92	11.5	15 46	15 43	22 18	3 55	3 57
7	1 24	+ 6.1	54.5	14.8	64	242	96	12.5	15 58	15 50	22 59	5 06	5 13
8	2 08	+11.3	54.2	14.8	76	243	99	13.5	16 11	15 58	23 41	6 18	6 29
9	2 53	+16.1	54.1	14.7	88	215	100	14.5	16 27	16 09	—	7 29	7 46
10	3 40	+20.2	54.0	14.7	100	73	99	15.5	16 48	16 24	0 26	8 42	9 04
11	4 29	+23.5	54.0	14.7	112	77	97	16.5	17 16	16 46	1 12	9 52	10 21
12	5 20	+25.8	54.1	14.7	124	82	92	17.5	17 53	17 20	2 01	10 57	11 31
13	6 13	+27.0	54.3	14.8	137	87	87	18.5	18 43	18 08	2 52	11 54	12 28
14	7 07	+26.9	54.6	14.9	149	93	80	19.5	19 45	19 13	3 44	12 39	13 11
15	8 00	+25.5	55.1	15.0	161	99	71	20.5	20 56	20 29	4 35	13 13	13 40
16	8 53	+22.9	55.7	15.2	173	105	62	21.5	22 12	21 52	5 26	13 38	13 59
17	9 45	+19.1	56.4	15.4	185	109	52	22.5	23 32	23 18	6 15	13 58	14 13
18	10 36	+14.4	57.3	15.6	197	113	42	23.5	—	—	7 03	14 14	14 23
19	11 26	+ 8.8	58.2	15.9	210	115	31	24.5	0 53	0 46	7 50	14 28	14 32
20	12 15	+ 2.6	59.2	16.1	222	116	21	25.5	2 16	2 15	8 38	14 42	14 40
21	13 07	− 3.9	60.1	16.4	234	116	13	26.5	3 42	3 47	9 28	14 56	14 49
22	14 00	−10.4	60.8	16.6	246	113	6	27.5	5 12	5 23	10 20	15 13	15 00
23	14 57	−16.5	61.3	16.7	258	108	1	28.5	6 46	7 05	11 17	15 36	15 16
24	15 58	−21.6	61.5	16.7	270	342	0	0.0	8 22	8 49	12 19	16 07	15 39
25	17 03	−25.2	61.3	16.7	283	285	2	1.0	9 52	10 25	13 24	16 52	16 18
26	18 10	−26.9	60.8	16.6	295	275	6	2.0	11 06	11 41	14 29	17 54	17 19
27	19 16	−26.7	60.0	16.4	307	267	13	3.0	11 59	12 31	15 33	19 11	18 40
28	20 19	−24.7	59.1	16.1	319	260	22	4.0	12 36	13 01	16 31	20 35	20 11
29	21 17	−21.3	58.2	15.9	331	254	32	5.0	13 00	13 19	17 24	21 58	21 41
30	22 11	−16.8	57.2	15.6	344	250	43	6.0	13 18	13 31	18 12	23 18	23 07

MERCURY

Day	RA h m	Dec. °	Diam. "	Phase %	Transit h m	5° high 52° h m	5° high 56° h m
1	14 39	−15.6	5	99	12 01	15 57	15 37
3	14 52	−16.8	5	99	12 06	15 54	15 32
5	15 04	−17.9	5	99	12 10	15 51	15 27
7	15 17	−19.0	5	98	12 15	15 48	15 22
9	15 29	−20.0	5	97	12 19	15 45	15 18
11	15 42	−20.9	5	97	12 24	15 43	15 13
13	15 54	−21.9	5	96	12 29	15 41	15 09
15	16 07	−22.5	5	95	12 34	15 40	15 05
17	16 20	−23.2	5	94	12 39	15 38	15 02
19	16 33	−23.9	5	93	12 44	15 38	14 59
21	16 46	−24.4	5	91	12 49	15 38	14 57
23	16 58	−24.9	5	90	12 54	15 38	14 55
25	17 11	−25.2	5	88	12 58	15 40	14 55
27	17 24	−25.5	5	86	13 03	15 42	14 55
29	17 36	−25.7	6	83	13 08	15 45	14 57
31	17 49	−25.8	6	81	13 12	15 48	15 00

VENUS

Day	RA h m	Dec. °	Diam. "	Phase %	Transit h m	5° high 52° h m	5° high 56° h m
1	15 41	−19.8	11	95	13 02	16 30	16 03
6	16 07	−21.3	11	94	13 09	16 24	15 54
11	16 33	−22.6	11	93	13 15	16 21	15 46
16	17 00	−23.6	11	92	13 22	16 19	15 42
21	17 27	−24.3	11	92	13 30	16 21	15 40
26	17 54	−24.7	11	91	13 37	16 25	15 43
31	18 22	−24.7	11	90	13 45	16 32	15 50

MARS

Day	RA h m	Dec. °	Diam. "	Phase %	Transit h m	5° high 52° h m	5° high 56° h m
1	22 40	−11.0	15	89	19 58	0 28	0 14
6	22 47	−10.0	14	89	19 45	0 21	0 08
11	22 54	− 8.9	13	88	19 33	0 15	0 03
16	23 02	− 7.8	13	88	19 22	0 10	23 58
21	23 11	− 6.7	12	88	19 11	0 05	23 55
26	23 20	− 5.5	12	87	19 00	0 01	23 52
31	23 29	− 4.3	11	87	18 50	23 56	23 49

SUNRISE AND SUNSET

	London 0°05' 51°30'		Bristol 2°35' 51°28'		Birmingham 1°55' 52°28'		Manchester 2°15' 53°28'		Newcastle 1°37' 54°59'		Glasgow 4°14' 55°52'		Belfast 5°56' 54°35'	
	h m	h m	h m	h m	h m	h m	h m	h m	h m	h m	h m	h m	h m	h m
1	6 53	16 34	7 03	16 44	7 03	16 39	7 07	16 37	7 09	16 30	7 22	16 38	7 25	16 49
2	6 55	16 32	7 05	16 42	7 05	16 37	7 09	16 35	7 11	16 28	7 25	16 36	7 27	16 47
3	6 57	16 31	7 06	16 41	7 07	16 35	7 11	16 33	7 13	16 26	7 27	16 33	7 29	16 45
4	6 58	16 29	7 08	16 39	7 08	16 33	7 13	16 32	7 15	16 24	7 29	16 31	7 31	16 43
5	7 00	16 27	7 10	16 37	7 10	16 32	7 15	16 30	7 17	16 22	7 31	16 29	7 33	16 41
6	7 02	16 25	7 12	16 35	7 12	16 30	7 17	16 28	7 19	16 20	7 33	16 27	7 35	16 39
7	7 04	16 24	7 13	16 34	7 14	16 28	7 19	16 26	7 21	16 18	7 35	16 25	7 37	16 37
8	7 05	16 22	7 15	16 32	7 16	16 26	7 20	16 24	7 23	16 16	7 37	16 23	7 39	16 35
9	7 07	16 21	7 17	16 31	7 18	16 25	7 22	16 23	7 25	16 14	7 39	16 21	7 41	16 33
10	7 09	16 19	7 19	16 29	7 19	16 23	7 24	16 21	7 27	16 13	7 41	16 19	7 43	16 31
11	7 11	16 17	7 20	16 28	7 21	16 21	7 26	16 19	7 29	16 11	7 44	16 18	7 45	16 30
12	7 12	16 16	7 22	16 26	7 23	16 20	7 28	16 18	7 31	16 09	7 46	16 16	7 47	16 28
13	7 14	16 14	7 24	16 25	7 25	16 18	7 30	16 16	7 33	16 07	7 48	16 14	7 49	16 26
14	7 16	16 13	7 26	16 23	7 27	16 17	7 32	16 14	7 35	16 06	7 50	16 12	7 51	16 24
15	7 18	16 12	7 27	16 22	7 28	16 15	7 34	16 13	7 37	16 04	7 52	16 10	7 53	16 23
16	7 19	16 10	7 29	16 20	7 30	16 14	7 36	16 11	7 39	16 02	7 54	16 09	7 55	16 21
17	7 21	16 09	7 31	16 19	7 32	16 13	7 37	16 10	7 41	16 01	7 56	16 07	7 57	16 20
18	7 23	16 08	7 32	16 18	7 34	16 11	7 39	16 08	7 43	15 59	7 58	16 05	7 59	16 18
19	7 24	16 06	7 34	16 17	7 35	16 10	7 41	16 07	7 45	15 58	8 00	16 04	8 01	16 17
20	7 26	16 05	7 36	16 15	7 37	16 09	7 43	16 06	7 47	15 56	8 02	16 02	8 03	16 15
21	7 28	16 04	7 37	16 14	7 39	16 07	7 45	16 04	7 49	15 55	8 04	16 01	8 04	16 14
22	7 29	16 03	7 39	16 13	7 41	16 06	7 46	16 03	7 51	15 54	8 06	15 59	8 06	16 13
23	7 31	16 02	7 41	16 12	7 42	16 05	7 48	16 02	7 53	15 52	8 08	15 58	8 08	16 11
24	7 32	16 01	7 42	16 11	7 44	16 04	7 50	16 01	7 55	15 51	8 10	15 57	8 10	16 10
25	7 34	16 00	7 44	16 10	7 46	16 03	7 51	16 00	7 56	15 50	8 12	15 56	8 12	16 09
26	7 36	15 59	7 45	16 09	7 47	16 02	7 53	15 59	7 58	15 49	8 13	15 54	8 13	16 08
27	7 37	15 58	7 47	16 08	7 49	16 01	7 55	15 58	8 00	15 48	8 15	15 53	8 15	16 07
28	7 39	15 57	7 48	16 07	7 50	16 00	7 56	15 57	8 02	15 46	8 17	15 52	8 17	16 06
29	7 40	15 57	7 50	16 07	7 52	15 59	7 58	15 56	8 03	15 45	8 19	15 51	8 18	16 05
30	7 42	15 56	7 51	16 06	7 53	15 59	8 00	15 55	8 05	15 45	8 21	15 50	8 20	16 04

JUPITER

Day	RA		Dec.		Transit		5° high			
							52°		56°	
	h	m	°	'	h	m	h	m	h	m
1	10	59.1	+7	32	8	18	2	13	2	10
11	11	04.9	+6	58	7	45	1	43	1	40
21	11	10.0	+6	29	7	11	1	11	1	09
31	11	14.3	+6	04	6	36	0	38	0	36

Diameters - equatorial 35" polar 32"

SATURN

Day	RA		Dec.		Transit		5° high			
							52°		56°	
	h	m	°	'	h	m	h	m	h	m
1	6	57.1	+22	03	4	17	20	48	20	32
11	6	56.2	+22	05	3	37	20	08	19	51
21	6	54.6	+22	07	2	56	19	27	19	10
31	6	52.3	+22	11	2	14	18	45	18	28

Diameters - equatorial 20" polar 18"
Rings - major axis 45" minor axis 19"

URANUS

Day	RA		Dec.		Transit		10° high			
							52°		56°	
	h	m	°	'	h	m	h	m	h	m
1	22	05.3	−12	34	19	23	23	02	22	40
11	22	05.2	−12	34	18	43	22	22	22	01
21	22	05.5	−12	33	18	04	21	44	21	22
31	22	06.0	−12	29	17	25	21	05	20	44

Diameter 4"

NEPTUNE

Day	RA		Dec.		Transit		10° high			
							52°		56°	
	h	m	°	'	h	m	h	m	h	m
1	20	51.5	−17	39	18	09	21	10	20	37
11	20	51.8	−17	37	17	30	20	31	19	58
21	20	52.4	−17	35	16	51	19	53	19	20
31	20	53.1	−17	32	16	13	19	15	18	42

Diameter 2"

December 2003

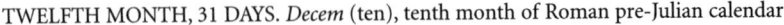

TWELFTH MONTH, 31 DAYS. *Decem* (ten), tenth month of Roman pre-Julian calendar

1	*Monday*	Samuel Courtauld d. 1947. James Baldwin d. 1987	*week* 48 *day* 335
2	*Tuesday*	Philip Larkin d. 1985. Opening of St Paul's Cathedral 1697	336
3	*Wednesday*	Robert Louis Stevenson d. 1894. Pierre Renoir d. 1919	337
4	*Thursday*	Frank Zappa d. 1993. First publication of "The Observer" 1791	338
5	*Friday*	Walt Disney b. 1901. Wolfgang Amadeus Mozart d. 1791	339
6	*Saturday*	Anthony Trollope d. 1882. Roy Orbison d. 1988	340
7	*Sunday*	**2nd S. in Advent.** Lord Darnley Henry Stuart b. 1545	341
8	*Monday*	Sammy Davis, Jnr b. 1925. John Lennon d. 1980	*week* 49 *day* 342
9	*Tuesday*	John Milton b. 1608. Sir Anthony van Dyck d. 1641	343
10	*Wednesday*	Luigi Pirandello d. 1936. Founding of Royal Academy 1768	344
11	*Thursday*	Willie Rushton d. 1996. USA declared war on Germany and Italy 1941	345
12	*Friday*	Sir Jean Anderson b. 1907. Joan Cross d. 1993	346
13	*Saturday*	Vassily Kandinsky d. 1944. Abel Tasman discovered New Zealand 1642	347
14	*Sunday*	**3rd S. in Advent.** Sir Stanley Spencer d. 1959	348
15	*Monday*	Izaak Walton d. 1683. Jan Vermeer d. 1675	*week* 50 *day* 349
16	*Tuesday*	Ludwig van Beethoven b. 1770. Boston Tea Party 1773	350
17	*Wednesday*	Dorothy L. Sayers d. 1957. Closure of Suez Canal 1956	351
18	*Thursday*	Paul Klee b. 1879. Sir John William Alcock d. 1919	352
19	*Friday*	Edith Piaf b. 1915. Masaru Ibuka d. 1997	353
20	*Saturday*	CHANUCAH begins. *Michaelmas Law Term* ends.	354
21	*Sunday*	**4th S. in Advent.** F. Scott Fitzgerald d. 1940	355
22	*Monday*	Giacomo Puccini b. 1858. Beatrix Potter d. 1943	*week* 51 *day* 356
23	*Tuesday*	Sir Richard Arkwright b. 1732. Ronnie Scott d. 1996	357
24	*Wednesday*	Christmas Eve. John Osborne d. 1994	358
25	*Thursday*	**Christmas Day.** *Bank Holiday in UK.*	359
26	*Friday*	**St Stephen.** Boxing Day. *Bank Holiday in UK.*	360
27	*Saturday*	**St John.** Marlene Dietrich b. 1901.	361
28	*Sunday*	**1st S. of Christmas. Holy Innocents.**	362
29	*Monday*	William E. Gladstone b. 1809. Harold Macmillan d. 1986	*week* 52 *day* 363
30	*Tuesday*	Romain Rolland d. 1944. Alfred North Whitehead d. 1947	364
31	*Wednesday*	Henri Matisse b. 1869. Elizabeth Arden b. 1884	365

ASTRONOMICAL PHENOMENA

d	h	
1	19	Mars in conjunction with Moon. Mars 4° N.
9	06	Mercury at greatest elongation E.21°
10	23	Saturn in conjunction with Moon. Saturn 5° S.
12	05	Pluto in conjunction
16	07	Jupiter in conjunction with Moon. Jupiter 3° S.
17	16	Mercury at stationary point
22	07	Sun's longitude 270° ♑
23	22	Mercury in conjunction with Moon. Mercury 5° N.
25	17	Venus in conjunction with Moon. Venus 3° N.
27	01	Mercury in inferior conjunction
30	10	Mars in conjunction with Moon. Mars 3° N.
31	21	Saturn at opposition

MINIMA OF ALGOL

d	h	d	h	d	h
2	14.6	14	01.9	25	13.2
5	11.4	16	22.7	28	10.0
8	08.2	19	19.5	31	06.8
11	05.1	22	16.3		

CONSTELLATIONS

The following constellations are near the meridian at

	d	h		d	h
November	1	24	December	16	21
November	15	23	January	1	20
December	1	22	January	16	19

Ursa Major (below the Pole), Ursa Minor (below the Pole), Cassiopeia, Andromeda, Perseus, Triangulum, Aries, Taurus, Cetus and Eridanus

THE MOON

Phases, Apsides and Node	d	h	m
○ Full Moon	8	20	37
☾ Last Quarter	16	17	42
● New Moon	23	09	43
☽ First Quarter	30	10	03
Apogee (406,278 km)	7	12	04
Perigee (358,338 km)	22	11	51

Mean longitude of ascending node on December 1, 49°

THE SUN   s.d. 16′.3

Day	Right Ascension h m s	Dec. – ° ′	Equation of Time m s	Rise 52° h m	Rise 56° h m	Transit h m	Set 52° h m	Set 56° h m	Sidereal time h m s	Transit of First Point of Aries h m s
1	16 26 28	21 42	+11 18	7 45	8 06	11 49	15 52	15 31	4 37 46	19 19 04
2	16 30 47	21 51	+10 55	7 46	8 08	11 49	15 52	15 30	4 41 42	19 15 08
3	16 35 06	22 00	+10 32	7 48	8 09	11 50	15 51	15 30	4 45 39	19 11 12
4	16 39 26	22 09	+10 09	7 49	8 11	11 50	15 51	15 29	4 49 35	19 07 16
5	16 43 47	22 17	+ 9 45	7 50	8 12	11 50	15 50	15 28	4 53 32	19 03 20
6	16 48 08	22 25	+ 9 20	7 52	8 14	11 51	15 50	15 28	4 57 28	18 59 25
7	16 52 30	22 32	+ 8 55	7 53	8 15	11 51	15 49	15 27	5 01 25	18 55 29
8	16 56 52	22 39	+ 8 30	7 54	8 17	11 52	15 49	15 26	5 05 21	18 51 33
9	17 01 14	22 45	+ 8 04	7 55	8 18	11 52	15 49	15 26	5 09 18	18 47 37
10	17 05 38	22 51	+ 7 37	7 56	8 19	11 53	15 49	15 26	5 13 15	18 43 41
11	17 10 01	22 57	+ 7 10	7 57	8 21	11 53	15 48	15 25	5 17 11	18 39 45
12	17 14 25	23 02	+ 6 42	7 59	8 22	11 54	15 48	15 25	5 21 08	18 35 49
13	17 18 50	23 06	+ 6 15	7 59	8 23	11 54	15 48	15 25	5 25 04	18 31 53
14	17 23 14	23 10	+ 5 46	8 00	8 24	11 54	15 48	15 25	5 29 01	18 27 57
15	17 27 39	23 14	+ 5 18	8 01	8 25	11 55	15 48	15 25	5 32 57	18 24 01
16	17 32 05	23 17	+ 4 49	8 02	8 26	11 55	15 49	15 25	5 36 54	18 20 05
17	17 36 30	23 20	+ 4 20	8 03	8 27	11 56	15 49	15 25	5 40 50	18 16 09
18	17 40 56	23 22	+ 3 51	8 04	8 27	11 56	15 49	15 25	5 44 47	18 12 14
19	17 45 22	23 24	+ 3 21	8 04	8 28	11 57	15 49	15 26	5 48 44	18 08 18
20	17 49 49	23 25	+ 2 52	8 05	8 29	11 57	15 50	15 26	5 52 40	18 04 22
21	17 54 15	23 26	+ 2 22	8 06	8 29	11 58	15 50	15 26	5 56 37	18 00 26
22	17 58 41	23 26	+ 1 52	8 06	8 30	11 58	15 51	15 27	6 00 33	17 56 30
23	18 03 08	23 26	+ 1 22	8 07	8 30	11 59	15 51	15 27	6 04 30	17 52 34
24	18 07 34	23 26	+ 0 52	8 07	8 31	11 59	15 52	15 28	6 08 26	17 48 38
25	18 12 01	23 25	+ 0 22	8 07	8 31	12 00	15 52	15 29	6 12 23	17 44 42
26	18 16 27	23 23	– 0 08	8 08	8 31	12 00	15 53	15 29	6 16 19	17 40 46
27	18 20 54	23 21	– 0 38	8 08	8 32	12 01	15 54	15 30	6 20 16	17 36 50
28	18 25 20	23 19	– 1 07	8 08	8 32	12 01	15 55	15 31	6 24 13	17 32 54
29	18 29 46	23 16	– 1 37	8 08	8 32	12 02	15 56	15 32	6 28 09	17 28 59
30	18 34 12	23 12	– 2 06	8 08	8 32	12 02	15 57	15 33	6 32 06	17 25 03
31	18 38 37	23 09	– 2 35	8 08	8 32	12 03	15 58	15 34	6 36 02	17 21 07

DURATION OF TWILIGHT (in minutes)

Latitude	52°	56°	52°	56°	52°	56°	52°	56°
	1 December		11 December		21 December		31 December	
Civil	40	45	41	47	41	47	41	47
Nautical	82	93	84	96	85	97	84	96
Astronomical	123	138	125	141	126	142	125	141

THE NIGHT SKY

Mercury remains too close to the Sun for observation throughout the month, inferior conjunction occurring on the 27th.

Venus, magnitude –4.0, is a bright early evening object, being gradually visible for longer and longer after sunset as the month progresses. It will still only be seen at a very low altitude above the south-western horizon. On the evening of the 25th, the thin crescent Moon, just over two days old, may be detected about 4 degrees below and to the left of the planet.

Mars continues to be visible as an evening object, magnitude –0.1, moving eastwards from Aquarius to Pisces early in the month. Mars is visible in the southern and south-western sky in the evenings. The Moon, near First Quarter, is near the planet on the evening of the 1st and again on the 29th and 30th.

Jupiter, magnitude –2.1, is a brilliant morning object, in the south-eastern sky. It is moving slowly eastwards in Leo. The Moon, at Last Quarter, passes 3 degrees north of the planet on the morning of the 16th.

Saturn, magnitude –0.4, reaches opposition on the 31st and thus is visible throughout the hours of darkness. Saturn is moving slowly retrograde in the constellation of Gemini. On the late evening of the 10th the waning gibbous Moon passes 4 degrees north of the planet.

Meteors. The maximum of the well-known Geminid meteor shower occurs on the 14th. Conditions for observation are rather unfavourable since the waning gibbous Moon is above the horizon from mid-evening until after sunrise.

THE MOON

Day	RA h m	Dec. °	Hor. par. '	Semi-diam. '	Sun's co-long. °	PA of Bright Limb °	Phase %	Age d	Rise 52° h m	Rise 56° h m	Transit h m	Set 52° h m	Set 56° h m
1	23 00	−11.7	56.4	15.4	356	247	53	7.0	13 32	13 39	18 56	—	—
2	23 46	− 6.3	55.7	15.2	8	245	63	8.0	13 44	13 47	19 37	0 33	0 28
3	0 30	− 0.7	55.1	15.0	20	245	72	9.0	13 55	13 53	20 18	1 45	1 45
4	1 14	+ 4.8	54.6	14.9	32	246	80	10.0	14 07	14 00	20 58	2 56	3 01
5	1 57	+10.1	54.3	14.8	44	248	87	11.0	14 19	14 08	21 40	4 07	4 17
6	2 41	+14.9	54.1	14.7	57	251	93	12.0	14 34	14 18	22 23	5 18	5 33
7	3 28	+19.2	54.0	14.7	69	257	97	13.0	14 53	14 31	23 09	6 30	6 51
8	4 16	+22.7	54.0	14.7	81	269	99	14.0	15 18	14 51	23 57	7 41	8 08
9	5 07	+25.3	54.1	14.7	93	27	100	15.0	15 53	15 20	—	8 49	9 21
10	6 00	+26.8	54.2	14.8	105	75	99	16.0	16 38	16 04	0 48	9 49	10 23
11	6 53	+27.0	54.5	14.8	117	86	96	17.0	17 37	17 04	1 40	10 38	11 11
12	7 47	+25.9	54.8	14.9	129	94	91	18.0	18 45	18 17	2 31	11 15	11 43
13	8 40	+23.6	55.2	15.0	141	100	85	19.0	20 00	19 38	3 22	11 43	12 05
14	9 32	+20.1	55.8	15.2	154	105	77	20.0	21 17	21 01	4 11	12 04	12 20
15	10 22	+15.7	56.4	15.4	166	109	68	21.0	22 35	22 26	4 58	12 20	12 32
16	11 10	+10.5	57.1	15.6	178	112	58	22.0	23 55	23 51	5 44	12 34	12 41
17	11 59	+ 4.6	57.9	15.8	190	114	47	23.0	—	—	6 30	12 48	12 48
18	12 48	− 1.6	58.7	16.0	202	114	36	24.0	1 16	1 18	7 17	13 01	12 57
19	13 38	− 7.9	59.6	16.2	214	112	26	25.0	2 40	2 48	8 06	13 16	13 06
20	14 32	−14.0	60.3	16.4	227	109	16	26.0	4 09	4 24	8 59	13 35	13 18
21	15 29	−19.4	60.8	16.6	239	103	9	27.0	5 42	6 04	9 56	14 00	13 37
22	16 32	−23.7	61.2	16.7	251	94	3	28.0	7 15	7 45	10 59	14 37	14 06
23	17 38	−26.3	61.1	16.7	263	65	0	29.0	8 39	9 14	12 05	15 30	14 55
24	18 45	−27.0	60.8	16.6	275	291	1	0.6	9 45	10 19	13 11	16 42	16 08
25	19 51	−25.7	60.2	16.4	288	271	4	1.6	10 30	10 59	14 14	18 06	17 38
26	20 54	−22.8	59.4	16.2	300	261	10	2.6	11 01	11 22	15 12	19 33	19 13
27	21 51	−18.5	58.5	15.9	312	255	17	3.6	11 22	11 37	16 03	20 57	20 44
28	22 43	−13.4	57.5	15.7	324	251	26	4.6	11 38	11 47	16 50	22 16	22 09
29	23 32	− 7.9	56.6	15.4	336	248	36	5.6	11 51	11 55	17 34	23 32	23 30
30	0 17	− 2.2	55.8	15.2	348	247	46	6.6	12 03	12 02	18 16	—	—
31	1 01	+ 3.4	55.1	15.0	1	247	56	7.6	12 14	12 09	18 56	0 44	0 47

MERCURY

Day	RA h m	Dec. °	Diam. "	Phase %	Transit h m	5° high 52° h m	5° high 56° h m
1	17 49	−25.8	6	81	13 12	15 48	15 00
3	18 01	−25.9	6	77	13 16	15 52	15 04
5	18 12	−25.8	6	73	13 19	15 57	15 09
7	18 23	−25.6	6	69	13 22	16 01	15 15
9	18 32	−25.3	7	63	13 23	16 06	15 21
11	18 41	−25.0	7	57	13 24	16 10	15 27
13	18 48	−24.6	7	50	13 22	16 12	15 32
15	18 52	−24.1	8	41	13 18	16 13	15 34
17	18 55	−23.6	8	33	13 12	16 11	15 34
19	18 54	−23.0	9	23	13 02	16 06	15 31
21	18 50	−22.5	9	15	12 50	15 58	15 25
23	18 43	−22.0	10	7	12 34	15 46	15 14
25	18 33	−21.5	10	2	12 15	15 31	15 01
27	18 21	−21.0	10	0	11 56	8 37	9 06
29	18 09	−20.7	10	2	11 37	8 15	8 43
31	17 59	−20.4	10	7	11 19	7 55	8 23

VENUS

Day	RA h m	Dec. °	Diam. "	Phase %	Transit h m	5° high 52° h m	5° high 56° h m
1	18 22	−24.7	11	90	13 45	16 32	15 50
6	18 49	−24.5	12	89	13 52	16 42	16 02
11	19 16	−24.0	12	88	14 00	16 55	16 17
16	19 43	−23.1	12	87	14 07	17 10	16 35
21	20 09	−22.0	12	86	14 13	17 27	16 55
26	20 35	−20.6	12	85	14 19	17 44	17 16
31	21 00	−19.0	13	84	14 25	18 02	17 38

MARS

Day	RA h m	Dec. °	Diam. "	Phase %	Transit h m	5° high 52° h m	5° high 56° h m
1	23 29	− 4.3	11	87	18 50	23 56	23 49
6	23 39	− 3.0	11	87	18 40	23 53	23 47
11	23 49	− 1.7	10	87	18 31	23 50	23 45
16	23 59	− 0.5	10	87	18 21	23 47	23 44
21	0 10	+ 0.8	9	87	18 12	23 44	23 42
26	0 21	+ 2.1	9	87	18 03	23 42	23 41
31	0 31	+ 3.4	8	87	17 54	23 40	23 40

SUNRISE AND SUNSET

	London 0°05′ 51°30′		Bristol 2°35′ 51°28′		Birmingham 1°55′ 52°28′		Manchester 2°15′ 53°28′		Newcastle 1°37′ 54°59′		Glasgow 4°14′ 55°52′		Belfast 5°56′ 54°35′	
	h m	h m	h m	h m	h m	h m	h m	h m	h m	h m	h m	h m	h m	h m
1	7 43	15 55	7 53	16 05	7 55	15 58	8 01	15 54	8 07	15 44	8 22	15 49	8 22	16 03
2	7 44	15 55	7 54	16 05	7 56	15 57	8 03	15 54	8 08	15 43	8 24	15 48	8 23	16 02
3	7 46	15 54	7 56	16 04	7 58	15 57	8 04	15 53	8 10	15 42	8 25	15 47	8 25	16 02
4	7 47	15 53	7 57	16 04	7 59	15 56	8 05	15 52	8 11	15 41	8 27	15 47	8 26	16 01
5	7 48	15 53	7 58	16 03	8 00	15 56	8 07	15 52	8 13	15 41	8 29	15 46	8 28	16 00
6	7 50	15 53	7 59	16 03	8 02	15 55	8 08	15 51	8 14	15 40	8 30	15 45	8 29	16 00
7	7 51	15 52	8 01	16 02	8 03	15 55	8 10	15 51	8 16	15 40	8 31	15 45	8 30	15 59
8	7 52	15 52	8 02	16 02	8 04	15 54	8 11	15 50	8 17	15 39	8 33	15 44	8 32	15 59
9	7 53	15 52	8 03	16 02	8 05	15 54	8 12	15 50	8 18	15 39	8 34	15 44	8 33	15 59
10	7 54	15 51	8 04	16 02	8 06	15 54	8 13	15 50	8 19	15 39	8 35	15 43	8 34	15 58
11	7 55	15 51	8 05	16 01	8 08	15 54	8 14	15 50	8 21	15 38	8 37	15 43	8 35	15 58
12	7 56	15 51	8 06	16 01	8 09	15 54	8 15	15 50	8 22	15 38	8 38	15 43	8 37	15 58
13	7 57	15 51	8 07	16 01	8 10	15 54	8 16	15 49	8 23	15 38	8 39	15 43	8 38	15 58
14	7 58	15 51	8 08	16 01	8 11	15 54	8 17	15 49	8 24	15 38	8 40	15 43	8 39	15 58
15	7 59	15 51	8 09	16 01	8 11	15 54	8 18	15 50	8 25	15 38	8 41	15 43	8 40	15 58
16	8 00	15 51	8 10	16 02	8 12	15 54	8 19	15 50	8 26	15 38	8 42	15 43	8 40	15 58
17	8 01	15 52	8 11	16 02	8 13	15 54	8 20	15 50	8 26	15 38	8 43	15 43	8 41	15 58
18	8 01	15 52	8 11	16 02	8 14	15 54	8 21	15 50	8 27	15 38	8 43	15 43	8 42	15 58
19	8 02	15 52	8 12	16 02	8 14	15 55	8 21	15 50	8 28	15 39	8 44	15 43	8 43	15 58
20	8 03	15 53	8 13	16 03	8 15	15 55	8 22	15 51	8 29	15 39	8 45	15 44	8 43	15 59
21	8 03	15 53	8 13	16 03	8 16	15 55	8 23	15 51	8 29	15 39	8 45	15 44	8 44	15 59
22	8 04	15 54	8 14	16 04	8 16	15 56	8 23	15 52	8 30	15 40	8 46	15 45	8 44	16 00
23	8 04	15 54	8 14	16 04	8 17	15 56	8 24	15 52	8 30	15 41	8 46	15 45	8 45	16 00
24	8 05	15 55	8 15	16 05	8 17	15 57	8 24	15 53	8 31	15 41	8 47	15 46	8 45	16 01
25	8 05	15 55	8 15	16 06	8 17	15 58	8 24	15 53	8 31	15 42	8 47	15 47	8 46	16 02
26	8 05	15 56	8 15	16 06	8 18	15 58	8 25	15 54	8 31	15 43	8 47	15 47	8 46	16 02
27	8 06	15 57	8 15	16 07	8 18	15 59	8 25	15 55	8 31	15 43	8 48	15 48	8 46	16 03
28	8 06	15 58	8 16	16 08	8 18	16 00	8 25	15 56	8 32	15 44	8 48	15 49	8 46	16 04
29	8 06	15 59	8 16	16 09	8 18	16 01	8 25	15 57	8 32	15 45	8 48	15 50	8 46	16 05
30	8 06	15 59	8 16	16 10	8 18	16 02	8 25	15 58	8 32	15 46	8 48	15 51	8 46	16 06
31	8 06	16 00	8 16	16 11	8 18	16 03	8 25	15 59	8 32	15 47	8 48	15 52	8 46	16 07

JUPITER

Day	RA		Dec.		Transit		5° high			
							52°		56°	
	h	m	°	′	h	m	h	m	h	m
1	11	14.3	+6	04	6	36	0	38	0	36
11	11	17.6	+5	46	6	00	0	03	0	02
21	11	19.9	+5	35	5	22	23	24	23	22
31	11	21.0	+5	31	4	44	22	46	22	44

Diameters - equatorial 38″ polar 35″

SATURN

Day	RA		Dec.		Transit		5° high			
							52°		56°	
	h	m	°	′	h	m	h	m	h	m
1	6	52.3	+22	11	2	14	18	45	18	28
11	6	49.4	+22	15	1	32	18	02	17	45
21	6	46.1	+22	20	0	49	17	19	17	02
31	6	42.6	+22	24	0	07	16	36	16	19

Diameters - equatorial 20″ polar 19″
Rings - major axis 46″ minor axis 20″

URANUS

Day	RA		Dec.		Transit		10° high			
							52°		56°	
	h	m	°	′	h	m	h	m	h	m
1	22	06.0	−12	29	17	25	21	05	20	44
11	22	06.9	−12	24	16	47	20	27	20	06
21	22	08.1	−12	17	16	09	19	50	19	29
31	22	09.5	−12	09	15	31	19	13	18	52

Diameter 4″

NEPTUNE

Day	RA		Dec.		Transit		10° high			
							52°		56°	
	h	m	°	′	h	m	h	m	h	m
1	20	53.1	−17	32	16	13	19	15	18	42
11	20	54.1	−17	29	15	34	18	37	18	04
21	20	55.2	−17	24	14	56	17	59	17	27
31	20	56.5	−17	19	14	18	17	22	16	50

Diameter 2″

RISING AND SETTING TIMES

TABLE 1. SEMI-DIURNAL ARCS (HOUR ANGLES AT RISING/SETTING)

Dec. Latitude	0°	10°	20°	30°	40°	45°	50°	52°	54°	56°	58°	60°	Dec.
	h m	h m	h m	h m	h m	h m	h m	h m	h m	h m	h m	h m	
0°	6 00	6 00	6 00	6 00	6 00	6 00	6 00	6 00	6 00	6 00	6 00	6 00	0°
1°	6 00	6 01	6 01	6 02	6 03	6 04	6 05	6 05	6 06	6 06	6 06	6 07	1°
2°	6 00	6 01	6 03	6 05	6 07	6 08	6 10	6 10	6 11	6 12	6 13	6 14	2°
3°	6 00	6 02	6 04	6 07	6 10	6 12	6 14	6 15	6 17	6 18	6 19	6 21	3°
4°	6 00	6 03	6 06	6 09	6 13	6 16	6 19	6 21	6 22	6 24	6 26	6 28	4°
5°	6 00	6 04	6 07	6 12	6 17	6 20	6 24	6 26	6 28	6 30	6 32	6 35	5°
6°	6 00	6 04	6 09	6 14	6 20	6 24	6 29	6 31	6 33	6 36	6 39	6 42	6°
7°	6 00	6 05	6 10	6 16	6 24	6 28	6 34	6 36	6 39	6 42	6 45	6 49	7°
8°	6 00	6 06	6 12	6 19	6 27	6 32	6 39	6 41	6 45	6 48	6 52	6 56	8°
9°	6 00	6 06	6 13	6 21	6 31	6 36	6 44	6 47	6 50	6 54	6 59	7 04	9°
10°	6 00	6 07	6 15	6 23	6 34	6 41	6 49	6 52	6 56	7 01	7 06	7 11	10°
11°	6 00	6 08	6 16	6 26	6 38	6 45	6 54	6 58	7 02	7 07	7 12	7 19	11°
12°	6 00	6 09	6 18	6 28	6 41	6 49	6 59	7 03	7 08	7 13	7 20	7 26	12°
13°	6 00	6 09	6 19	6 31	6 45	6 53	7 04	7 09	7 14	7 20	7 27	7 34	13°
14°	6 00	6 10	6 21	6 33	6 48	6 58	7 09	7 14	7 20	7 27	7 34	7 42	14°
15°	6 00	6 11	6 22	6 36	6 52	7 02	7 14	7 20	7 27	7 34	7 42	7 51	15°
16°	6 00	6 12	6 24	6 38	6 56	7 07	7 20	7 26	7 33	7 41	7 49	7 59	16°
17°	6 00	6 12	6 26	6 41	6 59	7 11	7 25	7 32	7 40	7 48	7 57	8 08	17°
18°	6 00	6 13	6 27	6 43	7 03	7 16	7 31	7 38	7 46	7 55	8 05	8 17	18°
19°	6 00	6 14	6 29	6 46	7 07	7 21	7 37	7 45	7 53	8 03	8 14	8 26	19°
20°	6 00	6 15	6 30	6 49	7 11	7 25	7 43	7 51	8 00	8 11	8 22	8 36	20°
21°	6 00	6 16	6 32	6 51	7 15	7 30	7 49	7 58	8 08	8 19	8 32	8 47	21°
22°	6 00	6 16	6 34	6 54	7 19	7 35	7 55	8 05	8 15	8 27	8 41	8 58	22°
23°	6 00	6 17	6 35	6 57	7 23	7 40	8 02	8 12	8 23	8 36	8 51	9 09	23°
24°	6 00	6 18	6 37	7 00	7 28	7 46	8 08	8 19	8 31	8 45	9 02	9 22	24°
25°	6 00	6 19	6 39	7 02	7 32	7 51	8 15	8 27	8 40	8 55	9 13	9 35	25°
26°	6 00	6 20	6 41	7 05	7 37	7 57	8 22	8 35	8 49	9 05	9 25	9 51	26°
27°	6 00	6 21	6 43	7 08	7 41	8 03	8 30	8 43	8 58	9 16	9 39	10 08	27°
28°	6 00	6 22	6 45	7 12	7 46	8 08	8 37	8 52	9 08	9 28	9 53	10 28	28°
29°	6 00	6 22	6 47	7 15	7 51	8 15	8 45	9 01	9 19	9 41	10 10	10 55	29°
30°	6 00	6 23	6 49	7 18	7 56	8 21	8 54	9 11	9 30	9 55	10 30	12 00	30°
35°	6 00	6 28	6 59	7 35	8 24	8 58	9 46	10 15	10 58	12 00	12 00	12 00	35°
40°	6 00	6 34	7 11	7 56	8 59	9 48	12 00	12 00	12 00	12 00	12 00	12 00	40°
45°	6 00	6 41	7 25	8 21	9 48	12 00	12 00	12 00	12 00	12 00	12 00	12 00	45°
50°	6 00	6 49	7 43	8 54	12 00	12 00	12 00	12 00	12 00	12 00	12 00	12 00	50°
55°	6 00	6 58	8 05	9 42	12 00	12 00	12 00	12 00	12 00	12 00	12 00	12 00	55°
60°	6 00	7 11	8 36	12 00	12 00	12 00	12 00	12 00	12 00	12 00	12 00	12 00	60°
65°	6 00	7 29	9 25	12 00	12 00	12 00	12 00	12 00	12 00	12 00	12 00	12 00	65°
70°	6 00	7 56	12 00	12 00	12 00	12 00	12 00	12 00	12 00	12 00	12 00	12 00	70°
75°	6 00	8 45	12 00	12 00	12 00	12 00	12 00	12 00	12 00	12 00	12 00	12 00	75°
80°	6 00	12 00	12 00	12 00	12 00	12 00	12 00	12 00	12 00	12 00	12 00	12 00	80°

TABLE 2. CORRECTION FOR REFRACTION AND SEMI-DIAMETER

	m	m	m	m	m	m	m	m	m	m	m	m	
0°	3	3	4	4	4	5	5	5	6	6	6	7	0°
10°	3	3	4	4	4	5	5	6	6	6	7	7	10°
20°	4	4	4	4	5	5	6	7	7	8	8	9	20°
25°	4	4	4	4	5	6	7	8	9	11	13	15	25°
30°	4	4	4	5	6	7	8	9	11	14	21	–	30°

NB: Regarding Table 1. If latitude and declination are of the same sign, take out the respondent directly. If they are of opposite signs, subtract the respondent from 12h.

Table 1 gives the complete range of declinations in case any user wishes to calculate semi-diurnal arcs for bodies other than the Sun and Moon.

Example:

Lat.	Dec.	Semi-diurnal arc
+52°	+20°	7h 51m
+52°	−20°	4h 09m

SUNRISE AND SUNSET

The local mean time of sunrise or sunset may be found by obtaining the hour angle from Table 1 and applying it to the time of transit. The hour angle is negative for sunrise and positive for sunset. A small correction to the hour angle, which always has the effect of increasing it numerically, is necessary to allow for the Sun's semi-diameter (16′) and for refraction (34′); it is obtained from Table 2. The resulting local mean time may be converted into the standard time of the country by taking the difference between the longitude of the standard meridian of the country and that of the place, adding it to the local mean time if the place is west of the standard meridian, and subtracting it if the place is east.

Example – Required the New Zealand Mean Time (12h fast on GMT) of sunset on May 23 at Auckland, latitude 36° 50′ S. (or minus), longitude 11h 39m E. Taking the declination as +20°.6 (page 35), we find:

	h	m
New Zealand Standard Time	+ 12	00
Longitude	– 11	39
Longitudinal Correction	+ 0	21
Tabular entry for Lat. 30° and Dec. 20°, opposite signs	+ 5	11
Proportional part for 6° 50′ of Lat.	–	15
Proportional part for 0°.6 of Dec.	–	2
Correction (Table 2)	+	5
Hour Angle	4	58
Sun transits (page 35)	11	57
Longitudinal correction	+	21
New Zealand Mean Time	17	16

MOONRISE AND MOONSET

It is possible to calculate the times of moonrise and moonset using Table 1, though the method is more complicated because the apparent motion of the Moon is much more rapid and also more variable than that of the Sun.

TABLE 3. LONGITUDE CORRECTION

X A	40m	45m	50m	55m	60m	65m	70m
h	m	m	m	m	m	m	m
1	2	2	2	2	3	3	3
2	3	4	4	5	5	5	6
3	5	6	6	7	8	8	9
4	7	8	8	9	10	11	12
5	8	9	10	11	13	14	15
6	10	11	13	14	15	16	18
7	12	13	15	16	18	19	20
8	13	15	17	18	20	22	23
9	15	17	19	21	23	24	26
10	17	19	21	23	25	27	29
11	18	21	23	25	28	30	32
12	20	23	25	28	30	33	35
13	22	24	27	30	33	35	38
14	23	26	29	32	35	38	41
15	25	28	31	34	38	41	44
16	27	30	33	37	40	43	47
17	28	32	35	39	43	46	50
18	30	34	38	41	45	49	53
19	32	36	40	44	48	51	55
20	33	38	42	46	50	54	58
21	35	39	44	48	53	57	61
22	37	41	46	50	55	60	64
23	38	43	48	53	58	62	67
24	40	45	50	55	60	65	70

The parallax of the Moon, about 57′, is near to the sum of the semi-diameter and refraction but has the opposite effect on these times. It is thus convenient to neglect all three quantities in the method outlined below.

Notation

ϕ	= latitude of observer
λ	= longitude of observer (measured positively towards the west)
T_{-1}	= time of transit of Moon on previous day
T_0	= time of transit of Moon on day in question
T_1	= time of transit of Moon on following day
δ_0	= approximate declination of Moon
δ_R	= declination of Moon at moonrise
δ_S	= declination of Moon at moonset
h_0	= approximate hour angle of Moon
h_R	= hour angle of Moon at moonrise
h_S	= hour angle of Moon at moonset
t_R	= time of moonrise
t_S	= time of moonset

Method

1. With arguments ϕ, δ_0 enter Table 1 on page 66 to determine h_0 where h_0 is negative for moonrise and positive for moonset.

2. Form approximate times from
$$t_R = T_0 + \lambda + h_0$$
$$t_S = T_0 + \lambda + h_0$$

3. Determine δ_R, δ_S for times t_R, t_S respectively.

4. Re-enter Table 1 on page 66 with
   (a) arguments ϕ, δ_R to determine h_R
   (b) arguments ϕ, δ_S to determine h_S

5. Form
$$t_R = T_0 + \lambda + h_R + AX$$
$$t_S = T_0 + \lambda + h_S + AX$$

where A = (λ + h)

and   X = ($T_0 - T_{-1}$)   if (λ + h)   is negative
      X = ($T_1 - T_0$)   if (λ + h)   is positive

AX is the respondent in Table 3.

Example – To find the times of moonrise and moonset at Vancouver (ϕ = +49°, λ = +8h 12m) on 2003 March 30. The starting data (page 28) are

T_{-1}	= 9h 51m
T_0	= 10h 35m
T_1	= 11h 17m
δ_0	= –11°

1. h_0 = 5h 08m
2. Approximate values
   t_R = 30d 10h 35m + 8h 12m + (-5h 08m)
       = 30d 13h 39m
   t_S = 30d 10h 35m + 8h 12m + (+5h 08m)
       = 30d 23h 55m
3. δ_R = –10°.6
   δ_S = –8°.5
4. h_R = –5h 10m
   h_S = +5h 20m
5. t_R = 30d 10h 35m + 8h 12m + (-5h 10m) + 5m
       = 30d 13h 42m
   t_S = 30d 10h 35m + 8h 12m + (+5h 20m) + 24m
       = 31d 00h 31m

To get the LMT of the phenomenon the longitude is subtracted from the GMT thus:

Moonrise = 30d 13h 42m – 8h 12m = 30d 05h 30m
Moonset = 31d 00h 31m – 8h 12m = 30d 16h 19m

ECLIPSES AND OCCULTATIONS 2003

ECLIPSES

There will be four eclipses in 2003, two of the Sun and two of the Moon. (Penumbral lunar eclipses are not mentioned in this section as they are too difficult to observe).

1. A total eclipse of the Moon on May 16 is visible from Madagascar, Africa, western Asia, Europe, the Atlantic Ocean and the Americas (except the extreme north-west). The partial eclipse begins at 02h 03m and ends at 05h 18m. Totality lasts from 03h 14m to 04h 06m.

2. An annular eclipse of the Sun on May 31 is visible as a partial eclipse from north-east Africa, the Middle East, Europe (except south-west France, Iberia, Eire, south-west England and south-west Wales), Asia (except the south), Greenland, extreme south-east Iceland and north-west N. America. The partial eclipse begins at 01h 46m and ends at 06h 30m. The path of annularity starts on the extreme south-eastern edge of Iceland at an altitude of only 3 degrees, and in the nearby Arctic Ocean at an altitude of 10 degrees or less. The annular phase begins at 03h 45m and ends at 04h 31m. The maximum duration is 3m 37s.

In the British Isles the partial phase begins before sunrise. However at this time most of the Sun is still eclipsed. At Greenwich the eclipse ends at 04h 31m and at Edinburgh it ends at 04h 40m.

3. A total eclipse of the Moon on November 9-10 is visible from the Indian Ocean (except the east), Africa, Europe, the Arctic Ocean, the Atlantic Ocean, Greenland, the Americas and the eastern Pacific Ocean. The partial eclipse begins at 23h 33m and ends at 03h 05m. Totality lasts from 01h 07m to 01h 30m.

4. A total eclipse of the Sun on November 23–24 is visible as a partial eclipse from Australia, New Zealand (except the north of North Island), the Southern Ocean and Antarctica. The partial phase begins at 20h 46m and ends at 00h 52m. The track of totality is confined to Antarctica. Totality begins at 22h 19m and ends at 23h 19m. The maximum duration is 1m 57s.

TRANSIT

There will be a transit of Mercury across the Sun on May 7, lasting from about 05h 13m (position angle 14 degrees) to 10h 32m (position angle 291 degrees), visible in its entirety from the British Isles. The least angular distance between the centres of the Sun and Mercury is 11.8 arcminutes.

LUNAR OCCULTATIONS

Observations of the times of occultations are made by both amateur and professional astronomers. Such observations are later analysed to yield accurate positions of the Moon; this is one method of determining the difference between terrestrial time and universal time.

Many of the observations made by amateurs are obtained with the use of a stop-watch which is compared with a time-signal immediately after the observation. Thus an accuracy of about one-fifth of a second is obtainable, though the observer's personal equation may amount to one-third or one-half of a second.

The list on page 69 includes most of the occultations visible under favourable conditions in the British Isles. No occultation is included unless the star is at least 10° above the horizon and the Sun sufficiently far below the horizon to permit the star to be seen with the naked eye or with a small telescope. The altitude limit is reduced from 10° to 2° for stars and planets brighter than magnitude 2.0 and such occultations are also predicted in daylight.

The column Phase shows (i) whether a disappearance (D) or reappearance (R) is to be observed; and (ii) whether it is at the dark limb (D) or bright limb (B). The column headed 'El. of Moon' gives the elongation of the Moon from the Sun, in degrees. The elongation increases from 0° at New Moon to 180° at Full Moon and on to 360° (or 0°) at New Moon again. Times and position angles (P), reckoned from the north point in the direction north, east, south, west, are given for Greenwich (lat. 51° 30′, long. 0°) and Edinburgh (lat. 56° 00′, long. 3° 12′ west).

The coefficients a and b are the variations in the GMT for each degree of longitude (positive to the west) and latitude (positive to the north) respectively; they enable approximate times (to within about 1m generally) to be found for any point in the British Isles. If the point of observation is $\Delta\lambda$ degrees west and $\Delta\phi$ degrees north, the approximate time is found by adding $a.\Delta\lambda + b.\Delta\phi$ to the given GMT.

Example: the disappearance of ZC466 on March 8 at Coventry, found from both Greenwich and Edinburgh.

	Greenwich	Edinburgh
	°	°
Longitude	0.0	+3.2
Long. of Coventry	+1.5	+1.5
$\Delta\lambda$	+1.5	−1.7
Latitude	+51.5	+56.0
Lat. of Coventry	+52.4	+52.4
$\Delta\phi$	+0.9	−3.6
	h m	h m
GMT	19 31.5	19 33.7
$a.\Delta\lambda$	−1.5	+1.5
$b.\Delta\phi$	+0.5	−6.8
	19 30.5	19 28.4

If the occultation is given for one station but not the other, the reason for the suppression is given by the following code:

N = star not occulted
A = star's altitude less than 10° (2° for bright stars and planets)
S = Sun not sufficiently below the horizon
G = occultation is of very short duration

In some cases the coefficients a and b are not given; this is because the occultation is so short that prediction for other places by means of these coefficients would not be reliable.

LUNAR OCCULTATIONS 2003

		ZC No.	Mag.	Phase	El. of Moon	GREENWICH UT h	m	a m	b m	P °	EDINBURGH UT h	m	a m	b m	P °
February	5	66	6.8	DD	51	19	50.6	−0.5	−1.1	74	19	44.9	−0.5	−0.7	58
	6	192	5.3	DD	62	21	46.6	G		130	21	30.9	−0.3	−2.5	105
	9	510	7.2	DD	95	21	35.2	G		4	N				
	9	517	6.4	DD	95	22	40.6	−0.6	−1.6	88	22	32.4	−0.7	−1.2	75
	10	633	5.4	DD	105	20	06.0	−1.5	+0.2	71	20	03.8	−1.3	+0.8	55
	10	642	6.9	DD	106	21	36.0	−1.2	−4.3	134	21	18.5	−1.2	−2.2	112
	11	789	6.9	DD	118	23	21.4	−1.0	−0.6	66	23	16.1	−1.1	−0.2	54
	13	1068	6.9	DD	139	18	05.0	−0.7	+1.8	75	18	12.1	−0.5	+2.3	60
March	5	128	7.3	DD	30	18	24.9	−0.4	+0.5	30	S				
	7	355	7.5	DD	52	18	47.7	−0.8	+1.0	28	18	53.4	G		4
	8	466	7.3	DD	63	19	31.5	−1.0	+0.6	37	19	33.7	−0.9	+1.9	17
	9	595	6.8	DD	74	19	46.6	−1.2	−1.0	80	19	39.7	−1.1	−0.4	66
	10	734	6.7	DD	85	20	53.1	−1.2	−0.5	64	20	48.6	−1.1	+0.1	50
	11	893	7.7	DD	98	24	03.6	−0.1	−1.6	93	23	55.8	−0.3	−1.5	87
April	6	688	6.8	DD	54	19	19.5	−1.2	+0.9	33	S				
	7	835	6.9	DD	67	22	37.5	+0.5	−2.5	134	22	27.7	+0.3	−2.4	126
	12	1484	3.6	DD	125	19	35.0	−1.7	+1.2	77	19	37.5	−1.7	+2.4	61
	13	1612	7.3	DD	140	23	03.4	−0.7	−1.8	145	22	53.4	−0.7	−1.5	141
May	6	1085	7.0	DD	60	22	58.4	−0.1	−0.9	59	22	53.5	−0.2	−1.0	56
	8	1334	7.0	DD	83	21	37.3	−0.9	−1.3	82	21	28.6	−1.0	−1.2	78
	9	1444	7.8	DD	94	20	27.8	−1.0	−1.7	124	S				
	10	1569	6.8	DD	108	22	46.9	−1.1	−1.3	83	22	37.7	−1.1	−1.2	81
June	3	1180	7.1	DD	42	21	57.9	+0.7	−1.9	146	S				
	6	1535	7.1	DD	78	21	22.6	−0.5	−1.8	110	S				
	6	1544	5.7	DD	79	23	11.6	G		55	23	04.6	G		53
	8	1758	7.0	DD	104	23	24.1	−0.4	−1.8	125	23	14.5	−0.5	−1.8	124
	9	1875	6.5	DD	117	22	34.4	−1.5	−1.0	71	22	25.3	−1.5	−0.9	70
	11	2117	5.3	DD	144	21	15.1	−1.0	−0.5	132	S				
	11	2118	2.9	DD	144	21	23.4	−1.0	−0.6	136	21	18.3	−0.9	−0.3	134
	11	2118	2.9	RB	145	22	30.7	−1.4	−0.7	282	22	24.0	−1.2	−0.5	283
July	4	1612	7.3	DD	62	21	11.0	−0.4	−1.6	87	S				
	7	1962	5.2	DD	101	23	12.7	−0.5	−1.8	123	23	03.0	−0.5	−1.8	121
	9	2217	5.5	DD	128	23	43.8	−0.8	−1.0	60	A				
	11	2524	6.0	DD	154	21	11.4	−1.7	+0.8	66	A				
August	8	2634	7.4	DD	137	21	06.9	−1.5	−0.2	115	A				
September	6	2914	5.0	DD	132	19	49.0	−1.5	+0.7	80	19	47.8	−1.2	+0.7	77
	6	2925	7.5	DD	134	22	03.8	−1.5	−0.5	91	A				
October	7	3413	6.4	DD	151	19	05.0	G		347	N				
	25	Mercury	−1.4	DB	2	12	21.4	−0.4	−1.8	171	12	13.0	−0.4	−1.4	170
	25	Mercury	−1.4	RB	2	13	15.0	−2.0	−0.7	256	13	06.2	−1.8	−0.5	256
	27	2290	2.5	DD	28	13	14.6	−1.4	+0.1	97	13	11.3	−1.2	+0.3	96
	27	2290	2.5	RB	29	14	23.1	−1.2	−0.7	307	14	16.9	−1.0	−0.4	308
November	2	3276	7.4	DD	111	21	54.0	−1.0	−0.6	69	21	48.9	−0.8	−0.4	56
	3	3396	7.9	DD	122	21	33.6	−2.1	−1.2	102	21	24.4	−1.5	−0.5	87
	10	660	4.4	RD	200	22	36.9	−1.1	+1.6	256	22	40.1	−1.1	+1.4	269
	28	3073	7.6	DD	65	17	19.8	−0.8	+0.5	28	17	20.1	−0.5	+0.5	18
	29	3215	7.7	DD	78	17	11.1	−2.2	−0.3	112	17	05.0	−1.6	+0.2	102
	30	3343	5.8	DD	90	17	01.9	−1.5	+0.8	76	17	01.6	−1.2	+1.0	69
	30	3349	4.2	DD	91	18	35.5	−1.0	+0.6	43	18	35.7	−0.8	+0.7	33
December	2	49	6.3	DD	115	20	40.3	−1.8	−0.6	89	20	34.2	−1.4	0.0	73
	21	2290	2.5	DB	333	12	19.4	−1.2	−0.9	73	12	11.8	−1.1	−0.8	71
	28	3438	7.5	DD	71	19	20.1	−1.2	−1.0	81	19	13.4	−0.9	−0.5	66
	28	3442	7.8	DD	72	20	23.4	−0.6	−0.4	55	20	20.7	−0.4	−0.1	39
	29	20	6.8	DD	84	21	37.2	−0.4	+0.2	37	21	38.4	−0.2	+0.8	18

MEAN PLACES OF STARS 2003.5

Name	Mag.	RA h m	Dec. ° '	Spectrum	Name	Mag.	RA h m	Dec. ° '	Spectrum
α And *Alpheratz*	2.1	0 08.6	+29 07	A0p	γ Corvi	2.6	12 16.0	−17 34	B8
β Cassiopeiae *Caph*	2.3	0 09.4	+59 10	F5	α Crucis	1.0	12 26.8	−63 07	B1
γ Pegasi *Algenib*	2.8	0 13.4	+15 12	B2	γ Crucis	1.6	12 31.4	−57 08	M3
β Mensae	2.9	0 25.9	−77 14	G0	γ Centauri	2.2	12 41.7	−48 59	A0
α Phoenicis	2.4	0 26.5	−42 17	K0	γ Virginis	2.7	12 41.8	− 1 28	F0
α Cassiopeiae *Schedar*	2.2	0 40.7	+56 33	K0	β Crucis	1.3	12 47.9	−59 42	B1
β Ceti *Diphda*	2.0	0 43.8	−17 58	K0	ε Ursae Majoris *Alioth*	1.8	12 54.2	+55 56	A0p
γ Cassiopeiae*	Var.	0 56.9	+60 44	B0p	α Canum Venaticorum	2.9	12 56.2	+38 18	A0p
β Andromedae *Mirach*	2.1	1 09.9	+35 38	M0	ζ Ursae Majoris *Mizar*	2.1	13 24.1	+54 54	A2p
δ Cassiopeiae	2.7	1 26.0	+60 15	A5	Virginis *Spica*	1.0	13 25.4	−11 11	B2
α Eridani *Achernar*	0.5	1 37.8	−57 13	B5	ε Centauri	2.6	13 40.1	−53 29	B1
β Arietis *Sheratan*	2.6	1 54.8	+20 49	A5	η Ursae Majoris *Alkaid*	1.9	13 47.7	+49 18	B3
γ Andromedae *Almak*	2.3	2 04.1	+42 21	K0	β Centauri *Hadar*	0.6	14 04.1	−60 23	B1
α Arietis *Hamal*	2.0	2 07.4	+23 29	K2	θ Centauri	2.1	14 06.9	−36 23	K0
α Ursae Minoris *Polaris*	2.0	2 35.8	+89 17	F8	α Bootis *Arcturus*	0.0	14 15.8	+19 10	K0
β Persei *Algol**	Var.	3 08.4	+40 58	B8	α Centauri *Rigil Kent*	0.1	14 39.8	−60 51	G0
α Persei *Mirfak*	1.8	3 24.6	+49 52	F5	ε Bootis	2.4	14 45.1	+27 04	K0
η Tauri *Alcyone*	2.9	3 47.7	+24 07	B5p	β UMi *Kochab*	2.1	14 50.7	+74 08	K5
α Tauri *Aldebaran*	0.9	4 36.1	+16 31	K5	γ Ursae Minoris	3.1	15 20.7	+71 49	A2
β Orionis *Rigel*	0.1	5 14.7	− 8 12	B8p	α CrB *Alphecca*	2.2	15 34.8	+26 42	A0
α Aurigae *Capella*	0.1	5 16.9	+46 00	G0	β Trianguli Australis	3.0	15 55.5	−63 26	F0
γ Orionis *Bellatrix*	1.6	5 25.3	+ 6 21	B2	δ Scorpii	2.3	16 00.5	−22 38	B0
β Tauri *Elnath*	1.7	5 26.5	+28 37	B8	β Scorpii	2.6	16 05.6	−19 49	B1
δ Orionis	2.2	5 32.2	− 0 18	B0	α Scorpii *Antares*	1.0	16 29.6	−26 26	M0
α Leporis	2.6	5 32.9	−17 49	F0	α Trianguli Australis	1.9	16 49.0	−69 02	K2
ε Orionis	1.7	5 36.4	− 1 12	B0	ε Scorpii	2.3	16 50.4	−34 18	K0
ζ Orionis	1.8	5 40.9	− 1 56	B0	α Herculis†	Var.	17 14.8	+14 23	M3
κ Orionis	2.1	5 47.9	− 9 40	B0	λ Scorpii	1.6	17 33.8	−37 06	B2
α Orionis *Betelgeuse**	Var.	5 55.4	+ 7 24	M0	α Ophiuchi *Rasalhague*	2.1	17 35.1	+12 33	A5
β Aurigae *Menkalinan*	1.9	5 59.8	+44 57	A0p	θ Scorpii	1.9	17 37.6	−43 00	F0
β CMa *Mirzam*	2.0	6 22.9	−17 57	B1	κ Scorpii	2.4	17 42.7	−39 02	B2
α Carinae *Canopus*	−0.7	6 24.0	−52 42	F0	γ Draconis	2.2	17 56.7	+51 29	K5
γ Geminorum *Alhena*	1.9	6 37.9	+16 24	A0	ε Sgr Kaus *Australis*	1.9	18 24.4	−34 23	A0
α Canis Majoris *Sirius*	−1.5	6 45.3	−16 43	A0	α Lyrae *Vega*	0.0	18 37.1	+38 47	A0
ε Canis Majoris	1.5	6 58.8	−28 59	B1	σ Sagittarii	2.0	18 55.5	−26 18	B3
δ Canis Majoris	1.9	7 08.5	−26 24	F8p	β Cygni *Albireo*	3.1	19 30.9	+27 58	K0
α Geminorum *Castor*	1.6	7 34.8	+31 53	A0	α Aquilae *Altair*	0.8	19 51.0	+ 8 53	A5
α CMi *Procyon*	0.4	7 39.5	+ 5 13	F5	α Capricorni	3.8	20 18.2	−12 32	G5
β Geminorum *Pollux*	1.1	7 45.5	+28 01	K0	γ Cygni	2.2	20 22.4	+40 16	F8p
ζ Puppis	2.3	8 03.7	−40 01	Od	α Pavonis	1.9	20 25.9	−56 43	B3
γ Velorum	1.8	8 09.6	−47 21	Oap	α Cygni *Deneb*	1.3	20 41.6	+45 18	A2p
ε Carinae	1.9	8 22.6	−59 31	K0	α Cephei *Alderamin*	2.4	21 18.7	+62 36	A5
δ Velorum	2.0	8 44.8	−54 43	A0	ε Pegasi	2.4	21 44.4	+ 9 53	K0
λ Velorum *Suhail*	2.2	9 08.1	−43 27	K5	δ Capricorni	2.9	21 47.2	−16 07	A5
β Carinae	1.7	9 13.2	−69 44	A0	α Gruis	1.7	22 08.5	−46 57	B5
ι Carinae	2.2	9 17.2	−59 17	F0	δ Cephei†	3.7	22 29.3	+58 26	†
κ Velorum	2.6	9 22.2	−55 02	B3	β Gruis	2.1	22 42.9	−46 52	M3
α Hydrae *Alphard*	2.0	9 27.8	− 8 40	K2	α PsA *Fomalhaut*	1.2	22 57.8	−29 36	A3
α Leonis *Regulus*	1.3	10 08.6	+11 57	B8	β Pegasi *Scheat*	2.4	23 03.9	+28 06	M0
γ Leonis *Algeiba*	1.9	10 20.2	+19 49	K0	α Pegasi *Markab*	2.5	23 04.9	+15 13	A0
β Ursae Majoris *Merak*	2.4	11 02.1	+56 22	A0					
α Ursae Majoris *Dubhe*	1.8	11 03.9	+61 44	K0					
δ Leonis	2.6	11 14.3	+20 30	A3					
β Leonis *Denebola*	2.1	11 49.2	+14 33	A2					
γ Ursae Majoris *Phecda*	2.4	11 54.0	+53 41	A0					

*γ Cassiopeiae, 2002 mag. 2.5. β Persei, mag. 2.1 to 3.4.
α Orionis, mag. 0.1 to 1.2.
†α Herculis, mag. 3.1 to 3.9. δ Cephei, mag. 3.7 to 4.4,
spectrum F5 to G0.

The positions of heavenly bodies on the celestial sphere are defined by two co-ordinates, right ascension and declination, which are analogous to longitude and latitude on the surface of the Earth. If we imagine the plane of the terrestrial equator extended indefinitely, it will cut the celestial sphere in a great circle known as the celestial equator. Similarly the plane of the Earth's orbit, when extended, cuts in the great circle called the ecliptic. The two intersections of these circles are known as the First Point of Aries and the First Point of Libra. If from any star a perpendicular is drawn to the celestial equator, the length of this perpendicular is the star's declination. The arc, measured eastwards along the equator from the First Point of Aries to the foot of this perpendicular, is the right ascension. An alternative definition of right ascension is that it is the angle at the celestial pole (where the Earth's axis, if prolonged, would meet the sphere) between the great circles to the First Point of Aries and to the star.

The plane of the Earth's equator has a slow movement, so that our reference system for right ascension and declination is not fixed. The consequent alteration in these quantities from year to year is called precession. In right ascension it is an increase of about 3 seconds a year for equatorial stars, and larger or smaller changes in either direction for stars near the poles, depending on the right ascension of the star. In declination it varies between +20″ and −20″ according to the right ascension of the star.

A star or other body crosses the meridian when the sidereal time is equal to its right ascension. The altitude is then a maximum, and may be deduced by remembering that the altitude of the elevated pole is numerically equal to the latitude, while that of the equator at its intersection with the meridian is equal to the co-latitude, or complement of the latitude.

Thus in London (lat. 51° 30′) the meridian altitude of Sirius is found as follows:

	°	′
Altitude of equator	38	30
Declination south	16	43
Difference	21	47

The altitude of Capella (Dec. +46° 00′) at lower transit is:

	°	′
Altitude of pole	51	30
Polar distance of star	44	00
Difference	7	30

The brightness of a heavenly body is denoted by its magnitude. Omitting the exceptionally bright stars Sirius and Canopus, the twenty brightest stars are of the first magnitude, while the faintest stars visible to the naked eye are of the sixth magnitude. The magnitude scale is a precise one, as a difference of five magnitudes represents a ratio of 100 to 1 in brightness. Typical second magnitude stars are Polaris and the stars in the belt of Orion. The scale is most easily fixed in memory by comparing the stars with Norton's Star Atlas. The stars Sirius and Canopus and the planets Venus and Jupiter are so bright that their magnitudes are expressed by negative numbers. A small telescope will show stars down to the ninth or tenth magnitude, while stars fainter than the twentieth magnitude may be photographed by long exposures with the largest telescopes.

MEAN AND SIDEREAL TIME

Acceleration					Retardation				
h	m	s	m	s	s	h	m	s	m	s	s
1	0	10	0	00	0	1	0	10	0	00	0
2	0	20	3	02	1	2	0	20	3	03	1
3	0	30	9	07	2	3	0	29	9	09	2
4	0	39	15	13	3	4	0	39	15	15	3
5	0	49	21	18	4	5	0	49	21	21	4
6	0	59	27	23	5	6	0	59	27	28	5
7	1	09	33	28	6	7	1	09	33	34	6
8	1	19	39	34	7	8	1	19	39	40	7
9	1	29	45	39	8	9	1	28	45	46	8
10	1	39	51	44	9	10	1	38	51	53	9
11	1	48	57	49	10	11	1	48	57	59	10
12	1	58	60	00		12	1	58	60	00	
13	2	08				13	2	08			
14	2	18				14	2	18			
15	2	28				15	2	27			
16	2	38				16	2	37			
17	2	48				17	2	47			
18	2	57				18	2	57			
19	3	07				19	3	07			
20	3	17				20	3	17			
21	3	27				21	3	26			
22	3	37				22	3	36			
23	3	47				23	3	46			
24	3	57				24	3	56			

The length of a sidereal day in mean time is 23h 56m 04s.09. Hence 1h MT = 1h+9s.86 ST and 1h ST = 1h−9s.83 MT.

To convert an interval of mean time to the corresponding interval of sidereal time, enter the acceleration table with the given mean time (taking the hours and the minutes and seconds separately) and add the acceleration obtained to the given mean time. To convert an interval of sidereal time to the corresponding interval of mean time, take out the retardation for the given sidereal time and subtract.

The columns for the minutes and seconds of the argument are in the form known as critical tables. To use these tables, find in the appropriate left-hand column the two entries between which the given number of minutes and seconds lies; the quantity in the right-hand column between these two entries is the required acceleration or retardation. Thus the acceleration for 11m 26s (which lies between the entries 9m 07s and 15m 13s) is 2s. If the given number of minutes and seconds is a tabular entry, the required acceleration or retardation is the entry in the right-hand column above the given tabular entry, e.g. the retardation for 45m 46s is 7s.

Example – Convert 14h 27m 35s from ST to MT

	h	m	s
Given ST	14	27	35
Retardation for 14h		2	18
Retardation for 27m 35s			5
Corresponding MT	14	25	12

For further explanation, *see* pages 75–6.

ECLIPSES AND SHADOW TRANSITS OF JUPITER'S SATELLITES 2003

GMT			*Sat.*	*Phen.*
d	*h*	*m*		
JANUARY				
1	03	00	I	Ec.D
1	03	51	IV	Sh.E
1	21	30	III	Sh.I
1	23	18	II	Ec.D
2	00	16	I	Sh.I
2	01	05	III	Sh.E
2	02	33	I	Sh.E
2	21	28	I	Ec.D
3	20	47	II	Sh.E
3	21	01	I	Sh.E
8	04	54	I	Ec.D
9	01	27	III	Sh.I
9	01	52	II	Ec.D
9	02	09	I	Sh.I
9	04	26	I	Sh.E
9	05	03	III	Sh.E
9	23	23	I	Ec.D
10	20	29	II	Sh.I
10	20	38	I	Sh.I
10	22	55	I	Sh.E
10	23	24	II	Sh.E
16	04	03	I	Sh.I
16	04	25	II	Ec.D
16	05	25	III	Sh.I
16	06	20	I	Sh.E
17	01	17	I	Ec.D
17	21	52	IV	Sh.E
17	22	31	I	Sh.I
17	23	05	II	Sh.I
18	00	48	I	Sh.E
18	02	00	II	Sh.E
18	19	45	I	Ec.D
19	19	28	III	Ec.D
23	05	56	I	Sh.I
24	03	11	I	Ec.D
25	00	25	I	Sh.I
25	01	42	II	Sh.I
25	02	42	I	Sh.E
25	04	37	II	Sh.E
25	21	40	I	Ec.D
26	00	45	IV	Ec.D
26	18	53	I	Sh.I
26	20	16	II	Ec.D
26	21	10	I	Sh.E
26	23	27	III	Ec.D
31	05	06	I	Ec.D
FEBRUARY				
1	02	19	I	Sh.I
1	04	19	II	Sh.I
1	04	36	I	Sh.E
1	23	34	I	Ec.D
2	20	47	I	Sh.I
2	23	04	I	Sh.E
3	01	42	II	Ec.R
3	20	21	I	Ec.R
4	20	33	II	Sh.E
6	20	57	III	Sh.E
8	04	12	I	Sh.I
9	03	47	I	Ec.R
9	22	41	I	Sh.I
10	00	58	I	Sh.E
10	04	16	II	Ec.R
10	22	16	I	Ec.R
11	19	27	I	Sh.E
11	20	15	II	Sh.I
11	23	09	II	Sh.E
11	23	41	IV	Ec.R
13	21	19	III	Sh.I
14	00	57	III	Sh.E
17	00	35	I	Sh.I
17	02	52	I	Sh.E
18	00	11	I	Ec.R
18	21	21	I	Sh.E
18	22	52	II	Sh.I
19	01	46	II	Sh.E
20	05	03	IV	Sh.I
20	20	08	II	Ec.R
21	01	18	III	Sh.I
21	04	55	III	Sh.E
24	02	29	I	Sh.I
24	04	47	I	Sh.E
25	02	06	I	Ec.R
25	20	58	I	Sh.I
25	23	15	I	Sh.E
26	01	28	II	Sh.I
26	04	23	II	Sh.E
26	20	34	I	Ec.R
27	22	42	II	Ec.R
MARCH				
3	04	24	I	Sh.I
3	23	02	III	Ec.R
4	04	01	I	Ec.R
4	22	52	I	Sh.I
5	01	10	I	Sh.E
5	04	06	II	Sh.I
5	22	29	I	Ec.R
6	19	38	I	Sh.E
7	01	17	II	Ec.R
8	20	18	II	Sh.E
8	23	05	IV	Sh.I
9	03	52	IV	Sh.E
11	03	02	III	Ec.R
12	00	47	I	Sh.I
12	03	04	I	Sh.E
13	00	24	I	Ec.R
13	21	33	I	Sh.E
15	20	01	II	Sh.I
15	22	54	II	Sh.E
18	03	22	III	Ec.D
19	02	42	I	Sh.I
20	02	19	I	Ec.R
20	21	10	I	Sh.I
20	23	27	I	Sh.E
21	20	48	I	Ec.R
21	20	51	III	Sh.E
22	22	38	II	Sh.I
23	01	31	II	Sh.E
25	21	53	IV	Sh.E
27	23	05	I	Sh.I
28	01	22	I	Sh.E
28	21	14	III	Sh.I
28	22	43	I	Ec.R
29	00	50	III	Sh.E
30	01	15	II	Sh.I
31	22	21	II	Ec.R
APRIL				
3	00	56	IV	Ec.D
4	01	00	I	Sh.I
5	00	38	I	Ec.R
5	01	13	III	Sh.I
5	21	45	I	Sh.E
8	00	56	II	Ec.R
12	21	24	I	Sh.I
12	23	40	I	Sh.E
13	21	02	I	Ec.R
15	23	00	III	Ec.R
16	22	39	II	Sh.E
19	23	19	I	Sh.I
19	23	52	IV	Ec.R
20	22	58	I	Ec.R
22	23	20	III	Ec.D
23	22	23	II	Sh.I
28	00	53	I	Ec.R
28	21	59	I	Sh.E
MAY				
2	22	03	II	Ec.R
5	23	54	I	Sh.E
12	23	33	I	Sh.I
13	23	11	I	Ec.R
14	23	11	IV	Sh.I
OCTOBER				
15	04	22	II	Sh.E
22	04	05	II	Sh.I
28	05	11	I	Sh.E
NOVEMBER				
4	04	48	I	Sh.I
6	04	15	III	Sh.E
7	04	19	II	Ec.D
12	03	49	I	Ec.D
13	03	26	I	Sh.E
13	04	41	III	Sh.I
15	05	11	IV	Sh.I
16	03	54	II	Sh.E
19	05	42	I	Ec.D
20	03	03	I	Sh.I
20	05	20	I	Sh.E
23	03	38	II	Sh.I
24	02	13	III	Ec.R
27	04	57	I	Sh.I
28	02	03	I	Ec.D
30	06	12	II	Sh.I
DECEMBER				
1	02	36	III	Ec.D
1	06	10	III	Ec.R
2	03	13	IV	Sh.E
5	03	56	I	Ec.D
6	03	34	I	Sh.E
9	03	55	II	Ec.D
12	05	49	I	Ec.D
13	03	12	I	Sh.I
13	05	27	I	Sh.E
18	00	38	II	Sh.I
18	03	28	II	Sh.E
19	03	59	III	Sh.E
20	05	05	I	Sh.I
21	02	11	I	Ec.D
22	01	49	I	Sh.E
25	03	12	II	Sh.I
25	06	03	II	Sh.E
26	04	27	III	Sh.I
27	01	28	IV	Ec.D
27	05	30	IV	Ec.R
28	04	04	I	Ec.D
29	01	26	I	Sh.I
29	03	42	I	Sh.E

Jupiter's satellites transit across the disk from east to west, and pass behind the disk from west to east. The shadows that they cast also transit across the disk. With the exception at times of Satellite IV, the satellites also pass through the shadow of the planet, i.e. they are eclipsed. Just before opposition the satellite disappears in the shadow to the west of the planet and reappears from occultation on the east limb. Immediately after opposition the satellite is occulted at the west limb and reappears from eclipse to the east of the planet. At times approximately two to four months before and after opposition, both phases of eclipses of Satellite III may be seen. When Satellite IV is eclipsed, both phases may be seen.

The times given refer to the centre of the satellite. As the satellite is of considerable size, the immersion and emersion phases are not instantaneous. Even when the satellite enters or leaves the shadow along a radius of the shadow, the phase can last for several minutes. With Satellite IV, grazing phenomena can occur so that the light from the satellite may fade and brighten again without a complete eclipse taking place.

The list of phenomena gives most of the eclipses and shadow transits visible in the British Isles under favourable conditions.

Ec. = Eclipse	R. = Reappearance
Sh. = Shadow transit	I. = Ingress
D. = Disappearance	E. = Egress

EXPLANATION OF ASTRONOMICAL DATA

Positions of the heavenly bodies are given only to the degree of accuracy required by amateur astronomers for setting telescopes, or for plotting on celestial globes or star atlases. Where intermediate positions are required, linear interpolation may be employed.

Definitions of the terms used cannot be given here. They must be sought in astronomical literature and textbooks.

A special feature has been made of the times when the various heavenly bodies are visible in the British Isles. Since two columns, calculated for latitudes 52° and 56°, are devoted to risings and settings, the range 50° to 58° can be covered by interpolation and extrapolation. The times given in these columns are Greenwich Mean Times for the meridian of Greenwich. An observer west of this meridian must add his/her longitude (in time) and vice versa.

In accordance with the usual convention in astronomy, + and − indicate respectively north and south latitudes or declinations.

All data are, unless otherwise stated, for 0h Greenwich Mean Time (GMT), i.e. at the midnight at the beginning of the day named. Allowance must be made for British Summer Time during the period that this is in operation (*see* pages 17 and 77).

PAGE ONE OF EACH MONTH
The calendar for each month is explained on page 17.

Under the heading Astronomical Phenomena will be found particulars of the more important conjunctions of the Sun, Moon and planets with each other, and also the dates of other astronomical phenomena of special interest.

Times of Minima of Algol are approximate times of the middle of the period of diminished light.

The Constellations listed each month are those that are near the meridian at the beginning of the month at 22h local mean time. Allowance must be made for British Summer Time if necessary. The fact that any star crosses the meridian 4m earlier each night or 2h earlier each month may be used, in conjunction with the lists given each month, to find what constellations are favourably placed at any moment. The table preceding the list of constellations may be extended indefinitely at the rate just quoted.

The principal phases of the Moon are the GMTs when the difference between the longitude of the Moon and that of the Sun is 0°, 90°, 180° or 270°. The times of perigee and apogee are those when the Moon is nearest to, and farthest from, the Earth, respectively. The nodes or points of intersection of the Moon's orbit and the ecliptic make a complete retrograde circuit of the ecliptic in about 19 years. From a knowledge of the longitude of the ascending node and the inclination, whose value does not vary much from 5°, the path of the Moon among the stars may be plotted on a celestial globe or star atlas.

PAGE TWO OF EACH MONTH
The Sun's semi-diameter, in arc, is given once a month.

The right ascension and declination (Dec.) is that of the true Sun. The right ascension of the mean Sun is obtained by applying the equation of time, with the sign given, to the right ascension of the true Sun, or, more easily, by applying 12h to the Sidereal Time. The direction in which the equation of time has to be applied in different problems is a frequent source of confusion and error. Apparent Solar Time is equal to the Mean Solar Time plus the Equation of Time. For example, at noon on August 8 the Equation of Time is −5m 41s and thus at 12h Mean Time on that day the Apparent Time is 12h −5m 41s = 11h 54m 19s.

The Greenwich Sidereal Time at 0h and the Transit of the First Point of Aries (which is really the mean time when the sidereal time is 0h) are used for converting mean time to sidereal time and vice versa.

The GMT of transit of the Sun at Greenwich may also be taken as the local mean time (LMT) of transit in any longitude. It is independent of latitude. The GMT of transit in any longitude is obtained by adding the longitude to the time given if west, and vice versa.

LIGHTING-UP TIME
The legal importance of sunrise and sunset is that the Road Vehicles Lighting Regulations 1989 (SI 1989 No. 1796) make the use of front and rear position lamps on vehicles compulsory during the period between sunset and sunrise. Headlamps on vehicles are required to be used during the hours of darkness on unlit roads or whenever visibility is seriously reduced. The hours of darkness are defined in these regulations as the period between half an hour after sunset and half an hour before sunrise.

In all laws and regulations 'sunset' refers to the local sunset, i.e. the time at which the Sun sets at the place in question. This common-sense interpretation has been upheld by legal tribunals. Thus the necessity for providing for different latitudes and longitudes, as already described, is evident.

SUNRISE AND SUNSET
The times of sunrise and sunset are those when the Sun's upper limb, as affected by refraction, is on the true horizon of an observer at sea-level. Assuming the mean refraction to be 34′, and the Sun's semi-diameter to be 16′, the time given is that when the true zenith distance of the Sun's centre is 90°+34′+16′ or 90°50′, or, in other words, when the depression of the Sun's centre below the true horizon is 50′. The upper limb is then 34′ below the true horizon, but is brought there by refraction. An observer on a ship might see the Sun for a minute or so longer, because of the dip of the horizon, while another viewing the sunset over hills or mountains would record an earlier time. Nevertheless, the moment when the true zenith distance of the Sun's centre is 90° 50′ is a precise time dependent only on the latitude and longitude of the place, and independent of its altitude above sea-level, the contour of its horizon, the vagaries of refraction or the small seasonal change in the Sun's semi-diameter; this moment is suitable in every way as a definition of sunset (or sunrise) for all statutory purposes. (For further information, *see* footnote on page 74.)

TWILIGHT
Light reaches us before sunrise and continues to reach us for some time after sunset. The interval between darkness and sunrise or sunset and darkness is called twilight. Astronomically speaking, twilight is considered to begin or end when the Sun's centre is 18° below the horizon, as no light from the Sun can then reach the observer. As thus defined twilight may last several hours; in high latitudes at the summer solstice the depression of 18° is not reached, and twilight lasts from sunset to sunrise.

The need for some sub-division of twilight is met by dividing the gathering darkness into four stages.

(1) *Sunrise or Sunset*, defined as above

(2) *Civil twilight*, which begins or ends when the Sun's centre is 6° below the horizon. This marks the time when operations requiring daylight may commence or must cease. In England it varies from about 30 to 60

minutes after sunset and the same interval before sunrise

(3) *Nautical twilight*, which begins or ends when the Sun's centre is 12° below the horizon. This marks the time when it is, to all intents and purposes, completely dark

(4) *Astronomical twilight*, which begins or ends when the Sun's centre is 18° below the horizon. This marks theoretical perfect darkness. It is of little practical importance, especially if nautical twilight is tabulated

To assist observers the durations of civil, nautical and astronomical twilights are given at intervals of ten days. The beginning of a particular twilight is found by subtracting the duration from the time of sunrise, while the end is found by adding the duration to the time of sunset. Thus the beginning of astronomical twilight in latitude 52°, on the Greenwich meridian, on March 11 is found as 06h 25m−113m = 04h 32m and similarly the end of civil twilight as 17h 57m+34m = 18h 31m. The letters TAN (twilight all night) are printed when twilight lasts all night.

Under the heading The Night Sky will be found notes describing the position and visibility of the planets and other phenomena.

PAGE THREE OF EACH MONTH

The Moon moves so rapidly among the stars that its position is given only to the degree of accuracy that permits linear interpolation. The right ascension (RA) and declination (Dec.) are geocentric, i.e. for an imaginary observer at the centre of the Earth. To an observer on the surface of the Earth the position is always different, as the altitude is always less on account of parallax, which may reach 1°.

The lunar terminator is the line separating the bright from the dark part of the Moon's disk. Apart from irregularities of the lunar surface, the terminator is elliptical, because it is a circle seen in projection. It becomes the full circle forming the limb, or edge, of the Moon at New and Full Moon. The selenographic longitude of the terminator is measured from the mean centre of the visible disk, which may differ from the visible centre by as much as 8°, because of libration.

Instead of the longitude of the terminator the Sun's selenographic co-longitude (Sun's co-long.) is tabulated. It is numerically equal to the selenographic longitude of the morning terminator, measured eastwards from the mean centre of the disk. Thus its value is approximately 270° at New Moon, 360° at First Quarter, 90° at Full Moon and 180° at Last Quarter.

The Position Angle (PA) of the Bright Limb is the position angle of the midpoint of the illuminated limb, measured eastwards from the north point on the disk. The Phase column shows the percentage of the area of the Moon's disk illuminated; this is also the illuminated percentage of the diameter at right angles to the line of cusps. The terminator is a semi-ellipse whose major axis is the line of cusps, and whose semi-minor axis is determined by the tabulated percentage; from New Moon to Full Moon the east limb is dark, and vice versa.

The times given as moonrise and moonset are those when the upper limb of the Moon is on the horizon of an observer at sea-level. The Sun's horizontal parallax (Hor. par.) is about 9″, and is negligible when considering sunrise and sunset, but that of the Moon averages about 57′. Hence the computed time represents the moment when the true zenith distance of the Moon is 90° 50′ (as for the Sun) minus the horizontal parallax. The time required for the Sun or Moon to rise or set is about four minutes (except in high latitudes). *See* also page 67 and footnote below.

The GMT of transit of the Moon over the meridian of Greenwich is given; these times are independent of latitude but must be corrected for longitude. For places in the British Isles it suffices to add the longitude if west, and vice versa. For other places a further correction is necessary because of the rapid movement of the Moon relative to the stars. The entire correction is conveniently determined by first finding the west longitude λ of the place. If the place is in west longitude, λ is the ordinary west longitude; if the place is in east longitude λ is the complement to 24h (or 360°) of the longitude and will be greater than 12h (or 180°). The correction then consists of two positive portions, namely λ and the fraction $\lambda/24$ (or $\lambda°/360$) multiplied by the difference between consecutive transits. Thus for Christchurch, New Zealand, the longitude is 11h 31m east, so $\lambda=$12h 29m and the fraction $\lambda/24$ is 0.52. The transit on the local date 2003 August 2 is found as follows:

	d	h m
GMT of transit at Greenwich August	1	14 54
λ		12 29
0.52×(14h 54m − 14h 06m)		25
GMT of transit at Christchurch	2	03 48
Corr. to NZ Standard Time		12 00
Local standard time of transit August	2	15 48

As is evident, for any given place the quantities λ and the correction to local standard time may be combined permanently, being here 24h 29m.

Positions of Mercury are given for every second day, and those of Venus and Mars for every fifth day; they may be interpolated linearly. The diameter (Diam.) is given in seconds of arc. The phase is the illuminated percentage of the disk. In the case of the inner planets this approaches 100 at superior conjunction and 0 at inferior conjunction. When the phase is less than 50 the planet is crescent-shaped or horned; for greater phases it is gibbous. In the case of the exterior planet Mars, the phase approaches 100 at conjunction and opposition, and is a minimum at quadratures.

Since the planets cannot be seen when on the horizon, the actual times of rising and setting are not given; instead, the time when the planet has an apparent altitude of 5° has been tabulated. If the time of transit is between 00h and 12h the time refers to an altitude of 5° above the eastern horizon; if between 12h and 24h, to the western horizon. The phenomenon tabulated is the one that occurs between sunset and sunrise. The times given may be interpolated for latitude and corrected for longitude, as in the case of the Sun and Moon.

The GMT at which the planet transits the Greenwich meridian is also given. The times of transit are to be corrected to local meridians in the usual way, as already described.

SUNRISE, SUNSET, MOONRISE AND MOONSET
The tables have been constructed for the meridian of Greenwich and for latitudes 52° and 56°. They give Greenwich Mean Time (GMT) throughout the year. To obtain the GMT of the phenomenon as seen from any other latitude and longitude in the British Isles, first interpolate or extrapolate for latitude by the usual rules of proportion. To the time thus found, the longitude (expressed in time) is to be added if west (as it usually is in Great Britain) or subtracted if east. If the longitude is expressed in degrees and minutes of arc, it must be converted to time at the rate of 1° = 4m and 15′ = 1m.

A method of calculating rise and set times for other places in the world is given on pages 66 and 67.

PAGE FOUR OF EACH MONTH

The GMTs of sunrise and sunset for seven cities, whose adopted positions in longitude (W.) and latitude (N.) are given immediately below the name, may be used not only for these phenomena, but also for lighting-up times (*see* page 73 for a fuller explanation).

The particulars for the four outer planets resemble those for the planets on Page Three of each month, except that, under Uranus and Neptune, times when the planet is 10° high instead of 5° high are given; this is because of the inferior brightness of these planets. The diameters given for the rings of Saturn are those of the major axis (in the plane of the planet's equator) and the minor axis respectively. The former has a small seasonal change due to the slightly varying distance of the Earth from Saturn, but the latter varies from zero when the Earth passes through the ring plane every 15 years to its maximum opening half-way between these periods. The rings were last open at their widest extent (and Saturn at its brightest) in 2002; this will occur again in 2017. The Earth passed through the ring plane in 1995–6 and will do so again in 2009.

TIME

From the earliest ages, the natural division of time into recurring periods of day and night has provided the practical time-scale for the everyday activities of the human race. Indeed, if any alternative means of time measurement is adopted, it must be capable of adjustment so as to remain in general agreement with the natural time-scale defined by the diurnal rotation of the Earth on its axis. Ideally the rotation should be measured against a fixed frame of reference; in practice it must be measured against the background provided by the celestial bodies. If the Sun is chosen as the reference point, we obtain Apparent Solar Time, which is the time indicated by a sundial. It is not a uniform time but is subject to variations which amount to as much as a quarter of an hour in each direction. Such wide variations cannot be tolerated in a practical time-scale, and this has led to the concept of Mean Solar Time in which all the days are exactly the same length and equal to the average length of the Apparent Solar Day.

The positions of the stars in the sky are specified in relation to a fictitious reference point in the sky known as the First Point of Aries (or the Vernal Equinox). It is therefore convenient to adopt this same reference point when considering the rotation of the Earth against background of the stars. The time-scale so obtained is known as Apparent Sidereal Time.

GREENWICH MEAN TIME

The daily rotation of the Earth on its axis causes the Sun and the other heavenly bodies to appear to cross the sky from east to west. It is convenient to represent this relative motion as if the Sun really performed a daily circuit around a fixed Earth. Noon in Apparent Solar Time may then be defined as the time at which the Sun transits across the observer's meridian. In Mean Solar Time, noon is similarly defined by the meridian transit of a fictitious Mean Sun moving uniformly in the sky with the same average speed as the true Sun. Mean Solar Time observed on the meridian of the transit circle telescope of the Old Royal Observatory at Greenwich is called Greenwich Mean Time (GMT). The mean solar day is divided into 24 hours and, for astronomical and other scientific purposes, these are numbered 0 to 23, commencing at midnight. Civil time is usually reckoned in two periods of 12 hours, designated a.m. (*ante meridiem*, i.e. before noon) and p.m. (*post meridiem*, i.e. after noon).

UNIVERSAL TIME

Before 1925 January 1, GMT was reckoned in 24 hours commencing at noon; since that date it has been reckoned from midnight. To avoid confusion in the use of the designation GMT before and after 1925, since 1928 astronomers have tended to use the term Universal Time (UT) or Weltzeit (WZ) to denote GMT measured from Greenwich Mean Midnight.

In precision work it is necessary to take account of small variations in Universal Time. These arise from small irregularities in the rotation of the Earth. Observed astronomical time is designated UT0. Observed time corrected for the effects of the motion of the poles (giving rise to a 'wandering' in longitude) is designated UT1. There is also a seasonal fluctuation in the rate of rotation of Earth arising from meteorological causes, often called the annual fluctuation. UT1 corrected for this effect is designated UT2 and provides a time-scale free from short-period fluctuations. It is still subject to small secular and irregular changes.

APPARENT SOLAR TIME

As mentioned above, the time shown by a sundial is called Apparent Solar Time. It differs from Mean Solar Time by an amount known as the Equation of Time, which is the total effect of two causes which make the length of the apparent solar day non-uniform. One cause of variation is that the orbit of the Earth is not a circle but an ellipse, having the Sun at one focus. As a consequence, the angular speed of the Earth in its orbit is not constant; it is greatest at the beginning of January when the Earth is nearest the Sun.

The other cause is due to the obliquity of the ecliptic; the plane of the equator (which is at right angles to the axis of rotation of the Earth) does not coincide with the ecliptic (the plane defined by the apparent annual motion of the Sun around the celestial sphere) but is inclined to it at an angle of 23° 26'. As a result, the apparent solar day is shorter than average at the equinoxes and longer at the solstices. From the combined effects of the components due to obliquity and eccentricity, the equation of time reaches its maximum values in February (−14 minutes) and early November (+16 minutes). It has a zero value on four dates during the year, and it is only on these dates (approximately April 15, June 14, September 1 and December 25) that a sundial shows Mean Solar Time.

SIDEREAL TIME

A sidereal day is the duration of a complete rotation of the Earth with reference to the First Point of Aries. The term sidereal (or 'star') time is a little misleading since the time-scale so defined is not exactly the same as that which would be defined by successive transits of a selected star, as there is a small progressive motion between the stars and the First Point of Aries due to the precession of the Earth's axis. This makes the length of the sidereal day shorter than the true period of rotation by 0.008 seconds. Superimposed on this steady precessional motion are small oscillations (nutation), giving rise to fluctuations in apparent sidereal time amounting to as much as 1.2 seconds. It is therefore customary to employ Mean Sidereal Time, from which these fluctuations have been removed. The conversion of GMT to Greenwich sidereal time (GST) may be performed by adding the value of the GST at 0h on the day in question (Page Two of each month) to the GMT converted to sidereal time using the table on page 71.

Example – To find the GST at August 8d 02h 41m 11s GMT

	h	m	s
GST at 0h	21	04	22
GMT	2	41	11
Acceleration for 2h			20
Acceleration for 41m 11s			7
Sum = GST =	23	46	00

If the observer is not on the Greenwich meridian then his/her longitude, measured positively westwards from Greenwich, must be subtracted from the GST to obtain Local Sidereal Time (LST). Thus, in the above example, an observer 5h east of Greenwich, or 19h west, would find the LST as 4h 46m 00s.

Ephemeris Time

An analysis of observations of the positions of the Sun, Moon and planets taken over an extended period is used in preparing ephemerides. (An ephemeris is a table giving the apparent position of a heavenly body at regular intervals of time, e.g. one day or ten days, and may be used to compare current observations with tabulated positions.) Discrepancies between the positions of heavenly bodies observed over a 300-year period and their predicted positions arose because the time-scale to which the observations were related was based on the assumption that the rate of rotation of the Earth is uniform. It is now known that this rate of rotation is variable. A revised time-scale, Ephemeris Time (ET), was devised to bring the ephemerides into agreement with the observations.

The second of ET is defined in terms of the annual motion of the Earth in its orbit around the Sun(1/31556925.9747 of the tropical year for 1900 January 0d 12h ET). The precise determination of ET from astronomical observations is a lengthy process as the requisite standard of accuracy can only be achieved by averaging over a number of years.

In 1976 the International Astronomical Union adopted Terrestrial Dynamical Time (TDT), a new dynamical time-scale for general use whose scale unit is the SI second (see Atomic Time). TDT was renamed Terrestrial Time (TT) in 1991. ET is now of little more than historical interest.

Terrestrial Time

The uniform time system used in computing the ephemerides of the solar system is Terrestrial Time (TT), which has replaced ET for this purpose. Except for the most rigorous astronomical calculations, it may be assumed to be the same as ET. During 2003 the estimated difference TT–UT is about 65 seconds.

Atomic Time

The fundamental standards of time and frequency must be defined in terms of a periodic motion adequately uniform, enduring and measurable. Progress has made it possible to use natural standards, such as atomic or molecular oscillations. Continuous oscillations are generated in an electrical circuit, the frequency of which is then compared or brought into coincidence with the frequency characteristic of the absorption or emission by the atoms or molecules when they change between two selected energy levels. The National Physical Laboratory (NPL) routinely uses clocks of high stability produced by locking a quartz oscillator to the frequencies defined by caesium or hydrogen atoms.

International Atomic Time (TAI), established through international collaboration, is formed by combining the readings of many caesium clocks and was set close to the

astronomically-based Universal Time (UT) near the beginning of 1958. It was formally recognized in 1971 and since 1988 January 1 has been maintained by the International Bureau of Weights and Measures (BIPM). The second markers are generated according to the International System (SI) definition adopted in 1967 at the 13th General Conference of Weights and Measures: 'The second is the duration of 9 192 631 770 periods of radiation corresponding to the transition between the two hyperfine levels of the ground state of the caesium-133 atom.'

Civil time in almost all countries is now based on Co-ordinated Universal Time (UTC), which was adopted for scientific purposes on 1972 January 1. UTC differs from TAI by an integer number of seconds (determined from studies of the rate of rotation of the Earth) and was designed to make both atomic time and UT accessible with accuracies appropriate for most users. The UTC time-scale is adjusted by the insertion (or, in principle, omission) of leap seconds in order to keep it within ±0.9s of UT. These leap seconds are introduced, when necessary, at the same instant throughout the world, either at the end of December or at the end of June. So, for example, the 22nd leap second occurred at 0h UTC on 1999 January 1. All leap seconds so far have been positive, with 61 seconds in the final minute of the UTC month. The time 23h 59m 60s UTC is followed one second later by 0h 0m 00s of the first day of the following month. Notices concerning the insertion of leap seconds are issued by the International Earth Rotation Service (IERS) at the Observatoire de Paris.

Radio Time-Signals

UTC is made generally available through time-signals and standard frequency broadcasts such as MSF in the UK, CHU in Canada and WWV and WWVH in the USA. These are based on national time-scales that are maintained in close agreement with UTC and provide traceability to the national time-scale and to UTC. The markers of seconds in the UTC scale coincide with those of TAI.

To disseminate the national time-scale in the UK, special signals are broadcast on behalf of the National Physical Laboratory from the BT radio station at Rugby (call-sign MSF). The signals are controlled from a caesium beam atomic frequency standard and consist of a precise frequency carrier of 60khz which is switched off, after being on for at least half a second, to mark every second. The first second of the minute begins with a period of 500 ms with the carrier switched off, to serve as a minute marker. In the other seconds the carrier is always off for at least one tenth of a second at the start and then it carries an on-off code giving the British clock time and date, together with information identifying the start of the next minute. Changes to and from summer time are made following government announcements. Leap seconds are inserted as announced by the IERS and information provided by them on the difference between UTC and UT is also signalled. Other broadcast signals in the UK include the BBC six pips signal, the BT Timeline ('speaking clock'), the NPL Truetime service for computers, and a coded time-signal on the BBC 198kHz transmitters which is used for timing in the electricity supply industry. From 1972 January 1 the six pips on the BBC have consisted of five short pips from second 55 to second 59 (six pips in the case of a leap second) followed by one lengthened pip, the start of which indicates the exact minute. From 1990 February 5 these signals have been controlled by the BBC with seconds markers referenced to the satellite-based US navigation system GPS (Global Positioning System) and time and day referenced to the MSF transmitter. Formerly they were

generated by the Royal Greenwich Observatory. The BT Timeline is compared daily with the National Physical Laboratory caesium beam atomic frequency standard at the Rugby radio station. The NPL Truetime service is directly connected to the national time scale.

Accurate timing may also be obtained from the signals of international navigation systems such as the ground-based Omega, or the satellite-based American GPS or Russian GLONASS systems.

STANDARD TIME

Since 1880 the standard time in Britain has been Greenwich Mean Time (GMT); a statute that year enacted that the word 'time' when used in any legal document relating to Britain meant, unless otherwise specifically stated, the mean time of the Greenwich meridian. Greenwich was adopted as the universal meridian on 13 October 1884. A system of standard time by zones is used world-wide, standard time in each zone differing from that of the Greenwich meridian by an integral number of hours, either fast or slow. The large territories of the USA and Canada are divided into zones approximately 7.5° on either side of central meridians.

Variations from the standard time of some countries occur during part of the year; they are decided annually and are usually referred to as Summer Time or Daylight Saving Time.

At the 180th meridian the time can be either 12 hours fast on Greenwich Mean Time or 12 hours slow, and a change of date occurs. The internationally recognised date or calendar line is a modification of the 180th meridian, drawn so as to include islands of any one group on the same side of the line, or for political reasons. The line is indicated by joining up the following co-ordinates:

Lat.	Long.	Lat.	Long.
60° S.	180°	48° N.	180°
51° S.	180°	53° N.	170° E.
45° S.	172.5° W.	65.5° N.	169° W.
15° S.	172.5° W.	75° N.	180°
5° S.	180°		

Changes to the date line would require an international conference.

BRITISH SUMMER TIME

In 1916 an Act ordained that during a defined period of that year the legal time for general purposes in Great Britain should be one hour in advance of Greenwich Mean Time. The Summer Time Acts 1922 and 1925 defined the period during which Summer Time was to be in force, stabilising practice until the Second World War.

During the war the duration of Summer Time was extended and in the years 1941 to 1945 and in 1947 Double Summer Time (two hours in advance of Greenwich Mean Time) was in force. After the war, Summer Time was extended each year in 1948–52 and 1961–4 by Order in Council.

Between 1968 October 27 and 1971 October 31 clocks were kept one hour ahead of Greenwich Mean Time throughout the year. This was known as British Standard Time.

The most recent legislation is the Summer Time Act 1972, which enacted that 'the period of summer time for the purposes of this Act is the period beginning at two o'clock, Greenwich mean time, in the morning of the day after the third Saturday in March or, if that day is Easter Day, the day after the second Saturday in March, and ending at two o'clock, Greenwich mean time, in the morning of the day after the fourth Saturday in October.'

The duration of Summer Time can be varied by Order in Council and in recent years alterations have been made to bring the operation of Summer Time in Britain closer to similar provisions in other countries of the European Union; for instance, since 1981 the hour of changeover has been 01h Greenwich Mean Time.

The duration of Summer Time in 2003 is:

March 30 01h GMT to October 26 01h GMT

MEAN REFRACTION

Alt.	Ref.		Alt.	Ref.		Alt.	Ref.	
°	′	′	°	′	′	°	′	′
1	20	21	3	12	13	7	54	6
1	30	20	3	34	12	9	27	5
1	41	19	4	00	11	11	39	4
1	52	18	4	30	10	15	00	3
2	05	17	5	06	9	20	42	2
2	19	16	5	50	8	32	20	1
2	35	15	6	44	7	62	17	0
2	52	14	7	54		90	00	
3	12							

The refraction table is in the form of a critical table (*see* page 71)

ASTRONOMICAL CONSTANTS

Solar parallax	8″.794
Astronomical unit	149597870 km
Precession for the year 2003	50″.291
Precession in right ascension	3s.075
Precession in declination	20″.043
Constant of nutation	9″.202
Constant of aberration	20″.496
Mean obliquity of ecliptic (2003)	23° 26′ 20″
Moon's equatorial hor. parallax	57′ 02″.70
Velocity of light in vacuo per second	299792.5 km
Solar motion per second	20.0 km
Equatorial radius of the Earth	6378.140 km
Polar radius of the Earth	6356.755 km
North galactic pole (IAU standard)	
	RA 12h 49m (1950.0). Dec. +27°.4 N.
Solar apex	RA 18h 06m Dec.+30

Length of year (in mean solar days)

Tropical	365.24219
Sidereal	365.25636
Anomalistic (perihelion to perihelion)	365.25964
Eclipse	346.62000

Length of month (mean values)	d	h	m	s
New Moon to New	29	12	44	02.9
Sidereal	27	07	43	11.5
Anomalistic (perigee to perigee)	27	13	18	33.2

ELEMENTS OF THE SOLAR SYSTEM

Orb	Mean distance from Sun (Earth=1)	Mean distance from Sun km 10⁶	Sidereal period days	Synodic period days	Incl. of orbit to ecliptic ° '	Diameter km	Mass (Earth=1)	Period of rotation on axis days
Sun	—	—	—	—	—	1,392,530	332,946	25–35*
Mercury	0.39	58	88.0	116	7 00	4,879	0.0553	58.646
Venus	0.72	108	224.7	584	3 24	12,104	0.8150	243.019r
Earth	1.00	150	365.3	—	—	12,756e	1.0000	0.997
Mars	1.52	228	687.0	780	1 51	6,794e	0.1074	10.26
Jupiter	5.20	778	4,332.6	399	1 18	{ 142,984e / 133,708p	317.89	{ 0.410e
Saturn	9.54	1427	10,759.2	378	2 29	{ 120,536e / 108,728e	95.18	{ 0.426e
Uranus	19.18	2870	30,684.6	370	0 46	51,118e	14.54	0.718r
Neptune	30.06	4497	60,191.0	367	1 46	49.528e	17.15	0.671
Pluto	39.80	5954	91,708.2	367	17 09	2,302	0.002	6.387

e equatorial, p polar, r retrograde, * depending on latitude

THE SATELLITES

Name		Star mag.	Mean distance from primary km	Sidereal period of revolution d		Name		Star mag.	Mean distance from primary km	Sidereal period of revolution d
EARTH						SATURN				
I	Moon	—	384,400	27.322		VI	Titan	8	1,221,850	15.945
						VII	Hyperion	14	1,481,100	21.277
MARS						VIII	Iapetus	11	3,561,300	79.330
I	Phobos	12	9,378	0.319		IX	Pheobe	16	12,952,000	550.48r
II	Deimos	13	23,459	1.262						
						URANUS				
JUPITER						VI	Cordelia	—	49,750	0.335
XVI	Metis	17	127,960	0.295		VII	Orphelia	—	53,760	0.376
XV	Adrastea	19	128,980	0.298		VIII	Bianca	—	59,170	0.435
V	Amalthea	14	181,300	0.498		IX	Cressida	—	61,780	0.464
XIV	Thebe	16	221,900	0.675		X	Desdemona	—	62,660	0.474
I	Io	5	421,600	1.769		XI	Juliet	—	64,360	0.493
II	Europa	5	670,900	3.552		XII	Portia	—	66,100	0.513
III	Ganymede	5	1,070,000	7.155		XIII	Rosalind	—	69,930	0.558
IV	Callisto	6	1,883,000	16.689		XIV	Belinda	—	75,260	0.624
XIII	Leda	20	11,094,000	239		XV	Puck	—	86,000	0.762
VI	Himalia	15	11,480,000	251		V	Miranda	17	129,800	1.413
X	Lysithea	18	11,720,000	259		I	Ariel	14	191,200	2.520
VII	Elara	17	11,737,000	260		II	Umbriel	15	266,000	4.144
XII	Ananke	19	21,200,000	631r		III	Titania	14	435,800	8.706
XI	Carme	18	22,600,000	692r		IV	Oberon	14	583,600	13.463
VIII	Pasiphae	17	23,500,000	735r		XVI	Caliban	—	7,164,600	579.4
IX	Sinope	18	23,700,000	758r		XX	Stephano	—	9,608,400	900
						XVII	Sycorax	—	12,174,700	1,283.7
SATURN						XVIII	Prospero	—	16,668,000	2,056
XVIII	Pan	—	133,583	0.575		XIX	Setebos	—	18,288,000	2,363
XV	Atlas	18	137,640	0.602						
XVI	Prometheus	16	139,353	0.613		NEPTUNE				
XVII	Pandora	16	141,700	0.629		III	Naiad	25	48,230	0.294
XI	Epimetheus	15	151,422	0.695		IV	Thalassa	24	50,070	0.311
X	Janus	14	151,472	0.695		V	Despina	23	52,530	0.335
I	Mimas	13	185,520	0.942		VI	Galatea	22	61,950	0.429
II	Enceladus	12	238,020	1.370		VII	Larissa	22	73,550	0.555
III	Tethys	10	294,660	1.888		VIII	Proteus	20	117,650	1.122
XIII	Telesto	19	294,660	1.888		I	Triton	13	354,760	5.877
XIV	Calypso	19	294,660	1.888		II	Nereid	19	5,513,400	360.136
IV	Dione	10	377,400	2.737						
XII	Helene	18	377,400	2.737		PLUTO				
V	Rhea	10	527,040	4.518		I	Charon	17	19,600	6.387

THE EARTH

The shape of the Earth is that of an oblate spheroid or solid of revolution whose meridian sections are ellipses not differing much from circles, whilst the sections at right angles are circles. The length of the equatorial axis is about 12,756 km, and that of the polar axis is 12,714 km. The mean density of the Earth is 5.5 times that of water, although that of the surface layer is less. The Earth and Moon revolve about their common centre of gravity in a lunar month; this centre in turn revolves round the Sun in a plane known as the ecliptic, that passes through the Sun's centre. The Earth's equator is inclined to this plane at an angle of 23.4°. This tilt is the cause of the seasons. In mid-latitudes, and when the Sun is high above the Equator, not only does the high noon altitude make the days longer, but the Sun's rays fall more directly on the Earth's surface; these effects combine to produce summer. In equatorial regions the noon altitude is large throughout the year, and there is little variation in the length of the day. In higher latitudes the noon altitude is lower, and the days in summer are appreciably longer than those in winter.

The average velocity of the Earth in its orbit is 30 km a second. It makes a complete rotation on its axis in about 23h 56m of mean time, which is the sidereal day. Because of its annual revolution round the Sun, the rotation with respect to the Sun, or the solar day, is more than this by about four minutes (*see* page 75). The extremity of the axis of rotation, or the North Pole of the Earth, is not rigidly fixed, but wanders over an area roughly 20 metres in diameter.

TERRESTRIAL MAGNETISM

The Earth's main magnetic field corresponds approximately to that of a very small bar magnet near the centre of the Earth, but with appreciable smooth spatial departures. The origin of the main field is not fully understood but is generally ascribed to electric currents associated with fluid motions in the Earth's core. As a result not only does the main field vary in strength and direction from place to place, but also with time. Superimposed on the main field are local and regional anomalies whose magnitudes may in places approach that of the main field; these are due to the influence of mineral deposits in the Earth's crust. A small proportion of the field is of external origin, mostly associated with electric currents in the ionosphere. The configuration of the external field and the ionisation of the atmosphere depend on the incident particle and radiation flux from the Sun. There are, therefore, short-term and non-periodic as well as diurnal, 27-day, seasonal and 11-year periodic changes in the magnetic field, dependent upon the position of the Sun and the degree of solar activity.

A magnetic compass points along the horizontal component of a magnetic line of force. These lines of force converge on the 'magnetic dip-poles', the places where the Earth's magnetic field is vertical. These poles move with time, and their present approximate adopted mean positions are 81°.7 N., 112°.0 W. and 64°.6 S., 138°.2 E.

There is also a 'magnetic equator', at all points of which the vertical component of the Earth's magnetic field is zero and a magnetised needle remains horizontal. This line runs between 2° and 12° north of the geographical equator in Asia and Africa, turns sharply south off the west African coast, and crosses South America through Brazil, Bolivia and Peru; it recrosses the geographical equator in mid-Pacific.

Reference has already been made to secular changes in the Earth's field. The following table indicates the changes in magnetic declination (or variation of the compass). Declination is the angle in the horizontal plane between the direction of true north and that in which a magnetic compass points. Similar, though much smaller, changes have occurred in 'dip' or magnetic inclination. Secular changes differ throughout the world. Although the London observations suggest a cycle with a period of several hundred years, an exact repetition is unlikely.

London		Greenwich	
1580	11° 15' E.	1900	16° 29' W.
1622	5° 56' E.	1925	13° 10' W.
1665	1° 22' W.	1950	9° 07' W.
1730	13° 00' W.	1975	6° 39' W.
1773	21° 09' W.	1998	3° 32' W.
1850	22° 24' W.		

In order that up-to-date information on declination may be available, many governments publish magnetic charts on which there are lines (isogonic lines) passing through all places at which specified values of declination will be found at the date of the chart.

In the British Isles, isogonic lines now run approximately north-east to south-west. Though there are considerable local deviations due to geological causes, a rough value of magnetic declination may be obtained by assuming that at 50° N. on the meridian of Greenwich, the value in 2003 is 2° 2' west and allowing an increase of 15' for each degree of latitude northwards and one of 27' for each degree of longitude westwards. For example, at 53° N., 5° W., declination will be about 2° 2'+45' + 135', i.e. 5° 2' west. The average annual change at the present time is about 10' decrease.

The number of magnetic observatories is about 180, irregularly distributed over the globe. There are three in Great Britain, run by the British Geological Survey: at Hartland, in north Devon; at Eskdalemuir, Dumfries and Galloway; and at Lerwick, Shetland Islands. The following are some recent annual mean values of the magnetic elements for Hartland.

Year	Declination West	Dip or inclination	Horizontal force	Vertical force
	° '	° '	gauss	gauss
1960	9 59	66 44	0.1871	0.4350
1965	9 30	66 34	0.1887	0.4354
1970	9 06	66 26	0.1903	0.4364
1975	8 32	66 17	0.1921	0.4373
1980	7 44	66 10	0.1933	0.4377
1985	6 56	66 08	0.1938	0.4380
1990	6 15	66 10	0.1939	0.4388
1995	5 33	66 07	0.1946	0.4395
2000	4 44	66 07	0.1951	0.4405
2001	4 34	66 06	0.1952	0.4407

As well as navigation at sea, in the air and on land by compass the oil industry depends on the Earth's magnetic field as a directional reference. They use magnetic survey tools when drilling well-bores and require accurate estimates of the local magnetic field, taking into account the crustal and external fields.

MAGNETIC STORMS

Occasionally, sometimes with great suddenness, the Earth's magnetic field is subject for several hours to marked disturbance. During a severe storm in 1989 the declination at Lerwick changed by almost 8° in less than an hour. In many instances such disturbances are accompanied by

widespread displays of aurorae, marked changes in the incidence of cosmic rays, an increase in the reception of 'noise' from the Sun at radio frequencies, and rapid changes in the ionosphere and induced electric currents within the Earth which adversely affect satellite operations, telecommunications and electric power transmission systems. The disturbances are caused by changes in the stream of ionised particles which emanates from the Sun and through which the Earth is continuously passing. Some of these changes are associated with visible eruptions on the Sun, usually in the region of sun-spots. There is a marked tendency for disturbances to recur after intervals of about 27 days, the apparent period of rotation of the Sun on its axis, which is consistent with the sources being located on particular areas of the Sun.

ARTIFICIAL SATELLITES

To consider the orbit of an artificial satellite, it is best to imagine that one is looking at the Earth from a distant point in space. The Earth would then be seen to be rotating about its axis inside the orbit described by the rapidly revolving satellite. The inclination of a satellite orbit to the Earth's equator (which generally remains almost constant throughout the satellite's lifetime) gives at once the maximum range of latitudes over which the satellite passes. Thus a satellite whose orbit has an inclination of 53° will pass overhead all latitudes between 53° S. and 53° N., would never be seen in the zenith of any place nearer the poles than these latitudes. If we consider a particular place on the earth, whose latitude is less than the inclination of the satellite's orbit, then the Earth's rotation carries this place first under the northbound part of the orbit and then under the southbound portion of the orbit, these two occurrences being always less than 12 hours apart for satellites moving in direct orbits (i.e. to the east). (For satellites in retrograde orbits, the words 'northbound' and 'southbound' should be interchanged in the preceding statement.) As the value of the latitude of the observer increases and approaches the value of the inclination of the orbit, so this interval gets shorter until (when the latitude is equal to the inclination) only one overhead passage occurs each day.

OBSERVATION OF SATELLITES

The regression of the orbit around the Earth causes alternate periods of visibility and invisibility, though this is of little concern to the radio or radar observer. To the visual observer the following cycle of events normally occurs (though the cycle may start in any position): invisibility, morning observations before dawn, invisibility, evening observations after dusk, invisibility, morning observations before dawn, and so on. With reasonably high satellites and for observers in high latitudes around the summer solstice, the evening observations follow the morning observations without interruption as sunlight passing over the polar regions can still illuminate satellites which are passing over temperate latitudes at local midnight. At the moment all satellites rely on sunlight to make them visible, though a satellite with a flashing light has been suggested for a future launching. The observer must be in darkness or twilight in order to make any useful observations. (For durations of twilight, and sunrise and sunset times, *see* Page Two of each month.)

Some of the satellites are visible to the naked eye and much interest has been aroused by the spectacle of a bright satellite disappearing into the Earth's shadow. The event is even more interesting telescopically as the disappearance occurs gradually as the satellite traverses the Earth's

penumbral shadow, and during the last few seconds before the eclipse is complete the satellite may change colour (in suitable atmospheric conditions) from yellow to red. This is because the last rays of sunlight are refracted through the denser layers of our atmosphere before striking the satellite.

Some satellites rotate about one or more axes so that a periodic variation in brightness is observed. This was particularly noticeable in several of the Soviet satellites.

Satellite research has provided some interesting results, including a revised value of the Earth's oblateness (1/298.2), and the discovery of the Van Allen radiation belts.

LAUNCHINGS

Apart from their names, e.g. Cosmos 6 Rocket, the satellites are also classified according to their date of launch. Thus 1961 α refers to the first satellite launching of 1961. A number following the Greek letter indicated the relative brightness of the satellites put in orbit. From the beginning of 1963 the Greek letters were replaced by numbers and the numbers by roman letters e.g. 1963–01A. For all satellites successfully injected into orbit the following table gives the designation and names of the main objects, the launch date and some initial orbital data. These are the inclination to the equator (i), the nodal period of revolution (P), and the apogee and perigee heights.

Although most of the satellites launched are injected into orbits less than 1,000 km high, there are an increasing number of satellites in geostationary orbits, i.e. where the orbital inclination is zero, the eccentricity close to zero, and the period of revolution is 1436.1 minutes. Thus the satellite is permanently situated over the equator at one selected longitude at a mean height of 35,786 km. This geostationary band is crowded. In one case there are six television satellites (Astra 2, 5, 6, 7, 1H and 2C) orbiting within a few tens of kilometres of each other. In the sky they appear to be separated by only a few arcminutes.

In 1997 a number of *Iridium* satellites were launched into high inclination orbits. These are owned by the mobile telephone company Cellnet. For visual observers, these satellites have the interesting characteristic that the large aerials they carry can, when in exactly the right orientation with respect to the Sun and the observer, give off a 'flare' in brightness which can on occasion attain a magnitude of –6, much brighter than Venus. The flare can be visible to the naked eye for nearly a minute.

The Russian Space Station, Mir, 1986–17A, which was launched in 1986 was successfully de-orbited on March 23 2001. The re-entry was carried out in several stages, the first small burn to lower the orbit occurring at 00h 33m. The main de-orbit burn began at 05h 07m, which lowered the perigee height to <80km. At 05h 50m observers in Fiji saw multiple bright re-entry bodies in the sky. The impact area was at about W. 160°, S. 40°. During its 15 years in orbit it had been visited by 111 spacecraft. The record for the longest spaceflight was set by Valeriy Polyakov in 1994-5 who spent 437 days in Mir.

The new International Space Station ISS, 1998–67A, is currently being assembled in an orbit of similar size and inclination to Mir. It will become even brighter as more parts are added to it. When passing over Britain it can appear to be almost as bright as Jupiter on favourable transits, though only visible for four or five minutes on each pass.

ARTIFICIAL SATELLITE LAUNCHES 2001–2002

Desig-nation	Satellite	Launch date	P	i	Apogee	Perigee
2001–			m	°	km	km
011	Eurobird, B-Sat 2A, rocket	March 8	1436.1	0.1	35769	35764
012	XM-2 Rock, rocket	March18	1435.8	0.1	38842	32678
013	Ekran 21, rocket, Breeze-M	April 7	1436.0	2.0	35774	35755
014	Mars Odyssey, PAM-D, rocket	April 7	Heliocentric orbit			
015	GSAT-1, rocket	April 18	1384.2	1.0	35715	33775
016	STS-100 Endeavour F16	April 19	92.4	51.6	385	360
017	Soyuz TM-32, rocket	April 28	92.4	51.6	384	361
018	XM-1 ROLL, rocket	May 5	1437.4	0.1	37090	34493
019	Panamsat PAS 10, rocket, platform, rocket	May 15	1436.1	0.1	35849	35684
020	USA 158, Geolite, rocket, rocket	May 18	No elements available			
021	Progress -M 16, rocket	May 20	92.3	51.6	377	353
022	Cosmos 2377, rocket	May 29	89.5	67.2	302	160
023	Cosmos 2378, rocket	June 8	104.9	83.0	992	945
024	Intelsat 901, rocket	June 9	1436.1	0.2	35774	35760
025	Astra 2C, rocket, rocket	June 16	1436.2	0.1	35787	35749
026	ICO F-2, rocket	June 19	351.4	45.0	10108	10085
027	M.A.P., rocket	June 30	Heliocentric orbit			
028	STS-104 Atlantis F24	July 12	92.4	51.6	399	381
029	Artemis, Bsat-2B, rocket,	July 12	1195.1	0.9	30940	30875
030	Molniya 3 K, rocket, Sylda	July 20	718.1	62.9	39906	425
031	Goes 12, rocket	July 23	1271.9	2.5	42248	22730
032	Coronas F, rocket	July 31	94.8	82.5	515	465
033	SP 21, rocket, rocket, rocket	August 6	No elements available			
034	Genesis, rocket, rocket	August 8	No elements available			
035	STS-105, Simplesat	August 10	92.3	51.6	400	385
036	Progress -M 45, rocket	August 21	92.5	51.7	381	369
037	Cosmos 2379, rocket, platform, rocket	August 24	1435.7	2.3	35804	35713
038	LRE, rocket	August 29	640.9	28.2	36186	264
039	Intelsat 902, rocket	August 30	1435.6	0.2	35777	35738
040	USA-160 Noss payload, rocket, dispenser	September 8	107.5	63.5	1168	1011
041	Progress DC-1, rocket	September 14	91.1	51.6	393	382
042	Atlantic Bird 2, rocket	September ?	1435.9	0.1	35776	35747
043	Starshine 3, Picosat 9, PCSAT, Sapphire, rocket	September 30	94.0	67.1	454	448
044	USA-161, rocket	October 5	No elements available			
045	Raduga 1-6, rocket, platform	October 6	1436.1	1.5	35778	35753
046	USA-162	October 11	No elements available			
047	Quickbird 2, rocket	October 18	93.8	97.3	443	439
048	Soyuz TM-33, rocket	October 21	92.4	51.7	377	364
049	TES, Proba-1, Bird 2, rocket	October 22	96.1	97.8	566	532
050	Molniya 3-52, rocket, platform, rocket	October 25	720.6	62.9	39858	597
051	Progress M1-7, rocket	November 26	92.2	51.7	367	353
052	DirecTV 4S, rocket	November 27	1413.4	0.1	36056	34584
053	Glonass, Glonass, rocket, rocket	December 1	675.3	64.9	19108	19090
054	STS-108 Endeavour F-17, Starshine II	December 5	92.1	51.6	383	369
055	Jason, Timed, rocket	December 7	112.1	66.0	1329	1321
056	Meteor 3M, Kompass, Badr-B, Maroc-Tubsat, reflector, rocket	December 10	105.2	99.6	1016	996
057	Cosmos 2383, rocket	December 21	92.8	65.0	417	405
058	Cosmos 2383-5, Gonets D-1, rocket	December 28	114.3	82.5	1432	1416

ARTIFICIAL SATELLITE LAUNCHES 2001–2002

Desig-nation	Satellite	Launch date	P	i	Apogee	Perigee
2002–			m	°	km	km
001	USA-164, rocket	January 16	1439.0	4.5	35848	35838
002	INSAT 3C, rocket	January 23	1014.6	0.8	35778	18360
003	MDS-1, DASH, VEP-3	February 4	635.5	28.5	35733	481
004	HESSI, rocket, rocket	February 5	96.5	38.0	605	579
005	Iridium 90, 91, 94, 95, 96, rocket	February 11	98.2	86.6	684	660
006	Echostar 7, rocket, rocket	February 21	1261.6	10.7	57001	7593
007	Intelsat 904, rocket	February 23	1146.8	0.6	35773	24057
008	Cosmos 2387, rocket	February 25	89.5	67.1	336	164
009	Envisat, rocket	March 1	100.3	98.5	786	764
010	STS 109	March 1	96.1	28.5	583	565

Time Measurement and Calendars

MEASUREMENTS OF TIME

Measurements of time are based on the time taken by the earth to rotate on its axis (day); by the moon to revolve round the earth (month); and by the earth to revolve round the sun (year). From these, which are not commensurable, certain average or mean intervals have been adopted for ordinary use.

THE DAY

The day begins at midnight and is divided into 24 hours of 60 minutes, each of 60 seconds. The hours are counted from midnight up to 12 noon (when the sun crosses the meridian), and these hours are designated a.m. (*ante meridiem*); and again from noon up to 12 midnight, which hours are designated p.m. (*post meridiem*), except when the 24-hour reckoning is employed. The 24-hour reckoning ignores a.m. and p.m., numbering the hours 0 to 23 from midnight.

Colloquially the 24 hours are divided into day and night, day being the time while the sun is above the horizon (including the four stages of twilight defined on page 73). Day is subdivided into morning, the early part of daytime, ending at noon; afternoon, from noon to about 6 p.m.; and evening, which may be said to extend from 6 p.m. until midnight. Night, the dark period between day and day, begins at the close of astronomical twilight (*see* page 74) and extends beyond midnight to sunrise the next day.

The names of the days are derived from Old English translations or adaptations of the Roman titles.

Sunday	Sun	Sol
Monday	Moon	Luna
Tuesday	Tiw/Tyr (god of war)	Mars
Wednesday	Woden/Odin	Mercury
Thursday	Thor	Jupiter
Friday	Frigga/Freyja (goddess of love)	Venus
Saturday	Saeternes	Saturn

THE MONTH

The month in the ordinary calendar is approximately the twelfth part of a year, but the lengths of the different months vary from 28 (or 29) days to 31.

THE YEAR

The equinoctial or tropical year is the time that the earth takes to revolve round the sun from equinox to equinox, i.e. 365.24219 mean solar days, or 365 days 5 hours 48 minutes and 45 seconds.

The calendar year usually consists of 365 days but a year containing 366 days is called bissextile (see Roman calendar, page 91) or leap year, one day being added to the month of February so that a date 'leaps over' a day of the week. In the Roman calendar the day that was repeated was the sixth day before the beginning of March, the equivalent of 24 February.

A year is a leap year if the date of the year is divisible by four without remainder, unless it is the last year of the century. The last year of a century is a leap year only if its number is divisible by 400 without remainder, e.g. the years 1800 and 1900 had only 365 days but the year 2000 has 366 days.

THE SOLSTICE

A solstice is the point in the tropical year at which the sun attains its greatest distance, north or south, from the Equator. In the northern hemisphere the furthest point north of the Equator marks the summer solstice and the furthest point south the winter solstice.

The date of the solstice varies according to locality. For example, if the summer solstice falls on 21 June late in the day by Greenwich time, that day will be the longest of the year at Greenwich though it may be by only a second, but it will fall on 22 June, local date, in Japan, and so 22 June will be the longest day there. The date of the solstice is also affected by the length of the tropical year, which is 365 days 6 hours less about 11 minutes 15 seconds. If a solstice happens late on 21 June in one year, it will be nearly six hours later in the next (unless the next year is a leap year), i.e. early on 22 June, and that will be the longest day.

This delay of the solstice does not continue because the extra day in leap year brings it back a day in the calendar. However, because of the 11 minutes 15 seconds mentioned above, the additional day in leap year brings the solstice back too far by 45 minutes, and the time of the solstice in the calendar is earlier, in a four-year pattern, as the century progresses. The last year of a century is in most cases not a leap year, and the omission of the extra day puts the date of the solstice later by about six hours too much. Compensation for this is made by the fourth centennial year being a leap year. The solstice has become earlier in date throughout this century and, because the year 2000 was a leap year, the solstice will get earlier still throughout the 21st century.

The date of the winter solstice, the shortest day of the year, is affected by the same factors as the longest day.

At Greenwich the sun sets at its earliest by the clock about ten days before the shortest day. The daily change in the time of sunset is due in the first place to the sun's movement southwards at this time of the year, which diminishes the interval between the sun's transit and its setting. However, the daily decrease of the Equation of Time causes the time of apparent noon to be continuously later day by day, which to some extent counteracts the first effect. The rates of the change of these two quantities are not equal or uniform; their combination causes the date of earliest sunset to be 12 or 13 December at Greenwich. In more southerly latitudes the effect of the movement of the sun is less, and the change in the time of sunset depends on that of the Equation of Time to a greater degree, and the date of earliest sunset is earlier than it is at Greenwich, e.g. on the Equator it is about 1 November.

THE EQUINOX

The equinox is the point at which the sun crosses the Equator and day and night are of equal length all over the world. This occurs in March and September.

DOG DAYS

The days about the heliacal rising of the Dog Star, noted from ancient times as the hottest period of the year in the northern hemisphere, are called the Dog Days. Their incidence has been variously calculated as depending on the Greater or Lesser Dog Star (Sirius or Procyon) and their duration has been reckoned as from 30 to 54 days. A generally accepted period is from 3 July to 15 August.

CHRISTIAN CALENDAR

In the Christian chronological system the years are distinguished by cardinal numbers before or after the birth of Christ, the period being denoted by the letters BC (Before Christ) or, more rarely, AC (*Ante Christum*), and AD (*Anno Domini* – In the Year of Our Lord). The correlative dates of the epoch are the fourth year of the 194th Olympiad, the 753rd year from the foundation of Rome, AM 3761 in Jewish chronology, and the 4714th year of the Julian period. The actual date of the birth of Christ is somewhat uncertain.

The system was introduced into Italy in the sixth century. Though first used in France in the seventh century, it was not universally established there until about the eighth century. It has been said that the system was introduced into England by St Augustine (AD 596), but it was probably not generally used until some centuries later. It was ordered to be used by the Bishops at the Council of Chelsea (AD 816).

THE JULIAN CALENDAR

In the Julian calendar (adopted by the Roman Empire in 45 BC, *see* page 91) all the centennial years were leap years, and for this reason towards the close of the 16th century there was a difference of ten days between the tropical and calendar years; the equinox fell on 11 March of the calendar, whereas at the time of the Council of Nicaea (AD 325), it had fallen on 21 March. In 1582 Pope Gregory ordained that 5 October should be called 15 October and that of the end-century years only the fourth should be a leap year (*see* page 83).

THE GREGORIAN CALENDAR

The Gregorian calendar was adopted by Italy, France, Spain and Portugal in 1582, by Prussia, the Roman Catholic German states, Switzerland, Holland and Flanders on 1 January 1583, by Poland in 1586, Hungary in 1587, the Protestant German and Netherland states and Denmark in 1700, and by Great Britain and Dominions (including the North American colonies) in 1752, by the omission of eleven days (3 September being reckoned as 14 September). Sweden omitted the leap day in 1700 but observed leap days in 1704 and 1708, and reverted to the Julian calendar by having two leap days in 1712; the Gregorian calendar was adopted in 1753 by the omission of eleven days (18 February being reckoned as 1 March). Japan adopted the calendar in 1872, China in 1912, Bulgaria in 1915, Turkey and Soviet Russia in 1918, Yugoslavia and Romania in 1919, and Greece in 1923.

In the same year that the change was made in England from the Julian to the Gregorian calendar, the beginning of the new year was also changed from 25 March to 1 January.

THE ORTHODOX CHURCHES

Some Orthodox Churches still use the Julian reckoning but the majority of Greek Orthodox Churches and the Romanian Orthodox Church have adopted a modified 'New Calendar', observing the Gregorian calendar for fixed feasts and the Julian for movable feasts.

The Orthodox Church year begins on 1 September. There are four fast periods and, in addition to Pascha (Easter), twelve great feasts, as well as numerous commemorations of the saints of the Old and New Testaments throughout the year.

THE DOMINICAL LETTER

The dominical letter is one of the letters A–G which are used to denote the Sundays in successive years. If the first day of the year is a Sunday the letter is A; if the second, B; the third, C; and so on. A leap year requires two letters, the first for 1 January to 29 February, the second for 1 March to 31 December (*see* page 86).

EPIPHANY

The feast of the Epiphany, commemorating the manifestation of Christ, later became associated with the offering of gifts by the Magi. The day was of great importance from the time of the Council of Nicaea (AD 325), as the primate of Alexandria was charged at every Epiphany feast with the announcement in a letter to the churches of the date of the forthcoming Easter. The day was also of importance in Britain as it influenced dates, ecclesiastical and lay, e.g. Plough Monday, when work was resumed in the fields, fell on the Monday in the first full week after Epiphany.

LENT

The Teutonic word Lent, which denotes the fast preceding Easter, originally meant no more than the spring season; but from Anglo-Saxon times at least it has been used as the equivalent of the more significant Latin term Quadragesima, meaning the 'forty days' or, more literally, the fortieth day. Ash Wednesday is the first day of Lent, which ends at midnight before Easter Day.

PALM SUNDAY

Palm Sunday, the Sunday before Easter and the beginning of Holy Week, commemorates the triumphal entry of Christ into Jerusalem and is celebrated in Britain (when palm is not available) by branches of willow gathered for use in the decoration of churches on that day.

MAUNDY THURSDAY

Maundy Thursday is the day before Good Friday, the name itself being a corruption of dies mandati (day of the mandate) when Christ washed the feet of the disciples and gave them the mandate to love one another.

EASTER DAY

Easter Day is the first Sunday after the full moon which happens on, or next after, the 21st day of March; if the full moon happens on a Sunday, Easter Day is the Sunday after.

This definition is contained in an Act of Parliament (24 Geo. II c. 23) and explanation is given in the preamble to the Act that the day of full moon depends on certain tables that have been prepared. These tables are summarised in the early pages of the Book of Common Prayer. The moon referred to is not the real moon of the heavens, but a hypothetical moon on whose 'full' the date of Easter depends, and the lunations of this 'calendar' moon consist of twenty-nine and thirty days alternately, with certain necessary modifications to make the date of its full agree as nearly as possible with that of the real moon, which is known as the Paschal Full Moon.

A FIXED EASTER

In 1928 the House of Commons agreed to a motion for the third reading of a bill proposing that Easter Day shall, in the calendar year next but one after the commencement of the Act and in all subsequent years, be the first Sunday after

the second Saturday in April. Easter would thus fall on the second or third Sunday in April, i.e. between 9 and 15 April (inclusive). A clause in the Bill provided that before it shall come into operation, regard shall be had to any opinion expressed officially by the various Christian churches. Efforts by the World Council of Churches to secure a unanimous choice of date for Easter by its member churches have so far been unsuccessful.

ROGATION DAYS

Rogation Days are the Monday, Tuesday and Wednesday preceding Ascension Day and from the fifth century were observed as public fasts with solemn processions and supplications. The processions were discontinued as religious observances at the Reformation, but survive in the ceremony known as 'beating the parish bounds'. Rogation Sunday is the Sunday before Ascension Day.

EMBER DAYS

The Ember Days at the four seasons are the Wednesday, Friday and Saturday (a) before the third Sunday in Advent, (b) before the second Sunday in Lent, and (c) before the Sundays nearest to the festivals of St Peter and of St Michael and All Angels.

TRINITY SUNDAY

Trinity Sunday is eight weeks after Easter Day, on the Sunday following Pentecost (Whit Sunday). Subsequent Sundays are reckoned in the Book of Common Prayer calendar of the Church of England as 'after Trinity'.

Thomas Becket (1118–70) was consecrated Archbishop of Canterbury on the Sunday after Whit Sunday and his first act was to ordain that the day of his consecration should be held as a new festival in honour of the Holy Trinity. This observance spread from Canterbury throughout the whole of Christendom.

MOVABLE FEASTS TO THE YEAR 2035

Year	Ash Wednesday	Easter	Ascension	Pentecost (Whit Sunday)	Advent Sunday
2003	5 March	20 April	29 May	8 June	30 November
2004	25 February	11 April	20 May	30 May	28 November
2005	9 February	27 March	5 May	15 May	27 November
2006	1 March	16 April	25 May	4 June	3 December
2007	21 February	8 April	17 May	27 May	2 December
2008	6 February	23 March	1 May	11 May	30 November
2009	25 February	12 April	21 May	31 May	29 November
2010	17 February	4 April	13 May	23 May	28 November
2011	9 March	24 April	2 June	12 June	27 November
2012	22 February	8 April	17 May	27 May	2 December
2013	13 February	31 March	9 May	19 May	1 December
2014	5 March	20 April	29 May	8 June	30 November
2015	18 February	5 April	14 May	24 May	29 November
2016	10 February	27 March	5 May	15 May	27 November
2017	1 March	16 April	25 May	4 June	3 December
2018	14 February	1 April	10 May	20 May	2 December
2019	6 March	21 April	30 May	9 June	1 December
2020	26 February	12 April	21 May	31 May	29 November
2021	17 February	4 April	13 May	23 May	28 November
2022	2 March	17 April	26 May	5 June	27 November
2023	22 February	9 April	18 May	28 May	3 December
2024	14 February	31 March	9 May	19 May	1 December
2025	5 March	20 April	29 May	8 June	30 November
2026	18 February	5 April	14 May	24 May	29 November
2027	10 February	28 March	6 May	16 May	28 November
2028	1 March	16 April	25 May	4 June	3 December
2029	14 February	1 April	10 May	20 May	2 December
2030	6 March	21 April	30 May	9 June	1 December
2031	26 February	13 April	22 May	1 June	30 November
2032	11 February	28 March	6 May	16 May	28 November
2033	2 March	17 April	26 May	5 June	27 November
2034	22 February	9 April	18 May	28 May	3 December
2035	7 February	25 March	3 May	13 May	2 December

NOTES

Ash Wednesday (first day in Lent) can fall at earliest on 4 February and at latest on 10 March

Mothering Sunday (fourth Sunday in Lent) can fall at earliest on 1 March and at latest on 4 April

Easter Day can fall at earliest on 22 March and at latest on 25 April

Ascension Day is forty days after Easter Day and can fall at earliest on 30 April and at latest on 3 June

Pentecost (Whit Sunday) is seven weeks after Easter and can fall at earliest on 10 May and at latest on 13 June

Trinity Sunday is the Sunday after Whit Sunday

Corpus Christi falls on the Thursday after Trinity Sunday

Sundays after Pentecost – there are not less than 18 and not more than 23

Advent Sunday is the Sunday nearest to 30 November

EASTER DAYS AND DOMINICAL LETTERS 1500 TO 2035

Dates up to and including 1752 are according to the Julian calendar. For dominical letters in leap years, *see* page 84

		1500–1599	1600–1699	1700–1799	1800–1899	1900–1999	2000–2035
March							
d	22	1573	1668	1761	1818		
e	23	1505/16	1600	1788	1845/56	1913	2008
f	24		1611/95	1706/99			1940
g	25	1543/54	1627/38/49	1722/33/44	1883/94	1951	2035
A	26	1559/70/81/92	1654/65/76	1749/58/69/80	1815/26/37	1967/78/89	
b	27	1502/13/24/97	1608/87/92	1785/96	1842/53/64	1910/21/32	2005/16
c	28	1529/35/40	1619/24/30	1703/14/25	1869/75/80	1937/48	2027/32
d	29	1551/62	1635/46/57	1719/30/41/52	1807/12/91	1959/64/70	
e	30	1567/78/89	1651/62/73/84	1746/55/66/77	1823/34	1902/75/86/97	
f	31	1510/21/32/83/94	1605/16/78/89	1700/71/82/93	1839/50/61/72	1907/18/29/91	2002/13/24
April							
g	1	1526/37/48	1621/32	1711/16	1804/66/77/88	1923/34/45/56	2018/29
A	2	1553/64	1643/48	1727/38	1809/20/93/99	1961/72	
b	3	1575/80/86	1659/70/81	1743/63/68/74	1825/31/36	1904/83/88/94	
c	4	1507/18/91	1602/13/75/86/97	1708/79/90	1847/58	1915/20/26/99	2010/21
d	5	1523/34/45/56	1607/18/29/40	1702/13/24/95	1801/63/74/85/96	1931/42/53	2015/26
e	6	1539/50/61/72	1634/45/56	1729/35/40/60	1806/17/28/90	1947/58/69/80	
f	7	1504/77/88	1667/72	1751/65/76	1822/33/44	1901/12/85/96	
g	8	1509/15/20/99	1604/10/83/94	1705/87/92/98	1849/55/60	1917/28	2007/12
A	9	1531/42	1615/26/37/99	1710/21/32	1871/82	1939/44/50	2023/34
b	10	1547/58/69	1631/42/53/64	1726/37/48/57	1803/14/87/98	1955/66/77	
c	11	1501/12/63/74/85/96	1658/69/80	1762/73/84	1819/30/41/52	1909/71/82/93	2004
d	12	1506/17/28	1601/12/91/96	1789	1846/57/68	1903/14/25/36/98	2009/20
e	13	1533/44	1623/28	1707/18	1800/73/79/84	1941/52	2031
f	14	1555/60/66	1639/50/61	1723/34/45/54	1805/11/16/95	1963/68/74	
g	15	1571/82/93	1655/66/77/88	1750/59/70/81	1827/38	1900/06/79/90	2001
A	16	1503/14/25/36/87/98	1609/20/82/93	1704/75/86/97	1843/54/65/76	1911/22/33/95	2006/17/28
b	17	1530/41/52	1625/36	1715/20	1808/70/81/92	1927/38/49/60	2022/33
c	18	1557/68	1647/52	1731/42/56	1802/13/24/97	1954/65/76	
d	19	1500/79/84/90	1663/74/85	1747/67/72/78	1829/35/40	1908/81/87/92	
e	20	1511/22/95	1606/17/79/90	1701/12/83/94	1851/62	1919/24/30	2003/14/25
f	21	1527/38/49	1622/33/44	1717/28	1867/78/89	1935/46/57	2019/30
g	22	1565/76	1660	1739/53/64	1810/21/32	1962/73/84	
A	23	1508	1671		1848	1905/16	2000
b	24	1519	1603/14/98	1709/91	1859		2011
c	25	1546	1641	1736	1886	1943	

HINDU CALENDAR

The Hindu calendar is a luni-solar calendar of twelve months, each containing 29 days, 12 hours. Each month is divided into a light fortnight (Shukla or Shuddha) and a dark fortnight (Krishna or Vadya) based on the waxing and waning of the moon. In most parts of India the month starts with the light fortnight, i.e. the day after the new moon, although in some regions it begins with the dark fortnight, i.e. the day after the full moon.

The new year begins in the month of Chaitra (March/April) and ends in the month of Phalgun (March). The twelve months, Chaitra, Vaishakh, Jyeshtha, Ashadh, Shravan, Bhadrapad, Ashvin, Kartik, Margashirsh, Paush, Magh and Phalgun, have Sanskrit names derived from twelve asterisms (constellations). There are regional variations to the names of the months but the Sanskrit names are understood throughout India.

Every lunar month must have a solar transit and is termed pure (shuddha). The lunar month without a solar transit is impure (mala) and called an intercalary month. An intercalary month occurs approximately every 32 lunar months, whenever the difference between the Hindu year of 360 lunar days (354 days 8 hours solar time) and the 365 days 6 hours of the solar year reaches the length of one Hindu lunar month (29 days 12 hours).

The leap month may be added at any point in the Hindu year. The name given to the month varies according to when it occurs but is taken from the month immediately following it. There is no leap month in 2003.

The days of the week are called Raviwar (Sunday), Somawar (Monday), Mangalwar (Tuesday), Budhawar (Wednesday), Guruwar (Thursday), Shukrawar (Friday) and Shaniwar (Saturday). The names are derived from the Sanskrit names of the Sun, the Moon and five planets, Mars, Mercury, Jupiter, Venus and Saturn.

Most fasts and festivals are based on the lunar calendar but a few are determined by the apparent movement of the Sun, e.g. Sankranti and Pongal (in southern India), which are celebrated on 14/15 January to mark the start of the Sun's apparent journey northwards and a change of season.

Festivals celebrated throughout India are Chaitra (the New Year), Raksha-bandhan (the renewal of the kinship bond between brothers and sisters), Navaratri (a nine-night festival dedicated to the goddess Parvati), Dasara

(the victory of Rama over the demon army), Diwali (a festival of lights), Makara Sankranti, Shivaratri (dedicated to Shiva), and Holi (a spring festival).

Regional festivals are Durga-puja (dedicated to the goddess Durga (Parvati)), Sarasvati-puja (dedicated to the goddess Sarasvati), Ganesh Chaturthi (worship of Ganesh on the fourth day (Chaturthi) of the light half of Bhadrapad), Ramanavami (the birth festival of the god Rama) and Janmashtami (the birth festival of the god Krishna).

The main festivals celebrated in Britain are Navaratri, Dasara, Durga-puja, Diwali, Holi, Sarasvati-puja, Ganesh Chaturthi, Raksha-bandhan, Ramanavami and Janmashtami.

For dates of the main festivals in 2003, *see* page 11.

JEWISH CALENDAR

The story of the Flood in the Book of Genesis indicates the use of a calendar of some kind and that the writers recognised thirty days as the length of a lunation. However, after the diaspora, Jewish communities were left in considerable doubt as to the times of fasts and festivals. This led to the formation of the Jewish calendar as used today. It is said that this was done in AD 358 by Rabbi Hillel II, though some assert that it did not happen until much later.

The calendar is luni-solar, and is based on the lengths of the lunation and of the tropical year as found by Hipparchus (c.120 BC), which differ little from those adopted at the present day. The year AM 5763 (2002–2003) is the 6th year of the 304th Metonic (Minor or Lunar) cycle of 19 years and the 23st year of the 206th Solar (or Major) cycle of 28 years since the Era of the Creation. Jews hold that the Creation occurred at the time of the autumnal equinox in the year known in the Christian calendar as 3760 BC (954 of the Julian period). The epoch or starting point of Jewish chronology corresponds to 7 October 3761 BC. At the beginning of each solar cycle, the Tekufah of Nisan (the vernal equinox) returns to the same day and to the same hour.

The hour is divided into 1080 minims, and the month between one new moon and the next is reckoned as 29 days, 12 hours, 793 minims. The normal calendar year, called a Regular Common year, consists of 12 months of 30 days and 29 days alternately. Since 12 months such as these comprise only 354 days, in order that each of them shall not diverge greatly from an average place in the solar year, a 13th month is occasionally added after the fifth month of the civil year (which commences on the first day of the month Tishri), or as the penultimate month of the ecclesiastical year (which commences on the first day of the month Nisan). The years when this happens are called Embolismic or leap years.

Of the 19 years that form a Metonic cycle, seven are leap years; they occur at places in the cycle indicated by the numbers 3, 6, 8, 11, 14, 17 and 19, these places being chosen so that the accumulated excesses of the solar years should be as small as possible.

A Jewish year is of one of the following six types:

Minimal Common	353 days
Regular Common	354 days
Full Common	355 days
Minimal Leap	383 days
Regular Leap	384 days
Full Leap	385 days

The Regular year has alternate months of 30 and 29 days. In a Full year, whether common or leap, Marcheshvan, the second month of the civil year, has 30 days instead of 29; in Minimal years Kislev, the third month, has 29 instead of 30. The additional month in leap years is called Adar I and precedes the month called Adar in Common years. Adar II is called Adar Sheni in leap years, and the usual Adar festivals are kept in Adar Sheni. Adar I and Adar II always have 30 days, but neither this, nor the other variations mentioned, is allowed to change the number of days in the other months, which still follow the alternation of the normal twelve.

These are the main features of the Jewish calendar, which must be considered permanent because as a Jewish law it cannot be altered except by a great Sanhedrin.

The Jewish day begins between sunset and nightfall. The time used is that of the meridian of Jerusalem, which is 2h 21m in advance of Greenwich Mean Time. Rules for the beginning of sabbaths and festivals were laid down for the latitude of London in the 18th century and hours for nightfall are now fixed annually by the Chief Rabbi.

JEWISH CALENDAR 5763–4

AM 5763 (763) is a Full leap year of 13 months, 55 sabbaths and 385 days. AM 5764 (764) is a Full Common year of 12 months, 51 sabbaths and 355 days.

Month (first day)	AM 5763	AM 5764
Tishri 1	7 September 2002	27 September 2003
Marcheshvan 1	7 October	27 October
Kislev 1	6 November	26 November
Tebet 1	6 December	26 December
Shebat 1	4 January 2003	24 January 2004
*Adar 1	3 February	23 February
†Adar II	5 March	
Nisan 1	3 April	23 March
Iyar 1	3 May	22 April
Sivan 1	1 June	21 May
Tammuz 1	1 July	20 June
Ab 1	30 July	19 July
Elul 1	29 August	18 August

*Known as Adar Rishon in leap years
†Known as Adar Sheni in leap years

JEWISH FASTS AND FESTIVALS

For dates of principal festivals in 2003, *see* page 11.

Tishri 1–2	Rosh Hashanah (New Year)
Tishri 3	*Fast of Gedaliah
Tishri 10	Yom Kippur (Day of Atonement)
Tishri 15–21	Succoth (Feast of Tabernacles)
Tishri 21	Hoshana Rabba
Tishri 22	Shemini Atseret (Solemn Assembly)
Tishri 23	Simchat Torah (Rejoicing of the Law)
Kislev 25	Chanucah (Dedication of the Temple) begins
Tebet 10	Fast of Tebet
†*Adar* 13	§Fast of Esther
†*Adar* 14	Purim
†*Adar* 15	Shushan Purim
Nisan 15–22	Pesach (Passover)
Sivan 6–7	Shavuot (Feast of Weeks)
Tammuz 17	*Fast of Tammuz
Ab 9	*Fast of Ab

*If these dates fall on the sabbath the fast is kept on the following day
†Adar Sheni in leap years
§This fast is observed on Adar 11 (or Adar Sheni 11 in leap years) if Adar 13 falls on a sabbath

THE MUSLIM CALENDAR

The Muslim era is dated from the *Hijrah*, or flight of the Prophet Muhammad from Mecca to Medina, the corresponding date of which in the Julian calendar is 16 July AD 622. The lunar *hijri* calendar is used principally in Iran, Egypt, Malaysia, Pakistan, Mauritania, various Arab states and certain parts of India. Iran uses the solar *hijri* calendar as well as the lunar *hijri* calendar. The dating system was adopted about AD 639, commencing with the first day of the month Muharram.

The lunar calendar consists of twelve months containing an alternate sequence of 30 and 29 days, with the intercalation of one day at the end of the twelfth month at stated intervals in each cycle of 30 years. The object of the intercalation is to reconcile the date of the first day of the month with the date of the actual new moon.

Some adherents still take the date of the evening of the first physical sighting of the crescent of the new moon as that of the first of the month. If cloud obscures the moon the present month may be extended to 30 days, after which the new month will begin automatically regardless of whether the moon has been seen. (Under religious law a month must have less than 31 days.) This means that the beginning of a new month and the date of religious festivals can vary from the published calendars.

In each cycle of 30 years, 19 years are common and contain 354 days, and 11 years are intercalary (leap years) of 355 days, the latter being called kabisah. The mean length of the Hijrah years is 354 days 8 hours 48 minutes and the period of mean lunation is 29 days 12 hours 44 minutes.

To ascertain if a year is common or kabisah, divide it by 30: the quotient gives the number of completed cycles and the remainder shows the place of the year in the current cycle. If the remainder is 2, 5, 7, 10, 13, 16, 18, 21, 24, 26 or 29, the year is kabisah and consists of 355 days.

MUSLIM CALENDAR 1423-24

Hijrah 1423 AH (remainder 13) is a kabisah year, 1424 AH (remainder 14) is a common year. Calendar dates below are estimates based on calculations of moon phases.

Month Length	1424 (1423)AH
Dhu'l-Qa'da (30)	4 January
Dhu'l-Hijjah (29 or 30)	3 February
Muharram (30)	4 March
Safar (29)	3 April
Rabi' I (30)	3 May
Rabi' II (29)	2 June
Jumada I (30)	1 July
Jumada II (29)	31 July
Rajab (30)	29 August
Sha'ban (29)	28 September
Ramadân (30)	27 October
Shawwâl (29)	25 November

MUSLIM FESTIVALS

Ramadan is a month of fasting for all Muslims because it is the month in which the revelation of the *Qur'an* (Koran) began. During Ramadan Muslims abstain from food, drink and sexual pleasure from dawn until after sunset throughout the month.

The two major festivals are *Id al-Fitr* and *Id al-Adha*. Id al-Fitr marks the end of the Ramadan fast and is celebrated on the day after the sighting of the new moon of the following month. Id al-Adha, the festival of sacrifice (also

known as the great festival), celebrates the submission of the Prophet Ibrahim (Abraham) to God. Id al-Adha falls on the tenth day of Dhul-Hijjah, coinciding with the day when those on *hajj* (pilgrimage to Mecca) sacrifice animals. Other days accorded special recognition are:

Muharram 1	New Year's Day
Muharram 10	Ashura (the day Prophet Noah left the Ark and Prophet Moses was saved from Pharaoh (Sunni), the death of the Prophet's grandson Husain (Shi'ite))
Rabi'u-l-Awwal (Rabi' I) 12	Mawlid al-Nabi (birthday of the Prophet Muhammad)
Rajab 27	Laylat al-Isra' wa'l-Mi'raj (The Night of Journey and Ascension)
Ramadân One of the odd-numbered nights in the last 10 of the month	Laylat al-Qadr (Night of Power)
Dhu'l-Hijjah 10	Id al-Adha (Festival of Sacrifice)

THE SIKH CALENDAR

The Sikh calendar is a lunar calendar of 365 days divided into 12 months. The length of the months varies between 29 and 32 days.

There are no prescribed feast days and no fasting periods. The main celebrations are Baisakhi Mela (the new year and the anniversary of the founding of the Khalsa), Diwali Mela (festival of light), Hola Mohalla Mela (a spring festival held in the Punjab), and the Gurpurbs (anniversaries associated with the ten Gurus).

For dates of the major celebrations in 2003, *see* page 11.

THAI CALENDAR

Thailand adopted the Suriyakati calendar, a modified version of the Gregorian calendar (Suriyakati) during the reign of King Rama V in 1888, using 1 April as the first day of the year. In 1940, the date of the new year was changed to 1 January. The years are counted from the beginning of the Buddhist era (BE), which is calculated to have commenced upon the death of the Lord Buddha, which is taken to have occurred in BC 543, so AD 2003 is BE 2546. The Chinese system of associating years with one of twelve animals is also in use in Thailand. The Chantarakati lunar calendar is used to determine religious holidays; the new year begins on the first day of the waxing moon in November or, if there is a leap month, in December.

CIVIL AND LEGAL CALENDAR

THE HISTORICAL YEAR

Before 1752, two calendar systems were used in England. The civil or legal year began on 25 March and the historical year on 1 January. Thus the civil or legal date 24 March 1658 was the same day as the historical date 24 March 1659; a date in that portion of the year is written as 24 March 165$\frac{8}{9}$, the lower figure showing the historical year.

THE NEW YEAR

In England in the seventh century, and as late as the 13th, the year was reckoned from Christmas Day, but in the 12th century the Church in England began the year with the feast of the Annunciation of the Blessed Virgin ('Lady Day') on 25 March and this practice was adopted generally in the 14th century. The civil or legal year in the British Dominions (exclusive of Scotland) began with Lady Day until 1751. But in and since 1752 the civil year has begun with 1 January. New Year's Day in Scotland was changed from 25 March to 1 January in 1600.

Elsewhere in Europe, 1 January was adopted as the first day of the year by Venice in 1522, German states in 1544, Spain, Portugal and the Roman Catholic Netherlands in 1556, Prussia, Denmark and Sweden in 1559, France in 1564, Lorraine in 1579, the Protestant Netherlands in 1583, Russia in 1725, and Tuscany in 1751.

REGNAL YEARS

Regnal years are the years of a sovereign's reign and each begins on the anniversary of his or her accession, e.g. regnal year 52 of the present Queen begins on 6 February 2003.

The system was used for dating Acts of Parliament until 1962. The Summer Time Act 1925, for example, is quoted as 15 and 16 Geo. V c. 64, because it became law in the parliamentary session which extended over part of both of these regnal years. Acts of a parliamentary session during which a sovereign died were usually given two year numbers, the regnal year of the deceased sovereign and the regnal year of his or her successor, e.g. those passed in 1952 were dated 16 Geo. VI and 1 Elizabeth II. Since 1962 Acts of Parliament have been dated by the calendar year.

QUARTER AND TERM DAYS

Holy days and saints days were the usual means in early times for setting the dates of future and recurrent appointments. The quarter days in England and Wales are the feast of the Nativity (25 December), the feast of Annunciation (25 March), the feast of St John the Baptist (24 June) and the feast of St Michael and All Angels (29 September).

The term days in Scotland are Candlemas (the feast of the Purification), Whitsunday, Lammas (Loaf Mass), and Martinmas (St Martin's Day). These fell on 2 February, 15 May, 1 August and 11 November respectively. However, by the Term and Quarter Days (Scotland) Act 1990, the dates of the term days were changed to 28 February (Candlemas), 28 May (Whitsunday), 28 August (Lammas) and 28 November (Martinmas).

RED-LETTER DAYS

Red-letter days were originally the holy days and saints days indicated in early ecclesiastical calendars by letters printed in red ink. The days to be distinguished in this way were approved at the Council of Nicaea in AD 325.

These days still have a legal significance, as judges of the Queen's Bench Division wear scarlet robes on red-letter days falling during the law sittings. The days designated as red-letter days for this purpose are:

Holy and saints days
The Conversion of St Paul, the Purification, Ash Wednesday, the Annunciation, the Ascension, the feasts of St Mark, SS Philip and James, St Matthias, St Barnabas, St John the Baptist, St Peter, St Thomas, St James, St Luke, SS Simon and Jude, All Saints, St Andrew

Civil calendar (for dates, *see* page 11)
The anniversaries of The Queen's accession, The Queen's birthday and The Queen's coronation, The Queen's official birthday, the birthday of the Duke of Edinburgh, the birthday of the Prince of Wales, St David's Day and Lord Mayor's Day.

PUBLIC HOLIDAYS

Public holidays are divided into two categories, common law and statutory. Common law holidays are holidays 'by habit and custom'; in England, Wales and Northern Ireland these are Good Friday and Christmas Day.

Statutory public holidays, known as bank holidays, were first established by the Bank Holidays Act 1871. They were, literally, days on which the banks (and other public institutions) were closed and financial obligations due on that day were payable the following day. The legislation currently governing public holidays in the UK, which is the Banking and Financial Dealings Act 1971, stipulates the days that are to be public holidays in England, Wales, Scotland and Northern Ireland.

Certain holidays (indicated by * below) are granted annually by royal proclamation, either throughout the UK or in any place in the UK. The public holidays are:

England and Wales
*New Year's Day
Easter Monday
*The first Monday in May
The last Monday in May
The last Monday in August
26 December, if it is not a Sunday
27 December when 25 or 26 December is a Sunday

Scotland
New Year's Day, or if it is a Sunday, 2 January
2 January, or if it is a Sunday, 3 January
Good Friday
The first Monday in May
*The last Monday in May
The first Monday in August
Christmas Day, or if it is a Sunday, 26 December
*Boxing Day – if Christmas Day falls on a Sunday, 26 December is given in lieu and an alternative day is given for Boxing Day

Northern Ireland
*New Year's Day
17 March, or if it is a Sunday, 18 March
Easter Monday
*The first Monday in May
The last Monday in May
* 12 July, or if it is a Sunday, 13 July
The last Monday in August
26 December, if it is not a Sunday
27 December if 25 or 26 December is a Sunday

For dates of public holidays in 2003 and 2004, *see* pages 12–13.

CHRONOLOGICAL CYCLES AND ERAS

SOLAR (OR MAYOR) CYCLE

The solar cycle is a period of twenty-eight years in any corresponding year of which the days of the week recur on the same day of the month.

METONIC (LUNAR, OR MINOR) CYCLE

In 432 BC, Meton, an Athenian astronomer, found that 235 lunations are very nearly, though not exactly, equal in duration to 19 solar years and so after 19 years the phases of the Moon recur on the same days of the month (nearly). The dates of full moon in a cycle of 19 years were inscribed in figures of gold on public monuments in Athens, and the number showing the position of a year in the cycle is called the golden number of that year.

JULIAN PERIOD

The Julian period was proposed by Joseph Scaliger in 1582. The period is 7980 Julian years, and its first year coincides with the year 4713 BC. The figure of 7980 is the product of the number of years in the solar cycle, the Metonic cycle and the cycle of the Roman indiction (28 x 19 x 15).

ROMAN INDICTION

The Roman indiction is a period of fifteen years, instituted for fiscal purposes about AD 300.

EPACT

The epact is the age of the calendar Moon, diminished by one day, on 1 January, in the ecclesiastical lunar calendar.

CHINESE CALENDAR

A lunar calendar was the sole calendar in use in China until 1911, when the government adopted the new (Gregorian) calendar for official and most business activities. The Chinese tend to follow both calendars, the lunar calendar playing an important part in personal life, e.g. birth celebrations, festivals, marriages; and in rural villages the lunar calendar dictates the cycle of activities, denoting the change of weather and farming activities.

The lunar calendar is used in Hong Kong, Singapore, Malaysia, Tibet and elsewhere in south-east Asia. The calendar has a cycle of 60 years. The new year begins at the first new moon after the sun enters the sign of Aquarius, i.e. the new year falls between 21 January and 19 February in the Gregorian calendar.

Each year in the Chinese calendar is associated with one of 12 animals: the rat, the ox, the tiger, the rabbit, the dragon, the snake, the horse, the goat or sheep, the monkey, the chicken or rooster, the dog, and the pig.

The date of the Chinese new year and the astrological sign for the years 2003–2007 are:

2003	1 February	Goat or Sheep
2004	22 January	Monkey
2005	9 February	Chicken or Rooster
2006	29 January	Dog
2007	18 February	Pig

COPTIC CALENDAR

In the Coptic calendar, which is used in parts of Egypt and Ethiopia, the year is made up of 12 months of 30 days each, followed, in general, by five complementary days. Every fourth year is an intercalary or leap year and in these years there are six complementary days. The intercalary year of the Coptic calendar immediately precedes the leap year of the Julian calendar. The era is that of Diocletian or the Martyrs, the origin of which is fixed at 29 August AD 284 (Julian date).

INDIAN ERAS

In addition to the Muslim reckoning, other eras are used in India. The Saka era of southern India, dating from 3 March AD 78, was declared the national calendar of the Republic of

India with effect from 22 March 1957, to be used currently with the Gregorian calendar. As revised, the year of the new Saka era begins at the spring equinox, with five successive months of 31 days and seven of 30 days in ordinary years, and six months of each length in leap years. The year AD 2003 is 1925 of the revised Saka era.

The year AD 2003 corresponds to the following years in other eras:

Year 2060 of the Vikram Samvat era
Year 1410 of the Bengali San era
Year 1179 of the Kollam era
Vedanga Jyotisa year 4 of the five-yearly cycle (386th cycle of Paitamah Siddhanta)
Year 6004 of the Kaliyuga era
Year 2547 of the Buddha Nirvana era

JAPANESE CALENDAR

The Japanese calendar is essentially the same as the Gregorian calendar, the years, months and weeks being of the same length and beginning on the same days as those of the Gregorian calendar. The numeration of the years is different, based on a system of epochs or periods each of which begins at the accession of an Emperor or other important occurrence. The method is not unlike the British system of regnal years, except that each year of a period closes on 31 December. The Japanese chronology begins about AD 650 and the three latest epochs are defined by the reigns of Emperors, whose actual names are not necessarily used:

Epoch
Taishō 1 August 1912 to 25 December 1926
Shōwa 26 December 1926 to 7 January 1989
Heisei 8 January 1989

The year Heisei 15 begins on 1 January 2003.

The months are known as First Month, Second Month, etc., First Month being equivalent to January. The days of the week are Nichiyōbi (Sun-day), Getsuyōbi (Moon-day), Kayōbi (Fire-day), Suiyōbi (Water-day), Mokuyōbi (Wood-day), Kinyōbi (Metal-day), Doyōbi (Earth-day).

THE MASONIC YEAR

Two dates are quoted in warrants, dispensations, etc., issued by the United Grand Lodge of England, those for the current year being expressed as Anno Domini 2000 – Anno Lucis 6000. This Anno Lucis (year of light) is based on the Book of Genesis 1:3, the 4000-year difference being derived, in modified form, from *Ussher's Notation*, published in 1654, which places the Creation of the World in 4004 BC.

OLYMPIADS

Ancient Greek chronology was reckoned in Olympiads, cycles of four years corresponding with the periodic Olympic Games held on the plain of Olympia in Elis once every four years. The intervening years were the first, second, etc., of the Olympiad, which received the name of the victor at the Games. The first recorded Olympiad is that of Choroebus, 776 BC.

ZOROASTRIAN CALENDAR

Zoroastrians, followers of the Iranian prophet Zarathushtra (known to the Greeks as Zoroaster) are mostly to be found in Iran and in India, where they are known as Parsees.

The Zoroastrian era dates from the coronation of the last Zoroastrian Sasanian king in AD 631. The Zoroastrian calendar is divided into twelve months, each comprising 30 days, followed by five holy days of the Gathas at the end of

each year to make the year consist of 365 days.

In order to synchronise the calendar with the solar year of 365 days, an extra month was intercalated once every 120 years. However, this intercalation ceased in the 12th century and the New Year, which had fallen in the spring, slipped back to August. Because intercalation ceased at different times in Iran and India, there was one month's difference between the calendar followed in Iran (Kadmi calendar) and that followed by the Parsees (Shenshai calendar). In 1906 a group of Zoroastrians decided to bring the calendar back in line with the seasons again and restore the New Year to 21 March each year (Fasli calendar).

The Shenshai calendar (New Year in August) is mainly used by Parsees. The Fasli calendar (New Year, 21 March) is mainly used by Zoroastrians living in Iran, in the Indian subcontinent, or away from Iran.

THE ROMAN CALENDAR

Roman historians adopted as an epoch the foundation of Rome, which is believed to have happened in the year 753 BC. The ordinal number of the years in Roman reckoning is followed by the letters AUC (*ab urbe condita*), so that the year 2003 is 2756 AUC (MMDCCLVI). The calendar that we know has developed from one said to have been established by Romulus using a year of 304 days divided into ten months, beginning with March. To this Numa added January and February, making the year consist of 12 months of 30 and 29 days alternately, with an additional day so that the total was 355. It is also said that Numa ordered an intercalary month of 22 or 23 days in alternate years, making 90 days in eight years, to be inserted after 23 February.

However, there is some doubt as to the origination and the details of the intercalation in the Roman calendar. It is certain that some scheme of this kind was inaugurated and not fully carried out, for in the year 46 BC Julius Caesar found that the calendar had been allowed to fall into some confusion. He sought the help of the Egyptian astronomer Sosigenes, which led to the construction and adoption (45 BC) of the Julian calendar, and, by a slight alteration, to the Gregorian calendar now in use. The year 46 BC was made to consist of 445 days and is called the Year of Confusion.

In the Roman (Julian) calendar the days of the month were counted backwards from three fixed points, or days, and an intervening day was said to be so many days before the next coming point, the first and last being counted. These three points were the Kalends, the Nones, and the Ides. Their positions in the months and the method of counting from them will be seen in the table below. The year containing 366 days was called *bissextillis annus*, as it had a doubled sixth day (*bissextus dies*) before the March Kalends on 24 February – *ante diem sextum Kalendas Martias*, or a.d. VI Kal. Mart.

Present days of the month	*March, May, July, October have thirty-one days*		*January, August, December have thirty-one days*		*April, June, September, November have thirty days*		*February has twenty-eight days, and in leap year twenty-nine*	
1	Kalendis		Kalendis		Kalendis		Kalendis	
2	VI ⎱		IV ⎱ ante		IV ⎱ ante		IV ⎱ ante	
3	V	ante	III ⎰ Nonas		III ⎰ Nonas		III ⎰ Nonas	
4	IV	Nonas	pridie Nonas		pridie Nonas		pridie Nonas	
5	III ⎰		Nonis		Nonis		Nonis	
6	pridie Nonas		VIII		VIII		VIII	
7	Nonis		VII		VII		VII	
8	VIII ⎱		VI ⎱ ante		VI ⎱ ante		VI ⎱ ante	
9	VII		V ⎰ Idus		V ⎰ Idus		V ⎰ Idus	
10	VI	ante	IV		IV		IV	
11	V	Idus	III		III		III	
12	IV		pridie Idus		pridie Idus		pridie Idus	
13	III ⎰		Idibus		Idibus		Idibus	
14	pridie Idus		XIX ⎱		XVIII ⎱		XVI	
15	Idibus		XVIII		XVII		XV	
16	XVII ⎱		XVII		XVI		XIV	
17	XVI		XVI		XV		XIII	
18	XV		XV		XIV		XII	
19	XIV		XIV		XIII		XI	
20	XIII		XIII		XII ⎱ ante Kalendas		X ⎱ ante Kalendas	
21	XII		XII ⎱ ante Kalendas		XI (of the month		IX ⎰ Martias	
22	XI	ante Kalendas	XI ⎰ (of the month		X following)		VIII	
23	X ⎰	(of the month	X following)		IX		VII	
24	IX	following)	IX		VIII		*VI	
25	VIII		VIII		VII		V ⎱	
26	VII		VII		VI		IV	
27	VI		VI		V		III ⎰	
28	V		V		IV ⎰		pridie Kalendas Martias	
29	IV ⎰		IV ⎰		III			
30	III ⎰		III ⎰		pridie Kalendas (Maias, Quinctilis, Octobris, Decembris)		* (repeated in leap year)	
31	pridie Kalendas (Aprilis, Iunias, Sextilis, Novembris)		pridie Kalendas (Februarias, Septembris, Ianuarias)					

Calendar for Any Year 1780–2040

To select the correct calendar for any year between 1780 and 2040, consult the index below
* leap year

1780 N*	1813 K	1846 I	1879 G	1912 D*	1945 C	1978 A	2011 M
1781 C	1814 M	1847 K	1880 J*	1913 G	1946 E	1979 C	2012 B*
1782 E	1815 A	1848 N*	1881 M	1914 I	1947 G	1980 F*	2013 E
1783 G	1816 D*	1849 C	1882 A	1915 K	1948 J*	1981 I	2014 G
1784 J*	1817 G	1850 E	1883 C	1916 N*	1949 M	1982 K	2015 I
1785 M	1818 I	1851 G	1884 F*	1917 C	1950 A	1983 M	2016 L*
1786 A	1819 K	1852 J*	1885 I	1918 E	1951 C	1984 B*	2017 A
1787 C	1820 N*	1853 M	1886 K	1919 G	1952 F*	1985 E	2018 C
1788 F*	1821 C	1854 A	1887 M	1920 J*	1953 I	1986 G	2019 E
1789 I	1822 E	1855 C	1888 B*	1921 M	1954 K	1987 I	2020 H*
1790 K	1823 G	1856 F*	1889 E	1922 A	1955 M	1988 L*	2021 K
1791 M	1824 J*	1857 I	1890 G	1923 C	1956 B*	1989 A	2022 M
1792 B*	1825 M	1858 K	1891 I	1924 F*	1957 E	1990 C	2023 A
1793 E	1826 A	1859 M	1892 L*	1925 I	1958 G	1991 E	2024 D*
1794 G	1827 C	1860 B*	1893 A	1926 K	1959 I	1992 H*	2025 G
1795 I	1828 F*	1861 E	1894 C	1927 M	1960 L*	1993 K	2026 I
1796 L*	1829 I	1862 G	1895 E	1928 B*	1961 A	1994 M	2027 K
1797 A	1830 K	1863 I	1896 H*	1929 E	1962 C	1995 A	2028 N*
1798 C	1831 M	1864 L*	1897 K	1930 G	1963 E	1996 D*	2029 C
1799 E	1832 B*	1865 A	1898 M	1931 I	1964 H*	1997 G	2030 E
1800 G	1833 E	1866 C	1899 A	1932 L*	1965 K	1998 I	2031 G
1801 I	1834 G	1867 E	1900 C	1933 A	1966 M	1999 K	2032 J*
1802 K	1835 I	1868 H*	1901 E	1934 C	1967 A	2000 N*	2033 M
1803 M	1836 L*	1869 K	1902 G	1935 E	1968 D*	2001 C	2034 A
1804 B*	1837 A	1870 M	1903 I	1936 H*	1969 G	2002 E	2035 C
1805 E	1838 C	1871 A	1904 L*	1937 K	1970 I	2003 G	2036 F*
1806 G	1839 E	1872 D*	1905 A	1938 M	1971 K	2004 J*	2037 I
1807 I	1840 H*	1873 G	1906 C	1939 A	1972 N*	2005 M	2038 K
1808 L*	1841 K	1874 I	1907 E	1940 D*	1973 C	2006 A	2039 M
1809 A	1842 M	1875 K	1908 H*	1941 G	1974 E	2007 C	2040 B*
1810 C	1843 A	1876 N*	1909 K	1942 I	1975 G	2008 F*	
1811 E	1844 D*	1877 C	1910 M	1943 K	1976 J*	2009 I	
1812 H*	1845 G	1878 E	1911 A	1944 N*	1977 M	2010 K	

A

January
Sun.	1	8	15	22	29
Mon.	2	9	16	23	30
Tue.	3	10	17	24	31
Wed.	4	11	18	25	
Thur.	5	12	19	26	
Fri.	6	13	20	27	
Sat.	7	14	21	28	

February
Sun.	5	12	19	26
Mon.	6	13	20	27
Tue.	7	14	21	28
Wed.	1	8	15	22
Thur.	2	9	16	23
Fri.	3	10	17	24
Sat.	4	11	18	25

March
Sun.	5	12	19	26	
Mon.	6	13	20	27	
Tue.	7	14	21	28	
Wed.	1	8	15	22	29
Thur.	2	9	16	23	30
Fri.	3	10	17	24	31
Sat.	4	11	18	25	

April
Sun.	2	9	16	23	30
Mon.	3	10	17	24	
Tue.	4	11	18	25	
Wed.	5	12	19	26	
Thur.	6	13	20	27	
Fri.	7	14	21	28	
Sat.	1	8	15	22	29

May
Sun.	7	14	21	28	
Mon.	1	8	15	22	29
Tue.	2	9	16	23	30
Wed.	3	10	17	24	31
Thur.	4	11	18	25	
Fri.	5	12	19	26	
Sat.	6	13	20	27	

June
Sun.	4	11	18	25	
Mon.	5	12	19	26	
Tue.	6	13	20	27	
Wed.	7	14	21	28	
Thur.	1	8	15	22	29
Fri.	2	9	16	23	30
Sat.	3	10	17	24	

July
Sun.	2	9	16	23	30
Mon.	3	10	17	24	31
Tue.	4	11	18	25	
Wed.	5	12	19	26	
Thur.	6	13	20	27	
Fri.	7	14	21	28	
Sat.	1	8	15	22	29

August
Sun.	6	13	20	27	
Mon.	7	14	21	28	
Tue.	1	8	15	22	29
Wed.	2	9	16	23	30
Thur.	3	10	17	24	31
Fri.	4	11	18	25	
Sat.	5	12	19	26	

September
Sun.	3	10	17	24	
Mon.	4	11	18	25	
Tue.	5	12	19	26	
Wed.	6	13	20	27	
Thur.	7	14	21	28	
Fri.	1	8	15	22	29
Sat.	2	9	16	23	30

October
Sun.	1	8	15	22	29
Mon.	2	9	16	23	30
Tue.	3	10	17	24	31
Wed.	4	11	18	25	
Thur.	5	12	19	26	
Fri.	6	13	20	27	
Sat.	7	14	21	28	

November
Sun.	5	12	19	26	
Mon.	6	13	20	27	
Tue.	7	14	21	28	
Wed.	1	8	15	22	29
Thur.	2	9	16	23	30
Fri.	3	10	17	24	
Sat.	4	11	18	25	

December
Sun.	3	10	17	24	31
Mon.	4	11	18	25	
Tue.	5	12	19	26	
Wed.	6	13	20	27	
Thur.	7	14	21	28	
Fri.	1	8	15	22	29
Sat.	2	9	16	23	30

B (LEAP YEAR)

January
Sun.	1	8	15	22	29
Mon.	2	9	16	23	30
Tue.	3	10	17	24	31
Wed.	4	11	18	25	
Thur.	5	12	19	26	
Fri.	6	13	20	27	
Sat.	7	14	21	28	

February
Sun.	5	12	19	26	
Mon.	6	13	20	27	
Tue.	7	14	21	28	
Wed.	1	8	15	22	29
Thur.	2	9	16	23	
Fri.	3	10	17	24	
Sat.	4	11	18	25	

March
Sun.	4	11	18	25	
Mon.	5	12	19	26	
Tue.	6	13	20	27	
Wed.	7	14	21	28	
Thur.	1	8	15	22	29
Fri.	2	9	16	23	30
Sat.	3	10	17	24	31

April
Sun.	1	8	15	22	29
Mon.	2	9	16	23	30
Tue.	3	10	17	24	
Wed.	4	11	18	25	
Thur.	5	12	19	26	
Fri.	6	13	20	27	
Sat.	7	14	21	28	

May
Sun.	6	13	20	27	
Mon.	7	14	21	28	
Tue.	1	8	15	22	29
Wed.	2	9	16	23	30
Thur.	3	10	17	24	31
Fri.	4	11	18	25	
Sat.	5	12	19	26	

June
Sun.	3	10	17	24	
Mon.	4	11	18	25	
Tue.	5	12	19	26	
Wed.	6	13	20	27	
Thur.	7	14	21	28	
Fri.	1	8	15	22	29
Sat.	2	9	16	23	30

July
Sun.	1	8	15	22	29
Mon.	2	9	16	23	30
Tue.	3	10	17	24	31
Wed.	4	11	18	25	
Thur.	5	12	19	26	
Fri.	6	13	20	27	
Sat.	7	14	21	28	

August
Sun.	5	12	19	26	
Mon.	6	13	20	27	
Tue.	7	14	21	28	
Wed.	1	8	15	22	29
Thur.	2	9	16	23	30
Fri.	3	10	17	24	31
Sat.	4	11	18	25	

September
Sun.	2	9	16	23	30
Mon.	3	10	17	24	
Tue.	4	11	18	25	
Wed.	5	12	19	26	
Thur.	6	13	20	27	
Fri.	7	14	21	28	
Sat.	1	8	15	22	29

October
Sun.	7	14	21	28	
Mon.	1	8	15	22	29
Tue.	2	9	16	23	30
Wed.	3	10	17	24	31
Thur.	4	11	18	25	
Fri.	5	12	19	26	
Sat.	6	13	20	27	

November
Sun.	4	11	18	25	
Mon.	5	12	19	26	
Tue.	6	13	20	27	
Wed.	7	14	21	28	
Thur.	1	8	15	22	29
Fri.	2	9	16	23	30
Sat.	3	10	17	24	

December
Sun.	2	9	16	23	30
Mon.	3	10	17	24	31
Tue.	4	11	18	25	
Wed.	5	12	19	26	
Thur.	6	13	20	27	
Fri.	7	14	21	28	
Sat.	1	8	15	22	29

EASTER DAYS

March 26	1815, 1826, 1837, 1967, 1978, 1989
April 2	1809, 1893, 1899, 1961
April 9	1871, 1882, 1939, 1950, 2023, 2034
April 16	1786, 1797, 1843, 1854, 1865, 1911, 1922, 1933, 1995, 2006, 2017
April 23	1905

EASTER DAYS

April 1	1804, 1888, 1956, 2040
April 8	1792, 1860, 1928, 2012
April 22	1832, 1984

C

	January	*February*	*March*
Sun.	7 14 21 28	4 11 18 25	4 11 18 25
Mon.	1 8 15 22 29	5 12 19 26	5 12 19 26
Tue.	2 9 16 23 30	6 13 20 27	6 13 20 27
Wed.	3 10 17 24 31	7 14 21 28	7 14 21 28
Thur.	4 11 18 25	1 8 15 22	1 8 15 22 29
Fri.	5 12 19 26	2 9 16 23	2 9 16 23 30
Sat.	6 13 20 27	3 10 17 24	3 10 17 24 31

	April	*May*	*June*
Sun.	1 8 15 22 29	6 13 20 27	3 10 17 24
Mon.	2 9 16 23 30	7 14 21 28	4 11 18 25
Tue.	3 10 17 24	1 8 15 22 29	5 12 19 26
Wed.	4 11 18 25	2 9 16 23 30	6 13 20 27
Thur.	5 12 19 26	3 10 17 24 31	7 14 21 28
Fri.	6 13 20 27	4 11 18 25	1 8 15 22 29
Sat.	7 14 21 28	5 12 19 26	2 9 16 23 30

	July	*August*	*September*
Sun.	1 8 15 22 29	5 12 19 26	2 9 16 23 30
Mon.	2 9 16 23 30	6 13 20 27	3 10 17 24
Tue.	3 10 17 24 31	7 14 21 28	4 11 18 25
Wed.	4 11 18 25	1 8 15 22 29	5 12 19 26
Thur.	5 12 19 26	2 9 16 23 30	6 13 20 27
Fri.	6 13 20 27	3 10 17 24 31	7 14 21 28
Sat.	7 14 21 28	4 11 18 25	1 8 15 22 29

	October	*November*	*December*
Sun.	7 14 21 28	4 11 18 25	2 9 16 23 30
Mon.	1 8 15 22 29	5 12 19 26	3 10 17 24 31
Tue.	2 9 16 23 30	6 13 20 27	4 11 18 25
Wed.	3 10 17 24 31	7 14 21 28	5 12 19 26
Thur.	4 11 18 25	1 8 15 22 29	6 13 20 27
Fri.	5 12 19 26	2 9 16 23 30	7 14 21 28
Sat.	6 13 20 27	3 10 17 24	1 8 15 22 29

EASTER DAYS

March 25	1883, 1894, 1951, 2035
April 1	1866, 1877, 1923, 1934, 1945, 2018, 2029
April 8	1787, 1798, 1849, 1855, 1917, 2007
April 15	1781, 1827, 1838, 1900, 1906, 1979, 1990, 2001
April 22	1810, 1821, 1962, 1973

E

	January	*February*	*March*
Sun.	6 13 20 27	3 10 17 24	3 10 17 24 31
Mon.	7 14 21 28	4 11 18 25	4 11 18 25
Tue.	1 8 15 22 29	5 12 19 26	5 12 19 26
Wed.	2 9 16 23 30	6 13 20 27	6 13 20 27
Thur.	3 10 17 24 31	7 14 21 28	7 14 21 28
Fri.	4 11 18 25	1 8 15 22	1 8 15 22 29
Sat.	5 12 19 26	2 9 16 23	2 9 16 23 30

	April	*May*	*June*
Sun.	7 14 21 28	5 12 19 26	2 9 16 23 30
Mon.	1 8 15 22 29	6 13 20 27	3 10 17 24
Tue.	2 9 16 23 30	7 14 21 28	4 11 18 25
Wed.	3 10 17 24	1 8 15 22 29	5 12 19 26
Thur.	4 11 18 25	2 9 16 23 30	6 13 20 27
Fri.	5 12 19 26	3 10 17 24 31	7 14 21 28
Sat.	6 13 20 27	4 11 18 25	1 8 15 22 29

	July	*August*	*September*
Sun.	7 14 21 28	4 11 18 25	1 8 15 22 29
Mon.	1 8 15 22 29	5 12 19 26	2 9 16 23 30
Tue.	2 9 16 23 30	6 13 20 27	3 10 17 24
Wed.	3 10 17 24 31	7 14 21 28	4 11 18 25
Thur.	4 11 18 25	1 8 15 22 29	5 12 19 26
Fri.	5 12 19 26	2 9 16 23 30	6 13 20 27
Sat.	6 13 20 27	3 10 17 24 31	7 14 21 28

	October	*November*	*December*
Sun.	6 13 20 27	3 10 17 24	1 8 15 22 29
Mon.	7 14 21 28	4 11 18 25	2 9 16 23 30
Tue.	1 8 15 22 29	5 12 19 26	3 10 17 24 31
Wed.	2 9 16 23 30	6 13 20 27	4 11 18 25
Thur.	3 10 17 24 31	7 14 21 28	5 12 19 26
Fri.	4 11 18 25	1 8 15 22 29	6 13 20 27
Sat.	5 12 19 26	2 9 16 23 30	7 14 21 28

EASTER DAYS

March 24	1799
March 31	1782, 1793, 1839, 1850, 1861, 1907
	1918, 1929, 1991, 2002, 2013
April 7	1822, 1833, 1901, 1985
April 14	1805, 1811, 1895, 1963, 1974
April 21	1867, 1878, 1889, 1935, 1946, 1957, 2019, 2030

D (LEAP YEAR)

	January	*February*	*March*
Sun.	7 14 21 28	4 11 18 25	3 10 17 24 31
Mon.	1 8 15 22 29	5 12 19 26	4 11 18 25
Tue.	2 9 16 23 30	6 13 20 27	5 12 19 26
Wed.	3 10 17 24 31	7 14 21 28	6 13 20 27
Thur.	4 11 18 25	1 8 15 22 29	7 14 21 28
Fri.	5 12 19 26	2 9 16 23	1 8 15 22 29
Sat.	6 13 20 27	3 10 17 24	2 9 16 23 30

	April	*May*	*June*
Sun.	7 14 21 28	5 12 19 26	2 9 16 23 30
Mon.	1 8 15 22 29	6 13 20 27	3 10 17 24
Tue.	2 9 16 23 30	7 14 21 28	4 11 18 25
Wed.	3 10 17 24	1 8 15 22 29	5 12 19 26
Thur.	4 11 18 25	2 9 16 23 30	6 13 20 27
Fri.	5 12 19 26	3 10 17 24 31	7 14 21 28
Sat.	6 13 20 27	4 11 18 25	1 8 15 22 29

	July	*August*	*September*
Sun.	7 14 21 28	4 11 18 25	1 8 15 22 29
Mon.	1 8 15 22 29	5 12 19 26	2 9 16 23 30
Tue.	2 9 16 23 30	6 13 20 27	3 10 17 24
Wed.	3 10 17 24 31	7 14 21 28	4 11 18 25
Thur.	4 11 18 25	1 8 15 22 29	5 12 19 26
Fri.	5 12 19 26	2 9 16 23 30	6 13 20 27
Sat.	6 13 20 27	3 10 17 24 31	7 14 21 28

	October	*November*	*December*
Sun.	6 13 20 27	3 10 17 24	1 8 15 22 29
Mon.	7 14 21 28	4 11 18 25	2 9 16 23 30
Tue.	1 8 15 22 29	5 12 19 26	3 10 17 24 31
Wed.	2 9 16 23 30	6 13 20 27	4 11 18 25
Thur.	3 10 17 24 31	7 14 21 28	5 12 19 26
Fri.	4 11 18 25	1 8 15 22 29	6 13 20 27
Sat.	5 12 19 26	2 9 16 23 30	7 14 21 28

EASTER DAYS

March 24	1940
March 31	1872, 2024
April 7	1844, 1912, 1996
April 14	1816, 1968

F (LEAP YEAR)

	January	*February*	*March*
Sun.	6 13 20 27	3 10 17 24	2 9 16 23 30
Mon.	7 14 21 28	4 11 18 25	3 10 17 24 31
Tue.	1 8 15 22 29	5 12 19 26	4 11 18 25
Wed.	2 9 16 23 30	6 13 20 27	5 12 19 26
Thur.	3 10 17 24 31	7 14 21 28	6 13 20 27
Fri.	4 11 18 25	1 8 15 22 29	7 14 21 28
Sat.	5 12 19 26	2 9 16 23	1 8 15 22 29

	April	*May*	*June*
Sun.	6 13 20 27	4 11 18 25	1 8 15 22 29
Mon.	7 14 21 28	5 12 19 26	2 9 16 23 30
Tue.	1 8 15 22 29	6 13 20 27	3 10 17 24
Wed.	2 9 16 23 30	7 14 21 28	4 11 18 25
Thur.	3 10 17 24	1 8 15 22 29	5 12 19 26
Fri.	4 11 18 25	2 9 16 23 30	6 13 20 27
Sat.	5 12 19 26	3 10 17 24 31	7 14 21 28

	July	*August*	*September*
Sun.	6 13 20 27	3 10 17 24 31	7 14 21 28
Mon.	7 14 21 28	4 11 18 25	1 8 15 22 29
Tue.	1 8 15 22 29	5 12 19 26	2 9 16 23 30
Wed.	2 9 16 23 30	6 13 20 27	3 10 17 24
Thur.	3 10 17 24 31	7 14 21 28	4 11 18 25
Fri.	4 11 18 25	1 8 15 22 29	5 12 19 26
Sat.	5 12 19 26	2 9 16 23 30	6 13 20 27

	October	*November*	*December*
Sun.	5 12 19 26	2 9 16 23 30	7 14 21 28
Mon.	6 13 20 27	3 10 17 24	1 8 15 22 29
Tue.	7 14 21 28	4 11 18 25	2 9 16 23 30
Wed.	1 8 15 22 29	5 12 19 26	3 10 17 24 31
Thur.	2 9 16 23 30	6 13 20 27	4 11 18 25
Fri.	3 10 17 24 31	7 14 21 28	5 12 19 26
Sat.	4 11 18 25	1 8 15 22 29	6 13 20 27

EASTER DAYS

March 23	1788, 1856, 2008
April 6	1828, 1980
April 13	1884, 1952, 2036
April 20	1924

G

	January	February	March
Sun.	5 12 19 26	2 9 16 23	2 9 16 23 30
Mon.	6 13 20 27	3 10 17 24	3 10 17 24 31
Tue.	7 14 21 28	4 11 18 25	4 11 18 25
Wed.	1 8 15 22 29	5 12 19 26	5 12 19 26
Thur.	2 9 16 23 30	6 13 20 27	6 13 20 27
Fri.	3 10 17 24 31	7 14 21 28	7 14 21 28
Sat.	4 11 18 25	1 8 15 22	1 8 15 22 29

	April	May	June
Sun.	6 13 20 27	4 11 18 25	1 8 15 22 29
Mon.	7 14 21 28	5 12 19 26	2 9 16 23 30
Tue.	1 8 15 22 29	6 13 20 27	3 10 17 24
Wed.	2 9 16 23 30	7 14 21 28	4 11 18 25
Thur.	3 10 17 24	1 8 15 22 29	5 12 19 26
Fri.	4 11 18 25	2 9 16 23 30	6 13 20 27
Sat.	5 12 19 26	3 10 17 24 31	7 14 21 28

	July	August	September
Sun.	6 13 20 27	3 10 17 24 31	7 14 21 28
Mon.	7 14 21 28	4 11 18 25	1 8 15 22 29
Tue.	1 8 15 22 29	5 12 19 26	2 9 16 23 30
Wed.	2 9 16 23 30	6 13 20 27	3 10 17 24
Thur.	3 10 17 24 31	7 14 21 28	4 11 18 25
Fri.	4 11 18 25	1 8 15 22 29	5 12 19 26
Sat.	5 12 19 26	2 9 16 23 30	6 13 20 27

	October	November	December
Sun.	5 12 19 26	2 9 16 23 30	7 14 21 28
Mon.	6 13 20 27	3 10 17 24	1 8 15 22 29
Tue.	7 14 21 28	4 11 18 25	2 9 16 23 30
Wed.	1 8 15 22 29	5 12 19 26	3 10 17 24 31
Thur.	2 9 16 23 30	6 13 20 27	4 11 18 25
Fri.	3 10 17 24 31	7 14 21 28	5 12 19 26
Sat.	4 11 18 25	1 8 15 22 29	6 13 20 27

EASTER DAYS

March 23	1845, 1913
March 30	1823, 1834, 1902, 1975, 1986, 1997
April 6	1806, 1817, 1890, 1947, 1958, 1969
April 13	1800, 1873, 1879, 1941, 2031
April 20	1783, 1794, 1851, 1862, 1919, 1930, 2003, 2014, 2025

I

	January	February	March
Sun.	4 11 18 25	1 8 15 22	1 8 15 22 29
Mon.	5 12 19 26	2 9 16 23	2 9 16 23 30
Tue.	6 13 20 27	3 10 17 24	3 10 17 24 31
Wed.	7 14 21 28	4 11 18 25	4 11 18 25
Thur.	1 8 15 22 29	5 12 19 26	5 12 19 26
Fri.	2 9 16 23 30	6 13 20 27	6 13 20 27
Sat.	3 10 17 24 31	7 14 21 28	7 14 21 28

	April	May	June
Sun.	5 12 19 26	3 10 17 24 31	7 14 21 28
Mon.	6 13 20 27	4 11 18 25	1 8 15 22 29
Tue.	7 14 21 28	5 12 19 26	2 9 16 23 30
Wed.	1 8 15 22 29	6 13 20 27	3 10 17 24
Thur.	2 9 16 23 30	7 14 21 28	4 11 18 25
Fri.	3 10 17 24	1 8 15 22 29	5 12 19 26
Sat.	4 11 18 25	2 9 16 23 30	6 13 20 27

	July	August	September
Sun.	5 12 19 26	2 9 16 23 30	6 13 20 27
Mon.	6 13 20 27	3 10 17 24 31	7 14 21 28
Tue.	7 14 21 28	4 11 18 25	1 8 15 22 29
Wed.	1 8 15 22 29	5 12 19 26	2 9 16 23 30
Thur.	2 9 16 23 30	6 13 20 27	3 10 17 24
Fri.	3 10 17 24 31	7 14 21 28	4 11 18 25
Sat.	4 11 18 25	1 8 15 22 29	5 12 19 26

	October	November	December
Sun.	4 11 18 25	1 8 15 22 29	6 13 20 27
Mon.	5 12 19 26	2 9 16 23 30	7 14 21 28
Tue.	6 13 20 27	3 10 17 24	1 8 15 22 29
Wed.	7 14 21 28	4 11 18 25	2 9 16 23 30
Thur.	1 8 15 22 29	5 12 19 26	3 10 17 24 31
Fri.	2 9 16 23 30	6 13 20 27	4 11 18 25
Sat.	3 10 17 24 31	7 14 21 28	5 12 19 26

EASTER DAYS

March 22	1818
March 29	1807, 1891, 1959, 1970
April 5	1795, 1801, 1863, 1874, 1885, 1931, 1942, 1953, 2015, 2026, 2037
April 12	1789, 1846, 1857, 1903, 1914, 1925, 1998, 2009
April 19	1829, 1835, 1981, 1987

H (LEAP YEAR)

	January	February	March
Sun.	5 12 19 26	2 9 16 23	1 8 15 22 29
Mon.	6 13 20 27	3 10 17 24	2 9 16 23 30
Tue.	7 14 21 28	4 11 18 25	3 10 17 24 31
Wed.	1 8 15 22 29	5 12 19 26	4 11 18 25
Thur.	2 9 16 23 30	6 13 20 27	5 12 19 26
Fri.	3 10 17 24 31	7 14 21 28	6 13 20 27
Sat.	4 11 18 25	1 8 15 22 29	7 14 21 28

	April	May	June
Sun.	5 12 19 26	3 10 17 24 31	7 14 21 28
Mon.	6 13 20 27	4 11 18 25	1 8 15 22 29
Tue.	7 14 21 28	5 12 19 26	2 9 16 23 30
Wed.	1 8 15 22 29	6 13 20 27	3 10 17 24
Thur.	2 9 16 23 30	7 14 21 28	4 11 18 25
Fri.	3 10 17 24	1 8 15 22 29	5 12 19 26
Sat.	4 11 18 25	2 9 16 23 30	6 13 20 27

	July	August	September
Sun.	5 12 19 26	2 9 16 23 30	6 13 20 27
Mon.	6 13 20 27	3 10 17 24 31	7 14 21 28
Tue.	7 14 21 28	4 11 18 25	1 8 15 22 29
Wed.	1 8 15 22 29	5 12 19 26	2 9 16 23 30
Thur.	2 9 16 23 30	6 13 20 27	3 10 17 24
Fri.	3 10 17 24 31	7 14 21 28	4 11 18 25
Sat.	4 11 18 25	1 8 15 22 29	5 12 19 26

	October	November	December
Sun.	4 11 18 25	1 8 15 22 29	6 13 20 27
Mon.	5 12 19 26	2 9 16 23 30	7 14 21 28
Tue.	6 13 20 27	3 10 17 24	1 8 15 22 29
Wed.	7 14 21 28	4 11 18 25	2 9 16 23 30
Thur.	1 8 15 22 29	5 12 19 26	3 10 17 24 31
Fri.	2 9 16 23 30	6 13 20 27	4 11 18 25
Sat.	3 10 17 24 31	7 14 21 28	5 12 19 26

EASTER DAYS

March 29	1812, 1964
April 5	1896
April 12	1868, 1936, 2020
April 19	1840, 1908, 1992

J (LEAP YEAR)

	January	February	March
Sun.	4 11 18 25	1 8 15 22 29	7 14 21 28
Mon.	5 12 19 26	2 9 16 23	1 8 15 22 29
Tue.	6 13 20 27	3 10 17 24	2 9 16 23 30
Wed.	7 14 21 28	4 11 18 25	3 10 17 24 31
Thur.	1 8 15 22 29	5 12 19 26	4 11 18 25
Fri.	2 9 16 23 30	6 13 20 27	5 12 19 26
Sat.	3 10 17 24 31	7 14 21 28	6 13 20 27

	April	May	June
Sun.	4 11 18 25	2 9 16 23 30	6 13 20 27
Mon.	5 12 19 26	3 10 17 24 31	7 14 21 28
Tue.	6 13 20 27	4 11 18 25	1 8 15 22 29
Wed.	7 14 21 28	5 12 19 26	2 9 16 23 30
Thur.	1 8 15 22 29	6 13 20 27	3 10 17 24
Fri.	2 9 16 23 30	7 14 21 28	4 11 18 25
Sat.	3 10 17 24	1 8 15 22 29	5 12 19 26

	July	August	September
Sun.	4 11 18 25	1 8 15 22 29	5 12 19 26
Mon.	5 12 19 26	2 9 16 23 30	6 13 20 27
Tue.	6 13 20 27	3 10 17 24 31	7 14 21 28
Wed.	7 14 21 28	4 11 18 25	1 8 15 22 29
Thur.	1 8 15 22 29	5 12 19 26	2 9 16 23 30
Fri.	2 9 16 23 30	6 13 20 27	3 10 17 24
Sat.	3 10 17 24 31	7 14 21 28	4 11 18 25

	October	November	December
Sun.	3 10 17 24 31	7 14 21 28	5 12 19 26
Mon.	4 11 18 25	1 8 15 22 29	6 13 20 27
Tue.	5 12 19 26	2 9 16 23 30	7 14 21 28
Wed.	6 13 20 27	3 10 17 24	1 8 15 22 29
Thur.	7 14 21 28	4 11 18 25	2 9 16 23 30
Fri.	1 8 15 22 29	5 12 19 26	3 10 17 24 31
Sat.	2 9 16 23 30	6 13 20 27	4 11 18 25

EASTER DAYS

March 28	1880, 1948, 2032
April 4	1920
April 11	1784, 1852, 2004
April 18	1824, 1976

K

	January	February	March
Sun.	3 10 17 24 31	7 14 21 28	7 14 21 28
Mon.	4 11 18 25	1 8 15 22	1 8 15 22 29
Tue.	5 12 19 26	2 9 16 23	2 9 16 23 30
Wed.	6 13 20 27	3 10 17 24	3 10 17 24 31
Thur.	7 14 21 28	4 11 18 25	4 11 18 25
Fri.	1 8 15 22 29	5 12 19 26	5 12 19 26
Sat.	2 9 16 23 30	6 13 20 27	6 13 20 27

	April	May	June
Sun.	4 11 18 25	2 9 16 23 30	6 13 20 27
Mon.	5 12 19 26	3 10 17 24 31	7 14 21 28
Tue.	6 13 20 27	4 11 18 25	1 8 15 22 29
Wed.	7 14 21 28	5 12 19 26	2 9 16 23 30
Thur.	1 8 15 22 29	6 13 20 27	3 10 17 24
Fri.	2 9 16 23 30	7 14 21 28	4 11 18 25
Sat.	3 10 17 24	1 8 15 22 29	5 12 19 26

	July	August	September
Sun.	4 11 18 25	1 8 15 22 29	5 12 19 26
Mon.	5 12 19 26	2 9 16 23 30	6 13 20 27
Tue.	6 13 20 27	3 10 17 24 31	7 14 21 28
Wed.	7 14 21 28	4 11 18 25	1 8 15 22 29
Thur.	1 8 15 22 29	5 12 19 26	2 9 16 23 30
Fri.	2 9 16 23 30	6 13 20 27	3 10 17 24
Sat.	3 10 17 24 31	7 14 21 28	4 11 18 25

	October	November	December
Sun.	3 10 17 24 31	7 14 21 28	5 12 19 26
Mon.	4 11 18 25	1 8 15 22 29	6 13 20 27
Tue.	5 12 19 26	2 9 16 23 30	7 14 21 28
Wed.	6 13 20 27	3 10 17 24	1 8 15 22 29
Thur.	7 14 21 28	4 11 18 25	2 9 16 23 30
Fri.	1 8 15 22 29	5 12 19 26	3 10 17 24 31
Sat.	2 9 16 23 30	6 13 20 27	4 11 18 25

EASTER DAYS

March 28	1869, 1875, 1937, 2027
April 4	1790, 1847, 1858, 1915, 1926, 1999, 2010, 2021
April 11	1819, 1830, 1841, 1909, 1971, 1982, 1993
April 18	1802, 1813, 1897, 1954, 1965
April 25	1886, 1943, 2038

M

	January	February	March
Sun.	2 9 16 23 30	6 13 20 27	6 13 20 27
Mon.	3 10 17 24 31	7 14 21 28	7 14 21 28
Tue.	4 11 18 25	1 8 15 22	1 8 15 22 29
Wed.	5 12 19 26	2 9 16 23	2 9 16 23 30
Thur.	6 13 20 27	3 10 17 24	3 10 17 24 31
Fri.	7 14 21 28	4 11 18 25	4 11 18 25
Sat.	1 8 15 22 29	5 12 19 26	5 12 19 26

	April	May	June
Sun.	3 10 17 24	1 8 15 22 29	5 12 19 26
Mon.	4 11 18 25	2 9 16 23 30	6 13 20 27
Tue.	5 12 19 26	3 10 17 24 31	7 14 21 28
Wed.	6 13 20 27	4 11 18 25	1 8 15 22 29
Thur.	7 14 21 28	5 12 19 26	2 9 16 23 30
Fri.	1 8 15 22 29	6 13 20 27	3 10 17 24
Sat.	2 9 16 23 30	7 14 21 28	4 11 18 25

	July	August	September
Sun.	3 10 17 24 31	7 14 21 28	4 11 18 25
Mon.	4 11 18 25	1 8 15 22 29	5 12 19 26
Tue.	5 12 19 26	2 9 16 23 30	6 13 20 27
Wed.	6 13 20 27	3 10 17 24 31	7 14 21 28
Thur.	7 14 21 28	4 11 18 25	1 8 15 22 29
Fri.	1 8 15 22 29	5 12 19 26	2 9 16 23 30
Sat.	2 9 16 23 30	6 13 20 27	3 10 17 24

	October	November	December
Sun.	2 9 16 23 30	6 13 20 27	4 11 18 25
Mon.	3 10 17 24 31	7 14 21 28	5 12 19 26
Tue.	4 11 18 25	1 8 15 22 29	6 13 20 27
Wed.	5 12 19 26	2 9 16 23 30	7 14 21 28
Thur.	6 13 20 27	3 10 17 24	1 8 15 22 29
Fri.	7 14 21 28	4 11 18 25	2 9 16 23 30
Sat.	1 8 15 22 29	5 12 19 26	3 10 17 24 31

EASTER DAYS

March 27	1785, 1842, 1853, 1910, 1921, 2005
April 3	1825, 1831, 1983, 1994
April 10	1803, 1814, 1887, 1898, 1955, 1966, 1977, 2039
April 17	1870, 1881, 1927, 1938, 1949, 2022, 2033
April 24	1791, 1859, 2011

L (LEAP YEAR)

	January	February	March
Sun.	3 10 17 24 31	7 14 21 28	6 13 20 27
Mon.	4 11 18 25	1 8 15 22 29	7 14 21 28
Tue.	5 12 19 26	2 9 16 23	1 8 15 22 29
Wed.	6 13 20 27	3 10 17 24	2 9 16 23 30
Thur.	7 14 21 28	4 11 18 25	3 10 17 24 31
Fri.	1 8 15 22 29	5 12 19 26	4 11 18 25
Sat.	2 9 16 23 30	6 13 20 27	5 12 19 26

	April	May	June
Sun.	3 10 17 24	1 8 15 22 29	5 12 19 26
Mon.	4 11 18 25	2 9 16 23 30	6 13 20 27
Tue.	5 12 19 26	3 10 17 24 31	7 14 21 28
Wed.	6 13 20 27	4 11 18 25	1 8 15 22 29
Thur.	7 14 21 28	5 12 19 26	2 9 16 23 30
Fri.	1 8 15 22 29	6 13 20 27	3 10 17 24
Sat.	2 9 16 23 30	7 14 21 28	4 11 18 25

	July	August	September
Sun.	3 10 17 24 31	7 14 21 28	4 11 18 25
Mon.	4 11 18 25	1 8 15 22 29	5 12 19 26
Tue.	5 12 19 26	2 9 16 23 30	6 13 20 27
Wed.	6 13 20 27	3 10 17 24 31	7 14 21 28
Thur.	7 14 21 28	4 11 18 25	1 8 15 22 29
Fri.	1 8 15 22 29	5 12 19 26	2 9 16 23 30
Sat.	2 9 16 23 30	6 13 20 27	3 10 17 24

	October	November	December
Sun.	2 9 16 23 30	6 13 20 27	5 12 19 26
Mon.	3 10 17 24 31	7 14 21 28	6 13 20 27
Tue.	4 11 18 25	1 8 15 22 29	7 14 21 28
Wed.	5 12 19 26	2 9 16 23 30	1 8 15 22 29
Thur.	6 13 20 27	3 10 17 24	2 9 16 23 30
Fri.	7 14 21 28	4 11 18 25	3 10 17 24 31
Sat.	1 8 15 22 29	5 12 19 26	4 11 18 25

EASTER DAYS

March 27	1796, 1864, 1932, 2016
April 3	1836, 1904, 1988
April 17	1808, 1892, 1960

N (LEAP YEAR)

	January	February	March
Sun.	2 9 16 23 30	6 13 20 27	5 12 19 26
Mon.	3 10 17 24 31	7 14 21 28	6 13 20 27
Tue.	4 11 18 25	1 8 15 22 29	7 14 21 28
Wed.	5 12 19 26	2 9 16 23	1 8 15 22 29
Thur.	6 13 20 27	3 10 17 24	2 9 16 23 30
Fri.	7 14 21 28	4 11 18 25	3 10 17 24 31
Sat.	1 8 15 22 29	5 12 19 26	4 11 18 25

	April	May	June
Sun.	2 9 16 23 30	7 14 21 28	4 11 18 25
Mon.	3 10 17 24	1 8 15 22 29	5 12 19 26
Tue.	4 11 18 25	2 9 16 23 30	6 13 20 27
Wed.	5 12 19 26	3 10 17 24 31	7 14 21 28
Thur.	6 13 20 27	4 11 18 25	1 8 15 22 29
Fri.	7 14 21 28	5 12 19 26	2 9 16 23 30
Sat.	1 8 15 22 29	6 13 20 27	3 10 17 24

	July	August	September
Sun.	2 9 16 23 30	6 13 20 27	3 10 17 24
Mon.	3 10 17 24 31	7 14 21 28	4 11 18 25
Tue.	4 11 18 25	1 8 15 22 29	5 12 19 26
Wed.	5 12 19 26	2 9 16 23 30	6 13 20 27
Thur.	6 13 20 27	3 10 17 24 31	7 14 21 28
Fri.	7 14 21 28	4 11 18 25	1 8 15 22 29
Sat.	1 8 15 22 29	5 12 19 26	2 9 16 23 30

	October	November	December
Sun.	1 8 15 22 29	5 12 19 26	3 10 17 24 31
Mon.	2 9 16 23 30	6 13 20 27	4 11 18 25
Tue.	3 10 17 24 31	7 14 21 28	5 12 19 26
Wed.	4 11 18 25	1 8 15 22 29	6 13 20 27
Thur.	5 12 19 26	2 9 16 23 30	7 14 21 28
Fri.	6 13 20 27	3 10 17 24	1 8 15 22 29
Sat.	7 14 21 28	4 11 18 25	2 9 16 23 30

EASTER DAYS

March 26	1780
April 2	1820, 1972
April 9	1944
April 16	2028
April 23	1848, 1916, 2000

GEOLOGICAL TIME

The earth is thought to have come into existence approximately 4,600 million years ago, but for nearly half this time, the Archean era, it was uninhabited. Life is generally believed to have emerged in the succeeding Proterozoic era. The Archean and the Proterozoic eras are often together referred to as the Precambrian.

Although primitive forms of life, e.g. algae and bacteria, existed during the Proterozoic era, it is not until the strata of Palaeozoic rocks is reached that abundant fossilised remains appear.

Since the Precambrian, there have been three great geological eras:

PALAEOZOIC ('ancient life')
c.570–c.245 million years ago
Cambrian – Mainly sandstones, slate and shales; limestones in Scotland. Shelled fossils and invertebrates, e.g. trilobites and brachiopods appear
Ordovician – Mainly shales and mudstones, e.g. in north Wales; limestones in Scotland. First fishes
Silurian – Shales, mudstones and some limestones, found mostly in Wales and southern Scotland
Devonian – Old red sandstone, shale, limestone and slate, e.g. in south Wales and the West Country
Carboniferous – Coal-bearing rocks, millstone grit, limestone and shale. First traces of land-living life
Permian – Marls, sandstones and clays. First reptile fossils

There were two great phases of mountain building in the Palaeozoic era: the Caledonian, characterised in Britain by NE–SW lines of hills and valleys; and the later Hercyian, widespread in west Germany and adjacent areas, and in Britain exemplified in E.–W. lines of hills and valleys.

The end of the Palaeozoic era was marked by the extensive glaciations of the Permian period in the southern continents and the decline of amphibians. It was succeeded by an era of warm conditions.

MESOZOIC ('middle forms of life')
c. 245–c.65 million years ago
Triassic – Mostly sandstone, e.g. in the West Midlands
Jurassic – Mainly limestones and clays, typically displayed in the Jura mountains, and in England in a NE–SW belt from Lincolnshire and the Wash to the Severn and the Dorset coast
Cretaceous – Mainly chalk, clay and sands, e.g. in Kent and Sussex

Giant reptiles were dominant during the Mesozoic era, but it was at this time that marsupial mammals first appeared, as well as *Archaeopteryx lithographica*, the earliest known species of bird. Coniferous trees and flowering plants also developed during the era, and, with the birds and the mammals, were the main species to survive into the Cenozoic era. The giant reptiles became extinct.

CENOZOIC ('recent life')
from c. 65 million years ago
Palaeocene ⎫ The emergence of new forms of life,
Eocene ⎬ including existing species
Oligocene – Fossils of a few still existing species
Miocene – Fossil remains show a balance of existing and extinct species
Pliocene – Fossil remains show a majority of still existing species
Pleistocene – The majority of remains are those of still existing species

Holocene – The present, post-glacial period. Existing species only, except for a few exterminated by man.

In the last 25 million years, from the Miocene through the Pliocene periods, the Alpine-Himalayan and the circum-Pacific phases of mountain building reached their climax. During the Pleistocene period ice-sheets repeatedly locked up masses of water as land ice; its weight depressed the land, but the locking-up of the water lowered the sea-level by 100—200 metres. The glaciations and interglacials of the Ice Age are difficult to date and classify, but recent scientific opinion considers the Pleistocene period to have begun approximately 1.64 million years ago. The last glacial retreat, merging into the Holocene period, was 10,000 years ago.

HUMAN DEVELOPMENT

Any consideration of the history of mankind must start with the fact that all members of the human race belong to one species of animal, i.e. *Homo sapiens*, the definition of a species being in biological terms that all its members can interbreed. As a species of mammal it is possible to group man with other similar types, known as the primates. Amongst these is found a sub-group, the apes, which includes, in addition to man, the chimpanzees, gorillas, orang-utans and gibbons. All lack a tail, have shoulder blades at the back, and a Y-shaped chewing pattern on the surface of their molars, as well as showing the more general primate characteristics of four incisors, a thumb which is able to touch the fingers of the same hand, and finger and toe nails instead of claws. The factors available to scientific study suggest that human beings have chimpanzees and gorillas as their nearest relatives in the animal world. However, there remains the possibility that there once lived creatures, now extinct, which were closer to modern man than the chimpanzees and gorillas, and which shared with modern man the characteristics of having flat faces (i.e. the absence of a pronounced muzzle), being bipedal, and possessing large brains.

There are two broad groups of extinct apes recognised by specialists. The ramapithecines, the remains of which, mainly jaw fragments, have been found in east Africa, Asia, and Turkey. They lived about 14 to 8 million years ago, and from the evidence of their teeth it seems they chewed more in the manner of modern man than the other presently living apes. The second group, the australopithecines, have left more numerous remains amongst which sub-groups may be detected, although the geographic spread is limited to south and east Africa. Living between 5 and 1.5 million years ago, they were closer relatives of modern man to the extent that they walked upright, did not have an extensive muzzle and had similar types of pre-molars. The first australopithecine remains were recognised at Taung in South Africa in 1924 and subsequent discoveries include those at the Olduvai Gorge in Tanzania. The most impressive discovery was made at Hadar, Ethiopia, in 1974 when about half a skeleton, known as 'Lucy', was found.

Also in east Africa, between 2 million and 1.5 million years ago, lived a hominid group which not only walked upright, had a flat face, and a large brain case, but also made simple pebble and flake stone tools. On present evidence these habilines seem to have been the first people to make tools, however crude. This facility is related to the larger brain size and human beings are the only animals to make implements to be used in other processes. These early pebble tool users, because of their distinctive

GEOLOGICAL TIME

Era	Period	Epoch	Date began*	Evolutionary stages
Cenozoic	Quaternary	Holocene	0.01	Man
		Pleistocene	1.64	
	Tertiary	Pliocene	5.2	
		Miocene	23.3	
		Oligocene	35.4	
		Eocene	56.5	
		Palaeocene	65.0	
Mesozoic	Cretaceous		145.6	
	Jurassic		208.0	First birds
	Triassic		245.0	First mammals
Palaeozoic	Permian		290.0	First reptiles
	Carboniferous		362.5	First amphibians and insects
	Devonian		408.5	
	Silurian		439.0	
	Ordovician		510.0	First fishes
	Cambrian		570.0	First invertebrates
Precambrian			4,600.0	First primitive life forms e.g. algae and bacteria

* millions of years ago

characteristics, have been grouped as a separate sub-species, now extinct, of the genus Homo and are known as *Homo habilis*.

The use of fire, again a human characteristic, is associated with another group of extinct hominids whose remains, about a million years old, are found in south and east Africa, China, Indonesia, north Africa and Europe. Mastery of the techniques of making fire probably helped the colonisation of the colder northern areas and in this respect the site of Vertesszollos in Hungary is of particular importance. *Homo erectus* is the name given to this group of fossils and it includes a number of famous individual discoveries, e.g. Solo Man, Heidelberg Man, and especially Peking Man who lived at the cave site at Choukoutien which has yielded evidence of fire and burnt bone.

The well-known group Neanderthal Man, or *Homo sapiens neandertalensis*, is an extinct form of modern man who lived between about 100,000 and 40,000 years ago, thus spanning the last Ice Age. Indeed, its ability to adapt to the cold climate on the edge of the ice-sheets is one of its characteristic features, the remains being found only in Europe, Asia and the Middle East. Complete neanderthal skeletons were found during excavations at Tabun in Israel, together with evidence of tool-making and the use of fire. Distinguished by very large brains, it seems that neanderthal man was the first to develop recognisable social customs, especially deliberate burial rites. Why the neanderthals became extinct is not clear but it may be connected with the climatic changes at the end of the Ice Ages, which would have seriously affected their food supplies; possibly they became too specialised for their own good.

The Swanscombe skull is the only known human fossil remains found in England. Some specialists see Swanscombe Man (or, more probably, woman) as a neanderthal. Others group these remains together with the Steinheim skull from Germany, seeing both as a separate sub-species. There is too little evidence as yet on which to form a final judgement.

Modern Man, *Homo sapiens sapiens*, the surviving sub-species of *Homo sapiens*, had evolved to our present physical condition and had colonised much of the world by about 30,000 years ago. There are many previously distinguished individual specimens, e.g. Cromagnon Man, which may now be grouped together as *Homo sapiens sapiens*. It was modern man who spread to the American continent by crossing the landbridge between Siberia and Alaska and thence moved south through North America and into South America. Equally it is modern man who over the last 30,000 years has been responsible for the major developments in technology, art and civilisation generally.

One of the problems for those studying fossil man is the lack in many cases of sufficient quantities of fossil bone for analysis. It is important that theories should be tested against evidence, rather than the evidence being made to fit the theory. The Piltdown hoax is a well-known example of 'fossils' being forged to fit what was seen in some quarters as the correct theory of man's evolution.

CULTURAL DEVELOPMENT

The Eurocentric bias of early archaeologists meant that the search for a starting point for the development and transmission of cultural ideas, especially by migration, trade and warfare, concentrated unduly on Europe and the Near East. The Three Age system, whereby pre-history was divided into a Stone Age, a Bronze Age and an Iron Age, was devised by Christian Thomsen, curator of the National Museum of Denmark in the early 19th century, to facilitate the classification of the museum's collections. The descriptive adjectives referred to the materials from which the implements and weapons were made and came to be regarded as the dominant features of the societies to which they related. The refinement of the Three Age system once dominated archaeological thought and remains a generally accepted concept in the popular mind. However, it is now seen by archaeologists as an inadequate model for human development.

Common sense suggests that there were no complete breaks between one so-called Age and another, any more than contemporaries would have regarded 1485 as a complete break between medieval and modern English history. Nor can the Three Age system be applied universally. In some areas it is necessary to insert a Copper Age, while in Africa south of the Sahara there would seem to be no Bronze Age at all; in Australia, Old Stone Age societies survived, while in South America, New Stone Age communities existed into modern times. The civilisations in other parts of the world clearly invalidate a Eurocentric theory of human development.

The concept of the 'Neolithic revolution', associated with the domestication of plants and animals, was a development of particular importance in the human cultural pattern. It reflected change from the primitive hunter/gatherer economies to a more settled agricultural way of life and therefore, so the argument goes, made possible the development of urban civilisation. However, it can no longer be argued that this 'revolution' took place only in one area from which all development stemmed. Though it appears that the cultivation of wheat and barley was first undertaken, together with the domestication of cattle and goats/sheep in the Fertile Crescent (the area bounded by the rivers Tigris and Euphrates), there is evidence that rice was first deliberately planted and pigs domesticated in south-east Asia, maize first cultivated in Central America and llamas first domesticated in South America. It has been recognised in recent years that cultural changes can take place independently of each other in different parts of the world at different rates and different times. There is no need for a general diffusionist theory.

Although scholars will continue to study the particular societies which interest them, it may be possible to obtain a reliable chronological framework, in absolute terms of years, against which the cultural development of any particular area may be set. The development and refinement of radio-carbon dating and other scientific methods of producing absolute chronologies is enabling the cross-referencing of societies to be undertaken. As the techniques of dating become more rigorous in application and the number of scientifically obtained dates increases, the attainment of an absolute chronology for prehistoric societies throughout the world comes closer to being achieved.

Tidal Tables

CONSTANTS

The constant tidal difference may be used in conjunction with the time of high water at a standard port shown in the predictions data (pages100–105) to find the time of high water at any of the ports or places listed below.

These tidal differences are very approximate and should be used only as a guide to the time of high water at the places below. More precise local data should be obtained for navigational and other nautical purposes.

All data allow high water time to be found in Greenwich Mean Time; this applies to data for the months when British Summer Time is in operation and the hour's time difference should be allowed for. Ports marked * are in a different time zone and the standard time zone difference also needs to be added/subtracted to give local time.

EXAMPLE

Required time of high water at Stranraer at 2 January 2003

Appropriate time of high water at Greenock

Afternoon tide 2 January		1204hrs
Tidal difference		−0020hrs
High water at Stranraer		1144hrs

The columns headed 'Springs' and 'Neaps' show the height, in metres, of the tide above datum for mean high water springs and mean high water neaps respectively.

Port		Diff. h m	Spring m	Neaps m
Aberdeen	Leith	−1 19	4.4	3.4
*Antwerp (Prosperpolder)	London	+0 50	5.8	4.8
Ardrossan	Greenock	−0 15	3.2	2.6
Avonmouth	London	−6 45	12.2	9.8
Ayr	Greenock	−0 25	3.0	2.5
Barrow (Docks)	Liverpool	0 00	9.3	7.1
Belfast	London	−2 47	3.5	3.0
Blackpool	Liverpool	−0 10	8.9	7.0
*Boulogne	London	−2 44	8.9	7.2
*Calais	London	−2 04	7.2	5.9
*Cherbourg	London	−6 00	6.4	5.0
Cobh	Liverpool	−5 55	4.2	3.2
Cowes	London	−2 38	4.2	3.5
Dartmouth	London	+4 25	4.9	3.8
*Dieppe	London	−3 03	9.3	7.3
Douglas, IoM	Liverpool	−0 04	6.9	5.4
Dover	London	−2 52	6.7	5.3
Dublin	London	−2 05	4.1	3.4
Dun Loaghaire	London	−2 10	4.1	3.4
*Dunkirk	London	−1 54	6.0	4.9
Fishguard	Liverpool	−4 01	4.8	3.4
Fleetwood	Liverpool	0 00	9.2	7.3
*Flushing	London	−0 15	4.7	3.9
Folkestone	London	−3 04	7.1	5.7
Galway	Liverpool	−6 08	5.1	3.9
Glasgow	Greenock	+0 26	4.7	4.0
Harwich	London	−2 06	4.0	3.4
*Le Havre	London	−3 55	7.9	6.6
Heysham	Liverpool	+0 05	9.4	7.4
Holyhead	Liverpool	−0 50	5.6	4.4

*Hook of Holland	London	−0 01	2.1	1.7
Hull (Albert Dock)	London	−7 40	7.5	5.8
Immingham	London	−8 00	7.3	5.8
Larne	London	−2 40	2.8	2.5
Lerwick	Leith	−3 48	2.2	1.6
Londonderry	London	−5 37	2.7	2.1
Lowestoft	London	−4 25	2.4	2.1
Margate	London	−1 53	4.8	3.9
Milford Haven	Liverpool	−5 08	7.0	5.2
Morecambe	Liverpool	+0 07	9.5	7.4
Newhaven	London	−2 46	6.7	5.1
Oban	Greenock	+5 43	4.0	2.9
*Ostend	London	−1 32	5.1	4.2
Plymouth	London	−5 05	5.5	4.4
Portland	London	+5 09	2.1	1.4
Portsmouth	London	−2 38	4.7	3.8
Ramsgate	London	−2 32	5.2	4.1
Richmond Lock	London	+1 00	4.9	3.7
Rosslare Harbour	Liverpool	−5 24	1.9	1.4
Rosyth	Leith	+0 09	5.8	4.7
*Rotterdam	London	+1 45	2.0	1.7
St Helier	London	+4 48	11.0	8.1
St Malo	London	+4 27	12.2	9.2
St Peter Port	London	+4 54	9.3	7.0
Scrabster	Leith	−6 06	5.0	4.0
Sheerness	London	−1 19	5.8	4.7
Shoreham	London	−2 44	6.3	4.9
Southampton (1st high water)	London	−2 54	4.5	3.7
Spurn Head	London	−8 25	6.9	5.5
Stornoway	Liverpool	−4 16	4.8	3.7
Stranraer	Greenock	−0 20	3.0	2.4
Stromness	Leith	−5 26	3.6	2.7
Swansea	London	−7 35	9.5	7.2
Tees (River Entrance)	Leith	+1 09	5.5	4.3
Tilbury	London	−0 49	6.4	5.4
Tobermory	Liverpool	−5 11	4.4	3.3
Tyne River (North Shields)	London	−10 30	5.0	3.9
Ullapool	Leith	−7 40	5.2	3.9
Walton-on-the-Naze	London	−2 10	4.2	3.4
Wick	Leith	−3 26	3.5	2.8
Zeebrugge	London	−0 55	4.8	3.9

PREDICTIONS

The data on pages 100–105 are daily predictions of the time and height of high water at London Bridge, Liverpool, Greenock and Leith. The time of the data is Greenwich Mean Time; this applies also to data for the months when British Summer Time is in operation and the hour's time difference should be allowed for. The datum of predictions for each port shows the difference of height, in metres from Ordnance data (Newlyn)

The tidal information for London Bridge, Liverpool, Greenock and Leith is reproduced with the permission of the UK Hydrographic Office and the Controller of HMSO. Crown copyright reserved.

JANUARY 2003   *High Water*   GMT

	LONDON BRIDGE *Datum of Predictions 3.20m below						LIVERPOOL *Datum of Predictions 4.93m below						GREENOCK *Datum of Predictions 1.62m below						LEITH *Datum of Predictions 2.90m below					
	hr	m	ht	hr	m	ht	hr	m	ht	hr	m	ht	hr	m	ht	hr	m	ht	hr	m	ht	hr	m	ht
1 Wednesday	—	—		12	15	6.7	09	47	9.0	22	11	9.1	11	18	3.4	23	28	3.4	00	45	5.3	13	11	5.3
2 Thursday	00	48	6.8	13	10	6.9	10	35	9.3	23	01	9.2	—	—		12	04	3.5	01	39	5.5	13	59	5.4
3 Friday	01	38	6.9	14	02	7.0	11	21	9.5	23	47	9.2	00	21	3.4	12	48	3.6	02	30	5.5	14	46	5.5
4 Saturday	02	24	6.9	14	51	7.1	—	—		12	05	9.5	01	10	3.4	13	30	3.7	03	19	5.5	15	31	5.5
5 Sunday	03	07	6.8	15	37	7.0	00	31	9.1	12	48	9.4	01	57	3.4	14	10	3.7	04	06	5.4	16	15	5.5
6 Monday	03	47	6.7	16	20	6.9	01	13	8.9	13	29	9.2	02	40	3.3	14	50	3.7	04	52	5.3	16	58	5.3
7 Tuesday	04	23	6.6	17	00	6.7	01	53	8.6	14	10	9.0	03	22	3.3	15	29	3.7	05	36	5.1	17	41	5.2
8 Wednesday	04	58	6.5	17	38	6.4	02	33	8.3	14	50	8.7	04	03	3.2	16	10	3.6	06	20	4.8	18	25	5.0
9 Thursday	05	35	6.3	18	18	6.2	03	13	8.0	15	33	8.3	04	45	3.1	16	51	3.4	07	04	4.6	19	11	4.8
10 Friday	06	16	6.1	19	00	6.0	03	58	7.6	16	21	7.9	05	29	3.1	17	36	3.2	07	51	4.4	20	03	4.6
11 Saturday	07	06	5.9	19	50	5.8	04	52	7.3	17	17	7.6	06	15	3.0	18	25	3.1	08	42	4.3	20	59	4.4
12 Sunday	08	05	5.7	20	47	5.7	05	57	7.1	18	23	7.4	07	04	2.9	19	20	2.9	09	38	4.3	21	59	4.4
13 Monday	09	11	5.6	21	51	5.7	07	07	7.2	19	31	7.5	08	03	2.9	20	30	2.9	10	37	4.3	23	01	4.4
14 Tuesday	10	20	5.7	22	55	5.9	08	10	7.5	20	32	7.8	09	16	2.9	21	52	2.9	11	39	4.5	—	—	
15 Wednesday	11	22	5.9	23	52	6.1	09	02	7.9	21	23	8.1	10	23	3.1	22	52	2.9	00	04	4.5	12	37	4.7
16 Thursday	—	—		12	18	6.2	09	47	8.4	22	08	8.4	11	11	3.2	23	39	3.0	01	00	4.7	13	26	4.9
17 Friday	00	43	6.4	13	08	6.4	10	28	8.7	22	50	8.7	11	50	3.3	—	—		01	47	4.9	14	08	5.1
18 Saturday	01	29	6.5	13	54	6.7	11	09	9.0	23	32	8.9	00	21	3.1	12	28	3.4	02	28	5.1	14	46	5.2
19 Sunday	02	13	6.7	14	38	6.8	11	50	9.2	—	—		01	04	3.1	13	07	3.5	03	07	5.3	15	23	5.4
20 Monday	02	54	6.7	15	22	7.0	00	14	9.1	12	32	9.4	01	47	3.1	13	46	3.6	03	46	5.4	16	00	5.5
21 Tuesday	03	34	6.8	16	05	7.0	00	57	9.2	13	15	9.4	02	29	3.1	14	27	3.7	04	26	5.5	16	39	5.5
22 Wednesday	04	13	6.8	16	48	7.0	01	41	9.2	13	59	9.4	03	11	3.1	15	08	3.7	05	08	5.5	17	21	5.5
23 Thursday	04	53	6.8	17	32	6.9	02	25	9.1	14	44	9.3	03	53	3.1	15	50	3.7	05	52	5.3	18	05	5.4
24 Friday	05	36	6.7	18	19	6.7	03	11	8.8	15	32	9.0	04	36	3.1	16	34	3.6	06	40	5.1	18	54	5.2
25 Saturday	06	21	6.5	19	09	6.4	04	01	8.5	16	24	8.6	05	22	3.0	17	23	3.4	07	33	4.9	19	52	5.0
26 Sunday	07	15	6.3	20	08	6.1	04	59	8.1	17	26	8.2	06	13	2.9	18	17	3.3	08	35	4.7	21	02	4.9
27 Monday	08	22	6.0	21	18	5.9	06	08	7.8	18	39	7.9	07	14	2.9	19	22	3.1	09	44	4.6	22	19	4.8
28 Tuesday	09	41	5.9	22	30	5.9	07	26	7.8	19	59	8.0	08	50	2.9	21	00	3.0	10	55	4.6	23	33	4.8
29 Wednesday	10	58	6.0	23	35	6.1	08	39	8.1	21	10	8.3	10	09	3.0	22	26	3.0	—	—		12	04	4.8
30 Thursday	—	—		12	04	6.3	09	38	8.6	22	07	8.6	11	05	3.2	23	27	3.1	00	41	5.0	13	05	5.0
31 Friday	00	33	6.4	13	02	6.6	10	28	9.0	22	56	8.9	11	53	3.4	—	—		01	39	5.2	13	55	5.2

FEBRUARY 2003   *High Water*   GMT

	LONDON BRIDGE						LIVERPOOL						GREENOCK						LEITH					
1 Saturday	01	25	6.6	13	54	6.9	11	12	9.3	23	39	9.0	00	20	3.2	12	38	3.5	02	28	5.3	14	40	5.4
2 Sunday	02	11	6.7	14	41	7.0	11	54	9.4	—	—		01	08	3.2	13	19	3.6	03	12	5.3	15	21	5.4
3 Monday	02	54	6.8	15	24	6.9	00	18	9.1	12	33	9.4	01	50	3.2	13	58	3.6	03	52	5.3	15	59	5.5
4 Tuesday	03	31	6.7	16	02	6.8	00	55	9.0	13	09	9.4	02	27	3.2	14	35	3.6	04	30	5.2	16	36	5.4
5 Wednesday	04	04	6.6	16	36	6.7	01	29	8.8	13	45	9.2	03	02	3.2	15	10	3.6	05	06	5.1	17	11	5.3
6 Thursday	04	35	6.6	17	07	6.6	02	03	8.6	14	20	8.9	03	35	3.2	15	44	3.5	05	42	4.9	17	47	5.1
7 Friday	05	07	6.5	17	40	6.4	02	37	8.4	14	55	8.6	04	09	3.2	16	19	3.4	06	20	4.7	18	25	4.9
8 Saturday	05	44	6.4	18	17	6.3	03	13	8.0	15	34	8.1	04	45	3.1	16	55	3.2	07	00	4.5	19	09	4.6
9 Sunday	06	25	6.2	18	58	6.1	03	54	7.6	16	20	7.7	05	24	3.0	17	37	3.0	07	46	4.4	19	59	4.4
10 Monday	07	13	5.9	19	47	5.8	04	46	7.2	17	18	7.3	06	08	2.9	18	26	2.8	08	41	4.2	21	00	4.2
11 Tuesday	08	10	5.7	20	46	5.6	05	55	7.0	18	31	7.1	07	01	2.8	19	28	2.7	09	43	4.1	22	10	4.1
12 Wednesday	09	17	5.5	21	57	5.6	07	17	7.1	19	50	7.3	08	08	2.8	20	51	2.6	10	51	4.2	23	24	4.2
13 Thursday	10	35	5.6	23	14	5.8	08	29	7.5	20	56	7.7	09	28	2.8	22	25	2.8	—	—		12	01	4.4
14 Friday	11	47	6.0	—	—		09	24	8.1	21	49	8.2	10	39	3.0	23	23	2.9	00	33	4.5	13	01	4.7
15 Saturday	00	16	6.1	12	46	6.4	10	09	8.6	22	34	8.7	11	26	3.2	—	—		01	26	4.8	13	47	5.0
16 Sunday	01	09	6.5	13	36	6.7	10	52	9.1	23	17	9.1	00	09	3.0	12	08	3.4	02	09	5.2	14	27	5.3
17 Monday	01	56	6.7	14	23	7.0	11	34	9.4	23	59	9.4	00	53	3.1	12	49	3.5	02	49	5.4	15	04	5.5
18 Tuesday	02	39	6.9	15	07	7.2	—	—		12	16	9.7	01	35	3.1	13	30	3.6	03	27	5.6	15	41	5.7
19 Wednesday	03	20	7.0	15	49	7.3	00	41	9.6	12	59	9.9	02	15	3.2	14	12	3.7	04	06	5.7	16	20	5.8
20 Thursday	03	58	7.1	16	31	7.2	01	23	9.6	13	41	9.9	02	53	3.2	14	52	3.8	04	47	5.7	16	59	5.8
21 Friday	04	37	7.1	17	12	7.1	02	05	9.5	14	24	9.6	03	29	3.2	15	33	3.8	05	30	5.5	17	45	5.6
22 Saturday	05	17	7.0	17	55	6.8	02	48	9.1	15	09	9.2	04	06	3.2	16	14	3.7	06	16	5.2	18	33	5.4
23 Sunday	06	00	6.8	18	40	6.4	03	34	8.6	15	58	8.8	04	44	3.1	16	58	3.5	07	05	4.9	19	24	5.0
24 Monday	06	48	6.4	19	31	5.9	04	27	8.1	16	59	7.9	05	30	3.0	17	47	3.2	08	04	4.6	20	42	4.7
25 Tuesday	07	50	5.9	20	43	5.5	05	38	7.5	18	19	7.4	06	24	2.8	18	46	2.9	09	17	4.4	22	06	4.5
26 Wednesday	09	22	5.5	22	08	5.5	07	07	7.4	19	54	7.4	07	54	2.7	20	56	2.7	10	37	4.4	23	30	4.6
27 Thursday	10	49	5.8	23	19	5.8	08	29	7.8	21	07	7.9	09	56	2.9	22	30	2.8	11	56	4.6	—	—	
28 Friday	11	55	6.2	—	—		09	29	8.3	22	01	8.4	10	53	3.1	23	27	3.0	00	43	4.8	13	01	4.9

MARCH 2003 *High Water* GMT

		LONDON BRIDGE				LIVERPOOL				GREENOCK				LEITH			
		*Datum of predictions 3.20m below				*Datum of predictions 4.93m below				*Datum of predictions 1.62m below				*Datum of predictions 2.90m below			
		hr m	ht	hr m	ht	hr m	ht	hr m	ht	hr m	ht	hr m	ht	hr m	ht	hr m	ht
1	Saturday	00 18	6.2	12 52	6.6	10 17	8.8	22 45	8.7	11 41	3.3	—	—	01 38	5.0	13 49	5.1
2	Sunday	01 10	6.5	13 42	6.9	10 59	9.2	23 24	9.0	00 14	3.1	12 24	3.4	02 22	5.2	14 30	5.3
3	Monday	01 56	6.7	14 26	7.0	11 37	9.4	23 59	9.0	00 57	3.1	13 04	3.5	02 58	5.2	15 05	5.4
4	Tuesday	02 37	6.8	15 06	6.9	—	—	12 12	9.4	01 33	3.1	13 41	3.5	03 32	5.3	15 38	5.4
5	Wednesday	03 12	6.7	15 39	6.8	00 30	9.0	12 45	9.3	02 05	3.1	14 15	3.5	04 04	5.2	16 10	5.4
6	Thursday	03 41	6.7	16 06	6.7	01 01	8.9	13 17	9.2	02 33	3.1	14 46	3.4	04 35	5.1	16 41	5.3
7	Friday	04 09	6.6	16 33	6.6	01 32	8.8	13 49	8.9	03 02	3.2	15 16	3.4	05 07	5.0	17 14	5.1
8	Saturday	04 39	6.6	17 04	6.6	02 02	8.6	14 20	8.6	03 31	3.2	15 47	3.3	05 41	4.8	17 50	4.9
9	Sunday	05 13	6.5	17 39	6.5	02 34	8.3	14 55	8.2	04 03	3.2	16 21	3.2	06 19	4.7	18 29	4.7
10	Monday	05 51	6.3	18 18	6.2	03 08	7.9	15 35	7.7	04 39	3.1	16 59	3.0	07 00	4.4	19 15	4.4
11	Tuesday	06 35	6.1	19 04	5.9	03 53	7.4	16 28	7.2	05 20	2.9	17 47	2.8	07 50	4.2	20 12	4.2
12	Wednesday	07 28	5.8	19 59	5.6	04 56	7.0	17 42	6.9	06 12	2.7	18 49	2.6	08 53	4.1	21 25	4.1
13	Thursday	08 32	5.6	21 07	5.5	06 23	6.8	19 12	6.9	07 19	2.6	20 12	2.5	10 08	4.1	22 46	4.2
14	Friday	09 51	5.6	22 34	5.6	07 53	7.2	20 30	7.5	08 44	2.7	22 00	2.6	11 26	4.3	—	—
15	Saturday	11 18	5.9	23 49	6.0	08 56	7.9	21 26	8.2	10 04	2.9	23 03	2.8	00 02	4.5	12 31	4.6
16	Sunday	—	—	12 22	6.4	09 45	8.6	22 12	8.8	10 57	3.1	23 49	3.0	01 00	4.9	13 20	5.0
17	Monday	00 44	6.4	13 14	6.8	10 29	9.2	22 55	9.3	11 42	3.3	—	—	01 44	5.3	14 00	5.4
18	Tuesday	01 32	6.8	14 01	7.2	11 12	9.7	23 37	9.6	00 32	3.1	12 26	3.5	02 24	5.6	14 38	5.7
19	Wednesday	02 16	7.0	14 45	7.3	11 54	10.0	—	—	01 13	3.2	13 09	3.6	03 03	5.8	15 16	5.9
20	Thursday	02 57	7.2	15 27	7.4	00 19	9.8	12 37	10.1	01 51	3.2	13 52	3.7	03 42	5.8	15 57	6.0
21	Friday	03 37	7.3	16 08	7.3	01 01	9.8	13 20	10.0	02 27	3.3	14 34	3.8	04 23	5.8	16 40	5.9
22	Saturday	04 17	7.3	16 49	7.1	01 42	9.6	14 03	9.7	03 01	3.4	15 14	3.8	05 06	5.6	17 26	5.7
23	Sunday	04 58	7.2	17 29	6.8	02 25	9.2	14 48	9.1	03 33	3.3	15 55	3.6	05 52	5.3	18 17	5.4
24	Monday	05 41	6.9	18 11	6.3	03 10	8.7	15 38	8.4	04 15	3.2	16 38	3.4	06 41	4.9	19 17	4.9
25	Tuesday	06 30	6.4	18 59	5.8	04 03	8.0	16 41	7.6	04 59	3.1	17 27	3.0	07 41	4.6	20 33	4.6
26	Wednesday	07 35	5.8	20 12	5.4	05 18	7.4	18 10	7.1	05 54	2.8	18 29	2.7	08 59	4.3	21 57	4.4
27	Thursday	09 16	5.6	21 49	5.4	06 52	7.3	19 45	7.2	07 19	2.7	21 10	2.6	10 23	4.3	23 23	4.5
28	Friday	10 36	5.8	22 59	5.7	08 11	7.7	20 52	7.7	09 37	2.8	22 23	2.8	11 43	4.5	—	—
29	Saturday	11 39	6.3	23 57	6.2	09 09	8.2	21 42	8.2	10 34	3.1	23 13	2.9	00 34	4.7	12 46	4.8
30	Sunday	—	—	12 32	6.7	09 56	8.7	22 24	8.6	11 20	3.3	23 55	3.0	01 24	5.0	13 32	5.1
31	Monday	00 47	6.6	13 21	7.0	10 37	9.0	23 00	8.9	—	—	12 02	3.4	02 04	5.1	14 10	5.2

APRIL 2003 *High Water* GMT

		LONDON BRIDGE				LIVERPOOL				GREENOCK				LEITH			
		hr m	ht	hr m	ht	hr m	ht	hr m	ht	hr m	ht	hr m	ht	hr m	ht	hr m	ht
1	Tuesday	01 33	6.8	14 03	7.0	11 13	9.2	23 32	8.9	00 33	3.1	12 42	3.4	02 37	5.2	14 43	5.3
2	Wednesday	02 13	6.8	14 40	6.9	11 46	9.2	—	—	01 06	3.1	13 17	3.3	03 07	5.2	15 13	5.4
3	Thursday	02 47	6.7	15 10	6.7	00 02	8.9	12 18	9.1	01 35	3.1	13 49	3.3	03 35	5.2	15 43	5.3
4	Friday	03 16	6.6	15 35	6.6	00 32	8.9	12 48	9.0	02 01	3.1	14 17	3.3	04 04	5.1	16 13	5.2
5	Saturday	03 43	6.6	16 01	6.6	01 01	8.8	13 18	8.8	02 28	3.2	14 47	3.2	04 35	5.0	16 47	5.1
6	Sunday	04 12	6.6	16 31	6.6	01 30	8.6	13 49	8.6	02 56	3.3	15 18	3.2	05 09	4.9	17 22	4.9
7	Monday	04 45	6.5	17 05	6.5	02 00	8.4	14 23	8.2	03 27	3.2	15 52	3.1	05 44	4.7	18 02	4.7
8	Tuesday	05 23	6.4	17 45	6.3	02 34	8.0	15 03	7.8	04 01	3.1	16 31	2.9	06 24	4.5	18 47	4.5
9	Wednesday	06 08	6.2	18 30	6.0	03 11	7.6	15 55	7.3	04 39	3.0	17 19	2.7	07 11	4.3	19 42	4.2
10	Thursday	07 01	5.9	19 25	5.7	04 17	7.1	17 06	6.9	05 28	2.8	18 24	2.5	08 11	4.1	20 51	4.1
11	Friday	08 05	5.7	20 32	5.5	05 40	6.9	18 36	7.0	06 37	2.6	19 49	2.5	09 29	4.1	22 11	4.2
12	Saturday	09 21	5.7	21 56	5.6	07 12	7.2	19 57	7.5	08 03	2.7	21 27	2.6	10 48	4.3	23 26	4.6
13	Sunday	10 47	6.0	23 13	6.0	08 21	7.9	20 55	8.2	09 26	2.9	22 33	2.8	11 54	4.6	—	—
14	Monday	11 53	6.5	—	—	09 14	8.7	21 43	8.9	10 25	3.1	23 21	3.0	00 25	5.0	12 45	5.1
15	Tuesday	00 11	6.5	12 46	6.9	10 01	9.3	22 27	9.4	11 14	3.3	—	—	01 13	5.3	13 28	5.4
16	Wednesday	01 01	6.8	13 34	7.2	10 45	9.8	23 11	9.8	00 04	3.1	12 00	3.5	01 55	5.6	14 09	5.8
17	Thursday	01 47	7.1	14 19	7.4	11 30	10.0	23 53	9.9	00 45	3.2	12 46	3.6	02 35	5.8	14 51	6.0
18	Friday	02 32	7.3	15 03	7.4	—	—	12 14	10.1	01 24	3.3	13 31	3.7	03 17	5.9	15 35	6.0
19	Saturday	03 15	7.4	15 45	7.3	00 36	9.9	12 59	9.9	02 02	3.4	14 14	3.6	04 00	5.8	16 22	5.9
20	Sunday	03 59	7.4	16 26	7.1	01 20	9.6	13 44	9.5	02 37	3.5	14 57	3.6	04 44	5.6	17 12	5.6
21	Monday	04 43	7.2	17 07	6.8	02 04	9.2	14 31	8.9	03 14	3.4	15 40	3.5	05 31	5.3	18 06	5.3
22	Tuesday	05 29	6.8	17 49	6.4	02 52	8.6	15 24	8.1	03 49	3.3	16 23	3.3	06 23	4.9	19 10	4.9
23	Wednesday	06 21	6.3	18 37	5.9	03 48	8.0	16 30	7.5	04 39	3.1	17 20	2.9	07 26	4.6	20 23	4.6
24	Thursday	07 32	5.9	19 54	5.5	05 03	7.5	17 55	7.1	05 37	2.9	18 33	2.7	08 43	4.4	21 40	4.4
25	Friday	09 02	5.7	21 23	5.6	06 27	7.4	19 17	7.2	07 03	2.8	20 48	2.6	10 01	4.4	22 59	4.5
26	Saturday	10 12	6.0	22 30	5.8	07 39	7.7	20 20	7.6	09 04	2.9	21 56	2.8	11 16	4.5	—	—
27	Sunday	11 11	6.3	23 26	6.2	08 37	8.1	21 10	8.0	10 04	3.0	22 43	2.9	00 06	4.7	12 17	4.8
28	Monday	—	—	12 04	6.7	09 25	8.5	21 52	8.4	10 51	3.2	23 23	3.0	00 56	4.8	13 03	5.0
29	Tuesday	00 17	6.5	12 51	6.9	10 06	8.8	22 28	8.6	11 33	3.2	23 59	3.0	01 35	5.0	13 42	5.1
30	Wednesday	01 03	6.7	13 33	6.9	10 43	8.9	23 01	8.8	—	—	12 12	3.2	02 08	5.1	14 15	5.2

MAY 2003   *High Water*   GMT

		London Bridge *Datum of Predictions 3.20m below hr m	ht	hr m	ht	Liverpool *Datum of Predictions 4.93m below hr m	ht	hr m	ht	Greenock *Datum of Predictions 1.62m below hr m	ht	hr m	ht	Leith *Datum of Predictions 2.90m below hr m	ht	hr m	ht
1	Thursday	01 43	6.7	14 08	6.8	11 17	8.9	23 31	8.8	00 32	3.1	12 48	3.2	02 37	5.1	14 46	5.2
2	Friday	02 18	6.7	14 38	6.7	11 49	8.9	—	—	01 02	3.1	13 19	3.1	03 06	5.2	15 17	5.2
3	Saturday	02 49	6.6	15 04	6.6	00 01	8.8	12 20	8.8	01 29	3.2	13 48	3.1	03 36	5.1	15 49	5.1
4	Sunday	03 18	6.5	15 32	6.6	00 31	8.7	12 51	8.7	01 57	3.2	14 19	3.1	04 07	5.1	16 24	5.0
5	Monday	03 49	6.5	16 04	6.6	01 02	8.6	13 24	8.5	02 27	3.3	14 54	3.0	04 41	5.0	17 01	4.9
6	Tuesday	04 24	6.5	16 39	6.5	01 35	8.4	14 01	8.2	02 59	3.3	15 31	2.9	05 17	4.8	17 42	4.7
7	Wednesday	05 04	6.4	17 19	6.3	02 12	8.2	14 43	7.9	03 34	3.2	16 13	2.8	05 57	4.7	18 27	4.6
8	Thursday	05 50	6.2	18 05	6.0	02 57	7.8	15 35	7.5	04 11	3.0	17 05	2.7	06 43	4.5	19 20	4.4
9	Friday	06 44	6.0	19 00	5.8	03 56	7.5	16 41	7.2	04 59	2.9	18 12	2.6	07 40	4.3	20 23	4.4
10	Saturday	07 47	5.9	20 06	5.7	05 11	7.3	18 01	7.3	06 07	2.8	19 28	2.6	08 53	4.3	21 37	4.5
11	Sunday	09 00	5.9	21 23	5.8	06 30	7.6	19 17	7.7	07 28	2.8	20 48	2.7	10 09	4.5	22 47	4.7
12	Monday	10 16	6.2	22 35	6.1	07 40	8.1	20 19	8.3	08 47	2.9	21 56	2.8	11 14	4.8	23 48	5.0
13	Tuesday	11 20	6.6	23 36	6.5	08 39	8.7	21 11	8.9	09 51	3.1	22 48	3.0	—	—	12 08	5.1
14	Wednesday	—	—	12 16	7.0	09 30	9.3	21 59	9.4	10 44	3.3	23 34	3.1	00 39	5.3	12 56	5.5
15	Thursday	00 29	6.9	13 06	7.2	10 19	9.7	22 44	9.7	11 34	3.5	—	—	01 25	5.6	13 42	5.7
16	Friday	01 20	7.1	13 54	7.3	11 06	9.8	23 29	9.8	00 17	3.2	12 22	3.5	02 09	5.7	14 29	5.9
17	Saturday	02 09	7.3	14 40	7.3	11 53	9.8	—	—	00 59	3.4	13 10	3.6	02 53	5.8	15 17	5.9
18	Sunday	02 56	7.4	15 24	7.2	00 15	9.7	12 41	9.6	01 39	3.5	13 58	3.6	03 38	5.7	16 08	5.8
19	Monday	03 44	7.3	16 07	7.0	01 01	9.5	13 29	9.2	02 18	3.5	14 44	3.5	04 25	5.5	17 01	5.5
20	Tuesday	04 31	7.1	16 50	6.7	01 48	9.1	14 19	8.7	02 58	3.5	15 31	3.3	05 15	5.3	17 57	5.2
21	Wednesday	05 20	6.8	17 33	6.4	02 38	8.7	15 12	8.1	03 40	3.4	16 22	3.1	06 09	5.0	18 58	4.9
22	Thursday	06 14	6.4	18 22	6.0	03 33	8.2	16 13	7.6	04 28	3.2	17 20	2.9	07 11	4.8	20 03	4.6
23	Friday	07 20	6.1	19 30	5.7	04 39	7.8	17 24	7.3	05 33	3.0	18 28	2.7	08 20	4.6	21 09	4.5
24	Saturday	08 33	5.9	20 47	5.7	05 51	7.6	18 35	7.2	06 38	2.9	19 47	2.7	09 28	4.5	22 16	4.4
25	Sunday	09 38	6.0	21 51	5.8	06 57	7.7	19 37	7.4	08 10	2.9	21 03	2.7	10 34	4.5	23 21	4.5
26	Monday	10 35	6.2	22 48	6.1	07 56	7.9	20 29	7.8	09 22	3.0	21 57	2.8	11 34	4.6	—	—
27	Tuesday	11 27	6.5	23 40	6.3	08 47	8.1	21 14	8.1	10 14	3.0	22 42	2.9	00 14	4.6	12 25	4.8
28	Wednesday	—	—	12 14	6.6	09 31	8.4	21 53	8.4	10 59	3.1	23 21	3.0	00 58	4.8	13 07	4.9
29	Thursday	00 27	6.5	12 57	6.7	10 11	8.5	22 28	8.5	11 40	3.0	23 58	3.1	01 34	4.9	13 45	5.0
30	Friday	01 10	6.6	13 34	6.7	10 47	8.6	23 01	8.6	—	—	12 16	3.0	02 07	5.0	14 20	5.0
31	Saturday	01 49	6.6	14 07	6.6	11 21	8.6	23 33	8.7	00 30	3.1	12 50	3.0	02 39	5.1	14 54	5.0

JUNE 2003   *High Water*   GMT

		London Bridge hr m	ht	hr m	ht	Liverpool hr m	ht	hr m	ht	Greenock hr m	ht	hr m	ht	Leith hr m	ht	hr m	ht
1	Sunday	02 24	6.5	14 39	6.6	11 55	8.6	—	—	01 00	3.2	13 22	2.9	03 11	5.1	15 29	5.0
2	Monday	02 58	6.5	15 11	6.5	00 06	8.7	12 30	8.5	01 31	3.3	13 57	2.9	03 45	5.1	16 06	5.0
3	Tuesday	03 33	6.5	15 45	6.5	00 41	8.6	13 07	8.5	02 04	3.3	14 36	2.9	04 20	5.0	16 44	5.0
4	Wednesday	04 11	6.5	16 22	6.4	01 19	8.5	13 47	8.3	02 39	3.3	15 18	2.9	04 57	4.9	17 25	4.9
5	Thursday	04 53	6.5	17 02	6.3	02 00	8.4	14 31	8.1	03 16	3.3	16 04	2.8	05 37	4.8	18 10	4.8
6	Friday	05 39	6.4	17 48	6.2	02 47	8.2	15 21	7.9	03 56	3.2	16 57	2.7	06 23	4.7	19 00	4.7
7	Saturday	06 31	6.2	18 41	6.1	03 42	8.0	16 20	7.7	04 44	3.1	17 57	2.7	07 15	4.6	19 57	4.6
8	Sunday	07 31	6.2	19 43	6.0	04 45	7.9	17 27	7.7	05 44	3.0	19 01	2.7	08 18	4.6	21 03	4.7
9	Monday	08 37	6.2	20 52	6.1	05 53	8.0	18 37	7.9	06 53	2.9	20 07	2.7	09 28	4.7	22 09	4.8
10	Tuesday	09 45	6.3	22 00	6.2	07 00	8.3	19 42	8.3	08 08	3.0	21 15	2.8	10 34	4.9	23 12	5.0
11	Wednesday	10 49	6.5	23 04	6.5	08 04	8.6	20 40	8.7	09 18	3.1	22 15	2.9	11 34	5.1	—	—
12	Thursday	11 48	6.8	—	—	09 02	9.0	21 33	9.1	10 18	3.3	23 07	3.1	00 07	5.2	12 29	5.4
13	Friday	00 03	6.8	12 42	7.0	09 56	9.3	22 22	9.4	11 12	3.3	23 55	3.2	00 59	5.4	13 22	5.6
14	Saturday	00 58	7.0	13 32	7.1	10 48	9.4	23 10	9.5	—	—	12 04	3.4	01 47	5.5	14 14	5.7
15	Sunday	01 51	7.1	14 20	7.1	11 38	9.4	23 58	9.5	00 40	3.3	12 56	3.4	02 34	5.6	15 04	5.7
16	Monday	02 43	7.2	15 07	7.0	—	—	12 28	9.3	01 23	3.4	13 47	3.3	03 22	5.6	15 58	5.6
17	Tuesday	03 32	7.2	15 52	6.9	00 45	9.4	13 17	9.0	02 05	3.5	14 37	3.3	04 11	5.5	16 50	5.5
18	Wednesday	04 21	7.1	16 35	6.8	01 34	9.2	14 05	8.7	02 47	3.5	15 26	3.2	05 00	5.3	17 43	5.2
19	Thursday	05 10	6.9	17 18	6.5	02 22	8.9	14 53	8.3	03 30	3.5	16 16	3.1	05 52	5.1	18 37	4.9
20	Friday	05 59	6.6	18 03	6.3	03 11	8.5	15 43	7.9	04 16	3.4	17 06	3.0	06 47	4.9	19 31	4.7
21	Saturday	06 52	6.3	18 53	6.1	04 03	8.1	16 37	7.5	05 06	3.2	17 57	2.9	07 44	4.6	20 26	4.5
22	Sunday	07 49	6.1	19 54	5.9	05 01	7.8	17 38	7.3	06 02	3.0	18 49	2.8	08 42	4.6	21 22	4.4
23	Monday	08 49	5.9	20 58	5.8	06 03	7.6	18 41	7.3	07 04	2.9	19 43	2.8	09 39	4.5	22 18	4.3
24	Tuesday	09 47	5.9	21 59	5.9	07 05	7.6	19 40	7.4	08 15	2.8	20 45	2.8	10 37	4.5	23 16	4.4
25	Wednesday	10 41	6.1	22 56	6.0	08 02	7.7	20 32	7.7	09 26	2.8	21 49	2.8	11 34	4.5	—	—
26	Thursday	11 31	6.2	23 49	6.2	08 53	7.9	21 17	8.0	10 22	2.9	22 41	2.9	00 09	4.6	12 28	4.6
27	Friday	—	—	12 17	6.4	09 38	8.1	21 58	8.3	11 08	2.9	23 25	3.0	00 57	4.7	13 15	4.7
28	Saturday	00 37	6.3	13 01	6.5	10 19	8.3	22 35	8.4	11 48	2.9	—	—	01 38	4.9	13 56	4.9
29	Sunday	01 21	6.4	13 41	6.6	10 58	8.4	23 12	8.6	00 02	3.1	12 26	2.9	02 15	5.0	14 35	5.0
30	Monday	02 03	6.5	14 19	6.6	11 36	8.5	23 48	8.7	00 36	3.2	13 03	2.9	02 52	5.1	15 12	5.0

JULY 2003 *High Water* GMT

	LONDON BRIDGE				LIVERPOOL				GREENOCK				LEITH			
	*Datum of Predictions 3.20m below				*Datum of Predictions 4.93m below				*Datum of Predictions 1.62m below				*Datum of Predictions 2.90m below			
	hr m	ht	hr m	ht	hr m	ht	hr m	ht	hr m	ht	hr m	ht	hr m	ht	hr m	ht
1 Tuesday	02 42	6.6	14 57	6.6	—	—	12 14	8.5	01 10	3.3	13 43	2.9	03 27	5.1	15 50	5.1
2 Wednesday	03 22	6.6	15 34	6.6	00 26	8.8	12 55	8.6	01 46	3.3	14 25	2.9	04 04	5.1	16 28	5.1
3 Thursday	04 02	6.6	16 11	6.5	01 07	8.8	13 36	8.6	02 23	3.4	15 09	2.9	04 41	5.1	17 08	5.1
4 Friday	04 44	6.7	16 51	6.5	01 50	8.8	14 19	8.5	03 02	3.4	15 54	2.9	05 20	5.1	17 51	5.1
5 Saturday	05 28	6.6	17 34	6.5	02 35	8.7	15 05	8.4	03 44	3.3	16 42	2.8	06 03	5.0	18 38	5.0
6 Sunday	06 16	6.5	18 21	6.4	03 24	8.6	15 56	8.2	04 29	3.3	17 32	2.8	06 51	5.0	19 30	4.9
7 Monday	07 10	6.4	19 16	6.3	04 18	8.4	16 53	8.0	05 20	3.2	18 24	2.8	07 45	4.9	20 29	4.8
8 Tuesday	08 09	6.2	20 18	6.2	05 19	8.3	17 58	8.0	06 19	3.1	19 22	2.8	08 49	4.9	21 33	4.8
9 Wednesday	09 14	6.2	21 27	6.2	06 24	8.2	19 07	8.0	07 26	3.0	20 31	2.8	09 59	4.9	22 39	4.8
10 Thursday	10 21	6.2	22 37	6.3	07 34	8.3	20 14	8.3	08 44	3.0	21 46	2.9	11 07	5.0	23 41	5.0
11 Friday	11 24	6.4	23 43	6.5	08 42	8.5	21 14	8.7	09 57	3.1	22 48	3.0	—	—	12 12	5.1
12 Saturday	—	—	12 22	6.6	09 43	8.8	22 09	9.0	10 59	3.2	23 40	3.2	00 40	5.1	13 12	5.3
13 Sunday	00 44	6.7	13 16	6.8	10 38	9.0	22 59	9.3	11 56	3.2	—	—	01 34	5.3	14 07	5.5
14 Monday	01 40	6.9	14 06	6.9	11 29	9.1	23 46	9.4	00 27	3.3	12 50	3.2	02 23	5.4	14 59	5.5
15 Tuesday	02 33	7.1	14 53	6.9	—	—	12 17	9.1	01 12	3.4	13 43	3.2	03 11	5.5	15 47	5.5
16 Wednesday	03 22	7.1	15 37	6.9	00 32	9.4	13 03	9.0	01 55	3.5	14 31	3.2	03 57	5.5	16 35	5.4
17 Thursday	04 09	7.1	16 18	6.8	01 17	9.3	13 46	8.8	02 36	3.5	15 15	3.1	04 43	5.4	17 20	5.2
18 Friday	04 52	6.9	16 57	6.7	01 59	9.1	14 26	8.5	03 17	3.5	15 56	3.1	05 28	5.3	18 05	5.0
19 Saturday	05 33	6.7	17 34	6.5	02 40	8.8	15 05	8.2	03 57	3.4	16 37	3.1	06 13	5.1	18 50	4.7
20 Sunday	06 13	6.4	18 12	6.3	03 21	8.4	15 46	7.8	04 38	3.3	17 17	3.0	06 58	4.9	19 35	4.5
21 Monday	06 54	6.1	18 57	6.1	04 06	8.0	16 32	7.5	05 21	3.1	17 59	2.9	07 47	4.7	20 24	4.4
22 Tuesday	07 40	5.9	19 49	5.9	04 57	7.6	17 28	7.2	06 07	3.0	18 43	2.9	08 40	4.5	21 16	4.3
23 Wednesday	08 34	5.7	20 51	5.7	05 58	7.3	18 36	7.1	07 01	2.8	19 33	2.8	09 38	4.3	22 14	4.3
24 Thursday	09 36	5.7	21 59	5.7	07 07	7.3	19 45	7.3	08 07	2.7	20 36	2.8	10 40	4.3	23 16	4.4
25 Friday	10 40	5.8	23 06	5.8	08 13	7.4	20 43	7.7	09 34	2.7	21 55	2.8	11 46	4.4	—	—
26 Saturday	11 39	6.0	—	—	09 09	7.7	21 32	8.1	10 42	2.8	22 54	3.0	00 18	4.5	12 47	4.5
27 Sunday	00 05	6.1	12 31	6.3	09 57	8.0	22 14	8.4	11 30	2.8	23 37	3.1	01 11	4.7	13 36	4.8
28 Monday	00 57	6.3	13 19	6.5	10 40	8.3	22 54	8.7	—	—	12 11	2.9	01 54	4.9	14 17	5.0
29 Tuesday	01 44	6.6	14 03	6.6	11 20	8.6	23 33	8.9	00 14	3.2	12 52	2.9	02 33	5.1	14 55	5.2
30 Wednesday	02 27	6.7	14 44	6.7	12 00	8.7	—	—	00 51	3.3	13 33	2.9	03 10	5.3	15 32	5.3
31 Thursday	03 09	6.8	15 23	6.7	00 12	9.1	12 41	8.9	01 29	3.4	14 15	3.0	03 46	5.4	16 09	5.4

AUGUST 2003 *High Water* GMT

	LONDON BRIDGE				LIVERPOOL				GREENOCK				LEITH			
	hr m	ht	hr m	ht	hr m	ht	hr m	ht	hr m	ht	hr m	ht	hr m	ht	hr m	ht
1 Friday	03 49	6.9	15 59	6.7	00 53	9.2	13 21	8.9	02 08	3.5	14 55	3.0	04 22	5.4	16 48	5.4
2 Saturday	04 30	6.9	16 36	6.8	01 34	9.2	14 02	8.9	02 47	3.5	15 35	3.0	05 00	5.4	17 30	5.3
3 Sunday	05 11	6.9	17 15	6.7	02 17	9.2	14 44	8.8	03 27	3.5	16 15	3.0	05 41	5.4	18 14	5.2
4 Monday	05 55	6.7	17 58	6.7	03 02	9.0	15 30	8.6	04 09	3.5	16 56	3.0	06 27	5.3	19 02	5.0
5 Tuesday	06 42	6.4	18 45	6.4	03 51	8.7	16 22	8.2	04 54	3.3	17 41	2.9	07 17	5.1	19 57	4.8
6 Wednesday	07 36	6.1	19 43	6.2	04 48	8.3	17 24	7.9	05 45	3.2	18 33	2.8	08 20	4.9	21 01	4.7
7 Thursday	08 41	5.9	20 56	5.9	05 56	7.9	18 40	7.7	06 46	3.0	19 41	2.7	09 36	4.8	22 13	4.6
8 Friday	09 55	5.8	22 19	5.9	07 16	7.8	20 00	7.9	08 13	2.9	21 28	2.8	10 54	4.8	23 26	4.7
9 Saturday	11 06	6.0	23 34	6.2	08 36	8.0	21 07	8.4	09 54	2.9	22 37	3.0	—	—	12 08	4.9
10 Sunday	—	—	12 09	6.3	09 41	8.4	22 02	8.8	11 02	3.0	23 30	3.2	00 32	5.0	13 13	5.1
11 Monday	00 37	6.5	13 04	6.6	10 34	8.7	22 50	9.2	11 58	3.1	—	—	01 28	5.2	14 05	5.3
12 Tuesday	01 33	6.9	13 54	6.8	11 21	9.0	23 34	9.4	00 17	3.4	12 49	3.1	02 16	5.4	14 51	5.4
13 Wednesday	02 23	7.1	14 39	6.9	—	—	12 04	9.0	01 01	3.5	13 35	3.2	02 59	5.5	15 33	5.5
14 Thursday	03 09	7.1	15 20	6.9	00 15	9.5	12 43	9.0	01 42	3.5	14 16	3.2	03 40	5.6	16 13	5.4
15 Friday	03 50	7.1	15 57	6.9	00 54	9.4	13 19	8.8	02 20	3.6	14 52	3.2	04 19	5.5	16 51	5.2
16 Saturday	04 27	6.9	16 29	6.8	01 30	9.2	13 52	8.6	02 56	3.5	15 25	3.2	04 57	5.4	17 29	5.0
17 Sunday	04 59	6.7	17 00	6.7	02 05	8.9	14 25	8.4	03 30	3.5	15 58	3.2	05 34	5.2	18 06	4.8
18 Monday	05 30	6.5	17 34	6.5	02 40	8.6	15 00	8.1	04 04	3.4	16 33	3.1	06 13	5.0	18 46	4.6
19 Tuesday	06 03	6.3	18 12	6.3	03 18	8.1	15 38	7.7	04 40	3.2	17 10	3.1	06 56	4.7	19 31	4.4
20 Wednesday	06 42	6.1	18 57	6.0	04 01	7.6	16 25	7.3	05 20	3.0	17 51	3.0	07 46	4.4	20 23	4.3
21 Thursday	07 29	5.8	19 51	5.7	04 56	7.2	17 28	7.0	06 08	2.8	18 40	2.8	08 45	4.2	21 23	4.2
22 Friday	08 26	5.6	20 56	5.5	06 09	6.9	18 53	7.0	07 10	2.6	19 40	2.8	09 53	4.1	22 30	4.2
23 Saturday	09 40	5.5	22 19	5.5	07 35	7.0	20 13	7.4	08 34	2.6	20 59	2.8	11 07	4.2	23 41	4.4
24 Sunday	11 01	5.7	23 36	5.9	08 45	7.5	21 09	7.9	10 26	2.7	22 21	2.9	—	—	12 19	4.4
25 Monday	—	—	12 05	6.1	09 37	8.0	21 54	8.4	11 17	2.9	23 10	3.1	00 43	4.7	13 13	4.8
26 Tuesday	00 33	6.3	12 57	6.4	10 21	8.4	22 34	8.9	11 58	3.0	23 50	3.3	01 31	5.0	13 55	5.1
27 Wednesday	01 23	6.7	13 43	6.7	11 01	8.8	23 13	9.2	—	—	12 38	3.0	02 11	5.2	14 32	5.4
28 Thursday	02 07	6.9	14 28	6.8	11 40	9.1	23 52	9.3	00 29	3.4	13 17	3.1	02 47	5.4	15 09	5.6
29 Friday	02 49	7.1	15 02	6.9	—	—	12 19	9.2	01 09	3.5	13 55	3.1	03 21	5.6	15 45	5.7
30 Saturday	03 29	7.1	15 39	7.0	00 32	9.6	12 59	9.3	01 49	3.6	14 32	3.2	03 58	5.8	16 24	5.7
31 Sunday	04 09	7.1	16 15	7.0	01 13	9.6	13 39	9.3	02 28	3.7	15 07	3.2	04 37	5.8	17 05	5.6

SEPTEMBER 2003 *High Water* GMT

	London Bridge 3.20m below				Liverpool 4.93m below				Greenock 1.62m below				Leith 2.90m below			
	hr m	ht	hr m	ht	hr m	ht	hr m	ht	hr m	ht	hr m	ht	hr m	ht	hr m	ht
1 Monday	04 48	7.0	16 53	7.0	01 55	9.5	14 20	9.1	03 07	3.7	15 42	3.2	05 19	5.7	17 49	5.4
2 Tuesday	05 28	6.8	17 33	6.8	02 38	9.2	15 04	8.7	03 47	3.6	16 19	3.2	06 05	5.5	18 36	5.1
3 Wednesday	06 11	6.4	18 19	6.5	03 26	8.6	15 54	8.2	04 29	3.4	17 01	3.1	06 57	5.2	19 29	4.8
4 Thursday	07 00	6.0	19 15	6.0	04 23	8.0	16 58	7.7	05 17	3.2	17 52	2.9	08 03	4.8	20 37	4.6
5 Friday	08 05	5.5	20 36	5.6	05 40	7.4	18 25	7.4	06 15	2.9	19 00	2.8	09 27	4.6	21 58	4.5
6 Saturday	09 37	5.4	22 15	5.7	07 17	7.3	19 55	7.7	08 06	2.7	21 20	2.8	10 53	4.6	23 19	4.6
7 Sunday	10 53	5.7	23 29	6.1	08 38	7.8	21 02	8.3	10 07	2.8	22 27	3.1	—	—	12 11	4.9
8 Monday	11 56	6.2	—	—	09 37	8.3	21 53	8.8	11 05	3.0	23 18	3.3	00 28	4.9	13 12	5.1
9 Tuesday	00 29	6.6	12 49	6.6	10 24	8.7	22 37	9.3	11 54	3.2	—	—	01 22	5.2	13 58	5.3
10 Wednesday	01 21	7.0	13 37	6.9	11 05	9.0	23 17	9.5	00 02	3.5	12 37	3.2	02 04	5.4	14 37	5.4
11 Thursday	02 07	7.2	14 19	7.0	11 42	9.1	23 53	9.5	00 44	3.5	13 16	3.2	02 42	5.6	15 12	5.4
12 Friday	02 49	7.2	14 57	7.0	—	—	12 16	9.0	01 23	3.6	13 50	3.2	03 17	5.6	15 46	5.4
13 Saturday	03 25	7.0	15 30	6.9	00 27	9.4	12 47	8.9	01 58	3.5	14 20	3.2	03 51	5.6	16 19	5.3
14 Sunday	03 55	6.8	15 59	6.8	00 59	9.2	13 17	8.7	02 30	3.5	14 49	3.3	04 25	5.4	16 52	5.1
15 Monday	04 21	6.7	16 27	6.7	01 30	8.9	13 47	8.5	03 00	3.5	15 18	3.3	04 59	5.2	17 26	5.0
16 Tuesday	04 49	6.6	16 59	6.6	02 02	8.6	14 19	8.3	03 31	3.4	15 50	3.3	05 35	5.0	18 03	4.8
17 Wednesday	05 20	6.4	17 35	6.4	02 37	8.2	14 53	7.9	04 04	3.2	16 25	3.2	06 16	4.7	18 45	4.6
18 Thursday	05 57	6.2	18 17	6.1	03 17	7.7	15 35	7.5	04 42	3.0	17 05	3.1	07 04	4.4	19 36	4.3
19 Friday	06 40	5.9	19 07	5.7	04 09	7.1	16 34	7.0	05 29	2.8	17 55	2.9	08 01	4.2	20 38	4.2
20 Saturday	07 33	5.6	20 09	5.5	05 21	6.8	17 59	6.8	06 33	2.6	18 58	2.8	09 12	4.1	21 50	4.2
21 Sunday	08 42	5.4	21 28	5.4	06 59	6.8	19 39	7.2	07 59	2.6	20 15	2.8	10 29	4.2	23 05	4.3
22 Monday	10 19	5.5	23 03	5.8	08 19	7.3	20 42	7.8	10 05	2.7	21 41	3.0	11 45	4.5	—	—
23 Tuesday	11 34	5.9	—	—	09 12	8.0	21 27	8.5	10 55	3.0	22 38	3.2	00 11	4.7	12 43	4.9
24 Wednesday	00 05	6.3	12 28	6.4	09 55	8.6	22 08	9.1	11 35	3.1	23 21	3.4	01 00	5.0	13 26	5.2
25 Thursday	00 55	6.8	13 13	6.7	10 34	9.1	22 47	9.5	—	—	12 13	3.2	01 40	5.4	14 04	5.6
26 Friday	01 40	7.1	13 55	6.9	11 14	9.4	23 27	9.8	00 03	3.5	12 51	3.3	02 17	5.7	14 41	5.8
27 Saturday	02 22	7.2	14 34	7.1	11 53	9.6	—	—	00 45	3.6	13 28	3.3	02 53	5.9	15 18	5.9
28 Sunday	03 03	7.3	15 13	7.2	00 07	9.9	12 34	9.7	01 26	3.7	14 03	3.4	03 32	6.0	15 58	5.9
29 Monday	03 43	7.2	15 52	7.2	00 49	9.9	13 14	9.5	02 07	3.8	14 37	3.5	04 13	6.0	16 40	5.7
30 Tuesday	04 22	7.1	16 32	7.1	01 32	9.6	13 56	9.2	02 47	3.8	15 12	3.5	04 58	5.8	17 24	5.5

OCTOBER 2003 *High Water* GMT

	London Bridge				Liverpool				Greenock				Leith			
1 Wednesday	05 02	6.8	17 15	6.9	02 17	9.1	14 41	8.8	03 27	3.7	15 50	3.4	05 48	5.5	18 12	5.1
2 Thursday	05 43	6.4	18 02	6.5	03 07	8.4	15 33	8.2	04 09	3.4	16 32	3.3	06 45	5.1	19 09	4.8
3 Friday	06 28	5.9	19 01	5.9	04 09	7.7	16 43	7.6	04 57	3.1	17 25	3.1	07 57	4.7	20 24	4.6
4 Saturday	07 34	5.4	20 36	5.5	05 37	7.2	18 18	7.4	06 01	2.8	18 40	2.9	09 23	4.6	21 49	4.5
5 Sunday	09 22	5.3	22 07	5.7	07 16	7.3	19 42	7.7	08 44	2.7	21 04	3.0	10 49	4.6	23 09	4.7
6 Monday	10 35	5.7	23 14	6.2	08 26	7.8	20 44	8.3	10 03	2.9	22 08	3.2	—	—	12 03	4.9
7 Tuesday	11 34	6.2	—	—	09 19	8.3	21 33	8.8	10 53	3.1	22 57	3.4	00 15	5.0	12 59	5.1
8 Wednesday	00 09	6.7	12 26	6.7	10 03	8.7	22 15	9.2	11 35	3.3	23 40	3.5	01 05	5.3	13 41	5.3
9 Thursday	00 59	7.1	13 12	6.9	10 41	9.0	22 52	9.4	—	—	12 13	3.3	01 45	5.4	14 16	5.4
10 Friday	01 43	7.2	13 54	7.0	11 14	9.0	23 26	9.4	00 20	3.6	12 47	3.3	02 19	5.5	14 47	5.4
11 Saturday	02 22	7.1	14 30	6.9	11 45	9.0	—	—	00 58	3.5	13 17	3.3	02 52	5.5	15 17	5.4
12 Sunday	02 55	6.9	15 01	6.8	—	—	12 14	8.9	01 31	3.5	13 45	3.4	03 23	5.5	15 47	5.3
13 Monday	03 21	6.7	15 29	6.7	00 28	9.1	12 43	8.8	12 01	3.4	14 13	3.4	03 55	5.4	16 18	5.2
14 Tuesday	03 44	6.6	15 57	6.6	00 58	8.8	13 13	8.7	02 31	3.4	14 42	3.5	04 29	5.2	16 57	5.0
15 Wednesday	04 12	6.6	16 29	6.5	01 30	8.6	13 44	8.4	03 01	3.3	15 14	3.5	05 06	5.0	17 27	4.9
16 Thursday	04 43	6.5	17 05	6.4	02 04	8.2	14 18	8.1	03 35	3.2	15 48	3.4	05 47	4.7	18 08	4.7
17 Friday	05 20	6.3	17 47	6.2	02 44	7.7	15 00	7.6	04 13	3.0	16 27	3.2	06 33	4.5	18 55	4.5
18 Saturday	06 02	6.0	18 37	5.9	03 35	7.2	15 57	7.2	05 00	2.8	17 15	3.1	07 27	4.3	19 55	4.3
19 Sunday	06 54	5.7	19 37	5.6	04 44	6.8	17 14	7.0	06 07	2.7	18 19	2.9	08 34	4.2	21 10	4.2
20 Monday	07 59	5.4	20 50	5.6	06 16	6.9	18 48	7.2	07 34	2.6	19 35	2.9	09 50	4.3	22 26	4.4
21 Tuesday	09 26	5.5	22 19	5.9	07 41	7.4	20 00	7.8	09 17	2.8	20 56	3.0	11 03	4.6	23 31	4.7
22 Wednesday	10 50	5.9	23 28	6.4	08 36	8.1	20 51	8.5	10 19	3.0	22 00	3.3	—	—	12 03	5.0
23 Thursday	11 47	6.3	—	—	09 21	8.7	21 35	9.2	11 03	3.2	22 49	3.5	00 22	5.1	12 51	5.3
24 Friday	00 21	6.8	12 36	6.7	10 03	9.3	22 18	9.7	11 42	3.3	23 37	3.6	01 05	5.5	13 32	5.6
25 Saturday	01 08	7.1	13 21	7.0	10 44	9.6	23 00	10.0	—	—	12 21	3.4	01 45	5.8	14 11	5.9
26 Sunday	01 53	7.3	14 05	7.2	11 26	9.8	23 43	10.0	00 19	3.7	12 59	3.5	02 25	6.0	14 51	5.9
27 Monday	02 36	7.3	14 48	7.3	—	—	12 08	9.8	01 04	3.8	13 36	3.6	03 08	6.1	15 33	5.9
28 Tuesday	03 18	7.2	15 32	7.3	00 28	9.9	12 52	9.7	01 47	3.8	14 13	3.7	03 54	6.0	16 16	5.8
29 Wednesday	03 59	7.1	16 17	7.2	01 14	9.5	13 37	9.3	02 30	3.8	14 50	3.7	04 43	5.8	17 03	5.5
30 Thursday	04 40	6.8	17 03	6.9	02 02	9.0	14 25	8.8	03 13	3.6	15 30	3.6	05 36	5.5	17 54	5.2
31 Friday	05 22	6.4	17 54	6.5	02 55	8.3	15 20	8.3	03 58	3.4	16 15	3.4	06 38	5.1	18 55	4.9

NOVEMBER 2003   *High Water*   GMT

		LONDON BRIDGE *Datum of Predictions 3.20m below				LIVERPOOL *Datum of Predictions 4.93m below				GREENOCK *Datum of Predictions 1.62m below				LEITH *Datum of Predictions 2.90m below			
		hr	ht m	hr	ht m	hr	ht m	hr	ht m	hr	ht m	hr	ht m	hr	ht m	hr	ht m
1	Saturday	06 09	5.9	18 59	6.0	04 01	7.6	16 32	7.7	04 52	3.1	17 11	3.2	07 52	4.8	20 13	4.7
2	Sunday	07 20	5.5	20 27	5.7	05 27	7.3	17 57	7.6	06 09	2.9	18 31	3.1	09 11	4.6	21 32	4.6
3	Monday	08 58	5.5	21 44	5.9	06 51	7.3	19 13	7.8	08 24	2.8	20 29	3.1	10 28	4.7	22 45	4.8
4	Tuesday	10 06	5.8	22 46	6.3	07 57	7.7	20 13	8.2	09 35	3.0	21 37	3.3	11 37	4.8	23 48	5.0
5	Wednesday	11 04	6.2	23 40	6.7	08 49	8.2	21 03	8.6	10 24	3.2	22 28	3.4	—	—	12 31	5.0
6	Thursday	11 55	6.6	—	—	09 33	8.6	21 46	8.9	11 04	3.3	23 12	3.5	00 37	5.2	13 14	5.1
7	Friday	00 29	7.0	12 42	6.8	10 10	8.8	22 24	9.1	11 40	3.3	23 52	3.5	01 19	5.3	13 49	5.2
8	Saturday	01 13	7.0	13 24	6.9	10 44	8.9	22 58	9.1	—	—	12 13	3.4	01 54	5.4	14 20	5.3
9	Sunday	01 50	7.0	14 01	6.8	11 15	9.0	23 30	9.0	00 29	3.4	12 44	3.4	02 27	5.4	14 49	5.3
10	Monday	02 22	6.8	14 34	6.7	11 44	8.9	—	—	01 03	3.4	13 14	3.5	02 59	5.3	15 19	5.3
11	Tuesday	02 48	6.7	15 03	6.6	00 00	8.9	12 15	8.9	01 34	3.3	13 43	3.6	03 32	5.2	15 50	5.2
12	Wednesday	03 13	6.6	15 33	6.5	00 32	8.8	12 46	8.7	02 05	3.3	14 13	3.6	04 07	5.1	16 23	5.1
13	Thursday	03 42	6.6	16 06	6.5	01 05	8.6	13 20	8.5	02 38	3.2	14 46	3.6	04 44	5.0	16 59	5.0
14	Friday	04 15	6.5	16 43	6.4	01 42	8.3	13 56	8.3	03 14	3.2	15 21	3.5	05 25	4.8	17 39	4.8
15	Saturday	04 52	6.4	17 26	6.2	02 23	7.9	14 39	7.9	03 54	3.0	15 59	3.4	06 09	4.6	18 24	4.6
16	Sunday	05 34	6.1	18 16	6.0	03 12	7.5	15 33	7.6	04 44	2.9	16 44	3.2	07 00	4.5	19 19	4.5
17	Monday	06 26	5.9	19 14	5.9	04 14	7.2	16 40	7.4	05 48	2.8	17 43	3.1	08 00	4.4	20 27	4.4
18	Tuesday	07 27	5.7	20 21	5.8	05 31	7.2	17 57	7.5	07 04	2.7	18 55	3.0	09 09	4.5	21 41	4.5
19	Wednesday	08 42	5.7	21 37	6	06 48	7.5	19 08	8.0	08 23	2.8	20 10	3.1	10 18	4.7	22 46	4.8
20	Thursday	10 00	6.0	22 46	6.4	07 52	8.1	20 08	8.6	09 32	3.0	21 19	3.3	11 20	5.0	23 41	5.1
21	Friday	11 04	6.4	23 45	6.7	08 44	8.7	21 01	9.1	10 25	3.2	22 16	3.5	—	—	12 13	5.3
22	Saturday	11 59	6.7	—	—	09 32	9.2	21 49	9.6	11 10	3.3	23 07	3.6	00 30	5.5	13 00	5.6
23	Sunday	00 37	7.0	12 51	7.0	10 17	9.6	22 37	9.8	11 52	3.5	23 56	3.7	01 16	5.7	13 43	5.7
24	Monday	01 25	7.2	13 40	7.2	11 02	9.8	23 24	9.9	—	—	12 33	3.6	02 03	5.9	14 27	5.8
25	Tuesday	02 12	7.2	14 29	7.3	11 48	9.8	—	—	00 44	3.8	13 15	3.7	02 50	6.0	15 12	5.8
26	Wednesday	02 57	7.2	15 18	7.3	00 12	9.7	12 35	9.7	01 32	3.7	13 55	3.8	03 40	5.9	15 58	5.7
27	Thursday	03 41	7.0	16 06	7.2	01 01	9.4	13 23	9.4	02 19	3.7	14 36	3.8	04 33	5.7	16 47	5.5
28	Friday	04 25	6.8	16 56	7.0	01 52	8.9	14 14	9.0	03 06	3.5	15 19	3.7	05 28	5.5	17 40	5.3
29	Saturday	05 09	6.5	17 49	6.6	02 46	8.4	15 08	8.6	03 57	3.3	16 06	3.6	06 29	5.1	18 41	5.0
30	Sunday	05 57	6.1	18 49	6.2	03 46	7.9	16 10	8.2	04 54	3.1	17 02	3.4	07 35	4.9	19 51	4.8

DECEMBER 2003   *High Water*   GMT

		LONDON BRIDGE				LIVERPOOL				GREENOCK				LEITH			
1	Monday	07 00	5.8	19 59	6.0	04 55	7.5	17 20	7.9	06 03	3.0	18 09	3.3	08 42	4.7	21 01	4.7
2	Tuesday	08 19	5.7	21 08	6.0	06 08	7.4	18 29	7.8	07 22	2.9	19 32	3.2	09 49	4.6	22 07	4.8
3	Wednesday	09 26	5.8	22 08	6.1	07 14	7.5	19 32	8.0	08 39	3.0	20 51	3.2	10 54	4.6	23 08	4.8
4	Thursday	10 25	6.1	23 03	6.3	08 10	7.8	20 26	8.2	09 37	3.1	21 50	3.3	11 51	4.7	—	—
5	Friday	11 19	6.3	23 53	6.5	08 57	8.2	21 13	8.5	10 23	3.2	22 40	3.3	00 01	4.9	12 39	4.9
6	Saturday	—	—	12 07	6.5	09 38	8.5	21 55	8.6	11 03	3.3	23 24	3.3	00 48	5.0	13 18	5.0
7	Sunday	00 37	6.6	12 52	6.6	10 14	8.7	22 31	8.7	11 41	3.4	—	—	01 29	5.1	13 53	5.1
8	Monday	01 16	6.7	13 33	6.6	10 48	8.8	23 05	8.8	00 04	3.3	12 16	3.4	02 06	5.1	14 26	5.2
9	Tuesday	01 50	6.6	14 09	6.6	11 20	8.9	23 38	8.7	00 40	3.2	12 48	3.5	02 41	5.1	14 58	5.2
10	Wednesday	02 21	6.6	14 43	6.5	11 53	8.9	—	—	01 13	3.2	13 18	3.6	03 15	5.1	15 30	5.2
11	Thursday	02 51	6.5	15 16	6.5	00 12	8.7	12 28	8.8	01 46	3.2	13 51	3.6	03 51	5.1	16 04	5.1
12	Friday	03 22	6.5	15 52	6.5	00 49	8.6	13 05	8.7	02 21	3.1	14 25	3.6	04 28	5.0	16 40	5.1
13	Saturday	03 56	6.5	16 30	6.5	01 27	8.4	13 43	8.6	03 00	3.1	15 02	3.5	05 07	5.0	17 18	5.0
14	Sunday	04 34	6.4	17 13	6.4	02 09	8.2	14 26	8.4	03 43	3.0	15 41	3.5	05 49	4.9	18 00	4.8
15	Monday	05 16	6.3	18 00	6.3	02 55	8.0	15 14	8.2	04 30	2.9	16 24	3.4	06 35	4.7	18 48	4.7
16	Tuesday	06 04	6.1	18 54	6.2	03 48	7.8	16 11	8.0	05 25	2.9	17 15	3.3	07 27	4.7	19 44	4.7
17	Wednesday	07 00	6.0	19 53	6.1	04 50	7.6	17 14	8.0	06 25	2.8	18 14	3.2	08 27	4.6	20 49	4.7
18	Thursday	08 04	6.0	20 59	6.1	05 58	7.7	18 20	8.1	07 29	2.9	19 20	3.2	09 33	4.7	21 57	4.8
19	Friday	09 15	6.1	22 08	6.3	07 06	8.0	19 26	8.4	08 38	2.9	20 34	3.2	10 37	4.9	23 01	5.0
20	Saturday	10 24	6.3	23 12	6.5	08 08	8.4	20 29	8.8	09 45	3.1	21 43	3.3	11 37	5.1	23 59	5.3
21	Sunday	11 28	6.5	—	—	09 04	8.9	21 26	9.2	10 40	3.2	22 42	3.4	—	—	12 31	5.3
22	Monday	00 09	6.7	12 28	6.8	09 56	9.3	22 20	9.4	11 29	3.4	23 38	3.5	00 55	5.5	13 21	5.5
23	Tuesday	01 03	6.9	13 23	7.0	10 46	9.6	23 11	9.6	—	—	12 15	3.6	01 48	5.7	14 09	5.6
24	Wednesday	01 53	7.0	14 16	7.2	11 35	9.7	—	—	00 31	3.6	13 00	3.7	02 40	5.8	14 57	5.7
25	Thursday	02 41	7.0	15 08	7.2	00 02	9.5	12 24	9.7	01 24	3.5	13 44	3.8	03 32	5.8	15 45	5.7
26	Friday	03 27	7.0	15 58	7.2	00 52	9.3	13 12	9.6	02 15	3.5	14 28	3.8	04 24	5.7	16 35	5.6
27	Saturday	04 12	6.8	16 46	7.1	01 41	9.1	14 00	9.3	03 04	3.4	15 12	3.8	05 16	5.5	17 26	5.4
28	Sunday	04 56	6.7	17 35	6.8	02 29	8.8	14 48	9.0	03 53	3.3	15 57	3.7	06 10	5.2	18 20	5.2
29	Monday	05 40	6.5	18 24	6.5	03 18	8.3	15 38	8.6	04 41	3.2	16 45	3.6	07 04	4.9	19 17	5.0
30	Tuesday	06 26	6.2	19 17	6.2	04 10	7.8	16 31	8.2	05 31	3.1	17 37	3.4	08 00	4.6	20 16	4.8
31	Wednesday	07 22	6.0	20 15	5.9	05 07	7.5	17 30	7.8	06 22	3.0	18 33	3.2	08 57	4.5	21 15	4.7

HM Coastguard

Founded in 1822, originally to guard the coasts against smuggling, HM Coastguard's role today is the very different one of search and rescue and accident prevention at sea and around the coast of the UK. The Service is responsible for co-ordinating all civil maritime search and rescue operations around the 10,500 mile coastline of Great Britain and Northern Ireland and 1,000 miles into the Atlantic. In addition, it co-operates with search and rescue organisations of neighbouring countries in western Europe and around the Atlantic seaboard. The Service maintains a 24-hour radar watch on the Dover Strait, providing a Channel navigation information service for all shipping in one of the busiest sea lanes in the world. It also liaises very closely with the offshore oil and gas industry and with merchant shipping companies.

HM Coastguard (HMCG) is part of the Maritime and Coastguard Agency (MCA), an executive agency of the Department for Transport. The MCA is organised into three regions, each with a Regional Director. Operational aspects of HMCG are the responsibility of Coastguard Regional Operations Managers (Search and Rescue). Each region is subdivided into Maritime Rescue Co-ordination Centres and Sub Centres (MRCC/MRSC) of which there are 19 in total. They are on 24-hour watch and are fitted with a comprehensive range of communications equipment. Each region is further sub-divided into sectors under the direction of a Sector Manager who is responsible for training the 3,250-strong Auxiliary Coastguard Service whose Rescue Teams are trained and equipped to carry out searches and cliff and mud rescues.

HM Coastguard co-ordinates on average around 12,000 incidents each year and the number of incidents to which a Search and Rescue Unit is despatched is around 6,500 a year. All distress radio and emergency telephone calls are centralised on the 19 co-ordination centres, which are on the alert for people or vessels in distress, shipping hazards and pollution incidents. Using telecommunications equipment, including satellite, they can alert and co-ordinate the most appropriate rescue facilities: RNLI lifeboats, Royal Navy, RAF or Coastguard helicopters and tugs, fixed-wing aircraft, vessels in the vicinity, or Coastguard Rescue Teams.

For those who regularly sail in local waters or make longer passages, the CG66 – Voluntary Safety Identification Scheme provides a valuable free service. Its aim is to give the Coastguard a record of the details of craft, their equipment fit, normal operating areas and shoreside contact details. The CG66 – Voluntary Safety Identification Scheme cards are available from all Coastguard stations, harbourmasters' offices, and most yacht clubs and marinas as well as Coastguard headquarters. Participants in the scheme are provided with a pack containing useful safety information and a card to leave with family members or friends advising how and when to contact the Coastguard should they become concerned for the safety of their craft.

Members of the public who see an accident or a potentially dangerous incident on or around the coast should dial 999 and ask for the Coastguard.

Maritime and Coastguard Headquarters and Office of the Director of Operations and Chief Coastguard, Spring Place, 105 Commercial Road, Southampton SO15 1EG. Tel: 023 8032 9100

The United Kingdom

UK Statistics

Royal Family

Kings and Queens

Precedence

Forms of Address

Peerage

Chiefs of Clans in Scotland

Privy Council

Parliament

The Government

Regional Government

Local Government

European Parliament

Law Courts and Offices

Tribunals

Police Service

Prison Service

Defence

Education

Health and Social Welfare

Utilities

Transport

Religion

Communications

Information Technology

Environment, Conservation and Heritage

Economic Statistics

Lotteries and Gaming

Finance

Taxation

Legal Notes

Intellectual Property

The Media

Trade Unions

Trade and Employers' Associations

National Academies and Research Councils

Sports Bodies

Clubs

Societies and Organisations

The United Kingdom

The United Kingdom comprises Great Britain (England, Wales and Scotland) and Northern Ireland. The Isle of Man and the Channel Islands are Crown dependencies with their own legislative systems, and not a part of the United Kingdom.

AREA

	Land miles²	km²	*Inland water miles²	km²	Total miles²	km²
United Kingdom	93,006	240,883	1,242	3,218	94,248	244,101
England	50,058	129,652	293	758	50,351	130,410
Wales	7,965	20,628	50	130	8,015	20,758
Scotland	29,767	77,097	653	1,692	30,420	78,789
†Northern Ireland	5,225	13,532	249	628	5,467	14,160
Isle of Man	221	572	—	—	221	572
Channel Islands	75	194	—	—	75	194

*Excluding tidal water.
†Excluding certain tidal waters that are parts of statutory areas in Northern Ireland.

POPULATION

The first official census of population in England, Wales and Scotland was taken in 1801 and a census has been taken every ten years since, except in 1941 when there was no census because of war. The last official census in the United Kingdom was taken on 29 April 2001 and the next is due in April 2011.

The first official census of population in Ireland was taken in 1841. However, all figures given below refer only to the area which is now Northern Ireland. Figures for Northern Ireland in 1921 and 1931 are estimates based on the censuses taken in 1926 and 1937 respectively.

Estimates of the population of England before 1801, calculated from the number of baptisms, burials and marriages, are:
1570 4,160,221   1670 5,773,646
1600 4,811,718   1700 6,045,008
1630 5,600,517   1750 6,517,035

Thousands	United Kingdom Total	Male	Female	England and Wales Total	Male	Female	Scotland Total	Male	Female	Northern Ireland Total	Male	Female
CENSUS RESULTS 1801–1991												
1801	—	—	—	8,893	4,255	4,638	1,608	739	869	—	—	—
1811	13,368	6,368	7,000	10,165	4,874	5,291	1,806	826	980	—	—	—
1821	15,472	7,498	7,974	12,000	5,850	6,150	2,092	983	1,109	—	—	—
1831	17,835	8,647	9,188	13,897	6,771	7,126	2,364	1,114	1,250	—	—	—
1841	20,183	9,819	10,364	15,914	7,778	8,137	2,620	1,242	1,378	1,649	800	849
1851	22,259	10,855	11,404	17,928	8,781	9,146	2,889	1,376	1,513	1,443	698	745
1861	24,525	11,894	12,631	20,066	9,776	10,290	3,062	1,450	1,612	1,396	668	728
1871	27,431	13,309	14,122	22,712	11,059	11,653	3,360	1,603	1,757	1,359	647	712
1881	31,015	15,060	15,955	25,974	12,640	13,335	3,736	1,799	1,936	1,305	621	684
1891	34,264	16,593	17,671	29,003	14,060	14,942	4,026	1,943	2,083	1,236	590	646
1901	38,237	18,492	19,745	32,528	15,729	16,799	4,472	2,174	2,298	1,237	590	647
1911	42,082	20,357	21,725	36,070	17,446	18,625	4,761	2,309	2,452	1,251	603	648
1921	44,027	21,033	22,994	37,887	18,075	19,811	4,882	2,348	2,535	1,258	610	648
1931	46,038	22,060	23,978	39,952	19,133	20,819	4,843	2,326	2,517	1,243	601	642
1951	50,225	24,118	26,107	43,758	21,016	22,742	5,096	2,434	2,662	1,371	668	703
1961	52,709	25,481	27,228	46,105	22,304	23,801	5,179	2,483	2,697	1,425	694	731
1971	55,515	26,952	28,562	48,750	23,683	25,067	5,229	2,515	2,714	1,536	755	781
1981	55,848	27,104	28,742	49,155	23,873	25,281	5,131	2,466	2,664	*1,533	750	783
1991	56,467	27,344	29,123	49,890	24,182	25,707	4,999	2,392	2,607	1,578	769	809

Census 2001 results were published on 30 September 2002. For further details visit www.statistics.gov.uk.

†RESIDENT POPULATION: PROJECTIONS (MID–YEAR)												
2001	59,987	29,605	30,382	53,174	26,286	26,888	5,109	2,484	2,625	1,705	836	869
2011	61,956	30,807	31,149	55,151	27,469	27,682	5,047	2,470	2,576	1,759	868	890
2021	64,105	31,953	32,151	57,329	28,621	28,707	4,973	2,439	2,534	1,803	893	910

*Figures include 44,500 non-enumerated persons.
† Projections are 2000 based.
Source: The Stationery Office – *Annual Abstract of Statistics 2002*; ONS – Census reports (Crown copyright).

ISLANDS: Census Results 1901–91

	Isle of Man			Jersey			*Guernsey		
	Total	Male	Female	Total	Male	Female	Total	Male	Female
1901	54,752	25,496	29,256	52,576	23,940	28,636	40,446	19,652	20,794
1911	52,016	23,937	28,079	51,898	24,014	27,884	41,858	20,661	21,197
1921	60,284	27,329	32,955	49,701	22,438	27,263	38,315	18,246	20,069
1931	49,308	22,443	26,865	50,462	23,424	27,038	40,643	19,659	20,984
1951	55,123	25,749	29,464	57,296	27,282	30,014	43,652	21,221	22,431
1961	48,151	22,060	26,091	57,200	27,200	30,000	45,068	21,671	23,397
1971	56,289	26,461	29,828	72,532	35,423	37,109	51,458	24,792	26,666
1981	64,679	30,901	33,778	77,000	37,000	40,000	53,313	25,701	27,612
1991	69,788	33,693	36,095	84,082	40,862	43,220	58,867	28,297	30,570

* Population of Guernsey, Herm, Jethou and Lithou. Figures for 1901–71 record all persons present on census night; census figures for 1981 and 1991 record all persons resident in the islands on census night
Source: 1991 Census.

RESIDENT POPULATION

Mid-Year Estimate

	1990	2000
United Kingdom	57,567,000	59,756,000
England	47,991,000	49,997,000
Wales	2,878,000	2,946,000
Scotland	5,102,000	5,115,000
Northern Ireland	1,596,000	1,698,000

Source: The Stationery Office – Annual Abstract of Statistics 2002 (Crown copyright).

By Age and Sex 2000*

Males	Under 18	65 and over
United Kingdom	6,942,000	3,875,000
England	5,787,000	3,256,000
Wales	342,000	212,000
Scotland	576,000	318,000
Northern Ireland	236,000	89,000

Females	Under 18	60 and over
United Kingdom	6,592,000	6,914,000
England	5,492,000	5,765,000
Wales	326,000	374,000
Scotland	550,000	606,000
Northern Ireland	224,000	170,000

* Estimated mid–year figures.
Source: The Stationery Office – Annual Abstract of Statistics 2002 (Crown copyright).

By Ethnic Group 2000

Ethnic group	Estimated population
Caribbean	529,000
African	440,000
Other black (non–mixed)	129,000
Other black (mixed)	178,000
Indian	985,000
Pakistani	675,000
Bangladeshi	257,000
Chinese	151,000
Other Asian (non–mixed)	242,000
Other (mixed)	240,000
Other (non–mixed)	219,000
Total ethnic minority groups	4,045,000
White	54,670,000
All ethnic groups†	58,731,000

†Includes ethnic groups not stated.
Source: The Stationery Office – Annual Abstract of Statistics 2002 (Crown copyright).

IMMIGRATION 2000
Acceptances for settlement in the UK by nationality

Region	Number of persons
Europe: total	15,110
European Economic Area	10
Remainder of Europe	15,100
Americas: total	11,520
USA	4,580
Canada	1,320
Africa: total	44,460
Asia: total	47,540
Indian sub-continent	22,730
Middle East	7,090
Oceania: total	4,900
British Overseas Citizens	630
Stateless	930
Total	125,090

Source: The Stationery Office – Annual Abstract of Statistics 2002 (Crown copyright).

LIVE BIRTHS AND BIRTH RATES 2000

	Live births	Male	Female	Birth rate*
United Kingdom	679,000	348,000	331,000	11.4
England and Wales	604,000	310,000	295,000	11.4
Scotland	53,000	27,000	26,000	10.4
Northern Ireland	22,000	11,000	10,000	12.7

*Live births per 1,000 population
Source: The Stationery Office – Annual Abstract of Statistics 2002 (Crown copyright).

LEGAL ABORTIONS 2000

Age group	England and Wales	Scotland†
15 and under	3,748	274
16-19	33,218	2,610
20-34	113,686	7,524
35-44	24,383	1,557
45 and over	459	28
All ages	175,542	11,933

† provisional
Source: The Stationery Office – Annual Abstract of Statistics 2002 (Crown copyright).

BIRTHS OUTSIDE MARRIAGE (UK)

Age group	1990	2000
Under 20	51,000	47,000
20-24	83,000	77,000
25-29	53,000	66,000
Over 30	37,000	78,000
Total	223,000	268,000

Source: The Stationery Office – *Annual Abstract of Statistics 2002* (Crown copyright).

MARRIAGE AND DIVORCE 1999

	Marriages	Divorces
United Kingdom	301,083	158,746
England and Wales	263,515	144,556
Scotland	29,940	11,864
Northern Ireland	7,628	2,326

Source: The Stationery Office – *Annual Abstract of Statistics 2002* (Crown copyright).

DEATHS and death rates 2000*

Males	Deaths	Death Rate*
United Kingdom	290,186	9.9
England and Wales	255,547	
Scotland	27,511	
Northern Ireland	7,128	
Females		
United Kingdom	318,180	10.5
England and Wales	280,117	
Scotland	30,288	
Northern Ireland	7,775	

* Death rate per 1,000 population
Source: The Stationery Office – *Annual Abstract of Statistics 2002* (Crown copyright).

INFANT MORTALITY 2000
Deaths of infants under 1 year of age per 1,000 live births

	Number
United Kingdom	5.6
England and Wales	5.6
Scotland	5.7
Northern Ireland	5.1

Source: The Stationery Office – *Annual Abstract of Statistics 2002* (Crown copyright).

LIFE EXPECTANCY   LIFE TABLES 1998-2000 (INTERIM FIGURES)

Age	England and Wales Male	England and Wales Female	Scotland Male	Scotland Female	Northern Ireland Male	Northern Ireland Female
0	75.4	80.2	72.8	78.2	74.5	79.6
5	70.9	75.7	68.4	73.7	70.0	75.1
10	66.0	70.7	63.4	68.7	65.1	70.1
15	61.0	65.7	58.5	63.7	60.1	65.2
20	56.2	60.8	53.7	58.8	55.4	60.3
25	51.4	55.9	49.0	53.9	50.6	55.4
30	46.6	51.0	44.3	49.1	45.9	50.5
35	41.8	46.1	39.6	44.2	41.1	45.6
40	37.1	41.3	34.9	39.4	36.4	40.7
45	32.4	36.5	30.4	34.7	31.7	36.0
50	27.9	31.9	25.9	30.1	27.2	31.4
55	23.5	27.3	21.7	25.7	22.8	26.9
60	19.3	23.0	17.9	21.4	18.7	22.5
65	15.6	18.9	14.4	17.5	15.0	18.4
70	12.2	15.0	11.3	13.9	11.7	14.6
75	9.3	11.6	8.6	10.7	8.9	11.2
80	7.0	8.7	6.5	7.9	6.6	8.3
85	5.2	6.3	4.8	5.6	4.9	6.0
90	3.9	4.7	3.5	3.8	4.0	4.2

Source: The Stationery Office – *Annual Abstract of Statistics 2002* (Crown copyright).

DEATHS ANALYSED BY CAUSE 2000

	England and Wales	Scotland	N. Ireland
TOTAL DEATHS	535,664	57,799	14,903
Deaths from natural causes	516,804	–	14,296
Infectious and parasitic diseases	3,767	476	73
Neoplasms	134,793	15,255	3,647
Malignant neoplasm of stomach	5,779	649	180
Malignant neoplasm of trachea, bronchus and lung	29,029	3,948	792
Malignant neoplasm of breast	11,433	1,122	289
Malignant neoplasm of uterus	1,333	128	33
Malignant neoplasm of cervix	1,106	117	30
Benign and unspecified neoplasms	1,733	–	60
Leukaemia	3,570	–	91
Endocrine, nutritional and metabolic diseases and immunity disorders	7,247	828	122
Diabetes mellitus	5,773	616	89
Nutritional deficiencies	60	–	2
Other metabolic and immunity disorders	1,054	–	22
Diseases of blood and blood-forming organs	1,791	114	122
Anaemias	554	–	13
Mental disorders	10,866	2,309	207
Diseases of the nervous system and sense organs	9,632	1,315	245
Meningitis	206	15	6
Diseases of the circulatory system	207,228	23,657	5,777
Rheumatic heart disease	1,551	–	33
Hypertensive disease	3,184	–	75
Ischaemic heart disease	108,417	12,412	3,235
Diseases of pulmonary circulation and other forms of heart disease	25,139	–	637
Cerebrovascular disease	52,516	6,803	527
Diseases of the respiratory system	92,461	6,547	942
Influenza	509	131	39
Pneumonia	56,329	2,312	2,026
Bronchitis, emphysema	2,981	–	75
Asthma	1,272	131	33
Diseases of the digestive system	22,134	2,922	531
Ulcer of stomach and duodenum	4,007	351	89
Appendicitis	139	–	5
Hernia of the abdominal cavity and other intestinal obstruction	2,117	–	44
Chronic liver disease and cirrhosis	4,770	956	101
Diseases of the genitourinary system	7,270	844	292
Nephritis, nephrotic syndrome and nephrosis	2,901	–	182
Hyperplasia of prostate	188	–	1
Complications of pregnancy, childbirth and the puerperium	38	–	–
Abortion	7	–	–
Diseases of the skin and subcutaneous tissue	1,266	89	21
Diseases of the musculo-skeletal system	3,407	405	40
Congenital anomalies	1,165	154	57
Certain conditions originating in the perinatal period	83	170	62
Birth trauma, hypoxia, birth asphyxia and other respiratory conditions	53	–	18
Signs, symptoms and ill-defined conditions	13,656	–	180
Sudden infant death syndrome	180	33	–
Deaths from injury and poisoning	16,525	2,384	607
All accidents	10,771	–	364
Motor vehicle accidents	2,889	345	138
Suicide and self-inflicted injury	3,479	648	163
All other external causes	2,275	–	80

Source: The Stationery Office – *Annual Abstract of Statistics 2002* (Crown copyright).

The National Flag

The national flag of the United Kingdom is the Union Flag, generally known as the Union Jack.

The Union Flag is a combination of the cross of St George, patron saint of England, the cross of St Andrew, patron saint of Scotland, and a cross similar to that of St Patrick, patron saint of Ireland.

Cross of St George: cross Gules in a field Argent (red cross on a white ground)

Cross of St Andrew: saltire Argent in a field Azure (white diagonal cross on a blue ground)

Cross of St Patrick: saltire Gules in a field Argent (red diagonal cross on a white ground)

The Union Flag was first introduced in 1606 after the union of the kingdoms of England and Scotland under one sovereign. The cross of St Patrick was added in 1801 after the union of Great Britain and Ireland.

FLYING THE UNION FLAG

The correct orientation of the Union Flag when flying is with the broader diagonal band of white uppermost in the hoist (i.e. near the pole) and the narrower diagonal band of white uppermost in the fly (i.e. furthest from the pole).

It is the practice to fly the Union Flag daily on some customs houses. In all other cases, flags are flown on government buildings by command of The Queen. It is now customary for the Union Flag to be flown at Buckingham Palace when The Queen is not present.

Days for hoisting the Union Flag are notified to the Department for Culture, Media and Sport by The Queen's command and communicated by the department to the other government departments. On the days appointed, the Union Flag is flown on government buildings in the United Kingdom from 8 a.m. to sunset.

DAYS FOR FLYING FLAGS

The Queen's Accession	6 February
Birthday of The Duke of York	19 February
*St David's Day (in Wales only)	1 March
Birthday of The Earl of Wessex	10 March
**Commonwealth Day (2003)	10 March
Birthday of The Queen	21 April
*St George's Day (in England only)	23 April
†Europe Day	9 May
Coronation Day	2 June
Birthday of The Duke of Edinburgh	10 June
The Queen's Official Birthday (2003)	14 June
Birthday of The Princess Royal	15 August
Remembrance Sunday (2003)	9 November
Birthday of The Prince of Wales	14 November
The Queen's Wedding Day	20 November
*St Andrew's Day (in Scotland only)	30 November

‡The opening of Parliament by The Queen
‡The prorogation of Parliament by The Queen

*Where a building has two or more flagstaffs, the appropriate national flag may be flown in addition to the Union Flag, but not in a superior position
**Commonwealth Day is always the second Monday in March
†The Union Flag should fly alongside the European flag. On government buildings that have only one flagpole, the Union Flag should take precedence
‡Flags are flown whether or not The Queen performs the ceremony in person. Flags are flown only in the Greater London area

FLAGS AT HALF-MAST

Flags are flown at half-mast (i.e. two-thirds up between the top and bottom of the flagstaff) on the following occasions:

(a) From the announcement of the death up to the funeral of the Sovereign, except on Proclamation Day, when flags are hoisted right up from 11 a.m. to sunset

(b) The funerals of members of the royal family, subject to special commands from The Queen in each case

(c) The funerals of foreign rulers, subject to special commands from The Queen in each case

(d) The funerals of prime ministers and ex-prime ministers of the UK, subject to special commands from The Queen in each case

(e) Other occasions by special command of The Queen

On occasions when days for flying flags coincide with days for flying flags at half-mast, the following rules are observed. Flags are flown:

(a) although a member of the royal family, or a near relative of the royal family, may be lying dead, unless special commands are received from The Queen to the contrary

(b) although it may be the day of the funeral of a foreign ruler

If the body of a very distinguished subject is lying at a government office, the flag may fly at half-mast on that office until the body has left (provided it is a day on which the flag would fly) and then the flag is to be hoisted right up. On all other government buildings the flag will fly as usual.

THE ROYAL STANDARD

The Royal Standard is hoisted only when The Queen is actually present in the building, and never when Her Majesty is passing in procession.

114

Archbishops of Canterbury since 1414

Henry Chichele (1362–1443), translated 1414
John Stafford (?–1452), translated 1443
John Kemp (c.1380–1454), translated 1452
Thomas Bourchier (c.1410–86), translated 1454
John Morton (c.1420–1500), translated 1486
Henry Deane (?–1503), translated 1501
William Warham (1450–1532), translated 1503
Thomas Cranmer (1489–1556), consecrated 1533
Reginald Pole (1500–58), consecrated 1556
Matthew Parker (1504–75), consecrated 1559
Edmund Grindal (c. 1519–83), translated 1576
John Whitgift (c.1530–1604), translated 1583
Richard Bancroft (1544–1610), translated 1604
George Abbot (1562–1633), translated 1611
William Laud (1573–1645), translated 1633
William Juxon (1582–1663), translated 1660
Gilbert Sheldon (1598–1677), translated 1663
William Sancroft (1617–93), consecrated 1678
John Tillotson (1630–94), consecrated 1691
Thomas Tenison (1636–1715), translated 1695
William Wake (1657–1737), translated 1716
John Potter (c.1674–1747), translated 1737
Thomas Herring (1693–1757), translated 1747
Matthew Hutton (1693–1758), translated 1757
Thomas Secker (1693–1768), translated 1758
Hon. Frederick Cornwallis (1713–83), translated 1768
John Moore (1730–1805), translated 1783
Charles Manners-Sutton (1755–1828), translated 1805
William Howley (1766–1848), translated 1828
John Bird Sumner (1780–1862), translated 1848
Charles Longley (1794–1868), translated 1862
Archibald Campbell Tait (1811–82), translated 1868
Edward White Benson (1829–96), translated 1883
Frederick Temple (1821–1902), translated 1896
Randall Davidson (1848–1930), translated 1903
Cosmo Lang (1864–1945), translated 1928
William Temple (1881–1944), translated 1942
Geoffrey Fisher (1887–1972), translated 1945
Michael Ramsey (1904–88), translated 1961
Donald Coggan (1909–2000), translated 1974
Robert Runcie (1921–2000), translated 1980
George Carey (1935–), translated 1991
Rowan Williams (1950–), translated 2002

The Royal Family

THE SOVEREIGN

ELIZABETH II, by the Grace of God, of the United Kingdom of Great Britain and Northern Ireland and of her other Realms and Territories Queen, Head of the Commonwealth, Defender of the Faith
Her Majesty Elizabeth Alexandra Mary of Windsor, elder daughter of King George VI and of HM Queen Elizabeth the Queen Mother
Born 21 April 1926, at 17 Bruton Street, London W1
Ascended the throne 6 February 1952
Crowned 2 June 1953, at Westminster Abbey
Married 20 November 1947, in Westminster Abbey, HRH The Prince Philip, Duke of Edinburgh
Official residences: Buckingham Palace, London SW1A 1AA; Windsor Castle, Berks; Palace of Holyroodhouse, Edinburgh
Private residences: Sandringham, Norfolk; Balmoral Castle, Aberdeenshire

HUSBAND OF THE QUEEN

HRH THE PRINCE PHILIP, DUKE OF EDINBURGH, KG, KT, OM, GBE, AC, QSO, PC, Ranger of Windsor Park
Born 10 June 1921, son of Prince and Princess Andrew of Greece and Denmark, naturalised a British subject 1947, created Duke of Edinburgh, Earl of Merioneth and Baron Greenwich 1947

CHILDREN OF THE QUEEN

HRH THE PRINCE OF WALES (Prince Charles Philip Arthur George), KG, KT, GCB, OM and Great Master of the Order of the Bath, AK, QSO, PC, ADC(P)
Born 14 November 1948, created Prince of Wales and Earl of Chester 1958, succeeded as Duke of Cornwall, Duke of Rothesay, Earl of Carrick and Baron Renfrew, Lord of the Isles and Prince and Great Steward of Scotland 1952
Married 29 July 1981 Lady Diana Frances Spencer (Diana, Princess of Wales (1961–97), youngest daughter of the 8th Earl Spencer and the Hon. Mrs Shand Kydd), marriage dissolved 1996
Issue:
(1) HRH Prince William of Wales (Prince William Arthur Philip Louis), *born* 21 June 1982
(2) HRH Prince Henry of Wales (Prince Henry Charles Albert David), *born* 15 September 1984
Residences of the Prince of Wales: St James's Palace, London SW1A 1BS; Highgrove, Doughton, Tetbury, Glos GL8 8TN

HRH THE PRINCESS ROYAL (Princess Anne Elizabeth Alice Louise), KG, GCVO
Born 15 August 1950, declared The Princess Royal 1987
Married (1) 14 November 1973 Captain Mark Anthony Peter Phillips, CVO (*born* 22 September 1948); marriage dissolved 1992; (2) 12 December 1992 Captain Timothy James Hamilton Laurence, MVO, RN (*born* 1 March 1955)
Issue:
(1) Peter Mark Andrew Phillips, *born* 15 November 1977
(2) Zara Anne Elizabeth Phillips, *born* 15 May 1981
Residence: Gatcombe Park, Minchinhampton, Glos

HRH THE DUKE OF YORK (Prince Andrew Albert Christian Edward), CVO, ADC(p)
Born 19 February 1960, created Duke of York, Earl of Inverness and Baron Killyleagh 1986
Married 23 July 1986 Sarah Margaret Ferguson, now Sarah, Duchess of York (*born* 15 October 1959, younger daughter of Major Ronald Ferguson and Mrs Hector Barrantes), marriage dissolved 1996
Issue:
(1) HRH Princess Beatrice of York (Princess Beatrice Elizabeth Mary), *born* 8 August 1988
(2) HRH Princess Eugenie of York (Princess Eugenie Victoria Helena), *born* 23 March 1990
Residences: Buckingham Palace, London SW1A 1AA; Sunninghill Park, Ascot, Berks

HRH THE EARL OF WESSEX (Prince Edward Antony Richard Louis), CVO
Born 10 March 1964, created Earl of Wessex, Viscount Severn 1999
Married 19 June 1999 Sophie Helen Rhys-Jones, now HRH The Countess of Wessex (*born* 20 January 1965, daughter of Mr and Mrs Christopher Rhys-Jones)
Residence: Bagshot Park, Bagshot, Surrey GU19 5HS

NEPHEW OF THE QUEEN

DAVID ALBERT CHARLES, VISCOUNT LINLEY, *born* 3 November 1961, *married* 8 October 1993 the Hon. Serena Stanhope, and has issue, Hon. Charles Patrick Inigo Armstrong-Jones, *born* 1 July 1999

NIECE OF THE QUEEN

LADY SARAH CHATTO (Sarah Frances Elizabeth), *born* 1 May 1964, *married* 14 July 1994 Daniel Chatto, and has issue, Samuel David Benedict Chatto, *born* 28 July 1996; Arthur Robert Nathaniel Chatto, *born* 5 February 1999
Residence: Kensington Palace, London W8 4PU

AUNT OF THE QUEEN

HRH PRINCESS ALICE, DUCHESS OF GLOUCESTER (Alice Christabel), GCB, CI, GCVO, GBE, Grand Cordon of Al Kamal
Born 25 December 1901, third daughter of the 7th Duke of Buccleuch and Queensberry
Married 6 November 1935 (as Lady Alice Montagu-Douglas-Scott) Prince Henry, Duke of Gloucester, third son of King George V
Residence: Kensington Palace, London W8 4PU

COUSINS OF THE QUEEN

HRH THE DUKE OF GLOUCESTER (Prince Richard Alexander Walter George), KG, GCVO, Grand Prior of the Order of St John of Jerusalem
Born 26 August 1944
Married 8 July 1972 Birgitte Eva van Deurs, now HRH The Duchess of Gloucester, GCVO (*born* 20 June 1946, daughter of Asger Henriksen and Vivian van Deurs)

Issue:
(1) Earl of Ulster (Alexander Patrick Gregers Richard), *born* 24 October 1974
(2) Lady Davina Windsor (Davina Elizabeth Alice Benedikte), *born* 19 November 1977
(3) Lady Rose Windsor (Rose Victoria Birgitte Louise), *born* 1 March 1980
Residence: Kensington Palace, London W8 4PU

HRH THE DUKE OF KENT (Prince Edward George Nicholas Paul Patrick), KG, GCMG, GCVO, ADC(p)
Born 9 October 1935
Married 8 June 1961 Katharine Lucy Mary Worsley, now HRH The Duchess of Kent, GCVO (*born* 22 February 1933, daughter of Sir William Worsley, Bt.)
Issue:
(1) Earl of St Andrews (George Philip Nicholas), *born* 26 June 1962, *married* 9 January 1988 Sylvana Tomaselli, and has issue, Edward Edmund Maximilian George, Baron Downpatrick, *born* 2 December 1988; Lady Marina Charlotte Alexandra Katharine Windsor, *born* 30 September 1992; Lady Amelia Sophia Theodora Mary Margaret Windsor, *born* 24 August 1995
(2) Lady Helen Taylor (Helen Marina Lucy), *born* 28 April 1964, *married* 18 July 1992 Timothy Taylor, and has issue, Columbus George Donald Taylor, *born* 6 August 1994; Cassius Edward Taylor, born 26 December 1996
(3) Lord Nicholas Windsor (Nicholas Charles Edward Jonathan), *born* 25 July 1970
Residence: Wren House, Palace Green, London W8 4PY

HRH PRINCESS ALEXANDRA, THE HON. LADY OGILVY (Princess Alexandra Helen Elizabeth Olga Christabel), GCVO
Born 25 December 1936
Married 24 April 1963 The Rt. Hon. Sir Angus Ogilvy, KCVO (*born* 14 September 1928, second son of 12th Earl of Airlie)
Issue:
(1) James Robert Bruce Ogilvy, *born* 29 February 1964, married 30 July 1988 Julia Rawlinson, and has issue, Flora Alexandra Ogilvy, *born* 15 December 1994; Alexander Charles Ogilvy, *born* 12 November 1996
(2) Marina Victoria Alexandra, Mrs Mowatt, *born* 31 July 1966, *married* 2 February 1990 Paul Mowatt (marriage dissolved 1997), and has issue, Zenouska May Mowatt, *born* 26 May 1990; Christian Alexander Mowatt, *born* 4 June 1993
Residence: Thatched House Lodge, Richmond Park, Surrey

HRH PRINCE MICHAEL OF KENT (Prince Michael George Charles Franklin), KCVO
Born 4 July 1942
Married 30 June 1978 Baroness Marie-Christine Agnes Hedwig Ida von Reibnitz, now HRH Princess Michael of Kent (*born* 15 January 1945, daughter of Baron Gunther von Reibnitz)
Issue:
(1) Lord Frederick Windsor (Frederick Michael George David Louis), *born* 6 April 1979
(2) Lady Gabriella Windsor (Gabriella Marina Alexandra Ophelia), *born* 23 April 1981
Residences: Kensington Palace, London W8 4PU; Nether Lypiatt Manor, Stroud, Glos GL6 7LS

ORDER OF SUCCESSION

1 HRH The Prince of Wales
2 HRH Prince William of Wales
3 HRH Prince Henry of Wales
4 HRH The Duke of York
5 HRH Princess Beatrice of York
6 HRH Princess Eugenie of York
7 HRH The Earl of Wessex
8 HRH The Princess Royal
9 Peter Phillips
10 Zara Phillips
11 Viscount Linley
12 Hon. Charles Armstrong-Jones
13 Lady Sarah Chatto
14 Samuel Chatto
15 Arthur Chatto
16 HRH The Duke of Gloucester
17 Earl of Ulster
18 Lady Davina Windsor
19 Lady Rose Windsor
20 HRH The Duke of Kent
21 Baron Downpatrick
22 Lady Marina Charlotte Windsor
23 Lady Amelia Windsor
24 Lord Nicholas Windsor
25 Lady Helen Taylor
26 Columbus Taylor
27 Cassius Taylor
28 Lord Frederick Windsor
29 Lady Gabriella Windsor
30 HRH Princess Alexandra, the Hon. Lady Ogilvy
31 James Ogilvy
32 Alexander Ogilvy
33 Flora Ogilvy
34 Marina, Mrs Paul Mowatt
35 Christian Mowatt
36 Zenouska Mowatt
37 The Earl of Harewood

The Earl of St Andrews and HRH Prince Michael of Kent both lost the right of succession to the throne through marriage to a Roman Catholic. Their children remain in succession provided that they are in communion with the Church of England.

Private Secretaries to the Royal Family

THE QUEEN

Office: Buckingham Palace, London SW1A 1AA
Tel: 020-7930 4832
Web: www.royal.gov.uk
Private Secretary to The Queen, The Rt. Hon. Sir Robin Janvrin, KCVO, CB

PRINCE PHILIP, THE DUKE OF EDINBURGH

Office: Buckingham Palace, London SW1A 1AA
Tel: 020-7930 4832
Private Secretary, Brig. M. Hunt-Davis, CVO, CBE

THE PRINCE OF WALES

Office: St James's Palace, London SW1A 1BS
Tel: 020-7930 4832
Private Secretary, Sir Michael Peat, KCVO

THE DUKE OF YORK

Office: Buckingham Palace, London SW1A 1AA
Tel: 020-7930 4832
Private Secretary, Miss C. Manley, OBE

THE EARL AND COUNTESS OF WESSEX

Office: The Old Stables, Bagshot Park, Surrey GU19 5PJ
Tel: 01276-700843/022
Private Secretary, Brigadier J. Smedley

THE PRINCESS ROYAL

Office: Buckingham Palace, London SW1A 1AA
Tel: 020-7930 4832
Private Secretary, N. Wright

PRINCESS ALICE, DUCHESS OF GLOUCESTER AND THE DUKE AND DUCHESS OF GLOUCESTER

Office: Kensington Palace, London W8 4PU
Tel: 020-7937 6374
Private Secretary, Maj. N. Barne, LVO

THE DUKE OF KENT

Office: St James's Palace, London, SW1A 1BQ
Tel: 020-7930 4872
Private Secretary, N. Adamson, OBE

THE DUCHESS OF KENT

Office: Palace Green, London, W8 4PU
Tel: 020-7937 2928
Personal Secretary, Miss V. Uttley,

PRINCE AND PRINCESS MICHAEL OF KENT

Office: Kensington Palace, London W8 4PU
Tel: 020-7938 3519
Private Secretary, N. Chance

PRINCESS ALEXANDRA, THE HON. LADY OGILVY

Office: Buckingham Palace, London SW1A 1AA
Tel: 020-7930 1860
Private Secretary, Lt.-Col. R. Macfarlane

Offices of the Royal Household

PRIVATE SECRETARY'S OFFICE

The Private Secretary, assisted by the three Assistant Private Secretaries, is responsible for:

– Informing and advising The Queen on constitutional, governmental and political matters in the UK, her other realms and the wider Commonwealth, including communications with the Prime Minister and Government Departments.
– Organising The Queen's domestic and overseas official programme, including the Presentation of Credentials by incoming foreign ambassadors from overseas countries.
– The Queen's speeches and messages, The Queen's patronage, The Queen's photographs and official presents, portraits of The Queen and dedications and congratulatory messages.

- Communications in connection with the role of the Royal Family and other members of the Royal Family and their households.
- Dealing with correspondence to The Queen from members of the public.
- Organising and co-ordinating Royal travel through the Royal Travel Office.
- Co-ordinating and initiating research to support engagements by members of the Royal Family through the Co-ordination and Research Unit.

The Private Secretary is also responsible for communications and media affairs. The Communications Secretary reports to the Private Secretary and is responsible for:

- Developing communications strategies to enhance the public understanding of the role of the royal family, including an education strategy, encompassing website development and other multi-media initiatives.
- Co-ordinating communications across the Households, including the publication of internal newsletters and related literature.
- The Buckingham Palace Press Office.

Within the Press Office, the Press Secretary, assisted by the Deputy Press Secretary and two Assistant Press Secretaries, is responsible for:

- Briefing the British and international media on the role and duties of The Queen and issues relating to the Royal Family.
- Responding to media enquiries.
- Arranging media facilities in the United Kingdom and overseas to support royal functions and engagements.
- The management of the Royal website.

The Private Secretary is Keeper of the Royal Archives and is responsible for the care of the records of the Sovereign and the Royal Household from previous reigns, which are preserved in the Royal Archives at Windsor, where they are managed by the Assistant Keeper (a post combined with that of the Librarian of the Royal Library, q.v.) and made available for historical research. As keeper, it is the Private Secretary's responsibility to ensure the proper management of the records of the present reign with a view to their transfer to the archives as and when appropriate.

The Private Secretary is an *ex officio* trustee of the Royal Collection Trust.

PRIVY PURSE AND TREASURER'S OFFICE

The Keeper of the Privy Purse and Treasurer to the Queen, assisted by the Deputy Treasurer (who is also Deputy Keeper of the Privy Purse) and the Assistant Keeper of the Privy Purse, is responsible for:

- The Queen's Civil List, which is the money paid from the Government's Consolidated Fund to meet official expenditure relating to the Queen's duties as Head of State and Head of the Commonwealth.
- Through the Director of Personnel, the identification, planning and management of personnel policy across the Household, the administration of all pension schemes provided for the Household and Private Estates employees, and the allocation of employee and pensioner housing.
- Information technology systems for the household.
- Internal audit services.
- All insurance matters.

- The Privy Purse, which is mainly financed by the net income of the Duchy of Lancaster, and which meets both official expenditure incurred by The Queen as Sovereign and private expenditure.
- Liaison with other members of the Royal Family and their Households on Financial matters.
- The Queen's private estates at Sandringham and Balmoral, The Queen's Racing Establishment and the Royal Studs and liaison with the Ascot Authority.
- The Home Park at Windsor and liaison with the Crown Estate Commissioners concerning the Home Park and the Great Park at Windsor.
- The Royal Philatelic Collection, which is managed by the Keeper of the Royal Philatelic Collection.
- Administrative aspects of the Military Knights of Windsor and the Royal Almonry.
- Administration of the Royal Victorian Order, of which the Keeper of the Privy Purse is Secretary, Long and Faithful Service Medals, and the Queen's Cups, Medals and Prizes, and Policy on Commemorative Medals.

The Keeper of the Privy Purse is one of three Royal Trustees (in respect of his responsibilities for the Civil List) and is Receiver General of the Duchy of Lancaster and a member of the Duchy's Council.

The Keeper of the Privy Purse is also responsible for property services for the Occupied Royal Palaces in England, which comprise Buckingham Palace, St James' Palace and Clarence House, Marlborough House Mews, the residential, office and general areas of Kensington Palace, Windsor Castle and related areas and buildings, Frogmore House, and Hampton Court Mews and Paddocks. The costs of property services for the Occupied Royal Palaces are met from a Grant-in-aid from the Department for Culture, Media and Sport.

The Director of Property Services, assisted by the Director of Finance, Property Services, has day to day responsibility for the Royal Household's Property Section, which is responsible for:

- Fire, health and safety issues.
- Repairs and refurbishment of buildings and new buildings work.
- Utilities and telephones.
- Putting up stages, flags and tents and other work in connection with ceremonial occasions and garden parties and other official functions.

The Property Section is also responsible, in effect on a sub-contract basis from the Department for Culture, Media and Sport, for the maintenance of Marlborough House (Which is occupied by the Commonwealth Secretariat).

The Keeper of the Privy Purse, assisted by the Director of Finance, Property Services, also oversees Royal Communications and Information expenditure, which is met from the Property Services Grant-in-aid.

The Keeper of the Privy Purse is responsible for the financial aspects of royal travel, which are overseen on a day to day basis by the Director of Finance, Royal Travel, who is also the Director of Finance, Property Services. The costs of official royal travel by aeroplane and train are met from a Grant-in-aid provided by the Department of Transport.

The Keeper of the Privy Purse is an *ex officio* trustee of the Royal Collection Trust and is also chairman of its trading subsidiary Royal Collection Enterprises Limited. He is also an *ex officio* trustee of the Historic Royal Palaces Trust.

The Queen's Civil List and the Grants-in-aid for property services and royal travel are provided by the Government in return for the surrender by the Sovereign of the net surplus from the Crown Estate and other hereditary revenues.

MASTER OF THE HOUSEHOLD'S DEPARTMENT

The Master of the Household, assisted by the Deputy Master of the Household (who is also Equerry to the Queen), is responsible for the staff and domestic arrangements at Buckingham Palace, Windsor Castle and the Palace of Holyroodhouse and at Balmoral Castle and Sandringham House when The Queen is in residence. These arrangements include:

- The provision of meals for The Queen and other members of the Royal Family, their guests and Royal Household employees.
- Service by liveried staff at meals, receptions and other events.
- Travel arrangements for employees and the movement of baggage between the Royal residences.
- Cleaning and laundry.
- Furnishings and the internal decorative appearance of the Occupied Royal Palaces in collaboration with the Director of the Royal Collection.
- Liaison with the Royalty and Diplomatic Protection Department of the Metropolitan Police concerning security procedures at the Occupied Royal Palaces.

The Master of the Household is responsible for The Queen's official entertaining, both at home and overseas, including preparation of guest lists, invitations and seating plans, and overseeing aspects of The Queen's private entertaining.

LORD CHAMBERLAIN'S OFFICE

The Comptroller, Lord Chamberlain's Office, assisted by the Assistant Comptroller, is responsible for:

- The organisation of all ceremonial engagements, including state visits to The Queen in the United Kingdom, royal weddings and royal funerals, the state opening of Parliament, Guards of Honour at Buckingham Palace, Investitures, and the Garter and Thistle ceremonies.
- Garden Parties at Buckingham Palace and Palace at Holyroodhouse (except for catering and tents).
- The Crown Jewels, which are part of the Royal Collection, when they are in use on state occasions.
- Co-ordination of the arrangements for The Queen to be represented at funerals and memorial services and at the arrival and departure of visiting Heads of State.
- Advising on matters of precedence, style and titles, dress, flying of flags, gun salutes, mourning and other ceremonial questions.
- Supervising the applications from tradesmen for Royal Warrants of Appointment.
- Advising on the commercial use of royal emblems and contemporary royal photographs.
- The Ecclesiastical Household, the Medical Household, the Body Guards and certain ceremonial appointments such as Gentlemen Ushers and Pages of Honour.
- The personal Lords in Waiting, who represent The Queen on various occasions and escort the visiting Head of State during incoming state visits.
- The Queen's Bargemaster and Watermen and The Queen's Swans.

The Comptroller, Lord Chamberlain's Office is also responsible for the Royal Mews, assisted by the Crown Equerry, who has day-to-day responsibility for:

- The provision of carriage processions for the State Opening of Parliament, State Visits, Trooping of the Colour, Royal Ascot, the Garter Ceremony, the Thistle Service, the Presentation of credentials to The Queen by incoming foreign Ambassadors and High Commissioners, and other state and ceremonial occasions.
- The provision of chauffeur-driven cars.
- Co-ordinating the travelling and transport arrangements by road in respect of The Queen's official engagements.
- Supervision and administration of the Royal Mews at Buckingham Palace, Windsor Castle, Hampton Court and the Palace of Holyroodhouse.

The Comptroller, Lord Chamberlain's Office also has overall responsibility for the Marshal of the Diplomatic Corps, who is responsible for the relationship between the Royal Household and the Diplomatic Heads of Mission in London; and the Secretary of the central chancery of the orders of Knighthood, who administers the Orders of Chivalry and their records, makes arrangements for the recipients at Investitures and the distribution of insignia, and ensures the proper public notification of awards through the London Gazette. The Secretary of the Central Chancery is also the Assistant Comptroller.

ROYAL COLLECTION DEPARTMENT

The Royal Collection, which contains a large number of works of art of all kinds, is held by The Queen as Sovereign in trust for her successors and the nation and is not owned by her as an individual. The administration, conservation and presentation of the Royal Collection are funded by the Royal Collection Trust solely from income from visitors to Windsor Castle, Buckingham Palace and the Palace of Holyroodhouse in Edinburgh. The Royal Collection Trust is chaired by the Prince of Wales. The Lord Chamberlain, the Private Secretary and the Keeper of the Privy Purse are *ex officio* trustees and there are three external trustees appointed by The Queen.

The Director of the Royal Collection is responsible for:

- The administration and custodial control of the Royal Collection in all royal residences.
- The care, display, conservation and restoration of items in the Collection.
- Initiating and assisting research into the Collection and publishing catalogues and books on the Collection.
- Making the Collection accessible to the public by display in places open to the public (including the unoccupied palaces), The Queen's Gallery at Buckingham Palace and the Queen's Gallery at the Palace of Holyroodhouse, by travelling exhibitions organised by museums and galleries in the United Kingdom and abroad.
- Educating and informing the public about the Collection.

The Director of the Royal Collection, who is at present also the Surveyor of The Queen's Works of Art, is assisted by the Surveyor of the Queen's Pictures, the Royal Librarian, the Deputy Surveyor of The Queen's Works of Art, the Managing Director, Royal Collection Enterprises, and the Finance Director, Royal Collection.

The Surveyor of the Queen's Pictures is responsible for pictures and miniatures, the Royal Librarian is responsible for all the books, manuscripts, coins and medals, insignia and works of art on paper including the watercolours, prints and drawings in the Print Room at Windsor Castle, and the Surveyor of the Queen's Works of art is responsible for furniture, ceramics and the other decorative arts in the Collection.

The Director of the Royal Collection has overall responsibility for the trading activities that fund the Royal Collection Department. These are administered by Royal Collection Enterprises Limited, the trading subsidiary of The Royal Collection Trust, which is run by the Managing Director, Royal Collection Enterprises. The company, whose chairman is the Keeper of the Privy Purse, is responsible for:

– Managing access by the public to Windsor Castle (including Frogmore House), Buckingham Palace (including the Royal Mews and The Queen's Gallery) and the Palace of Holyroodhouse.
– Running shops at each location.
– Managing the images and intellectual property rights of the Royal Collection.

The Director of the Royal Collection is also an *ex officio* trustee of the Historic Royal Palaces Trust.

Royal Salutes

ENGLAND

A salute of 62 guns is fired on the wharf at the Tower of London in conjunction with a 41 gun salute in Hyde Park on the following occasions:
(a) the anniversaries of the birth, accession and coronation of the Sovereign
(b) the anniversary of the birth of HRH Prince Philip, Duke of Edinburgh

A salute of 41 guns is fired in either Hyde Park, Green Park or the Tower of London on extraordinary and triumphal occasions, e.g. on the occasion of the Sovereign opening, proroguing or dissolving Parliament in person, or when passing through London in procession, except when otherwise ordered.

A salute of 41 guns is fired from two saluting stations in London (the Tower of London and Hyde Park) on the occasion of the birth of a royal infant.

Constable of the Royal Palace and Fortress of London, Gen. Sir Roger Wheeler, GCB, CBE
Lieutenant of the Tower of London, Lt.-Gen. Sir Roderick Cordy-Simpson, KBE, CB
Resident Governor and Keeper of the Jewel House, Maj.-Gen. Geoffrey Field, CB, OBE

Master Gunner of St James's Park, Gen. Sir Alex Harley, KBE, CB
Master Gunner within the Tower, Col. James Ferguson, TD

SCOTLAND

Royal salutes are authorised at Edinburgh Castle and Stirling Castle, although in practice Edinburgh Castle is the only operating saluting station in Scotland.

A salute of 21 guns is fired on the following occasions:
(a) the anniversaries of the birth, accession and coronation of the Sovereign
(b) the anniversary of the birth of HRH Prince Philip, Duke of Edinburgh

A salute of 21 guns is fired in Edinburgh on the occasion of the opening of the General Assembly of the Church of Scotland.

A salute of 21 guns may also be fired in Edinburgh on the arrival of HM The Queen or a member of the royal family who is a Royal Highness on an official visit.

Royal Finances

FUNDING

THE CIVIL LIST

The Civil List dates back to the late 17th century. It was originally used by the sovereign to supplement hereditary revenues for paying the salaries of judges, ambassadors and other government officers as well as the expenses of the royal household. In 1760 on the accession of George III it was decided that the Civil List would be provided by Parliament to cover all relevant expenditure in return for the King surrendering the hereditary revenues of the Crown. At that time Parliament undertook to pay the salaries of judges, ambassadors, etc. In 1831 Parliament agreed also to meet the costs of the royal palaces in return for a reduction in the Civil List. Each sovereign has agreed to continue this arrangement.

The Civil List paid to The Queen is charged on the Consolidated Fund. Until 1972, the amount of money allocated annually under the Civil List was set for the duration of a reign. The system was then altered to a fixed annual payment for ten years but from 1975 high inflation made an annual review necessary. The system of payments reverted to the practice of a fixed annual payment of £7.9m for ten years from 1 January 1991. In 2001 the payments were further fixed until 31 December 2010. In June 2002 the annual accounts for the Civil List were published for the first time and are to continue to be published annually instead of at 10-yearly intervals.

The Civil List Acts provide for other members of the royal family to receive parliamentary annuities from government funds to meet the expenses of carrying out their official duties. Since 1975 The Queen has reimbursed the Treasury for the annuities paid to the Duke of Gloucester, the Duke of Kent and Princess Alexandra. Since 1993 The Queen has reimbursed all the annuities except those paid to herself, Queen Elizabeth the Queen Mother and the Duke of Edinburgh.

The Prince of Wales does not receive a parliamentary annuity. He derives his income from the revenues of the Duchy of Cornwall and these monies meet the official and private expenses of the Prince of Wales and his family.

The annual payments for the years 2001–2011:

The Queen	£7,900,000
The Duke of Edinburgh	359,000
*The Duke of York	249,000
*†The Earl of Wessex	141,000
*The Princess Royal	228,000
*Princess Alice, Duchess of Gloucester	87,000
*The Duke and Duchess of Gloucester	175,000
*The Duke and Duchess of Kent	236,000
*Princess Alexandra	225,000
	9,600,000
*Refunded to the Treasury	1,341,000
Total	8,259,000

†The Earl of Wessex's annuity was increased from £96,000 upon his marriage in June 1999

GRANTS-IN-AID

The royal household receives grants-in-aid from two government departments to meet various official expenses. The Department for Culture, Media and Sport provides grant-in-aid to pay for the upkeep of English occupied royal palaces, the maintenance of Marlborough House and to meet the cost of royal media and information services. The Royal Travel grant-in-aid is provided by the Department for Transport to meet the cost of official royal travel by air and rail, using mainly aircraft from 32 (The Royal) Squadron, chartered commercial aircraft for major overseas state visits and the Royal Train.

Grants-in-aid 2001–2002:

Property Services, Royal Communications and Information and Maintenance of Marlborough House	£16,632,000
Royal Travel	6,010,000

THE PRIVY PURSE

The funds received by the Privy Purse pay for official expenses incurred by The Queen as head of state and for some of The Queen's private expenditure. The revenues of the Duchy of Lancaster are the principal source of income for the Privy Purse. The revenues of the Duchy were retained by George III in 1760 when the hereditary revenues were surrendered in exchange for the Civil List.

PERSONAL INCOME

The Queen's personal income derives mostly from investments, and is used to meet private expenditure.

DEPARTMENTAL VOTES

Items of expenditure connected with the official duties of the royal family which fall directly on votes of government departments include:

Ministry of Defence – equerries
Foreign and Commonwealth Office – Marshal of the Diplomatic Corps; costs (other than travel costs) associated with overseas visits at the request of government departments
HM Treasury – Central Chancery of the Orders of Knighthood
The Post Office – postal services

TAXATION

The sovereign is not legally liable to pay income tax or capital gains tax. After income tax was reintroduced in 1842, some income tax was paid voluntarily by the sovereign but over a long period these payments were phased out. In 1992 The Queen offered to pay tax on a voluntary basis from 6 April 1993, and the Prince of Wales offered to pay tax on a voluntary basis on his income from the Duchy of Cornwall. (He was already taxed in all other respects.)

The main provisions for The Queen and the Prince of Wales to pay tax, set out in a Memorandum of Understanding on Royal Taxation presented to Parliament on 11 February 1993, are that The Queen will pay income tax and capital gains tax in respect of her private income and assets, and on the proportion of the income and capital gains of the Privy Purse used for private purposes. Inheritance tax will be paid on The Queen's assets, except for those which pass to the next sovereign, whether automatically or by gift or bequest. The Prince of Wales will pay income tax on income from the Duchy of Cornwall used for private purposes.

The Prince of Wales has confirmed that he intends to pay tax on the same basis following his accession to the throne.

Other members of the royal family are subject to tax as for any taxpayer.

Military Ranks and Titles

THE QUEEN

Lord High Admiral of the United Kingdom
Colonel-in-Chief
The Life Guards; The Blues and Royals (Royal Horse Guards and 1st Dragoons); The Royal Scots Dragoon Guards (Carabiniers and Greys); The Queen's Royal Lancers; Royal Tank Regiment; Corps of Royal Engineers; Grenadier Guards; Coldstream Guards; Scots Guards; Irish Guards; Welsh Guards; The Royal Welsh Fusiliers; The Queen's Lancashire Regiment; The Argyll and Sutherland Highlanders (Princess Louise's); The Royal Green Jackets; Adjutant General's Corps; The Royal Mercian and Lancastrian Yeomanry; The

Governor General's Horse Guards (of Canada); The King's Own Calgary Regiment (Royal Canadian Armoured Corps); Canadian Forces Military Engineers Branch; Royal 22e Regiment (of Canada); Governor-General's Foot Guards (of Canada); The Canadian Grenadier Guards; Le Regiment de la Chaudiere (of Canada); 2nd Battalion Royal New Brunswick Regiment (North Shore); The 48th Highlanders of Canada; The Argyll and Sutherland Highlanders of Canada (Princess Louise's); The Calgary Highlanders; Royal Australian Engineers; Royal Australian Infantry Corps; Royal Australian Army Ordnance Corps; Royal Australian Army Nursing Corps; The Corps of Royal New Zealand Engineers; Royal New Zealand Infantry Regiment; The Malawi Rifles; The Royal Malta Artillery

Affiliated Colonel-in-Chief
The Queen's Gurkha Engineers

Captain-General
Royal Regiment of Artillery; The Honourable Artillery Company; Combined Cadet Force; Royal Regiment of Canadian Artillery; Royal Regiment of Australian Artillery; Royal Regiment of New Zealand Artillery; Royal New Zealand Armoured Corps

Patron
Royal Army Chaplains' Department

Air Commodore-in-Chief
Royal Auxiliary Air Force; Royal Air Force Regiment; Air Reserve (of Canada); Royal Australian Air Force Reserve; Territorial Air Force (of New Zealand)

Commandant-in-Chief
Royal Air Force College, Cranwell

Royal Hon. Air Commodore
Royal Air Force Marham; 603 (City of Edinburgh) Squadron Royal Auxiliary Air Force (Represented by The Rt. Hon. Lord Selkirk of Dougal, QC)

HRH THE PRINCE PHILIP, DUKE OF EDINBURGH

Admiral of the Fleet
Field Marshal
Marshal of the Royal Air Force

Admiral of the Fleet, Royal Australian Navy
Field Marshal, Australian Military Forces
Marshal of the Royal Australian Air Force

Admiral of the Fleet, Royal New Zealand Navy
Field Marshal, New Zealand Army
Marshal of the Royal New Zealand Air Force
Captain General, Royal Marines

Admiral
Royal Canadian Sea Cadets

Colonel-in-Chief
The Royal Gloucestershire, Berkshire and Wiltshire Regiment; The Highlanders (Seaforth, Gordons and Camerons); Corps of Royal Electrical and Mechanical Engineers; Intelligence Corps; Army Cadet Force Association; The Royal Canadian Regiment; The Royal Hamilton Light Infantry (Wentworth Regiment of Canada); The Cameron Highlanders of Ottawa; The Queen's Own Cameron Highlanders of Canada; The Seaforth Highlanders of Canada; The Royal Canadian Army Cadets; The Royal Australian Corps of Electrical and Mechanical Engineers; The Australian Army Cadet Corps

Deputy Colonel-in-Chief
The Queen's Royal Hussars (Queen's Own and Royal Irish)

Colonel
Grenadier Guards

Royal Hon. Colonel
City of Edinburgh University Officers' Training Corps; The Trinidad and Tobago Regiment

Air Commodore-in-Chief
Air Training Corps; Royal Canadian Air Cadets

Royal Hon. Air Commodore
Royal Air Force Kinloss

Member
Honourable Artillery Company

HRH THE PRINCE OF WALES

Rear Admiral, Royal Navy

Major-General, Army

Air Vice-Marshal, Royal Air Force

Colonel-in-Chief
The Royal Dragoon Guards; The 22nd (Cheshire) Regiment; The Royal Regiment of Wales (24th/41st Foot); The Parachute Regiment; The Royal Gurkha Rifles; Army Air Corps; The Royal Canadian Dragoons; Lord Strathcona's Horse (Royal Canadians); Royal Regiment of Canada (10th Royal Grenadiers); Royal Winnipeg Rifles; Royal Australian Armoured Corps; The Royal Pacific Islands Regiment; Air Reserve Group of Air Command (of Canada)

Deputy Colonel-in-Chief
The Highlanders (Seaforth, Gordons and Camerons)

Colonel
Welsh Guards

Royal Hon. Colonel
The Queen's Own Yeomanry

Air Commodore-in-Chief
Royal New Zealand Air Force

Royal Hon. Air Commodore
Royal Air Force Valley

HRH THE DUKE OF YORK

Commander (retd), Royal Navy

Admiral
Sea Cadet Corps

Colonel-in-Chief
The Staffordshire Regiment (The Prince of Wales's); The Royal Irish Regiment (27th (Inniskilling), 83rd, 87th and The Ulster Defence Regiment); The Queen's York Rangers (First Americans); Royal New Zealand Army Logistics Regiment

Royal Hon. Air Commodore
Royal Air Force Lossiemouth

HRH THE PRINCESS ROYAL

Rear Admiral
Chief Commandant for Women in the Royal Navy

Colonel-in-Chief
The King's Royal Hussars; Royal Corps of Signals; Royal Logistic Corps; The Worcestershire and Sherwood Foresters Regiment (29th/45th Foot); The Royal Scots (The Royal Regiment); 8th Canadian Hussars (Princess Louise's); Royal Newfoundland Regiment; Canadian Forces Communications and Electronics Branch; The Grey and Simcoe Foresters (Royal Canadian Armoured Corps); The Royal Regina Rifle Regiment; Royal Australian Corps of Signals; Royal New Zealand Corps of Signals; Royal New Zealand Nursing Corps

Colonel
The Blues and Royals (Royal Horse Guards and 1st Dragoons)

Affiliated Colonel-in-Chief
The Queen's Gurkha Signals; The Queen's Own Gurkha Transport Regiment

Royal Hon. Colonel
University of London Officers' Training Corps

Royal Hon. Air Commodore
Royal Air Force Lyneham; University of London Air Squadron

Commandant
First Aid Nursing Yeomanry (Princess Royal's Volunteer Corps)

HRH PRINCESS ALICE, DUCHESS OF GLOUCESTER

Air Chief Marshal

Colonel-in-Chief
The King's Own Scottish Borderers; Royal Australian Corps of Transport

Deputy Colonel-in-Chief
The King's Royal Hussars; The Royal Anglian Regiment

Air Chief Commandant
Women, Royal Air Force

HRH THE DUKE OF GLOUCESTER

Hon. Air Marshal

Deputy Colonel-in-Chief
The Royal Gloucestershire, Berkshire and Wiltshire Regiment; The Royal Logistic Corps

Royal Hon. Colonel
Royal Monmouthshire Royal Engineers (Militia)

Royal Hon. Air Commodore
Royal Air Force Odiham; No 501 (County of Gloucester) Squadron Royal Auxiliary Air Force

---

HRH THE DUCHESS OF GLOUCESTER

Colonel-in-Chief
Royal Australian Army Educational Corps; Royal New Zealand Army Educational Corps; Royal Army Dental Corps

Deputy Colonel-in-Chief
Adjutant-General's Corps

HRH THE DUKE OF KENT

Field Marshal

Hon. Air Chief Marshal

Colonel-in-Chief
The Royal Regiment of Fusiliers; The Devonshire and Dorset Regiment; Lorne Scots (Peel, Dufferin and Hamilton Regiment)

Deputy Colonel-in-Chief
The Royal Scots Dragoon Guards (Carabiniers and Greys)

Colonel
Scots Guards

Royal Hon. Air Commodore
Royal Air Force Leuchars

HRH THE DUCHESS OF KENT

Hon. Major-General

Colonel-in-Chief
The Prince of Wales's Own Regiment of Yorkshire

Deputy Colonel-in-Chief
The Royal Dragoon Guards; Adjutant-General's Corps; The Royal Logistic Corps

---

HRH PRINCE MICHAEL OF KENT

Colonel-in-Chief
Essex and Kent Scottish Regiment (Ontario)

Major (retd), The Royal Hussars (Prince of Wales's Own)

Hon. Commodore
Royal Naval Reserve

HRH PRINCESS ALEXANDRA, THE HON. LADY OGILVY

Patron
Queen Alexandra's Royal Naval Nursing Service

Patron and Air Chief Commandant
Princess Mary's Royal Air Force Nursing Service

Colonel-in-Chief
The King's Own Royal Border Regiment; The Queen's Own Rifles of Canada; The Canadian Scottish Regiment (Princess Mary's)

Deputy Colonel-in-Chief

The Queen's Royal Lancers; The Light Infantry Royal Hon. Air Commodore
Royal Air Force Cottesmore

Deputy Royal Hon. Colonel
The Royal Yeomanry

Patron and Air Chief Commandant
Princess Mary's Royal Air Force Nursing Service

The House of Windsor

King George V assumed by royal proclamation (17 July 1917) for his House and family, as well as for all descendants in the male line of Queen Victoria who are subjects of these realms, the name of Windsor.

KING GEORGE V (George Frederick Ernest Albert), second son of King Edward VII, *born* 3 June 1865; *married* 6 July 1893 HSH Princess Victoria Mary Augusta Louise Olga Pauline Claudine Agnes of Teck (Queen Mary, *born* 26 May 1867; *died* 24 March 1953); *succeeded* to the throne 6 May 1910; *died* 20 January 1936. *Issue:*

1. HRH PRINCE EDWARD Albert Christian George Andrew Patrick David, *born* 23 June 1894, *succeeded* to the throne as King Edward VIII, 20 January 1936; *abdicated* 11 December 1936; created *Duke of Windsor* 1937; *married* 3 June 1937, Mrs Wallis Simpson (Her Grace The Duchess of Windsor, *born* 19 June 1896; *died* 24 April 1986), *died* 28 May 1972

2. HRH PRINCE ALBERT Frederick Arthur George, *born* 14 December 1895, *created Duke of York* 1920; *married* 26 April 1923, Lady Elizabeth Bowes-Lyon, youngest daughter of the 14th Earl of Strathmore and Kinghorne (HM Queen Elizabeth the Queen Mother, *born* 4 August 1900; *died* 30 March 2002), *succeeded* to the throne as King George VI, 11 December 1936; *died* 6 February 1952, having had issue

3. HRH PRINCESS (Victoria Alexandra Alice) MARY, *born* 25 April 1897, *created* Princess Royal 1932; *married* 28 February 1922, Viscount Lascelles, later the 6th Earl of Harewood (1882–1947), *died* 28 March 1965. *Issue:*
   (1) George Henry Hubert Lascelles, 7th Earl of Harewood, KBE, *born* 7 February 1923; *married* (1) 1949, Maria (Marion) Stein (marriage dissolved 1967); *issue,* (*a*) David Henry George, Viscount Lascelles, *born* 1950; (*b*) James Edward,

born 1953; (*c*) (Robert) Jeremy Hugh, *born* 1955; (2) 1967, Mrs Patricia Tuckwell; *issue,* (*d*) Mark Hubert, *born* 1964
   (2) Gerald David Lascelles (1924–98), *married* (1) 1952, Miss Angela Dowding (marriage dissolved 1978); *issue,* (*a*) Henry Ulick, *born* 1953; (2) 1978, Mrs Elizabeth Colvin; *issue,* (*b*) Martin David, *born* 1962

4. HRH PRINCE HENRY William Frederick Albert, *born* 31 March 1900, *created* Duke of Gloucester, Earl of Ulster and Baron Culloden 1928, *married* 6 November 1935, Lady Alice Christabel Montagu-Douglas-Scott, daughter of the 7th Duke of Buccleuch (HRH Princess Alice, Duchess of Gloucester, *m.*); *died* 10 June 1974. *Issue:*
   (1) HRH Prince William Henry Andrew Frederick, *born* 18 December 1941; *accidentally killed* 28 August 1972
   (2) HRH Prince Richard Alexander Walter George (HRH The Duke of Gloucester)

5. HRH PRINCE GEORGE Edward Alexander Edmund, *born* 20 December 1902, *created* Duke of Kent, Earl of St Andrews and Baron Downpatrick 1934, *married* 29 November 1934, HRH Princess Marina of Greece and Denmark (*born* 30 November OS, 1906; *died* 27 August 1968); *killed on active service,* 25 August 1942. *Issue:*
   (1) HRH Prince Edward George Nicholas Paul Patrick (HRH The Duke of Kent)
   (2) HRH Princess Alexandra Helen Elizabeth Olga Christabel (HRH Princess Alexandra, the Hon. Lady Ogilvy)
   (3) HRH Prince Michael George Charles Franklin (HRH Prince Michael of Kent)

6. HRH PRINCE JOHN Charles Francis, *born* 12 July 1905; *died* 18 January 1919

Descendants of Queen Victoria

QUEEN VICTORIA (Alexandrina Victoria), *born* 24 May 1819; *succeeded* to the throne 20 June 1837; *married* 10 February 1840 (Francis) Albert Augustus Charles Emmanuel, Duke of Saxony, Prince of Saxe-Coburg and Gotha (HRH Albert, Prince Consort, *born* 26 August 1819, *died* 14 December 1861); *died* 22 January 1901.
Issue:
1. HRH PRINCESS VICTORIA Adelaide Mary Louisa (Princess Royal) (1840–1901); *m.* 1858, Friedrich III (1831–88), German Emperor March–June 1888. *Issue:*
   (1) HIM Wilhelm II (1859–1941), German Emperor 1888–1918, *m.* (1) 1881 Princess Augusta Victoria of Schleswig-Holstein-Sonderburg-Augustenburg (1858–1921); (2) 1922 Princess Hermine of Reuss (1887–1947). *Issue:*
   (*a*) Prince Wilhelm (1882–1951), Crown Prince 1888–1918, *m.* 1905 Duchess Cecilie of Mecklenburg-Schwerin; *Issue:* Prince Wilhelm (1906–40); Prince Louis Ferdinand (1907–94), *m.* 1938 Grand Duchess Kira; Prince Hubertus (1909–50); Prince Friedrich Georg (1911–66); Princess Alexandrine Irene (1915–80); Princess Cecilie (1917–75)
   (*b*) Prince Eitel-Friedrich (1883–1942), *m.* 1906 Duchess Sophie of Oldenburg (marriage dissolved 1926)
   (*c*) Prince Adalbert (1884–1948), *m.* 1914 Duchess Adelheid of Saxe-Meiningen; *issue:* Princess Victoria Marina (1917–81); Prince Wilhelm Victor (1919–89)
   (*d*) Prince August Wilhelm (1887–1949), *m.* 1908 Princess Alexandra of Schleswig-Holstein-Sonderburg-Glücksburg (marriage dissolved 1920); *Issue:* Prince Alexander (1912–85)
   (*e*) Prince Oskar (1888–1958), *m.* 1914 Countess von

Ruppin; *Issue:* Prince Oskar (1915–39); Prince Burchard (1917–88); Princess Herzeleide (1918–89); Prince Wilhelm-Karl (*b.* 1922)
   (*f*) Prince Joachim (1890–1920), *m.* 1916 Princess Marie of Anhalt; *Issue:* Prince (Karl) Franz Joseph (1916–75), and has issue
   (*g*) Princess Viktoria Luise (1892–1980), *m.* 1913 Ernst, Duke of Brunswick 1913–18 (1887–1953); *Issue:* Prince Ernst (1914–87); Prince Georg (*b.* 1915), *m.* 1946 Princess Sophie of Greece (*see* page 128) and has issue (two sons, one daughter); Princess Frederika (1917–81), *m.* 1938 Paul I, King of the Hellenes; Prince Christian (1919–81); Prince Welf Heinrich (*b.* 1923)
   (2) Princess Charlotte (1860–1919), *m.* 1878 Bernhard, Duke of Saxe-Meiningen 1914 (1851–1914). *Issue:* Princess Feodora (1879–1945), *m.* 1898 Prince Heinrich XXX of Reuss
   (3) Prince Heinrich (1862–1929), *m.* 1888 Princess Irene of Hesse. *Issue:*
   (*a*) Prince Waldemar (1889–1945), *m.* Princess Calixta Agnes of Lippe
   (*b*) Prince Sigismund (1896–1978), *m.*1919 Princess Charlotte of Saxe-Altenburg; *Issue:* Princess Barbara (1920–94); Prince Alfred (*b.* 1924)
   (*c*) Prince Heinrich (1900–4)
   (4) Prince Sigismund (1864–6)
   (5) Princess Victoria (1866–1929), *m.* (1) 1890, Prince Adolf of Schaumburg-Lippe (1859–1916); (2) 1927 Alexander Zubkov
   (6) Prince Waldemar (1868–79)

(7) Princess Sophie (1870–1932), *m.* 1889 Constantine I (1868–1923), King of the Hellenes 1913–17, 1920-3. *Issue:*
(*a*) George II (1890–1947), King of the Hellenes 1923–4 and 1935–47, *m.* 1921 Princess Elisabeth of Roumania (marriage dissolved 1935)
(*b*) Alexander I (1893–1920), King of the Hellenes 1917–20, *m.* 1919 Aspasia Manos; *Issue:* Princess Alexandra (1921–93), *m.* 1944 King Petar II of Yugoslavia
(*c*) Princess Helena (1896–1982), *m.* 1921 King Carol of Roumania (*see below*), (marriage dissolved 1928)
(*d*) Paul I (1901–64), King of the Hellenes 1947–64, *m.* 1938 Princess Frederika of Brunswick; *Issue:* King Constantine II (*b.* 1940), *m.* 1964 Princess Anne-Marie of Denmark and has issue (three sons, two daughters); Princess Sophie (*b.* 1938), *m.* 1962 Juan Carlos I of Spain; Princess Irene (*b.* 1942)
(*e*) Princess Irene (1904–74), *m.* 1939 4th Duke of Aosta; *Issue:* Prince Amedeo, 5th Duke of Aosta (*b.* 1943)
(*f*) Princess Katherine (Lady Katherine Brandram) (*b.* 1913), *m.* 1947 Major R. C. A. Brandram, MC, TD; *Issue:* R. Paul G. A. Brandram (*b.* 1948)
(8) Princess Margarethe (1872–1954), *m.* 1893 Prince Friedrich Karl of Hesse (1868–1940). *Issue:*
(*a*) Prince Friedrich Wilhelm (1893–1916)
(*b*) Prince Maximilian (1894–1914)
(*c*) Prince Philipp (1896–1980), *m.* 1925 Princess Mafalda of Italy; *Issue:* Prince Moritz (*b.* 1926); Prince Heinrich (1927–2000); Prince Otto (*b.* 1937); Princess Elisabeth (*b.* 1940)
(*d*) Prince Wolfgang (1896–1989), *m.* (1) 1924 Princess Marie Alexandra of Baden; (2) 1948 Ottilie Möller;
(*e*) Prince Richard (1901–69)
(*f*) Prince Christoph (1901–43), *m.* 1930 Princess Sophie of Greece (*see below*) and has issue (two sons, three daughters)

2. HRH PRINCE ALBERT EDWARD (HM KING EDWARD VII), *b.* 9 November 1841, *m.* 1863 HRH Princess Alexandra of Denmark (1844–1925), *succeeded* to the throne 22 January 1901, *d.* 6 May 1910. *Issue:*
(1) Albert Victor, Duke of Clarence and Avondale (1864–92)
(2) George (HM KING GEORGE V)
(3) Louise (1867–1931) Princess Royal 1905-31, *m.* 1889 1st Duke of Fife (1849–1912). *Issue:*
(*a*) Princess Alexandra, Duchess of Fife (1891–1959), *m.* 1913 Prince Arthur of Connaught
(*b*) Princess Maud (1893–1945), *m.* 1923 11th Earl of - Southesk (1893–1992); *Issue:* The Duke of Fife (*b.* 1929)
(4) Victoria (1868–1935)
(5) Maud (1869–1938), *m.* 1896 Prince Carl of Denmark (1872–1957), later King Haakon VII of Norway 1905–57. *Issue:*
(*a*) Olav V (1903–91), King of Norway 1957–91, *m.* 1929 Princess Märtha of Sweden (1901–54); *Issue:* Princess Ragnhild (*b.* 1930); Princess Astrid (*b.* 1932); Harald V, King of Norway (*b.* 1937)
(6) Alexander (6–7 April 1871)

3. HRH PRINCESS ALICE Maud Mary (1843–78), *m.* 1862 Prince Ludwig (1837–92), Grand Duke of Hesse 1877–92. *Issue:*
(1) Victoria (1863–1950), *m.* 1884 *Admiral of the Fleet* Prince Louis of Battenberg (1854–1921), *cr.* 1st Marquess of Milford Haven 1917. *Issue:*
(*a*) Alice (1885–1969), *m.* 1903 Prince Andrew of Greece (1882–1944); *Issue:* Princess Margarita (1905–81), *m.* 1931 Prince Gottfried of Hohenlohe-Langenburg (*see below*); Princess Theodora (1906–69) and has issue (two sons, one daughter); Princess Cecilie (1911–37), *m.* George, Grand Duke of Hesse (*see below*); Princess Sophie (*b.* 1914), *m.* (1) 1930 Prince Christoph of Hesse (*see above*); (2) 1946 Prince Georg of Hanover; Prince Philip, Duke of Edinburgh (*b.* 1921)
(*b*) Louise (1889–1965), *m.* 1923 Gustaf VI Adolf (1882–1973), King of Sweden 1950–73
(*c*) George, 2nd Marquess of Milford Haven (1892–1938), *m.* 1916 Countess Nadejda, daughter of Grand Duke Michael of Russia; *Issue:* Lady Tatiana (1917–88); David Michael, 3rd Marquess (1919–70)
(*d*) Louis, 1st Earl Mountbatten of Burma (1900–79), *m.* 1922 Edwina Ashley, daughter of Lord Mount Temple;

Issue: Patricia, Countess Mountbatten of Burma (*b.* 1924), Pamela (*b.* 1929)
(2) Elizabeth (1864–1918), *m.* 1884 Grand Duke Sergius of Russia (1857–1905)
(3) Irene (1866–1953), *m.* 1888 Prince Heinrich of Prussia
(4) Ernst Ludwig (1868–1937), Grand Duke of Hesse 1892–1918, *m.* (1) 1894 Princess Victoria Melita of Saxe-Coburg (*see below*) (marriage dissolved 1901); (2) 1905 Princess Eleonore of Solms-Hohensolmslich. *Issue:*
(*a*) Princess Elizabeth (1895–1903)
(*b*) George, Hereditary Grand Duke of Hesse (1906–37), *m.* Princess Cecilie of Greece (*see above*), and had issue, two sons, accidentally killed with parents 1937
(*c*) Ludwig, Prince of Hesse (1908–68), *m.* 1937 Margaret, daughter of 1st Lord Geddes
(5) Frederick William (1870–3)
(6) Alix (Tsaritsa of Russia) (1872–1918), *m.* 1894 Nicholas II (1868–1918) Tsar of All the Russias 1894–1917, assassinated 16 July 1918. *Issue:*
(*a*) Grand Duchess Olga (1895–1918)
(*b*) Grand Duchess Tatiana (1897–1918)
(*c*) Grand Duchess Marie (1899–1918)
(*d*) Grand Duchess Anastasia (1901–18)
(*e*) Alexis, Tsarevich of Russia (1904–18)
(7) Marie (1874–8)

4. HRH PRINCE ALFRED Ernest Albert, Duke of Edinburgh, *Admiral of the Fleet* (1844–1900), *m.* 1874 Grand Duchess Marie Alexandrovna of Russia (1853–1920); succeeded as Duke of Saxe-Coburg and Gotha 22 August 1893. *Issue:*
(1) Alfred, Prince of Saxe-Coburg (1874–99)
(2) Marie (1875–1938), *m.* 1893 Ferdinand (1865–1927), King of Roumania 1914–27. *Issue:*
(*a*) Carol II (1893–1953), King of Roumania 1930–40, *m.* (2) 1921 Princess Helena of Greece (*see below*) (marriage dissolved 1928); *Issue:* Michael (*b.* 1921), King of Roumania 1927–30, 1940–7, *m.* 1948 Princess Anne of Bourbon-Parma, and has issue (five daughters)
(*b*) Elisabeth (1894–1956), *m.* 1921 George II, King of the Hellenes
(*c*) Marie (1900–61), *m.* 1922 Alexander (1888–1934), King of Yugoslavia 1921–34; *Issue:* Petar II (1923–70), King of Yugoslavia 1934–45, *m.* 1944 Princess Alexandra of Greece (*see above*) and has issue (Crown Prince Alexander, b. 1945); Prince Tomislav (*b.* 1928), *m.* (1) 1957 Princess Margarita of Baden (daughter of Princess Theodora of Greece and Prince Berthold of Baden, *see above*); (2) 1982 Linda Bonney; and has issue (three sons, one daughter) Prince Andrej (1929–90), *m.* (1) 1956 Princess Christina of Hesse (daughter of Prince Christoph of Hesse and Princess Sophie of Greece, *see above*); (2) 1963 Princess Kira-Melita of Leiningen (*see below*); and has issue (three sons, two daughters)
(*d*) Prince Nicolas (1903–78)
(*e*) Princess Ileana (1909–91), *m.* (1) 1931 Archduke Anton of Austria; (2) 1954 Dr Stefan Issarescu; *Issue:* Archduke Stefan (*b.* 1932); Archduchess Maria Ileana (1933–59); Archduchess Alexandra (*b.* 1935); Archduke Dominic (*b.* 1937); Archduchess Maria Magdalena (*b.* 1939); Archduchess Elisabeth (*b.* 1942)
(*f*) Prince Mircea (1913–16)
(3) Victoria Melita (1876–1936), *m.* (1) 1894 Grand Duke Ernst Ludwig of Hesse (*see above*) (marriage dissolved 1901); (2) 1905 the Grand Duke Kirill of Russia (1876–1938). *Issue:*
(*a*) Marie Kirillovna (1907–51), *m.* 1925 Prince Friedrich Karl of Leiningen; *Issue:* Prince Emich (1926–91); Prince Karl (1928–90); Princess Kira-Melita (*b.* 1930), *m.* Prince Andrej of Yugoslavia (*see above*); Princess Margarita (*b.* 1932); Princess Mechtilde (*b.* 1936); Prince Friedrich (*b.* 1938)
(*b*) Kira Kirillovna (1909–67), *m.* 1938 Prince Louis Ferdinand of Prussia; *Issue:* Prince Friedrich Wilhelm (*b.* 1939); Prince Michael (*b.* 1940); Princess Marie (*b.* 1942); Princess Kira (*b.* 1943); Prince Louis Ferdinand (1944–77); Prince Christian (*b.* 1946); Princess Xenia (1949–92)
(*c*) Vladimir Kirillovich (1917–92), *m.* 1948 Princess Leonida Bagration-Mukhransky; *Issue:* Grand Duchess Maria (*b.* 1953), and has issue

(4) Alexandra (1878–1942), *m.* 1896 Ernst, Prince of Hohenlohe Langenburg. *Issue:*
　(a) Gottfried (1897–1960), *m.* 1931 Princess Margarita of Greece (*see* above); *Issue:* Prince Kraft (b. 1935), Princess Beatrice (1936–97), Prince Georg Andreas (b. 1938), Prince Ruprecht (1944–76); Prince Albrecht (1944–92)
　(b) Maria (1899–1967), *m.* 1916 Prince Friedrich of Schleswig-Holstein-Sonderburg-Glücksburg; *Issue:* Prince Peter (1922–80); Princess Marie (b. 1927)
　(c) Princess Alexandra (1901–63)
　(d) Princess Irma (1902–86)
(5) Princess Beatrice (1884–1966), *m.* 1909 Alfonso of Orleans, Infante of Spain. *Issue:*
　(a) Prince Alvaro (b. 1910), *m.* 1937 Carla Parodi-Delfino; *Issue:* Doña Gerarda (b. 1939); Don Alonso (1941–75); Doña Beatriz (b. 1943); Don Alvaro (b. 1947)
　(b) Prince Alonso (1912–36)
　(c) Prince Ataulfo (1913–74)

5. HRH PRINCESS HELENA Augusta Victoria (1846–1923), *m.* 1866 Prince Christian of Schleswig-Holstein-Sonderburg-Augustenburg (1831–1917). *Issue:*
　(1) Prince Christian Victor (1867–1900)
　(2) Prince Albert (1869–1931), Duke of Schleswig-Holstein 1921-31
　(3) Princess Helena (1870–1948)
　(4) Princess Marie Louise (1872–1956), *m.* 1891 Prince Aribert of Anhalt (marriage dissolved 1900)
　(5) Prince Harold (12–20 May 1876)

6. HRH PRINCESS LOUISE Caroline Alberta (1848–1939), *m.* 1871 the Marquess of Lorne, afterwards 9th Duke of Argyll (1845–1914); without issue

7. HRH PRINCE ARTHUR William Patrick Albert, Duke of Connaught, *Field Marshal* (1850-1942), *m.* 1879 Princess Louisa of Prussia (1860-1917). *Issue:*
　(1) Margaret (1882–1920), *m.* 1905 Crown Prince Gustaf Adolf (1882-1973), afterwards King of Sweden 1950-73. *Issue:*
　　(a) Gustaf Adolf, Duke of Västerbotten (1906-47), *m.* 1932 Princess Sibylla of Saxe-Coburg-Gotha (*see* below); *Issue:* Princess Margaretha (b. 1934); Princess Birgitta (b. 1937); Princess Désirée (b. 1938); Princess Christina (b. 1943); Carl XVI Gustaf, King of Sweden (b. 1946)
　　(b) Count Sigvard Bernadotte (b. 1907), *m.*; *Issue:* Count Michael (b. 1944)
　　(c) Princess Ingrid (Queen Mother of Denmark) (1910-2000), *m.* 1935 Frederick IX (1899-1972), King of Denmark 1947-72; *Issue:* Margrethe II, Queen of Denmark (b. 1940); Princess Benedikte (b. 1944); Princess Anne-Marie (b. 1946), *m.* 1964 Constantine II of Greece
　　(d) Prince Bertil, Duke of Halland (1912-97), *m.* 1976 Mrs Lilian Craig

　(e) Count Carl Bernadotte (b. 1916), *m.* (1) 1946 Mrs Kerstin Johnson; (2) 1988 Countess Gunnila Bussler
(2) Arthur (1883-1938), *m.* 1913 HH the Duchess of Fife. *Issue:*
　Alastair Arthur, 2nd Duke of Connaught (1914-13)
(3) (Victoria) Patricia (1886-1974), *m.* 1919 Adm. Hon. Sir Alexander Ramsay. *Issue:*
　Alexander Ramsay of Mar (1919–2000), *m.* 1956 Hon. Flora Fraser (Lady Saltoun)

8. HRH PRINCE LEOPOLD George Duncan Albert, Duke of Albany (1853–84), *m.* 1882 Princess Helena of Waldeck (1861–1922). *Issue:*
　(1) Alice (1883–1981), *m.* 1904 Prince Alexander of Teck (1874–1957), cr. 1st Earl of Athlone 1917. *Issue:*
　　(a) Lady May (1906–94), *m.* 1931 Sir Henry Abel-Smith, KCMG. KCVO, DSO; *Issue:* Anne (b. 1932); Richard (b. 1933); Elizabeth (b. 1936)
　　(b) Rupert, Viscount Trematon (1907–28)
　　(c) Prince Maurice (March-September 1910)
　(2) Charles Edward (1884–1954), Duke of Albany 1884 until title suspended 1917, Duke of Saxe-Coburg-Gotha 1900–18, *m.* 1905 Princess Victoria Adelheid of Schleswig-Holstein-Sonderburg-Glücksburg. *Issue:*
　　(a) Prince Johann Leopold (1906–72), and has issue
　　(b) Princess Sibylla (1908–72), *m.* 1932 Prince Gustav Adolf of Sweden (*see* above)
　　(c) Prince Dietmar Hubertus (1909–43)
　　(d) Princess Caroline (1912–83), and has issue
　　(e) Prince Friedrich Josias (b. 1918), and has issue

9. HRH PRINCESS BEATRICE Mary Victoria Feodore (1857–1944), *m.* 1885 Prince Henry of Battenberg (1858–96). *Issue:*
　(1) Alexander, 1st Marquess of Carisbrooke (1886–1960), *m.* 1917 Lady Irene Denison. *Issue:*
　　Lady Iris Mountbatten (1920–82), *m.*; *Issue:* Robin A. Bryan (b. 1957)
　(2) Victoria Eugénie (1887–1969), *m.* 1906 Alfonso XIII (1886–1941) King of Spain 1886–1931. *Issue:*
　　(a) Prince Alfonso (1907–38)
　　(b) Prince Jaime (1908–75), and has issue
　　(c) Princess Beatrice (b. 1909), and has issue
　　(d) Princess Maria (1911–96), and has issue
　　(e) Prince Juan (1913–93), Count of Barcelona; *Issue:* Princess Maria (b. 1936); Juan Carlos I, King of Spain (b. 1938), *m.* 1962 Princess Sophie of Greece and has issue (one son, two daughters); Princess Margarita *m.* 1939)
　　(f) Prince Gonzalo (1914–34)
　(3) Major Lord Leopold Mountbatten (1889–1922)
　(4) Maurice (1891–1914), died of wounds received in action

Kings and Queens

ENGLISH KINGS AND QUEENS 927 TO 1603

HOUSES OF CERDIC AND DENMARK

Reign

927–939　ÆTHELSTAN
　Son of Edward the Elder, by Ecgwynn, and grandson of Alfred
　Acceded to Wessex and Mercia c.924, established direct rule over Northumbria 927, effectively creating the Kingdom of England
　Reigned 15 years

939–946　EDMUND I
　Born 921, son of Edward the Elder, by Eadgifu
　Married (1) Ælfgifu (2) Æthelflæd
　Killed aged 25, reigned 6 years

946–955　EADRED
　Son of Edward the Elder, by Eadgifu
　Reigned 9 years

955–959　EADWIG
　Born before 943, son of Edmund and Ælfgifu
　Married Ælfgifu
　Reigned 3 years

959–975　EDGAR I
　Born 943, son of Edmund and Ælfgifu
　Married (1) Æthelflæd (2) Wulfthryth (3) Ælfthryth
　Died aged 32, reigned 15 years

975–978　EDWARD I (the Martyr)
　Born c.962, son of Edgar and Æthelflæd
　Assassinated aged c.16, *reigned* 2 years

978–1016　ÆTHELRED (the Unready)
　Born c.968/969, son of Edgar and Ælfthryth
　Married (1) Ælfgifu (2) Emma, daughter of Richard I, count of Normandy
　1013–14 dispossessed of kingdom by Swegn Forkbeard (king of Denmark 987–1014)
　Died aged c.47, *reigned* 38 years

1016　EDMUND II (Ironside)
　Born before 993, son of Æthelred and Ælfgifu
　Married Ealdgyth
　Died aged over 23, *reigned* 7 months (April–November)

1016–1035   CNUT (Canute)
*Born c.*995, son of Swegn Forkbeard, king of
Denmark, and Gunhild
Married (1) Ælfgifu (2) Emma, widow of
Æthelred the Unready
Gained submission of West Saxons 1015,
Northumbrians 1016, Mercia 1016, king of all
England after Edmund's death
King of Denmark 1019–35, king of Norway
1028–35
Died aged *c.*40, *reigned* 19 years

1035–1040   HAROLD I (Harefoot)
*Born c.*1016/17, son of Cnut and Ælfgifu
Married Ælfgifu
1035 recognised as regent for himself and his
brother Harthacnut; 1037 recognised
as king
Died aged *c.*23, *reigned* 4 years

1040–1042   HARTHACNUT
*Born c.*1018, son of Cnut and Emma
Titular king of Denmark from 1028
Acknowledged king of England 1035–7 with
Harold I as regent; effective king after
Harold's death
Died aged *c.*24, *reigned* 2 years

1042–1066   EDWARD II (the Confessor)
Born between 1002 and 1005, son of Æthelred the
Unready and Emma
Married Eadgyth, daughter of Godwine, earl of
Wessex
Died aged over 60, *reigned* 23 years

1066   HAROLD II (Godwinesson)
*Born c.*1020, son of Godwine, earl of Wessex, and
Gytha
Married (1) Eadgyth (2) Ealdgyth
Killed in battle aged *c.*46, *reigned* 10 months
(January–October)

THE HOUSE OF NORMANDY

1066–1087   WILLIAM I (the Conqueror)
Born 1027/8, son of Robert I, duke of Normandy;
obtained the Crown by conquest
Married Matilda, daughter of Baldwin, count of
Flanders
Died aged *c.*60, *reigned* 20 years

1087–1100   WILLIAM II (Rufus)
Born between 1056 and 1060, third son of William
I; succeeded his father in England only
Killed aged *c.*40, *reigned* 12 years

1100–1135   HENRY I (Beauclerk)
Born 1068, fourth son of William I
Married (1) Edith or Matilda, daughter of
Malcolm III of Scotland (2) Adela, daughter of
Godfrey, count of Louvain
Died aged 67, *reigned* 35 years

1135–1154   STEPHEN
Born not later than 1100, third son of Adela,
daughter of William I, and Stephen, count of
Blois
Married Matilda, daughter of Eustace, count of
Boulogne
1141 (February–November) held captive by
adherents   of Matilda, daughter of Henry I,
who contested the crown until 1153
Died aged over 53, *reigned* 18 years

THE HOUSE OF ANJOU (PLANTAGENETS)

1154–1189   HENRY II (Curtmantle)
Born 1133, son of Matilda, daughter of Henry I,
and Geoffrey, count of Anjou
Married Eleanor, daughter of William, duke of
Aquitaine, and divorced queen of Louis VII of
France
Died aged 56, *reigned* 34 years

1189–1199   RICHARD I (Coeur de Lion)
Born 1157, third son of Henry II
Married Berengaria, daughter of Sancho VI, king
of Navarre
Died aged 42, *reigned* 9 years

1199–1216   JOHN (Lackland)
Born 1167, fifth son of Henry II
Married (1) Isabella or Avisa, daughter of William,
earl of Gloucester (divorced) (2) Isabella,
daughter of Aymer, count of Angoulême
Died aged 48, *reigned* 17 years

1216–1272   HENRY III
Born 1207, son of John and Isabella of Angoulême
Married Eleanor, daughter of Raymond, count of
Provence
Died aged 65, *reigned* 56 years

1272–1307   EDWARD I (Longshanks)
Born 1239, eldest son of Henry III
Married (1) Eleanor, daughter of Ferdinand III,
king of Castile (2) Margaret, daughter of Philip III
of France
Died aged 68, *reigned* 34 years

1307–1327   EDWARD II
Born 1284, eldest surviving son of Edward I and
Eleanor
Married Isabella, daughter of Philip IV of France
Deposed January 1327, *killed* September 1327
aged 43, *reigned* 19 years

1327–1377   EDWARD III
Born 1312, eldest son of Edward II
Married Philippa, daughter of William, count of
Hainault
Died aged 64, *reigned* 50 years

1377–1399   RICHARD II
Born 1367, son of Edward (the Black Prince),
eldest son of Edward III
Married (1) Anne, daughter of Emperor Charles
IV (2) Isabelle, daughter of Charles VI of France
Deposed September 1399, *killed* February 1400
aged 3, *reigned* 22 years

THE HOUSE OF LANCASTER

1399–1413   HENRY IV
Born 1366, son of John of Gaunt, fourth son of
Edward III, and Blanche, daughter of Henry, duke
of Lancaster
Married (1) Mary, daughter of Humphrey, earl of
Hereford (2) Joan, daughter of Charles, king of
Navarre, and widow of John, duke of Brittany
Died aged *c.* 47, *reigned* 13 years

1413–1422   HENRY V
Born 1387, eldest surviving son of Henry IV and
Mary
Married Catherine, daughter of Charles VI of
France
Died aged 34, *reigned* 9 years

1422–1471   HENRY VI
Born 1421, son of Henry V
Married Margaret, daughter of René, duke of
Anjou and count of Provence
Deposed March 1461, restored October 1470
Deposed April 1471, *killed* May 1471 aged 49,
reigned 39 years

THE HOUSE OF YORK

1461–1483   EDWARD IV
Born 1442, eldest son of Richard of York
(grandson of Edmund, fifth son of Edward III,
and son of Anne, great-granddaughter of Lionel,
third son of Edward III)
Married Elizabeth Woodville, daughter of
Richard, Lord Rivers, and widow of Sir John Grey
Acceded March 1461, deposed October 1470,
restored April 1471
Died aged 40, *reigned* 21 years

1483   EDWARD V
Born 1470, eldest son of Edward IV
Deposed June 1483, *died* probably July–September
1483, aged 12, *reigned* 2 months (April–June)

1483–1485   RICHARD III
Born 1452, fourth son of Richard of York
Married Anne Neville, daughter of Richard, earl of
Warwick, and widow of Edward, Prince of Wales,
son of Henry VI
Killed in battle aged 32, *reigned* 2 years

THE HOUSE OF TUDOR

1485–1509   HENRY VII
Born 1457, son of Margaret Beaufort (great-granddaughter of John of Gaunt, fourth son of Edward III) and Edmund Tudor, earl of Richmond
Married Elizabeth, daughter of Edward IV
Died aged 52, reigned 23 years

1509–1547   HENRY VIII
Born 1491, second son of Henry VII
Married (1) Catherine, daughter of Ferdinand II, king of Aragon, and widow of his elder brother Arthur (divorced) (2) Anne, daughter of Sir Thomas Boleyn (executed) (3) Jane, daughter of Sir John Seymour (died in childbirth) (4) Anne, daughter of John, duke of Cleves (divorced) (5) Catherine Howard, niece of the Duke of Norfolk (executed) (6) Catherine, daughter of Sir Thomas Parr and widow of Lord Latimer
Died aged 55, reigned 37 years

1547–1553   EDWARD VI
Born 1537, son of Henry VIII and Jane Seymour
Died aged 15, reigned 6 years

1553   JANE
Born 1537, daughter of Frances (daughter of Mary Tudor, the younger daughter of Henry VII) and Henry Grey, duke of Suffolk
Married Lord Guildford Dudley, son of the Duke of Northumberland
Deposed July 1553, executed February 1554 aged 16, reigned 14 days

1553–1558   MARY I
Born 1516, daughter of Henry VIII and Catherine of Aragon
Married Philip II of Spain
Died aged 42, reigned 5 years

1558–1603   ELIZABETH I
Born 1533, daughter of Henry VIII and Anne Boleyn
Died aged 69, reigned 44 years

BRITISH KINGS AND QUEENS SINCE 1603

THE HOUSE OF STUART

Reign
1603–1625   JAMES I (VI OF SCOTLAND)
Born 1566, son of Mary, queen of Scots (granddaughter of Margaret Tudor, elder daughter of Henry VII), and Henry Stewart, Lord Darnley
Married Anne, daughter of Frederick II of Denmark
Died aged 58, reigned 22 years
(see also page 130)

1625–1649   CHARLES I
Born 1600, second son of James I
Married Henrietta Maria, daughter of Henry IV of France
Executed 1649 aged 48, reigned 23 years

COMMONWEALTH DECLARED 19 May 1649
1649–53 Government by a council of state
1653–8 Oliver Cromwell, Lord Protector
1658–9 Richard Cromwell, Lord Protector

1660–1685   CHARLES II
Born 1630, eldest son of Charles I
Married Catherine, daughter of John IV of Portugal
Died aged 54, reigned 24 years

1685–1688   JAMES II (VII of Scotland)
Born 1633, second son of Charles I
Married (1) Lady Anne Hyde, daughter of Edward, earl of Clarendon (2) Mary, daughter of Alphonso, duke of Modena

Reign ended with flight from kingdom December 1688
Died 1701 aged 67, reigned 3 years

INTERREGNUM 11 December 1688 to 12 February 1689

1689–1702   WILLIAM III
Born 1650, son of William II, prince of Orange, and Mary Stuart, daughter of Charles I
Married Mary, elder daughter of James II
Died aged 51, reigned 13 years

and

1689–1694   MARY II
Born 1662, elder daughter of James II and Anne
Died aged 32, reigned 5 years

1702–1714   ANNE
Born 1665, younger daughter of James II and Anne
Married Prince George of Denmark, son of Frederick III of Denmark
Died aged 49, reigned 12 years

THE HOUSE OF HANOVER

1714–1727   GEORGE I (Elector of Hanover)
Born 1660, son of Sophia (daughter of Frederick, elector palatine, and Elizabeth Stuart, daughter of James I) and Ernest Augustus, elector of Hanover
Married Sophia Dorothea, daughter of George William, duke of Lüneburg-Celle
Died aged 67, reigned 12 years

1727–1760   GEORGE II
Born 1683, son of George I
Married Caroline, daughter of John Frederick, margrave of Brandenburg-Anspach
Died aged 76, reigned 33 years

1760–1820   GEORGE III
Born 1738, son of Frederick, eldest son of George II
Married Charlotte, daughter of Charles Louis, duke of Mecklenburg-Strelitz
Died aged 81, reigned 59 years

REGENCY 1811–20
Prince of Wales regent owing to the insanity of George III

1820–1830   GEORGE IV
Born 1762, eldest son of George III
Married Caroline, daughter of Charles, duke of Brunswick-Wolfenbüttel
Died aged 67, reigned 10 years

1830–1837   WILLIAM IV
Born 1765, third son of George III
Married Adelaide, daughter of George, duke of Saxe-Meiningen
Died aged 71, reigned 7 years

1837–1901   VICTORIA
Born 1819, daughter of Edward, fourth son of George III
Married Prince Albert of Saxe-Coburg and Gotha
Died aged 81, reigned 63 years

THE HOUSE OF SAXE-COBURG AND GOTHA

1901–1910   EDWARD VII
Born 1841, eldest son of Victoria and Albert
Married Alexandra, daughter of Christian IX of Denmark
Died aged 68, reigned 9 years

THE HOUSE OF WINDSOR

1910–1936   GEORGE V
Born 1865, second son of Edward VII
Married Victoria Mary, daughter of Francis, duke of Teck
Died aged 70, reigned 25 years

1936   EDWARD VIII
Born 1894, eldest son of George V
Married (1937) Mrs Wallis Simpson
Abdicated 1936, died 1972 aged 77, reigned 10 months (20 January to 11 December)

1936–1952 GEORGE VI
  Born 1895, second son of George V
  Married Lady Elizabeth Bowes-Lyon, daughter of
  14th Earl of Strathmore and Kinghorne
  Died aged 56, *reigned* 15 years
1952– ELIZABETH II
  Born 1926, elder daughter of George VI
  Married Philip, son of Prince Andrew of Greece

KINGS AND QUEENS OF SCOTS 1016 TO 1603

Reign
1016–1034 MALCOLM II
  *Born c.*954, son of Kenneth II
  Acceded to Alba 1005, secured Lothian *c.*1016,
  obtained Strathclyde for his grandson Duncan
  *c.*1016, thus reigning over an area approximately
  the same as that governed by later rulers of
  Scotland
  Died aged *c.*80, *reigned* 18 years

THE HOUSE OF ATHOLL

1034–1040 DUNCAN I
  Son of Bethoc, daughter of Malcolm II, and
  Crinan, mormaer of Atholl
  Married a cousin of Siward, earl of Northumbria
  Reigned 5 years
1040–1057 MACBETH
  *Born c.*1005, son of a daughter of Malcolm II and
  Finlaec, mormaer of Moray
  Married Gruoch, granddaughter of Kenneth III
  Killed aged *c.*52, *reigned* 17 years
1057–1058 LULACH
  *Born c.*1032, son of Gillacomgan, mormaer of
  Moray, and Gruoch (and stepson of Macbeth)
  Died aged *c.*26, *reigned* 7 months (August–March)
1058–1093 MALCOLM III (Canmore)
  *Born c.*1031, elder son of Duncan I
  Married (1) Ingibiorg (2) Margaret (St Margaret),
  granddaughter of Edmund II of England
  Killed in battle aged *c.*62, *reigned* 35 years
1093–1097 DONALD III BÁN
  *Born c.*1033, second son of Duncan I
  Deposed May 1094, *restored* November 1094,
  deposed October 1097, *reigned* 3 years
1094 DUNCAN II
  *Born c.*1060, elder son of Malcolm III and
  Ingibiorg
  Married Octreda of Dunbar
  Killed aged *c.*34, *reigned* 6 months
  (May–November)
1097–1107 EDGAR
  *Born c.*1074, second son of Malcolm III and
  Margaret
  Died aged *c.*32, *reigned* 9 years
1107–1124 ALEXANDER I (The Fierce)
  *Born c.*1077, fifth son of Malcolm III and
  Margaret
  Married Sybilla, illegitimate daughter of Henry I
  of England
  Died aged *c.*47, *reigned* 17 years
1124–1153 DAVID I (The Saint)
  *Born c.*1085, sixth son of Malcolm III and
  Margaret
  Married Matilda, daughter of Waltheof, earl of
  Huntingdon
  Died aged *c.*68, *reigned* 29 years
1153–1165 MALCOLM IV (The Maiden)
  *Born c.*1141, son of Henry, earl of Huntingdon,
  second son of David I
  Died aged *c.*24, *reigned* 12 years
1165–1214 WILLIAM I (The Lion)
  *Born c.*1142, brother of Malcolm IV
  Married Ermengarde, daughter of Richard,
  viscount of Beaumont
  Died aged *c.*72, *reigned* 49 years

1214–1249 ALEXANDER II
  Born 1198, son of William I
  Married (1) Joan, daughter of John, king of
  England (2) Marie, daughter of Ingelram de
  Coucy
  Died aged 50, *reigned* 34 years
1249–1286 ALEXANDER III
  Born 1241, son of Alexander II and Marie
  Married (1) Margaret, daughter of Henry III of
  England (2) Yolande, daughter of the Count of
  Dreux
  Killed accidentally aged 44, *reigned* 36 years
1286–1290 MARGARET (The Maid of Norway)
  Born 1283, daughter of Margaret (daughter of
  Alexander III) and Eric II of Norway
  Died aged 7, *reigned* 4 years

  FIRST INTERREGNUM 1290–2
  Throne disputed by 13 competitors. Crown
  awarded to John Balliol by adjudication of
  Edward I of England

THE HOUSE OF BALLIOL

1292–1296 JOHN (Balliol)
  *Born c.*1250, son of Dervorguilla, great-great-
  granddaughter of David I, and John de Balliol
  Married Isabella, daughter of John, earl of Surrey
  Abdicated 1296, *died* 1313 aged *c.*63, *reigned* 3
  years

  SECOND INTERREGNUM 1296–1306
  Edward I of England declared John Balliol to have
  forfeited the throne for contumacy in 1296 and
  took the government of Scotland into his own
  hands

THE HOUSE OF BRUCE

1306–1329 ROBERT I (Bruce)
  Born 1274, son of Robert Bruce and Marjorie,
  countess of Carrick, and great-grandson of the
  second daughter of David, earl of Huntingdon,
  brother of William I
  Married (1) Isabella, daughter of Donald, earl of
  Mar (2) Elizabeth, daughter of Richard, earl of
  Ulster
  Died aged 54, *reigned* 23 years
1329–1371 DAVID II
  Born 1324, son of Robert I and Elizabeth
  Married (1) Joanna, daughter of Edward II of
  England (2) Margaret Drummond, widow of Sir
  John Logie (divorced)
  Died aged 46, *reigned* 41 years
  1332 Edward Balliol, son of John Balliol, crowned
  King of Scots September, expelled December
  1333–6 Edward Balliol restored as King of Scots

THE HOUSE OF STEWART

1371–1390 ROBERT II (Stewart)
  Born 1316, son of Marjorie (daughter of Robert I)
  and Walter, High Steward of Scotland
  Married (1) Elizabeth, daughter of Sir Robert
  Mure of Rowallan (2) Euphemia, daughter of
  Hugh,
  earl of Ross
  Died aged 74, *reigned* 19 years
1390–1406 ROBERT III
  *Born c.*1337, son of Robert II and Elizabeth
  Married Annabella, daughter of Sir John
  Drummond Stobhall
  Died aged *c.*69, *reigned* 16 years
1406–1437 JAMES I
  Born 1394, son of Robert III
  Married Joan Beaufort, daughter of John, earl of
  Somerset
  Assassinated aged 42, *reigned* 30 years

1437–1460	JAMES II
	Born 1430, son of James I
	Married Mary, daughter of Arnold, duke of Gueldres
	Killed accidentally aged 29, *reigned* 23 years
1460–1488	JAMES III
	Born 1452, son of James II
	Married Margaret, daughter of Christian I of Denmark
	Assassinated aged 36, *reigned* 27 years
1488–1513	JAMES IV
	Born 1473, son of James III
	Married Margaret Tudor, daughter of Henry VII of England
	Killed in battle aged 40, *reigned* 25 years
1513–1542	JAMES V
	Born 1512, son of James IV
	Married (1) Madeleine, daughter of Francis I of France (2) Mary of Lorraine, daughter of the Duc de Guise
	Died aged 30, *reigned* 29 years
1542–1567	MARY
	Born 1542, daughter of James V and Mary
	Married (1) the Dauphin, afterwards Francis II of France (2) Henry Stewart, Lord Darnley (3) James Hepburn, earl of Bothwell
	Abdicated 1567, prisoner in England from 1568, *executed* 1587, *reigned* 24 years
1567–1625	JAMES VI (and I of England)
	Born 1566, son of Mary, queen of Scots, and Henry, Lord Darnley
	Acceded 1567 to the Scottish throne, *reigned* 58 years
	Succeeded 1603 to the English throne, so joining the English and Scottish crowns in one person. The two kingdoms remained distinct until 1707 when the parliaments of the kingdoms became conjoined

WELSH SOVEREIGNS AND PRINCES

Wales was ruled by sovereign princes from the earliest times until the death of Llywelyn in 1282. The first English Prince of Wales was the son of Edward I, who was born in Caernarvon town on 25 April 1284. According to a discredited legend, he was presented to the Welsh chieftains as their prince, in fulfilment of a promise that they should have a prince who 'could not speak a word of English' and should be native *born*. This son, who afterwards became Edward II, was created 'Prince of Wales and Earl of Chester' at the Lincoln Parliament on 7 February 1301.

The title Prince of Wales is borne after individual conferment and is not inherited at birth, though some Princes have been declared and styled Prince of Wales but never formally so created (s.). The title was conferred on Prince Charles by The Queen on 26 July 1958. He was invested at Caernarvon on 1 July 1969.

INDEPENDENT PRINCES AD 844 TO 1282

844–878	Rhodri the Great
878–916	Anarawd, son of Rhodri
916–950	Hywel Dda, the Good
950–979	Iago ab Idwal (or Ieuaf)
979–985	Hywel ab Ieuaf, the Bad
985–986	Cadwallon, his brother
986–999	Maredudd ab Owain ap Hywel Dda
999–1008	Cynan ap Hywel ab Ieuaf
1018–1023	Llywelyn ap Seisyll
1023–1039	Iago ab Idwal ap Meurig
1039–1063	Gruffydd ap Llywelyn ap Seisyll
1063–1075	Bleddyn ap Cynfyn
1075–1081	Trahaern ap Caradog
1081–1137	Gruffydd ap Cynan ab Iago
1137–1170	Owain Gwynedd
1170–1194	Dafydd ab Owain Gwynedd
1194–1240	Llywelyn Fawr, the Great
1240–1246	Dafydd ap Llywelyn
1246–1282	Llywelyn ap Gruffydd ap Llywelyn

ENGLISH PRINCES SINCE 1301

1301	Edward (Edward II)
1343	Edward the Black Prince, son of Edward III
1376	Richard (Richard II), son of the Black Prince
1399	Henry of Monmouth (Henry V)
1454	Edward of Westminster, son of Henry VI
1471	Edward of Westminster (Edward V)
1483	Edward, son of Richard III (d. 1484)
1489	Arthur Tudor, son of Henry VII
1504	Henry Tudor (Henry VIII)
1610	Henry Stuart, son of James I (d. 1612)
1616	Charles Stuart (Charles I)
c.1638 (s.)	Charles Stuart (Charles II)
1688 (s.)	James Francis Edward Stuart (The Old Pretender), son of James II (d. 1766)
1714	George Augustus (George II)
1729	Frederick Lewis, son of George II (d. 1751)
1751	George William Frederick (George III)
1762	George Augustus Frederick (George IV)
1841	Albert Edward (Edward VII)
1901	George (George V)
1910	Edward (Edward VIII)
1958	Charles, son of Elizabeth II

PRINCESSES ROYAL

The style Princess Royal is conferred at the Sovereign's discretion on his or her eldest daughter. It is an honorary title, held for life, and cannot be inherited or passed on. It was first conferred on Princess Mary, daughter of Charles I, in approximately 1642.

c.1642	Princess Mary (1631–60), daughter of Charles I
1727	Princess Anne (1709–59), daughter of George II
1766	Princess Charlotte (1766–1828), daughter of George III
1840	Princess Victoria (1840–1901), daughter of Victoria
1905	Princess Louise (1867–1931), daughter of Edward VII
1932	Princess Mary (1897–1965), daughter of George V
1987	Princess Anne (b. 1950), daughter of Elizabeth II

Precedence

The Sovereign
The Prince Philip, Duke of
  Edinburgh
The Prince of Wales
The Sovereign's younger sons
The Sovereign's grandsons
The Sovereign's cousins
Archbishop of Canterbury
Lord High Chancellor
Archbishop of York
The Prime Minister
Lord President of the Council
Speaker of the House of Commons
Lord Privy Seal
Ambassadors and High
  Commissioners
Lord Great Chamberlain
Earl Marshal
Lord Steward of the Household
Lord Chamberlain of the Household
Master of the Horse
Dukes, according to their patent of
  creation:
  (1) of England
  (2) of Scotland
  (3) of Great Britain
  (4) of Ireland
  (5) those created since the Union
Ministers and Envoys
Eldest sons of Dukes of Blood Royal
Marquesses, according to their
  patent of creation:
  (1) of England
  (2) of Scotland
  (3) of Great Britain
  (4) of Ireland
  (5) those created since the Union
Dukes' eldest sons
Earls, according to their patent of
  creation:
  (1) of England
  (2) of Scotland
  (3) of Great Britain
  (4) of Ireland
  (5) those created since the Union
Younger sons of Dukes of Blood
  Royal
Marquesses' eldest sons
Dukes' younger sons
Viscounts, according to their patent
  of creation:
  (1) of England
  (2) of Scotland
  (3) of Great Britain
  (4) of Ireland
  (5) those created since the Union
Earls; eldest sons
Marquesses' younger sons
Bishops of London, Durham and
  Winchester
Other English Diocesan Bishops,
  according to seniority of
  consecration

Suffragan Bishops, according to
  seniority of consecration
Secretaries of State, if of the degree
  of a Baron
Barons, according to their patent of
  creation:
  (1) of England
  (2) of Scotland
  (3) of Great Britain
  (4) of Ireland
  (5) those created since the Union
Treasurer of the Household
Comptroller of the Household
Vice-Chamberlain of the Household
Secretaries of State under the degree
  of Baron
Viscounts' eldest sons
Earls' younger sons
Barons' eldest sons
Knights of the Garter
Privy Counsellors
Chancellor of the Exchequer
Chancellor of the Duchy of Lancaster
Lord Chief Justice of England
Master of the Rolls
President of the Family Division
Vice-Chancellor
Lords Justices of Appeal
Judges of the High Court
Viscounts' younger sons
Barons' younger sons
Sons of Life Peers
Baronets, according to date of patent
Knights of the Thistle
Knights Grand Cross of the Bath
Members of the Order of Merit
Knights Grand Commanders of the
  Star of India
Knights Grand Cross of St Michael
  and St George
Knights Grand Commanders of the
  Indian Empire
Knights Grand Cross of the Royal
  Victorian Order
Knights Grand Cross of the British
  Empire
Companions of Honour
Knights Commanders of the Bath
Knights Commanders of the Star of
  India
Knights Commanders of St Michael
  and St George
Knights Commanders of the Indian
  Empire
Knights Commanders of the Royal
  Victorian Order
Knights Commanders of the British
  Empire
Knights Bachelor
Vice-Chancellor of the County
  Palatine of Lancaster
Judges of the Technology and
  Construction Court
Circuit judges and judges of the
  Mayor's and City of London Court
Companions of the Bath

Companions of the Star of India
Companions of St Michael and St
  George
Companions of the Indian Empire
Commanders of the Royal Victorian
  Order
Commanders of the British Empire
Companions of the Distinguished
  Service Order
Lieutenants of the Royal Victorian
  Order
Officers of the British Empire
Companions of the Imperial Service
  Order
Eldest sons of younger sons of Peers
Baronets' eldest sons
Eldest sons of Knights, in the same
  order as their fathers
Members of the Royal Victorian
  Order
Members of the British Empire
Younger sons of the younger sons of
  Peers
Baronets' younger sons
Younger sons of Knights, in the same
  order as their fathers
Naval, Military, Air, and other
  Esquires by office

The Sovereign
The Prince Philip, Duke of
  Edinburgh
The Lord High Commissioner to the
  General Assembly (while that
  Assembly is sitting)
The Duke of Rothesay (eldest son of
  the Sovereign)
The Sovereign's younger sons
The Sovereign's cousins
Lord-Lieutenants
Lord Provosts of those Cities
Sheriffs Principal, successively, within
  their own localities and during
  holding of office
Lord Chancellor of Great Britain
Moderator of the General Assembly
  of the Church of Scotland
Keeper of the Great Seal
The Presiding Officer
The Secretary of State for Scotland
Hereditary Lord High Constable of
  Scotland
Hereditary Master of the Household
Dukes, in same order as in England
Eldest sons of Dukes of the Blood
  Royal
Marquesses, as in England
Dukes' eldest sons
Earls, as in England
Younger sons of Dukes of Blood
  Royal
Marquesses' eldest sons
Dukes' younger sons
Lord Justice General

Lord Clerk Register
Lord Advocate
The Advocate-General
Lord Justice Clerk
Viscounts, as in England
Earls' eldest sons
Marquesses' younger sons
Lord-Barons, as in England
Viscounts' eldest sons
Earls' younger sons
Lord-Barons' eldest sons
Knights of the Garter
Knights of the Thistle
Privy Counsellors
Senators of College of Justice (Lords
  of Session)
Viscounts' younger sons
Lord-Barons' younger sons
Sons of Life Peers
Baronets
Knights Grand Cross, Grand
Commander, and Knight
  Commanders, as in England
Solicitor-General for Scotland
Lord Lyon King of Arms
Sheriffs Principal, except as shown
  above
Knights Bachelor
Sheriffs
Companions of Orders, as in
  England
Commanders of the Royal Victorian
  Order
Commanders of the British Empire
Lieutenants of the Royal Victorian
  Order
Companions of the Distinguished
  Service Order
Eldest sons of younger sons of Peers
Baronets' eldest sons
Knights' eldest sons, as in England
Members of the Royal Victorian
  Order
Baronets' younger sons
Knights' younger sons
Queen's Counsel
Esquires
Gentlemen

WOMEN
Women take the same rank as their
husbands or as their brothers; but the
daughter of a peer marrying a
commoner retains her title as Lady or
Honourable. Daughters of peers rank
next immediately after the wives of
their elder brothers, and before their
younger brothers' wives. Daughters of
peers marrying peers of lower degree
take the same order of precedence as
that of their husbands; thus the
daughter of a Duke marrying a Baron
becomes of the rank of Baroness only,
while her sisters married to
commoners retain their rank and take
precedence of the Baroness. Merely

official rank on the husband's part
does not give any similar precedence
to the wife.

Peeresses in their own right take the
same precedence as peers of the same
rank, i.e. from their date of creation.

LOCAL PRECEDENCE
Scotland
The Lord Provosts of the city districts
of Aberdeen, Dundee, Edinburgh and
Glasgow are Lord Lieutenants for
those districts *ex officio* and take
precedence as such.

Forms of address

It is only possible to cover here the forms of address for peers, baronets and knights, their wife and children, and Privy Counsellors. Greater detail should be sought in one of the publications devoted to the subject.

Both formal and social forms of address are given where usage differs; nowadays, the social form is generally preferred to the formal, which increasingly is used only for official documents and on very formal occasions.

F_ represents forename
S_ represents surname

BARON – *Envelope (formal)*, The Right Hon. Lord _; *(social)*, The Lord _. *Letter (formal)*, My Lord; *(social)*, Dear Lord _. *Spoken*, Lord _.

BARON'S WIFE – *Envelope (formal)*, The Right Hon. Lady _; *(social)*, The Lady _. *Letter (formal)*, My Lady; *(social)*, Dear Lady _. *Spoken*, Lady _.

BARON'S CHILDREN – *Envelope*, The Hon. F_ S_. *Letter*, Dear Mr/Miss/Mrs S_. *Spoken*, Mr/Miss/Mrs S_.

BARONESS IN OWN RIGHT – *Envelope*, may be addressed in same way as a Baron's wife or, if she prefers *(formal)*, The Right Hon. the Baroness _; *(social)*, The Baroness _. Otherwise as for a Baron's wife.

BARONET – *Envelope*, Sir F_ S_, Bt. *Letter (formal)*, Dear Sir; *(social)*, Dear Sir F_. *Spoken*, Sir F_.

BARONET'S WIFE – *Envelope*, Lady S_. *Letter (formal)*, Dear Madam; *(social)*, Dear Lady S_. *Spoken*, Lady S_.

COUNTESS IN OWN RIGHT – As for an Earl's wife.

COURTESY TITLES – The heir apparent to a Duke, Marquess or Earl uses the highest of his father's other titles as a courtesy title. (For list, see pages 164-5.) The holder of a courtesy title is not styled The Most Hon. or The Right Hon., and in correspondence 'The' is omitted before the title. The heir apparent to a Scottish title may use the title 'Master' *(see* below).

DAME – *Envelope*, Dame F_ S_, followed by appropriate post-nominal letters. *Letter (formal)*, Dear Madam; *(social)*, Dear Dame F_. *Spoken*, Dame F_.

DUKE – *Envelope (formal)*, His Grace the Duke of _; *(social)*, The Duke of _. *Letter (formal)*, My Lord Duke; *(social)*, Dear Duke. *Spoken (formal)*, Your Grace; *(social)*, Duke.

DUKE'S WIFE – *Envelope (formal)*, Her Grace the Duchess of _; *(social)*, The Duchess of _. *Letter (formal)*, Dear Madam; *(social)*, Dear Duchess. *Spoken*, Duchess.

DUKE'S ELDEST SON – *see* Courtesy titles.

DUKE'S YOUNGER SON – *Envelope*, Lord F_ S_. *Letter (formal)*, My Lord; *(social)*, Dear Lord F_. *Spoken (formal)*, My Lord; *(social)*, Lord F_.

DUKE'S DAUGHTER – *Envelope*, Lady F_ S_. *Letter (formal)*, Dear Madam; *(social)*, Dear Lady F_. *Spoken*, Lady F_.

EARL – *Envelope (formal)*, The Right Hon. the Earl (of) _; *(social)*, The Earl (of) _. *Letter (formal)*, My Lord; *(social)*, Dear Lord _. *Spoken (formal)*, My Lord; *(social)*, Lord _.

EARL'S WIFE – *Envelope (formal)*, The Right Hon. the Countess (of) _; *(social)*, The Countess (of) _. *Letter (formal)*, Madam; *(social)*, Lady _. *Spoken (formal)*, Madam; *(social)*, Lady _.

EARL'S CHILDREN – Eldest son, *see* Courtesy titles. Younger sons, The Hon. F_ S_ (for forms of address, see Baron's children). Daughters, Lady F_ S_ (for forms of address, *see* Duke's daughter).

KNIGHT (BACHELOR) – *Envelope*, Sir F_ S_. *Letter (formal)*, Dear Sir; *(social)*, Dear Sir F_. *Spoken*, Sir F_.

KNIGHT (ORDERS OF CHIVALRY) – *Envelope*, Sir F_ S_, followed by appropriate post-nominal letters. Otherwise as for Knight Bachelor.

KNIGHT'S WIFE – As for Baronet's wife.

LIFE PEER – As for Baron/Baroness in own right.

LIFE PEER'S WIFE – As for Baron's wife.

LIFE PEER'S CHILDREN – As for Baron's children.

MARQUESS – *Envelope (formal)*, The Most Hon. the Marquess of _; *(social)*, The Marquess of _. *Letter (formal)*, My Lord; *(social)*, Dear Lord _. *Spoken (formal)*, My Lord; *(social)*, Lord _.

MARQUESS'S WIFE – *Envelope (formal)*, The Most Hon. the Marchioness of _; *(social)*, The Marchioness of _. *Letter (formal)*, Madam; *(social)*, Dear Lady _. *Spoken*, Lady _.

MARQUESS'S CHILDREN – Eldest son, *see* Courtesy titles. Younger sons, Lord F_ S_ (for forms of address, *see* Duke's younger sons). Daughters, Lady F_ S_ (for forms of address, *see* Duke's daughter).

MASTER – The title is used by the heir apparent to a Scottish peerage, though usually the heir apparent to a Duke, Marquess or Earl uses his courtesy title rather than 'Master'. *Envelope*, The Master of _. *Letter (formal)*, Dear Sir; *(social)*, Dear Master of _. *Spoken (formal)*, Master, or Sir; *(social)*, Master, or Mr S_.

MASTER'S WIFE – Addressed as for the wife of the appropriate peerage style, otherwise as Mrs S_.

PRIVY COUNSELLOR – *Envelope*, The Right Hon. (or Rt.) Hon. F_ S_. *Letter*, Dear Mr/Miss/Mrs S_. *Spoken*, Mr/Miss/Mrs S_. It is incorrect to use the letters PC after the name in conjunction with the prefix The Right Hon., unless the Privy Counsellor is a peer below the rank of Marquess and so is styled The Right Hon. because of his rank. In this case only, the post-nominal letters may be used in conjunction with the prefix The Right Hon.

VISCOUNT – *Envelope (formal)*, The Right Hon. the Viscount _; *(social)*, The Viscount _. *Letter (formal)*, My Lord; *(social)*, Dear Lord _. *Spoken*, Lord _.

VISCOUNT'S WIFE – *Envelope (formal)*, The Right Hon. the Viscountess _; *(social)*, The Viscountess _. *Letter (formal)*, Madam; *(social)*, Dear Lady _. *Spoken*, Lady _.

VISCOUNT'S CHILDREN – As for Baron's children.

The Peerage
and Members of the House of Lords

The rules which govern the creation and succession of peerages are extremely complicated. There are, technically, five separate peerages, the Peerage of England, of Scotland, of Ireland, of Great Britain, and of the United Kingdom. The Peerage of Great Britain dates from 1707 when an Act of Union combined the two kingdoms of England and Scotland and separate peerages were discontinued. The Peerage of the United Kingdom dates from 1801 when Great Britain and Ireland were combined under an Act of Union. Some Scottish peers have received additional peerages of Great Britain or of the United Kingdom since 1707, and some Irish peers additional peerages of the United Kingdom since 1801.

The Peerage of Ireland was not entirely discontinued from 1801 but holders of Irish peerages, whether pre-dating or created subsequent to the Union of 1801, were not entitled to sit in the House of Lords if they had no additional English, Scottish, Great Britain or United Kingdom peerage. However, they are eligible for election to the House of Commons and to vote in parliamentary elections. An Irish peer holding a peerage of a lower grade which enabled him to sit in the House of Lords was introduced there by the title which enabled him to sit, though for all other purposes he was known by his higher title.

In the Peerage of Scotland there is no rank of Baron; the equivalent rank is Lord of Parliament, abbreviated to 'Lord' (the female equivalent is 'Lady'). All peers of England, Scotland, Great Britain or the United Kingdom who are 21 years or over, and of British, Irish or Commonwealth nationality were entitled to sit in the House of Lords until the House of Lords Act 1999, when hereditary peers lost the right to sit. Ninety-two hereditaries are to remain in the House of Lords for a transitional period. In the list below, these peers are indicated by the **. Ten hereditary peers received Life Peerages in 1999 enabling them to remain in the reformed chamber, and two further hereditary peers reverted to sitting by virtue of the Life Peerages they already held.

HEREDITARY WOMEN PEERS

Most hereditary peerages pass on death to the nearest male heir, but there are exceptions, and several are held by women.

A woman peer in her own right retains her title after marriage, and if her husband's rank is the superior she is designated by the two titles jointly, the inferior one second. Her hereditary claim still holds good in spite of any marriage whether higher or lower. No rank held by a woman can confer any title or even precedence upon her husband but the rank of a hereditary woman peer in her own right is inherited by her eldest son (or in some cases daughter).

After the Peerage Act 1963, hereditary women peers in their own right were entitled to sit in the House of Lords, subject to the same qualifications as men, until the House of Lords Act 1999.

LIFE PEERS

Since 1876 non-hereditary or life peerages have been conferred on certain eminent judges to enable the judicial functions of the House of Lords to be carried out. These Lords are known as Lords of Appeal or law lords and, to date, such appointments have all been male.

Since 1958 life peerages have been conferred upon distinguished men and women from all walks of life, giving them seats in the House of Lords in the degree of Baron or Baroness. They are addressed in the same way as hereditary Lords and Barons, and their children have similar courtesy titles.

PEERAGES EXTINCT SINCE THE LAST EDITION

BARONIES: Macdonald of Gwaenysgor (cr. 1949)
LIFE PEERAGES: Bauer (cr. 1982); Brookes (cr. 1975); Carver (cr. 1977); Castle of Blackburn (cr. 1990); Fanshaw of Richmond (cr. 1983); Gibson-Watt (cr. 1979); Hailsham of St. Marylebone (cr. 1970); Holderness (1979); Ingrow (1982); Johnston of Rockport (cr. 1987); Keith of Kinkel (cr. 1977); Moyola (cr. 1971); Shore of Stepney (cr. 1997); Weinstock (cr.1980); Young (cr. 1971); Young of Darlington (cr. 1978)

DISCLAIMER OF PEERAGES

The Peerage Act 1963 enables peers to disclaim their peerages for life. Peers alive in 1963 could disclaim within twelve months after the passing of the Act (31 July 1963); a person subsequently succeeding to a peerage may disclaim within 12 months (one month if an MP) after the date of succession, or of reaching 21, if later. The disclaimer is irrevocable but does not affect the descent of the peerage after the disclaimant's death, and children of a disclaimed peer may, if they wish, retain their precedence and any courtesy titles and styles borne as children of a peer. The disclaimer permitted the disclaimant to sit in the House of Commons if elected as an MP. As the House of Lords Act 1999 removed hereditary peers from the House of Lords, they are now entitled to sit in the House of Commons without having to disclaim their titles.

The following peerages are currently disclaimed:

EARLDOMS: Durham (1970); Selkirk (1994)
VISCOUNTCIES: Stansgate (1963)
BARONIES: Merthyr (1977); Reith (1972); Sanderson of Ayot (1971); Silkin (1972)
PEERS WHO ARE MINORS (i.e. under 21 years of age)
EARLS: Craven (*b.* 1989); Cottenham (*b.* 1983)
VISCOUNTS: Selby (*b.* 1993)

CONTRACTIONS AND SYMBOLS

S. Scottish title
I. Irish title
* The peer holds also an Imperial title, specified after the name by Eng., Brit. or UK
** Hereditary peer remaining in the House of Lords for a transitional period
° there is no 'of' in the title
b. Born
s. Succeeded
m. Married
w. widower or widow
M.Minor
† heir not ascertained at time of going to press

Hereditary Peers

PEERS OF THE BLOOD ROYAL

Style, His Royal Highness The Duke of _/His Royal Highness the Earl of_
Style of address (formal) May it please your Royal Highness; *(informal)* Sir

Created	Title, order of succession, name, etc.	Heir
	Dukes	
1337	*Cornwall,* Charles, Prince of Wales, s. 1952	‡
1398	*Rothesay,* Charles, Prince of Wales, s. 1952	‡
1986	*York* (1st), The Prince Andrew, Duke of York	None
1928	*Gloucester* (2nd), Prince Richard, Duke of Gloucester, s. 1974	Earl of Ulster
1934	*Kent* (2nd), Prince Edward, Duke of Kent, s. 1942	Earl of St Andrews
	Earl	
1999	*Wessex* (1st), The Prince Edward, Earl of Wessex	None

‡ The title is not hereditary but is held by the Sovereign's eldest son from the moment of his birth or the Sovereign's accession

DUKES

Coronet, Eight strawberry leaves
Style, His Grace the Duke of _
Wife's style, Her Grace the Duchess of _
Eldest son's style, Takes his father's second title as a courtesy title
Younger sons' style, 'Lord' before forename and family name
Daughters' style, 'Lady' before forename and family name
For forms of address, *see* page 133

Created	Title, order of succession, name, etc.	Heir
1868 I.	*Abercorn (5th),* James Hamilton, KG, b. 1934, s. 1979, m., Lord Steward	Marquess of Hamilton, b. 1969
1701 S.*	*Argyll (13th) and 6th UK Duke Argyll,* 1892, Torquhil Campbell, b. 1968, s. 2001	Lord Colin Campbell, b. 1946
1703 S.	*Atholl (11th),* John Murray, b. 1929, s. 1996, m.	Marquess of Tullibardine, b. 1960
1682	*Beaufort (11th),* David Robert Somerset, b. 1928, s. 1984, w.,	Marquess of Worcester, b. 1952
1694	*Bedford (13th),* John Robert Russell, b. 1917, s. 1953, m.	Marquess of Tavistock, b. 1940
1663 S.*	*Buccleuch (9th) and Queensberry (11th)* (1684) *and 8th Eng. Earl, Doncaster,* 1662, Walter Francis John Montagu Douglas Scott, KT, VRD, b. 1923, s. 1973, m.	Earl of Dalkeith, b. 1954
1694	*Devonshire (11th),* Andrew Robert Buxton Cavendish, KG, MC, PC, b. 1920, s. 1950, m.	Marquess of Hartington, CBE, b. 1944
1947	*Edinburgh (1st),* HRH The Prince Philip, Duke of Edinburgh, *(see* page 115)	The Earl of Wessex §
1900	*Fife (3rd) and 12th Scott. Earl, Southesk,* 1633, (S. 1992), James George Alexander Bannerman Carnegie, b. 1929, s. 1959,	Earl of Southesk, b. 1961
1675	*Grafton (11th),* Hugh Denis Charles FitzRoy, KG, b. 1919, s. 1970,m.	Earl of Euston, b. 1947
1643 S.*	*Hamilton (15th) and Brandon (12th) (Brit. 1711),* Angus Alan Douglas Douglas-Hamilton, b. 1938, s. 1973, *Premier Peer of Scotland*	Marquess of Douglas and Clydesdale, b. 1978
1766 I.*	*Leinster (8th) and 8th Brit. Visct., Leinster,* 1747, Gerald FitzGerald, b. 1914, s. 1976, m., *Premier Duke and Marquess of Ireland*	Marquess of Kildare, b. 1948
1719	*Manchester (13th),* Alexander Charles David Drogo Montagu, b. 1962, s. 2002, m.	Viscount Mandeville, b. 1993
1702	*Marlborough* (11th), John George Vanderbilt Henry Spencer-Churchill, b. 1926, s. 1972, m.	Marquess of Blandford, b. 1955
1707 S.* **	*Montrose* (8th) and 6th Brit. Earl, Graham, 1722, James Graham, b. 1935, s. 1992, m.	Marquess of Graham, b. 1973
1483	***Norfolk (18th) and 13th Eng. Baron, Beaumont 1309,* s. 1971 and 5th UK Baron Howard of Glossop 1869,* s. 1972, Edward Wiliam Fitzalan-Howard, b. 1956, s. 2002, m., *Premier Duke and Earl Marshal* 1987	Earl of Arundel and Surrey, b. 1956
1766	*Northumberland (12th),* Ralph George Algernon Percy, b. 1956, s. 1995, m.	Earl Percy, b. 1984

§ In June 1999 Buckingham Palace revealed that the current Earl of Wessex would be given the Dukedom of Edinburgh when the present title returns to the Crown

Created	Title, order of succession, name, etc.	Heir
1675	*Richmond (10th) and Gordon (5th) (UK 1876) and Scott.* Duke Lennox (10th), Charles Henry Gordon Lennox, *b.* 1929, *s.*1989, *m.*	Earl of March and Kinrara, *b.* 1955
1707 S.*	*Roxburghe (10th) and 5th UK Earl, Innes, 1837,* Guy David Innes-Ker, *b.* 1954, *s.* 1974, *m., Premier Baronet of Scotland*	Marquess of Bowmont and Cessford, *b. 1981*
1703	*Rutland (11th),* David Charles Robert Manners, *b.* 1959, *s.* 1999, *m.*	Marquess of Granby, *b.* 1999
1684	*St Albans (14th),* Murray de Vere Beauclerk, *b.* 1939, *s.* 1988, *m.*	Earl of Burford, *b.* 1965
1547	*Somerset (19th),* John Michael Edward Seymour, *b.* 1952, *s.* 1984, *m.*	Lord Seymour, *b.* 1982
1833	*Sutherland (7th) and 6th UK Earl, Ellesmere, 1846,* Francis Ronald Egerton, *b.* 1940, *s.* 2000, *m.*	Marquess of Stafford, *b.* 1975
1814	*Wellington (8th) and 9th Irish Earl, Mornington, 1760,* Arthur Valerian Wellesley, KG, LVO, OBE, MC, *b.* 1915, *s.* 1972, *m.*	Marquess of Douro, *b.* 1945
1874	*Westminster (6th),* Gerald Cavendish Grosvenor, OBE, *b.* 1951, *s.* 1979, *m.*	Earl Grosvenor, *b.* 1991

MARQUESSES

Coronet, Four strawberry leaves alternating with four silver balls
Style, The Most Hon. the Marquess (of) _. In Scotland the spelling 'Marquis' is preferred for pre-Union creations
Wife's style, The Most Hon. the marchioness (of)_
Eldest son's style, Takes his father's second title as a courtesy title
Younger sons' style, 'Lord' before forename and family name
Daughters' style, 'Lady' before forename and family name
For forms of address, *see* page 133

Created	Title, order of succession, name, etc.	Heir
1916	*Aberdeen and Temair (7th) and Scott. Earl, Aberdeen* (1682), Alexander George Gordon, *b.* 1955, *s.* 2002, *m.*	Earl of Haddo, *b.* 1983
1876	*Abergavenny (6th),* Christopher George Charles Nevill, *b.* 1955, *s.* 2000, *m.*	David M. R. N., *b.* 1941
1821	*Ailesbury (8th),* Michael Sidney Cedric Brudenell-Bruce, *b.* 1926, *s.* 1974	Earl of Cardigan, *b.* 1952
1831	*Ailsa (8th) and 20th Scott. Earl, Cassillis,* 1509, Archibald Angus Charles Kennedy, *b.* 1956, *s.* 1994	Lord David Kennedy, *b.* 1958
1815	*Anglesey (7th),* George Charles Henry Victor Paget, *b.* 1922, *s.* 1947, *m.*	Earl of Uxbridge, *b.* 1950
1789	*Bath (7th),* Alexander George Thynn, *b.* 1932, *s.* 1992, *m.*	Viscount Weymouth, *b.* 1974
1826	*Bristol (8th),* Frederick William Augustus Hervey, *b.* 1979, *s.* 1999,	Timothy H. H., *b.* 1660
1796	*Bute (7th),* John Colum Crichton-Stuart, *b.* 1958, *s.* 1993, *m.*	Lord Mount Stuart, *b.* 1989
1812	° *Camden (6th),* David George Edward Henry Pratt, *b.* 1930, *s.* 1983	Earl of Brecknock, *b.* 1965
1815	** *Cholmondeley (7th) and 11th Irish Visct., Cholmondeley,* 1661, David George Philip Cholmondeley, *b.* 1960, *s.* 1990, *Lord Great Chamberlain*	Charles G. C., *b.* 1959
1816	° *Conyngham (7th) and 7th UK Baron, Minster,* 1821, Frederick William Henry Francis Conyngham, *b.* 1924, *s.* 1974, *m.*	Earl of Mount Charles, *b.* 1951
1791 I.*	*Donegall (7th) and 7th Brit. Baron, Fisherwick, 1970 and 6th Brit. Baron Templemore, 1831, s.* 1953, Dermot Richard Claud Chichester, LVO, *b.* 1916, *s.* 1975, *w.*	Earl of Belfast, *b.* 1952
1789 I.*	*Downshire (8th) and 8th Brit. Earl, Hillsborough,* 1772, (Arthur) Robin Ian Hill, *b.* 1929, *s.* 1989, *w.*	Earl of Hillsborough, *b.* 1959
1801 I.*	*Ely (8th) and 8th UK Baron, Loftus,* 1801, Charles John Tottenham, *b.* 1913, *s.* 1969, *w.*	Viscount Loftus, *b.* 1943
1801	*Exeter* (8th), (William) Michael Anthony Cecil, *b.* 1935, *s.* 1988, *m.,*	Lord Burghley, *b.* 1970
1800 I.*	*Headfort (6th) and 4th UK Baron, Kenlis,* 1831, Thomas Geoffrey Charles Michael Taylour, *b.* 1932, *s.* 1960, *m.*	Earl of Bective, *b.* 1959
1793	*Hertford (9th) and 10th Irish Baron, Conway,* 1712, Henry Jocelyn Seymour, *b.* 1958, *s.* 1997, *m.*	Earl of Yarmouth, *b.* 1993
1599 S.*	*Huntly (13th) and 5th UK Baron, Meldrum,* 1815, Granville Charles Gomer Gordon, *b.* 1944, *s.* 1987, *m., Premier Marquess of Scotland*	Earl of Aboyne, *b.* 1973
1784	*Lansdowne (9th) and 9th Irish Earl, Kerry,* 1723, Charles Maurice Mercer Nairne Petty-Fitzmaurice, *b.* 1941, *s.* 1999, *m.*	Earl of Shelburne, *b.* 1970
1902	*Linlithgow (4th) and 10th Scott. Earl, Hopetoun,* 1703, Adrian John Charles Hope, *b.* 1946, *s.* 1987, *m.*	Earl of Hopetown, *b.* 1969

Created	Title, order of succession, name, etc.	Heir
1816 I.*	Londonderry (9th) and 6th UK Earl, Vane, 1823, Alexander Charles Robert Vane-Tempest-Stewart, 1937, s. 1955, m.	Viscount Castlereagh, 1972
1701 S.*	Lothian (12th) and 6th UK Baron, Kerr, 1821, Peter Francis Walter Kerr, KCVO, b, 1922, s. 1940, m.	Earl of Ancram, PC, MP, b. 1945
1917	Milford Haven (4th), George Ivar Louis Mountbatten, b. 1961, s. 1970, m.	Earl of Medina, b. 1991
1838	Normanby (5th) and 9th Irish Baron, Mulgrave, 1767, Constantine Edmund Walter Phipps, b. 1954, s. 1994, m.	Earl of Mulgrave, b. 1994
1812	Northampton (7th), Spencer Douglas David Compton, b. 1946, s. 1978, m.	Earl Compton, b. 1973
1682 S.	Queensberry (12th), David Harrington Angus Douglas, b. 1929, s. 1954,	Viscount Drumlanrig, b. 1967
1926	Reading (4th), Simon Charles Henry Rufus Isaacs, b. 1942, s. 1980, m.	Viscount Erleigh, b. 1986
1789	Salisbury (6th), Robert Edward Peter Cecil, b. 1916, s. 1972, m.	Viscount Cranborne, PC, b. 1946 (see also Baron Cecil)
1800 I.*	Sligo (11th) and 11th UK Baron, Monteagle, 1806, Jeremy Ulick Browne, b. 1939, s. 1991, m.	Sebastian U. B., b. 1964
1787	° Townshend (7th), George John Patrick Dominic Townshend, b. 1916, s. 1921, w.	Viscount Raynham, b. 1945
1694	° Tweeddale (13th) and 4th UK Baron Tweeddale, 1881, Edward Douglas John Hay, b. 1947, s. 1979	Lord Charles D. M. H., b. 1947
1789 I.*	Waterford (8th) and 8th Brit. Baron Tyrone, 1786, John Hubert de la Poer Beresford, b. 1933, s. 1934, m.	Earl of Tyrone, b. 1958
1551	Winchester (18th), Nigel George Paulet, b. 1941, s. 1968, m., Premier Marquess of England	Earl of Wiltshire, b. 1969
1892	Zetland (4th) and 6th UK Earl, Zetland, 1838 and 7th Brit. Baron Dundas, 1794, Lawrence Mark Dundas, b. 1937, s. 1989, m.	Earl of Ronaldshay, b. 1965

EARLS

Coronet, Eight silver balls on stalks alternating with eight gold strawberry leaves
Style, The Right Hon. the Earl (of) _
Wife's style, The Right Hon. the Countess (of)_
Eldest son's style, Takes his father's second title as a courtesy title
Younger sons' style, 'The Hon.' before forename and family name
Daughters' style, 'Lady' before forename and family name
For forms of address, see page 133

Created	Title, order of succession, name, etc.	Heir
1639 S.	Airlie (13th), David George Coke Patrick Ogilvy, KT, GCVO, PC, Royal Victorian, b. 1926, s. 1968, m.	Lord Ogilvy, b. 1958
1696	Albemarle (10th), Rufus Arnold Alexis Keppel, b. 1965, s. 1979, m.	Crispian W. J. K., b. 1948
1952	° Alexander of Tunis (2nd), Shane William Desmond Alexander, b. 1935, s. 1969, m.	Hon. Brian J. A., b. 1939
1662	Annandale and Hartfell (11th), Patrick Andrew Wentworth Hope Johnstone, b. 1941, m., claim established 1985	Lord Johnstone, b. 1971
1789	° Annesley (10th), Patrick Annesley, b. 1924, s. 1979, m.	Hon. Philip H. A., b. 1927
1785	Antrim (9th), Alexander Randal Mark McDonnell, b. 1935, s. 1977, m.	Viscount Dunluce, b. 1967
1762	** Arran (9th) and 5th UK Baron Sudley, 1884, Arthur Desmond Colquhoun Gore, b. 1938, s. 1983, m.	Paul A. G., CMG, CVO, b.1921
1955	° ** Attlee (3rd), John Richard Attlee, b. 1956, s. 1991, m.	None
1714	Aylesford (11th), Charles Ian Finch-Knightley, b. 1918, s. 1958, w.	Lord Guernsey, b. 1947
1937	° ** Baldwin of Bewdley (4th), Edward Alfred Alexander Baldwin, b. 1938, s. 1976, m.	Viscount Corvedale, b.1973
1922	Balfour (4th), Gerald Arthur James Balfour, b. 1925, s. 1968, m.	Roderick F. A. G., b. 1948
1772	° Bathurst (8th), Henry Allen John Bathurst, b. 1927, s. 1943, m.	Lord Apsley, b. 1961
1919	° Beatty (3rd), David Beatty, b. 1946, s. 1972, m.	Viscount Borodale, b.1973
1797	Belmore (8th), John Armar Lowry-Corry, b. 1951, s. 1960, m.	Viscount Corry, b. 1985
1739	Bessborough (12th) and 9th UK Baron Duncannon, 1834, Myles Fitzhugh Longfield Ponsonby, b. 1941, s. 2002, m.	Viscount Duncannon, b. 1974
1815	Bradford (7th), Richard Thomas Orlando Bridgeman, b. 1947, s. 1981, m.	Viscount Newport, b. 1980
1469	Buchan (17th) and 8th UK Baron Erskine, 1806, Malcolm Harry Erskine, b. 1930, s. 1984, m.	Lord Cardross, b. 1960

Created	Title, order of succession, name, etc.	Heir
1746	*Buckinghamshire (10th)*, (George) Miles Hobart-Hampden, *b.* 1944, *s.* 1983, *m.*	Sir John Hobart, Bt., *b.*1945
1800	° *Cadogan (8th)*, Charles Gerald John Cadogan, *b.* 1937, *s.* 1997, *m.*	Viscount Chelsea, *b.* 1966
1878	° *Cairns (6th)*, Simon Dallas Cairns, CVO, CBE, *b.* 1939, *s.* 1989, *m.*	Viscount Garmoyle, *b.* 1965
1455	** *Caithness (20th)*, Malcolm Ian Sinclair, PC, *b.* 1948, *s.* 1965, w.	Lord Berriedale, *b.* 1981
1800	*Caledon (7th)*, Nicholas James Alexander, *b.* 1955, *s.* 1980, *m.*	Viscount Alexander, *b.* 1990
1661	*Carlisle (13th)* and *13th Scott. Baron Ruthven of Freeland*, 1651, George William Beaumont Howard, *b.* 1949, *s.* 1994,	Hon. Philip C. W. H., *b.* 1963
1793	*Carnarvon (8th)*, George Reginald Oliver Molyneux Herbert, *b.* 1956, *s.* 2001, *m.*	Lord Porchester, *b.* 1992
1748 I.*	*Carrick (10th)* and *4th UK Baron Butler*, 1912, David James Theobald Somerset Butler, *b.* 1953, *s.* 1992, *m.*	Viscount Ikerrin, *b.* 1975
1800 I.	° *Castle Stewart (8th)*, Arthur Patrick Avondale Stuart, *b.* 1928, *s.* 1961, *m.*	Viscount Stuart, *b.* 1953
1814	° *Cathcart (7th)* and *16th Scott. Baron Cathcart*, 1447, Charles Alan Andrew Cathcart, *b.* 1952, *s.* 1999, *m.*	Lord Greenock, *b.* 1986
1647	*Cavan*, The 12th Earl died in 1988. Heir had not established his claim to the title at the time of going to press	Roger C. Lambart, *b.* 1944
1827	° *Cawdor (7th)*, Colin Robert Vaughan Campbell, *b.* 1962, *s.* 1993, *m.*,	Hon. Frederick W. C., *b.* 1965
1801	*Chichester (9th)*, John Nicholas Pelham, *b.* 1944, *s.* 1944, *m.*	Richard A. H. P., *b.* 1952
1803 I.	*Clancarty (9th)* and *8th UK Visct. Clancarty*, 1823, Nicholas Power Richard Le Poer Trench, *b.* 1952, *s.* 1995,	None
1776 I.	*Clanwilliam (7th)* and *5th UK Baron Clanwilliam*, 1828, John Herbert Meade, *b.* 1919, *s.* 1989, *m.*	Lord Gillford, *b.* 1960
1776	*Clarendon (7th)*, George Frederick Laurence Hyde Villiers, *b.* 1933, *s.* 1955, *m.*	Lord Hyde, *b.* 1976
1620 I.	*Cork and Orrery (14th)* (*I.* 1660) and *10th Brit. Baron Boyle of Marston*, 1711, John William Boyle, DSC, *b.* 1916, *s.* 1995, *m.*	Viscount Dungarvan, *b.* 1945
1850 M.	*Cottenham (9th)*, Mark John Henry Pepys, *b.* 1983, *s.* 2000,	Hon. Sam R. P., *b.* 1986
1762 I.	** *Courtown (9th)* and *8th Brit. Baron Saltersford*, 1796, James Patrick Montagu Burgoyne Winthrop Stopford, *b.* 1954, *s.* 1975, *m.*	Viscount Stopford, *b.* 1988
1697	*Coventry (12th)*, Francis Henry Coventry, *b.* 1912, *s.* 2002, *m.*	Victor G. C., *b.* 1917
1857	° *Cowley (7th)*, Garret Graham Wellesley, *b.* 1934, *s.* 1975, *m.*	Viscount Dangan, *b.* 1965
1892	*Cranbrook (5th)*, Gathorne Gathorne-Hardy, *b.* 1933, *s.* 1978, *m.*	Lord Medway, *b.* 1968
1801 M.	*Craven (9th)*, Benjamin Robert Joseph Craven, *b.* 1989, *s.* 1990,	Rupert J. E. C., *b.* 1926
1398 S.*	*Crawford (29th)* and *Balcarres (12th)* (*s.* 1651) and *5th UK Baron, Wigan*, 1826 and *Baron Balniel* (*life peerage*, 1974), Robert Alexander Lindsay, KT, GCVO, PC, *b.* 1927, *s.* 1975, *m.*, *Premier Earl on Union Roll*	Lord Balniel, *b.* 1958
1861	*Cromartie (5th)*, John Ruaridh Blunt Grant Mackenzie, *b.* 1948, *s.* 1989, *m.*	Viscount Tarbat, *b.* 1987
1901	*Cromer (4th)*, Evelyn Rowland Esmond Baring, *b.* 1946, *s.* 1991, *m.*	Viscount Errington, b 1994
1633 S.*	*Dalhousie (17th)* and *5th UK Baron Ramsay*, 1875, James Hubert Ramsay, *b.* 1948, *s.* 1999, *m.*	Lord Ramsay, *b.* 1981
1725 I.	*Darnley (11th)* and *20th Engl. Baron Clifton of Leighton Bromswold*, 1608, Adam Ivo Stuart Bligh, *b.* 1941, *s.* 1980, *m.*	Lord Clifton, *b.* 1968
1711	*Dartmouth (10th)*, William Legge, *b.* 1949, *s.* 1997	Hon. Rupert L., *b.* 1951
1761	° *De La Warr (11th)*, William Herbrand Sackville, *b.* 1948, *s.* 1988, *m.*	Lord Buckhurst, *b.* 1979
1622	*Denbigh (12th)* and *Desmond (11th)* (*I.* 1622), Alexander Stephen Rudolph Feilding, *b.* 1970, *s.* 1995, *m.*	William D. F, *b.* 1939
1485	*Derby (19th)*, Edward Richard William Stanley, *b.* 1962, *s.* 1994, *m.*	Lord Stanley, *b.* 1998
1553	*Devon (18th)*, Hugh Rupert Courtenay, *b.* 1942, *s.* 1998, *m.*	Lord Courtenay, *b.* 1975
1800 I.*	*Donoughmore (8th)* and *8th UK Visct. Hutchinson*, 1821, Richard Michael John Hely-Hutchinson, *b.* 1927, *s.* 1981, w.	Viscount Suirdale, *b.* 1952
1661 I.*	*Drogheda (12th)* and *3rd UK Baron Moore*, 1954, Henry Dermot Ponsonby Moore, *b.* 1937, *s.* 1989, *m.*	Viscount Moore, *b.* 1983
1837	*Ducie (7th)*, David Leslie Moreton, *b.* 1951, *s.* 1991, *m.*	Lord Moreton, *b.* 1981
1860	*Dudley (4th)*, William Humble David Ward, *b.* 1920, *s.* 1969, *m.*	Viscount Ednam, *b.* 1947
1660 S.* **	*Dundee (12th)* and *2nd UK Baron Glassary*, 1954, Alexander Henry Scrymgeour, *b.* 1949, *s.* 1983, *m.*	Lord Scrymgeour, *b.* 1982
1669 S.	*Dundonald (15th)*, Iain Alexander Douglas Blair Cochrane, *b.* 1961, *s.* 1986, *m.*	Lord Cochrane, *b.* 1991
1686 S.	*Dunmore (12th)*, Malcolm Kenneth Murray, *b.* 1946, *s.* 1995, *m.*	Hon. Geoffrey C. M., *b.* 1949
1822 I.	*Dunraven and Mount-Earl (7th)*, Thady Windham Thomas Wyndham-Quin, *b.* 1939, *s.* 1965, *m.*	None
1833	*Durham (6th)*, Antony Claud Frederick Lambton, *b.* 1922, *s.* 1970, *m.*, Disclaimed for life 1970	Hon. Edward R. L. (Baron Durham), *b.* 1961
1837	*Effingham (7th)* and *17th Eng. Baron Howard of Effingham*, 1554, David Mowbray Algernon Howard, *b.* 1939, *s.* 1996, *m.*	Lord Howard of Effingham *b*, 1971
1507 S.*	*Eglinton (18th)* and *Winton (9th)* and *6th UK Earl Winton*, 1859, Archibald George Montgomerie, *b.* 1939, *s.* 1966, *m.*	Lord Montgomerie, *b.* 1966

Created	Title, order of succession, name, etc.	Heir
1733 I.*	Egmont (12th) and 10th Brit. Baron Lovel and Holland, 1762, Thomas Frederick Gerald Perceval, b. 1934, s. 2001	Philip E. P., MD, b. 1915
1821	Eldon (5th), John Joseph Nicholas Scott, b. 1937, s. 1976, m.	Viscount Encombe, b. 1962
1633 S.*	Elgin (11th) and Kincardine (15th) (s. 1647) and 4th UK Baron, Elgin, 1849, Andrew Douglas Alexander Thomas Bruce, KT, b. 1924, s. 1968, m.	Lord Bruce, b. 1961
1789 I.*	Enniskillen (7th) and 5th UK Baron, Grinstead, 1815, Andrew John Galbraith Cole, b. 1942, s. 1989, m.	Arthur G. C., b. 1920
1876 I.*	Erne (3rd) and 3rd UK Baron Fermanagh, 1876, Henry George Victor John Crichton, b. 1937, s. 1940, m.	Viscount Crichton, b. 1971
1452 S. **	Erroll (24th), Merlin Sereld Victor Gilbert Hay, b. 1948, s. 1978, m., Hereditary Lord High Constable and Knight Marischal of Scotland	Lord Hay, b. 1984
1661	Essex (10th), Robert Edward de Vere Capell, b. 1920, s. 1981, m.	Viscount Malden, b. 1944
1711	° ** Ferrers (13th), Robert Washington Shirley, PC, b. 1929, s. 1954, m.	Viscount Tamworth, b. 1952
1789	° Fortescue (8th), Charles Hugh Richard Fortescue, b. 1951, s. 1993, m.	Hon. Martin D. F., b. 1924
1841	Gainsborough (5th), Anthony Gerard Edward Noel, b. 1923, s. 1927, m.	Viscount Campden, b. 1950
1623 S.*	Galloway (13th) and 6th Brit. Baron of Garlies, 1796, Randolph Keith Reginald Stewart, b. 1928, s. 1978, w.	Andrew C. S., b. 1949
1703 S.*	Glasgow (10th) and 4th UK Baron, Fairlie, 1897, Patrick Robin Archibald Boyle, b. 1939, s. 1984, m.	Viscount of Kelburn, b. 1978
1806 I.*	Gosford (7th) and 5th UK Baron, Worlingham, 1835, Charles David Nicholas Alexander John Sparrow Acheson, b. 1942, s. 1966, m.	Hon. Patrick B. V. M. A., b. 1915
1945	Gowrie (2nd) and 3rd UK Baron Ruthven of Gowrie, 1919, Alexander Patric Greysteil Hore-Ruthven, PC, b. 1939, s. 1955, m.	Viscount Ruthven of Canberra, b. 1964
1684 I.*	Granard (10th) and 5th UK Baron, Granard, 1806, Peter Arthur Edward Hastings Forbes, b. 1957, s. 1992, m.	Viscount Forbes, b. 1981
1833	° Granville (6th), Granville George Fergus Leveson-Gower, b. 1959, s. 1996, m.	Hon. Niall J. L.-G., b. 1963
1806	° Grey (6th), Richard Fleming George Charles Grey, b. 1939, s. 1963, m.	Philip K. G., b. 1940
1752	Guilford (10th), Piers Edward Brownlow North, b. 1971, s. 1999, m.	Hon. Charles E. N., b. 1918
1619	Haddington (13th), John George Baillie-Hamilton, b. 1941, s. 1986, m.	Lord Binning, b. 1985
1919	° Haig (2nd), George Alexander Eugene Douglas Haig, OBE, b. 1918, s. 1928, m.	Viscount Dawick, b. 1961
1944	Halifax (3rd) and 5th UK Visct., Halifax, 1866, Charles Edward Peter Neil Wood, b. 1944, s. 1980, m.	Lord Irwin, b. 1977
1898	Halsbury (4th), Adam Edward Giffard, b. 1934, s. 2000, m.	None
1754	Hardwicke (10th), Joseph Philip Sebastian Yorke, b. 1971, s. 1974,	Charles E. Y., b. 1951
1812	Harewood (7th), George Henry Hubert Lascelles, KBE, b. 1923, s. 1947, m.	Viscount Lascelles, b. 1950,
1742	Harrington (11th) and 8th Brit. Visct. Stanhope of Mahon, 1717, William Henry Leicester Stanhope, b. 1922, s. 1929, m.	Viscount Petersham, b. 1945
1809	Harrowby (7th), Dudley Danvers Granville Coutts Ryder, TD, b. 1922, s. 1987, m.	Viscount Sandon, b. 1951
1605	** Home (15th), David Alexander Cospatrick Douglas-Home, CVO, b. 1943, s. 1995, m.	Lord Dunglass, b. 1987
1821	° ** Howe (7th), Frederick Richard Penn Curzon, b. 1951, s. 1984, m.	Viscount Curzon, b. 1994
1529	Huntingdon (16th), William Edward Robin Hood Hastings Bass, LVO, b. 1948, s. 1990, m.	Hon. Simon A. R. H. H. B., b. 1950
1885	Iddesleigh (4th), Stafford Henry Northcote, b. 1932, s. 1970, m.	Viscount St Cyres, b. 1957
1756	Ilchester (9th), Maurice Vivian de Touffreville Fox-Strangways, b. 1920, s. 1970, m.	Hon. Raymond G. F.-S., b. 1921
1929	Inchcape (4th), (Kenneth) Peter (Lyle) Mackay, b. 1943, s. 1994, m.	Viscount Glenapp, b. 1979
1919	Iveagh (4th), Arthur Edward Rory Guinness, b. 1969, s. 1992	Hon. Rory M. B. G., b. 1974
1925	° Jellicoe (2nd) and Baron Jellicoe of Southampton (life peerage, 1999), George Patrick John Rushworth Jellicoe, KBE, DSO, MC, PC, FRS, b. 1918, s. 1935, m.	Viscount Brocas, b. 1950
1697	Jersey (10th) and 13th Visct. Grandison, 1620, George Francis William Child Villiers, b. 1976, s. 1998	Hon. Jamie C. V., b. 1994
1822 I.	Kilmorey (6th), Richard Francis Needham, Kt., PC, b. 1942, s. 1977, m. (does not use title)	Viscount Newry and Morne, b. 1966
1866	Kimberley (5th), John Armine Wodehouse, b. 1951, s. 2002, m.	Lord Wodehouse, b.1978
1768 I.	Kingston (12th), Robert Charles Henry King-Tenison, b. 1969, s. 2002, m.	Viscount Kingsborough, b. 2000
1633 S.*	Kinnoull (15th) and 9th Brit. Baron Hay of Pedwardine, 1711, Arthur William George Patrick Hay, b. 1935, s. 1938, m.	Viscount Dupplin, b. 1962
1677 S.*	Kintore (13th) and 3rd UK Visct. Stonehaven, 1938, Michael Canning William John Keith, b. 1939, s. 1989, m.	Lord Inverurie, b. 1976
1914	° Kitchener of Khartoum (3rd), Henry Herbert Kitchener, TD, b. 1919, s. 1937	None
1624	Lauderdale (17th), Patrick Francis Maitland, b. 1911, s. 1968, m.	Viscount Maitland, b. 1937
1837	Leicester (7th), Edward Douglas Coke, b. 1936, s. 1994, m.	Viscount Coke, b. 1965

Created	Title, order of succession, name, etc.	Heir
1641 S.*	*Leven (14th) and Melville (13th) (s. 1690),* Alexander Robert Leslie Melville, *b.* 1924, *s.* 1947, *m.*	Lord Balgonie, *b.* 1954
1831	*Lichfield (5th),* Thomas Patrick John Anson, *b.* 1939, *s.* 1960,	Viscount Anson, *b.* 1978
1803 I.*	*Limerick (6th) and 6th UK Baron Foxford,* 1815, Patrick Edmund Pery, KBE, *b.* 1930, *s.* 1967, *m.*	Viscount Glentworth, *b.* 1963
1572	*Lincoln (19th),* Robert Edward Fiennes-Clinton, *b.* 1972, *s.* 2001	Hon. William R. F.-C., *b.* 1980
1633 S. **	*Lindsay (16th),* James Randolph Lindesay-Bethune, *b.* 1955, *s.* 1989, *m.*	Viscount Garnock, *b.* 1990
1626	*Lindsey (14th) and Abingdon (9th) (1682),* Richard Henry Rupert Bertie, *b.* 1931, *s.* 1963, *m.*	Lord Norreys, *b.* 1958
1776 I.	*Lisburne (8th),* John David Malet Vaughan, *b.* 1918, *s.* 1965, *m.*	Viscount Vaughan, *b.* 1945
1822 I.* **	*Listowel (6th) and 4th UK Baron Hare,* 1869, Francis Michael Hare, *b.* 1964, *s.* 1997, *m.*	Hon. Timothy P. H., *b.* 1966
1905	** *Liverpool (5th),* Edward Peter Bertram Savile Foljambe, *b.* 1944, *s.* 1969, *m.*	Viscount Hawkesbury, *b.* 1972
1945	° *Lloyd George of Dwyfor (3rd),* Owen Lloyd George, *b.* 1924, *s.* 1968, *m.*	Viscount Gwynedd, *b.* 1951
1785 I.*	*Longford (8th) and 2nd UK Baron Pakenham,* 1945, Thomas Frank Dermot Pakenham, *b.* 1933, *s.* 2001, *m.*	Edward M. P., *b.* 1970
1807	*Lonsdale (7th),* James Hugh William Lowther, *b.* 1922, *s.* 1953, *m.*	Viscount Lowther, *b.* 1949
1838	*Lovelace (5th) and 12th Brit. Baron King,* 1725, Peter Axel William Locke King, *b.* 1951, *s.* 1964, *m.*	None
1795 I.*	*Lucan (7th) and 3rd UK Baron Bingham,* 1934, Richard John Bingham, *b.* 1934, *s.* 1964, *m.*	Lord Bingham, *b.* 1967
1880	*Lytton (5th) and 18th Engl. Baron, Wentworth,* 1529, John Peter Michael Scawen Lytton, *b.* 1950, *s.* 1985, *m.*	Viscount Knebworth, *b.* 1989
1721	*Macclesfield (9th),* Richard Timothy George Mansfield Parker, *b.* 1943, *s.* 1992, *m.*	Hon. J. David G. P., *b.* 1945
1800	*Malmesbury (7th),* James Carleton Harris, *b.* 1946, *s.* 2000, *m.*	Viscount FitzHarris, *b.* 1970
1776 & 1792	*Mansfield and Mansfield (8th) and 14th Scott. Visct. Stormont,* 1621, William David Mungo James Murray, *b.* 1930, *s.* 1971, *m.*	Viscount Stormont, *b.* 1956
1565 S.* **	*Mar (14th) and Kellie (16th) (S. 1616) and Baron Erskine of Alloa Tower (life peerage, 2000),* James Thorne Erskine, *b.* 1949, *s.* 1994, *m.*	Hon. Alexander D. E., *b.* 1952
1785 I.	*Mayo (10th),* Terence Patrick Bourke, *b.* 1929, *s.* 1962	Lord Naas, *b.* 1953
1627 I.*	*Meath (15th) and 6th UK Baron, Chaworth,* 1831, John Anthony Brabazon, *b.* 1941, *s.* 1998, *m.*	Lord Ardee, *b.* 1941
1766	*Mexborough (8th),* John Christopher George Savile, *b.* 1931, *s.* 1980, *m.*	Viscount Pollington, *b.* 1959
1813	*Minto (6th),* Gilbert Edward George Lariston Elliot-Murray-Kynynmound, OBE, *b.* 1928, *s.* 1975, *m.*	Viscount Melgund, *b.* 1953
1562 S.*	*Moray (20th) and 12th Brit. Baron Stuart of Castle Stuart,* 1796, Douglas John Moray Stuart, *b.* 1928, *s.* 1974, *m.*	Lord Doune, *b.* 1966
1815	*Morley (6th),* John St Aubyn Parker, KCVO, *b.* 1923, *s.* 1962, *m.*	Viscount Boringdon, *b.* 1956
1458	*Morton (22nd),* John Charles Sholto Douglas, *b.* 1927, *s.* 1976, *m.*	Lord Aberdour, *b.* 1952
1789	*Mount Edgcumbe (8th),* Robert Charles Edgcumbe, *b.* 1939, *s.* 1982	Piers V. E., *b.* 1946
1805	° *Nelson (9th),* Peter John Horatio Nelson, *b.* 1941, *s.* 1981, *m.*	Viscount Merton, *b.* 1971
1660 S.	*Newburgh (12th),* Don Filippo Giambattista Camillo Francesco Aldo Maria Rospigliosi, *b.* 1942, *s.* 1986, *m.*	Princess Donna Benedetta F. M. R., *b.* 1974
1827 I.	*Norbury (7th),* Richard James Graham-Toler, *b.* 1967, *s.* 2000	†
1806 I.*	*Normanton (6th) and 9th Brit. Baron Mendip,* 1794 *and 4th UK Baron, Somerton,* 1873, Shaun James Christian Welbore Ellis Agar, *b.* 1945, *s.* 1967, *m.*	Viscount Somerton, *b.* 1982
1647 S. **	*Northesk (14th),* David John MacRae Carnegie, *b.* 1954, *s.* 1994, *m.*	Patrick C. C., *b.* 1940
1801 **	*Onslow (7th),* Michael William Coplestone Dillon Onslow, *b.* 1938, *s.* 1971, *m.*	Viscount Cranley, *b.* 1967
1696 S.	*Orkney (9th),* (Oliver) Peter St John, *b.* 1938, *s.* 1998, *m.*	Viscount Kirkwall, *b.* 1969
1328	*Ormonde and Ossory.* The marquessate of Ormonde became extinct in 1997 on the death of the 8th Marquess. Viscount Mountgarret is the senior known heir to the Earldoms of Ormonde and Ossory.	Viscount Mountgarret, (*see page* 144)
1925	*Oxford and Asquith (2nd),* Julian Edward George Asquith, KCMG, *b.* 1916, *s.* 1928, *w.*	Viscount Asquith, OBE, *b.* 1952
1929	° ** *Peel (3rd) and 4th UK Viscount Peel,* 1895, William James Robert Peel, *b.* 1947, *s.* 1969, *m.*	Viscount Clanfield, *b.* 1976
1551	*Pembroke (17th) and Montgomery (14th) (1605),* Henry George Charles Alexander Herbert, *b.* 1939, *s.* 1969	Lord Herbert, *b.* 1978
1605	*Perth (17th),* John David Drummond, PC, *b.* 1907, *s.* 1951, *w.*	Viscount Strathallan, *b.* 1935
1905	*Plymouth (3rd) and 15th Engl. Baron, Windsor,* 1529, Other Robert Ivor Windsor-Clive, *b.* 1923, *s.* 1943, *m.*	Viscount Windsor, *b.* 1951

Created	Title, order of succession, name, etc.	Heir
1785	*Portarlington (7th)*, George Lionel Yuill Seymour Dawson-Damer, *b.* 1938, *s.* 1959, *m.*	Viscount Carlow, *b.* 1965
1689	*Portland (12th)*, Count Timothy Charles Robert Noel Bentinck, *b.* 1953, *s.* 1997, *m.*	Viscount Woodstock, *b.* 1984
1743	*Portsmouth (10th)*, Quentin Gerard Carew Wallop, *b.* 1954, *s.* 1984, *m.*	Viscount Lymington, *b.* 1981
1804	*Powis (8th) and 9th Irish Baron, Clive,* 1762, John George Herbert, *b.* 1952, *s.* 1993, *m.*	Viscount Clive, *b.* 1979
1765	*Radnor (8th)*, Jacob Pleydell-Bouverie, Bt., *b.* 1927, *s.* 1968, *m.*	Viscount Folkestone, *b.* 1955
1831 I.*	*Ranfurly (7th) and 8th UK Baron, Ranfurly,* 1826, Gerald François Needham Knox, *b.* 1929, *s.* 1988, *m.*	Edward J. K., *b.* 1957
1771	*Roden (10th)*, Robert John Jocelyn, *b.* 1938, *s.* 1993, *m.*	Viscount Jocelyn, *b.* 1989
1801	*Romney (7th)*, Michael Henry Marsham, *b.* 1910, *s.* 1975, *w.*	Julian C. M., *b.* 1948
1703 S.*	*Rosebery (7th) and 3rd UK Earl Midlothian,* 1911, Neil Archibald Primrose, *b.* 1929, *s.* 1974, *m.*	Lord Dalmeny, *b.* 1967
1806 I.	*Rosse (7th)*, William Brendan Parsons, *b.* 1936, *s.* 1979, *m.*	Lord Oxmantown, *b.* 1969
1801	** *Rosslyn (7th)*, Peter St Clair-Erskine, *b.* 1958, *s.* 1977, *m.*	Lord Loughborough, *b.* 1986
1457 S.	*Rothes (21st)*, Ian Lionel Malcolm Leslie, *b.* 1932, *s.* 1975, *m.*	Lord Leslie, *b.* 1958
1861	° ** *Russell (5th)*, Conrad Sebastian Robert Russell, FBA, *b.* 1937, *s.* 1987, *m.*	Viscount Amberley, *b.* 1968
1915	° *St Aldwyn (3rd)*, Michael Henry Hicks Beach, *b.* 1950, *s.* 1992, *m.*	Hon. David S. H. B., *b.* 1955
1815	*St Germans (10th)*, Peregrine Nicholas Eliot, *b.* 1941, *s.* 1988	Lord Eliot, *b.* 1966
1660	** *Sandwich (11th)*, John Edward Hollister Montagu, *b.* 1943, *s.* 1995, *m.*	Viscount Hinchingbrooke, *b.* 1969
1690	*Scarbrough (12th) and 13th Irish Visct. Lumley,* 1628, Richard Aldred Lumley, *b.* 1932, *s.* 1969, *m.*	Viscount Lumley, *b.* 1973
1701 S.	*Seafield (13th)*, Ian Derek Francis Ogilvie-Grant, *b.* 1939, *s.* 1969, *m.*	Viscount Reidhaven, *b.* 1963
1882	** *Selborne (4th)*, John Roundell Palmer, KBE, FRS, *b.* 1940, *s.* 1971, *m.*	Viscount Wolmer, *b.* 1971
1646 S.	*Selkirk.* Disclaimed for life 1994. (*see* Lord Selkirk of Douglas, page 159)	Hon. John A. D.-H., *b.* 1978
1672	*Shaftesbury (10th)*, Anthony Ashley-Cooper, *b.* 1938, *s.* 1961, *m.*	Lord Ashley, *b.* 1977
1756 I.*	*Shannon (9th) and 8th Brit. Baron Carleton,* 1786, Richard Bentinck Boyle, *b.* 1924, *s.* 1963	Viscount Boyle, *b.* 1960
1442	** *Shrewsbury and Waterford (22nd) and 7th Eng. Earl Talbot,* 1784, Charles Henry John Benedict Crofton Chetwynd Chetwynd-Talbot, *b.* 1952, *s.* 1980, *m.*, *Premier Earl of England and Ireland*	Viscount Ingestre, *b.* 1978
1961	*Snowdon (1st) and Baron Armstrong-Jones (life peerage, 1999),* Antony Charles Robert Armstrong-Jones, GCVO, *b.* 1930, *s.*, *m.*, *Constable of Caernarfon Castle*	Viscount Linley, *b.* 1961
1765	° *Spencer (9th)*, Charles Edward Maurice Spencer, *b.* 1964, *s.* 1992	Viscount Althorp, *b.* 1994
1703 S.*	*Stair (14th) and 7th UK Baron, Oxenfoord,* 1841, John David James Dalrymple, *b.* 1961, *s.* 1996	Hon. David H. D., *b.* 1963
1984	*Stockton (2nd)*, Alexander Daniel Alan Macmillan, MEP, *b.* 1943, *s.* 1986, *m.*	Viscount Macmillan of Ovenden, *b.* 1974
1821	*Stradbroke (6th)*, Robert Keith Rous, *b.* 1937, *s.* 1983, *m.*	Viscount Dunwich, *b.* 1961
1847	*Strafford (8th)*, Thomas Edmund Byng, *b.* 1936, *s.* 1984, *m.*	Viscount Enfield, *b.* 1964
1606 S.*	*Strathmore and Kinghorne (18th) and 16th Scott. Earl, Strathmore, 1677 and 18th Scott. Earl, Kinghorne, 1606 and 5th UK Earl, Strathmore and Kinghorne,* 1937, Michael Fergus Bowes Lyon, *b.* 1957, *s.* 1987, *m.*	Lord Glamis, *b.* 1986
1603	*Suffolk (21st) and Berkshire (14th) (1626),* Michael John James George Robert Howard, *b.* 1935, *s.* 1941, *m.*	Viscount Andover, *b.* 1974
1955	*Swinton (2nd)*, David Yarburgh Cunliffe-Lister, *b.* 1937, *s.* 1972, *m.*	Hon. Nicholas J. C.-L., *b.* 1939
1714	*Tankerville (10th)*, Peter Grey Bennet, *b.* 1956, *s.* 1980	Revd the Hon. George A. G. B., *b.* 1925
1822	° *Temple of Stowe (8th)*, (Walter) Grenville Algernon Temple-Gore-Langton, *b.* 1924, *s.* 1988, *m.*	Lord Langton, *b.* 1955
1815	*Verulam (7th) and 11th Irish Visct. Grimston, 1719 and 16th Scott. Baron Forrester of Corstorphine,* 1633, John Duncan Grimston, *b.* 1951, *s.* 1973, *m.*	Viscount Grimston, *b.* 1978
1729	° *Waldegrave (13th)*, James Sherbrooke Waldegrave, *b.* 1940, *s.* 1995, *m.*	Viscount Chewton, *b.* 1986
1759	*Warwick (9th) and Brooke (9th) (Brit. 1746),* Guy David Greville, *b.* 1957, *s.* 1996, *m.*	Lord Brooke, *b.* 1982
1633 S.*	*Wemyss (12th) and March (8th) and 5th UK Baron Wemyss,* 1821, Francis David Charteris, KT, *b.* 1912, *s.* 1937, *m.*	Lord Neidpath, *b.* 1948
1621 I.	*Westmeath (13th)*, William Anthony Nugent, *b.* 1928, *s.* 1971, *m.*	Hon. Sean C. W. N., *b.* 1965
1624	*Westmorland (16th)*, Anthony David Francis Henry Fane, *b.* 1951, *s.* 1993, *m.*	Hon. Harry St C. F., *b.* 1953
1876	*Wharncliffe (5th)*, Richard Alan Montagu Stuart Wortley, *b.* 1953, *s.* 1987, *m.*	Viscount Carlton, *b.* 1980
1801	*Wilton (8th) and 6th Baron Ebury (1857),* Francis Egerton Grosvenor, *b.* 1934, *s.* 1999, *m.*	Viscount Grey de Wilton, *b.* 1959

Created	Title, order of succession, name, etc.	Heir
1628	Winchilsea (17th) and Nottingham (12th) (1681), Daniel James Hatfield Finch Hatton, b. 1967, s. 1999, m.	Hon. Robin H. F.-H., b. 1939
1766	° Winterton (8th), (Donald) David Turnour, b. 1943, s. 1991, m.	Robert C. T., b. 1950
1956	Woolton (3rd), Simon Frederick Marquis, b. 1958, s. 1969, m.	None
1837	Yarborough (8th), Charles John Pelham, b. 1963, s. 1991, m.	Lord Worsley, b. 1990

COUNTESSES IN THEIR OWN RIGHT

Style, The Right Hon. the Countess (of) _
Husband, Untitled
Children's style, As for children of an Earl
For forms of address, see page 133

Created	Title, order of succession, name, etc.	Heir
1643 S.	Dysart (11th in line), Rosamund Agnes Greaves, b. 1914, s. 1975	Lady Katherine Grant of Rothiemurchus, b. 1918
1633 S.	Loudoun (13th in line), Barbara Huddleston Abney-Hastings, b. 1919, s. 1960, m.	Lord Mauchline, b. 1942
c.1115 S.**	Mar (31st in line), Margaret of Mar, b. 1940, s. 1975, m., Premier Earldom of Scotland	Mistress of Mar, b. 1963
1947	° Mountbatten of Burma (2nd in line), Patricia Edwina Victoria Knatchbull, CBE, b. 1924, s. 1979, m.	Lord Romsey, b. 1947
c.1235 S.	Sutherland (24th in line), Elizabeth Millicent Sutherland, b. 1921, s. 1963, m.	Lord Strathnaver, b. 1947

VISCOUNTS

Coronet, Sixteen silver balls Style, The Right Hon. the Viscount _
Wife's style, The Right Hon. the Viscountess _
Children's style, 'The Hon.' before forename and family name
In Scotland, the heir apparent to a viscount may be styled 'The Master of _ (title of peer)'
For forms of address, see page 133

Created	Title, order of succession, name, etc.	Heir
1945	Addison (4th), William Matthew Wand Addison, b. 1945, s. 1992, m.	Hon. Paul W. A., b. 1973
1946	Alanbrooke (3rd), Alan Victor Harold Brooke, b. 1932, s. 1972,	None
1919	** Allenby (3rd), Lt.-Col. Michael Jaffray Hynman Allenby, b. 1931, s. 1984, m.	Hon. Henry J. H. A., b. 1968
1911	Allendale (3rd), Wentworth Hubert Charles Beaumont, b. 1922, s. 1956	Hon. Wentworth P. I. B., b. 1948
1642 S.	Arbuthnott (16th), John Campbell Arbuthnott, KT, CBE, DSC, FRSE, b. 1924, s. 1966, m.	Master of Arbuthnott, b. 1950
1751 I.	Ashbrook (11th), Michael Llowarch Warburton Flower, b. 1935, s. 1995, m.	Hon. Rowland F. W. F., b. 1975
1917	** Astor (4th), William Waldorf Astor, b. 1951, s. 1966, m.	Hon. William W. A., b. 1979
1781 I.	Bangor (8th), William Maxwell David Ward, b. 1948, s. 1993, m.	Hon. E. Nicholas W., b. 1953
1925	Bearsted (5th), Nicholas Alan Samuel, b. 1950, s. 1996, m.	Hon. Harry R. S., b. 1988
1963	Blakenham (2nd), Michael John Hare, b. 1938, s. 1982, m.	Hon. Caspar J. H., b. 1972
1935	** Bledisloe (3rd), Christopher Hiley Ludlow Bathurst, QC, b. 1934, s. 1979	Hon. Rupert E. L. B., b. 1964
1712	Bolingbroke (7th) and St John (8th) (1716), Kenneth Oliver Musgrave St John, b. 1927, s. 1974	Hon. Henry F. St J., b. 1957
1960	Boyd of Merton (2nd), Simon Donald Rupert Neville Lennox-Boyd, b. 1939, s. 1983, m.	Hon. Benjamin A. L.-B., b. 1964
1717 I.*	Boyne (11th) and 5th UK Baron Brancepeth, 1866, Gustavus Michael Stucley Hamilton-Russell, b. 1965, s. 1995, m.	Brian G. H.-R., b. 1940
1929	Brentford (4th), Crispin William Joynson-Hicks, b. 1933, s. 1983, m.	Hon. Paul W. J.-H., b. 1971

Created	Title, order of succession, name, etc.	Heir
1929	** *Bridgeman (3rd)*, Robin John Orlando Bridgeman, *b.* 1930, *s.* 1982, *m.*	Hon. Luke R. O. B., *b.* 1971
1868	*Bridport (4th) and 7th Duke, Bronte in Sicily, 1799 and 6th Irish Baron Bridport, 1794*, Alexander Nelson Hood, *b.* 1948, *s.* 1969, *m.*	Hon. Peregrine A. N. H., *b.* 1974
1952	** *Brookeborough (3rd)*, Alan Henry Brooke, *b.* 1952, *s.* 1987, *m.*	Hon. Christopher A. B., *b.* 1954
1933	*Buckmaster (3rd)*, Martin Stanley Buckmaster, OBE, *b.* 1921, *s.* 1974	Hon. Colin J. B., *b.* 1923
1939	*Caldecote (3rd)*, Piers James Hampden Inskip, *b.* 1947, *s.* 1999, *m.*	Hon. Thomas J. H. I., *b.* 1985
1941	*Camrose (4th)*, Adrian Michael Berry, *b.* 1937, *s.* 2001, *m.*	Hon. Jonathan W. B., *b.* 1970
1954	*Chandos (3rd) and Baron Lyttelton of Aldershot (life peerage, 2000)*, Thomas Orlando Lyttelton, *b.* 1953, *s.* 1980, *m.*	Hon. Oliver A. L., *b.* 1986
1665 I.*	*Charlemont (14th) and 18th Irish Baron Caulfeild of Charlemont, 1620*, John Day Caulfeild, *b.* 1934, *s.* 1985, *m.*	Hon. John D. C., *b.* 1966
1921	*Chelmsford (4th) and UK Baron Chelmsford, 1858*, Frederic Corin Piers Thesiger, *b.* 1962, *s.* 1999	To Barony only, Sir Wilfred P. T., KBE, *b.* 1910
1717 I.	*Chetwynd (10th)*, Adam Richard John Casson Chetwynd, *b.* 1935, *s.* 1965, *m.*	Hon. Adam D. C., *b.* 1969
1911	*Chilston (4th)*, Alastair George Akers-Douglas, *b.* 1946, *s.* 1982, *m.*	Hon. Oliver I. A.-D., *b.* 1973
1902	*Churchill (3rd) and 5th UK Baron Churchill, 1815*, Victor George Spencer, *b.* 1934, *s.* 1973	To Barony only, Richard H. R. S., *b.* 1926
1718	*Cobham (11th) and 8th Irish Baron Westcote, 1776*, John William Leonard Lyttelton, *b.* 1943, *s.* 1977, *m.*	Hon. Christopher C. L., *b.* 1947
1902	** *Colville of Culross (4th) and 13th Scott. Baron Colville of Culcross, 1604*, John Mark Alexander Colville, QC, *b.* 1933, *s.* 1945, *m.*	Master of Colville, *b.* 1959
1826	*Combermere (6th)*, Thomas Robert Wellington Stapleton-Cotton, *b.* 1969, *s.* 2001	Hon. David P. D., *b.* 1932
1917	*Cowdray (4th) and 4th UK Baron Cowdray, 1910*, Michael Orlando Weetman Pearson, *b.* 1944, *s.* 1995, *m.*	Hon. Peregrine J. D. P., *b.* 1994
1927	** *Craigavon (3rd)*, Janric Fraser Craig, *b.* 1944, *s.* 1974	None
1886	*Cross (3rd)*, Assheton Henry Cross, *b.* 1920, *s.* 1932	None
1943	*Daventry (4th)*, James Edward FitzRoy Newdegate, *b.* 1960, *s.* 2000, *m.*	Hon. Humphrey J. F. N., *b.* 1995
1937	*Davidson (2nd)*, John Andrew Davidson, *b.* 1928, *s.* 1970, *m.*	Hon. Malcolm W. M. D., *b.* 1934
1956	*De L'Isle (2nd) and 7th UK Baron de L'Isle and Dudley, 1835*, Philip John Algernon Sidney, MBE, *b.* 1945, *s.* 1991, *m.*	Hon. Philip W. E. S., *b.* 1985
1776 I.*	*De Vesci (7th) and 8th Irish Baron Knapton, 1750*, Thomas Eustace Vesey, *b.* 1955, *s.* 1983, *m.*	Hon. Oliver I. V., *b.* 1991
1917	*Devonport (3rd)*, Terence Kearley, *b.* 1944, *s.* 1973	Chester D. H. K., *b.* 1932
1964	*Dilhorne (2nd)*, John Mervyn Manningham-Buller, *b.* 1932, *s.* 1980, *m.*	Hon. James E. M.-B., *b.* 1956
1622 I.	*Dillon (22nd)*, Henry Benedict Charles Dillon, *b.* 1973, *s.* 1982	Hon. Richard A. L. D., *b.* 1948
1785 I.	*Doneraile (10th)*, Richard Allen St Leger, *b.* 1946, *s.* 1983, *m.*	Hon. Nathaniel W. R. St J. St L., *b.* 1971
1680 I.*	*Downe (12th) and 5th UK Baron Dawnay, 1897*, Richard Henry Dawnay, *b.* 1967, *s.* 2002	Thomas P. D., *b.* 1978
1959	*Dunrossil (3rd)*, Andrew William Reginald Morrison, *b.* 1953, *s.* 2000, *m.*	Hon. Callum A. B. M., *b.* 1994
1964	*Eccles (2nd)*, John Dawson Eccles, CBE, *b.* 1931, *s.* 1999, *m.*	Hon. William D. E., *b.* 1960
1897	*Esher (4th)*, Lionel Gordon Baliol Brett, CBE, *b.* 1913, *s.* 1963, *m.*	Hon. Christopher L. B. B., *b.* 1936
1816	*Exmouth (10th)*, Paul Edward Pellew, *b.* 1940, *s.* 1970, *m.*	Hon. Edward F. P., *b.* 1978
1620 S.	** *Falkland (15th)*, Lucius Edward William Plantagenet Cary, *b.* 1935, *s.* 1984, *m.*, *Premier Scottish Viscount on the Roll*	Master of Falkland, *b.* 1963
1720	*Falmouth (9th) and 26th Eng. Baron Le Despencer, 1264*, George Hugh Boscawen, *b.* 1919, *s.* 1962, *m.*	Hon. Evelyn A. H. B., *b.* 1955
1720 I.*	*Gage (8th) and 7th Brit. Baron Gage, 1790*, (Henry) Nicolas Gage, *b.* 1934, *s.* 1993, *m.*	Hon. Henry W. G., *b.* 1975
1727 I.	*Galway (12th)*, George Rupert Monckton-Arundell, *b.* 1922, *s.* 1980, *m.*	Hon. J. Philip M., *b.* 1952
1478 I.*	*Gormanston (17th) and 5th UK Baron Gormanston, 1868*, Jenico Nicholas Dudley Preston, *b.* 1939, *s.* 1940, *w.*, *Premier Viscount of Ireland*	Hon. Jenico F. T. P., *b.* 1974
1816 I.	*Gort (9th)*, Foley Robert Standish Prendergast Vereker, *b.* 1951, *s.* 1995, *m.*	Hon. Robert F. P. V., *b.* 1993
1900	** *Goschen (4th)*, Giles John Harry Goschen, *b.* 1965, *s.* 1977, *m.*	Hon. John A. G., *b.* 1992
1849	*Gough (5th)*, Shane Hugh Maryon Gough, *b.* 1941, *s.* 1951	None
1937	*Greenwood (3rd)*, Michael George Hamar Greenwood, *b.* 1923, *s.* 1998	None
1929	*Hailsham*, Douglas Martin Hogg, PC, QC, MP, *b.* 1945, *s.* 2001, *m.*	Hon. Quintin J. N. M. H., *b.* 1973
1891	*Hambleden (4th)*, William Herbert Smith, *b.* 1930, *s.* 1948, *m.*	Hon. William H. B. S., *b.* 1955
1884	*Hampden (6th)*, Anthony David Brand, *b.* 1937, *s.* 1975, *m.*	Hon. Francis A. B., *b.* 1970
1936	*Hanworth (3rd)*, David Stephen Geoffrey Pollock, *b.* 1946, *s.* 1996, *m.*	Hon. Richard C. S. P., *b.* 1951
1791 I.	*Harberton (10th)*, Thomas de Vautort Pomeroy, *b.* 1910, *s.* 1980, *w.*	Henry R. P., *b.* 1958
1846	*Hardinge (6th)*, Charles Henry Nicholas Hardinge, *b.* 1956, *s.* 1984, *m.*	Hon. Andrew H. H., *b.* 1960
1791 I.	*Hawarden (9th)*, (Robert) Connan Wyndham Leslie Maude, *b.* 1961, *s.* 1991, *m.*	Hon. Varian J. C. E. M., *b.* 1997
1960	*Head (2nd)*, Richard Antony Head, *b.* 1937, *s.* 1983, *m.*	Hon. Henry J. H., *b.* 1980

Created	Title, order of succession, name, etc.	Heir
1550	*Hereford (18th)*, Robert Milo Leicester Devereux, *b.* 1932, *s.* 1952, Premier Viscount of England	Hon. Charles R. de B. D., *b.* 1975
1842	*Hill (8th)*, Antony Rowland Clegg-Hill, *b.* 1931, *s.* 1974, *m.*	Peter D. R. C. C.-H., *b.* 1945
1796	*Hood (8th) and 7th Irish Baron, Hood*, 1782, Henry Lyttleton Alexander Hood, *b.* 1958, *s.* 1999, *m.*	Hon. Archibald L. S. H., *b.* 1993
1956	*Ingleby (2nd)*, Martin Raymond Peake, *b.* 1926, *s.* 1966, *w.*	None
1945	*Kemsley (3rd)*, Richard Gomer Berry, *b.* 1951, *s.* 1999, *m.*	Hon. Edward A. M., *b.* 1960
1911	*Knollys (3rd)*, David Francis Dudley Knollys, *b.* 1931, *s.* 1966, *m.*	Hon. Patrick N. M. K., *b.* 1962
1895	*Knutsford (6th)*, Michael Holland-Hibbert, *b.* 1926, *s.* 1986, *m.*	Hon. Henry T. H.-H., *b.* 1959
1954	*Leathers (3rd)*, Christopher Graeme Leathers, *b.* 1941, *s.* 1996, *m.*	Hon. James F. L., *b.* 1969
1781 I.	*Lifford (9th)*, (Edward) James Wingfield Hewitt, *b.* 1949, *s.* 1987, *m.*	Hon. James T. W. H., *b.* 1979
1921	*Long (4th)*, Richard Gerard Long, CBE, *b.* 1929, *s.* 1967, *m.*	Hon. James R. L., *b.* 1960
1957	*Mackintosh of Halifax (3rd)*, (John) Clive Mackintosh, *b.* 1958, *s.* 1980, *m.*	Hon. Thomas H. G. M., *b.* 1985
1955	*Malvern (3rd)*, Ashley Kevin Godfrey Huggins, *b.* 1949, *s.* 1978	Hon. M. James H., *b.* 1928
1945	*Marchwood (3rd)*, David George Staveley Penny, *b.* 1936, *s.* 1979, *w.*	Hon. Peter G. W. P., *b.* 1965
1942	*Margesson (2nd)*, Francis Vere Hampden Margesson, *b.* 1922, *s.* 1965, *m.*	Capt. Hon. Richard F. D. M., *b.* 1960
1660 I.*	*Massereene (14th) and Ferrard (7th) (1797) and 7th UK Baron, Oriel*, 1821, John David Clotworthy Whyte-Melville Foster Skeffington, *b.* 1940, *s.* 1992, *m.*	Hon. Charles J. C. W.-M. F. S., *b.* 1973
1802	*Melville (9th)*, Robert David Ross Dundas, *b.* 1937, *s.* 1971, *m.*	Hon. Robert H. K. D., *b.* 1984
1916	*Mersey (4th) and 13th Scott. Lord Nairne*, 1681 *s.* 1995, Richard Maurice Clive Bigham, *b.* 1934, *s.* 1979, *m.*	Master of Nairne, *b.* 1966
1717 I.*	*Midleton (12th) and 9th Brit. Baron Brodrick of Peper Harow*, 1796, Alan Henry Brodrick, *b.* 1949, *s.* 1988, *m.*	Hon. Ashley R. B., *b.* 1980
1962	*Mills (3rd)*, Christopher Philip Roger Mills, *b.* 1956, *s.* 1988, *m.*	None
1716 I.	*Molesworth (12th)*, Robert Bysse Kelham Molesworth, *b.* 1959, *s.* 1997	Hon. William J. C. M., *b.* 1960
1801 I.*	*Monck (7th) and 4th UK Baron, Monck*, 1866, Charles Stanley Monck, *b.* 1953, *s.* 1982. Does not use title	Hon. George S. M., *b.* 1957
1957	*Monckton of Brenchley (2nd)*, Maj.-Gen. Gilbert Walter Riversdale Monckton, CB, OBE, MC, *b.* 1915, *s.* 1965, *m.*	Hon. Christopher W. M., *b.* 1952
1946	*Montgomery of Alamein (2nd)*, David Bernard Montgomery, CBE, *b.* 1928, *s.* 1976, *m.*	Hon. Henry D. M., *b.* 1954
1550 I.*	*Mountgarret (17th) and 4th UK Baron Mountgarret*, 1911, Richard Henry Piers Butler, *b.* 1936, *s.* 1966, *m.*	Hon. Piers J. R. B., *b.* 1961
1952	*Norwich (2nd)*, John Julius Cooper, CVO, *b.* 1929, *s.* 1954, *m.*	Hon. Jason C. D. B. C., *b.* 1959
1651 S.	**Oxfuird (13th)*, George Hubbard Makgill, CBE, *b.* 1934, *s.* 1986, *m.*	Master of Oxfuird, *b.* 1969
1873	*Portman (10th)*, Christopher Edward Berkeley Portman, *b.* 1958, *s.* 1999, *m.*	Hon. Luke O. B. P., *b.* 1984
1743 I.*	*Powerscourt (10th) and 4th UK Baron Powerscourt*, 1885, Mervyn Niall Wingfield, *b.* 1935, *s.* 1973, *m.*	Hon. Mervyn A. W., *b.* 1963
1900	*Ridley (4th)*, Matthew White Ridley, KG, GCVO, TD, *b.* 1925, *s.* 1964, *m.*	Hon. Matthew W. R., *b.* 1958
1960	*Rochdale (2nd)*, St John Durival Kemp, *b.* 1938, *s.* 1993, *m.*	Hon. Jonathan H. D. K., *b.* 1961
1919	*Rothermere (4th)*, (Harold) Jonathan Esmond Vere Harmsworth, *b.* 1967, *s.* 1998, *m.*	Hon. Esmond V. H., *b.* 1967
1937	*Runciman of Doxford (3rd) and 4th UK Baron, Runciman*, 1933, Walter Garrison Runciman (Garry), CBE, FBA, *b.* 1934, *s.* 1989, *m.*	Hon. David W. R., *b.* 1967
1918	** *St Davids (3rd) and 20th Eng. Baron Strange of Knokin*, 1299 and 8th Engl. Baron, Hungerford, 1426 and Baron De Moleyns, 1445, Colwyn Jestyn John Philipps, *b.* 1939, *s.* 1991, *m.*	Hon. Rhodri C. P., *b.* 1966
1801	*St Vincent (7th)*, Ronald George James Jervis, *b.* 1905, *s.* 1940, *m.*	Hon. Edward R. J. J., *b.* 1951
1937	*Samuel (3rd)*, David Herbert Samuel, OBE, Ph.D., *b.* 1922, *s.* 1978, *m.*	Hon. Dan J. S., *b.* 1925
1911	*Scarsdale (4th) and 8th Brit. Baron Scarsdale*, 1761, Peter Ghislain Nathaniel Curzon, *b.* 1949, *s.* 2000, *m.*	Hon. David J. N. C., *b.* 1958
1905 M.	*Selby (6th)*, Christopher Rolf Thomas Gully, *b.* 1993, *s.* 2001	Hon. (James) Edward H. G. G., *b.* 1945
1805	*Sidmouth (7th)*, John Tonge Anthony Pellew Addington, *b.* 1914, *s.* 1976, *m.*	Hon. Jeremy F. A., *b.* 1947
1940	** *Simon (3rd)*, Jan David Simon, *b.* 1940, *s.* 1993, *m.*	None
1960	** *Slim (2nd)*, John Douglas Slim, OBE, *b.* 1927, *s.* 1970, *m.*	Hon. Mark W. R. S., *b.* 1960
1954	*Soulbury (2nd)*, James Herwald Ramsbotham, *b.* 1915, *s.* 1971, *w.*, GCVO, *b.* 1919	Hon. Sir Peter E. R., GCMG,
1776 I.	*Southwell (7th)*, Pyers Anthony Joseph Southwell, *b.* 1930, *s.* 1960, *m.*	Hon. Richard A. P. S., *b.* 1956
1942	*Stansgate*, Rt. Hon. Anthony Neil Wedgwood Benn, *b.* 1925, *s.* 1960, *w.* Disclaimed for life 1963.	Stephen M. W. B., *b.* 1951
1959	*Stuart of Findhorn (3rd)*, James Dominic Stuart, *b.* 1948, *s.* 1999, *m.*	Hon. Andrew M. S., *b.* 1957
1957	** *Tenby (3rd)*, William Lloyd George, *b.* 1927, *s.* 1983, *m.*	Hon. Timothy H. G. L. G., *b.* 1962

Created	Title, order of succession, name, etc.	Heir
1952	*Thurso (3rd)*, John Archibald Sinclair, *b.* 1953, *s.* 1995, *m.*	Hon. James A. R. S., *b.* 1984
1721	*Torrington (11th)*, Timothy Howard St George Byng, *b.* 1943, *s.* 1961, *m.*	John L. B., MC, *b.* 1919
1936	*Trenchard (3rd)*, Hugh Trenchard, *b.* 1951, *s.* 1987, *m.*	Hon. Alexander T. T., *b.* 1978
1921	*Ullswater (2nd)*, Nicholas James Christopher Lowther, PC, *b.* 1942, *s.* 1949, *m.*	Hon. Benjamin J. L., *b.* 1975
1621 I.	*Valentia (15th)*, Richard John Dighton Annesley, *b.* 1929, *s.* 1983, *m.*	Hon. Francis W. D. A., *b.* 1959
1952	** *Waverley (3rd)*, John Desmond Forbes Anderson, *b.* 1949, *s.* 1990,	Hon. Forbes A. R. A., *b.* 1996
1938	*Weir (3rd)*, William Kenneth James Weir, *b.* 1933, *s.* 1975, *m.*	Hon. James W. H. W., *b.* 1965
1918	*Wimborne (4th) and 5th UK Baron Wimborne*, 1880, Ivor Mervyn Vigors Guest, *b.* 1968, *s.* 1993	Hon. Julien J. G., *b.* 1945
1923	*Younger of Leckie (4th) and Baron Younger of Prestwick (life peerage, 1992)*, George Kenneth Hotson Younger, KT, KCVO, TD, PC, *b.* 1931, *s.* 1997, *m.*	Hon. James E. G. Y., *b.* 1955

BARONS/LORDS

Coronet, Six silver balls
Style, The Right Hon. the Lord _ . In the Peerage of Scotland there is no rank of Baron; the equivalent rank is Lord of Parliament (*see* page 134) and Scottish peers should always be styled 'Lord', never 'Baron'
Wife's style, The Right Hon. the Lady _
Children's style, 'The Hon.' before forename and family name
In Scotland, the heir apparent to a Lord may be styled 'The Master of _ (title of peer)'
For forms of address, *see* page 133

1911	*Aberconway (3rd)*, Charles Melville McLaren, *b.* 1913, *s.* 1953, *m.*	Hon. H. Charles M., *b.* 1948
1873	** *Aberdare (4th)*, Morys George Lyndhurst Bruce, KBE, PC, *b.* 1919, *s.* 1957, *m.*	Hon. Alastair J. L. B., *b.* 1947
1835	*Abinger (8th)*, James Richard Scarlett, *b.* 1914, *s.* 1943, *m.*	Hon. James H. S., *b.* 1959
1869	*Acton (4th) and Baron Acton of Bridgnorth (life peerage, 2000)*, Richard Gerald Lyon-Dalberg-Acton, *b.* 1941, *s.* 1989, *m.*	Hon. John C. F. H. L.-D.-A., *b.* 1966
1887	** *Addington (6th)*, Dominic Bryce Hubbard, *b.* 1963, *s.* 1982,	Hon. Michael W. L. H., *b.* 1965
1896	*Aldenham (6th) and Hunsdon of Hunsdon (4th) (1923)*, Vicary Tyser Gibbs, *b.* 1948, *s.* 1986, *m.*	Hon. Humphrey W. F. G., *b.* 1989
1962	*Aldington (2nd)*, Charles Harold Stuart Low, *b.* 1948, *s.* 2001, *m.*	Hon Philip T. A. L., *b.* 1990
1945	*Altrincham (2nd)*, Anthony Ulick David Dundas Grigg, *b.* 1934, *s.* 2000, *m.*	Hon. (Edward) Sebastian G., *b.* 1965
1929	*Alvingham (2nd)*, Maj.-Gen. Robert Guy Eardley Yerburgh, CBE, *b.* 1926, *s.* 1955, *m.*	Capt. Hon. Robert R. G. Y., *b.* 1956
1892	*Amherst of Hackney (4th)*, William Hugh Amherst Cecil, *b.* 1940, *s.* 1980, *m.*	Hon. H. William A. C., *b.* 1968
1881	** *Ampthill (4th)*, Geoffrey Denis Erskine Russell, CBE, PC, *b.* 1921, *s.* 1973	Hon. David W. E. R., *b.* 1947
1947	*Amwell (3rd)*, Keith Norman Montague, *b.* 1943, *s.* 1990, *m.*	Hon. Ian K. M., *b.* 1973
1863	*Annaly (6th)*, Luke Richard White, *b.* 1954, *s.* 1990, *m.*	Hon. Luke H. W., *b.* 1990
1885	*Ashbourne (4th)*, Edward Barry Greynville Gibson, *b.* 1933, *s.* 1983, *m.*	Hon. Edward C. d'O. G., *b.* 1967
1835	*Ashburton (7th)*, John Francis Harcourt Baring, KG, KCVO, *b.* 1928, *s.* 1991, *m.*	Hon. Mark F. R. B., *b.* 1958
1892	*Ashcombe (4th)*, Henry Edward Cubitt, *b.* 1924, *s.* 1962, *m.*	Mark E. C., *b.* 1964
1911	*Ashton of Hyde (3rd)*, Thomas John Ashton, TD, *b.* 1926, *s.* 1983, *m.*	Hon. Thomas H. A., *b.* 1958
1800 I.	*Ashtown (7th)*, Nigel Clive Crosby Trench, KCMG, *b.* 1916, *s.* 1990, *m.*	Hon. Roderick N. G. T., *b.* 1944
1956	** *Astor of Hever (3rd)*, John Jacob Astor, *b.* 1946, *s.* 1984, *m.*	Hon. Charles G. J. A., *b.* 1990
1789 I.	* *Auckland (10th) and 10th Brit. Baron Auckland*, 1793, Robert Ian Burnard Eden, *b.* 1962, *s.* 1997, *m.*	Hon. Ronald J. E., *b.* 1931
1313	*Audley*. Barony in abeyance between three co-heiresses since 1997	
1900	** *Avebury (4th)*, Eric Reginald Lubbock, *b.* 1928, *s.* 1971, *m.*	Hon. Lyulph A. J. L., *b.* 1954
1718 I.	*Aylmer (13th)*, Michael Anthony Aylmer, *b.* 1923, *s.* 1982, *m.*	Hon. A. Julian A., *b.* 1951
1929	*Baden-Powell (3rd)*, Robert Crause Baden-Powell, *b.* 1936, *s.* 1962, *m.*	Hon. David M. B.-P., *b.* 1940
1780	*Bagot (10th)*, (Charles Hugh) Shaun Bagot, *b.* 1944, *s.* 2000, *m.*	Richard C. V. B., *b.* 1941
1953	*Baillieu (3rd)*, James William Latham Baillieu, *b.* 1950, *s.* 1973, *m.*	Hon. Robert L. B., *b.* 1979
1607 S.	*Balfour of Burleigh (8th)*, Robert Bruce, FRSE, *b.* 1927, *s.* 1967, *m.*	Hon. Victoria B., *b.* 1973
1945	*Balfour of Inchrye (2nd)*, Ian Balfour, *b.* 1924, *s.* 1988, *m.*	None
1924	*Banbury of Southam (3rd)*, Charles William Banbury, *b.* 1953, *s.* 1981, *m.*	None

Created	Title, order of succession, name, etc.	Heir
1698	*Barnard (11th)*, Harry John Neville Vane, TD, *b.* 1923, *s.* 1964,	Hon. Henry F. C. V., *b.* 1959
1887	*Basing (5th)*, Neil Lutley Sclater-Booth, *b.* 1939, *s.* 1983, *m.*	Hon. Stuart W. S.-B., *b.* 1969
1917	*Beaverbrook (3rd)*, Maxwell William Humphrey Aitken, *b.* 1951, *s.* 1985, *m.*	Hon. Maxwell F. A., *b.* 1977
1647 S.	*Belhaven and Stenton (13th)*, Robert Anthony Carmichael Hamilton, *b.* 1927, *s.* 1961, *m.*	Master of Belhaven, *b.* 1953
1848 I.	*Bellew (7th)*, James Bryan Bellew, *b.* 1920, *s.* 1981, *w.*	Hon. Bryan E. B., *b.* 1943
1856	*Belper (5th)*, Richard Henry Strutt, *b.* 1941, *s.* 1999, *m.*	Hon. Michael H., *b.* 1969
1938	*Belstead (2nd) and Baron Ganzoni (life peerage, 1999)*, John Julian Ganzoni, PC, *b.* 1932, *s.* 1958	None
1421	*Berkeley (18th) and Baron Gueterbock (life peerage, 2000)*, Anthony Fitzhardinge Gueterbock, OBE, *b.* 1939, *s.* 1992, *m.*	Hon. Thomas F. G., *b.* 1969
1922	*Bethell (4th)*, Nicholas William Bethell, MEP, *b.* 1938, *s.* 1967, *m.*	Hon. James N. B., *b.* 1967
1938	*Bicester (3rd)*, Angus Edward Vivian Smith, *b.* 1932, *s.* 1968	Hugh C. V. S., *b.* 1934
1903	*Biddulph (5th)*, (Anthony) Nicholas Colin Maitland Biddulph, *b.* 1959, *s.* 1988, *m.*	Hon. Robert J. M. B., *b.* 1994
1938	*Birdwood (3rd)*, Mark William Ogilvie Birdwood, *b.* 1938, *s.* 1962, *m.*	None
1958	*Birkett (2nd)*, Michael Birkett, *b.* 1929, *s.* 1962, *w.*	Hon. Thomas B., *b.* 1982
1907	*Blyth (4th)*, Anthony Audley Rupert Blyth, *b.* 1931, *s.* 1977, *m.*	Hon. James A. I. B., *b.* 1970
1797	*Bolton (8th)*, Harry Algar Nigel Orde-Powlett, *b.* 1954, *s.* 2001, *m.*	Hon. Thomas O.-P., *b.* 1979
1452 S.	*Borthwick (24th)*, John Hugh Borthwick, *b.* 1940, *s.* 1997, *m.*	Hon. James H. A. B. of Glengelt, *b.* 1940
1922	*Borwick (4th)*, James Hugh Myles Borwick, MC, *b.* 1917, *s.* 1961, *m.*	Hon. Robin S. B., *b.* 1927
1761	*Boston (10th)*, Timothy George Frank Boteler Irby, *b.* 1939, *s.* 1978, *m.*	Hon. George W. E. B. I., *b.* 1971
1942	** *Brabazon of Tara (3rd)*, Ivon Anthony Moore-Brabazon, *b.* 1946, *s.* 1974, *m.*	Hon. Benjamin R. M.-B., *b.* 1983
1880	*Brabourne (7th)*, John Ulick Knatchbull, CBE, *b.* 1924, *s.* 1943, *m.*	Lord Romsey, *b.* 1947
1925	*Bradbury (3rd)*, John Bradbury, *b.* 1940, *s.* 1994, *m.*	Hon. John B., *b.* 1973
1962	*Brain (2nd)*, Christopher Langdon Brain, *b.* 1926, *s.* 1966, *m.*	Hon. Michael C. B., *b.* 1928
1938	*Brassey of Apethorpe (3rd)*, David Henry Brassey, OBE, *b.* 1932, *s.* 1967, *m.*	Hon. Edward B., *b.* 1964
1788	*Braybrooke (10th)*, Robin Henry Charles Neville, *b.* 1932, *s.* 1990, *m.*	George N., *b.* 1943
1957	** *Bridges (2nd)*, Thomas Edward Bridges, GCMG, *b.* 1927, *s.* 1969, *m.*	Hon. Mark T. B., *b.* 1954
1945	*Broadbridge (4th)*, Martin Hugh Broadbridge, *b.* 1929, *s.* 2000, *m.*	Hon. Richard J. M. B., *b.* 1959
1933	*Brocket (3rd)*, Charles Ronald George Nall-Cain, *b.* 1952, *s.* 1967, *m.*	Hon. Alexander C. C. N.-C., *b.* 1984
1860	** *Brougham and Vaux (5th)*, Michael John Brougham, CBE, *b.* 1938, *s.* 1967	Hon. Charles W. B., *b.* 1971
1945	*Broughshane (3rd)*, (William) Kensington Davison, DSO, DFC, *b.* 1914, *s.* 1995	None
1776	*Brownlow (7th)*, Edward John Peregrine Cust, *b.* 1936, *s.* 1978, *m.*	Hon. Peregrine E. Q. C., *b.* 1974
1942	*Bruntisfield (2nd)*, John Robert Warrender, OBE, MC, TD, *b.* 1921, *s.* 1993, *m.*	Hon. Michael J. V. W., *b.* 1949
1950	*Burden (3rd)*, Andrew Philip Burden, *b.* 1959, *s.* 1995	Hon. Fraser W. E. B., *b.* 1964
1529	*Burgh (7th)*, Alexander Peter Willoughby Leith, *b.* 1935, *s.* 1959, *m.*	Hon. A. Gregory D. L., *b.* 1958
1903	** *Burnham (6th)*, Hugh John Frederick Lawson, *b.* 1931, *s.* 1993, *m.*	Hon. Harry F. A. L., *b.* 1968
1897	*Burton (3rd)*, Michael Evan Victor Baillie, *b.* 1924, *s.* 1962, *m.*	Hon. Evan M. R. B., *b.* 1949
1643	*Byron (13th)*, Robert James Byron, *b.* 1950, *s.* 1989, *m.*	Hon. Charles R. G. B., *b.* 1990
1937	*Cadman (3rd)*, John Anthony Cadman, *b.* 1938, *s.* 1966, *m.*	Hon. Nicholas A. J. C., *b.* 1977
1945	*Calverley (3rd)*, Charles Rodney Muff, *b.* 1946, *s.* 1971, *m.*	Hon. Jonathan E. M., *b.* 1975
1383	*Camoys (7th)*, (Ralph) Thomas Campion George Sherman Stonor, GCVO, PC, *b.* 1940, *s.* 1976, *m.*	Hon. R. William R. T. S., *b.* 1974
1715 I.	*Carbery (11th)*, Peter Ralfe Harrington Evans-Freke, *b.* 1920, *s.* 1970, *m.*	Hon. Michael P. E.-F., *b.* 1942
1834 I.*	*Carew (7th) and 7th UK Baron*, Carew, 1838, Patrick Thomas Conolly-Carew, *b.* 1938, *s.* 1994, *m.*	Hon. William P. C.-C., *b.* 1973
1916	*Carnock (4th)*, David Henry Arthur Nicolson, *b.* 1920, *s.* 1982,	Nigel N., MBE, *b.* 1917
1796 I.*	*Carrington (6th) and 6th Brit. Baron Carrington, 1797 and Baron Carington of Upton (life peerage, 1999)*, Peter Alexander Rupert Carington, KG, GCMG, CH, MC, PC, *b.* 1919, *s.* 1938, *m.*	Hon. Rupert F. J. C., *b.* 1948
1812	*Castlemaine (8th)*, Roland Thomas John Handcock, MBE, *b.* 1943, *s.* 1973, *m.*	Hon. Ronan M. E. H., *b.* 1989
1936	*Catto (3rd)*, Innes Gordon Catto, *b.* 1950, *s.* 2001, *m.*	None
1918	*Cawley (4th)*, John Francis Cawley, *b.* 1946, *s.* 2001, *m.*	Hon. William R. H. C., *b.* 1981
1603	*Cecil*. A subsidiary title of the Marquess of Salisbury. His heir Viscount Cranborne was given a Writ in Acceleration in this title to enable him to sit in the House of Lords whilst his father is still alive.	

Created	Title, order of succession, name, etc.	Heir
1937	*Chatfield (2nd)*, Ernle David Lewis Chatfield, *b.* 1917, *s.* 1967, *m.*	None
1858	*Chesham (6th)*, Nicholas Charles Cavendish, *b.* 1941, *s.* 1989, *m.*	Hon. Charles G. C. C., *b.* 1974
1945	*Chetwode (2nd)*, Philip Chetwode, *b.* 1937, *s.* 1950, *m.*	Hon. Roger C., *b.* 1968
1945	*Chorley (2nd)*, Roger Richard Edward Chorley, *b.* 1930, *s.* 1978, *m.*	Hon. Nicholas R. D. C., *b.* 1966
1858	*Churston (5th)*, John Francis Yarde-Buller, *b.* 1934, *s.* 1991, *m.*	Hon. Benjamin F. A. Y.-B., *b.* 1974
1946	*Citrine (3rd)*, Ronald Eric Citrine, *b.* 1919, *s.* 1997, *m.* Does not use title	None
1800	*Clanmorris (8th)*, Simon John Ward Bingham, *b.* 1937, *s.* 1988, *m.*	Robert D. de B. B., *b.* 1942
1672	*Clifford of Chudleigh (14th)*, Thomas Hugh Clifford, *b.* 1948, *s.* 1988, *m.*	Hon. Alexander T. H. C., *b.* 1985
1299	*Clinton (22nd)*, Gerard Nevile Mark Fane Trefusis, *b.* 1934, *s.* 1965, *m.*	Hon. Charles P. R. F. T., *b.* 1962
1955	*Clitheroe (2nd)*, Ralph John Assheton, *b.* 1929, *s.* 1984, *m.*	Hon. Ralph C. A., *b.* 1962
1919	*Clwyd (3rd)*, (John) Anthony Roberts, *b.* 1935, *s.* 1987, *m.*	Hon. J. Murray R., *b.* 1971
1948	*Clydesmuir (3rd)*, David Ronald Colville, *b.* 1949, *s.* 1996, *m.*	Hon. Richard C., *b.* 1980
1960	** *Cobbold (2nd)*, David Antony Fromanteel Lytton Cobbold, *b.* 1937, *s.* 1987, *m.*	Hon. Henry F. L. C., *b.* 1962
1919	*Cochrane of Cults (4th)*, (Ralph Henry) Vere Cochrane, *b.* 1926, *s.* 1990, *m.*	Hon. Thomas H. V. C., *b.* 1957
1954	*Coleraine (2nd)*, (James) Martin (Bonar) Law, *b.* 1931, *s.* 1980, *m.*	Hon. James P. B. L., *b.* 1975
1873	*Coleridge (5th)*, William Duke Coleridge, *b.* 1937, *s.* 1984, *m.*	Hon. James D. C., *b.* 1967
1946	*Colgrain (3rd)*, David Colin Campbell, *b.* 1920, *s.* 1973, *m.*	Hon. Alastair C. L. C., *b.* 1951
1917	** *Colwyn (3rd)*, (Ian) Anthony Hamilton-Smith, CBE, *b.* 1942, *s.* 1966, *m.*	Hon. Craig P. H.-S., *b.* 1968
1956	*Colyton (2nd)*, Alisdair John Munro Hopkinson, *b.* 1958, *s.* 1996, *m.*	Hon. James P. M. H., *b.* 1983
1841	*Congleton (8th)*, Christopher Patrick Parnell, *b.* 1930, *s.* 1967, *m.*	Hon. John P. C. P., *b.* 1959
1927	*Cornwallis (3rd)*, Fiennes Neil Wykeham Cornwallis, OBE, *b.* 1921, *s.* 1982, *w.*	Hon. F. W. Jeremy C., *b.* 1946
1874	*Cottesloe (5th)*, Cdr. John Tapling Fremantle, *b.* 1927, *s.* 1994, *m.*	Hon. Thomas F. H. F., *b.* 1966
1929	*Craigmyle (4th)*, Thomas Columba Shaw, *b.* 1960, *s.* 1998, *m.*	Hon. Alexander F. S., *b.* 1988
1899	*Cranworth (3rd)*, Philip Bertram Gurdon, *b.* 1940, *s.* 1964, *w.*	Hon. Sacha W. R. G., *b.* 1970
1959	** *Crathorne (2nd)*, Charles James Dugdale, *b.* 1939, *s.* 1977, *m.*	Hon. Thomas A. J. D., *b.* 1977
1892	*Crawshaw (5th)*, David Gerald Brooks, *b.* 1934, *s.* 1997, *m.*	Hon. John P. B., *b.* 1938
1940	*Croft (3rd)*, Bernard William Henry Page Croft, *b.* 1949, *s.* 1997, *m.*	None
1797 I.	*Crofton (7th)*, Guy Patrick Gilbert Crofton, *b.* 1951, *s.* 1989, *m.*	Hon. E. Harry P. C., *b.* 1988
1375	*Cromwell (7th)*, Godfrey John Bewicke-Copley, *b.* 1960, *s.* 1982, *m.*	Hon. David G. B.-C., *b.* 1997
1947	*Crook (3rd)*, Robert Douglas Edwin Crook, *b.* 1955, *s.* 2001, *m.*	Hon. Matthew R. C., *b.* 1990
1920	*Cullen of Ashbourne (3rd)*, Edmund Willoughby Marsham Cokayne, *b.* 1916, *s.* 2000, *w.*	(Hon.) John O'B. M. C., *b.*1920
1914	*Cunliffe (3rd)*, Roger Cunliffe, *b.* 1932, *s.* 1963, *m.*	Hon. Henry C., *b.* 1962
1927	*Daresbury (4th)*, Peter Gilbert Greenall, *b.* 1953, *s.* 1996, *m.*	Hon. Thomas E. G., *b.* 1984
1924	*Darling (2nd)*, Robert Charles Henry Darling, *b.* 1919, *s.* 1936, *m.*	Hon. R. Julian H. D., *b.* 1944
1946	*Darwen (3rd)*, Roger Michael Davies, *b.* 1938, *s.* 1988, *m.*	Hon. Paul D., *b.* 1962
1932	*Davies (3rd)*, David Davies, *b.* 1940, *s.* 1944, *m.*	Hon. David D. D., *b.* 1975
1812 I.	*Decies (7th)*, Marcus Hugh Tristram de la Poer Beresford, *b.* 1948, *s.* 1992, *m.*	Hon. Robert M. D. de la P. B., *b.* 1988
1299	*de Clifford (27th)*, John Edward Southwell Russell, *b.* 1928, *s.* 1982, *m.*	Hon. William S. R., *b.* 1930
1851	*De Freyne (7th)*, Francis Arthur John French, *b.* 1927, *s.* 1935, *m.*	Hon. Fulke C. A. J. F., *b.* 1957
1821	*Delamere (5th)*, Hugh George Cholmondeley, *b.* 1934, *s.* 1979, *m.*	Hon. Thomas P. G. C., *b.* 1968
1838	*de Mauley (6th)*, Gerald John Ponsonby, *b.* 1921, *s.* 1962, *m.*	Hon. Col. Thomas M. P., *b.* 1930
1937	** *Denham (2nd)*, Bertram Stanley Mitford Bowyer, KBE, PC, *b.* 1927, *s.* 1948, *m.*	Hon. Richard G. G. B., *b.* 1959
1834	*Denman (5th)*, Charles Spencer Denman, CBE, MC, TD, *b.* 1916, *s.* 1971, *w.*	Hon. Richard T. S. D., *b.* 1946
1885	*Deramore (6th)*, Richard Arthur de Yarburgh-Bateson, *b.* 1911, *s.* 1964, *m.*	None
1887	*De Ramsey (4th)*, John Ailwyn Fellowes, *b.* 1942, *s.* 1993, *m.*	Hon. Freddie J. F., *b.* 1978
1264	*de Ros (28th)*, Peter Trevor Maxwell, *b.* 1958, *s.* 1983, *m.*, Premier Baron of England	Hon. Finbar J. M., *b.* 1988
1881	*Derwent (5th)*, Robin Evelyn Leo Vanden-Bempde-Johnstone, LVO, *b.* 1930, *s.* 1986, *m.*	Hon. Francis P. H. V.-B.-J., *b.* 1965
1831	*de Saumarez (7th)*, Eric Douglas Saumarez, *b.* 1956, *s.* 1991, *m.*	Hon. Victor T. S., *b.* 1956
1910	*de Villiers (3rd)*, Arthur Percy de Villiers, *b.* 1911, *s.* 1934	Hon. Alexander C. de V., *b.* 1940
1930	*Dickinson (2nd)*, Richard Clavering Hyett Dickinson, *b.* 1926, *s.* 1943, *m.*	Hon. Martin H. D., *b.* 1961
1620 I.*	*Digby (12th) and 5th Brit. Baron Digby*, 1765, Edward Henry Kenelm Digby, KCVO, *b.* 1924, *s.* 1964, *m.*	Hon. Henry N. K. D., *b.* 1954
1615	*Dormer (17th)*, Geoffrey Henry Dormer, *b.* 1920, *s.* 1995, *m.*	Hon. William R. D., *b.* 1960
1943	*Dowding (3rd)*, Piers Hugh Tremenheere Dowding, *b.* 1948, *s.* 1992	Hon. Mark D. J. D., *b.* 1949
1800 I.	*Dufferin and Clandeboye*, The 10th Baron died in 1991. Heir had not established his claim to the title at the time of going to press	Sir John Blackwood, Bt., *b.* 1944
1929	*Dulverton (3rd)*, (Gilbert) Michael Hamilton Wills, *b.* 1944, *s.* 1992	Hon. Robert A. H. W., *b.* 1983
1800 I.	*Dunalley (7th)*, Henry Francis Cornelius Prittie, *b.* 1948, *s.* 1992, *m.*	Hon. Joel H. P., *b.* 1981

Created	Title, order of succession, name, etc.	Heir
1324 I.	*Dunboyne (28th)*, Patrick Theobald Tower Butler, VRD, *b.* 1917, *s.* 1945, *m.*	Hon. John F. B., *b.* 1951
1892	*Dunleath (6th)*, Brian Henry Mulholland, *b.* 1950, *s.* 1997, *m.*	Hon. Andrew H. M., *b.* 1981
1439 I.	*Dunsany (20th)*, Edward John Carlos Plunkett, *b.* 1939, *s.* 1999, *m.*	Hon. Randal P., *b.* 1983
1780	*Dynevor (9th)*, Richard Charles Uryan Rhys, *b.* 1935, *s.* 1962	Hon. Hugo G. U. R., *b.* 1966
1963	*Egremont (2nd) and 7th UK Baron Leconfield*, 1859, John Max Henry Scawen Wyndham, *b.* 1948, *s.* 1972, *m.*	Hon. George R. V. W., *b.* 1983
1643	*Elibank (14th)*, Alan D'Ardis Erskine-Murray, *b.* 1923, *s.* 1973, *w.*	Master of Elibank, *b.* 1964
1802	*Ellenborough (8th)*, Richard Edward Cecil Law, *b.* 1926, *s.* 1945, *m.*	Maj. Hon. Rupert E. H. L., *b.* 1955
1509 S.*	*Elphinstone (19th) and 5th UK Baron Elphinstone*, 1885, Alexander Mountstuart Elphinstone, *b.* 1980, *s.* 1994	Hon. Angus J. E., *b.* 1982
1934 **	*Elton (2nd)*, Rodney Elton, TD, *b.* 1930, *s.* 1973, *m.*	Hon. Edward P. E., *b.* 1966
1627 S.	*Fairfax of Cameron (14th)*, Nicholas John Albert Fairfax, *b.* 1956, *s.* 1964, *m.*	Hon. Edward N. T. F., *b.* 1984
1961	*Fairhaven (3rd)*, Ailwyn Henry George Broughton, *b.* 1936, *s.* 1973, *m.*	Maj. Hon. James H. A. B., *b.* 1963
1916	*Faringdon (3rd)*, Charles Michael Henderson, *b.* 1937, *s.* 1977, *m.*	Hon. James H. H., *b.* 1961
1756	*Farnham (13th)*, Simon Kenlis Maxwell, *b.* 1933, *s.* 2001, *m.*	Hon. Robin S. M., *b.* 1965
1856	*Fermoy (6th)*, Patrick Maurice Burke Roche, *b.* 1967, *s.* 1984, *m.*	Hon. E. Hugh B. R., *b.* 1972
1826	*Feversham (6th)*, Charles Antony Peter Duncombe, *b.* 1945, *s.* 1963, *m.*	Hon. Jasper O. S. D., *b.* 1968
1798 I.	*ffrench (8th)*, Robuck John Peter Charles Mario ffrench, *b.* 1956, *s.* 1986, *m.*	Hon. John C. M. J. F. ff., *b.* 1928
1909	*Fisher (3rd)*, John Vavasseur Fisher, DSC, *b.* 1921, *s.* 1955, *m.*	Hon. Patrick V. F., *b.* 1953
1295	*Fitzwalter (21st)*, (Fitzwalter) Brook Plumptre, *b.* 1914, *m.*	Hon. Julian B. P., *b.* 1952
1776	*Foley (8th)*, Adrian Gerald Foley, *b.* 1923, *s.* 1927, *w.*	Hon. Thomas H. F., *b.* 1961
1445	*Forbes (22nd)*, Nigel Ivan Forbes, KBE, *b.* 1918, *s.* 1953, *m.*, Premier Lord of Scotland	Master of Forbes, *b.* 1946
1821	*Forester (8th)*, (George Cecil) Brooke Weld-Forester, *b.* 1938, *s.* 1977, *m.*	Hon. C. R. George W.-F., *b.* 1975
1922	*Forres (4th)*, Alastair Stephen Grant Williamson, *b.* 1946, *s.* 1978, *m.*	Hon. George A. M. W., *b.* 1972
1917	*Forteviot (4th)*, John James Evelyn Dewar, *b.* 1938, *s.* 1993, *m.*	Hon. Alexander J. E. D., *b.* 1971
1951 **	*Freyberg (3rd)*, Valerian Bernard Freyberg, *b.* 1970, *s.* 1993	None
1917	*Gainford (3rd)*, Joseph Edward Pease, *b.* 1921, *s.* 1971, *m.*	Hon. George P., *b.* 1926
1818	*Garvagh (5th)*, (Alexander Leopold Ivor) George Canning, *b.* 1920, *s.* 1956, *m.*	Hon. Spencer G. S. de R. C., *b.* 1953
1942 **	*Geddes (3rd)*, Euan Michael Ross Geddes, *b.* 1937, *s.* 1975, *m.*	Hon. James G. N. G., *b.* 1969
1876	*Gerard (5th)*, Anthony Robert Hugo Gerard, *b.* 1949, *s.* 1992, *m.*	Hon. Rupert B. C. G., *b.* 1981
1824	*Gifford (6th)*, Anthony Maurice Gifford, QC, *b.* 1940, *s.* 1961, *m.*	Hon. Thomas A. G., *b.* 1967
1917	*Gisborough (3rd)*, Thomas Richard John Long Chaloner, *b.* 1927, *s.* 1951, *m.*	Hon. T. Peregrine L. C., *b.* 1961
1960	*Gladwyn (2nd)*, Miles Alvery Gladwyn Jebb, *b.* 1930, *s.* 1996,	None
1899	*Glanusk (5th)*, Christopher Russell Bailey, *b.* 1942, *s.* 1997, *m.*	Hon. Charles H. B., *b.* 1976
1918 **	*Glenarthur (4th)*, Simon Mark Arthur, *b.* 1944, *s.* 1976, *m.*	Hon. Edward A. A., *b.* 1973
1911	*Glenconner (3rd)*, Colin Christopher Paget Tennant, *b.* 1926, *s.* 1983, *m.*	Hon. Cody T., *b.* 1994
1964	*Glendevon (2nd)*, Julian John Somerset Hope, *b.* 1950, *s.* 1996,	Hon. Jonathan C. H., *b.* 1952
1922	*Glendyne (3rd)*, Robert Nivison, *b.* 1926, *s.* 1967, *m.*	Hon. John N., *b.* 1960
1939 **	*Glentoran (3rd)*, (Thomas) Robin (Valerian) Dixon, CBE, *b.* 1935, *s.* 1995, *m.*	Hon. Daniel G. D., *b.* 1959
1909	*Gorell (4th)*, Timothy John Radcliffe Barnes, *b.* 1927, *s.* 1963, *m.*	Hon. Ronald A. H. B., *b.* 1931
1953	*Grantchester (3rd)*, Christopher John Suenson-Taylor, *b.* 1951, *s.* 1995, *m.*	Hon. Jesse D. S.-T., *b.* 1977
1782	*Grantley (8th)*, Richard William Brinsley Norton, *b.* 1956, *s.* 1995	Hon. Francis J. H. N., *b.* 1960
1794 I.	*Graves (9th)*, Evelyn Paget Graves, *b.* 1926, *s.* 1994, *m.*	Hon. Timothy E. G., *b.* 1960
1445 S.	*Gray (22nd)*, Angus Diarmid Ian Campbell-Gray, *b.* 1931, *s.* 1946, *m.*	Master of Grey, *b.* 1964
1950	*Greenhill (3rd)*, Malcolm Greenhill, *b.* 1924, *s.* 1989	None
1927 **	*Greenway (4th)*, Ambrose Charles Drexel Greenway, *b.* 1941, *s.* 1975, *m.*	Hon. Nigel. P. G., *b.* 1944
1902	*Grenfell (3rd) and Baron Grenfell of Kilvey (life peerage, 2000)*, Julian Pascoe Francis St Leger Grenfell, *b.* 1935, *s.* 1976, *m.*	Francis P. J. G., *b.* 1938
1944	*Gretton (4th)*, John Lysander Gretton, *b.* 1975, *s.* 1989	None
1397	*Grey of Codnor (6th)*, Richard Henry Cornwall-Legh, *b.* 1936, *s.* 1996, *m.*	Hon. Richard S. C. C.-L., *b.* 1976
1955	*Gridley (3rd)*, Richard David Arnold Gridley, *b.* 1956, *s.* 1996, *m.*	Hon. Carl R. G., *b.* 1981
1964	*Grimston of Westbury (2nd)*, Robert Walter Sigismund Grimston, *b.* 1925, *s.* 1979, *m.*	Hon. Robert J. S. G., *b.* 1951
1886	*Grimthorpe (4th)*, Christopher John Beckett, OBE, *b.* 1915, *s.* 1963, *m.*	Hon. Edward J. B., *b.* 1954
1945	*Hacking (3rd)*, Douglas David Hacking, *b.* 1938, *s.* 1971, *m.*	Hon. Douglas F. H., *b.* 1968
1950	*Haden-Guest (5th)*, Christopher Haden-Guest, *b.* 1948, *s.* 1996, *m.*	Hon. Nicholas H.-G., *b.* 1951
1886	*Hamilton of Dalzell (4th)*, James Leslie Hamilton, *b.* 1938, *s.* 1990, *m.*	Hon. Gavin G. H., *b.* 1968
1874	*Hampton (6th)*, Richard Humphrey Russell Pakington, *b.* 1925, *s.* 1974, *m.*	Hon. John H. A. P., *b.* 1964
1939	*Hankey (3rd)*, Donald Robin Alers Hankey, *b.* 1938, *s.* 1996, *m.*	Hon. Alexander M. A. H., *b.* 1947
1958	*Harding of Petherton (2nd)*, John Charles Harding, *b.* 1928, *s.* 1989, *m.*	Hon. William A. J. H., *b.* 1969
1910	*Hardinge of Penshurst (4th)*, Julian Alexander Hardinge, *b.* 1945, *s.* 1997	Hon. Hugh F. H., *b.* 1948
1876	*Harlech (6th)*, Francis David Ormsby-Gore, *b.* 1954, *s.* 1985, *m.*	Hon. Jasset D. C. O.-G., *b.* 1986

Created	Title, order of succession, name, etc.	Heir
1939	*Harmsworth (3rd)*, Thomas Harold Raymond Harmsworth, *b.* 1939, *s.* 1990, *m.*	Hon. Dominic M. E. H., *b.* 1973
1815	*Harris (8th)*, Anthony Harris, *b.* 1942, *s.* 1996, *m.*	Anthony J. T. H., *b.* 1915
1954	*Harvey of Tasburgh (2nd)*, Peter Charles Oliver Harvey, *b.* 1921, *s.* 1968, *w.*	Charles J. G. H., *b.* 1951
1295	*Hastings (22nd)*, Edward Delaval Henry Astley, *b.* 1912, *s.* 1956, *m.*	Hon. Delaval T. H. A., *b.* 1960
1835	*Hatherton (8th)*, Edward Charles Littleton, *b.* 1950, *s.* 1985, *m.*	Hon. Thomas E. L., *b.* 1977
1776	*Hawke (11th)*, Edward George Hawke, TD, *b.* 1950, *s.* 1992, *m.*	Hon. William M. T. H., *b.* 1995
1927	*Hayter (3rd)*, George Charles Hayter Chubb, KCVO, CBE, *b.* 1911, *s.* 1967, *m.*	Hon. G. William M. C., *b.* 1943
1945	*Hazlerigg (2nd)*, Arthur Grey Hazlerigg, MC, TD, *b.* 1910, *s.* 1949, *w.*	Hon. Arthur G. H., *b.* 1951
1943	*Hemingford (3rd)*, (Dennis) Nicholas Herbert, *b.* 1934, *s.* 1982, *m.*	Hon. Christopher D. C. H., *b.* 1973
1906	*Hemphill (5th)*, Peter Patrick Fitzroy Martyn Martyn-Hemphill, *b.* 1928, *s.* 1957, *m.*	Hon. Charles A. M. M.-H., *b.* 1954
1799 I.* **	*Henley (8th) and 6th UK Baron Northington*, 1885, Oliver Michael Robert Eden, *b.* 1953, *s.* 1977, *m.*	Hon. John W. O. E., *b.* 1988
1800 I.*	*Henniker (8th) and 4th UK Baron Hertsmere*,1866, John Patrick Edward Chandos Henniker-Major, KCMG, CVO, MC, *b.* 1916, *s.* 1980, *m.*	Hon. Mark I. P. C. H.-M., *b.* 1947
1461	*Herbert (19th)*, David John Seyfried, *b.* 1952, *s.* 2002, *m.* Title has been in abeyance since the death of 10th Duke of Beaufort in 1984, only called out of abeyance in 2002.	Hon. Dr. Oliver R. S., *b.* 1976
1886	*Herschell (3rd)*, Rognvald Richard Farrer Herschell, *b.* 1923, *s.* 1929, *m.*	None
1935	*Hesketh (3rd)*, Thomas Alexander Fermor-Hesketh, KBE, PC, *b.* 1950, *s.* 1955, *m.*	Hon. Frederick H. F.-H., *b.* 1988
1828	*Heytesbury (6th)*, Francis William Holmes à Court, *b.* 1931, *s.* 1971, *m.*	Hon. James W. H. à. C., *b.* 1967
1886	*Hindlip (6th)*, Charles Henry Allsopp, *b.* 1940, *s.* 1993, *m.*	Hon. Henry W. A., *b.* 1973
1950	*Hives (3rd)*, Matthew Peter Hives, *b.* 1971, *s.* 1997	Hon. Michael B. H., *b.* 1926
1912	*Hollenden (4th)*, Ian Hampden Hope-Morley, *b.* 1946, *s.* 1999, *m.*	Hon. Edward H.-M., *b.* 1981
1897	*HolmPatrick (4th)*, Hans James David Hamilton, *b.* 1955, *s.* 1991, *m.*	Hon. Ion H. J. H., *b.* 1956
1797 I.	*Hotham (8th)*, Henry Durand Hotham, *b.* 1940, *s.* 1967, *m.*	Hon. William B. H., *b.* 1972
1881	*Hothfield (6th)*, Anthony Charles Sackville Tufton, *b.* 1939, *s.* 1991, *m.*	Hon. William S. T., *b.* 1977
1597	*Howard de Walden.* The 9th Baron Howard de Walden died in 1999, leaving four co-heiresses.	
1930	*Howard of Penrith (3rd)*, Philip Esme Howard, *b.* 1945, *s.* 1999, *m.*	Hon. Thomas Philip H., *b.* 1974
1960	*Howick of Glendale (2nd)*, Charles Evelyn Baring, *b.* 1937, *s.* 1973, *m.*	Hon. David E. C. B., *b.* 1975
1796 I.	*Huntingfield (7th)*, Joshua Charles Vanneck, *b.* 1954, *s.* 1994, *m.*	Hon. Gerard C. A. V., *b.* 1985
1866 **	*Hylton (5th)*, Raymond Hervey Jolliffe, *b.* 1932, *s.* 1967, *m.*	Hon. William H. M. J., *b.* 1967
1933 I.	*Iliffe (3rd)*, Robert Peter Richard Iliffe, *b.* 1944, *s.* 1996, *m.*	Hon. Edward R. I., *b.* 1968
1543 I.	*Inchiquin (18th)*, Conor Myles John O'Brien, *b.* 1943, *s.* 1982, *m.*	Conor J. A. O'B., *b.* 1952
1962	*Inchyra (2nd)*, Robert Charles Reneke Hoyer Millar, *b.* 1935, *s.* 1989, *m.*	Hon. C. James C. H. M., *b.* 1962
1964 **	*Inglewood (2nd)*, (William) Richard Fletcher-Vane, MEP, *b.* 1951, *s.* 1989, *m.*	Hon. Henry W. F. F.-V., *b.* 1990
1919	*Inverforth (4th)*, Andrew Peter Weir, *b.* 1966, *s.* 1982	Hon. John V. W., *b.* 1935
1941	*Ironside (2nd)*, Edmund Oslac Ironside, *b.* 1924, *s.* 1959, *m.*	Hon. Charles E. G. I., *b.* 1956
1952	*Jeffreys (3rd)*, Christopher Henry Mark Jeffreys, *b.* 1957, *s.* 1986, *m.*	Hon. Arthur M. H. J., *b.* 1989
1906	*Joicey (5th)*, James Michael Joicey, *b.* 1953, *s.* 1993, *m.*	Hon. William J. J., *b.* 1990
1937	*Kenilworth (4th)*, (John) Randle Siddeley, *b.* 1954, *s.* 1981, *m.*	Hon. William R. J. S., *b.* 1992
1935	*Kennet (2nd)*, Wayland Hilton Young, *b.* 1923, *s.* 1960, *m.*	Hon. W. A. Thoby Y., *b.* 1957
1776 I.*	*Kensington (8th) and 5th UK Baron Kensington*, 1886, Hugh Ivor Edwardes, *b.* 1933, *s.* 1981, *m.*	Hon. W. Owen A. E., *b.* 1964
1951	*Kenswood (2nd)*, John Michael Howard Whitfield, *b.* 1930, *s.* 1963, *m.*	Hon. Michael C. W., *b.* 1955
1788	*Kenyon (6th)*, Lloyd Tyrell-Kenyon, *b.* 1947, *s.* 1993, *m.*	Hon. Lloyd N. T.-K., *b.* 1972
1947	*Kershaw (4th)*, Edward John Kershaw, *b.* 1936, *s.* 1962, *m.*	Hon. John C. E. K., *b.* 1971
1943	*Keyes (2nd)*, Roger George Bowlby Keyes, *b.* 1919, *s.* 1945, *w.*	Hon. Charles W. P. K., *b.* 1951
1909	*Kilbracken (3rd)*, John Raymond Godley, DSC, *b.* 1920, *s.* 1950	Hon. Christopher J. G., *b.* 1945
1900	*Killanin (4th)*, (George) Redmond Fitzpatrick Morris, *b.* 1947, *s.* 1999, *m.*	Hon. Luke M. G. M., *b.* 1975
1943	*Killearn (3rd)*, Victor Miles George Aldous Lampson, *b.* 1941, *s.* 1996, *m.*	Hon. Miles H. M. L., *b.* 1977
1789 I.	*Kilmaine (7th)*, John David Henry Browne, *b.* 1948, *s.* 1978, *m.*	Hon. John F. S. B., *b.* 1983
1831	*Kilmarnock (7th)*, Alastair Ivor Gilbert Boyd, *b.* 1927, *s.* 1975, *m.*	Hon. Robin J. B., *b.* 1941
1941	*Kindersley (3rd)*, Robert Hugh Molesworth Kindersley, *b.* 1929, *s.* 1976, *m.*	Hon. Rupert J. M. K., *b.* 1955
1223 I.	*Kingsale (35th)*, John de Courcy, *b.* 1941, *s.* 1969, *Premier Baron of Ireland*	Nevinson R. de C., *b.* 1920
1902	*Kinross (5th)*, Christopher Patrick Balfour, *b.* 1949, *s.* 1985, *m.*	Hon. Alan I. B., *b.* 1978
1951	*Kirkwood (3rd)*, David Harvie Kirkwood, PH.D., *b.* 1931, *s.* 1970, *m.*	Hon. James S. K., *b.* 1937
1800 I.	*Langford (9th)*, Col. Geoffrey Alexander Rowley-Conwy, OBE, *b.* 1912, *s.* 1953, *m.*	Hon. Owain G. R.-C., *b.* 1958
1942	*Latham (2nd)*, Dominic Charles Latham, *b.* 1954, *s.* 1970	Anthony M. L., *b.* 1954
1431	*Latymer (8th)*, Hugo Nevill Money-Coutts, *b.* 1926, *s.* 1987, *m.*	Hon. Crispin J. A. N. M.-C., *b.* 1955

Created	Title, order of succession, name, etc.	Heir
1869	*Lawrence (5th)*, David John Downer Lawrence, *b.* 1937, *s.* 1968	None
1947	*Layton (3rd)*, Geoffrey Michael Layton, *b.* 1947, *s.* 1989, *m.*	Hon. David L., *b.* 1914
1839	*Leigh (5th)*, John Piers Leigh, *b.* 1935, *s.* 1979, *m.*	Hon. Christopher D. P. L., *b.* 1960
1962	*Leighton of St Mellons (3rd)*, Robert William Henry Leighton Seager, *b.* 1955, *s.* 1998	Hon. Simon J. L. S., *b.* 1957
1797	*Lilford (7th)*, George Vernon Powys, *b.* 1931, *s.* 1949, *m.*	Hon. Mark V. P., *b.* 1975
1945	*Lindsay of Birker (3rd)*, James Francis Lindsay, *b.* 1945, *s.* 1994, *m.*	Alexander S. L., *b.* 1940
1758 I.	*Lisle (8th)*, Patrick James Lysaght, *b.* 1931, *s.* 1998	Hon. John N. G. L., *b.* 1960
1850	*Londesborough (9th)*, Richard John Denison, *b.* 1959, *s.* 1968, *m.*	Hon. James F. D., *b.* 1990
1541 I.	*Louth (16th)*, Otway Michael James Oliver Plunkett, *b.* 1929, *s.* 1950, *m.*	Hon. Jonathan O. P., *b.* 1952
1458 S.*	*Lovat (16th) and 5th UK Baron*, Lovat, 1837, Simon Fraser, *b.* 1977, *s.* 1995	Hon. Jack F., *b.* 1984
1946	*Lucas of Chilworth (3rd)*, Simon William Lucas, *b.* 1957, *s.* 2001, *m.*	Hon. John R. M. L., *b.* 1995
1663	** *Lucas (11th) and Dingwall (14th) (s. 1609)*, Ralph Matthew Palmer, *b.* 1951, *s.* 1991	Hon. Lewis E. P., *b.* 1987
1929	** *Luke (3rd)*, Arthur Charles St John Lawson-Johnston, *b.* 1933, *s.* 1996, *m.*	Hon. Ian J. St J. L.-J., *b.* 1963
1914	** *Lyell (3rd)*, Charles Lyell, *b.* 1939, *s.* 1943	None
1859	*Lyveden (7th)*, Jack Leslie Vernon, *b.* 1938, *s.* 1999, *m.*	Hon. Colin R. V., *b.* 1967
1959	*MacAndrew (3rd)*, Christopher Anthony Colin MacAndrew, *b.* 1945, *s.* 1989, *m.*	Hon. Oliver C. J. M., *b.* 1983
1776 I.	*Macdonald (8th)*, Godfrey James Macdonald of Macdonald, *b.* 1947, *s.* 1970, *m.*	Hon. Godfrey E. H. T. M., *b.* 1982
1937	*McGowan (3rd)*, Harry Duncan Cory McGowan, *b.* 1938, *s.* 1966, *m.*	Hon. Harry J. C. M., *b.* 1971
1922	*Maclay (3rd)*, Joseph Paton Maclay, *b.* 1942, *s.* 1969, *m.*	Hon. Joseph P. M., *b.* 1977
1955	*McNair (3rd)*, Duncan James McNair, *b.* 1947, *s.* 1989, *m.*	Hon. William S. A. M., *b.* 1958
1951	*Macpherson of Drumochter (2nd)*, (James) Gordon Macpherson, *b.* 1924, *s.* 1965, *m.*	Hon. James A. M., *b.* 1979
1937	** *Mancroft (3rd)*, Benjamin Lloyd Stormont Mancroft, *b.* 1957, *s.* 1987, *m.*	Hon. Arthur L. S. M., *b.* 1995
1807	*Manners (6th)*, John Hugh Robert Manners, *b.* 1956, *s.* 2001, *m.*	†
1922	*Manton (3rd)*, Joseph Rupert Eric Robert Watson, *b.* 1924, *s.* 1968, *m.*	Maj. Hon. Miles R. M. W., *b.* 1958
1908	*Marchamley (4th)*, William Francis Whiteley, *b.* 1968, *s.* 1994	None
1964	*Margadale (2nd)*, James Ian Morrison, TD, *b.* 1930, *s.* 1996, *m.*	Hon. Alastair J. M., *b.* 1958
1961	*Marks of Broughton (3rd)*, Simon Richard Marks, *b.* 1950, *s.* 1998, *m.*	Hon. Michael M., *b.* 1989
1964	*Martonmere (2nd)*, John Stephen Robinson, *b.* 1963, *s.* 1989	David A. R., *b.* 1965
1776 I.	*Massy (9th)*, Hugh Hamon John Somerset Massy, *b.* 1921, *s.* 1958, *m.*	Hon. David H. S. M., *b.* 1947
1935	*May (3rd)*, Michael St John May, *b.* 1931, *s.* 1950, *m.*	Hon. Jasper B. St J. M., *b.* 1965
1928	*Melchett (4th)*, Peter Robert Henry Mond, *b.* 1948, *s.* 1973	None
1925	*Merrivale (3rd)*, Jack Henry Edmond Duke, *b.* 1917, *s.* 1951, *w.*	Hon. Derek J. P. D., *b.* 1948
1911	*Merthyr*, Trevor Oswin Lewis, Bt., CBE, *b.* 1935, *s.* 1977, *m.* Disclaimed for life 1977.	David T. L., *b.* 1977
1919	*Meston (3rd)*, James Meston, *b.* 1950, *s.* 1984, *m.*	Hon. Thomas J. D. M., *b.* 1977
1838	** *Methuen (7th)*, Robert Alexander Holt Methuen, *b.* 1931, *s.* 1994, *m.*	James P. A. M.-C., *b.* 1952
1711	*Middleton (12th)*, (Digby) Michael Godfrey John Willoughby, MC, *b.* 1921, *s.* 1970, *m.*	Hon. Michael C. J. W., *b.* 1948
1939	*Milford (4th)*, Guy Wogan Philipps, *b.* 1961, *s.* 1999, *m.*	Hon. Roland A. P., *b.* 1962
1933	*Milne (2nd)*, George Douglass Milne, TD, *b.* 1909, *s.* 1948, *m.*	Hon. George A. M., *b.* 1941
1951	** *Milner of Leeds (2nd)*, Arthur James Michael Milner, AE, *b.* 1923, *s.* 1967, *w.*	Hon. Richard J. M., *b.* 1959
1947	*Milverton (2nd)*, Revd Fraser Arthur Richard Richards, *b.* 1930, *s.* 1978, *m.*	Hon. Michael H. R., *b.* 1936
1873	*Moncreiff (6th)*, Rhoderick Harry Wellwood Moncreiff, *b.* 1954, *s.* 2002, *m.*	Hon. Harry J. W. M., *b.* 1986
1884	*Monk Bretton (3rd)*, John Charles Dodson, *b.* 1924, *s.* 1933, *m.*	Hon. Christopher M. D., *b.* 1958
1885	*Monkswell (5th)*, Gerard Collier, *b.* 1947, *s.* 1984, *m.*	Hon. James A. C., *b.* 1977
1728	** *Monson (11th)*, John Monson, *b.* 1932, *s.* 1958, *m.*	Hon. Nicholas J. M., *b.* 1955
1885	** *Montagu of Beaulieu (3rd)*, Edward John Barrington Douglas-Scott-Montagu, *b.* 1926, *s.* 1929, *m.*	Hon. Ralph D.-S.-M., *b.* 1961
1839	*Monteagle of Brandon (6th)*, Gerald Spring Rice, *b.* 1926, *s.* 1946, *m.*	Hon. Charles J. S. R., *b.* 1953
1943	** *Moran (2nd)*, (Richard) John (McMoran) Wilson, KCMG, *b.* 1924, *s.* 1977, *m.*	Hon. James M. W., *b.* 1952
1918	*Morris (3rd)*, Michael David Morris, *b.* 1937, *s.* 1975, *m.*	Hon. Thomas A. S. M., *b.* 1982
1950	*Morris of Kenwood (2nd)*, Philip Geoffrey Morris, *b.* 1928, *s.* 1954, *m.*	Hon. Jonathan D. M., *b.* 1968
1831	*Mostyn (6th)*, Llewellyn Roger Lloyd-Mostyn, MC, *b.* 1948, *s.* 2000, *m.*	Hon. Gregory P. R. L.-M., *b.* 1984
1933	*Mottistone (4th)*, David Peter Seely, CBE, *b.* 1920, *s.* 1966, *m.*	Hon. Peter J. P. S., *b.* 1949
1945	*Mountevans (3rd)*, Edward Patrick Broke Evans, *b.* 1943, *s.* 1974, *m.*	Hon. Jeffrey de C. R. E., *b.* 1948
1283	** *Mowbray (26th), Segrave (27th) and Stourton (23rd) (1448)*, Charles Edward Stourton, CBE, *b.* 1923, *s.* 1965, *m.*	Hon. Edward W. S. S., *b.* 1953
1932	*Moyne (3rd)*, Jonathan Bryan Guinness, *b.* 1930, *s.* 1992, *m.*	Hon. Jasper J. R. G., *b.* 1954
1929	** *Moynihan (4th)*, Colin Berkeley Moynihan, *b.* 1955, *s.* 1997, *m.*	Hon. Nicholas E. B. M., *b.* 1994

Created	Title, order of succession, name, etc.	Heir
1781 I.	*Muskerry (9th)*, Robert Fitzmaurice Deane, *b.* 1948, *s.* 1988, *m.*	Hon. Jonathan F. D., *b.* 1986
1627 S.*	*Napier (14th) and Ettrick (5th) (UK 1872)*, Francis Nigel Napier, KCVO, *b.* 1930, *s.* 1954, *m.*	Master of Napier, *b.* 1962
1868	*Napier of Magdala (6th)*, Robert Alan Napier, *b.* 1940, *s.* 1987, *m.*	Hon. James R. N., *b.* 1966
1940	*Nathan (2nd)*, Roger Carol Michael Nathan, *b.* 1922, *s.* 1963, *m.*	Hon. Rupert H. B. N., *b.* 1957
1960	*Nelson of Stafford (3rd)*, Henry Roy George Nelson, *b.* 1943, *s.* 1995, *m.*	Hon. Alistair W. H. N., *b.* 1973
1959	*Netherthorpe (3rd)*, James Frederick Turner, *b.* 1964, *s.* 1982, *m.*	Hon. Andrew J. E. T., *b.* 1993
1946	*Newall (2nd)*, Francis Storer Eaton Newall, *b.* 1930, *s.* 1963, *m.*	Hon. Richard H. E. N., *b.* 1961
1776 I.	*Newborough (8th)*, Robert Vaughan Wynn, *b.* 1949, *s.* 1998, *m.*	Hon. Charles H. R. W., *b.* 1923
1892	*Newton (5th)*, Richard Thomas Legh, *b.* 1950, *s.* 1992, *m.*	Hon. Piers H. S., *b.* 1979
1930	*Noel-Buxton (3rd)*, Martin Connal Noel-Buxton, *b.* 1940, *s.* 1980, *m.*	Hon. Charles C. N.-B., *b.* 1975
1957	*Norrie (2nd)*, (George) Willoughby Moke Norrie, *b.* 1936, *s.* 1977, *m.*	Hon. Mark W. J. N., *b.* 1972
1884	** *Northbourne (5th)*, Christopher George Walter James, *b.* 1926, *s.* 1982, *m.*	Hon. Charles W. H. J., *b.* 1960
1866	** *Northbrook (6th)*, Francis Thomas Baring, *b.* 1954, *s.* 1990, *m.*	Peter B., *b.* 1939
1878	*Norton (8th)*, James Nigel Arden Adderley, *b.* 1947, *s.* 1993, *m.*	Hon. Edward J. A. A., *b.* 1982
1906	*Nunburnholme (6th)*, Stephen Charles Wilson, *b.* 1973, *s.* 2000	Hon. (David) Mark W., *b.* 1983
1950	*Ogmore (2nd)*, Gwilym Rees Rees-Williams, *b.* 1931, *s.* 1976, *m.*	Hon. Morgan R.-W., *b.* 1937
1870	*O'Hagan (4th)*, Charles Towneley Strachey, *b.* 1950, *s.* 1961	Hon. Richard T. S., *b.* 1950
1868	*O'Neill (4th)*, Raymond Arthur Clanaboy O'Neill, TD, *b.* 1933, *s.* 1944, *m.*	Hon. Shane S. C. O'N., *b.* 1965
1836 I.*	*Oranmore and Browne (5th) and 3rd UK Baron, Mereworth (1926)*, Dominick Geoffrey Thomas Browne, *b.* 1929, *s.* 2002,	Hon. Martin M. D. B., *b.* 1931
1933	** *Palmer (4th)*, Adrian Bailie Nottage Palmer, *b.* 1951, *s.* 1990, *m.*	Hon. Hugo B. R. P., *b.* 1980
1914	*Parmoor (4th)*, (Frederick Alfred) Milo Cripps, *b.* 1929, *s.* 1977	Michael L. S. C., *b.* 1942
1937	*Pender (3rd)*, John Willoughby Denison-Pender, *b.* 1933, *s.* 1965, *m.*	Hon. Henry J. R. D.-P., *b.* 1968
1866	*Penrhyn (6th)*, Malcolm Frank Douglas-Pennant, DSO, MBE, *b.* 1908, *s.* 1967, *w.*	Hon. Simon D.-P., *b.* 1938
1603	*Petre (18th)*, John Patrick Lionel Petre, *b.* 1942, *s.* 1989, *m.*	Hon. Dominic W. P., *b.* 1966
1918	*Phillimore (5th)*, Francis Stephen Phillimore, *b.* 1944, *s.* 1994, *m.*	Hon. Tristan A. S. P., *b.* 1977
1945	*Piercy (3rd)*, James William Piercy, *b.* 1946, *s.* 1981	Hon. Mark E. P. P., *b.* 1953
1827	*Plunket (8th)*, Robin Rathmore Plunket, *b.* 1925, *s.* 1975, *m.*	Hon. Shaun A. F. S. P., *b.* 1931
1831	*Poltimore (7th)*, Mark Coplestone Bampfylde, *b.* 1957, *s.* 1978, *m.*	Hon. Henry A. W. B., *b.* 1985
1690 S.	*Polwarth (10th)*, Henry Alexander Hepburne-Scott, TD, *b.* 1916, *s.* 1944, *m.*	Master of Polwarth, *b.* 1947
1930	*Ponsonby of Shulbrede (4th) and Baron Ponsonby of Roehampton (life peerage, 2000)*, Frederick Matthew Thomas Ponsonby, *b.* 1958, *s.* 1990	None
1958	*Poole (2nd)*, David Charles Poole, *b.* 1945, *s.* 1993, *m.*	Hon. Oliver J. P., *b.* 1972
1852	*Raglan (5th)*, FitzRoy John Somerset, *b.* 1927, *s.* 1964	Hon. Geoffrey S., *b.* 1932
1932	*Rankeillour (4th)*, Peter St Thomas More Henry Hope, *b.* 1935, *s.* 1967	Michael R. H., *b.* 1940
1953	*Rathcavan (3rd)*, Hugh Detmar Torrens O'Neill, *b.* 1939, *s.* 1994, *m.*	Hon. François H. N. O'N., *b.* 1984
1916	*Rathcreedan (3rd)*, Christopher John Norton, *b.* 1949, *s.* 1990, *m.*	Hon. Adam G. N., *b.* 1952
1868	*Rathdonnell (5th)*, Thomas Benjamin McClintock-Bunbury, *b.* 1938, *s.* 1959, *m.*	Hon. William L. M.-B., *b.* 1966
1911	*Ravensdale (3rd)*, Nicholas Mosley, MC, *b.* 1923, *s.* 1966, *m.*	Hon. Shaun N. M., *b.* 1949
1821	*Ravensworth (8th)*, Arthur Waller Liddell, *b.* 1924, *s.* 1950, *m.*	Hon. Thomas A. H. L., *b.* 1954
1821	*Rayleigh (6th)*, John Gerald Strutt, *b.* 1960, *s.* 1988, *m.*	Hon. John F. S., *b.* 1993
1937	** *Rea (3rd)*, John Nicolas Rea, MD, *b.* 1928, *s.* 1981, *m.*	Hon. Matthew J. R., *b.* 1956
1628 S.	** *Reay (14th)*, Hugh William Mackay, *b.* 1937, *s.* 1963, *m.*	Master of Reay, *b.* 1965
1902	*Redesdale (6th) and Baron Mitford (life peerage 2000)*, Rupert Bertram Mitford, *b.* 1967, *s.* 1991, *m.*	Hon. Bertram D. M., *b.* 2000
1940	*Reith*, Christopher John Reith, *b.* 1928, *s.* 1971, *m.* Disclaimed for life 1972	Hon. James H. J. R., *b.* 1971
1928	*Remnant (3rd)*, James Wogan Remnant, CVO, *b.* 1930, *s.* 1967, *m.*	Hon. Philip J. R., *b.* 1954
1806	*Rendlesham (9th)*, Charles William Brooke Thellusson, *b.* 1954, *s.* 1999, *m.*	Hon. Peter R. T., *b.* 1920
1933	*Rennell (3rd)*, (John Adrian) Tremayne Rodd, *b.* 1935, *s.* 1978, *m.*	Hon. James R. D. T. R., *b.* 1978
1964	*Renwick (2nd)*, Harry Andrew Renwick, *b.* 1935, *s.* 1973, *m.*	Hon. Robert J. R., *b.* 1966
1885	*Revelstoke (5th)*, John Baring, *b.* 1934, *s.* 1994	Hon. James C. B., *b.* 1938
1905	*Ritchie of Dundee (5th)*, (Harold) Malcolm Ritchie, *b.* 1919, *s.* 1978, *m.*	Hon. C. Rupert R. R., *b.* 1958
1935	*Riverdale (3rd)*, Anthony Robert Balfour, *b.* 1960, *s.* 1998	Hon. David R. B., *b.* 1938
1961	*Robertson of Oakridge (2nd)*, William Ronald Robertson, *b.* 1930, *s.* 1974, *m.*	Hon. William B. E. R., *b.* 1975
1938	*Roborough (3rd)*, Henry Massey Lopes, *b.* 1940, *s.* 1992, *m.*	Hon. Massey J. H. L., *b.* 1969
1931	*Rochester (2nd)*, Foster Charles Lowry Lamb, *b.* 1916, *s.* 1955, *w.*	Hon. David C. L., *b.* 1944
1934	*Rockley (3rd)*, James Hugh Cecil, *b.* 1934, *s.* 1976, *m.*	Hon. Anthony R. C., *b.* 1961
1782	*Rodney (10th)*, George Brydges Rodney, *b.* 1953, *s.* 1992, *m.*	Nicholas S. H. R., *b.* 1947
1651 S.*	*Rollo (14th) and 5th UK Baron Dunning, 1869*, David Eric Howard Rollo, *b.* 1943, *s.* 1997, *m.*	Master of Rollo, *b.* 1972
1959	*Rootes (3rd)*, Nicholas Geoffrey Rootes, *b.* 1951, *s.* 1992, *m.*	William B. R., *b.* 1944
1796 I.*	*Rossmore (7th) and 6th UK Baron, Rossmore, 1838*, William Warner Westenra, *b.* 1931, *s.* 1958, *m.*	Hon. Benedict W. W., *b.* 1983

Created	Title, order of succession, name, etc.	Heir
1939	** *Rotherwick (3rd)*, (Herbert) Robin Cayzer, *b.* 1954, *s.* 1996, *m.*	Hon. H. Robin C., *b.* 1989
1885	*Rothschild (4th)*, (Nathaniel Charles) Jacob Rothschild, GBE, *b.* 1936, *s.* 1990, *m.*	Hon. Nathaniel P. V. J. R., *b.* 1971
1911	*Rowallan (4th)*, John Polson Cameron Corbett, *b.* 1947, *s.* 1993,	Hon. Jason W. P. C. C., *b.* 1972
1947	*Rugby (3rd)*, Robert Charles Maffey, *b.* 1951, *s.* 1990, *m.*	Hon. Timothy J. H. M., *b.* 1975
1919	*Russell of Liverpool (3rd)*, Simon Gordon Jared Russell, *b.* 1952, *s.* 1981, *m.*	Hon. Edward C. S. R., *b.* 1985
1876	*Sackville (6th)*, Lionel Bertrand Sackville-West, *b.* 1913, *s.* 1965, *m.*	Robert B. S-W., *b.* 1958
1964	*St Helens (2nd)*, Richard Francis Hughes-Young, *b.* 1945, *s.* 1980, *m.*	Hon. Henry T. H.-Y., *b.* 1986
1559	** *St John of Bletso (21st)*, Anthony Tudor St John, *b.* 1957, *s.* 1978, *m.*	Hon. Oliver B. St J., *b.* 1995
1887	*St Levan (4th)*, John Francis Arthur St Aubyn, DSC, *b.* 1919, *s.* 1978, *m.*	Hon. O. Piers St. A., *b.* 1920
1885	*St Oswald (6th)*, Charles Rowland Andrew Winn, *b.* 1959, *s.* 1999, *m.*	Hon. Rowland C. S. H. W., *b.* 1986
1960	*Sanderson of Ayot*, Alan Lindsay Sanderson, *b.* 1931, *s.* 1971, *m.* Disclaimed for life 1971.	Hon. Michael S., *b.* 1959
1945	*Sandford (2nd)*, Revd John Cyril Edmondson, DSC, *b.* 1920, *s.* 1959, *m.*	Hon. James J. M. E., *b.* 1949
1871	*Sandhurst (6th)*, Guy Rees John Mansfield, *b.* 1949, *s.* 2002, *m.*	Hon. Edward J. M., *b.* 1982
1802	*Sandys (7th)*, Richard Michael Oliver Hill, *b.* 1931, *s.* 1961, *m.*	The Marquess of Downshire
1888	*Savile (3rd)*, George Halifax Lumley-Savile, *b.* 1919, *s.* 1931	John A. T. L-S., *b.* 1947
1447	*Saye and Sele (21st)*, Nathaniel Thomas Allen Fiennes, *b.* 1920, *s.* 1968, *m.*	Hon. Richard I. F., *b.* 1959
1826	*Seaford (6th)*, Colin Humphrey Felton Ellis, *b.* 1946, *s.* 1999, *m.*	Hon. Benjamin F. T. E., *b.* 1976
1932	** *Selsdon (3rd)*, Malcolm McEacharn Mitchell-Thomson, *b.* 1937, *s.* 1963, *m.*	Hon. Callum M. M. M.-T., *b.* 1969
1489 S.	*Sempill (21st)*, James William Stuart Whitemore Sempill, *b.* 1949, *s.* 1995, *m.*	Master of Semphill, *b.* 1979
1916	*Shaughnessy (3rd)*, William Graham Shaughnessy, *b.* 1922, *s.* 1938, *w.*	Hon. Michael J. S., *b.* 1946
1946	*Shepherd (3rd)*, Graham George Shepherd, *b.* 1949, *s.* 2001, *m.*	Hon. Patrick M. S.
1964	*Sherfield (2nd)*, Christopher James Makins, *b.* 1942, *s.* 1996, *m.*	Hon. Dwight W. M., *b.* 1951
1902	*Shuttleworth (5th)*, Charles Geoffrey Nicholas Kay-Shuttleworth, *b.* 1948, *s.* 1975, *m.*	Hon. Thomas E. K.-S., *b.* 1976
1950	*Silkin*, Arthur Silkin, *b.* 1916, *s.* 1972, *m.* Disclaimed for life 1972.	Hon. Christopher L. S., *b.* 1947
1963	*Silsoe (2nd)*, David Malcolm Trustram Eve, QC, *b.* 1930, *s.* 1976, *m.*	Hon. Simon R. T. E., *b.* 1966
1947	*Simon of Wythenshawe (2nd)*, Roger Simon, *b.* 1913, *s.* 1960, *m.*	Hon. Matthew S., *b.* 1955
1449 S.	*Sinclair (17th)*, Charles Murray Kennedy St Clair, CVO, *b.* 1914, *s.* 1957, *m.*	Master of Sinclair, *b.* 1968
1957	*Sinclair of Cleeve (3rd)*, John Lawrence Robert Sinclair, *b.* 1953, *s.* 1985	None
1919	*Sinha (6th)*, Arup Kumar Sinha, *b.* 1966, *s.* 1999	Hon. Dilip K. S., *b.* 1967
1828	** *Skelmersdale (7th)*, Roger Bootle-Wilbraham, *b.* 1945, *s.* 1973, *m.*	Hon. Andrew B.-W., *b.* 1977
1916	*Somerleyton (3rd)*, Savile William Francis Crossley, GCVO *b.* 1928, *s.* 1959, *m.*	Hon. Hugh F. S. C., *b.* 1971
1784	*Somers (9th)*, Philip Sebastian Somers Cocks, *b.* 1948, *s.* 1995	Alan B. C., *b.* 1930
1959	*Spens (4th)*, Patrick Nathaniel George Spens, *b.* 1968, *s.* 2001, *m.*	Hon. Peter L. S., *b.* 2000
1780	*Southampton (6th)*, Charles James FitzRoy, *b.* 1928, *s.* 1989, *m.*	Hon. Edward C. F., *b.* 1955
1640	*Stafford (15th)*, Francis Melfort William Fitzherbert, *b.* 1954, *s.* 1986, *m.*	Hon. Benjamin J. B. F., *b.* 1983
1938	*Stamp (4th)*, Trevor Charles Bosworth Stamp, MD, FRCP, *b.* 1935, *s.* 1987, *m.*	Hon. Nicholas C. T. S., *b.* 1978
1839	*Stanley of Alderley (8th) and Sheffield (8th) (I. 1738) and 7th UK Baron, Eddisbury*, 1848, Thomas Henry Oliver Stanley, *b.* 1927, *s.* 1971, *m.*	Hon. Richard O. S., *b.* 1956
1318	** *Strabolgi (11th)*, David Montague de Burgh Kenworthy, *b.* 1914, *s.* 1953, *m.*	Andrew D. W. K., *b.* 1967
1954	*Strang (2nd)*, Colin Strang, *b.* 1922, *s.* 1978, *m.*	None
1955	*Strathalmond (3rd)*, William Roberton Fraser, *b.* 1947, *s.* 1976, *m.*	Hon. William G. F., *b.* 1976
1936	*Strathcarron (2nd)*, David William Anthony Blyth Macpherson, *b.* 1924, *s.* 1937, *m.*	Hon. Ian D. P. M., *b.* 1949
1955	** *Strathclyde (2nd)*, Thomas Galloway Dunlop du Roy de Blicquy Galbraith, PC, *b.* 1960, *s.* 1985, *m.*	Hon. Charles W. du R. de B. G., *b.* 1962
1900	*Strathcona and Mount Royal (4th)*, Donald Euan Palmer Howard, *b.* 1923, *s.* 1959, *m.*	Hon. D. Alexander S. H., *b.* 1961
1836	*Stratheden (6th) and Campbell (6th) (1841)*, Donald Campbell, *b.* 1934, *s.* 1987, *m.*	Hon. David A. C., *b.* 1963
1884	*Strathspey (6th)*, James Patrick Trevor Grant of Grant, *b.* 1943, *s.* 1992 *m.*	Hon. Michael P. F. G., *b.* 1953
1838	*Sudeley (7th)*, Merlin Charles Sainthill Hanbury-Tracy, *b.* 1939, *s.* 1941	D. Andrew J. H.-T., *b.* 1928
1786	*Suffield (11th)*, Anthony Philip Harbord-Hamond, MC, *b.* 1922, *s.* 1951, *w.*	Hon. Charles A. A. H.-H., *b.* 1953
1893	*Swansea (4th)*, John Hussey Hamilton Vivian, *b.* 1925, *s.* 1934, *m.*	Hon. Richard A. H. V., *b.* 1957
1907	*Swaythling (5th)*, Charles Edgar Samuel Montagu, *b.* 1954, *s.* 1998, *m.*	Hon. Anthony T. S. M., *b.* 1931
1919	** *Swinfen (3rd)*, Roger Mynors Swinfen Eady, *b.* 1938, *s.* 1977, *m.*	Hon. Charles R. P. S. E., *b.* 1971
1935	*Sysonby (3rd)*, John Frederick Ponsonby, *b.* 1945, *s.* 1956	None
1831 I.	*Talbot of Malahide (10th)*, Reginald John Richard Arundell, *b.* 1931, *s.* 1987, *m.*	Hon. Richard J. T. A., *b.* 1957
1946	*Tedder (3rd)*, Robin John Tedder, *b.* 1955, *s.* 1994, *m.*,	Hon. Benjamin J. T., *b.* 1985
1884	*Tennyson (5th)*, Cdr. Mark Aubrey Tennyson, DSC, *b.* 1920, *s.* 1991, *m.*	David H. A. T., *b.* 1960
1918	*Terrington (6th)*, Christopher Richard James Woodhouse, MB, FRCS, *b.* 1946, *s.* 2001, *m.*	Hon. Jack H. L. W., *b.* 1978

Created	Title, order of succession, name, etc.	Heir
1940	*Teviot (2nd)*, Charles John Kerr, *b.* 1934, *s.* 1968, *m.*	Hon. Charles R. K., *b.* 1971
1616	*Teynham (20th)*, John Christopher Ingham Roper-Curzon, *b.* 1928, *s.* 1972, *m.*	Hon. David J. H. I. R.-C., *b.* 1965
1964	*Thomson of Fleet (2nd)*, Kenneth Roy Thomson, *b.* 1923, *s.* 1976, *m.*	Hon. David K. R. T., *b.* 1957
1792	*Thurlow (8th)*, Francis Edward Hovell-Thurlow-Cumming-Bruce, KCMG, *b.* 1912, *s.* 1971, *w.*	Hon. Roualeyn R. H.-T.-C.-B., *b.* 1952
1876	*Tollemache (5th)*, Timothy John Edward Tollemache, *b.* 1939, *s.* 1975, *m.*	Hon. Edward J. H. T., *b.* 1976
1564 S.	*Torphichen (15th)*, James Andrew Douglas Sandilands, *b.* 1946, *s.* 1975, *m.*	Douglas R. A. S., *b.* 1926
1947 **	*Trefgarne (2nd)*, David Garro Trefgarne, PC, *b.* 1941, *s.* 1960, *m.*	Hon. George G. T., *b.* 1970
1921	*Trevethin (4th) and Oaksey (2nd) (1947)*, John Geoffrey Tristram Lawrence, OBE, *b.* 1929, *s.* 1971, *m.*	Hon. Patrick J. T. L., *b.* 1960
1880	*Trevor (5th)*, Marke Charles Hill-Trevor, *b.* 1970, *s.* 1997, *m.*	Hon. Iain R. H.-T., *b.* 1971
1461 I.	*Trimlestown (21st)*, Raymond Charles Barnewall, *b.* 1930, *s.* 1997	None
1940	*Tryon (3rd)*, Anthony George Merrik Tryon, *b.* 1940, *s.* 1976	Hon. Charles G. B. T., *b.* 1976
1935	*Tweedsmuir (3rd)*, William de l'Aigle Buchan, *b.* 1916, *s.* 1996, *m.*	Hon. John W. H. de l'A. B., *b.* 1950
1523	*Vaux of Harrowden (11th)*, Anthony William Gilbey, *b.* 1940, *s.* 2002, *m.*	Hon. Richard H. G. G., *b.*1965
1800 I.	*Ventry (8th)*, Andrew Wesley Daubeny de Moleyns, *b.* 1943, *s.* 1987, *m.*	Hon. Francis W. D. de M., *b.* 1965
1762	*Vernon (11th)*, Anthony William Vernon-Harcourt, *b.* 1939, *s.* 2000, *m.*	Hon. Simon A. V.-H., *b.* 1969
1922	*Vestey (3rd)*, Samuel George Armstrong Vestey, *b.* 1941, *s.* 1954, *m.*	Hon. William G. V., *b.* 1983
1841 **	*Vivian (6th)*, Nicholas Crespigny Laurence Vivian, *b.* 1935, *s.* 1991, *m.*	Hon. Charles H. C. V., *b.* 1966
1934	*Wakehurst (3rd)*, (John) Christopher Loder, *b.* 1925, *s.* 1970, *m.*	Hon. Timothy W. L., *b.* 1958
1723 **	*Walpole (10th) and 8th Brit. Baron Walpole of Wolterton*, 1756, Robert Horatio Walpole, *b.* 1938, *s.* 1989, *m.*	Hon. Jonathan R. H. W., *b.* 1967
1780	*Walsingham (9th)*, John de Grey, *s.* 1989, *m.* MC, *b.* 1925, *s.* 1965, *m.*	Hon. Robert de. G., *b.* 1969
1936	*Wardington (2nd)*, Christopher Henry Beaumont Pease, *b.* 1924, *s.* 1950, *m.*	Hon. William S. P., *b.* 1925
1792 I.	*Waterpark (7th)*, Frederick Caryll Philip Cavendish, *b.* 1926, *s.* 1948, *m.*	Hon. Roderick A. C., *b.* 1959
1942	*Wedgwood (4th)*, Piers Anthony Weymouth Wedgwood, *b.* 1954, *s.* 1970, *m.*	John W., *b.* 1919
1861	*Westbury (6th)*, Richard Nicholas Bethell, MBE, *b.* 1950, *s.* 2001, *m.*	Hon. Alexander B., *b.* 1986
1944	*Westwood (3rd)*, (William) Gavin Westwood, *b.* 1944, *s.* 1991, *m.*	Hon. W. Fergus W., *b.* 1972
1544/5	*Wharton (12th)*, Myles Christopher David Robertson, *b.* 1964, *s.* 2000, *m.*	Hon. Christopher J. R., *b.* 1969
1935	*Wigram (2nd)*, (George) Neville (Clive) Wigram, MC, *b.* 1915, *s.* 1960, *w.*	Maj. Hon. Andrew F. C. W., *b.* 1949
1491 **	*Willoughby de Broke (21st)*, Leopold David Verney, *b.* 1938, *s.* 1986, *m.*	Hon. Rupert G. V., *b.* 1966
1946	*Wilson (2nd)*, Patrick Maitland Wilson, *b.* 1915, *s.* 1964, *w.*	None
1937	*Windlesham (3rd) and Baron Hennesy (life peerage, 1999)*, David James George Hennessy, CVO, PC, *b.* 1932, *s.* 1962, *w.*	Hon. James R. H., *b.* 1968
1951	*Wise (2nd)*, John Clayton Wise, *b.* 1923, *s.* 1968, *m.*	Hon. Christopher J. C. W., *b.* 1949
1869	*Wolverton (7th)*, Christopher Richard Glyn, *b.* 1938, *s.* 1988,	Hon. Andrew J. G., *b.* 1943
1928	*Wraxall (3rd)*, Sir Eustace Hubert Beilby Gibbs, KCVO, CMG, *b.* 1929, *s.* 2001, *m.*	Hon. Anthony H. G., *b.* 1958
1915	*Wrenbury (3rd)*, Revd John Burton Buckley, *b.* 1927, *s.* 1940, *m.*	Hon. William E. B., *b.* 1966
1838	*Wrottesley (6th)*, Clifton Hugh Lancelot de Verdon Wrottesley, *b.* 1968, Hon. Stephen J. W., *b.* 1955 *s.* 1977, *m.*	
1829	*Wynford (9th)*, John Philip Robert Best, *b.* 1950, *s.* 2002, *m.*	Hon. Harry R. F. B., *b.* 1987
1308	*Zouche (18th)*, James Assheton Frankland, *b.* 1943, *s.* 1965, *m.*	Hon. William T. A. F., *b.* 1984

BARONESSES/LADIES IN THEIR OWN RIGHT

Style, The Right Hon. the Lady _ , or The Right Hon. the Baroness _ , according to her preference. Either style may be used, except in the case of Scottish titles (indicated by S.), which are not baronies (see page 134) and whose holders are always addressed as Lady
Husband, Untitled
Children's style, As for children of a Baron
For forms of address, *see* page 133

Created	Title, order of succession, name, etc.	Heir
1664	*Arlington*, Jennifer Jane Forwood, *b.* 1939, *s.* 1999, *w.*, title called out of abeyance 1999	Hon. Patrick J. D. Forwood, *b.* 1967
1455	*Berners (16th)*, Pamela Vivien Kirkham, *b.* 1929, *s.* 1995, *m.*	Hon. Rupert W. T. K., *b.* 1953
1529	*Braye (8th)*, Mary Penelope Aubrey-Fletcher, *b.* 1941, *s.* 1985, *m.*	
1321	*Dacre (27th)*, Rachel Leila Douglas-Home, *b.* 1929, *s.* 1970, *w.*	Hon. James T. A. D.-H., *b.* 1952

154 The Peerage

Created	Title, order of succession, name, etc.	Heir
1332	** *Darcy de Knayth (18th)*, Davina Marcia Ingrams, DBE, *b.* 1938, *s.* 1943, *w.*	Hon. Caspar D. I., *b.* 1962
1439	*Dudley (14th)*, Barbara Amy Felicity Hamilton, *b.* 1907, *s.* 1972, m.	Hon. Jim A. H. Wallace , *b.* 1930
1490 S.	*Herries of Terregles (14th)*, Anne Elizabeth Fitzalan-Howard, *b.* 1938, *s.* 1975, *w.*	Lady Mary Mumford , *b.* 1940
1602 S.	*Kinloss (12th)*, Beatrice Mary Grenville Freeman-Grenville, b. 1922, *s.* 1944, *m.*	Master of Kinloss , *b.* 1953
1445 S.	** *Saltoun (20th)*, Flora Marjory Fraser, *b.* 1930, *s.* 1979, *w.*	Hon. Katharine I. M. I. F., *b.* 1957
1628	** *Strange (16th)*, (Jean) Cherry Drummond of Megginch, *b.* 1928, *s.* 1986, *m.*	Hon. Adam H. D. of M., *b.* 1953
1313	*Willoughby de Eresby (27th)*, (Nancy) Jane Marie Heathcote-Drummond-Willoughby, *b.* 1934, *s.* 1983,	Two co-heiresses

Life Peers

NEW LIFE PEERAGES *1 September 2001 to 31 August 2002:*
Amirali Bhatia, OBE; Conrad Moffat Black OC; Betty Boothroyd; Michael Chew Koon Chan, MBE; Susan Adele Greenfield; Sir David Hugh Alexander Hannay, GCMG; John David Taylor, PC

CREATED UNDER THE APPELLATE JURISDICTION ACT 1876 (AS AMENDED)

BARONS
Created

1986 Ackner, Desmond James Conrad Ackner, PC, b. 1920, m.
1980 Bridge of Harwich, Nigel Cyprian Bridge, PC, b. 1917, m.
1982 Brightman, John Anson Brightman, PC, b. 1911, m.
1991 Browne-Wilkinson, Nicolas Christopher Henry Browne-Wilkinson, PC, b. 1930, m.
1996 Clyde, James John Clyde, b. 1932, m.
1986 Goff of Chieveley, Robert Lionel Archibald Goff, PC, b. 1926, m.
1985 Griffiths, (William) Hugh Griffiths, MC, PC, b. 1923, m.
1998 Hobhouse of Woodborough, John Stewart Hobhouse, PC, b. 1932, Lord of Appeal in Ordinary
1995 Hoffmann, Leonard Hubert Hoffmann, PC, b. 1934, m. Lord of Appeal in Ordinary
1997 Hutton, (James) Brian (Edward) Hutton, PC, b. 1931, m. Lord of Appeal in Ordinary
1988 Jauncey of Tullichettle, Charles Eliot Jauncey, PC, b. 1925, m.
1979 Lane, Geoffrey Dawson Lane, AFC, PC, b. 1918, m.
1993 Lloyd of Berwick, Anthony John Leslie Lloyd, PC, b. 1929, m.
1998 Millett, Peter Julian Millett, PC, b. 1932, m. Lord of Appeal in Ordinary
1992 Mustill, Michael John Mustill, PC, b. 1931, m.
1994 Nicholls of Birkenhead, Donald James Nicholls, PC, b. 1933, m. Lord of Appeal in Ordinary
1994 Nolan, Michael Patrick Nolan, PC, b. 1928, m.
1986 Oliver of Aylmerton, Peter Raymond Oliver, PC, b. 1921, m.
1999 Phillips of Worth Matravers, Nicholas Addison Phillips, b. 1938, m. Master of the Rolls
1997 Saville of Newdigate, Mark Oliver Saville, PC, b. 1936, m. Lord of Appeal in Ordinary
1977 Scarman, Leslie George Scarman, OBE, PC, b. 1911, m.
1992 Slynn of Hadley, Gordon Slynn, PC, b. 1930, m. Lord of Appeal in Ordinary (due to retire from post Oct. 2002)
1995 Steyn, Johan van Zyl Steyn, PC, b. 1932, m. Lord of Appeal in Ordinary
1982 Templeman, Sydney William Templeman, MBE, PC, b. 1920, m.
1964 Wilberforce, Richard Orme Wilberforce, CMG, OBE, PC, b. 1907, m.
1992 Woolf, Harry Kenneth Woolf, PC, b. 1933, m. Lord Chief Justice of England and Wales

CREATED UNDER THE LIFE PEERAGES ACT 1958

* Hereditary peer who has been granted a life peerage. For further details, please refer to the Hereditary Peers section, pages 134–154. For example, life peer *Balniel* can be found under his hereditary title *Earl of Crawford and Balcarres.*

BARONS
Created

2000 * Acton of Bridgnorth, Lord Acton, b. 1941, m. (see Hereditary Peers)
2001 Adebowale, Victor Olufemi Adebowale, CBE, b. 1962
1998 Ahmed, Nazir Ahmed, b. 1957, m.
1996 Alderdice, John Thomas Alderdice, b. 1955, m.
1988 Alexander of Weedon, Robert Scott Alexander, QC, b. 1936, m.
1976 Allen of Abbeydale, Philip Allen, GCB, b. 1912, w.
1998 Alli, Waheed Alli, b. 1964
1997 Alton of Liverpool, David Patrick Paul Alton, b. 1951, m.
1992 Archer of Sandwell, Peter Kingsley Archer, PC, QC, b. 1926, m.
1992 Archer of Weston-super-Mare, Jeffrey Howard Archer, b. 1940, m.
1988 Armstrong of Ilminster, Robert Temple Armstrong, GCB, CVO, b. 1927, m.
1999 * Armstrong-Jones, Earl of Snowdon, GCVO, b. 1930, m. (see Hereditary Peers)
2000 Ashcroft, Michael Anthony Ashcroft, KCMG
2001 Ashdown of Norton-sub-Hamdon, Jeremy John Durham (Paddy) Ashdown, KBE, PC, b. 1941, m.
1992 Ashley of Stoke, Jack Ashley, CH, PC, b. 1922, m.
1993 Attenborough, Richard Samuel Attenborough, CBE, b. 1923, m.
1998 Bach, William Stephen Goulden Bach, b. 1946, m.
1997 Bagri, Raj Kumar Bagri, CBE, b. 1930, m.
1997 Baker of Dorking, Kenneth Wilfred Baker, CH, PC, b. 1934, m.
1974 * Balniel, The Earl of Crawford and Balcarres, b. 1927, m. (see Hereditary Peers)
1974 Barber, Anthony Perrinott Lysberg Barber, TD, PC, b. 1920, m.
1992 Barber of Tewkesbury, Derek Coates Barber, b. 1918, m.
1983 Barnett, Joel Barnett, PC, b. 1923, m.
1997 Bassam of Brighton, (John) Steven Bassam, b. 1953
1967 Beaumont of Whitley, Revd Timothy Wentworth Beaumont, b. 1928, m.
1998 Bell, Timothy John Leigh Bell, b. 1941, m.
2000 Bernstein of Craigweil, Alexander Bernstein, b. 1936, m.
2001 Best, Richard Stuart Best, OBE, b. 1945, m.
2001 Bhatia, Amirali Alibhai Bhatia, OBE, b. 1932, m.
1997 Biffen, (William) John Biffen, PC, b. 1930, m.
1996 Bingham of Cornhill, Thomas Henry Bingham, PC, b. 1933, m. Lord of Appeal in Ordinary
2000 Birt, John Francis Hodgess Birt, b. 1944, m.
2001 Black of Crossharbour, Conrad Moffat Black, OC, PC, b. 1944, m.

1997   *Blackwell,* Norman Roy Blackwell, *b.* 1952, *m.*

1971   *Blake,* Robert Norman William Blake, FBA, *b.* 1916, *w.*

1994   *Blaker,* Peter Allan Renshaw Blaker, KCMG, PC, *b.* 1922, *m.*

1978   *Blease,* William John Blease, *b.* 1914, *m.*

1995   *Blyth of Rowington,* James Blyth, *b.* 1940, *m.*

1980   *Boardman,* Thomas Gray Boardman, MC, TD, *b.* 1919, *m.*

1996   *Borrie,* Gordon Johnson Borrie, QC, *b.* 1931, *m.*

1976   *Boston of Faversham,* Terence George Boston, QC, *b.* 1930, *m.*

1996   *Bowness,* Peter Spencer Bowness, CBE, *b.* 1943, *m.*

1999   *Bradshaw,* William Peter Bradshaw, *b.* 1936, *m.*

1998   *Bragg,* Melvyn Bragg, *b.* 1939, *m.*

1987   *Bramall,* Edwin Noel Westby Bramall, KG, GCB, OBE, MC, *b.* 1923, *m.*

2000   *Brennan,* Daniel Joseph Brennan, QC, *b.* 1942, *m.*

1999   *Brett,* William Henry Brett, *b.* 1942, *m.*

1976   *Briggs,* Asa Briggs, FBA, *b.* 1921, *m.*

2000   *Brittan of Spennithorne,* Leon Brittan, PC, QC, *b.* 1939, *m.*

1997   *Brooke of Alverthorpe,* Clive Brooke, *b.* 1942, *m.*

2001   *Brooke of Sutton Mandeville,* Peter Leonard Brooke, CH, PC, *b.* 1934, *m.*

1998   *Brookman,* David Keith Brookman, *b.* 1937, *m.*

1979   *Brooks of Tremorfa,* John Edward Brooks, *b.* 1927, *m.*

2001   *Browne of Madingley,* Edmund John Phillip Browne, *b.* 1948

1974   *Bruce of Donington,* Donald William Trevor Bruce, *b.* 1912, *m.*

1976   *Bullock,* Alan Louis Charles Bullock, FBA, *b.* 1914, *m.*

1997   *Burlison,* Thomas Henry Burlison, *b.* 1936, *m.*

1998   *Burns,* Terence Burns, GCB, *b.* 1944, *m.*

1998   *Butler of Brockwell,* (Frederick Edward) Robin Butler, GCB, CVO, *b.* 1938, *m.*

1985   *Butterworth,* John Blackstock Butterworth, CBE, *b.* 1918, *m.*

1978   *Buxton of Alsa,* Aubrey Leland Oakes Buxton, KCVO, MC, *b.* 1918, *m.*

1987   *Callaghan of Cardiff,* (Leonard) James Callaghan, KG, PC, *b.* 1912, *m.*

1984   *Cameron of Lochbroom,* Kenneth John Cameron, PC, *b.* 1931, *m.*

1981   *Campbell of Alloway,* Alan Robertson Campbell, QC, *b.* 1917, *m.*

1974   *Campbell of Croy,* Gordon Thomas Calthrop Campbell, MC, PC, *b.* 1921, *m.*

2001   *Campbell-Savours,* Dale Norman Campbell-Savours, *b.* 1943, *m.*

1999   **Carington of Upton,* Lord Carrington, GCMG, *b.* 1919, *m.* (*see* Hereditary Peers)

1999   *Carlile of Berriew,* Alexander Charles Carlile, QC, *b.* 1948, *m.*

1987   *Carlisle of Bucklow,* Mark Carlisle, QC, PC, *b.* 1929, *m.*

1975   *Carr of Hadley,* (Leonard) Robert Carr, PC, *b.* 1916, *m.*

1987   *Carter,* Denis Victor Carter, PC, *b.* 1932, *m.*

1990   *Cavendish of Furness,* (Richard) Hugh Cavendish, *b.* 1941, *m.*

1996   *Chadlington,* Peter Selwyn Gummer, *b.* 1942, *m.*

1964   *Chalfont,* (Alun) Arthur Gwynne Jones, OBE, MC, PC, *b.* 1919, *m.*

2001   *Chan,* Michael Chew Koon Chan, MBE, *b.* 1940, *m.*

1985   *Chapple,* Francis (Frank) Joseph Chapple, *b.* 1921, *w.*

1987   *Chilver,* (Amos) Henry Chilver, FRS, FEng., *b.* 1926, *m.*

1977   *Chitnis,* Pratap Chidamber Chitnis, *b.* 1936, *m.*

1998   *Christopher,* Anthony Martin Grosvenor Christopher, CBE, *b.* 1925, *m.*

1992   *Clark of Kempston,* William Gibson Haig Clark, PC, *b.* 1917, *m.*

2001   *Clark of Windermere,* David George Clark, PC, Ph.D., *b.* 1939, *m.*

1998   *Clarke of Hampstead,* Anthony James Clarke, CBE, *b.* 1932, *m.*

1998   *Clement-Jones,* Timothy Francis Clement-Jones, CBE, *b.* 1949, *m.*

1990   *Clinton-Davis,* Stanley Clinton Clinton-Davis, PC, *b.* 1928, *m.*

1978   *Cockfield,* (Francis) Arthur Cockfield, PC, *b.* 1916, *w.*

2000   *Coe,* Sebastian Newbold Coe, OBE, *b.* 1956, *m.*

2001   *Condon,* Paul Leslie Condon, QPM, *m.*

1981   *Constantine of Stanmore,* Theodore Constantine, CBE, AE, *b.* 1910, *w.*

1992   *Cooke of Islandreagh,* Victor Alexander Cooke, OBE, *b.* 1920, *m.*

1996   *Cooke of Thorndon,* Robin Brunskill Cooke, KBE, PC, Ph.D., *b.* 1926, *m.*

1997   *Cope of Berkeley,* John Ambrose Cope, PC, *b.* 1937, *m.*

2001   *Corbett of Castle Vale,* Robin Corbett, *b.* 1933, *m.*

1991   *Craig of Radley,* David Brownrigg Craig, GCB, OBE, *b.* 1929, *m.*

1987   *Crickhowell,* (Roger) Nicholas Edwards, PC, *b.* 1934, *m.*

1978   *Croham,* Douglas Albert Vivian Allen, GCB, *b.* 1917, *w.*

1995   *Cuckney,* John Graham Cuckney, *b.* 1925, *m.*

1996   *Currie of Marylebone,* David Anthony Currie, *b.* 1946, *m.*

1979   *Dacre of Glanton,* Hugh Redwald Trevor-Roper, *b.* 1914, *w.*

1993   *Dahrendorf,* Ralf Dahrendorf, KBE, Ph.D., D.Phil., FBA, *b.* 1929, *m.*

1997   *Davies of Coity,* (David) Garfield Davies, CBE, *b.* 1935, *m.*

1997   *Davies of Oldham,* Bryan Davies, *b.* 1939, *m.*

1993   *Dean of Harptree,* (Arthur) Paul Dean, PC, *b.* 1924, *m.*

1998   *Dearing,* Ronald Ernest Dearing, *b.* 1930, *m.*

1986   *Deedes,* William Francis Deedes, KBE, MC, PC, *b.* 1913, *m.*

1991   *Desai,* Prof. Meghnad Jagdishchandra Desai, Ph.D., *b.* 1940, *m.*

1997   *Dholakia,* Navnit Dholakia, OBE, *b.* 1937, *m.*

1970   *Diamond,* John Diamond, PC, *b.* 1907, *m.*

1997   *Dixon,* Donald Dixon, PC, *b.* 1929, *m.*

1993   *Dixon-Smith,* Robert William Dixon-Smith, *b.* 1934, *m.*

1988   *Donaldson of Lymington,* John Francis Donaldson, PC, *b.* 1920, *m.*

1985   *Donoughue,* Bernard Donoughue, D.Phil., *b.* 1934

1987   *Dormand of Easington,* John Donkin Dormand, *b.* 1919, *m.*

1994   *Dubs,* Alfred Dubs, *b.* 1932, *m.*

1995   *Eames,* Robert Henry Alexander Eames, Ph.D., *b.* 1937, *m.*

1992   *Eatwell,* John Leonard Eatwell, Ph.D., *b.* 1945, *m.*

1983   *Eden of Winton,* John Benedict Eden, PC, *b.* 1925, *m.*

1999   *Elder,* Thomas Murray Elder, *b.* 1950

1992   *Elis-Thomas,* Dafydd Elis Elis-Thomas, *b.* 1946, *m.*

1985   *Elliott of Morpeth,* Robert William Elliott,
        b. 1920, *m.*
1981   *Elystan-Morgan,* Dafydd Elystan Elystan-
        Morgan, b. 1932, *m.*
1980   *Emslie,* George Carlyle Emslie, MBE, PC, FRSE,
        b. 1919, *m.*
2000   **Erskine of Alloa Tower,* Earl of Mar and Kellie ,
        b. 1949, *m. (see* Hereditary Peers)
1997   *Evans of Parkside,* John Evans, b. 1930, *m.*
2000   *Evans of Temple Guiting,* Matthew Evans, CBE,
        b. 1941, *m.*
1998   *Evans of Watford,* David Charles Evans, b. 1942,
        m.
1992   *Ewing of Kirkford,* Harry Ewing, b. 1931, *m.*
1983   *Ezra,* Derek Ezra, MBE, b. 1919, *m.*
1997   *Falconer of Thoroton,* Charles Leslie Falconer, QC,
        b. 1951, *m.*
1999   *Faulkner of Worcester,* Richard Oliver Faulkner,
        b. 1946, *m.*
2001   *Fearn,* Ronald Cyril Fearn, OBE, b. 1931, *m.*
1996   *Feldman,* Basil Feldman, b. 1926, *m.*
1999   *Fellowes,* Robert Fellowes, PC, GCB, GCVO,
        b. 1941, *m.*
1999   *Filkin,* David Geoffrey Nigel Filkin, CBE, b. 1944
1983   *Fitt,* Gerard Fitt, b. 1926, W.
1979   *Flowers,* Brian Hilton Flowers, FRS, b. 1924, *m.*
1999   *Forsyth of Drumlean,* Michael Bruce Forsyth,
        b. 1954, *m.*
1982   *Forte,* Charles Forte, b. 1908, *m.*
1999   *Foster of Thames Bank,* Norman Robert Foster,
        OM, b. 1935, *m.*
2001   *Fowler,* (Peter) Norman Fowler, PC, b. 1938, *m.*
1989   *Fraser of Carmyllie,* Peter Lovat Fraser, PC, QC,
        b. 1945, *m.*
1997   *Freeman,* Roger Norman Freeman, PC, b. 1942,
        m.
2000   *Fyfe of Fairfield,* George Lennox Fyfe, b. 1941, *m.*
1982   *Gallacher,* John Gallacher, b. 1920, *m.*
1999   **Ganzoni,* Lord Belstead, PC, b. 1932, *(see*
        Hereditary Peers)
1997   *Garel-Jones,* (William Armand) Thomas Tristan
        Garel-Jones, PC, b. 1941, *m.*
1999   **Gascoyne-Cecil,* The Viscount Cranborne , PC,
        b. 1946, *m. (see* Hereditary Peers)
1999   *Gavron,* Robert Gavron, CBE, b. 1930, *m.*
1992   *Geraint,* Geraint Wyn Howells, b. 1925, *m.*
1975   *Gibson,* (Richard) Patrick (Tallentyre) Gibson,
        b. 1916, *m.*
1997   *Gilbert,* John William Gilbert, PC, Ph.D., b. 1927,
        m.
1992   *Gilmour of Craigmillar,* Ian Hedworth John Little
        Gilmour, PC, b. 1926, *m.*
1994   *Gladwin of Clee,* Derek Oliver Gladwin, CBE,
        b. 1930, *m.*
1977   *Glenamara,* Edward Watson Short, CH, PC,
        b. 1912, *m.*
1999   *Goldsmith,* Peter Henry Goldsmith, QC, b. 1950,
        m.
1997   *Goodhart,* William Howard Goodhart, QC,
        b. 1933, *m.*
1997   *Gordon of Strathblane,* James Stuart Gordon,
        CBE, b. 1936, *m.*
1999   *Grabiner,* Anthony Stephen Grabiner, QC,
        b. 1945, *m.*
1983   *Graham of Edmonton,* (Thomas) Edward
        Graham, b. 1925, *m.*
1983   *Gray of Contin,* James (Hamish) Hector Northey
        Gray, PC, b. 1927, *m.*
2000   *Greaves,* Anthony Robert Greaves, b. 1942, *m.*

1974   *Greene of Harrow Weald,* Sidney Francis Greene,
        CBE, b. 1910, *m.*
1975   *Gregson,* John Gregson, b. 1924
2000   **Grenfell of Kilvey,* Lord Grenfell, b. 1935, *m. (see*
        Hereditary Peers)
1991   *Griffiths of Fforestfach,* Brian Griffiths, b. 1941,
        m.
2001   *Grocott,* Bruce Joseph Grocott, b. 1940, *m.*
2000   **Gueterbock,* Lord Berkley, OBE, b. 1939, *m. (see*
        Hereditary Peers)
2001   *Guthrie of Craigiebank,* Charles Ronald Llewelyn
        Guthrie, GCB, LVO, OBE, b. 1938, *m.*
1995   *Habgood,* Rt. Revd John Stapylton Habgood, PC,
        Ph.D., b. 1927, *m.*
1994   *Hambro,* Charles Eric Alexander Hambro,
        b. 1930, *m.*
2001   *Hannay of Chiswick,* David Hugh Alexander
        Hannay, GCMG, b. 1935, *m.*
1998   *Hanningfield,* Paul Edward Winston White,
        b. 1940
1983   *Hanson,* James Edward Hanson, b. 1922, *m.*
1997   *Hardie,* Andrew Rutherford Hardie, QC, PC,
        b. 1946, *m.*
1997   *Hardy of Wath,* Peter Hardy, b. 1931, *m.*
1998   *Harris of Haringey,* (Jonathan) Toby Harris,
        b. 1953, *m.*
1979   *Harris of High Cross,* Ralph Harris, b. 1924, *m.*
1996   *Harris of Peckham,* Philip Charles Harris,
        b. 1942, *m.*
1999   *Harrison,* Lyndon Henry Arthur Harrison,
        b. 1947, *m.*
1993   *Haskel,* Simon Haskel, b. 1934, *m.*
1998   *Haskins,* Christopher Robin Haskins, b. 1937, *m.*
1990   *Haslam,* Robert Haslam, b. 1923, *m.*
1997   *Hattersley,* Roy Sidney George Hattersley, PC,
        b. 1932, *m.*
1992   *Hayhoe,* Bernard John (Barney) Hayhoe, PC,
        b. 1925, *m.*
1992   *Healey,* Denis Winston Healey, CH, MBE, PC,
        b. 1917, *m.*
1999   **Hennessey,* Lord Windlesham, CVO, b. 1932, *m.*
        (see Hereditary Peers)
2001   *Heseltine,* Michael Ray Dibdin Heseltine, CH, PC,
        b. 1933, *m.*
1997   *Higgins,* Terence Langley Higgins, KBE, PC,
        b. 1928, *m.*
1979   *Hill-Norton,* Peter John Hill-Norton, GCB,
        b. 1915, *m.*
2000   *Hodgson of Astley Abbotts,* Robin Granville
        Hodgson, CBE, b. 1937, *m.*
1997   *Hogg of Cumbernauld,* Norman Hogg, b. 1938,
        m.
1991   *Hollick,* Clive Richard Hollick, b. 1945, *m.*
1990   *Holme of Cheltenham,* Richard Gordon Holme,
        CBE, b. 1936, *m.*
1979   *Hooson,* (Hugh) Emlyn Hooson, QC, b. 1925, *m.*
1995   *Hope of Craighead,* (James Arthur) David Hope,
        PC, b. 1938, *m. Lord of Appeal in Ordinary*
1992   *Howe of Aberavon,* (Richard Edward) Geoffrey
        Howe, CH, PC, QC, b. 1926, *m.*
1997   *Howell of Guildford,* David Arthur Russell
        Howell, PC, b. 1936, *m.*
1978   *Howie of Troon,* William Howie, b. 1924, *m.*
1997   *Hoyle,* (Eric) Douglas Harvey Hoyle, b. 1930, w.
1997   *Hughes of Woodside,* Robert Hughes, b. 1932, *m.*
2000   *Hunt of Chesterton,* Julian Charles Roland Hunt,
        CBE, b. 1941, *m.*
1997   *Hunt of Kings Heath,* Philip Alexander Hunt,
        OBE, b. 1949, *m.*

1980   *Hunt of Tanworth,* John Joseph Benedict Hunt, GCB, *b.* 1919, *m.*

1997   *Hunt of Wirral,* David James Fletcher Hunt, MBE, PC, *b.* 1942, *m.*

1997   *Hurd of Westwell,* Douglas Richard Hurd, CH, CBE, PC, *b.* 1930, *m.*

1996   *Hussey of North Bradley,* Marmaduke James Hussey, *b.* 1923, *m.*

1978   *Hutchinson of Lullington,* Jeremy Nicolas Hutchinson, QC, *b.* 1915, *m.*

1999   *Imbert,* Peter Michael Imbert, QPM, *b.* 1933, *m.*

1997   *Inge,* Peter Anthony Inge, GCB, *b.* 1935, *m.*

1987   *Irvine of Lairg,* Alexander Andrew Mackay Irvine, PC, QC, *b.* 1940, *m.*

1997   *Islwyn,* Royston John (Roy) Hughes, *b.* 1925, *m.*

1997   *Jacobs,* (David) Anthony Jacobs, *b.* 1931, *m.*

1997   *Janner of Braunstone,* Greville Ewan Janner, QC, *b.* 1928, *w.*

1999   **Jellicoe of Southampton,* Earl Jellicoe, KBE, *b.* 1918, *w. (see* Hereditary Peers)

1987   *Jenkin of Roding,* (Charles) Patrick (Fleeming) Jenkin, PC, *b.* 1926, *m.*

1987   *Jenkins of Hillhead,* Roy Harris Jenkins, OM, PC, *b.* 1920, *m.*

1981   *Jenkins of Putney,* Hugh Gater Jenkins, *b.* 1908, *w.*

2000   *Joffe,* Joel Goodman Joffe, CBE, *b.* 1932, *m.*

2001   *Jones,* (Stephen) Barry Jones, *b.* 1937, *m.*

1997   *Jopling,* (Thomas) Michael Jopling, PC, *b.* 1930, *m.*

2000   *Jordan,* William Brian Jordan, CBE, *b.* 1936, *m.*

1991   *Judd,* Frank Ashcroft Judd, *b.* 1935, *m.*

1980   *Keith of Castleacre,* Kenneth Alexander Keith, *b.* 1916, *m.*

1997   *Kelvedon,* (Henry) Paul Guinness Channon, PC, *b.* 1935, *m.*

2001   *Kilclooney,* John David Taylor, PC, *b.* 1937, *m.*

1996   *Kilpatrick of Kincraig,* Robert Kilpatrick, CBE, *b.* 1926, *m.*

1985   *Kimball,* Marcus Richard Kimball, *b.* 1928, *m.*

2001   *King of Bridgwater,* Thomas Jeremy King, CH, PC, *b.* 1933, *m.*

1983   *King of Wartnaby,* John Leonard King, *b.* 1918, *m.*

1999   *King of West Bromwich,* Tarsem King, *b.* 1937

1993   *Kingsdown,* Robert (Robin) Leigh-Pemberton, KG, PC, *b.* 1927, *m.*

1994   *Kingsland,* Christopher James Prout, TD, PC, QC, *b.* 1942

1999   *Kirkham,* Graham Kirkham, *b.* 1944, *m.*

1975   *Kirkhill,* John Farquharson Smith, *b.* 1930, *m.*

1987   *Knights,* Philip Douglas Knights, CBE, QPM, *b.* 1920, *m.*

1991   *Laing of Dunphail,* Hector Laing, *b.* 1923, *m.*

1999   *Laird,* John Dunn Laird, *b.* 1944, *m.*

1998   *Laming,* (William) Herbert Laming, CBE, *b.* 1936, *m.*

1998   *Lamont of Lerwick,* Norman Stewart Hughson Lamont, PC, *b.* 1942, *m.*

1990   *Lane of Horsell,* Peter Stewart Lane, *b.* 1925, *w.*

1997   *Lang of Monkton,* Ian Bruce Lang, PC, *b.* 1940, *m.*

1992   *Lawson of Blaby,* Nigel Lawson, PC, *b.* 1932, *m.*

2000   *Layard,* Peter Richard Grenville Layard, *b.* 1934, *m.*

1999   *Lea of Crondall,* David Edward Lea, OBE, *b.* 1937

1993   *Lester of Herne Hill,* Anthony Paul Lester, QC, *b.* 1936, *m.*

1997   *Levene of Portsoken,* Peter Keith Levene, KBE, *b.* 1941, *m.*

1997   *Levy,* Michael Abraham Levy, *b.* 1944, *m.*

1989   *Lewis of Newnham,* Jack Lewis, FRS, *b.* 1928, *m.*

1999   *Lipsey,* David Lawrence Lipsey, *b.* 1948, *m.*

1999   *Livsey,* Richard Livsey, CBE, *b.* 1948, *m.*

1997   *Lloyd-Webber,* Andrew Lloyd Webber, *b.* 1948, *m.*

1997   *Lofthouse of Pontefract,* Geoffrey Lofthouse, *b.* 1925, *w.*

2000   *Luce,* Richard Napier Luce, GCVO, PC, *b.* 1936, *m.*

2000   **Lyttleton of Aldershot,* The Viscount Chandos, *b.* 1953, *m. (see* Hereditary Peers)

1984   *McAlpine of West Green,* (Robert) Alistair McAlpine, *b.* 1942, *m.*

1988   *Macaulay of Bragar,* Donald Macaulay, QC, *b.* 1933, *m.*

1975   *McCarthy,* William Edward John McCarthy, D.Phil., *b.* 1925, *m.*

1976   *McCluskey,* John Herbert McCluskey, *b.* 1929, *m.*

1989   *McColl of Dulwich,* Ian McColl, CBE, FRCS, FRCSE, *b.* 1933, *m.*

1998   *Macdonald of Tradeston,* Angus John Macdonald, CBE, *b.* 1940, *m.*

1991   *Macfarlane of Bearsden,* Norman Somerville Macfarlane, KT, FRSE, *b.* 1926, *m.*

2001   *MacGregor of Pulham Market,* John Roddick Russell MacGregor, CBE, PC, *b.* 1937, *m.*

1982   *McIntosh of Haringey,* Andrew Robert McIntosh, *b.* 1933, *m.*

1979   *Mackay of Clashfern,* James Peter Hymers Mackay, KT, PC, FRSE, *b.* 1927, *m.*

1995   *Mackay of Drumadoon,* Donald Sage Mackay, PC, *b.* 1946, *m.*

1999   *Mackenzie of Culkein,* Hector Uisdean MacKenzie, *b.* 1940

1998   *Mackenzie of Framwellgate,* Brian Mackenzie, OBE, *b.* 1943, *m.*

1974   *Mackie of Benshie,* George Yull Mackie, CBE, DSO, DFC, *b.* 1919, *m.*

1996   *MacLaurin of Knebworth,* Ian Charter MacLaurin, *b.* 1937, *w.*

2001   *Maclennon of Rogart,* Robert Adam Ross Maclennan, PC, *b.* 1936, *m.*

1995   *McNally,* Tom McNally, *b.* 1943, *m.*

2001   *Maginnis of Drumglass,* Kenneth Wiggins Maginnis, *b.* 1938, *m.*

1991   *Marlesford,* Mark Shuldham Schreiber, *b.* 1931, *m.*

1981   *Marsh,* Richard William Marsh, PC, *b.* 1928, *m.*

1998   *Marshall of Knightsbridge,* Colin Marsh Marshall, *b.* 1933, *m.*

1987   *Mason of Barnsley,* Roy Mason, PC, *b.* 1924, *m.*

2001   *May of Oxford,* Robert McCredie May, *b.* 1936, *m.*

1997   *Mayhew of Twysden,* Patrick Barnabas Burke Mayhew, QC, PC, *b.* 1929, *m.*

1992   *Merlyn-Rees,* Merlyn Merlyn-Rees, PC, *b.* 1920, *m.*

1978   *Mishcon,* Victor Mishcon, QC, *b.* 1915, *m.*

2000   *Mitchell,* Parry Andrew Mitchell, *b.* 1943

2000   **Mitford,* Lord Redesdale, *b.* 1967, *m. (see* Hereditary Peers)

1997   *Molyneaux of Killead,* James Henry Molyneaux, KBE, PC, *b.* 1920

1997   *Monro of Langholm,* Hector Seymour Peter Monro, AE, PC, *b.* 1922, *m.*

1992   *Moore of Lower Marsh,* John Edward Michael Moore, PC, *b.* 1937, *m.*

1986   *Moore of Wolvercote,* Philip Brian Cecil Moore, GCB, GCVO, CMG, PC, *b.* 1921, *m.*

2000   *Morgan,* Kenneth Owen Morgan, *b.* 1934, *m.*

2001   *Morris of Aberavon,* John Morris, QC, *b.* 1931, *m.*

1997   *Morris of Manchester,* Alfred Morris, PC, *b.* 1928, *m.*

2001   *Moser,* Claus Adolf Moser, KCB, CBE, *b.* 1922, *m.*

1985   *Murray of Epping Forest,* Lionel Murray, OBE, PC, *b.* 1922, *m.*

1979   *Murton of Lindisfarne,* (Henry) Oscar Murton, OBE, TD, PC, *b.* 1914, *m.*

1997   *Naseby,* Michael Wolfgang Laurence Morris, PC, *b.* 1936, *m.*

1997   *Neill of Bladen,* (Francis) Patrick Neill, QC, *b.* 1926, *m.*

1997   *Newby,* Richard Mark Newby, OBE, *b.* 1953, *m.*

1997   *Newton of Braintree,* Antony Harold Newton, OBE, PC, *b.* 1937, *m.*

1994   *Nickson,* David Wigley Nickson, KBE, FRSE, *b.* 1929, *m.*

1975   *Northfield,* (William) Donald Chapman, *b.* 1923

1998   *Norton of Louth,* Philip Norton, *b.* 1951

2000   *Oakeshott of Seagrove Bay,* Matthew Alan Oakeshott, *b.* 1947, *m.*

1997   *Orme,* Stanley Orme, PC, *b.* 1923, *m.*

2001   *Ouseley,* Herman George Ouseley, *b.* 1945, *m.*

1992   *Owen,* David Anthony Llewellyn Owen, CH, PC, *b.* 1938, *m.*

1999   *Oxburgh,* Ernest Ronald Oxburgh, KBE, FRS, Ph.D., *b.* 1934, *m.*

1991   *Palumbo,* Peter Garth Palumbo, *b.* 1935, *m.*

2000   *Parekh,* Bhikhu Chhotalal Parekh, *b.* 1935, *m.*

1992   *Parkinson,* Cecil Edward Parkinson, PC, *b.* 1931, *m.*

1975   *Parry,* Gordon Samuel David Parry, *b.* 1925, *m.*

1999   *Patel,* Narendra Babubhai Patel, *b.* 1938

2000   *Patel of Blackburn,* Adam Hafejee Patel, *b.* 1940

1997   *Patten,* John Haggitt Charles Patten, PC, *b.* 1945, *m.*

1996   *Paul,* Swraj Paul, *b.* 1931, *m.*

1990   *Pearson of Rannoch,* Malcolm Everard MacLaren Pearson, *b.* 1942, *m.*

2001   *Pendry,* Thomas Pendry, *b.* 1934, *m.*

1979   *Perry of Walton,* Walter Laing Macdonald Perry, OBE, FRS, FRSE, *b.* 1921, *m.*

1987   *Peston,* Maurice Harry Peston, *b.* 1931, *m.*

1983   *Peyton of Yeovil,* John Wynne William Peyton, PC, *b.* 1919, *m.*

1998   *Phillips of Sudbury,* Andrew Wyndham Phillips, OBE, *b.* 1939, *m.*

1996   *Pilkington of Oxenford,* Revd Canon Peter Pilkington, *b.* 1933, *w.*

1992   *Plant of Highfield,* Prof. Raymond Plant, Ph.D., *b.* 1945, *m.*

1987   *Plumb,* (Charles) Henry Plumb, *b.* 1925, *m.*

1981   *Plummer of St Marylebone,* (Arthur) Desmond (Herne) Plummer, TD, *b.* 1914, *m.*

2000   ** Ponsonby of Roehampton,* Lord Ponsonby of Shulbrede, *b.* 1958, *(see* Hereditary Peers)

1990   *Porter of Luddenham,* George Porter, OM, FRS, *b.* 1920, *m.*

2000   *Powell of Bayswater,* Charles David Powell, KCMG, *b.* 1941

1987   *Prior,* James Michael Leathes Prior, PC, *b.* 1927, *m.*

1982   *Prys-Davies,* Gwilym Prys Prys-Davies, *b.* 1923, *m.*

1997   *Puttnam,* David Terence Puttnam, CBE, *b.* 1941, *m.*

1987   *Pym,* Francis Leslie Pym, MC, PC, *b.* 1922, *m.*

1982   *Quinton,* Anthony Meredith Quinton, FBA, *b.* 1925, *m.*

1994   *Quirk,* Prof. (Charles) Randolph Quirk, CBE, FBA, *b.* 1920, *m.*

2001   *Radice,* Giles Heneage Radice, PC, *b.* 1936

1997   *Randall of St Budeaux,* Stuart Jeffrey Randall, *b.* 1938, *m.*

1978   *Rawlinson of Ewell,* Peter Anthony Grayson Rawlinson, PC, QC, *b.* 1919, *m.*

1976   *Rayne,* Max Rayne, *b.* 1918, *m.*

1997   *Razzall,* (Edward) Timothy Razzall, CBE, *b.* 1943, *m.*

1987   *Rees,* Peter Wynford Innes Rees, PC, QC, *b.* 1926, *m.*

1988   *Rees-Mogg,* William Rees-Mogg, *b.* 1928, *m.*

1991   *Renfrew of Kaimsthorn,* (Andrew) Colin Renfrew, FBA, *b.* 1937, *m.*

1999   *Rennard,* Christopher John Rennard, MBE, *b.* 1960

1979   *Renton,* David Lockhart-Mure Renton, KBE, TD, PC, QC, *b.* 1908, *w.*

1997   *Renton of Mount Harry,* (Ronald) Timothy Renton, PC, *b.* 1932, *m.*

1997   *Renwick of Clifton,* Robin William Renwick, KCMG, *b.* 1937, *m.*

1990   *Richard,* Ivor Seward Richard, PC, QC, *b.* 1932, *m.*

1979   *Richardson,* John Samuel Richardson, LVO, MD, FRCP, *b.* 1910, *w.*

1983   *Richardson of Duntisbourne,* Gordon William Humphreys Richardson, KG, MBE, TD, PC, *b.* 1915, *m.*

1992   *Rix,* Brian Norman Roger Rix, CBE, *b.* 1924, *m.*

1997   *Roberts of Conwy,* (Ieuan) Wyn (Pritchard) Roberts, PC, *b.* 1930, *m.*

1999   *Robertson of Port Ellen,* George Islay MacNeill Robertson, PC, *b.* 1946, *m.*

1992   *Rodger of Earlsferry,* Alan Ferguson Rodger, PC, QC, FBA, *b.* 1944, *Lord of Appeal in Ordinary*

1992   *Rodgers of Quarry Bank,* William Thomas Rodgers, PC, *b.* 1928, *m.*

1999   *Rogan,* Dennis Robert David Rogan, *b.* 1942, *m.*

1996   *Rogers of Riverside,* Richard George Rogers, RA, RIBA, *b.* 1933, *m.*

1977   *Roll of Ipsden,* Eric Roll, KCMG, CB, *b.* 1907, *w.*

2001   *Rooker,* Jeffrey William Rooker, PC, *b.* 1941, *m.*

2000   *Roper,* John Francis Hodgess Roper, *b.* 1935, *m.*

1997   *Russell-Johnston,* (David) Russell Russell-Johnston, *b.* 1932, *m.*

1975   *Ryder of Eaton Hastings,* Sydney Thomas Franklin (Don) Ryder, *b.* 1916, *m.*

1997   *Ryder of Wensum,* Richard Andrew Ryder, OBE, PC, *b.* 1949, *m.*

1996   *Saatchi,* Maurice Saatchi, *b.* 1946, *m.*

1989   *Sainsbury of Preston Candover,* John Davan Sainsbury, KG, *b.* 1927, *m.*

1997   *Sainsbury of Turville,* David John Sainsbury, *b.* 1940, *m.*

1987   *St John of Fawsley,* Norman Antony Francis St John-Stevas, PC, *b.* 1929

1997   *Sandberg,* Michael Graham Ruddock Sandberg, CBE, *b.* 1927, *m.*

1985   *Sanderson of Bowden,* Charles Russell Sanderson, *b.* 1933, *m.*

1998   *Sawyer,* Lawrence (Tom) Sawyer, *b.* 1943

1979   *Scanlon,* Hugh Parr Scanlon, *b.* 1913, *m.*

2000   *Scott of Foscote,* Richard Rashleigh Folliott Scott, PC, *b.* 1934, *m. Lord of Appeal in Ordinary*

1997   *Selkirk of Douglas,* James Alexander Douglas-Hamilton, MSP, PC, QC, *b.* 1942, *m.*

1996   *Sewel,* John Buttifant Sewel, CBE, *b.* 1946

1999   *Sharman,* Colin Morven Sharman, OBE, *b.* 1943, *m.*

1994   *Shaw of Northstead,* Michael Norman Shaw, *b.* 1920, *m.*

1959	*Shawcross*, Hartley William Shawcross, GBE, PC, QC, *b.* 1902, *m.*
2001	*Sheldon*, Robert Edward Sheldon, PC, *b.* 1923, *m.*
1994	*Sheppard of Didgemere*, Allan John George Sheppard, KCVO, *b.* 1932, *m.*
1998	*Sheppard of Liverpool*, David Stuart Sheppard, *b.* 1929, *m.*
2000	*Shutt of Greetland*, David Trevor Shutt, OBE, *b.* 1942
1971	*Simon of Glaisdale*, Jocelyn Edward Salis Simon, PC, *b.* 1911, *m.*
1997	*Simon of Highbury*, David Alec Gwyn Simon, CBE, *b.* 1939, *m.*
1997	*Simpson of Dunkeld*, George Simpson, *b.* 1942, *m.*
1991	*Skidelsky*, Robert Jacob Alexander Skidelsky, D.Phil., *b.* 1939, *m.*
1997	*Smith of Clifton*, Trevor Arthur Smith, *b.* 1937, *m.*
1999	*Smith of Leigh*, Peter Richard Charles Smith, *b.* 1945, *m.*
1990	*Soulsby of Swaffham Prior*, Ernest Jackson Lawson Soulsby, Ph.D., *b.* 1926, *m.*
1983	*Stallard*, Albert William Stallard, *b.* 1921, *m.*
1997	*Steel of Aikwood*, David Martin Scott Steel, PC, KBE, MSP, *b.* 1938, *m.*
1991	*Sterling of Plaistow*, Jeffrey Maurice Sterling, GCVO, CBE, *b.* 1934, *m.*
1987	*Stevens of Ludgate*, David Robert Stevens, *b.* 1936, *m.*
1999	*Stevenson of Coddenham*, Henry Dennistoun Stevenson, CBE, *b.* 1945, *m.*
1992	*Stewartby*, (Bernard Harold) Ian (Halley) Stewart, RD, PC, FBA, FRSE, *b.* 1935, *m.*
1981	*Stodart of Leaston*, James Anthony Stodart, PC, *b.* 1916, *w.*
1983	*Stoddart of Swindon*, David Leonard Stoddart, *b.* 1926, *m.*
1969	*Stokes*, Donald Gresham Stokes, TD, FEng., *b.* 1914, *w.*
1997	*Stone of Blackheath*, Andrew Zelig Stone, *b.* 1942, *m.*
2001	*Sutherland of Houndwood*, Stewart Ross Sutherland, *b.* 1941, *m.*
1971	*Tanlaw*, Simon Brooke Mackay, *b.* 1934, *m.*
1996	*Taverne*, Dick Taverne, QC, *b.* 1928, *m.*
1978	*Taylor of Blackburn*, Thomas Taylor, CBE, *b.* 1929, *m.*
1996	*Taylor of Warwick*, John David Beckett Taylor, *b.* 1952, *m.*
1992	*Tebbit*, Norman Beresford Tebbit, CH, PC, *b.* 1931, *m.*
2001	*Temple-Morris*, Peter Temple-Morris, *b.* 1938, *m.*
1996	*Thomas of Gresford*, Donald Martin Thomas, OBE, QC, *b.* 1937, *m.*
1987	*Thomas of Gwydir*, Peter John Mitchell Thomas, PC, QC, *b.* 1920, *w.*
1997	*Thomas of Macclesfield*, Terence James Thomas, CBE, *b.* 1937, *m.*
1981	*Thomas of Swynnerton*, Hugh Swynnerton Thomas, *b.* 1931, *m.*
1977	*Thomson of Monifieth*, George Morgan Thomson, KT, PC, *b.* 1921, *m.*
1990	*Tombs*, Francis Leonard Tombs, FEng., *b.* 1924, *m.*
1998	*Tomlinson*, John Edward Tomlinson, MEP, *b.* 1939
1994	*Tope*, Graham Norman Tope, CBE, *b.* 1943, *m.*
1981	*Tordoff*, Geoffrey Johnson Tordoff, *b.* 1928, *m.*
1999	*Trotman*, Alexander Trotman, *b.* 1933

1993	*Tugendhat*, Christopher Samuel Tugendhat, *b.* 1937, *m.*
2000	*Turnberg*, Leslie Arnold Turnberg, Kt., MD, *b.* 1934, *m.*
1990	*Varley*, Eric Graham Varley, PC, *b.* 1932, *m.*
1996	*Vincent of Coleshill*, Richard Frederick Vincent, GBE, KCB, DSO, *b.* 1931, *m.*
1985	*Vinson*, Nigel Vinson, LVO, *b.* 1931, *m.*
1990	*Waddington*, David Charles Waddington, GCVO, PC, QC, *b.* 1929, *m.*
1990	*Wade of Chorlton*, (William) Oulton Wade, *b.* 1932, *m.*
1992	*Wakeham*, John Wakeham, PC, *b.* 1932, *m.*
1999	*Waldegrave of North Hill*, William Arthur Waldegrave, PC, *b.* 1946, *m.*
1997	*Walker of Doncaster*, Harold Walker, PC, *b.* 1927, *m.*
1992	*Walker of Worcester*, Peter Edward Walker, MBE, PC, *b.* 1932, *m.*
1974	*Wallace of Coslany*, George Douglas Wallace, *b.* 1906, *m.*
1995	*Wallace of Saltaire*, William John Lawrence Wallace, Ph.D., *b.* 1941, *m.*
1989	*Walton of Detchant*, John Nicholas Walton, TD, FRCP, *b.* 1922, *m.*
1998	*Warner*, Norman Reginald Warner, *b.* 1940, *m.*
1997	*Watson of Invergowrie*, Michael Goodall Watson, MSP, *b.* 1948, *m.*
1999	*Watson of Richmond*, Alan John Watson, CBE, *b.* 1941, *m.*
1992	*Weatherill*, (Bruce) Bernard Weatherill, PC, *b.* 1920, *m.*
1977	*Wedderburn of Charlton*, (Kenneth) William Wedderburn, FBA, QC, *b.* 1927, *m.*
1976	*Weidenfeld*, (Arthur) George Weidenfeld, *b.* 1919, *m.*
1978	*Whaddon*, (John) Derek Page, *b.* 1927, *m.*
1996	*Whitty*, John Lawrence (Larry) Whitty, *b.* 1943, *m.*
1974	*Wigoder*, Basil Thomas Wigoder, QC, *b.* 1921, *m.*
1985	*Williams* of Elvel, Charles Cuthbert Powell Williams, CBE, *b.* 1933, *m.*
1992	*Williams of Mostyn*, Gareth Wyn Williams, QC, PC, *b.* 1941, *m.*
1999	*Williamson of Horton*, David (Francis) Williamson, GCMG, CB, *b.* 1934, *m.*
1992	*Wilson of Tillyorn*, David Clive Wilson, KT, GCMG, Ph.D, *b.* 1935, *m.*
1995	*Winston*, Robert Maurice Lipson Winston, FRCOG, *b.* 1940, *m.*
1985	*Wolfson*, Leonard Gordon Wolfson, *b.* 1927, *m.*
1991	*Wolfson of Sunningdale*, David Wolfson, *b.* 1935, *m.*
1999	*Woolmer of Leeds*, Kenneth John Woolmer, *b.* 1940, *m.*
1994	*Wright of Richmond*, Patrick Richard Henry Wright, GCMG, *b.* 1931, *m.*
1984	*Young of Graffham*, David Ivor Young, PC, *b.* 1932, *m.*
1992	**Younger of Prestwick*, The Viscount Younger of Leckie, *b.* 1931, *m. (see* Hereditary Peers)

BARONESSES

Created

1997	*Amos*, Valerie Ann Amos, *b.* 1954
2000	*Andrews*, Elizabeth Kay Andrews, OBE, *b.* 1943, *m.*
1996	*Anelay of St Johns*, Joyce Anne Anelay, DBE, *b.* 1947, *m.*

1999   Ashton of Upholland, Catherine Margaret Ashton, b. 1956, m.
1999   Barker, Elizabeth Jean Barker, b. 1961
2000   Billingham, Angela Theodora Billingham, D.Phil., b. 1921, w.
1987   Blackstone, Tessa Ann Vosper Blackstone, Ph.D., b. 1942
1987   Blatch, Emily May Blatch, CBE, PC, b. 1937, m.
1999   Blood, May Blood, MBE, b. 1938
2001   Boothroyd, Betty Boothroyd, PC, b. 1929
1990   Brigstocke, Heather Renwick Brigstocke, b. 1929, m.
1998   Buscombe, Peta Jane Buscombe, b. 1954, m.
1996   Byford, Hazel Byford, DBE, b. 1941, m.
1982   Carnegy of Lour, Elizabeth Patricia Carnegy of Lour, b. 1925
1992   Chalker of Wallasey, Lynda Chalker, PC, b. 1942, m.
2000   Cohen of Pimlico, Janet Cohen, b. 1940, m.
1982   Cox, Caroline Anne Cox, b. 1937, m.
1998   Crawley, Christine Mary Crawley, MEP, b. 1950, m.
1990   Cumberlege, Julia Frances Cumberlege, CBE, b. 1943, m.
1978   David, Nora Ratcliff David, b. 1913, w.
1993   Dean of Thornton-le-Fylde, Brenda Dean, PC, b. 1943, m.
1974   Delacourt-Smith of Alteryn, Margaret Rosalind Delacourt-Smith, b. 1916, m.
1990   Dunn, Lydia Selina Dunn, DBE, b. 1940, m.
1990   Eccles of Moulton, Diana Catherine Eccles, b. 1933, m.
1972   Elles, Diana Louie Elles, b. 1921, m.
1997   Emerton, Audrey Caroline Emerton, DBE, b. 1935
1974   Falkender, Marcia Matilda Falkender, CBE, b. 1932
1994   Farrington of Ribbleton, Josephine Farrington, b. 1940, m.
2001   Finlay of Llandaff, Ilora Gillian Finlay, b. 1949, m.
1974   Fisher of Rednal, Doris Mary Gertrude Fisher, b. 1919, w.
1990   Flather, Shreela Flather, m.
1997   Fookes, Janet Evelyn Fookes, DBE, b. 1936
1999   Gale, Anita Gale, b. 1940
1981   Gardner of Parkes, (Rachel) Trixie (Anne) Gardner, b. 1927, m.
2000   Gibson of Market Rasen, Anne Gibson, OBE, b. 1940, m.
2001   Golding, Llinos Golding, b. 1933, m.
1998   Goudie, Mary Teresa Goudie, b. 1946, m.
1993   Gould of Potternewton, Joyce Brenda Gould, b. 1932, m.
2001   Greenfield, Susan Adele Greenfield, CBE, b. 1950, m.
2000   Greengross, Sally Ralea Greengross, OBE, b. 1935, m.
1991   Hamwee, Sally Rachel Hamwee, b. 1947
1999   Hanham, Joan Brownlow Hanham, CBE, b. 1939, m.
1999   Harris of Richmond, Angela Felicity Harris, b. 1944
1996   Hayman, Helene Valerie Hayman, PC, b. 1949, m.
1991   Hilton of Eggardon, Jennifer Hilton, QPM, b. 1936
1995   Hogg, Sarah Elizabeth Mary Hogg, b. 1946, m.
1990   Hollis of Heigham, Patricia Lesley Hollis, D.Phil., b. 1941, m.
1985   Hooper, Gloria Dorothy Hooper, b. 1939

2001   Howarth of Breckland, Valerie Georgina Howarth, OBE, b. 1940
2001   Howe of Idlicote, Elspeth Rosamond Morton Howe, CBE, b. 1932, m.
1999   Howells of St Davids, Rosalind Patricia-Anne Howells, b. 1931, m.
1965   Hylton-Foster, Audrey Pellew Hylton-Foster, DBE, b. 1908, w.
1991   James of Holland Park, Phyllis Dorothy White (P. D. James), OBE, b. 1920, w.
1992   Jay of Paddington, Margaret Ann Jay, PC, b. 1939, m.
1979   Jeger, Lena May Jeger, b. 1915, w.
1997   Kennedy of the Shaws, Helena Ann Kennedy, QC, b. 1950, m.
1997   Knight of Collingtree, (Joan Christabel) Jill Knight, DBE, b. 1923, w.
1997   Linklater of Butterstone, Veronica Linklater, b. 1943, m.
1996   Lloyd of Highbury, Prof. June Kathleen Lloyd, DBE, FRCP, FRCPE, FRCGP, b. 1928
1978   Lockwood, Betty Lockwood, b. 1924, w.
1997   Ludford, Sarah Ann Ludford, MEP, b. 1951
1979   McFarlane of Llandaff, Jean Kennedy McFarlane, b. 1926
1999   McIntosh of Hudnall, Genista Mary McIntosh, b. 1946
1997   Maddock, Diana Margaret Maddock, b. 1945, m.
1991   Mallalieu, Ann Mallalieu, QC, b. 1945, m.
1970   Masham of Ilton, Susan Lilian Primrose Cunliffe-Lister, b. 1935, m.
1999   Massey of Darwen, Doreen Elizabeth Massey, b. 1938, m.
2001   Michie of Gallanach, Janet Ray Michie, b. 1934, m.
1998   Miller of Chilthorne Domer, Susan Elizabeth Miller, b. 1954
1993   Miller of Hendon, Doreen Miller, MBE, b. 1933, m.
2001   Morgan of Huyton, Sally Morgan, b. 1959, m.
1997   Nicholson of Winterbourne, Emma Harriet Nicholson, MEP, b. 1941, m.
1982   Nicol, Olive Mary Wendy Nicol, b. 1923, m.
2000   Noakes, Shiela Valerie Masters, DBE, b. 1949, m.
2000   Northover, Lindsay Patricia Granshaw, b. 1954
1991   O'Cathain, Detta O'Cathain, OBE, b. 1938, m.
1999   O'Neill of Bengarve, Onora Sylvia O'Neill, CBE, Ph.D., b. 1941
1989   Oppenheim-Barnes, Sally Oppenheim-Barnes, PC, b. 1930, m.
1990   Park of Monmouth, Daphne Margaret Sybil Désirée Park, CMG, OBE, b. 1921
1991   Perry of Southwark, Pauline Perry, b. 1931, m.
1974   Pike, (Irene) Mervyn (Parnicott) Pike, DBE, b. 1918
1997   Pitkeathley, Jill Elizabeth Pitkeathley, OBE, b. 1940
1981   Platt of Writtle, Beryl Catherine Platt, CBE, FEng., b. 1923, m.
1999   Prashar, Usha Kumari Prashar, CBE, b. 1948, m.
1996   Ramsay of Cartvale, Margaret Mildred (Meta) Ramsay, b. 1936
1994   Rawlings, Patricia Elizabeth Rawlings, b. 1939
1997   Rendell of Babergh, Ruth Barbara Rendell, CBE, b. 1930, m.
1998   Richardson of Calow, Kathleen Margaret Richardson, OBE, b. 1938, m.
1997   Scotland of Asthal, Patricia Janet Scotland, QC, b. 1955, m.

2000   *Scott of Needham Market,* Rosalind Carol Scott, *b.* 1957

1991   *Seccombe,* Joan Anna Dalziel Seccombe, DBE, *b.* 1930, *m.*

1967   *Serota,* Beatrice Serota, DBE, *b.* 1919, *m.*

1998   *Sharp* of Guildford, Margaret Lucy Sharp, *b.* 1938, *m.*

1973   *Sharples,* Pamela Sharples, *b.* 1923, *m.*

1995   *Smith of Gilmorehill,* Elizabeth Margaret Smith, *b.* 1940, *w.*

1999   *Stern,* Vivien Helen Stern, CBE, *b.* 1941

1996   *Symons of Vernham Dean,* Elizabeth Conway Symons, *b.* 1951

1992   *Thatcher,* Margaret Hilda Thatcher, KG, OM, PC, FRS, *b.* 1925, *m.*

1994   *Thomas of Walliswood,* Susan Petronella Thomas, OBE, *b.* 1935, *m.*

1998   *Thornton,* (Dorothea) Glenys Thornton, *b.* 1952, *m.*

1980   *Trumpington,* Jean Alys Barker, PC, *b.* 1922, *w.*

1985   *Turner of Camden,* Muriel Winifred Turner, *b.* 1927, *m.*

1998   *Uddin,* Manzila Pola Uddin, *b.* 1959, *m.*

2000   *Walmsley,* Joan Margaret Walmsley, *b.* 1943

1985   *Warnock,* Helen Mary Warnock, DBE, *b.* 1924, *w.*

1999   *Warwick of Undercliffe,* Diana Mary Warwick, *b.* 1945, *m.*

1999   *Whitaker,* Janet Alison Whitaker, *b.* 1936

1996   *Wilcox,* Judith Ann Wilcox, *b.* 1940, *w.*

1999   *Wilkins,* Rosalie Catherine Wilkins, *b.* 1946

1993   *Williams of Crosby,* Shirley Vivien Teresa Brittain Williams, PC, *b.* 1930, *m.*

1997   *Young of Old Scone,* Barbara Scott Young, *b.* 1948

Lords Spiritual

The Lords Spiritual are the Archbishops of Canterbury and York and 24 diocesan bishops of the Church of England. The Bishops of London, Durham and Winchester always have seats in the House of Lords; the other 21 seats are filled by the remaining diocesan bishops in order of seniority. The Bishop of Sodor and Man and the Bishop of Gibraltar are not eligible to sit in the House of Lords.

ARCHBISHOPS

Style, The Most Revd and Right Hon. the Lord
Archbishop of _
Addressed as Archbishop, *or* Your Grace

Introduced to House of Lords

Awaiting Introduction	*Canterbury* (104th), Rowan Douglas Williams, D.Phil, *b.* 1950, *m., cons.* 1992, *elected* 2002, *trans.* 2000
1990	*York* (96th), David Michael Hope, KCVO, PC, D.Phil, LLD, *b.* 1940, *cons.* 1985, *elected* 1985, *trans.* 1995

BISHOPS

Style, The Right Revd the Lord Bishop of _
Addressed as My Lord
elected date of confirmation as diocesan bishop

Introduced to House of Lords (as at 31 August 2002)

1996	*London* (132nd), Richard John Carew Chartres, *b.* 1947, *m., cons.* 1992, *elected* 1995
1994	*Durham* (93rd), (Anthony) Michael (Arnold) Turnbull, *b.* 1935, *m., cons.* 1988, *elected* 1988, *trans.* 1994
1996	*Winchester* (96th), Michael Charles Scott-Joynt, *b.* 1943, *m., cons.* 1987, *elected* 1995
1989	*Lichfield* (97th), Keith Norman Sutton, *b.* 1934, *m., cons.* 1978, *elected* 1984
1990	*Bristol* (54th), Barry Rogerson, *b.* 1936, *m., cons.* 1979, *elected* 1985
1993	*Oxford* (41st), Richard Douglas Harries, *b.* 1936, *m., cons.* 1987, *elected* 1987
1995	*Blackburn* (7th), Alan David Chesters, *b.* 1937, *m., cons.* 1989, *elected* 1989
1997	*Hereford* (103rd), John Keith Oliver, *b.* 1935, *m., cons.* 1990, *elected* 1990
1997	*Southwark* (9th), Thomas Frederick Butler, *b.* 1940, *m., cons.* 1985, *elected* 1991, *trans.* 1998
1997	*Manchester* (11th) Nigel Simeon McCulloch, *b.* 1942, *m., cons.* 1986, *elected* 2002, *trans.* 2002
1998	*Salisbury* (77th), David Staffurth Stancliffe, *b.* 1942, *m., cons.* 1993, *elected* 1993
1998	*Gloucester* (39th), David Edward Bentley, *b.* 1935, *m., cons.* 1986, *elected* 1993
1999	*Rochester* (106th), Michael James Nazir-Ali, Ph.D., *b.* 1949, *m., cons.* 1984, *elected* 1994
1999	*Guildford* (8th), John Warren Gladwin, *b.* 1942, *m., cons.* 1994, *elected* 1994
1999	*Portsmouth* (8th), Kenneth William Stevenson, *b.* 1949, *m., cons.* 1995, *elected* 1995
1999	*Derby* (6th), Jonathan Sansbury Bailey, *b.* 1940, *m., cons.* 1992, *elected* 1995
1999	*St Albans* (9th), Christopher William Herbert, *b.* 1944, *m., cons.* 1995, *elected* 1995
2000	*Chelmsford* (8th), John Freeman Perry, *b.* 1935, *m., cons.* 1989, *elected* 1996
2001	*Peterborough* (37th), Ian Cundy, *b.* 1945, *m., cons.* 1992, *elected* 1996
2001	*Chester* (40th), Peter Robert Forster, Ph.D., *b.* 1950, *cons.* 1996, *elected* 1996
2002	*St Edmundsbury and Ipswich* (9th), (John Hubert) Richard Lewis, *b.* 1943, *m., cons.* 1992, *elected* 1997
Awaiting introduction	*Truro* (14th), William Ind, *b.* 1942, *m., cons.* 1987, *elected* 1997
Awaiting introduction	*Worcester* (112th), Peter Stephen Maurice Selby, *b.* 1941, *cons.* 1984, *elected* 1997
Awaiting introduction	*Newcastle* (11th), (John) Martin Wharton, *b.* 1944, *m., cons.* 1992, *elected* 1997

Bishops awaiting seats, in order of seniority
(as at 31 August 2002)

Sheffield (6th), John Nicholls, *b.* 1943, *m., cons.* 1990, *elected* 1997
Coventry (8th), Colin J. Bennetts, *b.* 1940, *m., cons.* 1994, *elected* 1998
Liverpool (7th), James Jones, *b.* 1948, *m., cons.* 1994, *elected* 1998
Leicester (6th), Timothy John Stevens, *b.* 1946, *m., cons.* 1999, *elected* 1999
Southwell (10th), George Henry Cassidy, *b.* 1942, *m., cons.* 1999, *elected* 1999
Norwich (71st), Graham R. James, *b.* 1951, *m., cons.* 1993, *elected* 1999
Exeter (70th), Michael L. Langrish, *b.* 1946, *m., cons.* 1993, *elected* 2000
Ripon and Leeds (12th), John R. Packer, *b.* 1946, *m., cons.*1996, *elected* 2000
Ely (68th) Dr. Anthony Russell, *b.* 1943, *m., cons.* 1988, *elected* 2000
Carlisle (65th) Graham Dow, *b.* 1942, *m., cons.* 1985, *elected* 2000
Chichester (102nd) John Hind, *b.* 1945, *cons.* 1991, *elected* 2000
Lincoln (71st) Dr John Saxbee *b.* 1946, *cons.* 1994, *elected* 2001
Bath & Wells (77th) Peter Price *b.* 1944, m., *cons.* 1997, *elected* 2002
Birmingham (8th) Dr John Tucker Mugabi Sentamu, Ph.D., *b.* 1949, *m., cons.* 1996, *elected* 2002
Wakefield (12th) *vacant*
Bradford (9th) David James *b.* 1945, *elected* 2002

COURTESY TITLES

From this list it will be seen that, for example, the Marquess of Blandford is heir to the Dukedom of Marlborough, and Viscount Amberley to the Earldom of Russell. Titles of second heirs are also given, and the courtesy title of the father of a second heir is indicated by *; e.g. Earl of Burlington, eldest son of *Marquess of Hartington
For forms of address, see page 133

MARQUESSES

* Blandford – Marlborough, D.
Bowmont and Cessford – Roxburghe, D.
Douglas and Clydesdale – Hamilton, D.
* Douro – Wellington, D.
Graham – Montrose, D.
Hamilton – Abercorn, D.
* Hartington – Devonshire, D.
Kildare – Leinster, D.
Stafford – Sutherland, D.
* Tavistock – Bedford, D.
Tullibardine – Atholl, D.
* Worcester – Beaufort, D.

EARLS

Aboyne – Huntly, M.
Ancram – Lothian, M.
Arundel and Surrey – Norfolk, D.
* Bective – Headfort, M.
* Belfast – Donegall, M.
Brecknock – Camden, M.
Burford – St Albans, D.
Burlington – *Hartington, M.
* Cardigan – Ailesbury, M.
Compton – Northampton, M.
* Dalkeith – Buccleuch, D.
* Euston – Grafton, D.
Glamorgan – *Worcester, M.
Grosvenor – Westminster, D.
Haddo – Aberdeen and Temair, M.
Hillsborough – Downshire, M.
Hopetoun – Linlithgow, M.
March and Kinrara – Richmond, D.
Medina – Milford Haven, M.
* Mount Charles – Conyngham, M.
Mornington – *Douro, M.
Mulgrave – Normanby, M.
Percy – Northumberland, D.
Ronaldshay – Zetland, M.
* St Andrews – Kent, D.
Shelburne – Lansdowne, M.
* Southesk – Fife, D.

Sunderland – *Blandford, M.
* Tyrone – Waterford, M.
Ulster – Gloucester, D.
* Uxbridge – Anglesey, M.
Wiltshire – Winchester, M.
Yarmouth – Hertford, M.

VISCOUNTS

Alexander – Caledon, E.
Althorp – Spencer, E.
Amberley – Russell, E.
Andover – Suffolk and Berkshire, E.
Anson – Lichfield, E.
Asquith – Oxford and Asquith, E.
Boringdon – Morley, E.
Borodale – Beatty, E.
Boyle – Shannon, E.
Brocas – Jellicoe, E.
Campden – Gainsborough, E.
Carlow – Portarlington, E.
Carlton – Wharncliffe, E.
Castlereagh – Londonderry, M.
Chelsea – Cadogan, E.
Chewton – Waldegrave, E.
Chichester – *Belfast, E.
Clanfield – Peel, E.
Clive – Powis, E.
Coke – Leicester, E.
Corry – Belmore, E.
Corvedale – Baldwin of Bewdley, E.
Cranborne – Salisbury, M.
Cranley – Onslow, E.
Crichton – Erne, E.
Curzon – Howe, E.
Dangan – Cowley, E.
Dawick – Haig, E.
Drumlanrig – Queensberry, M.
Duncannon – Bessborough, E.
Dungarvan – Cork and Orrery, E.
Dunluce – Antrim, E.
Dunwich – Stradbroke, E.
Dupplin – Kinnoull, E.
Ednam – Dudley, E.
Encombe – Eldon, E.
Enfield – Strafford, E.
Erleigh – Reading, M.
Errington – Cromer, E.
FitzHarris – Malmesbury, E.
Folkestone – Radnor, E.
Forbes – Granard, E.

Garmoyle – Cairns, E.
Garnock – Lindsay, E.
Glenapp – Inchcape, E.
Glentworth – Limerick, E.
Grey de Wilton – Wilton, E.
Grimstone – Verulam, E.
Gwynedd – Lloyd George of Dwyfor, E.
Hawkesbury – Liverpool, E.
Hinchingbrooke – Sandwich, E.
Ikerrin – Carrick, E.
Ingestre – Shrewsbury, E.
Ipswich – *Euston, E.
Jocelyn – Roden, E.
Kelburn – Glasgow, E.
Kilwarlin – Hillsborough, E.
Kingsborough – Kingston, E.
Kirkwall – Orkney, E.
Knebworth – Lytton, E.
Lascelles – Harewood, E.
Linley – Snowdon, E.
Loftus – Ely, M.
Lowther – Lonsdale, E.
Lumley – Scarbrough, E.
Lymington – Portsmouth, E.
Macmillan of Ovenden – Stockton, E.
Maitland – Lauderdale, E.
Malden – Essex, E.
Mandeville – Manchester, D.
Melgund – Minto, E.
Merton – Nelson, E.
Moore – Drogheda, E.
Newport – Bradford, E.
Newry and Mourne – Kilmorey, E.
Petersham – Harrington, E.
Pollington – Mexborough, E.
Raynham – Townshend, M.
Reidhaven – Seafield, E.
Ruthven of Canberra – Gowrie, E.
St Cyres – Iddesleigh, E.
Sandon – Harrowby, E.
Savernake – *Cardigan, E.
Slane – *Mount Charles, E.
Somerton – Normanton, E.
Stopford – Courtown, E.
Stormont – Mansfield, E.
Strathallan – Perth, E.
Stuart – Castle Stewart, E.
Suirdale – Donoughmore, E.
Tamworth – Ferrers, E.
Tarbat – Cromartie, E.
Vaughan – Lisburne, E.
Weymouth – Bath, M.

Windsor – Plymouth, E.
Wolmer – Selborne, E.
Woodstock – Portland, E.

BARONS (LORDS)

Aberdour – Morton, E.
Apsley – Bathurst, E.
Ardee – Meath, E.
Ashley – Shaftesbury, E.
Balgonie – Leven and Melville, E.
Balniel – Crawford and Balcarres, E.
Berriedale – Caithness, E.
Bingham – Lucan, E.
Binning – Haddington, E.
Brooke – Warwick, E.
Bruce – Elgin, E.
Buckhurst – De La Warr, E.
Burghley – Exeter, M.
Cardross – Buchan, E.
Carnegie – *Southesk, E.
Clifton – Darnley, E.
Cochrane – Dundonald, E.
Courtenay – Devon, E.
Dalmeny – Rosebery, E.
Doune – Moray, E.
Downpatrick – *St Andrews, E.
Dunglass – Home, E.
Eliot – St Germans, E.
Eskdail – *Dalkeith, E.
Formartine – *Haddo, E.
Gillford – Clanwilliam, E.
Glamis – Strathmore, E.
Greenock – Cathcart, E.
Guernsey – Aylesford, E.
Hay – Erroll, E.
Herbert – Pembroke, E.
Howard of Effingham – Effingham, E.
Howland – *Tavistock, M.
Hyde – Clarendon, E.
Inverurie – Kintore, E.
Irwin – Halifax, E.
Johnstone – Annandale and Hartfell, E.
Kenlis – *Bective, E.
Langton – Temple of Stowe, E.
La Poer – *Tyrone, E.
Leslie – Rothes, E.
Loughborough – Rosslyn, E.
Maltravers – *Arundel and Surrey, E.
Mauchline – Loudoun, C.
Medway – Cranbrook, E.
Montgomerie – Eglinton and Winton, E.
Moreton – Ducie, E.
Mount Stuart – Bute, M
Naas – Mayo, E.

Neidpath – *Wemyss and March*, E.
Norreys – *Lindsey and Abingdon*, E.
Ogilvy – *Airlie*, E.
Oxmantown – *Rosse*, E.

Paget de Beaudesert – *Uxbridge*, E.
Porchester – *Carnarvon*, E.
Ramsay – *Dalhousie*, E.
Romsey – *Mountbatten of Burma*, C

Scrymgeour – *Dundee*, E.
Seymour – *Somerset*, D.
Stanley – *Derby*, E.
Strathnaver – *Sutherland*, C.

Wodehouse – *Kimberley*, E.
Worsley – *Yarborough*, E.

PEERS' SURNAMES WHICH DIFFER FROM THEIR TITLES

The following symbols indicate the rank of the peer holding each title:

C.   Countess
D.   Duke
E.   Earl
M.   Marquess
V.   Viscount
*   Life Peer

Where no designation is given, the title is that of an hereditary Baron or Baroness

Abney-Hastings – *Loudoun*, C.
Acheson – *Gosford*, E.
Adderley – *Norton*
Addington – *Sidmouth*, V.
Adebowale – *A. of Thornes**
Agar – *Normanton*, E.
Aitken – *Beaverbrook*
Akers-Douglas – *Chilston*, V.
Alexander – *A. of Tunis*, E.
Alexander – *A. of Weedon**
Alexander – *Caledon*, E.
Allen – *A. of Abbeydale**
Allen – *Croham**
Allsopp – *Hindlip*
Alton – *A. of Liverpool**
Anderson – *Waverley*, V.
Anelay – *A. of St Johns**
Annesley – *Valentia*, V.
Anson – *Lichfield*, E.
Archer – *A. of Sandwell**
Archer – *A. of Weston-super-Mare**
Armstrong – *A. of Ilminster**
Armstrong-Jones – *Snowdon*, E.
Arthur – *Glenarthur*
Arundell – *Talbot of Malahide*
Ashdown – *A. of Norton-sub-Hamdon**
Ashley – *A. of Stoke**
Ashley-Cooper – *Shaftesbury*, E.
Ashton – *A. of Hyde*
Ashton – *A. of Upholland**
Asquith – *Oxford and Asquith*, E.
Assheton – *Clitheroe*
Astley – *Hastings*
Astor – *A. of Hever*
Aubrey-Fletcher – *Braye*

Bailey – *Glanusk*
Baillie – *Burton*
Baillie Hamilton – *Haddington*, E.
Baker – *B. of Dorking**
Baldwin – *B. of Bewdley*, E.
Balfour – *B. of Inchrye*
Balfour – *Kinross*
Balfour – *Riverdale*
Bampfylde – *Poltimore*
Banbury – *B. of Southam*
Barber – *B. of Tewkesbury**
Baring – *Ashburton*
Baring – *Cromer*, E.
Baring – *Howick of Glendale*
Baring – *Northbrook*
Baring – *Revelstoke*
Barker – *Trumpington**
Barnes – *Gorell*
Barnewall – *Trimlestown*
Bassam – *B. of Brighton**
Bathurst – *Bledisloe*, V.
Beauclerk – *St Albans*, D.
Beaumont – *Allendale*, V.
Beaumont – *B. of Whitley**
Beckett – *Grimthorpe*
Benn – *Stansgate*, V.
Bennet – *Tankerville*, E.
Bentinck – *Portland*, E.-
Beresford – *Decies*
Beresford – *Waterford*, M.
Bernstein – *B. of Craigweil**
Berry – *Camrose*, V.
Berry – *Kemsley*, V.
Bertie – *Lindsey*, E.
Best – *Wynford*
Bethell – *Westbury*
Bewicke-Copley – *Cromwell*
Bigham – *Mersey*, V.
Bingham – *B. of Cornhill**
Bingham – *Clanmorris*
Bingham – *Lucan*, E.
Black – *B. of Crossharbour**
Bligh – *Darnley*, E.
Blyth – *B. of Rowington**
Bootle-Wilbraham – *Skelmersdale*
Boscawen – *Falmouth*, V.
Boston – *B. of Faversham**
Bourke – *Mayo*, E.
Bowes Lyon – *Strathmore*, E.
Bowyer – *Denham*
Boyd – *Kilmarnock*
Boyle – *Cork and Orrery*, E.
Boyle – *Glasgow*, E.
Boyle – *Shannon*, E.
Brabazon – *Meath*, E.

Brand – *Hampden*, V.
Brassey – *B. of Apethorpe*
Brett – *Esher*, V.
Bridge – *B. of Harwich**
Bridgeman – *Bradford*, E.
Brittan – *B. of Spennithorne**
Brodrick – *Midleton*, V.
Brooke – *Alanbrooke*, V.
Brooke – *B. of Alverthorpe**
Brooke – *Brookeborough*, V.
Brooke – *B. of Sutton Mandeville**
Brooks – *B. of Tremorfa**
Brooks – *Crawshaw*
Brougham – *Brougham and Vaux*
Broughton – *Fairhaven*
Browne – *Kilmaine*
Browne – *B. of Madingley**
Browne – *Oranmore and Browne*
Browne – *Sligo*, M.
Bruce – *Aberdare*
Bruce – *Balfour of Burleigh*
Bruce – *B. of Donington**
Bruce – *Elgin and Kincardine*, E.
Brudenell-Bruce – *Ailesbury*, M.
Buchan – *Tweedsmuir*
Buckley – *Wrenbury*
Butler – *B. of Brockwell**
Butler – *Carrick*, E.
Butler – *Dunboyne*
Butler – *Mountgarret*, V.
Buxton – *B. of Alsa**
Byng – *Strafford*, E.
Byng – *Torrington*, V.
Callaghan – *C. of Cardiff**
Cambell-Savours – *C.-S. of Allerdale**
Cameron – *C. of Lochbroom**
Campbell – *Argyll*, D.
Campbell – *C. of Alloway**
Campbell – *C. of Croy**
Campbell – *Cawdor*, E.
Campbell – *Colgrain*
Campbell – *Stratheden and Campbell*
Campbell-Gray – *Gray*
Canning – *Garvagh*
Capell – *Essex*, E.
Carington – *Carrington*
Carlisle – *C. of Berriew**
Carlisle – *C. of Bucklow**
Carnegie – *Fife*, D.
Carnegie – *Northesk*, E.

Carr – *C. of Hadley**
Cary – *Falkland*, V.
Caulfeild – *Charlemont*, V.
Cavendish – *C. of Furness**
Cavendish – *Chesham*
Cavendish – *Devonshire*, D.
Cavendish – *Waterpark*
Cayzer – *Rotherwick*
Cecil – *Amherst of Hackney*
Cecil – *Exeter*, M.
Cecil – *Rockley*
Cecil – *Salisbury*, M.
Chalker – *C. of Wallasey**
Chaloner – *Gisborough*
Channon – *Kelvedon**
Charteris – *Wemyss and March*, E.
Chetwynd-Talbot – *Shrewsbury*, E.
Chichester – *Donegall*, M.
Child Villiers – *Jersey*, E.
Cholmondeley – *Delamere*
Chubb – *Hayter*
Clark – *C. of Kempston**
Clarke – *C. of Hampstead**
Clegg-Hill – *Hill*, V.
Clifford – *C. of Chudleigh*
Cochrane – *C. of Cults*
Cochrane – *Dundonald*, E.
Cocks – *Somers*
Cohen – *C. of Pimlico**
Cokayne – *Cullen of Ashbourne*
Coke – *Leicester*, E.
Cole – *Enniskillen*, E.
Collier – *Monkswell*
Colville – *Clydesmuir*
Colville – *C. of Culross*, V.
Compton – *Northampton*, M.
Condon – *C. of Langdon Green**
Conolly-Carew – *Carew*
Constantine – *C. of Stanmore**
Cooke – *C. of Islandreagh**
Cooke – *C. of Thorndon**
Cooper – *Norwich*, V
Cope – *C. of Berkeley**
Corbett – *C. of Castle Vale**.
Corbett – *Rowallan*
Cornwall-Leigh – *Grey of Condor*
Courtenay – *Devon*, E.
Craig – *C. of Radley**
Craig – *Craigavon*, V.
Crichton – *Erne*, E.
Crichton-Stuart – *Bute*, M.
Cripps – *Parmoor*

Crossley – *Somerleyton*
Cubitt – *Ashcombe*
Cunliffe-Lister – *Masham of Ilton**
Cunliffe-Lister – *Swinton, E.*
Currie – *C. of Marylebone**
Curzon – *Howe, E.*
Curzon – *Scarsdale, V.*
Cust – *Brownlow*
Dalrymple – *Stair, E.*
Daubeny de Moleyns – *Ventry*
Davies – *D. of Coity**
Davies – *Darwen*
Davies – *D. of Oldham**
Davison – *Broughshane*
Dawnay – *Downe, V.*
Dawson-Damer – *Portarlington, E.*
Dean – *D. of Harptree**
Dean – *D. of Thornton-le-Fylde**
Deane – *Muskerry*
de Courcy – *Kingsale*
de Grey – *Walsingham*
Delacourt-Smith – *Delacourt Smith of Alteryn**
Denison – *Londesborough*
Denison-Pender – *Pender*
Devereux – *Hereford, V.*
Dewar – *Forteviot*
De Yarburgh-Bateson – *Deramore*
Dixon – *Glentoran*
Dodson – *Monk Bretton*
Donaldson – *D. of Lymington**
Dormand – *D. of Easington**
Douglas – *Morton, E.*
Douglas – *Queensberry, M.*
Douglas-Hamilton – *Hamilton, D.*
Douglas-Hamilton – *Selkirk, E.*
Douglas-Hamilton – *Selkirk of Douglas**
Douglas-Home – *Dacre*
Douglas-Home – *Home, E.*
Douglas-Pennant – *Penrhyn*
Douglas-Scott-Montagu – *Montagu of Beaulieu*
Drummond – *Perth, E.*
Drummond of Megginch – *Strange*
Dugdale – *Crathorne*
Duke – *Merrivale*
Duncombe – *Feversham*
Dundas – *Melville, V.*
Dundas – *Zetland, M.*
Eady – *Swinfen*
Eccles – *E. of Moulton**
Eden – *Auckland*
Eden – *E. of Winton**
Eden – *Henley*
Edgcumbe – *Mount Edgcumbe, E.*

Edmondson – *Sandford*
Edwardes – *Kensington*
Edwards – *Crickhowell**
Egerton – *Sutherland, D.*
Eliot – *St Germans, E.*
Elliott - *E. of Morpeth**
Elliot-Murray-Kynynmound – *Minto, E.*
Ellis – *Seaford*
Erskine – *Buchan, E.*
Erskine – *Mar and Kellie, E.*
Erskine-Murray – *Elibank*
Evans – *E. of Parkside**
Evans – *E. of Temple Guiting**
Evans – *E. of Watford**
Evans – *Mountevans*
Evans-Freke – *Carbery*
Eve – *Silsoe*
Ewing – *E. of Kirkford**
Fairfax – *F. of Cameron*
Falconer – *F. of Thoroton**
Fane – *Westmorland, E.*
Farrington – *F. of Ribbleton**
Faulkner – *F. of Worcester**
Fearn – *F. of Southport**
Feilding – *Denbigh, E.*
Felton – *Seaford*
Fellowes – *De Ramsey*
Fermor-Hesketh – *Hesketh*
Fiennes – *Saye and Sele*
Fiennes-Clinton – *Lincoln, E.*
Finch Hatton – *Winchilsea, E.*
Finch-Knightley – *Aylesford, E.*
Finlay - *F. of Llandaff**
Fisher – *F. of Rednal**
Fitzalan-Howard – *Herries of Terregles*
Fitzalan-Howard – *Norfolk, D.*
FitzGerald – *Leinster, D.*
Fitzherbert – *Stafford*
FitzRoy – *Grafton, D.*
FitzRoy – *Southampton*
FitzRoy Newdegate – *Daventry, V.*
Fletcher-Vane – *Inglewood*
Flower – *Ashbrook, V.*
Foljambe – *Liverpool, E.*
Forbes – *Granard, E*
Forsyth – *F. of Drumlean**.
Forwood – *Arlington*
Foster – *F. of Thames Bank**
Fowler – *F. of Sutton Caulfield**
Fox-Strangways – *Ilchester, E.*
Frankland – *Zouche*
Fraser – *F. of Carmyllie**
Fraser – *F. of Kilmorack**
Fraser – *Lovat*
Fraser – *Saltoun*
Fraser – *Strathalmond*
Freeman-Grenville – *Kinloss*
Fremantle – *Cottesloe*

French – *De Freyne*
Fyfe – *F. of Fairfield**
Galbraith – *Strathclyde*
Ganzoni – *Belstead*
Gardner – *G. of Parkes**
Gathorne-Hardy – *Cranbrook, E.*
Gibbs – *Aldenham*
Gibbs – *Wraxall*
Gibson – *Ashbourne*
Gibson – *G. of Market Ransen**
Giffard – *Halsbury, E.*
Gilbey – *Vaux of Harrowden*
Gilmour – *G. of Craigmillar**
Gladwin – *G. of Clee**
Glyn – *Wolverton*
Godley – *Kilbracken*
Goff – *G. of Chieveley**
Golding – *G. of Newcastle-under-Lyme**
Gordon – *Aberdeen, M.*
Gordon – *G. of Strathblane**
Gordon – *Huntly, M.*
Gordon Lennox – *Richmond, D.*
Gore – *Arran, E.*
Gould – *G. of Potternewton**
Graham – *G. of Edmonton**
Graham – *Montrose, D.*
Graham-Toler – *Norbury, E.*
Granshaw – *Northover**
Grant of Grant – *Strathspey*
Granville – *G. of Eye**
Gray – *G. of Contin**
Greaves – *Dysart, C.*
Greenall – *Daresbury*
Greene – *G. of Harrow Weald**
Greville – *Warwick, E.*
Griffiths – *G. of Fforestfach**
Grigg – *Altrincham*
Grimston – *G. of Westbury*
Grimston – *Verulam, E.*
Grosvenor – *Westminster, D.*
Grosvenor – *Wilton and Ebury, E*
Guest – *Wimborne, V*
Gueterbock – *Berkeley*
Guinness – *Iveagh, E.*
Guinness – *Moyne*
Gully – *Selby, V.*
Gummer – *Chadlington**
Gurdon – *Cranworth*
Guthrie – *G. of Craigiebank**
Gwynne Jones – *Chalfont**
Hamilton – *Abercorn, D.*
Hamilton – *Belhaven and Stenton*
Hamilton – *Dudley*
Hamilton – *H. of Dalzell*
Hamilton – *Holm Patrick*

Hamilton-Russell – *Boyne, V.*
Hamilton-Smith – *Colwyn*
Hanbury-Tracy – *Sudeley*
Handcock – *Castlemaine*
Hannay – *H. of Chiswick**
Harbord-Hamond – *Suffield*
Harding – *H. of Petherton*
Hardinge – *H. of Penshurst*
Hardy – *H. of Wath**
Hare – *Blakenham, V.*
Hare – *Listowel, E.*
Harmsworth – *Rothermere, V.*
Harris – *H. of Haringey**
Harris – *H. of High Cross**
Harris – *H. of Peckham**
Harris – *H. of Richmond**
Harris – *Malmesbury, E.*
Harvey – *H. of Tasburgh*
Hastings Bass – *Huntingdon, E.*
Hay – *Erroll, E.*
Hay – *Kinnoull, E.*
Hay – *Tweeddale, M.*
Heathcote-Drummond-Willoughby – *Willoughby de Eresby*
Hely-Hutchinson – *Donoughmore, E.*
Henderson – *Faringdon*
Hennessy – *Windlesham*
Henniker-Major – *Henniker*
Hepburne-Scott – *Polwarth*
Herbert – *Carnarvon, E.*
Herbert – *Hemingford*
Herbert – *Pembroke, E.*
Herbert – *Powis, E.*
Hervey – *Bristol, M.*
Heseltine – *H. of Thenford**
Hewitt – *Lifford, V.*
Hicks Beach – *St Aldwyn, E.*
Hill – *Downshire, M.*
Hill – *Sandys*
Hill-Trevor – *Trevor*
Hilton – *H. of Eggardon**
Hobart-Hampden – *Buckinghamshire, E.*
Hobhouse – *H. of Woodborough**
Hodgson – *H. of Astley Abbotts**
Hogg – *Hailsham, V.*
Hogg – *H. of Cumbernauld**
Holland-Hibbert – *Knutsford, V.*
Hollis – *H. of Heigham**
Holme – *H. of Cheltenham**
Holmes à Court – *Heytesbury*
Hood – *Bridport, V.*
Hope – *Glendevon*
Hope – *H. of Craighead**
Hope – *Linlithgow, M.*
Hope – *Rankeillour*

Hope Johnstone – *Annandale and Hartfell, E.*
Hope-Morley – *Hollenden*
Hopkinson – *Colyton*
Hore Ruthven – *Gowrie, E.*
Hovell-Thurlow-Cumming-Bruce – *Thurlow*
Howard – *Carlisle, E.*
Howard – *Effingham, E.*
Howard – *H. of Penrith*
Howard – *Strathcona*
Howard – *Suffolk and Berkshire, E.*
Howarth – *H. of Breckland*
Howe – *H. of Aberavon*
Howe – *H. of Idlicote*
Howell – *H. of Guildford*
Howells – *Geraint*
Howells – *H. of St. Davids*
Howie – *H. of Troon*
Hubbard – *Addington*
Huggins – *Malvern, V.*
Hughes – *H. of Woodside*
Hughes – *Islwyn*
Hughes-Young – *St Helens*
Hunt – *H. of Chesterton*
Hunt – *H. of Kings Heath*
Hunt – *H. of Tanworth*
Hunt – *H. of Wirral*
Hurd – *H. of Westwell*
Hussey – *H. of North Bradley*
Hutchinson – *H. of Lullington*
Ingrams – *Darcy de Knayth*
Innes-Ker – *Roxburghe, D.*
Inskip – *Caldecote, V.*
Irby – *Boston*
Irvine – *I. of Lairg*
Isaacs – *Reading, M.*
James – *J. of Holland Park*
James – *Northbourne*
Janner – *J. of Braunstone*
Jauncey – *J. of Tullichettle*
Jay – *J. of Paddington*
Jebb – *Gladwyn*
Jenkin – *J. of Roding*
Jenkins – *J. of Hillhead*
Jenkins – *J. of Putney*
Jervis – *St Vincent, V.*
Jocelyn – *Roden, E.*
Jolliffe – *Hylton*
Jones - *J. of Deeside*
Joynson-Hicks – *Brentford, V.*
Kay-Shuttleworth – *Shuttleworth*
Kearley – *Devonport, V.*
Keith – *K. of Castleacre*
Keith – *Kintore, E.*
Kemp – *Rochdale, V.*
Kennedy – *Ailsa, M*
Kennedy – *K. of the Shaws*.
Kenworthy – *Strabolgi*
Keppel – *Albemarle, E.*
Kerr – *Lothian, M.*
Kerr – *Teviot*

Kilpatrick – *K. of Kincraig*
King – *Lovelace, E.*
King – *K. of Wartnaby*
King – *K. of West Bromwich*
King-Tenison – *Kingston, E.*
Kirkham – *Berners*
Kitchener – *K. of Khartoum, E.*
Knatchbull – *Brabourne*
Knatchbull – *Mountbatten of Burma, C.*
Knight – *K. of Collingtree*
Knox – *Ranfurly, E.*
Laing – *L. of Dunphail*
Lamb – *Rochester*
Lambton – *Durham, E.*
Lamont – *L. of Lerwick*
Lampson – *Killearn*
Lane – *L. of Horsell*
Lang – *L. of Monkton*
Lascelles – *Harewood, E.*
Law – *Coleraine*
Law – *Ellenborough*
Lawrence – *Trevethin and Oaksey*
Lawson – *Burnham*
Lawson – *L. of Blaby*
Lawson-Johnston – *Luke*
Lea – *L. of Crondall*
Leckie – *Younger of Prestwick*
Legge – *Dartmouth, E.*
Legh – *Grey of Codnor*
Legh – *Newton*
Leigh-Pemberton – *Kingsdown*
Leith – *Burgh*
Lennox-Boyd – *Boyd of Merton, V.*
Le Poer Trench – *Clancarty, E.*
Leslie – *Rothes, E.*
Leslie Melville – *Leven and Melville, E.*
Lester – *L. of Herne Hill*
Levene – *L. of Portsoken*
Leveson-Gower – *Granville, E.*
Lewis – *L. of Newnham*
Lewis – *Merthyr*
Liddell – *Ravensworth*
Lindesay-Bethune – *Lindsay, E.*
Lindsay – *Crawford, E.*
Lindsay – *L. of Birker*
Linklater – *L. of Butterstone*
Littleton – *Hatherton*
Lloyd – *L. of Berwick*
Lloyd – *L. of Highbury*
Lloyd George – *Lloyd George of Dwyfor, E.*
Lloyd George – *Tenby, V.*
Lloyd-Mostyn – *Mostyn*
Loder – *Wakehurst*
Lofthouse – *L. of Pontefract*
Lopes – *Roborough*
Lour – *Carnegy of Lour*

Low – *Aldington*
Lowry-Corry – *Belmore, E.*
Lowther – *Lonsdale, E.*
Lowther – *Ullswater, V.*
Lubbock – *Avebury*
Lucas – *L. of Chilworth*
Lumley – *Scarbrough, E.*
Lumley-Savile – *Savile*
Lyon-Dalberg-Acton – *Acton*
Lysaght – *Lisle*
Lyttelton – *Chandos, V.*
Lyttelton – *Cobham, V.*
Lytton Cobbold – *Cobbold*
McAlpine – *M. of West Green*
Macaulay – *M. of Bragar*
McClintock-Bunbury – *Rathdonnell*
McColl – *M. of Dulwich*
Macdonald – *M. of Tradeston*
McDonnell – *Antrim, E.*
Macfarlane – *M. of Bearsden*
McFarlane – *M. of Llandaff*
MacGregor – *M. of Pulham Market*
McIntosh – *M. of Haringey*
McIntosh – *M. of Hudnall*
Mackay – *Inchcape, E.*
Mackay – *M. of Clashfern*
Mackay – *M. of Drumadoon*
Mackay – *Reay*
Mackay – *Tanlaw*
MacKenzie – *M. of Culkein*
MacKenzie – *M. of Framwellgate*
Mackenzie – *Cromartie, E.*
Mackie – *M. of Benshie*
Mackintosh – *M. of Halifax, V.*
McLaren – *Aberconway*
MacLaurin – *M. of Knebworth*
MacLennan – *M. of Rogart*
Macmillan – *Stockton, E.*
Macpherson – *M. of Drumochter*
Macpherson – *Strathcarron*
Maffey – *Rugby*
Maginnis – *M. of Drumglass*
Maitland – *Lauderdale, E.*
Makgill – *Oxfuird, V.*
Makins – *Sherfield*
Manners – *Rutland, D.*
Manningham-Buller – *Dilhorne, V.*
Mansfield – *Sandhurst*
Marks – *M. of Broughton*
Marquis – *Woolton, E.*
Marshall – *M. of Knightsbridge*
Marsham – *Romney, E.*

Martyn-Hemphill – *Hemphill*
Mason – *M. of Barnsley*
Massey – *M. of Darwen*
Masters – *Noakes*
Maude – *Hawarden, V.*
Maxwell – *de Ros*
Maxwell – *Farnham*
May – *M. of Oxford*
Mayhew – *M. of Twysden*
Meade – *Clanwilliam, E.*
Mercer Nairne Petty-Fitzmaurice – *Lansdowne, M.*
Millar – *Inchyra*
Miller – *M. of Chiltorne Domer*
Miller – *M. of Hendon*
Milner – *M. of Leeds*
Mitchell-Thomson – *Selsdon*
Mitford – *Redesdale*
Molyneux – *M. of Killead*
Monckton – *M. of Brenchley, V.*
Monckton-Arundell – *Galway, V.*
Mond – *Melchett*
Money-Coutts – *Latymer*
Monro – *M. of Langholm*
Montagu – *Manchester, D.*
Montagu – *Sandwich, E.*
Montagu – *Swaythling*
Montagu Douglas Scott – *Buccleuch, D.*
Montagu Stuart Wortley – *Wharncliffe, E.*
Montague – *Amwell*
Montgomerie – *Eglinton, E.*
Montgomery – *M. of Alamein, V.*
Moore – *Drogheda, E.*
Moore – *M. of Lower Marsh*
Moore – *M. of Wolvercote*
Moore-Brabazon – *Brabazon of Tara*
Moreton – *Ducie, E*
Morgan – *M. of Huyton*.
Morris – *Killanin*
Morris – *M. of Aberavon*
Morris – *M. of Manchester*
Morris – *Naseby*
Morris – *M. of Kenwood*
Morrison – *Dunrossil, V.*
Morrison – *Margadale*
Moser – *M. of Regents Park*
Mosley – *Ravensdale*
Mountbatten – *Milford Haven, M.*
Muff – *Calverley*
Mulholland – *Dunleath*
Murray – *Atholl, D.*
Murray – *Dunmore, E.*
Murray – *Mansfield and Mansfield, E.*
Murray – *M. of Epping Forest*

Murton – *M. of Lindisfarne**
Nall-Cain – *Brocket*
Napier – *Napier and Ettrick*
Napier – *N. of Magdala*
Needham – *Kilmorey, E.*
Neill – *N. of Bladen**
Nelson – *N. of Stafford*
Nevill – *Abergavenny, M.*
Neville – *Braybrooke*
Newton – *N. of Braintree**
Nicholls – *N. of Birkenhead**
Nicolson – *Carnock*
Nicholson – *N. of Winterbourne**
Nivison – *Glendyne*
Noel – *Gainsborough, E.*
North – *Guilford, E.*
Northcote – *Iddesleigh, E.*
Norton – *Grantley*
Norton – *N. of Louth**
Norton – *Rathcreedan*
Nugent – *Westmeath, E.*
Oakeshott – *O. of Seagrove Bay**
O'Brien – *Inchiquin*
Ogilvie-Grant – *Seafield, E.*
Ogilvy – *Airlie, E.*
Oliver – *O. of Aylmerton**
O'Neill – *O'N of Bengarve**
O'Neill – *Rathcavan*
Orde-Powlett – *Bolton*
Ormsby-Gore – *Harlech*
Ouseley – *O. of Peckham Rye**
Page – *Whaddon**
Paget – *Anglesey, M.*
Pakenham – *Longford, E.*
Pakington – *Hampton*
Palmer – *Lucas and Dingwall*
Palmer – *Selborne, E.*
Park – *P. of Monmouth**
Parker – *Macclesfield, E.*
Parker – *Morley, E.*
Parnell – *Congleton*
Parsons – *Rosse, E.*
Patel – *P. of Blackburn**
Paulet – *Winchester, M.*
Peake – *Ingleby, V.*
Pearson – *Cowdray, V.*
Pearson – *P. of Rannoch**
Pease – *Gainford*
Pease – *Wardington*
Pelham – *Chichester, E.*
Pelham – *Yarborough, E.*
Pellew – *Exmouth, V*
Pendry – *P. of Stalybridge**.
Penny – *Marchwood, V.*
Pepys – *Cottenham, E.*
Perceval – *Egmont, E.*
Percy – *Northumberland, D.*
Perry – *P. of Southwark**
Perry – *P. of Walton**
Pery – *Limerick, E.*
Peyton – *P. of Yeovil**
Philipps – *Milford*
Philipps – *St Davids, V.*

Phillips – *P. of Sudbury**
Phillips – *P. of Worth Matravers**
Phipps – *Normanby, M.*
Pilkington – *P. of Oxenford**
Plant – *P. of Highfield**
Platt – *P. of Writtle**
Pleydell-Bouverie – *Radnor, E.*
Plummer – *P. of St Marylebone**
Plumptre – *Fitzwalter*
Plunkett – *Dunsany*
Plunkett – *Louth*
Pollock – *Hanworth, V.*
Pomeroy – *Harberton, V.*
Ponsonby – *Bessborough, E.*
Ponsonby – *de Mauley*
Ponsonby – *P. of Shulbrede*
Ponsonby – *Sysonby*
Porter – *P. of Luddenham**
Powell – *P. of Bayswater**
Powys – *Lilford*
Pratt – *Camden, M.*
Preston – *Gormanston, V.*
Primrose – *Rosebery, E.*
Prittie – *Dunalley*
Prout – *Kingsland**
Ramsay – *Dalhousie, E.*
Ramsay – *R. of Cartvale**
Ramsbotham – *Soulbury, V.*
Randall – *R. of St. Budeaux**
Rawlinson – *R. of Ewell**
Rees-Williams – *Ogmore*
Rendell – *R. of Babergh**
Renfrew – *R. of Kaimsthorn**
Renton – *R. of Mount Harry**
Renwick – *R. of Clifton**
Rhys – *Dynevor*
Richards – *Milverton*
Richardson – *R. of Calow**
Richardson – *R. of Duntisbourne**
Ritchie – *R. of Dundee*
Roberts – *Clwyd*
Roberts – *R. of Conway**
Robertson – *R. of Oakridge*
Robertson – *R. of Port Ellen**
Robertson – *Wharton*
Robinson – *Martonmere*
Roche – *Fermoy*
Rodd – *Rennell*
Rodger – *R. of Earlsferry**
Rodgers – *R. of Quarry Bank**
Rogers – *R. of Riverside**
Roll – *R. of Ipsden**
Roper-Curzon – *Teynham*
Rospigliosi – *Newburgh, E.*
Rous – *Stradbroke, E.*
Rowley-Conwy – *Langford*
Runciman – *R. of Doxford, V.*
Russell – *Ampthill*
Russell – *Bedford, D.*

Russell – *de Clifford*
Russell – *R. of Liverpool*
Ryder – *Harrowby, E.*
Ryder – *R. of Eaton Hastings**
Ryder – *R. of Wensum**
Sackville – *De La Warr, E.*
Sackville-West – *Sackville*
Sainsbury – *S. of Preston Candover**
Sainsbury – *S. of Turville**
St Aubyn – *St Levan*
St Clair – *Sinclair*
St Clair-Erskine – *Rosslyn, E.*
St John – *Bolingbroke and St John, V.*
St John – *St John of Blesso*
St John-Stevas – *St John of Fawsley**
St Leger – *Doneraile, V.*
Samuel – *Bearsted, V.*
Sanderson – *S. of Ayot*
Sanderson – *S. of Bowden**
Sandilands – *Torphichen*
Saumarez – *De Saumarez*
Savile – *Mexborough, E.*
Savile – *S. of Newdigate**
Scarlett – *Abinger*
Schreiber – *Marlesford**
Sclater-Booth – *Basing*
Scotland – *S. of Asthal**
Scott – *Eldon, E.*
Scott – *S. of Foscotte**
Scott – *S. of Needham Market**.
Scrymgeour – *Dundee, E.*
Seager – *Leighton of St Mellons*
Seely – *Mottistone*
Seyfried – *Herbert*
Seymour – *Hertford, M.*
Seymour – *Somerset, D.*
Sharp – *S. of Guildford**
Shaw – *Craigmyle*
Shaw – *S. of Northstead**
Sheldon – *S. of Ashdon-under-Lyne**
Sheppard – *S. of Didgemere**
Sheppard – *S. of Liverpool**
Shirley – *Ferrers, E.*
Short – *Glenamara**
Shutt – *S. of Greetland**
Siddeley – *Kenilworth*
Sidney – *De L'Isle, V.*
Simon – *S. of Glaisdale**
Simon – *S. of Highbury**
Simon – *S. of Wythenshawe*
Simpson – *S. of Dunkeld**
Sinclair – *Caithness, E.*
Sinclair – *S. of Cleeve*
Sinclair – *Thurso, V.*
Skeffington – *Massereene, V.*
Slynn – *S. of Hadley**
Smith – *Bicester*
Smith – *Hambleden, V.*
Smith – *Kirkhill**
Smith – *S. of Clifton**
Smith – *S. of Gilmorehill**

Smith – *S. of Leigh**
Somerset – *Beaufort, D.*
Somerset – *Raglan*
Soulsby – *S. of Swaffham Prior**
Spencer – *Churchill, V.*
Spencer-Churchill – *Marlborough, D.*
Spring Rice – *Monteagle of Brandon*
Stanhope – *Harrington, E.*
Stanley – *Derby, E.*
Stanley – *Stanley of Alderley and Sheffield*
Stapleton-Cotton – *Combermere, V.*
Steel – *S. of Aikwood**
Sterling – *S. of Plaistow**
Stevens – *S. of Ludgate**
Stevenson – *S. of Coddenham**
Stewart – *Galloway, E.*
Stewart – *Stewartby**
Stodart – *S. of Leaston**
Stoddart – *S. of Swindon**
Stone – *S. of Blackheath**
Stonor – *Camoys*
Stopford – *Courtown, E.*
Stourton – *Mowbray*
Strachey – *O'Hagan*
Strutt – *Belper*
Strutt – *Rayleigh*
Stuart – *Castle Stewart, E.*
Stuart – *Moray, E.*
Stuart – *S. of Findhorn, V.*
Suenson-Taylor – *Grantchester*
Sutherland – *S. of Houndwood**
Symons – *S. of Vernham Dean**
Taylor – *Kilclooney**
Taylor – *T. of Blackburn**
Taylor – *T. of Warwick**
Taylour – *Headfort, M.*
Temple-Gore-Langton – *Temple of Stowe, E*
Temple-Morris – *Temple-Morris of Llandaff**
Tennant – *Glenconner*
Thellusson – *Rendlesham*
Thesiger – *Chelmsford, V.*
Thomas – *T. of Gresford**
Thomas – *T. of Gwydir**
Thomas – *T. of Macclesfield**
Thomas – *T. of Swynnerton**
Thomas – *T. of Walliswood**
Thomson – *T. of Fleet*
Thomson – *T. of Monifieth**
Thynn – *Bath, M.*
Tottenham – *Ely, M.*
Trefusis – *Clinton*
Trench – *Ashtown*
Trevor-Roper – *Dacre of Glanton**
Tufton – *Hothfield*
Turner – *Netherthorpe*

Turner – *T. of Camden**
Turnour – *Winterton, E.*
Tyrell-Kenyon – *Kenyon*
Vanden-Bempde-
    Johnstone – *Derwent*
Vane – *Barnard*
Vane-Tempest-Stewart –
    Londonderry, M.
Vanneck – *Huntingfield*
Vaughan – *Lisburne, E.*
Vereker – *Gort, V.*
Verney – *Willoughby de
    Broke*
Vernon – *Lyveden*
Vesey – *De Vesci, V.*
Villiers – *Clarendon, E.*
Vincent – *V. of Coleshill**
Vivian – *Swansea*
Wade – *W. of Chorlton**
Waldegrave – *W. of North
    Hill**

Walker – *W. of Doncaster**
Walker – *W. of Worcester**
Wallace – *W. of Coslany**
Wallace – *W. of Saltaire**
Wallop – *Portsmouth, E.*
Walton – *W. of Detchant**
Ward – *Bangor, V.*
Ward – *Dudley, E.*
Warrender – *Bruntisfield*
Warwick – *W. of
    Undercliffe**
Watson – *W. of
    Invergowrie**
Watson – *Manton*
Watson – *W. of Richmond**
Webber – *Lloyd-Webber**
Wedderburn – *W. of
    Charlton**
Weir – *Inverforth*
Weld-Forester – *Forester*
Wellesley – *Cowley, E.*

Wellesley – *Wellington, D.*
Westenra – *Rossmore*
White – *Annaly*
White – *Haningfield**
Whiteley – *Marchamley*
Whitfield – *Kenswood*
Williams – *W. of Crosby**
Williams – *W. of Elve**
Williams – *W. of Mostyn**
Williamson – *Forres*
Williamson – *W. of
    Horton**
Willoughby – *Middleton*
Wills – *Dulverton*
Wilson – *Moran*
Wilson – *Nunburnholme*
Wilson – *W. of Tillyorn**
Windsor – *Gloucester, D.*
Windsor – *Kent, D.*
Windsor-Clive – *Plymouth,
    E.*

Wingfield – *Powerscourt, V.*
Winn – *St Oswald*
Wodehouse – *Kimberley, E.*
Wolfson – *W. of
    Sunningdale**
Wood – *Halifax, E.*
Woodhouse – *Terrington*
Woolmer – *W. of Leeds**
Wright – *W. of Richmond**
Wyndham – *Egremont and
    Leconfield*
Wyndham-Quin –
    Dunraven, E.
Wynn – *Newborough*
Yarde-Buller – *Churston*
Yerburgh – *Alvingham*
Yorke – *Hardwicke, E.*
Young – *Kennet*
Young – *Y. of Graffham**
Young – *Y. of Old Scone**
Younger – *Y. of Leckie, V.*

Orders of Chivalry

THE MOST NOBLE ORDER OF THE GARTER (1348)

KG
Ribbon, Blue
Motto, Honi soit qui mal y pense
(Shame on him who thinks evil of it)
The number of Knights Companions
is limited to 24

SOVEREIGN OF THE ORDER
The Queen

LADY OF THE ORDER
HRH The Princess Royal, 1994

ROYAL KNIGHTS
HRH The Prince Philip, Duke of
   Edinburgh, 1947
HRH The Prince of Wales, 1958
HRH The Duke of Kent, 1985
HRH The Duke of Gloucester, 1997

EXTRA KNIGHTS COMPANIONS
AND LADIES
HRH Princess Juliana of the
   Netherlands, 1958
Grand Duke Jean of Luxembourg,
   1972
HM The Queen of Denmark, 1979
HM The King of Sweden, 1983
HM The King of Spain, 1988
HM The Queen of the Netherlands,
   1989
HIM The Emperor of Japan, 1998
HM The King of Norway, 2001

KNIGHTS AND LADY
COMPANIONS

The Duke of Grafton, 1976
The Lord Richardson of
   Duntisbourne, 1983
The Lord Carrington, 1985
The Lord Callaghan of Cardiff, 1987
The Duke of Wellington, 1990
Field Marshal the Lord Bramall, 1990
Sir Edward Heath, 1992
The Viscount Ridley, 1992
The Lord Sainsbury of Preston
   Candover, 1992
The Lord Ashburton, 1994
The Lord Kingsdown, 1994
Sir Ninian Stephen, 1994
The Baroness Thatcher, 1995
Sir Edmund Hillary, 1995
The Duke of Devonshire, 1996
Sir Timothy Colman, 1996

The Duke of Abercorn, 1999
Sir William Gladstone, 1999
Field Marshal the Lord Inge, 2001
Sir Anthony Acland, 2001
Prelate, The Bishop of Winchester
Chancellor, The Lord Carrington, KG,
   GCMG, CH, MC
Register, The Dean of Windsor
Garter King of Arms, P. Gwynn-Jones,
   CVO
Gentleman Usher of the Black Rod, Lt.
   Gen. Sir Michael Willcocks, KCB
Secretary, D. H. B. Chesshyre, LVO

THE MOST ANCIENT AND MOST NOBLE ORDER OF THE THISTLE (revived 1687)

KT
Ribbon, Green
Motto, Nemo me impune lacessit *(No
   one provokes me with impunity)*
The number of Knights is limited to
16

SOVEREIGN OF THE ORDER
The Queen

LADY OF THE THISTLE
HRH The Princess Royal, 2000

ROYAL KNIGHTS
HRH The Prince Philip, Duke of
   Edinburgh, 1952
HRH The Prince of Wales, Duke of
   Rothesay, 1977

KNIGHTS AND LADIES
The Earl of Wemyss and March,
   1966
Sir Donald Cameron of Lochiel,
   1973
The Duke of Buccleuch and
   Queensberry, 1978
The Earl of Elgin and Kincardine,
   1981
The Lord Thomson of Monifieth,
   1981
The Earl of Airlie, 1985 Capt. Sir
   Iain Tennant, 1986
The Viscount Younger of Leckie,
   1995
The Viscount of Arbuthnott, 1996
The Earl of Crawford and Balcarres,
   1996
Lady Marion Fraser, 1996
The Lord Macfarlane of Bearsden,
   1996

The Lord Mackay of Clashfern, 1997
The Lord Wilson of Tillyorn, 2000
Chancellor, The Duke of Buccleuch
   and Queensberry, KT, VRD
Dean, The Very Revd G. I.
   Macmillan, CVO
*Secretary and Lord Lyon King of
   Arms,* R. O. Blair, LVO, WS
Usher of the Green Rod, Rear-Adm.
   C. H. Layman, CB, DSO, LVO

THE MOST HONOURABLE ORDER OF THE BATH (1725)

GCB *Military*   GCB *Civil*

GCB Knight (or Dame) Grand
        Cross
KCB Knight Commander
DCB Dame Commander
CB   Companion
Ribbon, Crimson
Motto, Tria juncta in uno *(Three
   joined in one)*

Remodelled 1815, and enlarged
many times since. The Order is
divided into civil and military
divisions. Women became eligible
for the Order from 1 January 1971

THE SOVEREIGN

GREAT MASTER AND FIRST OR
PRINCIPAL KNIGHT GRAND CROSS
HRH The Prince of Wales, KG, KT,
   GCB, OM

Dean of the Order, The Dean of
   Westminster
Bath King of Arms, Gen. Sir Brian
   Kenny, GCB, CBE
Registrar and Secretary, Air Vice-
   Marshal Sir Richard Peirse, KCVO,
   CB
Genealogist, P. Gwynn-Jones, CVO
Gentleman Usher of the Scarlet Rod,
   Rear-Adm. I. R. Henderson, CB,
   CBE
Deputy Secretary, The Secretary of
   the Central Chancery of the
   Orders of Knighthood
*Chancery, Central Chancery of the
   Orders of Knighthood,* St James's
   Palace, London SW1A 1BH

THE ORDER OF MERIT
(1902)

OM *Military*   OM *Civil*

OM

Ribbon, Blue and crimson

This Order is designed as a special distinction for eminent men and women without conferring a knighthood upon them. The Order is limited in numbers to 24, with the addition of foreign honorary members. Membership is of two kinds, military and civil, the badge of the former having crossed swords, and the latter oak leaves

THE SOVEREIGN

HRH The Prince Philip, Duke of
  Edinburgh, 1968
Sir George Edwards, 1971
Revd Prof. Owen Chadwick, KBE,
  1983
Sir Andrew Huxley, 1983
Dr Frederick Sanger, 1986
Dame Cicely Saunders, 1989
Prof. The Lord Porter of
  Luddenham, 1989
The Baroness Thatcher, 1990
Dame Joan Sutherland, 1991
Prof. Francis Crick, 1991
Sir Michael Atiyah, 1992
Lucian Freud, 1993
The Lord Jenkins of Hillhead, 1993
Sir Aaron Klug, 1995
The Lord Foster of Thames Bank,
  1997
Sir Denis Rooke, 1997
Sir James Black, 2000
Sir Anthony Caro, 2000
Prof. Sir Roger Penrose, 2000
Sir Tom Stoppard, 2000
HRH The Prince of Wales, 2002

Honorary Member, Nelson Mandela,
  1995
Secretary and Registrar, Sir Edward
  Ford, GCVO, KCB, ERD
Chancery, Central Chancery of the
  Orders of Knighthood, St James's
  Palace, London SW1A 1BH

THE MOST DISTINGUISHED ORDER OF ST MICHAEL AND ST GEORGE (1818)

GCMG   KCMG

GCMG   Knight (or Dame)
            Grand Cross
KCMG   Knight Commander
DCMG   Dame Commander
CMG   Companion
Ribbon, Saxon blue, with scarlet
  centre
Motto, Auspicium melioris aevi
  (*Token of a better age*)

THE SOVEREIGN

GRAND MASTER
HRH The Duke of Kent, KG, GCMG,
  GCVO, ADC

Prelate, The Rt. Revd Simon
  Barrington-Ward, KCMG
Chancellor, Sir Antony Acland, KG,
  GCMG, GCVO
Secretary, The Permanent Under-
  Secretary of State at the Foreign
  and Commonwealth Office and
  Head of the Diplomatic Service
Registrar, Lord Wilson of Tillyorn,
  KT, GCMG
King of Arms, Sir Ewen Fergusson,
  GCMG, GCVO
Gentleman Usher of the Blue Rod, Sir
  John Margetson, KCMG
Dean, The Dean of St Paul's
Deputy Secretary, The Secretary of
  the Central Chancery of the
  Orders of Knighthood
Chancery, Central Chancery of the
  Orders of Knighthood, St James's
  Palace, London SW1A 1BH

THE MOST EMINENT ORDER OF THE INDIAN EMPIRE (1878)

GCIE   Knight Grand Commander
KCIE   Knight Commander
CIE   Companion

Ribbon, Imperial purple
Motto, Imperatricis auspiciis (*Under
  the auspices of the Empress*)

THE SOVEREIGN

Registrar, The Secretary of the
  Central Chancery of the Orders
  of Knighthood
No conferments have been made
since 1947

THE IMPERIAL ORDER OF THE CROWN OF INDIA (1877) FOR LADIES

CI
Badge, the royal cipher in jewels
  within an oval, surmounted by an
  heraldic crown and attached to a
  bow of light blue watered ribbon,
  edged white

The honour does not confer any
rank or title upon the recipient
No conferments have been made
since 1947

HM The Queen, 1947
HRH Princess Alice, Duchess of
  Gloucester, 1937

THE ROYAL VICTORIAN ORDER (1896)

GCVO   KCVO
GCVO   Knight or Dame
            Grand Cross
KCVO   Knight
            Commander
DCVO   Dame
            Commander
CVO   Commander
LVO   Lieutenant
MVO   Member

Ribbon, Blue, with red and white
  edges
Motto, Victoria

THE SOVEREIGN

Chancellor, The Lord Chamberlain
Secretary, The Keeper of the Privy
  Purse
Registrar, The Secretary of the
  Central Chancery of the Orders
  of Knighthood
Chaplain, The Chaplain of the
  Queen's Chapel of the Savoy
Hon. Genealogist, D. H. B.
  Chesshyre, LVO

THE MOST EXCELLENT ORDER OF THE BRITISH EMPIRE (1917)

GBE   KBE

The Order was divided into military and civil divisions in December 1918

GBE   Knight or Dame Grand Cross
KBE   Knight Commander
DBE   Dame Commander
CBE   Commander
OBE   Officer
MBE   Member

Ribbon, Rose pink edged with pearl grey with vertical pearl stripe in centre (military division); without vertical pearl stripe (civil division)
Motto, For God and the Empire

THE SOVEREIGN

GRAND MASTER
HRH The Prince Philip, Duke of Edinburgh, KG, KT, OM, GBE, PC

Prelate, The Bishop of London
King of Arms, Air Chief Marshal Sir Patrick Hine, GCB, GBE
Registrar, The Secretary of the Central Chancery of the Orders of Knighthood
Secretary, The Secretary of the Cabinet and Head of the Home Civil Service
Dean, The Dean of St Paul's
Gentleman Usher of the Purple Rod, Sir Alexander Michael Graham, GBE, DCL
Chancery, Central Chancery of the Orders of Knighthood, St James's Palace, London SW1A 1BH

ORDER OF THE COMPANIONS OF HONOUR (1917)

CH

Ribbon, Carmine, with gold edges

This Order consists of one class only and carries with it no title. The number of awards is limited to 65 (excluding honorary members)

Anthony, Rt. Hon. John, 1981
Ashley of Stoke, The Lord, 1975
Attenborough, Sir David, 1995
Baker, Dame Janet, 1993

Baker of Dorking, The Lord, 1992
Birtwistle, Sir Harrison, 2001
Brenner, Sydney, 1986
Brook, Peter, 1998
Brooke of Sutton Mandeville, The Lord, 1992
Carrington, The Lord, 1983
Christie, Sir George, 2001
Davis, Sir Colin, 2001
De Chastelain, Gen. John, 1999
Doll, Prof. Sir Richard, 1995
Fraser, Rt. Hon. Malcolm, 1977
Freud, Lucian, 1983
Glenamara, The Lord, 1976
Hamilton, Richard, 1999
Hawking, Prof. Stephen, 1989
Healey, The Lord, 1979
Heseltine, The Lord, 1997
Hobsbawm, Prof. Eric, 1998
Hockney, David, 1997
Howard, Sir Michael Eliot, 2002
Howe of Aberavon, The Lord, 1996
Hurd of Westwell, The Lord, 1995
Jones, James, 1977
King of Bridgewater, The Lord, 1992
Lange, Rt. Hon. David, 1989
Lessing, Doris, 1999
Major, Rt. Hon. John, 1999
Owen, The Lord, 1994
Patten, Rt. Hon. Christopher, 1998
Pinter, Harold, 2002
Powell, Sir Philip, 1984
Riley, Bridget, 1999
Sanger, Frederick, 1981
Scofield, Paul, 2000
Sisson, Charles, 1993
Smith, Sir John, 1993
Somare, Rt. Hon. Sir Michael, 1978
Talboys, Rt. Hon. Sir Brian, 1981
Tebbit, The Lord, 1987
Varah, Rev. Dr. Chad, 1999

Honorary Members, Lee Kuan Yew, 1970; Prof. Anartya Sen, 2000; Bernard Haitink, 2002
Secretary and Registrar, The Secretary of the Central Chancery of the Orders of Knighthood

THE DISTINGUISHED SERVICE ORDER (1886)

DSO

Ribbon, Red, with blue edges

Bestowed in recognition of especial services in action of commissioned officers in the Navy, Army and Royal Air Force and (since 1942) Mercantile Marine. The members are Companions only. A Bar may be awarded for any additional act of service

THE IMPERIAL SERVICE ORDER (1902)

ISO

Ribbon, Crimson, with blue centre

Appointment as Companion of this Order is open to members of the Civil Services whose eligibility is determined by the grade they hold. The Order consists of The Sovereign and Companions to a number not exceeding 1,900, of whom 1,300 may belong to the Home Civil Services and 600 to Overseas Civil Services. The then Prime Minister announced in March 1993 that he would make no further recommendations for appointments to the Order.

Secretary, The Secretary of the Cabinet and Head of the Home Civil Service
Registrar, The Secretary of the Central Chancery of the Orders of Knighthood, St James's Palace, London SW1A 1BH

THE ROYAL VICTORIAN CHAIN (1902)

It confers no precedence on its holders

HM THE QUEEN

HRH Princess Juliana of the Netherlands, 1950
HM The King of Thailand, 1960
HM King Zahir Shah of Afghanistan, 1971
HM The Queen of Denmark, 1974
HM The King of Sweden, 1975
HM The Queen of the Netherlands, 1982
Gen. Antonio Eanes, 1985
HM The King of Spain, 1986
HM The King of Saudi Arabia, 1987
HE Richard von Weizsäcker, 1992
HM The King of Norway, 1994
The Earl of Airlie, 1997

Baronetage and Knightage

BARONETS

Style, 'Sir' before forename and surname, followed by 'Bt.'
Wife's style, 'Lady' followed by surname
For forms of address, *see* page 133

There are five different creations of baronetcies: Baronets of England (creations dating from 1611); Baronets of Ireland (creations dating from 1619); Baronets of Scotland or Nova Scotia (creations dating from 1625); Baronets of Great Britain (creations after the Act of Union 1707 which combined the kingdoms of England and Scotland); and Baronets of the United Kingdom (creations after the union of Great Britain and Ireland in 1801).

Badge of Baronets of the   *Badge of Baronets*
United Kingdom   *of Nova Scotia*

Badge of Ulster

The patent of creation limits the destination of a baronetcy, usually to male descendants of the first baronet, although special remainders allow the baronetcy to pass, if the male issue of sons fail, to the male issue of daughters of the first baronet. In the case of baronetcies of Scotland or Nova Scotia, a special remainder of 'heirs male and of tailzie' allows the baronetcy to descend to heirs general, including women. There are four existing Scottish baronets with such a remainder.

The Official Roll of Baronets is kept at the Lord Chancellor's Department by the Registrar of the Baronetage. Anyone who considers that he is entitled to be entered on the Roll may petition the Crown through the Lord Chancellor. Every person succeeding to a baronetcy must exhibit proofs of succession to the Lord Chancellor. A person whose name is not entered on the Official Roll will not be addressed or mentioned by the title of baronet in any official document, nor will he be accorded precedence as a baronet.

BARONETCIES EXTINCT SINCE THE LAST EDITION

Boulton (*cr.* 1905); Nepean (*cr.* 1802); Owen (*cr.* 1813)

Registrar of the Baronetage, P. Jenkins
Assistant Registrar, S. Johnson
Office, Lord Chancellor's Department, Room 1378, 50 Queen Anne's Gate, London SW1H 9AT. Tel: 020 7273 3537

KNIGHTS

Style, 'Sir' before forename and surname, followed by appropriate post-nominal initials if a Knight Grand Cross, Knight Grand Commander or Knight Commander

Wife's style, 'Lady' followed by surname
For forms of address, *see* page 133

The prefix 'Sir' is not used by knights who are clerics of the Church of England, who do not receive the accolade. Their wives are entitled to precedence as the wife of a knight but not to the style of 'Lady'.

ORDERS OF KNIGHTHOOD

Knight Grand Cross, Knight Grand Commander, and Knight Commander are the higher classes of the Orders of Chivalry (*see* pages 170–172). Honorary knighthoods of these Orders may be conferred on men who are citizens of countries of which The Queen is not head of state. As a rule, the prefix 'Sir' is not used by honorary knights.

KNIGHTS BACHELOR

The Knights Bachelor do not constitute a Royal Order, but comprise the surviving representation of the ancient State Orders of Knighthood. The Register of Knights Bachelor, instituted by James I in the 17th century, lapsed, and in 1908 a voluntary association under the title of The Society of Knights (now The Imperial Society of Knights Bachelor by Royal Command) was formed with the primary objects of continuing the various registers dating from 1257 and obtaining the uniform registration of every created Knight Bachelor. In 1926 a design for a badge to be worn by Knights Bachelor was approved and adopted; in 1974 a neck badge and miniature were added.

Knight Principal, Sir Richard Gaskell
Prelate, Rt. Revd and Rt. Hon. The Bishop of London
Registrar, Sir Robert Balchin, DL
Hon. Treasurer, Sir Paul Judge
Clerk to the Council, R. L. Jenkins, LVO, TD.
Office, 21 Old Buildings, Lincoln's Inn, London WC2A 3UJ

LIST OF BARONETS AND KNIGHTS

Revised to 31 August 2002
Peers are not included in this list

†	Not registered on the Official Roll of the Baronetage at the time of going to press
( )	The date of creation of the baronetcy is given in parenthesis
I	Baronet of Ireland
NS	Baronet of Nova Scotia
S	Baronet of Scotland

If a baronet or knight has a double-barrelled or hyphen-ated surname, he is listed under the final element of the name

A full entry in italic type indicates that the recipient of a knighthood died during the year in which the honour was conferred. The name is included for purposes of record

Abal, Sir Tei, Kt., CBE

Abbott, Sir Albert Francis, Kt., CBE

Abbott, *Adm.* Sir Peter Charles, GBE, KCB

Abdy, Sir Valentine Robert Duff, Bt. (1850)

Abel, Sir Seselo (Cecil) Charles Geoffrey, Kt., OBE

Abercromby, Sir Ian George, Bt. (S. 1636)

Acheson, *Prof.* Sir (Ernest) Donald, KBE

Ackers, Sir James George, Kt.

Ackroyd, Sir Timothy Robert Whyte, Bt. (1956)

Acland, *Lt.-Col.* Sir (Christopher) Guy (Dyke), Bt., MVO (1890)

Acland, Sir John Dyke, Bt. (1644)

Acland, *Maj.-Gen.* Sir John Hugh Bevil, KCB, CBE

Adam, Sir Christopher Eric Forbes, Bt. (1917)

Adams, Sir William James, KCMG

Adrien, *Hon.* Sir Maurice Latour-, Kt.

Adsetts, Sir William Norman, Kt., OBE

Adye, Sir John Anthony, KCMG

Agnew, Sir Crispin Hamlyn, Bt. (S. 1629)

Agnew, Sir John Keith, Bt. (1895)

Agnew, Sir Rudolph Ion Joseph, Kt.

Aiken, *Air Chief Marshal* Sir John Alexander Carlisle, KCB

Aikens, Sir Richard John Pearson, Kt., QC

†Ainsworth, Sir Anthony Thomas Hugh, Bt. (1916)

Aird, *Capt.* Sir Alastair Sturgis, GCVO

Aird, Sir (George) John, Bt. (1901)

Airy, *Maj.-Gen.* Sir Christopher John, KCVO, CBE

Aitchison, Sir Charles Walter de Lancey, Bt. (1938)

Akehurst, *Gen.* Sir John Bryan, KCB, CBE

Alberti, *Prof.* Sir Kurt George Matthew Mayer, Kt.

Albu, Sir George, Bt. (1912)

Alcock, *Air Chief Marshal* Sir (Robert James) Michael, GCB, KBE

Aldous, *Rt. Hon.* Sir William, Kt.

Alexander, Sir Charles Gundry, Bt. (1945)

Alexander, Sir Claud Hagart-, Bt. (1886)

†Alexander, Sir Patrick Desmond William Cable-, Bt. (1809)

Allan, Sir Anthony James Allan Havelock-, Bt. (1858)

Allen, *Prof.* Sir Geoffrey, Kt., Ph.D., FRS

Allen, Sir John Derek, Kt., CBE

Allen, *Hon.* Sir Peter Austin Philip Jermyn, Kt.

Allen, Sir Thomas Boaz, Kt., CBE

Allen, *Hon.* Sir William Clifford, KCMG, MP

Allen, Sir William Guilford, Kt.

Alleyne, Sir George Allanmoore Ogarren, Kt.

Alleyne, *Revd* Sir John Olpherts Campbell, Bt. (1769)

Alliance, Sir David, Kt., CBE

Allinson, Sir (Walter) Leonard, KCVO, CMG

Alliott, *Hon.* Sir John Downes, Kt.

Allison, *Air Chief Marshal* Sir John Shakespeare, KCB, CBE

Althaus, Sir Nigel Frederick, Kt.

Ambo, *Rt. Revd* George, KBE

Amet, *Hon.* Sir Arnold Karibone, Kt.

Amies, Sir (Edwin) Hardy, KCVO

Amory, Sir Ian Heathcoat, Bt. (1874)

Anderson, Sir John Anthony, KBE

Anderson, *Maj.-Gen.* Sir John Evelyn, KBE

Anderson, Sir John Muir, Kt., CMG

Anderson, *Hon.* Sir Kevin Victor, Kt.

Anderson, Sir Leith Reinsford Steven, Kt., CBE

Anderson, *Vice-Adm.* Sir Neil Dudley, KBE, CB

Anderson, *Prof.* Sir (William) Ferguson, Kt., OBE

Anderton, Sir (Cyril) James, Kt., CBE, QPM

Andrew, Sir Robert John, KCB

Andrews, Sir Derek Henry, KCB, CBE

Andrews, *Hon.* Sir Dormer George, Kt.

Angus, Sir Michael Richardson, Kt.

Annesley, Sir Hugh Norman, Kt., QPM

Anson, *Vice-Adm.* Sir Edward Rosebery, KCB

Anson, Sir John, KCB

Anson, *Rear-Adm.* Sir Peter, Bt., CB (1831)

†Anstruther, Sir Ian Fife Campbell, Bt., (S. 1694)

Antico, Sir Tristan Venus, Kt.

Antrobus, Sir Charles James, GCMG, OBE

Antrobus, Sir Edward Philip, Bt. (1815)

Appleyard, Sir Leonard Vincent, KCMG

Appleyard, Sir Raymond Kenelm, KBE

Arbuthnot, Sir Keith Robert Charles, Bt. (1823)

Arbuthnot, Sir William Reierson, Bt. (1964)

Arbuthnott, *Prof.* Sir John Peebles, Kt., Ph.D., FRSE

Archdale, *Capt.* Sir Edward Folmer, Bt., DSC, RN (1928)

Arculus, Sir Ronald, KCMG, KCVO

Armitage, *Air Chief Marshal* Sir Michael John, KCB, CBE

Armour, *Prof.* Sir James, Kt., CBE

Armstrong, Sir Christopher John Edmund Stuart, Bt., MBE (1841)

Armstrong, Sir Patrick John, Kt., CBE

Armytage, Sir John Martin, Bt. (1738)

Arnold, *Rt. Hon.* Sir John Lewis, Kt.

Arnold, Sir Malcolm Henry, Kt., CBE

Arnold, Sir Thomas Richard, Kt.

Arnott, Sir Alexander John Maxwell, Bt. (1896)

Arrindell, Sir Clement Athelston, GCMG, GCVO, QC

Arthur, *Lt.-Gen.* Sir (John) Norman Stewart, KCB

Arthur, Sir Stephen John, Bt. (1841)

Ash, *Prof.* Sir Eric Albert, Kt., CBE, FRS, FREng.

Ashburnham, Sir James Fleetwood, Bt. (1661)

Ashcroft, Sir Michael, KCMG

Ashley, Sir Bernard Albert, Kt.

Ashmore, *Admiral of the Fleet* Sir Edward Beckwith, GCB, DSC

†Aske, Sir Robert John Bingham, Bt. (1922)

Askew, Sir Bryan, Kt.

Asscher, *Prof.* Sir (Adolf) William, Kt., MD, FRCP

Astill, *Hon.* Sir Michael John, Kt.

Aston, Sir Harold George, Kt., CBE

Astwood, *Hon.* Sir James Rufus, KBE

Atcherley, Sir Harold Winter, Kt.

Atiyah, Sir Michael Francis, Kt., OM, Ph.D., FRS

Atkins, *Rt. Hon.* Sir Robert James, Kt.

Atkinson, *Prof.* Sir Anthony Barnes, Kt.

Atkinson, *Air Marshal* Sir David William, KBE

Atkinson, Sir Frederick John, KCB

Atkinson, Sir John Alexander, KCB, DFC

Atkinson, Sir Robert, Kt., DSC, FREng.

Atopare, Sir Sailas, GCMG

Attenborough, Sir David Frederick, Kt., CH, CVO, CBE, FRS

Audland, Sir Christopher John, KCMG

Audley, Sir George Bernard, Kt.

Augier, *Prof.* Sir Fitz-Roy Richard, Kt.

Auld, *Rt. Hon.* Sir Robin Ernest, Kt.

Austin, Sir Anthony Leonard, Bt. (1894)

Austin, *Vice-Adm.* Sir Peter Murray, KCB

Austin, *Air Marshal* Sir Roger Mark, KCB, AFC

Avei, Sir Moi, KBE

Axford, Sir William Ian, Kt.

Ayckbourn, Sir Alan, Kt., CBE

Aykroyd, Sir James Alexander Frederic, Bt. (1929)

Aykroyd, Sir William Miles, Bt., MC (1920)

Aylmer, Sir Richard John, Bt. (I. 1622)

Ayre, Sir Douglas, Kt., JP

Bacha, Sir Bhinod, Kt., CMG

Backhouse, Sir Jonathan Roger, Bt. (1901)

Bacon, Sir Nicholas Hickman Ponsonby, Bt. *Premier Baronet of England* (1611 and 1627)

Bacon, Sir Sidney Charles, Kt., CB, FREng.

Baddeley, Sir John Wolsey Beresford, Bt. (1922)

Baddiley, *Prof.* Sir James, Kt., Ph.D., D.Sc., FRS, FRSE

Badge, Sir Peter Gilmour Noto, Kt.

Badger, Sir Geoffrey Malcolm, Kt.

Baer, Sir Jack Mervyn Frank, Kt.

Bagge, Sir (John) Jeremy Picton, Bt. (1867)

Bagnall, *Air Marshal* Sir Anthony John Crowther, KCB, OBE

Bailey, Sir Alan Marshall, KCB

Bailey, Sir Brian Harry, Kt., OBE

Bailey, Sir Derrick Thomas Louis, Bt., DFC (1919)

Bailey, Sir John Bilsland, KCB

Bailey, Sir Richard John, Kt., CBE

Bailey, Sir Stanley Ernest, Kt., CBE, QPM

Bailhache, Sir Philip Martin, Kt.

Baillie, Sir Gawaine George Hope, Bt. (1823)

Bain, *Prof.* Sir George Sayers, Kt.

Baines, *Prof.* Sir George Grenfell-, Kt., OBE

†Baird, Sir Charles William Stuart, Bt. (1809)

†Baird, Sir James Andrew Gardiner, Bt. (S. 1695)

Baird, *Lt.-Gen.* Sir James Parlane, KBE, MD

Baird, *Air Marshal* Sir John Alexander, KBE

Baird, *Vice-Adm.* Sir Thomas Henry Eustace, KCB

Bairsto, *Air Marshal* Sir Peter Edward, KBE, CB

Baker, Sir Bryan William, Kt.

Baker, Sir Robert George Humphrey Sherston-, Bt. (1796)

Baker, *Hon.* Sir (Thomas) Scott (Gillespie), Kt.

Balchin, Sir Robert George Alexander, Kt.

Balderstone, Sir James Schofield, Kt.

Baldwin, *Prof.* Sir Jack Edward, Kt., FRS

Baldwin, Sir Peter Robert, KCB

Ball, *Air Marshal* Sir Alfred Henry Wynne, KCB, DSO, DFC

Ball, Sir Charles Irwin, Bt. (1911)

Ball, Sir Christopher John Elinger, Kt.

Ball, *Prof.* Sir Robert James, Kt., Ph.D.

Bamford, Sir Anthony Paul, Kt.

Band, *Vice-Adm.* Sir Jonathon, KCB

Banham, Sir John Michael Middlecott, Kt.

Bannerman, Sir David Gordon, Bt., OBE (S. 1682)

Bannister, Sir Roger Gilbert, Kt., CBE, DM, FRCP

Barber, Sir (Thomas) David, Bt. (1960)

Barbour, *Very Revd* Sir Robert Alexander Stewart, KCVO, MC

Barclay, Sir Colville Herbert Sanford, Bt. (S. 1668)

Barclay, Sir David Rowat, Kt.

Barclay, Sir Frederick Hugh, Kt.

Barclay, Sir Peter Maurice, Kt., CBE

Barder, Sir Brian Leon, KCMG

Baring, Sir John Francis, Bt. (1911)

Barker, Sir Colin, Kt.

Barker, *Hon.* Sir (Richard) Ian, Kt.

Barlow, Sir Christopher Hilaro, Bt. (1803)

Barlow, Sir Frank, Kt., CBE

Barlow, Sir (George) William, Kt., FREng.

Barlow, Sir John Kemp, Bt. (1907)

Barlow, Sir Thomas Erasmus, Bt., DSC (1902)

Barnard, Sir Joseph Brian, Kt.

Barnes, Sir (James) David (Francis), Kt., CBE

Barnes, Sir Kenneth, KCB

Barnewall, Sir Reginald Robert, Bt. (I. 1623)

Baron, Sir Thomas, Kt., CBE

Barraclough, *Air Chief Marshal* Sir John, KCB, CBE, DFC, AFC

Barran, Sir John Napoleon Ruthven, Bt. (1895)

Barratt, Sir Lawrence Arthur, Kt.

Barratt, Sir Richard Stanley, Kt., CBE, QPM

Barrett, *Lt.-Gen.* Sir David William Scott-, KBE, MC

Barrett, Sir Stephen Jeremy, KCMG

Barrington, Sir Alexander (Fitzwilliam Croker), Bt. (1831)

Barrington, Sir Nicholas John, KCMG, CVO

Barron, Sir Donald James, Kt.

Barrow, *Capt.* Sir Richard John Uniacke, Bt. (1835)

Barrowclough, Sir Anthony Richard, Kt., QC

Barry, Sir (Lawrence) Edward (Anthony Tress), Bt. (1899)

Barter, Sir Peter Leslie Charles, Kt., OBE

†Bartlett, Sir Andrew Alan, Bt. (1913)

Barttelot, *Col.* Sir Brian Walter de Stopham, Bt., OBE (1875)

Batchelor, Sir Ivor Ralph Campbell, Kt., CBE

Bate, Sir David Lindsay, KBE

Bates, Sir Geoffrey Voltelin, Bt., MC (1880)

Bates, Sir Malcolm Rowland, Kt.

Bates, Sir Richard Dawson Hoult, Bt. (1937)

Batho, Sir Peter Ghislain, Bt. (1928)

Bathurst, *Admiral of the Fleet* Sir (David) Benjamin, GCB

Bathurst, Sir Frederick John Charles Gordon Hervey-, Bt. (1818)

Bathurst, Sir Maurice Edward, Kt., CMG, CBE, QC

Batten, Sir John Charles, KCVO

Battersby, *Prof.* Sir Alan Rushton, Kt., FRS

Battishill, Sir Anthony Michael William, GCB

Batty, Sir William Bradshaw, Kt., TD

Baxendell, Sir Peter Brian, Kt., CBE, FREng.

Bayliss, Sir Richard Ian Samuel, KCVO, MD, FRCP

Bayne, Sir Nicholas Peter, KCMG

Baynes, Sir John Christopher Malcolm, Bt. (1801)

Bazley, Sir Thomas John Sebastian, Bt. (1869)

Beach, *Gen.* Sir (William Gerald) Hugh, GBE, KCB, MC

Beache, *Hon.* Sir Vincent Ian, KCMG

Beale, *Lt.-Gen.* Sir Peter John, KBE, FRCP

Beament, Sir James William Longman, Kt., Sc.D., FRS

Beamish, Sir Adrian John, KCMG

Beauchamp, Sir Christopher Radstock Proctor-, Bt. (1745)

Beaumont, *Capt. the Hon.* Sir (Edward) Nicholas (Canning), KCVO

Beaumont, Sir George (Howland Francis), Bt. (1661)

Beaumont, Sir Richard Ashton, KCMG, OBE

Beavis, *Air Chief Marshal* Sir Michael Gordon, KCB, CBE, AFC

Becher, Sir John William Michael Wrixon-, Bt. (1831)

Beck, Sir Edgar Philip, Kt.

Beckett, Sir Richard Gervase, Bt., QC (1921)

Beckett, Sir Terence Norman, KBE, FREng.

Beckwith, Sir John Lionel, Kt., CBE

Bedingfeld, *Capt.* Sir Edmund George Felix Paston-, Bt. (1661)

Beddoe, Sir David Sydney Rowe-, Kt.

Bedser, Sir Alec Victor, Kt., CBE

Beecham, Sir Jeremy Hugh, Kt.

Beecham, Sir John Stratford Roland, Bt. (1914)

Beetham, *Marshal of the Royal Air Force* Sir Michael James, GCB, CBE, DFC, AFC

Beevor, Sir Thomas Agnew, Bt. (1784)

Beldam, *Rt. Hon.* Sir (Alexander) Roy (Asplan), Kt.

Belich, Sir James, Kt.

Bell, Sir Brian Ernest, KBE

Bell, Sir John Lowthian, Bt. (1885)

Bell, *Prof.* Sir Peter Robert Frank, Kt.

Bell, *Hon.* Sir Rodger, Kt.

Bell, Sir William Hollin Dayrell Morrison-, Bt. (1905)

Bellamy, *Hon.* Sir Christopher William, Kt.

Bellew, Sir Henry Charles Gratton-, Bt. (1838)

Bellingham, Sir Anthony Edward Norman, Bt. (1796)

Bengough, *Col.* Sir Piers, KCVO, OBE

Benn, Sir (James) Jonathan, Bt. (1914)

Bennett, *Air Vice-Marshal* Sir Erik Peter, KBE, CB

Bennett, *Rt. Hon.* Sir Frederic Mackarness, Kt.

Bennett, *Hon.* Sir Hugh Peter Derwyn, Kt.

Bennett, *Gen.* Sir Phillip Harvey, KBE, DSO

Bennett, Sir Richard Rodney, Kt., CBE

Bennett, Sir Ronald Wilfrid Murdoch, Bt. (1929)

Benson, Sir Christopher John, Kt.

Benyon, Sir William Richard, Kt.

Beresford, Sir (Alexander) Paul, Kt., MP

Berger, *Vice-Adm.* Sir Peter Egerton Capel, KCB, LVO, DSC

Berghuser, *Hon.* Sir Eric, Kt., MBE

Beringer, *Prof.* Sir John Evelyn, Kt., CBE

Berman, Sir Franklin Delow, KCMG

Bernard, Sir Dallas Edmund, Bt. (1954)

Berney, Sir Julian Reedham Stuart, Bt. (1620)

Berridge, *Prof.* Sir Michael John, Kt., FRS

Berrill, Sir Kenneth Ernest, GBE, KCB

Berriman, Sir David, Kt.

Berry, *Prof.* Sir Colin Leonard, Kt., FRCPath.

Berry, *Prof.* Sir Michael Victor, Kt., FRS

Berthon, *Vice-Adm.* Sir Stephen Ferrier, KCB

Berthoud, Sir Martin Seymour, KCVO, CMG

Best, Sir Richard Radford, KCVO, CBE

Bethune, *Hon.* Sir (Walter) Angus, Kt.

Bett, Sir Michael, Kt., CBE

Bevan, Sir Martyn Evan Evans, Bt. (1958)

Bevan, Sir Nicolas, Kt., CB

Bevan, Sir Timothy Hugh, Kt.

Beverley, *Lt.-Gen.* Sir Henry York La Roche, KCB, OBE, RM

Bibby, Sir Derek James, Bt., MC (1959)

Bichard, Sir Michael George, KCB

Bick, *Hon.* Sir Martin James Moore-, Kt.

Bickersteth, *Rt. Revd* Sir John Monier, KCVO

Biddulph, Sir Ian D'Olier, Bt. (1664)

Bide, Sir Austin Ernest, Kt.

Bidwell, Sir Hugh Charles Philip, GBE

Biggam, Sir Robin Adair, Kt.

Biggs, Sir Norman Paris, Kt.

Bilas, Sir Angmai Simon, Kt., OBE

Billière, *Gen.* Sir Peter Edgar de la Cour de la, KCB, KBE, DSO, MC

Bingham, *Hon.* Sir Eardley Max, Kt., QC

Birch, Sir John Allan, KCVO, CMG

Birch, Sir Roger, Kt., CBE, QPM

Bird, Sir Richard Geoffrey Chapman, Bt. (1922)

Birkin, Sir John Christian William, Bt. (1905)

Birkin, Sir (John) Derek, Kt., TD

Birkmyre, Sir James, Bt. (1921)

Birrell, Sir James Drake, Kt.

Birtwistle, Sir Harrison, Kt. CH

Bischoff, Winfried Franz Wilhelm, Kt.

Bishop, Sir Frederick Arthur, Kt., CB, CVO

Bishop, Sir Michael David, Kt., CBE

Bisson, *Rt. Hon.* Sir Gordon Ellis, Kt.

Black, *Prof.* Sir Douglas Andrew Kilgour, Kt., MD, FRCP

Black, Sir James Whyte, Kt., OM, FRCP, FRS

Black, *Adm.* Sir (John) Jeremy, GBE, KCB, DSO

Black, Sir Robert David, Bt. (1922)

Blackburne, *Hon.* Sir William Anthony, Kt.

Blacker, *Gen.* Sir (Anthony Stephen) Jeremy, KCB, CBE

Blacker, *Gen.* Sir Cecil Hugh, GCB, OBE, MC

Blackett, Sir Hugh Francis, Bt. (1673)

Blackham, *Vice-Adm.* Sir Jeremy Joe, KCB

Blacklock, *Surgeon Capt. Prof.* Sir Norman James, KCVO, OBE

Blackman, Sir Frank Milton, KCVO, OBE

Blackwell, Sir Basil Davenport, Kt., FREng.

Blackwood, Sir John Francis, Bt. (1814)

Blair, *Lt.-Gen.* Sir Chandos, KCVO, OBE, MC

Blair, Sir Edward Thomas Hunter, Bt. (1786)

Blake, Sir Alfred Lapthorn, KCVO, MC

Blake, Sir Francis Michael, Bt. (1907)

Blake, Sir Peter Thomas, Kt, CBE

Blake, Sir (Thomas) Richard (Valentine), Bt. (I. 1622)

Blaker, Sir John, Bt. (1919)

Blakiston, Sir Ferguson Arthur James, Bt. (1763)

Blanch, Sir Malcolm, KCVO

Bland, Sir (Francis) Christopher (Buchan), Kt.

Bland, *Lt.-Col.* Sir Simon Claud Michael, KCVO

Blank, Sir Maurice Victor, Kt.

Blatherwick, Sir David Elliott Spiby, KCMG, OBE

Blelloch, Sir John Nial Henderson, KCB

Blennerhassett, Sir (Marmaduke) Adrian Francis William, Bt. (1809)

Blewitt, *Maj.* Sir Shane Gabriel Basil, GCVO

Blofeld, *Hon.* Sir John Christopher Calthorpe, Kt.

Blois, Sir Charles Nicholas Gervase, Bt. (1686)

Blomefield, Sir Thomas Charles Peregrine, Bt. (1807)

Bloomfield, Sir Kenneth Percy, KCB

Blosse, *Capt.* Sir Richard Hely Lynch-, Bt. (1622)

Blount, Sir Walter Edward Alpin, Bt., DSC (1642)

Blundell, Sir Thomas Leon, Kt., FRS

Blunden, Sir George, Kt.

†Blunden, Sir Philip Overington, Bt. (I. 1766)

Blunt, Sir David Richard Reginald Harvey, Bt. (1720)

Blyth, Sir Charles (Chay), Kt., CBE, BEM

Boardman, *Prof.* Sir John, Kt., FSA, FBA

Bodey, *Hon.* Sir David Roderick Lessiter, Kt., QC

Bodmer, Sir Walter Fred, Kt., Ph.D., FRS

Body, Sir Richard Bernard Frank Stewart, Kt., MP

Boevey, Sir Thomas Michael Blake Crawley-, Bt. (1784)

Bogan, Sir Nagora, KBE

Boileau, Sir Guy (Francis), Bt. (1838)

Boles, Sir Jeremy John Fortescue, Bt. (1922)

Boles, Sir John Dennis, Kt., MBE

Bolland, Sir Edwin, KCMG

Bollers, *Hon.* Sir Harold Brodie Smith, Kt.

Bolt, *Air Marshal* Sir Richard Bruce, KBE, CB, DFC, AFC

Bolton, Sir Frederic Bernard, Kt., MC

Bona, Sir Kina, KBE

Bonallack, Sir Michael Francis, Kt., OBE

Bond, Sir John Reginald Hartnell, Kt.

Bond, Sir Kenneth Raymond Boyden, Kt.

Bond, *Prof.* Sir Michael Richard, Kt., FRCPsych., FRCPGlas., FRCSE

Bondi, *Prof.* Sir Hermann, KCB, FRS

Bone, Sir Roger Bridgland, KCMG

Bonfield, Sir Peter Leahy, Kt., CBE, FREng.

Bonham, *Maj.* Sir Antony Lionel Thomas, Bt. (1852)

Bonington, Sir Christian John Storey, Kt., CBE

Bonsall, Sir Arthur Wilfred, KCMG, CBE

Bonsor, Sir Nicholas Cosmo, Bt. (1925)

Boolell, Sir Satcam, Kt.

Boord, Sir Nicolas John Charles, Bt. (1896)

Boorman, *Lt.-Gen.* Sir Derek, KCB

Booth, Sir Christopher Charles, Kt., MD, FRCP

Booth, *Hon.* Sir David Alwyn Gore-, KCMG, KCVO

Booth, Sir Douglas Allen, Bt. (1916)

Booth, Sir Gordon, KCMG, CVO

Booth, Sir Josslyn Henry Robert Gore-, Bt. (I. 1760)

Booth, Sir Michael Addison John Wheeler-, KCB

Boothby, Sir Brooke Charles, Bt. (1660)

Bore, Sir Albert, Kt.

Boreel, Sir Francis David, Bt. (1645)

Boreham, *Hon.* Sir Leslie Kenneth Edward, Kt.

Bornu, The Waziri of, KCMG, CBE

Borthwick, Sir John Thomas, Bt., MBE (1908)

Borysiewicz, *Prof.* Sir Leszek Krzysztof, Kt.

Bossom, *Hon.* Sir Clive, Bt. (1953)

Boswall, Sir (Thomas) Alford Houstoun-, Bt. (1836)

Boswell, *Lt.-Gen.* Sir Alexander Crawford Simpson, KCB, CBE

Bosworth, Sir Neville Bruce Alfred, Kt., CBE

Bottoms, *Prof.* Sir Anthony Edward, Kt.

Bottomley, Sir James Reginald Alfred, KCMG

Boughey, Sir John George Fletcher, Bt. (1798)

Boulton, Sir Clifford John, GCB

Boulton, Sir William Whytehead, Bt., CBE, TD (1944)

Bourn, Sir John Bryant, KCB

Bovell, *Hon.* Sir (William) Stewart, Kt.

Bowater, Sir Euan David Vansittart, Bt. (1939)

Bowater, Sir (John) Vansittart, Bt. (1914)

Bowden, Sir Andrew, Kt., MBE

†Bowden, Sir Nicholas Richard, Bt. (1915)

Bowen, Sir Geoffrey Fraser, Kt.

Bowen, Sir Mark Edward Mortimer, Bt. (1921)

Bowett, *Prof.* Sir Derek William, Kt., CBE, QC, FBA

†Bowlby, Sir Richard Peregrine Longstaff, Bt. (1923)

Bowman, Sir Jeffery Haverstock, Kt.

Bowman, Sir Paul Humphrey Armytage, Bt. (1884)

Bowness, Sir Alan, Kt., CBE

Boyce, Sir Graham Hugh, KCMG

Boyce, *Adm.* Sir Michael Cecil, GCB, OBE

Boyce, Sir Robert Charles Leslie, Bt. (1952)

Boyd, Sir Alexander Walter, Bt. (1916)

Boyd, Sir John Dixon Iklé, KCMG

Boyd, The *Hon.* Sir Mark Alexander Lennox-, Kt.

Boyd, *Prof.* Sir Robert Lewis Fullarton, Kt., CBE, D.Sc., FRS

Boyes, Sir Brian Gerald Barratt-, KBE

Boyle, Sir Stephen Gurney, Bt. (1904)

Boynton, Sir John Keyworth, Kt., MC

Boys, *Rt. Hon.* Sir Michael Hardie, GCMG

Boyson, *Rt. Hon.* Sir Rhodes, Kt.

Brabham, Sir John Arthur, Kt., OBE

Bradbeer, Sir John Derek Richardson, Kt., OBE, TD

Bradbury, *Surgeon Vice-Adm.* Sir Eric Blackburn, KBE, CB

Bradford, Sir Edward Alexander Slade, Bt. (1902)

Bradshaw, Sir Kenneth Anthony, KCB

Brain, Sir (Henry) Norman, KBE, CMG

Braithwaite, Sir (Joseph) Franklin Madders, Kt.

Braithwaite, *Rt. Hon.* Sir Nicholas Alexander, Kt., OBE

Braithwaite, Sir Rodric Quentin, GCMG

Bramley, *Prof.* Sir Paul Anthony, Kt.

Branson, Sir Richard Charles Nicholas, Kt.

Bratza, Sir Nicolas Dušan, Kt., QC

Brennan, *Hon.* Sir (Francis) Gerard, KBE

Brett, Sir Charles Edward Bainbridge, Kt., CBE

Brickwood, Sir Basil Greame, Bt. (1927)

Bridges, *Hon.* Sir Phillip Rodney, Kt., CMG

Brierley, Sir Ronald Alfred, Kt.

Bright, Sir Graham Frank James, Kt.

Bright, Sir Keith, Kt.

Brigstocke, *Adm.* Sir John Richard, KCB

Brinckman, Sir Theodore George Roderick, Bt. (1831)

†Brisco, Sir Campbell Howard, Bt. (1782)

Briscoe, Sir Brian Anthony, Kt.

Briscoe, Sir John Geoffrey James, Bt. (1910)

Brise, Sir John Archibald Ruggles-, Bt., CB, OBE, TD (1935)

Brittan, Sir Samuel, Kt.

Britton, Sir Edward Louis, Kt., CBE

†Broadbent, Sir Andrew George, Bt. (1893)

Brocklebank, Sir Aubrey Thomas, Bt. (1885)

Brodie, Sir Benjamin David Ross, Bt. (1834)

Broers, *Prof.* Sir Alec Nigel, Kt., Ph.D., FRS

Bromhead, Sir John Desmond Gonville, Bt. (1806)

Bromley, Sir Michael Roger, KBE

Bromley, Sir Rupert Charles, Bt. (1757)

Brook, *Prof.* Sir Richard John, Kt. OBE

†Brooke, Sir Alistair Weston, Bt. (1919)

Brooke, Sir Francis George Windham, Bt. (1903)

Brooke, *Rt. Hon.* Sir Henry, Kt.

Brooke, Sir (Richard) David Christopher, Bt. (1662)

Brooksbank, Sir (Edward) Nicholas, Bt. (1919)

Broom, *Air Marshal* Sir Ivor Gordon, KCB, CBE, DSO, DFC, AFC

Broomfield, Sir Nigel Hugh Robert Allen, KCMG

†Broughton, Sir David Delves, Bt. (1661)

Broun, Sir William Windsor, Bt. (S. 1686)

Brown, Sir Allen Stanley, Kt., CBE

Brown, Sir (Austen) Patrick, KCB

Brown, *Adm.* Sir Brian Thomas, KCB, CBE

Brown, Sir (Cyril) Maxwell Palmer, KCB, CMG

Brown, Sir David, Kt.

Brown, *Vice-Adm.* Sir David Worthington, KCB

Brown, Sir Derrick Holden-, Kt.

Brown, Sir Douglas Denison, Kt.

Brown, *Hon.* Sir Douglas Dunlop, Kt.

Brown, Sir George Francis Richmond, Bt. (1863)

Brown, Sir George Noel, Kt.

Brown, Sir John Gilbert Newton, Kt., CBE

Brown, Sir Martin, Kt.

Brown, Sir Mervyn, KCMG, OBE

Brown, Sir Peter Randolph, Kt.

Brown, *Hon.* Sir Ralph Kilner, Kt., OBE, TD

Brown, Sir Robert Crichton-, KCMG, CBE, TD

Brown, *Rt. Hon.* Sir Simon Denis, Kt.

Brown, *Rt. Hon.* Sir Stephen, GBE

Brown, Sir Stephen David Reid, KCVO

Brown, Sir Thomas, Kt.

Brown, Sir William Brian Piggott-, Bt. (1903)

Browne, Sir Anthony Arthur Duncan Montague-, KCMG, CBE, DFC

Browne, Sir Nicholas Walker, KBE, CMG

Brownrigg, Sir Nicholas (Gawen), Bt. (1816)

Browse, *Prof.* Sir Norman Leslie, Kt., MD, FRCS

Bruce, Sir (Francis) Michael Ian, Bt. (S. 1628)

Bruce, Sir Hervey James Hugh, Bt. (1804)

Brunner, Sir John Henry Kilian, Bt. (1895)

Brunton, Sir (Edward Francis) Lauder, Bt. (1908)

Brunton, Sir Gordon Charles, Kt.

Bryan, Sir Arthur, Kt.

Bryan, Sir Paul Elmore Oliver, Kt., DSO, MC

Bryce, *Hon.* Sir (William) Gordon, Kt., CBE

Bryson, *Adm.* Sir Lindsay Sutherland, KCB, FREng.

Buchan, Sir John, Kt., CMG

Buchanan, Sir Andrew George, Bt. (1878)

Buchanan, Sir Charles Alexander James Leith-, Bt. (1775)

Buchanan, *Vice-Adm.* Sir Peter William, KBE

Buchanan, Sir (Ranald) Dennis, Kt., MBE

Buchanan, Sir Robert Wilson (Robin), Kt.

Buck, Sir (Philip) Antony (Fyson), Kt., QC

Buckland, Sir Ross, Kt.

Buckley, Sir Michael Sidney, Kt.

Buckley, *Lt.-Cdr.* Sir (Peter) Richard, KCVO

Buckley, *Hon.* Sir Roger John, Kt.

Budd, Sir Alan Peter, Kt.
Budd, Sir Colin Richard, KCMG
Bulkeley, Sir Richard Thomas
Williams-, Bt. (1661)
Bull, Sir George Jeffrey, Kt.
Bull, Sir Simeon George, Bt. (1922)
Bullard, Sir Julian Leonard, GCMG
Bultin, Sir Bato, Kt., MBE
Bunbury, Sir Michael William, Bt.
(1681)
Bunbury, Sir (Richard David)
Michael Richardson-, Bt. (I. 1787)
Bunch, Sir Austin Wyeth, Kt., CBE
Bunyard, Sir Robert Sidney, Kt., CBE,
QPM
Burbidge, Sir Herbert Dudley, Bt.
(1916)
Burden, Sir Anthony Thomas, Kt.,
QPM
Burdett, Sir Savile Aylmer, Bt. (1665)
Burgen, Sir Arnold Stanley Vincent,
Kt., FRS
Burgess, Gen. Sir Edward Arthur,
KCB, OBE
Burgess, Sir (Joseph) Stuart, Kt.,
CBE, Ph.D., FRSC
Burgh, Sir John Charles, KCMG, CB
Burke, Sir James Stanley Gilbert, Bt.
(I. 1797)
Burke, Sir (Thomas) Kerry, Kt.
Burley, Sir Victor George, Kt., CBE
Burnet, Sir James William Alexander
(Sir Alastair Burnet), Kt.
Burnett, Air Chief Marshal Sir Brian
Kenyon, GCB, DFC, AFC
†Burnett, Sir Charles David, Bt.,
(1913)
Burnett, Sir John Harrison, Kt.
Burnett, Sir Walter John, Kt.
Burney, Sir Nigel Dennistoun, Bt.
(1921)
Burns, Sir (Robert) Andrew, KCMG
Burnton, Hon. Sir Stanley Jeffrey, Kt
Burrell, Sir John Raymond, Bt.
(1774)
Burston, Sir Samuel Gerald Wood,
Kt., OBE
Burt, Hon. Sir Francis Theodore
Page, KCMG
Burton, Sir Carlisle Archibald, Kt.,
OBE
Burton, Sir George Vernon Kennedy,
Kt., CBE
Burton, Lt.-Gen. Sir Edmund
Fortescue Gerard, KBE
Burton, Sir Graham Stuart, KCMG
Burton, Sir Michael John, Kt., QC
Burton, Sir Michael St Edmund,
KCVO, CMG
Bush, Adm. Sir John Fitzroy
Duyland, GCB, DSC
Butler, Rt. Hon. Sir Adam Courtauld,
Kt.
Butler, Hon. Sir Arlington Griffith,
KCMG
Butler, Sir Michael Dacres, GCMG
Butler, Sir (Reginald) Michael
(Thomas), Bt. (1922)
Butler, Sir Percy James, Kt., CBE, DL
Butler, Hon. Sir Richard Clive, Kt.

†Butler, Sir Richard Pierce, Bt.
(1628)
Butter, Maj. Sir David Henry, KCVO,
MC
Butterfield, Hon. Sir Alexander Neil
Logie, Kt.
Buxton, Sir Jocelyn Charles Roden,
Bt. (1840)
Buxton, Rt. Hon. Sir Richard Joseph,
Kt.
Buzzard, Sir Anthony Farquhar, Bt.
(1929)
Byatt, Sir Hugh Campbell, KCVO,
CMG
Byatt, Sir Ian Charles Rayner, Kt.
Byford, Sir Lawrence, Kt., CBE, QPM
Byron, Sir Charles Michael Dennis,
Kt.
Cadbury, Sir (George) Adrian
(Hayhurst), Kt.
Cadbury, Sir (Nicholas) Dominic,
Kt.
Cadogan, Prof. Sir John Ivan George,
Kt., CBE, FRS, FRSE
Cahn, Sir Albert Jonas, Bt. (1934)
Cain, Sir Henry Edney Conrad, Kt.
Caine, Sir Michael (Maurice
Micklewhite), Kt., CBE
Caines, Sir John, KCB
Calcutt, Sir David Charles, Kt., QC
Calderwood, Sir Robert, Kt.
Caldwell, Sir Edward George, KCB
Callan, Sir Ivan Roy, KCVO, CMG
Callaway, Prof. Sir Frank Adams, Kt.,
CMG, OBE
Calman, Prof. Sir Kenneth Charles,
KCB, MD, FRCP, FRCS, FRSE
Calne, Prof. Sir Roy Yorke, Kt., FRS
Calthorpe, Sir Euan Hamilton
Anstruther-Gough-, Bt. (1929)
Cameron of Lochiel, Sir Donald
Hamish, KT, CVO, TD
Cameron, Sir Hugh Roy Graham,
Kt., QPM
Campbell, Sir Alan Hugh, GCMG
Campbell, Prof. Sir Colin Murray,
Kt.
Campbell, Prof. Sir Donald, Kt., CBE,
FRCS, FRCPGlas.
Campbell, Sir Ian Tofts, Kt., CBE,
VRD
Campbell, Sir Ilay Mark, Bt. (1808)
Campbell, Sir James Alexander
Moffat Bain, Bt. (S. 1668)
Campbell, Sir Lachlan Philip
Kemeys, Bt. (1815)
Campbell, Sir Niall Alexander
Hamilton, Bt. (1831)
Campbell, Sir Robin Auchinbreck,
Bt. (S. 1628)
Campbell, Sir Alexander Thomas
Cockburn-, Bt. (1821)
Campbell, Hon. Sir Walter
Benjamin, Kt.
Campbell, Rt. Hon. Sir William
Anthony, Kt.
†Carden, Sir Christopher Robert, Bt.
(1887)
Carden, Sir John Craven, Bt.
(I. 1787)

Carew, Sir Rivers Verain, Bt. (1661)
Carey, Sir de Vic Graham, Kt.
Carey, Sir Peter Willoughby, GCB
Carlisle, Sir James Beethoven, GCMG,
GCQS
Carlisle, Sir John Michael, Kt.
Carlisle, Sir Kenneth Melville, Kt.
Carmichael, Sir David Peter William
Gibson-Craig-, Bt. (S. 1702 and
1831)
Carnac, Revd Canon Sir (Thomas)
Nicholas Rivett-, Bt. (1836)
Carnegie, Lt.-Gen. Sir Robin
Macdonald, KCB, OBE
Carnegie, Sir Roderick Howard, Kt.
Carnwath, Sir Robert John
Anderson, Kt., CVO
Caro, Sir Anthony Alfred, Kt., OM,
CBE
Carpenter, Lt.-Gen. the Hon. Sir
Thomas Patrick John Boyd-, KBE
Carr, Sir (Albert) Raymond
(Maillard), Kt.
Carrick, Hon. Sir John Leslie, KCMG
Carrick, Sir Roger John, KCMG, LVO
Carsberg, Prof. Sir Bryan Victor, Kt.
Carswell, Rt. Hon. Sir Robert
Douglas, Kt.
Carter, Prof. Sir David Craig, Kt.,
FRCSE, FRCSGlas., FRCPE
Carter, Gen. Sir Evelyn John Webb,
KCVO, OBE
Carter, Sir John, Kt., QC
Carter, Sir John Alexander, Kt.
Carter, Sir John Gordon Thomas, Kt.
Carter, Sir Philip David, Kt., CBE
Carter, Sir Richard Henry Alwyn, Kt.
Cartland, Sir George Barrington, Kt.,
CMG
Cartledge, Sir Bryan George, KCMG
Cary, Sir Roger Hugh, Bt. (1955)
Casey, Rt. Hon. Sir Maurice Eugene,
Kt.
Cash, Sir Gerald Christopher, GCMG,
GCVO, OBE
Cass, Sir Geoffrey Arthur, Kt.
Cassel, Sir Timothy Felix Harold, Bt.
(1920)
Cassels, Sir John Seton, Kt., CB
Cassels, Adm. Sir Simon Alastair
Cassillis, KCB, CBE
Cassidi, Adm. Sir (Arthur)
Desmond, GCB
Castell, Sir William Martin, Kt.
Cater, Sir Jack, KBE
Catford, Sir (John) Robin, KCVO, CBE
Catherwood, Sir (Henry) Frederick
(Ross), Kt.
Catling, Sir Richard Charles, Kt.,
CMG, OBE
Catto, Prof. Sir Graeme Robertson
Dawson, Kt.
Cave, Sir John Charles, Bt. (1896)
Cave, Sir Robert Cave-Browne-, Bt.
(1641)
Cayley, Sir Digby William David, Bt.
(1661)
Cayzer, Sir James Arthur, Bt. (1904)
Cazalet, Hon. Sir Edward Stephen,
Kt.
Cazalet, Sir Peter Grenville, Kt.

Cecil, *Rear-Adm.* Sir (Oswald) Nigel Amherst, KBE, CB

Chadwick, *Revd Prof.* Sir Henry, KBE

Chadwick, *Rt. Hon.* Sir John Murray, Kt., ED

Chadwick, Sir Joshua Kenneth Burton, Bt. (1935)

Chadwick, *Revd Prof.* Sir (William) Owen, OM, KBE, FBA

Chalmers, Sir Iain Geoffrey, Kt.

Chalmers, Sir Neil Robert, Kt.

Chalstrey, Sir (Leonard) John, Kt., MD, FRCS

Chan, *Rt. Hon.* Sir Julius, GCMG, KBE

Chance, Sir (George) Jeremy ffolliott, Bt. (1900)

Chandler, Sir Colin Michael, Kt.

Chandler, Sir Geoffrey, Kt., CBE

Chaney, *Hon.* Sir Frederick Charles, KBE, AFC

Chantler, *Prof.* Sir Cyril, Kt., MD, FRCP

Chaplin, Sir Malcolm Hilbery, Kt., CBE

Chapman, Sir David Robert Macgowan, Bt. (1958)

Chapman, Sir George Alan, Kt.

Chapman, Sir Sidney Brookes, Kt., MP

Chapman, *Lt-Gen.* Sir Timothy John Granville-, KCB, CBE

Chapple, *Field Marshal* Sir John Lyon, GCB, CBE

Charles, *Hon.* Sir Arthur William Hessin, Kt

Charles, Sir George Frederick Lawrence, KCMG, CBE

Charlton, Sir Robert (Bobby), Kt., CBE

Charnley, Sir (William) John, Kt., CB, FREng.

Chataway, *Rt. Hon.* Sir Christopher, Kt.

Chatfield, Sir John Freeman, Kt., CBE

Chaytor, Sir George Reginald, Bt. (1831)

Checketts, *Sqn. Ldr.* Sir David John, KCVO

Checkland, Sir Michael, Kt.

Cheshire, *Air Chief Marshal* Sir John Anthony, KBE, CB

Chessells, Sir Arthur David (Tim), Kt.

Chesterton, Sir Oliver Sidney, Kt., MC

Chetwood, Sir Clifford Jack, Kt.

Chetwynd, Sir Arthur Ralph Talbot, Bt. (1795)

Cheung, Sir Oswald Victor, Kt., CBE

Cheyne, Sir Joseph Lister Watson, Bt., OBE (1908)

Chichester, Sir (Edward) John, Bt. (1641)

Chilcot, Sir John Anthony, GCB

Child, Sir (Coles John) Jeremy, Bt. (1919)

Chilton, *Brig.* Sir Frederick Oliver, Kt., CBE, DSO

Chilwell, *Hon.* Sir Muir Fitzherbert, Kt.

Chinn, Sir Trevor Edwin, Kt., CVO

Chipperfield, Sir Geoffrey Howes, KCB

Chisholm, Sir John Alexander Raymond, Kt., FREng.

Chitty, Sir Thomas Willes, Bt. (1924)

Cholmeley, Sir Hugh John Frederick Sebastian, Bt. (1806)

Chow, Sir Chung Kong, Kt.

Chow, Sir Henry Francis, Kt., OBE

Christie, Sir George William Langham, Kt., CH

Christie, Sir William, Kt., MBE

Chung, Sir Sze-yuen, GBE, FREng.

Clapham, Sir Michael John Sinclair, KBE

Clark, Sir Francis Drake, Bt. (1886)

Clark, Sir John Stewart-, Bt., MEP (1918)

Clark, Sir Jonathan George, Bt. (1917)

Clark, Sir Robert Anthony, Kt., DSC

Clark, Sir Robin Chichester-, Kt.

Clark, Sir Terence Joseph, KBE, CMG, CVO

Clark, Sir Thomas Edwin, Kt.

Clarke, *Hon.* Sir Anthony Peter, Kt.

Clarke, Sir Arthur Charles, Kt., CBE

Clarke, Sir (Charles Mansfield) Tobias, Bt. (1831)

Clarke, Sir Ellis Emmanuel Innocent, GCMG

Clarke, Sir Jonathan Dennis, Kt.

Clarke, *Maj.* Sir Peter Cecil, KCVO

Clarke, Sir Robert Cyril, Kt.

Clarke, Sir Rupert William John, Bt., MBE (1882)

Clarke, Sir Stanley William, Kt., CBE

Clay, Sir Richard Henry, Bt. (1841)

Clayton, Sir David Robert, Bt. (1732)

Cleaver, Sir Anthony Brian, Kt.

Cleminson, Sir James Arnold Stacey, KBE, MC

Clerk, Sir John Dutton, Bt., CBE, VRD (s. 1679)

Clerke, Sir John Edward Longueville, Bt. (1660)

Clifford, Sir Roger Joseph, Bt. (1887)

Clifford, Sir Timothy Peter Plint, Kt.

Clothier, Sir Cecil Montacute, KCB, QC

Clucas, Sir Kenneth Henry, KCB

Clutterbuck, *Vice-Adm.* Sir David Granville, KBE, CB

Coates, Sir Anthony Robert Milnes, Bt. (1911)

Coates, Sir David Frederick Charlton, Bt. (1921)

Coats, Sir Alastair Francis Stuart, Bt. (1905)

Coats, Sir William David, Kt.

Cobham, Sir Michael John, Kt., CBE

Cochrane, Sir (Henry) Marc (Sursock), Bt. (1903)

Cockburn, Sir John Elliot, Bt. (s. 1671)

Cockshaw, Sir Alan, Kt., FREng.

Codrington, Sir Simon Francis Bethell, Bt. (1876)

Codrington, Sir William Alexander, Bt. (1721)

†Coghill, Sir Patrick Kendal Farley, Bt. (1778)

Coghlin, *Hon.* Sir Patrick, Kt.

Cohen, Sir Edward, Kt.

Cohen, Sir Ivor Harold, Kt., CBE, TD

Cohen, *Prof.* Sir Philip, Kt., Ph.D, FRS

Cohen, Sir Ronald, Kt.

Cohen, Sir Stephen Harry Waley-, Bt. (1961)

Coldstream, Sir George Phillips, GCB, KCVO, QC

Cole, Sir (Robert) William, Kt.

Coleridge, *Hon.* Mr Justice, Sir Paul James Duke, Kt.

Coles, Sir (Arthur) John, GCMG

Colfox, Sir (William) John, Bt. (1939)

Collett, Sir Christopher, GBE

Collett, Sir Ian Seymour, Bt. (1934)

Collins, *Hon.* Sir Andrew David, Kt.

Collins, Sir Bryan Thomas Alfred, Kt., OBE, QFSM

Collins, Sir John Alexander, Kt.

Collins, *Hon.* Sir Lawrence Antony, Kt.

Collyear, Sir John Gowen, Kt.

Colman, *Hon.* Sir Anthony David, Kt.

Colman, Sir Michael Jeremiah, Bt. (1907)

Colman, Sir Timothy, KG

Colquhoun of Luss, Sir Ivar Iain, Bt. (1786)

Colt, Sir Edward William Dutton, Bt. (1694)

Colthurst, Sir Richard La Touche, Bt. (1744)

Coltman, Sir (Arthur) Leycester Scott, KBE, CMG

Colvin, Sir Howard Montagu, Kt., CVO, CBE, FBA

Compton, *Rt. Hon.* Sir John George Melvin, KCMG

Conant, Sir John Ernest Michael, Bt. (1954)

Condon, Sir Paul Leslie, Kt., QPM

Connell, *Hon.* Sir Michael Bryan, Kt.

Connery, Sir Sean, Kt.

Conran, Sir Terence Orby, Kt.

Cons, *Hon.* Sir Derek, Kt.

Constable, Sir Frederic Strickland-, Bt. (1641)

Constantinou, Sir Georkios, Kt., OBE

Cook, *Prof.* Sir Alan Hugh, Kt.

Cook, Sir Christopher Wymondham Rayner Herbert, Bt. (1886)

Cooke, *Col.* Sir David William Perceval, Bt. (1661)

Cooke, Sir Howard Felix Hanlan, GCMG, GCVO

Cooke, *Hon.* Mr Justice, Sir Jeremy Lionel, Kt.

Cooke, *Prof.* Sir Ronald Urwick, Kt.

Cooksey, Sir David James Scott, Kt.

Cooper, Sir (Frederick Howard) Michael Craig-, Kt., CBE, TD

Cooper, *Gen.* Sir George Leslie Conroy, GCB, MC

Cooper, Sir Henry, Kt.

Cooper, Sir Louis Jacques Blom-, Kt., QC

†Cooper, Sir Alexander Paston Astley, Bt. (1821)

Cooper, Sir Richard Powell, Bt. (1905)

Cooper, Sir Robert George, Kt., CBE

Cooper, *Maj.-Gen.* Sir Simon Christie, GCVO

Cooper, Sir William Daniel Charles, Bt. (1863)

Coote, Sir Christopher John, Bt., *Premier Baronet of Ireland* (I. 1621)

Copas, *Most Revd* Sir Virgil, KBE, DD

Copisarow, Sir Alcon Charles, Kt.

Corbett, *Maj.-Gen.* Sir Robert John Swan, KCVO, CB

Corby, Sir (Frederick) Brian, Kt.

Corfield, *Rt. Hon.* Sir Frederick Vernon, Kt., QC

Corfield, Sir Kenneth George, Kt., FREng.

Cork, Sir Roger William, Kt.

Corley, Sir Kenneth Sholl Ferrand, Kt.

Cormack, Sir Patrick Thomas, Kt., MP

Corness, Sir Colin Ross, Kt.

Cornforth, Sir John Warcup, Kt., CBE, D.Phil., FRS

Cortazzi, Sir (Henry Arthur) Hugh, GCMG

Cory, Sir (Clinton Charles) Donald, Bt. (1919)

Cossons, Sir Neil, Kt., OBE

†Cotter, Sir Patrick Laurence Delaval Bt. (I. 1763)

Cotterell, Sir John Henry Geers, Bt. (1805)

Cotton, *Hon.* Sir Robert Carrington, KCMG

Cotton, Sir William Frederick, Kt., CBE

Cottrell, Sir Alan Howard, Kt., Ph.D., FRS, FREng.

†Cotts, Sir Richard Crichton Mitchell, Bt. (1921)

†Couper, Sir James George, Bt. (1841)

Court, *Hon.* Sir Charles Walter Michael, KCMG, OBE

Courtenay, Sir Thomas Daniel, Kt.

Cousins, *Air Chief Marshal* Sir David, KCB, AFC

Coutts, Sir David Burdett Money-, KCVO

Couzens, Sir Kenneth Edward, KCB

Covacevich, Sir (Anthony) Thomas, Kt., DFC

Coville, *Air Marshal* Sir Christopher Charles Cotton, KCB

Cowan, *Gen.* Sir Samuel, KCB, CBE

Coward, *Vice-Adm.* Sir John Francis, KCB, DSO

Cowen, *Rt. Hon. Prof.* Sir Zelman, GCMG, GCVO, QC

Cowie, Sir Thomas (Tom), Kt., OBE

Cowperthwaite, Sir John James, KBE, CMG

Cox, Sir Alan George, Kt., CBE

Cox, *Prof.* Sir David Roxbee, Kt., FRS

Cox, Sir Geoffrey Sandford, Kt., CBE

Cox, *Vice-Adm.* Sir John Michael Holland, KCB

Cradock, *Rt. Hon.* Sir Percy, GCMG

Craig, Sir (Albert) James (Macqueen), GCMG

Crane, *Hon.* Sir Peter Francis, Kt.

Craufurd, Sir Robert James, Bt. (1781)

Craven, Sir John Anthony, Kt.

Craven, *Air Marshal* Sir Robert Edward, KBE, CB, DFC

Crawford, *Prof.* Sir Frederick William, Kt., FREng.

Crawford, Sir (Robert) Stewart, GCMG, CVO

Crawford, *Vice-Adm.* Sir William Godfrey, KBE, CB, DSC

Crew, Sir (Michael) Edward, Kt., QPM

Cresswell, *Hon.* Sir Peter John, Kt.

Crick, *Prof.* Sir Bernard, Kt.

Crill, Sir Peter Leslie, KBE

Crisp, Sir (John) Peter, Bt. (1913)

Critchett, Sir Ian (George Lorraine), Bt. (1908)

Crocker, Sir Walter Russell, KBE

Croft, Sir Owen Glendower, Bt. (1671)

Croft, Sir Thomas Stephen Hutton, Bt. (1818)

†Crofton, Sir Hugh Denis, Bt. (1801)

Crofton, *Prof.* Sir John Wenman, Kt.

†Crofton, Sir Henry Edward Melville, Bt. (1838)

Crookenden, *Lt.-Gen.* Sir Napier, KCB, DSO, OBE

Cross, *Air Chief Marshal* Sir Kenneth Brian Boyd, KCB, CBE, DSO, DFC

Crossland, *Prof.* Sir Bernard, Kt., CBE, FREng.

Crossley, Sir Julian Charles, Bt. (1909)

Crowe, Sir Brian Lee, KCMG

Cruthers, Sir James Winter, Kt.

Cubbon, Sir Brian Crossland, GCB

Cubitt, Sir Hugh Guy, Kt., CBE

Cullen, Sir (Edward) John, Kt., FREng.

Culpin, Sir Robert Paul, Kt.

Cumming, Sir William Gordon Gordon-, Bt. (1804)

Cuninghame, Sir John Christopher Foggo Montgomery-, Bt. (NS 1672)

Cuningham, Sir Robert Henry Fairlie-, Bt. (S. 1630)

Cunliffe, Sir David Ellis, Bt. (1759)

Cunningham, *Lt.-Gen.* Sir Hugh Patrick, KBE

Cunynghame, Sir Andrew David Francis, Bt. (S. 1702)

†Currie, Sir Donald Scott, Bt. (1847)

Currie, Sir Neil Smith, Kt., CBE

Curry, Sir Donald Thomas Younger, Kt., CBE

Curtis, Sir Barry John, Kt.

Curtis, *Hon.* Sir Richard Herbert, Kt.

Curtis, Sir William Peter, Bt. (1802)

Curtiss, *Air Marshal* Sir John Bagot, KCB, KBE

Curwen, Sir Christopher Keith, KCMG

Cuschieri, *Prof.* Sir Alfred, Kt.

Cutler, Sir Charles Benjamin, KBE, ED

Dacie, *Prof.* Sir John Vivian, Kt., MD, FRS

Dain, Sir David John Michael, KCVO

Dalrymple, *Maj.* Sir Hew Fleetwood Hamilton-, Bt., GCVO, (S. 1697)

Dalton, Sir Alan Nugent Goring, Kt., CBE

Dalton, *Vice-Adm.* Sir Geoffrey Thomas James Oliver, KCB

Daly, *Lt.-Gen.* Sir Thomas Joseph, KBE, CB, DSO

Dalyell, Sir Tam (Thomas), Bt., MP (NS 1685)

Daniel, Sir Goronwy Hopkin, KCVO, CB, D.Phil.

Daniel, Sir John Sagar, Kt., D.Sc.

Daniel, Sir Wilred St Clair-, Kt., CBE, JP

Darby, Sir Peter Howard, Kt., CBE, QFSM

Darell, Sir Jeffrey Lionel, Bt., MC (1795)

Dargie, Sir William Alexander, Kt., CBE

Dark, Sir Anthony Michael Beaumont-, Kt.

Darling, Sir Clifford, GCVO

Darvall, Sir (Charles) Roger, Kt., CBE

Dasgupta, *Prof.* Sir Partha Sarathi, Kt.

†Dashwood, Sir Edward John Francis, Bt., *Premier Baronet of Great Britain* (1707)

Dashwood, Sir Richard James, Bt. (1684)

Daunt, Sir Timothy Lewis Achilles, KCMG

Davey, *Hon.* Sir David Herbert Penry-, Kt.

David, Sir Jean Marc, Kt., CBE, QC

David, *His Hon.* Sir Robin (Robert) Daniel George, Kt., QC

Davidge, Sir Leonard Edward, Kt.

Davidson, Sir Robert James, Kt., FREng.

†Davie, Sir Michael Ferguson-, Bt. (1847)

Davies, Sir Alan Seymour, Kt.

Davies, *Hon.* Sir (Alfred William) Michael, Kt.

Davies, Sir (Charles) Noel, Kt.

Davies, *Prof.* Sir David Evan Naughton, Kt., CBE, FRS, FREng.

Davies, *Hon.* Sir (David Herbert) Mervyn, Kt., MC, TD

Davies, Sir David John, Kt.

Davies, Sir Frank John, Kt., CBE

Davies, *Prof.* Sir Graeme John, Kt., FREng.

Davies, Sir John Howard, Kt.

Davies, Sir John Michael, KCB

Davies, *Vice-Adm.* Sir Lancelot Richard Bell, KBE

Davies, Sir Peter Maxwell, Kt., CBE

Davies, Sir Rhys Everson, Kt., QC

Davis, Sir Andrew Frank, Kt., CBE

Davis, Sir Colin Rex, Kt., CH, CBE

Davis, Sir (Ernest) Howard, Kt., CMG, OBE

Davis, Sir John Gilbert, Bt. (1946)

Davis, Hon. Mr Justice, Sir Nigel Anthony Lambert, Kt.

Davis, Sir Peter John, Kt.

Davis, Sir Thomas Robert Alexander Harries, KBE

Davison, Rt. Hon. Sir Ronald Keith, GBE, CMG

Davson, Sir Christopher Michael Edward, Bt. (1927)

Dawanincura, Sir John Norbert, Kt., OBE

Dawbarn, Sir Simon Yelverton, KCVO, CMG

Dawson, Hon. Sir Daryl Michael, KBE, CB

Dawson, Sir Hugh Michael Trevor, Bt. (1920)

Dawtry, Sir Alan (Graham), Kt., CBE, TD

Day, Sir Derek Malcolm, KCMG

Day, Air Chief Marshal Sir John Romney, KCB, OBE, ADC

Day, Sir (Judson) Graham, Kt.

Day, Sir Michael John, Kt., OBE

Day, Sir Simon James, Kt.

Deakin, Sir (Frederick) William (Dampier), Kt., DSO

Deane, Hon. Sir William Patrick, KBE

Dear, Sir Geoffrey James, Kt., QPM

Dearlove, Sir Richard Billing, KCMG, OBE

de Bellaigue, Sir Geoffrey, GCVO

†Debenham, Sir Thomas Adam Bt. (1931)

de Deney, Sir Geoffrey Ivor, KCVO

de Hoghton, Sir (Richard) Bernard (Cuthbert), Bt. (1611)

De la Bère, Sir Cameron, Bt. (1953)

de la Rue, Sir Andrew George Ilay, Bt. (1898)

Dellow, Sir John Albert, Kt., CBE

de Montmorency, Sir Arnold Geoffroy, Bt. (I. 1631)

Denholm, Sir John Ferguson (Ian), Kt., CBE

Denman, Sir (George) Roy, KCB, CMG

Denny, Sir Anthony Coningham de Waltham, Bt. (I. 1782)

Denny, Sir Charles Alistair Maurice, Bt. (1913)

Denton, Prof. Sir Eric James, Kt., CBE, FRS

Derbyshire, Sir Andrew George, Kt.

Derham, Sir Peter John, Kt.

de Trafford, Sir Dermot Humphrey, Bt. (1841)

Deverell, Lt.-Gen. Sir John Freegard, KCB, OBE

Devesi, Sir Baddeley, GCMG, GCVO

De Ville, Sir Harold Godfrey Oscar, Kt., CBE

Devitt, Sir James Hugh Thomas, Bt. (1916)

de Waal, Sir (Constant Henrik) Henry, KCB, QC

Dewar, Sir John James Evelyn, Bt. (1907)

Dewey, Sir Anthony Hugh, Bt. (1917)

Dewhurst, Prof. Sir (Christopher) John, Kt.

De Witt, Sir Ronald Wayne, Kt.

D'Eyncourt, Sir Mark Gervais Tennyson-, Bt. (1930)

Dhenin, Air Marshal Sir Geoffrey Howard, KBE, AFC, GM, MD

Dhrangadhra, HH the Maharaja Raj Saheb of, KCIE

Dibela, Hon. Sir Kingsford, GCMG

Dick, Maj.-Gen. Sir Iain Charles Mackay-, KCVO, MBE

Dickenson, Sir Aubrey Fiennes Trotman-, Kt.

Dickinson, Sir Harold Herbert, Kt.

Dickinson, Sir Samuel Benson, Kt.

Dilke, Sir Charles John Wentworth, Bt. (1862)

Dillon, Rt. Hon. Sir (George) Brian (Hugh), Kt.

Dixon, Sir Jeremy, Kt.

Dixon, Sir Jonathan Mark, Bt. (1919)

Djanogly, Sir Harry Ari Simon, Kt., CBE

Dobbs, Capt. Sir Richard Arthur Frederick, KCVO

Dobson, Vice-Adm. Sir David Stuart, KBE

Dobson, Gen. Sir Patrick John Howard-, GCB

Dodds, Sir Ralph Jordan, Bt. (1964)

Dodson, Sir Derek Sherborne Lindsell, KCMG, MC

Dodsworth, Sir John Christopher Smith-, Bt. (1784)

Doll, Prof. Sir (William) Richard (Shaboe), Kt., CH, OBE, FRS, DM, MD, D.Sc.

Dollery, Sir Colin Terence, Kt.

Donald, Sir Alan Ewen, KCMG

Donald, Air Marshal Sir John George, KBE

Donaldson, Prof. Sir Liam Joseph, Kt.

Donne, Hon. Sir Gaven John, KBE

Donne, Sir John Christopher, Kt.

Dookun, Sir Dewoonarain, Kt.

Dorey, Sir Graham Martyn, Kt.

Dorman, Sir Philip Henry Keppel, Bt. (1923)

Dougherty, Maj.-Gen. Sir Ivan Noel, Kt., CBE, DSO, ED

Doughty, Sir Graham Martin, Kt.

Doughty, Sir William Roland, Kt.

Douglas, Sir (Edward) Sholto, Kt.

Douglas, Hon. Sir Roger Owen, Kt.

Douglas, Rt. Hon. Sir William Randolph, KCMG

Dover, Prof. Sir Kenneth James, Kt., D.Litt., FBA, FRSE

Dowell, Sir Anthony James, Kt., CBE

Dowling, Sir Robert, Kt.

Down, Sir Alastair Frederick, Kt., OBE, MC, TD

Downes, Sir Edward Thomas, Kt., CBE

Downey, Sir Gordon Stanley, KCB

Downs, Sir Diarmuid, Kt., CBE, FREng.

Downward, Maj.-Gen. Sir Peter Aldcroft, KCVO, CB, DSO, DFC

Downward, Sir William Atkinson, Kt.

Dowson, Sir Philip Manning, Kt., CBE, PRA

Doyle, Sir Reginald Derek Henry, Kt., CBE

†D'Oyly, Sir Hadley Gregory Bt. (1663)

Drake, Hon. Sir (Frederick) Maurice, Kt., DFC

Drewry, Lt.-Gen. Sir Christopher Francis, KCB, CBE

Dreyer, Adm. Sir Desmond Parry, GCB, CBE, DSC

Drinkwater, Sir John Muir, Kt., QC

Driver, Sir Eric William, Kt.

Drummond, Sir John Richard Gray, Kt., CBE

Drury, Sir (Victor William) Michael, Kt., OBE

Dryden, Sir John Stephen Gyles, Bt. (1733 and 1795)

du Cann, Rt. Hon. Sir Edward Dillon Lott, KBE

†Duckworth, Sir Edward Richard Dyce, Bt. (1909)

du Cros, Sir Claude Philip Arthur Mallet, Bt. (1916)

Duffell, Lt.-Gen. Sir Peter Royson, KCB, CBE, MC

Duffus, Hon. Sir Herbert George Holwell, Kt.

Duffy, Sir (Albert) (Edward) Patrick, Kt., Ph.D.

Dugdale, Sir William Stratford, Bt., MC (1936)

Dummett, Prof. Sir Michael Anthony Eardley, Kt., FBA

Dunbar, Sir Archibald Ranulph, Bt. (S. 1700)

Dunbar, Sir David Hope-, Bt. (S. 1664)

Dunbar, Sir Robert Drummond Cospatrick, Bt. (S. 1698)

Dunbar, Sir James Michael, Bt. (S. 1694)

†Dunbar of Hempriggs, Sir Richard Francis, Bt. (S. 1706)

Duncan, Sir James Blair, Kt.

Duncombe, Sir Philip Digby Pauncefort-, Bt. (1859)

Dunlop, Sir Thomas, Bt. (1916)

Dunn, Air Marshal Sir Eric Clive, KBE, CB, BEM

Dunn, Air Marshal Sir Patrick Hunter, KBE, CB, DFC

Dunn, Rt. Hon. Sir Robin Horace Walford, Kt., MC

Dunne, Sir Thomas Raymond, KCVO

Dunning, Sir Simon William Patrick, Bt. (1930)

Dunstan, Lt.-Gen. Sir Donald Beaumont, KBE, CB

Dunt, *Vice-Adm.* Sir John Hugh, KCB

Duntze, Sir Daniel Evans Bt. (1774)

Dupre, Sir Tumun, Kt., MBE

Dupree, Sir Peter, Bt. (1921)

Durand, Sir Edward Alan Christopher David Percy, Bt. (1892)

Durant, Sir (Robert) Anthony (Bevis), Kt.

Durham, Sir Kenneth, Kt.

Durkin, *Air Marshal* Sir Herbert, KBE, CB

Durrant, Sir William Alexander Estridge, Bt. (1784)

Duthie, *Prof.* Sir Herbert Livingston, Kt.

Duthie, Sir Robert Grieve (Robin), Kt., CBE

Dwyer, Sir Joseph Anthony, Kt.

Dyer, *Prof.* Sir (Henry) Peter (Francis) Swinnerton-, Bt., KBE, FRS (1678)

Dyke, Sir David William Hart, Bt. (1677)

Dyson, *Hon.* Sir John Anthony, Kt.

Eady, *Hon.* Sir David, Kt.

Earle, Sir (Hardman) George (Algernon), Bt. (1869)

Easton, Sir Robert William Simpson, Kt., CBE

Eaton, *Adm.* Sir Kenneth John, GBE, KCB

Eberle, *Adm.* Sir James Henry Fuller, GCB

Ebrahim, Sir (Mahomed) Currimbhoy, Bt. (1910)

Echlin, Sir Norman David Fenton, Bt. (I. 1721)

Eckersley, Sir Donald Payze, Kt., OBE

Edge, *Capt.* Sir (Philip) Malcolm, KCVO

†Edge, Sir William, Bt. (1937)

Edmonstone, Sir Archibald Bruce Charles, Bt. (1774)

Edwardes, Sir Michael Owen, Kt.

Edwards, Sir Christopher John Churchill, Bt. (1866)

Edwards, Sir George Robert, Kt., OM, CBE, FRS, FREng.

Edwards, Sir Llewellyn Roy, Kt.

Edwards, *Prof.* Sir Samuel Frederick, Kt., FRS

Egan, Sir John Leopold, Kt.

Egerton, Sir John Alfred Roy, Kt.

Egerton, Sir (Philip) John (Caledon) Grey-, Bt. (1617)

Egerton, Sir Stephen Loftus, KCMG

Eichelbaum, *Rt. Hon.* Sir Thomas, GBE

Elias, Sir Patrick, Kt., QC

Eliott of Stobs, Sir Charles Joseph Alexander, Bt. (S. 1666)

Ellerton, Sir Geoffrey James, Kt., CMG, MBE

Elliot, Sir Gerald Henry, Kt.

Elliott, Sir Clive Christopher Hugh, Bt. (1917)

Elliott, Sir David Murray, KCMG, CB

Elliott, *Prof.* Sir John Huxtable, Kt., FBA

Elliott, Sir Randal Forbes, KBE

Elliott, *Prof.* Sir Roger James, Kt., FRS

Elliott, Sir Ronald Stuart, Kt.

Ellis, Sir Ronald, Kt., FREng.

Ellison, *Col.* Sir Ralph Harry Carr-, KCVO, TD

Elphinstone, Sir John, Bt. (S. 1701)

Elphinstone, Sir John Howard Main, Bt. (1816)

Elton, Sir Arnold, Kt., CBE

Elton, Sir Charles Abraham Grierson, Bt. (1717)

Elwes, Sir Jeremy Vernon, Kt., CBE

Elwood, Sir Brian George Conway, Kt., CBE

Elworthy, Sir Peter Herbert, Kt.

Emery, *Rt. Hon.* Sir Peter Frank Hannibal, Kt., MP

Empey, Sir Reginald Norman Morgan, Kt., OBE

Engle, Sir George Lawrence Jose, KCB, QC

English, Sir Terence Alexander Hawthorne, KBE, FRCS

Epstein, *Prof.* Sir (Michael) Anthony, Kt., CBE, FRS

Errington, *Col.* Sir Geoffrey Frederick, Bt., OBE (1963)

Errington, Sir Lancelot, KCB

Erskine, Sir (Thomas) David, Bt. (1821)

Esmonde, Sir Thomas Francis Grattan, Bt. (I. 1629)

Espie, Sir Frank Fletcher, Kt., OBE

Esplen, Sir John Graham, Bt. (1921)

Essenhigh, *Adm.* Sir Nigel Richard, GCB

Etherton, *Hon.* Sir Terence Michael Elkan Barnet, Kt.

Evans, Sir Anthony Adney, Bt. (1920)

Evans, *Rt. Hon.* Sir Anthony Howell Meurig, Kt., RD

Evans, *Prof.* Sir Christopher Thomas, Kt., OBE

Evans, *Air Chief Marshal* Sir David George, GCB, CBE

Evans, *Air Chief Marshal* Sir David Parry-, GCB, CBE

Evans, *Hon.* Sir David Roderick, Kt.

Evans, *Hon.* Sir Haydn Tudor, Kt.

Evans, *Prof.* Sir John Grimley, Kt., FRCP

Evans, Sir John Stanley, Kt., QPM

Evans, Sir Richard Harry, Kt., CBE

Evans, Sir Richard Mark, KCMG, KCVO

Evans, Sir Robert, Kt., CBE, FREng.

Evans, Sir (William) Vincent (John), GCMG, MBE, QC

Eveleigh, *Rt. Hon.* Sir Edward Walter, Kt., ERD

Everard, Sir Robin Charles, Bt. (1911)

Every, Sir Henry John Michael, Bt. (1641)

Ewans, Sir Martin Kenneth, KCMG

†Ewart, Sir William Michael, Bt. (1887)

Ewbank, *Hon.* Sir Anthony Bruce, Kt.

Ewin, Sir (David) Ernest Thomas Floyd, Kt., OBE, LVO

Ewing, Sir (Alistair) Simon Orr-, Bt. (1963)

Ewing, Sir Ronald Archibald Orr-, Bt. (1886)

Eyre, *Maj.-Gen.* Sir James Ainsworth Campden Gabriel, KCVO, CBE

Eyre, Sir Reginald Edwin, Kt.

Eyre, Sir Richard Charles Hastings, Kt., CBE

Faber, Sir Richard Stanley, KCVO, CMG

Fagge, Sir John William Frederick, Bt. (1660)

Fairbairn, Sir (James) Brooke, Bt. (1869)

Fairclough, Sir John Whitaker, Kt., FREng.

Fairhall, *Hon.* Sir Allen, KBE

Fairweather, Sir Patrick Stanislaus, KCMG

Falconer, *Hon.* Sir Douglas William, Kt., MBE

†Falkiner, Sir Benjamin Simon Patrick, Bt. (I. 1778)

Fall, Sir Brian James Proetel, GCVO, KCMG

Falle, Sir Samuel, KCMG, KCVO, DSC

Fang, *Prof.* Sir Harry, Kt., CBE

Fareed, Sir Djamil Sheik, Kt.

Farmer, Sir Thomas, Kt., CBE

Farquhar, Sir Michael Fitzroy Henry, Bt. (1796)

Farquharson, *Rt. Hon.* Sir Donald Henry, Kt.

Farquharson, Sir James Robbie, KBE

Farrell, Sir Terence, Kt., CBE

Farrer, Sir (Charles) Matthew, GCVO

Farrington, Sir Henry Francis Colden, Bt. (1818)

Fat, Sir (Maxime) Edouard (Lim Man) Lim, Kt.

Faulkner, Sir (James) Dennis (Compton), Kt., CBE, VRD

Fawcus, Sir (Robert) Peter, KBE, CMG

Fawkes, Sir Randol Francis, Kt.

Fay, Sir (Humphrey) Michael Gerard, Kt.

Fayrer, Sir John Lang Macpherson, Bt. (1896)

Fearn, Sir (Patrick) Robin, KCMG

Feilden, Sir Bernard Melchior, Kt., CBE

Feilden, Sir Henry Wemyss, Bt., (1846)

Fell, Sir David, KCB

Fender, Sir Brian Edward Frederick, Kt., CMG, Ph.D.

Fenn, Sir Nicholas Maxted, GCMG

Fennell, *Hon.* Sir (John) Desmond Augustine, Kt., OBE

Fennessy, Sir Edward, Kt., CBE

Fergus, Sir Howard Archibald, KBE, CBE

Ferguson, Sir Alexander Chapman, Kt., CBE

Ferguson, Sir Ian Edward Johnson-, Bt. (1906)

Fergusson of Kilkerran, Sir Charles, Bt. (S. 1703)

Fergusson, Sir Ewan Alastair John, GCMG, GCVO

Fergusson, Sir James Herbert Hamilton Colyer-, Bt. (1866)

Feroze, Sir Rustam Moolan, Kt., FRCS

Ferris, *Hon.* Sir Francis Mursell, Kt., TD

ffolkes, Sir Robert Francis Alexander, Bt, OBE (1774)

Field, Sir Malcolm David, Kt.

Field, *Hon* Mr Justice, Sir Richard Alan, Kt.

Fielding, Sir Colin Cunningham, Kt., CB

Fielding, Sir Leslie, KCMG

Fieldsend, *Hon.* Sir John Charles Rowell, KBE

Fiennes, Sir Ranulph Twisleton-Wykeham-, Bt., OBE (1916)

Figg, Sir Leonard Clifford William, KCMG

Figgis, Sir Anthony St John Howard, KCVO, CMG

Figures, Sir Colin Frederick, KCMG, OBE

Fingland, Sir Stanley James Gunn, KCMG

Finlay, Sir David Ronald James Bell, Bt. (1964)

Finney, Sir Thomas, Kt., OBE

Fisher, Sir George Read, Kt., CMG

Fisher, *Hon.* Sir Henry Arthur Pears, Kt.

Fison, Sir (Richard) Guy, Bt., DSC (1905)

†Fitzgerald, *Revd* (Sir) Daniel Patrick, Bt. (1903)

FitzGerald, Sir Adrian James Andrew, Bt. (1880)

FitzHerbert, Sir Richard Ranulph, Bt. (1784)

Fitzpatrick, *Gen.* Sir (Geoffrey Richard) Desmond, GCB, GCVO, DSO, MBE, MC

Fitzpatrick, *Air Marshal* Sir John Bernard, KBE, CB

Flanagan, Sir Ronald, GCB, OBE

Fletcher, Sir Henry Egerton Aubrey-, Bt. (1782)

Fletcher, Sir James Muir Cameron, Kt.

Floissac, *Hon.* Sir Vincent Frederick, Kt., CMG, OBE, QC

Floyd, Sir Giles Henry Charles, Bt. (1816)

Foley, *Lt.-Gen.* Sir John Paul, KCB, OBE, MC

Foley, Sir (Thomas John) Noel, Kt., CBE

Follett, *Prof.* Sir Brian Keith, Kt., FRS

Foot, Sir Geoffrey James, Kt.

Foots, Sir James William, Kt.

Forbes, *Maj.* Sir Hamish Stewart, Bt., MBE, MC (1823)

Forbes of Craigievar, Sir John Alexander Cumnock, Bt. (S. 1630)

Forbes, *Vice-Adm.* Sir John Morrison, KCB

Forbes, *Hon.* Sir Thayne John, Kt.

†Forbes, Sir William Daniel Stuart-, Bt. (S. 1626)

Ford, Sir Andrew Russell, Bt. (1929)

Ford, Sir David Robert, KBE, LVO, OBE

Ford, *Maj.* Sir Edward William Spencer, GCVO, KCB, ERD

Ford, *Air Marshal* Sir Geoffrey Harold, KBE, CB, FREng.

Ford, *Prof.* Sir Hugh, Kt., FRS, FREng.

Ford, Sir James Anson St Clair-, Bt. (1793)

Ford, Sir John Archibald, KCMG, MC

Ford, *Gen.* Sir Robert Cyril, GCB, CBE

Foreman, Sir Philip Frank, Kt., CBE, FREng.

Forman, Sir John Denis, Kt., OBE

Forrest, *Prof.* Sir (Andrew) Patrick (McEwen), Kt.

Forrest, *Rear-Adm.* Sir Ronald Stephen, KCVO

Forte, *Hon.* Sir Rocco John Vincent, Kt.

Forwood, Sir Peter Noel, Bt. (1895)

Foster, Sir Andrew William, Kt.

Foster, *Prof.* Sir Christopher David, Kt.

Foster, Sir John Gregory, Bt. (1930)

Foster, Sir Robert Sidney, GCMG, KCVO

Foulis, Sir Ian Primrose Liston-, Bt. (S. 1634)

Foulkes, Sir Arther Alexander, KCMG

Foulkes, Sir Nigel Gordon, Kt.

Fountain, *Hon.* Sir Cyril Stanley Smith, Kt.

Fowden, Sir Leslie, Kt., FRS

Fowke, Sir David Frederick Gustavus, Bt. (1814)

Fowler, Sir (Edward) Michael Coulson, Kt.

Fox, *Rt. Hon.* Sir Michael John, Kt.

Fox, Sir Paul Leonard, Kt., CBE

France, Sir Christopher Walter, GCB

Francis, Sir Horace William Alexander, Kt., CBE, FREng.

Frank, Sir Douglas George Horace, Kt., QC

Frank, Sir Robert Andrew, Bt. (1920)

Franklin, Sir Michael David Milroy, KCB, CMG

Franklin, Sir Michael George Charles, Kt.

Franks, Sir Arthur Temple, KCMG

Fraser, Sir Alasdair MacLeod, Kt.

Fraser, Sir Charles Annand, KCVO

Fraser, *Gen.* Sir David William, GCB, OBE

Fraser, Sir Iain Michael Duncan, Bt. (1943)

Fraser, Sir Ian James, Kt., CBE, MC

Fraser, Sir (James) Campbell, Kt.

Fraser, Sir James Murdo, KBE

Fraser, Sir William Kerr, GCB

Frayling, *Prof.* Sir Christopher John, Kt.

Frederick, Sir Christopher St John, Bt. (1723)

Freeland, Sir John Redvers, KCMG

Freeman, Sir James Robin, Bt. (1945)

Freer, *Air Chief Marshal* Sir Robert William George, GBE, KCB

French, *Hon.* Sir Christopher James Saunders, Kt.

Frere, *Vice-Adm.* Sir Richard Tobias, KCB

Fretwell, Sir (Major) John (Emsley), GCMG

Freud, Sir Clement Raphael, Kt.

Froggatt, Sir Leslie Trevor, Kt.

Froggatt, Sir Peter, Kt.

Frossard, Sir Charles Keith, KBE

Frost, Sir David Paradine, Kt., OBE

Frost, Sir Terence Ernest Manitou, Kt., RA

Fry, Sir Peter Derek, Kt.

Fuller, Sir James Henry Fleetwood, Bt. (1910)

Fuller, *Hon.* Sir John Bryan Munro, Kt.

Furness, Sir Stephen Roberts, Bt. (1913)

Gadsden, Sir Peter Drury Haggerston, GBE, FREng.

Gage, *Hon.* Sir William Marcus, Kt.

Gainsford, Sir Ian Derek, Kt., DDS

Gaius, *Rt. Revd* Saimon, KBE

Gallwey, Sir Philip Frankland Payne-, Bt. (1812)

Galsworthy, Sir Anthony Charles, KCMG

Galway, Sir James, Kt., OBE

Gam, *Rt. Revd* Sir Getake, KBE

Gamble, Sir David Hugh Norman, Bt. (1897)

Gambon, Sir Michael John, Kt., CBE

Garden, *Air Marshal* Sir Timothy, KCB

Gardiner, Sir George Arthur, Kt.

Gardiner, Sir John Eliot, Kt., CBE

Gardner, Sir Robert Henry Bruce-, Bt. (1945)

Gardner, Sir Roy Alan, Kt.

Garland, *Hon.* Sir Patrick Neville, Kt.

Garland, *Hon.* Sir Ransley Victor, KBE

Garlick, Sir John, KCB

Garner, Sir Anthony Stuart, Kt.

Garnett, *Vice-Adm.* Sir Ian David Graham, KCB

Garnier, *Rear-Adm.* Sir John, KCVO, CBE

Garrett, Sir Anthony Peter, Kt., CBE

Garrick, Sir Ronald, Kt., CBE, FREng.

Garrioch, Sir (William) Henry, Kt.

Garrod, *Lt.-Gen.* Sir (John) Martin Carruthers, KCB, OBE

Garthwaite, Sir (William) Mark (Charles), Bt. (1919)

Gaskell, Sir Richard Kennedy Harvey, Kt.

Gatehouse, *Hon.* Sir Robert Alexander, Kt.

Geno, Sir Makena Viora, KBE

Gent, Sir Christopher Charles, Kt.

George, Sir Arthur Thomas, Kt.

George, *Prof.* Sir Charles Frederick, MD, FRCP

George, Sir Edward, Kt.
George, *Rt. Hon.* Sir Edward Alan John, GBE
George, Sir Richard William, Kt., CVO
Gerken, *Vice-Adm.* Sir Robert William Frank, KCB, CBE
Gery, Sir Robert Lucian Wade-, KCMG, KCVO
Gethin, Sir Richard Joseph St Lawrence, Bt. (I. 1665)
Getty, Sir (John) Paul, KBE
Ghurburrun, Sir Rabindrah, Kt.
Gibb, Sir Francis Ross (Frank), Kt., CBE, FREng.
Gibbings, Sir Peter Walter, Kt.
Gibbons, Sir (John) David, KBE
Gibbons, Sir William Edward Doran, Bt. (1752)
Gibbs, *Rt. Hon.* Sir Harry Talbot, GCMG, KBE
Gibbs, *Hon.* Sir Richard John Hedley, Kt.
Gibbs, Sir Roger Geoffrey, Kt.
Gibbs, *Field Marshal* Sir Roland Christopher, GCB, CBE, DSO, MC
†Gibson, *Revd* Sir Christopher Herbert, Bt. (1931)
Gibson, Sir Ian, Kt., CBE
Gibson, *Rt. Hon.* Sir Peter Leslie, Kt.
Gibson, *Rt. Hon.* Sir Ralph Brian, Kt.
Giddings, *Air Marshal* Sir (Kenneth Charles) Michael, KCB, OBE, DFC, AFC
Giffard, Sir (Charles) Sydney (Rycroft), KCMG
Gilbert-Denham, *Lt.-Col.* Sir Seymour Vivian, KCVO
Gilbert, *Air Chief Marshal* Sir Joseph Alfred, KCB, CBE
Gilbert, Sir Martin John, Kt., CBE
†Gilbey, Sir Walter Gavin, Bt. (1893)
Giles, *Rear-Adm.* Sir Morgan Charles Morgan-, Kt., DSO, OBE, GM
Gill, Sir Anthony Keith, Kt., FREng.
Gillam, Sir Patrick John, Kt.
Gillen, *Hon.* Sir John de Winter, Kt.
Gillett, Sir Robin Danvers Penrose, Bt., RD (1959)
Gilmour, *Col.* Sir Allan Macdonald, KCVO, OBE, MC
Gilmour, Sir John Edward, Bt., DSO, TD (1897)
Gina, Sir Lloyd Maepeza, KBE
Gingell, *Air Chief Marshal* Sir John, GBE, KCB, KCVO
Girolami, Sir Paul, Kt.
Girvan, *Hon.* Sir (Frederick) Paul, Kt.
Gladstone, Sir (Erskine) William, Bt., KG (1846)
Glen, Sir Alexander Richard, KBE, DSC
Glenn, Sir (Joseph Robert) Archibald, Kt., OBE
Glidewell, *Rt. Hon.* Sir Iain Derek Laing, Kt.
Glover, Sir Victor Joseph Patrick, Kt.
Glyn, Sir Richard Lindsay, Bt. (1759 and 1800)

Goavea, Sir Sinaka Vakai, KBE
Gobbo, Sir James Augustine, Kt., AC
Godber, Sir George Edward, GCB, DM
Goff, Sir Robert (William) Davis-, Bt. (1905)
Goldberg, *Prof.* Sir Abraham, Kt., MD, D.Sc., FRCP
Goldberg, *Prof.* Sir David Paul Brandes, Kt.
Goldman, Sir Samuel, KCB
Goldring, Sir John Bernard, Kt.
Gomersall, Sir Stephen John, KCMG
Gooch, Sir Timothy Robert, Bt., MBE (1746)
Gooch, Sir Trevor Sherlock (Sir Peter), Bt. (1866)
Good, Sir John Kennedy-, KBE
Goodall, Sir (Arthur) David Saunders, GCMG
Goodall, *Air Marshal* Sir Roderick Harvey, KBE, CB, CBE, AFC RAF
Goode, *Prof.* Sir Royston Miles, Kt., CBE, QC
Goodenough, Sir Anthony Michael, KCMG
Goodenough, Sir William McLernon, Bt. (1943)
Goodhart, Sir Philip Carter, Kt.
Goodhart, Sir Robert Anthony Gordon, Bt. (1911)
Goodhew, Sir Victor Henry, Kt.
Gooding, Sir Alan, Kt.
Goodison, Sir Alan Clowes, KCMG
Goodison, Sir Nicholas Proctor, Kt.
Goodlad, *Rt. Hon.* Sir Alastair Robertson, KCMG
Goodman, Sir Patrick Ledger, Kt., CBE
Goodson, Sir Mark Weston Lassam, Bt. (1922)
Goodwin, Sir Matthew Dean, Kt., CBE
†Goold, Sir George William, Bt. (1801)
Gordon, Sir Andrew Cosmo Lewis Duff-, Bt. (1813)
Gordon, Sir Charles Addison Somerville Snowden, KCB
Gordon, Sir Gerald Henry, Kt., CBE, QC
Gordon, Sir Keith Lyndell, Kt., CMG
Gordon, Sir (Lionel) Eldred (Peter) Smith-, Bt. (1838)
Gordon, Sir Robert James, Bt. (S. 1706)
Gordon, Sir Sidney Samuel, Kt., CBE
Gordon Lennox, Lord Nicholas Charles, KCMG, KCVO
†Gore, Sir Nigel Hugh St George, Bt. (I. 1622)
Gorham, Sir Richard Masters, Kt., CBE, DFC
Goring, Sir William Burton Nigel, Bt. (1627)
Gorman, Sir John Reginald, Kt., CVO, CBE, MC
Gorst, Sir John Michael, Kt.
Goschen, Sir (Edward) Alexander Bt. (1916)

Gosling, Sir (Frederick) Donald, Kt.
Goswell, Sir Brian Lawrence, Kt.
Gough, Sir Charles Brandon, Kt.
Goulden, Sir (Peter) John, GCMG
Goulding, Sir Marrack Irvine, KCMG
Goulding, Sir (William) Lingard Walter, Bt. (1904)
Gourlay, *Gen.* Sir (Basil) Ian (Spencer), KCB, OBE, MC, RM
Gourlay, Sir Simon Alexander, Kt.
Govan, Sir Lawrence Herbert, Kt.
Gow, *Gen.* Sir (James) Michael, GCB
Gowans, Sir James Learmonth, Kt., CBE, FRCP, FRS
†Graaff, Sir David de Villiers, Bt. (1911)
Grabham, Sir Anthony Henry, Kt.
Graham, Sir Alexander Michael, GBE
Graham, Sir James Bellingham, Bt. (1662)
Graham, Sir James Fergus Surtees, Bt. (1783)
Graham, Sir James Thompson, Kt., CMG
Graham, Sir John Alexander Noble, Bt., GCMG (1906)
Graham, Sir John Alistair, Kt.
Graham, Sir John Moodie, Bt. (1964)
Graham, Sir Norman William, Kt., CB
Graham, Sir Peter, KCB, QC
Graham, Sir Peter Alfred, Kt., OBE
Graham, *Lt.-Gen.* Sir Peter Walter, KCB, CBE
†Graham, Sir Ralph Stuart, Bt. (1629)
Graham, *Hon.* Sir Samuel Horatio, Kt., CMG, OBE
Grandy, *Marshal of the Royal Air Force* Sir John, GCB, GCVO, KBE, DSO
Grant, Sir Archibald, Bt. (S. 1705)
Grant, Sir Clifford, Kt.
Grant, Sir (John) Anthony, Kt.
Grant, Sir Patrick Alexander Benedict, Bt. (S. 1688)
Grant, *Lt.-Gen.* Sir Scott Carnegie, KCB
Gray, *Hon.* Sir Charles Anthony St John, Kt., QC
Gray, *Prof.* Sir Denis John Pereira, Kt., OBE, FRCGP
Gray, Sir John Archibald Browne, Kt., Sc.D, FRS
Gray, Sir John Walton David, KBE, CMG
Gray, *Lt.-Gen.* Sir Michael Stuart, KCB, OBE
Gray, Sir Robert McDowall (Robin), Kt.
Gray, Sir William Hume, Bt. (1917)
Graydon, *Air Chief Marshal* Sir Michael James, GCB, CBE
Grayson, Sir Jeremy Brian Vincent Harrington, Bt. (1922)
Green, Sir Allan David, KCB, QC
Green, Sir Andrew Fleming, KCMG
Green, *Hon.* Sir Guy Stephen Montague, KBE

Green, Sir Kenneth, Kt.

Green, Sir Owen Whitley, Kt.

†Green, Sir Simon Lycett, Bt., TD (1886)

Greenaway, Sir John Michael Burdick, Bt. (1933)

Greenbury, Sir Richard, Kt.

Greene, Sir (John) Brian Massy-, Kt.

Greener, Sir Anthony Armitage, Kt.

Greengross, Sir Alan David, Kt.

Greening, *Rear-Adm.* Sir Paul Woollven, GCVO

Greenstock, Sir Jeremy Quentin, KCMG

Greenwell, Sir Edward Bernard, Bt. (1906)

Gregson, Sir Peter Lewis, GCB

Greig, Sir (Henry Louis) Carron, KCVO, CBE

Grenside, Sir John Peter, Kt., CBE

Grey, Sir Anthony Dysart, Bt. (1814)

Grierson, Sir Michael John Bewes, Bt. (S. 1685)

Grierson, Sir Ronald Hugh, Kt.

Griffin, *Maj.* Sir (Arthur) John (Stewart), KCVO

Griffin, Sir (Charles) David, Kt., CBE

Griffiths, Sir Eldon Wylie, Kt.

Griffiths, Sir John Norton-, Bt. (1922)

Grigson, *Hon.* Sir Geoffrey Douglas, Kt.

Grimshaw, Sir Nicholas Thomas, Kt., CBE

Grimwade, Sir Andrew Sheppard, Kt., CBE

Grindrod, *Most Revd* Sir John Basil Rowland, KBE

Grinstead, Sir Stanley Gordon, Kt.

Grose, *Vice-Adm.* Sir Alan, KBE

Gross, *Hon.* Mr Justice, Sir Peter Henry, Kt.

Grossart, Sir Angus MCFarlane McLeod, Kt., CBE

Grotrian, Sir Philip Christian Brent, Bt. (1934)

Grove, Sir Charles Gerald, Bt. (1874)

Grove, Sir Edmund Frank, KCVO

Grugeon, Sir John Drury, Kt.

Guinness, Sir Howard Christian Sheldon, Kt., VRD

Guinness, Sir John Ralph Sidney, Kt., CB

Guinness, Sir Kenelm Ernest Lee, Bt. (1867)

Guise, Sir John Grant, Bt. (1783)

Gull, Sir Rupert William Cameron, Bt. (1872)

Gumbs, Sir Emile Rudolph, Kt.

Gunn, Sir Robert Norman, Kt.

Gunn, Sir William Archer, KBE, CMG

†Gunning, Sir Charles Theodore, Bt. (1778)

Gunston, Sir John Wellesley, Bt. (1938)

Gurdon, *Prof.* Sir John Bertrand, Kt., D.Phil., FRS

Guthrie, Sir Malcolm Connop, Bt.(1936)

Guy, *Gen.* Sir Roland Kelvin, GCB, CBE, DSO

Habakkuk, Sir John Hrothgar, Kt., FBA

Haddacks, *Vice-Adm.* Sir Paul Kenneth, KCB

Hadfield, Sir Ronald, Kt., QPM

Hadlee, Sir Richard John, Kt., MBE

Hague, *Prof.* Sir Douglas Chalmers, Kt., CBE

Halberg, Sir Murray Gordon, Kt., MBE

Hall, Sir Basil Brodribb, KCB, MC, TD

Hall, Sir Douglas Basil, Bt., KCMG (S. 1687)

Hall, Sir Ernest, Kt., OBE

Hall, Sir Iain Robert, Kt.

Hall, Sir (Frederick) John (Frank), Bt. (1923)

Hall, Sir John, Kt.

Hall, Sir John Bernard, Bt. (1919)

Hall, Sir Laurence Charles Brodie-, Kt., AO, CMG

Hall, Sir Percival Burton Curtis, Kt.

Hall, Sir Peter Edward, KBE, CMG

Hall, *Prof.* Sir Peter Geoffrey, Kt., FBA

Hall, Sir Peter Reginald Frederick, Kt., CBE

Hall, Sir Robert de Zouche, KCMG

Hall, *Brig.* Sir William Henry, KBE, DSO, ED

Halliday, *Vice-Adm.* Sir Roy William, KBE, DSC

Halpern, Sir Ralph Mark, Kt.

Halsey, *Revd* Sir John Walter Brooke, Bt. (1920)

Halstead, Sir Ronald, Kt., CBE

Ham, Sir David Kenneth Rowe-, GBE

Hambling, Sir (Herbert) Hugh, Bt. (1924)

Hamer, *Hon.* Sir Rupert James, KCMG, ED

Hamilton, Sir Andrew Caradoc, Bt. (S. 1646)

Hamilton, *Rt. Hon.* Sir Archibald Gavin, Kt., MP

Hamilton, Sir Edward Sydney, Bt. (1776 and 1819)

Hamilton, Sir James Arnot, KCB, MBE, FREng.

Hamilton, Sir Malcolm William Bruce Stirling-, Bt. (S. 1673)

Hammick, Sir Stephen George, Bt. (1834)

Hammond, Sir Anthony Hilgrove, KCB, QC

Hampel, Sir Ronald Claus, Kt.

Hampshire, Sir Stuart Newton, Kt., FBA

Hampson, Sir Stuart, Kt.

Hampton, Sir (Leslie) Geoffrey, Kt.

Hancock, Sir David John Stowell, KCB

Hancock, *Air Marshal* Sir Valston Eldridge, KBE, CB, DFC

Hand, *Most Revd* Geoffrey David, KBE

Handley, Sir David John Davenport-, Kt., OBE

Hanham, Sir Michael William, Bt., DFC (1667)

Hanley, *Rt. Hon.* Sir Jeremy James, KCMG

Hanmer, Sir John Wyndham Edward, Bt. (1774)

Hann, Sir James, Kt., CBE

Hannam, Sir John Gordon, Kt.

Hanson, Sir (Charles) Rupert (Patrick), Bt. (1918)

Hanson, Sir John Gilbert, KCMG, CBE

Hardie, Sir Douglas Fleming, Kt., CBE

Harding, Sir George William, KCMG, CVO

Harding, *Marshal of the Royal Air Force* Sir Peter Robin, GCB

Harding, Sir Roy Pollard, Kt., CBE

Hardy, Sir David William, Kt.

Hardy, Sir James Gilbert, Kt., OBE

Hardy, Sir Richard Charles Chandos, Bt. (1876)

Hare, Sir David, Kt., FRSL

Hare, Sir Nicholas Patrick, Bt. (1818)

Harford, Sir (John) Timothy, Bt. (1934)

Hargroves, *Brig.* Sir Robert Louis, Kt., CBE

Harington, *Gen.* Sir Charles Henry Pepys, GCB, CBE, DSO, MC

Harington, Sir Nicholas John, Bt. (1611)

Harland, *Air Marshal* Sir Reginald Edward Wynyard, KBE, CB

Harley, *Gen.* Sir Alexander George Hamilton, KBE, CB

Harman, *Gen.* Sir Jack Wentworth, GCB, OBE, MC

Harman, *Hon.* Sir Jeremiah LeRoy, Kt.

Harman, Sir John Andrew, Kt.

Harmsworth, Sir Hildebrand Harold, Bt. (1922)

Harris, *Prof.* Sir Henry, Kt., FRCP, FRCPath., FRS

Harris, Sir Jack Wolfred Ashford, Bt. (1932)

Harris, *Air Marshal* Sir John Hulme, KCB, CBE

Harris, *Prof.* Sir Martin Best, Kt., CBE

Harris, Sir Thomas George, KBE, CMG,

Harris, Sir William Gordon, KBE, CB, FREng.

Harrison, Sir David, Kt., CBE, FREng.

Harrison, *Prof.* Sir Donald Frederick Norris, Kt., FRCS

Harrison, Sir Ernest Thomas, Kt., OBE

Harrison, Sir Francis Alexander Lyle, Kt., MBE, QC

Harrison, *Surgeon Vice-Adm.* Sir John Albert Bews, KBE

Harrison, *Hon.* Sir (John) Richard, Kt., ED

Harrison, *Hon.* Sir Michael Guy Vicat, Kt.

Harrison, Sir Michael James Harwood, Bt. (1961)

Harrison, Sir (Robert) Colin, Bt. (1922)

Harrison, Sir Terence, Kt., FREng

Harrop, Sir Peter John, KCB

Hart, Sir Graham Allan, KCB

Hart, *Hon.* Sir Michael Christopher Campbell, Kt.

Hartwell, Sir (Francis) Anthony Charles Peter, Bt. (1805)

Harvey, Sir Charles Richard Musgrave, Bt. (1933)

Harvie, Sir John Smith, Kt., CBE

Haselhurst, *Rt. Hon.* Sir Alan Gordon Barraclough, Kt., MP

Haskard, Sir Cosmo Dugal Patrick Thomas, KCMG, MBE

Haslam, *Rear-Adm.* Sir David William, KBE, CB

Hassett, *Gen.* Sir Francis George, KBE, CB, DSO, LVO

Hastings, Sir Max Macdonald, Kt.

Hastings, Sir Stephen Lewis Edmonstone, Kt., MC

Hatter, Sir Maurice, Kt.

Havelock, Sir Wilfrid Bowen, Kt.

Hawkins, Sir Paul Lancelot, Kt., TD

Hawkins, Sir Richard Caesar, Bt. (1778)

Hawley, Sir Donald Frederick, KCMG, MBE

†Hawley, Sir Henry Nicholas, Bt. (1795)

Haworth, Sir Philip, Bt. (1911)

Hawthorne, *Prof.* Sir William Rede, Kt., CBE, Sc.D, FRS, FREng.

Hay, Sir David Osborne, Kt., CBE, DSO

Hay, Sir David Russell, Kt., CBE, FRCP, MD

Hay, Sir Hamish Grenfell, Kt.

Hay, Sir James Brian Dalrymple-, Bt. (1798)

Hay, Sir John Erroll Audley, Bt. (S. 1663)

†Hay, Sir Ronald Frederick Hamilton, Bt. (S. 1703)

Hayes, Sir Brian, Kt., CBE, QPM

Hayes, Sir Brian David, GCB

Hayward, Sir Anthony William Byrd, Kt.

Hayward, Sir Jack Arnold, Kt., OBE

Haywood, Sir Harold, KCVO, OBE

Head, Sir Francis David Somerville, Bt. (1838)

Healey, Sir Charles Edward Chadwyck-, Bt. (1919)

Heap, Sir Peter William, KCMG

Heap, *Prof.* Sir Robert Brian, Kt., CBE, FRS

Hearne, Sir Graham James, Kt., CBE

Heath, *Rt. Hon.* Sir Edward Richard George, KG, MBE, MP

Heath, Sir Mark Evelyn, KCVO, CMG

Heathcote, *Brig.* Sir Gilbert Simon, Bt., CBE (1733)

Heathcote, Sir Michael Perryman, Bt. (1733)

Heatley, Sir Peter, Kt., CBE

Heaton, Sir Yvo Robert Henniker-, Bt. (1912)

Hedley, *Hon* Mr Justice, Sir Mark, Kt.

Heiser, Sir Terence Michael, GCB

Henao, *Revd* Sir Ravu, Kt., OBE

Henderson, Sir Denys Hartley, Kt.

Henderson, Sir (John) Nicholas, GCMG, KCVO

Henley, Sir Douglas Owen, KCB

Hennessy, Sir James Patrick Ivan, KBE, CMG

†Henniker, Sir Adrian Chandos, Bt. (1813)

Henriques, *Hon.* Sir Richard Henry Quixano, Kt.

Henry, *Rt. Hon.* Sir Denis Robert Maurice, Kt.

Henry, *Hon.* Sir Geoffrey Arama, KBE

†Henry, Sir Patrick Denis, Bt. (1923)

Henry, *Hon.* Sir Trevor Ernest, Kt.

Hepburn, Sir John Alastair Trant Kidd Buchan-, Bt. (1815)

Herbecq, Sir John Edward, KCB

Herbert, *Adm.* Sir Peter Geoffrey Marshall, KCB, OBE

Herbert, Sir Walter William, Kt.

Hermon, Sir John Charles, Kt., OBE, QPM

Heron, Sir Conrad Frederick, KCB, OBE

Heron, Sir Michael Gilbert, Kt.

Hervey, Sir Roger Blaise Ramsay, KCVO, CMG

Heseltine, *Rt. Hon.* Sir William Frederick Payne, GCB, GCVO

Hetherington, Sir Thomas Chalmers, KCB, CBE, TD, QC

Hewetson, Sir Christopher Raynor, Kt., TD

Hewett, Sir Richard Mark John, Bt. (1813)

Hewitt, Sir (Cyrus) Lenox (Simson), Kt., OBE

Hewitt, Sir Nicholas Charles Joseph, Bt. (1921)

Heygate, Sir Richard John Gage, Bt. (1831)

Heywood, Sir Peter, Bt. (1838)

Hezlet, *Vice-Adm.* Sir Arthur Richard, KBE, CB, DSO, DSC

Hibbert, Sir Jack, KCB

Hibbert, Sir Reginald Alfred, GCMG

Hickey, Sir Justin, Kt.

Hickman, Sir (Richard) Glenn, Bt. (1903)

Hicks, Sir Robert, Kt.

Hidden, *Hon.* Sir Anthony Brian, Kt.

Hielscher, Sir Leo Arthur, Kt.

Higgins, *Hon.* Sir Malachy Joseph, Kt.

Higginson, Sir Gordon Robert, Kt., Ph.D., FREng.

Hill, Sir Alexander Rodger Erskine-, Bt. (1945)

Hill, Sir Arthur Alfred, Kt., CBE

Hill, Sir Brian John, Kt.

Hill, Sir James Frederick, Bt. (1917)

Hill, Sir John McGregor, Kt., Ph.D., FREng.

Hill, Sir John Maxwell, Kt., CBE, DFC

†Hill, Sir John Rowley, Bt. (I. 1779)

Hill, *Vice-Adm.* Sir Robert Charles Finch, KBE, FREng.

Hillary, Sir Edmund, KG, KBE

Hillhouse, Sir (Robert) Russell, KCB

Hills, Sir Graham John, Kt.

Hine, *Air Chief Marshal* Sir Patrick Bardon, GCB, GBE

Hinston, Sir Harry Lee, Kt.

Hirsch, *Prof.* Sir Peter Bernhard, Kt., Ph.D., FRS

Hirst, *Rt. Hon.* Sir David Cozens-Hardy, Kt.

Hirst, Sir Michael William, Kt.

Hoare, *Prof.* Sir Charles Anthony Richard, Kt., FRS

Hoare, Sir Peter Richard David, Bt. (1786)

Hoare, Sir Timothy Edward Charles, Bt. (1784)

Hobart, Sir John Vere, Bt. (1914)

Hobbs, *Maj.-Gen.* Sir Michael Frederick, KCVO, CBE

Hobday, Sir Gordon Ivan, Kt.

Hobhouse, Sir Charles John Spinney, Bt. (1812)

Hockaday, Sir Arthur Patrick, KCB, CMG

Hockley, *Gen.* Sir Anthony Heritage Farrar-, GBE, KCB, DSO, MC

†Hodge, Sir Andrew Rowland, Bt. (1921)

Hodge, Sir James William, KCVO, CMG

Hodge, Sir Julian Stephen Alfred, Kt.

Hodges, *Air Chief Marshal* Sir Lewis MacDonald, KCB, CBE, DSO, DFC

Hodgkin, Sir Gordon Howard Eliot, Kt., CBE

Hodgkinson, *Air Chief Marshal* Sir (William) Derek, KCB, CBE, DFC, AFC

Hodgson, Sir Maurice Arthur Eric, Kt., FREng.

Hodgson, *Hon.* Sir (Walter) Derek (Thornley), Kt.

Hodson, Sir Michael Robin Adderley, Bt. (I. 1789)

Hoffenberg, *Prof.* Sir Raymond, KBE

Hogg, Sir Christopher Anthony, Kt.

Hogg, *Vice-Adm.* Sir Ian Leslie Trower, KCB, DSC

†Hogg, Sir Piers Michael James, Bt. (1846)

†Hogg, Sir Michael Edward Lindsay-, Bt. (1905)

Holcroft, Sir Peter George Culcheth, Bt. (1921)

Holderness, Sir Martin William, Bt. (1920)

Holden, Sir Edward, Bt. (1893)

Holden, Sir John David, Bt. (1919)

Holder, Sir John Henry, Bt. (1898)

Holdgate, Sir Martin Wyatt, Kt., CB, Ph.D.

Holdsworth, Sir (George) Trevor, Kt., CVO

Holland, *Hon.* Sir Alan Douglas, Kt.

Holland, *Hon.* Sir Christopher John, Kt.

Holland, Sir Clifton Vaughan, Kt.

Holland, Sir Geoffrey, KCB

Holland, Sir Kenneth Lawrence, Kt., CBE, QFSM

Holland, Sir Philip Welsby, Kt.

Holliday, *Prof.* Sir Frederick George Thomas, Kt., CBE, FRSE

Hollings, *Hon.* Sir (Alfred) Kenneth, Kt., MC

Hollis, *Hon.* Sir Anthony Barnard, Kt.

Hollom, Sir Jasper Quintus, KBE

Holloway, *Hon.* Sir Barry Blyth, KBE

Holm, Sir Carl Henry, Kt., OBE

Holm, Sir Ian (Ian Holm Cuthbert), Kt., CBE

Holman, *Hon.* Sir (Edward) James, Kt.

Holmes, *Prof.* Sir Frank Wakefield, Kt.

Holmes, Sir John Eaton, KBE, CMG, CVO

Holroyd, *Air Marshal* Sir Frank Martyn, KBE, CB, FREng.

Holt, *Prof.* Sir James Clarke, Kt.

Holt, Sir Michael, Kt., CBE

Home, Sir William Dundas, Bt. (S. 1671)

Hone, Sir Michael, Kt.

Honeycombe, *Prof.* Sir Robert William Kerr, Kt., FRS, FREng.

Honywood, Sir Filmer Courtenay William, Bt. (1660)

Hood, Sir Harold Joseph, Bt., TD (1922)

Hookway, Sir Harry Thurston, Kt.

Hooper, *Hon.* Sir Anthony, Kt.

Hope, Sir Colin Frederick Newton, Kt.

Hope, *Rt. Revd* and *Rt. Hon.* Sir David Michael, KCVO

Hope, Sir John Carl Alexander, Bt. (S. 1628)

Hopkin, Sir (William Aylsham) Bryan, Kt., CBE

Hopkins, Sir Anthony Philip, Kt., CBE

Hopkins, Sir Michael John, Kt., CBE, RA, RIBA

Hopwood, *Prof.* Sir David Alan, Kt., FRS

Hordern, *Rt. Hon.* Sir Peter Maudslay, Kt.

Horlick, *Vice-Adm.* Sir Edwin John, KBE, FREng.

Horlick, Sir James Cunliffe William, Bt. (1914)

Horlock, *Prof.* Sir John Harold, Kt., FRS, FREng.

Horn, *Prof.* Sir Gabriel, Kt., FRS

Hornby, Sir Derek Peter, Kt.

Hornby, Sir Simon Michael, Kt.

Horne, Sir Alan Gray Antony, Bt. (1929)

Horsfall, Sir John Musgrave, Bt., MC, TD (1909)

†Hort, Sir Andrew Edwin Fenton, Bt. (1767)

Horton, Sir Robert Baynes, Kt.

Hosker, Sir Gerald Albery, KCB, QC

Hoskyns, Sir Benedict Leigh, Bt. (1676)

Hoskyns, Sir John Austin Hungerford Leigh, Kt.

Hotung, Sir Joseph Edward, Kt.

Houghton, Sir John Theodore, Kt., CBE, FRS

Houldsworth, Sir Richard Thomas Reginald, Bt. (1887)

Hounsfield, Sir Godfrey Newbold, Kt., CBE

Hourston, Sir Gordon Minto, Kt.

House, *Lt.-Gen.* Sir David George, GCB, KCVO, CBE, MC

Houssemayne du Boulay, Sir Roger William, KCVO, CMG

Howard, Sir David Howarth Seymour, Bt. (1955)

Howard, Sir George Marshall, Kt.

Howard, *Prof.* Sir Michael Eliot, Kt., CH, CBE, MC

Howard, *Maj.-Gen.* Lord Michael Fitzalan-, GCVO, CB, CBE, MC

Howell, Sir Ralph Frederic, Kt.

Howells, Sir Eric Waldo Benjamin, Kt., CBE

Howes, Sir Christopher Kingston, KCVO, CB

Howlett, *Gen.* Sir Geoffrey Hugh Whitby, KBE, MC

Huggins, *Hon.* Sir Alan Armstrong, Kt.

Hughes, *Hon.* Sir Anthony Philip Gilson, Kt.

Hughes, Sir David Collingwood, Bt. (1773)

Hughes, *Hon.* Sir Davis, Kt.

Hughes, Sir Jack William, Kt.

Hughes, Sir Trevor Denby Lloyd-, Kt.

Hughes, Sir Trevor Poulton, KCB

Hull, *Prof.* Sir David, Kt.

Hulse, Sir Edward Jeremy Westrow, Bt. (1739)

Hume, Sir Alan Blyth, Kt., CB

Humphreys, Sir (Raymond Evelyn) Myles, Kt.

Hunt, Sir John Leonard, Kt.

Hunt, *Adm.* Sir Nicholas John Streynsham, GCB, LVO

Hunt, *Hon.* Sir Patrick James, Kt.

Hunt, Sir Rex Masterman, Kt., CMG

Hunt, Sir Robert Frederick, Kt., CBE, FREng.

Hunt, Sir Julian Charles Roland, CB, Bt.

Hunter, Sir Alistair John, KCMG

Hunter, Sir Ian Bruce Hope, Kt., MBE

Hunter, *Prof.* Sir Laurence Colvin, Kt., CBE, FRSE

Hurn, Sir (Francis) Roger, Kt.

Hurrell, Sir Anthony Gerald, KCVO, CMG

Hurst, Sir Geoffrey Charles, Kt., MBE

Husbands, Sir Clifford Straugh, GCMG

Hutchinson, *Hon.* Sir Ross, Kt., DFC

Hutchison, Sir James Colville, Bt. (1956)

Hutchison, *Rt. Hon.* Sir Michael, Kt.

Hutchison, Sir Robert, Bt. (1939)

Huxley, *Prof.* Sir Andrew Fielding, Kt., OM, FRS

Huxtable, *Gen.* Sir Charles Richard, KCB, CBE

Hyslop, Sir Robert John (Robin) Maxwell-, Kt.

Ibbs, Sir (John) Robin, KBE

Imray, Sir Colin Henry, KBE, CMG

Ingham, Sir Bernard, Kt.

Ingilby, Sir Thomas Colvin William, Bt. (1866)

Inglis, Sir Brian Scott, Kt.

Inglis of Glencorse, Sir Roderick John, Bt. (S. 1703)

Ingram, Sir James Herbert Charles, Bt. (1893)

Ingram, Sir John Henderson, Kt., CBE

Inkin, Sir Geoffrey David, Kt., OBE

†Innes, Sir David Charles Kenneth Gordon, Bt. (NS 1686)

Innes of Edinght, Sir Malcolm Rognvald, KCVO

Innes, Sir Peter Alexander Berowald, Bt. (S. 1628)

Irvine, Sir Donald Hamilton, CBE, MD, FRCGP

Irving, *Prof.* Sir Miles Horsfall, Kt., MD, FRCS, FRCSE

Irwin, *Lt.-Gen.* Sir Alistair Stuart Hastings, KCB, CBE

Isaacs, Sir Jeremy Israel, Kt.

Isham, Sir Ian Vere Gyles, Bt. (1627)

Jack, *Hon.* Sir Alieu Sulayman, Kt.

Jack, Sir David, Kt., CBE, FRS, FRSE

Jack, Sir David Emmanuel, GCMG, MBE

Jack, *Hon.* Sir Raymond Evan, Kt.

Jackling, Sir Roger Tustin, KCB. CBE

Jackson, Sir Barry Trevor, Kt.

Jackson, Sir Kenneth Joseph, Kt.

Jackson, *Lt.-Gen.* Sir Michael David, KCB, CBE

Jackson, Sir Michael Roland, Bt. (1902)

Jackson, Sir Nicholas Fane St George, Bt. (1913)

Jackson, Sir Keith Arnold, Bt. (1815)

Jackson, *Hon.* Sir Rupert Matthew, Kt., QC

Jackson, Sir William Thomas, Bt. (1869)

Jacob, *Hon.* Sir Robert Raphael Hayim (Robin), Kt.

Jacobi, Sir Derek George, Kt., CBE

Jacobi, Dr Sir James Edward, Kt., OBE

Jacobs, Sir Cecil Albert, Kt., CBE

Jacobs, *Hon.* Sir Kenneth Sydney, KBE

Jacomb, Sir Martin Wakefield, Kt.

Jaffray, Sir William Otho, Bt. (1892)

Jagger, Sir Michael Philip, Kt.

James, Sir Cynlais Morgan, KCMG

James, Sir Jeffrey Russell, KBE, CBE

James, Sir John Nigel Courtenay, KCVO, CBE

James, Sir Stanislaus Anthony, GCMG, OBE

Jamieson, *Air Marshal* Sir David Ewan, KBE, CB

Jansen, Sir Ross Malcolm, KBE

Jansen van Rensburg, *Lt.-Gen.* Sir Jurinus Lindo, Kt.

Janvrin, Sir Robin Berry, KCVO, CB

Jardine of Applegirth, Sir Alexander Maule, Bt. (S. 1672)

Jardine, Sir Andrew Colin Douglas, Bt. (1916)

Jardine, *Maj.* Sir (Andrew) Rupert (John) Buchanan-, Bt., MC (1885)

Jarman, *Prof.* Sir Brian, Kt., OBE

Jarratt, Sir Alexander Anthony, Kt., CB

Jarvis, Sir Gordon Ronald, Kt.

Jawara, *Hon.* Sir Dawda Kairaba, Kt.

Jay, Sir Antony Rupert, Kt., CVO

Jay, Sir Michael Hastings, KCMG

Jeewoolall, Sir Ramesh, Kt.

Jefferson, Sir George Rowland, Kt., CBE, FREng.

Jefferson, Sir Mervyn Stewart Dunnington-, Bt. (1958)

Jeffreys, *Prof.* Sir Alec John, Kt., FRS

Jeffries, *Hon.* Sir John Francis, Kt.

Jehangir, Sir Cowasji, Bt. (1908)

Jejeebhoy, Sir Jamsetjee, Bt. (1857)

Jenkins, Sir Brian Garton, GBE

Jenkins, Sir Elgar Spencer, Kt., OBE

Jenkins, Sir James Christopher, KCB, QC

Jenkins, Sir Michael Nicholas Howard, Kt., OBE

Jenkins, Sir Michael Romilly Heald, KCMG

Jenkinson, Sir John Banks, Bt. (1661)

Jenks, Sir Maurice Arthur Brian, Bt. (1932)

Jenner, *Air Marshal* Sir Timothy LVO, KCB

Jennings, Sir John Southwood, Kt., CBE, FRSE

Jennings, Sir Peter Neville Wake, Kt., CVO

Jennings, *Prof.* Sir Robert Yewdall, Kt., QC

Jephcott, Sir (John) Anthony, Bt. (1962)

Jessel, Sir Charles John, Bt. (1883)

Jewkes, Sir Gordon Wesley, KCMG

Job, Sir Peter James Denton, Kt.

John, Sir David Glyndwr, KCMG

John, Sir Elton Hercules (Reginald Kenneth Dwight), Kt., CBE

Johns, *Air Chief Marshal* Sir Richard Edward, GCB, CBE, LVO

Johnson, *Gen.* Sir Garry Dene, KCB, OBE, MC

Johnson, Sir John Rodney, KCMG

†Johnson, Sir Patrick Eliot, Bt. (1818)

Johnson, Sir Peter Colpoys Paley, Bt. (1755)

Johnson, *Hon.* Sir Robert Lionel, Kt.

Johnson, Sir Vassel Godfrey, Kt., CBE

Johnston, Sir John Baines, GCMG, KCVO

Johnston, *Lt.-Col.* Sir John Frederick Dame, GCVO, MC

Johnston, *Lt.-Gen.* Sir Maurice Robert, KCB, OBE

Johnston, Sir Thomas Alexander, Bt. (S. 1626)

Johnston, Sir William Robert Patrick Knox- (Sir Robin), Kt., CBE, RD

Johnstone, Sir Geoffrey Adams Dinwiddie, KCMG

Johnstone, Sir (George) Richard Douglas, Bt. (S. 1700)

Johnstone, Sir (John) Raymond, Kt., CBE

Jolliffe, Sir Anthony Stuart, GBE

Jolly, Sir Aurthur Richard, KCMG

Jonas, Sir John Peter Jens, Kt., CBE

Jones, *Gen.* Sir (Charles) Edward Webb, KCB, CBE

Jones, Sir Christopher Lawrence-, Bt. (1831)

Jones, Sir David Akers-, KBE, CMG

Jones, *Air Marshal* Sir Edward Gordon, KCB, CBE, DSO, DFC

Jones, Sir Harry George, Kt., CBE

Jones, Sir (John) Derek Alun-, Kt.

Jones, Sir John Henry Harvey-, Kt., MBE

Jones, Sir John Prichard-, Bt. (1910)

Jones, Sir Keith Stephen, Kt.

Jones, *Hon.* Sir Kenneth George Illtyd, Kt.

Jones, Sir Lyndon, Kt.

Jones, Sir (Owen) Trevor, Kt.

Jones, Sir (Peter) Hugh (Jefferd) Lloyd, Kt.

Jones, Sir Richard Anthony Lloyd-, KCB

Jones, Sir Robert Edward, Kt.

Jones, Sir Simon Warley Frederick Benton, Bt. (1919)

Jones, Sir William Gwynoro, Kt.

Jones, Sir Wynn Normington Hugh-, Kt., LVO

†Joseph, *Hon.* Sir James Samuel, Bt. (1943)

Jowitt, *Hon.* Sir Edwin Frank, Kt.

Joyce, *Lt.-Gen.* Sir Robert John Hayman-, KCB, CBE

Judge, *Rt. Hon.* Sir Igor, Kt.

Judge, Sir Paul Rupert, Kt.

Jugnauth, *Rt. Hon.* Sir Aneerood, KCMG, QC

Jungius, *Vice-Adm.* Sir James George, KBE

Jupp, *Hon.* Sir Kenneth Graham, Kt., MC

Kaberry, *Hon.* Sir Christopher Donald, Bt. (1960)

Kalms, Sir (Harold) Stanley, Kt.

Kalo, Sir Kwamala, Kt., MBE

Kan Yuet-Keung, Sir, GBE

Kapi, *Hon.* Sir Mari, Kt., CBE

Kaputin, Sir John Rumet, KBE, CMG

Katz, Sir Bernard, Kt., FRS

Kausimae, Sir David Nanau, KBE

Kavali, Sir Thomas, Kt., OBE

Kawashima, Sir Maurice Masaaki, Kt.

Kawharu, *Prof.* Sir Ian Hugh, Kt.

Kay, *Prof.* Sir Andrew Watt, Kt.

Kay, *Hon.* Sir John William, Kt.

Kay, *Hon.* Sir Maurice Ralph, Kt.

Kaye, Sir John Phillip Lister Lister-, Bt. (1812)

Kaye, Sir Paul Henry Gordon, Bt. (1923)

Keane, Sir Richard Michael, Bt. (1801)

Kearney, *Hon.* Sir William John Francis, Kt., CBE

Keeble, Sir (Herbert Ben) Curtis, Kt.

Keegan, Sir John Desmond Patrick, Kt., OBE GCM

Keene, *Hon.* Sir David Wolfe, Kt.

Keirlie, Sir Dennis Robert, Kt

Keith, *Hon.* Mr Justice, Sir Brian Richard, Kt.

Keith, *Prof.* Sir James, KBE

Kellett, Sir Stanley Charles, Bt. (1801)

Kelly, Sir Christopher William, KCB

Kelly, Sir David Robert Corbett, Kt., CBE

Kelly, *Rt. Hon.* Sir (John William) Basil, Kt.

Kemakeza, Sir Allan, Kt.

Kemball, *Air Marshal* Sir (Richard) John, KCB, CBE

Kemp, Sir (Edward) Peter, KCB

Kenilorea, *Rt. Hon.* Sir Peter, KBE

Kennaway, Sir John Lawrence, Bt. (1791)

Kennedy, Sir Francis, KCMG, CBE

Kennedy, *Hon.* Sir Ian Alexander, Kt.

Kennedy, *Prof.* Sir Ian McColl, Kt.

Kennedy, Sir Ludovic Henry Coverley, Kt.

†Kennedy, Sir Michael Edward, Bt., (1836)

Kennedy, *Rt. Hon.* Sir Paul Joseph Morrow, Kt.

Kennedy, *Air Chief Marshal* Sir Thomas Lawrie, GCB, AFC

Kenny, Sir Anthony John Patrick, Kt., D.Phil., D.Litt., FBA

Kenny, *Gen.* Sir Brian Leslie Graham, GCB, CBE

Kentridge, Sir Sydney Woolf, KCMG, QC

Kenyon, Sir George Henry, Kt.

Kermode, Sir (John) Frank, Kt., FBA

Kermode, Sir Ronald Graham Quale, KBE

Kerr, *Hon.* Sir Brian Francis, Kt.

Kerr, *Adm.* Sir John Beverley, GCB

Kerr, Sir John (Olav), GCMG, KCMG

Kerruish, Sir (Henry) Charles, Kt., OBE

Kerry, Sir Michael James, KCB, QC

Kershaw, *Prof.* Sir Ian, Kt.

Kershaw, Sir (John) Anthony, Kt., MC

Keswick, Sir John Chippendale Lindley, Kt.

Khan, Sir Sadruddin Aga, KBE

Kidd, Sir Robert Hill, KBE, CB

Kikau, Ratu Sir Jone Latianara, KBE

Killen, *Hon.* Sir Denis James, KCMG

Killick, Sir John Edward, GCMG

Kimber, Sir Charles Dixon, Bt. (1904)

King, Sir John Christopher, Bt. (1888)

King, *Vice-Adm.* Sir Norman Ross Dutton, KBE

King, Sir Wayne Alexander, Bt. (1815)

Kingman, *Prof.* Sir John Frank Charles, Kt., FRS

Kingsland, Sir Richard, Kt., CBE, DFC

Kingsley, Sir Ben, Kt.

Kinloch, Sir David, Bt. (S. 1686)

Kinloch, Sir David Oliphant, Bt. (1873)

Kipalan, Sir Albert, Kt.

Kirkpatrick, Sir Ivone Elliott, Bt. (S. 1685)

Kirkwood, *Hon.* Sir Andrew Tristram Hammett, Kt.

Kitcatt, Sir Peter Julian, Kt., CB

Kitson, *Gen.* Sir Frank Edward, GBE, KCB, MC

Kitson, Sir Timothy Peter Geoffrey, Kt.

Kleinwort, Sir Richard Drake, Bt. (1909)

Klug, Sir Aaron, Kt., OM

Kneller, Sir Alister Arthur, Kt.

Knight, Sir Arthur William, Kt.

Knight, Sir Harold Murray, KBE, DSC

Knight, *Air Chief Marshal* Sir Michael William Patrick, KCB, AFC

Knill, *Prof.* Sir John Lawrence, Kt., FREng.

†Knill, Sir Thomas John Pugin Bartholomew, Bt. (1893)

Knowles, Sir Charles Francis, Bt. (1765)

Knowles, Sir Durward Randolph, Kt., OBE

Knowles, Sir Richard Marchant, Kt.

Knox, Sir Bryce Muir, KCVO, MC, TD

Knox, Sir David Laidlaw, Kt.

Knox, *Hon.* Sir John Leonard, Kt.

Knox, *Hon.* Sir William Edward, Kt.

Koraea, Sir Thomas, Kt.

Kornberg, *Prof.* Sir Hans Leo, Kt., D.Sc., Sc.D, Ph.D., FRS

Korowi, Sir Wiwa, GCMG

Krebs, *Sir* John Richard, Kt., D.Phil., FRS

Kroto, *Prof.* Sir Harold Walter, Kt., FRS

Kulukundis, Sir Elias George (Eddie), Kt., OBE

Kurongku, *Most Revd* Peter, KBE

Lachmann, *Prof.* Peter Julius, Kt.

Lacon, Sir Edmund Vere, Bt. (1818)

Lacy, Sir Patrick Brian Finucane, Bt. (1921)

Lacy, Sir John Trend, Kt., CBE

Laddie, *Hon.* Sir Hugh Ian Lang, Kt.

Laidlaw, Sir Christophor Charles Fraser, Kt.

Laing, Sir (John) Martin (Kirby), Kt., CBE

Laing, Sir (John) Maurice, Kt.

Laing, Sir (William) Kirby, Kt., FREng.

Laird, Sir Gavin Harry, Kt., CBE

Lake, Sir (Atwell) Graham, Bt. (1711)

Laker, Sir Frederick Alfred, Kt.

Lakin, Sir Michael, Bt. (1909)

Laking, Sir George Robert, KCMG

Lamb, Sir Albert Thomas, KBE, CMG, DFC

Lambert, Sir Anthony Edward, KCMG

Lambert, Sir John Henry, KCVO, CMG

†Lambert, Sir Peter John Biddulph, Bt. (1711)

Lampl, Sir Frank William, Kt.

Lamport, Sir Stephen Mark Jeffrey, KCVO

Landale, Sir David William Neil, KCVO

Landau, Sir Dennis Marcus, Kt.

Lander, Sir Stephen James, KCB

Lane, *Prof.* Sir David Philip, Kt., FRS, FRSE

Langham, Sir James Michael, Bt. (1660)

Langlands, Sir Robert Alan, Kt.

Langley, *Hon.* Sir Gordon Julian Hugh, Kt.

Langley, *Maj.-Gen.* Sir Henry Desmond Allen, KCVO, MBE

Langrishe, Sir James Hercules, Bt. (I. 1777)

Lankester, Sir Timothy Patrick, KCB

Lapun, *Hon.* Sir Paul, Kt.

Larcom, Sir (Charles) Christopher Royde, Bt. (1868)

Large, Sir Andrew McLeod Brooks, Kt.

Large, Sir Peter, Kt., CBE

Latham, *Hon.* Sir David Nicholas Ramsey, Kt.

Latham, Sir Martin Stuart, Kt., OBE

Latham, Sir Michael Anthony, Kt.

Latham, Sir Richard Thomas Paul, Bt. (1919)

Latimer, Sir (Courtenay) Robert, Kt., CBE

Latimer, Sir Graham Stanley, KBE

Lauder, Sir Piers Robert Dick-, Bt. (S. 1690)

Laughton, Sir Anthony Seymour, Kt.

Laurantus, Sir Nicholas, Kt., MBE

Laurence, Sir Peter Harold, KCMG, MC

Laurie, Sir Robert Bayley Emilius, Bt. (1834)

Lauterpacht, Sir Elihu, Kt., CBE, QC

Lauti, *Rt. Hon.* Sir Toaripi, GCMG

Lavan, *Hon.* Sir John Martin, Kt.

Law, *Adm.* Sir Horace Rochfort, GCB, OBE, DSC

Lawes, Sir (John) Michael Bennet, Bt. (1882)

Lawler, Sir Peter James, Kt., OBE

Lawrence, Sir David Roland Walter, Bt. (1906)

Lawrence, Sir George Alexander Waldemar, Bt. (1858)

Lawrence, Sir Ivan John, Kt., QC

Lawrence, Sir John Patrick Grosvenor, Kt., CBE

Lawrence, Sir William Fettiplace, Bt. (1867)

Laws, *Rt. Hon.* Sir John Grant McKenzie, Kt.

Lawson, Sir Christopher Donald, Kt.

†Lawson, Sir Charles John Patrick, Bt. (1900)

Lawson, Sir John Philip Howard-, Bt. (1841)

Lawson, *Gen.* Sir Richard George, KCB, DSO, OBE

Layard, *Adm.* Sir Michael Henry Gordon, KCB, CBE

Lea, *Vice-Adm.* Sir John Stuart Crosbie, KBE

Lea, Sir Thomas William, Bt. (1892)

Leach, *Admiral of the Fleet* Sir Henry Conyers, GCB

Leahy, Sir Daniel Joseph, Kt.

Leahy, Sir John Henry Gladstone, KCMG

Leahy, Sir Terence Patrick, Kt.

Learmont, *Gen.* Sir John Hartley, KCB, CBE

Leask, *Lt.-Gen.* Sir Henry Lowther Ewart Clark, KCB, DSO, OBE

Leather, Sir Edwin Hartley Cameron, KCMG, KCVO

Leaver, Sir Christopher, GBE

Le Bailly, *Vice-Adm.* Sir Louis Edward Stewart Holland, KBE, CB

Le Cheminant, *Air Chief Marshal* Sir Peter de Lacey, GBE, KCB, DFC

†Lechmere, Sir Reginald Anthony Hungerford, Bt. (1818)

Ledger, Sir Philip Stevens, Kt., CBE, FRSE

Lee, Sir Arthur James, KBE, MC

Lee, *Air Chief Marshal* Sir David John Pryer, GBE, CB

Lee, *Brig.* Sir Leonard Henry, Kt., CBE

Lee, Sir Quo-wei, Kt., CBE

Leeds, Sir Christopher Anthony, Bt. (1812)

Lees, Sir David Bryan, Kt.

Lees, Sir Thomas Edward, Bt. (1897)

Lees, Sir Thomas Harcourt Ivor, Bt. (1804)

Lees, Sir (William) Antony Clare, Bt. (1937)

Leese, Sir John Henry Vernon, Bt. (1908)

Le Fanu, *Maj.* Sir (George) Victor (Sheridan), KCVO

le Fleming, Sir David Kelland, Bt. (1705)

Legard, Sir Charles Thomas, Bt. (1660)

Legg, Sir Thomas Stuart, KCB, QC

Leggatt, *Rt. Hon.* Sir Andrew Peter, Kt.

Leggatt, Sir Hugh Frank John, Kt.

Leggett, Sir Clarence Arthur Campbell, Kt., MBE

Leigh, Sir Geoffrey Norman, Kt.

Leigh, Sir Richard Henry, Bt. (1918)

Leighton, Sir Michael John Bryan, Bt. (1693)

Leitch, Sir George, KCB, OBE

Leith, Sir George Ian David Forbes-, Bt. (1923)

Le Marchant, Sir Francis Arthur, Bt. (1841)

Lemon, Sir (Richard) Dawnay, Kt., CBE

Leng, *Gen.* Sir Peter John Hall, KCB, MBE, MC

Lennard, *Revd* Sir Hugh Dacre Barrett-, Bt. (1801)

Leon, Sir John Ronald, Bt. (1911)

Leonard, *Rt. Revd* Monsignor and *Rt. Hon.* Graham Douglas, KCVO

Lepping, Sir George Geria Dennis, GCMG, MBE

Le Quesne, Sir (Charles) Martin, KCMG

Le Quesne, Sir (John) Godfray, Kt., QC

Leslie, Sir Colin Alan Bettridge, Kt.

Leslie, Sir John Norman Ide, Bt. (1876)

†Leslie, Sir (Percy) Theodore, Bt. (S. 1625)

Leslie, Sir Peter Evelyn, Kt.

Lester, Sir James Theodore, Kt.

Lethbridge, Sir Thomas Periam Hector Noel, Bt. (1804)

Lever, Sir Jeremy Frederick, KCMG, QC

Lever, Sir Paul, KCMG

Lever, Sir (Tresham) Christopher Arthur Lindsay, Bt. (1911)

Leveson, *Hon.* Sir Brian Henry, Kt.

Levey, Sir Michael Vincent, Kt., LVO

Levine, Sir Montague Bernard, Kt.

Levinge, Sir Richard George Robin, Bt. (I. 1704)

Lewando, Sir Jan Alfred, Kt., CBE

Lewinton, Sir Christopher, Kt.

Lewis, Sir David Courtenay Mansel, KCVO

Lewis, Sir Terence Murray, Kt., OBE, GM, QPM

Lewthwaite, *Brig.* Sir Rainald Gilfrid, Bt., CVO, OBE, MC (1927)

Ley, Sir Ian Francis, Bt. (1905)

Leyland, Sir Philip Vyvyan Naylor-, Bt. (1895)

Lickiss, Sir Michael Gillam, Kt.

Liddington, Sir Bruce, Kt.

Liggins, *Prof.* Sir Graham Collingwood, Kt., CBE, FRS

Lightman, *Hon.* Sir Gavin Anthony, Kt.

Lighton, Sir Thomas Hamilton, Bt. (I. 1791)

Likierman, *Prof.* Sir John Andrew, Kt.

Lilleyman, *Prof.* Sir John Stuart, Kt.

Limon, Sir Donald William, KCB

Linacre, Sir (John) Gordon (Seymour), Kt., CBE, AFC, dfm

Lindop, Sir Norman, Kt.

Lindsay, Sir James Harvey Kincaid Stewart, Kt.

Lindsay, *Hon.* Sir John Edmund Frederic, Kt.

Lindsay, Sir Ronald Alexander, Bt., (1962)

Lipton, Sir Stuart Anthony, Kt.

Lipworth, Sir (Maurice) Sydney, Kt.

Lithgow, Sir William James, Bt. (1925)

Little, *Most Revd* Sir Thomas Francis, KBE

Littler, Sir (James) Geoffrey, KCB

Livesay, *Adm.* Sir Michael Howard, KCB

Llewellyn, Sir David St Vincent, Bt. (1922)

Llewelyn, Sir John Michael Dillwyn-Venables-, Bt. (1890)

Lloyd, *Prof.* Sir Geoffrey Ernest Richard, Kt., FBA

Lloyd, Sir Ian Stewart, Kt.

Lloyd, Sir Nicholas Markley, Kt.

Lloyd, *Rt. Hon.* Sir Peter Robert Cable, Kt., MP

Lloyd, Sir Richard Ernest Butler, Bt. (1960)

Lloyd, *Hon.* Sir Timothy Andrew Wigram, Kt.

Loader, Sir Leslie Thomas, Kt., CBE

Loane, *Most Revd* Sir Marcus Lawrence, KBE

Lobo, Sir Rogerio Hyndman, Kt., CBE

Lockhart, Sir Simon John Edward Francis Sinclair-, Bt. (S. 1636)

†Loder, Sir Edmund Jeune, Bt. (1887)

Logan, Sir David Brian Carleton, KCMG

Logan, Sir Donald Arthur, KCMG

Logan, Sir Raymond Douglas, Kt.

Lokoloko, Sir Tore, GCMG, GCVO, OBE

Lombe, *Hon.* Sir Edward Christopher Evans-, Kt.

Longmore, *Hon.* Sir Andrew Centlivres, Kt.

Loram, *Vice-Adm.* Sir David Anning, KCB, CVO

Lord, Sir Michael Nicholson, Kt.

Lorimer, Sir (Thomas) Desmond, Kt.

Los, *Hon.* Sir Kubulan, Kt., CBE

Lovell, Sir (Alfred Charles) Bernard, Kt., OBE, FRS

Lovelock, Sir Douglas Arthur, KCB

Loveridge, Sir John Warren, Kt.

Lovill, Sir John Roger, Kt., CBE

Low, Sir James Richard Morrison-, Bt. (1908)

Lowe, *Air Chief Marshal* Sir Douglas Charles, GCB, DFC, AFC

Lowe, Sir Frank Budge, Kt.

Lowe, Sir Thomas William Gordon, Bt. (1918)

Lowson, Sir Ian Patrick, Bt. (1951)

Lowther, *Col.* Sir Charles Douglas, Bt. (1824)

Lowther, Sir John Luke, KCVO, CBE

Loyd, Sir Francis Alfred, KCMG, OBE

Loyd, Sir Julian St John, KCVO

Lu, Sir Tseng Chi, Kt.

Lucas, *Prof.* Sir Colin Renshaw, Kt.

Lucas, Sir Thomas Edward, Bt. (1887)

Lucy, Sir Edmund John William Hugh Cameron-Ramsay-Fairfax-, Bt. (1836)

Luddington, Sir Donald Collin Cumyn, KBE, CMG, CVO

Lumsden, Sir David James, Kt.

Lus, *Hon.* Sir Pita, Kt., OBE

Lush, *Hon.* Sir George Hermann, Kt.

Lushington, Sir John Richard Castleman, Bt. (1791)

Luttrell, *Col.* Sir Geoffrey Walter Fownes, KCVO, MC

Lyell, *Rt. Hon.* Sir Nicholas Walter, Kt., QC, MP

Lygo, *Adm.* Sir Raymond Derek, KCB

Lyle, Sir Gavin Archibald, Bt. (1929)

Lyne, Sir Roderic Michael John, KBE, CMG

Lyons, Sir Edward Houghton, Kt.

Lyons, Sir James Reginald, Kt.

Lyons, Sir John, Kt.

Lyons, Sir Michael Thomas, Kt.

McAlpine, Sir William Hepburn, Bt. (1918)

Macara, Sir Alexander Wiseman, Kt., FRCP, FRCGP

†Macara, Sir Hugh Kenneth, Bt. (1911)

Macartney, Sir John Barrington, Bt. (I. 1799)

MacCormick, *Prof.* Sir Donald Neil, Kt., MEP, QC

Maclean, Sir Murdo, Kt.

MacSween, *Prof.* Sir Roderick Norman McIver, Kt.

McAvoy, Sir (Francis) Joseph, Kt., CBE

McCaffrey, Sir Thomas Daniel, Kt.

McCall, Sir (Charles) Patrick Home, Kt., MBE, TD

McCallum, Sir Donald Murdo, Kt., CBE, FREng.

McCamley, Sir Graham Edward, KBE

McCarthy, *Rt. Hon.* Sir Thaddeus Pearcey, KBE

McCartney, Sir (James) Paul, Kt., MBE

MacCormac, Sir Richard Cornelius, Kt., CBE

McClellan, *Col.* Sir Herbert Gerard Thomas, Kt., CBE, TD

McClintock, Sir Eric Paul, Kt.

McColl, Sir Colin Hugh Verel, KCMG

McCollum, *Rt. Hon.* Sir William, Kt.

McCombe, *Hon.* Sir Richard George Bramwell, Kt.

McConnell, Sir Robert Shean, Bt. (1900)

McCorkell, *Col.* Sir Michael William, KCVO, OBE, TD

McCowan, *Rt. Hon.* Sir Anthony James Denys, Kt.

†McCowan, Sir David William, Bt. (1934)

McCullough, *Hon.* Sir (Iain) Charles (Robert), Kt.

MacDermott, *Rt. Hon.* Sir John Clarke, Kt.

McDermott, Sir (Lawrence) Emmet, KBE

Macdonald of Sleat, Sir Ian Godfrey Bosville, Bt. (S. 1625)

Macdonald, Sir Kenneth Carmichael, KCB

McDonald, Sir Tom, Kt., OBE

McDonald, Sir Trevor, Kt., OBE

MacDougall, Sir (George) Donald (Alastair), Kt., CBE, FBA

McDowell, Sir Eric Wallace, Kt., CBE

Mace, *Lt.-Gen.* Sir John Airth, KBE, CB

McEwen, Sir John Roderick Hugh, Bt. (1953)

McFarland, Sir John Talbot, Bt. (1914)

MacFarlane, *Prof.* Sir Alistair George James, Kt., CBE, FRS

Macfarlane, Sir (David) Neil, Kt.

Macfarlane, Sir George Gray, Kt., CB, FREng.

McFarlane, Sir Ian, Kt.

McGeoch, *Vice-Adm.* Sir Ian Lachlan Mackay, KCB, DSO, DSC

McGrath, Sir Brian Henry, GCVO

Macgregor, Sir Edwin Robert, Bt. (1828)

MacGregor of MacGregor, Sir Gregor, Bt. (1795)

McGregor, Sir Ian Alexander, Kt., CBE, FRS

McGrigor, *Capt.* Sir Charles Edward, Bt. (1831)

McIntosh, *Vice-Adm.* Sir Ian Stewart, KBE, CB, DSO, DSC

McIntosh, Sir Neil William David, Kt., CBE

McIntosh, Sir Ronald Robert Duncan, KCB

McIntyre, Sir Donald Conroy, Kt., CBE

McIntyre, Sir Meredith Alister, Kt.

Mackay, *Hon.* Sir Colin Crichton, Kt.

MacKay, *Prof.* Sir Donald Iain, Kt., FRSE

McKay, Sir John Andrew, Kt., CBE

McKay, Sir William Robert, KCB

Mackechnie, Sir Alistair John, Kt.

McKee, *Maj.* Sir (William) Cecil, Kt., ERD

McKellen, Sir Ian Murray, Kt., CBE

Mackenzie, Sir Alexander Alwyne Henry Charles Brinton Muir-, Bt. (1805)

Mackenzie, Sir (James William) Guy, Bt. (1890)

Mackenzie, *Gen.* Sir Jeremy John George, GCB, OBE

†Mackenzie, Sir Peter Douglas, Bt. (S. 1673)

†Mackenzie, Sir Roderick McQuhae, Bt. (S. 1703)

McKenzie, Sir Roy Allan, KBE

Mackerras, Sir (Alan) Charles (MacLaurin), Kt., CBE

Mackeson, Sir Rupert Henry, Bt. (1954)

McKillop, Sir Thomas Fulton Wilson, Kt.

MacKinlay, Sir Bruce, Kt., CBE

McKinnon, Sir James, Kt.

McKinnon, *Hon.* Sir Stuart Neil, Kt.

Mackintosh, Sir Cameron Anthony, Kt.

Mackworth, Sir Digby (John), Bt. (1776)

McLaren, Sir Robin John Taylor, KCMG

McLaughlin, *Hon.* Mr Justice, Sir Richard, Kt.

Maclean of Dunconnell, Sir Charles Edward, Bt. (1957)

Maclean, Sir Donald Og Grant, Kt.

MacLean, *Vice-Adm.* Sir Hector Charles Donald, KBE, CB, DSC

Maclean, Sir Lachlan Hector Charles, Bt. (NS 1631)

McLeod, Sir Charles Henry, Bt. (1925)

MacLeod, Sir (John) Maxwell Norman, Bt. (1924)

Macleod, Sir (Nathaniel William) Hamish, KBE

McLintock, Sir (Charles) Alan, Kt.

McLintock, Sir Michael William, Bt. (1934)

Maclure, Sir John Robert Spencer, Bt. (1898)

McMahon, Sir Brian Patrick, Bt. (1817)

McMahon, Sir Christopher William, Kt.

Macmillan, Sir (Alexander McGregor) Graham, Kt.

MacMillan, *Lt.-Gen.* Sir John Richard Alexander, KCB, CBE

McMullin, *Rt. Hon.* Sir Duncan Wallace, Kt.

McMurtry, Sir David, Kt., CBE

Macnaghten, Sir Patrick Alexander, Bt. (1836)

McNamara, *Air Chief Marshal* Sir Neville Patrick, KBE

Macnaughton, *Prof.* Sir Malcolm Campbell, Kt.

McNee, Sir David Blackstock, Kt., QPM

McNulty, Sir (Robert William) Roy, Kt., CBE

MacPhail, Sir Bruce Dugald, Kt.

Macpherson, Sir Ronald Thomas Steward (Tommy), CBE, MC, TD

Macpherson of Cluny, *Hon.* Sir William Alan, Kt., TD

McQuarrie, Sir Albert, Kt.

MacRae, Sir (Alastair) Christopher (Donald Summerhayes), KCMG

Macready, Sir Nevil John Wilfrid, Bt. (1923)

Mactaggart, Sir John Auld, Bt. (1938)

Macwhinnie, Sir Gordon Menzies, Kt., CBE

McWilliam, Sir Michael Douglas, KCMG

McWilliams, Sir Francis, GBE, FREng.

Madden, Sir Peter John, Bt. (1919)

Maddox, Sir John Royden, Kt.

Madel, Sir (William) David, Kt., MP

Madigan, Sir Russel Tullie, Kt., OBE

Magnus, Sir Laurence Henry Philip, Bt. (1917)

Mahon, Sir (John) Denis, Kt., CBE

Mahon, Sir William Walter, Bt. (1819)

Maiden, Sir Colin James, Kt., D.Phil.

Main, Sir Peter Tester, Kt., ERD

Maingard de la Ville ès Offrans, Sir Louis Pierre René, Kt., CBE

Maino, Sir Charles, KBE

†Maitland, Sir Charles Alexander, Bt. (1818)

Maitland, Sir Donald James Dundas, GCMG, OBE

Malbon, *Vice-Adm.* Sir Fabian Michael, KBE

Malcolm, Sir James William Thomas Alexander, Bt. (S. 1665)

Malet, Sir Harry Douglas St Lo, Bt. (1791)

Mallaby, Sir Christopher Leslie George, GCMG, GCVO

Mallick, *Prof.* Sir Netar Prakash, Kt., FRCP, FRCPED.

Mallinson, Sir William James, Bt. (1935)

Malpas, Sir Robert, Kt., CBE, FREng.

Mamo, Sir Anthony Joseph, Kt., OBE

Mance, *Hon.* Sir Jonathan Hugh, Kt.

Manchester, Sir William Maxwell, KBE

Mander, Sir Charles Marcus, Bt. (1911)

Manduell, Sir John, Kt., CBE

Mann, *Rt. Revd* Sir Michael Ashley, KCVO

Mann, Sir Rupert Edward, Bt. (1905)

Manning, Sir David Geoffrey, KCMG, CMG

Mansel, Sir Philip, Bt. (1622)

Mansfield, *Vice-Adm.* Sir (Edward) Gerard (Napier), KBE, CVO

Mansfield, *Prof.* Sir Peter, Kt., FRS

Mansfield, Sir Philip (Robert Aked), KCMG

Mantell, *Rt. Hon.* Sir Charles Barrie Knight, Kt.

Manton, Sir Edwin Alfred Grenville, Kt.

Manuella, Sir Tulaga, GCMG, MBE

Manzie, Sir (Andrew) Gordon, KCB

Mara, *Rt. Hon.* Ratu Sir Kamisese Kapaiwai Tuimacilai, GCMG, KBE

Margetson, Sir John William Denys, KCMG

Mark, Sir Robert, GBE

Markham, Sir Charles John, Bt. (1911)

Marling, Sir Charles William Somerset, Bt. (1882)

Marmot, *Prof.* Sir Michael Gideon, Kt.

Marr, Sir Leslie Lynn, Bt. (1919)

Marriner, Sir Neville, Kt., CBE

Marriott, Sir Hugh Cavendish Smith-, Bt. (1774)

†Marsden, Sir Simon Neville Llewelyn, Bt. (1924)

Marsh, *Prof.* Sir John Stanley, Kt., CBE

Marshall, Sir Arthur Gregory George, Kt., OBE

Marshall, Sir Denis Alfred, Kt.

Marshall, *Prof.* Sir (Oshley) Roy, Kt., CBE

Marshall, Sir Peter Harold Reginald, KCMG

Marshall, Sir (Robert) Michael, Kt.

Martin, Sir Clive Haydon, Kt., OBE

Martin, Sir George Henry, Kt., CBE

Martin, *Vice-Adm.* Sir John Edward Ludgate, KCB, DSC

Martin, *Prof.* Sir Laurence Woodward, Kt.

Martin, Sir (Robert) Bruce, Kt., QC

Marychurch, Sir Peter Harvey, KCMG

Masefield, Sir Charles Beech Gordon, Kt.

Masefield, Sir Peter Gordon, Kt.

Masire, Sir Ketumile, GCMG

Mason, *Hon.* Sir Anthony Frank, KBE

Mason, Sir (Basil) John, Kt., CB, D.Sc., FRS

Mason, *Prof.* Sir David Kean, Kt., CBE

Mason, Sir Frederick Cecil, KCVO, CMG

Mason, Sir Gordon Charles, Kt., OBE

Mason, Sir John Charles Moir, KCMG

Mason, Sir John Peter, Kt., CBE

Mason, Sir Peter James, KBE

Mason, *Prof.* Sir Ronald, KCB, FRS

Matane, Sir Paulias Nguna, Kt., CMG, OBE

Mather, Sir (David) Carol (Macdonell), Kt., MC

Mathers, Sir Robert William, Kt.

Matheson of Matheson, Sir Fergus John, Bt. (1882)

Mathewson, Sir George Ross, Kt., CBE, Ph.D., FRSE

Matthews, Sir Peter Alec, Kt.

Matthews, Sir Peter Jack, Kt., CVO, OBE, QPM

Matthews, Sir Terence Hedley, Kt., OBE

Maud, The *Hon.* Sir Humphrey John Hamilton, KCMG

Maughan, Sir Deryck, Kt.

Mawer, Sir Philip John Courtney, Kt.

Mawhinney, *Rt. Hon.* Sir Brian Stanley, Kt., MP

Maxwell, Sir Michael Eustace George, Bt. (S. 1681)

Maxwell, Sir Nigel Mellor Heron-, Bt. (S. 1683)

May, *Rt. Hon.* Sir Anthony Tristram Kenneth, Kt.

Maynard, *Hon.* Sir Clement Travelyan, Kt.

Mayne, *Very Revd* Sir Michael Clement Otway, KCVO

Meadow, *Prof.* Sir (Samuel) Roy, Kt., FRCP, FRCPE

Medlycott, Sir Mervyn Tregonwell, Bt. (1808)

Megarry, *Rt. Hon.* Sir Robert Edgar, Kt., FBA

Meldrum, Sir George William, LVO

Meldrum, Sir Graham, Kt., CBE, QFSM

Melhuish, Sir Michael Ramsay, KBE, CMG

Mellon, Sir James, KCMG

Melmouth, Sir Graham John, Kt.

Menter, Sir James Woodham, Kt., Ph.D., Sc.D, FRS

Menteth, Sir James Wallace Stuart-, Bt. (1838)

Merifield, Sir Anthony James, KCVO, CB

Meyer, Sir Anthony John Charles, Bt. (1910)

Meyer, Sir Christopher John Rome, KCMG

Meyjes, Sir Richard Anthony, Kt.

Meyrick, Sir David John Charlton, Bt. (1880)

Meyrick, Sir George Christopher Cadafael Tapps-Gervis-, Bt. (1791)

Miakwe, *Hon.* Sir Akepa, KBE

Michael, Sir Duncan, Kt.

Michael, Sir Peter Colin, Kt., CBE

Middleton, Sir John Maxwell, Kt.

Middleton, Sir Peter Edward, GCB

Miers, Sir (Henry) David Alastair Capel, KBE, CMG

Milbank, Sir Anthony Frederick, Bt. (1882)

Milburn, Sir Anthony Rupert, Bt. (1905)

Mildmay, Sir Walter John Hugh St John-, Bt. (1772)

Miles, Sir Peter Tremayne, KCVO

Miles, Sir William Napier Maurice, Bt. (1859)

Millais, Sir Geoffrey Richard Everett, Bt. (1885)

Millar, Sir Oliver Nicholas, GCVO, FBA

Millard, Sir Guy Elwin, KCMG, CVO

Miller, Sir Albert Joel, KCMG, MVO, MBE, QPM, CPM

Miller, Sir Donald John, Kt., FRSE, FREng.

Miller, Sir Harry Holmes, Bt. (1705)

Miller, Sir Hilary Duppa (Hal), Kt.

Miller, *Lt.-Col.* Sir John Mansel, GCVO, DSO, MC

Miller, Sir Jonathan Wolfe, Kt., CBE

Miller, Sir (Oswald) Bernard, Kt.

Miller, Sir Peter North, Kt.

Miller, Sir Ronald Andrew Baird, Kt., CBE

Miller of Glenlee, Sir Stephen William Macdonald, Bt. (1788)

Miller, Sir William R., Kt.

Millichip, Sir Frederick Albert (Bert), Kt.

Mills, *Vice-Adm.* Sir Charles Piercy, KCB, CBE, DSC

Mills, Sir Ian, Kt.

Mills, Sir Frank, KCVO, CMG

Mills, Sir John Lewis Ernest Watts, Kt., CBE

Mills, Sir Peter Frederick Leighton, Bt. (1921)

Milman, Sir David Patrick, Bt. (1800)

Milne, Sir John Drummond, Kt.

Milner, Sir Timothy William Lycett, Bt. (1717)

Mirrlees, *Prof.* Sir James Alexander, Kt., FBA

Mitchell, Sir David Bower, Kt.

Mitchell, Sir Derek Jack, KCB, CVO

Mitchell, *Prof.* Sir (Edgar) William John, Kt., CBE, FRS

Mitchell, *Rt. Hon.* Sir James FitzAllen, KCMG

Mitchell, *Very Revd* Sir Patrick Reynolds, KCVO

Mitchell, *Hon.* Sir Stephen George, Kt.

Mitting, *Hon.* Sir John Edward, Kt.

Moate, Sir Roger Denis, Kt.

Mobbs, Sir (Gerald) Nigel, Kt.

Moberly, Sir John Campbell, KBE, CMG

Moberly, Sir Patrick Hamilton, KCMG

Moffat, Sir Brian Scott, Kt., OBE

Moffat, *Lt.-Gen.* Sir (William) Cameron, KBE

†Moir, Sir Christopher Ernest, Bt. (1916)

†Molony, Sir Thomas Desmond, Bt. (1925)

Monck, Sir Nicholas Jeremy, KCB

Montagu, Sir Nicholas Lionel John, KCB

Montgomery, Sir (Basil Henry) David, Bt. (1801)

Montgomery, Sir (William) Fergus, Kt.

Moollan, Sir Abdool Hamid Adam, Kt.

Moollan, *Hon.* Sir Cassam (Ismael), Kt.

Moon, Sir Peter Wilfred Giles Graham-, Bt. (1855)

†Moon, Sir Roger, Bt. (1887)

Moore, *Most Revd* Sir Desmond Charles, KBE

Moore, Sir Francis Thomas, Kt.

Moore, *Maj.-Gen.* Sir (John) Jeremy, KCB, OBE, MC

Moore, Sir John Michael, KCVO, CB, DSC

Moore, *Vice Adm.* Sir Michael Antony Claës, KBE, LVO

Moore, *Prof.* Sir Norman Winfrid, Bt. (1919)

Moore, Sir Patrick Alfred Caldwell-, Kt., CBE

Moore, Sir Patrick William Eisdell-, Kt., OBE

Moore, Sir William Roger Clotworthy, Bt., TD (1932)

Morauta, Sir Mekere, Kt.

Mordaunt, Sir Richard Nigel Charles, Bt. (1611)

Moreton, Sir John Oscar, KCMG, KCVO, MC

Morgan, *Vice-Adm.* Sir Charles Christopher, KBE

Morgan, His *Hon. Maj.-Gen.* Sir David John Hughes-, Bt., CB, CBE (1925)

Morgan, Sir Graham, Kt.

Morgan, Sir John Albert Leigh, KCMG

Morison, *Hon.* Sir Thomas Richard Atkin, Kt.

Morland, *Hon.* Sir Michael, Kt.

Morland, Sir Robert Kenelm, Kt.

Morpeth, Sir Douglas Spottiswoode, Kt., TD

†Morris, Sir Allan Lindsay, Bt. (1806)

Morris, *Air Marshal* Sir Arnold Alec, KBE, CB, FREng.

Morris, Sir (James) Richard (Samuel), Kt., CBE, FREng.

Morris, Sir Keith Elliot Hedley, KBE, CMG

Morris, *Prof.* Sir Peter John, Kt., FRS

Morris, Sir Trefor Alfred, Kt., CBE, QPM

Morris, *Very Revd* Sir William James, KCVO, Ph.D.

Morrison, Sir (Alexander) Fraser, Kt., CBE

Morrison, *Hon.* Sir Charles Andrew, Kt.

Morrison, Sir Howard Leslie, Kt., OBE

Morrison, Sir Kenneth Duncan, Kt., CBE

Morritt, *Hon.* Sir (Robert) Andrew, Kt., CVO

Morrow, Sir Ian Thomas, Kt.

Morse, Sir Christopher Jeremy, KCMG

Mortimer, Sir Laird, Kt.

Mortimer, Sir John Clifford, Kt., CBE, QC

Morton, *Adm.* Sir Anthony Storrs, GBE, KCB

Morton, Sir (Robert) Alastair (Newton), Kt.

Moseley, Sir George Walker, KCB

Moses, *Hon.* Sir Alan George, Kt.

†Moss, Sir David John Edwards-, Bt. (1868)

Moss, Sir David Joseph, KCVO, CMG

Moss, Sir Stirling Craufurd, Kt., OBE

Mostyn, *Gen.* Sir (Joseph) David Frederick, KCB, CBE

†Mostyn, Sir William Basil John, Bt. (1670)

Mott, Sir John Harmer, Bt. (1930)

Mottram, Sir Richard Clive, KCB

†Mount, Sir (William Robert) Ferdinand, Bt. (1921)

Mountain, Sir Denis Mortimer, Bt. (1922)

Mountfield, Sir Robin, KCB

Mowbray, Sir John, Kt.

Mowbray, Sir John Robert, Bt. (1880)

Muir, Sir Laurence Macdonald, Kt.

†Muir, Sir Richard James Kay, Bt. (1892)

Mulcahy, Sir Geoffrey John, Kt.

Mullens, *Lt.-Gen.* Sir Anthony Richard Guy, KCB, OBE

Mummery, *Hon.* Sir John Frank, Kt.

Munby, *Hon.* Sir James Lawrence, Kt.

Munn, Sir James, Kt., OBE

Munro, Sir Alan Gordon, KCMG

†Munro, Sir Kenneth Arnold William, Bt. (S. 1634)

†Munro, Sir Keith Gordon, Bt. (1825)

Munro, Sir Sydney Douglas Gun-, GCMG, MBE

Muria, *Hon.* Sir Gilbert John Baptist, Kt.

Murphy, Sir Leslie Frederick, Kt.

Murray, *Rt. Hon.* Sir Donald Bruce, Kt.

Murray, Sir James, KCMG

Murray, *Prof.* Sir Kenneth, Kt., FRCPath., FRS, FRSE

Murray, Sir Nigel Andrew Digby, Bt. (S. 1628)

Murray, Sir Patrick Ian Keith, Bt. (S. 1673)

†Murray, Sir Rowland William, Bt. (S. 1630)

Mursell, Sir Peter, Kt., MBE

Musgrave, Sir Christopher John Shane, Bt. (1782)

Musgrave, Sir Christopher Patrick Charles, Bt. (1611)

Musson, *Gen.* Sir Geoffrey Randolph Dixon, GCB, CBE, DSO

Myers, Sir Philip Alan, Kt., OBE, QPM

Myers, *Prof.* Sir Rupert Horace, KBE

Mynors, Sir Richard Baskerville, Bt. (1964)

Naipaul, Sir Vidiadhar Surajprasad, Kt.

Nairn, Sir Michael, Bt. (1904)

Nairn, Sir Robert Arnold Spencer-, Bt. (1933)

Nairne, *Rt. Hon.* Sir Patrick Dalmahoy, GCB, MC

Naish, Sir (Charles) David, Kt.

Nall, Sir Edward William Joseph Bt. (1954)

Namaliu, *Rt. Hon.* Sir Rabbie Langanai, KCMG

†Napier, Sir Charles Joseph, Bt. (1867)

Napier, Sir John Archibald Lennox, Bt. (S. 1627)

Napier, Sir Oliver John, Kt.

Napier, *Rt. Hon.* Sir Richard, GCVO

Nasmith, *Prof.* Sir James Duncan Dunbar-, Kt., CBE, RIBA, FRSE

Neal, Sir Eric James, Kt., CVO

Neal, Sir Leonard Francis, Kt., CBE

Neale, Sir Gerrard Anthony, Kt.

Neave, Sir Paul Arundell, Bt. (1795)

Needham, *Rt. Hon.* Sir Richard (The Earl of Kilmorey)

Neill, *Rt. Hon.* Sir Brian Thomas, Kt.

Neill, *Rt. Hon.* Sir Ivan, Kt., PC (NI)

Neill, Sir (James) Hugh, KCVO, CBE, TD

†Nelson, Sir Jamie Charles Vernon Hope, Bt. (1912)

Nelson, *Hon.* Sir Robert Franklyn, Kt.

Neuberger, *Hon.* Sir David Edmond, Kt.

Neubert, Sir Michael John, Kt.

Neville, Sir Roger Albert Gartside, Kt., VRD

New, *Maj.-Gen.* Sir Laurence Anthony Wallis, KCB, CBE

Newall, Sir Paul Henry, Kt., TD

Newby, *Prof.* Sir Howard Joseph, Kt., CBE

Newington, Sir Michael John, KCMG

Newman, Sir Francis Hugh Cecil, Bt. (1912)

Newman, Sir Geoffrey Robert, Bt. (1836)

Newman, *Hon.* Sir George Michael, Kt.

Newman, Sir Kenneth Leslie, GBE, QPM

Newman, *Vice-Adm.* Sir Roy Thomas, KCB

Newman, *Col.* Sir Stuart Richard, Kt., CBE, TD

Newsam, Sir Peter Anthony, Kt.

Newton, Sir (Charles) Wilfred, Kt., CBE

Newton, Sir (Harry) Michael (Rex), Bt. (1900)

Newton, Sir Kenneth Garnar, Bt., OBE, TD (1924)

Ngata, Sir Henare Kohere, KBE

Nichol, Sir Duncan Kirkbride, Kt., CBE

Nicholas, Sir David, Kt., CBE

Nicholas, Sir John William, KCVO, CMG

Nicholls, *Air Marshal* Sir John Moreton, KCB, CBE, DFC, AFC

Nicholls, Sir Nigel Hamilton, KCVO, CBE

Nichols, Sir Richard Everard, Kt.

Nicholson, Sir Bryan Hubert, Kt.

†Nicholson, Sir Charles Christian, Bt. (1912)

Nicholson, *Rt. Hon.* Sir Michael, Kt.

Nicholson, Sir Paul Douglas, Kt.

Nicholson, Sir Robin Buchanan, Kt., Ph.D., FRS, FREng.

Nicoll, Sir William, KCMG

Nightingale, Sir Charles Manners Gamaliel, Bt. (1628)

Nightingale, Sir John Cyprian, Kt., CBE, BEM, QPM

Nixon, Sir Simon Michael Christopher, Bt. (1906)

Nixon, Sir Edwin Ronald, Kt., CBE

Noble, Sir David Brunel, Bt. (1902)

Noble, Sir Iain Andrew, Bt., OBE (1923)

Noble, Sir (Thomas Alexander) Fraser, Kt., MBE

Nombri, Sir Joseph Karl, Kt., ISO, BEM

Noon, Sir Gulam Kaderbhoy, Kt., MBE

Norman, Sir Arthur Gordon, KBE, DFC

Norman, Sir Mark Annesley, Bt. (1915)

Norman, Sir Robert Henry, Kt., OBE

Norman, Sir Ronald, Kt., OBE

Norrington, Sir Roger Arthur Carver, Kt., CBE

Norris, *Air Chief Marshal* Sir Christopher Neil Foxley-, GCB, DSO, OBE

Norris, Sir Eric George, KCMG

Norriss, *Air Marshal* Sir Peter Coulson, KBE, CB, AFC

North, Sir Peter Machin, Kt., CBE, QC, DCL, FBA

North, Sir Thomas Lindsay, Kt.

North, Sir (William) Jonathan (Frederick), Bt. (1920)

Norton, *Vice-Adm. Hon.* Sir Nicholas John Hill-, KCB

Nossal, Sir Gustav Joseph Victor, Kt., CBE

Nott, *Rt. Hon.* Sir John William Frederic, KCB

Nourse, *Rt. Hon.* Sir Martin Charles, Kt.

Nugent, Sir John Edwin Lavallin, Bt. (I. 1795)

Nugent, *Maj.* Sir Peter Walter James, Bt. (1831)

Nugent, Sir Robin George Colborne, Bt. (1806)

Nunn, Sir Trevor Robert, Kt., CBE

Nursaw, Sir James, KCB, QC

Nurse, Sir Paul Maxime, Kt., Ph.D.

Nuttall, Sir Nicholas Keith Lillington, Bt. (1922)

Nutting, Sir John Grenfell, Bt., QC (1903)

Oakeley, Sir John Digby Atholl, Bt. (1790)

Oakes, Sir Christopher, Bt. (1939)

Oakshott, *Hon.* Sir Anthony Hendrie, Bt. (1959)

Oates, Sir Thomas, Kt., CMG, OBE

O'Brien, Sir Frederick William Fitzgerald, Kt.

O'Brien, Sir Richard, Kt., DSO, MC

O'Brien, Sir Timothy John, Bt. (1849)

O'Brien, *Adm.* Sir William Donough, KCB, DSC

O'Connell, Sir Maurice James Donagh MacCarthy, Bt. (1869)

O'Dea, Sir Patrick Jerad, KCVO

Odell, Sir Stanley John, Kt.

Odgers, Sir Graeme David William, Kt.

O'Dowd, Sir David Joseph, Kt., CBE, QPM

Ogden, Sir (Edward) Michael, Kt., QC

Ogden, Sir Robert, Kt., CBE

Ogilvy, *Rt. Hon.* Sir Angus James Bruce, KCVO

Ogilvy, Sir Francis Gilbert Arthur, Bt. (S. 1626)

Ognall, *Hon.* Sir Harry Henry, Kt.

Ohlson, Sir Brian Eric Christopher, Bt. (1920)

Okeover, *Capt.* Sir Peter Ralph Leopold Walker-, Bt. (1886)

Olewale, *Hon.* Sir Niwia Ebia, Kt.

O'Loghlen, Sir Colman Michael, Bt. (1838)

Olson, Sir Ralph, Kt.

Olver, Sir Stephen John Linley, KBE, CMG

Omand, Sir David Bruce, KCB

O'Neil, *Hon.* Sir Desmond Henry, Kt.

O'Nions, *Prof.* Sir Robert Keith, Kt., FRS, Ph.D.

Onslow, Sir John Roger Wilmot, Bt. (1797)

Oppenheim, Sir Duncan Morris, Kt.

Oppenheimer, Sir Michael Bernard Grenville, Bt. (1921)

Orde, Sir John Alexander Campbell-, Bt. (1790)

O'Regan, Dr Sir Stephen Gerard (Tipene), Kt.

O'Reilly, Anthony John Francis, Kt.

Orr, Sir David Alexander, Kt., MC

Orr, Sir John, Kt., OBE

Osborn, Sir John Holbrook, Kt.

Osborn, Sir Richard Henry Danvers, Bt. (1662)

Osborne, Sir Peter George, Bt. (I. 1629)

Osifelo, Sir Frederick Aubarua, Kt., MBE

Osmond, Sir Douglas, Kt., CBE

Osmotherly, Sir Edward Benjamin Crofton, Kt., CB

O'Sullevan, Sir Peter John, Kt., CBE

Oswald, *Admiral of the Fleet* Sir (John) Julian Robertson, GCB

Oswald, Sir (William Richard) Michael, KCVO

Otton, Sir Geoffrey John, KCB

Otton, *Rt. Hon.* Sir Philip Howard, Kt.

Oulton, Sir Antony Derek Maxwell, GCB, QC

Ouseley, *Hon.* Sir Brian Walter, Kt.

Outram, Sir Alan James, Bt. (1858)

Overall, Sir John Wallace, Kt., CBE, MC

Owen, Sir Geoffrey, Kt.

Owen, Sir Hugo Dudley Cunliffe-, Bt. (1920)

Owen, *Hon.* Sir John Arthur Dalziel, Kt.

Owen, *Hon.* Sir Robert Michael, Kt.

Packer, Sir Richard John, KCB

Page, Sir (Arthur) John, Kt.

Page, Sir Frederick William, Kt., CBE, FREng.

Page, Sir John Joseph Joffre, Kt., OBE

Paget, Sir Julian Tolver, Bt., CVO (1871)

Paget, Sir Richard Herbert, Bt. (1886)

Pain, *Lt.-Gen.* Sir (Horace) Rollo (Squarey), KCB, MC

Pain, *Hon.* Sir Peter Richard, Kt.

Paine, Sir Christopher Hammon, Kt., FRCP, FRCR

Palin, *Air Chief Marshal* Sir Roger Hewlett, KCB, OBE

Palliser, *Rt. Hon.* Sir (Arthur) Michael, GCMG

Palmar, Sir Derek James, Kt.

Palmer, Sir (Charles) Mark, Bt. (1886)

Palmer, Sir Geoffrey Christopher John, Bt. (1660)

Palmer, *Rt. Hon.* Sir Geoffrey Winston Russell, KCMG

Palmer, Sir John Chance, Kt.

Palmer, Sir John Edward Somerset, Bt. (1791)

Palmer, *Maj.-Gen.* Sir (Joseph) Michael, KCVO

Palmer, Sir Reginald Oswald, GCMG, MBE

Pantlin, Sir Dick Hurst, Kt., CBE

Paolozzi, Sir Eduardo Luigi, Kt., CBE, RA

Parbo, Sir Arvi Hillar, Kt.

Park, *Hon.* Sir Andrew Edward Wilson, Kt.

Parker, Sir Alan William, Kt., CBE

Parker, Sir (Arthur) Douglas Dodds-, Kt.

Parker, Sir Eric Wilson, Kt.

Parker, Sir John, Kt.

Parker, *Hon.* Sir Jonathan Frederic, Kt.

Parker, *Maj.* Sir Michael John, KCVO, CBE

Parker, Sir Richard (William) Hyde, Bt. (1681)

Parker, *Rt. Hon.* Sir Roger Jocelyn, Kt.

Parker, Sir Thomas John, Kt.

Parker, *Vice-Adm.* Sir (Wilfred) John, KBE, CB, DSC

Parker, Sir William Peter Brian, Bt. (1844)

Parkes, Sir Edward Walter, Kt., FREng.

Parkinson, Sir Nicholas Fancourt, Kt.

Parry, Sir Emyr Jones, KCMG

Parsons, Sir John Christopher, KCVO

Parsons, Sir (John) Michael, Kt.

Parsons, Sir Richard Edmund (Clement Fownes), KCMG

Partridge, Sir Michael John Anthony, KCB

Pascoe, *Gen.* Sir Robert Alan, KCB, MBE

Pasley, Sir John Malcolm Sabine, Bt. (1794)

Paterson, Sir Dennis Craig, Kt.

Patnick, Sir (Cyril) Irvine, Kt., OBE

Patten, *Hon.* Mr Justice, Sir Nicholas John, Kt.

Pattie, *Rt. Hon.* Sir Geoffrey Edwin, Kt.

Pattinson, Sir (William) Derek, Kt.

Pattison, *Prof.* Sir John Ridley, Kt., DM, FRCPath.

Pattullo, Sir (David) Bruce, Kt., CBE

Paul, Sir John Warburton, GCMG, OBE, MC

Paul, *Air Marshal* Sir Ronald Ian Stuart-, KBE

Payne, Sir Norman John, Kt., CBE, FREng.

Peach, Sir Leonard Harry, Kt.

Peacock, *Prof.* Sir Alan Turner, Kt., DSC
Pearce, Sir Austin William, Kt., CBE, Ph.D., FREng.
Pearce, Sir (Daniel Norton) Idris, Kt., CBE, TD
Pearse, Sir Brian Gerald, Kt.
Pearson, Sir Francis Nicholas Fraser, Bt. (1964)
Pearson, *Gen.* Sir Thomas Cecil Hook, KCB, CBE, DSO
Peart, *Prof.* Sir William Stanley, Kt., MD, FRS
Pease, Sir (Alfred) Vincent, Bt. (1882)
Pease, Sir Richard Thorn, Bt. (1920)
Peat, Sir Gerrard Charles, KCVO
Peat, Sir Michael Charles Gerrard, KCVO
Peck, Sir Edward Heywood, GCMG
Peckham, *Prof.* Sir Michael John, Kt., FRCP, FRCPGlas., FRCR, FRCPath.
Pedder, *Air Marshal* Sir Ian Maurice, KCB, OBE, DFC
Peek, *Vice-Adm.* Sir Richard Innes, KBE, CB, DSC
Peek, Sir William Grenville, Bt. (1874)
Peel, Sir John Harold, KCVO
Peel, Sir (William) John, Kt.
Peirse, Sir Henry Grant de la Poer Beresford-, Bt. (1814)
Peirse, *Air Vice-Marshal* Sir Richard Charles Fairfax, KCVO, CB
Pelgen, Sir Harry Friedrich, Kt., MBE
Peliza, Sir Robert John, KBE, ED
Pelly, Sir Richard John, Bt. (1840)
Pemberton, Sir Francis Wingate William, Kt., CBE
Penrose, *Prof.* Sir Roger, Kt., OM, FRS
Pereira, Sir (Herbert) Charles, Kt., D.Sc., FRS
Perowne, *Vice-Adm.* Sir James Francis, KBE
Perring, Sir John Raymond, Bt. (1963)
Perris, Sir David (Arthur), Kt., MBE
Perry, Sir David Howard, KCB
Perry, Sir (David) Norman, Kt., MBE
Perry, Sir Michael Sydney, GBE
Pervez, Sir Mohammed Anwar, Kt., OBE
Pestell, Sir John Richard, KCVO
Peterkin, Sir Neville, Kt.
Peters, *Prof.* Sir David Keith, Kt., FRCP
Petersen, Sir Jeffrey Charles, KCMG
Petersen, Sir Johannes Bjelke-, KCMG
Peterson, Sir Christopher Matthew, Kt., CBE, TD
†Petit, Sir Jehangir, Bt. (1890)
Peto, Sir Henry George Morton, Bt. (1855)
Peto, Sir Michael Henry Basil, Bt. (1927)
Peto, *Prof.* Sir Richard, Kt., FRS
Petrie, Sir Peter Charles, Bt., CMG (1918)
Pettigrew, Sir Russell Hilton, Kt.
Pettit, Sir Daniel Eric Arthur, Kt.

Pettitt, Sir Dennis, Kt.
Philips, *Prof.* Sir Cyril Henry, Kt.
Phillips, Sir Fred Albert, Kt., CVO
Phillips, Sir (Gerald) Hayden, GCB
Phillips, Sir Henry Ellis Isidore, Kt., CMG, MBE
Phillips, Sir Horace, KCMG
Phillips, Sir John David, Kt., QPM
Phillips, Sir Peter John, Kt., OBE
Phillips, Sir Robin Francis, Bt. (1912)
Pickard, Sir (John) Michael, Kt.
Pickering, Sir Edward Davies, Kt.
Pickthorn, Sir James Francis Mann, Bt. (1959)
Pidgeon, Sir John Allan Stewart, Kt.
†Piers, Sir James Desmond, Bt. (I. 1661)
Pigot, Sir George Hugh, Bt. (1764)
Pigott, *Lt.-Gen.* Sir Anthony David, KCB, CBE
Pigott, Sir Berkeley Henry Sebastian, Bt. (1808)
Pike, *Lt.-Gen.* Sir Hew William Royston, KCB, DSO, MBE
Pike, Sir Michael Edmund, KCVO, CMG
Pike, Sir Philip Ernest Housden, Kt., QC
Pilditch, Sir Richard Edward, Bt. (1929)
Pile, Sir Frederick Devereux, Bt., MC (1900)
Pilkington, Sir Thomas Henry Milborne-Swinnerton-, Bt. (S. 1635)
Pill, *Rt. Hon.* Sir Malcolm Thomas, Kt.
Pilling, Sir Joseph Grant, KCB
Pinker, Sir George Douglas, KCVO
Pinsent, Sir Christopher Roy, Bt. (1938)
Pippard, *Prof.* Sir (Alfred) Brian, Kt., FRS
Pirie, *Gp Capt* Sir Gordon Hamish, Kt., CVO, CBE
Pitakaka, Sir Moses Puibangara, GCMG
Pitcher, Sir Desmond Henry, Kt.
Pitchford, *Hon.* Sir Christopher John, Kt.
Pitman, Sir Brian Ivor, Kt.
Pitoi, Sir Sere, Kt., CBE
Pitt, Sir Harry Raymond, Kt., Ph.D., FRS
Pitts, Sir Cyril Alfred, Kt.
Plastow, Sir David Arnold Stuart, Kt.
Platt, Sir Harold Grant, Kt.
Pledger, *Air Chief Marshal* Sir Malcolm David, KCB, OBE, AFC
Plumbly, Sir Derek John, KCMG
Pogo, *Rev.* Sir Ellison Leslie, Kt.
Pohai, Sir Timothy, Kt., MBE
Pole, Sir (John) Richard (Walter Reginald) Carew, Bt. (1628)
Pole, Sir Peter Van Notten, Bt. (1791)
Polkinghorne, *Revd* Canon Sir John Charlton, KBE, FRS
Pollard, Sir Charles, Kt.

Pollen, Sir John Michael Hungerford, Bt. (1795)
Pollock, Sir George Frederick, Bt. (1866)
Pollock, Sir Giles Hampden Montagu-, Bt. (1872)
Pollock, *Admiral of the Fleet* Sir Michael Patrick, GCB, LVO, DSC
Ponsonby, Sir Ashley Charles Gibbs, Bt., KCVO, MC (1956)
Poole, *Hon.* Sir David Anthony, Kt.
Poore, Sir Herbert Edward, Bt. (1795)
Pope, Sir Joseph Albert, Kt., D.Sc., Ph.D.
Popplewell, *Hon.* Sir Oliver Bury, Kt.
†Porritt, Sir Jonathon Espie, Bt. (1963)
Portal, Sir Jonathan Francis, Bt. (1901)
Porter, Sir John Simon Horsbrugh-, Bt. (1902)
Porter, Sir Leslie, Kt.
Porter, *Air Marshal* Sir (Melvin) Kenneth (Drowley), KCB, CBE
Porter, *Rt. Hon.* Sir Robert Wilson, Kt., PC (NI), QC
Posnett, Sir Richard Neil, KBE, CMG
Potter, *Rt. Hon.* Sir Mark Howard, Kt.
Potter, *Maj.-Gen.* Sir (Wilfrid) John, KBE, CB
Potts, *Hon.* Sir Francis Humphrey, Kt.
Pound, Sir John David, Bt. (1905)
Pountain, Sir Eric John, Kt.
Povey, Sir Keith, Kt., QPM
Powell, Sir (Arnold Joseph) Philip, Kt., CH, OBE, RA, FRIBA
Powell, Sir Nicholas Folliott Douglas, Bt. (1897)
Powell, Sir Richard Royle, GCB, KBE, CMG
Power, Sir Alastair John Cecil, Bt. (1924)
Power, *Hon.* Sir Noel Plunkett, Kt.
Prance, *Prof.* Sir Ghillean Tolmie, Kt., FRS
Prendergast, Sir (Walter) Kieran, KCVO, CMG
Prentice, *Hon.* Sir William Thomas, Kt., MBE
Prescott, Sir Mark, Bt. (1938)
†Preston, Sir Philip Charles Henry Hulton, Bt. (1815)
Prevost, Sir Christopher Gerald, Bt. (1805)
Price, Sir Charles Keith Napier Rugge-, Bt. (1804)
Price, Sir David Ernest Campbell, Kt.
Price, Sir Francis Caradoc Rose, Bt. (1815)
Price, Sir Frank Leslie, Kt.
Price, Sir Norman Charles, KCB
Price, Sir Robert John Green-, Bt. (1874)
Prickett, *Air Chief Marshal* Sir Thomas Other, KCB, DSO, DFC

Prideaux, Sir Humphrey Povah
Treverbian, Kt., OBE
†Primrose, Sir John Ure, Bt. (1903)
Pringle, *Air Marshal* Sir Charles
Norman Seton, KBE, FREng.
Pringle, *Hon.* Sir John Kenneth, Kt.
Pringle, *Lt.-Gen.* Sir Steuart
(Robert), Bt., KCB, RM (S. 1683)
Pritchard, Sir Neil, KCMG
Proby, Sir Peter, Bt. (1952)
Prosser, Sir Ian Maurice Gray, Kt.
Pryke, Sir Christopher Dudley, Bt.
(1926)
Puapua, *Rt. Hon.* Sir Tomasi, KBE
Pugh, Sir Idwal Vaughan, KCB
Pumfrey, *Hon.* Sir Nicholas Richard,
Kt.
Pumphrey, Sir (John) Laurence,
KCMG
Purchas, *Rt. Hon.* Sir Francis Brooks,
Kt.
Purves, Sir William, Kt., CBE, DSO
Purvis, *Vice-Adm.* Sir Neville, KCB
Quicke, Sir John Godolphin, Kt.,
CBE
Quigley, Sir (William) George
(Henry), Kt., CB, Ph.D.
Quilliam, *Hon.* Sir (James) Peter, Kt.
Quilter, Sir Anthony Raymond
Leopold Cuthbert, Bt. (1897)
Quinlan, Sir Michael Edward, GCB
Quinton, Sir James Grand, Kt.
Radcliffe, Sir Sebastian Everard, Bt.
(1813)
Radda, *Prof.* Sir George Karoly, Kt.,
CBE, FRS
Rae, *Hon.* Sir Wallace Alexander
Ramsay, Kt.
Raeburn, Sir Michael Edward
Norman, Bt. (1923)
Raikes, *Vice-Adm.* Sir Iwan Geoffrey,
KCB, CBE, DSC
Raison, *Rt. Hon.* Sir Timothy Hugh
Francis, Kt.
Ralli, Sir Godfrey Victor, Bt., TD
(1912)
Ramdanee, Sir Mookteswar
Baboolall Kailash, Kt.
Ramphal, Sir Shridath
Surendranath, GCMG
Ramphul, Sir Baalkhristna, Kt.
Ramphul, Sir Indurduth, Kt.
Ramsay, Sir Alexander William
Burnett, Bt. (1806)
Ramsay, Sir Allan John (Hepple),
KBE, CMG
Ramsbotham, *Gen.* Sir David John,
GCB, CBE
Ramsbotham, *Hon.* Sir Peter
Edward, GCMG, GCVO
Ramsden, Sir John Charles Josslyn,
Bt. (1689)
Randle, *Prof.* Sir Philip John, Kt.
Rank, Sir Benjamin Keith, Kt., CMG
Rankin, Sir Ian Niall, Bt. (1898)
Rasch, Sir Simon Anthony Carne, Bt.
(1903)
Rashleigh, Sir Richard Harry, Bt.
(1831)

Ratford, Sir David John Edward,
KCMG, CVO
Rattee, *Hon.* Sir Donald Keith, Kt.
Rattle, Sir Simon Dennis, Kt., CBE
Rault, Sir Louis Joseph Maurice, Kt.
Rawlins, *Surgeon Vice-Adm.* Sir John
Stuart Pepys, KBE
Rawlins, *Prof.* Sir Michael David,
Kt., FRCP, FRCPED.
Rawlinson, Sir Anthony Henry John,
Bt. (1891)
Read, *Air Marshal* Sir Charles
Frederick, KBE, CB, DFC, AFC
Read, Sir John Emms, Kt.
†Reade, Sir Kenneth Ray, Bt. (1661)
Reay, *Lt.-Gen.* Sir (Hubert) Alan
John, KBE
Redgrave, *Maj.-Gen.* Sir Roy Michael
Frederick, KBE, MC
Redgrave, Sir Steven Geoffrey, Kt.,
CBE
Redmayne, Sir Nicholas, Bt. (1964)
Redwood, Sir Peter Boverton, Bt.
(1911)
Reece, Sir Charles Hugh, Kt.
Rees, Sir David Allan, Kt., Ph.D.,
D.Sc., FRS
Rees, *Prof.* Sir Martin John, Kt., FRS
Reeve, Sir Anthony, KCMG, KCVO
Reeves, *Most Revd* Paul Alfred,
GCMG, GCVO
Reffell, *Adm.* Sir Derek Roy, KCB
Refshauge, *Maj.-Gen.* Sir William
Dudley, Kt., CBE
Reid, Sir Alexander James, Bt. (1897)
Reid, Sir (Harold) Martin (Smith),
KBE, CMG
Reid, Sir Hugh, Bt. (1922)
Reid, Sir Norman Robert, Kt.
Reid, Sir Robert Paul, Kt.
Reid, Sir William Kennedy, KCB
Reiher, Sir Frederick Bernard Carl,
KBE, CMG
Reilly, *Lt.-Gen.* Sir Jeremy Calcott,
KCB, DSO
Renals, Sir Stanley, Bt. (1895)
Renouf, Sir Clement William Bailey,
Kt.
Renshaw, Sir (Charles) Maurice
Bine, Bt. (1903)
Renwick, Sir Richard Eustace, Bt.
(1921)
Reporter, Sir Shapoor Ardeshirji,
KBE
Reynolds, Sir David James, Bt.
(1923)
Reynolds, Sir Peter William John,
Kt., CBE
Rhodes, Sir Basil Edward, Kt., CBE,
TD
Rhodes, Sir John Christopher
Douglas, Bt. (1919)
Rhodes, Sir Peregrine Alexander,
KCMG
Rice, *Maj.-Gen.* Sir Desmond Hind
Garrett, KCVO, CBE
Rice, Sir Timothy Miles Bindon, Kt.
Richard, Sir Cliff, Kt., OBE
Richards, Sir Brian Mansel, Kt., CBE,
Ph.D.

Richards, Sir (Francis) Brooks,
KCMG, DSC
Richards, Sir Francis Neville, KCMG,
CVO
Richards, *Lt.-Gen.* Sir John Charles
Chisholm, KCB, KCVO, RM
Richards, Sir Rex Edward, Kt., D.Sc.,
FRS
Richards, *Hon.* Sir Stephen Price, Kt.
Richardson, Sir Anthony Lewis, Bt.
(1924)
Richardson, *Rt. Hon.* Sir Ivor Lloyd
Morgan, Kt.
Richardson, Sir (John) Eric, Kt., CBE
Richardson, Sir Michael John de
Rougemont, Kt.
Richardson, *Lt.-Gen.* Sir Robert
Francis, KCB, CVO, CBE
Richardson, Sir Simon Alaisdair
Stewart-, Bt. (S. 1630)
Richardson, Sir Thomas Legh, KCMG
Richmond, *Prof.* Sir Mark Henry,
Kt., FRS
Ricketts, Sir Robert Cornwallis
Gerald St Leger, Bt. (1828)
Riddell, Sir John Charles Buchanan,
Bt., CVO (S. 1628)
Ridley, Sir Adam (Nicholas), Kt.
Ridley, Sir Michael Kershaw, KCVO
Ridsdale, Sir Julian Errington, Kt.,
CBE
Rifkind, *Rt. Hon.* Sir Malcolm Leslie,
KCMG, QC
Rigby, Sir Anthony John, Bt. (1929)
Rigby, Sir Peter, Kt.
Rimer, *Hon.* Sir Colin Percy
Farquharson, Kt.
Ringadoo, *Hon.* Sir Veerasamy,
GCMG
Ripley, Sir Hugh, Bt. (1880)
Risk, Sir Thomas Neilson, Kt.
Ritako, Sir Thomas Baha, Kt., MBE
Rix, *Hon.* Sir Bernard Anthony, Kt.
Rix, Sir John, Kt., MBE, FREng.
Robati, Sir Pupuke, KBE, OBE
Robb, Sir John Weddell, Kt.
Roberts, *Hon.* Sir Denys Tudor Emil,
KBE, QC
Roberts, Sir Derek Harry, Kt., CBE,
FRS, FREng.
Roberts, *Prof.* Sir Edward Adam,
KCMG
Roberts, Sir (Edward Fergus) Sidney,
Kt., CBE
Roberts, *Prof.* Sir Gareth Gwyn, Kt.,
FRS
Roberts, Sir Gilbert Howland
Rookehurst, Bt. (1809)
Roberts, Sir Gordon James, Kt., CBE
Roberts, Sir Hugh Ashley, KCVO, CVO
Roberts, Sir Ivor Anthony, KCMG
Roberts, Sir Samuel, Bt. (1919)
Roberts, Sir William James Denby,
Bt. (1909)
Robertson, Sir John Fraser, KCMG,
CBE
Robertson, Sir Lewis, Kt., CBE, FRSE
Robins, Sir Ralph Harry, Kt., FREng.
Robinson, Sir Albert Edward
Phineas, Kt.

†Robinson, Sir Christopher Philipse, Bt. (1854)

Robinson, Sir Dominick Christopher Lynch-, Bt. (1920)

Robinson, Sir Ian, Kt.

Robinson, Sir John James Michael Laud, Bt. (1660)

Robinson, Sir Wilfred Henry Frederick, Bt. (1908)

Robson, *Prof.* Sir James Gordon, Kt., CBE

Robson, Sir John Adam, KCMG

Robson, Sir Stephen Arthur, Kt., CB

Robson, Sir Robert William, Kt., CBE

Roch, *Rt. Hon.* Sir John Ormond, Kt.

Roche, Sir David O'Grady, Bt. (1838)

Roche, Sir Henry John, Kt.

Rodgers, Sir (Andrew) Piers (Wingate Aikin-Sneath), Bt. (1964)

Rodley, *Prof.* Sir Nigel, KBE

Rodrigues, Sir Alberto Maria, Kt., CBE, ED

Roe, *Air Chief Marshal* Sir Rex David, GCB, AFC

Rogers, Sir Frank Jarvis, Kt.

Rogers, *Air Chief Marshal* Sir John Robson, KCB, CBE

Rooke, Sir Denis Eric, Kt., OM, CBE, FRS, FREng.

Ropner, Sir John Bruce Woollacott, Bt. (1952)

Ropner, Sir Robert Douglas, Bt. (1904)

Rose, *Rt. Hon.* Sir Christopher Dudley Roger, Kt.

Rose, Sir Clive Martin, GCMG

Rose, Sir David Lancaster, Bt. (1874)

Rose, *Gen.* Sir (Hugh) Michael, KCB, CBE, DSO, QGM

Rose, Sir Julian Day, Bt. (1872 and 1909)

Ross, Sir (James) Keith, Bt., RD, FRCS (1960)

Ross, *Lt.-Gen.* Sir Robert Jeremy, KCB, OBE

Ross, *Lt.-Col.* Sir Walter Hugh Malcolm, KCVO, OBE

Rossi, Sir Hugh Alexis Louis, Kt.

Rotblat, *Prof.* Sir Joseph, KCMG, CBE, FRS

Roth, *Prof.* Sir Martin, Kt., MD, FRCP

Rothschild, Sir Evelyn Robert Adrian de, Kt.

Rougier, *Hon.* Sir Richard George, Kt.

Rowe, *Rear-Adm.* Sir Patrick Barton, KCVO, CBE

Rowland, *Air Marshal* Sir James Anthony, KBE, DFC, AFC

Rowland, Sir (John) David, Kt.

Rowlands, *Air Marshal* Sir John Samuel, GC, KBE

Rowley, Sir Charles Robert, Bt. (1836) (1786)

Rowlinson, *Prof.* Sir John Shipley, Kt., FRS

Roxburgh, *Vice-Adm.* Sir John Charles Young, KCB, CBE, DSO, DSC

Royden, Sir Christopher John, Bt. (1905)

Rudd, Sir (Anthony) Nigel (Russell), Kt.

Rudge, Sir Alan Walter, Kt., CBE, FRS

Rumbold, Sir Henry John Sebastian, Bt. (1779)

Runchorelal, Sir (Udayan) Chinubhai Madhowlal, Bt. (1913)

Rusby, *Vice-Adm.* Sir Cameron, KCB, LVO

†Russell, Sir (Arthur) Mervyn, Bt. (1812)

Russell, Sir Charles Dominic, Bt. (1916)

Russell, *Hon.* Sir David Sturrock West-, Kt.

Russell, Sir George, Kt., CBE

Russell, Sir Muir, KCB

Russell, *Prof.* Sir Peter Edward Lionel, Kt., D.Litt., FBA

Russell, Sir (Robert) Mark, KCMG

Russell, *Rt. Hon.* Sir (Thomas) Patrick, Kt.

Rutter, Sir Frank William Eden, KBE

Rutter, *Prof.* Sir Michael Llewellyn, Kt., CBE, MD, FRS

Ryan, Sir Derek Gerald, Bt. (1919)

Rycroft, Sir Richard John, Bt. (1784)

Ryrie, Sir William Sinclair, KCB

Sabola, *Hon.* Sir Joaquim Claudino Gonsalves-, Kt.

Sachs, *Hon.* Sir Michael Alexander Geddes, Kt.

Sainsbury, *Rt. Hon.* Sir Timothy Alan Davan, Kt.

†St Aubyn, Sir William Molesworth-, Bt. (1689)

†St George, Sir John Avenel Bligh, Bt. (I. 1766)

St Johnston, Sir Kerry, Kt.

Sainty, Sir John Christopher, KCB

Salisbury, Sir Robert William, Kt.

Salt, Sir Patrick MacDonnell, Bt. (1869)

Salt, Sir (Thomas) Michael John, Bt. (1899)

Sampson, Sir Colin, Kt., CBE, QPM

Samuel, Sir John Michael Glen, Bt. (1898)

Samuelson, Sir (Bernard) Michael (Francis), Bt. (1884)

Samuelson, Sir Sydney Wylie, Kt., CBE

Sanders, Sir John Reynolds Mayhew-, Kt.

Sanders, Sir Robert Tait, KBE, CMG

Sanders, Sir Ronald Michael, KCMG

Sanderson, Sir Frank Linton, Bt. (1920)

Sarei, Sir Alexis Holyweek, Kt., CBE

Satchwell, Sir Kevin Joseph, Kt.

Saunders, Sir Peter, Kt.

Savage, Sir Ernest Walter, Kt.

Savile, Sir James Wilson Vincent, Kt., OBE

Saxby, *Prof.* Sir Robin Keith, Kt.

Say, *Rt. Revd* Richard David, KCVO

Scheele, Sir Nicholas Vernon, KCMG

Schiemann, *Rt. Hon.* Sir Konrad Hermann Theodor, Kt.

Scholar, Sir Michael Charles, KCB

Scholey, Sir David Gerald, Kt., CBE

Scholey, Sir Robert, Kt., CBE, FREng.

Scholtens, Sir James Henry, KCVO

Schreier, Sir Bernard, Kt.

Schubert, Sir Sydney, Kt.

Scipio, Sir Hudson Rupert, Kt.

Scoon, Sir Paul, GCMG, GCVO, OBE

Scott, Sir Anthony Percy, Bt. (1913)

Scott, Sir David Aubrey, GCMG

Scott, Sir Dominic James Maxwell-, Bt. (1642)

Scott, Sir James Jervoise, Bt. (1962)

Scott, Sir Kenneth Bertram Adam, KCVO, CMG

Scott, Sir Michael, KCVO, CMG

Scott, *Rt. Hon.* Sir Nicholas Paul, KBE

Scott, Sir Oliver Christopher Anderson, Bt. (1909)

Scott, *Prof.* Sir Philip John, KBE

Scott, Sir Robert David Hillyer, Kt.

Scott, Sir Walter John, Bt. (1907)

Scott, *Rear-Adm.* Sir (William) David (Stewart), KBE, CB

Seale, Sir Clarence David, Kt.

Seale, Sir John Henry, Bt. (1838)

Seaman, Sir Keith Douglas, KCVO, OBE

Sebastian, Sir Cuthbert Montraville, GCMG, OBE

†Sebright, Sir Peter Giles Vivian, Bt. (1626)

Seccombe, Sir (William) Vernon Stephen, Kt.

Seconde, Sir Reginald Louis, KCMG, CVO

Sedley, *Rt. Hon.* Sir Stephen John, Kt.

Seely, Sir Nigel Edward, Bt. (1896)

Seeto, Sir Ling James, Kt., MBE

Seeyave, Sir Rene Sow Choung, Kt., CBE

Seligman, Sir Peter Wendel, Kt., CBE

Sellors, Sir Patrick John Holmes-, KCVO, FRCS

Semple, Sir John Laughlin, KCB

Sergeant, Sir Patrick, Kt.

Series, Sir (Joseph Michel) Emile, Kt., CBE

Serota, Sir Nicholas Andrew, Kt.

Serpell, Sir David Radford, KCB, CMG, OBE

†Seton, Sir Charles Wallace, Bt. (S. 1683)

Seton, Sir Iain Bruce, Bt. (S. 1663)

Severne, *Air Vice-Marshal* Sir John de Milt, KCVO, OBE, AFC

†Seymour, Sir Michael Patrick Culme-, Bt. (1809)

Shackleton, *Prof.* Sir Nicholas John, Kt., Ph.D., FRS

Shaffer, Sir Peter Levin, Kt., CBE

Shakerley, Sir Geoffrey Adam, Bt. (1838)

Shakespeare, Sir Thomas William, Bt. (1942)

Sharp, Sir Adrian, Bt. (1922)

Sharp, Sir George, Kt., OBE

Sharp, Sir Kenneth Johnston, Kt., TD

Sharp, Sir Leslie, Kt., QPM

Sharp, Sir Sheridan Christopher Robin, Bt. (1920)

Sharpe, Hon. Sir John Henry, Kt., CBE

Sharples, Sir James, Kt., QPM

Shattock, Sir Gordon, Kt.

Shaw, Sir Brian Piers, Kt.

Shaw, Sir (Charles) Barry, Kt., CB, QC

Shaw, Sir (George) Neville Bowman-, Kt.

Shaw, Prof. Sir John Calman, Kt., CBE, FRSE

Shaw, Sir John Michael Robert Best-, Bt. (1665)

Shaw, Sir Neil McGowan, Kt.

Shaw, Sir Robert, Bt. (1821)

Shaw, Sir Roy, Kt.

Shaw, Sir Run Run, Kt., CBE

Sheehy, Sir Patrick, Kt.

Sheen, Hon. Sir Barry Cross, Kt.

Sheffield, Sir Reginald Adrian Berkeley, Bt. (1755)

Shehadie, Sir Nicholas Michael, Kt., OBE

Sheil, Hon. Sir John, Kt.

Sheinwald, Sir Nigel Elton, KCMG

Sheldon, Hon. Sir (John) Gervase (Kensington), Kt.

Shelley, Sir John Richard, Bt. (1611)

Shelton, Sir William Jeremy Masefield, Kt.

Shepherd, Sir Colin Ryley, Kt.

Shepherd, Sir John Alan, KCVO, CMG

Shepperd, Sir Alfred Joseph, Kt.

Sher, Sir Antony, KBE

Sherman, Sir Alfred, Kt.

Shields, Sir Neil Stanley, Kt., MC

Shields, Prof. Sir Robert, Kt., MD

Shiffner, Sir Henry David, Bt. (1818)

Silber, Rt. Hon. Sir Stephen Robert, Kt.

Shinwell, Sir (Maurice) Adrian, Kt.

Shock, Sir Maurice, Kt.

Short, Sir Apenera Pera, KBE

Shortridge, Sir Jon Deacon, KCB

Shuckburgh, Sir Rupert Charles Gerald, Bt. (1660)

Siaguru, Sir Anthony Michael, KBE

Sidey, Air Marshal Sir Ernest Shaw, KBE, CB, MD

Sieff, Hon. Sir David, Kt.

Simeon, Sir John Edmund Barrington, Bt. (1815)

Simmons, Air Marshal Sir Michael George, KCB, AFC

Simmons, Sir Stanley Clifford, Kt., FRCS, FRCOG

Simms, Sir Neville Ian, Kt., FREng.

Simonet, Sir Louis Marcel Pierre, Kt., CBE

Simons, Sir Robert Stuart, Kt., QHP

Simpson, Hon. Sir Alfred Henry, Kt.

Simpson, Lt.-Gen. Sir Roderick Alexander Cordy-, KBE, CB

Simpson, Sir William James, Kt.

Sims, Sir Roger Edward, Kt.

Sinclair, Sir Clive Marles, Kt.

Sinclair, Sir George Evelyn, Kt., CMG, OBE

Sinclair, Sir Ian McTaggart, KCMG, QC

Sinclair, Sir Patrick Robert Richard, Bt. (S. 1704)

Sinclair, Sir Robert John, Kt.

Sinden, Sir Donald Alfred, Kt., CBE

Singer, Prof. Sir Hans Wolfgang, Kt.

Singer, Hon. Sir Jan Peter, Kt.

Singh, Hon. Sir Vijay Raghubir, Kt.

Sione, Sir Tomu Malaefone, GCMG, OBE

Sitwell, Sir (Sacheverell) Reresby, Bt. (1808)

Skeet, Sir Trevor Herbert Harry, Kt.

Skeggs, Sir Clifford George, Kt.

Skehel, Sir John James, Kt., FRS

Skingsley, Air Chief Marshal Sir Anthony Gerald, GBE, KCB

Skinner, Sir (Thomas) Keith (Hewitt), Bt. (1912)

Skipwith, Sir Patrick Alexander d'Estoteville, Bt. (1622)

Slack, Sir William Willatt, KCVO, FRCS

Slade, Sir Benjamin Julian Alfred, Bt. (1831)

Slade, Rt. Hon. Sir Christopher John, Kt.

Slaney, Prof. Sir Geoffrey, KBE

Slater, Adm. Sir John (Jock) Cunningham Kirkwood, GCB, LVO

Sleight, Sir Richard, Bt. (1920)

Sloan, Sir Andrew Kirkpatrick, Kt., QPM

Sloman, Sir Albert Edward, Kt., CBE

Smart, Prof. Sir George Algernon, Kt., MD, FRCP

Smart, Sir Jack, Kt., CBE

Smedley, Hon. Sir (Frank) Brian, Kt.

Smedley, Sir Harold, KCMG, MBE

Smiley, Lt.-Col. Sir John Philip, Bt. (1903)

Smith, Sir Alan, Kt., CBE, DFC

Smith, Sir Alexander Mair, Kt., Ph.D.

Smith, Hon. Sir Andrew Charles, Kt.

Smith, Sir Andrew Colin Hugh-, Kt.

Smith, Lt.-Gen. Sir Anthony Arthur Denison-, KBE

Smith, Sir Charles Bracewell-, Bt. (1947)

Smith, Prof. Sir Christopher Hubert Llewellyn-, Kt.

Smith, Sir Christopher Sydney Winwood, Bt. (1809)

Smith, Prof. Sir Colin Stansfield, Kt., CBE

Smith, Sir Cyril, Kt., MBE

Smith, Sir David Calvert-, QC

Smith, Prof. Sir David Cecil, Kt., FRS

Smith, Air Chief Marshal Sir David Harcourt-, GBE, KCB, DFC

Smith, Sir David Iser, KCVO

Smith, Sir Dudley (Gordon), Kt.

Smith, Prof. Sir Eric Brian, Kt., Ph.D.

Smith, Maj.-Gen. Sir (Francis) Brian Wyldbore-, Kt., CB, DSO, OBE

Smith, Prof. Sir Francis Graham-, Kt., FRS

Smith, Sir Geoffrey Johnson, Kt., MP

Smith, Sir John Alfred, Kt., QPM

Smith, Prof. Sir John Cyril, Kt., CBE, QC, FBA

Smith, Sir John Hamilton-Spencer-, Bt. (1804)

Smith, Sir John Jonah Walker-, Bt. (1960)

Smith, Sir John Lindsay Eric, Kt., CH, CBE

Smith, Sir John Rathbone Vassar-, Bt. (1917)

Smith, Sir Joseph William Grenville, Kt., MD, FRCP

Smith, Sir Leslie Edward George, Kt.

Smith, Maj.-Gen. Sir Michael Edward Carleton-, Kt., CBE

Smith, Sir Michael John Llewellyn, KCVO, CMG

Smith, Rt. Hon. Sir Murray Stuart-, Kt.

Smith, Sir (Norman) Brian, Kt., CBE, Ph.D.

Smith, Sir Peter Brierley, Kt., CBE

†Smith, Sir Peter Frank Graham Newson-, Bt. (1944)

Smith, Sir Raymond Horace, KBE

Smith, Sir Robert Courtney, Kt., CBE

Smith, Sir Robert Haldane, Kt

Smith, Sir Robert Hill, Bt., MP (1945)

Smith, Prof. Sir Roland, Kt.

Smith, Air Marshal Sir Roy David Austen-, KBE, CB, CVO, DFC

Smith, Gen. Sir Rupert Anthony, KCB, DSO, OBE

Smith, Sir (Thomas) Gilbert, Bt. (1897)

Smith, Sir (William) Antony (John) Reardon-, Bt. (1920)

Smith, Sir (William) Richard Prince-, Bt. (1911)

Smithers, Sir Peter Henry Berry Otway, Kt., VRD, D.Phil.

Smyth, Sir Thomas Weyland Bowyer-, Bt. (1661)

Smyth, Sir Timothy John, Bt. (1955)

Soakimori, Sir Frederick Pa-Nukuanca, KBE, CPM

Soame, Sir Charles John Buckworth-Herne-, Bt. (1697)

Sobers, Sir Garfield St Auburn, Kt.

Solomon, Sir Harry, Kt.

Somare, Rt. Hon. Sir Michael Thomas, GCMG, CH

Somerville, Brig. Sir John Nicholas, Kt., CBE

Somerville, Sir Quentin Charles Somerville Agnew-, Bt. (1957)

Sorrell, Sir Martin Stuart, Kt.

Soulsby, Sir Peter Alfred, Kt.

Soutar, Air Marshal Sir Charles John Williamson, KBE

South, Sir Arthur, Kt.

Southby, Sir John Richard Bilbe, Bt. (1937)

Southgate, Sir Colin Grieve, Kt.

Southgate, Sir William David, Kt.

Southward, Sir Leonard Bingley, Kt., OBE

Southwood, *Prof.* Sir (Thomas) Richard (Edmund), Kt., FRS

Souyave, *Hon.* Sir (Louis) Georges, Kt.

Sowrey, *Air Marshal* Sir Frederick Beresford, KCB, CBE, AFC

Sparkes, Sir Robert Lyndley, Kt.

Sparrow, Sir John, Kt.

Spearman, Sir Alexander Young Richard Mainwaring, Bt. (1840)

Spedding, *Prof.* Sir Colin Raymond William, Kt., CBE

Speed, Sir (Herbert) Keith, Kt., RD

Speelman, Sir Cornelis Jacob, Bt. (1686)

Speight, *Hon.* Sir Graham Davies, Kt.

Spencer, Sir Derek Harold, Kt., QC

Spencer, *Vice-Adm.* Sir Peter, KCB, ADC

Spicer, Sir James Wilton, Kt.

Spicer, Sir Nicholas Adrian Albert, Bt., MB (1906)

Spicer, Sir (William) Michael Hardy, Kt., MP

Spiers, Sir Donald Maurice, Kt., CB, TD

Spooner, Sir James Douglas, Kt.

Spratt, *Col.* Sir Greville Douglas, GBE, TD

Spring, Sir Dryden Thomas, Kt.

Squire, *Air Chief Marshal* Sir Peter Ted, GCB, DFC, AFC, ADC

Stabb, *Hon.* Sir William Walter, Kt., QC

Stainton, Sir (John) Ross, Kt., CBE

Stamer, Sir (Lovelace) Anthony, Bt. (1809)

Stanbridge, Air Vice-Marshal Sir Brian Gerald Tivy, KCVO, CBE, AFC

Standard, Sir Kenneth Livingstone, Kt., MD

Stanier, Sir Beville Douglas, Bt. (1917)

Stanier, *Field Marshal* Sir John Wilfred, GCB, MBE

Stanley, *Rt. Hon.* Sir John Paul, Kt., MP

Staples, Sir Richard Molesworth, Bt. (I. 1628)

Stark, Sir Andrew Alexander Steel, KCMG, CVO

Starkey, Sir John Philip, Bt. (1935)

Starrit, Sir James, KCVO

Staughton, *Rt. Hon.* Sir Christopher Stephen Thomas Jonathan Thayer, Kt.

Staveley, Sir John Malfroy, KBE, MC

Stear, *Air Chief Marshal* Sir Michael James Douglas, KCB, CBE

Steel, Sir David Edward Charles, Kt., DSO, MC, TD

Steel, *Hon.* Sir David William, Kt.

Steele, Sir (Philip John) Rupert, Kt.

Steere, Sir Ernest Henry Lee-, Kt.

Stephen, *Rt. Hon.* Sir Ninian Martin, KG, GCMG, GCVO, KBE

Stephens, Sir (Edwin) Barrie, Kt.

Stephenson, Sir Henry Upton, Bt. (1936)

Sternberg, Sir Sigmund, Kt.

Stevens, Sir Jocelyn Edward Greville, Kt., CVO

Stevens, Sir John, Kt.

Stevens, Sir Laurence Houghton, Kt., CBE

Stevenson, *Vice-Adm.* Sir (Hugh) David, KBE

Stevenson, Sir Simpson, Kt.

Stewart, Sir Alan, KBE

Stewart, Sir Alan d'Arcy, Bt. (I. 1623)

Stewart, Sir Brian John, Kt., CBE

Stewart, Sir David James Henderson-, Bt. (1957)

Stewart, Sir David John Christopher, Bt. (1803)

Stewart, Sir Edward Jackson, Kt.

Stewart, Sir Houston Mark Shaw-, Bt., MC, TD (S. 1667)

Stewart, Sir James Douglas, Kt.

Stewart, Sir James Moray, KCB

Stewart, Sir (John) Simon (Watson), Bt. (1920)

Stewart, Sir John Young, Kt., OBE

Stewart, *Lt.-Col.* Sir Robert Christie, KCVO, CBE, TD

Stewart, Sir Robertson Huntly, Kt., CBE

Stewart, Sir Robin Alastair, Bt. (1960)

Stewart, *Prof.* Sir William Duncan Paterson, Kt., FRS, FRSE

Stibbon, *Gen.* Sir John James, KCB, OBE

Stirling, Sir Alexander John Dickson, KBE, CMG

Stirling, Sir Angus Duncan Aeneas, Kt.

Stirrup, *Air Marshal* Sir Graham Eric, KCB, AFC

Stockdale, Sir Arthur Noel, Kt.

Stockdale, Sir Thomas Minshull, Bt. (1960)

Stoddart, *Wg Cdr.* Sir Kenneth Maxwell, KCVO, AE

Stoker, *Prof.* Sir Michael George Parke, Kt., CBE, FRCP, FRS, FRSE

Stokes, Sir John Heydon Romaine, Kt.

Stones, Sir William Frederick, Kt., OBE

Stonhouse, *Revd* Sir Michael Philip, Bt. (1628)

Stonor, *Air Marshal* Sir Thomas Henry, KCB

Stoppard, Sir Thomas, Kt., OM, CBE

Storey, *Hon.* Sir Richard, Bt., CBE (1960)

Stott, Sir Adrian George Ellingham, Bt. (1920)

Stoute, Sir Michael Ronald, Kt.

Stow, Sir Christopher Philipson-, Bt., DFC (1907)

Stowe, Sir Kenneth Ronald, GCB, CVO

Stracey, Sir John Simon, Bt. (1818)

Strachan, Sir Curtis Victor, Kt., CVO

Strachey, Sir Charles, Bt. (1801)

Strang Steel, Sir (Fiennes) Michael, Bt. (1938)

Strawson, *Prof.* Sir Peter Frederick, Kt., FBA

Street, *Hon.* Sir Laurence Whistler, KCMG

Streeton, Sir Terence George, KBE, CMG

Stringer, Sir Donald Edgar, Kt., CBE

Stringer, Sir Howard, Kt.

Strong, Sir Roy Colin, Kt., Ph.D., FSA

Stronge, Sir James Anselan Maxwell, Bt. (1803)

Stroud, *Prof.* Sir (Charles) Eric, Kt., FRCP

Strutt, Sir Nigel Edward, Kt., TD

Stuart, Sir James Keith, Kt.

Stuart, Sir Kenneth Lamonte, Kt.

Stuart, Sir Mark Moody-, KCMG

†Stuart, Sir Phillip Luttrell, Bt. (1660)

Stubbs, Sir William Hamilton, Kt., Ph.D.

Stucley, *Lt.* Sir Hugh George Coplestone Bampfylde, Bt. (1859)

Studd, Sir Edward Fairfax, Bt. (1929)

Studd, Sir Peter Malden, GBE, KCVO

Studholme, Sir Henry William, Bt. (1956)

†Style, Sir William Frederick, Bt. (1627)

Sugar, Sir Alan Michael, Kt.

Sugden, Sir Arthur, Kt.

Sullivan, *Hon.* Sir Jeremy Mirth, Kt.

Sullivan, Sir Richard Arthur, Bt. (1804)

Sulston, Sir John Edward, Kt.

Sumner, *Hon.* Sir Christopher John, Kt.

Sutherland, Sir John Brewer, Bt. (1921)

Sutherland, Sir William George MacKenzie, Kt.

Suttie, Sir James Edward Grant-, Bt. (S. 1702)

Sutton, Sir Frederick Walter, Kt., OBE

Sutton, *Air Marshal* Sir John Matthias Dobson, KCB

Sutton, Sir Richard Lexington, Bt. (1772)

Swaffield, Sir James Chesebrough, Kt., CBE, RD

Swaine, Sir John Joseph, Kt., CBE

Swan, Sir Conrad Marshall John Fisher, KCVO, Ph.D.

Swan, Sir John William David, KBE

Swann, Sir Michael Christopher, Bt., TD (1906)

Swanwick, Sir Graham Russell, Kt., MBE

Swartz, *Hon.* Sir Reginald William Colin, KBE, ED

Sweeney, Sir George, Kt.

Sweeting, *Prof.* Sir Martin Nicholas, Kt., OBE, FRS

Sweetnam, Sir (David) Rodney, KCVO, CBE, FRCS

Swinburn, *Lt.-Gen.* Sir Richard Hull, KCB

Swinson, Sir John Henry Alan, Kt., OBE

Swinton, *Maj.-Gen.* Sir John, KCVO, OBE
Swire, Sir Adrian Christopher, Kt.
Swire, Sir John Anthony, Kt., CBE
Sykes, Sir David Michael, Bt. (1921)
Sykes, Sir Francis John Badcock, Bt. (1781)
Sykes, Sir Hugh Ridley, Kt.
Sykes, *Prof.* Sir (Malcolm) Keith, Kt.
Sykes, Sir Richard, Kt.
Sykes, Sir Tatton Christopher Mark, Bt. (1783)
Symington, *Prof.* Sir Thomas, Kt., MD, FRSE
Symons, *Vice-Adm.* Sir Patrick Jeremy, KBE
Synge, Sir Robert Carson, Bt. (1801)
Tait, *Adm.* Sir (Allan) Gordon, KCB, DSC
Talbot, *Hon.* Sir Hilary Gwynne, Kt.
Talboys, *Rt. Hon.* Sir Brian Edward, CH, KCB
Tancred, Sir Henry Lawson-, Bt. (1662)
Tangaroa, *Hon.* Sir Tangoroa, Kt., MBE
Tapsell, Sir Peter Hannay Bailey, Kt., MP
Tate, Sir (Henry) Saxon, Bt. (1898)
Tavaiqia, *Ratu* Sir Josaia, KBE
Tavare, Sir John, Kt., CBE
Tavener, *Prof.* Sir John Kenneth, Kt.
Taylor, *Lt.-Gen.* Sir Allan Macnab, KBE, MC
Taylor, Sir (Arthur) Godfrey, Kt.
Taylor, Sir Cyril Julian Hebden, Kt.
Taylor, Sir Edward Macmillan (Teddy), Kt., MP
Taylor, *Rt. Revd* John Bernard, KCVO
Taylor, Sir John Lang, KCMG
Taylor, Sir Nicholas Richard Stuart, Bt. (1917)
Taylor, *Prof.* Sir William, Kt., CBE
Teagle, *Vice-Adm.* Sir Somerford Francis, KBE
Tebbit, Sir Donald Claude, GCMG
Tebbit, Sir Kevin Reginald, KCB, CMG
Telford, Sir Robert, Kt., CBE, FREng.
Temple, *Maj.* Sir Richard Anthony Purbeck, Bt., MC (1876)
Templeton, Sir John Marks, Kt.
Tenison, Sir Richard Hanbury-, KCVO
Tennant, Sir Anthony John, Kt.
Tennant, *Capt.* Sir Iain Mark, KT
Terry, *Air Marshal* Sir Colin George, KBE, CB
Terry, Sir Michael Edward Stanley Imbert-, Bt. (1917)
Terry, *Air Chief Marshal* Sir Peter David George, GCB, AFC
Thatcher, Sir Denis, Bt., MBE, TD (1990)
Thesiger, Sir Wilfred Patrick, KBE, DSO
Thomas, Sir Derek Morison David, KCMG
Thomas, Sir (Godfrey) Michael (David), Bt. (1694)
Thomas, Sir Jeremy Cashel, KCMG
Thomas, Sir (John) Alan, Kt.

Thomas, *Prof.* Sir John Meurig, Kt., FRS
Thomas, Sir Keith Vivian, Kt.
Thomas, Sir Quentin Jeremy, Kt., CB
Thomas, Sir Robert Evan, Kt.
Thomas, *Hon.* Sir Roger John Laugharne, Kt.
Thomas, *Hon.* Sir Swinton Barclay, Kt.
Thomas, Sir William James Cooper, Bt., TD (1919)
Thomas, Sir (William) Michael (Marsh), Bt. (1918)
Thompson, Sir Christopher Peile, Bt. (1890)
Thompson, Sir Clive Malcolm, Kt.
Thompson, Sir David Albert, KCMG
Thompson, Sir Donald, Kt.
Thompson, Sir Gilbert Williamson, Kt., OBE
Thompson, *Surgeon Vice-Adm.* Sir Godfrey James Milton-, KBE
Thompson, Sir (Humphrey) Simon Meysey-, Bt. (1874)
Thompson, *Prof.* Sir Michael Warwick, Kt., D.Sc
Thompson, Sir Nicholas Annesley, Bt. (1963)
Thompson, Sir Nigel Cooper, KCMG, CBE
Thompson, Sir Paul Anthony, Bt. (1963)
Thompson, Sir Peter Anthony, Kt.
Thompson, Sir Thomas d'Eyncourt John, Bt. (1806)
Thomson, Sir (Frederick Douglas) David, Bt. (1929)
Thomson, Sir John Adam, GCMG
Thomson, Sir John (Ian) Sutherland, KBE, CMG
Thomson, Sir Mark Wilfrid Home, Bt. (1925)
Thomson, Sir Thomas James, Kt., CBE, FRCP
Thorn, Sir John Samuel, Kt., OBE
Thorne, Sir Neil Gordon, Kt., OBE, TD
Thorne, Sir Peter Francis, KCVO, CBE
Thornton, Sir (George) Malcolm, Kt.
Thornton, Sir Peter Eustace, KCB
Thornton, Sir Richard Eustace, KCVO, OBE
†Thorold, Sir (Anthony) Oliver, Bt. (1642)
Thorpe, *Hon.* Sir Mathew Alexander, Kt.
Thouron, Sir John Rupert Hunt, KBE
Thwaites, Sir Bryan, Kt., Ph.D.
Tibbits, *Capt.* Sir David Stanley, Kt., DSC
Tickell, Sir Crispin Charles Cervantes, GCMG, KCVO
Tidbury, Sir Charles Henderson, Kt.
Tikaram, Sir Moti, KBE
Tilt, Sir Robin Richard, Kt.
Timmins, *Col.* Sir John Bradford, KCVO, OBE, TD
Tims, Sir Michael David, KCVO
Tindle, Sir Ray Stanley, Kt., CBE

Tippet, *Vice-Adm.* Sir Anthony Sanders, KCB
†Tipping, Sir David Gwynne Evans-, Bt. (1913)
Tirvengadum, Sir Harry Krishnan, Kt.
Titman, Sir John Edward Powis, KCVO
Tod, *Vice-Adm.* Sir Jonathan James Richard, KCB, CBE
Todd, *Prof.* Sir David, Kt., CBE
Todd, Sir Ian Pelham, KBE, FRCS
Todd, *Hon.* Sir (Reginald Stephen) Garfield, Kt.
Tollemache, Sir Lyonel Humphry John, Bt. (1793)
Tololo, Sir Alkan, KBE
Tomkins, Sir Edward Emile, GCMG, CVO
Tomkys, Sir (William) Roger, KCMG
Tomlinson, *Prof.* Sir Bernard Evans, Kt., CBE
Tomlinson, *Hon.* Sir Stephen Miles, Kt.
Tooley, Sir John, Kt.
Tooth, Sir (Hugh) John Lucas-, Bt. (1920)
ToRobert, Sir Henry Thomas, KBE
Tory, Sir Geofroy William, KCMG
Touche, Sir Anthony George, Bt. (1920)
Touche, Sir Rodney Gordon, Bt. (1962)
Toulson, *Hon.* Sir Roger Grenfell, Kt.
Tovey, Sir Brian John Maynard, KCMG
ToVue, Sir Ronald, Kt., OBE
Towneley, Sir Simon Peter Edmund Cosmo William, KCVO
Townsend, Sir Cyril David, Kt.
Traill, Sir Alan Towers, GBE
Trant, *Gen.* Sir Richard Brooking, KCB
Treacher, *Adm.* Sir John Devereux, KCB
Treitel, *Prof.* Sir Guenter Heinz, Kt., FBA, QC
Trelawny, Sir John Barry Salusbury-, Bt. (1628)
Trench, Sir Peter Edward, Kt., CBE, TD
Trescowthick, Sir Donald Henry, KBE
†Trevelyan, Sir Edward (Norman), Bt. (1662)
Trevelyan, Sir Geoffrey Washington, Bt. (1874)
Trezise, Sir Kenneth Bruce, Kt., OBE
Trippier, Sir David Austin, Kt., RD
Tritton, Sir Anthony John Ernest, Bt. (1905)
Trollope, Sir Anthony Simon, Bt. (1642)
Trotter, Sir Neville Guthrie, Kt.
Trotter, Sir Ronald Ramsay, Kt.
Troubridge, Sir Thomas Richard, Bt. (1799)
Troup, *Vice-Adm.* Sir (John) Anthony (Rose), KCB, DSC
Trowbridge, *Rear-Adm.* Sir Richard John, KCVO

Truscott, Sir George James Irving, Bt. (1909)

Tsang, Sir Donald Yam-keun, KBE

Tuck, Sir Bruce Adolph Reginald, Bt. (1910)

Tucker, Hon. Sir Richard Howard, Kt.

Tuckey, Hon. Sir Simon Lane, Kt.

Tuita, Sir Mariano Kelesimalefo, Kt., OBE

Tuite, Sir Christopher Hugh, Bt., Ph.D. (1622)

Tuivaga, Sir Timoci Uluiburotu, Kt.

Tully, Sir William Mark, KBE, OBE

Tumim, His Hon. Sir Stephen, Kt.

Tupper, Sir Charles Hibbert, Bt. (1888)

Turbott, Sir Ian Graham, Kt., CMG, CVO

Turing, Sir John Dermot, Bt. (S. 1638)

Turnbull, Sir Andrew, KCB, CVO

Turner, Sir Colin William Carstairs, Kt., CBE, DFC

Turner, Hon. Sir Michael John, Kt.

Turnquest, Sir Orville Alton, GCMG, QC

Tuti, Revd Dudley, KBE

Tweedie, Prof. Sir David Philip, Kt.

Tyree, Sir (Alfred) William, Kt., OBE

Tyrwhitt, Sir Reginald Thomas Newman, Bt. (1919)

Unsworth, Hon. Sir Edgar Ignatius Godfrey, Kt., CMG

Unwin, Sir (James) Brian, KCB

Ure, Sir John Burns, KCMG, LVO

Urquhart, Sir Brian Edward, KCMG, MBE

Urwick, Sir Alan Bedford, KCVO, CMG

Usher, Sir Andrew John, Bt. (1899)

Usher, Sir Leonard Gray, KBE

Ustinov, Sir Peter Alexander, Kt., CBE

Utting, Sir William Benjamin, Kt., CB

Vai, Sir Mea, Kt., CBE, ISO

Vallance, Sir Iain David Thomas, Kt.

Vallat, Sir Francis Aimé, GBE, KCMG, QC

Vallings, Vice-Adm. Sir George Montague Francis, KCB

Vanderfelt, Sir Robin Victor, KBE

Vane, Sir John Robert, Kt., D.Phil., D.Sc., FRS

Vardy, Sir Peter, Kt.

Vasquez, Sir Alfred Joseph, Kt., CBE, QC

Vaughan, Sir Gerard Folliott, Kt., FRCP

Vavasour, Sir Eric Michael Joseph Marmaduke, Bt. (1828)

Veale, Sir Alan John Ralph, Kt., FREng.

Venner, Sir Kenneth Dwight Vincent, KBE

Vereker, Sir John Michael Medlicott, KCB

†Verney, Sir John Sebastian, Bt. (1946)

Verney, Hon. Sir Lawrence John, Kt.,

TD

†Verney, SirEdmund Ralph, Bt. (1818)

Vernon, Sir Nigel John Douglas, Bt. (1914)

Vernon, Sir (William) Michael, Kt.

Vestey, Sir (John) Derek, Bt. (1921)

Vickers, Lt.-Gen. Sir Richard Maurice Hilton, KCB, CVO, OBE

Vincent, Sir William Percy Maxwell, Bt. (1936)

Vineall, Sir Anthony John Patrick, Kt.

Vinelott, Hon. Sir John Evelyn, Kt.

Vines, Sir William Joshua, Kt., CMG

von Schramek, Sir Eric Emil, Kt.

†Vyvyan, Sir Ralph Ferrers Alexander, Bt. (1645)

Waddell, Sir James Henderson, Kt., CB

Wade, Prof. Sir Henry William Rawson, Kt., QC, FBA

Waine, Rt. Revd John, KCVO

Waite, Rt. Hon. Sir John Douglas, Kt.

Wake, Sir Hereward, Bt., MC (1621)

Wakefield, Sir (Edward) Humphry (Tyrell), Bt. (1962)

Wakefield, Sir Norman Edward, Kt.

Wakefield, Sir Peter George Arthur, KBE, CMG

Wakeford, Air Marshal Sir Richard Gordon, KCB, OBE, LVO, AFC

Wakeley, Sir John Cecil Nicholson, Bt., FRCS (1952)

†Wakeman, Sir Edward Offley Bertram, Bt. (1828)

Wales, Sir Robert Andrew, Kt.

Walford, Sir Christopher Rupert, Kt.

Walker, Revd Alan Edgar, Kt., OBE

Walker, Sir Alfred Cecil, Kt.

Walker, Gen. Sir Antony Kenneth Frederick, KCB

Walker, Sir Baldwin Patrick, Bt. (1856)

Walker, Sir David Alan, Kt.

Walker, Sir Harold Berners, KCMG

Walker, Maj. Sir Hugh Ronald, Bt. (1906)

Walker, Sir James Graham, Kt., MBE

Walker, Sir James Heron, Bt. (1868)

Walker, Sir John Ernest, Kt., D.Phil., FRS

Walker, Air Marshal Sir John Robert, KCB, CBE, AFC

Walker, Gen. Sir Michael John Dawson, GCB, CMG, CBE, ADC

Walker, Sir Michael Leolin Forestier-, Bt. (1835)

Walker, Sir Miles Rawstron, Kt., CBE

Walker, Sir Patrick Jeremy, KCB

Walker, Rt. Hon. Sir Rodney Myerscough, Kt.

Walker, Hon. Sir Timothy Edward, Kt.

Wall, Sir John Anthony, Kt., CBE

Wall, Sir (John) Stephen, KCMG, LVO

Wall, Hon. Sir Nicholas Peter Rathbone, Kt.

Wall, Sir Robert William, Kt., OBE

Wallace, Lt.-Gen. Sir Christopher Brooke Quentin, KBE

Wallace, Sir Ian James, Kt., CBE

Waller, Hon. Sir (George) Mark, Kt.

Waller, Sir Robert William, Bt. (I. 1780)

Walley, Sir John, KBE, CB

Wallis, Sir Peter Gordon, KCVO

Wallis, Sir Timothy William, Kt.

Walmsley, Vice-Adm. Sir Robert, KCB

Walsh, Prof. Sir John Patrick, KBE

†Walsham, Sir Timothy John, Bt. (1831)

Walters, Prof. Sir Alan Arthur, Kt.

Walters, Sir Dennis Murray, Kt., MBE

Walters, Sir Frederick Donald, Kt.

Walters, Sir Peter Ingram, Kt.

Walters, Sir Roger Talbot, KBE, FRIBA

Wamiri, Sir Akapite, KBE

Wan, Sir Wamp, Kt., MBE

Wanstall, Hon. Sir Charles Gray, Kt.

Ward, Rt. Hon. Sir Alan Hylton, Kt.

Ward, Sir John Devereux, Kt., CBE

Ward, Sir Joseph James Laffey, Bt. (1911)

Ward, Maj.-Gen. Sir Philip John Newling, KCVO, CBE

Ward, Rt. Rev. Simon Barrington-, KCMG

Ward, Sir Timothy James, Kt.

Wardale, Sir Geoffrey Charles, KCB

Wardlaw, Sir Henry (John), Bt. (S. 1631)

Waring, Sir (Alfred) Holburt, Bt. (1935)

Warmington, Sir David Marshall, Bt. (1908)

Warner, Sir (Edward Courtenay) Henry, Bt. (1910)

Warner, Prof. Sir Frederick Edward, Kt., FRS, FREng.

Warner, Sir Gerald Chierici, KCMG

Warner, Hon. Sir Jean-Pierre Frank Eugene, Kt.

Warren, Sir (Frederick) Miles, KBE

Warren, Sir Kenneth Robin, Kt.

†Warren, Sir Michael Blackley, Bt. (1784)

Wass, Sir Douglas William Gretton, GCB

Waterhouse, Hon. Sir Ronald Gough, GBE

Waterlow, Sir Christopher Rupert, Bt. (1873)

Waterlow, Sir (James) Gerard, Bt. (1930)

Waters, Gen. Sir (Charles) John, GCB, CBE

Waters, Sir (Thomas) Neil (Morris), Kt.

Wates, Sir Christopher Stephen, Kt.

Watkins, Rt. Hon. Sir Tasker, VC, GBE

Watson, Sir Andrew Michael Milne-, Bt. (1937)

Watson, Sir Bruce Dunstan, Kt.

Watson, Prof. Sir David John, Kt., Ph.D.

Watson, Sir (James) Andrew, Bt. (1866)

Watson, Sir John Forbes Inglefield-, Bt. (1895)

Watson, *Vice-Adm.* Sir Philip Alexander, KBE, LVO

Watson, Sir Ronald Matthew, Kt., CBE

Watt, *Surgeon Vice-Adm.* Sir James, KBE, FRCS

Watt, Sir James Harvie-, Bt. (1945)

Watts, Sir John Augustus Fitzroy, KCMG, CBE

Watts, Sir Arthur Desmond, KCMG

Watts, *Lt.-Gen.* Sir John Peter Barry Condliffe, KBE, CB, MC

Wauchope, Sir Roger (Hamilton) Don-, Bt. (S. 1667)

Weatherall, *Prof.* Sir David John, Kt., FRS

Weatherall, *Vice-Adm.* Sir James Lamb, KCVO, KBE

Weatherstone, Sir Dennis, KBE

Webb, *Prof.* Sir Adrian Leonard, Kt.

Webb, Sir Thomas Langley, Kt.

Webster, *Very Revd* Alan Brunskill, KCVO

Webster, *Vice-Adm.* Sir John Morrison, KCB

Webster, *Hon.* Sir Peter Edlin, Kt.

Wedderburn, Sir Andrew John Alexander Ogilvy-, Bt. (1803)

Wedgwood, Sir (Hugo) Martin, Bt. (1942)

Weekes, Sir Everton DeCourcey, KCMG, OBE

Weinberg, Sir Mark Aubrey, Kt.

Weir, Sir Michael Scott, KCMG

Weir, Sir Roderick Bignell, Kt.

Welby, Sir (Richard) Bruno Gregory, Bt. (1801)

Welch, Sir John Kemp-, Kt.

Welch, Sir John Reader, Bt. (1957)

Weldon, Sir Anthony William, Bt. (I. 1723)

Weller, Sir Arthur Burton, Kt., CBE

Wellings, Sir Jack Alfred, Kt., CBE

†Wells, Sir Christopher Charles, Bt. (1944)

Wells, Sir John Julius, Kt.

Wells, Sir William Henry Weston, Kt., FRICS

West, *Adm.* Sir Alan William John, KCB, DSC

Westbrook, Sir Neil Gowanloch, Kt., CBE

Weston, Sir Michael Charles Swift, KCMG, CVO

Weston, Sir (Philip) John, KCMG

Whalen, Sir Geoffrey Henry, Kt., CBE

Wheeler, Sir Harry Anthony, Kt., OBE

Wheeler, *Air Chief Marshal* Sir (Henry) Neil (George), GCB, CBE, DSO, DFC, AFC

Wheeler, *Rt. Hon.* Sir John Daniel, Kt.

Wheeler, Sir John Hieron, Bt. (1920)

Wheeler, *Gen.* Sir Roger Neil, GCB, CBE

Wheler, Sir Edward Woodford, Bt. (1660)

Whishaw, Sir Charles Percival Law, Kt.

Whitaker, Sir John James Ingham (Jack), Bt. (1936)

White, *Prof.* Sir Christopher John, Kt., CVO

White, Sir Christopher Robert Meadows, Bt. (1937)

White, *Hon.* Sir Christopher Stuart Stuart-, Kt.

White, Sir David Harry, Kt.

White, Sir Frank John, Kt.

White, Sir George Stanley James, Bt. (1904)

White, *Wg Cdr.* Sir Henry Arthur Dalrymple-, Bt., DFC (1926)

White, *Adm.* Sir Hugo Moresby, GCB, CBE

White, *Hon.* Sir John Charles, Kt., MBE

White, Sir John Albert

White, Sir John Woolmer, Bt. (1922)

White, Sir Lynton Stuart, Kt., MBE, TD

White, Sir Nicholas Peter Archibald, Bt. (1802)

White, *Adm.* Sir Peter, GBE

Whitehead, Sir John Stainton, GCMG, CVO

Whitehead, Sir Rowland John Rathbone, Bt. (1889)

Whiteley, Sir Hugo Baldwin Huntington-, Bt. (1918)

Whiteley, *Gen.* Sir Peter John Frederick, GCB, OBE, RM

Whitfield, Sir William, Kt., CBE

Whitmore, Sir Clive Anthony, GCB, CVO

Whitmore, Sir John Henry Douglas, Bt. (1954)

Whitney, Sir Raymond William, Kt., OBE, MP

Whitson, Sir Keith Roderick, Kt.

Wickerson, Sir John Michael, Kt.

Wicks, Sir Nigel Leonard, GCB, CVO, CBE

†Wigan, Sir Michael Iain, Bt. (1898)

Wiggin, Sir Alfred William (Jerry), Kt., TD

†Wiggin, Sir Charles Rupert John, Bt. (1892)

Wigram, *Maj.* Sir Edward Robert Woolmore, Bt. (1805)

Wignall, Sir Trevor Charles, Kt.

Wilbraham, Sir Richard Baker, Bt. (1776)

Wilford, Sir (Kenneth) Michael, GCMG

Wilkes, *Prof.* Sir Maurice Vincent, Kt.

Wilkes, *Gen.* Sir Michael John, KCB, CBE

Wilkins, Sir Graham John, Kt.

Wilkinson, Sir (David) Graham (Brook) Bt. (1941)

Wilkinson, *Prof.* Sir Denys Haigh, Kt., FRS

Wilkinson, Sir Philip William, Kt.

Willcocks, Sir David Valentine, Kt., CBE, MC

Willcocks, *Lt.-Gen.* Sir Michael Alan, Kt., CB

Williams, Sir Alastair Edgcumbe James Dudley-, Bt. (1964)

Williams, Sir Alwyn, Kt., Ph.D., FRS, FRSE

Williams, Sir Arthur Dennis Pitt, Kt.

Williams, Sir (Arthur) Gareth Ludovic Emrys Rhys, Bt. (1918)

Williams, *Prof.* Sir Bernard Arthur Owen, Kt., FBA

Williams, *Prof.* Sir Bruce Rodda, KBE

Williams, Sir Charles Othniel, Kt.

Williams, Sir Daniel Charles, GCMG, QC

Williams, *Adm.* Sir David, GCB

Williams, *Prof.* Sir David Glyndwr Tudor, Kt.

Williams, Sir David Innes, Kt.

Williams, Sir David Reeve, Kt., CBE

Williams, *Hon.* Sir Denys Ambrose, KCMG

Williams, Sir Donald Mark, Bt. (1866)

Williams, *Prof.* Sir (Edward) Dillwyn, Kt., FRCP

Williams, *Hon.* Sir Edward Stratten, KCMG, KBE

Williams, Sir Francis Owen Garbett, Kt., CBE

Williams, *Prof.* Sir Glanmor, Kt., CBE, FBA

Williams, Sir Henry Sydney, Kt., OBE

Williams, Sir (John) Kyffin, Kt., OBE, DL, RA

Williams, Sir (Lawrence) Hugh, Bt. (1798)

Williams, Sir Leonard, KBE, CB

Williams, Sir Osmond, Bt., MC (1909)

Williams, Sir Peter Michael, Kt.

Williams, *Prof.* Sir Robert Evan Owen, Kt., MD, FRCP

Williams, Sir (Robert) Philip Nathaniel, Bt. (1915)

Williams, Sir Robin Philip, (1953)

Williams, Sir (William) Maxwell (Harries), Kt.

Williamson, *Marshal of the Royal Air Force* Sir Keith Alec, GCB, AFC

Williamson, Sir Robert Brian, Kt., CBE

Willink, Sir Charles William, Bt. (1957)

Willis, *Vice-Adm.* Sir (Guido) James, KBE

Willis, *Air Chief Marshal* Sir John Frederick, GBE, KCB

Willison, *Lt.-Gen.* Sir David John, KCB, OBE, MC

Willison, Sir John Alexander, Kt., OBE

Wills, Sir David James Vernon, Bt. (1923)

Wills, Sir David Seton, Bt. (1904)

Wilmot, Sir David, Kt., QPM

Wilmot, Sir Henry Robert, Bt. (1759)

Wilmot, Sir Michael John Assheton Eardley-, Bt. (1821)
Wilsey, *Gen.* Sir John Finlay Willasey, GCB, CBE
Wilshaw, Sir Michael, Kt.
Wilson, *Prof.* Sir Alan Geoffrey, Kt.
Wilson, *Lt.-Gen.* Sir (Alexander) James, KBE, MC
Wilson, Sir Anthony, Kt.
Wilson, *Vice-Adm.* Sir Barry Nigel, KCB
Wilson, *Lt.-Col.* Sir Blair Aubyn Stewart-, KCVO
Wilson, Sir Charles Haynes, Kt.
Wilson, *Prof.* Sir Colin Alexander St John, Kt., RA, FRIBA
Wilson, Sir David, Bt. (1920)
Wilson, Sir David Mackenzie, Kt.
Wilson, Sir Geoffrey Masterman, KCB, CMG
Wilson, Sir James William Douglas, Bt. (1906)
Wilson, *Brig.* Sir Mathew John Anthony, Bt., OBE, MC (1874)
Wilson, *Hon.* Sir Nicholas Allan Roy, Kt.
Wilson, Sir Patrick Michael Ernest David McNair-, Kt.
Wilson, Sir Richard Thomas James, KCB, GCB
Wilson, Sir Robert Peter, KCMG
Wilson, *Air Chief Marshal* Sir (Ronald) Andrew (Fellowes), KCB, AFC
Wilson, *Hon.* Sir Ronald Darling, KBE, CMG
Wilton, Sir (Arthur) John, KCMG, KCVO, MC
Wingate, *Capt.* Sir Miles Buckley, KCVO
Winkley, Sir David Ross, Kt.
Winnington, Sir Francis Salwey William, Bt. (1755)
Winskill, Air Cdre Sir Archibald Little, KCVO, CBE, DFC
Winterton, Sir Nicholas Raymond, Kt.
Wisdom, Sir Norman, Kt., OBE
Wiseman, Sir John William, Bt. (1628)
Wolfendale, *Prof.* Sir Arnold Whittaker, Kt., FRS
Wolfson, Sir Brian Gordon, Kt.
Wolseley, Sir Charles Garnet Richard Mark, Bt. (1628)
†Wolseley, Sir James Douglas, Bt. (I. 1745)
Wolstenholme, Sir Gordon Ethelbert Ward, Kt., OBE
Wombwell, Sir George Philip Frederick, Bt. (1778)
Womersley, Sir Peter John Walter, Bt. (1945)
Woo, Sir Leo Joseph, Kt.
Woo, Sir Po-Shing, Kt.
Wood, Sir Alan Marshall Muir, Kt., FRS, FREng.
Wood, Sir Andrew Marley, GCMG

Wood, Sir Anthony John Page, Bt. (1837)
Wood, Sir Frederick Ambrose Stuart, Kt.
Wood, Sir Ian Clark, Kt., CBE
Wood, *Prof.* Sir John Crossley, Kt., CBE
Wood, *Hon.* Sir John Kember, Kt., MC
Wood, Sir Martin Francis, Kt., OBE
Wood, Sir Russell Dillon, KCVO, VRD
†Wood, Sir Samuel Thomas Hill-, Bt. (1921)
Wood, Sir William Alan, KCVO, CB
Woodard, *Rear Adm.* Sir Robert Nathaniel, KCVO
Woodcock, Sir John, Kt., CBE, QPM
Woodhead, *Vice-Adm.* Sir (Anthony) Peter, KCB
Woodhouse, *Rt. Hon.* Sir (Arthur) Owen, KBE, DSC
Wooding, Sir Norman Samuel, Kt., CBE
Woodroffe, *Most Revd* George Cuthbert Manning, KBE
Woods, Sir Robert Kynnersley, Kt., CBE
Woodward, *Hon.* Sir (Albert) Edward, Kt., OBE
Woodward, *Adm.* Sir John Forster, GBE, KCB
Worsley, *Gen.* Sir Richard Edward, GCB, GBE
Worsley, Sir (William) Marcus (John), Bt. (1838)
Worsthorne, Sir Peregrine Gerard, Kt.
Wratten, *Air Chief Marshal* Sir William John, GBE, CB, AFC
Wraxall, Sir Charles Frederick Lascelles, Bt. (1813)
Wrey, Sir George Richard Bourchier, Bt. (1628)
Wrigglesworth, Sir Ian William, Kt.
Wright, Sir Allan Frederick, KBE
Wright, Sir David John, GCMG, LVO
Wright, Sir Denis Arthur Hepworth, GCMG
Wright, Sir Edward Maitland, Kt., D.Phil., LL D, D.Sc., FRSE
Wright, *Hon.* Sir (John) Michael, Kt.
Wright, Sir (John) Oliver, GCMG, GCVO, DSC
Wright, Sir Paul Hervé Giraud, KCMG, OBE
Wright, Sir Peter Robert, Kt., CBE
Wright, Sir Richard Michael Cory-, Bt. (1903)
Wrightson, Sir Charles Mark Garmondsway, Bt. (1900)
Wrigley, *Prof.* Sir Edward Anthony (Sir Tony), Kt., Ph.D., PBA
Wu, Sir Gordon Ying Sheung, KCMG
Wynn, Sir David Watkin Williams-, Bt. (1688)
Yacoub, *Prof.* Sir Magdi Habib, Kt., FRCS
Yaki, Sir Roy, KBE
Yang, *Hon.* Sir Ti Liang, Kt.
Yapp, Sir Stanley Graham, Kt.

Yardley, Sir David Charles Miller, Kt., LL D
Yarranton, Sir Peter George, Kt.
Yarrow, Sir Eric Grant, Bt., MBE (1916)
Yellowlees, Sir Henry, KCB
Yocklunn, Sir John (Soong Chung), KCVO
Yoo Foo, Sir (François) Henri, Kt.
Young, Sir Anthony Ian, Kt.
Young, Sir Brian Walter Mark, Kt.
Young, Sir Colville Norbert, GCMG, MBE
Young, Sir Dennis Charles, KCMG
Young, *Rt. Hon.* Sir George Samuel Knatchbull, Bt., MP (1813)
Young, *Hon.* Sir Harold William, KCMG
Young, Sir Jimmy Leslie Ronald, Kt., CBE
Young, Sir John Kenyon Roe, Bt. (1821)
Young, *Hon.* Sir John McIntosh, KCMG
Young, Sir John Robertson, KCMG
Young, Sir Leslie Clarence, Kt., CBE
Young, Sir Nicholas Charles, Kt.
Young, Sir Richard Dilworth, Kt.
Young, Sir Robin Urquhart, KCB
Young, Sir Roger William, Kt.
Young, Sir Stephen Stewart Templeton, Bt. (1945)
Young, Sir William Neil, Bt. (1769)
†Younger, Sir Julian William Richard, Bt.(1911)
Yuwi, Sir Matiabe, KBE
Zeeman, *Prof.* Sir (Erik) Christopher, Kt., FRS
Zissman, Sir Bernard Philip, Kt.
Zochonis, Sir John Basil, Kt.
Zoleveke, Sir Gideon Pitabose, KBE
Zunz, Sir Gerhard Jacob (Jack), Kt., FREng.
Zurenuoc, Sir Zibang, KBE

Patron Saints

ST GEORGE
Patron Saint of England

St George is believed to have been born in Cappadocia, of Christian parents, in the latter part of the third century and to have served with distinction as a soldier under the Emperor Diocletian, including a visit to England on a military mission. When the persecution of Christians was ordered, St George sought a personal interview to remonstrate with the Emperor and after a profession of faith resigned his military commission. Arrest and torture followed and he was martyred at Nicomedia on 23 April 303, a day ordered to be kept in remembrance as a national festival by the Council of Oxford in 1222, although it was not until the reign of Edward III that he was made patron saint of England.

St George's connection with a dragon seems to date from the close of the sixth century and to be due to the transfer of his remains from Nicomedia to Lydda, close to the scene of the legendary exploit of Perseus in rescuing Andromeda and slaying the sea monster, credit for which became attached to the Christian martyr.

ST DAVID
Patron Saint of Wales

St David is believed to have been born towards the beginning and to have died towards the end of the sixth century. St David was an eloquent preacher, who founded the monastery at Menevia, now St David's. He became the patron saint of Wales, but there is no record of any papal canonisation before 1181. His annual festival is observed on 1 March.

ST ANDREW
Patron Saint of Scotland

St Andrew, one of the apostles and brother of Simon Peter, was born at Bethsaida on the sea of Galilee and lived at Capernaum. He preached the Gospel in Asia Minor and Scythia along the shores of the Black Sea and became the patron sait of Russia. It is believed that he suffered crucifixion at Patras in Achae, on a *crux decussasta* (now known as St Andrew's Cross) and that his relics were removed from Patras to Constantinople and thence to St. Andrews, probably in the eighth century, since which time he has been the patron saint of Scotland. The festival of St Andrew is held on 30 November.

ST PATRICK
Patron Saint of Ireland

St Patrick was born, probably in England, about 389 and was carried off to Ireland as a slave about 16 years later, escaping to Gaul at the age of 22. He was ordained deacon at Auxerre and having been consecrated Bishop in 432 was dispatched to Wicklow to reorganise the Christian communities in Ireland. He founded the see of Armagh and introduced Latin into Ireland as the language of the Church. He died *c*.461 and his festival is celebrated on 17 March.

Dames Grand Cross and Dames Commanders

Style, 'Dame' before forename and surname, followed by appropriate post-nominal initials. Where such an award is made to a lady already in enjoyment of a higher title, the appropriate initials follow her name
Husband, Untitled
For forms of address, *see* page 133

Dame Grand Cross and Dame Commander are the higher classes for women of the Order of the Bath, the

Order of St Michael and St George, the Royal Victorian Order, and the Order of the British Empire. Dames Grand Cross rank after the wives of Baronets and before the wives of Knights Grand Cross. Dames Commanders rank after the wives of Knights Grand Cross and before the wives of Knights Commanders.

Honorary Dames Commanders may be conferred on women who are citizens of countries of which The Queen is not head of state.

LIST OF DAMES
Revised to 31 August 2002

Women peers in their own right and life peers are not included in this list. Female members of the royal family are not included in this list; details of the orders they hold are given within the Royal Family section.

If a dame has a double barrelled or hyphenated surname, she is listed under the final element of the name. A full entry in italic type indicates that the recipient of an honour died during the year in which the honour was conferred. The name is included for the purposes of record.

Abaijah, Dame Josephine, DBE
Abel Smith, Lady, DCVO
Abergavenny, The Marchioness of, DCVO
Airlie, The Countess of, DCVO
Albemarle, The Countess of, DBE
Albon, Dame Yvonne Jeanne, DBE
Allen, *Prof.* Dame Ingrid Victoria, DBE, CBE, DL
Anderson, *Brig.* Hon. Dame Mary Mackenzie (Mrs Pihl), DBE
Andrews, Dame Julie, DBE
Anglesey, The Marchioness of, DBE
Anson, Lady (Elizabeth Audrey), DBE
Anstee, Dame Margaret Joan, DCMG
Arden, *Hon.* Dame Mary Howarth (Mrs Mance), DBE
Bainbridge, Dame Beryl, DBE
Baker, Dame Janet Abbott (Mrs Shelley), CH, DBE
Ballin, Dame Reubina Ann, DBE
Barletta, Dame Nelia, DBE
Barrow, Dame Jocelyn Anita (Mrs Downer), DBE
Barstow, Dame Josephine Clare (Mrs Anderson), DBE
Bassey, Dame Shirley, DBE
Beaurepaire, Dame Beryl Edith, DBE
Beer, *Prof.* Dame Gillian Patricia Kempster, DBE, FBA
Bergquist, *Prof.* Dame Patricia Rose, DBE
Berry, Dame Alice Miriam, DBE

Bewley, Dame Beulah Rosemary, DBE
Black, *Hon.* Dame Jill Margaret, DBE
Blaize, Dame Venetia Ursula, DBE
Blaxland, Dame Helen Frances, DBE
Booth, *Hon.* Dame Margaret Myfanwy Wood, DBE
Bowman, Dame (Mary) Elaine Kellett-, DBE
Bowtell, Dame Ann Elizabeth, DCB
Boyd, Dame Vivienne Myra, DBE
Barbour, Dame Margaret (Mrs Ash), DBE
Bracewell, *Hon.* Dame Joyanne Winifred (Mrs Copeland), DBE
Brain, Dame Margaret Anne (Mrs Wheeler), DBE
Brazill, Dame Josephine (Sister Mary Philippa), DBE
Bridges, Dame Mary Patricia, DBE
Browne, Lady Moyra Blanche Madeleine, DBE
Bryans, Dame Anne Margaret, DBE
Buttfield, Dame Nancy Eileen, DBE
Byatt, Dame Antonia Susan, DBE, FRSL
Bynoe, Dame Hilda Louisa, DBE
Caldicott, Dame Fiona, DBE, FRCP, FRCPsych.
Cartwright, Dame Silvia Rose, DBE
Cates, Dame Emma De-, DBE
Charles, Dame (Mary) Eugenia, DBE
Chesterton, Dame Elizabeth Ursula, DBE
Clark, *Prof.* Dame Jill MacLeod, DBE
Clark, *Prof.* Dame (Margaret) June, DBE, Ph.D.
Collins, Dame Diana Clavering, DBE
Clay, Dame Marie Mildred, DBE
Clayton, Dame Barbara Evelyn (Mrs Klyne), DBE
Coll, Dame Elizabeth Anne Loosemore Esteve-, DBE
Collarbone, Dame Patricia, DBE
Corsar, The *Hon.* Dame Mary Drummond, DBE
Davies, Dame Audrey Joan, DBE
Davies, Dame Wendy Patricia, DBE
Davis, Dame Karlene Cecile, DBE

Daws, Dame Joyce Margaretta, DBE
Deech, Dame Ruth Lynn, DBE
Dell, Dame Miriam Patricia, DBE
Dench, Dame Judith Olivia (Mrs Williams), DBE
Descartes, Dame Marie Selipha Sesenne, DBE, BEM
Devonshire, The Duchess of, DCVO
Digby, Lady, DBE
Donaldson, Dame (Dorothy) Mary (Lady Donaldson of Lymington), GBE
Duffield, Dame Vivien Louise, DBE, CBE
Dugdale, Kathryn, Lady, DCVO
Dumont, Dame Ivy Leona, DCMG
Dyche, Dame Rachael Mary, DBE
Elcoat, Dame Catherine Elizabeth, DBE
Ellison, Dame Jill, DBE
Else, Dame Jean, DBE
Engel, Dame Pauline Frances (Sister Pauline Engel), DBE
Evans, Dame Anne Elizabeth Jane, DBE
Evans, Dame Lois Marie Browne-, DBE
Evans, Dame Hilda Mary, DBE, BEM
Evison, Dame Helen June Patricia, DBE
Fenner, Dame Peggy Edith, DBE
Fielding, Dame Pauline, DBE
Fitton, Dame Doris Alice (Mrs Mason), DBE
Fort, Dame Maeve Geraldine, DCMG, DCVO
Fraser, Dame Dorothy Rita, DBE
Friend, Dame Phyllis Muriel, DBE
Fritchie, Dame Irene Tordoff (Dame Rennie Fritchie), DBE
Frost, Dame Phyllis Irene, DBE
Fry, Dame Margaret Louise, DBE
Gallagher, Dame Monica Josephine, DBE
Gardiner, Dame Helen Louisa, DBE, MVO
Gibson, Dame Alice Emily, DBE
Giles, *Air Comdt.* Dame Pauline (Mrs Parsons), DBE, RRC

Goltra, Dame Seipp, DBE
Goodman, Dame Barbara, DBE
Gordon, Dame Minita Elmira, GCMG, GCVO
Gow, Dame Jane Elizabeth (Mrs Whiteley), DBE
Grafton, The Duchess of, GCVO
Grant, Dame Mavis, DBE
Green, Dame Mary Georgina, DBE
Grey, Dame Beryl Elizabeth (Mrs Svenson), DBE
Grimthorpe, The Lady, DCVO
Guilfoyle, Dame Margaret Georgina Constance, DBE
Guthardt, *Revd Dr* Dame Phyllis Myra, DBE
Haig, Dame Mary Alison Glen-, DBE
Hale, *Hon.* Dame Brenda Marjorie (Mrs Farrand), DBE
Hallett, Dame Heather Carol, DBE, QC
Harper, Dame Elizabeth Margaret Way, DBE
Heilbron, *Hon.* Dame Rose, DBE
Herbison, Dame Jean Marjory, DBE, CMG
Hercus, *Hon.* Dame (Margaret) Ann, DCMG
Higgins, *Prof.* Dame Julia Stretton, DBE, CBE, FRS
Higgins, *Prof.* Dame Rosalyn, DBE, QC
Hill, *Air Cdre* Dame Felicity Barbara, DBE
Hiller, Dame Wendy (Mrs Gow), DBE
Hine, Dame Deirdre Joan, DBE, FRCP
Hird, Dame Thora (Mrs Scott), DBE
Hogg, *Hon.* Dame Mary Claire (Mrs Koops), DBE
Hollows, Dame Sharon, DBE
Hurley, *Prof.* Dame Rosalinde (Mrs Gortvai), DBE
Hussey, Lady Susan Katharine (Lady Hussey of North Bradley), DCVO
Imison, Dame Tamsyn, DBE
Isaacs, Dame Albertha Madeline, DBE
James, Dame Naomi Christine (Mrs Haythorne), DBE
Jenkins, Dame (Mary) Jennifer (Lady Jenkins of Hillhead), DBE
Jones, Dame Gwyneth (Mrs Haberfeld-Jones), DBE
Jones, Dame (Lilian) Pauline Neville-, DCMG
Keegan, Dame Geraldine Mary Marcella, DBE, OBE
Kekedo, Dame Rosalina Violet, DBE
Kelleher, Dame Joan, DBE
Kelly, Dame Lorna May Boreland, DBE
Kershaw, Dame Janet Elizabeth Murray (Dame Betty), DBE
Kettlewell, *Comdt.* Dame Marion Mildred, DBE
King, Dame Thea, DBE, OBE
Kirby, Dame Georgina Kamiria, DBE
Kirk, Dame (Lucy) Ruth, DBE
Kramer, *Prof.* Dame Leonie Judith,

DBE
Laine, Dame Cleo (Clementine) Dinah (Mrs Dankworth), DBE
Lamb, Dame Dawn Ruth, DBE
Lewis, Dame Edna Leofrida (Lady Lewis), DBE
Litchfield, Dame Ruby Beatrice, DBE
Lott, Dame Felicity Ann Emwhyla (Mrs Woolf), DBE
Louisy, Dame (Calliopa) Pearlette, GCMG
Lympany, Dame Moura, DBE
Lynn, Dame Vera (Mrs Lewis), DBE
Mackinnon, Dame (Una) Patricia, DBE
McKechnie, Dame Sheila Marshall, DBE, OBE
McLaren, Dame Anne Laura, DBE, FRCOG, FRS
Macmillan of Ovenden, Katharine, Viscountess, DBE
Mayhew, Dame Judith, DBE
Major, Dame Malvina Lorraine (Mrs Fleming), DBE
Major, Dame Norma Christina Elizabeth, DBE
Markova, Dame Alicia, DBE
Metcalf, Dame Helen, DBE
Metge, *Dr* Dame (Alice) Joan, DBE
Middleton, Dame Elaine Madoline, DCMG, MBE
Miller, Dame Mary Elizabeth Hedley-, DCVO, CB
Mills, Dame Barbara Jean Lyon, DBE, QC
Mitchell, Dame Mona, DCVO
Moores, Dame Yvonne, DBE
Morrison, *Hon.* Dame Mary Anne, DCVO
Muirhead, Dame Lorna Elizabeth Fox, DBE
Muldoon, Thea Dale, Lady, DBE, QSO
Mumford, Lady Mary Katharine, DCVO
Munro, Dame Alison, DBE
Murdoch, Dame Elisabeth Joy, DBE
Murray, Dame (Alice) Rosemary, DBE, D.Phil.
Ogilvie, Dame Bridget Margaret, DBE, Ph.D., D.Sc.
Oliver, Dame Gillian Frances, DBE
Ollerenshaw, Dame Kathleen Mary, DBE, D.Phil.
Oxenbury, Dame Shirley Anne, DBE
Park, Dame Merle Florence (Mrs Bloch), DBE
Paterson, Dame Betty Fraser Ross, DBE
Peake, *Air Cdre* Dame Felicity Hyde, DBE, AE
Penhaligon, Dame Annette (Mrs Egerton), DBE
Peters, Dame Mary Elizabeth, DBE, CBE
Poole, Dame Avril Anne Barker, DBE
Porter, Dame Shirley (Lady Porter), DBE
Powell, Dame Sally Ann Vickers, DBE
Prendergast, Dame Simone Ruth, DBE

Prentice, Dame Winifred Eva, DBE
Preston, Dame Frances Olivia Campbell-, DCVO
Price, Dame Margaret Berenice, DBE
Purves, Dame Daphne Helen, DBE
Pyke, Lady, DBE
Quinn, Dame Sheila Margaret Imelda, DBE
Rafferty, *Hon.* Anne Judith, DBE
Rawson, *Prof.* Dame Jessica Mary, DBE,
Rees, *Prof.* Dame Lesley Howard, DBE
Reeves, Dame Helen May, DBE
Richardson, Dame Mary, DBE
Riddelsdell, Dame Mildred, DCB, CBE
Ridley, Dame (Mildred) Betty, DBE
Ridsdale, Dame Victoire Evelyn Patricia (Lady Ridsdale), DBE
Rigg, Dame Diana, DBE
Rimington, Dame Stella, DCB
Ritterman, Dame Janet, DBE
Robottom, Dame Marlene, DBE
Roe, Dame Raigh Edith, DBE
Rothschild, *Hon.* Dame Miriam Louisa, DBE, FRS
Rue, Dame (Elsie) Rosemary, DBE
Rumbold, *Rt. Hon.* Dame Angela Claire Rosemary, DBE
Runciman of Doxford, The Viscountess, DBE
Salas, Dame Margaret Laurence, DBE
Salmond, *Prof.* Dame Mary Anne, DBE
Saunders, Dame Cicely Mary Strode, OM, DBE, FRCP
Sawyer, *Hon.* Dame Joan Augusta, DBE
Schwarzkopf, Dame Elisabeth Friederike Marie Olga Legge-, DBE
Scott, Barbara, DBE
Scott, Dame Jean Mary Monica Maxwell-, DCVO
Seward, Dame Margaret Helen Elizabeth, DBE
Shenfield, Dame Barbara Estelle, DBE
Shirley, Dame Stephanie, DBE
Shovelton, Dame Helena, DBE
Sibley, Dame Antoinette (Mrs Corbett), DBE
Sloss, *Rt. Hon.* Dame (Ann) Elizabeth (Oldfield) Butler-, DBE
Smieton, Dame Mary Guillan, DBE
Smith, Dame Dela, DBE
Smith, *Hon.* Dame Janet Hilary (Mrs Mathieson), DBE
Smith, Dame Margaret Natalie (Maggie) (Mrs Cross), DBE
Smith, Dame Margot, DBE
Smyth, Dame Frances Mary, DBE
Soames, Mary, Lady, DBE
Southgate, *Prof.* Dame Lesley Jill, DBE
Spark, Dame Muriel Sarah, DBE
Spencer, Dame Rosemary Jane, DCMG

Steel, *Hon.* Dame (Anne) Heather
(Mrs Beattie), DBE
Strachan, Dame Valerie Patricia
Marie, DCB
Strathern, *Prof.* Dame Anne Marilyn,
DBE
Sutherland, Dame Joan (Mrs
Bonynge), OM, DBE
Sutherland, Dame Veronica Evelyn,
DBE, CMG
Szaszy, Dame Miraka Petricevich,
DBE
Taylor, Dame Elizabeth, DBE
Taylor, Dame Jean Elizabeth, DCVO
Taylor, Dame Meg, DBE
Te Atairangikaahu, Te Arikinui,
Dame, DBE
Te Kanawa, Dame Kiri Janette, DBE
Thomas, Dame Maureen Elizabeth
(Lady Thomas), DBE
Thorneycroft, Carla, Lady, DBE
Tinson, Dame Sue, DBE
Tizard, Dame Catherine Anne,
GCMG, GCVO, DBE
Tokiel, Dame Rosa, DBE
Trotter, Dame Janet Olive, DBE
Uprichard, Dame Mary Elizabeth,
DBE
Varley, Dame Joan Fleetwood, DBE
Wagner, Dame Gillian Mary
Millicent (Lady Wagner), DBE
Wall, (Alice) Anne, (Mrs Michael
Wall), DCVO
Wallis, Dame Sheila Ann, DBE
Warburton, Dame Anne Marion,
DCVO, CMG
Warwick, Dame Margaret Elizabeth
Harvey Turner-, DBE, FRCP,
FRCPEd.
Waterhouse, Dame Rachel Elizabeth,
DBE, Ph.D.
Webb, *Prof.* Dame Patricia, DBE
Weir, Dame Gillian Constance (Mrs
Phelps), DBE
Weston, Dame Margaret Kate, DBE
Williamson, Dame (Elsie) Marjorie,
DBE, Ph.D.
Winstone, Dame Dorothy Gertrude,
DBE, CMG
Wong Yick-ming, Dame Rosanna,
DBE
Wright, Dame Clarice Betty, DBE
Wright, Dame Gail, DBE

Decorations and Medals

PRINCIPAL DECORATIONS AND MEDALS
In order of precedence

VICTORIA CROSS (VC), 1856 (see below)
GEORGE CROSS (GC), 1940 (see below)

BRITISH ORDERS OF KNIGHTHOOD AND
DISTINGUISHED SERVICE ORDER
Baronet's Badge
Knight Bachelor's Badge

DECORATIONS
Conspicuous Gallantry Cross (CGC), 1995
Royal Red Cross Class I (RRC), 1883
Distinguished Service Cross (DSC), 1914. For all ranks for
actions at sea
Military Cross (MC), December 1914. For all ranks for
actions on land
Distinguished Flying Cross (DFC), 1918. For all ranks for
acts of gallantry when flying in active operations against
the enemy
Air Force Cross (AFC), 1918. For all ranks for acts of
courage when flying, although not in active operations
against the enemy
Royal Red Cross Class II (ARRC)
Order of British India
Kaisar-i-Hind Medal
Order of St John

MEDALS FOR GALLANTRY AND DISTINGUISHED
CONDUCT
Union of South Africa Queen's Medal for Bravery, in Gold
Distinguished Conduct Medal (DCM), 1854
Conspicuous Gallantry Medal (CGM), 1874
Conspicuous Gallantry Medal (Flying)
George Medal (GM), 1940
Queen's Police Medal for Gallantry
Queen's Fire Service Medal for Gallantry
Royal West African Frontier Force Distinguished Conduct
Medal
King's African Rifles Distinguished Conduct Medal
Indian Distinguished Service Medal
Union of South Africa Queen's Medal for Bravery, in Silver
Distinguished Service Medal (DSM), 1914
Military Medal (MM), 1916
Distinguished Flying Medal (DFM), 1918
Air Force Medal (AFM)
Constabulary Medal (Ireland)
Medal for Saving Life at Sea
Sea Gallantry Medal
Indian Order of Merit (Civil)
Indian Police Medal for Gallantry
Ceylon Police Medal for Gallantry
Sierra Leone Police Medal for Gallantry
Sierra Leone Fire Brigades Medal for Gallantry
Colonial Police Medal for Gallantry (CPM)
Queen's Gallantry Medal (QGM), 1974
Royal Victorian Medal (RVM), Gold, Silver and Bronze
British Empire Medal (BEM), (formerly the Medal of the
Order of the British Empire, for Meritorious Service;
also includes the Medal of the Order awarded before 29
December 1922)
Canada Medal
Queen's Police (QPM) and Queen's Fire Service Medals
(QFSM) for Distinguished Service

Queen's Volunteer Reserves Medal
Queen's Medal for Chiefs

WAR MEDALS AND STARS (in order of date)

Polar Medals (in order of date)

POLICE MEDALS FOR VALUABLE SERVICE

JUBILEE, CORONATION AND DURBAR MEDALS
King George V, King George VI and Queen Elizabeth II Long
and Faithful Service Medals

EFFICIENCY AND LONG SERVICE DECORATIONS AND
MEDALS
Medal for Meritorious Service
Accumulated Campaign Service Medal
The Medal for Long Service and Good Conduct (Military)
Naval Long Service and Good Conduct Medal
Royal Marines Meritorious Service Medal
Royal Air Force Meritorious Service Medal
Royal Air Force Long Service and Good Conduct Medal
Medal for Long Service and Good Conduct (Ulster Defence
Regiment)
Police Long Service and Good Conduct Medal
Fire Brigade Long Service and Good Conduct Medal
Colonial Police and Fire Brigades Long Service Medals
Colonial Prison Service Medal
Hong Kong Disciplined Services Medal
Army Emergency Reserve Decoration (ERD), 1952
Volunteer Officers' Decoration (VD)
Volunteer Long Service Medal
Volunteer Officers' Decoration for India and the Colonies
Volunteer Long Service Medal for India and the Colonies
Colonial Auxiliary Forces Officers' Decoration
Colonial Auxiliary Forces Long Service Medal
Medal for Good Shooting (Naval)
Militia Long Service Medal
Imperial Yeomanry Long Service Medal
Territorial Decoration (TD), 1908
Efficiency Decoration (ED)
Territorial Efficiency Medal
Efficiency Medal
Special Reserve Long Service and Good Conduct Medal
Decoration for Officers, Royal Navy Reserve (RD), 1910
Decoration for Officers, RNVR (VRD)
Royal Naval Reserve Long Service and Good Conduct
Medal
RNVR Long Service and Good Conduct Medal
Royal Naval Auxiliary Sick Berth Reserve Long Service and
Good Conduct Medal
Royal Fleet Reserve Long Service and Good Conduct
Medal
Royal Naval Wireless Auxiliary Reserve Long Service and
Good Conduct Medal
Air Efficiency Award (AE), 1942
Volunteer Reserves Service Medal
Ulster Defence Regiment Medal
Northern Ireland Home Service Medal
The Queen's Medal. For champion shots in the RN, RM,
RNZN, Army, RAF
Cadet Forces Medal, 1950
Coastguard Auxiliary Service Long Service Medal
(formerly Coast Life Saving Corps Long Service
Medal)
Special Constabulary Long Service Medal
Royal Observer Corps Medal

Civil Defence Long Service Medal
Ambulance Service (Emergency Duties) Long Service and
  Good Conduct Medal
Royal Fleet Auxiliary Service Medal
Rhodesia Medal
Royal Ulster Constabulary Service Medal
Northern Ireland Prison Service Medal
Service Medal of the Order of St John
Badge of the Order of the League of Mercy
Voluntary Medical Service Medal, 1932
Women's Voluntary Service Medal
Colonial Special Constabulary Medal

FOREIGN ORDERS, DECORATIONS AND MEDALS (IN
ORDER OF DATE)

THE VICTORIA CROSS (1856)
FOR CONSPICUOUS BRAVERY

VC

Ribbon, Crimson, for all Services (until 1918 it was blue
for the Royal Navy)

Instituted on 29 January 1856, the Victoria Cross was
awarded retrospectively to 1854, the first being held by Lt.
C. D. Lucas, RN, for bravery in the Baltic Sea on 21 June
1854 (gazetted 24 February 1857). The first 62 Crosses
were presented by Queen Victoria in Hyde Park, London,
on 26 June 1857.
  The Victoria Cross is worn before all other
decorations, on the left breast, and consists of a cross-
pattée of bronze, one and a half inches in diameter, with
the Royal Crown surmounted by a lion in the centre, and
beneath there is the inscription *For Valour*. Holders of the
VC receive a tax-free annuity of £1,300, irrespective of
need or other conditions. In 1911, the right to receive the
Cross was extended to Indian soldiers, and in 1920 to
matrons, sisters and nurses, and the staff of the Nursing
Services and other services pertaining to hospitals and
nursing, and to civilians of either sex regularly or
temporarily under the orders, direction or supervision of
the naval, military, or air forces of the Crown.

SURVIVING RECIPIENTS OF THE VICTORIA CROSS
as at August 2002

Annand, *Capt.* R. W. (Durham Light Infantry)
1940 *World War*
Bhan Bhagta Gurung, *Havildar* (2nd Gurkha Rifles)
1945 *World War*
Cruickshank, *Flt. Lt.* J. A. (RAFVR)
1944 *World War*
Fraser, *Lt.-Cdr.* I. E., DSC (RNR)
1945 *World War*
Gardner, *Capt.* P. J., MC (Royal Tank Regiment)
1941 *World War*
Kenna, *Pte.* E. (Australian Military Forces, 2/4th (NSW))
1945 *World War*
Lachhiman Gurung, *Havildar* (8th Gurkha Rifles)
1945 *World War*
Norton, *Capt.* G. R., MM (South African Forces, Kaffrarian
Rifles)
1944 *World War*

Payne, *WO* K., DSC (USA) (Australian Army Training
Team)
1969 *Vietnam*
Rambahadur Limbu, *Capt.*, MVO (10th Princess Mary's
Gurkha Rifles)
1965 *Sarawak*
Smith, *Sgt.* E. A., CD (Seaforth Highlanders of Canada)
1944 *World War*
Speakman-Pitts, *Sgt.* W. (Black Watch, attached KOSB)
1951 *Korea*
Tulbahadur Pun, *Lt.* (6th Gurkha Rifles)
1944 *World War*
Umrao Singh, *Sub Major* (Royal Indian Artillery)
1944 *World War*
Watkins, *Maj. Rt. Hon.* Sir Tasker, GBE (Welch Regiment)
1944 *World War*
Wilson, *Lt.-Col.* E. C. T. (East Surrey Regiment)
1940 *World War*

THE GEORGE CROSS (1940)
FOR GALLANTRY

GC

Ribbon, Dark blue, threaded through a bar adorned with
laurel leaves
Instituted 24 September 1940 (with amendments,
3 November 1942)

The George Cross is worn before all other decorations
(except the VC) on the left breast (when worn by a
woman it may be worn on the left shoulder from a ribbon
of the same width and colour fashioned into a bow). It
consists of a plain silver cross with four equal limbs, the
cross having in the centre a circular medallion bearing a
design showing St George and the Dragon. The
inscription *For Gallantry* appears round the medallion
and in the angle of each limb of the cross is the Royal
cypher 'G VI' forming a circle concentric with the
medallion. The reverse is plain and bears the name of the
recipient and the date of the award. The cross is
suspended by a ring from a bar adorned with laurel leaves
on dark blue ribbon one and a half inches wide.
  The cross is intended primarily for civilians; awards to
the fighting services are confined to actions for which
purely military honours are not normally granted. It is
awarded only for acts of the greatest heroism or of the
most conspicuous courage in circumstances of extreme
danger. From 1 April 1965, holders of the Cross have
received a tax-free annuity, which is now £1,300. The
cross has twice been awarded collectively rather than to
an individual: to Malta (1942) and the Royal Ulster
Constabulary (1999).
  The royal warrant which ordained that the grant of the
Empire Gallantry Medal should cease authorised holders
of that medal to return it to the Central Chancery of the
Orders of Knighthood and to receive in exchange the
George Cross. A similar provision applied to posthumous
awards of the Empire Gallantry Medal made after the
outbreak of war in 1939. In October 1971 all surviving
holders of the Albert Medal and the Edward Medal
exchanged those decorations for the George Cross.

SURVIVING RECIPIENTS OF THE GEORGE CROSS
as at August 2002

If the recipient originally received the Empire Gallantry
Medal (EGM), the Albert Medal (AM) or the Edward Medal
(EM), this is indicated by the initials in parenthesis.

Archer, *Col.* B. S. T., GC, OBE, ERD, 1941
Bamford, J., GC, 1952
Beaton, J., GC, CVO, 1974
Bridge, *Lt.-Cdr.* J., GC, GM and BAR, 1944
Butson, *Lt.-Col.* A. R. C., GC, CD, MD (AM), 1948
Bywater, R. A. S., GC, GM, 1944
Errington, H., GC, 1941
Farrow, K., GC (AM), 1948
Flintoff, H. H., GC (EM), 1944
Gledhill, A. J., GC, 1967
Gregson, J. S., GC (AM), 1943
Johnson, *WO1 (SSM)* B., GC, 1990
Kinne, D. G., GC, 1954
Lowe, A. R., GC (AM), 1949
Lynch, J., GC, BEM (AM), 1948
Moore, R. V., GC, CBE, 1940
Naughton, F., GC (EGM), 1937
Pratt, M. K., GC, 1978
Purves, Mrs M., GC (AM), 1949
Raweng, Awang anak, GC, 1951
Riley, G., GC (AM), 1944
Rowlands, *Air Marshal* Sir John, GC, KBE, 1943
Stevens, H. W., GC, 1958
Styles, *Lt.-Col.* S. G., GC, 1972
Walker, C., GC, 1972
Walker, C. H., GC (AM), 1942
Walton, E. W. K., GC (AM), DSO, 1948
Wilcox, C., GC (EM), 1949
Wiltshire, S. N., GC (EGM), 1930
Wooding, E. A., GC (AM), 1945

Chiefs of Clans and Names in Scotland

Only chiefs of whole Names or Clans are included, except certain special instances (marked *) who, though not chiefs of a whole name, were or are for some reason (e.g. the Macdonald forfeiture) independent. Under decision (*Campbell-Gray*, 1950) that a bearer of a 'double or triple-barrelled' surname cannot be held chief of a part of such, several others cannot be included in the list at present.

THE ROYAL HOUSE: HM THE QUEEN

AGNEW: Sir Crispin Agnew of Lochnaw, Bt., QC, 6 Palmerston Road, Edinburgh EH9 1TN

ANSTRUTHER: vacant

ARBUTHNOTT: The Viscount of Arbuthnott, KT, CBE, DSC, Arbuthnott House, Laurencekirk, Kincardineshire AB30 1PA

BARCLAY: Peter C. Barclay of Towie Barclay and of that Ilk, 69 Oakwood Court, W14 8JF

BORTHWICK: The Lord Borthwick, Crookston, Heriot, Midlothian EH38 5YS

BOYD: The Lord Kilmarnock, MBE, 194 Regent's Park Road, London NW1 8XP

BOYLE: The Earl of Glasgow, Kelburn, Fairlie, Ayrshire KA29 0BE

BRODIE: Ninian Brodie of Brodie, Brodie Castle, Forres, Morayshire IV36 0TE

BRUCE: The Earl of Elgin and Kincardine, Broomhall, Dunfermline, Fife KY11 3DU

BUCHAN: David S. Buchan of Auchmacoy, Auchmacoy House, Ellon, Aberdeenshire

BURNETT: J. C. A. Burnett of Leys, Crathes Castle, Banchory, Kincardineshire

CAMERON: Sir Donald Cameron of Lochiel, KT, CVO, TD, Achnacarry, Spean Bridge, Inverness-shire

CAMPBELL: The Duke of Argyll, Inveraray, Argyll PA32 8XF

CARMICHAEL: Richard J. Carmichael of Carmichael, Carmichael, Thankerton, Biggar, Lanarkshire

CARNEGIE: The Duke of Fife, Elsick House, Stonehaven, Kincardineshire AB3 2NT

CATHCART: The Earl Cathcart, 18 Smith Terrace, SW3 4DL

CHARTERIS: The Earl of Wemyss and March, KT, Gosford House, Longniddry, East Lothian EH32 0PX

CLAN CHATTAN: K. Mackintosh of Clan Chattan, Fairburn, Felixkyg, Zimbabwe

CHISHOLM: Hamish Chisholm of Chisholm (*The Chisholm*), Elmpine, Beck Row, Bury St Edmunds, Suffolk IP28 8BT

COCHRANE: The Earl of Dundonald, Lochnell Castle, Ledaig, Argyllshire

COLQUHOUN: Sir Ivar Colquhoun of Luss, Bt., Camstraddan, Luss, Dunbartonshire G83 8NX

CRANSTOUN: David A. S. Cranstoun of that Ilk, Corehouse, Lanark

CRICHTON: vacant

CUMMING: Sir Alastair Cumming of Altyre, Bt., Altyre, Forres, Moray

DARROCH: Capt. Duncan Darroch of Gourock, The Red House, Branksome Park Road, Camberley, Surrey

DAVIDSON: Alister G. Davidson of Davidston, 21 Winscombe Street, Auckland, New Zealand

DEWAR: Michael Dewar of that Ilk and Vogrie, Rectory Farm House, Wincanton, Somerset BA9 8ET

DRUMMOND: The Earl of Perth, PC, Stobhall, Perth PH2 6DR

DUNBAR: Sir James Dunbar of Mochrum, Bt., 211 Gardenville Drive, Yorktown, VA 23693, USA

DUNDAS: David D. Dundas of Dundas, 3 Crane Close,

Tokai 7945, Cape Town, South Africa

DURIE: Andrew Durie of Durie, CBE, Finnich Malise, Croftamie, Stirlingshire G63 0HA

ELIOTT: Mrs Margaret Eliott of Redheugh, Redheugh, Newcastleton, Roxburghshire

ERSKINE: The Earl of Mar and Kellie, Erskine House, Kirk Wynd, Alloa, Clackmannan FK10 4JF

FARQUHARSON: Capt. A. Farquharson of Invercauld, MC, Invercauld, Braemar, Aberdeenshire AB35 5TT

FERGUSSON: Sir Charles Fergusson of Kilkerran, Bt., Kilkerran, Maybole, Ayrshire

FORBES: The Lord Forbes, KBE, Balforbes, Alford, Aberdeenshire AB33 8DR

FORSYTH: Alistair Forsyth of that Ilk, Ethie Castle, by Arbroath, Angus DD11 5SP

FRASER: The Lady Saltoun, Inverey House, Braemar, Aberdeenshire AB35 5YB

*FRASER (of Lovat): The Lord Lovat, Beaufort Lodge, Beauly, Inverness-shire IV4 7AZ

GAYRE: R. Gayre of Gayre and Nigg, Minard Castle, Minard, Inverary, Argyll PA32 8YB

GORDON: The Marquess of Huntly, Aboyne Castle, Aberdeenshire AB34 5JP

GRAHAM: The Duke of Montrose, Buchanan Auld House, Drymen, Stirlingshire

GRANT: The Lord Strathspey, The School House, Lochbuie, Mull, Argyllshire PA62 6AA

GRIERSON: Sir Michael Grierson of Lag, Bt., 40C Palace Road, London SW2 3NJ

GUTHRIE: Alexander Guthrie of Guthrie, 22 William Street, Shenton Park, Perth, Western Australia

HAIG: The Earl Haig, OBE, Bemersyde, Melrose, Roxburghshire TD6 9DP

HALDANE: Martin Haldane of Gleneagles, Gleneagles, Auchterarder, Perthshire

HANNAY: David Hannay of Kirkdale and of that Ilk, Cardoness House, Gatehouse-of-Fleet, Kirkcudbrightshire

HAY: The Earl of Erroll, Woodbury Hall, Sandy, Beds

HENDERSON: John Henderson of Fordell, 7 Owen Street, Toowoomba, Queensland, Australia

HUNTER: Pauline Hunter of Hunterston, Plovers Ridge, Lon Cecrist, Treaddur Bay, Holyhead, Gwynedd

IRVINE OF DRUM: David C. Irvine of Drum, Holly Leaf Cottage, Banchory, Aberdeenshire AB31 4BR

JARDINE: Sir Alexander Jardine of Applegirth, Bt., Ash House, Thwaites, Millom, Cumbria LA18 5HY

JOHNSTONE: The Earl of Annandale and Hartfell, Raehills, Lockerbie, Dumfriesshire

KEITH: The Earl of Kintore, The Stables, Keith Hall, Inverurie, Aberdeenshire AB51 0LD

KENNEDY: The Marquess of Ailsa, Cassillis House, Maybole, Ayrshire

KERR: The Marquess of Lothian, KCVO, Ferniehurst Castle, Jedburgh, Roxburghshire TN8 6NX

KINCAID: Arabella Kincaid of Kincaid Stoneyeld, Downton, Ludlow, Shropshire

LAMONT: Peter N. Lamont of that Ilk, 209 Bungarribee Road, Blacktown, Australia

LEASK: Madam Leask of Leask, 1 Vincent Road, Sheringham, Norfolk

LENNOX: Edward J. H. Lennox of that Ilk, Tods Top Farm, Downton on the Rock, Ludlow, Shropshire

LESLIE: The Earl of Rothes, Tanglewood, West Tytherley, Salisbury, Wilts SP5 1LX

LINDSAY: The Earl of Crawford and Balcarres, KT, GCVO, PC, Balcarres, Colinsburgh, Fife

LOCKHART: Angus H. Lockhart of the Lee, Newholme, Dunsyre, Lanark

LUMSDEN: Gillem Lumsden of that Ilk and Blanerne, Stapely Howe, Hoe Benham, Newbury, Berks

MACALESTER: William St J. S. McAlester of Loup and Kennox, 27 Durnham Road, Christchurch, Dorset BH23 7ND

MACARTHUR; James MacArthur of that Ilk, 14 Hillpark Wood, Edinburgh

MCBAIN: J. H. McBain of McBain, 7025 North Finger Rock Place, Tucson, Arizona, USA

MACDONALD: The Lord Macdonald (*The Macdonald of Macdonald*), Kinloch Lodge, Sleat, Isle of Skye

*MACDONALD OF CLANRANALD: Ranald A. Macdonald of Clanranald, Mornish House, Killin, Perthshire FK21 8TX

*MACDONALD OF SLEAT (Clan Husteain): Sir Ian Macdonald of Sleat, Bt., Thorpe Hall, Rudston, Driffield, N. Humberside YO25 0JE

* MACDONELL OF GLENGARRY: Ranald MacDonell of Glengarry, Elonbank, Castle Street, Fortrose, Ross-shire IV10 8TH

MACDOUGALL: vacant

MACDOWALL: Fergus D. H. Macdowall of Garthland, 16 Rowe Road, Ottawa, Ontario K29 2ZS

MACGREGOR: Brig. Sir Gregor MacGregor of MacGregor, Bt., Bannatyne, Newtyle, Blairgowrie, Perthshire PH12 8TR

MACINTYRE: James W. MacIntyre of Glenoe, 15301 Pine Orchard Drive, Apartment 3H, Silver Spring, Maryland, USA

MACKAY: The Lord Reay, 98 Oakley Street, London SW3

MACKENZIE: The Earl of Cromartie, Castle Leod, Strathpeffer, Ross-shire IV14 9AA

MACKINNON: Madam Anne Mackinnon of Mackinnon, 3 Anson Way, Bridgewater, Somerset TA6 3TB

MACKINTOSH: John Mackintosh of Mackintosh (*The Mackintosh of Mackintosh*), Moy Hall, Inverness IV13 7YQ

MACLAREN: Donald MacLaren of MacLaren and Achleskine, Achleskine, Kirkton, Balquhidder, Lochearnhead

MACLEAN: The Hon. Sir Lachlan Maclean of Duart, Bt., CVO, Arngask House, Glenfarg, Perthshire PH2 9QA

MACLENNAN: Ruaraidh MacLennan of MacLennan, Oldmill, Dores, Inverness-shire IV2 6R

MACLEOD: John MacLeod of MacLeod, Dunvegan Castle, Isle of Skye

MACMILLAN: George MacMillan of MacMillan, Finlaystone, Langbank, Renfrewshire

MACNAB: J. C. Macnab of Macnab (*The Macnab*), Leuchars Castle Farmhouse, Leuchars, Fife KY16 0EY

MACNAGHTEN: Sir Patrick Macnaghten of Macnaghten and Dundarave, Bt., Dundarave, Bushmills, Co. Antrim

MACNEACAIL: Iain Macneacail of Macneacail and Scorrybreac, 12 Fox Street, Ballina, NSW, Australia

MACNEIL OF BARRA: Ian R. Macneil of Barra (*The Macneil of Barra*), 95/6 Grange Loan, Edinburgh

MACPHERSON: The Hon. Sir William Macpherson of Cluny, TD, Newton Castle, Blairgowrie, Perthshire

MACTAVISH: E. S. Dugald MacTavish of Dunardry, 2519 Vivaldi Lane, Four Seasons Estates, Gambrills, MD21 054, USA

MACTHOMAS: Andrew P. C. MacThomas of Finegand, c/o Roslin Cottage, Pitmedden, Aberdeenshire AB41 7NY

MAITLAND: The Earl of Lauderdale, 12 St Vincent Street, Edinburgh

MAKGILL: The Viscount of Oxfuird, Kemback, Stoke, Nr Andover, Hampshire SP11 ONP

MALCOLM (MacCallum): Robin N. L. Malcolm of Poltalloch, Duntrune Castle, Lochgilphead, Argyll

MAR: The Countess of Mar, St Michael's Farm, Great Witley, Worcs WR6 6JB

MARJORIBANKS: Andrew Marjoribanks of that Ilk, 10 Newark Street, Greenock

MATHESON: Maj. Sir Fergus Matheson of Matheson, Bt., Old Rectory, Hedenham, Bungay, Suffolk NR35 2LD

MENZIES: David R. Menzies of Menzies, 42 Panorama Drive, Preston Beach, Western Australia 6215

MOFFAT: Madam Moffat of that Ilk, St Jasual, Bullocks Farm Lane, Wheeler End Common, High Wycombe

MONCREIFFE: The Hon. Peregrine Moncreiffe of Moncreiffe, Easter Moncreiffe, Bridge of Earn, Perthshire

MONTGOMERIE: The Earl of Eglinton and Winton, Balhomie, Cargill, Perth PH2 6DS

MORRISON: Dr Iain M. Morrison of Ruchdi, Magnolia Cottage, The Street, Walberton, Sussex

MUNRO: Hector W. Munro of Foulis, Foulis Castle, Evanton, Ross-shire IV16 9UX

MURRAY: The Duke of Atholl, Blair Castle, Blair Atholl, Perthshire

NESBITT (or Nisbet): Mark Nesbitt of that Ilk, 114 Cambridge Road, Teddington, Middlesex TW11 8DJ

NICOLSON: The Lord Carnock, 90 Whitehall Court, London SW1A 2EL

OGILVY: The Earl of Airlie, KT, GCVO, PC, Cortachy Castle, Kirriemuir, Angus

RAMSAY: The Earl of Dalhousie, Brechin Castle, Brechin, Angus DD7 6SH

RATTRAY: James S. Rattray of Rattray, Craighall, Rattray, Perthshire

RIDDELL: Sir John Riddell of Riddell, CB, CVO, Hepple, Morpeth, Northumberland

ROBERTSON: Alexander G. H. Robertson of Struan (*Struan-Robertson*), The Breach Farm, Goudhurst Road, Cranbrook, Kent

ROLLO: The Lord Rollo, Pitcairns, Dunning, Perthshire

ROSE: Miss Elizabeth Rose of Kilravock, Kilravock Castle, Croy, Inverness

ROSS: David C. Ross of that Ilk and Balnagowan, Shandwick, Perth Road, Stanley, Perthshire

RUTHVEN: The Earl of Gowrie, PC, 34 King Street, Covent Garden, London WC2

SCOTT: The Duke of Buccleuch and Queensberry, KT, VRD, Bowhill, Selkirk

SCRYMGEOUR: The Earl of Dundee, Birkhill, Cupar, Fife

SEMPILL: The Lord Sempill, 3 Vanburgh Place, Edinburgh, eh6 8ae

SHAW: John Shaw of Tordarroch, East Craig an Ron, 22 Academy Mead, Fortrose IV10 8TW

SINCLAIR: The Earl of Caithness, 137 Claxton Grove, London W6 8HB

SKENE: Danus Skene of Skene, Orwell House, Manse Road, Milnathort, Fife KY13 9YQ

STIRLING: Fraser J. Stirling of Cader, 44A Oakley Street, London SW3 5HA

STRANGE: Maj. Timothy Strange of Balcaskie, Little Holme, Porton Road, Amesbury, Wilts

SUTHERLAND: The Countess of Sutherland, House of Tongue, Brora, Sutherland

SWINTON: John Swinton of that Ilk, 123 Superior Avenue SW, Calgary, Alberta, Canada

TROTTER: Alexander Trotter of Mortonhall, Charterhall, Duns, Berwickshire

URQUHART: Kenneth T. Urquhart of Urquhart, 507 Jefferson Park Avenue, Jefferson, New Orleans, La. 70121, USA

WALLACE: Ian F. Wallace of that Ilk, 5 Lennox Street, Edinburgh EH4 1QB

WEDDERBURN OF THAT ILK: The Master of Dundee, Birkhill, Cupar, Fife

WEMYSS: David Wemyss of that Ilk, Invermay, Forteviot, Perthshire

The Privy Council

The Sovereign in Council, or Privy Council, was the chief source of executive power until the system of Cabinet government developed in the 18th century. Now the Privy Council's main functions are to advise the Sovereign and to exercise its own statutory responsibilities independent of the Sovereign in Council.

Membership of the Privy Council is automatic upon appointment to certain government and judicial positions in the United Kingdom, e.g. Cabinet ministers must be Privy Counsellors and are sworn in on first assuming office. Membership is also accorded by The Queen to eminent people in the UK and independent countries of the Commonwealth of which Her Majesty is Queen, on the recommendation of the British Prime Minister. Membership of the Council is retained for life, except for very occasional removals.

The administrative functions of the Privy Council are carried out by the Privy Council Office under the direction of the President of the Council, who is always a member of the Cabinet.

President of the Council, The Rt. Hon. Robin Cook, MP
Clerk of the Council, A. Galloway

MEMBERS *as at August 2002*

HRH The Duke of Edinburgh, 1951
HRH The Prince of Wales, 1977

Aberdare, Lord, 1974
Ackner, Lord, 1980
Airlie, Earl of, 1984
Aldous, Sir William, 1995
Alebua, Ezekiel, 1988
Alison, Michael, 1981
Ampthill, Lord, 1995
Ancram, Michael, 1996
Anderson, Donald, 2000
Anthony, Douglas, 1971
Arbuthnot, James, 1998
Archer of Sandwell, Lord, 1977
Arden, Dame Mary, 2000
Armstrong, Hilary, 1999
Arnold, Sir John, 1979
Arthur, Hon. Owen, 1995
Ashdown of Norton-sub-Hamdon, Lord, 1989
Ashley of Stoke, Lord, 1979
Atkins, Sir Robert, 1995
Auld, Sir Robin, 1995
Baker of Dorking, Lord, 1984
Barber, Lord, 1963
Barnett, Lord, 1975

Barron, Kevin, 2001
Beckett, Margaret, 1993
Beith, Alan, 1992
Beldam, Sir Roy, 1989
Belstead, Lord, 1983
Benn, Anthony, 1964
Bennett, Sir Frederic, 1985
Biffen, Lord, 1979
Bingham of Cornhill, Lord, 1986
Birch, William, 1992
Bisson, Sir Gordon, 1987
Blackstone, Baroness, 2001
Blair, Tony, 1994
Blaker, Lord, 1983
Blanchard, Peter, 1998
Blatch, Baroness, 1993
Blunkett, David, 1997
Boateng, Paul, 1999
Bolger, James, 1991
Booth, Albert, 1976
Boothroyd, Baroness, 1992
Boscawen, Hon. Robert, 1992
Bottomley, Virginia, 1992
Boyd, Colin, 2000
Boyson, Sir Rhodes, 1987
Bradley, Keith, 2001
Brathwaite, Sir Nicholas, 1991
Bridge of Harwich, Lord, 1975
Brightman, Lord, 1979
Brittan of Spennithorne, Lord, 1981
Brook, Sir Henry, 1996
Brooke of Sutton Mandeville, Lord, 1988
Brown, Gordon, 1996
Brown, Nicholas, 1997
Brown, Sir Simon, 1992
Brown, Sir Stephen, 1983
Browne-Wilkinson, Lord, 1983
Butler, Sir Adam, 1984
Butler-Sloss, Dame Elizabeth, 1988
Buxton, Sir Richard, 1997
Byers, Stephen, 1998
Caborn, Richard, 1999
Caithness, Earl of, 1990
Callaghan of Cardiff, Lord, 1964
Cameron of Lochbroom, Lord, 1984
Camoys, Lord, 1997
Campbell of Croy, Lord, 1970
Campbell, Walter Menzies, 1999
Campbell, Sir William, 1999
Carey, George, 1991
Carlisle of Bucklow, Lord, 1979
Carnwath, Sir Robert, 2002
Carr of Hadley, Lord, 1963
Carrington Lord, 1959
Carswell, Sir Robert, 1993
Carter, Lord, 1997
Casey, Sir Maurice, 1986
Chadwick, Sir John, 1997
Chalfont, Lord, 1964
Chalker of Wallasey, Baroness, 1987
Chan, Sir Julius, 1981
Chataway, Sir Christopher, 1970
Clark of Windermere, Lord, 1997
Clark, Helen, 1990

Clark of Kempston, Lord, 1990
Clarke, Sir Anthony, 1998
Clarke, Charles, 2001
Clarke, Kenneth, 1984
Clarke, Thomas, 1997
Clinton-Davis, Lord, 1998
Clyde, Lord, 1996
Cockfield, Lord, 1982
Colman, Fraser, 1986
Compton, Sir John, 1983
Concannon, John, 1978
Cook, Robin, 1996
Cooke of Thorndon, Lord, 1977
Cope of Berkeley, Lord, 1988
Corfield, Sir Frederick, 1970
Coulsfield, Lord, 2000
Cowen, Sir Zelman, 1981
Cradock, Sir Percy, 1993
Cranborne, Viscount, 1994
Crawford and Balcarres, Earl of, 1972
Creech, Hon. Wyatt, 1999
Crickhowell, Lord, 1979
Croom-Johnson, Sir David, 1984
Cullen, Hon. Lord, 1997
Cunningham, Jack, 1993
Curry, David, 1996
Darling, Alistair, 1997
Davies, Denzil, 1978
Davies, Ronald, 1997
Davis, David, 1997
Davis, Terence, 1999
Davison, Sir Ronald, 1978
Dean of Harptree, Lord, 1991
Dean of Thornton-le-Fylde, Baroness, 1998
Deedes, Lord, 1962
Denham, John, 2000
Denham, Lord, 1981
Devonshire, Duke of, 1964
Diamond, Lord, 1965
Dillon, Sir Brian, 1982
Dixon, Lord, 1996
Dobson, Frank, 1997
Donaldson of Lymington, Lord, 1979
Dorrell, Stephen, 1994
Douglas, Sir William, 1977
du Cann, Sir Edward, 1964
Duncan Smith, Iain, 2001
Dunn, Sir Robin, 1980
Dyson, Sir John, 2001
East, Paul, 1998
Eden of Winton, Lord, 1972
Eggar, Timothy, 1995
Eichelaum, Sir Thomas, 1989
Elias, Hon. Dame, Sian, 1999
Emery, Sir Peter, 1993
Emslie, Lord, 1972
Erroll of Hale, Lord, 1960
Esquivel, Manuel, 1986
Evans, Sir Anthony, 1992
Eveleigh, Sir Edward, 1977
Farquharson, Sir Donald, 1989
Fellowes, Lord, 1990
Ferrers, Earl, 1982
Field, Frank, 1997

Floissac, Sir Vincent, 1992
Foot, Michael, 1974
Forsyth of Drumlean, The Lord, 1995
Forth, Eric, 1997
Foster, Derek, 1993
Foulkes, George, 2002
Fowler, Lord, 1979
Fox, Sir Michael, 1981
Fraser, Malcolm, 1976
Fraser of Carmyllie, Lord, 1989
Freeman, John, 1966
Freeman, Lord, 1993
Freeson, Reginald, 1976
Garel-Jones, Lord, 1992
Gault, Thomas, 1992
George, Bruce, 2000
George, Sir Edward, 1999
Georges, Telford, 1986
Gibbs, Sir Harry, 1972
Gibson, Sir Peter, 1993
Gibson, Sir Ralph, 1985
Gilbert, Lord, 1978
Gill, Lord, 2002
Gilmour of Craigmillar, Lord, 1973
Glenamara, Lord, 1964
Glidewell, Sir Iain, 1985
Goff of Chieveley, Lord, 1982
Goldsmith, Lord, 2002
Goodlad, Sir Alastair, 1992
Gowrie, Earl of, 1984
Graham, Sir Douglas, 1998
Graham of Edmonton, Lord, 1998
Gray of Contin, Lord, 1982
Griffiths, Lord, 1980
Gummer, John, 1985
Habgood, Rt. Revd Lord, 1983
Hague, William, 1995
Hain, Peter, 2001
Hale, Dame Brenda, 1999
Hamilton, Sir Archie, 1991
Hamilton, Lord, 2002
Hanley, Sir Jeremy, 1994
Hardie, Lord, 1997
Hardie Boys, Sir Michael, 1989
Harman, Harriet, 1997
Harrison, Walter, 1977
Haselhurst, Sir Alan, 1999
Hattersley, Lord, 1975
Hayhoe, Lord, 1985
Hayman, Baroness, 2000
Healey, Lord, 1964
Heath, Sir Edward, 1955
Heathcoat-Amory, David, 1996
Henry, Sir Denis, 1993
Henry, John, 1996
Heseltine, Lord, 1979
Heseltine, Sir William, 1986
Hesketh, Lord, 1991
Hewitt, Patricia, 2001
Higgins, Lord, 1979
Hirst, Sir David, 1992
Hobhouse of Woodborough, Lord, 1993
Hoffmann, Lord, 1992
Hogg, Hon. Douglas, 1992
Hollis of Heigham, Baroness, 1999
Holme of Cheltenham, Lord, 2000
Hoon, Geoffrey, 1999
Hope of Craighead, Lord, 1989
Hordern, Sir Peter, 1993
Howard, Michael, 1990

Howarth, Alan, 2000
Howe of Aberavon, Lord, 1972
Howell of Guildford, Lord, 1979
Hunt, Jonathan, 1989
Hunt of Wirral, Lord, 1990
Hurd of Westwell, Lord, 1982
Hutchison, Sir Michael, 1995
Hutton, Lord, 1988
Hutton, John, 2001
Ingraham, Hubert, 1993
Ingram, Adam, 1999
Irvine of Lairg, Lord, 1997
Jack, Michael, 1997
Janvrin, Sir Robin, 1998
Jauncey of Tullichettle, Lord, 1988
Jay of Paddington, Baroness, 1998
Jellicoe, Earl, 1963
Jenkin of Roding, Lord, 1973
Jenkins of Hillhead, Lord, 1964
Johnson Smith, Sir Geoffrey, 1996
Jones, Aubrey, 1955
Jones, Lord, 1999
Jopling, Lord, 1979
Jowell, Tessa, 1998
Judge, Sir Igor, 1996
Jugnauth, Sir Aneerood, 1987
Kaufman, Gerald, 1978
Kay, Sir John, 2000
Keene, Sir David, 2000
Keith, Sir Kenneth, 1998
Kelly, Sir Basil, 1984
Kelvedon, Lord, 1980
Kenilorea, Sir Peter, 1979
Kennedy, Charles, 1999
Kennedy, Sir Paul, 1992
King of Bridgwater, Lord, 1979
Kingsdown, Lord, 1987
Kingsland, Lord, 1994
Kinnock, Neil, 1983
Kirkwood, Lord, 2000
Knight, Gregory, 1995
Lamont of Lerwick, Lord, 1986
Lane, Lord, 1975
Lang of Monkton, Lord, 1990
Lange, David, 1984
Latasi, Kamuta, 1996
Latham, Sir David, 2000
Lauti, Sir Toaripi, 1979
Laws, Sir John, 1999
Lawson of Blaby, Lord, 1981
Lawton, Sir Frederick, 1972
Leggatt, Sir Andrew, 1990
Leonard, Rt. Revd Graham, 1981
Letwin, Oliver, 2002
Liddell, Mrs Helen, 1998
Lilley, Peter, 1990
Lloyd of Berwick, Lord, 1984
Lloyd, Sir Peter, 1994
London, The Bishop of, 1995
Longmore, Sir Andrew, 2001
Louisy, Allan, 1981
Luce, Lord, 1986
Lyell, Sir Nicholas, 1990
Mabon, Dickson, 1977
McCartney, Ian, 1999
McCollum, Sir Liam, 1997
McConnell, Jack, 2001
McCowan, Sir Anthony, 1989
MacDermott, Sir John, 1987
Macdonald of Tradeston, Lord, 1999
MacGregor of Pulham Market, Lord, 1985

MacIntyre, Duncan, 1980
Mackay, Andrew, 1998
McIntosh of Haringey, Lord, 2002
McKay, Ian, 1992
Mackay of Clashfern, Lord, 1979
Mackay of Drumadoon, Lord, 1996
McKinnon, Donald, 1992
Maclean, David, 1995
Maclean, Lord, 2001
McLeish, Henry, 2000
Maclennan of Rogart, Lord, 1997
McMullin, Sir Duncan, 1980
Major, John, 1987
Mance, Sir Jonathan, 1999
Mandelson, Peter, 1998
Mantell, Sir Charles, 1997
Mara, Ratu Sir Kamisese, 1973
Marnoch, Lord, 2001
Marsh, Lord, 1966
Martin, Michael, 2000
Mason of Barnsley, Lord, 1968
Maude, Hon. Francis, 1992
Mawhinney, Sir Brian, 1994
May, Sir Anthony, 1998
Mayhew of Twysden, Lord, 1986
Meacher, Michael, 1997
Megarry, Sir Robert, 1978
Mellor, David, 1990
Merlyn-Rees, Lord, 1974
Michael, Alun, 1998
Milburn, Alan, 1998
Millan, Bruce, 1975
Millett, Lord, 1994
Milligan, Lord, 2000
Mitchell, Sir James, 1985
Molyneaux of Killead, Lord, 1983
Monro of Langholm, Lord, 1995
Moore, Michael, 1990
Moore of Lower Marsh, Lord, 1986
Moore of Wolvercote, Lord, 1977
Morgan, Rhodri, 2000
Morris, Charles, 1978
Morris, Estelle, 1999
Morris of Aberavon, Lord, 1970
Morris of Manchester, Lord, 1979
Morritt, Sir Robert, 1994
Mowlam, Marjorie, 1997
Moyle, Roland, 1978
Mummery, Sir John, 1996
Murphy, Paul, 1998
Murray, Hon. Lord, 1974
Murray, Sir Donald, 1989
Murray of Epping Forest, Lord, 1976
Murton of Lindisfarne, Lord, 1976
Mustill, Lord, 1985
Nairne, Sir Patrick, 1982
Namaliu, Sir Rabbie, 1989
Naseby, Lord, 1994
Needham, Sir Richard, 1994
Neill, Sir Brian, 1985
Newton of Braintree, Lord, 1988
Nicholls of Birkenhead, Lord, 1995
Nicholson, Sir Michael, 1995
Nolan, Lord, 1991
Nott, Sir John, 1979
Nourse, Sir Martin, 1985
Oakes, Gordon, 1979
O'Connor, Sir Patrick, 1980
O'Donnell, Turlough, 1979
O'Flynn, Francis, 1987
Ogilvy, Sir Angus, 1997
Oliver of Aylmerton, Lord, 1980

Oppenheim-Barnes, Baroness, 1979
Orme, Lord, 1974
Osbourne, Lord, 2001
Otton, Sir Philip, 1995
Owen, Lord, 1976
Paeniu, Bikenibeu, 1991
Palliser, Sir Michael, 1983
Palmer, Sir Geoffrey, 1986
Parker, Sir Jonathan, 2000
Parker, Sir Roger, 1983
Parkinson, Lord, 1981
Patten, Christopher, 1989
Patten, Lord, 1990
Patterson, Percival, 1993
Pattie, Sir Geoffrey, 1987
Pendry, Lord, 2000
Penrose, Lord, 2000
Perth, Earl of, 1957
Peters, Winston, 1998
Peyton of Yeovil, Lord, 1970
Phillips of Worth Matravers, Lord, 1995
Pill, Sir Malcolm, 1995
Pindling, Sir Lynden, 1976
Portillo, Michael, 1992
Potter, Sir Mark, 1996
Prescott, John, 1994
Price, George, 1982
Primarolo, Dawn, 2002
Prior, Lord, 1970
Prosser, Lord, 2000
Puapua, Sir Tomasi, 1982
Purchas, Sir Francis, 1982
Pym, Lord, 1970
Quin, Ms Joyce, 1998
Radice, Lord, 1999
Raison, Sir Timothy, 1982
Ramsden, James, 1963
Rawlinson of Ewell, Lord, 1964
Raynsford, Nick, 2001
Redwood, John, 1993
Rees, Lord, 1983
Reid, John, 1998
Renton, Lord, 1962
Renton of Mount Harry, Lord, 1989
Richard, Lord, 1993
Richardson, Sir Ivor, 1978
Richardson of Duntisbourne, Lord, 1976
Rifkind, Sir Malcolm, 1986
Rix, Sir Bernard, 2000
Roberts of Conwy, Lord, 1991

Robertson of Port Ellen, Lord, 1997
Roch, Sir John, 1993
Rodger of Earlsferry, Lord, 1992
Rodgers of Quarry Bank, Lord, 1975
Rooker, Lord, 1999
Rose, Sir Christopher, 1992
Ross, Hon. Lord, 1985
Rumbold, Dame Angela, 1991
Russell, Sir Patrick, 1987
Ryder of Wensum, Lord, 1990
Sainsbury, Sir Timothy, 1992
St John of Fawsley, Lord, 1979
Sandiford, Erskine, 1989
Saville of Newdigate, Lord, 1994
Scarman, Lord, 1973
Schiemann, Sir Konrad, 1995
Scott, Sir Nicholas, 1989
Scott of Foscote, Lord, 1991
Scotland of Asthal, Baroness, 2001
Seaga, Edward, 1981
Sedley, Sir Stephen, 1999
Selkirk of Douglas, Lord, 1996
Shawcross, Lord, 1946
Shearer, Hugh, 1969
Sheldon, Lord, 1977
Shephard, Gillian, 1992
Shipley, Jennifer, 1998
Short, Clare, 1997
Simmonds, Kennedy, 1984
Simon of Glaisdale, Lord, 1961
Sinclair, Ian, 1977
Slade, Sir Christopher, 1982
Slynn of Hadley, Lord, 1992
Smith, Andrew, 1997
Smith, Christopher, 1997
Somare, Sir Michael, 1977
Spellar, John, 2001
Stanley, Sir John, 1984
Staughton, Sir Christopher, 1988
Steel of Aikwood, Lord, 1977
Stephen, Sir Ninian, 1979
Stewartby, Lord, 1989
Steyn, Lord, 1992
Stodart of Leaston, Lord, 1974
Strang, Gavin, 1997
Strathclyde, Lord, 1995
Straw, Jack, 1997
Stuart-Smith, Sir Murray, 1988
Sutherland, Lord, 2000
Symons of Vernham Dean, Baroness, 2001
Talboys, Sir Brian, 1977

Taylor, Ann, 1997
Tebbit, Lord, 1981
Templeman, Lord, 1978
Thatcher, Baroness, 1970
Thomas, Edmund, 1996
Thomas of Gwydir, Lord, 1964
Thomas, Sir Swinton, 1994
Thomson of Monifieth, Lord, 1966
Thorpe, Jeremy, 1967
Thorpe, Sir Matthew, 1995
Tipping, Andrew, 1998
Tizard, Robert, 1986
Trefgarne, Lord, 1989
Trimble, David, 1997
Trumpington, Baroness, 1992
Tuckey, Sir Simon, 1998
Ullswater, Viscount, 1994
Upton, Simon, 1999
Varley, Lord, 1974
Waddington, Lord, 1987
Waite, Sir John, 1993
Wakeham, Lord, 1983
Waldegrave of North Hill, Lord, 1990
Walker of Doncaster, Lord, 1979
Walker of Worcester, Lord, 1970
Walker, Sir Robert, 1997
Wallace, James, 2000
Waller, Sir Mark, 1996
Ward, Sir Alan, 1995
Watkins, Sir Tasker, 1980
Weatherill, Lord, 1980
Wheeler, Sir John, 1993
Widdecombe, Ann, 1997
Wigley, Dafydd, 1997
Wilberforce, Lord, 1964
Williams, Alan, 1977
Williams of Crosby, Baroness, 1974
Williams of Mostyn, Lord
Windlesham, Lord, 1973
Winti, Paias, 1987
Withers, Reginald, 1977
Wolfe, Sir David, 2000
Woodhouse, Sir Owen, 1974
Woolf, Lord, 1986
Wylie, Hon. Lord, 1970
York, The Archbishop of, 1991
Young, Baroness, 1981
Young, Sir George, 1993
Young of Graffham, Lord, 1984
Younger of Leckie, Viscount, 1979
Zacca, Edward, 1992

The Privy Council of Northern Ireland

The Privy Council of Northern Ireland had responsibilities in Northern Ireland similar to those of the Privy Council in Great Britain until the Northern Ireland Act 1974 instituted direct rule and a UK Cabinet minister became responsible for the functions previously exercised by the Northern Ireland government.
 Membership of the Privy Council of Northern Ireland is retained for life. Since the Northern Ireland Constitution Act 1973 no further appointments have been made. The postnominal initials PC (NI) are used to differentiate its members from those of the Privy Council.

MEMBERS *as at August 2002*

Bailie, Robin, 1971
Bleakley, David, 1971

Craig, William, 1963
Dobson, John, 1969
Kelly, Sir Basil, 1969
Kirk, Herbert, 1962
Long, William, 1966
McIvor, Basil, 1971
Neill, Sir Ivan, 1950
Porter, Sir Robert, 1969
Taylor, John, mp, 1970
West, Henry, 1960

Parliament

The United Kingdom constitution is not contained in any single document but has evolved in the course of time, formed partly by statute, partly by common law and partly by convention. A constitutional monarchy, the United Kingdom is governed by Ministers of the Crown in the name of the Sovereign, who is head both of the state and of the government.

The organs of government are the legislature (Parliament), the executive and the judiciary. The executive consists of HM Government (Cabinet and other Ministers), government departments, local authorities (*see* Local Government and Government Departments and Public Offices). The judiciary (*see* Law Courts and Offices) pronounces on the law, both written and unwritten, interprets statutes and is responsible for the enforcement of the law; the judiciary is independent of both the legislature and the executive.

THE MONARCHY

The Sovereign personifies the state and is, in law, an integral part of the legislature, head of the executive, head of the judiciary, commander-in-chief of all armed forces of the Crown and 'Supreme Governor' of the Church of England. The seat of the monarchy is in the United Kingdom. In the Channel Islands and the Isle of Man, which are Crown dependencies, the Sovereign is represented by a Lieutenant-Governor. In the member states of the Commonwealth of which the Sovereign is head of state, her representative is a Governor-General; in UK dependencies the Sovereign is usually represented by a Governor, who is responsible to the British Government.

Although in practice the powers of the monarchy are now very limited, restricted mainly to the advisory and ceremonial, there are important acts of government which require the participation of the Sovereign. These include summoning, proroguing and dissolving Parliament, giving royal assent to bills passed by Parliament, appointing important office-holders, e.g. government ministers, judges, bishops and governors, conferring peerages, knighthoods and other honours, and granting pardon to a person wrongly convicted of a crime. The Sovereign appoints the Prime Minister; by convention this office is held by the leader of the political party which enjoys, or can secure, a majority of votes in the House of Commons. In international affairs the Sovereign as head of state has the power to declare war and make peace, to recognise foreign states and governments, to conclude treaties and to annex or cede territory. However, as the Sovereign entrusts executive power to Ministers of the Crown and acts on the advice of her Ministers, which she cannot ignore, royal prerogative powers are in practice exercised by Ministers, who are responsible to Parliament.

Ministerial responsibility does not diminish the Sovereign's importance to the smooth working of government. She holds meetings of the Privy Council (*see* below), gives audiences to her Ministers and other officials at home and overseas, receives accounts of Cabinet decisions, reads dispatches and signs state papers; she must be informed and consulted on every aspect of national life; and she must show complete impartiality.

COUNSELLORS OF STATE

In the event of the Sovereign's absence abroad, it is necessary to appoint Counsellors of State under letters patent to carry out the chief functions of the Monarch, including the holding of Privy Councils and giving royal assent to acts passed by Parliament. The normal procedure is to appoint as Counsellors three or four members of the royal family among those remaining in the UK.

In the event of the Sovereign on accession being under the age of 18 years, or at any time unavailable or incapacitated by infirmity of mind or body for the performance of the royal functions, provision is made for a regency.

THE PRIVY COUNCIL

The Sovereign in Council, or Privy Council, was the chief source of executive power until the system of Cabinet government developed. Its main function is to advise the Sovereign to approve Orders in Council and to advise on the issue of royal proclamations. The Council's own statutory responsibilities (independent of the powers of the Sovereign in Council) include powers of supervision over the registering bodies for the medical and allied professions. A full Council is summoned only on the death of the Sovereign or when the Sovereign announces his or her intention to marry. (For a full list of Counsellors, *see* The Privy Council section.)

There are a number of advisory Privy Council committees, whose meetings the Sovereign does not attend. Some are prerogative committees, such as those dealing with legislative matters submitted by the legislatures of the Channel Islands and the Isle of Man or with applications for charters of incorporation; and some are provided for by statute, e.g. those for the universities of Oxford and Cambridge and the Scottish universities.

The Judicial Committee of the Privy Council is the court of final appeal from courts of the UK dependencies, courts of independent Commonwealth countries which have retained the right of appeal and courts of the Channel Islands and the Isle of Man.

It also has certain jurisdiction within the United Kingdom, the most important of which is that it is the court of final appeal for 'devolution issues,' i.e. issues as to the legal competences and functions of the legislative and executive authorities established in Scotland, Wales and Northern Ireland by the devolution legislation of 1998.

The Committee is composed of Privy Counsellors who hold, or have held, high judicial office, although usually only three or five hear each case.

Administrative work is carried out by the Privy Council Office under the direction of the President of the Council, a Cabinet Minister.

PARLIAMENT

Parliament is the supreme law-making authority and can legislate for the UK as a whole or for any parts of it separately (the Channel Islands and the Isle of Man are Crown dependencies and not part of the UK). The main functions of Parliament are to pass laws, to provide (by voting taxation) the means of carrying on the work of government and to scrutinise government policy and administration, particularly proposals for expenditure. International treaties and agreements are by custom presented to Parliament before ratification.

Parliament emerged during the late 13th and early 14th centuries. The officers of the King's household and the King's judges were the nucleus of early Parliaments, joined by such ecclesiastical and lay magnates as the King might summon to form a prototype 'House of Lords', and occasionally by the knights of the shires, burgesses and proctors of the lower clergy. By the end of Edward III's reign a 'House of Commons' was beginning to appear; the first known Speaker was elected in 1377.

Parliamentary procedure is based on custom and precedent, partly formulated in the Standing Orders of both Houses of Parliament, and each House has the right to control its own internal proceedings and to commit for contempt. The system of debate in the two Houses is similar; when a motion has been moved, the Speaker proposes the question as the subject of a debate. Members speak from wherever they have been sitting. Questions are decided by a vote on a simple majority. Draft legislation is introduced, in either House, as a bill. Bills can be introduced by a Government Minister or a private Member, but in practice the majority of bills which become law are introduced by the Government. To become law, a bill must be passed by each House and then sent to the Sovereign for the royal assent, after which it becomes an Act of Parliament.

Proceedings of both Houses are public, except on extremely rare occasions. The minutes (called Votes and Proceedings in the Commons, and Minutes of Proceedings in the Lords) and the speeches (*The Official Report of Parliamentary Debates, Hansard*) are published daily. Proceedings are also recorded for transmission on radio and television and stored in the Parliamentary Recording Unit before transfer to the National Sound Archive. Television cameras have been allowed into the House of Lords since 1985 and into the House of Commons since 1989; committee meetings may also be televised.

By the Parliament Act of 1911, the maximum duration of a Parliament is five years (if not previously dissolved), the term being reckoned from the date given on the writs for the new Parliament. The maximum life has been prolonged by legislation in such rare circumstances as the two world wars (31 January 1911 to 25 November 1918; 26 November 1935 to 15 June 1945). Dissolution and writs for a general election are ordered by the Sovereign on the advice of the Prime Minister. The life of a Parliament is divided into sessions, usually of one year in length, beginning and ending most often in October or November.

DEVOLUTION

The Scottish Parliament has legislative power over all devolved matters, i.e. matters not reserved to Westminster or otherwise outside its powers. The National Assembly for Wales has power to make secondary legislation in the areas where executive functions have been transferred to it. The Northern Ireland Assembly has legislative

authority in the fields previously administered by the Northern Ireland departments. For further information, *see* Regional Government section

THE HOUSE OF LORDS

London SW1A 0PW
Tel: 020-7219 3000
Information Office: 020-7219 3107
Email: hlinfo@parliament.uk
Web: www.parliament.uk

The members of the House of Lords comprise life peers created under the Life Peerages Act 1958, 92 hereditary peers elected under the House of Lords Act 1999 and those Lords of Appeal in Ordinary created life peers under the Appellate Jurisdiction Act 1876, as amended (i.e. Law Lords), the Archbishops of Canterbury and York, the Bishops of London, Durham and Winchester, and the 21 senior diocesan bishops of the Church of England.

The House of Lords Act provides for 92 hereditary peers (42 Conservative, 28 cross-bench, three Liberal Democrat, two Labour, the Earl Marshal, the Lord Great Chamberlain and 15 office holders) to remain in the House of Lords until longer-term reform of the House has been carried out; elections to select those who remain were held in October and November 1999.

Peers are disqualified from sitting in the House if they are:

– aliens, i.e. any peer who is not a British citizen, a Commonwealth citizen (under the British Nationality Act 1981) or a citizen of the Republic of Ireland
– under the age of 21
– undischarged bankrupts or, in Scotland, those whose estate is sequestered
– convicted of treason

Bishops retire at the age of 70 and cease to be members of the house at that time.

Peers who do not wish to attend sittings of the House of Lords may apply for leave of absence for the duration of a Parliament.

The House of Lords is the second chamber of the 'Upper House' of the UK's bi-cameral parliament. Until the beginning of this century the House of Lords had considerable power, being able to veto any bill submitted to it by the House of Commons. Today the main functions of the House of Lords are to revise legislation, to act as a check on the Government, to provide a forum of independent expertise, and to act as a final court of appeal.

The House of Lords also has a number of Select Committees. Some relate to the internal affairs of the House – such as its management and administration – while others carry out important investigative work on matters of public interest. There are four main areas of work – Europe, Science, the Economy and the Constitution. Unlike the Commons, Lords investigative committees do not look at the work of particular Government departments.

The House of Lords has judicial powers as the ultimate Court of Appeal for courts in Great Britain and Northern Ireland, except for criminal cases in Scotland. These powers are exercised by the Lord Chancellor and the Lords of Appeal in Ordinary (the Law Lords) (*see* Law Courts and Officers section).

Members of the House of Lords are unpaid. However, they are entitled to reimbursement of travelling expenses on parliamentary business within the UK and certain other expenses incurred for the purpose of attendance at

sittings of the House, within a maximum for each day of £122.00 for overnight subsistence, £61.00 for day subsistence and incidental travel, and £51.00 for secretarial costs, postage and certain additional expenses as at 1 August 2002.

COMPOSITION *as at 1 August 2002**

Archbishops and Bishops, 26
Life peers under the Appellate Jurisdiction Act 1876, 27
Life peers under the Life Peerages Act 1958, 557
(112 women)
Peers under the House of Lords Act 1999, 91 (4 women)
Total 701

*Excluding 12 Peers, 11 are on leave of absence from the House and one (elected hereditary) is bankrupt and cannot attend)

STATE OF PARTIES *as at 1 August 2002**

Conservative, 219
Labour, 191
Liberal Democrats, 65
Cross-bench, 179
Archbishops and Bishops, 26
Other, 8
Total: 688

* Excluding peers on leave of absence from the House

OFFICERS

The House is presided over by the Lord Chancellor, who is *ex officio* Speaker of the House. A panel of deputy Speakers is appointed by Royal Commission. The first deputy Speaker is the Chairman of Committees, appointed at the beginning of each session, a salaried officer of the House who takes the chair in committee of the whole House and in some select committees. He is assisted by a panel of deputy chairmen, headed by the salaried Principal Deputy Chairman of Committees, who is also chairman of the European Communities Committee of the House.

The permanent officers include the Clerk of the Parliaments, who is the Accounting Officer and the chief permanent official responsible for the administration of the House; the Gentleman Usher of the Black Rod, who as well as his responsibility for security and other services also has royal duties as secretary to the Lord Great Chamberlain.

Speaker (£180,045), The Lord Irvine of Lairg, PC, QC
Private Secretary, Ms E. Hutchinson
Chairman of Committees (£74,040), The Lord Tordoff
Principal Deputy Chairman of Committees (£69,267),
The Lord Brabazon of Tara

DEPARTMENT OF THE CLERK OF THE PARLIAMENTS

Clerk of the Parliaments (£132,603), Sir Michael Davies, KCB
Clerk Assistant (£64,768–£104,292), P. D. G. Hayter
Reading Clerk and Principal Finance Officer (£64,768–£104,292), M. G. Pownall
Counsel to Chairman of Committees (£64,768–£104,292), Allan D. Roberts; Dr C. S. Kerse; D. W. Saunders
Principal Clerks (£59,088–£98,494), B. P. Keith,
(*Judicial Office and Fourth Clerk at the Table*);
D. R. Beamish, (*Journals*); Dr R. H. Walters,
(*Committees and Overseas Office*)
Chief Clerks (£48,552–£77,869), E. C. Ollard,
(*Establishment Officer*); T. V. Mohan (*Public Bills*);
S. P. Burton (*Committee Office*); A. Makower
(*Seconded to Government Whips, as Private Secretary to*

the Leader of the House and Government Chief Whip)
Senior Clerks (£32,931–£49,896) Miss M. B. Robertson
(*Committee Office*); T. E. Radice; D. J. Batt;
E. R. Morgan; J. A. Vaughan; Miss C. Salmon;
A. Rawsthorne; A. J Mackersie; Miss K. Ball; I. Mackley
Clerks (£20,540–£28,243), R. A. McLean; C. S. Johnson;
Miss C. K. S. K. Mawson (*Seconded to Government
Whips Office as Assistant Private Secretary*); T. Elias;
Miss A. Murphy; R. R. Neal; R. R. McLean
Clerk of the Records (£48,552–£77,869), S. K. Ellison
Assistant Clerks of the Records (£33,919–£51,393),
D. L. Prior; Dr C. Shenton; F. P. Grey
Librarian (£53,534–£87,598), D. L. Jones
Deputy Librarian (£38,412–£62,324), Dr P. G. Davis
Senior Library Clerks (£33,919–£51,393), Dr I. L.
Victory; S. Kennedy; H. C. Deadman
Library Clerk (£20,540–£28,243), I. S. Cruse;
A. J. C. Brocklehurst
Examiners of Petitions for Private Bills
(£48,552–£77,869), to be announced; F. A. Cranmer
Editor, Official Report (Hansard), (£48,552–£77,869),
Mrs C. J. Boden
Deputy Editor, Official Report (£38,412–£62,324),
Miss J. A. Bradshaw

DEPARTMENT OF THE GENTLEMAN USHER OF THE BLACK ROD

Gentleman Usher of the Black Rod and Serjeant-at-Arms
(£64,768–£104,292), Lt.-Gen. Sir Michael Willcocks
*Yeoman Usher of the Black Rod and Deputy
Serjeant-at-Arms* (£33,919–£51,393), Brig. H. D. C.
Duncan, MBE

SELECT COMMITTEES

The main House of Lords select committees, as at June 2002, are as follows:
European Union – Chair, The Lord Brabazon of Tara;
Clerk, S. Burton
European Union – Sub-committees:
A (*Economic and Financial Affairs, Trade and External
Relations*) – *Chair*, The Lord Grenfell; *Clerk*,
R. McLean
B (*Energy, Industry and Transport*) – *Chair*, The Lord
Brook of Alverthorpe; *Clerk*, P. Wogan
C (*Common Foreign and Security Policy*) – *Chair*,
The Lord Jopling; *Clerk*, D. Batt
D (*Environment, Agriculture, Public Health and
Consumer Protection*) – *Chair*, The Earl of Selborne;
Clerk, T. Radice
E (*Law and Institutions*) – *Chair*, The Lord Scott of
Foscote; *Clerk*, R. McLean
F (*Social Affairs, Education and Home Affairs*) – *Chair*,
Baroness Harris of Richmond; *Clerk*, T. Rawsthorne
Animals in Scientific Procedures – *Chair*, The Lord Smith
of Clifton
Constitution Committee – *Chair*, The Lord Norton of
Louth; *Clerk*, A. Mackersie
Delegated Powers and Regulatory Reform – *Chair*,
The Lord Dahrendorf; *Clerk*, T. Moham
Economic Affairs-Chair, The Lord Peston; *Clerk*,
Ms C. Salmon
Science and Technology – *Chair*, Lord Oxburgh, FRCOG;
Clerk, Ms M. Robertson

THE HOUSE OF COMMONS

London SW1A 0AA
Tel: 020-7219 3000
Information Office: Tel: 020-7219 4272
Forthcoming business: Tel: 020-7219 5532
Email: hcinfo@parliament.uk
Web: www.parliament.uk

The members of the House of Commons are elected by universal adult suffrage. For electoral purposes, the United Kingdom is divided into constituencies, each of which returns one member to the House of Commons, the member being the candidate who obtains the largest number of votes cast in the constituency. To ensure equitable representation, the four Boundary Commissions keep constituency boundaries under review and recommend any redistribution of seats which may seem necessary because of population movements, etc. The number of seats was raised to 640 in 1945, reduced to 625 in 1948, and subsequently rose to 630 in 1955, 635 in 1970, 650 in 1983, 651 in 1992 and 659 in 1997. Of the present 659 seats, there are 529 for England, 40 for Wales, 72 for Scotland and 18 for Northern Ireland. The number of Scottish MPs at Westminster is likely to be cut by about 12 by 2007.

An electoral reform commission headed by Lord Jenkins of Hillhead proposed in October 1998 that the 'first-past-the-post' system of electing members of the House of Commons should be replaced by an alternative vote top-up system, under which 80–85 per cent of MPs would be elected by an alternative vote method and the remaining 15–20 per cent by an open-list system of proportional representation. A referendum will be held on the proposals at an unspecified future date.

ELECTIONS

Elections are by secret ballot, each elector casting one vote; voting is not compulsory. For entitlement to vote in parliamentary elections, *see* Legal Notes section. When a seat becomes vacant between general elections, a by-election is held.

British subjects and citizens of the Irish Republic can stand for election as Members of Parliament (MPs) provided they are 21 or over and not subject to disqualification. Those disqualified from sitting in the House include:

– undischarged bankrupts
– people sentenced to more than one year's imprisonment
– members of the House of Lords (but hereditary peers not sitting in the Lords are eligible)
– holders of certain offices listed in the House of Commons Disqualification Act 1975, e.g. members of the judiciary, Civil Service, regular armed forces, police forces, some local government officers and some members of public corporations and government commissions

A candidate does not require any party backing but his or her nomination for election must be supported by the signatures of ten people registered in the constituency. A candidate must also deposit with the returning officer £500, which is forfeit if the candidate does not receive more than 5 per cent of the votes cast. All election expenses at a general election, except the candidate's personal expenses, are subject to a statutory limit of £5,483, plus 4.6 pence for each elector in a borough constituency or 6.2 pence for each elector in a county constituency.

See pages 227–235 for an alphabetical list of MPs, pages 237–270 for the results of the last general election, and page 271 for the results of by-elections since the general election.

STATE OF PARTIES *as at 25 June 2002*

Conservative, 164 (14 women)
Labour, 410 (94 women)
Liberal Democrats, 53 (5 women)
Plaid Cymru, 4
Scottish Nationalist, 5 (1 woman)
Sinn Fein (have not taken their seats), 4 (1 woman)
Social Democratic Labour, 3
Democratic Unionist Party, 5 (1 woman)
Ulster Unionist, 6 (1 woman)
Independent (Dr Richard Taylor-Wyre Forest), 1
The Speaker and three Deputy Speakers, 4
Total, 659 (118 women)

BUSINESS

The week's business of the House is outlined each Thursday by the Leader of the House, after consultation between the Chief Government Whip and the Chief Opposition Whip. A quarter to a third of the time will be taken up by the Government's legislative programme and the rest by other business. As a rule, bills likely to raise political controversy are introduced in the Commons before going on to the Lords, and the Commons claims exclusive control in respect of national taxation and expenditure. Bills such as the Finance Bill, which imposes taxation, and the Consolidated Fund Bills, which authorise expenditure, must begin in the Commons. A bill of which the financial provisions are subsidiary may begin in the Lords; and the Commons may waive its rights in regard to Lords' amendments affecting finance.

The Commons has a public register of MPs' financial and certain other interests; this is published annually as a House of Commons paper. Members must also disclose any relevant financial interest or benefit in a matter before the House when taking part in a debate, in certain other proceedings of the House, or in consultations with other MPs, with Ministers or with civil servants.

MEMBERS' PAY AND ALLOWANCES

Since 1911 members of the House of Commons have received salary payments; facilities for free travel were introduced in 1924. Salary rates since 1911 are as follows:

1911	£400 p.a.	1984 Jan	£16,106 p.a.
1931	360	1985 Jan	16,904
1934	380	1986 Jan	17,702
1935	400	1987 Jan	18,500
1937	600	1988 Jan	22,548
1946	1,000	1989 Jan	24,107
1954	1,250	1990 Jan	26,701
1957	1,750	1991 Jan	28,970
1964	3,250	1992 Jan	30,854
1972 Jan	4,500	1994 Jan	31,687
1975 June	5,750	1995 Jan	33,189
1976 June	6,062	1996 Jan	34,085
1977 July	6,270	1996 July	43,000
1978 June	6,897	1997 April	43,860
1979 June	9,450	1998 April	45,066
1980 June	11,750	1999 April	47,008
1981 June	13,950	2000 April	48,371
1982 June	14,510	2001 April	49,822
1983 June	15,308	2002 April	55,118

In 1969 MPs were granted an allowance for secretarial and research expenses, now known as the Office Costs Allowance. From April 2002 the allowance is £53,446 a year. This will cease to exist after March 2003. Instead most Members now receive an Incidental Expenses Provision (£18,234) and a staffing allowance (between £61,980 and £72,310).

Since 1972 MPs have been able to claim reimbursement for the additional cost of staying overnight away from their main residence while on parliamentary business; this is known as the Additional Costs Allowance and from April 2001 is £19,722 a year.

Members' of staff who are paid out of the allowances can benefit from a sum not exceeding 10 per cent of their gross salary which is paid into a pension scheme of their choice. This sum comes from a central budget.

MEMBERS' PENSIONS

Pension arrangements for MPs were first introduced in 1964. The arrangements currently provide a pension of one-fiftieth of salary for each year of pensionable service with a maximum of two-thirds of salary at age 65. Pension is payable normally at age 65, for men and women, or on later retirement. Pensions may be paid earlier, e.g. on retirement due to ill health or at age 60 after 20 years' service. The widow/widower of a former MP receives a pension of five-eighths of the late MPs pension. Pensions are index-linked. Members currently contribute six per cent of salary to the pension fund; there is an Exchequer contribution, currently slightly more than the amount contributed by MPs.

The House of Commons Members' Fund provides for annual or lump sum grants to ex-MPs, their widows or widowers, and children whose incomes are below certain limits or who are experiencing severe hardship. Members contribute £24 a year and the Exchequer £215,000 a year to the fund.

OFFICERS AND OFFICIALS

The House of Commons is presided over by the Speaker, who has considerable powers to maintain order in the House. A deputy Speaker, called the Chairman of Ways and Means, and two Deputy Chairmen may preside over sittings of the House of Commons; they are elected by the House, and, like the Speaker, neither speak nor vote other than in their official capacity.

The staff of the House are employed by a Commission chaired by the Speaker. The heads of the six House of Commons departments are permanent officers of the House, not MPs. The Clerk of the House is the principal adviser to the Speaker on the privileges and procedures of the House, the conduct of the business of the House, and committees. The Serjeant-at-Arms is responsible for security, ceremonial, and for accommodation in the Commons part of the Palace of Westminster.

Speaker (£124,979), The Rt. Hon. Michael J. Martin, MP (Glasgow Springburn)
Chairman of Ways and Means (£91,538), Sir Alan Haselhurst, MP (Saffron Walden)
First Deputy Chairman of Ways and Means (£86,968), Sylvia Heal, MP (Halesowen and Rowley Regis)
Second Deputy Chairman of Ways and Means (£86,968), Sir Michael Lord, MP (Suffolk Central and Ipswich North)

OFFICES OF THE SPEAKER AND CHAIRMAN OF WAYS AND MEANS

Speaker's Secretary (£53,534–£87,598), Sir Nicolas Bevan, CB
Chaplain to the Speaker, Revd Canon R. Wright
Secretary to the Chairman of Ways and Means (£33,095–£49,291), M. Hennessy

DEPARTMENT OF THE CLERK OF THE HOUSE

Clerk of the House of Commons (£132,603), W. R. McKay, CB

Clerk Assistant (£70,905–£110,428), R. B. Sands
Clerk of Committees (£70,905–£110,428), G. Cubie
Clerk of Legislation (£70,905–£110,428), D. G. Millar
Principal Clerks (£64,768–£104,292)
  Journals, Dr M. R. Jack
  Table Office, Ms H. E. Irwin
Principal Clerks (£53,534–£87,598)
  Overseas Office, Mrs J. Sharpe
  Bills, F. A. Cranmer
  Select Committees, R. W. G. Wilson; D. L. Natzler; D. W. N. Doig
  Delegated Legislation, W. A. Proctor
Deputy Principal Clerks (£48,552–£77,869), Ms A. Barry; Dr C. R. M. Ward; A. Sandall; A. R. Kennon; L. C. Laurence Smyth; S. J. Patrick; D. J. Gerhold; C. J. Poyser; D. F. Harrison; S. J. Priestley; A. H. Doherty; P. A. Evans; R. I. S. Phillips; Dr R. G. James; D. R. Lloyd; B. M. Hutton; J. S. Benger, D.Phil.; Ms E. C. Samson; N. P. Walker; Mrs E. J. Flood; C. G. Lee; C. D. Stanton; Miss L. M. Gardner; F. J. Reid; C. A. Shaw; P. G. Moon; T. W. P. Healey; P. Aylett
Senior Clerks (£33,095–£49,291), M. Clark; M. Hennessy; G. R. Devine; Mrs J. N. St J. Mulley; J. D. Whatley; K. C. Fox; J. D. W. Rhys; Ms E. S. Payne; Miss S. McGlashen; Mrs C. Oxborough; T. Goldsmith; H. A. Yardley; Ms K. Emms; N. P. Wright; M. Hillyard; J. H. Davies; M. P. Atkins; M. Egan; J. S. Fox; S. T. Fiander (*acting*); D. H. Griffiths (*acting*); Ms R. Melling, CBE (*acting*); G. K. Clarke; D. Lees; A. Kidner
Examiners of Petitions for Private Bills, F. A. Cranmer; Dr F. P. Tudor
Registrar of Members' Interests (£53,534–£87,598), Ms A. Barry
Taxing Officer, F. A. Cranmer

VOTE OFFICE

Deliverer of the Vote (£48,552–£77,869), J. F. Collins
Deputy Deliverers of the Vote (£33,095–£49,291), O. B. T. Sweeney (*Parliamentary*); F. W. Hallett (*Production*); R. Brook (*Development*)

LEGAL SERVICES OFFICE

Speaker's Counsel and Head of Legal Services Office (£64,768–£104,292), J. E. G. Vaux
Counsel for European Legislation (£53,534–£87,598), M. Carpenter
Counsel for Legislation, A. D. Preston
Assistant Counsel (£48,552–£77,869), A. Akbar; P. Brooksbank

DEPARTMENT OF THE SERJEANT-AT-ARMS

Serjeant-at-Arms (£64,768–£104,292), M. J. A. Cummins
Deputy Serjeant-at-Arms (£48,552–£77,869), R. M. Morton
Assistant Serjeants-at-Arms (£37,484–£59,764), P. A. J. Wright; J. M. Robertson; M. Harvey

DEPARTMENT OF THE LIBRARY

Librarian (£64,768–£104,292), Miss P. Baines
Directors (£48,552–£77,869), K. G. Cuninghame; R. Clements; Miss E. M. McInnes; B. Twigger
Heads of Sections (£37,484–£59,764), Dr C. Pond; Mrs C. Andrews; Mrs J. Lourie; C. Barclay; Mrs C. Gillie; Mrs G. Allen; R. Cracknell; E. Wood; Dr P. Richards

Senior Library Clerks (£33,095–£49,291), Ms F. Poole;
T. Edmonds; Dr D. Gore; Mrs H. Holden;
Mrs P. Carling; S. Wise; Mrs K. Greener;
Ms P. Strickland; Miss V. Miller; Ms J. Roll;
Ms W. Wilson; Dr P. Bowers; A. Seely; Mrs J. Hough;
Dr G. Danby; B. Morgan; Ms K. Wright;
Miss L. Conway; C. Blair; C. Sear; Ms F. Whittle;
K. Parry; Dr A. Sleator; Mrs B. Brevitt; Mrs D. Clark;
T. Youngs; Dr S. McGinness; P. Bolton; S. Kennedy

DEPARTMENT OF FINANCE AND ADMINISTRATION

Director of Finance and Administration
(£64,768–£104,292), A. J. Walker
Director of Operations (£53,534–£87,598), A. A. Cameron
Director of Personnel Policy (£48,552–£77,869)
Ms S. Craig
Director of Finance Policy (£53,534–£87,598), M. Barram
Director of Internal Review Services (£37,484–£59,764),
R. Russell

DEPARTMENT OF THE OFFICIAL REPORT

Editor (£53,534–£87,598), I. Church
Deputy Editors (£44,038–£69,178), W. G. Garland;
Miss L. Sutherland; Ms C. Fogarty

REFRESHMENT DEPARTMENT

Director of Catering Services (£53,534–£87,598),
Mrs S. Harrison
Catering Operations Manager (Outbuildings)
(£33,095–£49,291), Ms D. Herd
Food and Beverage Operations Manager, R. Gibbs
Executive Chef (£33,095–£49,291), D. Dorricott
Finance and Administration Manager (£33,095–£49,291),
Mrs J. Rissen

SELECT COMMITTEES

The more significant committees, as at May 2002, are:

DEPARTMENTAL COMMITTEES

Accommodation and Works – Chair, Derek Conway, MP;
Clerk, Ms S. McGlashan
Administration – Chair, Mrs M. Roe; Clerk,
Ms S. McGlashan
Culture, Media and Sport – Chair, Rt. Hon.
Gerald Kaufman, MP; Clerks, F. Reid; Miss N. Welfoot
Defence – Chair, Bruce George, MP; Clerks,
Mrs C. Oxborough; Mr Hutton
Education and Skills – Chair, Barry Sheerman, MP,
Clerks, L. Smyth; Miss S. Jones
Environment, Food and Rural Affairs – Chair, Rt. Hon.
David Curry, MP; Clerks, Miss K. Emms; G. Devine
Foreign Affairs – Chair, Rt. Hon. Donald Anderson, MP;
Clerks, Ms S. Priestley; S. Mark
Health – Chair, David Hinchliffe, MP; Clerks, Dr J. S.
Benger; J. Davies
Home Affairs – Chair, Chris Mullin, MP; Clerks,
A. R. Kennon; Ms S. F. Ioannou
International Development – Chair, Tony Baldry, MP;
Clerks, A. H. Doherty; G. K. Clarke
Northern Ireland – Chair, Michael Mates, MP; Clerk,
Ms E. Payne
Scottish Affairs – Chair, Mrs I. Adams; Clerk,
J. D. Whatley
Trade and Industry – Chair, Martin O'Neill, MP; Clerks,
Mrs E. J. Flood; D. Lees
Transport – Chair, Hon. Gwyneth Dunwoody, MP;
Clerk, Mr Cook
Treasury – Chair, Rt. Hon. John McFall, MP; Clerks,
Dr C. Ward; A. Kidner

Urban Affairs sub committee: – Chair, Andrew
Bennett, MP; Clerks; Dr D. Harrison; Ms S. Hartwell
Welsh Affairs – Chair, Martyn Jones, MP; Clerk,
T. Healey
Work and Pensions – Chair, Archy Kirkwood, MP; Clerks,
P. Moon; G. Farrar

NON-DEPARTMENTAL COMMITTEES

Selection – Chair, John McWilliam, MP; Clerk, Dr Egan
Statutory Instruments – Chair, David Tredinnick, MP;
Clerks, H. Yardley; Ms C. Mawson
Deregulation and Regulatory Reform – Chair,
Peter Pike, MP; Clerk, H. Yardley
Environmental Audit – Chair, John Horam, MP; Clerk,
Mrs J. Mulley
European Scrutiny – Chair, Jimmy Hood, MP; Clerk,
D. Gerhold
Human Rights (Joint Committee) – Chair, Jean Carston;
Clerks, P. Evans; A. Mackenzie
Modernisation of the House of Commons – Chair,
Rt. Hon. Robin Cook, MP; Clerks, G. Cubie; A. Sandall
Procedure – Chair, Nicholas Winterton, MP; Clerks,
Dr. R. G. James; M. Atkins
Public Accounts – Chair, Edward Leigh, MP; Clerk,
N. Wright
Public Administration – Chair, Tony Wright, MP; Clerk,
P. Aylett

PARLIAMENTARY INFORMATION

The following is a short glossary of aspects of the work of
Parliament. Unless otherwise stated, references are to
House of Commons procedures.

BILL – Proposed legislation is termed a bill. The stages
of a public bill in the House of Commons are as follows:
First Reading: This stage merely constitutes an order to
have the bill printed
Second Reading: The debate on the principles of the bill
Committee Stage: The detailed examination of a bill, clause
by clause. In most cases this takes place in a standing
committee, or the whole House may act as a committee. A
special standing committee may take evidence before
embarking on detailed scrutiny of the bill. Very rarely, a
bill may be examined by a select committee.
Report Stage: Detailed review of a bill as amended in
committee
Third Reading: Final debate on a bill. Public bills go
through the same stages in the House of Lords, except
that in almost all cases the committee stage is taken in
committee of the whole House.
A bill may start in either House, and has to pass
through both Houses to become law. Both Houses have to
agree the same text of a bill, so that the amendments
made by the second House are then considered in the
originating House, and if not agreed, sent back or
themselves amended, until agreement is reached.

CHILTERN HUNDREDS – A nominal office of profit
under the Crown, the acceptance of which requires an
MP to vacate his/her seat. The Manor of Northstead is
similar. These are the only means by which an MP may
resign.

CONSOLIDATED FUND BILL – A bill to authorise issue
of money to maintain Government services. The bill is
dealt with without debate.

EARLY DAY MOTION – A motion put on the notice
paper by an MP without in general the real prospect of its
being debated. Such motions are expressions of backbench opinion.

FATHER OF THE HOUSE – The Member whose continuous service in the House of Commons is the longest. The present Father of the House is the Rt. Hon. Tam Dalyell.

HOURS OF MEETING – The House of Commons normally meets Monday, Tuesday and Wednesday at 2.30 p.m., Thursdays at 11.30 a.m. and some Fridays at 9.30 a.m. There are ten Fridays without sittings in each session. (*See also* Westminster Hall Sittings, below). The House of Lords normally meets at 2.30 p.m. Monday to Wednesday and at 3 p.m. on Thursday. In the latter part of the session, the House of Lords sometimes sits on Fridays at 11 a.m.

LEADER OF THE OPPOSITION – In 1937 the office of Leader of the Opposition was recognised and a salary was assigned to the post. Since April 2002 this has been £117,597 (including parliamentary salary of £55,118). The present leader of the Opposition is Iain Duncan Smith.

THE LORD CHANCELLOR – The Lord High Chancellor of Great Britain is (*ex officio*) the Speaker of the House of Lords. Unlike the Speaker of the House of Commons, he is a member of the Government, takes part in debates and votes in divisions. He has none of the powers to maintain order that the Speaker in the Commons has, these powers being exercised in the Lords by the House as a whole. The Lord Chancellor sits in the Lords on one of the Woolsacks, couches covered with red cloth and stuffed with wool. If he wishes to address the House in any way except formally as Speaker, he leaves the Woolsack.

NORTHERN IRELAND GRAND COMMITTEE – The Northern Ireland Grand Committee consists of all MPs representing constituencies in Northern Ireland, together with not more than 25 other MPs nominated by the Committee of Selection. The business of the committee includes questions, short debates, ministerial statements, bills, legislative proposals and other matters relating exclusively to Northern Ireland, and delegated legislation. The Northern Ireland Affairs Committee is one of the departmental select committees, empowered to examine the expenditure, administration and policy of the Northern Ireland Office and the administration and expenditure of the Crown Solicitor's Office.

OPPOSITION DAY – A day on which the topic for debate is chosen by the Opposition. There are 20 such days in a normal session. On 17 days, subjects are chosen by the Leader of the Opposition; on the remaining three days by the leader of the next largest opposition party.

PARLIAMENT ACTS 1911 AND 1949 – Under these Acts, bills may become law without the consent of the Lords, though the House of Lords has the power to delay a public bill for 13 months from its first second reading in the House of Commons.

PRIME MINISTER'S QUESTIONS – The Prime Minister answers questions from 3.00 to 3.30 p.m. on Wednesdays.

PRIVATE BILL A bill promoted by a body or an individual to give powers additional to, or in conflict with, the general law, and to which a special procedure applies to enable people affected to object.

PRIVATE MEMBER'S BILL – A public bill promoted by a Member who is not a member of the Government.

PRIVATE NOTICE QUESTION – A question adjudged of urgent importance on submission to the Speaker (in the Lords, the Leader of the House), answered at the end of oral questions, usually at 3.30 p.m.

PRIVILEGE – The following are covered by the privilege of Parliament:
(i) freedom from interference in going to, attending at, and going from, Parliament
(ii) freedom of speech in parliamentary proceedings
(iii) the printing and publishing of anything relating to the proceedings of the two Houses is subject to privilege
(iv) each House is the guardian of its dignity and may punish any insult to the House as a whole

QUESTION TIME – Oral questions are answered by Ministers in the Commons from 2.30 to 3.30 p.m. Monday to Wednesday and 11.30 a.m. to 12.30 p.m. on Thursdays. Questions are also taken at the start of the Lords sittings, with a daily limit of four oral questions.

ROYAL ASSENT – The royal assent is signified by letters patent to such bills and measures as have passed both Houses of Parliament (or bills which have been passed under the Parliament Acts 1911 and 1949). The Sovereign has not given royal assent in person since 1854. On occasion, for instance in the prorogation of Parliament, royal assent may be pronounced to the two Houses by Lords Commissioners. More usually royal assent is notified to each House sitting separately in accordance with the Royal Assent Act 1967. The old French formulae for royal assent are then endorsed on the acts by the Clerk of the Parliaments.

The power to withhold assent resides with the Sovereign but has not been exercised in the UK since 1707.

SELECT COMMITTEES – Consisting usually of ten to fifteen members of all parties, select committees are a means used by both Houses in order to investigate certain matters.

Most select committees in the House of Commons are tied to departments: each committee investigates subjects within a government department's remit. There are other select committees dealing with public accounts (i.e. the spending by the Government of money voted by Parliament) and European legislation, and also domestic committees dealing, for example, with privilege and procedure. Major select committees usually take evidence in public; their evidence and reports are published by The Stationery Office. House of Commons select committees are reconstituted after a general election. For main committees, *see* page 221.

The principal select committee in the House of Lords is that on the European Communities, which has, at present, six sub-committees dealing with all areas of Community policy. The House of Lords also has a select committee on science and technology, which appoints sub-committees to deal with specific subjects, and a select committee on delegated powers and deregulation. For committees, *see* page 218. In addition, *ad hoc* select committees have been set up from time to time to investigate specific subjects. There are also some joint committees of the two Houses, e.g. the committees on statutory instruments and on parliamentary privilege.

THE SPEAKER – The Speaker of the House of Commons is the spokesman and chairman of the Chamber. He or she is elected by the House at the beginning of each Parliament or when the previous Speaker retires or dies. The Speaker neither speaks in debates nor votes in divisions except when the voting is equal.

VACANT SEATS – When a vacancy occurs in the House of Commons during a session of Parliament, the writ for the by-election is moved by a Whip of the party to which the member whose seat has been vacated belonged. If the House is in recess, the Speaker can issue a warrant for a writ, should two members certify to him that a seat is vacant.

WELSH AFFAIRS COMMITTEE – The Welsh Affairs Committee was empowered to examine the expenditure, administration and policy of the Welsh Office. Following devolution, the role of the committee has been questioned. If it continues, it will be concerned with the role and responsibilities of the relevant Secretary of State and the policy of the UK departments as it affects Wales.

WESTMINSTER HALL SITTINGS – Following a report by the Modernisation of the House of Commons Select Committee, the Commons decided in May 1999 to set up a second debating forum. It is known as 'Westminster Hall' and sittings are in the Grand Committee Room on Tuesdays from 10 a.m. to 1 p.m., Wednesdays from 9.30 a.m. to 2 p.m. and Thursdays from 2.30 p.m. for up to three hours. Sittings will be open to the public at the times indicated.

WHIPS – In order to secure the attendance of Members of a particular party in Parliament, particularly on the occasion of an important vote, Whips (originally known as 'Whippers-in') are appointed. The written appeal or circular letter issued by them is also known as a 'whip', its urgency being denoted by the number of times it is underlined. Failure to respond to a three-line whip is tantamount in the Commons to secession (at any rate temporarily) from the party. Whips are provided with office accommodation in both Houses, and Government and some Opposition Whips receive salaries from public funds.

PARLIAMENTARY EDUCATION UNIT – Norman Shaw Building (North), London SW1A 2TT
   Tel: 020-7219 2105; Email: edunit@parliament.uk
   Web: www.explore-parliament.uk

GOVERNMENT OFFICE

The Government is the body of Ministers responsible for the administration of national affairs, determining policy and introducing into Parliament any legislation necessary to give effect to government policy. The majority of Ministers are members of the House of Commons but members of the House of Lords or of neither House may also hold ministerial responsibility. The Lord Chancellor is always a member of the House of Lords. The Prime Minister is, by current convention, always a member of the House of Commons.

THE PRIME MINISTER

The office of Prime Minister, which had been in existence for nearly 200 years, was officially recognised in 1905 and its holder was granted a place in the table of precedence. The Prime Minister, by tradition also First Lord of the Treasury and Minister for the Civil Service, is appointed by the Sovereign and is usually the leader of the party which enjoys, or can secure, a majority in the House of Commons. Other Ministers are appointed by the Sovereign on the recommendation of the Prime Minister, who also allocates functions amongst Ministers and has the power to obtain their resignation or dismissal individually. The Prime Minister informs the Sovereign of state and political matters, advises on the dissolution of Parliament, and makes recommendations for important Crown appointments, the award of honours, etc.

As the chairman of Cabinet meetings and leader of a political party, the Prime Minister is responsible for translating party policy into government activity. As leader of the Government, the Prime Minister is responsible to Parliament and to the electorate for the policies and their implementation.

The Prime Minister also represents the nation in international affairs, e.g. summit conferences.

THE CABINET

The Cabinet developed during the 18th century as an inner committee of the Privy Council, which was the chief source of executive power until that time. The Cabinet is composed of about 20 Ministers chosen by the Prime Minister, usually the heads of government departments (generally known as Secretaries of State unless they have a special title, e.g. Chancellor of the Exchequer), the leaders of the two Houses of Parliament, and the holders of various traditional offices.

The Cabinet's functions are the final determination of policy, control of government and co-ordination of government departments. The exercise of its functions is dependent upon enjoying majority support in the House of Commons. Cabinet meetings are held in private, taking place once or twice a week during parliamentary sittings and less often during a recess. Proceedings are confidential, the members being bound by their oath as Privy Counsellors not to disclose information about the proceedings.

The convention of collective responsibility means that the Cabinet acts unanimously even when Cabinet Ministers do not all agree on a subject. The policies of departmental Ministers must be consistent with the policies of the Government as a whole, and once the Government's policy has been decided, each Minister is expected to support it or resign.

The convention of ministerial responsibility holds a Minister, as the political head of his or her department, accountable to Parliament for the department's work. Departmental Ministers usually decide all matters within their responsibility, although on matters of political importance they normally consult their colleagues collectively. A decision by a departmental Minister is binding on the Government as a whole.

POLITICAL PARTIES

Before the reign of William and Mary the principal officers of state were chosen by and were responsible to the Sovereign alone and not to Parliament or the nation at large. Such officers acted sometimes in concert with one another but more often independently, and the fall of one did not, of necessity, involve that of others, although all were liable to be dismissed at any moment.

In 1693 the Earl of Sunderland recommended to William III the advisability of selecting a ministry from the political party which enjoyed a majority in the House of Commons and the first united ministry was drawn in 1696 from the Whigs, to which party the King owed his throne. This group became known as the Junto and was regarded with suspicion as a novelty in the political life of the nation, being a small section meeting in secret apart from the main body of Ministers. It may be regarded as the forerunner of the Cabinet and in course of time it led to the establishment of the principle of joint responsibility of Ministers, so that internal disagreement caused a change of personnel or resignation of the whole body of Ministers.

The accession of George I, who was unfamiliar with the English language, led to a disinclination on the part of the Sovereign to preside at meetings of his Ministers and caused the appearance of a Prime Minister, a position first acquired by Robert Walpole in 1721 and retained by him without interruption for 20 years and 326 days.

DEVELOPMENT OF PARTIES

In 1828 the Whigs became known as Liberals, a name originally given to it by its opponents to imply laxity of principles, but gradually accepted by the party to indicate its claim to be pioneers and champions of political reform and progressive legislation. In 1861 a Liberal Registration Association was founded and Liberal Associations became widespread. In 1877 a National Liberal Federation was formed, with headquarters in London. The Liberal Party was in power for long periods during the second half of the 19th-century and for several years during the first quarter of the 20th-century, but after a split in the party the numbers elected were small from 1931. In 1988, a majority of the Liberals agreed on a merger with the Social Democratic Party under the title Social and Liberal Democrats; since 1989 they have been known as the Liberal Democrats. A minority continue separately as the Liberal Party.

Soon after the change from Whig to Liberal the Tory Party became known as Conservative, a name believed to have been invented by John Wilson Croker in 1830 and to have been generally adopted about the time of the passing of the Reform Act of 1832 to indicate that the preservation of national institutions was the leading principle of the party. After the Home Rule crisis of 1886 the dissentient Liberals entered into a compact with the Conservatives, under which the latter undertook not to contest their seats, but a separate Liberal Unionist organisation was maintained until 1912, when it was united with the Conservatives.

Labour candidates for Parliament made their first appearance at the general election of 1892, when there were 27 standing as Labour or Liberal-Labour. In 1900 the Labour Representation Committee was set up in order to establish a distinct Labour group in Parliament, with its own whips, its own policy, and a readiness to co-operate with any party which might be engaged in promoting legislation in the direct interest of labour. In 1906 the LRC became known as the Labour Party.

The Council for Social Democracy was announced by four former Labour Cabinet Ministers in January 1981 and in March 1981 the Social Democratic Party was launched. Later that year the SDP and the Liberal Party formed an electoral alliance. In 1988 a majority of the SDP agreed on a merger with the Liberal Party but a minority continued as a separate party under the SDP title. In 1990 it was decided to wind up the party organisation and its three sitting MPs were known as independent social democrats. None were returned at the 1992 general election.

Plaid Cymru was founded in 1926 to provide an independent political voice for Wales and to campaign for self-government in Wales.

The Scottish National Party was founded in 1934 to campaign for independence for Scotland.

The Social Democratic and Labour Party was founded in 1970, emerging from the civil rights movement of the 1960s, with the aim of promoting reform, reconciliation and partnership across the sectarian divide in Northern Ireland and of opposing violence from any quarter.

The Democratic Unionist Party was founded in 1971 to resist moves by the Ulster Unionist Party which were considered a threat to the Union. Its aim is to maintain Northern Ireland as an integral part of the UK.

The Ulster Unionist Council first met formally in 1905. Its objectives are to maintain Northern Ireland as an integral part of the UK and to promote the aims of the Ulster Unionist Party.

GOVERNMENT AND OPPOSITION

The government of the day is formed by the party which wins the largest number of seats in the House of Commons at a general election, or which has the support of a majority of members in the House of Commons. By tradition, the leader of the majority party is asked by the Sovereign to form a government, while the largest minority party becomes the official Opposition with its own leader and a 'Shadow Cabinet'. Leaders of the Government and Opposition sit on the front benches of the Commons with their supporters (the back-benchers) sitting behind them.

FINANCIAL SUPPORT

Financial support to Opposition parties in the House of Commons was introduced in 1975 and is commonly known as Short Money, after Edward Short, the Leader of the House at that time, who introduced the scheme. Short money allocation for 2002–3 is:

Conservative	£3,459,536.50
Liberal Democrats	1,174,410.37
Plaid Cymru	69,897.25
SNP	113,091.76
SDLP	55,112.74
Democratic Unionists	80,017.07
Ulster Unionists	95,832.96

A specific allocation for the Leader of the Opposition's office was introduced in April 1999 and has been set at £531,621.39 for 2002–3.

Financial support to the Opposition parties in the House of Lords was introduced in 1996 and is commonly known as Cranborne Money.

The parties included here are those with MPs sitting in the House of Commons in the present Parliament. Addresses of other political parties may be found in the Societies and Institutions section.

CONSERVATIVE PARTY

Conservative Central Office, 32 Smith Square, London SW1P 3HH
Tel: 020-7222 9000; Fax: 020-7222 1135;
Email: info@conservatives.com
Web: www.conservatives.com

SHADOW CABINET *as at 1 August 2002*
Leader of the Opposition, Iain Duncan Smith, MP
Deputy Leader and Secretary of State for Foreign and Commonwealth Affairs, Rt. Hon. Michael Ancram, QC, MP
Agriculture (Minister), John Hayes, MP
*Attorney General, Bill Cash, MP
Chancellor of the Exchequer, Rt. Hon. Michael Howard, QC, MP
Party Chairman, Mrs Theresa May, MP
Chief Secretary to the Treasury, Howard Flight, MP
Secretary of State for Culture, Media and Sport, John Whittingdale, OBE, MP
Secretary of State for Defence, Hon. Bernard Jenkin, MP
Secretary of State for Education and Skills, Damian Green, MP
Secretary of State for Environment, Food and Rural Affairs, David Lidington, MP
Secretary of State for Health, Dr Liam Fox, MP
Secretary of State for Home Department, Rt. Hon. Oliver Letwin, MP

Secretary of State for International Development,
Mrs Caroline Spelman, MP
Leader of the House of Commons, Rt. Hon. Eric Forth, MP
Leader of the House of Lords, Rt. Hon. Lord Strathclyde
Lord Chancellor's Department, Rt. Hon.
Lord Kingsland, QC
Secretary of State for Northern Ireland,
Quentin Davies, MP
Secretary of State for Office of the Deputy Prime Minister,
Rt. Hon. David Davis, MP
Secretary of State for Scotland, Mrs Jacqui Lait, MP
Secretary of State for Trade and Industry, Tim Yeo, MP
Secretary of State for Transport, Tim Collins, CBE, MP
Secretary of State for Wales, Nigel Evans, MP
Secretary of State for Work and Pensions,
David Willetts, MP
Whip (House of Commons), Rt. Hon. David Maclean, MP
Whip (House of Lords), Rt. Hon. Lord Cope of Berkeley
*not a member of the shadow cabinet but attends at the
invitation of the Leader

SCOTTISH CONSERVATIVE AND UNIONIST PARTY

83 Princes Street, Edinburgh EH2 2ER
Tel: 0131-247 6890; Fax: 0131-247 6891;
Email: central.office@scottishtories.org.uk
Web: www.scottishtories.org.uk
Chairman, David Mitchell, CBE
Deputy Chairman, Mrs M. Goodman
Hon. Treasurer, Mrs J. Slater
Campaign Executive, Mark Neeham

LABOUR PARTY

Millbank Tower, Millbank, London SW1P 4GT
Tel: 0870-590 0200; Fax: 020-7802 1234;
Email: join@labour.org.uk; Web: www.labour.org.uk

Parliamentary Party Leader, Rt. Hon. Anthony
(Tony) Blair, MP
Deputy Party Leader, Rt. Hon. John Prescott, MP
Leader in the Lords, Lord Williams of Mostyn, QC
Chair, Ms Jean Corston, MP
Vice-Chairs, Anne Clwyd, MP; Helen Jackson, MP
General Secretary, D. Triesman
General Secretary, Scottish Labour Party, L. Quinn

LIBERAL DEMOCRATS

4 Cowley Street, London SW1P 3NB
Tel: 020-7222 7999; Fax: 020-7799 2170;
Email: libdems@cix.co.uk
Web: www.libdems.org.uk

President, Lord Dholakia
Hon. Treasurer, Reg Clark
Chief Executive, Hugh Rickard
Parliamentary Party Leader, Rt. Hon.
Charles Kennedy, MP
Shadow Leader in the House of Commons, Paul Tyler, MP
Leader in the Lords, Baroness Williams of Grosby

LIBERAL DEMOCRAT SPOKESMEN *as at August 2002*
Deputy Leader, Rt. Hon. Alan Beith, MP
Culture, Media and Sport, Constitution,
Nick Harvey, MP
Defence, Paul Keetch, MP
Education and Skills, Phil Willis, MP
Environment, Food and Rural Affairs, Malcolm Bruce, MP
Foreign Affairs, Rt. Hon. Menzies Campbell, MP
Home Affairs, Simon Hughes, MP
Health, Dr Evan Harris, MP
International Development, Dr Jenny Tonge, MP

Scotland, John Thurso, MP
Trade and Industry, Dr Vincent Cable, MP
Transport, Don Foster, MP
Treasury, Matthew Taylor, MP
Wales and Northern Ireland, Lembit Opik, MP
Work and Pensions, Prof. Steve Webb, MP
Chair of the Parliamentary Party, Mark Oaten, MP

LIBERAL DEMOCRAT WHIPS
House of Lords, The Lord Roper of Thorney Island
House of Commons, Andrew Stunell, MP (*Chief Whip*)

SCOTTISH LIBERAL DEMOCRATS

4 Clifton Terrace, Edinburgh EH12 5DR
Tel: 0131-337 2314; Fax: 0131-337 3566;
Email: administration@scotlibdems.org.uk
Web: www.scotlibdems.org.uk

Party President, Malcolm Bruce, MP
Party Leader, Jim Wallace, MSP
Convener, Cllr Ian Yuill
Vice-Conveners, Neil Wallace; Moira Craig
Treasurer, D. R. Sullivan
Chief Executive, Kilvert Croft

WELSH LIBERAL DEMOCRATS

Bay View House, 102 Bute Street, Cardiff CF10 5AD
Tel: 029-2031 3400; Fax: 029-2031 3401;
Email: ldwales@cix.co.uk
Web: www.welshlibdems.org.uk

Party President, Rob Humphreys
Party Leader, Lembit Opik, MP
Chairman, Rob Humphreys
Treasurer, Phill Lloyd
Secretary, Brain Lopez
Administrative Officer, Jeni Batchelor
Chief Executive, Chris Lines

PLAID CYMRU – THE PARTY OF WALES

18 Park Grove, Cardiff CF10 3BN
Tel: 029-2064 6000;
Fax: 029-2064 6001;
Email: post@plaidcymru.org
Web: www.plaidcymru.org

Party President, Ieuan Wyn Jones, AM
Chairman, Elin Jones, AM
Hon. Treasurer, Jeff Canning
Chief Executive/General Secretary, Dafydd Trystan

SCOTTISH NATIONAL PARTY

107 McDonald Road, Edinburgh EH7 4NW
Tel: 0131-525 8900;
Fax: 0131-525 8901;
Web: www.snp.org

Parliamentary Party Leader, John Swinney, MSP
Chief Whip, Kay Ullrich, MSP
National Convener, John Swinney, MSP
Senior Vice-Convener, Roseanna Cunningham, MSP
National Treasurer, Jim Mather
National Secretary, Stewart Hosie
Chief Executive, Peter Murrell

NORTHERN IRELAND

DEMOCRATIC UNIONIST PARTY

91 Dundela Avenue, Belfast BT4 3BU
Tel: 028-9047 1155;
Fax: 028-9047 1797;
Email: info@dup.org.uk
Web: www.dup.org.uk

Parliamentary Party Leader, Ian Paisley, MP, MEP, MLA
Deputy Leader, Peter Robinson, MP, MLA
Chairman, Maurice Morrow, MLA
Chief Executive, Allan Ewart
Hon. Treasurer, Gregory Campbell, MP, MLA
Party Secretary, Nigel Dodds, MP, MLA

SINN FEIN

53 Falls Road, Belfast BT12 4PD
Tel: 028-9030 1719; Fax: 028-9022 3002;
Web: www.sinnfein.ie

Party President, Gerry Adams, MP, MLA
Vice-President, Pat Doherty, MP, MLA
Chief Negotiator, Martin McGuinnes, MP, MLA

SOCIAL DEMOCRATIC AND LABOUR PARTY

121 Ormeau Road, Belfast BT7 1SH
Tel: 028-9024 7700;
Fax: 028-9023 6699;
Email: sdlp@indigo.ie
Web: www.sdlp.ie

Parliamentary Party Leader, Mark Durkan, MLA
Deputy Leader, Ms Brid Rodgers, MLA
Chief Whip, Eddie McGrady, MP
Chairman, Alex Attwood, MLA

Hon. Treasurer, Gerard O'Hare
General Secretary, Geraldine Cosgrove

ULSTER UNIONIST PARTY

429 Holywood Road, Belfast BT4 2LN
Tel: 028-9076 5500;
Fax: 028-9076 9419;
Email: uup@uup.org;
Web: www.uup.org

Party Leader, Rt. Hon. David Trimble, MP, MLA
Chief Whip, Ald. Roy Beggs, MP

ULSTER UNIONIST COUNCIL

President, Revd Martin Smyth, MP
Leader, Rt. Hon. David Trimble, MP, MLA
Chairman of the Executive Committee, James Cooper
Hon. Treasurer, Jack Allen, OBE
Vice-Chairman, Donn McConnell, OBE
Vice Presidents, Jeffrey Donaldson, MP; Sir Reg Empey,
  OBE, MLA; Lord Maginnis of Drumglass;
  Jim Nicolson, MEP
Hon. Secretaries, Lord Rogan of Lower Iveagh;
  Arlene Foster; Cllr Jim Rodgers; Dermot Nesbitt, MLA
Assistant Honorary Treasurer, May Steele, MBE

MEMBERS OF PARLIAMENT

*Abbott, Ms Diane (b. 1953) Lab., Hackney North and Stoke Newington, Maj. 13,651
*Adams, Gerard (Gerry) (b. 1948) SF, Belfast West, Maj. 19,342
*Adams, Mrs K. Irene (b. 1948) Lab., Paisley North, Maj. 9,321
*Ainger, Nicholas R. (b. 1949) Lab., Carmarthen West and Pembrokeshire South, Maj. 4,538
*Ainsworth, Peter M. (b. 1956) C., Surrey East, Maj. 13,203
*Ainsworth, Robert W. (b. 1952) Lab., Coventry North East, Maj. 15,751
*Alexander, Douglas G. (b. 1967) Lab., Paisley South, Maj. 11,910
Allan, Richard B. (b. 1966) LD, Sheffield Hallam, Maj. 9,347
*Allen, Graham W. (b. 1953) Lab., Nottingham North, Maj. 12,240
*Amess, David A. A. (b. 1952) C., Southend West, Maj. 7941
*Ancram, Rt. Hon. Michael A. F. J. K. (Earl of Ancram) (b. 1945) C., Devizes, Maj. 11,896
*Anderson, Rt. Hon. Donald (b. 1939) Lab., Swansea East, Maj. 16,148
*Anderson, Mrs Janet (b. 1949) Lab., Rossendale and Darwen, Maj. 5,223
*Arbuthnot, Rt. Hon. James N. (b. 1952) C., Hampshire North East, Maj. 13,257
*Armstrong, Rt. Hon. Hilary J. (b. 1945) Lab., Durham North West, Maj. 16,333
Atherton, Ms Candy K. (b. 1955) Lab., Falmouth and Camborne, Maj. 4,527
Atkins, Ms Charlotte (b. 1950) Lab., Staffordshire Moorlands, Maj. 5,838
*Atkinson, David A. (b. 1940) C., Bournemouth East, Maj. 3,434
*Atkinson, Peter L. (b. 1943) C., Hexham, Maj. 2,529
*Austin, John E. (b. 1944) Lab., Erith and Thamesmead, Maj. 11,167
Bacon, Richard (b. 1962) C., Norfolk South, Maj. 6,893
*Bailey, Adrian (b. 1945) Lab. Co-op., West Bromwich West, Maj. 11,355
Baird, Vera (b. 1950) Lab., Redcar, Maj. 13,443
*Baker, Norman (b. 1957) LD, Lewes, Maj. 9,710
*Baldry, Anthony B. (b. 1950) C., Banbury, Maj. 5,219
*Banks, Anthony L. (b. 1943) Lab., West Ham, Maj. 15,645
Barker, Gregory (b. 1966) C., Bexhill and Battle, Maj. 10,503
*Barnes, Harold (b. 1936) Lab., Derbyshire North East, Maj. 12,258
Baron, John (b. 1959) C., Billericay, Maj. 5,013
Barrett, John (b. 1954) LD, Edinburgh West, Maj. 7,589
*Barron, Rt. Hon. Kevin J. (b. 1946) Lab., Rother Valley, Maj. 14,882
*Battle, John D. (b. 1951) Lab., Leeds West, Maj. 14,935
*Bayley, Hugh (b. 1952) Lab., City of York, Maj. 13,779
Beard, Nigel C. (b. 1936) Lab., Bexleyheath and Crayford, Maj. 1,472
*Beckett, Rt. Hon. Margaret (b. 1943) Lab., Derby South, Maj. 13,855
Begg, Ms Anne (b. 1955) Lab., Aberdeen South, Maj. 4,388
*Beggs, Roy (b. 1936) UUP, Antrim East, Maj. 128
*Beith, Rt. Hon. Alan J. (b. 1943) LD, Berwick upon Tweed, Maj. 8,458

*Bell, Stuart (b. 1938) Lab., Middlesbrough, Maj. 16,330
Bellingham, Henry (b. 1,955) Lab., Norfolk North West, Maj. 3,485
*Benn, Hilary J. (b. 1953) Lab., Leeds Central, Maj. 14,381
*Bennett, Andrew F. (b. 1939) Lab., Denton and Reddish, Maj. 15,330
*Benton, Joseph E. (b. 1933) Lab., Bootle, Maj. 19,043
Bercow, John S. (b. 1963) C., Buckingham, Maj. 13,325
*Beresford, Sir Paul (b. 1946) C., Mole Valley, Maj. 10,153
*Berry, Dr Roger D.Phil. (b. 1948) Lab., Kingswood, Maj. 13,962
*Best, Harold (b. 1939) Lab., Leeds North West, Maj. 5,236
*Betts, Clive J. C. (b. 1950) Lab., Sheffield Attercliffe, Maj. 18,844
Blackman, Ms Elizabeth M. (b. 1949) Lab., Erewash, Maj. 6,932
*Blair, Rt. Hon. Anthony C. L. (b. 1953) Lab., Sedgefield, Maj. 17,713
Blears, Hazel A. (b. 1956) Lab., Salford, Maj. 11,012
Blizzard, Robert J. (b. 1950) Lab., Waveney, Maj. 8,553
*Blunkett, Rt. Hon. David (b. 1947) Lab., Sheffield Brightside, Maj. 17,049
Blunt, Crispin J. R. (b. 1960) C., Reigate, Maj. 8,025
*Boateng, Rt. Hon. Paul Y. (b. 1951) Lab., Brent South, Maj. 17,380
Borrow, David S. (b. 1952) Lab., Ribble South, Maj. 3,792
*Boswell, Timothy E. (b. 1942) C., Daventry, Maj. 9,649
*Bottomley, Peter J. (b. 1944) C., Worthing West, Maj. 9,037
*Bottomley, Rt. Hon. Virginia H. B. M. (b. 1948) C., Surrey South West, Maj. 861
*Bradley, Rt. Hon. (b. 1950) Lab., Manchester Withington, Maj. 11,524
Bradley, Peter C. S. (b. 1953) Lab., The Wrekin, Maj. 3,587
Bradshaw, Benjamin P. J. (b. 1960) Lab., Exeter, Maj. 11,759
*Brady, Graham (b. 1967) C., Altrincham and Sale West, Maj. 2,941
Brake, Thomas A. (b. 1962) LD, Carshalton and Wallington, Maj. 4,547
*Brazier, Julian W. H. TD (b. 1953) C., Canterbury, Maj. 2,069
Breed, Colin E. (b. 1947) LD, Cornwall South East, Maj. 5,375
Brennan, Kevin (b. 1959) Lab., Cardiff West, Maj. 11,321
Brooke, Annette (b. 1947) LD, Dorset Mid and Poole North, Maj. 384
*Brown, Rt. Hon. J. Gordon Ph.D. (b. 1951) Lab., Dunfermline East, Maj. 15,063
*Brown, Rt. Hon. Nicholas H. (b. 1950) Lab., Newcastle upon Tyne East and Wallsend, Maj. 14,223
Brown, Russell L. (b. 1951) Lab., Dumfries, Maj. 8,834
Browne, Desmond (b. 1952) Lab., Kilmarnock and Loudoun, Maj. 10,334
*Browning, Mrs Angela F. (b. 1946) C., Tiverton and Honiton, Maj. 6,284
*Bruce, Malcolm G. (b. 1944) LD, Gordon, Maj. 7,879
Bryant, Chris (b. 1962) Lab., Rhondda, Maj. 16,047
Buck, Ms Karen P. (b. 1958) Lab., Regent's Park and Kensington North, Maj. 10,266
*Burden, Richard H. (b. 1954) Lab., Birmingham Northfield, Maj. 7,798
Burgon, Colin (b. 1948) Lab., Elmet, Maj. 4,171

Burnett, John P. A. (*b.* 1945) *LD, Devon West and Torridge,* Maj. 1,194

*Burnham, Andy (*b.* 1970) *Lab., Leigh,* Maj. 16362

*Burns, Simon H. M. (*b.* 1952) *C., Chelmsford West,* Maj. 6,261

Burnside, David (*b.* 1952) *UUP, Antrim South,* Maj. 1,011

Burstow, Paul K. (*b.* 1962) *LD, Sutton and Cheam,* Maj. 4,304

Burt, Alastair (*b.* 1955) *C., Bedfordshire North East,* Maj. 8,577

*Butterfill, John V. (*b.* 1941) *C., Bournemouth West,* Maj. 4,718

*Byers, Rt. Hon. Stephen J. (*b.* 1953) *Lab., Tyneside North,* Maj. 20,668

Cable, Dr J. Vincent (*b.* 1943) *LD, Twickenham,* Maj. 7,655

*Caborn, Rt. Hon. Richard G. (*b.* 1943) *Lab., Sheffield Central,* Maj. 12,544

Cairns, David (*b.* 1966) *Lab., Greenock and Inverclyde,* Maj. 9,890

Calton, Patsy (*b.* 1948) *LD, Cheadle,* Maj. 33

Cameron, David (*b.* 1966) *C., Witney,* Maj. 7,973

Campbell, Alan (*b.* 1957) *Lab., Tynemouth,* Maj. 8,678

*Campbell, Mrs Anne (*b.* 1940) *Lab., Cambridge,* Maj. 8,579

*Campbell, Ronald (*b.* 1943) *Lab., Blyth Valley,* Maj. 12,188

*Campbell, Rt. Hon. W. Menzies CBE, QC (*b.* 1941) *LD, Fife North East,* Maj. 9,736

Campbell, Gregory (*b.* 1953) *DUP, Londonderry East,* Maj. 1,901

*Caplin, Ivor K. (*b.* 1958) *Lab., Hove,* Maj. 3,171

Carmichael, Alistair (*b.* 1965) *LD, Orkney and Shetland,* Maj. 3475

Casale, Roger M. (*b.* 1960) *Lab., Wimbledon,* Maj. 3,744

*Cash, William N. P. (*b.* 1940) *C., Stone,* Maj. 6,036

Caton, Martin P. (*b.* 1951) *Lab., Gower,* Maj. 7,395

*Cawsey, Ian A. (*b.* 1960) *Lab., Brigg and Goole,* Maj. 3,961

Challen, Colin (*b.* 1953) *Lab., Morley and Rothwell,* Maj. 12,090

*Chapman, J. K. (Ben) (*b.* 1940) *Lab., Wirral South,* Maj. 5,049

*Chapman, Sir Sydney (*b.* 1935) *C., Chipping Barnet,* Maj. 2,701

*Chaytor, David M. (*b.* 1949) *Lab., Bury North,* Maj. 6,532

*Chidgey, David W. G. (*b.* 1942) *LD, Eastleigh,* Maj. 3,058

*Chope, Christopher R. OBE (*b.* 1947) *C., Christchurch,* Maj. 13,544

*Clapham, Michael (*b.* 1943) *Lab., Barnsley West and Penistone,* Maj. 12,352

*Clappison, W. James (*b.* 1956) *C., Hertsmere,* Maj. 4,902

Clark, Ms Helen R. (*b.* 1954) *Lab., Peterborough,* Maj. 384

Clark, Dr Lynda M. QC (*b.* 1949) *Lab., Edinburgh Pentlands,* Maj. 1,742

Clark, Paul G. (*b.* 1957) *Lab., Gillingham,* Maj. 2,272

Clarke, Anthony R. (*b.* 1963) *Lab., Northampton South,* Maj. 885

*Clarke, Rt. Hon. Charles R. (*b.* 1950) *Lab., Norwich South,* Maj. 8,816

*Clarke, Rt. Hon. Kenneth H. QC (*b.* 1940) *C., Rushcliffe,* Maj. 7,357

*Clarke, Rt. Hon. Thomas CBE (*b.* 1941) *Lab., Coatbridge and Chryston,* Maj. 15,314

*Clelland, David G. (*b.* 1943) *Lab., Tyne Bridge,* Maj. 14,889

*Clifton-Brown, Geoffrey R. (*b.* 1953) *C., Cotswold,* Maj. 11,983

*Clwyd, Anne (*b.* 1937) *Lab., Cynon Valley,* Maj. 12,998

*Coaker, Vernon R. (*b.* 1953) *Lab., Gedling,* Maj. 5,598

*Coffey, Ms M. Ann (*b.* 1946) *Lab., Stockport,* Maj. 11,569

*Cohen, Harry M. (*b.* 1949) *Lab., Leyton and Wanstead,* Maj. 12,904

Coleman, Iain (*b.* 1958) *Lab., Hammersmith and Fulham,* Maj. 2,015

Collins, Timothy W. G. CBE (*b.* 1964) *C., Westmorland and Lonsdale,* Maj. 3,147

Colman, Anthony (*b.* 1943) *Lab., Putney,* Maj. 2,771

*Connarty, Michael (*b.* 1947) *Lab., Falkirk East,* Maj. 10,712

Conway, Derek (*b.* 1953) *C., Old Bexley and Sidcup,* Maj. 3,345

*Cook, Frank (*b.* 1935) *Lab., Stockton North,* Maj. 14,647

*Cook, Rt. Hon. R. F. (Robin) (*b.* 1946) *Lab., Livingston,* Maj. 10,616

Cooper, Ms Yvette (*b.* 1969) *Lab., Pontefract and Castleford,* Maj. 16,378

*Corbyn, Jeremy *b.* (*b.* 1949) *Lab., Islington North,* Maj. 12,958

*Cormack, Sir Patrick FSA (*b.* 1939) *C., Staffordshire South,* Maj. 6,881

*Corston, Ms Jean A. (*b.* 1942) *Lab., Bristol East,* Maj. 13,392

Cotter, Brian J. (*b.* 1938) *LD, Weston-super-Mare,* Maj. 338

*Cousins, James M. (*b.* 1944) *Lab., Newcastle upon Tyne Central,* Maj. 11,605

*Cox, Thomas M. (*b.* 1930) *Lab., Tooting,* Maj. 10,400

*Cran, James D. (*b.* 1944) *C., Beverley and Holderness,* Maj. 781

Cranston, Ross F. QC (*b.* 1948) *Lab., Dudley North,* Maj. 6,800

*Crausby, David A. (*b.* 1946) *Lab., Bolton North East,* Maj. 8,422

Cruddas, Jon (*b.* 1965) *Lab., Dagenham,* Maj. 8,693

Cryer, Mrs C. Ann (*b.* 1939) *Lab., Keighley,* Maj. 4,005

Cryer, John R. (*b.* 1964) *Lab., Hornchurch,* Maj. 1,482

*Cummings, John S. (*b.* 1943) *Lab., Easington,* Maj. 21,949

*Cunningham, Rt. Hon. Dr J. A. (Jack) Ph.D. (*b.* 1939) *Lab., Copeland,* Maj. 4,964

*Cunningham, James D. (*b.* 1941) *Lab., Coventry South,* Maj. 8,279

Cunningham, Tony (*b.* 1952) *Lab., Workington,* Maj. 10,850

*Curry, Rt. Hon. David M. (*b.* 1944) *C., Skipton and Ripon,* Maj. 12,930

Curtis-Thomas, Ms Claire (*b.* 1958) *Lab., Crosby,* Maj. 8,353

Daisley, Paul (*b.* 1957) *Lab., Brent East,* Maj. 13,047

*Dalyell, Tam (*b.* 1932) *Lab., Linlithgow,* Maj. 9,129

*Darling, Rt. Hon. Alistair M. (*b.* 1953) *Lab., Edinburgh Central,* Maj. 8,142

Davey, Edward J. (*b.* 1965) *LD, Kingston and Surbiton,* Maj. 15,676

Davey, Ms Valerie (*b.* 1940) *Lab., Bristol West,* Maj. 4,426

David, Wayne (*b.* 1957) *Lab., Caerphilly,* Maj. 14,425

*Davidson, Ian G. (*b.* 1950) *Lab. Co-op., Glasgow Pollok,* Maj. 11,268

*Davies, Rt. Hon. D. J. Denzil (*b.* 1938) *Lab., Llanelli,* Maj. 6,403

Davies, Geraint R. (*b.* 1960) *Lab., Croydon Central,* Maj. 3,984

*Davies, J. Quentin (*b.* 1944) *C., Grantham and Stamford,* Maj. 4,518

*Davis, Rt. Hon. David M. (*b.* 1948) *C., Haltemprice and Howden,* Maj. 1,903

*Davis, Rt. Hon. Terence A. G. (*b.* 1938) *Lab., Birmingham Hodge Hill,* Maj. 11,618

Dawson, T. Hilton (*b.* 1953) *Lab., Lancaster and Wyre,* Maj. 481

Dean, Ms Janet E. A. (*b.* 1949) *Lab., Burton,* Maj. 4,849

*Denham, Rt. Hon. John Y. (*b.* 1953) *Lab., Southampton Itchen,* Maj. 11,223

*Dhanda, Parmjit (*b.* 1971) *Lab., Gloucester,* Maj. 3,880

*Dismore, Andrew H. (*b.* 1954) *Lab., Hendon,* Maj. 7,417

Djanogly, Jonathan (*b.* 1965) *C., Huntingdon,* Maj. 12,792

Dobbin, James (*b.* 1941) *Lab. Co-op., Heywood and Middleton,* Maj. 11,670

*Dobson, Rt. Hon. Frank G. (*b.* 1940) *Lab., Holborn and St Pancras,* Maj. 11,175

Dodds, Nigel MLA (*b.* 1958) *DUP, Belfast North,* Maj. 6,387

Donaldson, Jeffrey M. (*b.* 1962) *UUP, Lagan Valley,* Maj. 18,342

Doherty, Pat (*b.* 1945) *SF, Tyrone West,* Maj. 5,040

*Donohoe, Brian H. (*b.* 1948) *Lab., Cunninghame South,* Maj. 11,230

Doran, Frank (*b.* 1949) *Lab., Aberdeen Central,* Maj. 6,646

*Dorrell, Rt. Hon. Stephen J. (*b.* 1952) *C., Charnwood,* Maj. 7,739

Doughty, Sue (*b.* 1955) *LD, Guildford,* Maj. 538

*Dowd, James P. (*b.* 1951) *Lab., Lewisham West,* Maj. 11,920

Drew, David E. (*b.* 1952) *Lab. Co-op., Stroud,* Maj. 5,039

Drown, Ms Julia K. (*b.* 1962) *Lab., Swindon South,* Maj. 7,341

*Duncan, Alan J. C. (*b.* 1957) *C., Rutland and Melton,* Maj. 8,612

Duncan, Peter (*b.* 1965) *C., Galloway and Upper Nithsdale,* Maj. 74

*Duncan Smith, G. Iain (*b.* 1954) *C., Chingford and Woodford Green,* Maj. 5487

*Dunwoody, Hon. Mrs Gwyneth P. (*b.* 1930) *Lab., Crewe and Nantwich,* Maj. 9,906

*Eagle, Ms Angela (*b.* 1961) *Lab., Wallasey,* Maj. 12,276

Eagle, Ms Maria (*b.* 1961) *Lab., Liverpool Garston,* Maj. 12,494

Edwards, Huw W. E. (*b.* 1953) *Lab., Monmouth,* Maj. 384

Efford, Clive S. (*b.* 1958) *Lab., Eltham,* Maj. 6,996

*Ellman, Ms Louise J. (*b.* 1945) *Lab. Co-op., Liverpool Riverside,* Maj. 13,950

*Ennis, Jeffrey (*b.* 1952) *Lab., Barnsley East and Mexborough,* Maj. 16,789

*Etherington, William (*b.* 1941) *Lab., Sunderland North,* Maj. 13,354

*Evans, Nigel M. (*b.* 1957) *C., Ribble Valley,* Maj. 11,238

Ewing, Annabelle (*b.* 1960) *SNP, Perth,* Maj. 48

*Fabricant, Michael L. D. (*b.* 1950) *C., Lichfield,* Maj. 4,426

*Fallon, Michael C. (*b.* 1952) *C., Sevenoaks,* Maj. 10,154

Farrelly, Paul (*b.* 1962) *Lab., Newcastle under Lyme,* Maj. 9,986

*Field, Rt. Hon. Frank (*b.* 1942) *Lab., Birkenhead,* Maj. 15,591

*Field, Mark (*b.* 1934) *C., Cities of London and Westminster,* Maj. 4,499

*Fisher, Mark (*b.* 1944) *Lab., Stoke-on-Trent Central,* Maj. 11,845

*Fitzpatrick, James (*b.* 1952) *Lab., Poplar and Canning Town,* Maj. 14,104

*Fitzsimons, Ms Lorna (*b.* 1967) *Lab., Rochdale,* Maj. 5,655

*Flight, Howard E. (*b.* 1948) *C., Arundel and South Downs,* Maj. 13,704

*Flint, Ms Caroline L. (*b.* 1961) *Lab., Don Valley,* Maj. 9,520

Flook, Adrian (*b.* 1963) *C., Taunton,* Maj. 235

*Flynn, Paul P. (*b.* 1935) *Lab., Newport West,* Maj. 9,304

Follett, Ms D. Barbara (*b.* 1942) *Lab., Stevenage,* Maj. 8,566

*Forth, Rt. Hon. Eric (*b.* 1944) *C., Bromley and Chislehurst,* Maj. 9,037

*Foster, Rt. Hon. Derek (*b.* 1937) *Lab., Bishop Auckland,* Maj. 13,926

*Foster, Donald M. E. (*b.* 1947) *LD, Bath,* Maj. 9,894

*Foster, Michael J. (*b.* 1946) *Lab., Hastings and Rye,* Maj. 4,308

Foster, Michael (*b.* 1963) *Lab., Worcester,* Maj. 5,766

*Foulkes, George (*b.* 1942) *Lab. Co-op., Carrick, Cumnock and Doon Valley,* Maj. 14,856

*Fox, Dr Liam (*b.* 1961) *C., Woodspring,* Maj. 8,798

Francis, David, Hywel (*b.* 1946) *Lab., Aberavon,* Maj. 16,108

Francois, Mark Ph.D. (*b.* 1965) *C., Rayleigh,* Maj. 8,290

*Gale, Roger J. (*b.* 1943) *C., Thanet North,* Maj. 6,650

*Galloway, George (*b.* 1954) *Lab., Glasgow Kelvin,* Maj. 7,260

*Gapes, Michael J. (*b.* 1952) *Lab. Co-op., Ilford South,* Maj. 13,997

Gardiner, Barry S. (*b.* 1957) *Lab., Brent North,* Maj. 10,205

*Garnier, Edward H. QC (*b.* 1952) *C., Harborough,* Maj. 5,252

George, Andrew H. (*b.* 1958) *LD, St Ives,* Maj. 10,053

*George, Rt. Hon. Bruce T. (*b.* 1942) *Lab., Walsall South,* Maj. 9,931

*Gerrard, Neil F. (*b.* 1942) *Lab., Walthamstow,* Maj. 15,181

*Gibb, Nicholas J. (*b.* 1960) *C., Bognor Regis and Littlehampton,* Maj. 5,643

*Gibson, Dr Ian (*b.* 1938) *Lab., Norwich North,* Maj. 5863

*Gidley, Sandra (*b.* 1957) *LD, Romsey,* Maj. 2,370

Gildernew, Michelle (*b.* 1970) *SF, Fermanagh and South Tyrone,* Maj. 53

*Gillan, Mrs Cheryl E. K. (*b.* 1952) *C., Chesham and Amersham,* Maj. 11,882

Gilroy, Mrs Linda (*b.* 1949) *Lab. Co-op., Plymouth Sutton,* Maj. 7,517

*Godsiff, Roger D. (*b.* 1946) *Lab., Birmingham Sparkbrook and Small Heath,* Maj. 16,246

Goggins, Paul G. (*b.* 1953) *Lab., Wythenshawe and Sale East,* Maj. 12,608

Goodman, Paul (*b.* 1960) *C., Wycombe,* Maj. 3,168

Gray, James W. (*b.* 1954) *C., Wiltshire North,* Maj. 3,878

Grayling, Chris (*b.* 1962) *C., Epsom and Ewell,* Maj. 10,080

Green, Damian H. (*b.* 1956) *C., Ashford,* Maj. 7,359

Green, Mathew (*b.* 1970) *LD, Ludlow,* Maj. 1,630

*Greenway, John R. (*b.* 1946) *C., Ryedale,* Maj. 4,875

*Grieve, Dominic C. R. (*b.* 1956) *C., Beaconsfield,* Maj. 11,065

*Griffiths, Ms Jane P. (*b.* 1954) *Lab., Reading East,* Maj. 5,588

*Griffiths, Nigel (*b.* 1955) *Lab., Edinburgh South,* Maj. 5,499

*Griffiths, Winston J. (*b.* 1943) *Lab., Bridgend,* Maj. 10,045

Grogan, John T. (*b.* 1961) *Lab., Selby,* Maj. 2,138

*Gummer, Rt. Hon. John S. (*b.* 1939) *C., Suffolk Coastal,* Maj. 4,326

*Hague, Rt. Hon. William J. (*b.* 1961) *C., Richmond,* Maj. 16,319

*Hain, Rt. Hon. Peter G. (*b.* 1950) *Lab., Neath,* Maj. 14,816

*Hall, Michael T. (*b.* 1952) *Lab., Weaver Vale,* Maj. 9,637

Hall, Patrick (*b.* 1951) *Lab., Bedford,* Maj. 6,157

Hamilton, David (*b.* 1950) *Lab., Midlothian,* Maj. 9,014

*Hamilton, Fabian (*b.* 1955) *Lab., Leeds North East,* Maj. 7,089

Hammond, Philip (*b.* 1955) *C., Runnymede and Weybridge,* Maj. 8,360

*Hancock, Michael T. CBE (*b.* 1946) *LD, Portsmouth South,* Maj. 6,094

*Hanson, David G. (*b.* 1957) *Lab., Delyn,* Maj. 8,065

*Harman, Rt. Hon. Harriet QC (*b.* 1950) *Lab., Camberwell and Peckham,* Maj. 14,123

*Harris, Dr Evan (*b.* 1965) *LD, Oxford West and Abingdon,* Maj. 9,185

Harris, Tom (*b.* 1964) *Lab., Glasgow Cathcart,* Maj. 10,816

Harvard, Dai (*b.* 1949) *Lab., Merthyr Tydfil and Rhymney,* Maj. 14,923

*Harvey, Nicholas B. (*b.* 1961) *LD, Devon North,* Maj. 2,984

*Haselhurst, Rt. Hon. Sir Alan (*b.* 1937) *C., Saffron Walden,* Maj. 12,004

Hawkins, Nick (*b.* 1957) *C., Surrey Heath,* Maj. 10,819

Hayes, John H. (*b.* 1958) *C., South Holland and the Deepings,* Maj. 11,099

*Heal, Mrs Sylvia L (*b.* 1942) *Lab., Halesowen and Rowley Regis,* Maj. 7,359

*Heald, Oliver (*b.* 1954) *C., Hertfordshire North East,* Maj. 3,444

Healey, John (*b.* 1960) *Lab., Wentworth,* Maj. 16,449

Heath, David W. CBE (*b.* 1954) *LD, Somerton and Frome,* Maj. 668

*Heathcoat-Amory, Rt. Hon. David P. (*b.* 1949) *C., Wells,* Maj. 2,796

*Henderson, Douglas J. (*b.* 1949) *Lab., Newcastle upon Tyne North,* Maj. 14,450

Henderson, Ivan J. (*b.* 1958) *Lab., Harwich,* Maj. 2,596

*Hendrick, Mark (*b.* 1958) *Lab.Co-op., Preston,* Maj. 12,268

Hendry, Charles (*b.* 1959) *C., Wealden,* Maj. 13,772

Hepburn, Stephen (*b.* 1959) *Lab., Jarrow,* Maj. 17,595

*Heppell, John (*b.* 1948) *Lab., Nottingham East,* Maj. 10,320

Hermon, Lady Sylvia (*b.* 1956) *UUP, Down North,* Maj. 7,324

Hesford, Stephen (*b.* 1957) *Lab., Wirral West,* Maj. 4,035

Hewitt, Rt. Hon. Patricia H. (*b.* 1948) *Lab., Leicester West,* Maj. 9,639

Heyes, David (*b.* 1946) *Lab., Ashton under Lyne,* Maj. 15,518

*Hill, T. Keith (*b.* 1943) *Lab., Streatham,* Maj. 14,270

*Hinchliffe, David M. (*b.* 1948) *Lab., Wakefield,* Maj. 7,954

Hoban, Mark (*b.* 1964) *C., Fareham,* Maj. 7,009

*Hodge, Mrs Margaret E. MBE (*b.* 1944) *Lab., Barking,* Maj. 9,534

*Hoey, Ms Catharine (Kate) L. (*b.* 1946) *Lab., Vauxhall,* Maj. 13,018

*Hogg, Rt. Hon. Douglas M. QC (*b.* 1945) *C., Sleaford and North Hykeham,* Maj. 8,622

Holmes, Paul (*b.* 1957) *LD, Chesterfield,* Maj. 2,586

*Hood, James (*b.* 1948) *Lab., Clydesdale,* Maj. 7,794

*Hoon, Rt. Hon. Geoffrey W. (*b.* 1953) *Lab., Ashfield,* Maj. 13,268

Hope, Philip I. (*b.* 1955) *Lab. Co-op., Corby, Maj.* 5,700

Hopkins, Kelvin P. (*b.* 1941) *Lab., Luton North,* Maj. 9,977

*Horam, John R. (*b.* 1939) *C., Orpington,* Maj. 269

*Howard, Rt. Hon. Michael QC (*b.* 1941) *C., Folkestone and Hythe,* Maj. 5,907

*Howarth, Rt. Hon. Alan CBE (*b.* 1967) *Lab., Newport East,* Maj. 9,874

*Howarth, George E. (*b.* 1949) *Lab., Knowsley North and Sefton East,* Maj. 18,927

Howarth, J. Gerald D. (*b.* 1947) *C., Aldershot,* Maj. 6,564

*Howells, Dr Kim S. Ph.D. (*b.* 1946) *Lab., Pontypridd,* Maj. 17,684

Hoyle, Lindsay H. (*b.* 1957) *Lab., Chorley,* Maj. 8444

*Hughes, Ms Beverley J. (*b.* 1950) *Lab., Stretford and Urmston,* Maj. 13,239

*Hughes, Kevin M. (*b.* 1952) *Lab., Doncaster North,* Maj. 15,187

*Hughes, Simon H. W. (*b.* 1951) *LD, Southwark North and Bermondsey,* Maj. 9,632

Humble, Mrs Jovanka (Joan) (*b.* 1951) *Lab., Blackpool North and Fleetwood,* Maj. 5,721

*Hume, John MEP (*b.* 1937) *SDLP, Foyle,* Maj. 11,550

*Hunter, Andrew R. F. (*b.* 1943) *C., Basingstoke,* Maj. 880

Hurst, Alan A. (*b.* 1945) *Lab., Braintree,* Maj. 358

*Hutton, Rt. Hon. John MP. (*b.* 1955) *Lab., Barrow and Furness,* Maj. 9,889

Iddon, Brian (*b.* 1940) *Lab., Bolton South East,* Maj. 12,871

*Illsley, Eric E. (*b.* 1955) *Lab., Barnsley Central,* Maj. 15,130

*Ingram, Rt. Hon. Adam P. (*b.* 1947) *Lab., East Kilbride,* Maj. 12,755

Irranca-Davies, Huw (*b.* 1963) *Lab., Ogmore,* Maj. 5,721

*Jack, Rt. Hon. J. Michael (*b.* 1946) *C., Fylde,* Maj. 9,610

*Jackson, Ms Glenda M. CBE (*b.* 1936) *Lab., Hampstead and Highgate,* Maj. 7,876

*Jackson, Mrs Helen M. (*b.* 1939) *Lab., Sheffield Hillsborough,* Maj. 14,569

*Jackson, Robert V. (*b.* 1946) *C., Wantage,* Maj. 5,600

*Jamieson, David C. (*b.* 1947) *Lab., Plymouth Devonport,* Maj. 13,033

*Jenkin, Hon., Bernard C. (*b.* 1959) *C., Essex North,* Maj. 7,186

*Jenkins, Brian D. (*b.* 1942) *Lab., Tamworth,* Maj. 4,598

*Johnson, Alan A. (*b.* 1950) *Lab., Hull West and Hessle,* Maj. 10,951

Johnson, Boris (*b.* 1964) *C., Henley,* Maj. 8,458

Johnson, Ms Melanie J. (*b.* 1955) *Lab., Welwyn Hatfield,* Maj. 11,96

Jones, Ms Helen M. Ph.D. (*b.* 1954) *Lab., Warrington North,* Maj. 15,156

*Jones, Jonathan O. (*b.* 1954) *Lab. Co-op., Cardiff Central,* Maj. 659

Jones, Kevan (*b.* 1964) *Lab., Durham North,* Maj. 18,683

*Jones, Ms Lynne M. Ph.D. (*b.* 1951) *Lab., Birmingham Selly Oak,* Maj. 10,339

*Jones, Martyn D. (*b.* 1947) *Lab., Clwyd South,* Maj. 8,898

*Jones, Nigel D. (*b.* 1948) *LD, Cheltenham,* Maj. 5,255

*Jowell, Rt. Hon. Tessa J. H. D. (*b.* 1947) *Lab., Dulwich and West Norwood,* Maj. 12,310

*Joyce, Eric (*b.* 1960) *Lab., Falkirk West,* Maj. 8,532

*Kaufman, Rt. Hon. Gerald *b.* (*b.* 1930) *Lab., Manchester Gorton,* Maj. 11,304

Keeble, Ms Sally C. (*b.* 1951) *Lab., Northampton North,* Maj. 7,893

Keen, Mrs Ann L. (*b.* 1948) *Lab.Co-op., Brentford and Isleworth,* Maj. 10,318

*Keen, D. Alan (*b.* 1937) *Labour Co-op., Feltham and Heston,* Maj. 12,657

*Keetch, Paul S. (*b.* 1961) *LD, Hereford,* Maj. 968

*Kelly, Ms Ruth M. (*b.* 1968) *Lab., Bolton West,* Maj. 5,518

*Kemp, Fraser (*b.* 1958) *Lab., Houghton and Washington East,* Maj. 19,818

*Kennedy, Rt. Hon., Charles P. (*b.* 1959) *LD, Ross, Skye and Inverness West,* Maj. 12,952

*Kennedy, Mrs Jane E. (*b.* 1958) *Lab., Liverpool Wavertree,* Maj. 12,319

*Key, S. Robert (*b.* 1945) *C., Salisbury,* Maj. 8,703

*Khabra, Piara S. (*b.* 1922) *Lab., Ealing Southall,* Maj. 13,683

*Kidney, David N. (*b.* 1955) *Lab., Stafford,* Maj. 5,032

*Kilfoyle, Peter (*b.* 1946) *Lab., Liverpool Walton,* Maj. 17,996

King, Andrew (*b.* 1948) *Lab., Rugby and Kenilworth,* Maj. 2,877

*King, Ms Oona T. (*b.* 1967) *Lab., Bethnal Green and Bow,* Maj. 10,057

*Kirkbride, Miss Julie (*b.* 1960) *C., Bromsgrove,* Maj. 8,158

*Kirkwood, Archibald J. (*b.* 1946) *LD, Roxburgh and Berwickshire,* Maj. 7,511

Knight, Jim (*b.* 1965) *Lab., Dorset South,* Maj. 153

Knight, Rt. Hon. Greg (*b.* 1949) *C., Yorkshire East,* Maj. 4,682

*Kumar, Dr Ashok (*b.* 1956) *Lab., Middlesbrough South and Cleveland East,* Maj. 9,351

*Ladyman, Dr Stephen J. (*b.* 1952) *Lab., Thanet South,* Maj. 1,792

Laing, Mrs Eleanor F. (*b.* 1958) *C., Epping Forest,* Maj. 8,426

*Lait, Ms Jacqueline A. H. (*b.* 1947) *C., Beckenham,* Maj. 4,959

Lamb, Norman (*b.* 1957) *LD, Norfolk North,* Maj. 483

*Lammy, David (*b.* 1972) *Lab., Tottenham,* Maj. 16,916

*Lansley, Andrew D. CBE (*b.* 1956) *C., Cambridgeshire South,* Maj. 8,403

*Lawrence, Mrs Jacqueline R. (*b.* 1948) *Lab., Preseli Pembrokeshire,* Maj. 2,946

Laws, David (*b.* 1965) *LD, Yeovil,* Maj. 3,928

*Laxton, Robert (*b.* 1944) *Lab., Derby North,* Maj. 6,982

Lazarowicz, Mark (*b.* 1953) *Lab. Co-op., Edinburgh North and Leith,* Maj. 8,817

*Leigh, Edward J. E. (*b.* 1950) *C., Gainsborough,* Maj. 8,071

*Lepper, David (*b.* 1945) *Lab. Co-op., Brighton Pavilion,* Maj. 9,643

Leslie, Christopher M. (*b.* 1972) *Lab., Shipley,* Maj. 1,428

Letwin, Oliver (*b.* 1956) *C., Dorset West,* Maj. 1,414

*Levitt, Tom (*b.* 1954) *Lab., High Peak,* Maj. 4,489

*Lewis, Ivan (*b.* 1967) *Lab., Bury South,* Maj. 12,772

*Lewis, Dr Julian M. (*b.* 1951) *C., New Forest East,* Maj. 3,829

*Lewis, Terence (*b.* 1935) *Lab., Worsley,* Maj. 11,787

*Liddell, Rt. Hon. Helen (*b.* 1950) *Lab., Airdrie and Shotts,* Maj. 12,340

Liddell-Grainger, Ian (*b.* 1959) *C., Bridgwater,* Maj. 4,987

*Lidington, David R. Ph.D. (*b.* 1956) *C., Aylesbury,* Maj. 10,009

*Lilley, Rt. Hon. Peter *b.* (*b.* 1943) *C., Hitchin and Harpenden,* Maj. 6,663

Linton, J. Martin (*b.* 1944) *Lab., Battersea,* Maj. 5,053

*Lloyd, Anthony J. (*b.* 1950) *Lab., Manchester Central,* Maj. 13,742

*Llwyd, Elfyn (*b.* 1951) *PC, Meirionnydd nant Conwy,* Maj. 5,684

*Lord, Sir Michael N. (*b.* 1938) *C., Suffolk Central and Ipswich North,* Maj. 3,469

*Loughton, Timothy P. (*b.* 1962) *C., Worthing East and Shoreham,* Maj. 6,139

*Love, Andrew (*b.* 1949) *Lab. Co-op., Edmonton,* Maj. 9,772

Lucas, Ian (*b.* 1960) *Lab., Wrexham,* Maj. 9,188

*Luff, Peter J. (*b.* 1955) *C., Worcestershire Mid,* Maj. 10,627

Luke, Ian (*b.* 1951) *Lab., Dundee East,* Maj. 4,475

Lyons, John (*b.* 1950) *Lab., Strathkelvin and Bearsden,* Maj. 11,717

*MacDonald, Calum A. Ph.D. (*b.* 1956) *Lab., Western Isles,* Maj. 1,074

*MacDougall, John (*b.* 1947) *Lab., Fife Central,* Maj. 10,075

*Mackay, Rt. Hon. Andrew J. (*b.* 1949) *C., Bracknell,* Maj. 6,713

*Mackinlay, Andrew S. (*b.* 1949) *Lab., Thurrock,* Maj. 9,997

*Maclean, Rt. Hon. David J. (*b.* 1953) *C., Penrith and the Border,* Maj. 14,677

*MacShane, Denis Ph.D. (*b.* 1948) *Lab., Rotherham,* Maj. 13,077

Mactaggart, Ms Fiona M. (*b.* 1953) *Lab., Slough,* Maj. 12,508

Mahmood, Khalid (*b.* 1961) *Lab., Birmingham Perry Barr,* Maj. 8,753

*Mahon, Mrs Alice (*b.* 1937) *Lab., Halifax,* Maj. 6,129

Malins, Humfrey J. CBE (*b.* 1945) *C., Woking,* Maj. 6,759

*Mallaber, Ms C. Judith (*b.* 1951) *Lab., Amber Valley,* Maj. 7,227

*Mallon, Seamus (*b.* 1936) *SDLP, Newry and Armagh,* Maj. 3,575

*Mandelson, Rt. Hon. Peter B. (*b.* 1953) *Lab., Hartlepool,* Maj. 14,571

Mann, John (*b.* 1960) *Lab., Bassetlaw,* Maj. 9,748

*Maples, John C. (*b.* 1943) *C., Stratford-upon-Avon,* Maj. 11,802

Morris, Robert (*b.* 1955) *Lab., Wolverhampton South West,* Maj. 3,487

*Marsden, Gordon (*b.* 1953) *Lab., Blackpool South,* Maj. 8,262

*Marsden, Paul W. B. (*b.* 1968) *Lab., Shrewsbury and Atcham,* Maj. 3,579

*Marshall, David Ph.D (*b.* 1941) *Lab., Glasgow Shettleston,* Maj. 9,818

*Marshall, James Ph.D. (*b.* 1941) *Lab., Leicester South,* Maj. 13,243

*Marshall-Andrews, Robert G. QC (*b.* 1944) *Lab., Medway,* Maj. 3,780

*Martin, Rt. Hon. Michael J. (*b.* 1945) *The Speaker, Glasgow Springburn,* Maj. 11,378

*Martlew, Eric A. (*b.* 1949) *Lab., Carlisle,* Maj. 5,702

*Mates, Michael J. (*b.* 1934) *C., Hampshire East,* Maj. 8,890

*Maude, Rt. Hon. Francis A. A. (*b.* 1953) *C., Horsham,* Maj. 13,666

*Mawhinney, Rt. Hon. Sir Brian Ph.D. (*b.* 1940) *C., Cambridgeshire North West,* Maj. 8,101

*May, Mrs Theresa M. (*b.* 1956) *C., Maidenhead,* Maj. 3,284

*McAvoy, Thomas M. (*b.* 1943) *Lab. Co-op., Glasgow Rutherglen,* Maj. 12,625

*McCabe, Stephen J. (*b.* 1955) *Lab., Birmingham Hall Green,* Maj. 6,648

*McCafferty, Ms Christine (*b.* 1945) *Lab., Calder Valley,* Maj. 3,094

*McCartney, Rt. Hon. Ian (*b.* 1951) *Lab., Makerfield,* Maj. 17,750

McDonagh, Ms Siobhain A. (*b.* 1960) *Lab., Mitcham and Morden*, Maj. 13,785

McDonnell, John M. (*b.* 1951) *Lab., Hayes and Harlington*, Maj. 13,466

*McFall, John (*b.* 1944) *Lab. Co-op., Dumbarton*, Maj. 9,575

*McGrady, Edward K. (*b.* 1935) *SDLP, Down South*, Maj. 13,858

McGuinness, Martin (*b.* 1950) *SF, Ulster Mid*, Maj. 9,953

McGuire, Anne (*b.* 1949) *Lab., Stirling*, Maj. 6,274

*McIntosh, Miss Anne C. B. (*b.* 1954) *C., Vale of York*, Maj. 12,517

McIsaac, Ms Shona (*b.* 1960) *Lab., Cleethorpes*, Maj. 5,620

McKechin, Anne (*b.* 1961) *Lab., Glasgow Maryhill*, Maj. 9,888

McKenna, Ms Rosemary CBE (*b.* 1941) *Lab., Cumbernauld and Kilsyth*, Maj. 7,520

*McLoughlin, Patrick A. (*b.* 1957) *C., Derbyshire West*, Maj. 7,370

*McNamara, J. Kevin (*b.* 1934) *Lab., Hull North*, Maj. 10,721

*McNulty, Anthony J. (*b.* 1958) *Lab., Harrow East*, Maj. 11,124

*McWalter, Tony (*b.* 1945) *Lab. Co-op., Hemel Hempstead*, Maj. 3,742

*McWilliam, John D. (*b.* 1941) *Lab., Blaydon*, Maj. 7,809

*Meacher, Rt. Hon. Michael H. (*b.* 1939) *Lab., Oldham West and Royton*, Maj. 13,365

*Meale, J. Alan (*b.* 1949) *Lab., Mansfield*, Maj. 11,038

Mercer, Patrick OBE (*b.* 1956) *C., Newark*, Maj. 4,073

*Merron, Ms Gillian J. (*b.* 1959) *Lab., Lincoln*, Maj. 8,420

*Michael, Rt. Hon. Alun E. (*b.* 1943) *Lab. Co-op., Cardiff South and Penarth*, Maj. 12,287

*Milburn, Rt. Hon. Alan (*b.* 1958) *Lab., Darlington*, Maj. 9,529

Miliband, David (*b.* 1966) *Lab., South Shields*, Maj. 14,090

*Miller, Andrew P. (*b.* 1949) *Lab., Ellesmere Port and Neston*, Maj. 10,861

Mitchell, Andrew (*b.* 1956) *C., Sutton Coldfield*, Maj. 10,104

*Mitchell, Austin V. D.Phil. (*b.* 1934) *Lab., Great Grimsby*, Maj. 11,484

*Moffatt, Mrs Laura J. (*b.* 1954) *Lab., Crawley*, Maj. 6,770

Mole, Chris (*b.* 1958) *Lab., Ipswich*, Maj. 4,087

*Moore, Michael (*b.* 1965) *LD, Tweeddale, Ettrick and Lauderdale*, Maj. 5,157

*Moran, Ms Margaret (*b.* 1955) *Lab., Luton South*, Maj. 10,133

Morgan, Ms Julie (*b.* 1944) *Lab., Cardiff North*, Maj. 6,165

*Morley, Elliot A. (*b.* 1952) *Lab., Scunthorpe*, Maj. 10,372

*Morris, Rt. Hon., Estelle (*b.* 1952) *Lab., Birmingham Yardley*, Maj. 2,578

*Moss, Malcolm D. (*b.* 1943) *C., Cambridgeshire North East*, Maj. 6,373

Mountford, Ms Kali C. J. (*b.* 1954) *Lab., Colne Valley*, Maj. 4,639

*Mudie, George E. (*b.* 1945) *Lab., Leeds East*, Maj. 12,643

*Mullin, Christopher J. (*b.* 1947) *Lab., Sunderland South*, Maj. 13,667

Munn, Meg (*b.* 1959) *Lab. Co-op., Sheffield Heeley*, Maj. 11,704

Murphy, Denis (*b.* 1948) *Lab., Wansbeck*, Maj. 13,101

Murphy, Jim (*b.* 1967) *Lab., Eastwood*, Maj. 9,141

*Murphy, Rt. Hon, Paul P. (*b.* 1948) *Lab., Torfaen*, Maj. 16,280

Murrison, Andrew (*b.* 1961) *C., Westbury*, Maj. 5,294

Naysmith, J. Douglas (*b.* 1941) *Lab. Co-op., Bristol North West*, Maj. 11,087

Norman, Archibald J. (*b.* 1954) *C., Tunbridge Wells*, Maj. 9,730

Norris, Dan (*b.* 1960) *Lab., Wansdyke*, Maj. 5,113

*Oaten, Mark (*b.* 1964) *LD, Winchester*, Maj. 9,634

*O'Brien, Michael (*b.* 1954) *Lab., Warwickshire North*, Maj. 9,639

*O'Brien, Stephen (*b.* 1957) *C., Eddisbury*, Maj. 4,568

*O'Brien, William (*b.* 1929) *Lab., Normanton*, Maj. 9,937

*O'Hara, Edward (*b.* 1937) *Lab., Knowsley South*, Maj. 21,316

*Olner, William J. (*b.* 1942) *Lab., Nuneaton*, Maj. 7,535

*O'Neill, Martin J. (*b.* 1945) *Lab., Ochil*, Maj. 5,349

Opik, Lembit (*b.* 1965) *LD, Montgomeryshire*, Maj. 6,234

*Organ, Ms Diana M. (*b.* 1952) *Lab., Forest of Dean*, Maj. 2,049

Osborne, George (*b.* 1971) *C., Tatton*, Maj. 8,611

Osborne, Mrs Sandra C. (*b.* 1956) *Lab., Ayr*, Maj. 2,545

*Ottaway, Richard G. J. (*b.* 1945) *C., Croydon South*, Maj. 8,697

*Owen, Albert (*b.* 1960) *Lab., Ynys Môn*, Maj. 800

*Page, Richard L. (*b.* 1941) *C., Hertfordshire South West*, Maj. 8,181

*Paice, James E. T. (*b.* 1949) *C., Cambridgeshire South East*, Maj. 8,990

*Paisley, Revd Ian R. K. MEP (*b.* 1926) *DUP, Antrim North*, Maj. 14,224

Palmer, Nicholas D. (*b.* 1950) *Lab., Broxtowe*, Maj. 5,873

*Paterson, Owen W. (*b.* 1956) *C., Shropshire North*, Maj. 6,241

*Pearson, Ian P. Ph.D. (*b.* 1959) *Lab., Dudley South*, Maj. 6,817

*Perham, Ms Linda (*b.* 1947) *Lab., Ilford North*, Maj. 2,115

Picking, Anne (*b.* 1958) *Lab., East Lothian*, Maj. 10,830

*Pickles, Eric J. (*b.* 1952) *C., Brentwood and Ongar*, Maj. 2,821

*Pickthall, Colin (*b.* 1944) *Lab., Lancashire West*, Maj. 9,643

*Pike, Peter L. (*b.* 1937) *Lab., Burnley*, Maj. 10,498

*Plaskitt, James A. (*b.* 1954) *Lab., Warwick and Leamington*, Maj. 5,953

Pollard, Kerry P. (*b.* 1944) *Lab., St Albans*, Maj. 4,466

*Pond, Christopher R. (*b.* 1952) *Lab., Gravesham*, Maj. 4,862

*Pope, Gregory J. (*b.* 1960) *Lab., Hyndburn*, Maj. 8,219

*Portillo, Rt. Hon. Michael (*b.* 1953) *C., Kensington and Chelsea*, Maj. 8,771

Pound, Stephen P. (*b.* 1948) *Lab., Ealing North*, Maj. 11,837

*Prentice, Ms Bridget T. (*b.* 1952) *Lab., Lewisham East*, Maj. 8,959

*Prentice, Gordon (*b.* 1951) *Lab., Pendle*, Maj. 4,275

*Prescott, Rt. Hon. John L. (*b.* 1938) *Lab., Hull East*, Maj. 15,325

Price, Adam (*b.* 1968) *PC, Carmarthen East and Dinefwr*, Maj. 2,590

*Primarolo, Ms Dawn (*b.* 1954) *Lab., Bristol South*, Maj. 14,181

*Prisk, Mark (*b.* 1962) *C., Hertford and Stortford*, Maj. 5,603

*Prosser, Gwynfor M. (*b.* 1943) *Lab., Dover*, Maj. 5,199

Pugh, John (*b.* 1949) *LD, Southport*, Maj. 3,007

*Purchase, Kenneth (*b.* 1939) *Lab. Co-op., Wolverhampton North East*, Maj. 9,965

Purnell, James (*b.* 1970) *Lab., Stalybridge and Hyde,* Maj. 8,859

*Quin, Rt. Hon. Joyce G. (*b.* 1944) *Lab., Gateshead East and Washington West,* Maj. 17,904

*Quinn, Lawrence W. (*b.* 1956) *Lab., Scarborough and Whitby,* Maj. 3,585

*Rammell, William E. (*b.* 1959) *Lab., Harlow,* Maj. 5,228

*Randall, A. John (*b.* 1955) *C., Uxbridge,* Maj. 2,098

Rapson, Sydney N. J. (*b.* 1942) *Lab., Portsmouth North,* Maj. 5,134

*Raynsford, Rt. Hon., W. R. N. (Nick) (*b.* 1945) *Lab., Greenwich and Woolwich,* Maj. 13,433

*Redwood, Rt. Hon. John A. D.Phil. (*b.* 1951) *C., Wokingham,* Maj. 5,994

Reed, Andrew J. (*b.* 1964) *Lab., Loughborough,* Maj. 6,378

Reid, Alan (*b.* 1954) *LD, Argyll and Bute,* Maj. 1,653

*Reid, Rt. Hon. John Ph.D. (*b.* 1947) *Lab., Hamilton North and Bellshill,* Maj. 13,561

*Rendel, David D. (*b.* 1949) *LD, Newbury,* Maj. 2,415

*Robathan, Andrew R. G. (*b.* 1951) *C., Blaby,* Maj. 6,209

Robertson, Angus (*b.* 1945) *SNP, Moray,* Maj.

Robertson, Hugh (*b.* 1962) *C., Faversham and Mid Kent,* Maj. 4,183

*Robertson, John (*b.* 1952) *Lab., Glasgow Anniesland,* Maj. 11,054

Robertson, Laurence A. (*b.* 1958) *C., Tewkesbury,* Maj. 8,663

*Robinson, Geoffrey (*b.* 1938) *Lab., Coventry North West,* Maj. 10,874

Robinson, Iris MLA (*b.* 1949) *DUP, Strangford,* Maj. 1,110

*Robinson, Peter D. (*b.* 1948) *DUP, Belfast East,* Maj. 7,117

*Roche, Mrs Barbara M. R. (*b.* 1954) *Lab., Hornsey and Wood Green,* Maj. 10,614

*Roe, Mrs Marion A. (*b.* 1936) *C., Broxbourne,* Maj. 8,993

*Rooney, Terence H. (*b.* 1950) *Lab., Bradford North,* Maj. 8,969

Rosindell, Andrew (*b.* 1966) *C., Romford,* Maj. 5,977

*Ross, Ernest (*b.* 1942) *Lab., Dundee West,* Maj. 6,800

*Roy, Frank (*b.* 1958) *Lab., Motherwell and Wishaw,* Maj. 10,956

*Ruane, Christopher S. (*b.* 1958) *Lab., Vale of Clwyd,* Maj. 5,761

*Ruddock, Mrs Joan M. (*b.* 1943) *Lab., Lewisham Deptford,* Maj. 15,293

Ruffley, David L. (*b.* 1962) *C., Bury St Edmunds,* Maj. 2,503

Russell, Ms Christine M. (*b.* 1945) *Lab., City of Chester,* Maj. 6,894

*Russell, Robert E. (*b.* 1946) *LD, Colchester,* Maj. 5,553

*Ryan, Ms Joan M. (*b.* 1955) *Lab., Enfield North,* Maj. 2,291

*Salmond, Alexander E. A. (*b.* 1954) *SNP, Banff and Buchan,* Maj. 10,503

Salter, Martin J. (*b.* 1954) *Lab., Reading West,* Maj. 8,849

*Sanders, Adrian M. (*b.* 1959) *LD, Torbay,* Maj. 6,708

*Sarwar, Mohammad (*b.* 1952) *Lab., Glasgow Govan,* Maj. 6,400

*Savidge, Malcolm K. (*b.* 1946) *Lab., Aberdeen North,* Maj. 4,449

*Sawford, Philip A. (*b.* 1950) *Lab., Kettering,* Maj. 665

*Sayeed, Jonathan (*b.* 1948) *C., Bedfordshire Mid,* Maj. 8,066

*Sedgemore, Brian C. J. (*b.* 1937) *Lab., Hackney South and Shoreditch,* Maj. 15,049

Selous, Andrew (*b.* 1962) *C., Bedfordshire South West,* Maj. 776

*Shaw, Jonathan R. (*b.* 1966) *Lab., Chatham and Aylesford,* Maj. 4,340

*Sheerman, Barry J. (*b.* 1940) *Lab. Co-op., Huddersfield,* Maj. 10,046

*Shephard, Rt. Hon. Gillian P. (*b.* 1940) *C., Norfolk South West,* Maj. 9,366

*Shepherd, Richard C. S. (*b.* 1942) *C., Aldridge-Brownhills,* Maj. 3,768

Sheridan, Jim (*b.* 1952) *Lab., Renfrewshire West,* Maj. 8,575

*Shipley, Ms Debra A. (*b.* 1957) *Lab., Stourbridge,* Maj. 3,812

*Short, Rt. Hon. Clare (*b.* 1946) *Lab., Birmingham Ladywood,* Maj. 18,143

Simmonds, Mark (*b.* 1964) *C., Boston and Skegness,* Maj. 515

Simon, Sion (*b.* 1969) *Lab., Birmingham Erdington,* Maj. 9,962

*Simpson, Alan J. (*b.* 1948) *Lab., Nottingham South,* Maj. 9,989

*Simpson, Keith (*b.* 1949) *C., Norfolk Mid,* Maj. 4,562

Singh, Marsha (*b.* 1954) *Lab., Bradford West,* Maj. 4,165

*Skinner, Dennis E. (*b.* 1932) *Lab., Bolsover,* Maj. 18,777

*Smith, Rt. Hon. Andrew D. (*b.* 1951) *Lab., Oxford East,* Maj. 10,344

*Smith, Ms Angela E. (*b.* 1959) *Lab. Co-op., Basildon,* Maj. 7,738

*Smith, Rt. Hon. Christopher R. Ph.D. (*b.* 1951) *Lab., Islington South and Finsbury,* Maj. 7,280

*Smith, Ms Geraldine (*b.* 1961) *Lab., Morecambe and Lunesdale,* Maj. 5,092

*Smith, Ms Jacqui (*b.* 1962) *Lab., Redditch,* Maj. 2,484

*Smith, John W. P. (*b.* 1951) *Lab., Vale of Glamorgan,* Maj. 4,700

*Smith, Llewellyn T. (*b.* 1944) *Lab., Blaenau Gwent,* Maj. 19,313

*Smith, Sir Robert Bt. (*b.* 1958) *LD, Aberdeenshire West and Kincardine,* Maj. 4,821

*Smyth, Revd, W. Martin (*b.* 1931) *UUP, Belfast South,* Maj. 5,399

*Soames, Hon. A. Nicholas W. (*b.* 1948) *C., Sussex Mid,* Maj. 6,898

*Soley, Clive S. (*b.* 1939) *Lab., Ealing Acton and Shepherd's Bush,* Maj. 10,789

Southworth, Ms Helen M. (*b.* 1956) *Lab., Warrington South,* Maj. 7,387

*Spellar, Rt. Hon. John F. (*b.* 1947) *Lab., Warley,* Maj. 11,850

Spelman, Mrs Caroline A. (*b.* 1958) *C., Meriden,* Maj. 3,784

*Spicer, Sir Michael (*b.* 1943) *C., Worcestershire West,* Maj. 5,374

Spink, Dr Robert (*b.* 1948) *C., Castle Point,* Maj. 985

*Spring, Richard J. G. (*b.* 1946) *C., Suffolk West,* Maj. 4,295

*Squire, Ms Rachel A. (*b.* 1954) *Lab., Dunfermline West,* Maj. 10,980

*Stanley, Rt. Hon. Sir John (*b.* 1942) *C., Tonbridge and Malling,* Maj. 8,250

Starkey, Dr Phyllis M. (*b.* 1947) *Lab., Milton Keynes South West,* Maj. 6,978

*Steen, Anthony (*b.* 1939) *C., Totnes,* Maj. 3,597

*Steinberg, Gerald N. (*b.* 1945) *Lab., City of Durham,* Maj. 13,441

*Stevenson, George W. (*b.* 1938) *Lab., Stoke-on-Trent South,* Maj. 10,489

*Stewart, David J. (*b.* 1956) *Lab., Inverness East, Nairn and Lochaber,* Maj. 4,716

*Stewart, Ian (*b.* 1950) *Lab., Eccles,* Maj. 14,528

*Stinchcombe, Paul D. (*b.* 1962) *Lab., Wellingborough,*
Maj. 2,355

*Stoate, Dr Howard G. A. (*b.* 1954) *Lab., Dartford,*
Maj. 3,306

*Strang, Rt.Hon Dr Gavin (*b.* 1943) *Lab., Edinburgh East
and Musselburgh,* Maj. 12,168

*Straw, Rt. Hon. J. W. (Jack) (*b.* 1946) *Lab., Blackburn,*
Maj. 9,249

*Streeter, Gary N. (*b.* 1955) *C., Devon South West,*
Maj. 7,144

*Stringer, Graham E. (*b.* 1950) *Lab., Manchester Blackley,*
Maj. 14,464

*Stuart, Mrs Gisela G. (*b.* 1955) *Lab., Birmingham
Edgbaston,* Maj. 4,698

*Stunell, Andrew (*b.* 1942) *LD, Hazel Grove,* Maj. 8,435

*Sutcliffe, Gerard (*b.* 1953) *Lab., Bradford South,*
Maj. 9,662

Swayne, Desmond A. (*b.* 1956) *C., New Forest West,*
Maj. 13,191

Swire, Hugo (*b.* 1959) *C., Devon East,* Maj. 8,195

*Syms, Robert A. R. (*b.* 1956) *C., Poole,* Maj. 7,166

Tami, Mark (*b.* 1963) *Lab., Alyn and Deeside,* Maj. 9,222

*Tapsell, Sir Peter (*b.* 1930) *C., Louth and Horncastle,*
Maj. 7,554

*Taylor, Rt. Hon. Ann (*b.* 1947) *Lab., Dewsbury,*
Maj. 7,449

*Taylor, Ms Dari J. (*b.* 1944) *Lab., Stockton South,*
Maj. 9,086

Taylor, David L. (*b.* 1946) *Lab. Co-op., Leicestershire
North West,* Maj. 8,157

*Taylor, Sir Edward (Teddy) (*b.* 1937) *C., Rochford and
Southend East,* Maj. 7,034

*Taylor, Ian C. MBE (*b.* 1945) *C., Esher and Walton,*
Maj. 11,538

*Taylor, John M. (*b.* 1941) *C., Solihull,* Maj. 9,407

*Taylor, Matthew O. J. (*b.* 1963) *LD, Truro and St Austell,*
Maj. 8,065

Taylor, Dr Richard (*b.* 1935) *KHHC, Wyre Forest,*
Maj. 17,630

Thomas, Gareth (*b.* 1954) *Lab., Clwyd West,* Maj. 1,115

*Thomas, Gareth R. (*b.* 1967) *Lab., Harrow West,*
Maj. 6,156

*Thomas, Simon (*b.* 1963) *PC, Ceredigion,* Maj. 3,944

*Thurso, John (*b.* 1953) *LD, Caithness, Sutherland and
Easter Ross,* Maj. 2,744

*Timms, Stephen C. (*b.* 1955) *Lab., East Ham,*
Maj. 21,032

*Tipping, S. P. (Paddy) (*b.* 1949) *Lab., Sherwood,*
Maj. 9,373

Todd, Mark W. (*b.* 1954) *Lab., Derbyshire South,*
Maj. 7,851

Tonge, Dr Jennifer L. (*b.* 1941) *LD, Richmond Park,*
Maj. 4,964

*Touhig, J. Donnelly (Don) (*b.* 1947) *Lab. Co-op., Islwyn,*
Maj. 15,309

*Tredinnick, David A. S. (*b.* 1950) *C., Bosworth,*
Maj. 2,280

*Trend, Hon. Michael St J. CBE (*b.* 1952) *C., Windsor,*
Maj. 8,889

*Trickett, Jon H. (*b.* 1950) *Lab., Hemsworth,* Maj. 15,636

*Trimble, Rt. Hon. W. David (*b.* 1944) *UUP, Upper
Bann,* Maj. 2,058

Truswell, Paul A. (*b.* 1955) *Lab., Pudsey,* Maj. 5,626

Turner, Andrew (*b.* 1953) *C., Isle of Wight,* Maj. 2,826

*Turner, Dennis (*b.* 1942) *Lab. Co-op., Wolverhampton
South East,* Maj. 12,464

Turner, Desmond S. (*b.* 1939) *Lab., Brighton Kemptown,*
Maj. 4,922

*Turner, Neil (*b.* 1945) *Lab., Wigan,* Maj. 13,743

*Twigg, J. Derek (*b.* 1959) *Lab., Halton,* Maj. 17,428

*Twigg, Stephen (*b.* 1966) *Lab., Enfield Southgate,*
Maj. 5,546

*Tyler, Paul A. CBE (*b.* 1941) *LD, Cornwall North,*
Maj. 9,832

*Tynan, Bill (*b.* 1940) *Lab., Hamilton South,* Maj. 10,775

*Tyrie, Andrew G. (*b.* 1957) *C., Chichester,* Maj. 11,355

*Vaz, N. Keith A. S. (*b.* 1956) *Lab., Leicester East,*
Maj. 13,422

*Viggers, Peter J. (*b.* 1938) *C., Gosport,* Maj. 2,621

*Vis, R. J. (Rudi) (*b.* 1941) *Lab., Finchley and Golders
Green,* Maj. 3,716

*Walley, Ms Joan L. (*b.* 1949) *Lab., Stoke-on-Trent North,*
Maj. 11,784

*Walter, Robert J. (*b.* 1948) *C., Dorset North,* Maj. 3,797

*Ward, Ms Claire M. (*b.* 1972) *Lab., Watford,* Maj. 5,555

*Wareing, Robert N. (*b.* 1930) *Lab., Liverpool West
Derby,* Maj. 15,853

*Waterson, Nigel C. (*b.* 1950) *C., Eastbourne,* Maj. 2,154

Watkinson, Angela (*b.* 1941) *C., Upminster,* Maj. 1,241

*Watson, Tom (*b.* 1967) *Lab., West Bromwich East,*
Maj. 9,763

Watts, David L. (*b.* 1951) *Lab., St Helens North,*
Maj. 15,901

Webb, Prof. Steven J. (*b.* 1965) *LD, Northavon,*
Maj. 9,877

Weir, Michael (*b.* 1957) *SNP, Angus,* Maj. 3,611

White, Brian A. R. (*b.* 1957) *Lab., Milton Keynes North
East,* Maj. 1,829

*Whitehead, Alan P. V. (*b.* 1950) *Lab., Southampton Test,*
Maj. 11,207

*Whittingdale, John F. L. OBE (*b.* 1959) *C., Maldon and
Chelmsford East,* Maj. 8,462

*Wicks, Malcolm H. (*b.* 1947) *Lab., Croydon North,*
Maj. 16,858

*Widdecombe, Rt. Hon. Ann N. (*b.* 1947) *C., Maidstone
and the Weald,* Maj. 10,318

Wiggin, Bill (*b.* 1966) *C., Leominster,* Maj. 10,367

*Wilkinson, John A. D. (*b.* 1940) *C., Ruislip-Northwood,*
Maj. 7,537

*Willetts, David L. (*b.* 1956) *C., Havant,* Maj. 4,207

*Williams, Rt. Hon. Alan J. (*b.* 1930) *Lab., Swansea West,*
Maj. 9,550

*Williams, Betty (*b.* 1944) *Lab., Conwy,* Maj. 6,219

Williams, Hywel (*b.* 1953) *PC, Caernarfon,* Maj. 3,511

Williams, Roger (*b.* 1948) *LD, Brecon and Radnorshire,*
Maj. 751

*Willis, G. Philip (*b.* 1941) *LD, Harrogate and
Knaresborough,* Maj. 8,845

Wills, Michael D. (*b.* 1952) *Lab., Swindon North,*
Maj. 8,105

*Wilshire, David (*b.* 1943) *C., Spelthorne,* Maj. 3,262

*Wilson, Brian D. H. (*b.* 1948) *Lab., Cunninghame
North,* Maj. 8,398

*Winnick, David J. (*b.* 1933) *Lab., Walsall North,*
Maj. 9,391

*Winterton, Mrs J. Ann (*b.* 1941) *C., Congleton,*
Maj. 7,134

*Winterton, Nicholas R. (*b.* 1938) *C., Macclesfield,*
Maj. 7,200

Winterton, Ms Rosalie (*b.* 1958) *Lab., Doncaster Central,*
Maj. 11,999

Wishart, Peter (*b.* 1962) *SNP, Tayside North,* Maj. 3,283

*Wood, Michael R. (*b.* 1946) *Lab., Batley and Spen,*
Maj. 5,064

Woodward, Shaun (*b.* 1958) *Lab., St Helens South,*
Maj. 8,985

*Woolas, Philip J. (*b.* 1959) *Lab., Oldham East and
Saddleworth,* Maj. 2,726

*Worthington, Anthony (*b.* 1941) *Lab., Clydebank and Milngavie,* Maj. 10,724

*Wray, James (*b.* 1938) *Lab., Glasgow Baillieston,* Maj. 9,839

*Wyatt, Derek M. (*b.* 1949) *Lab., Sittingbourne and Sheppey,* Maj. 3,509

Wright, Anthony D. (*b.* 1954) *Lab., Great Yarmouth,* Maj. 4,564

*Wright, Anthony W. D.Phil. (*b.* 1948) *Lab., Cannock Chase,* Maj. 10,704

Wright, David (*b.* 1967) *Lab., Telford, Maj.* 8,383

*Yeo, Timothy S. K. (*b.* 1945) *C., Suffolk South,* Maj. 5,081

*Young, Rt. Hon. Sir George Bt. (*b.* 1941) *C., Hampshire North West,* Maj. 12,009

Younger-Ross, Richard (*b.* 1953) *LD, Teignbridge,* Maj. 3,011

*Sitting MPs

For By-elections since 2001 *see* page 271

GENERAL ELECTION STATISTICS

PARLIAMENTS SINCE 1970

Assembled	Dissolved	Duration		
		yr	m	d
29 June 1970	8 February 1974	3	7	10
6 March 1974	20 September 1974	0	6	14
22 October 1974	7 April 1979	4	5	16
9 May 1979	13 May 1983	4	0	4
15 June 1983	18 May 1987	3	11	3
17 June 1987	16 March 1992	4	8	28
27 April 1992	8 April 1997	4	11	12
7 May 1997	14 May 2001	4	0	7
13 June 2001				

GENERAL ELECTION TURNOUT

	2001	1997
England	59.4	71.4
Wales	61.6	73.5
Scotland	58.2	71.3
Northern Ireland	68.0	67.1

VOTES CAST 1997 AND 2001

	1997	2001
Conservative	9,600,940	8,357,622
Labour	13,517,911	10,724,895
Liberal Democrats	5,243,440	4,812,833
Scottish Nationalist	622,260	464,305
Plaid Cymru	161,030	195,892
N. Ireland parties	780,920	635,735
Others	1,361,701	1,177,516
Total	31,287,702	26,368,798

DISTRIBUTION OF SEATS BY COUNTRY 2001

	England	Wales	Scotland	N. Ireland
Conservative	165	–	1	–
Labour	323	34	55	–
Lib. Dem.	40	2	10	–
SNP	–	–	5	–
Plaid Cymru	–	4	–	–
Other	1	–	1*	18

* The Speaker

PARLIAMENTARY CONSTITUENCIES AS AT 7 JUNE 2001

The results of voting in each parliamentary division at the general election of 7 June 2001 are given below. The majority in the 1997 general election and by-elections between 1997 and 2001 are given below the 2001 result.

Symbols
* Sitting MP
† Previously MP in another seat

Abbreviations

AL	Asian League
Alliance	Alliance
Anti-Corrupt	Anti-Corruption Forum
BNP	British National Party
Bean	New Millennium Bean
CPA	Christian Peoples Alliance
Ch. D.	Christian Democrat
Choice	People's Choice
Comm.	Communist Party
Community	Independent Community Candidate Empowering Change
C.	Conservative
Country	Countryside Party
Customer	Direct Customer Service Party
Def Welfare	Defend the Welfare State Against Blairism
DUP	Democratic Unionist Party
English Independence Party	English Independence Party
Elvis	Church of the Militant Elvis Party
Ext. Club	Extinction Club
FDP	Fancy Dress Party
Free	Freedom Party
Green	Green Party
Grey	Grey Party

IOW	Isle of Wight Party
Ind.	Independent
Ind. UU	Independent United Unionist
Ind. Vote	Independent - Vote for Yourself Party
JLDP	John Lillburne Democratic Party
JP	Justice Party
KHHC	Kidderminster Hospital and Health Concern
Lab.	Labour
Lab. Co-op	Labour and Co-operative
LCA	Legalise Cannabis Alliance
LD	Liberal Democrat
LP	Liberated Party
Left All	All Left Alliance
Lib.	Liberal
Loony	Monster Raving Loony Party
Low Excise	Lower Excise Duty Party
Marxist	Marxist Party
Meb. Ker.	Mebyon Kernow
Muslim	Muslim Party
NBP	New Britain Party
NF	National Front
NI Unionist	Northern Ireland Unionist
NI WC	Northern Ireland Women's Coalition
PC	Plaid Cymru
PF	Pathfinders
PJP	People's Justice Party
PUP	Progressive Unionist Party
Pacifist	Pacifist for Peace, Justice, Cooperation, Environment
Pensioner	Pensioner Coalition
Pro Euro C	Pro Euro Conservative Party
ProLife	ProLife Alliance
Prog Dem	Progress Democratic Party Members Decide Policy
Qari	Qari
R & R Loony	Rock & Roll Loony Party

RP	Rate Payer
Ref. UK	Reform UK
Reform	Reform 2000
Res. Motor	Motor Residents and Motorists of Great Britain
SDLP	Social Democratic and Labour Party
SF	Sinn Fein
SNP	Scottish National Party
SSP	Scottish Socialist Party
Scot. Ref.	Scottish Freedom Referendum Party
Scot. U.	Scottish Unionist
Soc.	Socialist Party
Soc. All.	Socialist Alliance
Soc. Alt.	Socialist Alternative Party
Soc. Lab.	Socialist Labour Party
Socialist	Socialist
Speaker	The Speaker
Stuck	Stuckist
Sunrise	Chairman of Sunrise Radio
Tatton	Tatton Group Independent
Third	Third Way
Truth	Truth Party
UK Ind.	UK Independence Party
UKU	United Kingdom Unionist
UUAP	United Unionist Assembly Party
UUP	Ulster Unionist Party
Unrep.	Unrepresented People's Party
WSA	Welsh Socialist Alliance
Wessex Reg.	Wessex Regionalist
WFLOE	Women for Life on Earth
Women's Co.	Women's Coalition
WP	Workers' Party
WRP	Workers' Revolutionary Party
Wrestling	Jam Wrestling Party

ENGLAND

ALDERSHOT
E.78,262 T. 45,315 (57.90%)   C. hold
*Gerald Howarth, C.   19,106
Adrian Collett, LD   12,542
Luke Akehurst, Lab.   11,391
Derek Rumsey, UK Ind.   797
Adam Stacey, Green   630
Arthur Pendragon, Ind.   459
Alan Hope, Loony   390
C. majority 6,564 (14.49%)
1.13% swing LD to C.
(1997: C. maj. 6,621 (12.22%))

ALDRIDGE-BROWNHILLS
E.62,388 T. 37,810 (60.60%)   C. hold
*Richard Shepherd, C.   18,974
Ian Geary, Lab.   15,206
Mrs Monica Howes, LD   3,251
John Rothery, Soc. All.   379
C. majority 3,768 (9.97%)
2.26% swing Lab. to C.
(1997: C. maj. 2,526 (5.44%))

ALTRINCHAM & SALE WEST
E.71,820 T. 43,568 (60.66%)   C. hold
*Graham Brady, C.   20,113
Ms Janet Baugh, Lab.   17,172
Christopher Gaskell, LD   6,283
C. majority 2,941 (6.75%)
1.92% swing Lab. to C.
(1997: C. maj. 1,505 (2.91%))

AMBER VALLEY
E.73,798 T. 44,513 (60.32%) Lab. hold
*Ms Judy Mallaber, Lab.   23,101
Ms Gillian Shaw, C.   15,874
Ms Kate Smith, LD   5,538
Lab. majority 7,227 (16.24%)
2.49% swing Lab. to C.
(1997: Lab. maj. 11,613 (21.21%))

ARUNDEL & SOUTH DOWNS
E.70,956 T. 45,889 (64.67%)   C. hold
*Howard Flight, C.   23,969
Derek Deedman, LD   10,265
Charles Taylor, Lab.   9,488
Robert Perrin, UK Ind.   2,167
C. majority 13,704 (29.86%)
1.26% swing LD to C.
(1997: C. maj. 14,035 (27.34%))

ASHFIELD
E.73,428 T. 39,350 (53.59%) Lab. hold
*Rt. Hon. G. Hoon, Lab.   22,875
Julian Leigh, C.   9,607
Bill Smith, LD   4,428
Melvin Harby, Ind.   1,471
George Watson, Soc. All.   589
Ms Katrina Howse, Soc. Lab.   380
Lab. majority 13,268 (33.72%)
5.60% swing Lab. to C.
(1997: Lab. maj. 22,728 (44.91%))

ASHFORD
E.76,699 T. 47,937 (62.50%)   C. hold
*Damien Green, C.   22,739
John Adams, Lab.   15,380
Keith Fitchett, LD   7,236
Richard Boden, Green   1,353
David Waller, UK Ind.   1,229

C. majority 7,359 (15.35%)
2.84% swing Lab. to C.
(1997: C. maj. 5,355 (9.68%))

ASHTON UNDER LYNE
E.72,820 T. 35,764 (49.11%) Lab. hold
David Heyes, Lab.   22,340
Tim Charlesworth, C.   6,822
Mrs Kate Fletcher, LD   4,237
Roger Woods, BNP   1,617
Nigel Rolland, Green   748
Lab. majority 15,518 (43.39%)
2.59% swing Lab. to C.
(1997: Lab. maj. 22,965 (48.57%))

AYLESBURY
E.80,002 T. 49,087 (61.36%)   C. hold
*David Lidington, C.   23,230
Peter Jones, LD   13,221
Keith White, Lab.   11,388
Justin Harper, UK Ind.   1,248
C. majority 10,009 (20.39%)
2.88% swing LD to C.
(1997: C. maj. 8,419 (14.63%))

BANBURY
E.83,392 T. 51,515 (61.77%)   C. hold
*Tony Baldry, C.   23,271
Leslie Sibley, Lab.   18,052
Tony Worgan, LD   8,216
Bev Cotton, Green   1,281
Stephen Harris, UK Ind.   695
C. majority 5,219 (10.13%)
1.02% swing Lab. to C.
(1997: C. maj. 4,737 (8.10%))

BARKING
E.55,229 T. 25,126 (45.49%) Lab. hold
*Mrs Margaret Hodge, Lab.   15,302
Mike Weatherley, C.   5,768
Anura Keppetipola, LD   2,450
Mark Toleman, BNP   1,606
Lab. majority 9,534 (37.94%)
5.14% swing Lab. to C.
(1997: Lab. maj. 15,896 (48.22%))

BARNSLEY CENTRAL
E.60,086 T. 27,543 (45.84%) Lab. hold
*Eric Illsley, Lab.   19,181
Alan Hartley, LD   4,051
Ian McCord, C.   3,608
Henry Rajch, Soc. All.   703
Lab. majority 15,130 (54.93%)
6.26% swing Lab. to C.
(1997: Lab. maj. 24,501 (67.15%))

BARNSLEY EAST & MEXBOROUGH
E.65,655 T. 32,509 (49.51%) Lab. hold
*Jeff Ennis, Lab.   21,945
Mrs Sharron Brook, LD   5,156
Matthew Offord, C.   4,024
Terry Robinson, Soc. Lab.   722
George Savage, UK Ind.   662
Lab. majority 16,789 (51.64%)
5.57% swing Lab. to LD
(1997: Lab. maj. 26,763 (61.76%))

BARNSLEY WEST & PENISTONE
E.65,291 T. 34,564 (52.94%) Lab. hold
*Michael Clapham, Lab.   20,244
William Rowe, C.   7,892

Miles Crompton, LD   6,428
Lab. majority 12,352 (35.74%)
2.59% swing Lab. to C.
(1997: Lab. maj. 17,267 (40.91%))

BARROW & FURNESS
E.64,746 T. 39,020 (60.27%) Lab. hold
*Rt. Hon. J. Hutton, Lab.   21,724
James Airey, C.   11,835
Barry Rabone, LD   4,750
John Smith, UK Ind.   711
Lab. majority 9,889 (25.34%)
2.36% swing Lab. to C.
(1997: Lab. maj. 14,497 (30.06%))

BASILDON
E.74,121 T. 40,875 (55.15%)Lab Co-op
hold
*Ms Angela Smith, Lab. Co-op.   21,551
Dominic Schofield, C.   13,813
Ms Jane Smithard, LD   3,691
Frank Mallon, UK Ind.   1,397
Dick Duane, Soc. All.   423
Lab Co-op majority 7,738 (18.93%)`
3.04% swing Lab Co-op to C.
(1997: Lab. maj. 13,280 (25.02%))

BASINGSTOKE
E.79,110 T. 47,995 (60.67%)   C. hold
*Andrew Hunter, C.   20,490
Jon Hartley, Lab.   19,610
Steve Sollitt, LD   6,693
Mrs Kim-Elisbeth Graham,
UK Ind.   1,202
C. majority 880 (1.83%)
1.18% swing C. to Lab.
(1997: C. maj. 2,397 (4.19%))

BASSETLAW
E.68,302 T. 38,895 (56.95%) Lab. hold
John Mann, Lab.   21,506
Mrs Alison Holley, C.   11,758
Neil Taylor, LD   4,942
Kevin Meloy, Soc. Lab.   689
Lab. majority 9,748 (25.06%)
5.68% swing Lab. to C.
(1997: Lab. maj. 17,460 (36.43%))

BATH
E.71,372 T. 46,296 (64.87%)   LD hold
*Don Foster, LD   23,372
Ashley Fox, C.   13,478
Ms Marilyn Hawkings, Lab.   7,269
Mike Boulton, Green   1,469
Andrew Tettenborn, UK Ind.   708
LD majority 9,894 (21.37%)
2.06% swing C. to LD
(1997: LD maj. 9,319 (17.26%))

BATLEY & SPEN
E.63,665 T. 38,542 (60.54%) Lab. hold
*Mike Wood Lab.   19,224
Mrs Elizabeth Peacock C.   14,160
Ms Kath Pinnock, LD   3,989
Clive Lord, Green   595
Allen Burton, UK Ind.   574
Lab. majority 5,064 (13.14%)
0.03% swing C. to Lab.
(1997: Lab. maj. 6,141 (13.08%))

BATTERSEA
E.67,495 T. 36,804 (54.53%) Lab. hold
*Martin Linton, *Lab.*   18,498
Mrs Lucy Shersby, *C.*   13,445
Ms Siobhan Vitelli, *LD*   4,450
Thomas Barber, *Ind.*   411
Lab. majority 5,053 (13.73%)
1.21% swing C. to Lab.
(1997: Lab. maj. 5,360 (11.31%))

BEACONSFIELD
E.68,378 T. 42,044 (61.49%) C. hold
*Dominic Grieve *C.*   22,233
Stephen Lathrope, *Lab.*   9,168
Stephen Lloyd, *LD*   9,017
Andrew Moffatt, *UK Ind.*   1,626
C. majority 13,065 (31.07%)
0.95% swing Lab. to C.
(1997: C. maj. 13,987 (27.86%))

BECKENHAM
E.72,241 T. 45,562 (63.07%) C. hold
*Mrs Jacqui Lait *C.*   20,618
Richard Watts, *Lab.*   15,659
Alex Feakes, *LD*   7,308
Ms Karen Moran, *Green*   961
Christopher Pratt, *UK Ind.*   782
Rif Winfield *Lib.*   234
C. majority 4,959 (10.88%)
0.89% swing Lab. to C.
(1997 Nov by-election: C. maj. 1,227
(3.85%); (1997: C. maj. 4,953 (9.11%))

BEDFORD
E.67,763 T. 40,579 (59.88%) Lab. hold
*Patrick Hall, *Lab.*   19,454
Mrs Nicky Attenborough, *C.*   13,297
Michael Headley, *LD*   6,425
Dr Richard Rawlins, *Ind.*   973
Mrs Jennifer Lo Bianco, *UK Ind.*   430
Lab. majority 6,157 (15.17%)
0.89% swing Lab. to C.
(1997: Lab. maj. 8,300 (16.96%))

BEDFORDSHIRE MID
E.70,594 T. 46,638 (66.07%) C. hold
*Jonathan Sayeed, *C.*   22,109
James Valentine, *Lab.*   14,043
Graham Mabbutt, *LD*   9,205
Christopher Laurence, *UK Ind.*   1,281
C. majority 8,066 (17.29%)
1.89% swing Lab. to C.
(1997: C. maj. 7,090 (13.51%))

BEDFORDSHIRE NORTH EAST
E.69,451 T. 45,246 (65.15%) C. hold
Alastair Burt, *C.*   22,586
Philip Ross, *Lab.*   14,009
Dan Rogerson, *LD*   7,409
Ms Ros Hill, *UK Ind.*   1,242
C. majority 8,577 (18.96%)
3.64% swing Lab. to C.
(1997: C. maj. 5,883 (11.68%))

BEDFORDSHIRE SOUTH WEST
E.72,126 T. 43,854 (60.80%) C. hold
Andrew Selous, *C.*   18,477
Andrew Date, *Lab.*   17,701
Martin Pantling, *LD*   6,473
Tom Wise, *UK Ind.*   1,203
C. majority 776 (1.77%)
0.76% swing Lab. to C.
(1997: C. maj. 132 (0.24%))

BERWICK-UPON-TWEED
E.56,918 T. 36,308 (63.79%) LD hold
*Rt. Hon. A. Beith *LD*   18,651
Glen Sanderson, *C.*   10,193
Martin Walker, *Lab.*   6,435
John Pearson, *UK Ind.*   1,029
LD majority 8,458 (23.30%)
0.94% swing C. to LD
(1997: LD maj. 8,042 (19.24%))

BETHNAL GREEN & BOW
E.79,192 T. 38,470 (48.58%) Lab. hold
*Ms Oona King, *Lab.*   19,380
Shahagir Faruk, *C.*   9,323
Ms Janet Ludlow, *LD*   5,946
Ms Anna Bragga, *Green*   1,666
Michael Davidson, *BNP*   1,267
Dennis Deldlerfield, *NBP*   888
Lab. majority 10,057 (26.14%)
0.44% swing C. to Lab.
(1997: Lab. maj. 11,285 (25.26%))

BEVERLEY & HOLDERNESS
E.75,146 T. 46,375 (61.71%) C. hold
*James Cran, *C.*   19,168
Ms Pippa Langford, *Lab.*   18,387
Stewart Willie, *LD*   7,356
Stephen Wallis, *UK Ind.*   1,464
C. majority 781 (1.68%)
0.08% swing Lab. to C.
(1997: C. maj. 811 (1.53%))

BEXHILL & BATTLE
E.69,010 T. 44,783 (64.89%) C. hold
Greg Barker, *C.*   21,555
Stephen Hardy, *LD*   11,052
Ms Anne Moore-Williams, *Lab.*   8,702
Nigel Farage, *UK Ind.*   3,474
C. majority 10,503 (23.45%)
0.40% swing LD to C.
(1997: C. maj. 11,100 (22.66%))

BEXLEYHEATH & CRAYFORD
E.63,580 T. 40,378 (63.51%) Lab. hold
*Nigel Beard, *Lab.*   17,593
David Evennett, *C.*   16,121
Nickolas O'Hare, *LD*   4,476
Colin Smith, *BNP*   1,408
John Dunford, *UK Ind.*   780
Lab. majority 1,472 (3.65%)
1.72% swing Lab. to C.
(1997: Lab. maj. 3,415 (7.08%))

BILLERICAY
E.78,528 T. 45,598 (58.07%) C. hold
John Baron, *C.*   21,608
Ms Amanda Campbell, *Lab.*   16,595
Frank Bellard, *LD*   6,323
Nick Yeomans, *UK Ind.*   1,072
C. majority 5,013 (10.99%)
4.27% swing Lab. to C.
(1997: C. maj. 1,356 (2.45%))

BIRKENHEAD
E.60,726 T. 28,967 (47.70%) Lab. hold
*Rt. Hon. F. Field, *Lab.*   20,418
Brian Stewart, *C.*   827
Roy Wood, *LD*   3,722
Lab. majority 15,591 (53.82%)
0.86% swing Lab. to C.
(1997: Lab. maj. 21,843 (55.55%))

BIRMINGHAM EDGBASTON
E.67,405 T. 37,749 (56.00%) Lab. hold
*Ms Gisela Stuart *Lab.*   18,517
Nigel Hastilow, *C.*   13,819
Ms Nicola Davies, *LD*   4,528
John Gretton, *Pro Euro C*   454
Sam Brackenbury, *Soc. Lab.*   431
Lab. majority 4,698 (12.45%)
1.23% swing C. to Lab.
(1997: Lab. maj. 4,842 (9.99%))

BIRMINGHAM ERDINGTON
E.65,668 T. 30,604 (46.60%) Lab. hold
Sion Llewelyn Simon, *Lab.*   17,375
Oliver Lodge, *C.*   7,413
Ms Sandra Johnson, *LD*   3,602
Michael Shore, *NF*   681
Steve Goddard, *Soc. All.*   669
Mark Nattrass, *UK Ind.*   521
Ms Judith Sambrook-Marshall,
Soc. Lab.   343
Lab. majority 9,962 (32.55%)
0.62% swing Lab. to C.
(1997: Lab. maj. 12,657 (31.32%))

BIRMINGHAM HALL GREEN
E.57,563 T. 33,084 (57.47%) Lab. hold
*Stephen McCabe, *Lab.*   18,049
Chris White, *C.*   11,441
Punjab Singh, *LD*   2,926
Peter Johnson, *UK Ind.*   708
Lab. majority 6,648 (20.09%)
0.02% swing Lab. to C.
(1997: Lab. maj. 8,420 (20.14%))

BIRMINGHAM HODGE LODGE
E.55,254 T. 26,465 (47.90%) Lab. hold
*Rt. Hon. T. Davis, *Lab.*   16,901
Mrs Debbie Lewis, *C.*   5,283
Alistair Dow, *LD*   2,147
Lee Windridge, *BNP*   889
Parwez Hussain, *PJP*   561
Dennis Cridge, *Soc. Lab.*   284
Harvey Vivian, *UK Ind.*   275
Ayub Khan, *Muslim*   125
Lab. majority 11,618 (43.90%)
1.16% swing C. to Lab.
(1997: Lab. maj. 14,200 (41.58%))

BIRMINGHAM LADYWOOD
E.71,113 T. 31,493 (44.29%) Lab. hold
*Rt. Hon. Ms C. Short, *Lab.*   21,694
Benjamin Prentice, *C.*   3,551
Mahmood Chaudhry, *LD*   2,586
Allah Ditta, *PJP*   2,112
Surinder Virdee, *Soc. Lab.*   443
Mahmood Hussain, *Muslim*   432
James Caffery, *(ProLife)*   392
Dr Anneliese Nattrass, *UK Ind.*   283
Lab. majority 18,143 (57.61%)
1.59% swing Lab. to C.
(1997: Lab. maj. 23,082 (60.78%))

BIRMINGHAM PERRY BARR
E.71,121 T. 37,417 (52.61%) Lab. hold
Khalid Mahmood, *Lab.*   17,415
David Binns, *C.*   8,662
Jon Hunt, *LD*   8,566
Avtar Singh Jouh, *Soc. Lab.*   1,544
Ms Caroline Johnson, *Soc. All.*   465
Ms Natalya Nattrass, *UK Ind.*   352
Michael Roche, *Marxist*   221

Robert Davidson, *Muslim*   192
Lab. majority 8,753 (23.39%)
8.96% swing Lab. to C.
(1997: Lab. maj. 18,957 (41.32%))

BIRMINGHAM SELLY OAK
E. 71,237 T. 40,100 (56.29%) Lab. hold
*Dr Lynne Jones, *Lab.*   21,015
Ken Hardeman, *C.*   10,676
David Osborne, *LD*   6,532
Barney Smith, *Green*   1,309
Mrs Beryl Williams, *UK Ind.*   568
Lab. majority 10,339 (25.78%)
1.04% swing Lab. to C.
(1997: Lab. maj. 14,088 (27.87%))

BIRMINGHAM SPARKBROOK & SMALL HEATH
E.74,358 T. 36,647 (49.28%) Lab. hold
*Roger Godsiff, *Lab.*   21,087
Qassim Afzal, *LD*   4,841
Shafaq Hussain, *PJP*   4,770
Iftkhar Hussain, *C.*   3,948
Gul Mohammed, *Ind.*   662
Wayne Vincent, *UK Ind.*   634
Abdul Aziz, *Muslim*   401
Salman Mirza, *Soc. All.*   304
Lab. majority 16,246 (44.33%))
5.31% swing Lab. to LD
(1997: Lab. maj. 19,526 (46.76%)

BIRMINGHAM YARDLEY
E.52,444 T. 30,013 (57.23%) Lab. hold
*Rt. Hon. Ms E. Morris *Lab.*   14,085
John Hemming, *LD*   11,507
Barrie Roberts, *C.*   3,941
Alan Ware, *UK Ind.*   329
Colin Wren, *Soc. Lab.*   151
Lab. majority 2,578 (8.59%)
2.74% swing Lab. to LD
(1997: Lab. maj. 5,315 (14.07%))

BISHOP AUCKLAND
E.67,377 T. 38,559 (57.23%) Lab. hold
*Rt. Hon. D. Foster, *Lab.*   22,680
Mrs Fiona McNish, *C.*   8,754
Chris Foote-Wood, *LD*   6,073
Carl Bennett, *Green*   1,052
Lab. majority 13,926 (36.12%)
4.85% swing Lab. to C.
(1997: Lab. maj. 21,064 (45.82%))

BLABY
E.73,907 T. 47,642 (64.46%)   C. hold
*Andrew Robathan, *C.*   22,104
David Morgan, *Lab.*   15,895
Geoff Welsh, *LD*   8,286
Edward Scott, *BNP*   1,357
C. majority 6,209 (13.03%)
0.48% swing Lab. to C.
(1997: C. maj. 6,474 (12.08%))

BLACKBURN
E.72,621 T. 40,484 (55.75%) Lab. hold
*Rt. Hon. J. Straw, *Lab.*   21,808
John Cotton, *C.*   12,559
Imtiaz Patel, *LD*   3,264
Mrs Dorothy Baxter, *UK Ind.*   1,185
Paul Morris, *Ind.*   577
Terence Cullen, *Soc. Lab.*   559
Frederick Nichol, *Socialist*   532
Lab. majority 9,249 (22.85%)
3.79% swing Lab. to C.

(1997: Lab. maj. 14,451 (30.43%))

BLACKPOOL NORTH & FLEETWOOD
E.74,456 T. 42,581 (57.19%) Lab. hold
*Ms Joan Humble, *Lab.*   21,610
Alan Vincent, *C.*   15,889
Steven Bate, *LD*   4,132
Colin Porter, *UK Ind.*   950
Lab. majority 5,721 (13.44%)
1.60% swing Lab. to C.
(1997: Lab. maj. 8,946 (16.64%))

BLACKPOOL SOUTH
E. 74,311 T. 38,792 (52.20%) Lab. hold
*Gordon Marsden, *Lab.*   21,060
David Morris, *C.*   12,798
Ms Doreen Holt, *LD*   4,115
Mrs VAL Cowell, *UK Ind.*   819
Lab. majority 8,262 (21.30%)
0.67% swing Lab. to C.
(1997: Lab. maj. 11,616 (22.63%))

BLAYDON
E.64,574 T. 37,086 (57.43%) Lab. hold
*John McWilliam, *Lab.*   20,340
Peter Maughan, *LD*   12,531
Mark Watson, *C.*   4,215
Lab. majority 7,809 (21.06%)
7.55% swing Lab. to LD
(1997: Lab. maj. 16,605 (36.16%))

BLYTH VALLEY
E.63,274 T. 34,550 (54.60%) Lab. hold
*Ronnie Campbel, *Lab.*   20,627
Jeff Reid, *LD*   8,439
Wayne Daley, *C.*   5,484
Lab. majority 12,188 (35.28%)
3.24% swing Lab. to LD
(1997: Lab. maj. 17,736 (41.75%))

BOGNOR REGIS & LITTLEHAMPTON
E. 66,903 T. 38,968 (58.25%)   C. hold
*Nick Gibb, *C.*   17,602
George O'Neill, *Lab.*   11,959
Ms Pamela Peskett, *LD*   6,846
George Stride, *UK Ind.*   1,779
Ms Lilias Rider Haggard Cheyne, *Green*   782
C. majority 5,643 (14.48%)
0.64% swing C. to Lab.
(1997: C. maj. 7,321 (15.76%))

BOLSOVER
E. 67,537 T. 38,271 (56.67%) Lab. hold
*Dennis Skinner, *Lab.*   26,249
Simon Massey, *C.*   7,472
Ms Marie Bradley, *LD*   4,550
Lab. majority 18,777 (49.06%)
4.10% swing Lab. to C.
(1997: Lab. maj. 27,149 (57.26%))

BOLTON NORTH EAST
E. 69,514 T. 38,950 (56.03%) Lab. hold
*David Crausby, *Lab.*   21,166
Michael Winstanley, *C.*   12,744
Tim Perkins, *LD*   4,004
Kenneth McIvor, *Green*   629
Ms Lynne Lowe, *Soc. Lab.*   407
Lab. majority 8,422 (21.62%)
2.06% swing Lab. to C.
(1997: Lab. maj. 12,669 (25.74%))

BOLTON SOUTH EAST
E. 68,140 T. 34,154 (50.12%) Lab. hold
*Dr Brian Iddon, *Lab.*   21,129
Haroon Rashid, *C.*   8,258
Frank Harasiwka, *LD*   3,941
Dr William John Kelly, *Soc. Lab.*   826
Lab. majority 12,871 (37.69%)
5.74% swing Lab. to C.
(1997: Lab. maj. 21,311 (49.16%))

BOLTON WEST
E. 66,033 T. 41,214 (62.41%) Lab. hold
*Ms Ruth Kelly, *Lab.*   19,381
James Stevens, *C.*   13,863
Ms Barbara Ronson, *LD*   7,573
David Toomer, *Soc. All.*   397
Lab. majority 5,518 (13.39%)
0.50% swing Lab. to C.
(1997: Lab. maj. 7,072 (14.39%))

BOOTLE
E. 56,320 T. 27,594 (49.00%) Lab. hold
*Joe Benton *Lab.*   21,400
Jim Murray, *LD*   2,357
Miss Judith Symes, *C.*   2,194
Dave Flynn, *Soc. Lab.*   971
Peter Glover, *Soc. All.*   672
Lab. majority 19,043 (69.01%)
4.05% swing Lab. to LD
(1997: Lab. maj. 28,421 (74.36%))

BOSTON & SKEGNESS
E. 69,010 T. 40,313 (58.42%)   C. hold
Mark Simmonds, *C.*   17,298
Ms Elaine Bird, *Lab.*   16,783
Duncan Moffatt, *LD*   4,994
Cyril Wakefield, *UK Ind.*   717
Martin Harrison, *Green*   521
C. majority 515 (1.28%)
0.06% swing C. to Lab.
(1997: C. maj. 647 (1.39%))

BOSWORTH
E. 69,992 T. 45,106 (64.44%)   C. hold
*David Tredinnick, *C.*   20,030
Andrew Furlong, *Lab.*   17,750
Jon Ellis, *LD*   7,326
C. majority 2,280 (5.05%)
1.54% swing Lab. to C.
(1997: C. maj. 1,027 (1.97%))

BOURNEMOUTH EAST
E. 60,454 T. 35,799 (59.22%)   C. hold
*David Atkinson, *C.*   15,501
Andrew Garratt, *LD*   12,067
Paul Nicholson, *Lab.*   7,107
George Chamberlaine, *UK Ind.*   1,124
C. majority 3,434 (9.59%)
0.21% swing C. to LD
(1997: C. maj. 4,346 (10.01%))

BOURNEMOUTH WEST
E.62,038 T. 33,648 (54.24%)   C. hold
*John Butterfill, *C.*   14,417
David Stokes, *Lab.*   9,699
Ms Fiona Hornby, *LD*   8,468
Mrs Cynthia Blake, *UK Ind.*   1,064
C. majority 4,718 (14.02%)
1.54% swing C. to Lab.
(1997: C. maj. 5,710 (13.90%))

BRACKNELL
E.81,118 T. 49,225 (60.68%)   C. hold
*Rt. Hon. A. Mackay, *C.*   22,962
Ms Janet Keene, *Lab.*   16,249
Ray Earwicker, *LD*   8,424
Lawrence Boxall, *UK Ind.*   1,266
Ms Dominica Roberts, *ProLife*   324
C. majority 6,713 (13.64%)
1.97% swing C. to Lab.
(1997: C. maj. 10,387 (17.58%))

BRADFORD NORTH
E.66,454 T. 35,017 (52.69%) Lab. hold
*Terry Rooney, *Lab.*   17,419
Zahid Iqbal, *C.*   8,450
David Ward, *LD*   6,924
John Brayshaw, *BNP*   1,613
Steven Schofield, *Green*   611
Lab. majority 8,969 (25.61%)
2.44% swing Lab. to C.)

BRADFORD SOUTH
E.68,450 T. 35,137 (51.33%) Lab. hold
*Gerry Sutcliffe, Lab   19,603
Graham Tennyson, *C.*   9,941
Alexander Wilson-Fletcher, *LD*   3,717
Peter North, *UK Ind.*   783
Tony Kelly, *Soc. Lab.*   571
Ateeq Siddique, *Soc. All.*   302
George Riseborough,
Def Welfare   220
Lab. majority 9,662 (27.50%)
0.61% swing Lab. to C.
(1997: Lab. maj. 12,936 (28.71%))

BRADFORD WEST
E.71,620 T. 38,370 (53.57%) Lab. hold
*Marsha Singh, *Lab.*   18,401
Mohammed Riaz, *C.*   14,236
John Robinson, *Green*   2,672
Abdul Rauf Khan, *LD*   2,437
Imran Hussain, *UK Ind.*   427
Farhan Khokhar, *AL*   197
Lab. majority 4,165 (10.85%)
1.17% swing C. to Lab.
(1997: Lab. maj. 3,877 (8.51%))

BRAINTREE
E.79,157 T. 50,315 (63.56%) Lab. hold
*Alan Hurst, *Lab.*   21,123
Brooks Newmark, *C.*   20,765
Peter Turner, *LD*   5,664
James Abbott, *Green*   1,241
Michael Nolan, *LCA*   774
Charles Cole, *UK Ind.*   748
Lab. majority 358 (0.71%)
0.95% swing Lab. to C.
(1997: Lab. maj. 1,451 (2.61%))

BRENT EAST
E.58,095 T. 28,992 (49.90%) Lab gain
Paul Daisley, *Lab.*   18,325
David Gauke, *C.*   5,278
Ms Nowsheen Bhatti, *LD*   3,065
Ms Simone Aspis, *Green*   1,361
Ms Sarah Macken, *ProLife*   392
Ms Iris Cremer, *Soc. Lab.*   383
Ashwin Tanna, *UK Ind.*   188
*Lab. majority*13,047 (45.00%)
0.01% swing Lab. to C.
(1997: Lab. maj. 15,882 (45.03%))

BRENT NORTH
E.58,789 T. 33,939 (57.73%) Lab. hold
*Barry Gardiner, *Lab.*   20,149
Philip Allott, *C.*   9,944
Paul Lorber, *LD*   3,846
Lab. majority 10,205 (30.07%)
9.77% swing C. to Lab.
(1997: Lab. maj. 4,019 (10.53%))

BRENT SOUTH
E.55,891 T. 28,637 (51.24%) Lab. hold
*Rt. Hon. P. Boateng, *Lab.*   20,984
Carupiah Selvarajah, *C.*   3,604
Havard Hughes, *LD*   3,098
Mick McDonnell, *Soc. All.*   491
Thomas Mac Stiofain, *Res. Motor*   460
Lab. majority 17,380 (60.69%)
1.81% swing C. to Lab.
(1997: Lab. maj. 19,691 (57.08%))

BRENTFORD & ISLEWORTH
E.84,049 T. 44,514 (52.96%) Lab. hold
*Ms Ann Keen *Lab.*   23,275
Tim Mack, *C.*   12,957
Gareth Hartwell, *LD*   5,994
Nic Ferriday, *Green*   1,324
Gerald Ingram, *UK Ind.*   412
Danny Faith, *Soc. All.*   408
Asa Khaira, *Ind.*   144
Lab. majority 10,318 (23.18%)
1.26% swing Lab. to C.
(1997: Lab. maj. 14,424 (25.70%))

BRENTWOOD & ONGAR
E.64,695 T. 43,542 (67.30%)   C. hold
*Eric Pickles, *C.*   16,558
†Martin Bell, *Ind Bell*   13,737
David Kendall, *LD*   6,772
Ms Diana Johnson, *Lab.*   5,505
Ken Gulleford, *UK Ind.*   611
Peter Pryke, *Ind.*   239
David Bishop, *Elvis*   68
Tony Appleton, *Ind.*   52
C. majority 2,821 (6.48%)
(1997: C. maj. 9,690 (19.10%))

BRIDGWATER
E.74,079 T. 47,847 (64.59%)   C. hold
Ian Liddell-Grainger, *C.*   19,354
Ian Thorn, *LD*   14,367
William Monteith, *Lab.*   12,803
Ms Vicky Gardner, *UK Ind.*   1,323
C. majority 4,987 (10.42%)
3.57% swing LD to C.
(1997: C. maj. 1,796 (3.28%))

BRIGG & GOOLE
E.63,536 T. 41,054 (64.62%) Lab. hold
*Ian Cawsey, *Lab.*   20,066
Don Stewart, *C.*   16,105
David Nolan, *LD*   3,796
Godfrey Bloom, *UK Ind.*   688
Michael Kenny, *Soc. Lab.*   399
Lab. majority 3,961 (9.65%)
2.00% swing Lab. to C.
(1997: Lab. maj. 6,389 (13.65%))

BRIGHTON KEMPTOWN
E.67,621 T. 39,203 (57.97%) Lab. hold
*Dr Desmond Turner, *Lab.*   18,745
Geoffrey Theobald, *C.*   13,823
Ms Jan Marshall, *LD*   4,064

Hugh Miller, *Green*   1,290
Dr James Chamberlain-
Webber, *UK Ind.*   543
John McLeod, *Soc. Lab.*   364
Dave Dobbs, *Free*   227
Ms Elaine Cook, *ProLife*   147
Lab. majority 4,922 (12.56%)
2.45% swing C. to Lab.
(1997: Lab. maj. 3,534 (7.66%))

BRIGHTON PAVILION
E.69,200 T. 40,723 (58.85%)Lab Co-op
hold
*David Lepper, *Lab. Co-op.*   19,846
David Gold, *C.*   10,203
Ms Ruth Berry, *LD*   5,348
Keith Taylor, *Green*   3,806
Ian Fyvie, *Soc. Lab.*   573
Bob Dobbs, *Free*   409
Stuart Hutchin, *UK Ind.*   361
Ms Marie Paragallo, *ProLife*   177
Lab Co-op majority 9,643 (23.68%)
1.63% swing Lab Co-op to C.
(1997: Lab. maj. 13,181 (26.93%))

BRISTOL EAST
E.70,279 T. 40,334 (57.39%) Lab. hold
*Ms Jean Corston, *Lab.*   22,180
Jack Lo-Presti, *C.*   8,788
Brian Niblett, *LD*   6,915
Geoff Collard, *Green*   1,110
Roger Marsh, *UK Ind.*   572
Mike Langley, *Soc. Lab.*   438
Andy Pryor, *Soc. All.*   331
Lab. majority 13,392 (33.20%)
0.16% swing Lab. to C.
(1997: Lab. maj. 16,159 (33.52%))

BRISTOL NORTH WEST
E.76,756 T. 46,692 (60.83%)Lab Co-op
hold
*Doug Naysmith *Lab. Co-op.*   24,436
Charles Hansard, *C.*   13,349
Peter Tyzack, *LD*   7,387
Miss Diane Carr, *UK Ind.*   1,149
Vince Horrigan, *Soc. Lab.*   371
Lab Co-op majority 11,087 (23.74%)
1.57% swing to Lab. Co-op
(1997: Lab. maj. 11,382 (20.60%))

BRISTOL SOUTH
E.72,490 T. 40,970 (56.52%) Lab. hold
*Ms Dawn Primarolo, *Lab.*   23,299
Richard Eddy, *C.*   9,118
James Main, *LD*   6,078
Glenn Vowles, *Green*   1,233
Brian Drummond, *Soc. All.*   496
Chris Prasad, *UK Ind.*   496
Giles Shorter, *Soc. Lab.*   250
Lab. majority 14,181 (34.61%)
2.08% swing Lab. to C.
(1997: Lab. maj. 19,328 (38.77%))

BRISTOL WEST
E.84,821 T. 55,665 (65.63%) Lab. hold
*Ms Valerie Davey, *Lab.*   20,505
Stephen Williams, *LD*   16,079
Mrs Pamela Chesters, *C.*   16,040
John Devaney, *Green*   1,961
Bernard Kennedy, *Soc. Lab.*   590
Simon Muir, *UK Ind.*   490

Lab. majority 4,426 (7.95%)
0.37% swing LD to Lab.
(1997: Lab. maj. 1,493 (2.38%))

BROMLEY & CHISLEHURST
E.68,763 T.43,231 (62.87%)   C. hold
*Rt. Hon. E. Forth C.   21,412
Ms Sue Polydorou, Lab.   12,375
Geoff Payne, LD   8,180
Rob Bryant, UK Ind.   1,264
C. majority 9,037 (20.90%)
0.09% swing C. to Lab.
(1997: C. maj. 11,118 (21.08%))

BROMSGROVE
E.68,115 T.45,684 (67.07%)   C. hold
*Miss Julie Kirkbride, C.   23,640
Peter McDonald, Lab.   15,502
Mrs Margaret Rowley, LD   5,430
Ian Gregory, UK Ind.   1,112
C. majority 8,138 (17.81%)
4.22% swing Lab. to C.
(1997: C. maj. 4,895 (9.38%))

BROXBOURNE
E.68,982 T. 37,845 (54.86%)   C. hold
*Mrs Marion Roe, C.   20,487
David Prendergast, Lab.   11,494
Ms Julia Davies, LD   4,158
Martin Harvey, UK Ind.   858
John Cope, BNP   848
C. majority 8,993 (23.76%)
4.80% swing Lab. to C.
(1997: C. maj. 6,653 (14.16%))

BROXTOWE
E.73,675 T.49,004 (66.51%) Lab. hold
*Nick Palmer, Lab.   23,836
Mrs Pauline Latham, C.   17,963
David Watts, LD   7,205
Lab. majority 5,873 (11.98%)
1.20% swing C. to Lab.
(1997: Lab. maj. 5,575 (9.59%))

BUCKINGHAM
E.65,270 T.45,272 (69.36%)   C. hold
*John Bercow, C.   24,296
Mark Seddon, Lab.   10,971
Ms Isobel Wilson, LD   9,037
Christopher Silcock, UK Ind.   968
C. majority 13,325 (29.43%)
2.18% swing Lab. to C.
(1997: C. maj. 12,386 (25.08%))

BURNLEY
E.66,393 T. 36,884 (55.55%) Lab. hold
*Peter Pike, Lab.   18,195
Robert Frost, C.   7,697
Paul Wright, LD   5,975
Steven Smith, BNP   4,151
Richard Buttrey, UK Ind.   866
Lab. majority 10,498 (28.46%)
4.62% swing Lab. to C.
(1997: Lab. maj. 17,062 (37.71%))

BURTON
E.75,194 T.46,457 (61.78%) Lab. hold
*Ms Janet Dean, Lab.   22,783
Mrs Maggie Punyer, C.   17,934
David Fletcher, LD   4,468
Ian Crompton, UK Ind.   984
John Taylor, ProLife   288

Lab. maority 4,849 (10.44%)
0.59% swing Lab. to C.
(1997: Lab. maj. 6,330 (11.62%))

BURY NORTH
E.71,108 T.44,788 (62.99%) Lab. hold
*David Chaytor, Lab.   22,945
John Walsh, C.   16,413
Bryn Hackley, LD   5,430
Lab. majority 6,532 (14.58%)
0.15% swing C. to Lab.
(1997: Lab. maj. 7,866 (14.29%))

BURY SOUTH
E.67,276 T.39,539 (58.77%) Lab. hold
*Ivan Lewis Lab.   .23,406
Mrs Nicola Le Page, C.   10,634
Tim Pickstone, LD   5,499
Lab. majority 12,772 (32.30%)
3.80% swing C. to Lab.
(1997: Lab. maj. 12,433 (24.70%))

BURY ST EDMUNDS
E.76,146 T. 50,257 (66.00%)   C. hold
*David Ruffley C.   21,850
Mark Ereira, Lab.   19,347
Richard Williams, LD   6,998
John Howlett, UK Ind.   831
Mike Brundle, Ind.   651
Michael Benwell, Soc. Lab.   580
C. majority 2,503 (4.98%)
2.16% swing Lab. to C.
(1997: C. maj. 368 (0.66%))

CALDER VALLEY
E.75,298 T. 47,425 (62.98%) Lab. hold
*Mrs Christine McCafferty, Lab. 20,244
Mrs Sue Robson-Catling, C.   17,150
Michael Taylor, LD   7,596
Steve Hutton, Green   1,034
John Nunn, UK Ind.   729
Philip Lockwood, LCA   672
Lab. majority 3,094 (6.52%)
2.27% swing Lab. to C.
(1997: Lab. maj. 6,255 (11.07%))

CAMBERWELL & PECKHAM
E.53,694 T. 25,104 (46.75%) Lab. hold
*Rt. Hon. Ms H. Harman, Lab.   17,473
Donnachadh McCarthy, LD   3,350
Jonathan Morgan, C.   2,740
Storm Poorun, Green   805
John Mulrenan, Soc. All.   478
Robert Adams, Soc. Lab.   188
Frank Sweeney, WRP   70
Lab. majority 14,123 (56.26%)
0.91% swing Lab. to LD
(1997: Lab. maj. 16,351 (57.43%))

CAMBRIDGE
E.70,663 T. 42,836 (60.62%) Lab. hold
*Ms Anne Campbell, Lab.   19,316
David Howarth, LD   10,737
Graham Stuart, C.   9,829
Stephen Lawrence, Green   1,413
Howard Senter, Soc. All.   716
Len Baynes, UK Ind.   532
Ms Clare Underwood, ProLife   232
Ms Margaret Courtney, WRP   61
Lab. majority 8,579 (20.03%)
8.64% swing Lab. to LD
(1997: Lab. maj. 14,137 (27.54%))

CAMBRIDGESHIRE NORTH EAST
E.79,891 T. 48,051 (60.15%)   C. hold
*Malcolm Moss, C.   23,132
Dil Owen, Lab.   16,759
Richard Renaut, LD   6,733
John Stevens, UK Ind.   1,189
Tony Hoey, ProLife   238
C. majority 6,373 (13.26%)
2.03% swing Lab. to C.
(1997: C. maj. 5,101 (9.20%))

CAMBRIDGESHIRE NORTH WEST
E.70,569 T. 43,956 (62.29%)   C. hold
*Rt. Hon. Sir B. Mawhinney, C. 21,895
Ms Anthea Cox, Lab.   13,794
Alastair Taylor, LD   6,957
Barry Hudson, UK Ind.   881
David Hall, Ind.   429
C. majority 8,101 (18.43%)
1.27% swing Lab. to C.
(1997: C. maj. 7,754 (15.88%))

CAMBRIDGESHIRE SOUTH
E.72,095 T. 48,341 (67.05%)   C. hold
*Andrew Lansley C.   21,387
Ms Amanda Taylor, LD   12,984
Dr Joan Herbert, Lab.   11,737
Simon Saggers, Green   1,182
Mrs Helene Davies, UK Ind.   875
Ms Beata Klepacka, ProLife   176
C. majority 8,403 (17.38%)
0.58% swing LD to C.
(1997: C. maj. 8,712 (16.23%))

CAMBRIDGESHIRE SOUTH EAST
E.81,663 T. 51,886 (63.54%)   C. hold
*James Paice, C.   22,927
Ms Sal Brinton, LD   13,937
Andrew Inchley, Lab.   13,714
Neil Scarr, UK Ind.   1,308
C. majority 8,990 (17.33%)
0.27% swing C. to LD
(1997: C. maj. 9,349 (16.46%))

CANNOCK CHASE
E.73,423 T. 41,064 (55.93%) Lab. hold
*Dr Tony Wright, Lab.   23,049
Gavin Smithers, C.   12,345
Stewart Reynolds, LD   5,670
Lab. majority 10,704 (26.07%)
0.79% swing Lab. to C.
(1997: Lab. maj. 14,478 (27.65%))

CANTERBURY
E.74,159 T. 45,132 (60.86%)   C. hold
*Julian Brazier, C.   18,711
Ms Emily Thornberry, Lab.   16,642
Peter Wales, LD   8,056
Ms Hazel Dawe, Green   920
Ms Lisa Moore, UK Ind.   803
C. majority 2,069 (4.58%)
1.37% swing C. to Lab.
(1997: C. maj. 3,964 (7.33%))

CARLISLE
E.58,811 T. 34,909 (59.36%) Lab. hold
*Eric Martlew, Lab.   17,856
Mike Mitchelson, C.   12,154
John Guest, LD   4,076
Colin Paisley, LCA   554
Paul Wilcox, Soc. All.   269
Lab. majority 5,702 (16.33%)

6.04% swing Lab. to C.
(1997: Lab. maj. 12,390 (28.41%))

CARSHALTON & WALLINGTON
E. 67,337 T. 40,612 (60.31%) LD hold
*Tom Brake, LD   18,289
Ken Andrew C.   13,742
Ms Margaret Cooper, Lab.   7,466
Simon Dixon, Green   614
Martin Haley, UK Ind.   501
LD majority 4,547 (11.20%)
3.26% swing C. to LD
(1997: LD maj. 2,267 (4.68%))

CASTLE POINT
E.68,108 T. 39,763 (58.38%) Con gain
Dr Robert Spink, C.   17,738
*Ms Christine Butler, Lab.   16,753
Billy Boulton, LD   3,116
Ron Hurrell, UK Ind.   1,273
Douglas Roberts, Ind.   663
Nik Searle, Truth   220
C. majority 985 (2.48%)
2.39% swing Lab. to C.
(1997: Lab. majority 1,116 (2.30%))

CHARNWOOD
E.74,836 T. 48,265 (64.49%)   C. hold
*Rt. Hon. S. Dorrell, C.   23,283
Sean Sheahan, Lab.   15,544
Ms Susan King, LD   7,835
Jamie Bye, UK Ind.   1,603
C. majority 7,739 (16.03%)
2.77% swing Lab. to C.
(1997: C. maj. 5,900 (10.50%))

CHATHAM & AYLESFORD
E.69,759 T. 39,735 (56.96%) Lab. hold
*Jonathan Shaw, Lab.   19,180
Sean Holden, C.   14,840
David Lettington, LD   4,705
Gregory Knopp, UK Ind.   1,010
Lab. majority 4,340 (10.92%)
2.62% swing C. to Lab.
(1997: Lab. maj. 2,790 (5.68%))

CHEADLE
E.69,002 T. 43,606 (63.20%)   LD gain
Ms Patsy Calton, LD   18,477
*Stephen Day, C.   18,444
Howard Dawber, Lab.   6,086
Vincent Cavanagh, UK Ind.   599
LD majority, 33 (0.08%)
3.07% swing C. to LD
(1997: C. maj. 3,189 (6.07%))

CHELMSFORD WEST
E. 78,291 T. 48,143 (61.49%)   C. hold
*Simon Burns, C.   20,446
Adrian Longden, Lab.   14,185
Stephen Robinson, LD   11,197
Mrs Eleanor Burgess, Green   837
Ken Wedon, UK Ind.   785
Christopher Philbin, LCA   693
C. majority 6,261 (13.01%)
0.62% swing C. to Lab.
(1997: C. maj. 6,691 (11.42%))

CHELTENHAM
E.67,563 T. 41,835 (61.92%)   LD hold
*Nigel Jones, LD   19,970
Rob Garnham, C.   14,715

Andy Erlam, Lab.   5,041
Keith Bessant, Green   735
Dancing Ken Hanks, Loony   513
Jim Carver UK Ind.   482
Anthony Gates, ProLife   272
Roger Everest, Ind.   107
LD majority 5,255 (12.56%)
0.32% swing LD to C.
(1997: LD maj. 6,645 (13.21%))

CHESHAM & AMERSHAM
E.70,021 T. 45,283 (64.67%)   C. hold
*Mrs Cheryl Gillan, C.   22,867
John Ford, LD   10,985
Ken Hulme, Lab.   8,497
Ian Harvey, UK Ind.   1,367
Nick Wilkins, Green   1,114
Ms Gillian Duval, ProLife   453
C. majority 11,882 (26.24%)
0.16% swing C. to LD
(1997: C. maj. 13,859 (26.55%))

CHESTER, CITY OF
E.70,382 T. 44,877 (63.76%) Lab. hold
*Ms Christine Russell Lab.   21,760
David Jones, C.   14,866
Tony Dawson, LD   6,589
Allan Weddell, UK Ind.   899
George Rogers, Ind.   763
Lab. majority 6,894 (15.36%)
1.70% swing Lab. to C.
(1997: Lab. maj. 10,553 (18.76%))

CHESTERFIELD
E.73,252 T. 44,441 (60.67%)   LD gain
Paul Holmes, LD   21,249
Reg Race, Lab.   18,663
Simon Hitchcock, C.   3,613
Ms Jeannie Robinson, Soc. All.   437
Bill Harrison, Soc. Lab.   295
Christopher Rawson, Ind.   184
LD majority 2,586 (5.82%)
8.53% swing Lab. to LD
(1997: Lab. maj. 5,775 (11.24%))

CHICHESTER
E.77,703 T. 49,512 (63.72%)   C. hold
*Andrew Tyrie C.   23,320
Ms Lynne Ravenscroft, LD   11,965
Ms Celia Barlow, Lab.   10,627
Douglas Denny, UK Ind.   2,308
Gavin Graham, Green   1,292
C. majority 11,355 (22.93%)
2.74% swing LD to C.
(1997: C. maj. 9,734 (17.45%))

CHINGFORD & WOODFORD GREEN
E.63,252 T. 36,982 (58.47%)   C. hold
*Iain Duncan Smith, C.   17,834
Ms Jessica Webb, Lab.   12,347
John Beanse, LD   5,739
Ms Jean Griffin, BNP   1,062
C. majority 5,487 (14.84%)
0.99% swing Lab. to C.
(1997: Lab. maj. 5,714 (12.85%))

CHIPPING BARNET
E.70,217 T. 42,456 (60.46%)   C. hold
*Sir Sydney Chapman, C.   19,702
Damien Welfare, Lab.   17,001
Sean Hooker, LD   5,753

C. majority 2,701 (6.36%)
2.14% swing Lab. to C.
(1997: C. maj. 1,035 (2.09%))

CHORLEY
E.77,036 T. 47,952 (62.25%) Lab. hold
*Lindsay Hoyle, Lab.   25,088
Peter Booth, C.   6,644
Stephen Fenn, LD   5,372
Graham Frost, UK Ind.   848
Lab. majority 8,444 (17.61%)
0.25% swing C. to Lab.
(1997: Lab. maj. 9,870 (17.10%))

CHRISTCHURCH
E.73,503 T. 49,567 (67.44%)   C. hold
*Christopher Chope, C.   27,306
Ms Dorothy Webb, LD   13,762
Ms Judith Begg, Lab.   7,506
Ms Margaret Strange, UK Ind.   993
C. majority 13,544 (27.32%)
11.74% swing LD to C.
(1997: C. maj. 2,165 (3.85%))

CITIES OF LONDON & WESTMINSTER
E.71,935 T. 33,975 (47.23%)   C. hold
Mark Field, C.   15,737
Michael Katz, Lab.   11,238
Martin Horwood, LD   5,218
Hugo Charlton, Green   1,318
Colin Merton, UK Ind.   464
C. majority 4,499 (13.24%)
0.54% swing Lab. to C.
(1997: C. maj. 4,881 (12.16%))

CLEETHORPES
E.68,392 T. 42,418 (62.02%) Lab. hold
*Ms Shona McIsaac, Lab.   21,032
Stephen Howd, C.   15,412
Gordon Smith, LD   5,080
Ms Janet Hatton, UK Ind.   894
Lab. majority 5,620 (13.25%)
2.47% swing Lab. to C.
(1997: Lab. maj. 9,176 (18.18%))

COLCHESTER
E.78,955 T. 43,736 (55.39%)   LD hold
*Bob Russell, LD   18,627
Kevin Bentley, C.   13,074
Chris Fegan, Lab.   10,925
Roger Lord, UK Ind.   631
Leonard Overy-Owen, Grey   479
LD maj. 5,553 (12.70%)
4.83% swing C. to LD
(1997: LD maj. 1,581 (3.04%))

COLNE VALLEY
E.74,192 T. 46,987 (63.33%) Lab. hold
*Ms Kali Mountford Lab.   18,967
Philip Davies, C.   14,328
Gordon Beever, LD   11,694
Richard Plunkett, Green   1,081
Dr Arthur Quarmby, UK Ind.   917
Lab. majority 4,639 (9.87%)
0.65% swing Lab. to C.
(1997: Lab. maj. 4,840 (8.58%))

CONGLETON
E.71,941 T. 45,083 (62.67%)   C. hold
*Mrs Ann Winterton, C.   20,872
John Flanagan, Lab.   13,738

David Lloyd-Griffiths, *LD*   9,719
Bill Young, *UK Ind.*   754
C. majority 7,134 (15.82%)
1.08% swing Lab. to C.
(1997: C. maj. 6,130 (11.48%))

COPELAND
*E.*53,526 *T.* 34,750 (64.92%) Lab. hold
*Rt. Hon. Dr J. Cunningham,
Lab.   17,991
Mike Graham, *C.*   13,027
Mark Gayler, *LD*   3,732
Lab. majority 4,964 (14.28%)
7.30% swing Lab. to C.
(1997: Lab. maj. 11,944 (28.89%))

CORBY
*E.*72,304 *T.* 47,222 (65.31%)Lab Co-op
hold
*Phil Hope, *Lab. Co-op.*   23,283
Andrew Griffith, *C.*   17,583
Kevin Scudder, *LD*   4,751
Ian Gillman, *UK Ind.*   855
Andrew Dickson, *Soc. Lab.*   750
Lab Co-op majority 5,700 (12.07%)
4.95% swing Lab Co-op to C.
(1997: Lab. maj. 11,860 (21.98%))

CORNWALL NORTH
*E.*84,662 *T.* 53,983 (63.76%) LD hold
*Paul Tyler, *LD*   28,082
John Weller, *C.*   18,250
Mike Goodman, *Lab.*   5,257
Steve Protz, *UK Ind.*   2,394
LD majority 9,832 (18.21%)
2.79% swing LD to C.
(1997: LD maj. 13,933 (23.79%))

CORNWALL SOUTH EAST
*E.*79,090 *T.* 51,753 (65.44%) LD hold
*Colin Breed, *LD*   23,756
Ashley Gray, *C.*   18,381
Bill Stevens, *Lab.*   6,429
Graham Palmer, *UK Ind.*   1,978
Dr Ken George, *Meb. Ker.*   1,209
LD majority 5,375 (10.39%)
0.45% swing LD to C.
(1997: LD maj. 6,480 (11.28%))

COTSWOLD
*E.*68,154 *T.* 45,981 (67.47%) C. hold
*Geoffrey Clifton-Brown, *C.*   23,133
Ms Angela Lawrence, *LD*   11,150
Richard Wilkins, *Lab.*   10,383
Mrs Jill Stopps, *UK Ind.*   1,315
C. majority 11,983 (26.06%)
1.33% swing LD to C.
(1997: C. maj. 11,965 (23.41%))

COVENTRY NORTH EAST
*E.*73,998 *T.* 37,265 (50.36%) Lab. hold
Bob Ainsworth, *Lab.*   22,739
Gordon Bell, *C.*   6,988
Geoffrey Sewards, *LD*   4,163
Dave Nellist, *Soc. All.*   2,638
Edward Sheppard, *BNP*   737
Lab. majority 15,751 (42.27%)
2.34% swing Lab. to C.
(1997: Lab. maj. 22,569 (46.94%))

COVENTRY NORTH WEST
*E.*76,652 *T.* 42,551 (55.51%) Lab. hold
*Geoffrey Robinson, *Lab.*   21,892

Andrew Fairburn, *C.*   11,018
Napier Penlington, *LD*   5,832
Ms Christine Oddy, *Ind.*   3,159
Mark Benson, *UK Ind.*   650
Lab. majority 10,874 (25.56%)
2.50% swing Lab. to C.
(1997: Lab. maj. 16,601 (30.56%))

COVENTRY SOUTH
*E.*72,527 *T.* 40,096 (55.28%) Lab. hold
*Jim Cunningham, *Lab.*   20,125
Ms Heather Wheeler, *C.*   11,846
Vincent McKee, *LD*   5,672
Rob Windsor, *Soc. All.*   1,475
Ms Irene Rogers, *Ind.*   564
Timothy Logan, *Soc. Lab.*   414
Lab. majority 8,279 (20.65%)
0.61% swing Lab. to C.
(1997: Lab. maj. 10,953 (21.86%))

CRAWLEY
*E.*71,626 *T.* 39,522 (55.18%) Lab. hold
*Ms Laura Moffatt, *Lab.*   19,488
Henry Smith, *C.*   12,718
Ms Linda Seekings, *LD*   5,009
Brian Galloway, *UK Ind.*   1,137
Ms Claire Staniford, *Loony*   388
Arshad Khan, *JP*   271
Karl Stewart, *Soc. Lab.*   260
Ms Muriel Hirsch, *Soc. All.*   251
Lab. majority 6,770 (17.13%)
3.05% swing Lab. to C.
(1997: Lab. maj. 11,707 (23.22%))

CREWE & NANTWICH
*E.*69,040 *T.* 41,547 (60.18%) Lab. hold
*Mrs Gwyneth Dunwoody, *Lab.* 22,556
Donald Potter, *C.*   2,650
David Cannon, *LD*   5,595
Roger Croston, *UK Ind.*   746
Lab. majority 9,906 (23.84%)
3.69% swing Lab. to C.
(1997: Lab. maj. 15,798 (31.22%))

CROSBY
*E.*57,375 *T.* 36,866 (64.25%) Lab. hold
*Ms Claire Curtis-Thomas, *Lab.* 20,327
Robert Collinson, *C.*   11,974
Tim Drake, *LD*   4,084
Mark Holt, *Soc. Lab.*   481
Lab. majority 8,353 (22.66%)
3.19% swing C. to Lab.
(1997: Lab. maj. 7,182 (16.27%))

CROYDON CENTRAL
*E.*77,567 *T.* 45,860 (59.12%) Lab. hold
*Geraint Davies, *Lab.*   21,643
David Congdon, *C.*   17,659
Paul Booth, *LD*   5,156
James Feisenberger, *UK Ind.*   545
Ms Lynda Miller, *BNP*   449
John Cartwright, *Loony*   408
Lab. majority 3,984 (8.69%)
0.85% swing C. to Lab.
(1997: Lab. maj. 3,897 (6.99%))

CROYDON NORTH
*E.*76,600 *T.* 41,882 (54.68%) Lab. hold
*Malcolm Wicks, *Lab.*   26,610
Simon Allison, *C.*   9,752
Ms Sandra Lawman, *LD*   4,375
Alan Smith, *UK Ind.*   606
Don Madgwick, *Soc. All.*   539

Lab. majority 16,858 (40.25%)
2.63% swing C. to Lab.
(1997: Lab. maj. 18,398 (35.00%))

CROYDON SOUTH
*E.*73,402 *T.* 45,060 (61.39%) C. hold
*Richard Ottaway, *C.*   22,169
Gerry Ryan, *Lab.*   13,472
Ms Anne Gallop, *LD*   8,226
Mrs Kathleen Garner, *UK Ind.*   998
Mark Samuel, *Choice*   195
C. majority 8,697 (19.30%)
1.35% swing C. to Lab.
(1997: C. maj. 11,930 (22.01%))

DAGENHAM
*E.*59,340 *T.* 27,580 (46.48%) Lab. hold
Jon Cruddas, *Lab.*   15,784
Michael White, *C.*   7,091
Adrian Gee-Turner, *LD*   2,820
David Hill, *BNP*   1,378
Berlyne Hamilton, *Soc. All.*   262
Robert Siggins, *Soc. Lab.*   245
Lab. majority 8,693 (31.52%)
7.82% swing Lab. to C.
(1997: Lab. maj. 17,054 (47.16%))

DARLINGTON
*E.*64,328 *T.* 40,754 (63.35%) Lab. hold
*Rt. Hon. A. Milburn, *Lab.*   22,479
Tony Richmond, *C.*   12,950
Robert Adamson, *LD*   4,358
Alan Docherty, *Soc. All.*   469
Craig Platt, *Ind.*   269
Ms Amanda Rose, *Soc. Lab.*   229
Lab. majority 9,529 (23.38%)
4.94% swing Lab. to C.
(1997: Lab. maj. 16,025 (33.27%))

DARTFORD
*E.*72,258 *T.* 44,740 (61.92%) Lab. hold
*Howard Stoate, *Lab.*   21,466
Bob Dunn, *C.*   18,160
Graham Morgan, *LD*   3,781
Mark Croucher, *UK Ind.*   989
Keith Davenport, *FDP*   344
Lab. majority 3,306 (7.39%)
0.47% swing Lab. to C.
(1997: Lab. maj. 4,328 (8.32%))

DAVENTRY
*E.*86,537 *T.* 56,684 (65.50%) C. hold
*Tim Boswell, *C.*   27,911
Kevin Quigley, *Lab.*   18,262
Jamie Calder, *LD*   9,130
Peter Baden, *UK Ind.*   1,381
C. majority 9,649 (17.02%)
2.54% swing Lab. to C.
(1997: C. maj. 7,378 (11.95%))

DENTON & REDDISH
*E.*69,236 *T.* 33,593 (48.52%) Lab. hold
*Andrew Bennett, *Lab.*   21,913
Paul Newman, *C.*   6,583
Roger Fletcher, *LD*   4,152
Alan Cadwallender, *UK Ind.*   945
Lab. majority 15,330 (45.63%)
0.78% swing C. to Lab.
(1997: Lab. maj. 20,311 (44.08%))

DERBY NORTH
*E.*76,489 *T.* 44,054 (57.60%) Lab. hold
*Bob Laxton, *Lab.*   22,415

Barrie Holden, *C.*   15,433
Robert Charlesworth, *LD*   6,206
Lab. majority 6,982 (15.85%)
1.53% swing Lab. to C.
(1997: Lab. maj. 10,615 (18.91%))

DERBY SOUTH
*E.*77,366 *T.* 43,075 (55.68%) Lab. hold
*Rt. Hon. Mrs M. Beckett, *Lab.* 24,310
Simon Spencer, *C.*   10,455
Anders Hanson, *LD*   8,310
Lab. majority 13,855 (32.16%)
0.54% swing C. to Lab.
(1997: Lab. maj. 16,106 (31.08%))

DERBYSHIRE NORTH EAST
*E.*71,527 *T.* 42,124 (58.89%) Lab. hold
*Harry Barnes, *Lab.*   23,437
James Hollingsworth, *C.*   11,179
Mark Higginbottom, *LD*   7,508
Lab. majority 12,258 (29.10%)
3.08% swing Lab. to C.
(1997: Lab. maj. 18,321 (35.25%))

DERBYSHIRE SOUTH
*E.*81,010 *T.* 51,945 (64.12%) Lab. hold
*Mark Todd, *Lab.*   26,338
James Hakewill, *C.*   18,487
Russell Eagling, *LD*   5,233
John Blunt, *UK Ind.*   1,074
Paul Liversuch, *Soc. Lab.*   564
James Taylor, *Ind.*   249
Lab. majority 7,851 (15.11%)
4.09% swing Lab. to C.
(1997: Lab. maj. 13,967 (23.29%))

DERBYSHIRE WEST
*E.*75,067 *T.* 50,589 (67.39%) C. hold
*Patrick McLoughlin, *C.*   24,280
Stephen Clamp, *Lab.*   16,910
Jeremy Beckett, *LD*   7,922
Stuart Bavester, *UK Ind.*   672
Nick Delves, *Loony*   472
Robert Goodall, *Ind.*   333
C. majority 7,370 (14.57%)
2.99% swing Lab. to C.
(1997: C. maj. 4,885 (8.59%))

DEVIZES
*E.*83,655 *T.* 53,249 (63.65%) C. hold
*Rt. Hon. M. Ancram, *C.*   25,159
Jim Thorpe, *Lab.*   13,263
Ms Helen Frances, *LD*   11,756
Alan Wood, *UK Ind.*   1,521
Ludovic Kennedy, *Ind.*   1,078
Ms Vanessa Potter, *Loony*   472
C. majority 11,896 (22.34%)
1.88% swing Lab. to C.
(1997: C. maj. 9,782 (16.29%))

DEVON EAST
*E.*70,278 *T.* 47,837 (68.07%) C. hold
Hugo Swire, C.22,681
Tim Dumper, *LD*   14,486
Phil Starr, *Lab.*   7,974
David Wilson, *UK Ind.*   2,696
C. majority 8,195 (17.13%)
1.44% swing LD to C.
(1997: C. maj. 7,489 (14.25%))

DEVON NORTH
*E.*72,100 *T.* 49,254 (68.31%) LD hold
*Nick Harvey, *LD*   21,784
Clive Allen, *C.*   18,800
Ms Viv Gale, *Lab.*   4,995
Roger Knapman, *UK Ind.*   2,484
Tony Bown, *Green*   1,191
LD majority 2,984 (6.06%)
2.61% swing LD to C.
(1997: LD maj. 6,181 (11.27%))

DEVON SOUTH WEST
*E.*70,922 *T.* 46,904 (66.13%) C. hold
*Gary Streeter, *C.*   21,970
Christopher Mavin, *Lab.*   14,826
Phil Hutty, *LD*   8,616
Roger Bullock, *UK Ind.*   1,492
C. majority 7,144 (15.23%)
0.58% swing Lab. to C.
(1997: C. maj. 7,433 (14.07%))

DEVON WEST & TORRIDGE
*E.*78,976 *T.* 55,684 (70.51%) LD hold
*John Burnett, *LD*   23,474
Geoffrey Cox, *C.*   22,280
David Brenton, *Lab.*   5,959
Bob Edwards, *UK Ind.*   2,674
Martin Quinn, *Green*   1,297
LD majority 1,194 (2.14%)
0.58% swing Lab. to LD.
(1997: LD maj. 1,957 (3.31%))

DEWSBURY
*E.*62,344 *T.* 36,651 (58.79%) Lab. hold
*Rt. Hon. Mrs A. Taylor, *Lab.*   18,524
Robert Cole, *C.*   11,075
Ian Cuthbertson, *LD*   4,382
Russell Smith, *BNP*   1,632
Ms Brenda Smithson, *Green*   560
David Peace, *UK Ind.*   478
Lab. majority 7,449 (20.32%)
0.50% swing C. to Lab.
(1997: Lab. maj. 8,323 (19.33%))

DON VALLEY
E. 66,244 *T.* 36,630 (55.30%) Lab. hold
*Ms Caroline Flint, *Lab.*   20,009
James Browne, *C.*   10,489
Phillip Smith, *LD*   4,089
Tony Wilde, *Ind.*   800
David Cooper, *UK Ind.*   777
Nigel Ball, *Soc. Lab.*   466
Lab. majority 9,520 (25.99%)
3.84% swing Lab. to C.
(1997: Lab. maj. 14,659 (33.66%))

DONCASTER CENTRAL
*E.*65,087 *T.* 33,902 (52.09%) Lab. hold
*Ms Rosie Winterton, *Lab.*   20,034
Gary Meggitt, *C.*   8,035
Michael Southcombe, *LD*   4,390
David Gordon, *UK Ind.*   926
Ms Janet Terry, *Soc. All.*   517
Lab. majority 11,999 (35.39%)
2.85% swing Lab. to C.
(1997: Lab. maj. 17,856 (41.10%))

DONCASTER NORTH
*E.*62,124 *T.* 31,363 (50.48%) Lab. hold
*Kevin Hughes, *Lab.*   19,788
Mrs Anita Kapoor, *C.*   4,601
Colin Ross, *LD*   3,323

Martin Williams, *Ind.*   2,926
John Wallis, *UK Ind.*   725
Lab. majority 15,187 (48.42%)
3.28% swing Lab. to C.
(1997: Lab. maj. 21,937 (54.99%))

DORSET MID & POOLE NORTH
*E.*66,675 *T.* 43,718 (65.57%) LD gain
Ms Annette Brooke, *LD*   18,358
*Christopher Fraser, *C.*   17,974
James Selby-Bennett, *Lab.*   6,765
Jeff Mager, *UK Ind.*   621
LD majority 384 (0.88%)
1.11% swing C. to LD
(1997: C. maj. 681 (1.34%))

DORSET NORTH
*E.*72,140 *T.* 47,821 (66.29%) C. hold
*Robert Walter, *C.*   22,314
Miss Emily Gasson, *LD*   18,517
Mark Wareham, *Lab.*   5,334
Peter Jenkins, *UK Ind.*   1,019
Joseph Duthie, *Low Excise*   391
Mrs Cora Bone, *Ind.*   246
C. majority 3,797 (7.94%)
1.36% swing LD to C.
(1997: C. maj. 2,746 (5.23%))

DORSET SOUTH
*E.*69,233 *T.* 45,345 (65.50%) Lab gain
Jim Knight, *Lab.*   19,027
*Ian Cameron Bruce, *C.*   18,874
Andrew Canning, *LD*   6,531
Laurence Moss, *UK Ind.*   913
Lab. majority 153 (0.34%)
0.25% swing C. to Lab.
(1997: C. maj. 77 (0.16%))

DORSET WEST
*E.*74,016 *T.* 49,571 (66.97%) C. hold
*Oliver Letwin, *C.*   22,126
Simon Green, *LD*   20,712
Richard Hyde, *Lab.*   6,733
C. majority 1,414 (2.85%)
0.29% swing C. to LD
(1997: C. maj. 1,840 (3.44%))

DOVER
*E.*69,025 *T.* 44,960 (65.14%) Lab. hold
*Gwyn Prosser, *Lab.*   21,943
Paul Watkins, *C.*   16,744
Antony Hook, *LD*   5,131
Lee Speakman, *UK Ind.*   1,142
Lab. majority 5,199 (11.56%)
5.05% swing Lab. to C.
(1997: Lab. maj. 11,739 (21.66%))

DUDLEY NORTH
*E.*68,964 *T.* 38,564 (55.92%) Lab. hold
*Ross Cranston, *Lab.*   20,095
Andrew Griffiths, *C.*   13,295
Richard Burt, *LD*   3,352
Simon Darby, *BNP*   1,822
Lab. majority 6,800 (17.63%)
1.08% swing Lab. to C.
(1997: Lab. maj. 9,457 (19.79%))

DUDLEY SOUTH
*E.*65,578 *T.* 36,344 (55.42%) Lab. hold
*Ian Pearson, *Lab.*   18,109
Jason Sugarman, *C.*   11,292
Ms Lorely Burt, *LD*   5,421

John Westwood, *UK Ind.* 859
Ms Angela Thompson *Soc. All.* 663
Lab. majority 6,817 (18.76%)
4.22% swing Lab. to C.
(1997: Lab. maj. 13,027 (27.19%))

DULWICH & WEST NORWOOD

*E.*70,497 *T.* 38,247 (54.25%) Lab. hold
*Rt. Hon. Ms T. Jowell, *Lab.* 20,999
Nick Vineall, *C.* 8,689
Ms Caroline Pidgeon, *LD* 5,806
Ms Jenny Jones, *Green* 1,914
Brian Kelly, *Soc. All.* 839
Lab. majority 12,310 (32.19%)
2.29% swing Lab. to C.
(1997: Lab. maj. 16,769 (36.76%))

DURHAM NORTH

*E.*67,610 *T.* 38,568 (57.04%) Lab. hold
Kevan Jones, *Lab.* 25,920
Matthew Palmer, C .7,237
Ms Carole Field, *LD* 5,411
Lab. majority 18,683 (48.44%)
3.65% swing Lab. to C.
(1997: Lab. maj. 26,299 (55.75%))

DURHAM NORTH WEST

*E.*67,062 *T.* 39,226 (58.49%) Lab. hold
*Rt. Hon. Ms H. Armstrong,
  Lab. 24,526
William Clouston, *C.* 8,193
Alan Ord, *LD* 5,846
Ms Joan Hartnell, *Soc. Lab.* 661
Lab. majority 16,333 (41.64%)
5.90% swing Lab. to C.
(1997: Lab. maj. 24,754 (53.44%))

DURHAM, CITY OF

*E.*69,633 *T.* 41,486 (59.58%) Lab. hold
*Gerry Steinberg, *Lab.* 23,254
Ms Carol Woods, *LD* 9,813
Nick Cartmell, *C.* 7,167
Mrs Chris Williamson, *UK Ind.* 1,252
Lab. majority 13,441 (32.40%)
7.82% swing Lab. to LD
(1997: Lab. maj. 22,504 (45.80%))

EALING ACTON & SHEPHERD'S BUSH

*E.*70,697 *T.* 37,201 (52.62%) Lab. hold
*Clive Soley, *Lab.* 20,144
Miss Justine Greening, *C.* 9,355
Martin Tod, *LD* 6,171
Nick Grant, *Soc. All.* 529
Andrew Lawrie, *UK Ind.* 476
Carlos Rule, *Soc. Lab.* 301
Ms Rebecca Ng, *ProLife* 225
Lab. majority 10,789 (29.00%)
1.77% swing Lab. to C.
(1997: Lab. maj. 15,647 (32.55%))

EALING NORTH

*E.*77,524 *T.* 44,957 (57.99%) Lab. hold
*Stephen Pound, *Lab.* 25,022
Charles Walker, *C.* 13,185
Francesco Fruzza, *LD* 5,043
Ms Astra Seibe, *Green* 1,039
Daniel Moss, *UK Ind.* 668
Lab. majority 11,837 (26.33%)
4.94% swing C. to Lab.
(1997: Lab. maj. 9,160 (16.44%))

EALING SOUTHALL

*E.*82,373 *T.* 46,828 (56.85%) Lab. hold
*Piara Khabra, *Lab.* 22,239
Daniel Kawczynski, *C.* 8,556
Avtar Lit, *Sunrise* 5,764
Baldev Sharma, *LD* 4,680
Ms Jane Cook, *Green* 2,119
Salvinder Dhillon, *Community* 1,214
Mushtaq Choudhry, *Ind.* 1,166
Harpal Brar, *Soc. Lab.* 921
Mohammed Bhutta, *Qari* 169
Lab. majority 13,683 (29.22%)
5.00% swing Lab. to C.
(1997: Lab. maj. 21,423 (39.21%))

EASINGTON

*E.*61,532 *T.* 33,010 (53.65%) Lab. hold
*John Cummings, *Lab.* 25,360
Philip Lovel, *C.* 3,411
Christopher, Ord *LD* 3,408
Dave Robinson, *Soc. Lab.* 831
Lab. majority 21,949 (66.49%)
2.57% swing Lab. to C.
(1997: Lab. maj. 30,012 (71.64%))

EAST HAM

*E.*71,255 *T.* 37,277 (52.31%) Lab. hold
*Stephen Timms, *Lab.* 27,241
Peter Campbell, *C.* 6,209
Ms Bridget Fox, *LD* 2,600
Rod Finlayson, *Soc. Lab.* 783
Ms Johinda Pandhal, *UK Ind.* 444
Lab. majority 21,032 (56.42%)
3.95% swing C. to Lab.
(1997: Lab. maj. 19,358 (48.53%))

EASTBOURNE

*E.*73,784 *T.* 44,770 (60.68%) C. hold
*Nigel Waterson, *C.* 19,738
Chris Berry, *LD* 17,584
Ms Gillian Roles, *Lab.* 5,967
Barry Jones, *UK Ind.* 907
Ms Theresia Williamson, *Lib.* 574
C. majority 2,154 (4.81%)
0.51% swing LD to C.
(1997: C. maj. 1,994 (3.79%))

EASTLEIGH

*E.*74,603 *T.* 47,573 (63.77%) LD hold
*David Chidgey, *LD* 19,360
Conor Burns, *C.* 16,302
Sam Jaffa, *Lab.* 10,426
Stephen Challis, *UK Ind.* 849
Ms Martha Lyn, *Green* 636
LD majority 3,058 (6.43%)
2.54% swing C. to LD
(1997: LD maj. 754 (1.35%))

ECCLES

*E.*68,764 *T.* 33,182 (48.25%) Lab. hold
*Ian Stewart, *Lab.* 21,395
Peter Caillard, *C.* 6,867
Bob Boyd, *LD* 4,920
Lab. majority 14,528 (43.78%)
2.09% swing Lab. to C.
(1997: Lab. maj. 21,916 (47.96%))

EDDISBURY

*E.*69,181 *T.* 44,387 (64.16%) C. hold
*Stephen O'Brien, *C.* 20,556
Bill Eyres, *Lab.* 15,988
Paul Roberts, *LD* 6,975

David Carson, *UK Ind.* 868
C. majority 4,568 (10.29%)
3.95% swing Lab. to C.
1999 Jul by-election: C. maj. 1,606
(1997: C. maj. 1,185 (2.39%))

EDMONTON

*E.*62,294, *T.* 34,774 (55.82%)Lab Co-op hold
*Andy Love, *Lab. Co-op.* 20,481
David Burrowes, *C.* 10,709
Douglas Taylor, *LD* 2,438
Miss Gwyneth Rolph, *UK Ind.* 406
Erol Basarik, *Reform* 344
Howard Medwell, *Soc. All.* 296
Dr Ram Saxena, *Ind.* 100
Lab Co-op majority 9,772 (28.10%)
0.97% swing Lab Co-op to C.
(1997: Lab. maj. 13,472 (30.04%)

ELLESMERE PORT & NESTON

*E.*68,147 *T.* 41,528 (60.94%) Lab. hold
*Andrew Miller, *Lab.* 22,964
Gareth Williams, *C.* 12,103
Stuart Kelly, *LD* 4,828
Henry Crocker, *UK Ind.* 824
Geoff Nicholls, *Green* 809
Lab. majority 10,861 (26.15%)
2.18% swing Lab. to C.
(1997: Lab. maj. 16,036 (30.51%))

ELMET

*E.*70,041 *T.* 45,937 (65.59%) Lab. hold
*Colin Burgon, *Lab.* 22,038
Andrew Millard, *C.* 17,867
Ms Madeleine Kirk, *LD* 5,001
Andrew Spence, *UK Ind.* 1,031
Lab. majority 4,171 (9.08%)
3.57% swing Lab. to C.
(1997: Lab. maj. 8,779 (16.22%))

ELTHAM

*E.*57,519 *T.* 33,792 (58.75%) Lab. hold
*Clive Efford, *Lab.* 17,855
Mrs Sharon Massey, *C.* 10,859
Martin Morris, *LD* 4,121
Terry Jones, *UK Ind.* 706
Andrew Graham, *Ind.* 251
Lab. majority 6,996 (20.70%)
1.37% swing Lab. to C.
(1997: Lab. maj. 10,182 (23.45%))

ENFIELD NORTH

*E.*67,756 *T.* 38,143 (56.29%) Lab. hold
*Ms Joan Ryan, *Lab.* 17,888
Nick De Bois, *C.* 15,597
Ms Hilary Leighter, *LD* 3,355
Ramon Johns, *BNP* 605
Brian Hall, *UK Ind.* 247
Michael Akerman, *ProLife* 241
Richard Course, *Ind.* 210
Lab. majority 2,291 (6.01%)
4.15% swing Lab. to C.
(1997: Lab. maj. 6,822 (14.31%))

ENFIELD SOUTHGATE

*E.*66,418 *T.* 41,908 (63.10%) Lab. hold
*Stephen Twigg, *Lab.* 21,727
John Flack, *C.* 16,181
Wayne Hoban, *LD* 2,935
Ms Elaine Graham-Leigh, *Green* 662
Roy Freshwater, *UK Ind.* 298

Andrew Malakouna, *Ind.* 105
Lab. majority 5,546 (13.23%)
5.08% swing C. to Lab.
(1997: Lab. maj. 1,433 (3.08%))

EPPING FOREST
E.72,645 T. 42,414 (58.39%) C. hold
*Mrs Eleanor Laing, *C.* 20,833
Christopher Naylor, *Lab.* 12,407
Michael Heavens, *LD* 7,884
Andrew Smith, *UK Ind.* 1,290
C. majority 8,426 (19.87%)
4.98% swing Lab. to C.
(1997: C. maj. 5,252 (9.91%))

EPSOM & EWELL
E.74,266 T. 46,643 (62.81%) C. hold
Chris Grayling, *C.* 22,430
Charles Mansell, *Lab.* 12,350
John Vincent, *LD* 10,316
G. Webster-Gardiner, *UK Ind.* 1,547
C. majority 10,080 (21.61%)
0.17% swing Lab. to C.
(1997: C. maj. 11,525 (21.27%))

EREWASH
E.78,484 T. 48,596 (61.92%) Lab. hold
*Ms Liz Blackman, *Lab.* 23,915
Gregor MacGregor, *C.* 16,983
Martin Garnett, *LD* 5,586
Ms Louise Smith, *UK Ind.* 692
Steven Belshaw, *BNP* 591
R U Seerius, *Loony* 428
Peter Waldock, *Soc. Lab.* 401
Lab. majority 6,932 (14.26%)
0.44% swing C. to Lab.
(1997: Lab. maj. 9,135 (15.14%))

ERITH & THAMESMEAD
E.66,371 T. 33,351 (50.25%) Lab. hold
*John Austin, *Lab.* 19,769
Mark Brooks, *C.* 8,602
James Kempton, *LD* 3,800
Hardev Dhillon, *Soc. Lab.* 1,180
Lab. majority 11,167 (33.48%)
4.21% swing Lab. to C.
(1997: Lab. maj. 17,424 (41.90%))

ESHER & WALTON
E.73,541 T. 45,531 (61.91%) C. hold
*Ian Taylor, *C.* 22,296
Joe McGowan, *Lab.* 10,758
Mark Marsh, *LD* 10,241
Bernard Collignon, *UK Ind.* 2,236
C. majority 11,538 (25.34%)
0.86% swing C. to Lab.
(1997: C. maj. 14,528 (27.07%))

ESSEX NORTH
E.71,680 T. 44,944 (62.70%) C. hold
*Bernard Jenkin, *C.* 21,325
Philip Hawkins, *Lab.* 14,139
Trevor Ellis *LD* 7,867
George Curtis, *UK Ind.* 1,613
C. majority 7,186 (15.99%)
2.65% swing Lab. to C.
(1997: C. maj. 5,476 (10.69%))

EXETER
E.81,942 T. 52,616 (64.21%) Lab. hold
*Ben Bradshaw, *Lab.* 26,194
Mrs Anne Jobson, *C.* 14,435
Richard Copus, *LD* 6,512
David Morrish, *Lib.* 2,596

Paul Edwards, *Green* 1,240
John Stuart, *UK Ind.* 1,109
Francis Choules, *Soc. All.* 530
Lab. majority 11,759 (22.35%)
1.71% swing C. to Lab.
(1997: Lab. maj. 11,705 (18.92%))

FALMOUTH & CAMBORNE
E.72,833 T. 46,820 (64.28%) Lab. hold
*Ms Candy Atherton, *Lab.* 18,532
Nick Serpell, *C.* 14,005
Julian Brazil, *LD* 11,453
John Browne, *UK Ind.* 1,328
Ms Hilda Wasley, *Meb. Ker.* 853
Paul Holmes, *Lib.* 649
Lab. majority 4,527 (9.67%)
2.33% swing C. to Lab.
(1997: Lab. maj. 2,688 (5.01%))

FAREHAM
E.72,678 T. 45,447 (62.53%) C. hold
Mark Hoban, *C.* 21,389
James Carr, *Lab.* 14,380
Hugh Pritchard, *LD* 8,503
William O'Brien, *UK Ind.* 1,175
C. majority 7,009 (15.42%)
2.21% swing C. to Lab.
(1997: C. maj. 10,358 (19.85%))

FAVERSHAM & KENT MID
E.67,995 T. 41,051 (60.37%) C. hold
Hugh Robertson, *C.* 18,739
Grahame Birchall, *Lab.* 14,556
Mike Sole, *LD* 5,529
Jim Gascoyne, *UK Ind.* 828
Ms Penny Kemp, *Green* 799
Norman Davidson, *R & R Loony* 600
C. majority 4,183 (10.19%)
0.89% swing Lab. to C.
(1997: C. maj. 4,173 (8.41%))

FELTHAM & HESTON
E.73,229 T. 36,177 (49.40%) Lab Co-op hold
*Alan Keen, *Lab. Co-op.* 21,406
Mrs Liz Mammatt, *C.* 8,749
Andy Darley, *LD* 4,998
Surinder Cheema, *Soc. Lab.* 651
Warwick Prachar, *Ind.* 204
Asa Khaira, *Ind.* 169
Lab Co-op majority 12,657 (34.99%)
1.11% swing C. to Lab. Co-op
(1997: Lab. maj. 15,273 (32.76%))

FINCHLEY & GOLDERS GREEN
E.76,175 T. 43,675 (57.34%) Lab. hold
*Rudi Vis, *Lab.* 20,205
John Marshall, *C.* 16,489
Ms Sarah Teather, *LD* 5,266
Ms Miranda Dunn, *Green* 1,385
John de Roeck, *UK Ind.* 330
Lab. majority 3,716 (8.51%)
1.08% swing C. to Lab.
(1997: Lab. maj. 3,189 (6.34%))

FOLKESTONE & HYTHE
E.71,503 T. 45,855 (64.13%) C. hold
*Rt. Hon. M. Howard, *C.* 20,645
Peter Carroll, *LD* 14,738
Albert Catterall, *Lab.* 9,260
John Baker, *UK Ind.* 1,212
C. majority 5,907 (12.88%)
0.36% swing LD to C.
(1997: C. maj. 6,332 (12.17%))

FOREST OF DEAN
E.66,240 T. 44,607 (67.34%) Lab. hold
*Ms Diana Organ, *Lab.* 19,350
Mark Harper, *C.* 17,301
David Gayler, *LD* 5,762
Simon Pickering, *Green* 1,254
Allen Prout, *UK Ind.* 661
Gerald Morgan, *Ind.* 279
Lab. majority 2,049 (4.59%)
4.02% swing Lab. to C.
(1997: Lab. maj. 6,343 (12.64%))

FYLDE
E.72,207 T. 44,737 (61.96%) C. hold
*Rt. Hon. M. Jack, *C.* 23,383
John Stockton, *Lab.* 13,773
John Begg, *LD* 6,599
Mrs Lesley Brown, *UK Ind.* 982
C. majority 9,610 (21.48%)
2.13% swing Lab. to C.
(1997: C. maj. 8,963 (17.22%))

GAINSBOROUGH
E.65,871 T. 42,319 (64.25%) C. hold
*Edward Leigh, *C.* 19,555
Alan Rhodes, *Lab.* 11,484
Steve Taylor, *LD* 11,280
C. majority 8,071 (19.07%)
2.39% swing Lab. to C.
(1997: C. maj. 6,826 (14.29%))

GATESHEAD EAST &
WASHINGTON WEST
E.64,041 T. 33,615 (52.49%) Lab. hold
*Rt. Hon. Ms J. Quin, *Lab.* 22,903
Ron Beadle, *LD* 4,999
Ms Elizabeth Campbell, *C.* 4,970
Martin Rouse, *UK Ind.* 743
Lab. majority 17,904 (53.26%)
4.04% swing Lab. to LD
(1997: Lab. maj. 24,950 (57.92%))

GEDLING
E.68,540 T. 43,816 (63.93%) Lab. hold
*Vernon Coaker, *Lab.* 22,383
Jonathan Bullock, *C.* 16,785
Tony Gillam, *LD* 4,648
Lab. majority 5,598 (12.78%)
2.74% swing C. to Lab.
(1997: Lab. maj. 3,802 (7.29%))

GILLINGHAM
E.70,898 T. 42,212 (59.54%) Lab. hold
*Paul Clark, *Lab.* 18,782
Tim Butcher, *C.* 16,510
Jonathan Hunt, *LD* 5,755
Tony Scholefield, *UK Ind.* 933
Wynford Vaughan, *Soc. All.* 232
Lab. majority 2,272 (5.38%)
0.74% swing C. to Lab.
(1997: Lab. maj. 1,980 (3.91%))

GLOUCESTER
E.81,144 T. 48,223 (59.43%) Lab. hold
Parmjit Dhanda, *Lab.* 22,067
Paul James, *C.* 18,187
Tim Bullamore, *LD* 6,875
Terry Lines, *UK Ind.* 822
Stewart Smyth, *Soc. All.* 272
Lab. majority 3,880 (8.05%)
3.11% swing Lab. to C.
(1997: Lab. maj. 8,259 (14.26%))

GOSPORT
E.69,626 T. 39,789 (57.15%)   C. hold
*Peter Viggers, C.   17,364
Richard Williams, Lab.   14,743
Roger Roberts, LD   6,011
John Bowles, UK Ind.   1,162
Kevin Chetwynd, Soc. Lab.   509
C. majority 2,621 (6.59%)
3.18% swing C. to Lab.
(1997: C. maj. 6,258 (12.94%))

GRANTHAM & STAMFORD
E.74,459 T. 46,289 (62.17%)   C. hold
*Quentin Davies, C.   21,329
John Robinson, Lab.   16,811
Ms Jane Carr, LD   6,665
Miss Marilyn Swain, UK Ind.   1,484
C. majority 4,518 (9.76%)
2.34% swing Lab. to C.
(1997: C. maj. 2,692 (5.08%))

GRAVESHAM
E.69,590 T. 43,639 (62.71%) Lab. hold
*Chris Pond, Lab.   21,773
Jacques Arnold, C.   16,911
Bruce Parmenter, LD   4,031
William Jenner, UK Ind.   924
Lab. majority 4,862 (11.14%)
0.15% swing C. to Lab.
(1997: Lab. maj. 5,779 (10.85%))

GREAT GRIMSBY
E.63,157 T. 33,017 (52.28%) Lab. hold
*Austin Mitchell, Lab.   19,118
James Cousins, C.   7,634
Andrew de Freitas, LD   6,265
Lab. majority 11,484 (34.78%)
1.46% swing Lab. to C.
(1997: Lab. maj. 16,244 (37.70%))

GREAT YARMOUTH
E.69,131 T. 40,366 (58.39%) Lab. hold
*Tony Wright, Lab.   20,344
Charles Reynolds, C.   15,780
Maurice Leeke, LD   3,392
Bertie Poole, UK Ind.   850
Lab. majority 4,564 (11.31%)
3.21% swing Lab. to C.
(1997: Lab. maj. 8,668 (17.73%))

GREENWICH & WOOLWICH
E.62,530 T. 32,536 (52.03%) Lab. hold
*RT. Hon. N. Raynsford, Lab.   19,691
Richard Forsdyke, C.   6,258
Russell Pyne, LD   5,082
Stan Gain UK, Ind.   672
Miss Kirstie Paton, Soc. All.   481
Ms Margaret Sharkey, Soc. Lab.   352
Lab. majority 13,433 (41.29%)
1.79% swing Lab. to C.
(1997: Lab. maj. 18,128 (44.87%))

GUILDFORD
E.76,046 T. 47,842 (62.91%)   LD gain
Ms Sue Doughty, LD   20,358
*Nick St Aubyn, C.   19,820
Ms Joyce Still, Lab.   6,558
Ms Sonya Porter, UK Ind.   736
John Morris, Pacifist   370
LD majority 538 (1.12%)
4.77% swing C. to LD
(1997: C. maj. 4,791 (8.41%))

HACKNEY NORTH & STOKE
NEWINGTON
E.60,444 T. 29,621 (49.01%) Lab. hold
*Ms Diane Abbott, Lab.   18,081
Mrs Pauline Dye, C.   4,430
Ms Meral Ece, LD   4,170
Chit Yen Chong, Green   2,184
Sukant Chandan, Soc. Lab.   756
Lab. majority 13,651 (46.09%)
0.74% swing Lab. to C.
(1997: Lab. maj. 15,627 (47.57%))

HACKNEY SOUTH &
SHOREDITCH
E.63,990 T. 30,347 (47.42%) Lab. hold
*Brian Sedgemore, Lab.   19,471
Tony Vickers, LD   4,422
Paul White, C.   4,180
Ms Cecilia Prosper, Soc. All.   1,401
Saim Kokshal, Reform   471
Ivan Beavis, Comm.   259
William Rogers, WRP   143
Lab. majority 15,049 (49.59%)
2.60% swing LD to Lab.
(1997: Lab. maj. 14,980 (44.39%))

HALESOWEN & ROWLEY REGIS
E.65,683 T. 39,274 (59.79%) Lab. hold
*Ms Sylvia Heal, Lab.   20,804
Les Jones, C.   13,445
Patrick Harley, LD   4,089
Alan Sheath, UK Ind.   936
Lab. majority 7,359 (18.74%)
1.23% swing Lab. to C.
(1997: Lab. maj. 10,337 (21.20%))

HALIFAX
E.69,870 T. 40,390 (57.81%) Lab. hold
*Ms Alice Mahon, Lab.   19,800
James Walsh, C.   13,671
John Durkin, LD   5,878
Mrs Helen Martinek, UK Ind.   1,041
Lab. majority 6,129 (15.17%)
3.50% swing Lab. to C.
(1997: Lab. maj. 11,212 (22.18%))

HALTEMPRICE & HOWDEN
E.67,055 T. 43,928 (65.51%)   C. hold
*Rt. Hon. D. Davis, C.   18,994
John Neal, LD   17,091
Leslie Howell, Lab.   6,898
Ms Joanne Robinson, UK Ind.   945
C. majority 1,903 (4.33%)
5.41% swing C. to LD
(1997: C. maj. 7,514 (15.16%))

HALTON
E.63,673 T. 34,470 (54.14%) Lab. hold
*Derek Twigg, Lab.   23,841
Chris Davenport, C.   6,413
Peter Walker, LD   4,216
Lab. majority 17,428 (50.56%)
1.33% swing Lab. to C.
(1997: Lab. maj. 23,650 (53.22%))

HAMMERSMITH & FULHAM
E.79,302 T. 44,700 (56.37%) Lab. hold
*Iain Coleman, Lab.   19,801
Matthew Carrington, C.   17,786
Jon Burden, LD   5,294
Daniel Lopez Dias, Green   1,444
Gerald Roberts, UK Ind.   375
Lab. majority 2,015 (4.51%)

1.30% swing Lab. to C.
(1997: Lab. maj. 3,842 (7.11%))

HAMPSHIRE EAST
E.78,802 T. 50,289 (63.82%)   C. hold
*Michael Mates, C.   23,950
Robert Booker, LD   15,060
Ms Barbara Burfoot, Lab.   9,866
Stephen Coles, UK Ind.   1,413
C. majority 8,890 (17.68%)
1.13% swing C. to LD
(1997: C. maj. 11,590 (19.93%))

HAMPSHIRE NORTH EAST
E.71,323 T. 43,947 (61.62%)   C. hold
*Rt. Hon. J. Arbuthnot, C.   23,379
Mike Plummer, LD   10,122
Barry Jones, Lab.   8,744
Graham Mellstrom, UK Ind.   1,702
C. majority 13,257 (30.17%)
1.00% swing LD to C.
(1997: C. maj. 14,398 (28.17%))

HAMPSHIRE NORTH WEST
E.76,359 T. 48,631 (63.69%)   C. hold
*Rt. Hon. Sir G. Young, C.   24,374
Mick Mumford, Lab.   12,365
Alex Bentley, LD   10,329
Stanley Oram, UK Ind.   1,563
C. majority 12,009 (24.69%)
1.53% swing Lab. to C.
(1997: C. maj. 11,551 (21.13%))

HAMPSTEAD & HIGHGATE
E.65,309 T. 35,407 (54.21%) Lab. hold
*Ms Glenda Jackson, Lab.   16,601
Andrew Mennear, C.   8,725
Jonathan Simpson, LD   7,273
Andrew Cornwell, Green   1,654
Ms Helen Cooper, Soc. All.   559
Thomas McDermott, UK Ind.   316
Ms Sister Xnunoftheabove, Ind.   144
Ms Mary Teale, ProLife   92
Amos Klein, Ind.   43
Lab. majority 7,876 (22.24%)
3.96% swing Lab. to C.
(1997: Lab. maj. 13,284 (30.17%))

HARBOROUGH
E.73,300 T. 46,427 (63.34%)   C. hold
*Edward Garnier, C.   20,748
Ms Jill Hope, LD   15,496
Raj Jethwa, Lab.   9,271
David Knight, UK Ind.   912
C. majority 5,252 (11.31%)
0.49% swing C. to LD
(1997: C. maj. 6,524 (12.30%))

HARLOW
E.67,074 T. 40,115 (59.81%) Lab. hold
*Bill Rammell, Lab.   19,169
Robert Halfon, C.   13,941
Ms Lorna Spenceley, LD   5,381
Tony Bennett, UK Ind.   1,223
John Hobbs, Soc. All.   401
Lab. majority 5,228 (13.03%)
4.48% swing Lab. to C.
(1997: Lab. maj. 10,514 (21.99%))

HARROGATE &
KNARESBOROUGH
E.65,185 T. 42,179 (64.71%)   LD hold
*Phil Willis, LD   23,445

Andrew Jones, *C.* 14,600
Alastair MacDonald, *Lab.* 3,101
Bill Brown, *UK Ind.* 761
John Cornforth, *ProLife* 272
LD majority 8,845 (20.97%)
3.94% swing C. to LD
(1997: LD maj. 6,236 (13.09%))

HARROW EAST
*E.*81,575 *T.* 48,077 (58.94%) Lab. hold
*Tony McNulty, *Lab.* 26,590
Peter Wilding, *C.* 15,466
George Kershaw, *LD* 6,021
Lab. majority 11,124 (23.14%)
3.02% swing C. to Lab.
(1997: Lab. maj. 9,738 (17.09%))

HARROW WEST
*E.*73,505 *T.* 46,648 (63.46%) Lab. hold
*Gareth Thomas, *Lab.* 23,142
Danny Finkelstein, *C.* 16,986
Christopher Noyce, *LD* 5,995
Peter Kefford, *UK Ind.* 525
Lab. majority 6,156 (13.20%)
5.42% swing C. to Lab.
(1997: Lab. maj. 1,240 (2.36%))

HARTLEPOOL
*E.*67,652 *T.* 38,051 (56.25%) Lab. hold
*Rt. Hon. P. Mandelson, *Lab.* 22,506
Gus Robinson, *C.* 7,935
Nigel Boddy, *LD* 5,717
Arthur Scargill, *Soc. Lab.* 912
Ian Cameron, *Ind.* 557
John Booth, *Ind.* 424
Lab. majority 14,571 (38.29%)
0.54% swing Lab. to C.
(1997: Lab. maj. 17,508 (39.38%))

HARWICH
*E.*77,539 *T.* 48,115 (62.05%) Lab. hold
*Ivan Henderson, *Lab.* 21,951
Ian Sproat, *C.* 19,355
Peter Wilcock, *LD* 4,099
Tony Finnegan-Butler, *UK Ind.* 2,463
Clive Lawrance, *Ind.* 247
Lab. majority 2,596 (5.40%)
1.56% swing C. to Lab.
(1997: Lab. maj. 1,216 (2.28%))

HASTINGS & RYE
*E.*70,632 *T.* 41,218 (58.36%) Lab. hold
*Michael Foster, *Lab.* 19,402
Mark Coote, *C.* 15,094
Graem Peters, *LD* 4,266
Alan Coomber, *UK Ind.* 911
Ms Sally Phillips, *Green* 721
Mrs Gillian Bargery, Ind. 486
John Ord-Clarke, *Loony* 198
Brett McLean, *R & R Loony* 140
Lab. majority 4,308 (10.45%)
2.62% swing C. to Lab.
(1997: Lab. maj. 2,560 (5.21%))

HAVANT
*E.*70,246 *T.* 40,437 (57.56%) C. hold
*David Willetts, *C.* 17,769
Peter Guthrie, *Lab.* 13,562
Ms Helena Cole, *LD* 7,508
Kevin Jacks, *Green* 793
Tim Cuell, *UK Ind.* 561
Roy Stanley, *Ind.* 244

C. majority 4,207 (10.40%)
1.34% swing Lab. to C.
(1997: C. maj. 3,729 (7.72%))

HAYES & HARLINGTON
*E.*57,561 *T.* 32,403 (56.29%) Lab. hold
*John McDonnell, *Lab.* 21,279
Robert McLean, *C.* 7,813
Ms Nahid Boethe, *LD* 1,958
Gary Burch, *BNP* 705
Wally Kennedy, *Soc. Alt.* 648
Lab. majority 13,466 (41.56%)
3.39% swing C. to Lab.
(1997: Lab. maj. 14,291 (34.78%))

HAZEL GROVE
*E.*65,107 *T.* 38,478 (59.10%) LD hold
*Andrew Stunell, *LD* 20,020
Ms Nadine Bargery, *C.* 11,585
Martin Miller, *Lab.* 6,230
Gerald Price, *UK Ind.* 643
LD majority 8,435 (21.92%)
1.01% swing LD to C.
(1997: LD maj. 11,814 (23.95%))

HEMEL HEMPSTEAD
*E.*72,086 *T.* 45,833 (63.58%)Lab Co-op
hold
*Tony McWalter, *Lab. Co-op.* 21,389
Paul Ivey, *C.* 17,647
Neil Stuart, *LD* 5,877
Barry Newton, *UK Ind.* 920
Lab Co-op majority 3,742 (8.16%)
0.78% swing C. to Lab. Co-op
(1997: Lab. maj. 3,636 (6.60%))

HEMSWORTH
*E.*67,948 *T.* 35,227 (51.84%) Lab. hold
*Jon Trickett, *Lab.* 23,036
Mrs Elizabeth Truss, *C.* 7,400
Ed Waller, *LD* 3,990
Paul Turek, *Soc. Lab.* 801
Lab. majority 15,636 (44.39%)
4.19% swing C. to Lab.
(1997: Lab. maj. 23,992 (52.76%))

HENDON
*E.*78,212 *T.* 40,851 (52.23%) Lab. hold
*Andrew Dismore, *Lab.* 21,432
Richard Evans, *C.* 14,015
Wayne Casey, *LD* 4,724
Craig Crosbie, *UK Ind.* 409
Ms Stella Taylor, *WRP* 164
Michael Stewart, *Prog Dem* 107
Lab. majority 7,417 (18.16%)
2.93% swing C. to Lab.
(1997: Lab. maj. 6,155 (12.30%))

HENLEY
*E.*69,081 *T.* 44,401 (64.27%) C. hold
Boris Johnson, *C.* 20,466
Ms Catherine Bearder, *LD* 12,008
Ms Janet Mathews, *Lab.* 9,367
Philip Collings, *UK Ind.* 1,413
Oliver Tickell, *Green* 1,147
C. majority 8,458 (19.05%)
1.31% swing C. to LD
(1997: C. maj. 11,167 (21.66%))

HEREFORD
*E.*70,305 *T.* 44,624 (63.47%) LD hold
*Paul Keetch, *LD* 18,244

Mrs Virginia Taylor, *C.* 17,276
David Hallam, *Lab.* 6,739
Clive Easton, *UK Ind.* 1,184
David Gillett, *Green* 1,181
LD majority 968 (2.17%)
5.24% swing LD to C.
(1997: LD maj. 6,648 (12.65%))

HERTFORD & STORTFORD
*E.*75,141 *T.* 47,176 (62.78%) C. hold
Mark Prisk, *C.* 21,074
Simon Speller, *Lab.* 15,471
Ms Mione Gold Spink, *LD* 9,388
Stuart Rising, *UK Ind.* 1,243
C. majority 5,603 (11.88%)
0.37% swing C. to Lab.
(1997: C. maj. 6,885 (12.62%))

HERTFORDSHIRE NORTH EAST
*E.*68,790 *T.* 44,645 (64.90%) C. hold
*Oliver Heald, *C.* 19,695
Ivan Gibbons, *Lab.* 16,251
Ms Alison Kingman, *LD* 7,686
Michael Virgo, *UK Ind.* 1,013
C. majority 3,444 (7.71%)
0.89% swing Lab. to C.
(1997: C. maj. 3,088 (5.94%))

HERTFORDSHIRE SOUTH WEST
*E.*73,367 *T.* 47,269 (64.43%) C. hold
*Richard Page, *C.* 20,933
Graham Dale, *Lab.* 12,752
Ed Featherstone, *LD* 12,431
Colin Dale-Mills, *UK Ind.* 847
Ms Julia Goffin, *ProLife* 306
C. majority 8,181 (17.31%)
0.39% swing C. to Lab.
(1997: C. maj. 10,021 (18.08%))

HERTSMERE
*E.*68,780 *T.* 41,505 (60.34%) C. hold
*James Clappison, *C.* 19,855
Ms Hilary Broderick, *Lab.* 14,953
Paul Thompson, *LD* 6,300
James Dry, *Soc. Lab.* 397
C. majority 4,902 (11.81%)
2.85% swing Lab. to C.
(1997: C. maj. 3,075 (6.11%))

HEXHAM
*E.*59,807 *T.* 42,413 (70.92%) C. hold
*Peter Atkinson, *C.* 18,917
Paul Brannen, *Lab.* 16,388
Philip Latham, *LD* 6,380
Alan Patterson, *UK Ind.* 728
C. majority 2,529 (5.96%)
2.74% swing Lab. to C.
(1997: C. maj. 222 (0.49%))

HEYWOOD & MIDDLETON
*E.*73,005 *T.* 38,779 (53.12%)Lab Co-op
hold
*Jim Dobbin, *Lab. Co-op.* 22,377
Mrs Marilyn Hopkins, *C.* 10,707
Ian Greenhalgh, *LD* 4,329
Philip Burke, *Lib.* 1,021
Ms Christine West, *Ch. D.* 345
Lab Co-op majority 11,670 (30.09%)
2.30% swing Lab Co-op to C.
(1997: Lab. maj. 17,542 (34.70%))

HIGH PEAK
E.73,774 T. 48,114 (65.22%) Lab. hold
*Tom Levitt, Lab.   22,430
Simon Chapman, C.   17,941
Peter Ashenden, LD   7,743
Lab. majority 4,489 (9.33%)
3.03% swing Lab. to C.
(1997: Lab. maj. 8,791 (15.38%))

HITCHIN & HARPENDEN
E.67,196 T. 44,924 (66.86%)   C. hold
*Rt. Hon. P. Lilley, C.   21,271
Alan Amos, Lab.   14,608
John Murphy, LD   8,076
John Saunders, UK Ind.   606
Peter Rigby, Ind.   363
C. majority 6,663 (14.83%)
1.06% swing Lab. to C.
(1997: C. maj. 6,671 (12.72%))

HOLBORN & ST PANCRAS
E.62,813 T. 31,129 (49.56%) Lab. hold
*Rt. Hon. F. Dobson, Lab.   16,770
Nathaniel Green, LD   5,595
Mrs Roseanne Serelli, C.   5,258
Rob Whitley, Green   1,875
Ms Candy Udwin, Soc. All.   971
Joti Brar, Soc. Lab.   359
Magnus Nielsen, UK Ind.   301
Lab. majority 11,175 (35.90%)
8.31% swing Lab. to LD
(1997: Lab. maj. 17,903 (47.11%))

HORNCHURCH
E.61,008 T. 35,557 (58.28%) Lab. hold
*John Cryer, Lab.   16,514
Robin Squire, C.   15,032
Ms Sarah Lea, LD   2,928
Lawrence Webb, UK Ind.   893
Mr David Durant, Third   190
Lab. majority 1,482 (4.17%)
4.38% swing Lab. to C.
(1997: Lab. maj. 5,680 (12.93%))

HORNSEY & WOOD GREEN
E.75,967 T. 44,063 (58.00%) Lab. hold
*Ms Barbara Roche, Lab.   21,967
Ms Lynne Featherstone, LD   11,353
Jason Hollands, C   .6,921
Ms Jayne Forbes, Green   2,228
Ms Louise Christian, Soc. All.   1,106
Ms Ella Rule, Soc. Lab.   294
Erdil Ataman, Reform   194
Lab. majority 10,614 (24.09%)
13.21% swing Lab. to C.
(1997: Lab. maj. 20,499 (39.82%))

HORSHAM
E.79,604 T. 50,770 (63.78%)   C. hold
*Rt. Hon. F. Maude, C.   26,134
Hubert Carr, LD   12,468
Ms Janet Sully, Lab.   10,267
Hugo Miller, UK Ind.   1,472
Jim Duggan, Ind.   429
C. majority 13,666 (26.92%)
0.46% swing Lab. to C.
(1997: C. maj. 14,862 (26.00%))

HOUGHTON & WASHINGTON EAST
E.67,946 T.33,641 (49.51%) Lab. hold
*Fraser Kemp, Lab.   24,628
Tony Devenish, C.   4,810

Richard Ormerod, LD   4,203
Lab. majority 19,818 (58.91%)
2.29% swing Lab. to C.
(1997: Lab. maj. 26,555 (63.49%))

HOVE
E.70,889 T. 41,988 (59.23%) Lab. hold
*Ivor Caplin, Lab.   19,253
Mrs Jenny Langston, C.   16,082
Harold de Souza, LD   3,823
Ms Anthea Ballam, Green   1,369
Andy Richards Soc. All.   531
Richard Franklin, UK Ind.   358
Nigel Donovan, Lib.   316
Simon Dobbshead, Free   196
Thomas Major, Ind.   60
Lab. majority 3,171 (7.55%)
0.34% swing Lab. to C.
(1997: Lab. maj. 3,959 (8.23%))

HUDDERSFIELD
E.64,349 T. 35,383 (54.99%)Lab Co-op hold
*Barry Sheerman, Lab. Co-op.   18,840
Paul Baverstock, C.   8,794
Neil Bentley, LD   5,300
John Phillips, Green   1,254
Mrs Judith Longman, UK Ind.   613
Graham Hellawell, Soc. All.   374
George Randall, Soc. Lab.   208
Lab Co-op majority 10,046 (28.39%)
3.59% swing Lab Co-op to C.
(1997: Lab. maj. 15,848 (35.57%))

HULL EAST
E.66,473 T. 30,875 (46.45%) Lab. hold
*Rt. Hon. J. Prescott, Lab.   19,938
Ms Jo Swinson, LD   4,613
Ms Sandip Verma, C.   4,276
Ms Jeanette Jenkinson, UK Ind.   1,218
Ms Linda Muir, Soc. Lab.   830
Lab. majority 15,325 (49.64%)
5.94% swing Lab. to LD
(1997: Lab. maj. 23,318 (57.60%))

HULL NORTH
E.63,022 T. 28,633 (45.43%) Lab. hold
*Kevin McNamara, Lab.   16,364
Ms Simone Butterworth, LD   5,643
Paul Charlson, C.   4,902
Ms Tineka Robinson, UK Ind.   655
Roger Smith, Soc. All.   490
Carl Wagner, LCA   478
Christopher Veasey, Ind.   101
Lab. majority 10,721 (37.44%)
6.89% swing Lab. to LD
(1997: Lab. maj. 19,705 (50.79%))

HULL WEST & HESSLE
E.63,077 T. 28,916 (45.84%) Lab. hold
*Alan Johnson, Lab.   16,880
John Sharp, C.   5,929
Ms Angela Wastling, LD   4,364
John Cornforth, UK Ind.   878
David Harris, Ind.   512
David Skinner, Soc. Lab.   353
Lab. majority 10,951 (37.87%)
1.38% swing Lab. to C.
(1997: Lab. maj. 15,525 (40.48%))

HUNTINGDON
E.78,604 T. 49,089 (62.45%)   C. hold
Jonathan Djanogly, C.   24,507

Michael Pope, LD   11,715
Takki Sulaiman, Lab.   11,211
Derek Norman, UK Ind.   1,656
C. majority 12,792 (26.06%)
7.26% swing C. to LD
(1997: C. maj. 18,140 (31.84%))

HYNDBURN
E.66,445 T. 38,243 (57.56%) Lab. hold
*Greg Pope, Lab.   20,900
Peter Britcliffe, C.   12,681
Bill Greene, LD   3,680
John Tomlin, UK Ind.   982
Lab. majority 8,219 (21.49%)
1.11% swing Lab. to C.
(1997: Lab. maj. 11,448 (23.71%))

ILFORD NORTH
E.68,893 T. 40,234 (58.40%) Lab. hold
*Ms Linda Perham, Lab.   18,428
Vivian Bendall, C.   16,313
Gavin Stollar, LD   4,717
Martin Levin, UK Ind.   776
Lab. majority 2,115 (5.26%)
0.67% swing Lab. to C.
(1997: Lab. maj. 3,224 (6.60%))

ILFORD SOUTH
E.76,025 T. 41,295 (54.32%)Lab Co-op hold
*Mike Gapes, Lab. Co-op.   24,619
Suresh Kuma, C.   10,622
Ralph Scott, LD   4,647
Harun Khan, UK Ind.   1,407
Lab Co-op majority 13,997 (33.90%)
2.75% swing C. to Lab. Co-op
(1997: Lab. maj. 14,200 (28.39%))

IPSWICH
E.68,198 T. 38,873 (57.00%) Lab. hold
*Jamie Cann, Lab.   19,952
Edward Wild, C.   11,871
Terry Gilbert, LD   5,904
William Vinyard, UK Ind.   624
Peter Leach, Soc. All.   305
Shaun Gratton, Soc. Lab.   217
Lab. majority 8,081 (20.79%)
0.40% swing Lab. to C.
(1997: Lab. maj. 10,439 (21.58%))

ISLE OF WIGHT
E.106,305 T. 63,482 (59.72%)   C. gain
Andrew Turner, C.   25,223
*Dr Peter Brand, LD   22,397
Ms Deborah Gardiner, Lab.   9,676
David Lott, UK Ind.   2,106
David Holmes, Ind.   1,423
Paul Scivier, Green   1,279
Philip Murray, IOW   1,164
James Spensley, Soc. All.   214
C. majority 2,826 (4.45%)
6.61% swing LD to C.
(1997: LD maj. 6,406 (8.76%))

ISLINGTON NORTH
E.61,970 T. 30,216 (48.76%) Lab. hold
*Jeremy Corbyn, Lab.   18,699
Ms Laura Willoughby, LD   5,741
Neil Rands, C.   3,249
Chris Ashby, Green   1,876
Steve Cook, Soc. Lab.   512
Emine Hassan, Reform   139
Lab. majority 12,958 (42.88%)

6.38% swing Lab. to LD
(1997: Lab. maj. 19,955 (55.64%))

ISLINGTON SOUTH & FINSBURY
E.59,515 T. 28,206 (47.39%) Lab. hold
*Rt. Hon. C. Smith, *Lab.*   15,217
Keith Sharp, *LD*   7,937
Mrs Nicky Morgan, *C.*   3,860
Ms Janine Booth, *Soc. All.*   817
Thomas McCarthy, *Ind.*   267
Charles Thomson, *Stuck*   108
Lab. majority 7,280 (25.81%)
7.71% swing Lab. to LD
(1997: Lab. maj. 14,563 (41.24%))

JARROW
E.63,172 T. 34,479 (54.58%) Lab. hold
*Stephen Hepburn, *Lab.*   22,777
James Selby, *LD*   5,182
Donald Wood, *C.*   5,056
Alan Badger, *UK Ind.*   716
Alan Le Blond, *Ind.*   391
John Bissett, *Soc.*   357
Lab. majority 17,595 (51.03%)
1.37% swing Lab. to LD
(1997: Lab. maj. 21,933 (49.91%))

KEIGHLEY
E.68,349 T. 43,333 (63.40%) Lab. hold
*Ms Ann Cryer, *Lab.*   20,888
Simon Cooke, *C.*   16,883
Mike Doyle, *LD*   4,722
Michael Cassidy, *UK Ind.*   840
Lab. majority 4,005 (9.24%)
2.30% swing Lab. to C.
(1997: Lab. maj. 7,132 (13.85%))

KENSINGTON & CHELSEA
E.62,007 T. 28,038 (45.22%) C. hold
*Rt. Hon. M. Portillo, *C.*   15,270
Simon Stanley, *Lab.*   6,499
Ms Kishwer Falkner, *LD*   4,416
Ms Julia Stephenson, *Green*   1,158
Nicholas Hockney, *UK Ind.*   416
Ms Josephine Quintavalle, *ProLife*   179
Ginger Crab, *Wrestling*   100
C. majority 8,771 (31.28%)
2.81% swing Lab. to C.
(1999 Nov by-election: C. maj. 6,706
(34.37%); 1997: C. maj. 9,519
(25.66%))

KETTERING
E.79,697 T. 53,752 (67.45%) Lab. hold
*Philip Sawford, *Lab.*   24,034
Philip Hollobone, *C.*   23,369
Roger Aron, *LD*   5,469
Barry Mahoney, *UK Ind.*   880
Lab. majority 665 (1.24%)
0.45% swing C. to Lab.
(1997: Lab. maj. 189 (0.33%))

KINGSTON & SURBITON
E.72,687 T. 49,093 (67.54%) LD hold
*Edward Davey, *LD*   29,542
David Shaw, *C.*   13,866
Phil Woodford, *Lab.*   4,302
Chris Spruce, *Green*   572
Miss Amy Burns, *UK Ind.*   438
John Hayball, *Soc. Lab.*   319
Jeremy Middleton, *Unrep.*   54
LD majority 15,676 (31.93%)

15.92% swing C. to LD
(1997: LD maj. 56 (0.10%))

KINGSWOOD
E.80,531 T. 52,676 (65.41%) Lab. hold
*Dr Roger Berry, *Lab.*   28,903
Robert Marven, *C.*   14,941
Christopher Greenfield, *LD*   7,747
David Smith, *UK Ind.*   1,085
Lab. majority 13,962 (26.51%)
1.35% swing C. to Lab.
(1997: Lab. maj. 14,253 (23.80%))

KNOWSLEY NORTH & SEFTON
EAST
E.70,781 T. 37,517 (53.00%) Lab. hold
*George Howarth, *Lab.*   25,035
Keith Chapman, *C.*   6,108
Richard Roberts, *LD*   5,173
Ron Waugh, *Soc. Lab.*   574
Thomas Rossiter, *Ind.*   356
David Jones, *Ind.*   271
Lab. majority 18,927 (50.45%)
1.08% swing Lab. to C.
(1997: Lab. maj. 26,147 (52.61%))

KNOWSLEY SOUTH
E.70,681 T. 36,590 (51.77%) Lab. hold
*Eddie O'Hara, *Lab.*   26,071
David Smithson, *LD*   4,755
Paul Jemetta, *C.*   4,250
Alan Fogg, *Soc. Lab.*   1,068
Ms Mona McNee, *Ind.*   446
Lab. majority 21,316 (58.26%)
5.27% swing Lab. to LD
(1997: Lab. maj. 30,708 (64.53%))

LANCASHIRE WEST
E.72,858 T. 42,971 (58.98%) Lab. hold
*Colin Pickthall, *Lab.*   23,404
Jeremy Myers, *C.*   13,761
John Thornton, *LD*   4,966
David Hill, *Ind.*   523
David Braid, *Ind.*   317
Lab. majority 9,643 (22.44%)
4.42% swing Lab. to C.
(1997: Lab. maj. 17,119 (31.28%))

LANCASTER & WYRE
E.78,964 T. 52,350 (66.30%) Lab. hold
*Hilton Dawson, *Lab.*   22,556
Steve Barclay, *C.*   22,075
Ms Liz Scott, *LD*   5,383
Prof John Whitelegg, *Green*   1,595
Dr John Whittaker, *UK Ind.*   741
Lab. majority 481 (0.92%)
0.64% swing Lab. to C.
(1997: Lab. maj. 1,295 (2.20%))

LEEDS CENTRAL
E.65,497 T. 27,306 (41.69%) Lab. hold
*Hilary Benn, *Lab.*   18,277
Miss Victoria Richmond, *C.*   3,896
Stewart Arnold, *LD*   3,607
David Burgess, *UK Ind.*   775
Steve Johnson, *Soc. All.*   751
Lab. majority 14,381 (52.67%)
1.62% swing Lab. to C.
(1999 Jun by-election: Lab. maj. 2,293
(17.39%); 1997: Lab. maj. 20,689
(55.90%))

LEEDS EAST
E.56,400 T. 29,055 (51.52%) Lab. hold
*George Mudie, *Lab.*   18,290
Barry Anderson, *C.*   5,647
Brian Jennings, *LD*   3,923
Raymond Northgreaves, *UK Ind.*   634
Mark King, *Soc. Lab.*   419
Peter Socrates, *Ind.*   142
Lab. majority 12,643 (43.51%)
2.64% swing Lab. to C.
(1997: Lab. maj. 17,466 (48.80%))

LEEDS NORTH EAST
E.64,123 T. 39,773 (62.03%) Lab. hold
*Fabian Hamilton, *Lab.*   19,540
Owain Rhys, *C.*   12,451
Jonathan Brown, *LD*   6,325
Ms Celia Foote, *Left All*   770
Jeffrey Miles, *UK Ind.*   382
Colin Muir, *Soc. Lab.*   173
Mohammed Zaman, *Ind.*   132
Lab. majority 7,089 (17.82%)
1.27% swing C. to Lab.
(1997: Lab. maj. 6,959 (15.29%))

LEEDS NORTH WEST
E.72,945 T. 42,451 (58.20%) Lab. hold
*Harold Bes,t *Lab.*   17,794
Adam Pritchard, *C.*   12,558
David Hall-Matthews, *LD*   11,431
Simon Jones, *UK Ind.*   668
Lab. majority 5,236 (12.33%)
2.27% swing C. to Lab.
(1997: Lab. maj. 3,844 (7.79%))

LEEDS WEST
E.64,218 T. 32,094 (49.98%) Lab. hold
*John Battle, *Lab.*   19,943
Kris Hopkins, *C.*   5,008
Darren Finlay, *LD*   3,350
David Blackburn, *Green*   2,573
William Finley, *UK Ind.*   758
Noel Nowosielski, *Lib.*   462
Lab. majority 14,935 (46.54%)
1.31% swing Lab. to C.
(1997: Lab. maj. 19,771 (49.16%))

LEICESTER EAST
E.65,527 T. 40,661 (62.05%) Lab. hold
*Keith Vaz *Lab.*   23,402
John Mugglestone *C.*   9,960
Ms Harpinder Athwal, *LD*   4,989
Dave Roberts, *Soc. Lab.*   837
Clive Potter, *BNP*   772
Shirley Bennett, *Ind.*   701
Lab. majority 13,442 (33.06%)
4.22% swing Lab. to C.
(1997: Lab. maj. 18,422 (41.49%))

LEICESTER SOUTH
E.72,671 T. 42,142 (57.99%) Lab. hold
*Jim Marshall, *Lab.*   22,958
Richard Hoile, *C.*   9,715
Parmjit Singh Gill, *LD*   7,243
Ms Margaret Layton, *Green*   1,217
Arnold Gardner, *Soc. Lab.*   676
Kirti Ladwa, *UK Ind.*   333
Lab. majority 13,243 (31.42%)
1.43% swing Lab. to C.
(1997: Lab. maj. 16,493 (34.28%))

LEICESTER WEST

E.65,267 T.33,219 (50.90%) Lab. hold
*Rt. Hon. Ms P. Hewitt, *Lab.*   18,014
Chris Shaw, *C.*   8,375
Andrew Vincent, *LD*   5,085
Matthew Gough, *Green*   1,074
Sean Kirkpatrick, *Soc. Lab.*   350
Steve Score, *Soc. All.*   321
Lab. majority 9,639 (29.02%)
1.21% swing Lab. to C.
(1997: Lab. maj. 12,864 (31.44%))

LEICESTERSHIRE NORTH WEST

E.68,414 T.45,009 (65.79%) Lab Co-op
hold
*David Taylor, *Lab. Co-op.*   23,431
Nick Weston, *C.*   15,274
Charlie Fraser-Fleming, *LD*   4,651
William Nattrass, *UK Ind.*   1,021
Robert Nettleton, *Ind.*   632
Lab Co-op majority 8,157 (18.12%)
3.64% swing Lab Co-op to C.
(1997: Lab. maj. 13,219 (25.41%))

LEIGH

E.71,054 T.35,298 (49.68%) Lab. hold
Andrew Burnham, *Lab.*   22,783
Andrew Oxley, *C.*   6,421
Ray Atkins, *LD*   4,524
William Kelly, *Soc. Lab.*   820
Chris Best, *UK Ind.*   750
Lab. majority 16,362 (46.35%)
3.50% swing Lab. to C.
(1997: Lab. maj. 24,496 (53.35%))

LEOMINSTER

E.68,695 T.46,729 (68.02%) Con gain
Bill Wiggin, *C.*   22,879
Ms Celia Downie, *LD*   12,512
Stephen Hart, *Lab.*   7,872
Ms Pippa Bennett, *Green*   1,690
Christopher Kingsley, *UK Ind.*   1,590
John Haycock, *Ind.*   186
C. majority 10,367 (22.19%)
2.35% swing LD to C.
(1997: C. maj. 8,835 (17.48%))

LEWES

E.66,332 T.45,433 (68.49%) LD hold
*Norman Baker, *LD*   25,588
Simon Sinnatt, *C.*   15,878
Paul Richards, *Lab.*   3,317
John Harvey, *UK Ind.*   650
LD majority 9,710 (21.37%)
9.36% swing C. to LD
(1997: LD maj. 1,300 (2.65%))

LEWISHAM DEPTFORD

E.62,869 T.29,107 (46.30%) Lab. hold
*Joan Ruddock, *Lab.*   18,915
Ms Cordelia McCartney, *C.*   3,622
Andrew Wiseman, *LD*   3,409
Darren Johnson, *Green*   1,901
Ian Page, *Soc. All.*   1,260
Lab. majority 15,293 (52.54%)
1.78% swing Lab. to C.
(1997: Lab. maj. 18,878 (56.11%))

LEWISHAM EAST

E.58,302 T.30,040 (51.52%) Lab. hold
*Ms Bridget Prentice, *Lab.*   16,116
David McInnes, *C.*   7,157
David Buxton, *LD*   4,937

Barry Roberts, *BNP*   1,005
Ms Jean Kysow, *Soc. All.*   464
Maurice Link, *UK Ind.*   361
Lab. majority 8,959 (29.82%)
1.30% swing Lab. to C.
(1997: Lab. maj. 12,127 (32.42%))

LEWISHAM WEST

E.60,947 T.30,815 (50.56%) Lab. hold
*Jim Dowd, *Lab.*   18,816
Gary Johnson, *C.*   .6,896
Richard Thomas, *LD*   4,146
Frederick Pearson, *UK Ind.*   485
Nick Long, *Ind.*   472
Lab. majority 11,920 (38.68%)
0.25% swing C. to Lab.
(1997: Lab. maj. 14,337 (38.19%))

LEYTON & WANSTEAD

E.61,549 T.33,718 (54.78%) Lab. hold
*Harry Cohen, *Lab.*   19,558
Edward Heckels, *C.*   6,654
Alex Wilcock, *LD*   5,389
Ashley Gunstock, *Green*   1,030
Ms Sally Janner, *Soc. All.*   709
M. Skaife D'Ingerthorp, *UK Ind.*   378
Lab. majority 12,904 (38.27%)
0.17% swing Lab. to C.
(1997: Lab. maj. 15,186 (38.62%))

LICHFIELD

E.63,794 T.41,680 (65.34%)   C. hold
*Michael Fabricant, *C.*   20,480
Martin Machray, *Lab.*   16,054
Phillip Bennion, *LD*   4,462
John Phazey, *UK Ind.*   684
C. majority 4,426 (10.62%)
5.06% swing Lab. to C.
(1997: C. maj. 238 (0.49%))

LINCOLN

E.66,299 T.37,125 (56.00%) Lab. hold
*Ms Gillian Merron, *Lab.*   20,003
Mrs Christine Talbot, *C.*   11,583
Ms Lisa Gabriel, *LD*   4,703
Roger Doughty, *UK Ind.*   836
Lab. majority 8,420 (22.68%)
0.61% swing Lab. to C.
(1997: Lab. maj. 11,130 (23.91%))

LIVERPOOL GARSTON

E.65,094 T.32,651 (50.16%) Lab. hold
*Ms Maria Eagle, *Lab.*   20,043
Ms Paula Keaveney, *LD*   7,549
Miss Helen Sutton, *C.*   5,059
Lab. majority 12,494 (38.27%)
2.05% swing Lab. to LD
(1997: Lab. maj. 18,417 (42.36%))

LIVERPOOL RIVERSIDE

E.74,827 T.25,503 (34.08%) Lab Co-
op hold
*Ms Louise Ellman, *Lab. Co-op.* 18,201
Richard Marbrow, *LD*   4,251
Miss Judith Edwards, *C.*   2,142
Ms Cathy Wilson, *Soc. All.*   909
Lab Co-op majority 13,950 (54.70%)
1.23% swing Lab Co-op to LD
(1997: Lab. maj. 21,799 (57.16%))

LIVERPOOL WALTON

E.66,237 T.28,458 (42.96%) Lab. hold
*Peter Kilfoyle, *Lab.*   22,143

Kiron Reid, *LD*   4,147
Stephen Horgan, *C.*   1,726
Paul Forrest, *UK Ind.*   442
Lab. majority 17,996 (63.24%)
2.00% swing Lab. to LD
(1997: Lab. maj. 27,038 (67.24%))

LIVERPOOL WAVERTREE

E.72,555 T.32,138 (44.29%) Lab. hold
*Ms Jane Kennedy, *Lab.*   20,155
Christopher Newby, *LD*   7,836
Geoffrey Allen, *C.*   3,091
Michael Lane, *Soc. Lab.*   359
Mark O'Brien, *Soc. All.*   349
Neil Miney, *UK Ind.*   348
Lab. majority 12,319 (38.33%)
2.29% swing Lab. to LD
(1997: Lab. maj. 19,701 (42.91%))

LIVERPOOL WEST DERBY

E.67,921 T.30,907 (45.50%) Lab. hold
*Robert Wareing, *Lab.*   20,454
Steve Radford, *Lib.*   4,601
Patrick Moloney, *LD*   3,366
Bill Clare, *C.*   2,486
Lab. majority 15,853 (51.29%)
5.15% swing Lab. to Lib.
(1997: Lab. maj. 25,965 (61.59%))

LOUGHBOROUGH

E.70,077 T.44,254 (63.15%)   Lab Co-
op hold
*Andy Reed, *Lab. Co-op.*   22,016
Neil Lyon, *C.*   15,638
Ms Julie Simons, *LD*   5,667
John Bigger, *UK Ind.*   933
Lab Co-op majority 6,378 (14.41%)
1.75% swing C. to Lab. Co-op
(1997: Lab. maj. 5,712 (10.91%))

LOUTH & HORNCASTLE

E.71,556 T.44,460 (62.13%)   C. hold
*Sir Peter Tapsell, *C.*   21,543
David Bolland, *Lab.*   13,989
Ms Fiona Martin, *LD*   8,928
C. majority 7,554 (16.99%)
1.59% swing Lab. to C.
(1997: C. maj. 6,900 (13.81%))

LUDLOW

E.63,053 T.43,124 (68.39%)   LD gain
Matthew Green, *LD*   18,620
Martin Taylor-Smith, *C.*   16,990
Nigel Knowles, *Lab.*   5,785
Jim Gaffney, *Green*   871
Phil Gutteridge, *UK Ind.*   858
LD majority 1,630 (3.78%)
8.27% swing C. to LD
(1997: C. maj. 5,909 (12.77%))

LUTON NORTH

E.65,998 T.39,126 (59.28%) Lab. hold
*Kelvin Hopkins, *Lab.*   22,187
Mrs Amanda Sater, *C.*   12,210
Dr Bob Hoyle, *LD*   3,795
Colin Brown, *UK Ind.*   934
Lab. majority 9,977 (25.50%)
2.58% swing C. to Lab.
(1997: Lab. maj. 9,626 (20.34%))

LUTON SOUTH

E.68,985 T.39,351 (57.04%) Lab. hold
*Ms Margaret Moran, *Lab.*   21,719

Gordon Henderson, *C.* 11,586
Rabi Martins, *LD* 4,292
Marc Scheimann, *Green* 798
Charles Lawman, *UK Ind.* 578
Joe Hearne, *Soc. All.* 271
Robert Bolton, *WRP* 107
Lab. majority 10,133 (25.75%)
1.13% swing C. to Lab.
(1997: Lab. maj. 11,319 (23.49%))

MACCLESFIELD
*E.*73,123　*T.* 45,585 (62.34%)　C. hold
*Nicholas Winterton, *C.* 22,284
Stephen Carter, *Lab.* 15,084
Mike Flynn, *LD* 8,217
C. majority 7,200 (15.79%)
0.09% swing C. to Lab.
(1997: C. maj. 8,654 (15.97%))

MAIDENHEAD
*E.*68,130　*T.* 43,318 (63.58%)　C. hold
*Mrs Theresa May, *C.* 19,506
Ms Kathryn Newbound, *LD* 16,222
John O'Farrell, *Lab.* 6,577
Dr Denis Cooper, *UK Ind.* 741
Lloyd Clarke, *Loony* 272
C. majority 3,284 (7.58%)
7.98% swing C. to LD
(1997: C. maj. 11,981 (23.54%))

MAIDSTONE & THE WEALD
*E.*74,002　*T.* 45,577 (61.59%)　C. hold
*Rt. Hon. Miss A. Widdecombe,
C. 22,621
Mark Davis, *Lab.* 12,303
Ms Allison Wainman, *LD* 9,064
John Botting, *UK Ind.* 978
Neil Hunt, *Ind.* 611
C. majority 10,318 (22.64%)
2.36% swing Lab. to C.
(1997: C. maj. 9,603 (17.91%))

MAKERFIELD
*E.*68,457　*T.* 34,856 (50.92%) Lab. hold
*Rt. Hon. Ian McCartney, *Lab.* 23,879
Mrs Jane Brooks, *C.* 6,129
David Crowther, *LD* 3,990
Malcolm Jones, *Soc. All.* 858
Lab. majority 17,750 (50.92%)
3.61% swing Lab. to C.
(1997: Lab. maj. 26,177 (58.15%))

MALDON & CHELMSFORD EAST
*E.*69,201　*T.* 44,100 (63.73%)　C. hold
*John Whittingdale, *C.* 21,719
Russell Kennedy, *Lab.* 13,257
Ms Jane Jackson, *LD* 7,002
Geoffrey Harris, *UK Ind.* 1,135
Walter Schwarz, *Green* 987
C. majority 8,462 (19.19%)
0.37% swing C. to Lab.
(1997: C. maj. 10,039 (19.92%))

MANCHESTER BLACKLEY
*E.*59,111　*T.* 26,523 (44.87%) Lab. hold
*Graham Stringer, *Lab.* 18,285
Lance Stanbury, *C.* 3,821
Gary Riding, *LD* 3,015
Kevin Barr, *Soc. Lab.* 485
Ms Karen Reissmann, *Soc. All.* 461
Aziz Bhatti, *Anti-Corrupt* 456
Lab. majority 14,464 (54.53%

0.13% swing Lab. to C.
(1997: Lab. maj. 19,588 (54.79%))

MANCHESTER CENTRAL
*E.*66,268　*T.* 25,928 (39.13%) Lab. hold
*Tony Lloyd, *Lab.* 17,812
Philip Hobson, *LD* 4,070
Aaron Powell, *C.* 2,328
Ms Vanessa Hall, *Green* 1,018
Ron Sinclair, *Soc. Lab.* 484
Ms Terrenia Brosnan, *ProLife* 216
Lab. majority 13,742 (53.00%)
2.84% swing Lab. to LD
(1997: Lab. maj. 19,682 (58.69%))

MANCHESTER GORTON
*E.*63,834　*T.* 27,229 (42.66%) Lab. hold
*Rt. Hon. G. Kaufman, *Lab.* 17,099
Ms Jackie Pearcey, *LD* 5,795
Christopher Causer, *C.* 2,705
Bruce Bingham, *Green* 835
Rashid Bhatti, *UK Ind.* 462
Ms Kirsty Muir, *Soc. Lab.* 333
Lab. majority 11,304 (41.51%)
3.12% swing Lab. to LD
(1997: Lab. maj. 17,342 (47.76%))

MANCHESTER WITHINGTON
*E.*67,480　*T.* 35,050 (51.94%) Lab. hold
*Rt. Hon. K. Bradley, *Lab.* 19,239
Ms Yasmin Zalzala, *LD* 7,715
Julian Samways, *C.* 5,349
Ms Michelle Valentine, *Green* 1,539
John Clegg, *Soc. All.* 1,208
Lab. majority 11,524 (32.88%)
7.53% swing Lab. to LD
(1997: Lab. maj. 18,581 (42.20%))

MANSFIELD
*E.*66,748　*T.* 36,852 (55.21%) Lab. hold
*Alan Meale, *Lab.* 21,050
William Wellesley, *C.* 10,012
Tim Hill, *LD* 5,790
Lab. majority 11,038 (29.95%)
6.65% swing Lab. to C.
(1997: Lab. maj. 20,518 (43.26%))

MEDWAY
*E.*64,930　*T.* 38,610 (59.46%) Lab. hold
*Robert Marshall-Andrews, *Lab.*18,914
Mark Reckless, *C.* 15,134
Geoffrey Juby, *LD* 3,604
Ms Nikki Sinclaire, *UK Ind.* 958
Lab. majority 3,780 (9.79%)
1.08% swing Lab. to C.
(1997: Lab. maj. 5,354 (11.96%))

MERIDEN
*E.*74,439　*T.* 44,559 (59.86%)　C. hold
*Mrs Caroline Spelman, *C.* 21,246
Ms Christine Shawcroft, *Lab.* 17,462
Nigel Hicks, *LD* 4,941
Richard Adams, *UK Ind.* 910
C. majority 3,784 (8.49%)
3.71% swing Lab. to C.
(1997: C. maj. 582 (1.07%))

MIDDLESBROUGH
*E.*67,659　*T.* 33,717 (49.83%) Lab. hold
*Stuart Bell, *Lab.* 22,783
Alex Finn, *C.* 6,453
Keith Miller, *LD* 3,512

Geoff Kerr-Morgan, *Soc. All.* 577
Kai Andersen, *Soc. Lab.* 392
Lab. majority 16,330 (48.43%)
2.92% swing Lab. to C.
(1997: Lab. maj. 25,018 (54.28%))

MIDDLESBROUGH SOUTH &
CLEVELAND EAST
*E.*71,485　*T.* 43,991 (61.54%) Lab. hold
*Dr Ashok Kumar, *Lab.* 24,321
Mrs Barbara Harpham, *C.* 14,970
Ms Linda Parrish, *LD* 4,700
Lab. majority 9,351 (21.26%)
0.73% swing C. to Lab.
(1997: Lab. maj. 10,607 (19.79%))

MILTON KEYNES NORTH EAST
*E.*75,526　*T.* 47,094 (62.35%) Lab. hold
*Brian White, *Lab.* 19,761
Mrs Marion Rix, *C.* 17,932
David Yeoward, *LD* 8,375
Michael Phillips, *UK Ind.* 1,026
Lab. majority 1,829 (3.88%)
1.71% swing C. to Lab.
(1997: Lab. maj. 240 (0.47%))

MILTON KEYNES SOUTH WEST
*E.*76,607　*T.* 45,384 (59.24%) Lab. hold
*Dr Phyllis Starkey, *Lab.* 22,484
Iain Stewart, *C.* 15,506
Nazar Mohammad, *LD* 4,828
Alan Francis, *Green* 957
Clive Davies, *UK Ind.* 848
Patrick Denning, *LCA* 500
Dave Bradbury, *Soc. All.* 261
Lab. majority 6,978 (15.38%)
2.45% swing Lab. to C.
(1997: Lab. maj. 10,292 (20.28%))

MITCHAM & MORDEN
*E.*65,671　*T.* 37,961 (57.80%) Lab. hold
*Ms Siobhain McDonagh, *Lab.* 22,936
Harry Stokes, *C.* 9,151
Nicholas Harris, *LD* 3,820
Tom Walsh, *Green* 926
John Tyndall, *BNP* 642
Adrian Roberts, *UK Ind.* 486
Lab. majority 13,785 (36.31%)
3.83% swing C. to Lab.
(1997: Lab. maj. 13,741 (28.66%))

MOLE VALLEY
*E.*67,770　*T.* 47,072 (69.46%)　C. hold
*Sir Paul Beresford, *C.* 23,790
Ms Celia Savage, *LD* 13,637
Dan Redford, *Lab.* 7,837
Ron Walters, *UK Ind.* 1,333
William Newton, *ProLife* 475
C. majority 10,153 (21.57%)
1.41% swing LD to C.
(1997: C. maj. 10,221 (18.74%))

MORECAMBE & LUNESDALE
*E.*68,607　*T.* 41,655 (60.72%) Lab. hold
*Ms Geraldine Smith, *Lab.* 20,646
David Nuttall, *C.* 15,554
Chris Cotton, *LD* 3,817
Gregg Beaman, *UK Ind.* 935
Ms Cherith Adams, *Green* 703
Lab. majority 5,092 (12.22%)
0.05% swing C. to Lab.
(1997: Lab. maj. 5,965 (12.12%))

MORLEY & ROTHWELL
E.71,815 T. 38,442 (53.53%) Lab. hold
Colin Challen, *Lab.*   21,919
David Schofield, *C.*   9,829
Stewart Golton, *LD*   5,446
John Bardsley, *UK Ind.*   1,248
Lab. majority 12,090 (31.45%)
0.35% swing Lab. to C.
(1997: *Lab. majority* 14,750 (32.14%))

NEW FOREST EAST
E.66,767 T. 42,178 (63.17%)   C. hold
*Dr Julian Lewis, *C.*   17,902
Brian Dash, *LD*   14,073
Alan Goodfellow, *Lab.*   9,141
William Howe, *UK Ind.*   1,062
C. majority 3,829 (9.08%)
0.78% swing C. to LD
(1997: C. maj. 5,215 (10.63%))

NEW FOREST WEST
E.67,806 T. 44,087 (65.02%)   C. hold
*Desmond Swayne, *C.*   24,575
Mike Bignell, *LD*   11,384
Ms Crada Onuegbu, *Lab.*   6,481
Michael Clark, *UK Ind.*   1,647
C. majority 13,191 (29.92%)
3.57% swing LD to C.
(1997: C. maj. 11,332 (22.78%))

NEWARK
E.71,089 T. 45,147 (63.51%)   Con gain
Patrick Mercer, *C.*   20,983
*Ms Fiona Jones, *Lab.*   16,910
David Harding-Price, *LD*   5,970
Donald Haxby, *Ind.*   822
Ian Thomson, *Soc. All.*   462
C. majority 4,073 (9.02%)
7.41% swing Lab. to C.
(1997: *Lab. majority* 3,016 (5.80%))

NEWBURY
E.75,490 T. 50,807 (67.30%)   LD hold
*David Rendel, *LD*   24,507
Richard Benyon, *C.*   22,092
Steve Billcliffe, *Lab.*   3,523
Ms Delphine Gray-Fisk, *UK Ind.*   685
LD majority 2,415 (4.75%)
5.16% swing LD to C.
(1997: LD maj. 8,517 (15.08%))

NEWCASTLE UPON TYNE CENTRAL
E.67,970 T. 34,870 (51.30%) Lab. hold
*Jim Cousins, *Lab.*   19,169
Stephen Psallidas, *LD*   7,564
Aidan Ruff, *C.*   7,414
Gordon Potts, *Soc. Lab.*   723
Lab. majority 11,605 (33.28%)
5.44% swing Lab. to LD
(1997: *Lab. majority* 16,480 (35.75%))

NEWCASTLE UPON TYNE EAST & WALLSEND
E.61,494 T. 32,694 (53.17%) Lab. hold
*Rt. Hon. N. Brown, *Lab.*   20,642
David Ord, *LD*   6,419
Tim Troman, *C.*   ,873
Andrew Gray, *Green*   651
Dr Harash Narang, *Ind.*   563
Ms Blanch Carpenter, *Soc. Lab.*   420
Martin Levy, *Comm.*   126
Lab. majority 14,223 (43.50%)

8.53% swing Lab. to LD
(1997: *Lab. maj.* 23,811 (57.25%))

NEWCASTLE UPON TYNE NORTH
E.63,208 T. 36,368 (57.54%) Lab. hold
*Doug Henderson, *Lab.*   21,874
Phillip Smith, *C.*   7,424
Graham Soult, *LD*   7,070
Lab. majority 14,450 (39.73%)
1.50% swing Lab. to C.
(1997: *Lab. maj.* 19,332 (42.74%))

NEWCASTLE-UNDER-LYME
E.65,739 T. 38,674 (58.83%) Lab. hold
Paul Farrelly, *Lab.*   0,650
Mike Flynn, *C.*   10,664
Jerry Roodhouse, *LD*   5,993
Robert Fyson, *Ind.*   773
Paul Godfrey, *UK Ind.*   594
Lab. majority 9,986 (25.82%)
4.60% swing Lab. to C.
(1997: *Lab. maj.* 17,206 (35.02%))

NORFOLK MID
E.74,911 T. 52,548 (70.15%)   C. hold
*Keith Simpson, *C.*   23,519
Daniel Zeichner, *Lab.*   .18,957
Ms V. Clifford-Jackson, *LD*   7,621
John Agnew, *UK Ind.*   1,333
Peter Reeve, *Green*   1,118
C. majority 4,562 (8.68%)
3.18% swing Lab. to C.
(1997: C. maj. 1,336 (2.33%))

NORFOLK NORTH
E.80,061 T. 56,220 (70.22%)   LD gain
Norman Lamb, *LD*   23,978
*David Prior, *C.*   23,495
Michael Gates, *Lab.*   7,490
Mike Sheridan, *Green*   649
Paul Simison, *UK Ind.*   608
LD majority 483 (0.86%)
1.53% swing C. to LD
(1997: C. maj. 1,293 (2.20%))

NORFOLK NORTH WEST
E.77,387 T. 51,203 (66.16%)   Con gain
Henry Bellingham, *C.*   24,846
*Dr George Turner, *Lab.*   21,361
Dr Ian Mack, *LD*   4,292
Ian Durrant, *UK Ind.*   704
C. majority 3,485 (6.81%)
4.57% swing Lab. to C.
(1997: *Lab. maj.* 1,339 (2.33%))

NORFOLK SOUTH
E.82,710 T. 55,929 (67.62%)   C. hold
Richard Bacon, *C.*   23,589
Dr Anne Lee, *LD*   16,696
Mark Wells, *Lab.*   13,719
Ms Stephanie Ross-Wagenknecht,
  Green   1,069
Joseph Neal, *UK Ind.*   856
C. majority 6,893 (12.32%)
0.22% swing LD to C.
(1997: C. maj. 7,378 (11.88%))

NORFOLK SOUTH WEST
E.83,903 T. 52,949 (63.11%)   C. hold
*Rt. Hon. Mrs G. Shephard, *C.*   27,633
Ms Anne Hanson, *Lab.*   18,267
Gordon Dean, *LD*   5,681

Ian Smith, *UK Ind.*   1,368
C. majority 9,366 (17.69%)
6.75% swing Lab. to C.
(1997: C. maj. 2,464 (4.19%))

NORMANTON
E.65,392 T. 34,155 (52.23%) Lab. hold
*William O'Brien, *Lab.*   19,152
Graham Smith, *C.*   9,215
Stephen Pearson, *LD*   4,990
Mick Appleyard, *Soc. Lab.*   798
Lab. majority 9,937 (29.09%)
3.93% swing Lab. to C.
(1997: *Lab. maj.* 15,893 (36.96%))

NORTHAMPTON NORTH
E.74,124 T. 41,494 (55.98%) Lab. hold
*Ms Sally Keeble, *Lab.*   20,507
John Whelan, *C.*   12,614
Richard Church, *LD*   7,363
Dusan Torbica, *UK Ind.*   596
Gordon White, *Soc. All.*   414
Lab. majority 7,893 (19.02%)
0.16% swing Lab. to C.
(1997: *Lab. maj.* 10,000 (19.34%))

NORTHAMPTON SOUTH
E.85,271 T. 51,029 (59.84%) Lab. hold
*Tony Clarke, *Lab.*   21,882
Shailesh Vara, *C.*   20,997
Andrew Simpson, *LD*   6,355
Derek Clark, *UK Ind.*   1,237
Miss Tina Harvey, *LP*   362
Ms Clare Johnson, *ProLife*   196
Lab. majority 885 (1.73%)
0.22% swing C. to Lab.
(1997: *Lab. maj.* 744 (1.30%))

NORTHAVON
E.78,841 T. 55,758 (70.72%)   LD hold
*Steve Webb, *LD*   29,217
Dr Carrie Ruxton, *C.*   19,340
Robert Hall, *Lab.*   6,450
Mrs Carmen Carver, *UK Ind.*   751
LD majority 9,877 (17.71%)
7.15% swing C. to LD
(1997: LD maj. 2,137 (3.42%))

NORWICH NORTH
E.74,911 T. 45,614 (60.89%) Lab. hold
*Dr Ian Gibson, *Lab.*   21,624
Ms Kay Mason, *C.*   15,761
Ms Moira Toye, *LD*   6,750
Robert Tinch, *Green*   797
Guy Cheyney, *UK Ind.*   471
Michael Betts, *Ind.*   211
Lab. majority 5,863 (12.85%)
2.17% swing Lab. to C.
(1997: *Lab. maj.* 9,470 (17.20%))

NORWICH SOUTH
E.65,792 T. 42,592 (64.74%) Lab. hold
*Rt. Hon. C. Clarke, *Lab.*   19,367
Andrew French, *C.*   10,551
Andrew Aalders-Dunthorne, *LD* 9,640
Adrian Holmes, *Green*   1,434
Alun Buffrey, *LCA*   620
Edward Manningham, *Soc. All.*   507
Tarquin Mills, *UK Ind.*   473
Lab. majority 8,816 (20.70%)
3.67% swing Lab. to C.
(1997: *Lab. maj.* 14,239 (28.03%))

NOTTINGHAM EAST
E.65,339 T. 29,731 (45.50%) Lab. hold
*John Heppell, *Lab.*   17,530
Richard Allan, *C.*   7,210
Tim Ball, *LD*   3,874
Pete Radcliff, *Soc. All.*   1,117
Lab. majority 10,320 (34.71%)
2.04% swing Lab. to C.
(1997: Lab. maj. 15,419 (38.80%))

NOTTINGHAM NORTH
E.64,281 T. 30,042 (46.74%) Lab. hold
*Graham Allen, *Lab.*   19,392
Martin Wright, *C.*   7,152
Rob Lee, *LD*   3,177
Andrew Botham, *Soc. Lab.*   321
Lab. majority 12,240 (40.74%)
2.34% swing Lab. to C.
(1997: Lab. maj. 18,801 (45.42%))

NOTTINGHAM SOUTH
E.73,049 T. 36,605 (50.11%) Lab. hold
*Alan Simpson, *Lab.*   19,949
Mrs Wendy Manning, *C.*   9,960
Kevin Mulloy, *LD*   6,064
David Bartrop, *UK Ind.*   632
Lab. majority 9,989 (27.29%)
0.13% swing Lab. to C.
(1997: Lab. maj. 13,364 (27.55%))

NUNEATON
E.72,101 T. 43,312 (60.07%) Lab. hold
*Bill Olner, *Lab.*   22,577
Mark Lancaster, *C.*   15,042
Tony Ferguson, *LD*   4,820
Brian James, *UK Ind.*   873
Lab. majority 7,535 (17.40%)
3.95% swing Lab. to C.
(1997: Lab. maj. 13,540 (25.30%))

OLD BEXLEY & SIDCUP
E.67,841 T. 42,133 (62.11%)   C. hold
Derek Conway, *C.*   19,130
Jim Dickson, *Lab.*   15,785
Ms Belinda Ford, *LD*   5,792
Mrs Janice Cronin, *UK Ind.*   1,426
C. majority 3,345 (7.94%)
0.49% swing Lab. to C.
(1997: C. maj. 3,569 (6.95%))

OLDHAM EAST &
SADDLEWORTH
E.74,511 T. 45,420 (60.96%) Lab. hold
*Phil Woolas, *Lab.*   17,537
Howard Sykes, *LD*   14,811
Craig Heeley, *C.*   .7,304
Michael Treacy, *BNP*   5,091
Ms Barbara Little, *UK Ind.*   677
Lab. majority 2,726 (6.00%)
0.13% swing Lab. to LD
(1997: Lab. maj. 3,389 (6.26%))

OLDHAM WEST & ROYTON
E.69,409 T. 39,962 (57.57%) Lab. hold
*Rt. Hon. M. Meacher, *Lab.*   20,441
Duncan Reed, *C.*   7,076
Nick Griffin, *BNP*   6,552
Marc Ramsbottom, *LD*   4,975
David Roney, *Green*   918
Lab. majority 13,365 (33.44%)
0.99% swing Lab. to C.
(1997: Lab. maj. 16,201 (35.42%))

ORPINGTON
E.74,423 T. 50,912 (68.41%)   C. hold
*John Horam, *C.*   2,334
Chris Maines, *LD*   22,065
Chris Purnell, *Lab.*   5,517
John Youles, *UK Ind.*   996
C. majority 269 (0.53%)
2.19% swing C. to LD
(1997: C. maj. 2,952 (4.91%))

OXFORD EAST
E.74,421 T. 39,848 (53.54%) Lab. hold
*Rt. Hon. A. Smith, *Lab.*   19,681
Steve Goddard, *LD*   9,337
Ms Cheryl Potter, *C.*   7,446
Pritam Singh, *Green*   1,501
John Lister, *Soc. All.*   708
Peter Gardner, *UK Ind.*   570
Fahim Ahmed, *Soc. Lab.*   274
Ms Linda Hodge, *ProLife*   254
Pathmanathan Mylvaganan, *Ind.*   77
Lab. majority 10,344 (25.96%)
8.08% swing Lab. to LD
(1997: Lab. maj. 16,665 (34.81%))

OXFORD WEST & ABINGDON
E.79,915 T. 51,568 (64.53%)   LD hold
*Dr Evan Harris, *LD*   24,670
Ed Matts, *C.*   15,485
Ms Gillian Kirk, *Lab.*   9,114
Mike Woodin, *Green*   1,423
Marcus Watney, *UK Ind.*   451
Ms Sigrid Shreeve, *Ind.*   332
Robert Twigger, *Ext. Club*   93
LD majority 9,185 (17.81%)
3.77% swing C. to LD
(1997: LD maj. 6,285 (10.27%))

PENDLE
E.62,870 T. 39,732 (63.20%) Lab. hold
*Gordon Prentice, *Lab.*   17,729
Rasjid Skinner, *C.*   13,454
David Whipp, *LD*   5,479
Christian Jackson, *BNP*   1,976
Graham Cannon, *UK Ind.*   1,094
Lab. majority 4,275 (10.76%)
6.13% swing Lab. to C.
(1997: Lab. maj. 10,824 (23.02%))

PENRITH & THE BORDER
E.67,776 T. 44,249 (65.29%)   C. hold
*Rt. Hon. D. Maclean, *C.*   24,302
Kenneth Geyve Walker, *LD*   9,625
Michael Boaden, *Lab.*   8,177
Thomas Lowther, *UK Ind.*   938
Mark Gibson, *LCA*   870
John Moffat, *Ind.*   337
C. majority 14,677 (33.17%)
6.13% swing LD to C.
(1997: C. maj. 10,233 (20.90%))

PETERBOROUGH
E.64,918 T. 39,812 (61.33%) Lab. hold
*Mrs Helen Brinton, *Lab.*   17,975
Stewart Jackson, *C.*   15,121
Nick Sandford, *LD*   5,761
Julian Fairweather, *UK Ind.*   955
Lab. majority 2,854 (7.17%)
3.98% swing Lab. to C.
(1997: Lab. maj. 7,323 (15.12%))

PLYMOUTH DEVONPORT
E.73,666 T. 41,719 (56.63%) Lab. hold
*David Jamieson, *Lab.*   24,322
John Glen, *C.*   11,289
Keith Baldry, *LD*   4,513
Michael Parker, *UK Ind.*   958
Tony Staunton, *Soc. All.*   334
Rob Hawkins, *Soc. Lab.*   303
Lab. majority 13,033 (31.24%)
2.73% swing Lab. to C.
(1997: Lab. maj. 19,067 (36.70%))

PLYMOUTH SUTTON
E.68,438 T. 39,073 (57.09%) Lab Co-
op hold
*Mrs Linda Gilroy, *Lab. Co-op.* 19,827
Oliver Colvile, *C.*   12,310
Alan Connett, *LD*   5,605
Alan Whitton, *UK Ind.*   970
Henry Leary, *Soc. Lab.*   361
Lab Co-op majority 7,517 (19.24%)
0.29% swing Lab Co-op to C.
(1997: Lab. maj. 9,440 (19.81%))

PONTEFRACT & CASTLEFORD
E.63,181 T. 31,391 (49.68%) Lab. hold
*Ms Yvette Cooper, *Lab.*   21,890
Ms Pamela Singleton, *C.*   5,512
Wesley Paxton, *LD*   2,315
John Burdon, *UK Ind.*   739
Trevor Bolderson, *Soc. Lab.*   605
John Gill, *Soc. All.*   330
Lab. majority 16,378 (52.17%)
4.99% swing Lab. to C.
(1997: Lab. maj. 25,725 (62.15%))

POOLE
E.64,644 T. 39,233 (60.69%)   C. hold
*Robert Syms, *C.*   17,710
David Watt, *Lab.*   10,544
Nick Westbrook, *LD*   10,011
John Bass, *UK Ind.*   968
C. majority 7,166 (18.27%)
1.15% swing C. to Lab.
(1997: C. maj. 5,298 (11.32%))

POPLAR & CANNING TOWN
E.75,173 T. 34,108 (45.37%) Lab. hold
*Jim Fitzpatrick, *Lab.*   20,862
Robert Marr, *C.*   6,758
Ms Alexi Sugden, *LD*   3,795
Paul Borg, *BNP*   1,743
Dr Kambiz Boomla, *Soc. All.*   950
Lab. majority 14,104 (41.35%)
3.41% swing Lab. to C.
(1997: Lab. maj. 18,915 (48.17%))

PORTSMOUTH NORTH
E.64,256 T. 36,866 (57.37%) Lab. hold
*Syd Rapson, *Lab.*   18,676
Chris Day, *C.*   13,542
Darren Sanders, *LD*   3,795
William McCabe, *UK Ind.*   559
Brian Bundy, *Ind.*   294
Lab. majority 5,134 (13.93%)
2.19% swing C. to Lab.
(1997: Lab. maj. 4,323 (9.55%))

PORTSMOUTH SOUTH
E.77,095 T. 39,215 (50.87%)   LD hold
*Mike Hancock, *LD*   17,490

Philip Warr, *C.* 11,396
Graham Heaney, *Lab.* 9,361
John Molyneux, *Soc. All.* 647
Michael Tarrant, *UK Ind.* 321
LD majority 6,094 (15.54%)
3.58% swing C. to LD
(1997: LD maj. 4,327 (8.37%))

PRESTON
*E.*72,077 *T.* 36,041 (50.00%)Lab Co-op hold
*Mark Hendrick, *Lab. Co-op.* 20,540
Graham O'Hare, *C.* 8,272
Bill Chadwick, *LD* 4,746
Bilal Patel, *Ind.* 1,241
Richard Merrick, *Green* 1,019
The Revd David Braid, *Ind.* 223
Lab Co-op majority 12,268 (34.04%)
2.41% swing Lab Co-op to C.
(2000 Nov by-election: Lab. maj. 4,426)
(1997: Lab. maj. 18,680 (38.86%)))

PUDSEY
*E.*71,405 *T.* 45,175 (63.27%) Lab. hold
*Paul Truswell, *Lab.* 21,717
John Procter, *C.* 16,091
Stephen Boddy, *LD* 6,423
David Sewards, *UK Ind.* 944
Lab. majority 5,626 (12.45%)
0.34% swing C. to Lab.
(1997: Lab. maj. 6,207 (11.77%))

PUTNEY
*E.*60,643 *T.* 34,254 (56.48%) Lab. hold
*Tony Colman, *Lab.* 15,911
Michael Simpson, *C.* 13,140
Tony Burrett, *LD* 4,671
Ms Pat Wild, *UK Ind.* 347
Ms Yvonne Windsor, *ProLife* 185
Lab. majority 2,771 (8.09%)
0.66% swing C. to Lab.
(1997: Lab. maj. 2,976 (6.76%))

RAYLEIGH
*E.*70,073 *T.* 42,773 (61.04%) C. hold
Mark Francois, *C.* 21,444
Paul Clark, *Lab.* 13,144
Geoff Williams, *LD* 6,614
Colin Morgan, *UK Ind.* 1,581
C. majority 8,290 (19.38%)
0.72% swing C. to Lab.
(1997: C. maj. 10,684 (20.83%))

READING EAST
*E.*74,637 *T.* 43,618 (58.44%) Lab. hold
*Ms Jane Griffiths, *Lab.* 19,531
Barry Tanswell, *C.* 13,943
Tom Dobrashian, *LD* 8,078
Ms Miriam Kennett, *Green* 1,053
Miss Amy Thornton, *UK Ind.* 525
Darren Williams, *Soc. All.* 394
Peter Hammerson, *Ind.* 94
Lab. majority 5,588 (12.81%)
2.63% swing C. to Lab.
(1997: Lab. maj. 3,795 (7.55%))

READING WEST
*E.*71,688 *T.* 41,986 (58.57%) Lab. hold
*Martin Salter, *Lab.* 22,300
Stephen Reid, *C.* 13,451
Ms Polly Martin, *LD* 5,387
David Black, *UK Ind.* 848
Lab. majority 8,849 (21.08%)

7.44% swing C. to Lab.
(1997: Lab. maj. 2,997 (6.20%))

REDCAR
*E.*66,179 *T.* 38,198 (57.72%) Lab. hold
Ms Vera Baird, *Lab.* 23,026
Chris Main, *C.* 9,583
Stan Wilson, *LD* 4,817
John Taylor, *Soc. Lab.* 772
Lab. majority 13,443 (35.19%)
4.53% swing Lab. to C.
(1997: Lab. maj. 21,664 (44.25%))

REDDITCH
*E.*62,543 *T.* 37,032 (59.21%) Lab. hold
*Ms Jacqui Smith, *Lab.* 16,899
Mrs Karen Lumley, *C.* 14,415
Michael Ashall, *LD* 3,808
George Flynn, *UK Ind.* 1,259
Richard Armstrong, *Green* 651
Lab. majority 2,484 (6.71%)
3.49% swing Lab. to C.
(1997: Lab. maj. 6,125 (13.69%))

REGENT'S PARK & KENSINGTON NORTH
*E.*75,886 *T.* 37,052 (48.83%) Lab. hold
*Ms Karen Buck, *Lab.* 20,247
Peter Wilson, *C.* 9,981
David Boyle, *LD* 4,669
Dr Paul Miller, *Green* 1,268
China Mieville, *Soc. All.* 459
Alan Crisp, *UK Ind.* 354
Ms Charlotte Regan, *Ind.* 74
Lab. majority 10,266 (27.71%)
1.63% swing Lab. to C.
(1997: Lab. maj. 14,657 (30.96%))

REIGATE
*E.*65,023 *T.* 39,474 (60.71%) C. hold
*Crispin Blunt, *C.* 18,875
Simon Charleton, *Lab.* 10,850
Ms Jane Kulka, *LD* 8,330
Stephen Smith, *UK Ind.* 1,062
Harold Green, *Ref. UK* 357
C. majority 8,025 (20.33%)
2.13% swing Lab. to C.
(1997: C. maj. 7,741 (16.07%))

RIBBLE SOUTH (SOUTH RIBBLE)
*E.*73,794 *T.* 46,130 (62.51%) Lab. hold
*David Borrow, *Lab.* 21,386
Adrian Owens, *C.* 17,594
Mark Alcock, *LD* 7,150
Lab. majority 3,792 (8.22%)
0.49% swing Lab. to C.
(1997: Lab. maj. 5,084 (9.20%))

RIBBLE VALLEY
*E.*74,319 *T.* 49,171 (66.16%) C. hold
*Nigel Evans, *C.* 25,308
Mike Carr, *LD* 14,070
Marcus Johnstone, *Lab.* 9,793
C. majority 11,238 (22.85%)
5.63% swing LD to C.
(1997: C. maj. 6,640 (11.60%))

RICHMOND (YORKS)
*E.*65,360 *T.* 44,034 (67.37%) C. hold
*Rt. Hon. W. Hague, *C.* 25,951
Ms Fay Tinnion, *Lab.* 9,632
Edward Forth, *LD* 7,890
Mrs Melodie Staniforth, *Loony* 561
C. majority 16,319 (37.06%)

8.00% swing Lab. to C.
(1997: C. maj. 10,051 (21.05%))

RICHMOND PARK
*E.*72,663 *T.* 49,151 (67.64%) LD hold
*Dr Jenny Tonge, *LD* 23,444
Tom Harris, *C.* 18,480
Barry Langford, *Lab.* 5,541
James Page, *Green* 1,223
Peter St John Howe, *UK Ind.* 348
Raymond Perrin, *Ind.* 115
LD majority 4,964 (10.10%)
2.45% swing C. to LD
(1997: LD maj. 2,951 (5.19%))

ROCHDALE
*E.*69,506 *T.* 39,412 (56.70%) Lab. hold
*Ms Lorna Fitzsimons, *Lab.* 19,406
Paul Rowen, *LD* 13,751
Ms Elaina Cohen, *C.* 5,274
Nick Harvey, *Green* 728
Mohammed Salim, *Ind.* 253
Lab. majority 5,655 (14.35%)
2.45% swing LD to Lab.
(1997: Lab. maj. 4,545 (9.45%))

ROCHFORD & SOUTHEND EAST
*E.*69,991 *T.* 37,452 (53.51%) C. hold
*Sir Teddy Taylor, *C.* 20,058
Chris Dandridge, *Lab.* 13,024
Stephen Newton, *LD* 2,780
Adrian Hedges, *Green* 990
Brian Lynch, *Lib.* 600
C. majority 7,034 (18.78%)
4.86% swing Lab. to C.
(1997: C. maj. 4,225 (9.07%))

ROMFORD
*E.*59,893 *T.* 35,701 (59.61%) C. gain
Andrew Rosindell, *C.* 18,931
*Ms Eileen Gordon, *Lab.* 12,954
Nigel Meyer, *LD* 2,869
Stephen Ward, *UK Ind.* 533
Frank McAllister, *BNP* 414
C. majority 5,977 (16.74%)
9.14% swing Lab. to C.
(1997: Lab. maj. 649 (1.54%))

ROMSEY
*E.*70,584 *T.* 48,459 (68.65%) LD hold
*Mrs Sandra Gidley, *LD* 22,756
Paul Raynes, *C.* 20,386
Stephen Roberts, *Lab.* 3,986
Anthony McCabe, *UK Ind.* 730
Derrick Large, *LCA* 601
LD majority 2,370 (4.89%)
10.73% swing C. to LD
(2000 May by-election: LD maj. 3,311
(8.55%); 1997: C. maj. 8,585 (16.56%))

ROSSENDALE & DARWEN
*E.*70,280 *T.* 41,358 (58.85%) Lab. hold
*Ms Janet Anderson, *Lab.* 20,251
George Lee, *C.* 15,028
Brian Dunning, *LD* 6,079
Lab. majority 5,223 (12.63%)
4.38% swing Lab. to C.
(1997: Lab. maj. 10,949 (21.38%))

ROTHER VALLEY
*E.*69,174 *T.* 36,803 (53.20%) Lab. hold
*Rt. Hon. K. Barron, *Lab.* 22,851
James Duddridge, *C.* 7,969
Ms Win Knight, *LD* 4,603

David Cutts, *UK Ind.* 1,380
Lab. majority 14,882 (40.44%)
5.22% swing Lab. to C.
(1997: Lab. maj. 23,485 (50.88%))

ROTHERHAM
*E.*57,931 *T.* 29,354 (50.67%) Lab. hold
*Denis MacShane, *Lab.* 18,759
Richard Powell, *C.* 5,682
Charles Hall, *LD* 3,117
Peter Griffith, *UK Ind.* 730
Dick Penycate, *Green* 577
Ms Freda Smith, *Soc. All.* 352
Geoffrey Bartholomew, *JLDP* 137
Lab. majority 13,077 (44.55%)
6.24% swing Lab. to C.
(1997: Lab. maj. 21,469 (57.02%))

RUGBY & KENILWORTH
*E.*79,764 *T.* 53,796 (67.44%) Lab. hold
*Andy King, *Lab.* 24,221
David Martin, *C.* 21,344
Ms Gwen Fairweather, *LD* 7,444
Paul Garratt, *UK Ind.* 787
Lab. majority 2,877 (5.35%)
2.27% swing C. to Lab.
(1997: Lab. maj. 495 (0.81%))

RUISLIP-NORTHWOOD
*E.*60,788 *T.* 37,141 (61.10%) C. hold
*John Wilkinson, *C.* 18,115
Ms Gillian Travis, *Lab.* 10,578
Mike Cox, *LD* 7,177
Graham Lee, *Green* 724
Ian Edward, *BNP* 547
C. majority 7,537 (20.29%)
1.46% swing Lab. to C.
(1997: C. maj. 7,794 (17.38%))

RUNNYMEDE & WEYBRIDGE
*E.*75,569 *T.* 42,426 (56.14%) C. hold
*Philip Hammond, *C.* 0,646
Ms Jane Briginshaw, *Lab.* 6,924
Christopher Browne, *UK Ind.* 1,332
Charles Gilman, *Green* 1,238
C. majority 8,360 (19.70%)
0.27% swing Lab. to C.
(1997: C. maj. 9,875 (19.16%))

RUSHCLIFFE
*E.*81,839 *T.* 54,446 (66.53%) C. hold
*Rt. Hon. K. Clarke, *C.* 25,869
Paul Fallon, *Lab.* 18,512
Jeremy Hargreaves, *LD* 7,395
Ken Browne, *UK Ind.* 1,434
Ashley Baxter, *Green* 1,236
C. majority 7,357 (13.51%)
2.69% swing Lab. to C.
(1997: C. maj. 5,055 (8.14%))

RUTLAND & MELTON
*E.*72,448 *T.* 47,056 (64.95%) C. hold
*Alan Duncan, *C.* 22,621
Matthew O'Callaghan, *Lab.* 14,009
Kim Lee, *LD* 8,386
Peter Baker, *UK Ind.* 1,223
Christopher Davies, *Green* 817
C. majority 8,612 (18.30%)
0.76% swing Lab. to C.
(1997: C. maj. 8,836 (16.78%))

RYEDALE
*E.*66,543 *T.* 43,899 (65.97%) C. hold
*John Greenway, *C.* 20,711
Keith Orrell, *LD* 15,836
David Ellis, *Lab.* 6,470
Stephen Feaster, *UK Ind.* 882
C. majority 4,875 (11.11%)
0.37% swing LD to C.
(1997: C. maj. 5,058 (10.37%))

SAFFRON WALDEN
*E.*76,724 *T.* 50,040 (65.22%) C. hold
*Rt. Hon. Sir A. Haselhurst, *C.* 24,485
Mrs E. Tealby-Watson, *LD* 12,481
Ms Tania Rogers, *Lab.* 11,305
Richard Glover, *UK Ind.* 1,769
C. majority 12,004 (23.99%)
2.73% swing LD to C.
(1997: C. maj. 10,573 (18.53%))

SALFORD
*E.*54,152 *T.* 22,514 (41.58%) Lab. hold
*Ms Hazel Blears, *Lab.* 14,649
Norman Owen, *LD* 3,637
Chris King,*C.* 3,446
Peter Grant, *Soc. All.* 414
Ms Hazel Wallace, *Ind.* 216
Roy Masterson, *Ind.* 152
Lab. majority 11,012 (48.91%)
4.89% swing Lab. to LD
(1997: Lab. maj. 17,069 (51.53%))

SALISBURY
*E.*80,538 *T.* 52,603 (65.31%) C. hold
*Robert Key, *C.* 24,527
Ms Yvonne Emmerson-Peirce,
LD 15,824
Ms Sue Mallory, *Lab.* 9,199
Malcolm Wood, *UK Ind.* 1,958
Hamish Soutar, *Green* 1,095
C. majority 8,703 (16.54%)
2.88% swing LD to C.
(1997: C. maj. 6,276 (10.78%))

SCARBOROUGH & WHITBY
*E.*75,213 *T.* 47,523 (63.18%) Lab. hold
*Lawrie Quinn, *Lab.* 22,426
John Sykes, *C.* 18,841
Tom Pearce, *LD* 3,977
Jonathan Dixon, *Green* 1,049
John Jacob, *UK Ind.* 970
Ms Theresa Murray, *ProLife* 260
Lab. majority 3,585 (7.54%)
0.94% swing Lab. to C.
(1997: Lab. maj. 5,124 (9.43%))

SCUNTHORPE
*E.*59,689 *T.* 33,625 (56.33%) Lab. hold
*Elliot Morley, *Lab.* 20,096
Bernard Theobald, *C.* 9,724
Bob Tress, *LD* 3,156
John Cliff, *UK Ind.* 347
David Patterson, *Ind.* 302
Lab. majority 10,372 (30.85%)
1.62% swing Lab. to C.
(1997: Lab. maj. 14,173 (34.09%))

SEDGEFIELD
*E.*64,925 *T.* 40,258 (62.01%) Lab. hold
*Rt. Hon. T. Blair, *Lab.* 26,110
Douglas Carswell, *C.* 8,397
Andrew Duffield, *LD* 3,624

Andrew Spence, *UK Ind.* 974
Brian Gibson, *Soc. Lab.* 518
Christopher Driver, *R & R Loony* 375
Ms Helen John *WFLOE* 260
Lab. majority 17,713 (44.00%)
4.69% swing Lab. to C.
(1997: Lab. maj. 25,143 (53.37%))

SELBY
*E.*77,924 *T.* 50,272 (64.51%) Lab. hold
*John Grogan, *Lab.* 22,652
Michael Mitchell, *C.* 20,514
Jeremy Wilcock, *LD* 5,569
Ms Helen Kenwright, *Green* 902
Bob Lewis, *UK Ind.* 635
Lab. majority 2,138 (4.25%)
1.28% swing Lab. to C.
(1997: Lab. maj. 3,836 (6.81%))

SEVENOAKS
*E.*66,648 *T.* 42,614 (63.94%) C. hold
*Michael Fallon, *C.* 21,052
Ms Caroline Humphreys, *Lab.* 10,898
Clive Gray, *LD* 9,214
Mrs Lisa Hawkins, *UK Ind.* 1,155
Mark Ellis, *PF* 295
C. majority 10,154 (23.83%)
1.48% swing Lab. to C.
(1997: C. maj. 10,461 (20.86%))

SHEFFIELD ATTERCLIFFE
*E.*68,386 *T.* 35,824 (52.38%) Lab. hold
*Clive Betts, *Lab.* 24,287
John Perry, *C.* 5,443
Ms Gail Smith, *LD* 5,092
Ms Pauline Arnott, *UK Ind.* 1,002
Lab. majority 18,844 (52.60%)
1.69% swing C. to Lab.
(1997: Lab. maj. 21,818 (49.23%))

SHEFFIELD BRIGHTSIDE
*E.*54,711 *T.* 25,552 (46.70%) Lab. hold
*Rt. Hon. D. Blunkett, *Lab.* 19,650
Matthew Wilson, *C.* 2,601
Ms Alison Firth, *LD* 2,238
Brian Wilson, *Soc. All.* 361
Robert Morris, *Soc. Lab.* 354
Mark Suter, *UK Ind.* 348
Lab. majority 17,049 (66.72%)
0.81% swing C. to Lab.
(1997: Lab. maj. 19,954 (58.92%))

SHEFFIELD CENTRAL
*E.*62,018 *T.* 30,069 (48.48%) Lab. hold
Rt. Hon. R. Caborn, *Lab.* 18,477
Ali Qadar, *LD* 5,933
Miss Noelle Brelsford, *C.* 3,289
Bernard Little, *Green* 1,008
Nick Riley, *Soc. All.* 754
David Hadfield, *Soc. Lab.* 289
Ms Charlotte Schofield, *UK Ind.* 257
Michael Driver *WRP* 62
Lab. majority 12,544 (41.72%)
2.36% swing Lab. to LD
(1997: Lab. maj. 16,906 (46.43%))

SHEFFIELD HALLAM
*E.*60,288 *T.* 38,246 (63.44%) LD hold
*Richard Allan, *LD* 21,203
John Harthman, *C.* 11,856
Ms Gillian Furniss, *Lab.* 4,758
Leslie Arnott, *UK Ind.* 429

LD majority 9,347 (24.44%)
3.12% swing C. to LD
(1997: LD maj. 8,271 (18.19%))

SHEFFIELD HEELEY
E.62,758 *T.* 34,139 (54.40%) Lab. hold
Ms Meg Munn, *Lab.*   19,452
David Willis, *LD*   7,748
Ms Carolyn Abbott, *C.*   4,864
Rob Unwin, *Green*   774
Brian Fischer, *Soc. Lab.*   667
David Dunn, *UK Ind.*   634
Lab. majority 11,704 (34.28%)
2.60% swing Lab. to LD
(1997: Lab. maj. 17,078 (39.48%))

SHEFFIELD HILLSBOROUGH
E.75,097 *T.* 42,536 (56.64%) Lab. hold
*Ms Helen Jackson, *Lab.*   24,170
John Commons, *LD*   9,601
Graham King, *C.*   7,801
Peter Webb, *UK Ind.*   964
Lab. majority 14,569 (34.25%)
1.62% swing LD to Lab.
(1997: Lab. maj. 16,451 (31.02%))

SHERWOOD
E.75,670 *T.* 45,900 (60.66%) Lab. hold
*Paddy Tipping, *Lab.*   24,900
Brandon Lewis, *C.*   15,527
Peter Harris, *LD*   5,473
Lab. majority 9,373 (20.42%)
4.66% swing Lab. to C.
(1997: Lab. maj. 16,812 (29.74%))

SHIPLEY
E.69,577 *T.* 46,020 (66.14%) Lab. hold
*Christopher Leslie, *Lab.*   20,243
David Senior, *C.*   18,815
Ms Helen Wright, *LD*   4,996
Martin Love, *Green*   1,386
Walter Whitacker, *UK Ind.*   580
Lab. majority 1,428 (3.10%)
1.28% swing Lab. to C.
(1997: Lab. maj. 2,996 (5.67%))

SHREWSBURY & ATCHAM
E.74,964 *T.* 49,909 (66.58%) Lab. hold
*Paul Marsden, *Lab.*   22,253
Miss Anthea McIntyre, *C.*   18,674
Jonathan Rule, *LD*   6,173
Henry Curteis, UK *Ind.*   1,620
Ms Emma Bullard, *Green*   931
James Gollins, *Ind.*   258
Lab. majority 3,579 (7.17%)
2.08% swing C. to Lab.
(1997: Lab. maj. 1,670 (3.02%))

SHROPSHIRE NORTH
E.73,716 *T.* 46,520 (63.11%)   C. hold
*Owen Paterson, *C.*   22,631
Michael Ion, *Lab.*   16,390
Ben Jephcott, *LD*   5,945
David Trevanion, *UK Ind.*   1,165
Russell Maxfield, *Ind.*   389
C. majority 6,241 (13.42%)
4.58% swing Lab. to C.
(1997: C. maj. 2,195 (4.26%))

SITTINGBOURNE & SHEPPEY
E.65,825 *T.* 37,858 (57.51%) Lab. hold
*Derek Wyatt, *Lab*   .17,340
Adrian Lee, *C.*   13,831
Ms Elvie Lowe, *LD*   5,353

Michael Young, *R & R Loony*   673
Robert Oakley, *UK Ind.*   661
Lab. majority 3,509 (9.27%)
2.54% swing C. to Lab.
(1997: Lab. maj. 1,929 (4.18%))

SKIPTON & RIPON
E.75,201 *T.* 49,126 (65.33%)   C. hold
*Rt. Hon. D. Curry, *C.*   25,736
Bernard Bateman, *LD*   12,806
Michael Dugher, *Lab.*   8,543
Mrs Nancy Holdsworth,
   UK *Ind.*   2,041
C. majority 12,930 (26.32%)
2.47% swing LD to C.
(1997: C. maj. 11,620 (21.38%))

SLEAFORD & NORTH HYKEHAM
E.74,561 *T.* 48,719 (65.34%)   C. hold
*Rt. D. Hogg, *C.*   24,190
Ms Elizabeth Donnelly, *Lab.*   15,568
Robert Arbon, *LD*   7,894
Michael Ward-Barrow, *UK Ind.* 1,067
C. majority 8,622 (17.70%)
4.03% swing Lab. to C.
(1997: C. maj. 5,123 (9.64%))

SLOUGH
E.72,429 *T.* 38,998 (53.84%) Lab. hold
*Ms Fiona Mactaggart, *Lab.*   22,718
Mrs Diana Coad, *C.*   10,210
Keith Kerr, *LD*   4,109
Michael Haines, *Ind.*   859
John Lane, *UK Ind.*   738
Choudry Nazir, *Ind.*   364
Lab. majority 12,508 (32.07%)
2.34% swing C. to Lab.
(1997: Lab. maj. 13,071 (27.39%))

SOLIHULL
E.77,094 *T.* 48,271 (62.61%)   C. hold
*John Taylor, *C.*   21,935
Ms Jo Byron, *LD*   12,528
Brendan O'Brien, *Lab.*   12,373
Andy Moore, *UK Ind.*   1,061
Ms Stephanie Pyne, *ProLife*   374
C. majority 9,407 (19.49%)
0.07% swing LD to C.
(1997: C. maj. 11,397 (19.35%))

SOMERTON & FROME
E.74,991 *T.* 52,684 (70.25%) LD hold
*David Heath, *LD*   22,983
Jonathan Marland, *C.*   22,315
Andrew Perkins, *Lab.*   6,113
Peter Bridgwood, *UK Ind.*   919
Ms Jean Pollock, *Lib.*   354
LD majority 668 (1.27%)
0.52% swing C. to LD
(1997: LD maj. 130 (0.23%))

SOUTH HOLLAND & THE DEEPINGS
E.73,880 *T.* 46,202 (62.54%)   C. hold
*John Hayes, *C.*   25,611
Graham Walker, *Lab.*   14,512
Ms Grace Hill, *LD*   4,761
Malcolm Charlesworth, *UK Ind.* 1,318
C. majority 11,099 (24.02%)
4.04% swing Lab. to C.
(1997: C. maj. 7,991 (15.94%))

SOUTH SHIELDS
E.61,802 *T.* 30,448 (49.27%) Lab. hold

David Miliband, *Lab.*   19,230
Miss Joanna Gardner, *C.*   5,140
Marshall Grainger, *LD*   5,127
Alan Hardy, *UK Ind.*   689
Roger Nettleship, *Ind.*   262
Lab. majority 14,090 (46.28%)
5.28% swing Lab. to C.
(1997: Lab. maj. 22,153 (56.84%))

SOUTHAMPTON ITCHEN
E.76,603 *T.* 41,373 (54.01%) Lab. hold
*Rt. Hon. J. Denham, *Lab.*   22,553
Mrs Caroline Nokes, *C.*   .11,330
Mark Cooper, *LD*   6,195
Kim Rose, UK *Ind.*   829
Gavin Marsh, *Soc. All.*   241
Michael Holmes, *Soc. Lab.*   225
Lab. majority 11,223 (27.13%)
0.37% swing C. to Lab.
(1997: Lab. maj. 14,209 (26.38%))

SOUTHAMPTON TEST
E.73,893 *T.* 41,575 (56.26%) Lab. hold
*Alan Whitehead, *Lab.*   21,824
Richard Gueterbock, *C.*   10,617
John Shaw, *LD*   7,522
Garry Rankin-Moore, *UK Ind.*   792
Mark Abel, *Soc. All.*   442
Paramjit Bahia, *Soc. Lab.*   378
Lab. majority 11,207 (26.96%)
0.43% swing C. to Lab.
(1997: Lab. maj. 13,684 (26.10%))

SOUTHEND WEST
E.64,116 *T.* 37,375 (58.29%)   C. hold
*David Amess, *C.*   17,313
Paul Fisher, *Lab.*   9,372
Richard de Ste Croix, *LD*   9,319
Brian Lee, *UK Ind.*   1,371
C. majority 7,941 (21.25%)
2.64% swing Lab. to C.
(1997: C. maj. 2,615 (5.62%))

SOUTHPORT
E.70,785 *T.* 41,153 (58.14%) LD hold
John Pugh, *LD*   18,011
Laurence Jones, *C.*   15,004
Paul Brant, *Lab.*   6,816
David Green, *Lib.*   767
Gerry Kelley, *UK Ind.*   555
LD majority 3,007 (7.31%)
2.44% swing LD to C.
(1997: LD maj. 6,160 (12.18%))

SOUTHWARK NORTH & BERMONDSEY
E.73,527 *T.* 36,862 (50.13%) LD hold
*Simon Hughes, *LD*   20,991
Kingsley Abrams, *Lab.*   11,359
Ewan Wallace, *C.*   2,800
Ms Ruth Jenkins, *Green*   752
Ms Lianne Shore, *NF*   612
Rob McWhirter, *UK Ind.*   271
John Davies, *Ind.*   77
LD majority 9,632 (26.13%)
8.91% swing Lab. to LD
(1997: LD majority 3,387 (8.30%))

SPELTHORNE
E.68,731 *T.* 41,794 (60.81%)   C. hold
*David Wilshire, *C.*   18,851
Andrew Shaw, *Lab.*   15,589
Martin Rimmer, *LD*   6,156
Richard Squire, *UK Ind.*   1,198

C. majority 3,262 (7.80%)
0.56% swing Lab. to C.
(1997: C. maj. 3,473 (6.69%))

ST ALBANS
E.66,040 T. 43,761 (66.26%) Lab. hold
*Kerry Pollard, *Lab.*   19,889
Charles Elphicke, *C.*   15,423
Nick Rijke, *LD*   7,847
Christopher Sherwin, *UK Ind.*   602
Lab. majority 4,466 (10.21%)
0.71% swing C. to Lab.
(1997: Lab. maj. 4,459 (8.78%))

ST HELENS NORTH
E.70,545 T. 37,601 (53.30%) Lab. hold
*Dave Watts, *Lab.*   22,977
Simon Pearce, *C.*   7,076
John Beirne, *LD*   6,609
Stephen Whatham, *Soc. Lab.*   939
Lab. majority 15,901 (42.29%)
2.64% swing Lab. to C.
(1997: Lab. maj. 23,417 (47.57%))

ST HELENS SOUTH
E.65,122 T. 33,804 (51.91%) Lab. hold
†Shaun Woodward, *Lab.* 16,799
Brian Spencer, *LD*   7,814
Dr Lee Rotherham, *C.*   4,675
Neil Thompson, *Soc. All.*   2,325
Mike Perry, *Soc. Lab.*   1,504
Bryan Slater, *UK Ind.*   336
Michael Murphy, *Ind.*   271
David Braid, *Ind.*   80
Lab. majority 8,985 (26.58%)
14.33% swing Lab. to LD
(1997: Lab. maj. 23,739 (53.63%))

ST IVES
E.74,256 T. 49,266 (66.35%) LD hold
*Andrew George, *LD*   25,413
Miss Joanna Richardson, *C.*   15,360
William Morris, *Lab.*   6,567
Mick Faulkner, *UK Ind.*   1,926
LD majority 10,053 (20.41%)
3.55% swing C. to LD
(1997: LD maj. 7,170 (13.30%))

STAFFORD
E.67,934 T. 44,366 (65.31%) Lab. hold
*David Kidney, *Lab.*   21,285
Philip Cochrane, *C.*   16,253
Ms Jeanne Pinkerton, *LD*   4,205
Earl of Bradford, *UK Ind.*   2,315
Michael Hames, *R & R Loony*   308
LD majority 5,032 (11.34%)
1.50% swing C. to Lab.
(1997: Lab. maj. 4,314 (8.34%))

STAFFORDSHIRE MOORLANDS
E.66,760 T. 42,658 (63.90%) Lab. hold
*Ms Charlotte Atkins, *Lab.*   20,904
Marcus Hayes, *C.*   15,066
John Redfern, *LD*   5,928
Paul Gilbert, *UK Ind.*   760
Lab. majority 5,838 (13.69%)
2.99% swing Lab. to C.
(1997: Lab. maj. 10,049 (19.66%))

STAFFORDSHIRE SOUTH
E.69,925 T. 42,180 (60.32%) C. hold
*Sir Patrick Cormack, *C.*   21,295

Paul Kalinauckas, *Lab.*   14,414
Ms Jo Harrison, *LD*   4,891
Mike Lynch, *UK Ind.*   1,580
C. majority 6,881 (16.31%)
0.51% swing Lab. to C.
(1997: C. maj. 7,821 (15.30%))

STALYBRIDGE & HYDE
E.66,265 T. 32,046 (48.36%) Lab. hold
James Purnell, *Lab.*   17,781
Andrew Reid, *C.*   8,922
Brendon Jones, *LD*   4,327
Frank Bennett, *UK Ind.*   1,016
Lab. majority 8,859 (27.64%)
3.36% swing Lab. to C.
(1997: Lab. maj. 14,806 (34.36%))

STEVENAGE
E.69,203 T. 42,453 (61.35%) Lab. hold
*Ms Barbara Follett, *Lab.*   22,025
Graeme Quar, *C.*   13,459
Harry Davies, *LD*   6,027
Steve Glennon, *Soc. All.*   449
Antal Losonczi, *Ind.*   320
Ms Sarah Bell, *ProLife*   173
Lab. majority 8,566 (20.18%)
1.18% swing Lab. to C.
(1997: Lab. maj. 11,582 (22.54%))

STOCKPORT
E.66,397 T. 35,383 (53.29%) Lab. hold
*Ms Ann Coffey, *Lab.*   20,731
John Allen, *C.*   9,162
Mark Hunter, *LD*   5,490
Lab. majority 11,569 (32.70%)
3.91% swing Lab. to C.
(1997: Lab. maj. 18,912 (40.52%))

STOCKTON NORTH
E.65,192 T. 35,427 (54.34%) Lab. hold
*Frank Cook, *Lab.*   22,470
Ms Amanda Vigar, *C.*   7,823
Ms Mary Wallace, *LD*   4,208
Bill Wennington, *Green*   926
Lab. majority 14,647 (41.34%)
3.34% swing Lab. to C.
(1997: Lab. maj. 21,357 (48.02%))

STOCKTON SOUTH
E.71,026 T. 44,209 (62.24%) Lab. hold
*Ms Dari Taylor, *Lab.*   23,414
Tim Devlin, *C.*   14,328
Mrs Suzanne Fletcher, *LD*   6,012
Lawrie Coombes, *Soc. All.*   455
Lab. majority 9,086 (20.55%)
0.84% swing Lab. to C.
(1997: Lab. maj. 11,585 (22.23%))

STOKE-ON-TRENT CENTRAL
E.59,750 T. 28,300 (47.36%) Lab. hold
*Mark Fisher, *Lab.*   17,170
Ms Jill Clark, *C.*   5,325
Gavin Webb, *LD*   4,148
Richard Wise, *Ind.*   1,657
Lab. majority 11,845 (41.86%)
3.83% swing Lab. to C.
(1997: Lab. maj. 19,924 (49.51%))

STOKE-ON-TRENT NORTH
E.57,998 T. 30,115 (51.92%) Lab. hold
*Ms Joan Walley, *Lab.*   17,460
Benjamin Browning, *C.*   5,676

Henry Jebb, *LD*   3,580
Lee Wanger, *Ind.*   3,399
Lab. majority 11,784 (39.13%)
2.92% swing Lab. to C.
(1997: Lab. maj. 17,392 (44.98%))

STOKE-ON-TRENT SOUTH
E.70,032 T. 36,028 (51.45%) Lab. hold
*George Stevenson, *Lab.*   19,366
Philip Bastiman, *C.*   8,877
Christopher Coleman, *LD*   4,724
Adrian Knapper, *Ind.*   1,703
Steven Batkin, *BNP*   1,358
Lab. majority 10,489 (29.11%)
5.23% swing Lab. to C.
(1997: Lab. maj. 18,303 (39.58%))

STONE
E.68,847 T. 45,642 (66.29%) C. hold
*William Cash, *C.*   22,395
John Palfreyman, *Lab.*   16,359
Brendan McKeown, *LD*   6,888
C. majority 6,036 (13.22%)
3.01% swing Lab. to C.
(1997: C. maj. 3,818 (7.20%))

STOURBRIDGE
E.64,610 T. 39,924 (61.79%) Lab. hold
*Ms Debra Shipley, *Lab.*   18,823
Stephen Eyre, *C.*   15,011
Chris Bramall, *LD*   4,833
John Knotts, *UK Ind.*   763
Mick Atherton, *Soc. Lab.*   494
Lab. majority 3,812 (9.55%)
0.91% swing Lab. to C.
(1997: Lab. maj. 5,645 (11.36%))

STRATFORD-ON-AVON
E.85,241 T. 54,914 (64.42%) C. hold
*John Maples, *C.*   27,606
Dr Susan Juned, *LD*   15,804
Mushtaq Hussain, *Lab.*   9,164
Ronald Mole, *UK Ind.*   1,184
Mick Davies, *Green*   1,156
C. majority 11,802 (21.49%)
0.61% swing C. to LD
(1997: C. maj. 14,106 (22.72%))

STREATHAM
E.76,021 T. 36,998 (48.67%) Lab. hold
*Keith Hill, *Lab.*   21,041
Roger O'Brien, *LD*   6,771
Stephen Hocking, *C.*   6,639
Mohammed Sajid, *Green*   1,641
Greg Tucker, *Soc. All.*   906
Lab. majority 14,270 (38.57%)
5.33% swing Lab. to LD
(1997: Lab. maj. 18,423 (41.04%))

STRETFORD & URMSTON
E.70,924 T. 38,973 (54.95%) Lab. hold
*Ms Beverley Hughes, *Lab.*   23,804
Jonathan Mackie, *C.*   10,565
John Bridges, *LD*   3,891
Ms Katie Price, *Ind.*   713
Lab. majority 13,239 (33.97%)
2.98% swing C. to Lab.
(1997: Lab. maj. 13,640 (28.01%))

STROUD
E.78,878 T. 55,175 (69.95%) Lab Co-op
hold

*David Drew, *Lab. Co-op.*   25,685
Neil Carmichael, *C.*   20,646
Ms Janice Beasley, *LD*   6,036
Kevin Cranston, *Green*   1,913
Adrian Blake, *UK Ind.*   895
Lab Co-op majority 5,039 (9.13%)
2.24% swing C. to Lab. Co-op
(1997: Lab. maj. 2,910 (4.66%))

SUFFOLK CENTRAL & IPSWICH NORTH

E.74,200 T. 47,104 (63.48%)   C. hold
*Michael Lord, *C.*   20,924
Ms Carole Jones, *Lab.*   17,455
Mrs Ann Elvin, *LD*   7,593
Jonathan Wright, *UK Ind.*   1,132
C. majority 3,469 (7.36%)
0.33% swing Lab. to C.
(1997: C. maj. 3,538 (6.70%))

SUFFOLK COASTAL

E.75,963 T. 50,407 (66.36%)   C. hold
*Rt. Hon. J. Gummer, *C.*   21,847
Nigel Gardner, *Lab*   .17,521
Tony Schur, *LD*   9,192
Michael Burn, *UK Ind.*   1,847
C. majority 4,326 (8.58%)
1.40% swing Lab. to C.
(1997: C. maj. 3,254 (5.79%))

SUFFOLK SOUTH

E.68,408 T. 45,293 (66.21%)   C. hold
*Tim Yeo, *C.*   18,748
Marc Young, *Lab.*   13,667
Mrs Tessa Munt, *LD*   11,296
Derek Allen, *UK Ind.*   1,582
C. majority 5,081 (11.22%)
1.59% swing Lab. to C.
(1997: C. maj. 4,175 (8.03%))

SUFFOLK WEST

E.71,220 T. 42,445 (59.60%)   C. hold
*Richard Spring, *C.*   20,201
Michael Jeffreys, *Lab.*   15,906
Robin Martlew, *LD*   5,017
Will Burrows, *UK Ind.*   1,321
C. majority 4,295 (10.12%)
3.16% swing Lab. to C.
(1997: C. maj. 1,867 (3.80%))

SUNDERLAND NORTH

E.60,846 T. 29,820 (49.01%)   Lab. hold
*Bill Etherington, *Lab.*   18,685
Michael Harris, *C.*   5,331
John Lennox, *LD*   3,599
Neil Herron, *Ind.*   1,518
David Guynan, *BNP*   687
Lab. majority 13,354 (44.78%)
3.38% swing Lab. to C.
(1997: Lab. maj. 19,697 (51.55%))

SUNDERLAND SOUTH

E.64,577 T. 31,187 (48.29%)   Lab. hold
*Chris Mullin, *Lab.*   19,921
Jim Boyd, *C.*   6,254
Mark Greenfield, *LD*   3,675
Joseph Dobbie, *BNP*   576
Joseph Moore, *UK Ind.*   470
Ms Rosalyn Warner, *Loony*   291
LD majority 13,667 (43.82%)
2.68% swing Lab. to C.
(1997: Lab. maj. 19,638 (49.18%))

SURREY EAST

E.75,049 T. 47,049 (62.69%)   C. hold
*Peter Ainsworth, *C.*   24,706
Jeremy Pursehouse, *LD*   11,503
Ms Jo Tanner, *Lab.*   8,994
Anthony Stone, *UK Ind.*   1,846
C. majority 13,203 (28.06%)
0.23% swing LD to C.
(1997: C. maj. 15,093 (27.61%))

SURREY HEATH

E.75,858 T. 45,102 (59.46%)   C. hold
*Nicholas Hawkins, *C.*   22,401
Mark Lelliott, *LD*   11,582
James Norman, *Lab.*   9,640
Nigel Hunt, *UK Ind.*   1,479
C. majority 10,819 (23.99%)
2.89% swing C. to LD
(1997: C. maj. 16,287 (29.76%))

SURREY SOUTH WEST

E.74,127 T. 49,592 (66.90%)   C. hold
*Rt. Hon. Mrs V. Bottomley, *C.*   22,462
Simon Cordon, *LD*   21,601
Martin Whelton, *Lab.*   4,321
Timothy Clark, *UK Ind.*   1,208
C. majority 861 (1.74%)
1.52% swing C. to LD
(1997: C. maj. 2,694 (4.77%))

SUSSEX MID

E.70,632 T. 45,822 (64.87%)   C. hold
*Nicholas Soames, *C.*   21,150
Ms Lesley Wilkins, *LD*   14,252
Paul Mitchell, *Lab.*   8,693
Petrina Holsworth *UK Ind.*   1,126
Peter Berry, *Loony*   601
C. majority 6,898 (15.05%)
1.12% swing LD to C.
(1997: C. maj. 6,854 (12.82%))

SUTTON & CHEAM

E.63,648 T. 39,723 (62.41%)   LD hold
*Paul Burstow, *LD*   19,382
Lady Olga Maitland, *C.*   15,078
Ms Lisa Homan, *Lab.*   5,263
LD majority 4,304 (10.84%)
3.19% swing C. to LD
(1997: LD maj. 2,097 (4.45%))

SUTTON COLDFIELD

E.71,856 T. 43,452 (60.47%)   C. hold
Andrew Mitchell, *C.*   21,909
Robert Pocock, *Lab.*   11,805
Martin Turner, *LD*   8,268
Mike Nattrass, *UK Ind.*   1,186
Ian Robinson, *Ind.*   284
C. majority 10,104 (23.25%)
2.58% swing C. to Lab.
(1997: C. maj. 14,885 (28.41%))

SWINDON NORTH

E.69,335 T. 42,328 (61.05%)   Lab. hold
*Michael Wills, *Lab.*   22,371
Nick Martin, *C.*   14,266
David Nation, *LD*   4,891
Brian Lloyd, *UK Ind.*   800
Lab. majority 8,105 (19.15%)
1.61% swing C. to Lab.
(1997: Lab. maj. 7,688 (15.93%))

SWINDON SOUTH

E.71,080 T. 43,384 (61.04%)   Lab. hold
*Ms Julia Drown, *Lab.*   22,260
Simon Coombs, *C.*   14,919
Geoff Brewer, *LD*   5,165
Mrs Vicki Sharp, *UK Ind.*   713
Roly Gillard, *R & R Loony*   327
Lab. majority 7,341 (16.92%)
2.94% swing C. to Lab.
(1997: Lab. maj. 5,645 (11.04%))

TAMWORTH

E.69,596 T. 40,250 (57.83%)   Lab. hold
*Brian Jenkins, *Lab.*   19,722
Ms Luise Gunter, *C.*   15,124
Ms Jennifer Pinkett, *LD*   4,721
Paul Sootheran, *UK Ind.*   683
Lab. majority 4,598 (11.42%)
1.81% swing Lab. to C.
(1997: Lab. maj. 7,496 (15.04%))

TATTON

E.64,954 T. 41,278 (63.55%)   C. gain
George Osborne, *C.*   19,860
Steve Conquest, *Lab.*   11,249
Mike Ash, *LD*   7,685
Mark Sheppard, *UK Ind.*   769
Peter Sharratt, *Ind.*   734
Mrs Viviane Allinson, *Tatton*   505
John Batchelor *Ind.*   322
Jonathan Boyd Hunt *Ind.*   154
C. majority 8,611 (20.86%)
(1997: Ind. maj. 11,077 (22.70%))

TAUNTON

E.81,651 T. 55,225 (67.64%)   C. gain
Adrian Flook, *C.*   23,033
*Mrs Jackie Ballard, *LD*   22,798
Andrew Govier, *Lab.*   8,254
Michael Canton, *UK Ind.*   1,140
C. majority 235 (0.43%)
2.21% swing LD to C.
(1997: LD maj. 2,443 (4.00%))

TEIGNBRIDGE

E.85,533 T. 59,310 (69.34%)   LD gain
Richard Younger-Ross, *LD*   26,343
*Patrick Nicholls, *C.*   23,332
Christopher Bain, *Lab.*   7,366
Paul Viscount Exmouth, *UK Ind.* 2,269
LD majority 3,011 (5.08%)
2.76% swing C. to LD
(1997: C. maj. 281 (0.45%))

TELFORD

E.59,486 T. 30,875 (51.90%)   Lab. hold
David Wright, *Lab.*   16,854
Andrew Henderson, *C.*   8,471
Ms Sally Wiggin, *LD*   3,983
Ms Nicola Brookes, *UK Ind.*   1,098
Mike Jeffries, *Soc. All.*   469
Lab. majority 8,383 (27.15%)
1.63% swing Lab. to C.
(1997: Lab. maj. 11,290 (30.42%))

TEWKESBURY

E.70,276 T. 45,195 (64.31%)   C. hold
*Laurence Robertson, *C.*   20,830
Keir Dhillon, *Lab.*   12,167
Stephen Martin, *LD*   11,863
Charles Vernall, *Ind.*   335
C. majority 8,663 (19.17%)
0.19% swing C. to Lab.
(1997: C. maj. 9,234 (17.71%))

THANET NORTH
E.70,581 T. 41,868 (59.32%)   C. hold
*Roger Gale, C.   21,050
James Stewart Laing, Lab.   14,400
Seth Proctor, LD   4,603
John Moore, UK Ind.   980
David Shortt, Ind.   440
Thomas Holmes, NF   395
C. majority 6,650 (15.88%)
5.12% swing Lab. to C.
(1997: C. maj. 2,766 (5.65%))

THANET SOUTH
E.61,462 T. 39,431 (64.16%)   Lab. hold
*Dr Stephen Ladyman, Lab.   18,002
Mark Macgregor, C.   16,210
Guy Voizey, LD   3,706
William Baldwin, Ind.   770
Terry Eccott, UK Ind.   501
Bernard Franklin, NF   242
Lab. majority 1,792 (4.54%)
0.92% swing Lab. to C.
(1997: Lab. maj. 2,878 (6.39%))

THURROCK
E.76,524 T. 37,362 (48.82%)   Lab. hold
*Andrew Mackinlay, Lab.   21,121
Mike Penning, C.   11,124
John Lathan, LD   3,846
Christopher Sheppard, UK Ind.   1,271
Lab. majority 9,997 (26.76%)
4.90% swing Lab. to C.
(1997: Lab. maj. 17,256 (36.55%))

TIVERTON & HONITON
E.80,646 T. 55,784 (69.17%)   C. hold
*Mrs Angela Browning, C.   26,258
Jim Barnard, LD   19,974
Ms Isabel Owen, Lab.   6,647
Alan Langmaid, UK Ind.   1,281
Matthew Burgess, Green   1,030
Mrs Jennifer Roach, Lib.   594
C. majority 6,284 (11.26%)
4.23% swing LD to C.
(1997: C. maj. 1,653 (2.80%))

TONBRIDGE & MALLING
E.65,939 T. 42,436 (64.36%)   C. hold
*Rt. Hon. Sir J. Stanley, C.   20,956
Ms Victoria Hayman, Lab.   12,706
Ms Merilyn Canet, LD   7,605
Ms Lynn Croucher, UK Ind.   1,169
C. majority 8,250 (19.44%)
0.67% swing C. to Lab.
(1997: C. maj. 10,230 (20.78%))

TOOTING
E.68,447 T. 37,591 (54.92%)   Lab. hold
*Tom Cox, Lab.   20,332
Alexander Nicoll, C.   9,932
Simon James, LD   5,583
Matthew Ledbury, Green   1,744
Lab. majority 10,400 (27.67%)
2.45% swing Lab. to C.
(1997: Lab. maj. 15,011 (32.56%))

TORBAY
E.72,409 T. 47,569 (65.69%)   LD hold
*Adrian Sanders, LD   24,015
Christian Sweeting, C.   17,307
John McKay, Lab.   4,484
Graham Booth, UK Ind.   1,512

Ms Pam Neale, Ind.   251
LD majority 6,708 (14.10%)
7.04% swing C. to LD
(1997: LD maj. 12 (0.02%))

TOTNES
E.72,548 T. 49,246 (67.88%)   C. hold
*Anthony Steen, C.   21,914
Ms Rachel Oliver, LD   18,317
Thomas Wildy, Lab.   6,005
Craig Mackinlay, UK Ind.   3,010
C. majority 3,597 (7.30%)
2.84% swing C. to Lab.
(1997: C. maj. 877 (1.63%))

TOTTENHAM
E.65,567 T. 31,601 (48.20%)   Lab. hold
*David Lammy, Lab.   21,317
Ms Uma Fernandes, C.   4,401
Ms Meher Khan, LD   3,008
Peter Budge, Green   1,443
Weyman Bennett, Soc. All.   1,162
Unver Shefki, Reform   270
LD majority 16,916 (53.53%)
0.03% swing Lab. to C.
(2000 Jun by-election: Lab. maj. 5,646
(34.39%); 1997: Lab. maj. 20,200
(53.58%))

TRURO & ST AUSTELL
E.79,219 T. 50,295 (63.49%)   LD hold
*Matthew Taylor, LD   24,296
Tim Bonner, C.   16,231
David Phillips, Lab.   6,889
James Wonnacott, UK Ind.   1,664
Conan Jenkin, Meb. Ker.   1,137
John Lee, Ind.   78
LD majority 8,065 (16.04%)
3.00% swing LD to C.
(1997: LD maj. 12,501 (22.03%))

TUNBRIDGE WELLS
E.64,534 T. 40,201 (62.29%)   C. hold
*Archie Norman, C.   19,643
Keith Brown, LD   9,913
Ian Carvell, Lab.   9,332
Victor Webb, UK Ind.   1,313
C. majority 9,730 (24.20%)
4.34% swing LD to C.
(1997: C. maj. 7,506 (15.52%))

TWICKENHAM
E.74,135 T. 49,938 (67.36%)   LD hold
*Dr Vincent Cable, LD   24,344
Nick Longworth, C.   16,689
Dean Rogers, Lab.   6,903
Ms Judy Maciejowska, Green   1,423
Ray Hollebone, UK Ind.   579
LD majority 7,655 (15.33%)
3.98% swing C. to
(1997: LD maj. 4,281 (7.36%))

TYNE BRIDGE
E.58,900 T. 26,032 (44.20%)   Lab. hold
*David Clelland, Lab.   18,345
James Cook, C.   3,456
Jonathan Wallace, LD   3,213
James Fitzpatrick, Soc. Lab.   533
Samuel Robson, Soc. All.   485
Lab. majority 14,889 (57.19%)
4.27% swing Lab. to C.
(1997: Lab. maj. 22,906 (65.73%))

TYNEMOUTH
E.65,184 T. 43,903 (67.35%)   Lab. hold
*Alan Campbell, Lab.   23,364
Karl Poulsen, C.   14,686
Ms Penny Reid, LD   5,108
Michael Rollings, UK Ind.   745
Lab. majority 8,678 (19.77%)
1.14% swing Lab. to C.
(1997: Lab. maj. 11,273 (22.04%))

TYNESIDE NORTH
E.64,914 T. 37,569 (57.88%)   Lab. hold
*Rt. Hon. S. Byers, Lab.   26,127
Mark Ruffell, C.   5,459
Simon Reed, LD   4,649
Alan Taylor, UK Ind.   770
Pete Burnett, Soc. All.   324
Ken Capstick, Soc. Lab.   240
Lab. majority 20,668 (55.01%)
2.02% swing Lab. to C.
(1997: Lab. maj. 26,643 (59.05%))

UPMINSTER
E.56,829 T. 33,851 (59.57%)   C. gain
Mrs Angela Watkinson, C.   5,410
*Keith Darvill, Lab.   14,169
Peter Truesdale, LD   3,183
Terry Murray, UK Ind.   1,089
C. majority 1,241 (3.67%)
5.18% swing Lab. to C.
(1997: Lab. maj. 2,770 (6.70%))

UXBRIDGE
E.58,066 T. 33,418 (57.55%)   C. hold
*John Randall, C.   15,751
David Salisbury-Jones, Lab.   13,653
Ms Catherine Royce, LD   3,426
Paul Cannons, UK Ind.   588
C. majority 2,098 (6.28%)
2.26% swing Lab. to C.
(1997 Jul by-election: C. maj. 3,766
(11.82%); 1997: C. maj. 724 (1.75%))

VALE OF YORK
E.73,335 T. 48,490 (66.12%)   C. hold
*Miss Anne McIntosh, C.   25,033
Christopher Jukes, Lab.   12,516
Greg Stone, LD   9,799
Peter Thornber, UK Ind.   1,142
C. majority 12,517 (25.81%)
3.78% swing Lab. to C.
(1997: C. maj. 9,721 (18.25%))

VAUXHALL
E.74,474 T. 33,392 (44.84%)   Lab. hold
*Ms Kate Hoey, Lab.   19,738
Anthony Bottrall, LD   6,720
Gareth Compton, C.   4,489
Shane Collins, Green   1,485
Ms Theresa Bennett, Soc. All.   853
Martin Boyd, Ind.   107
Lab. majority 13,018 (38.99%)
4.39% swing Lab. to LD
(1997: Lab. maj. 18,660 (47.77%))

WAKEFIELD
E.75,750 T. 41,254 (54.46%)   Lab. hold
*David Hinchcliffe, Lab.   20,592
Mrs Thelma Karran, C.   12,638
Douglas Dale, LD   5,097
Ms Sarah Greenwood, Green   1,075
Ms Janice Cannon, UK Ind.   677

Abdul Aziz, *Soc. Lab.* 634
Mick Griffiths, *Soc. All.* 541
Lab. majority 7,954 (19.28%)
4.82% swing Lab. to C.
(1997: Lab. maj. 14,604 (28.93%))

WALLASEY
E.64,889 T. 37,346 (57.55%) Lab. hold
*Ms Angela Eagle, *Lab.* 22,718
Mrs Lesley Rennie, *C.* 10,442
Peter Reisdorf, *LD* 4,186
Lab. majority 12,276 (32.87%)
3.92% swing Lab. to C.
(1997: Lab. maj. 19,074 (40.72%))

WALSALL NORTH
E.66,020 T. 32,312 (48.94%) Lab. hold
*David Winnick, *Lab.* 18,779
Melvin Pitt, *C.* 9,388
Michael Heap, *LD* 2,923
Mrs Jenny Mayo, *UK Ind.* 812
Dave Church, *Soc. All.* 410
Lab. majority 9,391 (29.06%)
(1997: Lab. maj. 12,588 (29.07%))

WALSALL SOUTH
E.62,657 T. 34,899 (55.70%) Lab. hold
*Rt. Hon. B. George, *Lab.* 20,574
Mike Bird, *C.* 10,643
Bill Tomlinson, *LD* 2,365
Derek Bennett, *UK Ind.* 974
Peter Smith, *Soc. All.* 343
Lab. majority 9,931 (28.46%)
1.15% swing C. to Lab.
(1997: Lab. maj. 11,312 (26.16%))

WALTHAMSTOW
E.64,403 T. 34,429 (53.46%) Lab. hold
*Neil Gerrard, *Lab.* 21,402
Nick Boys Smith, *C.* 6,221
Peter Dunphy, *LD* 5,024
Simon Donovan, *Soc. Alt.* 806
William Phillips, *BNP* 389
Ms Gerda Mayer, *UK Ind.* 298
Ms Barbara Duffy *ProLife* 289
Lab. majority 15,181 (44.09%)
0.64% swing C. to Lab.
(1997: Lab. maj. 17,149 (42.81%))

WANSBECK
E.62,989 T. 37,419 (59.41%) Lab. hold
*Denis Murphy, *Lab.* 21,617
Alan Thompson, *C.* 8,516
Mrs Rachael Lake, *C.* 4,774
Michael Kirkup, *Ind.* 1,076
Dr Nic Best, *Green* 954
Gavin Attwell, *UK Ind.* 482
Lab. majority 13,101 (35.01%)
7.25% swing Lab. to LD
(1997: Lab. maj. 22,367 (49.52%))

WANSDYKE
E.70,728 T. 49,047 (69.35%) Lab. hold
*Dan Norris, *Lab.* 22,706
Chris Watt, *C.* 17,593
Ms Gail Coleshill, *LD* 7,135
Francis Hayden, *Green* 958
Peter Sandell, *UK Ind.* 655
Lab. majority 5,113 (10.42%)
0.83% swing C. to Lab.
(1997: Lab. maj. 4,799 (8.77%))

WANTAGE
E.76,129 T. 49,129 (64.53%) C. hold
*Robert Jackson, *C.* 19,475
Stephen Beer, *Lab.* 13,875
Neil Fawcett, *LD* 13,776
David Brooks-Saxl, *Green* 1,062
Count Nicholai Tolstoy, *UK Ind.* 941
C. majority 5,600 (11.40%)
0.31% swing Lab. to C.
(1997: C. maj. 6,039 (10.77%))

WARLEY
E.58,071 T. 31,415 (54.10%) Lab. hold
*Rt. Hon. J. Spellar, *Lab.* 19,007
Mark Pritchard, *C.* 7,157
Ron Cockings, *LD* 3,315
Harbhajan Dardi, *Soc. Lab.* 1,936
Lab. majority 11,850 (37.72%)
1.00% swing Lab. to C.
(1997: Lab. maj. 15,451 (39.73%))

WARRINGTON NORTH
E.72,445 T. 38,910 (53.71%) Lab. hold
*Ms Helen Jones, *Lab.* 24,026
James Usher, *C.* 8,870
Roy Smith, *LD* 5,232
Jack Kirkham, *UK Ind.* 782
Lab. majority 15,156 (38.95%)
0.43% swing C. to Lab.
(1997: Lab. maj. 19,527 (38.10%))

WARRINGTON SOUTH
E.74,283 T. 45,487 (61.23%) Lab. hold
*Ms Helen Southworth, *Lab.* 22,409
Ms Caroline Mosley, *C.* 15,022
Roger Barlow, *LD* 7,419
Mrs Joan Kelley, *UK Ind.* 637
Lab. majority 7,387 (16.24%)
1.69% swing Lab. to C.
(1997: Lab. maj. 10,807 (19.62%))

WARWICK & LEAMINGTON
E.81,405 T. 53,539 (65.77%) Lab. hold
*James Plaskitt, *Lab.* 26,108
David Campbell Bannerman, *C.* 20,155
Ms Linda Forbes, *LD* 5,964
Ms Clare Kime, *Soc. All.* 664
Greville Warwick, *UK Ind.* 648
Lab. majority 5,953 (11.12%)
2.73% swing C. to Lab.
(1997: Lab. maj. 3,398 (5.65%))

WARWICKSHIRE NORTH
E.73,828 T. 44,409 (60.15%) Lab. hold
*Mike O'Brien, *Lab.* 24,023
Geoff Parsons, *C.* 14,384
William Powell, *LD* 5,052
John Flynn, *UK Ind.* 950
Lab. majority 9,639 (21.71%)
2.76% swing C. to Lab.
(1997: Lab. maj. 14,767 (27.23%))

WATFORD
E.75,724 T. 46,372 (61.24%) Lab. hold
*Ms Claire Ward, *Lab.* 20,992
Michael McManus, *C.* 15,437
Duncan Hames, *LD* 8,088
Ms Denise Kingsley, *Green* 900
Edmund Stewart-Mole, *UK Ind.* 535
Jon Berry, *Soc. All.* 420
Lab. majority 5,555 (11.98%)
0.75% swing C. to Lab.
(1997: Lab. maj. 5,792 (10.48%))

WAVENEY
E.76,585 T. 47,167 (61.59%) Lab. hold
*Bob Blizzard, *Lab.* 23,914
Lee Scott, *C.* 15,361
David Young, *LD* 5,370
Brian Aylett, *UK Ind.* 1,097
Graham Elliot, *Green* 983
Rupert Mallin, *Soc. All.* 442
Lab. majority 8,553 (18.13%)
1.93% swing Lab. to C.
(1997: Lab. maj. 12,453 (21.99%))

WEALDEN
E.83,066 T. 52,756 (63.51%) C. hold
Charles Hendry, *C.* 26,279
Steve Murphy, *LD* 12,507
Ms Kathy Fordham, *Lab.* 10,705
Keith Riddle, *UK Ind.* 1,539
Julian Salmon, *Green* 1,273
Cyril Thornton, *Pensioner* 453
C. majority 13,772 (26.11%)
1.03% swing LD to C.
(1997: C. maj. 14,204 (24.04%))

WEAVER VALE
E.68,236 T. 39,271 (57.55%) Lab. hold
*Mike Hall, *Lab.* 20,611
Carl Cross, *C.* 10,974
Nigel Griffiths, *LD* 5,643
Michael Cooksley, *Ind.* 1,484
Jim Bradshaw, *UK Ind.* 559
Lab. majority 9,637 (24.54%)
1.65% swing Lab. to C.
(1997: Lab. maj. 13,448 (27.84%))

WELLINGBOROUGH
E.77,389 T. 51,006 (65.91%) Lab. hold
*Paul Stinchcombe, *Lab.* 23,867
Peter Bone, *C.* .21,512
Peter Gaskell, *LD* 4,763
Anthony Ellwood, *UK Ind.* 864
Lab. majority 2,355 (4.62%)
2.14% swing C. to Lab.
(1997: Lab. maj. 187 (0.33%))

WELLS
E.74,189 T. 51,314 (69.17%) C. hold
*Rt. Hon. D. Heathcoat-Amory,
   C. 22,462
Graham Oakes, *LD* 19,666
Andy Merryfield, *Lab.* 7,915
Steve Reed, *UK Ind.* 1,104
Colin Bex, *Wessex Reg.* 167
C. majority 2,796 (5.45%)
2.25% swing LD to C.
(1997: C. maj. 528 (0.94%))

WELWYN HATFIELD
E.67,004 T. 42,821 (63.91%) Lab. hold
*Ms Melanie Johnson, *Lab.* 18,484
Grant Shapps, *C.* 17,288
Daniel Cooke, *LD* 6,021
Malcolm Biggs, *UK Ind.* 798
Ms Fiona Pinto, *ProLife* 230
Lab. majority 1,196 (2.79%)
3.89% swing Lab. to C.
(1997: Lab. maj. 5,595 (10.57%))

WENTWORTH
E.64,033 T. 33,778 (52.75%) Lab. hold
*John Healey, *Lab.* 22,798
Mike Roberts, *C.* 6,349

David Wildgoose, *LD* 3,652
John Wilkinson, *UK Ind.* 979
Lab. majority 16,449 (48.70%)
4.32% swing Lab. to C.
(1997: Lab. maj. 23,959 (57.34%))

WEST BROMWICH EAST
*E.*61,198 *T.* 32,664 (53.37%) Lab. hold
Tom Watson, *Lab.* 18,250
David MacFarlane, *C.* 8,487
Ian Garrett, *LD* 4,507
Steven Grey, *UK Ind.* 835
Sheera Johal, *Soc. Lab.* 585
Lab. majority 9,763 (29.89%)
1.43% swing Lab. to C.
(1997: Lab. maj. 13,584 (32.74%))

WEST BROMWICH WEST
*E.*66,777 *T.* 31,840 (47.68%)Lab Co-op
hold
*Adrian Bailey, *Lab. Co-op.* 19,352
Mrs Karen Bissell, *C.* 7,997
Mrs Sadie Smith, *LD* 2,168
John Salvage, *BNP* 1,428
Kevin Walker, *UK Ind.* 499
Baghwant Singh, *Soc. Lab.* 396
Lab Co-op majority 11,355 (35.66%)
(2000 Nov by-election: Lab. maj. 3,232
(17.12%); 1997: Speaker majority
15,423 (42.03%))

WEST HAM
*E.*59,828 *T.* 29,273 (48.93%) Lab. hold
*Tony Banks, *Lab.* 20,449
Syed Kamall, *C.* 4,804
Paul Fox, *LD* 2,166
Ms Jackie Chandler Oatts, *Green* 1,197
Gerard Batten, *UK Ind.* 657
Lab. majority 15,645 (53.45%)
2.24% swing Lab. to C.
(1997: *Lab. majority* 19,494 (57.92%))

WESTBURY
*E.*75,911 *T.* 50,628 (66.69%) C. hold
Dr Andrew Murrison, *C.* 21,299
David Vigar, *LD* 16,005
Ms Sarah Cardy, *Lab.* 10,847
Charles Booth-Jones, *UK Ind.* 1,261
Bob Gledhill, *Green* 1,216
C. majority 5,294 (10.46%)
0.12% swing C. to LD
(1997: C. maj. 6,068 (10.69%))

WESTMORLAND & LONSDALE
*E.*70,637 *T.* 47,903 (67.82%) C. hold
*Tim Collins, *C.* 22,486
Tim Farron, *LD* 19,339
John Bateson, *Lab.* 5,234
Robert Gibson, *UK Ind.* 552
Tim Bell, *Ind.* 292
C. majority 3,147 (6.57%)
1.17% swing C. to LD
(1997: C. maj. 4,521 (8.90%))

WESTON-SUPER-MARE
*E.*74,343 *T.* 46,680 (62.79%) LD hold
*Brian Cotter, *LD* 18,424
John Penrose, *C.* 18,086
Derek Kraft, *Lab.* 9,235
Bill Lukins, *UK Ind.* 650
John Peverelle, *Ind.* 206
Richard Sibley, *Ind.* 79

LD majority 338 (0.72%)
0.83% swing LD to C.
(1997: LD maj. 1,274 (2.39%))

WIGAN
*E.*64,040 *T.* 33,591 (52.45%) Lab. hold
*Neil Turner, *Lab.* 20,739
Mark Page, *C.* 6,996
Trevor Beswick, *LD* 4,970
Dave Lowe, *Soc. All.* 886
Lab. majority 13,743 (40.91%)
5.38% swing Lab. to C.
(1999 Sept by-election: Lab. maj. 6,729)
(1997: Lab. maj. 22,643 (51.67%))

WILTSHIRE NORTH
*E.*79,524 *T.* 52,948 (66.58%) C. hold
*James Gray, *C.* 24,090
Hugh Pym, *LD* 20,212
Ms Jo Garton, *Lab.* 7,556
Neil Dowdney, *UK Ind.* 1,090
C. majority 3,878 (7.32%)
0.67% swing LD to C.
(1997: C. maj. 3,475 (5.99%))

WIMBLEDON
*E.*63,930 *T.* 41,109 (64.30%) Lab. hold
*Roger Casale, *Lab.* 18,806
Stephen Hammond, *C.* 15,062
Martin Pierce, *LD* 5,341
Rajeev Thacker, *Green* 1,007
Roger Glencross, *CPA* 479
Ms Mariana Bell, *UK Ind.* 414
Lab. majority 3,744 (9.11%)
1.47% swing C. to Lab.
(1997: Lab. maj. 2,980 (6.17%))

WINCHESTER
*E.*81,852 *T.* 59,158 (72.27%) LD hold
*Mark Oaten, *LD* 32,282
Andrew Hayes, *C.* 22,648
Stephen Wyeth, *Lab.* .3,498
Ms Joan Martin, *UK Ind.* 664
Ms Henrietta Rouse, *Wessex Reg.* 66
LD majority 9,634 (16.29%)
8.14% swing C. to LD
(1997 Nov by-election: LD maj. 21,556
(39.64%))
(1997: LD maj. 2 (0.00%))

WINDSOR
*E.*69,136 *T.* 42,110 (60.91%) C. hold
*Michael Trend, *C.* 19,900
Nick Pinfield, *LD* 11,011
Mark Muller, *Lab.* 10,137
John Fagan, *UK Ind.* 1,062
C. majority 8,889 (21.11%)
0.79% swing LD to C.
(1997: C. maj. 9,917 (19.53%))

WIRRAL SOUTH
*E.*60,653 *T.* 39,818 (65.65%) Lab. hold
*Ben Chapman, *Lab.* 18,890
Anthony Millard, *C.* 13,841
Phillip Gilchrist, *LD* 7,087
Lab. majority 5,049 (12.68%)
0.94% swing Lab. to C.
(1997: Lab. maj. 7,004 (14.56%))

WIRRAL WEST
*E.*62,294 *T.* 40,475 (64.97%) Lab. hold
*Stephen Hesford, *Lab.* 19,105

Chris Lynch, *C.* 15,070
Simon Holbrook, *LD* 6,300
Lab. majority 4,035 (9.97%)
2.06% swing C. to Lab.
(1997: Lab. maj. 2,738 (5.84%))

WITNEY
*E.*74,624 *T.* 49,203 (65.93%) C. gain
David Cameron, *C.* 22,153
Michael Bartlet, *Lab.* 14,180
Gareth Epps, *LD* 10,000
Mark Stevenson, *Green* 1,100
Barry Beadle, *Ind.* 1,003
Kenneth Dukes, *UK Ind.* 767
C. majority 7,973 (16.20%)
1.87% swing Lab. to C.
(1997: C. maj. 7,028 (12.46%))

WOKING
*E.*71,163 *T.* 42,910 (60.30%) C. hold
*Humfrey Malins, *C.* 19,747
Alan Hilliar, *LD* 12,988
Sabir Hussain, *Lab.* 8,714
Michael Harvey, *UK Ind.* 1,461
C. majority 6,759 (15.75%)
2.30% swing LD to C.
(1997: C. maj. 5,678 (11.15%))

WOKINGHAM
*E.*68,430 *T.* 43,848 (64.08%) C. hold
*Rt. Hon. J. Redwood, *C.* 20,216
Dr Royce Longton, *LD* 14,222
Matthew Syed, *Lab.* 7,633
Franklin Carstairs, *UK Ind.* 897
Peter "Top Cat" Owen *Loony* 880
C. majority 5,994 (13.67%)
2.51% swing C. to LD
(1997: C. maj. 9,365 (18.69%))

WOLVERHAMPTON NORTH EAST
*E.*60,486 *T.* 31,494 (52.07%)Lab Co-op
hold
*Ken Purchase, *Lab. Co-op.* 18,984
Ms Maria Miller, *C.* 9,019
Steven Bourne, *LD* 2,494
Thomas McCartney, *UK Ind.* 997
Lab Co-op majority 9,965 (31.64%)
0.14% swing C. to Lab. Co-op
(1997: Lab. maj. 12,987 (31.37%))

WOLVERHAMPTON SOUTH EAST
*E.*53,931 *T.* 27,297 (50.61%) Lab Co-op
hold
*Dennis Turner, *Lab. Co-op.* 18,409
Adrian Pepper, *C.* 5,945
Peter Wild, *LD* 2,389
James Barry, *NF* 554
Lab Co-op majority 12,464 (45.66%)
1.04% swing C. to Lab. Co-op
(1997: Lab. maj. 15,182 (43.58%))

WOLVERHAMPTON SOUTH WEST
*E.*67,171 *T.* 40,897 (60.88%) Lab. hold
Robert Marris, *Lab.* 19,735
David Chambers, *C.* 16,248
Mike Dixon, *LD* 3,425
Ms Wendy Walker, *Green* 805
Doug Hope, *UK Ind.* 684
Lab. majority 3,487 (8.53%)
0.97% swing Lab. to C.
(1997: Lab. maj. 5,118 (10.46%))

WOODSPRING
E.71,023 T. 48,758 (68.65%)   C. hold
*Dr Liam Fox, C.   21,297
Chanel Stevens, Lab.   12,499
Colin Eldridge, LD   11,816
David Shopland, Ind.   1,412
Dr Richard Lawson, Green   1,282
Fraser Crean, UK Ind.   452
C. majority 8,798 (18.04%)
2.86% swing C. to Lab.
(1997: C. maj. 7,734 (14.08%))

WORCESTER
E.71,255 T. 44,210 (62.04%) Lab. hold
*Michael Foster, Lab.   21,478
Richard Adams, C.   15,712
Paul Chandler, LD   5,578
Richard Chamings, UK Ind.   1,442
Lab. majority 5,766 (13.04%)
0.67% swing Lab. to C.
(1997: Lab. maj. 7,425 (14.38%))

WORCESTERSHIRE MID
E.71,985 T. 44,897 (62.37%)   C. hold
*Peter Luff, C.   22,937
David Bannister, Lab.   12,310
R. Woodthorpe-Browne, LD   8,420
Tony Eaves, UK Ind.   1,230
C. majority 10,627 (23.67%)
2.57% swing Lab. to C.
(1997: C. maj. 9,412 (18.52%))

WORCESTERSHIRE WEST
E.66,769 T. 44,807 (67.11%)   C. hold
*Sir Michael Spicer, C.   20,597
Mike Hadley, LD   15,223
Waquar Azmi, Lab.   6,275
Ian Morris, UK Ind.   1,574
Malcolm Victory, Green   1,138
C. majority 5,374 (11.99%)
2.10% swing LD to C.
(1997: C. maj. 3,846 (7.80%))

WORKINGTON
E.65,965 T. 41,822 (63.40%) Lab. hold
Tony Cunningham, Lab.   23,209
Tim Stoddart, C.   12,359
Ian Francis, LD   5,214
John Peacock, LCA   1,040
Lab. majority 10,850 (25.94%)
6.93% swing Lab. to C.
(1997: Lab. maj. 19,656 (39.81%))

WORSLEY
E.69,300 T. 35,363 (51.03%) Lab. hold
*Terry Lewis, Lab   20,193
Tobias Ellwood, C.   8,406
Robert Bleakley, LD   6,188
Ms Dorothy Entwistle, Soc. Lab.   576
Lab. majority 11,787 (33.33%)
2.30% swing Lab. to C.
(1997: Lab. maj. 17,741 (37.93%))

WORTHING EAST & SHOREHAM
E.71,890 T. 43,068 (59.91%)   C. hold
*Tim Loughton, C.   18,608
Daniel Yates, Lab.   12,469
Paul Elgood, LD   9,876
Jim McCulloch, UK Ind.   1,195
Christopher Baldwin, LCA   920
C. majority 6,139 (14.25%)
1.14% swing C. to Lab.
(1997: C. maj. 5,098 (9.89%))

WORTHING WEST
E.72,419 T. 43,209 (59.67%)   C. hold
*Peter Bottomley, C.   20,508
James Walsh, LD   11,471
Alan Butcher, Lab.   9,270
Tim Cross, UK Ind.   1,960
C. majority 9,037 (20.91%)
2.96% swing LD to C.
(1997: C. maj. 7,713 (15.00%))

WREKIN, THE
E.65,837 T. 41,490 (63.02%) Lab. hold
*Peter Bradley, Lab.   19,532
Jacob Rees-Mogg, C.   15,945
Ian Jenkins, LD   4,738
Denis Brookes, UK Ind.   1,275
Lab. majority 3,587 (8.65%)
0.98% swing C. to Lab.
(1997: Lab. maj. 3,025 (6.69%))

WYCOMBE
E.74,647 T. 44,974 (60.25%)   C. hold
Paul Goodman, C.   19,064
Chauhdry Shafique, Lab.   15,896
Ms Dee Tomlin, LD   7,658
Christopher Cooke, UK Ind.   1,059
John Laker, Green   1,057
David Fitton, Ind.   240
C. majority 3,168 (7.04%)
1.26% swing Lab. to C.
(1997: C. maj. 2,370 (4.53%))

WYRE FOREST
E.72,152 T. 49,062 (68.00%) KHHC gain
Dr Richard Taylor, KHHC   28,487
*David Lock, Lab.   10,857
Mark Simpson, C.   9,350
James Millington, UK Ind.   368
KHHC majority 17,630 (35.93%)
(1997: Lab. maj. 6,946 (12.62%))

WYTHENSHAWE & SALE EAST
E.72,127 T. 35,055 (48.60%) Lab. hold
*Paul Goggins, Lab.   21,032
Mrs Susan Fildes, C.   8,424
Ms Vanessa Tucker, LD   4,320
Lance Crookes, Green   869
Fred Shaw, Soc. Lab.   410
Lab. majority 12,608 (35.97%)
1.49% swing C. to Lab.
(1997: Lab. maj. 15,019 (32.99%))

YEOVIL
E.75,977 T. 48,132 (63.35%)   LD hold
David Laws, LD   21,266
Marco Forgione, C.   17,338
Joe Conway, Lab.   7,077
Neil Boxall, UK Ind.   1,131
Alex Begg, Green   786
Tony Prior, Lib.   534
LD majority 3,928 (8.16%)
6.47% swing LD to C.
(1997: LD maj. 11,403 (21.10%))

YORK, CITY OF
E.80,431 T. 47,980 (59.65%) Lab. hold
*Hugh Bayley, Lab.   25,072
Michael McIntyre, C.   11,293
Andrew Waller, LD   8,519
Bill Shaw, Green   1,465
Frank Ormston, Soc. All.   674
Richard Bate, UK Ind.   576
Graham Cambridge, Loony   381
Lab. majority 13,779 (28.72%)
3.23% swing Lab. to C.
(1997: Lab. maj. 20,523 (35.17%))

YORKSHIRE EAST
E.72,342 T. 43,314 (59.87%)   C. hold
Rt. Hon. G. Knight, C.   19,861
Ms Tracey Simpson-Laing, Lab.   15,179
Ms Mary-Rose Hardy, LD   6,300
Trevor Pearson, UK Ind.   1,661
Paul Dessoy, Ind.   313
C. majority 4,682 (10.81%)
1.99% swing Lab. to C.
(1997: C. maj. 3,337 (6.82%))

WALES

ABERAVON
E.49,660 T. 30,190 (60.79%) Lab. hold
Hywel Francis, Lab.   19,063
Ms Lisa Turnbull, PC   2,955
Chris Davies, LD   2,933
Ali Miraj, C.   2,296
Andrew Tutton, RP   1,960
Captain Beany, Bean   727
Mr Martin Chapman, Soc. All.   256
Lab. majority 16,108 (53.36%)
6.08% swing Lab. to PC
(1997: Lab. maj. 21,571 (59.98%))

ALYN & DEESIDE
E.60,478 T. 35,421 (58.57%) Lab. hold
Mark Tami, Lab.   18,525
Mark Isherwood, C.   9,303
Derek Burnham, LD   4,585
Richard Coombs, PC   1,182
Klaus Armstrong-Braun, Green   881
William Crawford, UK Ind.   481
Max Cooksey, Ind.   253
Glyn Davies, Comm.   211
Lab. majority 9,222 (26.04%)
6.53% swing Lab. to C.
(1997: Lab. maj. 16,403 (39.10%))

BLAENAU GWENT
E.53,353 T. 31,725 (59.46%) Lab. hold
*Llew Smith, Lab.   22,855
Adam Rykala, PC   3,542
Edward Townsend, LD   2,945
Huw Williams, C.   2,383
Lab. majority 19,313 (60.88%)
6.68% swing Lab. to PC
(1997: Lab. maj. 28,035 (70.74%))

BRECON & RADNORSHIRE
E.52,247 T. 37,516 (71.81%)   LD hold
Roger Williams, LD   13,824
Dr Felix Aubel, C.   13,073
Huw Irranca-Davis, Lab.   8,024

Brynach Parri, *PC* 1,301
Ian Mitchell, *Ind.* 762
Mrs Elizabeth Phillips, *UK Ind.* 452
Robert Nicholson, *Ind.* 80
LD majority 751 (2.00%)
4.94% swing LD to C.
(1997: LD maj. 5,097 (11.89%))

BRIDGEND
*E.*61,496 *T.* 37,004 (60.17%) Lab. hold
*Win Griffiths, *Lab.* 19,422
Ms Tania Brisby, *C.* 9,377
Ms Jean Barraclough, *LD* 5,330
Ms Monica Mahoney, *PC* 2,652
Ms Sara Jeremy, *ProLife* 223
Lab. majority 10,045 (27.15%)
4.05% swing Lab. to C.
(1997: Lab. maj. 15,248 (35.24%))

CAERNARFON
*E.*47,354 *T.* 29,053 (61.35%) PC hold
Hywel Williams, *PC* 12,894
Martin Eaglestone, *Lab.* 9,383
Ms Bronwen Naish, *C.* 4,403
Melab Owain, *LD* 1,823
Ifor Lloyd, *UK Ind.* 550
PC majority 3,511 (12.08%)
4.75% swing PC to Lab
(1997: PC maj. 7,449 (21.59%))

CAERPHILLY
*E.*67,593 *T.* 38,831 (57.45%) Lab. hold
Wayne David, *Lab.* 22,597
Lindsay Whittle, *PC* 8,172
David Simmonds, *C.* 4,413
Rob Roffe, *LD* 3,649
Lab. majority 14,425 (37.15%)
10.49% swing Lab. to PC
(1997: Lab. maj. 25,839 (57.08%))

CARDIFF CENTRAL
*E.*59,785 *T.* 34,842 (58.28%) Lab. Co-op.
hold
*Jon Owen Jones, *Lab. Co-op.* 13,451
Ms Jenny Willott, *LD* 12,792
Gregory Walker, *C.* 5,537
Richard Grigg, *PC* 1,680
Stephen Bartley, *Green* 661
Julian Goss, *Soc. All.* 283
Frank Hughes, *UK Ind.* 221
Ms Madeleine Jeremy, *ProLife* 217
Lab. Co-op. majority 659 (1.89%)
8.43% swing Lab. Co-op. to LD
(1997: Lab. maj. 7,923 (18.75%))

CARDIFF NORTH
*E.*62,634 *T.* 43,240 (69.04%) Lab. hold
*Ms Julie Morgan, *Lab.* 19,845
Alastair Watson, *C.* 13,680
John Dixon, *LD* 6,631
Sion Jobbins, *PC* 2,471
Don Hulston, *UK Ind.* 613
Lab. majority 6,165 (14.26%)
1.25% swing Lab. to C.
(1997: Lab. maj. 8,126 (16.76%))

CARDIFF SOUTH & PENARTH
*E.*62,125 *T.* 35,751 (57.55%)Lab. Co-op.
hold
*Rt. Hon. A. Michael, *Lab. Co-op.* 20,094
Ms Maureen Kelly Owen, *C.* 7,807
Dr Rodney Berman, *LD* 4,572
Ms Lila Haines, *PC* 1,983

Justin Callan, *UK Ind.* 501
Dave Bartlett, *Soc. All.* 427
Ms Anne Savoury, *ProLife* 367
Lab. Co-op. majority 12,287 (34.37%)
0.81% swing C. to Lab. Co-op.
(1997: Lab. maj. 13,881 (32.74%))

CARDIFF WEST
*E.*58,348 *T.* 34,083 (58.41%) Lab. hold
Kevin Brennan, *Lab.* 18,594
Andrew Davies, *C.* 7,273
Ms Jacqui Gasson, *LD* 4,458
Delme Bowen, *PC* 3,296
Ms Joyce Jenking, *UK Ind.* 462
Lab. majority 11,321 (33.22%)
2.79% swing Lab. to C.
(1997: Lab. maj. 15,628 (38.80%))

CARMARTHEN EAST & DINEFWR
*E.*54,035 *T.* 38,053 (70.42%) PC gain
Adam Price, *PC* 16,130
*Alan Williams, *Lab.* 13,540
David N Thomas, *C.* 4,912
Doiran Evans, *LD* 2,815
Mike Squires, *UK Ind.* 656
PC majority 2,590 (6.81%)
7.54% swing Lab. to PC
(1997: Lab. maj. 3,450 (8.27%))

CARMARTHEN WEST &
PEMBROKESHIRE SOUTH
*E.*56,518 *T.* 36,916 (65.32%) Lab. hold
*Nick Ainger, *Lab.* 15,349
Robert Wilson, *C.* 10,811
Llyr Hughes Griffiths, *PC* 6,893
William Jeremy, *LD* 3,248
Ian Phillips, *UK Ind.* 537
Nick Turner, *Customer* 78
Lab. majority 4,538 (12.29%)
5.14% swing Lab. to C.
(1997: Lab. maj. 9,621 (22.57%))

CEREDIGION
*E.*56,118 *T.* 34,606 (61.67%) PC hold
*Simon Thomas, *PC* 13,241
Mark Williams, *LD* 9,297
Paul Davies, *C.* 6,730
David Grace, *Lab.* 5,338
PC majority 3,944 (11.40%)
6.89% swing PC to LD
(2000 Feb by-election: PC maj. 4,948
(19.74%); 1997: PC maj. 6,961
(17.33%))

CLWYD SOUTH
*E.*53,680 *T.* 33,496 (62.40%) Lab. hold
*Martyn Jones, *Lab.* 17,217
Tom Biggins, *C.* 8,319
Dyfed Edwards, *PC* 3,982
David Griffiths, *LD* 3,426
Mrs Edwina Theunissen, *UK Ind.* 552
Lab. majority 8,898 (26.56%)
4.25% swing Lab. to C.
(1997: Lab. maj. 13,810 (35.07%))

CLWYD WEST
*E.*53,960 *T.* 34,600 (64.12%) Lab. hold
*Gareth Thomas, *Lab.* 13,426
Jimmy James, *C.* 2,311
Elfed Williams, *PC* 4,453
Ms Bobbie Feeley, *LD* 3,934
Matthew Guest, *UK Ind.* 476
Lab. majority 1,115 (3.22%)

0.68% swing Lab. to C.
(1997: Lab. maj. 1,848 (4.59%))

CONWY
*E.*54,751 *T.* 34,366 (62.77%) Lab. hold
*Mrs Betty Williams, *Lab.* 14,366
David Logan, *C.* 8,147
Ms Vicky Macdonald, *LD* 5,800
Ms Ann Owen, *PC* 5,665
Alan Barham, *UK Ind.* 388
Lab. majority 6,219 (18.10%)
3.66% swing C. to Lab
(1997: Lab. maj. 1,596 (3.84%))

CYNON VALLEY
*E.*48,591 *T.* 26,958 (55.48%) Lab. hold
*Ms Ann Clwyd, *Lab.* 17,685
Steven Cornelius, *PC* 4,687
Ian Parry, *LD* 2,541
Julian Waters, *C.* 2,045
Lab. majority 12,998 (48.22%)
5.44% swing Lab. to PC
(1997: Lab. maj. 19,755 (59.10%))

DELYN
*E.*54,732 *T.* 34,636 (63.28%) Lab. hold
*David Hanson, *Lab.* 17,825
Paul Brierley, *C.* 9,220
Tudor Jones, *LD* 5,329
Paul Rowlinson, *PC* 2,262
Lab. majority 8,605 (24.84%)
2.29% swing Lab. to C.
(1997: Lab. maj. 11,693 (29.42%))

GOWER
*E.*58,943 *T.* 37,353 (63.37%) Lab. hold
*Martin Caton, *Lab.* 17,676
John Bushell, *C.* 10,281
Ms Sheila Waye, *LD* 4,507
Ms Sian Caiach, *PC* 3,865
Ms Tina Shrewsbury, *Green* 607
Darran Hickery, *Soc. Lab.* 417
Lab. majority 7,395 (19.80%)
5.11% swing Lab. to C.
(1997: Lab. maj. 13,007 (30.02%))

ISLWYN
*E.*51,230 *T.* 31,691 (61.86%)Lab. Co-op.
hold
*Don Touhig, *Lab. Co-op.* 19,505
Kevin Etheridge, *LD* 4,196
Leigh Thomas, *PC* 3,767
Philip Howells, *C.* 2,543
Paul Taylor, *Ind.* 1,263
Ms Mary Millington, *Soc. Lab.* 417
Lab. Co-op. majority 15,309 (48.31%)
8.71% swing Lab. Co-op. to LD
(1997: Lab. maj. 23,931 (65.73%))

LLANELLI
*E.*58,148 *T.* 36,198 (62.25%) Lab. hold
*Rt. Hon. D. Davies, *Lab.* 17,586
Dyfan Jones, *PC* 11,183
Simon Hayes, *C.* 3,442
Ken Rees, *LD* 3,065
Ms Jan Cliff, *Green* 515
John Willock, *Soc. Lab.* 407
Lab. majority 6,403 (17.69%)
10.62% swing Lab. to PC
(1997: Lab. maj. 16,039 (38.92%))

MEIRIONNYDD NANT CONWY
*E.*33,175 *T.* 21,068 (63.51%) PC hold
*Elfyn Llwyd, *PC* 10,459

Ms Denise Idris Jones, *Lab.*   4,775
Ms Lisa Francis, *C.*   3,962
Dafydd Raw-Rees, *LD*   1,872
PC majority 5,684 (26.98%)
0.36% swing PC to Lab.
(1997: PC maj. 6,805 (27.69%))

MERTHYR TYDFIL & RHYMNEY
*E.*55,368 *T.* 31,684 (57.22%) Lab. hold
Dai Havard, *Lab.*   19,574
Robert Hughes, *PC*   4,651
Keith Rogers, *LD*   2,385
Richard Cuming, *C.*   2,272
Jeff Edwards, *Ind.*   1,936
Ken Evans, *Soc. Lab.*   692
Anthony Lewis, *ProLife*   174
Lab. majority 14,923 (47.10%)
11.80% swing Lab. to PC
(1997: Lab. maj. 27,086 (69.20%))

MONMOUTH
*E.*62,202 *T.* 44,462 (71.48%) Lab. hold
*Huw Edwards, *Lab.*   19,021
Roger Evans, *C.*   18,637
Neil Parker, *LD*   5,080
Marc Hubbard, *PC*   1,068
David Rowlands, *UK Ind.*   656
Lab. majority 384 (0.86%)
3.83% swing Lab. to C.
(1997: Lab. maj. 4,178 (8.52%))

MONTGOMERYSHIRE
*E.*44,243 *T.* 28,983 (65.51%) LD hold
*Lembit Opik, *LD*   14,319
David Jones, *C.*   8,085
Paul Davies, *Lab.*   3,443
David Senior, *PC*   1,969
David William Rowlands, *UK Ind.* 786
Miss Ruth Davies, *ProLife*   210
Reg Taylor, *Ind.*   171
LD majority 6,234 (21.51%)
0.88% swing C. to LD
(1997: LD maj. 6,303 (19.74%))

NEATH
*E.*56,107 *T.* 35,020 (62.42%) Lab. hold
*Rt. Hon. P. Hain, *Lab.*   21,253
Alun Llywelyn, *PC*   6,437
David Davies, *LD*   3,335
David Devine, *C.*   3,310
Huw Pudner, *Soc. All.*   483
Gerardo Brienza, *ProLife*   202
Lab. majority 14,816 (42.31%)
11.56% swing Lab. to PC
(1997: Lab. maj. 26,741 (64.84%))

NEWPORT EAST
*E.*56,118 *T.* 31,282 (55.74%) Lab. hold
*Rt. Hon. A. Howarth, *Lab.*   17,120
Ian Oakley, *C.*   7,246
Alistair Cameron, *LD*   4,394
Madoc Batcup, *PC*   1,519
Ms Liz Screen, *Soc. Lab.*   420
NeAL Reynolds, *UK Ind.*   410
Robert Griffiths, *Comm.*   173
Lab. majority 9,874 (31.56%)
2.36% swing Lab. to C.
(1997: Lab. maj. 13,523 (36.29%))

NEWPORT WEST
*E.*59,742 *T.* 35,063 (58.69%) Lab. hold
*Paul Flynn, *Lab.*   18,489
Dr William Morgan, *C.*   9,185

Ms Veronica Watkins, *LD*   4,095
Anthony Salkeld, *PC*   2,510
Hugh Moelwyn-Hughes, *UK Ind.*   506
Terry Cavill, *BNP*   278
Lab. majority 9,304 (26.54%)
4.81% swing Lab. to C.
(1997: Lab. maj. 14,537 (36.16%))

OGMORE
*E.*52,185 *T.* 30,353 (58.16%) Lab. hold
*Sir Ray Powell, *Lab.*   18,833
Ms Angela Pulman, *PC*   4,259
Ian Lewis, *LD*   3,878
Richard Hill, *C.*   3,383
Lab. majority 14,574 (48.02%)
9.46% swing Lab. to PC
(1997: Lab. maj. 24,447 (64.22%))

PONTYPRIDD
*E.*66,105 *T.* 38,309 (57.95%) Lab. hold
*Dr Kim Howells, *Lab.*   22,963
Bleddyn Hancock, *PC*   5,279
Ms Prudence Dailey, *C.*   .5,096
Eric Brooke, *LD*   4,152
Ms Sue Warry, *UK Ind.*   603
Joseph Biddulph, *ProLife*   216
Lab. majority 17,684 (46.16%)
5.61% swing Lab. to PC
(1997: Lab. maj. 23,129 (50.44%))

PRESELI PEMBROKESHIRE
*E.*54,283 *T.* 36,777 (67.75%) Lab. hold
*Ms Jackie Lawrence, *Lab.*   15,206
Stephen Crabb, *C.*   12,260
Rhys Sinnet, *PC*   4,658
Alexander Dauncey, *LD*   3,882
Ms Trish Bowen, *Soc. Lab.*   452
Hugh Jones, *UK Ind.*   319
Lab. majority 2,946 (8.01%)
6.29% swing Lab. to C.
(1997: Lab. maj. 8,736 (20.60%))

RHONDDA
*E.*56,059 *T.* 34,002 (60.65%) Lab. hold
Chris Bryant, *Lab.*   23,230
Ms Leanne Wood, *PC*   7,183
Peter Hobbins, *C.*   1,557
Gavin Cox, *LD*   1,525
Glyndwr Summers, *Ind.*   507
Lab. majority 16,047 (47.19%)
6.95% swing Lab. to PC
(1997: Lab. maj. 24,931 (61.09%))

SWANSEA EAST
*E.*57,273 *T.* 30,072 (52.51%) Lab. hold
*Rt. Hon. D. Anderson, *Lab.*   19,612
John Ball, *PC*   3,464
Robert Speht, *LD*   3,064
Paul Morris, *C.*   3,026
Tony Young, *Green*   463
Tim Jenkins, *UK Ind.*   443
Lab. majority 16,148 (53.70%)
9.15% swing Lab. to PC
(1997: Lab. maj. 25,569 (66.12%))

SWANSEA WEST
*E.*57,074 *T.* 32,100 (56.24%) Lab. hold
*Rt. Hon. A. Williams, *Lab.*   15,644
Ms Margaret Harper, *C.*   6,094
Mike Day, *LD*   5,313
Ian Titherington, *PC*   3,404
Richard Lewis, *UK Ind.*   653
Martyn Shrewsbury, *Green*   626

Alec Thraves, *Soc. All.*   366
Lab. majority 9,550 (29.75%)
2.99% swing Lab. to C.
(1997: Lab. maj. 14,459 (35.73%))

TORFAEN
*E.*61,110 *T.* 35,242 (57.67%) Lab. hold
*Rt. Hon. P. Murphy, *Lab.*   21,883
Jason Evans, *C.*   5,603
Alan Masters, *LD*   3,936
Stephen Smith, *PC*   2,720
Mrs Brenda Vipass, *UK Ind.*   657
Steve Bell, *Soc. All.*   443
Lab. majority 16,280 (46.19%)
5.27% swing Lab. to C.
(1997: Lab. maj. 24,536 (56.74%))

VALE OF CLWYD
*E.*51,247 *T.* 32,346 (63.12%) Lab. hold
*Chris Ruane, *Lab.*   16,179
Brendan Murphy, *C.*   10,418
Graham Rees, *LD*   3,058
John Penri Williams, *PC*   2,300
William Campbell, *UK Ind.*   391
Lab. majority 5,761 (17.81%)
2.54% swing Lab. to C.
(1997: Lab. maj. 8,955 (22.89%))

VALE OF GLAMORGAN
*E.*67,071 *T.* 45,184 (67.37%) Lab. hold
*John Smith, *Lab.*   20,524
Lady Susan Inkin, *C.*   15,824
Dewi Smith, *LD*   5,521
Chris Franks, *PC*   2,867
Niall Warry, *UK Ind.*   448
Lab. majority 4,700 (10.40%)
4.57% swing Lab. to C.
(1997: Lab. maj. 10,532 (19.54%))

WREXHAM
*E.*50,465 *T.* 30,048 (59.54%) Lab. hold
Ian Lucas, *Lab.*   15,934
Ms Felicity Elphick, *C.*   6,746
Ron Davies, *LD*   5,153
Malcolm Evans, *PC*   1,783
Mrs Jane Brookes, *UK Ind.*   432
Lab. majority 9,188 (30.58%)
0.86% swing Lab. to C.
(1997: Lab. maj. 11,762 (32.30%))

YNYS MON
*E.*53,117 *T.* 34,018 (64.04%) Lab. gain
Albert Owen, *Lab.*   11,906
Eilian Williams, *PC*   11,106
Albie Fox, *C.*   7,653
Nick Bennett, *LD*   2,772
Francis Wykes, *UK Ind.*   359
Ms Nona Donald, *Ind.*   222
Lab. majority 800 (2.35%)
4.28% swing PC to Lab
(1997: PC maj. 2,481 (6.21%))

SCOTLAND

ABERDEEN CENTRAL
E.50,098 T. 26,429 (52.75%) Lab. hold
*Frank Doran, *Lab.* 12,025
Wayne Gault, *SNP* 5,379
Ms Eleanor Anderson, *LD* 4,547
Stewart Whyte, *C.* 3,761
Andy Cumbers, *SSP* 717
Lab. majority 6,646 (25.15%)
4.24% swing Lab. to SNP
(1997: Lab. maj. 10,801 (30.32%))

ABERDEEN NORTH
E.52,746 T. 30,357 (57.55%) Lab. hold
*Malcolm Savidge, *Lab.* 13,157
Dr Alasdair Allan, *SNP* 8,708
Jim Donaldson, *LD* 4,991
Richard Cowling, *C.* 3,047
Ms Shona Forman, *SSP* 454
Lab. majority 4,449 (14.66%)
5.70% swing Lab. to SNP
(1997: Lab. maj. 10,010 (26.06%))

ABERDEEN SOUTH
E.58,907 T. 36,890 (62.62%) Lab. hold
*Ms Anne Begg, *Lab.* 14,696
Ian Yuill, *LD* 10,308
Moray Macdonald, *C.* 7,098
Ian Angus, *SNP* 4,293
David Watt, *SSP* 495
Lab. majority 4,388 (11.89%)
2.13% swing LD to Lab.
(1997: Lab. maj. 3,365 (7.64%))

ABERDEENSHIRE WEST & KINCARDINE
E.61,180 T. 37,914 (61.97%) LD hold
*Sir Robert Smith, *LD* 16,507
Tom Kerr, *C.* 11,686
Kevin Hutchens, *Lab.* 4,669
John Green, *SNP* 4,634
Alan Manley, *SSP* 418
LD majority 4,821 (12.72%)
3.28% swing C. to LD
(1997: LD maj. 2,662 (6.16%))

AIRDRIE & SHOTTS
E.58,349 T. 31,736 (54.39%) Lab. hold
*Rt. Hon. Ms H. Liddell, *Lab.* 18,478
Ms Alison Lindsay, *SNP* 6,138
John Love, *LD* 2,376
Gordon McIntosh, *C.* 1,960
Ms Mary Dempsey, *Scot. U.* 1,439
Kenny McGuigan, *SSP* 1,171
Chris Herriot, *Soc. Lab.* 174
Lab. majority 12,340 (38.88%)
0.73% swing SNP to Lab.
(1997: Lab. maj. 15,412 (37.42%))

ANGUS
E.59,004 T. 35,013 (59.34%) SNP hold
Michael Weir, *SNP* 12,347
Marcus Booth, *C.* 8,736
Ian McFatridge, *Lab.* 8,183
Peter Nield, *LD* 5,015
Bruce Wallace, *SSP* 732
SNP majority 3,611 (10.31%)
6.67% swing SNP to C.
(1997: SNP maj. 10,189 (23.66%))

ARGYLL & BUTE
E.49,175 T. 30,957 (62.95%) LD hold

Alan Reid, *LD* 9,245
Hugh Raven, *Lab.* 7,592
David Petrie, *C.* 6,436
Ms Agnes Samuel, *SNP* 6,433
Des Divers, *SSP* 1,251
LD majority 1,653 (5.34%)
9.60% swing LD to Lab.
(1997: LD maj. 6,081 (17.03%))

AYR
E.55,630 T. 38,560 (69.32%) Lab. hold
*Ms Sandra Osborne, *Lab.* 16,801
Phil Gallie, *C.* 14,256
Jim Mather, *SNP* 4,621
Stuart Ritchie, *LD* 2,089
James Stewart, *SSP* 692
Joseph Smith, *UK Ind.* 101
Lab. majority 2,545 (6.60%)
4.01% swing Lab. to C.
(1997: Lab. maj. 6,543 (14.62%))

BANFF & BUCHAN
E.56,496 T. 30,806 (54.53%) SNP hold
*Alex Salmond, *SNP* 16,710
Alexander Wallace, *C.* 6,207
Edward Harris, *Lab.* 4,363
Douglas Herbison, *LD* 2,769
Ms Alice Rowan, *SSP* 447
Eric Davidson, *UK Ind.* 310
SNP majority 10,503 (34.09%)
1.06% swing C. to SNP
(1997: SNP maj. 12,845 (31.97%))

CAITHNESS, SUTHERLAND & EASTER ROSS
E.41,225 T. 24,867 (60.32%) LD hold
Viscount John Thurso, *LD* 9,041
Michael Meighan, *Lab.* .6,297
John Macadam, *SNP* 5,273
Robert Rowantree, *C.* 3,513
Ms Karn Mabon, *SSP* 544
Gordon Campbell, *Ind.* 199
LD majority 2,744 (11.03%)
1.64% swing Lab. to LD
(1997: LD maj. 2,259 (7.75%))

CARRICK, CUMNOCK & DOON VALLEY
E.64,919 T. 40,107 (61.78%)Lab Co-op hold
*George Foulkes, *Lab Co-op* 22,174
Gordon Miller, *C.* 7,318
Tom Wilson, *SNP* 6,258
Ms Amy Rogers, *LD* 2,932
Ms Amanda McFarlane, *SSP* 1,058
James McDaid, *Soc. Lab.* 367
Lab. Co-op majority 14,856 (37.04%)
2.90% swing Lab Co-op to C.
(1997: Lab. maj. 21,062 (42.84%))

CLYDEBANK & MILNGAVIE
E.52,534 T. 32,491 (61.85%) Lab. hold
*Tony Worthington, *Lab.* 17,249
Jim Yuill, *SNP* 6,525
Rod Ackland, *LD* 3,909
Dr Catherine Pickering, *C.* 3,514
Ms Dawn Brennan, *SSP* 1,294
Lab. majority 10,724 (33.01%)
0.54% swing Lab. to SNP
(1997: Lab. maj. 13,320 (34.08%))

CLYDESDALE
E.64,423 T. 38,222 (59.33%) Lab. hold

*Jimmy Hood, *Lab.* 17,822
Jim Wright, *SNP* 10,028
Kevin Newton, *C.* 5,034
Ms Moira Craig, *LD* 4,111
Paul Cockshott, *SSP* 974
Donald MacKay, *UK Ind.* 253
Lab. majority 7,794 (20.39%)
5.01% swing Lab. to SNP
(1997: Lab. maj. 13,809 (30.41%))

COATBRIDGE & CHRYSTON
E.52,178 T. 30,311 (58.09%) Lab. hold
*Rt. Hon. T. Clarke, *Lab.* 19,807
Peter Kearney, *SNP* 4,493
Alistair Tough, *LD* 2,293
Patrick Ross-Taylor, *C.* 2,171
Ms Lynne Sheridan, *SSP* 1,547
Lab. majority 15,314 (50.52%)
0.39% swing Lab. to SNP
(1997: Lab. maj. 19,295 (51.30%))

CUMBERNAULD & KILSYTH
E.49,739 T. 29,699 (59.71%) Lab. hold
*Ms Rosemary McKenna, *Lab.* 16,144
David McGlashan, *SNP* 8,624
John O'Donnell, *LD* 1,934
Ms Alison Ross, *C.* 1,460
Kenny McEwan, *SSP* 1,287
Thomas Taylor, *Scot. Ref.* 250
Lab. majority 7,520 (25.32%)
2.78% swing Lab. to SNP
(1997: Lab. maj. 11,128 (30.89%))

CUNNINGHAME NORTH
E.54,993 T. 33,816 (61.49%) Lab. hold
*Brian Wilson, *Lab.* 15,571
Campbell Martin, *SNP* 7,173
Richard Wilkinson, *C.* 6,666
Ross Chmiel, *LD* 3,060
Sean Scott, *SSP* 964
Ms Louise McDaid, *Soc. Lab.* 382
Lab. majority 8,398 (24.83%)
3.51% swing Lab. to SNP
(1997: Lab. maj. 11,039 (26.84%))

CUNNINGHAME SOUTH
E.49,982 T. 28,009 (56.04%) Lab. hold
*Brian Donohoe, *Lab.* 16,424
Bill Kidd, *SNP* 5,194
Mrs Pam Paterson, *C.* 2,682
John Boyd, *LD* 2,094
Ms Rosemary Byrne, *SSP* 1,233
Bobby Cochrane, *Soc. Lab.* 382
Lab. majority 11,230 (40.09%)
0.93% swing Lab. to SNP
(1997: Lab. maj. 14,869 (41.95%))

DUMBARTON
E.56,267 T. 33,994 (60.42%)Lab Co-op hold
*John McFall, *Lab Co-op* 16,151
Iain Robertson, *SNP* 6,576
Eric Thompson, *LD* 5,265
Peter Ramsay, *C.* 4,648
Les Robertson, *SSP* 1,354
Lab. Co-op majority 9,575 (28.17%)
0.89% swing SNP to Lab. Co-op
(1997: Lab. maj. 10,883 (26.38%))

DUMFRIES
E.62,931 T. 42,586 (67.67%) Lab. hold
*Russell Brow, *Lab.* 20,830
John Charteris, *C.* 11,996

John Ross Scott, *LD* 4,955
Gerry Fisher, *SNP* 4,103
John Dennis, *SSP* 702
Lab. majority 8,834 (20.74%)
0.64% swing C. to Lab.
(1997: Lab. maj. 9,643 (19.47%))

DUNDEE EAST
*E.*56,535 *T.* 32,358 (57.24%) Lab. hold
Iain Luke, *Lab.* 14,635
Stewart Hosie, *SNP* 10,160
Alan Donnelly, C. 3,900
Raymond Lawrie, *LD* 2,784
Harvey Duke, *SSP* 879
Lab. majority 4,475 (13.83%)
5.38% swing Lab. to SNP
(1997: Lab. maj. 9,961 (24.58%))

DUNDEE WEST
*E.*53,760 *T.* 29,242 (54.39%) Lab. hold
*Ernie Ross, *Lab.* 14,787
Gordon Archer, *SNP* 7,987
Ian Hail, C. 2,656
Ms Elizabeth Dick, *LD* 2,620
Jim McFarlane, *SSP* 1,192
Lab. majority 6,800 (23.25%)
3.65% swing Lab. to SNP
(1997: Lab. maj. 11,859 (30.56%))

DUNFERMLINE EAST
*E.*52,811 *T.* 30,086 (56.97%) Lab. hold
*Rt. Hon. G. Brown, *Lab.* 19,487
John Mellon, *SNP* 4,424
Stuart Randall, C. 2,838
John Mainland, *LD* 2,281
Andy Jackson, *SSP* 770
Tom Dunsmore, *UK Ind.* 286
Lab. majority 15,063 (50.07%)
0.60% swing Lab. to SNP
(1997: Lab. maj. 18,751 (51.26%))

DUNFERMLINE WEST
*E.*54,293 *T.* 30,975 (57.05%) Lab. hold
*Ms Rachel Squire, *Lab.* 16,370
Brian Goodall, *SNP* 5,390
Russell McPhate, *LD* 4,832
James Mackie, C. 3,166
Ms Kate Stewart, *SSP* 746
Alastair Harper, *UK Ind.* 471
Lab. majority 10,980 (35.45%)
0.77% swing SNP to Lab.
(1997: Lab. maj. 12,354 (33.91%))

EAST KILBRIDE
*E.*66,572 *T.* 41,690 (62.62%) Lab. hold
*Rt. Hon. A. Ingram, *Lab.* 22,205
Archie Buchanan, *SNP* 9,450
Ewan Hawthorn, *LD* 4,278
Mrs Margaret McCulloch, C. 4,238
David Stevenson, *SSP* 1,519
Lab. majority 12,755 (30.59%)
2.52% swing Lab. to SNP
(1997: Lab. maj. 17,384 (35.63%))

EAST LOTHIAN
*E.*58,987 *T.* 36,871 (62.51%) Lab. hold
Mrs Anne Picking, *Lab.* 17,407
Hamish Mair, C. 6,577
Ms Judy Hayman, *LD* 6,506
Ms Hilary Brown, *SNP* 5,381
Derrick White, *SSP* 624
Jake Herriot, *Soc. Lab.* 376
Lab. majority 10,830 (29.37%)

1.68% swing Lab. to C.
(1997: Lab. maj. 14,221 (32.74%))

EASTWOOD
*E.*68,378 *T.* 48,368 (70.74%) Lab. hold
*Jim Murphy, *Lab.* 23,036
Raymond Robertson, C. 13,895
Allan Steele, *LD* 6,239
Stewart Maxwel, *SNP* 4,137
Peter Murray, *SSP* 814
Dr Manar Tayan, *Ind.* 247
Lab. majority 9,141 (18.90%)
6.35% swing C. to Lab.
(1997: Lab. maj. 3,236 (6.19%))

EDINBURGH CENTRAL
*E.*66,089 *T.* 34,390 (52.04%) Lab. hold
*Rt. Hon. A. Darling, *Lab.* 14,495
Andrew Myles, *LD* 6,353
Alastair Orr, C. 5,643
Dr Ian McKee, *SNP* 4,832
Graeme Farmer, *Green* 1,809
Kevin Williamson, *SSP* 1,258
Lab. majority 8,142 (23.68%)
5.15% swing Lab. to LD
(1997: Lab. maj. 11,070 (25.90%))

EDINBURGH EAST & MUSSELBURGH
*E.*59,241 *T.* 34,454 (58.16%) Lab. hold
*Rt. Hon. Dr G. Strang, *Lab.* 18,124
Rob Munn, *SNP* 5,956
Gary Peacock, *LD* 4,981
Peter Finnie, C. 3,906
Derek Durkin, *SSP* 1,487
Lab. majority 12,168 (35.32%)
0.41% swing SNP to Lab.
(1997: Lab. maj. 14,530 (34.50%))

EDINBURGH NORTH & LEITH
*E.*62,475 *T.* 33,234 (53.20%) Lab. hold
Mark Lazarowicz, *Lab.* 15,271
Sebastian Tombs, *LD* 6,454
Ms Kaukab Stewart, *SNP* 5,290
Iain Mitchell, C. 4,626
Ms Catriona Grant, *SSP* 1,334
Don Jacobsen, *Soc. Lab.* 259
Lab. majority 8,817 (26.53%)
3.67% swing Lab. to LD
(1997: Lab. maj. 10,978 (26.81%))

EDINBURGH PENTLANDS
*E.*59,841 *T.* 38,932 (65.06%) Lab. hold
*Dr Lynda Clark, *Lab.* 15,797
Sir Malcolm Rifkind, C. 14,055
David Walker, *LD* 4,210
Stewart Gibb, *SNP* 4,210
James Mearns, *SSP* 555
William McMurdo, *UK Ind.* 105
Lab. majority 1,742 (4.47%)
3.08% swing Lab. to C.
(1997: Lab. maj. 4,862 (10.63%))

EDINBURGH SOUTH
*E.*64,012 *T.* 37,166 (58.06%) Lab. hold
*Nigel Griffiths, *Lab.* 15,671
Ms Marilyne MacLaren, *LD* 10,172
Geoffrey Buchan, C. 6,172
Ms Heather Williams, *SNP* 3,683
Colin Fox, *SSP* 933
Ms Linda Hendry, *LCA* 535
Lab. majority 5,499 (14.80%)
7.19% swing Lab. to LD
(1997: Lab. maj. 11,452 (25.54%))

EDINBURGH WEST
*E.*61,895 *T.* 39,478 (63.78%) LD hold
John Barrett, *LD* 16,719
Ms Elspeth Alexandra, *Lab.* 9,130
Iain Whyte, C. 8,894
Alyn Smith, *SNP* 4,047
Bill Scott, *SSP* 688
LD majority 7,589 (19.22%)
2.59% swing LD to Lab.
(1997: LD maj. 7,253 (15.22%))

FALKIRK EAST
*E.*57,633 *T.* 33,702 (58.48%) Lab. hold
*Michael Connarty, *Lab.* 18,536
Ms Isabel Hutton, *SNP* 7,824
Bill Stevenson, C. 3,252
Ms Karen Utting, *LD* 2,992
Tony Weir, C. 725
Raymond Stead, *Soc. Lab.* 373
Lab. majority 10,712 (31.78%)
0.20% swing Lab. to SNP
(1997: Lab. maj. 13,385 (32.18%))

FALKIRK WEST
*E.*53,583 *T.* 30,891 (57.65%) Lab. hold
*Eric Joyce, *Lab.* 16,022
David Kerr, *SNP* 7,490
Simon Murray, C. 2,321
Hugh O'Donnell, *LD* 2,203
William Buchanan, *Ind.* 1,464
Ms Mhairi McAlpine, *SSP* 707
Hugh Lynch, *Ind.* 490
Ronnie Forbes, *Soc. Lab.* 194
Lab. majority 8,532 (27.62%)
4.15% swing Lab. to SNP
2000 Dec. by-election: Lab. maj. 705 (3.61%)
(1997: Lab. majority 13,783 (35.92%))

FIFE CENTRAL
*E.*59,597 *T.* 32,512 (54.55%) Lab. hold
John MacDougall, *Lab.* 18,310
David Alexander, *SNP* 8,235
Ms Elizabeth Riches, *LD* 2,775
Jeremy Balfour, C. 2,351
Ms Morag Balfour, *SSP* 841
Lab. majority 10,075 (30.99%)
1.33% swing Lab. to SNP
(1997: Lab. maj. 13,713 (33.64%))

FIFE NORTH EAST
*E.*61,900 *T.* 34,692 (56.05%) LD hold
*Rt. Hon. M. Campbell, *LD* 17,926
Mike Scott-Hayward, C. 8,190
Ms Claire Brennan, *Lab.* 3,950
Ms Kris Murray-Browne, *SNP* 3,596
Keith White, *SSP* 610
Mrs Leslie Von Goetz, *LCA* 420
LD majority 9,736 (28.06%)
1.66% swing C. to LD
(1997: LD maj. 10,356 (24.75%))

GALLOWAY & UPPER NITHSDALE
*E.*52,756 *T.* 35,914 (68.08%) C. gain
Peter Duncan, C. 12,222
Malcolm Fleming, *SNP* 12,148
Thomas Sloan, *Lab.* 7,258
Neil Wallace, *LD* 3,698
Andy Harvey, *SSP* 588
C. majority 74 (0.21%)
6.80% swing SNP to C.
(1997: SNP maj. 5,624 (13.39%))

GLASGOW ANNIESLAND
*E.*53,290 *T.* 26,722 (50.14%) Lab. hold
*John Robertson, *Lab.* 15,102
Grant Thoms, *SNP* 4,048
Christopher McGinty, *LD* 3,244
Stewart Connell, *C.* 2,651
Charlie McCarthy, *SSP* 1,486
Ms Katherine McGavigan, *Soc. Lab.* 191
Lab. majority 11,054 (41.37%)
1.68% swing Lab. to SNP
2000 Nov. by-election: Lab. maj. 6,337
(31.35%)
(1997: Lab. maj. 15,154 (44.73%))

GLASGOW BAILLIESTON
*E.*49,268 *T.* 23,261 (47.21%) Lab. hold
*Jimmy Wray, *Lab.* 14,200
Lachlan McNeill, *SNP* 4,361
David Comrie, *C.* 1,580
Jim McVicar, *SSP* 1,569
Charles Dundas, *LD* 1,551
Lab. majority 9,839 (42.30%)
2.15% swing Lab. to SNP
(1997: Lab. maj. 14,840 (46.59%))

GLASGOW CATHCART
*E.*52,094 *T.* 27,386 (52.57%) Lab. hold
Tom Harris, *Lab.* 14,902
Mrs Josephine Docherty, *SNP* 4,086
Richard Cook, *C.* 3,662
Tom Henery, *LD* 3,006
Ronnie Stevenson, *SSP* 1,730
Lab. majority 10,816 (39.49%)
1.80% swing SNP to Lab.
(1997: Lab. maj. 12,245 (35.90%))

GLASGOW GOVAN
*E.*54,068 *T.* 25,284 (46.76%) Lab. hold
*Mohammad Sarwar, *Lab.* 12,464
Ms Karen Neary, *SNP* 6,064
Bob Stewart, *LD* 2,815
Mark Menzies, *C.* 2,167
Willie McGartland, *SSP* 1,531
John Foster, *Comm.* 174
Badar Mirza, *Ind.* 69
Lab. majority 6,400 (25.31%)
8.14% swing SNP to Lab.
(1997: Lab. maj. 2,914 (9.04%))

GLASGOW KELVIN
*E.*61,534 *T.* 26,802 (43.56%) Lab. hold
*George Galloway, *Lab.* 12,014
Ms Tamsin Mayberry, *LD* 4,754
Frank Rankin, *SNP* 4,513
Miss Davina Rankin, *C.* 2,388
Ms Heather Ritchie, *SSP* 1,847
Tim Shand, *Green* 1,286
Lab. majority 7,260 (27.09%)
4.85% swing Lab. to LD
(1997: Lab. maj. 9,665 (29.60%))

GLASGOW MARYHILL
*E.*55,431 *T.* 22,231 (40.11%) Lab. hold
Ms Ann McKechin, *Lab.* 13,420
Alex Dingwall, *SNP* 3,532
Stuart Callison, *LD* 2,372
Gordon Scott, *SSP* 1,745
Gawain Towler, *C.* 1,162
Lab. majority 9,888 (44.48%)
1.76% swing Lab. to SNP
(1997: Lab. maj. 14,264 (47.99%))

GLASGOW POLLOK
*E.*49,201 *T.* 25,277 (51.37%) Lab Co-op
hold
*Ian Davidson, *Lab Co-op* 15,497
David Ritchie, *SNP* 4,229
Keith Baldssara, *SSP* 2,522
Ms Isabel Nelson, *LD* 1,612
Rory O'Brien, *C.* 1,417
Lab Co-op majority 11,268 (44.58%)
1.27% swing SNP to Lab. Co-op
(1997: Lab. maj. 13,791 (42.04%))

GLASGOW RUTHERGLEN
*E.*51,855 *T.* 29,213 (56.34%)Lab Co-op
hold
*Tommy McAvoy, *Lab Co-op* 16,760
Ms Anne McLaughlin, *SNP* 4,135
David Jackson, *LD* 3,689
Malcolm Macaskill, *C.* 3,301
Bill Bonnar, *SSP* 1,328
Lab. Co-op majority 12,625 (43.22%)
0.48% swing SNP to Lab. Co-op
(1997: Lab. maj. 15,007 (42.25%))

GLASGOW SHETTLESTON
*E.*51,557 *T.* 20,465 (39.69%) Lab. hold
*David Marshall, *Lab.* 13,235
Jim Byrne, *SNP* 3,417
Ms Rosie Kane, *SSP* 1,396
Lewis Hutton, *LD* 1,105
Campbell Murdoch, *C.* 1,082
Murdo Ritchie, *Soc. Lab.* 230
Lab. majority 9,818 (47.97%)
5.60% swing Lab. to SNP
(1997: Lab. maj. 15,868 (59.18%))

GLASGOW SPRINGBURN
*E.*55,192 *T.* 24,104 (43.67%) Speaker
hold
*Rt. Hon. M. Martin, *Speaker* 16,053
Sandy Bain, *SNP* 4,675
Ms Carolyn Leckie, *SSP* 1,879
Daniel Houston, *Scot. U.* 1,289
Richard Silvester, *Ind.* 208
Speaker majority 11,378 (47.20%)
(1997: Lab. maj. 17,326 (54.87%))

GORDON
*E.*59,996 *T.* 35,001 (58.34%) LD hold
*Malcolm Bruce, *LD* 15,928
Mrs Nanette Milne, *C.* 8,049
Mrs Rhona Kemp, *SNP* 5,760
Ellis Thorpe, *Lab.* 4,730
John Sangster, *SSP* 534
LD majority 7,879 (22.51%)
2.97% swing C. to LD
(1997: Lab. maj. 6,997 (16.57%))

GREENOCK & INVERCLYDE
*E.*47,884 *T.* 28,419 (59.35%) Lab. hold
David Cairns, *Lab.* 14,929
Chic Brodie, *LD* 5,039
Andrew Murie, *SNP* 4,248
Alistair Haw, *C.* 3,000
Davey Landels, *SSP* 1,203
Lab. majority 9,890 (34.80%)
3.77% swing Lab. to LD
(1997: Lab. maj. 13,040 (37.59%))

HAMILTON NORTH & BELLSHILL
*E.*53,539 *T.* 30,404 (56.79%) Lab. hold
*Rt. Hon. Dr J. Reid, *Lab.* 18,786
Chris Stephens, *SNP* 5,225

Bill Frain Bell, *C.* 2,649
Keith Legg, *LD* 2,360
Ms Shareen Blackall, *SSP* 1,189
Steve Mayes, *Soc. Lab.* 195
Lab. majority 13,561 (44.60%)
0.16% swing Lab. to SNP
(1997: Lab. maj. 17,067 (44.92%))

HAMILTON SOUTH
*E.*46,665 *T.* 26,750 (57.32%) Lab. hold
*Bill Tynan, *Lab.* 15,965
John Wilson, *SNP* 5,190
John Oswald, *LD* 2,381
Neil Richardson, *C.* ,876
Ms Gena Mitchell, *SSP* 1,187
Ms Janice Murdoch, *UK Ind.* 151
Lab. majority 10,775 (40.28%)
3.85% swing Lab. to SNP
1999 Sep. by-election: Lab. maj. 556
(2.86%)
(1997: Lab. maj. 15,878 (47.98%))

INVERNESS EAST, NAIRN & LOCHABER
*E.*67,139 *T.* 42,461 (63.24%) Lab. hold
*David Stewart, *Lab.* 15,605
Angus MacNeil, *SNP* 10,889
Ms Patsy Kenton, *LD* 9,420
Richard Jenkins, *C.* 5,653
Steve Arnott, *SSP* 894
Lab. majority 4,716 (11.11%)
3.10% swing SNP to Lab.
(1997: Lab. maj. 2,339 (4.90%))

KILMARNOCK & LOUDOUN
*E.*61,049 *T.* 37,665 (61.70%) Lab. hold
*Des Browne, *Lab.* 19,926
John Brady, *SNP* 9,592
Donald Reece, *C.* 3,943
John Stewart, *LD* 3,177
Jason Muir, *SSP* 1,027
Lab. majority 10,334 (27.44%)
6.07% swing SNP to Lab.
(1997: Lab. maj. 7,256 (15.30%))

KIRKCALDY
*E.*51,559 *T.* 28,157 (54.61%)Lab Co-op
hold
*Dr Lewis Moonie, *Lab Co-op* 15,227
Ms Shirley-Anne Somerville, *SNP* 6,264
Scott Campbell, *C.* 3,013
Andrew Weston, *LD* 2,849
Dougie Kinnear, *SSP* 804
Lab. Co-op majority 8,963 (31.83%)
0.60% swing SNP to Lab. Co-op
(1997: Lab. maj. 10,710 (30.63%))

LINLITHGOW
*E.*54,599 *T.* 31,655 (57.98%) Lab. hold
*Tam Dalyell, *Lab.* 17,207
Jim Sibbald, *SNP* 8,078
Gordon Lindhurst, *C.* 2,836
Martin Oliver, *LD* 2,628
Eddie Cornoch, *SSP* 695
Ms Helen Cronin, *R & R Loony* 211
Lab. majority 9,129 (28.84%)
0.75% swing Lab. to SNP
(1997: Lab. maj. 10,838 (27.33%))

LIVINGSTON
*E.*64,850 *T.* 36,033 (55.56%) Lab. hold
*Rt. Hon. R. Cook, *Lab.* 19,108
Graham Sutherland, *SNP* 8,492

Gordon Mackenzie, *LD* 3,969
Ian Mowat, *C.* 2,995
Ms Wendy Milne, *SSP* 1,110
Robert Kingdon, *UK Ind.* 359
Lab. majority 10,616 (29.46%)
1.02% swing SNP to Lab.
(1997: Lab. maj. 11,747 (27.43%))

MIDLOTHIAN
*E.*48,625 *T.* 28,724 (59.07%) Lab. hold
David Hamilton, *Lab.* 15,145
Ian Goldie, *SNP* 6,131
Ms Jacqueline Bell, *LD* 3,686
Robin Traquair, *C.* 2,748
Bob Goupillot, *SSP* 837
Terence Holden, *ProLife* 177
Lab. majority 9,014 (31.38%)
1.69% swing SNP to Lab.
(1997: Lab. maj. 9,870 (28.00%))

MORAY
*E.*58,008 *T.* 33,223 (57.27%) SNP hold
Angus Robertson, *SNP* 10,076
Mrs Catriona Munro, *Lab.* 8,332
Frank Spencer-Nairn, *C.* 7,677
Ms Linda Gorn, *LD* 5,224
Ms Norma Anderson, *SSP* 821
Bill Jappy, *Ind.* 802
Nigel Kenyon, *UK Ind.* 291
SNP majority 1,744 (5.25%)
8.25% swing SNP to Lab.
(1997: SNP maj. 5,566 (14.00%))

MOTHERWELL & WISHAW
*E.*52,418 *T.* 29,673 (56.61%) Lab. hold
*Frank Roy, *Lab.* 16,681
Jim McGuigan, *SNP* 5,725
Mark Nolan, *C.* 3,155
Iain Brown, *LD* 2,791
Stephen Smellie, *SSP* 1,260
Ms Claire Watt, *Soc. Lab.* 61
Lab. majority 10,956 (36.92%)
1.00% swing SNP to Lab.
(1997: Lab. maj. 12,791 (34.93%))

OCHIL
*E.*57,554 *T.* 35,303 (61.34%) Lab. hold
*Martin O'Neill, *Lab.* 16,004
Keith Brown, *SNP* 10,655
Alasdair Campbell, *C.* 4,235
Paul Edie, *LD* 3,253
Ms Pauline Thompson, *SSP* 751
Flash Gordon Approaching, *Loony* 405
Lab. majority 5,349 (15.15%)
2.26% swing SNP to Lab.
(1997: Lab. maj. 4,652 (10.63%))

ORKNEY & SHETLAND
*E.*31,909 *T.* 16,733 (52.44%) LD hold
Alistair Carmichael, *LD* 6,919
Robert Mochrie, *Lab.* 3,444
John Firth, *C.* 3,121
John Mowat, *SNP* 2,473
Peter Andrews, *SSP* 776
LD majority 3,475 (20.77%)
6.48% swing LD to Lab.
(1997: LD maj. 6,968 (33.72%))

PAISLEY NORTH
*E.*47,994 *T.* 27,153 (56.58%) Lab. hold
*Ms Irene Adams, *Lab.* 15,058
George Adam, *SNP* 5,737
Ms Jane Hook, *LD* 2,709
Craig Stevenson, *C.* 2,404
Jim Halfpenny, *SSP* 982
Robert Graham, *ProLife* 263
Lab. majority 9,321 (34.33%)
1.61% swing Lab. to SNP
(1997: Lab. maj. 12,814 (37.54%))

PAISLEY SOUTH
*E.*53,351 *T.* 30,536 (57.24%) Lab. hold
*Douglas Alexander, *Lab.* 17,830
Brian Lawson, *SNP* 5,920
Brian O'Malley, *LD* 3,178
Andrew Cossar, *C.* 2,301
Ms Frances Curran, *SSP* 835
Ms Patricia Graham, *ProLife* 346
Terence O'Donnell, *Ind.* 126
Lab. majority 11,910 (39.00%)
2.44% swing Lab. to SNP
(1997 Nov by-election: Lab. maj. 2,731)
(1997: Lab. maj. 12,750 (34.13%))

PERTH
*E.*61,497 *T.* 37,816 (61.49%) SNP hold
Ms Annabelle Ewing, *SNP* 11,237
Miss Elizabeth Smith, *C.* 11,191
Ms Marion Dingwall, *Lab.* 9,638
Ms Vicki Harris, *LD* 4,853
Frank Byrne, *SSP* 899
SNP majority 48 (0.13%)
3.46% swing SNP to C.
(1997: SNP maj. 3,141 (7.05%))

RENFREWSHIRE WEST
*E.*52,889 *T.* 33,497 (63.33%) Lab gain
James Sheridan, *Lab.* 15,720
Ms Carol Puthucheary, *SNP* 7,145
David Sharpe, *C.* 5,522
Ms Clare Hamblen, *LD* 4,185
Ms Arlene Nunnery, *SSP* 925
Lab. majority 8,575 (25.60%)
2.77% swing SNP to Lab.
(1997: Lab. maj. 7,979 (20.05%))

ROSS, SKYE & INVERNESS WEST
*E.*56,522 *T.* 34,812 (61.59%) LD hold
*Rt. Hon. C. Kennedy, *LD* 18,832
Donald Crichton, *Lab.* 5,880
Ms Jean Urquhart, *SNP* 4,901
Angus Laing, *C.* 3,096
Dr Eleanor Scott, *Green* 699
Stuart Topp, *SSP* 683
Philip Anderson, *UK Ind.* 456
James Crawford, *Country* 265
LD majority 12,952 (37.21%)
13.57% swing Lab. to LD
(1997: LD maj. 4,019 (10.06%))

ROXBURGH & BERWICKSHIRE
*E.*47,059 *T.* 28,797 (61.19%) LD hold
*Archy Kirkwood, *LD* 14,044
George Turnbull, *C.* 6,533
Ms C. Maxwell-Stuart, *Lab.* 4,498

Roderick Campbell, *SNP* 2,806
Ms Amanda Millar, *SSP* 463
Peter Neilson, *UK Ind.* 453
LD majority 7,511 (26.08%)
1.73% swing C. to LD
(1997: LD maj. 7,906 (22.63%))

STIRLING
*E.*53,097 *T.* 35,930 (67.67%) Lab. hold
*Ms Anne McGuire, *Lab.* 15,175
Geoff Mawdsley, *C.* 8,901
Ms Fiona Macaulay, *SNP* 5,877
Clive Freeman, *LD* 4,208
Dr Clarke Mullen, *SSP* 1,012
Mark Ruskell, *Green* 757
Lab. majority 6,274 (17.46%)
1.27% swing C. to Lab.
(1997: Lab. maj. 6,411 (14.93%))

STRATHKELVIN & BEARSDEN
*E.*62,729 *T.* 41,486 (66.14%) Lab. hold
John Lyons, *Lab.* 19,250
Gordon Macdonald, *LD* 7,533
Calum Smith, *SNP* 6,675
Murray Roxburgh, *C.* 6,635
Willie Telfer, *SSP* 1,393
Lab. majority 11,717 (28.24%)
7.44% swing Lab. to LD
(1997: Lab. maj. 16,292 (32.77%))

TAYSIDE NORTH
*E.*61,645 *T.* 38,517 (62.48%) SNP hold
Peter Wishart, *SNP* 15,441
Murdo Fraser, *C.* 12,158
Thomas Docherty, *Lab.* 5,715
Ms Julia Robertson, *LD* 4,363
Ms Rosie Adams, *SSP* 620
Ms Tina MacDonald, *Ind.* 220
SNP majority 3,283 (8.52%)
0.30% swing SNP to C.
(1997: SNP maj. 4,160 (9.13%))

TWEEDDALE, ETTRICK & LAUDERDALE
*E.*51,966 *T.* 33,217 (63.92%) LD hold
*Michael Moore, *LD* 14,035
Keith Geddes, *Lab.* 8,878
Andrew Brocklehurst, *C* .5,118
Richard Thomson, *SNP* 4,108
Norman Lockhart, *SSP* 695
John Hein, *Lib.* 383
LD majority 5,157 (15.53%)
5.86% swing Lab. to LD
(1997: LD maj. 1,489 (3.81%))

WESTERN ISLES
*E.*21,807 *T.* 13,159 (60.34%) Lab. hold
*Calum MacDonald, *Lab.* 5,924
Alasdair Nicholson, *SNP* 4,850
Douglas Taylor, *C.* 1,250
John Horne, *LD* 849
Ms Joanne Telfer, *SSP* 286
Lab. majority 1,074 (8.16%)
7.02% swing Lab. to SNP
(1997: Lab. majority 3,576 (22.20%))

NORTHERN IRELAND

ANTRIM EAST
*E.*60,897 *T.* 36,000 (59.12%) UUP hold
*Roy Beggs, UUP	13,101
Sammy Wilson, DUP	12,973
John Mathews, Alliance	4,483
Danny O'Connor, SDLP	2,641
Robert Mason, Ind.	1,092
Ms Jeanette Graffin, SF	903
Alan Greer, C.	807

UUP majority 128 (0.36%)
9.48% swing UUP to DUP
(1997: UUP maj. 6,389 (18.60%)))

ANTRIM NORTH
*E.*74,451 *T.* 49,217 (66.11%) DUP hold
*Revd Ian Paisley, DUP	24,539
Lexie Scott, UUP	10,315
Sean Farren, SDLP	8,283
John Kelly, SF	4,822
Miss Jayne Dunlop, Alliance	1,258

DUP majority 14,224 (28.90%)
3.01% swing UUP to DUP
(1997: DUP maj. 10,574 (22.89%)))

ANTRIM SOUTH
*E.*70,651 *T.* 44,158 (62.50%) UUP gain
David Burnside, UUP	16,366
*Revd Robert McCrea, DUP	15,355
Sean McKee, SDLP	5,336
Martin Meehan, SF	4,160
David Ford, Alliance	1,969
Norman Boyd, NI Unionist	972

UUP majority 1,011 (2.29%)
10.21% swing UUP to DUP
(2000 Sep. by-election: DUP maj. 822)
(1997: UUP maj. 16,611 (41.33%)))

BELFAST EAST
*E.*58,455 *T.* 36,829 (63.00%) DUP hold
*Peter Robinson, DUP	15,667
Tim Lemon, UUP	8,550
Dr David Alderdice, Alliance	5,832
David Ervine, PUP	3,669
Joe O'Donnell, SF	1,237
Ms Ciara Farren, SDLP	880
Terry Dick, C.	800
Joe Bell, WP	123
Rainbow George Weiss, Ind. Vote	71

DUP majority 7,117 (19.32%)
1.01% swing UUP to DUP
(1997: DUP maj. 6,754 (17.30%)))

BELFAST NORTH
*E.*60,941 *T.* 40,932 (67.17%) DUP gain
Nigel Dodds, DUP	16,718
Gerry Kelly, SF	10,331
Alban Maginness, SDLP	8,592
*Cecil Walker, UUP	4,904
Ms Marcella Delaney, WP	253
Rainbow George Weiss, Ind. Vote	134

DUP majority 6,387 (15.60%)
(1997: UUP maj. 13,024 (31.42%)))

BELFAST SOUTH
*E.*59,436 *T.* 37,952 (63.85%) UUP hold
*Revd M. Smyth, UUP	17,008
Dr Alasdair McDonnell, SDLP	11,609
Prof Monica McWilliams, Women's Co.	2,968

Alex Maskey, SF	2,894
Ms Geraldine Rice, Alliance	2,042
Ms Dawn Purvis, PUP	1,112
Paddy Lynn, WP	204
Rainbow George Weiss, Ind. Vote	115

UUP majority 5,399 (14.23%)
1.29% swing SDLP to UUP
(1997: UUP maj. 4,600 (11.65%))

BELFAST WEST
*E.*59,617 *T.* 40,982 (68.74%) SF hold
*Gerry Adams, SF	27,096
Alex Attwood, SDLP	7,754
The Rev Eric Smyth, DUP	2,641
Chris McGimpsey, UUP	2,541
John Lowry, WP	736
Mr David Kerr, Third	116
Rainbow George Weiss, Ind. Vote	98

SF majority 19,342 (47.20%)
14.98% swing SDLP to SF
(1997: SF maj. 7,909 (17.24%))

DOWN NORTH
*E.*63,212 *T.* 37,189 (58.83%) UUP gain
Lady Sylvia Hermon, UUP	20,833
*Robert McCartney, UKU	13,509
Ms Marietta Farrell, SDLP	1,275
Julian Robertson, C.	815
Chris Carter, Ind.	444
Eamon McConvey, SF	313

UUP majority 7,324 (19.69%)
11.83% swing UKU to UUP
(1997: UKU maj. 1,449 (3.96%))

DOWN SOUTH
*E.*73,519 *T.* 52,074 (70.83%) SDLP hold
*Eddie McGrady, SDLP	24,136
Mick Murphy, SF	10,278
Dermot Nesbitt, UUP	9,173
Jim Wells, DUP	7,802
Ms Betty Campbell, Alliance	685

SDLP majority 13,858 (26.61%)
7.97% swing SDLP to SF
(1997: SDLP maj. 9,933 (20.08%))

FERMANAGH & SOUTH TYRONE
*E.*66,640 *T.* 51,974 (77.99%) SF gain
Ms Michelle Gildernew, SF	17,739
James Cooper, UUP	17,686
Tommy Gallagher, SDLP	9,706
Jim Dixon, Ind. UU	6,843

SF majority 53 (0.10%)
14.22% swing UUP to SF
(1997: UUP maj. 13,688 (28.34%))

FOYLE
*E.*70,943 *T.* 48,879 (68.90%) SDLP hold
*John Hume, SDLP	24,538
Mitchel McLaughlin, SF	12,988
William Hay, DUP	7,414
Andrew Davidson, UUP	3,360
Colm Cavanagh, Alliance	579

SDLP majority 11,550 (23.63%)
2.47% swing SDLP to SF
(1997: SDLP maj. 13,664 (28.57%))

LAGAN VALLEY
*E.*72,671 *T.* 45,941 (63.22%) UUP hold
*Jeffrey Donaldson, UUP	25,966
Seamus Close, Alliance	7,624
Edwin Poots, DUP	6,164

Ms Patricia Lewsley, SDLP	3,462
Paul Butler, SF	2,725

UUP majority 18,342 (39.93%)
0.86% swing Alliance to UUP
(1997: UUP maj. 16,925 (38.20%))

LONDONDERRY EAST
*E.*60,276 *T.* 39,869 (66.14%) DUP gain
Gregory Campbell, DUP	12,813
*William Ross, UUP	10,912
John Dallat, SDLP	8,298
Francie Brolly, SF	6,221
Mrs Yvonne Boyle, Alliance	1,625

DUP majority 1,901 (4.77%)
7.36% swing UUP to DUP
(1997: UUP maj. 3,794 (9.95%))

NEWRY & ARMAGH
*E.*72,466 *T.* 55,621 (76.75%) SDLP hold
*Seamus Mallon, SDLP	20,784
Conor Murphy, SF	17,209
Paul Berry, DUP	10,795
Mrs Sylvia McRoberts, UUP	6,833

SDLP majority 3,575 (6.43%)
7.75% swing SDLP to SF
(1997: SDLP maj. 4,889 (9.17%))

STRANGFORD
*E.*72,192 *T.* 43,254 (59.92%) DUP gain
Mrs Iris Robinson, DUP	18,532
*David McNarry, UUP	17,422
Kieran McCarthy, Alliance	2,902
Danny McCarthy, SDLP	2,646
Liam Johnstone, SF	930
Cedric Wilson, NI Unionist	822

DUP majority 1,110 (2.57%)
8.32% swing UUP to DUP
(1997: UUP maj. 5,852 (14.07%))

TYRONE WEST
*E.*60,739 *T.* 48,530 (79.90%) SF gain
Pat Doherty, SF	19,814
*William Thompson, UUP	14,774
Ms Brid Rodgers, SDLP	13,942

SF majority 5,040 (10.39%)
7.05% swing UUP to SF
(1997: UUP maj. 1,161 (2.51%))

ULSTER MID
*E.*61,390 *T.* 49,936 (81.34%) SF hold
*Martin McGuinness, SF	25,502
Ian McCrea, DUP	15,549
Ms Eilis Haughey, SDLP	8,376
Francie Donnelly, WP	509

SF majority 9,953 (19.93%)
8.11% swing DUP to SF
(1997: SF maj. 1,883 (3.71%))

UPPER BANN
*E.*72,574 *T.* 51,036 (70.32%) UUP hold
*Rt. Hon. D. Trimble, UUP	17,095
David Simpson, DUP	15,037
Dr Dara O'Hagan, SF	10,770
Ms Dolores Kelly, SDLP	7,607
Tom French, WP	527

UUP majority 2,058 (4.03%)
14.05% swing UUP to DUP
(1997: UUP maj. 9,252 (19.36%))

IPSWICH
(22 November 2001)
*E.*68,244 *T.* 40.2 %

Chris Mole, *Lab.*	11,881
Paul West, *C.*	7,794
Ms Tessa Munt, *LD*	6,146
Dave Cooper, *CPA*	581
Jonathan Wright, *UK Ind.*	276
Tony Slade, *Green*	255
John Ramirez, *LCA*	236
Peter Leech, *Soc. All.*	152
Nicholas Winskill, *English Independence Party*	84
Lab. majority	4,087

OGMORE
(14 February 2002)
*E.*52,209 *T.*35.2%

Huw Irranca-Davies, *Lab.*	9,548
Bleddyn Hancock, *PC*	3,827
Veronica Watkins, *LD*	1,608
Guto Bebb, *C.*	1,377
Christopher Herriot, *Soc. Lab.*	1,152
Jonathan Spink, *Green*	250
Jeff Hurford, *WSA*	205
Leslie Edwards, *Loony*	187
Captain Beany, *Bean*	122
Revd David Braid, *Ind.*	100
Lab. majority	5,721

The Government

Prime Minister, First Lord of the Treasury and Minister for the Civil Service
The Rt. Hon. Anthony (Tony) Blair, MP, since May 1997
Deputy Prime Minister and First Secretary of State
The Rt. Hon. John Prescott, MP, *Deputy Prime Minister* since May 1997 and *First Secretary of State* since June 2001
Chancellor of the Exchequer
The Rt. Hon. Gordon Brown, MP, since May 1997
President of the Council and Leader of the House of Commons
The Rt. Hon. Robin Cook, MP, since June 2001
Lord Chancellor
The Rt. Hon. The Lord Irvine of Lairg, PC, QC, since May 1997
Secretary of State for Foreign and Commonwealth Affairs
The Rt. Hon. Jack Straw, MP, since June 2001
Secretary of State for the Home Department
The Rt. Hon. David Blunkett, MP, since June 2001
Secretary of State for Environment, Food and Rural Affairs
The Rt. Hon. Margaret Beckett, MP, since June 2001
Secretary of State for International Development
The Rt. Hon. Clare Short, MP, since May 1997
Secretary of State for Transport
The Rt. Hon. Alistair Darling, MP, since May 2002
Secretary of State for Health
The Rt. Hon. Alan Milburn, MP, since October 1999
Secretary of State for Northern Ireland
The Rt. Hon. Dr John Reid, MP, since January 2001
Secretary of State for Wales
The Rt. Hon. Paul Murphy, MP, since July 1999
Secretary of State for Defence
The Rt. Hon. Geoff Hoon, MP, since October 1999
Secretary of State for Work and Pensions
The Rt. Hon. Andrew Smith, MP, since May 2002
Secretary of State for Scotland
The Rt. Hon. Helen Liddell, MP, since January 2001
Lord Privy Seal and Leader of the House of Lords
The Rt. Hon. The Lord Williams of Mostyn, QC, since June 2001
Secretary of State for Trade and Industry
The Rt. Hon. Patricia Hewitt, MP, since June 2001
Secretary of State for Education and Skills
The Rt. Hon. Estelle Morris, MP, since June 2001
Secretary of State for Culture, Media and Sport
The Rt. Hon. Tessa Jowell, MP, since June 2001
Parliamentary Secretary to the Treasury (Chief Whip)
The Rt. Hon. Hilary Armstrong, MP, since June 2001
Minister Without Portfolio and Party Chair
The Rt. Hon. Charles Clarke, MP, since June 2001
Chief Secretary to the Treasury
The Rt. Hon. Paul Boateng, MP, since May 2002

The Minister of State at the Department for Work and Pensions with responsibility for Work, and the Government Chief Whip in the House of Lords attend Cabinet meetings although they are not members of the Cabinet.

LAW OFFICERS

Attorney-General
The Rt. Hon. Lord Goldsmith, QC, since June 2001
Lord Advocate
Colin Boyd, QC, since February 2000
Solicitor-General
The Rt. Hon. Harriet Harman, MP, QC, since June 2001
Solicitor-General for Scotland
Mrs Elish Angiolini, QC, since November 2001
Advocate-General for Scotland
Dr Lynda Clark, QC, MP, since May 1999

MINISTERS OF STATE

Cabinet Office
Douglas Alexander, MP
The Rt. Hon. The Lord MacDonald of Tradeston, CBE (*Chancellor of the Duchy of Lancaster*)
Culture, Media and Sport
The Rt. Hon. Richard Caborn, MP (*Sport*)
The Rt. Hon. The Baroness Blackstone (*Arts and Spokesperson in the House of Lords*)
Defence
The Rt. Hon. Adam Ingram, MP (*Armed Forces*)
Office of the Deputy Prime Minister
The Rt. Hon. Lord Rooker (*Housing and Planning*)
The Rt. Hon. Nick Raynsford, MP (*Local Government and the Regions*)
Ms Barbara Roche, MP (*Social Exclusion, Regional Co-ordination and Deputy Minister for Women*)
Education and Skills
David Miliband, MP (*School Standards*)
Margaret Hodge, MBE, MP (*Lifelong Learning and Higher Education*)
Environment, Food and Rural Affairs
The Rt. Hon. Michael Meacher, MP (*Environment*)
The Rt. Hon. Alun Michael, MP (*Rural Affairs*)
Foreign and Commonwealth Office
The Rt. Hon. Peter Hain, MP (*Europe*)
The Rt. Hon. The Baroness Symons of Vernham Dean (*Trade*)
Health
The Rt. Hon. John Hutton, MP (*NHS and Delivery*)
Jacqui Smith, MP (*Social and Long Term Care, Disability and Mental Health*)
Home Office
The Rt. Hon. The Lord Falconer of Thoroton, QC (*Criminal Justice, Sentencing and Law Reform*)
The Rt. Hon. John Denham, MP (*Police and Crime Reduction, Community Safety and Young People*)
Beverley Hughes, MP (*Citizenship, Immigration and Community Cohesion*)
Northern Ireland Office
Jane Kennedy, MP (*Security, Policing and Prisons*)
Trade and Industry
Stephen Timms, MP (*E-Commerce and Competitiveness*)
The Rt. Hon. The Baroness Symons of Vernham Dean (*Trade and Investment*)

Brian Wilson, MP (*Energy and Construction*)
Alan Johnson, MP (*Employment Relations, Industry and the Regions*)
Transport
The Rt. Hon. John Spellar, MP (*Transport*)
Treasury
The Rt. Hon. Dawn Primarolo, MP (*Paymaster-General*)
Ms Ruth Kelly, MP (*Financial Secretary*)
John Healey, MP (*Economic Secretary*)
Work and Pensions
The Rt. Hon. Nick Brown, MP (*Work*)
The Rt. Hon. Ian McCartney, MP (*Pensions*)

UNDER-SECRETARIES OF STATE

Culture, Media and Sport
Dr Kim Howells, MP (*Tourism, Film and Broadcasting*)
Defence
Dr Lewis Moonie, MP (*Veterans*)
The Lord Bach of Lutterworth (*Defence Procurement*)
Office of the Deputy Prime Minister
Tony McNulty, MP (*Housing, Planning and Urban Policy*)
Christopher Leslie, MP (*Fire Service, Building Regulations and E-Local Government*)
Education and Skills
The Baroness Ashton of Upholland (*Early Years and School Standards*)
Ivan Lewis, MP (*Adult Learning*)
Stephen Twigg, MP (*Young People and Learning*)
Environment, Food and Rural Affairs
Elliot Morley, MP (*Animal Health and Welfare, Fisheries, Whaling, Forestry, Agri-environment Schemes, Floods and Coastal Defence*)
The Lord Whitty of Camberwell (*Food, Farming and Waterways*)
Foreign and Commonwealth Office
Mike O'Brien, MP (*Middle East, North Africa, South and South East Asia and Arms Control*)
The Baroness Amos (*Sub-Saharan Africa*)
Dr Denis MacShane, MP (*South East Europe and Latin America*)
Health
Ms Hazel Blears, MP (*Public Health*)
The Lord Hunt of Kings Heath, OBE (*Performance and Quality in the House of Lords*)
David Lammy, MP (*Emergency Care and Public Involvement*)
Home Office
Hilary Benn, MP (*Community and Custodial Provision*)
Robert Ainsworth, MP (*Anti-Drugs Co-ordination and Organised Crime*)
Michael Wills, MP (*Criminal Justice System – Information Technology*)
The Lord Filkin, CBE (*Race Equality, Community, European and International Policy*)
International Development
Ms Sally Keeble, MP
Northern Ireland Office
Desmond Browne, MP (*Criminal Justice, Victims and Human Rights*)
Scotland
Ms Anne McGuire, MP
Trade and Industry
The Lord Sainsbury of Turville, KG (*Science and Innovation*)

Ms Melanie Johnson, MP (*Competition, Consumers and Markets*)
Nigel Griffiths, MP, (*Small Business*)
Transport
David Jamieson, MP
Wales Office
Don Touhig, MP
Work and Pensions
The Rt. Hon. The Baroness Hollis of Heigham
Malcolm Wicks, MP (*Work*)
Ms Maria Eagle, MP (*Disabled People*)

GOVERNMENT WHIPS

HOUSE OF LORDS
Captain of the Honourable Corps of the Gentlemen-at-Arms (*Chief Whip*)
The Lord Grocott
Captain of The Queen's Bodyguard of the Yeomen of the Guard (*Deputy Chief Whip*)
The Rt. Hon The Lord McIntosh of Haringey
Lords-in-Waiting
Lord Davies of Oldham
The Lord Bassam of Brighton
Baronesses-in-Waiting
The Baroness Farrington of Ribbleton
The Baroness Andrews, OBE
The Baroness Crawley

HOUSE OF COMMONS
Parliamentary Secretary to the Treasury (*Chief Whip*)
The Rt. Hon. Hilary Armstrong, MP
Treasurer of HM Household (*Deputy Chief Whip*)
Keith Hill, MP
Comptroller of HM Household
Thomas McAvoy, MP
Vice-Chamberlain of HM Household
Gerry Sutcliffe, MP
Lords Commissioners of HM Treasury
John Heppell, MP; Nick Ainger, MP; Ian Pearson, MP; Jim Fitzpatrick, MP; Philip Woolas, MP
Assistant Whips
Fraser Kemp, MP; Angela Smith, MP; Ivor Caplin, MP; Dan Norris, MP; Jim Murphy, MP; Derek Twigg, MP; Joan Ryan, MP

Government Departments and Public Offices

This section covers central Government departments, executive agencies, regulatory bodies, other statutory independent organisations, and bodies which are government-financed or whose head is appointed by a Government Minister.

THE CIVIL SERVICE

Under the Next Steps programme, launched in 1988, many semi-autonomous executive agencies were established to carry out much of the work of the Civil Service. Executive agencies operate within a framework set by the responsible minister which specifies policies, objectives and available resources. All executive agencies are set annual performance targets by their Minister. Each agency has a chief executive, who is responsible for the day-to-day operations of the agency and who is accountable to the minister for the use of resources and for meeting the agency's targets. The minister accounts to Parliament for the work of the agency. Nearly 80 per cent of civil servants now work in executive agencies. In April 2001 there were about 506,450 permanent civil servants.

The Senior Civil Service was created in 1996 and on 1 April 2001 comprised 3,850 staff from Permanent Secretary to the former Grade 5 level, including all agency chief executives. All Government departments and executive agencies are now responsible for their own pay and grading systems for civil servants outside the Senior Civil Service. In practice the grades of the former Open structure are still in use in some organisations. The Open structure represented the following:

Grade	Title
1	Permanent Secretary
1A	Second Permanent Secretary
2	Deputy Secretary
3	Under-Secretary
4	Chief Scientific Officer B, Professional and Technology Directing A
5	Assistant Secretary, Deputy Chief Scientific Officer, Professional and Technology Directing B
6	Senior Principal, Senior Principal Scientific Officer, Professional and Technology Superintending Grade
7	Principal, Principal Scientific Officer, Principal Professional and Technology Officer

SALARIES – 2002–3

MINISTERIAL SALARIES *from 1 April 2002*

Ministers who are Members of the House of Commons receive a parliamentary salary (£55,118) in addition to their ministerial salary.

Prime Minister	£116,436
Cabinet minister (Commons)	£69,861
†Cabinet minister (Lords)	£94,826
Minister of State (Commons)	£36,240
Minister of State (Lords)	£74,040
Parliamentary Under-Secretary (Commons)	£27,506
Parliamentary Under-Secretary (Lords)	£64,485

† Except the Lord Chancellor, who receives a salary of £180,045

SPECIAL ADVISORS' SALARIES *from 1 April 2002*

Special advisers to Government Ministers are paid out of public funds; their salaries are negotiated individually, but are usually in the range £34,001 to £90,000.

CIVIL SERVICE SALARIES *from 1 April 2002*

Senior Civil Service (SCS)

Secretary of the Cabinet and Head of the Home Civil Service as at January 2002	£175,000–£179,999
Permanent Secretary	£115,000–£245,000
Band 3	£87,125–£184,500
Band 2	£70,725–£148,625
Band 1	£51,250–£107,625

A new Senior Civil Service pay system was introduced from 1 April 2002 with three rather than nine pay bands.

Staff are placed in pay bands according to their level of responsibility and taking account of other factors such as experience and marketability. Movement within and between bands is based on performance.

Other Civil Servants

Following the delegation of responsibility for pay and grading to Government departments and agencies from 1 April 1996, it is no longer possible to show service-wide pay rates for staff outside the Senior Civil Service. The following table will however give an indication of the percentage of civil servants at a given salary level.

Non-Industrial Staff by Gross Salary Band
as at 1 April 2001

Salary Band	Total Non SCS	Per Cent of Total
£5,001–£10,000	21,460	5.13
£10,001–£15,000	146,220	34.97
£15,001–£20,000	108,000	25.83
£20,001–£25,000	76,420	18.28
£25,001–£30,000	31,460	7.52
£30,001–£35,000	14,830	3.55
£35,001–£40,000	8,070	1.93
£40,001–£45,000	5,910	1.41
£45,001–£50,000	3,150	0.75
£50,001–£55,000	1,820	0.43
£55,001–£60,000	690	0.17
£60,001–£65,000	70	0.02
£65,001–£70,000	20	0.00
£70,001–£75,000	10	0.00
£75,001 +	0	0.00

Source: Civil Service Statistics 2001

GOVERNMENT DEPARTMENTS

THE CABINET OFFICE
70 Whitehall, London SW1A 2AS
Tel: 020-7270 1234
Web: www.cabinet-office.gov.uk

The Cabinet Office has four main roles: to support the Prime Minister in leading the Government; to support the Government in transacting its business; to lead and support the reform and delivery programme and to co-ordinate security and intelligence. The Department is headed by the Minister for the Cabinet Office (and Chancellor of the Duchy of Lancaster) and has one Minister of State. The Cabinet Office has two Executive Agencies: The Government Car and Despatch Agency (GCDA) and the Central Office of Information (COI) which is a department in its own right.

Prime Minister and Minister for the Civil Service, The Rt. Hon. Anthony (Tony) Blair, MP
  Parliamentary Private Secretary, David Hanson, MP
Minister for the Cabinet Office and Chancellor of the Duchy of Lancaster, The Rt. Hon. The Lord Macdonald of Tradeston, CBE
  Principal Private Secretary (SCS), Mark Kieran
  Parliamentary Private Secretary, Alan Campbell, MP
Minister of State, Douglas Alexander, MP
  Private Secretary, Louisa-Jayne O'Neill
  Parliamentary Private Secretary, Lawrie Quinn, MP
Minister without Portfolio and Party Chair, The Rt. Hon. Charles Clarke, MP
  Parliamentary Private Secretary, Gareth Thomas, MP
Secretary of the Cabinet and Head of the Home Civil Service, Sir Andrew Turnbull, KCB, CVO
  Principal Private Secretary (SCS), Ian Fletcher
Chief Scientific Adviser, Prof. D. King
Security and Intelligence Co-ordinator and Permanent Secretary, Sir David Omand
  Principal Private Secretary (SCS), Sebastian Madden

ECONOMIC AND DOMESTIC SECRETARIAT
Head (SCS), P. Britton, CB
Deputy Head (SCS), Ms L. Bell

DEFENCE AND OVERSEAS AFFAIRS SECRETARIAT
Prime Minister's Foreign Policy Adviser and Head of Secretariat, Sir David Manning, KCMG
Deputy Head (SCS), T. McKane

EUROPEAN SECRETARIAT
Prime Minister's European Policy Adviser and Head of Secretariat, Sir Stephen Wall, KCMG, LVO
Deputy Head (SCS), M. Donnelly, CMG

CEREMONIAL SECRETARIAT
Ashley House, 2 Monck Street, London SW1P 2BQ.
Tel: 020-7276 2728
Honours Nomination Unit: Tel: 020-7276 2775
Ceremonial Officer (SCS), G. Catto

CIVIL CONTINGENCIES SECRETARIAT
10 Great George Street, London SW1P 3AE.
Head (SCS), M. Granatt, CB
Deputy Head (SCS), Dr J. Fuller

MACHINERY OF GOVERNMENT SECRETARIAT
Director (SCS), Ms H. Ghosh
Deputy Director (SCS), Ms S. Gray

OFFICE OF THE COMMISSIONER FOR PUBLIC APPOINTMENTS (OCPA)
3rd Floor, 35 Great Smith Street, London SW1P 3BQ.
Tel: 020-7276 2625
The Commissioner for Public Appointments is responsible for monitoring, regulating and providing advice to departments on ministerial appointments to public bodies. The Commissioner publishes a Code of Practice, guidance for departments and an annual report. The Commissioner has the right to investigate and will also deal with complaints.
Commissioner for Public Appointments, Dame Rennie Fritchie, DBE
Secretary to the Commissioner and Head of the Office (SCS), J. Barron

OFFICE OF THE CIVIL SERVICE COMMISSIONERS (OCSC)
3rd Floor, 35 Great Smith Street, London SW1P 3BQ.
Tel: 020-7276 2615
The independent Civil Service Commissioners are the custodians of the rules for selection on merit by fair and open competition; they publish a Recruitment Code and audit departments and agencies' performance against it. When senior posts are opened to people from outside the Service the Commissioners normally chair the recruitment process. The Commissioners also act as an independent appeals body under the Civil Service Code.
First Commissioner, Baroness Usha Prashar, CBE
Commissioners (part-time), D. Bell; P. Bounds; J. Boyle; Ms B. Curtis; Ms S. Forbes, CBE; Dame Rennie Fritchie; Prof. E. Gallagher, CBE; H. Hamill, CB; G. Lemos, CMG; A. MacDonald, CB; G. Maddrell; Ms G. Peacock; Dr M. Semple, OBE
Secretary to the Commissioners and Head of the Office (SCS), Jim Barron

REGULATORY IMPACT UNIT
3rd Floor, 35 Great Smith Street, London SW1P 3BQ.
Tel: 020-7276 2193
The Regulatory Impact Unit assists Government Ministers and Departments in finding the right balance between under-regulating (and so failing to protect the public) and over-regulating (and so failing to preserve freedoms, or creating excessive burdens on business). The Unit also investigates ways of reducing bureaucracy and red tape in the public and private sectors, and works with and supports the Better Regulation Task Force.
Director (SCS), P. Wynn Owen
Deputy Directors (SCS), M. Courtney; Ms J. Cruickshank; Ms S. Grey; Ms C. Potts; Dr P. Rushbrook

THE PRIME MINISTER'S DELIVERY UNIT
53 Parliament Street, London SW1A 2NG.
Tel: 020-7276 3515
To strengthen the capacity of Whitehall to deliver the Government's key objectives the Prime Minister established the Delivery Unit – based in the Cabinet Office in June 2001. The Unit reports to the Prime Minister under the day-to-day supervision of the Minister for the Cabinet Office, Lord Macdonald. The role of the Unit is to ensure that the Government achieves its priority objectives during this Parliament across the key areas of public service: health, education, crime, asylum and transport. The Unit's remit will expand later in 2002 to include priorities in the other main domestic service delivery departments. The Unit's work is carried out by a team of staff with experience of delivery, drawn

from the public and private sectors.
Prime Minister's Chief Adviser on Delivery, Prof. M.
   Barber
Deputy Head of Unit (SCS), W. Jordan

OFFICE OF THE E-ENVOY

Stockley House, 130 Wilton Road, Victoria, London
SW1V 1LQ. Tel: 020-7276 3300
The Office of the E-Envoy was set-up in September 1999.
In 2000, the Central IT Unit, Knowledge Network, and
New Media Team were incorporated into the work of the
Office of the E-Envoy (OEE). Its purpose is to promote
the use of e-technology to catalyse transformation in the
public sector and to support the Prime Minister on the
Government's overall strategy for making the UK a
leading online economy. The Office works with partners
in the public, private and voluntary sectors and
internationally.
E-Envoy, A. Pinder

STRATEGY UNIT

Admiralty Arch, The Mall, London SW1A 2WH
The Strategy Unit (SU) is the result of a merger between
the Performance and Innovation Unit (PIU) and the
Prime Minister's Forward Strategy Unit (PMFSU). The
PIU was created in 1998 to improve the capacity of
Government to address strategic, crosscutting issues and
promote innovation in the development of policy and in
the delivery of the Government's objectives. The PMFSU
was created in July 2001 to provide the Prime Minister
with long-range policy analysis and thinking. The merged
units continue to play the same role, tackling issues on a
project basis, and focussing on long term problems that
cross public sector institutional boundaries.
Director (SCS), G. Mulgan
Deputy Director (SCS), J. Rentoul

THE PRIME MINISTER'S OFFICE OF PUBLIC SERVICES
REFORM

53 Parliament Street, London SW1A 2NG.
Tel: 020-7276 3528
The reform and modernisation of the public services is
the Government's top priority. To strengthen the
Government's ability to deliver the change in public
services, the Prime Minister established the Office of
Public Services Reform based in the Cabinet Office. This
new Unit reports directly to the Prime Minister through
the Cabinet Secretary. The Office's role is to advise the
Prime Minister and Departments on how the
Government's commitment to radical reform of the Civil
Service and public services can be taken forward. It will
cover the full range of public services, including those
provided by central and local government, as well as other
public bodies.
Prime Minister's Chief Adviser on Public Services Reform,
Ms W. Thomson

CIVIL SERVICE CORPORATE MANAGEMENT AND
REFORM

Head of CSCMR (SCS), Ms A. Perkins, CB
Directors (SCS), J. Barker; Ms S. Hinkley, CBE
Deputy Directors (SCS), Ms J. Thorne; T. Bird; Ms R.
   Griggs; M. Herron; D. Pain, CBE; S. Fryer; Ms L. Davis

CENTRE FOR MANAGEMENT AND POLICY STUDIES
(CMPS)

Admiralty Arch, The Mall, London SW1A 2WH.
Tel: 020-7276 1313
CMPS works to ensure that the Civil Service is cultivating
the right skills, culture and approaches to perform its

task; to ensure that policy makers across government has
access to the best research, evidence and international
experience; and to help Government learn better. CMPS
includes the Civil Service College, which is based in
Sunningdale, Berkshire.
Director-General, Prof. R. Amman
Directors (SCS), P. Tebby; E. Wooldridge, R. Green; Ms S.
   Duncan

GOVERNMENT INFORMATION AND COMMUNICATION
SERVICES

10 Great George St, London SW1P 3AE.
Tel: 020-7276 0014
Office of the Head of the Government Information and
Communication Service. Responsible for the standards of
the service provided by the GICS to Whitehall
Departments and their Agencies. Supports the Head of
the Civil Service's work. Provides guidance on the
strategic development of the GICS, its professional
practice, recruitment and promotion. Focuses on cross-
departmental communication and management of the
central GICS units.
Head of Government Information and Communication
   Service (SCS), Mike Granatt, CB
Deputy Head of GICS (Corporate and HR Strategy)
   (SCS), Ms S. Jenkins
Director of GICS Development Centre (SCS), T. Dunmore
Director of Operations, Ms L. Salisbury
Head of Government News Network, R. Haslam
Regional Director, Eastern, Ms M. Basham
   2nd Floor, Block A1, Westbrook Centre, Milton Road,
   Cambridge CB4 1YG.
Regional Director, East Midlands, P. Smith
   The Belgrave Centre, Talbot Street, Nottingham NG1
   5GG.
Regional Director, West Midlands, B. Garner
   Five Ways House, Islington Row, Middleway,
   Edgbaston, Birmingham B15 1SH.
Regional Director, North East, C. Child
   Wellbar House, Gallowgate, Newcastle upon Tyne NE1 4TB.
Regional Director, North West, Ms E. Jones
   Sunley Tower, Piccadilly Plaza, Manchester M1 4BD.
Regional Director, London and South East, Ms V. Burdon
   Hercules Road, London SE1 7DU.
Regional Director, South West, P. Whitbread
   The Pithay, Bristol BS1 2PB.
Regional Director, Yorkshire and the Humber, Ms W.
   Miller
   City House, New Station Street, Leeds LS1 4JG.

CORPORATE SERVICES GROUP

9 Whitehall, London SW1A 2DD.
Director of Corporate Services and Principal Establishment
   and Finance Officer, P. Wardle
Deputy Director, Human Resources, Ms C. Francis
Deputy Director, Financial Management, Ms S. Budden
Deputy Director, Business Development, J. Sweetman
Deputy Director, Infrastructure, E. Hepburn
Deputy Director, Histories and Records, Ms T. Stirling

HER MAJESTY'S STATIONERY OFFICE

St Clements House, 2–16 Colegate, Norwich NR3 1BQ.
   Tel: 01603-621000
Controller, Ms C. Tullo

COMMUNICATION GROUP

70 Whitehall, London SW1A 2AS.
Tel: 020-7276 1272/0311/0432
Advises on presentation of departmental policy and
activity. Handles media and public relations activities

other than recruitment publicity and advertising.
Director of Communication, Ms L. Austin
Head of News, J. Bretherton

EXECUTIVE AGENCY

GOVERNMENT CAR AND DESPATCH AGENCY

46 Ponton Road, London SW8 5AX.
Tel: 020-7217 3839; Fax: 020-7217 3840
The Agency provides secure transport and mail distribution to Government and the public sector.
Chief Executive, N. Matheson

PRIME MINISTER'S OFFICE

10 Downing Street, London SW1A 2AA
Tel: 020-7270 3000; Fax: 020-7925 0918;
Web: www.number-10.gov.uk
Prime Minister, The Rt. Hon Anthony (Tony) Blair, MP
   Principal Private Secretary and Head of Policy Directorate, Jeremy Heywood, CB
   Parliamentary Private Secretary, David Hanson, MP
   Chief of Staff, Jonathan Powell
Personal Assistant to Prime Minister (Diary), Katie Kay
Political Secretary, Robert Hill
Head of Policy Directorate, Andrew Adonis
Policy Directorate; Carey Oppenheim; Ed Richards; Simon Virley; Geoffrey Norris; Mike Emmerich; Sarah Hunter; Simon Stevens; Justin Russell; Clare Sumner; Alasdair McGowan; Derek Scott; Matthew Elson; Patrick Diamond; Martin Hurst
Foreign Policy, Matthew Rycroft; Anna Wechberg; Liz Lloyd; Roger Liddle; Francis Campbell
Head of Delivery Unit, Prof. Michael Barber
Head of the Office of Public Services Reform, Wendy Thompson
Head of Strategy, Geoff Mulgan
Research and Information Unit, Phil Bassett
Director of Communications and Strategy, Alastair Campbell
Corporate Communications, James Humphreys
Strategic Communications Unit, Peter Hyman
Direct Communications Unit, Jan Taylor
Prime Minister's Official Spokesmen (PMOS); Godric Smith; Tom Kelly
Director of Events and Visits, Fiona Millar
Director of Government Relations, The Baroness Margaret Morgan of Huyton
Secretary for Appointments, William Chapman
Advisor on Foreign Policy and Head of the Overseas and Defence Secretariat, Sir David Manning
Advisor on European Union Affairs and Head of the European Secretariat, Sir Stephen Wall
Parliamentary Clerk, Nicholas Howard

CENTRAL OFFICE OF INFORMATION

Hercules Road, London SE1 7DU
Tel: 020-7928 2345; Fax: 020-7928 5037

The Central Office of Information (COI) is a Government department which offers consultancy, procurement and project management services to central Government for publicity. Administrative responsibility for the COI rests with the Minister for the Cabinet Office.
Chief Executive, vacant
   Senior Personal Secretary, Mrs Ira MacMull
Deputy Chief Executive, P. Buchanan

MANAGEMENT BOARD

Members, I. Hamilton; Mrs S. Whetton; B. McDonald
Secretary, Mrs I. MacMull

DIRECTORS

Director, Client Services, I. Hamilton
Director, Marketing Communications, P. Buchanan
Director, Films, Radio and Events, Mrs S. Whetton
Director, Publications, I. Hamilton
Director, Central Services, B. McDonald

DEPARTMENT FOR CULTURE, MEDIA AND SPORT

2–4 Cockspur Street, London SW1Y 5DH
Tel: 020-7211 6200; Fax: 020-7211 6032
Web: www.culture.gov.uk

The Department for Culture, Media and Sport was established in July 1997 and is responsible for Government policy relating to the arts, broadcasting, the press, museums and galleries, libraries, sport and recreation, historic buildings and ancient monuments, tourism, and the music industry.
Secretary of State for Culture, Media and Sport, The Rt. Hon. Tessa Jowell, MP
   Principal Private Secretary, Simon Cooper
   Private Secretary, Hugh Ind
   Special Adviser, Bill Bush
   Parliamentary Private Secretary, Bill Rammell, MP
Minister of State, The Rt. Hon. The Baroness Blackstone (Arts and spokesperson in the House of Lords)
   Private Secretary, David McLaren
   Parliamentary Private Secretary, Martin Linton, MP
Minister of State, The Rt. Hon. Richard Caborn, MP (Sport)
   Private Secretary, Graheme Cornell
   Parliamentary Private Secretary, Ben Chapman, MP
Parliamentary Under-Secretary, Dr Kim Howells, MP
   Private Secretary, Garath Maybury
Permanent Secretary (SCS), Sue Street

MUSEUMS, GALLERIES, LIBRARIES AND HERITAGE GROUP

Head of Group (SCS), Ms A. Stewart
Head, Museums, Libraries and Archives (SCS), Ms J. Evans
Head, Buildings, Monuments and Sites (SCS), C. Pillman
Head, Museums and Libraries Sponsorship, R. Hartman
Head, Cultural Property, Ms H. Bauer
Director, Government Art Collection (SCS), Ms P. Johnson

STRATEGY AND COMMUNICATION GROUP

Head of Group (SCS), Ms S. Kenny
Head of News, P. Feeny
Head of Policy, Innovation and Delivery, J. Zeff
Head of Promotions and Publicity, G. Newsom

CORPORATE SERVICES GROUP

Head of Group (SCS), N. Kroll
Head, Finance and Planning Division (SCS), A. McLellan
Head, Personnel and Central Services Division (SCS), P. Heron
Head, Central Appointments, S. Roberts
Head, Internal Audit, M. Kirk
Head, Golden Jubilee Unit, Ms H. Bayne

CREATIVE INDUSTRIES, MEDIA AND BROADCASTING GROUP

Head of Group (SCS), A. Ramsay
Head, Broadcasting Division (SCS), Ms D. Kahn
Head, Creative Industries Division (SCS), M. Seeney
Head, Gambling and National Lottery Licensing, E. Grant

REGIONS, TOURISM, MILLENNIUM AND
INTERNATIONAL GROUP
Head of Group, B. Leonard
Head, Tourism Division (SCS), S. Broadley
Head, National Lottery Distribution and Communities,
   Ms B. Lodge
Head, Local, Regional and International Division, M.
   Ferrero

EDUCATION, TRAINING, ARTS AND SPORT
Head of Group, Ms P. Drew
Head, Arts Division (SCS), A. Davey
Head, Sports and Recreation Division (SCS), H. Reeves
Head, Education and Social Policy, P. Clapp
Head, Commonwealth Games Unit, R. Raine

EXECUTIVE AGENCY

ROYAL PARKS AGENCY
The Old Police House, Hyde Park, London W2 2UH
Tel: 020-7298 2000; Fax: 020-7298 2005
The agency is responsible for maintaining and developing
the royal parks.
Chief Executive (G5), W. Weston

OFFICE OF THE DEPUTY PRIME MINISTER
26 Whitehall, London, SW1A 2WH
Tel: 020-7944 4400
Web: www.odpm.gov.uk

The Office of the Deputy Prime Minister was created in
May 2002 taking on responsibility for policy areas from
both the Department for Transport, Local Government
and the Regions and the Cabinet Office. The Department
brings together regional and local government (including
the Regional Government Offices), housing, planning
and regeneration, social exclusion and neighbourhood
renewal.
   The department also has responsibility for transport
issues not undertaken by the recently formed
Department for Transport. Regional and local
government and the Government's cross-cutting agenda
for neighbourhood renewal and social inclusion are
administered by a single department under the Deputy
Prime Minister, who will also assume responsibility for
implementing the Regional Government and Local
Government White Papers. The Deputy Prime Minister
will continue to act as the Prime Minister's deputy across
the full range of domestic and international business,
chairing a range of key Cabinet committees.
Deputy Prime Minister and First Secretary of State, The
   Rt. Hon. John Prescott, MP
   Principal Private Secretary, David Prout
Minister of State, The Rt. Hon. Nick Raynsford, MP
   (Local Government and the Regions)
   Private Secretary, Sarah Sturrock
Minister of State, The Rt. Hon. Lord Rooker (Housing,
   Planning and Regeneration)
   Private Secretary, Julie Penton

Minister of State, Ms Barbara Roche, MP (Social
   Exclusion, Regional Co-ordination and Deputy
   Minister for Women)
   Private Secretary, Mark Livesey
Parliamentary Under-Secretary, Christopher Leslie, MP
   (Local Government and the Regions)
   Private Secretary, Steve Kelly
Parliamentary Under-Secretary, Tony McNulty, MP
   (Housing, Planning and Regeneration)
   Private Secretary, Claire Skipsey
Permanent Secretary, Mavis McDonald
   Private Secretary, Julie Eason

DIRECTORATE OF COMMUNICATION
Director (acting), Ms L. Austin

CENTRAL POLICY GROUP
Admiralty Arch, The Mall, London SW1A 2WH.
Tel: 020-7276 3559. Director, P. Unwin

HOUSING, HOMELESSNESS, URBAN
POLICY AND PLANNING
Director-General (SCS), Ms G. Turton
Directors, M. Gahagan (Housing Directorate); Ms L.
   Casey (Homelessness Directorate); B. Hackland
   (Planning Directorate); D. Lunts (Urban Policy Unit)

LEGAL DIRECTORATE
Director-General, D. Hogg, CB
Directors, Ms S. Unerman (Planning, Local Government,
   Housing and Employment Directorate)

LOCAL AND REGIONAL GOVERNMENT GROUP
Director-General, P. Wood
Directors, C. Norris (Fire, Health and Safety Directorate);
   A. Whetnall (Local Government Directorate);
   B. Linnard (Local Government Finance Directorate);
   R. Allan (Regional Policy Unit); P. Ward (Local
   Government Performance Unit)

NEIGHBOURHOOD RENEWAL UNIT
Director-General, J. Montgomery
Director, A. Riddell

REGIONAL CO-ORDINATION UNIT
River Walk House, Millbank, London SW1P 4RR
Tel: 020-7217 3550
Director-General, R. Smith
Director, A. Wells
Regional Directors, D. Morrison (Government Office for
   the East Midlands); Ms L. Meek (Government Office
   for London); J. Blackie (Government Office for the
   North East); K. Barnes (Government Office for the
   North West); D. Saunders (Government Office for the
   South East); Ms J. Henderson (Government Office for
   the South West); G. Garbutt (Government Office for
   the West Midlands); Ms F. Everiss (Government Office
   for Yorkshire and the Humber)

SOCIAL EXCLUSION UNIT
35 Great Smith Street, London SW1P 3BQ
Tel: 020-7276 2050
Director, Ms C. Tyler

STRATEGY AND CORPORATE SERVICES
Director-General, R. Dudding
Directors, M. Sykes (Commercial Directorate); C. Riley
   (Strategy and Economics Directorate); D. Fisk (Chief
   Scientist); M. Bailey (Human Resources Directorate)
   (acting)

EXECUTIVE AGENCIES

FIRE SERVICE COLLEGE

Moreton-in-Marsh, Gloucestershire, GL56 0RH
Tel: 01608-650831; Fax: 01608-651788;
Web: www.fireservicecollege.ac.uk

The Fire Service College provides unique facilities for both practical and theoretical fire fighting, fire safety and accident and emergency training.
Chief Executive (acting), A. R. Currie

ORDNANCE SURVEY

Romsey Road, Maybush, Southampton, SO16 4GU.
Tel: 023-8079 2000; Fax: 023-8079 2660
Web: www.ordsvy.gov.uk

The Ordnance Survey department carries out official surveying and definitive mapping of Great Britain.
Chief Executive, V. Lawrence

PLANNING INSPECTORATE

Crown Buildings, Cathays Park, Cardiff CF10 3NQ.
Tel: 029-2082 3866; Fax; 029-2082 5150
Web: www.planning-inspectorate.gov.uk

The Inspectorate deals with appeals against the decisions of local authorities on planning applications and appeals against local authority enforcement notices. It also provides inspectors to hold inquiries into objections to local authority planning.
Chief Executive and Chief Planning Inspector, C. Shepley

THE QUEEN ELIZABETH II CONFERENCE CENTRE

Broad Sanctuary, London SW1P 3EE
Tel: 020-7222 5000; Fax: 020-7798 4200
Web: www.qeiicc.co.uk

The Centre provides secure conference facilities for national and international government and private sector use.
Chief Executive, Kirk Albrow

THE RENT SERVICE

Clifton House, 1st Floor, 87–113 Euston Road, London NW1 2RA Tel: 020-7554 2450; Fax: 020-7554 2490
Web: www.vca.gov.uk

The Agency combines 77 independent units previously administered by local authorities.
Chief Executive, Miss C. Copeland

DEPARTMENT FOR EDUCATION AND SKILLS

Sanctuary Buildings, Great Smith Street, London SW1P 3BT Tel: 0870-001 2345; Fax: 020-7925 6000
Email: info@dfes.gsi.gov.uk
Web: www.dfes.gov.uk
Caxton House, Tothill Street, London SW1H 9NA
Tel: 020-7273 3000; Fax: 020-7273 5124
Castle View House, East Lane, Runcorn, WA7 2DN.
Tel: 0114-275 3275; Fax: 0114-259 4724
Mowden Hall, Staindrop Road, Darlington DL3 9BG.
Tel: 0870-001 2345

The Department for Education and Skills aims to help build a competitive economy and inclusive society by creating opportunities for everyone to develop their learning potential and achieve excellence in standards of education and levels of skills. The department's main objectives are to give children an excellent start in education and enable young people and adults to develop and equip themselves with the skills, knowledge and personal qualities needed for life and work.

The Department also sponsors eleven non-departmental public bodies across a variety of professional disciplines and educational services.
Secretary of State for Education and Skills, The Rt. Hon. Estelle Morris, MP
  Principal Private Secretary, Chris Wormald
  Deputy Principal Private Secretary, Kim Sibley
  Private Secretaries, Jane Whitfield; Claire Carroll; Dean Creamer
  Special Advisers, Chris Boffey; Dr Will Cavendish
  Parliamentary Private Secretary, Vernon Coaker, MP
Minister of State (School Standards), David Miliband, MP
  Private Secretary, Nick Carson
  Parliamentary Private Secretary, Ian Cawsey, MP
Minister of State (Lifelong Learning and Higher Education), Margaret Hodge, MBE, MP
  Private Secretary, Nicole Kett
  Parliamentary Private Secretary, Mike Foster, MP
Parliamentary Under-Secretary of State, Ivan Lewis, MP *(Adult Learning and Skills)*
  Private Secretary, Jo Bewley
Parliamentary Under-Secretary of State, Stephen Twigg, MP *(Young People and Learning)*
  Private Secretary, Steve Bartlett
Parliamentary Under-Secretary of State, The Baroness Catherine Ashton of Upholland *(Early Years and School Standards)*
  Private Secretary, Hannah Woodhouse
Permanent Secretary, David Normington, CB
  Private Secretary, Claudette Sutton

STRATEGY AND COMMUNICATIONS DIRECTORATE (SCD)
Director, P. Wanless
Heads of Divisions, T. Cook *(Press Office);* D.-J. Collins *(News)*
Divisional Managers, Ms Y. Diamond *(Corporate Communications);* B. Glickman *(Effective Partnerships);* J. Ross *(Publicity);* M. Haroon *(Regional Policy)*

SCHOOLS DIRECTORATE
Director-General, P. Housden
Head of Schools Communication Unit, R. Graham
Divisional Managers, J. Coles *(Education Bill);* Ms C. Bienkowska *(Strategy and Performance)*

STANDARDS AND EFFECTIVENESS UNIT
Director, D. Hopkins
Director of Operations, S. Crowne
Divisional Managers, L. Longstone *(School Diversity);* S. Adamson *(Pupil Standards);* B. Shaw *(School Improvement and Excellence);* Ms S. Imbriano *(Local Implementation) (acting);* R. Wood *(Local Standards Policy);* D. Woods *(Transforming Standards Advisers)*

SCHOOL ORGANISATION AND FUNDING
Director, Ms H. Williams
Divisional Managers, A. Wye *(School and LEA Funding);* K. Beeton *(School Capital and Building);* M. Patel *(Schools Building and Design Unit);* Ms C. Macready *(Schools Admissions, Organisation and Governance)*

SCHOOL WORKFORCE UNIT
Director, S. Kershaw
Director of Central Groups, S. Edwards
Deputy Directors, R. Harrison *(Recruitment);* S. Hillier *(Quality and Status);* G. Holley *(Workload and Retention);* M. Willams *(Pay, Pensions and Performance)*

CHILDREN AND FAMILIES

Director, T. Jeffery
Divisional Managers, Ms K. Driver (School Inclusion); M. Phipps (Schools Plus); Ms P. Jones (Pupil Support and Independent Schools); Ms A. Gross (Special Education Needs); Ms S. Scales (Behaviour and Youth at Risk)

EARLY YEARS AND CHILDCARE UNIT

Head of Unit, A. Cranston
Divisional Managers, D. Jeffrey (Quality and Standards); N. Tooze (Affordability and Accessibility Division)

SURE START UNIT

Director, Ms N. Eisenstadt
Policy Divisional Manager (acting), Ms S. Lewis
Operations Divisional Manager, J. Doughty

CHILDREN AND YOUNG PEOPLE'S UNIT

Director, Ms A. Efunshile
Divisional Managers, A. McCully (Policy and Strategy); Ms K. Bundred (Local Partnerships)

ASSESSMENT, CURRICULUM AND E-LEARNING IN SCHOOLS

Director, Ms I. Wilde
Divisional Managers, Ms M. Watts (Curriculum); D. Brown; (ICT in Schools); N. Baxter (Parents and Performance)

YOUTH DIRECTORATE

Director-General, P. Shaw
Divisional Managers, Ms C. Hunter (Youth Co-ordination); J. Temple (Strategy and Funding)

ASSESSMENT, CURRICULUM AND E-LEARNING IN SCHOOLS

Director, Ms I. Wilde
Divisional Managers, G. McKenzie (Post 16 E-Learning Task Force); Ms A. Wright (E-Learning Strategy Unit)

CONNEXIONS SERVICE NATIONAL UNIT

Chief Executive, Ms A. Weinstock
Divisional Managers, Ms J. Pugh (Strategy and Communications); G. McKenzie (Operational Policy); S. Geary (Delivery and Quality); Ms J. Haywood (Activities for Young People and Volunteering)

QUALIFICATIONS AND YOUNG PEOPLE

Director, R. Hull
Divisional Managers, Ms S. Marshall (Qualifications for Work); Ms C. Johnson (School and College Qualifications); T. Fellowes (Young People Learner Support); A. Davies (Young People's Policy)

JOINT INTERNATIONAL UNIT

Director, C. Tucker
Divisional Managers, W. Harris (European Union); Ms J. Evans (European Social Fund); Ms M. Niven (International Relations)

LIFELONG LEARNING DIRECTORATE (LLD)

Director-General, Ms J. Shiner
Divisional Managers, A. Clarke (Prisoners' Learning and Skills Unit)

ADULT SKILLS STRATEGY UNIT

Director, Ms S. Pember
Deputy Directors, Ms M. Boo (Strategy); B. Brooks (Standards, Quality and Curriculum)

ADULT LEARNING GROUP

Director, S. Marston
Divisional Managers, T. Down (Access to Learning for Adults); Ms M. Bennett (Lifelong Learning and Technologies); S. Perryman (Skills for Employment and Sector Skills Council); H. Tollyfield (Workplace Learning); O. Couch; Ms S. Orr (ILA Project)

HIGHER EDUCATION GROUP

Director, N. Sanders, CB
Divisional Mangers, M. Hipkins (HE Funding and Organisation); P. Cohen (Quality and Employability); N. Flint (Student Support 1); Ms N. Graham (Student Support 2); Ms S. Todd, P. Swift (HE Project); C. Barnham (HE Delivery Programme Unit)

LEARNING DELIVERY AND STANDARDS GROUP

Director, P. Lauener
Divisional Managers, P. Mucklow (FE and Partnerships); J. Turner (LSC Unit); S. Baddeley; J. Mackey (Raising Standards); H. Coussens (Tec Transition Unit); D. Taylor (FE Strategy Project)

CORPORATE SERVICES AND DEVELOPMENT DIRECTORATE

Director, Ms S. Thomas
Divisional Managers, G. Archer (Leadership and Personnel); Ms A.-M. Lawlor (Change); Ms S. Edgar; Ms B. Moyes (Learning Academy); R. Hinchcliffe (Information Services); P. Neill (Commercial Services); Ms D. Jarvis (Equality and Diversity)

PROJECT DEVELOPMENT DIRECTORATE (LLD)

Director, D. Grover

LEGAL ADVISER'S OFFICE

Legal Adviser, J. Jones
Divisional Managers, D. Aries (Lifelong Learning and Schools Admissions); F. Clarke (Effectiveness and Admissions); P. Kilgarriff (Governance and Finance); N. Ash (Special Needs and Curriculum); Ms C. Davies (Equality, Establishment and European Commission); Ms S. McGibbon (Teachers)

FINANCE AND ANALYTICAL SERVICES DIRECTORATE (FASD)

Director-General, P. Makeham
Divisional Managers, N. Thirtle (Internal Audit); M. McClelland (Programme and Project Management Unit)

FINANCE

Director, Ms R. Thompson
Divisional Managers, P. Houten (Programmes); Ms M. Maddox (Efficiency); P. Connor, CBE (Financial Accounting)

ANALYTICAL SERVICES

Director, P. Johnson
Divisional Managers, M. Britton (Qualifications, Pupil Assessment and IT); J. Elliot (Youth); Ms K. Hancock (Higher Education); B. Butcher (Adults); Ms A. Brown (Schools 1); R. Bartholomew (Schools 2)

DEPARTMENT FOR ENVIRONMENT, FOOD AND RURAL AFFAIRS
Nobel House, 17 Smith Square, London SW1P 3JR
Tel: 020-7238 3000; Fax: 020-7238 6591
Web: www.defra.gov.uk

The Department for Environment, Food, and Rural Affairs is responsible for Government policies on agriculture, horticulture and fisheries in England and for policies relating to the food chain. In association with the agriculture departments of the Scottish Executive, the National Assembly for Wales and the Northern Ireland Office, and with the Intervention Board, the department is responsible for negotiations in the EU on the common agricultural and fisheries policies, and for single European market questions relating to its responsibilities. Its remit also includes international agricultural and food trade policy.

The department exercises responsibilities for policies on climate change and international negotiations on sustainable development. It is also responsible for a range of pollution issues relating to waste and recycling, the protection and enhancement of the countryside and the marine environment, flood defence, GM crops, hunting, rural development and other rural issues. It is the licensing authority for veterinary medicines and the registration authority for pesticides. It administers policies relating to the control of animal, plant and fish diseases. It provides scientific, technical and professional services and advice to farmers, growers and ancillary industries, and commissions research to assist in the formulation and assessment of policy and to underpin applied research and development work done by industry. Responsibility for food safety and standards was transferred to the Food Standards Agency in April 2000.

Secretary of State for Environment, Food and Rural Affairs, The Rt. Hon. Margaret Beckett, MP
Principal Private Secretary (G7), Gavin Ross
Private Secretaries, Alexia Flowerday; Davinder Lail; Joe Bray
Special Advisers, Sheila Watson; Nicci Collins
Parliamentary Private Secretary, Andrew Reed, MP
Minister of State (Environment), The Rt. Hon. Michael Meacher, MP
Private Secretaries, Gabriel Edwards; Belinda Gordon
Parliamentary Private Secretary, Terry Rooney, MP
Minister of State (Rural Affairs), The Rt. Hon. Alun Michael, MP
Private Secretary, Becky Taylor
Parliamentary Private Secretary, Peter Bradley, MP
Parliamentary Under-Secretary, Elliot Morley, MP
Private Secretaries, Robert Hitchen; Bradley Bates
Parliamentary Under-Secretary, The Lord Whitty of Camberwell
Senior Private Secretary, Teresa Hart
Private Secretary, Emily Garner
Permanent Secretary (SCS), Brian Bender, CB
Private Secretary, Suzie Daykin

ESTABLISHMENTS GROUP
Director of Corporate Services (SCS), R. Allen

CORPORATE SERVICES DIVISION
Head of Division (SCS), B. Jones

PERSONNEL DIVISION
Head of Division (SCS), Ms T. Newell

BUILDING AND ESTATE MANAGEMENT
Eastbury House, 30–34 Albert Embankment, London SE1 7TL
Tel: 020-7238 6000
Head of Division (SCS), J. A. S. Nickson

INFORMATION TECHNOLOGY DIRECTORATE
Government Buildings, Epsom Road, Guildford, Surrey GU1 2LD Tel: 01483-403757

E-BUSINESS
E-Business Director, D. Rossington
IT Director, S. Soper
Assistant Director (Applications), P. Barber
Assistant Director (Infrastructure), D. Brown
Assistant Director (E-Business), A. Hill

COMMUNICATIONS DIRECTORATE
Nobel House, 17 Smith Square, London SW1P 3JR
Tel: 020-7238 6000; Helpline: 0645-335577

Director of Communications (SCS), L. Hudson
Head of News, M. Smith
Chief Publicity Officer (G7), N. Wagstaffe
Principal Librarian (G7), P. McShane

AGENCY OWNERSHIP UNIT
1A Page Street, London SW1P 4PQ
Head of Unit (SCS), Dr M. Tas

FINANCE DEPARTMENT
3–8 Whitehall Place (West Block), London SW1A 2HH
Tel: 020-7238 6000

Finance Director, (SCS), A. Burchell

FINANCIAL MANAGEMENT AND INFORMATION
Head of Division (SCS), C. Ridley

PROCUREMENT AND CONTRACTS DIVISION
19–29 Woburn Place, London WC1H 0LU
Tel: 020-7273 3000
Head of Division (SCS), D. Rabey

AUDIT, CONSULTANCY AND MANAGEMENT SERVICES
19–29 Woburn Place, London WC1H 0LU
Tel: 020-7273 3000
Director of Audit (SCS), D. V. Fisher

RESOURCE MANAGEMENT STRATEGY UNIT
19–29 Woburn Place, London WC1H 0LU
Tel: 020-7273 3000
Head of Unit (SCS), D. V. Fisher

RESOURCE MANAGEMENT DIVISION
Foss House, Kings Pool, 1–2 Peasholme Green, York YO1 7PX Tel: 01904-455328
Head of Division (G6), R. Atkinson

BUSINESS IMPROVEMENT DIVISION
Head of Unit (G7), Ms. J. Flint and G. Holt

LEGAL DEPARTMENT
55 Whitehall, London SW1A 2EY
Tel: 020-7238 6000

Legal Adviser and Solicitor (SCS), D. Macrae
Principal Assistant Solicitors (SCS), S. Parker; Ms C. A. Crisham

LEGAL DIVISIONS

Assistant Solicitor, Division A1, C. Allen
Assistant Solicitor, Division A2, Ms A. Werbicki
Assistant Solicitor, Division A3, C. Gregory
Assistant Solicitor, Division A4, N. Lefton
Assistant Solicitor, Division A5, B. Dickinson
Assistant Solicitor, Division A6, B. Dickinson
Assistant Solicitor, Division B1, Ms S. Spence
Assistant Solicitor, Division B2, M. Patel
Assistant Solicitor, Division B3, C. Burke

INVESTIGATION UNIT

Chief Investigation Officer (G7), Miss J. Panting

ECONOMICS AND STATISTICS
3–8 Whitehall Place (West Block), London SW1A 2HH
Tel: 020-7238 6000
Director of Economics and Statistics Group (SCS), D. Thompson
Divisions Senior Economic Adviser, Economics and Statistics (Farm Business) (G6), J. Watson
Senior Economic Advisers, Economics (International) (SCS), Dr S. Harding; J. P. Muriel

STATISTICS DIVISION

Foss House, Kings Pool, 1–2 Peasholme Green, York YO1 7PX Tel: 01904-455332

Chief Statistician (Commodities and Food) (SCS), S. Platt
Chief Statistician (Census and Surveys) (SCS), P. F. Helm

CHIEF SCIENTIST'S GROUP
Cromwell House, Dean Bradley Street, London, SW1P 3JH. Tel: 020- 7238 6000

Chief Scientist (SCS), Prof. H. Dalton

DIVISIONS

Head, Agriculture, Environment and Food Technology (SCS), Dr J. C. Sherlock
Head, Veterinary, Food and Aquatic Science (SCS), Dr N. Coulson
Head, Research Policy and International (SCS), A. R. Burne

FISHERIES DEPARTMENT
Nobel House, 17 Smith Square, London SW1P 3JR

Fisheries Director (SCS), S. Wentworth

DIVISIONS

Head, Fisheries I (SCS), P. M. Boyling
Head, Fisheries II (SCS), R. Cowan
Head, Fisheries III (SCS), C. Ryder
Head, Fisheries IV (SCS), B. S. Edwards
Chief Inspector, Sea Fisheries Inspectorate (G6), S. G. Ellson

FOOD, FARMING AND FISHERIES
3–8 Whitehall Place (West Block), London SW1A 2HH
Tel: 020-7238 6000

Director General (SCS), A. J. Lebrecht

AGRICULTURAL STRATEGY, EUROPEAN UNION AND INTERNATIONAL POLICY
Director (SCS), D. Hunter

DIVISIONS

Head, European Union and Co-ordination Agriculture (SCS), T. Eddy, CBE
Head, European Union and International Division (SCS),

D. Dawson
Head, Cap Schemes Policy, D. Littler
Head, Horticulture, Potatoes and HMI (SCS), D. Jones
Head Genetic Modification and Industrial Crops, Ms S. Henry
Head, Arable Crops (SCS), A. Kuyk
Head, Beef and Sheep (SCS), I. Llewelyn
Head, Livestock Schemes (SCS), A. Taylor
Head, Milk, Pigs, Eggs and Poultry (SCS), A. Slade
Head, Plant Health and PHSI, S. Hunter

FOOD INDUSTRY, COMPETITIVENESS AND CONSUMERS
Director, (SCS), J. Robbs

DIVISIONS

Head, Food and Drinks Industry (SCS), C. Young
Head, International Relations and Export Promotion (SCS), N. Denton
Head, Agricultural Resources and Better Regulations (SCS), L. Harris
Head, Marketing, Competition and Consumers (SCS), Ms J. Allfrey
Head, Flood Management (SCS), Miss S. Nason

PLANT VARIETY RIGHTS OFFICE AND SEED DIVISION
White House Lane, Huntingdon Road, Cambridge CB3 0LF
Head of Office (SCS), H. Hamilton

POLICY AND CORPORATE STRATEGY
Cromwell House, Dean Bradley Street, London SW1P 3JH
Tel: 020-7238 6000

Director, B. Harding
East of England, Building A, Westbrook Centre, Milton Road, Cambridge, CB4 1YG. Tel: 01223-346700. *Rural Director,* J. Rabagliati
East Midlands, The Belgrave Centre, Talbot Street, Nottingham, NG1 5GG. *Rural Director,* G. Norbury
North East, Welbar House, Gallowgate, Newcastle-upon-Tyne, NE1 4TD. Tel: 0191-201 3300. *Rural Director,* J. Bainton
North West, Sunley Tower, Picadilly Plaza, Manchester, M1 4BE. Tel: 0161-952 4000. *Regional Director,* N. Cumberlidge
South-East, Bridge House, 1 Walnut Tree Close, Guildford, Surrey, GU1 4GA. Tel: 01483-882255. *Regional Director,* Ms A. Parker
South-West, 4th and 5th Floors, The Pithay, Bristol, BS1 2PB. Tel: 0117-900 1700. *Regional Director,* T. Render
West Midlands, 77 Paradise Circus, Queensway, Birmingham, B1 2DT. Tel: 0121-212 5000. *Regional Director,* B. Davies
Yorkshire and the Humberside, PO Box 213, City House, New Station Street, Leeds, LS1 4US. Tel: 0113-280 0600. *Regional Director (acting),* G. Kingston

LAND MANAGEMENT AND RURAL DEVELOPMENT
Head of Group, Mrs K. A. J. Brown

DIVISIONS

Head, Conservation Management, J. Osmond
Head, Rural Development Division, M. Nesbitt
Head, Organics, Forestry and Industrial Crops, A. Perrins
Head, Land Management Improvement, P. Cleasby
Head, Corporate Strategy Unit, Ms A. Tarran

RURAL DEVELOPMENT SERVICE

Head of Group, J. Adams
Technical Advice, A. Hooper
Business Process Director, J. Robinson

RURAL DEVELOPMENT CENTRES

East, Government Buildings, Brooklands Avenue Cambridge, CB2 2DR, Tel: 01223-462727. *Regional Manager*, M. Edwards
East-Midlands, Block 7, Government Buildings, Chalfont Drive, Nottingham, NG8 3SN. Tel: 0115-929 1191. *Regional Manager*, S. Buckenham
North-East, Government Buildings Kenton Bar, Newcastle-upon-Tyne, NE5 3EW. Tel: 0191-286 3377. *Regional Manager*, F. Gough
North-West, Electra Way, Crewe Business Park, Crewe, Cheshire, CW1 6GJ. Tel: 01270-754000. *Regional Manager*, T. Percival
South-East, Government Buildings, Coley Park, Reading, Berkshire, RG1 6DT. Tel: 0118-958 1222, *Regional Manager*, N. Beard
South-West, Block 3, Government Buildings, Burghill Road, Westbury-on-Trym, Bristol, BS10 6NJ. Tel: 0117-959 1000. *Regional Manager*, D. Sisson
West Midlands, Block C, Government Buildings, Whittington Road, Worcester, WR5 2LQ. Tel: 01905-763355. *Regional Manager*, C. Deakin
Yorkshire and The Humberside, Government Buildings, Otley Road, Lawnswood, Leeds, LS16 5QT. Tel: 0113-261 3333. *Regional Manager*, M. Silverwood

ANIMAL HEALTH GROUP

1A Page Street, London SW1P 4PQ. Tel: 020-7904 6000

Head of Group (SCS), N. Thornton

DIVISIONS

Head of Animal Identification and Animal International Trade, Miss J. Wordley
Animal Movements and Exotic Diseases, R. Hathaway
Head Animal Health Services, Ms C. Harold
Animal Welfare, G. Noble
TSE Group Director, P. Nash
Head, BSE and Scrapie, J. A. Bailey
Head, Sheep TSE, N. Cleary

ANIMAL HEALTH AND ENVIRONMENT DIRECTORATE

Nobel House, 17 Smith Square, London, SW1P 3JR

Director-General, Ms. J. Bacon

WILDLIFE AND COUNTRYSIDE GROUP

Ergon House, 17 Smith Square, London, SW1P 3JR, Tel: 020-7238-6000.

Director, Ms S. Lamberet

DIVISIONS

Countryside, S. Carter
European Wildlife, M. Capstick
Global Wildlife, M. Brasher
Rural Development, H. Cleary
Rural Task Force Secretariat, C. Dunabin

CHIEF VETERINARY OFFICER'S GROUP

1A Page Street, London SW1P 4PQ. Tel: 020-7904 6000

Chief Veterinary Officer (SCS), J. M. Scudamore
Deputy Chief Veterinary Officer (Services) (SCS), R. Cawthorne

DIVISIONS

Head of Veterinary Services East (SCS), G. Jones
Head of Veterinary Services West (SCS), J. Cross
Head of Veterinary Services North (SCS), R. Drummond
Head of Veterinary Services Resources (SCS), Ms B. Phillip
Assistant Chief Veterinary Officer (Scotland), L. Gardner
Head of Veterinary Services (Scotland) (SCS), D. McIntosh
Assistant Chief Veterinary Officer (Wales), A. Edwards
Deputy Chief Veterinary Officer (Policy) (SCS), R. Cawthorne
Head, Veterinary International Trade Team (SCS), R. A. Bell
Head, Veterinary Notifiable Disease Team (Exotic Diseases) (SCS), Dr D. Matthews
Head, Veterinary Notifiable Disease Team (Endemic Animal Diseases and Zoonosis) (SCS), vacant
Head, Welfare Team (SCS), D. Pritchard

EXECUTIVE AGENCIES

CENTRAL SCIENCE LABORATORY (CSL)

Sand Hutton, York YO41 1LZ
Tel: 01904-462000; Fax: 01904-462111

The Central Science Laboratory (CSL) provides advice, technical and enforcement support, underpinned by appropriate research, to meet both the statutory and policy objectives of DEFRA; and it provides research and development and advice on a commercial basis to other government departments and to public and private sector organisations both overseas and UK-based.
CSL's main work areas are: safeguarding food supplies through the identification and control of invertebrate pests, plant pests and diseases; the management of vertebrate wildlife, food and consumer safety with the emphasis on the microbiological and chemical safety, and the quality and nutritional value of food.
CSL is also concerned with environmental protection through the investigation of the impact of agriculture on the environment, and the promotion of biodiversity in agricultural habitats.

Chief Executive (G3), Prof. M. Roberts
Research Directors (G5), Prof. Tony Hardy (*Agriculture and Environment*); Prof. John Gilbert (*Food*)
Commercial Director, Dr Robert Bolton
Corporate Services Director, Dr Helen Crews
Finance and Procurement Director, Richard Shaw

CENTRE FOR ENVIRONMENT, FISHERIES AND AQUACULTURE SCIENCE

Pakefield Road, Lowestoft, Suffolk NR33 0HT
Tel: 01502-562244; Fax: 01502-513865

The Agency, established in April 1997, provides research and consultancy services in fisheries science and management, aquaculture, fish health and hygiene, environmental impact assessment, and environmental quality assessment.

Chief Executive, Dr P. Greig-Smith

PESTICIDES SAFETY DIRECTORATE

Mallard House, Kings Pool, 3 Peasholme Green, York YO1 7PX. Tel: 01904-640500; Fax: 01904-455733

The Pesticides Safety Directorate is responsible for the evaluation and approval of agricultural pesticides and the development of policies relating to them, in order to protect consumers, users and the environment.

Chief Executive (SCS), Dr H. K. Wilson
Director (Policy) (SCS), Dr S. Popple
Director (Approvals) (SCS), R. Davis

RURAL PAYMENTS AGENCY

Corporate Headquarters, Kings House, 33 Kings Road, Reading RG1 3BU. Tel: 0118-958 3626; Fax: 0118-959 7736

The Rural Payments Agency (RPA) became an executive agency of DEFRA in October 2001. It is responsible for Common Agricultural Policy (CAP) schemes in England and for certain other schemes throughout the UK.

The RPA brings together the CAP payment functions of the intervention Board and DEFRA for the first time.

Chief Executive, J. McNeil
Director (IS), A. McDermott
Director (Operations), H. MacKinnon
Director (Human Resources), R. Gregg
Director (Finance), A. Kerr
Director (Business), S. Vry
Director (CAP), A. Sutton

VETERINARY LABORATORIES AGENCY

Woodham Lane, New Haw, Addlestone, Surrey KT15 3NB
Tel: 01932-341111; Fax: 01932-347046

The Veterinary Laboratories Agency provides scientific and technical expertise in animal and public health.

Chief Executive, Prof. S. Edwards
Director of Research, Prof. J. A. Morris
Director of Surveillance and Laboratory Services, R. Hancock
Director of Finance, C. Morrey
Laboratory Secretary, C. Edwards

VETERINARY MEDICINES DIRECTORATE

Woodham Lane, New Haw, Addlestone, Surrey KT15 3LS
Tel: 01932-336911; Fax: 01932-336618

The Veterinary Medicines Directorate is responsible for all aspects of the authorisation and control of veterinary medicines, including post-authorisation surveillance of residues in animals and animal products, and the provision of policy advice to Ministers.
Chief Executive (G4), S. Dean
Director (Policy) (G5), J. Fitzgerald
Directors (Licensing) (G5), J. O'Brien; D. Mackay
Director of Corporate Business (G6), C. Bean

FOREIGN AND COMMONWEALTH OFFICE

King Charles Street, London SW1A 2AH
Tel: 020-7270 1500; Web: www.fco.gov.uk

The Foreign and Commonwealth Office provides, through its staff in the UK and through its diplomatic missions abroad, the means of communication between the British Government and other governments and international governmental organisations on all matters falling within the field of international relations.

It is responsible for alerting the British Government to the implications of developments overseas; for promoting British interests overseas; for protecting British citizens abroad; for explaining British policies to, and cultivating relationships with, governments overseas; for the discharge of British responsibilities to the overseas territories; for entry clearance UK Visas, with the Home Office and for promoting British business overseas (jointly with the Department of Trade and Industry through British Trade International).

Secretary of State for Foreign and Commonwealth Affairs, The Rt. Hon. Jack Straw, MP
Principal Private Secretary, Simon McDonald
Special Advisers, Michael Williams; Ed Owen
Parliamentary Private Secretary, Colin Pickthall, MP

Minister of State, The Rt. Hon. Peter Hain, MP (Europe)
Private Secretary, James Morrison
Parliamentary Private Secretary, Caroline Flint, MP
Minister of State, The Rt. Hon. The Baroness Symons of Vernham Dean *(Trade and Investment)*
Private Secretary, Matthew Taylor
Parliamentary Private Secretary, Charlotte Atkins, MP
Parliamentary Under-Secretary of State, Mike O'Brien, MP
Private Secretary, Nick Astbury
Parliamentary Under-Secretary of State, Dr Denis MacShane, MP
Private Secretary, David Dunn
Parliamentary Under-Secretary of State, The Baroness Amos
Private Secretary, Tom Fletcher
Permanent Under-Secretary of State and Head of HM Diplomatic Service, Sir Michael Jay, KCMG
Private Secretary, Susan Hyland
Chief Executive, British Trade International, Sir David Wright, KCMG, LVO
Deputy Under-Secretaries, Peter Collecott *(Chief Clerk);* Michael Arthur, CMG *(Economic Director);* Michael Wood, CMG *(Legal Adviser);* Peter Ricketts, CMG *(Political Director);* Stephen Wright, CMG *(Defence Intelligence);* Graham Fry *(Wider World)*

DIRECTORS

Africa, M. Lyall Grant
Americas/Overseas Territories, R. Wilkinson, CVO
International Security, W. Ehrman
Wider Europe, J. Macgregor, CVO
European Union, K. Darroch, CMG
Chief Executive FCO Services, S. Sage
Global Issues, N. Brewer
South East Europe and Gibraltar, J. Bevan
Middle East and North Africa, E. Chaplin
Asia Pacific, R. Marsden
British Trade International, D. Hall, CMG
Personnel, D. Holt
Public Services, R. Stagg
Resources, S. Gass, CMG, CVO

HEADS OF DEPARTMENTS

African Department (Equatorial), F. Baker
African Department (Southern), A. Pocock
Aviation and Maritime Department, C. Segar
Central and North-West European Department, Sir John Ramsden
China/Hong Kong Department, A. Seaton
Common Foreign and Security Policy Department, T. Barrow
Commonwealth Co-ordination, C. Bright
Consular Division, J. Watt
Counter-Terrorism Policy Department, K. Bloomfield
Cultural Relations Department, Dr M. Reilly
Diplomatic Service Families Association, E. Salvesen
Diplomatic Service Trade Union Side (DSTUS), S. Watson
Drugs and International Crime Department, M. Ryder
Eastern Department, S. Butt
Eastern Adriatic Department, S. Wordsworth
Economic Policy, C. Butler
Environment Policy, J. Ashton
Estate Strategy, J. Metcalfe
European Unit (Bi-lateral), K. Pierce
European Union Department (External), S. Featherstone
European Union Department (Internal), N. Beard
Financial Compliance Unit, D. Major
FCO Association, D. Burns, CMG *(Chairman)*
FCO Services, J. Clark *(Head, Conference and Visits Group);* J. Elgie *(Head, Estates Group);* J. Thompson, MBE *(Head, Information Management Group);* V. Life

(Head Management Consultancy Services); V. Davies *(Head Language Group)*; Ms J. Link *(Head, Resource Management Group)*; M. Carr *(Head, Support Group)*; N. Stickells *(Head, Technical Group)*
Human Rights Policy, Dr C. Browne
Internal Audit (FCO/DFID), R. Elias
IT Strategy Unit, N. Westcott
UK Visas Joint Entry Clearance Unit (Joint FCO/Home Office Unit), R. Brinkley
Latin America and Caribbean Department, J. Dew
Legal Advisers, M. Wood, CMG
Middle East Department, C. Gray
National Audit Office, J. Pearce
Near East and North Africa Department, N. Archer
News, J. Williams
Non-Proliferation Department, T. Dowse
North America Department, N. Armour
North-East Asia and Pacific Department, S. Smith
Organisation for Security Co-operation in Europe, P. January
Overseas Territories Department, A. Huckle
Parliamentary Relations and Devolution, M. Hamlyn
Personnel Command, T. Simmons *(Performance and Development)*; Ms E. Kennedy *(Assistant Director, *Medical and Welfare)*; P. Jones *(Personnel Management)*; S. Wightman *(Personnel Policy)*; R. White *(Personnel Services)*; C. Edgerton; T. Malcomson *(Prosper)*; A. Cookson-Hall *(Recruitment)*; G. Deacon *(Interchange)*; C. Dharwarker *(Training)*; R. Clarke *(Policy Planning Staff)*
Protocol Department, Mrs K. F. Colvin
Public Diplomacy, J. Buck
Purchasing Directorate, M. Gower
Quality and Efficiency, K. Jackson
Records and Historical, H. Yasamee
Research Analysis, A. Noble
Resource Accounting, M. Brown
Resource Budgeting, M. Williamson
Science and Technology, R. Barnett
Security Strategy Unit, J. Macgregor
Security Policy, A. M. Thomson
South Asia, S. Smith
South-East Asian Department, R. Gordon
Southern European, G. Gillham
United Nations, S. Pattison
Whitehall Liaison Department, M. Kidd

* Joint Foreign and Commonwealth Office/Department for International Development department

BRITISH TRADE INTERNATIONAL

CENTRAL SERVICES GROUP

Group Director, D. Hall

REGIONAL GROUP

Group Director, I. Jones

INTERNATIONAL GROUP

Group Director, Q. Quayle

BUSINESS GROUP

Group Director, D. Warren

STRATEGY AND COMMUNICATIONS GROUP

Group Director, S. Lyle Smythe
Invest UK Chief Executive, W. Pedder

EXECUTIVE AGENCIES

WILTON PARK CONFERENCE CENTRE

Wiston House, Steyning, W. Sussex BN44 3DZ
Tel: 01903-815020; Fax: 01903-879647

Wilton Park organises international affairs conferences and is hired out to Government departments and commercial users.

Chief Executive, C. B. Jennings

CORPS OF QUEEN'S MESSENGERS

Support Group, Foreign and Commonwealth Office, London SW1A 2AH. Tel: 020-7270 2779

Superintendent of the Corps of Queen's Messengers, A. C. Brown
Queen's Messengers, P. Allen; R. Allen; Maj. A. N. D. Bols; Maj. P. C. H. Dening-Smitherman; Sqn. Ldr. J. S. Frizzell; Maj. D. A. Griffiths; Sqn Ldr A. Hill; R. Long; Maj. K. J. Rowbottom; Maj. M. R. Senior; Maj. J. E. A. Andre; W. Lisle; Maj. J. H. Steele; J. A. Hatfield; Sqn Ldr P. J. Hearn; S. J. Addy; Lt.-Col. R. I. S. Burgess

DEPARTMENT OF HEALTH

Richmond House, 79 Whitehall, London SW1A 2NL
Tel: 020-7210 3000;
Web: www.doh.gov.uk

The Department of Health is responsible for the provision of the National Health Service in England and for social care. The department's aims are to support, protect, promote and improve the nation's health; to secure the provision of comprehensive, high quality care for all those who need it, regardless of their ability to pay or where they live or their age; and to provide responsive social care and child protection for those who lack the support they need.
Secretary of State for Health, The Rt. Hon. Alan Milburn, MP
  Principal Private Secretary, Heather Rodgers
  Private Secretaries, Sammy Sinclair; Stephen Waring; Alistair Finney; Wendy Brown
  Special Advisers, Prof. Paul Corrigan; Darren Murphy
  Parliamentary Private Secretary, Mike Hall, MP
Minister of State, The Rt. Hon. John Hutton, MP *(NHS and Delivery)*
  Private Secretary, Paul Richardson
  Parliamentary Private Secretary, Claire Ward, MP
Minister of State, Jacqui Smith, MP *(Community)*
  Private Secretary, Will Niblett
  Parliamentary Private Secretary, Andy Love, MP
Parliamentary Under-Secretary of State, David Lammy, MP
  Private Secretary, Mary Agnew
Parliamentary Under-Secretary of State (Lords), The Lord Hunt of Kings Heath, OBE
  Private Secretary, David McNeil
Parliamentary Under-Secretary of State (Health), Hazel Blears, MP
  Private Secretary, Kevin Holton
Parliamentary Clerk, Neil Townley
Permanent Secretary (SCS), Nigel Crisp
  Private Secretary, Mark Davies
Chief Medical Officer (SCS), Sir Liam Donaldson, FRCSED, FRCPED
  Private Secretary, Rachel Dickson
Deputy Chief Medical Officer, Dr Pat Troop, CBE
Director of National Cancer Services, Prof. Michael Richards, FRCP

CHIEF NURSING OFFICER'S DIRECTORATE

Chief Nursing Officer and Director of Nursing–Private Office London and Leeds, Ms S. Mullally
Division Head, Ms F. Goldhill
Assistant Chief Nursing Officer (Clinical Practice); Ms K. Billingham
Assistant Chief Nursing Officer (Corporate Management), D. Moore
Assistant Chief Nursing Officer (Nursing and Midwifery Policy); Ms G. Stephens
Branch Heads, P. Allanson; Ms A. Imison, P. Hampshire; Ms A. Humphrey; A. Sheehan; J. Mahoney; R. Thompson; I. Berry; Ms S. White
Principal Medical Officer, Dr J. Graham

DIRECTORATE OF ACCESS AND CHOICE

Director of Access and Choice, Ms M. Edwards
Branch Heads; Dr S. Lowden; M. Morrison; B. Ricketts; R. Webster; G. Hetherington; P. Jenkins

COMMUNICATIONS DIRECTORATE

Director of Communications, Ms S. Jarvis
Deputy Director of Strategic Communications Group (acting), R. Langford
Deputy Director of Marketing Communications Group, W. Roberts
Head of Corporate Development, Ms M. King
Assistant Director (News), J. Hibbs
Branch Heads, N. Court; R. Langford

DIRECTORATE OF CHILDREN, OLDER PEOPLE AND SOCIAL CARE SERVICES

Chief Inspector, Ms D. Platt
Deputy Chief Inspector (SSI Inspection), Ms A. Nottage
Deputy Director and Head of Social Care Policy, G. Denham
Director of the Change Agent Team, R. Humphries
National Clinical Director for Children, Prof. A. Aynsley-Green
National Director for Older People's Services, Prof. I. Philp
Social Care Quality Programme Co-ordinator, Prof. D. Gardiner
Branch Heads, Ms A. Smith; D. Holmes; Ms K. Tyson; B. Clark; Ms J. Grauberg; Ms J. Shersby; Ms C. Phillips; Ms A. Parker, CBE; R. Campbell; A. McNeil; Ms H. Robinson; C. Muir; Ms A. McDonald; Ms C. Brock
Assistant Chief Inspectors, G. Mason; J. Fraser; R. Jones; Ms L. Hoare; J. Phillips; M. Rourke; P. Brearley; J. Cypher; Ms J. Owen; S. Pitt; J. Bolton *(Consultant)*

DIRECTORATE OF EXTERNAL AND CORPORATE AFFAIRS

Director of External and Corporate Affairs, H. Taylor
Division Heads, D. Clark; Ms E. Al-Khalifa; A. McKeon; Ms O. Senior; Dr A. Holt
Branch Heads, Dr J. Smith; Ms J. Howe; Dr P. Clappison; C. Dobson; Prof. C. Ham; P. Stocks; J. Middleton, Ms W. Honeyghan-Williams; Ms J. Taylor; P. Lemmey; M. Collyer; Ms R. Jenkins; B. Mussenden; Ms L. Yee; M. Rainsford; C. Horsey; P. Charman *(Consultant);* Ms L. Wishart; Ms J. Dainty; A. Angilley; S. Gallagher; K. Guinness; M. Brownlee; Ms K. James; R. Cienciala; R. Carter; C. Dowse

FINANCE AND INVESTMENT DIRECTORATE

Director of Finance, R. Douglas
Deputy Directors of Finance, Ms C. Daws; M. Harris, CBE
Director of Counter Fraud Services, J. Gee
Branch Heads, M. Sturges; J. Stopes-Roe; J. Tomlinson; P. Kendall; Ms P. Taylor; A. MacLellan; B. Burleigh; P. Coates; Ms L. Eccles; I. Ellul

MODERNISATION AGENCY

Director of Modernisation Agency, D. Fillingham
Director of Corporate Development, Ms K. Barnard
Head of Clinical Governance Support Team, Prof. A. Halligan
Head of National Primary Care Development Team, Dr J. Oldham
Director of NHS Collaboratives, K. Cottrell
Director of NHS Leadership Centre, Ms B. Harris
Director of Changing Workforce Programme, Ms J. Hargadon
Head of Human Resources, Ms C. Corrigan
Head of Whole Systems Development, Ms M. Lawless
Head of Pay Modernisation Unit, R. Mailly
Project Manager, Ms L. Postle
Associate Director Strategic Programmes Management (NHS Leadership Centre), Ms C. Pond
Director National Nurse Leadership Project (NHS Leadership Centre), Dr J. Faugier
Division Head, M. Scott
Consultant, M. Davidge
Branch Heads, Dr S. Lowden; Ms B. Aworinde *(Consultant);* Dr V. Day; Dr K. Harmond, Dr P. Zollinger-Read *(Consultant);* B. Gowland *(Consultant);* Dr H. Bevan; N. Patten; Dr I. Rutter

NHS HUMAN RESOURCES DIRECTORATE

Director of Human Resources, A. Foster
Deputy Directors of Human Resources, M. Stainforth; D. Amos
Deputy Director of Human Resources and Head of Learning and Personnel Development Division, Prof. M. Pearson
Branch Heads, R. Mundon; Dr R. Moore; N. Offley; R. Heron, CBE; P. Loveland; J. Ennis; Ms H. Fields; Ms S. Goulding; Ms D. Mellor, OBE; B. Dyson; Dr J. Moore; T. Sands

PUBLIC HEALTH AND CLINICAL QUALITY DIRECTORATE

Director of Public Health and Clinical Quality Directorate; Chief Medical Officer, Sir Liam Donaldson
Deputy Chief Medical Officer (Public Health), Dr P. Troop, CBE
Head of Clinical Quality (Ethics and Genetics), Ms M. Fry
Head of Public Health Division, Prof. D. Nutbeam
Branch Heads, Dr Pui-Ling Li; N. Dean; Ms L. Woodeson; Ms J. Walden; J. Brookes; N. Boyd; Ms E. Johnson; Dr D. Harper, CBE; Dr M. O'Mahony; Ms C. Hamlyn; Ms N. Ishmael, OBE; E. Waterhouse; Ms I. Sharp

RESEARCH ANALYSIS AND INFORMATION DIRECTORATE

Director of Research Analysis and Information Directorate and Head of Research and Development Division, Sir J. Pattison
Under-Secretary and Chief Economic Adviser, B. McCormick
Head of Information Policy Unit, Dr P. Drury
Director of Statistics, Dr J. Fox
Assistant Director of Research and Development, Dr P. Greenaway
Branch Heads, Ms A. Kauder; N. York; Dr G. Royston; Dr S. Harding; A. Hare; S. Old; J. Thorp; M. Freeman; Dr P. Westley; Ms A. Kauder; Ms J. Griffin; Dr J. Stephenson; M. Taylor; G. Phillpotts; J. Stokoe; R. Willmer; Ms A. Roberts; R. Staton; A. Sutherland

SPECIALIST HEALTH SERVICES DIRECTORATE

Director of Specialist Health Services and Deputy Chief Medical Officer, vacant
Chief Dental Officer, Dame Margaret Seward, DBE
Senior Dental Officer, C. Audrey
Head of Coronary Heart Disease and Cancer, Ms H. Gwynn
Director of Prison Health and Head of the Prison Health Policy Unit, Dr F. Harvey
Head of Prison Health Task Force, J. Boyington
Head of Specialist Services, D. Hewlett
Branch Heads, Ms L. Percival; Ms M. Furr; Ms H. Shirley-Quirk; Ms J. McKessack; Dr M. McGovern; Dr J. Carpenter; Dr S. Hadjipavlou; Dr M. Piper; Ms S. Foley; Dr C. Howells; Ms L. Bates; R. Daly; A. Mithani; Dr G. Chapman; Ms A. Stephenson; Ms C. Imison; P. Whiteside

HER MAJESTY'S INSPECTOR OF ANATOMY

Branch Head, Dr J. Metters

SHARED SERVICES

Chief Executive and Programme Director, P. Hewitson

NHS APPOINTMENTS COMMISSION

Chair, Sir William Wells

SOLICITOR'S OFFICE DEPARTMENT FOR WORK AND PENSIONS

Solicitor, Ms M. Morgan, CB
Director of Legal Services, Mrs G. Kerrigan

DIRECTORS OF HEALTH AND SOCIAL CARE

Director of Operations, A. Doran; J. Bacon *(London)*; D. Nicholson *(Midlands and East)*; P. Garland, CB *(North)*; Ms R. Carnall *(South)*; vacant *(Corporate Development Team)*

OPERATIONS DIVISION

Director of Operations, A. Doran
Branch Heads, S. Emslie; S. Peck

ADVISORY COMMITTEES

ADVISORY COMMITTEE ON THE MICROBIOLOGICAL SAFETY OF FOOD, Room 808C, Aviation House, 125 Kingsway, London, WC2B 6NH. Tel: 020-7276 8947. *Chairman*, Prof. D. Georgala, CBE
COMMITTEE ON THE SAFETY OF MEDICINES, Market Towers, 1 Nine Elms Lane, London SW8 5NQ. Tel: 020-7273 0000. *Director*, I. Hudson Breckenridge, CBE, FRCP, FRCPEd, FRSE
MEDICINES COMMISSION, Market Towers, 1 Nine Elms Lane, London SW8 5NQ. Tel: 020-7273 0652. *Chairman*, Prof. P. Kumar, FRCP

SPECIAL HEALTH AUTHORITIES

DENTAL VOCATIONAL TRAINING AUTHORITY, Master's House, Temple Grove, Compton Place Road, Eastbourne, E. Sussex BN20 8AD. Tel: 01323-431189. *Chairman*, R. Davies; *Secretary*, Ms J. Verity
FAMILY HEALTH SERVICES APPEAL AUTHORITY (SHA), 30 Victoria Avenue, Harrogate HG1 5PR. Tel: 01423-530280. *Chief Executive (acting)*, P. Burns
HEALTH DEVELOPMENT AGENCY, Holborn Gate, 330 High Holborn, London WC1V 7BA. Tel: 020-7430 0850. *Chair*, Ms Y. Buckland; *Chief Executive*, Prof. R. Parish

MICROBIOLOGICAL RESEARCH AUTHORITY, Porton Down, Salisbury, Wilts SP4 0JG. Tel: 01980-612100. *Chairman*, Sir William Stewart, FRSE, FRS; *Director*, Dr R. H. Gilmour
NATIONAL BLOOD SERVICE, Oak House, Reeds Crescent, Watford, Herts WD24 4QN. Tel: 01923-486800. *Chairman*, M. Fogden, CB; *Chief Executive*, M. Gorham
NATIONAL INSTITUTE OF CLINICAL EXCELLENCE, 11 The Strand, London WC2N 5HR. Tel: 020-7766 9191. *Chairman*, Sir Michael Rawlins; *Chief Executive*, A. Dillon
NHS INFORMATION AUTHORITY, Aqueous II, Aston Cross, Rocky Lane, Birmingham B6 5RQ. Tel: 0121-333 0333. *Chairman*, Prof. A. Bellingham, CBE; *Chief Executive*, Dr G. Thomas
NHS LITIGATION AUTHORITY, Mapier Health, 24-28 High Holborn, London WC13 6AZ. Tel: 020-7430 8700. *Chief Executive*, S. Walker
PRESCRIPTION PRICING AUTHORITY, Bridge House, 152 Pilgrim Street, Newcastle upon Tyne NE1 6SN. Tel: 0191-232 5371. *Chairman*, Mrs A. Galbraith; *Chief Executive*, N. Scholte
UK TRANSPLANT, Fox Den Road, Stoke Gifford, Bristol BS34 8RR. Tel: 0117-975 7575. *Chairman*, Mrs G. Flower; *Chief Executive*, Mrs S. Sutherland

SPECIAL HOSPITALS

ASHWORTH HOSPITAL, Parkbourn, Maghull, Merseyside L31 1HW. Tel: 0151-473 0303. *Chief Executive*, C. Flynn
BROADMOOR HOSPITAL, Crowthorne, Berks RG45 7EG. Tel: 01344 773111.
RAMPTON HOSPITAL, Retford, Notts DN22 0PD. Tel: 01777-248321. *Chief Executive*, J. Taylor

EXECUTIVE AGENCIES

MEDICINES CONTROL AGENCY (MCA)

Market Towers, 1 Nine Elms Lane, London SW8 5NQ
Tel: 020-7273 0000; Fax: 020-7273 0353

The MCA is responsible for safeguarding public health by ensuring all medicines on the UK market meet appropriate standards of safety, quality and efficacy. This is achieved by a system of licensing, inspection, enforcement and monitoring of medicines after they have been licensed.
Chief Executive, Dr K. H. Jones, CB

MEDICAL DEVICES AGENCY

Hannibal House, Elephant and Castle, London SE1 6TQ
Tel: 020-7972 8000; Fax: 020-7972 8108
Web: www.medical-devices.gov.uk

The Agency safeguards the performance, quality and safety of medical devices and ensures that they comply with relevant EU directives.
Chief Executive, Dr D. Jefferys

NHS ESTATES

1 Trevelyan Square, Boar Lane, Leeds LS1 6AE
Tel: 0113-254 7000; Fax: 0113-254 7299;

NHS Estates provides advice and guidance in the area of healthcare estate and facilities management to the NHS and the healthcare industry.
Chief Executive (acting), P. Wearmouth

NHS PENSIONS

Hesketh House, 200–220 Broadway, Fleetwood, Lancs FY7 8LG. Tel: 01253-774774; Fax: 01253-774860

NHS Pensions administers the NHS occupational pension scheme.
Chief Executive (acting), Mrs P. Corless

NHS PURCHASING AND SUPPLY AGENCY
Premier House, 60 Caversham Road, Reading, Berks RG1 7EB. Tel 0118-980 8600.

The agency is responsible for ensuring that the NHS makes the most effective use of its resources by getting the best value for money possible when purchasing goods and services.
Chief Executive, D. Eaton

HOME OFFICE
Home Office, 50 Queen Anne's Gate, London SW1H 9AT
Tel: 0870-000 1585; Fax: 020-7273 2065
Web: www.homeoffice.gov.uk

The Home Office deals with those internal affairs in England and Wales which have not been assigned to other Government departments. The Home Secretary is the link between The Queen and the public and exercises certain powers on her behalf, including that of the royal pardon.

The Home Office's objectives are: to build a safe, just and tolerant society, to maintain and enhance public security and protection; to support and mobilise communities so that they are able to shape policy and improvement for their locality, overcome nuisance, anti-social behaviour, maintain and enhance social cohesion and enjoy their homes and public spaces peacefully; to deliver departmental policies and responsibilities fairly, effectively and efficiently; and to make the best use of resources. These objectives reflect the priorities of the Government and the Home Secretary in areas of crime, citizenship and communities, namely: to reduce crime and the fear of crime; to reduce organised and international crime; to combat terrorism and other threats to national security; to ensure the effective delivery of justice; to deliver effective custodial and community sentences; to reduce re-offending and protect the public; to reduce the availability and abuse of dangerous drugs; to regulate entry to and settlement in the UK effectively in the interests of sustainable growth and social inclusion; and to support strong active communities in which people of all races and backgrounds are valued and participate on equal terms.

The Home Office delivers these aims through the prison, probation and immigration services, its agencies and non-departmental public bodies, and by working with partners in private, public and voluntary sectors, individuals and communities.

The Home Secretary is also the link between the UK Government and the governments of the Channel Islands and the Isle of Man.

Secretary of State for the Home Department, The Rt. Hon. David Blunkett, MP
  Principal Private Secretary (SCS), Jonathan Sedgwick
  Private Secretaries, Gareth Hills; Kirsty Wildgoose; Emily Miles; Simon Watkin; Rebecca Razavi
  Special Advisers, Nick Pearce; Katherine Raymond; Sophie Linden; Huw Evans
Minister of State, The Rt. Hon. John Denham, MP
  (Crime Reduction, Policing, Community Safety and Young People)
  Private Secretary, Richard Riley
Minister of State, Beverley Hughes, MP *(Citizenship, Immigration and Community Cohesion)*
  Private Secretary, Neil Roberts

Minister of State, The Rt. Hon. The Lord Falconer of Thoroton, QC *(Criminal Justice System, Sentencing and Law Reform)*
  Private Secretary, Tom Walker
Parliamentary Under-Secretary of State, Bob Ainsworth, MP *(Anti–Drugs Co-ordination and Organised Crime)*
  Private Secretary, Peter Grime
Parliamentary Under-Secretary of State, Hilary Benn, MP, *(Community and Custodial Provision)*
  Private Secretary, Sabita Sharma
Parliamentary Under-Secretary of State, The Lord Filkin, CBE *(Race Equality, Community and European International Policy)*
  Private Secretary, Kishor Mistry
Permanent Secretary of State (SCS), John Grieve
  Private Secretary, Philip Colligan
Parliamentary Under-Secretary of State, Michael Wills, MP *(Criminal Justice Systems IT and Performance of the Correspondence System)*
  Private Secretary, Jessie Laurie
Parliamentary Clerk, Diana Luchford

COMMUNICATION DIRECTORATE
Director (SCS), B. Butler
Assistant Director (Head of Direct Communications Unit), G. Sampher
Customer Communications Manager, Ms J. Speight
Deputy Director Press Office and (Head of News), Ms J. Simpson
Head of Strategic Communications (SCS), Ms P. Teare
Head of Internal Communications Unit (SCS), P. Samuels
Head of Information Services Unit (G6), P. Griffiths
Head of Marketing Communications Unit, G. Hooper

COMMUNITY POLICY DIRECTORATE
Director (SCS), Ms H. Jackson
Deputy Director and Head of Active Community Unit, Ms H. Edwards, CBE

Head of Animal Procedures and Coroners Unit, T. Cobley

SCIENTIFIC PROCEDURES INSPECTORATE
Chief Inspector (SCS), Dr J. Richmond
Superintendent Inspector (SCS), Dr J. Anderson

Heads of Units

Community Cohesion, J. Kohli
Commission for Racial Equality Chair, vacant
Deputy Chair, Ms B. Bernard
Entitlement Card, S. Harrison
Family Policy, R. Woodland
Strategic Support Group, R. Jenkins
Race Equality, R. Weatherill
Regions and Renewals, Ms B. Moxon

CORPORATE DEVELOPMENT AND SERVICES GROUP
Grenadier House, 99–105 Horseferry Road, London SW1P 2DD. Tel: 0870-000 1585
Queen Anne's Gate, London SW1H 9AT
Tel: 0870-000 1585

Director (SCS), C. Everett
Personnel Director, Ms D. Loudon
Heads of Units, G. Jones *(Assessment and Consultancy)*; T. Edwards *(Building and Estate Management)*; A. Honeyman *(Business Support and Communications)*; J. Potts *(Central Personnel Management)*; vacant *(Opportunities Training and Development)*; D. McDonough *(Departmental Security)*; N. Benger

(Corporate Support Service); B. Gudgin *(Information Management and Technology)*
Records Management, R. Thompson
President of HO Sports and Social Association, J. Gieve
Chair, Ms D. Loudon
Human Resource Equality, vacant
Merseyside Personnel Management Unit, S. Wharton

CRIMINAL POLICY GROUP

Group Directors *(SCS)*, Ms M. Wallace
Directors, D. Cooke *(CJS Performance)*; M. Boyle *(Criminal Law and Policy)*; Ms C. Steward *(Correctional and Rehabilitation Policy)*; Ms J. Wright *(Criminal Justice System IT)*
Heads of Units *(SCS)*, H. Tams *(Adult Offenders and Rehabilitaion)*; vacant *(Correctional Service Standards)*; Ms A.-M. Field *(Criminal Justice Joint Planning)*; F. Galliono *(Criminal Justice Integration Programme)*; M. Gladwyn *(Criminal Justice Integration)*; I. Chisholm *(Criminal Justice Reform Unit)*; Ms J. Furniss *(Justice and Victims)*; Ms E. Moody, Ms F. Spencer *(Mental Health)*; S. Hickson *(Juvenile Offenders)*; Ms D. Grice *(Sentencing and Offenders)*; Ms A. Owens *(HM Inspector of Prisons)* C. Allen *(Deputy Inspector)*; Prof. R. Morgan *(HM Inspector of Probation)*; Ms F. Flaxington *(Deputy Chief Inspector)*; J. Hutchings *(Assistant Chief Inspector)*; S. Shaw *(Prisons and Probation Ombudsman)*; Ms S. Marshall *(Criminal Justice White Paper)*; Ms C. Stewart *(Correctional Service Standards)*; B. Griffith-Williams *(Sentencing Advisory Panel)*; Ms C. French *(Sentencing Framework Implementation Team)*; Lord Norman Warner *(Youth Justice)*

IMMIGRATION AND NATIONALITY DIRECTORATE, AND EUROPEAN AND INTERNATIONAL UNIT

Advance House, 15 Wellesley Road, Croydon, Surrey CR9 3LY Tel: 020-8760 3023.
Apollo House, 36 Wellesley Road, Croydon, Surrey CR9 3RR Tel: 0870-000 1585
50 Queen Anne's Gate, London SW1H 9AT
Tel: 020-7273 4000
India Buildings, 3rd Floor, Water Street, Liverpool L2 0QN
Tel: 0151-237 5200

Director-General *(SCS)*, B. Jeffery
Deputy Director General *(Operation)*, C. Mace; R. Halwood
Directors, P. Wench *(Policy Director)*; C. Allars *(New Policy Team)*; S. Barnett *(Human Resources Directorate)*; K. Brewer *(Detention and Procurement)*; S. Calvard *(Business Information System and Technology Directorate)*; B. Caffarey *(Immigration and Nationality Policy Directorate)*; Ms F. Clarkson *(Asylum and Appeals Policy Directorate)*; B. Eagle *(National Immigration Asylum Bill Team)*; C. Hudson *(Integrated Casework Directorate (Croydon)*; G. James *(Control and Removals Directorate)*; Ms J. Rimble *(International Directorate)*; Ms A. Simkins *(Finance and Service Directorate)*; Ms F. Chaloner *(National Asylum Support Service)*; A. Underwood *(Integrated Casework Directorate (North))*

WORK PERMITS UK

Moorfort, Sheffield, S1 4PQ.

Director, A. Underwood
Deputy Directors, M. Seal *(Operations)*; S. Lamb *(Operations Management)*; Ms S. Hannah *(Operations

Support Management)*; R. Saxby *(Managed Migration)*; N. Hughes *(Charging Development)*

LEGAL ADVISERS' BRANCH

Legal Adviser *(SCS)*, D. Seymour
Deputy Legal Advisers *(SCS)*, D. Noble; C. Osborne
Assistant Legal Advisers *(SCS)*, R. Clayton; J. O'Meara; S. Bramley; H. Carter; Ms S. Weston; Ms R. Collins-Rice; Ms R. Davies; K. Norris; S. Braviner Roman

ORGANISED AND INTERNATIONAL CRIME DIRECTORATE

Director *(SCS)*, S. Boys-Smith
Deputy Directors, Dr K. Collins *(Organised Crime)*; P. Storr *(International)*; Ms S. Killen *(Drugs)*
Heads of Unit, V. Hogg *(Communities and Law Enforcement)*; Ms C.-A. Sweeney *(Corporate Services)*; Ms R. Morle *(Drugs Prevention Advisory Service)*; Ms J. Youell *(Strategic Co-ordination and Planning)*; Ms J. Lempriere *(Treatment, Young People and Local Delivery (Drugs Unit))*; P. Regan *(Extradition Bill Team)*; L. Pallett *(European and International)*; J. Bradley *(Finance and Planning)*; G. Stadlen *(Financial Crime Team)*; S. Webb *(Policing Organised Crime)*; C. Welsh *(Judicial Co-ordination)*; I. Humphreys *(National Technical Assistant Centre)*

PLANNING, FINANCE AND PERFOMANCE GROUP

50 Queen Anne's Gate, London SW1H 9AT
Tel: 020-7273 4000
Horseferry House, Dean Ryle Street, London SW1P 2AW
Tel: 020-7273 4000

Director *(SCS)*, L. Haugh *(Finance)*
Heads of Units *(G7)*, P. Nagel *(Audit and Assurance)*; A. Cory *(Accounting and Finance)*; Ms B. Sandars *(Special Conference Centre)*; R. Scotland *(Commercial and Procurement)*; Ms A. Barnett *(Group Resource)*; S. Jenner *(Performance, Delivery and Strategy Team)*; N. Roche *(Strategic Policy Team)*; V. Clayton *(Spending Review 2002 Project Team)*

POLICING AND CRIME REDUCTION GROUP

Director General *(SCS)*, J. Lyon
Directors *(SCS)*, S. Rimmer *(Policing)*; K. Bond *(Police Standards)*; J. Daniell *(Crime)*
Heads of Unit, J. Duke-Evans *(Action Against Crime and Disorder)*; Ms L. Wickstead *(Crime Reduction Programmes and Partnerships)*; Sir Keith Povey *(HM Inspector of Constabulary)*; P. Wheelhouse *(Information Communication and Technology)*; R. McCool *(Performance and Strategic Management)*; P. Pugh *(Police Leadership and Powers)*; Ms C. Byrne *(Police Personnel)*; Ms T. Burnhams *(Police Reform Bill and Implementation)*; A. Ford *(Police Resource)*; B. Coleman *(Police Scientific Development Branch)*; Ms E. Arney, T. Pearman *(Police Standards)*; P. Edwards *(Property Road Crime Reduction)*; J. Sanders *(Security Industry Authority and Implementation)*; Dr A. Whitehead *(Science Policy)*; K. Sutton *(Street Crime Action Team)*; M. Gillespie *(Violent and Youth Crime Reduction)*

CENTREX (CENTRAL POLICE TRAINING AND DEVELOPMENT AUTHORITY)

Chief Executive, C. Mould

NATIONAL POLICE TRAINING

Bramshill House, Bramshill, Hook, Hants RG27 0JW
Tel: 01256-602100

Directors, A. Humphreys; Ms V. Vaughan-Dick;
 I. McDonald

RESEARCH, DEVELOPMENT AND
STATISTICS DIRECTORATE

Director (SCS), Dr P. Wiles
Heads of Unit, D. Moxon *(Crime and Criminal Justice);*
 vacant *(Corporate Management);* Ms C. Lehman
 (Communications and Development Unit); M. Foster
 (Economics and Resource Analysis); Prof. D. Pyle
 (Drugs and Alcohol Research); C. Lewis *(Offenders and
 Correctional);* P. Ward *(Immigration and Community);*
 Ms C. Wills *(Policing and Reducing Crime Unit)*

EXECUTIVE AGENCIES

UK PASSPORT SERVICES
Globe House, 89 Ecclestone Square, London SW1V 1PN
Advice line: 0870-521 0410
Chief Executive (SCS), B. Herdan
Deputy Chief Executive and Director of Operations (G6),
 K. Sheehan
Director of Systems (G6), J. Davies
Director Finance, Ms A. Cook
Director of Human Resources, R. Mycroft

CRIMINAL RECORDS BUREAU, Horton House,
 Exchange Flags, Liverpool L2 3YL Tel: 0151-236 8068
Chief Executive, Bernard Herdan
Director of Operation, K. Broadbent

FORENSIC SCIENCE SERVICE
see Police Service section

HM PRISION SERVICE
see Prison Service section

PAROLE BOARD FOR ENGLAND AND WALES
see Prison Service section

PRISIONS AND PROBATIONS OMBUDSMAN FOR
ENGLAND AND WALES
see Prison Service section

DEPARTMENT FOR INTERNATIONAL
DEVELOPMENT
1 Palace Street, London SW1E 5HE
Tel: 020-7023 0000; 0845-300 400 Fax: 020-7023 0634
Email: enquiry@dfid.gov.uk; Web: www.dfid.gov.uk
Abercrombie House, Eaglesham Road, East Kilbride,
Glasgow G75 8EA
Tel: 01355-843632; Fax: 01355-843246

The Department for International Development (DFID)
is the UK Government department responsible for
promoting development and the reduction of poverty.
The government's aim is to strengthening the
department and increase its budget. The central focus of
the Government's policy, set out in the 1997 White Paper
on International Development, is a commitment to the
internationally agreed target to halve the proportion of
people living in extreme poverty by 2015, together with
associated targets, including basic health care provision
and universal access to primary education, by the same
date. A second White Paper on International
Development, published in December 2000, reaffirmed

this commitment, while focusing specifically on how to
manage the process of globalisation to benefit poor
people. DFID seeks to work in partnership with
governments committed to these targets, and with
business, civil society and the research community.
 DFID also works with multilateral institutions
including the World Bank, United Nations agencies and
the European Community. The bulk of assistance is
concentrated on the poorest countries in Asia and sub-
Saharan Africa. DFID also contributes to poverty
elimination and sustainable development in middle-
income countries in Latin America, the Caribbean and
elsewhere. In the transition countries of central and
Eastern Europe, DFID is working to ensure the process of
change brings benefits to all people, and particularly to
the poorest.

Secretary of State for International Development, The Rt.
 Hon. Clare Short, MP
 Private Secretary, Anna Bewes
 Special Advisers, Susannah Cox; Ruth Driscoll
 Parliamentary Private Secretary, Dennis Turner, MP
Parliamentary Under-Secretary, Sally Keeble, MP
 Private Secretary, James Price
Permanent Secretary (SCS), Suma Chakrabarti
 Private Secretary, Joanna Graham
 Parliamentary Clerk, Ian Ruff
House of Lords Spokesperson, Baroness Amos
Liaison Peer, Baroness Whittaker

SENIOR MANAGEMENT
Director-General (SCS), Ms N. Brewer *(Programmes and
 International)*
Director-General (SCS), B. R. Ireton, CB *(Knowledge
 Sharing and Special Initiatives)*
Director-General (SCS), R. G. Manning, CB *(Policy)*

AFRICA DIVISION
Director of Division (SCS), G. Stegmann
Heads of Departments, T. Craddock *(SCS) (Africa Great
 Lakes and Horn);* O. Barder *(Africa Policy);* B.
 Thomson *(SCS) (West and North Africa)*
Heads of Offices, M. Wood *(SCS) (Malawi);* J. Winter
 (Central Africa); E. Cassidy *(Mozambique);* Ms H.
 Mealins *(Zambia);* M. Wyatt *(Eastern Africa);* D. Bell
 (Kenya); Ms C. Sergeant *(Tanzania);* M. Hammond
 (Uganda); Ms W. Phillips *(Nigeria);* S. Sharpe
 (Southern Africa)
Heads of Field Offices, J. Riley *(Botswana);* Mrs I. Thorn
 (Lesotho)
Head of Unit, Ms R. Malone *(Namibia)*
Programme Support Officer, Ms K. Wells *(Swaziland)*

ASIA AND PACIFIC DIVISION
Director of Division (SCS), M. Dinham
Heads of Departments (SCS), P. Grant *(Asia Regional
 Economics and Policy);* Ms M. H. Vowles *(SCS)
 (Eastern Asia and Pacific);* C. Austin *(Western Asia)*
Heads of Offices, P. Ackroyd *(SCS) (Bangladesh);* R.
 Graham-Harrison *(SCS) (India);* D. Wood *(Nepal);* J.
 Medhurst *(Pacific);* M. Mallalieu *(SCS) (South East
 Asia);* A. Johnson *(Vietnam);* Ms F. McConnon
 (China)
Development Secretaries, J. Carpy *(Indonesia);* D.
 Arghiros *(Cambodia);* Ms P. Thorpe *(Sri Lanka)*

EASTERN EUROPE AND WESTERN HEMISPHERE
DIVISION

Director of Division (SCS), Ms C. Miller
Heads of Departments (SCS), Ms B. Killen *(Americas and Transition Economies Policy)*; S. Ray *(SCS) (Central and South Eastern Europe)*; D. Batt *(SCS) (Eastern Europe and Central Asia)*; G. Duffy *(Latin America)*; Ms R. Eyben *(SCS) (Bolivia)*; Mrs S. Warner *(Belize)*; Ms J. Alston *(Caribbean)*; S. Mills *(Brazil)*; Ms G. Taylor *(Central America)*; C. Warren *(Overseas Territories)*; Ms J. Chambers *(Honduras)*; M. Lewis *(Peru)*
Development Secretaries, J. McCredie *(Guyana)*; G. Saggers *(Jamaica)*

INTERNATIONAL DIVISION

Director of Division (SCS), J. A. L. Faint
Heads of Departments (SCS), A. Smith *(European Union)*; Dr M. Kapila *(Conflict and Humanitarian Affairs)*; Ms M. Cund *(International Financial Institutions)*; M. Mosselmans *(United Nations and Commonwealth)*

ECONOMICS, BUSINESS AND STATISTICS DIVISION

Director of Division, Prof. A. Wood
Heads of Departments, P. Landymore *(Economics Policy and Research)*; Ms C. Seymour-Smith *(International Trade)*; Ms V. Harris *(Private Sector Policy)*; P. Spray *(Social Science Research Unit)*; C. Kirk *(Evaluation)*
Chief Enterprise Development Adviser, D. J. Stanton
Chief Statistician, T. Williams

FINANCE DIVISION

Director of Division, M. Lowcock
Heads of Departments, Ms S. Wardell *(Development Policy)*; K. Sparkhall *(Finance)*; M. Smithson *(Accounts)*; R. Elias *(Internal Audit)*; S. Chard *(Procurement)*

HUMAN RESOURCES

Director (SCS), D. Fish
Heads of Departments (SCS) J. Anning *(Human Resources Operations)*; D. Richards *(Human Resources Policy)*; P. Brough *(Overseas Pensions)*

RURAL LIVELIHOODS AND ENVIRONMENTAL
DIVISION

Head of Division, A. J. Bennett, CMG
Heads of Departments, A. Davis *(Environment Policy)*; J. Michael Scott *(Rural Livelihoods)*

INFORMATION DIVISION

Director (SCS), vacant
Heads of Departments, R. Calvert *(Information and Civil Society)*; D. Gillett *(Information Systems and Services)*

OTHER RELATED ORGANISATIONS

CDC CAPITAL PARTNERS

One Bessborough Gardens, London SW1V 2JQ
Tel: 020-7828 4488; Fax: 020-7282 6505

CDC Capital Partners provides equity finance to private sector businesses in emerging markets. It has over 20 offices located across Latin America, Africa, South Asia and Asia Pacific. CDC is a public limited company with the Department for International Development as its 100 per cent shareholder.
Chairman, The Lord Cairns, CBE
Deputy Chairman, Ms J. Almond
Chief Executive, Dr A. Gillespie

LORD CHANCELLOR'S DEPARTMENT

Selborne House, 54–60 Victoria Street, London SW1E 6QW
Tel: 020-7210 8500
Web: www.lcd.gov.uk

The Lord Chancellor appoints Justices of the Peace (except in the Duchy of Lancaster) and advises the Crown on the appointment of most members of the higher judiciary. He is responsible for promoting general reforms in the civil law, for the procedure of the civil courts and for the Community Legal Service. He is a member of the Cabinet. He also has ministerial responsibility for magistrates' courts, which are administered locally. Administration of the Supreme Court and county courts in England and Wales was taken over by the Court Service, an executive agency of the department, in 1995.

The Lord Chancellor is also responsible for ensuring that letters patent and other formal documents are passed in the proper form under the Great Seal of the Realm, of which he is the custodian. The work in connection with this is carried out under his direction in the Office of the Clerk of the Crown in Chancery.

The Lord Chancellor is also the senior Lord of Appeal in Ordinary and speaker of the House of Lords.
Lord Chancellor (£180,045), The Rt. Hon. The Lord Irvine of Lairg, QC
  Principal Private Secretary, Sarah Albon
  Special Adviser, Gary Hart
  Parliamentary Private Secretaries, Laura Moffat, MP; Gordon Marsden, MP
Parliamentary Secretary, The Rt. Hon. Baroness Scotland of Asthal, QC
  Private Secretary, Brett Regan
Parliamentary Secretary, Yvette Cooper, MP
  Private Secretary, Grant Morris
Parliamentary Secretary, Rosie Winterton, MP
  Private Secretary, David Liddemore
Permanent Secretary, Sir Hayden Phillips, GCB
  Private Secretary, Helen Smith

CROWN OFFICE

House of Lords, London SW1A 0PW
Tel: 020-7219 4713

Clerk of the Crown in Chancery, Sir Hayden Phillips, KCB
Deputy Clerk of the Crown in Chancery, vacant
Clerk of the Chamber, C. I. P. Denyer

JUDICIAL GROUP

Tel: 020-7210 8500
Director General, Mrs J. Williams

Directors (SCS), Mrs E. J. Grimsey; D. Nooney
Heads of Divisions, A. Shaw; J. Powell *(Courts Division (JC))*; P. Farmer; R. Sams *(Tribunals) (JT))*; D. Staff *(Pay, Pensions and Terms and Conditions (JP))*; Ms M. Pigot *(Judical Appointments Policy Secretariat (JS))*; Ms J. Killick

JUDICIAL STUDIES BOARD

9th Floor, Millbank Tower, London SW1P 4QW
Tel: 020-7217 4706
Secretary (SCS), E. S. Adams

POLICY GROUP

Tel: 020-7210 8719
Director-General (SCS), Dr J. Spencer
Heads of Divisions (SCS), A. Cogbill *(Civil Justice and*

Legal Services Directorate); J. Tanner *(Civil Justice)*; A. Frazer *(Civil Law Development)*; D. A. Hill *(Public Legal Services)*; C. Myerscough *(Criminal Courts Reform)*; P. Harris *(Legal Services Development)*; Ms A. Finlay *(Public and Private Rights Directorate)*; Ms S. Field; Mrs R. Pratt; Ms S. Johnson *(Family Policy 1 and 2)*; B. Wells *(Administrative Justice)*; vacant *(Constitutional Directorate)*; Lee Hughes *(Freedom Of Information and Data Protection)*; Rick Evans *(Constitutional Policy)*; M. de Pulford *(Human Rights Division)*; N. Smedley *(Criminal Justice Group)*; vacant *(Criminal Justice)*; A. Frazer *(Civil Law Development)*; L. Hughes *(FOI and Data Protection)*; M. Goulding *(IT and Business Change)*; A. McDonald *(Tribunals for Users Programme)*; A. Shaw *(Land Registration and E-Conveyancing)*; Ms M. Shaw *(Asylum Policy)*; D. Watts *(Support and Analysis)*

LEGAL AND INTERNATIONAL GROUP

Tel: 020-7210 0711

Legal Adviser to the Lord Chancellor's Department and Director-General of Legal Group (SCS), P. Jenkins
Heads of Divisions (SCS), P. Fish *(Legal Advice and Litigation)*; R. Heaton *(Constitutional Law)*; Ms C. Johnston *(Legal Advice and Legislation)*; M. Collon *(Drafting Services)*; A. Wallace *(International)*; R. Evans *(Constitutional Policy)*

COMMUNICATIONS GROUP

Tel: 020-7210 8672

Director of Communications (SCS), A. Percival, LVO
Head of External Communications (SCS), M. Wicksteed

CORPORATE SERVICES GROUP

Tel: 020-7210 8503

Director of Corporate Services (SCS), Ms. J. Rowe
Heads of Divisions (SCS), S. Smith *(Finance)*; A. Pay *(Accountancy)*; A. Rummins *(Internal Assurance)*; A. Maulltby *(Information Management)*; R. Atkinson *(Facilities and Support Services)*; K. Garett *(Statutory Publications)*; vacant *(Information Technology)*; B. Eadie, R. Moore *(Corporate Services Secretariat)*; P. Jacob *(Change Unit)*; K. Chivers *(Magistrates Courts' Service Inspectorate)*; Ms M. Field *(Corporate Diversity Unit)*; D. Gladwell *(International Departmental Review of Immunity from Prosecution)*

ECCLESIASTICAL PATRONAGE

10 Downing Street, London SW1A 2AA
Tel: 020-7930 4433

Secretary for Ecclesiastical Patronage, J. H. Holroyd, CB
Assistant Secretary for Ecclesiastical Patronage, N. C. Wheeler

LORD CHANCELLOR'S ADVISORY COMMITTEE ON STATUTE LAW

Room 6.06, Selborne House, 54–60 Victoria Street, London SW1E 6QW
Tel: 020-7210 2615; Fax: 020-7210 2678

The Advisory Committee advises the Lord Chancellor on all matters relating to the revision, modernisation and publication of the statute book.
Chairman, The Lord Chancellor, The Rt. Hon. The Lord Irvine of Lairg, QC
Deputy Chairman, Sir Hayden Phillips, KCB
Members, The Hon. Mr Justice Carnwath, CVO; The Hon. Lord Gill; J. M. Davies; J. C. McCluskie, CB, QC; R. Henderson; P. Jenkins; Mrs C. Tullo; W. R. McKay, CB; K. Garrett; E. G. Cauldwell, CB; P. J. Layden, TD; G.

Gray; Miss J. Wheldon, CB, QC; Ms J. Rowe; A. Pawsey
Secretary, N. Hodgett

EXECUTIVE AGENCY

THE COURT SERVICE

Southside, 105 Victoria Street, London SW1E 6QT
Tel: 020-7210 1646; Fax: 020-7210 2059
Web: www.courtservice.gov.uk

The Court Service provides administrative support to the Supreme Court, the Crown Court, county courts and a number of tribunals in England and Wales.
Chief Executive (SCS), I. Magee
Director of Field Services, P. Handcock
Director of Operational Policy (SCS), Miss B. Kenny
Director of Finance (SCS), P. Commins
Director of Purchasing and Contract Management (SCS), C. Lyne
Director of Information Services and Communications Technologies (SCS), Ms A. Vernon
Director of Human Resources (acting) (SCS), Ms H. Dudley
Director of Civil and Family Modernisation, J. Sills
Customer Service Director (SCS), M. Camley
Programme Delivery Directors (SCS), D. Barr; J. Lane
Head of Magistrate's Courts Administrative Division (SCS), N. Haighton
Programme Director Magistrates' Courts IT Division and LIBRA Project (SCS), N. Haighton
Director of Tribunals (SCS), S. Smith

SUPREME COURT GROUP

Strand, London WC2A 2LL
Tel: 020-7936 6000
Director (SCS), I. Hyams

NORTHERN IRELAND OFFICE

11 Millbank, London SW1P 4PN
Tel: 020-7210 3000
Castle Buildings, Stormont, Belfast BT4 3SG
Tel: 01232-520700; Fax: 01232-528195
Web: www.nio.gov.uk

The Northern Ireland Office was established in 1972, when the Northern Ireland (Temporary Provisions) Act transferred the legislative and executive powers of the Northern Ireland Parliament and Government to the UK Parliament and a Secretary of State.
The Northern Ireland Office is responsible primarily for security issues, law and order and prisons, and for matters relating to the political and constitutional future of the province. It also deals with international issues as they affect Northern Ireland.
Under the terms of the 1998 Good Friday Agreement, power was devolved to the Northern Ireland Assembly in 1999. The Assembly has taken on responsibility for the relevant areas of work previously undertaken by the departments of the Northern Ireland Office covering agriculture and rural development, the environment, regional development, social development, education, higher education, training and employment, enterprise, trade and investment, culture, arts and leisure, health, social services and public safety and finance and personnel.
Secretary of State for Northern Ireland, The Rt. Hon. Dr John Reid, MP
  Parliamentary Private Secretary, Gillian Merron, MP
Minister of State, Jane Kennedy, MP
  Parliamentary Private Secretary, Shona McIsaac, MP

Parliamentary Under-Secretary of State, Desmond Browne, MP
Permanent Under-Secretary of State, Sir Joseph Pilling, KCB
Head of the Northern Ireland Civil Service, Gerry Loughran

NORTHERN IRELAND INFORMATION SERVICE

Castle Buildings, Stormont, Belfast BT4 3SG
Tel: 028-9052 0700

EXECUTIVE AGENCIES

COMPENSATION AGENCY, Royston House, Upper Queen Street, Belfast BT1 6FD. Tel: 01232-2499444
FORENSIC SCIENCE AGENCY, Seapark, 151 Belfast Road, Carrickfergus, Co. Antrim BT38 8PL
Tel: 01232-365744
NORTHERN IRELAND PRISON SERVICE, *see* Prison Service section

SCOTLAND OFFICE
Dover House, Whitehall, London SW1A 2AU
Tel: 020-7270 6754; Fax: 020-7270 6812
Email: scottish.secretary@scotland.gov.uk
Web: www.scottishsecretary.gov.uk

The Scotland Office is the department of the Secretary of State for Scotland, who represents Scottish interests in the Cabinet on matters reserved to the UK Parliament, i.e. constitutional matters, financial and economic matters, defence and international relations, immigration, social security, various matters relating to the single market with the UK (energy, transport, consumer protection) and employment. It also supports the Advocate General, the legal adviser to the UK Government on Scottish law. *See also* Regional Government section.
Secretary of State for Scotland, The Rt. Hon. Helen Liddell, MP
 Private Secretary, Ms J. Colquhoun
 Parliamentary Private Secretary, Sandra Osborne, MP
Parliamentary Under-Secretary of State, Anne McGuire, MP
 Private Secretary, Chloe Squire
 Parliamentary Private Secretary, Sandra Osborne MP
Advocate-General for Scotland, Dr Lynda Clark, QC, MP
 Private Secretary, Gary Whyte
Spokesperson in the House of Lords, Lord McIntosh of Haringey

DEPARTMENT OF TRADE AND INDUSTRY
1 Victoria Street, London SW1H 0ET
Tel: 020-7215 5000; Fax: 020-7222 0612;
Web: www.dti.gov.uk

The Department of Trade and Industry works with businesses, employees and consumers to increase UK productivity and competitiveness. The department's aim is to make the UK a more prosperous country and close the gap with international competitors.
 This is achieved by making it easier and more attractive to start and grow new businesses. There is a strong focus on innovation to help more firms to grow and capture new markets, ensuring fair and open markets at home and overseas to support successful UK businesses and the creation of jobs, and better support for scientific excellence.
Secretary of State for Trade and Industry, The Rt. Hon. Patricia Hewitt, MP
 Principal Private Secretary, Erica Zimmer

 Private Secretaries, Eleanor Brooks; Sarah Hodgetts
 Parliamentary Private Secretaries, Anne Campbell, MP; Andrew Miller, MP *Minister of State,* Stephen Timms, MP *(E-Commerce and Competitiveness)*
 Private Secretary, Alison Walker
 Parliamentary Private Secretary, Lawrie Quinn, MP
Minister of State, The Rt. Hon. The Baroness Symons of Vernham Dean *(Trade and Investment and Deputy Leader of the House of Lords)*
 Private Secretary, Mathew Taylor
 Parliamentary Private Secretary, Charlotte Atkins, MP
Minister of State, Brian Wilson, QC, MP *(Energy and Construction)*
 Private Secretary, Maria Bazell
 Parliamentary Private Secretary, Ian Stewart, MP
Minister of State, Alan Johnson, MP *(Employment Relations, Industry and the Regions)*
 Private Secretary, Giles Smith
 Parliamentary Private Secretary, Bob Laxton, MP
Parliamentary Under-Secretary of State, Melanie Johnson, MP *(Competition, Consumers and Markets)*
 Private Secretary, Emma Ward
Parliamentary Under-Secretary of State, The Lord Sainsbury of Turville§ *(Science and Innovation)*
 Private Secretary, Charlotte DuBern
Parliamentary Under-Secretary of State, Nigel Griffiths, MP *(Small Business)*
 Private Secretary, Louise Robson
Permanent Secretary, Robin Young, CB
 Private Secretary, Fergus Harradence
Parliamentary Clerk, Tim Williams
Chief Scientific Adviser and Head of Office of Science and Technology, Prof. David King
 Private Secretary, Juliet Griffin
Chief Executive British Trade International, Sir David Wright, KCMG, LVO
 Private Secretary, Gavin Scott
§ Unpaid

STRATEGY UNIT
Director of Strategy Unit (SCS), S. Lyle-Smythe
Chief Economic Adviser (SCS), Ms V. Pryce
Director of Strategic Planning (SCS), Ms C. Normand
Director of Communications (SCS), I. Plewhite
Director of Economic Analysis (SCS), K. Warwick
Director of Performance and Evaluation (SCS), A. Rees
Director of Statistical Analysis (SCS), G. Everett

INNOVATION GROUP
Director-General (acting), A. Keddie
Director, Facilitating Innovation, J. Rhodes
Directors, I. Eddison; Mrs P. Jackson; D. Reed; P. Burke

BRITISH NATIONAL SPACE CENTRE
Director-General (SCS), Dr C. Hicks
Deputy Director-General (SCS), D. Leadbeater
Directors (SCS), A. Cooper; Dr D. Hall; Miss P. Freedman

NATIONAL WEIGHTS AND MEASURES LABORATORY
Director and Chief Executive (SCS), J. Llewellyn

PATENT OFFICE
Chief Executive (SCS), Ms A. Brimelow

ENERGY GROUP
Director-General, Miss J. MacNaughton

COAL

Director of Coal (SCS), R. Wright
Directors (SCS), P. Mason; Mrs A. Taylor

ENERGY POLICY

Deputy Director-General (SCS), N. Hirst
Directors (SCS), N. Peace; J. Doddrell; Dr A. Gault; G. C. White; G. Bryce

ENGINEERING INSPECTORATE

Director of Engineering Inspectorate (SCS), Dr P. Fenwick

NUCLEAR INDUSTRIES

Director of Nuclear Liabilities and BNFL (SCS), Ms H. Leisner
Directors (SCS), Dr D. Walker; S. Spivey

NUCLEAR LIABILITIES AND BNFL

Director of Nuclear Industries (SCS), Ms A. Lambert
Directors (SCS), J. R. V. Brookes, CBE; Dr A. Eggington; S. Toole; J. Campbell

OIL AND GAS

Director of Oil and Gas (SCS), G. Dart
Directors (SCS), J. R. V. Brooks, CBE; Dr A. Eggington; S. Toole; J. Campbell

BUSINESS GROUP

Director-General, M. Gibson

BUSINESS RELATIONS

Director of Business Relations (SCS), J. Alty
Directors (SCS), Mrs S. Morris; H. Brown

AEROSPACE AND DEFENCE INDUSTRIES

Director, (SCS), J. Hunt

AUTOMOTIVE

Director (SCS), Ms S. Chambers

BIOSCIENCE

Director (SCS), Ms M. Darnborough

CHEMICALS

Director (SCS), Dr D. Jennings

CONSTRUCTION INDUSTRIES

Director (SCS), Ms E. Whatmore

CONSUMER GOODS AND SERVICES

Director (SCS), B. Hopson

JOINT ENVIRONMENTAL MARKETS UNIT

Director (SCS), D. Prior

MARINE

Director (SCS), Ms S. Bishop

MATERIALS

Director (SCS), Ms N. Carter

BUSINESS RELATIONS - COMMUNICATION AND INFORMATION INDUSTRIES

Director of Communication and Information Industries (SCS), D. Hendon
Directors (SCS), N. Worman; D. Lumley; D. Love; C. Holmes; Mrs G. Alliston; S. Pride

BUSINESS RELATIONS - POSTAL SERVICES

Director of Postal Services (SCS), D. Davis
Directors (SCS), Ms H. Merrifield; M. Higson

BUSINESS SUPPORT

Director of Business Support (SCS), D. Saunders
Director (SCS), M. Hilton

RADIO COMMUNICATIONS AGENCY

Chief Executive (SCS), Ms R. Anderson

REGIONS

Deputy Director-General, Regions (SCS), P. MacIntyre
Directors (SCS), A. Steele; J. Neve; P. Bunn; W. Arnold

SMALL BUSINESS SERVICE

Chief Executive (SCS), M. Wynn Griffith
Deputy Chief Executive (SCS), Dr D. Evans
Directors (SCS), Dr K. Poulter; A. Piper; P. Williams; Mrs M. Mayer

SERVICES GROUP

Director-General, Dr C. Bell

ESTATES AND FACILITIES MANAGEMENT

Director (SCS), M. Coolican

EXPORT CONTROL AND NON PROLIFERATION

Director of Export Control and Non Proliferation (SCS), M. O'Shea
Directors (SCS), J. Clayton; D. Figuera

FINANCE AND RESOURCE MANAGEMENT

Director of Finance and Resource Management, (SCS), E. Hosker
Directors (SCS), A. Wright; Dr P. Lloyd; C. Juman; Ms H. Taylor

HUMAN RELATIONS AND CHANGE MANAGEMENT

Director of Human Resources and Change Management (SCS), Ms S. Haird
Directors (SCS), T. Soane; H. Ewing; Ms R. Heyhoe

INFORMATION MANAGEMENT AND PROCESS ENGINEERING

Director (SCS), D. Wheeler

FAIR MARKETS GROUP

Director-General, S. Haddrill

COMPANY LAW AND INVESTIGATIONS

Director of Company Law and Investigations (SCS), R. Rogers
Directors (SCS), R. Burns; J. Grewe; K. Masson; G. Harp; J. Gardner; J. Sibley; Ms B. Chase; A. Robertshaw; C. Callaghan

COMPETITION AND CONSUMER AFFAIRS

Director of Competition and Consumer Affairs (SCS), J. Rees
Directors (SCS), P. Sellers; D. Miner; T. Shearer; Ms J. Swift; Ms P. Wilson; Ms C. Durkin; Ms B. Habberjam

EMPLOYMENT RELATIONS

Director of Employment Relations (SCS), Ms J. Munday
Directors (SCS), M. Beatson; Mrs S. Rhodes; Mrs R. McCarthy-Ward

LOW PAY COMMISSION

Secretary (SCS), Ms K. Harre

WOMEN AND EQUALITY UNIT

10 Great George Street, London SW1P 3AE
Tel: 020-7273 8880
Head of Unit (SCS), Dr S. Atkins
Deputy Director (SCS), Ms L. Chennells; Ms H. Samson-Barry

EUROPEAN AND WORLD TRADE POLICY
Director-General, R. Cardon

Directors (SCS), Dr E. Draige; H. Savill; T. Abraham; D. Andrews; A. Berry; C. Moir; M. Cocks

LEGAL SERVICES

The Solicitor and Director-General, A. Inglese
Director of Legal Resources (SCS), C. Warren
Director of Legal Services A (SCS), Ms T. Dunstan
Legal Directors (SCS), J. Roberts; S. Hyett; C. Norris; Ms E. Race
Director of Legal Services B (SCS), Ms A. Brett-Holt
Legal Directors (SCS), R. Baker; R. Perkins; Ms S. Hardy; R. Green; R. Swede
Director of Legal Services C (SCS), P. Bovey
Legal Directors (SCS), M. Bucknil; A. Woods; M. Smith; T. Susman; B. Welch; C. Raikes
Director of Legal Services D (SCS), S. Milligan
Legal Directors (SCS), L. Newbatt; A. Faucett

OFFICE OF SCIENCE AND TECHNOLOGY

Chief Scientific Adviser and Head of Office of Science and Technology, Prof. D. King
Director-General of Research Councils, Dr J. Taylor, OBE, FRS
Director of Science and Engineering Base (SCS), C. Henshall
Directors (SCS), Dr F. Saunders; S. Speed; Dr S. De Souza
Director of Transdepartmental Science and Technology (SCS), Ms J. Durning
Directors (SCS), A. Wootton; Ms J. Carney; Mrs J. Britton; E. Quilty; R. Abel

BRITISH TRADE INTERNATIONAL

Kingsgate House, 66–74 Victoria Street, London SW1E 6SW
Tel: 020-7215 5000

British Trade International brings together the Department of Trade and Industry and the Foreign and Commonwealth Office export and investment operations.

Chair, The Rt. Hon. The Baroness Symons of Vernham Dean
Vice-Chairmen, Sir David Brown, Sir David John, KCMG
Group Members, R. Turner, OBE; V. Brown; A. Summers; K. Pathak, OBE; W. Thompson, OBE; D. Jones; M. Gibson; Sir Peter Mason, KBE; A. Hingston; G. Fry; S. Hampson; Ms S. Pirie, OBE; Ms J. Stevens; P. Barron, CBE; Dr J. Bridge
Special Representative for Investment and Trade, HRH The Duke of York GCMG, GCVO

TRADE PARTNERS UK

The Trade Partners UK network provides services to British exporters and investors at home and overseas.
Chief Executive, Sir David Wright, KCMG, LVO
Deputy Chief Executive and Group Director (SCS), I. Jones *(Regions)*
Group Directors (SCS), Q. Quayle *(International)*; D. Warren *(Business)*; J. Reynolds *(Strategy and Communications)*

INVEST UK

Chief Executive (SCS), W. Pedder
Directors (SCS), S. O. Leary *(Operations)*; M. Uden *(International)*

EXECUTIVE AGENCIES

COMPANIES HOUSE

Crown Way, Cardiff CF14 3UZ
Tel: 0870-333 3636; Fax: 029-2038 0517;
Email: genenquiries@companieshouse.gov.uk
Web: www.companieshouse.gov.uk
London Information Centre, 21 Bloomsbury Street, London WC1B 3XD Tel: 0870-333 3636;
Fax: 020-2038 0517
Edinburgh, 37 Castle Terrace, Edinburgh EH1 2EB
Tel: 0870-333 3636; Fax: 029-380 517
Birmingham, Central Library, Chamberlain Square, Birmingham B33 3HQ
Tel: 0870-333 3636; Fax: 029-2038 0517
Leeds, 25 Queen Street, Leeds, LS1 2TW
Tel: 0870-333 3636; Fax: 029-2038 0517
Manchester, 75 Mosley Street, Manchester, M2 2HR
Tel: 0870-333 3636; Fax: 029-2038 0517

Companies House incorporates companies, registers company documents and provides company information.
Registrar of Companies for England and Wales, C. Clancey
Registrar for Scotland, J. Henderson

EMPLOYMENT TRIBUNALS SERVICE

19–29 Woburn Place, London WC1H 0LU
Tel: 020-7273 8666; Fax: 020-7273 8670

The Service became an executive agency in 1997 and brought together the administrative support for the employment tribunals and the Employment Appeal Tribunal.
Chief Executive, R. Heathcote

THE INSOLVENCY SERVICE

PO Box 203, 21 Bloomsbury Street, London WC1B 3QW
Tel: 020-7637 1110; Fax: 020-7636 4709

The Service administers and investigates the affairs of bankrupts and companies in compulsory liquidation; deals with the disqualification of directors in all corporate failures; regulates insolvency practitioners and their professional bodies; provides banking and investment services for bankruptcy and liquidation estates; and advises Ministers on insolvency policy issues.
Inspector-General and Chief Executive, D. J. Flynn
Deputy Inspectors-Generals, G. Horne; L. T. Cramp

NATIONAL WEIGHTS AND MEASURES LABORATORY (NWML)

Stanton Avenue, Teddington, Middx TW11 0JZ
Tel: 020-8943 7272; Fax: 020-8943 7270;
Web: www.nwml.gov.uk

The Laboratory administers weights and measures legislation, carries out type examination, calibration and testing, and runs courses on legal metrology.
Chief Executive, Dr J. Llewellyn

PATENT OFFICE

see Intellectual Property section

RADIOCOMMUNICATIONS AGENCY

Wyndham House, 189 Marsh Wall, London E14 9SX
Tel: 020-7211 0211; Fax: 020-7211 0507;
Web: www.radio.gov.uk

The Agency is responsible for the management of the radio spectrum used for civilian purposes within the UK. It also represents UK radio interests internationally.

The Office of Communications (OFCOM), will become the new regulator for the communications sector in 2003.

Chief Executive, Ms R. Anderson

DEPARTMENT FOR TRANSPORT

Great Minster House, 76 Marsham Street, London SW1P 4DR
Ashdown House, 123 Victoria Street, London SW1E 6DE
Tel: 020-7944 8300
Web: www.dft.gov.uk

The Department for Transport was established in May 2002 following the de-merger of the Department of Transport, Local Government and the Regions.

The department's main responsibilities are aviation, freight, health and safety, integrated and local transport, London Underground, maritime, mobility and inclusion, railways, roads and road safety, shipping and vehicles.

The department's Ministers are based at Great Minster House.

Secretary of State for Transport, The Rt. Hon Alistair Darling, MP
   Private Secretary, Andrew Campbell
Minister of State, The Rt. Hon. John Spellar, MP
   (Transport)
   Private Secretary, Phil West
Parliamentary Under-Secretary of State, David Jamieson, MP *(Transport)*
   Private Secretary, Shane Snow
Permanent Secretary, Rachel Lomax
   Private Secretary, Jessica Bowles

† Based at Ashdown House
‡ Based at Great Minster House

‡DIRECTORATE OF COMMUNICATION

Director (acting), C. Skinner

†FINANCE ACCOUNTING SERVICES

Divisional Manager, A. Beard

‡HUMAN RESOURCES DIRECTORATE

Director, Ms H. Parker-Brown

‡LEGAL TRANSPORT DIRECTORATE

Director, C. Muttukumaru

‡RAILWAYS AND AVIATION

Director-General (SCS), D. Rowlands
Directors, R. Griffins *(Aviation Directorate);* R. Bennett *(London Underground Task Group);* M. Lambirth *(Rail Delivery Directorate);* D. McMillan *(Rail Restructuring Directorate);* I. Devlin *(Transport Security Division)*
Deputy Director, J. Grubb *(Transport Security Division)*

‡TRANSPORT STRATEGY, ROADS, LOCAL AND MARITIME

Director-General (SCS), W. Rickett
Directors, J. Plowman *(Driver, Vehicle and Operator Group);* A. Davis *(Integrated and Local Transport Directorate);* B. Wadsworth *(Logistics and Maritime Transport Directorate);* D. Roberts *(Road Transport Directorate);* P. McCarthy *(Transport Finance Directorate);* Ms D. Phillips *(Transport Strategy Directorate)*
Branch Heads, J. Hart *(Dangerous Goods Branch);* A. Aitchison *(Transport Finance Branch 1);* Ms M. Stallebrass *(Transport Finance Branch 2);* M. Lowe *(Transport Finance Branch 3);* L. Stark *(Transport Delivery Branch 2);* R. Phillips *(Transport Delivery Branch 3)*

‡STRATEGY AND CORPORATE SERVICES

Director-General, R. Dudding
Directors, M. Sykes *(Commercial Directorate);* C. Riley *(Strategy and Economics Directorate);* D. Fisk *(Chief Scientist)*

‡HEALTH AND SAFETY SPONSORSHIP

Divisional Manager, G. Williams

EXECUTIVE AGENCIES

DRIVER AND VEHICLE LICENSING AGENCY

Longview Road, Morriston, Swansea SA6 7JL
Tel: 01792-782341; Fax: 01792-782793;
Web: www.dvla.gov.uk

The Agency is responsible for registering and licensing drivers and vehicles, and the collection and enforcement of vehicle exercise duty.

Chief Executive, C. Bennett

DRIVING STANDARDS AGENCY

Stanley House, Talbot Street, Nottingham NG1 5GU
Tel: 0115-901 2500; Fax: 0115-901 2940;
Web: www.dsa.gov.uk

The Agency is responsible for carrying out theory and practical driving tests for car drivers, motorcyclists, bus and lorry drivers and for maintaining the registers of Approved Driving Instructors and Large Goods Vehicle Instructors, as well as supervising Compulsory Basic Training (CBT) for learner motorcyclists. There are five area offices, which manage over 430 practical test centres across Britain.

Chief Executive, G. Austin

HIGHWAYS AGENCY

St Christopher House, Southwark Street, London SE1 0TE
Tel: 020-7921 4574; Fax: 020-7921 4592
Web: www.highways.gov.uk

The Agency is responsible for delivering the Transport Department's road programme and for maintaining the national road network in England.

Chief Executive, T. Matthews

MARITIME AND COASTGUARD AGENCY

Spring Place, 105 Commercial Road, Southampton SO15 1EG
Tel: 023-8032 9100; Fax: 023-8032 9298;
Web: www.mcga.gov.uk

The agency's aim is to be a world-class organisation that is committed to preventing loss of life, continuously improving maritime safety and protecting the marine environment.

Chief Executive, M. Storey
Chief Coastguard, J. Astbury

VEHICLE CERTIFICATION AGENCY

1 Eastgate Office Centre, Eastgate Road, Bristol BS5 6XX
Tel: 0117-951 5151; Fax: 0117-952 4103;
Web: www.vca.gov.uk

The agency is the UK authority responsible for ensuring that vehicles and vehicle parts have been designed and constructed to meet internationally agreed standards of safety and environmental protection.
Chief Executive, D. W. Harvey

VEHICLE INSPECTORATE (VI)

Berkeley House, Croydon Street, Bristol BS5 0DA
Tel: 0117-954 3200; Fax: 0117-954 3212
Web: www.via.gov.uk

The Agency tests and certifies the roadworthiness of heavy goods and public service vehicles and supervises MOT testing.
Chief Executive, M. R. Newey

HM TREASURY

1 Horse Guards Road, London SW1A 2HQ
Tel: 020-7270 5000
Email: public.enquiries@hm-treasury.gov.uk
Web: www.hm-treasury.gov.uk

The Office of the Lord High Treasurer has been continuously in commission for well over 200 years. The Lord High Commissioners of HM Treasury are the First Lord of the Treasury (who is also the Prime Minister), the Chancellor of the Exchequer and five junior Lords. This Board of Commissioners is assisted at present by the Chief Secretary, the Parliamentary Secretary (who is also the Government Chief Whip in the House of Commons), the Paymaster-General, the Financial Secretary, and the Economic Secretary. The Prime Minister as First Lord is not primarily concerned in the day-to-day aspects of Treasury business; neither are the Parliamentary Secretary and the Junior Lords as Government Whips. Treasury business is managed by the Chancellor of the Exchequer and the other Treasury Ministers, assisted by the Permanent Secretary.

The Chief Secretary is responsible for public expenditure planning and control; public sector pay; value for money in the public services; public service agreements; public/private partnerships and procurement policy; strategic oversight of banking, financial services and insurance; departmental investment strategies including the Capital Modernisation Fund and Invest to Save Budget; welfare reform; devolution; and resource accounting and budgeting.

The Paymaster-General is responsible for the Inland Revenue and the Valuation Office, with overall responsibility for the Finance Bill. She leads on personal taxation, business taxation, European and international tax issues.

The Economic Secretary is responsible for Customs and Excise; growth and productivity; science, research and development; competition and deregulation policy; export credit; VAT and road and fuel duties; and parliamentary financial business (Public Accounts Committee, National Audit Office).

The Financial Secretary is responsible for National Savings and Investments, the Debt Management Office, the Office of National Statistics, the Royal Mint, and the Government Actuary's Department; banking, financial services and insurance; foreign exchange reserves; debt management policy; financial services tax issues and

charity taxation. She provides support to the Chancellor on EU issues.

Prime Minister and First Lord of the Treasury, The Rt. Hon. Anthony (Tony) Blair, MP
Chancellor of the Exchequer, The Rt. Hon. Gordon Brown, MP
  Principal Private Secretary, Mark Bowman
  Private Secretaries, Beth Russell; Will Price
  Parliamentary Private Secretary, Anne Keen, MP
  Chief Economic Adviser to the Treasury, Ed Balls
  Special Advisers, Ed Miliband; Ian Austin; Nicola Murphy; Spencer Livermore
  Council of Economic Advisers, Chris Wales; Paul Gregg; Ms Shriti Vadera; Maeve Sherlock; Stewart Wood
Chief Secretary to the Treasury, The Rt. Hon. Paul Boateng, MP
  Private Secretary, Lucy Makinson
  Parliamentary Private Secretary, Helen Southworth, MP
Paymaster-General, The Rt. Hon. Dawn Primarolo, MP
  Private Secretary, Andy Gordon
  Parliamentary Private Secretary, Chris Pond, MP
Financial Secretary to the Treasury, Ruth Kelly, MP
  Private Secretary, Rob Gregory
  Parliamentary Private Secretary, Tony Wright, MP
Economic Secretary to the Treasury, John Healey, MP
  Private Secretary, Helen Watson
Permanent Secretary to the Treasury, Gus O'Donnell, CB
  Parliamentary Clerk, David Martin
Parliamentary Secretary to the Treasury and Government Chief Whip, The Rt. Hon. Hilary Armstrong, MP
  Private Secretary, Roy Stone
Treasurer of HM Household and Deputy Chief Whip, Keith Hill, MP
Comptroller of HM Household, Thomas McAvoy, MP
Vice-Chamberlain of HM Household, Gerry Sutcliffe, MP
Lord Commissioners of HM Treasury (Whips), Ian Pearson, MP; John Heppel, MP; Nick Ainger, MP; Jim Fitzpatrick, MP; Philip Woolas, MP
Assistant Whips, Jim Murphy, MP; Fraser Kemp, MP; Angela Smith, MP; Ivor Caplin, MP; Joan Ryan, MP; Derek Twigg MP; Dan Norris, MP

DIRECTORATES

Head of Ministerial Support Team (SCS), M. Bowman
Head of Communications and Strategy Team (SCS), M. Ellam

MACROECONOMIC POLICY AND INTERNATIONAL FINANCE

Managing Director, J. Cunliffe
Directors (SCS), S. Brooks; S. Pickford; I. Rogers; S. Owen
Heads of Teams (SCS), C. M. Kelly; A. Kilpatrick; D. Ramsden; M. Glycopantis; P. Mills; G. Lloyd; R. Lawrence K. Peters; A. Lewis; M. Manuel; R. Woods; J. de Berker

BUDGET AND PUBLIC FINANCES

Managing Director (SCS), R. Culpin
Director (SCS), N. Holgate
Heads of Teams (SCS), P. Betts; I. Taylor; G. Parker; A. Gibbs; D. Deaton; P. Rankin; M. Swan; D. Richardson; J. Richardson; H. John

PUBLIC SERVICES

Managing Director, N. Macpherson
Directors, L. de Groot; A. Sharples; J. Grice; J. Stephens

Heads of Teams, R. Brown; A. Bridges; R. Dunn; M. Wheatley; P. Brook; A. Charlesworth; A. Sharples; A. Ritchie; A. Graham; W. Nye; L. Atter; P. Johnston; H. Tuffs; M. Dawes; D. Gordon; I. Walker

CORPORATE SERVICES AND DEVELOPMENT (CSD)

Managing Director (SCS), H. Douglas, CB
Heads of Teams (SCS), C. Pearson; J. Dodds; P. Pelger; S. Norris; R. Brightwell

FINANCIAL MANAGEMENT, REPORTING AND AUDIT

Managing Director (SCS), A. Likierman
Director and Head of Treasury Office of Accounts Team (SCS), B. Glicksman
Heads of Teams (SCS), D. Loweth; K. Ross; I. Carruthers; C. Butler; B. Glicksman; A. M. Jones

FINANCE, REGULATION AND INDUSTRY

Managing Director (SCS), to be appointed
Directors (SCS), H. J. Bush, CB; R. Fellgett
Heads of Teams (SCS), S. Meek; J. Halligan; J. Kingman; R. Bent; S. Beckett; D. Storey; C. Maxwell; S. Catchpole; D. Lawton; J. Close; R. Price; G. Spence

EXECUTIVE AGENCIES

NATIONAL SAVINGS AND INVESTMENTS
see Finance section

OFFICE FOR NATIONAL STATISTICS
see Public Bodies section

ROYAL MINT
see Public Bodies section

UNITED KINGDOM DEBT MANAGEMENT OFFICE

Eastcheap Court, 11 Philpot Lane, London, EC3M 8UD
Tel: 020-7862 6500; Fax: 020- 7862 6509

The UK Debt Management Office was launched as an executive agency of the Treasury in April 1998. The office has two main functions: it is the Government's debt manager (issuing gilts, managing the gilt market); and the Government's cash manager (balancing the Exchequer's cash flow on a daily basis by issuing Treasury bills and through other transactions in the sterling money markets).
Chief Executive, M. L. Williams

OTHER BODIES

OFFICE OF GOVERNMENT COMMERCE (OGC)
Trevelyan House, 26-30 Great Peter Street, London SW1P 2BY
Tel: 0845-000 4999
Web: www.ogc.gov.uk

The Office of Government Commerce was set up on the 1 April 2000. It is a unique body within government, overseen by a supervisory board of Ministers and officials from across the departments of government. Its aim is to achieve the best value for money for the Government's commercial relationships and coherence of purchasing activity across 200 Government departments, non-governmental bodies and agencies. The OGC is an office of HM Treasury.
Chief Executive, P. Gershon
Deputy Chief Executive, B. Rigby

OGC BUYING SOLUTIONS

Royal Liver Building, Pier Head, Liverpool L3 1PE
Tel: 0151-227 4262; Fax: 0151-258 1249
Web: www. ogcbuyingsolutions.gov.uk

The Agency provides a professional purchasing service to Government departments and other public bodies. From April 2000 it became part of the Office of Government Commerce reporting to the Chief Secretary to the Treasury.
Chief Executive (SCS), D. J. Court

THE TREASURY SOLICITOR
DEPARTMENT OF HM PROCURATOR-GENERAL AND TREASURY SOLICITOR

Queen Anne's Chambers, 28 Broadway, London SW1H 9JS
Tel: 020-7210 3000; Fax: 020-7210 3004

The Treasury Solicitor's Department provides legal services for many Government departments. Those without their own lawyers are provided with legal advice, and both they and other departments are provided with litigation services. The Treasury Solicitor is also the Queen's Proctor, and is responsible for collecting Bona Vacantia on behalf of the Crown. The Department became an executive agency in 1996.
HM Procurator-General and Treasury Solicitor (SCS), Juliet Wheldon

LITIGATION DIVISION

(SCS), R. Aitken; Mrs D. Babar; P. Bennett; D. Pearson; L. John-Charles; A. D. Lawton; ; B. McKay; P. R. Messer; D. Palmer; R. Phillips; A. J. Sandal; P. Kent; H. Giles; S. Cochrane; A. Chapman; P. Whitehurst; M. Truran

QUEEN'S PROCTOR DIVISION

Queen's Proctor (SCS), Juliet Wheldon
Assistant Queen's Proctor (SCS), Sue Cochrane

DIRECTORATE OF CORPORATE STRATEGY

Director of Corporate Strategy (SCS), M. Fuhr
Assistant Director Establishments (G7), Ms H. Donnelly
Assistant Director Finance (G7), C. A. Woolley
Assistant Director Information Systems (G6), M. Gabbidon
Business Support Manager (SEO), E. Blishen
Assistant Director Human Resources (G6), Ms M. Esplin

BONA VACANTIA DIVISION

(G6), J. Davis

EUROPEAN DIVISION

(SCS), J. E. Collins; A. Ridout; M. C. P. Thomas

CULTURE, MEDIA AND SPORT DIVISION

(SCS), Ms I. Letwin

CABINET OFFICE AND CENTRAL ADVISORY DIVISION

(SCS), Ms R. Jeffreys, C. House

MINISTRY OF DEFENCE ADVISORY DIVISION

Metropole Building, Northumberland Avenue, London WC2N 5BL Tel: 020-7218 4691

(SCS), V. Rose; L. Nicoll; H. Morrison; Mrs V. Collett; M. Hemming

DEPARTMENT FOR EDUCATION AND SKILLS DIVISION

Caxton House, Tothill Street, London SW1H 9NA
Tel: 020-7273 3000

(SCS), F. D. W. Clarke; P. Kilgarriff; D. Macrae; D. Aries; N. Ash

HM Treasury Advisory Division
1 Horse Guards Road, London SW1A 2HQ
Tel: 020-7270 3000

(SCS), M. A. Blythe; J. R. J. Braggins; J. Jones; P. Henderson; A. Stewart; S. Cochran

---

WALES OFFICE
Gwydyr House, Whitehall, London SW1A 2ER
Tel: 020-7270 0549; Fax: 020-7270 0568
Email: wales.office@wales.gov.uk
Web: www.walesoffice.gov.uk

The Wales Office is the department of the Secretary of State for Wales, who represents Welsh interests in the Cabinet.

Secretary of State for Wales, The Rt. Hon. Paul Murphy, MP
Principal Private Secretary, Simon Morris
Parliamentary Private Secretary, Gareth Thomas, MP
Parliamentary Under-Secretary, Don Touhig, MP
Head of Office, Alison Jackson

DEPARTMENT FOR WORK AND PENSIONS
Richmond House, 79 Whitehall, London SW1A 2NS
Tel: 020-7238 0800; Fax: 020-7238 0763
Email: ministers@dwp.gsi.gov.uk
Web: www.dwp.gov.uk

The Department for Work and Pensions was formed on 8 June 2001 from parts of the former Department of Social Security and Department for Education and Employment and the Employment Service. The department helps unemployed people of working age into work, helps employers to fill their vacancies and provides financial support to people unable to help themselves through back to work programmes. The department also administers the Child Support system, social security benefits and the social fund. In addition, the department has reciprocal social security arrangements with other countries.

In April 2002 the Benefits Agency and the Employment Service was replaced by the Jobcentre Plus network (responsible for helping people to find jobs and paying benefits to people of working age), and the Pension Service which administers the Benefits Agency's pension-related services.

Secretary of State for Work and Pensions, The Rt. Hon. Andrew Smith, MP
Principal Private Secretary, Neil Couling
Private Secretaries, Alan Wardel; Emily Ackroyd; Jo Littleton; Louise Stitson
Special Adviser, Andrew Maugham
Parliamentary Private Secretary, Anne Coffey, MP
Minister of State, The Rt. Hon. Nick Brown, MP *(Work)*
Parliamentary Private Secretary, Bob Blizzard, MP
Special Adviser, Kieran Simpson
Private Secretary, Dan Jefferson
Minister of State, The Rt. Hon. Ian McCartney, MP *(Pensions)*
Private Secretary, Denise Whitehead
Parliamentary Private Secretary, Neil Turner, MP
Parliamentary Under-Secretary of State (Lords), The Rt. Hon. The Baroness Hollis of Heigham, DL *(Children and the Family)*
Private Secretary, Mary Curran
Parliamentary Under-Secretary of State, Malcolm Wicks, MP *(Work)*
Private Secretary, Jenny Shellens

Parliamentary Under-Secretary of State, Maria Eagle, MP *(Disabled People)*
Private Secretary, Emma Davies
Permanent Secretary (SCS), Rachel Lomax
Private Secretary, Judith Tunstall
Parliamentary Clerk, Tim Elms

WORKING AGE AND CHILDREN GROUP
Group Director (SCS), Ms U. Brennan
Director, Work and Welfare Strategy, M. Richardson
Director, Fraud, Planning and Presentation Strategy, R. Clark
Director, National Employment Panel, Ms C. Stratton
Director, Children and Housing, M. Neale
Director, Child Benefit Centre, Ms J. Ritchie

PENSIONS AND DISABILITY GROUP
Managing Director, P. Gray
Director, Pensions Strategy and Client Programme, Ms H. Reynolds
Director, Private Pensions, J. Hughes
Director, Private Pensions II, Ms J. Hill
Director, Pensions Stewardship, R. D'Souza
Director, Disability and Carers, D. Brereton, CB
Director, Disability and Carers Service, J. Sumner
Director, Joint International Unit (also for Department for Education and Skills), C. Tucker

CORPORATE AND SHARED SERVICES GROUP FINANCE
Group Director and Principal Finance Officer (SCS), J. Codling
Director, Financial Services, P. Robinson
Director, Financial Management, M. Davison
Director, Internal Assurance Services, C. Turner
Director, Commercial, D. Smith
Director, Corporate Management Information, B. Hayward

CORPORATE DEVELOPMENT GROUP
Group Director, Dr S. Hickey
Director, Planning and Performance, R. Devereux
Director, Universal Banking, Ms S. Trundle
Director, Payment Modernisation, Ms C. Goodfellow

PROGRAMME AND SYSTEMS DELIVERY GROUP
Group Director, R. Westcott
Director, Project Management, G. Hextall
Director, Joint Programme Management, Ms S. Newton
Director, Planning and Finance, K. Palmer
Director, Technology Office, P. Cook
Director, External Supply, P. Crahan
Director, Digital Infrastructure, A. Stott

HUMAN RESOURCES GROUP
Group Director, K. White
Diversity Director, Ms B. Burford
Head of Department, Senior Civil Service, Ms M. Helson
Head of Department, Training Services, B. Gormley
Head of Department, Workforce Planning, Ms S. Rice
Head of Department, Development, J. Ashe
Head of Department, HR Services, O. Thorpe
Head of Department, HR Change Programme, Ms G. Adey
Head of Department, Occupational Psychology, Dr M. Dalgliesh

MEDICAL POLICY AND CORPORATE MEDICAL GROUP

Chief Medical Adviser and Medical Director, Dr M. Aylward, CB
Policy Manager, State Incapacity Benefits, Dr P. Sawney
Policy Manager, Disability and Carer Benefits, Dr R. Thomas
EU of Medical Advisers in Social Security (UEMASS), Dr P. Stidolph
Contractorisation of Medical Services (IMPACT) Project, Dr M. Henderson

LAW AND SPECIAL POLICY GROUP

Head of Group, Ms M. Morgan, CB
Director of Legal Services, J. Catlin
Assistant Director, SOL Prosecutions, Ms S. Edwards
Assistant Director, Commercial Branch, R. Powell
Assistant Director, SOL Litigation, Ms A. James

ANALYTICAL SERVICES DIVISION (ASD)

Director, D. Stanton, CB
Policy Mangers, Welfare to Work Strategy, Ms B. O'Gorman
Policy Mangers, Ajudicational and Constitutional Reform, J. Griffiths
Policy Mangers, Pension Provision Group, G. Fiegehen

COMMUNICATIONS DIRECTORATE

Director, S. MacDowall
Head of Media Relations, Ms S. Dodd
Head of Corporate Communications, K. Young
Head of Marketing, S. O'Neill

EXECUTIVE AGENCIES

APPEALS SERVICE AGENCY
see Tribunals Section

CHILD SUPPORT AGENCY

Long Benton, Benton Park Road, Newcastle upon Tyne NE98 1YX
Tel: CSA Helpline: 08457-133 133

The Agency was set up in April 1993. It is responsible for the administration of the Child Support Act and for the assessment, collection and enforcement of maintenance payments for all new cases.
Chief Executive, D. Smith

Non-Executive Director, Ms M. Brown, MBE
Deputy Chief Executive and Director of Operations, M. Isaac
Directors, M. Neale; G. Keenan; Ms E. Fox; V. Gaskell; P. Hedley

JOBCENTRE PLUS

Richmond House, 79 Whitehall, London SW1A 2NS
Tel: 020-7238 0800; Fax: 020-7238-0763
Web: www.jobcentreplus.gov.uk

Jobcentre Plus was formed in April 2002 following the merger of the Employment Service and some parts of the Benefits Agency. The agency administers claims for and payments of social security benefits to help people gain employment or improve their prospects for work as well as helping employers to fill their vacancies.
Chief Executive, L. Lewis, CB

THE PENSION SERVICE

Richmond House, 79 Whitehall, London SW1A 2NS
Tel: Public Enquiries: 020-7712 2171

The Pension Service was created in April 2002 to deliver services to pensioners through a network of twenty-six pension centres.
Chief Executive, Ms A. Cleveland

VETERANS AGENCY

Norcross, Blackpool, Lancs FY5 3WP
Tel: 0800-162 2277
Email: help@veteransagency.mod.uk
Web: www.veteransagency.mod.uk

The Agency administers the payment of war disablement and war widows' pensions and provides welfare services and support to war disablement pensioners, war widows and their dependants and carers.
Chief Executive (acting), A. Burnham

ADVISORY BODIES

SOCIAL SECURITY ADVISORY COMMITTEE
New Court, 48 Carey Street, London WC2A 2LS.
Tel: 020-7412 1508; Fax: 020-7412 1570;
Email: ssac@dwp.gsi.gov.uk; Web: www.ssac.org.uk
Chairman, Sir Thomas Boyd-Carpenter, KBE
Secretary, Ms G. Saunders

PUBLIC OFFICES

ADJUDICATOR'S OFFICE
Haymarket House, 28 Haymarket, London SW1Y 4SP
Tel: 020-7930 2292; Fax: 020-7930 2298
Web: www.adjucatorsoffice.gov.uk

The Adjudicator's Office opened in 1993 and investigates complaints about the way the Inland Revenue (including the Valuation Office Agency), Customs and Excise and the Public Guardianship Office have handled a person's affairs.
The Adjudicator, Dame Barbara Mills, DBE, QC
Head of Office, C. Gordon

ADVISORY, CONCILIATION AND ARBITRATION SERVICE
Brandon House, 180 Borough High Street, London SE1 1LW 4SP Tel: 020-7210 3613; Fax: 020-7210 3708
Web: www.acas.org.uk

The Advisory, Conciliation and Arbitration Service (ACAS) was set up under the Employment Protection Act 1975 (the provisions now being found in the Trade Union and Labour Relations (Consolidation) Act 1992).
ACAS is directed by a Council consisting of a full-time chairman and part-time employer, trade union and independent members, all appointed by the Secretary of State for Trade and Industry. The functions of the Service are to promote the improvement of industrial relations in general, to provide facilities for conciliation, mediation and arbitration as means of avoiding and resolving industrial disputes, and to provide advisory and information services on industrial relations matters to employers, employees and their representatives.
ACAS has regional offices in Birmingham, Bristol, Cardiff, Fleet, Glasgow, Leeds, Liverpool, London, Manchester, Newcastle upon Tyne and Nottingham.
Chairman, R. Donaghy, OBE
National Conciliator (G6), T. Lippiatt

ANCIENT MONUMENTS BOARD FOR SCOTLAND
Longmore House, Salisbury Place, Edinburgh EH9 1SH
Tel: 0131-668 8764; Fax: 0131-668 8765;
Email: ancient.monuments@scotland.gov.uk
Web: www. historic-scotland.net

The Ancient Monuments Board for Scotland advises the Scottish Ministers on the exercise of their functions, under the Ancient Monuments and Archaeological Areas Act 1979, of providing protection for monuments of national importance.
Chairman, Prof. Michael Lynch, FRSE
Members, R. J. Mercer, FRSE, FSA; Miss L. M. Thoms; J. C. Higgitt, FSA; Dr C. Swanson, Ph.D.; M. Baughan; Dr J. E. Cannizzo, Ph.D.; Dr S. Peake, Ph.D.; M. J. Taylor; Ms J. Harden; A. Saville, FSA; Cllr J. A. McFadden, CBE; Cllr E. F. Scott; Prof. C. D. Morris, FRSE, FSA; A. P. K. Wright, OBE; Dr C. E. Batey, Ph.D.
Secretary, R. A. J. Dalziel
Assistant Secretary, D. M. Tulloch
Assessor, Dr. D. J. Breeze, Ph.D, FRSE, FSA

ANCIENT MONUMENTS BOARD FOR WALES (CADW)
Crown Buildings, Cathays Park, Cardiff CF10 3NQ
Tel: 029-2050 0200; Fax: 029-2082 6375;
Email: cadw@wales.gsi.gov.uk
Web: www.cadw.wales.gov.uk

The Ancient Monuments Board for Wales advises the National Assembly for Wales on its statutory functions in respect of ancient monuments.
Chairman, Prof. R. R. Davies, CBE, FBA, D.Phil
Members, R. G. Keen; Prof. W. Davies, FBA, FSA; M. J. Garner; Prof. R. A. Griffiths, D.Litt.; R. Brewer, FSA; Prof. A. Whittle, FBA, D.Phil; C. Musson, MBE, FSA; Prof. M. Aldhouse-Green, FSA
Secretary, Mrs J. Booker

ARTS COUNCILS

The Arts Council of Great Britain was established as an independent body in 1946 to be the principal channel for the Government's support of the arts. In 1994 the Scottish and Welsh Arts Councils became autonomous and the Arts Council of Great Britain became the Arts Council of England.
The Arts Councils are responsible for the distribution of the proceeds of the National Lottery allocated to the arts. (*see* Lotteries and Gaming Section).

ARTS COUNCIL OF ENGLAND
14 Great Peter Street, London SW1P 3NQ
Tel: 020-7333 0100; Fax: 020-7973 6590;
Web: www.artscouncil.org.uk

The Arts Council is the national, strategic policy body for the arts. It commissions new work, conducts research, provides advice and information, promotes the case for publicly funded arts, creates partnerships and accesses new money for artistic activity. It receives funding from Government, but is an independent non-political body working at arm's length from the Government.
On 1 April 2002, the Arts Council of England and the 10 regional arts boards joined together to form a single development organisation for the arts.
The Government grant for 2002–2003 is £296 million.
Chairman, G. Robinson
Members, Sir Norman Adsetts; T. Bloxham; Ms D. Bull, CBE; P. Collard; Ms D. Grubb; Ms S. Woodford Hollick; Prof. A. Livingston; S. Lowe; Prof. J. McGregor; B. McMaster, CBE; Ms E. Owusu; W. Sieghart; S. Timperley; Ms D. Wilson
Chief Executive, P. Hewitt

REGIONAL ARTS COUNCILS
Web: www.arts.org.uk

EAST ENGLAND ARTS, Cherry Hinton Hall, Cherry Hinton Road, Cambridge CB1 8DW. Tel: 01223-215355. *Chair,* Prof. S. Timperley
EAST MIDLANDS ARTS, Mountfields House, Epinal Way, Loughborough, Leics LE11 0QE. Tel: 01509-218292. *Chair (acting),* S. Lowe
LONDON ARTS, 2 Pear Tree Court, London, EC1R 0DS. Tel: 020-7608 6100. *Chair,* Lady Hollick
NORTHERN ARTS, Central Square, Forth Street, Newcastle upon Tyne NE1 3PJ. Tel: 0191-255 8500. *Chair,* P. Collard
NORTH-WEST ARTS, Manchester House, 22 Bridge Street, Manchester M3 3AB. Tel: 0161-834 6644. *Chair,* T. Bloxham, MBE

SOUTHERN AND SOUTH-EAST ARTS, Tunbridge Wells Office, Union House, Eridge Road, Tunbridge Wells, Kent TN4 8HF. Tel: 01892-507200. *Chair,* Ms D. Grubb Winchester Office, 13 St Clement Street, Winchester SO23 9DQ. Tel: 01962-855099. *Chair,* D. Astor
SOUTH-WEST ARTS, Bradninch Place, Gandy Street, Exeter EX4 3LS. Tel: 01392-218188.
Chair, Prof. A. Livingston
WEST MIDLANDS ARTS, 82 Granville Street, Birmingham B1 2LH. Tel: 0121-631 3121.
Chair, Ms D. Wilson
YORKSHIRE ARTS, 21 Bond Street, Dewsbury, W. Yorks WF13 1AX. Tel: 01924-455555.
Chair, Sir Norman Adsetts

SCOTTISH ARTS COUNCIL

12 Manor Place, Edinburgh EH3 7DD
Tel: 0131-226 6051; Fax: 0131-225 9833;
Email: administrator@scottisharts.org.uk
Web: www.scottisharts.org.uk
The Scottish Arts Council funds arts organisations in Scotland. Its grant for 2002–3 from the Scottish Executive was £34.3 million. It has also received additional funds of £500,000 for traditional arts and £1.1 million for drama. The Scottish Arts Council also receives National Lottery funding to support and develop artistic excellence and creativity throughout Scotland.
Chairman, J. Boyle
Vice-Chair, Ms D. Idiens
Members, Ms S. Ainsley; Cllr E. Cameron; R. Chester; W. English; J. Faulds; Ms M. Marshall; Dr A. Matheson, OBE; J. Scott Moncrieff; W. Speirs; Ms J. Baker; Ms L. Mitchell; Ms D. Idien
Director, G. Berry

ARTS COUNCIL OF WALES

9 Museum Place, Cardiff CF10 3NX
Tel: 029-2037 6500; Fax: 029-2022 1447
Web: www.ccc-acw.org.uk
The Arts Council of Wales funds arts organisations in Wales and is funded by the National Assembly for Wales. The grant for 2002–2003 was £20.783 million.
Chairman, Ms S. Crouch
Members, D. Davies; Dr H. Walford Davies; E. Fivet; S. Garrett; E. AP Gwyn; H. James; D. Jones; P. Ryan, OBE; R. Davies; Ms M. A. Elis; Ms J. Roberts; D. W. Walters
Chief Executive, P. Tyndall
Deputy Chief Executive, F. Medley

ARTS COUNCIL OF NORTHERN IRELAND

MacNeice House, 77 Malone Road, Belfast BT9 6AQ
Tel: 028-9038 5200; Fax: 028-9066 1715;
Email: publicaffairs@artscouncil-ni.org
Web: www.artscouncil-ni.org
The Arts Council of Northern Ireland is the prime distributor of Government funds in support of the arts in Northern Ireland. It is funded by the Department of Culture, Arts and Leisure, and the grant for 2002–2003 is £7.4 million.
Chairman, Prof. B. Walker
Vice-Chair, Ms E. O'Baoill
Members, Mrs M. Armstrong; D. Boyd; Cllr M. Bradley; Dr M. Crozier; R. Dunn, OBE; Dr T. Maginess; D. Hyndman; Ms J. Jordan; J. Kerr; Dr T. Maginess; Prof. B. McClelland; Ms G. Moriarty; A. Shortt; Mrs. M. Yeomans
Chief Executive, Ms R. McDonough

ART GALLERIES AND ASSOCIATED BODIES

NATIONAL GALLERIES OF SCOTLAND

The Mound, Edinburgh EH2 2EL
Tel: 0131-624 6200; Fax: 0131-343 3250;
The National Galleries of Scotland comprise the National Gallery of Scotland, the Scottish National Portrait Gallery, the Scottish National Gallery of Modern Art and the Dean Gallery. There are also outstations at Paxton House, Berwickshire, and Duff House, Banffshire. Total Government grant-in-aid for 2002–2003 is £12.28 million.

TRUSTEES
Chairman of the Trustees, Mr B. Ivory, CBE
Trustees, Ms V. Atkinson; J. Hunter Blair; Ms A. Bonnar; G. J. N. Gemmell, CBE; Lord Gordon of Strathblane, CBE; A. P. Leitch; Prof. C. Lodder; Dr I. McKenzie Smith, OBE; G. Weaver; Prof. I. Whyte

OFFICERS
Director-General (G4), Sir T. Clifford, FRSE
Keeper of Conservation (G6), M. Gallagher
Head of Press and Information (G7), P. Convery
Head of Education (G7), M. Finn
Registrar (G7), Miss A. Buddle
Buildings (G7), R. Galbraith
Director, National Gallery of Scotland (G6), M. Clarke
Director, Scottish National Portrait Gallery (G6), J. Holloway
Curator of Photography, Miss S. F. Stevenson
Director, Scottish National Gallery and Dean Gallery (G6), R. Calvocoressi

NATIONAL GALLERY

Trafalgar Square, London WC2N 5DN
Tel: 020-7839 3321; Fax: 020-7747 2403;
Web: www.nationalgallery.org.uk
The National Gallery, which houses a permanent collection of western painting from the 13th to the 20th century, was founded in 1824, following a parliamentary grant of £60,000 for the purchase and exhibition of the Angerstein collection of pictures. The present site was first occupied in 1838; an extension to the north of the building with a public entrance in Orange Street was opened in 1975, and the Sainsbury wing was opened in 1991. Total Government grant-in-aid for 2002–2003 was £20.449 million.

BOARD OF TRUSTEES
Chairman, P. Scott, QC
Trustees, P. Hughes, CBE; C. Le Brun; Dr D. Landau; Sir Colin Southgate; J. Snow; Prof. Dawn Ades; Lady Hopkins; M. Getty; R. Sondhi; Prof. J. Higgins, DBE; D. Moore; Sir John Kerr, GCMG

OFFICERS
Director, Dr C. Saumarez Smith
Keeper, Dr N. Penny
Head of Curational Department, Dr S. Foister
Senior Curator, Dr D. Jaffé
Chief Restorer, M. H. Wyld, CBE
Head of Exhibitions, M. J. Wilson
Scientific Adviser, Dr A. Roy
Director of Administration, J. MacAuslan
Head of Education, K. Adler

NATIONAL PORTRAIT GALLERY

St Martin's Place, London WC2H 0HE
Tel: 020-7306 0055; Fax: 020-7306 0056;
Web: www.npg.org.uk

A grant was made in 1856 to form a gallery of the portraits of the most eminent persons in British history. The present building was opened in 1896 and the Ondaatje wing; including a new Balcony Gallery, Tudor Gallery, IT Gallery, Lecture Theatre, and roof-top restaurant opened in May 2000. There are three regional partnerships displaying portraits in appropriate settings: Montacute House, Beningbrough Hall and Bodelwyddan Castle. Total Government grant-in-aid for 2002–2003 was £5.462 million.

BOARD OF TRUSTEES

Chairman, Sir David Scholey, CBE
Trustees, The Rt. Hon. Robin Cook, MP; Prof. P. King, CBE, PRA; Ms. F. Fraser; Mrs T. Green; M. Hastings; T. Phillips, RA; Prof. The Earl Russell, FBA; Mrs. C. Tomalin, FRSL; D. Scholey, CBE; Mrs A. Shulman; Sir John Weston, KCMG; Baroness Willoughby de Eresby; Prof. D. Cannadine; Prof. L. Jordanova; Dr C. Ondaatje, CBE
Director (G3), S. Nairne

ROYAL FINE ART COMMISSION FOR SCOTLAND

Bakehouse Close, 146 Canongate, Edinburgh EH8 8DD
Tel: 0131-556 6699; Fax: 0131-556 6633;
Web: www.royfinartcomforsco.gov.uk

The Commission was established in 1927 and advises Ministers and local authorities on the visual impact and quality of design of construction projects. It is an independent body and gives its opinions impartially.
Chairman, The Rt. Hon. The Lord Cameron of Lochbroom, PC, FRSE
Commissioners, Ms J. Malvenan; R. G. Maund; M. Murray; D. Page; B. Rae; Prof. R. Russell; M. Turnbull; A. Wright; Ms K. Anderson; Mrs M. Hickish; P. Stallan
Secretary, C. Prosser

TATE BRITAIN

Millbank, London SW1P 4RG
Tel: 020-7887 8008; Fax: 020-7887 8007;
Web: www.tate.org.uk

Tate Britain displays the national collection of British art. The gallery opened in 1897, the cost of erection (£80,000) being defrayed by Sir Henry Tate, who also contributed the nucleus of the present collection. The Turner wing was opened in 1910, and further galleries and a new sculpture hall followed in 1937. In 1979 a further extension was built, and the Clore Gallery, for the Turner collection, was opened in 1987. Tate consists of four galleries: Tate Britain and Tate Modern in London, Tate Liverpool and Tate St Ives.

BOARD OF TRUSTEES

Chairman, D. Verey
Trustees, Prof. D. Ades; Ms V. Barnsley; Prof. J. Latto; Sir Christopher Mallaby, GCMG, GCVO; J. Snow; J. Studzinski; Ms G. Wearing; C. Ofili; Ms J. Opie; Sir Richard Carew Poole; Sir Howard Davies

OFFICERS

Director, Sir Nicholas Serota
Director of National Programmes, vacant

Director of Collections, vacant
Director, Tate Modern, V. Todoli
Director, Tate Britain, S. Deuchar
Curator, Tate Liverpool, C. Gruneberg
Curator, Tate St Ives, S. Daniel-McElvoy

TATE MODERN

Bankside, London SE1 9TG
Tel: 020-7887 8008;
Web: www.tate.org.uk

Opened on 11 May 2000, Tate Modern displays the Tate collection of international modern art dating from 1900 to the present day. It includes works by Dalí, Picasso, Matisse and Warhol as well as many contemporary works. It is housed in the former Bankside Power Station in London, redesigned by the Swiss architects Herzog & de Meuron.
Director, V. Todoli

WALLACE COLLECTION

Hertford House, Manchester Square, London W1M 6BN
Tel: 020-7563 9500; Fax: 020-7224 2155;
Web: www.wallace-collection.org.uk

The Wallace Collection was bequeathed to the nation by the widow of Sir Richard Wallace, Bt., in 1897, and Hertford House was subsequently acquired by the Government. Total Government grant-in-aid for 2002–2003 was £2.463 million.
Director, Miss R. J. Savill
Head of Finance and Administration, Ms. S. Logan *(acting)*

ASSEMBLY OMBUDSMAN FOR NORTHERN IRELAND AND NORTHERN IRELAND COMMISSIONER FOR COMPLAINTS

Progressive House, 33 Wellington Place, Belfast BT1 6HN Tel: 028-9023 3821; Fax: 028-9023 4912;
Email: ombudsman@ni-ombudsman.org.uk
Web: www.ni-ombudsman.org.uk

The Ombudsman is appointed under legislation with powers to investigate complaints by people claiming to have sustained injustice in consequence of maladministration arising from action taken by a Northern Ireland Government department, or any other public body within his remit. Staff are presently seconded from the Northern Ireland Civil Service.
Ombudsman, T. Frawley
Deputy Ombudsman, J. MacQuarrie
Directors, C. O'Hare; R. Doherty; H. Mallon

AUDIT COMMISSIONS

AUDIT COMMISSION FOR LOCAL AUTHORITIES AND THE NATIONAL HEALTH SERVICE IN ENGLAND AND WALES

1 Vincent Square, London SW1P 2PN
Tel: 020-7828 1212; Fax: 020-7976 6187
Web: www.audit-commission.gov.uk

The Audit Commission was set up in 1983 and is responsible for appointing external auditors to local authorities, including the Greater London Authority, and local National Health Service bodies in England and Wales. It is also responsible for promoting the proper stewardship of public finances and value for money in the services provided by local authorities and health bodies.

The Commission has a chairman, a deputy chairman and up to 18 members who are appointed by the Office of the Deputy Prime Minister in consultation with the Secretary of State for Wales and the Health Secretaries in England and Wales.

Acting Chair, Ms A. Fresko

Members, Dr. P. Lane; G. Lemos; Cllr N. Skellett; C. Swinson; D. Moss; Cllr R. Arthur; Sir. David Williams; Prof. S. Richards; Dr J. Curson; Sir Graham Hart, KCB; Ms E. Filkin; B. Wolfe; Ms J. Baddeley; J. Bowen; R. Hoyle

Controller of Audit, A. Foster

Commission Secretary, B. Taylor

Chief Executive of District Audit Service, A. Meekings

AUDIT SCOTLAND

110 George Street, Edinburgh EH2 4LH
Tel: 0131-477 1234; Fax: 0131-477 4567;
Web: www.audit-scotland.gov.uk
Audit Scotland was set up on 1 April 2000 to provide services to the Accounts Commission and the Auditor General for Scotland. Together they help to ensure that the Scottish Executive and public sector bodies in Scotland are held accountable for the proper, efficient and effective use of around £17 billion of public funds.

Audit Scotland's work covers over 200 bodies including local authorities, police and fire boards; NHS boards and trusts; further education colleges; the water authority; departments of the Scottish Executive; executive agencies such as the Prison Service and non-departmental public bodies such as Scottish Enterprise.

Audit Scotland carries out financial and regularity audits to ensure that the public sector bodies adhere to the highest standards of financial management and governance. It also performs audits to ensure that these bodies achieve the best value for money. All of Audit Scotland's work in connection with local authorities, fire and police boards is carried out for the Accounts Commission while its other work is undertaken for the Auditor General.

Auditor General, R. W. Black

Accounts Commission Chairman, A. MacNish

Secretary, W. F. Magee

BANK OF ENGLAND

Threadneedle Street, London EC2R 8AH
Tel: 020-7601 4444; Fax: 020-7601 4771;
Email: enquiries@bankofengland.co.uk
Web: www.bankofengland.co.uk

The Bank of England was incorporated in 1694 under royal charter. It is the banker of the Government and it manages the note issue. Since May 1997 it has been operationally independent and its Monetary Policy Committee has had responsibility for setting short-term interest rates to meet the Government's inflation target. As the central reserve bank of the country, the Bank keeps the accounts of British banks, who maintain with it a proportion of their cash resources, and of most overseas central banks. The Bank has three main areas of activity: Monetary Stability, Market Operations and Financial Stability. Its responsibility for banking supervision has been transferred to the Financial Services Authority. (*See also* Financial Services Regulation section).

Governor, The Rt. Hon. E. A. J. George

Deputy Governors, D. Clementi; M. A. King

Non-Executive Directors, R. E. Bailie, OBE; Sir David Cooksey; Sir Howard Davies; Sir Ian Gibson, CBE; Dame Sheila McKechnie, DBE; Dr J. Neill, CBE; N. I.

Simms; J. Stretton; Ms K. A. O'Donovan; G. Hall; Dr D. Julius, CBE; Sir. John Bond; Mrs M. Francis; Ms B. Blow; Sir Brian Moffat, OBE; W. Norris; Mrs L. Powers-Freeling

Monetary Policy Committee, The Governor; the Deputy Governors; Prof. S. Nickell, C. J. Allsopp; C. Bean; Ms K. Barker; Ms M. Bell; P. Tucker

Advisers to the Governor, Sir Peter Petrie; M. Glover; C. Goodhart

Chief Cashier and Deputy Director, Banking and Market Services, Ms M. V. Lowther

Chief Registrar, G. P. Sparkes

General Manager, Printing Works, M. Thompson

Secretary, P. D. Rodgers

The Auditor, K. Butler

BOARD OF INLAND REVENUE

Somerset House, Strand, London WC2R 1LB
Tel: 020-7438 6622; Fax: 020-7438 7562;
Email: library.ir.sh@gtnet.gov.uk
Web: www.inlandrevenue.gov.uk

The Board of Inland Revenue was constituted under the Inland Revenue Board Act 1849. The Board administers and collects direct taxes – income tax, corporation tax, capital gains tax, inheritance tax, stamp duty, and petroleum revenue tax – and advises the Chancellor of the Exchequer on policy questions involving them. The Department's Valuation Office is an executive agency responsible for valuing property for tax purposes. The Contributions Agency of the Department for Work and Pensions which is responsible for the collection of contributions under the National Insurance scheme, became part of the Inland Revenue in April 1999 and is now an executive office called the National Insurance Contributions Office. The Contributions Unit of the Social Security Agency in Northern Ireland also transferred to the Inland Revenue in April 1999.

THE BOARD

Chairman (G1), Sir Nicholas Montagu, KCB

Deputy Chairmen (G2), T. J. Flesher; Ms A. Chant

Director-General, Policy and Technical, D. Hartnett

Chief Executive, Valuation Office Agency, M. Johns

DIVISIONS

Director, Human Resources Division (G3), A. Walker

Director of Business (G3), J. Yard

Head, Strategy and Planning, S. Norris

Principal of Financial Institutions (G3), R. R. Martin

Director, Business Operations (G3), S. Banyard

Director of Analysis Research, (G3), Prof. D. Ulph

Director Business Tax (G3), Ms M. Hay

Director International (G3), G. Makhlouf

Director of Special Compliance, J. Middleton

Director, Personal Tax (G3), T. Orhinal

Director, Capital and Savings (G3), M. Williams

Head, Revenue Policy (G3), D. Hartnett

EXECUTIVE OFFICES

ACCOUNTS OFFICE (CUMBERNAULD), St Mungo's Road, Cumbernauld, Glasgow G70 5TR. *Director*, J. Brown

ACCOUNTS OFFICE (SHIPLEY), Shipley, Bradford, W. Yorks BD98 8AA. *Director*, P. Gronow

CAPITAL TAXES OFFICE (SCOTLAND), Meldrum House, 15 Drumshugh Gardens, Edinburgh, EH3 7UG. *Registrar*, Mrs J. Templeton

CENTRE FOR NON-RESIDENTS, St John's House,
Merton Road, Bootle L26 9BB; Fitz Roy House,
PO Box 46, Castle Meadow, Nottingham NG2 1BD.
Director, J. Johnson
ENFORCEMENT OFFICE, Durrington Bridge House,
Barrington Road, Worthing, W. Sussex BN12 4SE.
Director, D. Ellis
FINANCIAL ACCOUNTING OFFICE, South Block,
Barrington Road, Worthing, W. Sussex BN12 4XH.
Director, Ms M. McLeish
INLAND REVENUE CAPITAL TAXES, Ferrers House, PO
Box 38, Castle Meadow Road, Nottingham NG2 1BB.
Director, J. Lee Pemberton
INTERNAL AUDIT OFFICE, 2nd Floor (North), 22
Kingsway, London WC2B 6NR. *Director*, N. R. Buckley
MARKETING AND COMMUNICATIONS, Ground Floor,
New Wing Somerset House, Strand, London WC2R
1LB. *Director of Communications*, I. Schoolar
NATIONAL INSURANCE CONTRIBUTIONS OFFICE,
DWP Longbenton, Benton Park Road, Newcastle
upon Tyne NE98 1ZZ. *Chief Executive (G3)*,
B. Woodley
OIL TAXATION OFFICE, Melbourne House, Aldwych,
London WC2B 4LL. *Director*, R. Dyall
SAVINGS, PENSIONS AND SHARES, Yorke House, PO
Box 62, Castle Meadow Road, Nottingham NG2 1BG.
Director, R. Hurcombe
SOLICITOR'S OFFICE, East Wing, Somerset House,
London WC2R 1LB. *Solicitor (G2)*, P. Ridd
SOLICITOR'S OFFICE (SCOTLAND), Clarendon House,
114-116 George Street, Edinburgh EH2 4LH. *Solicitor*,
I. K. Laing
SPECIAL COMPLIANCE OFFICE, Angel Court, 199
Borough High Street, London SE1 1HZ. *Director*,
J. Middleton
STAMP OFFICE, Ground Floor, PO Box 38, Ferrers
House, Castle Meadow, Nottingham NG2 1BB.
Director, C. Lester
TRAINING OFFICE, Lawress Hall, Riseholme Park,
Lincoln LN2 2BJ. *Director*, Ms L. Hinnigan

REGIONAL EXECUTIVE OFFICES

INLAND REVENUE CENTRAL ENGLAND, Churchgate,
New Road, Peterborough PE1 1TD.
Director, E. McKeegan
INLAND REVENUE LARGE BUSINESS OFFICE, 1st Floor
North, 22 Kingsway, London WC2B 6NR.
Director, S. Jones
INLAND REVENUE LONDON, New Court, Carey Street,
London WC2A 2JE. *Director*, C. R. Massingale
INLAND REVENUE NORTHERN ENGLAND, The Triad,
Stanley Road, Bootle, Merseyside L75 2DD.
Director, R. Cooke
INLAND REVENUE NORTHERN IRELAND, Dorchester
House, 52–58 Great Victoria Street, Belfast BT2 7QE.
Director, Ms. N. Ferguson
INLAND REVENUE SCOTLAND, Clarendon House,
114–116 George Street, Edinburgh EH2 4LH.
Director, D. Hinstridge
INLAND REVENUE SOUTHERN ENGLAND 4th Floor,
Dukes Court, Dukes Street, Woking GU21 5XR.
Director, T. Sleeman
INLAND REVENUE WALES, 1st Floor, Phase II Building,
Ty Glas Avenue, Llanishen, Cardiff CF14 5TS.
Director, K. Cartwright

VALUATION OFFICE AGENCY

New Court, 48 Carey Street, London WC2A 2JE
Tel: 020-7506 1700; Fax: 020-7506 1998;
Web: www.voa.gov.uk

50 Frederick Street, Edinburgh EH2 1NG
Tel: 0131-465 0700; Fax: 0131-465 0799;
Chief Executive, M. A. Johns
Chief Valuer, Scotland, A. Ainslie
Chief Valuer, Wales, P. Clement

BOUNDARY COMMISSIONS

The Commissions are constituted under the
Parliamentary Constituencies Act 1986. The Speaker of
the House of Commons is ex officio chairman of all four
commissions in the UK. Each of the four commissions is
required by law to keep the parliamentary constituencies
in their part of the UK under review. The latest Boundary
Commission report for England was completed in April
1995 and its proposals took effect at the 1997 general
election. The next report must be submitted before April
2006. The latest Scottish report was completed in
December 1994, with the European constituencies
completed in April 1996.

ENGLAND

1 Drummond Gate, London SW1V 2QQ
Tel: 020-7533 5177; Fax: 020-7533 5176
Deputy Chairman, The Hon. Mr Justice Harrison
Joint Secretaries, R. Farrance; M. Barnett

WALES

1st Floor, Caradog House, 1–6 St Andrews Place, Cardiff
CF10 3BE
Tel: 029-2039 5031; Fax: 029-2039 5250
Deputy Chairman, The Hon. Mr Justice Richards
Joint Secretaries, E. H. Lewis; M. Barnett

SCOTLAND

3 Drumsheugh Gardens, Edinburgh EH3 7QJ
Tel: 0131-538 7200; Fax: 0131-538 7240
Deputy Chairman, The Hon. Lady Cosgrove
Secretary, R. Smith

NORTHERN IRELAND

RIR Division, 11 Millbank, London SW1P 4QE
Tel: 020-7210 6569; Fax: 020-7533 5176
Deputy Chairman, The Hon. Mr Justice Coghlin
Secretary, Mrs L. Rogers

BRITISH BROADCASTING CORPORATION

Broadcasting House, Portland Place, London W1A 1AA
Tel: 020-7580 4468; BBC Information Line: 0870-010
0222; Web: www.bbc.co.uk
Television Centre, Wood Lane, London W12 7RJ

The BBC was incorporated under royal charter in 1926 as
successor to the British Broadcasting Company Ltd. The
BBC's current charter came into force on 1 May 1996 and
extends to 31 December 2006. The chairman, vice-
chairman and other governors are appointed by The
Queen-in-Council. The BBC is financed by revenue from
receiving licences for the home services and by grant-in-
aid from Parliament for the World Service (radio).

BOARD OF GOVERNORS

Chairman, G. Davies
Vice-Chairman, R. Ryder
National Governors, Prof. F. Monds (*N. Ireland*); R. S.
Jones, OBE (*Wales*); Sir Robert Smith (*Scotland*)
Governors, Sir Richard Eyre, CBE; D. Glecson; Dame
Pauline Neville-Jones, DCMG; A. Young; Baroness
Hogg; R. Sondhi

BOARD OF MANAGEMENT
EXECUTIVE COMMITTEE
Director-General and Editor-in-Chief, G. Dyke
Directors, Ms J. Bennett (*Television*); Ms J. Abramsky
(*Radio*); M. Byford (*BBC World Service*); R.
Sambrook (*News*); Ms G. Benson (*Joint Director,
Factual and Learning*); A. Yentob (*Drama,
Entertainment and Children*); P. Loughrey (*Nations
and Regions*); J. Smith (*Finance and Business Affairs*);
S. Dando (*Human Resources and Internal
Communications*); A. Duncan (*Marketing and
Communications*); M. Stevenson (*Joint Director,
Factual and Learning*); P. Salmon (*Sport*); Ms C.
Thomson (*Public Policy*); Ms C. Fairbairn (*Strategy
and Distribution*), A. Highfield (*New Media*)
Chief Executives, R. Gavin (*BBC Worldwide*); R. Flynn,
(*BBC Ventures*)

OTHER SENIOR STAFF
Controller, BBC1, L. Heggessey
Controller, BBC2, Ms J. Root
Controller, Radio 1, A. Parfitt
Controller, Radio 2, J. Moir
Controller, Radio 3, R. Wright
Controller, Radio 4, H. Boaden
Controller, Radio 5 Live, B. Shennan
Controller, BBC Scotland, J. McCormick
Controller, BBC Wales, M. Richards
Controller, BBC N. Ireland, A. Carragher
Controller, English Regions, A. Griffee
Secretary, G. Milner

THE BRITISH COUNCIL
10 Spring Gardens, London SW1A 2BN
Tel: 020-7930 8466; Fax: 020-7839 6347
Bridgewater House, 58 Whitworth Street,
Manchester M1 6BB Tel: 0161-957 7000
Portland Place, London W1B 1EJ
Tel: 020-7930 3194; Fax: 020-7389 3199

The British Council was established in 1934,
incorporated by Royal Charter in 1940 and granted a
supplemental charter in 1993. It is an independent, non-
political organisation which promotes Britain abroad. It
is the UK's international organisation for educational and
cultural relations. The British Council is represented in
218 towns and cities in 109 countries. Total income in
2001–2002, including Foreign and Commonwealth Office
grants and contracted money, was £440.795 million.
Chairman, The Baroness Kennedy of The Shaws, QC
Deputy Chairman, Sir Tim Lankester, KCB
Director-General, D. Green, CMG

BRITISH FILM COMMISSION
10 Little Portland Street, London W1N 5DF
Tel: 020-7861 7860; Fax: 020-7861 7864
Email: info@bfc.co.uk; Web: www.bfc.co.uk

Originally established in 1991, the British Film
Commission (BFC) is now a division of the Film Council.
Its remit is to attract inward investment by promoting the
UK as an international production centre to the film and
television industries and encouraging the use of British
locations, services, facilities and personnel. Working with
the UK Screen Agencies, the BFC also provides overseas
producers with a bespoke information service and offers
practical help and advice to those filming in the UK.
Commissioner, S. Norris

BRITISH FILM INSTITUTE
21 Stephen Street, London W1T 1LN
Tel: 020-7255 1444; Fax: 020-7436 0439
Web: www.bfi.org.uk

The British Film Institute (BFI) offers opportunities for
people throughout the UK to experience, learn and
discover more about the world of film and moving image
culture. The BFI incorporates the BFI National Library,
the monthly magazine *Sight and Sound,* the BFI National
Film Theatre, the annual London Film Festival and the
BFI London IMAX, and provides advice and support for
regional cinemas and film festivals across the UK. The
BFI also undertakes the preservation of, and promotes
access to films, television programmes, computer games,
museum collections, stills, posters and designs, and other
special collections.
Chairman, Ms J. Bakewell, CBE
Director, J. Teckman
Deputy Director, A. Wootton

BRITISH PHARMACOPOEIA COMMISSION
Market Towers, 1 Nine Elms Lane, London SW8 5NQ
Tel: 020-7273 0561; Fax: 020-7273 0566

The British Pharmacopoeia Commission sets standards
for medicinal products used in human and veterinary
medicines and is responsible for publication of the British
Pharmacopoeia (a publicly available statement of the
standard that a product must meet throughout its shelf-
life), the British Pharmacopoeia (Veterinary) and the
selection of British Approved Names. It has 15 members
who are appointed by the Secretary of State for Health,
the Minister for Environment, Food and Rural Affairs, the
Scottish Ministers, the National Assembly for Wales, and
the relevant Northern Ireland departments.
Chairman, Prof. D. Calam, OBE, D.Phil.
Vice-Chairman, Prof. J. A. Goldsmith
Secretary and Scientific Director, Dr M. G. Lee

BRITISH STANDARDS INSTITUTION (BSI)
389 Chiswick High Road, London W4 4AL
Tel: 020-8996 9000; Fax: 020-8996 7344

The British Standards Institution is the recognised
authority in the UK for the preparation and publication
of national standards for industrial and consumer
products. About 90 per cent of its standards work is now
internationally linked. British Standards are issued for
voluntary adoption, though in a number of cases
compliance with a British Standard is required by
legislation. Industrial and consumer products certified as
complying with the relevant British Standard may carry
the Institution's certification trade mark, known as the
'Kitemark.'
Chairman, V. E. Thomas, CBE

BRITISH TOURIST AUTHORITY
Thames Tower, Black's Road, London W6 9EL
Tel: 020-8846 9000; Fax: 020-8563 0302
Web: www.britishtouristauthority.org

Established under the Development of Tourism Act 1969,
the British Tourist Authority is responsible for promoting
tourism to Britain from overseas. It also has a general
responsibility for the promotion and development of
tourism and tourist facilities within Britain as a whole,

and for advising the Secretary of State for Culture, Media and Sport on tourism matters.
Chairman, D. Quarmby
Chief Executive, T. Wright

BRITISH WATERWAYS
Willow Grange, Church Road, Watford, Herts WD17 4QA Tel: 01923-226422; Fax: 01923-201400
Email: enquirieshq@britishwaterways.co.uk
Web: www.britishwaterways.co.uk

British Waterways conserves and manages over 2,000 miles of canals and rivers in England, Scotland and Wales. It is responsible to the Secretary of State for Environment, Food and Rural Affairs.
Its responsibilities include maintaining the waterways and structures on and around them; looking after wildlife and the waterway environment; and ensuring that canals and rivers are safe and enjoyable places to visit.
Chairman (part-time), Dr G. Greener
Members (part-time), D. Langslow; I. Darling; Ms H. Gorden; P. Soulsby; C. Christie; Ms S. Achmatowicz; G. Fleming; Ms J. Lewis-Jones; Ms A. Malik; T. Tricker
Chief Executive, D. Fletcher

BROADCASTING STANDARDS COMMISSION
7 The Sanctuary, London SW1P 3JS
Tel: 020-7808 1000; Fax: 020-7233 0397

The Commission was established in April 1997 under the Broadcasting Act 1996. It is an independent organisation representing the interests of the consumer, and its remit covers all television and radio broadcasting. The Commission considers the portrayal of violence and sexual conduct and matters of taste and decency. It also provides redress for people who believe they have been unfairly treated or subjected to unwarranted infringement of privacy. The Commission conducts research into standards and fairness in broadcasting and produces codes of practice, and it considers and adjudicates on complaints. Members of the Commission are appointed by the Secretary of State for Culture, Media and Sport. The appointments are part-time. In 2003 the British Standards Commission is due to be replaced by Ofcom, the Office of Communications.
Chair (£50,990), Lord Dubs of Battersea
Deputy Chair (£38,500), Lady S. Warner
Commissioners (each £16,310), D. Boulton; U. Dholakia; G. Elliott; S. Heppel, CB; Revd Rose Hudson Wilkin; Rt. Revd R. Holloway; Ms M. Redfern; Ms S. O'Sullivan; Ms K. Worrall; R. M. Jones
Director, P. Bolt

THE BROADS AUTHORITY
Thomas Harvey House, 18 Colegate, Norwich NR3 1BQ
Tel: 01603-610734; Fax: 01603-765710
Web: www.broads-authority.gov.uk

The Broads Authority is a special statutory authority set up under the Norfolk and Suffolk Broads Act 1988. The functions of the Authority are to conserve and enhance the natural beauty of the Broads; to provide integrated management of the land and water space of the area; to promote the enjoyment of the Broads by the public; and to protect the interests of navigation. The Authority comprises 35 members, appointed by the local authorities in the area covered, environmental conservation bodies, the Environment Agency, and the Great Yarmouth Port Authority. *Chairman*, The Viscountess Knollys
Chief Executive, Dr J. Packman

CENTRAL ARBITRATION COMMITTEE
Third Floor, Discovery House,
28–42 Banner Street, London, EC1Y 8QE
Tel: 020-7251 9747; Fax: 020-7251 3114
Web: www.cac.gov.uk

The Central Arbitration Committee determines claims for statutory recognition and de-recognition of trade unions under the Employment Relations Act 1999, it also adjudicates on disclosure of information cases, issues relating to the European Works Council Directive and arbitrates on trade disputes.
Chairman, Sir Michael Burton
Chief Executive, Ms K. Elliott

CERTIFICATION OFFICE FOR TRADE UNIONS AND EMPLOYERS' ASSOCIATIONS
180 Borough High Street, London SE1 1LW
Tel: 020-7210 3734/5; Fax: 020-7210 3612

The Certification Office is an independent statutory authority. The Certification Officer is appointed by the Secretary of State for Trade and Industry and is responsible for receiving and scrutinising annual returns from trade unions and employers' associations; for determining complaints concerning trade union elections, certain ballots and certain breaches of trade union rules; for ensuring observance of statutory requirements governing mergers between trade unions and employers' associations; for overseeing the political funds and finances of trade unions and employers' associations; and for certifying the independence of trade unions.
Certification Officer, Mr Cockburn
Assistant Certification Officer, G. Walker

SCOTLAND

58 Frederick Street, Edinburgh EH2 1NB
Tel: 0131-226 3224; Fax: 0131-200 1300
Assistant Certification Officer for Scotland, J. L. J. Craig

CHARITY COMMISSION
Harmsworth House, 13–15 Bouverie Street,
London EC4Y 8DP Tel: 0800-333 0123;
Fax: 020-7674 2310;
2nd Floor, 20 King's Parade, Queen's Dock,
Liverpool L3 4DQ Tel: 0800-333 0123;
Fax: 0151-703 1555
Woodfield House, Tangier, Taunton, Somerset TA1 4BL
Tel: 0800-333 0123; Fax: 01823-345003
Web: www.charitycommission.gov.uk

The Charity Commission for England and Wales is the Government Department whose aim is to give the public confidence in the integrity of charities. It also carries out the functions of the registration, monitoring and support of charities and the investigation of alleged wrong-doing. The Commission maintains a computerised register of some 187,000 charities. It is accountable to the courts and for its efficiency to the Home Secretary. There are five Commissioners appointed by the Home Office for a fixed term and the Commission has Offices in London, Liverpool and Taunton.
Chief Commissioner (G3), J. Stoker

Legal Commissioner (*G3*), M. Carpenter
Commissioners (*part-time*) (*G4*), D. Taylor;
   Ms J. Warburton; Ms J. Unwin
Heads of Legal Sections (*G5*), J. A. Dutton;
   G. S. Goodchild; K. M. Dibble; S. Slack
Director of Operations (*G4*), S. Gillespie
Head of Policy Division (*G5*), Ms R. Chapman
Establishment Officer (*G5*), Ms C. Stewart
Information Systems Controller (*G5*), K. Chaun

The offices responsible for charities in Scotland and
   Northern Ireland are:
SCOTLAND - Scottish Charities Office, Crown Office,
   25 Chambers Street, Edinburgh EH1 1LA.
   Tel: 0131-226 2626
NORTHERN IRELAND - Department for Social
   Development, Charities Branch, 5th Floor, Churchill
   House, Victoria Square, Belfast BT1 4SD

CHURCH COMMISSIONERS
1 Millbank, London SW1P 3JZ
Tel: 020-7898 1000; Fax: 020-7898 1131
Email: commissioners.enquiry@c-of-e.org
Web: www.churchcommissioners.org

The Church Commissioners were established in 1948 by
the amalgamation of Queen Anne's Bounty (established
1704) and the Ecclesiastical Commissioners (established
1836). They are responsible for the management of the
majority of the Church of England's assets, the income
from which is predominantly used to help pay for the
stipend and pension of the clergy. The Commissioners
own 125,000 acres of agricultural land, a number of
residential estates in central London, and commercial
property in Great Britain. They also carry out
administrative duties in connection with pastoral
reorganisation and redundant churches.

The Commissioners are: the Archbishops of
Canterbury and York; four bishops, three clergy and
four lay persons elected by the respective houses of the
General Synod; two deans or provosts elected by all the
deans and provosts; three persons nominated by The
Queen; three persons nominated by the Archbishops of
Canterbury and York; three persons nominated by the
Archbishops after consultation with others including the
lord mayors of London and York and the vice-chancellors
of the universities of Oxford and Cambridge; the First
Lord of the Treasury; the Lord President of the Council;
the Home Secretary; the Lord Chancellor; the Secretary
of State for Culture, Media and Sport; and the Speaker of
the House of Commons.

INCOME AND EXPENDITURE
for year ended 31 December 2001

	£million
Net income	118.5
Investments	69.0
Property	43.2
Interest from loans, etc.	11.4
Total expenditure	159.5
Parish ministry support	22
Bishop and cathedral clergy stipends	7.1
Bishops' housing	3.3
Grants to cathedrals	2.6
Financial provision for resigning clergy	1.2
Clergy pensions and CHARM subsidy	95.3
Transitional support for pension contributions	7.1
Church buildings	1.4
Bishops' working cost	9.6
Commissioners' administration of national church functions	4.7
Administration costs of other church bodies	1.8

CHURCH ESTATES COMMISSIONERS
First, A. Whittam Smith
Second, S. Bell, MP
Third, The Viscountess Brentford

OFFICERS

Secretary, H. H. Hughes
Deputy Secretary (Finance and Investment), C. W. Daws
Official Solicitor, S. Jones
Assistant Secretaries:
   The Accountant, M. Adams
   Management Accountant, B. J. Hardy
   Chief Surveyor and Deputy Secretary, A. C. Brown
   Computer Manager, J. W. Ferguson
   Investments Manager, M. Chaloner
   Pastoral, Houses and Redundant Churches, M. D.
     Elengorn

CIVIL AVIATION AUTHORITY
CAA House, 45–59 Kingsway, London WC2B 6TE
Tel: 020-7379 7311
Web: www.caa.co.uk

The CAA is responsible for the economic regulation of
UK airlines and for the safety regulation of UK civil
aviation by the certification of airlines and aircraft and by
licensing aerodromes, flight crew and aircraft engineers.

The CAA advises the Government on aviation issues,
represents consumer interests, conducts economic and
scientific research, produces statistical data, and provides
specialist services and other training and consultancy
services to clients world-wide. It also regulates UK
airspace and runs the ATOL flight and air holiday
protection scheme.
Chairman, Sir Roy McNulty
Secretary, R. J. Britton

THE COAL AUTHORITY
200 Lichfield Lane, Mansfield, Notts NG18 4RG
Tel: 01623-427162; Fax: 01623-622072
Email: thecoalauthority@coal.gov.uk
Web: www.coal.gov.uk

The Coal Authority was established under the Coal
Industry Act 1994 to manage certain functions previously
undertaken by British Coal, including ownership of
unworked coal. It is responsible for licensing coal mining
operations and for providing information on coal
reserves and past and future coal mining. It settles
subsidence claims not falling on coal mining operators. It
deals with the management and disposal of property, and
with surface hazards such as abandoned coal mine shafts.
Chairman, J. Harris
Chief Executive, Dr I. Roxburgh

COLLEGE OF ARMS (OR HERALDS' COLLEGE)
Queen Victoria Street, London EC4V 4BT
Tel: 020-7248 2762; Fax: 020-7248 6448;
Email: enquiries@college-of-arms.gov.uk
Web: www.college-of-arms.gov.uk

The Sovereign's Officers of Arms (Kings, Heralds' and
Pursuivants of Arms) were first incorporated by Richard
III. The powers vested by the Crown in the Earl Marshal
(the Duke of Norfolk) with regard to state ceremonial are
largely exercised through the College. The College is also
the official repository of the arms and pedigrees of
English, Welsh, Northern Irish and Commonwealth

(except Canadian) families and their descendants, and its records include official copies of the records of Ulster King of Arms, the originals of which remain in Dublin. The 13 officers of the College specialise in genealogical and heraldic work for their respective clients.

Arms have been and still are granted by letters patent from the Kings of Arms. A right to arms can only be established by the registration in the official records of the College of Arms of a pedigree showing direct male line descent from an ancestor already appearing therein as being entitled to arms, or by making application through the College of Arms for a grant of arms. Grants are made to corporations as well as to individuals.

Earl Marshal, The Duke of Norfolk, KG, GCVO, CB, CBE, MC
Deputy Earl Marshal, Earl of Arundel and Surrey

KINGS OF ARMS

Garter, P. L. Gwynn-Jones, CVO, FSA
Clarenceux, D. H. B. Chesshyre, LVO, FSA
Norroy and Ulster, T. Woodcock, LVO, FSA

HERALDS

Richmond (and Earl Marshal's Secretary), P. L. Dickinson
York, H. E. Paston-Bedingfeld
Chester (and Registrar), T. H. S. Duke
Lancaster, R. J. B. Noel
Windsor, W. G. Hunt, TD

PURSUIVANTS

Rouge Croix, D. V. White
Rouge Dragon, C. E. A. Cheesman

COMMISSION FOR ARCHITECTURE AND THE BUILT ENVIRONMENT
The Tower Building, 11 York Road, London, SE1 7NX
Tel: 020-7960 2400; Fax: 020-7960 2444
Email: enquiries@cabe.org.uk
Web: www.cabe.org.uk

The Commission for Architecture and the Built Environment (CABE) is responsible for promoting the importance of high quality architecture and urban design and encouraging the understanding of architecture through educational and regional initiatives. CABE offers free advice to local authorities, public sector clients and others embarking on building projects of any size or purpose.
Chairman, Sir Stuart Lipton
Chief Executive, J. Rouse

COMMISSION FOR INTEGRATED TRANSPORT
Romney House, 5th Floor, Tufton Street, London
SW1P 3RA Tel: 020-7944 4101; Fax: 020-7944 2919
Email: cfit@dtft.gsi.gov.uk
Web: www.cfit.gov.uk

The Commission for Integrated Transport was proposed in the 1998 Transport White Paper and was set up in June 1999. Its role is to provide independent expert advice to the Government in order to achieve a transport system that supports sustainable development. Members of the Commission are appointed by the Secretary of State for Transport.
Chairman (£30,000), Prof. D. Begg
Vice-Chairman (£24,000), Sir Trevor Chinn
Members (£5,431 each), L. Christensen, CBE; N. Gavron; S. Joseph; D. Leeder; Ms L. Matson; W. Morris; J. O'Brien; Ms V. Palmer; M. Parker; Baroness Scott; M. Hodgkinson

Ex-Officio Members, Sir Roy McNulty, (*Chairman, Civil Aviation Authority*); T. Matthews (*Chief Executive, Highways Agency*); R. Bowker (*Chairman, British Railways Board and Head, Strategic Rail Authority*); Ms J. Wilmot (*Chair, Disabled Persons Transport Advisory Committee*)
Secretary (*G6*), A. Braithwaite

COMMISSION FOR RACIAL EQUALITY
Elliot House, 10–12 Allington Street,
London SW1E 5EH
Tel: 020-7828 7022; Fax: 020-7630 7605

The Commission was established in 1977 under the Race Relations Act 1976. Its duties are to work towards the elimination of discrimination and promote equality of opportunity, to encourage good relations between different racial groups and to monitor the working of the Race Relations Act. It is funded by the Home Office.
Chairman, Ms. B. Bernard (*acting*)
Deputy Chairs, Ian Barr (*acting*); Khurshid Ahmed (*acting*)
Commissioners, K. Ahmed; I. Barr; K. Hampton; Ms G. Mills; P. Passley; Ms S. Patel; Ms C. Short; Dr J. Singh Gundara; Ms G. Sootarsing; K. Jandu; Ms S. Spencer
Chief Executive (*acting*), D. Housley

COMMITTEE ON STANDARDS IN PUBLIC LIFE
35 Great Smith Street, London SW1P 3BQ
Tel: 020-7276 2595; Fax: 020-7276 2585
Web: www.public-standards.gov.uk

The Committee on Standards in Public Life was set up in October 1994. It is a standing body whose chairman and members are appointed by the Prime Minister; three members are nominated by the leaders of the three main political parties. The committee's remit is to examine concerns about standards of conduct of all holders of public office, including arrangements relating to financial and commercial activities, and to make recommendations as to any changes in present arrangements which might be required to ensure the highest standards of propriety in public life. It is also charged with reviewing issues in relation to the funding of political parties. The committee does not investigate individual allegations of misconduct.
Chair, Sir Nigel Wicks
Members, Ms A. Abraham; Prof. A. Brown; Sir Anthony Cleaver, OBE; The Lord Goodhart, QC; F. Heaton; The Rt. Hon. Lord MacGregor of Pulham Market, OBE; R. Donaghy, OBE; Rabbi Julia Neuberger; The Rt. Hon. Chris Smith, MP
Secretary (*SCS*), Mrs S. Tyerman

COMMONWEALTH INSTITUTE
Kensington High Street, London W8 6NQ
Tel: 020-7603 4535; Fax: 020-7602 7374
Email: crc@commonwealth.org.uk
Web: www.commonwealth.org.uk

The Commonwealth Institute is an independent agency working with young people across the Commonwealth.

Central to the Institute's mission is running schools education programmes, supplying learning resources and support to schools, teachers and young people, on citizenship, development and issues dealing with managing and celebrating cultural diversity.

The Institute houses the Commonwealth Resource

Centre, (open to the public six days a week), the Commonwealth Literature Library and the Commonwealth Conference and Events Centre.

In January 2000, the Institute became an Independent Commonwealth agency after forty years as an agency of the Foreign and Commonwealth Office. It is a registered charity and a company limited by guarantee. It is controlled by a Board of Trustees elected by a Board of Governors. All the Commonwealth High Commissioners in London are ex-officio governors of the Institute in addition to other governors appointed by the Board of Trustees.

Chairman, Ms J. Hanratty, OBE
Vice-Chairman, The Rt. Hon. Lord Fellowes, GCB, GCVO
Chief Executive, D. French
Commercial Director, P. Kennedy
Director of Education, S. Brace
Finance Director, Ms. J. Curry
Head of Public Affairs, P. Harry

COMMONWEALTH WAR GRAVES COMMISSION

2 Marlow Road, Maidenhead, Berks SL6 7DX
Tel: 01628-634221; Fax: 01628-771208
Email: general.enq@cwgc.org
Web: www.cwgc.org

The Commonwealth War Graves Commission (formerly Imperial War Graves Commission) was founded by royal charter in 1917. It is responsible for the commemoration of 1,694,714 members of the forces of the Commonwealth who fell in the two world wars. More than one million graves are maintained in 23,237 burial grounds throughout the world. Over three-quarters of a million men and women who have no known grave or who were cremated are commemorated by name on memorials built by the Commission.

The funds of the Commission are derived from the six participating governments, i.e. the UK, Canada, Australia, New Zealand, South Africa and India.

President, HRH The Duke of Kent, KG, GCMG, GCVO, ADC
Chairman, The Secretary of State for Defence in the UK
Vice-Chairman, Gen. Sir John Wilsey, GCB, CBE
Members, The High Commissioners in London for Australia, Canada, South Africa, New Zealand and India. Baroness Golding; J. Wilkinson, MP; Sir John Gray, KBE, CMG; P. D. Orchard-Lisle, CBE, TD; Air Chief Marshal Sir Michael Stear, KCB, CBE; Dame Susan Tinson, DBE; Sir John Keegan, OBE; Adm. Sir Peter Abbott, GBE, KCB
Director-General and Secretary to the Commission, R. E. Kellaway
Deputy Director-General, R. J. Dalley, CBE
Legal Adviser and Solicitor, G. C. Reddie
Directors, D. R. Parker (*Information and Secretariat*); A. Coombe (*Works*); R. D. Wilson (*Administration*); D. C. Parker (*Horticulture*); D. G. Stacey (*Personnel*)

IMPERIAL WAR GRAVES ENDOWMENT FUND

Trustees, A. C. Barker (*Chairman*); C. G. Clarke; Gen. Sir John Wilsey, GCB, CBE
Secretary to the Trustees, R. D. Wilson, GCB, CBE

COMMUNITY FUND

St Vincent House, 16 Suffolk Street, London SW1Y 4NL
Tel: 020-7747 5299; Fax: 020-7747 5220
Web: www.community-fund.org.uk

The Fund was set up under the National Lottery Act 1993 to distribute funds from the Lottery to support charitable, benevolent and philanthropic organisations. The chair and members are appointed by the Secretary of State for Culture, Media and Sport. The Fund's aim is to meet the needs of those at greatest disadvantage in society and also to improve the quality of life in the community.

It has UK-wide, county and regional priorities for its general grants programmes and runs two specialist programmes for research and international grants.

Chair, Lady Brittan, CBE
Deputy Chairman, Dame Valerie Strachan, DCB
Members, E. Appelbee; R. Bevan; S. Burkeman; J. Carroll; P. Cavanagh; D. Graham; K. Hampton; Prof. J. Kearney; L. MacLeod; S. Malley; R. Martineau; J. Strachan; E. Watkins; B. Whitaker, CBE
Chief Executive, R. Buxton

COMMUNITIES SCOTLAND

Thistle House, 91 Haymarket Terrace,
Edinburgh EH12 5HE
Tel: 0131-313 0044; Fax: 0131-313 2680
Web: www.communitiesscotland.gov.uk

Communities Scotland, formerly Scottish Homes, plays an important role in delivering Scottish ministers' policies to promote social justice through neighbourhood renewal, community empowerment and housing investment. As an executive agency, it reports directly to ministers in the Scottish Parliament.

A residuary body, retaining the name Scottish Homes, manages the houses which have not yet transferred from Scottish Homes to community ownership. These houses are expected to transfer as tenants vote in local ballots over the next few years.

Chairman, J. Ward, CBE
Chief Executive, B. Millar

COMPETITION COMMISSION

New Court, 48 Carey Street, London WC2A 2JT
Tel: 020-7271 0100; Fax: 020-7271 0367

The Commission was established in 1948 as the Monopolies and Restrictive Practices Commission (later the Monopolies and Mergers Commission); it became the Competition Commission in April 1999 under the Competition Act 1998. Its role is to investigate and report on matters which are referred to it by the Secretary of State for Trade and Industry or the Director-General of Fair Trading or, in the case of regulated utilities, by the appropriate regulator. It has no power to initiate its own investigations.

The Appeal Tribunals of the Competition Commission hears appeals against decisions by the Director-General of Fair Trading and the utility regulators in respect of the prohibitions on anti-competitive agreements and abuse of a dominant position.

The Commission has a full-time chairman, president and two part-time deputy chairmen. There are about 50 reporting panel members and 23 specialist panel members to carry out investigations and 21 appeal panel members. All are appointed by the Secretary of State for Trade and Industry.

Chairman, Dr D. Morris
Deputy Chairmen, Prof. P. Geroski; Mrs D. Kingsmill, CBE
President, Appeal Tribunals, His Hon. Sir Christopher Bellamy, QC
Members; Prof. J. Baillie; R. Bertram; Mrs S. Brown; Prof. M. Cave; C. Clarke; A. Clothier; Dr J. Collings; Dr D. Coyle; C. Darke; L. Elks; Dr G. Flower; C. Goodall;

N. Garthwaite; Prof. C. Graham; Prof. A. Gregory;
Mrs D. Guy; G. Hadley; Prof. A. Hamlin; Ms J.
Hanratty; Prof. J. Haskel; P. Hazell; C. Henderson, CB;
R. Holroyd; Prof. P. Klemperer; P. MacKay; Dame
Barbara Mills DBE, QC; Prof. P. Moizer; Dr E. Monck;
R. Munson; Prof. D. Newbery, FBA; Dr G. Owen; Prof.
D. Parker; A. Pryor, CB; R. Rawlinson; Prof. J. Rees;
T. S. Richmond, MBE, TD; J. Rickford, CBE; E. Seddon;
Dame Helena Shovelton, DBE; C. Smallwood;
D. Stark; Prof. A. Steele; P. Stoddart, FCA; R. Turgoose;
Prof. C. Waddams; S. Walzer; M. Webster;
Prof. S. Wilks; A. M. Young
Appeal Panel Members, Prof. A. Bain, OBE; M. Blair, QC;
P. Clayton; B. Colgate; M. Davey; P. Grant-
Hutchinson; Prof. P. Grinyer; Mrs S. Hewitt; Ms A.
Kelly; Hon. A. Lewis; G. Mathers; Prof. J. Pickering;
R. Prosser, OBE; Dr A. Pryor, CB; Ms P. Quigley, WS;
A. Scott, TD; Mrs V. Smith-Hillman; Prof. P.
Stoneman; D. Summers; Prof. G. Zellick
Appeal Panel Registrar, C. Dhanowa
Secretary, R. Foster

CONSIGNIA

148 Old Street, London EC1V 9HQ
Tel: 020-7250 2888
Web: www.consignia.com

Crown services for the carriage of Government
dispatches were set up in about 1516. The conveyance of
public correspondence began in 1635 and the mail service
was made a parliamentary responsibility with the setting
up of a Post Office in 1657. Telegraphs came under Post
Office control in 1870 and the Post Office Telephone
Service began in 1880. The National Girobank service of
the Post Office began in 1968. The Post Office ceased to
be a Government department in 1969 when
responsibility for the running of the postal,
telecommunications, giro and remittance services was
transferred to a public authority called The Post Office.
The 1981 British Telecommunications Act separated the
functions of the Post Office, making it solely responsible
for postal services and Girobank. Girobank was privatised
in 1990. The Postal Services Act 2000 turned The Post
Office into a wholly owned public limited company
establishing a regulatory regime under the Postal Service
Commission. The Post Office Group changed its name to
Consignia plc on 26 March 2001 when its new corporate
structure took effect.

The chairman, chief executive and members of the
Consignia Board are appointed by the Secretary of State
for Trade and Industry but responsibility for the running
of Consignia as a whole rests with the Board in its
corporate capacity.

CONSIGNIA BOARD

Chairman, A. Leighton
Chief Executive, J. Roberts, CBE
Members, M. Cassoni (*Group Finance Director*); J. Cope
  (*Group Managing Director Mail Services*)
Non Executive Directors, M. Templeman; Ms R. Thorne;
  J. Lloyd
Secretary, J. Evans

COUNCIL ON TRIBUNALS

81 Chancery Lane, London WC2A 1BQ
Tel: 020-7855 5200; Fax: 020-7855 5201
Web: www.council-on-tribunals.gov.uk

The Council on Tribunals is an independent body that
operates under the Tribunals and Inquiries Act 1992. It
consists of 16 members appointed by the Lord Chancellor
and the Scottish Ministers; one member is appointed to
represent the interests of people in Wales. The Scottish
Committee of the Council generally considers Scottish
tribunals and matters relating only to Scotland.

The Council advises on and keeps under review the
constitution and working of administrative tribunals as
listed in the Tribunals Inquiries Act, and considers and
reports on administrative procedures relating to statutory
inquiries. Some 80 tribunals are currently under the
Council's supervision. It is consulted by and advises
Government departments on a wide range of subjects
relating to adjudicative procedures.

Chairman, The Rt. Hon. The Lord Newton of Braintree
Members, The Parliamentary Commissioner for
  Administration (*ex officio*); R. J. Elliot, WS (*Chairman
  of the Scottish Committee*); Mrs C. Berkeley; S. M. D.
  Brown; J. H. Eames; Mrs A. Galbraith; Mrs S. R.
  Howdle; I. J. Irvine; S. Jones, CBE; Prof. G.
  Richardson; E. P. Roberts; P. A. A. Waring;
  S. D. Mannion, OPM; S. Russell, CB
Secretary, Mrs P. J. Fairbairn

SCOTTISH COMMITTEE OF THE COUNCIL ON TRIBUNALS

44 Palmerston Place, Edinburgh EH12 5BJ
Tel: 0131-220 1236; Fax: 0131-225 4271;
Email: sccot@gtnet.gov.uk

Chairman, R. J. Elliot
Members, The Parliamentary Commissioner for
  Administration (*ex officio*); Mrs. M. Wood
Secretary, Mrs E. M. MacRae

COUNTRYSIDE AGENCY

John Dower House, Crescent Place,
Cheltenham, Glos GL50 3RA
Tel: 01242-521381; Fax: 01242-584270

The Countryside Agency was set up in April 1999 by the
merger of the Countryside Commission with parts of the
Rural Development Commission. It is a Government
agency which promotes the conservation and
enhancement of the countryside in England and
undertakes activities aimed at stimulating job creation
and the provision of essential services in the countryside.
The Agency is funded by an annual grant from the
Department for Environment, Food and Rural Affairs
and board members are appointed by the Secretary of
State.

Chairman, E. Cameron
Deputy Chair, Ms P. Warhurst
Members, Ms K. Ashbrook; Ms J. Bradbury; Rt. Revd
  Bishop of Norwich; Sir Martin Doughty;
  Dr V. Edwards; P. Fane; A. Hams, OBE; Prof. P. Lowe;
  L. Frank-Riley; Ms F. Rowe; Ms. S. Stapley; J. Varley
Chief Executive, R. G. Wakeford
Directors, Miss M. A. Clark, OBE; D. Coleman;
  J. Tomlinson; S. Sleet

COUNTRYSIDE COUNCIL FOR WALES/CYNGOR CEFN GWLAD CYMRU
Maes y Ffynnon, Penrhosgarnedd, Bangor, Gwynedd LL57 2DN
Tel: 01248-385500; Fax: 01248-385505

The Countryside Council for Wales is the Government's statutory adviser on sustaining natural beauty, wildlife and the opportunity for outdoor enjoyment in Wales and its inshore waters. It is funded by the National Assembly for Wales and accountable to the First Secretary, who appoints its members.
Chairman, J. Lloyd Jones, OBE
Chief Executive, R. Thomas
Senior Director and Chief Scientist, Dr M. E. Smith
Director, Countryside Policy, Dr J. Taylor
Director, Conservation, Dr D. Parker
Director, Corporate Affairs, L. Warmington

COURT OF THE LORD LYON
HM New Register House, Edinburgh EH1 3YT
Tel: 0131-556 7255; Fax: 0131-557 2148

The Court of the Lord Lyon is the Scottish Court of Chivalry (including the genealogical jurisdiction of the Ri-Sennachie of Scotland's Celtic Kings). The Lord Lyon King of Arms has jurisdiction, subject to appeal to the Court of Session and the House of Lords, in questions of heraldry and the right to bear arms. The Court also administers the Scottish Public Register of All Arms and Bearings and the Public Register of All Genealogies. Pedigrees are established by decrees of Lyon Court and by letters patent. As Royal Commissioner in Armory, the Lord Lyon grants patents of arms (which constitute the grantee and heirs noble in the Noblesse of Scotland) to 'virtuous and well-deserving' Scotsmen and to petitioners (personal or corporate) in The Queen's overseas realms of Scottish connection, and issues birthbrieves.
Lord Lyon King of Arms, R. O. Blair, LVO, WS
Heralds' Albany, J. A. Spens, MVO, RD, WS
Rothesay, Sir Crispin Agnew of Lochnaw, Bt., QC
Ross, C. J. Burnett, FSA Scot.
Pursuivants Unicorn, Alastair Campbell of Airds
Carrick, Mrs C. G. W. Roads, MVO
Bute, W. D. H. Sellar

EXTRAORDINARY OFFICERS

Orkney Herald Extrordinary, Sir Malcolm Innes of Edingight, KCVO, WS
Linlithgow Pursuivant Extraordinary, J. C. G. George
Lyon Clerk and Keeper of Records, Mrs C. G. W. Roads, MVO, FSA Scot.
Procurator-Fiscal, vacant
Herald Painter, Mrs J. Phillips
Macer, H. M. Love

COVENT GARDEN MARKET AUTHORITY
Covent House, New Covent Garden Market,
London SW8 5NX Tel: 020-7720 2211; Fax: 020-7622 5307
Email: info@cgma.gov.uk
Web: www.cgma.gov.uk

The Covent Garden Market Authority is constituted under the Covent Garden Market Acts 1961 to 1977, the members being appointed by the Minister of Environment, Food and Rural Affairs. The Authority owns and operates the 56-acre New Covent Garden Markets (fruit, vegetables, flowers) which have been trading since 1974.
Chairman (part-time), L. Mills, CBE
General Manager, Dr P. M. Liggins
Secretary, C. Farey

CRIMINAL CASES REVIEW COMMISSION
Alpha Tower, Suffolk Street Queensway,
Birmingham B1 1TT
Tel: 0121-633 1800; Fax: 0121-633 1823/1804

The Criminal Cases Review Commission is an independent body set up under the Criminal Appeal Act 1995. It is a non-departmental public body reporting to Parliament via the Home Secretary. It is responsible for investigating suspected miscarriages of justice in England, Wales and Northern Ireland, and deciding whether or not to refer cases back to an appeal court. Membership of the Commission is by royal appointment; the senior executive staff are appointed by the Commission.
Chairman, Sir Frederick Crawford, FREng
Members, B. Capon; L. Elks; A. Foster; Ms F. King; J. Knox; D. Kyle; Prof. L. Leigh; J. MacKeith; K. Singh; B. Skitt; E. Weiss; D. Jessel
Chief Executive, Ms J. Courtney
Director of Finance and Personnel, D. Robson
Legal Advisers, J. Wagstaff; M. Aspinall
Police Adviser, R. Barrington

CRIMINAL INJURIES COMPENSATION AUTHORITY (CICA)
Morley House, 26–30 Holborn Viaduct,
London EC1A 2JQ
Tel: 020-7842 6800; Fax: 020-7436 0804
Web: www.cica.gov.uk
Tay House, 300 Bath Street, Glasgow G2 4JR
Tel: 0141-331 2726; Fax: 0141-331 2287

All applications for compensation for personal injury arising from crimes of violence in England, Scotland and Wales are dealt with at the above locations. (Separate arrangements apply in Northern Ireland.) Applications received up to 31 March 1996 are assessed on the basis of common law damages under the 1990 compensation scheme. Applications received later than 1 April 1996 are assessed under a tariff-based scheme, made under the Criminal Injuries Compensation Act 1995, by the Criminal Injuries Compensation Authority (CICA). There is a separate avenue of appeal to the Criminal Injuries Compensation Appeals Panel (CICAP). In 2000–2001 total compensation paid was around £207.874 million.
Chief Executive, Howard Webber
Deputy Chief Executive, E. McKeown
Head of Legal Services, Ms A. M. Johnstone
Press enquiries, Mrs L. Fidler

CRIMINAL INJURIES COMPENSATION APPEALS PANEL (CICAP)
11th Floor, Cardinal Tower, 12 Farringdon Road,
London EC1M 3HS
Tel: 020-7549 4600; Fax: 020-7549 4643;
Email: info@cicap.gov.uk; Web: www.cicap.gov.uk
Chairman, R. Goodier
Chief Executive and Secretary to the Panel, R. Burke

CROFTERS COMMISSION
4-6 Castle Wynd, Inverness IV2 3EQ
Tel: 01463-663450; Fax: 01463-711820
Email: info@crofterscommission.org.uk

The Crofters Commission was established in 1955 under the Crofters (Scotland) Act. It advises the Scottish Ministers on all matters relating to crofting. It develops and promotes thriving crofting communities and simplifies relevant legislation. It administers the Crofting Counties Agricultural Grants Scheme, Livestock Improvement Schemes and the Croft Entrant Scheme. It also provides a free enquiry service.
Chairman, I. MacAskill
Chief Executive, S. Rankin

CROWN ESTATE
16 Carlton House Terrace, London SW1Y 5AH
Tel: 020-7210 4377; Fax: 020-7930 8187
Web: www.crownestate.co.uk

The Crown Estate includes substantial blocks of urban property, primarily in London, almost 120,000 hectares of agricultural land and extensive marine holdings throughout the United Kingdom. Its origins go back to the reign of King Edward the Confessor and, until the accession of King George III, the Sovereign received its rents and profits. However, since 1760 the annual surplus, after deducting management expenses, has been surrendered by the Sovereign to Parliament to help meet the cost of civil government. In return, the Sovereign receives the Civil List and the Government meets other official expenditure incurred in support of the Sovereign.

In the year ended 31 March 2002, the gross revenue from the Crown Estate totalled £223.5 million and £163.3 million was paid to the Exchequer as surplus revenue.
First Commissioner and Chairman (part-time), Sir Denys Henderson
Second Commissioner and Chief Executive, R. Bright
Commissioners (part-time), I. D. Grant, CBE; Mrs H. M. R. Chapman, CBE; R. R. Spinney, FRICS; Sir Donald Curry, KB, CBE; H. Duberly, CBE; M. Moore
Director of Urban Estates, D. A. Bickmore
Rural Estate, C. Bourchier
Urban, Central London Estate, Ms E. Miller
Urban, Regent Street Strategy, D. Shaw
Urban, Regent Street Estate, A. Meakin
Urban, Regional Estate, M. Dillon
Urban, Residential Estate, R. Wyatt
Urban, Special Projects, L. Colgan
Marine Estate, F. G. Parrish
Finance and Information Systems, J. G. Lelliott
Internal Audit, J. Ford
Corporate Planning and Human Resources, M. J. Gravestock
Human Resources Manager, Ms V. Burns
Communications Manager, I. Belcher

SCOTLAND

10 Charlotte Square, Edinburgh EH2 4BR
Tel: 0131-226 7241; Fax: 0131-220 1366
Head of Scottish Estate, M. Cunliffe

WINDSOR ESTATE

The Great Park, Windsor, Berks SL4 2HT
Tel: 01753-860222; Fax: 01753-859617
Deputy Ranger, P. Everett

HM CUSTOMS AND EXCISE
New King's Beam House, 22 Upper Ground, London SE1 9PJ
Tel: 020-7620 1313; National Advice Service: 0845-010 900
Web: www.hmce.gov.uk

Commissioners of Customs were first appointed in 1671 and housed by the King in London. The Excise Department was formerly under the Inland Revenue Department and was amalgamated with the Customs Department in 1909.

HM Customs and Excise is responsible for collecting and administering customs and excise duties and VAT, and advises the Chancellor of the Exchequer on any matters connected with them. The Department is also responsible for preventing and detecting the evasion of revenue laws and for enforcing a range of prohibitions and restrictions on the importation of certain classes of goods. In addition, the Department undertakes certain agency work on behalf of other departments, including the compilation of UK overseas trade statistics from customs import and export documents.

THE BOARD

Chairman (G1), R. Broadbent
Private Secretary, Ms D. Morris
Commissioners, Director General Business Services and Taxes (G2), M. J. Eland
Director General Law Enforcement (G2), T. Byrne
Director Logistics (G3), A. Fraser
Director Finance and Strategy (G3), M. Hanson
Director Intelligence (G3), M. N. Norgrove
Non Executive Directors, Ms R. Pickavance; D. Spencer; B. Quirk; T. Hall; Sir Stephen Lander
Solicitor (G2), D. Pickup, CB

DEER COMMISSION FOR SCOTLAND
Knowsley, 82 Fairfield Road, Inverness IV3 5LH
Tel: 01463-231751; Fax: 01463-712931
Email: deercom@aol.com
Web: www.dcs.gov.uk

The Deer Commission for Scotland has the general functions of furthering the conservation and control of deer in Scotland. It has the statutory duty, with powers, to prevent damage to agriculture, forestry and the habitat by deer. It is funded by the Scottish Executive.
Chairman (part-time), A. Raven
Director, N. Reiter
Technical Director, D. Balharry

DESIGN COUNCIL
34 Bow Street, London WC2E 7DL
Tel: 020-7420 5200; Fax: 020-7420 5300

The Design Council is a campaigning and lobbying organisation which works with partners in business, education and Government to promote the effective use of good design. It is a registered charity with a Royal Charter and is funded by grant-in-aid from the Department of Trade and Industry.
Chairman, C. Frayling
Chief Executive, A. Summers

DISABILITY RIGHTS COMMISSION (DRC)
DRC, Stratford upon Avon CV37 9BR
DRC Helpline: 0845-762 2633
Web: www.drc-gb.org

The Commission is an executive non-departmental public body established in April 2000. Its role is to advise Government on issues of discrimination against disabled people and the operation of the Disability Discrimination Act 1995. It promotes good practice to employers and service providers and provides advice, information and sometimes legal support to disabled people.
Chair, B. Massie, CBE
Chief Executive, B. Niven
Commissioners, S. Alam; Ms K. Allen; M. Burton; Ms. J. Campbell, MBE; M. Devenney; R. Exell, OBE; Dr K. Fitzpatrick; C. Holmes, MBE; J. Hougham, CBE; Mrs E. Noad; Ms E. Rank-Petruzzietto; L. Rellon; Ms P. Russell, CBE; Ms J. White, MBE

THE DUCHY OF CORNWALL
10 Buckingham Gate, London SW1E 6LA
Tel: 020-7834 7346; Fax: 020-7931 9541

The Duchy of Cornwall was created by Edward III in 1337 for the support of his eldest son Edward, later known as the Black Prince. It is the oldest of the English duchies. The duchy is acquired by inheritance by the sovereign's eldest son either at birth or on the accession of his parent to the throne, whichever is the later. The primary purpose of the estate remains to provide an income for the Prince of Wales. The estate is mainly agricultural and based in the south-west of England. A recent purchase has increased the landholding to approximately 150,000 acres in 26 counties. The duchy also has some residential property, a number of shops and offices, and a Stock Exchange portfolio. Prince Charles is the 24th Duke of Cornwall.

THE PRINCE'S COUNCIL

Chairman, HRH The Prince of Wales
Lord Warden of the Stannaries, The Earl Peel
Receiver-General, The Rt. Hon. J. H. Leigh-Pemberton
Attorney-General to the Prince of Wales, N. Underhill, QC
Secretary and Keeper of the Records, W. R. A. Ross
Other members, R. Broadhurst; Mrs. J. Coode; W. N. Hood, CBE; Sir Christopher Howes, CB; S. Lamport; J. E. Pugsley; The Duke of Westminster

OTHER OFFICERS

Auditors, G. N. C. Ward; R. Hughes
Sheriff (2002–2003), Mrs J. Cooke

THE DUCHY OF LANCASTER
Lancaster Place, Strand, London WC2E 7ED
Tel: 020-7836 8277; Fax: 020-7836 3098

The estates and jurisdiction known as the Duchy of Lancaster have belonged to the reigning monarch since 1399 when John of Gaunt's son came to the throne as Henry IV. As the Lancaster Inheritance it goes back as far as 1265 when Henry III granted his youngest son Edmund lands and possessions following the Baron's war. In 1267 Henry gave Edmund the County, Honor and Castle of Lancaster and created him the first Earl of Lancaster. In 1351 Edward III created Lancaster a County Palatine.

The Chancellor of the Duchy of Lancaster is responsible for the administration of the Duchy, the appointment of justices of the peace in Lancashire, Greater Manchester and Merseyside and ecclesiastical patronage in the Duchy gift.
Chancellor of the Duchy of Lancaster (and Minister for the Cabinet Office), The Rt. Hon. The Lord Macdonald of Tradeston, CBE
Chairman of the Duchy Council, Sir Michael Bunbury, BT
Attorney-General, M. T. J. Briggs, QC
Receiver-General, A. Reid
Clerk of the Council and Chief Executive, P. R. Clarke
Secretary for Appointments, Mrs L. M. Addison

ECGD (EXPORT CREDITS GUARANTEE DEPARTMENT)
PO Box 2200, 2 Exchange Tower, Harbour Exchange Square, London E14 9GS
Tel: 020-7512 7000; Fax: 020-7512 7649

ECGD (Export Credits Guarantee Department), the UK's official export credit agency, is a Government department responsible to the Secretary of State for Trade and Industry and functions under the Export and Investment Guarantees Act 1991. This enables ECGD to facilitate UK exports by making available export credit insurance to firms engaged in selling overseas and to guarantee repayment to banks providing finance for capital goods. The Act also empowers ECGD to insure UK companies investing overseas against political risks such as war, expropriation and restrictions on remittances.
Chief Executive, H. V. B. Brown
Group Directors (G3), V. P. Lunn-Rockliffe (*Portfolio Asset Management*); J. R. Weiss (*Business*); T. M. Jaffray (*Risk Asset Management*)

DIVISIONS

Director, Finance (G5), I. Dickson
Director, Central Services (G5), S. R. Dodgson
Directors, Business Divisions (G5), G. G. Welsh (*Division A*); R. Gotts (*Division B*); M. D. Pentecost (*Division C*); J. C. W. Croall (*Capital Management*)
Director, Office of the General Counsel (G5), N. Ridley
Director, International Debt (G5), Ms L. Woods
Director, Claims (G5), R. F. Lethbridge
Director, Active Portfolio Management, Y. Tamir
Director, Strategy and Communications, J. Ormerod
Director, Risk Management, P. J. Radford
Director, IT Services (G6), E. J. Walsby
Director, Internal Audit (G6), G. Cassell
Director, Operational Research (G6), Ms R. Kaufman

EXPORT GUARANTEES ADVISORY COUNCIL

Chairman, E. L. Airey
Other Members, J. Armitt; A. Brown; J. Elkington; Prof. J. Kydd; D. MacLachlan; Prof. K. Phylaktis; A. Shepherd; Dr R. Thamotheram; Sir David Wright

ENGLISH HERITAGE (HISTORIC BUILDINGS AND MONUMENTS COMMISSION FOR ENGLAND)
23 Savile Row, London W1S 2ET
Tel: 020-7973 3000; Fax: 020-7973 3001
Web: www.english-heritage.org.uk

English Heritage was established under the National Heritage Act 1983. On 1 April 1999 it merged with the Royal Commission on the Historical Monuments of

England to become the new lead body for England's historic environment. Its duties are to carry out and sponsor archaeological, architectural and scientific survey and research designed to increase the understanding of England's past and its changing condition; to offer expert advice and skills and give grants to secure the preservation of listed buildings, cathedrals, churches, archaeological sites, ancient monuments and historic houses of England; to encourage the imaginative re-use of historic buildings to aid regeneration of the centres of cities, towns and villages; to manage the historic monuments and historic buildings in England; and to curate and make publicly accessible the National Monuments Record, whose records of over one million historic sites and buildings, and collections of more that 12 million photographs, maps, drawings and reports constitute the central database and archive to England's historic environment.

Chairman, Sir Neil Cossons
Commissioners, M. Cairns; Prof. D. Cannadine; Mrs G. Drummond; A. Fane; P. Gough, CBE; J. Grenville; L. Grossman; The Earl of Leicester; R. Morris, FSA; L. Sparks; Miss S. Underwood
Chief Executive, Dr S. Thurley

NATIONAL MONUMENTS RECORD, National Monuments Record Centre, Kemble Drive, Swindon SN2 2GZ. Tel: 01793-414600; Fax: 01793-414606. *London Search Room:* 55 Blandford Street, London SW1H 3AF. Tel: 020-7208 8200; Fax: 020-7224 5333

ENGLISH NATURE
Northminster House, Peterborough PE1 1UA
Tel: 01733-455000; Fax: 01733-568834
Web: www.english-nature.org.uk

English Nature was established in 1991 and is responsible for advising the Secretary of State for the Environment, Food and Rural Affairs on nature conservation in England. It promotes, directly and through others, the conservation of England's wildlife and natural features. It selects, establishes and manages National Nature Reserves and identifies and notifies Sites of Special Scientific Interest. It provides advice and information about nature conservation, and supports and conducts research relevant to these functions. Through the Joint Nature Conservation Committee, it works with its sister organisations in Scotland and Wales on UK and international nature conservation issues.

Chairman, M. Doughty
Chief Executive, D. Arnold-Forster
Directors, Dr K. L. Duff; Miss C. E. M. Wood; Ms S. Collins; A. E. Brown

THE ENVIRONMENT AGENCY
Rio House, Waterside Drive, Aztec West, Almondsbury, Bristol BS32 4UD
Tel: 01454-624400; Fax: 01454-624409
Email: enquiries@environment-agency.gov.uk
Web: www.environment-agency.gov.uk

The Environment Agency was established in 1996 under the Environment Act 1995 and is a non-departmental public body sponsored by the Department of the Environment, Food and Rural Affairs and the National Assembly for Wales. The Agency is responsible for pollution prevention and control in England and Wales, and for the management and use of water resources, including flood defences, fisheries and navigation. It has

head offices in London and Bristol and eight regional offices.

THE BOARD
Chairman, Sir John Harman
Members, C. Beardwood; A. J. P. Dalton; A. Dare, CBE; E. Gallagher; N. Haigh, OBE; C. Hampson, CBE; Prof. R. Macrory; Prof. J. McGlade; G. Manning, OBE; Dr A. Powell; Prof. D. Ritchie; A. Rogers; G. Wardell

THE EXECUTIVE
Chief Executive, B. Young
Director of Finance, N. Reader
Director of Personnel, G. Duncan
Director of Environmental Protection, Dr P. Leinster
Director of Water Management, G. Mance
Director of Operations, A. Robertson
Director of Corporate Affairs, H. McCallum
Director of Legal Services, R. Navarro
Chief Scientist, Dr John Murlis

EQUAL OPPORTUNITIES COMMISSION
Arndale House, Arndale Centre, Manchester M4 3EQ
Tel: 0845-601 5901; Fax: 0161-838 1733
Email: info@eoc.org.uk; Web: www.eoc.org.uk

Press Office, 36 Broadway, London SW1H 0BH.
Tel: 020-7222 0004
Other Offices, St Stephens House, 279 Bath Street, Glasgow G2 4JL Tel: 0845-601 5901; Windsor House, Windsor Lane, Cardiff CF10 3GE
Tel: 029-2034 3552

The Commission was established under the Sex Discrimination Act in 1975, as an independent statutory body. It works towards the elimination of discrimination on the grounds of sex or marital status, to promote equality of opportunity between men and women generally and to provide advice and legal assistance to individuals who have been discriminated against. It is responsible to The Department for Trade and Industry.
Chair, Ms J. Mellor
Deputy Chair, Ms J. Watson
Commissioners, Ms T. Akpeki; Ms S. Ashtiany; Ms K. Carberry; Ms F. Cannon; Ms J. Drake; Ms A. Mason; ; Ms S. Pierce; Prof. T. Rees; Ms S. Sharma; D. Smith; Ms T. Woodcraft;
Chief Executive, C. Slocock

EQUALITY COMMISSION FOR NORTHERN IRELAND
Equality House, 7–9 Shaftesbury Square, Belfast, BT2 7DP.
Tel: 028-9050 0600; Fax: 028-9033 1544
Email: information@equalityni.org
Web: www.equalityni.org

The Equality Commission was set up in 1999 and is responsible for promoting equality and eliminating discrimination on the grounds of race, disability, gender, religion and political opinion.
Chief Commissioner, Ms J. Harbison
Chief Executive, E. Collins

FILM COUNCIL
10 Little Portland Street, London W1W 7JG Tel: 020-7861 7861; Fax: 020-7861 7862
Email: info@filmcouncil.org.uk

The Council was created in April 2000 by the Department for Culture, Media and Sport to develop a coherent strategy for the development and leadership of film culture and the film industry. It is responsible for the majority of the Department for Culture, Media and Sport funding for film as well as lottery and grant-in-aid (with the exception of the National Film and Television School).
Chairman, A. Parker
Deputy Chairman, S. Till
Chief Executive, J. Woodward

FOOD STANDARDS AGENCY (UK)
Aviation House, 125 Kingsway, London, WC2B 6NH
Tel: 020-7276 8000; Fax: 020-7276 8004
Web: www.food.gov.uk

The Food Standards Agency (FSA) was established by an Act of Parliament (the Food Standards Act 1999) in April 2000 to protect public health from risks arising in connection with the consumption of food, and otherwise to protect the interests of consumers in relation to food. The Agency has the general function of developing policy in these areas and provides information and advice to the Government, other public bodies and consumers. It also sets standards for and monitors food law enforcement by local authorities. The Agency is a UK-wide non-ministerial Government body which is led by a board, which has been appointed to act in the public interest. It has executive offices in Scotland, Wales and Northern Ireland. It is advised by advisory committees on food safety matters of special interest to each of these areas.
Chairman, Prof. Sir John Krebs, MD
Deputy Chairman, Ms S. Leather
Chief Executive, G. Podger

EXECUTIVE AGENCY

MEAT HYGIENE SERVICE
Kings Pool, Peasholme Green, York YO1 7PR
Tel: 01904-455500; Fax: 01904-455502

The Agency was launched in April 1995 and from the 1 April 2000 became an executive agency of the Food Standards Agency. It protects public health and promotes animal welfare through veterinary supervision and meat inspection in licensed fresh meat establishments.
Chief Executive (G4), C. J. Lawson

FOOD STANDARDS AGENCY SCOTLAND
St Magnus House, 25 Guild Street, Aberdeen, AB11 6NJ
Tel: 01224-285100; Fax: 01224-285167;
Email: scotland@foodstandards.gsi.gov.uk
Web: www food.gov.uk

FOOD STANDARDS AGENCY WALES
1st Floor, Southgate House, Wood Street, Cardiff CF10 1EW
Tel: 029-2067 8999;
Email: wales@foodstandards.gsi.gov.uk
Web: www.food.gov.uk
Advisory Committee for Wales Chair, Ms A. Hemingway

FOOD STANDARDS AGENCY NORTHERN IRELAND
10B and 10C Clarendon Road, Belfast, BT1 3BG
Tel: 028-9041 7700; Fax: 028-9041 7726
Email: infosani@foodstandards.gsi.gov.uk
Web: www.food.gov.uk
Advisory Committee for Northern Ireland,
Chairman, M. Walker

FOREIGN COMPENSATION COMMISSION
Room SG/III, Old Admiralty Building, Whitehall, London, SW1A 2PA
Tel: 020-7008 1321; Fax: 020-7008 0160

The Commission was set up by the Foreign Compensation Act 1950 primarily to distribute, under Orders in Council, funds received from other governments in accordance with agreements to pay compensation for expropriated British property and other losses sustained by British nationals.
Chairman, A. W. E. Wheeler, CBE
Secretary, A. N. Grant

FORESTRY COMMISSION
231 Corstorphine Road, Edinburgh EH12 7AT
Tel: 0845-367 3787; Fax: 0131-316 4891
Email: enquiries@forestry.gsi.gov.uk
Web: www.forestry.gov.uk

The Forestry Commission is the Government department responsible for forestry policy in Great Britain. It reports directly to forestry Ministers (i.e. the Minister of Environment, Food and Rural Affairs, the Scottish Ministers and the National Assembly for Wales), to whom it is responsible for advice on forestry policy and for the implementation of that policy.

The Commission's principal objectives are to protect Britain's forests and woodlands; expand Britain's forest area; enhance the economic value of the forest resources; conserve and improve the biodiversity, landscape and cultural heritage of forests and woodlands; develop opportunities for woodland recreation; and increase public understanding of and community participation in forestry. Forest Enterprise, a trading body operating as an executive agency of the Commission, manages its forestry estate on a multi-use basis.
Chairman (part-time), The Rt. Hon. Lord Clark of Windermere
Director-General and Deputy Chairman (G2), D. J. Bills, CBE
Secretary to the Commissioners (G5), F. Strang

FOREST ENTERPRISE HEADQUARTERS, 231 Corstorphine Road, Edinburgh EH12 7AT. Tel: 0845-367 3787. *Chief Executive,* Dr B. McIntosh
FOREST RESEARCH, Alice Holt Lodge, Wrecclesham, Farnham, Surrey GU10 4LU. Tel: 01420-222555; Northern Research Station, Roslin, Midlothian EH25 9SY. Tel: 0131-445 2176. *Chief Executive,* vacant

GAMING BOARD FOR GREAT BRITAIN

Berkshire House, 168–173 High Holborn, London WC1V 7AA
Tel: 020-7306 6200; Fax: 020-7306 6266
Email: enqs@gbggb.org.uk
Web: www.gbgb.org.uk

The Board was established in 1968 and is responsible to the Secretary of State for Culture, Media and Sport. It is the regulatory body for casinos, bingo clubs, gaming machines and the larger society and all local authority lotteries in Great Britain. Its functions are to ensure that those involved in organising gaming and lotteries are fit and proper to do so and to keep gaming free from criminal infiltration; to ensure that gaming and lotteries are run fairly and in accordance with the law; and to advise the Secretary of State on developments in gaming and lotteries.
Chairman (part-time) (£40,000–£45,000), P. Dean, CBE
Secretary, T. Kavanagh

GOVERNMENT ACTUARY'S DEPARTMENT

New King's Beam House, 22 Upper Ground, London SE1 9RJ
Tel: 020-7211 2601; Fax: 020-7211 2640/2650
Email: enquiries@gad.gov.uk
Web: www.gad.gov.uk

The Government Actuary provides a consulting service to Government departments, the public sector, and overseas governments. The actuaries advise on social security schemes and superannuation arrangements in the public sector at home and abroad, on population and other statistical studies, and on supervision of insurance companies and pension funds.
Government Actuary, C. D. Daykin, CB
Directing Actuaries, D. G. Ballantine; A. G. Young
Chief Actuaries, E. I. Battersby; I. A. Boonin; A. I. Johnston; D. Lewis; G. T. Russell

GOVERNMENT HOSPITALITY

Lancaster House, Stable Yard, St James's, London SW1A 1BB
Tel: 020-7008 8196; Fax: 020-7210 4301

The Government Hospitality Fund was instituted in 1908 for the purpose of organising official hospitality on a regular basis with a view to the promotion of international goodwill.
Government Hospitality is now incorporated as part of the Foreign and Commonwealth Office's Conference and Visitors Group.
Minister, Dr D. MacShane
Head of Government Hospitality, R. Alexander

GOVERNMENT OFFICES FOR THE REGIONS

The Government Offices for the Regions manage expenditure programmes amounting to over £7 billion per year for various Government departments. The programmes cover areas such as; sustainable development, neighbourhood renewal, social inclusion, regeneration, competitiveness and rural affairs.
Government Offices handle land use planning, housing and countryside work, road schemes decisions, local transport priorities, transport interaction with land uses

planning and statutory casework. Government Offices have a sponsorship role for the eight Regional Development Agencies and the London Development Agency and are also involved in training and education and business support issues.

REGIONAL CO-ORDINATION UNIT, Riverwalk House, 157–161 Millbank, London SW1P 4RR Tel: 020-7217 3029; Fax: 020-7217 3471
Director General; R. Smith
Director (G3), A. Wells
Directors, A. Modu *(Corporate Relations);* A. Sargeant *(Strategy);* T. Vokes *(Business Development)*

EAST MIDLANDS

Secretariat: The Belgrave Centre, Stanley Place, Talbot Street, Nottingham NG1 5GG
Tel: 0115-971 2757; Fax: 0115-971 2412;
Email: enquiries.goem@go-regions.gsi.gov.uk
Web: www.go-em.gov.uk

Regional Director (G3), D. Morrison
Directors (G5), Dr S. Kennett *(Infrastructure and Community Affairs);* S. Brookes *(Regional Crime Reduction);* G. Norbury *(European and Rural Affairs Policy);* R. Poole *(Industry, Education and Skills, Leicestershire and Derby);* R. Smith *(Corporate Affairs)*

EAST OF ENGLAND

Secretariat: Building A, Westbrook Centre, Milton Road, Cambridge CB4 1YG
Tel: 01223-346708; Fax: 01223-346705

Regional Director (G3), C. Whitworth *(acting)*
Directors (G5), Ms C. Bowdler *(Planning and Transport);* M. Oldham *(Business and Europe);* J. Street *(Learning and Local Government);* J. Rabagliati *(DEFRA, Agriculture, Countryside and Sustainability);* H. Cooper *(Temporary Strategy and Services);* H. Tam *(HO Community Safety and Regeneration)*

LONDON

Secretariat: Riverwalk House, 157–161 Millbank, London SW1P 4RR
Tel: 020-7217 3029; Fax: 020-7217 3471

Regional Director (G3), L. Meek
Directors (G3), J. Anderson and S. Webber *(Job Share Government/FGLA Liaison Unit);* S. Ebanja *(Local Government and Europe);* C. Lyons *(Corporate and Change Management);* A. Melville *(London Co-Ordination and Environment Division);* E. Roy *(Crime Reduction);* K. Timmins *(Trade and Industry);* R. Wragg *(Skills and Education)*

NORTH-EAST

Secretariat: Wellbar House, Gallow Gate, Newcastle upon Tyne NE1 4TD
Tel: 0191-202 3811; Fax: 0191-202 3830
Email: general.enquiries.gone@go-regions.gsi.gov.uk
Regional Director (G3), J. Blackie
Directors (G5), J. Darlington *(Planning, Environment and Transport);* D. Caudle *(Education, Skills, Enterprise and Regeneration);* J. Bainton *(DEFRA);* A. Brown *(Crime Reduction);* D. Pearce *(Strategy and Resources);* D. Slater *(Competitiveness in Europe)*

NORTH-WEST

Secretariat: 12th Floor, Sunley Tower, Piccadilly Plaza, Manchester M1 4BE
Tel: 0161-952 4010; Fax: 0161-952 4019

Regional Director (G3), K. Barnes
Directors, (G5), P. Styche (Communities); Dr D.
Highham (Business and Europe); (G6), I. Jamieson
(Business and Europe); Ms S. Yates (Europe and
Liverpool); E. Hughes (Planning and
Environment/Regional Policy and Co-ordination); D.
Duff, OBE (Tec Transition); D. Hopewell (Corporate
Services); N. Burke (Education and Social Exclusion);
M. Hill (Commonwealth Games); J. Flannon
(Objective 1); Dr D. Higham (Business Connexions); T.
Walker (Small Business Team)

SOUTH-EAST

Secretariat: 2nd Floor, Bridge House, 1 Walnut Tree Close,
Guildford, Surrey GU1 4GA
Tel: 01483-882470; Fax: 01483-882269

Regional Director (G3), Ms C. Dixon
Directors (G5), C. Byrne (Hants/IOW); S. Burt (Skills and
Enterprise Berks/Oxon/Bucks); A. Campbell
(Regeneration, Housing and Environment, Kent); A.
Parker (DEFRA and Europe, Surrey and Sussex); C.
Dixon (Transport and Strategy); P. Craggs (Finance
and Corporate Management); H. Marriage (Crime
Reduction)

SOUTH-WEST

Secretariat: 2 Rivergate, Temple Quay, Bristol BS1 6ED
Tel: 0117-900 1701; Fax: 0117-900 1901
Web: www.gosw.gov.uk

Regional Director (G3), Ms J. Henderson
Directors (G5), R. Bayly (Transport, Devon and
Cornwall); C. Carrington (Local Government and
Neighbourhood Renewal-Former West/West of
England); T. Shearer (Enterprise Intelligence and Young
People-Gloucestershire/Wiltshire); (G6) M. Davey
(Corporate Services); P. Rowlandson (Crime
Reduction); T. Render (Food Farming and Rural
Development, Somerset and Dorset)

WEST MIDLANDS

Secretariat: 6th Floor, 77 Paradise Circus, Queensway,
Birmingham B1 2DT
Tel: 0121-212 5226; Fax: 0121-212 5224
Email: enquiries.gowm@go-regions.gsi.gov.uk

Regional Director (G3), G. Garbutt
Directors (G5), C. Marsh (Corporate Affairs and Europe);
P. Holland (Local Government); (G6) C. Beesley
(Business and Learning Division); B. Davies (DEFRA);
M. Greary (Crime Reduction)

YORKSHIRE AND THE HUMBER

Secretariat: PO Box 213, City House, New Station Street,
Leeds LS1 4US
Tel: 0113-283 6681; Fax: 0113-283 5210
Email: enquiries.goyh@go-regions.gsi.gov.uk

Regional Director (G3), F. Everiss
Directors (G5), G. Dyche (HO Crime Reduction and
Voluntary Sector); S. Perryman (People and
Communities); (G6), J. Jarvis (Regional Affairs);
N. Best (Corporate Services); G. Kingston (DEFRA-
Rural); I. Mills (Europe); S. Yates (Objective 1);
M. Jackson (Competitiveness and Sensibilities)

HEALTH AND SAFETY COMMISSION
Rose Court, 2 Southwark Bridge, London SE1 9HS
Tel: 020-7717 6000; Fax: 020-7717 6644
Email: hseinformationservices@natbrit.com
Web: www.hse.gov.uk

The Health and Safety Commission was created under
the Health and Safety at Work etc. Act 1974, with duties
to reform health and safety law, to propose new
regulations, and generally to promote the protection of
people at work and the public from hazards arising from
industrial and commercial activity, including major
industrial accidents and the transportation of hazardous
materials. Its nine members are nominated by
organisations representing employers, employees, local
authorities and others.
Chairman, B. Callaghan
Members, J. Donovan; M. Rooney; Ms J. Edmond-Smith;
G. Brumwell; Ms M. Burns; A. Chowdry; O. Tudor; J.
Longworth; J. Hackitt
Secretary, M. Dempsey

HEALTH AND SAFETY EXECUTIVE
Rose Court, 2 Southwark Bridge, London SE1 9HS
Tel: 020-7717 6000; Fax: 020-7717 6717

The Health and Safety Executive is the Health and Safety
Commission's major instrument. Through its
inspectorates it enforces health and safety law in the
majority of industrial premises. The Executive advises the
Commission in its major task of laying down safety
standards through regulations and practical guidance for
many industrial processes. The Executive is also the
licensing authority for nuclear installations and the
reporting officer on the severity of nuclear incidents in
Britain, and it is responsible for the Channel Tunnel
Safety Authority.
Director-General, T. Walker
Deputy Director-General, Policy, K. Timms
Deputy Director-General, Operations, J. McCracken
Director, Field Operations Unit, Dr A. Ellis
Director, Safety Policy Directorate, N. Starling
Director, Health Directorate, S. Caldwell
Director and HM Chief Inspector of the Nuclear
  Installations Inspectorate, L. Williams
Director, Strategy and Analytical Support Directorate, Dr
  P. Graham
Director, Hazardous Installations Directorate and Chief
  Scientist, Dr P. Davies
Director, Resource and Planning Directorate, R. Hillier
HM Chief Inspector of Railways, Dr A. Sefton

HIGHLANDS AND ISLANDS ENTERPRISE
Cowan House, Inverness Retail and Business Park,
Inverness, Scotland IV2 7GF
Tel: 01463-234171; Fax: 01463-244469
Email: hie.general@hient.co.uk
Web: www.hie.co.uk

Highlands and Islands Enterprise (HIE) was set up under
the Enterprise and New Towns (Scotland) Act 1991. Its
role is to design, direct and deliver enterprise
development, training, environmental and social projects
and services. HIE is made up of a strategic core body and
ten Local Enterprise Companies (LECs) to which many of
its individual functions are delegated.
Chairman, Dr J. Hunter
Chief Executive, I. J. R. S Cumming

HISTORIC BUILDINGS COUNCIL FOR SCOTLAND
Longmore House, Salisbury Place, Edinburgh EH9 1SH
Tel: 0131-668 8799; Fax: 0131-668 8788

The Historic Buildings Council for Scotland is the advisory body to the Scottish Ministers on matters related to buildings of special architectural or historical interest and in particular to proposals for awards by them of grants for the repair of buildings of outstanding architectural or historical interest or lying within outstanding conservation areas.
Chairman, Cllr P. Chalmers
Members, Cllr R. Cairns; Archbishop M. Conti; Ms L. Davidson; Mrs A. Dundas-Bekker; The Very Revd G. Forbes; Dr J. Frew; M. Hopton; Ms F. Sinclair
Secretary, Mrs S. Williamson

HISTORIC BUILDINGS COUNCIL FOR WALES
Cathays Park, Cardiff CF10 3NQ
Tel: 029-2050 0200; Fax: 029-2082 6375

The Council's function is to advise the National Assembly for Wales on the historic buildings through Cadw: Welsh Historic Monuments, which is an executive agency of the Assembly.
Chairman, T. Lloyd, FSA
Members, Prof. P. Morgan; Mrs S. Furse; Dr S. Unwin; Dr E. William; Miss E. Evans; Dr R. Wools
Secretary, Mrs J. Booker

HISTORIC ROYAL PALACES
Hampton Court Palace, East Molesey, Surrey KT8 9AU
Tel: 020-8781 9500; Fax: 020-8781 9754
Web: www.hrp.org.uk

Historic Royal Palaces is a non-departmental public body with charitable status. The Secretary of State for Culture, Media and Sport is still accountable to Parliament for the care, conservation and presentation of the palaces, which are owned by the Sovereign in right of the Crown. The chairman of the trustees is appointed by The Queen on the advice of the Secretary of State.
  Historic Royal Palaces is responsible for the Tower of London, Hampton Court Palace, Kensington Palace State Apartments and the Royal Ceremonial Dress Collection, Kew Palace with Queen Charlotte's Cottage, and the Banqueting House, Whitehall.

TRUSTEES

Chairman, The Earl of Airlie, KT, GCVO, PC
Appointed by The Queen, A. Reid; Sir Hugh Roberts, KCVO, FSA; Field Marshal The Lord Inge, KG, GCB (*Constable of the Tower of London*)
Appointed by the Secretary of State, M. Herbert, CBE; Ms A. Heylin, OBE; S. Jones, LVO; Mrs. G. Woolfe, MBE
Ex officio, Sir Roger Wheeler, GCB, CBE

OFFICERS

Chief Executive, A. Coppin
Director of Finance, Ms A. McLeish
Director of Human Resources, G. Josephs
Director, Palaces Group, H. Player
Resident Governor, HM Tower of London, Maj.-Gen. G. Field, CB, OBE

Retail Director, Ms A. Boyes
Marketing Director, D. Homan
Director of Conservation, J. Barnes

HOME-GROWN CEREALS AUTHORITY
Caledonia House, 223 Pentonville Road, London N1 9HY
Tel: 020-7520 3926; Fax: 020-7520 3954

Set up under the Cereals Marketing Act 1965, the HGCA Board consists of seven members representing UK cereal growers, seven representing dealers in, or processors of, grain and two independent members. HGCA's functions are to improve the production and marketing of UK-grown cereals and oilseeds through a research and development programme, to provide a market information service, and to promote UK cereals in export markets.
Chairman (part-time), A. Pike
Chief Executive, P. V. Biscoe

HONOURS SCRUTINY COMMITTEE
Ashley House, 2 Monck Street, London SW1P 2BQ
Tel: 020-7276 2770; Fax: 020-7276 2766

The Honours Scrutiny Committee is a committee of Privy Counsellors. The Prime Minister submits certain particulars to the Committee about persons proposed to be recommended for honour at any level other than a peerage for their political services, or for an honour at the level of Knight or Dame for non-political services. The Committee, after such enquiry as it thinks fit, reports to the Prime Minister whether, so far as it believes, the political candidates are fit and proper persons to be recommended and for any non-political candidate, who may have made a political donation, whether this was a factor in the recommendation for an honour.
Chairman, The Lord Thomson of Monifieth, KT, PC
Members, The Baroness Dean of Thornton-le-Fylde, PC; The Lord Hurd of Westwell, CH, CBE
Secretary, Mrs P. G. W. Catto

HORSERACE TOTALISATOR BOARD
Tote House, 74 Upper Richmond Road, London SW15 2SU
Tel: 020-8874 6411; Fax: 020-8874 6107
Web: www.tote.co.uk

The Horserace Totalisator Board (the Tote) was established by the Betting, Gaming and Lotteries Act 1963. Its function is to operate totalisators on approved racecourses in Great Britain, and it also provides on and off-course cash and credit offices. Under the Horserace Totalisator and Betting Levy Board Act 1972, it is further empowered to offer bets at starting price (or other bets at fixed odds) on any sporting event, and under the Horserace Totalisator Board Act 1997 to take bets on any event, except the National Lottery. The chairman and members of the Board are appointed by the Secretary of State, Department of Culture, Media and Sport.
  The Government announced in March 2001 that the Tote would be sold to a racing trust, subject to the necessary legislation going through Parliament.
Chairman, P. I. Jones
Chief Executive, W. J. Heaton

HOUSING CORPORATION

Maple House, 149 Tottenham Court Road, London
W1T 7BN
Tel: 020-7393 2000; Fax: 020-7393 2111
Web: www.housingcorp.gov.uk

Established by Parliament in 1964, the Housing
Corporation regulates and funds registered social
landlords, non-profit making bodies run by voluntary
committees. There are over 2,000 registered social
landlords, most of which are housing associations, who
provide homes for more than 1.5 million people. Under
the Housing Act 1996, the Corporation's regulatory role
was widened to embrace new types of landlords, in
particular local housing companies. The Corporation is
funded by the Office of the Deputy Prime Minister.
Chairman, The Rt. Hon. The Baroness Dean of
   Thornton-le-Fylde
Deputy Chairman, E. Armitage
Chief Executive, Dr N. Perry

HUMAN FERTILISATION AND
EMBRYOLOGY AUTHORITY

Paxton House, 30 Artillery Lane, London E1 7LS
Tel: 020-7377 5077; Fax: 020-7377 1871
Web: www.hfea.gov.uk

The Human Fertilization and Embryology Authority
(HFEA) was established under the Human Fertilisation
and Embryology Act 1990. Its function is to license the
following activities: the creation or use of embryos
outside the body in the provision of infertility treatment
services; the use of donated gametes in infertility
treatment; the storage of gametes or embryos; and
research on human embryos. It maintains a confidential
database of all such treatments and of egg and sperm
donors, and provides information to patients, clinics and
the public. The HFEA also keeps under review
information about embryos and, when requested to do
so, gives advice to the Secretary of State for Health.
Chairman, S. Leather
Deputy Chairman, Ms J. Tugendhat
Members, Dr S. Avery; Prof. T. Baldwin; Prof. D. Barlow;
   Prof. P. Braude; I. Brecker; Prof. I. Cameron; J.
   Denton; Prof. C. Gosden; Prof. A. Grubb; S. Jenkins;
   Prof. H. Leese; Prof. S. Lewis; Ms S. Nathan; Ms S.
   Nebhrajani; Rt. Revd The Lord Bishop of Rochester;
   Dr F. Shenfield; Mrs L. Woods
Chief Executive, Dr M. Dalziel

HUMAN GENETICS COMMISSION

Area 652C, Skipton House, 80 London Road,
London, SE1 6LH
Tel: 020-7972 1518; Fax: 020-7972 1717
Email: hgc@doh.gov.uk
Web: www.hgc.gov.uk

The Human Genetics Commission was established in
1999, subsuming three previous advisory committees. Its
remit is to give Ministers strategic advice on how
developments in human genetics will impact on people
and health care, focusing in particular on the special and
ethical implications.
Chairman, Baroness H. Kennedy of the Shaws, QC
Vice-Chair, Prof. A. McCall Smith
Members; Dr W. Albert, Prof. E. Anionwu; Dr S. Bain;
   Prof. J. Burn; Ms R. Evans; Dr H. Harris; Prof. J.
   Harris; Ms S. Leather; Ms H. Newiss; Revd Dr. J.

Polkinghorne; Prof. M. Richards; Dr G. Samuels; Dr
S. Singleton; Mr G. Watts; Mr P. Webb; Prof. V. van
Heyningen; Dr Patrick Morrison; Dr R. Skinner
Head of Secretariat, M. Bale

INDEPENDENT HOUSING OMBUDSMAN

Norman House, 105–109 Strand, London WC2R 0AA
Tel: 020-7836 3630; Fax: 020-7836 3900
Email: ombudsman@ihos.org.uk
Web: www.ihos.org.uk

The Independent Housing Ombudsman (IHO) was
established in 1997 under the Housing Act 1996. The
Ombudsman deals with complaints against registered
social landlords (not including local authorities) and
some private landlords. IHO is also managing the pilot
Tenancy Deposit Scheme aimed at protecting the deposits
of private tenants and resolving any disputes over their
return quickly, cheaply and fairly.
Ombudsman, M. Biles
Chair of Board, G. Lewis
General Manager, L. Greenberg

INDEPENDENT INTERNATIONAL
COMMISSION ON DECOMMISSIONING

Dublin Castle, Block M, Ship Street, Dublin 2
Tel: 00 353 1-478 0111; Fax: 00 353 1-478 0600
Rosepark House, Upper Newtownards Road, Belfast
BT4 3NX
Tel: 028-9048 8600; Fax: 028-9048 8601

The Commission was established by agreement between
the British and Irish Governments in August 1997. Its
objective is to facilitate the decommissioning of illegally-
held firearms and explosives in accordance with the
relevant legislation in both jurisdictions. Its members are
appointed jointly by the two Governments; staff are
appointed by the Commission. All are drawn from
countries other than the UK and the Republic of Ireland.
Chairman, Gen. J. de Chastelain *(Canada)*
Commissioners, A. Sens *(USA)*
Staff Director, A. Suonio

INDEPENDENT REVIEW SERVICE FOR THE
SOCIAL FUND

4th Floor, Centre City Podium, 5 Hill Street,
Birmingham B5 4UB
Tel: 0121-606 2100; Fax: 0121-606 2180

The Social Fund Commissioner is appointed by the
Secretary of State for Work and Pensions. The
Commissioner appoints Social Fund Inspectors, who
provide an independent review of decisions made by
Social Fund Officers in the Department of Work and
Pensions.
Social Fund Commissioner, Sir Richard Tilt

INDEPENDENT TELEVISION COMMISSION

33 Foley Street, London W1W 7TL
Tel: 0845-601 3608; Fax: 020-7306 7800
Email: publicaffairs@itc.org.uk
Web: www.itc.org.uk

The Independent Television Commission replaced the
Independent Broadcasting Authority in 1991. The
Commission is responsible for licensing and regulating all
commercially funded television services broadcast from

the UK. Members are appointed by the Secretary of State for Culture, Media and Sport.

The Office of Communications, OFCOM, is due to become the new regulator for the communications sector in 2003.

Chairman, Sir Robin Biggam
Deputy Chairman, Baroness Janet Whitaker
Members, A. Balls, CB; C. Brendish, CBE; Ms B. Donoghue; Sir Michael Checkland; J. Goffe; J. Kelly, OBE; Dr C. Bharucha, FRCPath. (*Member for Northern Ireland*); Prof. D. L. Morgan, D.Phil. (*Member for Wales*); M. Shea, CVO (*Member for Scotland*)
Chief Executive, P. Hodgson
Secretary and Director of Development, M. Redley

INDUSTRIAL INJURIES ADVISORY COUNCIL

6th Floor, The Adelphi, 1–11 John Adam Street, London WC2N 6HT
Tel: 020-7962 8066; Fax: 020-7712 2255
Email: iiac@dial.pipex.com
Web: www.iiac.org.uk

The Industrial Injuries Advisory Council is a statutory body under the Social Security Administration Act 1992. It considers and advises the Secretary of State for Work and Pensions on regulations and other questions relating to industrial injuries benefits or their administration.
Chairman, Prof. A. J. Newman Taylor, OBE, FRCP
Administrative Secretary, M. Rigby

INFORMATION COMMISSIONER'S OFFICE

Wycliffe House, Water Lane, Wilmslow, Cheshire SK9 5AF
Tel: 01625-545745; Fax: 01625-524510
Email: data@dataprotection.gov.uk
Web: www.dataprotection.gov.uk

The Data Protection Act 1998 sets rules for processing personal information and applies to some paper records as well as those held on computers.

The Data Protection Act works in two ways; it says that those who record and use personal information (data controllers) must be open about how the information is used and must follow the eight principles of 'good information handling'. It also gives data subjects (individuals who are the subject of personal data) certain rights.

The Commissioner has a number of specific duties under the Act. She is given discretion in the manner in which she fulfils those duties and much of her work, and that of her staff involves informal advice and consultation with data controllers, and data subjects and the various bodies that represent them.

It is the Commissioner's duty to compile and maintain the register of data controllers, and provide facilities for members of the public to examine the register; promote observance of the data protection principles; and disseminate information to the public about the Act and her function under the Act. The Commissioner also has the power to produce codes of practice.

The Commissioner reports annually to parliament on the performance of her functions under the Act and has obligations to assess breaches of the Act.

The Information Commissioner is also responsible for Freedom of Information.
Commissioner, Mrs E. France

JOINT NATURE CONSERVATION COMMITTEE

Monkstone House, City Road, Peterborough PE1 1JY
Tel: 01733-562626; Fax: 01733-555948

The Committee was established under the Environmental Protection Act 1990. It advises the Government and others on UK and international nature conservation issues and disseminates knowledge on these subjects. It establishes common standards for the monitoring of nature conservation and research, and provides guidance to English Nature, Scottish Natural Heritage, the Countryside Council for Wales and the Department of the Environment for Northern Ireland.
Chairman (acting), Prof. O. W. Heal
Managing Director, D. Steer
Director, Dr M. A. Vincent

LAND REGISTRIES

HM LAND REGISTRY

Lincoln's Inn Fields, London WC2A 3PH
Tel: 020-7917 8888; Fax: 020-7955 0110
Email: enquiries.pic@landreg.gov.uk
Web: www.landreg.gov.uk

The registration of title to land was first introduced in England and Wales by the Land Registry Act 1862; HM Land Registry operates today under the Land Registration Acts 1925 to 1997. The object of registering title to land is to create and maintain a register of landowners whose title is guaranteed by the state and so to simplify the transfer, mortgage and other dealings with real property. Registration on sale is now compulsory throughout England and Wales. The register has been open to inspection by the public since 1990.

HM Land Registry is an executive agency and Trading Fund administered under the Lord Chancellor by the Chief Land Registrar.

HEADQUARTERS OFFICE

Chief Land Registrar and Chief Executive, P. Collis
Solicitor to Land Registry, J. V. Timothy
Director of Corporate Services, E. G. Beardsall
Director of Operations, A. Howarth
Director of Practice, J. V. Timothy
Director of Information Systems, I. Johnson
Director of Facilities, A. Elston
Head of Personnel, J. Hodder
Director of Finance, Ms H. Jackson
Director of Communication, A. Pemberton
Director of Service Development, P. Norman

COMPUTER SERVICES DIVISION

Burrington Way, Plymouth PL5 3LP
Tel: 01752-635600
Head of IT Services Division, P. A. Maycock
Head of IT Development Division, J. Formby
Head of IT Management Services, K. Deards

LAND CHARGES AND AGRICULTURAL CREDITS DEPARTMENT

Plumer House, Tailyour Road, Crownhill, Plymouth PL6 5HY
Tel: 01752-636666
Superintendent, Ms M. Taylor

DISTRICT LAND REGISTRIES

BIRKENHEAD (OLD MARKET) – Old Market House, Hamilton Street, Birkenhead CH41 5FL. Tel: 0151-473 1110. *District Land Registrar*, P. J. Brough

BIRKENHEAD (ROSEBRAE) – Rosebrae Court, Woodside Ferry Approach, Birkenhead CH41 6DU. Tel: 0151-472 6666. *District Land Registrar*, M. J. Garwood

COVENTRY – Leigh Court, Torrington Avenue, Tile Hill, Coventry CV4 9XZ. Tel: 024-7686 0860. *District Land Registrar*, Mrs D. M. Weaver

CROYDON – Sunley House, Bedford Park, Croydon CR9 3LE. Tel: 020-8781 9100. *District Land Registrar*, F. M. Twambley

DURHAM (BOLDON HOUSE) – Boldon House, Wheatlands Way, Pity Me, Durham DH1 5GJ. Tel: 0191-301 2345. *District Land Registrar*, R. B. Fearnley

DURHAM (SOUTHFIELD HOUSE) – Southfield House, Southfield Way, Durham DH1 5TR. Tel: 0191-301 3500. *District Land Registrar*, P. J. Timothy

GLOUCESTER – Twyver House, Bruton Way, Gloucester GL1 1DQ. Tel: 01452-511111. *District Land Registrar*, Mrs J. Jenkins

HARROW – LYON HOUSE, Lyon Road, Harrow, Middx HA1 2EU. Tel: 020-8235 1181. *District Land Registrar*, C. Tate

KINGSTON UPON HULL – Earle House, Portland Street, Hull HU2 8JN. Tel: 01482-223244. *District Land Registrar*, S. R. Coveney

LANCASHIRE – Wrea Brook Court, Lytham Road, Warton, Preston, PR4 1TE. Tel: 01772-836 700 *District Land Registrar*, Mrs L. Wallwork

LEICESTER – Westbridge Place, Leicester LE3 5DR. Tel: 0116-265 4000. *District Land Registrar*, Mrs J. A. Goodfellow

LYTHAM – Birkenhead House, East Beach, Lytham St Annes, Lancs FY8 5AB. Tel: 01253-849849. *District Land Registrar*, J. Griffiths

NOTTINGHAM (EAST) – Robins Wood Road, Nottingham NG8 3RQ. Tel: 0115-906 5353. *District Land Registrar*, Ms A. M. Goss

NOTTINGHAM (WEST) – Chalfont Drive, Nottingham NG8 3RN. Tel: 0115-935 1166. *District Land Registrar*, P. A. Brown

PETERBOROUGH – Touthill Close, City Road, Peterborough PE1 1XN. Tel: 01733-288288. *District Land Registrar*, C. W. Martin

PLYMOUTH – Plumer House, Tailyour Road, Crownhill, Plymouth PL6 5HY. Tel: 01752-636000. *District Land Registrar*, A. J. Pain

PORTSMOUTH – St Andrew's Court, St Michael's Road, Portsmouth PO1 2JH. Tel: 023-9276 8888. *District Land Registrar*, S. R. Sehrawat

STEVENAGE – Brickdale House, Swingate, Stevenage, Herts SG1 1XG. Tel: 01438-788888. *District Land Registrar*, M. Croker

SWANSEA – Tŷ Bryn Glas, High Street, Swansea SA1 1PW. Tel: 01792-458877. *District Land Registrar*, G. A. Hughes

TELFORD – Parkside Court, Hall Park Way, Telford TF3 4LR. Tel: 01952-290355. *District Land Registrar*, A. M. Lewis

TUNBRIDGE WELLS – Forest Court, Forest Road, Tunbridge Wells, Kent TN2 5AQ. Tel: 01892-510015. *District Land Registrar*, G. R. Tooke

WALES – Tŷ Cwm Tawe, Phoenix Way, Llansamlet, Swansea SA7 9FQ. Tel: 01792-355000. *District Land Registrar*, T. M. Lewis

WEYMOUTH – Melcombe Court, 1 Cumberland Drive, Weymouth, Dorset DT4 9TT. Tel: 01305-363636. *District Land Registrar*, Mrs P. M. Reeson

YORK – James House, James Street, York YO10 3YZ. Tel: 01904-450000. *District Land Registrar*, Mrs R. F. Lovel

REGISTERS OF SCOTLAND

Meadowbank House, 153 London Road, Edinburgh EH8 7AU
Tel: 0131-659 6111; Fax: 0131-479 3688
Customer Service Centre: 0845-607 0161

Registers of Scotland is the executive agency responsible for framing and maintaining records relating to property and other legal documents in Scotland. The agency holds 15 registers: two property registers (General Register of Sasines and Land Register of Scotland) and 13 chancery and judicial registers (Register of Deeds in the Books of Council and Session; Register of Protests; Register of Judgements; Register of Service of Heirs; Register of the Great Seal; Register of the Quarter Seal; Register of the Prince's Seal; Register of Crown Grants; Register of Sheriffs' Commissions; Register of the Cachet Seal; Register of Inhibitions and Adjudications; Register of Entails; and Register of Hornings).

Chief Executive and Keeper of the Registers of Scotland, A. W. Ramage
Deputy Keeper, A. G. Rennie
Managing Director, F. Manson

LAW COMMISSION

Conquest House, 37–38 John Street, London WC1N 2BQ
Tel: 020-7453 1220; Fax: 020-7453 1297
Web: www.lawcom.gov.uk

The Law Commission was set up in 1965, under the Law Commissions Act 1965, to make proposals to the Government for the examination of the law in England and Wales and for its revision where it is unsuited for modern requirements, obscure, or otherwise unsatisfactory. It recommends to the Lord Chancellor programmes for the examination of different branches of the law and suggests whether the examination should be carried out by the Commission itself or by some other body. The Commission is also responsible for the preparation of Consolidation and Statute Law (Repeals) Bills.

Chairman, The Hon. Mr Justice Toulson
Commissioners, Judge A. Wilkie, QC; Prof. H. Beale, QC; Prof. M. Partington; S. Bridge
Secretary, M. W. Sayers

LAW OFFICERS' DEPARTMENTS

Legal Secretariat to the Law Officers, Attorney-General's Chambers, 9 Buckingham Gate, London SW1E 6JP
Tel: 020-7271 2400; Fax: 020-7271 2430
Email: lslo@gtnet.gov.uk
Web: www.lslo.gov.uk
Attorney-General's Chambers, Royal Courts of Justice, Belfast BT1 3JY
Tel: 028-9054 6082; Fax: 028-9054 6049

The Law Officers of the Crown for England and Wales are the Attorney-General and the Solicitor-General. The Attorney-General, assisted by the Solicitor-General, is the chief legal adviser to the Government and is also ultimately responsible for all Crown litigation. He has overall responsibility for the work of the Law Officers' Departments (the Treasury Solicitor's Department, the Crown Prosecution Service, the Serious Fraud Office and

the Legal Secretariat to the Law Officers). He has a specific statutory duty to superintend the discharge of their duties by the Director of Public Prosecutions (who heads the Crown Prosecution Service) and the Director of the Serious Fraud Office. The Director of Public Prosecutions for Northern Ireland is also responsible to the Attorney-General for the performance of his functions. The Attorney-General has additional responsibilities in relation to aspects of the civil and criminal law.

Attorney-General (*£99,200), The Rt. Hon. The Lord Goldsmith, QC
    Private Secretary, C. Bartlett
Parliamentary Private Secretary, M. Foster, MP
Solicitor-General, The Rt. Hon. Harriet Harman, QC, MP
Legal Secretary (G2), D. Brummell
Deputy Legal Secretary (G3), S. Parkinson

*In addition to a parliamentary salary of £55,118

LEARNING AND SKILLS COUNCIL

Cheylesmore House, Quinton Road, Coventry, West Midlands, CV1 2WT
Tel: 0845-019 4170; Fax: 024-7649 3600
Email: info@lsc.gov.uk; Web: www.lsc.gov.uk

The Learning and Skills Council (LSC) was established in April 2001 to replace the Further Education Funding and the Training and Enterprise Councils. It is a non-departmental public body responsible for the planning and funding of post-16 education and training. It has an annual budget of £7.3 billion. Its remit is to ensure that high quality post-16 provision is available to meet the needs of employers, individuals and communities. The LSC operates through a national office based in Coventry and 47 local offices.

Chairman, B. Sanderson
Chief Executive, J. Harwood

LEGAL SERVICES COMMISSION

85 Gray's Inn Road, London WC1X 8TX
Tel: 020-7759 0000
Web: www.legalservices.gov.uk

On 1 April 2000, the Legal Aid Board was replaced by the Legal Services Commission (LSC), which runs two schemes - the civil scheme for funding civil cases as part of the Community Legal Service, and the Criminal Defence Service. The Criminal Defence Services provides access to advice, assistance and representation to people accused of a crime, as the interests of justice require.

The LSC has an important role in co-ordinating and working in a partnership with other funders of legal services, such as local authorities. The LSC also directly funds legal services for eligible clients.

Chairman, P. G. Birch, CBE
Members, S. Orchard, CBE (*Chief Executive*); A. Edwards; P. Ely; B. Harvey (*Director of Resources and Supplier Development*); Ms J. Herzog; Ms S. Hewitt; Ms Y. Mosquito; R. Penn; J. Shearer; Ms M. Richards

LIBRARIES

THE BRITISH LIBRARY

96 Euston Road, London NW1 2DB
Tel: 020-7412 7000
Email: visitor-services@bl.uk; Web: www.bl.uk

The British Library was established in 1973. It is the UK's national library and occupies a key position in the library and information network. The Library aims to serve scholarship, research, industry, commerce and all other major users of information. Its services are based on collections which include over 16 million volumes, 1 million discs, and 55,000 hours of tape recordings. The Library is now based at two sites: London (St Pancras and Colindale) and Boston Spa, W. Yorks. Government-grant-in-aid to the British Library in 2002–2003 is £85.09 million. The Library's sponsoring department is the Department for Culture, Media and Sport.

Access to the reading rooms at St Pancras is limited to holders of a British Library Reader's Pass; information about eligibility is available from the Reader Admissions Office. The exhibition galleries and public areas are open to all, free of charge.

Opening hours of services vary and specific information should be checked by telephone.

BRITISH LIBRARY BOARD

Chairman, Lord Eatwell
Chief Executive and Deputy Chairman, Ms L. Brindley
Part-time Members, H. Boyd-Carpenter, CVO; Prof. M. Anderson, OBE, FBA, FRSE; Dr C. G. R. Leach; Dame Jessica Rawson, DBE, FBA; J. Ritblat; P. Scherer; Prof. L. Colley; S. Olswang

BRITISH LIBRARY, BOSTON SPA

Boston Spa, Wetherby, W. Yorks LS23 7BQ
Tel: 01937-546000

BRITISH LIBRARY, ST PANCRAS

96 Euston Road, London NW1 2DB
Tel: 020-7412 7000

PRESS AND PUBLIC RELATIONS. Tel: 020-7412 7111
EXHIBITIONS SERVICE AND VISITOR SERVICES.
    Tel: 020-7412 7332
EDUCATION SERVICE. Tel: 020-7412 7797

SCHOLARSHIP AND COLLECTIONS

Reader Services, Tel: 020-7412 7676
Asia, Pacific and African Collections, Tel: 020-7412 7873
British Collections, Tel: 020-7412 7676
    Western Manuscripts, Tel: 020-7412 7513
    Map Library, Tel: 020-7412 7702
    Music Library, Tel: 020-7412 7772
    Philatelic Collections, Tel: 020-7412 7635
    National Sound Archive, Tel: 020-7412 7440
    Newspaper Library, Colindale Avenue, London
    NW9 5HE. Tel: 020-7412 7353
European and American Collections, Tel: 020-7412 7676

OPERATIONS AND SERVICES

Reader Admissions, Tel: 020-7412 7677

SCIENCE, TECHNOLOGY AND INFORMATION SERVICE

Physical Sciences, Tel: 020-7412 7494/7496
    British and EPO Patents, Tel: 020-7412 7919
    Foreign Patents, Tel: 020-7412 7902
    Business, Tel: 020-7412 7454
    Social Policy Information Service, Tel: 020-7412 7536

NATIONAL PRESERVATION OFFICE. Tel: 020-7412 7612

NATIONAL LIBRARY OF SCOTLAND

George IV Bridge, Edinburgh EH1 1EW
Tel: 0131-226 4531; Fax: 0131-622 4803
Email: enquiries@nls.uk; Web: www.nls.uk

The Library, which was founded as the Advocates' Library in 1682, became the National Library of Scotland in 1925. It is funded by the Scottish Executive. It contains about

seven million books and pamphlets, 20,000 current periodicals, 350 newspaper titles and 120,000 manuscripts. It has an unrivalled Scottish collection.

The Reading Room is for reference and research which cannot conveniently be pursued elsewhere. Admission is by ticket issued to an approved applicant. Opening hours: Reading Room, weekdays, 9.30–8.30 (Wednesday, 10–8.30); Saturday 9.30–1 Map Library, weekdays, 9.30–5 (Wednesday, 10–5); Saturday 9.30–1 Exhibition, weekdays, 10–5; Saturday 10–5; Sunday 2–5

Chairman of the Trustees, Prof. Michael Anderson, OBE, FBA, FRSE
Librarian and Secretary to the Trustees (G4), M. Wade
Secretary of the Library (G6), M. C. Graham
Director of General Collections, C. Newton
Director of Special Collections, M. C. T. Simpson
Director of Public Services, A. M. Marchbank

NATIONAL LIBRARY OF WALES/LLYFRGELL GENEDLAETHOL CYMRU

Aberystwyth SY23 3BU
Tel: 01970-632800; Fax: 01970-615709
Web: www.llgc.org.uk

The National Library of Wales was founded by royal charter in 1907 and is funded by the National Assembly for Wales. It contains about four million printed books, 40,000 manuscripts, four million deeds and documents, numerous maps, prints and drawings, and a sound and moving image collection. It specialises in manuscripts and books relating to Wales and the Celtic peoples. It is the repository for pre-1858 Welsh probate records, manorial records and tithe documents, and certain legal records. Readers' room open weekdays, 9.30–6 (Saturday 9.30–5); closed first week of October. Admission by reader's ticket to the Reading Rooms but free entry to the exhibition programme.

President, Dr R. Brinley Jones
Librarian (G4), A. M. W. Green
Heads of Departments (G6), M. W. Mainwaring *(Corporate Services)*; G. Jenkins *(Collection Services)*; Dr W. R. M. Griffiths *(Public Services)*

LIGHTHOUSE AUTHORITIES

CORPORATION OF TRINITY HOUSE

Trinity House, Tower Hill, London EC3N 4DH
Tel: 020-7481 6900; Fax: 020-7480 7662
Web: www.trinityhouse.co.uk

Trinity House, the first general lighthouse and pilotage authority in the kingdom, was granted its first charter by Henry VIII in 1514. The Corporation is the general lighthouse authority for England, Wales and the Channel Islands and maintains 72 lighthouses, 13 major floating aids to navigation (e.g. light vessels) and more than 420 buoys. The Corporation also has certain statutory jurisdiction over aids to navigation maintained by local harbour authorities and is responsible for dealing with wrecks dangerous to navigation, except those occurring within port limits or wrecks of HM ships.

The Trinity House Lighthouse Service is maintained out of the General Lighthouse Fund which is provided from light dues levied on ships calling at ports of the UK and the Republic of Ireland. The Corporation is also a deep-sea pilotage authority and a charitable organisation.

The affairs of the Corporation are controlled by a board of Elder Brethren and the Secretary. A separate board, which comprises Elder Brethren, senior staff and outside representatives, currently controls the Lighthouse Service. The Elder Brethren also act as nautical assessors in marine cases in the Admiralty Division of the High Court of Justice.

ELDER BRETHREN

Master, HRH The Prince Philip, Duke of Edinburgh, KG, KT, PC
Deputy Master and Executive Chairman, Rear-Adm. J. M. de Halpert, CBE
Wardens, Capt. C. M. C. Stewart *(Rental)*; Cdr. M. J. Rivett-Carnac, RN *(Nether)*
Elder Brethren, HRH The Prince of Wales, KG, KT; HRH The Duke of York, CVO, ADC; Capt. Sir David Tibbits, DSC, RN; Capt. D. A. G. Dickens; Capt. J. E. Bury; Capt. J. A. N. Bezant, DSC, RD; Capt. D. J. Cloke; Capt. Sir Miles Wingate, KCVO; The Rt. Hon. Sir Edward Heath, KG, MBE; Capt. P. F. Mason, CBE; Capt.T. Woodfield, OBE; The Rt. Hon. The Lord Simon of Glaisdale; Capt. D. T. Smith, OBE, RN; Cdr. Sir Robin Gillett, Bt., GBE, RD; Capt. Sir Malcolm Edge, KCVO; The Rt. Hon. The Lord Cuckney of Millbank; Capt. D. J. Orr; The Rt. Hon.The Lord Carrington, KG, GCMG, CH, MC; The Rt. Hon. The Lord Mackay of Clashfern, KT; Sir Adrian Swire, AE; The Rt. Hon. The Lord Sterling of Plaistow, CBE; Adm. Sir Jock Slater, GCB, LVO; Capt. J. R. Burton-Hall, RD; Capt. I. Gibb; P. J. Melson, CBE, RN; Capt. D. C. Glass; D. Porter Capt. P. Richards, RD; S. P. Sherrard; The Lord Brown of Madingley; The Rt. Hon. The Lord Robertson of Port Ellen

OFFICERS

Secretary, R. F. Dobb
Director of Finance, K. W. Clark
Director of Engineering, D. Golden
Director of Administration, D. I. Brewer
Legal and Insurance Manager, J. D. Price
Navigation Manager, Mrs K. Hossain
Head of Marketing and Management Services, S. J. W. Dunning
Senior Inspector of Shipping, J. R. Dunnett
Media and Communication Officer, H. L. Cooper
Head of Human Resources, P. F. Morgan

NORTHERN LIGHTHOUSE BOARD

84 George Street, Edinburgh EH2 3DA
Tel: 0131-473 3100; Fax: 0131-220 2093
Email: enquiries@nlb.org.uk; Web: www.nlb.org.uk

The Lighthouse Board is the general lighthouse authority for Scotland and the Isle of Man. The board owes its origin to an Act of Parliament passed in 1786. At present the Commissioners operate under the Merchant Shipping Act 1995 and are 19 in number.

The Commissioners control 83 major automatic lighthouses, 118 minor lights and many lighted and unlighted buoys. They have a fleet of two motor vessels.

COMMISSIONERS

The Lord Advocate; the Solicitor-General for Scotland; the Lord Provosts of Edinburgh, Glasgow and Aberdeen; the Provost of Inverness; the Convener of Argyll and Bute Council; the Sheriffs-Principal of North Strathclyde, Tayside, Central and Fife, Grampian, Highlands and Islands, South Strathclyde, Dumfries and Galloway, Lothians and Borders and Glasgow and Strathkelvin; Capt. D. M. Cowell; Adm. Sir Michael Livesay, KCB; The Lord Maclay; P. MacKay, CB; Capt. K. MacLeod

OFFICERS
Chief Executive, Capt. J. B. Taylor, RN
Director of Finance, D. Gorman
Director of Engineering, M. Waddell
Director of Operations and Navigational Requirements, G. Platten

LOCAL COMMISSIONERS

COMMISSION FOR LOCAL ADMINISTRATION IN ENGLAND
21 Queen Anne's Gate, London SW1H 9BU
Tel: 020-7915 3210; Fax: 020-7233 0396

Local Commissioners (local government ombudsmen) are responsible for investigating complaints from members of the public against local authorities (but not town and parish councils); English Partnerships (planning matters only); Housing Action Trusts; education appeal panels; police authorities and certain other authorities. The Commissioners are appointed by the Crown on the recommendation of the Secretary of State for Transport, Local Government, and the Regions.

Certain types of action are excluded from investigation, including personnel matters and commercial transactions unless they relate to the purchase or sale of land. Complaints can be sent direct to the Local Government Ombudsman or through a councillor, although the Local Government Ombudsman will not consider a complaint unless the council has had an opportunity to investigate and reply to a complainant.

A free leaflet *'Complaint about the council? How to complain to the Local Government Ombudsman'* is available from the Commission's offices.
Chairman and Chief Executive of the Commission and Local Commissioner (£137,377), T. Redmond
Vice-Chairman and Local Commissioner (£103,999), Mrs P. A. Thomas
Local Commissioner (£102,999), J. R. White
Member (ex officio), The Parliamentary Commissioner for Administration
Deputy Chief Executive and Secretary (£66,797), N. J. Karney

COMMISSION FOR LOCAL ADMINISTRATION IN WALES
Derwen House, Court Road, Bridgend CF31 1BN
Tel: 01656-6613257; Fax: 01656-673279
Email: enquiries@ombudsman-wales.org
Web: www.ombudsman-wales.org

The Local Commissioner for Wales has similar powers to the Local Commissioners in England, but since the end of 2001 he has also had additional powers (similar to the Standards Board for England) to investigate allegations made against local authority members of misconduct. The Commissioner is appointed by the Crown on the recommendation of the Secretary of State for Wales. A free leaflet 'Your Local Government Ombudsman in Wales' is available from the Commissioners office.
Local Commissioner, E. R. Moseley
Secretary, D. Bowen
Member (ex officio), The Parliamentary Commissioner for Administration

LONDON REGIONAL TRANSPORT
55 Broadway, London SW1H 0BD
Tel: 020-7222 5600
Web: www.londontransport.co.uk

Subject to the financial objectives and principles approved by the Secretary of State for Transport. London Regional Transport has a general duty to provide or secure the provision of public transport services for Greater London.
Chairman (non-executive), Sir Malcolm Bates
Member, and Managing Director of London Underground Ltd, P. Godier

LORD GREAT CHAMBERLAIN'S OFFICE
House of Lords, London SW1A 0PW
Tel: 020-7219 3100; Fax: 020-7219 2500

The Lord Great Chamberlain is a Great Officer of State, the office being hereditary since the grant of Henry I to the family of De Vere, Earls of Oxford. It is now a joint hereditary office between the Cholmondeley and Carington families. The Lord Great Chamberlain is responsible for the royal apartments of the Palace of Westminster, i.e. The Queen's Robing Room, the Royal Gallery and, in conjunction with the Lord Chancellor and the Speaker, Westminster Hall. The Lord Great Chamberlain has particular responsibility for the internal administrative arrangements within the House of Lords for State Openings of Parliament.
Lord Great Chamberlain, The Marquess of Cholmondeley
Secretary to the Lord Great Chamberlain, Lt.-Gen. Sir Michael Willcocks, KCB
Clerks to the Lord Great Chamberlain, Ms J. Perodeau; Ms A. Feuz

LORD PRIVY SEAL'S OFFICE
Cabinet Office, 70 Whitehall, London SW1A 2AT
Tel: 020-7270 3000
Web: www. cabinetoffice.gov.uk

The Lord Privy Seal is a member of the Cabinet and Leader of the House of Lords. He has no departmental portfolio, but is a member of a number of Cabinet committees. He is responsible to the Prime Minister for the organisation of Government business in the House and has a responsibility to the House itself to advise it on procedural matters and other difficulties which arise.
Lord Privy Seal, Leader of the House of Lords, The Rt. Hon. The Lord Williams of Mostyn, QC
Principal Private Secretary, P. Richardson
Private Secretary (House of Lords), Miss M. Robertson

MENTAL HEALTH ACT COMMISSION
Maid Marian House, 56 Hounds Gate, Nottingham NG1 6BG
Tel: 0115-943 7100; Fax: 0115-943 7101
Web: www.mhac.trent.nhs.uk

The Mental Health Act Commission was established in 1983. Its functions are to keep under review the operation of the Mental Health Act 1983; to visit and meet patients detained under the Act; to investigate complaints falling within the Commission's remit; to operate the consent to treatment safeguards in the Mental Health Act; to publish a biennial report on its activities; to monitor the

implementation of the Code of Practice; and to advise Ministers. Commissioners are appointed by the Secretary of State for Health.

Chairman, Miss M. Clayton
Vice-Chairman, Prof. K. Patel
Chief Executives, P. Hampshire

MILLENNIUM COMMISSION

Portland House, Stag Place, London SW1E 5EZ
Tel: 020-7880 2001; Fax: 020-7880 2000
Email: info@millennium.gov.uk

The Millennium Commission was established in February 1994 and is accountable to the Department for Culture, Media and Sport. It is an independent body which distributes money from National Lottery proceeds to projects to mark the millennium.

Chair, The Rt. Hon. Tessa Jowell, MP
Members, Dr H. Couper; The Earl of Dalkeith; Ms F. Benjamin; The Rt. Hon. M. Heseltine, MP; Ms J. Donovan, CBE; M. D' Ancona; Lord Gletoran; Ms Barbara Roche, MP
Director, M. O'Connor

MUSEUMS

THE BRITISH MUSEUM

Great Russell Street, London WC1B 3DG
Tel: 020-7323 8000; Fax: 020-7323 8616
Email: information@thebritishmuseum.ac.uk
Web: www.thebritishmuseum.ac.uk

The British Museum houses the national collection of antiquities, ethnography, coins and paper money, medals, prints and drawings. The British Museum may be said to date from 1753, when Parliament approved the holding of a public lottery to raise funds for the purchase of the collections of Sir Hans Sloane and the Harleian manuscripts, and for their proper housing and maintenance. The building (Montagu House) was opened in 1759. The present buildings were erected between 1823 and the present day, and the original collection has increased to its present dimensions by gifts and purchases. Total government grant-in-aid for 2002–2003 is £36.869 million.

BOARD OF TRUSTEES

Appointed by the Sovereign, HRH The Duke of Gloucester, KG, GCVO
Appointed by the Prime Minister, C. Allen-Jones *(Oriental Antiquities);* H. Askari; N. Barber *(Greek and Roman Antiquities);* Dame Prof. Gillian Beer, DBE, FBA *(Ancient Egypt and Sudan);* Sir John Boyd, KCMG *(Japanese Antiquities);* Lord Browne of Madingley, FREng; The Rt. Hon Countess of Dalkeith; Sir Michael Hopkins, CBE, RA; ; Sir Joseph Hotung *(Ancient Near East);* Prof. M. Kemp, FBA *(Education);* D. Lindsell; C. McCall, QC; Sir Martin Rees, FRS *(Conservation),* Dr A. Ritchie *(Coins and Medals);* E. Salama *(Nominated by the Learned Societies);* Prof. Jean Thomas, CBE *(Scientific Research (Nominated by the Royal Society);* T. Phillips, RA *(Ethnography) (Nominated by the Royal Academy);* Sir Keith Thomas, FBA *((Prints and Drawings) Nominated by the British Academy);* Prof. B. Cunliffe, CBE *(Prehistory and Early Europe (Nominated by the Society of Antiquaries of London))*

Appointed by the Trustees of the British Museum, G. C. Greene, CBE *(Chair);* The Hon. Phillip Lader; Lord Powell of Bayswater, KCMG; Dr J. Montagu, FBA *(Medieval and Modern Europe);* J. Tusa

OFFICERS

Director, Neil MacGregor
Director of Marketing and Public Affairs, Dr C. Homden
Director of Resources, D. Austwick, OBE
Secretary, T. Doubleday
Head of Exhibitions, G. A. L. House
Head of Media Relations, A. E. Hamilton
Head of Design, Miss M. Hall, OBE
Head of Education, J. F. Reeve
Director of Operations, C. E. I. Jones
Head of Building Development and Planning, K. T. Stannard
Head of Building Management, T. R. A. Giles
Head of Finance, D. Allcorn
Head of Visitor Services, Ms L. Lee
Head of Membership Development, Ms M. Fenn
Head of Marketing Communications, M. Ladds

KEEPERS

Senior Keeper, Dr B. J. Mack
Keeper of Prints and Drawings, A. V. Griffiths
Keeper of Coins and Medals, Dr A. M. Burnett
Keeper of Egyptian Antiquities, W. V. Davies
Keeper of Ancient Near East Antiquities, Dr J. E. Curtis
Keeper of Greek and Roman Antiquities, Dr D. J. R. Williams
Keeper of Medieval and Modern Europe, J. Cherry
Keeper of Prehistory and Early Europe, Dr C. Malone
Keeper of Japanese Antiquities, V. T. Harris
Keeper of Oriental Antiquities, R. J. Knox
Keeper of Ethnography, Dr B. Durrans
Keeper of Scientific Research, Dr S. G. E. Bowman
Keeper of Conservation, W. A. Oddy

IMPERIAL WAR MUSEUM

Lambeth Road, London SE1 6HZ
Tel: 020-7416 5320; Fax: 020-7416 5374

The Museum, founded in 1917, illustrates and records all aspects of the two world wars and other military operations involving Britain and the Commonwealth since 1914. It was opened in its present home, formerly Bethlem Hospital, in 1936. The Museum is a multi-branch organisation which also includes: the Cabinet War Rooms in Whitehall, HMS Belfast in the Pool of London, Imperial War Museum Duxford in Cambridgeshire and Imperial War Museum North in Trafford. The total grant-in-aid (including grants for special projects) for 2002–3 is £16.350 million.

OFFICERS

Chairman of Trustees, Adm. Sir Jock Slater, GCB, LVO
Director-General, R. W. K. Crawford, CBE
Secretary and Director of Finance, J. Card
Director of HMS Belfast, J. Wenzel
Director, Imperial War Museum, Duxford, E. Inman, OBE
Director, Imperial War Museum, North, J. Forrester
Director of Public Services, Dr C. Dowling
Director of Collections, Ms J. Carmichael
Director of Corporate Services, A. Stoneman
Director of Development, Ms V. Cornwall
Director of the Cabinet War Rooms, P. Reed

MUSEUM OF LONDON

London Wall, London EC2Y 5HN
Tel: 020-7600 3699; Fax: 020-7600 1058

Email: info@museumoflondon.org.uk
Web: www.museumoflondon.org.uk

The Museum of London illustrates the history of London from prehistoric times to the present day. It opened in 1976 and is based on the amalgamation of the former Guildhall Museum and London Museum. The Museum is controlled by a Board of Governors, appointed (nine each) by the Government and the Corporation of London. The Museum is currently funded by a grant of £6.293 million from the Department for Culture, Media and Sport and a grant of £4.519 million from the Corporation of London for 2002–3.
Chairman of Board of Governors, R. Hambro
Director (acting), Ms G. Cowcher

NATIONAL ARMY MUSEUM
Royal Hospital Road, London SW3 4HT
Tel: 020-7730 0717; Fax: 020-7823 6573
Email: info@national-army-museum.ac.uk
Web: www.national-army-museum.ac.uk

The National Army Museum covers the history of five centuries of the British Army. It was established by royal charter in 1960. Total Government grant-in-aid for 2001–2 was £4.684 million.
Director, I. G. Robertson
Assistant Directors, D. K. Smurthwaite; A. J. Guy; P. B. Boyden

NATURAL HISTORY MUSEUM
Cromwell Road, London SW7 5BD
Tel: 020-7942 5000

The Natural History Museum originates from the natural history departments of the British Museum, which grew extensively during the 19th century; in 1860 the natural history collection was moved from Bloomsbury to a new location. Part of the site of the 1862 International Exhibition in South Kensington was acquired for the new museum, and the Museum opened to the public in 1881. In 1963 the Natural History Museum became completely independent with its own board of trustees. The Walter Rothschild Zoological Museum, Tring, bequeathed by the second Lord Rothschild, has formed part of the Museum since 1938. The Geological Museum merged with the Natural History Museum in 1985. Total Government grant-in-aid for 2002–3 is £38.085 million.

BOARD OF TRUSTEES

Appointed by the Prime Minister, The Lord Oxburgh, KBE, Ph.D., FRS *(Chairman);* Sir Crispin Tickell, GCMG, KCVO; Dame Anne McLaren, DBE, FRS, FRCOG; Sir Richard Sykes, FRS; Miss J. Mayhew; Ms J. Bennett, OBE; Prof. M. Hassell, FRS; O. Stocken; Prof. J. McGlade
Appointed by the Secretary of State for Culture, Media and Sport, Prof. C. Leaver, CBE, FRS
Appointed by the Trustees of the Natural History Museum, The Lord Palumbo; Prof. Sir K. O'Nions, FRS; Prof. Linda Partridge, FRS, FRSE

SENIOR STAFF

Director, Dr N. R. Chalmers
Director of Science, Prof. P. Henderson, D.Phil.
Head of Audit and Review, D. Thorpe
Keeper of Botany, Dr R. Bateman
Director of Communications and Development, Ms S. Ament
Keeper of Entomology, Dr R. Vane-Wright
Director of Estates, K. Rellis
Director of Finance, N. Greenwood

Head of Library and Information Services, G. Higley
Keeper of Mineralogy, Prof. A. Fleet
Keeper of Palaeontology, Dr N. MacLeod
Director of Human Resources, D. Hill
Head of Visitor and Operational Services, D. Candlin
Keeper of Zoology, Prof. P. Rainbow
Director, Tring Zoological Museum, Mrs T. Wild

NATIONAL MARITIME MUSEUM
Greenwich, London SE10 9NF
Tel: 020-8858 4422; Fax: 020-8312 6632

Established by Act of Parliament in 1934, the National Maritime Museum illustrates the maritime history of Great Britain in the widest sense, underlining the importance of the sea and its influence on the nation's power, wealth, culture, technology and institutions. The Museum is in three groups of buildings in Greenwich Park – the main building, the Queen's House (built by Inigo Jones, 1616-35) and the Royal Observatory (including Wren's Flamsteed House). In May 1999, a £20 million Heritage Lottery supported project opened 16 new galleries in a glazed courtyard in the Museum's west wing. Total Government grant-in-aid for 2002–3 is £13.681 million.
Director, R. Clare

NATIONAL MUSEUMS AND GALLERIES ON MERSEYSIDE
PO Box 33, 127 Dale Street, Liverpool L69 3LA
Tel: 0151-207 0001; Fax: 0151-478 4790

The Board of Trustees of the National Museums and Galleries on Merseyside is responsible for the Liverpool Museum, the Merseyside Maritime Museum (incorporating HM Customs and Excise National Museum), the Museum of Liverpool Life, the Lady Lever Art Gallery, the Walker, Sudley House and the Conservation Centre. Total Government grant-in-aid for 2002–2003 is £16.569 million.
Chairman of the Board of Trustees, D. McDonnell
Director, Dr David Fleming
Keeper of Art Galleries, J. Treuherz
Keeper of Conservation, A. Durham
Keeper, Liverpool Museum, Ms L. Knowles
Keeper, Merseyside Maritime Museum and Museum of Liverpool Life, M. Stammers

NATIONAL MUSEUMS AND GALLERIES OF WALES/AMGUEDDFEYDD AC ORIELAU CENEDLAETHOL CYMRU
Cathays Park, Cardiff CF10 3NP
Tel: 029-2039 7951; Fax: 029-2037 3219
Email: post@nmgw.ac.uk; Web: www.nmgw.ac.uk

The National Museums and Galleries of Wales comprise the National Museum and Gallery Cardiff, the Museum of Welsh Life St Fagans, Big Pit National Museum of Wales, Blaenafon, the Roman Legionary Museum Caerleon, Turner House Gallery Penarth, the Welsh Slate Museum Llanberis, the Segontium Roman Museum Caernarfon and the Museum of the Welsh Woollen Industry Dre-fach, Felindre. Total funding from the Welsh Assembly for 2002–3 is £19.350 million.
President, M. C. T. Prichard, CBE
Vice-President, R. G. Thomas, OBE

OFFICERS

Director, A. Southall
Directors, Dr E. Wiliam (*Collections and Education and Deputy Director*); J. Williams-Davies (*Museum of Welsh Life*); M. Tooby (*National Museum and*

Gallery); R. Gwyn (*Strategic Communications*);
M. Richards (*Resource Planning*)
Keeper of Geology, Dr M. G. Bassett
Keeper of Bio-diversity and Systematic Biology, Dr P. G.
Oliver
Keeper of Art, O. Fairclough
Keeper of Archaeology, R. Brewer
Manager, Roman Legionary Museum, B. Lewis
Keeper in Charge, Turner House Gallery, O. Fairclough
*Keeper, Welsh Slate Museum and Segontium Roman
Museum*, Dr D. Roberts
Manager, Museum of the Welsh Woollen Industry, S. Moss
Manager, Big Pit National Museum of Wales, P. Walker

NATIONAL MUSEUMS OF SCOTLAND
Chambers Street, Edinburgh EH1 1JF
Tel: 0131-225 7534; Fax: 0131-220 4819

The National Museums of Scotland comprise the Royal
Museum of Scotland, the National War Museum of
Scotland, the Museum of Scottish County Life, the
Museum of Flight, Shambellie House Museum of
Costume and the Museum of Scotland. Total funding
from the Scottish Executive for 2001–2 was £17 million.

BOARD OF TRUSTEES

Chairman, The Lord Wilson of Tillyorn, GCMG
Members, G. Johnston, OBE, TD; Ms C. Macaulay;
N. McIntosh, CBE; Mrs N. Mahal; Prof. A. Manning,
OBE; Prof. J. Murray; Dr A. Ritchie, OBE; I. Smith

OFFICERS

Director, Dr G. Rintoul
Development Director, C. McCallum
Keeper of Archaeology, D. V. Clarke, FSA
Keeper of Geology and Zoology, M. Shaw, D.Phil.
Keeper of Social and Technological History, G. Sprott
Head of Public Affairs, Ms M. Bryden
Head of Technical Services, S. R. Elson
Keeper of History and Applied Art, Dr D. Caldwell, FSA

RESOURCE: THE COUNCIL FOR MUSEUMS,
ARCHIVES AND LIBRARIES
16 Queen Anne's Gate, London SW1H 9AA
Tel: 020-72733 1444; Fax: 020-72733 1404
Web: www.resource.gov.uk

Resource: The Council for Museums, Archives and
Libraries provides strategic guidance, advice and
advocacy across the whole of Government on museum,
archive and library matters. It is a non-departmental
public body sponsored by the Department for Culture,
Media and Sport. Resource came into being in April 2000,
replacing the Museums and Galleries Commission
(MGC) and the Library and Information Commission
(LIC), and now includes archives within its portfolio.
Chairman, Lord Evans
Chief Executive (acting), L. Batt, OBE
Board Members, L. Grossman; V. Gray; M. Wood; A.
Chowdhury; Dr M. Crozier; V. Griffiths; N. Hodgson;
M. Jones; N. MacGregor; J. Ryder; M. Stevenson; Prof.
L. Young; A. Watkin; D. Barrie

ROYAL AIR FORCE MUSEUM
Grahame Park Way, London NW9 5LL
Tel: 020-8205 2266; Fax: 020-8200 1751

Situated on the former airfield at RAF Hendon, the
Museum illustrates the development of aviation from
before the Wright brothers to the present-day RAF. Total
Government grant-in-aid for 2002–2003, including

funding for the outstation at Cosford, is £6.053 million.
Director-General, Dr M. A. Fopp
Directors, H. Hall; A. Wright; S. Garman; K. Ifould
Senior Keeper, P. Elliott

THE SCIENCE MUSEUM
Exhibition Road, London SW7 2DD
Tel: 0870 870 4868; Fax: 020-7942 4447

The Science Museum, part of the National Museum of
Science and Industry, houses the national collections of
science, technology, industry and medicine. The Museum
began as the science collection of the South Kensington
Museum and first opened in 1857. In 1883 it acquired the
collections of the Patent Museum and in 1909 the science
collections were transferred to the new Science Museum,
leaving the art collections with the Victoria and Albert
Museum. The Wellcome Wing was opened in July 2000.
Some of the Museum's commercial aircraft, agricultural
machinery, and road and rail transport collections are at
Wroughton, Wilts. The National Museum of Science and
Industry also incorporates the National Railway
Museum, York and the National Museum of
Photography, Film and Television, Bradford.
Total Government grant-in-aid for 2001–2 was £26.678
million.

BOARD OF TRUSTEES

Chairman, The Rt. Hon. Lord Waldegrave of North Hill
Members, Prof. Sir Ron U. Cooke, DSC; Prof. A. Dowling,
CBE, FREng; G. Dyke; Baroness Susan Greenfield, CBE,
D.Phil.; Dr A. Grocock; Mrs J. Kennedy, OBE, FREng; Dr
N. Myhrvold; Dr B. Ogilvie, DBE; The Lord Puttnam,
CBE; D. E. Rayner, CBE; Prof. M. Richards, MD, FRCP;
M. G. Smith; Prof. R. A. Smith, Ph.D., FREng

OFFICERS

Director, Dr. L. Sharp
Head of Science Museum, J. Tucker
Interim Head of Change Management, A. Mather
Head of Finance, Ms A. Caine
Head of IT, M. Burns
Head of Estates, J. Bevin
Head of Physical Sciences and Engineering Group (acting),
Dr A. Q. Morton
Head of Commercial Development, M. Sullivan
Head of Design, T. Molloy
Head of National Railway Museum, A. Scott
*Head of National Museum of Photography, Film and
Television*, Ms A. Nevill

VICTORIA AND ALBERT MUSEUM
Cromwell Road, London SW7 2RL
Tel: 020-7942 2000; Web: www.vam.ac.uk

The Victoria and Albert Museum is the national museum
of fine and applied art and design. It descends directly
from the Museum of Manufactures, which opened in
Marlborough House in 1852 after the Great Exhibition of
1851. The Museum was moved in 1857 to become part of
the South Kensington Museum. It was renamed the
Victoria and Albert Museum in 1899. It also houses the
National Art Library and Print Room.
The Museum administers three branch museums: the
Museum of Childhood at Bethnal Green, the Theatre
Museum in Covent Garden, and the Wellington Museum at
Apsley House. The museum in Bethnal Green was opened
in 1872 and the building is the most important surviving
example of the type of glass and iron construction used by
Paxton for the Great Exhibition. Total Government grant-
in-aid for 2002–2003 is £34.621 million.

National Heritage Memorial Fund 329

BOARD OF TRUSTEES

Chairman, Ms P. Ridley
Deputy Chairman, J. Scott, CBE, FSA
Members, Prof. M. Buck; Viscountess Cobham; R.
Dickins; Prof. Sir Christopher Frayling, Ph.D.; Sir
Terence Heiser, GCB; Mrs J. Gordon Clark; Lady
Heseltine; R. Mathers; P. Rogers; P. Ruddock; Prof. Sir
Christopher White, CVO, FBA
Secretary to the Board of Trustees (acting), J. F. Rider

OFFICERS

Director, M. Jones, MA
Deputy Director, J. W. Close
Director of Collections and Keeper of Asian Department,
Dr D. Swallow
Director of Apsley House, the Wellington Museum, Miss A.
Robinson
Keeper of Furniture, Textiles and Fashion Department, C.
Wilk
*Keeper of Sculpture, Metalwork, Ceramics and Glass
Department,* Dr P. E. D. Williamson
Director of the Theatre Museum, Miss M. Benton
Keeper of Word and Image Department, Ms S. B. Lambert
Director of Collections Services, N. Umney
Head of Conservation Department, vacant
Head of Exhibitions Department, Mrs L. Lloyd Jones
Head of Regional Outreach and Purchase Grant Fund,
Miss J. Daviess
Head of Photographic Studio, J. Stevenson
Head of Records and Collections Services Department, A.
Seal
Director of Development, vacant
Director of Finance, I. Blatchford
Director of Learning and Visitor Services, D. Anderson,
OBE
Director of Personnel, Mrs G. Henchley
Director of Projects and Estate, Mrs G. F. Miles
Director of Public Affairs, D. Whitmore
Managing Director of V&A Enterprises Ltd, M. Cass
Head of Research Department, Ms C. Sargentson
Director of the Museum of Childhood, Ms D. Lees

NATIONAL AUDIT OFFICE

157-197 Buckingham Palace Road, London SW1W 9SP
Tel: 020-7798 7000; Fax: 020-7798 7070
Audit House, 23-24 Park Place, Cardiff CF1 3BA
Tel: 029-2067 8500; Fax: 029-2067 8501
Email: enquiries@nao.gsi.gov.uk
Web: www.nao.gov.uk

The National Audit Office came into existence under the
National Audit Act 1983 to replace and continue the work
of the former Exchequer and Audit Department. The Act
reinforced the Office's total financial and operational
independence from the Government and brought its
head, the Comptroller and Auditor-General, into a closer
relationship with Parliament as an officer of the House of
Commons.
The National Audit Office provides independent
information, advice and assurance to Parliament and the
public about all aspects of the financial operations of
Government departments and many other bodies
receiving public funds. It does this by examining and
certifying the accounts of these organisations and by
regularly publishing reports to Parliament on the results
of its value for money investigations of the economy,
efficiency and effectiveness with which public resources
have been used. The National Audit Office is also the

auditor by agreement of the accounts of certain
international and other organisations. In addition, the
Office authorises the issue of public funds to Government
departments.
Comptroller and Auditor-General, Sir John Bourn, KCB
Private Secretary, N. Sayers
Deputy Comptroller and Auditor-General, T. Burr
Deputy Auditor-General, M. C. Pfleger
Assistant Auditors-General, J. Colman; Miss C.
Mawhood; M. Sinclair; Ms W. Kenway-Smith; M.
Whitehouse

NATIONAL CONSUMER COUNCIL

20 Grosvenor Gardens, London SW1W 0DH
Tel: 020-7730 3469; Fax: 020-7730 0191
Email: info@ncc.org.uk; Web: www.ncc.org.uk

The National Consumer Council (NCC) was set up by the
Government in 1975 to give an independent voice to
consumers in the UK. Its role is to advocate the consumer
interest to decision-makers in national and local
government, industry and regulatory bodies, business
and the professions. It does this through a combination of
research and campaigning. NCC is a non-profit making
company limited by guarantee and is largely funded by
grant-in-aid from the Department of Trade and Industry.
Chair, Mrs D. Hutton, CBE
Director, Ms A. Bradley

NATIONAL ENDOWMENT FOR SCIENCE,
TECHNOLOGY AND THE ARTS (NESTA)

Fishmongers' Chambers, 110 Upper Thames Street,
London EC4R 3TW
Tel: 020-7645 9500; Fax: 020-7645 9501

The National Endowment for Science, Technology and
the Arts (NESTA) was established under the National
Lottery Act 1998 with a £200 million endowment from
the proceeds of the National Lottery. Its aims are to help
talented individuals; to enable innovative ideas to be
successfully commercially exploited; and to promote
public knowledge of science, technology and the arts.
Chairman, The Lord Puttnam of Queensgate, CBE
Trustees, F. Matarasso; The Baroness McIntosh of
Hudnall; Prof. J. Kirkpatrick; D. Alexander; Dr Y.
Barnett; D. Wanless; P. Daniel; Dr K. Gramich; Ms N.
Rothwell; G. Ross Russell; S. Singh
Chief Executive, J. Newton

NATIONAL HERITAGE MEMORIAL FUND

7 Holbein Place, London SW1W 8NR
Tel: 020-7591 6000; Fax: 020-7591 6001

The National Heritage Memorial Fund was set up under
the National Heritage Act 1980 in memory of people who
have given their lives for the United Kingdom. The Fund
provides grants (and sometimes loans) to organisations
based in the United Kingdom, mainly so they can buy
items of outstanding interest and of importance to the
national heritage. These must either be at risk or have a
memorial character. The Fund is administered by 13
trustees who are appointed by the Prime Minister.
The National Lottery Act 1993 designated the Fund as
distributor of the heritage share of proceeds from the
National Lottery. As a result, the Fund now operates two
funds: the Heritage Memorial Fund and the Heritage

Lottery Fund. The Heritage Memorial Fund receives an annual grant from the Department for Culture, Media and Sport; the grant for 2001–2002 was £5 million.
Chairman, L. Forgan
Trustees, Prof. C. Baines; N. Dodd; Sir Angus Grossart, CBE; G. Waterfield; Mrs P. Lankester; Ms P. Wilson; Ms S. Palmer; Earl of Dalkeith; Prof. T. Pritchard; J. Wright; Dr M. Phillips; Dr D. Langslow
Director, Ms A. Case

NATIONAL LOTTERY COMMISSION
2 Monck Street, London SW1P 2BQ
Tel: 020-7016 3400; Fax: 020-72016 3401
Web: www.natlotcomm.gov.uk

The National Lottery Commission replaced the Office of the National Lottery (OFLOT) in April 1999 under the National Lottery Act 1998. The Commission is responsible for the granting, varying and enforcing of licences to run the National Lottery. Its duties are to ensure that the National Lottery is run with all due propriety, that the interests of players are protected, and, subject to these two objectives, that returns to the 'good causes' are maximised.
Chairman, Lord Terry Burns
Commissioners, Ms H. Spicer; B. Pomeroy; R. Gilmore; T. Hornsby; Ms M. Black
Chief Executive, M. Harris
Director of Licensing, K. Jones
Director of Compliance and Resources, Ms M. Phillips

NATIONAL PHYSICAL LABORATORY
Queens Road, Teddington, Middx TW11 0LW
Tel: 020-8977 3222; Fax: 020-8943 6458

The Laboratory is the UK's national standards laboratory. It develops, maintains and disseminates national measurement standards for physical quantities such as mass, length, time, temperature, voltage, force and pressure. It also conducts underpinning research on engineering materials and information technology and disseminates good measurement practice. It is Government-owned but contractor-operated.
Managing Director, Dr B. McGuiness
Director of Marketing and Strategic Planning, D. C. Richardson

NATIONAL RADIOLOGICAL PROTECTION BOARD
Chilton, Didcot, Oxon OX11 0RQ
Tel: 01235-831600; Fax: 01235-833891
Email: nrpb@nrpb.org
Web: www.nrpb.orgk

The National Radiological Protection Board is an independent statutory body created by the Radiological Protection Act 1970. It is the national point of authoritative reference on radiological protection for both ionising and non-ionising radiations, and has issued recommendations on limiting human exposure to electromagnetic fields and radiation from a range of sources, including X-rays, the Sun, base stations and mobile phones. Its sponsoring department is the Department of Health.
Chairman, Sir Walter Bodmer, Ph.D., FRCPath., FRS.
Director, Prof. R. H. Clarke

NATIONAL SAVINGS AND INVESTMENTS
375 Kensington High Street, London W14 8SD
Tel: 020-7348 9200; Fax: 020-7048 9755
Web: www.nsandi.com

National Savings and Investments was established as a Government department in 1969. It became an executive agency of the Treasury in 1996 and is responsible for the design, marketing and administration of savings and investment products for personal savers and investors. In April 1999 Siemens Business Services took over all the back office functions at National Savings and Investments.
Chief Executive, A. Cook
Personnel Director, D. S. Speedie
Finance Director, T. Bayley
Commercial Director, G. Cattanach
Partnerships and Operations Director, S. Owen

For details of schemes, *see* National Savings section

NEW OPPORTUNITIES FUND
1 Plough Place, London EC4A 1DE
Tel: 020-7211 1800; Fax: 020-7211 1750
Email: enquiries@nof.org.uk
Web: www.nof.org.uk

The New Opportunities Fund provides lottery funding for health, education and environment projects in order to help create lasting improvements to the quality of life, particularly in disadvantaged communities.
    The Fund works with national, regional and local partners from the public, private and voluntary sectors to fund initiatives, with particular focus on the needs of those who are most disadvantaged in society.
Chair of the Board, The Baroness Pitkeathley
Members of the Board, Ms J. Barrow *(Member for England)*; Prof. E. Bolton, CB; Prof. A. Patmore, CBE; D. Mackie; D. Campbell, CBE *(Member for Scotland)*; Prof. S. Griffiths, OBE; Prof. B. Gadd, CBE *(Member for Northern Ireland)*; T. Davies *(Member for Wales)*; D. Carrington; Ms P. Hudson; Ms B. Stephens; G. Thompson, MBE
Chief Executive, S. Dunmore

NORTHERN IRELAND AUDIT OFFICE
106 University Street, Belfast BT7 1EU
Tel: 028-9025 1000; Fax: 028-9025 1106
Email: auditoffice@nics.gov.uk
Web: www.niauditoffice.gov.uk

The primary aim of the Northern Ireland Audit Office is to provide independent assurance, information and advice to the Northern Ireland Assembly on the proper accounting for Northern Ireland departmental and certain other public expenditure, revenue, assets and liabilities; on regularity and propriety; and on the economy, efficiency and effectiveness of the use of resources.
Comptroller and Auditor-General for Northern Ireland, J. M. Dowdall

NORTHERN IRELAND HUMAN RIGHTS COMMISSION

Temple Court, 39–41 North Street, Belfast BT1 1NA
Tel: 028-9024 3987; Fax: 028-9024 7844
Email: nihrc@belfast.org.uk
Web: www.nihrc.org

The Northern Ireland Human Rights Commission was set up in March 1999. Its main functions are to keep under review the law and practice relating to human rights in Northern Ireland, to advise the Government and to promote an awareness of human rights in Northern Ireland. It can also take cases to court. The Commission currently consists of one full-time commissioner and twelve part-time commissioners, all appointed by the Secretary of State for Northern Ireland.

Chief Commissioner (£60,000), Prof. B. Dickson
Commissioners (£10,000), Prof. C. Bell; Mrs M. A.
   Dinsmore, QC; T. Donnelly, MBE; Lady Christine
   Eames; Revd H. Good, OBE; Prof. T. Hadden; Ms P.
   Kelly; Dr I. McCormack; Dr C. McGimpsey; K.
   McLaughlin; F. McGuinness; P. Yu

OCCUPATIONAL PENSIONS REGULATORY AUTHORITY

Invicta House, Trafalgar Place, Brighton BN1 4DW
Tel: 01273-627600; Fax: 01273-627760
Email: helpdesk@opra.gov.uk
Web: www.opra.gov.uk

The Occupational Pensions Regulatory Authority (OPRA) was set up under the Pensions Act 1995 and became fully operational on 6 April 1997. It is the UK regulator of pension arrangements offered by employers. It maintains a register of stakeholder pensions and regulates payments into stakeholder and personal pensions.

Chairman, H. Maunsell, OBE
Chief Executive, T. Hobman

OFFICE FOR NATIONAL STATISTICS

1 Drummond Gate, London SW1V 2QQ
Tel: 020-7533 5888
Email: info@statistics.gov.uk
Web: www.statistics.gov.uk

The Office for National Statistics was created in 1996 by the merger of the Central Statistical Office and the Office of Population Censuses and Surveys. It is both a Government department and an executive agency of the Treasury and is responsible for preparing and interpreting key economic statistics for Government policy; collecting and publishing business statistics; publishing annual and monthly statistical digests; providing researchers, analysts and other customers with a statistical service; administration of the marriage laws and local registration of births, marriages and deaths in England and Wales; provision of population estimates and projections and statistics on health and other demographic matters in England and Wales; population censuses in England and Wales; surveys for Government departments and public bodies; and promoting these functions within the UK, the European Union and internationally to provide a statistical service to meet European Union and international requirements.

Following the publication of the White Paper, 'Building Trust in Statistics', National Statistics was launched in June 2000. Headed by the National Statistician, with an independent Statistics Commission, providing assurance to Parliament about the integrity of official statistics and statistical practice. The National Statistics brand encompasses the output of the ONS, plus many of the key public interest statistics produced by other Government departments.

*National Statistician, Registrar General for England and
   Wales and the Head of the Government Statistical
   Service*, L. Cook
Directors, Ms S. Linacre *(Method and Quality)*; vacant;
   J. Kidgell *(Economic Statistics)*; J. Pullinger *(Social
   Statistics)*; P. Walton *(Business Change)*; Ms S. Young
   (Human Resources)
Principal Establishment Officer, Ms J. Wyman
Head of Communication, Ms H. Rafalowska
Parliamentary Clerks, A. Eltonwall; R. Smith

OFFICE FOR STANDARDS IN EDUCATION (OFSTED)

Alexandra House, 33 Kingsway, London WC2B 6SE
Tel: 020-7421 6800; Early Years Helpline: 0845-601
4771; Fax: 020-7421 6707
Email: geninfo@ofsted.gov.uk
Web: www.ofsted.gov.uk

OFSTED is a non-ministerial Government department established under the Education (Schools Act) 1992. Since April 2001 OFSTED has been responsible for inspecting all educational provision for 16-19 year olds.to establish and monitor an independent inspection system for maintained schools in England. Its inspection role also includes the inspection of local education authorities, teacher training institutions and youth work. In September 2001, OFSTED took over the regulation of childcare providers, from 150 local authorities.

HM Chief Inspector, D. Bell
Directors of Inspection, D. Taylor; E. Passmore, OBE
Director of Policy, Planning and Resources, R. Green
Director of Early Years, M. Smith
Director of Finance, P. Jolly
Director of Corporate Services, R. Knight

DIVISION MANAGERS

Personnel Management, A. White
Contracts, C. Clarke
Communications, Media and Public Relations, J. Lawson
Information Systems, M. Worthy
Administrative Support and Estate Management, K.
   Francis
Early Years Inspection Quality, D. Bradley
Inspection Quality (Schools), P. Matthews
LEA Inspections, D. Singleton
School Improvement, K. Cross
Primary, K. Lloyd
Secondary, M. Raleigh
Curriculum Advice and Inspection, B. McCafferty
Post-Compulsory, vacant
Research, Analysis and International, G. Goodwin
Teacher Education, C. Gould

OFFICE FOR THE REGULATION OF ELECTRICITY AND GAS
Brookmount Buildings, 42 Fountain Street, Belfast
BT1 5EE
Tel: 028-9031 1575 (Electricity); 028-9031 4212 (Gas); Fax: 028-9031 1740
Email: ofreg@nics.gov.uk
Web: www.nics.gov.uk/ofreg

The Office for the Regulation of Electricity and Gas (OFREG) is the combined regulatory body for the electricity and gas supply industries in Northern Ireland.
Director-General of Electricity Supply and Director-General of Gas for Northern Ireland, D. McIldoon

OFFICE OF GAS AND ELECTRICITY MARKETS
9 Millbank, London, SW1P 3GE
Tel: 020-7901 7000; Fax: 020-7901 7066
Scotland: Regent Court, 70 West Regent Street, Glasgow G2 2QZ
Tel: 0141-331 2678; Fax: 0141-331 2777

The Office of Gas and Electricity Markets (Ofgem) regulates the gas and electricity industries in England, Scotland and Wales.
Ofgem's aim is to promote and protect the interests of gas and electricity customers by promoting competition and regulating monopolies. Ofgem is governed by an authority and its powers are provided for under the Gas Act 1986, the Electricity Act 1989 and the Utilities Act 2000.
Chief Executive, C. McCarthy
Managing Directors, J. Neilson *(Customers and Supply);* Dr E. Marshall, CBE *(Competition and Trading Arrangements);* R. Ramsay *(Regulation and Financial Affairs);* C. Coulthard *(Scotland)*
Chief Operating Officer, Ms G. Whittington

OFFICE OF FAIR TRADING
Fleetbank House, 2–6 Salisbury Square, London EC4Y 8JX
Tel: 020-7211 8000; Fax: 020-7211 8800
Email: enquiries@oft.gov.uk
Web: www.oft.gov.uk

The Office of Fair Trading is a non-ministerial Government department headed by the Director-General of Fair Trading. It keeps commercial activities in the UK under review and seeks to protect consumers against unfair trading practices. The Director-General's consumer protection duties under the Fair Trading Act 1973, together with his responsibilities under the Consumer Credit Act 1974, the Estate Agents Act 1979, the Control of Misleading Advertisements Regulations 1988, the Consumer Protection (Distance Selling) Regulations 2000, the Stop Now Orders (EC Directive) Regulations 2001 and the Unfair Terms in Consumer Contracts Regulations 1999 are administered by the Office's Consumer Regulation Enforcement Division. The Competition Enforcement Division is concerned with monopolies and mergers (under the Fair Trading Act 1973) and the Director-General's other responsibilities for competition matters, including those under the Competition Act 1998, the Financial Services Act 1986 and the Broadcasting Act 1990. The Markets and Policy Initiatives Division was instigated in October 2001 to carry out investigations into markets, and co-ordinate

the OFT's overall relationships with Government departments and other bodies involved with consumer and competition issues. A further role of the new Division is to identify and assess the impact of Government regulations on competition.
Director-General, J. Vickers

CONSUMER REGULATION ENFORCEMENT DIVISION
Divisional Director (G3), Miss C. Banks
Branch Directors (G5), S. Wood; R. Watson COMPETITION ENFORCEMENT DIVISION
Divisional Director (G3), Mrs M. J. Bloom
Branch Directors (G5), J. Coombes; A. Walker-Smith; V. Smith; S. Priddis; Dr D. Mason; Dr G. Davis; A. Williams

MARKETS AND POLICY INITIATIVES DIVISION
Divisional Director (G3), J. May
Branch Directors, (G5), M. Graham; C. Rawlins
Chief Economist, Ms A. Fletcher

LEGAL DIVISION
Divisional Director (G3), Miss P. Edwards
Branch Directors (G5), M. A. Khan; S. Brindley

COMMUNICATIONS DIVISION
Director of Communications (Chief Information Officer), (G5) M. Ricketts

RESOURCES AND SERVICES
Director of Resources and Services (Chief Establishment and Finance Officer), (G5) D. Fisher

OFFICE OF MANPOWER ECONOMICS
Oxford House, 8th Floor, 76 Oxford Street, London W1D 1BS
Tel: 020-7467 7244; Fax: 020-7467 7248
Web: www.ome.uk.com

The Office of Manpower Economics was set up in 1971. It is an independent non-statutory organisation which is responsible for servicing independent review bodies which advise on the pay of various public service groups, the Pharmacists Review Panel and the Police Negotiating and Advisory Boards. The Office is also responsible for servicing *ad hoc* bodies of inquiry and for undertaking research into pay and associated matters as requested by the Government.
OME Director, M. J. Horsman
Director, Health Secretariats, Office Services and OME Deputy Director, G. S. Charles
Director, Armed Forces' Secretariat, C. Haworth
Director, Senior Salaries and Police Negotiating and Advisory Boards Secretariat, vacant
Director, School Teachers' Secretariat, Mrs E. M. Melling
Director, Prison Service Secretariat, M. C. Cahill
Press Liaison Officer, C. P. Jordan

OFFICE OF TELECOMMUNICATIONS (OFTEL)
50 Ludgate Hill, London EC4M 7JJ
Tel: 020-7634 8700; Fax: 020-7634 8943
Web: www.oftel.gov.uk

The Office of Telecommunications (Oftel) is the regulator, for the UK telecommunications industry. Oftel is a Government department but is independent of ministerial control. Oftel's aim is for consumers to get the best deal in terms of quality, choice and value for money for their telecoms services. Its strategy to achieve this goal is through four objectives: effective competition benefiting consumers; well informed consumers;

adequately protected consumers; and prevention of significant anti-competitive practice. Oftel is responsible for ensuring that holders of telecommunications licences comply with their licence conditions, and has powers under the Competition Act 1998 to deal with anti-competitive practices . The Director-General has a duty to consider all reasonable complaints about telecommunications services.

If the Communications Bill 2002 is passed, Oftel, along with the Independent Television Commission, the Broadcasting Standards Commission, the Radio Authority and the Radiocommunications Agency will merge to become the Office of Communications, Ofcom, the new regulator for the communications sector, in 2003.

Director-General, D. Edmonds
Director of Operations, P. Waller
Director of Regulatory Policy, P. Rutnam
Director of Compliance, C. Kenny
Director of Technology, P. Walker
Director of Strategy and Forecasting, A. Bell
Director of Business Support, D. Smith
Director of Communications, D. Stroud

OFFICE OF THE LEGAL SERVICES OMBUDSMAN

3rd Floor, Sunlight House, Quay Street, Manchester M3 3JZ
Tel: 0845-601 0794; Fax: 0161-832 5446;
Email: lso@olso.gsi.gov.uk
Web: www.olso.org

The Legal Services Ombudsman is appointed by the Lord Chancellor under the Courts and Legal Services Act 1990 to oversee the handling of complaints against solicitors, barristers, licensed conveyancers, legal executives and patent agents by their professional bodies. A complainant must first complain to the relevant professional body before raising the matter with the Ombudsman. The Ombudsman is independent of the legal profession and her services are free of charge.

Legal Services Ombudsman, Ms A. Abraham
Service Manager, S. D. Entwistle

OFFICE OF THE SCOTTISH LEGAL SERVICES OMBUDSMAN

17 Waterloo Place, Edinburgh, EH1 3DL
Tel: 0131-244 3055; Fax: 0131-244 3065
Email: ombudsman@slso.org.uk
Web: www.slso.org.uk

The Ombudsman investigates complaints about the way in which Scottish professional bodies have handled a complaint against a legal practitioner.

The Ombudsman also examines complaints about the unwillingness of a professional body to investigate a complaint against a legal practitioner.

Scottish Legal Services Ombudsman, Ms L. Costelloe Baker

OFFICE OF THE LORD ADVOCATE

Crown Office, 25 Chambers Street, Edinburgh EH1 1LA
Tel: 0131-226 2626; Fax: 0131-226 6920

The Law Officers for Scotland are the Lord Advocate and the Solicitor-General for Scotland.

Lord Advocate, The Rt. Hon. Colin Boyd, QC
Solicitor-General for Scotland, Ms E. Angiolini, QC
 Private Secretary to the Lord Advocate, Ms K. Davidson
 Private Secretary to the Solicitor General, R. Kent

OFFICE OF THE PARLIAMENTARY COMMISSIONER FOR ADMINISTRATION AND HEALTH SERVICE COMMISSIONER

Millbank Tower, Millbank, London SW1P 4QP
Tel: 0845-015 4033; Fax: 020-7217 4160
Email: opca.enquiries@ombudsman.gsi.gov.uk
Web: www.ombudsman.org.uk
Health Service Ombudsman Tel: 0845-015 4033;
Fax: 020-7217 4940
Email: ohsc.enquiries@ombudsman.gsi.gov.uk

The Parliamentary Commissioner for Administration (the Parliamentary Ombudsman) is independent of Government and is an officer of Parliament. He is responsible for investigating complaints referred to him by MPs from members of the public who claim to have sustained injustice in consequence of maladministration by or on behalf of Government departments and certain non-departmental public bodies. In March 1999 an additional 158 public bodies were brought within the jurisdiction of the Parliamentary Commissioner. Certain types of action by Government departments or bodies are excluded from investigation. The Parliamentary Commissioner is also responsible for investigating complaints, referred by MPs, alleging that access to official information has been wrongly refused under the Code of Practice on Access to Government Information 1994.

The Health Service Commissioners (the Health Service Ombudsmen) for England and for Wales are responsible for investigating complaints against National Health Service authorities and trusts that are not dealt with by those authorities to the satisfaction of the complainant. Complaints can be referred direct by the member of the public who claims to have sustained injustice or hardship in consequence of the failure in a service provided by a relevant body, failure of that body to provide a service or in consequence of any other action by that body. The Ombudsmens' jurisdiction now covers complaints about family doctors, dentists, pharmacists and opticians, and complaints about actions resulting from clinical judgement.

The Health Service Ombudsmen are also responsible for investigating complaints that information has been wrongly refused under the Code of Practice on Openness in the National Health Service 1995. The two offices are presently held by the Parliamentary Commissioner.

Parliamentary Commissioner and Health Service Commissioner (G1), M. S. Buckley
Deputy Parliamentary Commissioner (G3), A. Watson
Deputy Health Service Commissioner (G3), Ms H. Scott
Directors, Parliamentary Commissioner (G5), G. Monk; D. Reynolds; Ms C. Corrigan
Directors, Health Service Commissioners (G5), Ms H. Bainbridge; N. J. Jordan; D. R. G. Pinchin; L. Charlton
Finance and Establishment Officer (G5), J. Stevens

OFFICE OF THE PENSIONS OMBUDSMAN

6th Floor, 11 Belgrave Road, London SW1V 1RB
Tel: 020-7834 9144; Fax: 020-7821 0065

The Pensions Ombudsman is appointed under the Pension Schemes Act 1993 as amended by the Pensions Act 1995. He independently investigates and decides complaints and disputes concerning pension schemes.

Pensions Ombudsman, D. Laverick

OFFICE OF THE RAIL REGULATOR
1 Waterhouse Square, 138–142 Holborn, London
EC1N 2TQ
Tel: 020-7282 2000; Fax: 020-7282 2047
Web: www.rail-reg.gov.uk

The Office of the Rail Regulator was set up under the Railways Act 1993. It is headed by the Rail Regulator, who is independent of ministerial control. The Regulator's principal function is to regulate Railtrack's stewardship of the national network and to provide the economic regulation of the monopoly and dominant elements of the rail industry. The Regulator also licenses operators of railway assets, approves agreements for access by those operators to track, stations and light maintenance depots, and enforces domestic competition law. The International Rail Regulator is a statutory office separate from that of the Rail Regulator. The International Rail Regulator licenses the operation of certain international rail services in the European Economic Area, and access to railway infrastructure in Great Britain for the purpose of the operation of such services. The Office of The International Rail Regulator is co-located with the Office of the Rail Regulator, who fulfils both functions.
Rail Regulator, T. Winsor
Director of Strategy Planning and Communications, K. Webb
Director of Network Regulation, M. Beswick
Director of Access, Competition and Licensing, S. Gooding
Chief Economist and Director of Economics and Finance, T. Martin
Chief Legal Adviser and Director of Legal Services, Ms G. Richmond

OFFICE OF WATER SERVICES
Centre City Tower, 7 Hill Street, Birmingham B5 4UA
Tel: 0121-625 1300; Fax: 0121-625 1400
Email: enquiries@ofwat.gsi.gov.uk
Web: www.ofwat.gov.uk

The Office of Water Services (Ofwat) was set up under the Water Act 1989 and is a non-ministerial Government department headed by the Director-General of Water Services. It is the independent economic regulator of the water and sewerage companies in England and Wales. Ofwat's main duties are to ensure that the companies can finance and carry out the functions specified in the Water Industry Act 1991 and to protect the interests of water customers. There are ten WaterVoice committees which are concerned solely with the interests of water customers. Representation of customer interests at national and European level is the responsibility of the WaterVoiceCouncil .
Director-General of Water Services, P. Fletcher
Chairman, WaterVoice Council, M. Terry

ORDNANCE SURVEY
Romsey Road, Maybush, Southampton SO16 4GU
Tel: 023-8079 2000; Fax: 023-8079 2615

Ordnance Survey is the national mapping agency for Great Britain. It is a Government department and executive agency operating as a Trading Fund and reporting to the Office of the Deputy Prime Minister.
Director-General and Chief Executive, Ms V. Lawrence

PARADES COMMISSION
12th Floor, Windsor House, 6-12 Bedford Street, Belfast BT2 7EL
Tel: 028-9054 8900; Fax: 028-9032 2988
Email: info@paradescommission.com
Web: www.paradescommission.org

The Parades Commission was set up under the Public Processions (Northern Ireland) Act 1998. Its function is to encourage and facilitate local accommodation on contentious parades; where this is not possible, the Commission is empowered to make legal determinations about such parades, which may include imposing conditions on aspects of the notified parade.
The chairman and members are appointed by the Secretary of State for Northern Ireland; the membership must, as far as is practicable, be representative of the community in Northern Ireland.
Chairman, A. J. Holland
Members, J. Cousins; Revd R. Magee; W. Martin; P. Osborne; Sir John Pringle, P. Quinn
Secretary (G5), A. Elliott

PARLIAMENTARY COMMISSIONER FOR STANDARDS
House of Commons, London SW1A 0AA
Tel: 020-7219 0320; Fax: 020-7219 0490

Following recommendations of the Committee on Standards in Public Life, the House of Commons agreed to the appointment of an independent Parliamentary Commissioner for Standards with effect from November 1995. The Commissioner has responsibility for maintaining and monitoring the operation of the Register of Members' Interests; advising Members of Parliament and the Select Committee on Standards and Privileges; interpreting the rules on disclosure and advocacy, and on other questions of propriety. and the Commissioner also receives and investigates complaints about the conduct of MPs.
Parliamentary Commissioner for Standards, P. Mawer

PARLIAMENTARY COUNSEL
36 Whitehall, London SW1A 2AY
Tel: 020-7210 6611; Fax: 020-7210 6632
Web: www.parliamentary-counsel.gov.uk

Parliamentary Counsel draft all Government bills (i.e. primary legislation) except those relating exclusively to Scotland. They also advise on all aspects of parliamentary procedure in connection with such bills and draft Government amendments to them as well as any motions (including financial resolutions) necessary to secure their introduction into, and passage through, Parliament.
First Parliamentary Counsel (SCS), E. G. Bowman, CB
Counsel (SCS), G. B. Sellers, CB; E. R. Sutherland, CB; P. F. A. Knowles, CB; S. C. Laws, CB; R. S. Parker, CB; Miss C. E. Johnston, CB; P. J. Davies, CB; J. M. Sellers

PAROLE BOARD FOR ENGLAND AND WALES
Abell House, John Islip Street, London SW1P 4LH
Tel: 020-7217 5314; Fax: 020-7217 5793
Email: info@paroleboard.gov.uk
Web: www.paroleboard.gov.uk

The duty of the Parole Board is to advise the Home Secretary with respect to matters referred to it by him

which are connected with the early release or recall of prisoners. Its functions include giving directions concerning the release on licence of prisoners serving discretionary life sentences and of certain prisoners serving long-term determinate sentences.

Chairman, D. Hatch, CBE
Vice-Chairman, The Hon. Mr Justice Scott Baker
Chief Executive, C. Glenn

PAROLE BOARD FOR SCOTLAND
Saughton House, Broomhouse Drive, Edinburgh EH11 3XD
Tel: 0131-244 8473; Fax: 0131-244 6974

The Board directs and advises the Scottish Minister on the release of prisoners on licence, and related matters.
Chairman, Dr J. J. McManus
Vice-Chairman, Mrs M. Casserly
Secretary, H. P. Boyle

PATENT OFFICE
Concept House, Cardiff Road, Newport NP10 8QQ
Tel: 0845-950 0505; Fax: 01633-814444
Email: enquiries@patent.gov.uk
Web: www.patent.gov.uk

The Patent Office is an executive agency of the Department of Trade and Industry. The duties of the Patent Office are to administer the Patent Acts, the Registered Designs Act and the Trade Marks Act, and to deal with questions relating to the Copyright, Designs and Patents Act 1988. The Search and Advisory Service carries out commercial searches through patent information.
Comptroller-General, Ms A. Brimelow
Director, Intellectual Property Policy Directorate,
    G. Jenkins
Director, Patents and Designs, R. J. Marchant
Director and Assistant Registrar of Trade Marks,
    P. Lawrence
*Director, Administration and Resources and Secretary to
    the Patent Office*, Ms C. Fullerton
Director, Copyright, A. Murphy
Director, Finance, J. Thompson

PENSIONS COMPENSATION BOARD
11 Belgrave Road, London SW1V 1RB
Tel: 020-7828 9794; Fax: 020-7931 7239

The Pensions Compensation Board was established under the Pensions Act 1995 and is funded by a levy paid by all eligible occupational pension schemes. Its function is to compensate occupational pension schemes for losses due to dishonesty where the employer is insolvent.
Chairman, Sir Bryan Carsberg
Secretary, M. Lydon

POLICE COMPLAINTS AUTHORITY
10 Great George Street, London SW1P 3AE
Tel: 020-7273 6450; Fax: 020-7273 6401
Email: info@pca.gov.uk
Web: www.pca.gov.uk

The Police Complaints Authority was established under the Police and Criminal Evidence Act 1984 to provide an independent system for dealing with complaints by members of the public against police officers in England and Wales. It is funded by the Home Office. The authority has powers to supervise the investigation of certain categories of serious complaints and examines all completed investigations to decide whether officers should face misconduct proceedings. It does not deal with police operational matters; these are usually dealt with by the Chief Constable of the relevant force.
Chairman, Sir Alistair Graham
Deputy Chair, I. Bynoe
2nd Deputy Chair, Ms W. Towers
Members, Mrs A. Boustred; D. Gear; Miss M. Mian;
    D. Petch; S. Swindell; D. Hughes; D. Glass;
    L. Pilkington; A. Macdougall; S. Hawkins;
    M. Williams; E. Rassaby; N. Williams; A. Barker;
    J. Rodgers

POLICE OMBUDSMAN FOR NORTHERN IRELAND
New Cathedral Buildings, St Anne's Square, Belfast BT1 1PG
Tel: 028-9082 8600; Fax: 028-9082 8659;
Email: info@policeombudsman.org
Web: www.policeombudsman.org

Founded in November 2000 under the Police (Northern Ireland) Act 1998, the function of the Police Ombudsman for Northern Ireland is to investigate complaints against the police in an impartial, efficient, effective and (as far as possible) transparent way, to win the confidence of the public and the police. It must report on trends in complaints and react to incidents involving the police, where it is in the public interest, even if no individual complaint has been made.
Ombudsman, N. O'Loan

PORT OF LONDON AUTHORITY
Bakers Hall, 7 Harp Lane, London EC3R 6LB
Tel: 020-7743 7900; Fax: 020-7743 7999
Web: www.portoflondon.co.uk

The Port of London Authority (PLA) is the port authority for the 93 miles of the tidal River Thames from the Estuary to Teddington. It provides navigational and pilotage services for ships using the Port of London, including the maintenance of shipping channels. The PLA is also actively engaged in the promotion of the Port of London. The Port of London is one of the UK's main three ports, handling over 50 million tonnes of cargo each year. The port comprises over 80 independently owned terminals and port facilities, which handle a very wide range of cargoes.
    The PLA is a public trust constituted under the Port of London Act 1908 and subsequent legislation.
Chairman, S. P. Sherrard
Vice-Chairman, R. D. Clegg
Chief Executive, S. C. Cuthbert
Secretary, D. Cartlidge

PRISONS AND PROBATION OMBUDSMAN FOR ENGLAND AND WALES
Ashley House, 2 Monck Street, London SW1P 2BQ
Tel: 020-7276 2876; Fax: 020-7276 2860
Email: mail@ppo.gsi.gov.uk

The Ombudsman is appointed by the Home Secretary. He provides a free and independent adjudication service for prisoners and those under probation supervision who have been unable to resolve their grievances with the Prison and Probation Services.
Prisons Ombudsman, S. Shaw

PRIVY COUNCIL OFFICE
2 Carlton Gardens, London SW1Y 5AA
Tel: 020-7210 1033; Fax: 020-7210 1071

The Office is responsible for the arrangements leading to the making of all royal proclamations and Orders in Council; for certain formalities connected with ministerial changes; for considering applications for the granting (or amendment) of royal charters; for the scrutiny and approval of by-laws and statutes of chartered bodies; and for the appointment of high sheriffs and many Crown and Privy Council appointments to governing bodies.

President of the Council (and Leader of the House of Commons), The Rt. Hon. Robin Cook, MP
  Private Secretaries, S. Hillcoat; Ms C. Nalty (*Parliamentary Affairs*); G. Jones (*Policy and Legislation*)
Parliamentary Secretary, Stephen Twigg, MP
  Private Secretary, Ms F. Slee
Clerk of the Council, A. Galloway
Deputy Clerk of the Council, G. Donald
Senior Clerk, Ms M. McCullagh
Registrar, J. Watherston

PUBLIC HEALTH LABORATORY SERVICE
61 Colindale Avenue, London NW9 5DF
Tel: 020-8200 1295; Fax: 020-8358 3130/3131
Email: phls@phls.nhs.uk

The Public Health Laboratory Service comprises eight groups of laboratories, the Central Public Health Laboratory, the Communicable Disease Surveillance Centre, a Regional Epidemiology service and the headquarters. The PHLS seeks to protect the population from infection through detection, diagnosis, surveillance, prevention and control of infections and communicable diseases. It keeps track of what infections are appearing where, advises on remedial or preventive action and provides clinical diagnostic services.

Chairman (acting), R. Tabor
Director, Prof. B. I. Duerden, FRCPath (*Corporate Planning and Resources*)
Deputy Director, K. M. Saunders

CENTRAL PUBLIC HEALTH LABORATORY

Colindale Avenue, London NW9 5HT
Director, Prof. S. P. Borriello

COMMUNICABLE DISEASE SURVEILLANCE CENTRE

Colindale Avenue, NW9 5EQ
Director, Dr A. Nicoll

PHLS GROUPS OF LABORATORIES AND GROUP DIRECTORS

East, Dr P. M. B. White
Midlands, Dr R. E. Warren
North, Dr N. F. Lightfoot
North-West, Dr I. Farrell
South-West, Prof. K. A. V. Cartwright
London and South-East, Dr R. Gross
Trent, Dr P. J. Wilkinson
Wales, Dr A. J. Howard

OTHER SPECIAL LABORATORIES AND UNITS
ANAEROBE REFERENCE UNIT, Public Health Laboratory, Cardiff. *Head*, Prof. B. I. Duerden
ANTIVIRAL SUSCEPTIBILITY REFERENCE UNIT, Public Health Laboratory, Birmingham. *Head*, Dr D. P. Pillay
CRYPTOSPRORIDIUM REFERENCE UNIT, Public Health Laboratory, Swansea. *Head*, Dr Rachel Chalmers
GENITO-URINARY INFECTIONS REFERENCE LABORATORY, Public Health Laboratory, Bristol. *Head*, Dr A. J. Herring
LEPTOSPIRA REFERENCE LABORATORY, Public Health Laboratory, Hereford. Director, Dr T. J. Coleman
LYME DISEASE REFERENCE UNIT, Public Health Laboratory, Southampton. *Head*, Dr S. O'Connell
MALARIA REFERENCE LABORATORY, London School of Hygiene and Tropical Medicine, London WC1E 7HT. *Directors*, Prof. D. J. Bradley; Dr D. C. Warhurst
MENINGOCOCCAL REFERENCE LABORATORY, Public Health Laboratory, Manchester. *Director*, Dr E. Kaczmarski
MYCOBACTERIUM REFERENCE UNIT, Public Health Laboratory, Dulwich, London. *Director*, Prof. F. Drobniewski
MYCOLOGY REFERENCE LABORATORY, Public Health Laboratory, Bristol. *Head*, Dr E. M. Johnson
PARASITOLOGY REFERENCE LABORATORY, Hospital for Tropical Diseases, London. *Director*, Dr P. L. Chiodini
TOXOPLASMA REFERENCE LABORATORY, Public Health Laboratory, Swansea. *Head*, D. H. M. Joynson

PUBLIC GUARDIANSHIP OFFICE
Archway Tower, 2 Junction Road, London N19 5SZ
Tel: 020-7664 7000; Fax: 020-7664 7705
Email: custerv@guardianship.gov.uk
Web: www.guardianship.gov.uk

The Public Guardianship Office (PGO) is the administrative arm of the Court of Protection, based within the Lord Chancellor's Department.

Established on the 1 April 2001, it has taken over the mental health functions previously undertaken by the Public Trust Office (PTO), which also provides services that promote the financial and social well being of people with mental incapacity.

Chief Executive (Accountant-General), D. Lye
Director of Finance, I. Rees
Director of Client Services, K. Launchbury
Director of Client Services (acting), Ms W. Mason
Director of Human Resource, H. Daley
Director of Communications, L. Joy

QUEST (THE QUALITY, EFFICIENCY AND STANDARDS TEAM)
c/o Department for Culture, Media and Sport, 2–4 Cockspur Street, London SW1Y 5DH
Tel: 020-7273 8708; Fax: 020-7273 8700

Quest was established in 1999. Its role is to monitor the quality of performance in organisations sponsored by the Department for Culture, Media and Sport and to provide independent advice to the Secretary of State.
Chief Executive, vacant

THE RADIO AUTHORITY

Holbrook House, 14 Great Queen Street,
London WC2B 5DG
Tel: 020-7430 2724; Fax: 020-7405 7062
Web: www.radioauthority.org.uk

The Radio Authority was established in 1991 under the Broadcasting Act 1990. It is the regulator and licensing authority for all independent radio services. Members of the Authority are appointed by the Secretary of State for Culture, Media and Sport; senior executive staff are appointed by the Authority.

The Office of Communications, OFCOM, is due to become the new regulator for the communications sector in 2003.

Chairman, R. Hooper
Deputy Chairman, D. Witherow
Members, M. Adair; T. Prag; G. Talfan Davies; F. Sharkey; Ms S. Hewitt; Ms S. Nathan; Ms K. O'Rourke
Chief Executive, T. Stoller
Deputy Chief Executive, D. Vick
Secretary to the Authority and Director of Legal Affairs, Ms E. Salomon

RECORD OFFICES

ADVISORY COUNCIL ON PUBLIC RECORDS

Secretariat: Public Record Office, Kew, Surrey TW9 4DU
Tel: 020-8392 5381; Fax: 020-8392 5295
Council members are appointed by the Lord Chancellor, under the Public Records Act 1958, to advise him on matters concerning public records in general and in particular, on those aspects of the work of the Public Record Office which affect members of the public who make use of it.

Chairman, The Rt. Hon. Lord Phillips
Secretary, T. R. Padfield

CORPORATION OF LONDON RECORDS OFFICE

PO Box 270, Guildhall, London EC2P 2EJ
Tel: 020-7332 1251; Fax: 020-7710 8682;
Email: clro@corpoflondon.gov.uk;
Web: www.cityoflondon.gov.uk/archives/clro

The Corporation of London Records Office contains the municipal archives of the City of London which are regarded as the most complete collection of ancient municipal records in existence. The collection includes charters of William the Conqueror, Henry II, and later kings and queens to 1957; ancient custumals: Liber Horn, Dunthorne, Custumarum, Ordinacionum, Memorandorum and Albus, Liber de Antiquis Legibus, and collections of statutes; continuous series of judicial rolls and books from 1252 and Council minutes from 1275; records of the Old Bailey and Guildhall sessions from 1603; financial records from the 16th century; the records of London Bridge from the 12th century; and numerous subsidiary series and miscellanea of historical interest. The Readers' Room is open Monday–Friday, 9.30 a.m.–4.45 p.m.

Keeper of the City Records, The Town Clerk
City Archivist, J. R. Sewell, OBE
Deputy City Archivist, J. M. Bankes

HISTORICAL MANUSCRIPTS COMMISSION

Quality House, Quality Court, Chancery Lane, London WC2A 1HP
Tel: 020-7242 1198; Fax: 020-7831 3550
Email: nra@hmc.gov.uk; Web: www.hmc.gov.uk

The Commission was set up by royal warrant in 1869 to enquire and report on collections of papers of value for the study of history which were in private hands. In 1959 a new warrant enlarged these terms of reference to include all historical records, wherever situated, outside the Public Records and gave it added responsibilities as a central co-ordinating body to promote, assist and advise on their proper preservation and storage. The Commission is sponsored by the Department for Culture, Media and Sport.

The Commission also maintains the National Register of Archives (NRA), which contains over 43,000 unpublished lists and catalogues of manuscript collections describing the holdings of local record offices, national and university libraries, specialist repositories and others in the UK and overseas. The NRA can be searched using computerised indices which are available in the Commission's search room.

The Commission also administers the Manorial and Tithe Documents Rules on behalf of the Master of the Rolls.

In April 2003 the Historical Manuscripts Commission and the Public Record Office are combining to form the National Archives.

Chairman, The Lord Bingham of Cornhill, PC
Commissioners, Sir Patrick Cormack, FSA, MP; Sir Matthew Farrer, GCVO; Sir John Sainty, KCB, FSA; Very Revd H. E. C. Stapleton, FSA; Sir Keith Thomas, FBA; The Earl of Scarbrough; A. Dundas-Bekker; Dr S. J. Davies; Prof. P. Clarke; V. Gray; Miss R. Dunhill, FSA; Dr C. Barron, FSA; Prof. T. C. Smout, CBE, FBA, FRSE
Secretary, Dr C. J. Kitching, FSA

HOUSE OF LORDS RECORD OFFICE (THE PARLIAMENTARY ARCHIVES)

House of Lords, London SW1A 0PW
Tel: 020-7219 3074; Fax: 020-7219 2570
Email: hlro@parliament.uk; Web: www.parliament.uk

Since 1497, the records of Parliament have been kept within the Palace of Westminster. They are in the custody of the Clerk of the Parliaments. In 1946 a record department was established to supervise their preservation and their availability to the public. The search room of the office is open to the public Monday–Friday, 9.30 a.m.–5 p.m. (Tuesday to 8 p.m.) by appointment.

Some three million documents are preserved, including Acts of Parliament from 1497, journals of the House of Lords from 1510, minutes and committee proceedings from 1610, and papers laid before Parliament from 1531. Amongst the records are the Petition of Right, the Death Warrant of Charles I, the Declaration of Breda, and the Bill of Rights. The House of Lords Record Office also has charge of the journals of the House of Commons (from 1547), and other surviving records of the Commons (from 1572), including documents relating to private bill legislation from 1818. Among other documents are the records of the Lord Great Chamberlain, the political papers of certain members of the two Houses, and documents relating to Parliament acquired on behalf of the nation. A permanent exhibition was established in the Royal Gallery in 1979.

Clerk of the Records, S. K. Ellison
Assistant Clerks of the Records, D. L. Prior; Dr C. Shenton; Ms F. P. Grey (Freedom of Information Officer)

NATIONAL ARCHIVES OF SCOTLAND

HM General Register House, Edinburgh EH1 3YY
Tel: 0131-535 1314; Fax: 0131-535 1360
Email: enquiries@nas.gov.uk; Web: www.nas.gov.uk

The history of the national archives of Scotland can be traced back to the 13th century. The National Archives of Scotland (formerly the Scottish Record Office) is an executive agency of the Scottish Executive and keeps the administrative records of pre-Union Scotland, the registers of central and local courts of law, the public registers of property rights and legal documents, and many collections of local and church records and private archives. Certain groups of records, mainly the modern records of Government departments in Scotland, the Scottish railway records, the plans collection, and private archives of an industrial or commercial nature, are preserved in the branch repository at West Register House in Charlotte Square. The search rooms in both buildings are open Monday-Friday, 9 a.m.–4.45 p.m. A permanent exhibition at West Register House and changing exhibitions at General Register House are open to the public on weekdays, 10 a.m.–4 p.m. The National Register of Archives Scotland is based in the West Register House.

Keeper of the Records of Scotland, G. P. MacKenzie
Deputy Keepers, Dr P. D. Anderson; D. Brownlee

THE PUBLIC RECORD OFFICE

Kew, Richmond, Surrey TW9 4DU
Tel: 020-8876 3444; Fax: 020-8878 8905
Web: www.pro.gov.uk

The Public Record Office, originally established in 1838 under the Master of the Rolls, was placed under the direction of the Lord Chancellor in 1958; it became an executive agency in 1992. The Lord Chancellor appoints a Keeper of Public Records, whose duties are to co-ordinate and supervise the selection of records of Government departments and the law courts for permanent preservation, to safeguard the records and to make them available to the public. There is a separate record office for Scotland, now called the National Archives of Scotland.

The Office holds records of central Government dating from the Domesday Book (1086) to the present. Under the Public Records Act 1967 they are normally open to inspection when 30 years old, and are then available, without charge, in the reading rooms (Monday, Wednesday, Friday, Saturday, 9.30 a.m.–5 p.m.; Tuesday 10 a.m.–7 p.m.; Thursday 9.30 a.m.–7 p.m.).

In April 2003 the Public Records Office and the Historical Manuscripts Commission are combining to form the National Archives.

Keeper of Public Records (G3), Mrs S. Tyacke, CB
Director of Public Services (G5), Dr E. Hallam Smith
Director of Government and Archival Services (G5), Dr D. Simpson
Director of Corporate Services, Mrs W. Jones

PUBLIC RECORD OFFICE OF NORTHERN IRELAND

66 Balmoral Avenue, Belfast BT9 6NY
Tel: 028-9025 1318; Fax: 028-9025 5999

The Public Record Office of Northern Ireland is responsible for identifying and preserving Northern Ireland's archival heritage and making it available to the public. It is an executive agency of the Department of Culture, Arts and Leisure. The search room is open on weekdays, 9.15 a.m.–4.45 p.m. (Thursday, 9.15 a.m.–8.45 p.m., first Thursday of each month 10.00 a.m.–8.45 p.m.).
Chief Executive, Dr G. Slater

SCOTTISH RECORDS ADVISORY COUNCIL

HM General Register House, Edinburgh EH1 3YY
Tel: 0131-535 1403; Fax: 0131-535 1360
Web: www.nas.gov.uk

The Council was established under the Public Records (Scotland) Act 1937. Its members are appointed by the First Minister and it may submit proposals or make representations to the First Minister, the Lord Justice General or the Lord President of the Court of Session on questions relating to the public records of Scotland.
Chairman, Prof. H. MacQueen
Secretary, Dr A. Rosie

REGISTRAR OF PUBLIC LENDING RIGHT

Richard House, Sorbonne Close, Stockton on Tees; TS17 6DA
Tel: 01642-604699; Fax: 01642-615641
Email: registrar@plr.uk.com
Web: www.plr.uk.com

Under the Public Lending Right system, in operation since 1983, payment is made from public funds to authors whose books are lent out from public libraries. Payment is made once a year and the amount each author receives is proportionate to the number of times (established from a sample) that each registered book has been lent out during the previous year. The Registrar of PLR, who is appointed by the Secretary of State for Culture, Media and Sport, compiles the register of authors and books. Authors resident in all EC countries are eligible to apply. (The term 'author' covers writers, illustrators, translators, and some editors/compilers.)

A payment of 2.67 pence was made in 2001–2002 for each estimated loan of a registered book, up to a top limit of £6,000 for the books of any one registered author; the money for loans above this level is used to augment the remaining PLR payments. In February 2002, the sum of £4,503,593 million was made available for distribution to 34,220 registered authors and assignees as the annual payment of PLR.
Registrar, Dr J. G. Parker
Chairman of Advisory Committee, C. Francis

REVIEW BODIES

The secretariat for these bodies is provided by the Office of Manpower Economics.

ARMED FORCES PAY

The Review Body on Armed Forces Pay was appointed in 1971. It advises the Prime Minister and Government on the pay and allowances of members of naval, military and air forces of the Crown.
Chairman, The Baroness Dean of Thornton-le-Fylde, PC
Members, N. Sherlock; Vice-Adm. Sir Peter Woodhead; Dr A. Wright; J. Davies; The Lord Gladwin of Clee, CBE; Prof. D. Greenaway; Prof. The Lord Patel of Dunkeld; M. Ward

DOCTORS' AND DENTISTS'

The Review Body on Doctors' and Dentists' Remuneration was set up in 1971. It advises the Prime Minister and Government on the remuneration of doctors and dentists taking any part in the National Health Service.
Chairman, M. Blair, QC
Members, Prof. F. Burchill; Prof. A. Dow; A. Hawksworth; H. Donaldson; Ms D. Page; Dr G. Jones; R. Malone

NURSING STAFF, MIDWIVES, HEALTH VISITORS AND PROFESSIONS ALLIED TO MEDICINE

The Review Body for nursing staff, midwives, health visitors and professions allied to medicine was set up in 1983. It advises the Prime Minister and Government on the remuneration of nursing staff, midwives and health visitors employed in the National Health Service; and also of physiotherapists, radiographers, occupational therapists, orthoptists, chiropodists, dieticians and related grades employed in the National Health Service.
Chairman, Prof. C. Booth
Members, M. Banerjee; J. Bartlett; W. MacPherson; C. Monks, OBE; Prof. P. Weetman; D. Evans; Sir Patrick Symons, KBE

SCHOOL TEACHERS

The School Teachers' Review Body (STRB) was set up under the School Teachers' Pay and Conditions Act 1991. It is required to examine and report on such matters relating to the statutory conditions of employment of school teachers in England and Wales as may be referred to it by the Secretary of State for Education and Skills.
Chairman, W. Cockburn, CBE
Members, C. Ferguson; R. Gardner; Dr B. Roberts; R. Pearson; J. Singh; Mrs P. Sloane

SENIOR SALARIES

The Senior Salaries Review Body (formerly the Top Salaries Review Body) was set up in 1971 to advise the Prime Minister on the remuneration of the judiciary, senior civil servants and senior officers of the armed forces. In 1993 its remit was extended to cover the pay, pensions and allowances of MPs, Ministers and others whose pay is determined by a Ministerial and Other Salaries Order and the allowances of peers. It also advises on the pay of officers and members of the devolved Parliament and Assemblies.
Chairman, J. Baker, CBE
Members, D. Clayman; Prof. S. Dawson; The Baroness Dean of Thornton-le-Fylde, PC; Sir Terry Heiser, GCB; Prof. Sir David Williams, QC; George Staple, CB, QC; J. Rubin

PRISON SERVICE

The Prison Service Pay Review Body (PSPRB) was set up in 2001. It makes independent recommendations on the pay of prison governors, prison officers and related grades for the Prison Service in England and Wales and for the Northern Ireland Prison Service.
Chairman, Sir Toby Frere, KCB
Members, D. Bourn; B. Brewer; A. Faulder; A. Gallico; P. Heard; F. Horisk; Prof. A. Smith; P. Tett

ROYAL BOTANIC GARDEN EDINBURGH

20A Inverleith Row, Edinburgh EH3 5LR
Tel: 0131-552 7171; Fax: 0131-248 2901
Email: info@rbge.org.uk
Web: www.rbge.org.uk

The Royal Botanic Garden Edinburgh (RBGE) originated as the Physic Garden, established in 1670 beside the Palace of Holyroodhouse. The Garden moved to its present 28-hectare site at Inverleith, Edinburgh, in 1821. There are also three Regional Gardens: Benmore Botanic Garden, near Dunoon, Argyll; Logan Botanic Garden, near Stranraer, Wigtownshire; and Dawyck Botanic Garden, near Stobo, Peeblesshire. Since 1986 RBGE has been administered by a board of trustees established under the National Heritage (Scotland) Act 1985. It receives an annual grant from the Environment and Rural Affairs Department of the Scottish Executive.

RBGE is an international centre for scientific research on plant diversity and for horticulture education and conservation. It has an extensive library, a herbarium with over two million preserved plant specimens, and over 16,500 species in the living collections. Public opening hours: Edinburgh site, daily (except Christmas Day and New Year's Day) November–January 10 a.m.– 4 p.m.; February and October 10 a.m.–5 p.m.; March and September 10 a.m.–6 p.m.; April–August 10 a.m.–7 p.m.; Benmore and Logan Botanic Garden, 1 March– 31 October 10 a.m.–6 p.m.; Dawyck Botanic Garden open: 14 February–17 November; 10 a.m.–6 p.m. Admission free to Edinburgh site; admission charge to Regional Gardens.
Chairman of the Board of Trustees, Dr P. Nicholson
Regius Keeper, Prof. S. Blackmore, FRSE

ROYAL BOTANIC GARDENS KEW

Richmond, Surrey TW9 3AB
Tel: 020-8332 5000; Fax: 020-8332 5197
Wakehurst Place, Ardingly, nr Haywards Heath,
W. Sussex RH17 6TN
Tel: 01444-89000; Fax: 01444-894069

The Royal Botanic Gardens (RBG) Kew were originally laid out as a private garden for Kew House for George III's mother, Princess Augusta, in 1759. They were much enlarged in the 19th century, notably by the inclusion of the grounds of the former Richmond Lodge. In 1965 the garden at Wakehurst Place was acquired; it is owned by the National Trust and managed by RBG Kew. Under the National Heritage Act 1983 a board of trustees was set up to administer the gardens, which in 1984 became an independent body supported by grant-in-aid from the Department of Environment, Food and Rural Affairs.

The functions of RBG Kew are to carry out research into plant sciences, to disseminate knowledge about plants and to provide the public with the opportunity to gain knowledge and enjoyment from the gardens' collections. There are extensive national reference collections of living and preserved plants and a comprehensive library and archive. The main emphasis is on plant conservation and bio-diversity.

The gardens are open daily (except Christmas Day and New Year's Day) from 9.30 a.m. (Wakehurst, 10 a.m.). The closing hour varies from 4 p.m. in mid-winter to 6 p.m. on weekdays and 7.30 p.m. on Sundays and Bank Holidays in mid-summer. Admission, 2002, £6.50 adults (free for children under 16), concessionary schemes available. Glasshouses (Kew only), 9.30 a.m.–4.30 p.m. (winter); 9.30 a.m.–5.30 p.m. (summer). No dogs except guide-dogs for the blind.

ROYAL COMMISSION FOR THE EXHIBITION OF 1851

Sherfield Building, Imperial College of Science, Technology and Medicine, London SW7 2AZ
Tel: 020-7594 8790; Fax: 020-7594 8794
Email: royalcom1851@ic.ac.uk
Web: www.royalcommission1851.org.uk

The Royal Commission was incorporated by supplemental charter as a permanent commission after winding up the affairs of the Great Exhibition of 1851. Its object is to promote scientific and artistic education by means of funds derived from its Kensington estate, purchased with the surplus left over from the Great Exhibition. Annual charitable expenditure on educational grants is about £1 million.

President, HRH The Prince Philip, Duke of Edinburgh, KG, KT, PC
Chairman, Board of Management, Sir Alan Rudge, CBE, FRS, FREng
Secretary to Commissioners, M. C. Shirley

ROYAL COMMISSION ON ENVIRONMENTAL POLLUTION

3rd Floor, The Sanctuary, Westminster, London SW1P 3JS
Tel: 020-7799 8970 Email:enquiries@rcep.org.uk
Web: www.rcep.org.uk

The Commission was set up in 1970 to advise on national and international matters concerning the pollution of the environment.

Chairman, Prof. Sir Tom Blundell, FRS
Members, Dr I. Graham-Bryce; CBE; Prof. R. Clift, OBE, FREng; J. Flemming, CBE; Sir Brian Folett, FRS; Prof. B. Hoskins, CBE, FRS; Prof. R. Macrory, CBE; Mrs C. Miller; Dr S. Owens, OBE; Prof. J. Plant, CBE; Prof. P. Ekins; Prof. S. Holgate; J. Speirs; Prof. J. Sprent
Secretary, Dr P. Hinchcliffe

ROYAL COMMISSION ON THE ANCIENT AND HISTORICAL MONUMENTS OF SCOTLAND

John Sinclair House, 16 Bernard Terrace, Edinburgh EH8 9NX
Tel: 0131-662 1456; Fax: 0131-662 1477
Web: www. www.rcahms.gov.uk

The Royal Commission was established in 1908 and is appointed to provide for the survey and recording of ancient and historical monuments connected with the culture, civilisation and conditions of life of the people in Scotland from the earliest times. It is funded by the Scottish Executive. The Commission compiles and maintains the National Monuments Record of Scotland as the national record of the archaeological and historical environment. The National Monuments Record is open for reference Monday–Friday 9.30–4.30.

Chairman, Mrs K. Dalyell
Commissioners, Prof. R. A. Paxton, MBE, FRSE; Dr B. E. Crawford, FSA; Miss A. C. Riches, OBE, FSA; J. W. T. Simpson; Dr M. A. Mackay; Dr J. Murray; Dr A. Macdonald; Prof. C. D. Morris, FSA, FRSE; Dr S. Nenadic
Secretary, R. J. Mercer, FSA, FRSE

ROYAL COMMISSION ON THE ANCIENT AND HISTORICAL MONUMENTS OF WALES

Crown Building, Plas Crug, Aberystwyth SY23 1NJ
Tel: 01970-621200; Fax: 01970-627701;
Email: admin@rcahmw.org.uk
Web: www.rcahmw.org.uk

The Royal Commission was established in 1908 and is currently empowered by a Royal Warrant of 2001 to survey, record, publish and maintain a database of ancient and historical and maritime sites and structures, and landscapes in Wales. The Commission is funded by the National Assembly for Wales and is also responsible for the National Monuments Record of Wales, which is open daily for public reference, for the supply of archaeological information to the Ordnance Survey, for the co-ordination of archaeological aerial photography in Wales, and for sponsorship of the regional Sites and Monuments Records.

Chairman, Prof. R. A. Griffiths, D.Litt.
Commissioners, Prof. A. D. Carr, FSA; D. W. Crossley, FSA; N. Harries; J. W. Lloyd, CB; J. Newman, FSA; Prof. F. Sims-Williams, FBA; Dr L. O. W. Smith; Prof. G. J. Wainwright, MBE, FSA; Dr E. William, FSA;
Secretary, P. R. White, FSA

THE ROYAL MINT

Llantrisant, Pontyclun CF72 8YT
Tel: 01443-623148; Fax: 01443-623185
Email: secretariat@royalmint.gov.uk
Web: www.royalmint.com

The prime responsibility of the Royal Mint is the provision of United Kingdom coinage, but it actively competes in world markets for a share of the available circulating coin business and about half of the coins and blanks it produces annually are exported. The Mint also manufactures special proof and uncirculated quality coins in gold, silver and other metals; military and civil decorations and medals; commemorative and prize medals; and royal and official seals.

The Royal Mint became an executive agency of the Treasury in 1990. The Government announced in July 1999 that the Royal Mint would be given greater commercial freedom to expand its business into new areas and develop partnerships with the private sector.

Master of the Mint, The Chancellor of the Exchequer (*ex officio*)
Chief Executive, G. Sheehan

THE ROYAL NATIONAL THEATRE

South Bank, London, SE1 9PX
Tel: 020-7452 3333; Fax: 020-7452 3344
Web: www.nationaltheatre.org.uk

Chairman, Sir Christopher Hogg
Members, Ms J. Bakewell, CBE; The Hon. P. Benson, LVO; Sir David Hancock, KCB; G. Hutchings; Ms K. Jones; Ms S. MacGregor, OBE; B. Okri; The Rt. Hon. Chris Smith, MP; Sir Tom Stoppard, OM, CBE; E. Walker-Arnott; P. Wiegand; Prof. L. Young; A. Ptaszynski
Company Secretary, Mrs M. McGregor
Director, T. Nunn, CBE
Executive Director, The Baroness McIntosh of Hudnall

RURAL PAYMENTS AGENCY (RPA)

Kings House, Kings Road, Reading, Berkshire RG1 3BU
Tel: 0118-958 3626; Fax: 0118-953 1370;
Email: enquiries@rpa.gsi.gov.uk
Web:www.rpa.gov.uk

Rural Payments Agency (RPA) was established as an executive agency of the Department for Environment, Food and Rural Affairs. It is the single paying agency responsible for Common Agricultural Policy (CAP) schemes in England and for certain schemes throughout the UK. RPA brings together the CAP paying functions of the former Ministry of Agriculture Fisheries and Food Regional Service Centres and the Intervention Board.
Chief Executive (G3), J. McNeill
Directors (G5), H. MacKinnon (*Operations*); A. Kerr, (*Finance*); R. Gregg (*Human Resources*); A. MacDermott (*Interim Information Systems*); S. Vry (*Business Development*); I. Pearson (*Operations Development*); A. Sutton (*CAP Schemes*); Ms G. Robinson (*Head of Internal Audit*); B. Stedman (*Head of Inspectorate*); Ms S. Milum (*Group Manager Counter Fraud and Compliance Unit*)

SCOTTISH CRIMINAL CASES REVIEW COMMISSION

5th Floor, Portland House, 17 Renfield Street, Glasgow G2 5AH Tel: 0141-270 7030; Fax: 0141-270 7040
Web: www.sccrc.org.uk

The Commission is a non-departmental public body which started operating on 1 April 1999. It took over from the Secretary of State for Scotland powers to consider alleged miscarriages of justice in Scotland and refer cases meeting the relevant criteria to the High Court for review. Members are appointed by Her Majesty The Queen on the recommendation of the First Minister; senior executive staff are appointed by the Commission.
Chairperson, The Very Revd G. Forbes
Members, Prof. P. Duff; Sir Gerald Gordon, CBE, QC; W. Taylor, QC; R. Anderson, QC; D. Belfall; J. Mackay, QPM
Chief Executive, Ms C. A. Kelly

SCOTTISH ENTERPRISE

120 Bothwell Street, Glasgow G2 7JP
Tel: 0141-248 2700; Fax: 0141-221 3217

Scottish Enterprise was established in 1991 and its purpose is to create jobs and prosperity for the people of Scotland. It is funded largely by the Scottish Executive and is responsible to the Scottish Ministers. Working in partnership with the private and public sectors, Scottish Enterprise aims to further the development of Scotland's economy, to enhance the skills of the Scottish workforce and to promote Scotland's international competitiveness. Through Locate in Scotland, Scottish Enterprise is concerned with attracting firms to Scotland, and through Scottish Trade International it helps Scottish companies to compete in world export markets. Scottish Enterprise has a network of 12 Local Enterprise Companies that deliver economic development services at local level.
Chairman (£33,883), Sir Ian Robinson, CBE
Chief Executive, Dr R. Crawford

SCOTTISH ENVIRONMENT PROTECTION AGENCY

Erskine Court, The Castle Business Park, Stirling FK9 4TR
Tel: 01786-457700; Hotline: 0800 80 70 60
Fax: 01786-446885;
Web: www.sepa.org.uk

The Scottish Environment Protection Agency (SEPA) is the public body responsible for environmental protection in Scotland. It regulates potential pollution to land, air and water, the storage, transport and disposal of controlled waste and the safe keeping and disposal of radioactive materials. It does this within a complex legislative framework of Acts of Parliament, EC Directives and Regulations, granting licenses to operations of industrial processes and waste disposal.
SEPA also operates Floodline, 0845-988 1188, a public information service providing information on possible risk of flooding 24 hours a day, 365 days a year.
Chairman, K. Collins
Chief Executive, M. P. Henton
Director of Finance and Corporate Support, J. Ford
Director of Strategic Planning, C. Gemmell
Director of Operations, W. Halcrow
Director of Public Affairs and Corporate Communications, J. Beveridge

SCOTTISH LAW COMMISSION

140 Causewayside, Edinburgh EH9 1PR
Tel: 0131-668 2131; Fax: 0131-662 4900
Email: info@scotlawcom.gov.uk
Web: www. scotlawcom.gov.uk

The Commission keeps the law in Scotland under review and makes proposals for its development and reform. It is responsible to the Scottish Ministers through the Scottish Executive Justice Department.
Chairman (*part-time*), The Hon. Lord Gill
Commissioners (*full-time*), Prof. G. Maher; Prof. K. G. C. Reid; Prof. J. M. Thomson; (*part-time*) P. S. Hodge, QC
Secretary, Miss J. McLeod

SCOTTISH LEGAL AID BOARD

44 Drumsheugh Gardens, Edinburgh EH3 7SW
Tel: 0131-226 7061; Fax: 0131-220 4878
Email: general@slab.org.uk
Web: www.scotlegalaid.gov.uk

The Scottish Legal Aid Board was set up under the Legal Aid (Scotland) Act 1986. It is responsible for ensuring that advice, assistance and representation are available in accordance with the Act. Members are appointed by Scottish Ministers.
Chairman, Mrs J. Couper
Members, W. Gallagher; Sheriff A. Jessop; N. Kuenssberg; G. Mckinstry; D. J. C. Nicol; Prof. J. P. Percy; Mrs Y. Osman; Mrs M. Scanlan; M. C. Thomson, QC; A. F. Wylie, QC
Chief Executive, L. Montgomery

SCOTTISH NATURAL HERITAGE
12 Hope Terrace, Edinburgh EH9 2AS
Tel: 0131-447 4784; Fax: 0131-446 2277
Email: enquiries@snh.gov.uk
Web: www.snh.org.uk

Scottish Natural Heritage was established in 1992 under the Natural Heritage (Scotland) Act 1991. It provides advice on nature conservation to all those whose activities affect wildlife, landforms and features of geological interest in Scotland, and seeks to develop and improve facilities for the enjoyment and understanding of the Scottish countryside. It is funded by the Scottish Executive.

Chairman, Dr J. Markland, CBE
Chief Executive, I. Jardine
Chief Scientific Adviser, C. Galbraith
Directors of Operations, J. Thomson (*West*); A. Bachell (*East*); J. Watson (*North*)
Director of Corporate Services, I. Edgeler

SCOTTISH PRISONS COMPLAINTS COMMISSION
Government Buildings, Broomhouse Drive, Edinburgh EH11 3XD
Tel: 0131-244 8423; Fax: 0131-244 8430

The Commission was established in 1994. It is an independent body to which prisoners in Scottish prisons can make application in relation to any matter where they have failed to obtain satisfaction from the Scottish Prison Service's internal grievance procedures. Clinical judgements made by medical officers, matters which are the subject of legal proceedings and matters relating to sentence, conviction and parole decision-making are excluded from the Commission's jurisdiction. The Commissioner is appointed by the First Minister.

Commissioner, Miss J. N. Aitken

SCOTTISH PUBLIC SERVICES OMBUDSMAN

Under the Scottish Public Services Ombudsman Act 2002, the Scottish parliamentary, health service, local government and housing association ombudsmen will be abolished and replaced by the Scottish Public Services Ombudsman. On 27 June 2002, Prof. Alice Brown's nomination for the role of Ombudsman was approved by the Scottish Parliament.

SEAFISH INDUSTRY AUTHORITY
18 Logie Mill, Logie Green Road, Edinburgh EH7 4HG
Tel: 0131-558 3331; Fax: 0131-558 1442
Email: seafish@seafish.co.uk
Web: www.seafish.co.uk

Established under the Fisheries Act 1981, Seafish promotes the efficiency of the seafood industry. It carries out research relating to the industry and gives advice on related matters. It provides training, seafood marketing and business advice. It is responsible to the Department of the Environment, Food and Rural Affairs.

Chairman, A. Dewar-Durie
Chief Executive, J. Rutherford

THE SECURITY AND INTELLIGENCE SERVICES

Under the Intelligence Services Act 1994, the Intelligence and Security Committee of Parliamentarians was established to oversee the work of GCHQ, MI5 and MI6; in 1999 an Investigator was appointed to the committee in order to reinforce the authority of its findings and establish public confidence in the oversight system. The Act also established the Intelligence Services Tribunal, which hears complaints made against GCHQ and MI6. The Security Service Tribunal and Commissioner (see below) investigate complaints about MI5.

DEFENCE INTELLIGENCE STAFF
see Defence section

GOVERNMENT COMMUNICATIONS HEADQUARTERS (GCHQ)
Priors Road, Cheltenham, Glos GL52 5AJ
Tel: 01242-221491; Fax: 01242-574349

GCHQ produces signals intelligence in support of national security and the UK's economic wellbeing, and in the prevention or detection of serious crime. Additionally, GCHQ Communications-Electronics Security Group (CESG) provides advice and assistance to Government departments, the armed forces and other national infrastructure bodies on the security of their communications and information systems. GCHQ was placed on a statutory footing by the Intelligence Services Act 1994 and is headed by a director who is directly accountable to the Foreign Secretary. A new building to house GCHQ is being constructed in Cheltenham, with the anticipated completion date of early 2003.

Director, F. N. Richards, CVO, CMG

INVESTIGATORY POWERS TRIBUNAL
PO Box 33220, London, SW1H 9ZQ
Tel: 020-7273 4515

The Investigatory Powers Tribunal replaces the Interception of Communications Tribunal, the Intelligence Services Tribunal, the Security Services Tribunal and the complaints function of the Commissioner appointed under the Police Act 1997.
The Regulation of Investigatory Powers Act 2000 provides for a Tribunal made up of senior members of the legal profession, independent of the Government and appointed by The Queen, to consider all complaints against the intelligence services and those against public authorities in respect of powers covered by RIPA; and to consider proceedings brought under section 7 of the Human Rights Act 1998 against the intelligence services and law enforcement agencies in respect of these powers.

President, The Rt. Hon. Lord Justice John Mummery
Vice-President, Mr Justice Michael Burton
Members, W. Carmichael; Sir David Calcutt, QC; Sir Richard Gaskell; Sheriff Principal J. McInnes, QC; Sir John Pringle, QC; P. Scott, QC; R. Seabrook, QC
Secretary, Mr D. Payne

NATIONAL CRIMINAL INTELLIGENCE SERVICE
PO Box 8000, London SE11 5EN
Tel: 020-7238 8000; Web: www.ncis.gov.uk

The National Criminal Intelligence Service (NCIS) provides intelligence about serious and organised crime

to law enforcement, government and other relevant national and international agencies.
Director-General, J. Abbott, QPM, CBE
Deputy Director-General, D. Bolt
Director, International Division, N. Bailey
Director, UK Division, V. Harvey
Director, Resources Division, N. Beard

SERVICE AUTHORITY

PO Box 2600, London SW1V 2WG
Tel: 020-7238 2600

The Service Authority for NCIS is responsible for ensuring its effective operation. It operates with the Service Authority for the National Crime Squad. There are 26 members of the authorities, of whom the chairman and nine others serve as 'core members' on both authorities.
Chairman, D. Lock
Clerk, T. Simmons
Treasurer, P. Derrick

THE SECRET INTELLIGENCE SERVICE (MI6)

PO Box 1300, London SE1 1BD

The Secret Intelligence Service produces secret intelligence in support of the Government's security, defence, foreign and economic policies. It was placed on a statutory footing by the Intelligence Services Act 1994 and is headed by a chief, known as 'C', who is directly accountable to the Foreign Secretary.
Chief, Sir R. B. Dearlove, OBE, KCMG

THE SECURITY SERVICE (MI5)

PO Box 3255, London SW1P 1AE
Tel: 020-7930 9000

The function of the Security Service is the protection of national security, in particular against threats from espionage, terrorism, sabotage and the proliferation of weapons of mass destruction, from the activities of agents of foreign powers, and from actions intended to overthrow or undermine parliamentary democracy by political, industrial or violent means. It is also the Service's function to safeguard the economic well-being of the UK against threats posed by the actions or intentions of persons outside the British Islands. In 1996 the Service's role was extended to support the police and customs in the prevention and detection of serious crime.
Director-General, Ms E. Manningham-Buller

INTELLIGENCE SERVICES COMMISSIONER

c/o PO Box 33220, London SW1H 9ZQ
Tel: 020-7273 4514

The Commissioner is appointed by the Prime Minister. He keeps under review the issue of warrants by the Secretaries of State as detailed under the Regulation of Investigatory Powers Act (RIPA) 2000. The Commissioner is also required to submit an annual report on the discharge of his functions to the Prime Minister.
Commissioner, The Rt. Hon. Lord Justice Simon Brown
Private Secretary, D. Payne

SENTENCE REVIEW COMMISSIONERS

5th Floor, Windsor House, 12–16 Bedford Street, Belfast BT2 7SR
Tel: 028-9054 9412; Fax: 028-9054 9427
Email: sentrev@belfast.org.uk
Web: www.sentencereview.org.uk

The Sentence Review Commissioners are appointed by the Secretary of State for Northern Ireland to consider applications from prisoners serving sentences in Northern Ireland for declarations that they are entitled to early release in accordance with the provisions of the Northern Ireland (Sentences) Act 1998. The commissioners have been appointed until 31 July 2005 and are served by staff seconded from the Northern Ireland Office.
Joint Chairmen, Sir John Belloch, KCB; B. Currin
Commissioners, Dr S. Casale; Dr P. Curran; I. Dunbar, CB; Mrs M. Gilpin; Dr A. Grounds; D. McFerran; Ms C. McGrory; Dr D. Morrow

SERIOUS FRAUD OFFICE

Elm House, 10–16 Elm Street, London WC1X 0BJ
Tel: 020-7239 7272; Fax: 020-7837 1689
Email: public.enquiries@sfo.gsi.gov.uk

The Serious Fraud Office works under the superintendence of the Attorney-General. Its remit is to investigate and prosecute serious and complex fraud. (Other fraud cases are handled by the fraud divisions of the Crown Prosecution Service.) The scope of its powers covers England, Wales and Northern Ireland. The staff includes lawyers, accountants and other support staff investigating teams work closely with the police.
Director, Mrs R. Wright, CB

SMALL BUSINESS COUNCIL

Victoria Street, London SW1H 0ET
Tel: 020-7215 5399
Email: sbcsecretariat@sbs.gsi.gov.uk
Web: www.businessadviceonline.org

The Small Business Council was set up in March 2000. It is a non-departmental public body reporting to the Secretary for Trade and Industry on the needs of small businesses. It produces and annual report.
Chairman, W. Sargent
Members, Ms S. Anderson, CBE; J. Braithwaite. CBE; Dr M. Carter; Ms S. Gemmell; P. Morgan; Ms M. Rigby; K. Patel; I. Rees; M. Snyder; Prof. D. Storey; Mrs. M. Tarn; Ms Y. Thompson; J. Torrance; Ms B. Webster, OBE; Mrs S. Brownson, OBE; P. Harrod; B. Jeffrey; J. Karia; G. Osborne; R. Reed; M. Robinson; S. Topman

SMALL BUSINESS SERVICE

Kingsgate House, 66–74 Victoria Street, London SW1E 6SW
Tel: 0114-259 7788; Fax: 0114-259 7330;
Web: www.sbs.gov.uk

The Small Business Service was set up in March 2000. It is an advisory Non-Departmental Public Body reporting to the Secretary for Trade and Industry on the needs of small businesses. It produces an annual report. There are 45 local Business Link franchises throughout England

largely coterminous in their boundaries with the new Learning and Skills.

Chairman, W. Sargent

Members, Ms S. Anderson, CBE; J. Braithwaite, CBE; Ms S. Brownson, OBE; Dr M. Carter; Ms S. Gemmell; P. Harrod; B. Jeffrey; J. Karia; P. Morgan; G. Osborne; K. Patel; R. Reed; I. Rees; Ms M. Rigby; M. Robinson; M. Snyder; Prof. D. Storey; Mrs M. Tarn; Ms Y. Thompson; S. Topman; J. Torrance; Mrs B. Webster, OBE

STATISTICS COMMISSION
10 Great George Street, London SW1P 3AE
Tel: 020-7273 8008;
Email: statscom@statscom.org.uk
Web:www.statscom.org.uk

The Statistics Commission has been set up to advise on the quality, quality assurance and priority-setting for National Statistics, and on the procedures designed to deliver statistical integrity, to help ensure National Statistics are trustworthy and responsive to public needs. It is independent of both Ministers and the producers of National Statistics. It operates in a transparent way with the minutes of its meetings, correspondence and evidence it receives, and advice it gives, all normally publicly available for scrutiny.

Chairman, Sir John Kingman, FRS

Members, Miss C. Bowe; Sir Kenneth Calman, KCB; Ms P. Hodgson; Prof. D. Rhind; Mrs J. Trewsdale; D. Wanless; M. Weale

STRATEGIC RAIL AUTHORITY
55 Victoria Street, London SW1H 0EU
Tel: 020-7654 6000; Fax: 020-7654 6010

The Strategic Rail Authority (SRA) formally came into being on 1 February 2001 following the passage of the Transport Act 2000. On 14 January 2002 it published its Strategic Plan, setting out the strategic priorities for Britain's railways over the next ten years.

As well as providing overall strategic direction for Britain's railways, the SRA has responsibility for consumer protection, the development of rail freight and administering freight grants, and for steering forward investment projects aimed at opening up bottlenecks and expanding network capacity. It is directly responsible for letting and managing passenger rail franchises.

The SRA manages all public sector expenditure in the rail industry and operates under directions and guidance issued by the Secretary of State for Transport. In Scotland it is subject to directions and guidance from the Secretary of State for Transport. In Scotland it is also subject to directions and guidance from the Scottish Minister for Transport, and is also subject to directions and guidance from the Mayor of London in respect of services operating within the capital.

Chairman and Chief Executive, R. Bowker

Non-executive members, L. D. Adams, OBE; D. A. Begg; W. Gallagher; D. Grayson, CBE; P. H. Kent, CBE; J. Mayhew; D. A. Quarmby

Secretary, P. Trewin

TOURISM BODIES

The English Tourism Council, VisitScotland Tourist Board, the Wales Tourist Board and the Northern Ireland Tourist Board are responsible for developing and marketing the tourist industry in their respective countries.

ENGLISH TOURISM COUNCIL, Thames Tower, Black's Road, London W6 9EL. Tel: 020-8563 3000; Fax: 020-8563-0302; Web: www.englishtourism.org.uk
Chief Executive, Ms M. Lynch

VISIT SCOTLAND, 23 Ravelston Terrace, Edinburgh EH4 3TP. Tel: 0131-332 2433; Thistle House, Beechwood Park North, Inverness IV2 3ED Tel: 01463-716996; Web: www.visitscotland.com; *Chairman*, P. Lederer; *Chief Executive*, P. Riddle

WALES TOURIST BOARD, Brunel House, 2 Fitzalan Road, Cardiff CF24 0UY. Tel: 029-2049 9909; Fax: 029-2048 5031; Email: info@tourism.wales.gov.uk; Web: www.visitwales.com *Chief Executive*, J. Jones

NORTHERN IRELAND TOURIST BOARD, St Anne's Court, 59 North Street, Belfast BT1 1NB. Tel: 028-9023 1221; Fax: 028-9024 0960; Email: info@nitb.com; Web: www.discovernorthernireland.com
Chief Executive, A. Clarke

UNITED KINGDOM SPORTS COUNCIL (UK SPORT)
40 Bernard Street, London WC1N 1ST
Tel: 020-7211 5100; Fax: 020-7841 8850
Web: www.uksport.gov.uk

The UK Sports Council (UK Sport) was established by Royal Charter in January 1997. Its role is to focus on high performance sport at UK level, with the aim of achieving sporting excellence in world competition. It works to combat drug misuse, deals with international relations and supports major events. It also distributes the funds allocated to sport from the proceeds of the National Lottery.

Chairman, Sir Rodney Walker

Chief Executive, R. Callicott

UNRELATED LIVE TRANSPLANT
REGULATORY AUTHORITY
c/o Department of Health, Room 339, Wellington House, 133–155 Waterloo Road, London SE1 8UG
Tel: 020-7972 4812; Fax: 020-7972 4852
Web: www.doh.gov.uk/ultra.htm

The Unrelated Live Transplant Regulatory Authority (ULTRA) is a statutory body established in 1990. In every case where the transplant of an organ within the definition of the Human Organ Transplants Act 1989 is proposed between a living donor and a recipient who are not genetically related, the proposal must be referred to ULTRA. Applications must be made by registered medical practitioners.

The Authority comprises a chairman and ten members appointed by the Secretary of State for Health. The secretariat is provided by Department of Health officials.

Chairman, Prof. Sir Roddy MacSween

Members, Prof. J. A. Bradley; Mrs J. H. Callman; Dr J. F. Douglas; Dr H. Draper; Miss P. M. Franklin; Dr S. Fuggle; Dr R. Gokal; A. J. Hooker; Prof. A. Rees; Mrs S. J. Sullivan

Administrative Secretary, E. Scarlett

Medical Secretary, Dr P. Doyle

UK ATOMIC ENERGY AUTHORITY

Harwell, Didcot, Oxon OX11 0RA
Tel: 01235-820220; Fax: 01235-436401
Web: www.ukaea.org.uk

The UKAEA was established by the Atomic Energy Authority Act 1954 and took over responsibility for the research and development of the civil nuclear power programme. The Authority's commercial arm, AEA Technology plc, was privatised in 1996. UKAEA is now responsible for the safe management and decommissioning of its radioactive plant and for maximising the income from the buildings and land on its sites. UKAEA also undertakes special nuclear tasks for the Government, including the UK's contribution to the international fusion programme.
Chairman, D. Tunnicliffe, CBE
Chief Executive, Dr J. McKeown

WALES YOUTH AGENCY

Leslie Court, Lon-y-Llyn, Caerphilly CF83 1BQ
Tel: 029-2085 5700; Fax: 029-2085 5701
Email: wya@wya.org.uk
Web: www.wya.org.uk

The Wales Youth Agency is an independent organisation funded by the National Assembly for Wales to support the youth service in Wales. Its functions include the encouragement and development of the partnership between statutory and voluntary agencies relating to young people; the promotion of staff development and training; and the extension of marketing and information services in the relevant fields. The board of directors does not receive a salary.
Chairman of the Board of Directors, G. Davies
Vice-Chairman of the Board of Directors, Dr H. Williamson, CBE
Chief Executive, B. Williams

WELSH ADMINISTRATION OMBUDSMAN

5th Floor, Capital Tower, Greyfriars Road, Cardiff
CF10 3AG
Tel: 0845-601 0987; Fax: 029-2022 6909
Email: wao.enquiries@ombudsman.gsi.gov.uk
Web: www.ombudsman.org.uk

The Welsh Administration Ombudsman was appointed in July 1999 to investigate complaints by members of the public who have suffered an injustice through maladministration by the National Assembly for Wales and certain public bodies involved in devolved Welsh affairs.
Welsh Administration Ombudsman, vacant

WELSH DEVELOPMENT AGENCY

Plas Glyndwr, Kingsway, Cardiff CF10 3AH
Tel: 0845-777 5577; Fax: 01443-845589

The Agency was established under the Welsh Development Agency Act 1975. Its remit is to help further the regeneration of the economy and improve the environment in Wales. Under the Government of Wales Act 1998, the Land Authority for Wales and the Development Board for Rural Wales merged with the Welsh Development Agency. The Agency is sponsored by the National Assembly for Wales.
The Agency's priorities are to create new businesses and to encourage existing small firms to grow. Its main activities include promoting Wales as a location for inward investment, helping to boost the growth, profitability and competitiveness of indigenous Welsh companies, providing investment capital for industry, encouraging investment by the private sector in property development, grant-aiding land reclamation, and stimulating quality urban and rural development.
Chairman, R. Jones, OBE
Deputy Chairman, T. G. Jones, CBE
Chief Executive, G. Hawker, CBE

WOMEN'S NATIONAL COMMISSION

Room 56/4, Cabinet Office, Horse Guards Road, London SW1P 3AL
Tel: 020-7238 0386; Fax: 020-7238 0387

The Women's National Commission is an independent advisory committee to the Government. Its remit is to ensure that the informed opinions of women are given their due weight in the deliberations of the Government and in public debate on matters of public interest including those of special interest to women. The Commission's sponsoring department is the Cabinet Office.
Chair, vacant
Director, Ms J. Veitch

Regional Government

GREATER LONDON AUTHORITY (GLA)

City Hall, The Queen's Walk, London SE1 2AA
Tel: 020-7983 4000; Press Office: 020-7983 4071/4072/
4090/4067/4228; Email: mayor@london.gov.uk
Web: www.london.gov.uk

On the 7 May 1998 London voted in favour of the formation of the Greater London Authority. The first elections to the GLA were on Thursday, 4 May 2000 and the new Authority took over its responsibilities on 3 July 2000. On 15 July 2002 the GLA moved to one of London's most spectacular new buildings, built on a brown field site on the south bank on the river Thames, adjacent to Tower Bridge.

The structure and objectives of the GLA stem from its eight main areas of responsibility. These are transport, planning, economic development and regeneration, the environment, police, fire and emergency planning, culture and health. The bodies that co-ordinate these functions and report to the GLA are: Transport for London (TfL), the London Development Agency (LDA), the Metropolitan Police Authority (MPA) and the London Fire and Emergency Planning Authority (LFEPA). The GLA also absorbed a number of other London bodies, such as the London Planning Advisory Committee, the London Ecology Unit and the London Research Centre.

The GLA consists of a directly elected Mayor, The Mayor of London, and a separately elected assembly, The London Assembly. The Mayor has the key role of decision making with the Assembly performing the tasks of regulating and scrutinising these decisions. In addition, the GLA has around 400 permanent staff to support the activities of the Mayor and the Assembly, which are overseen by a Head of Paid Service. The Mayor may appoint two political advisors but he/she may not appoint the Chief Executive the Monitoring Officer or the Chief Finance Officer. These must be appointed by the Assembly.

The Mayor is also responsible for appointing an advisory Cabinet. The Cabinet functions as part of the Mayor's objective of eliminating barriers to effective decision making and enabling the GLA to speak with one voice on behalf of London. The function of the Mayor's Cabinet is to provide the Mayor with the most sound advice on policy and strategy. Meetings of the Cabinet are designed to be a powerful forum for discussing the issues affecting Londoners. The Cabinet is not intended to fit the Whitehall Cabinet model in that GLA members will not be bound by the convention of collective responsibility, the absence of which does not mean that the Mayor will devolve or federalise his powers. All decisions are made by the Mayor acting on the honest advice of his Cabinet. Cabinet members can be broadly categorised into (a) those with specific policy brief (e.g. in the areas of planning, policing or fire and civil defence) and (b) those who have been chosen to give advice and/or reflect political breadth.

The role of the Mayor can be broken down into a number of key areas: to represent and promote London at home and abroad and speak up for Londoners; to devise strategies and plans to tackle London-wide issues, such as transport, economic development and regeneration, air quality, noise, waste, bio-diversity, planning and culture; to set budgets for Transport for London, the London Development Agency, the Metropolitan Police Authority and the London Fire and Emergency Planning Authority; to control new transport and economic development bodies and appoint their members; to make appointments to the new police and fire authorities; and to publish regular reports on the state of the environment in London.

The role of the Assembly can be broken down into a number of key areas:

- to provide a check and balance on the Mayor
- to scrutinise the Mayor
- to have the power to amend the Mayor's budget by a majority of 2/3
- to investigate issues of London-wide significance and make proposals to the Mayor
- to provide the Deputy Mayor and the members serving on the police, fire and emergency planning authorities with advice

ELECTIONS AND THE VOTING SYSTEMS

The Assembly will be elected every four years at the same time as the Mayor and consists of 25 members. There is one member from each of the 14 GLA constituencies topped up with 11 London members who are representatives of political parties or individuals standing as independent candidates. The next election will be in May 2004.

The GLA constituencies are: Barnet and Camden; Bexley and Bromley; Brent and Harrow; City and East, covering Barking and Dagenham, the City of London, Newham and Tower Hamlets; Croydon and Sutton; Ealing and Hillingdon; Enfield and Haringey; Greenwich and Lewisham; Havering and Redbridge; North East, covering Hackney, Islington and Waltham Forest; Lambeth and Southwark; West Central, covering Hammersmith and Fulham, Kensington and Chelsea and Westminster; South West, covering Hounslow, Kingston upon Thames and Richmond upon Thames; Merton and Wandsworth.

Two distinct voting systems were used to appoint the existing Mayor and the Assembly. The Mayor was elected using the Supplementary Vote System (SV). With the SVS electors have two votes; one to give the first choice for Mayor and one to give the second choice. Electors cannot vote twice for the same candidate. If one candidate gets more than half of all the first choice votes, he or she becomes Mayor. If no candidate gets more than half the first choice votes, the two candidates with the most first choice votes remain in the election and all the other candidates drop out. The second choice votes on the ballot papers of the candidates who drop out are then counted. Where these second choice votes are for the two remaining candidates they are added to the first choice votes these candidates already have. The candidate with the most first and second choice votes combined would become the Mayor of London.

The Assembly was appointed using the Additional Member System (AM). Under AMS, electors have two votes. The first vote is for a constituency candidate. The second vote is for a party list or individual candidate contesting the London-wide Assembly seats. The 14 constituency members were elected under the first-past-the-post system, the same system used in general and local elections. Electors vote for one candidate and the candidate with the most votes wins. The Additional (London) Members were drawn from party lists or were independent candidates who stood as London Members.

The Greater London Returning Officer (GLRO) was the independent official responsible for running the first election in London. The GLRO had overall responsibility for running a free, fair and efficient election. He was supported in this by Returning Officers in each of the 14 London Constituencies.

GLRO, Robert V. Hughes, CBE

FUNCTIONS AND STRUCTURE

Every aspect of the Assembly and its activities must be open to the view of the public and therefore accountable. Assembly meetings are open to the public and the reports it produces are available to the public. Other measures such as a twice yearly 'people's question time' also take place. The meetings where the Assembly questions the Mayor are also open to the public.

TRANSPORT FOR LONDON (TfL)

TfL is run by a board of 8-15 members appointed by the Mayor. Its role is:

• to manage the buses, Croydon Tramlink and the Docklands Light Railway (DLR)
• to manage the underground once Public Private partnership contracts are in place
• to manage an important network of roads to be known as the GLA Road Network
• to regulate taxis and minicabs
• to run the London River Services and promote the river for passenger and freight movement
• to help to co-ordinate the Dial-a-Ride and Taxicard schemes for door-to-door services for transport users with mobility problems
• to take responsibility for traffic lights

London Borough Councils maintain the role of highway and traffic authorities for 95 per cent of London's roads. A £5 congestion charge for motorists driving into central London is set to be introduced in February 2003.
Transport Commissioner for London, Robert Kiley

SPATIAL DEVELOPMENT STRATEGY (SDS)

The Mayor of London is responsible for strategic planning in London in the form of a Spatial Planning Strategy (The London Plan). This sets priorities and provides direction for the future development of London. It replaces regional planning guidance provided by the Office of the Deputy Prime Minister. The SDS incorporates the key aspects of the many other areas of the Mayor's responsibility including sustainable development, transport, economic development, housing, the built environment, the natural and open environment, waste, town centres, cultural and community facilities, London's Capital and World City roles and the River Thames. London Borough Councils continue to deal with all planning applications and produce development plans.

LONDON DEVELOPMENT AGENCY (LDA)

The LDA promotes economic development and regeneration. It is one of the eight regional development agencies set up around the country to perform this task. The key aspects of the LDA's role are:

• to promote business efficiency, investment and competitiveness
• to promote employment
• to enhance the skills of local people
• to create sustainable development

The London Boroughs retain powers to promote economic development in their local areas.

THE ENVIRONMENT

The Mayor is required to formulate strategies to tackle London's environmental issues including the quality of water, air and land; the use of energy and London's contribution to climate change targets; ground water levels and traffic emissions; and municipal waste management.

METROPOLITAN POLICE AUTHORITY (MPA)

This body, which oversees the policing of London consists of 12 members of the assembly, including the deputy Mayor, 4 magistrates and 7 independents. One of the independents was appointed by the Home Secretary. The role of the MPA is:

• to maintain an efficient and effective police force
• to publish an annual policing plan
• to set police targets and monitor performance
• to be part of the appointment, discipline and removal of senior officers
• to be responsible for the performance budget

The boundaries of the metropolitan police districts have been changed to be in line with the 32 London boroughs. Areas beyond the GLA remit have been incorporated into the Surrey, Hertfordshire and Essex police areas. The City of London has its own police force.

LONDON FIRE AND EMERGENCY PLANNING AUTHORITY (LFEPA)

On 3 July 2000 the existing London Fire and Civil Defence Authority became the London Fire and Emergency Planning Authority. It consists of 17 members, 9 drawn from the assembly and 8 from the London Boroughs. The role of LFEPA is:

• to set the strategy for the provision of fire services
• to ensure that the fire brigade can meet all the normal requirements efficiently
• to ensure that effective arrangements are made for the fire brigade to receive emergency calls and deal with them promptly
• to ensure that information useful to the development of the fire brigades is gathered
• to assist the boroughs with their emergency planning training and exercises

THE CULTURAL STRATEGY GROUP FOR LONDON (CSGL)

The GLA aims to provide a wide ranging culture strategy, encompassing the arts, sport and tourism. The CSGL provides advice and guidance to the GLA on this matter. Its role is:

• to produce a strategy for the cultural development of London
• to endorse and bid for major sporting events which London may host
• to develop the creative industries' contribution to the London economy
• to take over management of Trafalgar Square and Parliament Square
• to develop a policy for the development of tourism in London

SALARIES *as at July 2002*

Mayor	£108,000
Deputy Mayor	£67,150
Assembly Member	£45,950

MAYOR'S ADVISORY CABINET

Deputy Mayor and Spatial Development and Strategic
  Planning, Nicky Gavron
Chair, Cultural Strategy, Yasmin Anwar
Chair, London Fire and Emergency Planning Authority,
  Val Shawcross
Chair, London Development Agency, George Barlow
City and Business, Judith Mayhew
Community Partnerships, Richard Stone
Disability Rights, Caroline Gooding
Environment, Victor Anderson
Health, Sue Atkinson
Homelessness, Glenda Jackson
Human Rights and Equalities, Graham Tope
Lesbian and Gay Issues, Angela Mason
Liberal Democrats, Lynne Featherstone
Older People, Graeme Matthews
Police, Lord Harris of Haringey
Race Relations, Lee Jasper
Regeneration, Kumar Murshid
Trade Unions, Rod Robertson
Urban Strategy, Richard Rogers
Women and Equality, Diane Abbott

GREATER LONDON ASSEMBLY MEMBERS
AS AT 31 JULY 2002

The Mayor, Ken Livingstone, (Ind.)
Anderson, Victor (Green), London List
Arnold, Jennette (Lab.), London List
Arbour, Anthony (C.), South West, maj. 7,059
Barnes, Richard (C.), Ealing and Hillingdon, maj. 6,812
Biggs, John (Lab.), City and East, maj. 26,121
Bray, Angie (C.), West Central, maj. 18,279
Coleman, Brian (C.), Barnet and Camden, maj. 551
Duvall, Len (Lab.), Greenwich and Lewisham, maj. 17,985
Evans, Jeremy Roger (C.), Havering and Redbridge, maj.
  8,269
Featherstone, Lynne (LD), London List
Gavron, Nicky (Lab.), Enfield and Haringey, maj. 3,302
Hamwee, Baroness Sally (LD), London List
Harris, Lord Toby (Lab.), Brent and Harrow, maj. 4,380
Heath, Samantha (Lab.), London List
Hillier, Meg (Lab.), North East, maj. 17,603
Howlett, Elizabeth (C.), Merton and Wandsworth, maj.
  12,870
Johnson, Darren (Green), London List
Jones, Jennifer (Green), London List
Neill, Bob (C.), Bexley and Bromley, maj. 34,559
Ollerenshaw, Eric (C.), London List
Pelling, Andrew John (C.), Croydon and Sutton, maj.
  17,087
Phillips, Trevor (Lab.), London List
Shawcross, Valerie (Lab.), Lambeth and Southwark, maj.
  15,493
Tope, Graham (LD), London List
*Tuffrey, Mike (LD), London List
*Replaced Louise Bloom (LD) London List

THE NATIONAL ASSEMBLY FOR WALES

Cathays Park, Cardiff CF1 3NQ
Tel: 029-2082 5111;
National Assembly Information Line: 029-2089 8200
Email: webmaster@wales.gov.uk
Web: www.wales.gov.uk
In July 1997 the Government announced plans to
establish a National Assembly for Wales. In a referendum
on 18 September 1997 about 50 per cent of the electorate
voted, of whom 50.3 per cent voted in favour of the
Assembly. Elections are to be held every four years. The
First elections were held on 6 May 1999 when about 46
per cent of the electorate voted.
  The Assembly has 60 members (including the Presiding
Officer), comprising 40 constituency members and 20
additional regional members from party lists. It can
introduce only secondary legislation and has no power to
raise or lower income tax.
  The National Assembly for Wales has responsibility in
Wales for ministerial functions relating to health and
personal social services; education, except for terms and
conditions of service and student awards; training; the
Welsh language, arts and culture; the implementation of
the Citizen's Charter in Wales; local government; housing;
water and sewerage; environmental protection; sport;
agriculture and fisheries; forestry; land use, including
town and country planning and countryside and nature
conservation; new towns; non-departmental public
bodies and appointments in Wales; ancient monuments
and historic buildings and the Welsh Arts Council; roads;
tourism; financial assistance to industry; the Strategic
Development Scheme in Wales and the Programme for
the Valleys; and the operation of the European Regional
Development Fund in Wales and other European Union
matters. See also Office of the Secretary of State for Wales.

SALARIES FROM 1 APRIL 2002:

†First Minister	£69,862
†Minister/Presiding Officer	£36,241
Assembly Members	£41,500*

* Reduced by two-thirds if the member is already an MP or an
  MEP
† First Minister, Ministers and Presiding Officer also receive
  the Assembly Member salary

THE WELSH ASSEMBLY GOVERNMENT
First Minister of the Assembly, Rhodri Morgan, AM
  Principal Private Secretary, L. Conway
  Special Advisers, P. Griffiths; M. Drakeford; Dr R.
    Jones; L. Punter; N. Bennett; M. Hines
Deputy First Minister and Minister for Rural Development
  and Wales Abroad, Michael German, OBE, AM
Minister for Economic Development, Andrew Davies, AM
Minister for Education and Lifelong Learning, Jane
  Davidson, AM
Minister for Environment, Planning and Transport, Sue
  Essex, AM
Minister for Finance and Communities, Edwina Hunt, AM
Minister for Health and Social Services, Jane Hutt, AM
Minister for Open Government, Carwyn Jones, AM
Minister for Sport, Culture and the Welsh Language,
  Jenny Randerson, AM
Permanent Secretary (G1), J. D. Shortridge KCB

OFFICE OF THE PRESIDING OFFICER
Clerk to the Assembly, P. Silk, CB

COMMITTEE SECRETARIAT
Grade 5, Ms M. Knox

CABINET SECRETARIAT
Grade 5, L. Conway

OFFICE OF THE COUNSEL GENERAL
Counsel General, W. Roddick, QC

COMMUNICATIONS DIRECTORATE
Head, M. Brooke

STRATEGIC POLICY UNIT
Head, M. Quinn

*Personnel, Management and Business Services Group
(G3)*, P. Gregory
Heads of Divisions (G5), G. A. Thomas, M. Harper,
  Mrs M. Evans; N. Finlayson
Chief Statistician (G5), W. R. L. Alldritt
Head of Health Statistics and Analysis Unit (G6),
  P. Demery

FINANCE GROUP
Principal Finance Officer (G3), D. T. Richards
Head of Division (G5), L. A. Pavelin
Senior Economic Adviser (G5), M. G. Phelps
Head of Internal Audit (G6), D. A. McNeill

ECONOMIC AFFAIRS, TRANSPORT,
PLANNING AND ENVIRONMENT
Senior Director (G2), D. W. Jones

AGRICULTURE AND RURAL AFFAIRS DEPARTMENT
Head of Department (G3), H. D. Brodie
Heads of Division (G5), M. Dunn; G. Jones;
  R. O'Sullivan; R. C. Williams

ECONOMIC DEVELOPMENT DEPARTMENT
Head of Department (G3), D. Pritchard
Heads of Divisions (G5), M. J. Clancy; M. Cochlin;
  W. G. Davies; R. Loveland

SOCIAL POLICY AND LOCAL
GOVERNMENT
Senior Director (G2), G. C. G. Craig

TRAINING AND EDUCATION DEPARTMENT
Head of Department (G3), R. J. Davies
Heads of Divisions (G5), R. Thomas; D. R. Adams;
  J. Howells; Mrs E. A. Taylor; A. Lansdown; R. Keveren

OFFICE OF HM CHIEF INSPECTOR FOR SCHOOLS IN
WALES – ESTYN
Chief Inspector (G4), Miss S. Lewis
Staff Inspectors (G5), M. G. Haines; C. Abbott
There are 45 Grade 6 Inspectors.
Head of Administration (G7), Mrs S. Howells

SOCIAL SERVICES AND COMMUNITIES GROUP
Director, Ms H. Thomas

LOCAL GOVERNMENT GROUP
Head of Group (G3), A. Peat
Heads of Divisions (G5), Ms K. Cassidy; A. Thornton

NHS DIRECTORATE
Director (G3), Mrs A. Lloyd
Heads of Divisions (G5), Ms S. Beaver; J. Morgan,
  S. Redmond; Ms J. Gregory; M. Ponton; R. Phillips;
  Dr B. Fuge

HEALTH PROTECTION AND IMPROVEMENT
DIRECTORATE
Chief Medical Officer (G3), Dr R. Hall
Principal Medical Officers (G4), Dr B. Fuge;
  Dr M. Ponton
Senior Medical Officers (G5), Dr J. Ludlow;
  Dr H. N. Williams; Dr D. Salter
Chief Dental Officer (G5), P. Langmaid
Chief Scientific Adviser (G5), Dr J. A. V. Pritchard
Deputy Scientific Adviser (G6), Dr E. O. Crawley
Chief Pharmaceutical Adviser (G5), Miss C. W. Howells
Chief Environmental Health Adviser (G5), R. Alexander
Deputy Environmental Health Adviser (G6),
  D. Worthington

NURSING DIVISION
Chief Nursing Officer, Miss R. Kennedy
Nursing Officers, P. Johnson; M. F. Tonkin; Mrs H. Wood;
  Mrs R. Johnson; Miss M. Parker; Mrs T. Donnelly;
  Mrs H. Wood

TRANSPORT, PLANNING AND ENVIRONMENT GROUP
Head of Group (G3), M. L. Evans
Director of Transport (G4), R. Shaw
Heads of Divisions (G5), J. R. Rees (*Roads Construction
  Grade 7*), R. H. Powell; I. P. Davies; R. K. Cones; K. J.
  A. Tengy; T. J. Collins; S. C. Shouler; M. J. Gilbert; T.
  C. Dorken; M. J. A. Parker; I. A. Grindulis; A. D.
  Perry; Dr M. C. Dunn

EXECUTIVE AGENCIES

CADW: WELSH HISTORIC MONUMENTS

FARMING AND RURAL CONSERVATION AGENCY

INTERVENTION BOARD

PLANNING INSPECTORATE

MEMBERS OF THE WELSH ASSEMBLY
AS AT MAY 2002

Barrett, Ms Lorraine, *Lab. Co-op., Cardiff South and
  Penarth*, maj. 6,803
Bates, Mick, *LD, Montgomeryshire*, maj. 5,504
Black, Peter, *LD, South Wales West region*
Bourne, Prof. Nicholas, *C., Wales Mid and West region*
Burnham, Eleanor, *LD, Wales North region*
Butler, Ms Rosemary, *Lab., Newport West*, maj. 4,710
Cairns, Alun, *C., South Wales West region*
Chapman, Ms Christine, *Lab. Co-op., Cynon Valley*, maj.
  677
Dafis, Cynog G., *PC, Wales Mid and West region*
Davidson, Ms Jane, *Lab., Pontypridd*, maj. 1,575
Davies, Andrew, *Lab., Swansea West*, maj. 1,926
Davies, David, *C., Monmouth*, maj. 2,712
Davies, Geraint, *PC, Rhondda*, maj. 2,285
Davies, Glyn, *C., Wales Mid and West region*
Davies, Ms Janet, *PC, South Wales West region*
Davies, Ms Jocelyn, *PC, South Wales East region*
Davies, Rt. Hon. Ronald, *Lab., Caerphilly*, maj. 2,861
Edwards, Richard, *Lab., Preseli Pembrokeshire*, maj. 2,738
Elis Thomas, Dafydd, *PC, Meirionnydd Nant Conwy*,
  maj. 8,742
Essex, Ms Sue, *Lab., Cardiff North*, maj. 2,304
Evans, Delyth, *Lab., Wales Mid and West region*
German, Michael, *LD, South Wales East region*
Gibbons, Brian, *Lab., Aberavon*, maj. 6,743
Graham, William, *C., South Wales East region*
Gregory, Ms Janice, *Lab., Ogmore*, maj. 4,565
Griffiths, John, *Lab. Co-op., Newport East*, maj. 5,111

Gwyther, Ms Christine, *Lab., Carmarthen West and Pembrokeshire South*, maj. 1,492
Halford, Ms Alison, *Lab., Delyn*, maj. 5,417
Hancock, Brian, *PC, Islwyn*, maj. 604
Hart, Ms Edwina, *Lab., Gower*, maj. 3,160
Hutt, Ms Jane, *Lab., Vale of Glamorgan*, maj. 926
Jarman, Ms Pauline, *PC, South Wales Central region*
Jones, Ms Ann, *Lab., Vale of Clwyd*, maj. 3,341
Jones, Carwyn, *Lab., Bridgend*, maj. 4,258
Jones, Elin, *PC, Ceredigion*, maj. 10,249
Jones, Gareth, *PC, Conwy*, maj. 114
Jones, Ms Helen Mary, *PC, Llanelli*, maj. 688
Jones, Ieuan W., *PC, Ynys Môn*, maj. 9,288
Law, Peter, *Lab. Co-op., Blaenau Gwent*, maj. 10,568
Lewis, Huw, *Lab. Co-op., Merthyr Tydfil and Rhymney*, maj. 4,214
Lloyd, Dr David, *PC, South Wales West region*
*Lloyd, Ms Val, *Lab., Swansea East*, maj. 5,019
Marek, Dr John, *Lab., Wrexham*, maj. 6,472
Melding, David, *C., South Wales Central region*
Middlehurst, Tom, *Lab., Alyn and Deeside*, maj. 6,359
Morgan, H. Rhodri, *Lab., Cardiff West*, maj. 10,859
Morgan, Jonathan, *C., South Wales Central region*
Neagle, Ms Lynne, *Lab., Torfaen*, maj. 5,285
Pugh, Alun, *Lab., Clwyd West*, maj. 760
Randerson, Ms Jenny, *LD, Cardiff Central*, maj. 3,168

Richards, Rod, *C., Wales North region*
Rogers, Peter, *C., Wales North region*
Ryder, Ms Janet, *PC, Wales North region*
Sinclair, Ms Karen, *Lab., Clwyd South*, maj. 3,685
Thomas, Ms Gwenda, *Lab., Neath*, maj. 2,618
Thomas, Owen John, *PC, South Wales Central region*
Thomas, Rhodri, *PC, Carmarthen East and Dinefwr*, maj. 6,980
Wigley, Rt. Hon. Dafydd, *PC, Caernarfon*, maj. 12,273
Williams, Ms Kirsty, *LD, Brecon and Radnorshire*, maj. 5,852
Williams, Dr Phil, *PC, South Wales East region*

* Val Feld died on 17 July 2001. She was replaced by Val Lloyd.

STATE OF THE PARTIES AS AT MAY 2002

	Constituency AMs	Regional AMs	Total
Labour	27	1	28
Plaid Cymru	8†	8	16†
Conservative	1	8	9
Liberal Democrats	3	3	6
The Presiding Officer (The Lord Elis-Thomas)	1	0	1

† Excludes the Presiding Officer, who has no party allegiance while in post

Welsh Assembly AS AT MAY 1999

CONSTITUENCIES

ABERAVON (S. WALES WEST)
E. 49,786 *T.* 46.79%
B. Gibbons, *Lab.*	11,941
Ms J. Davies, *PC*	5,198
K. Davies, *LD*	3,165
Ms M. E. Davies, *C.*	1,624
Capt. Beany, *Bean*	849
D. Pudner, *United Soc.*	517
Lab. majority 6,743

ALYN AND DEESIDE (WALES N.)
E. 59,386 *T.* 32.04%
T. Middlehurst, *Lab.*	9,772
N. Formstone, *C.*	3,413
Ms A. Owen, *PC*	2,304
J. Clarke, *LD*	1,879
J. Cooksey, *Ind.*	1,333
G. Davies, *Comm.*	329
Lab. majority 6,359

BLAENAU GWENT (S. WALES EAST)
E. 53,919 *T.* 48.21%
P. Law, *Lab. Co-op.*	16,069
P. Williams, *PC*	5,501
K. Rogers, *LD*	2,980
D. Thomas, *C.*	1,444
Lab. Co-op. majority 10,568

BRECON AND RADNORSHIRE (WALES MID AND W.)
E. 51,166 *T.* 57.10%
Ms K. Williams, *LD*	13,022
N. Bourne, *C.*	7,170
I. Janes, *Lab. Co-op.*	5,165
D. Patterson, *PC*	2,356
M. Shaw, *Ind.*	1,502
LD majority 5,852

BRIDGEND (S. WALES WEST)
E. 60,234 *T.* 41.56%
C. Jones, *Lab.*	9,321
A. Cairns, *C.*	5,063
J. Canning, *PC*	4,919
R. Humphreys, *LD*	3,910
A. Jones, *Ind.*	1,819
Lab. majority 4,258

CAERNARFON (WALES N.)
E. 47,213 *T.* 60.32%
D. Wigley, *PC*	18,748
T. Jones, *Lab.*	6,475
Ms B. Naish, *C.*	2,464
D. Shankland, *LD*	791
PC majority 12,273

CAERPHILLY (S. WALES EAST)
E. 65,997 *T.* 43.20%
R. Davies, *Lab.*	12,602
R. Gough, *PC*	9,741
M. German, *LD*	3,543
Ms M. Taylor, *C.*	2,213
T. Richards, *United Soc.*	412
Lab. majority 2,861

CARDIFF CENTRAL (S. WALES CENTRAL)
E. 57,815 *T.* 44.75%
Ms J. Randerson, *LD*	10,937
M. Drakeford, *Lab.*	7,769
O. J. Thomas, *PC*	3,795
S. Jones, *C.*	3,034
J. Goss, *United Soc.*	338
LD majority 3,168

CARDIFF NORTH (S. WALES CENTRAL)
E. 61,398 *T.* 51.33%
Ms S. Essex, *Lab.*	12,198
J. Morgan, *C.*	9,894
A. Meikle, *LD*	5,088
C. Mann, *PC*	4,337
Lab. majority 2,304

CARDIFF SOUTH AND PENARTH (S. WALES CENTRAL)
E. 61,149 *T.* 37.67%
Ms L. Barrett, *Lab. Co-op.*	11,057
Ms M. Davies, *C.*	4,254
J. Rowlands, *PC*	3,931
Ms J. Maw-Cornish, *LD*	2,890
D. Bartlett, *United Soc.*	355
J. Foreman, *Ind. Lab.*	339
T. Davies, *Celtic All.*	210
Lab. Co-op. majority 6,803

CARDIFF WEST (S. WALES CENTRAL)
E. 57,717 *T.* 40.22%
R. Morgan, *Lab.*	14,305
Ms M. Boult, *C.*	3,446
Ms E. Bush, *PC*	3,402
D. Garrow-Smith, *LD*	2,063
Lab. majority 10,859

CARMARTHEN EAST AND DINEFWR (WALES MID AND W.)
E. 53,634 *T.* 60.88%
R. Thomas, *PC*	17,328
C. Llewellyn, *Lab.*	10,348
Ms H. Stoddart, *C.*	2,776
Ms J. Hughes, *LD*	2,202
PC majority 6,980

CARMARTHEN WEST AND PEMBROKESHIRE SOUTH (WALES MID AND W.)
E. 55,655 *T.* 50.58%
Ms C. Gwyther, *Lab.*	9,891
R. Llewellyn, *PC*	8,399
D. Edwards, *C.*	5,079
E. Davies, *Ind.*	2,090
R. Williams, *LD*	1,875
G. Fry, *TFPW*	815
Lab. majority 1,492

CEREDIGION (WALES MID AND W.)
E. 55,311 *T.* 57.67%

E. Jones, *PC*	15,258
Ms M. Battle, *Lab.*	5,009
D. Lloyd Evans, *Ind.*	4,114
D. Evans, *LD*	3,571
H. Lloyd Davies, *C.*	2,944
D. Bradney, *Green*	1,002
PC majority 10,249	

CLWYD SOUTH (WALES N.)
E. 53,843 *T.* 40.51%

Ms K. Sinclair, *Lab.*	9,196
H. Williams, *PC*	5,511
D. R. Jones, *C.*	4,167
D. Burnham, *LD*	2,432
M. Jones, *United Soc.*	508
Lab. majority 3,685	

CLWYD WEST (WALES N.)
E. 53,952 *T.* 46.77%

A. Pugh, *Lab.*	7,824
R. Richards, *C.*	7,064
Ms E. Williams, *PC*	6,886
Ms R. Feeley, *LD*	3,462
Lab. majority 760	

CONWY (WALES N.)
E. 55,189 *T.* 49.11%

G. Jones, *PC*	8,285
Ms C. Sherrington, *Lab.*	8,171
D. I. Jones, *C.*	5,006
*Ms C. Humphreys, *LD*	4,480
G. Edwards, *Ind.*	1,160
PC majority 114	

* C. Humphreys resigned in April 2001. Replaced by Ms E. Burnham.

CYNON VALLEY (S. WALES CENTRAL)
E. 47,619 *T.* 45.50%

Ms C. Chapman, *Lab. Co-op.*	9,883
P. Richards, *PC*	9,206
Ms A. Willott, *LD*	1,531
E. Hayward, *C.*	1,046
Lab. Co-op. majority 677	

DELYN (WALES N.)
E. 54,047 *T.* 44.13%

Ms A. Halford, *Lab.*	10,672
Ms K. Lumley, *C.*	5,255
Ms M. Ellis, *PC*	4,837
Ms E. Burnham, *LD*	3,089
Lab. majority 5,417	

GOWER (S. WALES WEST)
E. 58,523 *T.* 47.33%

Ms E. Hart, *Lab.*	9,813
D. Jones, *PC*	6,653
A. Jones, *C.*	3,912
H. Evans, *LD*	3,260
R. Lewis, *Ind.*	2,307
I. Richard, *PRP*	1,755
Lab. majority 3,160	

ISLWYN (S. WALES EAST)
E. 50,600 *T.* 47.29%

B. Hancock, *PC*	10,042
S. Williams, *Lab.*	9,438
Ms C. Bennett, *LD*	2,351
C. Stevens, *C.*	1,621

I. Thomas, *United Soc.*	475
PC majority 604	

LLANELLI (WALES MID AND W.)
E. 58,371 *T.* 48.63%

Ms H. M. Jones, *PC*	11,973
Ms A. Garrard, *Lab. Co-op.*	11,285
T. Dumper, *LD*	2,920
B. Harding, *C.*	1,864
A. Popham, *Ind.*	345
PC majority 688	

MEIRIONNYDD NANT CONWY (WALES MID AND W.)
E. 32,922 *T.* 57.33%

D. Elis Thomas, *PC*	12,034
Ms D. Jones, *Lab.*	3,292
O. J. Williams, *C.*	2,170
G. Worley, *LD*	1,378
PC majority 8,742	

MERTHYR TYDFIL AND RHYMNEY (S. WALES EAST)
E. 55,858 *T.* 44.91%

H. Lewis, *Lab. Co-op.*	11,024
A. Cox, *PC*	6,810
A. Rogers, *Ind.*	3,746
E. Jones, *LD*	1,682
Ms C. Hyde, *C.*	1,246
M. Jenkins, *United Soc.*	580
Lab. Co-op. majority 4,214	

MONMOUTH (S. WALES EAST)
E. 61,999 *T.* 51.13%

D. Davies, *C.*	12,950
Ms C. Short, *Lab.*	10,238
C. Lines, *LD*	4,639
M. Hubbard, *PC*	1,964
A. Carrington, *TFPW*	1,911
C. majority 2,712	

MONTGOMERYSHIRE (WALES MID AND W.)
E. 43,386 *T.* 49.41%

M. Bates, *LD*	10,374
G. Davies, *C.*	4,870
D. Senior, *PC*	3,554
C. Hewitt, *Lab.*	2,638
LD majority 5,504	

NEATH (S. WALES WEST)
E. 56,085 *T.* 47.95%

Ms G. Thomas, *Lab.*	12,234
T. Jones, *PC*	9,616
D. Davies, *LD*	2,631
Ms J. Chambers, *C.*	1,895
N. Duncan, *United Soc.*	519
Lab. majority 2,618	

NEWPORT EAST (S. WALES EAST)
E. 54,196 *T.* 35.45%

J. Griffiths, *Lab. Co-op.*	9,497
M. Major, *C.*	4,386
A. Cameron, *LD*	2,684
C. Holland, *PC*	2,647
Lab. Co-op. majority 5,111	

NEWPORT WEST (S. WALES EAST)
E. 57,243 *T.* 42.34%

Ms R. Butler, *Lab.*	11,538
W. Graham, *C.*	6,828
R. Vickery, *PC*	3,053

Ms V. Watkins, *LD*	2,820
Lab. majority 4,710	

OGMORE (S. WALES WEST)
E. 51,998 *T.* 41.54%

Ms J. Gregory, *Lab.*	10,407
J. Rogers, *PC*	5,842
R. Hughes, *Ind.*	2,439
Ms S. Waye, *LD*	1,496
C. Smart, *C.*	1,415
Lab. majority 4,565	

PONTYPRIDD (S. WALES CENTRAL)
E. 64,597 *T.* 45.71%

Ms J. Davidson, *Lab.*	11,330
B. Hancock, *PC*	9,755
G. Orsi, *LD*	5,240
Ms S. Ingerfield, *C.*	2,485
P. Phillips, *Ind.*	436
R. Griffiths, *Comm.*	280
Lab. majority 1,575	

PRESELI PEMBROKESHIRE (WALES MID AND W.)
E. 54,225 *T.* 53.63%

R. Edwards, *Lab.*	9,977
C. Bryant, *PC*	7,239
F. Aubel, *C.*	6,585
D. Lloyd, *LD*	3,338
A. Luke, *Ind.*	1,944
Lab. majority 2,738	

RHONDDA (S. WALES CENTRAL)
E. 55,398 *T.* 50.22%

G. Davies, *PC*	13,558
W. David, *Lab.*	11,273
M. Williams, *LD*	1,303
G. Summers, *Ind.*	913
P. Hobbins, *C.*	774
PC majority 2,285	

SWANSEA EAST (S. WALES WEST)
E. 57,766 *T.* 36.07%

*Ms V. Feld, *Lab.*	9,495
J. Ball, *PC*	5,714
P. Black, *LD*	3,963
W. Hughes, *C.*	1,663
Lab. majority 3,781	

*By-election held in September 2001 due to death of Ms Feld

SWANSEA WEST (S. WALES WEST)
E. 59,369 *T.* 39.97%

A. Davies, *Lab.*	8,217
D. Lloyd, *PC*	6,291
P. Valerio, *C.*	3,643
J. Newbury, *LD*	3,543
D. Evans, *Ind.*	996
J. Harris, *PRP*	774
A. Thraves, *United Soc.*	263
Lab. majority 1,926	

TORFAEN (S. WALES EAST)
E. 61,037 *T.* 39.19%

Ms L. Neagle, *Lab.*	9,080
M. Gough, *Ind. Lab.*	3,795
Ms I. Nutt, *LD*	2,828
N. Turner, *PC*	2,614
Ms J. Gray, *LD*	2,614
Ms K. Thomas, *C.*	2,152

S. Smith, *Local Soc.*   839
Lab. majority 5,285

VALE OF CLWYD (WALES N.)
E. 51,124 T. 43.43%

Ms A. Jones, *Lab.*	8,359
R. Salisbury, *C.*	5,018
Ms S. Brynach, *PC*	4,295
G. Clague, *Dem. All.*	1,908
P. Lloyd, *LD*	1,376
D. Roberts, *Ind.*	661
D. Pennant, *Ind.*	586

Lab. majority 3,341

VALE OF GLAMORGAN (S. WALES CENTRAL)
E. 67,804 T. 48.31%

Ms J. Hutt, *Lab.*	11,448
D. Melding, *C.*	10,522
C. Franks, *PC*	7,848
F. Little, *LD*	2,938

Lab. majority 926

WREXHAM (WALES N.)
E. 50,932 T. 34.19%

J. Marek, *Lab.*	9,239
Ms C. O'Toole, *LD*	2,767
Ms F. Elphick, *C.*	2,747
Ms J. Ryder, *PC*	2,659

Lab. majority 6,472

YNYS MON (WALES N.)
E. 52,571 T. 59.56%

I. W. Jones, *PC*	16,469
A. Owen, *Lab.*	7,181
P. Rogers, *C.*	6,031
J. Clarke, *LD*	1,630

PC majority 9,288

BY-ELECTIONS

SWANSEA EAST (S. WALES WEST)
(27 September 2001)
E. 57,057 T. 22.62%

V. Lloyd, *Lab.*	7,484
J. Ball, *PC*	2,465
R. Speht, *LD*	1,592
G. Rowbottom, *C.*	675
T. Jenkins, *UKIP*	243

M. Shrewsbury, *GP*	206
A. Thompson, *WSA*	173
Capt. Beany, *NMBP*	37

Lab. majority 5,019

REGIONS

SOUTH WALES CENTRAL
E. 473,494 T. 45.51%

Lab.	79,564 (36.92%)
PC	58,080 (26.95%)
C.	34,944 (16.22%)
LD	30,911 (14.35%)
Green	5,336 (2.48%)
Soc. Lab.	2,822 (1.31%)
Ind. Matt.	1,524 (0.71%)
NLP	665 (0.31%)
Comm.	652 (0.30%)
United Soc.	602 (0.28%)
Ind. Phill.	378 (0.18%)

Lab. majority 21,484
(May 1997, *Lab.* maj. 131,398)
Additional Members: J. Morgan, *C.*;
   D. Melding, *C.*; Ms P. Jarman,
   PC; O. J. Thomas, *PC*

SOUTH WALES EAST
E. 460,846 T. 43.95%

Lab.	83,953 (41.45%)
PC	49,139 (24.26%)
C.	33,947 (16.76%)
LD	24,757 (12.22%)
Soc. Lab.	4,879 (2.41%)
Green	4,055 (2.00%)
United Soc.	903 (0.45%)
NLP	898 (0.44%)

Lab. majority 34,814
(May 1997, *Lab.* maj. 163,134)
Additional Members: W. Graham,
   C.; M. German, *LD*; Ms J. Davies,
   PC; Dr P. Williams, *PC*

SOUTH WALES WEST
E. 393,758 T. 42.44%

Lab.	70,625 (42.26%)
PC	50,757 (30.37%)
C.	20,993 (12.56%)

LD	18,527 (11.09%)
Green	4,082 (2.44%)
United Soc.	1,257 (0.75%)
NLP	676 (0.40%)
PRP	204 (0.12%)

Lab. majority 19,868
(May 1997, Lab. maj. 142,286)
Additional Members: A. Cairns, *C.*;
   P. Black, *LD*; Dr D. Lloyd, *PC*; Ms
   J. Davies, *PC*

WALES MID AND WEST
E. 404,667 T. 54.21%

PC	84,554 (38.55%)
Lab.	53,842 (24.55%)
C.	36,622 (16.70%)
LD	31,683 (14.44%)
Green	7,718 (3.52%)
Soc. Lab.	3,019 (1.38%)
Ind. Turner	1,214 (0.55%)
NLP	705 (0.32%)

PC majority 30,712
(May 1997, Lab. maj. 52,382)
Additional Members: G. Davies, *C.*;
   Prof. N. Bourne, *C.*; *A. Michael,
   Lab.*; C. Dafis, *PC*

* A. Michael resigned in March 2000.
Replaced by D. Evans.

WALES NORTH
E. 478,252 T. 45.06%

Lab.	73,673 (34.19%)
PC	69,518 (32.26%)
C.	41,700 (19.35%)
LD	22,130 (10.27%)
Green	4,667 (2.17%)
Rhuddlan	1,353 (0.63%)
NLP	917 (0.43%)
United Soc.	828 (0.38%)
Comm.	714 (0.33%)

Lab. majority 4,155
(May 1997, Lab. maj. 80,590)
Additional Members: P. Rogers, *C.*;
   R. Richards, *C.*; Ms C.
   Humphreys, *LD*; Ms J. Ryder, *PC*

* C. Humpreys resigned in April 2001.
Replaced by Ms E. Burnham.

THE SCOTTISH PARLIAMENT
Edinburgh EH99 1SP. Tel: 0131-348 5000;
Email: sp.info@scottish.parliament.uk
Web: www.scottish.parliament.uk

In July 1997 the Government announced plans to establish a Scottish Parliament. In a referendum on 11 September 1997 about 62 per cent of the electorate voted, of whom 74.3 per cent voted in favour of the Parliament and 63.5 in favour of its having tax-raising powers. Elections are to be held every four years. The first elections were held on 6 May 1999 when about 59 per cent of the electorate voted. The first session was held on 12 May 1999 and the Scottish Parliament was officially opened on 1 July 1999 at the Edinburgh Assembly Hall; a new building to house the Parliament is under construction in Edinburgh.

The Scottish Parliament has 129 members (including the Presiding Officer), comprising 73 constituency members and 56 additional regional members from party lists. It can introduce primary legislation and has the power to raise or lower the basic rate of income tax by up to three pence in the pound.

The Scottish Parliament is responsible for: education, health, law, environment, economic development, local government, housing, police, fire services, planning, financial assistance to industry, tourism, some transport, heritage and the arts, agriculture, forestry and food standards.

SALARIES FROM 1 APRIL 2002:

First Minister	£69,861*
Ministers	£36,240*
Lord Advocate	£47,349*
Solicitor-General for Scotland	£34,237*
Junior Ministers	£22,699*
MSPs	£48,228†
Presiding Officer	£36,240*
Deputy Presiding Officers	£22,699*

* In addition to the MSP salary of £48,228
† Reduced by two-thirds if the member is already an MP or an MEP

THE SCOTTISH EXECUTIVE

St Andrew's House, Regent Road, Edinburgh EH1 3DG
Tel: 0131-556 8400. Email: ceu@scotland.gov.uk
Web: www.scotland.gov.uk

The Scottish Executive is the devolved government for Scotland. It is responsible for most of the issues of day-to-day concern to the people of Scotland, including health, education, justice, rural affairs and transport and manages an annual budget of around £20 billion.

The Executive was established in 1999, following the first elections to the Scottish Parliament. It is a coalition between the Scottish Labour Party and the Scottish Liberal Democrat Party.

The Executive is led by a First Minister who is nominated by the Parliament and in turn appoints the other Scottish Ministers.

Scottish Executive civil servants are accountable to Scottish Ministers, who are themselves accountable to the Scottish Parliament.

First Minister, Jack McConnell, MSP *(Lab.)*
Deputy First Minister and Minister for Justice, Jim Wallace, QC, MSP *(LD)*
Minister for Education and Young People, Cathy Jamieson, MSP *(Lab. Co-op.)*
Minister for Enterprise, Transport and Lifelong Learning, Iain Gray, MSP *(Lab.)*
Minister for Environment and Rural Development, Ross Finnie, MSP *(LD)*
Minister for Finance and Public Services, Andy Kerr, MSP *(Lab.)*
Minister for Health and Community Care, Malcolm Chisholm, MSP *(Lab.)*
Minister for Parliamentary Business, Patricia Ferguson, MSP *(Lab.)*
Minister for Social Justice, Margaret Curran, MSP *(Lab.)*
Minister for Tourism, Culture and Sport, Mike Watson, MSP *(Lab.)*
Lord Advocate, Colin Boyd, QC
Solicitor-General, Elish Angiolini, QC

JUNIOR MINISTERS (NOT MEMBERS OF THE SCOTTISH EXECUTIVE)

Deputy Minister for Education and Young People; Nicol Stephen, MSP *(LD)*
Deputy Minister for Enterprise, Transport and Lifelong Learning, Lewis Macdonald, MSP *(Lab.)*
Deputy Minister for Environment and Rural Development, Allan Wilson, MSP *(Lab.)*
Deputy Minister for Finance and Public Services, Peter Peacock, MSP *(Lab.)*
Deputy Ministers for Health and Community, Hugh Henry, MSP *(Lab.); Mary Mulligan, MSP *(Lab.)*
Deputy Minister for Justice, Richard Simpson, MSP *(Lab.)*
Deputy Minister for Parliamentary Business, Euan Robson, MSP *(LD)*
Deputy Minister for Social Justice, Margaret Curran, MSP *(Lab.)*
Deputy Minister for Tourism, Culture and Sport, Elaine Murray, MSP *(Lab.)*

SCOTTISH EXECUTIVE CORPORATE SERVICES

Saughton House, Broomhouse Drive, Edinburgh EH1 3XD
Tel: 0131-556 8400

Principal Establishment Officer (SCS), Mrs A. Robson
Director of Personnel and Pay (SCS), Dr I. Clayden
Director of Development and Training (SCS), D. Bolger

DIRECTORATE OF ADMINISTRATIVE SERVICES
Director of Information Technology (SCS), P. Gray
Director of Accomodation, P. Rhodes
Chief Estates Adviser, A. Andrews

SECURITY BRANCH
Governors House, Regents Road, Edinburgh EH1 3DE
Tel: 0131-244 3685
Departmental Security Officer, K. Jenkinson

BUILDING DIVISION
Area 2-J, Victoria Quay, Edinburgh EH6 6QQ
Tel: 0131-244 7473
Chief Quantity Surveyor (SCS), A. J. Wyllie

FINANCE AND CENTRAL SERVICES DEPARTMENT (FCSD)

St Andrew's House, Regent Road, Edinburgh EH13DG
Tel: 0131-556 8400

Head of Department, J. Elvidge
Principal Finance Officer (SCS), P. S. Collings
Chief Economic Adviser and Head of Analytical Services Group, A. W. Goudie
Head of Local Government, Europe and External Relations Group, D. Middleton
Head, Public Service Delivery Group, Ms B. Campbell
Head, New Media and Presentation, Roger Williams
Head of Secretariat, Ms L. Lewis
Departmental Secretariat, J. Dryden; S. Sutherland; Ms B. Begbie

MEDIA COMMUNICATIONS GROUP
Head of New Media and Presentation (SCS), R. Williams
Head of Press Office and FCSD, C. Imrie
Head of News, A. Baird

SOLICITOR'S OFFICE
Solicitor (SCS), R. M. Henderson
Deputy Solicitors (SCS), S. Foubister; Ms L. Towers
Divisional Solicitors (SCS), G. C. Duke; I. H. Harvie; H. F. Macdiarmid

SCOTTISH EXECUTIVE RURAL AFFAIRS DEPARTMENT

Pentland House, 47 Robb's Loan, Edinburgh EH14 1TY
Tel: 0131-556 8400

Head of Department (SCS), J. S. Graham
Group Heads (SCS), A. J. Rushworth *(Agriculture and Biological Research);* M. B. Foulis *(Environment);* D. J. Crawley *(Food and Agriculture)*
Division/Unit Heads, Ms J. Dalgleish; A. G. Dickson; Ms E. Mitchell; D. Rodgers *(Environment Group);* J. Hutchinson *(Fisheries Group);* I. R. Anderson; D. R. Dickson; D. J. Greig; Ms J. Polley; A. E. Sim; Dr J. R. Wildgoose; *(Food and Agriculture Group)*
Assistant Chief Agricultural Officers, W. A. Aitken; J. Henderson; A. Robb
Chief Agricultural Economist, A. Moxey
Chief Food and Dairy Officer, S. Hodge

EXECUTIVE AGENCIES

FISHERIES RESEARCH SERVICES
SCOTTISH AGRICULTURAL SCIENCE AGENCY
SCOTTISH FISHERIES PROTECTION AGENCY

SCOTTISH EXECUTIVE DEVELOPMENT DEPARTMENT

Victoria Quay, Edinburgh EH6 6QQ
Tel: 0131-244 0759

Head of Department (SCS), Mrs N. Munro
Heads of Groups (SCS), M. Neilson *(Housing and Area Regeneration);* J. Mackinnon *(Planning and Building Standards);* M. Batho *(Social Justice);* J. Martin *(Transport)*
Heads of Divisions, J. Barton; P. Cornish; A. Denham; F. Duffy; I. Duncan; R. Grant; D. Hart; K. Hogg;

J. Howison; G. Huggins; M. McGinn L. Mason;
J. Pryce; J. Ross; T. Williamson
Heads of Units (SCS), Ms Y. Strachan *(Equality)*;
K. Barton *(Social Inclusion)*; N. Mackay *(Voluntary
Issues)*
Communities Scotland, Head, B. Millar
Senior Economic Adviser (SCS), N. Jackson
Chief Reporter (Inquiry Unit), J. McCulloch

SCOTTISH EXECUTIVE EDUCATION DEPARTMENT
Victoria Quay, Edinburgh EH6 6QQ
Tel: 0131-556 8400

Secretary (SCS), M. Ewart
Heads of Groups, Ms G. Stewart *(Children and Young
People)*; P. Rycroft *(Schools)*; J. Mason *(Tourism,
Culture and Sport)*
Heads of Divisions, Ms S. Smith *(Children and Families)*;
Ms V. Cox *(Early Education and Childcare Division)*;
Ms E. Emberson *(New Educational Developments)*;
J. Fraser *(Pupil Support and Inclusion)*; Ms F. Osowska
(Qualifications Assessment and Curriculum); B. Irvine
(Sport, Arts and Culture); D. Henderson *(Teachers)*;
Ms R. Gwyon *(Young People and Looked After
Children)*
Heads of Units, I. Gilzean *(SCS) (Architectural Policy)*;
A. Merrill *(Information Analysis and Communication)*;
Ms L. Fraser *(Major Events)*; N. Stewart *(Tourism)*

HM INSPECTORS OF EDUCATION
Senior Chief Inspector (SCS), D. A. Osler

SOCIAL WORK SERVICES INSPECTORATE
Chief Inspector of Social Work and Services in Scotland,
A. Skinner

EXECUTIVE AGENCIES
HISTORIC SCOTLAND

SCOTTISH PUBLIC PENSIONS AGENCY

SCOTTISH EXECUTIVE ENTERPRISE AND LIFELONG LEARNING DEPARTMENT
Meridian Court, 5 Cadogan Street, Glasgow G2 6AT
Tel: 0141-242 5505; Fax: 0141-242 0208
Europa Building, 450 Argyll Street, Glasgow G2 8LT
Tel: 0141-242 0207; Fax: 0141-242 0208
Atlantic Quay, 150 Broomielaw, Glasgow G2 8LU
Tel: 0141-248 2367 Fax: 0141-248 2086

Secretary (SCS), E. W. Frizzell, CB
Private Secretary, Ms D. Sheldon
Heads of Groups, G. Dickson *(Enterprise and Industrial
Affairs)*; E. J. Weeple *(Lifelong Learning)*
Heads of Divisions, J. Ireland *(Analytical Services)*;
I. Howie *(Business Growth and Innovation)*; R.
Naysmith *(Energy, Telecommunications and Corporate
Services)*; D. Stewart *(Enterprise and Industry)*;
J. Morgan *(Enterprise Networks)*; J. Rigg *(Funding for
Learners)*; G. Toup *(Further and Adult Education)*;
L. Hunter *(Higher Education and Science)*; W. Malone
(Investment Assistance); M. Togneri *(Scottish
Development International)*; H. Jones *(Skills and
Learning Opportunitites)*; K. Doran *(Transitions to
Work)*

EXECUTIVE AGENCY
STUDENT AWARDS AGENCY FOR SCOTLAND

SCOTTISH EXECUTIVE HEALTH DEPARTMENT
St Andrew's House, Edinburgh EH1 3DG
Tel: 0131-244 2410

*National Health Service in Scotland and Head of
Department (SCS)*, T. Jones
Director of Performance Management and Finance (SCS),
J. Aldridge
Director of Human Resources (SCS), M. Butler
Director of Service Policy and Planning, G. Robinson
Chief Nursing Officer, Miss A. Jarvie
Chief Medical Officer, Dr M. Armstrong
Heads of Community Care, T. Teale; A. Rennie
Head of Information Services, NHS, C. Knox
Head of Estates, David Hastie
Head of Public Health Policy (SCS), J. T. Brown
Chief Pharmacist (SCS), W. Scott
Chief Scientist, Prof. R. Young
Chief Dental Officer, T. R. Watkins
Chief Medical Officer (SCS), Dr M. Armstrong
Deputy Chief Medical Officer (SCS), Dr A. Keel
Principal Medical Officers, Dr J. B. Loudon; Dr R.
Skinner
Senior Medical Officers, Dr A. Anderson; Dr I. Bashford;
Dr K. Brotherston; Dr R. Cairncross; Miss A. S.
Campbell; Dr D. Campbell; Dr M. Cornbleet; Dr M.
Donaghy; Dr A. Johnston; Dr M. Mishra; Dr E.
Stewart; Dr H. Whyte

SCOTTISH EXECUTIVE JUSTICE DEPARTMENT
Saughton House, Broomhouse Drive,
Edinburgh EH11 3XD
Tel: 0131-556 8400; Fax: 0131-244 8240

Secretary (SCS), J. Gallagher
Under-Secretaries (SCS), C. Baxter; M. H. Brannan;
V. Macniven
Assistant Secretaries (SCS), P. Beaton; E. Carmichael;
W. Dickson; D. Henderson; A. McIntosh; R. Menlowe;
A. Quinn; J. Rowell; R. Scott; I. Snedden; D. Stewart

OTHER APPOINTMENTS
HM Chief Inspector of Constabulary, Sir Roy Cameron,
QPM
HM Chief Inspector of Prisons, Dr A. McLellan
Director, Scottish Police College, D. Garbutt, QPM.
HM Chief Inspector of Fire Services, D. Davis, CBE, QFSM
Head of Training, Scottish Fire Service Training School,
J. Robson

OFFICE OF THE SCOTTISH PARLIAMENTARY COUNSEL
Victoria Quay, Edinburgh EH6 6QQ. Tel: 0131-244 1672

First Scottish Parliamentary Counsel, J. C. McCluskie,
CB, QC
Scottish Parliamentary Counsel, G. M. Clark; C. A. M.
Wilson; Miss M. MacKenzie
Assistant Scottish Parliamentary Counsel, Mrs D. F.
Barbirou; A. W. Beattie; W. Ferrie; A. C. Gordon;
I. B. Young;

PRIVATE LEGISLATION OFFICE UNDER THE PRIVATE LEGISLATION PROCEDURE (SCOTLAND) ACT 1936
50 Frederick Street, Edinburgh EH2 1EN
Tel: 0131-226 6499
Senior Counsel, J. S. Bevan

EXECUTIVE AGENCIES
NATIONAL ARCHIVES OF SCOTLAND

REGISTERS OF SCOTLAND

SCOTTISH PRISON SERVICE

GENERAL REGISTER OFFICE FOR SCOTLAND

**MENTAL WELFARE COMMISSION
FOR SCOTLAND**
K Floor, Argyle House, 3 Lady Lawson Street,
Edinburgh EH3 9SH
Tel: 0131-222 6111
Chairman, I. J. Miller, OBE
Vice-Chairman, Mrs M. Ross

MEMBERS OF THE SCOTTISH PARLIAMENT
as at July 2002

Adam, Brian, *SNP, Scotland North East region*
Aitken, William, *C., Glasgow region*
Alexander, Ms Wendy, *Lab., Paisley North,* maj. 4,616
Baillie, Ms Jackie, *Lab., Dumbarton,* maj. 4,758
Barrie, Scott, *Lab., Dunfermline West,* maj. 5,021
Boyack, Ms Sarah, *Lab., Edinburgh Central,* maj. 4,626
Brankin, Ms Rhona, *Lab. Co-op., Midlothian,* maj. 5,525
Brown, Robert, *LD, Glasgow region*
Butler, Bill, *Lab., Glasgow Anniesland,* maj. 5,376
Campbell, Colin, *SNP, Scotland West region*
Canavan, Dennis A., *MP, Lab., Falkirk West,* maj. 12,192
Chisholm, Malcolm G. R., *MP, Lab., Edinburgh North and Leith,* maj. 7,736
Craigie, Ms Cathy, *Lab., Cumbernauld and Kilsyth,* maj. 4,259
Crawford, Bruce, *SNP, Scotland Mid and Fife region*
Cunningham, Ms Roseanna, *MP, SNP, Perth,* maj. 2,027
Curran, Ms Margaret, *Lab., Glasgow Baillieston,* maj. 3,072
Davidson, David, *C., Scotland North East region*
Deacon, Ms Susan, *Lab., Edinburgh East and Musselburgh,* maj. 6,714
Douglas-Hamilton, The Lord, PC, QC, *C., Lothians region*
Eadie, Ms Helen, *Lab. Co-op., Dunfermline East,* maj. 8,699
‡Elder, Ms Dorothy, *Ind., Glasgow region*
Ewing, Fergus, *SNP, Inverness East, Nairn and Lochaber,* maj. 441
Ewing, Mrs Margaret A., *MP, SNP, Moray,* maj. 4,129
Ewing, Dr Winnifred, *SNP, Highlands and Islands region*
Fabiani, Ms Linda, *SNP, Scotland Central region*
Ferguson, Ms Patricia, *Lab., Glasgow Maryhill,* maj. 4,326
Fergusson, Alex, *C., Scotland South region*
Finnie, Ross, *LD, Scotland West region*
Fitzpatrick, Brian, *Lab., Strathkelvin and Bearsden,* maj. 7,829
Gallie, Phil, *C., Scotland South region*
Gibson, Kenneth, *SNP, Glasgow region*
Gillon, Ms Karen, *Lab., Clydesdale,* maj. 3,880 (elected as Karen Turnbull)
Godman, Ms Patricia, *Lab., Renfrewshire West,* maj. 2,893
Goldie, Miss Annabel, *C., Scotland West region*
Gorrie, Donald C. E., *MP, OBE, LD, Scotland Central region*
Grahame, Ms Christine, *SNP, Scotland South region* (elected as Christine Creech)
Grant, Ms Rhoda, *Lab., Highlands and Islands region*
Gray, Iain, *Lab., Edinburgh Pentlands,* maj. 2,885
Hamilton, Duncan, *SNP, Highlands and Islands region*
Harding, Keith, *C., Scotland Mid and Fife region*
Harper, Robin, *Green, Lothians region*
Henry, Hugh, *Lab., Paisley South,* maj. 4,495
Home Robertson, John D., *MP, Lab., East Lothian,* maj. 10,946
Hughes, Ms Janis, *Lab., Glasgow Rutherglen,* maj. 7,287
Hyslop, Ms Fiona, *SNP, Lothians region*

Ingram, Adam, *SNP, Scotland South region*
Jackson, Gordon, QC, *Lab., Glasgow Govan,* maj. 1,756
Jackson, Dr Sylvia, *Lab., Stirling,* maj. 3,981
Jamieson, Ms Cathy, *Lab. Co-op., Carrick, Cumnock and Doon Valley,* maj. 8,803
Jamieson, Ms Margaret, *Lab., Kilmarnock and Loudoun,* maj. 2,760
Jenkins, Ian, *LD, Tweeddale, Ettrick and Lauderdale,* maj. 4,478
Johnstone, Alex, *C., Scotland North East region*
Kerr, Andy, *Lab., East Kilbride,* maj. 6,499
Lamont, Johann, *Lab. Co-op., Glasgow Pollock,* maj. 4,642
Livingstone, Ms Marilyn, *Lab. Co-op., Kirkcaldy,* maj. 4,475
Lochhead, Richard, *SNP, Scotland North East region*
Lyon, George, *LD, Argyll and Bute,* maj. 2,057
McAllion, John, *MP, Lab., Dundee East,* maj. 2,854
MacAskill, Kenny, *SNP, Lothians region*
McAveety, Frank, *Lab. Co-op., Glasgow Shettleston,* maj. 5,467
McCabe, Tom, *Lab., Hamilton South,* maj. 7,176
McConnell, Jack, *Lab., Motherwell and Wishaw,* maj. 5,076
Macdonald, Lewis, *Lab., Aberdeen Central,* maj. 2,696
MacDonald, Ms Margo, *SNP, Lothians region*
MacGrigor, Jamie, *C., Highlands and Islands region*
McGugan, Ms Irene, *SNP, Scotland North East region*
Macintosh, Ken, *Lab., Eastwood,* maj. 2,125
McIntosh, Mrs Lindsay, *C., Scotland Central region*
Mackay, Angus, *Lab., Edinburgh South,* maj. 5,424
MacLean, Ms Kate, *Lab., Dundee West,* maj. 121
McLeish, Henry B., *MP, Lab., Fife Central,* maj. 8,675
McLeod, Ms Fiona, *SNP, Scotland West region*
McLetchie, David, *C., Lothians region*
McMahon, Michael, *Lab., Hamilton North and Bellshill,* maj. 5,606
Macmillan, Ms Maureen, *Lab., Highlands and Islands region*
McNeil, Duncan, *Lab., Greenock and Inverclyde,* maj. 4,313
McNeill, Ms Pauline, *Lab., Glasgow Kelvin,* maj. 4,408
McNulty, Des, *Lab., Clydebank and Milngavie,* maj. 4,710
Martin, Paul, *Lab., Glasgow Springburn,* maj. 7,893
Marwick, Ms Tricia, *SNP, Scotland Mid and Fife region*
Matheson, Michael, *SNP, Scotland Central region*
Monteith, Brian, *C., Scotland Mid and Fife region*
Morgan, Alasdair N., *MP, SNP, Galloway and Upper Nithsdale,* maj. 3,201
Morrison, Alasdair, *Lab., Western Isles,* maj. 2,093
Muldoon, Bristow, *Lab., Livingston,* maj. 3,904
Mulligan, Ms Mary, *Lab., Linlithgow,* maj. 2,928
Mundell, David, *C., Scotland South region*
Munro, John Farquhar, *LD, Ross, Skye and Inverness West,* maj. 1,539
Murray, Dr Elaine, *Lab., Dumfries,* maj. 3,654
Neil, Alex, *SNP, Scotland Central region*
Oldfather, Ms Irene, *Lab., Cunninghame South,* maj. 6,541
Paterson, Gil, *SNP, Scotland Central region*
Peacock, Peter, *Lab., Highlands and Islands region*
Peattie, Ms Cathy, *Lab., Falkirk East,* maj. 4,139
Quinan, Lloyd, *SNP, Scotland West region*
Radcliffe, Ms Nora, *LD, Gordon,* maj. 4,195
Raffan, Keith, *LD, Scotland Mid and Fife region*
Reid, George, *SNP, Scotland Mid and Fife region*
Robison, Ms Shona, *SNP, Scotland North East region*
Robson, Euan, *LD, Roxburgh and Berwickshire,* maj. 3,585
Rumbles, Mike, *LD, Aberdeenshire West and Kincardine,* maj. 2,289
Russell, Michael, *SNP, Scotland South region*

Scanlon, Mrs Mary, *C., Highlands and Islands region*
Scott, John, *C., Ayr*, maj. 3,344
Scott, Tavish, *LD, Shetland*, maj. 3,194
Sheridan, Tommy, *SSP, Glasgow region*
Simpson, Dr Richard, *Lab., Ochil*, maj. 1,303
Smith, Ms Elaine, *Lab., Coatbridge and Chryston*, maj. 10,404
Smith, Iain, *LD, Fife North East*, maj. 5,064
Smith, Ms Margaret, *LD, Edinburgh West*, maj. 4,583
Steel, Rt. Hon. Sir David (The Lord Steel of Aikwood), KBE, PC, *LD, Lothians region*
Stephen, Nicol, *LD, Aberdeen South*, maj. 1,760
Stevenson, Stewart, *SNP, Banff and Buchan*
Stone, Jamie, *LD, Caithness, Sutherland and Easter Ross*, maj. 4,391
Sturgeon, Ms Nicola, *SNP, Glasgow region*
Swinney, John R., mp, *SNP, Tayside North*, maj. 4,192
Thomson, Ms Elaine, *Lab., Aberdeen North*, maj. 398
Tosh, Murray, *C., Scotland South region*
Ullrich, Ms Kay, *SNP, Scotland West region*
Wallace, Ben, *C., Scotland North East region*
Wallace, James R., MP, QC, *LD, Orkney*, maj. 4,619
Watson, Mike (The Lord Watson of Invergowrie), *Lab., Glasgow Cathcart*, maj. 5,374
Welsh, Andrew P., MP, *SNP, Angus*, maj. 8,901
White, Ms Sandra, *SNP, Glasgow region*
Whitefield, Ms Karen, *Lab., Airdrie and Shotts*, maj. 8,985

Wilson, Allan, *Lab., Cunninghame North*, maj. 4,796
Wilson, Andrew, *SNP, Scotland Central region*
Young, John, OBE, *C., Scotland West region*

STATE OF THE PARTIES *as at July 2002*†

	Constituency MSPs	Regional MSPs	Total
Scottish Labour Party	52	3	55
Scottish National Party	7	27	34
Scottish Conservative and Unionist Party	1	18	19
Scottish Liberal Democrats	12	4†	16†
Scottish Green Party	0	1	1
Scottish Socialist Party	0	1	1
Independent (Dennis Canavan and ‡Dorothy-Grace Elder)	1	1	2
The Presiding Officer (Rt. Hon. Sir David Steel, KBE, MSP)	0	1	1

Deputy Presiding Officers, Murray Tosh, MSP *(C.);* George Reid, MSP *(SNP)*

† Excludes the Presiding Officer, who has no party allegiance while in post

‡ a Glasgow list MSP, who resigned from the SNP to sit as an Independent

Scottish Parliament AS AT MAY 1999

CONSTITUENCIES

ABERDEEN CENTRAL
(Scotland North East region)
E. 52,715 T. 50.26%

L. Macdonald, *Lab.*	10,305
R. Lochhead, *SNP*	7,609
Ms E. Anderson, *LD*	4,403
T. Mason, *C.*	3,655
A. Cumbers, *SSP*	523
Lab. majority 2,696	

ABERDEEN NORTH
(Scotland North East region)
E. 54,553 T. 51.00%

Ms E. Thomson, *Lab.*	10,340
B. Adam, *SNP*	9,942
J. Donaldson, *LD*	4,767
I. Haughie, *C.*	2,772
Lab. majority 1398	

ABERDEEN SOUTH
(Scotland North East region)
E. 60,579 T. 57.26%

N. Stephen, *LD*	11,300
M. Elrick, *Lab.*	9,540
Ms N. Milne, *C.*	6,993
Ms I. McGugan, *SNP*	6,651
S. Sutherland, *SWP*	206
LD majority 1,760	

ABERDEENSHIRE WEST AND KINCARDINE
(Scotland North East region)
E. 60,702 T. 58.87%

M. Rumbles, *LD*	12,838
B. Wallace, *C.*	10,549
Ms M. Watt, *SNP*	7,699

G. Guthrie, *Lab.*	4,650
LD majority 2,289	

AIRDRIE AND SHOTTS
(Scotland Central region)
E. 58,481 T. 56.79%

Ms K. Whitefield, *Lab.*	18,338
G. Paterson, *SNP*	9,353
P. Ross-Taylor, *C.*	3,177
D. Miller, *LD*	2,345
Lab. majority 8,985	

ANGUS
(Scotland North East region)
E. 59,891 T. 57.66%

A. Welsh, *SNP*	16,055
R. Harris, *C.*	7,154
I. McFatridge, *Lab.*	6,914
R. Speirs, *LD*	4,413
SNP majority 8,901	

ARGYLL AND BUTE
(Highlands and Islands region)
E. 49,609 T. 64.86%

G. Lyon, *LD*	11,226
D. Hamilton, *SNP*	9,169
H. Raven, *Lab.*	6,470
D. Petrie, *C.*	5,312
LD majority 2,057	

AYR
(Scotland South region)
E. 56,338 T. 66.48%

*I. Welsh, *Lab.*	14,263
P. Gallie, *C.*	14,238
R. Mullin, *SNP*	7,291
Ms E. Morris, *LD*	1,662
Lab. majority 25	

*I. Welsh resigned on 21 December 1999. By-election held on 16 March 2000 see p359

BANFF AND BUCHAN
(Scotland North East region)
E. 57,639 T. 55.06%

*A. Salmond, *SNP*	16,695
D. Davidson, *C.*	5,403
M. Mackie, *LD*	5,315
Ms M. Harris, *Lab.*	4,321
SNP majority 11,292	

*A. Salmond resigned 14 May 2001. By-election held on 7 June 2001 see p359

CAITHNESS, SUTHERLAND AND EASTER ROSS
(Highlands and Islands region)
E. 41,581 T. 62.60%

J. Stone, *LD*	10,691
J. Hendry, *Lab.*	6,300
Ms J. Urquhart, *SNP*	6,035
R. Jenkins, *C.*	2,167
J. Campbell, *Ind.*	554
E. Stewart, *Ind.*	282
LD majority 4,391	

CARRICK, CUMNOCK AND DOON VALLEY
(Scotland South region)
E. 65,580 T. 62.66%

Ms C. Jamieson, *Lab. Co-op.*	19,667
A. Ingram, *SNP*	10,864
J. Scott, *C.*	8,123
D. Hannay, *LD*	2,441
Lab. Co-op. majority 8,803	

CLYDEBANK AND MILNGAVIE
(Scotland West region)
E. 52,461 T. 63.55%

D. McNulty, *Lab.*	15,105
J. Yuill, *SNP*	10,395
R. Ackland, *LD*	4,149

Ms D. Luckhurst, *C.* 3,688
Lab. majority 4,710

CLYDESDALE
(Scotland South region)
E. 64,262 T. 60.61%
Ms K. Turnbull, *Lab.* 16,755
Ms A. Winning, *SNP* 12,875
C. Cormack, *C.* 5,814
Ms S. Grieve, *LD* 3,503
Lab. majority 3,880

COATBRIDGE AND CHRYSTON
(Scotland Central region)
E. 52,178 T. 57.87%
Ms E. Smith, *Lab.* 17,923
P. Kearney, *SNP* 7,519
G. Lind, *C.* 2,867
Ms J. Hook, *LD* 1,889
Lab. majority 10,404

CUMBERNAULD AND KILSYTH
(Scotland Central region)
E. 49,395 T. 61.97%
Ms C. Craigie, *Lab.* 15,182
A. Wilson, *SNP* 10,923
H. O'Donnell, *LD* 2,029
R. Slack, *C.* 1,362
K. McEwan, *SSP* 1,116
Lab. majority 4,259

CUNNINGHAME NORTH
(Scotland West region)
E. 55,867 T. 59.95%
A. Wilson, *Lab.* 14,369
Ms K. Ullrich, *SNP* 9,573
M. Johnston, *C.* 6,649
C. Irving, *LD* 2,900
Lab. majority 4,796

CUNNINGHAME SOUTH
(Scotland South region)
E. 50,443 T. 56.06%
Ms I. Oldfather, *Lab.* 14,936
M. Russell, *SNP* 8,395
M. Tosh, *C.* 3,229
S. Ritchie, *LD* 1,717
Lab. majority 6,541

DUMBARTON
(Scotland West region)
E. 56,090 T. 61.86%
Ms J. Baillie, *Lab.* 15,181
L. Quinan, *SNP* 10,423
D. Reece, *C.* 5,060
P. Coleshill, *LD* 4,035
Lab. majority 4,758

DUMFRIES
(Scotland South region)
E. 63,162 T. 60.93%
Ms E. Murray, *Lab.* 14,101
D. Mundell, *C.* 10,447
S. Norris, *SNP* 7,625
N. Wallace, *LD* 6,309
Lab. majority 3,654

DUNDEE EAST
(Scotland North East region)
E. 57,222 T. 55.33%
J. McAllion, *Lab.* 13,703
Ms S. Robison, *SNP* 10,849

I. Mitchell, *C.* 4,428
R. Lawrie, *LD* 2,153
H. Duke, *SSP* 530
Lab. majority 2,854

DUNDEE WEST
(Scotland North East region)
E. 55,725 T. 52.19%
Ms K. MacLean, *Lab.* 10,925
C. Cashley, *SNP* 10,804
G. Buchan, *C.* 3,345
Ms E. Dick, *LD* 2,998
J. McFarlane, *SSP* 1,010
Lab. majority 121

DUNFERMLINE EAST
(Scotland Mid and Fife region)
E. 52,087 T. 56.94%
Ms H. Eadie, *Lab. Co-op.* 16,576
D. McCarthy, *SNP* 7,877
Ms C. Ruxton, *C.* 2,931
F. Lawson, *LD* 2,275
Lab. Co-op. majority 8,699

DUNFERMLINE WEST
(Scotland Mid and Fife region)
E. 53,112 T. 57.75%
S. Barrie, *Lab.* 13,560
D. Chapman, *SNP* 8,539
Ms E. Harris, *LD* 5,591
J. Mackie, *C.* 2,981
Lab. majority 5,021

EAST KILBRIDE
(Scotland Central region)
E. 66,111 T. 62.49%
A. Kerr, *Lab.* 19,987
Ms L. Fabiani, *SNP* 13,488
C. Stevenson, *C.* 4,465
E. Hawthorn, *LD* 3,373
Lab. majority 6,499

EAST LOTHIAN
(Scotland South region)
E. 58,579 T. 64.16%
J. Home Robertson, *Lab.* 19,220
C. Miller, *SNP* 8,274
Ms C. Richard, *C.* 5,941
Ms J. Hayman, *LD* 4,147
Lab. majority 10,946

EASTWOOD
(Scotland West region)
E. 67,248 T. 67.51%
K. Macintosh, *Lab.* 16,970
J. Young, *C.* 14,845
Ms R. Findlay, *SNP* 8,760
Ms A. McCurley, *LD* 4,472
M. Tayan, *Ind.* 349
Lab. majority 2,125

EDINBURGH CENTRAL
(Lothians region)
E. 65,945 T. 56.73%
Ms S. Boyack, *Lab.* 14,224
I. McKee, *SNP* 9,598
A. Myles, *LD* 6,187
Ms J. Low, *C.* 6,018
K. Williamson, *SSP* 830
B. Allingham, *Ind. Dem.* 364
W. Wallace, *Braveheart* 191
Lab. majority 4,626

EDINBURGH EAST AND MUSSELBURGH
(Lothians region)
E. 60,167 T. 61.48%
Ms S. Deacon, *Lab.* 17,086
K. MacAskill, *SNP* 10,372
J. Balfour, *C.* 4,600
Ms M. Thomas, *LD* 4,100
D. White, *SSP* 697
M. Heavey, *Ind. You* 134
Lab. majority 6,714

EDINBURGH NORTH AND LEITH
(Lothians region)
E. 62,976 T. 58.19%
M. Chisholm, *Lab.* 17,203
Ms A. Dana, *SNP* 9,467
J. Sempill, *C.* 5,030
S. Tombs, *LD* 4,039
R. Brown, *SSP* 907
Lab. majority 7,736

EDINBURGH PENTLANDS
(Lothians region)
E. 60,029 T. 65.97%
I. Gray, *Lab.* 14,343
D. McLetchie, *C.* 11,458
S. Gibb, *SNP* 8,770
I. Gibson, *LD* 5,029
Lab. majority 2,885

EDINBURGH SOUTH
(Lothians region)
E. 64,100 T. 62.61%
A. MacKay, *Lab.* 14,869
Ms M. MacDonald, *SNP* 9,445
M. Pringle, *LD* 8,961
I. Whyte, *C.* 6,378
W. Black, *SWP* 482
Lab. majority 5,424

EDINBURGH WEST
(Lothians region)
E. 61,747 T. 67.34%
Ms M. Smith, *LD* 15,161
Lord J. Douglas-Hamilton, *C.* 10,578
Ms C. Fox, *Lab.* 8,860
G. Sutherland, *SNP* 6,984
LD majority 4,583

FALKIRK EAST
(Scotland Central region)
E. 57,345 T. 61.40%
Ms C. Peattie, *Lab.* 15,721
K. Brown, *SNP* 11,582
A. Orr, *C.* 3,399
G. McDonald, *LD* 2,509
R. Stead, *Soc. Lab.* 1,643
V. MacGrain, *SFPP* 358
Lab. majority 4,139

FALKIRK WEST
(Scotland Central region)
E. 53,404 T. 63.04%
D. Canavan, *Falkirk W.* 18,511
R. Martin, *Lab.* 6,319
M. Matheson, *SNP* 5,986
G. Miller, *C.* 1,897
A. Smith, *LD* 954
Falkirk W. majority 12,192

FIFE CENTRAL
(Scotland Mid and Fife region)
E. 58,850 *T.* 55.82%

H. McLeish, *Lab.*	18,828
Ms P. Marwick, *SNP*	10,153
Ms J. A. Liston, *LD*	1,953
K. Harding, *C.*	1,918
Lab. majority 8,675	

FIFE NORTH EAST
(Scotland Mid and Fife region)
E. 60,886 *T.* 59.03%

I. Smith, *LD*	13,590
E. Brocklebank, *C.*	8,526
C. Welsh, *SNP*	6,373
C. Milne, *Lab.*	5,175
D. Macgregor, *Ind.*	1,540
R. Beveridge, *Ind.*	737
LD majority 5,064	

GALLOWAY AND UPPER
NITHSDALE
(Scotland South region)
E. 53,057 *T.* 66.56%

A. Morgan, *SNP*	13,873
A. Fergusson, *C.*	10,672
J. Stevens, *Lab.*	7,209
Ms J. Mitchell, *LD*	3,562
SNP majority 3,201	

GLASGOW ANNIESLAND
(Glasgow region)
E. 54,378 *T.* 52.37%

*D. Dewar, *Lab.*	16,749
K. Stewart, *SNP*	5,756
W. Aitken, *C.*	3,032
I. Brown, *LD*	1,804
Ms A. Lynch, *SSP*	1,000
E. Boyd, *Soc. Lab.*	139
Lab. majority 10,993	

*By-election held on 23 November 2000
due to the death of Donald Dewar on
11 October 2000, see p359

GLASGOW BAILLIESTON
(Glasgow region)
E. 49,068 *T.* 48.32%

Ms M. Curran, *Lab.*	11,289
‡Ms D. Elder, *SNP*	8,217
J. McVicar, *SSP*	1,864
Ms K. Pickering, *C.*	1,526
Ms J. Fryer, *LD*	813
Lab. majority 3,072	

GLASGOW CATHCART
(Glasgow region)
E. 51,338 *T.* 52.55%

M. Watson, *Lab.*	12,966
Ms M. Whitehead, *SNP*	7,592
Ms M. Leishman, *C.*	3,311
C. Dick, *LD*	2,187
R. Slorach, *SWP*	920
Lab. majority 5,374	

GLASGOW GOVAN
(Glasgow region)
E. 53,257 *T.* 49.52%

G. Jackson, *Lab.*	11,421
Ms N. Sturgeon, *SNP*	9,665
Ms T. Ahmed-Sheikh, *C.*	2,343
M. Aslam Khan, *LD*	1,479

C. McCarthy, *SSP*	1,275
J. Foster, *Comm. Brit.*	190
Lab. majority 1,756	

GLASGOW KELVIN
(Glasgow region)
E. 61,207 *T.* 46.34%

Ms P. McNeill, *Lab.*	12,711
Ms S. White, *SNP*	8,303
Ms M. Craig, *LD*	3,720
A. Rasul, *C.*	2,253
Ms H. Ritchie, *SSP*	1,375
Lab. majority 4,408	

GLASGOW MARYHILL
(Glasgow region)
E. 56,469 *T.* 40.75%

Ms P. Ferguson, *Lab.*	11,455
W. Wilson, *SNP*	7,129
Ms C. Hamblen, *LD*	1,793
G. Scott, *SSP*	1,439
M. Fry, *C.*	1,194
Lab. majority 4,326	

GLASGOW POLLOCK
(Glasgow region)
E. 47,970 *T.* 54.37%

J. Lamont, *Lab. Co-op.*	11,405
K. Gibson, *SNP*	6,763
T. Sheridan, *SSP*	5,611
R. O'Brien, *C.*	1,370
J. King, *LD*	931
Lab. Co-op. majority 4,642	

GLASGOW RUTHERGLEN
(Glasgow region)
E. 51,012 *T.* 56.89%

Ms J. Hughes, *Lab.*	13,442
T. Chalmers, *SNP*	6,155
R. Brown, *LD*	5,798
I. Stewart, *C.*	2,315
W. Bonnar, *SSP*	832
J. Nisbet, *Soc. Lab.*	481
Lab. majority 7,287	

GLASGOW SHETTLESTON
(Glasgow region)
E. 50,592 *T.* 40.58%

F. McAveety, *Lab. Co-op.*	11,078
J. Byrne, *SNP*	5,611
Ms R. Kane, *SSP*	1,640
C. Bain, *C.*	1,260
L. Clarke, *LD*	943
Lab. Co-op. majority 5,467	

GLASGOW SPRINGBURN
(Glasgow region)
E. 55,670 *T.* 43.77%

P. Martin, *Lab.*	14,268
J. Brady, *SNP*	6,375
M. Roxburgh, *C.*	1,293
M. Dunnigan, *LD*	1,288
J. Friel, *SSP*	1,141
Lab. majority 7,893	

GORDON
(Scotland North East region)
E. 59,497 *T.* 56.51%

Ms N. Radcliffe, *LD*	12,353
A. Stronach, *SNP*	8,158
A. Johnstone, *C.*	6,602

Ms G. Carlin-Kulwicki, *Lab.*	3,950
H. Watt, *Ind.*	2,559
LD majority 4,195	

GREENOCK AND INVERCLYDE
(Scotland West region)
E. 48,584 *T.* 58.95%

D. McNeil, *Lab.*	11,817
R. Finnie, *LD*	7,504
I. Hamilton, *SNP*	6,762
R. Wilkinson, *C.*	1,699
D. Landels, *SSP*	857
Lab. majority 4,313	

HAMILTON NORTH AND
BELLSHILL
(Scotland Central region)
E. 53,992 *T.* 57.82%

M. McMahon, *Lab.*	15,227
Ms K. McAlorum, *SNP*	9,621
S. Thomson, *C.*	3,199
Ms J. Struthers, *LD*	2,105
Ms K. McGavigan, *Soc. Lab.*	1,064
Lab. majority 5,606	

HAMILTON SOUTH
(Scotland Central region)
E. 46,765 *T.* 55.43%

T. McCabe, *Lab.*	14,098
A. Ardrey, *SNP*	6,922
Ms M. Mitchell, *C.*	2,918
J. Oswald, *LD*	1,982
Lab. majority 7,176	

INVERNESS EAST, NAIRN AND
LOCHABER
(Highlands and Islands region)
E. 66,285 *T.* 63.10%

F. Ewing, *SNP*	13,825
Ms J. Aitken, *Lab.*	13,384
D. Fraser, *LD*	8,508
Ms M. Scanlon, *C.*	6,107
SNP majority 441	

KILMARNOCK AND LOUDOUN
(Scotland Central region)
E. 61,454 *T.* 64.03%

Ms M. Jamieson, *Lab.*	17,345
A. Neil, *SNP*	14,585
L. McIntosh, *C.*	4,589
J. Stewart, *LD*	2,830
Lab. majority 2,760	

KIRKCALDY
(Scotland Mid and Fife region)
E. 51,640 *T.* 54.88%

Ms M. Livingstone, *Lab. Co-op.*	13,645
S. Hosie, *SNP*	9,170
M. Scott-Hayward, *C.*	2,907
J. Mainland, *LD*	2,620
Lab. Co-op. majority 4,475	

LINLITHGOW
(Lothians region)
E. 54,262 *T.* 62.26%

Ms M. Mulligan, *Lab.*	15,247
S. Stevenson, *SNP*	12,319
G. Lindhurst, *C.*	3,158
J. Barrett, *LD*	2,643
Ms I. Ovenstone, *Ind.*	415
Lab. majority 2,928	

LIVINGSTON
(Lothians region)
E. 62,060 T. 58.93%
B. Muldoon, *Lab.* 17,313
G. McCarra, *SNP* 13,409
D. Younger, *C.* 3,014
M. Oliver, *LD* 2,834
Lab. majority 3,904

MIDLOTHIAN
(Lothians region)
E. 48,374 T. 61.51%
Ms R. Brankin, *Lab. Co-op.* 14,467
A. Robertson, *SNP* 8,942
J. Elder, *LD* 3,184
G. Turnbull, *C.* 2,544
D. Pryde, *Ind.* 618
Lab. Co-op. majority 5,525

MORAY
(Highlands and Islands region)
E. 58,388 T. 57.50%
Mrs M. Ewing, *SNP* 13,027
A. Farquharson, *Lab.* 8,898
A. Findlay, *C.* 8,595
Ms P. Kenton, *LD* 3,056
SNP majority 4,129

MOTHERWELL AND WISHAW
(Scotland Central region)
E. 52,613 T. 57.71%
J. McConnell, *Lab.* 13,955
J. McGuigan, *SNP* 8,879
W. Gibson, *C.* 3,694
J. Milligan, *Soc. Lab.* 1,941
R. Spillane, *LD* 1,895
Lab. majority 5,076

OCHIL
(Scotland Mid and Fife region)
E. 57,083 T. 64.58%
R. Simpson, *Lab.* 15,385
G. Reid, *SNP* 14,082
*N. Johnston, *C.* 4,151
Earl of Mar and Kellie, *LD* 3,249
Lab. majority 1,303

*N. Johnston resigned on 10 August
2001. He was replaced by Murdo Fraser

ORKNEY
(Highlands and Islands region)
E. 15,658 T. 56.95%
J. Wallace, *LD* 6,010
C. Zawadzki, *C.* 1,391
J. Mowat, *SNP* 917
A. Macleod, *Lab.* 600
LD majority 4,619

PAISLEY NORTH
(Scotland West region)
E. 49,020 T. 56.61%
Ms W. Alexander, *Lab.* 13,492
I. Mackay, *SNP* 8,876
P. Ramsay, *C.* 2,242
Ms T. Mayberry, *LD* 2,133
Ms F. Macdonald, *SSP* 1,007
Lab. majority 4,616

PAISLEY SOUTH
(Scotland West region)
E. 53,637 T. 57.15%

H. Henry, *Lab.* 13,899
W. Martin, *SNP* 9,404
S. Callison, *LD* 2,974
Ms S. Laidlaw, *C.* 2,433
P. Mack, *Ind.* 1,273
Ms J. Forrest, *SWP* 673
Lab. majority 4,495

PERTH
(Scotland Mid and Fife region)
E. 61,034 T. 61.27%
Ms R. Cunningham, *SNP* 13,570
I. Stevenson, *C.* 11,543
Ms J. Richards, *Lab.* 8,725
C. Brodie, *LD* 3,558
SNP majority 2,027

RENFREWSHIRE WEST
(Scotland West region)
E. 52,452 T. 64.89%
Ms P. Godman, *Lab.* 12,708
C. Campbell, *SNP* 9,815
Ms A. Goldie, *C.* 7,243
N. Ascherson, *LD* 2,659
A. McGraw, *Ind.* 1,136
P. Clark, *SWP* 476
Lab. majority 2,893

ROSS, SKYE AND INVERNESS WEST
(Highlands and Islands region)
E. 55,845 T. 63.42%
J. Farquhar-Munro, *LD* 11,652
D. Munro, *Lab.* 10,113
J. Mather, *SNP* 7,997
J. Scott, *C.* 3,351
D. Briggs, *Ind.* 2,302
LD majority 1,539

ROXBURGH AND BERWICKSHIRE
(Scotland South region)
E. 47,639 T. 58.52%
E. Robson, *LD* 11,320
A. Hutton, *C.* 7,735
S. Crawford, *SNP* 4,719
Ms S. McLeod, *Lab.* 4,102
LD majority 3,585

SHETLAND
(Highlands and Islands region)
E. 16,978 T. 58.77%
T. Scott, *LD* 5,435
J. Wills, *Lab.* 2,241
W. Ross, *SNP* 1,430
G. Robinson, *C.* 872
LD majority 3,194

STIRLING
(Scotland Mid and Fife region)
E. 52,904 T. 67.68%
Ms S. Jackson, *Lab.* 13,533
Ms A. Ewing, *SNP* 9,552
B. Monteith, *C.* 9,158
I. Macfarlane, *LD* 3,407
S. Kilgour, *Ind.* 155
Lab. majority 3,981

STRATHKELVIN AND BEARSDEN
(Scotland West region)
E. 63,111 T. 67.17%
*S. Galbraith, *Lab.* 21,505
Ms F. McLeod, *SNP* 9,384
C. Ferguson, *C.* 6,934

Ms A. Howarth, *LD* 4,144
Ms M. Richards, *Anti-Drug* 423
Lab. majority 12,121

*S. Galbraith resigned on 14 May 2001.
By-election held on 7 June 2001
see p360

TAYSIDE NORTH
(Scotland Mid and Fife region)
E. 61,795 T. 61.58%
J. Swinney, *SNP* 16,786
M. Fraser, *C.* 12,594
Ms M. Dingwall, *Lab.* 5,727
P. Regent, *LD* 2,948
SNP majority 4,192

TWEEDDALE, ETTRICK AND LAUDERDALE
(Scotland South region)
E. 51,577 T. 65.37%
I. Jenkins, *LD* 12,078
Ms C. Creech, *SNP* 7,600
G. McGregor, *Lab.* 7,546
J. Campbell, *C.* 6,491
LD majority 4,478

WESTERN ISLES
(Highlands and Islands region)
E. 22,412 T. 62.26%
A. Morrison, *Lab.* 7,248
A. Nicholson, *SNP* 5,155
J. MacGrigor, *C.* 1,095
J. Horne, *LD* 456
Lab. majority 2,093

BY-ELECTIONS

AYR (16 March 2000)
T. 57%
J. Scott, *C.* 12,580
J. Mather, *SNP* 9,236
R. Millar, *Lab.* 7,054
J. Stewart, *SSP* 1,345
S. Ritchie, *LD* 800
G. Corbett, *Green* 460
W. Botcherby, *Ind.* 186
A. McConnachie, *UK Ind* 113
R. Graham, *ProLife* 111
K. Dhillon, *Ind* 15
C. majority 3,344

GLASGOW ANNIESLAND (23 NOVEMBER 2000)
T. 20,221
Bill Butler, *Lab.* 9,838
Tom Chalmers, *SNP,* 4,462
Kate Pickering, *Scottish Conservative and Unionist,* 2,148
R. Kane, *SSP,* 1,429
Judith Fryer, *LD,* 1,384
Alasdair Whitelaw, *Green,* 662
Murdo Ritchie, *SLP.* 298
Lab. majority, 5,376

BANFF AND BUCHAN (7 June 2001)
T. 30,838
Stewart Stevenson, *SNP,* 15,386
Ted Brocklebank *C.,* 6,819

Megan Harris, *Lab.*, 4,597
Canon Kenyon Wright, *LD*, 3,231
Peter Anderson, *SSP*, 682
SNP majority, 8,567

STRATHKELVIN AND BEARSDEN (7 June 2001)
T. 41,734
*Brian Fitzpatrick, *Lab.*, 15,401
Jean M. Turner, *Ind.*, 7,275
John Morrison, *LD*, 7,147
Janet E. Law, *SNP*, 6,457
Charles Ferguson, *C.*, 5,037
Lab. majority, 8,126

REGIONS

GLASGOW
E. 531,956 *T.* 48.19%

Lab.	112,588	(43.92%)
SNP	65,360	(25.50%)
C.	20,239	(7.90%)
SSP	18,581	(7.25%)
LD	18,473	(7.21%)
Green	10,159	(3.96%)
Soc. Lab.	4,391	(1.71%)
ProLife	2,357	(0.92%)
SUP	2,283	(0.89%)
Comm. Brit.	521	(0.20%)
Humanist	447	(0.17%)
NLP	419	(0.16%)
SPGB	309	(0.12%)
Choice	221	(0.09%)

Lab. majority 47,228
(May 1997, Lab. maj. 166,061)
Additional Members: W. Aitken, *C.*; R. Brown, *LD*; Ms D. Elder, *SNP*; Ms S. White, *SNP*; Ms N. Sturgeon, *SNP*; K. Gibson, *SNP*; T. Sheridan, *SSP*

HIGHLANDS AND ISLANDS
E. 326,553 *T.* 61.76%

SNP	55,933	(27.73%)
Lab.	51,371	(25.47%)
LD	43,226	(21.43%)
C.	30,122	(14.94%)
Green	7,560	(3.75%)
Ind. Noble	3,522	(1.75%)
Soc. Lab.	2,808	(1.39%)
Highlands	2,607	(1.29%)
SSP	1,770	(0.88%)
Mission	1,151	(0.57%)
Int. Ind.	712	(0.35%)
NLP	536	(0.27%)
Ind. R.	354	(0.18%)

SNP majority 4,562
(May 1997, LD maj. 1,388)
Additional Members: J. MacGrigor, *C.*; Mrs M. Scanlon, *C.*; Ms M. MacMillan, *Lab.*; P. Peacock, *Lab.*; Ms R. Grant, *Lab.*; Mrs W. Ewing, *SNP*; D. Hamilton, *SNP*

LOTHIANS
E. 539,656 *T.* 61.25%

Lab.	99,908	(30.23%)
SNP	85,085	(25.74%)
C.	52,067	(15.75%)
LD	47,565	(14.39%)
Green	22,848	(6.91%)
Soc. Lab.	10,895	(3.30%)
SSP	5,237	(1.58%)
Lib.	2,056	(0.62%)
Witchery	1,184	(0.36%)
ProLife	898	(0.27%)
Rights	806	(0.24%)
NLP	564	(0.17%)
Braveheart	557	(0.17%)
SPGB	388	(0.12%)
Ind. Voice	256	(0.08%)
Ind. Ind.	145	(0.04%)
Anti-Corr.	54	(0.02%)

Lab. majority 14,823
(May 1997, Lab. maj. 101,991)
Additional Members: Lord James Douglas Hamilton, *C.*; ,D. McLetchie, *C.*; Rt. Hon. Sir David Steel, *LD*; K. MacAskill, *SNP*; Ms M. MacDonald, *SNP*; Ms F. Hyslop, *SNP*; R. Harper, *Green*

SCOTLAND CENTRAL
E. 551,733 *T.* 59.90%

Lab.	129,822	(39.28%)
SNP	91,802	(27.78%)
C.	30,243	(9.15%)
Falkirk W.	27,700	(8.38%)
LD	20,505	(6.20%)
Soc. Lab.	10,956	(3.32%)
Green	5,926	(1.79%)
SSP	5,739	(1.74%)
SUP	2,886	(0.87%)
ProLife	2,567	(0.78%)
SFPP	1,373	(0.42%)
NLP	719	(0.22%)
Ind. Prog.	248	(0.08%)

Lab. majority 38,020
(May 1997, Lab. maj. 143,376)
Additional Members: Mrs L. McIntosh, *C.*; D. Gorrie, *LD*; A. Neil, *SNP*; M. Matheson, *SNP*; Ms L. Fabiani, *SNP*; A. Wilson, *SNP*; G. Paterson, *SNP*

SCOTLAND MID AND FIFE
E. 509,387 *T.* 60.01%

Lab.	101,964	(33.36%)
SNP	87,659	(28.68%)
C.	56,719	(18.56%)
LD	38,896	(12.73%)
Green	11,821	(3.87%)
Soc. Lab.	4,266	(1.40%)
SSP	3,044	(1.00%)
ProLife	735	(0.24%)
NLP	558	(0.18%)

Lab. majority 14,305
(May 1997, Lab. maj. 54,087)
Additional Members: *N. Johnston, *C.*; B. Monteith, *C.*; K. Harding, *C.*; K. Raffan, *LD*; B. Crawford, *SNP*; G. Reid, *SNP*; Ms P. Marwick, *SNP*

*N. Johnston resigned on 10 August 2001. He was replaced by Murdo Fraser

SCOTLAND NORTH EAST
E. 518,521 *T.* 55.05%

SNP	92,329	(32.35%)
Lab.	72,666	(25.46%)
C.	52,149	(18.27%)
LD	49,843	(17.46%)
Green	8,067	(2.83%)
Soc. Lab.	3,557	(1.25%)
SSP	3,016	(1.06%)
Ind. Watt.	2,303	(0.81%)
Ind. SB	770	(0.27%)
NLP	746	(0.26%)

SNP majority 19,663
(May 1997, Lab. maj. 17,518)
Additional Members: D. Davidson, *C.*; A. Johnstone, *C.*; B. Wallace, *C.*; R. Lochhead, *SNP*; Ms S. Robison, *SNP*; B. Adam, *SNP*; Ms I. McGugan, *SNP*

SCOTLAND SOUTH
E. 510,634 *T.* 62.35%

Lab.	98,836	(31.04%)
SNP	80,059	(25.15%)
C.	68,904	(21.64%)
LD	38,157	(11.99%)
Soc. Lab.	13,887	(4.36%)
Green	9,468	(2.97%)
Lib.	3,478	(1.09%)
SSP	3,304	(1.04%)
UK Ind.	1,502	(0.47%)
NLP	775	(0.24%)

Lab. majority 18,777
(May 1997, Lab. maj. 79,585)
Additional Members: P. Gallie, *C.*; D. Mundell, *C.*; M. Tosh, *C.*; A. Fergusson, *C.*; M. Russell, *SNP*; A. Ingram, *SNP*; Ms C. Creech, *SNP*

SCOTLAND WEST
E. 498,466 *T.* 62.27%

Lab.	119,663	(38.55%)
SNP	80,417	(25.91%)
C.	48,666	(15.68%)
LD	34,095	(10.98%)
Green	8,175	(2.63%)
SSP	5,944	(1.91%)
Soc. Lab.	4,472	(1.44%)
ProLife	3,227	(1.04%)
Individual	2,761	(0.89%)
SUP	1,840	(0.59%)
NLP	589	(0.19%)
Ind. Water	565	(0.18%)

Lab. majority 39,246
(May 1997, Lab. maj. 115,995)
Additional Members: Miss A. Goldie, *C.*; J. Young, *C.*; R. Finnie, *LD*; L. Quinan, *SNP*; Ms F. McLeod, *SNP*; Ms K. Ullrich, *SNP*; C. Campbell, *SNP*

‡A Glasgow List MSP, who resigned from the SNP to sit as an independent.

NORTHERN IRELAND ASSEMBLY
Parliament Buildings, Stormont, Belfast BT4 3XX
Tel: 028-9052 1333; Fax: 028-9052 1961
Web: www.ni-assembly.gov.uk

The Assembly has 108 members elected by single transferable vote (six from each of the 18 Westminster constituencies). The first elections took place on 25 June 1998 and members met for the first time on 1 July. Safeguards ensure that key decisions have cross-community support. The executive powers of the Assembly are discharged by an Executive Committee comprising a First Minister and Deputy First Minister (jointly elected by the Assembly on a cross-community basis) and up to ten ministers with departmental responsibilities. Ministerial posts are allocated on the basis of the number of seats each party holds.

The Assembly met in shadow form, pending the establishment of an Executive and the transfer of powers from Parliament. Following devolution it has executive and legislative authority over those areas formerly the responsibility of the Northern Ireland government departments. Its powers might be extended further in future.

Power was initially due to be transferred to the new Executive on 10 March 1999, but disagreements emerged over whether Sinn Fein should be allowed to enter the Executive before IRA weapons had been decommissioned. Further deadlines of 2 April and 30 June were also missed. On 15 July the Assembly met to nominate ministers, with the transfer of power to follow on 18 July. However, as the decommissioning issue had still not been resolved, Unionists failed to nominate ministers (the UUP boycotting the meeting itself) and the process collapsed. On 20 July the two prime ministers announced a review of the implementation of the Agreement to be facilitated by Senator George Mitchell. The scope of the review was tightly drawn, focusing only on the practical implementation of the three principles set out above, effectively decommissioning the Executive. The timing of the review dove-tailed with the inevitably sensitive publication of the Patten Commission's report on policing.

Following a series of meetings involving the parties in London, Mitchell's interim report of 15 November stated that he was increasingly more confident that the parties could find a way through the impasse.

On 18 November, following statements from the UUP, Sinn Fein and one from the IRA, Senator Mitchell concluded the review indicating that he now believed there was a basis for devolution to occur, for the institutions to be established and for decommissioning to take place as soon as possible. He concluded that devolution should take effect, the Executive Committee should meet and paramilitary organisations should appoint their authorised representatives to the IICD in that order and all in the same day. On 20 November the Secretary of State announced support for the Mitchell proposals and stated that the assembly should meet on 29 November for the purpose of running d'Hondt procedure for appointing shadow ministers and devolution should take effect after the necessary Parliamentary procedures had been completed on 2 December 1999.

Powers were devolved to Assembly and other institutions established on 2 December on a basis agreed by the parties during the Mitchell review. The Mitchell review created the expectation that the establishment of the institutions and the appointment of authorised

representatives produced conditions in which Sinn Fein could influence bringing about the start of decommissioning. But it was a matter of political reality that if decommissioning did not occur by the end of January it would be very difficult for David Trimble to continue as leader of the Ulster Unionist Party beyond this. In Late November the Council of the UUP had endorsed the Mitchell outcome but, reflecting the political reality, also recommend that progress on the timing and modalities of decommissioning be reviewed at the end of January 2000 through reports presented to the two governments by the IICD.

Devolution and the institutions were able to flourish on the basis of sufficient cross community support. Unfortunately that support began to ebb when the anticipated progress on decommissioning failed to materialise at the end of January. The two Governments took receipt of General de Chastelain's 31 January report but held back publication in order to explore any hope of credible progress on decommissioning. Both governments tried further efforts to gain clarity on the decommissioning issue.

The Secretary of State announced the suspension legislation on 3 February and warned publicly that it would come into effect on Friday 11 February . On the morning of 11 February, there was some sign that a new IRA proposal was emerging. The Irish Government presented a new position from its leadership. There were still only words and no timescale, but it did include clearer and less equivocal words than before. Unfortunately this was not enough to avert the collapse of the institutions.

Suspension meant that the Assembly could not meet or conduct any business. Parliament Buildings remained open for use by Assembly Members for the purpose of carrying out constituency work and they continued to be paid salaries and allowances – set at the lower pre-devolution shadow rate to reflect the suspension of Assembly business.

Following a period of intensive discussions with pro-Agreement parties during 4 and 5 May at Hillsborough, the Prime Minister and Taoiseach issued a joint statement committing both Government's proposals. On May 6, the IRA responded with a significant and forthcoming statement in which they recognised that:
- the implementation of what the Governments had agreed would provide a new context in which Republicans could pursue their political objectives peacefully.
- in that new context the IRA leadership would initiate a process that would completely and verifiably put arms beyond use.
- the IRA would renew contact with the Decommissioning Commission.
- agreed, as a confidence building measure, to open a number of arms dumps to independent inspectors reporting to the Decommissioning Commission on a regular basis to verify that arms remain secure.
The pro-Agreement parties welcomed these developments. The UUP leader, David Trimble said that the IRA statement "appeared to break new ground". The Prime Minister and the Taoiseach announced on 8 May that they were asking the former Finnish President Martti Ahtisaari and Cyril Ramaphosa, the ANC negotiator, to become the independent inspectors. On 9 May, the Chief Constable of the RUC recognised that the IRA statement marked a significant reduction in the overall threat and announced a number of measures, spread across Northern Ireland, designed as a return to more normal policing.

The Government published the Police Bill on 16 May and gave assurances to Unionists that the legal description of the new police service would incorporate the RUC, while the operational and working name would change to Police Service of Northern Ireland. The Government also took an enabling power to resolve the flying of flags over Government buildings if the devolved Executive could not.

A week later than originally envisaged the Ulster Unionist Council endorsed the Government's proposals on 27 May and devolved government was restored to Northern Ireland with effect from midnight on 29 May 2000.

Following considerable political unrest, David Trimble resigned as Northern Ireland First Minister on 1 July 2001, followed on 18 October by other UUP Ministers. His resignation was an ultimatum to encourage the IRA to start decommissioning their weapons. The administrative elements of his post passed to Sir Reg Empey.

To allow time to resolve this situation the Secretary of State for Northern Ireland ordered 24-hour suspensions of the Assembly on 10 August and 22 September 2001. On 5 November 2001 this period was concluded when David Trimble was elected as First Minister and Mark Durkan was elected as Deputy First Minister to replace Seamus Mallon who had retired.

The next elections to the Northern Ireland Assembly will take place on 1 May 2003.

SALARIES AS AT APRIL 2002

First Minister	£111,183*
Deputy First Minister	£111,183*
Assembly Member	£41,321

*Includes their Assembly Member salary

NORTHERN IRELAND EXECUTIVE

Castle Buildings, Stormont, Belfast BT4 3SG
Tel 028-9052 0700; Fax 028-9052 8195
Web: www.northernireland.gov.uk

First Minster, David Trimble, MLA
Deputy First Minister, Mark Durkan, MLA
Minister of Agriculture and Rural Development, Brid Rogers, MLA
Minster for Culture and Arts and Leisure, Michael McGimpsey, MLA
Minister of Education, Martin McGuiness, MLA
Minister for Enterprise, Trade and Investment, Sir Reg Empey, MLA
Minister for Environment, Dermot Nesbitt, MLA
Minister for Finance and Personnel, Dr Sean Farren, MLA
Minister of Health, Social Services and Public Safety, Bairbre de Brún, MLA
Minister for Employment and Learning, Carmel Hanna, MLA
Minister for Regional Development, Peter Robinson, MLA
Minister for Social Development, Nigel Dodds, MLA

OFFICE OF THE FIRST MINISTER AND DEPUTY MINISTER

Castle Buildings, Stormont Estate, Belfast BT4 3SR
Tel: 028-9052 8400

First Minister, David Trimble, MLA
Deputy First Minister, Mark Durkan, MLA

DEPARTMENT OF AGRICULTURE AND RURAL DEVELOPMENT

Dundonald House, Upper Newtownards Road, Belfast BT4 3SB
Tel: 028-9052 4999; Fax: 028-9052 5003;
Web: www.dardni.gov.uk

Minister for Agriculture and Rural Development, Brid Rodgers, MLA
Permanent Secretary (SCS), Peter Small
Under-Secretaries (SCS), Roy McEnaghan *(Agri-Food Development)*; Pat Toal *(Central Services and Rural Development)*; Tony McCusker *(Food, Farming and Environmental Policy)*; Robert Houston *(Veterinary)*; Dr George McIroy *(Science)*

EXECUTIVE AGENCIES

RIVERS AGENCY

FOREST SERVICE

DEPARTMENT OF CULTURE, ARTS AND LEISURE

20–24 York Street, Belfast BT15 1AQ
Tel: 028-9025 8825

Minister for Culture, Arts and Leisure, Michael McGimpsey, MLA
Permanent Secretary (SCS), Dr Aideen McGinley

DEPARTMENT OF EDUCATION

Rathgael House, 43 Balloo Road,
Bangor, Co. Down BT19 7PR
Tel: 028-9127 9279; Fax 028-9127 9100

Minister of Education, Martin McGuinness, MLA
Permanent Secretary (SCS), Jerry McGinn
Deputy Secretaries (SCS), (Schools) Stephen Pover
Chief Inspector (SCS), Marion Matchett *(Education and Training Inspectorate)*

DEPARTMENT OF ENTERPRISE, TRADE AND INVESTMENT

Netherleigh, Massey Avenue, Belfast BT4 2JP
Tel: 028-9052 9900; Fax 028-9052 9550

Minister for Enterprise, Trade and Investment, Sir Reg Empey, MLA
Permanent Secretary (SCS), Bruce Robinson
Under-Secretaries (SCS), Greg McConnell *(Policy Group)*; R. Hamilton *(Management Services Group)*

EXECUTIVE AGENCY

INVEST NORTHERN IRELAND

DEPARTMENT OF THE ENVIRONMENT FOR NORTHERN IRELAND

Clarence Court, 10-18 Adelaide Street, Belfast BT2 8GB
Tel: 028-90540 540

Minister for the Environment, Dermot Nesbitt, MLA
Permanent Secretary (SCS), Stephen Quinn
Under-Secretaries (SCS), C. Smith *(Local Government and Planning)*; F. Dillon *(Environment and Heritage, Road Safety, DVT (NI), DVL (NI) and Environmental Policy)*

EXECUTIVE AGENCIES

DRIVER AND VEHICLE LICENSING AGENCY (NORTHERN IRELAND)
DRIVER AND VEHICLE TESTING AGENCY (NORTHERN IRELAND)

ENVIRONMENT AND HERITAGE SERVICE
PLANNING SERVICE

DEPARTMENT OF FINANCE AND PERSONNEL

Rathgael House, Balloo Road, Bangor BT19 7NA
Tel: 028-9127 9279

Minister of Finance and Personnel, Dr Sean Farren, MLA
Permanent Secretary (SCS), P. Carvill
Under-Secretaries (SCS), Dr A. McCormick *(Central Finances Group)*; Carol Moore *(Central Personnel Group)* G. Johnston *(Law Reform)*
GENERAL REGISTER OFFICE (NORTHERN IRELAND), Oxford House, 49-55 Chichester Street, Belfast BT1 4HH. Tel: 028-9025 2000.
Registrar-General, Dr N. Caven

EXECUTIVE AGENCIES

BUSINESS DEVELOPMENT SERVICE
LAND REGISTERS OF NORTHERN IRELAND
NORTHERN IRELAND STATISTICS AND RESEARCH AGENCY
RATE COLLECTION AGENCY
VALUATION AND LANDS AGENCY

DEPARTMENT OF HEALTH SOCIAL SERVICES AND PUBLIC SAFETY NORTHERN IRELAND

Castle Buildings, Stormont, Belfast BT4 3SJ
Tel: 028-9052 0000; Fax: 028-9052 0573

Minister for Health, Social Services and Public Safety: Bairbre de Brún, MLA
Permanent Secretary (SCS) Clive Gowdy
Chief Medical Officer (SCS) Dr H. Campbell
Under-Secretaries (SCS), D. Hill *(Planning and Resources Group)*; P. Simpson *(HPSS Management Group)*

EXECUTIVE AGENCY

NORTHERN IRELAND HEALTH AND SOCIAL SERVICES ESTATES AGENCY

DEPARTMENT FOR EMPLOYMENT AND LEARNING

Adelaide House, Adelaide Street, Belfast BT2 8FD
Tel: 028-9025 7777; Fax: 028-9025 7783

Minister for Employment and Learning, Carmel Hanna, MLA
Private Secretary (SCS), Ms M. Stevenson
Permanent Secretary (SCS) Alan Shannon

DEPARTMENT FOR REGIONAL DEVELOPMENT

Clarence Court, 10–18 Adelaide Street, Belfast BT2 8GB
Tel: 028-9054 0540; Fax: 028-9054 0064

Minister for Regional Development, Peter Robinson, mla
Permanent Secretary (SCS) N. Hamilton
Deputy Secretaries (SCS), Paul Swinney *(Strategic Planning, Transport and Finance)*; Linda Brown *(Roads, Water, Personnel and Management Services)*

DEPARTMENT FOR SOCIAL DEVELOPMENT

Churchill House, Victoria Square, Belfast BT2 4BA
Tel: 028-9056 9100

Minister for Social Development, Nigel Dodds, MP, MLA
Permanent Secretary (SCS) John Hunter
Deputy Secretaries (SCS), Cliff Radcliffe *(Urban Regeneration and Community Development)*; D. Baker *(Resources, Housing and Social Group)*

NORTHERN IRELAND ASSEMBLY MEMBERS
as at 31 July 2002

Adams, Gerry, *(SF), West Belfast*
Adamson, Dr Ian, *(UUP), East Belfast*
*Agnew, Fraser, *(UUAP), North Belfast*
Alderdice, Lord, *(Speaker), East Belfast*
††Armitage, Ms Pauline, *(Ind. Unionist), East Londonderry*
Armstrong, Billy, *(UUP), Mid Ulster*
Attwood, Alex, *(SDLP), West Belfast*
Beggs, Roy, *(UUP), East Antrim*
Bell, Billy, *(UUP), Lagan Valley*
Bell, Eileen, *(All.), North Down*
Berry, Paul, *(DUP), Newry and Armagh*
Birnie, Dr Esmond, *(UUP), South Belfast*
†Boyd, Norman, *(NIUP), South Antrim*
Bradley, P. J., *(SDLP), South Down*
Brún, Ms Bairbre de, *(SF), West Belfast*
Byrne, Joe, *(SDLP), West Tyrone*
Campbell, Gregory, *(DUP), East Londonderry*
Carrick, Mervyn, *(DUP), Upper Bann*
Carson, Ms Joan, *(UUP), Fermanagh and South Tyrone*
Close, Seamus, *(All.), Lagan Valley*
Clyde, Wilson, *(DUP), South Antrim*
Cobain, Fred, *(UUP), North Belfast*
Coulter, Revd Robert, *(UUP), North Antrim*
**Courtney, Anne, *(SDLP), Foyle*
Dallat, John, *(SDLP), East Londonderry*
Davis, Ivan, *(UUP), Lagan Valley*
Dodds, Nigel, *(DUP), North Belfast*
Doherty, Arthur, *(SDLP), East Londonderry*
Doherty, Pat, *(SF), West Tyrone*
*Douglas, Boyd, *(UUAP), East Londonderry*
Durkan, Mark, *(SDLP), Foyle*
Empey, Sir Reg, *(UUP), East Belfast*
Ervine, David, *(PUP), East Belfast*
Farren, Dr Sean, *(SDLP), North Antrim*
Fee, John, *(SDLP), Newry and Armagh*
Ford, David, *(All.), South Antrim*
Foster, Sam, *(UUP), Fermanagh and South Tyrone*
Gallagher, Tommy, *(SDLP), Fermanagh and South Tyrone*
Gibson, Oliver, *(DUP), West Tyrone*
Gildernew, Michelle, *(SF), Fermanagh and South Tyrone*
‡Gorman, Sir John, *(UUP), North Down*
Hanna, Carmel. *(SDLP), South Belfast*
***Hamilton, Tom, *(UUP), Strangford*
Haughey, Denis, *(SDLP), Mid Ulster*
Hay, William, *(DUP), Foyle*
Hendron, Dr Joe, *(SDLP), West Belfast*
Hilditch, David, *(DUP), East Antrim*
Hussey, Derek, *(UUP), West Tyrone*
Hutchinson, Bill, *(PUP), North Belfast*
§Hutchinson, Roger, *(Ind Unionist), East Antrim*
Kane, Gardiner, *(DUP), North Antrim*
Kelly, Gerry, *(SF), North Belfast*
Kelly, John, *(SF), Mid Ulster*
Kennedy, Danny, *(UUP), Newry and Armagh*
Leslie, James, *(UUP), North Antrim*
Lewsley, Patricia, *(SDLP), Lagan Valley*
Maginnis, Alban, *(SDLP), North Belfast*
Mallon, Séamus, *(SDLP), Newry and Armagh*
Maskey, Alex, *(SF), West Belfast*
McCarthy, Keiran, *(All.), Strangford*
McCartney, Robert, *(UKUP), North Down*
McClarty, David, *(UUP), East Londonderry*
McCrea, Revd William, *(DUP), Mid Ulster*
‡McClelland, Donovan, *(SDLP), South Antrim*
McDonnell, Dr Alasdair, *(SDLP), South Belfast*
McElduff, Barry, *(SF), West Tyrone*

McFarland, Alan, *(UUP), North Down*
Mcgimpsey, Michael, *(UUP), South Belfast*
McGrady, Eddie, *(SDLP), South Down*
McGuiness, Martin, *(SF), Mid Ulster*
McHugh, Gerry, *(SF), Fermanagh and South Tyrone*
McLaughlin, Mitchel, *(SF), Foyle*
McMenamin, Eugene, *(SDLP), West Tyrone*
McNamee, Pat, *(SF), Newry and Armagh*
McWilliams, Prof. Monica, *(NIWC), South Belfast*
Molloy, Francie, *(SF), Mid Ulster*
Murphy, Connor, *(SF), Newry and Armagh*
Murphy, Mick, *(SF), South Down*
‡Morrice, Ms Jane, *(NIWC), North Down*
Morrow, Maurice, *(DUP), Fermanagh and South Tyrone*
Neeson, Sean, *(All.), East Antrim*
Nelis, Ms Mary, *(SF), Foyle*
Nesbitt, Dermot, *(UUP), South Down*
O'Connor, Danny, *(SDLP), East Antrim*
O'Hagan, Dara, *(SF), Upper Bann*
O'Neill, Eamon, *(SDLP), South Down*
Paisley, Revd Dr Ian, *(DUP), North Antrim*
Poots, Edwin, *(DUP), Lagan Valley*
Ramsey, Sue, *(SF), West Belfast*
Robinson, Iris, *(DUP), Strangford*
Robinson, Ken, *(UUP), East Anrtim*
Robinson, Mark, *(DUP), South Belfast*
Robinson, Peter, *(DUP), East Belfast*
†Roche, Patrick, *(NIUP), Lagan Valley*
Rodgers, Brid, *(SDLP), Upper Bann*
Savage, George, *(UUP), Upper Bann*
Shannon, Jim, *(DUP), Strangford*
Shipley-Dalton, Duncan, *(UUP), South Antrim*
Taylor, The Rt. Hon. John, *(UUP), Strangford*
Tierney, John, *(SDLP), Foyle*
Trimble, The Rt. Hon. David, *(UUP), Upper Bann*
Watson, Denis, *(UUAP), Upper Bann*
§§Weir, Peter, *(DUP), North Down*
Wells, Jim, *(DUP), South Down*
†Wilson, Cedric, *(NIUP), Strangford*
Wilson, Jim, *(UUP) South Antrim*
Wilson, Sammy, *(DUP), East Belfast*
* Elected as independent candidates, formed the United
  Unionist Assembly Party (UUAP) with effect from 21
  September 1998
† Elected as UK Unionist Candidates, formed Northern
  Ireland Unionist Party (NIUP) with effect from 15 January
  1999
‡ Elected as Deputy Speakers of the Northern Ireland
  Assembly 31 January 2000
§ Roger Hutchinson was expelled from the Northern Ireland
  Unionist Party (NIUP) with effect from 2 December 1999
** John Hume, MP, MEP, resigned from the Northern Ireland
  Assembly with effect from 1 December 2000. He was
  replaced by Anne Courtney
*** Tom Benson died on 24 December 2000. He was replaced
  by Tom Hamilton
†† Pauline Armitage was suspended from the UUP with effect
  from 9 November 2001 and became an Independent
  Unionist with effect from 30 April 2002
§§ Peter Weir ceased to be a member of the UUP with effect
  from 9 November 2001 and became a member of the DUP
  with effect from 30 April 2002

POLITICAL COMPOSITION

UUP	Ulster Unionist Party	26
SDLP	Social Democratic and Labour Party	24
DUP	Democratic Unionist Party	21
SF	Sinn Féin	18
All	Alliance	6
NIUP	Northern Ireland Unionist Party	3
UUAP	United Unionist Assembly Party	3
NIWC	Northern Ireland Women's Coalition	2
PUP	Progressive Unionist Party	2
UKUP	UK Unionist Party	1
Ind Unionist	Independent Unionist	2

Local Government

Major changes in local government were introduced in England and Wales in 1974 and in Scotland in 1975 by the Local Government Act 1972 and the Local Government (Scotland) Act 1973. Further significant alterations were made in England by the Local Government Acts of 1985, 1992 and 2000.

The structure in England was based on two tiers of local authorities (county councils and district councils) in the non-metropolitan areas; and a single tier of metropolitan councils in the six metropolitan areas of England and London borough councils in London.

Following reviews of the structure of local government in England by the Local Government Commission, 46 unitary (all-purpose) authorities were created between April 1995 and April 1998 to cover certain areas in the non-metropolitan counties. The remaining county areas continue to have two tiers of local authorities. The county and district councils in the Isle of Wight were replaced by a single unitary authority on 1 April 1995; the former counties of Avon, Cleveland, Humberside and Berkshire have been replaced by unitary authorities; and Hereford and Worcester was replaced by a new county council for Worcestershire (with district councils) and a unitary authority for Herefordshire.

The Local Government (Wales) Act 1994 and the Local Government etc. (Scotland) Act 1994 abolished the two-tier structure in Wales and Scotland with effect from 1 April 1996, replacing it with a single tier of unitary authorities.

Local authorities are empowered or required by various Acts of Parliament to carry out functions in their areas. The legislation concerned comprises public general Acts and 'local' Acts which local authorities have promoted as private bills.

ELECTIONS

Local elections are normally held on the first Thursday in May. Generally, all British subjects, citizens of the Republic of Ireland, Commonwealth and other European Union citizens who are 18 years or over and resident on the qualifying date in the area for which the election is being held, are entitled to vote at local government elections. A register of electors is prepared and published annually by local electoral registration officers.

A returning officer has the overall responsibility for an election. Voting takes place at polling stations, arranged by the local authority and under the supervision of a presiding officer specially appointed for the purpose. Candidates, who are subject to various statutory qualifications and disqualifications designed to ensure that they are suitable persons to hold office, must be nominated by electors for the electoral area concerned.

In England, the Boundary Committee for England is responsible for carrying out periodic reviews of electoral arrangements and making recommendations to the Electoral Commission. In Wales and Scotland these matters are the responsibility of the Local Government Boundary Commission for Wales and the Local Government Boundary Commission for Scotland respectively. The Local Government Act 2000 provided for the Secretary of State to change the frequency and phasing of elections.

THE BOUNDARY COMMITTEE FOR ENGLAND, Trevelyan House, Great Peter Street, London SW1P 2HW. Tel: 020-7271 0500

LOCAL GOVERNMENT BOUNDARY COMMISSION FOR WALES, Caradog House, 1–6 St Andrew's Place, Cardiff CF10 3BE. Tel: 029-2039 5031

LOCAL GOVERNMENT BOUNDARY COMMISSION FOR SCOTLAND, 3 Drumsheugh Gardens, Edinburgh EH3 7QJ. Tel: 0131-538 7510

INTERNAL ORGANISATION

The council as a whole is the final decision-making body within any authority. Councils are free to a great extent to make their own internal organisational arrangements. The Local Government Act, given Royal assent on 28 July 2000, allows councils to adopt one of three broad categories of a new constitution which include a separate executive.

These three categories are:

– A directly elected mayor with a cabinet selected by that mayor.

– A cabinet, either elected by the council or appointed by its leader.

– A directly elected mayor and council manager.

Normally, questions of policy are settled by the full council, while the administration of the various services is the responsibility of committees of councillors. Day-to-day decisions are delegated to the council's officers, who act within the policies laid down by the councillors.

FINANCE

Local government in England, Wales and Scotland is financed from four sources: the council tax, non-domestic rates, government grants, and income from fees and charges for services.

COUNCIL TAX

Under the Local Government Finance Act 1992, from 1 April 1993 the council tax replaced the community charge (which had been introduced in April 1989 in Scotland and April 1990 in England and Wales in place of domestic rates).

The council tax is a local tax levied by each local council. Liability for the council tax bill usually falls on the owner-occupier or tenant of a dwelling which is their sole or main residence. Council tax bills may be reduced because of the personal circumstances of people resident in a property, and there are discounts in the case of dwellings occupied by fewer than two adults.

In England, each county council, each district council and each police authority sets its own council tax rate. The district councils collect the combined council tax, and the county councils and police authorities claim their share from the district councils' collection funds. In Wales, each unitary authority and each police authority sets its own council tax rate. The unitary authorities collect the combined council tax and the police authorities claim their share from the funds. In Scotland, each local authority sets its own rate of council tax.

The tax relates to the value of the dwelling. Each dwelling is placed in one of eight valuation bands, ranging from A to H, based on the property's estimated market value as at 1 April 1991.

The valuation bands and ranges of values in England, Wales and Scotland are:

England

A	Up to £40,000	E	£88,001–£120,000
B	£40,001–£52,000	F	£120,001–£160,000
C	£52,001–£68,000	G	£160,001–£320,000
D	£68,001–£88,000	H	Over £320,000

Wales

A	Up to £30,000	E	£66,001–£90,000
B	£30,001–£39,000	F	£90,001–£120,000
C	£39,001–£51,000	G	£120,001– £240,000
D	£51,001–£66,000	H	Over £240,000

Scotland

A	Up to £27,000	E	£58,001–£80,000
B	£27,001–£35,000	F	£80,001–£106,000
C	£35,001–£45,000	G	£106,001–£212,000
D	£45,001–£58,000	H	Over £212,000

The council tax within a local area varies between the different bands according to proportions laid down by law. The charge attributable to each band as a proportion of the Band D charge set by the council is approximately:

A	67%	E	122%
B	78%	F	144%
C	89%	G	167%
D	100%	H	200%

The band D rate is given in the tables on the following pages. There may be variations from the given figure within each district council area because of different parish or community precepts being levied.

NON-DOMESTIC RATES

Non-domestic (business) rates are collected by billing authorities; these are the district councils in those areas of England with two tiers of local government and unitary authorities in other parts of England, in Wales and in Scotland. In respect of England and Wales, the Local Government Finance Act 1988 provides for liability of rates to be assessed on the basis of a poundage (multiplier) tax on the rateable value of property (hereditaments). Separate multipliers are set by the Office of the Deputy Prime Minister in England, the National Assembly for Wales and the Scottish Executive, and rates are collected by the billing authority for the area where a property is located. Rate income collected by billing authorities is paid into a national non-domestic rating (NNDR) pool and redistributed to individual authorities on the basis of the adult population figure as prescribed by the Office of the Deputy Prime Minister, the National Assembly for Wales or the Scottish Executive. The rates pools are maintained separately in England, Wales and Scotland. Actual payment of rates in certain cases is subject to transitional arrangements, to phase in the larger increases and reductions in rates resulting from the effects of the 2000 revaluation.

Rates are levied in Scotland in accordance with the Local Government (Scotland) Act 1975. For 1995–6, the Secretary of State for Scotland prescribed a single non-domestic rates poundage to apply throughout the country at the same level as the uniform business rate (UBR) in England. Rate income is pooled and redistributed to local authorities on a per capita basis. For the year 1995–6 payment of rates was subject to transitional arrangements to phase in the effect of the 1995 revaluation.

Rateable values for the 2000 rating lists came into force on 1 April 2000. They are derived from the rental value of property as at 1 April 1993 and determined on certain

statutory assumptions by the Valuation Office Agency in England and Wales, and by Regional Assessors in Scotland. New property which is added to the list, and significant changes to existing property, necessitate amendments to the rateable value on the same basis. Rating lists (valuation rolls in Scotland) remain in force until the next general revaluation. Such revaluations take place every five years, the next being in 2005.

Certain types of property are exempt from rates, e.g. agricultural land and buildings, certain businesses and places of public religious worship. Charities and other non-profit-making organisations may receive full or partial relief. Empty property is liable to pay rates at 50 per cent, except for certain specified classes which are exempt entirely.

GOVERNMENT GRANTS

In addition to specific grants in support of revenue expenditure on particular services, central government pays revenue support grant to local authorities. This grant is paid to each local authority so that if each authority spends at the level of its standard spending assessment, all authorities in the same class can set broadly the same council tax.

COMPLAINTS

Local Government Ombudsmen are responsible for investigating complaints from members of the public who claim to have suffered as a consequence of maladministration in local government or in certain local bodies.

The Northern Ireland Commissioner for Complaints fulfils a similar function in Northern Ireland, investigating complaints about local authorities and certain public bodies.

Complaints are made to the relevant local authority in the first instance and complainants may approach the Commissioners if not satisfied. Complaints may also be made directly to the Commissioners.

The Local Government Act 2000 established a Standards Board and Adjudication Panel in England. The Standards Board investigates any allegations that councillors have breached the council's Code of Conduct and if there is evidence of wrongdoing the Adjudication Panel will consider the report of investigations and if it is upheld, impose a penalty. In Wales the Commission for Local Administration in Wales undertakes the role of the Standards Board.

THE QUEEN'S REPRESENTATIVES

The Lord-Lieutenant of a county is the permanent local representative of the Crown in that county. The appointment of Lord-Lieutenants is now regulated by the Lieutenancies Act 1997. They are appointed by the Sovereign on the recommendation of the Prime Minister. The retirement age is 75. The office of Lord-Lieutenant dates from 1551, and its holder was originally responsible for the maintenance of order and for local defence in the county. The duties of the post include attending on royalty during official visits to the county, performing certain duties in connection with armed forces of the Crown (and in particular the reserve forces), and making presentations of honours and awards on behalf of the Crown. In England, Wales and Northern Ireland, the Lord-Lieutenant usually also holds the office of *Custos Rotulorum*. As such, he or she acts as head of the county's commission of the peace (which recommends the appointment of magistrates).

The office of Sheriff (from the Old English shire-reeve) of a county was created in the tenth century. The Sheriff

was the special nominee of the Sovereign, and the office reached the peak of its influence under the Norman kings. The Provisions of Oxford (1258) laid down a yearly tenure of office. Since the mid-16th century the office has been purely civil, with military duties taken over by the Lord-Lieutenant of the county. The Sheriff (commonly known as 'High Sheriff') attends on royalty during official visits to the county, acts as the returning officer during parliamentary elections in county constituencies, attends the opening ceremony when a High Court judge goes on circuit, executes High Court writs, and appoints under-sheriffs to act as deputies. The appointments and duties of the High Sheriffs in England and Wales are laid down by the Sheriffs Act 1887.

The serving High Sheriff submits a list of names of possible future sheriffs to a tribunal which chooses three names to put to the Sovereign. The tribunal nominates the High Sheriff annually on 12 November and the Sovereign picks the name of the Sheriff to succeed in the following year. The term of office runs from 25 March to the following 24 March (the civil and legal year before 1752). No person may be chosen twice in three years if there is any other suitable person in the county.

CIVIC DIGNITIES

District councils in England may petition for a royal charter granting borough or 'city' status to the district. Local councils in Wales may petition for a royal charter granting county borough or 'city' status to the council.

In England and Wales the chairman of a borough or county borough council may be called a mayor, and the chairman of a city council may be called a Lord Mayor if Lord Mayoralty has been conferred on that city. Parish councils in England and community councils in Wales may call themselves 'town councils', in which case their chairman is the town mayor.

In Scotland the chairman of a local council may be known as a convenor; a provost is the equivalent of a mayor. The chairmen of the councils for the cities of Aberdeen, Dundee, Edinburgh and Glasgow are Lord Provosts.

ENGLAND

There are currently 34 non-metropolitan counties; all are divided into non-metropolitan districts. In addition, there are 45 unitary authorities (13 created in April 1996, 13 in April 1997 and 19 in April 1998). At present there are 238 non-metropolitan districts. The populations of most of the new unitary authorities are in the range of 100,000 to 300,000. The non-metropolitan districts have populations broadly in the range of 60,000 to 100,000; some, however, have larger populations, because of the need to avoid dividing large towns, and some in mainly rural areas have smaller populations.

The main conurbations outside Greater London – Tyne and Wear, West Midlands, Merseyside, Greater Manchester, West Yorkshire and South Yorkshire – are divided into 36 metropolitan districts, most of which have a population of over 200,000.

There are also about 10,000 parishes, in 219 of the non-metropolitan and 18 of the metropolitan districts.

ELECTIONS

For districts, non-metropolitan counties and for about 8,000 parishes, there are elected councils, consisting of directly elected councillors. The councillors elect annually one of their number as chairman.

Generally, councillors serve four years and there are no elections of district and parish councillors in county election years. In metropolitan districts, one-third of the councillors for each ward are elected each year except in the year when county elections take place elsewhere. Non-metropolitan districts can choose whether to have elections by thirds or whole council elections. In the former case, one-third of the council, as nearly as may be, is elected in each year of metropolitan district elections. If whole council elections are chosen, these are held in the year midway between county elections.

FUNCTIONS

In non-metropolitan areas, functions are divided between the districts and counties, those requiring the larger area or population for their efficient performance going to the county. The metropolitan district councils, with the larger population in their areas, already had wider functions than non-metropolitan councils, and following abolition of the metropolitan county councils were also given most of their functions. A few functions continue to be exercised over the larger area by joint bodies, made up of councillors from each district.

The allocation of functions is as follows:

County councils: education; strategic planning; traffic, transport and highways; fire service; consumer protection; refuse disposal; smallholdings; social services; libraries

Non-metropolitan district councils: local planning; housing; highways (maintenance of certain urban roads and off-street car parks); building regulations; environmental health; refuse collection; cemeteries and crematoria

Unitary councils: their functions are all those listed above, except that the fire service is exercised by a joint body

Concurrently by county and district councils: recreation (parks, playing fields, swimming pools); museums; encouragement of the arts, tourism and industry

The Police and Magistrates Court Act 1994 set up police authorities in England and Wales separate from the local authorities.

PARISH COUNCILS

Parishes with 200 or more electors must generally have parish councils, which means that over three-quarters of the parishes have councils. A parish council comprises at least five members, the number being fixed by the district council. Elections are held every four years, at the time of the election of the district councillor for the ward including the parish. All parishes have parish meetings, comprising the electors of the parish. Where there is no council, the meeting must be held at least twice a year.

Parish council functions include: allotments; encouragement of arts and crafts; community halls; recreational facilities (e.g. open spaces, swimming pools), cemeteries and crematoria; and many minor functions. They must also be given an opportunity to comment on planning applications. They may, like county and district councils, spend limited sums for the general benefit of the parish. They levy a precept on the district councils for their funds.

The Local Government and Rating Act 1997 gave additional powers to parish councils to spend money on community transport initiatives and crime prevention equipment.

FINANCE

Aggregate external finance for 2002–3 has been determined at £47,344 million. Of this, special and specific grants were estimated at £10,829 million; £19,889

million was in respect of Revenue Support Grant and £16,626 million was support from the national non-domestic rate pool.

In England, the average council tax per dwelling for 2002–3 is £804, an increase from £741 in 2001–2. The average council tax is £828 in shire areas, £819 in London and £722 in metropolitan areas. In England, the average council tax bill for a band D dwelling (occupied by two adults) for 2002–3 is £976. The average band D council tax is £984 in shire areas, £895 in London and £1,017 in metropolitan areas.

The provisional amount estimated to be raised from national non-domestic rates from central and local lists is £15,733 million. Total rateable value held on local authority and central lists at 31 December 2001 was £41,866 million. The amount of national non-domestic rates to be redistributed to authorities from the pool in 2002–3 is £16,626 million. The national non-domestic rate multiplier, or poundage, for 2002–3 is 43.7p.

Under the Local Government and Housing Act 1989, local authorities have four main ways of paying for capital expenditure: borrowing and other forms of extended credit; capital grants from central government towards some types of capital expenditure; 'usable' capital receipts from the sale of land, houses and other assets; and revenue.

The amount of capital expenditure which a local authority can finance by borrowing (or other forms of credit) is effectively limited by the credit approvals issued to it by central government. Most credit approvals can be used for any kind of local authority capital expenditure; these are known as basic credit approvals. Others (supplementary credit approvals) can be used only for the kind of expenditure specified in the approval, and so are often given to fund particular projects or services.

Local authorities can use all capital receipts from the sale of property or assets for capital spending, except in the case of sales of council houses. Generally, the 'usable' part of a local authority's capital receipts consists of 25 per cent of receipts from the sale of council houses and 50 per cent of other housing assets such as shops or vacant land. The balance has to be set aside as provision for repaying debt and meeting other credit liabilities.

EXPENDITURE

Local authority budgeted net revenue expenditure for 2001–2 was (2001–2 cash prices):

Service	£m
Education	25,813
Personal social services	11,076
Police	7,861
Highway maintenance	1,615
Fire	1,842
Emergency Planning and other Home Office services	105
Magistrates courts	324
Public transport and parking	972
Housing benefit administration	6,167
Non-housing revenue account housing	434
Libraries, culture and heritage	1,201
Sport	557
Local environmental services	4,696
Other services	2,427
Net current expenditure	65,073
Capital charges	2,050
Capital charged to revenue	699
Other non-current expenditure	2,378
Interest receipts	−809

Gross revenue expenditure	69,390
Specific and special grants outside AEF	−8,119
Revenue expenditure	61,270
Specific and special grants inside AEF	−5,431
Net revenue expenditure	55,839

AEF = aggregate external finance

LONDON

Since the abolition of the Greater London Council in 1986, the Greater London area has not had a single local government body. The area is divided into 32 borough councils, which have a status similar to the metropolitan district councils in the rest of England, and the Corporation of the City of London.

In March 1998 the Government announced proposals for a Greater London Authority (GLA) covering the area of the 32 London boroughs and the City of London, which would comprise a directly elected mayor and a 25-member assembly. A referendum was held in London on 7 May 1998; the turnout was approximately 34 per cent, of whom 72 per cent voted in favour of the GLA. The independent candidate for London Mayor, Ken Livingstone, was elected on 4 May 2000 and the Authority assumed its responsibilities on 3 July 2000. The GLA is responsible for transport, economic development, strategic planning, culture, health, the environment, the police and fire and emergency planning. The separately elected assembly scrutinise the mayor's activities and approve plans and budgets. There are 14 Constituency Assembly members, each representing a separate area of London (each constituency is made up of two or three complete London boroughs). Eleven additional members, making up the total Assembly complement of 25 members, are elected on a London-wide basis, either as independents or from party political lists on the basis of proportional representation. Parties or independent candidates must secure at least five per cent of the vote to be entitled to additional seats.

LONDON BOROUGH COUNCILS

The London boroughs have whole council elections every four years, in the year immediately following the county council election year. The most recent elections took place on 2 May 2002.

The borough councils have responsibility for the following functions: building regulations; cemeteries and crematoria; consumer protection; education; youth employment; environmental health; electoral registration; food; drugs; housing; leisure services; libraries; local planning; local roads; museums; parking; recreation (parks, playing fields, swimming pools); refuse collection and street cleansing; social services; town planning; and traffic management.

THE CORPORATION OF LONDON

The Corporation of London is the local authority for the City of London. Its legal definition is 'The Mayor and Commonalty and Citizens of the City of London'. It is governed by the Court of Common Council, which consists of the Lord Mayor, 24 other aldermen, and 130 common councilmen. The Lord Mayor and two sheriffs are nominated annually by the City guilds (the livery companies) and elected by the Court of Aldermen. Aldermen and councilmen are elected from the 25 wards into which the City is divided; councilmen must stand for re-election annually. The Council is a legislative assembly, and there are no political parties.

The Corporation has the same functions as the London borough councils. In addition, it runs the City of London Police; is the health authority for the Port of London; has health control of animal imports throughout Greater London, including at Heathrow airport; owns and manages public open spaces throughout Greater London; runs the Central Criminal Court; and runs Billingsgate, Smithfield and Spitalfields markets.

THE CITY GUILDS (LIVERY COMPANIES)

The livery companies of the City of London grew out of early medieval religious fraternities and began to emerge as trade and craft guilds, retaining their religious aspect, in the 12th century. From the early 14th century, only members of the trade and craft guilds could call themselves citizens of the City of London. The guilds began to be called livery companies, because of the distinctive livery worn by the most prosperous guild members on ceremonial occasions, in the late 15th century.

By the early 19th century the power of the companies within their trades had begun to wane, but those wearing the livery of a company continued to play an important role in the government of the City of London. Liverymen still have the right to nominate the Lord Mayor and sheriffs, and most members of the Court of Common Council are liverymen.

WALES

The Local Government (Wales) Act 1994 abolished the two-tier structure of eight county and 37 district councils which had existed since 1974, and replaced it, from 1 April 1996, with 22 unitary authorities. The new authorities were elected in May 1995. Each unitary authority has inherited all the functions of the previous county and district councils, except fire services (which are provided by three combined fire authorities, composed of representatives of the unitary authorities) and National Parks (which are the responsibility of three independent National Park authorities).

The Police and Magistrates Courts Act 1994 set up four police authorities with effect from 1 April 1995: Dyfed-Powys, Gwent, North Wales, and South Wales.

COMMUNITY COUNCILS

In Wales community councils are the equivalent of parishes in England. Unlike England, where many areas are not in any parish, communities have been established for the whole of Wales, approximately 865 communities in all. Community meetings may be convened as and when desired.

Community councils exist in 735 communities and further councils may be established at the request of a community meeting. Community councils have broadly the same range of powers as English parish councils. Community councillors are elected for a term of four years.

FINANCE

Aggregate external finance for 2002–3 (excluding specific grants) is £2,989 million. This comprises revenue support grant of £2,341 million, support from the national non-domestic rate pool of £643 million, and £4.75 million in council tax reduction grants. Total standard spending by local authorities considered for grant purposes is £3,684 million.

The average Band D council tax levied in Wales for 2002–3 is £762, comprising unitary authorities £650,

police authorities £94, community councils £19 and an average grant reduction of £4.6.

EXPENDITURE

Local authority budgeted net revenue expenditure for 2002–3 is:

Service	£m
Education	1,694.5
Personal social services	836.4
Police	453.6
Fire	110.4
Other law, order and protective services	26.9
Roads and Transport	228.3
Council tax benefit and administration	16.7
Non-housing revenue account housing, including housing benefit	290.9
Libraries, culture, heritage, sport and recreation	140.6
Local environmental services	255.1
National Parks	12.9
Debt financing costs	259.6
Other services	293.0
Gross Revenue Expenditure	4,618.9
Less specific government grants	−644.4
Net revenue expenditure	3,974.5

SCOTLAND

The Local Government etc. (Scotland) Act 1994 abolished the two-tier structure of nine regional and 53 district councils which had existed since 1975 and replaced it, from 1 April 1996, with 29 unitary authorities on the mainland; the three islands councils remained. The new authorities were elected in April 1995. Each unitary authority has inherited all the functions of the regional and district councils, except water and sewerage and reporters panels.

In July 1999 the Scottish Parliament assumed responsibility for legislation on local government. The Government had established a Commission on Local Government and the Scottish Parliament (the McIntosh Commission) to make recommendations on the relationship between local authorities and the new Parliament and on increasing local authorities' accountability. The Commission published its reports in July 1999.

Following this report, the Scottish Executive established the 'Renewing Local Democracy' working group to consider ways in which to make council membership more attractive and councils more representative of their communities. The group would also advise on appropriate membership levels for each council, looking at modernising management practices and local concerns. They also investigated which method of election would be most appropriate, taking account of the following criteria; proportionality and the councillor-ward link, fair provision for independents, allowance for geographical diversity and a close fit between council wards and natural communities, and advise on an appropriate system of remuneration for councillors, taking account of available resources.

The Scottish Executive also set up the Leadership Advisory Panel in August 1999 following the recommendations of the McIntosh Report. The panel worked closely with Scottish local authorities helping them to conduct a self-review of their political management structures and to implement its recommendations.

The Local Government in Scotland Bill was introduced to the Scottish Parliament in May 2002. This Bill centres on three integrated core elements:
- A power for local authorities to promote and improve well-being of their area and/or persons in it
- Statutory underpinning for community planning through the introduction of a duty on local authorities and key partners, including police, health boards and enterprise agencies
- A duty to secure best value

The overall aim of the bill is to provide a framework for more responsive public services, giving councils more flexibility and responsibility to act in the best interests of their communities.

ELECTIONS

The unitary authorities consist of directly elected councillors. The Scottish Local Government (Elections) Act 2002 moved elections from a three-year to a four-year cycle; the next elections will take place in May 2003. In 2001 the register showed 3,984,306 electors in Scotland.

FUNCTIONS

The functions of the councils and islands councils are: education; social work; strategic planning; the provision of infrastructure such as roads; consumer protection; flood prevention; coast protection; valuation and rating; the police and fire services; civil defence; electoral registration; public transport; registration of births, deaths and marriages; housing; leisure and recreation; development control and building control; environmental health; licensing; allotments; public conveniences; and the administration of district courts.

COMMUNITY COUNCILS

Scottish community councils differ from those in England and Wales. Their purpose as defined in statute is to ascertain and express the views of the communities they represent, and to take in the interests of their communities such action as appears to be expedient or practicable. Over 1,000 community councils have been established under schemes drawn up by local authorities in Scotland.

Since April 1996 community councils have had an enhanced role, becoming statutory consultees on local planning issues and on the decentralisation schemes which the new councils have to draw up for delivery of services.

FINANCE

Figures for 2001–2 show total receipts from non-domestic rates of £1,664,910,260 (provisional). The unified small business rate for 2001–2 was 45p for property with a rateable value of less than £10,000 and 47.8p otherwise. The average Band D council tax payable in 2001–2 was £929.

EXPENDITURE

The 2002–3 budget estimates for local authorities in Scotland are:

Service	£m
Education	3,616.7
Arts and Libraries	131.9
Social Work Services	1,473.6
Law, order and protective services	1,063.7
Roads and transport	407.6
Other environmental services	805.7
Tourism	9.5
Housing	4.2
Sub-total	7,512.9
Sheltered employment	9.9
Housing benefit administration	45.2
Consumer protection	18.9
Total	7,586.8

NORTHERN IRELAND

For the purpose of local government Northern Ireland has a system of 26 single-tier district councils.

ELECTIONS

Council members are elected for periods of four years at a time on the principle of proportional representation.

FUNCTIONS

The district councils have three main roles. These are:
Executive: responsibility for a wide range of local services including building regulations; community services; consumer protection; cultural facilities; environmental health; miscellaneous licensing and registration provisions, including dog control; litter prevention; recreational and social facilities; refuse collection and disposal; street cleansing; and tourist development
Representative: nominating representatives to sit as members of the various statutory bodies responsible for the administration of regional services such as drainage, education, fire, health and personal social services, housing, and libraries
Consultative: acting as the medium through which the views of local people are expressed on the operation in their area of other regional services, notably conservation (including water supply and sewerage services), planning and roads, provided by those departments of central government which have an obligation, statutory or otherwise, to consult the district councils about proposals affecting their areas

FINANCE

Local government in Northern Ireland is funded by a system of rates (a local property tax calculated by using the rateable value of a property multiplied by an amount per pound of rateable value). Rates are collected by the Rate Collection Agency, an executive agency within the Department of Finance and Personnel. A general revaluation of non-domestic properties became effective on 1 April 1997 and the results of a further revaluation will be effective from 1 April 2003. Separate regional rates are made at standard uniform amounts by the Department of Finance and Personnel for both domestic and non-domestic sectors. District councils strike their individual district rates on the same basis.

In 2001–2 approximately £647.8 million was raised in rates. The average domestic poundage levied was 241.26p and the average non-domestic rate poundage was 48.94p.

Political Composition of Local Councils

As at July 2002

Abbreviations

BNP	British National Party
C.	Conservative
CU	Conservative and Unionist
Green	Green
Ind.	Independent
Ind. All.	Independent Alliance
IKHHC	Independent Kidderminster Hospital and Health Concern
Lab.	Labour
LD	Liberal Democrat
Lib.	Liberal
NP	Non-Political/Non-Party
PC	Plaid Cymru
SD	Social Democrat
SNP	Scottish National Party
Soc.	Socialist
SSIG	South Shropshire Independent Group

ENGLAND

COUNTY COUNCILS

Bedfordshire	*C.* 26; *Lab.* 13; *LD* 10
Buckinghamshire	*C.* 40; *LD* 9; *Lab.* 5
Cambridgeshire	*C.* 34; *LD* 16; *Lab.* 9
Cheshire	*C.* 28; *Lab.* 17; *LD* 5; *Ind.* 1
Cornwall	*LD* 36; *Ind.* 25; *C.* 9; *Lab.* 9
Cumbria	*Lab.* 40; *C.* 33; *LD* 10; *Ind.* 1
Derbyshire	*Lab.* 43; *C.* 13; *LD* 7; *Ind.* 1
Devon	*C.* 23; *LD* 21; *Lab.* 5; *Ind.* 3; *Lib.* 2
Dorset	*C.* 23; *LD* 14; *Lab.* 4; *Ind.* 1
Durham	*Lab.* 53; *LD* 4; *C.* 2; *Ind.* 2
East Sussex	*C.* 24; *LD* 13; *Lab.* 6
Essex	*C.* 49; *Lab.* 18; *LD* 10; *Ind.* 2
Gloucestershire	*C.* 27; *Lab.* 19; *LD* 16; *Ind.* 1
Hampshire	*C.* 46; *LD* 19; *Lab.* 9
Hertfordshire	*C.* 40; *Lab.* 27; *LD* 10
Kent	*C.* 52; *Lab.* 22; *LD* 10
Lancashire	*Lab.* 44; *C.* 26; *LD* 6; *Green* 1; *Other* 1
Leicestershire	*C.* 28; *Lab.* 15; *LD* 10; *Ind.* 1
Lincolnshire	*C.* 49; *Lab.* 21; *LD* 4; *Ind.* 3
Norfolk	*C.* 47; *Lab.* 26; *LD* 11
Northamptonshire	*Lab.* 39; *C.* 33; *LD* 1
Northumberland	*Lab.* 36; *C. and Ind.* 19; *LD* 11
North Yorkshire	*C.* 41; *LD* 17; *Lab.* 11; *Ind.* 5
Nottinghamshire	*Lab.* 40; *C.* 20; *LD* 3
Oxfordshire	*C.* 26; *Lab.* 24; *LD* 18; *Green* 2
Shropshire	*C.* 18; *Lab.* 11; *LD* 9; *Other* 6
Somerset	*LD* 29; *C.* 24; *Lab.* 5
Staffordshire	*Lab.* 36; *C.* 24; *LD* 2
Suffolk	*Lab.* 35; *C.* 31; *LD* 12; *Ind.* 1; *Other* 1
Surrey	*C.* 50; *Lab.* 13; *Lab.* 6; *Other* 4; *Ind.* 2
Warwickshire	*Lab.* 28; *C.* 20; *LD* 13; *Other* 1
West Sussex	*C.* 42; *LD* 18; *Lab.* 11
Wiltshire	*C.* 28; *LD* 13; *Lab.* 3; *Ind.* 3
Worcestershire	*C.* 26; *Lab.* 14; *LD* 8; *Other* 10; *Ind.* 1

METROPOLITAN BOROUGH COUNCILS

Barnsley	*Lab.* 49; *Ind.* 9; *C.* 4; *LD* 3; *NP* 1
Birmingham	*Lab.* 67; *C.* 31; *LD* 15; *Other* 4
Bolton	*Lab.* 31; *C.* 16; *LD* 13
Bradford	*Lab.* 38; *C.* 38; *LD* 12; *Green* 2
Bury	*Lab.* 33; *C.* 12; *LD* 3
Calderdale	*C.* 25; *LD* 15; *Lab.* 13; *Ind.* 1
Coventry	*Lab.* 31; *C.* 19; *Soc.* 3; *LD* 1
Doncaster	*Lab.* 41; *LD* 8; *C.* 6; *Other* 5; *Ind.* 2; *Vacant* 1
Dudley	*Lab.* 37; *C.* 24; *LD* 11
Gateshead	*Lab.* 46; *LD* 20
Kirklees	*LD* 28; *Lab.* 26; *C.* 14; *Green* 3
Knowsley	*Lab.* 57; *LD* 8; *Other* 2
Leeds	*Lab.* 56; *LD* 20; *C.* 16; *Green* 3; *Ind.* 1
Liverpool	*LD* 66; *Lab.* 26; *Other* 5; *Ind.* 2
Manchester	*Lab.* 75; *LD* 22; *Other* 1; *Vacant* 1
Newcastle upon Tyne	*Lab.* 57; *LD* 19
North Tyneside	*Lab.* 33; *C.* 18; *LD* 8; *Vacant* 1
Oldham	*LD* 30; *Lab.* 27; *C.* 2; *Green* 1
Rochdale	*Lab.* 31; *LD* 21; *C.* 7
Rotherham	*Lab.* 58; *C.* 4; *Ind.* 3
Salford	*Lab.* 51; *LD* 6; *C.* 2; *Ind.* 1
Sandwell	*Lab.* 55; *LD* 7; *C.* 7; *Ind.* 1
Sefton	*Lab.* 25; *LD* 21; *C.* 17; *Other* 3
Sheffield	*LD* 43; *Lab.* 43; *C.* 1
Solihull	*C.* 29; *Lab.* 13; *LD* 9
South Tyneside	*Lab.* 45; *LD* 11; *Other* 4
St. Helens	*Lab.* 33; *LD* 15; *C.* 5; *Ind.* 1
Stockport	*LD* 33; *Lab.* 19; *C.* 8; *Other* 3
Sunderland	*Lab.* 62; *C.* 11; *LD* 2
Wolverhampton City	*Lab.* 35; *C.* 21; *LD* 4
Tameside	*Lab.* 46; *C.* 6; *LD* 2; *Other* 2; *Ind.* 1
Trafford	*Lab.* 32; *C.* 28; *LD* 3
Wakefield	*Lab.* 53; *C.* 5; *Ind.* 3; *LD* 2
Walsall	*Lab.* 28; *C.* 24; *LD* 7
Wigan	*Lab.* 65; *LD* 3; *C.* 2; *Other* 2
Wirral	*Lab.* 31; *C.* 20; *LD* 14; *Ind.* 1

DISTRICT COUNCILS

Adur	*C.* 25; *Lab.* 11; *LD* 3
Allerdale	*Lab.* 36; *C.* 8; *LD* 8; *Ind.* 4
Alnwick	*Ind.* 13; *LD* 11; *Lab.* 2; *C.* 2; *Other* 1; *Vacant* 1
Amber Valley	*C.* 25; *Lab.* 19; *Vacant* 1
Arun	*C.* 37; *LD* 9; *Lab.* 8; *Ind.* 2
Ashfield	*Lab.* 30; *Ind.* 2; *C.* 1
Ashford	*C.* 23; *LD* 7; *Lab.* 8; *Other* 7; *Ind. LD* 2; *Ind.* 2;
Aylesbury Vale	*C.* 26; *LD* 24; *Ind.* 7; *Lab.* 1
Babergh	*Ind.* 13; *LD* 13; *C.* 10; *Lab.* 5; *Other* 1
Barrow-in-Furness	*Lab.* 19; *C.* 15; *Barrow Ind.* 3; *Other* 1
Basildon	*C.* 21; *Lab.* 18; *LD* 3
Basingstoke and Deane	*C.* 25; *LD* 17; *Lab.* 15; *Ind.* 3
Bassetlaw	*Lab.* 28; *C.* 16; *LD* 3; *Ind.* 1
Bedford	*C.* 24; *Lab.* 14; *LD* 12; *Ind.* 4
Berwick-upon-Tweed	*LD* 16; *Ind.* 10; *C.* 3
Blaby	*C.* 26; *LD* 7; *Lab.* 6
Blyth Valley	*Lab.* 36; *LD* 10; *Ind.* 2; *C.* 2
Bolsover	*Lab.* 32; *Ind.* 4; *Other* 1
Boston	*C.* 14; *Lab.* 10; *Ind.* 5; *LD* 3
Braintree	*Lab.* 31; *C.* 17; *Ind.* 4; *LD* 3; *Other* 3; *Green* 2
Breckland	*C.* 34; *Lab.* 13; *Ind.* 4; *LD* 2
Brentwood	*LD* 20; *C.* 14; *Lab.* 2

Bridgnorth	*Ind. Alliance* 14; *C. with Ind. C.* 11; *Lab.* 4; *Other* 3
Broadland	*C.* 26; *LD* 10; *Other* 7; *Lab.* 6;
Bromsgrove	*C.* 28; *Lab.* 8; *Other* 2; *Ind. C.* 1
Broxbourne	*C.* 35; *Lab.* 2; *Other* 1
Broxtowe	*Lab.* 25; *C.* 12; *LD* 11; *Ind.* 1
Burnley	*Lab.* 27; *LD* 8; *C.* 4; *Ind.* 3; *BNP* 3
Cambridge	*LD* 24; *Lab.* 16; *C.* 2
Cannock Chase	*Lab.* 23; *C.* 10; *LD* 9
Canterbury	*C.* 19; *LD* 17; *Lab.* 13
Caradon	*Ind.* 19; *LD* 19; *Lab.* 2; *C.* 1
Carlisle	*C.* 27; *Lab.* 18; *LD* 5; *Ind.* 2
Carrick	*LD* 29; *Ind.* 6; *C.* 6; *Lab.* 2; *Other* 2
Castle Morpeth	*Ind.* 10; *Lab.* 8; *LD* 8; *C.* 4; *Ind. Lab.* 1; *Green* 1; *Vacant* 1
Castle Point	*Lab.* 22; *C.* 16; *Other* 1
Charnwood	*Lab.* 23; *C.* 20; *LD* 6; *Ind.* 1; *Vacant* 1
Chelmsford	*LD*s 26; *C.*s 22; *Lab.* 5; *Other* 3
Cheltenham	*LD* 21; *C.* 13; *Other* 4; *Lab.* 2
Cherwell	*C.* 37; *Lab.* 11; *LD* 2
Chester	*Lab.* 21; *LD* 19; *C.* 19; *Ind.* 1
Chester-le-Street	*Lab.* 30; *LD* 1; *Ind.* 1; *C.* 1
Chesterfield	*Lab.* 28; *LD* 19
Chichester	*C.* 29; *LD* 19; *Ind.* 2
Chiltern	*C.* 29; *LD* 19; *Other* 2
Chorley	*Lab.* 22; *C.* 16; *LD* 6; *Ind.* 3
Christchurch	*C.* 17; *LD* 5; *Ind.* 3
Colchester	*LD* 27; *C.* 24; *Lab.* 6; *Ind.* 4
Congleton	*C.* 22; *LD* 14; *Lab.* 3; *Other* 9
Copeland	*Lab.* 30; *C.* 17; *Ind.* 3; *LD* 1
Corby	*Lab.* 25; *C.* 3; *Ind.* 1
Cotswold	*Ind.* 16; *C.* 14; *LD* 8; *Ind. C.* 2; *Lab.* 1; *Other* 3
Craven	*C.* 13; *LD* 9; *Ind.* 8
Crawley	*Lab.* 23; *C.* 7; *LD* 2
Crewe and Nantwich	*Lab.* 26; *C.* 21; *LD* 5; *Ind.* 1; *Other* 3
Dacorum	*C.* 27; *Lab.* 20; *LD* 4; *Ind.* 1
Dartford	*Lab.* 29; *C.* 13; *Ind.* 5
Daventry	*C.* 26; *Lab.* 10; *LD* 1; *Ind.* 1
Derbyshire Dales	*C.* 21; *LD* 9; *Lab.* 6; *Ind.* 3
Derwentside	*Lab.* 47; *Ind.* 8
Dover	*Lab.* 28; *C.* 26; *LD* 1; *Ind.* 1
Durham City	*Lab.* 32; *LD* 13; *Ind.* 3; *Other* 1
Easington	*Lab.* 45; *Ind.* 5; *Lib.* 1
Eastbourne	*C.* 12; *LD* 15
East Cambridgeshire	*LD* 20; *Ind.* 12; *Lab.* 4; *C.* 1
East Devon	*C.* 37; *LD* 15; *Ind.* 6; *Lab.* 1; *Lib.* 1
East Dorset	*C.* 26; *LD* 9; *Ind.* 1
East Hampshire	*C.* 22; *LD* 17; *Ind.* 3
East Hertfordshire	*C.* 32; *LD* 9; *Lab.* 7; *Ind.* 2
Eastleigh	*LD* 31; *C.* 9; *Lab.* 4
East Lindsey	*95 Group* 36; *Lab.* 8; *C.* 8; *LD* 8
East Northamptonshire	*C.* 21; *Lab.* 15
East Staffordshire	*Lab.* 29; *C.* 14; *LD* 3
Eden	*Ind.* 31; *LD* 3; *C.* 2; *Lab.* 1
Ellesmere Port and Neston	*Lab.* 33; *C.* 8; *LD* 2
Elmbridge	*RA* 31; *C.* 20; *LD* 8; *Lab.* 1
Epping Forest	*C.* 26; *LD* 13; *Ind.* 10; *Lab.* 9
Epsom and Ewell	*RA* 27; *LD* 9; *Lab.* 3
Erewash	*Lab.* 29; *C.* 16; *Ind.* 4; *LD* 3
Exeter City	*Lab.* 22; *LD* 8; *C.* 6; *Lib.* 4
Fareham	*C.* 17; *LD* 14
Fenland	*C.* 29; *Lab.* 7; *Ind.* 3; *LD* 1
Forest Heath	*C.* 21; *LD* 2; *Lab.* 1; *Ind.* 1

Forest of Dean	*Lab.* 28; *Ind.* 14; *LD* 6; *C.* 2
Fylde	*C.* 22; *Ind.* 13; *RA* 9; *LD* 3; *Lab.* 2
Gedling	*C.* 28; *Lab.* 19; *LD* 7; *Ind.* 3
Gloucester	*C.* 16; *Lab.* 11; *LD* 10; *Ind.* 1
Gosport	*Lab.* 12; *LD* 12; *C.* 10
Gravesham	*Lab.* 29; *C.* 15
Great Yarmouth	*C.* 28; *Lab.* 20
Guildford	*LD* 19; *C.* 17; *Lab.* 6; *Ind.* 3
Hambleton	*C.* 35; *Ind.* 6; *LD* 4; *Lab.* 2
Harborough	*C.* 18; *LD* 13; *Ind.* 3; *Lab.* 3
Harlow	*C.* 12; *LD* 12; *Lab.* 9
Harrogate	*LD* 27; *C.* 26; *Ind.* 1
Hart	*C.* 22; *LD* 10; *Ind.* 3
Hastings	*Lab.* 21; *C.* 10; *LD* 1
Havant	*Lab.* 17; *C.* 10; *LD* 12;
Hertsmere	*C.* 25; *Lab.* 9; *LD* 5; *Ind. Lab.* 2
High Peak	*Lab.* 27; *C.* 10; *LD* 5; *Ind.* 2
Hinckley and Bosworth	*LD* 14; *C.* 11; *Lab.* 9
Horsham	*C.* 24; *LD* 15; *Ind.* 4
Huntingdonshire	*C.* 37; *LD* 13; *Ind.* 3
Hyndburn	*Lab.* 18; *C.* 17
Ipswich	*Lab.* 34; *C.* 9; *LD* 3;
Kennet	*C.* 23; *Ind.* 11; *Lab.* 4; *LD* 2
Kerrier	*Ind.* 20; *LD* 10; *Lab.* 9; *C.* 4; *Vacant* 1
Kettering	*Lab.* 23; *C.* 16; *Ind.* 5; *Lib.* 1
King's Lynn and West Norfolk	*Lab.* 27; *C./Ind.* 27; *LD* 6
Lancaster	*Ind.* 17; *Lab.* 16; *C.* 11; *LD* 7; *Green* 6; *Other* 3
Lewes	*LD* 28; *C.* 17; *Ind.* 3
Lichfield	*C.* 19; *Lab.* 11
Lincoln	*Lab.* 26; *C.* 6
Macclesfield	*C.* 35; *LD* 15; *Lab.* 6; *RA* 3; *Ind.:* 1
Maidstone	*LD* 21; *C.* 19; *Lab.* 12; *Ind.* 3
Maldon	*C.* 19; *Ind.* 6; *Lab.* 5
Malvern Hills	*C. Ind.* 24; *LD Green* 12; *Other* 5; *Vacant* 1
Mansfield	*Lab.* 38; *C.* 4; *LD* 2; *Ind.* 1; *Vacant* 1
Melton	*C.* 10; *Lab.* 9; *Ind.* 7
Mendip	*C.* 18; *Lab.* 10; *LD* 16; *Ind.* 2
Mid Bedfordshire	*C.* 35; *Lab.* 7; *LD* 6; *Ind.* 5
Mid Devon	*Ind.* 18; *LD* 18; *C.* 2; *Lab.* 1; *Lib.* 1
Mid Suffolk	*C. Ind.* 17; *LD* 13; *Lab.* 6; *Ind. Lab.* 2; *Other* 1; *Vacant* 1
Mid Sussex	*C.* 29; *LD* 21; *Ind.* 2; *Lab.* 2
Mole Valley	*C.* 18; *LD* 15; *Ind.* 7; *Lab.* 1
Newark and Sherwood	*Lab.* 25; *C.* 21; *LD* 5; *Ind.* 3
Newcastle-under-Lyme	*Lab.* 29; *LD* 18; *C.* 10; *Vacant* 3
New Forest	*C.* 32; *LD* 23; *Ind.* 3
Northampton	*Lab.* 27; *LD* 11; *C.* 8; *Ind.* 1
North Cornwall	*Ind.* 24; *LD* 11; *C.* 3
North Devon	*LD* 27; *Ind.* 10; *C.* 5; *Other* 2
North Dorset	*C.* 15; *LD* 10; *Ind.* 8
North East Derbyshire	*Lab.* 39; *C.* 9; *LD* 3; *Ind.* 2
North Hertfordshire	*C.* 28; *Lab.* 17; *LD* 4
North Kesteven	*C.* 15; *Other* 9; *LD* 7; *Lab.* 6; *Ind.* 3
North Norfolk	*C. and Ind. Alliance* 17; *LD* 12; *Lab.* 7; *Ind.* 7; *Ind. Lab.* 3
North Shropshire	*Other* 13; *C.* 12; *Ind.* 9; *Lab.* 5; *LD* 1
North Warwickshire	*Lab.* 22; *C.* 9; *LD* 2; *Ind.* 1
North West Leicestershire	*Lab.* 31; *C.* 8; *Ind.* 1
North Wiltshire	*LD* 28; *C.* 19; *Lab.* 4; *Ind.* 1

Norwich	*LD* 30; *Lab.* 29; *C.* 1
Nuneaton and Bedworth	*Lab.* 26; *C.* 8
Oadby and Wigston	*LD* 21; *C.* 5
Oswestry	*Lab.* 5; *LD* 6; *C.* 4; *Ind.* 3; *Other* 10; *Vacant* 1
Oxford	*Lab.* 29; *LD* 15; *Green* 3; *Other* 1
Pendle	*Lab.* 19; *LD* 19; *C.* 11
Penwith	*C.* 10; *Ind.* 8; *LD* 7; *Other* 4; *Lab.* 3
Preston	*Lab.* 25; *C.* 19; *LD* 11; *Ind.* 2
Purbeck	*C.* 16; *LD* 4; *Ind.* 3; *Vacant* 1
Redditch	*Lab.* 14; *C.* 12; *LD* 3
Reigate and Banstead	*C.* 33; *Lab.* 6; *LD* 6; *RA* 6
Restormel	*LD* 18; *C.* 13; *Other* 12; *Lab.* 1
Ribble Valley	*C.* 19; *LD* 16 ; *Ind.* 3; *Lab.* 1
Richmondshire	*RAIC* 12; *LD* 8; *C.* 7; *Ind.* 4; *Other* 1
Rochford	*C.* 28; *Lab.* 4; *LD* 4; *Ind.* 2; *Other* 1
Rossendale	*Lab.* 23; *C.* 12;
Rother	*C.* 29; *LD* 8; *Lab.* 4; *Ind.* 4; *Vacant* 2
Rugby	*Lab.* 17; *C.* 17; *LD* 10; *Ind.* 4
Runnymede	*C.* 31; *Other* 6; *Lab.* 4
Rushcliffe	*C.* 30; *LD* 12; *Lab.* 11; *Ind.* 1
Rushmoor	*C.* 24; *LD* 10; *Lab.* 6; *Other* 1
Ryedale	*C.* 11; *Ind.* 6; *LD* 5; *Lab.* 1
Salisbury	*C. and Ind.* 29; *LD* 15; *Lab.* 11; *Ind.* 3
Scarborough	*C.* 19; *Ind.* 13; *Lab.* 11; *LD* 5; *Vacant* 1
Sedgefield	*Lab.* 42; *Ind.* 3; *LD* 2; *Vacant* 2
Sedgemoor	*C.* 31; *Lab.* 16; *LD* 3
Selby	*Lab.* 20; *C.* 15; *Ind.* 6
Sevenoaks	*C.* 33; *Lab.* 7; *LD* 9; *Ind.* 4
Shepway	*C.* 29; *LD* 16; *Lab.* 10, *Vacant* 1
Shrewsbury and Atcham	*Lab.* 9; *C.* 22; *LD* 6; *Ind.* 3
South Bedfordshire	*C.* 28; *LD* 15; *Lab.* 7
South Bucks	*C.* 28; *Ind.* 8; *LD* 2; *Vacant* 2
South Cambridgeshire	*C.* 22; *LD* 17; *Ind.* 10; *Lab.* 6
South Derbyshire	*Lab.* 24; *C.* 10
South Hams	*C.* 29; *LD* 5; *Ind.* 4; *Lab.* 2
South Holland	*C.* 19; *Ind.* 11; *Lab.* 3; *Other* 5
South Kesteven	*C.* 30; *Ind.* 13; *Lab.* 11; *LD* 3; *Other* 1
South Lakeland	*LD* 21; *C.* 19; *Lab.* 9; *Ind.* 3
South Norfolk	*LD* 27; *C.* 16; *Lab.* 2; *Ind.* 2
South Northamptonshire	*C.* 29; *Lab.* 6; *Ind.* 4; *LD* 3
South Oxfordshire	*LD* 18; *C.* 21; *Lab.* 7; *Ind.* 4;
South Ribble	*Lab.* 21; *C.* 18; *LD* 12; *Other* 3
South Shropshire	*LD and Progressive Group* 17; *SSIG* 15; *Other* 8
South Somerset	*LD* 41; *C.* 12; *Ind.* 7
South Staffordshire	*C.* 37; *Lab.* 9; *Ind.* 3; *LD* 1
Spelthorne	*C.* 27; *Lab.* 9; *LD* 4
St. Albans	*C.* 21; *LD* 20; *Lab.* 15; *Ind.* 1; *Vacant* 1
St. Edmundsbury	*C.* 21; *Lab.* 17; *Ind.* 2; *LD* 2; *Ind.* 2
Stafford	*Lab.* 28; *C.* 22; *LD* 8; *Ind.* 1; *Vacant* 1
Staffordshire Moorlands	*C.* 17, *Lab.* 14; *LD* 10; *RA* 12; *Ind.* 3
Stevenage	*Lab.* 33; *C.* 3; *LD* 3
Stratford-on-Avon	*C.s* 27; *LD* 18; *Ind* 3; *Lab.* 2
Stroud	*C.* 28; *Lab.* 10; *LD* 4; *Green* 4; *Ind.* 2; *Other* 1

Suffolk Coastal	*C.* 37; *LD* 10; *Lab.* 7; *Ind.* 1
Swale	*C.* 25; *LD* 12; *Lab.* 10
Tamworth	*Lab.* 22; *C.* 8
Tandridge	*C.* 29; *LD* 10; *Lab.* 3
Taunton Deane	*LD* 23; *C.* 20; *Lab.* 5; *Ind.* 5; *Vacant* 1
Teesdale	*Teesdale Ind.* 11; *Lab.* 9; *Other* 8; *C.* 3
Teignbridge	*Ind.* 22; *C.* 20; *Ind. LD* 9; *Other* 6; *Lab.* 1
Tendring	*Lab.* 21; *C.* 16; *LD* 10; *Ind.* 5; *RA* 3; *Ind. C.* 3; *Other* 1
Test Valley	*C.* 29; *LD* 13; *Ind.* 1; *Other* 1
Tewkesbury	*C.* 16; *Lab.* 8; *Ind.* 8; *LD* 4
Thanet	*Lab.* 33; *C.* 18; *Ind.* 3
Three Rivers	*LD* 26; *C.* 15; *Lab.* 7
Tonbridge and Malling	*C.* 27; *LD* 21; *Lab.* 7
Torridge	*Ind.* 14; *LD* 11; *Other* 9; *Lab.* 2
Tunbridge Wells	*C.* 34; *LD* 11; *Lab.* 3
Tynedale	*C.* 23; *Lab.* 12; *LD* 11; *Ind.* 6
Uttlesford	*LD* 18; *C.* 15; *Ind.* 6; *Lab.* 2; *Other* 1
Vale of White Horse	*LD* 32; *C.* 15; *Lab.* 2; *Ind.* 1; *Vacant* 1
Vale Royal	*Lab.* 32; *C.* 16; *LD* 8; *Ind.* 1
Wansbeck	*Lab.* 25; *LD* 19; *Ind.* 1
Warwick	*Lab.* 17; *LD* 13; *C.* 10; *Ind.* 5
Watford	*Lab.* 15; *LD* 12; *C.* 7; *Ind.* 1; *Vacant* 1
Waveney	*Lab.* 22; *C.* 20; *LD* 3; *Ind.* 3
Waverley	*C.* 31; *LD* 24; *Lab.* 2
Wear Valley	*Lab.* 30; *Ind.* 6; *LD* 4
Welwyn Hatfield	*C.* 26; *Lab.* 22
West Devon	*Ind.* 11; *C.* 8; *LD* 8; *Other* 2; *Vacant* 1
West Dorset	*C.* 22; *LD* 15; *Other* 14; *Lab.* 4
West Lancashire	*C.* 30; *Lab.* 24
West Lindsey	*C.* 13; *LD* 13; *Ind.* 8; *Lab.* 3
West Oxfordshire	*C.* 32; *LD* 10; *Ind.* 5; *Lab.* 2
West Somerset	*C.* 20; *Ind.* 8; *Lab.* 2; *LD* 1
West Wiltshire	*LD* 25; *C.* 11; *Other* 3; *Lab.* 2; *Ind.* 2
Weymouth and Portland	*Lab.* 15; *LD* 10; *C.* 6; *Other* 4
Winchester	*LD* 35; *C.* 14; *Ind.* 5; *Lab.* 3
Woking	*C.* 17; *LD* 13; *Lab.* 5; *Ind.* 1
Worcester	*C.* 18; *Lab.* 12; *Ind.* 4; *LD* 1; *Ind. C.* 1
Worthing	*LD* 19; *C.* 17
Wychavon	*C.* 33; *LD* 10; *Lab.* 4; *Ind.* 1; *Vacant* 1
Wycombe	*C.* 41; *Lab.* 9; *LD* 7; *Ind.* 2; *Vacant* 1
Wyre	*C.* 35; *Lab.* 19; *LD* 2
Wyre Forest	*IKKHC* 21; *C.* 7; *Lab.* 5; *Other* 5; *LD* 2; *Ind.* 2
Wealden	*C.s* 35; *LD* 20; *Ind.* 2; *Vacant* 1

UNITARY COUNCILS

Bath and North East Somerset	*LD* 30; *Lab.* 17; *C.* 16; *Ind. Lab.* 2
Blackburn with Darwen	*Lab.* 36; *C.* 17; *LD* 9
Blackpool	*Lab.* 25; *C.* 15; *LD* 4
Bournemouth	*C.* 27; *LD* 18; *Lab.* 6; *Ind.* 6
Bracknell Forest	*C.* 31; *Lab.* 9
Brighton and Hove	*Lab.* 45; *C.* 21; *LD* 5; *Green* 3; *Ind.* 1
Bristol	*Lab.* 36; *LD* 24; *C.* 9
Darlington	*Lab.* 35; *C.* 15; *LD* 2
Derby	*Lab.* 27; *C.* 11; *LD* 12

East Riding of Yorkshire *C.* 27; *LD* 22; *Lab.* 11; *Ind.* 4;
    SD 2; *Ind. Lab.* 1
Halton *Lab.* 47; *LD* 7; *C.* 2
Hartlepool *Lab.* 23; *LD* 12; *C.* 8; *Ind.* 4
Herefordshire *C.* 22; *LD* 17; *Ind.* 15; *Lab.* 5;
    NP 1
Isle of Wight *LD* 19; *C.* 12; *Ind.* 11; *Lab.* 5;
    Other 1
Kingston upon Hull *LD* 29; *Lab.* 24; *Ind.* 4; *C.* 2;
Leicester *Lab.* 29; *LD* 17; *C.* 10
Luton *Lab.* 36; *LD* 9; *C.* 3
Medway *C.* 38; *Lab.* 25; *LD* 15; *Ind. LD* 2
Middlesbrough *Lab.* 42; *LD* 6; *C.* 4; *Ind.* 1
Milton Keynes *Lab.* 15; *LD* 27; *C.* 7;
North East Lincolnshire *Lab.* 23; *C.* 10; *LDs* 5; *Ind.* 3
North Somerset *C.* 30; *Lab.* 14; *LD* 12; *Ind.* 4;
    Green 1
Nottingham *Lab.* 40; *C.* 11; *LD* 4
North Lincolnshire *Lab.* 23; *C.* 19
Peterborough *C.* 30; *Lab.* 18; *LD* 4; *Lib.* 3;
    Other 2
Plymouth *C.* 38; *Lab.* 21; *LD* 1
Poole *LD* 19; *C.* 17; *Lab.* 3
Portsmouth *C.* 15; *Lab.* 14; *LD* 13
Reading *Lab.* 36; *LD* 6; *C.* 3
Redcar and Cleveland *Lab.* 30; *C.* 14; *LD* 10; *Other.* 1
Rutland *Ind.* 11; *LD* 4; *Other* 1; *Lab.* 1;
    Green 1: *C.* 1; *Vacant* 1
Slough *Lab.* 27; *C.* 6; *Lib.* 3; *Ind.* 2;
    Other 2; *LD* 1
South Gloucestershire *Lab.* 22; *LD* 37; *C.* 10; *Vacant* 1
Southampton *Lab.* 19; *LD* 18; *C.* 11
Southend on Sea *C.* 33; *Lab.* 11; *LD* 7
Stockton-on-Tees *Lab.* 36; *C.* 12; *LD* 5; *Vacant* 2
Stoke-on-Trent *Lab.* 22; *Ind.* 20; *LD* 7; *C.* 5;
    Other 1
Swindon *Lab.* 29; *C.* 22; *LD* 8
Telford and Wrekin *Lab.* 30; *C.* 11; *LD* 4; *Ind.* 4;
    Other 4; *RA* 1
Thurrock *Lab.* 36; *C.* 9; *LD* 1; *Ind.* 2
Torbay *C.* 30; *LD* 6
Warrington *Lab.* 41; *LD* 15; *C.* 4
West Berkshire *LD* 28; *C.* 25; *Ind.* 1
Windsor and
    Maidenhead *C.* 29; *LD* 21; *RA* 7; *Lab.* 1
Wokingham *C.* 30; *LD* 22; *Lab.* 1; *Ind.* 1
York *LD* 24; *Lab.* 25; *C.* 3; *Ind.* 1

LONDON BOROUGH COUNCILS

Barking and Dagenham *Lab.* 42; *RA* 4; *LD* 3; *C.* 2
Barnet *C.* 33; *Lab.* 24; *LD* 6
Bexley *Lab.* 32; *C.* 30; *LD* 1
Brent *Lab.* 35; *C.* 16; *LD* 6
Bromley *C.* 41; *LD* 13; *Lab.* 6
Camden *Lab.* 35; *C.* 11; *LD* 8
Croydon *Lab.* 37; *C.* 32; *LD* 1
Ealing *Lab.* 45; *C.* 17; *LD* 4
Enfield *C.* 39; *Lab.* 24
Greenwich *Lab.* 38; *C.* 9; *LD* 4
Hackney *Lab.* 45; *C.* 9; *LD* 3
Hammersmith and
    Fulham *Lab.* 28; *C.* 18
Haringey *Lab.* 42; *LD* 15
Harrow *Lab.* 31; *C.* 29; *LD* 3
Havering *C.* 26; *RA* 18; *Lab.* 9; *LD* 1
Hillingdon *C.* 31; *Lab.* 27; *LD* 7
Hounslow *Lab.* 36; *C.* 15; *LD* 5; *Other* 4
Islington *LD* 38; *Lab.* 10
Kensington and Chelsea *C.* 42; *Lab.* 12
Kingston upon Thames *LD* 30; *C.* 15; *Lab.* 3

Lambeth *LD* 28; *Lab.* 28; *C.* 7
Lewisham *Lab.* 45; *LD* 4; *C.* 2; *Green* 1;
    Other 2
Merton *Lab.* 32; *C.* 25; *RA* 3
Newham *Lab.* 59; *Other* 1
Redbridge *C.* 33; *Lab.* 21; *LD* 9
Richmond upon
    Thames *C.* 39; *LD* 15
Southwark *LD* 30; *Lab.* 28; *C.* 5
Sutton *LD* 43; *C.* 8; *Lab.* 3
Tower Hamlets *Lab.* 35; *LD* 16
Waltham Forest *Lab.* 29; *C.* 18; *LD* 13
Westminster *C.* 42; *Lab.* 12
Wandsworth *C.* 50; *Lab.* 10

WALES

Blaenau Gwent *Lab.* 33; *Ind. RA* 4; *Ind.* 2;
    Ind. Lab. 1; *LD* 2
Bridgend *Lab.* 40; *LD* 6; *Ind.* 6; *C.* 1
Caerphilly *PC* 38; *Lab.* 28; *Ind.* 4; *LD* 3;
Cardiff *Lab.* 49; *LD* 19; *C.* 5; *PC* 1;
    Ind. 1
Carmarthenshire *Lab.* 31; *Ind.* 24; *PC* 16;
    Ind. Lab. 1; *RA* 1; *LD* 1
Ceredigion *Ind.* 21; *PC* 12; *LD* 8; *Other* 1;
    Lab. 1
Conwy *Lab.* 19; *Ind.* 15; *LD* 13; *PC* 7;
    C. 5
Denbighshire *Lab.* 14; *Ind.* 13; *PC* 7; *Other* 5;
    C. 2; *LD* 1
Flintshire *Lab.* 42; *Alliance* 16; *LD* 7; *PC* 2;
    Other 3
Gwynedd *PC* 43; *Ind.* 20; *Lab.* 12; *LD* 6;
    Ind. Nationalist 2
Isle of Anglesey *Ind.* 19; *PC* 8; *Lab.* 4; *Ind. All.* 4;
    Other 5
Merthyr Tydfil *Lab.* 15; *Ind.* 14; *PC* 4
Monmouthshire *Lab.* 19; *C.* 18; *Ind.* 4; *LD* 1
Neath Port Talbot *Lab.* 40; *PC* 10; *RA* 5; *SD* 3;
    Ind. 3; *LD* 2; *Other.* 1
Newport *Lab.* 39; *C.* 5; *Other* 2; *LD* 1
Pembrokeshire *Ind.* 41; *Lab.* 13; *LD* 4; *PC* 2
Powys *Ind.* 57; *LD* 9; *Lab.* 6; *C.* 1
Rhondda Cynon Taff *PC* 38; *Lab.* 26: *Other* 8; *Ind.* 3
Swansea, City and
    County *Lab.* 45; *LD* 11: *Ind.* 7: *C.* 4;
    PC 2; *Other* 1
Torfaen *Lab.* 39; *Ind.* 3; *C.* 1; *LD* 1
Vale of Glamorgan *C.* 22; *Lab.* 18; *PC* 6; *LD* 1
Wrexham *Lab.* 24; *Ind.* 11; *LD* 9; *C.* 4;
    Other 4

SCOTLAND

Aberdeen *Lab.* 22; *LD* 12; *C.* 6; *SNP* 3
Aberdeenshire *LD* 27; *SNP* 23; *Ind.* 10; *CU* 8
Angus *SNP* 21; *LD* 2; *C.* 2; *Other* 2;
    Lab. 1; *Ind.* 1
Argyll and Bute *NP* 19; *LD* 6; *SNP* 4; *C.* 4; *Ind.* 3
Clackmannanshire *SNP* 10; *Lab.* 7; *C.* 1
Dumfries and Galloway *Lab.* 12; *Ind.* 11; *CU* 9; *LD* 7;
    SNP 5; *Other* 3
Dundee *Lab.* 12; *SNP* 11; *C.* 4;
    Ind. Lab. 1; *LD* 1
East Ayrshire *Lab.* 16; *SNP* 9; *C.* 1; *Vacant* 1
East Dunbartonshire *Lab.* 11; *LD* 10; *C.* 3
East Lothian *Lab.* 16; *C.* 5; *SNP*

East Renfrewshire	*Lab.* 9; *C.* 8; *LD* 2; *RA* 1
Eilean Siar	
(Western Isles)	NP 13; *Ind. Forum* 11; *Lab.* 4; *SNP* 3
Edinburgh	*Lab.* 31; *C.* 13; *LD* 13; *SNP* 1
Falkirk	*Lab.* 14; *SNP* 10; *Other* 4; *C.* 2; *Ind.* 2
Fife	*Lab.* 40; *LD* 21; *SNP* 11; *C.* 3; *Other* 2; *Ind.* 1
Glasgow	*Lab.* 74; *SNP* 2; *C.* 1; *LD* 1; *Soc.* 1
Highland	*Ind.* 50; *Lab.* 11; *LD.* 10; *SNP* 9
Inverclyde	*Lab.* 10; *LD* 9; *C.* 1
Midlothian	*Lab.* 17; *LD* 1
Moray	*Ind.* 13; *Lab.* 6; *Other* 2; *Lib.* 2; *SNP* 2; *CU* 1
North Ayrshire	*Lab.* 25; *SNP* 2; *C.* 2; *Ind.* 1
North Lanarkshire	*Lab.* 56; *SNP* 12; *Ind.* 2
Orkney	*Ind.* 21
Perth and Kinross	*SNP* 15; *C.* 11; *LD* 7; *Lab.* 6; *Ind.* 2
Renfrewshire	*Lab.* 21; *SNP* 15; *LD* 3; *C.* 1
Scottish Borders	*Ind.* 14; *LD* 14; *SNP* 3; *C.* 1; *Lab.* 1; *Vacant* 1
Shetland	*Ind.* 13; *LD* 9
South Ayrshire	*Lab.* 15; *C.* 13; *Ind.* 2
South Lanarkshire	*Lab.* 48; *SNP* 10; *Lab. and Co-op* 4; *C.* 2; *LD* 1
Stirling	*Lab.* 11; *C.* 10; *SNP* 1
West Dunbartonshire	*Lab.* 10; *SNP* 7; *Ind.* 4; *Other* 1
West Lothian	*Lab.* 20; *SNP* 10; *C.* 1; *Ind.* 1

England

The Kingdom of England lies between 55° 46′ and 49° 57′ 30″ N. latitude (from a few miles north of the mouth of the Tweed to the Lizard), and between 1° 46′ E. and 5° 43′ W. (from Lowestoft to Land's End). England is bounded on the north by the Cheviot Hills; on the south by the English Channel; on the east by the Straits of Dover (Pas de Calais) and the North Sea; and on the west by the Atlantic Ocean, Wales and the Irish Sea. It has a total area of 50,351 sq. miles (130,410 sq. km): land 50,058 sq. miles (129,652 sq. km); inland water 293 sq. miles (758 sq. km).

POPULATION

The population at the 1991 census was 47,055,204. Census 2001 results were available from 30 September 2002. The average density of the population in 1991 was 3.6 persons per hectare.

FLAG

The flag of England is the cross of St George, a red cross on a white field (cross gules in a field argent). The cross of St George, the patron saint of England, has been used since the 13th century.

RELIEF

There is a marked division between the upland and lowland areas of England. In the extreme north the Cheviot Hills (highest point, The Cheviot, 2,674 ft) form a natural boundary with Scotland. Running south from the Cheviots, though divided from them by the Tyne Gap, is the Pennine range (highest point, Cross Fell, 2,930 ft), the main orological feature of the country. The Pennines culminate in the Peak District of Derbyshire (Kinder Scout, 2,088 ft). West of the Pennines are the Cumbrian mountains, which include Scafell Pike (3,210 ft), the highest peak in England, and to the east are the Yorkshire Moors, their highest point being Urra Moor (1,490 ft).

In the west, the foothills of the Welsh mountains extend into the bordering English counties of Shropshire (Wrekin, 1,334 ft; Long Mynd, 1,694 ft) and Hereford and Worcester (the Malvern Hills – Worcestershire Beacon, 1,394 ft). Extensive areas of highland and moorland are also to be found in the south-western peninsula formed by Somerset, Devon and Cornwall: principally Exmoor (Dunkery Beacon, 1,704 ft), Dartmoor (High Willhays, 2,038 ft) and Bodmin Moor (Brown Willy, 1,377 ft). Ranges of low, undulating hills run across the south of the country, including the Cotswolds in the Midlands and south-west, the Chilterns to the north of London, and the North (Kent) and South (Sussex) Downs of the south-east coastal areas.

The lowlands of England lie in the Vale of York, East Anglia and the area around the Wash. The lowest-lying are the Cambridgeshire Fens in the valleys of the Great Ouse and the River Nene, which are below sea-level in places. Since the 17th century extensive drainage has brought much of the Fens under cultivation. The North Sea coast between the Thames and the Humber, low-lying and formed of sand and shingle for the most part, is subject to erosion and defences against further incursion have been built along many stretches.

HYDROGRAPHY

The Severn is the longest river in Great Britain, rising in the north-eastern slopes of Plynlimon (Wales) and entering England in Shropshire with a total length of 220 miles (354 km) from its source to its outflow into the Bristol Channel, where it receives on the east the Bristol Avon, and on the west the Wye, its other tributaries being the Vyrnwy, Tern, Stour, Teme and Upper (or Warwickshire) Avon. The Severn is tidal below Gloucester, and a high bore or tidal wave sometimes reverses the flow as high as Tewkesbury (13½; miles above Gloucester). The scenery of the greater part of the river is very picturesque and beautiful, and the Severn is a noted salmon river, some of its tributaries being famous for trout. Navigation is assisted by the Gloucester and Berkeley Ship Canal (16¼ miles), which admits vessels of 350 tons to Gloucester. The Severn Tunnel was begun in 1873 and completed in 1886 at a cost of £2 million and after many difficulties from flooding. It is 4 miles 628 yards in length (of which 2¼ miles are under the river). The Severn road bridge between Haysgate, Gwent, and Almondsbury, Glos, with a centre span of 3,240 ft, was opened in 1966.

The longest river wholly in England is the Thames, with a total length of 215 miles (346 km) from its source in the Cotswold hills to the Nore, and is navigable by ocean-going ships to London Bridge. The Thames is tidal to Teddington (69 miles from its mouth) and forms county boundaries almost throughout its course; on its banks are situated London, Windsor Castle, Eton College and Oxford University.

Of the remaining English rivers, those flowing into the North Sea are the Tyne, Wear, Tees, Ouse and Trent from the Pennine Range, the Great Ouse (160 miles), which rises in Northamptonshire, and the Orwell and Stour from the hills of East Anglia. Flowing into the English Channel are the Sussex Ouse from the Weald, the Itchen from the Hampshire Hills, and the Axe, Teign, Dart, Tamar and Exe from the Devonian hills. Flowing into the Irish Sea are the Mersey, Ribble and Eden from the western slopes of the Pennines and the Derwent from the Cumbrian mountains.

The English Lakes, noteworthy for their picturesque scenery and poetic associations, lie in Cumbria, the largest being Windermere (10 miles long), Ullswater and Derwent Water.

ISLANDS

The Isle of Wight is separated from Hampshire by the Solent. The capital, Newport, stands at the head of the estuary of the Medina, Cowes (at the mouth) being the chief port. Other centres are Ryde, Sandown, Shanklin, Ventnor, Freshwater, Yarmouth, Totland Bay, Seaview and Bembridge.

Lundy (the name means Puffin Island), 11 miles north-west of Hartland Point, Devon, is about two miles long and about half a mile wide on average, with a total area of about 1,116 acres, and a population of about 20. It became the property of the National Trust in 1969 and is now principally a bird sanctuary.

The Isles of Scilly consist of about 140 islands and skerries (total area, 6 sq. miles/10 sq. km) situated 28 miles south-west of Land's End, Cornwall. Only five are inhabited: St Mary's, St Agnes, Bryher, Tresco and St Martin's. The population is c. 2,000. The entire group has been designated a Conservation Area, a Heritage Coast, and an Area of Outstanding Natural Beauty, and has been given National Nature Reserve status by the Nature Conservancy Council because of its unique flora and fauna. Tourism and the winter/spring flower trade for the home market form the basis of the economy of the Isles. The island group is a recognised rural development area.

EARLY HISTORY

Archaeological evidence suggests that England has been inhabited since at least the Palaeolithic period, though the extent of the various Palaeolithic cultures was dependent upon the degree of glaciation. The succeeding Neolithic and Bronze Age cultures have left abundant remains throughout the country, the best-known of these being the henges and stone circles of Stonehenge (ten miles north of Salisbury, Wilts) and Avebury (Wilts), both of which are believed to have been of religious significance. In the latter part of the Bronze Age the Goidels, a people of Celtic race, and in the Iron Age other Celtic races of Brythons and Belgae, invaded the country and brought with them Celtic civilisation and dialects, place names in England bear witness to the spread of the invasion over the whole kingdom.

THE ROMAN CONQUEST

The Roman conquest of Gaul (57–50 BC) brought Britain into close contact with Roman civilisation, but although Julius Caesar raided the south of Britain in 55 BC and 54 BC, conquest was not undertaken until nearly 100 years later. In AD 43 the Emperor Claudius dispatched Aulus Plautius, with a well-equipped force of 40,000, and himself followed with reinforcements in the same year. Success was delayed by the resistance of Caratacus (Caractacus), the British leader from AD 48–51, who was finally captured and sent to Rome, and by a great revolt in AD 61 led by Boudicca (Boadicea), Queen of the Iceni; but the south of Britain was secured by AD 70, and Wales and the area north to the Tyne by about AD 80.

In AD 122, the Emperor Hadrian visited Britain and built a continuous rampart, since known as Hadrian's Wall, from Wallsend to Bowness (Tyne to Solway). The work was entrusted by the Emperor Hadrian to Aulus Platorius Nepos, legate of Britain from ad 122 to 126, and it was intended to form the northern frontier of the Roman Empire.

The Romans administered Britain as a province under a Governor, with a well-defined system of local government, each Roman municipality ruling itself and its surrounding territory, while London was the centre of the road system and the seat of the financial officials of the Province of Britain. Colchester, Lincoln, York, Gloucester and St Albans stand on the sites of five Roman municipalities, and Wroxeter, Caerleon, Chester, Lincoln and York were at various times the sites of legionary fortresses. Well-preserved Roman towns have been uncovered at or near Silchester (Calleva Atrebatum), ten miles south of Reading, Wroxeter (Viroconium Cornoviorum), near Shrewsbury, and St Albans (Verulamium) in Hertfordshire.

Four main groups of roads radiated from London, and a fifth (the Fosse) ran obliquely from Lincoln through Leicester, Cirencester and Bath to Exeter. Of the four groups radiating from London, one ran south-east to Canterbury and the coast of Kent, a second to Silchester and thence to parts of western Britain and south Wales, a third (later known as Watling Street) ran through Verulamium to Chester, with various branches, and the fourth reached Colchester, Lincoln, York and the eastern counties.

In the fourth century Britain was subject to raids along the east coast by Saxon pirates, which led to the establishment of a system of coastal defences from the Wash to Southampton Water, with forts at Brancaster, Burgh Castle (Yarmouth), Walton (Felixstowe), Bradwell, Reculver, Richborough, Dover, Lympne, Pevensey and Porchester (Portsmouth). The Irish (Scoti) and Picts in the north were also becoming more aggressive; from about AD 350 incursions became more frequent and more formidable. As the Roman Empire came under attack increasingly towards the end of the fourth century, many troops were removed from Britain for service in other parts of the empire. The island was eventually cut off from Rome by the Teutonic conquest of Gaul, and with the withdrawal of the last Roman garrison early in the fifth century, the Romano-British were left to themselves.

SAXON SETTLEMENT

According to legend, the British King Vortigern called in the Saxons to defend him against the Picts, the Saxon chieftains being Hengist and Horsa, who landed at Ebbsfleet, Kent, and established themselves in the Isle of Thanet; but the events during the one-and-a-half centuries between the final break with Rome and the re-establishment of Christianity are unclear. However, it would appear that in the course of this period the raids turned into large-scale settlement by invaders traditionally known as Angles (England north of the Wash and East Anglia), Saxons (Essex and southern England) and Jutes (Kent and the Weald), which pushed the Romano-British into the mountainous areas of the north and west. Celtic culture outside Wales and Cornwall survives only in topographical names. Various kingdoms established at this time attempted to claim overlordship of the whole country, hegemony finally being achieved by Wessex (capital, Winchester) in the ninth century. This century also saw the beginning of raids by the Vikings (Danes), which were resisted by Alfred the Great (871–899), who fixed a limit to the advance of Danish settlement by the Treaty of Wedmore (878), giving them the area north and east of Watling Street, on condition that they adopt Christianity.

In the tenth century the kings of Wessex recovered the whole of England from the Danes, but subsequent rulers were unable to resist a second wave of invaders. England paid tribute (Danegeld) for many years, and was invaded in 1013 by the Danes and ruled by Danish kings from 1016 until 1042, when Edward the Confessor was recalled from exile in Normandy. On Edward's death in 1066 Harold Godwinson (brother-in-law of Edward and son of Earl Godwin of Wessex) was chosen King of England. After defeating (at Stamford Bridge, Yorkshire, 25 September) an invading army under Harald Hadraada, King of Norway (aided by the outlawed Earl Tostig of Northumbria, Harold's brother), Harold was himself defeated at the Battle of Hastings on 14 October 1066, and the Norman conquest secured the throne of England for Duke William of Normandy, a cousin of Edward the Confessor.

CHRISTIANITY

Christianity reached the Roman province of Britain from Gaul in the third century (or possibly earlier); Alban, traditionally Britain's first martyr, was put to death as a Christian during the persecution of Diocletian (22 June 303), at his native town Verulamium; and the Bishops of Londinium, Eboracum (York), and Lindum (Lincoln) attended the Council of Arles in 314. However, the Anglo-Saxon invasions submerged the Christian religion in England until the sixth century when conversion was undertaken in the north from 563 by Celtic missionaries from Ireland led by St Columba, and in the south by a mission sent from Rome in 597 which was led by St Augustine, who became the first archbishop of Canterbury. England appears to have been converted again by the end of the seventh century and followed,

after the Council of Whitby in 663, the practices of the Roman Church, which brought the kingdom into the mainstream of European thought and culture.

PRINCIPAL CITIES

BATH

Bath stands on the River Avon between the Cotswold Hills to the North and the Mendips to the south. In the early eighteenth century, Bath became England's premier spa town where the rich and celebrated members of fashionable society gathered to 'take the waters' and enjoy the town's theatres and concert rooms. During this period the architect John Wood laid the foundations for a new Georgian city to be built using the honey-coloured stone that Bath is famous for today.

Today Bath is a thriving tourist destination and remains a leading cultural, religious and historical centre with many art galleries and historic sites including; the Pump Room (1790), The Royal Crescent (1767), the Circus (1754), the eighteenth century Assembly Rooms, housing the Museum of Costume, Pulteney Bridge (1771), the Guildhall and the Abbey, now over 500 years old, which is built on the site of the Saxon monastery.

BIRMINGHAM

Birmingham is Britain's second city with a population of nearly one million. The generally accepted derivation of 'Birmingham' is the *ham* (dwelling-place) of the *ing* (family) of *Beorma*, presumed to have been Saxon. During the Industrial Revolution the town grew into a major manufacturing centre and in 1889 was granted city status.

Recent developments include the Millennium Point, incorporating the science museum, Thinktank and Brindleyplace. The Eastside of the city is currently undergoing a massive reconstruction.

The principal buildings are the Town Hall (1834–50); the Council House (1879); Victoria Law Courts (1891); Birmingham University (1906–9); the 13th-century Church of St Martin-in-the-Bull-Ring (rebuilt 1873); Our Lady, Help of Christians Church; the Cathedral (formerly St Philip's Church) (1711); the Roman Catholic Cathedral of St Chad (1839–41); the assay office (1773) and the National Exhibition Centre (1976). There is also the Birmingham Museum and Art Gallery including the Waterhall Gallery which opened in 2001.

BRISTOL

Bristol was a Royal Borough before the Norman Conquest. The earliest form of the name is *Bricgstow*. In 1373 Edward III granted Bristol county status.

The chief buildings include the 12th-century Cathedral (with later additions), with Norman chapter house and gateway, the 14th-century Church of St Mary Redcliffe, Wesley's Chapel, Broadmead, the Merchant Venturers' Almshouses, the Council House (1956), Guildhall, Exchange (erected from the designs of John Wood in 1743), Cabot Tower, the University and Clifton College. The Roman Catholic Cathedral at Clifton was opened in 1973.

The Clifton Suspension Bridge, with a span of 702 feet over the Avon, was projected by Brunel in 1836 but was not completed until 1864. Brunel's SS *Great Britain*, the first ocean-going propeller-driven ship, is now being restored in the City Docks from where she was launched in 1843. The docks themselves have been extensively restored and redeveloped and are becoming a focus for the arts and recreation.

CAMBRIDGE

Cambridge, a settlement far older than its ancient University, lies on the River Cam or Granta. The city is a county town and regional headquarters. Its industries include high technology research and development, and biotechnology. Among its open spaces are Jesus Green, Sheep's Green, Coe Fen, Parker's Piece, Christ's Pieces, the University Botanic Garden, and the Backs, or lawns and gardens through which the Cam winds behind the principal line of college buildings. Historical sites east of the Cam include; King's Parade, Great St Mary's Church, Gibbs' Senate House and King's College Chapel.

University and college buildings provide the outstanding features of Cambridge architecture but several churches (especially St Benet's, the oldest building in the city, and St Sepulchre's, the Round Church) are also notable. The Guildhall (1937) stands on a site of which at least part has held municipal buildings since 1224.

CANTERBURY

Canterbury, the Metropolitan City of the Anglican Communion, dates back to prehistoric times. It was the Roman *Durovernum Cantiacorum* and the Saxon *Cant-wara-byrig* (stronghold of the men of Kent). Here in 597 St Augustine began the conversion of the English to Christianity, when Ethelbert, King of Kent, was baptised.

Of the Benedictine St Augustine's Abbey, burial place of the Jutish Kings of Kent, only ruins remain. St Martin's Church, on the eastern outskirts of the city, is stated by Bede to have been the place of worship of Queen Bertha, the Christian wife of King Ethelbert, before the advent of St Augustine.

In 1170 the rivalry of Church and State culminated in the murder in Canterbury Cathedral, by Henry II's knights, of Archbishop Thomas Becket. His shrine became a great centre of pilgrimage, as described in Chaucer's *Canterbury Tales*. After the Reformation pilgrimages ceased, but the prosperity of the city was strengthened by an influx of Huguenot refugees, who introduced weaving. The poet and playwright Christopher Marlowe was born and reared in Canterbury, and there are also literary associations with Defoe, Dickens, Joseph Conrad and Somerset Maugham.

The Cathedral, with architecture ranging from the 11th to the 15th centuries, is world famous. Modern pilgrims are attracted particularly to the Martyrdom, the Black Prince's Tomb, the Warriors' Chapel and the many examples of medieval stained glass.

The medieval city walls are built on Roman foundations and the 14th-century West Gate is one of the finest buildings of its kind in the country.

The 1,000-seat Marlowe Theatre is a centre for the Canterbury Arts Festival each autumn.

CARLISLE

Carlisle is situated at the confluence of the River Eden and River Caldew, 309 miles north-west of London and about ten miles from the Scottish border. It was granted a charter in 1158.

The city stands at the western end of Hadrian's Wall and dates from the original Roman settlement of *Luguvalium*. Granted to Scotland in the tenth century, Carlisle is not included in the Domesday Book. William Rufus reclaimed the area in 1092 and the castle and city walls were built to guard Carlisle and the western border; the citadel is a Tudor addition to protect the south of the city. Border disputes were common until the problem of the Debateable Lands was settled in 1552. During the Civil War the city remained Royalist; in 1745 Carlisle was besieged for the last time by the Young Pretender (Bonnie Prince Charlie).

The Cathedral, originally a 12th-century Augustinian priory, was enlarged in the 13th and 14th centuries after the diocese was created in 1133. To the south is a restored Tithe Barn and nearby the 18th-century church of St Cuthbert, the third to stand on a site dating from the seventh century.

Carlisle is the major shopping, commercial and agricultural centre for the area, and industries include the manufacture of metal goods, biscuits and textiles. However, the largest employer is the services sector, notably in central and local government, retailing and transport. The city has an important communications position at the centre of a network of major roads, as a stage on the main west coast rail services, and with its own airport at Crosby-on-Eden.

CHESTER

Chester is situated on the River Dee, and was granted borough and city status in 1974. Its recorded history dates from the first century when the Romans founded the fortress of *Deva*. The city's name is derived from the Latin *castra* (a camp or encampment). During the Middle Ages, Chester was the principal port of north-west England but declined with the silting of the Dee estuary and competition from Liverpool. The city was also an important military centre, notably during Edward I's Welsh campaigns and the Elizabethan Irish campaigns. During the Civil War, Chester supported the King and was besieged from 1643 to 1646. Chester's first charter was granted *c.* 1175 and the city was incorporated in 1506. The office of Sheriff is the earliest created in the country (*c.* 1120s), and in 1992 the Mayor was granted the title of Lord Mayor. He/she also enjoys the title 'Admiral of the Dee'.

The city's architectural features include the city walls (an almost complete two-mile circuit), the unique 13th-century Rows (covered galleries above the street-level shops), the Victorian Gothic Town Hall (1869), the Castle (rebuilt 1788 and 1822) and numerous half-timbered buildings. The Cathedral was a Benedictine abbey until the Dissolution. Remaining monastic buildings include the chapter house, refectory and cloisters and there is a modern free-standing bell tower. The Norman church of St John the Baptist was a cathedral church in the early Middle Ages.

COVENTRY

Coventry is an important industrial centre, producing vehicles, machine tools, agricultural machinery, man-made fibres, aerospace components and telecommunications equipment. New investment has come from financial services, power transmission, professional services, leisure and education.

The city owes its beginning to Leofric, Earl of Mercia, and his wife Godiva who, in 1043, founded a Benedictine monastery. The guildhall of St Mary dates from the 14th century, three of the city's churches date from the 14th and 15th centuries, and 16th-century almshouses may still be seen. Coventry's first cathedral was destroyed at the Reformation, its second in the 1940 blitz (the walls and spire remain) and the new cathedral designed by Sir Basil Spence, consecrated in 1962, now draws numerous visitors.

Coventry is the home of the University of Warwick, Coventry University, the Westwood Business Park, the Cable and Wireless College, the Museum of British Road Transport and the Skydome Arena.

DERBY

Derby stands on the banks of the River Derwent, and its name dates back to 880 when the Danes settled in the locality and changed the original Saxon name of *Northworthy* to *Deoraby*.

Derby has a wide range of industries including aero engines, cars, pipework, specialised mechanical engineering equipment, textiles, chemicals, plastics and the Royal Crown Derby porcelain. The city is an established centre of railway excellence with rail research, engineering, safety testing, infrastructure and train-operating companies.

Buildings of interest include St Peter's Church and the Old Abbey Building (14th century), the Cathedral (1525), St Mary's Roman Catholic Church (1839) and the Industrial Museum, formerly the Old Silk Mill (1721). The traditional city centre is complemented by the Eagle Centre and 'out-of-centre' retail developments. In addition to the Derby Playhouse and the mutli-purpose venue Assembly Rooms, Pride Park Stadium is the home of Derby County Football Club, opened by the Queen in 1997.

The first charter granting a Mayor and Aldermen was that of Charles I in 1637. Previous charters date back to 1154. It was granted city status in 1977.

DURHAM

The city of Durham is a district in the county of Durham and a major tourist attraction because of its prominent Norman Cathedral and Castle set high on a wooded peninsula overlooking the River Wear. The Cathedral was founded as a shrine for the body of St Cuthbert in 995. The present building dates from 1093 and among its many treasures is the tomb of the Venerable Bede (673–735). Durham's Prince Bishops had unique powers up to 1836, being lay rulers as well as religious leaders. As a palatinate, Durham could have its own army, nobility, coinage and courts. The Castle was the main seat of the Prince Bishops for nearly 800 years; it is now used as a college by the University. The University, founded on the initiative of Bishop William Van Mildert, is England's third oldest.

Among other buildings of interest is the Guildhall in the Market Place which dates originally from the 14th century. Work has been carried out to conserve this area as part of the city's contribution to the Council of Europe's Urban Renaissance Campaign. Annual events include Durham's Regatta in June (claimed to be the oldest rowing event in Britain) and the Annual Gala (formerly Durham Miners' Gala) in July.

The economy has undergone a significant change with the replacement of mining as the dominant industry by 'white collar' employment. Although still a predominantly rural area, the industrial and commercial sector is growing and a wide range of manufacturing and service industries are based on industrial estates in and around the city. A research and development centre, linked to the University, also plays an important role in the local economy.

380   Local Government

EXETER

Exeter lies on the River Exe ten miles from the sea and was granted a charter by Henry II. The Romans founded *Isca Dumnoniorum* in the first century AD as a legionary fortress, and in the third century a stone wall (much of which remains) was built, providing protection against Saxon, and then Danish invasions. After the Conquest, the city led a resistance to William in the west until reduced by siege. The Normans built the ringwork castle of Rougemont, the gatehouse and towers remain, although the rest was pulled down in 1784. The first bridge across the Exe was built in the early 13th century. The city's main port was situated downstream at Topsham until the construction in the 1560s of the first true canal in England The redevelopment of the canal in 1700 brought seaborne trade directly into the city. Exeter was the Royalist headquarters in the west during the Civil War.

The diocese of Exeter was established by Edward the Confessor in 1050, although a minster existed near the Cathedral site from the late seventh century. A new cathedral was built in the 12th century but the present building, incorporating the Norman Towers, was begun *c.* 1275 and completed about a century later. The Guildhall dates from the 12th century and there are many other medieval buildings in the city, as well as architecture in the Georgian and Regency styles, and the Custom House (1680). Damage suffered by bombing in 1942 led to the redevelopment of the city centre.

Exeter's prosperity from medieval times was based on trade in wool, commemorated by Tuckers Hall. The wool trade flourished until the late 18th century when export trade was hit by the French wars. Subsequently Exeter has developed as an administrative and commercial centre, notably in the distributive trades, light manufacturing industries and tourism.

KINGSTON UPON HULL

Hull (officially Kingston upon Hull) lies at the junction of the River Hull with the Humber, 22 miles from the North Sea, it has an estimated population of 257,900. It is one of the major seaports of the United Kingdom. The port provides a wide range of cargo services, including ro-ro and container traffic, and handles a million passengers annually on daily sailings to Rotterdam and Zeebrugge. There is a variety of manufacturing and service industries.

The city, restored after heavy air raid damage during the Second World War, has good educational facilities with both the University of Hull and the University of Lincoln being within its boundaries. Hull has been granted Urban Regeneration Company Status, current projects include Hull's £45.5 million Millennium Project and the world's only Submarium. Future developments include the Kingston Communications Stadium with a seating capacity for 25,000 and the £25 million BBC regional centre.

Tourism is a major growth industry and the old town area has been renovated and includes Museums, a marina and shopping complex. Just west of the city is the Humber Bridge, until recently the world's longest single-span suspension bridge.

Kingston upon Hull was so named by Edward I. City status was accorded in 1897 and the office of Mayor raised to the dignity of Lord Mayor in 1914.

LANCASTER

Lancaster was originally a Roman fort and in Anglo-Saxon times a church was built within the ruins of the fort.

In the late 17th century, Lancaster began to trade with the West Indies and the new American colonies. This trade meant the 18th century was an age of great prosperity for the city and there are many splendid buildings dating from this period, including the complete port facility of St George's Quay, with the Custom House and numerous warehouses.

In the Victorian age, Lancaster began to specialise in textiles and two major manufacturing firms, Storeys and Williamsons, dominated the industry, the latter having a world reputation for the production of linoleum.

Lancaster was originally a market town and a borough, gaining its first charter in 1193. In 1937 Lancaster was awarded city status on King George VI's Coronation Day. Today, Lancaster has mainly technology and service industries and is an important centre for education.

LEEDS

Leeds, situated in the lower Aire Valley, is a junction for road, rail, canal and air services and an important manufacturing and commercial centre.

The principal buildings are the Civic Hall (1933), the Town Hall (1858), the Municipal Buildings and Art Gallery (1884) with the Henry Moore Gallery (1982), the Corn Exchange (1863) and the University. The Parish Church (St Peter's) was rebuilt in 1841; the 17th-century St John's Church has a fine interior with a famous English Renaissance screen; the last remaining 18th-century church in the city is Holy Trinity in Boar Lane (1727). Kirkstall Abbey (about three miles from the centre of city), founded by Henry de Lacy in 1152, is one of the most complete examples of Cistercian houses now remaining. Temple Newsam, birthplace of Lord Darnley, was acquired by the Council in 1922. The present house was largely rebuilt by Sir Arthur Ingram in about 1620. Adel Church, about five miles from the centre of the city, is a fine Norman structure. The new Royal Armouries - Museum houses the collection of antique arms and armour formerly held at the Tower of London.

Leeds was first incorporated by Charles I in 1626. The earliest forms of the name are *Loidis* or *Ledes*, the origins of which are obscure.

LEICESTER

Leicester is situated geographically in the centre of England. The city was an important Roman settlement and also one of the five Danish boroughs of Danelaw. In 1485 Richard III was buried in Leicester following his death at the nearby Battle of Bosworth. In 1589 Queen Elizabeth I granted a charter to the city and the ancient title was confirmed by letters patent in 1919.

The textile industry, responsible for Leicester's early expansion, has declined in recent years, although the city still maintains a strong manufacturing base. Cotton mills and factories are now undergoing extensive regeneration and are being converted into offices, apartments, bars and restaurants. The principal buildings include the two universities, the University of Leicester and De Montfort University, as well as the Town Hall, the 13th century Guildhall, De Montfort Hall, Leicester Cathedral, the Jewry Wall (the UK's highest standing Roman wall), St Nicholas Church and St Mary de Castro church. The motte and Great Hall of Leicester can be seen from the castle gardens, situated next to the ancient River Soar.

LINCOLN

Situated 40 miles inland on the River Witham, Lincoln derives its name from a contraction of *Lindum Colonia*, the settlement founded in AD 48 by the Romans to command the crossing of Ermine Street and Fosse Way.

Sections of the third-century Roman city wall can be seen, including an extant gateway (Newport Arch), and excavations have discovered traces of a sewerage system unique in Britain. The Romans also drained the surrounding fenland and created a canal system, laying the foundations of Lincoln's agricultural prosperity and also the city's importance in the medieval wool trade as a port and Staple town.

As one of the Five Boroughs of Danelaw, Lincoln was an important trading centre in the ninth and tenth centuries and medieval prosperity from the wool trade lasted until the 14th century. This wealth enabled local merchants to build parish churches (of which three survive), and attracted a Jewish community (Jew's House and Court, Aaron's House) in the 12th century. However, the removal of the Staple to Boston in 1369 heralded a decline, from which the city only recovered fully in the 19th century, when improved fen drainage made Lincoln agriculturally important. Improved canal and rail links led to industrial development, mainly in the manufacture of machinery, components and engineering products.

The castle was built shortly after the Conquest and is unusual in having two mounds; on one motte stands a Keep (Lucy's Tower) added in the 12th century. It currently houses one of the four surviving copies of the Magna Carta. The Cathedral was begun c. 1073 when the first Norman bishop moved the see of Lindsey to Lincoln, but was mostly destroyed by fire and earthquake in the 12th century. Rebuilding was begun by St Hugh and completed over a century later. Other notable architectural features are the 12th-century High Bridge, the oldest in Britain still to carry buildings, and the Guildhall situated above the 15th–16th-century Stonebow gateway.

LIVERPOOL

Liverpool, on the north bank of the River Mersey, three miles from the Irish Sea, is the United Kingdom's foremost port for Atlantic trade. Tunnels link Liverpool with Birkenhead and Wallasey.

There are 2,100 acres of dockland on both sides of the river and the Gladstone and Royal Seaforth Docks can accommodate Panamax-sized vessels. Liverpool Free Port was opened in 1984.

Liverpool was created a free borough in 1207 and a city in 1880. From the early 18th century it expanded rapidly with the growth of industrialisation and the Atlantic trade. Surviving buildings from this period include the Bluecoat Chambers (1717, formerly the Bluecoat School), the Town Hall (1754, rebuilt to the original design 1795), and buildings in Rodney Street, Canning Street and the suburbs. Notable from the 19th and 20th centuries are the Anglican Cathedral, built from the designs of Sir Giles Gilbert Scott (the foundation stone was laid in 1904, and the building was completed only in 1980), the Catholic Metropolitan Cathedral (designed by Sir Frederick Gibberd, consecrated 1967) and St George's Hall (1842, regarded as one of the finest modern examples of classical architecture. The refurbished Albert Dock (designed by Jesse Hartley) contains the Merseyside Maritime Museum and Tate Gallery, Liverpool.

In 1852 an Act was obtained for establishing a public library, museum and art gallery; as a result Liverpool had one of the first public libraries in the country. The Brown, Picton and Hornby libraries now form one of the country's major libraries. The Victoria Building of Liverpool University, the Royal Liver, Cunard and Mersey Docks & Harbour Company buildings at the Pier Head, the Municipal Buildings and the Philharmonic Hall are other examples of the city's fine architecture.

MANCHESTER

Manchester (the *Mamucium* of the Romans, who occupied it in AD 79) is a commercial and industrial centre with a population engaged in the engineering, chemical, clothing, food processing and textile industries and in education. Banking, insurance and a growing leisure industry are among the prime commercial activities. The city is connected with the sea by the Manchester Ship Canal, opened in 1894, 35.5 miles long, and accommodating ships up to 15,000 tons. In 2001 Manchester Airport handled just over 19 million terminal, transit, scheduled and charter passengers.

The principal buildings are the Town Hall, erected in 1877 from the designs of Alfred Waterhouse, with a large extension of 1938; the Royal Exchange (1869, enlarged 1921); the Central Library (1934); Heaton Hall; the 17th-century Chetham Library; the Rylands Library (1900), which includes the Althorp collection; the University precinct; the 15th-century Cathedral (formerly the parish church) and G-MEX exhibition centre. Recent developments include the Manchester Arena, the largest indoor arena in Europe, and the Bridgewater Hall. Manchester is the home of the Hallé Orchestra, the Royal Northern College of Music, the Royal Exchange Theatre and seven public art galleries. Metrolink, the light rail system, opened in 1992.

To accommodate The Commonwealth Games held in Manchester in 2002 new sports facilities were built including a stadium, swimming pool complex and the National Cycling Centre.

The town received its first charter of incorporation in 1838 and was created a city in 1853.

NEWCASTLE UPON TYNE

Newcastle upon Tyne, on the north bank of the River Tyne, is eight miles from the North Sea. A cathedral and university city, it is the administrative, commercial and cultural centre for north-east England and the principal port. It is an important manufacturing centre with a wide variety of industries.

The principal buildings include the Castle Keep (12th century), Black Gate (13th century), Blackfriars (13th century), West Walls (13th century), St Nicholas's Cathedral (15th century, fine lantern tower), St Andrew's Church (12th–14th century), St John's (14th–15th century), All Saints (1786 by Stephenson), St Mary's Roman Catholic Cathedral (1844), Trinity House (17th century), Sandhill (16th-century houses), Guildhall (Georgian), Grey Street (1834–9), Central Station (1846–50), Laing Art Gallery (1904), University of Newcastle Physics Building (1962) and Medical Building (1985), Civic Centre (1963), Central Library (1969) and Eldon Square Shopping Development (1976). Open spaces include the Town Moor (927 acres) and Jesmond Dene. Ten bridges span the Tyne at Newcastle.

The city's name is derived from the 'new castle' (1080) erected as a defence against the Scots. In 1400 it was made a county, and in 1882 a city.

NORWICH

Norwich grew from an early Anglo-Saxon settlement near the confluence of the Rivers Yare and Wensum, and now serves as provincial capital for the predominantly agricultural region of East Anglia. The name is thought to relate to the most northerly of a group of Anglo-Saxon villages or *wics*. The city's first known charter was granted in 1158 by Henry II.

Norwich serves its surrounding area as a market town and commercial centre, banking and insurance being

prominent among the city's businesses. From the 14th century until the Industrial Revolution, Norwich was the regional centre of the woollen industry, but now the biggest single industry is financial services and principal trades are engineering, printing, shoemaking, double glazing, the production of chemicals and clothing, food processing and technology. Norwich is accessible to seagoing vessels by means of the River Yare, entered at Great Yarmouth, 20 miles to the east.

Among many historic buildings are the Cathedral (completed in the 12th century and surmounted by a 15th-century spire 315 feet in height), the keep of the Norman castle (now a museum and art gallery), the 15th-century flint-walled Guildhall, some thirty medieval parish churches, St Andrew's and Blackfriars' Halls, the Tudor houses preserved in Elm Hill and the Georgian Assembly House. The University of East Anglia is on the city's western boundary.

NOTTINGHAM

Nottingham stands on the River Trent and is connected by canal with the Atlantic Ocean and the North Sea. *Snotingaham* or *Notingeham*, literally the homestead of the people of Snot, is the Anglo-Saxon name for the Celtic settlement of *Tigguocobauc*, or the house of caves. In 878, Nottingham became one of the Five Boroughs of Danelaw. William the Conqueror ordered the construction of Nottingham Castle, while the town itself developed rapidly under Norman rule. Its laws and rights were later formally recognised by Henry II's charter in 1155. The Castle became a favoured residence of King John. In 1642 King Charles I raised his personal standard at Nottingham Castle at the start of the Civil War.

Nottingham is home to Notts County FC (the world's oldest football league side), Nottingham Forest FC, Nottingham Racecourse, Trent Bridge cricket ground and the National Watersports Centre. The principal industries include textiles, pharmaceuticals, food manufacturing, engineering and telecommunications. There are two universities within the city boundaries.

Architecturally, Nottingham has a wealth of notable buildings, particularly those designed in the Victorian era by T. C. Hine and Watson Fothergill. The City Council owns the Castle, of Norman origin but restored in 1878, Wollaton Hall (1580–8), Newstead Abbey (home of Lord Byron), the Guildhall (1888) and Council House (1929). St Mary's, St Peter's and St Nicholas's Churches are of interest, as is the Roman Catholic Cathedral (Pugin, 1842–4).

Nottingham was granted city status in 1897.

OXFORD

Oxford is a university city, an important industrial centre, and a market town. Industry played a minor part in Oxford until the motor industry was established in 1912.

Oxford is known for its architecture, its oldest specimens being the reputedly Saxon tower of St Michael's church, the remains of the Norman castle and city walls, and the Norman church at Iffley. It also has many Gothic buildings, such as the Divinity Schools, the Old Library at Merton College, William of Wykeham's New College, Magdalen College and Christ Church and many other college buildings. Later centuries are represented by the Laudian quadrangle at St John's College, the Renaissance Sheldonian Theatre by Wren, Trinity College Chapel, and All Saints Church; Hawksmoor's mock-Gothic at All Souls College, and the 18th-century Queen's College. In addition to individual buildings, High Street and Radcliffe Square both form interesting architectural compositions. Most of the

Colleges have gardens, those of Magdalen, New College, St John's and Worcester being the largest.

ST ALBANS

The origins of St Albans, situated on the River Ver, stem from the Roman town of *Verulamium*. Named after the first Christian martyr in Britain, who was executed here, St Albans has developed around the Norman Abbey and Cathedral Church (consecrated 1115), built partly of materials from the old Roman city. The museums house Iron Age and Roman artefacts and the Roman Theatre, unique in Britain, has a stage as opposed to an amphitheatre. Archaeological excavations in the city centre have revealed evidence of pre-Roman, Saxon and medieval occupation.

The town's significance grew to the extent that it was a signatory and venue for the drafting of the Magna Carta. It was also the scene of riots during the Peasants' Revolt, the French King John was imprisoned there after the Battle of Poitiers, and heavy fighting took place there during the Wars of the Roses.

Previously controlled by the Abbot, the town achieved a charter in 1553 and city status in 1877. The street market, first established in 1553, is still an important feature of the city, as are many hotels and inns, surviving from the days when St Albans was an important coach stop. Tourist attractions include historic churches and houses, and a 15th-century clock tower.

The city now contains a wide range of firms, with special emphasis on information and legal services. In addition, it is the home of the Royal National Rose Society, and of Rothamsted Park, the agricultural research centre.

SALISBURY

The history of Salisbury centres around the Cathedral and Cathedral Close. The city evolved from an Iron Age camp a mile to the north of its current position which was strengthened by the Romans and called *Serviodunum*. The Normans built a castle and cathedral on the site and renamed it Sarum. In AD 1220, Bishop Richard Poore and the architect Elias de Derham decided to build a new Gothic style cathedral. The cathedral was completed 38 years later and a community known as New Sarum, now called Salisbury, grew around it. Originally the cathedral had a squat tower. The 404 ft spire that makes the cathedral the tallest medieval structure in the world was added *c.* 1315. A walled Close with houses for the clergy was built around the cathedral, the Medieval Hall still stands today, alongside buildings dating from the 13th to the 20th century; including some designed by Sir Christopher Wren.

A prosperous wool and cloth trade allowed Salisbury to flourish until the 17th century. When the wool trade declined new crafts were established including cutlery, leather and basket work, saddlery, lacemaking, joinery and malting. By 1750 it had become an important road junction and coaching centre and in the Victorian era the railways created a new age of expansion and prosperity. Today Salisbury is a thriving tourist centre.

SHEFFIELD

Sheffield is situated at the junction of the Sheaf, Porter, Rivelin and Loxley valleys with the River Don. Though its cutlery, silverware and plate have long been famous, Sheffield has other and now more important industries: special and alloy steels, engineering, tool-making, medical equipment and media-related industries (in its new Cultural Industries Quarter). Sheffield has two universities and is an important research centre.

The parish church of St Peter and St Paul, founded in the 12th century, became the Cathedral Church of the Diocese of Sheffield in 1914. The Roman Catholic Cathedral Church of St Marie (founded 1847) was created Cathedral for the new diocese of Hallam in 1980. Parts of the present building date from c.1435. The principal buildings are the Town Hall (1897), the Cutlers' Hall (1832), City Hall (1932), Graves Art Gallery (1934), Mappin Art Gallery, the Crucible Theatre and the restored 19th-century Lyceum theatre, which dates from 1897 and was reopened in 1990. Three major sports venues were opened in 1990 to 1991. These are Sheffield Arena, Don Valley Stadium and Pond's Forge. The Millennium Galleries opened in 2001.

Sheffield was created a city in 1893.

STOKE-ON-TRENT

Stoke-on-Trent, standing on the River Trent and familiarly known as The Potteries, is the main centre of employment for the population of north Staffordshire. The city is the largest clayware producer in the world (china, earthenware, sanitary goods, refractories, bricks and tiles) and also has a wide range of other manufacturing industry, including steel, chemicals, engineering and tyres. Extensive reconstruction has been carried out in recent years.

The city was formed by the federation of the separate municipal authorities of Tunstall, Burslem, Hanley, Stoke, Fenton, and Longton in 1910 and received its city status in 1925.

WINCHESTER

Winchester, the ancient capital of England, is situated on the River Itchen. The city is rich in architecture of all types but the Cathedral takes pride of place. The cathedral was built in 1079–93 and exhibits examples of Norman, Early English and Perpendicular styles. The author Jane Austen is buried in the Cathedral. Winchester College, founded in 1382, is one of the most famous public schools, the original building (1393) remaining largely unaltered. St Cross Hospital, another great medieval foundation, lies one mile south of the city. The almshouses were founded in 1136 by Bishop Henry de Blois, and Cardinal Henry Beaufort added a new almshouse of 'Noble Poverty' in 1446. The chapel and dwellings are of great architectural interest, and visitors may still receive the 'Wayfarer's Dole' of bread and ale.

Excavations have done much to clarify the origins and development of Winchester. Part of the forum and several of the streets from the Roman town have been discovered; excavations in the Cathedral Close have uncovered the entire site of the Anglo-Saxon cathedral (known as the Old Minster) and parts of the New Minster which was built by Alfred's son Edward the Elder and is the burial place of the Alfredian dynasty. The original burial place of St Swithun, before his remains were translated to a site in the present cathedral, was also uncovered.

Excavations in other parts of the city have thrown much light on Norman Winchester, notably on the site of the Royal Castle (adjacent to which the new Law Courts have been built) and in the grounds of Wolvesey Castle, where the great house built by Bishops Giffard and Henry de Blois in the 12th century has been uncovered. The Great Hall, built by Henry III between 1222 and 1236 survives and houses the Arthurian Round Table.

YORK

The city of York is an archiepiscopal seat. Its recorded history dates from AD 71, when the Roman Ninth Legion established a base under Petilius Cerealis later becoming the fortress of *Eburacum*. In Anglo-Saxon times the city was the royal and ecclesiastical centre of Northumbria, and after capture by a Viking army in AD 866 it became the capital of the Viking kingdom of Jorvik. By the 14th century the city had become a great mercantile centre, mainly because of its control of the wool trade, and was used as the chief base against the Scots. Under the Tudors its fortunes declined, though Henry VIII made it the headquarters of the Council of the North. Excavations on many sites, including Coppergate, have greatly expanded knowledge of Roman, Viking and medieval urban life.

With its development as a railway centre in the 19th century the commercial life of York expanded. The principal industries are the manufacture of chocolate, scientific instruments and sugar. It is the location of several government departments.

The city is rich in examples of architecture of all periods. The earliest church was built in AD 627 and, in the 12th to 15th centuries, the present Minster was built in a succession of styles. Other examples within the city are the medieval city walls and gateways, churches and guildhalls. Domestic architecture includes the Georgian mansions of The Mount, Micklegate and Bootham.

There are 50 cities in England and space constraints prevent us from including a profile of them all. The above is intended merely to represent a selection of England's principal cities – other cities (with date city status conferred) are: Bradford (pre-1900), Brighton and Hove (2000), Chichester (pre-1900), Ely (pre-1900), Gloucester (pre-1900), Hereford (pre-1900), London (pre-1900), Lichfield (pre-1900), Peterborough (pre-1900), Plymouth (1928), Portsmouth (1926), Preston (2002), Ripon (pre-1900), Salford (1926), Southampton (1964), Sunderland (1992), Truro (pre-1900), Wakefield (pre-1900), Wells (pre-1900), Westminster (pre-1900), Wolverhampton (2000) and Worcester (pre-1900).

Certain cities have also been granted a Lord Mayoralty–this grant confers no additional powers or functions and is purely honorific. Cities with Lord Mayors are: Birmingham, Bradford, Bristol, Canterbury, Chester, Coventry, Exeter, Kingston-Upon-Hull, Leeds, Leicester, Liverpool, London, Manchester, Newcastle-upon-Tyne, Norwich, Nottingham, Oxford, Plymouth, Portsmouth, Sheffield and Stoke-on-Trent.

English Counties and Shires

LORD-LIEUTENANTS AND HIGH SHERIFFS

County/Shire	Lord-Lieutenant	High Sheriff, 2002–3
Bedfordshire	S. C. Whitbread	Lt.-Col. C. R. Mason
Berkshire	P. L. Wroughton	T. Dawson
Bristol	J. Tidmarsh, mbe	J. Savage
Buckinghamshire	Sir Nigel Mobbs	The Hon. Rupert Carington
Cambridgeshire	J. G. P. Crowden *(due to retire early 2003)*	Mrs J Lewin Smith
Cheshire	W. A. Bromley-Davenport	J. Richards
Cornwall	Lady Mary Holborow	Ms J. A. Coode
Cumbria	J. A. Cropper	D. Trimble
Derbyshire	J. K. Bather	Mrs D. Jeffrey
Devon	E. Dancer, CBE	Maj. Gen. N. Ansell, CB, OBE
Dorset	Capt. M. Fulford-Dobson, RN	J. Boughey
Durham	Sir Paul Nicholson	A. Martell
East Riding of Yorkshire	R. Marriott, TD	R. Byass
East Sussex	P. Stewart-Roberts.	The Hon. David Pennock
Essex	The Lord Braybrooke	D. Boyle
Gloucestershire	H. W. G. Elwes	J. Woolley
Greater London	The Lord Imbert, QPM	Countess Nicoló S. Di Monteluce
Greater Manchester	Col. J. B. Timmins, OBE, TD	Prof. Sir Netar Mallick
Hampshire	Mrs F. M. Fagan	C. Murray
Herefordshire	Sir Thomas Dunne, KCVO	Col. Sir Piers Bengough, KCVO, OBE
Hertfordshire	S. A. Bowes Lyon	The Countess of Verulam
Isle of Wight	C. D. J. Bland	Mrs A. Springman
Kent	A. Willett, CBE	C. Dawes
Lancashire	The Lord Shuttleworth	Sir T. G. Bowring
Leicestershire	T. G. M. Brooks *(due to retire end 2002)*	R. Everard
Lincolnshire	Mrs B. K. Cracroft-Eley	C. Ferens
Merseyside	A. W. Waterworth	Lady Pilkington
Norfolk	Sir Timothy Colman, KG	R. Gurney
Northamptonshire	Lady Juliet Townsend, LVO	J. Pearson
Northumberland	Sir John Riddel, CVO	Sir Francis Blake
North Yorkshire	The Lord Crathorne	M. Evans
Nottinghamshire	Sir Andrew Buchanan, Bt.	Col. T. Richmond, MBE, TD
Oxfordshire	H. L. J. Brunner	Brig. J. Mogg
Rutland	Air Chief Marshal Sir Thomas Kennedy, GCB, AFC	J. Paton
Shropshire	A. E. H. Heber-Percy	J. Bishop
Somerset	Lady Gass	R. Hoddell
South Yorkshire	The Earl of Scarbrough	Mrs M. Rae
Staffordshire	J. A. Hawley, TD	M. Hurdle
Suffolk	The Lord Belstead, PC	R. Rous
Surrey	Mrs S. J. F. Goad	Miss P. Keith
Tyne and Wear	N. Sherlock	Dr G. Banerjee
Warwickshire	M. Dunne	W. Dugdale
West Midlands	R. R. Taylor, OBE	G. Allen
West Sussex	H. Wyatt	M. Burrell
West Yorkshire	J. Lyles, CBE	J. Dent
Wiltshire	Lt.-Gen. Sir Maurice Johnston, KCB, OBE	Sir Christopher Benson
Worcestershire	M. Brinton	Col. Sir Piers Bengough, KCVO, OBE

COUNTY COUNCILS: AREA, POPULATION

Council	Administrative Headquarters	Telephone	Area (Hectares)	Population
Bedfordshire	County Hall, Bedford	01234-363222	119,220	560,000
Buckinghamshire	County Hall, Aylesbury	01296-395000	156,538	475,000
Cambridgeshire	Shire Hall, Cambridge	01223-717111	305,399	550,000
Cheshire	County Hall, Chester	0845-760 3456	208,344	670,700
Cornwall	County Hall, Truro	01872-322000	354,810	492,600
Cumbria	The Courts, Carlisle	01228-606060	681,000	491,039
Derbyshire	County Hall, Matlock	01629-580000	262,858	741,500
Devon	County Hall, Exeter	01392-382000	670,343	704,600
Dorset	County Hall, Dorchester	01305-251000	254,375	389,000
Durham	County Hall, Durham	0191-386 4411	223,180	487,600
East Sussex	Pelham House, St Andrew's Lane, Lewes	01273-481000	172,500	496,200
Essex	County Hall, Chelmsford	01245-492211	344,781	1,605,600
Gloucestershire	Shire Hall, Gloucester	01452-425000	265,535	557,257
Hampshire	The Castle, Winchester	01962-841841	367,915	1,523,742
Hertfordshire	County Hall, Hertford	01992-555555	164,306	1,024,800
Kent	County Hall, Maidstone	01622-694000	354,296	1,318,000
Lancashire	County Hall, Preston	01772-254868	289,780	30,000
Leicestershire	County Hall, Leicester	0116-265 6284	208,380	611,200
Lincolnshire	County Offices, Lincoln	01522-552222	588,000	619,400
Norfolk	County Hall, Norwich	01603-222222	537,234	783,000
Northamptonshire	County Hall, Northampton	01609 780 780	236,737	604,400
Northumberland	County Hall, Morpeth	01604-236236	502,594	310,000
North Yorkshire	County Hall, Northallerton	01670 533 000	830,399	569,800
Nottinghamshire	County Hall, Nottingham	0115-982 3823	208,510	748,100
Oxfordshire	County Hall, Oxford	01865-792422	260,595	626,200
Shropshire	The Shirehall, Shrewsbury	01743-251000	319,736	280,500
Somerset	County Hall, Taunton	01823-355455	345,233	494,600
Staffordshire	County Buildings, Stafford	01785-223121	262,355	800,000
Suffolk	County Hall, Ipswich	01473-583000	380,207	660,000
Surrey	County Hall, Kingston Upon Thames	020-8541 8800	167,011	1,057,137
Warwickshire	Shire Hall, Warwick	01926-410410	510,000	510,000
West Sussex	County Hall, Chichester	01243-777100	759,600	762,930
Wiltshire	County Hall, Trowbridge	01225-713000	431,000	534,285
Worcestershire	County Hall, Worcester	01905-763763	545,000	431,068

COUNTY COUNCILS: Standard Spending Assessment and Chief Officers

Council	Standard Spending Assessment 2002–3 (£ million)	Chief Executive	Chief Finance Officer
Bedfordshire	285.197	Dick Wilkinson	Bill Dodds
Buckinghamshire	344.817	Chris Wilson	Martin Shefferd
Cambridgeshire	371.234	Alan Barnish	Matthew Rowe
Cheshire	478.816	Colin Cheesman	vacant
Cornwall	377.674	Peter Stethridge	Frank Twyning
Cumbria	372.488	Louis Victory	Bob Mather
Derbyshire	528.221	Nick Hodgson	Peter Swaby
Devon	505.794	Philip Jenkinson	Jan Stanhope
Dorset	262.256	David Jenkins	Paul Kent
Durham	390.237	Kingsley Smith	John Kirby
East Sussex	373.452	Cheryl Miller	Sean Nolan
Essex	1,006.918	Stewart Ashurst	Keith Neale
Gloucestershire	400.039	Joyce Redfearn	Bob Potter
Hampshire	863.186	Peter Robertson	Jon Pittam
Hertfordshire	813.388	W. Ogley	Chris Sweeney
Kent	1,055.565	Michael Pitt	David Lewis
Lancashire	875.582	Chris Trinick	Brian Aldred
Leicestershire	410.854	J. B. Sinnott	A. Yould
Lincolnshire	474.291	David Bowles	Peter Moore
Norfolk	570.018	Tim Byles	Bob Summers
North Yorkshire	465.141	Jeremy Walker	John Moore
Northamptonshire	239.044	Peter Gould	Dennis Coeggett *acting*
Northumberland	412.901	Alan Clarke	Clive Burns
Nottinghamshire	540.926	Roger Latham	Arthur Deakin
Oxfordshire	418.076	Richard Shaw	Chris Gray
Shropshire	206.319	Nigel Pursey	Laura Rowley
Somerset	355.806	Michael Jennings	Chris Bilsland
Staffordshire	570.180	Bernard Price	Richard Tettenborn
Suffolk	475.154	Lin Homer	William Banks
Surrey	722.101	Paul Coen	N. Skelett
Warwickshire	348.109	Ian Caulfield	David Clarke
West Sussex	533.100	Paul Rigg	Helen Kilpatrick
Wiltshire	366.245	Keith Robinson	David Chalker
Worcestershire	293.232	Rob Sykes	Mike Weaver

Metropolitan Borough Councils

Metropolitan Council	Telephone	Population	Band D Charge*	Chief Executive
Barnsley	01226-770770	226,700	£956	Philip Coppard
BIRMINGHAM CITY	0121-303 9944	1,000,000	£1,026	Stewart Dobson
Bolton	01204-333333	226,100	£1,031	Bernard Knight
BRADFORD CITY	01274-752111	480,750	£931	Ian Stewart
Bury	0161-253 5000	182,400	£970	Mark Sanders
Calderdale	01422-357257	193,000	£1,018	Paul Sheehan
COVENTRY CITY	024-7683 3333	30,000	£1,114	Stella Manzie
Doncaster	01302 734444	288,854	£917	David Marlow
Dudley	01384-818181	311,468	£947	Andrew Sparke
Gateshead	0191-433 3000	200,000	£1,128	Leslie Elton
Kirklees	01484-221000	392,300	£1,006	Tony Elson
Knowsley	0151-443 3772	153,252	£1,078	Stephen Gallagher
LEEDS CITY	0113-234 8080	727,000	£900	Paul Rogerson
LIVERPOOL CITY	0151-225 2319	468,000	£1,136	David Henshaw
MANCHESTER CITY	0161-234 7125	431,052	£1,052	Howard Berstein
NEWCASTLE UPON TYNE CITY	0191-232 8520	270,500	£1,129	Ian Stratford
North Tyneside	0191-200 6565	198,000	£1,079	David Wright
Oldham	0161-911 3000	220,000	£1,089	Andrew Kilburn
Rochdale	01706-647474	208,500	£1,020	Roger Ellis
Rotherham	01709-822770	253,706	£1,001	Ged Fitzgerald
SALFORD CITY	0161-793 3410	229,300	£1,139	John Willis
Sandwell	0121-569 2200	288,400	£1,028	Nigel Summers
Sefton	0151-922 4040	290,000	£1,087	Graham Haywood
SHEFFIELD CITY	0114-272 6444	530,000	£1,066	R. Kerslake
Solihull	0121-704 6000	205,600	£910	Katherine Kerswell
South Tyneside	0191-427 1717	154,057	£1,049	Irene Lucas
St. Helens	01744-456166	179,000	£1,103	Carole Hudson
Stockport	0161-480 4949	292,000	£1,079	John Schultz
SUNDERLAND CITY	0191-553 1000	290,700	£974	Colin Sinclair
Tameside	0161-342 8355	219,403	£1,024	Michael Greenwood
Trafford	0161-912 1212	230,000	£817	Carole Hassan
WAKEFIELD CITY	01924-306090	319,600	£891	John Edwards
Walsall	01922-650000	261,600	£997	Hardial Bhogal
Wigan	01942-244991	310,000	£1,009	Stephen Jones
Wirral	0151-6387070	326,000	£1,077	Stephen Maddox
WOLVERHAMPTON CITY	01902-556556	240,900	£1,089	Derrick Anderson

Council tax figures have been rounded to the nearest £
SMALL CAPITALS = City status

Unitary Councils

Unitary Council	Telephone	Population	Band D Charge*	Chief Executive
Bath and North East Somerset	01225-477000	170,238	£993	John Everitt
Blackburn with Darwen	01254-585585	138,078	£1,060	Phil Watson
Blackpool	01253-477477	150,020	£951	Mr G. Essex-Crosby
Bournemouth	01202-451451	162,000	£963	David Newell
Bracknell Forest	01344-424642	111,500	£870	Gordon Mitchell
BRIGHTON AND HOVE CITY	01273-290000	258,100	£923	David Panter
BRISTOL CITY	0117-922 2000	400,600	£1,071	Carew Reynell
Darlington	01325-380651	100,501	£935	Barry Keel
DERBY CITY	01332-293111	235,000	£929	Ray Cowlishaw
East Riding of Yorkshire	01482-887700	318,938	£1,053	Darryl Stephenson
Halton	0151-424 2061	123,038	£866	Mike Cuff
Hartlepool	01429-266522	90,000	£1,141	Brian Dinsdale, OBE
Herefordshire	01432-260000	167,000	£937	Neil Pringle
Isle of Wight	01983-821000	126,000	£982	Alan Kaye *acting*

Unitary Council	Telephone	Population	Band D Charge*	Chief Executive
KINGSTON UPON HULL CITY	01482-300300	254,339	£938	Ian Crookham
LEICESTER CITY	0116-232 3232	290,900	£985	Rodney Green
Luton	01582-546000	180,600	£922	Darra Singh
Medway	01634-306000	244,800	£819	Judith Armitt
Middlesbrough	01642-245432	145,000	£953	John E. Foster
Milton Keynes	01908-691691	215,000	£922	Howard Miller
North East Lincolnshire	01472-313131	155,189	£1,070	Jim Leivers
North Lincolnshire	01724-296296	152,287	£1,119	Michael Garnett
North Somerset	01934-888888	189,776	£919	Graham Turner
NOTTINGHAM CITY	0115-915 5555	282,900	£1,057	John Jackson
PETERBOROUGH CITY	01733-563141	156,000	£963	Paul Martin
PLYMOUTH CITY	01752-668000	250,000	£896	Alison Stone
Poole	01202-633633	139,000	£936	John McBride
PORTSMOUTH CITY	023-9282 2251	188,800	£827	Nick Gurney
Reading	0118-939 0900	143,520	£1,051	Trish Haines
Redcar and Cleveland	01642-444000	138,200	£1,108	Colin Moore
Rutland	01572-722577	35,000	£1,164	Keith Franklin
Slough	01753-552288	111,000	£841	Cheryl Coppell
South Gloucestershire	01454-868686	252,000	£1019	Mike Robinson
SOUTHAMPTON CITY	023-8022 3855	215,273	£908	Bradley Roynon
Southend on Sea	01702-215000	176,000	£813	George Krawiec
Stockton-on-Tees	01642-393939	178,300	£1,020	George Garlick
STOKE-ON-TRENT CITY	01782-234567	253,200	£916	Dr Ita O'Donovan
Swindon	01793-463000	181,500	£909	Paul Doherty
Telford and Wrekin	01952-202100	153,000	£990	Michael Frater
Thurrock	01375-390000	150,000	£844	Eric Nath
Torbay	01803-201201	124,100	£947	Tony Hodgkiss
Warrington	01925-444400	193,000	£892	Steven Broomhead
West Berkshire	01635-424000	145,000	£1,022	Jim Graham
Windsor and Maidenhead	01628-798888	140,500	£888	David Lunn
Wokingham	0118-974 6000	146,252	£1,017	Jane Earl
YORK CITY	01904-613161	178,800	£874	David Atkinson

*Council tax figures have been rounded to the nearest £
SMALL CAPITALS = City status

District Councils

District Council	Telephone	Population	Band D Charge*	Chief Executive
Adur, W. Sussex	01273-263000	59,180	£989	Ian Lowrie
Allerdale, Cumbria	01900-326333	95,980	£1,027	Patrick Leonard
Alnwick, Northumberland	01665-510505	31,400	£1,078	Bill Batey
Amber Valley, Derbys	01773-570222	119,000	£1,084	Peter Carney
Arun, W. Sussex	01903-737500	143,800	£947	I. Sumnall
Ashfield, Notts	01623-450000	106,760	£1,134	Neil Bernasconi
Ashford, Kent	01233-637311	102,180	£939	David Hill
Aylesbury Vale, Bucks	01296-585858	156,600	£944	Richard Carr
Babergh, Suffolk	01473-822801	80,790	£977	Patricia Barnes
Barrow-in-Furness, Cumbria	01229-894990	71,000	£1,066	Tom Campbell
Basildon, Essex	01268-533333	166,990	£1,027	John Robb
Basingstoke and Deane, Hants	01256-844844	150,200	£907	Katrine Sporle
Bassetlaw, Notts	01909-533533	106,600	£1,116	James Molloy
Bedford, Beds	01234-267422	140,700	£1,050	Shaun Field
Berwick-upon-Tweed, Northumberland	01289-330044	26,730	£1,067	Jane Pannell
Blaby, Leics	0116-275 0555	86,400	£1,017	P. Dolan
Blyth Valley, Northumberland	01670-542102	79,900	£1,067	Geoff Paul
Bolsover, Derbys	01246-240000	71,000	£1,116	John Fotherby
Boston, Lincs	01205-314200	54,150	£964	Nicola Bulbeck
Braintree, Essex	01376-552525	132,300	£983	Annie Ralph
Breckland, Norfolk	01362-695333	122,000	£944	Rob Garnett

District Council	Telephone	Population	Band D Charge*	Chief Executive
Brentwood, Essex	01277-261111	71,400	£974	Bob McLintock
Bridgnorth, Shrops	01746-713100	52,300	£978	Trudi Elliott
Broadland, Norfolk	01603-431133	119,500	£977	Colin Bland
Bromsgrove, Worcs	01527-873232	85,210	£978	R. F.Lewis
Broxbourne, Herts	01992-785555	83,000	£879	M. Walker
Broxtowe, Notts	0115-917 7777	110,320	£1,134	Melvyn Brown
Burnley, Lancs	01282-425011	89,900	£1,123	Gillian Taylor
CAMBRIDGE, CAMBS	01223-457000	122,920	£942	Robert Hammond
Cannock Chase, Staffs	01543-462621	91,000	£963	Stephen Brown
CANTERBURY, KENT	01227-862000	123,900	£956	Colin Carmichael
Caradon, Cornwall	01579-341000	81,600	£941	Byron Davies
CARLISLE, CUMBRIA	01228-817000	102,320	£1,055	Peter Stybelski
Carrick, Cornwall	01872-224400	85,300	£952	John Winskill
Castle Morpeth, Northumberland	01670-514351	50,000	£1,099	Peter Wilson
Castle Point, Essex	01268-882200	84,800	£1,020	B. Rollinson
Charnwood, Leics	01509-263151	155,400	£1,001	Geoff Henshall
Chelmsford, Essex	01245-606606	156,000	£987	Martin Easteal
Cheltenham, Glos	01242-262626	103,120	£973	Christine Laird
Cherwell, Oxon	01295-252535	140,000	£978	Grahame Handley
CHESTER, DERBYS	01244-324324	118,700	£1,037	Paul Durham
Chester-le-Street, Co Durham	0191-387 1919	57,850	£1,033	Mick Waterson
Chesterfield, Derbys	01246-345345	101,000	£1,051	D. Shaw
Chichester, W. Sussex	01243-785166	110,110	£927	John Marsland
Chiltern, Bucks	01494-729000	91,682	£959	Alan Goodrum
Chorley, Lancs	01257-515151	100,240	£1,065	J. W. Davies
Christchurch, Dorset	01202-495000	44,330	£1,012	Mike Turvey
Colchester, Essex	01206-282222	159,000	£976	Andrea Hill
Congleton, Cheshire	01270-763231	88,400	£1,036	Peter Cooper
Copeland, Cumbria	01946-852585	69,800	£1,044	John Stanforth
Corby, Northants	01536-402551	53,000	£974	Nigel Rudd
Cotswold, Glos	01285-623000	83,000	£983	Clive Abbott
Craven, N. Yorks	01756-700600	52,100	£964	Rachel Mann
Crawley, W. Sussex	01293-438000	97,000	£936	Michael Coughlin
Crewe and Nantwich, Cheshire	01270-537777	116,800	£1,028	Alan Wenham
Dacorum, Herts	01442-228000	137,000	£920	Paul Walker
Dartford, Kent	01322-343434	86,000	£965	Graham Harris
Daventry, Northants	01327-871100	69,000	£950	Steve Atkinson
Derbyshire Dales, Derbys	01629-761100	71,300	£1,083	David Wheatcroft
Derwentside, Co Durham	01207-218000	87,300	£1,124	Mike Clark
Dover, Kent	01304-821199	107,300	£968	John Moir
DURHAM CITY, CO DURHAM	0191-386 6111	80,670	£1,061	Colin Shersmith
Easington, Co Durham	0191-527 0501	93,000	£1,171	Paul Wilding
East Cambridgeshire, Cambs	01353-665555	92,650	£958	John Hill
East Devon, Devon	01395-516551	68,900	£947	M. Williams
East Dorset, Dorset	01202-886201	130,600	£1,045	Alan Breakwell
East Hampshire, Hants	01730-266551	83,000	£958	Philip Burton
East Hertfordshire, Herts	01279-655261	112,430	£939	Roger Bailey
East Lindsey, Lincs	01507-601111	124,000	£942	Paul Haigh
East Northamptonshire, Northants	01832-742000	115,000 111,180	£970	Graham Wise
East Staffordshire, Staffs	01283-508000	124,170	£970	William Saunders
Eastbourne, E. Sussex	01323-410000	76,760	£979	Martin Ray
Eastleigh, Hants	023-8068 8000	103,700	£961	Chris Tapp
Eden, Cumbria	01768-864671	50,670	£1,033	Ian Bruce
Ellesmere Port and Neston, Cheshire	0151-356 6789	81,200	£1,037	Stephen Ewbank
Elmbridge, Surrey	01372-474474	132,000	£955	Mike Lockwood
Epping Forest, Essex	01992-554000	120,800	£991	John Burgess
Epsom and Ewell, Surrey	01372-732000	70,000	£935	David Smith
Erewash, Derbys	0115-907 2244	108,160	£1,067	Tony Harris
EXETER CITY, DEVON	01392-277888	112,360	£933	Philip Bostock
Fareham, Hants	01329-236100	107,000	£920	Alan Davies
Fenland, Cambs	01354-654321	81,900	£971	Norman Topliss
Forest Heath, Suffolk	01638-719000	70,770	£977	David Burnip
Forest of Dean, Glos	01594-810000	75,350	£1,008	Meg Holborow
Fylde, Lancs	01253-721222	74,970	£1,054	K. Lee

District Council	Telephone	Population	Band D Charge*	Chief Executive
Gedling, Notts	0115-901 3901	110,130	£1,109	*Shared role split between 3 persons*
GLOUCESTER, GLOS	01452-522232	101,610	£976	Paul Smith
Gosport, Hants	023-9258 4242	78,040	£959	Malcolm Crocker
Gravesham, Kent	01474-564422	92,450	£946	Rosemary Ledley
Great Yarmouth, Norfolk	01493-856100	90,300	£968	Richard Packham
Guildford, Surrey	01483-505050	129,200	£947	David Williams
Hambleton, N. Yorks	01609-779977	86,500	£896	Peter Simpson
Harborough, Leics	01858-821100	75,300	£1,018	Mike Wilson
Harlow, Essex	01279-446611	74,630	£1,061	Doug Patterson
Harrogate, N. Yorks	01423-500600	153,620	£981	Mick Walsh
Hart, Hants	01252-622122	80,920	£968	Chris James
Hastings, E. Sussex	01424-781066	84,500	£1,011	Roy Mawford
Havant, Hants	023-9247 4174	120,110	£942	Vacant
Hertsmere, Herts	020-8207 2277	99,100	£918	Ron Higgins
High Peak, Derbys	0845-129 7777	88,000	£1,080	Peter Sloman
Hinckley and Bosworth, Leics	01455-238141	98,400	£972	Jim Corry
Horsham, W. Sussex	01403-215100	125,700	£924	Martin Pearson
Huntingdonshire, Cambs	01480-388388	153,000	£953	David Monks
Hyndburn, Lancs	01254-388111	78,390	£1,098	M. Chambers
Ipswich, Suffolk	01473-432000	116,960	£1,062	James Hehir
Kennet, Wilts	01380-724911	79,500	£982	Mark Boden
Kerrier, Cornwall	01209-614000	90,500	£957	Geoffrey Cox
Kettering, Northants	01536-410333	84,000	£982	David Cook
King's Lynn and West Norfolk, Norfolk	01553-616200	133,420	£981	Geoff Chilton
LANCASTER, LANCS	01524-582000	137,000	£1,064	Mark Cullinan
Lewes, E. Sussex	01273-471600	85,860	£1,020	John Crawford
Lichfield, Staffs	01543-308000	29,000	£941	Peter Young
LINCOLN, LINCS	01522-881188	170,000	£989	Andrew Taylor
Macclesfield, Cheshire	01625 500500	152,000	£1,018	D. W. Parr
Maidstone, Kent	01622 602000	142,000	£1,000	David Petford
Maldon, Essex	01621-854477	57,300	£983	S. Packham
Malvern Hills, Worcs	01684-892700	74,011	£986	Chris Bocock
Mansfield, Notts	01623 463463	100,000	£1,148	Richard Goad
Melton, Leics	01664 502502	47,900	£1,008	J. Delwyn Burbidge
Mendip, Somerset	01749-343399	100,000	£998	Graham Jeffs
Mid Bedfordshire, Beds	01525-402051	125,700	£1,061	Jaki Salisbury
Mid Devon, Devon	01884-255255	68,600	£991	P. Edwards
Mid Suffolk, Suffolk	01449-720711	85,720	£974	Andrew Good
Mid Sussex, W. Sussex	01444-458166	126,000	£938	Bill Hatton
Mole Valley, Surrey	01306-885001	79,000	£925	Heather Kerswell
New Forest, Notts	023-8028 5000	104,010	£972	Dave Yates
Newark and Sherwood, Staffs	01636-650000	123,300	£1,177	Richard Dix
Newcastle-under-Lyme, Hants	01782-717717	172,740	£946	Felix Harley
North Cornwall, Cornwall	01208-893333	198,300	£958	David Brown
North Devon, Devon	01271-327711	81,000	£985	David Cunliffe
North Dorset, Dorset	01258-454111	87,740	£998	Alan Greaves
North East Derbyshire, Derbys	01246-231111	62,000	£1124	Carol Gilby
North Hertfordshire, Herts	01462-474000	99,000	£943	Stuart Philp
North Kesteven, Lincs	0115-925449	113,500	£976	Ruth Marlow
North Norfolk, Norfolk	01263-513811	92,450	£981	Bruce Barnett
North Shropshire, Shrops	01939-232771	100,900	£1,005	R. J. Hughes
North Warwickshire, Warks	01827 715 341	54,100	£1,097	Jerrry Hutchinson
North West Leicestershire, Leics	01530 454 545	479,210	£1,035	Malcolm Diaper
North Wiltshire, Wilts	01249-706111	86,770	£1,014	Bob Marshall
Northampton, Northants	01604 233 500	139,350	£997	Roger Morris
NORWICH, NORFOLK	01603-622233	123,500	£1,029	Anne Seex
Nuneaton and Bedworth, Warks	024-7637 6376	117,060	£1,062	Christine Kerr
Oadby and Wigston, Leics	0116 288 8961	53,570	£1,020	Ruth Hyde
Oswestry, Shrops	01691-671111	33,510	£1,032	Paul Shevlin
OXFORD, OXON	01865-249811	146,100	£1,041	Marion Headicar
Pendle, Lancs	01282-661661	83,000	£1,117	Stephen Barnes
Penwith, Cornwall	01736-362341	60,110	£921	Jim McKenna
PRESTON, LANCS	01772-906000	135,000	£1,126	Jim Carr
Purbeck, Dorset	01929-556561	46,400	£1,023	Paul Croft
Redditch, Worcs	01527-64252	77,000	£996	Chris Smith

District Council	Telephone	Population	Band D Charge*	Chief Executive
Reigate and Banstead, Surrey	01737-276000	119.000	£962	Nigel Clifford
Restormel, Cornwall	01726-223300	93,800	£925	Patricia Crowson
Ribble Valley, Lancs	01200-425111	52,440	£1,051	David Morris
Richmondshire, N. Yorks	01748-829100	51,300	£985	Harry Tabiner
Rochford, Essex	01702-546366	79,220	£999	Paul Warren
Rossendale, Lancs	01706-217777	65,000	£1,108	J. Hartley
Rother, E. Sussex	01424-787878	92,000	£984	Derek Stevens
Rugby, Warks	01788-533533	87,000	£1,056	Diane Colley
Runnymede, Surrey	01932-838383	76,630	£887	Tim Williams
Rushcliffe, Notts	0115-981 9911	105,000	£1,107	Keith Beaumont
Rushmoor, Hants	01252-398398	89,000	£939	Andrew Lloyd
Ryedale, N. Yorks	01653-600666	49,000	£988	Harold Mosley
SALISBURY, WILTS	01722-336272	115,000	£976	Richard Sheard
Scarborough, N. Yorks	01723-232323	106,070	£975	John Trebble
Sedgefield, Co Durham	01388-816166	89,500	£1,194	Norman Vaulks
Sedgemoor, Somerset	01278-435435	104,000	£969	Kerry Rickards
Selby, N. Yorks	01757-705101	72,800	£978	Martin Connor
Sevenoaks, Kent	01732-227000	111,000	£999	Nigel Howells
Shepway, Kent	01303-850388	96,460	£990	Ronald Thompson
Shrewsbury and Atcham, Shrops	01743-281000	97,400	£979	Robin Hooper
South Bedfordshire, Beds	01582-472222	111,260	£1,113	Jon Ruddick
South Bucks, Berks	01753-533333	63,000	£942	Chris Furness
South Cambridgeshire, Cambs	01223-443000	126,000	£931	John Ballantyne
South Derbyshire, Derbys	01283-221000	81,200	£1,063	Frank McArdle
South Hams, Devon	01803-861234	82,600	£961	Ruth Bagley
South Holland, Lincs	01775-761161	75,200	£966	Chris Simpkins
South Kesteven, Lincs	01476-406080	120,000	£935	Chris Farmer
South Lakeland, Cumbria	01539-733333	103,210	£1,035	Philip Cunliffe
South Norfolk, Norfolk	01508-533633	110,000	£997	Geoffrey Rivers
South Northamptonshire, Northants	01327-322322	78,800	£988	Rob Tinlin
South Oxfordshire, Oxon	01491-823000	125,000	£992	David Buckle
South Ribble, Lancs	01772-421491	104,300	£1,066	Jean Hunter
South Shropshire, Shrops	01584-813000	41,500	£1,030	Graham Biggs
South Somerset, Somerset	01935-462462	155,700	£995	Elaine Peters
South Staffordshire, Staffs	01902-696000	102,320	£912	L. Barnfield
Spelthorne, Surrey	01784-451499	87,500	£930	Michael Taylor
ST. ALBANS, HERTS	01727-866100	126,000	£957	Peter Lerner
St. Edmundsbury, Suffolk	01284-763233	97,000	£974	Deborah Cadman
Stafford, Staffs	01785-619000	127,000	£940	David Rawlings
Staffordshire Moorlands, Staffs	01538-483483	95,070	£959	Simon Baker
Stevenage, Herts	01438-242242	77,000	£939	Ian Paske
Stratford-on-Avon, Warks	01789-267575	114,000	£999	Paul Lankester
Stroud, Glos	01453-766321	108,000	£1,030	David Hagg
Suffolk Coastal, Suffolk	01394-383789	121,000	£966	Tom Griffin
Surrey Heath, Surrey	01276-707100	85,000	£953	Barry Catchpole
Swale, Kent	01795-424341	120,000	£962	Chris Edwards
Tamworth, Staffs	01827-709709	77,000	£912	David Weatherley
Tandridge, Surrey	01883-722000	81,240	£955	Philip Thomas
Taunton Deane, Somerset	01823-356356	100,000	£965	Stephen Fletcher
Teesdale, Co Durham	01833-690000	24,990	£1,059	Charles Anderson
Teignbridge, Devon	01626-361101	123,500	£976	H. Davis
Tendring, Essex	01255-425501	134,470	£970	John Hawkins
Test Valley, Hants	01264-368000	111,000	£914	Alan Jones
Tewkesbury, Glos	01684-295010	74,480	£941	Teri Turner
Thanet, Kent	01843-577000	127,000	£984	Richard Samuel
Three Rivers, Herts	01923-776611	89,100	£948	Alastair Robertson
Tonbridge and Malling, Kent	01732-844522	106,300	£974	David Hughes
Torridge, Devon	01237-428700	56,840	£959	R. Brasington
Tunbridge Wells, Kent	01892-526121	102,740	£947	Rodney Stone
Tynedale, Northumberland	01434-652200	58,180	£1,083	Peter Kemp
Uttlesford, Essex	01799-510510	69,800	£985	Elizabeth Forbes
Vale of White Horse, Oxon	01235-520202	113,940	£954	Terry Stock
Vale Royal, Cheshire	01606-862862	119,600	£1,037	Anne Bingham-Holmes
Wansbeck, Northumberland	01670-532200	63,170	£1,077	R. Stephenson
Warwick, Warks	01926-450000	123,800	£1,016	Janie Barrett
Watford, Herts	01923-226400	81,000	£1,017	Alan Clarke

District Council	Telephone	Population	Band D Charge*	Chief Executive
Waveney, Suffolk	01502-562111	110,100	£940	Mari McLean
Waverley, Surrey	01483-523333	113,210	£962	Christine Pointer
Wealden, E. Sussex	01892-653311	143,400	£1,026	Charlie Lant
Wear Valley, Co Durham	01388-765555	62,750	£1,075	Iain Phillips
Wellingborough, Northants	01933-229777	70,400	£950	Tony McArdle
Welwyn Hatfield, Herts	01707-357000	92,370	£958	Michel Saminaden
West Devon, Devon	01822-813600	47,720	£1,003	David Incoll
West Dorset, Dorset	01305-251010	92,240	£1,023	Clive Rennison
West Lancashire, Lancs	01695-577177	110,200	£1,086	Bill Taylor
West Lindsey, Lincs	01427-615411	77,270	£982	Robert Nelsey
West Oxfordshire, Oxon	01993-702941	99,000	£919	Geoff Bonner
West Somerset, Somerset	01984-632291	32,700	£989	Tim Howes
West Wiltshire, Wilts	01225-776655	108,000	£1,010	Jeffrey Ligo
Weymouth and Portland, Dorset	01305-761222	63,000	£1,028	Tom Grainger
WINCHESTER, HANTS	01962-840222	110,000	£943	David Cowan
Woking, Surrey	01483-755855	93,500	£971	Paul Russell
WORCESTER, WORCS	01905-723471	95,500	£954	David Wareing
Worthing, W. Sussex	01903-239999	100,000	£937	Sheryl Grady
Wychavon, Worcs	01386-565000	113,440	£949	Sid Pritchard
Wycombe, Bucks	01494-461000	162,000	£946	R. Cummins
Wyre, Lancs	01253-891000	106,240	£1,060	Michael Brown
Wyre Forest, Worcs	01562-820505	94,810	£994	Walter Delin

*Council tax figures have been rounded to the nearest £
SMALL CAPITALS = City status

1   Stockton-on-Tees
2   Middlesbrough
3   Blackpool
4   Blackburn
    with Darwen
5   Bolton
6   Bury
7   Rochdale
8   Salford
9   Oldham
10 Liverpool
11 Knowsley
12 St Helens
13 Halton
14 Warrington
15 Trafford
16 Manchester
17 Tameside
18 Stockport
19 Nottingham
20 Telford and
    Wrekin
21 Wolverhampton

22 Walsall
23 Sandwell
24 Dudley
25 Birmingham
26 Solihull
27 Coventry
28 Peterborough
29 South Glos
30 Bristol
31 Bath and
    NE Somerset
32 Windsor and
    Maidenhead
33 Slough
34 Reading
35 Wokingham
36 Bracknell Forest
37 Thurrock
38 Southend
39 Medway
40 Plymouth
41 Torbay

LONDON

1   Hillingdon
2   Harrow
3   Barnet
4   Enfield
5   Waltham Forest
6   Redbridge
7   Barking and Dagenham
8   Havering
9   Ealing
10 Brent
11 Camden
12 Haringey
13 Islington
14 Hackney
15 Newham
16 Hounslow
17 Hammersmith and Fulham
18 Kensington and Chelsea
19 City of Westminster
20 City of London
21 Tower Hamlets
22 Richmond upon Thames
23 Wandsworth
24 Lambeth
25 Southwark
26 Lewisham
27 Greenwich
28 Bexley
29 Kingston upon Thames
30 Merton
31 Sutton
32 Croydon
33 Bromley

London

THE CORPORATION OF LONDON

The City of London is the historic centre at the heart of London known as 'the square mile' around which the vast metropolis has grown over the centuries. The City's residential population is 5,500. The civic government is carried on by the Corporation of London through the Court of Common Council.

The City is an international financial centre, generating over £20 billion a year for the British economy. It includes the head offices of the principal banks, insurance companies and mercantile houses, in addition to buildings ranging from the historic Roman Wall and the 15th-century Guildhall, to the massive splendour of St Paul's Cathedral and the architectural beauty of Wren's spires.

The City of London was described by Tacitus in AD 62 as 'a busy emporium for trade and traders'. Under the Romans it became an important administration centre and hub of the road system. Little is known of London in Saxon times, when it formed part of the kingdom of the East Saxons. In 886 Alfred recovered London from the Danes and reconstituted it a burgh under his son-in-law. In 1066 the citizens submitted to William the Conqueror who in 1067 granted them a charter, which is still preserved, establishing them in the rights and privileges they had hitherto enjoyed.

THE MAYORALTY

The Mayoralty was probably established about 1189, the first Mayor being Henry Fitz Ailwyn who filled the office for 23 years and was succeeded by Fitz Alan (1212–14). A new charter was granted by King John in 1215, directing the Mayor to be chosen annually, which has ever since been done, though in early times the same individual often held the office more than once. A familiar instance is that of 'Whittington, thrice Lord Mayor of London' (in reality four times, 1397, 1398, 1406, 1419); and many modern cases have occurred. The earliest instance of the phrase 'Lord Mayor' in English is in 1414. It was used more generally in the latter part of the 15th century and became invariable from 1535 onwards. At Michaelmas the liverymen in Common Hall choose two Aldermen who have served the office of Sheriff for presentation to the Court of Aldermen, and one is chosen to be Lord Mayor for the following mayoral year.

LORD MAYOR'S DAY

The Lord Mayor of London was previously elected on the feast of St Simon and St Jude (28 October), and from the time of Edward I, at least, was presented to the King or to the Barons of the Exchequer on the following day, unless that day was a Sunday. The day of election was altered to 16 October in 1346, and after some further changes was fixed for Michaelmas Day in 1546, but the ceremonies of admittance and swearing-in of the Lord Mayor continued to take place on 28 and 29 October respectively until 1751. In 1752, at the reform of the calendar, the Lord Mayor was continued in office until 8 November, the 'New Style' equivalent of 28 October. The Lord Mayor is now presented to the Lord Chief Justice at the Royal Courts of Justice on the second Saturday in November to make the final declaration of office, having been sworn in at Guildhall on the preceding day. The procession to the Royal Courts of Justice is popularly known as the Lord Mayor's Show.

REPRESENTATIVES

Aldermen are mentioned in the 11th century and their office is of Saxon origin. They were elected annually between 1377 and 1394, when an Act of Parliament of Richard II directed them to be chosen for life.

The Common Council, elected annually on the first Friday in December, was, at an early date, substituted for a popular assembly called the Folkmote. At first only two representatives were sent from each ward, but the number has since been greatly increased. The Corporation is reducing the number of Common Councilmen from 130 to 100 through natural wastage. The Government has introduced legislation to remove anomalies from the election system and to extend the non-resident franchise.

OFFICERS

Sheriffs were Saxon officers; their predecessors were the wic-reeves and portreeves of London and Middlesex. At first they were officers of the Crown, and were named by the Barons of the Exchequer; but Henry I (in 1132) gave the citizens permission to choose their own Sheriffs, and the annual election of Sheriffs became fully operative under King John's charter of 1199. The citizens lost this privilege, as far as the election of the Sheriff of Middlesex was concerned, by the Local Government Act 1888; but the liverymen continue to choose two Sheriffs of the City of London, who are appointed on Midsummer Day and take office at Michaelmas.

The office of Chamberlain is an ancient one, the first contemporary record of which is 1237. The Town Clerk (or Common Clerk) is mentioned in 1274.

ACTIVITIES

The work of the Corporation is assigned to a number of committees which present reports to the Court of Common Council. These Committees are: Barbican Centre; Barbican Residential; Board of Govenors of the City of London Freeman's School, the City of London School, London School for Girls, the Guildhall School of Music and Drama and the Museum of London; Bridge House Grants; City Lands and Bridge House Estates; Managers of West Ham Park; Community Services; Education; Epping Forest and Open Spaces; Establishment; Finance; Gresham (city side); Guildhall Yard East Building; Hampstead Heath Management; Libraries; Guildhall Art Galleries and Archives; Markets; Planning and Transportation; Police; Policy and Resources; Port Health and Environmental Services; Queen's Park and Highgate Wood Management and Standards Committees..

The City's estate, in the possession of which the Corporation of London differs from other municipalities, is managed by the City Lands and Bridge House Grants Estates Committee, the chairmanship of which carries with it the title of Chief Commoner.

The Honourable the Irish Society, which manages the Corporation's estates in Ulster, consists of a Governor and five other Aldermen, the Recorder, and 19 Common Councilmen, of whom one is elected Deputy Governor.

THE LORD MAYOR 2001–2*

The Rt. Hon. the Lord Mayor, Alderman Michael Oliver, TD *Private Secretary*, P. Tribe

* The Lord Mayor for 2002–3 was elected on Michaelmas Day. *See* Stop-press

THE SHERIFFS 2002–3

David Brewer *(Alderman Bassishaw)*; Martin Clarke

OFFICERS, ETC.

Town Clerk, T. Simmons
Chamberlain, P. Derrick
Chief Commoner (2002), J. Charkham
Clerk, The Honourable the Irish Society, S. Waley, The Irish Chamber, 1st Floor, 75 Watling Street, London EC4M 9BJ

THE ALDERMEN

Name and Ward	CC	Ald.	Shff.	Lord Mayor
Sir Alan Traill,				
GBE, *Langbourn*	1970	1975	1982	1984
Sir David Rowe-Ham,				
GBE, *Bridge and*				
Bridge Wt.	–	1976	1984	1986
Sir Alexander Graham,				
GBE, *Queenhithe*	1978	1979	1986	1990
Sir Brian Jenkins,				
GBE, *Cordwainer*	–	1980	1987	1991
Sir Paul Newall,				
TD, *Walbrook*	1980	1981	1989	1993
Sir Roger Cork, *Tower*	1978	1983	1992	1996
Richard Nichols,				
Candlewick	1983	1984	1994	1997
Lord Levene of Portsoken,				
KBE, *Portsoken*	1983	1984	1995	1998
Sir Clive Martin, *Aldgate*	–	1985	1996	1999
Sir David Howard, BT	1972	1986	1997	2000

All the above have passed the Civic Chair

Michael Oliver, *Bishopsgate*	1980	1987	1997
Gavyn Arthur, *Cripplegate*	1988	1991	1998
Robert Finch, *Coleman Street*	–	1992	1999
Michael Savory, *Bread Street*	1980	1996	2001
Richard Agutter,			
Castle Baynard	–	1995	2000
David Brewer, *Bassishaw*	1992	1996	
Nicholas Anstee, *Aldersgate*	1987	1996	
John Hughesdon, *Billingsgate*	1991	1997	
Anthony Bull, *Cheap*	1968	1984	
Simon Walsh, *Farringdon Wt*	1989	2000	
John Stuttard, *Lime Street*	–	2001	
Dr Andrew Parmley, *Vintry*	1992	2001	
David Lewis, *Broad Street*	–	2001	
Robert Hall, *Farringdon Wn*	1995	2002	
Mrs Alison Gowman,			
Dowgate	1991	2002	

THE COMMON COUNCIL

Deputy: Each Common Councilman so described serves as deputy to the Alderman of her/his ward.

Abrahams, G. (2000)	*Farringdon Wt*
Absalom, J. D. (1994)	*Farringdon Wt.*
Altman, L. P., CBE (1996)	*Cripplegate Wn.*
Angell, E. H. (1991)	*Cripplegate Wt.*
Archibald, *Deputy* W. W. (1986)	*Cornhill*
Ayers, K. E. (1996)	*Bassishaw*
Balls, H. D. (1970)	*Castle Baynard*
Barker, *Deputy* J. A. (1981)	*Cripplegate Wn.*
Barter, S. (1999)	*Langbourn*
Beale, Deputy M. J. (1979)	*Lime Street*
Bird, J. L., OBE (1977)	*Bridge*
Bradshaw, D. J. (1991)	*Cripplegate Wn.*
Bramwell, F. M. (1983)	*Langbourn*

Brewster, J. W., OBE (1994)	*Bassishaw*
Brooks, W. I. B. (1988)	*Billingsgate*
Byllam-Barnes, J. C. F. B. (1997)	*Cheap*
Campbell-Taylor, Father W. G. (2001)	*Portsoken*
Caspi, D. R. (1994)	*Bridge*
Cassidy, *Deputy* M. J. (1989)	*Coleman Street*
Catt, B. F. (1982)	*Farringdon Wn.*
Chadwick, R. A. H. (1994)	*Tower*
Charkham, J. P. (1996)	*Farringdon Wt.*
Cohen, Mrs C. M. (1986)	*Lime Street*
Cotgrove, D. (1991)	*Lime Street*
Currie, *Deputy* Miss S. E. M. (1985)	*Cripplegate Wt.*
Daily-Hunt, R. B. (1989)	*Cripplegate Wt.*
Darwin, G. E. (1995)	*Farringdon Wt.*
Davis, C. B. (1991)	*Bread Street*
Dove, W. H., MBE (1993)	*Bishopsgate*
Duckworth, S. (2000)	*Bishopsgate*
Dudley, The Revd Dr M. R. (2002)	*Aldersgate*
Dunitz, A. A. (1984)	*Portsoken*
Eskenzi, *Deputy* A. N., CBE (1970)	*Farringdon Wn.*
Eve, R. A. (1980)	*Cheap*
Everett, K. M. (1984)	*Candlewick*
Falk, F. A., TD (1997)	*Broad Street*
Farr, M. C. (1998)	*Walbrook*
Farrow, *Deputy* M. W. W. (1996)	*Farringdon Wt.*
Farthing, R. B. C. (1981)	*Aldgate*
FitzGerald, *Deputy* R. C. A. (1981)	*Bread Street*
Forbes, G. B. (1993)	*Bishopsgate*
Fraser, S. J. (1993)	*Coleman Street*
Fraser, *Deputy* W. B. (1981)	*Vintry*
Galloway, *Deputy* A. D. (1981)	*Broad Street*
Gillon, G. M. F. (1995)	*Cordwainer*
Ginsburg, S. (1990)	*Bishopsgate*
Graves, A. C. (1985)	*Bishopsgate*
Halliday, *Deputy* Mrs P. (1992)	*Walbrook*
Hardwick, Dr P. B. (1987)	*Aldgate*
Harris, B. N. (1996)	*Broad Street*
Harris-Jones, Dr R. D. L. (2001)	*Farringdon Wt.*
Hart, *Deputy* M. G. (1970)	*Bridge*
Haynes, J. E. H. (1986)	*Cornhill*
Henderson-Begg, M. (1977)	*Coleman Street*
Hoffman, T. (2002)	*Vintry*
Holland, *Deputy* J., CBE (1972)	*Aldgate*
Holliday, Mrs E. H. L. (1987)	*Vintry*
Hook, J. W. (2000)	*Walbrook*
Jackson, L. St J. T. (1978)	*Bread Street*
Kellett, Mrs M. W. F. (1986)	*Tower*
Kemp, D. L. (1984)	*Coleman Street*
King, A. (1999)	*Queenhithe*
Knowles, *Deputy* S. K. (1984)	*Candlewick*
Leck, P. (1998)	*Aldersgate*
Lee, The Revd Dr B. J. (2001)	*Portsoken*
Littlechild, Mrs V. (1998)	*Cripplegate Wt.*
Lord, C. E. (2000)	*Coleman Street*
Luder, I. D. (1998)	*Farringdon Wt.*
McGuinness, C. (1997)	*Castle Baynard*
McNeil, I. D. (1977)	*Lime Street*
Malins, J. H., QC (1981)	*Farringdon Wt.*
Martinelli, *Deputy* P. J. (1994)	*Bassishaw*
Mayhew, *Deputy* Dame Judith (1986)	*Queenhithe*
Mayhew, J. P. (1996)	*Aldersgate*
Mead, Mrs W. (1997)	*Farringdon Wt.*
Mitchell, *Deputy* C. R. (1971)	*Castle Baynard*
Mobsby, *Deputy* D. J. L. (1985)	*Billingsgate*
Montgomery, B. (1999)	*Dowgate*
Mooney, B. D. F. (1998)	*Queenhithe*
Moss, A. D. (1989)	*Tower*
Moys, Mrs S. (2000)	*Aldgate*
Nash, *Deputy* Mrs J. C. (1983)	*Aldersgate*
Newman, Mrs P. B. (1989)	*Aldersgate*

Owen, Mrs J. (1975)	Langbourn
Owen-Ward, J. R. (1983)	Bridge
Page, M. (2002)	Farringdon Wn.
Pembroke, *Deputy* Mrs A. M. F. (1978)	Cheap
Pollard, J. H. G. (2002)	Dowgate
Price, E. E. (1996)	Farringdon Wt.
Pulman, *Deputy* G. A. G. (1983)	Tower
Punter, C. (1993)	Cripplegate Wn.
Quilter, S. D. (1998)	Cripplegate Wt.
Regan, R. D. (1998)	Farringdon Wn.
Robinson, Mrs D. C. (1989)	Bishopsgate
Roney, *Deputy* E. P. T., CBE (1974)	Bishopsgate
Salinger, S. (2002)	Cripplegate Wn.
Samuel, *Deputy* Mrs I., MBE (1971)	Portsoken
Sargant, K. A. (1991)	Cornhill
Scott, J. (1999)	Broad Street
Scriven, R. G., CBE (1984)	Candlewick
Shalit, *Deputy* D. M. (1972)	Farringdon Wn.
Sherlock, *Deputy* M. R. C. (1992)	Dowgate
Snyder, *Deputy* M. J. (1986)	Cordwainer
Stevenson, F. P. (1994)	Cripplegate Wn.
Taylor, J. A. F., TD (1991)	Bread Street
Thorp, C. R. (1996)	Billingsgate
Thorp, D. (2000)	Farringdon Wt.
Trotter, J. (1993)	Billingsgate
Willoughby, *Deputy* P. J. (1985)	Bishopsgate
Wilmot, R. T. D. (1973)	Cordwainer

The City Guilds (Livery Companies)

The constitution of the livery companies has been unchanged for centuries. There are three ranks of membership: freemen, liverymen and assistants. A person can become a freeman by patrimony (through a parent having been a freeman); by servitude (through having served an apprenticeship to a freeman); or by redemption (by purchase).

Election to the livery is the prerogative of the company, who can elect any of its freemen as liverymen. Assistants are usually elected from the livery and form a Court of Assistants which is the governing body of the company. The Master (in some companies called the Prime Warden) is elected annually from the assistants. As at June 2002, 23,339 liverymen of the guilds were entitled to vote at elections at Common Hall.

The order of precedence, omitting extinct companies, is given in parenthesis after the name of each company in the list below. In certain companies the election of Master or Prime Warden for the year does not take place until the autumn. In such cases the Master or Prime Warden for 2001–2 is given.

THE TWELVE GREAT COMPANIES
In order of civic precedence

MERCERS *(1)*. Mercers Hall, Ironmonger Lane, London, EC2V 8HE. Livery, 229. Clerk, C. H. Parker. Master, Wg Cdr. M. G. Dudgeon, OBE.

GROCERS *(2)*. Grocers Hall, Princes Street, London, EC2R 8AD. Livery, 323. Clerk, Brig. P. P. Rawlins, MBE. Master, N. J. A. V. Taylor.

DRAPERS *(3)*. Drapers Hall, Throgmorton Avenue, London, EC2N 2DQ. Livery, 268. Clerk, Rear-Admiral A. B. Ross CB, CBE. Master, Lord Luke, DL.

FISHMONGERS *(4)*. Fishmongers Hall, London Bridge, London, EC4R 9EL. Livery, 356. Clerk, K. S. Waters. Prime Warden, Sir Thomas Stockdale, Bt.

GOLDSMITHS *(5)*. Goldsmiths Hall, Foster Lane, London, EC2V 6BN. Livery, 275. Clerk, R. D. Buchanan-Dunlop, CBE. Prime Warden, R. P. T. Came.

MERCHANT TAYLORS *(6/7)*. 30 Threadneedle Street, London, EC2R 8JB. Livery, 328. Clerk, D. A. Peck. Master, J. R. Owens.

SKINNERS *(6/7)*. Skinners Hall, 8 Dowgate Hill, London, EC4R 2SP. Livery, 390. Clerk, Capt. D. Hart Dyke, CBE, LVO, RN. Master, C. Everett, CBE.

HABERDASHERS *(8)*. 18 East Smithfield, London, EC1A 9HQ. Livery, 301. Clerk, Capt. R. J. Fisher, RN. Master, (from 23 November 2002) The Hon. L. B. Hacking.

SALTERS *(9)*. Salters Hall, 4 Fore Street, London, EC2Y 5DE. Livery, 164. Clerk, Col. M. P. Barneby. Master, J. C. Russell.

IRONMONGERS *(10)*. Ironmongers Hall, Shaftesbury Place, Barbican, London, EC2Y 8AA. Livery, 129. Clerk, J. A. Oliver. Master, T. P. C. Oliver.

VINTNERS *(11)*. Vintners Hall, Upper Thames Street, London, EC4V 3BG. Livery, 295. Clerk, Brig. M. Smythe, OBE. Master, A. Platt.

CLOTHWORKERS *(12)*. Clothworkers Hall, Dunster Court, Mincing Lane, London EC3R 7AH. Livery, 210. Clerk, A. C. Blessley. Master, R. Saunders

OTHER CITY GUILDS
In alphabetical order

ACTUARIES *(91)*. 81 Worrin Road, Shenfield, Brentwood, Essex CM15 8JN. Livery, 198. Clerk, Mrs J. V. Evans. Master, R. W. Michaelson

AIR PILOTS AND AIR NAVIGATORS *(81)*. Cobham House, 9 Warwick Court, Grays Inn, London WC1R 5DJ. Livery, 500. Clerk, C. L. Hodgkinson. Master, D. M. S. Simpson, OBE, CEng. Grand Master, HRH The Duke of York, CVO, ADC

APOTHECARIES *(58)*. Apothecaries Hall, 14 Black Friars Lane, London EC4V 6EJ. Livery, 1,700. Clerk, Lt.-Col. R. J. Stringer. Master, M. H. Jourdan

ARBITRATORS *(93)*. 13 Hall Gardens, Colney Heath, St Albans, Herts AL4 0QF. Livery, 150. Clerk, Mrs G. Duffy. Master, Miss Victoria Russell

ARMOURERS AND BRASIERS *(22)*. Armourers Hall, 81 Coleman Street, London EC2R 5BJ. Livery, 122. Clerk, Cdr. T. J. K. Sloane, OBE, RN. Master, R. A. Crabb

BAKERS *(19)*. Bakers Hall, Harp Lane, London EC3R 6DP. Livery, 365. Clerk, R. E. B. Sawyer. Master, A. G. Cavan

BARBERS *(17)*. Barber-Surgeons' Hall, Monkwell Square, Wood Street, London EC2Y 5BL. Livery, 200. Clerk, Brig. A. F. Eastburn. Master, J. T. Back, MA

BASKETMAKERS *(52)*. 48 Seymour Walk, London SW10 9NF. Livery, 308. Clerk, Maj. G. J. Flint-Shipman, TD. Prime Warden, G. F. O. Alford

BLACKSMITHS *(40)*. 48 Upwood Road, London SE12 8AN. *Livery,* 226. *Clerk,* C. Jeal. *Prime Warden,* P. R. Allcard

BOWYERS *(38)*. 11 Aldermans Hill, London N13 4YD. *Livery,* 103. *Clerk,* J. R. Owen-Ward (until October 2002). *Master,* C. N. G. Arding

BREWERS *(14)*. Brewers Hall, Aldermanbury Square, London EC2V 7HR. *Livery,* 154. *Clerk,* Brig. D. J. Ross CBE. *Master,* T. D. M. Hart, CA

BRODERERS *(48)*. Ember House, 35–37 Creek Road, East Molesey, Surrey KT8 9BE. *Livery,* 178. *Clerk,* P. J. C. Crouch. *Master,* W. H. Sowerby

BUILDERS MERCHANTS *(88)*. 4 College Hill, London EC4R 2RB. Livery, 200. *Clerk,* Miss S. M. Robinson, TD. *Master,* J. P. B. Cheele

BUTCHERS *(24)*. Butchers Hall, 87 Bartholomew Close, London EC1A 7EB. *Livery,* 594. *Clerk,* G. J. Sharp. *Master,* M. J. Richardson, MBE

CARMEN *(77)*. 8 Little Trinity Lane, London EC4V 2AN. *Livery,* 457. *Clerk,* Cdr. R. M. H. Bawtree, OBE, RN. *Master,* C. J. A. Barrett

CARPENTERS *(26)*. Carpenters Hall, 1 Throgmorton Avenue, London EC2N 2JJ. *Livery,* 150. *Clerk,* Maj.-Gen. P. T. Stevenson, OBE. *Master,* M. I. Montague-Smith

CHARTERED ACCOUNTANTS IN ENGLAND AND WALES *(86)*. The Rustlings, Valley Close, Studham, Dunstable LU6 2QN. *Livery,* 340. *Clerk,* C. Bygrave. *Master,* P. Brennan, OBE

CHARTERED ARCHITECTS *(98)*. 82A Muswell Hill Road, London N10 3JR. *Livery,* 161. *Clerk,* D. Cole-Adams. *Master,* B. Waters

CHARTERED SECRETARIES AND ADMINISTRATORS *(87)*. Sadlers House, Gutter Lane, London EC2V 6BR. *Livery,* 215. *Clerk,* G. E. L. Lintott MA, ACIS. *Master,* P. M. Marcell, LLB, FCIS, FFA

CHARTERED SURVEYORS *(85)*. 75 Meadway Drive, Horsell, Woking, Surrey GU21 4TF. *Livery,* 350. *Clerk,* Mrs A. L. Jackson. *Master,* G. M. F. Gillon, FRICS, CC

CLOCKMAKERS *(61)*. Room 66–67 Albert Buildings, 49 Queen Victoria Street, London EC4N 4SE. *Livery,* 230. *Clerk,* Gp Capt. P. H. Gibson, MBE. *Master,* M. M. Smith

COACHMAKERS AND COACH HARNESS MAKERS *(72)*. 8 Chandlers Court, Burwell, Cambridge CB5 0AZ. *Livery,* 400. *Clerk,* Gp Capt. G. Bunn, CBE. *Master,* Hon. Air Commodore V. Gauntlett

CONSTRUCTORS *(99)*. 181 Fentiman Road, London SW8 1JY. *Livery,* 130. *Clerk,* L. L. Brace. *Master,* P. Lacey

COOKS *(35)*. Registry Chambers, The Old Deanery, Deans Court, London EC4V 5AA. *Livery,* 75. *Clerk,* M. C. Thatcher. *Master,* M. J. Messeat

COOPERS *(36)*. Coopers Hall, 13 Devonshire Square, London EC2M 4TH. *Livery,* 260. *Clerk,* A. G. R. Carroll. *Master,* K. C. Brown

CORDWAINERS *(27)*. 8 Warwick Court, Grays Inn, London WC1R 5DJ. *Livery,* 161. *Clerk,* Lt.-Col. J. R. Blundell, RM. *Master,* D. M. B. Skinner

THE COMPANY OF CURRIERS *(29)*. Kestrel Cottage, East Knoyle, Salisbury SP3 6AD. *Livery,* 95. *Clerk,* Gp Capt. F. J. Hamilton. *Master,* P. D. MacCorkindale

CUTLERS *(18)*. Cutlers Hall, Warwick Lane, London EC4M 7BR. *Livery,* 100. *Clerk,* J. P. Allen. *Master,* R. D. Regan, CC

DISTILLERS *(69)*. 71 Lincolns Inn Fields, London WC2A 3JF. *Livery,* 270. *Clerk,* C. V. Hughes. *Master,* G. M. W. Milsom, OBE

DYERS *(13)*. Dyers Hall, 10 Dowgate Hill, London EC4R 2ST. *Livery,* 127. *Clerk,* J. R. Chambers, FCA. *Prime Warden,* R. P. Back

ENGINEERS *(94)*. Kiln Bank, Bodle Street Green, Hailsham, E. Sussex BN27 4UA. *Livery,* 292. *Clerk,* Cdr. B. D. Gibson, RN. *Master,* R. J. R. Cousins

ENVIRONMENTAL CLEANERS *(97)*. 6 Grange Meadows, Elmswell, Bury St Edmunds, Suffolk IP30 9GE. *Livery,* 250. *Clerk,* M. A. Bizley. *Master,* L. E. Daniel

FAN MAKERS *(76)*. Skinners Hall, 8 Powgate Hill, London EC4R 2SP. *Livery,* 216. *Clerk,* K. J. Patterson. *Master,* G. D Payne

FARMERS *(80)*. Chislehurst Business Centre, 1 Bromley Lane, Chislehurst, Kent BR7 6LH. *Livery,* 300. *Clerk,* Miss M. L. Winter. *Master,* H. R. H. The Princess Royal

FARRIERS *(55)*. 19 Queen Street, Chipperfield, Kings Langley, Herts WD4 9BT. *Livery,* 345. *Clerk,* Mrs C. C. Clifford. *Master,* R. E. Greatorex, FCA

FELTMAKERS OF LONDON *(63)*. The Old Post House, Upton Grey, Basingstoke, Hampshire RG25 2RL. *Livery,* 173. *Clerk,* Maj. J. T. H. Coombs. *Master,* W. Horsham

FIREFIGHTERS *(103)*. The Insurance Hall, 20 Aldermanbury, London EC2V 7GF. *Freemen,* 55. *Clerk,* Mrs M. Holland Prior. *Master,* J. Garrett

FLETCHERS *(39)*. Farmers and Fletchers Hall, 3 Cloth Street, London EC1A 7LD. *Livery,* 130. *Clerk,* M. Johnson. *Master,* J. R Fenner, OBE

FOUNDERS *(33)*. Founders Hall, Number One, Cloth Fair, London EC1A 7JQ. *Livery,* 175. *Clerk,* A. J. Gillett. *Master,* N. V. Turnbull

FRAMEWORK KNITTERS *(64)*. Whitegarth Chambers, 37 The Uplands, Loughton, Essex IG10 1NQ. *Livery,* 220. *Clerk,* H. W. H. Ellis. *Master,* J. C. Strange

FRUITERERS *(45)*. Chapelstones, 84 High Street, Codford St Mary, Warminster BA12 0ND. *Livery,* 280. *Clerk,* Lt.-Col. L. G. French. *Master,* G. A. T Turnbull

FUELLERS *(95)*. 22 Broadfields, Headstone Lane, Hatch End, Middx HA2 6NH. *Livery,* 90. *Clerk,* R. A. Riley. *Master,* A. Bainbridge

FURNITURE MAKERS *(83)*. Painters Hall, 9 Little Trinity Lane, London EC4V 2AD. *Livery,* 296. *Clerk,* Mrs J. A. Wright. *Master,* C. P. Claxton Steven

GARDENERS *(66)*. 25 Luke Street, London EC2A 4AR. *Livery,* 263. *Clerk,* Col. N. G. S. Gray. *Master,* T. H. J. Gough

GIRDLERS *(23)*. Girdlers Hall, Basinghall Avenue, London EC2V 5DD. *Livery,* 80. *Clerk,* Lt.-Col. R. Sullivan. *Master,* J. O. Udal

GLASS SELLERS *(71)*. 43 Aragon Avenue, Thames Ditton, Surrey KT7 0PY. *Livery,* 230. Hon. *Clerk,* B. J. Rawles. *Master,* Prof. J. R. Whiteman, Ph.D., FIMA, FRSA

GLAZIERS AND PAINTERS OF GLASS *(53)*. Glaziers Hall, 9 Montague Close, London SE1 9DD. *Livery,* 248. *Clerk,* Col. D. W. Eking. *Master,* R. C. Shrimplin

GLOVERS *(62)*. 71 Ifield Road, London SW10 9AU. *Livery,* 260. *Clerk,* Mrs M. Hood. *Master,* A. Howarth

GOLD AND SILVER WYRE DRAWERS *(74)*. Twizzletwig, The Ballands South, Fetcham, Leatherhead, Surrey KT22 9EP. *Livery,* 310. *Clerk,* T. J. Waller. *Master,* K. F. Blundell

GUNMAKERS *(73)*. The Proof House, 48–50 Commercial Road, London E1 1LP. *Livery,* 238. *Clerk,* S. Duckworth. *Master,* R. Wilkin

HORNERS *(54)*. Flat 5, 15 Greycoat Place, London SW1P 1SB. *Livery,* 235. *Clerk,* A. R. Layard. *Master,* D. W. S. Beynon

INFORMATION TECHNOLOGISTS *(100)*. Information Technologists Hall, 39A Bartholomew Close, London EC1A 7JN. *Livery,* 255. *Clerk,* Mrs G. Davies. *Master,* J. C. Carrington

INNHOLDERS *(32)*. Innholders Hall, 30 College Street, London EC4R 2RH. *Livery,* 141. *Clerk,* D. E. Bulger. *Master,* T. C. Wood

INSURERS *(92)*. The Hall, 20 Aldermanbury, London EC2V 7HY. *Livery,* 358. *Clerk,* L. J. Walters. *Master,* C. J. Hart

JOINERS AND CEILERS *(41)*. 75 Meadway Drive, Horsell, Woking, Surrey GU21 4TF. *Livery,* 124. *Clerk,* Mrs A. L. Jackson. *Master,* J. Snelling

LAUNDERERS *(89)*. Launderers Hall, 9 Montague Close, London Bridge, London SE1 9DD. *Livery,* 250. *Clerk,* Mrs J. Polek. *Master,* D. M. Hart

LEATHERSELLERS *(15)*. The Hall, 15 St Helens Place, London EC3A 6DQ. *Livery,* 150. *Clerk,* Capt. J. G. F. Cooke, OBE, RN. *Master,* G. H. J. Nicholson

LIGHTMONGERS *(96)*. Crown Wharf, 11A Coldharbour, Blackwall Reach, London E14 9NS. *Livery,* 194. *Clerk,* D. B. Wheatley. *Master,* B. Hurst

LORINERS *(57)*. 8 Portland Square, London E1W 2QR. *Livery,* 355. *Clerk,* G. B. Forbes. *Master,* P. A. Lusty FCA

MAKERS OF PLAYING CARDS *(75)*. Flat 5, 15 Greycoat Place, London SW1P 1SB. *Livery,* 141. *Clerk,* A. R. Layard. *Master,* R. G. W. Somerville

MARKETORS *(90)*. 13 Hall Gardens, Colney Heath, St Albans, Herts AL4 0QF. *Livery,* 231. *Clerk,* Mrs G. Duffy. *Master,* I. Blythe

MASONS *(30)*. 22 Cannon Hill, Southgate, London N14 6LG. *Livery,* 116. *Clerk,* P. F. Clark. *Master,* P. J. Johnson

MASTER MARINERS *(78)*. HQS Wellington, Temple Stairs, Victoria Embankment, London WC2R 2PN. *Livery,* 210. *Senior Warden,* Capt. S. Culshaw. *Master,* Capt. A. Rawcliffe, MRIN. *Admiral,* HRH The Prince Philip, Duke of Edinburgh, KG, KT, OM, GBE, PC

MUSICIANS *(50)*. 6th Floor, 2 London Wall Building, London EC2M 5PP. *Livery,* 374. *Clerk,* Col. T. P. B. Hoggarth. *Master,* G. G. C. Barrett

NEEDLEMAKERS *(65)*. 5 Staple Inn, London WC1V 7QH. *Livery,* 230. *Clerk,* M. G. Cook. *Master,* D. Hubert

PAINTER-STAINERS *(28)*. Painters Hall, 9 Little Trinity Lane, London EC4V 2AD. *Livery,* 320. *Clerk,* Col. W. J. Chesshyre. *Master,* Dr R. G. Glover

PARISH CLERKS *(No livery)*. Acreholt, 33 Medstead Road, Beech, Alton, Hampshire GU34 4AD. *Members,* 95. *Clerk,* Lt. Col. B. J. N. Coombes. *Master,* C. J. Cleugh

PATTENMAKERS *(70)*. 3 The High Street, Sutton Valence, Kent ME17 3AG. *Livery,* 200. *Clerk,* Lt. Col. R. W. Murfin TD. *Master,* N. J. Linstead

PAVIORS *(56)*. 3 Ridgemount Gardens, Enfield, Middx EN2 8QL. *Livery,* 230. *Clerk,* J. L. White. *Master,* A. I. Nellist

PEWTERERS *(16)*. Pewterers Hall, Oat Lane, London EC2V 7DE. *Livery,* 120. *Clerk,* Lt. Col. M. Reeve-Tucker, OBE. *Master,* K. D. N. Kearney

THE COMPANY OF PLASTERERS *(46)*. 6th Floor, 19 Great Winchester Street, London EC2N 2BH. *Livery,* 212. *Clerk,* Mrs. H. Machtus. *Master,* R. P. Doran

PLUMBERS *(31)*. Room 28, 49 Queen Victoria Street, London EC4N 4SA. *Livery,* 336. *Clerk,* Lt. Col. R. J. A. Paterson-Fox. *Master,* A. K. Woollaston. *Grand Master,* P. Lerwill

POULTERS *(34)*. The Old Butchers, Station Road, Groombridge, Kent TN3 9QX. *Livery,* 178. *Clerk,* Mrs G. W. Butcher. *Master,* J. M. Morris

SADDLERS *(25)*. Saddlers Hall, 40 Gutter Lane, London EC2V 6BR. *Livery,* 75. *Clerk,* Gp Capt. W. S. Brereton Martin, CBE. *Master,* D. T. L. Hardy

SCIENTIFIC INSTRUMENT MAKERS *(84)*. 9 Montague Close, London SE1 9DD. *Livery,* 240. *Clerk,* N. J. Watson. *Master,* Dr D. Cornish

SCRIVENERS *(44)*. HQS Wellington, Temple Stairs, Victoria Embankment, London WC2R 2PN. *Livery,* 228. *Clerk,* A. Hill. *Master,* N. P. Ready

SHIPWRIGHTS *(59)*. Ironmongers Hall, Barbican, London EC2Y 8AA. *Livery,* 400. *Clerk,* Capt. R. F. Channon, RN. *Prime Warden,* D. B Cobb, CBE. *Permanent Master,* HRH The Prince Philip, Duke of Edinburgh, KG, KT, OM, GBE, PC

THE CITY OF LONDON SOLICITORS COMPANY *(79)*. 4 College Hill, London EC2R 2RB. *Livery,* 200. *Clerk,* N. Cameron. *Master,* M. J. Cassidy

SPECTACLE MAKERS *(60)*. Apothecaries Hall, Black Friars Lane, London EC4V 6EL. *Livery,* 353. *Clerk,* Lt.-Col. J. A. B. Salmon, OBE, LLB. *Master,* N. C. Sebag-Montefiore, MA

STATIONERS AND NEWSPAPER MAKERS *(47)*. Stationers Hall, Ave Maria Lane, London EC4M 7DD. *Livery,* 452. *Clerk,* Brig. D. G. Sharp, AFC. *Master,* M. A. Pelham

TALLOW CHANDLERS *(21)*. Tallow Chandlers Hall, 4 Dowgate Hill, London EC4R 2SH. *Livery,* 180. *Clerk,* Brig. R. W. Wilde, CBE. *Master,* P. J. Purton, OBE

TAX ADVISERS *(No Livery)*. 504 Bryer Court, Barbican, London EC2Y 8DE. *Freemen,* 130. *Clerk,* C. E. Lord, CC. *Master,* P. W. Murcott

TIN PLATE WORKERS ALIAS WIRE WORKERS *(67)*. Bartholomew House, 66 Westbury Road, New Malden, Surrey KT3 5AS. *Livery,* 195. *Clerk,* M. Henderson-Begg, CC. *Master,* I. Boss

TOBACCO PIPE MAKERS AND TOBACCO BLENDERS *(82)*. Hackhurst Farm, Lower Dicker, Hailsham, E. Sussex BN27 4BP. *Livery,* 156. *Clerk,* N. J. Hallings-Pott. *Master,* M. M. Walter

TURNERS *(51)*. 182 Temple Chambers, Temple Avenue, London EC4Y 0HP. *Livery,* 160. *Clerk,* E. A. Windsor Clive. *Master,* N. A. Crooks-Meredith

THE TYLERS AND BRICKLAYERS COMPANY *(37)*. 11 Manchester Square, London W1U 3PL. *Livery,* 172. *Acting Clerk,* I. J. H. M. Grimshaw. *Master,* J. L. Martin

UPHOLDERS *(49)*. Hall in the Wood, 46 Quail Gardens, Selsdon Vale, Croydon CR2 8TF. *Livery,* 225. *Clerk,* J. P. Cody. *Master,* T. R. Usher

WATERMEN AND LIGHTERMEN *(No livery)*. Watermens Hall, 16 St Mary-at-Hill, London EC3R 8EF. *Craft Owning Freemen,* 366. *Clerk,* C. Middlemiss. *Master,* J. S. Allan

WATER CONSERVATORS *(102)*. Watermens Hall, 16 St Mary-at-Hill, London EC2R 8EF. *Livery,* 175. *Clerk,* R. A. Riley. *Master,* Prof. G. Noone, MBE

WAX CHANDLERS *(20)*. Wax Chandlers Hall, Gresham Street, London EC2V 7AD. *Livery,* 121. *Master,* P. J. Scott

WEAVERS *(42)*. Saddlers House, Gutter Lane, London EC2V 6BR. *Livery,* 125. *Clerk,* Mr. J. Snowdan. *Upper Bailiff,* J. G. Ouvry

WHEELWRIGHTS *(68)*. Ember House, 35–37 Creek Road, East Molesey, Surrey KT8 9BE. *Livery,* 206. *Clerk,* P. J. C. Crouch. *Master,* N. A. Joseph

WOOLMEN *(43)*. Hollands, Hedsor Road, Bourne End, Bucks SL8 5EE. *Livery,* 135. *Clerk,* F. Allen. *Master,* J. B. Whitaker

WORLD TRADERS *(101)*. 36 Ladbroke Grove, London W11 2PA. *Livery,* 148. *Clerk,* N. R. Pullman. *Master,* J. L. Stace

Council	Administrative Headquarters	Telephone	Population	Band D charge 2002*	Chief Executive
Barking and Dagenham	Dagenham, RM10 7BN	020-8592 4500	156,000	£911	Graham Farrant
Barnet	Hendon, NW4 4BG	020-8359 2480	345,500	£915	Leo Boland
Bexley	Bexleyheath, DA6 7LB	020-8303 7777	219,000	£938	Christopher Duffield
Brent	Wembley, HA9 9HX	020-8937 1234	243,025	£878	Gareth Daniel
Bromley	Bromley, BR1 3UH	020-8464 3333	297,600	£880	David Bartlett
Camden	Judd Street, WC1H 9JE	020-7974 4444	192,000	£1,006	Steve Bundred
CORPORATION OF LONDON	Guildhall, EC2P 2EJ	020-7606 3030	6,800	£620	Tom Simmons
Croydon	Park Lane, Croydon, CR9 3JS	020-8686 4433	340,000	£854	David Wechsler
Ealing	New Broadway, W5 2BY	020-8579 2424	298,000	£885	Gillian Guy
Enfield	Silver Street, EN1 3XA	020-8366 6565	260,000	£955	David Plank
Greenwich	Wellington Street, SE18 6PW	020-8854 8888	207,650	£954	Mary Nay
Hackney	Mare Street, E8 1EA	020-8356 3000	195,000	£1,023	Max Caller
Hammersmith and Fulham	King Street, W6 9JU	020-8748 3020	157,000	£946	Richard Harbord
Haringey	High Road, N22 8LE	020-8489 0000	223,700	£983	David Warwick
Harrow	Harrow, HA1 2XF	020-8424 1103	220,000	£1,009	Joyce Markham
Havering	Romford, RM1 3BD	01708-434343	229,800	£1,037	Harold Tinworth
Hillingdon	Uxbridge, UB8 1UW	01895-250111	231,602	£992	Dorian Leatham
Hounslow	Lampton Road Hounslow TW3 4DN	020-8583 2000	205,000	£1,022	Mark Gilks
Islington	Upper Street, N1 2UD	020-7527 2000	176,393	£867	Leisha Fullick
Kensington and Chelsea	Hornton Street, W8 7NX	020-7937 5464	179,200	£772	Derek Myers
Kingston upon Thames	Kingston upon Thames, KT1 1EU	020-8546 2121	144,313	£1,060	Bruce McDonald
Lambeth	Brixton, SW2 1RW	020-7926 1000	272,500	£810	L. Casey
Lewisham	Catford Road, SE6 4RU	020-8314 6000	241,500	£957	Barry Quirk
Merton	London Road, Morden SM4 5DX	020-8543 2222	187,229	£1,018	Roger Paine
Newham	Barking Road, E6 2RP	020-8430 2000	230,000	£885	Dave Burbage
Redbridge	Ilford, IG1 1DD	020-8554 5000	232,500	£930	Roger Hampson
Richmond upon Thames	Twickenham, TW1 3BZ	020-8891 1411	182,766	£1,097	Gillian Norton
Southwark	Peckham Road, SE5 8UB	020-7525 5000	237300	£950	R. Coomber
Sutton	St. Nicholas Way, Sutton, SM1 1EA	020-8770 5000	178,737	£955	Joanna Simons
Tower Hamlets	Clove Crescent, E14 2BG	020-7364 5000	176,035	£816	Christine Gilbert
Waltham Forest	Forest Road, E17 4JF	020-8527 5544	219,000	£979	Simon White
Wandsworth	Wandsworth High Street, SW18 2PU	020-8871 6000	266,300	£403	G. Jones
WESTMINSTER	Victoria Street, SW1E 6QP	020-7641 6000	174,814	£445	Peter Rogers

*Council tax figures have been rounded to the nearest £
SMALL CAPITALS = City status

Wales

The Principality of Wales (Cymru) occupies the extreme west of the central southern portion of the island of Great Britain, with a total area of 8,015 sq. miles (20,758 sq. km): land 7,965 sq. miles (20,628 sq. km); inland water 50 sq. miles (130 sq. km). It is bounded on the north by the Irish Sea, on the south by the Bristol Channel, on the east by the English counties of Cheshire, Shropshire, Worcestershire and Gloucestershire, and on the west by St George's Channel.

Across the Menai Straits is the island of Anglesey (Ynys Môn) (276 sq. miles), communication with which is facilitated by the Menai Suspension Bridge (1,000 ft long) built by Telford in 1826, and by the tubular railway bridge (1,100 ft long) built by Stephenson in 1850. Holyhead harbour, on Holy Isle (north-west of Anglesey), provides accommodation for ferry services to Dublin (70 miles).

POPULATION

The population at the 1991 census was 2,835,073 (males 1,370,104; females 1,464,969). The average density of population in 1991 was 1.36 persons per hectare. Census 2001 results were available from 30 September 2002.

RELIEF

Wales is a country of extensive tracts of high plateau and shorter stretches of mountain ranges deeply dissected by river valleys. Lower-lying ground is largely confined to the coastal belt and the lower parts of the valleys. The highest mountains are those of Snowdonia in the north-west (Snowdon, 3,559 ft), Berwyn (Aran Fawddwy, 2,971 ft), Cader Idris (Pen y Gadair, 2,928 ft), Dyfed (Plynlimon, 2,467 ft), and the Black Mountain, Brecon Beacons and Black Forest ranges in the south-east (Carmarthen Van, 2,630 ft, Pen y Fan, 2,906 ft, Waun Fâch, 2,660 ft).

HYDROGRAPHY

The principal river rising in Wales is the Severn, which flows from the slopes of Plynlimon to the English border. The Wye (130 miles) also rises in the slopes of Plynlimon. The Usk (56 miles) flows into the Bristol Channel, through Gwent. The Dee (70 miles) rises in Bala Lake and flows through the Vale of Llangollen, where an aqueduct (built by Telford in 1805) carries the Pontcysyllte branch of the Shropshire Union Canal across the valley. The estuary of the Dee is the navigable portion, 14 miles in length and about five miles in breadth, and the tide rushes in with dangerous speed over the 'Sands of Dee'. The Towy (68 miles), Teifi (50 miles), Taff (40 miles), Dovey (30 miles), Taf (25 miles) and Conway (24 miles), the last named broad and navigable, are wholly Welsh rivers.

The largest natural lake is Bala (Llyn Tegid) in Gwynedd, nearly four miles long and about one mile wide. Lake Vyrnwy is an artificial reservoir, about the size of Bala, and forms the water supply of Liverpool; Birmingham is supplied from reservoirs in the Elan and Claerwen valleys.

WELSH LANGUAGE

According to the 1991 census results, the percentage of persons of three years and over able to speak Welsh was:

Clwyd	18.2	Powys	20.2
Dyfed	43.7	S. Glamorgan	6.5
Gwent	2.4	W. Glamorgan	15.0
Gwynedd	61.0		
Mid Glamorgan	8.5	Wales	18.7

The 1991 figure represents a slight decline from 18.9 per cent in 1981 (1971, 20.8 per cent; 1961, 26 per cent).

FLAG

The flag of Wales, the Red Dragon (Y Ddraig Goch), is a red dragon on a field divided white over green (per fess argent and vert a dragon passant gules). The flag was augmented in 1953 by a royal badge on a shield encircled with a riband bearing the words Ddraig Goch Ddyry Cychwyn and imperially crowned, but this augmented flag is rarely used.

EARLY HISTORY

The earliest inhabitants of whom there is any record appear to have been subdued or exterminated by the Goidels (a people of Celtic race) in the Bronze Age. A further invasion of Celtic Brythons and Belgae followed in the ensuing Iron Age. The Roman conquest of southern Britain and Wales was for some time successfully opposed by Caratacus (Caractacus or Caradog), chieftain of the Catuvellauni and son of Cunobelinus (Cymbeline). South-east Wales was subjugated and the legionary fortress at Caerleon-on-Usk established by about AD 75–77; the conquest of Wales was completed by Agricola about AD 78. Communications were opened up by the construction of military roads from Chester to Caerleon-on-Usk and Caerwent, and from Chester to Conwy (and thence to Carmarthen and Neath). Christianity was introduced during the Roman occupation, in the fourth century.

ANGLO-SAXON ATTACKS

The Anglo-Saxon invaders of southern Britain drove the Celts into the mountain stronghold of Wales, and into Strathclyde (Cumberland and south-west Scotland) and Cornwall, giving them the name of Waelisc (Welsh), meaning 'foreign'. The West Saxons' victory of Deorham (AD 577) isolated Wales from Cornwall and the battle of Chester (AD 613) cut off communication with Strathclyde and northern Britain. In the eighth century the boundaries of the Welsh were further restricted by the annexations of Offa, King of Mercia, and counter-attacks were largely prevented by the construction of an artificial boundary from the Dee to the Wye (Offa's Dyke).

In the ninth century Rhodri Mawr (844–878) united the country and successfully resisted further incursions of the Saxons by land and raids of Norse and Danish pirates by sea, but at his death his three provinces of Gwynedd (north), Powys (mid) and Deheubarth (south) were divided among his three sons, Anarawd, Mervyn and Cadell. Cadell's son Hywel Dda ruled a large part of Wales and codified its laws but the provinces were not united again until the rule of Llewelyn ap Seisyllt (husband of the heiress of Gwynedd) from 1018 to 1023.

THE NORMAN CONQUEST

After the Norman conquest of England, William I created palatine counties along the Welsh frontier, and the Norman barons began to make encroachments into Welsh territory. The Welsh princes recovered many of their losses during the civil wars of Stephen's reign and in the early 13th century Owen Gruffydd, prince of Gwynedd, was the dominant figure in Wales. Under Llywelyn ap Iorwerth (1194–1240) the Welsh united in

powerful resistance to English incursions and Llywelyn's privileges and de facto independence were recognised in the Magna Carta. His grandson, Llywelyn ap Gruffydd, was the last native prince; he was killed in 1282 during hostilities between the Welsh and English, allowing Edward I of England to establish his authority over the country. On 7 February 1301, Edward of Caernarvon, son of Edward I, was created Prince of Wales, a title subsequently borne by the eldest son of the sovereign.

Strong Welsh national feeling continued, expressed in the early 15th century in the rising led by Owain Glyndŵr, but the situation was altered by the accession to the English throne in 1485 of Henry VII of the Welsh House of Tudor. Wales was politically assimilated to England under the Act of Union of 1535, which extended English laws to the Principality and gave it parliamentary representation for the first time.

EISTEDDFOD

The Welsh are a distinct nation, with a language and literature of their own, and the national bardic festival (Eisteddfod), instituted by Prince Rhys ap Griffith in 1176, is still held annually. These Eisteddfodau (sessions) form part of the Gorsedd (assembly) and are believed to date from the time of Prydian, a ruling prince in an age many centuries before the Christian era.

PRINCIPAL CITIES

CARDIFF

Cardiff, at the mouth of the Rivers Taff, Rhymney and Ely, is the capital city of Wales with a population of over 325,000 and was granted city status in 1905. The city has changed dramatically in recent years following the regeneration of Cardiff Bay and construction of a barrage, which has created a permanent freshwater lake and waterfront for the city. As the capital city of Wales, Cardiff is home to the National Assembly for Wales and is a major administrative, retail, business and cultural centre.

The civic centre, is home to many fine buildings including, the City Hall, Castell Coch, Cardiff Castle, Llandaff Cathedral, National Museum of Wales, University Buildings, Law Courts and Temple of Peace and Health andthe Millennium Stadium which opened in 1999.

SWANSEA

Swansea (Abertawe) is a city and a seaport. The Gower peninsula was brought within the city boundary under local government reform in 1974.

The principal buildings are the Norman Castle (rebuilt c.1330), the Royal Institution of South Wales, founded in 1835 (including Library), the University of Wales Swansea at Singleton, and the Guildhall, containing Frank Brangwyn's British Empire panels. The Dylan Thomas Centre, formerly the old Guildhall, was restored in 1995. More recent buildings include the County Hall, the new Maritime Quarter Marina and leisure centre.

Swansea was chartered by the Earl of Warwick, c. 1158–84, and further charters were granted by King John, Henry III, Edward II, Edward III and James II, Cromwell (two) and the Marcher Lord William de Breos. It was formally invested with city status in 1969 by HRH The Prince of Wales.

Including the above, there are five places with city status in Wales. The other three (with date city status conferred) are; Bangor (pre-1900), St David's (1994) and Newport which was awarded city status in (2002).

Cardiff and Swansea have also been granted Lord Mayoralities.

LOCAL COUNCILS

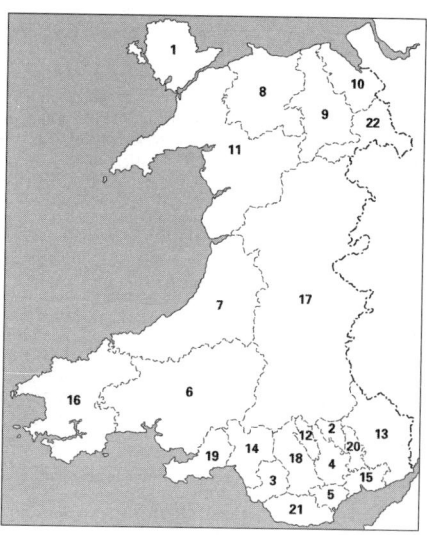

Key	County
1	Anglesey
2	Blaenau Gwent
3	Bridgend
4	Caerphilly
5	Cardiff
6	Carmarthenshire
7	Ceredigion
8	Conwy
9	Denbighshire
10	Flintshire
11	Gwynedd
12	Merthyr Tydfil
13	Monmouthshire
14	Neath Port Talbot
15	Newport
16	Pembrokeshire
17	Powys
18	Rhondda, Cynon, Taff
19	Swansea
20	Torfaen
21	Vale of Glamorgan
22	Wrexham

LORD-LIEUTENANTS AND HIGH SHERIFFS

County/Shire	Lord-Lieutenant	High Sheriff, 2002–3
Clwyd	T. Jones, CBE	Cdr. F. Bradshaw
Dyfed	Sir David Mansel Lewis, KCVO	S. Rees
Gwent	S. Boyle	W. Waters
Gwynedd	Prof. E. Sunderland, OBE	Mrs P. Hughes
Mid Glamorgan	M. A. McLaggan	G. Coleman
Powys	The Hon. Mrs E. S. Legge-Bourke, LVO	Mrs S. Blain
S. Glamorgan	Capt. N. Lloyd-Edwards	C. Richards
W. Glamorgan	R. C. Hastie, CBE	R. Phelps

LOCAL COUNCILS

Council	Administrative Headquarters	Telephone	Population	Band D charge 2002*	Chief Executive
Blaenau Gwent	Ebbw Vale	01495-350555	73,000	£879	Roger Leadbeter
Bridgend	Bridgend	01656-643643	131,500	£829	Keri Lewis
Caerphilly	Hengoed	01443-815588	176,000	£756	Malgwyn Davies
CARDIFF CITY	Cardiff	029-2087 2000	324,370	£748	Byron Davies
Carmarthenshire	Carmarthen	01267-234567	170,000	£801	Mark James
Ceredigion	Aberaeron	01545-570881	71,700	£802	Owen Watkin
Conwy	Conwy	01492-574000	112,700	£655	D. Barker
Denbighshire	Ruthin	01824-706000	90,000	£843	Ian Miller
Flintshire	Mold	01352-752121	148,300	£752	Philip McGreevy
Gwynedd	Caernarfon	01286-672255	116,000	£761	Geraint Jones
Isle of Anglesey	Llangefni	01248-750057	65,400	£711	Geraint Edwards
Merthyr Tydfil	Merthyr Tydfil	01685-725000	56,800	£939	Garry Meredith
Monmouthshire	Cwmbran	01633-644644	86,000	£730	Elizabeth Raikes
Neath Port Talbot	Port Talbot	01639-763333	139,650	£960	Ken Sawyers
NEWPORT	Newport	01633-244491	139,000	£597	Chris Freegard
Pembrokeshire	Haverfordwest	01437-764551	113,720	£628	Bryn Parry-Jones
Powys	Llandrindod Wells	01597-826000	126,000	£713	Jacky Tonge
Rhondda Cynon Taff	Clydach Vale	01443-424000	240,117	£853	Kim Ryley
SWANSEA, CITY AND COUNTY	Swansea	01792-636000	231,180	£755	Vivienne Sugar
Torfaen	Pontypool	01495-762200	90,500	£716	Clive Grace
Vale of Glamorgan	Barry	01446-700111	121,300	£709	John Maitland-Evans
Wrexham	Wrexham	01978-292000	125,750	£784	Derek Griffin

* Council tax figures have been rounded to the nearest £

SMALL CAPS = City status

Scotland

The Kingdom of Scotland occupies the northern portion of the main island of Great Britain and includes the Inner and Outer Hebrides, and the Orkney, Shetland, and many other islands. It lies between 60° 51′ 30″ and 54° 38′ N. latitude and between 1° 45′ 32″ and 6° 14′ W. longitude, with England to the south, the Atlantic Ocean on the north and west, and the North Sea on the east.

The greatest length of the mainland (Cape Wrath to the Mull of Galloway) is 274 miles, and the greatest breadth (Buchan Ness to Applecross) is 154 miles. The customary measurement of the island of Great Britain is from the site of John o' Groats house, near Duncansby Head, Caithness, to Land's End, Cornwall, a total distance of 603 miles in a straight line and approximately 900 miles by road.

The total area of Scotland is 30,420 sq. miles (78,789 sq. km); land 29,767 sq. miles (77,097 sq. km), inland water 653 sq. miles (1,692 sq. km).

POPULATION

The population at the 1991 census was 4,998,567 (males 2,391,961; females 2,606,606). The average density of the population in 1991 was 0.65 persons per hectare. Census 2001 results available from 30 September 2002.

RELIEF

There are three natural orographic divisions of Scotland. The southern uplands have their highest points in Merrick (2,766 ft), Rhinns of Kells (2,669 ft), and Cairnsmuir of Carsphairn (2,614 ft) in the west; and the Tweedsmuir Hills in the east (Hartfell 2,651 ft, Dollar Law 2,682 ft, Broad Law 2,756 ft).

The central lowlands, formed by the valleys of the Clyde, Forth and Tay, divide the southern uplands from the northern Highlands, which extend almost from the extreme north of the mainland to the central lowlands, and are divided into a northern and a southern system by the Great Glen.

The Grampian Mountains, which entirely cover the southern Highland area, include in the west Ben Nevis (4,406 ft), the highest point in the British Isles, and in the east the Cairngorm Mountains (Cairn Gorm 4,084 ft, Braeriach 4,248 ft, Ben Macdui 4,296 ft). The north-western Highland area contains the mountains of Wester and Easter Ross (Carn Eige 3,880 ft, Sgurr na Lapaich 3,775 ft).

Created, like the central lowlands, by a major geological fault, the Great Glen (60 miles long) runs between Inverness and Fort William, and contains Loch Ness, Loch Oich and Loch Lochy. These are linked to each other and to the north-east and south-west coasts of Scotland by the Caledonian Canal, providing a navigable passage between the Moray Firth and the Inner Hebrides.

HYDROGRAPHY

The western coast is fragmented by peninsulas and islands, and indented by fjords (sea-lochs), the longest of which is Loch Fyne (42 miles long) in Argyll. Although the east coast tends to be less fractured and lower, there are several great drowned inlets (firths), e.g. Firth of Forth, Firth of Tay, Moray Firth, as well as the Firth of Clyde in the west.

The lochs are the principal hydrographic feature. The largest in Scotland and in Britain is Loch Lomond (27 sq. miles), in the Grampian valleys; the longest and deepest is Loch Ness (24 miles long and 800 feet deep), in the Great

Glen; and Loch Shin (20 miles long) and Loch Maree in the Highlands.

The longest river is the Tay (117 miles), noted for its salmon. It flows into the North Sea, with Dundee on the estuary, which is spanned by the Tay Bridge (10,289 ft) opened in 1887 and the Tay Road Bridge (7,365 ft) opened in 1966. Other noted salmon rivers are the Dee (90 miles) which flows into the North Sea at Aberdeen, and the Spey (110 miles), the swiftest flowing river in the British Isles, which flows into Moray Firth. The Tweed, which gave its name to the woollen cloth produced along its banks, marks in the lower stretches of its 96-mile course the border between Scotland and England.

The most important river commercially is the Clyde (106 miles), formed by the junction of the Daer and Portrail water, which flows through the city of Glasgow to the Firth of Clyde. During its course it passes over the picturesque Falls of Clyde, Bonnington Linn (30 ft), Corra Linn (84 ft), Dundaff Linn (10 ft) and Stonebyres Linn (80 ft), above and below Lanark. The Forth (66 miles), upon which stands Edinburgh, the capital, is spanned by the Forth Railway Bridge (1890), which is 5,330 feet long, and the Forth Road Bridge (1964), which has a total length of 6,156 feet (over water) and a single span of 3,000 feet.

The highest waterfall in Scotland, and the British Isles, is Eas a'Chùal Aluinn with a total height of 658 feet (200 m), which falls from Glas Bheinn in Sutherland. The Falls of Glomach, on a head-stream of the Elchaig in Wester Ross, have a drop of 370 feet.

GAELIC LANGUAGE

According to the 1991 census, 1.4 per cent of the population of Scotland, mainly in the Highlands and western coastal regions, were able to speak the Scottish form of Gaelic.

LOWLAND SCOTTISH LANGUAGE

Several regional Lowland Scottish dialects, known variously as Scots, Scotch, Lallans or Doric, are widely spoken. The General Register Office (Scotland) has estimated that 1.5 million people, or 30 per cent of the population, are Scots speakers.

FLAG

The flag of Scotland is known as the Saltire. It is a white diagonal cross on a blue field (saltire argent in a field azure) and represents St Andrew, the patron saint of Scotland.

THE SCOTTISH ISLANDS

ORKNEY

The Orkney Islands (total area 375.5 sq. miles) lie about six miles north of the mainland, separated from it by the Pentland Firth. Of the 90 islands and islets (holms and skerries) in the group, about one-third are inhabited.

The total population at the 1991 census was 19,612; the 1991 populations of the islands shown here include those of smaller islands forming part of the same civil parish.

Mainland, 15,128	Rousay, 291
Burray, 363	Sanday, 533
Eday, 166	Shapinsay, 322
Flotta and Fara, 126	South Ronaldsay, 943
Graemsay and Hoy, 477	Stronsay, 382

North Ronaldsay, 92   Westray, 704
Papa Westray, 85

The islands are rich in prehistoric and Scandinavian remains, the most notable being the Stone Age village of Skara Brae, the burial chamber of Maeshowe, the many brochs (towers) and the 12th-century St Magnus Cathedral. Scapa Flow, between the Mainland and Hoy, was the war station of the British Grand Fleet from 1914 to 1919 and the scene of the scuttling of the surrendered German High Seas Fleet (21 June 1919).

Most of the islands are low-lying and fertile, and farming (principally beef cattle) is the main industry. Flotta, to the south of Scapa Flow, is the site of the oil terminal for the Piper, Claymore and Tartan fields in the North Sea.

The capital is Kirkwall (population 6,881) on Mainland.

SHETLAND

The Shetland Islands have a total area of 551 sq. miles and a population at the 1991 census of 22,522. They lie about 50 miles north of the Orkneys, with Fair Isle about half-way between the two groups. Out Stack, off Muckle Flugga, one mile north of Unst, is the most northerly part of the British Isles (60° 51′ 30″ N. lat.).

There are over 100 islands, of which 16 are inhabited. Populations at the 1991 census were:

Mainland, 17,596   Muckle Roe, 115
Bressay, 352   Trondra, 117
East Burra, 72   Unst, 1,055
Fair Isle, 67   West Burra, 857
Fetlar, 90   Whalsay, 1,041
Housay, 85   Yell, 1,075

Shetland's many archaeological sites include Jarlshof, Mousa and Clickhimin, and its long connection with Scandinavia has resulted in a strong Norse influence on its place-names and dialect.

Industries include fishing, knitwear and farming. In addition to the fishing fleet there are fish processing factories, while the traditional handknitting of Fair Isle and Unst is supplemented now with machine-knitted garments. Farming is mainly crofting, with sheep being raised on the moorland and hills of the islands. Latterly the islands have become a centre of the North Sea oil industry, with pipelines from the Brent and Ninian fields running to the terminal at Sullom Voe, the largest of its kind in Europe. Lerwick is the main centre for supply services for offshore oil exploration and development.

The capital is Lerwick (population 7,901) on Mainland.

THE HEBRIDES

Until the late 13th century the Hebrides included other Scottish islands in the Firth of Clyde, the peninsula of Kintyre (Argyll), the Isle of Man, and the (Irish) Isle of Rathlin. The origin of the name is stated to be the Greek Eboudai, latinised as Hebudes by Pliny, and corrupted to its present form. The Norwegian name Sudreyjar (Southern Islands) was latinised as Sodorenses, a name that survives in the Anglican bishopric of Sodor and Man.

There are over 500 islands and islets, of which about 100 are inhabited, though mountainous terrain and extensive peat bogs mean that only a fraction of the total area is under cultivation. Stone, Bronze and Iron Age settlement has left many remains, including those at Callanish on Lewis, and Norse colonisation influenced language, customs and place-names. Occupations include farming (mostly crofting and stock-raising), fishing and the manufacture of tweeds and other woollens. Tourism is also an important factor in the economy.

The Inner Hebrides lie off the west coast of Scotland and relatively close to the mainland. The largest and best-known is Skye (area 643 sq. miles; pop. 8,868; chief town, Portree), which contains the Cuillin Hills (Sgurr Alasdair 3,257 ft), the Red Hills (Beinn na Caillich 2,403 ft), Bla Bheinn (3,046 ft) and The Storr (2,358 ft). Skye is also famous as the refuge of the Young Pretender in 1746. Other islands in the Highland council area include Raasay (pop. 163), Rum, Eigg and Muck.

Further south the Inner Hebridean islands include Arran (pop. 4,474) containing Goat Fell (2,868 ft); Coll and Tiree (pop. 940); Colonsay and Oronsay (pop. 106); Islay (area 235 sq. miles; pop. 3,538); Jura (area 160 sq. miles; pop. 196) with a range of hills culminating in the Paps of Jura (Beinn-an-Oir, 2,576 ft, and Beinn Chaolais, 2,477 ft); and Mull (area 367 sq. miles; pop. 2,708; chief town Tobermory) containing Ben More (3,171 ft).

The Outer Hebrides, separated from the mainland by the Minch, now form the Eilean Siar Western Isles Islands Council area (area 1,119 sq. miles; population at the 1991 census 29,600). The main islands are Lewis with Harris (area 770 sq. miles, pop. 21,737), whose chief town, Stornoway, is the administrative headquarters; North Uist (pop. 1,404); South Uist (pop. 2,106); Baleshare (55); Benbecula (pop. 1,803) and Barra (pop. 1,244). Other inhabited islands include Bernera (262), Berneray (141), Eriskay (179), Grimsay (215), Scalpay (382) and Vatersay (72).

EARLY HISTORY

There is evidence of human settlement in Scotland dating from the third millennium BC, the earliest settlers being Middle Stone Age hunters and fishermen. Early in the second millennium BC, New Stone Age farmers began to cultivate crops and rear livestock; their settlements were on the west coast and in the north, and included Skara Brae and Maeshowe (Orkney). Settlement by the Early Bronze Age 'Beaker folk', so-called from the shape of their drinking vessels, in eastern Scotland dates from about 1800 BC. Further settlement is believed to have occurred from 700 BC onwards, as tribes were displaced from further south by new incursions from the Continent and the Roman invasions from AD 43.

Julius Agricola, the Roman governor of Britain AD 77–84, extended the Roman conquests in Britain by advancing into Caledonia, culminating with a victory at Mons Graupius, probably in AD 84; he was recalled to Rome shortly afterwards and his forward policy was not pursued. Hadrian's Wall, mostly completed by AD 30, marked the northern frontier of the Roman empire except for the period between about AD 144 and 190 when the frontier moved north to the Forth–Clyde isthmus and a turf wall, the Antonine Wall, was manned.

After the Roman withdrawal from Britain, there were centuries of warfare between the Picts, Scots, Britons, Angles and Vikings. The Picts, believed to be a non-Indo-European race, occupied the area north of the Forth. The Scots, a Gaelic-speaking people of northern Ireland, colonised the area of Argyll and Bute (the kingdom of Dalriada) in the fifth century AD and then expanded eastwards and northwards. The Britons, speaking a Brythonic Celtic language, colonised Scotland from the south from the first century BC; they lost control of south-eastern Scotland (incorporated into the kingdom of Northumbria) to the Angles in the early seventh century but retained Strathclyde (south-western Scotland and Cumbria). Viking raids from the late eighth century were followed by Norse settlement in the western and

northern isles, Argyll, Caithness and Sutherland from the mid-ninth century onwards.

UNIFICATION

The union of the areas which now comprise Scotland began in AD 843 when Kenneth mac Alpin, king of the Scots from c. 834, became also king of the Picts, joining the two lands to form the kingdom of Alba (comprising Scotland north of a line between the Forth and Clyde rivers). Lothian, the eastern part of the area between the Forth and the Tweed, seems to have been leased to Kenneth II of Alba (reigned 971–995) by Edgar of England c. 973/4, and Scottish possession was confirmed by Malcolm II's victory over a Northumbrian army at Carham c.1016. At about this time Malcolm II (reigned 1005–34) placed his grandson Duncan on the throne of the British kingdom of Strathclyde, bringing under Scots rule virtually all of what is now Scotland.

The Norse possessions were incorporated into the kingdom of Scotland from the 12th century onwards. An uprising in the mid-12th century drove the Norse from most of mainland Argyll. The Hebrides were ceded to Scotland by the Treaty of Perth in 1266 after a Norwegian expedition in 1263 failed to maintain Norse authority over the islands. Orkney and Shetland fell to Scotland in 1468–9 as a pledge for the unpaid dowry of Margaret of Denmark, wife of James III, though Danish claims of suzerainty were relinquished only with the marriage of Anne of Denmark to James VI in 1590.

From the 11th century, there were frequent wars between Scotland and England over territory and the extent of England's political influence. The failure of the Scottish royal line with the death of Margaret of Norway in 1290 led to disputes over the throne which were resolved by the adjudication of Edward I of England. He awarded the throne to John Balliol in 1292 but Balliol's refusal to be a puppet king led to war. Balliol surrendered to Edward I in 1296 and Edward attempted to rule Scotland himself. Resistance to Scotland's loss of independence was led by William Wallace, who defeated the English at Stirling Bridge (1297), and Robert Bruce, crowned in 1306, who held most of Scotland by 1311 and routed Edward II's army at Bannockburn (1314). England recognised the independence of Scotland in the Treaty of Northampton in 1328. Subsequent clashes include the disastrous battle of Flodden (1513) in which James IV and many of his nobles fell.

THE UNION

In 1603 James VI of Scotland succeeded Elizabeth I on the throne of England (his mother, Mary Queen of Scots, was the great-granddaughter of Henry VII), his successors reigning as sovereigns of Great Britain. Political union of the two countries did not occur until 1707.

THE JACOBITE REVOLTS

After the abdication (by flight) in 1688 of James VII and II, the crown devolved upon William III (grandson of Charles I) and Mary II (elder daughter of James VII and II). In 1689 Graham of Claverhouse roused the Highlands on behalf of James VII and II, but died after a military success at Killiecrankie.

After the death of Anne (younger daughter of James VII and II), the throne devolved upon George I (great-grandson of James VI and I). In 1715, armed risings on behalf of James Stuart (the Old Pretender, son of James VII and II) led to the indecisive battle of Sheriffmuir, and the Jacobite movement died down until 1745, when Charles Stuart (the Young Pretender) defeated the Royalist troops at Prestonpans and advanced to Derby (1746). From Derby,

the adherents of 'James VIII and III' (the title claimed for his father by Charles Stuart) fell back on the defensive and were finally crushed at Culloden (16 April 1746).

PRINCIPAL CITIES

ABERDEEN

Aberdeen, 130 miles north-east of Edinburgh, received its charter as a Royal Burgh in 1124. Scotland's third largest city, Aberdeen lies between two rivers, the Dee and the Don facing the North Sea, the city has a strong maritime history and today is a main centre for offshore oil exploration and production. It is also an ancient university town and distinguished research centre. Other industries include engineering, food processing, textiles, paper manufacturing and chemicals.

Places of interest include King's College, St Machar's Cathedral, Brig o' Balgownie, Duthie Park and Winter Gardens, Hazlehead Park, the Kirk of St Nicholas, Mercat Cross, Marischal College and Marischal Museum, Provost Skene's House, Art Gallery, Gordon Highlanders Museum, Satrosphere Hands-On Discovery Centre, and Aberdeen Maritime Museum.

DUNDEE

The unique City Churches – three churches under one roof, together with the 15th-century St Mary's Tower – are the most prominent architectural feature. Dundee has two historic ships: the Dundee-built RRS Discovery which took Capt. Scott to the Antarctic lies alongside Discovery Quay, and the frigate Unicorn, the only British-built wooden warship still afloat, is moored in Victoria Dock. Places of interest include Mills Public Observatory, the Tay road and rail bridges, Dundee Contemporary Arts Centre, McManus Galleries, Claypotts Castle, Broughty Castle, Verdant Works (Textile Heritage Centre) and the Sensation science centre.

EDINBURGH

Edinburgh is the capital of and seat of government in Scotland. The city is built on a group of hills and contains in Princes Street one of the most beautiful thoroughfares in the world.

The principal buildings are the Castle, which now houses the Stone of Scone and also includes St Margaret's Chapel, the oldest building in Edinburgh, and near it, the Scottish National War Memorial; the Palace of Holyroodhouse; Parliament House, the present seat of the judicature; three universities (Edinburgh, Heriot-Watt, Napier); St Giles' Cathedral; St Mary's (Scottish Episcopal) Cathedral (Sir George Gilbert Scott); the General Register House (Robert Adam); the National and the Signet Libraries; the National Gallery of Scotland; the Royal Scottish Academy; the Scottish National Portrait Gallery; and the Edinburgh International Conference Centre. A new Scottish Parliament building is currently under construction at Holyrood.

GLASGOW

Glasgow, a Royal Burgh, is Scotland's largest city and its principal commercial and industrial centre. The city occupies the north and south banks of the Clyde, formerly one of the chief commercial estuaries in the world. The main industries include engineering, electronics, finance, chemicals and printing. The city is also a key tourist and conference destination.

The chief buildings are the 13th-century Gothic Cathedral, the University (Sir George Gilbert Scott), the

City Chambers, the Royal Concert Hall, St Mungo Museum of Religious Life and Art, Pollok House, the School of Art (Mackintosh), Kelvingrove Art Galleries, the Gallery of Modern Art, the Burrell Collection museum and the Mitchell Library. The city is home to the Scottish National Orchestra, Scottish Opera, Scottish Ballet and BBC Scotland and Scottish Television.

INVERNESS

Inverness was granted city status in January 2001. The city's name is derived from the Gaelic for 'the mouth of the Ness', referring to the river on which it lies. Inverness is recorded as being at the junction of the old trade routes since 565AD. Today the city is the main administrative centre for the north of Scotland and is the capital of the Highlands. Tourism is one of the city's main industries.

Among the city's most notable buildings is Abertarff House, built in 1593 and the oldest secular building remaining in Inverness. Balnain House, built as a town house in 1726 is a fine example of early Georgian architecture. Once a hospital for Hanoverian soldiers after the battle of Culloden and as billets for the Royal Engineers when completing the 1st Ordnance Survey, today Balnain House is the National Trust for Scotland's regional HQ. The Old High Church, on St Michael's Mount, is the original Parish Church of Inverness and is built on the sight of the earliest Christian church in the city. Parts of the church date back to the 14th century.

Stirling was granted city status in 2002.
Aberdeen, Dundee, Edinburgh and Glasgow have also been granted Lord Mayoralty/Lord Provostship.

LORD-LIEUTENANTS

Title	Name	Title	Name
Aberdeenshire	A. D. M. Farquharson, OBE	Nairn	E. J. Brodie
Angus	Mrs G. L. Osborne	Orkney	G. R. Marwick
Argyll and Bute	K. A. Mackinnon, GQ, RD	Perth and Kinross	Sir David Montgomery, BT.
Ayrshire and Arran	Maj. R. Y. Henderson, TD	Renfrewshire	C. H. Parker, OBE
Banffshire	J. A. S. McPherson, CBE	Ross and Cromarty	Capt. R. W. K. Stirling of
Berwickshire	Maj. A. R. Trotter		Fairburn, TD
Caithness	Maj. G. T. Dunnett, TD	Roxburgh, Ettrick and	Dr June Paterson-Brown, CBE
Clackmannan	Mrs S. G. Cruickshank	Lauderdale	
Dumfries	Capt. R. C. Cunningham-	Shetland	J. H. Scott
	Jardine	Stirling and Falkirk	Lt.-Col. J. Stirling of Garden,
Dunbartonshire	Brig. D. D. G. Hardie, TD		CBE, TD
East Lothian	W. Garth Morrison, CBE	Sutherland	Maj.-Gen. D. Houston, CBE
Eilean Siar/Western Isles	A. Matheson, OBE	The Stewartry of	Lt.-Gen. Sir Norman Arthur,
Fife	Mrs C. M. Dean	Kirkcudbright	kcb
Inverness	Vacant	Tweeddale	Capt. D. Younger
Kincardineshire	J. D. B. Smart	West Lothian	Mrs I. B. Brydie, MBE
Lanarkshire	G. Cox, MBE	Wigtown	Maj. E. S. Orr-Ewing
Midlothian	Capt. G. W. Burnet, LVO		
Moray	Air Vice-Marshal G. A. Chesworth, CB, OBE, DFC		

The Lord Provosts of the four city districts of Aberdeen, Dundee, Edinburgh and Glasgow are Lord-Lieutenants for those districts *ex officio*.

LOCAL COUNCILS

Council	Administrative Headquarters	Telephone	Population	Band D charge 2002*	Chief Executive
Aberdeen	Aberdeen	01224-522000	217,260	£981	Douglas Paterson
Aberdeenshire	Aberdeen	01467-620981	227,200	£919	Alan Campbell
Angus	Forfar	01307-461460	112,000	£881	Sandy Watson
Argyll and Bute	Lochgilphead	01546-602127	90,000	£1,009	James McLellan
Clackmannanshire	Alloa	01259-452000	49,000	£978	Keir Bloomer
Dumfries and Galloway	Dumfries	01387-260000	145,000	£899	Philip Jones
Dundee	Dundee	01382-434000	145,000	£1,079	Alex Stephen
East Ayrshire	Kilmarnock	01563-576000	123,230	£967	David Montgomery
East Dunbartonshire	Kirkintilloch	0141-578 8000	110,000	£915	Vicki Nash
East Lothian	Haddington	01620-827827	91,280	£955	John Lindsay
East Renfrewshire	Gifnock	0141-577 3000	89,280	£910	Peter Daniels
Edinburgh	Edinburgh	0131-200 2000	448,850	£1,001	Tom Aitchison
Eilean Siar (Western Isles)	Stornoway	01851-703773	27,560	£815	Bill Howat
Falkirk	Falkirk	01324-506070	142,000	£863	Mary Pitcaithly
Fife	Glenrothes	01592-414141	350,000	£935	Douglas Sinclair
Glasgow	Glasgow	0141-287 2000	612,000	£1,141	James Andrews
Highland	Inverness	01463-702000	208,000	£939	Arthur McCourt

Council	Administrative Headquarters	Telephone	Population	Band D charge 2002*	Chief Executive
Inverclyde	Greenock	01475-717171	85,000	£1,062	Robert Cleary
Midlothian	Dalkeith	0131-270 7500	82,000	£1,036	Trevor Muir
Moray	Elgin	01343-543451	85,000	£865	Alastair Keddie
North Ayrshire	Irvine	01294-324100	139,000	£927	Bernard Devine
North Lanarkshire	Motherwell	01698-302222	327,600	£939	Gavin Whitefield
Orkney	Kirkwall	01856 873 535	19,810	£824	Alistair Buchan
Perth and Kinross	Perth	01738-475000	133,620	£936	Harry Robertson
Renfrewshire	Paisley	0141-842 5000	176,970	£941	Tom Scholes
Scottish Borders	Melrose	01835-824000	106,000	£864	David Hume
Shetland	Lerwick	01595-693535	23,000	£810	Morgan Goodlad
South Ayrshire	Ayr	01292-612406	48,000	£918	George Thorley
South Lanarkshire	Hamilton	01698-454444	301,070	£947	Michael Docherty
Stirling	Stirling	01786-443322	84,700	£1,011	Keith Yates
West Dunbartonshire	Dumbarton	01389-737000	93,977	£1,050	Tim Huntingford
West Lothian	Livingston	01506-777000	152,000	£951	Alex Linkston

*Council tax figures have been rounded to the nearest £
SMALL CAPS = City status

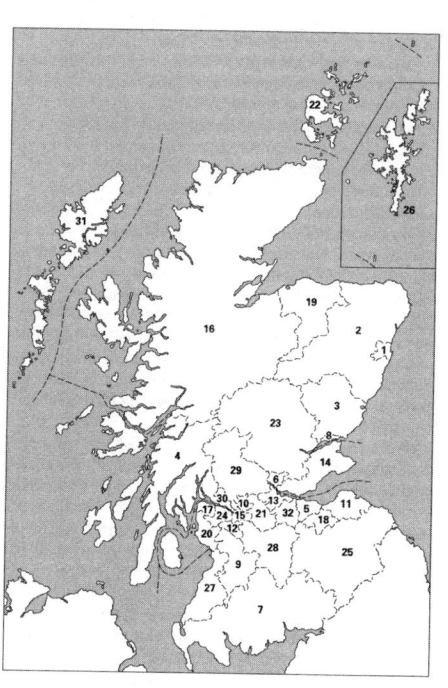

Key	Council
1	Aberdeen City
2	Aberdeenshire
3	Angus
4	Argyll and Bute
5	City of Edinburgh
6	Clackmannanshire
7	Dumfries and Galloway
8	Dundee City
9	East Ayrshire
10	East Dunbartonshire
11	East Lothian
12	East Renfrewshire
13	Falkirk
14	Fife
15	Glasgow City
16	Highland
17	Inverclyde
18	Midlothian
19	Moray
20	North Ayrshire
21	North Lanarkshire
22	Orkney
23	Perth and Kinross
24	Renfrewshire
25	Scottish Borders
26	Shetland
27	South Ayrshire
28	South Lanarkshire
29	Stirling
30	West Dunbartonshire
31	Western Isles (Eilean Siar)
32	West Lothian

Northern Ireland

Northern Ireland has a total area of 5,467 sq. miles (14,144 sq. km): land, 5,225 sq. miles (13,532 sq. km); inland water and tideways, 249 sq. miles (628 sq. km).

The population of Northern Ireland at the 1991 census was 1,577,836 (males, 769,071; females, 808,765). The average density of population in 1991 was 1.11 persons per hectare.

In 1991 the number of persons in the various religious denominations (expressed as percentages of the total population) were: Roman Catholic, 38.4; Presbyterian, 21.4; Church of Ireland, 17.7; Methodist, 3.8; others 7.7; none, 3.7; not stated, 7.3.

The latest census took place on 29 April 2001. Results available from 30 September 2002.

FLAG

The official national flag of Northern Ireland is now the Union Flag. The flag formerly in use (a white, six-pointed star in the centre of a red cross on a white field, enclosing a red hand and surmounted by a crown) has not been used since the imposition of direct rule.

PRINCIPAL CITIES

BELFAST

Belfast, the administrative centre of Northern Ireland, is situated at the mouth of the River Lagan at its entrance to Belfast Lough. The city grew, owing to its easy access by sea to Scottish coal and iron, to be a great industrial centre.

The principal buildings are of a relatively recent date and include the Parliament Buildings at Stormont, the City Hall, Waterfront Hall, the Law Courts, the Public Library and the Museum and Art Gallery.

Belfast received its first charter of incorporation in 1613 and was created a city in 1888; the title of Lord Mayor was conferred in 1892.

LONDONDERRY

Londonderry (originally Derry) is situated on the River Foyle, and has important associations with the City of London. The Irish Society was created by the City of London in 1610, and under its royal charter of 1613 it fortified the city and was for a long time closely associated with its administration. Because of this connection the city was incorporated in 1613 under the new name of Londonderry.

The city is famous for the great siege of 1688–9, when for 105 days the town held out against the forces of James II until relieved by sea. The city walls are still intact and form a circuit of almost a mile around the old city.

Interesting buildings are the Protestant Cathedral of St Columb's (1633) and the Guildhall, reconstructed in 1912 and containing a number of beautiful stained glass windows, many of which were presented by the livery companies of London.

Three other places in Northern Ireland have been granted city status: Armagh (1994), Newry (2002) and Lisburn (2002).

CONSTITUTIONAL DEVELOPMENTS

Northern Ireland is subject to the same fundamental constitutional provisions which apply to the rest of the United Kingdom. It had its own parliament and government from 1921 to 1972, but after increasing civil unrest the Northern Ireland (Temporary Provisions) Act 1972 transferred the legislative and executive powers of the Northern Ireland parliament and government to the UK Parliament and a Secretary of State. The Northern Ireland Constitution Act 1973 provided for devolution in Northern Ireland through an assembly and executive, but a power-sharing executive formed by the Northern Ireland political parties in January 1974 collapsed in May 1974. Since then Northern Ireland has been governed by direct rule under the provisions of the Northern Ireland Act 1974. This allows Parliament to approve all laws for Northern Ireland and places the Northern Ireland department under the direction and control of the Secretary of State for Northern Ireland.

Attempts were made by successive governments to find a means of restoring a widely acceptable form of devolved government to Northern Ireland. In 1985 the governments of the United Kingdom and the Republic of Ireland signed the Anglo-Irish Agreement, establishing an intergovernmental conference in which the Irish government may put forward views and proposals on certain aspects of Northern Ireland affairs.

Discussions between the British and Irish governments and the main Northern Ireland parties began in 1991. It was agreed that any political settlement would need to address relationships within Northern Ireland, within the island of Ireland (north/south) and between the British and Irish governments (east/west). Although round table talks ended in 1992 the process continued from September 1993 as separate bilateral discussions with three of the Northern Ireland parties (the DUP declined to participate).

In December 1993 the British and Irish governments published the Joint Declaration complementing the political talks, and making clear that any settlement would need to be founded on principles of democracy and consent. The declaration also stated that all democratically mandated parties could be involved in political talks as long as they permanently renounced paramilitary violence.

The provisional IRA and loyalist paramilitary groups announced cease-fires on 31 August and 13 October 1994 respectively. The Government initiated exploratory meetings with Sinn Fein and loyalist representatives in December 1994.

In February 1995 the then Prime Minister (John Major) launched A Framework for Accountable Government in Northern Ireland and, with the Irish Prime Minister, A New Framework for Agreement. These outlined what a comprehensive political settlement might look like. The ideas were intended to facilitate multilateral dialogue involving the Northern Ireland parties and the British government.

In autumn 1995 the Prime Minister said that Sinn Fein would not be invited to all-party talks until the IRA had decommissioned its arms; the IRA ruled out any decommissioning of weapons in advance of a political settlement. An international body chaired by a former US senator, George Mitchell, reported in January 1996 that

no weapons would be decommissioned before the start of all-party talks and that a compromise agreement was necessary under which weapons would be decommissioned during negotiations. The Prime Minister accepted the report and proposed the election of representatives to conduct all-party talks. On 9 February 1996 the IRA called off its cease-fire.

PEACE TALKS

Following elections on 30 May 1996, all-party talks opened at Stormont Castle on 10 June 1996 which included nine of the ten parties returned at the election; Sinn Fein representatives were turned away because the IRA had failed to reinstate its cease-fire. On 29 July 1996 the all-party talks were suspended after disagreements over the issue of decommissioning arms. An opening agenda for the talks was agreed in October 1996.

On 25 June 1997 the newly-elected Labour Government said that substantive negotiations should begin in September 1997 with a view to reaching conclusions by May 1998. The British and Irish governments issued a joint paper outlining their proposals for resolving the decommissioning issue. The Government also indicated that if the IRA were to call a cease-fire, it would assess whether it was genuine over a period of six weeks, and if satisfied that it was so, would then invite Sinn Fein to the talks. An IRA cease-fire was declared on 20 July 1997.

When the UK Government announced in August 1997 that Sinn Fein would be present when the substantive talks opened on 15 September, the Unionist and loyalist parties, unhappy at the terms on which Sinn Fein had been admitted, boycotted the opening session. The Ulster Unionist Party, the Progressive Unionist Party and the Ulster Democratic Party re-entered the negotiations on 17 September. Full-scale peace talks began on 7 October. The parties had agreed to concentrate on constitutional issues, with the issue of decommissioning terrorist weapons to be handled by a new independent commission.

On 12 January 1998 the British and Irish governments issued a joint document, Propositions on Heads of Agreement, proposing the establishment of various new cross-border bodies; further proposals were presented on 27 January. A draft peace settlement was issued by the talks' chairman, Sen. George Mitchell, on 6 April 1998 but was rejected by the Unionists the following day. On 10 April agreement was reached between the British and Irish governments and the eight Northern Ireland political parties still involved in the talks (the Good Friday Agreement). The agreement provided for an elected New Northern Ireland Assembly; a North/South Ministerial Council, and a British-Irish Council comprising representatives of the British, Irish, Channel Islands and Isle of Man governments and members of the new assemblies for Scotland, Wales and Northern Ireland. Further points included the abandonment of the Republic of Ireland's constitutional claim to Northern Ireland; the decommissioning of weapons; the release of paramilitary prisoners; and changes in policing.

Referendums on the agreement were held in Northern Ireland and the Republic of Ireland on 22 May 1998. In Northern Ireland the turnout was 81 per cent, of which 71.12 per cent voted in favour of the agreement. In the Republic of Ireland, the turnout was about 55 per cent, of which 94.4 per cent voted in favour of both the agreement and the necessary constitutional change. In the UK, the Northern Ireland Act 1998, enshrining the provisions of the Agreement, received Royal Assent in November 1998.

For details of the Northern Ireland Assembly and the further political developments in Northern Ireland, see the Regional Government section.

OTHER BODIES

Consultations between the First Minister and Deputy First Minister, the British and Irish Governments and the political parties concluded in early 1999 with an agreement to establish six areas for cross-border bodies and a further six areas for co-operation. Treaties between the British and Irish governments establishing the bodies and parallel domestic legislation to underpin them are now in place.

The Good Friday Agreement also provided for a British-Irish Intergovernmental Conference to promote bilateral co-operation at all levels on matters of mutual interest, with a particular focus on non-devolved Northern Ireland matters, and supported by a joint standing Secretariat.

The British-Irish Council will operate on the basis of consensus and may reach agreements and pursue common policies in areas of mutual interest.

FINANCE

Northern Ireland's expenditure is funded by the Northern Ireland Consolidated Fund (NICF). Up to date of devolution on 2 December 1999, the NICF was largely financed by Northern Ireland's attributed share of UK taxation and supplemented by a grant-in-aid. From devolution, these separate elements have been subsumed into a single Block Grant. In 2001–2 the provisional outturn for public expenditure falling within the Northern Ireland Departmental Expenditure Limit was £5,637 million. For 2002–3 the provisional estimate of required funds is £6,131 million.

NORTHERN IRELAND COUNTIES

County	Area* (sq. miles)	Lord-Lieutenant
Antrim	1,093	The Lord O'Neill, TD
Armagh	484	The Earl of Caledon
Belfast City	25	Lady Carswell, OBE
Down	945	Maj. W. J. Hall
Fermanagh	647	The Earl of Erne
Londonderry	798	J. Eaton, TD
Londonderry City	3.4	D. F. Desmond, CBE
Tyrone	1,211	The Duke of Abercorn

DISTRICT COUNCILS

Council	Telephone	Population	Band D charge 2002*	Chief Executive
Antrim, Co. Down	028-9446 3113	47,000	£501.24	Samuel Magee
Ards, Co. Down	028-9182 4000	72,300	£465.32	David Fallows
Armagh, Co. Armagh	028-3752 9600	54,000	£487.61	Victor Brownlees
Ballymena, Co. Antrim	028-2566 0300	57,300	£467.73	M. Rankin
Ballymoney, Co. Antrim	028-2766 2280	25,900	£446.32	John Dempsey
Banbridge, Co. Down	028-4066 0600	39,300	£483.66	Robert Gilmore
Belfast, Co. Antrim and Co. Down	028-9032 0202	297,100	£447.81	Peter McNaney
Carrickfergus, Co. Antrim	028-9335 1604	38,000	£449.12	Alan Cardwell
Castlereagh, Co. Down	028-9049 4500	66,000	£443.70	Adrian Donaldson
Coleraine, Co. Londonderry	028-7034 7034	55,682	£516.13	Wavell Moore
Cookstown, Co. Tyrone	028-8676 2205	32,000	£414.02	Michael McGuckin
Craigavon, Co. Armagh	028-3831 2400	79,600	£513.22	Trevor Reaney
Derry, Co. Londonderry	028-7136 5151	106,600	£471.17	Cathal Logue
Down, Co. Down	028-4461 0800	63,000	£495.61	John McGrillen
Dungannon, Co. Tyrone	028-8772 0300	48,500	£384.69	William Beattie
Fermanagh, Co. Fermanagh	028-6632 5050	57,200	£394.79	Rodney Connor
Larne, Co. Antrim	028-2827 2313	30,000	£422.87	Colm McGarry
Limavady, Co. Londonderry	028-7772 2226	32,000	£467.82	John Stevenson
Lisburn, Co. Antrim	028-9250 9250	111,500	£481.11	Norman Davidson
Magherafelt, Co. Londonderry	028-7939 7979	39,000	£462.35	John McLaughlin
Moyle, Co. Antrim	028-2076 2225	15,000	£489.73	R. Lewis
Newry and Mourne, Co. Down and Co. Armagh	028-3031 3031	88,000	£475.20	Thomas McCall
Newtownabbey, Co. Antrim	028-9034 0000	82,000	£552.38	Norman Dunn
North Down, Co. Down	028-9127 0371	75,800	£545.43	Trevor Polley
Omagh, Co. Tyrone	028 8224 5321	48,000	£468.33	Danny Sorley
Strabane, Co. Tyrone	028-7138 2204	37,300	£400.51	Philip Faithfull

* This figure is calculated by taking the total sum of rates assessed for occupied domestic properties in each council area and dividing that sum by the number of occupied domestic properties. District councils determine district rates to reflect their revenue needs while the regional rate is uniform. The type and volume of property in each council district affects the average rate bill and as such the overall average.

The Isle of Man

Ellan Vannin

The Isle of Man is an island situated in the Irish Sea, in latitude 54° 3′–54° 25′ N. and longitude 4° 18′–4° 47′ W., nearly equidistant from England, Scotland and Ireland. Although the early inhabitants were of Celtic origin, the Isle of Man was part of the Norwegian Kingdom of the Hebrides until 1266, when this was ceded to Scotland. Subsequently granted to the Stanleys (Earls of Derby) in the 15th century and later to the Dukes of Atholl, it was brought under the administration of the Crown in 1765. The island forms the bishopric of Sodor and Man.

The total land area is 221 sq. miles (572 sq. km). The report on the 2001 census showed a resident population of 76,315 (males, 37,372; females, 38,943). The main language in use is English. There are no remaining native speakers of Manx Gaelic but 1,527 people are able to speak the language.

CAPITAL – ΨDouglas; population (2001), 25,347.

ΨCastletown (3,100) is the ancient capital; the other towns are ΨPeel (3,785) and ΨRamsey (7,322)

FLAG – A red flag charged with three conjoined armoured legs in white and gold

TYNWALD DAY – 5 July

GOVERNMENT

The Isle of Man is a self-governing Crown dependency, having its own parliamentary, legal and administrative system. The British Government is responsible for international relations and defence. Under the UK Act of Accession, Protocol 3, the island's relationship with the European Union is limited to trade alone and does not extend to financial aid. The Lieutenant-Governor is The Queen's personal representative on the island.

The legislature, Tynwald, is the oldest parliament in the world in continuous existence. It has two branches: the Legislative Council and the House of Keys. The Council consists of the President of Tynwald, the Bishop of Sodor and Man, the Attorney-General (who does not have a vote) and eight members elected by the House of Keys. The House of Keys has 24 members, elected by universal adult suffrage. The branches sit separately to consider legislation and sit together, as Tynwald Court, for most other parliamentary purposes.

The presiding officer of Tynwald Court is the President of Tynwald, elected by the members, who also presides over sittings of the Legislative Council. The presiding officer of the House of Keys is Mr Speaker, who is elected by members of the House.

The principal members of the Manx Government are the Chief Minister and nine departmental ministers, who comprise the Council of Ministers.

Lieutenant-Governor, HE Air-Marshal I. MacFadyen, CB, OBE

ADC to the Lieutenant-Governor, C. J. Tummon

President of Tynwald, The Hon. N. Q. Cringle

Speaker, House of Keys, The Hon. J. A. Brown, SHK

The First Deemster and Clerk of the Rolls, His Honour T. W. Cain, QC

Clerk of Tynwald, Secretary to the House of Keys and Counsel to the Speaker, Mr Malachy Cornwell-Kelly

Clerk of the Legislative Council and Deputy Clerk of Tynwald, Mrs M. Cullen

Attorney-General, W. J. H. Corlett, QC

Chief Minister, The Hon. R. K. Corkill, MHK

Chief Secretary, Mrs M. Williams

ECONOMY

Most of the income generated in the island is earned in the services sector with financial and professional services accounting for just over half of the national income. Tourism and manufacturing are also major generators of income whilst the island's other traditional industries of agriculture and fishing now play a smaller role in the economy.

Under the terms of Protocol 3, the island has tariff-free access to EU markets for its goods.

The island's unemployment rate is approximately 0.5 per cent and price inflation is around 2.4 per cent per annum.

FINANCE

The budget for 2002–3 provided for net revenue expenditure of £388 million. The principal sources of government revenue are taxes on income and expenditure. Income tax is payable at a rate of 10 per cent on the first £10,000 of taxable income for single resident individuals and 18 per cent on the balance, after personal allowances of £8,000. These bands are doubled for married couples. The rate of income tax is 10 per cent on the first £500,000 of taxable income of resident trading companies, rising to 15 per cent on the balance. By agreement with the British Government, the island keeps most of its rates of indirect taxation (VAT and duties) the same as those in the United Kingdom. However, VAT on tourist accommodation, property, repairs and renovations is charged at 5 per cent. A reciprocal agreement on national insurance benefits and pensions exists between the governments of the Isle of Man and the United Kingdom. Taxes are also charged on property (rates), but these are comparatively low.

The major government expenditure items are health, social security and education, which account for 60 per cent of the government budget. The island makes an annual contribution to the United Kingdom for defence and other external services.

The island has a special relationship with the European Union and neither contributes money to nor receives funds from the EU budget.

The Channel Islands

The Channel Islands, situated off the north-west coast of France (at distances from ten to 30 miles), are the only portions of the Dukedom of Normandy still belonging to the Crown, to which they have been attached since the Norman Conquest of 1066. They were the only British territory to come under German occupation during the Second World War, following invasion on 30 June to 1 July 1940. The islands were relieved by British forces on 9 May 1945, and 9 May (Liberation Day) is now observed as a bank and public holiday.

The islands consist of Jersey (28,717 acres/11,630 ha), Guernsey (15,654 acres/6,340 ha), and the dependencies of Guernsey: Alderney (1,962 acres/795 ha), Brechou (74/30), Great Sark (1,035/419), Little Sark (239/97), Herm (320/130), Jethou (44/18) and Lihou (38/15) – a total of 48,083 acres/19,474 ha, or 75 sq. miles/194 sq. km. The 2001 census showed the population of Jersey is 87,186; Guernsey, 59,807 and Alderney, 2,294. Sark did not complete the same census but a recent informal census gave their population figure as 591. The official languages are English and French but French is being supplanted by English, which is the language in daily use. In country districts of Jersey and Guernsey and throughout Sark a Norman-French *patois* is also in use, though to a declining extent.

GOVERNMENT

The islands are Crown dependencies with their own legislative assemblies (the States in Jersey, Guernsey and Alderney, and the Court of Chief Pleas in Sark), and systems of local administration and of law, and their own courts. Acts passed by the States require the sanction of The Queen-in-Council. The British Government is responsible for defence and international relations. The Channel Islands have trading rights alone within the European Union; these rights do not include financial aid.

In both Bailiwicks the Lieutenant-Governor and Commander-in-Chief, who is appointed by the Crown, is the personal representative of The Queen and the channel of communication between the Crown (via the Privy Council) and the island's government.

The government of each Bailiwick is conducted by committees appointed by the States, although in 2001 the States of Jersey decided to move to a ministerial system of government combined with a system of scrutiny, this decision is expected to be implemented within the next two years. Justice is administered by the Royal Courts of Jersey and Guernsey, each consisting of the Bailiff and 12 elected Jurats. The Bailiffs of Jersey and Guernsey, appointed by the Crown, are President of the States and of the Royal Courts of their respective islands.

Each Bailiwick constitutes a deanery under the jurisdiction of the Bishop of Winchester.

ECONOMY

A mild climate and good soil have led to the development of intensive systems of agriculture and horticulture, which form a significant part of the economy. Equally important are invisible earnings, principally from tourism and banking and finance, the low rate of income tax (20p in the £ in Jersey and Guernsey; no tax of any kind in Sark) and the absence of super-tax and death duties, making the islands an important offshore financial centre.

Principal exports are agricultural produce and flowers; imports are chiefly machinery, manufactured goods, food, fuel and chemicals. Trade with the UK is regarded as internal.

British currency is legal tender in the Channel Islands but each Bailiwick issues its own coins and notes (see Finance section). They also issue their own postage stamps; UK stamps are not valid.

JERSEY

Lieutenant-Governor and Commander-in-Chief of Jersey, Chief Marshall Sir John Cheshire, KBE, CB, *apptd* 2001
Secretary and ADC, Lt.-Col. A. J. C. Woodrow, OBE, MC
Bailiff of Jersey, Sir Philip Bailhache, Kt.
Deputy Bailiff, M. C. St J. Birt
Attorney-General, W. J. Bailhache, QC
Receiver-General, Gp Capt. R. Green, OBE
Solicitor-General, Miss S. C. Nicolle, QC
Greffier of the States, M. N. de la Haye
States Treasurer, Mr I. Black

FINANCE

Year to 31 Dec.	2000	2001
Revenue income	£518,177,000	£541,759,000
Revenue expenditure	446,605,000	£470,063,000
Capital expenditure	51,861,000	£80,700,000
Public debt	0	0

CHIEF TOWN – ΨSt Helier, on the south coast of Jersey
FLAG – A white field charged with a red saltire cross, and the arms of Jersey in the upper centre

GUERNSEY AND DEPENDENCIES

Lieutenant-Governor and Commander-in-Chief of the Bailiwick of Guernsey and its Dependencies, HE Lieutenant-General Sir John Foley, KCB, OBE, MC, *apptd* 2000
Secretary and ADC, Colonel R. H. Graham, MBE
Bailiff of Guernsey, de V. G. Carey
Deputy Bailiff, G. R. Rowland, QC
HM Procureur and Receiver-General, J. N. van Leuven
HM Comptroller, H. E. Roberts, QC
States Supervisor, M. J. Brown

FINANCE

Year to 31 Dec.	2000	2001
Revenue	£257,600,000	£280,200,000
Expenditure	204,400,000	£222,900,000

CHIEF TOWNS – ΨSt Peter Port, on the east coast of Guernsey; St Anne on Alderney
FLAG – White, bearing a red cross of St George, with a gold cross overall in the centre

ALDERNEY

President of the States, Sir Norman Browse
Clerk of the States, R. L. Barnwell
Clerk of the Court, Mrs S. Kelly

SARK

Seigneur of Sark, J. M. Beaumont, OBE
The Seneschal, Lieutenant-Colonel R. J. Guille, MBE
The Greffier, J. P. Hamon

OTHER DEPENDENCIES

Herm and Lihou are owned by the States of Guernsey; Herm is leased. Jethou is leased by the Crown to the States of Guernsey and is sub-let by the States. Brecqhou is within the legislative and judicial territory of Sark.

European Parliament

European Parliament elections take place at five-yearly intervals; the first direct elections to the Parliament were held in 1979. In mainland Britain MEPs were elected in all constituencies on a first-past-the-post basis until the elections of June 1999; in Northern Ireland three MEPs have been elected by the single transferable vote system of proportional representation since 1979. From 1979 to 1994 the number of seats held by the UK in the European Parliament was 81. At the June 1994 election the number of seats increased to 87 (England 71, Wales 5, Scotland 8, Northern Ireland 3).

At the European Parliament elections held on 10 June 1999, all British MEPs were elected under a 'closed-list' regional system of proportional representation, with England being divided into nine regions and Scotland and Wales each constituting a region. Parties submitted a list of candidates for each region in their own order of preference. Voters voted for a party or an independent candidate, and the first seat in each region was allocated to the party or candidate with the highest number of votes. The rest of the seats in each region were then allocated broadly in proportion to each party's share of the vote. Each region returned the following number of members: East Midlands, 6; Eastern, 8; London, 10; North East, 4; North West, 10; South East, 11; South West, 7; West Midlands, 8; Yorkshire and the Humber, 7; Wales, 5; Scotland, 8.

If a vacancy occurs due to the resignation or death of an MEP, the vacancy is filled by the next available person on that party's list. If an independent MEP resigns or dies, a by-election is held. Where an MEP leaves the party on whose list he/she was elected, there is no requirement to resign and he/she can remain in office until the next election.

British subjects and citizens of the Irish Republic are eligible for election to the European Parliament provided they are 21 or over and not subject to disqualification. Since 1994, nationals of member states of the European Union have had the right to vote in elections to the European Parliament in the UK as long as they are entered on the electoral register.

MEPs currently receive a salary from the parliaments or governments of their respective member states, set at the level of the national parliamentary salary and subject to national taxation rules. British MEPs receive a salary of £55,118. MPs who are also MEPs do not receive both salaries in full. Instead they receive the full MPs' salary plus a 'duality rate' equal to one third of the MEP's salary. Thus their total salary is £73,491, (comprising of £55,118 plus £18,373).

A proposal that all MEPs should be paid the same rate of salary out of the EU budget, and subject to the EC tax rate, was under negotiation between the European Parliament and the Council of Ministers at the time of going to press.

UK MEMBERS AS AT 28 JULY 2002

* Denotes membership of the last European Parliament
† Replacements since the last election
‡ Previously a member of the UK Independence Party
** Previously a member of the Conservative Party
†† Previously a member of the Labour Party and sits with the Conservatives

†Adam, Gordon J. (b. 1934), C., North East
Atkins, Rt. Hon. Sir Robert (b. 1946), C., North West
Attwooll, Ms Elspeth M. A. (b. 1943), LD, Scotland
*††Balfe, Richard A. (b. 1944), C., London
Beazley, Christopher J. P. (b. 1952), C., Eastern
Bethell, The Lord (b. 1938), C., London
*Bowe, David R. (b. 1955), Lab., Yorkshire and the Humber
Bowis, John C., OBE (b. 1945), C., London
Bradbourn, Philip, OBE (b. 1951), C., West Midlands
Bushill-Matthews, Philip (b. 1943), C., West Midlands
Callanan, Martin (b. 1961), C., North East
Cashman, Michael (b. 1950), Lab., West Midlands
*Chichester, Giles B. (b. 1946), C., South West
Clegg, Nicholas W. P. (b. 1967), LD, East Midlands
*Corbett, Richard (b. 1955), Lab., Yorkshire and the Humber
*Corrie, John A. (b. 1935), C., West Midlands
Davies, Christopher G. (b. 1954), LD, North West
Deva, Niranjan J. A. (Nirj), FRSA (b. 1948), C., South East
Dover, Den (b. 1938), C., North West
Duff, Andrew N. (b. 1950), LD, Eastern
*Elles, James E. M. (b. 1949), C., South East
Evans, Ms Jillian R. (b. 1959), PC, Wales
Evans, Jonathan P., FRSA (b. 1950), C., Wales
*Evans, Robert J. E. (b. 1956), Lab., London
Farage, Nigel P. (b. 1964), UK Ind., South East
*Ford, J. Glyn (b. 1950), Lab., South West
Foster, Mrs Jacqui (b. 1947), C., North West
Gill, Ms Neena (b. 1956), Lab., West Midlands
Goodwill, Robert (b. 1956), C., Yorkshire and the Humber
Hannan, Daniel J. (b. 1971), C., South East
Harbour, Malcolm (b. 1947), C., West Midlands
Heaton-Harris, Christopher (b. 1967), C., East Midlands
Helmer, Roger (b. 1944), C., East Midlands
‡Holmes, Michael J. (b. 1938), Ind., South West
†Honeyball, Mary Mrs (b. 1952), Lab., London
*Howitt, Richard (b. 1961), Lab., Eastern
Hudghton, Ian (b. 1951), SNP, Scotland
*Hughes, Stephen (b. 1952), Lab., North East
Huhne, Christopher M. P., OBE (b. 1954), LD, South East
*Hume, John, MP (b. 1937), SDLP, Northern Ireland
Inglewood, The Lord (b. 1951), C., North West
*Jackson, Mrs Caroline F., D.Phil. (b. 1946), C., South West
Khanbhai, Bashir (b. 1945), C., Eastern
*Kinnock, Mrs Glenys (b. 1944), Lab., Wales
Kirkhope, Timothy J. R. (b. 1945), C., Yorkshire and the Humber
Lambert, Ms Jean D. (b. 1950), Green, London
Lucas, Dr Caroline. (b. 1960), Green, South East
Ludford, The Baroness (b. 1951), LD, London
Lynne, Ms Elizabeth (b. 1948), LD, West Midlands
*McAvan, Ms Linda (b. 1962), Lab., Yorkshire and the Humber
*McCarthy, Ms Arlene (b. 1960), Lab., North West
MacCormick, Prof. D. Neil, FBA (b. 1941), SNP, Scotland
*McMillan-Scott, Edward H. C. (b. 1949), C., Yorkshire and the Humber
*McNally, Mrs Eryl M. (b. 1942), Lab., Eastern
*Martin, David W. (b. 1954), Lab., Scotland
*Miller, William (b. 1954), Lab., Scotland
Moraes, Claude (b. 1965), Lab., London

*Morgan, Ms Eluned (b. 1967), Lab., Wales
*Murphy, Dr Simon F. (b. 1962), Lab., West Midlands
**Newton Dunn, William F. (Bill) (b. 1941), LD, East Midlands
Nicholson of Winterbourne, The Baroness (b. 1941), LD, South East
*Nicholson, James (b. 1945), UUP, Northern Ireland
O'Toole, Ms Barbara M. (b. 1960), Lab., North East
*Paisley, Revd Ian R. K., MP (b. 1926), DUP, Northern Ireland
Parish, Neil (b. 1956), C., South West
*Perry, Roy J. (b. 1943), C., South East
*Provan, James L. C. (b. 1936), C., South East
Purvis, John R., CBE (b. 1938), C., Scotland
*Read, Ms I. M. (b. 1939), Lab., East Midlands
*Simpson, Brian (b. 1953), Lab., North West
*Skinner, Peter W. (b. 1959), Lab., South East
Stevenson, Struan (b. 1948), C., Scotland

Stihler, Catherine D. (elected Catherine Taylor) (b. 1973), Lab., Scotland
Stockton, The Earl of (b. 1943), C., South West
*Sturdy, Robert W. (b. 1944), C., Eastern
Sumberg, David (b. 1941), C., North West
Tannock, Dr Charles (b. 1957), C., London
Titford, Jeffrey (b. 1933), UK Ind., Eastern
*Titley, Gary (b. 1950), Lab., North West
Van Orden, Geoffrey (b. 1945), C., Eastern
Villiers, Ms Theresa (b. 1968), C., London
Wallis, Ms Diana (b. 1954), LD, Yorkshire and the Humber
*Watson, Graham R. (b. 1956), LD, South West
*Watts, Mark F. (b. 1964), Lab., South East
*Whitehead, Philip (b. 1937), Lab., East Midlands
Wyn, Eurig (b. 1944), PC, Wales
*Wynn, Terence (b. 1946), Lab., North West

UK REGIONS AS AT 10 JUNE 1999

Abbreviations
ACPFCA	Anti-Corruption Pro Family Christian Alliance
AHRPE	Architect Human Rights Peace in Europe
Anti VAT	Independent Anti Value Added Tax
EFP	English Freedom Party
Ind. Profit	Independent Making a Profit in Europe
Ind. Stable	Independent Open Democracy for Stability
Lower Tax	Account for Lower Scottish Taxes
MEP Ind.	MEP Independent Labour
Soc. All.	Socialist Alliance
SSP	Scottish Socialist Party
WW	Weekly Worker

For other abbreviations, *see* UK General Election Results, page 234.

EASTERN

E. 4,019,916	T. 24.74%
C.	425,091 (42.75%)
Lab.	250,132 (25.15%)
LD	118,822 (11.95%)
UK Ind.	88,452 (8.89%)
Green	61,334 (6.17%)
Lib.	16,861 (1.70%)
Pro Euro C.	16,340 (1.64%)
BNP	9,356 (0.94%)
Soc. Lab.	6,143 (0.62%)
NLP	1,907 (0.19%)
C. majority	174,959
(June 1994, Lab. maj. 90,087)	

MEMBERS ELECTED

*R. Sturdy, C.
C. Beazley, C.
B. Khanbhai, C.
G. Van Orden, C.
*Ms E. McNally, Lab.
*R. Howitt, Lab.
A. Duff, LD
J. Titford, UK Ind.

EAST MIDLANDS

E. 3,170,517	T. 22.83%
C.	285,662 (39.47%)
Lab.	206,756 (28.57%)
LD	92,398 (12.77%)
UK Ind.	54,800 (7.57%)
Green	38,954 (5.38%)
Alt. Lab.	17,409 (2.41%)
Pro Euro C.	11,359 (1.57%)
BNP	9,342 (1.29%)
Soc. Lab.	5,528 (0.76%)
NLP	1,525 (0.21%)
C. majority	78,906
(June 1994, Lab. maj. 229,680)	

MEMBERS ELECTED

R. Helmer, C.
**W. Newton Dunn, LD
C. Heaton-Harris, C.
*Ms M. Read, Lab.
*P. Whitehead, Lab.
N. Clegg, LD

LONDON

E. 4,940,493	T. 23.10%
Lab.	399,466 (35.00%)
C.	372,989 (32.68%)
LD	133,058 (11.66%)
Green	87,545 (7.67%)
UK Ind.	61,741 (5.41%)
Soc. Lab.	19,632 (1.72%)
BNP	17,960 (1.57%)
Lib.	16,951 (1.49%)
Pro Euro C.	16,383 (1.44%)
AHRPE	4,851 (0.43%)
Anti VAT	2,596 (0.23%)
Hum.	2,586 (0.23%)
Hemp	2,358 (0.21%)
NLP	2,263 (0.20%)
WW	846 (0.07%)
Lab. majority	26,477
(June 1994, Lab. maj. 346,850)	

MEMBERS ELECTED

Miss T. Villiers, C.
Dr C. Tannock, C.

The Lord Bethell, C.
J. Bowis, C.
*Ms P. Green, Lab.
C. Moraes, Lab.
*R. Evans, Lab.
*††R. Balfe, Lab.
Ms S. Ludford, LD
Ms J. Lambert, Green

NORTH EAST

E. 1,954,076	T. 19.74%
Lab.	162,573 (42.15%)
C.	105,573 (27.37%)
LD	52,070 (13.50%)
UK Ind.	34,063 (8.83%)
Green	18,184 (4.71%)
Soc. Lab.	4,511 (1.17%)
BNP	3,505 (0.91%)
Pro Euro C.	2,926 (0.76%)
SPGB	1,510 (0.39%)
NLP	826 (0.21%)
Lab. majority	57,000
(June 1994, Lab. maj. 330,689)	

MEMBERS ELECTED

M. Callanan, C.
*A. Donnelly, Lab.
*S. Hughes, Lab.
Ms M. O'Toole, Lab.

NORTHERN IRELAND

E. 1,190,160	T. 57.77%
First Count	
*Revd I. Paisley, DUP	192,762 (28.40%)
*J. Hume, SDLP	190,731 (28.10%)
*J. Nicholson, UUP	119,507 (17.61%)
M. McLaughlin, SF	117,643 (17.33%)
D. Ervine, PUP	22,494 (3.31%)
R. McCartney, UKU	20,283 (2.99%)
S. Neeson, All.	14,391 (2.12%)
J. Anderson, NLP	998 (0.15%)

MEMBERS ELECTED

*Revd I. Paisley, *DUP*
*J. Hume, *SDLP*
*J. Nicholson, *UUP* (elected on third count)

NORTH WEST

E. 5,170,524	*T.* 19.67%
C.	360,027 (35.39%)
Lab.	350,511 (34.46%)
LD	119,376 (11.74%)
UK Ind.	66,779 (6.57%)
Green	56,828 (5.59%)
Lib.	22,640 (2.23%)
BNP	13,587 (1.34%)
Soc. Lab.	11,338 (1.11%)
Pro Euro C.	9,816 (0.97%)
ACPFCA	2,251 (0.22%)
NLP	2,114 (0.21%)
Ind. Hum.	1,049 (0.10%)
WW	878 (0.09%)
C. majority	9,516
(June 1994, Lab. maj. 444,569)	

MEMBERS ELECTED

The Lord Inglewood, *C.*
Sir Robert Atkins, *C.*
D. Sumberg, *C.*
D. Dover, *C.*
Mrs J. Foster, *C.*
*Ms A. McCarthy, *Lab.*
*G. Titley, *Lab.*
*T. Wynn, *Lab.*
*B. Simpson, *Lab.*
C. Davies, *LD*

SCOTLAND

E. 3,979,845	*T.* 24.83%
Lab.	283,490 (28.68%)
SNP	268,528 (27.17%)
C.	195,296 (19.76%)
LD	96,971 (9.81%)
Green	57,142 (5.78%)
SSP	39,720 (4.02%)
Pro Euro C.	17,781 (1.80%)
UK Ind.	12,549 (1.27%)
Soc. Lab.	9,385 (0.95%)
BNP	3,729 (0.38%)
NLP	2,087 (0.21%)
Lower Tax	1,632 (0.17%)
Lab. majority	14,962
(June 1994, Lab. maj. 148,718)	

MEMBERS ELECTED

S. Stevenson, *C.*
J. Purvis, *C.*
*D. Martin, *Lab.*
*W. Miller, *Lab.*
Ms C. Taylor, *Lab.*
Ms E. Attwooll, *LD*
*I. Hudghton, *SNP*
Prof. N. MacCormick, *SNP*

SOUTH EAST

E. 5,972,945	*T.* 24.95%
C.	661,931 (44.42%)
Lab.	292,146 (19.61%)
LD	228,136 (15.31%)
UK Ind.	144,514 (9.70%)
Green	110,571 (7.42%)

Pro Euro C.	27,305 (1.83%)
BNP	12,161 (0.82%)
Soc. Lab.	7,281 (0.49%)
NLP	2,767 (0.19%)
Ind. Stable	1,857 (0.12%)
Ind. Profit	1,400 (0.09%)
C. majority	369,785
(June 1994, C. maj. 230,122)	

MEMBERS ELECTED

*J. Provan, *C.*
*R. Perry, *C.*
D. Hannan, *C.*
*J. Elles, *C.*
N. Deva, *C.*
*P. Skinner, *Lab.*
*M. Watts, *Lab.*
The Baroness Nicholson of Winterbourne, *LD*
C. Huhne, *LD*
Dr Caroline Lucas, *Green*
N. Farage, *UK Ind.*

SOUTH WEST

E. 3,747,620	*T.* 27.81%
C.	434,645 (41.70%)
Lab.	188,362 (18.07%)
LD	171,498 (16.45%)
UK Ind.	111,012 (10.65%)
Green	86,630 (8.31%)
Lib.	21,645 (2.08%)
Pro Euro C.	11,134 (1.07%)
BNP	9,752 (0.94%)
Soc. Lab.	5,741 (0.55%)
NLP	1,968 (0.19%)
C. majority	246,283
(June 1994, LD maj. 3,796)	

MEMBERS ELECTED

*Dr Caroline Jackson, *C.*
*G. Chichester, *C.*
The Earl of Stockton, *C.*
N. Parish, *C.*
*G. Ford, *Lab.*
*G. Watson, *LD*
M. Holmes, *UK Ind.*

WALES

E. 2,211,162	*T.* 28.33%
Lab.	199,690 (31.88%)
PC	185,235 (29.57%)
C.	142,631 (22.77%)
LD	51,283 (8.19%)
UK Ind.	19,702 (3.15%)
Green	16,146 (2.58%)
Pro Euro C.	5,834 (0.93%)
Soc. Lab.	4,283 (0.68%)
NLP	1,621 (0.26%)
Lab. majority	14,455
(June 1994, Lab. maj. 368,271)	

MEMBERS ELECTED

J. Evans, *C.*
*Ms G. Kinnock, *Lab.*
*Ms E. Morgan, *Lab.*
Ms J. Evans, *PC*
E. Wyn, *PC*

WEST MIDLANDS

E. 4,001,942	*T.* 21.21%
C.	321,719 (37.91%)
Lab.	237,671 (28.00%)
LD	95,769 (11.28%)
UK Ind.	49,621 (5.85%)
Green	49,440 (5.83%)
MEP Ind.	36,849 (4.34%)
Lib.	14,954 (1.76%)
BNP	14,344 (1.69%)
Pro Euro C.	11,144 (1.31%)
Soc. All.	7,203 (0.85%)
Soc. Lab.	5,257 (0.62%)
EFP	3,066 (0.36%)
NLP	1,647 (0.19%)
C. majority	84,048
(June 1994, Lab. maj. 268,888)	

MEMBERS ELECTED

*J. Corrie, *C.*
P. Bushill-Matthews, *C.*
M. Harbour, *C.*
P. Bradbourn, *C.*
*S. Murphy, *Lab.*
M. Cashman, *Lab.*
Ms N. Gill, *Lab.*
Ms E. Lynne, *LD*

YORKSHIRE AND THE HUMBER

E. 3,767,227	*T.* 19.75%
C.	272,653 (36.64%)
Lab.	233,024 (31.32%)
LD	107,168 (14.40%)
UK Ind.	52,824 (7.10%)
Green	42,604 (5.73%)
Alt. Lab.	9,554 (1.28%)
BNP	8,911 (1.20%)
Pro Euro C.	8,075 (1.09%)
Soc. Lab.	7,650 (1.03%)
NLP	1,604 (0.22%)
C. majority	39,629
(June 1994, Lab. maj. 344,310)	

MEMBERS ELECTED

*E. McMillan-Scott, *C.*
T. Kirkhope, *C.*
R. Goodwill, *C.*
*Ms L. McAvan, *Lab.*
*D. Bowe, *Lab.*
*R. Corbett, *Lab.*
Ms D. Wallis, *LD*

For further information about the European Parliament visit www.europarl.org.uk.
For information about which areas of the country are covered by a particular region, please visit www.homeoffice.gov.uk.

Law Courts and Offices

THE JUDICIAL COMMITTEE OF THE PRIVY COUNCIL

The Judicial Committee of the Privy Council is primarily the final court of appeal for the United Kingdom overseas and those independent Commonwealth countries which have retained this avenue of appeal (Antigua and Barbuda, The Bahamas, Barbados, Belize, Brunei, Dominica, Grenada, Jamaica, Kiribati, Mauritius, New Zealand, St Christopher and Nevis, St Lucia, St Vincent and the Grenadines, Trinidad and Tobago, and Tuvalu). The Committee also hears appeals from the Channel Islands and the Isle of Man and appeals against pastoral schemes under the Pastoral Measure 1983.

Under the devolution legislation enacted in 1998, the Judicial Committee of the Privy Council is the final arbiter in disputes as to the legal competence of things done or proposed by the devolved legislative and Executive authorities in Scotland, Wales and Northern Ireland.

In 2001 the Judicial Committee heard a total of 86 appeals and dealt with 58 petitions for special leave to appeal.

The members of the Judicial Committee include the Lord Chancellor, the Lords of Appeal in Ordinary other Privy Counsellors who hold or have held high judicial office and certain judges from the Commonwealth countries from which appeals lie to the Judicial Committee.

JUDICIAL COMMITTEE OF THE PRIVY COUNCIL,
Downing Street, London SW1A 2AJ.
Tel: 020-7276 0483/5.
Registrar of the Privy Council, J. A. C. Watherston
Chief Clerk, F. G. Hart

The Judicature of England and Wales

The legal system of England and Wales is separate from those of Scotland and Northern Ireland and differs from them in law, judicial procedure and court structure, although there is a common distinction between civil law (disputes between individuals) and criminal law (acts harmful to the community).

The supreme judicial authority for England and Wales is the House of Lords, which is the ultimate Court of Appeal from all courts in Great Britain and Northern Ireland (except criminal courts in Scotland) for all cases except those concerning the interpretation and application of European Community law, including preliminary rulings requested by British courts and tribunals, which are decided by the European Court of Justice (*see* European Union section). Under the Human Rights Act 1998, which came into force on 2 October 2000, the European Convention on Human Rights is incorporated into British law; unresolved cases are still referred to the European Court of Human Rights. As a Court of Appeal the House of Lords consists of the Lord Chancellor and the Lords of Appeal in Ordinary (law lords).

SUPREME COURT OF JUDICATURE

The Supreme Court of Judicature comprises the Court of Appeal, the High Court of Justice and the Crown Court. The High Court of Justice is the superior civil court and is divided into three divisions. The Chancery Division is concerned mainly with equity, bankruptcy and contentious probate business. The Queen's Bench Division deals with commercial and maritime law, serious personal injury and medical negligence cases, cases involving a breach of contract and professional negligence actions. The Family Division deals with matters relating to family law. Sittings are held at the Royal Courts of Justice in London or at 126 District Registries outside the capital. High Court judges sit alone to hear cases at first instance. The Restrictive Practices Court, set up under the Restrictive Trade Practices Act 1956, and the Technology and Construction Court, which deals with cases which require expert evidence on technical and other issues concerning mainly the construction industry, defective products, property valuations, and landlord and tenant disputes, are also currently part of the High Court, although the Restrictive Practices Court is due to be abolished following the establishment of the Competition Commission. Appeals from the High Court are heard in the Court of Appeal (Civil Division), presided over by the Master of the Rolls, and may go on to the House of Lords.

In December 1999 the Lord Chancellor began a wide ranging, independent review of the criminal courts in England and Wales. Lord Justice Auld lead the review into how the criminal courts work at every level. The report *Review of the Criminal Courts of England and Wales* was published in October 2001 and assesses what should be done to modernise and improve the criminal justice system so that its aims can be achieved more effectively.

CRIMINAL CASES

In criminal matters the decision to prosecute in the majority of cases rests with the Crown Prosecution Service, the independent prosecuting body in England and Wales. The Service is headed by the Director of Public Prosecutions, who works under the superintendence of the Attorney-General. Certain categories of offence continue to require the Attorney-General's consent for prosecution.

The Crown Court sits in about 90 centres, divided into six circuits, and is presided over by High Court judges, full-time circuit judges, and part-time recorders, sitting with a jury in all trials which are contested. Since 12 April 2000, the distinction between assistant recorders and recorders has changed. Consequently, there are now only full recorders. The post of Assistant Recorder remains on the statute book but appointments are no longer made. There were 1,325 full recorders at 1 June 2002. The Crown Court deals with trials of the more serious criminal offences, the sentencing of offenders committed for sentence by magistrates' courts (when the magistrates consider their own power of sentence inadequate), and appeals from magistrates' courts. Magistrates usually sit with a circuit judge or recorder to deal with appeals and committals for sentence. Appeals from the Crown Court, either against sentence or conviction, are made to the Court of Appeal (Criminal Division), presided over by the Lord Chief Justice. A further appeal from the Court of

Appeal to the House of Lords can be brought if a point of law of general public importance is considered to be involved.

Minor criminal offences (summary offences) are dealt with in magistrates' courts, which usually consist of three unpaid lay magistrates (justices of the peace) sitting without a jury, who are advised on points of law and procedure by a legally-qualified clerk to the justices. There were 24,520 justices of the peace at 1 April 2002. In busier courts a full-time, salaried and legally-qualified stipendiary magistrate presides alone. Cases involving people under 18 are heard in youth courts, specially constituted magistrates' courts. Preliminary proceedings in a serious case to decide whether there is evidence to justify committal for trial in the Crown Court are also dealt with in the magistrates' courts. Appeals from magistrates' courts against sentence or conviction are made to the Crown Court. Appeals upon a point of law are made to the High Court, and may go on to the House of Lords.

CIVIL CASES

Most minor civil cases are dealt with by the county courts, of which there are around 222 (details may be found in the local telephone directory). Cases are heard by circuit judges, courts or district judges (magistrates courts). There were 413 district judges and 103 District Judges (magistrates courts) at 1 June 2002. For cases involving small claims there are special simplified procedures. Where there are financial limits on county court jurisdiction, claims which exceed those limits may be tried in the county courts with the consent of the parties, subject to the Court's agreement, or in certain circumstances on transfer from the High Court. Outside London, bankruptcy proceedings can be heard in designated county courts. Magistrates' courts can deal with certain classes of civil case and committees of magistrates license public houses, clubs and betting shops. For the implementation of the Children Act 1989, a new structure of hearing centres was set up in 1991 for family proceedings cases, involving magistrates' courts (family proceedings courts), divorce county courts, family hearing centres and care centres. Appeals in family matters heard in the family proceedings courts go to the Family Division of the High Court; affiliation appeals and appeals from decisions of the licensing committees of magistrates go to the Crown Court. Appeals from county courts may be heard in the High Court of Appeal (civil division) and may go on to the House of Lords.

CORONERS' COURTS

Coroners' courts investigate violent and unnatural deaths or sudden deaths where the cause is unknown. Cases may be brought before a local coroner (a senior lawyer or doctor) by doctors, the police, various public authorities or members of the public. Where a death is sudden and the cause is unknown, the coroner may order a post-mortem examination to determine the cause of death rather than hold an inquest in court.

Judicial appointments are made by The Queen; the most senior appointments are made on the advice of the Prime Minister and other appointments on the advice of the Lord Chancellor.

Under the provisions of the Criminal Appeal Act 1995, a Commission was set up to direct and supervise investigations into possible miscarriages of justice and to refer cases to the courts on the grounds of conviction and sentence; these functions were formerly the responsibility of the Home Secretary.

THE HOUSE OF LORDS
AS FINAL COURT OF APPEAL

The Lord High Chancellor (£180,045)
The Rt. Hon. the Lord Irvine of Lairg, *born* 1940, *apptd* 1997
LORDS OF APPEAL IN ORDINARY (each £163,376)
Style, The Rt. Hon. Lord—

Rt. Hon. Lord Bingham of Cornhill, *born* 1933, *apptd* 2000
Rt. Hon. Lord Slynn of Hadley, *born* 1930, *apptd* 1992
Rt. Hon. Lord Nicholls of Birkenhead, *born* 1933, *apptd* 1994
Rt. Hon. Lord Steyn, *born* 1932, *apptd* 1995
Rt. Hon. Lord Hoffmann, *born* 1934, *apptd* 1995
Rt. Hon. Lord Hope of Craighead, *born* 1938, *apptd* 1996
Rt. Hon. Lord Hutton, *born* 1931, *apptd* 1997
Rt. Hon. Lord Saville of Newdigate, *born* 1936, *apptd* 1997
Rt. Hon. Lord Hobhouse of Woodborough, *born* 1932, *apptd* 1998
Rt. Hon. Lord Millett, *born* 1932, *apptd* 1998
Rt. Hon. Lord Scott Foscote, *born* 1934, *apptd* 1998
Rt. Hon. Lord Roger of Earlsferry, *born* 1944, *apptd* 2001

Judicial Office of the House of Lords, House of Lords, London SW1A 0PW. Tel: 020-7219 3111
Registrar, The Clerk of the Parliaments

SUPREME COURT OF JUDICATURE

COURT OF APPEAL

The Master of the Rolls (£169,089), The Rt. Hon. Lord Phillips of Worth Matravers, *born* 1938, *apptd* 2000
Secretary, Mrs L. Grace
Clerk, Ms J. Jones

LORDS JUSTICES OF APPEAL (each £155,293)
Style, The Rt. Hon. Lord/Lady Justice [surname]

Rt. Hon. Sir Paul Kennedy, *born* 1935, *apptd* 1992
Rt. Hon. Sir Simon Brown, *born* 1937, *apptd* 1992
Rt. Hon. Sir Christopher Rose, *born* 1937, *apptd* 1992
Rt. Hon. Sir Peter Gibson, *born* 1934, *apptd* 1993
Rt. Hon. Sir Robin Auld, *born* 1937, *apptd* 1995
Rt. Hon. Sir Malcolm Pill, *born* 1938, *apptd* 1995
Rt. Hon. Sir William Aldous, *born* 1936, *apptd* 1995
Rt. Hon. Sir Alan Ward, *born* 1936, *apptd* 1995
Rt. Hon. Sir Konrad Schiemann, *born* 1937, *apptd* 1995
Rt. Hon. Sir Mathew Thorpe, *born* 1938, *apptd* 1995
Rt. Hon. Sir Mark Potter, *born* 1937, *apptd* 1996
Rt. Hon. Sir Henry Brooke, *born* 1936, *apptd* 1996
Rt. Hon. Sir Igor Judge, *born* 1941, *apptd* 1996
Rt. Hon. Sir Mark Waller, *born* 1940, *apptd* 1996
Rt. Hon. Sir John Mummery, *born* 1938, *apptd* 1996
Rt. Hon. Sir Charles Mantell, *born* 1937, *apptd* 1997
Rt. Hon. Sir John Chadwick, ED, *born* 1941, *apptd* 1997
Rt. Hon. Sir Robert Walker, *born* 1938, *apptd* 1997
Rt. Hon. Sir Richard Buxton, *born* 1938, *apptd* 1997
Rt. Hon. Sir Anthony May, *born* 1940, *apptd* 1997
Rt. Hon. Sir Simon Tuckey, *born* 1941, *apptd* 1997
Rt. Hon. Sir Anthony Clarke, *born* 1943, *apptd* 1998

418   Law Courts and Offices

Rt. Hon. Sir John Laws, *born* 1945, *apptd* 1999
Rt. Hon. Sir Stephen Sedley, *born* 1939, *apptd* 1999
Rt. Hon. Sir Jonathan Mance, *born* 1943, *apptd* 1999
Rt. Hon. Dame Brenda Hale, DBE, *born* 1945, *apptd* 1999
Rt. Hon. Sir David Latham, *born* 1942, *apptd* 2000
Rt. Hon. Sir John William Kay, *born* 1943, *apptd* 2000
Rt. Hon. Sir Bernard Anthony Rix, *born* 1943, *apptd* 2000
Rt. Hon. Sir Jonathan Parker, *born* 1937, *apptd* 2000
Rt. Hon. Dame Mary Howarth Arden, DBE, *born* 1947, *apptd* 2000
Rt. Hon. Sir David Wolfe Keene, *born* 1941, *apptd* 2000
Rt. Hon. Sir John Anthony Dyson, *born* 1943, *apptd* 2001
Rt. Hon. Sir Andrew Centlivres Longmore, *born* 1944, *apptd* 2001
Rt. Hon. Sir Robert John Carnwath, CVO, *born* 1945, *apptd* 2002
Ex officio Judges, The Lord High Chancellor; the Lord Chief Justice of England; the Master of the Rolls; the President of the Family Division; and the Vice-Chancellor

COURT OF APPEAL (CIVIL DIVISION)
Vice-President, The Rt. Hon. Lord Justice Nourse

COURT OF APPEAL (CRIMINAL DIVISION)
Vice-President, The Rt. Hon. Lord Justice Rose
Judges, The Lord Chief Justice of England; the Master of the Rolls; Lords Justices of Appeal; and Judges of the High Court of Justice

COURTS-MARTIAL APPEAL COURT
Judges, The Lord Chief Justice of England; the Master of the Rolls; Lords Justices of Appeal; and Judges of the High Court of Justice

HIGH COURT OF JUSTICE

CHANCERY DIVISION
President, The Lord High Chancellor
The Vice-Chancellor (£163,376), The Rt. Hon. Sir Andrew Moritt, CVO, *born* 1938 *apptd* 2000
Clerk, W. Northfield, BEM

JUDGES (each £137,377)
Style, The Hon. Mr/Mrs Justice [surname]
Hon. Sir Francis Ferris, TD, *born* 1932, *apptd* 1990
Hon. Sir John Lindsay, *born* 1935, *apptd* 1992
Hon. Sir Edward Evans-Lombe, *born* 1937, *apptd* 1993
Hon. Sir Robin Jacob, *born* 1941, *apptd* 1993
Hon. Sir William Blackburne, *born* 1944, *apptd* 1993
Hon. Sir Gavin Lightman, *born* 1939, *apptd* 1994
Hon. Sir Colin Rimer, *born* 1944, *apptd* 1994
Hon. Sir Hugh Laddie, *born* 1946, *apptd* 1995
Hon. Sir Timothy Lloyd, *born* 1946, *apptd* 1996
Hon. Sir David Neuberger, *born* 1948, *apptd* 1996
Hon. Sir Andrew Park, *born* 1939, *apptd* 1997
Hon. Sir Nicholas Pumfrey, *born* 1951, *apptd* 1997
Hon. Sir Michael Hart, *born* 1948, *apptd* 1998
Hon. Sir Lawrence Collins, *born* 1941, *apptd* 2000
Hon. Sir Nicholas John Patten, *born* 1950, *apptd* 2000
Hon. Sir Terence Michael Barnet Etherton, *born* 1951, *apptd* 2001
Hon. Sir Peter Winston Smith, *born* 1952, *appt* 2002

HIGH COURT OF JUSTICE IN BANKRUPTCY
Judges, The Vice-Chancellor and judges of the Chancery Division of the High Court

COMPANIES COURT
Judges, The Vice-Chancellor and judges of the Chancery Division of the High Court

PATENT COURT (APPELLATE SECTION)
Judge, The Hon. Mr Justice Jacob

QUEEN'S BENCH DIVISION
The Lord Chief Justice of England and Wales (£177,545)
The Rt. Hon. the Lord Woolf, *born* 1933, *apptd* 2000
Private Secretary, E. Adams
Clerk, J. Bond
Vice-President, The Rt. Hon. Lord Justice May, *born* 1940, *apptd* 2002

JUDGES (each £137,377)
Style, The Hon. Mr/Mrs Justice [surname]
Hon. Sir Stuart McKinnon, *born* 1938, *apptd* 1988
Hon. Sir Douglas Dunlop Brown, *born* 1931, *apptd* 1996
Hon. Sir Michael Morland, *born* 1929, *apptd* 1989
Hon. Sir Roger Buckley, *born* 1939, *apptd* 1989
Hon. Sir Anthony Hidden, *born* 1936, *apptd* 1989
Hon. Sir Michael Wright, *born* 1932, *apptd* 1990
Hon. Sir Peter Cresswell, *born* 1944, *apptd* 1991
Hon. Sir Christopher Holland, *born* 1937, *apptd* 1992
Hon. Sir Richard Curtis, *born* 1933, *apptd* 1992
Hon. Dame Janet Smith, DBE, *born* 1940, *apptd* 1992
Hon. Sir Anthony Colman, *born* 1938, *apptd* 1992
Hon. Sir Thayne Forbes, *born* 1938, *apptd* 1993
Hon. Sir Scott Baker, *born* 1937, *apptd* 1993
Hon. Sir Michael Sachs, *born* 1932, *apptd* 1993
Hon. Sir Stephen Mitchell, *born* 1941, *apptd* 1993
Hon. Sir Rodger Bell, *born* 1939, *apptd* 1993
Hon. Sir Michael Harrison, *born* 1939, *apptd* 1993
Hon. Sir William Gage, *born* 1938, *apptd* 1993
Hon. Sir Thomas Morison, *born* 1939, *apptd* 1993
Hon. Sir Andrew Collins, *born* 1942, *apptd* 1994
Hon. Sir Maurice Kay, *born* 1942, *apptd* 1995
Hon. Sir Anthony Hooper, *born* 1937, *apptd* 1995
Hon. Sir Alexander Butterfield, *born* 1942, *apptd* 1995
Hon. Sir George Newman, *born* 1941, *apptd* 1995
Hon. Sir David Poole, *born* 1938, *apptd* 1995
Hon. Sir Martin Moore-Bick, *born* 1946, *apptd* 1995
Hon. Sir Gordon Langley, *born* 1943, *apptd* 1995
Hon. Sir Roger Thomas, *born* 1947, *apptd* 1996
Hon. Sir Robert Nelson, *born* 1942, *apptd* 1996
Hon. Sir Roger Toulson, *born* 1946, *apptd* 1996
Hon. Sir Michael Astill, *born* 1938, *apptd* 1996
Hon. Sir Alan Moses, *born* 1945, *apptd* 1996
Hon. Sir David Eady, *born* 1943, *apptd* 1997
Hon. Sir Jeremy Sullivan, *born* 1945, *apptd* 1997
Hon. Sir David Penry-Davey, *born* 1942, *apptd* 1997
Hon. Sir Stephen Richards, *born* 1950, *apptd* 1997
Hon. Sir David Steel, *born* 1943, *apptd* 1998
Hon. Sir Charles Gray, born 1942, *apptd* 1998
Hon. Sir Nicolas Bratza, *born* 1945, *apptd* 1998
Hon. Sir Michael Burton, *born* 1946, *apptd* 1998
Hon. Sir Rupert Jackson, *born* 1948, *apptd* 1999
Hon. Dame Heather Hallett, DBE, *born* 1949, *apptd* 1999
Hon. Sir Patrick Elias, *born* 1947, *apptd* 1999
Hon. Sir Richard Aikens, *born* 1948, *apptd* 1999
Hon. Sir Stephen Silber, *born* 1944, *apptd* 1999
Hon. Sir John Goldring, *born* 1944, *apptd* 1999
Hon. Sir Peter Crane, *born* 1940, *apptd* 2000
Hon. Dame Anne Rafferty, DBE, *born* 1950, *apptd* 2000
Hon. Sir Geoffrey Grigson, *born* 1944, *apptd* 2000
Hon. Sir Richard Gibbs, *born* 1941, *apptd* 2000
Hon. Sir Richard Henriques, *born* 1943, *apptd* 2000
Hon. Sir Stephen Tomlinson, *born* 1952, *apptd* 2000

Hon. Sir Andrew Smith, *born 1947, apptd* 2000
Hon. Sir Stanley Burnton, *born 1942, apptd* 2000
Hon. Sir Patrick Hunt, *born 1943, apptd* 2000
Hon. Sir Christopher Pitchford, *born 1947, apptd* 2000
Hon. Sir Brian Leveson, *born 1949, apptd* 2000
Hon. Sir Duncan Ouseley, *born 1950, apptd* 2000
Hon. Sir Raymond Jack, *born 1942, apptd* 2000
Hon. Sir Richard McCombe, *born 1952, apptd* 2001
Hon. Sir Robert Owen, *born 1944, apptd* 2001
Hon. Sir Colin Mackay, *born 1943, apptd* 2001
Hon. Sir John Mitting, *born 1947, apptd* 2001
Hon. Sir David Evans, *born 1946, apptd* 2001
Hon. Sir Nigel Davis, *born 1951, apptd* 2001
Hon. Sir Peter Gross, *born 1952, apptd* 2001
Hon. Sir Brian Keith, *born 1944, apptd* 2001
Hon. Sir Jeremy Cooke, *born 1949, apptd* 2001
Hon. Sir Richard Field, *born 1947, apptd* 2002
Hon. Sir Christopher Pitchers, *born 1942, apptd* 2002
Hon. Sir Roger Royce, *born 1944, apptd* 2002
Hon. Sir Colman Treacy, *born 1949, apptd* 2002
Hon. Sir Peregrine Simon, *born 1950, apptd* 2002

FAMILY DIVISION

President (£163,376), The Rt. Hon. Dame Elizabeth
  Butler-Sloss, DBE, *born 1933, apptd* 1999
Secretary, Mrs S. Leung
Clerk, Mrs S. Bell

JUDGES (each £137,377)

Style, The Hon. Mr/Mrs Justice [surname]

Hon. Sir Robert Johnson, *born 1933, apptd* 1989
Hon. Dame Joyanne Bracewell, DBE, *born 1934, apptd*
  1990
Hon. Sir Peter Singer, *born 1944, apptd* 1993
Hon. Sir Nicholas Wilson, *born 1945, apptd* 1993
Hon. Sir Nicholas Wall, *born 1945, apptd* 1993
Hon. Sir Andrew Kirkwood, *born 1944, apptd* 1993
Hon. Sir Hugh Bennett, *born 1943, apptd* 1995
Hon. Sir Edward Holman, *born 1947, apptd* 1995
Hon. Dame Mary Hogg, DBE, *born 1947, apptd* 1995
Hon. Sir Christopher Sumner, *born 1939, apptd* 1996
Hon. Sir Anthony Hughes, *born 1948, apptd* 1997
Hon. Sir Arthur Charles, *born 1948, apptd* 1998
Hon. Sir David Bodey, *born 1947,* apptd 1999
Hon. Dame Jill Black, DBE, *born 1954, apptd* 1999
Hon. Sir James Munby, *born 1948, apptd* 2000
Hon. Sir Paul Coleridge, *born 1949, apptd* 2000
Hon. Sir Mark Hedley, *born 1946, apptd* 2002

TECHNOLOGY AND CONSTRUCTION COURT

St Dunstan's House, 133–137 Fetter Lane, London
  EC4A 1HD. Tel: 020-7947 7427

JUDGES (each £111,210)

The Hon. Mr Justice Forbes (*Presiding Judge*)
His Hon. Judge Bowsher, QC
His Hon. Judge Havery, QC
His Hon. Judge Lloyd, QC
His Hon. Judge Thornton, QC
His Hon. Judge Wilcox
His Hon. Judge Toulmin, CMG, QC
His Hon. Judge Seymour, QC

Court Manager, Ms L. Fletcher

LORD CHANCELLOR'S DEPARTMENT

see Government Departments and Public Offices section

SUPREME COURT DEPARTMENTS AND OFFICES

Royal Courts of Justice, London WC2A 2LL
Tel: 020-7947 6000

DIRECTOR'S OFFICE

Director, I. Hyams
Group Manager and Deputy Director, J. Selch
Group Manager, Family Proceedings and Probate Service,
  R. P. Knight
Finance and Performance Officer, K. Richardson

ADMIRALTY AND COMMERCIAL REGISTRY AND
MARSHAL'S OFFICE

Registrar*(£86,639), P. Miller
Admiralty Marshal and Court Manager, K. Houghton

BANKRUPTCY DEPARTMENT

Chief Registrar (£102,999), W. S. James
Bankruptcy Registrars*(£86,639), S. Baister; G. W. Jaques
  W. S. James; J. A. Simmonds; P. J. S. Rawson;
Court Manager, Mrs J. O'Connor

CENTRAL OFFICE OF THE SUPREME COURT

*Senior Master of the Supreme Court (QBD), and Queen's
  Remembrancer* (£102,999), R. L. Turner
Masters of the Supreme Court (QBD) *(£86,639), G. H.
  Hodgson; J. Trench; M. Tennant; P. Miller; N. O. G.
  Murray; I. H. Foster; G. H. Rose; P. G. A. Eyre; H. J.
  Leslie; J. G. G. Ungley; S. Whittaker; B. Yoxall
Court Manager, M. A. Brown

CHANCERY CHAMBERS

Chief Master of the Supreme Court (£102,999), J. I.
  Winegarten
Masters of the Supreme Court *(£86,639), J. A.
  Moncaster; R. A. Bowman; N. W. Bragge; T. J. Bowles
Court Manager, G. Robinson
Conveyancing Counsel of the Supreme Court, W. D.
  Ainger; H. M. Harrod; A. C. Taussig

COMPANIES COURT

Registrar*(£86,639), W. James
Court Manager, Mrs O'Connel

COURT OF APPEAL CIVIL DIVISION

Head of the Civil Appeals Office, R. A. Venne
Court Manager, Mrs S. Morson

COURT OF APPEAL CRIMINAL DIVISION

Registrar (£102,999), M. McKenzie, CB, QC
Deputy Registrar, Mrs L. G. Knapman
Chief Clerk, M. Bishop

CROWN OFFICE OF THE SUPREME COURT

*Master of the Crown Office, and Queen's Coroner and
  Attorney* (£102,999), M. McKenzie, CB, QC
Head of Crown Office, Mrs L. G. Knapman
Chief Clerk, M. Bishop

EXAMINERS OF THE COURT

Empowered to take examination of witnesses in all
Divisions of the High Court.

Examiners, A. G. Dyer; A. W. Hughes; Mrs G. M. Kenne;
  R. M. Planterose; Miss V. E. I. Selvaratnam

SUPREME COURT COSTS OFFICE

Senior Cost Judge (£102,999), P. T. Hurst

Masters of the Supreme Court*(£86,639), M. Ellis; T. H. Seager-Berry; C. C. Wright; P. R. Rogers; G. N. Pollard; J. E. O'Hare; C. D. N. Campbell
Court Manager, D. O'Riordan
*salary includes £4,000 inner London weighting

COURT OF PROTECTION
Archway Towers, 11th Floor, 2 Junction Road, London N19 5SZ
Tel: 020-7664 7317
Master (£102,999), D. A. Lush

ELECTION PETITIONS OFFICE
Room E113, Royal Courts of Justice, Strand, London WC2A 2LL. Tel: 020-7947 6131
The office accepts petitions and deals with all matters relating to the questioning of parliamentary, European Parliament and local government elections, and with applications for relief under the Representation of the People legislation.
Prescribed Officer, R. L. Turner
Chief Clerk, Miss J. L. Waine

OFFICE OF THE LORD CHANCELLOR'S VISITORS
Archway Towers, 11th Floor, 2 Junction Road, London N19 5SZ. Tel 020-7664 7317
Legal Visitor, A. R. Tyrrell
Medical Visitors, K. Khan; W. B. Sprey; E. Mateu; S. E. Mahapatra; A. Bailey; A. Kaeser

OFFICIAL RECEIVERS' DEPARTMENT
21 Bloomsbury Street, London WC1B 3SS
Tel: 020-7323 3090
Senior Official Receiver, M. C. A. Osborne
Official Receivers, M. J. Pugh; L. T. Cramp; J. Norris

OFFICIAL SOLICITOR'S DEPARTMENT
81 Chancery Lane, London WC2B 6HD
Tel: 020-7911 7127
Official Solicitor to the Supreme Court, L. C. Oates
Deputy Official Solicitor, E. Solomons
Chief Clerk, R. Lancaster

PRINCIPAL REGISTRY (FAMILY DIVISION)
First Avenue House, 42–49 High Holborn, London WC1V 6NP. Tel: 020-7947 6000
Senior District Judge (£102,999), G. B. N. A. Angel
District Judges (£86,639) salary includes £4,000 inner London weighting
A. R. S. Bassett-Cross; M. C. Berry; H. Black; Miss S. M. Bowman; Miss H. C. Bradley; G. C. Brasse; R. Conn; Miss P. Cushing; K. E. Green; N. A. Grove; R. Harper; B. P. F. Kenworthy-Browne; G. J. Maple; C. Million; Mrs K. T. Moorhouse; Miss I. M. Plumstead; Miss D. C. Redgrave; Miss L. D. Roberts M. J. Segal; K. J. White; P. Waller
Family and Probate Service Group Manager, R. P. Knight

District Probate Registrars
Birmingham and Stoke-on-Trent, P. Burch (*deputy*)
Brighton and Maidstone, P. Ellwood
Bristol, Exeter and Bodmin, R. H. P. Joyce
Cardiff, Bangor and Carmarthen, P. Curran (*deputy*)
Ipswich, Norwich and Peterborough, D. N. Mee
Leeds, Lincoln and Sheffield, A. P. Dawson
Liverpool, Lancaster and Chester, C. Fox
Manchester and Nottingham, M. A. Moran
Newcastle, Carlisle, York and Middlesborough, P. Sanderson

Oxford, Gloucester and Leicester, R. R. Da Costa
Winchester, A. K. Biggs

JUDGE ADVOCATES

THE JUDGE ADVOCATE OF THE FLEET
c/o Chichester Combined Court, Southgate, Chichester PO19 1SX. Tel: 01243-520741
Judge Advocate of the Fleet (£102,999), His Hon. Judge Sessions

OFFICE OF THE JUDGE ADVOCATE-GENERAL OF THE FORCES
(*Joint Service for the Army and the Royal Air Force*)
81 Chancery Lane, London WC2A 1BQ
Tel: 020-7218 8089
Judge Advocate-General (£102,999), His Hon. Judge J. W. Rant, CB, QC
Vice-Judge Advocate-General (£99,110), E. G. Moelwyn-Hughes
Judge Advocates *(£86,639), M. A. Hunter; J. P. Camp; C. R. Burn; R. C. C. Seymour; I. H. Pearson; R. G. Chapple; J. F. T. Bayliss; M. R. Elsom
Style for Judge Advocates, Judge Advocate [surname]
*salary includes £4,000 inner London weighting

HIGH COURT AND CROWN COURT CENTRES

First-tier centres deal with both civil and criminal cases and are served by High Court and circuit judges. Second-tier centres deal with criminal cases only and are served by High Court and circuit judges. Third-tier centres deal with criminal cases only and are served only by circuit judges.

MIDLAND CIRCUIT
First-tier – Birmingham, Lincoln, Nottingham, Stafford, Warwick
Second-tier – Leicester, Northampton, Shrewsbury, Worcester, Wolverhampton
Third-tier – Coventry, Derby, Hereford, Stoke-on-Trent
Circuit Administrator, P. Risk, The Priory Courts, 6th Floor, 33 Bull Street, Birmingham B4 6DS.
Tel: 0121-681 3201
Group Managers: Mrs D. Ponsonby, *West Midlands/Warwickshire Group;* D. Bennett, *Staffordshire/West Mercia Group;* A. Phillips; *East Midlands Group*

NORTH-EASTERN CIRCUIT
First-tier- Leeds, Newcastle upon Tyne, Sheffield, Teesside
Second-tier – Bradford, York
Third-tier – Doncaster, Durham, Kingston-upon-Hull; Great Grimsby
Circuit Administrator, P. J. Farmer, 18th Floor, West Riding House, Albion Street, Leeds LS1 5AA.
Tel: 0113-251 1200
Group Managers: P. M. Norris, *North and West Yorkshire Group;* Miss S. Proudlock, *Tyne Tees Group;* D. Keane, *Humberside and South Yorkshire Group*

NORTHERN CIRCUIT
First-tier – Carlisle, Liverpool, Manchester (Crown Square), Preston

Third-tier – Barrow-in-Furness, Bolton, Burnley, Lancaster; Manchester (Minshull Street)
Circuit Administrator, C. A. Meyer, 15 Quay Street, Manchester M60 9FD. Tel: 0161-833 1005
Group Managers: Miss G. Hague, *Greater Manchester Group*; R. Knott, *Merseyside Group*; S. McNally, *Lancashire and Cumbria Group*

SOUTH-EASTERN CIRCUIT

First-tier – Chelmsford, Lewes, Norwich
Second-tier – Ipswich, London (Central Criminal Court), Luton, Maidstone, Reading, St Albans
Third-tier – Aylesbury, Basildon, Bury St Edmunds, Cambridge, Canterbury, Chichester, Croydon, Guildford, King's Lynn, London (Blackfriars, Harrow, Inner London Sessions House, Isleworth, Kingston, Middlesex Guildhall, Snaresbrook, Southwark, Wood Green, Woolwich), Southend
Circuit Administrator, K. Pogson, New Cavendish House, 18 Maltravers Street, London WC2R 3EU. Tel: 020-7947 7235
Group Managers: K. Budgen *(London Crown)*; D. Thompson *(London County)*; L. Lennon *(Kent and Sussex)*; M. Littlewood *(East Anglia, Bedfordshire and Hertfordshire)*; S. Townley *(Thames Valley, Surrey and Oxford)*
The High Court in Greater London sits at the Royal Courts of Justice.

WALES AND CHESTER CIRCUIT

First-tier – Caernarfon, Cardiff, Chester, Mold, Swansea
Second-tier – Carmarthen, Merthyr Tydfil, Newport, Welshpool
Third-tier – Dolgellau, Haverfordwest, Knutsford, Warrington
Circuit Administrator, N. Chipnall, Churchill House, Churchill Way, Cardiff CF10 4HH. Tel: 029-2041 5500
Group Managers: G. Pickett, *South Wales Group*; G. Kenney, *North Wales and Cheshire Group*; Mrs D. Thomas, *Swansea Group*

WESTERN CIRCUIT

First-tier – Bristol, Exeter, Truro, Winchester
Second-tier – Dorchester, Gloucester, Plymouth, Weymouth
Third-tier – Barnstaple, Bournemouth, Newport (IOW), Portsmouth, Salisbury, Southampton, Swindon, Taunton
Circuit Administrator, D. Ryan, Bridge House, Sion Place, Clifton, Bristol BS8 4BN. Tel: 0117-974 3763
Group Managers: N. Jeffery, *East Group*; D. Gentry, *West Group*

CIRCUIT JUDGES

*Senior Circuit Judges, each £111,210
Circuit Judges at the Central Criminal Court, London (Old Bailey Judges), each £111,210
Circuit Judges, each £102,999
Style, His/Her Hon. Judge [surname]
Senior Presiding Judge, The Rt. Hon. Lord Justice Judge

MIDLAND CIRCUIT

Presiding Judges, The Hon. Mr Justice Goldring; The Hon. Mr Justice Hughes

I. D. G. Alexander, QC; Miss C. Alton; B. Appleby, QC; M. Asokan; D. Bennett; R. Benson; R. Bray; D. Brunning; J. Burgess; Miss J. Butler, QC; J. Cavell; F. Chapman; M. Coates; R. Cole; N. B. Coles, QC; I. Collis; T. Corrie; P. de Mille (shared with South-Eastern Circuit); D. D. Douce;

C. H. Durman; M.R. Eades; P. Eccles, QC; T. Faber; Miss E. Fisher; J. Fletcher; A. Geddes; R. Griffith-Jones; J. Hall; V. Hall; D. Hamilton; S. Hammond; Miss A. W. Hampton; C. Harris, QC; M. Heath; E. Hindley, QC; C. Hodson; H. Hughes; R. Inglis; R. Jenkins; F. Kirkham; P. McCahill, QC; D. McCarthy; A. McCreath; D. McEvoy, QC; M. McKenna; J. Machin; L. Marshall; W. D. Matthews; H. R. Mayor, QC; C. Metcalf; A. Mitchell; N. Mitchell; P. Morrell; I. Morris; M. Mott; A. H. Norris, QC; A. Nicholl; R. O'Rorke; S. Oliver-Jones, QC; R. Onions; R. Orme; J. Orrell; D. Perrett, QC; *R. Pollard; D. Pugsley; J. Pyke; J. Rubery; R. Rundell; J. Shand; D. Stanley; M. Stokes, QC; P. Stretton; G. Styler; A. Taylor; J. Teare; S. Tonking; S. Waine; *J. Wait; R. Wakerley, QC *(Recorder of Birmingham)*; J. Warner; C. Wide, QC

NORTH-EASTERN CIRCUIT

Presiding Judges, The Hon. Mr Justice Henriques; The Hon. Mr Justice Bennett (until 1 January 2003 when The Hon. Mr Justice Andrew Smith will take office)

NORTH AND WEST YORKSHIRE GROUP

R. Adams; R. Bartfield; G. N. Barr Young; J. E. Barry; C. O. J. Behrens; P. Benson; B. Bush; P. J. Charlesworth; G. Cliffe; P. J. Cockroft; J. Dobkin; A. C. Finnerty; M. S. Garner; R. A. Grant; S. P. Grenfell; S. J. Gullick; T. S. A. Hawkesworth, QC; P. M. L. Hoffman; P. Hunt; R. Ibbotson; N. H. Jones, QC; G. H. Kamil; T. D. Kent-Jones, TD; P. Langan, QC; K. M. P. Macgill; A. G. McCallum; C. I. McGonigal; J. T. Milford, QC; J. Prophet; R. M. Scott; J. Spencer, QC; S. M. Spencer, QC, J. S. H. Stewart, QC; R. C. Taylor; T. Walsh; J. S. Wolstenholme

TYNE TEES GROUP

P. J. B. Armstrong; B. Bolton; P. H. Bowers; A. N. J. Briggs; D. M. A. Bryant; M. C. Carr; M. L. Cartlidge; E. J. Faulks; P. J. Fox, QC; T. Hewitt; D. Hodson; A. T. Lancaster; P. R. Lowden; J. T. Milford, QC; J. P. Moir; M. G. C. Moorhouse; L. Spittle; M. Taylor; C. T. Walton; J. De G. Walford; G. Whitburn, QC; D. R. Wood

HUMBERSIDE AND SOUTH YORKSHIRE GROUP

T. W. Barber; R. Bartfield; D. R. Bentley, QC; J. W. Bullimore; A. C. Carr; J. Crabtree; M. T. Cracknell; J. Davies; J. Dowse; A. R. Goldsack, QC; P. Heppel, QC; T. Hewitt; L. Hull; P. Jones; K. R. Keen, QC; S. W. Lawler, QC; M. K. Mettyear; R. J. Moore; M. J. A. Murphy, QC; J. H. Reddihough; P. E. Robertshaw; J. Shipley; L. Sutcliffe; J. A. Swanson

NORTHERN CIRCUIT

Presiding Judges, The Hon. Mr Justice Penry-Davey; The Hon. Mr Justice Leveson

M. P. Allweis; J. F. Appleton; E. K. Armitage, QC; R. K. Atherton; Miss P. H. Badley; S. W. Baker; R. C. W. Bennett; A. N. H. Blake; C. Bloom, QC; D. Boulton; L. F. M. Brown; R. Brown; J. K. Burke, QC; M. D. Byrne; I. B. Campbell; B. I. Caulfield; D. Clark; *D. C. Clarke, QC *(Recorder of Liverpool)*; G. M. Clifton; C. J. Cornwall; I. W. Crompton; Miss J. M. P. Daley; *Sir R. Davies, QC *(Recorder of Manchester)*; B. R. Duckworth; S. B. Duncan; Miss D. B. Eaglestone; T. K. Earnshaw; G. A. Ensor; D. Marshall Evans, QC; S. J. D. Fawcus; P. S. Fish; Miss B.A. Forrester; J. R. B. Geake; D. S. Gee; W. George; J. A. D. Gilliland, QC; N. B. D. Gilmour, QC; C. L. Goldstone, QC; I. M. Hamilton; J. A. Hammond; D. Harris, QC; T. B. Hegarty, QC; M. J. Henshell; F. R. B. Holloway; R. C. Holman; A. D. Hope; N. J. G. Howarth; G. W. Humphries; C. James; M. Kershaw, QC *(Commercial Circuit Judge)*; E. M. Knopf;

Miss L. J. Kushner, QC; P. M. Lakin; B. L. Lever; B. Lewis; J. Lewis; A. C. Lowcock; A. P. Lyon; D. Lynch; D. I. Mackay; J. B. Macmillan; D. G. Maddison; B. C. Maddocks; C. J. Mahon; J. A. Morgan; W. P. Morris; T. J. Mort; L. A. Newton; *C. P. L. Openshaw, QC; F. D. Owen; J. A. Phillips; J. C. Phipps; P. R. Raynor, QC; J. H. Roberts; Miss M. Roddy; Miss G. D. Ruaux; M. W. Rudland; A. A. Rumbelow, QC; H. Singer; E. Slinger; A. Smith; P. Smith; Miss E. M. Steel; M. T. Steiger, QC; D. R. Swift; P. Sycamore; C. B. Tetlow; I. J. C. Trigger; Miss B. J. Watson; K. Wilkinson; B. Woodward

SOUTH-EASTERN CIRCUIT

Presiding Judges, The Hon. Mr Justice Aikens; The Hon. Mr Justice Moses (until 1 January 2003 when The Hon. Mrs Justice Rafferty will take office); The Hon. Mr Justice Bell

M. F. Addison; P. C. Ader; J. Altman; Mrs S. C. Andrew; A. R. L. Ansell; M. G. Anthony; S. A. Anwyl, QC; E. H. Bailey; M. F. Baker; C. G. Ball, QC; A. F. Balston; G. S. Barham; B. J. Barker, QC; C. J. A. Barnett, QC; W. E. Barnett, QC; R. A. Barratt, QC; K. Bassingthwaighte; *G. A. Bathurst-Norman; P. J. L. Beaumont, QC *(Common Serjeant)*; N. E. Beddard; R. V. M. E. Behar; Mrs C. V. Bevington; N. C. van der Bijl; I. G. Bing; M. G. Binning; J. E. Bishop; B. M. B. Black; H. O. Blacksell; J. G. Boal, QC; A. V. Bradbury; P. N. Brandt; G. B. Breen; R. G. Brown; J. M. Bull, QC; J. P. Burke; The Hon. C. W. Byers; H. J. Byrt, QC; J. Q. Campbell; M. J. Carroll; M. T. Caterson; B. E. F. Catlin; C. L. Clark; P. C. Clegg; Miss S. Coates; N. J. Coleman; S. H. Colgan; *P. H. Collins, CBE; C. C. Colston, QC; S. S. Coltart; C. D. Compston; T. A. C. Coningsby, QC; J. G. Connor; R. D. Connor; M. J. Cook; R. A. Cooke; M. R. Coombe; P. E. Copley; T. G. E. Corrie; P. Crawford, QC; Dr E. Cotran; P. R. Cowell; R. C. Cox; M. L. S. Cripps; C. A. Critchlow; J. F. Crocker; D. L. Croft, QC; D. M. Cryan; P. Curl; Mrs P. M. T. Dangor; A. M. Darroch; M. Dean, QC; P. G. Dedman; J. E. Devaux; M. N. Devonshire, TD; P. Dodgson; P. H. Downes; W. H. Dunn, QC; C. M. Edwards; D. R. Ellis; R. C. Elly; C. Elwen; F. P. L. Evans; Miss D. Faber; D. J. Farnworth; P. Fingret; P. E. J. Focke, QC; J. Ford; G. C. F. Forrester; Ms D. A. Freedman; L. Gerber; C. A. H. Gibson; Miss A. F. Goddard, QC; S. A. Goldstein; C. G. M. Gordon; J. B. Gosschalk; A. A. Goymer; B. S. Green, QC; A. E. Greenwood; P. Grobel; TD, VRD; D. A. B. R. Hallgarten, QC; Miss G. Hallon; J. Hamilton; Miss S. Hamilton, QC; C. R. H. Hardy; C. Harris, QC; M. F. Harris; A. M. Harvey; W. G. Hawkesworth; R. G. Hawkins, QC; J. M. Haworth; R. J. Haworth; R. M. Hayward; A. N. Hitching; H. E. G. Hodge, OBE; K. M. J. Hollis; J. F. Holt; A. C. W. Hordern, QC; K. A. D. Hornby; M. Hucker; J. C. A. Hughes; J. G. Hull; QC; M. J. Hyam *(Recorder of London)*; D. A. Inman; A. B. Issard-Davies; D. G. A. Jackson; Miss S. Jackson; Dr P. J. E. Jackson; T. J. C. Joseph; I. G. F. Karsten; S. S. Katkhuda; C. J. B. Kemp; M. Kennedy, QC; W. A. Kennedy; G. M. P. F. Khayat, QC; A. W. P. King; T. R. King; B. J. Knight, QC; P. E. Knowles; L. G. Krikler; L. H. C. Lait; Capt. J. B. R. Langdon, RN; P. H. Latham; R. Laurie; T. Lawrence; D. M. Levy, QC; C. C. D. Lindsay, QC; S. H. Lloyd; F. R. Lockhart; N. G. E. Loraine-Smith; J. A. M. Lowen; Mrs C. M. Ludlow; Capt. S. Lyons; A. G. McDowall; R. J. McGregor-Johnson; B. McIntyre; K. A. Machin, QC; R. G. McKinnon; W. N. McKinnon; N. A. McKittrick; J. McMullen, QC; K. C. Macrae; T. Maher; F. J. M. Marr-Johnson; D. N. N. Martineau; D. Matheson, QC; N. A. Medawar, QC; D. B. Meier; D. J. Mellor; G. D. Mercer; P. N. De Mille; D. Q. Miller; Miss A. E. Mitchell; D. C. Mitchell; F. I. Mitchell; H. M. Morgan; D. Morton Jack; C. J. Moss, QC; R. T. Moss;

Miss M. J. S. Mowat; G. S. Murdoch, QC; T. M. E. Nash; M. H. D. Neligan; Mrs M. F. Norrie; Brig. A. P. Norris, OBE; P. W. O'Brien; M. A. Oppenheimer; D. C. J. Paget, QC; D. J. Parry; A. Patience, QC; Mrs N. Pearce; Prof. D. S. Pearl; Miss V. A. Pearlman; B. P. Pearson; R. Penton, QC; P. R. Pescod; N. A. J. Philpot; T. D. Pillay; D. C. Pitman; A. B. Pitts; J. R. Platt; J. R. Playford, QC; Miss I. M. Plumstead; P. B. Pollock; T. G. Pontius; W. D. C. Poulton; S. Pratt; R. J. C. V. Prendergast; D. W. Radford; J. W. Rant, CB, QC; E. V. P. Reece; D. J. Rennie; J. R. Reid, QC; M. P. Reynolds; M. S. Rich, QC; D. J. Richardson; N. P. Riddell; G. Rivlin, QC; S. D. Robbins; J. M. Roberts; D. A. H. Rodwell, QC; G. H. Rooke, TD, QC; W. M. Rose; T. R. G. Ryland; J. E. A. Samuels, QC; R. B. Sanders; A. R. G. Scott-Gall; J. S. Sennitt; D. Serota, QC; J. L. Sessions; D. R. A. Sich; A. G. Simmons; K. T. Simpson; P. R. Simpson; S. P. Sleeman; C. M. Smith, QC; S. A. R. Smith; Miss Z. P. Smith; E. Southwell; S. B. Spence; S. M. Stephens, QC; Mrs L. J. Stern, QC; J. Stewart, QC; N. A. Stewart; D. M. A. Stokes, QC; G. Stone, QC; T. M. F. Stow, QC; J. B. C. Tanzer, QC; A. M. Tapping; C. Thomas; A. G. Y. Thorpe; C. H. Tilling; C. J. M. Tyrer; J. E. van der Werff; T. L. Viljoen; J. P. Wadsworth, QC; Miss A. P. Wakefield; R. Wakefield; R. Walker; S. P. Waller; A. R. Webb; C. S. Welchman; K. Wilding; A. F. Wilkie, QC; S. R. Wilkinson; Miss J. A. Williams; R. J. Winstanley; R. L. J. Wood; S. E. Woollam; D. Worsley; M. P. Yelton; M. K. Zeidman, QC K. H. Zucker, QC

WALES AND CHESTER CIRCUIT

Presiding Judges, The Hon. Mr Justice Richards; The Hon. Mr Justice Pitchford

K. E. Barnett; M. R. Burr; J. R. Case; N. M. Chambers, QC; S. Clarke; J. Curran; Miss J. M. P. Daley; H. Daniel; D. Davies; R. L. Denyer, QC; J. B. S. Diehl, QC; R. Dutton; E. Edwards; G. O. Edwards, QC; M. Farmer; M. Furness; W. Gaskell; D. Halbert; D. Hale; Miss J. E. Hayward; G. R. Hickinbottom; R. P. Hughes; M. Hughes, QC; G. Jones; H. Jones; G. Kilfoil; C. Llewellyn-Jones, QC; C. Masterman; The Lord Elystan Morgan of Aberteifi; D. W. Morgan; D. G. Morris; D. C. Morton; H. Moseley, QC; I. C. Parry; G. A. L. Price, QC; P. Price, QC; E. M. Rees; D. W. Richards; D. Richards; J. M. T. Rogers, QC; *J. G. Williams, QC; N. F. Woodward

WESTERN CIRCUIT

Presiding Judges, The Hon. Mrs Justice Hallett; The Hon. Mr Justice Toulson (until 1 January 2003 when The Hon. Mr Justice David Steel will take office)

P. R. Barclay; J. F. Beashel; R. Bond; J. G. Boggis, QC; J. Bonvin; C. L. Boothman; M. J. L. Brodrick; J. M. Burford, QC; R. D. Bursell, QC; G. W. A. Cottle; M. G. Cotterill; *T. Crowther, QC; K. C. Cutler; P. Darlow; S. Darwall Smith; Mrs L. Davies; J. Foley; F. Gilbert, QC; D. L. Griffiths; J. D. Griggs; C. M. A. Hagen; A. M. Havelock-Allan, QC; R. Hooton; M. K. Harington; I. Hughes, QC; G. Hume Jones; G. B. Hutton; J. R. Jarvis; C. Leigh, QC; T. Longbotham; T. Mackean; I. S. McKintosh; D. MacLaren Webster, QC; J. G. McNaught; The Lord Meston, QC; T. J. Milligan; J. O. Neligan; S. K. O'Malley; S. K. Overend; R. Price; R. C. Pryor, QC; M. W. Roach; R. Rucker; J. Rudd; A. Rutherford; A. O. H. Sander; D. H. Selwood; R. M. Shawcross; D. Smith, QC; W. E. M. Taylor; A. A. R. Thompson, QC; D. K. Ticehurst, QC; D. I. H. Tyzack, QC; N. Vincent; R. C. B. Wade; J. H. Weeks, QC; J. S. Wiggs

RECORDERS (EACH £488 PER DAY)

F. A. Abbott; M. A. Abelson; J. J. Acton Davis; R. D. I. Adam; F. T. Ahmed; N. J. Ainley; J. R. Aitken; J. F. Akast; R.

Akenhead; G. L. Aldous; C. D. Allan; C. J. Alldis; J. H. Allen; R. G. B. Allen; D. M. Altaras; G. T. Amakye; W. P. Andreae-Jones; G. M. Andrews, QC; P. J. Andrews; R. A. Anelay; J. M. Appleby; L. E. Appleby, QC; B. J. Argyle; L. E. Armitage; G. K. Arran; G. F. Arthur; T. M. Ashe; S. J. Ashurst; I. D. Atherton; P. Atherton; C. E. S. Atkins; C. L. Atkinson; N. J. Atkinson; C. B. Attwooll; D. J. M. Aubrey; D. S. Aubrey; J. A. J. Aucott; M. G. Austin-Smith; M. J. S. Axtell; W. S. Aylen; P. D. Babb; I. J. F. Badenoch; A. B. Baillie; J. S. Baird; I. M. Baker; J. L. Baker; J. R. Baker; M. A. Baker; N. R. J. Baker; D. J. Balcombe; A. Ball, QC; P. R. Ball; A. Barker; S. G. H. Barker; G. E. Barling; D. N. Barnard; H. J. Barnes; S. E. Barnes; T. P. Barnes; A. J. Barnett; J. V. Barnett; F. J. Baron, QC; P. A. S. Barrie; D. A. Bartlett; D. J. Batcup; D. C. Bate; J. R. A. Bate-Williams; S. D. Batten; P. D. Batty; J. J. Baughan; J. F. T. Bayliss; R. A. Bayliss; T. W. Bayliss; J. C. Bazley; C. M. Beale; D. M. Bean; J. Beatson, QC; G. M. Bebb; M. W. D. Beddoe; S. J. Bedford; R. W. Belben; C. W. Bellamy, QC; J. M. Bellamy; S. H. G. T. Bellamy; S.A. Bennett-Jenkins; J. K. Benson; J. T. Benson; R. A. Benson; H. L. Bentham; D. N. Berkley; C. R. Berry; R. S. Berry; M. Bethel; J. P. V. Bevan; M. O. Bickford-Smith; N. Bidder; N. L. Biddle; P. V. Birkett; M. I. Birnbaum; W. J. Birtles; P. W. Birts; M. A. Bishop; M. L. Bishop; M. J. Black; J. Blackett; S. J. Blackford; B. G. D. Blair; P. M. Blair; W. J. L. Blair; J. A. Blair-Gould; N. J. G. Blake; P. E. Bleasdale; R. H. L. Blomfield; D. J. Blunt; O. S. P. Blunt; E. J. Bond; G. T. K. Boney; A. J. Booth; C. Booth, QC; J. J. Boothby; I. M. Bourne; S. N. Bourne-Arton; M. J. Bowerman; M. A. Bowes; M. R. Bowron; W. H. Boyce; H. C. Bradley; S. F. Bradley, QC; D. L. Bradshaw; N. J. Braslavsky; G. C. Brasse; G. D. Brasse; D. J. Brennan, QC; T. R. Brennan; A. J. Brigden; A. J. Bright; C. J. Bright; D. R. Bright; M. J. Brindle; C. Briscoe; R. P. Brittain; R. A. Britton; E. L. Broadbent; J. S. Brock; J. S. Brodwell; R. B. D. Bromilow; J. Bromley-Davenport; M. E. M. Brooke; J. Brooke-Smith; E. F. T. Brown; R. A. Brown; S. C. Brown; S. S. Brown; B. J. Browne; D. J. M. Browne; J. N. Browne; D. M. Brunnen; A. J. N. Brunner; R. V. Bryan; K. R. B. Buckingham; B. M. Bucknall, QC; C. R. Budden; A. De P. J. M. Bueno; G. Bull; J. E. Bullen; P. E. Bullock; J. M. Burbidge; L. S. Burn; I. D. Burnett; R. H. Burns; F. G. Burrell; A. S. Burrows; M. P. Burrows; A. C. Burton; F. Burton; K. Bush; R. H. Bush; C. M. Butler; P. A. Butler; D. W. Caddick; S. E. M. Cahill; R. C. Pratt; B. A. Cameron; N. St.Clair Cameron; A. B. Campbell; A. N. Campbell; A. S. Campbell; N. C. W. Campbell; S. G. Campbell; A. Campbell-Tiech; J. M. Caplan; M. G. Caplan; Martin John Cardinal; G. M. C. Carey; J. R. P. Carey; R. J. Carey-Hughes; A. C. Carlile; D. C. Carr; P. Carr; J. J. Carter-Manning; D. C. H. Cartwright; R. Carus; P. D. Cattan; J. A. Caudle; P. M. Cawson; P. Chaisty; R. M. Challinor; M. L. Chambers; D. C. Champion; C. B. Chandler; V. R. Chapman; R. G. Chapple; J. M. Cherry; D. J. Chinery; A. N. Chinn; A. C. Chippindall; C. F. Chruszcz; C. H. Clark; T. N. Clark; C. S. C. Clarke; N. S. Clarke; P. W. Clarke; P. R. J. Clarkson; E. G. Claxton; T. Clayson; A. S. L. Cleary; W. Clegg; P. M. Clements; G. H. Cliff; S. Climie; A. Clover; W. P. Coates; Y. A. Coen, QC; J. J. Coffey; T. A. Coghlan; E. M. Cohen; J. L. Cohen; L. F. R. Cohen; W. J. Coker; A. J. S. Coleman; B. R. Coleman; A. R. Collender; P. N. Collier; G. D. Conlin; A. D. Conrad; N. Orton Cooke; K. B. Coonan; A. E. M. Cooper; Y. R. Coppel; J. P. Corbett; J. V. Corless; P. J. Cosgrove; D. R. Cotton, QC; J. V. Cousins; P. S. Mc Crea Cowan; J. S. Coward; T. G. Cowling; B. R. Cox; K. P. Cox; L. M. Cox, QC; P. Crampin; M. D. G. Cran; R. D. Crawford; L. S. Crawford, OBE; M. L. Creed; N. Crichton; D. I. Crigman; D. R. Crome; S. R. Crookenden; S. M. Crosbie; J. D. Crowley; J. E. Crowley, QC; H. K. Crowson; T. S. Culver; P. D. Curran; P. P. S. Curran; J. W. O. Curtis;

M. J. Curwen; A. T. Dallas; A. J. G. Dalziel; J. M. Darbyshire; N. M. Davey; A. M. Davies; A. R. M. Davies; D. O. H. Davies; F. A. Davies; H. Davies; J. T. L. Davies; L. J. Davies; N. V. Davies, QC; P. Davies; R. L. Davies; V. E. M. Davies; R. S. Davis; W. E. Davis; A. W. Dawson; J. Dawson; S. E. Dawson; D. H. Day; A. P. De Freitas; M. R. de Haas, QC; P. A. De La Piquerie; M. A. De Navarro; H. A. D. De Silva; A. R. de Wilde; N. A. Dean; J. L. DeCamp; M. J. Dennis; J. A. Denniss; N. C. J. Dennys; P. A. Derbyshire; D. J. Desmond; G. D. M. Dickinson; L. E. Dickinson; P. N. Digney; C. E. Dines; A. D. Dinkin; J. W. Dixon; D. R. Dobbin; J. S. Dodd; R. S. Dodds; R. A. M. Doggett; D. T. Donaldson; A. M. Donne; J. N. Donne, RD; C. J. Donnellan; A. F. S. Donovan; A. K. Dooley; M. J. Douglas; J. M. R. Dowell; R. E. Downing; S. D. Draycott; M. J. Dudley; E. C. Duff; J. R. Duggan; P. R. Dunkels; J. D. D. Hall; T. J. Dutton; S. L. Earlam; D. T. Eccles; C. N. Edelman; A. J. C. Edis; M. J. S. Edmunds; A. H. Edwards; S. M. Edwards, QC; A. J. C. Edwards-Stuart; M. F. Egan; C. W. Ekins; G. Elias; A. J. Elleray; E. A. Elliott; D. Ellis, QC; M. C. Ellison; M. R. Elsom; J. A. Elvidge; D. J. Elvin; R. M. Englehart; D. C. L. Etherington; D. A. Evans; D. H. Evans; E. M. Evans, QC; F. W. H. Evans; G. R. W. Evans; I. Evans; M. Evans; M. J. Evans; R. K. Evans; M. A. Everall; W. F. Everard; S. G. Everett; I. S. Fairwood; R. B. Farley; D. A. Farrell; D. J. Farrer; E. P. L. Faulks; W. A. Featherby; C. S. Feeny; P. E. Feinberg; J. F. Q. Fenwick; R. Fernyhough; J. M. Ferris; D. J. Field; M. C. Field; P. J. Field; J. E. Finestein; B. G. Finucane; D. T. Fish; D. P. Fisher; M. D. G. Fitton; E. H. Fitzgerald; G. D. Flather; J. M. Flaux; N. Flewitt; R. A. Flowerdew; C. D. Floyd; N. M. Ford; B. C. Forster; M. D. P. Fortune; D. R. Foskett; I. H. Foster; J. R. Foster; R. J. S. Foster; M. G. Fowler; C. R. Fox; J. L. Foy; P. N. Francis; R A. Francis; R. W. Fraser; C. M. Frazer; B. C. Freedman; J. S. Freedman; S. D. Freeland; C. E. Freeman; D. P. Friedman; A. B. Fulford; J. P. M. Fuller; H. J. Furness; S. A. Furst; J. N. C. Gaisman; R. Gaitskell; S. Gal; J. D. Gallagher; C. E. Gardner; M. Nicholas; G. Jones; C. J. Gargan; M. P. Gargan; P. R. Garlick; K. M. Garnett; N. S. Garnham; E. H. Garnier; C. R. Garside; J. B. Gateshill; I. A. Gatt; A. H. Gee; N. S. M. Gee; D. S. Geey; C. R. George; S. M. Gerlis; J. S. Gibbons; M. T. P. Gibney; C. A. W. Gibson; J. H. Gibson; A. J. Gilbart; K. Gillance; R. P. Glancy; A. T. Glass; M. G. Gledhill; I. D. Glen; P. A. Glenn; I. B. Glick; H. B. Globe; E. Gloster, QC; J. E. Glynn, QC; H. A. Godfrey; N. G. Godsmark; J. S. Gold; J. J. Goldberg; I. S. Goldrein; A. J. Goldstaub; A. J. J. Gompertz; D. F. Good; C. J. Goodchild; R. M. Goode; D. N. Goodin; J. N. Goose; D. M. Gordon; R. J. F. Gordon; A. P. Gore; J. V. R. Gosling; J. R. W. Goss; T. J. C. Goudie; G. Gozem; I. D. Graham; D. E. B. Grant; C. J. Gratwicke; D. J. M. Green; H. Green; J. E. G. Greenberg, QC; P. J. Gregory; P. J. J. Gregory; J. G. Grenfell; A. K. Grice; T. J. Grice; M. R. C. Grieve; M. L. Griffith; D. E. Griffith-Jones; C. D. Mc Vay Griffiths; J. P. G. Griffiths; T. V. Griffiths; M. S. E. Grime; P. H. J. Grumbar; N. L. J. Grundy; P. M. Grundy; P. L. Guest; B. P. Gulbenkian; U. Gupta; J. D. Guthrie; C. A. Haddon-Cave; N. S. Haggan; J. W. Haines; N. J. Hall; S. J. Hall; J. P. N. Hallam; L. Hallam; N. A. Hamblen; M. H. K. Hamer; F. W. Hamilton, QC; P. L. Hamlin; V. L. Hammerton; P. Hampton; J. L. Hand; W. J. Harbage; A. J. Harding; S. M. Harman; G. T. Harrap; P. J. Harrington; R. D. Harrison; R. M. Harrison; H. M. Harrod; J. M. Harrow; W. S. Hart; P. K. Hartley-Davies; J. G. Harvey; M. L. T. Harvey; J. A. Harvie; D. W. Hatton; A. J. V. Hawks; R. W. P. H. Hay; A. P. Hayden; R. H. Smith; J. P. T. Head; N. H. Williams; R. Hedgeland; A. T. Hedworth; R. A. Henderson; R. St Clair M. Henderson; C. Henry; D. C. Herbert; R. C. Herman; D. A. Hernandez; D. A. Hershman; M. S. Heslop; R. R. Hetherington; S. R. G. Hickey; D. E. A. Higgins; J. A. Higham; M. C. Hildyard,

QC; J. M. Hill; R. N. Hill; J. R. Hill-Baker; J. M. Hillen; N. R. M. Hilliard; J. W. Hillyer; A. J. H. Hilton; P. N. Hinchliffe; J. W. Hirst; W. T. J. Hirst; J. G. Hobson; S. A. Hockman; D. R. Hodge; A. J. C. Hoggett; D. J. Holgate; M. F. R. Holland; C. S. Hollander; T. V. Holroyde; R. M. Hone; G. A. J. Hooper; T. J. A. Hooper; A. D. Hope; S. J. Hopkins; M. A. P. Hopmeier; T. J. Horlock; M. Horowitz; M. A. Horton; R. Horwood-Smart, QC; C. P. Hotten; B. F. Houlder; M. N. Howard; C. I. Howells; D. T. Howker; M. J Hubbard; C. J. Hudson; A. W. Hughes; D. L. Hughes; K. L. Hughes; M. A. Hughes; P. T. Hughes; D. R. Humphrey; J. C. Humphryes; W. G. B. Hungerford; D. R. N. Hunt; M. A. Hunter; W. R. Hunter; P. T. Hurst; G. N. N. Huskinson; M. Hussain; J. G. K. Hyland; M. D. Inman; S. J. Irwin; P. R. Isaacs; S. L. Isaacs; S. M. Jack; S. E. Jacklin; P. A. B. Jackson; R. E. Jackson; I. E. Jacob; R. M. Jameson; J. M. Jarman; N. F. B. Jarman; J. M. Jarvis; R. M. Jay; A. H. Jeffreys; E. N. Jenkins; J. D. Jenkins; T. A. Jenkins; D. H. T. Jeremy; S. A. John; T. A. John; M. S. Johnson; P. T. Johnson; A. M. Jolles; D. A. F. Jones; D. L. Jones; E. B. Jones; J. R. Jones; N. D. Jones; R. H. Jones; S. E. Jones; W. J. Jones; R. C. Jose; W. R. Joseph, QC; H. M. Joy; P. S. L. Joyce; R. W. S. Juckes; M. L. Kallipetis; L. N. Kamill; T. V. W. Kark; P. A. J. Katz; M. J. Kay; S. W. Kay; R. G. Kaye; G. S. J. Kealey; C. B. Kealy; G. A. Kearl; M. J. Keehan; S. M.Keen; A. M. Kelbrick; D. Kelly; P. J. Kelson; D. Kennett-Brown; M. H. Kent; D. M. Kerr; A. Kershaw; J. C. Kershaw, QC; L. D. Kershen; A. J. Keyser; K. S. Khalil; M. I. Khan; A. A. S. Khangure; M. A. Khokhar; S. J. Killeen; C. A. Kinch; G. P. King; T. R. A. King; C. J. Kingsland, QC; P. G. Kirtley; M. S. Knott; R. St John Knowles; C. J. Knox; B. I. Kogan; J. C. M. Korner; QC; S. E. Kramer; M. Kushner; P. E. Kyte; J. Lafferty; J. J. Laidlaw; E. M. C. Laing; E. A. Lamb; T. R. Lamb; N. R. W. Lambert; P. J. L. Lambert; D. C. Lamdin; D. A. Landau; D. G. Lane; A. D. Langdon; B. F. J. Langstaff; M. D. Laprell; K. P. E. Lasok; R. B. Latham; G. F. Laurence; E. A. Lawson, QC; M. H. Lawson; G. S. Lawson-Rogers; A. W. Layton; J. H. C. Lea; P. L. O. Leaver; D. Lederman; I. Leeming; M. P. G. Leeming; A. J. Lees; G. A. M. Leggatt; S. C. Lennard; A. J. Leonard; M. J. Lerego; H. B. G. Lett; S. Levene; J. Lever; B. H. Leveson; M. N. Levett; M. Levy; A. W. Lewis; D. R. Lewis; J. T. Lewis; P. K. Lewis; K. M. A. J. Lewison; N. J. D. Lickley; K. J. Lindblom; S. J. Linehan; R. A. Lissack; N. M. L. Lithman; G. W. Little; B. J. E. Livesey; H. C. Lloyd; L. J. R. Lobo; D. H. R. Lochrane; C. J. Lockhart-Mummery; P. N. Lodder; A. J. C. Lodge; A. P. Long; M. J. Longman; P. A. Lopez; D. C. Lovell-Pank; G. J. Lowe; G. W. Lowe; N. M. Lowe; J. M. A. Luba; N. J. M. Lucas; B. A. Lunt; R. D. Lynagh; P. Lynch, QC; C. M. Lyon; V. L. Lyon; A. N. MacDonald; C. A. Macdonald; K. D. J. Macdonald; R. D. Machell; D. L. Mackie; Julia Macur, QC; N. J. Madge; S. R. Maidment; P. R. Main; A. G. Mainds; A. H. R. Maitland; A. R. Malcolm; A. Malek; S. M. Males; H. J. Malins; J. H. Malins; D. E. Manley; G. A. Mann; M. E. Mann; P. Mann; C. Manning; D. V. Manning-Davies; G. R. J. Mansfield; R. L. Marks; J. W. Marrin; A. L. Marriott; G. M. Marriott; A. S. Marron; A. G. Marsden; P. D. Marshall; R. G. Marshall-Andrews; G. C. Marson; N. R. Marston; G. J. Martin; H. R. A. Martineau; S. A. Maskrey; C. P. Mather; J. D. Matthews; P. R. Matthews; S. P. Matthews, QC; P. B. Mauleverer; A. R. M. Maw; R. M. Mawhinney; R. B. Mawrey; J. F. M. Maxwell; R. Maxwell; J. M. May; N. May; P. R. May; V. Mayer; I. Mayes; D. W. Mayhew; R. J. McCarthy; A. E. McCooey; G. F. McDermott; A. E. McFarlane; M. P. McGowan, QC; R. P. J. McGrane; I. A. B. McLaren; J. McLeod; A. J. McLoughlin; M. Meeke; G. M. Mercer; N. F. Merriman; R. J. Merz; R. St. Barbe Methuen; H. Mifflin; J. E. M. Miller, QC; K. S. H. Miller; P. W. Miller; R. A. Miller; S. M. Miller; C. J. Millington; C. E. Million; J. B. M. Milmo; D. C. Milne; C. J. M. Miskin; C. M. Miskin; A. R.

Mitchell; C. R. Mitchell; G. C. M. Mitchell; A. Mithani; E. G. Moelwyn-Hughes; C. R. D. Moger; P. M. J. Moloney; A. Molyneux; C. P. Montgomery, QC; D. M. Moore; A. G. Moran; L. Morgan; P. B. Morgan; A. J. Morris; A. P. Morris; S. N. Morris; C. Morris-Coole; R. F. Morrison; H. A. Morrison, OBE; G. E. Morrow; M. G. Mcewan Morse; P. J. Moss; N. A. J. G. Mostyn; P. C. Mott; T. J. Mousley; T. R. Mowschenson; R. W. Moxon-Brown; J. H. Muir; F. J. Muller; A. H. Munday; S. B. Mcleod Munro, QC; G. S. Murdoch, QC; C. A. C. Murfitt; I. P. Murphy; N. J. Murphy; P. J. Murphy; S. P. Murphy; A. C. Murray; C. M. Murray; J. M. A. Murray; N. J. Mylne; H. H. G. Narayan; P. J. Nathan; S. A. Nathan; A. Nawaz; S. P. Newell; A. R. H. Newman; C. M. Newman, QC; R. B. Newton; A. I. Niblett; G. Nice; A. G. L. Nicol; A. M. Nield; A. E. R. Noble; B. Nolan; M. C. Norman; J. M. Norris; P. H. Norris; O. E. Nsugbe; J. G. Nutting, QC; F. M. T. Oldham, QC; R. J. Oldham; C. A. Otton-Goulder, QC; G. A. Owen; R. F. Owen; T. W. Owen; D. R. Owen-Jones; D. P. O'Brien; P. O'Brien; M. P. O'Dwyer; C. E. O'Leary; J. M. O'Mahony; Ms S. J. O'Neill, QC; M. N. O'Sullivan; A. J. O'Toole; N. D. Padfield; A. May Page, QC; A. O. Palmer; P. J. S. Palmer; S. R. Paneth; D. P. Pannick; A. D. W. Pardoe; S. A. B. Parish; C. J. F. Parker; J. M. F. Parker, QC; K. B. Parker; P. L. Parker; R. J. B. Parkes; J. Parkin; G. C. Parkins; M. P. Parroy; N. I. Parry; N. S. K. Pascoe; I. F. Paton; F. S. Patterson, QC; S. Patterson; A. E. H. Pauffley, QC; W. E. Pawlak; F. M. Pearce; D. J. Pearce-Higgins; R. J. P. Wheatley; I. H. Pearson; I. D. E. Peart; S. K. Peat; I. J. C. Peddie; J. V. Pegden; T. Pepper; C. G. Perry; M. Pert; N. M. Peters; J. R. D. Philips; D. J. Phillips; M. P. Phillips; P,. J. M. D. Phillips; S. E. Phillips; W. B. Phillips; J. K. Pickup; M. T. Picton; P. J. Pimm; J. P. Pini; B. M. D. Pitt; D. M. Pittaway; E. F. Platt, QC; C. G. Platts; R. Platts; R. O. Plender; J. C. Plumptre; J. C. Plumstead; A. C. Plunkett; R. Polden; M. P. H. Pooles; S. D. Popat; R. M. Poulet; J. L. Powell; J. M. H. Powell; S. R. Powles, QC; S. O. F. Pownall; R. J. Pratt; S. R. Prevezer, QC; D. Price; J. A. Price; J. C. Price; N. P. L. Price; R. P. Lewis; C. J. Prince; I. D. Pringle; R. B. L. Prior; F. S. K. Privett; H. W. Prosser; K. J. Prosser S. R. S. Proudman, QC; A. C. Pugh; G. V. Pugh, QC; G. F. Pulman; C. P. B. Purchas; R. M. Purchas; N. R. Purnell; Q. C. W. Querelle; N. J. Quinn; A. A. Radcliffe; D. A. Radcliffe; N. P. Radford, QC; S. Rafferty; T. W. H. Raggatt; D. Railton; S. P. N. Rainey; P. J. H. Ralls; E. A. Ralphs; V. A. Ramsey; J. Y. Randall; J. J. B. Rawkins; J. E. R. James; M. A. Read; S. J. H. Readhead; D. G. Readings; M. H. Redfern; A. R. F. Redgrave; D. Reed; D. W. Rees; G. W. Rees; P. Rees; C. E. Reese; P. C. Reid; P. W. Reid; A. L. Reynolds; R. E. Rhodes; J. S. Richards; J. W. Richardson; G. B. Richmond; T. Rigby; S. V. Riordan; G. Risius; J. H. Ritchie, QC; A. A. Riza; Ms J. M. Roberts; T. D. Roberts; M. L. Robertshaw; A. J. Robertson; G. R. Robertson; G. Robinson; V. Robinson; D. E. H. Robson; G. W. Roddick; D. J. Rodgers; M. N. Rogers; S. E. Rogers; P. F. G. Rook; E. J. Roscoe; J. L. Rose; M. H. Rosen; S. Ross; P. M. Ross; J. G. R. Martyn; P. M. Roth; P. C. Rouch; J. M. Rowe; R. P. Rowlands; M. Royall; M. W. Rudland; P. E. B. M. Rueff; N. J. Rumfitt; A. P. Russell; S. C. Russell-Flint; T. P. F. Ryan; E. N. Ryder; A. J. Ryder; T. R. Ryder; J. R. T. Rylance; M. E. Rylands; P. J. Sales; C. R. A. Sallon; C. N. Salmon; T. P. Saloman; V. E. S. Salomonsen; D. A. Salter; R. Salter; A. T. Sander; N. H. Sangster; P. A. Sapsford; N. L. Sarony; J. H. B. Saunders; M. P. Sayers; D. Schofield; J. Scholes; P. J. Scotland, QC; T. J. W. Scott; P. Scriven, QC; R. J. Seabrook; C. Seagroatt; B. Searle; N. J. Seed; M. R. Selfe; W. P. L. Sellick; O. M. Sells; V. E. Selvaratnam, QC; H. J. Setright; A. J. S Llewellyn; N. K. Shant; A. R. F. Sharp; V. M. Sharp, QC; A. M. N. Shaw; P. P. Shears; G. E. Shelton; A. Shepherd; S. J. Sher; D. A. Sherwin; J. M. Shorrock; W. R. Siberry; M. A. Simmons, QC; J. Simpkiss; M. J.

Simpson; P. F. Singer; S. L. Singleton; E. A. Slade, QC; J. C. N. Slater; M. N. Slater; P. K. Sloan; D. Smith; M. A. Smith; R. D. H. Smith; R. L. Smith; R. S. Smith; S. M. Smith; W. T. C. Smith; C. J. Smyth; S. M. J. A. Smyth; S. M. Solley; G. Solomons; M. A. Soole; R. Spearman; M. B. Spencer; M. G. Spencer; R. G. Spencer; T. J. Spencer; R. V. S. Bernard; D. Patrick Spens; R. W. Spon-Smith; P. S. St John-Stevens; N. F. Stadlen; S. E. Staite; E. Stary; R. J. Stead; T. H. Stead; J. B. Steel; D. Steer; I. M. Stern; A. W. Stevenson; R. P. D. Stewart; S. P. Stewart; W. R. Stewart-Smith; A. C. Steynor; G. J. C. Still; D. A. Stockdale; D. M Stocken; C. T. Storey; J. B. Storey; P. M. Storey; D. M. A. Strachan; T. D. Straker; N. A. Strauss; M. Stuart-Moore; J. H. Stuart-Smith; T. Sullivan; Ms L. E. Sullivan, QC; M. A. Supperstone; P. J. Susman; A. H. Sutcliffe; R. P. Sutton; R. H. Swain; N. H. Sweeney; D. A. Sweeting; C. J. Swift, QC; J. P. Swift; C. J. M. Symons; E. Tabachnik; J. P. Tabor; J. A. Tackaberry; P. C. Tain; C. Tait; P. J. Talbot; R. K. K. Talbot; R. B. Tansey; G. F. Tattersall; D. F. Taylor; D. W. Taylor; J. A. Taylor; T. Teague; N. J. M. Teare; R. H. Tedd; A. D. Temple; V. B. A. Temple; M. H. Tennant; P. T. Testar; L. M. Theis; K. M. Thirlwall, QC; J. A. F. Thom; C. S. Thomas, QC; K. G. Thomas; N. M. Thomas; P. A. Thomas; P. H. Thomas; R. L. Thomas; R. M. Thomas; S. M. Thomas; C. F. J. Thompson; R. E. Thorn; A. R. Thornton; P. R. Thornton; I. S. Thorp; A. C. Tickle; A. H. Tidbury; M. B. Tillett; J. H. H. Tillyard; R. S. Tolson; D. R. Tomlinson; M. J. Topolski; P. J. H. Towler; J. B. S. Townend; J. N. Townsend; D. Tremberg; H. B. Trethowan; A. J. Trevaskis; G. D. Treverton-Jones; R. D. T. Jones; A. D. H. Trollope; D. W. Tucker; M. G. Tugendhat; H. W. Turcan; D. A. Turner; D. G. P. Turner; J. Turner; J. C. Turner; M. G. Turner; T. J. Turner; P. A. Twigg; R. W. Twomlow; R. T. Tyson; R. P. A. Ullstein; N. E. Underhill; J. G. G. Ungley; P. C. Upward; H. V. C. Vagg; N. P. Valios; V. V. Veeder; J. M. Venters; M. J. D. Vere-Hodge; C. J. Vosper; Ms J. A. Waddicor; D. M. Waksman; W. F. Waldron; R. A. Walker; R. J. Walker; J. J. Walker-Smith; M. A. Wall; P. S. Wallis; B. G. Wallwork; M. F. Walsh; J. J. Wardlow; A. C. B. Warner; B. B. Warner; S. C. Warner; A. R. L. Warnock; J. Warren; M. J. D. Warren; N. J. Warren; N. R. Warren; S. Wass, QC; P. H. Wassall; D. E. B. Waters; P. J. Watkins; P. Watson; H. J. Watson; A. Watson; B. J. Waylen; B. R. Weatherill; N. J. D. Webb; A. S. Webster; A. G. Weekes, QC; L. West; M. R. West; L. J. West-Knights; G. B. N. White; D. R. B. Whitehouse; R. P. Whitehurst; P. G. Whiteman; D. E. Wickham; S. J. P. Widdup; R. Wigglesworth; J. Wigoder; D. C. Wilby; M. J. Wilby; S. R. Wildblood; N. V. M. Wilkinson; E. Willers; C. D. C. Williams; D. H. Williams; G. W. Williams, QC; J. L. Williams; J. R. S. Williams; L. Williams; W. L. Williams; H. E. Williamson, QC; P. J. Williamson; S. W. Williamson; R. J. C. Wilmot-Smith; A. J. D. Wilson; A. M. Wilson; I. K. R. Wilson; M. C. Wilson; C. Wilson-Smith; G. Wingate-Saul; H. Wolton; G. N. Wood; J. A. D. Wood; M. M. Wood; N. A. Wood; N. M. Wood; S. E. Wood; W. R. Wood; S. Woodley, QC; J. T. Woods; W. C. Woodward; A. P. L. Woolman; T. H. Workman; A. M. Worrall, QC; P. F. Worsley; D. J. S. Worster; S. A. Worthington; D. J. F. Wright; J. J. Wright; N. A. Wright; P. D. Wright; P. M. Wright; P. D. Wulwik; R. N. L. Wyand; G. W. Walters; J. R. Yearwood

---

DISTRICT JUDGES

District Judges (each £82,639)

MIDLAND CIRCUIT

M. Asokan; P. Atkinson; C. Beale; A. Brown; A. Butler; M. Cardinal; D. Cernik; R. Chapman; A. Cleary;

J. Cochrane; R. Cole; D. J. Cooke; T. Cotterill; T. Davies; E. Dickinson; D. D. Douce; P. Dowling; L. Eaton; M. Ellery; A. Elliott; S. Gailey; F. Goddard; R. Hearne; R. L. Hudson; J. Jack; A. Jenkins; A. Jones; P. Kesterton; K. Lacy; D. Lipman; J. Ilsley; P. McHale; P. Mackenzie; A. Marston; G. Martin, OBE, A. Maw; R. Merriman; D. Millard; A. Mithani; R. J. Morton; D. O'Regan; B. Oliver; D. Owen; M. Parry; P. Rank; F. Reeson; T. Ridgway; S. Rogers; P. Sanghera; R. Sankey; R. Savage; L. H. Schroeder; V. Sehdev; V. Stamenkovich; R. Stevens, OBE, A. F. Suckling; R. J. Toombs; W. A. Vincent; P. Wartnaby; P. Waterworth; G. Weston ; R. Whitehurst

NORTH-EASTERN CIRCUIT

S. T. Alderson; H. Anderson; C. A. Arkless; I. D. Atherton; A. M. Babbington; H. J. Bailey; C. W. Bellamy; I. P. Besford; C. M. Birkby; J. Bower; J. A. Buchan; P. E. Bullock (*Recorder*); P. Cuthbertson; G. J. Edwards; A. R. Elliott; J. M. C. Evans; I. S. Fairwood; J. Flanagan; P. R. Giles; M. M. Glentworth; N. W. Goudie; S. J. Greenwood; M. F. Handley; R. V. M. Hall; J. E. Harrison; P. G. Hawksworth; H. F. Heath; N. G. Hickinbottom; R. N. Hill; T. W. Hill; J. R. A. Howard; R. A. Jordan; D. Kirkham; A. M. Large; D. E. Lascelles; P. E. Lawton; G. Y. Lingard; R. Loomba; G. Lord; J. E. Mainwaring-Taylor; G. M. Marley; P. C. Mort; D. A. Oldham; J. F. W. Peters; A. P. Powell; M. F. Rhodes; D. M. Robertson; J. S. Robinson; S. Rodgers; D. Scott-Phillips; I. F. Slim; S. E. Spencer; B. D. Stapely; D. M. Stocken (*Recorder*); J. A. Taylor; P. W. J. Traynor; D. J. R. Weston; P. J. E. Wildsmith; J. S. Wilson; H. P. Wood; M. J. Young

NORTHERN CIRCUIT

G. R. Ashton; R. R. P. Ackroyd; I. Bennett; P. H. Berkson; Ms A. J. C. Brazier; R Bryce; M. E. Buckley; Ms V. Buckley; D. B. Chapman; J. L. Clark; J. R. Clegg; P. St J. Dignan; E. Donnelly; J. F. Duerden; C. R. Fairclough; G. J. Fitzgerald; R. M. Forrester; C. R. Fox; C. E. Freeman; B. N. Gaunt; J. M. Geedes; M. Gosnell; M. J. Gregory; M. Griffiths; A. J. J. Harrison; N. Harrison; L. Henthorn; J. D. Heyworth; J. Horan; M. A. Hovington; G. A. Humphreys-Roberts; S. C. Jackson; J. A. James; E. Johnson; A. Jones; E. R. Jones; E. M. Knopf; G. A. Needham; G. Nuttall; N. A. Law; R. A. McCullagh; B. V. McGrath; Ms M. A. Mornington; L. C. Osborne; J. K. Park; M. I. Peake; I. J. Pickup; J. J. B. Rawkins; D. E. Russell; A. M. Saffman; D. J. Shannon; Ms J. Shaw; M. J. Simpson; R. Smedley; W. H. Stansfield; Ms P. S. Stockton; L. G. Sykes; C M Swindley; R. Talbot; B. W. Travers; J. G. Turner; M. W. Turner; M. J. Wilby; P. T. Wilby; S. Wright

SOUTH-EASTERN CIRCUIT

J. L. Allen; Anthony; P. R. Ayers; Balson; J. D. Banks; R. A. Barratt, QC; Barnett, QC; P. W. Bazley-White; J. L. Beattie; R. H. L. Blomfield; A. J. Blundson, M. Birchall; G. Brett; B. T. Bowman; G. H. Burgess; L. M. Burgess; D. W. Caddick; A. R. Campbell; P. R. Carr; C. B. Chandler; J. H.G. Chrispin; E. Cohen; S. Coates; L. Cohen; J. I. Collier; S. Coltart; B. R. J. Cole; A. J. Coni; Croft, QC; C. N. Darbyshire; C. Dabezies; R. A. Davis; A. S. F. Davies; J. R. Davidson; I. M. Diamond; K. H. Dimmick; R. D. Dudley; C. M. Edwards; C. Enzer; I. Evans; D. Eynon; M. Fawcett; G. B. Field; S. H. D. Fink; N. G. Freeborough; J. M. Fortgang; V. W. Gatter; P. Gamba; S. M. Gerlis; M. C. Gilchrist; P. S. Gill; J. Gittens; P. M. L. Glover; S. G. Gold; G. A. Green; N. J. Gregory; E. J. Habershon; D. F. Hallett; C. Hamilton; S. Hasan; M. J. Haselgrove; D. N. Hayes; A. M. Harvey; Hayward; M. G. Hawthorne; R. M. Henry; S.

Henson; P. F. Hewetson-Brown; M. Hickman; R. S. Hicks;
R. M. Jacey; N. E. Jackson; G. S. Jackson; T. H. N. Jenkins;
S. V. Jones; J. I. Karet; J. L. C. Kirby; Kemp; D. C. Lamdin;
Langdon; M. Langley; I. H. Lay; Lee; C. J. Letham; H. A. J.
Letts; S. E. Levinson; B. G. Lightman; S. Lloyd;
McKinnon; N. Madge; H. L. Manners; R. Matthews; J. S.
Merrick; L. D. Millard; A. J. Mills; E. C. Millward; R. J.
Mitchell; S. R. Mitchell; C. B. Molle; S. I. Morley; A.
Morris; P. Mostyn; B. Mullis; R. M. Naqvi; M. F. Norrie;
M. J. Parker; M. J. Payne; G. L. Pearl; P. Pearl; P. H. Pelly;
S. Plaskow; Polder; K. A. Price; A. L. Raeside; M. A. Read;
J. M. Rhodes; J. T. Robinson; P. Rogers; M. Royall; B. I.
Rutland; Scott-Gam; Sessions; F. W. Shanks; I. Sheratte; G.
Silverman; H. Silverman; M. N. Skerratt; E. J. Silverwood-
Cope; M. M. Short; R. Southcombe; R. G. Sparrow; C. A.
Sonnex; E. Stary; P. R. Statman; G. M. Stephenson; D.
Steel; P. A. Sturdy; J. R. K. Taylor; R. P. Taylor R. P. Taylor;
A. K. Taylor; E. R. W. Temple; R. C. Tetlow; I. G. Tilbury;
M. Trent; M. Walker; A. S. Wharton; A. N. Wicks; C. P.
Wigfield; F. J. Wilkinson; E. Willers; S. L. Williams; F.
Wright; A. J. Worthinghton; M. Zimmels

WALES AND CHESTER CIRCUIT

D. J. Asplin; V. S. Batcup; C. F. Beattie; G. H. F. Carson; J.
L. Davies; C. R. Dawson; H. Dawson; J. M. Doel; P. M.
Evans; R. Evans; I. G. Ewing; J. E. Garland-Thomas; W. H.
Godwin; S. G. Harrison; R. L. Hendicott; R. A. Hoffman;
D. L. Hughes; D. P. Jenkins; T. A. John; T. J. Lewis; P. H.
Llewellyn, obe; C. W. Newman; A. T. North; Mrs C. E.
O'Leary; E. O. Parry; C. G. Perry; D. W. Rees; V. Reeves; J.
E. Regan; S. Rogers; R. Singh, cbe; A. A. Wallace; A. J.
P. Weaver; O. W. Williams

WESTERN CIRCUIT

C. M. Ackner; C. E. H. Ackroyd; R. D. I. Adam; J D.
Ainsworth; R. C. Bird; D. Carney; B. R. Carron; G. F.
Cawood; M. T. Cooper; P. W. Corrigan; J. P. Crosse; M.
Dancey; M. P. H. Daniel; J. M. R. Dowell; Ms J. Exton; D.
J. Field; J. Freeman; J .W. Frenkel; C. Fuller; R. A. F. Griggs;
J. Hurley; J. R. Ing; R. D. S. James; P. D. Jolly; B. G.
Meredith; P. Mildred; A. D. Moon; N. J. Murphy; R. F. D.
Naylor; S. Raskin; M. Rutherford; A. L. Simons; P. N.
Singleton; B. J. A. Smith; J. Sparrow; Mrs G. Stuart Brown;
M. H. Tennant; A. B. Thomas; J. L. Thomas; C. J. Tromans;
J. Turner; A. J. Wainwright; A. Walker; I. E. Weintroub; D.
R. White; R. A. Wilson

DISTRICT JUDGES (MAGISTRATES COURTS)

The provisional and metropolitan Division has now been
changed, all former Provincial and Metropolitan
Stipendiary Magistrates can serve nationally within any
district and are now called District Judges (Magistrates
Courts).

District Judges (each £86,639) salary includes £4,000
inner London weighting

M. A. Abelson; Mrs J. H. Alderson; R. W. Anderson; Mrs
A. Arnold; A. Berg; J. A. Browne; P. H. R. Browning; N. R.
Cadbury; A. L. Callaway; J. J. Charles ; D. J. Chinery; R. F.
S. Clancy ; T. G. Cowling; C. R. Darnton; S. N. Day; Mrs
S. E. Driver; P. K. Dodd, OBE; T. English ; P. R. Farmer; J.
Finestein; P. J. Firth; J. G. Foster; M. J. Friel; I. Gillespie; K.
A. Gray; M. L. R. Harris; N. P. Heley; R. Holland; E. E.
Jellema; R. D. Kitson; Ms B. A. Knight; I. S. Lomax; C. M.
McColl; D. V. Manning-Davies; Ms K. J. Marshall; D. M.
Meredith; B. Morgan ; L. Morgan; P. T. Nuttall; J. B.
Prowse; P. B. Richardson; P. G. G. Richards; M. A.

Rosenberg; F. J. Rutherford; Mrs F. M. Shelvey; S. L. Sims;
P. C. Tain; D. R. G. Tapp; D. L. Thomas; W. D. Thomas; M.
J. Walker; P. Ward; P. H. Wassall; G. R. Watkins; Miss P. J.
Watkins; C. S. Wiles; J. I. Woollard; R. J. Zara

METROPOLITAN DISTRICTS

Bow Street, P. Hewitt *(Senior District Judge)*; T. H.
  Workman *(Deputy Senior District Judge)*; G. E.
  Parkinson; H. N. Evans
Camberwell Green, K. I. Grant; P. M. Davidson; H. Gott;
  S. V. Green; R. K. House; A. J. Sawetz
Greenwich, D. A. Cooper M. Kelly; H. C. Riddle; P. S.
  Wallis
Highbury Corner, P. A. M. Clark; M. A. Johnstone; J. V.
  Perkins; Miss D. Quick; R. A. McPhee
Horseferry Road, A. R. Davies; A. T. Evans; Mrs K. R.
  Keating; C. S. R. Tubbs; G. L. Wicks
Inner London and City Family Proceedings Court,
  N. Crichton
Marylebone, Ms G. Babington-Browne; D. Kennett
  Brown; Miss E. Roscoe
North East London, G. E. Cawdron
South East London, F. J. McIvor
South-Western, A. W. Ormerod; Miss D. Wickham
Thames, I. M. Baker; A. C. Baldwin; Mrs J. Comyns; S. E.
  Dawson; A. M. Rose
Tower Bridge, G. S. F. Black; M. J. Read; S. Somjee; J. A.
  Zani
West London Magistrates' Court, J. B. Coleman; S. N.
  Cooper; Miss D. Lachhar; B. Loosley; K. L. Maitland-
  Davies; J. R. D. Philips; D. Simpson; S. F. Williams

GREATER LONDON MAGISTRATES' COURTS AUTHORITY

185 Marylebone Road, London, NW1 5QL. Tel: 0845 601
3600

Justices' Chief Executive and Clerk to the Committee,
  Maj.-Gen. A. Truluck, CB, CBE
Training Manager, Mrs R. Marsh
Director of Human Resources, Miss S. Campbell
Director of Finance, T. Summers
Director of Legal Operations, M. Eldridge

CROWN PROSECUTION SERVICE

50 Ludgate Hill, London EC4M 7EX
Tel: 020-7796 8000;
Email: enquiries@cps.gov.uk
Web: www.cps.gov.uk

The Crown Prosecution Service (CPS) is responsible for
the independent review and conduct of criminal
proceedings instituted by police forces in England and
Wales, with the exception of cases conducted by the
Serious Fraud Office and certain minor offences.

The Service is headed by the Director of Public
Prosecutions (DPP), who works under the
superintendence of the Attorney General, and a Chief
Executive. The Service comprises a headquarters and 42
Areas, each Area corresponding to a police area in
England and Wales. Each Area is headed by a Chief
Crown Prosecutor, supported by an Area Business
Manager.

Director of Public Prosecutions (SCS), Sir David Calvert-
  Smith, QC
Chief Executive (SCS), R. Foster
Directors (SCS), C. Newell *(Casework);* G. Patten *(Policy);*
  J. Graham *(Finance);* L. Carey *(Business Information
  Systems);* I. Seehra *(Human Resources)*

Head of Communications (SCS), Mrs S. Cunningham
Head of Management Audit Services (SCS), R. Capstick

CPS AREAS

ENGLAND

CPS AVON AND SOMERSET 2nd Floor, Froomsgate House, Rupert Street, Bristol BS1 2QJ. Tel: 0117-930 2800. *Chief Crown Prosecutor* (SCS), D. Archer

CPS BEDFORDSHIRE Sceptre House, 7–9 Castle Street, Luton LU1 3AJ. Tel: 01582-816600. *Chief Crown Prosecutor* (SCS), R. Newcombe

CPS CAMBRIDGESHIRE Justinian House, Spitfire Close, Ermine Business Park, Huntingdon, Cambs PE29 6XY. Tel: 01480-825200. *Chief Crown Prosecutor* (SCS), R. Crowley

CPS CHESHIRE 2nd Floor, Windsor House, Pepper Street, Chester CH1 1TD. Tel: 01244-408600. *Chief Crown Prosecutor* (SCS), B. Hughes

CPS CLEVELAND 5 Linthorpe Road, Middlesbrough, Cleveland TS1 1TX. Tel: 01642-204500. *Chief Crown Prosecutor* (SCS), D. Magson

CPS CUMBRIA 1st Floor, Stocklund House, Castle Street, Carlisle CA3 8SY. Tel: 01228-882900. *Chief Crown Prosecutor* (SCS), D. Farmer

CPS DERBYSHIRE 7th Floor, St Peter's House, Gower Street, Derby DE1 1SB. Tel: 01332-614000. *Chief Crown Prosecutor* (SCS), D. Adams

CPS DEVON AND CORNWALL Hawkins House, Pynes Hill, Rydon Lane, Exeter EX2 5SS. Tel: 01392-288000. *Chief Crown Prosecutor* (SCS), A. Cresswell

CPS DORSET 1st Floor, Oxford House, Oxford Road, Bournemouth BH8 8HA. Tel: 01202-498700. *Chief Crown Prosecutor* (SCS), J. Revell

CPS DURHAM Elvet House, Hallgarth Street, Durham DH1 3AT. Tel: 0191-383 5800. *Chief Crown Prosecutor* (SCS), J. Corrighan

CPS ESSEX County House, 100 New London Road, Chelmsford cm2 0rg. Tel: 01245-455800. Chief Crown Prosecutor (SCS), J. Bell

CPS GLOUCESTERSHIRE 2 Kimbrose Way, Gloucester GL1 2DB. Tel: 01452-872400. *Chief Crown Prosecutor* (SCS), W. Cole

CPS GREATER MANCHESTER PO Box 237, 8th Floor, Sunlight House, Quay Street, Manchester M60 3PS. Tel: 0161-827 4700. *Chief Crown Prosecutor* (SCS), T. Taylor

CPS HAMPSHIRE AND ISLE OF WIGHT 3rd Floor, Black Horse House, 810 Leigh Road, Eastleigh, Hants SO50 9FH. Tel: 02380-673800. *Chief Crown Prosecutor* (SCS), R. Daw

CPS HERTFORDSHIRE Queen's House, 58 Victoria Street, St Albans, Herts AL1 3HZ.Tel: 01727-798700. *Chief Crown Prosecutor* (SCS), C. Ingham

CPS HUMBERSIDE 2nd Floor, King William House, Market Place Lowgate, Kingston-upon-Hull HU1 1RS. Tel: 01482-621000. *Chief Crown Prosecutor* (SCS), B. Marshall

CPS KENT Priory Gate, 29 Union Street, Maidstone, Kent ME14 1PT. Tel: 01622-356300. *Chief Crown Prosecutor* (SCS), Ms E. Howe

CPS LANCASHIRE 3rd Floor, Unicentre, Lord's Walk, Preston PR1 1DH. Tel: 01772-208100. *Chief Crown Prosecutor* (SCS), D. Dickenson

CPS LEICESTERSHIRE Princes Court, 34 York Road, Leicester LE1 5TU. Tel: 0116-204 6700. *Chief Crown Prosecutor* (SCS), M. Howard

CPS LINCOLNSHIRE Crosstrend House, 10A Newport, Lincoln LN1 3DF. Tel: 01522-585900. *Chief Crown Prosecutor* (SCS), Ms A. Kerr

CPS LONDON 2nd Floor, The Flagship, 142 Holborn, London EC1N 2NQ. Tel: 020-7796 8000. *Chief Crown Prosecutor* (SCS), Ms D. Sharpling

CPS MERSEYSIDE 7th Floor (South), Royal Liver Building, Pier Head, Liverpool L3 1HN. Tel: 0151-239 6400. *Chief Crown Prosecutor* (SCS), J. Holt

CPS NORFOLK Haldin House, Old Bank of England Court, Queen Street, Norwich NR2 4SX. Tel: 01603-693000. *Chief Crown Prosecutor* (SCS), P. Tidey

CPS NORTH YORKSHIRE 6th Floor, Ryedale Building, 60 Piccadilly, York YO1 1NS. Tel: 01904-731700. *Chief Crown Prosecutor* (SCS), R. Turnbull

CPS NORTHAMPTONSHIRE Beaumont House, Cliftonville, Northampton NN1 5BE. Tel: 01604-823600. *Chief Crown Prosecutor* (SCS), C. Chapman

CPS NORTHUMBRIA 1st Floor, Benton House, 136 Sandyford Road, Newcastle upon Tyne NE2 1QE. Tel: 0191-260 4200. *Chief Crown Prosecutor* (SCS), Ms N. Reasbeck

CPS NOTTINGHAMSHIRE 2 King Edward Court, King Edward Street, Nottingham NG1 1EL. Tel: 0115-852 3300. *Chief Crown Prosecutor* (SCS), P. Lewis

CPS SOUTH YORKSHIRE Greenfield House, 32 Scotland Street, Sheffield S3 7DQ. Tel: 0114-229 8600. *Chief Crown Prosecutor* (SCS), Mrs J. Walker

CPS STAFFORDSHIRE 11A Princes Street, Stafford ST16 2EU. Tel: 01785-272200. *Chief Crown Prosecutor* (SCS), H. Ireland

CPS SUFFOLK Saxon House, 1 Cromwell Square, Ipswich IP1 1TS. Tel: 01473-282100. *Chief Crown Prosecutor* (SCS), C. Yule

CPS SURREY One Onslow Street, Guildford, Surrey GU1 4YA. Tel: 01483-468200. *Chief Crown Prosecutor* (SCS), Ms S. Hebblethwaite

CPS SUSSEX Unit 3, Clifton Mews, Clifton Hill, Brighton BN1 3HR. Tel: 01273-765600. *Chief Crown Prosecutor* (SCS), Mrs A. Saunders

CPS THAMES VALLEY The Courtyard, Lombard Street, Abingdon, Oxon OX14 5SE. Tel: 01235-551900. *Chief Crown Prosecutor* (SCS), S. Clements

CPS WARWICKSHIRE Rossmore House, 10 Newbold Terrace, Leamington Spa, Warks CV32 4EA. Tel: 01926-455000. *Chief Crown Prosecutor* (SCS), M. Lynn

CPS WEST MERCIA Artillery House, Heritage Way, Droitwich, Worcester WR9 8YB. Tel: 01905-825000. *Chief Crown Prosecutor* (SCS), J. England

CPS WEST MIDLANDS 14th Floor, Colmore Gate, 2 Colmore Row, Birmingham B3 2QA. Tel: 0121-262 1300. *Chief Crown Prosecutor* (SCS), D. Blundell

CPS WEST YORKSHIRE Oxford House, Oxford Row, Leeds LS1 3BE Tel: 0113-290 2700. *Chief Crown Prosecutor* (SCS), N. Franklin

CPS WILTSHIRE 2nd Floor, Fox Talbot House, Bellinger Close, Malmesbury Road, Chippenham, Wilts SN15 1BN. Tel: 01249-766100. *Chief Crown Prosecutor* (SCS), N. Hawkins

WALES

CPS DYFED POWYS Heol Penlanffos, Tanerdy, Carmarthen, Dyfed SA31 2EZ. Tel: 01267-242100. *Chief Crown Prosecutor* (SCS), S. Rowlands

CPS GWENT 6th Floor, Chartist Tower, Upper Dock Street, Newport, Gwent NP9 1DW. Tel: 01633-261100. *Chief Crown Prosecutor* (SCS), C. Woolley

CPS NORTH WALES Bromfield House, Ellice Way, Wrexham LL13 7YW. Tel: 01978 346000. *Chief Crown Prosecutor* (SCS), P. Whittaker

CPS South Wales 20th Floor, Capital House,
Greyfriars Road, Cardiff CF1 3PL. Tel: 029-2080 3900.
Chief Crown Prosecutor (SCS), H. Heycock

The Scottish Judicature

Scotland has a legal system separate from and differing
greatly from the English legal system in enacted law,
judicial procedure and the structure of courts.

In Scotland the system of public prosecution is headed
by the Lord Advocate and is independent of the police,
who have no say in the decision to prosecute. The Lord
Advocate, discharging his functions through the Crown
Office in Edinburgh, is responsible for prosecutions in
the High Court, sheriff courts and district courts.
Prosecutions in the High Court are prepared by the
Crown Office and conducted in court by one of the law
officers, by an advocate-depute, or by a solicitor advocate.
In the inferior courts the decision to prosecute is made
and prosecution is preferred by procurators fiscal, who
are lawyers and full-time civil servants subject to the
directions of the Crown Office. A permanent legally-
qualified civil servant known as the Crown Agent is
responsible for the running of the Crown Office and the
organisation of the Procurator Fiscal Service, of which he
is the head.

Scotland is divided into six sheriffdoms, each with a
full-time sheriff principal. The sheriffdoms are further
divided into sheriff court districts, each of which has a
legally-qualified resident sheriff or sheriffs, who are the
judges of the court.

In criminal cases sheriffs principal and sheriffs have the
same powers; sitting with a jury of 15 members, they may
try more serious cases on indictment, or, sitting alone,
may try lesser cases under summary procedure. Minor
summary offences are dealt with in district courts which
are administered by the district and the islands local
government authorities and presided over by lay justices
of the peace (of whom there are about 4,000) and, in
Glasgow only, by district judges (magistrates courts).
Juvenile offenders (children under 16) may be brought
before an informal children's hearing comprising three
local lay people. The superior criminal court is the High
Court of Justiciary which is both a trial and an appeal
court. Cases on indictment are tried by a High Court
judge, sitting with a jury of 15, in Edinburgh and on
circuit in other towns. Appeals from the lower courts
against conviction or sentence are heard also by the High
Court, which sits as an appeal court only in Edinburgh.
There is no further appeal to the House of Lords in
criminal cases.

In civil cases the jurisdiction of the sheriff court extends
to most kinds of action. Appeal against decisions of the
sheriff may be made to the sheriff principal and thence to
the Court of Session, or direct to the Court of Session,
which sits only in Edinburgh. The Court of Session is
divided into the Inner and the Outer House. The Outer
House is a court of first instance in which cases are heard
by judges sitting singly, sometimes with a jury of 12. The
Inner House, itself subdivided into two divisions of equal
status, is mainly an appeal court. Appeals may be made to
the Inner House from the Outer House as well as from the
sheriff court. An appeal may be made from the Inner
House to the House of Lords.

The judges of the Court of Session are the same as those
of the High Court of Justiciary, the Lord President of the
Court of Session also holding the office of Lord Justice
General in the High Court. Senators of the College of
Justice are Lords Commissioners of Justiciary as well as

judges of the Court of Session. On appointment, a
Senator takes a judicial title, which is retained for life.
Although styled 'The Hon./Rt. Hon. Lord –', the Senator
is not a peer.

The office of coroner does not exist in Scotland. The
local procurator fiscal inquires privately into sudden or
suspicious deaths and may report findings to the Crown
Agent. In some cases a fatal accident inquiry may be held
before the sheriff.

COURT OF SESSION and HIGH COURT OF JUSTICIARY

The Lord President and Lord Justice General (£169,089)
The Rt. Hon. the Lord Cullen, *born* 1935, *apptd* 2001
Private Secretary, A. Maxwell

INNER HOUSE
Lords of Session (each £155,293)

First Division
The Lord President
Rt. Hon. Lord Cameron of Lochbroom, (Cameron of
Lochbroom) *born* 1931, *apptd* 1989
Rt. Hon. Lord Marnoch (Michael Bruce), *born* 1938, *apptd* 1990
Rt. Hon. Lord Penrose, (George Penrose) *born* 1938, *apptd* 1990
Rt. Hon. Lord Hamilton (Arthur Hamilton), *born* 1942, *apptd* 1995

Second Division
Lord Justice Clerk (£163,376), The Rt. Hon. Lord Gill
(Brian Gill), *born* 1942, *apptd* 2001
Rt. Hon. Lord Kirkwood (Ian Kirkwood), *born* 1932, *apptd* 1987
Hon. Lord MacLean (Ranald MacLean), *born* 1938, *apptd* 1990
Hon. Lord Osborne (Kenneth Osborne), *born* 1937, *apptd* 1990

OUTER HOUSE
Lords of Session (each £137,377)
Hon. Lord Abernethy (Alistair Cameron), *born* 1938, *apptd* 1992
Hon. Lord Johnston (Alan Johnston), *born* 1942, *apptd* 1994
Hon. Lord Dawson (Thomas Dawson), *born* 1948, *apptd* 1995
Hon. Lord Macfadyen (Donald Macfadyen), *born* 1945, *apptd* 1995
Hon. Lady Cosgrove (Hazel Aronson), *born* 1946, *apptd* 1996
Hon. Lord Nimmo Smith (William Nimmo Smith), *born* 1942, *apptd* 1996
Hon. Lord Philip (Alexander Philip), *born* 1942, *apptd* 1996
Hon. Lord Kingarth (Derek Emslie), *born* 1949, *apptd* 1997
Hon. Lord Bonomy (Iain Bonomy), *born* 1946, *apptd* 1997
Hon. Lord Eassie (Ronald Mackay), *born* 1945, *apptd* 1997
Hon. Lord Reed (Robert Reed), *born* 1956, *apptd* 1998
Hon. Lord Wheatley (John Wheatley), *born* 1941, *apptd* 2000

Hon. Lady Paton (Ann Paton), *born* 1952, *apptd* 2000
Hon. Lord Carloway (Colin Sutherland), *born* 1954, *apptd* 2000
Hon. Lord Clarke (Matthew Clarke), *born* 1947, *apptd* 2000
Rt. Hon. The Lord Hardie (Andrew Hardie), *born* 1946, *apptd* 2000
Rt. Hon. The Lord Mackay of Drumadoon (Donald Mackay), *born* 1946, *apptd* 2000
Hon. Lord McEwan (Robin McEwan), *born* 1943, *apptd* 2000
Hon. Lord Menzies (Duncan Menzies), *born* 1953, *apptd* 2001
Hon. Lord Drummond Young (James Drummond Young), *born* 1950, *apptd* 2001
Hon. Lord Emslie (Nigel Emslie), *born* 1947, *apptd* 2001
Hon. Lady Smith (Anne Smith), *born* 1955, *apptd* 2001

COURT OF SESSION AND HIGH COURT OF JUSTICIARY

Parliament House, Parliament Square, Edinburgh EH1 1HQ Tel 0131-225 2595

Principal Clerk of Session and Justiciary (£41,620–£57,701), J. L. Anderson
Deputy Principal Clerk of Justiciary (£32,249–£46,766), N. Dowie
Deputy Principal Clerk of Session and Principal Extractor (£32,249–£46,766), D. Shand
Deputy in Charge of Offices of Court, (£23,972–£30,565), Mrs P. McFarlane
Deputy Principal Clerk (Keeper of the Rolls) (£32,249–£46,766), D. Shand
Deputy Clerks of Session and Justiciary (£23,972–£30,565), I. F. Smith; T. Higgins; T. B. Cruickshank; Q. A. Oliver; F. Shannly; A. S. Moffat; G. G. Ellis; W. Dunn; A. Finlayson; C. Armstrong; M. Weir; R. M. Sinclair; B. Watson; D. W. Cullen; I. D. Martin; N. McGinley; J. Lynn; Mrs E. Dickson; K. O. Carter; G. Combe; R. T. MacPherson; P. A. Johnston; D. Bruton; J. Mclean; A. Whyte; D. MacLeod; A. McKay; C. McGrane; L. MacLachlan; A. Thompson

SCOTTISH EXECUTIVE JUSTICE DEPARTMENT

Hayweight House, 23 Lauriston Street, Edinburgh EH3 9DQ
Tel: 0131-229 9200

The Judicial Appointments and Finance Division is responsible for the provision of sufficient Judges and Sheriffs to meet the needs of the business of the supreme and Sheriffs Court in Scotland. It is also responsible for providing the Secretariat for the independent Judicial Appointments Board for Scotland as well as providing resources for the efficient administration of a number of specialist courts and tribunals.
Head of Judicial Appointments and Finance Division (SCS), D. Stewart

SCOTTISH COURT SERVICE

Hayweight House, 23 Lauriston Street, Edinburgh EH3 9DQ. Tel: 0131-229 9200

The Scottish Court Service is an executive agency within the Scottish Executive Justice Department. It is responsible to the Scottish Ministers for the provision of staff, court houses and associated services for the Supreme and Sheriff Courts.
Chief Executive, J. Ewing

SHERIFF COURT OF CHANCERY

27 Chambers Street, Edinburgh EH1 1LB

Tel: 0131-225 2525

The Court deals with service of heirs and completion of title in relation to heritable property.
Sheriff of Chancery, C. G. B. Nicholson, CBE, QC

HM COMMISSARY OFFICE

27 Chambers Street, Edinburgh EH1 1LB
Tel: 0131-225 2525

The Office is responsible for issuing confirmation, a legal document entitling a person to execute a deceased person's will, and other related matters.
Commissary Clerk, W. M. McCulloch

SCOTTISH LAND COURT

1 Grosvenor Crescent, Edinburgh EH12 5ER
Tel: 0131-225 3595

The court deals with disputes relating to agricultural and crofting land in Scotland.
Chairman (£111,210), The Hon. Lord McGhie (James McGhie), QC
Members, D. J. Houston; D. M. Macdonald; J. Kinloch (*part-time*)
Principal Clerk, K. H. R. Graham, WS

SHERIFFDOMS

SALARIES

Sheriff Principal	£111,210
Sheriff	£102,999
Area Director	£32,293–£63,490
Sheriff Clerk	£12,719–£43,873
*Floating Sheriff	

GLASGOW AND STRATHKELVIN

Sheriff Principal, E. F. Bowen, QC
Area Director West, I. Scott

SHERIFFS AND SHERIFF CLERKS

Glasgow, B. Kearney; B. A. Lockhart; Mrs A. L. A. Duncan; A. C. Henry; J. K. Mitchell; A. G. Johnston; Miss S. A. O. Raeburn, QC; D. Convery; I. A. S. Peebles, QC; C. W. McFarlane, QC; K. M. Maciver; H. Matthews, QC; J. A. Baird; Miss R. E. A. Rae, QC; A. W. Noble; J. D. Friel; Mrs D. M. MacNeill, QC; J. A. Taylor; C. A. L. Scott; *S. Cathcart; *Ms L. M. Ruxton; I. H. L. Miller; Mrs F. L. Reith; W. J. Totten; *M. G. O'Grady; W. H. Holligan
Sheriff Clerk, C. Binning

GRAMPIAN, HIGHLANDS AND ISLANDS

Sheriff Principal, Sir Stephen S. T. Young, Bt., QC
Area Director North, J. Robertson

SHERIFFS AND SHERIFF CLERKS

Aberdeen and Stonehaven, A. S. Jessop; Mrs A. M. Cowan; C. J. Harris, QC; P. M. Bowman; G. K. Buchanan; D. J. Cusine; *A. L. MacFadyen; *Sheriff Clerks,* Mrs E. Laing (*Aberdeen*); A. Hempseed (*Stonehaven*)
Elgin, I. A. Cameron; *Sheriff Clerk,* M. McBey
Fort William, W. D. Small (also *Oban*); *Sheriff Clerk Depute,* S. McKenna
Inverness, Lochmaddy, Portree, Stornoway, Dingwall, Tain, Wick and Dornoch, D. Booker-Milburn; A. Pollock; D. O. Sutherland; *Sheriff Clerks,* A. Bayliss (*Inverness*);

M. McBey (*Dingwall*); *Sheriff Clerks Depute,* Miss M.
Campbell (*Lochmaddy and Portree*); Miss A. B.
Armstrong (*Stornoway*); L. MacLachlan (*Tain*); Mrs J.
McEwan (*Wick*); K. Kerr (*Dornoch*)
Kirkwall and Lerwick, C. S. Mackenzie; *Sheriff Clerks
Depute,* A. Moore (*Kirkwall*); M. Flanagan (*Lerwick*)
Peterhead and Banff, K. A. McLernan; *M. Garden *Sheriff
Clerk Depute,* Mrs F. L. MacPherson (*Banff*)

LOTHIAN AND BORDERS

Sheriff Principal, C. G. B. Nicholson, CBE, QC
Area Director East, M. Bonar

SHERIFFS AND SHERIFF CLERKS

Edinburgh, R. G. Craik, QC (also *Peebles*); R. J. D. Scott
(also *Peebles*); Miss I. A. Poole; A. M. Bell; J. M. S.
Horsburgh, QC; G. W. S. Presslie (also *Haddington*);
J. A. Farrell; A. Lothian; I. D. Macphail, QC; C. N.
Stoddart; M. McPartlin; J. D. Allan; N. M. P.
Morrison, QC; Miss M. M. Stephen; Mrs M. L. E.
Jarvie, QC; *Mrs K. E. C. Mackie; *N. J. MacKinnon;
*D. W. M. McIntyre; S. M. Sinclair; M. G. R.
Edington; *Sheriff Clerk,* J. Ross
Linlithgow, H. R. MacLean; G. R. Fleming; P. Gillam; *W.
D. Muirhead; *Sheriff Clerk,* R. D. Sinclair
Haddington, G. W. S. Presslie (also *Edinburgh*); *Sheriff
Clerk,* J. O'Donnell
Jedburgh and Duns, T. A. K. Drummond, QC; *Sheriff
Clerk,* I. W. Williamson
Peebles, R. G. Craik, QC (also *Edinburgh*); R. J. D. Scott
(also *Edinburgh*); *Sheriff Clerk Depute,* M. L.
Kubeczka
Selkirk, T. A. K. Drummond, QC; *Sheriff Clerk Depute,* L.
McFarlane

NORTH STRATHCLYDE

Sheriff Principal, B. A. Kerr, QC
Area Director West, I. Scott

SHERIFFS AND SHERIFF CLERKS

Campbeltown, *W. Dunlop (also *Paisley*); *Sheriff Clerk
Depute,* Miss E. Napier Dumbarton, J. T. Fitzsimons;
T. Scott; S. W. H. Fraser; *Sheriff Clerk,* S. Bain
Dunoon, Mrs C. M. A. F. Gimblett; *Sheriff Clerk Depute,*
J. McGraw
Greenock, J. Herald (also *Rothesay*); V. J. Canavan; *Mrs
R. Swanney; *Sheriff Clerk,* J. Tannahill
Kilmarnock, T. M. Croan; T. F. Russell; Mrs I. S.
McDonald (also *Paisley*); *Sheriff Clerk,* G. Waddell
Oban, W. D. Small (also *Fort William*); *Sheriff Clerk
Depute,* D. Irwin
Paisley, J. Spy; N. Douglas; D. J. Pender; *W. Dunlop; G.
C. Kavanagh (also *Campbeltown*); Mrs I. S.
McDonald (also *Kilmarnock*); *C. W. Pettigrew;
Sheriff Clerk, Miss S. Hindes
Rothesay, J. Herald (also *Greenock*); *Sheriff Clerk Depute,*
Mrs C. K. McCormick

SOUTH STRATHCLYDE, DUMFRIES AND GALLOWAY

Sheriff Principal, J. C. McInnes, QC
Area Director West, I. Scott

SHERIFFS AND SHERIFF CLERKS

Airdrie, R. H. Dickson; I. C. Simpson; J. C. Morris, QC;
A. D. Vannet (also *Lanark*) *Sheriff Clerk,* D. Forrester
Ayr, N. Gow, QC; C. B. Miller; J. McGowan; *Sheriff Clerk,*
Miss C. D. Cockburn
Dumfries, K. G. Barr; K. A. Ross; *Sheriff Clerk,* P.

McGonigle
Hamilton, D. C. Russell; W. E. Gibson; J. H. Stewart; Miss
J. Powie; H. S. Neilson; S. C. Pender; T. Welsh, QC;
D. M. Bicket; *Mrs M. Smart; *H. K. Small; *Mrs M.
Gailbraith; *Sheriff Clerk,* P. Feeney
Lanark, Ms N. C. Stewart; A. D. Vannett (also *Airdrie*);
Sheriff Clerk, Mrs M. McLean
Stranraer and Kirkcudbright, J. R. Smith; *Sheriff Clerks,*
W. McIntosh (*Stranraer*); B. Lindsay (*Kirkcudbright*)

TAYSIDE, CENTRAL AND FIFE

Sheriff Principal, R. A. Dunlop, QC
Area Director East, M. Bonar

SHERIFFS AND SHERIFF CLERKS

Alloa, W. M. Reid; *Sheriff Clerk,* R. G. McKeand
Arbroath and Forfar, K. A. Veal; C. N. R. Stein; *Sheriff
Clerks,* M. Herbertson (*Arbroath*); S. Munro (*Forfar*)
Cupar, G. J. Evans; *Sheriff Clerk,* A. Nicol
Dundee, R. A. Davidson; A. L. Stewart, QC; J. P. Scott;
*P. P. Davies; F. R. Crowe; *Sheriff Clerk,* D. Nicoll
Dunfermline, J. S. Forbes; Mrs I. G. McColl; *R. J.
Macleod; D. M. Mackie; *Sheriff Clerk,* W. McCulloch
Falkirk, A. V. Sheehan; A. J. Murphy; *C. Caldwell; *Sheriff
Clerk,* R. McMillan
Kirkcaldy, F. J. Keane; G. W. M. Liddle; *B. G. Donald;
Sheriff Clerk, W. Jones
Perth, M. J. Fletcher; J. K, Tierney; L. D. R. Foulis; *D. C.
W. Pyle; *Sheriff Clerk,* J. Murphy
Stirling, The Hon. R. E. G. Younger; A. W. Robertson
Sheriff Clerk,

STIPENDIARY MAGISTRATES

GLASGOW
R. Hamilton, *apptd* 1984; J. B. C. Nisbet, *apptd* 1984; R. B.
Christie, *apptd* 1985; Mrs J. A. M. MacLean, *apptd* 1990

CROWN OFFICE AND PROCURATOR FISCAL SERVICE

CROWN OFFICE

25 Chambers Street, Edinburgh EH1 1LA
Tel: 0131-226 2626; Web: www.crownoffice.gov.uk

Crown Agent Designate (£96,700), N. McFadyen
Deputy Crown Agent (£76,369), W. A. Gilchrist

PROCURATORS FISCAL

SALARIES

Area Fiscals   £51,250–£184,500
District Procurator Fiscal, upper level   £51,250–£117,875
District Procurator Fiscal, lower level   £42,750–£52,300

GRAMPIAN AREA
Area Procurator Fiscal, J. Watt
Procurators Fiscal, Miss C. Frame; A. J. M. Colley; D. J.
Dickinson; A. B. Hutchinson; E. K. Barbour; (*Inverness
vacant*)

HIGHLAND AND ISLANDS AREA
Area Procurator Fiscal, G. Napier
Procurators Fiscal, R. W. Urquhart; Ms A. Wyllie; Ms S.
Foard; J. F. Bamber; D. S. Teale; G. Aitken

LANARKSHIRE AREA
Area Procurator Fiscal, J. Brisbane
Procurators Fiscal, D. Spiers; Mrs A. C. Donaldson; S. Houston

CENTRAL AREA
Area Procurator Fiscal, Mrs G. M. Watt
Procurators Fiscal; W. J. Gallacher; (*Alloa and Stirling vacant*)

TAYSIDE AREA
Area Procurator Fiscal, B. Heywood
Procurators Fiscal, N. Orr; A. J. Wheelan; J. I. Craigen; I. A. MacLeod

FIFE AREA
Area Procurator Fiscal, C. Ritchie
Procurator Fiscal; E. B. Russell; Miss H. Clark; (*Kirkaldy vacant*)

LOTHIAN AND BORDERS AREA
Area Procurator Fiscal, D. Brown
Procurators Fiscal, A. R. G. Fraser; F. Mulholland; A. J. P. Reith; A. J. R. Fraser; R. Stott; Mrs L.E. Thomson

AYRSHIRE AREA
Area Procurator Fiscal, Mrs J. E. Cameron
Procurators Fiscal; I. L. Murray; (*Kilmarnock vacant*)

ARGYLL AREA
Area Procurator Fiscal, J. Miller
Procurators Fiscal, F. Redman; C. C. Donnelly; D. L. Webster; W. S. Carnegie; B. R. Maguire; G. F. Williams

DUMFRIES AND GALLOWAY
Area Procurator Fiscal, D. Howdle
Procurators Fiscal, J. Robertson; (*Dumfries and Kircudbright vacant*)

GLASGOW AREA
Area Procurator Fiscal, L. A. Higson (*Glasgow*)

Northern Ireland Judicature

In Northern Ireland the legal system and the structure of courts closely resemble those of England and Wales; there are, however, often differences in enacted law.

The Supreme Court of Judicature of Northern Ireland comprises the Court of Appeal, the High Court of Justice and the Crown Court. The practice and procedure of these courts is similar to that in England. The superior civil court is the High Court of Justice, from which an appeal lies to the Northern Ireland Court of Appeal; the House of Lords is the final civil court.

The Crown Court, served by High Court and county court judges, deals with criminal trials on indictment. Cases are heard before a judge and, except those involving offences specified under emergency legislation, a jury. Appeals from the Crown Court against conviction and sentence are heard by the Northern Ireland Court of Appeal; the House of Lords is the final court of appeal.

The decision to prosecute in cases tried on indictment and in summary cases of a serious nature rests in Northern Ireland with the Director of Public Prosecutions, who is responsible to the Attorney-General. Minor summary offences are prosecuted by the police.

Minor criminal offences are dealt with in magistrates' courts by a legally qualified resident magistrate and,

where an offender is under 17, by juvenile courts each consisting of a resident magistrate and two lay members specially qualified to deal with juveniles (at least one of whom must be a woman). On 19 August 2002 there were 878 justices of the peace in Northern Ireland. Appeals from magistrates' courts are heard by the county court, or by the Court of Appeal on a point of law or an issue as to jurisdiction.

Magistrates' courts in Northern Ireland can deal with certain classes of civil case but most minor civil cases are dealt with in county courts. Judgments of all civil courts are enforceable through a centralised procedure administered by the Enforcement of Judgments Office.

SUPREME COURT OF JUDICATURE

The Royal Courts of Justice, Belfast BT1 3JF
Tel 028-9023 5111
Lord Chief Justice of Northern Ireland (£169,089)
The Rt. Hon. Sir Robert Carswell, *born* 1934, *apptd* 1997
Principal Secretary, S. T. A. Rogers

LORDS JUSTICES OF APPEAL (each £177,545)
Style, The Rt. Hon. Lord Justice [surname]
Rt. Hon. Sir Michael Nicholson, *born* 1933, *apptd* 1995
Rt. Hon. Sir William McCollum, *born* 1933, *apptd* 1997
Rt. Hon. Sir Anthony Campbell, *born* 1936, *apptd* 1998

PUISNE JUDGES (each £137,377)
Style, The Hon. Mr Justice [surname]
Hon. Sir John Sheil, *born* 1938, *apptd* 1989
Hon. Sir Brian Kerr, *born* 1948, *apptd* 1993
Hon. Sir Malachy Higgins, *born* 1944, *apptd* 1993
Hon. Sir Paul Girvan, *born* 1948, *apptd* 1995
Hon. Sir Patrick Coghlin, *born* 1945, *apptd* 1997
Hon. Sir John Gillen, *born* 1947, *apptd* 1998
Hon. Sir Richard McLaughlin, *born* 1947, *apptd* 1999
Hon. Sir Ronald Weatherup, *born* 1947, *apptd* June 2001

MASTERS OF THE SUPREME COURT (each £82,639)
Master, Queen's Bench and Appeals and Clerk of the Crown, J. W. Wilson, QC
Master, High Court, C. J. McCorry
Master, Office of Care and Protection, F. B. Hall
Master, Chancery Office, R. A. Ellison
Master, Bankruptcy and Companies Office, C. W. G. Redpath
Master, Probate and Matrimonial Office, Miss M. McReynolds
Master, Taxing Office, J. C. Napier

OFFICIAL SOLICITOR
Official Solicitor to the Supreme Court of Northern Ireland, Miss B. M. Donnelly

COUNTY COURTS

JUDGES (each £102,999)
Style, His/Her Hon. Judge [surname]
Judge Brady, QC; Judge Burgess, Judge Curran, QC; Judge Finnegan; Judge Foote, QC; Judge Gibson, QC; Judge Lockie; Judge Markey, QC; Judge McFarland; Judge McKay, QC; Judge Martin (*Chief Social Security and Child Support Commissioner*); Her Hon. Judge Kennedy; Judge Smyth, QC

RECORDERS
Belfast (£125,248), Judge Hart, QC
Londonderry, Her Hon. Judge Philpott, QC

MAGISTRATES' COURTS

RESIDENT MAGISTRATES (EACH £82,639)
There are 19 resident magistrates in Northern Ireland.

CROWN SOLICITOR'S OFFICE
PO Box 410, Royal Courts of Justice, Belfast BT1 3JY
Tel: 028-9054 2555
Crown Solicitor, O. G. Paulin

DEPARTMENT OF THE DIRECTOR OF PUBLIC PROSECUTIONS
Royal Courts of Justice, Belfast BT1 3NX
Tel: 028-9054 2444
Director of Public Prosecutions, Sir Alasdair Fraser, CB, QC
Deputy Director of Public Prosecutions, W. R. Junkin

NORTHERN IRELAND COURT SERVICE
Windsor House, Bedford Street, Belfast BT2 7LT
Tel: 028-9032 8594
Director (G3), D. A. Lavery

Tribunals

AGRICULTURAL LAND TRIBUNALS
c/o Department of Environment,
Food and Rural Affairs,
Nobel House, 17 Smith Square, London SW1P 3JR
Tel: 020-7238 5677; Fax: 020-7238 6553

Agricultural Land Tribunals settle disputes and other issues between agricultural landlords and tenants, and drainage disputes between neighbours.

There are seven tribunals covering England and one covering Wales. For each tribunal the Lord Chancellor appoints a chairman and one or more deputies (barristers or solicitors of at least seven years standing). The Lord Chancellor also appoints lay members to three statutory panels: the 'landowners' panel, the 'farmers' panel and the 'drainage' panel.

Each tribunal is an independent statutory body with jurisdiction only within its own area. A separate tribunal is constituted for each case, and consists of a chairman (who may be the chairman or one of the deputy chairmen) and two lay members nominated by the chairman.

Chairmen (England) (£300 a day), W. D. M. Wood; P. A. de la Piquerie; N. Thomas; G. L. Newsom; His Hon. Judge Robert Taylor; J. H. Weatherill; Hon. Judge W. H. R. Crawford, QC

Deputy Chairmen (£300 a day), Ms A. M. Scifert; T. D. Bowles; J. E. Mitting; P. Bleasdale; W. M. Kingston; J. Hogson; M. E. Haywood; S. Evans

Chairman (Wales) (£300 a day), W. J. Owen

Deputy Chairman (Wales) (£300 a day), B. L. Y. Richards

THE APPEALS SERVICE
5th Floor, Fox Court, 14 Grays Inn Road,
London WC1 8HN
Tel: 020-7712 2600

The Appeals Service arranges and hears appeals on decisions on social security, child support, housing benefit, council tax benefit, vaccine damage, tax credits and compensation recovery.

Judicial authority for the Service rests with the president, while administrative responsibility is exercised by the Appeals Service Agency, which is an executive agency of the Department for Work and Pensions.

President (£111,210), His Hon. Judge Michael Harris

Chief Executive, Appeals Service Agency, N. Ward

COMMONS COMMISSIONERS
Room Zone 1/05B, Temple Quay House,
2 The Square, Temple Quay, Bristol BS1 6EB
Tel: 0117-372 8928

The Commons Commissioners are responsible for deciding disputes arising under the Commons Registration Act 1965. They also enquire into the ownership of unclaimed common land and village greens. Commissioners are appointed by the Lord Chancellor.

Chief Commons Commissioner (part-time), E. F. Cousins

Clerk, N. Wilson

COPYRIGHT TRIBUNAL
Harmsworth House, 13–15 Bouverie Street,
London EC4Y 8DP
Tel: 020-7596 6510; Minicom: 0845-922 2250;
Fax: 020-7596 6526
Email: copyright.tribunal@patent.gov.uk
Web: www.patent.gov.uk/copy/tribunal/index.htm

The Copyright Tribunal resolves disputes over copyright licences, principally where there is collective licensing.

The chairman and two deputy chairmen are appointed by the Lord Chancellor. Up to eight ordinary members are appointed by the Secretary of State for Trade and Industry.

Chairman, C. P. Tootal

Secretary, Miss J. E. M. Durdin

EMPLOYMENT TRIBUNALS

THE EMPLOYMENT TRIBUNALS
(ENGLAND AND WALES)
19–29 Woburn Place, London WC1H 0LU
Tel: 020-7273 8666; Fax: 020-7273 8686
Web: www.employmenttribunals.gov.uk

Employment Tribunals for England and Wales sit in 12 regions. The tribunals deal with matters of employment law, redundancy, dismissal, contract disputes, sexual, racial and disability discrimination and related areas of dispute which may arise in the workplace. A public register of applications is held at Southgate Street, Bury St Edmunds, Suffolk IP33 2AQ. The tribunals are funded by the Department of Trade and Industry; administrative support is provided by the Employment Tribunals Service.

Chairmen, who may be full-time or part-time, are legally qualified. They are appointed by the Lord Chancellor. Tribunal members are appointed by the Secretary of State for Trade and Industry.

President (£111,210), to be appointed

CENTRAL OFFICE OF THE EMPLOYMENT TRIBUNALS (SCOTLAND)
Eagle Building, 215 Bothwell Street, Glasgow G2 7TS
Tel: 0141-204 0730; Fax: 0141-204 0732

Tribunals in Scotland have the same remit as those in England and Wales. Chairmen are appointed by the Lord President of the Court of Session and lay members by the Secretary of State for Trade and Industry.

President (£111,210), C. M. Milne

Regional Chairman, (£102,999) S. F. R. Patrick

EMPLOYMENT APPEAL TRIBUNAL
Central Office: Audit House, 58 Victoria Embankment, London EC4Y 0DS
Tel: 020-7273 1040; Fax: 020-7273 1045
Divisional Office: 52 Melville Street, Edinburgh EH3 7HF
Tel: 0131-225 3963; Fax: 0131-220 6694
Web: www.employmentappeals.gov.uk

The Employment Appeal Tribunal hears appeals on a question of law arising from any decision of an employment tribunal. A tribunal consists of a judge and two lay members, one from each side of industry. They are appointed by The Queen on the recommendation of the Lord Chancellor and the Secretary of State for Trade and Industry. Administrative support is provided by the Employment Tribunals Service.
President (£111,210), The Hon. Mr Justice Lindsay
Scottish Chairman, The Hon. Lord Johnston
Registrar, P. Donleavy
Deputy Registrar, Ms J. Johnson

GENERAL COMMISSIONERS OF INCOME TAX
Lord Chancellor's Department, Selborne House, 54–60 Victoria Street, London SW1E 6QW
Tel: 020-7210 0680; Fax: 020-7210 0660

General Commissioners of Income Tax operate under the Taxes Management Act 1970. They are unpaid judicial officers who sit in some 390 Divisions throughout the United Kingdom to hear appeals against decisions by the Inland Revenue on a variety of taxation matters. The Commissioners' jurisdiction was extended in 1999 to hear National Insurance appeals. The Lord Chancellor appoints General Commissioners (except in Scotland, where they are appointed by the Scottish Executive). There are approximately 2,700 General Commissioners appointed throughout the United Kingdom. In each Division, Commissioners appoint a Clerk, who is normally legally qualified, who makes the administrative arrangements for appeal hearings and advises the Commissioners on points of law and procedure. The Lord Chancellor's Department pays the Clerks' remuneration.

Appeals from the General Commissioners are by way of case stated, on a point of law, to the High Court (the Court of Session in Scotland or the Court of Appeal in Northern Ireland).

In 2001, approximately 50,000 cases were listed before the General Commissioners.

IMMIGRATION APPELLATE AUTHORITY
Taylor House, 88 Rosebery Avenue, London EC1R 4QU
Tel: 0845-600 0877
Web: www.iaa.gov.uk

The Immigration Appellate Authorities' powers are now derived from the immigration and Asylum Act 1999. Immigration Adjudicators hear appeals from immigration decisions concerning the need for, and the refusal of, leave to enter or remain in the UK, refusals to grant asylum, decisions to make deportation orders and directions to remove persons subject to immigration control from the UK.

The Immigration Appeal Tribunal provides a second appellate level for those dissatisfied with an Adjudicator's decision. Leave to appeal needs to be obtained. From the Tribunal there is an appeal to the Court of Appeal on a point of law only.

An adjudicator sits alone. The Tribunal sits in divisions of three, normally a legally qualified member and two lay members.

IMMIGRATION APPEAL TRIBUNAL
Field House, 15 Bream's Buildings, Chancery Lane, London EC4A 1DZ
Tel: 020-7073 4200
President, The Hon. Mr Justice Collins
Deputy President, C. M. G. Ockelton
Vice-Presidents, J. Barnes; K. Eshun; J. R. A. Fox; M. W. Rapinet; G. Warr; Dr H. H. W. Storey; J. G. Freeman; D. K. Allen; K. Drabu; P. Moulden; A. Mackey; H. J. E. Latter; S. L. Batiste; J. A. J. C. Gleesen
Vice-Presidents (acting), Prof. D. B. Casson; D. J. Parke

IMMIGRATION APPEAL ADJUDICATORS
Chief Adjudicator, His Hon. Judge H. Hodge, OBE
Deputy Chief Adjudicator, E. Arfon-Jones

IMMIGRATION SERVICES TRIBUNAL
48–49 Chancery Lane, London WC2A 1JR
Tel: 020-7947 7200; Fax: 020-7947 7215

The Immigration Services Tribunal is an independent judicial body set up to provide a forum in which appeals against decisions of the Immigration Services Commissioner and complaints made by the Immigration Services Commissioner can be heard and determined. The cases exclusively concern people providing advice and representation services in connection with immigration matters.

The Tribunal forms part of the Court Service. It is the responsibility of the Lord Chancellor. There is a president, who is the judicial head; other judicial members, who must be legally qualified; lay members who must have substantial experience in immigration services or in the law and procedure relating to immigration; and a secretary who is responsible for administration. The tribunal can sit anywhere in the UK.
President, Hon. Judge Seddon Crisp
Members; D. Bean, QC; G. Marriott; P. Barnett; O. Conway; M. Hoare; S. Maguire; A. Montgomery; I. Newton; M. Quayum; S. Rowland; P. Fisher
Immigration Services Tribunal Staff, D. Duncan

INDUSTRIAL TRIBUNALS AND THE FAIR EMPLOYMENT TRIBUNAL
(NORTHERN IRELAND)
Long Bridge House, 20–24 Waring Street, Belfast BT1 2EB
Tel: 028-9032 7666; Fax: 028-9023 0184

The industrial tribunal system in Northern Ireland was set up in 1965 and has a similar remit to the employment tribunals in the rest of the UK. There is also a Fair Employment Tribunal, which hears and determines individual cases of alleged religious or political discrimination in employment. Employers can appeal to the Fair Employment Tribunal if they consider the directions of the Equality Commission to be unreasonable, inappropriate or unnecessary, and the Equality Commission can make application to the Tribunal for the enforcement of undertakings or directions with which an employer has not complied.

The president, vice-president and part-time chairmen of the Fair Employment Tribunal are appointed by the

Lord Chancellor. The full-time chairman and the part-time chairmen of the industrial tribunals and the panel members to both the industrial tribunals and the Fair Employment Tribunal are appointed by the Department of Higher and Further Education Training and Employment.

President of the Industrial Tribunals and the Fair Employment Tribunal (£102,999), J. Maguire, CBE
Vice-President of the Industrial Tribunals and the Fair Employment Tribunal, Mrs M. P. Price
Secretary, Miss A. Loney

INFORMATION TRIBUNAL
c/o The Lord Chancellor's Department, Selborne House, 54–60 Victoria Street, London SW1E 6QN
Tel: 020-7210 2668; Fax: 020-7210 1415
Email: roger.hartley@lcdhq.gsi.gov.uk

The Information Tribunal determines appeals against notices issued by the Information Commissioner. The chairman and deputy chairman are appointed by the Lord Chancellor and must be legally qualified. Lay members are appointed by the Lord Chancellor to represent the interests of data users or data subjects. A tribunal consists of a chairman sitting with equal numbers of the lay members. There is a separate panel of the tribunal which hears national security appeals; the president of this panel is the Rt. Hon. Sir Anthony Evans, RD.

Chairman, to be appointed
Secretary, R. Hartley
Information Commissioner, R. Thomas

LANDS TRIBUNAL
48–49 Chancery Lane, London WC2A 1JR
Tel: 020-7947 7200; Fax: 020-7947 7215

The Lands Tribunal is an independent judicial body which determines questions relating to the valuation of land, rating appeals from valuation tribunals, the discharge or modification of restrictive covenants, and compulsory purchase compensation. The tribunal may also arbitrate under references by consent. The president and members are appointed by the Lord Chancellor.

President (£111,210), G. R. Bartlett, QC
Members (£99,110), P. H. Clarke, FRICS; N. J. Rose, FRICS; P. R. Francis
Member (part-time), His Hon. Judge Rich, QC
Registrar, D. Scannell

LANDS TRIBUNAL FOR SCOTLAND
1 Grosvenor Crescent, Edinburgh EH12 5ER
Tel: 0131-225 7996

The Lands Tribunal for Scotland has the same remit as the tribunal for England and Wales but also covers questions relating to tenants' rights to buy their homes under the Housing (Scotland) Act 1987. The president is appointed by the Lord President of the Court of Session.

President (£111,210), The Hon. Lord McGhie, QC
Members (£99,110), A. R. MacLeary, FRICS
Member (part-time) (£33,409), J. N. Wright, QC; R. F. Durman, FRICS
Clerk, N. M. Tainsh

MENTAL HEALTH REVIEW TRIBUNALS
Secretariat: Health Service Directorate, Room 320 Wellington House, 133–155 Waterloo Road, London SE1 8UG
Tel: 020-7972 4577; Fax: 020-7972 4884

The Mental Health Review Tribunals are independent judicial bodies which review the cases of patients compulsorily detained under the provisions of the Mental Health Act 1983. They have the power to discharge the patient, to recommend leave of absence, delayed discharge, transfer to another hospital or that a guardianship order be made, to reclassify both restricted and unrestricted patients, and to recommend consideration of a supervision application. There are four tribunals in England, each headed by a regional chairman who is appointed by the Lord Chancellor on a part-time basis. Each tribunal is made up of at least three members, and must include a lawyer, who acts as president, a medical member and a lay member.

There are five regional offices:

LIVERPOOL, 3rd Floor, Cressington House, 249 St Mary's Road, Garston, Liverpool L19 0NF. Tel: 0151-728 5400
LONDON (NORTH), Spur 3, Block 1, Government Buildings, Honeypot Lane, Stanmore, Middx HA7 1AY. Tel: 020-7972 3754
LONDON (SOUTH), Block 3, Crown Offices, Kingston Bypass Road, Surbiton, Surrey KT6 5QN. Tel: 020-8268 4549
NOTTINGHAM, Spur A, Block 5, Government Buildings, Chalfont Drive, Western Boulevard, Nottingham NG8 3RZ. Tel: 0115-942 8308
WALES, 4th Floor, Crown Buildings, Cathays Park, Cardiff CF1 3NQ. Tel: 029-2082 5328

NATIONAL HEALTH SERVICE TRIBUNAL (SCOTLAND)
40 Craiglockhart Road, North, Edinburgh EH14 1BT
Tel/Fax: 0131-443 2575

The tribunal considers representations that the continued inclusion of a doctor, dentist, optometrist or pharmacist on a health board's list would be prejudicial to the efficiency of the service concerned. The tribunal sits when required and is composed of a chairman, one lay member, and one practitioner member drawn from a representative professional panel. The chairman is appointed by the Lord President of the Court of Session, and the lay member and the members of the professional panel are appointed by the First Minister.

Chairman, M. G. Thomson, QC
Lay member, J. D. M. Robertson, CBE
Clerk to the Tribunal, W. Bryden

PENSIONS APPEAL TRIBUNAL
CENTRAL OFFICE (ENGLAND AND WALES), 48–49 Chancery Lane, London WC2A 1JF
Tel: 020-7947 7034; Fax: 020-7947 7492

The Pensions Appeal Tribunals are responsible for hearing appeals from ex-servicemen or women and widows who have had their claims for a war pension rejected by the Secretary of State for Work and Pensions. The Entitlement Appeal Tribunals hear appeals in cases where the Secretary of State has refused to grant a war pension. The Assessment Appeal Tribunals hear appeals

against the Secretary of State's assessment of the degree of disablement caused by an accepted condition. The tribunal members are appointed by the Lord Chancellor.
President, Dr H. M. G. Concannon
Tribunal Manager, Miss L. Nay

PENSIONS APPEAL TRIBUNALS FOR SCOTLAND
20 Walker Street, Edinburgh EH3 7HS
Tel: 0131-220 1404
President, C. N. McEachran, QC

OFFICE OF THE SOCIAL SECURITY AND CHILD SUPPORT COMMISSIONERS

5th Floor, Newspaper House, 8–16 Great New Street, London EC4A 3BN
Tel: 020-7353 5145; Fax: 020-7936 2171
23 Melville Street, Edinburgh EH3 7PW
Tel: 0131-225 2201

The Social Security Commissioners are the final statutory authority to decide appeals relating to entitlement to social security benefits. The Child Support Commissioners are the final statutory authority to decide appeals relating to child support. Appeals may be made in relation to both matters only on a point of law. The Commissioners' jurisdiction covers England, Wales and Scotland. There are 17 commissioners; they are all qualified lawyers.
Chief Social Security Commissioner and Chief Child Support Commissioner (£111,210), His Hon. Judge Michael Harris
Secretary, J. Arckron (London); S. Niven (Edinburgh)

OFFICE OF THE SOCIAL SECURITY COMMISSIONERS AND CHILD SUPPORT COMMISSIONERS FOR NORTHERN IRELAND

1st Floor, Headline Building, 10–14 Victoria Street, Belfast BT1 3GG
Tel: 028-9033 2344; Fax: 028-9031 3510
Email: socialsecuritycommissioners@courtsni.gov.uk
Web: www.courtsni.gov.uk

The role of Northern Ireland Social Security Commissioners and Child Support Commissioners is similar to that of the Commissioners in Great Britain. There are two commissioners for Northern Ireland.
Chief Commissioner (£111,210), His Hon. Judge Martin, QC
Commissioner, Mrs M. F. Brown
Registrar of Appeals, W. R. Brown

THE SOLICITORS' DISCIPLINARY TRIBUNAL

3rd Floor, Gate House, 1 Farringdon Street, London EC4M 7NS
Tel: 020-7329 4808; Fax: 020-7329 4833
Email: enquiries@solicitorsdt.com
Web: www.solicitorstribunal.org.uk

The Solicitors' Disciplinary Tribunal is an independent statutory body whose members are appointed by the Master of the Rolls. The tribunal considers applications made to it alleging either professional misconduct and/or a breach of the statutory rules by which solicitors are bound against an individually named solicitor, former solicitor, registered foreign lawyer, or solicitor's clerk. The president and solicitor members do not receive

remuneration.
President, A. Isaacs
Clerk, Mrs S. C. Elson

THE SCOTTISH SOLICITORS' DISCIPLINE TRIBUNAL

22 Rutland Square, Edinburgh EH1 2BB
Tel: 0131-229 5860; Fax: 0131-229 0255

The Scottish Solicitors' Discipline Tribunal is an independent statutory body with a panel of 18 members, ten of whom are solicitors; members are appointed by the Lord President of the Court of Session. Its principal function is to consider complaints of misconduct against solicitors in Scotland.
Chairman, G. F. Ritchie
Clerk, J. V. Lea, WS

SPECIAL COMMISSIONERS

15–19 Bedford Avenue, London WC1B 3AS
Tel: 020-7631 4242; Fax: 020-7436 4150/4151

The Special Commissioners are an independent body appointed by the Lord Chancellor to hear complex appeals against decisions of the Board of Inland Revenue and its officials.
Presiding Special Commissioner (£111,210) His Hon. Stephen Oliver, QC
Clerk, R. P. Lester

SPECIAL IMMIGRATION APPEALS COMMISSION

Taylor House, 88 Rosebery Avenue, London EC1R 4QU
Tel: 020-7862 4200

The Commission was set up under the Special Immigration Appeals Commission Act 1998. Its main function is to consider appeals against orders for deportations in cases which involve, in the main, considerations of national security. Members are appointed by the Lord Chancellor.
Chairman, The Hon. Mr Justice Collins

TRAFFIC COMMISSIONERS

c/o Scottish Traffic Area, Argyle House, 3 Lady Lawson Street, Edinburgh EH3 9SE
Tel: 0131-200 4955; Fax: 0131-529 8501

The Traffic Commissioners are responsible for licensing operators of heavy goods and public service vehicles. There are seven Commissioners in the eight traffic areas covering Britain. Each Traffic Commissioner constitutes a tribunal for the purposes of the Tribunals and Inquiries Act 1992.
Senior Traffic Commissioner, M. W. Betts, CBE

TRANSPORT TRIBUNAL

48–49 Chancery Lane, London WC2A 1JR
Tel: 020-7947 7200; Fax: 020-7947 7798

The Transport Tribunal hears appeals against decisions made by Traffic Commissioners at public inquiries. The tribunal consists of a legally qualified president, two legal members who may sit as chairmen, and five lay members. The president and legal members are appointed by the Lord Chancellor and the lay members by the Secretary of State for Transport.

President (part-time), H. B. H. Carlisle, QC
Legal members (part-time), His Hon. Judge Brodrick;
    J. Beech
Lay members, D. Yeomans; J. W. Whitworth; P. Steel;
    P. Rogers; L. Milliken; G. Inch; S. James; J. Robinson
Secretary, E. Miles

VALUATION TRIBUNALS

Valuation Tribunal Management Board,
2nd Floor, Walton House, 11 Parade,
Leamington Spa, Warks CV32 4DG
Tel: 01926-423825; Fax: 01926-423 207
Web: www.valuation-tribunals.gov.uk

The Valuation Tribunals hear appeals concerning the council tax, non-domestic rating and land drainage rates in England and Wales. There are 56 tribunals in England and four in Wales; those in England are funded by the Office of the Deputy Prime Minister and those in Wales by the National Assembly for Wales. A separate tribunal is constituted for each hearing, and normally consists of a chairman and two other members. Members are appointed by a representative of the local authorities and the Valuation Tribunal president and serve on a voluntary basis. The Valuation Tribunal Management Board considers all matters affecting valuation tribunals in England, and the Council of Wales Valuation Tribunals performs the same function in Wales.

Chairman, Valuation Tribunal Management Board,
    P. Wood, OBE
Valuation Tribunals National Officer, B. P. Massen, MBE
President, Council of Wales Valuation Tribunals,
    J. H. Owens

VAT AND DUTIES TRIBUNALS

15–19 Bedford Avenue, London WC1B 3AS
Tel: 020-7631 4242; Fax: 020-7436 4150/4151

VAT and Duties Tribunals are administered by the Lord Chancellor in England and Wales, and by the First Minister in Scotland. They are independent and decide disputes between taxpayers and Customs and Excise. In England and Wales, the president and chairmen are appointed by the Lord Chancellor and members by the Treasury. Chairmen in Scotland are appointed by the Lord President of the Court of Session.

President, His Hon. Stephen Oliver, QC
Vice-President, England and Wales, J. D. Demack
Vice-President, Scotland, T. G. Coutts, QC
Vice-President, Northern Ireland, His Hon. J. McKee, QC
Registrar, R. P. Lester

TRIBUNAL CENTRES

EDINBURGH, 44 Palmerston Place, Edinburgh EH12 5BJ.
    Tel: 0131-226 3551
LONDON (including Belfast), 15–19 Bedford Avenue,
    London WC1B 3AS. Tel: 020-7631 4242
MANCHESTER, 9th Floor, Westpoint, 501 Chester Road,
    Manchester M16 5HU. Tel: 0161-868 6600

The Police Service

There are 52 police forces in the United Kingdom. Most forces' area is coterminous with one or more local authority areas. Policing in London is carried out by the Metropolitan Police and the City of London Police; in Northern Ireland by the Police Service of Northern Ireland; and by the Isle of Man, States of Jersey and Guernsey forces in their respective islands and bailiwicks. National services include the National Crime Squad (NCS) and the National Criminal Intelligence Service (NCIS).

The police authorities of English and Welsh forces comprise local councillors, magistrates and independent members. In Scotland, there are six joint police boards made up of local councillors; the other two police authorities are councils. In London the Metropolitan Police Authority oversees police operations. A committee of the Corporation of London including councillors and magistrates oversees the City of London Police. In Northern Ireland the Secretary of State appoints the policing board.

Police authorities in England, Scotland and Wales are financed by central and local government grants and a precept on the council tax. The Northern Ireland Policing Board is wholly funded by central government. The police authorities, subject to the approval of the Home Secretary (in England and Wales), the Secretary of State for Northern Ireland and to regulations, are responsible for appointing the Chief Constable. In England and Wales they are responsible for publishing annual policing plans and annual reports, setting local objectives and a budget, and levying the precept. The police authorities in Scotland are responsible for setting a budget, providing the resources necessary to police the area adequately, appointing officers of the rank of Assistant Chief Constable and above, and determining the number of officers and civilian staff in the force. The Northern Ireland Policing Board exercises these functions in Northern Ireland.

The Home Secretary, the Secretary of State for Northern Ireland and the Scottish Executive are responsible for the organisation, administration and operation of the police service. They make regulations covering matters such as police ranks, discipline, hours of duty and pay and allowances. All police forces are subject to inspection by HM Inspectors of Constabulary, who report to the Home Secretary, Scottish Executive or Secretary of State for Northern Ireland.

COMPLAINTS

The investigation and resolution of a serious complaint against a police officer in England and Wales is subject to the scrutiny of the Police Complaints Authority. An officer who is dismissed, required to resign or reduced in rank, whether as a result of a complaint or not, may appeal to a police appeals tribunal established by the relevant police authority. In Scotland, Chief Constables are obliged to investigate a complaint against one of their officers; if there is a suggestion of criminal activity, the complaint is investigated by an independent public prosecutor. In Northern Ireland complaints are investigated by the Police Ombudsman.

BASIC RATES OF PAY *since 1 September 2001*

Chief Constable of Police Services of Northern Ireland	
No fixed term	£116,559–£125,283
Fixed term appointment	£122,556–£131,718
Chief Constables of Greater Manchester, Strathclyde and West Midlands	
No fixed term	£103,044–£116,286
Fixed term appointment	£108,066–£121,962
Chief Constable	
No fixed term	£78,480–£112,224
Fixed term appointment	£82,407–£117,699
Deputy Chief Constable	
No fixed term	80% of their Chief Constable's pay or £75,171, whichever is higher
Fixed term appointment	80% of their Chief Constable's pay or £78,930, whichever is higher
Assistant Chief Constable	
No fixed term	£65,484–£75,171
Fixed term appointment	£68,760–£78,930
Chief Superintendent*	£56,547–£59,823
Superintendent*	£47,649–£55,581
Chief Inspector†	£39,153–£43,911
Inspector†	£35,034–£40,761
Sergeant	£27,084–£31,590
Constable	£17,733–£28,062

*The rank of Chief Superintendent was re-introduced on 1 January 2002 and so pay arrangements take effect from that date. Superintendents who were not given the rank of Chief Superintendent on its re-introduction will receive full protection of their existing Superintendent range 2 salary (£55,581–£59,151).

†Includes London salary range, applicable only to officers in the Metropolitan and City of London polices forces.

Metropolitan Police

Commissioner	£158,544–£170,400
Deputy Commissioner	£128,793–£138,423
Assistant Commissioner	£109,482–£122,556
Deputy Assistant Commissioner*	80% of the basic salary of the assistant commissioner
Commander	
No fixed term	£65,484–£75,171
Fixed term appointment	£68,760–£78,930

*This rank was formally introduced on 1 January 2002, pay arrangements take effect from that date

City of London Police

Commissioner	
No fixed term	£89,754–£104,268
Fixed term appointment	£94,245–£109,482
Assistant Commissioner	
No fixed term	80% of the basic salary of the commissioner or £75,171, whichever is higher
Fixed term appointment	80% of the basic salary of the commisioner or £78,930, whichever is higher

THE SPECIAL CONSTABULARY

Each police force has its own special constabulary, made up of volunteers who work in their spare time. Special Constables have full police powers.

NATIONAL CRIME SQUAD

The National Crime Squad (NCS) was established on 1 April 1998, replacing the six regional crime squads in England and Wales. It investigates national and international organised and serious crime. It also supports police forces investigating serious crime. The Squad is accountable to the National Crime Squad Service Authority.
Headquarters: PO Box 2500, London SW1V 2WF. Tel: 020-7238 2500
Director General, W. Hughes, QPM

NCS AND NCIS SERVICE AUTHORITIES

The Service Authorities are responsible for ensuring the effective operation of the National Crime Squad and National Criminal Intelligence Service. Each Authority has eleven members, of whom eight sit on both Authorities as core members. The Service Authorities are non-departmental public bodies.
Headquarters: PO Box 2600, London SW1V 2WG. Tel: 020-7238 2600
Chairman, D. Lock, *Clerk,* T. Simmons

NATIONAL MISSING PERSONS BUREAU

The Police National Missing Persons Bureau (PNMPB) acts as a central clearing house of information, receiving reports about vulnerable missing persons that are still outstanding after 14 days and details of unidentified persons or remains within 48 hours of being found from all forces in England and Wales. Reports are also received from Scottish police forces, the Police Services of Northern Ireland and foreign police forces via Interpol. The Bureau also manages the Missing Kids website, www.missingkids.com.
Headquarters: New Scotland Yard, Broadway, London SW1H 0BG. Tel: 020-7230 2153
Director, G. Pugh

POLICE INFORMATION TECHNOLOGY ORGANISATION

The Police Information Technology Organisation (PITO) is a non-departmental public body funded by grant-in-aid from central Government and by charges from the services provided. It provides information technology, communications systems and services to the police and other criminal justice organisations in the UK and also has a role in the purchasing of goods and services for the police.
Headquarters: New Kings Beam House, 22 Upper Ground, London SE1 9QY. Tel: 020-8358 5678
Chairman, Sir Edmund Burton
Chief Executive, V. Dews

FORENSIC SCIENCE SERVICE

The Forensic Science Service (FSS) is an executive agency of the Home Office providing forensic science services to the police forces in England and Wales. It employs over 2,500 people, including over 1,600 trained scientists and has seven laboratories throughout the country.
Headquarters: Priory House, Gooch Street North, Birmingham B5 6QQ. Tel: 0121-607 6800
Chief Executive, D. Werrett

POLICE FORCES AND AUTHORITIES

Strength: actual strength of force as at mid 2002

ENGLAND

AVON AND SOMERSET CONSTABULARY, PO Box 37, Valley Road, Portishead, North Somerset BS20 8QJ. Tel: 01275-818181; Fax: 01275-816112; *Strength,* 3,072; *Chief Constable,* S. Pilkington, QPM

BEDFORDSHIRE POLICE, Police Headquarters, Woburn Road, Kempston, Bedford MK43 9AX. Tel: 01234-841212; Fax: 01234-842006; *Strength,* 1,120; *Chief Constable,* P. Hancock, QPM

CAMBRIDGESHIRE CONSTABULARY, Hinchingbrooke Park, Huntingdon, Cambs PE29 6NP. Tel: 01480-456111; Fax: 01480-422447; *Strength,* 1,362; *Chief Constable,* T. Lloyd

CHESHIRE CONSTABULARY, Police Headquarters, Nuns Road, Chester CH1 2PP. Tel: 01244-350000; Fax: 01244-612269; *Strength,* 2,107; *Chief Constable,* N. K. Burgess, QPM

CLEVELAND POLICE, Police HQ, PO Box 70, Ladgate Lane, Middlesbrough TS8 9EH. Tel: 01642-326326; Fax: 01642-301200; *Strength,* 1,448; *Chief Constable,* B. Shaw

CUMBRIA CONSTABULARY, Carleton Hall, Penrith, Cumbria CA10 2AU. Tel: 01768-891999; Fax: 01768-217099; *Strength,* 1,100; *Chief Constable,* M. Baxter

DERBYSHIRE CONSTABULARY, Butterley Hall, Ripley, Derbyshire DE5 3RS. Tel: 01773-570100; Fax: 01773-572225; *Strength,* 1,913; *Chief Constable,* D. F. Coleman

DEVON AND CORNWALL CONSTABULARY, Middlemoor, Exeter EX2 7HQ. Tel: 08705-777444; Fax: 08705-452346; *Strength,* 3,126; *Chief Constable,* Sir John Evans, QPM

DORSET POLICE HEADQUARTERS, Winfrith, Dorchester, Dorset DT2 8DZ. Tel: 01929-462727; Fax: 01202-223987; *Strength,* 1,378; *Chief Constable,* Mrs J. Stichbury

DURHAM CONSTABULARY, Aykley Heads, Durham City DH1 5TT. Tel: 0191-386 4929; Fax: 0191-375 2160; *Strength,* 1,614; *Chief Constable,* G. Hedges, QPM

ESSEX POLICE, PO Box 2, Springfield, Chelmsford, Essex CM2 6DA. Tel: 01245-491491; Fax: 01245-452259; *Strength,* 2,963; *Chief Constable,* D. F. Stevens, QPM, LLB

GLOUCESTERSHIRE CONSTABULARY, Holland House, Lansdown Road, Cheltenham, Glos GL51 6QH. Tel: 0845-0901234; Fax: 01242-221362; *Strength,* 1,180; *Chief Constable,* T. Brain

GREATER MANCHESTER POLICE, PO Box 22 (S West PDO), Chester House, Boyer Street, Manchester M16 0RE. Tel: 0161-872 5050; Fax: 0161-856 2666; *Strength,* 7,240; *Chief Constable,* Sir David Wilmot

HAMPSHIRE CONSTABULARY, Police Headquarters, West Hill, Winchester, Hampshire SO22 5DB. Tel: 0845-045 4545; Fax: 01962-871204; *Strength,* 3,465; *Chief Constable,* P. R. Kernaghan, QPM, LLB

HERTFORDSHIRE CONSTABULARY, Stanborough Road, Welwyn Garden City, Herts AL8 6XF. Tel: 01707-354200; Fax: 01707-354409; *Strength,* 1,847; *Chief Constable,* P. Acres

HUMBERSIDE POLICE, Queens Gardens, Kingston upon Hull HU1 3DJ. Tel: 01482-326111; Fax: 01482-220037; *Strength,* 2,053; *Chief Constable,* D. Westwood, QPM

KENT CONSTABULARY, Sutton Road, Maidstone, Kent ME15 9BZ. Tel: 01622-690690; Fax: 01622-690511; *Strength,* 3,341; *Chief Constable,* Sir David Phillips, QPM

LANCASHIRE CONSTABULARY, PO Box 77, Hutton, Preston, Lancashire PR4 5SB. Tel: 01772-614444; Fax: 01772-618843; *Strength*, 3,327; *Chief Contstable*, Mrs P. Clare, QPM

LEICESTERSHIRE CONSTABULARY, St John's, Enderby, Leicester LE19 2BX. Tel: 0116-222 2222; Fax: 0116-248 2227; *Strength*, 2,065; *Chief Constable*, D. J. Wyrko, QPM

LINCOLNSHIRE POLICE, PO Box 999, Lincoln LN5 7PH. Tel: 01522-532222; Fax: 01522-558229; *Strength*, 1,228; *Chief Constable*, R. J. N. Childs

MERSEYSIDE POLICE, PO Box 59, Liverpool L69 1JD. Tel: 0151-709 6010; Fax: 0151-777 8999; *Strength*, 4,109; *Chief Constable*, N. Bettison, QPM

NORFOLK CONSTABULARY, Police Headquarters, Jubilee House, Wymondham, Norfolk NR18 0WW. Tel: 01953-424242; Fax: 01953-424241; *Strength*, 1,475; *Chief Constable*, K. Williams

NORTHAMPTONSHIRE POLICE, Wootton Hall, Northampton NN4 0JQ. Tel: 01604-700700; Fax: 01604-703028; *Strength*, 1,120; *Chief Executive*, C. Fox

NORTHUMBRIA POLICE, Force Headquarters, North Road, Ponteland, Newcastle upon Tyne NE20 0BL. Tel: 01661-872555; Fax: 01661-868928; *Strength*, 3,927; *Chief Constable*, C. Strachan

NORTH YORKSHIRE POLICE, Newby Wiske Hall, Newby Wiske, Northallerton, N. Yorks DL7 9HA. Tel: 01609-783131; Fax: 01609-789213; *Strength*, 1,420; *Chief Constable*, D. R. Kenworthy

NOTTINGHAMSHIRE POLICE, Sherwood Lodge, Arnold, Nottingham NG5 8PP. Tel: 0115-967 0999; Fax: 0115-967 0900; *Strength*, 2,347; *Chief Constable*, S. M. Green

SOUTH YORKSHIRE POLICE, Snig Hill, Sheffield S3 8LY. Tel: 0114-220 2020; Fax: 0114-252 3154; *Strength*, 3,200; *Chief Constable*, M. Hedges

STAFFORDSHIRE POLICE, Cannock Road, Stafford ST17 0QG. Tel: 01785-257717(S)/232425(D); Fax: 01785-232313; *Strength*, 2,172; *Chief Constable*, J. Giffard

SUFFOLK CONSTABULARY HEADQUARTERS, Force Headquarters, Portal Avenue, Martlesham Heath, Ipswich IP5 3QS. Tel: 01473-613500; Fax: 01473-610876; *Strength*, 1,191; *Chief Constable*, P. J. Scott-Lee, QPM

SURREY POLICE, Mount Browne, Sandy Lane, Guildford, Surrey GU3 1HG. Tel: 01483-571212; Fax: 01483-300279; *Strength*, 1,994; *Chief Constable*, D. O'Connor

SUSSEX POLICE, Malling House, Church Lane, Lewes, E. Sussex BN7 2DZ. Tel: 0845-60 70 999; Fax: 01273-404274; *Strength*, 2,964; *Chief Constable*, K. Jones

THAMES VALLEY POLICE, Oxford Road, Kidlington, Oxon OX5 2NX. Tel: 01865-846000; Fax: 01865-846160; *Strength*, 3,778; *Chief Constable*, P. Neyroud

WARWICKSHIRE POLICE, PO Box 4, Leek Wootton, Warwick CV35 7QB. Tel: 01926-415000; Fax: 01926-415188; *Strength*, 969; *Chief Constable*, J. Burbeck, QPM, FIMGT

WEST MERCIA CONSTABULARY, Hindlip Hall, PO Box 55, Worcester WR3 8SP. Tel: 01905-723000; Fax: 01905-454226; *Strength*, 2,018; *Chief Constable*, P. Hampson, QPM

WEST MIDLANDS POLICE, PO Box 52, Lloyd House, Colmore Circus, Queensway, Birmingham B4 6NQ. Tel: 0845-113 5000; Fax: 0121-626 5695; *Strength*, 7,711; *Chief Constable*, Sir Edward Crew, QPM, OStJ, DL, CI MGT

WEST YORKSHIRE POLICE, PO Box 9, Laburnum Road, Wakefield, W. Yorks WF1 3QP. Tel: 01924-375222; Fax: 01924-292182; *Strength*, 4,899; *Chief Constable*, G. Moore

WILTSHIRE CONSTABULARY, Police Headquarters, London Road, Devizes, Wilts SN10 2DN. Tel: 01380-722341; Fax: 01380-734176; *Strength*, 1,128; *Chief Constable*, Miss E. Neville

WALES

DYFED-POWYS POLICE, PO Box 99, Llangunnor, Carmarthen, Carmarthenshire SA31 2PF. Tel: 01267-222020; Fax: 01267-222185; *Strength*, 1,128; *Chief Constable*, T. Grange QPM, MSC

GWENT POLICE, Police Headquarters, Turnpike Road, Croesyceiliog, Cwmbran, Gwent NP44 2XJ. Tel: 01633-838111; Fax: 01633-865211; *Strength*, 1,260; *Chief Constable*, K. Turner, O ST J, QPM

NORTH WALES POLICE, Glan-y-don, Colwyn Bay, Conwy LL29 8AW. Tel: 0845-607 1002; Fax: 01492-511232; *Strength*, 1,426; *Chief Constable*, R. Brunstrom

SOUTH WALES POLICE, Police Headquarters, Cowbridge Road, Bridgend CF31 3SU. Tel: 01656-655555; Fax: 01656-869399; *Strength*, 3,243; *Chief Constable*, Sir Anthony Burden, QPM

SCOTLAND

CENTRAL SCOTLAND POLICE, Randolphfield, Stirling FK8 2HD. Tel: 01786-456000; Fax: 01786-451177; *Strength*, 712; *Chief Constable*, A. Cameron, QPM

DUMFRIES AND GALLOWAY CONSTABULARY, Police Headquarters, Cornwall Mount, Dumfries DG1 1PZ. Tel: 01387-252112; Fax: 01387-260501; *Strength*, 490; *Chief Constable*, D. Strang

FIFE CONSTABULARY, Police Headquarters, Detroit Road, Glenrothes, Fife KY6 2RJ. Tel: 01592-418888; Fax: 01592-418444; *Strength*, 892; *Chief Constable*, P. M. Wilson, QPM, LLB

GRAMPIAN POLICE, Force Headquarters, Queen Street, Aberdeen AB10 1ZA. Tel: 01224-386000; Fax: 01224-643366; *Strength*, 1,228; *Chief Constable*, A. G. Brown, QPM

LOTHIAN AND BORDERS POLICE, Fettes Avenue, Edinburgh EH4 1RB. Tel: 0131-311 3131; Fax: 0131-311 3580; *Strength*, 2,582; *Chief Constable*, P. Tomkins

NORTHERN CONSTABULARY, Police Headquarters, Old Perth Road, Inverness IV2 3SY. Tel: 01463-715555; Fax: 01463-720373; *Strength*, 684; *Chief Constable*, W. Robertson

STRATHCLYDE POLICE, HQ, 173 Pitt Street, Glasgow G2 4JS. Tel: 0141-532 2000; Fax: 0141-532 2475; *Strength*, 7,200; *Chief Constable*, W. Rae, QPM

TAYSIDE POLICE, PO Box 59, 4 West Bell Street, Dundee DD1 9JU. Tel: 01382-223200; Fax: 01382-200449; *Strength*, 1,164; *Chief Constable*, J. Vine

NORTHERN IRELAND

POLICE SERVICE OF NORTHERN IRELAND, Police Headquarters, Brooklyn, 65 Knock Road, Belfast BT5 6LE. Tel: 028-9065 0222; Fax: 028-9070 0124; *Strength*, 9,218; *Chief Constable*, H. Orde

ISLANDS

ISLAND POLICE FORCE, Hospital Lane, St Peter Port, Guernsey GY1 2QN. Tel: 01481-725111; Fax: 01481-245136; *Strength*, 166; *Chief Constable*, M. H. Wyeth

STATES OF JERSEY POLICE, Rouge Bouillon, PO Box 789, St Helier, Jersey JE2 3ZA. Tel: 01534-612612; Fax: 01534-612116; *Strength*, 240; *Chief Officer*, G. Power

ISLE OF MAN CONSTABULARY, Police Headquarters, Glencrutchery Road, Douglas, Isle of Man IM2 4RG. Tel: 01624-631212; Fax: 01624-628113; *Strength*, 244; *Chief Constable*, M. Culverhouse

METROPOLITAN POLICE SERVICE
New Scotland Yard, Broadway, London SW1H 0BG
Tel 020-7230 1212

Strength: (July 2001), 25,485

Commissioner, Sir John Stevens, QPM, LLB, MPhil
Deputy Commissioner, Ian Blair, QPM, MA (Oxon)

OPERATIONAL AREAS

Assistant Commissioners, T. Ghaffur, QPM *(Policy, Review and Standards)*; M. Todd, QPM *(Territorial Policing)*

SPECIALIST OPERATIONS DEPARTMENT

Assistant Commissioner, D. Veness, CBE, QPM
Deputy Assistant Commissioners, P. J. Clarke; M. A. Fuller; W. I. Griffiths, BEM, QPM, C. A Howlett, QPM
Commanders, A. J. Brown; R. C. Pearce

CITY OF LONDON POLICE
37 Wood Street, London EC2P 2NQ
Tel 020-7601 2222

Strength: (February 2002), 735

Though small, the City of London includes one of the most important financial centres in the world and the force has particular expertise in areas such as fraud investigation as well as the areas required of any police force. The force has a wholly elected police authority, the police committee of the Corporation of London, which appoints the Commissioner.
Commissioner, P. Nove, QPM
Assistant Commissioner, J. Hart, QPM
Commander, F. Armstrong
Chairman of Police Committee, S. Walsh

BRITISH TRANSPORT POLICE
15 Tavistock Place, London WC1H 9SJ
Tel 020-7388 7541

Strength: (March 2002), 2,123

British Transport Police is the national police force for the railways in England, Wales and Scotland, including the London Underground system, Docklands Light Railway, Midland Metro Tram system and Croydon Tramlink. The Chief Constable reports to the British Transport Police Committee. The members of the Committee are appointed by the Strategic Rail Authority.
Chief Constable, I. Johnston, CBE, QPM
Deputy Chief Constable, J. A. Lake

MINISTRY OF DEFENCE POLICE
MDP Wethersfield, Braintree, Essex CM7 4AZ
Tel 01371-854115

Strength: (March 2002), 3,755

The Ministry of Defence Police is a civilian police force geared to meeting the requirements of the MOD and other customers including visiting forces and the Royal Mint. Other specialist services include marine policing, dogs, firearms and Police Search Teams. The Force also has its own Criminal Investigation Department with specialist officers working in the field of fraud investigation and can also offer crime prevention advice.
Chief Constable, D. L. Clarke, QPM
Deputy Chief Constable, D. A. Ray, QPM, MA, LLM
Head of Secretariat, P. A. Crowther

ROYAL PARKS CONSTABULARY
The Old Police House, Hyde Park, London W2 2UH
Tel 020-7298 2000

Strength: (August 2002), 154

The Royal Parks Constabulary is maintained by the Royal Parks Agency, an executive agency of the Department for Culture, Media and Sport, and is responsible for the policing of eight royal parks in and around London.
Chief Officer (acting), D. Pollock
Deputy Chief Officer, K. Quinn

UNITED KINGDOM ATOMIC ENERGY AUTHORITY CONSTABULARY
Building E6, Culham Science Centre, Abingdon, Oxon OX14 3DB Tel 01235-463760

Strength: (February 2002), 531

The Constabulary is responsible for policing the United Kingdom Atomic Energy Authority, URENCO (Uranium Enrichment Services Worldwide) and British Nuclear Fuels plc establishments and for escorting nuclear material between establishments within the UK and worldwide.
Chief Constable, W. F. Pryke
Deputy Chief Constable, P. P. Crossan

STAFF ASSOCIATIONS

Police officers are not permitted to join a trade union or to take strike action. All ranks have their own staff associations.
ASSOCIATION OF CHIEF POLICE OFFICERS OF ENGLAND, Wales and Northern Ireland, 7th Floor, 25 Victoria Street, London SW1H 0EX. Tel: 020-7227 3434. *Chief Executive,* Miss M. C. E. Barton, OBE
THE POLICE SUPERINTENDENTS' ASSOCIATION OF ENGLAND AND WALES, 67A Reading Road, Pangbourne, Reading RG8 7JD. Tel: 0118-984 4005. *National Secretary,* Chief Supt. D. Palmer
THE POLICE FEDERATION OF ENGLAND AND WALES, 15–17 Langley Road, Surbiton, Surrey KT6 6LP. Tel: 020-8399 2224. *General Secretary,* C. Elliott
ASSOCIATION OF CHIEF POLICE OFFICERS IN SCOTLAND, Police Headquarters, 173 Pitt Street, Glasgow G2 4JS. Tel: 0141-532 2052. *Hon. Secretary,* W. Rae, QPM
THE ASSOCIATION OF SCOTTISH POLICE SUPERINTENDENTS, Secretariat, 173 Pitt Street, Glasgow G2 4JS. Tel: 0141-221 5796. *President,* Chief Supt. A. Shanks
THE SCOTTISH POLICE FEDERATION, 5 Woodside Place, Glasgow G3 7QF. Tel: 0141-332 5234. *General Secretary,* D. J. Keil, QPM
THE SUPERINTENDENTS' ASSOCIATION OF NORTHERN IRELAND, 77–79 Garnerville Road, Belfast BT4 2NX. Tel: 028-9070 0660. *Hon. Secretary,* Supt. H. R. Phillips, MCIPD
THE POLICE FEDERATION FOR NORTHERN IRELAND, 77–79 Garnerville Road, Belfast BT4 2NX. Tel: 028-9076 4200. *Secretary,* D. A. McClurg

The Prison Service

The prison services in the United Kingdom are the responsibility of the Home Secretary, the Scottish Executive Justice Department and the Secretary of State for Northern Ireland. The chief director generals (Chief Executive in Scotland), officers of the Prison Service, the Scottish Prison Service and the Northern Ireland Prison Service are responsible for the day-to-day running of the system.

There are 140 prison establishments in England and Wales, 20 in Scotland and four in Northern Ireland. Convicted prisoners are classified according to their assessed security risk and are housed in establishments appropriate to that level of security. There are no open prisons in Northern Ireland. Female prisoners are housed in women's establishments or in separate wings of mixed prisons. Remand prisoners are, where possible, housed separately from convicted prisoners. Offenders under the age of 21 are usually detained in a young offender institution, which may be a separate establishment or part of a prison.

Nine prisons are now run by the private sector, and in England and Wales all escort services have been contracted out to private companies. Two prisons are being built and financed under the Private Finance Initiative and will also be run by private contractors. In Scotland, one prison (Kilmarnock) was built and financed by the private sector and is being operated by private contractors.

There are independent prison inspectorates in England and Wales and Scotland which report annually on conditions and the treatment of prisoners. HM Chief Inspector of Prisons for England and Wales also performs an inspectorate role for prisons in Northern Ireland. Every prison establishment also has an independent board of visitors or visiting committee made up of local volunteers. Any prisoner whose complaint is not satisfied by the internal complaints procedures may complain to the Prisons Ombudsman for England and Wales or the Scottish Prisons Complaints Commission. There is no Prisons Ombudsman for Northern Ireland, but complaints by prisoners regarding maladministration may be made to the Parliamentary Commissioner for Administration.

AVERAGE PRISON POPULATION 2001–2002(UK)

	Remand	Sentenced	Other
ENGLAND AND WALES			
Male	10,826	51,834	900
Female	828	3,038	46
Total	11,654	54,872	946
SCOTLAND			
Male	–	–	–
Female	–	–	–
Total	1,018	5,168	–
N. IRELAND			
Male	268	634	6
Female	7	10	1
Total	275	644	7
UK TOTAL	12,947	60,684	953

The projected prison population for 2007 in England and Wales is 78,100 if custody rates and sentence lengths remain at 2001 levels.

Sources: Home Office – Research Development Statistics; Scottish Prison Service – Annual Report and Accounts 2001–2002; Northern Ireland Prison Service – Annual Report 2001–2002

SENTENCED PRISON POPULATION BY SEX AND OFFENCE (ENGLAND AND WALES) *as at 30 April 2002*

	Male	Female
Violence against the person	11,604	510
Sexual offences	5,179	20
Burglary	8,806	210
Robbery	6,861	298
Theft, handling	4,632	527
Fraud and forgery	899	120
Drugs offences	8,636	1,310
Other offences	6,098	262
Offence not known	936	79
In default of payment of a fine	32	2
*TOTAL	53,683	3,338

*Figures do not include civil (non-criminal) prisoners
Source: Home Office – Research Development Statistics

AVERAGE SENTENCED POPULATION BY LENGTH OF SENTENCE 2001–2002 (ENGLAND AND WALES)

	Adults	Young Offenders
Less than 12 months	7,075	2,366
12 months to less than 4 years	16,175	4,220
4 years to less than 10 years	17,094	1,353
10 years less than life	2,543	22
Life	4,832	137
*TOTAL	47,719	8,098

*Figures include fine defaulters and non-criminals
Source: Home Office – Research Development Statistics

AVERAGE DAILY SENTENCED POPULATION BY LENGTH OF SENTENCE 2001–2002 (SCOTLAND)

	Adults	Young Offenders
Less than 4 years	2,108	460
4 years or over (including life)	2,431	168
TOTAL	4,539	628

Source: Scottish Prison Service – Annual Report and Accounts 2001–2002

PRISON SUICIDES 2002 (ENGLAND AND WALES)

Males	67
Females	8
TOTAL	75
Rate per 1,000 prisoners in custody	1.11

Source: Home Office – Research Development Statistics

AVERAGE NUMBER OF PRISON SERVICE STAFF 2001–2002 (GREAT BRITAIN)

	England and Wales	Scotland
No. of prison service staff	44,155	4,538

Sources: HM Prison Service – Annual Report and Accounts 2001–2002; Scottish Prison Service – Annual Report and Accounts 2001–2002

OPERATING COSTS OF PRISON SERVICE IN ENGLAND
AND WALES 2001–2002

	£
Staff costs	1,138,398,000
Other administrative costs	1,164,180,000
Operating income	(205,295,000)
Net operating costs for the year	2,245,313,000
Charge on capital employed	284,930,000
Net operating costs	2,245,313,000
Average cost per prisoner place	
(reflecting establishment costs only)	36,377

Source: HM Prison Service – Annual Report and Accounts
2001–2002

OPERATING COSTS OF SCOTTISH PRISON SERVICE
2001–2002

	£
Total income	2,374,000
Total expenditure	199,114,000
Staff costs	122,228,000
Running costs	55,983,000
Other current expenditure	20,903,000
Operating cost	(196,740,000)
Cost of capital charges	(21,671,000)
Interest payable and similar charges	(11,000)
Interest receivable	110,000
Lockerbie Trial Costs	2,810,000
Deficit for financial year	(221,122,000)
Average annual cost per prisoner per place	28,110

Source: Scottish Prison Service – Annual Report and Accounts
2001–2002

OPERATING COSTS OF NORTHERN IRELAND PRISON
SERVICE 2001–2

	£
Income	(128,000)
Staff Costs	70,867,000
Depreciation and other charges	7,544,000
Other Operating Costs	20,605,000
Total Expenditure	99,016,000
Net cost of Operations	98,888,000
Average annual cost per prisoner place	71,475

Source: Northern Ireland Prison Service – Annual Report and
Accounts 2001–2002

THE PRISON SERVICES

HM PRISON SERVICE

Cleland House, Page Street, London SW1P 4LN
Tel: 020-7217 6000; Fax: 020-7217 6403

SALARIES 2001–2

Senior Manager A	£44,520–£64,287
Senior Manager B	£42,960–£61,351
Senior Manager C	£38,240–£55,239
Senior Manager D	£34,050–£50,584
Manager E	£24,100–£38,069
Manager F	£19,910–£32,250
Manager G	£18,860–£26,430

THE PRISON SERVICE MANAGEMENT BOARD

Director-General (SCS), M. Narey
  Private Secretary, D. Drew
  Staff Officer, C. Sturt

Prisons and Probation Minister, Chairman of the Strategy
Board for Correctional Services, Beverley J. Hughes, MP
Director, Criminal Policy Group, Home Office, Ms S.
  Street
Deputy Director-General (SCS), P. Wheatley
Director of High Security Prisons (SCS), P. Atherton
Director of Security (SCS), B. Clark
Director of Personnel (SCS), G. Hadley
Director of Finance and Procurement (SCS), J. Steele
Director of Corporate Affairs (SCS), D. Howard
Director of Resettlement (SCS) (acting), C. Harnett
Head of the Prison Health Policy Unit (SCS), Dr F.
  Harvey
Non-Executive Members, Sir Duncan Nichol, CBE;
  P. Carter; R. Rosser
Board Secretary and Head of Secretariat, R. Yates
Chaplain-General and Archdeacon of the Prison Service,
  W. Noblett
Muslim Advisor, M. Ahmed
Race Equality Advisor, Ms J. Clements
Legal Adviser, S. Bramley

AREA MANAGERS (SCS)

Eastern, M. Spurr; East Midlands (North), D. Shaw; East
  Midlands (South), B. Perry; London, B. Duff; North
  East, M. Egan; North West, I. Lockwood; South East
  (Thames Valley and Hampshire), Mrs S. Payne; South
  East (Kent Surrey and Sussex), A. Smith; South West,
  J. Petherick; Wales, J. May; West Midlands, B.Payling;
  Yorkshire and Humberside, P. Earnshaw
Operational Manager for Women's Prisons, N. Clifford
Operational Manager for Juvenile Estate, D. Waplington
Operational Manager for High Security Prisons,
  P. Atherton

PRISON ESTABLISHMENTS – ENGLAND AND WALES

CNA Average number of in use certified normal
accommodation places without overcrowding 2001–2
Prisoners, 63,813
Prisoners/Young Offenders Average number of
prisoners/young offenders 2001–2002, Prisoners,
55,530, Young Offenders 10,994
ACKLINGTON, Morpeth, Northumberland NE65 9XH.
  CNA, 780. Prisoners, 759. Governor, R. Atkinson
ALBANY, Newport, Isle of Wight PO30 5RS. CNA, 446.
  Prisoners, 438. Governor, C. Allison
ALTCOURSE (PRIVATE PRISON), Higher Lane, Fazakerley,
  Liverpool L9 7AG. CNA, 600. Prisoners, 841. Director, W.
  MacGowan
†‡ASHFIELD, Shortwood Road, Pucklechurch, Bristol
  BS16 9QT. CNA, 400. Prisoners, 346. Director, (acting), J.
  Mullens
ASHWELL, Oakham, Leics LE15 7LF. CNA, 484. Prisoners,
  369. Governor (acting), D. Walmsley
*‡ASKHAM GRANGE, Askham Richard, York YO2 3PT.
  CNA, 132. Prisoners and Young Offenders, 120.
  Governor, I. Simmonds
‡AYLESBURY, Bierton Road, Aylesbury, Bucks HP20 1EH.
  CNA, 418. Young Offenders, 347. Governor, M. Bell
BEDFORD, St Loyes Street, Bedford MK40 1HG. CNA, 324.
  Prisoners, 440. Governor, A. Cross
†BELMARSH, Western Way, Thamesmead, London SE28
  0EB. CNA, 843. Prisoners, 699. Governor, G. Hughes
BIRMINGHAM, Winson Green Road, Birmingham B18
  4AS. CNA, 722. Prisoners, 836. Governor, M. Shann
BLAKENHURST, Hewell Lane, Redditch, Worcs B97 6QS.
  CNA, 647. Prisoners, 842. Governor, M. Lomas
BLANTYRE HOUSE, Goudhurst, Cranbrook, Kent TN17
  2NH. CNA, 120. Prisoners, 120. Governor, C. Bartlett

BLUNDESTON, Lowestoft, Suffolk NR32 5BG. *CNA*, 424. *Prisoners*, 412. *Governor*, J. Knight

†‡BRINSFORD, New Road, Featherstone, Wolverhampton WV10 7PY. *CNA*, 477. *Young Offenders*, 460. *Governor*, T. Watson

BRISTOL, Cambridge Road, Bristol BS7 8PS. *CNA*, 490. *Prisoners*, 586. *Governor*, N. Wall

BRIXTON, PO Box 369, Jebb Avenue, London SW2 5XF. *CNA*, 651. *Prisoners*, 766. *Governor*, S. Twinn

*†‡BROCKHILL, Redditch, Worcs B97 6RD. *CNA*, 159. *Prisoners and Young Offenders*, 155. *Governor*, D. Elaine

BUCKLEY HALL (PRIVATE PRISON), Buckley Farm Lane, Rochdale, Lancs OL12 9DP. *CNA*, 350. *Prisoners*, 367 *Governor*, S. Morrison

BULLINGDON, PO Box 50, Bicester, Oxon OX6 0PR. *CNA*, 767. *Prisoners*, 913. *Acting Governor*, S. Sanders

*‡BULLWOOD HALL, High Road, Hockley, Essex SS5 4TE. *CNA*, 180. *Prisoners and Young Offenders*, 169. *Governor*, T. Hassall

CAMP HILL, Newport, Isle of Wight PO30 5PB. *CNA*, 481 *Prisoners*, 525. *Governor*, S. Metcalf

CANTERBURY, 46 Longport, Canterbury CT1 1PJ. *CNA*, 196. *Prisoners*, 290. *Governor*, Ms H. Rinaldi

†‡CARDIFF, Knox Road, Cardiff CF2 1UG. *CNA*, 435. *Prisoners and Young Offenders*, 645. *Governor*, J. Thomas-Ferrand

‡CASTINGTON, Morpeth, Northumberland NE65 9XG. *CNA*, 400. *Young Offenders*, 262. *Governor*, M. Lees

CHANNINGS WOOD, Denbury, Newton Abbott, Devon TQ12 6DW. *CNA*, 594. *Prisoners*, 587. *Governor*, N. Evans

†‡CHELMSFORD, 200 Springfield Road, Chelmsford, Essex CM2 6LQ. *CNA*, 450. *Prisoners and Young Offenders*, 459. *Governor*, P. Haley

COLDINGLEY, Bisley, Woking, Surrey GU24 9EX. *CNA*, 370. *Prisoners*, 368. *Governor*, J. Dixon

*COOKHAM WOOD, Rochester, Kent ME1 3LU. *CNA*, 120. *Prisoners*, 146. *Governor*, S. West

DARTMOOR, Princetown, Yelverton, Devon PL20 6RR. *CNA*, 691. *Prisoners*, 636. *Governor*, G. Johnson

‡DEERBOLT, Bowes Road, Barnard Castle, Co. Durham DL12 9BG. *CNA*, 472. *Young Offenders*, 456. *Governor*, P. Copple

†‡DONCASTER (PRIVATE PRISON), Off North Bridge, Marshgate, Doncaster DN5 8UX. *CNA*, 771. *Prisoners and Young Offenders*, 1,103. *Director*, K. Rogers

†‡DORCHESTER, North Square, Dorchester DT1 1JD. *CNA*, 172. *Prisoners and Young Offenders*, 272. *Governor*, R. Bateman

DOVEGATE (PRIVATE PRISON), Uttoxeter, ST14 8XR. *CNA*, 800, *Prisoners*, 698. *Director*, P. Wright.

‡DOVER, The Citadel, Western Heights, Dover CT17 9DR. *CNA*, 316. *Young Offenders*, 288. *Governor*, C. Kershaw

DOWNVIEW, Sutton Lane, Sutton, Surrey SM2 5PD. *CNA*, 294. *Prisoners*, 262. *Governor*, D. Lancaster

*‡DRAKE HALL, Eccleshall, Staffs ST21 6LQ. *CNA*, 267. *Prisoners and Young Offenders*, 241. *Governor*, P. Tidball

*†DURHAM, Old Elvet, Durham DH1 3HU. *CNA*, 632. *Prisoners*, 711. *Governor*, M. Newell

*‡EAST SUTTON PARK, Sutton Valence, Maidstone, Kent ME17 3DF. *CNA*, 94. *Prisoners and Young Offenders*, 94. *Governor*, Revd R. Carter

*†‡EASTWOOD PARK, Falfield, Wotton-under-Edge, Glos GL12 8DB. *CNA*, 295. *Prisoners and Young Offenders*, 303. *Governor*, P. Winkley.

ELMLEY, Church Road, Eastchurch, Sheerness, Kent ME12 4AY. *CNA*, 763. *Prisoners*, 894. *Governor*, B. Pollett

ERLESTOKE, Devizes, Wilts SN10 5TU. *CNA*, 326. *Prisoners*, 315. *Governor*, Mrs J. Blake

EVERTHORPE, Brough, E. Yorks HU15 1RB. *CNA*, 438. *Prisoners*, 380. *Governor*, P. Midgley

†‡EXETER, New North Road, Exeter EX4 4EX. *CNA*, 321. *Prisoners and Young Offenders*, 469. *Governor*, G. Deighton

FEATHERSTONE, New Road, Wolverhampton WV10 7PU. *CNA*, 597. *Prisoners*, 593. *Governor*, M. Pascoe

†‡FELTHAM, Bedfont Road, Feltham, Middx TW13 4ND. *CNA*, 712. *Prisoners and Young Offenders*, 660. *Governor*, N. Pascoe

FORD, Arundel, W. Sussex BN18 0BX. *CNA*, 501. *Prisoners*, 498. *Governor*, K. Kan

FOREST BANK, Agecroft Road, Pendlebury, Manchester M27 8UE. *CNA*, 800. *Prisoners*, 817. *Director*, M. Goodwin

*‡FOSTON HALL, Foston, Derbys DE65 5DN. *CNA*, 214. *Prisoners*, 208. *Governor*, Ms P. Scriven

FRANKLAND, Brasside, Durham DH1 5YD. *CNA*, 653. *Prisoners*, 629. *Governor*, I. Woods

FULL SUTTON, Full Sutton, York YO41 1PS. *CNA*, 595. *Prisoners*, 584. *Governor*, D. Roberts

GARTH, Ulnes Walton Lane, Leyland, Preston PR5 3NE. *CNA*, 633. *Prisoners*, 618. *Governor*, J. Illingsworth

GARTREE, Gallow Field Road, Market Harborough, Leics LE16 7RP. *CNA*, 366. *Prisoners*, 276. *Governor*, S. McAllister

†‡GLEN PARVA, Tigers Road, Wigston, Leicester LE8 4TN. *CNA*, 664. *Prisoners*, 794. *Governor*, C. Bushell

†‡GLOUCESTER, Barrack Square, Gloucester GL1 2JN. *CNA*, 236. *Prisoners and Young Offenders*, 270. *Governor*, D. Chalmers

GRENDON/SPRING HILL, Grendon Underwood, Aylesbury, Bucks HP18 0TL. *CNA*, 497. *Prisoners*, 434. *Governor*, W. Payne

‡GUYS MARSH, Shaftesbury, Dorset SP7 0AH. *CNA*, 442. *Prisoners and Young Offenders*, 507. *Governor*, Mrs D. Calvert

‡HATFIELD, Thorne Road, Hatfield, Doncaster DN7 6EL. *CNA*, 180. *Young Offenders*, 169. *Governor*, T. Watson

HAVERIGG, Millom, Cumbria LA18 4NA. *CNA*, 564. *Prisoners*, 556. *Governor*, G. Brunskill

HEWELL GRANGE, Redditch, Worcs B97 6QQ. *CNA*, 187. *Prisoners*, 185. *Governor*, N. Croft

HIGH DOWN, Sutton Lane, Sutton, Surrey SM2 5PJ. *CNA*, 645. *Prisoners*, 645. *Governor*, T. Butt

*HIGHPOINT, Stradishall, Newmarket, Suffolk CB8 9YG. *CNA*, 850. *Prisoners*, 222. *Governor*, S. Doolan

†‡HINDLEY, Gibson Street, Bickershaw, Wigan, Lancs WN2 5TH. *CNA*, 535. *Prisoners*, 446. *Governor*, J. Heavens

‡HOLLESLEY BAY COLONY, Woodbridge, Suffolk IP12 3JW. *CNA*, 463. *Prisoners and Young Offenders*, 311. *Governor*, S. Robinson

*†‡HOLLOWAY, Parkhurst Road, London N7 0NU. *CNA*, 508. *Prisoners and Young Offenders*, 467. *Governor*, E. Willetts

HOLME HOUSE, Holme House Road, Stockton-on-Tees TS18 2QU. *CNA*, 874. *Prisoners*, 971. *Governor*, R. Crouch

†‡HULL, Hedon Road, Hull HU9 5LS. *CNA*, 466. *Prisoners and Young Offenders*, 628. *Governor*, S. Wagstaffe

‡HUNTERCOMBE, Huntercombe Place, Nuffield, Henley-on-Thames RG9 5SB. *CNA*, 360. *Young Offenders*, 314. *Governor*, E. Jones

KINGSTON, 122 Milton Road, Portsmouth PO3 6AS. *CNA*, 193. *Prisoners*, 181. *Governor*, A. Munro

KIRKHAM, Freckleton Road, Preston PR4 2RN. *CNA*, 561. *Prisoners*, 479. *Governor*, D. Thomas

KIRKLEVINGTON GRANGE, Yarm, Cleveland TS15 9PA. *CNA*, 183. *Prisoners*, 179. *Governor*, Ms S. Anthony

LANCASTER, The Castle, Lancaster LA1 1YL. *CNA*, 240 *Prisoners*, 229. *Governor*, T. Williams

†‡LANCASTER FARMS, Far Moor Lane, Stone Row Head, off Quernmore Road, Lancaster LA1 3QZ. *CNA,* 496. *Prisoners and Young Offenders,* 457. *Governor,* R. McColm

LATCHMERE HOUSE, Church Road, Ham Common, Richmond, Surrey TW10 5HH. *CNA,* 193. *Prisoners,* 169. *Governor,* T. Hinchliffe

LEEDS, Armley, Leeds LS12 2TJ. *CNA,* 770. *Prisoners,* 1,256. *Governor,* S. Tasker

LEICESTER, Welford Road, Leicester LE2 7AJ. *CNA,* 193. *Prisoners,* 361. *Governor,* R. Kellett

†‡LEWES, Brighton Road, Lewes, E. Sussex BN7 1EA. *CNA,* 485. *Prisoners and Young Offenders,* 525. *Governor,* P. Carroll

LEYHILL, Wotton-under-Edge, Glos GL12 8BT. *CNA,* 422. *Prisoners,* 432. *Governor,* R. Booty

LINCOLN, Greetwell Road, Lincoln LN2 4BD. *CNA,* 374. *Prisoners,* 546. *Governor,* R. Peacock

§LINDHOLME, Bawtry Road, Hatfield Woodhouse, Doncaster DN7 6EE. *CNA,* 649 *Prisoners,* 644. *Governor,* M. Read

LITTLEHEY, Perry, Huntingdon, Cambs PE18 0SR. *CNA,* 624. *Prisoners,* 627. *Governor,* J. Morgan

LIVERPOOL, 68 Hornby Road, Liverpool L9 3DF. *CNA,* 1,216. *Prisoners,* 1,257. *Governor,* C. Sheffield

LONG LARTIN, South Littleton, Evesham, Worcs WR11 5TZ. *CNA,* 599. *Prisoners,* 448. *Governor,* J. Mullen

LOWDHAM GRANGE (PRIVATE PRISON), Lowdham, Notts NG14 7TA. *CNA,* 504. *Prisoners,* 489. *Director,* A. Bramley

*†‡LOW NEWTON, Brasside, Durham DH1 5SD. *CNA,* 247. *Prisoners and Young Offenders,* 293. *Governor,* D. Thompson

MAIDSTONE, 36 County Road, Maidstone ME14 1UZ. *CNA,* 452. *Prisoners,* 438. *Governor,* J. Galbally

MANCHESTER, Southall Street, Manchester M60 9AH. *CNA,* 953. *Prisoners,* 1,105. *Governor,* J. Smith

‡MOORLAND, Bawtry Road, Hatfield Woodhouse, Doncaster DN7 6BW. *CNA,* 770. *Prisoners,* 754. *Governor,* B. McCourt

MORTON HALL, Swinderby, Lincoln LN6 9PS. *CNA,* 192. *Prisoners,* 180. *Governor,* L. Saunders

THE MOUNT, Molyneaux Avenue, Bovingdon, Hemel Hempstead HP3 0NZ. *CNA,* 704. *Prisoners,* 758. *Governor,* P. Wailen

*†‡NEW HALL, Dial Wood, Flockton, Wakefield WF4 4AX. *CNA,* 327. *Prisoners and Young Offenders,* 378. *Governor,* V. Bird, OBE

†‡NORTHALLERTON, 15A East Road, Northallerton, N. Yorks DL6 1NW. *CNA,* 153. *Prisoners,* 222. *Governor,* M. Ward

NORTH SEA CAMP, Freiston, Boston, Lincs PE22 0QX. *CNA,* 208. *Prisoners,* 199. *Governor,* M. A. Lewis

†‡NORWICH, Mousehold, Norwich NR1 4LU. *CNA,* 561. *Prisoners and Young Offenders,* 722. *Governor,* M. Knight

NOTTINGHAM, Perry Road, Sherwood, Nottingham NG5 3AG. *CNA,* 398. *Prisoners,* 508. *Governor,* K. Beaumont

‡ONLEY, Willoughby, Rugby, Warks CV23 8AP. *CNA,* 640. *Young Offenders,* 576. *Governor,* R. Fielder

†‡PARC (PRIVATE PRISON), Heol Hopcyn John, Bridgend CF35 6AR. *CNA,* 844. *Prisoners and Young Offenders,* 869. *Director,* J. Evans

PARKHURST, Newport, Isle of Wight PO30 5NX. *CNA,* 482. *Prisoners,* 427. *Governor,* D. Kennedy

PENTONVILLE, Caledonian Road, London N7 8TT. *CNA,* 897. *Prisoners,* 1,122. *Governor,* G. Davies

‡PORTLAND, Easton, Portland, Dorset DT5 1DL. *CNA,* 512. *Young Offenders,* 480. *Governor,* K. Lockyer

‡PRESCOED, 47 Maryport Street, Usk, Gwent NP5 1XP. *CNA,* 120. *Prisoners and Young Offenders,* 111

Governor, R. J. Comber

PRESTON, 2 Ribbleton Lane, Preston PR1 5AB. *CNA,* 434. *Prisoners,* 542. *Governor,* A. Scott

RANBY, Ranby, Retford, Notts DN22 8EV. *CNA,* 679. *Prisoners,* 738. *Governor,* V. Hart

†‡READING, Forbury Road, Reading RG1 3HY. *CNA,* 195. *Prisoners and Young Offenders,* 247. *Governor,* N. Leader

*RISLEY, Risley, Warrington WA3 6BP. *CNA,* 819. *Prisoners,* 800. *Governor,* C. McConnell

†‡ROCHESTER, 1 Fort Road, Rochester, Kent ME1 3QS. *CNA,* 355. *Prisoners and Young Offenders,* 45. *Governor,* J. Robinson

RYE HILL (PRIVATE PRISON), Onley, Rugby CV23 8AM. *CNA,* 600. *Prisoners and Young Offenders,* 596. *Director,* A. Rose-Quirie

*SEND, Ripley Road, Send, Woking, Surrey GU23 7LJ. *CNA,* 220. *Prisoners,* 216. *Governor,* T. Beeston

SHEPTON MALLET, Cornhill, Shepton Mallet, Somerset BA4 5LU. *CNA,* 195. *Prisoners,* 150. *Governor,* B. McAlley

SHREWSBURY, The Dana, Shrewsbury SY1 2HR. *CNA,* 184. *Prisoners,* 325. *Governor,* M. Bolton

HMP SPRING HILL, Grendon Underwood, Aylesbury, Bucks, HP18 0TH

STAFFORD, 54 Gaol Road, Stafford ST16 3AW. *CNA,* 627. *Prisoners,* 619. *Governor,* L. Taylor

STANDFORD HILL, Church Road, Eastchurch, Isle of Sheppey, Kent ME12 4AA. *CNA,* 384. *Prisoners,* 332. *Governor,* J. Robinson

STOCKEN, Stocken Hall Road, Stretton, nr Oakham, Leics LE15 7RD. *CNA,* 556. *Prisoners,* 578. *Governor,* B. Edwards

‡STOKE HEATH, Stoke Heath, Market Drayton, Shropshire TF9 2JL. *CNA,* 564. *Prisoners,* 546. *Governor,* C. James

*‡STYAL, Wilmslow, Cheshire SK9 4HR. *CNA,* 412. *Prisoners and Young Offenders,* 436. *Governor,* Ms M. Moulden

SUDBURY, Ashbourne, Derbys DE6 5HW. *CNA,* 511. *Prisoners,* 506. *Governor,* C. Davidson

SWALESIDE, Brabazon Road, Eastchurch, Isle of Sheppey, Kent ME12 4AX. *CNA,* 747. *Prisoners,* 746. *Governor,* M. Conway

†SWANSEA, 200 Oystermouth Road, Swansea SA1 3SR. *CNA,* 251. *Prisoners,* 346. *Governor,* Miss V. O'Dea

‡SWINFEN HALL, Lichfield, Staffs WS14 9QS. *CNA,* 320. *Young Offenders,* 308 *Governor,* Ms J. Mosley

‡THORN CROSS, Arley Road, Appleton Thorn, Warrington WA4 4RL. *CNA,* 316. *Young Offenders,* 212. *Governor,* C. Davies

USK, 47 Maryport Street, Usk, Gwent NP5 1XP. *CNA,* 128. *Prisoners,* 216. *Governor,* R. J. Comber

THE VERNE, Portland, Dorset DT5 1EQ. *CNA,* 552. *Prisoners,* 562. *Governor,* M. Cook

WAKEFIELD, 5 Love Lane, Wakefield WF2 9AG. *CNA,* 561. *Prisoners,* 558. *Governor,* J. Slater

WANDSWORTH, Heathfield Road, London SW18 3HS. *CNA,* 1,163. *Prisoners,* 1,301. *Governor,* J. Heavens

WAYLAND, Griston, Thetford, Norfolk IP25 6RL. *CNA,* 618. *Prisoners,* 623. *Governor,* Mrs K. Crawley

WEALSTUN, Wetherby, W. Yorks LS23 7AZ. *CNA,* 632. *Prisoners,* 583. *Governor,* S. Tilley

WEARE, Portland Dock, Castletown, Portland, Dorset DT5 1PZ. *CNA,* 400. *Prisoners,* 374. *Governor,* Ms S. F. McCormick

WELLINGBOROUGH, Millers Park, Doddington Road, Wellingborough, Northants NN8 2NH. *CNA,* 518. *Prisoners,* 449. *Governor,* Dr P. Bennett

‡WERRINGTON, Werrington, Stoke-on-Trent ST9 0DX. *CNA,* 132. *Young Offenders,* 122. *Governor,* J. Hughes

‡WETHERBY, York Road, Wetherby, W. Yorks LS22 5ED. CNA, 360. *Young Offenders,* 347. *Governor,* S. McEwan

WHATTON, 14 Cromwell Road, Nottingham NG13 9FQ. CNA, 275. *Prisoners,* 272. *Governor,* B. Greenberry

WHITEMOOR, Longhill Road, March, Cambs PE15 0PR. CNA, 500. *Prisoners,* 418. *Governor,* B. Perry

*WINCHESTER, Romsey Road, Winchester SO22 5DF. CNA, 437. *Prisoners* 528. *Governor,* J. Gomersall

THE WOLDS (PRIVATE PRISON), Everthorpe, Brough, E. Yorks HU15 2JZ. CNA, 360. *Prisoners,* 397. *Director,* D. McDonnell

†‡§WOODHILL, Tattenhoe Street, Milton Keynes MK4 4DA. CNA, 677. *Prisoners and Young Offenders,* 743. *Governor,* B. Mullen

WORMWOOD SCRUBS, PO Box 757, Du Cane Road, London W12 0AE. CNA, 952. *Prisoners,* 947. *Governor,* K. Munns

WYMOTT, Ulnes Walton Lane, Leyland, Preston PR5 3LW. CNA, 809. *Prisoners,* 793. *Governor,* A. Scott

Note: HMP Peterborough opening 2003

SCOTTISH PRISON SERVICE

Calton House, 5 Redheughs Rigg, Edinburgh EH12 9HW Tel: 0131-556 8400

SALARIES 2001–2

Senior managers in the Scottish Prison Service, including governors and deputy governors of prisons, are paid across three pay bands:

Band I	£48,000-£68,000
Band H	£38,100-£48,100
Band G	£30,000-£40,000

Chief Executive of Scottish Prison Service, A. Cameron
Director, Human Resources, B. Allison
Director, Finance and Information Systems, W. Pretswell
Director, Strategy and Business Performance, K. Thomson
Deputy Director, Rehabilitation and Care, A. Spencer
Deputy Director, Estates and Buildings, D. Williams
Operations Director, South and West, M. Duffy
Operations Director, North and East, P. Withers
Head of Training, Scottish Prison Service College, vacant
Head of Communications, T. Fox

PRISON ESTABLISHMENTS

Prisoners/ Young Offenders Average number of prisoners/young offenders 2001–2

*ABERDEEN, Craiginches, Aberdeen AB9 2HN. *Prisoners,* 197. *Governor,* A. Mooney

BARLINNIE, Barlinnie, Glasgow G33 2QX. *Prisoners,* 1,089. *Governor,* W. McKinlay

CASTLE HUNTLY, Castle Huntly, Longforgan, nr Dundee DD2 5HL. *Prisoners,* 136. *Governor,* I. Whitehead

*‡CORNTON VALE, Cornton Road, Stirling FK9 5NY. *Prisoners and Young Offenders,* 201. *Governor,* S. Swan

*‡DUMFRIES, Terregles Street, Dumfries DG2 9AX. *Young Offenders,* 51. *Governor,* C. McGeever

EDINBURGH, 33 Stenhouse Road, Edinburgh EH1 3LN. *Prisoners,* 688. *Governor,* R. MacCowan

‡GLENOCHIL, King O'Muir Road, Tullibody, Clackmannanshire FK10 3AD. *Prisoners and Young Offenders,* 485. *Governor,* K. Donegan

GREENOCK, Gateside, Greenock PA16 9AH. *Prisoners,* 317. *Governor,* vacant

*INVERNESS, Porterfield, Inverness IV2 3HH. *Prisoners,* 133. *Governor,* A. MacDonald

KILMARNOCK (PRIVATE PRISON), Bowhouse, Mauchline Road, Kilmarnock KA1 5JH. *Prisoners,* 535.

Director, N. Cameron

LOW MOSS, Low Moss, Bishopbriggs, Glasgow G64 2QB. *Prisoners,* 325. *Governor,* I. Bannatyne

NORANSIDE, Noranside, Fern, by Forfar, Angus DD8 3QY. *Prisoners,* 102. *Governor,* I. Whitehead

PERTH, 3 Edinburgh Road, Perth PH2 8AT. *Prisoners,* 492. *Governor,* W. Millar

PETERHEAD, Salthouse Head, Peterhead, Aberdeenshire AB4 6YY. *Prisoners,* 291. *Governor,* I. Gunn

‡POLMONT, Brightons, Falkirk, Stirlingshire FK2 0AB. *Young Offenders,* 443. *Governor,* D. Gunn

SHOTTS, Shotts ML7 4LF. *Prisoners,* 512. *Governor,* A. Park

NORTHERN IRELAND PRISON SERVICE

Dundonald House, Upper Newtownards Road, Belfast BT4 3SU. Tel: 028-9052 2922; Fax: 028-9052 5100; Email: info@niprisonservice.gov.uk; Web: www.niprisonservice.gov.uk

SALARIES 2001–2

Governor 1	£55,536-£57,453
Governor 2	£50,148,-£51,687
Governor 3	£43,309-£44,532
Governor 4	£36,317-£38,249
Governor 5	£25,461-£34,261

A Northern Ireland allowance is also payable

PRISON ESTABLISHMENTS

Prisoners/ Young Offenders Average number of prisoners/young offenders as at August 2002

‡HYDEBANK WOOD YOC, Hospital Road, Belfast BT8 8NA. *Young Offenders,* 144

*‡MAGHABERRY, Old Road, Ballinderry Upper, Lisburn, Co. Antrim BT28 2PT. *Prisoners and Young Offenders,* 555

§MAGILLIGAN, Point Road, Magilligan, Co. Londonderry BT49 0LR. *Prisoners,* 319

* Women's establishment or establishment with units for women
† Remand Centre or establishment with units for remand prisoners
‡ Young Offender Institution or establishment with units for young offenders
§ Immigration Holding Centre

Defence

The armed forces of the United Kingdom comprise the Royal Navy, the Army and the Royal Air Force. The Queen is commander-in-chief of all the armed forces. The Ministry of Defence, headed by a Secretary of State, provides the support structure for the armed forces. Within the Ministry of Defence, the Defence Council has overall responsibility for running the armed forces. The Chief of Staff of each service reports through the Chief of the Defence Staff to the Secretary of State on matters relating to the running of his service. The Chief of Staff also chairs the executive committee of the appropriate service board, which manages the service in accordance with centrally determined objectives and budgets. The military-civilian Central Staffs, headed by the Vice-Chief of the Defence Staff and the Second Permanent Under-Secretary of State, are responsible for policy, operational requirements, commitments, financial management, resource planning and civilian personnel management. The Defence Procurement Agency is responsible for purchasing equipment. The Defence Scientific Staff and the Defence Intelligence Staff also form part of the Ministry of Defence.

A permanent Joint Headquarters for the conduct of joint operations was set up at Northwood in 1996. The Joint Headquarters connects the policy and strategic functions of the MoD Head Office with the conduct of operations and is intended to strengthen the policy/executive division. A Joint Rapid Deployment Force was established in August 1996 and a Joint Rapid Reaction Force was set up in April 1999.

Britain pursues its defence and security policies through its membership of NATO (to which most of its armed forces are committed), the Western European Union, the European Union, the Organisation for Security and Co-operation in Europe and the UN (see International Organisations section).

ARMED FORCES STRENGTHS as at 1 July 2002

All Services	203,680
Men	186,550
Women	17,140
Royal Naval Services	41,460
Army	109,470
Royal Air Force	52,750

Source: Ministry of Defence; Defence Analytical Service Agency

SERVICE PERSONNEL

1 August 2002

	Royal Navy	Army	RAF	All Services
1975 strength	76,200	167,100	95,000	338,300
1990 strength	63,200	152,800	89,700	305,700
1999 strength	43,700	113,500	55,200	212,400
2001 strength	41,864	108,475	53,391	203,730
2002 strength	41,460	109,470	52,750	203,680

Source: Ministry of Defence; Defence Analytical Service Agency

CIVILIAN PERSONNEL

1975 level	316,700
1990 level	172,300
1999 level	117,700
2000 level	99,142
2001 level	98,384
2002 level	89,288

Source: UK Defence Statistics 2002

DEPLOYMENT OF UK PERSONNEL

SERVICE PERSONNEL IN UK as at July 2002

	England	Wales	Scotland	N. Ireland	Unknown
All Services	141,720	2,290	14,250	7,660	5,420
Officers	23,850	300	1,830	770	1,360
Other Ranks	117,870	1,890	12,410	6,900	4,050
Army[2]	70,750	910	3,710	6,480	3,200
Officers	9,830	110	530	620	180
Ranks	60,920	800	3,180	5,860	3,020
Navy[1,2]	31,620	20	4,670	150	30
Officers	6,190	10	550	10	20
Ranks	25,430	10	4,120	140	10
RAF[2]	39,350	1,370	5,870	1,030	2,200
Officers	7,830	180	760	130	1,170
Other Ranks	31,520	1,190	5,110	900	1,030

[1] Naval Service personnel on sea service in home waters are included against the local authority containing the home port of their ship.
[2] The titles Naval Service, Army and Royal Air Force include Nursing services.
[3] The Home battalions of the Royal Irish Regiment are excluded from the UK Northern Ireland figures.

Source: Ministry of Defence: Defence Analytical Service Agency

SERVICE PERSONNEL OVERSEAS as at 1 April 2002

	Breakdown	Total
All Services		40,806
Officers	5,951	
Other Ranks	34,855	
Army		31,290
Officers	3,876	
Ranks	27,414	
Royal Navy		3,739
Officers	736	
Ranks	3,003	
RAF		5,777
Officers	1,339	
Ranks	4,438	

Source: Ministry of Defence: Defence Analytical Service Agency

NUCLEAR FORCES

Britain's nuclear forces comprise four ballistic missile submarines carrying Trident missiles and equipped with nuclear warheads. All nuclear free-fall bombs have been taken out of service.

ARMS CONTROL

The 1990 Conventional Armed Forces in Europe (CFE) Treaty, which commits all NATO and former Warsaw Pact members to limiting their holdings of 5 major classes of conventional weapons, has been adapted to reflect the changed geo-strategic environment and negotiations continue for its implementation. The Open Skies Treaty, which the UK signed in 1992 and entered into force in 2002, allows for the overflight of States Parties by other States Parties using unarmed observation aircraft.

In 1968 the UK signed and ratified the Nuclear Non-Proliferation Treaty, which came into force in 1970 and was indefinitely and unconditionally extended in 1995. In 1996 the UK signed the Comprehensive Nuclear Test Ban Treaty and ratified it in 1998. The UK is a party to the

1972 Biological and Toxin Weapons Convention, which provides for a world-wide ban on biological weapons, and the 1993 Chemical Weapons Convention, which came into force in 1997 and provides for a verifiable world-wide ban on chemical weapons.

DEFENCE BUDGET

Estimated Outturn	£ billion
2000–2001	22.820
2001–2002	23.408
2002–2003	24.036
2003–2004	24.816

Source: Ministry of Defence: Defence Analytical Service Agency

The 2000 Spending Review agreed plans for defence spending to rise to almost £25 billion by 2003–2004. This represented an increase of some 1per cent in real terms over three years, and was the first sustained real increase in defence spending since the end of the Cold War. By 2003–4 defence spending as a share of GDP is expected to have fallen from 2.4 per cent to 2.3 per cent, reflecting strong growth in the economy, though representing around 6 per cent of total Government expenditure.

MINISTRY OF DEFENCE

Old War Office, Whitehall, London SW1A 2EU
Tel 020-7218 9000
Public Enquiry Office: Tel 020-7218 6645
Web: www.mod.uk

Officers promoted in an acting capacity to a more senior rank are listed under the more senior rank. Promotion to five-star rank is no longer usual in peacetime.

GRADE EQUIVALENTS

Grade 1 equivalents: (5*) Admiral of the Fleet, (5*) Field Marshal, (5*) Marshal of the RAF. (4*) Admiral, (4*) General, (4*) Air Chief Marshal.
Grade 2 equivalents: (3*) Vice Admiral, (3*) Lieutenant General, (3*) Air Marshal

Secretary of State for Defence, The Rt. Hon. Geoffrey Hoon, MP
 Private Secretary (SCS), P. Watkins
 Special Advisers, R. Taylor; A. Hood
 Parliamentary Private Secretary, Liz Blackman, MP
Minister of State for the Armed Forces, The Rt. Hon. Adam Ingram, MP
 Parliamentary Private Secretaries, Stephen Ladyman, MP; Miss D. Taylor, MP
 Private Secretary (SCS), G. Dean
Parliamentary Under-Secretary of State for Defence and Minister for Defence Procurement, Lord Bach of Lutterworth
 Private Secretary (SCS), B. Palmer
Parliamentary Under-Secretary of State for Defence and Minister for Veterans, Dr Lewis Moonie, MP
 Private Secretary (SCS), Miss T. Kent
Permanent Under-Secretary of State (SCS), Sir Kevin Tebbit, KCB, CMG
Second Permanent Under-Secretary, Ian Andrews, CBE, TD
Chief of Defence Staff, Adm. Sir Michael Boyce, GCB, OBE, ADC (until April 2003, when Sir Michael Walker GCB, CMG, CBE, ADC will take office)

THE DEFENCE COUNCIL

The Defence Council is the Senior Committee of the Ministry of Defence, which was established by Royal Prerogative under the Letters Patent in April 1964. The Letters Patent confer on the Defence Council the command over all of the Armed Forces and charge the Council with such matters relating to the administration of the Armed Forces as the Secretary of State for Defence should direct them to execute. It is chaired by the Secretary of State for Defence and consists of the Minister of State for the Armed Forces, the Parliamentary Under-Secretary of State for Defence and Minister for Defence Procurement, the Parliamentary Under-Secretary of State for Defence and Minister for Veterans, the Permanent Under-Secretary of State, the Chief of the Defence Staff, the Chief of the Naval Staff and First Sea Lord, the Chief of the General Staff, the Chief of the Air Staff, the Vice-Chief of the Defence Staff, the Second Permanent Under-Secretary of State, the Chief Scientific Advisor, the Chief of Defence Procurement, and the Chief of Defence Logistics.

CHIEFS OF STAFF

CHIEF OF THE NAVAL STAFF

First Sea Lord and Chief of the Naval Staff (4),* Adm. Sir Alan West, KCB, DSC
Asst Chief of the Naval Staff (2),* Rear-Adm. T. P. McClement, OBE

CHIEF OF THE GENERAL STAFF

Chief of the General Staff (4),* Gen. Sir Michael Walker, GCB, CMG, CBE, ADC (until February 2003, when Gen. Sir Mike Jackson, KCB, CBE, DSO, ADC takes office)
Asst Chief of the Defence Staff (2),* Maj.-Gen. F. R. Dannatt, CBE, MC
Director-General, Development and Doctrine (2),* Maj.-Gen. J. B. A. Bailey, MBE

CHIEF OF THE AIR STAFF

Chief of the Air Staff (4),* Air Chief Marshal Sir Peter Squire, GCB, DFC, AFC, ADC
Asst Chief of the Air Staff (2),* Air Vice-Marshal P. O. Sturley, CB, MBE
British-American Community Relations Co-ordinator (2),* Air Marshal Sir John Kemball, KCB, CBE, RAF (retd)
Head of Air Historical Branch (RAF) and Publications Clearance Branch (Air) (SCS), S. Cox
Chairman Joint Air Navigation Services Council, Sir M. Field
Director, Airspace Policy (2),* J. R. D. Arscott

CENTRAL STAFFS

Vice-Chief of the Defence Staff, Air Chief Marshal Sir Anthony Bagnall, KCB, OBE
Second Permanent Under-Secretary of State (SCS), I. Andrews, CBE, TD
Deputy CDS (Equipment Capability) (3),* Air Marshal Sir Jock Stirrup, KCB, CB, AFC
Capability Manager (Information Superiority) (SCS), Maj.-Gen. R. H. G. Fulton, RM
Capability Manager (Strategic Deployment) (2),* Rear-Adm. R. G. J. Ward
Director of Science (Strategic/Deployment) (SCS), Dr J. B. Jones
Capability Manager (Manoeuvre) (2),* Maj.-Gen. A. C. Figgures, CBE
Director of Science (Manoeuvre) (SCS), Dr D. J. Ferbrache
Capability Manager (Strike) (2),* Air Vice-Marshal N. J. Day, CBE

Asst CDS (Resources and Plans), Rear-Adm. R. A. I. McLean, OBE

Director-General (Service Personnel Policy), Cdre. N. Preston-Jones

Defence Housing Executive (SCS), J. Wilson

Director of Finance and Secretariat (Defence Housing Executive) (SCS), R. Mansell

Surgeon-General (3*), Surgeon Vice-Adm. I. L. Jenkins, CVO, QHS, FRCS

Chief of Staff to the Surgeon-General (2*), Air Vice-Marshal D. C. Couzens

Director General (Resources and Plans) (SCS), T. Woolley

Director of Defence Resources and Plans (SCS), G. Lester

Director of Capability Resources and Scrutiny (SCS), D. Williams

Director of Performance and Analysis (SCS), D. Stephens

Director General Equipment (SCS), N. Witney

Director of Equipment Secretariat (SCS), D. Kirk

Director-General (Financial Management) (SCS), B. Mann

Director of Finance Policy (SCS), B. Davis

Corporate Financial Controller (SCS), D. Dick

Senior Economic Adviser (SCS), N. V. Davies

Director-General Central Budget, C. Sandars

Chief Executive, Defence Bills Agency (SCS), N. Swanney

Director-General of Corporate Communication (SCS), M. Howard

Director News (SCS), D. Plews

Director of Corporate Communications Services (SCS), C. Williams

Secretary to the Defence Press and Broadcasting Advisory Committee (2*), Adm. N. J. Wilkinson, (retd)

Director of Reserve Forces and Cadets, Brig. T. H. Lang

Director of Resettlement, Brig. D. Godsal

Deputy CDS (Commitments) (3*), Lt-Gen. Sir Anthony D. Pigott, KCB, CBE

Asst. Chief of the Defence Staff (Operations) (2*), Air Vice-Marshal P. B. Walker, CBE, AFC

Director General Operational Policy (SCS), D. Bowen

Head of Balkans Secretariat (SCS), J. Tesh

Head of Overseas Secretariat (SCS), S. Pollard

Head of Gulf Veterans Illness Unit (SCS), D. J. S. Applegate

Policy Director (SCS), S. Webb

Asst. Chief of the Defence Staff (Policy) (2*), Air Vice-Marshal D. A. Hobart

Director of Defence Policy and Planning (SCS), P. Turner

Personnel Director, R. Hatfield

Director General Management and Organisation (SCS), O. G. Muirhead

Director of Management and Consultancy Services (SCS), S. A. Marsh

Director of Organisation and Management Development (SCS), G. N. Lewitt

Head of Framework Team (SCS), C. H. O. D. Alexander

Director General Civilian Policy (SCS), J. Pitt-Brooke

Chief Constable/Chief Executive, MOD Police, D. L. Clarke

Director of Claims and Legal (Finance and Secretariat) (SCS), Mrs J. Alexander

Chief Executive, Defence Estates (SCS), Vice-Adm. P. A. Dunt

Commandant Joint Services Command and Staff College (2*), Rear-Adm. R. J. Lippiett, MBE

DEFENCE INTELLIGENCE STAFF

Old War Office Building, Whitehall, London SW1A 2EU
Tel 020-7218 6645; Fax 020-7218 1562

Chief of Defence Intelligence (3*), Air Marshal J. C. French, CBE

Deputy Chief of Defence Intelligence (SCS), A. J. Cragg, CMG

Director Intelligence Programmes and Resources (SCS), P. I. Bailey

Head of Defence Intelligence Secretariat and Communications Information Systems (SCS), C. A. Younger

Director, Intelligence Global Issues (SCS), J. M. Cunningham

Director Intelligence Scientific and Technical (SCS), P. H. West

Director-General, Intelligence (Assessments) (2*), Maj.-Gen. M. Laurie, CBE

DEFENCE SCIENTIFIC STAFF

Chief Scientific Adviser (SCS) (Grade 1A), Prof. Sir Keith O'Nions, FRS

Deputy Under-Secretary Of State (Science and Technology) (Grade 2), G. H. B Jordan

Head of Finance and Secretariat (SCS), R. Mansell

Director General (Scrutiny and Analysis) (SCS), N. J. Bennett

Director General (Research and Technology) (SCS), M. S. Markin

Director of Strategic Technologies (SCS), P. W. Roper

SECOND SEA LORD/COMMANDER-IN-CHIEF NAVAL HOME COMMAND

Second Sea Lord and C.-in-C. Naval Home Command, Vice-Adm. Sir P. Spencer, KCB, ADC (until January 2003, when Vice-Adm. J. M. Burnell-Nugent, CBE will take office)

Director-General, Naval Personnel (Strategy and Plans) and Chief of Staff to Second Sea Lord and C.-in-C. Naval Home Command, Rear-Adm. R. G. Lockwood

Asst Under-Secretary of State (Naval Personnel) (SCS), P. W. D. Hatt

Flag Officer Training and Recruiting and Chief Executive, Naval Recruiting and Training Agency, Rear-Adm. J. Chadwick

Naval Secretary and Chief Executive, Naval Manning Agency, Rear-Adm. M. W. G. Kerr

Medical Director, General Navy Surgeon, RearAdm. R. D. Curr, FRCGP

Director-General, Naval Chaplaincy Services, Revd Dr C. Stewart

COMMANDER-IN-CHIEF FLEET

C.-in-C. Fleet, Adm. Sir Jonathon Band

Chief of Staff (Operations) and Flag Officer Submarines, Rear-Adm. N. S. R. Kilgour

Chief of Staff (Corporate Development), Rear-Adm. P. D. Greenish

Flag Officer Sea Training and Flag Officer Surface Flotilla, Rear-Adm. A. K. Backus, OBE

Commander, UK Maritime Force, Rear-Adm. D. G. Snelson

Commodore Naval Aviation Commodore, C. H. T Clayton

Commandant-General, Royal Marines, Maj.-Gen. R. A. Fry, MBE

ADJUTANT-GENERAL'S DEPARTMENT

Adjutant-General, Lt.-Gen. T. J. Granville-Chapman, KCB, CBE

Deputy Adjutant-General and Director General Service Conditions (Army), Maj.-Gen. M. A. Charlton-Weedy, CBE

Chief of Staff, Maj-Gen. K. H. Cima

Head, Command Secretariat (SCS), M. E. McLoughlin

Director-General, Army Training and Recruiting and Chief Executive, Army Training and Recruiting Agency, Lt.-Gen. A. M. D. Palmer, CBE
Chaplain-General, The Ven J. Blackburn
Director-General, Army Medical Services, Maj.-Gen. D. S. Jolliffe, QHP
Director, Army Legal Services, Maj.-Gen. G. Risius, CB
Military Secretary and Chief Executive, Army Personnel Centre, Maj-Gen. A. P. Grant-Peterkin
Commandant, Royal Military Academy, Sandhurst, Maj.-Gen. P. C. C. Trousdell, CB

COMMANDER-IN-CHIEF LAND COMMAND

C.-in-C., Land Command, Gen. Sir Michael Jackson, KCB, CBE, DSO *(Commander-in-Chief Headquarters Land Command)* (until February 2003 when Lt.-Gen. Sir Timothy Granville-Chapman takes over)
Deputy C.-in-C., Land Command, and Inspector-General, Territorial Army and C-in-C Allied Forces Northern Europe, Lt.-Gen. C. N. G. Delves, CBE, DSO
Chief of Staff, HQ Land Command, Maj.-Gen. F. R. Viggers, MBE
Commander Regional Forces, Lt.-Gen. J. P. Kiszely, MC

HQ STRIKE COMMAND

Air Officer Commanding-in-Chief, Air Chief Marshal Sir John Day, KCB, OBE, ADC
Chief of Air Staff, Air Chief Marshal Sir Peter Squire
Deputy Chief of Staff Operations, Air Vice-Marshal N. J. Sudborough OBE
Air Officer Logistics and Communications Information Systems, Air Vice-Marshal P. J. Scott
Air Officer Administration, Air Vice-Marshal A. J. Burton
Head, Command Secretariat (SCS), I. G. McEwen
Air Officer Commanding, No. 1 Group, Air Vice-Marshal A. D. White
Air Officer Commanding No 3 Group, Rear Adm. S. Lidbetter
Air Office Commanding, No. 38 Group, Air Vice-Marshal K. D. Filbey, CBE
Deputy Commander-in-Chief Strike Command, Air Marshal B. K. Burridge

HQ PERSONNEL AND TRAINING COMMAND

Air Member for Personnel and Commander-in-Chief Personnel and Training Command and Commander-in-Chief Strike Command, Air Chief Marshal Sir John Day
Chief of Staff, Air Vice-Marshal G. Jones, CBE, MBE
Chief Executive, Training Group Defence Agency, Air Vice-Marshal A. Miller
Air Officer Administration and Air Officer Commanding Directly Administered Units, Air Vice-Marshal A. J. Burton
Air Commodore Policy and Plans, Air Cdre D. N. Case
Commandant, RAF College, Cranwell, Air Vice-Marshall A. J. Smith, OBE
Air Secretary and Chief Executive, RAF Personnel Management Agency, Air Vice-Marshal I. M. Stewart, AFC
Director-General, Medical Services (RAF), Air Vice-Marshal W. J. Pike
Director, Legal Services (RAF), Air Vice-Marshal J. Weeden
Chaplain-in-Chief (RAF), Ven. R. D. Hesketh
Command Secretary (SCS), R. Rooks

DEFENCE PROCUREMENT AGENCY (DPA)

215 MOD Abbey Wood, Bristol BS34 8JH
Tel 0117-913 0249; Fax 0117-913 0902

Chief of Defence Procurement and Chief Executive, DPA, Sir Robert Walmsley, KCB
Deputy Chief Executive (SCS), David Gould
Non-Executive Director, T. McGuffog
Executive Director 1 (SCS), I. Fauset
Executive Director 2, Maj.-Gen. P. Gilchrist
Executive Director 3 (SCS), Air Vice-Marshal B. M. Thornton
Executive Director 4, and Controller of the Navy, Rear-Adm. N. Guild
Executive Director 5 (SCS), S. Porter
Executive Director 6 (SCS), Ms S. Scholefield

EXECUTIVE AGENCIES

DEFENCE LOGISTICS ORGANISATION (DLO)
DLO Headquarters, Spur 4, E Block, Ensleigh, Bath BA1 5AB
Chief of Defence Logistics, Air Chief Marshal Sir Malcolm Pledger, KCB, OBE, AFC
DLO'S BUSINESS UNITS
ARMY BASE REPAIR ORGANISATION (ABRO), Building 200, Monxton Road, Andover, Hampshire SP11 8HT. Tel: 01264-383295.
BRITISH FORCES POST OFFICE (BFPO), Inglis Barracks, Mill Hill, London NW7 1PX. Tel: 020-8818 6310.
CORPORATE TECHNICAL SERVICES (CTS), DLO, Monxton Road, Andover SP11 8HT. Tel: 01264-382515.
DEFENCE CATERING GROUP, Block F, Room 102, Ensleigh, Bath BA1 5AB. Telephone: 01225-468088.
DEFENCE COMMUNICATION SERVICES AGENCY (DCSA), Basil Hill Site, Park Lane, Corsham, Wilts SN13 9NR. Tel: 01225-814785.
DEFENCE FUELS GROUP, Defence Petroleum Centre, West Moors, Wimborne, Dorset BH21 6QS. Tel: 01202-654351.
DEFENCE MUNITIONS, Spur 12, Beckford, Ensleigh, Bath BA1 5AB. Tel: 01225-467670.
DEFENCE STORAGE AND DISTRIBUTION AGENCY, Ploughley Road, Lower Arncott, Bicester, Oxon OX25 2LD. Tel: 01869-256840.
DEFENCE SUPPLY CHAIN, Monxton Road, Andover, Hampshire SP11 8HT. Tel: 01264-383846.
DEFENCE TRANSPORT AND MOVEMENTS AGENCY, (DTMA), Building 211, DLO Andover, Monxton, Road, Andover, Hampshire SPE11 8HT. Tel: 01480-452451
EQUIPMENT SUPPORT (AIR), DLO, Building J103, Cranswick House, RAF Wyton, Huntingdon, Cambs PE28 2EA. Tel: 01480-452451.
EQUIPMENT SUPPORT (LAND), Building 300, DLO, Monxton Road, Andover, Hampshire SP11 8HT. Tel: 01264-383512.
PAY AS YOU DINE PROJECT, Building 209, DLO Andover, Monxton Road, Andover, Hants SP11 8HT. Tel: 01264-348051.
WARSHIP SUPPORT AGENCY, B Block, Management Suite, Foxhill, Bath BA1 5AB. Tel: 01225-882348; Fax: 01225-884313.

OTHER EXECUTIVE AGENCIES

ARMED FORCES PERSONNEL ADMINISTRATION AGENCY (AFPAA), Building 182, RAF Innsworth, Gloucester GL3 1HW. Tel: 01452-712612

ARMY PERSONNEL CENTRE, Kentigern House, 65 Brown Street, Glasgow G2 8EX. Tel: 0141-224 2023

ARMY TRAINING AND RECRUITING AGENCY, Trenchard Lines, Upavon, Pewsey, Wilts SN9 6BE. Tel: 01980-618009

DEFENCE ANALYTICAL SERVICES AGENCY (DASA), Room 1/124, St Christopher House, Southwark Street, London SE1 OTD. Tel: 020-7305 2193

DEFENCE AVIATION REPAIR AGENCY, (DARA) Head Office, Building 145, St Athan, Barry, Vale of Glamorgan CF62 4WA. Tel: 01446-798893

DEFENCE BILLS AGENCY (DBA), Room 410, Mersey House, Drury Lane, Liverpool L2 7PX. Tel: 0151-242 2519

DEFENCE DENTAL AGENCY (DDA), RAF Halton, Aylesbury, Bucks HP22 5PG. Tel: 01296-623535

DEFENCE ESTATES, Blakemore Drive, Sutton Coldfield, W. Midlands B75 7RL. Tel: 0121-311 2140

DEFENCE GEOGRAPHIC AND IMAGERY INTELLIGENCE AGENCY (DGIA), Watson Building, Elmwood Avenue, Feltham, Middx TW13 7AH Tel: 020-8818 2133

DEFENCE HOUSING EXECUTIVE, 8th Floor, St Christopher House, Southwark Street, London SE1 0TD. Tel: 020-7305 2035

DEFENCE INTELLIGENCE AND SECURITY CENTRE (DISC), Chicksands, Shefford, Beds SG17 5PR. Tel: 01462-752125

DEFENCE MEDICAL TRAINING ORGANISATION, Building 87, Fort Blockhouse, Gosport, Hants PO12 2AB. Tel: 023-9276 5284

DEFENCE PROCUREMENT AGENCY (DPA), Maple #1, 2120, MOD Abbey Wood, Bristol BS34 8JH. Tel: 0117-913 0000

DEFENCE SCIENCE AND TECHNOLOGY LABORATORY (DSTL), Porton Down, Salisbury SP4 OJQ. Tel: 01980-613121

DEFENCE SECONDARY CARE AGENCY, Room 4/168, St Christopher House, Southwark Street, London, SE1 OTD. Tel: 020-7305 6042

DEFENCE VETTING AGENCY, Building 107, Imphal Barracks, Fulford Road, York YO10 4AS. Tel: 01904-662444

DISPOSAL SERVICES AGENCY, 2nd Floor, St Georges Court, 2–12 Bloomsbury Way, London WC1A 2SH. Tel: 020-7305 3279; Fax: 020-7305 3242

THE DUKE OF YORK'S ROYAL MILITARY SCHOOL (DYRMS), Dover, Kent CT15 5EQ. Tel: 01304-245024, Web: www.dukeofyorkschool.com

MEDICAL SUPPLIES AGENCY, Drummond Barracks, Ludgershall, Andover, Hants SP11 9RU. Tel: 01264-798622

MET OFFICE, London Road, Bracknell, Berks RG12 2SZ. Tel: 0845-300 0300; Web: www.metoffice.com

MINISTRY OF DEFENCE POLICE, Wethersfield, Braintree, Essex CM7 4AZ. Tel: 01371-854000

NAVAL MANNING AGENCY, Victory Building, HM Naval Base, Portsmouth PO1 3LS. Tel: 023-9272 7408

NAVAL RECRUITING AND TRAINING AGENCY (NRTA), Victory Building, HM Naval Base, Portsmouth PO1 3LS. Tel: 023-9272 7600; Fax: 023-9272 7613

PAY AND PERSONNEL AGENCY, PO Box 99, Bath BA1 5AA. Tel: 01225-828105

QUEEN VICTORIA SCHOOL, Dunblane, Perthshire FK15 0JY. Tel: 01786-822288

QINETIQ Ively Road, Farnborough, Hampshire GU14 0LX. Tel: 01252-392000

RAF PERSONNEL MANAGEMENT AGENCY, RAF Innsworth, Gloucester GL3 1EZ. Tel: 01452-712612

RAF TRAINING GROUP DEFENCE AGENCY, RAF Innsworth, Gloucester GL3 1EZ. Tel: 01452-712612

SERVICE CHILDREN'S EDUCATION, HQ UKSCE, Building 5, Wegberg Military Complex, BFPO 40. Tel: 00-49 2161-908 2372

UK NATIONAL CODIFICATION BUREAU, Room 2.4.23, Kentigern House, 65 Brown Street, Glasgow G2 8EX. Tel: 0141-224 2164

UNITED KINGDOM HYDROGRAPHIC OFFICE, Admiralty Way, Taunton, Somerset TA1 2DN. Tel: 01823-337900. Web: www.ukho.gov.uk

VETERANS AGENCY, Tomlinson House, Norcross, Blackpool FY5 3WP. Freephone: 0800-1692277

The Royal Navy

LORD HIGH ADMIRAL OF THE UNITED KINGDOM HM The Queen

ADMIRALS OF THE FLEET

HRH The Prince Philip, Duke of Edinburgh, KG, KT, OM, GBE, AC, QSO, PC, *apptd* 1953
The Lord Hill-Norton, GCB, *apptd* 1971
Sir Michael Pollock, GCB, LVO, DSC, *apptd* 1974
Sir Edward Ashmore, GCB, DSC, *apptd* 1977
Sir Henry Leach, GCB, *apptd* 1982
Sir Julian Oswald, GCB, *apptd* 1993
Sir Benjamin Bathurst, GCB, *apptd* 1995

ADMIRALS

Boyce, Sir Michael, GCB, OBE, ADC (*Chief of Defence Staff until April 2003*)
West, Sir Alan, KCB, DSC (*First Sea Lord and Chief of Naval Staff*)
Forbes, I. A., CBE (*Deputy Supreme Allied Commander Atlantic*)
Band, Sir Jonathon (*C.-in-C. Fleet*)
Garnett, Sir Ian, KCB (*Chief of Staff Supreme Headquarters Allied Powers Europe*)

VICE-ADMIRALS

Haddacks, Sir Paul, KCB (*Director of International Military Staff, NATO*)
Spencer, Sir Peter, KCB, ADC (*Second Sea Lord and C.-in-C. Naval Home Command*)
Dunt, P., CB (*Chief Executive Defence Estate Agency*)
Burnell-Nugent, J. M., CBE (*from January 2003 Second Sea Lord and Commander-in-Chief Naval Home Command*)
Jenkins, I. L., CVO, QHS (*Surgeon-General*)

REAR-ADMIRALS

HRH The Prince of Wales, KG, KT, OM, GCB, AK, QSO, PC, ADC(P)
HRH The Princess Royal, KG, KT, GCVO (*Chief Commandant for Women in the Royal Navy*)
Lippiett, R. J., MBE (*Commandant Joint Services Command and Staff College*)
Chadwick, J. (*Flag Officer Training and Recruiting and Chief Executive, Naval Recruiting and Training Agency*)

Davies, P. R. *(Flag Officer Training and Recruiting and Chief Executive, Naval Recruiting and Training Agency)*

Stevens, R. P., CB *(Chief of Staff to Commander Allied Naval Forces, Southern Europe)*

Kerr, M. W. G. *(Naval Secretary and Chief Executive, Naval Manning Agency)*

Wood, M. G., CBE *(Director-General Defence Logistics (Operations and Business Development) and Chief Naval Engineer Officer)*

Ward, R. G. J. *(Capability Manager (Strategic Deployment), Chief Executive, Defence Communications Services Agency)*

Backus, A. K., OBE *(Flag Officer Surface Flotilla)*

Snelson, D. G., *(Commander UK Maritime Forces and Commander Anti Submarine Warfare Striking Force)*

Guild, N. C. F. *(Executive Director 4, Defence Procurement Agency, Controller of the Navy)*

Dymock, A. K. *(Defence Attaché and Head of British Defence Staff, Washington)*

Reeve, J. *(Deputy Chief Executive, Warship Support Agency)*

Stanhope, M., OBE *(Cabinet Office)*

Anthony, D. J., MBE *(Flag Officer Scotland, N. England and N. Ireland, and Naval Base Commander Clyde)* (until May 2003, when Rear-Adm. N. H. L. Harris takes office)

Lockwood, R. G. *(Director-General, Naval Personnel (Strategy and Plans) and Chief of Staff to Second Sea Lord and C.-in-C. Naval Home Command)*

Greenish, P. D. *(Chief of Staff (Corporate Development))*

McLean, R. A. I., OBE *(Asst Chief of the Defence Staff (Resources and Planning))*

McClement, T. P., OBE *(Asst Chief of the Naval Staff)*

Lidbetter, S., *(Air Officer Commanding No. 3 Group)*

Kilgour, N. S. R., *(Flag Officer Submarines and Chief of Staff (Operations) to C.-in-C. Fleet)*

Rapp, J. C., *(Flag Officer Sea Training)*

Style, C. R., *(Capability Manager (Strategic Deployment), DCDS (ES))*

Edleston, H. A.H. G., *(Military Adviser to the High Representative Bosnia and Hercegovina)*

Curr, FRCGP, R. D. *(Medical Director, General Navy Surgeon)*

Goodall, Sir Roderick, KBE, CB, ADC *(Director-General Training and Education)*

HM Fleet *as at 31 March 2001*

SUBMARINES

Trident	Vanguard, Vengeance, Victorious, Vigilant
Fleet	*Sceptre, *Sovereign, *Spartan, *Splendid, *Superb, *Talent, *Tireless, *Torbay, *Trafalgar, *Trenchant, Triumph, *Turbulent
AIRCRAFT CARRIERS	*Ark Royal, Illustrious, Invincible
LANDING PLATFORM DOCK	Fearless, *Intrepid
LANDING PLATFORM HELICOPTER	Ocean

DESTROYERS

Type 42	Cardiff, Edinburgh, Exeter, Glasgow, Gloucester, *Liverpool, *Manchester, *Newcastle, Nottingham, Southampton, York

FRIGATES

Type 23	Argyll, Grafton, *Iron Duke, Kent, Lancaster, Marlborough, Monmouth, Montrose, *Norfolk, Northumberland, *Portland, Richmond, Somerset, Sutherland, Westminster
Type 22	Campbeltown, Chatham, Cornwall, Coventry, Cumberland, Sheffield

OFFSHORE PATROL

Castle Class	*Dumbarton Castle, Leeds Castle
Island Class	Alderney, Anglesey, Guernsey, Lindisfarne, Shetland

MINEHUNTERS

Hunt Class	*Atherstone, Brecon, Brocklesby, Cattistock, Chiddingfold, Cottesmore, Dulverton, Hurworth, Ledbury, Middleton, Quorn
Sandown Class	Bangor, *Blyth, Bridport, Cromer, Grimsby, Inverness, Pembroke, Penzance, *Sandown, *Shoreham, Walney, Ramsey

PATROL CRAFT

Coastal Training Craft	Archer, Biter, Blazer, Charger, Dasher, Example, Exploit, Explorer, Express, Puncher, Pursuer, Raider, Smiter, Tracker
Gibraltar Search and Rescue Craft	Ranger, Trumpeter
ICE PATROL SHIP	Endurance
SURVEY SHIPS	Beagle, Bulldog, Gleaner, Herald, Roebuck, Scott

*undergoing refit or held at a low level of readiness

OTHER PARTS OF THE NAVAL SERVICE

ROYAL MARINES

The Royal Marines were formed in 1664 and are part of the Naval Service. Their primary purpose is to conduct amphibious and land warfare. The principal operational units are 3 Commando Brigade Royal Marines, an amphibious all-arms brigade trained to operate in arduous environments, which is a core element of the UK's Joint Rapid Reaction Force; Comacchio Group Royal Marines, which is responsible for the security of nuclear weapon facilities; and Special Boat Service Royal Marines, the maritime special forces. The Royal Marines also provide detachments for warships and land-based naval parties as required. The headquarters of the Royal Marines is at Portsmouth and principal bases are at Plymouth, Arbroath, Poole, Taunton and Chivenor. The Corps of Royal Marines is about 6,500 strong.

Capability Manager (Information Superiority), Maj.-Gen. R. H. G. Fulton, RM

Commandant-General, Royal Marines, Maj-Gen. R. A. Fry, MBE

Chief of Staff, NATO Joint Headquarters North, Maj.-Gen. D. Wilson, OBE

Director-General, Joint Doctrine and Concepts Centre, Maj.-Gen. A. A. Milton, CB, OBE, ADC

ROYAL MARINES RESERVE (RMR)

The Royal Marines Reserve is a commando-trained volunteer force with the principal role, when mobilised, of supporting the Royal Marines. There are RMR centres in London, Glasgow, Bristol, Liverpool and Newcastle. The current strength of the RMR is about 1,000.

Director, RMR, Col. M. Sturman, OBE

ROYAL FLEET AUXILIARY SERVICE (RFA)

The Royal Fleet Auxiliary Service is a civilian-manned flotilla of 21 ships. Its primary role is to supply the Royal Navy at sea with fuel, ammunition, food and stores, enabling it to maintain operations away from its home ports. It also provides secure logistic support and amphibious operations for the Army and Royal Marines, and forward ship maintenance and repair and sea-borne aviation training facilities for the Royal Navy.

FLEET AIR ARM

The Fleet Air Arm (FAA) provides the Royal Navy with a multi-role aviation combat capability able to operate autonomously at short notice world-wide in all environments, over the sea and land. The FAA has some 6200 people, which comprises 11.5 per cent of the total Royal Naval strength. It operates some 200 combat aircraft and more than 50 support/training aircraft. Its Sea Harrier fighters provide air defence/strike capability for the fleet, and the Sea King, Merlin and Lynx helicopters provide commando support, anti-submarine, anti-surface, airborne early warning and search and rescue capability.

ROYAL NAVAL RESERVE (RNR)

The Royal Naval Reserve is an integral part of the Naval Service. It comprises up to 3,850 men and women nation-wide who volunteer to train in their spare time to enable the Royal Navy to meet its operational commitments, at sea and ashore, in crisis or war.

The standard annual training commitment is 24 days, including 12 days' continuous operational training. Daily pay scales range from £31 to £200 for officers and from £17 to £69 for ratings. A tax-free bounty is also payable, the amount depending on the length of service.

Director Naval Reserves, Capt. C. G. Massie-Taylor, OBE, RN

QUEEN ALEXANDRA'S ROYAL NAVAL NURSING SERVICE

The first nursing sisters were appointed to naval hospitals in 1884 and the Queen Alexandra's Royal Naval Nursing Service (QARNNS) gained its current title in 1902. Nursing ratings were introduced in 1960 and men were integrated into the Service in 1982; QARNNS recruits qualified nurses as both officers and ratings and student nurse training can be undertaken in the Service. Female medical assistants were introduced between 1987–1998, although no longer recruited some continue to serve in QARNNS.

Patron, HRH Princess Alexandra, the Hon. Lady Ogilvy, GCVO

Matron-in-Chief and Director of Naval Nursing Services, Capt. M. Bowen

The Army

THE QUEEN

FIELD MARSHALS

HRH The Prince Philip, Duke of Edinburgh, KG, KT, OM, GBE, AC, QSO, PC, *apptd* 1953

HRH The Duke of Kent, KG, GCMG, GCVO, ADC, *apptd* 1993

The Lord Carver, GCB, CBE, DSO, MC, *apptd* 1973

Sir Roland Gibbs, GCB, CBE, DSO, MC, *apptd* 1979

The Lord Bramall, KG, GCB, OBE, MC, *apptd* 1982

The Lord Vincent GBE, KCB, DSO

Sir John Stanier, GCB, MBE, *apptd* 1985

Sir John Chapple, GCB, CBE, *apptd* 1992

The Lord Inge, KG, GCB (Col. Green Howards, Col. Cmdt. APTC), *apptd* 1994

GENERALS

Walker, Sir Michael, GCB, CMG, CBE, ADC *(Chief of the General Staff until Feb 2003, when he retires)*

Jackson, Sir Mike, KCB, CBE, DSO, ADC, Col. Cmdt. Parachute Regiment, Col. Cmdt. AG Corps, Hon. Col. The Rifle Volunteers *(Chief of the General Staff from February 2003)*

Deverell, Sir John, KCB, OBE, Col. Cmdt. LI, Col. Cmdt. SASC *(C.-in-C. Allied Forces Northern Europe)*

LIEUTENANT-GENERALS

Drewry, Sir Christopher F., KCB, CBE *(Commander, ACE Rapid Reaction Corps)*

Menzies, R. C., CB, OBE, QHS Surgeon-General

Pigott, Sir Anthony D., KCB, CBE, Col. The Queen's Gurkha Engineers, Col. Cmdt. RE *(Deputy CDS (Commitments))*

Granville-Chapman, Sir Timothy J., KCB, CBE *(Commander-in-Chief, Land)*

Irwin, A. S. H., KCB, CBE, *(Adjutant-General)*

Delves, C. N. G., CBE, DSO *(Commander Field Army)*

O'Donoghue, K., CBE *(UK Military Representative at HQ NATO)*

Reith, J. G., CB, CBE *(Chief of Joint Operations)*

Kiszely J. P., MC *(Commander Regional Forces Land Command)*

Palmer, A. M. D., CBE *(Director-General, Army Training and Recruiting and Chief Executive, Army Training and Recruiting Agency)*

MAJOR-GENERALS

Denaro, A. G., CBE, *(Middle Eastern Adviser to the Secretary of State for Defence, General Officer Commanding 5th Division)*

Trousdell, P. C. C., CB *(General Officer Commanding Northern Ireland)*

Searby, R. V. *(Senior British Loan Service Officer, Oman)*

Risius, G., CB *(Director, Army Legal Services)*

Elliott, C. H., CBE, *(Defence Services Secretary)*

Raper, A. J., CBE *(Director General Capability Defence Logistics Organisation)*

Ridgway, A. P., CB, CBE *(Head of Defence Training Review Implementation)*

Watt, C. R., CBE, *(GOC London District and Major General Commanding the Household Division)*

HRH The Prince of Wales, KG, KT, GCB and Great Master of the Order of the Bath, OM, QSO, PC, ADC(P)

Grant-Peterkin, A. P., OBE *(Military Secretary and Chief Executive, Army Personnel Centre)*

Dannatt, F. R., CBE, MC *(Asst Chief of the General Staff)*
Viggers, F. R., MBE *(Chief of Staff, HQ Land Command)*
Moore-Bick, J. D., CBE, *(GOC United Kingdom Support Command Germany)*
Gordon, R. D. S., CBE *(GOC HQ 2 Division and Governor of Edinburgh Castle)*
Plummer, B. P. CBE, *(Director General Training Support, HQ Land Command)*
Judd, D. L. *(Quartermaster General and Director General of Equipment Support (Land))*
Brims, R. V., CBE, *(GOC 1st (UK) Armoured Division)*
Gilchrist, P. *(Master General of the Ordnance, Col Cmdt RAC Executive Director 2, Defence Procurement Agency)*
Jolliffe, D. S. QHP, FRCP *(Director General, Army Medical Services)*
Cross, T. CBE *(Director General of Defence Supply Chain)*
Messervy-Whiting, G. G, MBE *(Head Interim Military Staff EU Brussels)*
Figgures, A. C., CBE *(Capability Manager (Manoeuvre) DCDS (Equipment Capability))*
Laurie, M. I., CBE, *(Director General of Intelligence (Assessments))*
McColl, J. C., CBE, *(GOC 3rd (UK) Division)*
Charlton-Weedy, M. A. CBE, *(Deputy Adjutant-General)*
Gamon, J. A., QHDS *(Chief Executive of the Defence Dental Agency)*
Richards, D. J., CBE, DSO *(Chief of Staff, HQ, ACE Rapid Reaction Corps)*
Skempton, K., CBE *(Asst Chief of Staff HQ Allied Forces South)*
Shaw, J. M., MBE *(GOC Theatre Troops Land Command)*
Monro, S. H. R. H., CBE *(Deputy Commander High Readiness Force (Land) (Italy))*
Baxter, R., CBE *(Commandant RMCS)*
Ritchie, A.S., CBE *(GOC 4th Division)*
Bailey, J. B. A., MBE *(Director-General Development and Doctrine)*
Cima, K. H., *(Senior Army Member, Royal College of Defence Studies)*
Williams, P. G., OBE *(Head of NATO Military Liaison Mission Moscow)*
Short, J. H. T., OBE, *(Chief of Staff Joint Headquarters (North)*

CONSTITUTION OF THE ARMY

The regular forces include the following arms, branches and corps. They are listed in accordance with the order of precedence within the British Army. All enquiries with regard to records of serving personnel (Regular and Territorial Army) should be directed to Relations with the Public, Army Personnel Office, Kentigern House, 65 Brown Street, Glasgow G2 8EX. Tel: 0141-224 2023/3303.

THE ARMS

HOUSEHOLD CAVALRY – The Household Cavalry Regiment (The Life Guards and The Blues and Royals)
ROYAL ARMOURED CORPS – Cavalry Regiments: 1st The Queen's Dragoon Guards; The Royal Scots Dragoon Guards (Carabiniers and Greys); The Royal Dragoon Guards; The Queen's Royal Hussars (The Queen's Own and Royal Irish); 9th/12th Royal Lancers (Prince of Wales's); The King's Royal Hussars; The Light Dragoons; The Queen's Royal Lancers; Royal Tank Regiment, comprising two regular regiments
ARTILLERY – Royal Regiment of Artillery
ENGINEERS – Corps of Royal Engineers

SIGNALS – Royal Corps of Signals

THE INFANTRY

The Foot Guards and regiments of Infantry of the Line are grouped in divisions as follows:
GUARDS DIVISION – Grenadier, Coldstream, Scots, Irish and Welsh Guards. *Divisional Office,* HQ Infantry, Warminster Training Centre, Warminster, Wilts. *Training Centre,* Infantry Training Centre, Vimy Barracks, Catterick, N. Yorks
SCOTTISH DIVISION – The Royal Scots (The Royal Regiment); The Royal Highland Fusiliers (Princess Margaret's Own Glasgow and Ayrshire Regiment); The King's Own Scottish Borderers; The Black Watch (Royal Highland Regiment); The Highlanders (Seaforth, Gordons and Camerons); The Argyll and Sutherland Highlanders (Princess Louise's). *Divisional Office,* HQ Infantry, Warminster Training Centre, Warminster, Wilts. *Training Centre,* Infantry Training Centre, Vimy Barracks, Catterick, N. Yorks
QUEEN'S DIVISION – The Princess of Wales's Royal Regiment (Queen's and Royal Hampshire's); The Royal Regiment of Fusiliers; The Royal Anglian Regiment. *Divisional Office,* HQ Infantry, Warminster Training Centre, Warminster, Wilts. *Training Centre,* Infantry Training Centre, Vimy Barracks, Catterick, N. Yorks
KING'S DIVISION – The King's Own Royal Border Regiment; The King's Regiment; The Prince of Wales's Own Regiment of Yorkshire; The Green Howards (Alexandra, Princess of Wales's Own Yorkshire Regiment); The Queen's Lancashire Regiment; The Duke of Wellington's Regiment (West Riding). *Divisional Office,* HQ Infantry, Warminster Training Centre, Warminster, Wilts. *Training Centre,* Infantry Training Centre, Vimy Barracks, Catterick, N. Yorks
PRINCE OF WALES'S DIVISION – The Devonshire and Dorset Regiment; The Cheshire Regiment; The Royal Welch Fusiliers; The Royal Regiment of Wales (24th/41st Foot); The Royal Gloucestershire, Berkshire and Wiltshire Regiment; The Worcestershire and Sherwood Foresters Regiment (29th/45th Foot); The Staffordshire Regiment (The Prince of Wales's). *Divisional Office,* HQ Infantry, Warminster Training Centre, Warminster, Wilts. *Training Centre,* Infantry Training Centre, Vimy Barracks, Catterick, N. Yorks
LIGHT DIVISION – The Light Infantry; The Royal Green Jackets. *Divisional Office,* HQ Infantry, Warminster Training Centre, Warminster, Wilts. *Training Centre,* Infantry Training Centre, Vimy Barracks, Catterick, N. Yorks
THE ROYAL IRISH REGIMENT (one general service and three home service battalions) 27th (Inniskilling), 83rd, 87th and the Ulster Defence Regiment. *Regimental HQ* and *Training Centre,* St Patrick's Barracks, BFPO 808
BRIGADE OF GURKHAS – The Royal Gurkha Rifles; The Queen's Gurkha Engineers; Queen's Gurkha Signals; The Queen's Own Gurkha Logistic Regiment. *Regimental HQ,* Airfield Camp, Netheravon, Wilts. *Gurkha Company,* Infantry Training Centre, Vimy Barracks, Catterick, N. Yorks
THE PARACHUTE REGIMENT (three regular battalions) – *Regimental HQ,* Flagstaff House, Colchester, Essex. *Training Centre,* Infantry Training Centre, Vimy Barracks, Catterick, N. Yorks
SPECIAL AIR SERVICE REGIMENT – Stirling Lines, Hereford

ARMY AIR CORPS – *Regimental HQ and Training Centre*, Middle Wallop, Stockbridge, Hants

SERVICES/ARMS

Royal Army Chaplains' Department – *Regimental HQ*, HQ AG, Upavon, Pewsey, Wilts. *Training Centre*, Armed Forces Chaplaincy Centre, Amport House, Amport, Andover, Hants

The Royal Logistic Corps – *Regimental HQ*, Blackdown Barracks, Deepcut, Camberley, Surrey. *Training Centre*, Princess Royal Barracks, Deepcut, Camberley, Surrey

Royal Army Medical Corps – *Regimental HQ*, former Army Staff College, Slim Road, Cambereley, Surrey and *Training Centre*, Defence Medical Services Keogh Barracks, Ash Vale, Aldershot, Hants

Corps of Royal Electrical and Mechanical Engineers – *Regimental HQ* and *Training Centre*, Hazebrouck Barracks, Isaac Newton Road, Arborfield, Reading, Berks

Adjutant-General's Corps – Staff and Personnel Support Branch (SPS), Provost Branch (Royal Military Police and Military Provost Staff Corps (RMP and MPS), Educational and Training Services Branch (ETS), Army Legal Services Branch (ALS), Regimental HQ, Worthy Down, Winchester, Hants. *Traininning Centres*, SPS and (ETS) Worthy Down, Winchester, Hants; RMP and MPS, Roussillon Barracks, Chichester, West Sussex.

Royal Army Veterinary Corps – *Regimental HQ*, former Army Staff College, Slim Road, Camberley, Surrey, *Training Centre*, Defence Animal Centre, Melton Mowbray, Leics.

Royal Army Dental Corps – *Regimental HQ*, former Army Staff College, Slim Road, Camberley, Surrey, *Training Centre*, Evelyn Woods Road, Aldershot, Hants

Intelligence Corps – *Directorate HQ* and *Training Centre*, Chicksands, Shefford, Beds

Army Physical Training Corps – *Regimental HQ*, Trenchard Lines, Upavon, Pewsey, Wilts, *Training Centre*, Army School of Physical Training, Fox Lines, Queen's Avenue, Aldershot, Hants

Queen Alexandra's Royal Army Nursing Corps – *Regimental HQ*, former Army Staff College, Slim Road, Cambereley, *Training Centres*, Army Nursing Training is carried out at Universities Birmingham and Portsmouth

Surrey Corps of Army Music – *Directorate HQ* and *Training Centre*, Army School of Music, Kneller Hall, Kneller Road, Twickenham, Middx

ARMY EQUIPMENT HOLDINGS *as at August 2002*

Tanks	386
Armoured combat vehicles	2,978
Artillery pieces	302
Landing craft	8
Helicopters	296

THE TERRITORIAL ARMY (TA)

The Territorial Army provides formed units and individuals as an essential part of the Army's order of battle for operations across all military tasks in order to ensure that the Army is capable of mounting and sustaining operations at nominated states of readiness. It also provides a basis for regeneration, while at the same time maintaining links with the local community and society at large. From 1 July 1999 its established strength has been 41,204.

Members of the TA receive pay at the rate appropriate to their rank. From 1 April 2002, the minimum daily pay for an officer is £49.63 and for a soldier is £28.32. Pay rises with rank and length of service. Members who complete their annual training requirements (27 and 19 days respectively for members of the Independent and Specialist TA) and are certified as efficient receive a single bounty ranging from £110 to £1,290.

Inspector-General, Lt.-Gen. J.P. Kiszely, MC

QUEEN ALEXANDRA'S ROYAL ARMY NURSING CORPS

The Queen Alexandra's Royal Army Nursing Corps (QARANC) was founded in 1902 as Queen Alexandra's Imperial Military Nursing Service (QAIMNS) and gained its present title in 1949. The QARANC has trained nurses for the register since 1950 and also trains and employs Health Care Assistants to Level 3 NVQ. The Corps recruits qualified nurses as Officers and other ranks and in 1992 male nurses already serving in the Army were transferred to the QARANC.

Director of Army Nursing Services (DANS) and Matron in Chief Army, Col. K. George

The Royal Air Force

THE QUEEN

MARSHALS OF THE ROYAL AIR FORCE

HRH The Prince Philip, Duke of Edinburgh, KG, KT, OM, GBE, AC, QSO, PC, *apptd* 1953

Sir John Grandy, GCB, GCVO, KBE, DSO, *apptd* 1971

Sir Michael Beetham, GCB, CBE, DFC, AFC, *apptd* 1982

Sir Keith Williamson, GCB, AFC, *apptd* 1985

The Lord Craig of Radley, GCB, OBE, *apptd* 1988

AIR CHIEF MARSHALS

HRH Princess Alice, Duchess of Gloucester, GCB, CI, GCVO, GBE

Squire, Sir Peter, GCB, DFC, AFC, ADC *(Chief of Air Staff)*

Bagnall, Sir Anthony, KCB, OBE *(Vice Chief of Defence Staff)*

Day, Sir John, KCB, OBE, ADC *(C.-in-C. RAF Strike Command)*

Pledger, Sir Malcolm, KCB, OBE, AFC *(Chief of Defence Logistics)*

AIR MARSHALS

Coville, Sir Christopher, KCB *(Air Member for Personnel and C.-in-C. Personnel and Training Command))*

Spink, C. R., CB, CBE *(Director-General, Saudi Arabia Armed Forces Project)*

Stirrup, Sir Jock, KCB, CB, AFC *(Deputy Chief of Defence Staff (Equipment Capability)*

French, J. C., CBE *(Chief of Defence Intelligence)*

Burridge, B. K., CBE *(Deputy C.-in-C. RAF Strike Command)*

AIR VICE-MARSHALS

HRH The Prince of Wales, KG, KT, GCB, OM, QSO, PC, ADC(P)

Stewart, I. M., CB, AFC *(Air Secretary and Chief Executive, RAF Personnel Management Agency)*

Wright, R. A., AFC *(Asst Chief of Staff Policy and Requirements, SHAPE)*

Filbey, K. D., CBE *(AOC No. 2 Group)*

Sturley, P.O., CB, MBE *(Asst Chief of the Air Staff)*

Niven, D. M., CB, CBE *(Commander, Joint Helicopter Command)*
Rimmer, T. W., CB, OBE *(Commander British Forces Cyprus and Administrator of the Sovereign Base Areas of Akrotiri and Dhekelia)*
Couzens, D. C. *(Chief of Staff to the Surgeon-General)*
Burton, A. J., OBE *(Air Officer Administration, RAF Personnel and Training Command)*
Liddell, P., CB *(Director-General of Equipment Support (Air) Defence Logistics Organisation)*
Scott, P. J. *(Air Officer Logistics and Communications Information Systems, RAF Strike Command)*
Roser, P. W., MBE *(Senior Directing Staff (Air), Royal College of Defence Studies)*
Vallance, A. G. B., OBE *(Executive Asst to Chief of Staff Command Structure Implementation SHAPE)*
Thornton, B. M. *(Executive Director-3/ Controller Aircraft, Defence Procurement Agency)*
Hobart, D. A. *(Assistant Chief of the Defence Staff (Policy))*
Sudborough, N. J., CB, OBE, *(Deputy Chief of Staff (Operations) RAF Strike Command)*
Walker, P. B., CBE *(Assistant Chief of the Defence Staff (Operations))*
Day, N. J., CBE *(Capability Manager (Strike))*
Willis, G. E. *(Project Alexander Implementation Team Leader)*
Weeden, J. *(Director, Legal Services (RAF))*
Pike, W. J., QHP *(Director-General, Medical Services (RAF))*
R. D. Hesketh, The Ven. *(Chaplain-in-Chief to the Royal Air Force) (Holds rank relative to Air Vice-Marshal)*
Miller, G. A., *(Air Officer Training and Chief Executive, Training Group Defence Agency)*
Robinson, P. A., OBE *(Commander Joint Force Operational Readiness and Training, PJHQ)*
Jones, G., CBE, MBE *(Chief of Staff, RAF, Personnel and Training Command)*
Smith, A. J., OBE *(AOC & Commandant, RAF College, Cranwell)*

CONSTITUTION OF THE ROYAL AIR FORCE

The RAF consists of two commands, Strike Command and Personnel and Training Command.

Strike Command is responsible for all the RAF's front line forces. Restructured on 1 April 2000, the Command consists of three groups each organised around specific operational duties. No 1 Group comprises the tactical fast jet forces responsible for attack, offensive support and air defence operations, No 2 Group provides the overarching enabling forces – Air Transport, Air Refuelling and Strategic Reconnaissance, whilst No 3 Group comprises the Maritime Patrol Aircraft, Search and Rescue Squadrons and Joint Force Harrier, the combined force of Royal Navy Sea Harriers and RAF Harrier GR7s.

Personnel and Training Command (PTC), created on 1 April 1994, is responsible for all aspects of recruiting, training, career management, welfare, conditions of service, and resettlement of RAF regular and reserve forces. Two Agencies form an integral part of PTC. The RAF Training Group Defence Agency deals with the recruitment and selection of all RAF personnel and delivery of RAF non-operational flying and ground training, whilst the RAF Personnel Management Agency (RAF PMA), is responsible for the management of the careers of uniformed personnel serving in the Regular and Reserve Air Forces, and posts and deploys personnel to meet the Services military tasks in times of war, crisis and peace.

RAF EQUIPMENT *as at 1 July 2002*

AIRCRAFT

Tornado	177
Harrier	53
Jaguar	46
Canberra	5
Nimrod	24
VC10	19
Tristar	8
Hercules	50
BAe 125	5
BAe 146	2
Sentry E-3D	6
Hawk	98
Dominie	8
Islander	1
Jetstream	10
Tucano	74
C-17	4

HELICOPTERS

Chinook	31
Puma	33
Sea King	19
Wessex	11
Gazelle	2
Merlin	22
Squirrel	26
Twin Squirrel	3
Griffin	9

ROYAL AUXILIARY AIR FORCE (RAuxAF)

The Auxiliary Air Force was formed in 1924 to train an elite corps of civilians to serve their country in flying Squadrons in their spare time. By 1939, there were 20 Auxiliary Air Force fighter and bomber flying Squadrons and 47 Balloon Squadrons. In 1947 the Force was awarded the prefix 'Royal' in recognition of its distinguished war service and The Sovereign's Colour for the Royal Auxiliary Air Force was presented in 1989. Today the RAuxAF continues to recruit highly motivated civilian personnel to train as Reservists in their spare-time, mainly in the evenings and at weekends, to enable them to support military operations when required.
Air Commodore-in-Chief, HM The Queen
Honorary Inspector-General Royal Auxiliary Air Force, AVM. B. H. Newton, CB, OBE

PRINCESS MARY'S ROYAL AIR FORCE NURSING SERVICE

The Princess Mary's Royal Air Force Nursing Service (PMRAFNS) was formed on 1st June 1918 as the Royal Air Force Nursing Service. In June 1923, His Majesty King George V gave his Royal Assent for the Royal Air Force Nursing Service to be known as the Princess Mary's Royal Air Force Nursing Service. Men were integrated into the PMRAFNS in 1980 and now serve as officers and other ranks. Student nurse training is undertaken and qualified RN's, RM's and RMN's are recruited to the commissioned branches of the PMRAFNS.
Patron and Air Chief Commandant, HRH Princess Alexandra, the Hon. Lady Ogilvy, GCVO
Matron-in-Chief and Director RAF Nursing Service, Air Cdre R. H. Williams

SERVICE SALARIES

The following rates of pay apply from 1 April 2002. Annual salaries are derived from daily rates in whole pence and rounded to the nearest £.

The pay rates shown are for Army personnel. The rates apply also to personnel of equivalent rank and pay band in the other services (*see* below for table of relative ranks

Rank	Daily	Annual	Rank	Daily	Annual
Second Lieutenant	£53.41	£19,494.65	Lieutenant-Colonel		
Lieutenant			On appointment	£145.44	£53,085.60
On appointment	£64.20	£23,433.00	After 1 year in rank	£147.36	£53,786.40
After 1 year in rank	£65.89	£24,049.85	After 2 years in rank	£149.28	£54,487.20
After 2 years in rank	£67.58	£24,666.70	After 3 years in rank	£151.18	£55,180.70
After 3 years in rank	£69.29	£25,279.90	After 4 years in rank	£153.10	£55,881.50
After 4 years in rank	£70.95	£25,896.75	After 5 years in rank	£155.01	£56,578.65
Captain			After 6 years in rank	£156.93	£57,279.45
On appointment	£82.26	£30,024.90	After 7 years in rank	£158.84	£57,976.60
After 1 year in rank	£84.47	£30,831.55	After 8 years in rank	£160.77	£58,681.05
After 2 years in rank	£86.70	£31,645.50	Colonel		
After 3 years in rank	£88.93	£32,459.45	On appointment	£168.42	£61,473.30
After 4 years in rank	£91.15	£33,269.75	After 1 year in rank	£170.64	£62,283.60
After 5 years in rank	£93.38	£34,083.70	After 2 years in rank	£172.86	£63,093.90
After 6 years in rank	£95.60	£34,894.00	After 3 years in rank	£175.07	£63,900.55
After 7 years in rank	£96.72	£35,302.80	After 4 years in rank	£177.29	£64,710.85
After 8 years in rank	£97.83	£35,707.95	After 5 years in rank	£179.50	£65,517.50
Major			After 6 years in rank	£181.71	£66,324.15
On appointment	£103.62	£37,821.30	After 7 years in rank	£183.93	£67,134.45
After 1 year in rank	£106.18	£38,755.70	After 8 years in rank	£186.15	£67,944.75
After 2 years in rank	£108.73	£39,686.45	Brigadier		
After 3 years in rank	£111.30	£40,624.50	On appointment	£202.02	£73,737.30
After 4 years in rank	£113.86	£41,558.90	After 1 year in rank	£204.17	£74,552.05
After 5 years in rank	£116.42	£42,493.30	After 2 years in rank	£206.32	£75,306.80
After 6 years in rank	£118.98	£43,427.70	After 3 years in rank	£208.47	£76,091.55
After 7 years in rank	£121.54	£44,362.10	After 4 years in rank	£210.63	£76,879.95
After 8 years in rank	£124.10	£45,296.50			

PERFORMANCE MANAGEMENT AND PAY SYSTEM FOR SENIOR MILITARY OFFICERS

Revised pay rates effective from 1 April 2002 for all military officers of 2-Star rank and above (excluding medical and dental officers). Officers enter relevant scale at scale points, provided they have served a minimum of 6 months in rank and, subject to satisfactory performance, become eligible for an incremental award on 1 April of each year.

Major-General (2-Star)		
Scale 1	£228.22	£83,300
Scale 2	£232.78	£84,965
Scale 3	£237.35	£86,631
Scale 4	£241.91	£88,297
Scale 5	£246.47	£89,962
Scale 6	£251.04	£91,628
Scale 7	£255.60	£93,293
Lieutenant-General (3-Star)		
Scale 1	£266.45	£97,255
Scale 2	£273.11	£99,684
Scale 3	£279.76	£102,114
Scale 4	£286.42	£104,543
Scale 5	£293.07	£106,972
Scale 6	£299.73	£109,401
Scale 7	n/a	n/a

General (4-Star)		
Scale 1	£328.10	£119,758
Scale 2	£336.61	£122,864
Scale 3	£345.12	£125,970
Scale 4	£353.63	£129,076
Scale 5	£362.14	£132,182
Scale 6	£370.65	£135,288
Scale 7	n/a	n/a

Field Marshal – appointments to this rank are not usually made in peace time. The salary for holders of the rank is equivalent to the salary of a 5-Star General, a salary level available only in times of war. In peace time, the equivalent rank to Field Marshal is the Chief of Defence Staff. From 1 April 2002, the annual salary for the Chief of Defence Staff is £178,000.

SALARIES OF OFFICERS COMMISSIONED FROM THE RANKS (LIEUTENANTS AND CAPTAINS ONLY)

YEARS OF COMMISSIONED SERVICE	YEARS OF NON-COMMISSIONED SERVICE FROM AGE 18					
	Less than 12 years		over 12 but less than 15 years		15 years or more	
	Daily	Annual	Daily	Annual	Daily	Annual
On commissioning	£90.24	£32,937.60	£94.78	£34,594.70	£99.32	£36,251.80
After 1 year's service	£92.51	£33,766.15	£97.05	£35,423.25	£101.15	£36,919.75
After 2 years' service	£94.78	£34,594.70	£99.32	£36,251.80	£102.62	£37,456.30
After 3 years' service	£97.05	£35,423.25	£101.15	£36,919.75	£104.09	£37,992.85
After 4 years' service	£99.32	£36,251.80	£102.62	£37,456.30	£105.56	£38,529.40
After 5 years' service	£101.15	£36,919.75	£104.09	£37,992.85	£107.02	£39,062.30
After 6 years' service	£102.62	£37,456.30	£105.56	£38,529.40	£108.49	£39,598.85
After 8 years' service	£104.09	£37,992.85	£107.02	£39,062.30	£109.96	£40,135.40
After 10 years' service	£105.56	£38,529.40	£108.49	£39,598.85	£109.96	£40,135.40
After 12 years' service	£107.02	£39,062.30	£109.96	£40,135.40	£109.96	£40,135.40
After 14 years' service	£108.49	£39,598.85	£109.96	£40,135.40	£109.96	£40,135.40
After 16 years' service	£109.96	£40,135.40	£109.96	£40,135.40	£109.96	£40,135.40

SOLDIERS' SALARIES

The pay structure below officer level is divided into pay bands. Jobs at each rank are allocated to bands according to their score in the job evaluation system. Length of service is from age 18.

Scale A: committed to serve for less than 6 years, or those with less than 9 years' service who are serving on Open Engagement

Scale B: committed to serve for 6 years but less than 9 years

Scale C: committed to serve for 9 years or more, or those with more than 9 years' service who are serving on Open Engagement

Rates of pay effective from 1 April 2002 are:

RANK	SCALE A			
	Lower Band		Higher Band	
	Daily	Annual	Daily	Annual
Private				
Level 1	£34.46	£12,577.90	£34.46	£12,577.90
Level 2	£36.49	£13,318.85	£39.80	£14,527.00
Level 3	£38.51	£14,056.15	£43.93	£16,034.45
Level 4	£41.89	£15,289.85	£47.24	£17,242.60
Lance Corporal (levels 5–7 also applicable to Privates)				
Level 5	£44.14	£16,111.10	£52.24	£19,067.60
Level 6	£45.98	£16,782.70	£54.78	£19,994.70
Level 7	£47.96	£17,505.40	£57.29	£20,910.85
Level 8	£50.15	£18,304.75	£59.86	£21,848.90
Level 9	£51.97	£18,969.05	£62.79	£22,918.35

	SCALE B			
	Lower Band		Higher Band	
	Daily	Annual	Daily	Annual
Corporal				
Level 1	£56.29	£20,545.85	£58.46	£21,337.90
Level 2	£58.91	£21,502.15	£62.17	£22,692.05
Level 3	£59.94	£21,878.10	£65.86	£24,038.90
Level 4	£61.76	£22,542.40	£67.39	£24,597.35
Level 5	£62.70	£22,885.50	£69.03	£25,195.95
Level 6	£63.45	£23,159.25	£70.46	£25,717.90
Level 7	£64.31	£23,473.15	£72.00	£26,280.00

	SCALE C			
	Lower Band		Higher Band	
	Daily	Annual	Daily	Annual
Sergeant				
Level 1	£65.13	£23,772.45	£71.08	£25,944.20
Level 2	£66.82	£24,389.30	£72.91	£26,612.15
Level 3	£68.50	£25,002.50	£74.76	£27,287.40
Level 4	£69.20	£25,258.00	£75.70	£27,630.50
Level 5	£70.44	£25,710.60	£77.17	£28,167.05
Level 6	£71.87	£26,232.55	£78.65	£28,707.25
Level 7	£73.55	£26,845.75	£80.12	£29,243.80

	Lower Band		Higher Band	
	Daily	Annual	Daily	Annual
Staff Sergeant				
Level 1	£72.09	£26,312.85	£80.17	£29,262.05
Level 2	£73.03	£26,655.95	£82.12	£29,973.80
Level 3	£75.40	£27,521.00	£84.07	£30,685.55
Level 4	£77.16	£28,163.40	£86.02	£31,397.30
Warrant Officer II				
(levels 5–7 also applicable to Staff Sergeants)				
Level 5	£78.22	£28,550.30	£87.98	£32,112.70
Level 6	£80.17	£29,262.05	£89.92	£32,820.80
Level 7	£82.12	£29,973.80	£91.22	£33,295.30
Level 8	£84.07	£30,685.55	£92.53	£33,773.45
Level 9	£85.98	£31,382.70	£93.84	£34,251.60

	Lower Band		Higher Band	
	Daily	Annual	Daily	Annual
Warrant Officer I				
Level 1	£83.74	£30,565.10	£91.30	£33,324.50
Level 2	£85.37	£31,160.05	£93.10	£33,981.50
Level 3	£87.09	£31,787.85	£94.70	£34,565.50
Level 4	£88.82	£32,419.30	£96.43	£35,196.95
Level 5	£90.55	£33,050.75	£98.16	£35,828.40
Level 6	£93.10	£33,981.50	£99.90	£36,463.50
Level 7	£95.72	£34,937.80	£101.43	£37,021.95

RELATIVE RANK – ARMED FORCES

Royal Navy	Army	Royal Air Force
1 Admiral of the Fleet	1 Field Marshal	1 Marshal of the RAF
2 Admiral (Adm.)	2 General (Gen.)	2 Air Chief Marshal
3 Vice-Admiral (Vice-Adm.)	3 Lieutenant-General (Lt.-Gen.)	3 Air Marshal
4 Rear-Admiral (Rear-Adm.)	4 Major-General (Maj.-Gen.)	4 Air Vice-Marshal
5 Commodore (Cdre)	5 Brigadier (Brig.)	5 Air Commodore (Air Cdre)
6 Captain (Capt.)	6 Colonel (Col.)	6 Group Captain (Gp Capt.)
7 Commander (Cdr.)	7 Lieutenant-Colonel (Lt.-Col.)	7 Wing Commander (Wg Cdr.)
8 Lieutenant-Commander (Lt.-Cdr.)	8 Major (Maj.)	8 Squadron Leader (Sqn Ldr)
9 Lieutenant (Lt.)	9 Captain (Capt.)	9 Flight Lieutenant (Flt. Lt.)
10 Sub-Lieutenant (Sub-Lt.)	10 Lieutenant (Lt.)	10 Flying Officer (FO)
11 Acting Sub-Lieutenant (Acting Sub-Lt.)	11 Second Lieutenant (2nd Lt.)	11 Pilot Officer (PO)

SERVICE RETIRED PAY ON COMPULSORY RETIREMENT

Those who leave the services having served at least five years, but not long enough to qualify for the appropriate immediate pension, now qualify for a preserved pension and terminal grant, both of which are payable at age 60. The tax-free resettlement grants shown below are payable on release to those who qualify for a preserved pension and who have completed nine years service from age 21 (officers) or 12 years from age 18 (other ranks).

The annual rates for army personnel are given. The rates apply also to personnel of equivalent rank in the other services, including the nursing services.

OFFICERS

Applicable to officers who give full pay service on the active list on or after 31 March 2002. Pensionable earnings for Senior Officers (*) is defined as the total amount of basic pay received during the year ending on the day prior to retirement, or the amount of basic pay received during any 12 month period within 3 years prior to retirement, which ever is the higher. Figures given for Senior Officers are percentage rates of pensionable earnings on final salary arrangements on or after 31 March 2002.

No. of years reckonable service over age 21	Capt. and below	Major	Lt.-Col.	Colonel	Brigadier	Major-General*	Lieutenant-General*	General*
16	£9,945	£11,844	£15,529	£17,982	£21,462	—	—	—
17	£10,403	£12,407	£16,247	£18,814	£22,299	—	—	—
18	£10,861	£12,969	£16,966	£19,645	£23,136	—	—	—
19	£11,320	£13,532	£17,684	£20,477	£23,973	—	—	—
20	£11,778	£14,094	£18,403	£21,309	£24,809	—	—	—
21	£12,236	£14,657	£19,121	£22,140	£25,646	—	—	—
22	£12,695	£15,219	£19,839	£22,972	£26,483	—	—	—
23	£13,153	£15,782	£20,558	£23,804	£27,320	—	—	—
24	£13,611	£16,344	£21,276	£24,636	£28,156	38.5%	—	—
25	£14,070	£16,907	£21,995	£25,467	£28,993	39.7%	—	—
26	£14,528	£17,469	£22,713	£26,299	£29,830	40.8%	—	—
27	£14,986	£18,031	£23,431	£27,131	£30,667	42.0%	42.0%	—
28	£15,445	£18,594	£245,10	£27,963	£31,503	43.1%	43.1%	—
29	£15,903	£19,156	£24,868	£28,794	£32,340	44.3%	44.3%	—
30	£16,361	£19,719	£25,587	£29,626	£33,177	45.4%	45.4%	45.4%
31	£16,820	£20,281	£26,305	£30,458	£34,014	46.6%	46.6%	46.6%
32	£17,278	£20,844	£27,023	£31,290	£34,850	47.7%	47.7%	47.7%
33	£17,736	£21,406	£27,742	£32,121	£35,687	48.9%	48.9%	48.9%
34	£18,195	£21,969	£28,460	£32,953	£36,524	50.0%	50.0%	50.0%

WARRANT OFFICERS, NCOs AND PRIVATES

Applicable to soldiers who give full pay service on or after 31 March 2002.

No. of years reckonable service	Below Corporal	Corporal	Sergeant	Staff Sergeant	Warrant Officer Level II	Warrant Officer Level I
22	£5,852	£7,503	£8,323	£9,480	£9,881	£10,561
23	£6,056	£7,765	£8,613	£9,811	£10,226	£10,930
24	£6,260	£8,027	£8,904	£10,142	£10,571	£11,298
25	£6,465	£8,289	£9,194	£10,473	£10,916	£11,667
26	£6,669	£8,551	£9,485	£10,804	£11,261	£12,036
27	£6,873	£8,812	£9,775	£11,134	£11,606	£12,404
28	£7,078	£9,074	£10,066	£11,465	£11,951	£12,773
29	£7,282	£9,336	£10,356	£11,796	£12,296	£13,142
30	£7,486	£9,598	£10,647	£12,127	£12,641	£13,510
31	£7,690	£9,860	£10,937	£12,458	£12,986	£13,879
32	£7,895	£10,122	£11,228	£12,789	£13,331	£14,248
33	£8,099	£10,384	£11,518	£13,120	£13,675	£14,616
34	£8,303	£10,646	£11,809	£13,451	£14,020	£14,985
35	£8,507	£10,908	£12,099	£13,782	£14,365	£15,353
36	£8,712	£11,169	£12,390	£14,113	£14,710	£15,722
37	£8,916	£11,431	£12,680	£14,443	£15,055	£16,091

RESETTLEMENT GRANTS

Terminal grants are in each case three times the rate of retired pay or pension. There are special rates of retired pay for certain other ranks not shown above. Lower rates are payable in cases of voluntary retirement.

A gratuity of £3,380 is payable for officers with short service commissions for each year completed. Resettlement grants are: officers £11,631; non-commissioned ranks £7,857.

Education

Responsibility for education in England lies with the Secretary of State for Education and Skills (formerly of Education and Employment); in Wales, with the First Secretary of the National Assembly for Wales; in Scotland, with Scottish Ministers; and in Northern Ireland with Education Ministers.

The main concerns of the education departments (the Department for Education and Skills (DfES) in England; the National Assembly for Wales Training and Education Department; the Scottish Executive Department of Education and Department of Enterprise, Transport and Lifelong Learning; the Department of Education (DED) and Department for Employment and Learning (DEL) in the Northern Ireland Executive) are the formulation of national policies for education and the maintenance of consistency in educational standards. They are responsible for the broad allocation of resources for education, for the rate and distribution of educational building and for the supply, training and superannuation of teachers (in England through the Teacher Training Agency).

EXPENDITURE

In the UK in 1999–2000, expenditure on education was (£ million):

Schools and under-fives	27,564.7
Further and higher education	11,913.1
Other education and related expenditure	1,411.0

Most of this expenditure, except that for higher and further education in England, Wales and Scotland (which is met by the respective funding agencies), is incurred by local authorities, which make their own expenditure decisions according to their local situations and needs. Expenditure on education by central government departments, in real terms, was (£ million):

	2001–2 estimated outturn	2002–3 planned
DfES	17,469.0	21,015.0
National Assembly for Wales	958.1	1,072.4
Scottish Executive	1,059.4	1,604.0
Northern Ireland Assembly	1,802.5	1,824.0

Planned spending on education in the UK as a proportion of gross national product in 2001–2 was 5 per cent and will rise to a projected 5.3 per cent in 2003–4.

The bulk of direct expenditure by the DfES, the National Assembly for Wales and the Scottish Executive is directed towards supporting higher education in universities and colleges through the Higher Education Funding Councils (HEFCs) and further education and, in England and Wales, sixth form colleges, through the funding councils for that sector. In addition, the DfES funds student support in England and Wales, the City Technology Colleges, the City College for the Technology of the Arts, and pays grants under the specialist schools programme.

In Wales the National Assembly also funds curriculum development, educational services and research and supports bilingual education. In Scotland the main elements of central government expenditure, in addition to those outlined above, are grant-aided special schools, student awards and bursaries (through the Student Awards Agency for Scotland), teachers, curriculum development, special educational needs and community education. In Northern Ireland the DED also administers the teachers' superannuation scheme, pays teachers' salaries and funds grant-maintained integrated and voluntary grammar schools. DEL directly funds higher education, student awards and further education.

Current net expenditure on education by local education authorities in England, Wales, and Scotland, and education and library boards in Northern Ireland is (£ million):

	2001–2 estimated outturn	2002–3 planned
England	22,513	22,502
Wales	1,586	1,695
Scotland	3,022.9	3,312.7
Northern Ireland	1,015	1,018

LOCAL EDUCATION ADMINISTRATION

In England and Wales the education service is administered by local education authorities (LEAs), which have day-to-day responsibility for providing most state primary and secondary education in their areas. They share with the appropriate funding bodies the duty to provide adult education to meet local needs.

The LEAs own and maintain most schools and some colleges, build new ones and provide equipment. LEAs are financed largely from the council tax and aggregate external finance from the Office of the Deputy Prime Minister in England and the National Assembly for Wales.

All LEA-maintained schools manage their own budgets. The LEA allocates funds to the school, largely on the basis of pupil numbers, and the school governing body is responsible for overseeing spending and for most aspects of staffing, including appointments and dismissals. LEAs have powers to monitor, maintain and improve standards. An Education Association can be set up to take over the management of failing schools where both the LEA and the governing body have not brought about improvements identified as necessary by inspection.

The duty of providing education locally in Scotland rests with the education authorities. They are responsible for the construction of buildings, the employment of teachers and other staff and the provision of equipment and materials. Devolved School Management is in place for all primary, secondary and special schools. Education authorities are required to establish school boards consisting of parents and teachers as well as co-opted members, responsible, among other things, for the appointment of staff.

Education is administered locally in Northern Ireland by five education and library boards, who fund controlled and maintained schools and whose costs are met in full by the Northern Ireland Executive. All grant-aided schools include elected parents and teachers on their boards of governors. Provision has been made for schools wishing to provide integrated education to have grant-maintained integrated status from the outset, funded directly by the Department of Education. All schools and colleges of further education have full responsibility for their own budgets, including staffing costs. The Council for Catholic Maintained Schools forms an upper tier of management for Catholic schools and provides advice on matters relating to management and administration.

THE INSPECTORATE

The Office for Standards in Education (OFSTED) is a non-ministerial government department in England headed by HM Chief Inspector of Schools (HMCI). OFSTED's remit is to regularly inspect and report on all maintained schools in England, local education authorities (supported by the Audit Commission), teacher training institutions. youth work and all 16–19 education, including sixth form and further education colleges. OFSTED also has responsibility for the regulation of early years childcare including childminders.

Teams of OFSTED-trained accredited inspectors, including educationalists and lay people, carry out inspections in schools according to the Framework for Inspection of Schools to ensure consistency in the process of inspection and the criteria used. HM Inspectors (HMI) within OFSTED report on good practice in schools and on other educational issues based on inspection evidence. Schools are inspected at least once every six years. A summary of the inspection report must be sent to the parents of each pupil by the school, followed by a copy of the governors' action plan.

There are about 200 HMIs and about 1,600 childcare inspectors on OFSTED's permanent staff. About 1,500 registered inspectors, 7,500 team inspectors, and 700 lay inspectors work on contract to OFSTED.

Estyn: Arolygiaeth Ei Mawrhydi dros Addysg a Hyfforddiant yng Nghymru (Her Majesty's Inspectorate for Education and Training in Wales) inspects nursery provision, maintained schools, local education authorities, teacher education and training, work-based training, careers companies, adult and youth education, and colleges of further education in Wales. Its remit also includes advice to the National Assembly for Wales on a wide range of education and training matters.

There are 56 HMIs, 191 registered inspectors and 566 team members in Wales.

HM Inspectorate of Education (HMIE) is an executive agency of the Scottish Executive. HM Inspectors (HMI) inspect or review and report on education in pre-school centres, nursery, primary, secondary and special schools, further education institutions (under contract to the Scottish Further Education Funding Council), initial teacher education, community learning; care and welfare of pupils; the education functions of local authorities; and in other contexts as necessary. HMIs work in teams alongside lay members and associate assessors, who are practising teachers seconded for the inspection. The inspection of higher education is the responsibility of inspectors appointed to the Higher Education Funding Council for Scotland. There are one senior chief inspector, one depute senior chief inspector, five chief inspectors and 80 inspectors in Scotland.

Inspection is carried out in Northern Ireland by the Education and Training Inspectorate which provides services for the Department of Education and the Department for Employment and Learning, among others. Schools are inspected currently once every five to seven years. In further education and training, extended inspections are carried out once every eight years and focused inspections at least every four years. In addition, the Inspectorate provides advice to Ministers and Departments to assist in the formulation of policies in education and training.

The Inspectorate comprises a Chief Inspector, four assistant chief inspectors, 10 managing inspectors and 49 inspectors. Inspectorate teams also include on occasion lay persons and associate assessors.

SCHOOLS AND PUPILS

Full-time education is compulsory in Great Britain for all children between five and 16 years and between four and 16 years in Northern Ireland. About 94 per cent of children receive free education from public funds and the rest attend fee-paying schools or are educated at home. Provision is being increased for pre-school children and many pupils remain at school after the minimum leaving age. No fees are charged in any publicly maintained school in England, Wales and Scotland. In Northern Ireland, fees may be charged in voluntary schools and are paid by pupils in preparatory departments of grammar schools, but pupils admitted to the secondary departments of grammar schools, unless they come from outside the province, do not pay fees.

The 'Parents' Charter', available free from education departments, is a booklet telling parents about the education system. Schools are now required to make available information about themselves, their truancy rates, destinations of leavers, public examination and national test results. Parents in England and Wales must receive a written yearly progress report on all aspects of their child's achievements. There is a similar commitment for Northern Ireland. In Scotland the school report card gives parents information on their child's progress.

FALL AND RISE IN NUMBERS

In primary education, and increasingly in secondary education, pupil numbers in the UK increased through the 1990s. In maintained primary schools they stood at 4.9 million in 1991, had risen to 5.3 million by 2001 but are expected to decline slightly to 5.2 million by 2007. In secondary schools pupil numbers stood at 3.5 million in 1991, had risen to 3.9 million by 2001 and are projected to rise to 4.1 million by 2010.

ENGLAND AND WALES

There are two main types of school in England and Wales: publicly maintained schools, which charge no fees; and independent schools, which charge fees. Publicly maintained schools, with the exception in England of City Technology Colleges, are maintained by local education authorities (LEAs).

Publicly funded schools are classified as community, voluntary or foundation schools. Community (formerly county) schools are owned by LEAs and wholly funded by them. They are non-denominational and provide primary and secondary education. Schools in the voluntary category provide primary and secondary education and many have a particular religious ethos. Although the buildings are in many cases provided by the voluntary bodies, they are financially maintained by a LEA. The voluntary category comprises two subdivisions, voluntary controlled and voluntary aided. In the case of voluntary controlled schools the LEA bears all costs. In voluntary aided schools, although the managers or governors are responsible for repairs, improvements and alterations to the building, central government may reimburse up to 85 per cent of approved capital expenditure, while the LEA pays for internal maintenance and other running costs. That subdivision also includes schools formerly classed as special agreement and those former grant-maintained schools which were originally voluntary aided or special agreement schools or were founded by promoters. In the case of former special agreement schools, the LEA may, by special agreement, pay between one-half and three-quarters of the cost of building a new or extending an existing school, usually a

secondary school. Foundation schools are former grant-maintained schools which were originally county or voluntary controlled schools or were established by the Funding Agency for Schools. Under the previous administration all secondary and primary schools, whether maintained or independent, were eligible to apply for grant-maintained status subject to a ballot of parents. Grant-maintained schools were maintained directly by the Secretary of State (through the Funding Agency for Schools) and the former Welsh Office, not the LEA; those arrangements no longer apply and they are now included in LEA funding arrangements. They are wholly run by their own governing body. About 60 per cent of schools established were secondary schools.

The number of schools by category in 2001 was:

	England	Wales
Maintained schools	22,514	1,860
Community	14,612	1,573
Voluntary	7,038	275
aided	4,270	160
controlled	2,768	115
Foundation	864	12
CTCs and CCTAs*	15	–
Independent schools	2,200	54
TOTAL	24,729	1,914

* In England only

Under the Local Management of Schools initiative, LEAs are required to delegate the entire school budget, including staffing costs, directly to those schools that wish it. LEAs continue to retain responsibility for various common services, including transport and special educational needs units. The LEA acts as admission authority for most community and some voluntary schools.

Governing bodies – All publicly maintained schools have a governing body, usually made up of a number of parent and local community representatives, governors appointed by the LEA if the school is LEA maintained, the headteacher (unless he or she chooses otherwise), and serving teachers. Schools can appoint up to four sponsor governors from business who will be expected to provide financial and managerial assistance. Governing bodies are responsible for the overall policies of schools and their academic aims and objectives. They also control matters of school discipline, the appointment and dismissal of staff and act as the admission authority for voluntary aided and all foundation schools.

City Technology Colleges CTCs and City Colleges for the Technology of the Arts CCTAs (in England only) are state-aided but independent of LEAs. Their aim is to widen the choice of secondary education in disadvantaged urban areas and to teach a broad curriculum with an emphasis on science, technology, business understanding and arts technologies. Capital costs are shared by government and business sponsors, and running costs are covered by a per capita grant from the DfES in line with comparable costs in an LEA maintained school. The first city technology college opened in 1988 in Solihull. The first CCTA, known as Britschool, opened in Croydon in 1991.

The Specialist Schools Programme is open to all state secondary schools in England, which wish to specialise in the teaching of a particular subject area (technology, mathematics and science, modern foreign languages, sports and the arts). The schools must raise £50,000 sponsorship, prepare four-year development plans with measurable targets in the specialist subject area and make provision for sharing resources and good practice with

other schools and the wider community. In return, in addition to the normal funding arrangements, the schools receive business sponsorship (up to four sponsor governors may sit on governing bodies) and a capital grant of up to £100,000 from central government, together with extra annual funding of £123 per pupil (for four years initially) to assist the delivery of an enhanced curriculum. By September 2002, there were 443 technology colleges, 173 arts colleges, 161 sports colleges, 157 language colleges, 24 science colleges, 18 business and enterprise colleges, 12 mathematics and computing colleges and 4 engineering colleges.

City Academies – The first City Academies, publicly funded independent secondary schools involving sponsors from the private and voluntary sectors, opened in September 2001. Twenty partnerships were in place by September 2002. They are usually in deprived communities and replace either seriously failing schools with poor examination results or are established to meet a demand for places.

Excellence in Cities and Beacon Schools are two initiatives launched to address educational problems in under-achieving urban areas. They aim to raise standards by sharing and spreading good practice for which the Government has provided additional financial support.

Education Action Zones were established to help raise standards in deprived inner-city areas by working in partnership with the local community and other organisations.

SCOTLAND

Education authority schools (known as public schools) are financed by local government, partly through revenue support grants from central government, and partly from local taxation. Devolved management from the local authority to the school is in place for more than 88 per cent of all school level expenditure. A small number of grant-aided schools, mainly in the special sector, are conducted by boards of managers and receive grants directly from the Scottish Executive Education Department.

Independent schools charge fees and receive no direct grant, but are subject to inspection and registration.

The number of schools by category in 2001 was:

Publicly maintained schools	5,448
Independent schools	164
TOTAL	5,612

NORTHERN IRELAND

Controlled schools are maintained by the education and library boards with all costs paid from public funds. Voluntary maintained schools, mainly under Roman Catholic management, receive grants towards capital costs and running costs in whole or in part. Voluntary grammar schools may be under denominational or non-denominational management and receive grants from the Department for Education. Voluntary maintained and voluntary grammar schools can apply for designation as a new category of voluntary school, which is eligible for a grant of 100 per cent as opposed to 85 per cent. Such schools are managed by a board of governors on which no single interest group has a majority of nominees. All grant-aided schools include elected parents and teachers on their boards of governors, whose responsibilities also include financial management under the Local Management of Schools initiative. All schools now have fully delegated budgets. The majority of children in Northern Ireland are educated in schools which have a

464 Education

religious affiliation. Integrated schools exist to educate Protestant and Roman Catholic children together. There are two types: grant-maintained integrated schools which are funded by DED and controlled integrated schools funded by the education and library boards. Procedures are in place for balloting parents in existing religiously affiliated schools to determine whether they want their school to become integrated, subject to the satisfaction of certain criteria. By September 2002, 47 integrated schools had been established, 17 of them secondary.

The number of schools by category in 2001–2 was:

Publicly-funded schools:	1,282
Controlled	641
Maintained	540
Voluntary grammar	54
Integrated schools	47
Independent schools	25
TOTAL	1,307

THE STATE SYSTEM

PRE-SCHOOL EDUCATION – for children from two to five years, it is not compulsory, although a free place is available for each four-year-old who requires it and provision for three-year-olds in the public sector is being increased. Northern Ireland has a compulsory school starting age of four as of September each year, but from March 2003 one year of pre-school education will be available for each child whose parents wish it. Pre-school education takes place variously in nursery schools (2,864 in the public sector in 2001), nursery classes in primary schools, or pre-school education centres. The proportion of three- and four-year-olds enrolled was 63 per cent in the UK in 2000–1, distributed as follows (thousands):

Maintained schools	
nursery	152.2
primary	103.3
special	6.9
Non-maintained schools	
nursery	71.2
special	0.1
TOTAL	333.7

Education authorities are responsible for planning, co-ordinating and delivering nursery education in their areas using a range of providers on the basis of an Early Years Development Plan, in partnership with parents and the private and voluntary sectors. All providers of pre-school education are subject to inspection.

PRIMARY EDUCATION – begins at five years in Great Britain and four years in Northern Ireland. In England, Wales and Northern Ireland the transfer to secondary school is generally made at 11 years. In Scotland, the primary school course lasts for seven years and pupils transfer to secondary courses at about the age of 12.

Primary schools consist mainly of infant schools for children aged five to seven, junior schools for those aged seven to 11, and combined junior and infant schools for both age groups. First schools in some parts of England cater for ages five to ten as the first stage of a three-tier system: first, middle and secondary.

Primary schools (UK) 2000–1	
No. of primary schools	22,902
No. of pupils (000s)	4,444.0
Pupils aged 2-4 years (000s)	103.3

Pupil-teacher ratios in maintained primary schools were:

	1999–2000	2000–1
England	23.3	22.9
Wales	22.3	21.5
Scotland	19.1	19.0
Northern Ireland	20.2	20.1
UK	22.7	20.8

The average size of classes 'as taught' was 25.0 in 2000–1.

MIDDLE SCHOOLS – take children from first schools, mostly in England, cover varying age ranges between eight and 14 and usually lead on to comprehensive upper schools.

SECONDARY EDUCATION – Secondary schools are for children aged 11 to 16 and for those who choose to stay on to 18. At 16, many students prefer to move on to tertiary or sixth form colleges. Most secondary schools in England, Wales and Scotland are co-educational. The largest secondary schools have over 1,500 pupils, but only 5.8 per cent of schools take over 1,000 pupils.

Secondary schools 2000–1

	England	Wales	Scotland	N. Ireland
No. of pupils (000s)	3,231.8	210.4	319.1	155.6
Average class size	22.1	21.3	n/a	n/a
Pupil-teacher ratio	17.1	16.6	13.0	14.5

In England and Wales the main types of maintained secondary schools (January 2001) were: comprehensive schools (87 per cent of pupils in England, 100 per cent in Wales), whose admission arrangements are without reference to ability or aptitude; deemed middle schools for children aged between eight and 14 years who then move on to senior comprehensive schools at 12, 13 or 14 (4.2 per cent of pupils in England); secondary modern schools (3.5 per cent of pupils in England) providing a general education with a practical bias; secondary grammar schools (4.4 per cent of pupils in England) with selective intake providing an academic course from 11 to 16–18 years; and technical schools (0.07 per cent of pupils in England), providing an integrated academic and technical education.

In Scotland all pupils in education authority secondary schools attend schools with a comprehensive intake. Most of these schools provide a full range of courses appropriate to all levels of ability from first to sixth year.

In most areas of Northern Ireland there is a selective system of secondary education with pupils transferring either to grammar schools (35 per cent of pupils in 2001) or secondary schools (65 per cent of pupils in 2001) at 10–11 years of age. Parents can choose the school they would like their children to attend and all those who apply must be admitted if they meet the criteria. If a school is over-subscribed beyond its statutory admissions number, selection is on the basis of published criteria, which, for most grammar schools, place emphasis on performance in the transfer procedure tests which are set and administered by the Northern Ireland Council for the Curriculum, Examinations and Assessment. When parents consider that a school has not applied its criteria fairly they have access to independent appeals tribunals. Grammar schools provide an academic type of secondary education with A-levels at the end of the seventh year, while secondary non-grammar schools follow a curriculum suited to a wider range of aptitudes and abilities.

SPECIAL EDUCATION – Wherever possible, taking parents' wishes into account, children with special educational needs (SEN) are educated in ordinary schools, which are required to publish their policy for pupils with such needs. Local education authorities in England and Wales and education and library boards in Northern Ireland are required to identify and secure provision for the needs of children with learning difficulties, to involve the parents in any decision and, in cases where they deem that that they should determine a child's education, draw up a formal statement of the child's special educational needs and how they intend to meet them, all within statutory time limits.

In Scotland, school placing is a matter of agreement between education authorities and parents. Parents have the right to say which school they want their child to attend, and a right of appeal where their wishes are not being met. Whenever possible, children with special needs are integrated into ordinary schools.

Maintained special schools are run by education authorities which pay all the costs of maintenance, but under the terms of Local Management of Schools, those able and wishing to manage their own budgets may choose to do so. Non-maintained special schools are run by voluntary bodies; they may receive some grant from central government for capital expenditure and for equipment but their current expenditure is met primarily from the fees charged to education authorities for pupils placed in the schools. Some independent schools provide education wholly or mainly for children with special educational needs and are required to meet similar standards to those for maintained and non-maintained special schools.

In January 2001 the number of pupils in maintained schools identified as having SEN was (thousands):

In special schools:

	England	Wales	Scotland	N. Ireland
Special schools	91.0	3.8	8.3	4.7
% with SEN statements	96.1%	97.2%	80.4%	82.9%
Mainstream schools	1,670.7	103.4	30.5	n/a
% with SEN statements	4.2%	5.4%	2.6%	1.5%

ALTERNATIVE PROVISION

There is no legal obligation on parents in the UK to educate their children at school provided that the local education authority is satisfied that the child is receiving full-time education suited to its age, abilities and aptitudes. The education authority need not be informed that a child is being educated at home unless the child is already registered at a state school. In that case the parents must arrange for the child's name to be removed from the school's register (by writing to the headteacher) before education at home can begin. Failure to do so leaves the parents liable to prosecution for condoning non-attendance.

INDEPENDENT SCHOOLS

Independent schools charge fees and are owned and managed under special trusts, with profits being used for the benefit of the schools concerned. About 6 per cent of children in the UK attend independent schools. There is a wide variety of provision, from kindergartens to large day and boarding schools, and from experimental schools to traditional institutions. A number of independent schools have been instituted by religious and ethnic minorities.

The term public schools is applied to those independent schools in membership of the Headmasters' and Headmistresses' Conference, the Governing Bodies Association or the Governing Bodies of Girls' Schools Association.

Most independent schools in Scotland follow the same examination system as England, Wales and Northern Ireland, i.e. GCSE followed by A-levels.

Preparatory schools are so-called because they prepare pupils for the common entrance examination to senior independent schools. Most cater for pupils from about seven to 13 years. The common entrance examination is set by the Common Entrance Examination Board, but marked by the independent school to which the pupil intends to go. It is taken at 13 by boys, and between 11 and 13 by girls.

The Assisted Places Scheme was funded by central government in England, Wales and Scotland and enabled children to attend independent secondary schools which their parents could not otherwise afford. It ceased to operate after the September 1997 intake but pupils holding their places at the beginning of the 1997–8 school year will keep them until they have completed their education at their current school.

In 2000–1, the number of independent schools and pupils was:

	No. of Schools	No. of pupils (000s)	% of school population	Pupil-teacher ratio
England	2,205	586.2	7.5	9.7
Wales	54	9.5	1.9	9.6
Scotland	129	29.2	3.4	10.1
N. Ireland	26	1.2	0.3	9.3

THE CURRICULUM

ENGLAND

The national curriculum was introduced in primary and secondary schools between autumn 1989 and autumn 1996, for the period of compulsory schooling from five to 16. It is mandatory in all maintained schools. A review was completed in August 1999 and a revised curriculum was introduced in schools from September 2000.

The statutory subjects are:

Core subjects	Foundation subjects
English	Design and technology
Mathematics	Information and
Science	communication technology
	History
	Geography
	Art and design
	Music
	Physical education

At key stage three (11- to 14-year-olds) a modern foreign language is introduced. At key stage four (14- to 16-year-olds) pupils are required to continue to study the core subjects, plus physical education, design and technology and information and communication technology. Citizenship is a compulsory subject for secondary pupils. Other foundation subjects are optional and other subjects, such as drama, dance and classical languages, are taught when the resources of individual schools permit. Religious education must be taught across all key stages, following a locally agreed syllabus; parents have the right to remove their children if they wish.

Statutory assessment takes place on entry to primary school and national tests and tasks in English and mathematics at key stage one (five- to seven-year-olds),

with the addition of science at key stages two (seven- to 11-year-olds) and three, are in place. Teachers make their own assessments of their pupils' progress to set alongside the test results. At key stage four the GCSE and vocational equivalents are the main form of assessment.

The DfES publishes tables showing pupils' performance in A-level, AS-level, GCSE, GNVQ and Vocational A-level examinations school by school. LEAs are required to publish similar information in November each year showing the results of national curriculum tests and teacher assessments for seven, 11 and 14-year-olds. Approximately 600,000 pupils in each of the age groups take the tests each year.

NATIONAL TESTING (TEACHERS' ASSESSMENT RESULTS IN PARENTHESIS) IN CORE SUBJECTS 2001

Percentage of pupils reaching or exceeding the expected level of performance at that age:

	Key stage 1 7-year olds (level 2)	Key stage 2 11-year-olds (level 4)	Key stage 3 14-year-olds (level 5)
English	81.6 (85)	75 (72)	64 (65)
Mathematics	91 (89)	71 (74)	66 (68)
Science	– (89)	87 (82)	66 (64)

National targets for 2004 proposed for 11-year-olds are: 85 per cent to reach level four in English and mathematics and 35 per cent to reach level five. Targets for 14-year-olds are: 75 per cent to reach level five in English, mathematics and information and communication technology and 70 per cent in science by 2004; by 2007, 85 and 80 per cent respectively.

The Qualifications and Curriculum Authority (QCA) is an independent government agency funded by the DfES. It is responsible for ensuring that the curriculum and qualifications available to young people and adults are of high quality, coherent and flexible and its remit ranges from the under-fives to higher level vocational qualifications.

WALES

The national curriculum was introduced simultaneously in Wales and, although it is broadly similar, has separate and distinctive characteristics which are reflected, where appropriate, in the programmes of study. A review of the curriculum in Wales has been completed and changes were introduced from September 2000. Welsh is compulsory for pupils at all key stages, either as a first or as a second language. In 2000–1 some 27 per cent of primary schools used Welsh as the sole or main medium of instruction and 67.7 per cent taught Welsh as a first language. Over 22 per cent of secondary schools taught Welsh both as a first and second language, while 68.6 per cent taught it as a second language only.

Schools perform tests and tasks in all the national curriculum subjects except at key stage 1, where teacher assessment is the sole means of assessing attainment. Approximately 38,000 pupils in each of the key stages 2 and 3 take the tests each year. Information about pupils' performance in examinations and national curriculum tests is made available by schools to parents but is no longer published.

NATIONAL TESTING (TEACHERS' ASSESSMENT RESULTS IN PARENTHESIS) IN CORE SUBJECTS 2001

Percentage of pupils reaching or exceeding the expected level of performance at that age:

	Key stage 1 7-year-olds (level 2)	Key stage 2 11-year-olds (level 4)	Key stage 3 14-year-olds (level 5)
English	(83.0)	73.0 (77.0)	63.0 (62.0)
Welsh (first language)	(87.0)	70.0 (71.0)	70.0 (71.0)
Mathematics	(89.0)	75.0 (74.0)	65.0 (62.0)
Science	(88.0)	81.0 (82.0)	63.0 (63.0)

National targets have been set as follows: by 2004 80-85 per cent of 11-year-olds to reach level four or better and 80-85 per cent of 14-year-olds to reach level five or better in English, Welsh (first language), mathematics and science.

Awdurdod Cymwysterau, Cwricwlwm ac Asesu Cymru (ACCAC)/the Qualifications, Curriculum and Assessment Authority for Wales advises government on the matters within its remit. ACCAC is funded by the National Assembly for Wales.

SCOTLAND

The content and management of the curriculum in Scotland are not prescribed by statute but are the responsibility of education authorities and individual headteachers. Advice and guidance are provided by the Scottish Executive Education Department and Learning and Teaching Scotland, which also has a developmental role. Those bodies have produced guidelines on the structure and balance of the curriculum as well as for each of the curriculum areas for the five to 14 age group. There are also guidelines on assessment across the whole curriculum, on reporting to parents, and on standardised national tests for English language and mathematics at five levels. Testing is carried out on a voluntary basis when the teacher deems it appropriate; most pupils are expected to move from one level to the next at roughly two-year intervals. National testing is largely in place in most primary schools but secondary school participation rates are lower.

The curriculum for 14- to 16-year-olds includes study within each of eight modes: language and communication; mathematical studies; science; technology; social studies; creative activities; physical education; and religious and moral education. There is a recommended percentage of time to be devoted to each area over the two years. Provision is made for teaching in Gaelic in Gaelic-speaking areas.

For 16- to 18-year-olds National Qualifications, a unified framework of courses and awards, which brings together both academic and vocational courses, was introduced in 1999. The Scottish Qualifications Authority awards the certificates.

NORTHERN IRELAND

A curriculum common to all grant-aided schools exists. Pupils are required to study religious education and, depending on which key stage they have reached, certain subjects from six broad areas of study: English, mathematics, science and technology; the environment and society; creative and expressive studies and, in key stages three and four, language studies. A revised statutory curriculum is to be introduced from September 2004. Six cross-curricular educational themes, which include information technology and education for

mutual understanding, are woven through the main subjects of the curriculum. Irish is a foundation subject in schools that use it as a medium of instruction.

The assessment of pupils is broadly in line with practice in England and Wales and takes place at the ages of eight, 11 and 14. The GCSE is used to assess 16-year-olds. From 2001 the Department of Education ceased to publish the national testing results, as a consultation exercise showed that parents and others preferred the option of individual schools providing information to parents.

National targets have been set as follows for achievement by 2004: for key stage 2 (11-year-olds), 77 per cent to reach level four or above in English and 80 per cent in mathematics; and for key stage 3 (14-year-olds), 72 per cent in English and mathematics and 70 per cent in science to reach level five and above.

The Council for the Curriculum, Examinations and Assessment (CCEA) monitors and advises the Department of Education and teachers on all matters relating to the curriculum, assessment arrangements and examinations in grant-aided schools. It conducts GCSE, A- and AS-level examinations, pupil assessment at key stages one, two and three and administers the transfer procedure tests.

PUBLIC EXAMINATIONS AND QUALIFICATIONS

ENGLAND, WALES AND NORTHERN IRELAND

Until the end of 1987, most secondary school pupils at the end of compulsory schooling around the age of 16, and others, took the General Certificate of Education (GCE) Ordinary-level or the Certificate of Secondary Education (CSE). From 1988 these were replaced by a single system of examinations, the General Certificate of Secondary Education (GCSE), which is usually taken after five years of secondary education. The GCSE is the main method of assessing the performance of pupils at age 16 in all national curriculum subjects required to be assessed at the end of compulsory schooling, as well as a range of subjects which are commonly taught in schools but fall outside the National Curriculum requirements. The structure of the examination reflects national curriculum requirements where these apply. GCSE short-course qualifications are available in some subjects. As a rule the syllabus comprises half the content of a full GCSE course.

The GCSE differs from its predecessors in that there are syllabuses based on national criteria covering course objectives, content and assessment methods; differentiated assessment (i.e. different papers or questions for different ranges of ability) and grade-related criteria (i.e. grades awarded on absolute rather than relative performance). The GCSE certificates are awarded on an eight-point scale, A* to G. Grades A to C are the equivalent of the corresponding O-level grades A to C or CSE grade 1. Grades D–G record achievement at least as high as that represented by CSE grades 2 to 5. All GCSE syllabuses, assessments and grading procedures are monitored by the Qualifications and Curriculum Authority to ensure that they conform to the national criteria

In the UK in 1999–2000, 50.4 per cent of all 15 to 16-year-old entrants achieved five or more results at grade C or better, while only 5.5 per cent of pupils achieved no graded results.

Students are increasingly encouraged to continue their education post-16. For those who do so, in addition to the vocational qualifications outlined below, there are General Certificate of Education (GCE) Advanced (A-level) examinations. A-level courses usually last two years

and have traditionally provided the foundation for entry to higher education. The new A-level qualification, introduced for first teaching from September 2000, is normally composed of six units (three A2 units and three AS units), the latter being less demanding and constituting the new AS-level qualification, which represents the first half of a full A-level. Students who go on to complete the full A-level will be assessed on their attainment in all six units, which may be taken either in stages or all at the end of the course. Candidates have the choice between end-of-course or staged assessment, with limits on coursework. A-levels and AS-levels are marked on a six-point scale: from A to E (pass) and U (unclassified) which is not certificated. The Advanced Subsidiary (AS) level examinations, introduced for examination in summer 2001, represent the first half of the full A Level, but are also a qualification in their own right. Students can take the AS and then decide whether to continue with the subject to the A Level or to leave at that point with their AS result. AS results earn points for potential use in applying for higher education and have been used as a means of diversifying the range of subjects chosen by students post-16. The government made some changes in response to the criticism that the introduction of AS-level examinations had imposed too heavy a burden in the first year of the A-level course on students and teachers. These changes were generally to reduce the length of examination papers so that more than one exam could be fitted into a single examination timetable session.

There is also the opportunity for A-level candidates to take additional papers of greater difficulty, known as Advanced Extension Awards (which replaced Special-level or Scholarship-level). Papers are available in most of the traditional academic subjects and are marked on a two-point scale (merit and distinction).

Alongside A-Levels are the Vocational Certificate of Education (VCE). These are offered in a range of vocationally orientated subjects such as Health and Social Care, Manufacturing and Travel and Tourism. Introduced at the same time as the unitised A-Levels, the VCE is available in a 3-unit (AS), 6-unit (full award) and 12-unit (double award) format. The emphasis in VCE is on practical skills and a greater proportion of the assessment is carried out through portfolio work, assessed by the centre and externally moderated by the awarding body.

Many maintained schools offer BTEC Firsts and an increasing number offer BTEC Nationals. National Vocational Qualifications (NVQs) in the form of General NVQs (GNVQs) are also available to students in schools. The Vocational Certificates of Education (VCE) exist at Advanced and AS levels.

In the UK in 1999–2000, 34.5 per cent of young students in schools and colleges achieved two or more passes at A-level or SCE H-grade (an increase of 0.8 per cent on the previous year). Of those in the UK who entered for A-level or SCE H-grade examinations, the greatest number of entries were in the following subjects:

	all entrants (%)	boys (%)	girls (%)
Mathematics	11.8	50.4	49.6
English	11.4	50.0	50.0
English literature	8.9	47.9	52.1
Science double award	8.7	49.4	50.6
Design and technology	8.0	53.7	46.3

The various examining boards in England have combined into three Unitary Awarding Bodies (UABs), which offer both academic and vocational qualifications: GNVQs, GCSEs, AS and A-levels. The new bodies are: the Assessment and Qualifications Alliance (AQA); Edexcel;

and Oxford, Cambridge and RSA Examinations (OCR). The UABs are separate bodies, although they work together in many ways to meet the needs of schools and colleges. The Joint Council for General Qualifications (JCGQ) comprises the three English UABs, the Welsh Joint Education Committee and the Northern Ireland Council for the Curriculum, Examinations and Assessment.

SCOTLAND

Scotland has its own system of public examinations. In 1999 a new system, Higher Still, was introduced to provide a range of National Qualifications for learners whatever their abilities or interests. The new system has been implemented for all pupils in the fifth and sixth year of secondary education (post-16).

Five levels of study are offered to learners through Higher Still: Access, Intermediate 1, Intermediate 2, Higher and Advanced Higher. The new Higher National course and Advanced Higher National course are direct replacements for the old SCE Higher grade and Certificate of Sixth Year Studies respectively.

National Courses consist of blocks of study called National Units. A Unit usually consists of around 40 hours of study and there are three Units in a course. Unit awards demonstrate that a learner has achieved competence in a particular area of study.

National Course awards are graded by external assessment, which consists of an examination, coursework or performance, or a combination of two or more of these. National Course awards also require candidates to pass all Unit assessments of the course. A typical National Course external assessment requires candidates to demonstrate long-term retention of knowledge, high levels of problem solving, integration of knowledge across a whole course and an ability to apply knowledge and skills in novel situations. The range of subjects has been expanded to include vocational qualifications and some new subjects have been introduced.

The new National Qualifications system has been introduced in a few schools for pupils in their fourth year of secondary education, but the majority of this lower age group still take the traditional Standard Grade examinations at the end of a two-year course. Each Standard Grade normally has two or three elements, each of which has an assessment attached to it which may take the form of an examination, coursework or performance. The mark for each element is aggregated to give the overall grade.

Awards at Standard Grade are set at three levels: Credit (leading to awards at grade 1 or 2); General (leading to awards at grade 3 or 4); and Foundation (leading to awards at grade 5 or 6). Grade 7 is awarded to those who, although they have completed the course, have not attained any of these levels. Normally pupils will take examinations covering two pairs of grades, either grades 1–4 or grades 3–6. Most candidates take seven or eight Standard Grade examinations.

The qualifications system is administered and quality assured by the Scottish Qualifications Authority (SQA).

THE INTERNATIONAL BACCALAUREATE

The International Baccalaureate is an internationally recognised two-year pre-university course and examination designed to facilitate the mobility of students and to promote international understanding. There are 51 schools and colleges in the UK which offer the International Baccalaureate diploma.

RECORDS OF ACHIEVEMENT

The National Record of Achievement will be phased out by 2004, when the Progress File will replace it in England, Wales and Northern Ireland. In Scotland the Scottish Qualifications Authority issues a Scottish Qualifications Certificate recording all qualifications achieved at all levels which it has either awarded or accredited.

TEACHERS

ENGLAND AND WALES

New entrants to the teaching profession in state primary and secondary schools are required to be graduates and to have Qualified Teacher Status (QTS). QTS is achieved by successfully completing a course of initial teacher training, traditionally either a Bachelor of Education (BEd) degree or the Postgraduate Certificate of Education (PGCE) at an accredited institution. A third route into teaching enables students on traditional academic degree courses to undertake QTS modules at the same time. New entrants are statutorily required to serve a one-year induction period during which they will have a structured programme of support. In recent years various employment-based routes to QTS have been developed. The Graduate Teacher Programme allows those who has qualified as teachers overseas or graduates of at least 24 years of age with teaching experience to undergo between one term's and one year's school-based training. The schools involved receive up to £13,000 to cover the trainee's salary in addition to a grant of up to £4,000 for undertaking training. "Training only" grants are also available to schools which themselves fund trainees' salaries. The Registered Teacher Scheme is designed to attract into the teaching profession entrants over 24 years of age without a degree or formal teaching qualification but with at least two years of higher education and with relevant experience; entrants are paid a salary and complete a degree while undergoing training.

All teacher training is now largely school-based, with student teachers spending about two-thirds of their training in the classroom and schools are given a role in course design and delivery. Individual schools or consortia of schools and CTCs can bid for funds from the DfES to carry out their own teacher training, including recruitment of students, subject to approval of their proposed training programme by the Teacher Training Agency (TTA) and monitoring and evaluation by OFSTED and Estyn. Funds are given to schools to meet the costs of designing and delivering the courses.

Teachers in further education are not required to have QTS, though roughly half have a teaching qualification and most have industrial, commercial or professional experience. A qualification for aspiring head-teachers, the National Professional Qualification for Headship, has been introduced. The National College for School Leadership administers this qualification and others and acts as a focus for development and support.

The government has introduced various schemes in an attempt to address the shortage of teachers in England and Wales. Eligible graduates training for the PGCE receive an annual training salary of £6,000 (£150 per week). Teachers who then go on to teach shortage subjects (English, Welsh (in Wales), modern foreign languages, mathematics, science and technology) receive a further £4,000 as a lump sum after completing their first year of work and will moreover be assisted to pay off their student loans over 10 years if certain conditions are met. Some teachers are eligible for help to buy homes in areas where housing costs are high. Providers of initial teacher training in England and Wales may receive funds from

the TTA to help promote courses in certain subjects and to offer financial support to students undertaking them. The subjects are: design and technology; geography; information technology; mathematics; modern languages; music; religious education; science; and Welsh in Wales. A training salary for trainee teachers in post-16 non-degree craft subjects is being trialled.

The TTA administers a returners' programme for qualified teachers who wish to refresh their skills before returning to the profession. They benefit from the waiving of course fees, a grant of up to £150 per week while studying and supplementary grants for childcare.

The TTA funds all types of teacher training in England, whether run by universities, colleges or schools, and some educational research. In Wales funding is undertaken by the Higher Education Funding Council for Wales (HEFCW). On an integrated England and Wales basis the TTA also acts as a central source of information and advice about entry to teaching, and has responsibilities relating to the continuing professional development of teachers. The General Teaching Council, an independent professional council, advises the Secretary of State and the TTA, with a separate council for Wales.

The Specialist Teacher Assistant (STA) scheme provides trained support to qualified teachers in the teaching of reading, writing and arithmetic to young pupils.

SCOTLAND

The General Teaching Council (GTC) for Scotland advises central government on matters relating to teacher supply and the professional suitability of all teacher training courses. The GTC is also the body responsible for disciplinary procedures in cases of professional misconduct. All teachers in maintained schools must be registered with the GTC, initially for a two-year probationary period which can be extended if necessary. Only graduates are accepted as entrants to the profession; primary school teachers undertake either a four-year vocational degree course or a one-year postgraduate course, while teachers of academic subjects in secondary schools undertake the latter. There is also a combined degree sometimes known as a concurrent degree. Most initial teacher training is classroom-based. The Scottish Qualification for Headship has been introduced for aspiring head teachers. The colleges of education provide both in-service and pre-service training for teachers which is subject to inspection by HM Inspectorate of Education. The colleges are funded by the Scottish Higher Education Funding Council, which also sets intake levels for teacher education courses.

NORTHERN IRELAND

All new entrants to teaching in grant-aided schools are graduates and hold an approved teaching qualification. Initial teacher training, provided by the two universities and two colleges of education, is integrated with induction and early in-service training, the latter over a period of three years. The colleges are concerned with teacher education mainly for the primary school sector. They also provide BEd courses for intending secondary school teachers of religious education, commercial studies and craft, design and technology. With these exceptions, the professional training of teachers for secondary schools is provided in the education departments of the universities. A review of primary and secondary teacher training has taken place as a result of which all student teachers spend more time in the classroom. The General Teaching Council for Northern Ireland advises government on professional issues, maintains a register of professional teachers and acts as a disciplinary body.

ACCREDITATION OF TRAINING INSTITUTIONS

Advice to central government on the accreditation, content and quality of initial teacher training courses is given in England by the TTA, in Wales by the HEFCW and in Northern Ireland by the Department of Education. These bodies also monitor and disseminate good practice, assisted in Northern Ireland by the Teacher Education Committee. The GTC performs those functions in Scotland.

SERVING TEACHERS 1999–2000 *(full-time)* (thousands):

Public sector schools	E&W	Scotland	NI*	Total UK
Nursery and primary	181.4	21.5	8.1	211.1
Secondary	190.3	22.6	10.2	223.0
Special (public sector and non-maintained)	13.8	2.9	0.7	16.6
Independent schools	48.4	2.7	0.1	51.2
TOTAL	433.9	48.9	19.2	502.0

*Provisional

SALARIES

Qualified teachers in England, Wales and Northern Ireland, other than the leadership group (which includes headteachers, deputy headteachers, and advanced skills teachers) are paid on an 11-point scale, six points on the main pay scale and five on the upper scale. Entry points and placement depend on qualifications and experience. There are additional cash allowances for management responsibilities, special needs work and recruitment and retention factors as calculated by the relevant body, i.e. the governing body or the LEA. The "advanced skills teacher" grade was introduced to enhance prospects in the classroom for the most able teachers. High-performing teachers as assessed against national standards receive a performance-related pay increase. There is a statutory superannuation scheme in maintained schools.

Salary scales for teachers in England, Wales and Northern Ireland are as follows:

Head	£34,575–£85,704
Deputy head	from £30,564
Advanced skills teacher	£28,950–£46,164
Teacher	£17,628–£32,250

Teachers in Scotland are paid on a seven-point scale. The entry point depends on type of qualification and additional allowances are payable under a range of circumstances.

Salary scales for teachers in Scotland are

	1 August 2002	1 April 2003
Head	£33,828–£62,661	£36,414–£67,449
Depute Head	£33,828–£46,887	£36,414–£50,469
Principal teacher	£30,090–£35,100	£32,338–£37,782
Senior teacher	£27,480–£29,073	£31,229
Teacher	£16,644–£26,670	£18,000–£28,707

POST-16 EDUCATION

In the United Kingdom about 70 per cent of 16-year-olds continue in full-time education either in school sixth forms, sixth form colleges or further education colleges.

ENGLAND AND WALES

Further education and sixth form colleges are funded directly by central government through the Learning and Skills Council in England, which operates through 47 regional centres, and the National Council for Education and Training in Wales. The Councils have a duty to secure provision of adequate facilities in their areas and are also responsible for the assessment of quality, in which their inspectors play a key role. Further education colleges are controlled by autonomous further education corporations, which include substantial representation from industry and commerce, and which own their own assets and employ their own staff. Their funding is determined in part by the number of students enrolled and their level of achievement.

Teaching staff in further education establishments are not necessarily required to have teaching qualifications although many do so, but they are subject to regular appraisal of teaching performance. It is planned to introduce a mandatory professional qualification for college principals.

Much further education tends to be broadly vocational in purpose and employers are often involved in designing courses. It ranges from lower-level technical and commercial courses and government-sponsored training, through courses for those aiming at higher-level posts in industry, commerce and administration, to professional courses. Facilities exist for GCE A- and AS-levels, GCSEs, GNVQs and a full range of vocational qualifications. These courses can form the foundation for progress to higher education qualifications. Many students attend part-time, either through day or block release from employment, or in the evenings.

The main courses and examinations in the vocational field, all of which link in with the National Vocational Qualification (NVQ) framework, are offered by the following bodies, but there are also many others.

Edexcel resulted from the merger of the Business and Technology Education Council (BTEC) and London Examinations. It provides programmes of study across a wide range of subject areas. Qualifications offered include GNVQs, NVQs, GCSEs, AS and A-levels, National and Higher National diplomas and certificates and other BTEC qualifications.

City & Guilds specialise in developing qualifications and assessments for work-related and leisure qualifications. They offer nationally and internationally recognised certificates in over 500 vocational qualifications. The progressive structure of awards spans seven levels, from foundation to the highest level of professional competence.

Oxford, Cambridge and RSA Examinations cover the full range of academic and vocational qualifications. The latter include accounting, business administration, customer service, management, language schemes, information technology and teaching qualifications. A wide range of NVQs and GNVQs are offered and a policy operates of credit accumulation, so that candidates can take a single unit or complete qualifications.

There are 411 further education establishments (of which 105 are sixth form colleges) in England and 24 in Wales. In England (1999–2000) there were 932.0 thousand full-time and sandwich-course students and 2,502.7 thousand part-time students. In Wales (1999–2000) there were 45.3 thousand full-time and sandwich students and 181.5 thousand part-time students.

SCOTLAND

Responsibility for further education lies with the Scottish Executive under the Minister for Enterprise, Transport and Lifelong Learning. The Executive liaises with the Scottish Further Education Funding Council. There are 46 further education colleges run by their own boards of management. The boards include the principal and staff and student representatives among their ten to 16 members; at least half of whom must have experience of commerce, industry or professional practice. Two colleges, on Orkney and Shetland, are under Islands Council control and two others, Sabhal Mor Ostaig (the Gaelic college on Skye) and Newbattle Abbey are run by trustees.

The Scottish Qualifications Authority (SQA) is the statutory awarding body for qualifications in the national education and training system in Scotland. It is both the main awarding body for qualifications for work including Scottish Vocational Qualifications (SVQs) and is also their accrediting body. The SQA is by statute required clearly to separate its awarding and accrediting functions.

There are three main qualification families in Scottish further education: National Qualifications; Higher National Qualifications (HNC and HND); and SVQs. In addition to Standard Grade qualifications, National Qualifications are available at five levels: Access, Intermediate 1, Intermediate 2, Higher and Advanced Higher. Another feature of the qualifications system is the Scottish Group Award (SGA). SGAs are built up unit by unit and allow opportunity for credit transfer from other qualifications (such as Standard Grade or SVQ) providing a further option for learners, especially adult returners.

SVQs are competence-based qualifications suitable for work-place delivery but they can also be taken in further education colleges and other centres where work-place conditions can be simulated.

The Scottish Credit and Qualifications Framework (SCQF) includes qualifications across academic and vocational sectors in a single credit-based framework and comprises 12 levels covering all mainstream qualifications from Access level in National Qualifications to postgraduate qualifications. It includes SVQs. Individual qualifications are allocated credits and levels and learners are able to transfer credits from one qualification to another in appropriate subjects.

In the academic year 1999–2000 there were 38,200 full-time and sandwich-course students and 273,700 part-time students on non-advanced vocational courses of further education in further education colleges (excluding Newbattle Abbey College).

NORTHERN IRELAND

All further education colleges are independent corporate bodies like their counterparts in the rest of the UK. Responsibility for the sector lies with the Department for Employment and Learning, which funds the colleges directly. The colleges own their own property, are responsible for their own services and employ their own staff.

The governing bodies of the colleges must include at least 50 per cent membership from the professions, local business or industry, or other fields of employment relevant to the activities of the college.

In 2001–2 Northern Ireland had 17 institutions of further education, and there were 21,267 full-time and 55,783 part-time enrolments on vocational further education courses.

STUDENT SUPPORT

The means-tested Education Maintenance Allowance (EMA) for eligible 16- to 19-year-old students continuing their education beyond school leaving age is being piloted in certain areas in England and Scotland, where there are

problems of poverty and low staying-on rates. It is a weekly allowance worth up to £40, which is payable subject to conditions laid out under a learning agreement. Bonuses may be paid for satisfactory attendance, progression and achievement. Also available to students in that age group are means-tested discretionary payments from LEAs and free or subsidised travel to and from school or college, while adults may apply for funds, which also cover financial help with childcare, allocated by central government through the funding bodies. The discretionary access fund also exists, administered by the institutions.

Eligible Welsh-domiciled students aged over 18 on further education courses, whether full-time or part-time (subject to a minimum contact requirement), receive a means-tested non-repayable Assembly Learning Grant. The grant is administered by local education authorities. Discretionary Financial Contingency Funds are also available to all students suffering hardship and are administered by the institutions themselves.

Full-time students over 19 years of age and resident in Northern Ireland, on certain vocational courses, may benefit from discretionary non-repayable Access Bursaries of up to £1,500. The bursaries are administered by the Education and Library Boards. Discretionary Access Funds exist, administered by the institutions themselves, for which any students suffering hardship are eligible to apply.

NATIONAL VOCATIONAL QUALIFICATIONS

National Vocational Qualifications (NVQs) are work-place based occupational qualifications. General National Vocational Qualifications (GNVQs) provide a vocational alternative to academic qualifications in colleges and schools. GNVQs cover six broad categories in the NVQ framework and are aimed at those wishing to familiarise themselves with a range of opportunities. The Vocational A-level, which replaced Advanced GNVQs, operates at three levels: the three unit vocational A-level (known as Vocational AS), equivalent to one GCE AS-level; the 6 unit Vocational A-level, equivalent to one GCE A-level; and the 12 unit Vocational A-level (double award) equivalent to two A-levels (formerly Advanced GNVQ). Part one GNVQ comprises Intermediate GNVQ, equivalent to two GCSEs at A* to C grade and Foundation GNVQ, equivalent to two GCSEs at D to G grade. The full GNVQ, also at Intermediate and Foundation level, is similarly equivalent to four GCSEs.

HIGHER EDUCATION

The term higher education is used to describe education above A-level, Higher and Advanced Higher Grade and their equivalent, which is provided in universities, colleges of higher education and in some further education colleges.

The Further and Higher Education Act 1992 and parallel legislation in Scotland removed the distinction between higher education provided by the universities and that provided in England and Wales by the former polytechnics and colleges of higher education and in Scotland by the former central institutions and others. It allowed all polytechnics, and other higher education institutions which satisfy the necessary criteria, to award their own taught course and research degrees and to adopt the title of university. All the polytechnics, art colleges and some colleges of higher education have since done so. The change of name does not affect the legal constitution of the institutions. Funding is by the Higher

Education Funding Councils for England, Wales and Scotland and directly by the Department for Employment and Learning in Northern Ireland.

The number of students in higher education in the UK in 2000–1 was (thousands):

Full-time, sandwich	1,276.3
% female	53.5%
Part-time	791.0
% female	56.2%
TOTAL	2,067.3
of which overseas	11.1%

The proportion of the 18- to 21-year-old population undertaking full-time and part-time courses in higher education was about 30 per cent in England and Wales, about 40 per cent in Scotland and about 45 per cent in Northern Ireland in 2000–1. In the same year about 28 per cent of undergraduates in the first year of a first degree course were aged 21 years or over, while over 50 per cent of first year postgraduate students were aged 30 years or over; 56.9 per cent of the UK domiciled student population were female (57.7 per cent of UK domiciled undergraduates).

Women formed the majority of students in subjects allied to medicine (83.3 per cent), education (72.6 per cent), veterinary science (69.6 per cent), languages (68.4 per cent), information science (62.7 per cent), social, economic and political studies (61.8 per cent) and biological sciences (61.6 per cent). Men formed the majority of those studying engineering and technology (84.9 per cent), computer science (73.9 per cent), architecture, building and planning (71.7 per cent), mathematical sciences (62.5 per cent) and physical sciences (61.7 per cent).

Responsibility for universities rests in England with the Secretary of State for Education and Skills and with Education Ministers in Scotland, Northern Ireland and Wales. Advice to government on matters relating to the universities is provided by the Higher Education Funding Councils for England, Wales and Scotland, and by the Higher Education Council in Northern Ireland. The former receive a block grant from central government which they allocate to the universities and colleges. The grant is allocated directly to institutions by the Department for Employment and Learning in Northern Ireland on the advice of the Northern Ireland Higher Education Council.

There are now 88 universities in the UK, where only 47 existed prior to the Further and Higher Education Acts 1992. Of the 88, 71 are in England (including one federal university), two (one a federal institution) in Wales, 13 in Scotland and two in Northern Ireland. There are also 64 colleges of higher education, some of which are multidisciplinary while others specialise, for example, in teacher training. Some award their own degrees and qualifications, while others are validated by a university or a national body.

The pre-1992 universities each have their own system of internal government but broad similarities exist. Most are run by two main bodies: the senate, which deals primarily with academic issues and consists of members elected from within the university; and the council, which is the supreme body and is responsible for all appointments and promotions, and bidding for and allocation of financial resources. At least half the members of the council are drawn from outside the university. Joint committees of senate and council are common.

Those universities which were formerly polytechnics (38) or other higher education institutions (three) and the colleges of higher education (61) are run by higher

education corporations, which are controlled by boards of governors. At least half the members of each board must be drawn from industry, business, commerce and the professions.

The non-residential Open University provides courses nationally leading to degrees, diplomas and certificates. Teaching is through a combination of specially produced textbooks, television programmes, audio- and videotapes, correspondence, tutorials, short residential courses and computer software. No qualifications are needed for entry. The Open University offers a modular programme of undergraduate courses by credit accumulation and post-experience and postgraduate courses, including a programme of higher degrees which comprises BPhil, MPhil and PhD through research, and MA, MBA and MSc through taught courses. The Open University in England, Wales and Northern Ireland is funded by the Higher Education Funding Council for England (HEFCE) and in Scotland by the Scottish Higher Education Funding Council (SHEFC). The Open University's recurrent grant for 2000–1 was £127.0 million from the HEFCE, £12.8 million from SHEFC and £0.6 million from the Teacher Training Agency. In 2002 about 145,000 undergraduates were registered of whom about 55 per cent were women. Estimated cost (2002) of a six-credit degree was around £4,600 including course fees of about £3,400.

The University for Industry (UfI) promotes learning ranging from basic skills to specialised technological and management skills. UfI operates through learning centres. The Scottish UfI operates within the distinctive Scottish system.

The independent University of Buckingham receives no public funding and provides a two-year course (four terms per year) leading to a bachelor's degree. Its tuition fees from October 2002 and from January 2003 are £2,700 and £2,730 per term respectively.

ENGLAND AND WALES

In 2000–1 full-time and part-time student enrolments were (thousands):

England

Undergraduates	1,278.9
% overseas	7.8%
Postgraduates	377.8
% overseas	25.4%

Wales

Undergraduates	87.5
% overseas	6.6%
Postgraduates	19.8
% overseas	20.1%

Higher education courses funded by the funding bodies are also taught in some further education colleges. In England in 2000–1 there were about 68.6 thousand full-time and part-time students (4.4 per cent of total higher education student numbers) on such courses and 1,296 enrolments (1.3 per cent of higher education student numbers) in Wales.

SCOTLAND

The Scottish Higher Education Funding Council (SHEFC) funds 20 institutions of higher education, including 13 universities. The universities are broadly managed as described above and the remaining colleges are managed by independent governing bodies which include representatives of industrial, commercial, professional and educational interests. Most of the courses outside the universities have a vocational

orientation and a substantial number are sandwich courses.

Student numbers in 2000–1 in universities and other higher education institutions were (thousands):

Undergraduates	139.5
% overseas	7.4%
Postgraduates	40.7
% overseas	23.0%

There were about 73,000 students on higher education courses in further education colleges, constituting about 27.8 per cent of the total higher education student number.

NORTHERN IRELAND[1]

In Northern Ireland higher education is provided in the 17 colleges of further education, the two universities and the two university colleges. These institutions offer a range of courses, including first and postgraduate degrees, PGCEs, undergraduate diplomas and certificates, and professional qualifications.

Enrolments in higher education institutions in 2001–2 were (thousands):

Undergraduates	34.4
% overseas* students	1.6%
Postgraduates	7.9
% overseas* students	9.0%

*classified as not domiciled in the UK or Republic of Ireland

In addition to the above, in 2001–2 there were 12,188 enrolments on higher education courses in Northern Ireland institutions of further education, which equated to 22.4 per cent of all higher education enrolments in Northern Ireland.

[1] Higher education figures provisional

ACADEMIC STAFF

Each university and college appoints its own academic staff on its own conditions. However, there is a common salary structure and, except for Oxford and Cambridge, a common career structure in the pre-1992 universities and a common salary structure for the post-1992 universities. The Universities and Colleges Employers Association acts as a pay agency for universities and colleges.

Teaching staff in higher education require no formal teaching qualification, but the Institute of Teaching and Learning in Higher Education, funded by the funding Councils, has been established to set up an accreditation scheme for higher education teachers and to encourage innovation in teaching and learning. Teacher trainers are required to spend a certain amount of time in schools to ensure that they have sufficient recent practical experience.

In 2000–1, there were 139.9 thousand full-time and part-time academic staff (UK nationals) in institutions of higher education in the UK, of which 69.3 per cent were wholly institutionally financed.

Salary scales for staff in the pre-1992 universities differ from those in the former polytechnics and colleges; it is planned eventually to amalgamate them. The salary scales for non-clinical academic staff in the pre-1992 universities throughout the UK are (2001–2):

Professor	from £39,394
Senior lecturer	£34,158–£41,732
Lecturer grade B	£25,455–£36,355
Lecturer grade A	£20,470–£24,435

The salaries of clinical academic staff are kept broadly comparable to those of doctors and dentists in the National Health Service.

Salary scales for lecturers in the former polytechnics, now universities, and colleges of higher education in England, Wales and Northern Ireland are:

Head of Department	from £26,304
Principal lecturer	£31,129–£39,141
Senior lecturer	£24,906–£32,910
Lecturer	£19,575–£26,686

and in Scotland:

Head of Department	£46,154–£52,094
Senior Lecturer	£29,709–£40,578
Lecturer	£22,522–£36,355

FINANCE

Although universities and colleges are expected to look to a wider range of funding sources than before, and to generate additional revenue in collaboration with industry, they are still largely financed, directly or indirectly, from government resources.

In 2000–1 the total income of institutions of higher education in the UK was £13,493.9 million (£12,711.7 million in 1999–2000) comprising (*percentage of income in parenthesis*):

	1999–2000 £ million	2000–1 £ million

Funding
  Council
  grants
	£5,140.3 (40.4%)	£5,355.7 (39.7%)

Tuition fees and
  education
  contracts
	£2,858.9 (22.5%)	£3,048.6 (22.6%)

Research grants and contracts	£1,969.9 (15.5%)	£2,207.2 (16.4%)
Other income*	£2,450.2 (19.3%)	£2,589.9 (19.2%)

*includes fees, services, endowments and investments

In the academic year 2000–1 the HEFCE's and HEFCW's recurrent grant to institutions outside their sector for the provision of higher education courses was £140.0 million.

COURSES

In the UK all universities and some colleges award their own degrees and other qualifications and may act as awarding and validating bodies for neighbouring colleges which are not yet accredited. The Quality Assurance Agency for Higher Education, funded by institutional contributions, advises government on applications for degree-awarding powers.

Facilities exist for full-time and part-time study, day release, sandwich or block release. Credit accumulation and transfer (CATS) is a system of study which allows a student to achieve a final qualification by accumulating credits for courses of study successfully achieved, or even professional experience, over a period. Credit transfer information and values are carried on an electronic database called ECCTIS 2000, which is available in most careers offices and many schools and colleges.

Higher education courses comprise: first degree and postgraduate (including research); Diploma in Higher Education (DipHE); Higher National Diploma (HND) and Higher National Certificate (HNC); and preparation for professional examinations. The in-service training of teachers is also included, but is funded in England by the Teacher Training Agency, not the HEFCE.

The Diploma of Higher Education (DipHE) is a two-year diploma usually intended to serve as a stepping-stone to a degree course or other further study. The DipHE is awarded by the institution itself if it is accredited; by an accredited institution of its choice if not. The BTEC Higher National Certificate (HNC) is awarded after two years part-time study. The BTEC Higher National Diploma (HND) is awarded after two years full-time, or three years sandwich-course or part-time study.

The foundation degree is a vocational degree which forms either a self-contained qualification or a basis for further study leading to an honours degree or further professional qualifications. It features non-traditional and flexible delivery arrangements.

Undergraduate courses lead to the title of Bachelor, Bachelor of Arts (BA) and Bachelor of Science (BSc) being the most common, except in certain Scottish universities where master is sometimes used for a first degree in arts subjects. For a higher degree the titles are Master of Arts (MA), Master of Science (MSc) and the research degrees of Master of Philosophy (MPhil) and Doctor of Philosophy (PhD or, at a few universities, DPhil).

Most undergraduate courses at universities and colleges of higher education run for three years, but some take up to four years. They include modern language courses and honours courses at Scottish universities and the University of Keele. Professional courses in subjects such as medicine, veterinary science and architecture take longer.

Postgraduate studies vary in length. Certificates, diplomas or masters degrees usually take one year full-time or two years part-time. Research degrees take from two to three years full-time.

Post-experience short courses form a large part of higher education provision, reflecting the need to update professional and technical training. Most of these courses fund themselves.

ADMISSIONS

The target proportion of 18- to 30-year-olds entering full-time higher education by 2010 is set at 50 per cent. Institutions suffer financial penalties if the number of students laid down for them by the funding Councils is exceeded, but the individual university or college decides which students to accept. The formal entry requirements to most degree courses are two A-levels at grade E or above (or equivalent), and to HND courses one A-level (or equivalent). In practice, most offers of places require qualifications in excess of this, higher requirements usually reflecting the popularity of a course or institution. These requirements do not, however, exclude applications from students with a variety of non-GCSE qualifications or unquantified experience and skills.

For admission to a degree, DipHE or HND, potential students apply through a central clearing house, the Universities and Colleges Admission Service (UCAS). Applicants are supplied with an application form and the UCAS Handbook, available from schools, colleges and careers offices or direct from UCAS, and may apply to a maximum of six institutions/courses. The only exception among universities is the Open University, which conducts its own admissions.

Applications for undergraduate teacher training courses are made through UCAS. Details of initial teacher training courses in Scotland can be obtained from colleges of education and those universities offering such courses, and from the Committee of Scottish Higher Education Principals (COSHEP).

For admission as a postgraduate student, universities and colleges normally require a good first degree in a

subject related to the proposed course of study or research, but other experience and qualifications will be considered on merit. Most applications are made to individual institutions but there are two clearing houses of relevance. All postgraduate teacher training courses in England and Wales and most of those in Scotland utilise the Graduate Teacher Training Registry. Applications for post graduate certificate of education (PGCE) courses at institutions in Northern Ireland are made directly to the institutions. For social work the Social Work Admissions System operates.

FEES

Entrants to undergraduate courses domiciled in England, Wales and Northern Ireland pay, directly to the institution, an annual contribution to their fees (up to £1,100 in 2002–3) depending on their own level of income or that of their spouse or parents. The fee contribution represents about a quarter of the average cost of a higher education course in the UK and the balance is paid by the education authority or, in Northern Ireland, by the Education and Libraries Board. Students from EU member countries pay fees at home student rates and, if studying at institutions in England, Wales and Northern Ireland, are liable to make an annual contribution to fees assessed against family income. Among the classes of students exempt from payment are: Scottish domiciled and EU students at Scottish institutions; students from England, Wales and Northern Ireland in the fourth year of a four-year degree course at a Scottish institution; existing students with mandatory awards (see below), for whom the grant-awarding body pays; students on certain courses of initial teacher training; medical students in the fifth year of their course; health professionals on National Health Service bursaries; and full-time or part-time students on benefit or low incomes.

Universities and colleges are free to set their own charges for students from non-EU countries, whose fees are meant to cover the cost of their education. Financial help is available under a number of schemes.

For postgraduate students, the maximum tuition fee that will be reimbursed through the awards system in 2002–3 is £2,870 full-time or £1,435 part-time.

STUDENT SUPPORT

LOANS

The means-tested interest-free loan is the main form of support for most undergraduate students in the UK who started full-time or sandwich undergraduate courses of higher education from the academic year commencing in September 1998. Students apply through LEAs in England and Wales, education and library boards in Northern Ireland and the Students Awards Agency in Scotland. The maximum loan available to full-time students in 2002–3 is £4,815, of which 75 per cent is not subject to means testing.

Loan rates for 2002–3 (final year rates in parenthesis):
Living in college/
　　lodgings in London area　　　£4,815 (£4,175)
Living in college/
　　lodgings elsewhere　　　　　£3,905 (£3,390)
Living in parental home　　　　　£3,090 (£2,700)

Extra income assessed loans are available to students whose courses last over 30 term-time weeks or who need to study abroad in certain high-cost countries. Loans of up to £500 are available to part-time students on low incomes or with dependent children.

Loans are available to students on designated courses, which comprise those full-time or sandwich courses leading to: a degree; the Diploma of Higher Education; the Higher National Diploma; initial teacher-training courses (not in Scotland), including those for the PGCE and the art teachers' certificate or diploma; a university certificate or diploma course lasting at least three years; and other qualifications which are specifically designated as being comparable to first degree courses. Certain residency conditions also apply. In 2000–1, 759.0 thousand loans were taken up, to the value of £2,119.0 million.

Repayment arrangements differ for students who embarked upon higher education courses before the 1998–9 academic year and those starting thereafter. The former normally repay on a mortgage-style basis over five to seven years, although repayment can be deferred if annual income is at or below 85 per cent of national average earnings. The latter are not required to make repayments until their annual income is above £10,000 when nine per cent of the income above that amount is taken to repay the loan. Interest on the loan is linked to inflation in line with the Retail Prices Index. Providing repayments have been kept up, the loan is automatically cancelled on death; if the recipient becomes permanently disabled; or at age 65.

NON-REPAYABLE GRANTS AND ALLOWANCES

Eligible students, such as single parents, others with dependants, or those leaving care, are entitled to apply for various additional means-tested supplementary grants for help in meeting certain living and other costs, for childcare and for each child at school. Disabled students are eligible for non means-tested Disabled Students' Allowances.

Eligible Scottish-domiciled students from low income families at institutions in Scotland may apply for a Young Students' Bursary. The maximum available in 2002–3 is £2,050.

Eligible Welsh-domiciled undergraduates from low income families, whether on full-time or part-time courses, receive a means-tested non-repayable Assembly Learning Grant of up to £1,500 per year. The grant is administered by local education authorities.

Full-time students on low income resident in Northern Ireland may benefit from discretionary non-repayable Access Bursaries of up to £1,500. The award of a bursary carries a reduction in student loan entitlement. The bursaries are administered by the Education and Library Boards.

MANDATORY GRANTS

Students who started their courses before September 1998 and certain others continue, for the duration of their course, to be eligible for means-tested maintenance grants from which a parental contribution is deductible on a sliding scale dependent on income or, for married students, from their spouse's income. However, a parental contribution is not deducted from the grant to students over 25 years of age who have been self-supporting for any three years before the beginning of their course.

Grants are paid by the local education authority for the area in which the student lives in England, Wales and Northern Ireland. The cost is reimbursed by central government. For students resident in Scotland grants are made by central government through the Student Awards Agency.

The means-tested maintenance grant, usually paid once a term, covers periods of attendance during term as well as the Christmas and Easter vacations, but not the summer vacation.

The basic grant rates for 2002–3 (rates for Scottish students in parenthesis) are:

Living in College/lodgings in London

area	£2,450 (£2,365)
College/lodgings outside London area	£1,990 (£1,915)
Parental home	£1,625 (£1,465)

Additional allowances are available if, for example, the course requires a period of study abroad.

Expenditure on mandatory awards in 2000–1 was £406.8 million.

ACCESS FUNDS

Funds, variously known as hardship or access funds (Financial Contingency Funds in Wales) are allocated by central government to the appropriate funding Councils in England and Wales and to the Student Awards Agency in Scotland and administered by further and higher education institutions. In Northern Ireland they are allocated by central government directly to the institution. All students, whether full- or part-time, undergraduate or postgraduate, may apply but those whose courses attract a student loan must already have applied for their full entitlement before applying to the hardship funds. Payment may be made as a short-term loan but is usually made as a grant. The amount payable depends on individual circumstances and on the amount the institution has available. Some colleges offer non-repayable bursaries from hardship funds, i.e. a payment for each year of the course, to students who might be prevented from completing their studies due to financial problems.

POSTGRADUATE AWARDS

Grants for postgraduate study are discretionary and competition for them is fierce. They comprise maintenance grants for students undertaking doctoral research or taught masters degrees, are not means-tested and are dependent on the class of first degree (especially for research degrees); and flat-rate maintenance grants which replaced the former 30-week bursaries for new entrants from the academic year 2000–1. There are additional allowances for disabled students, those with dependants and for fieldwork expenses. Postgraduate students, with the exception of students in England, Wales and Northern Ireland on loan-bearing diploma courses such as teacher training, are not eligible to apply for student loans.

Awards are funded by The British Academy, the Higher Education Funding Councils for England and Wales, the Department for Employment and Learning (DEL) for Northern Ireland, and the Scottish Higher Education Funding Council.

Prospective students should apply for awards (depending on the subject domain) to the following bodies: the Arts and Humanities Research Board or to one of the six Research Councils in England, Wales and Northern Ireland (where application may also be made to DEL) and to the Student Awards Agency in Scotland.

The rates of awards in 2002–3 are:

	London	Elsewhere
Doctoral	£10,000	£8,000
Masters, 12 months	£9,700	£7,700
9 months	£7,275	£5,775
Professional and vocational	£5,230	£4,410

ADULT AND CONTINUING EDUCATION

In the UK, the duty of securing adult and continuing education leading to academic or vocational qualifications is statutory. The Learning and Skills Council in England, the National Council for Education

and Training in Wales and the Further Education Funding Council in Scotland are responsible for and fund those courses which take place in their sector and lead to academic and vocational qualifications, prepare students to undertake further or higher education courses, or confer basic skills; the Higher Education Funding Councils fund advanced courses of continuing education. The LEAs have the power, although not the duty, to provide those courses which do not fall within the remit of the funding bodies. Funding in Northern Ireland is through the education and library boards.

Adult education is provided in adult education centres and colleges run by LEAs (England and Wales), further education colleges and evening centres (Scotland), community schools (Northern Ireland), and the adult studies departments of higher education institutions.

The involvement of universities in adult education and continuing education has diversified considerably. Birkbeck College in the University of London caters solely for part-time students. The post-1992 universities and the colleges of higher education, because of their range of courses and flexible patterns of student attendance, provide opportunities in the field of adult and continuing education. The Forum for the Advancement of Continuing Education promotes collaboration between institutions of higher education active in this area. The Open University, in partnership with the BBC, provides distance teaching leading to first degrees, and also offers post-experience and higher degree courses.

Of the voluntary bodies, the biggest is the Workers' Educational Association (WEA) which operates throughout the UK, reaching about 150,000 adult students annually. The further education funding bodies and LEAs make grants towards provision.

NIACE, the National Organisation for Adult Learning, has a broad remit to promote lifelong learning opportunities for adults. NIACE works to develop increased participation in education and training. It does this through research and project work, conferences, publications and the provision of an information service to educational providers. NIACE Cymru, the Welsh committee, receives financial support from the National Assembly for Wales, support in kind from local authorities, and advises government, voluntary bodies and education providers on adult continuing education and training matters in Wales. In Scotland advice on adult and community education, and promotion thereof, is provided by Community Learning Scotland. In Northern Ireland those functions are undertaken by the Department for Employment and Learning.

The Universities' Association for Continuing Education (UACE) represents the continuing education community within higher education and is open to universities and higher education institutions in the UK with additional provision for international, associate and individual members.

GRANTS

Adult education bursaries for students at the long-term residential colleges of adult education are the responsibility of the colleges themselves. The awards are administered for the colleges by the Awards Officer of the Residential Colleges Committee for students resident in England. They are funded for colleges in England and Wales by the respective Councils; for colleges in Scotland by the Department for Lifelong Learning and administered by the Scottish Further Education Funding Council; and for colleges in Northern Ireland by the Department for Employment and Learning and administered by the education and library boards.

Education Directory

LOCAL EDUCATION AUTHORITIES

ENGLAND

COUNTY COUNCILS

BEDFORDSHIRE, County Hall, Cauldwell Street, Bedford MK42 9AP. Tel: 01234-363222; Web: www.bedfordshire.gov.uk. *Director,* David Doran

BUCKINGHAMSHIRE, County Hall, Walton Street, Aylesbury HP20 1UA. Tel: 01296-382603. *Chief Education Officer,* P. J. Mooney

CAMBRIDGESHIRE, Box ELH 1500, Shire Hall, Castle Hill, Cambridge CB3 0AP. Tel: 01223-717667; Web: www.cambridgeshire.gov.uk. *Director,* A. Baxter

CHESHIRE, County Hall, Chester CH1 1SQ. Tel: 01244-602424; Web: www.cheshire.gov.uk. *Director of Education,* D. Cracknell

CORNWALL, County Hall, Truro TR1 3AY. Tel: 01872-322000; Web: www.cornwall.gov.uk. *Director,* J. Harris

CUMBRIA, 5 Portland Square, Carlisle CA1 1PU. Tel: 01228-606877; Web: www.cumbria.gov.uk/education. *Director of Education,* J. Nellist

DERBYSHIRE, County Hall, Matlock DE4 3AG. Tel: 01629-585814; Web: www.derbyshire.gov.uk. *Chief Education Officer,* R. V. Taylor

DEVON, County Hall, Topsham Road, Exeter EX2 4QG. Tel: 01392-382059; Web: www.devon.gov.uk. *Director,* A. G. Smith

DORSET, County Hall, Colliton Park, Dorchester DT1 1XJ. Tel: 01305-224110; Web: www.dorset-cc.gov.uk. *Director,* D. Goddard

DURHAM, County Hall, Durham DH1 5UJ. Tel: 0191-383 3319; Web: www.durham.gov.uk. *Director,* K. Mitchell

EAST SUSSEX, PO Box 4, County Hall, St Anne's Crescent, Lewes BN7 1SG. Tel: 01273-481000; Web: www.eastsussexcc.gov.uk. *Director of Education,* Ms D. Stokoe

ESSEX, PO Box 47, Chelmsford CM2 6WN. Tel: 01245-492211; Web: www.essexccc.gov.uk. *Director,* P. A. Lincoln

GLOUCESTERSHIRE, Shire Hall, Westgate Street, Gloucester GL1 2TG. Tel: 01452-425300; Web: www.gloscc.gov.uk. *Interim Director of Education,* Margaret Davies

HAMPSHIRE, The Castle, Winchester SO23 8UG. Tel: 01962-846452; Web: www.hantsnet2000.hants.gov.uk. *County Education Officer,* A. J. Seber

HERTFORDSHIRE, County Hall, Pegs Lane, Hertford SG13 8DE. Tel: 01992-555555; Web: www.hertscc.gov.uk. *Director,* R. Shostak

ISLE OF WIGHT, County Hall, High Street, Newport PO30 1UD. Tel: 01983-823400; Web: www.iwight.com. *Director,* A. Kaye

KENT, Sessions House, County Hall, Maidstone ME14 1XQ. Tel: 01622-671411; Web: www.kent.gov.uk. *Strategic Director,* Graham Badman

LANCASHIRE, PO Box 61, County Hall, Preston PR1 8RJ. Tel: 01772-254868; Web: www.lancashire.gov.uk. *Director,* J. Bennett

LEICESTERSHIRE, County Hall, Glenfield, Leicester LE3 8RF. Tel: 0116-265 6301; Web: www.leics.gov.uk. *Director,* Mrs J. A. M. Strong

LINCOLNSHIRE, County Offices, Newland, Lincoln LN1 1YQ. Tel: 01522-552222; Web: www.lincolnshire.gov.uk. *Director,* Dr C. Berry

NORFOLK, County Hall, Martineau Lane, Norwich NR1 2DL. Tel: 01603-222146; Web: www.norfolk.gov.uk. *Director,* Dr B. C. Slater

NORTH YORKSHIRE, County Hall, Northallerton, N. Yorks DL7 8AE. Tel: 01609-780780. *Director,* Miss C. Welbourn

NORTHAMPTONSHIRE, PO Box 216, John Dryden House, 8–10 The Lakes, Northampton NN4 7DD. Tel: 01604-236252; Web: www.northamptonshire.gov.uk. *Corporate Director,* Mrs B. Bignold

NORTHUMBERLAND, County Hall, Morpeth NE61 2EF. Tel: 01670-533601. *Director,* Dr L. Davis

NOTTINGHAMSHIRE, County Hall, West Bridgford, Nottingham NG2 7QP. Tel: 0115-982 3823; Web: www.nottscc.gov.uk/education. *Director,* P. Tulley

OXFORDSHIRE, Education Department, Macclesfield House, New Road, Oxford OX1 1NA. Tel: 01865-815449; Web: www.oxfordshire.gov.uk. *Acting Chief Education Officer,* R. Smith

SHROPSHIRE, The Shirehall, Abbey Foregate, Shrewsbury SY2 6ND. Tel: 01743-254307. *Corporate Director,* Mrs E. Nicholson

SOMERSET, County Hall, Taunton TA1 4DY. Tel: 01823-355455; Web: www.somerset.gov.uk. *Corporate Director - Education,* M. Jennings

STAFFORDSHIRE, Tipping Street, Stafford ST16 2DH. Tel: 01785-223121; Web: www.staffordshire.gov.uk. *Director,* Mrs J. C. Hawkins

SUFFOLK, St Andrew House, County Hall, Ipswich IP4 1LJ. Tel: 01473-584631; Web: www.suffolkcc.gov.uk. *Director,* D. J. Peachey

SURREY, County Hall, Penrhyn Road, Kingston upon Thames KT1 2DJ. Tel: 0845-600 9009; Web: www.surreycc.gov.uk. *Director,* Dr P. Gray

WARWICKSHIRE, 22 Northgate Street, Warwick CV34 4SP. Tel: 01926-410410; Web: www.warwickshire.gov.uk. *County Education Officer,* E. Wood

WEST SUSSEX, County Hall, Chichester PO19 1RF. Tel: 01243-777750; Web: www.westsussex.gov.uk. *Director,* R. Back

WILTSHIRE, County Hall, Bythesea Road, Trowbridge BA14 8JB. Tel: 01225-713000; Web: www.wiltshire.gov.uk. *Chief Education Officer,* R. W. Wolfson

WORCESTERSHIRE, Educational Services Directorate, PO Box 73, County Hall, Spetchley Road, Worcester WR5 2YA. Tel: 01905-766859; Web: www.worcestershire.gov.uk. *Director,* J. Kramer

UNITARY AND METROPOLITAN BOROUGH COUNCILS

BARNSLEY, Berneslai Close, Barnsley S70 2HS. Tel: 01226-773500. *Executive Director, Education,* Ms J. Potter

BATH AND NORTH-EAST SOMERSET, PO Box 25, Riverside, Temple Street, Keynsham, Bristol BS31 1DN. Tel: 01225-477000; Web: www.bathnes.gov.uk. *Education Director,* D. Williams

BIRMINGHAM, Education Offices, Margaret Street, Birmingham B3 3BU. Tel: 0121 303 2550; Web: www.bgfl.org. *Chief Education Officer,* Prof. T. Brighouse

BLACKBURN WITH DARWEN, Town Hall, Blackburn BB1 7DY. Tel: 01254-585541; Web: www.blackburn.gov.uk. *Director,* Peter Morgan

BLACKPOOL, Progress House, Clifton Road, Blackpool FY4 4US. Tel: 01253-476555. *Corporate Director,* Dr D. Sanders

BOLTON, Paderborn House, Civic Centre, Bolton BL1 1JW. Tel: 01204-333333. *Director,* Mrs M. Blenkinsop

BOURNEMOUTH, Dorset House, 20–22 Christchurch Road, Bournemouth BH1 3NL. Tel: 01202-456219. *Director,* P. Deshpande

BRACKNELL FOREST, Edward Elgar House, Skimped Hill Lane, Bracknell, Berks RG12 1LY. Tel: 01344-424642; Web: www.bracknell-forest.gov.uk. *Director of Education,* T. Eccleston

BRADFORD, Support Office, Flockton Road, Bradford BD4 7RY. Tel: 01274-751840; Web: www.educationbradford.com. *Managing Director,* Mark Pattison

BRIGHTON AND HOVE, PO Box 2503, Kings House, Grand Avenue, Hove BN3 2SU. Tel: 01273-290000; Web: www.brighton-hove.gov.uk. *Strategic Director,* David. Hawker

BRISTOL, The Council House, College Green, Bristol BS99 7EB. Tel: 0117-903 7961; Web: www.bristol-lea.org.uk.

BURY, Athenaeum House, Market Street, Bury BL9 0SW. Tel: 0161-253 5652. *Chief Education Officer,* H. Williams

CALDERDALE, Northgate House, Northgate, Halifax HX1 1UN. Tel: 01422-357257; Web: www.calderdale.gov.uk. *Group Director,* Ms C. White

COVENTRY, Council Offices, Earl Street, Coventry CV1 5RS. Tel: 024-7683 1511; Web: www.coventry.gov.uk. *Strategic Director,* Ms C. Goodwin

DARLINGTON, Town Hall, Darlington DL1 5QT. Tel: 01325-380651; Web: www.darlington.gov.uk. *Director,* G. Pennington

DERBY, Middleton House, 27 St Mary's Gate, Derby DE1 3NN. Tel: 01332-716924; Web: www.derby.gov.uk. *Director,* A. Flack

DONCASTER, Directorate of Education and Culture, The Council House, College Road, Doncaster DN1 3AD. Tel: 01302-737103. *Acting Executive Director,* M. S. Eales

DUDLEY, Westox House, 1 Trinity Road, Dudley DY1 1JQ. Tel: 01384-814225; Web: www.dudley.gov.uk. *Director,* John Freeman

EAST RIDING OF YORKSHIRE, County Hall, Beverley HU17 9BA. Tel: 01482-392020; Web: www.eastriding.gov.uk. *Director,* Jon Mager

GATESHEAD, Civic Centre, Regent Street, Gateshead NE8 1HH. Tel: 0191-433 3000; Web: www.gateshead.gov.uk. *Director,* Brian H. Edwards

HALTON, Grosvenor House, Halton Lea, Runcorn WA7 2WD. Tel: 0151-424 2061. *Director,* G. Talbot

HARTLEPOOL, Civic Centre, Victoria Road, Hartlepool TS24 8AY. Tel: 01429-266522; Web: www.hartlepool.gov.uk. *Director,* J. J. Fitt

HEREFORDSHIRE, Education and Conference Centre, Po Box 185, 4 Blackfriars Street, Hereford HR4 9ZR. Tel: 01432-260000; Web: www.education.herefordshire.gov.uk. *Director,* Dr E. Oram

KINGSTON UPON HULL, Essex House, Manor Street, Kingston upon Hull HU1 1YD. Tel: 01482-613161. *Acting Group Director,* P. Fletcher, OBE

KIRKLEES, Oldgate House, 2 Oldgate, Huddersfield HD1 6QW. Tel: 01484-225242; Web: www.kirkleesmc.gov.uk. *Director,* G. Tonkin

KNOWSLEY, Education Offices, Huyton Hey Road, Huyton, Knowsley L36 9YH. Tel: 0151-443 3220; Web: www.knowsley.gov.uk. *Director,* S. Munby

LEEDS, Merrion House, 110 Merrion Centre, Leeds LS2 8DT. Tel: 0113-247 5590; Web: www.leeds.gov.uk/educate.html. *Chief Executive,* C. Edwards

LEICESTER, Marlborough House, 38 Welford Road, Leicester LE2 7AA. Tel: 0116-252 7807. *Director,* S. Andrews

LIVERPOOL, 4th Floor, Lewis Buildings, 4 Renshaw Street, Liverpool L1 4AD. Tel: 0151-233 3000; Web: www.liverpool.gov.uk. *Executive Director,* C. Hilton

LUTON, Unity House, 111 Stuart Street, Luton LU1 5NP. Tel: 01582-546000; Web: www.luton.gov.uk. *Corporate Director,* T. Dessent

MANCHESTER, Overseas House, Quay Street, Manchester M3 3BB. Tel: 0161-234 5000. *Chief Education Officer,* D. Johnston

MEDWAY, Civic Centre, Strood, Rochester, Kent ME2 4AY. Tel: 01634-306000; Web: www.medway.gov.uk. *Director of Education,* R. Bolsin

MIDDLESBROUGH, PO Box 504, Vancouver House, Gurney Street, Middlesbrough TS1 1EL. Tel: 01642-265432. *Corporate Director,* Barbara Comiskey

MILTON KEYNES, Civic Offices, Saxon Court, 505 Avebury Boulevard, Milton Keynes MK9 3HS. Tel: 01908-253325; Web: www.mkweb.co.uk. *Head of Education and Chief Education Officer,* J. McElligott

NEWCASTLE UPON TYNE, Civic Centre, Newcastle upon Tyne NE1 8PU. Tel: 0191-232 8520 ext. 5301; Web: www.newcastle.gov.uk. *Director,* P. Turner

NORTH EAST LINCOLNSHIRE, 7 Eleanor Street, Grimsby DN32 9DU. Tel: 01472-323025; Web: www.nelincs.gov.uk. *Director,* G. Hill

NORTH LINCOLNSHIRE, PO Box 35, Hewson House, Station Road, Brigg DN20 8XJ. Tel: 01724-297240; Web: www.northlincs.gov.uk. *Director,* Dr T. W. Thomas

NORTH SOMERSET, PO Box 51, Town Hall, Weston-super-Mare BS23 1ZZ. Tel: 01934-888888; Web: www.n-somerset.gov.uk. *Director,* Colin Diamond

NORTH TYNESIDE, Town Hall, High Street East, Wallsend, Tyne & Wear NE28 7RR. Tel: 0191-200 6565; Web: www.northtyneside.gov.uk. *Chief Education Officer,* Anne Marie Carrie

NOTTINGHAM CITY, Sandfield Centre, Sandfield Road, Lenton, Nottingham NG7 1QH. Tel: 0115-915 0706; Web: www.nottinghamcity.gov.uk. *Director,* Heather Tomlinson

OLDHAM, PO Box 40, Civic Centre, West Street, Oldham OL1 1XJ. Tel: 0161-911 4200; Web: www.oldham.gov.uk. *Executive Director,* C. Berry

PETERBOROUGH, Bayard Place, Broadway, Peterborough PE1 1FB. Tel: 01733-748000; Web: www.peterborough.gov.uk. *Director,* R. Clayton

PLYMOUTH, City of Plymouth, Plymouth PL1 2AA. Tel: 01752-307400; Web: www.plymouth.gov.uk. *Director,* S. Faruqi

POOLE, Civic Centre, Poole, Dorset BH15 2RU. Tel: 01202-633202; Web: www.boroughofpoole.com. *Policy Director – Education,* Dr S. Goodwin

PORTSMOUTH, Civic Offices, Guildhall Square, Portsmouth PO1 2AL. Tel: 023-9284 1209; Web: www.portsmouthcc.gov.uk. *Chief Education Officer,* J. Gaskin

READING, Civic Centre, PO Box 2623, Reading RG1 7WA. Tel: 0118-939 0900; Web: www.reading.gov.uk. *Director,* A. J. Daykin

REDCAR AND CLEVELAND, Council Offices, Kirkleatham Street, Redcar TS10 1YA. Tel: 01642-444342; Web: www.redcar-cleveland.gov.uk. *Director,* Jenny Lewis
ROCHDALE, PO Box 70, Municipal Offices, Smith Street, Rochdale OL16 1YD. Tel: 01706-647474. *Director of Education,* T. Piggott
ROTHERHAM, Education Office, Norfolk House, Walker Place, Rotherham S65 1AS. Tel: 01709-382121; Web: www.rotherham.gov.uk. *Executive Director,* Ms D. Billups
RUTLAND, Catmose, Oakham, Rutland LE15 6HP. Tel: 01572-722577; Web: www.rutnet.co.uk. *Director,* Ms C. Chambers
SALFORD, Minerva House, Pendlebury Road, Swinton, Manchester. Tel: 0161-778 0123; Web: www.salford.gov.uk. *Director,* Mrs J. Baker
SANDWELL, PO Box 41, Shaftesbury House, 402 High Street, West Bromwich, West Midlands B70 9LT. Tel: 0121-525 7366; Web: www.lea.sandwell.gov.uk. *Executive Director,* E. Griffiths
SEFTON, Town Hall, Oriel Road, Bootle, Merseyside L20 7AE. Tel: 0151-922 4040; Web: www.sefton.gov.uk/education. *Director,* Elaine Simpson
SHEFFIELD, Education Directorate, Town Hall, Sheffield S1 2HH. Tel: 0114-273 5722; Web: www.sheffield.gov.uk. *Executive Director of Education,* J. Crossley-Holland
SLOUGH, Town Hall, Bath Road, Slough SL1 3UQ. Tel: 01753-875712. *Director of Learning and Cultural Services,* Christopher Spencer
SOLIHULL, PO Box 20, Council House, Solihull B91 3QU. Tel: 0121-704 6656; Web: www.solihull.gov.uk. *Director of Education,* K. Crompton
SOUTH GLOUCESTERSHIRE, Bowling Hill, Chipping Sodbury, S. Glos BS37 6JX. Tel: 01454-868686; Web: www.southglos.gov.uk. *Director of Education,* Ms T. Gillespie
SOUTH TYNESIDE, Town Hall and Civic Offices, Westoe Road, South Shields NE33 2RL. Tel: 0191-427 1717. *Director,* Ms B. Hughes
SOUTHAMPTON, Southampton City Council, 5th Floor, Frobisher House, Nelson Gate, Southampton SO15 1QZ. Tel: 023-80 832771; Web: www.southampton.gov.uk. *Executive Director,* I. Sandbrook
SOUTHEND, Civic Centre, Victoria Avenue, Southend-on-Sea SS2 6ER. Tel: 01702-215890. *Director,* Lorraine O'Reilly
ST HELENS, Rivington Centre, Rivington Road, St Helens WA10 4ND. Tel: 01744-455328; Web: www.sthelens.gov.uk. *Director,* Ms S. Richardson
STOCKPORT, Town Hall, Stockport SK1 3XE. Tel: 0161-474 3808. *Director for Education,* Kathy August
STOCKTON-ON-TEES, Municipal Buildings, PO Box 228, Church Road, Stockton-on-Tees TS18 1XE. Tel: 01642-393441; Web: www.stockton.gov.uk. *Director,* S. T. Bradford
STOKE-ON-TRENT, Floor 2, Civic Centre, Glebe Street, Stoke-on-Trent ST4 1HH. Tel: 01782-232014. *Director,* N. Rigby
SUNDERLAND, PO Box 101, Civic Centre, Sunderland SR2 7DN. Tel: 0191-553 1000; Web: www.sunderland.gov.uk. *Director of Education and Community Services,* Dr J. A. Williams
SWINDON, Sanford House, Sanford Street, Swindon SN1 1QH. Tel: 01793-463069. *Acting Director,* John Simpson

TAMESIDE, Council Offices, Wellington Road, Ashton under Lyne, Lancs OL6 6DL. Tel: 0161-342 2201; Web: www.tameside.gov.uk. *Strategic Director,* P. Lawday
TELFORD AND WREKIN, Civic Offices, Telford, Shropshire TF3 4WF. Tel: 01952-202402. *Corporate Director,* Mrs C. Davies
THURROCK, PO Box 118, Grays, Essex RM17 6GF. Tel: 01375-652652; Web: www.thurrock.gov.uk/education. *Director,* Steve Beynon
TORBAY, Oldway Mansion, Paignton, Devon TQ3 2TE. Tel: 01803-208208. *Strategic Director of Education,* Frank Weeple
TRAFFORD, PO Box 40, Trafford Town Hall, Talbot Road, Stretford, Trafford, Greater Manchester M32 0EL. Tel: 0161-912 1212. *Executive Director,* C. Pratt
WAKEFIELD, County Hall, Bond Street, Wakefield WF1 2QL. Tel: 01924-306090; Web: www.wakefield.gov.uk. *Chief Education Officer,* J. McLeod
WALSALL, Civic Centre, Darwall Street, Walsall WS1 1TP. TEL: 01922-652301; Web: www.walsall.gov.uk. *Director,* C. Green
WARRINGTON, New Town House, Buttermarket Street, Warrington, Cheshire WA1 2NJ. Tel: 01925-442971. *Director,* M. L. Roxburgh
WEST BERKSHIRE, Avonbank House, West Street, Newbury, Berks RG14 1BZ. Tel: 01635-519722; Web: www.westberks.gov.uk. *Corporate Director,* Richard Hubbard
WIGAN, Gateway House, Standishgate, Wigan, Lancs WN1 1AE. Tel: 01942-828891; Web: www.wiganmbc.gov.uk. *Director,* R. J. Clark
WINDSOR AND MAIDENHEAD, Town Hall, St Ives Road, Maidenhead, Berks SL6 1RF. Tel: 01628-796367; Web: www.rbwm.gov.uk. *Director,* M. Peckham
WIRRAL, Hamilton Building, Conway Street, Birkenhead CH41 4FD. Tel: 0151-666 2121. *Director,* C. Rice
WOKINGHAM, Wokingham District Council, Shute End, Wokingham, Berks RG40 1WN. Tel: 0118-974 6100; Web: www.wokingham.gov.uk. *Director,* A. Roberts
WOLVERHAMPTON, Wolverhampton City Council, St Peter's Square, Wolverhampton WV1 1RR. Tel: 01902-554100; Web: www.wolverhampton.gov.uk. *Co-ordinating Director,* Roy Lockwood
YORK, 10–12 George Hudson Street, York YO1 6ZG. Tel: 01904-613161; Web: www.york.gov.uk. *Director,* Patrick Scott

LONDON

*Inner London borough

BARKING AND DAGENHAM, Town Hall, Barking, Essex IG11 7LU. Tel: 020-8227 3181/3662; Web: www.bardaglea.org.uk. *Director,* A. Larbalestier
BARNET, The Old Town Hall, Friern Barnet Lane, London N11 3DL. Tel: 020-8359 3048; Web: www.barnet.gov.uk. *Chief Education Officer,* Miss L. Stone
BEXLEY, Hill View, Hill View Drive, Welling, Kent DA16 3RY. Tel: 020-8303 7777; Web: www.bexley.gov.uk. *Director,* P. McGee
BRENT, Chesterfield House, 9 Park Lane, Wembley, Middx HA9 7RW. Tel: 020-8937 3190; Web: www.brent.gov.uk. *Acting Director,* Nick Boxer
BROMLEY, Civic Centre, Stockwell Close, Bromley BR1 3UH. Tel: 020-8313 4066; Web: www.bromley.gov.uk. *Director,* K. Davis
*CAMDEN, Crowndale Centre, 218–220 Eversholt Street, London NW1 1BD. Tel: 020-7974 1505. *Director,* R. Litchfield

*CITY OF LONDON, Education Service, Corporation of London, PO Box 270, Guildhall, London EC2P 2EJ. Tel: 020-7332 1750. *City Education Officer*, D. Smith

*CITY OF WESTMINSTER, City Hall, 64 Victoria Street, London SW1E 6QP. Tel: 020-7641 1947; Web: www.westminster.gov.uk. *Director*, J. Harris

CROYDON, Taberner House, Park Lane, Croydon CR9 1TP. Tel: 020-8760 5452; Web: www.croydon.gov.uk. *Director*, D. Sands

EALING, Perceval House, 14–16 Uxbridge Road, London W5 2HL. Tel: 020-8758 5410; Web: www.ealing.gov.uk. *Director*, A. Parker

ENFIELD, PO Box 56, Civic Centre, Silver Street, Enfield, Middx EN1 3XQ. Tel: 020-8379 3201. *Director*, Ms E. Graham

*GREENWICH, Riverside House, Woolwich High Street, London SE18 6DF. Tel: 020-8921 8238; Web: www.greenwich.gov.uk. *Director*, G. Gyte

*HACKNEY, Hackney Technology and Learning Centre, 1 Reading Lane, London E8 1GQ. Tel: 020-8356 8436. *Director*, Mr A. Wood

*HAMMERSMITH, Town Hall, King Street, London W6 9JU; Web: www.lbhf.gov.uk. *Director*, Ms C. Whatford

HARINGEY, 48 Station Road, Wood Green, London N22 7TY. Tel: 020-8489 0000; Web: www.haringey.gov.uk. *Director*, P. Roberts

HARROW, PO Box 22, Civic Centre, Station Road, Harrow HA1 2UW. Tel: 020-8863 5611; Web: www.harrow.gov.uk. *Director*, P. A. Osburn

HAVERING, The Broxhill Centre, Broxhill Road, Harold Hill, Romford RM4 1XN. Tel: 01708-432488. *Executive Director*, S. Evans

HILLINGDON, Civic Centre, High Street, Uxbridge UB8 1UW. Tel: 01895-250528. *Corporate Director*, P. O'Hear

HOUNSLOW, Civic Centre, Lampton Road, Hounslow, Middx TW3 4DN. Tel: 020-8583 2000; Web: www.hounslow.gov.uk. *Director*, J. D. Tricket

*ISLINGTON, Laycock Street, Islington, London N1 1TH. Tel: 020-7527 5666; Web: www.islington.gov.uk. *Director of Education and Deputy Chief Executive*, N. Mehmet

*KENSINGTON AND CHELSEA, Town Hall, Hornton Street, London W8 7NX. Tel: 020-7361 3303; Web: www.rbkc.gov.uk. *Executive Director*, Jacky Griffin

KINGSTON UPON THAMES, Guildhall 2, Kingston upon Thames KT1 1EU. Tel: 020-8546 2121; Web: www.kingston.gov.uk. *Director*, Mr J. Braithwaite

*LAMBETH, International House, Canterbury Crescent, London SW9 7QE. Tel: 020-7926 1000. *Acting Director*, A. Wood

*LEWISHAM, 3rd Floor, Laurence House, 1 Catford Road, London SE6 4RU. Tel: 020-8314 8527; Web: www.lewisham.gov.uk. *Executive Director*, Ms F. Sulke

MERTON, Civic Centre, London Road, Morden, Surrey SM4 5DX. Tel: 020-8545 3251; Web: www.merton.gov.uk. *Director of Education, Leisure and Libraries*, Mrs Sue Evans

NEWHAM, Broadway House, 322 High Street, Stratford, London E15 1AJ. Tel: 020-8430 2000. *Director*, Ms P. Maddison

REDBRIDGE, Lynton House, 255–259 High Road, Ilford, Essex IG1 1NN. Tel: 020-8478 3020; Web: www.redbridge.gov.uk. *Director*, E. Grant

RICHMOND UPON THAMES, 1st Floor, Regal House, London Road, Twickenham TW1 3QS. Tel: 020-8891 7500; Web: www.richmond.gov.uk. *Chief Education Officer*, Anji Phillips

*SOUTHWARK, John Smith House, 144–152 Walworth Road, London SE17 1JL. Tel: 020-7525 5050/5001; Web: www.southwark.gov.uk/learning. *Strategic Director*, Dr Roger Smith

SUTTON, The Grove, Carshalton, Surrey SM5 3AL. Tel: 020-8770 5000; Web: www.sutton.gov.uk. *Strategic Director*, Dr I. Birnbaum

*TOWER HAMLETS, Town Hall, Mulberry Place, 5 Clove Crescent, London E14 2BG. Tel: 020-7364 5000; Web: www.towerhamlets.gov.uk. *Corporate Director – Education*, Stephen Grix

WALTHAM FOREST, Leyton Municipal Offices, High Road, Leyton, London E10 5QJ. Tel: 020-8527 5544 ext. 5015. *Director*, Graham Moss

*WANDSWORTH, Town Hall, Wandsworth High Street, London SW18 2PU. Tel: 020-8871 8013; Web: www.wandsworth.gov.uk. *Director*, P. Robinson

WALES

ANGLESEY, Swyddfa'r Sir, Llangefni, Anglesey LL77 7EY. Tel: 01248-752921; Web: www.ynysmon.gov.uk. *Director*, R. P. Jones

BLAENAU GWENT, Victoria House, Victoria Business Park, Ebbw Vale, Blaenau Gwent NP23 6ER. Tel: 01495-355434. *Director*, B. Mawby

BRIDGEND, Sunnyside, Bridgend CF31 4AR; Web: www.bridgend.gov.uk. *Director*, D. Matthews

CAERPHILLY, Council Offices, Caerphilly Road, Ystrad Mynach, Hengoed CF82 7EP. Tel: 01443-815588. *Director*, D. Hopkins

CARDIFF, County Hall, Atlantic Wharf, Cardiff CF10 4UW. Tel: 029-2087 2700; Web: www.cardiff.gov.uk. *Head of Service*, H. Knight

CARMARTHENSHIRE, Pibwrlwyd, Carmarthen SA31 2NH. Tel: 01267-224501; Web: www.carmathenshire.gov.uk. *Director*, Alun G. Davies

CEREDIGION, Swyddfa'r Sir, Marine Terrace, Aberystwyth SY23 2DE. Tel: 01970-633600. *Director*, R. J. Williams

CONWY, Government Buildings, Dinerth Road, Colwyn Bay LL28 4UL. Tel: 01492-575031/032; Web: www.conwy.gov.uk. *Director*, R. E. Williams

DENBIGHSHIRE, Caledfryn, Smithfield Road, Denbigh, Denbighshire LL16 3RJ. Tel: 01824-706777; Web: www.denbighshire.gov.uk. *Director*, S. Bowen

FLINTSHIRE, County Hall, Mold CH7 6ND. Tel: 01352-704010; Web: www.flintshire.gov.uk. *Director*, John R. Clutton

GWYNEDD, Shirehall Street, Caernarfon LL55 1SH. Tel: 01286-672255; Web: www.gwynedd.gov.uk. *Director*, D. Whittall

MERTHYR TYDFIL, Ty Keir Hardie, Riverside Court, Avenue De Clichy, Merthyr Tydfil CF47 8XD. Tel: 01685-724600; Web: www.mnet2000.org.uk. *Corporate Chief Officer*, W. V. Morgan

MONMOUTHSHIRE, County Hall, Cwmbran NP44 2XH. Tel: 01633-644487. *Director*, P. Cooke

NEATH PORT TALBOT, Civic Centre, Port Talbot SA13 1PJ. Tel: 01639-763298; Web: www.neath-porttalbot.gov.uk. *Director*, K Napieralla

NEWPORT, CIVIC CENTRE, Newport NP20 4UR. Tel: 01633-232257; Web: www.newport.gov.uk. *Chief Education Officer*, D. Griffiths

PEMBROKESHIRE, County Hall, Haverfordwest SA61 1TP. Tel: 01437-764551; Web: www.pembrokeshire.gov.uk. *Director*, G. Davies

POWYS, County Hall, Llandrindod Wells LD1 5LG. Tel: 01597-826422. *Group Director*, M. Barker

RHONDDA, CYNON TAFF, Education Centre, Grawen Street, Porth CF39 0BU. Tel: 01443-687666. *Group Director,* D. Jones, MSc.

SWANSEA, County Hall, Oystermouth Road, Swansea SA1 3SN. Tel: 01792-636351. *Director,* R. Parry

TORFAEN, County Hall, Croesyceiliog, Cwmbran, Torfaen NP44 2WN. Tel: 01633-648610. *Director,* M. de Val

VALE OF GLAMORGAN, Civic Offices, Holton Road, Barry CF63 4RU. Tel: 01446-709138; Web: www.valeofglamorgan.gov.uk. *Director,* B. Jeffreys

WREXHAM, Ty Henblas, Queen's Square, Wrexham LL13 8AZ. Tel: 01978-297421; Web: www.wrexham.gov.uk. *Director,* Terry Garner

SCOTLAND

ABERDEEN CITY, Summerhill Education Centre, Stronsay Drive, Aberdeen AB15 6JA. Tel: 01224-346060; Web: www.aberdeen-education.org.uk. *Corporate Director,* J. Stodter

ABERDEENSHIRE, Woodhill House, Westburn Road, Aberdeen AB16 5GJ. Tel: 01224-664630; Web: www.aberdeenshire.gov.uk. *Director,* H. Vernal

ANGUS, County Buildings, Market Street, Forfar DD8 3WE. Tel: 01307-461460; Web: www.angus.gov.uk. *Director of Education,* J. Anderson

ARGYLL AND BUTE, Argyll House, Alexandra Parade, Dunoon, Argyll PA23 8AJ. Tel: 01369-704000. *Director of Education,* A. C. Morton

CITY OF EDINBURGH, Wellington Court, 10 Waterloo Place, Edinburgh EH1 3EG. Tel: 0131-469 3000. *Director, Education,* Mr R. Jobson

CLACKMANNANSHIRE, Lime Tree House, Castle Street, Alloa FK10 1EX. Tel: 01259-452374. *Director,* Dave Jones

DUMFRIES AND GALLOWAY, Education Department, 30 Edinburgh Road, Dumfries DG1 1JG. Tel: 01387-260419. *Director for Education,* F. Sanderson

DUNDEE CITY, Floor 8, Tayside House, Crichton Street, Dundee DD1 3RJ. Tel: 01382-433088; Web: www.dundeecity.gov.uk. *Director of Education,* Mrs A. Wilson

EAST AYRSHIRE, Council Headquarters, London Road, Kilmarnock KA3 7BU. Tel: 01563-576017; Web: www.east-ayrshire.gov.uk. *Director,* J. Mulgrew

EAST DUNBARTONSHIRE, Boclair House, 100 Milngavie Road, Bearsden, Glasgow G61 2TQ. Tel: 0141-578 8000; Web: www.eastdunbarton.gov.uk. *Strategic Director - Community,* Ms S. Bruce

EAST LOTHIAN, John Muir House, Haddington EH41 3HA. Tel: 01620-827562; Web: www.eastlothian.gov.uk. *Director,* A. Blackie

EAST RENFREWSHIRE, Council Offices, Eastwood Park, Rouken Glen Road, Giffnock G46 6UG. Tel: 0141-577 3431; Web: www.eastrenfrewshire.gov.uk. *Director,* John Wilson

FALKIRK, McLaren House, Marchmont Avenue, Polmont, Falkirk FK2 0NZ. Tel: 01324-506600; Web: www.falkirk.gov.uk. *Director,* Dr G. Young

FIFE, Fife House, North Street, Glenrothes KY7 5PN. Tel: 01592-413667. *Head of Education,* A. McKay

GLASGOW CITY, Nye Bevan House, 20 India Street, Glasgow G2 4PF. Tel: 0141-287 6898; Web: www.glasgow.gov.uk. *Director,* K. Corsar

HIGHLAND, Council Buildings, Glenurquhart Road, Inverness IV3 5NX. Tel: 01463-702802. *Director,* B. Robertson

INVERCLYDE, 105 Dalrymple Street, Greenock PA15 1HT. Tel: 01475-712824. *Director,* B. McLeary

MIDLOTHIAN, Fairfield House, 8 Lothian Road, Dalkeith EH22 3ZG. Tel: 0131-270 7500; Web: www.midlothian.gov.uk. *Director,* D. MacKay

MORAY, Council Offices, High Street, Elgin IV30 1BX. Tel: 01343-563171. *Director,* D. M. Duncan

NORTH AYRSHIRE, Cunninghame House, Irvine KA12 8EE. Tel: 01294-324400; Web: www.north-ayrshire.gov.uk. *Corporate Director,* J. Travers

NORTH LANARKSHIRE, Municipal Buildings, Kildonan Street, Coatbridge ML5 3BT. Tel: 01236-812222; Web: www.northlan.gov.uk. *Director,* M. O'Neill

ORKNEY ISLANDS, Council Offices, School Place, Kirkwall, Orkney KW15 1NY. Tel: 01856-873535. *Director,* L. Manson

PERTH AND KINROSS, Pullar House, 35 Kinnoull Street, Perth PH1 5GD. Tel: 01738-476200. *Acting Director,* George Waddell

RENFREWSHIRE, Council Headquarters, South Building, Cotton Street, Paisley PA1 1LE. Tel: 0141-842 5601; Web: www.renfrewshire.gov.uk. *Director,* Ms S. Rae

SCOTTISH BORDERS, Council Headquarters, Newtown St Boswells, Melrose, Roxburghshire TD6 0SA. Tel: 01835-824000; Web: www.scottishborders.gov.uk. *Director,* J. Christie

SHETLAND ISLANDS, Hayfield House, Hayfield Lane, Lerwick, Shetland ZE1 0QD. Tel: 01595-744000; Web: www.shetland.gov.uk. *Head of Education Service,* M. Payton

SOUTH AYRSHIRE, County Buildings, Wellington Square, Ayr KA7 1DR. Tel: 01292-612201; Web: www.south-ayrshire.gov.uk. *Director,* M. McCabe

SOUTH LANARKSHIRE, Council Headquarters, Almada Street, Hamilton ML3 0AE. Tel: 01698-454545; Web: www.southlanarkshire.gov.uk. *Executive Director,* Ms M. Allan

STIRLING, Viewforth, Stirling FK8 2ET. Tel: 01786-442678. *Director,* Gordon Jeyes

WEST DUNBARTONSHIRE, Garshake Road, Dumbarton G82 3PU. Tel: 01389-737301. *Director,* I. McMurdo

WESTERN ISLES/EILEAN SIAR, Council Offices, Sandwick Road, Stornoway, Isle of Lewis HS1 2BW. Tel: 01851-703773. *Director of Education,* M. Macleod

WEST LOTHIAN, Lindsay House, South Bridge Street, Bathgate EH48 1TS. Tel: 01506-776000. *Corporate Manager,* R. Stewart

NORTHERN IRELAND

BELFAST, 40 Academy Street, Belfast BT1 2NQ. Tel: 028-9056 4000; Web: www.belb.org.uk. *Chief Executive,* David Cargo

NORTH EASTERN, County Hall, 182 Galgorm Road, Ballymena, Co. Antrim BT42 1HN. Tel: 028-2565 3333; Web: www.neelb.org.uk. *Chief Executive,* G. Topping

SOUTH EASTERN, Headquarters Offices, Grahamsbridge Road, Dundonald, Belfast BT16 2HS. Tel: 028-9056 6200; Web: www.seelb.org.uk. *Chief Executive,* J. B. Fitzsimons

SOUTHERN, 3 Charlemont Place, The Mall, Armagh BT61 9AX. Tel: 028-3751 2200; Web: www.selb.org. *Chief Executive,* Mrs H. McClenaghan

WESTERN, 1 Hospital Road, Omagh, Co. Tyrone BT79 0AW. Tel: 028-8241 1411; Web: www.welbni.org. *Chief Executive,* P. J. Martin

ISLANDS

GUERNSEY, The Grange, St Peter Port, Guernsey GY1 1RQ. Tel: 01481-710821. *Director,* D. T. Neale

ISLE OF MAN, St. George's Court, Upper Church Street, Douglas, Isle of Man IM1 2SG. Tel: 01624-685820; Web: www.gov.im. *Director,* John Cain

ISLES OF SCILLY, Town Hall, St Mary's, Isles of Scilly TR21 0LW. Tel: 01720-422537 ext. 145. *Secretary for Education,* P. S. Hygate

JERSEY, PO Box 142, Jersey JE4 8QJ. Tel: 01534-509500; Web: www.education.gov.je. *Director,* T. W. McKeon

ADVISORY BODIES

SCHOOLS

BRITISH EDUCATIONAL COMMUNICATIONS AND TECHNOLOGY AGENCY, Milburn Hill Road, Science Park, Coventry CV4 7JJ. Tel: 024-7641 6994; Web: www.becta.org.uk. *Chief Executive,* O. Lynch

EDUCATION OTHERWISE, PO Box 7420, London N9 9SG. Helpline: 0870-730 0074; Web: www.education-otherwise.org

INTERNATIONAL BACCALAUREATE ORGANISATION, Peterson House, Malthouse Avenue, Cardiff Gate, Cardiff CF23 8GL. Tel: 029-2054 7777; Web: www.ibo.org. *Academic Director,* Prof. J. Thompson

LEARNING AND SKILLS COUNCIL, Cheylesmore House, Quinton Road, Coventry CV1 2WT. Tel: 0845-019 4170; 101 Lockhurst Lane, Coventry CV6 5SF. Tel: 024-7670 3241; Web: www.lsc.gov.uk. *Chief Executive,* John Harwood

SPECIAL EDUCATIONAL NEEDS TRIBUNAL, 7th Floor, Windsor House, 50 Victoria Street, London SW1H 0NW. Tel: 01325 392555; Web: www.sentribunal.gov.uk. *President,* T. Aldridge, *Secretary,* K. Mullany

INDEPENDENT SCHOOLS

GOVERNING BODIES ASSOCIATION, The Ancient Foresters, Bush End, Takeley, Bishop's Stortford, Herts CM22 6NN. Tel: 01279-871865; Web: www.governingbodies.org. *Secretary,* F. V. Morgan

GOVERNING BODIES OF GIRLS' SCHOOLS ASSOCIATION, The Ancient Foresters, Bush End, Takeley, Bishop's Stortford, Herts CM22 6NN. Tel: 01279-871865; Web: www.governingbodies.org. *Secretary,* F. V. Morgan

INDEPENDENT SCHOOLS COUNCIL, Grosvenor Gardens House, 35–37 Grosvenor Gardens, London SW1W 0BS. Tel: 020-7 798 1500; Web: www.isis.uk.net. *General Secretary,* Dr A. B. Cooke

INDEPENDENT SCHOOLS EXAMINATIONS BOARD, Jordan House, Christchurch Road, New Milton, Hants BH25 6QJ. Tel: 01425-621111; Web: www.iseb.co.uk. *General Secretary,* Mrs J. Williams

FURTHER EDUCATION

LEARNING AND SKILLS DEVELOPMENT AGENCY, 19–25 Argyll Street, London W1F 7LS. Tel: 020-7297 9000; Web: www.lsda.org.uk. *Chief Executive,* C. Hughes, *Chair,* T. Melia, CBE

Regional Advisory Councils

ASSOCIATION OF COLLEGES IN THE EASTERN REGION, Suite 1, Lancaster House, Meadow Lane, St Ives, Huntingdon, Cambs PE27 4LG. Tel: 01480-468198; Web: www.acer.ac.uk. *Chief Executive,* Veronica Windmill

AOSEC (ASSOCIATION OF SOUTH EAST COLLEGES), Building 33, The University of Reading, London Road, Reading RG1 5AQ. Tel: 0118-931 6320; Web: www.aosec.org.uk. *Chief Executive,* B. Knowles, *Chair,* Rob Fryatt

CENTRA (EDUCATION AND TRAINING SERVICES) LTD, Duxbury Park, Duxbury Hall Road, Chorley, Lancs PR7 4AT. Tel: 01257-241428; Web: www.centra.org.uk. *Chief Executive,* P. Wren, *Chairman,* R. Dowd

EMFEC (EAST MIDLAND FURTHER EDUCATION COUNCIL), Robins Wood House, Robins Wood Road, Aspley, Nottingham NG8 3NH. Tel: 0115-854 1616; Web: www.emfec.co.uk. *Chief Executive,* Ms J. Gardiner

NCFE, Portland House, New Bridge Street, Newcastle upon Tyne NE1 8AN. Tel: 0191-201 3100; Web: www.ncfe.org.uk. *Chief Executive,* I. M. Sutcliffe, *Director of Business Innovation,* C. Jackland

SOUTH WEST ASSOCIATION FOR EDUCATION AND TRAINING, Bishops Hull House, Bishops Hull, Taunton, Somerset TA1 5EP. Tel: 01823-335491

WELSH JOINT EDUCATION COMMITTEE, 245 Western Avenue, Cardiff CF5 2YX. Tel: 029-2026 5000; Web: www.wjec.co.uk. *Chief Executive,* Wyn G. Roberts, *Director of Examinations,* Derec Stockey

HIGHER EDUCATION

ASSOCIATION OF COMMONWEALTH UNIVERSITIES, John Foster House, 36 Gordon Square, London WC1H 0PF. Tel: 020-7380 6700; Web: www.acu.ac.uk. *Secretary-General,* Prof. M. G. Gibbons,

UNIVERSITIES SCOTLAND, 53 Hanover Street, Edinburgh EH2 2PJ. Tel: 0131-226 1111; Web: www.universities-scotland.ac.uk. *Director,* D. Caldwell

UNIVERSITIES UK, Woburn House, 20 Tavistock Square, London WC1H 9HQ. Tel: 020-7419 4111; Web: www.universitiesuk.ac.uk. *President,* Prof. R. Floud, *Chief Executive,* Baroness Warwick

NORTHERN IRELAND HIGHER EDUCATION COUNCIL, 4th Floor, Room 407, Adelaide House, 39–49 Adelaide Street, Belfast BT2 8FD. *Chairman,* Tony Hopkins, CBE

QUALITY ASSURANCE AGENCY FOR HIGHER EDUCATION, Southgate House, Southgate Street, Gloucester GL1 1UB. Tel: 01452-557000; Web: www.qaa.ac.uk. *Chief Executive,* P. Williams

CURRICULUM COUNCILS

AWDURDOD CYMWYSTERAU, CWRICWLWM AC ASESU CYMRU/QUALIFICATIONS, CURRICULUM AND ASSESSMENT AUTHORITY FOR WALES, Castle Buildings, Womanby Street, Cardiff CF10 1SX. Tel: 029-20 375400; Web: www.accac.org.uk. *Chief Executive,* J. V. Williams

COUNCIL FOR THE CURRICULUM, EXAMINATIONS AND ASSESSMENT, Clarendon Dock, 29 Clarendon Road, Belfast BT1 3BG. Tel: 028-9026 1200; Web: www.ccea.org.uk. *Chief Executive,* G. Boyd

QUALIFICATIONS AND CURRICULUM AUTHORITY, 83 Piccadilly, London W1Y 8QA. Tel: 020-7509 5555; Web: www.qca.org.uk. *Chairman,* Sir William Stubbs, Ph.D *Chief Executive,* Sir William Stubbs

LEARNING AND TEACHING SCOTLAND, Gardyne Road, Dundee DD5 1NY. Tel: 01382-443600; Web: www.ltscotland.com. *Chief Executive,* M. Baughan

EXAMINING BODIES

ASSESSMENT AND QUALIFICATIONS ALLIANCE (AQA), Devas Street, Manchester M15 6EX. Tel: 0161-953 1180; Fax: 0161-273 7572; Web: www.aqa.org.uk. *Director General*, C. R. Adams

EDEXCEL, Stewart House, 32 Russell Square, London WC1B 5DN. Tel: 0870 240 9800; Fax: 020-7758 6960; Web: www.edexcel.org.uk

OCR (OXFORD CAMBRIDGE AND RSA EXAMINATIONS), Head Office, 1 Regent Street, Cambridge CB2 1GG. Tel: 01223-552552; Fax: 01223-552553; Web: www.ocr.org.uk. *Chief Executive*, Gregor Watson, *Director-General*, M. Cross

NORTHERN IRELAND COUNCIL FOR THE CURRICULUM, Examinations and Assessment, 29 Clarendon Road, Belfast, County Antrim BT1 3BG. Tel: 028-9026 1200; Fax: 028-9026 1234; Web: www.ccea.org.uk. *Chief Executive*, Dr A. Walker

SCOTTISH QUALIFICATIONS AUTHORITY Hanover House, 24 Douglas Street, Glasgow G2 7NQ. Helpdesk: 0141-242 2214; Fax: 0141-242 2244 Web: www.sqa.org.uk

WELSH JOINT EDUCATION COMMITTEE, 245 Western Avenue, Cardiff CF5 2YX. Tel: 029-2026 5000; Fax: 029-2057 5894; Web: www.wjec.co.uk. *Chief Executive*, Derec Stockey

GSCE

AQA, *see above*
EDEXCEL, *see above*
NORTHERN IRELAND COUNCIL FOR THE CURRICULUM EXAMINATIONS AND ASSESSMENT, *see above*
WELSH JOINT EDUCATION COMMITTEE, *see above*

A-LEVEL

AQA, *see above*
EDEXCEL, *see above*
NORTHERN IRELAND COUNCIL FOR THE CURRICULUM EXAMINATIONS AND ASSESSMENT, *see above*
OCR, *see above*
WELSH JOINT EDUCATION COMMITTEE, *see above*

FURTHER EDUCATION

CITY & GUILDS, 1 Giltspur Street, London EC1A 9DD. Tel: 020-7294 2468; Fax: 020-7294 2400 Web: www.city-and-guilds.co.uk *Director-General*: C. Humphries OBE
EDEXCEL, *see above*
OCR, *see above*

FUNDING COUNCILS

FURTHER EDUCATION

LEARNING AND SKILLS COUNCIL, Cheylesmore House, Quinton Road, Coventry CV1 2WT. Tel: 0845-019 4170; Web: www.lsc.gov.uk. *Chief Executive*, J. Harwood

NATIONAL COUNCIL - ELWA, Linden Court, The Orchards, Ilex Close, Cardiff CF14 5DZ. Tel: 029-2076 1861; Web: www.elwa.org.uk. *Chief Executive*, S. Martin

SCOTTISH FUNDING COUNCILS FOR FURTHER AND HIGHER EDUCATION, Donaldson House, 97 Haymarket Terrace, Edinburgh EH12 5HD. Tel: 0131-313 6500; Web: www.sfc.ac.uk. *Chief Executive*, Roger McClure

HIGHER EDUCATION

HIGHER EDUCATION FUNDING COUNCIL FOR ENGLAND, Northavon House, Coldharbour Lane, Bristol BS16 1QD. Tel: 0117-931 7317; Web: www.hefce.ac.uk. *Chief Executive*, Sir Howard Newby

HIGHER EDUCATION COUNCIL - ELWA, Linden Court, The Orchards, Ilex Close, Cardiff CF14 5DZ. Tel: 029-2076 1861; Web: www.elwa.org.uk. *Chief Executive*, S. Martin

SCOTTISH FUNDING COUNCILS FOR FURTHER AND HIGHER EDUCATION, Donaldson House, 97 Haymarket Terrace, Edinburgh EH12 5HD. Tel: 0131-313 6500; Web: www.shefc.ac.uk. *Chief Executive*, Roger McClure

STUDENT AWARDS AGENCY FOR SCOTLAND, Gyleview House, 3 Redheughs Rigg, Edinburgh EH12 9HH. Tel: 0131-476 8212; Web: www.student-support-saas.gov.uk. *Chief Executive*, D. Stephen

STUDENT LOANS COMPANY LTD, 100 Bothwell Street, Glasgow G2 7JD. Tel: 0141-306 2000; Web: www.slc.co.uk. *Chief Executive*, C. Ward

TEACHER TRAINING AGENCY, Portland House, Stag Place, London SW1E 5TT. Tel: 020-7925 3700; Web: www.teach-tta.gov.uk. *Chairman*, Prof. C. Booth

ADMISSIONS AND COURSE INFORMATION

CAREERS RESEARCH AND ADVISORY CENTRE, Sheraton House, Castle Park, Cambridge CB3 0AX. Tel: 01223-460277; Web: www.crac.org.uk, *Chief Executive*, D. Thomas

UNIVERSITIES SCOTLAND, 53 Hanover Street, Edinburgh EH2 2PJ. Tel: 0141-353 1880; Web: www.universities-scotland.ac.uk, *Director*, D. Caldwell

GRADUATE TEACHER TRAINING REGISTRY, ROSEHILL, New Barn Lane, Cheltenham, Glos GL52 3LZ. Tel: 01242-544600; Web: www.gttr.ac.uk, *GTTR Unit Manager*, Mrs J. Pearce

SOCIAL WORK ADMISSIONS SYSTEM, Rosehill, New Barn Lane, Cheltenham, Glos GL52 3LZ. Tel: 01242-544600, *SWAS Unit Manager*, Mrs J. Pearce

UNIVERSITIES AND COLLEGES ADMISSIONS SERVICE, Rosehill, New Barn Lane, Cheltenham, Glos GL52 3LZ. Tel: 01242-222444; Web: www.ucas.com, *Chief Executive*, M. A. Higgins

UNIVERSITIES

UNIVERSITY OF ABERDEEN (1495)
King's College, Aberdeen AB24 3FX.
Tel: 01224-272000; Fax: 01224-272086;
Web: www.abdn.ac.uk
Academic Registrar, Dr T. Webb
Chancellor, The Lord Wilson of Tillyorn, GCMG (1997)
Rector, Miss C. Dickson Wright
Secretary, S. Cannon
Vice-Chancellor and Principal, Prof. C. D. Rice

UNIVERSITY OF ABERTAY DUNDEE (1994)
Bell Street, Dundee DD1 1HG.
Tel: 01382-308000; Fax: 01382-308877;
Web: www.abertay.ac.uk
Chancellor, The Rt. Hon. Earl of Airlie, KT, GCVO, PC (1994)
Registrar, Philip Henry
University Secretary and Director of Operations, Ms C. Lamb
Vice-Chancellor, Prof. B. King

ANGLIA POLYTECHNIC UNIVERSITY (1992)
Rivermead Campus, Bishop Hall Lane, Chelmsford, Essex CM1 1SQ.
Tel: 01245-493131; Fax: 01245-495419;
Web: www.anglia.ac.uk
Chancellor, Lord Ashcroft, KCMG
Secretary and Clerk, S. G. Bennett
Vice-Chancellor, M. Malone-Lee, CB

ASTON UNIVERSITY (1895)
Aston Triangle, Birmingham B4 7ET.
Tel: 0121-359 3611; Fax: 0121-359 3611;
Web: www.aston.ac.uk
Chancellor, Sir Adrian Cadbury (1979)
Registrar and Secretary, R. D. A. Packham
Vice-Chancellor, Prof. M. Wright

UNIVERSITY OF BATH (1966)
Claverton Down, Bath BA2 7AY.
Tel: 01225-388388; Fax: 01225-386709;
Web: www.bath.ac.uk
Chancellor, The Lord Tugendhat (1998)
Registrar, J. A. Bursey
Vice-Chancellor, Prof. G. Breakwell

UNIVERSITY OF BIRMINGHAM (1900)
Edgbaston, Birmingham BH15 2TT.
Tel: 0121-414 3344; Fax: 0121-414 3971;
Web: www.bham.ac.uk
Chancellor, Sir Dominic Cadbury (2002)
Registrar and Secretary, David Allen
Vice-Chancellor, Prof. Michael Sterling, DEng, FREng

BOURNEMOUTH UNIVERSITY (1992)
Fern Barrow, Poole, Dorset BH12 5BB.
Tel: 01202-524111; Fax: 01202-702736;
Web: www.bournemouth.ac.uk
Chancellor, Lord John Taylor of Warwick (1992)
Registrar, N. O. G. Richardson
Vice-Chancellor, Prof. G. Slater

UNIVERSITY OF BRADFORD (1966)
Richmond Building, Richmond Road, Bradford, W. Yorks BD7 1DP.
Tel: 01274-232323; Fax: 01274-235300;
Web: www.brad.ac.uk
Chancellor, The Baroness Lockwood of Dewsbury (1997)
Registrar and Secretary, N. J. Andrew
Vice-Chancellor, Prof. C. Taylor

UNIVERSITY OF BRIGHTON (1992)
Mithras House, Lewes Road, Brighton BN2 4AT.
Tel: 01273-600900; Fax: 01273-642010;
Web: www.bton.ac.uk/university.html
Chairman of the Board, Sir Michael Checkland
Director, Prof. Sir David Watson
Registrar and Secretary, Ms C. E. Moon

UNIVERSITY OF BRISTOL (1909)
Senate House, Tyndall Avenue, Bristol BS8 1TH.
Tel: 0117-928 9000;
Web: www.bristol.ac.uk
Chancellor, Sir Jeremy Morse, KCMG (1989)
Registrar, D. Pretty
Secretary, Dr K. McKenzie, D.Phil.
Vice-Chancellor, Prof. Eric Thomas

BRUNEL UNIVERSITY (1966)
Uxbridge, Middx UB8 3PH.
Tel: 01895-274000; Fax: 01895-232806;
Web: www.brunel.ac.uk
Academic and Principal Registrar, J. B. Alexander
Chancellor, The Rt. Hon Lord Wakeham, (1998)
Vice-Chancellor and Principal, Prof. Steven Schwartz

UNIVERSITY OF BUCKINGHAM (1983)
Buckingham MK18 1EG.
Tel: 01280-814080; Fax: 01280-822245;
Web: www.buckingham.ac.uk
Chancellor, Sir Martin Jacomb (1998)
Registrar and Secretary, S. Cooksey
Vice-Chancellor, Dr Terence Kealey

UNIVERSITY OF CAMBRIDGE
The Old Schools, Trinity Lane, Cambridge CB2 1TN.
Tel: 01223-337733; Fax: 01223-332332;
Web: www.cam.ac.uk

UNIVERSITY OFFICERS, ETC

Chancellor, HRH The Prince Philip, Duke of Edinburgh, KG, KT, OM, GBE, PC (1977)
Commissary, The Lord Mackay of Clashfern, KT, PC, FRSE (2002)
Deputy High Steward, The Lord Richardson of Duntisbourne, MBE, TD, PC (1983)
Academic Secretary: G. P. Allen (Wolfson)
Director of the Fitzwilliam Museum, D. D. Robinson (Magdalene)(1995)
High Steward, Dame Bridget Ogilvie (Girton)(2001)
Librarian, P. K. Fox (Selwyn), (1994)
Orator, A. J. Bowen, (Jesus), (1993)
Registrary, T. J. Mead, Ph.D. (Wolfson) (1997)
Secretary-General of the Faculties, D. A. Livesey, Ph.D. (Emmanuel)
Treasurer, Mrs J. Womack (Trinity Hall) (1993)
Vice-Chancellor, Prof. Sir Alec Broers, FRS, FREng (Trinity)(1996)

COLLEGES AND HALLS *with dates of foundation*

CHRIST'S (1505) *Master*, Prof. Malcolm Bowie, D.Phil. FBA (2002)
CHURCHILL (1960) *Master*, Sir John Boyd, KCMG (1996)
CLARE (1326) *Master*, Prof. B. A. Hepple, LL D (1993)
CLARE HALL (1966) *President*, Prof. Ekhart Salje, Ph.D. FRS (2001)
CORPUS CHRISTI (1352) *Master*, Prof. H. Ahmed, FREng (2000)
DARWIN (1964) *Master*, Prof. W. A. Brown (2000)
DOWNING (1800) *Master*, Dr S. G. Fleet, Ph.D. (2001)
EMMANUEL (1584) *Master*, Prof. J. E. Ffowcs-Williams, (1996)

FITZWILLIAM (1966) *Master,* Prof. B. F. G. Johnson,
Ph.D. FRS (1999)
GIRTON (1869) *Mistress,* Prof. Dame Marylin Strathern,
Ph.D., FBA (1998)
GONVILLE AND CAIUS (1348) *Master,* N. McKendrick
(1996)
HOMERTON (1824) (for B.Ed. Students) *Principal,* Dr
K. B. Pretty (1991)
HUGHES HALL (1885) (for post-graduate students)
President, Prof. P. Richards, MD, Ph.D. (1998
JESUS (1496) *Master,* Prof. R. Mair, Ph.D, FREng (2001)
KING'S (1441) *Provost,* Prof. P. P. G. B. Bateson, FRS
(1987)
*LUCY CAVENDISH COLLEGE (1965) (for women
research students and mature and affiliated
undergraduates) *President,* Dame Veronica
Sutherland, CMG (2001)
MAGDALENE (1542) *Master,* D. D. Robinson (2002)
*NEW HALL (1954) *President,* Mrs A. Lonsdale (1996)
*NEWNHAM (1871) *Principal,* Baroness O'Neill of
Bengarve, CBE (1992)
PEMBROKE (1347) *Master,* Sir Roger Tomkys, KCMG
(1992)
PETERHOUSE (1284) *Master,* Lord Wilson of Tillyorn,
KT, GCMG, Ph.D. FRSE (2002)
QUEENS' (1448) *President,* The Lord Eatwell (1997)
ROBINSON (1977) *Warden,* A. D. Yates (2001)
ST CATHARINE'S (1473) *Master,* Prof. D. S. Ingram
(2000)
ST EDMUND'S (1896) *Master,* Prof. Sir Brian Heap, FRS
(1996)
ST JOHN'S (1511) *Master,* Prof. P. Goddard, FRS (1994)
SELWYN (1882) *Master,* Prof. R. J. Bowring, Litt.D.
(2000), *Proctors,* Dr D. J. Chivers
SIDNEY SUSSEX (1596) MASTER, Prof. S. J. N. Dawson
(1999)
TRINITY (1546) *Master,* Prof. A. K. Sen, Ph.D. (1998)
TRINITY HALL (1350) Master, Prof. P. F. Clarke, Lit.D.,
FBA (1984)
WOLFSON (1965) *President,* G. Johnson, Ph.D. (1994),
Academic Secretary, G. P. Allen (Wolfson) (2002)

*College for women only

UNIVERSITY OF CENTRAL ENGLAND IN BIRMINGHAM (1992)

Perry Barr, Birmingham B42 2SU.
Tel: 0121-331 5000; Fax: 0121-331 6740;
Web: www.uce.ac.uk
Chancellor, James Wilson
Registrar and Secretary, Ms M. Penlington
Vice-Chancellor, Dr P. C. Knight, CBE

UNIVERSITY OF CENTRAL LANCASHIRE (1992)

Preston PR1 2HE.
Tel: 01772-201201; Fax: 01772-892911;
Web: www.uclan.ac.uk
Academic Registrar, Lesley Munro
Chancellor, Sir Richard Evans, CBE, DL (2002)
Registrar, Ms L. Munro
Vice-Chancellor, Dr Malcolm McVicar

CITY UNIVERSITY (1966)

Northampton Square, London EC1V 0HB.
Tel: 020-7040 5060; Fax: 020-7040 8560;
Web: www.city.ac.uk
Academic Registrar, Ms F. Owen
Chancellor, The Rt. Hon. the Lord Mayor of London
Secretary, I. Creagh
Vice-Chancellor, Prof. D. W. Rhind, Ph.D., DSc

COVENTRY UNIVERSITY (1992)

Priory Street, Coventry CV1 5FB.
Tel: 024-7688 7688; Fax: 024-7688 8638;
Web: www.coventry.ac.uk
Academic Registrar (acting), J. Coleman, Ph.D.
Chancellor, The Lord Plumb, DL (1995)
Secretary, J. Gledhill, Ph.D.
Vice-Chancellor, M. Goldstein, CBE, Ph.D

CRANFIELD UNIVERSITY (1969)

Cranfield, Beds MK43 0AL.
Tel: 01234-750111; Fax: 01234-750875;
Web: www.cranfield.ac.uk
Academic Registrar and Secretary, D. J. Buck
Chancellor, The Lord Vincent of Coleshill, GBE, KCB, DSO
(1998)
Vice-Chancellor, Prof. F. R. Hartley

DE MONTFORT UNIVERSITY (1992)

The Gateway, Leicester LE1 9BH.
Tel: 0116-255 1551; Fax: 0116-257 7515;
Web: www.dmu.ac.uk
Academic Registrar, V. E. Critchlow
Chancellor, Baroness Prashar of Runnymede, CBE (1998)
Chief Executive and Vice-Chancellor, Prof. P. Tasker
Secretary, Ms Linda Jones

UNIVERSITY OF DERBY (1992)

Kedleston Road, Derby DE22 1GB.
Tel: 01332-590500; Fax: 01332-622772;
Web: www.derby.ac.uk
Chancellor, vacant
Registrar, Mrs J. M. Fry
Secretary, Richard Gillis
Vice-Chancellor, Prof. R. Waterhouse

UNIVERSITY OF DUNDEE (1967)

Dundee DD1 4HN.
Tel: 01382-344000; Fax: 01382-201604;
Web: www.dundee.ac.uk
Academic Secretary, Dr I. K. Francis
Chancellor, Sir James Black, FRCP, FRS (1992)
Vice-Chancellor, Sir Alan Langlands

UNIVERSITY OF DURHAM (1832)

The University Office, Durham DH1 3HP.
Tel: 0191-374 2000; Fax: 0191-374 7250;
Web: www.dur.ac.uk
Chancellor, Sir Peter Ustinov, CBE, FRSL, FRSA, FRSL
Registrar and Secretary, J. V. Hogan, Ph.D.
Vice-Chancellor, Prof. Sir Kenneth Calman, KCB, MD,
Ph.D., FRCP, FRCGP, FRCR, FRSE

COLLEGES

COLLINGWOOD, *Principal,* Jane H. M. Taylor, D.Phil.
(2001)
GRADUATE SOCIETY, *Principal,* M. J. Rowell, Ph.D.
(2000)
GREY, *Master,* V. E. Watts (1989)
HATFIELD, *Master,* Prof. T. P. Burt, Ph.D. (1996)
ST AIDAN'S, *Principal,* J. S. Ashworth, (1998)
ST CHAD'S, *Principal,* Revd J. P. M. Cassidy, Ph.D. (1997)
ST CUTHBERT'S SOCIETY, *Principal,* D. J. Robson, Ph.D.
(2001)
ST HILD AND ST BEDE, *Principal,* J. A. Pearson, Ph.D.
(2000)
ST JOHN'S, *Principal,* Rt. Revd. Prof. S. W. Sykes (1999)
ST MARY'S, *Principal,* Miss J. L. Hobbs (1999)
TREVELYAN, *Principal,* N. Martin, Ph.D. (2000)
UNIVERSITY, *Master,* Prof. M. E. Tucker, Ph.D. (1998)
USHAW, *President,* Revd J. O'Keefe (1996)
VAN MILDERT, *Principal,* G. Patterson (2000)

UNIVERSITY OF EAST ANGLIA (1963)
Norwich NR4 7TJ.
Tel: 01603-456161; Fax: 01603-458553;
Web: www.uea.ac.uk
Chancellor, Sir Geoffrey Allen, FRS, FREng. (1994)
Registrar and Secretary, B. Summers
Vice-Chancellor, Prof. David Eastwood

UNIVERSITY OF EAST LONDON (1898)
Longbridge Road, Dagenham, Essex RM8 2AS.
Tel: 020-8223 3000; Fax: 020-8590 7799;
Web: www.uel.ac.uk
Chancellor, The Lord Rix, CBE, DL. (1997)
Registrar and Secretary, A. Ingle
Vice-Chancellor, Prof. M. Thorne

UNIVERSITY OF EDINBURGH (1583)
Old College, South Bridge, Edinburgh EH8 9YL.
Tel: 0131-650 1000; Fax: 0131-650 2147;
Web: www.ed.ac.uk
Chancellor, HRH The Prince Philip, Duke of Edinburgh,
    KG, OM, GBE, PC, FRS (1952)
Principal and Vice-Chancellor, Prof. Lord Stewart
    Sutherland of Houndwood, FBA, FRSE
Rector, R. Harper, MSP
Secretary, Melvyn Cornish
Vice-Principals, Prof. M. Anderson; Prof. G. S. Bouldon;
    Prof. A. Brown; G. S. Field

UNIVERSITY OF ESSEX (1964)
Wivenhoe Park, Colchester CO4 3SQ.
Tel: 01206-873333; Fax: 01206-873598;
Web: www.essex.ac.uk
Chancellor, The Lord Nolan, PC (1997)
Registrar and Secretary, T. Rich, Ph.D.
Vice-Chancellor, Prof. I. Crewe

UNIVERSITY OF EXETER (1955)
Northcote House, The Queen's Drive, Exeter EX4 4QJ.
Tel: 01392-661000; Fax: 01392-263108;
Web: www.exeter.ac.uk
Chancellor, The Lord Alexander of Weedon (1998), QC
Registrar and Secretary, I. H. C. Powell
Vice-Chancellor, Prof. S. Smith

UNIVERSITY OF GLAMORGAN (1992)
Pontypridd CF37 1DL.
Tel: 01443-480480; Freephone: 0800-716925;
Fax: 01443-480558; Web: www.glam.ac.uk
Chancellor, The Rt. Hon. the Lord Morris of Aberavon,
    QC (1994)
Registrar, J. O'Shea
Secretary, J. L. Bracegirdle
Vice-Chancellor, Prof. Sir Adrian Webb

UNIVERSITY OF GLASGOW (1451)
Gilbert Scott Building, University Avenue, Glasgow G12
8QQ. Tel: 0141-339 8855; Fax: 0141-330 4808;
Web: www.gla.ac.uk
Chancellor, Sir William Kerr Fraser, GCB, LL D, FRSE
Rector, G. Hemphill
Secretary, D. Mackie, FRSA
Vice-Chancellor, Prof. Sir Graeme Davies, FREng, FRSE

GLASGOW CALEDONIAN UNIVERSITY (1993)
City Campus, Cowcaddens Road, Glasgow G4 0BA.
Tel: 0141-331 3000; Fax: 0141-331 3005;
Web: www.caledonian.ac.uk
Principal and Vice-Chancellor, Dr I. A. Johnston, Ph.D.,
    CB, FIPO, FRSA
Pro Vice Chancellor Learning, Prof. P. Abbott, KBE (1993)
Secretary to University Court, B. M. Murphy

UNIVERSITY OF GLOUCESTERSHIRE (2001)
PO Box 220, The Park, Cheltenham, Glos GL50 2QF.
Tel: 01242-532700; Web: www.glos.ac.uk

UNIVERSITY OF GREENWICH (1992)
Old Royal Naval College, Park Row, Greenwich, London
SE10 9LS. Tel: 020-8331 8000; Fax: 020-8331 8145;
Web: www.gre.ac.uk
Academic Registrar, Miss C. Rose
Chancellor, The Rt. Hon. Lord Holme of Cheltenham,
    CBE
Secretary, L. Cording
Vice-Chancellor, Prof. R. Trainor

HERIOT-WATT UNIVERSITY (1966)
Edinburgh EH14 4AS.
Tel: 0131-449 5111; Fax: 0131-445 3441;
Web: www.hw.ac.uk
Chancellor, The Lord Mackay of Clashfern, KT, PC (1979)
Secretary, P. L. Wilson
Vice-Chancellor, Prof. J. S. Archer, FREng.

UNIVERSITY OF HERTFORDSHIRE (1992)
College Lane, Hatfield, Herts AL10 9AB.
Tel: 01707-284000; Fax: 01707-284115;
Web: www.herts.ac.uk
Chancellor, The Lord MacLaurin of Knebworth (1996)
Registrar and Secretary, P. E. Waters
Vice-Chancellor, Prof. N. K. Buxton

UNIVERSITY OF HUDDERSFIELD (1992)
Queensgate, Huddersfield HD1 3DH.
Tel: 01484-422288; Fax: 01484-516151;
Web: www.hud.ac.uk
Chancellor, Sir Ernest Hall, OBE (1996)
Secretary, T. Mears
Vice-Chancellor, Prof. J. R. Tarrant

UNIVERSITY OF HULL (1954)
Cottingham Road, Hull HU6 7RX.
Tel: 01482-346311; Fax: 01482-465194;
Web: www.hull.ac.uk
Chancellor, The Lord Armstrong of Ilminster, GCB, CVO
    (1994)
Registrar and Secretary, David Lock
Vice-Chancellor, Prof. David Drewry

KEELE UNIVERSITY (1962)
Keele, Staffs ST5 5BG.
Tel: 01782-621111; Fax: 01782-584165;
Web: www.keele.ac.uk
Chancellor, vacant
Registrar and Secretary, S. J. Morris
Vice-Chancellor, Prof. J. V. Finch, CBE, DL, Ph.D.

UNIVERSITY OF KENT AT CANTERBURY (1965)
Canterbury, Kent CT2 7NZ.
Tel: 01227-764000;
Web: www.ukc.ac.uk
Chancellor, Sir Crispin Tickell, GCMG, KCVO
Registrar and Secretary, N. A. McHard
Vice-Chancellor, Prof. D. Melville, Ph.D

KINGSTON UNIVERSITY (1992)
River House, 53-57 High Street, Kingston upon Thames,
Surrey KT1 1LQ.
Tel: 020-8547 2000; Fax: 020-8547 7178;
Web: www.kingston.ac.uk
Chancellor, Sir Peter Hall
Secretary, R. S. Abdula, MBE
Vice-Chancellor, Prof. P. Scott

UNIVERSITY OF LANCASTER (1964)
Bailrigg, Lancaster LA1 4YW.
Tel: 01524-65201; Fax: 01542-63806;
Web: www.lancs.ac.uk
Chancellor, HRH Princess Alexandra, the Hon. Lady
 Ogilvy, GCVO (1964)
Secretary, Miss F. Aiken
Vice-Chancellor, P. W. Wellings, Ph.D.

UNIVERSITY OF LEEDS (1904)
Leeds LS2 9JT.
Tel: 0113-243 1751; Fax: 0113-244 3923;
Web: www.leeds.ac.uk
Chancellor, Lord Bragg of Wigton
Secretary, J. Roger Gair
Vice-Chancellor, Prof. A. G. Wilson

LEEDS METROPOLITAN UNIVERSITY (1992)
City Campus, Leeds LS1 3HE.
Tel: 0113-283 2600; Web: www.lmu.ac.uk
Chancellor, Leslie Silver, OBE (1989)
Secretary, Steve Denton
Vice-Chancellor, Prof. Leslie Wagner, CBE

UNIVERSITY OF LEICESTER (1957)
University Road, Leicester LE1 7RH.
Tel: 0116-252 2522; Fax: 0116-252 2200;
Web: www.le.ac.uk
Chancellor, Sir Michael Atiyah, OM, FRS, Ph.D. (1995)
Registrar and Secretary, K. J. Julian
Vice-Chancellor, Prof. R. Burgess, Ph.D.

UNIVERSITY OF LINCOLN (1992)
Brayford Pool, Lincoln LN7 6TS.
Tel: 01522-882000; Fax: 01522-882088;
Web: www.ulh.ac.uk
Chancellor, Dame Elizabeth Esteve-Coll
Registrar (acting), Paul Walsh
Vice-Chancellor, Prof. David Chiddick

UNIVERSITY OF LIVERPOOL (1903)
Senate House, Abercromby Square, Liverpool L69 3BX.
Tel: 0151-794 2000; Fax: 0151 708 6502;
Web: www.liv.ac.uk
Chancellor, The Rt. Hon. Lord Owen, CH, PC (1996)
Registrar and Secretary, M. D. Carr
Vice-Chancellor, Prof. J. D. Bone, FRSA

LIVERPOOL JOHN MOORES UNIVERSITY
(1992)
Egerton Court, 2 Rodaney Street, Liverpool L3 5UX.
Tel: 0151-231 2121;
Web: www.livjm.ac.uk
Chancellor, Ms C. Booth, QC
Registrar and Secretary, Ms A. Wild
Vice-Chancellor, Prof. M. Brown

UNIVERSITY OF LONDON (1836)
Senate House, Malet Street, London WC1E 7HU.
Tel: 020-7862 8000; Fax: 020-7862 8358;
Web: www.lon.ac.uk
Academic Registrar, Mrs G. F. Roberts
Chairman of Convocation, D. D. A. Leslie
Chairman of the Council, The Lord Woolf, PC
Chancellor, HRH The Princess Royal, KG, GCVO, FRS
 (1981)
Director of Administration, J. R. Davidson
Vice-Chancellor, Prof. G. Zellick, Ph.D.
Visitor, HM The Queen in Council

COLLEGES

BIRKBECK, Malet Street, London WC1E 7HX. *Master,*
 Prof. T. O'Shea, Ph.D. (1998)
GOLDSMITHS COLLEGE, Lewisham Way, New Cross,
 London SE14 6NW. *Warden,* Prof. B. Pimlott, FBA
 (1998)
HEYTHROP COLLEGE, Kensington Square, London W8
 5HQ. *Principal,* Revd Dr J. McDade, SJ, BD (1999)
IMPERIAL COLLEGE OF SCIENCE, TECHNOLOGY AND
 MEDICINE (includes Imperial College Schools of
 Medicine at Charing Cross, Hammersmith and St
 Mary's hospitals and at the National Heart and Lung
 Institute), South Kensington, London SW7 2AZ. *Rector,*
 Sir Richard Sykes, FRS (2001)
INSTITUTE OF EDUCATION, 20 Bedford Way, London
 WC1H 0AL. *Director,* Prof. G. Whitty (2000)
KING'S COLLEGE LONDON, (includes Guy's, King's and
 St Thomas' Schools of Medicine, Dentistry and
 Biomedical Sciences), Strand, London WC2R 2LS.
 Principal, Prof. A. Lucas, Ph.D. (1993)

ASSOCIATED INSTITUTES

LONDON BUSINESS SCHOOL, Sussex Place, Regent's
 Park, London NW1 4SA. *Dean,* Prof. L. D'Andrea
 Tyson (2002)
LONDON SCHOOL OF ECONOMICS AND POLITICAL
 SCIENCE, Houghton Street, London WC2A 2AE.
 Director, Prof. A. Giddens (1997)
LONDON SCHOOL OF HYGIENE AND TROPICAL
 MEDICINE, Keppel Street, London WC1E 7HT.
 Dean, Prof. A. Haines (2001)
QUEEN MARY, Mile End Road, London E1 4NS.
 Principal, Prof. A. Smith, FRS, Ph.D. (1998)
ROYAL HOLLOWAY, (incorporating St Bartholomew's
 and the Royal London School of Medicine and
 Dentistry), Egham Hill, Egham, Surrey TW20 0EX.
 Principal, Prof. D. Bone, FRSA (2000)
ROYAL VETERINARY COLLEGE, Royal College Street,
 London NW1 0TU.
 Principal and Dean, Prof. L. E. Lanyon, CBE (1989)
ST GEORGE'S HOSPITAL MEDICAL SCHOOL, Cranmer
 Terrace, London SW17 0RE.
 Principal, Prof. R. Boyd (1996)
SCHOOL OF ORIENTAL AND AFRICAN STUDIES,
 Thornhaugh Street, Russell Square, London
 WC1H 0XG. *Director,* Prof. C. Bundy (2001)
SCHOOL OF PHARMACY, 29–39 Brunswick Square,
 London WC1N 1AX. *Dean,* Prof. A. T. Florence, CBE,
 Ph.D. (1989)
ROYAL ACADEMY OF MUSIC, Marylebone Road,
 London NW1 5HT. Principal, Prof. Curtis Price, Ph.D.,
 FKC (1995)
UNIVERSITY COLLEGE LONDON, Gower Street,
 London WC1E 6BT. *Provost and President,* Prof. Sir C.
 Llewellyn-Smith, FRS (1998)

PROGRAMMES

EXTERNAL PROGRAMME, Senate House, Malet Street,
 London WC1E 7HU. *Director,* J McConnell (1992)
PHILOSOPHY PROGRAMME, Senate House, Malet Street,
 London WC1E 7HU. *Director,* Dr T. Crane (1998)

INSTITUTES AND ASSOCIATE INSTITUTIONS

BRITISH INSTITUTE IN PARIS, 9–11 rue de Constantine,
 75340 Paris, Cedex 07, France. *London office:* Senate
 House, Malet Street, London WC1E 7HU. *Director,*
 Prof. C. L. Campos OBE, Ph.D. (1978)
CENTRE FOR DEFENCE STUDIES, Senate House, Malet
 Street, London WC1E 7HU. *Honorary Director,* Prof. L.
 Freedman, CBE, FBA (1990)

COURTAULD INSTITUTE OF ART, *Director,* Prof. E. C. Fernie, CBE, FSA, FRSE (1995)

INSTITUTE OF CANCER RESEARCH, Royal Cancer Hospital, Chester Beatty Laboratories, 17A Onslow Gardens, London SW7 3AL.
Chief Executive, Dr P. Rigby

INSTITUTE OF ENGLISH STUDIES, Senate House, Malet Street, London WC1E 7HU. *Director,* Prof. W. Gould (2000)

UNIVERSITY MARINE BIOLOGICAL STATION, Isle of Cumbrae, Scotland KA28 0EG

SCHOOL OF ADVANCED STUDY

INSTITUTE OF ADVANCED LEGAL STUDIES, Charles Clore House, 17 Russell Square, London WC1B 5DR. *Director,* Prof. B. A. K. Rider (1995)

INSTITUTE OF CLASSICAL STUDIES, Senate House, Malet Street, London WC1E 7HU. *Director,* Prof. G. B. Waywell, FSA (1996)

INSTITUTE OF COMMONWEALTH STUDIES, 27–28 Russell Square, London EC1B 5DS. *Director,* Prof. T. Shaw (2001)

INSTITUTE OF GERMANIC STUDIES, 29 Russell Square, London WC1B 5DP. *Director,* Prof. R. Görner, Ph.D. (1999)

INSTITUTE OF HISTORICAL RESEARCH, Senate House, Malet Street, London WC1E 7HU, *Director,* Prof. D. Cannadine (1998)

INSTITUTE OF LATIN AMERICAN STUDIES, 31 Tavistock Square, London WC1H 9HA, *Director,* Prof. J. Dunkerley (1998)

INSTITUTE OF ROMANCE STUDIES, Senate House, Malet Street, London WC1E 7HU, *Director,* Prof. J. Labanyi (1997)

INSTITUTE OF UNITED STATES STUDIES, Senate House, Malet Street, London WC1E 7HU. *Director,* Prof. G. L. McDowell, Ph.D. (1992)

WARBURG INSTITUTE, Woburn Square, London WC1H 0AB, *Director,* C. Hope, Ph.D. (2002)

LONDON METROPOLITAN UNIVERSITY (2002)
31 Jewry Street, London E1 7QA.
Tel: 020-7320 1000; Fax: 020-7320 1163;
Web: www.londonmet.ac.uk
Academic Registrar, Ms J. Grinstead
Chancellor, The Earl of Limerick
Patron, HRH The Prince Philip, Duke of Edinburgh, KG, KT, OM, GBE, PC (1952)
Secretary and Clerk to the Board of Governors, J. McParland

LOUGHBOROUGH UNIVERSITY (1966)
Admin 2, Loughborough, Leics LE11 3TU.
Tel: 01509-263171; Fax: 01509-223901;
Web: www.lboro.ac.uk
Chancellor, Sir Denis Rooke, CBE, FRS, FREng. (1989)
Registrar and Secretary, J. M. Town
Vice-Chancellor, Prof. D. J. Wallace, FRS, FRSE

UNIVERSITY OF LUTON (1993)
Park Square, Luton LU1 3JU.
Tel: 01582-734111; Fax: 01582-486260;
Web: www.luton.ac.uk
Chancellor, Sir Robin Biggam (2001)
Vice-Chancellor, Dr Day John

UNIVERSITY OF MANCHESTER (1851)
Oxford Road, Manchester M13 9PL.
Tel: 0161-275 2000; Fax: 0161-275 2209;
Web: www.man.ac.uk

Chancellor, A. Ford (1994)
Registrar and Secretary, E. Newcomb, FRSA, OBE
Vice-Chancellor, Prof. Sir Martin Harris, CBE, DL, Ph.D

UNIVERSITY OF MANCHESTER INSTITUTE OF SCIENCE AND TECHNOLOGY (UMIST) (1824)
PO Box 88, Manchester M60 1QD.
Tel: 0161-236 3311; Fax: 0161-955 8066;
Web: www.umist.ac.uk
Chancellor, Sir Terry Leahy, Ph.D. (1995)
Registrar and Secretary, Jon Baldwin
Secretary, Renata Halsted
Vice-Chancellor, Prof. John Garside, Ph.D.

MANCHESTER METROPOLITAN UNIVERSITY (1992)
All Saints, Manchester M15 6BH.
Tel: 0161-247 2000; Fax: 0161-247 6390;
Web: www.mmu.ac.uk
Academic Registrar, J. D. M. Karczewski-Slowikowski
Chancellor, The Duke of Westminster, OBE, TD, D.Litt (1993)
Secretary, S. Heaton
Vice-Chancellor, Mrs A. V. Burslem, OBE, JP, FRSA

MIDDLESEX UNIVERSITY (1992)
White Hart Lane, London N17 8HR.
Tel: 020-8411 5000; Fax: 020-8411 5649;
Web: www.mdx.ac.uk
Chancellor, The Rt. Hon. Lord Sheppard of Didgemere, KGVC
Registrar, vacant
Vice-Chancellor, Prof. M. Driscoll, FRSA

NAPIER UNIVERSITY (1992)
Craighouse Campus, Craighouse Road, Edinburgh EH10 5DT. Tel: 0131-444 2266; Fax: 0131-455 4666;
Web: www.napier.ac.uk
Academic Registrar, Mrs L. Fraser
Chancellor, The Rt Hon. Viscount Younger of Leckie, KT, KCVO, TD, PC, FRSE (1993)
Secretary, Dr G. Webber
Vice-Chancellor, Prof. J. Mavor

UNIVERSITY OF NEWCASTLE UPON TYNE (1834)
6 Kensington Terrace, Newcastle upon Tyne NE1 7RU.
Tel: 0191-222 6000; Fax: 0191-222 6229;
Web: www.ncl.ac.uk
Chancellor, Rt. Hon. C. Patten, CH
Registrar, D. E. T. Nicholson
Vice-Chancellor, Prof. C. R. W. Edwards

UNIVERSITY OF NORTHUMBRIA AT NEWCASTLE (1992)
Ellison Building, Ellison Place, Newcastle upon Tyne NE1 8ST. Tel: 0191-232 6002; Fax: 0191-227 4017;
Web: www.northumbria.ac.uk
Chancellor, The Lord Glenamara, CH, PC (1984)
Registrar, Mrs C. Penna
Secretary, R. A. Bott
Vice-Chancellor, Kel Fidler

UNIVERSITY OF NOTTINGHAM (1948)
University Park, Nottingham NG7 2RD.
Tel: 0115-951 5151; Fax: 0115-951 3666;
Web: www.nottingham.ac.uk
Chancellor, Prof. F. Yang, Litt.D. (1993)
Registrar, K. H. Jones
Vice-Chancellor, Prof. Sir Colin Campbell, DL, FRSA, LL D

NOTTINGHAM TRENT UNIVERSITY (1992)
Burton Street, Nottingham NG1 4BU.
Tel: 0115-941 8418;
Web: www.ntu.ac.uk
Chairman of the Board of Governors, John Peace
Registrar, D. W. Samson
Secretary, S. Smith
Vice-Chancellor, Prof. R. Cowell, Ph.D

OPEN UNIVERSITY (1969)
Walton Hall, Milton Keynes MK7 6AA.
Tel: 01908-274066; Fax: 01908-652247;
Web: www.open.ac.uk
Chancellor, Baroness Betty Boothroyd, MP
Head of Student Services Registry, Ms H. Niven
Secretary, F. Woodburn
Vice-Chancellor, Prof. Brenda Gourley

UNIVERSITY OF OXFORD
University Offices, Wellington Square, Oxford OX1 2JD.
Tel: 01865-270000; Fax: 01865-270708;
Web: www.ox.ac.uk
Assessor, Dr S. R. Parkinson (Linacre), elected 2002
Bodley's Librarian, R. P. Carr (Balliol), elected 1997
Chancellor, The Lord Jenkins of Hillhead (Balliol), elected 1987, OM, PC
Director of the Ashmolean Museum, Dr C. Brown (Worcester), elected 1998
High Steward, The Lord Goff of Chieveley (Lincoln) and (New College), elected 1990, PC
Keeper of Archives, S. Bailey, elected 2000
Proctors, Dr T. P. Softley (Merton); Ms E. A. Chapman (Somerville), elected 2002
Public Orator, Prof. J. Griffin (Balliol), elected 1992
Registrar of the University, D. R. Holmes (St John's), elected 1998
Secretary of the Chest, J. R. Clements (Merton), elected 1995
Secretary of the Faculties and Academic Registrar, A. P. Weale (Worcester), elected 1984
Surveyor to the University, P. M. R. Hill (St Cross), elected 1993
Vice-Chancellor, Dr C. R. Lucas (Balliol), elected 1997

OXFORD COLLEGES AND HALLS *with dates of foundation*

ALL SOULS (1438) *Warden,* Prof. J. Davis, FBA, Ph.D (1995)
BALLIOL (1263) *Master,* A. Graham (1998)
BLACKFRIARS (1221) *Regent,* Revd F. G. Kerr (1998)
BRASENOSE (1509) *Principal,* The Lord Windlesham, Bt. CVO, PC, D.Litt (1989)
CAMPION HALL (1896) *Master,* Revd Dr. G. J. Hughes (1998)
CHRIST CHURCH (1546) *Dean,* Very Revd J. H. Drury (1991)
CORPUS CHRISTI (1517) *President,* Sir Timothy Lankester, KCB (2001)
EXETER (1314) *Rector,* Prof. M. Butler (1993)
GREEN (1979) *Warden,* Sir John Hanson, KCMG, CBE (1997)
GREYFRIARS (1910) *Warden,* Revd Dr. T. G. Weinady (1996)
HARRIS MANCHESTER (1786) *Principal,* Revd R. Waller, Ph.D. (1988)
HERTFORD (1874) *Principal,* Sir Walter Bodmer, FRS, FRCPath. (1996)
JESUS (1571) *Principal,* Sir Peter North, CBE, QC, FBA (1984)
KEBLE (1868) *Warden,* Prof. A. Cameron, CBE, Ph.D., FBA, FSA (1994)

KELLOGG (1990) *President,* Dr G. P. Thomas (1990)
LADY MARGARET HALL (1878) *Principal,* Sir Brian Fall, GVCO, KCMG (1995)
LINACRE (1962) *Principal,* Prof. P. A. Slack, FBA (1996)
LINCOLN (1427) *Rector,* Prof. P. Langford (2000)
MAGDALEN (1458) *President,* A. D. Smith, CBE (1988)
MANSFIELD (1886) *Principal,* Dr D. Walford, FRCPath, FRCP, FFPHM (1996)
MERTON (1264) *Warden,* Prof. Dame J. Rawson, CBE, FBA (1994)
NEW COLLEGE (1379) *Warden,* Prof. A. J. Ryan, FBA (1996)
NUFFIELD (1958) *Warden,* Sir Tony Atkinson, FBA (1994)
ORIEL (1326) *Provost,* Dr E. W. Nicholson, DD, FBA (1990)
PEMBROKE (1624) *Master,* Giles Henderson, CBE (2001)
QUEEN'S (1340) *Provost,* Sir Alan Budd (1999)
REGENT'S PARK (1810) *Principal,* Revd Dr. P. S. Fiddes (1989)
ST ANNE'S (1952) (Society of Oxford Home-Students (1879)) *Principal,* Mrs R. L. Deech (1991)
ST ANTONY'S (1953) *Warden,* Sir Marrack Goulding, KCMG (1997)
ST BENET'S HALL (1897) *Master,* Revd H. Wansbrough, OSB (1991)
ST CATHERINE'S (1963) *Master,* Sir Peter Williams, CBE, FREng., FRS (2000)
ST CROSS (1965) *Master,* Dr R. C. Repp (1987)
ST EDMUND HALL (c.1278) *Principal,* Prof. D. M. P. Mingos, FRS, FRSC (1999)
*ST HILDA'S (1893) *Principal,* Dr J. Milne, MRCP, MRCPsych (2001)
ST HUGH'S (1886) *Principal,* D. Wood, CBE, QC (1991)
ST JOHN'S (1555) *President,* Sir Michael Scholar, KCB (2001)
ST PETER'S (1929) *Master,* Dr J. P. Barron, FSA (1991)
SOMERVILLE (1879) *Principal,* Dame Fiona Caldicott, DBE, FRCP, FRCPsych., FRCPI (1996)
TEMPLETON (1965) *President,* Sir David Rowland (1998)
TRINITY (1554) *President,* The Hon. Michael J. Beloff, QC, FRSA (1996)
UNIVERSITY (1249) *Master,* Lord Butler of Brockwell, CCB, CVO (1998)
WADHAM (1610) *Warden,* J. S. Flemming, FBA, CBE (1993)
WOLFSON (1966) *President,* Prof. Sir Gareth Roberts, FRS, Ph.D (2000)
WORCESTER (1714) *Provost,* R. G. Smethurst, (1991)
WYCLIFFE HALL (1877) *Principal,* Revd Dr. A. E. McGrath (1995)
*Women only

OXFORD BROOKES UNIVERSITY (1992)
Gipsy Lane, Oxford OX3 0BP.
Tel: 01865-484848; Fax: 01865-483616;
Web: www.brookes.ac.uk
Academic Registrar, Steve Marshall
Chancellor, John Snow
Vice-Chancellor, Prof. G. Upton

UNIVERSITY OF PAISLEY (1992)
Paisley PA1 2BE.
Tel: 0141-848 3000; Fax: 0141-848 3333;
Web: www.paisley.ac.uk
Chancellor, Sir Robert Easton, CBE (1993)
Registrar and Deputy Secretary, D. Rigg
Secretary, J. Fraser
Vice-Chancellor and Principal, Prof. J. Macklin, CBE

UNIVERSITY OF PLYMOUTH (1992)
Drake Circus, Plymouth PL4 8AA.
Tel: 01752-600600; Fax: 01752-232141;
Web: www.plymouth.ac.uk
Academic Registrar and University Secretary, Miss J. Hopkinson
Vice-Chancellor, Prof. J. Levinsky

UNIVERSITY OF PORTSMOUTH (1992)
University House, Winston Churchill Avenue, Portsmouth PO1 2UP.
Tel: 023-9284 8484; Fax: 023-9284 2733;
Web: www.port.ac.uk
Academic Registrar, A. Rees
Chancellor, The Lord Palumbo of Walbrook (1992)
Vice-Chancellor, Prof. J. Craven

QUEEN'S UNIVERSITY OF BELFAST (1908)
Belfast BT7 1NN.
Tel: 028-9024 5133; Fax: 028-9024 7895;
Web: www.qub.ac.uk
Chancellor, Sen. G. Mitchell
Registrar, J. O'Kane
Vice-Chancellor, Prof. G. Bain

UNIVERSITY OF READING (1926)
Whiteknights, PO Box 217, Reading RG6 6AH.
Tel: 0118-987 5123; Fax: 0118-931 8924;
Web: www.reading.ac.uk
Chancellor, The Lord Carrington, KG, GCMG, CH, MC, PC (1992)
Registrar, D. C. R. Frampton
Vice-Chancellor, Prof. R. Williams

ROBERT GORDON UNIVERSITY (1992)
Schoolhill, Aberdeen AB10 1FR.
Tel: 01224-262000; Fax: 01224-263000;
Web: www.rgu.ac.uk
Chancellor, Sir Bob Reid (1993)
Registrar, Ms Hilary Douglas
Secretary, Dr Adrian Graves, D.Phil.
Vice-Chancellor and Principal, Prof. William Stevely, DPhil.

UNIVERSITY OF SURREY ROEHAMPTON
Whitelands College, West Hill, London SW15 3SN.
Tel: 020-8392 3000/3232; Fax: 020-8392 3148/3470;
Web: www.roehampton.ac.uk
Chancellor, HRH The Duke of Kent, KG
Secretary, A. Skinner
Vice Chancellor, B. Porter, Ph.D.

ROYAL COLLEGE OF ART (1837)
Kensington Gore, London SW7 2EU.
Tel: 020-7590 4444; Fax: 020-7590 4500;
Web: www.rca.ac.uk
Provost, The Earl of Snowdon, GCVO (1995)
Rector and Vice Provost, Prof. Sir Christopher Frayling, Ph.D. *Registrar,* A. Selby

ROYAL COLLEGE OF MUSIC
Prince Consort Road, London SW7 2BS.
Tel: 020-7589 3643; Fax: 020-7589 7740;
Web: www.rcm.ac.uk
Dean and Deputy Director, Dr J. Cox
Director, Dr J. Ritterman
Registrar and Secretary, K. A. Porter

UNIVERSITY OF ST ANDREWS (1411)
College Gate, St Andrews, Fife KY16 9AJ.
Tel: 01334-476161; Fax: 01334-462570;
Web: www.st-and.ac.uk
Chancellor, Sir Kenneth Dover, D.Litt., FRSE, FBA (1981)
Rector, A. Neil (2000-2003)
Secretary and Registrar, D. J. Corner
Vice-Chancellor, Dr B. Lang

UNIVERSITY OF SALFORD (1967)
Salford, Greater Manchester M5 4WT.
Tel: 0161-295 5000; Fax: 0161-295 5999;
Web: www.salford.ac.uk
Chancellor, Sir Walter Bodmer, Ph.D., FRS
Registrar, Dr M. D. Winton, Ph.D.
Vice-Chancellor, Prof. M. Harloe

UNIVERSITY OF SHEFFIELD (1905)
Western Bank, Sheffield, S10 2TN.
Tel: 0114-222 2000; Fax: 0114-279 8603;
Web: www.shef.ac.uk
Chancellor, Sir Peter Middleton, GCB
Registrar and Secretary, Dr D. E. Fletcher, Ph.D
Vice-Chancellor, Prof. R. F. Boucher, CBE, Ph.D., FREng

SHEFFIELD HALLAM UNIVERSITY (1992)
Howard Street, Sheffield S1 1WB.
Tel: 0114-225 5555; Fax: 0114-225 3398;
Web: www.shu.ac.uk
Acting Registrar, Mrs G. Arnold
Chancellor, Lord Robert Winston (1992)
Secretary, Ms R. Seyd
Vice-Chancellor, Prof. D. Green

UNIVERSITY OF SOUTHAMPTON (1952)
Highfield, Southampton SO17 1BJ.
Tel: 023-8059 5000; Fax: 023-8059 3285;
Web: www.soton.ac.uk
Chancellor, Lord Selbourne, KBE, FRS (1996)
Registrar and Secretary, J. F. D. Lauwerys
Vice-Chancellor, Prof. Bill Wakeham

SOUTH BANK UNIVERSITY (1992)
103 Borough Road, London SE1 0AA.
Tel: 020-7928 8989; Fax: 020-7815 8155;
Web: www.sbu.ac.uk
Chancellor, Sir Trevor McDonald, OBE
Registrar, Dr Noel Morrison
Secretary, Ms K. Stephenson
Vice-Chancellor, Prof. D. Hopkin

STAFFORDSHIRE UNIVERSITY (1992)
College Road, Stoke-on-Trent ST4 2DE.
Tel: 01782-294000; Fax: 01782-745422;
Web: www.staffs.ac.uk
Chancellor, The Lord Ashley of Stoke, CH, PC (1993)
Dean of Students and Academic Registrar, Ms F. Francis
Secretary, K. Sproston
Vice-Chancellor, Prof. C. E. King, Ph.D., DL, D.Litt, FRSA

UNIVERSITY OF STIRLING (1967)
Stirling FK9 4LA.
Tel: 01786-473171; Fax: 01786-463000;
Web: www.stir.ac.uk
Chancellor, Dame Diana Rigg, DBE
Principal and Academic Registrar, D. G. Wood
Secretary, K. J. Clarke
Vice-Chancellor, Prof. Colin Bell, FRSE, FRSA

UNIVERSITY OF STRATHCLYDE (1796)
McCance Building, John Anderson Campus, Glasgow
G1 1XQ. Tel: 0141-552 4400; Fax: 0141-552 0775;
Web: www.strath.ac.uk
Academic Registrar, Dr S. M. Mellows
Chairman of Court, A. S. Hunter
Chancellor, The Rt. Hon. Lord Hope of Craighead,
(1998)
Secretary, Dr P. W. A. West
Vice-Chancellor, Prof. A. Hamnett

UNIVERSITY OF SUNDERLAND (1992)
Langham Tower, Ryhope Road, Sunderland SR2 7EE.
Tel: 0191-515 2000;
Web: www.sunderland.ac.uk
Chancellor, The Lord Puttnam of Queensgate, CBE
(1998)
Rector, Revd P. Hutchinson
Secretary, J. D. Pacey
Vice-Chancellor, Prof. P. Fidler, MBE

UNIVERSITY OF SURREY (1966)
Guildford, Surrey GU2 7XH.
Tel: 01483-300800; Fax: 01483-300803;
Web: www.surrey.ac.uk
Chancellor, HRH The Duke of Kent, KG, GCMG, GCVO
(1977)
Secretary and Registrar, H. W. B. Davies, FRSA
Vice-Chancellor, Prof. P. J. Dowling, CBE, FRS, FREng, FRS

UNIVERSITY OF SUSSEX (1961)
Sussex House, Falmer, Brighton BN1 9RH.
Tel: 01273-606755; Fax: 01273-678335;
Web: www.sussex.ac.uk
Chancellor, The Lord Attenborough, CBE (1998)
Registrar, N. Gershon
Vice-Chancellor, Prof. M. A. M. Smith

UNIVERSITY OF TEESSIDE (1992)
Middlesbrough TS1 3BA.
Tel: 01642-218121; Fax: 01642-342067;
Web: www.tees.ac.uk
Chancellor, Lord Leon Brittan of Spennithorn, QC (1993)
Registrar, Ms J. Walters
Secretary, J. M. McClintock
Vice-Chancellor, Prof. D. Fraser

THAMES VALLEY UNIVERSITY (1992)
St Mary's Road, Ealing, London W5 5RF.
Tel: 020-8579 5000; Fax: 020-8566 1353;
Web: www.tvu.ac.uk
Chancellor, Sir William Stubbs
Secretary, A. M. Dalton
Vice-Chancellor, Prof. K. Barker, CBE

UNIVERSITY OF ULSTER (1984)
Cromore Road, Coleraine, Co. Londonderry BT52 1SA.
Tel: 08700 400 700;
Web: www.ulster.ac.uk
Chancellor, vacant
Registrar, Mrs I. Aston
Secretary, J. Hunter
Vice-Chancellor, Prof. P. G. McKenna, Ph.D.

UNIVERSITY OF WALES (1893)
King Edward VII Avenue, Cathays Park,
Cardiff CF10 3NS.
Tel: 029-2038 2656; Fax: 029-2039 6040;
Web: www.wales.ac.uk
Chancellor, HRH The Prince of Wales, KG, KT, GCB, OM,
PC (1976)
Secretary-General, Lynne E. Williams, Ph.D.
Senior Vice-Chancellor, Prof. D. Llwyd Morgan, D.Phil.,
D.Litt.

MEMBER INSTITUTES
UNIVERSITY OF WALES, Aberystwyth, Old College,
King Street, Aberystwyth SY23 2AX. Tel: 01970-623111.
Vice-Chancellor, Prof. D. Llwyd Morgan, D.Phil., D.Litt
(1995)
UNIVERSITY OF WALES BANGOR, Bangor, LL57 2DG.
Tel: 01248-351151. *Vice-Chancellor,* Prof. H. R. Evans,
Ph.D., FREng (1995)
UNIVERSITY OF WALES, CARDIFF, PO Box 920, Cardiff
CF10 3XP. Tel: 01222-874000. *Vice-Chancellor,* Dr D.
Grant, CBE, FEng. (2001)
UNIVERSITY OF WALES COLLEGE, NEWPORT, Caerleon
Campus, PO Box 179, Newport NP6 1YG. Tel: 01633-
430088. *Principal,* Prof. J. R. Lusty, Ph.D., FRSC (2002)
UNIVERSITY OF WALES COLLEGE OF MEDICINE,
Heath Park, Cardiff CF14 4XN. Tel: 01222-747747.
Vice-Chancellor, Prof. S. Tomlinson, MD, FRCP (2001)
UNIVERSITY OF WALES INSTITUTE, CARDIFF, Llandaff
Centre, Western Avenue, Cardiff CF5 2SG. Tel: 01222-
506070. *Principal,* A. J. Chapman, Ph.D. (1998)
UNIVERSITY OF WALES, LAMPETER, Lampeter SA48
7ED. Tel: 01570-422351. *Vice-Chancellor,* Prof. K. G.
Robbins, D.Litt., D.Phil, FRSED (1992)
UNIVERSITY OF WALES SWANSEA, Singleton Park,
Swansea SA2 8PP. Tel: 01792-205678. *Vice-Chancellor,*
Prof. R. H. Williams, Ph.D., FRS (1994)

UNIVERSITY OF WARWICK (1965)
Coventry CV4 7AL.
Tel: 024-7652 3523; Fax: 024-7646 1606;
Web: www.warwick.ac.uk
Administrative Secretary, Ms C. Charlton
Chancellor, Sir Nicholas Scheele (1989)
Registrar, Dr J. W. Nicholls
Vice-Chancellor, Prof. V. D. Vandelinde, FRS

UNIVERSITY OF WESTMINSTER (1992)
309 Regent Street, London W1B 2UW.
Tel: 020-7911 5000;
Web: www.wmin.ac.uk
Academic Registrar, Ms E. Green
Secretary, C. Mainstone
Vice-Chancellor and Rector, Dr G. M. Copland (1996)

UNIVERSITY OF THE WEST OF ENGLAND (1992)
Frenchay Campus, Coldharbour Lane, Bristol BS16 1QY.
Tel: 0117-965 6261; Fax: 0117-344 2341;
Web: www.uwe.ac.uk
Academic Secretary, Ms C. Webb
Chancellor, The Rt. Hon. Dame Elizabeth Butler-Sloss,
DBE (1993)
Vice-Chancellor, A. C. Morris

UNIVERSITY OF WOLVERHAMPTON (1992)
Wulfruna Street, Wolverhampton WV1 1SB.
Tel: 01902-321000; Fax: 01902-322680;
Web: www.wlv.ac.uk
Chancellor, Lord Paul of Marylebone
Registrar, J. Nelson
University Secretary and Clerk to the Board of Governors,
A. W. Lee
Vice-Chancellor, Prof. J. S. Brooks, Ph.D.

UNIVERSITY OF YORK (1963)
Heslington, York YO10 5DD.
Tel: 01904-430000; Fax: 01904-433433;
Web: www.york.ac.uk
Chancellor, Dame Janet Baker, CH, DBE (1991)
Registrar and Secretary, D. J. Foster
Vice-Chancellor, Prof. B. Cantor, Ph.D., FREng, FIM, FRMS

COLLEGES

It is not possible to name here all the colleges offering course of higher or further education. The list does not include colleges forming part of a university. The English colleges that follow are confined to those in the higher education courses, some with HEFCFE funding.

The list of colleges in Wales, Scotland and Northern Ireland include institutions providing at least one full-time course leading to a first degree granted by an accredited validating body.

ENGLAND

BATH SPA UNIVERSITY COLLEGE, Newton Park, Newton St Loe, Bath BA2 9BN. Tel: 01225-875875; Fax: 01225-875444; www.bathspa.ac.uk.

BISHOP GROSSETESTE COLLEGE, Newport, Lincoln LN1 3DY. Tel: 01522-527347; Fax: 01522-530243; Web: www.bgc.ac.uk. *Principal,* Prof. E. Baker

BOLTON INSTITUTE OF HIGHER EDUCATION, Deane Road, Bolton BL3 5AB. Tel: 01204-528851; Fax: 01204-399074; Web: www.bolton.ac.uk. *Principal,* Mrs M. Temple

BUCKINGHAMSHIRE CHILTERNS UNIVERSITY COLLEGE, Queen Alexandra Road, High Wycombe, Bucks HP11 2JZ. Tel: 01494-522141; Fax: 01494-524392; Web: www.bcuc.ac.uk. *Director,* Prof. P. B. Mogford

CANTERBURY CHRIST CHURCH UNIVERSITY COLLEGE, North Holmes Road, Canterbury, Kent CT1 1QU. Tel: 01227-767700; Fax: 01227-470442; Web: www.cant.ac.uk. *Principal,* Prof. M. Wright

THE CENTRAL SCHOOL OF SPEECH AND DRAMA, Embassy Theatre, Eton Avenue, London NW3 3HY. Tel: 020-7722 8183; Fax: 020-7722 4132; Web: www.cssd.ac.uk.
Principal, Prof. G. Crossley

DARTINGTON COLLEGE OF ARTS, Totnes, Devon TQ9 6EJ. Tel: 01803-862224; Fax: 01803-863569; Web: www.dartington.ac.uk.
Principal and Chief Executive, Prof. K. Thompson

EDGE HILL COLLEGE OF HIGHER EDUCATION, St Helens Road, Ormskirk, Lancs L39 4QP. Tel: 01695-575171; Fax: 01695-579997; Web: www.edgehill.ac.uk. *Chief Executive,* Dr J. Cater

FALMOUTH COLLEGE OF ARTS, Woodlane, Falmouth, Cornwall TR11 4RH. Tel: 01326-211077; Fax: 01326-212261; Web: www.falmouth.ac.uk. *Principal,* Prof. A. G. Livingston

HARPER ADAMS UNIVERSITY COLLEGE, Edgmond, Newport, Shropshire TF10 8NB. Tel: 01952-820280; Fax: 01952-814783; Web: www.harper-adams.ac.uk. *Principal,* Prof. E. W. Jones

KENT INSTITUTE OF ART AND DESIGN, Oakwood Park, Maidstone, Kent ME16 8AG. Tel: 01622-757286; Fax: 01622-621100; Web: www.kiad.ac.uk. *Director,* Prof. V. Grylls

KING ALFRED'S COLLEGE, Sparkford Road, Winchester, Hants SO22 4NR. Tel: 01962-841515; Fax: 01962-842280; Web: www.wkac.ac.uk. *Principal,* Prof. P. Light

LIVERPOOL HOPE, Hope Park, Liverpool L16 9JD. Tel: 0151-291 3000; Fax: 0151-291 3100; Web: www.hope.ac.uk. *Rector and Chief Executive,* Prof. S. Lee

THE LONDON INSTITUTE, 65 Davies Street, London W1Y 2AA. Tel: 020-7514 6000; Fax: 020-7514 6131; Web: www.linst.ac.uk. *Rector,* Sir Michael Bichard

RCN INSTITUTE, The Royal College of Nursing, 20 Cavendish Square, London W1G 0RN. Tel: 020-7409 3333; Fax: 020-7647 3442; Web: www.rcn.org.uk. *Director,* Prof. A. L. Kitson

ROSE BRUFORD COLLEGE, Lamorbey Park, Sidcup, Kent DA15 9DF. Tel: 020-8 300 3024; Fax: 020-8 308 0542; Web: www.bruford.ac.uk. *Principal,* Prof. A. Pearce

ROYAL AGRICULTURAL COLLEGE, Cirencester, Glos GL7 6JS. Tel: 01285-652531; Fax: 01285-650219; Web: www.royagcol.ac.uk. *Principal,* Prof. J. B. Dent

ROYAL NORTHERN COLLEGE OF MUSIC, 124 Oxford Road, Manchester M13 9RD. Tel: 0161-907 5200; Fax: 0161-273 7611; Web: www.rncm.ac.uk. *Principal,* Prof. E. Gregson

ST MARTIN'S COLLEGE, Lancaster LA1 3JD. Tel: 01524-384384; Fax: 01524-384385; Web: www.ucsm.ac.uk. *Principal and Chief Executive,* Prof. C. J. Carr

SOUTHAMPTON INSTITUTE, East Park Terrace, Southampton SO14 0YN. Tel: 023-8031 9000; Fax: 023-8022 2259; Web: www.solent.ac.uk. *Principal,* Dr R. Brown

SURREY INSTITUTE OF ART AND DESIGN, University College, Falkner Road, Farnham, Surrey GU9 7DS. Tel: 01252-722441; Fax: 01252-892616; Web: www.surrart.ac.uk. *Director,* Prof. E. Thomas

TRINITY AND ALL SAINTS' COLLEGE, Brownberrie Lane, Horsforth, Leeds LS18 5HD. Tel: 0113-283 7100; Fax: 0113-283 7200; Web: www.tasc.ac.uk. *Principal,* Dr M. J. Coughlan

CHESTER COLLEGE OF HIGHER EDUCATION, Parkgate Road, Chester CH1 4BJ. Tel: 01244-375444; Fax: 01244-392820; Web: www.chester.ac.uk. *Principal,* Prof. T. J. Wheeler

UNIVERSITY COLLEGE CHICHESTER, Bishop Otter Campus, College Lane, Chichester, W. Sussex PO19 4PE. Tel: 01243-816000; Fax: 01243-816080; Web: www.ucc.ac.uk. *Director,* P. E. D. Robinson

UNIVERSITY COLLEGE NORTHAMPTON, Park Campus, Boughton Green Road, Northampton NN2 7AL. Tel: 01604-735500; Fax: 01604-720636; Web: www.northampton.ac.uk. *Rector,* Dr S. M. Gaskell

THE COLLEGE OF ST MARK AND ST JOHN, Derriford Road, Plymouth PL6 8BH. Tel: 01752-636700; Fax: 01752-636820; Web: www.marjon.ac.uk. *Principal,* Dr W. J. Rea

UNIVERSITY COLLEGE WORCESTER, Henwick Grove, Worcester WR2 6AJ. Tel: 01905-855000; Fax: 01905-855132; Web: www.worc.ac.uk. *Principal,* Ms D. Urwin

WINCHESTER SCHOOL OF ART, Park Avenue, Winchester, Hants SO23 8DL. Tel: 023-8059 6900; Fax: 023-8059 6901; Web: www.soton.ac.uk/~wsart/. *Head of School,* Prof. Katharine Crouan

YORK ST JOHN COLLEGE, Lord Mayor's Walk, York YO31 7EX. Tel: 01904-624624; Fax: 01904-612512; Web: www.yorksj.ac.uk. *Principal,* Prof. D. Willcocks

WALES

CARMARTHENSHIRE COLLEGE, Graig Campus, Sandy Road, Llanelli SA15 4DN. Tel: 01554-748000; Fax: 01554-758189; Web: www.ccta.ac.uk. *Principal and Chief Executive,* B. Robinson

COLEG LLANDRILLO, Llandudno Road, Rhos-on-Sea, Colwyn Bay, Conwy LL28 4HZ. Tel: 01492-546666; Fax: 01492-543052; Web: www.llandrillo.ac.uk. *Principal,* W. S. H. Evans

NORTH EAST WALES INSTITUTE OF HIGHER EDUCATION, Plas Coch, Mold Road, Wrexham LL11 2AW. Tel: 01978-290666; Fax: 01978-290008; Web: www.newi.ac.uk. *Principal and Chief Executive,* Prof. M. Scott

SWANSEA INSTITUTE OF HIGHER EDUCATION, Mount Pleasant, Swansea SA1 6ED. Tel: 01792-481000; Fax: 01792-481085; Web: www.sihe.ac.uk. *Principal,* Prof. D. Warner

TRINITY COLLEGE, College Road, Carmarthen SA31 3EP. Tel: 01267-676767; Fax: 01267-676777; Web: www.trinity-cm.ac.uk. *Principal,* Dr M. Hughes

WELSH COLLEGE OF MUSIC AND DRAMA, Castle Grounds, Cathays Park, Cardiff CF10 3ER. Tel: 029-2034 2854; Fax: 029-2039 1304; Web: www.wcmd.ac.uk. *Principal,* E. Fivet

SCOTLAND

BELL COLLEGE OF TECHNOLOGY, Almada Street, Hamilton, Lanarkshire ML3 0JB. Tel: 01698-283100; Fax: 01698-282131; Web: www.bell.ac.uk. *Principal,* Dr K. J. MacCallum

DUMFRIES AND GALLOWAY COLLEGE, Heathhall, Dumfries DG1 3QZ. Tel: 01387-261261; Fax: 01387-250006; Web: www.dumgal.ac.uk. *Principal,* Tony Jakimciw

FIFE COLLEGE OF FURTHER AND HIGHER EDUCATION, St Brycedale Avenue, Kirkcaldy, Fife KY1 1EX. Tel: 01592-268591; Fax: 01592-640225; Web: www.fife.ac.uk. *Principal,* Mrs J. S. R. Johnston

GLASGOW SCHOOL OF ART, 167 Renfrew Street, Glasgow G3 6RQ. Tel: 0141-353 4500; Fax: 0141-353 4746; Web: www.gsa.ac.uk. *Director,* Professor Seona Reid

INVERNESS COLLEGE, 3 Longman Road, Inverness IV1 1SA. Tel: 01463-273000; Fax: 01463-711977; Web: www.uhi.ac.uk/inverness. *Principal,* Prof. John Little

LEWS CASTLE COLLEGE, Stornoway, Isle of Lewis HS2 0XR. Tel: 01851-770000; Fax: 01851-770001; Web: www.lews.uhi.ac.uk. *Principal,* David Green

MORAY COLLEGE, Moray Street, Elgin, Moray IV30 1JJ. Tel: 01343-576000; Fax: 01343-576001; Web: www.moray.ac.uk. *Principal,* Dr Jim Logan

ORKNEY COLLEGE, Kirkwall, Orkney KW15 1LX. Tel: 01856-569000; Fax: 01856-569001; Web: www.uhi.ac.uk/orkney.htm. *Principal,* Dr William Rose

QUEEN MARGARET UNIVERSITY COLLEGE, Clerwood Terrace, Edinburgh EH12 8TS. Tel: 0131-317 3000; Fax: 0131-317 3256; Web: www.qmuc.ac.uk. *Principal,* Prof. Joan Stringer, CBE

ROYAL SCOTTISH ACADEMY OF MUSIC AND DRAMA, 100 Renfrew Street, Glasgow G2 3DB. Tel: 0141-332 4101; Fax: 0141-332 8901; Web: www.rsamd.ac.uk. *Principal,* Prof. John Wallace, OBE

SÀBHAL MOR OSTAIG, Sleat, Isle of Skye IV44 8RQ. Tel: 01471-888000; Fax: 01471-888001; Web: www.uhi.ac.uk/smo.htm.

SAC (SCOTTISH AGRICULTURAL COLLEGE), Central Office, West Mains Road, Edinburgh EH9 3JG. Tel: 0131-535 4000; Fax: 0131-535 4242; Web: www.sac.ac.uk. *Principal and Chief Executive,* Prof. William A. C. McKelvey

NORTH ISLAND COLLEGE, Ormlie Road, Thurso, Caithness KW14 7EE. Tel: 01847-896161; Fax: 01847-893872; Web: www.uhi.ac.uk/thurso.htm. *Principal,* H. Logan

NORTHERN IRELAND

ST MARY'S UNIVERSITY COLLEGE, 191 Falls Road, Belfast BT12 6FE. Tel: 028-9032 7678; Fax: 028-9033 3719; Web: www.stmarys-belfast.ac.uk. *Principal,* Very Revd Prof. M. O'Callaghan

ADULT CONTINUING EDUCATION

CO-OPERATIVE COLLEGE, Holyoake House, Hanover Street, Manchester M60 0AS; Fax: 0161-246 2909; Web: www.co-op.ac.uk. *Chief Executive and Principal,* M. Wilson

COMMUNITY LEARNING SCOTLAND, Rosebery House, 9 Haymarket Terrace, Edinburgh EH12 5EZ; Fax: 0131-313 2488; Web: www.communitylearning.org. *Chief Executive,* C. McConnell

FACE, Regional Office, Widening Participation Unit, University of East London, Romford Road, London E15 4LZ; Fax: 020-8223 4936; Web: www.face.sbu.ac.uk. *Chair,* John Storan

NATIONAL INSTITUTE OF ADULT CONTINUING EDUCATION, 21 De Montfort Street, Leicester LE1 7GE; Fax: 0116-204 4200; Web: www.niace.org.uk. *Director,* A. Tuckett

NIACE DYSGU CYMRU, Ground Floor, 35 Cathedral Road, Cardiff CF11 9HB; Fax: 029-2037 0900; Web: www.niacedc.org.uk. *Acting Director,* Rhoslyn Griffiths

THE RESIDENTIAL COLLEGES COMMITTEE, c/o Ruskin College, Oxford OX1 2HE; Fax: 01865-556360; Web: www.ruskin.ac.uk. *Awards Officer,* Mrs C. Gregory

THE UNIVERSITIES ASSOCIATION FOR CONTINUING EDUCATION, University of Cambridge Institute of Continuing Education, Madingley Hall, Madingley, Cambridge CB3 8AQ; Fax: 01954-280279; Web: www.uace.org.uk. *Chair,* Prof. Timothy O'Shea

WORKERS' EDUCATIONAL ASSOCIATION, Temple House, 17 Victoria Park Square, London E2 9PB; Fax: 020-8983 1515; Web: www.wea.org.uk. *General Secretary,* R. Lochrie

LONG-TERM RESIDENTIAL COLLEGES FOR ADULT EDUCATION

COLEG HARLECH/WEA(N), Harlech, Gwynedd LL46 2PU; Fax: 01766-780363; Web: www.harlech.ac.uk. *Principal,* A. Williams

FIRCROFT COLLEGE, 1018 Bristol Road, Selly Oak, Birmingham B29 6LH; Fax: 0121-472 0116; Web: www.fircroft.ac.uk. *Principal,* Ms F. Larden

HILLCROFT COLLEGE (WOMEN), South Bank, Surbiton, Surrey KT6 6DF; Fax: 020-8399 2688; Web: www.hillcroft.ac.uk. *Principal,* Mrs J. Ireton

NEWBATTLE ABBEY COLLEGE, Newbattle Road, Dalkeith, Midlothian EH22 3LL; Fax: 0131-663 1921; Web: www.newbattleabbeycollege.co.uk. *Principal,* Ms A. Southwood

NORTHERN COLLEGE, Wentworth Castle, Stainborough, Barnsley, S. Yorks S75 3ET; Fax: 01226-776000. *Principal and Chief Executive,* Prof. J. A. Jowitt

PLATER COLLEGE, Pullens Lane, Oxford OX3 0DT; Fax: 01865-740500; Web: www.plater.ac.uk. *Principal,* R. Beckinsale

RUSKIN COLLEGE, Walton Street, Oxford OX1 2HE; Fax: 01865-554331; Web: www.ruskin.ac.uk. *Principal,* J. Durcan

PROFESSIONAL EDUCATION
Excluding postgraduate study

The organisations listed below are those which, by providing specialist training or conducting examinations, control entry into a profession, or are responsible for maintaining a register of those with professional qualifications in their sector.

EU RECOGNITION

It is now possible for those with professional qualifications obtained in the UK to have these recognised in other European Union countries. A booklet, Europe Open for Professions, and further information can be obtained from:

DEPARTMENT OF TRADE AND INDUSTRY, Bay 212, Kingsgate House, 66–74 Victoria Street, London SW1E 6SW. Tel: 020-7215 4648. *Contact*, Mrs P. Campbell

ACCOUNTANCY

The main bodies granting membership on examination after a period of practical work are:

ASSOCIATION OF CHARTERED CERTIFIED ACCOUNTANTS (ACCA), 29 Lincoln's Inn Fields, London WC2A 3EE. Tel: 020-7396 7000; Fax: 020-7396 7070; Email: info@accaglobal.com; Web: www.accaglobal.com. *Chief Executive*, Anthea Rose

CIMA (THE CHARTERED INSTITUTE OF MANAGEMENT ACCOUNTANTS), 26 Chapter Street, London SW1P 4NP. Tel: 020-7663 5441; Fax: 020-7663 5442; Web: www.cimaglobal.com. *Chief Executive*, Charles Tilley

INSTITUTE OF CHARTERED ACCOUNTANTS IN ENGLAND AND WALES, Chartered Accountants' Hall, PO Box 433, Moorgate Place, London EC2P 2BJ. Tel: 020-7920 8100; Fax: 020-7920 0547; Email: comms@icaew.co.uk; Web: www.icaew.co.uk. *Secretary General*, Peter Owen

INSTITUTE OF CHARTERED ACCOUNTANTS OF SCOTLAND, CA House, 21 Haymarket Yards, Edinburgh EH12 5BH. Tel: 0131-347 0100; Fax: 0131-347 0105; Email: enquiries@icas.org.uk; Web: www.icas.org.uk. *Chief Executive*, David Brew

ACTUARIAL SCIENCE

The UK actuarial profession is controlled by the Institute of Actuaries in London and the faculty of Actuaries in Edinburgh. The Faculty and the Institute together set examinations, continuing professional development, professional codes and disciplinary standards. They issue technical guidance and run Boards and UK qualified actuaries may be Fellows of either organisation.

INSTITUTE OF ACTUARIES, Staple Inn Hall, High Holborn, London WC1V 7QJ. Tel: 020-7632 2100; Fax: 020-7632 2111; Email: institute@actuaries.org.uk; Web: www.actuaries.org.uk. *Secretary General*, Caroline Instance, *President*, Jeremy Goford, FIA

THE FACULTY OF ACTUARIES IN SCOTLAND, Maclaurin House, 18 Dublin Street, Edinburgh EH1 3PP. Tel: 0131-240 1300; Fax: 0131-240 1313; Email: faculty@actuaries.org.uk; Web: www.actuaries.org.uk. *Secretary*, Richard Machonachie

ARCHITECTURE

The Education Committee of the Royal Institute of British Architects sets standards and guides the whole system of architectural education throughout the UK. The Architects Registration Board is the independent regulator for the architects' profession in the UK. It was established to simultaneously protect the interest of consumers and to safeguard the reputation of architects. RIBA recognises courses at 36 schools of architecture in the UK for exemption from their own examinations as well as 55 courses overseas.

ROYAL INSTITUTE OF BRITISH ARCHITECTS, 66 Portland Place, London W1N 4AD. Tel: 020-7580 5533; Fax: 020-7251 1541; Email: admin@inst.riba.org; Web: www.architecture.com

ARCHITECTS REGISTRATION BOARD, 8 Weymouth Street, London W1W 5BU. Tel: 020-7580 5861; Fax: 020-7436 5269; Email: info@arb.org.uk; Web: www.arb.org.uk. *Chief Executive and Registrar*, Robin Vaughan

THE ARCHITECTURAL ASSOCIATION (INC.), 34–36 Bedford Square, London WC1B 3ES. Tel: 020-7887 4000; Fax: 020-7414 0782; Email: arch-assoc@arch-assoc.org.uk; Web: www.aaschool.ac.uk. *Secretary*, Edouard Le Maistre

BANKING

Professional organisations granting qualifications after examination are:

THE INSTITUTE OF FINANCIAL SERVICES, IFS House, 4/9 Burgate Lane, Canterbury CT1 2XJ. Tel: 01227-762600; Fax: 01227-763788; Email: institute@ifslearning.com; Web: www.ifslearning.com. *Chief Executive Officer*, G. Shreeve

THE CHARTERED INSTITUTE OF BANKERS IN SCOTLAND, Drumsheugh House, 38B Drumsheugh Gardens, Edinburgh EH3 7SW. Tel: 0131-473 7777; Fax: 0131-473 7788; Email: info@ciobs.org.uk; Web: www.ciobs.org.uk. *Chief Executive*, Prof. Charles Munn, FCIBS

BUILDING

Examinations are conducted by:

RICS (ROYAL INSTITUTION OF CHARTERED SURVEYORS), 12 Great George Street, Parliament Square, London SW1P 3AD. Tel: 020-7222 7000; Fax: 020-7222 9430; Email: info@rics.org.uk; Web: www.rics.org.uk. *Chief Executive*, J. Armstrong

THE CHARTERED INSTITUTE OF BUILDING, Englemere, Kings Ride, Ascot, Berks SL5 7TB. Tel: 01344-630700; Fax: 01344-630777; Email: reception@ciob.org.uk; Web: www.ciob.org.uk. *Chief Executive*, Chris Blythe

THE INSTITUTE OF CLERKS OF WORKS OF GREAT BRITAIN, 1st and 2nd Floors, The Old House, The Lawns, 33 Thorpe Road, Peterborough PE3 6AD. Tel: 01733-564033; Fax: 01733-564632; Web: www.icwgb.com. *General Secretary*, D. McGeorge

BUSINESS, MANAGEMENT AND ADMINISTRATION

Professional bodies conducting training and/or examinations include:

THE ASSOCIATION OF MBAS, 15 Duncan Terrace, London N1 8BZ. Tel: 020-7837 3375; Fax: 020-7278 3634; Email: info@mba.org.uk; Web: www.mba.org.uk. *Director-General*, M. A. Jones

THE CAM FOUNDATION, Moor Hall, Cookham, Maidenhead, Berks SL6 9QH. Tel: 01628-427180; Fax: 01628-427159; Web: www.camfoundation.com. *Registrar*, Daisy Magday

THE CHARTERED INSTITUTE OF HOUSING, Octavia House, Westwood Business Park, Westwood Way, Coventry CV4 8JP. Tel: 024-7685 1700; Fax: 024-7669 5110; Email: customer.services@cih.org; Web: www.cih.org. *Chief Executive*, D. Butler

THE CHARTERED INSTITUTE OF MARKETING, Moor Hall, Cookham, Maidenhead, Berks. Tel: 01628-427500

CHARTERED INSTITUTE OF PERSONNEL AND DEVELOPMENT, CIPD House, Camp Road, London SW19 4UX. Tel: 020-8971 9000; Fax: 020-8263 3333; Email: cipd@cipd.co.uk; Web: www.cipd.co.uk. *Director-General*, G. Armstrong

THE CHARTERED INSTITUTE OF PURCHASING AND SUPPLY, Easton House, Easton on the Hill, Stamford, Lincs PE9 3NZ. Tel: 01780-756777; Fax: 01780-751610; Email: info@cips.org; Web: www.cips.org. *Chief Executive*, Ken James

CHARTERED MANAGEMENT INSTITUTE, Management House, Cottingham Road, Corby, Northants NN17 1TT. Tel: 01536-204222; Fax: 01536-401013; Email: marketing@imgt.org.uk; Web: www.inst-mgt.org.uk. *Director-General*, Mary Chapman

HENLEY MANAGEMENT COLLEGE, Greenlands, Henley on Thames, Oxon RG9 3AU. Tel: 01491-571454; Fax: 01491-571635; Web: www.henleymc.ac.uk. *Principal*, Prof. Stephen Watson

THE INSTITUTE OF ADMINISTRATIVE MANAGEMENT, 16 Park Crescent, London, W1B 1BA. Tel: 020-7612 7099; Fax: 020-7612 7094; Email: enquiries@instam.org; Web: www.instam.org. *Chief Executive*, David Woodgate

INSTITUTE OF CHARTERED SHIPBROKERS, 3 St Helen's Place, London EC3A 6EJ. Tel: 020-7628 5559; Fax: 020-7628 5445; Email: info@ics.org.uk; Web: www.ics.org.uk. *Director-General*, Alan Phillips

THE INSTITUTE OF EXPORT, Export House, Minerva Business Park, Lynch Wood, Peterborough PE2 6FT. Tel: 01733-404400; Fax: 01733-404444; Email: institute@export.org.uk; Web: www.export.org.uk. *Chief Executive*, Hugh Allen

THE INSTITUTE OF HEALTHCARE MANAGEMENT, PO Box 33239, London SW1W 0WN. Tel: 020-7881 9235; Fax: 020-7881 9236; Email: enquiries@ihm.org.uk; Web: www.ihm.org.uk. *Chief Executive*, S. Marples

INSTITUTE OF QUALITY ASSURANCE, 12 Grosvenor Crescent, London SW1X 7EE. Tel: 020-7245 6722; Fax: 020-7245 6788; Email: iqa@iqa.org; Web: www.iqa.org. *Chief Executive*, Frank Steer, MBE

CHIROPRACTIC

The General Chiropractic Council (GCC) is the statutory regulatory body for chiropractors and its role and remit is defined in the Chiropractors Act 1994. The GCC's register of chiropractors opened in June 1999 and over 2000 chiropractors are expected to be registered with the GCC by the end of 2002.

BRITISH CHIROPRACTIC ASSOCIATION, Blagrave House, Blagrave Street, Reading, Berks RG1 1QB. Tel: 0118-950 5950; Fax: 0118-958 8946; Email: enquiries@chiropractic-uk.co.uk; Web: www.chiropractic-uk.co.uk

COLLEGE OF CHIROPRACTORS, PO Box 2739, 106 London Street, Reading RG1 4BF. Tel: 0118-950 2070; Fax: 0118-950 2074; Email: admin@colchiro.co.uk.

GENERAL CHIROPRACTIC COUNCIL, 344-354 Gray's Inn Road, London WC1X 8BP. Tel: 020-7713 5155; Fax: 020-7713 5844; Email: enquiries@gcc-uk.org; Web: www.gcc-uk.org

SCOTTISH CHIROPRACTIC ASSOCIATION, 16 Jenny Moores Road, St Boswells, Roxburghshire TD6 0AL. Tel: 01835-824026; Fax: 01835-824046; Email: sca@scottishborders.co.uk; Web: www.sca-chiropractic.org.uk. *Administrator*, Miss A. Butler

UNITED CHIROPRACTIC ASSOCIATION, Chichester House, 145A London Road, Kingston upon Thames, Surrey KT2 6SR. Tel: 020-8939 4599; Fax: 020-8546 6616; Email: uca@bthcc.co.uk. *Chairman*, Neil Folker

DANCE

The Council for Dance Education and Training (CDET) accredits courses at the following: ArtsEdLondon, Arts Educational Tring Park; Central School of Ballet; Bird College of Performing Arts; Elmhurst – The School for Dance and Performing Arts; The Hammond School; The Italia Conti Academy of Theatre Arts Ltd; Laban Centre, London; Laine Theatre Arts Ltd; London Contemporary Dance School; London Studio Centre; Midlands Academy of Dance and Drama; Merseyside Dance and Drama Centre; Northern Ballet School; Performers College; Stella Mann College; Studios La Pointe; Royal Academy of Dancing; The Urdang Academy.

The accreditation of a course in a school does not necessarily imply that other courses of a different type or duration in the same school are also accredited.

CDET has approved the teacher registration systems of the following: British Ballet Organisation; British Theatre Dance Association; Cecchetti Society; Imperial Society of Teachers of Dancing; Royal Academy of Dancing.

IMPERIAL SOCIETY OF TEACHERS OF DANCING, Imperial House, 22-26 Paul Street, London EC2A 4QE. Tel: 020-7377 1577; Fax: 020-7247 8979; Email: admin@istd.org; Web: www.istd.org. *Chief Executive*, Michael J. Browne

INTERNATIONAL DANCE TEACHERS' ASSOCIATION, International House, 76 Bennett Road, Brighton BN2 5JL. Tel: 01273-685652; Fax: 01273-674388; Email: info@idta.co.uk; Web: www.idta.co.uk.

ROYAL ACADEMY OF DANCE, 36 Battersea Square, London SW11 3RA. Tel: 020-7326 8000; Fax: 020-7924 3129; Email: info@rad.org.uk; Web: www.rad.org.uk. *Chief Executive*, L. Rittner, *Artistic Director*, Ms L. Wallis

ROYAL BALLET SCHOOL, 155 Talgarth Road, London W14 9DE. Tel: 020-8748 6335; Fax: 020-8563 0649; Web: www.royalballetschool.co.uk. *Director*, Ms G. Stock, AM

DEFENCE

ROYAL COLLEGE OF DEFENCE STUDIES, Seaford House, 37 Belgrave Square, London SW1X 8NS. Tel: 020-7915 4800; Fax: 020-7915 4999; Email: dsupport@rcds.ac.uk; Web: www.mod.uk/rcds/index.html. *Commandant*, Lt Gen (Retd) Sir Christopher Wallace, KBE

JOINT SERVICES COMMAND AND STAFF COLLEGE, Faringdon Road, Watchfield, Swindon, Wilts SN6 8TS. Tel: 01793-788555; Email: registry@jscsc.org.uk; Web: www.jscsc.org.uk. *Commandant*, Rear-Adm. R. J. Lippiett, MBE

ROYAL NAVAL COLLEGE

BRITANNIA ROYAL NAVAL COLLEGE, Dartmouth, Devon TQ6 0HJ. Tel: 01803-677108; Fax: 01803-677015. *Commodore*, Cdre M. W. G. Kerr, RN

MILITARY COLLEGES

DIRECTORATE OF EDUCATIONAL AND TRAINING SERVICES (ARMY), Trenchard Lines, Upavon, Pewsey, Wilts SN9 6BE. Tel: 01980-618719/618701; Fax: 01980-618705; Email: dets_a@gtnet.gov.uk; Web: www.agc-ets.co.uk. *Director,* Brig. P. S. Purves

ROYAL MILITARY ACADEMY SANDHURST, Camberley, Surrey GU15 4PQ. Tel: 01276-63344; Fax: 01276-412249. *Commandant,* Maj. Gen. P. C. C. Trousdell, CB, *Chief of Staff,* Col. Maj. Vacher OBE

ROYAL MILITARY COLLEGE OF SCIENCE, Cranfield University, RMCS Shrivenham, Swindon SN6 8LA. Tel: 01793-782551; Fax: 01793-783369; Email: m.r.penny@rmcs.cranfield.ac.uk; Web: www.rmcs.cranfield.ac.uk.

ROYAL AIR FORCE COLLEGES

The Royal Airforce College provides initial training for all officer entrants to the RAF. Also provides initial specialist and postgraduate training for engineering and supply officers. The RAF College is the site of the Joint Elementary Flying School for pilots of all three services, Number 3 Flying Training School and the RAF Central Flying School. It is also the headquarters for the RAF University Air Squadrons, and is responsible for supervision of the Air Cadet Organisation.

ROYAL AIR FORCE COLLEGE, Cranwell, Sleaford, Lincs NG34 8HB. Tel: 01400-261201; Fax: 01400-262532; Email: aoc.college@dial.pipex.com; Web: www.cranwell.raf.mod.uk/

TRAINING, DEVELOPMENT AND SUPPORT UNIT, RAF Halton, Aylesbury, Bucks HP22 5PG. Tel: 01296-623535 ext. 6210; Fax: 01296-696972; Email: octdsu@raf-tdsu.demon.co.uk. *Commanding Officer,* Gp Capt P. D. J. Turner, RAF

DENTISTRY

In order to practise in the UK, a dentist must be registered with the General Dental Council. To be registered a person must be qualified in one of the following ways: hold the degree or diploma in dental surgery of a university in the UK or hold the licentiate in dental surgery awarded by one of the Royal Surgical Colleges in the UK; have completed the Council's International Qualifying Examination (IQE); be a European Community or European Economic Area national holding an appropriate European diploma; hold a registered overseas diploma or be an EEA national holding a primary dental qualification from outside the EEA but has acquired a right to practise in the EEA. The holder of a dental degree or diploma other than those referred to above may be eligible for temporary registration to enable him or her to practise dentistry in the United Kingdom for a limited period and in specified posts without the need to take further examinations. The Dentists Register and Rolls of Dental Auxiliaries are maintained by:

GENERAL DENTAL COUNCIL, 37 Wimpole Street, London W1G 8DQ. Tel: 020-7887 3800; Fax: 020-7224 3294; Email: information@gdc-uk.org; Web: www.gdc-uk.org.

DIETETICS

See also FOOD AND NUTRITION SCIENCE
The professional association is the British Dietetic Association. Full membership is open to dieticians holding a recognised qualification, who may also become State Registered Dieticians through the Council for Professions Supplementary to Medicine (see Medicine).

THE BRITISH DIETETIC ASSOCIATION, 5th Floor, Charles House, 148–149 Craig Charles Street, Queensway, Birmingham B3 3HT. Tel: 0121-200 8080; Fax: 0121-200 8081; Web: www.bda.uk.com.

DRAMA

The national validating body for courses providing training in drama for the professional theatre is the National Council for Drama Training. It currently has accredited courses at the following: Academy of Live and Recorded Arts; Arts Educational Schools; Birmingham School of Speech Training and Dramatic Art; Bristol Old Vic Theatre School; Central School of Speech and Drama; Drama Centre, London; Drama Studio, London; Guildford School of Acting; Guildhall School of Music and Drama, London; London Academy of Music and Dramatic Art; Manchester Metropolitan University School of Theatre; Mountview Theatre School; Oxford School of Drama, Woodstock; Queen Margaret University College, Edinburgh; Rose Bruford College, Sidcup; Royal Academy of Dramatic Art, London; Royal Scottish Academy of Music and Drama; Webber Douglas Academy of Dramatic Art, London; Welsh College of Music and Drama.

The accreditation of a course in a school does not necessarily imply that other courses of different type or duration in the same school are also accredited.

NATIONAL COUNCIL FOR DRAMA TRAINING, 5 Tavistock Place, London WC1H 9SS. Tel: 020-7387 3650; Fax: 020-7681 4733; Email: info@ncdt.co.uk; Web: www.ncdt.co.uk.

ENGINEERING

The Engineering and Technology Board came into being on the 1 January 2002 with the aim of supporting, serving and adding value to the wider engineering and technology community in the UK.

The Council's register of over 250,000 professionals, qualified to internationally recognised standards, reflects engineers and technicians across the broad spectrum of the industry. Working with and through the institutions, the Council sets the standards for the registration of individuals, and also the accreditation for academic courses in universities and colleges and the practical training in industry.

The principal qualifying bodies are:

BRITISH COMPUTER SOCIETY, 1 Sanford Street, Swindon SN1 1HJ. Tel: 01793-417417; Fax: 01793-480270; Email: bcshq@hq.bcs.org.uk; Web: www.bcs.org. *Chief Executive,* David Clark

CHARTERED INSTITUTE OF BUILDING SERVICES ENGINEERS, 222 Balham High Road, London SW12 9BS. Tel: 020-8675 5211; Fax: 020-8675 5449; Web: www.cibse.org. *Chief Executive,* Julian Amey

THE ENGINEERING AND TECHNOLOGY BOARD, 10 Maltravers Street, London WC2R 3ER. Tel: 020-7240 7333; Fax: 020-7240 6014; Email: staff@etechb.co.uk; Web: www.etechb.co.uk.

THE INSTITUTE OF MARINE ENGINEERING, SCIENCE AND TECHNOLOGY, 80 Coleman Street, London EC2R 5BJ. Tel: 020-7382 2600; Fax: 020-7382 2670; Email: imare@imarest.org; Web: www.imarest.org. *Director-General,* K. F. Read

THE INSTITUTE OF MATERIALS, 1 Carlton House Terrace, London SW1Y 5DB. Tel: 020-7451 7300; Fax: 020-7839 1702; Email: admin@materials.org.uk; Web: www.materials.org.uk. *Chief Executive,* Dr B. Rickinson

THE INSTITUTE OF MEASUREMENT AND CONTROL, 87 Gower Street, London WC1E 6AF. Tel: 020-7387

4949; Fax: 020-7388 8431; Email: education@instmc.org.uk; Web: www.instmc.org.uk. *Secretary*, M. J. Yates

THE INSTITUTE OF PHYSICS, 76 Portland Place, London W1B 1NT. Tel: 020-7470 4800; Fax: 020-7470 4848; Email: physics@iop.org; Web: www.iop.org. *Chief Executive*, Julia King

INSTITUTION OF CHEMICAL ENGINEERS, Davis Building, 165–189 Railway Terrace, Rugby, Warks CV21 3HQ. Tel: 01788-578214; Fax: 01788-560833; Web: www.icheme.org. *Chief Executive*, Dr Trevor Evans

THE INSTITUTION OF CIVIL ENGINEERS, 1 Great George Street, London SW1P 3AA. Tel: 020-7222 7722; Fax: 020-7976 7610; Email: library@ice.org.uk; Web: www.ice.org.uk. *Acting Chief Executive*, Amar Bhogal

INSTITUTION OF ELECTRICAL ENGINEERS, Savoy Place, London WC2R 0BL. Tel: 020-7240 1871; Fax: 020-7240 7735; Web: www.iee.org.uk. *Chief Executive*, Dr A. Roberts

INSTITUTION OF GAS ENGINEERS AND MANAGERS, 21 York Gate, London NW1 4QG. Tel: 020-7487 0650; Fax: 020-7224 4762; Email: general@igem.org.uk; Web: www.igaseng.com. *Chief Executive Officer*, G. Davies

INSTITUTION OF MECHANICAL ENGINEERS, 1 Birdcage Walk, London SW1H 9JJ. Tel: 020-7222 7899; Fax: 020-7222 4557; Email: enquiries@imeche.org.uk; Web: www.imeche.org.uk. *Director-General*, Sir Michael Moore, KBE, LVO

INSTITUTION OF MINING AND METALLURGY, Danum House, South Parade, Doncaster, S. Yorks DN1 2DY. Tel: 01302-320486; Fax: 01302-380900; Email: hq@imm.org.uk; Web: www.imm.org.uk. *Secretary*, Dr G. J. M. Woodrow

INSTITUTION OF STRUCTURAL ENGINEERS, 11 Upper Belgrave Street, London SW1X 8BH. Tel: 020-7235 4535; Fax: 020-7235 4294; Email: mail@istructe.org.uk; Web: www.istructe.org.uk. *Chief Executive and Secretary*, Dr K. J. Eaton

INSTITUTION OF STRUCTURAL ENGINEERS, (SCOTTISH BRANCH), 15 Beresford Place, East Trinity Road, Edinburgh EH5 3SL. Tel: 0131-552 8852; Fax: 0131-552 8852; Email: mail@istructe.org.uk; Web: www.istructe.org.uk. *Chief Executive and Secretary*, Dr K. J. Eaton

ROYAL AERONAUTICAL SOCIETY, 4 Hamilton Place, London W1J 7BQ. Tel: 020-7670 4300; Fax: 020-7499 6230; Email: raes@raes.org.uk; Web: www.raes.org.uk. *Director*, K. Mans

ROYAL INSTITUTION OF NAVAL ARCHITECTS, 10 Upper Belgrave Street, London SW1X 8BQ. Tel: 020-7235 4622; Fax: 020-7259 5912; Email: hq@rina.org.uk; Web: www.rina.org.uk. *Chief Executive*, T. Blakeley

FILM AND TELEVISION

Postgraduate training for those intending to make a career in film, television and media production is provided by the National Film and Television School, which provides courses in animation direction, documentary direction, fiction direction, producing, screenwriting, screen design, editing, cinematography, screen sound, screen music and television producing/direction. Short courses enabling professionals to update or expand their skills, are run by the National Short Course Training Programme. There is also the Finishing School, a new industry-accredited, Digital Post-Production training workshop and creative laboratory.

NATIONAL FILM AND TELEVISION SCHOOL, Station Road, Beaconsfield, Bucks HP9 1LJ. Tel: 01494-731 425; Fax: 01494-674042; Email: admin@nftsfilm-tv.ac.uk; Web: www.nftsfilm-tv.ac.uk. *Director*, S. Bayly

FOOD AND NUTRITION SCIENCE

See also DIETETICS
Scientific and professional bodies include:
THE BRITISH DIETETIC ASSOCIATION, 5th Floor, Charles House, 148–149 Craig Charles Street Queensway, Birmingham B3 3HT. Tel: 0121-200 8080; Fax: 0121-200 8081; Web: www.bda.uk.com.

FORESTRY AND TIMBER STUDIES

Professional organisations include:
COMMONWEALTH FORESTRY ASSOCIATION, c/o Oxford Forestry Institute, South Parks Road, Oxford OX1 3RB. Tel: 01865-271037; Fax: 01865-275074; Email: cfa_oxford@hotmail.com. *Chairman*, Dr J. S. Maini

INSTITUTE OF CHARTERED FORESTERS, 7A St Colme Street, Edinburgh EH3 6AA. Tel: 0131-225 2705; Fax: 0131-220 6128; Email: icf@charteredforesters.org; Web: www.charteredforesters.org. *Executive Director*, Mrs M. W. Dick, FRSA, OBE

ROYAL FORESTRY SOCIETY OF ENGLAND, WALES AND NORTHERN IRELAND, 102 High Street, Tring, Herts HP23 4AF. Tel: 01442-822028; Fax: 01442-890395; Email: rfshq@rfs.org.uk; Web: www.rfs.org.uk. *Director*, Dr J. E. Jackson

ROYAL SCOTTISH FORESTRY SOCIETY, Hagg-on-Esk, Canonbie, Dumfriesshire DG14 0BE. Tel: 01387-371518; Fax: 01387-371418; Email: rsfs@ednet.co.uk; Web: www.rsfs.org. *President*, P. J. Fothergill, *Director*, A. G. Little

FUEL AND ENERGY SCIENCE

The principal professional body is:
THE INSTITUTE OF PETROLEUM, 61 New Cavendish Street, London W1G 7AR. Tel: 020-7467 7100; Fax: 020-7255 1472; Email: ip@petroleum.co.uk; Web: www.petroleum.co.uk. *Director-General*, J. Pym

HOTELKEEPING, CATERING AND INSTITUTIONAL MANAGEMENT

See also DIETETICS, AND FOOD AND NUTRITION SCIENCE
The qualifying professional body in these areas is:
HOTEL AND CATERING INTERNATIONAL MANAGEMENT ASSOCIATION, 34 West Street, Sutton, Surrey. Email: general@hcima.co.uk; Web: www.hcima.org.uk. *Chief Executive*, Philip Rossiter

INSURANCE

Organisations conducting examinations and awarding diplomas are:
ASSOCIATION OF AVERAGE ADJUSTERS, The Baltic Exchange, St Mary Axe, London EC3A 8BH. Tel: 020-7623 5501; Fax: 020-7369 1623; Email: aaa@balticexchange.com; Web: www.average-adjusters.com. *Chairman*, Tim Madge

THE CHARTERED INSTITUTE OF LOSS ADJUSTERS, Peninsular House, 36 Monument Street, London EC3R 8LJ. Tel: 020-7337 9960; Fax: 020-7929 3082; Email: info@cila.co.uk; Web: www.cila.co.uk. *Executive Director*, Graham Cave

THE CHARTERED INSURANCE INSTITUTE,
20 Aldermanbury, London EC2V 7HY. Tel: 020-8989
8464; Fax: 020-8530 3052; Email:
customer.serv@cii.co.uk; Web: www.cii.co.uk.
Director-General, Dr Sandy Scott

JOURNALISM

Courses for trainee newspaper journalists are available at
30 centres. One-year full-time courses are available for
selected students, three-year degree programmes and 18-
week courses for graduates. Particulars of all these
courses are available from the National Council for the
Training of Journalists. Short courses for mid-career
development can be arranged, as can various distance
learning courses. The NCTJ also offers NVQs.

For periodical journalists, there are nine centres
running courses approved by the Periodicals Training
Council (PTC). The PTC also provides career
information for people wishing to join the industry.

NATIONAL COUNCIL FOR THE TRAINING OF
JOURNALISTS, Latton Bush Centre, Southern Way,
Harlow, Essex CM18 7BL. Tel: 01279-430009;
Fax: 01279-438008; Email: info@nctj.com;
Web: www.nctj.com.

THE PERIODICALS TRAINING COUNCIL, Queens
House, 55–56 Lincoln Inn Field, London WC2A 3LJ.
Tel: 020-7400 7509; Fax: 020-7404 4167; Email:
training@ppa.co.uk; Web: www.ppa.co.uk/ptc.

LAW

THE BAR

Admission to the Bar of England and Wales is controlled
by the Bar Council, called by the Inns of Court.
Admission to the Bar of Northern Ireland by the
Honorable Society of the Inn of Court of Northern
Ireland and admission as an Advocate of the Scottish Bar
is controlled by the Faculty of Advocates. The governing
body of the barristers' branch of the legal profession in
England and Wales is the General Council of the Bar (the
Bar Council). The governing body in Northern Ireland is
the Honorable Society of the Inn of Court of Northern
Ireland, and the Faculty of Advocates is the governing
body of the Scottish Bar. The education and examination
of students training for the Bar of England and Wales is
regulated by the General Council of the Bar. Those who
intend to practise at the Bar of England and Wales must
pass the Bar's vocational course. The Inns of Court
School of Law (now part of the Institute of Law at City
University) is the largest provider of the Bar Vocational
Course that trains barristers, but several other
institutions have been validated to provide the course.
Applications are handled by the Bar Council's Centralised
Applications Clearing House (CACH).

CACH, THE GENERAL COUNCIL OF THE BAR, 2–3
Curistor Street, London EC4A 1NE. Tel: 020-7440
4000; Fax: 020-7440 4002; Email:
cach@barcouncil.org.uk;
Web: www.barcouncil.org.uk.
Chief Executive, N. Morison

FACULTY OF ADVOCATES, Advocates Library,
Parliament House, Edinburgh EH1 1RF. Tel: 0131-226
5071; Fax: 0131-225 3642;
Web: www.advocates.org.uk.
Dean, G. N. H. Emslie, QC

THE GENERAL COUNCIL OF THE BAR, 3 Bedford Row,
London WC1R 4DB. Tel: 020-7242 0082; Fax: 020-7831
4778; Email: chiefexec@barcouncil.org.uk;
Web: www.barcouncil.org.uk.

THE HONORABLE SOCIETY OF THE INN OF COURT
OF NORTHERN IRELAND, The Under-treasurer's
Office, Royal Courts of Justice, Belfast BT1 3JF.
Tel: 028-9072 4699.

INNS OF COURT SCHOOL OF LAW, 4 Gray's Inn Place,
Gray's Inn, London WC1R 5DX. Tel: 020-7404 5787;
Fax: 020-7831 4188; Email: icslcourses@city.ac.uk;
Web: www.city.ac.uk.

The Inns of Court

GRAY'S INN, 8 South Square, London WC1R 5ET. Tel:
020-7458 7800; Fax: 020-7458 7801;
Web: www.graysinn.org.uk. Treasurer, The Rt. Hon.
Sir Paul Kennedy, QC, Under-Treasurer, Maj.-Gen. D.
Jenkins, CB, CBE

INNER TEMPLE, London EC4Y 7HL. Tel: 020-7797 8250;
Fax: 020-7797 8178; Web: www.innertemple.org.uk.
Treasurer, Richard Southwell, QC

HONORABLE SOCIETY OF LINCOLN'S INN, Treasury
Office, Lincoln's Inn, London WC2A 3TL. Tel: 020-7405
1393; Fax: 020-7831 1839;
Email: mail@lincolnsinn.org.uk;
Web: www.lincolnsinn.org.uk.
Under-Treasurer, Col. D. Hills, MBE

MIDDLE TEMPLE, London EC4Y 9AT. Tel: 020-7427
4800; Fax: 020-7427 4801; Email:
studentenquiries@middletemple.org.uk;
Web: www.middletemple.org.uk.
Treasurer, Rt. Hon. Lord Justice Rose, QC

SOLICITORS

The College of Law is one of the leading providers of
training that enables graduates to be come a solicitor,
however, there are a number of institutions offering the
necessary courses, namely the Legal Practice Course and
the Common Professional Examination (conversion
course for non-law graduates). The Law Society of
England and Wales, the Law Society of Scotland and the
Law Society of Northern Ireland control the education
and examination of trainee solicitors and the admission
of solicitors.

THE COLLEGE OF LAW, Braboeuf Manor, Portsmouth
Road, St Catherine's, Guildford, Surrey GU3 1HA.
Tel: 01483-460200; Fax: 01483-460305;
Web: www.lawcol.org.uk.

THE LAW SOCIETY OF ENGLAND AND WALES,
113 Chancery Lane, London WC2A 1PL.
Tel: 020-7242 1222; Web: www.lawsociety.org.uk.

LAW SOCIETY OF SCOTLAND, 26 Drumsheugh
Gardens, Edinburgh EH3 7YR. Tel: 0131-476
8155/8126/8173; Fax: 0131-225 2934; Email:
legaleduc@lawscot.org.uk; Web: www.lawscot.org.uk.

LAW SOCIETY OF NORTHERN IRELAND, Law Society
House, 98 Victoria Street, Belfast BT1 3JZ.
Tel: 028-9023 1614; Fax: 028-9023 2606;
Email: info@lawsoc-ni.org; Web: www.lawsoc-ni.org.
Chief Executive and Secretary, J. W. Bailie

LIBRARIANSHIP AND INFORMATION
SCIENCE/MANAGEMENT

The Library Association (part of the Chartered Institute
of Library and Information Professionals since April
2002) accredits degree and postgraduate courses in
library and information science which are offered by 17
universities in the UK. A full list of accredited degree and
postgraduate courses is available from its Professional
Qualifications Department and on its web site (*see*
below).

CHARTERED INSTITUTE OF LIBRARY AND
INFORMATION PROFESSIONALS, 7 Ridgmount Street,
London WC1E 7AE. Tel: 020-7255 0500; Fax: 020-7255
0501; Web: www.cilip.org.uk.

MEDICINE

All doctors must be registered with the General Medical Council (GMC), which is responsible for protecting the public by setting standards for professional practice, overseeing medical education, keeping a register of qualified doctors and taking action where a doctor's fitness to practise is in doubt. A doctor not registered with the GMC is not a legally qualified medical practitioner for the purposes of the Medical Act 1983. In order to be eligible for registration, doctors must obtain a primary medical qualification recognised by the GMC and have satisfactorily completed a year of general clinical training. Special arrangements apply to doctors qualified outside the UK. Once registered, doctors undertake general professional and basic specialist training as senior house officers. Further specialist training is provided by the royal colleges, faculties and societies listed below.

The United Examining Board holds qualifying examinations for candidates who have trained overseas. These candidates must also have spent a period at a UK medical school.

FACULTY OF PHARMACEUTICAL MEDICINE,
1 St Andrew's Place, London NW1 4LB.
Tel: 020-7224 0343; Fax: 020-7224 5381;
Email: fpm@fpm.org.uk; Web: www.fpm.org.uk.
Faculty Administrator, Mrs K. Swanston

GENERAL MEDICAL COUNCIL, 178 Great Portland Street, London W1N 6JE. Tel: 020-7580 7642; Fax: 020-7915 3641; Web: www.gmc-uk.org.

JOINT COMMITTEE ON POSTGRADUATE TRAINING FOR GENERAL PRACTICE, 14 Princes Gate, London SW7 1PU. Tel: 020-7581 3232; Fax: 020-7589 5047; Email: enquiry@jcptgp.org.uk;
Web: www.jcptgp.org.uk.

ROYAL COLLEGE OF GENERAL PRACTITIONERS, 14 Princes Gate, London SW7 1PU. Tel: 020-7581 3232; Fax: 020-7225 3047; Email: info@rcgp.org.uk; Web: www.rcgp.org.uk. *Hon. Secretary,* Dr M. Baker

SCOTTISH COUNCIL FOR POSTGRADUATE MEDICAL AND DENTAL EDUCATION, 2nd Floor, Hanover Buildings, 66 Rose Street, Edinburgh EH2 2NN. Tel: 0131-225 4365; Fax: 0131-225 5891.

UNITED EXAMINING BOARD, Apothecaries Hall, Black Friars Lane, London EC4V 6EJ. Tel: 020-7236 1180; Fax: 020-7329 3177;
Email: examoffice@apothecaries.org.
Chairman, Prof J. S. P. Lumley

COLLEGES/SOCIETIES HOLDING POSTGRADUATE MEMBERSHIP AND DIPLOMA EXAMINATIONS

FACULTY OF ACCIDENT AND EMERGENCY MEDICINE, 35–43 Lincoln's Inn Fields, London WC2A 3PE.
Tel: 020-7405 7071; Fax: 020-7405 0318;
Email: faem@compuserve.com;
Web: www.faem.org.uk. *President,* I. W. R. Anderson, *Registrar,* Dr E. Glucksman

FACULTY OF PUBLIC HEALTH MEDICINE, 4 St Andrews Place, London NW1 4LB. Tel: 020-7935 0243; Fax: 020-7224 6973; Email: enquiries@fphm.org.uk; Web: www.fphm.org.uk.
Faculty Secretary, P. Scourfield

ROYAL COLLEGE OF ANAESTHETISTS, 48–49 Russell Square, London WC1B 4JY. Tel: 020-7813 1900; Fax: 020-7813 1876; Email: info@rcoa.ac.uk; Web: www.rcoa.ac.uk.
The College Secretary, Kevin Story

ROYAL COLLEGE OF OBSTETRICIANS AND GYNAECOLOGISTS, 27 Sussex Place, Regent's Park, London NW1 4RG. Tel: 020-7772 6200; Fax: 020-7723 0575; Email: coll.sec@rcog.org.uk;
Web: www.rcog.org.uk. *College Secretary,* P. A. Barnett

ROYAL COLLEGE OF PAEDIATRICS AND CHILD HEALTH, 50 Hallam Street, London W1W 6DE.
Tel: 020-7307 5600; Fax: 020-7307 5601; Email: enquiries@rcpch.ac.uk; Web: www.rcpch.ac.uk.
College Secretary, Len Tyler

ROYAL COLLEGE OF PATHOLOGISTS, 2 Carlton House Terrace, London SW1Y 5AF. Tel: 020-7451 6700; Fax: 020-7451 6701; Email: info@rcpath.org; Web: www.rcpath.org. *Chief Executive,* D. Ross

ROYAL COLLEGE OF PHYSICIANS, 11 St Andrews Place, Regent's Park, London NW1 4LE. Tel: 020-7935 1174; Fax: 020-7487 5218; Web: www.rcplondon.ac.uk. *President,* Prof. Sir George Alberti, *Chief Executive,* P. Masterton-Smith

ROYAL COLLEGE OF PHYSICIANS AND SURGEONS OF GLASGOW, 232–242 St Vincent Street, Glasgow G2 5RJ. Tel: 0141-221 6072; Fax: 0141-221 1804; Email: registrar@rcpsglasg.ac.uk; Web: www.rcpsglasg.ac.uk. *President,* Prof. A. R. Lorimer, PRCPS Glasg.

ROYAL COLLEGE OF PHYSICIANS OF EDINBURGH, 9 Queen Street, Edinburgh EH2 1JQ. Tel: 0131-225 7324; Fax: 0131-220 3939; Web: www.rcpe.ac.uk. *President,* Dr N. D. C. Finlayson, OBE

ROYAL COLLEGE OF PSYCHIATRISTS, 17 Belgrave Square, London SW1X 8PG. Tel: 020-7235 2351; Fax: 020-7245 1231; Email: rcpsych@rcpsych.ac.uk; Web: www.rcpsych.ac.uk. *President,* Dr M. Shooter

ROYAL COLLEGE OF RADIOLOGISTS, 38 Portland Place, London W1N 4JQ. Tel: 020-7636 4432; Fax: 020-7323 3100; Email: enquiries@rcr.ac.uk;
Web: www.rcr.ac.uk. *President,* Dr D. V. Ash

ROYAL COLLEGE OF SURGEONS OF EDINBURGH, Nicolson Street, Edinburgh EH8 9DW. Tel: 0131-527 1600; Fax: 0131-557 6406; Email: information@rcsed.ac.uk; Web: www.rcsed.ac.uk. *Chief Executive,* J. R. C. Foster

THE ROYAL COLLEGE OF SURGEONS OF ENGLAND, 35–43 Lincoln's Inn Fields, London WC2A 3PE. Tel: 020-7405 3474; Fax: 020-7831 9438; Web: www.rcseng.ac.uk.
Chief Executive, Craig Duncan

SOCIETY OF APOTHECARIES OF LONDON, 14 Black Friars Lane, London EC4V 6EJ. Tel: 020-7236 1189; Fax: 020-7329 3177; Email: clerk@apothecaries.org; Web: www.apothecaries.org. *The Clerk,* R. J. Stringer

PROFESSIONS SUPPLEMENTARY TO MEDICINE

The standard of professional education in art, drama and music therapies, biomedical sciences, chiropody, dietetics, occupational therapy, orthoptics, prosthetics and orthotics, physiotherapy and radiography is the responsibility of nine professional boards, which also publish an annual register of qualified practitioners. The work of the boards is co-ordinated by the Council for Professions Supplementary to Medicine.

In January 2000 three new boards were established, covering speech and language therapists, clinical scientists and paramedics.

COUNCIL FOR PROFESSIONS SUPPLEMENTARY TO MEDICINE, Park House, 184 Kennington Park Road, London SE11 4BU. Tel: 020-7582 0866; Fax: 020-7820 9684; Web: www.cpsm.org.uk.

ART, DRAMA AND MUSIC THERAPIES

A postgraduate qualification in the relevant therapy is required. There are six institutions in the UK offering courses in art therapy and six offering courses in music therapy.

ASSOCIATION OF PROFESSIONAL MUSIC THERAPISTS,
26 Hamlyn Road, Glastonbury, Somerset BA6 8HT.
Tel: 01458-834919; Fax: 01458-834919; Email:
apmtoffice@aol.com; Web: www.apmt.org.uk.
Administrator, Mrs D. Asbridge

BRITISH ASSOCIATION OF ART THERAPISTS, Mary
Ward House, 5 Tavistock Place, London WC1H 9SN.
Tel: 020-7383 3774; Web: www.baat.co.uk.

BRITISH ASSOCIATION OF DRAMA THERAPISTS,
41 Broomhouse Lane, London SW6 3DP.
Tel: 020-7731 0160; Email: gillian@badth.demon.co.uk.

BIOMEDICAL SCIENCES

Qualifications from higher education establishments and
training in medical laboratories are required for
membership of the Institute of Biomedical Science.

INSTITUTE OF BIOMEDICAL SCIENCES, 12 Coldbath
Square, London EC1R 5HL. Tel: 020-7713 0214;
Fax: 020-7436 4946; Email: mail@ibms.org;
Web: www.ibms.org.

CHIROPODY

Professional recognition is granted by the Society of
Chiropodists and Podiatrists to students who are awarded
BSc degrees in Podiatry or Podiatric Medicine after
attending a course of full-time training for three or four
years at one of the 13 recognised schools in the UK (ten
in England and Wales, two in Scotland and one in
Northern Ireland). Qualifications granted and degrees
recognised by the Society are approved for the purpose of
State Registration, which is a condition of employment
within the National Health Service.

SOCIETY OF CHIROPODISTS AND PODIATRISTS,
1 Fellmongers Path, Tower Bridge Road, London SE1
3LY. Tel: 020-7234 8620; Fax: 020-7234 8621;
Email: enq@scpod.org; Web: www.feetforlife.org.
Chief Executive, Ms Hilary De Lyon

OCCUPATIONAL THERAPY

The professional qualification and eligibility for state
registration may be obtained upon successful completion
of a validated course in any of the institutions approved
by the College of Occupational Therapists. The courses
are normally degree-level courses based in higher
education institutions.

COLLEGE OF OCCUPATIONAL THERAPISTS, 106–114
Borough High Street, London SE1 1LB. Tel: 020-7357
6480; Fax: 020-7450 2299; Email: cot@cot.co.uk;
Web: www.cot.co.uk.

FACULTY OF OCCUPATIONAL MEDICINE, 6 St
Andrew's Place, London NW1 4LB. Tel: 020-7317 5890;
Fax: 020-7317 5899; Email: fom@facoccmed.ac.uk;
Web: www.facoccmed.ac.uk.
President, Dr W J Gunnyeon

ORTHOPTICS

Orthoptists undertake the diagnosis and treatment of all
types of squint and other anomalies of binocular vision,
working in close collaboration with ophthalmologists.
The training and maintenance of professional standards
are the responsibility of the Orthoptists Board of the
Council for the Professions Supplementary to Medicine.
The professional body is the British Orthoptic Society.
Training is at degree level.

THE BRITISH ORTHOPTIC SOCIETY, Tavistock House
North, Tavistock Square, London WC1H 9HX.
Tel: 020-7387 7992; Fax: 020-7383 2584;
Web: www.orthoptics.org.uk.
Hon. Chairman, C. Timms

PHYSIOTHERAPY

Full-time three- or four-year degree courses are available
at 30 higher education institutions in the UK.
Information about courses leading to eligibility for
Membership of the Chartered Society of Physiotherapy
and to State Registration is available from the Chartered
Society of Physiotherapy.

THE CHARTERED SOCIETY OF PHYSIOTHERAPY, 14
Bedford Row, London WC1R 4ED. Tel: 020-7306 6666;
Fax: 020-7306 6611; Email:
careersadviser@csphysio.org.uk;
Web: www.csphysio.org.uk.

PROSTHETICS AND ORTHOTICS

Prosthetists provide artificial limbs, while orthotists
provide devices to support or control a part of the body.
It is necessary to obtain an honours degree to become a
prosthetist/orthotist. Training is centred at two UK
universities, University of Salford and University of
Strathclyde.

BRITISH ASSOCIATION OF PROSTHETISTS AND
ORTHOTISTS, Sir James Clark Building, Abbey Mill
Business Centre, Paisley PA1 1TJ. Tel: 0141-561 7217;
Fax: 0141-561 7218; Email: admin@bapo.com;
Web: www.bapo.com.

RADIOGRAPHY AND RADIOTHERAPY

In order to practise both diagnostic and therapeutic
radiography in the UK, it is necessary to have successfully
completed a course of education and training recognised
by the Privy Council. Such courses are offered by
universities throughout the UK and lead to the award of
a degree in radiography. Further information is available
from the college.

THE SOCIETY AND COLLEGE OF RADIOGRAPHERS,
207 Providence Square, Mill Street, London SE1 2EW.
Tel: 020-7740 7200; Fax: 020-7740 7204;
Email: info@sor.org; Web: www.sor.org.

COMPLEMENTARY MEDICINE

Professional courses are validated by:

INSTITUTE FOR COMPLEMENTARY MEDICINE,
PO Box 194, London SE16 7QZ. Tel: 020-7237 5165;
Fax: 020-7237 5175; Email: icm@icmedicine.co.uk;
Web: www.icmedicine.co.uk.

MERCHANT NAVY TRAINING SCHOOLS

OFFICERS

WARSASH MARITIME CENTRE, Southampton Institute,
Newtown Road, Warsash, Southampton SO31 9ZL.
Tel: 01489-576161; Fax: 01489-573988;
Email: wmc@solent.ac.uk;
Web: www.solent.ac.uk/wmc/ *Head,* J. Milligan

SEAFARERS

NATIONAL SEA TRAINING CENTRE, North West Kent
College, Dering Way, Gravesend, Kent DA12 2JJ.
Tel: 01322-629600; Fax: 01322-629687.
Director of Faculty - NSTC, I. R. Goodwin, *Principal -
North West Kent College,* M. Bell

MUSIC

The Associated Board of The Royal Schools of Music
conducts graded music examinations in over 80 countries
and provides other services to music education through
its professional development department and publishing
company.

ASSOCIATED BOARD OF THE ROYAL SCHOOLS OF
MUSIC, 24 Portland Place, London W1B 1LU.
Tel: 020-7636 5400; Fax: 020-7637 0234;
Email: abrsm@abrsm.ac.uk; Web: www.abrsm.ac.uk;
www.abrsmpublishing.co.uk. *Chief Executive*, R.
Morris

GUILDHALL SCHOOL OF MUSIC & DRAMA, Silk
Street, Barbican, London EC2Y 8DT. Tel: 020-7628
2571; Fax: 020-7256 9438; Web: www.gsmd.ac.uk.
Principal, Baroness McIntosh of Hudnall

LONDON COLLEGE OF MUSIC AND MEDIA, Thames
Valley University, St Mary's Road, London W5 5RF.
Tel: 020-8231 2304; Fax: 020-8231 2546;
Web: www.elgar.tvu.ac.uk.
The Dean, Prof. Colin Lawson

ROYAL ACADEMY OF MUSIC, Marylebone Road,
London NW1 5HT. Tel: 020-7873 7373;
Fax: 020-7873 7374; Email: registry@ram.ac.uk;
Web: www.ram.ac.uk. *Principal*, Prof. Curtis Price

ROYAL COLLEGE OF ORGANISTS, 7 St Andrew Street,
London EC4A 3LQ. Tel: 020-7936 3606; Fax: 020-7353
8244; Email: admin@rco.org.uk;
Web: www.rco.org.uk.
The Registrar, Gordon St. J. Clarke

ROYAL NORTHERN COLLEGE OF MUSIC, 124 Oxford
Road, Manchester M13 9RD. Tel: 0161-907 5200; Fax:
0161-273 7611; Email: info@rncm.ac.uk;
Web: www.rncm.ac.uk. *Principal*, Prof. E. Gregson

ROYAL SCOTTISH ACADEMY OF MUSIC AND DRAMA,
100 Renfrew Street, Glasgow G2 3DB.
Tel: 0141-332 4101; Fax: 0141-332 8901;
Email: registry@rsamd.ac.uk; Web: www.rsamd.ac.uk.
Principal, John Wallace, OBE

TRINITY COLLEGE OF MUSIC, King Charles Court, Old
Royal Naval College, London SE10 9JF. Tel: 020-8305
3888; Fax: 020-8305 3999; Email: info@ tcm.ac.uk;
Web: www.tcm.ac.uk. *Principal*, G. Henderson

NURSING

All nurses must be registered with the Nursing and
Midwifery Council. Courses leading to registration as a
nurse or midwife are at least three years in length. There
are also some programmes which are combined with
degrees. Students study in colleges of nursing or in
institutions of higher education. Courses offer a combination of theoretical and practical experience in a
variety of settings. Different courses lead to different
types of registration, including Registered Nurse (RN),
Registered Mental Nurse (RMN), Registered Learning
Disabilities Nurse (RLDN), Registered Sick Children's
Nurse (RSCN), Registered Midwife (RM) and Registered
Health Visitor (RHV). The various national boards, listed
below, are responsible for validating courses in nursing.
In February 1999 the Government announced plans to
replace these boards and the UK Central Council with a
single UK-wide body. Health visitors will continue to
have separate registration and representation on the new
body.

The Royal College of Nursing is the largest professional
union representing nurses and provides higher education
through its Institute.

UK CENTRAL COUNCIL FOR NURSING, MIDWIFERY
AND HEALTH VISITING, 23 Portland Place, London
W1N 4JT. Tel: 020-7637 7181; Fax: 020-7436 2924;
Email: communications@nmc-uk.org;
Web: www.nmc-uk.org.

OPHTHALMIC AND DISPENSING OPTICS

Professional bodies are:

THE ASSOCIATION OF BRITISH DISPENSING
OPTICIANS, Godmersham Park, Godmersham,
Kent CT4 7DT. Tel: 01227-738829; Fax: 01227-733900;
Email: general@abdo.org.uk; Web: www.abdo.org.uk.
The registrar, Derek Baker

THE COLLEGE OF OPTOMETRISTS, 42 Craven Street,
London WC2N 5NG. Tel: 020-7839 6000;
Fax: 020-7839 6800;
Email: optometry@college-optometrists.org;
Web: www.college-optometrists.org.
Chief Executive, P. D. Leigh

OSTEOPATHY

Osteopathy is the first of the professions previously
outside conventional medical services to achieve
statutory recognition under a new body the General
Osteopathic Council. Since May 2000 all practising
osteopaths have had to be registered with the General
Osteopathic Council and the title 'osteopath' is protected
by law. To gain entry to the register all newly qualified
osteopaths have to be in possession of a recognised
qualification from a course of training accredited by the
General Osteopathic Council. The General Osteopathic
Council is responsible for regulating, developing, and
promoting the profession.

GENERAL OSTEOPATHIC COUNCIL, Osteopathy House,
176 Tower Bridge Road, London SE1 3LU.
Tel: 020-7357 6655; Fax: 020-7357 0011;
Email: info@osteopathy.org.uk;
Web: www.osteopathy.org.uk.
Chief Executive & Registrar, Miss M. J. Craggs

PHARMACY

The Royal Pharmaceutical Society of Great Britain is the
regulatory and professional body for pharmacists in all
aspects of practice. It has a statutory duty to maintain the
registers of pharmacists and pharmacy premises. The
Society also operates widely to promote the development
of the science and practice of pharmacy. To be eligible to
register students must have a degree in pharmacy
followed by one year pre-registration training at a
premises recognised by the Society.

ROYAL PHARMACEUTICAL SOCIETY OF GREAT
BRITAIN, 1 Lambeth High Street, London SE1 7JN.
Tel: 020-7735 9141; Fax: 020-7735 7629;
Email: enquiries@rpsgb.org.uk;
Web: www.rpsgb.org.uk. *Secretary and Registrar*, Ms
A. M Lewis

PHOTOGRAPHY

The professional body is:

BRITISH INSTITUTE OF PROFESSIONAL
PHOTOGRAPHY, Fox Talbot House, Amwell End,
Ware, Herts SG12 9HN. Tel: 01920-464011;
Fax: 01920-487056; Email: bipp@compuserve.com;
Web: www.bipp.com. *Chief Executive*, Alex Mair

PRINTING

Details of training courses in printing can be obtained
from the Institute of Printing and the British Printing
Industries Federation. In addition to these examining and
organising bodies, examinations are held by various
independent regional examining boards in further
education.

INSTITUTE OF PRINTING, The Mews, Hill House,
Clanricarde Road, Tunbridge Wells, Kent TN1 1PJ.
Tel: 01892-538118; Fax: 01892-518028;
Email: admin@iop.ftech.co.uk;
Web: www.instituteofprinting.org.

BRITISH PRINTING INDUSTRIES FEDERATION, Farringdon Point, 29–35 Farringdon Road, London EC1M 3JF. Tel: 020-7915 8300; Fax: 020-7405 7784; Email: info@bpif.org.uk; Web: www.bpif.org.uk.

SCIENCE

Professional qualifications are awarded by:
THE INSTITUTE OF BIOLOGY, 20–22 Queensberry Place, London SW7 2DZ. Tel: 020-7581 8333; Fax: 020-7823 9409; Email: info@iob.org; Web: www.iob.org. *Chief Executive*, Prof. Alan Malcolm
THE ROYAL SOCIETY OF CHEMISTRY, Burlington House, Piccadilly, London W1J 0BA. Tel: 020-7437 8656; Fax: 020-7437 8883; Email: rsc@rsc.org; Web: www.rsc.org. *Secretary-General and Chief Executive*, Dr D. Giachardi

SPEECH AND LANGUAGE THERAPY

The Royal College of Speech and Language Therapists accredits education and training courses leading to qualification as a speech and language therapist.
ROYAL COLLEGE OF SPEECH AND LANGUAGE THERAPISTS, 2 White Hart Yard, London SE1 1NX. Tel: 020-7378 1200; Fax: 020-7403 7254; Email: info@rcslt.org; Web: www.rcslt.org.

SURVEYING

The qualifying professional bodies include:
ARCHITECTURE AND SURVEYING INSTITUTE, St Mary House, 15 St Mary Street, Chippenham, Wilts SN15 3WD. Tel: 01249-444505; Fax: 01249-443602; Email: mail@asi.org.uk; Web: www.asi.org.uk. *Chief Executive*, Ian Norris
ASSOCIATION OF BUILDING ENGINEERS, Lutyens House, Billing Brook Road, Weston Favell, Northampton NN3 8NW. Tel: 01604-404121; Fax: 01604-784220; Email: building.engineers@abe.org.uk; Web: www.abe.org.uk. *Chief Executive*, David Gibson
INSTITUTE OF REVENUES, RATING AND VALUATION, 41 Doughty Street, London WC1N 2LF. Tel: 020-7831 3505; Fax: 020-7831 2048; Email: enquiries@irrv.org.uk; Web: www.irrv.org.uk. *Director*, David Magor
THE ROYAL INSTITUTION OF CHARTERED SURVEYORS, 12 Great George Street, Parliament Square, London SW1P 3AD. Tel: 020-7222 7000; Fax: 020-7222 9430; Email: info@rics.org.uk; Web: www.rics.org. *Chief Executive*, J. H. A. J. Armstrong

TEACHING

To work as a qualified teacher in a school in England and Wales, Qualified Teacher Status (QTS) must be acquired by completing a programme of Initial Teacher Training. Teaching is an all-graduate profession. Those without a first degree may take a Bachelor of Education (BEd) or a Bachelor of Arts/Science (BA/BSc) with QTS, full-time for three or four years, depending on the programme followed. These degrees combine subject and professional studies with teaching practice.

For those who already have a first degree, the most common route is through a one-year Postgraduate Certificate of Education (PGCE). This may be taken full-time or part-time, or as a distance-learning programme. Postgraduates may also gain QTS through training in a school (School-Centred Initial Teacher Training). Graduates aged 24 or above can apply to train through the Graduate Teacher Programme which offers a salary while employed in a school as a trainee teacher, usually for one year.

Further information about how to become a teacher in England and Wales is available on the Teacher Training Agency's website (see below) or in *The Initial Teacher Training Handbook* (£9.99 plus p&p) available from UCAS on +44 (0)1242 544610. Further personal advice is available from the Teaching Information Line, 0845 600 0991. The Higher Education Funding Council for Wales funds initial teacher training and accredits providers of initial teacher training in Wales. They also produce Performance Information on Initial Teacher Training Providers in Wales. Details of courses in Scotland can be obtained from universities and the Graduate Teacher Training Registry (GTTR). Details of courses in Northern Ireland can be obtained from the Department of Education for Northern Ireland.
TEACHER TRAINING AGENCY, Portland House, Stag Place, London SW1E 5TT. Tel: 020-7925 3700; Fax: 020-7925 3799; Web: www.canteach.gov.uk.

TEXTILES

THE TEXTILE INSTITUTE, 4th Floor, St James's Buildings, Oxford Street, Manchester M1 6FQ. Tel: 0161-237 1188; Fax: 0161-236 1991; Email: tiihq@textileinst.org; Web: www.texi.org.

THEOLOGICAL COLLEGES

ANGLICAN

COLLEGE OF THE RESURRECTION, Mirfield, W. Yorks WF14 0BW. Tel: 01924-490441; Fax: 01924-492738; Web: www.mirfield.org.uk. *Principal*, Revd C. Irvine
CRANMER HALL, ST JOHN'S COLLEGE, Durham DH1 3RJ. Tel: 0191-374 3579; Fax: 0191-374 3573; Web: www.dur.ac.uk/cranmer. *Warden*, The Revd Dr S. J. L. Croft
OAK HILL COLLEGE, Chase Side, Southgate, London N14 4PS. Tel: 0208-449 0467; Fax: 0208-441 5996; Web: www.oakhill.ac.uk. *Principal*, Revd Dr D. Peterson
RIDLEY HALL, Cambridge CB3 9HG. Tel: 01223-741080; Fax: 01223-741081; Web: www.ridley.cam.ac.uk. *Principal*, The Revd Canon Dr Christopher Cocksworth
RIPON COLLEGE, Cuddesdon, Oxford OX44 9EX. Tel: 01865-874595; Fax: 01865-875431; Web: www.ripon-cuddesdon.ac.uk. *Principal*, Canon J. Clarke
ST JOHN'S COLLEGE, Chilwell Lane, Bramcote, Nottingham NG9 3DS. Tel: 0115-925 1114; Fax: 0115-943 6438; Web: www.stjohns-nottm.ac.uk. *Principal*, Canon Dr C. Baxter
ST MICHAEL'S THEOLOGICAL COLLEGE, Llandaff, Cardiff CF5 2YJ. Tel: 029-2056 3379; Fax: 029-2083 8008; Web: www.stmichaels.ac.uk. *Principal*, Revd Dr J. Holdsworth
ST STEPHEN'S HOUSE, 16 Marston Street, Oxford OX4 1JX. Tel: 01865-247874; Fax: 01865-794338; Web: www.ststephenshouse.ac.uk. *Principal*, Revd Dr J. P. Sheehy
THEOLOGICAL INSTITUTE OF THE SCOTTISH EPISCOPAL CHURCH, Old Coates House, 32 Manor Place, Edinburgh EH3 7EB. Tel: 0131-220 2272; Fax: 0131-220 2294. *Principal*, Revd Canon Dr M. Fuller
WESTCOTT HOUSE, Jesus Lane, Cambridge CB5 8BP. Tel: 01223-741000; Fax: 01223-741002; Web: www.ely.anglican.org/westcott. *Principal*, Revd M. Roberts

WYCLIFFE HALL THEOLOGICAL COLLEGE,
54 Banbury Road, Oxford OX2 6PW. Tel: 01865-
274200; Fax: 01865-274215;
Web: www.wycliffe.ox.ac.uk.
Principal, Revd Prof. A. E. McGrath

BAPTIST

BRISTOL BAPTIST COLLEGE, The Promenade, Clifton,
Bristol BS8 3NF. Tel: 0117-946 7050;
Fax: 0117-946 7787; Web: www.bristol-baptist.ac.uk.
Principal, Revd C. Ellis
NORTHERN BAPTIST COLLEGE, Luther King House,
Brighton Grove, Rusholme, Manchester M14 5JP.
Tel: 0161-224 6404; Fax: 0161-248 9201;
Web: www.northern.org.uk.
Principal, Revd Dr R. Kidd
NORTH WALES BAPTIST COLLEGE, Ffordd Ffriddoedd,
Bangor LL57 2EH. Tel: 01248-362608; Fax: 01248-
383759; Web: www.bangor.ac.uk/rs/gttest.html.
Warden, Revd Dr D. D. Morgan
REGENT'S PARK COLLEGE, Oxford OX1 2LB.
Tel: 01865-288120; Fax: 01865-288121;
Web: www.rpc.ox.ac.uk.
Principal, Revd Dr P. S. Fiddes
THE SCOTTISH BAPTIST COLLEGE, 12 Aytoun Road,
Glasgow G41 5RN. Tel: 0141-848 3988;
Fax: 0141-848 3989;
Web: www.scottishbaptistcollege.org.uk.
Principal, Dr K. B. E. Roxburgh
SOUTH WALES BAPTIST COLLEGE, 54 Richmond
Road, Cardiff CF24 3UR. Tel: 029-2025 6066;
Fax: 029-2041 1566;
Web: www.welshbaptists.com.
Principal, Revd Dr J. Weaver

CHURCH OF SCOTLAND

CHRIST'S COLLEGE, 25 High Street, Old Aberdeen,
Aberdeen AB24 3EE. Tel: 01224-272138;
Fax: 01224-272136;
Master, Revd Prof. Iain R. Torrance
NEW COLLEGE, Mound Place, Edinburgh EH1 2LX.
Tel: 0131-650 8916/8900; Fax: 0131-650 6579;
Web: www.divinity.ed.ac.uk.
Principal, Revd Dr D. Lyall
TRINITY COLLEGE, Faculty of Divinity, University of
Glasgow, Glasgow G12 8QQ. Tel: 0141-330 4990;
Fax: 0141-330 4943. *Principal,* Prof. J. Houston

CONGREGATIONAL

SCOTTISH CONGREGATIONAL COLLEGE, 340 Cathedral
Street, Glasgow G1 2BQ. Tel: 0141-332 7667;
Fax: 0141-332 8463. *Principal,* Revd J. W. Dyce

METHODIST

EDGHILL THEOLOGICAL COLLEGE, 9 Lennoxvale,
Belfast BT9 5BY. Tel: 028-9066 5870;
Fax: 028-9068 7204;
Web: www.edgehilltheologicalcollege.org.
Principal, Revd Dr D. Cooke
HARTLEY VICTORIA COLLEGE, Luther King House,
Brighton Grove, Rusholme, Manchester M14 5JP.
Tel: 0161-249 2516; Fax: 0161-248 9201.
Principal, Revd Dr J. A. Harrod
WESLEY COLLEGE, College Park Drive, Henbury Road,
Bristol BS10 7QD. Tel: 0117-959 1200;
Fax: 0117-950 1277;
Web: www.wesley-college-bristol.ac.uk.
Principal, Revd Dr J. H. Pye

WESLEY STUDY CENTRE, St John's College, South
Bailey, Durham DH1 3RJ. Tel: 0191-374 3580; Fax:
0191-374 3573; Web: www.dur.ac.uk/st-johns.college.
Director, Revd R. Walton
WESLEY THEOLOGICAL COLLEGE, Wesley House, Jesus
Lane, Cambridge CB5 8BJ. Tel: 01223-741033;
Fax: 01223-321177;
Principal, Revd Dr P. Luscombe

NON-DENOMINATIONAL

SPURGEON'S COLLEGE, South Norwood Hill, London
SE25 6DJ. Tel: 020-8653 0850; Fax: 020-8771 0959;
Web: www.spurgeons.ac.uk.
Principal, Revd Dr N. G. Wright
ST MARY'S COLLEGE, The University, St Andrews, Fife
KY16 9JU. Tel: 01334-462850; Fax: 01334-462852;
Web: www.st-andrews.ac.uk.
Principal, The Revd Professor T. A. Hart
TRINITY COLLEGE, Stoke Hill, Bristol BS9 1JP.
Tel: 0117-968 2803; Fax: 0117-968 7470;
Web: www.trinity-bris.ac.uk.
Principal, Revd Dr F. Bridger

PRESBYTERIAN

UNION THEOLOGICAL COLLEGE, 108 Botanic Avenue,
Belfast BT7 1JT. Tel: 028-9020 5080;
Fax: 028-9058 0040; Web: www.union.ac.uk.
Principal, Revd J. C. McCullough

PRESBYTERIAN CHURCH OF WALES

UNITED THEOLOGICAL COLLEGE, Aberystwyth,
Ceredigion SY23 2LT. Tel: 01970-624574;
Fax: 01970-626350; Web: www.ebcpcw.org.uk.
Principal, Revd Dr J. Tudno Williams

ROMAN CATHOLIC

ALLEN HALL, 28 Beaufort Street, London SW3 5AA.
Tel: 020-7349 5600; Fax: 020-7349 5601.
Rector, Revd P. McGinn
CAMPION HOUSE COLLEGE, 112 Thornbury Road,
Isleworth, Middx TW7 4NN. Tel: 020-8560 1924;
Fax: 020-8569 9645;
Web: www.campionhouse.org.uk.
Principal, Revd M. Barrow, SJ
OSCOTT COLLEGE, Chester Road, Sutton Coldfield,
West Midlands B73 5AA. Tel: 0121-321 5000;
Fax: 0121-321 5002. *Rector,* Fr. Mark Crisp
SCOTUS COLLEGE, 2 Chesters Road, Bearsden, Glasgow
G61 4AG. Tel: 0141-942 8384; Fax: 0141-943 1767.
Rector, Revd N. Donnachie
ST JOHN'S SEMINARY, Wonersh, Guildford, Surrey GU5
0QX. Tel: 01483-892217; Fax: 01483-894531;
Web: www.dspacc.dial.pipex.com/town/venue/aba24/.
Rector, Revd Canon K. Haggerty
USHAW COLLEGE, Durham DH7 9RH. Tel: 0191-373
8501; Fax: 0191-373 8504;
Web: www.dur.ac.uk/ushaw.
President, Revd J. O'Keefe

UNITARIAN

UNITARIAN COLLEGE, Luther King House, Brighton
Grove, Rusholme, Manchester M14 5JP.
Tel: 0161-224 2849; Fax: 0161-248 9201.
Principal, Revd Ann Peart

UNITED REFORMED

NORTHERN COLLEGE, Luther King House, Brighton Grove, Rusholme, Manchester M14 5JP. Tel: 0161-249 2506; Fax: 0161-248 9201.
Principal, Revd Dr D. R. Peel

WESTMINSTER COLLEGE, Madingley Road, Cambridge CB3 0AA. Tel: 01223-741084; Fax: 01223-300765; Web: www.westminster.cam.ac.uk.
Principal, Revd Dr S. Orchard

JEWISH

LEO BAECK COLLEGE, Sternberg Centre for Judaism, 80 East End Road, London N3 2SY. Tel: 020-8349 5600; Fax: 020-8343 2558; Web: www.lbc.ac.uk.
Principal, Rabbi Prof. J. Magonet

LONDON SCHOOL OF JEWISH STUDIES, Schaller House, 44a Albert Road, London NW4 2SJ. Tel: 020-8203 6427; Fax: 020-8203 6420; Web: www.lsjs.ac.uk.
Principal, Dr A. Weiss, *Director*, Dr I. Rabinowitz

THE QUEEN'S FOUNDATION FOR ECUMENICAL THEOLOGICAL EDUCATION, Somerset Road, Edgbaston, Birmingham B15 2QH. Tel: 0121-454 1527; Fax: 0121-454 8171; Web: www.queens.ac.uk.
Principal, Revd Canon P. Fisher

VETERINARY MEDICINE

The regulatory body for veterinary medicine is the Royal College of Veterinary Surgeons, which keeps the register of those entitled to practise veterinary medicine.

Holders of recognised degrees from any of the six UK university veterinary schools or from certain EU or overseas universities are entitled to be registered, and holders of certain other degrees may tale a statutory membership examination.

The British Veterinary Association is the professional body representing veterinary surgeons. The British Veterinary Nursing Association is the professional body representing veterinary nurses.

ROYAL COLLEGE OF VETERINARY SURGEONS, Belgravia House, 62–64 Horseferry Road, London SW1P 2AF. Tel: 020-7222 2001; Fax: 020-7222 2004; Email: admin@rcvs.org.uk; Web: www.rcvs.org.uk.

BRITISH VETERINARY NURSING ASSOCIATION, Level 15, Terminus House, Terminus Street, Harlow, Essex CM20 1XA. Tel: 01279-450567; Fax: 01279-420866; Email: bvna@bvna.co.uk; Web: www.bvna.org.uk.

Independent Schools

The following pages list those independent schools (UK and overseas) whose Head is a member of the *Headmasters' and Headmistresses' Conference*, the *Society of Headmasters and Headmistresses* or the *Girls' School Association*. The list includes name of school, location, date founded, number of pupils, termly fees (day and boarding) and the name of Head (with date of appointment). This section has been compiled with the assistance of the *Guide to Independent Schools 2003*.

School	Date Founded	No of pupils	Termly fees		Head (with date of appointment)
			Day	Boarding	
ENGLAND					
The Abbey School, Berkshire	1887	990	£2,350	–	Mrs B. E. Stanley (2002)
Abbotsholme School, Staffordshire	1889	252	£3,627	£5,425	Mrs K. Warde (Acting, 2002)
Abingdon School, Oxfordshire	1256	796	£2,850	£5,200	M. Turner (2002)
Ackworth School, West Yorkshire	1779	501	£2,599	£4,612	M. Dickinson (1995)
Adcote School for Girls, Shropshire	1907	95	£2,700	£4,790	R. E. D. Case (2002)
Aldenham School, Hertfordshire	1597	405	£3,890	£5,590	R. Harman (2000)
Alderley Edge School for Girls, Cheshire	1999	650	£1,825	–	Mrs K. Mills (1999)
The Alice Ottley School, Worcestershire	1883	640	£2,424	–	Mrs M. Chapman (1999)
Alleyn's School, London	1619	922	£2,846	–	C. Diggory (2002)
Ampleforth College, York	1802	517	£3,160	£6,030	Rev G. F. L. Chamberlain (1992)
Ardingly College, West Sussex	1858	710	£4,310	£5,750	J. Franklin (1998)
Arnold School, Lancashire	1896	1169	£1,835	–	W. T. Gillen (1994)
The Arts Educational School, Hertfordshire	–	263	£4,950	£6,150	S. Anderson (2002)
Ashford School, Kent	1898	488	£3,035	£5,270	Mrs P. Holloway (2000)
Ashville College, North Yorkshire	1877	840	£2,424	£4,594	M. H. Crosby (1987)
The Atherley School, Hampshire	1926	450	£2,220	–	Mrs M. Bradley (1999)
Austin Friars School, Cumbria	1951	272	£2,283	–	N. J. B. O'Sullivan (2000)
Bablake School, Coventry	1344	1000	£1,951	–	Dr S. Nuttall (1991)
Badminton School, Bristol	1858	395	£3,395	£6,030	Mrs J. Scarrow (1997)
Bancroft's School, Essex	1737	989	£2,823	–	Dr P. Scott (1996)
Barnard Castle School, Durham	1883	660	£2,468	£4,169	M. D. Featherstone (1997)
Batley Grammar School, West Yorkshire	1612	447	£2,047	–	B. Battye (1998)
Battle Abbey School, East Sussex	1912	276	£2,900	£4,680	R. Clark (1998)
Bearwood College, Berkshire	1827	356	£2,995	£5,075	S. G. G. Aiano (1998)
Bedales School, Hampshire	1893	405	£4,540	£6,369	K. Budge (2001)
Bedford School, Bedfordshire	1552	1090	£3,540	£5,585	Dr I. P. Evans (1990)
Bedford High School, Bedfordshire	1882	880	£2,615	£5,232	Mrs G. Piotrowska (2000)
Bedford Modern School, Bedfordshire	1566	1100	£2,481	–	S. Smith (1996)
Bedgebury School, Kent	1860	366	£3,350	£5,390	Mrs H. Moriarty (2000)
Beechwood School, Kent	1915	300	£3,025	£4,925	N. Beesley (1999)
The Belvedere School, Liverpool	1880	600	£1,945	–	Mrs G. Richards (1997)
Benenden School, Kent	1923	450	–	£6,500	Mrs C. Oulton (2000)
Berkhamsted Collegiate School, Hertfordshire	1541	1460	£3,372	£5,364	Dr P. Chadwick (1996)
Bethany School, Kent	1866	315	£3,113	£5,172	N. Dorey (1997)
Birkdale School, Sheffield	915	800	£2,191	–	R. J. Court (1998)
Birkenhead School, Wirral	1860	832	£1,998	–	S. Haggett (1988)
Birkenhead High School, Merseyside	1901	860	£1,814	–	Mrs C. Evans (1997)
Bishop's Stortford College, Hertfordshire	1868	390	£3,375	£4,681	J. G Trotman (1996)
Blackheath High School, London	1880	630	£2,385	–	Mrs E. Laws (2000)
Bloxham School, Oxfordshire	1860	365	£4,670	£5,995	M. E. Allbrook (2002)
Blundell's School, Devon	1604	520	£3,500	£5,585	J. Leigh (1991)
Bolton School Boys' Division, Lancashire	1524	1070	£2,166	–	M. Brooker (2003)
Bolton School Girls' Division, Lancashire	1877	1187	£2,166	–	Miss E. J. Panton (1993)
Bootham School, York	1823	420	£3,170	£4,849	I. Small (1988)
Box Hill School, Surrey	1959	320	£2,710	£4,642	Dr R. Atwood (1987)
Bradfield College, Berkshire	1850	610	£5,000	£6,250	P. Smith (1986)
Bradford Girls' Grammar School, West Yorkshire	1875	809	£2,195	–	Mrs L. J. Warrington (1987)
Bradford Grammar School, West Yorkshire	1548	1050	£2,184	–	S. Davidson (1996)
Brentwood School, Essex	1557	1101	£3,016	£5,223	J. Kelsall (1993)
Brighton College, East Sussex	1845	643	£3,749	£5,812	Dr A. Seldon (1997)
Bristol Cathedral School, Bristol	1542	425	£2,072	–	K. J. Riley (1993)
Bristol Grammar School, Bristol	1532	1249	£2,062	–	D. Mascord (1999)
Bromley High School, Kent	1883	901	£2,385	–	Mrs L. Duggleby (2001)
Bromsgrove School, Worcestershire	1548	1117	£3,015	£5,150	T. M. Taylor (1986)
Bruton School for Girls, Somerset	1900	560	£2,510	£4,280	Mrs B. Bates (1999)
Bryanston School, Dorset	1928	640	£5,127	£6,409	T. Wheare (1983)

School	Date Founded	No of pupils	Termly fees		Head (with date of appointment)
			Day	Boarding	
Burgess Hill School for Girls, West Sussex	1906	720	£2,775	£4,850	Mrs S. Gorham (2001)
Bury Grammar School, Lancashire	1726	826	£1,845	–	K. Richards (1990)
Bury Grammar School (Girls), Lancashire	1884	1045	£1,845	–	Miss C. H. Thompson (1998)
Canford School, Dorset	1923	571	£4,625	£6,165	J. D. Lever (1992)
Casterton School, Cumbria	1823	352	£2,772	£4,633	A. F. Thomas (1990)
Caterham School, Surrey	1811	982	£2,921	£5,415	R. Davey (1995)
Central Newcastle High School, Newcastle upon Tyne	1895	993	£1,945	–	Mrs L. J. Griffin (2000)
Channing School, London	1885	527	£2,785	–	Mrs E. Radice (1999)
Charterhouse, Surrey	1611	701	£5,255	£6,360	Revd J. Witheridge (1996)
Cheadle Hulme School, Cheshire	1855	1379	£2,106	–	P. Dixon (2001)
Cheltenham College, Gloucestershire	1841	535	£4,670	£6,210	P. A. Chamberlain (1997)
The Cheltenham Ladies' College, Gloucestershire	1853	850	£3,900	£5,800	Mrs V. Tuck (1996)
Chetham's School of Music, Manchester	1653	285	£5,296	£6,842	Mrs C. Moreland (1999)
Chigwell School, Essex	1629	760	£3,021	£4,096	D. Gibbs (1995)
Christ's Hospital, West Sussex	1552	820	Means tested	–	Dr P. Southern (1996)
Churcher's College, Hampshire	1722	743	£2,430	–	G. W. Buttle (1988)
City of London School, London	1442	900	£2,979	–	D. Levin (1999)
City of London Freemen's School, Surrey	1854	814	£3,063	£4,875	D. C. Haywood (1987)
City of London School for Girls, London	1894	682	£2,787	–	Dr Y. Burne (1995)
Claremont Fan Court School, Surrey	1978	600	£2,905	£4,825	Mrs P. Farrar
Clayesmore School, Dorset	1896	301	£3,977	£5,564	M. Cooke (2000)
Clifton College, Bristol	1862	650	£3,580	£5,225	S. Spurr (2000)
Clifton High School, Bristol	1877	773	£2,235	£3,860	Mrs M. C. Culligan (1998)
Cobham Hall School, Kent	1962	205	£3,870	£5,670	Mrs R. McCarthy (1990)
Colfe's School, London	1652	1041	£2,748	–	A. Chicken (2001)
Colston's Collegiate School, Bristol	1710	858	£1,955	£4,201	D. G. Crawford (1995)
Colston's Girls' School, Bristol	1891	453	£1,933	–	Mrs J. P Franklin (1989)
Combe Bank School, Kent	1924	483	£3,125	–	Mrs R. Martin (2000)
Concord College, Shropshire	1949	280	£1,910	£5,400	A. Morris (1975)
Cranleigh School, Surrey	1865	545	£4,810	£6,170	G. Waller (1997)
Croham Hurst School, Surrey	1899	545	£2,425	–	Miss S. Budgen (1994)
Croydon High School, Surrey	1874	930	£2,385	–	Miss L. M. Ogilvie (1998)
Culford School, Suffolk	1881	680	£3,563	£5,474	J. Richardson (1992)
The Dame Alice Harpur School, Bedfordshire	1882	975	£2,398	–	Mrs J. Berry (2000)
Dauntsey's School, Wiltshire	1542	678	£3,260	£5,454	S. B. Roberts (1997)
Dean Close School, Gloucestershire	1886	456	£4,185	£5,965	Rev T. M. Hastie-Smith (1998)
Denstone College, Staffordshire	1868	419	£2,733	£4,200	D. Derbyshire (1997)
Derby High School, Derbyshire	1892	600	£2,055	–	Dr G. H. Goddard (1983)
Dover College, Kent	1871	330	£2,930	£5,200	H. Blackett (1997)
Downe House, Berkshire	1907	536	£4,500	£6,210	Mrs E. McKendrick (1997)
Downside School, Bath	1606	310	£2,796	£5,358	D. A. Sutch (1995)
Duke of York Royal Military School, Kent	1803	500	–	£500	J. Cummings (1999)
Dulwich College, London	1619	1450	£3,110	£6,150	G. G. Able (1997)
Dunottar School, Surrey	1926	420	£2,530	–	Mrs J. Hobson (2001)
Durham School, Durham	1414	338	£3,119	£4,765	N. G. Kern (1997)
Durham High School for Girls, Durham	1884	550	£2,160	–	Mrs A. J. Templeman (1998)
Eastbourne College, East Sussex	1867	527	£3,815	£5,900	C. M. P. Bush (1993)
Edgbaston High School for Girls, Birmingham	1876	930	£2,025	–	E. Mullinger (1998)
Ellesmere College, Shropshire	1884	472	£3,392	£5,194	B. J. Wignall (1996)
Elmhurst, Surrey	c1910	171	£3,557	£4,561	J. McNamara (1995)
Eltham College, London	1842	780	£2,900	£5,980	P. Henderson (2000)
Emanuel School, London	1594	753	£2,853	–	Mrs A.-M. Sutcliffe (1998)
Embley Park School, Hampshire	1946	450	£2,835	£4,635	D. Chapman (1987)
Epsom College, Surrey	1855	683	£4,320	£6,123	S. Borthwick (1999)
Eton College, Berkshire	1440	1287	–	£6,366	A. R. M. Little (2002)
Exeter School, Devon	1633	835	£2,125	–	N. Gamble (1992)
Farlington School, West Sussex	1896	423	£2,920	£4,670	Mrs T. Mawer (1992)
Farnborough Hill, Hampshire	1889	475	£2,305	–	Miss J. Thomas (1997)
Farringtons & Stratford House, Kent	1994	550	£2,580	£4,930	Mrs C. James (1999)
Felsted School, Essex	1564	432	£4,025	£5,835	S.Roberts (1993)
Forest School, London	1834	1170	£2,916	£4,567	A. G. Boggis (1992)
Framlingham College, Suffolk	1864	419	£3,252	£5,058	Mrs G. Randall (1994)
Francis Holland School, London, NW1	1878	380	£2,900	–	Mrs G. Low (1998)
Francis Holland School, London, SW1	1878	450	£3,100	–	Miss S. Pattenden (1997)

School	Date Founded	No of pupils	Termly fees		Head (with date of appointment)
			Day	Boarding	
Frensham Heights School, Surrey	1925	470	£3,770	£5,640	P. M. de Voil (1993)
Friends' School, Essex	1702	340	£2,940	£4,899	A. Waters (2001)
Fulneck School, West Yorkshire	1994	416	£2,270	£4,175	Mrs H. Gordon (1996)
Giggleswick School, North Yorkshire	1512	492	£3,837	£5,782	G. Boult (2001)
The Godolphin School, Wiltshire	1726	410	£3,300	£5,420	Miss J. Horsburgh (1996)
Godolphin & Latymer School, London	1905	700	£2,845	–	Miss M. Rudland (1986)
The Grange School, Cheshire	1933	1100	£1,765	–	J. Stephen (1997)
Greenacre School for Girls, Surrey	1933	410	£2,480	–	Mrs P. Wood (1990)
Gresham's School, Norfolk	1555	523	£4,410	£5,690	J. Arkell (1991)
Guildford High School, Surrey	1888	905	£2,695	–	Mrs F. Boulton (2002)
Haberdashers' Aske's Boy's School, Hertfordshire	1690	1300	£2,925	–	P. Hamilton (2002)
Haberdashers' Aske's, School for Girls, Hertfordshire	1690	1107	£2,350	–	Mrs P. Penney (1991)
Haileybury, Hertfordshire	1862	687	£4,590	£6,215	S. Westley (1996)
Hampton School, Middlesex	1556	1065	£2,755	–	B. Martin (1997)
Harrogate Ladies' College, North Yorkshire	1893	380	£2,900	£4,750	Dr M. J. Hustler (1996)
Harrow School, Middlesex	1572	785	–	£6,375	B. Lenon (1999)
Headington School, Oxfordshire	1915	833	£2,645	£4,895	Mrs H. Fender (1996)
Heathfield School, Berkshire	1899	220	–	£6,235	Mrs H. Wright (2001)
Heathfield School, Middlesex	1900	560	£2,385	–	Miss C. Juett (1997)
Hereford Cathedral School, Hereford	1384	900	£2,300	–	Dr H. Tomlinson (1987)
Hethersett Old Hall School, Norfolk	1928	273	£2,375	£4,700	Mrs J. Mark (2000)
Highgate School, London	1565	1100	£3,475	–	R. Kennedy (1989)
The Hulme Grammar School, Lancashire	1611	720	£1,807	–	K. Jones (2000)
Hurstpierpoint College, West Sussex	1849	346	£4,250	£5,490	S. Meek (1995)
Hymers College, Hull	1893	968	£1,845	–	J. Morris (1990)
Ipswich School, Suffolk	1390	685	£2,460	£4,279	I. G. Galbraith (1992)
Ipswich High School, Suffolk	1878	700	£1,945	–	Miss V. MacCuish (1993)
James Allen's Girls' School, London	1741	770	£2,810	–	Mrs M. Gibbs (1994)
The John Lyon School, Middlesex	1876	525	£2,820	–	Dr C. Ray (2001)
Kelly College, Devon	1877	360	£3,600	£5,650	M. Stead (2001)
Kent College, Canterbury, Kent	1885	686	£3,294	£5,655	G. G. Carminati (2002)
Kent College, Tunbridge Wells, Kent	1886	570	£3,360	£5,425	Mrs A. Upton (2002)
King Edward VII & Queen Mary School, Lancashire	1999	875	£1,816	–	J. Wilde (1993)
King Edward's School, Bath	1552	983	£2,365	–	Miss C. Thompson (2002)
King Edward's School, Birmingham	1552	875	£2,175	–	R. Dancey (1998)
King Edward VI High School for Girls, Birmingham	1883	550	£2,120	–	Miss S. Evans (1996)
King Edward VI School, Hampshire	1553	950	£2,282	–	J. Thould (2002)
King Edward's School, Surrey	1553	478	£3,360	£4,910	K. Fulton-Peebles (2000)
King Henry VIII School, Coventry	1545	1089	£1,951	–	G. Fisher (2000)
King's School, Somerset	1519	355	£3,985	£5,415	R. I. Smyth (1992)
The King's School, Kent	597	774	£4,530	£6,445	K. Wilkinson (1996)
The King's School, Chester	1541	703	£2,190	–	T. J. Turvey (2000)
The King's School, Cambridgeshire	970	928	£3,840	£5,560	R. Youdale (1991)
The King's School, Gloucestershire	1072	500	£2,900	£4,300	P. Lacey (1992)
The King's School, Cheshire	1502	1400	£2,047	–	S. Coyne (2000)
King's School, Kent	1541	700	£3,610	£6,210	Dr I. R. Walker (1986)
King's College, Somerset	1522	430	£3,685	£5,595	C. Ramsey (2002)
King's High School for Girls, Warwickshire	1879	550	£2,176	–	E. Surber (2001)
The King's School, Worcestershire	1541	1230	£2,526	–	T. H. Keyes (1998)
King's College School, London	1829	720	£3,560	–	T. Evans (1997)
Kingsley School, Warwickshire	1884	617	£2,145	–	Mrs C. Mannion Watson (1997)
Kingston Grammar School, Surrey	c1310	600	£2,855	–	C. D. Baxter (1991)
Kingswood School, Bath	1748	572	£3,172	£5,363	G. M. Best (1987)
Kirkham Grammar School, Lancashire	1549	950	£1,860	£3,515	B. Stacey (1991)
La Sagesse High School, Newcastle upon Tyne	1912	400	£2,123	–	Miss L. C. (1994)
Lady Eleanor Holles School, Middlesex	1711	885	£2,791	–	Miss E. Candy (1981)
Lancing College, West Sussex	1848	410	£4,160	£5,985	P. M. Tinniswood (1998)
Langley School, Norfolk	1910	350	£2,500	£4,785	J. G. Malcolm (1997)
Latymer Upper School, London	1624	980	£3,160	–	P. Winter (2002)
Lavant House Rosemead, West Sussex	1995	130	£2,745	£4,745	Mrs M. Scott (2001)
Leeds Grammar School, Leeds	1552	1380	£2,415	–	Dr M. Bailey (1999)
Leeds Girls' High School, Leeds	1876	982	£2,252	–	Ms S. Fishburn (1997)
Leicester Grammar School, Leicestershire	1981	700	£2,155	–	C. King (2001)

School	Date Founded	No of pupils	Termly fees		Head (with date of appointment)
			Day	Boarding	
Leicester High School for Girls, Leicestershire	1906	435	£2,105	–	Mrs P. A. Watson (1992)
Leighton Park School, Berkshire	1890	380	£3,974	£5,676	J. Dunston (1996)
The Leys School, Cambridge	1875	525	£4,250	£5,700	Rev Dr J. C. A. Barrett (1990)
Licensed Victuallers' School, Berkshire	1803	800	£2,655	£4,680	I. Mullins (1996)
Lincoln Minster School, Lincolnshire	1997	617	£2,370	£4,485	C. Rickart (1999)
Liverpool College, Liverpool	1840	1050	£2,165	–	B. Christian (2002)
Longridge Towers School, Northumberland	1983	292	£2,000	£4,000	Dr M. Barron (1983)
Lord Wandsworth College, Hampshire	1920	495	£3,900	£5,235	I. Power (1997)
Loughborough Grammar School, Leicestershire	1495	990	£2,262	£3,900	P. Fisher (1998)
Loughborough High School, Leicestershire	1495	555	£2,058	–	Miss B. O'Connor (2002)
Magdalen College School, Oxfordshire	1480	600	£2,572	–	A. D. Halls (1998)
Malvern College, Worcestershire	1865	533	£4,140	£6,240	H. Carson (1997)
Malvern Girls' College, Worcestershire	1893	410	£4,083	£6,127	Mrs P. M. C. Leggate (1997)
The Manchester Grammar School, Manchester	1515	1440	£1,976	–	Dr G. M. Stephen (1994)
Manchester High School for Girls, Manchester	1874	933	£1,940	–	Mrs C. Lee-Jones (1998)
Marlborough College, Wiltshire	1843	844	£4,725	£6,300	Edward Gould (1993)
Marymount International School, Surrey	1955	202	£3,800	£6,483	Sister R. Sheridan (1990)
The Maynard School, Devon	1658	470	£2,224	–	Dr D. West (2000)
Merchant Taylors' School, Liverpool	1620	894	£1,869	–	S. Dawkins (1986)
Merchant Taylors' School, Middlesex	1561	775	£3,240	–	J. Gabitass (1991)
Merchant Taylors' School for Girls, Liverpool	1888	900	£1,869	–	Mrs J. I. Mills (1994)
Mill Hill School, London	1807	600	£3,715	£5,724	W. R. Winfield (1996)
Millfield School, Somerset	1935	1225	£4,185	£6,375	P. M. Johnson (1998)
Milton Abbey School, Dorset	1954	220	£4,444	£5,924	W. J. Hughes-D'Aeth (1995)
Moira House Girls School, East Sussex	1875	350	£3,200	£5,450	Mrs A. Harris (1997)
Monkton Combe School, Bath	1868	350	£3,970	£5,820	M. Cuthbertson (1990)
Moreton Hall, Shropshire	1913	270	£3,985	£5,695	J. Forster (1992)
The Mount School, York	1785	428	£3,035	£4,830	Mrs D. Gant (2001)
Mount St Mary's College, Derbyshire	1842	285	£2,500	£4,500	P. MacDonald (1998)
New Hall School, Essex	1642	634	£3,150	£4,860	Mrs K. A. Jeffrey (2002)
Newcastle Church High School, Newcastle upon Tyne	1885	633	£2,032	–	Mrs L. G. Smith (1996)
Newcastle-under-Lyme School, Staffordshire	1602	1100	£1,815	–	Mr R. Dillow (2002)
North Foreland Lodge, Staffordshire	1909	180	£3,600	£5,775	Miss S. Cameron (1996)
North London Collegiate School, Middlesex	1850	1009	£2,764	–	Mrs B. McCabe (1997)
Northampton High School, Northamptonshire	1878	842	£2,150	–	Mrs L. A. Mayne (1988)
Northamptonshire Grammar School, Northamptonshire	1989	380	£2,500		S. Larter (1996)
Northwood College, Middlesex	1878	776	£2,484	–	Mrs R. Mercer (2002)
Norwich School, Norfolk	1547	792	£2,216	–	J. B. Hawkins (2002)
Norwich High School for Girls, Norfolk	1875	874	£1,945	–	Mrs V. Bidwell (1985)
Notre Dame Senior School, Surrey	1937	360	£2,545	–	Mrs M. McSwiggan (1999)
Notting Hill and Ealing High School, London	1873	830	£2,385	–	Mrs S. Whitfield (1991)
Nottingham High School, Nottinghamshire	1513	804	£2,320	–	C. Parker CBE (1995)
Nottingham High School for Girls, Nottinghamshire	1875	1113	£1,945	–	Mrs A. Rees (1996)
Oakham School, Leicestershire	1584	1051	£3,210	£5,370	Dr J. A. F. Spence (2002)
Old Palace School, Surrey	1889	850	£2,116	–	Mrs J. Hancock (2000)
The Oratory School, Berkshire	1859	389	£3,495	£5,975	C. Dytor (2001)
Oswestry School, Shropshire	1407	453	£2,825	£4,739	P. Stockdale (2001)
Oundle School, Cambridgeshire	1556	1050	£2,948	£5,753	Dr R. Townsend (1999)
Our Lady's Convent Senior School, Oxfordshire	1860	360	£2,165	–	Mrs G. Butt (1996)
Oxford High School, Oxfordshire	1875	917	£1,945	–	Miss F. Lusk (1997)
Pangbourne College, Berkshire	1917	399	£4,030	£5,745	Dr K. Greig (2000)
Parsons Mead School, Surrey	1897	290	£2,679	£4,671	Mrs P. Taylor (2000)
The Perse School, Cambridgeshire	1615	580	£2,758	–	N. Richardson (1994)
Perse School for Girls, Cambridgeshire	1881	715	£2,540	–	Miss T. Kelleher (2001)
Peterborough High School, Cambridgeshire	1895	350	£2,407	£4,385	Mrs S. Dixon (1999)
Pipers Corner School, Buckinghamshire	1930	450	£2,745	£4,580	Mrs V. Stattersfield (1996)
Pocklington School, York	1514	733	£2,579	£4,339	N. Clements (2000)
Polam Hall School, Durham	1854	455	£2,175	£4,470	Mrs H. Hamilton (1987)
The Portsmouth Grammar School, Hampshire	1732	884	£2,421	–	Dr T. Hands (1997)
Portsmouth High School, Hampshire	1882	608	£1,945	–	Miss P. Hulse (1999)
The Princess Helena College, Hertfordshire	1820	136	£3,450	£5,050	A.-M. Hodgekiss (1998)
Prior Park College, Bath	1830	500	£2,891	£5,213	G. Mercer (1996)
Prior's Field School, Surrey	1902	285	£3,116	£4,660	Mrs J. Dwyer (1999)
Priory School, Birmingham	1933	320	£1,995	–	Mrs E. Brook (2001)

School	Date Founded	No of pupils	Termly fees Day	Boarding	Head (with date of appointment)
The Purcell School, Hertfordshire	1962	167	£4,801	£6,142	J. Tolputt (1999)
Putney High School, London	1893	800	£2,385	–	Dr D. Lodge (2002)
Queen Anne's School, Berkshire	1894	330	£3,863	£5,720	Mrs D. Forbes (1993)
Queen Elizabeth's Grammar School, Lancashire	1509	794	£2,105	–	Dr D. Hempsall (1995)
Queen Elizabeth Grammar School, West Yorkshire	1591	900	£2,166	–	M. Gibbons (2001)
Queen Elizabeth's Hospital, Bristol	1590	560	£2,021	£3,725	S. Holliday (2000)
Queen Margaret's School, York	1901	368	£2,988	£4,716	Dr G. A. H. Chapman (1992)
The Queen's School, Cheshire	1878	621	£2,015	–	Mrs C. M. Buckley (2001)
Queen's College, London	1848	380	£3,040	–	Miss M. M. Connell (1999)
Queen's College, Somerset	1843	672	£3,063	£4,719	C. J. Alcock (2001)
Queenswood, Hertfordshire	1894	375	£3,765	£5,560	C. Farr (1996)
Radley College, Oxfordshire	1847	620	–	£6,350	A. McPhail (2000)
Ratcliffe College, Leicestershire	1847	560	£2,891	£4,354	P. Farrar (1999)
Read School, North Yorkshire	1667	260	£1,875	£4,055	R. Hadfield (1996)
Reading Blue Coat School, Berkshire	1646	617	£2,673	–	S. J. W. McArthur (1997)
The Red Maids' School, Bristol	1634	440	£1,905	£3,900	Mrs I. Tobias (2001)
Redland High School, Bristol	1882	674	£2,090	–	Mrs C. Lear (1990)
Reed's School, Surrey	1813	456	£3,729	£4,933	D. W. Jarrett (1997)
Reigate Grammar School, Surrey	1675	850	£2,596	–	D. Thomas (2001)
Rendcomb College, Gloucestershire	1920	350	£3,985	£5,030	G. Holden (1999)
Repton School, Derbyshire	1557	542	£3,970	£5,355	G. E. Jones (1987)
Rishworth School, West Yorkshire	1724	540	£2,320	£4,490	R. Baker (1999)
RNIB New College, Worcestershire	–	110	£7,314	£10,538	N. Ratcliffe (2000)
Roedean School, East Sussex	1885	426	£3,600	£6,390	C. Shaw (2003)
Rossall School, Lancashire	1844	415	£2,695	£6,060	T. Wilbur (2001)
The Royal Grammar School, Surrey	1509	850	£2,930	–	T. Young (1992)
Royal Grammar School, Newcastle upon Tyne	1510	1100	£1,950	–	J. F. X. Miller (1994)
Royal Grammar School, Worcestershire	1291	983	£2,238	–	W. A. Jones (1993)
The Royal High School, Bath	1997	900	£1,945	£3,815	J. Graham-Brown (2000)
Royal Hospital School, Suffolk	1712	680	£2,793	£4,332	N. Ward (1995)
Royal Masonic School, Hertfordshire	1788	762	£2,430	£3,994	Mrs D. Rose (2002)
Royal Russell School, Surrey	1853	780	£2,750	£5,300	Dr J. Jennings (1996)
The Royal School, Surrey	1840	344	£3,126	£4,938	Mrs L. Taylor-Gooby (1999)
Rugby School, Warwickshire	1567	790	£3,780	£6,300	P. Derham (2001)
Ryde School, Isle of Wight	1921	720	£2,075	£4,235	Dr N. J. England (1997)
Rye St Antony School, Oxfordshire	1930	400	£2,500	£4,250	Miss A. Jones (1990)
St Albans School, Hertfordshire	1100	730	£2,848	–	A. Grant (1993)
St Albans High School, Hertfordshire	1889	855	£2,385	–	Mrs C. Y. Daly (1994)
St Antony's-Leweston School, Dorset	1891	252	£3,353	£5,042	H. J. MacDonald (1999)
St Bede's School, East Sussex	1978	630	£3,390	£5,520	S. Cole (2001)
St Bees School, Cumbria	1583	300	£3,435	£5,585	P. J. Capes (2000)
St Benedict's School, London	1902	551	£2,580	–	C. J. Cleugh (2002)
St Catherine's School, Surrey	1885	691	£2,815	£4,625	Mrs A. Phillips (2000)
St Christopher School, Hertfordshire	1915	592	£3,100	£5,450	C. Reid (1981)
St David's School, Middlesex	1716	412	£2,570	£4,525	Ms P. A. Bristow (1999)
St Dominic's Priory School, Staffordshire	1934	360	£1,853	–	Mrs J. Hildreth (1994)
St Dunstan's College, London	c1446	938	£2,895	–	I. Davies (1998)
St Dunstan's Abbey, Devon	1867	330	£2,336	£4,536	Mrs T. Smith (2001)
St Edmund's School, Kent	1749	562	£3,618	£5,605	A. N. Ridley (1994)
St Edward's School, Gloucestershire	1987	788	£2,620	–	Dr A. J. Nash (2001)
St Edward's School, Oxfordshire	1863	615	£4,650	£6,200	D. Christie (1988)
St Elphin's School, Derbyshire	1844	230	£2,915	£4,780	Mrs E. Taylor (2001)
St Felix School, Suffolk	1897	162	£3,230	£4,890	Mr R. Williams (1998)
St George's School, Berkshire	c1900	300	£3,675	£5,740	Mrs J. Grant-Peterkin (1999)
St George's College, Surrey	1869	850	£3,040	–	J. A. Peake (1994)
The School of St Helen & St Katharine, Oxfordshire	1903	613	£2,265	–	Mrs C. Hall (1993)
St Helen's School, Middlesex	1899	966	£2,600	£4,850	Mrs M. Morris (2000)
St James's School, Worcestershire	c1979	128	£3,516	£5,725	S. Kershaw (1997)
St John's School, Surrey	1851	450	£3,904	£5,540	C. Tongue (1992)
St Joseph's College, Suffolk	1937	595	£2,410	£4,980	Mrs S. Grant (2002)
St Lawrence College in Thanet, Kent	1879	472	£3,720	£5,825	M. Slater (1996)
St Leonards-Mayfield School, East Sussex	1863	383	£3,477	£5,342	Mrs J. Dalton (2000)
St Mary's School, Berkshire	1885	350	£3,995	£5,890	Mrs M. Breen (1999)
St Mary's School, Wiltshire	1873	290	£4,086	£6,087	Mrs C. J. Shaw (1996)
St Mary's School, Cambridgeshire	1898	459	£2,420	£5,190	Mrs J. Triffitt (2001)
St Mary's College, Merseyside	1919	1009	£1,820	–	W. Hammond (1991)

School	Date Founded	No of pupils	Termly fees Day	Boarding	Head (with date of appointment)
St Mary's School, Buckinghamshire	1872	310	£2,645	–	Mrs F. Balcombe (1995)
St Mary's School, Dorset	1945	330	£3,350	£5,145	Mrs S. Pennington (1998)
St Mary's School, Oxfordshire	1872	200	£3,979	£5,968	Mrs S. Sowden (1994)
St Paul's School, London	1509	814	£3,915	£5,825	R. S. Baldock (1992)
St Paul's Girls' School, London	1509	675	£3,161	–	Miss E. Diggory (1998)
St Peter's School, York	627	500	£3,174	£5,042	A. Trotman (1995)
St Swithun's School, Hampshire	1884	462	£3,305	£5,460	Dr H. L. Harvey (1995)
St Teresa's School, Surrey	1928	340	£2,890	£4,660	Mrs M. Prescott (1997)
Scarborough College, North Yorkshire	1898	510	£2,256	£3,250	T. L. Kirkup (1996)
Seaford College, West Sussex	1884	360	£3,500	£5,265	T. J. Mullins (1997)
Sedbergh School, Cumbria	1525	400	£3,820	£5,165	C. Hirst (1995)
Sevenoaks School, Kent	1432	962	£3,554	£5,829	Mrs C. Ricks (2002)
Sheffield High School, Sheffield	1878	950	£1,945	–	Mrs M. Houston (1990)
Sherborne School, Dorset	1550	520	£4,800	£6,315	S. F. Eliot (2000)
Sherborne School for Girls, Dorset	1899	350	£4,630	£6,215	Mrs G. Kerton-Johnson (1999)
Shiplake College, Oxfordshire	1959	290	£3,703	£5,490	N. V. Bevan (1988)
The Schools, Shropshire	1552	700	£4,295	£6125	J. Goulding (2001)
Shrewsbury High School, Shropshire	1885	647	£1,945	–	Mrs M. Cass (2000)
Sibford School, Oxfordshire	1842	379	£2,394	£4,830	S. Freestone (1997)
Sir William Perkins's School, Surrey	1725	580	£2,386	–	Miss S. Ross (1994)
Solihull School, West Midlands	1560	966	£2,134	–	J. Claughton (2001)
South Hampstead High School, London	1876	937	£2,385	–	Mrs V. L. Ainley (2001)
Stamford School, Lincolnshire	1532	624	£2,324	£4,520	Dr P. Mason (1997)
Stamford High School, Lincolnshire	1877	635	£2,324	£4,520	Dr P. Mason (1997)
Stanbridge Earls School, Hampshire	1952	199	£4,300	£5,800	N. Hall (2001)
Stockport Grammar School, Cheshire	1487	1410	£1,956	–	I. Mellor (1996)
Stonar, Cottles Park, Wiltshire	1895	400	£2,496	£4,450	Mrs C. Osborne (2002)
Stonyhurst College, Lancashire	1593	397	£3,332	£5,648	A. Aylward (1996)
Stover School, Devon	1932	410	£2,095	£4,395	P. Bujak (1995)
Stowe School, Buckinghamshire	1923	588	£4,695	£6,260	J. Nichols (1989)
Streatham Hill & Clapham High School, London	1887	810	£2,385	–	Mrs S. Mitchell (2002)
Sunderland High School, Sunderland	1993	600	£1,830	–	Dr A. Slater (1998)
Surbiton High School, Surrey	1884	1159	£2,365	–	Dr J. Longhurst (2001)
Sutton High School, Surrey	1884	760	£2,385	–	Mrs A. Coutts (1995)
Sutton Valence School, Kent	1576	790	£3,660	£5,800	J. Davies (2001)
Sydenham High School for Girls, London	1887	700	£2,385	–	Ms C. Pullen (2002)
Talbot Heath, Dorset	1886	664	£2,430	£4,140	Mrs C. Dipple (1991)
Teesside High School, Stockton-on-Tees	1970	470	£1,985	–	Mrs H. French (2000)
Tettenhall College, West Midlands	1863	470	£2,618	£4,367	Dr P. C. Bodkin (1994)
Tonbridge School, Kent	1553	720	£4,509	£6,381	J. M. Hammond (1990)
Tormead School, Surrey	1905	720	£2,390	–	Mrs S. Marks (2001)
Trinity School of John Whitgift, Surrey	1596	875	£2,800	–	C. Tarrant (1999)
Truro School, Cornwall	1880	788	£2,296	£4,479	P. K. Smith (2001)
Truro High School, Cornwall	1880	485	£1,980	£3,710	M. McDowell (2000)
Tudor Hall School, Oxfordshire	1850	269	£3,260	£5,220	Miss N. Godfrey (1984)
University College School, London	1830	900	£3,250	–	K. Durham (1996)
Uppingham School, Leicestershire	1584	710	£4,310	£6,152	Dr S. Winkley (1991)
Wakefield Girls' High School, West Yorkshire	1878	670	£2,166	–	Mrs P. Langham (1987)
Walthamstow Hall, Kent	1838	452	£3,275	–	Mrs J. Milner (2002)
Warminster School, Wiltshire	1973	525	£2,665	£4,630	D. Dowdles (1998)
Warwick School, Warwickshire	c914	1019	£2,229	£4,757	E. Halse (2002)
Wellingborough School, Northamptonshire	1595	781	£2,610	–	R. Ullmann (1993)
Wellington College, Berkshire	1853	785	£4,520	£5,870	A. H. Munro (2000)
Wellington School, Somerset	1837	850	£2,230	£4,050	A. J. Rogers (1990)
Wells Cathedral School, Somerset	c1150	736	£3,080	£5,190	E. Cairncross (2000)
Wentworth College, Dorset	1871	235	£2,660	£4,220	Miss S. D. Coe (1990)
West Buckland School, Devon	1858	674	£2,520	£4,420	J. Vick (1997)
Westfield School, Newcastle upon Tyne	1959	360	£2,099	–	Mrs M. Farndale (1992)
Westholme School, Lancashire	1923	1106	£1,701	–	Mrs L. Croston (1988)
Westminster School, London	1560	680	£4,724	£6,288	T. Jones-Parry (1998)
Westonbirt School, Gloucestershire	1928	200	£3,871	£5,555	Mrs M. Henderson (1999)
Whitgift School, Surrey	1596	1150	£3,080	–	Dr C. Barnett (1991)
William Hulme's Grammar School, Manchester	1887	690	£2,062	–	S. R. Patriarca (2000)
Wimbledon High School, London	1880	900	£2,385	–	Mrs P. Wilkes (2001)
Winchester College, Hampshire	1382	680	£6,221	£6,548	Dr N. Tate (2000)
Windermere St Anne's School, Cumbria	1863	402	£2,449	£4,432	Miss W. A. Ellis (2000)
Withington Girls' School, Manchester	1890	640	£1,920	–	Mrs J. Pickering (2000)

School	Date Founded	No of pupils	Termly fees		Head (with date of appointment)
			Day	Boarding	
Woldingham School, Surrey	1842	530	£3,480	£5,820	Miss D. Vernon (2000)
Wolverhampton Grammar School, West Midlands	1512	739	£2,400	–	Dr B. Trafford (1991)
Woodbridge School, Suffolk	1577	885	£2,810	£4,860	S. H. Cole (1994)
Woodhouse Grove School, West Yorkshire	1812	650	£2,520	£4,370	D. Humphreys (1996)
Worksop College, Nottinghamshire	1890	380	£3,440	£5,025	R. A. Collard (1994)
Worth School, West Sussex	1933	430	£3,926	£5,331	Fr C. Jamison (1992)
Wrekin College, Shropshire	1880	400	£3,250	£5,380	S. Drew (1998)
Wychwood School, Oxfordshire	1897	150	£2,390	£3,740	Mrs S. M. P. Wingfield – Digby (1997)
Wycliffe College, Gloucestershire	1882	804	£3,905	£6,505	Dr T. Collins (1998)
Wycombe Abbey School, Buckinghamshire	1896	542	£4,650	£6,200	Mrs P. Davies (1998)
Yarm School, Cleveland	1978	865	£2,492	–	D. M. Dunn (1999)
The Yehudi Menuhin School, Surrey	1963	60	£8,235	£8,455	N. Chisholm (1988)

WALES

School	Date Founded	No of pupils	Termly fees		Head (with date of appointment)
Christ College, Brecon	1541	310	£3,752	£4,838	D. P. Jones (1996)
Haberdashers' Monmouth School, Monmouth	1892	680	£2,521	£4,339	Dr B. Despontin (1997)
Howell's School, Denbigh	1540	340	£2,645	£3,945	Mrs L. Robinson (2001)
Howell's School, Cardiff	1860	735	£1,945	–	Mrs J. Fitz (1991)
Llandovery College, Carmarthenshire	1847	260	£3,014	£4,505	P. Hogan (2000)
Monmouth School, Monmouth	1614	669	£2,564	£4,274	T. Haynes (1995)
Rougemont School, Gwent	1920	705	£1,781	–	I. Brown (1995)
Rydal Penrhos Senior School, Colwyn Bay	1880s	400	£3,036	£5,088	M. S. James (1998)

SCOTLAND

School	Date Founded	No of pupils	Termly fees		Head (with date of appointment)
Craigholme School, Glasgow	1894	538	£2,070	–	Mrs G. Burt (1990)
High School of Dundee, Dundee	1239	1070	£2,108	–	A. M. Duncan (1997)
The Edinburgh Academy, Edinburgh	1824	777	£2,400	£5,116	John Light (1995)
Fettes College, Edinburgh	1870	592	£4,063	£6,022	M. Spens (1998)
George Heriot's School, Edinburgh	1628	1547	£2,062	–	A. Hector (1998)
George Watson's College, Edinburgh	1741	2278	£2,175	£4,475	G. H. Edwards (2001)
The Glasgow Academy, Glasgow	1846	1110	£2,145	–	D. Comins (1994)
The High School of Glasgow, Glasgow	1124	1060	£2,172	–	R. Easton (1983)
Glenalmond College, Perthshire	1841	405	£3,995	£5,920	I. Templeton (1992)
Hutchesons' Grammar School, Glasgow	1976	2080	£2,002	–	J. Knowles (1999)
Kelvinside Academy, Glasgow	1878	640	£2,135	–	J. Broadfoot (1998)
Kilgraston School, Perthshire	1920	232	£3,150	£5,330	Mrs J. L Austin (1993)
Lomond School, Argyll & Bute	1977	509	£2,220	£4,750	A. Macdonald (1986)
Loretto School, Midlothian	1827	370	£3,929	£5,888	M. Mavor (2001)
The Mary Erskine School, Edinburgh	1694	681	£2,036	£4,295	D. Gray (2000)
Merchiston Castle School, Edinburgh	1833	420	£4,125	£5,885	A. Hunter (1998)
Morrison's Academy, Perthshire	1860	530	£2,154	£5,322	I. Bendall (2001)
Robert Gordon's College, Aberdeen	1732	1450	£2,110	–	B. Lockhart (1996)
St Columba's School, Renfrewshire	1897	684	£2,033	–	A. H. Livingstone (1987)
St George's School for Girls, Edinburgh	1888	980	£2,175	£4,275	Dr J. McClure (1994)
St Margaret's School for Girls, Aberdeen	1846	396	£2,085	–	Mrs L. McKay (2001)
St Margaret's School, Edinburgh	1998	560	£2,120	£4,430	Mrs E. Davis (2001)
Stewart's Melville College, Edinburgh	1972	745	£2,285	£4,426	D. Gray (2000)
Strathallan School, Perth	1913	444	£3,760	£5,460	B. K. Thompson (2000)

NORTHERN IRELAND

School	Date Founded	No of pupils	Termly fees		Head (with date of appointment)
Belfast Royal Academy, Belfast	1785	1582	£80	–	W. S. F. Young (2000)
Campbell College, Belfast	1894	665	£533	£2,072	Dr I. Pollock (1987)
Coleraine Academical Institution, Coleraine	1860	790	£25	–	R. S. Forsythe (1984)
The Methodist College, Belfast	1868	2350	£80	£2,890	Dr W. Mulryne (1988)
The Royal Belfast, Academical Institution, Belfast	1810	1050	£210	–	M. Ridley (1990)
The Royal School, Northland Row, Dungannon	1614	660	£37	£4,555	P. D. Hewitt (1984)

CHANNEL ISLANDS

School	Date Founded	No of pupils	Termly fees		Head (with date of appointment)
Elizabeth College, Guernsey	1563	740	£1,250	–	Dr N. D. Argent (2001)
Victoria College, St Helier, Jersey	1852	900	£994	–	R. Cook (2000)

School	Date Founded	No of pupils	Termly fees Day	Boarding	Head (with date of appointment)

BELGIUM

| British School of Brussels vzw, Leuvensesteenweg 19, 3080 Tervuren, Belgium | 1969 | 1105 | €6,900 | | – M. A. Gibbons (2001) |

FRANCE

| International School of Paris, High School and Business Office, 6 rue Beethoven, 75016 Paris, France | 1964 | 430 | €5,443 | | – G. Jones (1998) |

ITALY

| St George's British International School, Via Cassia La Storta, 00123 Rome, Italy | 1958 | 571 | €4,166 | | – Ms B. Gardener (1994) |
| Sir James Henderson, British School of Milan, Via Pisani Dossi 16, 20134 Milano, Italy | 1969 | 670 | €3,233 | | – T. Church (2002) |

NETHERLANDS

| British School in the Netherlands, Jan van Hooflaan 3 2252 BG Voorschoten, Netherlands | 1935 | 1812 | €3,640 | | – T. Rowell (1999) |

PORTUGAL

| St Julian's School, 2777-601 Carcavelos, Codex, Portugal | 1932 | 850 | €4,667 | | – D. Smith (2000) |

SPAIN

| King's College, Paseo de los Andes 35, Soto de Vinuelas, 28761 Madrid, Spain | 1969 | 1300 | €2,476 | €4,459 | C. T. G. Leech (1997) |

SWITZERLAND

| Aiglon College, 1885 Chesieres-Villars, Switzerland | 1949 | 330 | SFr13,745 | SFr20,860 | Rev Dr J.Long (2000) |

Health

SELECTED CAUSES OF DEATH, BY GENDER AND
AGE 1999 (UNITED KINGDOM)

	Under 1*	1–14	15–24	25–34	35–54	55–64	65–74	75 and over	All ages
Males									
Circulatory diseases	28	64	90	368	6,969	13,097	31,293	67,821	119,730
Cancer	6	195	207	426	6,109	12,320	24,727	34,820	78,810
Respiratory diseases	94	93	76	143	1,245	2,944	9,675	34,640	48,910
Injury and poisoning	39	280	1,613	2,387	3,666	1,156	1,056	2,175	12,372
Infectious diseases	77	64	54	100	386	222	395	805	2,103
Other causes	2,074	336	598	1,092	4,420	3,599	6,590	19,734	38,443
All males (number)	2,318	1,032	2,638	4,516	22,795	33,338	73,763	159,995	300,368
Females									
Circulatory diseases	23	44	90	214	2,629	5,365	18,852	103,349	130,566
Cancer	8	137	132	509	7,285	10,304	18,887	36,404	73,666
Respiratory diseases	51	70	62	97	929	2,118	7,525	50,024	60,876
Injury and poisoning	30	153	414	543	1,134	499	719	3,712	7,204
Infectious diseases	69	50	51	42	168	165	327	1,183	2,055
Other causes*	1,546	319	277	519	2,654	2,594	5,930	43,485	57,327
All females (number)	1,727	773	1,026	1,924	14,802	21,045	52,240	238,157	331,694

* Deaths at under 28 days are not assigned a specific cause and are entered under 'other'.
Source: Office for National Statistics, Mortality Statistics Section, GRO Scotland and NISRA

NOTIFICATIONS OF INFECTIOUS DISEASES
(UK) 2000

Measles	2,865
Mumps	3,367
Rubella	2,064
Whooping cough	866
Scarlet fever	2,544
Dysentery	1,613
Food poisoning	98,076
Typhoid and paratyphoid fevers	205
Hepatitis	4,530
Tuberculosis	7,100
Malaria	1,166

Source: The Stationery Office – *Annual Abstract of Statistics 2002*
(Crown copyright)

HIV/AIDS AND SEXUALLY TRANSMITTED
DISEASES (ENGLAND)

	1987	2000
HIV cases diagnosed	1,917	3,551
Exposure category		
Homosexual intercourse	73%	39%
Heterosexual intercourse	9%	49%
Injecting drug use	12%	2.6%
Blood products	2%	0.6%
Mother to infant	—	2.4%
Other/undetermined	4%	6.4%
Aids cases diagnosed	640	718

Source: Public Health Laboratory Service

CURRENT SMOKERS (UK)
By gender and socio-economic group
Percentage

Males	
16-19	30
20-24	42
25-34	37
35-49	32
50-59	27
60 and over	16
All men aged 16 and over	28

Females	
16-19	31
20-24	39
25-34	33
35-49	29
50-59	27
60 and over	16
All women aged 16 and over	26

Source: The Stationery Office – *Social Trends 32* (Crown copyright).

LIFETIME EXPERIENCE OF STRESSFUL LIFE
EVENTS, BY EVENT AND GENDER, GREAT
BRITAIN (2000) *Percentage* †

	Men	Women
Death of a close friend or other relative	68	73
Death of a close relative*	51	55
Being sacked or made redundant	40	19
Serious or life threatening illness/ injury	30	22
Separation due to marital difficulties or breakdown of a steady relationship	25	29
Bullying	19	17
Serious money problems	14	8
Violence at work	6	2
Running away from home	5	5
Violence at home	4	10
Being homeless	4	3
Being expelled from school	2	1
Sexual abuse	2	5

*Parent, spouse or partner, child or sibling.
†Percentage of people aged 16–74 who reported experiencing each event.
Source: The Stationery Office – *Social Trends 32* (Crown copyright).

Social Welfare

National Health Service

The National Health Service (NHS) came into being on 5 July 1948 under the National Health Service Act 1946, covering England and Wales, and under separate legislation for Scotland and Northern Ireland. The NHS is now administered by the Secretary of State for Health (in England), the National Assembly for Wales, the Scottish Executive and the Secretary of State for Northern Ireland.

The function of the NHS is to provide a comprehensive health service designed to secure improvement in the physical and mental health of the people and to prevent, diagnose and treat illness. It was founded on the principle that treatment should be provided according to clinical need rather than ability to pay, and should be free at the point of delivery. However, prescription charges were provided for by legislation in 1949 and implemented in 1952, and charges for some dental and ophthalmic treatment have also been introduced.

The NHS covers a comprehensive range of hospital, specialist, family practitioner (medical, dental, ophthalmic and pharmaceutical), artificial limb and appliance, ambulance, and community health services. Everyone normally resident in the UK is entitled to use any of these services.

STRUCTURE

The structure of the NHS remained relatively stable for the first 30 years of its existence. In 1974, a three-tier management structure comprising Regional Health Authorities, Area Health Authorities and District Management Teams was introduced in England, and the NHS became responsible for community health services. In 1979 Area Health Authorities were abolished and District Management Teams were replaced by District Health Authorities.

The National Health Service and Community Care Act 1990 provided for more streamlined Regional Health Authorities and District Health Authorities, and for the establishment of Family Health Services Authorities (FHSAs) and NHS Trusts. The concept of the 'internal market' was introduced into health care, whereby care was provided through NHS contracts where health authorities or boards and GP fundholders (the purchasers) were responsible for buying health care from hospitals, non-fundholding GPs, community services and ambulance services (the providers).

NHS Trusts operate as self-governing health care providers independent of health authority control and responsible to the Secretary of State. Until 1999 they derived their income principally from contracts to provide services to health authorities and fund-holding GPs. In Northern Ireland, 20 health and social services trusts are responsible for providing health and social services in an organisational model unique to Northern Ireland.

The Act also paved the way for the Community Care reforms, which were introduced in April 1993 and changed the way care is administered for elderly people, the mentally ill, the physically handicapped and people with learning disabilities.

The eight Regional Health Authorities in England were abolished in April 1996 and replaced by eight regional offices which, together with the headquarters in Leeds, formed the NHS Executive. In April 2002 the eight regional offices were replaced by four Directorates of Health and Social Care. These provide the link between the Department of Health and the frontline NHS and social services.

In April 1996 the District Health Authorities and Family Health Service Authorities were merged to form 100 unified Health Authorities (HAs) in England. In April 2002 as part of the NHS Reform and Health Care Professions Bill, twenty eight new Health Authorities, called Strategic Health Authorities (StHAs) were formed from the existing HAs. This streamlined service means that increased power and responsibility will be devolved to people working on the frontline. Primary Care Trusts will have the majority of the responsibility for commissioning services, whilst StHAs will deal with solving local problems, holding local health services to account and encouraging greater autonomy for NHS Trusts and Primary Care Trusts.

In Wales the chairman and non-executive members of the five HAs which replaced the former 17 HAs and FHSAs in April 1996 are appointed by the First Secretary. Health Solutions Wales provides a range of specialist services to the NHS in Wales. In Scotland there are 15 Health Boards with similar responsibilities to those of HAs. In Northern Ireland there are four Health and Social Services Boards.

There are also Community Health Councils (called Local Health Councils in Scotland and Health and Social Services Councils in Northern Ireland) throughout the UK; their role is to represent the interests of the public to health authorities and boards. The Government announced in March 1998 that public consultation and patient representation in the NHS would be increased.

Under the Health Act 1999 the NHS internal market in England was replaced by teams of GPs and community nurses working together in primary care groups. In Scotland, the Act replaced the internal market with Local Health Care Co-operatives from 1 April 1999. In Wales the internal market was replaced by a system of Local Health Groups. In England from April 2000, Primary Care Trusts (PCTs) replaced the primary care group structure. PCTs have become the cornerstone of the NHS, enabling professionals and local communities to make decisions about their local health services.

In March 2000 the government launched The NHS Plan, an extensive programme of reforms intended to modernise the NHS. Under a system of 'earned autonomy' power over spending will be devolved to local health organisations that achieve the government's targets for providing healthcare and they will have access to a £500 million performance fund. Increased overlap between the social services and the NHS will be co-ordinated by the care trusts, with a focus on providing care for the elderly in their own homes. The Plan also outlines a concordat with private healthcare providers whereby the NHS will pay for the use of facilities in private hospitals.

FINANCE

The NHS is still funded mainly through general taxation, although in recent years more reliance has been placed on the NHS element of National Insurance contributions, patient charges and other sources of income. In the April 2002 Budget, the Chancellor announced an annual funding increase for the NHS of 7.4 per cent in real terms for a five-year period. The new provision for NHS spending allocates £72.1 billion for 2003–4, £79.3 billion for 2004–5, £87.2 billion for 2005–6, £95.9 billion for 2006–7 and £105.6 billion for 2007–8. Provision for 2002–3 had already been set at £65.4 billion under previous plans. The new provisions will be funded by increases in National Insurance contributions for both employers and employees.

In April 2002, the Secretary of State published the document *Delivering the NHS Plan: next steps on investment, next steps on reform,* which included: major expansions in NHS capacity (buildings, beds and staff) with the aim of dramatically reducing waiting times for treatment; structural changes and the creation of "foundation" hospitals which will enjoy greater independence; financial incentives to penalise local authorities whose delays lead to delayed patient discharge; and the creation of a new health inspectorate, the Commission for Healthcare Audit and Inspection (CHAI), which will undertake various commission roles and further co-operation with the private sector.

NATIONAL HEALTH CURRENT EXPENDITURE
2000–2001

	£ million
National Health Service:	
Hospitals, Community Health	
Services and Family Health Services	52,599
Departmental administration	324
Less payments by patients	(1,068)
TOTAL	51,855

PERSONAL SOCIAL SERVICES CURRENT EXPENDITURE
2000–2001

	£ million
Central government	49
Local authorities running expenses	12,048
Capital expenditure	128
TOTAL	12,225

Source: The Stationery Office – *Annual Abstract of Statistics 2002* (Crown copyright)

TOTAL NHS EXPENDITURE PER HEAD OF
POPULATION 2000–1

	Net £	Gross £
UK	967	906
England	949	885
Scotland	1,094	1,026
Wales	976	958
Northern Ireland	912	898

Source: Department of Health

ORGANISATIONS

DIRECTORATES OF HEALTH AND SOCIAL CARE (ENGLAND)

In April 2002 the eight NHS executive regional offices were replaced by four Directorates of Health and Social Care. The Directorates provide the link between the Department of Health and 28 Strategic Health Authorities.

NORTH DIRECTORATE OF HEALTH AND SOCIAL CARE, *Director,* P. Garland. *Geographical Responsibilities,* Cumbria, Durham, Yorkshire, Lancashire, North Lincolnshire, Cheshire, Tyne & Wear, Teeside, Merseyside, Greater Manchester

MIDLANDS AND THE EAST DIRECTORATE OF HEALTH AND SOCIAL CARE, *Director,* D. Nicholson. *Geographical Responsibilities,* Derbyshire, Nottinghamshire, Lincolnshire (except the far North), Leicestershire, Staffordshire, Shropshire, Worcestershire, Herefordshire, the West Midlands, Warwickshire, Northamptonshire, Cambridgeshire, Norfolk, Suffolk, Bedfordshire, Hertfordshire, Essex

SOUTH DIRECTORATE OF HEALTH AND SOCIAL CARE, *Director,* Ms R. Carnall. *Geographical Responsibilities,* Cornwall, Devon, Somerset, Dorset, Wiltshire, Avon, Gloucestershire, Oxfordshire, Berkshire, Buckinghamshire, Hampshire, Surrey, Sussex, Kent

LONDON DIRECTORATE OF HEALTH AND SOCIAL CARE, *Director,* J. Bacon. *Geographical Responsibilities,* Greater London

For further information contact the Department of Health Public Enquiry Office, Tel: 0207-210 4850; Email: dhmail@doh.gsi.gov.uk; Web: www.doh.gov.uk

NHS BOARDS (SCOTLAND)

ARGYLL AND CLYDE, Ross House, Hawkhead Road, Paisley PA2 7BN. Tel: 0141-842 7200. *Chief Executive,* N. McConachie

AYRSHIRE AND ARRAN, Boswell House, 10 Arthur Street, AYR KA7 1QJ. Tel: 01292-611040. *Chief Executive,* W. Y. Hatton

BORDERS, Newstead, Melrose, Roxburghshire TD6 9BD. Tel: 01896-825500. *Chief Executive,* Dr L. Burley

DUMFRIES AND GALLOWAY, Grierson House, The Crichton Royal, Bankend Road, Dumfries DG1 4ZG. Tel: 01387-272700. *Chief Executive,* M. Wright

FIFE, Springfield House, Cupar KY15 5UP. Tel: 01334-656200. *Chief Executive,* G. Brechin

FORTH VALLEY, 33 Spittal Street, Stirling FK8 1DX. Tel: 01786-463031. *Chief Executive,* F. Mackenzie

GRAMPIAN, Summerfield House, 2 Eday Road, Aberdeen AB15 6RE. Tel: 01224-663456. *Chief Executive,* N. Campbell

GREATER GLASGOW, Dalian House, 350 St Vincent Street, Glasgow G3 8YZ. Tel: 0141-201 4444. *Chief Executive,* T. A. Divers

HIGHLAND, Assynt House, Beechwood Park, Inverness IV2 3HG. Tel: 01463-717123. *General Manager,* R. Gibbins

LANARKSHIRE, 14 Beckford Street, Hamilton, Lanarkshire ML3 0TA. Tel: 01698-281313. *Chief Executive,* D. Pigott

LOTHIAN, Deaconess House, 148 Pleasance, Edinburgh EH8 9RS. Tel: 0131-536 9000. *Chief Executive,* J. Barbour, OBE

ORKNEY, Garden House, New Scapa Road, Kirkwall, Orkney KW15 1BQ. Tel: 01856-885400. *Chief Executive,* J. Wellden

SHETLAND, Brevik House, South Road, Lerwick ZE1 0TG. Tel: 01595-696767. *Chief Executive,* Miss S. Laurenson

TAYSIDE, Kings Cross, Clepington Road, Dundee DD3 8EA. Tel: 01382-818479. *Chief Executive,* Prof. T. Wells

WESTERN ISLES, 37 South Beach Street, Stornoway, Isle of Lewis HS1 2BN. Tel: 01851-702997. *Chief Executive,* M. Macmannan

HEALTH AUTHORITIES* (WALES)

BRO TAF, 17 Churchill House, Churchill Way, Cardiff CF10 2TW. Tel: 029-2040 2402. *Chief Executive,* Mrs J. Williams

DYFED POWYS, PO Box 13, St David's Hospital, Carmarthen SA31 3YH. Tel: 01267-225225. *Chief Executive,* S. Gray

GWENT, Mamhilad House, Mamhilad Park Estate, Pontypool NP4 0YP. Tel: 01495-765065. *Chief Executive,* B. Hudson

IECHYD MORGANNWG, 41 High Street, Swansea SA1 1LT. Tel: 01792-458066. *Chief Executive,* Ms B. Hughes

NORTH WALES, Preswylfa, Hendy Road, Mold CH7 1PZ. Tel: 01352-700227. *Chief Executive,* D. Hands

HEALTH SOLUTIONS WALES, 14th Floor, Brunnell House, 2 Fitzellen Road, Cardiff CF24 0HA. Tel: 029-2050 0500.

*From 1 April 2003, Health Authorities in Wales are to be replaced by Local Health Boards

NORTHERN IRELAND HEALTH AND SOCIAL SERVICES BOARDS

EASTERN, Champion House, 12–22 Linenhall Street, Belfast BT2 8BS. Tel: 028-9032 1313. *Chief Executive,* Dr M. P. J. Kilbane, FRCP

NORTHERN, County Hall, 182 Galgorm Road, Ballymena BT42 1QB. Tel: 028-2565 3333. S. MacDonnell

SOUTHERN, Tower Hill, Armagh BT61 7DR. Tel: 028-3741 0041. *Acting Chief Executive,* C. Donaghy

WESTERN, 15 Gransha Park, Clooney Road, Londonderry BT47 6FN. Tel: 028-7186 0086. *Chief Executive,* S. Lindsay

HEALTH PROMOTION AUTHORITIES

HEALTH Promotion Wales, Welsh Assembly Government, Cathays Park, Cardiff, CF10 3NQ. Tel: 029-2082 3315. *Head of Division,* C. Tudor-Smith

HEALTH EDUCATION BOARD FOR SCOTLAND, Woodburn House, Canaan Lane, Edinburgh EH10 4SG. Tel: 0131-536 5500. *Acting Chief Executive,* G. Robertson

HEALTH PROMOTION AGENCY FOR NORTHERN IRELAND, 18 Ormeau Avenue, Belfast BT2 8HS. Tel: 028-9031 1611; *Chief Executive,* Dr B. Gaffney

EMPLOYEES AND SALARIES

EMPLOYEES

NHS HOSPITAL AND COMMUNITY HEALTH SERVICE STAFF *(England, Wales and Scotland) 2000*

Medical and dental	74,000
Nursing, midwifery and health visitors	425,000
Other non-medical staff	176,000
General medical practitioners	37,000
General dental practitioners	21,000

Source: National Statistics – *Social Trends 2002 (Crown copyright)*

SALARIES *as at 1 April 2002*
General Practitioners (GPs), dentists, optometrists and pharmacists are self-employed, and are employed by the NHS under contract. GPs are paid for their NHS work in accordance with a scheme of remuneration which includes a basic practice allowance, capitation fees, reimbursement of certain practice expenses and payments for out-of-hours work. Dentists receive payment for items of treatment for individual adult patients and, in addition, a continuing care payment for those registered with them. Optometrists receive approved fees for each sight test they carry out. Pharmacists receive professional fees from the NHS and are refunded the cost of prescriptions supplied.

Consultant	£52,640–£68,505
Specialist Registrar	£25,920–£37,775
Registrar	£25,920–£31,435
Senior House Officer	£23,190–£32,520
House Officer	£18,585–£20,975
GP	*£66,280
Nursing Grades H–I (Modern Matron)†	£25,005–£32,760
Nursing Grades G–I (Senior Ward Sister)†	£22,385–£32,760
Nursing Grade F (Ward Sister)†	£18,970– £24,565
Nursing Grade E (Senior Staff Nurse)	£ 17,105–£20,655
Nursing Grade D (Staff Nurse)	£16,005–£17,670
Nursing Grade C (Enrolled Nurse and some Nursing auxiliary staff)	£13,040–£16,005
Nursing Grades A–B	£9,735–£13,485

* average intended net remuneration
† Including discretionary points

HEALTH SERVICES

PRIMARY AND COMMUNITY HEALTH CARE

Primary and community health care services comprise the family health services (i.e. the general medical, personal medical, pharmaceutical, dental, and ophthalmic services) and community services (including preventive activities such as vaccination, immunisation and fluoridation). Nursing services including practice nurses, district nurses and health visitors, community psychiatric nurses, school nurse and ante- and post-natal care, also form an integral part of primary and community health care.

FAMILY DOCTOR SERVICE
In England and Wales the Family Doctor Service is now the responsibility of Primary Care Trusts (PCT). GPs contract to provide services to the NHS in two ways: by providing general medical services or by applying to become Personal medical service pilots. In late 1999 a pilot scheme of 19 walk-in centres, where people may consult a nurse or, in some cases, a doctor without an appointment between the hours of 7 a.m. and 10 p.m., was introduced. The scheme has since been expanded to cover 43 walk-in centres around the country.

Any vocationally trained doctor may provide general or personal medical services and 27,700 GPs in England do so. The distribution of GPs is controlled by Primary Care Trusts. The average number of patients on a doctor's list in the UK as at August 2001 was 1,853. GPs may also have private fee-paying patients, but not if that patient is already an NHS patient on that doctor's patient list.

From 1 April 2000, Primary Care Trusts became operational in England. PCTs have key responsibilities aimed at improving the health of the community including: community development, health promotion and education. They are free-standing statutory bodies undertaking many of the functions previously exercised by Health Authorities, such as securing the provision of high quality services and integrating health and social care. Each PCT is overseen by a lay board, comprising a Chair and a majority of non-executives who are appointed by the NHS Appointments Commission and who are members of the local community to be served by the PCT. The Board's role is to provide strategic oversight and verification to the work of the Executive, including monitoring the progress against the Health Improvement Modernisation Programme (HIMP) and is where the detailed work of the trust is carried out. The Executive committee guides the Board on the detailed thinking on priorities, service policies and investment plans.

In Scotland, fundholding was replaced by over 70 Local Health Care Co-operatives on 1 April 1999. These, consisting of GPs and others involved in primary care, are responsible for developing health care in their area.

In Wales 22 Local Health Groups were set up by the Health Authorities and began work in April 1999. They are coterminous with local authority areas. At present, they advise Health Authorities but in the future they will assume responsibility for commissioning services and devising strategies for improved health. They will also integrate the delivery of primary and community care. A governing body including GPs and other health professionals, social services and community representatives administers each group.

Everyone aged 16 or over can choose their doctor (parents or guardians choose for children under 16); the doctor is free to accept or refuse an individual. Should a patient have difficulty in registering with a doctor, PCTs have powers to assign the patient to a GP. A person may change their doctor if they wish, by going to the surgery of a GP of their choice who is willing to accept them, either handing in their medical card to register or filling in a form. When people are away from home they can still use the Family Doctor Service if they ask to be treated as temporary residents, and in an emergency, any doctor in the service will give treatment and advice. A number of drop-in medical centres have been set up where anyone can consult a doctor.

PHARMACEUTICAL SERVICE

Patients may obtain medicines, appliances and oral contraceptives prescribed under the NHS from any pharmacy whose owner has entered into arrangements with the PCT to provide this service; the number of these pharmacies in England and Wales in December 2000 was 12,257. There are also some appliance suppliers who only provide special appliances. In rural areas, where access to a pharmacy may be difficult, patients may be able to obtain medicines, etc., from their doctor.

Except for contraceptives (for which there is no charge), a charge of £6.20 is payable for each item

supplied unless the patient is exempt and the declaration on the back of the prescription form is completed. Prepayment certificates (£32.40 valid for four months, £89.00 valid for a year) may be purchased by those patients not entitled to exemption who require frequent prescriptions.

The following people are exempt from prescription charges:
– children under 16
– full-time students under 19
– young people under 25 in Wales
– men and women aged 60 and over
– pregnant women who hold an exemption certificate
– women who have had a baby in the last 12 months and who hold an exemption certificate
– people suffering from certain medical conditions or have a continuing physical disability and need help from another person who hold an exemption certificate
– people and their partners who receive income support, Working Families' Tax Credit who are named on a Tax Credit Exemption Certificate, Disabled Person's Tax Credit who are named on a Tax Credit Exemption Certificate or income-based Jobseeker's Allowance
– people who are named on an HC2 certificate issued by the Health Benefits Division
– war pensioners (for their accepted disabilities)
– NHS in-patients
– NHS out-patients if medication is taken whilst being treated at the hospital
– people who get prescriptions dispensed by a hospital for the treatment of an STD

Booklet HC11, available from main post offices and local social security offices, gives further details.

DENTAL SERVICE

Dentists, like doctors, may take part in the NHS and also have private patients. About 17,000 dentists in England provide NHS general dental services. They are responsible to the PCTs in whose areas they provide services. Patients may go to any dentist who is taking part in the NHS and is willing to accept them. Patients are required to pay 80 per cent of the cost of NHS dental treatment. Since 1 April 2002 the maximum charge for a course of treatment has been £366. There is no charge for arrest of bleeding or repairs to dentures; home visits by the dentist or re-opening a surgery in an emergency are charged for as treatment given in the normal way. The following people are exempt from dental charges or have charges remitted:
– people under 18
– full-time students under 19
– women who were pregnant when accepted for treatment
– women who have had a child in the previous 12 months
– people and their partners who receive Income Support, Working Families' Tax Credit and named on a Tax Credit NHS Exemption Certificate, Disabled Person's Tax Credit and named on a Tax Credit NHS Exemption Certificate, or income-based Jobseeker's Allowance.
– people who are named on an HC2 certificate issued by the Health Benefits Division
– NHS in-patients (if the treatment is carried out by a hospital dentist)
– people named on a HC3 may also get help

Booklet HC11, available from main post offices and local social security offices, gives further details.

GENERAL DENTAL SERVICE 2001–2 (ENGLAND)

Number of dentists	18,254
Number of patients registered	
Adults	16,800,000
Children	6,800,000
Number of courses of treatment	
Adults	26,300,000
Expenditure (£ million)	
Gross expenditure	1,600
Paid by patients	500
Paid out of public funds	1,200

Source: Department of Health

GENERAL OPHTHALMIC SERVICES

General Ophthalmic Services are administered by PCTs. Testing of sight may be carried out by any ophthalmic medical practitioner or ophthalmic optician (optometrist). The optician must give the prescription to the patient, who can take this to any supplier of glasses to have them dispensed. Only registered opticians can supply glasses to children and to people registered as blind or partially sighted. At the end of March 2001 there were 7,548 practising Optometrists in Great Britain. 16.5 million sight tests were carried out in 2000–1.

The NHS sight test costs £16.72. Those on a low income may qualify for help with the cost. The test is available free to:

– people aged 60 or over
– children under 16*
– full-time students under 19*
– people and their partners who receive Income Support, income-based Jobseeker's Allowance, Working Families' Tax Credit and named on a Tax Credit NHS Exemption Certificate, Disabled Person's Tax Credit and named on a Tax Credit NHS Exemption Certificate *
– people who are named on an HC2 certificate issued by the Health Benefits Division*
– people prescribed complex lenses*
– people registered as blind or partially sighted
– diagnosed diabetic and glaucoma patients
– people over 40 who are a parent, sibling or child of a diagnosed glaucoma patient and people advised by an ophthalmologist that they are at risk of glaucoma
– people whose sight test is carried out through the Hospital Eye Department as part of the management of their eye condition
– people named on a HC3 certificate may also get help*

The categories indicated by * above are automatically entitled to help with the purchase of glasses under an NHS voucher scheme, as are people whose spectacles are lost or damaged as a result of illness. Booklet HC11, available from main post offices and local social security offices, gives further details.

Diagnosis and specialist treatment of eye conditions, and the provision of special glasses, are available through the Hospital Eye Service.

COMMUNITY CHILD HEALTH SERVICES

Pre-school services at GP surgeries or child health clinics provide regular monitoring of children's physical, mental and emotional health and development, and advice to parents on their children's health and welfare.

The School Health Service provides for the medical and dental examination of schoolchildren, and advises the local education authority, the school, the parents and the pupil of any health factors which may require special consideration during the pupil's school life. GPs are increasingly undertaking child health monitoring in order to improve the preventive health care of children.

HEALTH ACTION ZONES

Health Action Zones were set up by the government in areas of deprivation and poor health to tackle health inequalities and modernise services. The 26 zones have populations ranging from 180,000 to 1.4 million in certain areas. In total Health Action Zones cover over 13 million people.

HOSPITALS AND OTHER SERVICES

Hospital, medical, dental, nursing, ophthalmic and ambulance services are provided by the NHS to meet all reasonable requirements. Facilities for the care of expectant and nursing mothers and young children, and other services required for the diagnosis and treatment of illness, are also provided. Rehabilitation services (occupational therapy, physiotherapy and speech therapy) may also be provided, and surgical and medical appliances are supplied where appropriate. Specialists and consultants who work in NHS hospitals can also engage in private practice, including the treatment of their private patients in NHS hospitals although, under the terms of the NHS plan, newly qualified consultants are unable to do private work for up to seven years.

PRIVATE FINANCE INITIATIVE

The Private Finance Initiative (PFI) was launched in 1992, and involves the private sector in designing, building, financing and operating new hospitals, which are then leased to the NHS. The NHS Plan committed the NHS to entering into a new public private partnership, Partnerships for Health, a joint venture between the Department of Health and Partnerships UK plc (PUK) established in September 2001. Both parties committed an initial £5 million of equity funding to the company and £195 million has been earmarked for the NHS Local Improvement Finance Trust (LIFT). LIFT will build and refurbish primary care premises, which it will own and then rent to GPs on a lease basis (as well as other parties such as chemists, opticians, dentists etc).

CHARGES

NHS trusts can provide accommodation in single rooms or small wards, if not required for patients who need privacy for medical reasons. The patient is still an NHS patient, but there may be a charge for these additional facilities. NHS trusts can charge for certain patient services that are considered to be additional treatments over and above the normal service provision. There is no blanket policy to cover this and each case should be considered in the light of the patient's clinical need. However, if an item or service is considered to be an integral part of a patient's treatment by their clinician, then a charge should not be made. In some NHS hospitals, accommodation and services are available for the treatment of private patients where it does not interfere with care for NHS patients. Income generated by treating private patients is then put back into the local NHS services. Private patients undertake to pay the full costs of medical treatment, accommodation, medication and other related services. Charges for private patients are set locally.

AMBULANCE SERVICE

The NHS provides emergency ambulance services free of charge via the 999 emergency telephone service. There are 35 ambulance services in the UK. Helicopter ambulances are used in some areas where access may be difficult or heavy traffic could hinder road progress, and an air ambulance service is available throughout Scotland. Non-

emergency ambulance services are provided free of charge to patients who are deemed to require them on medical grounds.

In 2001–2 in England approximately 4.7 million emergency calls were made to the ambulance service, an increase of 7 per cent on the previous year. There were about 3.1 million emergency patient journeys. By 1 April 2001 all services had introduced call prioritisation. The prioritisation procedures require all emergency calls to be classified as either immediately life threatening (category A) or other emergency (category B/C). Services are expected to reach 75 per cent of Category A calls within eight minutes and 95 per cent of category B/C calls within 19 minutes in rural areas and 14 minutes in urban areas. In 2001–2, 14 services met or exceeded the 75 per cent target for responding to category A calls within 8 minutes. For category B/C calls, 16 services responded to 95 per cent or more calls within 14 or 19 minutes.

NHS DIRECT

NHS Direct is a telephone service staffed by nurses which gives patients advice on how to look after themselves as well as directing them to the appropriate part of the NHS for treatment if necessary. Tel: 0845-4647.

BLOOD SERVICES

There are four national bodies which co-ordinate the blood donor programme in the UK. About two million donations of blood are given each year; donors give blood at local centres on a voluntary basis.

NATIONAL BLOOD SERVICE, Oak House, Reeds Crescent, Watford, Herts WD24 4QN. Tel: 01923-486800. *Chief Executive*, M. Gorham

SCOTTISH NATIONAL BLOOD TRANSFUSION SERVICE, 21 Ellens Glen Road, Edinburgh EH17 7QT. Tel: 0131-536 5700. *National Director*, A. Macmillan Douglas

WELSH BLOOD SERVICE, Ely Valley Road, Talbot Green, Pontyclun CF72 9WB. Tel: 01443-622000. *Director*, Dr F. G. Williams

NORTHERN IRELAND BLOOD TRANSFUSION SERVICE, Belfast City Hospital Complex, Lisburn Road, Belfast BT9 7TS. Tel: 028-9032 1414. *Chief Executive*, Dr W. M. McClelland

HOSPICES

Hospice or palliative care may be available for patients with life-threatening illnesses. It may be provided at the patient's home or in a voluntary or NHS hospice or in hospital, and is intended to ensure the best possible quality of life for the patient during their illness, and to provide help and support to both the patient and the patient's family. The National Council for Hospices and Specialist Palliative Care Services co-ordinates NHS and voluntary services in England, Wales and Northern Ireland; the Scottish Partnership Agency for Palliative and Cancer Care performs the same function in Scotland.

NATIONAL COUNCIL FOR HOSPICE AND SPECIALIST PALLIATIVE CARE SERVICES, 1st Floor, 34-44 Britannia Street, London WC1X 9JG. Tel: 020-7520 8299. *Chief Executive*, Ms E. S. Richardson

SCOTTISH PARTNERSHIP FOR PALLIATIVE CARE, 1a Cambridge Street, Edinburgh EH1 2DY. Tel: 0131-229 0538. *Director*, Mrs P. Wallace

NUMBER OF BEDS AND PATIENT ACTIVITY 2000

	England	Wales
In-patients:		
Average daily available beds	186,000	14,600
Average daily occupation of beds	156,000	11,700
Persons waiting for admission at 31 March	1,007,000	61,100
Day-case admissions	3,593,000*	216,200
Ordinary admissions	8,604,000*	513,800
Out-patient attendances:		
New attendances	12,466,000	699,200
Total attendances	43,569,000	737,200
Accident and emergency:		
New cases	12,953,000	853,700
Total attendances	14,293,000	986,200
Ward attendances	1,078,000	n/a

* 1999 figures

SCOTLAND

In-patients:	
Average available staffed beds	33,500
Average occupied beds	26,900
Out-patient attendances:	
New patients	2,766,000
Total attendances	6,451,000

Source: The Stationery Office – *Annual Abstract of Statistics 2002* (Crown copyright)

WAITING LISTS

At the end of March 2002 the total number of patients waiting to be admitted to NHS hospitals in England was 1,034,719, a decrease of 1.0 per cent on the previous year. The number of patients who had been waiting more than one year was 22,182, a decrease of 30 per cent on the previous year. Under the Patient's Charter, patients guaranteed admission within 18 months of being placed on a waiting list. Only 13 patients had been waiting longer than 18 months at the end of March 2002 compared to 356 at end June 2001.

NHS CHARTERS

The original Patient's Charter was published in 1991 and came into force in 1992; an expanded version was published in 1995. The Charter sets out the rights of patients in relation to the NHS (i.e. the standards of service which all patients will receive at all times); and patients' reasonable expectations (i.e. the standards of service that the NHS aims to provide, even if they cannot in exceptional circumstances be met). The Charter covers areas such as access to services, personal treatment of patients, the provision of information, registering with a doctor, hospital waiting times, care in hospitals, community services, ambulance waiting times, dental, optical and pharmaceutical services, and maternity services. In England there are separate Patient's Charter leaflets setting out standards in relation to services for children and young people, maternity services, mental health services and blood donation. Further information is available free of charge from NHS Direct (Tel 0845-4647).

Health authorities and boards, NHS Trusts and GP practices may also have their own local charters setting out the standard of service they aim to provide.

COMPLAINTS

The Patient's Charter includes the right to have any complaint about the service provided by the NHS dealt with quickly, with a full written reply being provided by a relevant chief executive. There are two levels to the NHS complaints procedure: the first level involves resolution of a complaint locally, following a direct approach to the relevant service provider; the second level involves an independent review procedure if the complaint is not resolved locally. As a final resort, patients may approach the Health Service Commissioner or Ombudsman (in Northern Ireland, the Commissioner for Complaints) if they are dissatisfied with the response of the NHS to a complaint. In 2000–1 there were 95,994 written complaints about hospital and community health services, of which 55.6 per cent were resolved locally within the target period of four weeks; only 0.3 per cent of complainants requested an independent review. Hospital and Community Trusts received 94 per cent of the total number of complaints with Ambulance Trusts receiving four per cent and Health Authorities two per cent.

RECIPROCAL ARRANGEMENTS

Citizens of countries in the European Economic Area (EEA – see European Union section) who are resident in the UK are entitled to receive emergency health care either free of charge or for a reduced charge when they are temporarily visiting other member states of the EEA. Form E111, available at post offices, should be obtained before travelling. There are also bilateral agreements with several other countries, including Australia and New Zealand, for the provision of urgent medical treatment either free of charge or for a reduced charge. EEA nationals visiting the UK and visitors from other countries with which the UK has bilateral healthcare agreements, are entitled to receive emergency healthcare on the NHS on the same terms as it is available to UK residents.

Personal Social Services

The Secretary of State for Health is responsible, under the Local Authority Social Services Act 1970, for the provision of social services for elderly people, disabled people, families and children, and those with mental disorders. Personal Social Services are administered by local authorities according to policies and standards set by central government. Each authority has a Director of Social Services and a Social Services Committee responsible for the social services functions placed upon them. Local authorities provide, enable and commission care after assessing the needs of their population. The private and voluntary sectors also play an important role in the delivery of social services, and an estimated six million people in Great Britain provide substantial regular care for a member of their family.

Under the Care Standards Act 2000, the National Care Standards Commission (NCSC) was set up to regulate social, private and voluntary care services throughout England. From 1 April 2002 NCSC took responsibility for the registration and inspection of services replacing the system of inspection by local authority and Health Authority inspection units. Care homes, children's homes, domiciliary care agencies, residential family centres, voluntary adoption agencies, independent

fostering agencies, private and voluntary hospitals and clinics, exclusively private doctors and nurses agencies all have to register with the NCSC. The Commission is also responsible for inspecting Local Authority fostering and adoption services and the welfare aspects of boarding schools.

The Community Care reforms introduced in 1993 were intended to enable vulnerable groups to live in the community rather than in residential homes wherever possible, and to offer them as independent a lifestyle as possible.

FINANCE

The Personal Social Services programme is financed partly by central government, with decisions on expenditure allocations being made at local authority level.

STAFF

STAFF OF LOCAL AUTHORITY SOCIAL SERVICES DEPARTMENTS 2000 (England)
Full-time equivalents

Area office/field work staff	108,800
Residential care staff	56,600
Day care staff	30,800
Central/strategic HQ staff	19,400
Other staff	1,500
Total staff	217,200

Source: Department of Health

ELDERLY PEOPLE

Services for elderly people are designed to enable them to remain living in their own homes for as long as possible. Local authority services include advice, domestic help, meals in the home, alterations to the home to aid mobility, emergency alarm systems, day and/or night attendants, laundry services and the provision of day centres and recreational facilities. Charges may be made for these services. Respite care may also be provided in order to allow carers temporary relief from their responsibilities. Local authorities and the private sector also provide 'sheltered housing' for elderly people, sometimes with resident wardens. If an elderly person is admitted to a residential home, charges are made according to a means test; if the person cannot afford to pay, the costs are met by the local authority.

DISABLED PEOPLE

Services for disabled people are designed to enable them to remain living in their own homes wherever possible. Local authority services include advice, adaptations to the home, meals in the home, help with personal care, occupational therapy, educational facilities and recreational facilities. Respite care may also be provided in order to allow carers temporary relief from their responsibilities. Special housing may be available for disabled people who can live independently, and residential accommodation for those who cannot.

FAMILIES AND CHILDREN

Local authorities are required to provide services aimed at safeguarding the welfare of children in need and, wherever possible, allowing them to be brought up by their families. Services include advice, counselling, help in the home and the provision of family centres. Many authorities also provide short-term refuge accommodation for women and children.

DAY CARE

In allocating day-care places to children, local authorities give priority to children with special needs, whether in terms of their health, learning abilities or social needs. They also provide a registration and inspection service in relation to childminders, play groups and private day nurseries in the local authority area. In 2000 in England, Wales and Northern Ireland there were 279,000 registered day nurseries, 353,000 registered child-minders, and 392,000 play groups. Out of school clubs have been introduced in recent years and in 2000 there were 153,000 such places in England, Wales and Northern Ireland.

CHILD PROTECTION

Children considered to be at risk of physical injury, neglect or sexual abuse are placed on the local authority's child protection register. Local authority social services staff, school nurses, health visitors and other agencies work together to prevent and detect cases of abuse. In England at 31 March 2000 there were 30,300 children on child protection registers, a five per cent decrease from March 1999. Of these, 46 per cent were at risk of neglect, 29 per cent of physical injury, 18 per cent of sexual abuse and 18 per cent of emotional abuse.

LOCAL AUTHORITY CARE

Local authorities are required to provide accommodation for children who have no parent or guardian or whose parents or guardians are unable or unwilling to care for them. A family proceedings court may also issue a care order in cases where a child is being neglected or abused, or is not attending school; the court must be satisfied that this would positively contribute to the well-being of the child. The welfare of children in local authority care must be properly safeguarded. Children may be placed with foster families, who receive payments to cover the expenses of caring for the child or children, or in residential care. Children's homes may be run by the local authority or by the private or voluntary sectors; all homes are subject to inspection procedures.

ADOPTION

Local authorities are required to provide an adoption service, either directly or via approved voluntary societies. In England and Wales in 2000, around 2,800 children were placed for adoption.

PEOPLE WITH LEARNING DISABILITIES

Services for people with learning disabilities (i.e. mental handicap) are designed to enable them to remain living in the community wherever possible. Local authority services include short-term care, support in the home, the provision of day care centres, and help with other activities outside the home. Residential care is provided for the severely or profoundly disabled.

MENTALLY ILL PEOPLE

Under the Care Programme Approach, mentally ill people should be assessed by specialist services and receive a care plan, and a key worker should be appointed for each patient. Regular reviews of the patient's progress should be conducted. Local authorities provide help and advice to mentally ill people and their families, and places in day centres and social centres. Social workers can apply for a mentally disturbed person to be compulsorily detained in hospital. Where appropriate, mentally ill people are provided with accommodation in special hospitals, local authority accommodation, or homes run

by private or voluntary organisations. Patients who have been discharged from hospitals may be placed on a supervision register.

National Insurance and Related Cash Benefits

The state insurance and assistance schemes, comprising schemes of national insurance and industrial injuries insurance, national assistance, and non-contributory old age pensions, came into force from 5 July 1948. The Ministry of Social Security Act 1966 replaced national assistance and non-contributory old age pensions with a scheme of non-contributory benefits. These and subsequent measures relating to social security provision in Great Britain were consolidated by the Social Security Act 1975, the Social Security (Consequential Provisions) Act 1975, and the Industrial Injuries and Diseases (Old Cases) Act 1975. Corresponding measures were passed for Northern Ireland. The Social Security Pensions Act 1975 introduced a new state pensions scheme in 1978, and the graduated pension scheme 1961 to 1975 has been wound up, existing rights being preserved. Under the Pensions Act 1995 the age of retirement is to be 65 for both men and women, this being phased in between 2010 and 6 April 2020. The Pensioners' Payments and Social Security Act 1979 provided for a Christmas bonus for pensioners in 1979 and in succeeding years. The Child Benefit Act 1975 replaced family allowances (introduced 1946) with child benefit and one-parent benefit. Some of this legislation has been superseded by the provisions of the Social Security Acts 1969 to 1992. The Government is reforming the social security system. The Welfare Reform and Pensions Act became law on 11 November 1999. Changes in benefits came into effect from April 2001.

NATIONAL INSURANCE SCHEME

The National Insurance (NI) scheme operates under the Social Security Contributions and Benefits Act 1992 and the Social Security Administration Act 1992, and orders and regulations made thereunder. The scheme is financed by contributions payable by earners, employers and others (see below) and by a Treasury grant. Money collected under the scheme is used to finance the National Insurance Fund (from which contributory benefits are paid) and to contribute to the cost of the National Health Service.

NATIONAL INSURANCE FUND

Estimated receipts and payments of the National Insurance Fund for 2001–2:

Receipts	£'000s
National Insurance contributions	54,805,000
Compensation from Consolidated Fund for Statutory Sick Pay and Statutory Maternity Pay recoveries	683,000
Income from investments	1,112,000
State scheme premiums	137,000
Other receipts	205,000
	56,942,000

Payments	£'000s
Benefits (at present rates)	47,539,000
Benefits increase due to proposed change	2,965,000
Personal pensions contracted-out rebates	2,518,000

Age-related rebates for contracted-out money purchase schemes	115,000
Transfers to Northern Ireland	110,000
Administration	36,000
Redundancy fund payments (net)	156,000
Other payments	20,000
	54,558,000

Balances	£'000s
Opening balance	18,420,000
Excess of receipts over payments	2,384,000
Balance at end of year	20,804,000

CONTRIBUTIONS

There are six classes of NI contributions:

Class 1	paid by employees and their employers
Class 1A	paid by employers who provide employees with certain benefits in kind for private use, such as company cars
Class 1B	paid by employers in value of any items included on a PAYE settlement with the Inland Revenue
Class 2	paid by self-employed people
Class 3	voluntary contributions paid to protect entitlement to the State Pension and who do not pay enough NI contributions in another class
Class 4	paid by the self-employed on their taxable profits over a set limit. These are normally paid by self-employed people in addition to Class 2 contributions. Class 4 contributions do not count towards benefits.

The lower and upper earnings limits and the percentage rates referred to below apply from April 2002 to April 2003 unless otherwise stated.

CLASS 1

Class 1 contributions are paid where a person:

- is an employed earner (employee), office holder (e.g. company director) or employed under a contract of service
- is 16 or over and under state pension age
- earns at or above the Primary Threshold of £89.00 per week (including overtime pay, bonus, commission, etc., without deduction of superannuation contributions)

Class 1 contributions are made up of primary and secondary contributions. Primary contributions are those paid by the employee and these are deducted from earnings by the employer. From 6 April 2001 the employee's earnings threshold has been raised to the same level as the employer's earnings threshold, they will now be referred to as the earnings threshold. Primary contributions are not paid on earnings below the earnings threshold of £89.00. Contributions are payable at the rate of ten per cent on earnings between the earnings threshold and the upper earnings limit of £585.00 per week (8.4 per cent for contracted-out employment). Some married women or widows pay a reduced rate of 3.85 per cent on earnings between the lower and upper earnings limits. It is no longer possible to elect to pay the reduced rate but those who had reduced liability before 12 May 1977 may retain it so long as certain conditions are met. *See* leaflet CA09 (widows) or leaflet CA13 (married women). Secondary contributions are paid by employers of employed earners at the rate of 11.8 per cent on all earnings at or above the earnings threshold of £89.00 per week. Employers operating contracted-out salary related schemes pay reduced contributions of 11.4 per cent; those with contracted-out money-purchase schemes pay 11.7 per cent. There is no upper earnings limit for employers' contributions. The contracted-out rate applies only to that portion of earnings between the earnings threshold and the upper earnings limits. Employers' contributions below and above those respective limits are assessed at the appropriate not contracted-out rate.

CLASS 2

Class 2 contributions are paid where a person is self-employed and is 16 or over and under state pension age. Contributions are paid at a flat rate of £2.00 per week regardless of the amount earned. However, those with earnings of less than £4,025 a year can apply for Small Earnings Exception, e.g. exemption from liability to pay Class 2 contributions. Those granted exemption from Class 2 contributions may pay Class 2 or Class 3 contributions voluntarily. Self-employed earners (whether or not they pay Class 2 contributions) may also be liable to pay Class 4 contributions based on profits. There are special rules for those who are concurrently employed and self-employed.

Married women and widows can no longer choose not to pay Class 2 contributions but those who elected not to pay Class 2 contributions before 12 May 1977 may retain the right so long as certain conditions are met.

Class 2 contributions are collected by the National Insurance Contributions Office (NICO), an executive agency of the Inland Revenue, by direct debit or quarterly bills. *See* leaflets CWL2 and CA02.

CLASS 3

Class 3 contributions are voluntary flat-rate contributions of £6.85 per week payable by persons over the age of 16 who would otherwise be unable to qualify for retirement pension and certain other benefits because they have an insufficient record of Class 1 or Class 2 contributions. This may include those who are not working, those not liable for Class 1 or Class 2 contributions or those excepted from Class 2 contributions. Married women and widows who on or before 11 May 1977 elected not to pay Class 1 (full rate) or Class 2 contributions cannot pay Class 3 contributions while they retain this right. Class 3 contributions are collected by the NICO by quarterly bills or direct debit. *See* leaflet CA08.

CLASS 4

Self-employed people whose profits and gains are over £4,615 a year pay Class 4 contributions in addition to Class 2 contributions. This applies to self-employed earners over 16 and under the state pension age. Class 4 contributions are calculated at seven per cent of annual profits or gains between £4,615 and £30,420. Class 4 contributions are assessed and collected by the Inland Revenue together with Schedule D tax. It is possible, in some circumstances, to apply for exceptions from liability to pay Class 4 contributions or to have the amount of contribution reduced (where Class 1 contributions are payable on earnings assessed for Class 4 contributions). *See* leaflet CWL2.

PENSIONS

The Social Security Pensions Act (1975) came into force in 1978. It aimed to:
– reduce reliance on means-tested benefit in old age, widowhood and chronic ill-health
– ensure that occupational pension schemes which are contracted out of the state scheme fulfil the conditions of a good scheme
– ensure that pensions are adequately protected against inflation
– ensure that men and women are treated equally in state and occupational schemes

Legislation and regulations introduced since 1978 go further towards fulfilling these aims and more changes came into effect in April 1997. One of the changes is to equalise the state pension age for men (currently 65 years) and women (currently 60 years) from 6 April 2020. The change will be phased in over the ten years leading up to 6 April 2020. As a result the state pension age is as follows:
– the pension age for men remains at 65
– the pension age for women born on or before 5 October 1950 remains at 60
– the pension age for women born on or between 6 October 1950 and 5 October 1951 is 61
– the pension age for women born on or between 6 October 1951 and 5 October 1952 is 62
– the pension age for women born on or between 6 October 1952 and 5 October 1953 is 63
– the pension age for women born on or between 6 October 1953 and 5 October 1954 is 64
– the pension age for women born on 6 October 1954 or later is 65

STATE PENSION SCHEME

The state pension scheme consists of the basic flat-rate pension and the State Second Pension, also known as the Additional Pension, which reformed the State Earnings-Related Pension Scheme (SERPS) from 6 April 2002.

The amount of basic pension paid is dependent on the number of 'qualifying years' a person has in their 'working life'. A 'qualifying year' is a tax year in which a person pays Class 1 (at the standard rate), 2 or 3 NI contributions for the whole year (see above). Those in receipt of Invalid Care Allowance, Disabled Person's Tax Credit, Jobseeker's Allowance, Incapacity Benefit, Severe Disablement Allowance or approved training have contributions credited to them for each week they receive benefit or fulfil certain other conditions. For those reaching pensionable age on or after 6 April 1999, a Class 3 credit of earnings will be awarded for each week from 6 April 1995 that Family Credit or, subsequently, Working Families' Tax Credit, has been received. 'Working life' is counted from the start of the tax year in which a person reaches 16 to the end of the tax year before the one in which they reach pensionable age: for men this is normally 49 years and for women this varies between 44 and 49 years depending on birth date (see above). To get the full rate (100 per cent) basic pension a person must have qualifying years for about 90 per cent of their working life. To get the minimum basic pension (25 per cent) a person will need ten or eleven qualifying years. Married women who are not entitled to a pension on their own contributions may get a pension on their husband's contributions. It is possible for people who are unable to work because they care for children or a sick or disabled person at home to reduce the number of

qualifying years required. This is called home responsibilities protection (HRP) and can be given for any tax year since April 1978; the number of years for which HRP is given is deducted from the number of qualifying years needed. From April 2002, HRP may also qualify the recipient for Additional Pension through the State Second Pension.

The amount of Additional Pension or SERPS paid depends on the amount of earnings a person has, or is treated as having, between the lower and upper earnings limits for each complete tax year between 6 April 1978 (when the scheme started) and the tax year before they reach state pension age. The right to Additional Pension does not depend on the person's right to basic pension. The amount of Additional Pension paid also depends on when a person reaches retirement; changes phased in from 6 April 1999 mean that pensions are calculated differently from that date. Men or women widowed before 6 October 2002 inherit all their late spouse's additional pension. From 6 October 2002, the maximum percentage of SERPS that a person can inherit from a late spouse will depend on their late spouse's date of birth:

Maximum % SERPS entitlement for surviving spouse	d.o.b (men)	d.o.b. (women)
100%	5/10/37 or earlier	5/10/42 or earlier
90%	6/10/37 to 5/10/39	6/10/42 to 5/10/44
80%	6/10/39 to 5/10/41	6/10/44 to 5/10/46
70%	6/10/41 to 5/10/43	6/10/46 to 5/10/48
60%	6/10/43 to 5/10/45	6/10/48 to 5/7/50
50%	6/10/45 or later	6/7/50 or later

The maximum Additional Pension – Second State Pension a person can inherit from a late spouse is 50 per cent.

There are four categories of state pension provided under the Social Security Contributions and Benefits Act 1992:
– Category A, a contributory pension made up of a Basic Pension dependent on the number of qualifying years in your working life and an Additional Pension dependent on earnings since April 1978.
– Category B, a contributory pension made up of basic and additional elements, payable to married women, widows and widowers based on their spouse's qualifying years and earnings. From 6 April 2010 both men and women will be able to get a Basic Pension based on their spouse's National Insurance contributions, if this is better than the pension based on their own contribution record.
– Category C, this pension is now obsolete.
– Category D, a non-contributory pension for those aged 80 and over.

Graduated retirement benefit is also available to those who paid graduated NI contributions into the scheme when it existed between April 1961 and April 1975.

The Pension Service provides a state pension forecasting service, for more information telephone: 0191-218 7280.

From 1978 to 2002, Additional Pension was called the State Earnings-Related Pension Scheme (SERPS). SERPS covered all earnings by employees from 6 April 1978 to 5 April 1997 on which standard rate class 1 National Insurance had been paid and earnings between 6 April

1997 and 5 April 2002 if the standard rate class 1 contributions had been contracted-in.

In 2002 The Welfare Reform and Pensions Act 1999 replaced SERPS with an Additional Pension, – the State Second Pension, targeted towards low and moderate earners and certain carers and people with long-term illness or disability. If earnings are above the annual National Insurance Lower Earnings Limit (£3,900 for 2002–3) but below the new low earnings threshold (£10,800 a year for 2002–3), the State Second Pension regards this as earnings of £10,800 and it is treated equivalently. Carers and people with long term illness and disability will be considered as at the low earnings threshold for each complete tax year even if they do not work at all, or earn less than the annual Lower Earnings Limit.

CONTRACTED-OUT OCCUPATIONAL AND PERSONAL PENSION SCHEMES

Since July 1988, an employee has been able to start a personal pension which, if it meets certain conditions, can be used in place of Additional Pension. Part of this pension takes the place of Additional Pension and is known as Protected Rights. A contracted-out deduction will be made from Additional Pension built up from 6 April 1987 to 5 April 1997. The reduction may be more or less than the pension provided by the scheme. From 6 April 1997 to 5 April 2002, any Additional Pension will not be built up during the period of membership to a contracted-out personal pension. A contracted-out deduction does not apply to any pension built up from and including 6 April 1997. From 6 April 2002, employees contracted-out into a personal pension and earning between the lower earnings limit and the low earnings threshold (£3,900 and £10,800 in 2002–3) may get an Additional Pension through the State Second Pension as well as their personal pension.

There are two main types of contracted-out occupational schemes.

Contracted-Out Salary-Related (COSR) Scheme
- this scheme provides a pension related to earnings
- any notional additional pension built up from 6 April 1978 to 5 April 1997 will be reduced by the amount of Guaranteed Minimum Pension (GMP) built up during that period (the contracted-out deduction)
- from 6 April 1997 these schemes no longer provide a GMP but do have to satisfy a reference scheme test as a condition of contracting out.

Contracted-Out Money Purchase (COMP) Scheme
- this scheme provides a pension based on the value of the fund built up, i.e. the money paid in, along with returns from investment
- part of the pension, known as Protected Rights, takes the place of the Additional Pension. A contracted-out deduction, which may be more or less than the pension provided by the scheme, will be made from any additional pension built up from 6 April 1988 to 5 April 1997. Protected Rights are the part of the pension fund derived from NIC rebates and their investment return.
- From 6 April 1997 to 5 April 2002 no Additional Pension can be earned during the period of membership to a COMP scheme.

From and including 6 April 1997, a contracted-out deduction does not apply to any pension accrued. From April 2002, employees contracted-out into an occupational pension and earning between £3,900 and £24,600 (in 2002–3 terms) may get Additional Pension

through the State Second Pension as well as their occupational pension.

Contracted-Out Mixed Benefit (COMB) Scheme
A mixed benefit scheme has two active sections, one salary related and the other money purchase. Scheme rules set out which section individual employees may join and the circumstances (if any) in which members may move between sections. Each section must satisfy the respective contracting-out conditions for COSR and COMP schemes.

Appropriate Personal Pension Schemes
The option of a personal pension scheme is open to all employees, even if their employer has an occupational pension scheme. A personal pension scheme must provide a pension based on the value of the fund built up, i.e. the money paid in, along with returns from investment. Part of the pension, known as Protected Rights, takes the place of Additional Pension. A contracted-out deduction, which may be more or less than the pension provided by the scheme, will be made from any additional pension earned from 6 April 1987 to 5 April 1997. Employees who are members of a personal pension plan and their employers pay NI contributions at the full rate and the Inland Revenue pays the difference between the full rate and the contracted-out rate into the personal pension scheme. The rebate age is related and increases with age.

Stakeholder Pensions
Stakeholder pensions became available in April 2001. It is possible to invest up to £3,600 (including tax relief) annually in a stakeholder pension scheme without evidence of earnings. The minimum contribution cannot be set higher than £20 and providers are prohibited from levying a charge of more than 1 per cent of the value of the individual fund annually. The charge is taken directly from the fund. People who are already members of occupational pension schemes may also contribute to a stakeholder pension scheme and it is possible to contribute to a scheme that is not your own, for example that of a non-working partner. As with a personal pension, if it meets certain conditions, it can be used in place of the Additional Pension. For further information contact the Office of the Pensions Advisory Service on 020-7233 8080. The Pensions Advisory Service (OPAS) gives free help and advice to people who have problems with occupational or personal pensions. A Pensions Ombudsman deals with complaints regarding maladministration of pensions schemes. The Occupational Pensions Regulatory Authority (OPRA) was set up by parliament to help make sure occupational pension schemes are safe and well run, it can impose penalties where there are breaches of the law. *See* leaflet NP46.

BENEFITS

Leaflets relating to the various benefits and contribution conditions for different benefits are available from local social security offices; leaflets NI196 *Social Security Benefit Rates*, FB2 *Which Benefit?* and MG1 *A Guide to Benefits* are general guides to benefits, benefit rates and contributions. The benefits payable under the Social Security Acts are:

CONTRIBUTORY BENEFITS

Jobseeker's Allowance (contribution-based)
Incapacity Benefit
Maternity Allowance
Widow's Benefit and Bereavement Benefit
Retirement pensions, categories A and B

NON-CONTRIBUTORY BENEFITS AND TAX CREDITS

Child Benefit
Guardian's Allowance
Jobseeker's Allowance (income-based)
Carer's Allowance
Severe Disablement Allowance
Attendance Allowance
Disability Living Allowance
Disabled Person's Tax Credit
Retirement Pensions, categories C and D
Income Support
Working Families' Tax Credit
Housing Benefit
Council Tax Benefit
Social Fund

BENEFITS FOR INDUSTRIAL INJURIES AND
DISABLEMENT

Other
Statutory Sick Pay
Statutory Maternity Pay

TAX CREDITS

Under the Tax Credits Act 1999, Family Credit and
Disability Working Allowance (both non-contributory
benefits) were replaced by Working Families' Tax Credit
and Disabled Person's Tax Credit from 5 October 1999.
Both of these are administered by the Inland Revenue.
People receiving Family Credit or Disability Working
Allowance on 5 October 1999 continued to receive their
benefits until the award expired, when they were able to
change to the new tax credits. Couples receiving Working
Families' Tax Credit can choose which partner is the
applicant. For awards starting from April 2000 applicants
who are employees receive the credits from their
employer along with their wages or salary. Self-employed
applicants and applicants who are not in work, are paid
direct by the Inland Revenue.

Working Families' Tax Credit and Disabled Person's Tax
Credit, along with the Children's Tax Credit, will cease at
the end of 2003–4 and be replaced by new tax credits:
Working Tax Credit and Child Tax Credit. Both Working
Families' Tax Credit and Disabled Person's Tax Credit are
usually paid at the same rate for 26 weeks. However, to
help ensure a smooth transition to Working Tax Credit
and Child Tax Credit at April 2003, all awards starting
from 4 June 2002 will run until 7 April 2003.

Further information and application forms are
available from Inland Revenue Tax Enquiry Centres,
Benefits Agency offices, Jobcentres, post offices and
Citizens' Advice Bureaux.

WORKING FAMILIES' TAX CREDIT

Working Families' Tax Credit is a tax credit paid to
couples (married or unmarried) or lone parents who
have at least one child living with them and where at least
one partner works at least 16 hours per week. The credit
is not payable if any savings exceed £8,000.

There are six elements for awards starting from June
2002:
– a basic credit of £62.50 per family per week

– enhanced disability tax credit (where applicant or
partner is entitled to the highest rate care component
of Disability Living Allowance) of £16.25 per week
– a credit of £11.65 per week where one earner works at
least 30 hours per week
– a credit for each child at the rate of £26.45 per week
from birth and £27.20 from the September following
their 16th birthday up to the day before their 19th
birthday
– a disabled child's tax credit of £35.50 per week, or an
enhanced disabled child's credit of £46.75 for each
severely disabled child
– a childcare tax credit (in certain circumstances) of up
to 70 per cent of eligible childcare costs up to a
maximum of £135 per week for one child and £200 per
week for two or more children

If net income is below £94.50 per week, the maximum tax
credit is payable. If net income exceeds £94.50 per week,
the total tax credit is reduced by 55p for each £1.00 above
£94.50.

DISABLED PERSON'S TAX CREDIT

Disabled Person's Tax Credit is a tax credit for people who
are working at least 16 hours per week but have an illness
or disability which puts them at a disadvantage in getting
a job. To qualify, a person must have one of the 'qualifying
benefits' or have had them up to 182 days before
applying. The credit is not payable if any savings exceed
£16,000.

There are six elements for awards starting from June
2002:
– a basic credit of £61.10 per week for a single person or
£95.30 for a couple or lone parent
– enhanced disability tax credit (where applicant or
partner is entitled to the highest rate care component of
Disability Living Allowance) of £11.25 per week for a
single person or £16.25 for a couple or lone parent.
– a credit of £11.65 per week where the applicant works
at least 30 hours per week
– a credit for each child at the rate of £26.45 from birth
and £27.20 from the September following their 16th
birthday up to the day before their 19th birthday
– a disabled child's tax credit of £35.50 per week or an
enhanced disabled child's credit of £46.75 for each
severely disabled child.
– a childcare tax credit (in certain circumstances) of up to
70 per cent of eligible childcare costs up to a maximum
of £135 per week for one child and £200 per week for
two or more children

If net income is below £73.50 per week for a single person
or £94.50 per week for a couple or lone parent, the
maximum tax credit is payable. If net income exceeds
these thresholds, the total tax credit is reduced by 55p for
each £1.00 above the threshold.

CONTRIBUTORY BENEFITS

Entitlement to contributory benefits depends on
contribution conditions being satisfied either by the
claimant or by some other person (depending on the kind
of benefit). The class or classes of contribution which for
this purpose are relevant to each benefit are:

Jobseeker's Allowance (contribution-based)	Class 1
Incapacity Benefit	Class 1 or 2
Maternity Allowance	Class 1 or 2
Widow's Benefits	Class 1, 2 or 3
Retirement pensions, categories A and B	Class 1, 2 or 3

The system of contribution conditions relates to yearly
levels of earnings on which contributions have been paid.

JOBSEEKER'S ALLOWANCE

Jobseeker's allowance (JSA) replaced unemployment benefit and income support for unemployed people under pension age from 7 October 1996. There are two routes of entitlement. Contribution-based JSA is paid as a personal rate (i.e. additional benefit for dependants is not paid) to those who have made sufficient NI contributions in two particular tax years. Savings and partner's earnings are not taken into account and payment can be made for up to six months. Rates of JSA correspond to income support rates.

Claims for this benefit are made through Jobcentre Plus and Jobcentres. A person wishing to claim JSA must be unemployed, capable of work and available for any work which they can reasonably be expected to do, usually for at least 40 hours per week. They must agree and sign a 'jobseeker's agreement', which will set out each claimant's plans to find work, and must actively seek work. If they refuse work or training their benefit may be suspended for between two and four weeks.

A person will be disqualified from JSA if they have left a job voluntarily or through misconduct, if they refuse to take up an offer of employment or if they fail to attend a training scheme or employment programme. In these circumstances, it may be possible to receive hardship payments, particularly where the claimant or their family is vulnerable, e.g. if sick or pregnant, or for those with children or caring responsibilities. *See* leaflet JSAL5.

INCAPACITY BENEFIT

Incapacity benefit is available to those who are incapable of work but cannot get statutory sick pay from their employer. It is not payable to those over state pension age. However, people who are already in receipt of short-term incapacity benefit when they reach state pension age may continue to receive this benefit for up to 52 weeks. Eligibility for incapacity benefit is restricted to people who have paid National Insurance contributions for one of the previous three years, although some exceptions do apply. The amount of incapacity benefit payable may be reduced where a claimant receives more than a specified amount of occupational or personal pension. Severely disabled people aged between 16 and 19 should receive incapacity benefit without meeting the national insurance contribution conditions. There are three rates of incapacity benefit:

- short-term lower rate for the first 28 weeks of sickness
- short-term higher rate from weeks 29 to 52
- long-term rate from week 53 onwards

The terminally ill and those entitled to the highest rate care component of disability living allowance are paid the long-term rate after 28 weeks. Incapacity benefit is taxable after 28 weeks.

Two rates of age addition are paid with long-term benefit based on the claimant's age when incapacity started. The higher rate is payable where incapacity for work commenced before the age of 35; and the lower rate where incapacity commenced before the age of 45. Increases for dependants are also payable with short and long-term incapacity benefit.

There are two medical tests of incapacity: the 'own occupation' test and the 'personal capability' assessment. Those who worked before becoming incapable of working will be assessed, for the first 28 weeks of incapacity, on their ability to do their own job. After 28 weeks (or from the start of incapacity for those who were not working) claimants are assessed on their ability to carry out a range of work-related activities. *See* leaflets IB1 and IB214. From October 2001 all new benefit claimants in the 51 Jobcentre Plus areas receive a service combining jobs and benefits advice and support. The government plans to extend this as Jobcentre Plus is rolled out nationally. New Incapacity Benefit claimants will be invited back for work-focused interviews at intervals of not longer than three years. The interviews are not medical tests, but if the claimant is due for a medical test around the same time, their local office will aim to schedule both together. People who are severely disabled and those who are terminally ill will not be asked to attend these interviews.

MATERNITY ALLOWANCE

Maternity Allowance (MA) covers women who are self-employed or otherwise do not qualify for statutory maternity pay. In order to qualify, the woman must have been working and have average weekly earnings of at least £30 per week for at least 26 weeks in the 66-week period which ends with the week before the week in which the baby is due. A woman can choose to start receiving MA between the beginning of the 11th week before the week in which the baby is due and the Sunday after the baby is born, depending on when she stops working. MA is paid for a period of up to 18 weeks. MA is only paid while the woman is not working. *See* leaflet NI17A.

BEREAVEMENT BENEFITS

Bereavement benefits replaced widows' benefits on 9 April 2001. Those claiming widows' benefits before this date will continue to receive them under the old scheme for as long as they qualify. The new system provides bereavement benefits for widows and widowers providing that their deceased spouse paid National Insurance contributions. The new system offers benefits in three forms:

Bereavement payment – may be received by a man or woman who is under the state pension age at the time of their spouse's death, or whose husband or wife was not entitled to a Category A retirement pension when he or she died. It is a single tax-free lump sum of £2,000 payable immediately on becoming a widow or widower.

Widowed parent's allowance – a taxable benefit payable to the surviving partner if he or she is entitled or treated as entitled to child benefit, or to a widow if she is expecting her husband's baby

Bereavement allowance – a taxable weekly benefit paid for 52 weeks after the spouse's death. A widow or widower may receive this pension if aged 45 or over at the time of his or her spouse's death (40 or over if widowed before 11 April 1988) or when his or her widowed parent's allowance ends. If aged 55 or over he or she will receive the full bereavement allowance

It is not possible to receive widowed parent's allowance and bereavement allowance at the same time, and bereavement benefit in any form ceases upon remarriage or during a period of cohabitation as man and wife without being legally married. *See* leaflet NP45.

RETIREMENT PENSION: CATEGORIES A AND B

Category A pension is payable for life to men and women who reach state pension age and who satisfy the contributions conditions. Category B pension is payable for life to a spouse and is based on their wife's or husband's contributions. It becomes payable only when the wife or husband has claimed their pension and the spouse has reached state pension age. It is also payable on widowhood after the state retirement age regardless of whether the wife or husband had qualified for their pension. There are special rules for those who are widowed before reaching pensionable age.

A person may defer claiming their pension for five years after state pension age. In doing so they may earn increments which will increase the weekly amount paid when they claim their pension. If a married man defers his Category A pension, his wife cannot claim a Category B pension on his contributions but she may earn increments on her pension during this time. A woman can defer her Category B pension, and earn increments, even if her husband is claiming his Category A pension.

The basic state pension is £75.50 per week plus any additional (earnings-related) pension the person may be entitled to. An increase of £45.20 is paid for an adult dependant, providing the dependant's earnings do not exceed the rate of Jobseeker's Allowance for a single person (*see* below). It is also possible to get an increase of Category A and B pensions for a child or children. An age addition of 25p per week is payable if a retirement pensioner is aged 80 or over.

Since 1989 pensioners have been allowed to have unlimited earnings without affecting their retirement pension. Income support is payable on top of a pension where a pension does not give the person enough to live on and to those who are entitled to retirement pension but who have not claimed it. Pensioners may also be entitled to housing and council tax benefits.

GRADUATED RETIREMENT BENEFIT

Graduated NI contributions were first payable from 1961 and were calculated as a percentage of earnings between certain bands. They were discontinued in 1975. Any graduated pension which an employed person over 18 and under 70 (65 for a woman) had earned by paying graduated contributions will be paid when the contributor claims retirement pension or at 70 (65 for a woman), in addition to any retirement pension for which he or she qualifies. A husband or wife can only get a graduated pension in return for his/her own graduated contributions, but not for his/her spouse's.

Graduated retirement benefit is at a weekly rate for each 'unit' of graduated contributions paid by the employee (half a unit or more counts as a whole unit); the rate varies from person to person. A unit of graduated pension can be calculated by adding together all graduated contributions and dividing by 7.5 (men) or 9.0 (women). If a person defers making a claim beyond 65 (60 for a woman), entitlement may be increased by one seventh of a penny per £1 of its weekly rate for each complete week of deferred retirement, as long as the retirement is deferred for a minimum of seven weeks.

In April 2002 the Pension Service, part of the Department for Work and Pensions was set up and is due to be expanded over the next two years. This organisation aims to provide an improved service for pensioners, enabling pensioners to contact the nearest pension centre by telephone, email, post or face to face without going through the local social security office.

WEEKLY RATES OF BENEFIT

from April 2002

Jobseeker's Allowance (contribution-based)

Person under 18	£32.50
Person aged 18–24	42.70
Person aged 25 to state pension age	53.95

Short-term Incapacity Benefit

Person under pension age – lower rate	53.50
*Person under pension age – higher rate	63.25
Increase for adult dependant	33.10
*Person over pension age	68.05
Increase for adult dependant	33.10

Long-term Incapacity Benefit

Person (under or over pension age)	70.95
Increase for adult dependant	42.45
Age addition – lower rate	7.45
Age addition – higher rate	14.90

Invalidity Allowance: maximum amount payable

Higher rate	14.90
Middle rate	9.50
Lower rate	4.75

Maternity Allowance

Employed	£75.00
Maternity rate threshold	30.00

Widow's Benefits (before 9 April 2001)

Widow's payment (lump sum)	1,000.00
Widowed mother's allowance	72.50
Widow's pension	72.50

Bereavement Benefit (from 9 April 2001)

Bereavement payment (lump sum)		2,000.00
*Widowed parents allowance		75.50
*Bereavement allowance		75.50
*Age related	54	70.22
	53	64.93
	52	59.65
	51	54.36
	50	49.08
	49	43.79
	48	38.51
	47	33.22
	46	27.94
	45	22.65

Retirement pension: categories A and B

Single person	75.50
Increase for adult dependant	45.20

*These benefits attract an increase for each dependant child (in addition to child benefit) of £9.65 for the first or only child and £11.35 for each subsequent child

NON-CONTRIBUTORY BENEFITS

These benefits are paid from general taxation and are not dependent on NI contributions. Unless otherwise stated, a benefit is tax-free and is not means tested.

JOBSEEKER'S ALLOWANCE (INCOME-BASED)

Those who do not qualify for contribution-based Job Seeker's Allowance (JSA), those who have exhausted their entitlement to contribution-based JSA or those for whom contribution-based JSA provides insufficient income may qualify for income-based JSA. The amount paid depends on age, number of dependants, amount of income and savings. Income-based JSA comprises of three parts:

– a personal allowance for the jobseeker and his/her partner and an allowance for each child or young person for whom they are responsible
– premiums for people with special needs
– premiums for housing costs.

The rules of entitlement are the same as for contribution-based JSA.

CHILD BENEFIT

Child Benefit is payable for virtually all children aged under 16, and for those aged 16 to 18 who are studying full-time up to and including A-level or equivalent standard. It is also payable for a short period if the child has left school recently and is registered for work or work-based training for young people at a careers office.

A higher rate of benefit, Child Benefit (Lone Parent) may be paid to a person who is responsible for bringing

up one or more children on his/her own. It is a flat rate benefit payable for the eldest child only. Since 6 July 1998 Child Benefit (Lone Parent) has not been available to new lone parents but it may still be payable in certain circumstances. See leaflets CH1 and CH11.

GUARDIAN'S ALLOWANCE

Where the parents of a child are dead, the person who has the child in his/her family may claim a Guardian's Allowance in addition to Child Benefit. In exceptional circumstances the allowance is payable on the death of only one parent. See leaflet NI14.

CARER'S ALLOWANCE

Carer's Allowance (CA) is a benefit payable to people who spend at least 35 hours per week caring for a severely disabled person. To qualify for CA a person must be caring for someone in receipt of one of the following benefits:

- the middle or highest rate of disability living allowance care component
- either rate of attendance allowance
- constant attendance allowance, paid at not less than the normal maximum rate, under the industrial injuries or war pension schemes

See leaflets FB31 and SD1.

SEVERE DISABLEMENT ALLOWANCE

From April 2001 Severe Disablement Allowance (SDA) has not been available to new claimants. Those claiming SDA before that date will continue to receive it for as long as they qualify. See leaflet NI252.

ATTENDANCE ALLOWANCE

This is payable to disabled people who claim after the age of 65 and who need a lot of care or supervision because of physical or mental disability for a period of at least six months. Attendance Allowance has two rates: the lower rate is for day or night care, and the higher rate is for day and night care. People not expected to live for more than six months because of an illness can receive the highest rate of Attendance Allowance straight away. See leaflets DS702 and SD1.

DISABILITY LIVING ALLOWANCE

This is payable to disabled people who claim before the age of 65 who have personal care and mobility needs because of an illness or disability for a period of at least three months and are likely to have those needs for a further six months or more. The allowance has two components: the care component, which has three rates, and the mobility component, which has two rates. The rates depend on the care and mobility needs of the claimant. People not expected to live for more then six months because of an illness will automatically receive the highest rate of the care component. See leaflets DS704 and SD1.

RETIREMENT PENSION: CATEGORY D

Category D pension is provided for people aged 80 and over if they are not entitled to another category of pension or are entitled to less than the Category D rate.

WEEKLY RATES OF BENEFIT
from April 2002

Jobseeker's Allowance (income-based)

Person under 18, living with family	£32.50
Person under 18, living away from home	42.70
Person aged 18–24	42.70
Person aged 25 to state pension age	53.95
Couple with one or both under 18	32.50-84.65
	(depending on circumstances)
Couple aged 18 to state pension age	84.65
Dependant children and young persons	
premium up to 16	£33.50
16–19 years	34.30
Family premium (lone parent)	15.90

Child Benefit

Eldest child	15.75
Eldest child of certain lone parents	17.55
Each subsequent child	10.55

Guardian's allowance

Eldest child	9.85
Each subsequent child	11.35

*Carer's Allowance

Increase for dependant adult	42.45
	25.35

*Severe Disablement Allowance

†Basic rate	42.85
Under 40	14.90
40–49	9.50
50–59	4.75
Additions may be payable for dependant adults	

Attendance allowance

Higher rate	56.25
Lower rate	37.65

Disability living allowance

Care component	
Higher rate	56.25
Middle rate	37.65
Lowest rate	14.90
Mobility component	
Higher rate	39.30
Lower rate	14.90

Retirement pension: category D

Single person	43.40
Increase for wife/other adult dependant	24.95

* These benefits attract an increase for each dependant child (in addition to child benefit) of £9.65 for the first or only child and £11.35 for each subsequent child
† The age addition applies to the age when incapacity began

INCOME SUPPORT

Income support is a benefit for those aged 16 and over whose income is below a certain level. It can be paid to people who are not expected to sign on as unemployed (income support for unemployed people was replaced by jobseeker's allowance in October 1996) and who are:

- incapable of work due to sickness or disability
- bringing up children alone
- 60 or over
- looking after a person who has a disability
- registered blind

Some people who are not in these categories may also be able to claim income support.

Income support is also payable to people who work for less than 16 hours a week on average (or 24 hours for a partner). Some people can claim income support if they work longer hours.

Income support is not payable if the claimant, or claimant and partner, have capital or savings in excess of £8,000. For capital and savings in excess of £3,000, a deduction of £1 is made for every £250 or part of £250 held. Different limits apply to people permanently in residential care and nursing homes: the upper limit is £16,000 and deductions apply for capital in excess of £10,000.

Sums payable depend on fixed allowances laid down by law for people in different circumstances. If both partners are entitled to income support, either may claim it for the couple. People receiving income support may be able to receive housing benefit, help with mortgage or home loan interest and help with health care. They may also be eligible for help with exceptional expenses from the Social Fund. Special rates may apply to some people living in residential care or nursing homes. Leaflet IS20 gives a detailed explanation of income support.

In October 1998 the Government's voluntary New Deal for Lone Parents programme became available throughout the UK. All lone parents receiving income support are assigned a personal adviser at a Jobcentre who will provide guidance and support with a view to enabling the claimant to find work.

INCOME SUPPORT PREMIUMS

Income support premiums are additional weekly payments for those with special needs. People qualifying for more than one premium will normally only receive the highest single premium for which they qualify. However, family premium, disabled child premium, severe disability premium and carer premium are payable in addition to other premiums.

People with children may qualify for:
- the family premium if they have at least one child (a higher rate is paid to lone parents, although from 6 April 1998 it has not been available to new claimants)
- the disabled child premium if they have a child who receives disability living allowance or is registered blind

Carers may qualify for:
- the carer premium if they or their partner are in receipt of invalid care allowance

Long-term sick or disabled people may qualify for:
- the disability premium if they or their partner are receiving certain benefits because they are disabled or cannot work; are registered blind; or if the claimant has been incapable of work or receiving statutory sick pay for at least 364 days (196 days if the person is terminally ill), including periods of incapacity separated by eight weeks or less
- the severe disability premium if the person lives alone and receives attendance allowance or the middle or higher rate of disability living allowance care component and no one receives invalid care allowance for caring for that person. This premium is also available to couples where both partners meet the above conditions

People aged 60 and over may qualify for:
- the pensioner premium if they or their partner are aged 60 to 74
- the enhanced pensioner premium if they or their partner are aged 75 to 79
- the higher pensioner premium if they or their partner are aged 80 or over. This is also available to people over

60 who receive attendance allowance, disability living allowance, long-term incapacity benefit or severe disablement allowance, or who are registered blind

WEEKLY RATES OF BENEFIT

from April 2002

Income support

Single person	
under 18	£32.50
under 18 (higher)	42.70
aged 18–24	42.70
aged 25 and over	53.95
aged under 18 and a single parent (lower)	£32.50
aged under 18 and a single parent (higher)	42.70
aged 18 and over and a single parent	53.95
Couples*	
Both under 18	64.45
one or both aged 18 or over	84.65
For each child in a family from birth until September following 16th birthday	33.50
†from September following 16th birthday to day before 19th birthday	34.30

Premiums

Family premium	14.75
Family (lone parent) premium	15.90
Disabled child premium	35.50
Carer premium	24.80
Disability premium	
Single	23.00
Couple	32.80
Enhanced disability premium	
Single	11.25
Enhanced disabled child premium	11.25
Severe disability premium	
Lower rate (single person and some couples)	42.25
Higher rate (couples)	84.50
Pensioner premium	
Single	44.20
Couple	65.15
Higher pensioner premium	
Single	44.20
Couple	65.15
Enhanced pensioner premium	
Single	44.20
Couple	65.15
Bereavement premium	19.45

* Where one or both partners are aged under 18, their personal allowance will depend on their situation
† If in full-time education up to A-level or equivalent standard

HOUSING BENEFIT

Housing benefit is designed to help people with rent (including rent for accommodation in guesthouses, lodgings or hostels). It does not cover mortgage payments. The amount of benefit paid depends on:

- the income of the claimant, and partner if there is one, including earned income, unearned income (any other income including some other benefits) and savings
- number of dependants
- certain extra needs of the claimant, partner or any dependants
- number and gross income of people sharing the home who are not dependent on the claimant
- how much rent is paid

Housing benefit is not payable if the claimant, or claimant and partner, have savings of over £16,000. The

amount of benefit is affected if savings held exceed £3,000. Housing benefit is not paid for meals, fuel or certain service charges that may be included in the rent. Deductions are also made for most non-dependants who live in the same accommodation as the claimant (and their partner).

The maximum amount of benefit (which is not necessarily the same as the amount of rent paid) may be paid where the claimant is in receipt of income support or income-based jobseeker's allowance or where the claimant's income is less than the amount allowed for their needs. Any income over that allowed for their needs will mean that their benefit is reduced.

See leaflets GL16 and RR2.

COUNCIL TAX BENEFIT

Nearly all the rules which apply to housing benefit apply to council tax benefit, which helps people on low incomes to pay council tax bills. The amount payable depends on how much council tax is paid and who lives with the claimant. The benefit may be available to those receiving income support or income-based Jobseeker's Allowance or to those whose income is less than that allowed for their needs. Any income over that allowed for their needs will mean that their council tax benefit is reduced. Deductions are made for non-dependants.

The maximum amount that is payable for those living in properties in council tax bands A to E is 100 per cent of the claimant's council tax liability. This also applies to those living in properties in bands F to H who were in receipt of the benefit at 31 March 1998 if they have remained in the same property. From 1 April 1998 council tax benefit for new claimants living in property bands F to H (or existing claimants moving into these bands) was restricted to the level payable for band E.

If a person shares a home with one or more adults (not their partner) who are on a low income, it may be possible to claim a second adult rebate. Those who are entitled to both council tax benefit and second adult rebate will be awarded whichever is the greater. Second adult rebate may be claimed by those not in receipt of council tax benefit.

THE SOCIAL FUND

The Social Fund helps people with expenses which are difficult to meet from regular income. Regulated maternity and funeral payments are decided by Decision Makers; cold weather payments and winter fuel payments are made automatically. These payments are not limited by a budget. Regulations prescribe the circumstances and amounts payable. Discretionary community care grants, and budgeting and crisis loans are decided by appropriate officers and come out of the grants and loans budget allocated to each district on 1 April each year.

See leaflet SB16.

REGULATED PAYMENTS

Sure Start Maternity Grant
The Sure Start Maternity Grant (SSMG) is a one-off payment of £500 for parents on low incomes to buy essential items for new babies. To qualify, mothers and expectant mothers must also receive health and welfare advice for themselves and their child from an approved health professional. SSMG can be claimed any time from the 29th week of pregnancy until the child is three months old. Those eligible are mothers or their partners in receipt of Income Support, income-based Jobseeker's Allowance, Disabled Person's Tax Credit and Working Families' Tax Credit.

Funeral Payments
Payable for the necessary cost of burial or cremation, plus other funeral expenses reasonably incurred up to £600, to people receiving Income Support, income-based Jobseeker's Allowance, Disabled Person's Tax Credit, Working Families' Tax Credit, Council Tax Benefit or Housing Benefit who have good reason for taking responsibility for the funeral expenses. These payments are recoverable from any estate of the deceased.

Cold Weather Payments
A payment of £8.50 when the average temperature over seven consecutive days is recorded as or forecast to be 0°C or below in their area. Payments are made to people on Income Support or income-based Jobseeker's Allowance and who have a child under five or whose benefit includes a pensioner or disability premium. They do not have to be repaid.

Winter Fuel Payments
An annual payment of £200 per household paid to most people aged 60 or over. The majority of eligible people are paid automatically before Christmas, although a few need to claim. Payments do not have to be repaid.

DISCRETIONARY PAYMENTS

Community Care Grants
These are intended to help people on Income Support or income-based Jobseeker's Allowance (or those likely to receive these benefits on leaving residential or institutional accommodation) to live as independently as possible in the community; ease exceptional pressures on families; care for a prisoner or young offender released on temporary licence; help people set up home as part of a resettlement programme and/or assist with certain travelling expenses. They do not have to be repaid.

Budgeting Loans
These are interest-free loans to people who have been receiving income support or income-based Jobseeker's Allowance for at least 26 weeks, for intermittent expenses that may be difficult to budget for.

Crisis Loans
These are interest-free loans to anyone, whether receiving benefit or not, who is without resources in an emergency, where there is no other means of preventing serious damage or serious risk to their health or safety.

SAVINGS

Savings over £500 (£1,000 for people aged 60 or over) are taken into account for Community Care Grants and Budgeting Loans. All savings are taken into account for Crisis Loans. Savings are not taken into account for Cold Weather or Winter Fuel Payments.

INDUSTRIAL INJURIES AND DISABLEMENT BENEFITS

The industrial injuries scheme, administered under the Social Security Contributions and Benefits Act 1992, provides a range of benefits designed to compensate for disablement resulting from an industrial accident (i.e. an accident arising out of and in the course of an employed earner's employment) or from a prescribed disease due to the nature of a person's employment. Those who are self-employed are not covered by this scheme.

INDUSTRIAL INJURIES DISABLEMENT BENEFIT

A person must be at least 14 per cent disabled (except for certain respiratory diseases) in order to qualify for this benefit. The amount paid depends on the degree of disablement:

– those assessed as 14–19 per cent disabled are paid at the 20 per cent rate
– those with disablement of over 20 per cent will have the percentage rounded up or down to the nearest ten per cent, e.g. a disablement of 44 per cent will be paid at the 40 per cent rate while a disablement of 45 per cent will be paid at the 50 per cent rate

Benefit is payable 15 weeks (90 days) after the date of the accident or onset of the disease and may be payable for a limited period or for life. The benefit is payable whether the person works or not and those who are incapable of work are entitled to draw statutory sick pay or incapacity benefit in addition to industrial injuries disablement benefit. It may also be possible to claim the following allowances:

– reduced earnings allowance for those who are unable to return to their regular work or work of the same standard and who had their accident (or whose disease started) before 1 October 1990
– retirement allowance for those who were entitled to reduced earnings allowance who have reached state pension age
– constant attendance allowance for those with a disablement of 100 per cent who need constant care. There are four rates of allowance depending on how much care the person needs
– exceptionally severe disablement allowance for those who are entitled to constant care attendance allowance at one of the higher rates and who need constant care permanently

See leaflets SD6, SD7 and SD8.

OTHER BENEFITS

People who are disabled because of an accident or disease that was the result of work that they did before 5 July 1948 are not entitled to industrial injuries disablement benefit. They may, however, be entitled to payment under the workmen's compensation scheme or the pneumoconiosis, byssinosis and miscellaneous diseases benefit scheme. *See* leaflet GL23.

WEEKLY RATES OF BENEFIT

from April 2002
*Disablement benefit/pension
Degree of disablement

100 per cent	£114.80
90	103.32
80	91.84
70	80.36
60	68.88
50	57.40
40	45.92
30	34.44
20	22.96
†Unemployability supplement	70.95
Addition for adult dependant	40.40
(subject to earnings rule)	
Reduced earnings allowance (maximum)	45.92
Retirement allowance (maximum)	11.29
Constant attendance allowance	46.00
(normal maximum rate)	
Exceptionally severe disablement allowance	46.00

* There is a weekly benefit for those under 18 with no dependants which is set at a lower rate

† This benefit attracts an increase for each dependent child (in addition to child benefit) of £9.65 for the first child and £11.35 for each subsequent child

CLAIMS AND QUESTIONS

With a few exceptions, claims and questions relating to social security benefits are decided in agencies. *See* leaflets GL24 and NI260(DMA).

Entitlement to benefit (including disablement questions) and regulated Social Fund payments is determined by Decision Makers. A claimant who is dissatisfied with that decision can ask for an explanation and review of the decision. If they are still dissatisfied they can go to the Appeals Service, an independent tribunal. There is a further right of appeal to a Social Security Commissioner against the tribunal's decision but leave to appeal must first be obtained. Appeals to the Commissioner must be on a point of law. Provision is also made for the determination of certain questions by the Secretary of State for Work and Pensions.

Decisions on applications to the discretionary Social Fund are made by Social Fund Officers. Applicants can ask for a review within 28 days of the date on the decision letter. The Social Fund Review Officer will review the case and there is a further right of review to an independent Social Fund Inspector.

Reviews of Housing and Council Tax Benefit decisions are dealt with initially by the council. The claimant must ask for a review within six weeks of being told how much benefit they will receive. Further reviews are dealt with by an independent review board or the Appeals Tribunal.

OTHER BENEFITS

STATUTORY SICK PAY

Employers usually pay statutory sick pay (SSP) to their employees for up to 28 weeks of sickness in any period of incapacity for work that lasts longer than four days. SSP is paid at £63.25 per week and is subject to PAYE tax and NI deductions. Employees who cannot obtain SSP may be able to claim incapacity benefit. Employers may be able to recover some SSP costs. *See* leaflets NI244 and NI245.

STATUTORY MATERNITY PAY

In general, employers pay statutory maternity pay (SMP) to pregnant women who have been employed by them full or part-time for at least 26 weeks into the 15th week before the week the baby is due, and whose earnings on average at least equal the lower earnings limit applied to NI contributions (£75 per week from April 2002). All women who meet these conditions receive payment of 90 per cent of their average earnings for six weeks, followed by a maximum of 12 weeks at £62.75. SMP can be paid from the beginning of the 11th week before the week in which the baby is due, but women can decide to begin maternity leave later than this. SMP is not payable for any week in which the woman works. Employers are reimbursed for 92 per cent of the SMP they pay. Small employers with annual gross NI payments of £40,000 or less recover 100 per cent of the SMP paid out plus 4.5 per cent in compensation for the secondary National Insurance Contributions paid on SMP. *See* Leaflet NI17A.

War Pensions

The War Pensions Agency, which became an executive agency of the Ministry of Defence in June 2001, and now known as the Veteran's Agency, awards war pensions under The Naval, Military and Air Forces, Etc. (Disablement and Death) Service Pensions Order 1983 to

members of the armed forces in respect of disablement due to service. There is also a scheme for civilians and civil defence workers in respect of the 1939–45 war, and other schemes for groups such as merchant seamen and Polish armed forces who served under British command, during World War II.

PENSIONS

War disablement pension is awarded for the disabling effects of any injury, wound or disease which is the result of, or has been aggravated by, conditions of service in the armed forces. It can only be paid once the person has left the armed forces. The amount of pension paid depends on the severity of disablement, which is assessed by comparing the health of the claimant with that of a healthy person of the same age and sex. The person's earning capacity or occupation are not taken into account in this assessment. A pension is awarded if the person has a disablement of 20 per cent or more and a lump sum is usually payable to those with a disablement of less than 20 per cent. No award is made for noise-induced sensorineural hearing loss where the assessment of disablement is less than 20 per cent.

War widow/widower's pension is payable where the spouse's death was due to, or hastened by, service in the armed forces or where the spouse was in receipt of a war disablement pension constant attendance allowance (or would have been had if not in hospital). A war widow/widower's pension is also payable if the spouse was getting unemployability supplement at the time of death and pensionable disablement was at least 80 per cent. Most war widows/widowers receive a standard rank-related rate but a lower weekly rate is payable to war widows/widowers of Personnel below the rank of Lieutenant-Colonel who are under the age of 40, without children and capable of maintaining themselves. This is increased to the standard rate at age 40. Allowances are paid for children (in addition to child benefit) and adult dependants. An age allowance may also be given when the widow/widower reaches 65 and increased at age 70 and age 80.

All war pensions and war widow/widower's pensions are tax-free and pensioners living overseas receive the same amount as those resident in the UK.

SUPPLEMENTARY ALLOWANCES

A number of supplementary allowances may be awarded to a war pensioner which are intended to meet various needs which may result from disablement or death and take account of its particular effect on the pensioner or spouse. The principal supplementary allowances are unemployability supplement, allowance for lowered standard of occupation and constant attendance allowance. Others include exceptionally severe disablement allowance, severe disablement occupational allowance, treatment allowance, mobility supplement, comforts allowance, clothing allowance, age allowance and widow/widower's age allowance. There is a rent allowance available on a war widow/widower's pension.

DEPARTMENT FOR WORK AND PENSIONS BENEFITS

Most benefits are paid in addition to the basic war disablement pension or war widow/widower's pension. Any retirement pension for which a war widow/widower qualifies on their own NI contribution record can be paid in addition to war widow/widower's pension.

A war pensioner or war widow/widower who claims income support, working families tax credit or disabled person's tax credit has the first £10 a week of pension disregarded. A similar provision operates for housing benefit and council tax benefit; but the local authority may, at its discretion, disregard any or all of the balance.

CLAIMS AND QUESTIONS

To claim a war pension it is necessary to contact the nearest war pensioners' welfare service office, the address of which is available from local social security offices, or to write to the Veteran's Agency, Norcross, Blackpool FY5 3WP. Claims can also be made through authorised agents, usually ex-service organisations such as the RBL, BLESMA etc. General advice on any war pensions matter can be obtained by ringing the War pensions Freeline (UK only) on 0800-169 2277.

If living overseas, call (00 44) (125) 386-6043;
Email: help@veteransagency.mod.uk
Web: www.veteransagency.mod.uk

The Water Industry

ENGLAND AND WALES

The water industry supplies 58 million people 18,000 million litres of water every day. Around 2.8 million tests are carried out to check drinking water quality every year and 99.86 per cent of samples meet all British/European standards. In England and Wales the Secretary of State for Environment, Food and Rural Affairs and the National Assembly for Wales have overall responsibility for water policy and oversee environmental standards for the water industry. The Drinking Water Inspectorate acts on their behalf as the regulator of drinking water quality.

The Director-General of Water Services, as the independent economic regulator, is responsible for ensuring that the private water companies are able to fulfil their statutory obligation to provide water supply and sewerage services, and for protecting the interests of consumers.

The Secretary of State for Environment, Food and Rural Affairs and the National Assembly for Wales are responsible for policy relating to land drainage, flood protection, sea defences and the protection and development of fisheries.

The Environment Agency is responsible for environmental water quality and the control of pollution, the management of water resources and nature conservation.

THE WATER COMPANIES

Until 1989 nine regional water authorities in England and the Welsh Water Authority in Wales were responsible for water supply and the development of water resources, sewerage and sewage disposal, pollution control, freshwater fisheries, flood protection, water recreation and environmental conservation. The Water Act 1989 provided for the creation of a privatised water industry under public regulation. The functions of the regional water authorities were taken over by ten holding companies and the regulatory bodies and have since been consolidated into the Water Industry Act 1991.

Of the 99 per cent of the population of England and Wales who are connected to a public water supply, 78 per cent are supplied by the water companies (through their principal operating subsidiaries, the water service companies). The remaining 22 per cent are supplied by statutory water companies which were already in the private sector. Most of these have public limited company (PLC) status and many are now in foreign ownership or are part of larger multi-utility companies. They are represented by Water UK, which also represents the ten water service companies responsible for sewerage and sewage disposal in England and Wales, and the state-owned water authorities of Scotland and Northern Ireland. Water UK is the trade association for all the water service companies.

Limited competition exists in the water industry, with large users of water being able to negotiate separate supply arrangements and water services. Discussions are underway to determine the feasibility and future extent of competition.

WATER UK, 1 Queen Anne's Gate, London, SW1H 9BT. Tel: 020-7344 1844 Web: www.water.org.uk. Chief Executive, Ms P. Taylor

Water Service Companies

ANGLIAN WATER SERVICES LTD (part of AWG PLC), Anglian House, Ambury Road, Huntingdon, Cambs PE29 3NZ. Tel: 01480-323000; Web: www.anglianwater.co.uk

DWR CYMRU CYFYNGEDIG (WELSH WATER), Pentwyn Road, Nelson, Treharris, Mid Glamorgan CF46 6LY. Tel: 01443-452300; Web: www.dwrcymru.co.uk

NORTHUMBRIAN WATER LTD (ONDEO GROUP), Abbey Road, Pity Me, Durham DH1 5FJ. Tel: 0191-383 2222; Web: www.nwl.co.uk

SEVERN TRENT PLC, 2297 Coventry Road, Sheldon, Birmingham B26 3PU. Tel: 0121-722 4000; Web: www.severn-trent.com

WATER SUPPLY AND CONSUMPTION 2000–1

	Supply		Consumption			
	Supply from treatment works (*Ml/day*)	Total leakage (*Ml/day*)	Household (*l/head/day*) Unmetered	Non-household (*l/prop/day*) Metered	Unmetered	Metered
WATER SERVICE COMPANIES						
Anglian	1,133.9	194.2	155.2	113.9	564.0	3,267
Dwr Cymru (Welsh)	899.3	260.2	146.9	138.1	754.0	2,486
North West	1,935.3	463.3	140.8	135.1	901.0	4,866
Northumbrian	750.1	163.6	147.6	129.9	703.0	2,689
Severn Trent	1,868.0	340.2	139.9	131.4	600.0	2,269
South West	429.1	83.6	156.8	128.5	824.0	1,617
Southern	578.4	91.7.	158.0	141.7	545.0	2,611
Thames	2,600.3	687.9	166.6	154.4	939.0	3,492
Wessex	373.2	84.2	143.0	130.0	2,401.0	2,389
Yorkshire	1,274.4	304.4	140.2	130.7	146.0	2,822
Total	11,841.9	2,673.2	–	–	–	–
Average	–	–	149.0	131.6	762.5	2,792.1
WATER COMPANIES						
Total	3,149.2	569.6	–	–	–	–
Average	–	–	161.4	142.6	841.6	2,799.4

Source: Office of Water Services

SOUTHERN WATER, Southern House, Yeoman Road,
Worthing, W. Sussex BN13 3NX. Tel: 01903-264444;
Web: www.southernwater.co.uk

SOUTH WEST WATER LTD (part of PENNON GROUP
PLC), Peninsula House, Rydon Lane, Exeter EX2 7HR.
Tel: 01392-446688; Web: www.swwater.co.uk

THAMES WATER UTILITIES LTD (part of RWE),
Gainsborough House, Manor Farm Road, Reading
RG2 0JN. Tel: 0118-959 1159;
Web: www.thames-water.com

UNITED UTILITIES WATER PLC, Dawson House,
Liverpool Road, Great Sankey, Warrington WA5 3LW.
Tel: 01925-234000; Web: www.unitedutilities.com

WESSEX WATER SERVICES LTD, Claverton Down Road,
Claverton Down, Bath BA2 7WW. Tel: 01225-526000;
Web: wessexwater.co.uk

YORKSHIRE WATER SERVICES LTD (part of KELDA
GROUP), Western House, Western Way, Halifax Road,
Bradford BD6 2LZ. Tel: 01274-600111;
Web: www.yorkshirewater.com

REGULATORY BODIES

The Office of Water Services (Ofwat) was set up under
the Water Act 1989 and is the independent economic
regulator of the water and sewerage companies in
England and Wales. Ofwat's main duty is to ensure that
the companies can finance and carry out their statutory
functions and to protect the interests of water customers.
Ofwat is a non-ministerial government department
headed by the Director General of Water Services, who is
appointed by the Secretary of State for Environment,
Food and Rural Affairs and the Secretary of State for
Wales. Under the Competition Act 1998, from 1 March
2000 the Competition Commission has heard appeals
against the regulator's decisions regarding anti-
competitive agreements and abuse of a dominant
position in the marketplace.

The Environment Agency has statutory duties and
powers in relation to water resources, pollution control,
flood defence, fisheries, recreation, conservation and
navigation in England and Wales.

The Drinking Water Inspectorate (DWI) is the drinking
water quality regulator for England and Wales,
responsible for assessing the quality of the drinking water
supplied by the water companies and investigating any
incidents affecting drinking water quality, initiating
prosecution where necessary. The DWI also provides
scientific advice on drinking water policy issues to the
Department of the Environment, Food and Rural Affairs
and the National Assembly for Wales.

METHODS OF CHARGING

In England and Wales, most domestic customers still pay
for domestic water supply and sewerage services through
charges based on the old rateable value of their property.
It is expected that in 2002–3 about 23 per cent of
householders will be charged according to consumption,
which is recorded by meter. Industrial and most
commercial customers are charged according to
consumption.

Under the Water Industry Act 1999, water companies
can continue basing their charges on the old rateable
value of property. Domestic customers can continue
paying on an unmeasured basis unless they choose to pay
according to consumption. After having a meter installed
(which is free of charge), a customer can revert to
unmeasured charging within 12 months. Domestic,
school and hospital customers cannot be disconnected
for non-payment.

In November 1999 Ofwat set new price limits for the
period 2000–5. Ofwat will set price limits for 2005–10 in
November 2004.

SCOTLAND

Overall responsibility for national water policy in
Scotland rested with the Secretary of State for Scotland
until July 1999 when it was devolved to the Scottish
Ministers. Until The Local Government (Scotland) Act
1994, water supply and sewerage services were local
authority responsibilities. The Central Scotland Water
Development Board had the function of developing new
sources of water supply for the purpose of providing
water in bulk to water authorities whose limits of supply
were within the board's area. Under the Act, three new
public water authorities, covering the north, east and west
of Scotland respectively, took over the provision of water
and sewerage services from April 1996. The Central
Scotland Water Development Board was then abolished.
The new authorities were accountable to the Secretary of
State for Scotland, and since July 1999 have been
accountable to the Scottish Ministers. The Act also
established the Scottish Water and Sewerage Customers
Council representing consumer interests. It monitored
the performance of the authorities; approved charges
schemes; investigated complaints; and advised the
Secretary of State. The Water Industry Act 1999, whose
Scottish provisions were accepted by the Scottish
Executive, abolished the Scottish Water and Sewerage
Customers Council and replaced it in November 1999 by
a Water Industry Commissioner.

The Water Industry (Scotland) Act 2002 resulted from
the Scottish Executive's proposal that a single authority
was better placed than three separate authorities to
harmonise changes across the Scottish water industry.
This lead to Scottish Water replacing the three existing
water authorities, East of Scotland Water, North of
Scotland Water and West of Scotland Water, from 31
March 2002. Scottish Water is a public sector company,
structured and managed like a private company, but
remains answerable to the Scottish Parliament. Scottish
Water is regulated by the Water Industry Commissioner
for Scotland, the Scottish Environment Protection
Agency (SEPA), and the Drinking Water Quality
Regulator for Scotland. The Water Industry
Commissioner is responsible for regulating all aspects of
economic and customer service performance, including
water and sewerage charges and SEPA is responsible for
environmental issues, including controlling pollution and
promoting the cleanliness of Scotland's rivers, lochs and
coastal waters.

WATER RESOURCES 1999

	No.	Yield (Ml/day)
Reservoirs and lochs	322	3,099
Feeder intakes	23	–
River intakes	249	452
Bore-holes	45	100
Underground springs	84	27
TOTAL	*723	3,678

* Including compensation reservoirs

WATER CONSUMPTION 1999

Total (Ml/day)	2,363
Potable	2,352.3
Unmetered	1,912.3
Metered	520.2
Non-potable†	10.7
TOTAL (l/head/day)	474.4
Unmetered	383.9
Metered and non-potable†	106.3

† 'Non-potable' supplied for industrial purposes. Metered
supplies in general relate to commercial and industrial use and
unmetered to domestic use
Source: The Scottish Office; *Public Water Supplies in Scotland
1999–2000*

Scottish Water, PO Box 8855, Edinburgh EH10 6YQ.
Tel: 0845-601 8855; Web: www.esw.co.uk
The Water Industry Commissioner for
Scotland, Ochil House, Springkerse Business Park,
Stirling, FK7 7XE. Tel: 01786-430200;
Web: www.watercommissioner.co.uk
Scottish Environment Protection Agency,
Erskine Court, Castle Business Park, Stirling FK9 4TR.
Tel: 01786-457700; Web: www.sepa.org.uk

Methods of Charging

Scottish Water sets charges for domestic and non-domestic water and sewerage provision through charges schemes which have to be approved by the Water Industries Commissioner.

NORTHERN IRELAND

In Northern Ireland ministerial responsibility for water services lies with The Minister of the Department for Regional Development. The Water Service, which is an executive agency of the Department for Regional Development, is responsible for policy and co-ordination with regard to supply, distribution and cleanliness of water, and the provision and maintenance of sewerage services.

The Water Service is divided into four regions, the Eastern, Northern, Western and Southern Divisions. These are based in Belfast, Ballymena, Londonderry and Craigavon respectively.

Methods of Charging

Until last year the Water Service was funded mainly through the regional rate (part of which was appropriated in-aid of the Department) and direct charges principally for metered water. However, the regional rate is no longer appropriated-in-aid and following devolution the Water service is now funded by parliamentary vote and direct charges. All properties which are not exclusively domestic are metered. They are, however, granted an allowance of 200 cubic metres per annum to reflect domestic usage – this is known as the domestic usage allowance. Customers are charged only for water used in excess of the domestic usage allowance together with a standing charge, which is intended to cover the costs of meter provision, maintenance, reading and billing. This allowance is not granted if rates are not paid on the property. Traders operating from rated premises are required to pay for the treatment and disposal of trade effluent which they discharge into the public sewer.

Northern Ireland Water Service, Northland House, 3 Frederick Street, Belfast, BT1 2NR.
Tel: 028-9024 4711; Web: www.doeni.gov.uk/water

Energy

The main primary sources of energy in Britain are oil, natural gas, coal, nuclear power and water power. The main secondary sources (e.g. sources derived from the primary sources) are electricity, coke and smokeless fuels and petroleum products. The Department for the Environment, Food and Rural Affairs (DEFRA) is responsible for promoting energy efficiency.

INDIGENOUS PRODUCTION OF PRIMARY FUELS

Million tonnes of oil equivalent

	2001
Coal	21.0
Petroleum	127.8
Natural gas	105.8
Primary electricity	21.2
Total*	277.6

* Includes renewables

INLAND ENERGY CONSUMPTION BY PRIMARY FUEL

Million tonnes of oil equivalent, seasonally adjusted

	2001
Coal	41.5
Petroleum	76.5
Natural gas	95.1
Primary electricity (mainly nuclear)	22.0
Renewables and waste	2.7
Total	237.7

TRADE IN FUELS AND RELATED MATERIALS 2001

	Quantity*	Value†
IMPORTS		
Coal and other solid fuel	24.8	1,196
Crude petroleum	42.7	5,038
Petroleum products	23.2	3,696
Natural gas	2.4	181
Electricity	0.9	165
Total	94.1	10,276
Total (fob)‡	—	7,195
EXPORTS		
Coal and other solid fuel	0.7	70
Crude petroleum	91.4	10,754
Petroleum products	33.8	4,263
Natural gas	8.4	718
Electricity	—	3
Total	134.3	15,807
Total (fob)‡	—	15,807

* Million tonnes of oil equivalent
† £ million
‡ Adjusted to exclude estimated costs of insurance, freight, etc.
Source: Department of Trade and Industry

OIL

Until the 1960s Britain imported almost all its oil supplies. In 1969 oil was discovered in the Arbroath field of the UK Continental Shelf (UKCS). The first oilfield to be brought into production was the Argyll field in 1975, and since the mid-1970s Britain has been a major producer of crude oil.

Licences for exploration and production are granted to companies by the Department of Trade and Industry; the leading British oil companies are British Petroleum (BP) and Shell. At the end of 2001, 1,030 Seaward Production Licences and 101 onshore Petroleum Exploration and Development Licences had been awarded, and there were 144 offshore oilfields in production. In 2001 there were 9 oil refineries and three smaller refining units processing crude and process oils. There are estimated to be reserves of 1,400 million tonnes of oil remaining in the UKCS. Royalties are payable on fields approved before April 1982 and petroleum revenue tax is levied on fields approved between 1975 and March 1993.

DRILLING ACTIVITY 2001

Number of wells started	Offshore	Onshore
Exploration and appraisal	60	5
Exploration	24	—
Appraisal	36	—
Development	282	20

VALUE OF UKCS OIL AND GAS PRODUCTION AND INVESTMENT

£ million

	2000	2001
Total income	25,518	24,493
Operating costs	4,359	4,335
Gross trading profits*	20,906	20,079
Percentage contribution to GVA	2.6	2.4
Exploration expenditure	348	411
Other Capital investment	2,748	3,509
Percentage contribution to industrial investment	12	15

* Net of stock appreciation

INDIGENOUS PRODUCTION AND REFINERY RECEIPTS

	2000	2001
Indigenous production	126,245	116,679
(thousand tonnes)		
Crude oil	117,882	108,387
NGLs*	8,363	8,292
Refinery receipts (thousand tonnes)		
Indigenous	37,687	29,403
Other†	3,493	4,328
Net foreign imports	45,771	50,613

* Natural gas liquids: condensates and petroleum gases derived at onshore treatment plants
† Mainly recycled products

DELIVERIES OF PETROLEUM PRODUCTS FOR INLAND
CONSUMPTION BY ENERGY USE
Thousand tonnes

	2000	2001
Industry	5,493	6,029
Transport	49,759	48,965
Domestic	2,920	3,164
Other	2,109	2,311
Total	60,281	60,469

Source: Department of Trade and Industry

GAS

From the late 18th-century gas in Britain was produced
from coal. In the 1960s town gas began to be produced
from oil-based feedstocks using imported oil. In 1965 gas
was discovered in the North Sea in the West Sole field,
which became the first gasfield in production in 1967,
and from the late 1960s natural gas began to replace town
gas. Britain is now the world's fourth largest producer of
gas and in 1998 only 1.5 per cent of gas available for
consumption in the UK was imported. From October
1998 Britain was connected to the continental European
gas system via a pipeline from Bacton, Norfolk to
Zeebrugge, Belgium.

By the end of 1998 there were 80 offshore gasfields
producing natural gas and associated gas (mainly
methane). There is estimated to be 1,795,000 million
cubic metres of recoverable gas reserves. There are about
9,419km of major submarine pipelines for transporting
hydrocarbons and onshore pipelines for carrying refined
products and chemicals. Natural gas is transported
around Britain by about 273,000km of pipelines supplied
by seven coastal terminals. This pipeline system is owned
by Transco and licensed gas shippers are allowed access
under a network code. New arrangements for trading
within the pipeline system were introduced on 1 October
1999.

The Office of Gas and Electricity Markets (OFGEM) is
the regulator for the gas industry. It was formed in 1999
by the merger of the Office of Gas Supply and the Office
of Electricity Regulation. Under the Competition Act
1998, from 1 March 2000 the Competition Commission
has heard appeals against the regulator's decisions
regarding anti-competitive agreements and abuse of a
dominant position in the marketplace. In 2002, OFGEM
removed all domestic price controls from British Gas,
allowing competition to regulate prices.

The gas industry in Britain was nationalised in 1949
and operated as the Gas Council. The Gas Council was
replaced by the British Gas Corporation in 1972 and the
industry became more centralised. The British Gas
Corporation was privatised in 1986 as British Gas plc.

In 1993 the Monopolies and Mergers Commission
found that British Gas's integrated business in Great
Britain as a gas trader and the owner of the gas
transportation system could be expected to operate
against the public interest. In February 1997, British Gas
demerged its trading arm to become two separate
companies. BG plc is responsible for the Transco pipeline
business in Britain and oil and gas exploration and
production in the UK and abroad. Centrica plc runs the
trading and services operations under the British Gas
brand name in Great Britain. In October 2000 Transco
became part of Lattice Group plc.

Competition was gradually introduced into the
industrial gas market from 1986. Supply of gas to the
domestic market was opened to companies other than
British Gas, starting in April 1996 with a pilot project in
the West Country and Wales. From spring 1997
competition was progressively introduced throughout the
rest of Britain in stages which were completed in May
1998. With the electricity market also open, many
suppliers now offer their customers both gas and
electricity. Some gas companies have become part of
larger multi-utility companies, often operating
internationally.

NATURAL GAS PRODUCTION AND SUPPLY
GWh

	1999	2000
Gross gas production	1,152,154	1,258,549
Exports	84,433	146,342
Imports	12,862	26,032
Gas available	1,011,157	1,062,187
Gas transmitted‡	1,011,284	1,061,953

‡ Figures differ from gas available mainly because of stock
changes

NATURAL GAS CONSUMPTION
GWh

	1999	2000
Electricity generators	313,319	323,371
Iron and steel industry	22,664	22,383
Other industries	180,950	193,244
Domestic	356,067	373,400
Public administration, commerce and agriculture	121,560	122,277
Total	994,560	1,034,675

Source: Department of Trade and Industry

COAL

Coal has been mined in Britain for centuries and the
availability of coal was crucial to the industrial revolution
of the 18th-and 19th-centuries. Mines were in private
ownership until 1947 when they were nationalised and
came under the management of the National Coal Board,
later the British Coal Corporation. In addition to
producing coal at its own deep-mine and opencast sites,
of which there were 850 in 1955, British Coal was
responsible for licensing private operators.

Under the Coal Industry Act 1994, the Coal Authority
was established to take over ownership of coal reserves
and to issue licences to private mining companies as part
of the privatisation of British Coal. The Coal Authority
also deals with the physical legacy of mining, e.g.
subsidence damage claims, and is responsible for holding
and making available all existing records. The mines were
sold as five separate businesses in 1994 and coal
production in the UK is now undertaken entirely in the
private sector. At the end of March 2002 there were 15
large deep mines in operation.

The main UK customer for coal is the electricity supply
industry. A review of energy policy was undertaken
during 1998 and the Government announced measures
in its October 1998 Energy White Paper which included a
freeze on new applications to build gas-fired power
stations in order to increase opportunities for coal-fired
power stations. The moratorium on new gas-fired power
stations was lifted in 2000 in the light of two measures to

improve the competitiveness of coal fired generation. Firstly the government reached agreement with the European Commission to make available temporary state aid for the coal industry; such aid to end with the termination of the European Coal and Steel Community Treaty in 2002. Secondly there was the reform of the electricity wholesale market and the replacement of The Pool with the New Electricity Trading Arrangements (NETA) which took effect from 27 March 2001.

COAL PRODUCTION AND FOREIGN TRADE

Thousand tonnes

	2000	2001p
Total production	31,198	31,930
Deep-mined	17,188	17,347
Opencast	13,412	14,166
Imports	23,445	35,542
Exports	661	550

p provisional

INLAND COAL USE

Thousand tonnes

	2000	2001
Fuel producers		
Collieries	12	10
Electricity generators	46,201	50,996
Coke ovens and blast furnaces	8,685	7,896
Other conversion industries	1,205	1,205
Final users		
Industry	694	1,743
Domestic	1,907	2,538
Public administration, commerce and agriculture	156	147
Total	58,860	64,535

Source: Department of Trade and Industry

ELECTRICITY

The first power station in Britain generating electricity for public supply began operating in 1882. In the 1930s a national transmission grid was developed and it was reconstructed and extended in the 1950s and 1960s. Power stations were operated by the Central Electricity Generating Board.

Under the Electricity Act 1989, 12 regional electricity companies (RECs), which are responsible for the distribution of electricity from the national grid to consumers, were formed from the former area electricity boards in England and Wales. Four companies were formed from the Central Electricity Generating Board: three generating companies (National Power PLC, Nuclear Electric PLC and PowerGen PLC) and the National Grid Company PLC, which owns and operates the transmission system. National Power and PowerGen were floated on the stock market in 1991. National Power was demerged in October 2000 to form two separate companies: International Power PLC and Innogy PLC, which manages the bulk of National Power's UK assets. Nuclear Electric was split into two parts in 1995; the part comprising the more modern nuclear stations was incorporated into a new company, British Energy, which was floated on the stock market in 1996. Magnox Electric, which owns the magnox nuclear reactors, remained in the public sector and was integrated into British Nuclear Fuels (BNFL) in 1999. Ownership of the National Grid Company was transferred to the RECs and it was subsequently floated in 1995.

Generators and suppliers participate in a competitive wholesale trading market known as NETA (New Electricity Trading Arrangements) which began in March 2001, replacing the Electricity Pool. The introduction of competition into the domestic electricity market was completed in May 1999. With the gas market also open, many suppliers now offer their customers both gas and electricity.

Some electricity companies have bought others and there is a trend towards larger multi-utility companies, often operating internationally.

In Scotland, three new companies were formed under the Electricity Act 1989: Scottish Power PLC and Scottish Hydro-Electric PLC, which are responsible for generation, transmission, distribution and supply; and Scottish Nuclear Ltd. Scottish Power and Scottish Hydro-Electric were floated on the stock market in 1991 (the latter merged with Southern Electric in 1998 to become Scottish and Southern Energy PLC); Scottish Nuclear was incorporated into British Energy in 1995.

In Northern Ireland, Northern Ireland Electricity plc was set up in 1993 under a 1991 Order in Council. It is responsible for transmission, distribution and supply and has been floated on the stock market. There is no Pool in Northern Ireland; three private companies are responsible for electricity generation and the electricity is sold to Northern Ireland Electricity under a series of power purchase agreements.

The Office of Gas and Electricity Markets is the regulator for the electricity industry. It was formed in 1999 by the merger of the Office of Electricity Regulation and the Office of Gas Supply. Under the Competition Act 1998, the Competition Commission hears appeals against the regulator's decisions regarding anti-competitive agreements and abuse of a dominant position in the marketplace.

The Electricity Association is the electricity industry's main trade association, providing representational and professional services for the electricity companies. EA Technology Ltd provides distribution and utilisation research, development and technology transfer.

NUCLEAR POWER

Nuclear reactors began to supply electricity to the national grid in 1956. It is generated at six magnox reactors, seven advanced gas-cooled reactors (AGRs) and one pressurised water reactor (PWR), Sizewell 'B' in Suffolk. Nuclear stations now generate about 17 per cent of the UK's electricity.

In preparation for privatisation, the nuclear industry was restructured in December 1995. A holding company, British Energy PLC, was formed with two operational subsidiaries, Nuclear Electric Ltd and Scottish Nuclear Ltd. Nuclear Electric operates the five AGRs and the PWR in England and Wales; Scottish Nuclear operates the two AGRs in Scotland. British Energy was floated on the stock market in 1996. The Magnox reactors were transferred to Magnox Electric PLC and later to British Nuclear Fuels Ltd (BNFL). BNFL is in public ownership, providing reprocessing, waste management and effluent treatment services. The UK Atomic Energy Authority is responsible for the decommissioning of nuclear reactors and other nuclear facilities used in research and development. UK Nirex, which is owned by the nuclear generating companies and the Government, is responsible for the disposal of intermediate and some low-level nuclear waste. The Nuclear Installations Inspectorate of the Health and Safety Executive is the nuclear industry's regulator.

ELECTRICITY AND GAS SUPPLIERS*
AMERADA, Selectapost 620, Claypit Lane, Leeds LS2 8QL.
Tel: 0845-305 5000
ATLANTIC ELECTRIC & GAS LTD, Southgate House,
Southgate Street, Gloucester GL1 1UW.
Tel: 01452-551155
BG PLC, 100 Thames Valley Park Drive,
Reading RG6 1PT. Tel: 0118-935 3222.
Chairman, R. V. Giordano; *Chief Executive*,
F. Chapman
BRITISH GAS, Helmont House, Churchill Way,
Cardiff CF1 4NB. Tel: 0845-760 0200
CAMBRIDGE GAS & ELECTRICITY COMPANY,
PO Box 79, Cambridge CB3 8GD. Tel: 0845-071 1515
CENTRICA PLC, Millstream, Maidenhead Road,
Windsor, Berkshire SL4 56D Tel: 01753-494000.
Chief Executive, Sir Roy Gardner
COUNTRYWIDE ENERGY, Defford Mill, Earls Croome,
Worcester WR8 9DF. Tel: 01386-757333
CROWN ENERGY, Bury New Road, Heap Bridge, Bury,
Lancashire BL6 7HY. Tel: 0161-797 3334
LATTICE GROUP PLC, 130 Jermyn Street, London SW1
4UR. Tel: 020 7389 3200. *Chairman*, Sir John Parker
LONDON ELECTRICITY GROUP, Admail 1025,
London WC1V 6LA. Tel: 0800-096 9000
NORTH WALES ENERGY/ENERGY SUPPLIES UK LTD,
Packsaddle, Wrexham Road, Rhostyllen,
Wrexham LL14 4EH. Tel: 01978-833233
NORTHERN ELECTRIC & GAS LTD, Carliol House,
Market Street, Newcastle upon Tyne NE1 6NE.
Tel: 08457-199696
NPOWER, Birchfield House, Joseph Street, Oldbury,
West Midlands B69 2AQ. Tel: 0870-161 1031
POWERGEN RETAIL LTD, Raw Dykes Road,
Leicester LE2 7JY. Tel: 0800-363363
SCOTTISH AND SOUTHERN ENERGY PLC,
PO Box 6009, Basingstoke, RG21 8ZH.
Tel: 0845-744 4555
SCOTTISH GAS, 4 Marine Drive, Edinburgh EH5 1YB.
Tel: 0845-708 9502
SCOTTISHPOWER PLC, PO Box 3865, Glasgow G44 4GG.
Tel: 0845-270 0700
SEEBOARD ENERGY LTD, 329 Portland Road, Hove,
East Sussex BN3 5SY. Tel: 0800-056 8888
SOUTH WESTERN ELECTRICITY PLC, Osprey Road,
Sowton, Exeter, Devon, EV2 7HZ.Tel: 08457-650650
SEVERN TRENT ENERGY, Selectapost 640, Claypit Lane,
Leeds LS2 8EW. Tel: 0845-207 7777
TELECOM PLUS PLC, Dryden House, The Edge Business
Centre, Humber Road, London NW2 6EW.
Tel: 020-8955 5555
THE GAS SUPPLY COMPANY, Woolpit Business Park,
Woolpit, Bury St Edmunds, Suffolk IP30 9UQ
TXU ENERGI, Caxton Road, Bedford MK41 0EW.
Tel: 0845-722 6226
UTILITY LINK LTD, 16 Avon Reach, Monkton Hill,
Chippenham, Wiltshire SN15 1EE. Tel: 0845-601 2421
YORKSHIRE ELECTRICITY GROUP PLC, Freepost 2081,
LS1 1PG. Tel: 0800-073 4343
* This list represents just a selection of the companies that
supply gas and electricity.

ELECTRICITY ASSOCIATION LTD, 30 Millbank,
London SW1P 4RD. Tel: 020-7963 5700
EA TECHNOLOGY LTD, Capenhurst, Chester CH1 6ES.
Tel: 0151-339 4181

ELECTRICITY GENERATION, SUPPLY AND
CONSUMPTION
GWh

	1999	2000
Electricity generated: total	368,364	374,900
Major power producers: total	336,486	341,785
Conventional thermal, gas turbines	118,762	131,032
and oil engines		
Nuclear stations	95,133	85,063
Combined cycle gas turbine stations	114,620	117,965
Hydro-electric stations:		
Natural flow	4,431	4,331
Pumped storage	2,902	2,694
Renewables other than hydro	638	700
Other generators	31,878	33,115
Electricity used on works: total	16,693	16,260
Major generating companies	15,338	14,953
Other generators	1,355	1,307
Electricity supplied (gross): total	351,671	358,640
Major power producers: total	321,148	326,832
Conventional thermal, gas turbines	112,920	124,924
and oil engines		
Nuclear stations	87,672	78,334
Combined cycle gas turbine stations	112,768	116,110
Hydro-electric stations:		
Natural flow	4,410	4,316
Pumped storage	2,804	2,603
Renewables other than hydro	574	640
Other generators	30,523	31,808
Electricity used in pumping		
Major power producers	3,774	3,499
Electricity supplied (net): total	345,568	355,141
Major power producers	317,374	323,333
Other generators	30,523	31,808
Net imports	14,244	14,174
Electricity available	362,141	369,315
Losses in transmission, etc.	29,789	30,796
Electricity consumption: total	332,352	338,519
Fuel industries	8,310	8,426
Final users: total	324,042	330,093
Industrial sector	112,128	114,674
Domestic sector	110,308	111,842
Other sectors	101,606	103,577

Source: The Stationery Office – Annual Abstract of Statistics
2002 (Crown Copyright)

RENEWABLE SOURCES

Renewable sources of energy principally include biofuels,
hydro, wind and solar. Renewable sources accounted for
3.1 million tonnes of oil equivalent of primary energy use
in 2001; of this, about 2.4 million tonnes was used to
generate electricity and about 0.7 million tonnes to
generate heat.
    The Non-Fossil Fuel Obligation (NFFO) Renewables
Orders have been the Government's principal mechanism
for developing renewable energy sources. NFFO
Renewables Orders require the regional electricity
companies to buy specified amounts of electricity from
specified non-fossil fuel sources.
    Since February 2000 the United Kingdom's renewables
policy has consisted of four key strands:
– A new obligation for all electricity suppliers in Great
    Britain to supply a specific proportion of electricity
    from eligible renewables.
– The exemption of renewable electricity sources from
    the Climate Change Levy.
– An expanded support programme for new and
    renewable energy, including capital grants and an

expanded research and development programme.
–   Development of a regional strategic approach to
    planning and targets for renewables.
The aim of the Renewables Obligation is to increase the
contribution of electricity from renewables in the United
Kingdom so that by 2010, 10 per cent of licensed UK
electricity sales should be from renewable sources eligible
under the obligation.

RENEWABLE ENERGY SOURCES 2001

	Percentages
Biofuels and wastes	85.6
Landfill gas	27.0
Sewage gas	5.4
Wood combustion	15.1
Straw combustion	4.8
Waste combustion	21.5
Other biofuels	11.8
Hydro	11.3
Large-scale	10.7
Small-scale	0.6
Wind and wave	2.7
Geothermal and active solar heating	0.4
Total	100

Source: Department of Trade and Industry

Transport

CIVIL AVIATION

Since the privatisation of British Airways in 1987, UK airlines have been operated entirely by the private sector. In 2001, total capacity of British airlines amounted to 42 billion tonne-km, of which 32 billion tonne-km was on scheduled services. In 2000 British airlines carried 105.2 million passengers, 71.8 million on scheduled services and 33.4 million on charter flights. After the 11 September terrorist attacks passenger traffic fell by 6 per cent (to December 2001). The five main London airports suffered a 2 per cent drop in passenger traffic during 2001 but regional airports saw a growth of 6 per cent, largely due to the expansion of no-frills airlines. The number of passengers is estimated to be growing at 5 per cent each year.

Leading British airlines include British Airways, Britannia Airways, BMI British Midland, Air 2000, Airtours, JMC, Monarch, Virgin Atlantic, Go Fly and Easyjet.

There are 145 licensed civil aerodromes in Britain, with Heathrow and Gatwick handling the highest volume of passengers. BAA PLC owns and operates the seven major airports: Heathrow, Gatwick, Stansted, Southampton, Glasgow, Edinburgh and Aberdeen, which between them handle about 70 per cent of air passengers and 80 per cent of air cargo traffic in Britain. Many other airports, including Manchester, are controlled by local authorities or private companies.

The Civil Aviation Authority (CAA), an independent statutory body, is responsible for the regulation of UK airlines. This includes economic and airspace regulation, air safety, consumer protection and environmental research and consultancy. All commercial airline companies must be granted an Air Operator's Certificate, which is issued by the CAA to operators meeting the required safety standards. The CAA also issues airport safety licences, which must be obtained by any airport used for public transport and training flights. All British-registered aircraft must be granted an airworthiness certificate, and the CAA also issues professional licences to pilots, flight crew, ground engineers and air traffic controllers. The CAA also manages the Air Travel Organiser's License (ATOL), the UK's principal travel protection scheme. The CAA's costs are met entirely from charges on those whom it regulates, there is no direct Government funding of the CAA's work.

The Transport Act, passed by parliament on 29 November 2000, separated the CAA from its subsidiary, National Air Traffic Services (NATS), which plans and provides air traffic control services throughout the United Kingdom and over the North Atlantic – more than a million square miles – and at most of Britain's major airports. In March 2001, the Airline Group, comprising 7 of Britain's major airlines, was selected by the government as its strategic partner for NATS. The Airline Group plans to invest 1 billion of private capital in NATS over 10 years. In July 2001, under the terms of a Public Private Partnership, 46 per cent of shares in NATS were sold to The Airline Group, 5 per cent to staff and 49 per cent were retained by the government.

AIR PASSENGERS 2001*

ALL UK AIRPORTS: TOTAL	182,317,425
LONDON AREA AIRPORTS: TOTAL	113,790,381
Battersea Heliport	5,259
Gatwick (BAA)	31,181,770
Heathrow (BAA)	60,764,924
London City	1,618,833
Luton	6,555,155
Southend	4,366
Stansted (BAA)	13,665,333
OTHER UK AIRPORTS: TOTAL	68,521,785
Aberdeen (BAA)	2,529,218
Barra	8,512
Barrow-in-Furness	54
Belfast City	1,192,897
Belfast International	3,618,671
Benbecula (HIAL)†	34,235
Biggin Hill	3,611
Birmingham	7,808,562
Blackpool	80,501
Bournemouth	265,758
Bristol	2,694,464
Cambridge	18,245
Campbeltown (HIAL)	8,164
Cardiff	1,543,782
Carlisle	75
Coventry	1,485
Dundee	49,183
East Midlands	2,387,060
Edinburgh (BAA)	6,067,333
Exeter	344,025
Glasgow (BAA)	7,292,327
Gloucestershire	64
Hawarden	3,175
Humberside	435,473
Inverness (HIAL)	363,704
Islay (HIAL)	19,586
Isle of Man	706,985
Kent International	5,921
Kirkwall (HIAL)	93,857
Leeds/Bradford	1,530,227
Lerwick (Tingwall)	1,971
Liverpool	2,253,398
Londonderry	187,519
Lydd	65
Manchester	19,307,261
Newcastle upon Tyne	3,431,393
Norwich	390,460
Penzance Heliport	128,044
Plymouth	171,908
Prestwick	1,240,004
St Mary's, Isles of Scilly	133,333
Scatsta	247,131
Sheffield City	32,956
Shoreham	924
Southampton (BAA)	857,670
Stornoway (HIAL)	87,933
Sumburgh (HIAL)	137,490
Teesside	733,617
Tiree (HIAL)	5,309
Tresco, Isles of Scilly (Heliport)	40,286
Unst	252
Wick (HIAL)	25,707

CHANNEL IS. AIRPORTS: TOTAL   2,542,793
    Alderney   72,111
    Guernsey   911,022
    Jersey   1,559,660
*Total terminal, transit, scheduled and charter passengers

† Highlands and Islands Airports Ltd

Source: Civil Aviation Authority

RAILWAYS

Britain pioneered railways and a railway network was developed across Britain by private companies in the course of the 19th-century. In 1948 the main railway companies were nationalised and were run by a public authority, the British Transport Commission. The Commission was replaced by the British Railways Board in 1963, operating as British Rail. On 1 April 1994, responsibility for managing the track and railway infrastructure passed to a newly-formed company, Railtrack; the British Railways Board continued as operator of all train services until 1996–7 when they were sold or franchised to the private sector.

OTHER RAIL SYSTEMS

Plans for a public-private partnership (PPP) for London Underground were pushed through by the government in February 2002 despite opposition from the Mayor of London and a range of transport organisations. Under PPP London Underground will remain responsible for all aspects of operations and safety, in the public sector. Three long-term contracts for maintenance and renewal of infrastructure will be awarded to private sector companies. There are two groupings of 'deep tube' lines and one group for the sub-surface lines. A proposed £13 billion is to be invested in overhauling the rail network over the first 15 years of the scheme. In 2001–2 there were 953 million passenger journeys on the London Underground, down 2 per cent on the previous year.

Britain has seven other metro systems; those in Birmingham, Glasgow, Newcastle, Manchester, Sheffield and the Croydon Tramlink and Docklands Light Railway in London. The latest to open was the Croydon Tramlink in May 2000.

Light rail and metro systems in Great Britain contributed to the growth in public transport, with 134 million passenger journeys in 2000–1, up 23 per cent on the previous year. The Government's 10-year Transport Plan target is to double light rail use in England over the next decade. The Nottingham Express Transit (NET) and Leeds Supertram are currently under construction.

RAIL REGULATOR

Under the Railways Act 1993 and the Transport Act 2000 the Rail Regulator exercises statutory powers to regulate the national rail infrastructure network (track, signalling, bridges, tunnels and stations). The network is operated under a network licence, which is issued by the Government but enforced by the Regulator who is independent of the Government. The Regulator also ensures the network provider has the necessary funds to maintain, renew and expand the network, that all train operators are ensured fair access to the network and under the Competition Act 1998, prevents anti-competitive practices.

Regulations, which took effect on 28 June 1998, established licensing and access arrangements for certain international train services in Great Britain; these are overseen by the International Rail Regulator.

The Strategic Rail Authority (SRA) was created to provide strategic leadership to the rail industry and formally came into being on 1 February 2001 following the passing of the Transport Act 2000. In addition to its co-ordinating role, the SRA is responsible for allocating Government funding to the railways, awarding and monitoring the franchises for operating rail services, as well as a number of other statutory functions; particularly relating to customer protection.

SERVICES

For privatisation, domestic passenger services were divided into 25 train-operating units, which have been franchised to private sector operators via a competitive tendering process overseen by the Strategic Rail Authority (SRA). The franchise agreements were for between five and 15 years. The Government continues to subsidise loss-making but socially necessary rail services. The SRA is responsible for monitoring the performance of the franchisees, allocating and administering government subsidy payments, proposing closures to the Rail Regulator and designating experimental services.

There are currently 25 train operating companies (TOCs): Anglia Railways; Arriva Trains Merseyside; Arriva Trains Northern; c2c; Central Trains; Chiltern Railways; Connex South Eastern; First Great Eastern; First Great Western; First North Western; Gatwick Express; Great North Eastern Railway; Island Line (Isle of Wight); Midland Mainline; Scotrail; Silverlink; South Central; South West Trains; Thameslink; Thames Trains; Virgin Crosscountry; Virgin West Coast; Wales and Borders; Wessex Trains and West Anglia Great Northern Railway.

In addition to these 25 franchised TOCs, Eurostar and Eurotunnel provide services through the channel tunnel, but are not subject to the franchise process. The first phase of the Channel Tunnel high-speed link through Kent is due to open in 2003 and the second stage through to St Pancras is due to open in 2007. The Heathrow Express service is a subsidiary of the airports group BAA. The SRA is currently reviewing the franchising process.

Railtrack publishes a national timetable which contains details of rail services operated over the Railtrack network, coastal shipping information and connections with Ireland, the Isle of Man, the Isle of Wight, the Channel Islands and some European destinations.

The national rail enquiries service offers information about train times and fares for any part of the country:

National Rail Enquiries   08457-484950;
                            Web: www.nationalrail.co.uk
Transport for London   020-7941 4500;
                    Web: www.transportforlondon.gov.uk
Eurostar   08705-186186;
                                Web: www.eurostar.com

Rail Users' Consultative Committees monitor the policies and performance of train and station operators in their area (there are nine, covering Britain). They are statutory bodies and have a legal right to make recommendations for changes. The London Regional Passengers Committee represents users of buses, the Underground, Croydon Tramlink and the Docklands Light Railway as well as the users of rail services in the London area. In summer 2000 the Greater London Assembly and Mayor established Transport for London with a view to developing a strategy for transport in the capital.

On privatisation, British Rail's bulk freight haulage companies and Rail Express Systems, which carries Royal Mail traffic, were sold to English, Welsh and Scottish Railways (EWS), which also purchased Railfreight Distribution (international freight) in 1997. In 2000–1 95.4 million tonnes of freight was transported by EWS and other freight companies, using an average of 1,600 trains a day.

RAILTRACK, Railtrack House, Euston Square, London NW1 2EE. Tel: 020-7557 8000. Web: www.railtrack.co.uk *Chairman*, J. Robinson. *Chief Executive*, J. Armitt
ASSOCIATION OF TRAIN OPERATING COMPANIES, 40 Bernard Street, London WC1N 1BY. Tel: 020-7904 3010. Web: www.atoc.org.uk *Chairman*, C. Garnett
OFFICE OF THE RAIL REGULATOR (ORR) 1 Waterhouse Square, 138–142 Holborn, London EC1N 2TQ. Tel: 020-7282 2000. Web: www.rail-reg.gov.uk *Rail Regulator*, T. Winsor
STRATEGIC RAIL AUTHORITY, 55 Victoria Street, London, SW1H 0EU. Tel: 020-7654 6000 Web: www.sra.gov.uk *Chairman*, R. Bowker

RAILTRACK

At 31 March 2001, Railtrack had about 20,000 miles of standard gauge lines and sidings in use, representing 10,347 miles of route of which 3,210 miles were electrified. Standard rail on main line has a weight of 110 lb per yard. Railtrack owns around 2,500 stations, 90 light maintenance depots, about 40,000 bridges, viaducts and tunnels, and over 9,000 level crossings.

Passenger journeys made in 2000–1 totalled 957 million, including 407 million made by season ticket holders. This national total was the largest since the early 1960s. Passenger kilometres in the year totalled 38.7 billion, earning a total revenue of £3,413 million. On 5 October 2001, Railtrack PLC was put into administration under the Railways Act 1993. Ernst and Young were appointed as Railway Administrators.

RAIL SAFETY

The Railways (Safety Case) Regulations 1994 require infrastructure controllers (e.g. Railtrack, London Underground) to have systems in place to manage safety on the railway networks for which they are responsible. Each infrastructure controller is required to present a Railway Safety Case (RSC) to the Railway Inspectorate (part of the Health and Safety Executive). The RSC must be accepted by the Inspectorate, and is subject to regular compliance audits.

The infrastructure controllers require companies wishing to operate services to present an RSC. The RSC must be accepted by the infrastructure controller before a train or station operator can receive a licence and begin to provide services. If any revision is required, the RSC must be re-presented. RSCs must be thoroughly reviewed at least every three years. The Inspectorate may examine the RSC of train and service operators as part of its general inspection activities.

Following consultation the Railways (Safety Case) Regulations were amended to transfer the responsibility for acceptance of RSCs of train and station operators from the infrastructure controllers to the Health and Safety Executive. The new regulations and guidance came into force on 31 December 2000.

ACCIDENTS ON RAILWAYS

	1999–2000	2000–2001
Train accidents: total	1,893	1,801
Persons killed: total	33	17
Passengers	29	10
Railway staff	2	4
Others	2	3
Persons injured: total	332	252
Passengers	290	188
Railway staff	23	46
Others	19	18
Other accidents through movement of railway vehicles		
Persons killed	27	17
Persons injured	908	949
Other accidents on railway premises		
Persons killed	5	5
Passengers	4	3
Railway staff	1	1
Others	0	1
Persons injured	3,992	4,130
Trespassers and suicides		
Persons killed	274	299
Persons injured	144	177

Source: Department for Transport

THE CHANNEL TUNNEL

The earliest recorded scheme for a submarine transport connection between Britain and France was in 1802. Tunnelling has begun simultaneously on both sides of the Channel three times: in 1881, in the early 1970s, and on 1 December 1987, when construction workers began to bore the first of the three tunnels which form the Channel Tunnel. They 'holed through' the first tunnel (the service tunnel) on 1 December 1990 and tunnelling was completed in June 1991. The tunnel was officially inaugurated by The Queen and President Mitterrand of France on 6 May 1994.

The submarine link comprises three tunnels. There are two rail tunnels, each carrying trains in one direction, which measure 24.93 ft (7.6 m) in diameter. Between them lies a smaller service tunnel, measuring 15.75 ft (4.8 m) in diameter. The service tunnel is linked to the rail tunnels by 130 cross-passages for maintenance and safety purposes. The tunnels are 31 miles (50 km) long, 24 miles (38 km) of which is under the sea-bed at an average depth of 132 ft (40 m). The rail terminals are situated at Folkestone and Calais, and the tunnels go underground at Shakespeare Cliff, Dover, and Sangatte, west of Calais.

Eurostar is the high speed passenger train connecting London with Paris in three hours and Brussels in two hours 40 minutes, via the Channel Tunnel. There are up to 24 trains each way per day on the Paris route and eight each way per day on the Brussels route. Some trains stop en route at Ashford (Kent), Calais and Lille. Vehicle shuttle services operate between Folkestone and Calais.

RAIL LINKS

The route for the British Channel Tunnel Rail Link will run from Folkestone to a new terminal at St Pancras station, London, with new intermediate stations at Ebbsfleet, Kent, and Stratford, East London; at present services run into a terminal at Waterloo station, London.

Construction of the rail link is being financed by the private sector with a substantial government contribution. A private sector consortium, London and Continental Railways Ltd (LCR), is responsible for the design, construction and ownership of the rail link, and comprises Union Railways and the UK operator of

Eurostar. Construction was expected to be completed in 2003, but on 28 January 1998 LCR informed the Government that it was unable to fulfil its obligations. On 3 June 1998 the Government announced a new funding agreement with LCR. The rail link will be constructed in two phases: phase one, from the Channel Tunnel to Fawkham Junction (where an existing connection allows trains to continue to Waterloo), began in October 1998 and will be completed in 2003; phase two, from Fawkham Junction to St Pancras, will be built between 2001 and 2007. Infrastructure developments in France have been completed and high-speed trains run from Calais to Paris and from Lille to the South of France.

ROADS

HIGHWAY AUTHORITIES

The powers and responsibilities of highway authorities in England and Wales are set out in the Highways Act 1980; for Scotland there is separate legislation.

Responsibility for trunk road motorways and other trunk roads in Great Britain rests in England with the Secretary of State for Transport, in Scotland with the Scottish Executive, and in Wales with the Welsh Assembly. The costs of construction, improvement and maintenance are paid for by central government in England and by the Welsh Assembly in Wales. The highway authority for non-trunk roads in England, Wales and Scotland is, in general, the local authority in whose area the roads lie. With the establishment of the Greater London Authority in July 2000, Transport for London became the highway authority for all former trunk roads in London.

In Northern Ireland the Department for Regional Development is the statutory road authority responsible for public roads and their maintenance and construction; the Roads Service carries out these functions on behalf of the Department.

FINANCE

In England all aspects of trunk road and motorway funding are provided directly by the Government to the Highways Agency which operates, maintains and improves the trunk road network on behalf of the Secretary of State. For the financial year 2002–3 the Highways Agency was allocated £1,680 million of which £740 million was for maintenance, £698 million for major new roads including private finance payments and £242 million on smaller improvements and traffic management measures.

Central Government support for local authority capital expenditure on roads and other transport infrastructure is provided through grant and credit approvals as part of the Local Transport Plan (LTP). Local Authorities bid for resources on the basis of a five-year programme built around delivering integrated transport strategies. As well as covering the structural maintenance of local roads and the construction of major new road schemes, LTP funding also includes smaller-scale safety and traffic management measures with associated improvements for public transport, cyclists and pedestrians.

For the financial year 2001–2 local authorities were allocated £39 million in the form of a Transport Supplementary Grant, a £19 million public Transport Liabilities Grant and £1,178 million in credit approvals including Annual Capital Guidelines. For 2000–1 the estimated outturn figure was £759 million. The costs of repayment and interest on the borrowing are funded through the Revenue Support Grant Settlement (RSG).

Support for the routine maintenance of local roads is also provided through the RSG system. For 2002–3 the amount identified for local highway maintenance by Central Government was £1,955 million (£1,905 million in 2001–2). However, RSG is a general, unhypothecated grant and local authorities set their own spending priorities.

In Wales total expenditure on trunk roads, motorways and transport services in 2000–1 was £117.9 million and estimated expenditure in 2001–2 is £131.2 million.

Until 1999 the Scottish Office received a block vote from Parliament and the Secretary of State for Scotland determined how much was spent on roads. Since 1 July 1999 all decisions on transport expenditure have been devolved to the Scottish Executive. Total planned expenditure on building and maintaining trunk roads in Scotland was estimated at £205.7 million in 2001–2.

In Northern Ireland estimated expenditure on roads for 2001–2 was £180.9 million and £191.1 million has been allocated for expenditure in 2002–3.

The Transport Act 2000 gave Welsh and English local authorities (outside London) powers to introduce road user charging or workplace parking levy schemes. The Act requires that the net revenue raised is used to improve local transport services and facilities for at least ten years. The aim is to reduce congestion and encourage greater use of alternative modes of transport. Schemes developed by local authorities require Government approval. The Government's Ten-Year Plan for Transport assumes that 8 large road user charging and 12 large workplace parking levy schemes will be developed by 2010. Charging schemes in London are allowed under the 1999 Greater London Authority Act.

PRIVATE FINANCE

Private finance is being increasingly used to help finance road schemes. The current targeted programme of road improvements plans to design, build, finance and operate road contracts with a capital value of £360 million which will deliver five of the road schemes in the Government's targeted programme of improvements. In Scotland the M77 and Glasgow Southern Orbital Road is a £100 million joint Private Public Partnership (PPP) with East Renfrewshire Council.

TARGETED PROGRAMME OF IMPROVEMENTS (TPI)

The 1998 Roads Review increased the emphasis given to making better use of the existing road network and improving road maintenance. In addition a carefully targeted programme of major trunk road improvements was announced. This currently contains 55 schemes with the value of around £26 billion. The first scheme, the A27 Polegate Bypass, opened in June 2002. A series of studies are also underway looking at transport problems across all modes. Road schemes that emerge from these studies will be progressed through the regional planning guidance (RPG) system. This is now the method by which truck road schemes will enter the TPI.

ROAD LENGTHS
(in miles) 2001

	Total roads	Trunk roads (including Motorways)	Motorways*
England	177,420	6,598	1,804
Wales	20,932	1,061	82
Scotland	33,121	2,024	229
N. Ireland	15,691	781	83

*There were in addition 26.1 miles of local authority motorways in England

MOTORWAYS

England and Wales:

M1	London to Yorkshire
M2	London to Faversham
M3	London to Southampton
M4	London to South Wales
M5	Birmingham to Exeter
M6	Catthorpe to Carlisle
M10	St Albans spur
M11	London to Cambridge
M18	Rotherham to Goole
M20	London to Folkestone
M23	London to Gatwick
M25	London orbital
M26	M20 to M25 spur
M27	Southampton bypass
M32	M4 to Bristol spur
M40	London to Birmingham
M41	London to West Cross
M42	South-west of Birmingham to Measham
M45	Dunchurch spur
M50	Ross spur
M53	Chester to Birkenhead
M54	M6 to Telford
M55	Preston to Blackpool
M56	Manchester to Chester
M57	Liverpool outer ring
M58	Liverpool to Wigan
M60	Manchester ring road
M61	Manchester to Preston
M62	Liverpool to Hull
M65	Calder Valley
M67	Manchester Hyde to Denton
M69	Coventry to Leicester
M180	South Humberside

Scotland:

M8	Edinburgh-Newhouse, Baillieston-West Ferry Interchange
M9	Edinburgh to Dunblane
M73	Maryville to Mollinsburn
M74	Glasgow-Gretna
M77	Ayr Road Route
M80	Stirling to Haggs/Glasgow (M8) to Stepps
M90	Inverkeithing to Perth
M876	Dennyloanhead (M80) to Kincardine Bridge

Northern Ireland:

M1	Belfast to Dungannon
M2	Belfast to Antrim
M2	Ballymena bypass
M3	Belfast Cross Harbour Bridge
M5	M2 to Greencastle
M12	M1 to Craigavon
M22	Antrim to Randalstown

ROAD USE

ESTIMATED TRAFFIC ON ALL ROADS
(GREAT BRITAIN) 2000

Million vehicle kilometres

All motor vehicles	468,700
Cars and taxis	380,400
Two-wheeled motor vehicles	4,400
Buses and coaches	4,900
Light vans	50,300
Other goods vehicles	28,600
Total goods vehicles	78,900
Pedal cycles	4,100

ROAD GOODS TRANSPORT (GREAT BRITAIN) 2000

Analysis by mode of working and by gross weight of vehicle

Estimated tonne kilometres (thousand million)	150.5
Own account	37.5
Public haulage	113.0
By gross weight of vehicle (billion tonne kilometres)	
Estimated tonnes lifted (millions)	1,593
Own account	556
Public haulage	1038
By gross weight of vehicle (million tonnes)	
Not over 25 tonnes	325
Over 25 tonnes	1,268

ROAD PASSENGER SERVICES

Until 1988 most road passenger transport services in Great Britain were provided by the public sector; the National Bus Company was the largest bus and coach operator in England and Wales and the Scottish Bus Group the largest operator in Scotland. The privatisation of the National Bus Company was completed in 1988 and that of the Scottish Bus Group in 1991. London Transport's bus operating subsidiaries were privatised by the end of 1994. Almost all bus and coach services in Great Britain are now provided by private sector companies.

Bus services outside London were deregulated in 1986, although local authorities can subsidise the provision of socially necessary services after competitive tendering. In London, Transport for London retains overall responsibility for the running of the bus network.

The largest bus operators in Great Britain are Stagecoach Holdings, First Group (formerly FirstBus) and Arriva (formerly Cowie British Bus), which between them account for over 50 per cent of all bus services (by turnover). There are also 17 municipal bus companies in the UK, and thousands of smaller private sector operators. National Express runs a national network of coach routes, operating through a number of contractors.

In Northern Ireland, almost all passenger transport services are provided by Ulsterbus Limited and Citybus Limited, two wholly owned subsidiaries of the Northern Ireland Transport Holding Company. Along with Northern Ireland Railways, Ulsterbus and Citybus operate under the brand name of Translink and are publicly owned. Ulsterbus operates long distance, rural, town and Londonderry City bus services while Citybus provide the bulk of internal bus services in Greater Belfast. There are also 136 small private sector operators.

The Transport Act 2000 outlines a 10-year transport plan intended to promote bus use, through agreements between local authorities and bus operators and to improve the standard and efficiency of services. The 10-year plan sets targets for bus patronage and reliability of services in England.

There are about 70,000 licensed taxis in Great Britain, of which about 20,000 are in London. There are also around 83,000 licensed private hire vehicles in England and Wales outside London, and an estimated 60,000 in London (where there has been no licensing system). The Greater London Assembly and Mayor control the licensing of taxis and private hire vehicles, through the Public Carriage Office. Licensing of private hire vehicle operators in London is in progress.

BUSES AND COACHES (GREAT BRITAIN) 1999–2000

Number of vehicles (31 March 2000)	80,000
Vehicle kilometres (millions)	4,016
Local bus passenger journeys (millions)	4,279
Passenger receipts (£ million)	4,043

ROAD SAFETY

The Government in 1987 set a target of reducing road traffic casualties by a third by the year 2000 compared to the average for 1981–5. Measures to achieve this were successful in reducing the number of deaths on the road by 39 per cent by 2000, and the number of serious casualties by 49 per cent. The total number of casualties, however, fell only very slightly because of a 16 per cent rise in slight injuries. Nevertheless, this represented a 37 per cent fall in the casualty rate due to a 57 per cent rise in traffic over the same period.

In March 2000, the Government published a new road safety strategy, *Tomorrow's Roads – Safer for Everyone*, which set new casualty reduction targets for 2010. The new targets include a 40 per cent reduction in the overall number of people killed or seriously injured in road accidents, a 50 per cent reduction in the number of children killed or seriously injured and a 10 per cent reduction in the slight casualty rate, all compared with the average for 1994–8.

ROAD ACCIDENT CASUALTIES 2001*

	Fatal	Serious	Slight	All Severities
England	2,909	32,164	244,354	279,427
Wales	187	1,535	12,053	13,775
Scotland	347	3,395	16,102	19,844
Great Britain	3,443	37,094	272,509	313,046

	Killed	Injured
1965	7,952	389,985
1970	7,499	355,869
1975	6,366	318,584
1980	6,010	323,000
1985	5,165	312,359
1990	5,217	335,924
1995	3,621	306,885
1996	3,598	316,704
1997	3,599	323,945
1998	3,421	321,791
1999	3,423	316,887
2000	3,409	316,872
2001*	3,443	309,603

* Provisional

Source: Department for Transport

DRIVING LICENCES

It is necessary to hold a valid full licence in order to drive unaccompanied on public roads in the UK. Learner drivers must obtain a provisional driving licence before starting to learn to drive and must then pass theory and practical tests to obtain a full driving licence.

There are separate tests for motor cycles, cars, passenger-carrying vehicles (PCVs) and large goods vehicles (LGVs). Drivers must hold full car entitlement before they can apply for PCV or LGV entitlements.

The Driver and Vehicle Licensing Agency (DVLA) no longer issues paper licences, however, those currently in circulation will remain valid until they expire or the details on them change. The photocard driving licence was introduced to comply with the second EC directive on driving licences. This requires a photograph of the driver to be included on all UK licences issued from July 2001. In March 2000 the DVLA ceased issuing paper licences and over 15.5 million photocards have since been issued. Some 39 million people in the UK (21 million male, 18 million female) hold either a valid provisional or full driving licence.

To apply for a first photocard driving licence, individuals are required to complete the forms *Application for a Driving Licence* (D1) and *Application for a Photocard Driving Licence* (D750). Application forms are available from post offices.

The minimum age for driving motor cars, light goods vehicles up to 3.5 tonnes and motor cycles is 17 (moped, 16). Since June 1997, drivers who collect six or more penalty points within two years of qualifying lose their licence and are required to take another test. A leaflet, *What You Need to Know About Driving Licences* (form D100), is available from post offices.

The DVLA is responsible for issuing driving licences, registering and licensing vehicles, and collecting excise duty in Great Britain. In Northern Ireland the Driver and Vehicle Licensing Agency (Northern Ireland) has similar responsibilities.

DRIVING LICENCE FEES *as at 1 April 2002*

First provisional licence	£29.00
Changing a provisional to a full licence after passing a driving test	£12.00
Renewal of licence	£6.00
Renewal of licence including PCV or LGV entitlements	£29.00
Renewal after disqualification	£35.00
Renewal after drinking and driving disqualification	£50.00
Medical renewal	Free
Medical renewal (over 70)	Free
Duplicate Licence	£17.00
Exchange licence	£18.00
Removing endorsements	£18.00
Replacement (change of name or address)	Free

DRIVING TESTS

The Driving Standards Agency is responsible for carrying out driving tests and approving driving instructors in Great Britain. In Northern Ireland the Driver and Vehicle Testing Agency (Northern Ireland) is responsible for testing drivers and vehicles.

In 2000–2001, almost 1.1 million driving tests were conducted, resulting in 480,017 passes which equals a 43.92 per cent pass rate. 61,776 vocational tests (lorries and buses) were taken, the pass rate was 52.01 per cent. In the motorcycle category, almost 91,000 tests were taken with a pass rate of 66.19 per cent. In the same period 1.3 million theory tests were conducted. At the end of 2001 there were 29,962 people on the Register of Approved Driving Instructors.

Since 1 March 1997 driving test candidates have been required to produce photographic confirmation of their identity.

DRIVING TEST FEES (weekday rate/evening and Saturday rate) *since August 2001*

For cars	£38.00/£47.00
†For motor cycles	£46.50/£56.00
For lorries, buses	£76.00/£94.00
Extended Test for cars (after disqualification)	£76.00/£94.00
Extended Test for motorcycles (after disqualification)	£93.00/£112.00
Motorcycle Compulsory Basic Training (CBT)	£8.00
Theory Test for all categories	£15.50

MOTOR VEHICLES

Vehicles must be licensed by the DVLA or the DVLNI before they can be driven on public roads. They must also be approved as roadworthy by the Vehicle Certification Agency. The Vehicle Inspectorate carries out annual testing and inspection of goods vehicles, buses and coaches.

There were approximately 27 million vehicles licensed at the DVLA at March 2001: (approximate figures)

Private and light goods	23,900,000
Motor cycles, scooters, mopeds	800,000
Coaches and buses	83,500
Large goods vehicles	450,000
Electric vehicles	10,200
Others	1,750,000
TOTAL:	27,000,000

Source: DVLA

VEHICLES LICENCES

Registration and first licensing of vehicles is through local offices of the Driver and Vehicle Licensing Agency in Swansea. Local facilities for relicensing are available at any post office which deals with vehicle licensing. Applicants will need to take their vehicle registration document; if this is not available the applicant must complete form V62 which is held at post offices. Postal applications can be made to the post offices shown in the V100 booklet, available at any post office. This V100 also provides guidance on registering and licensing vehicles.

Details of the present duties chargeable on motor vehicles are available at post offices and Local Offices. The Vehicle Excise and Registration Act 1994 provides *inter alia* that any vehicle kept on a public road but not used on roads is chargeable to excise duty as if it were in use. All non-commercial vehicles constructed before 1 January 1973 are exempt from vehicle excise duty.

VEHICLE EXCISE DUTY RATES *from 1 May 2002*
REGISTERED BEFORE 1 MARCH 2001

	Twelve months £	Six months £
Motor Cars		
Light vans, cars, taxis, etc		
Under 1549cc	105.00	57.75
Over 1549cc	160.00	88.00
Motor Cycles		
With or without sidecar, not over 150cc	15.00	–
151-400 cc	30.00	–
401-600 cc	45.00	–
Over 600 cc	60.00	–
Tricycles (not over 450 kg unladen)		
Not over 150cc	15.00	–
All others	60.00	33.00
*Buses**		
Seating 9–16 persons	165.00	90.75
	(160.00)	(88.00)
Seating 17-35	220.00	121.00
	(160.00)	(88.00)
Seating 36-60	330.00	181.50
	(160.00)	(88.00)
Seating over 60 persons	500.00	275.00
	(160.00)	(88.00)

* Figures in parentheses refer to reduced pollution vehicles.

REGISTERED ON OR AFTER 1 MARCH 2001

	Diesel Car		
Band	CO^2 Emissions (g/km)	12 month rate £	6 month rate £
A	Up to 120	80.00	44.00
B	121-150	110.00	60.50
C	151-165	130.00	71.50
D	166-185	150.00	82.50
E	Over 185	160.00	88.00

Petrol Car		Alternative Fuel Car	
12 month rate £	6 month rate £	12 month rate £	6 month rate £
70.0	38.50	60.00	33.00
100.00	55.00	90.00	49.50
120.00	66.00	110.00	60.50
140.00	77.00	130.00	71.50
155.00	82.25	150.00	82.50

MoT TESTING

Cars, motor cycles, motor caravans, light goods and dual-purpose vehicles more than three years old must be covered by a current MoT test certificate. However, some vehicles i.e. minibuses may require a certificate at one year old. All certificates must be renewed annually. The MoT testing scheme is administered by the Vehicle Inspectorate on behalf of the Secretary of State for Transport.

A fee is payable to MoT testing stations, which must be authorised to carry out tests. The maximum fees, which are prescribed by regulations, are:

For cars and light vans	£37.60	
For solo motor cycles	£14.25	
For motor cycle combinations	£23.50	
For three-wheeled vehicles	£27.50	
Private passenger vehicles and ambulances		
With 9-12 passenger seats	£39.75	£44.70*
13-16 passenger seats	£43.35	£55.95*
Over 16 passenger seats	£52.35	£87.30*
For light goods vehicles between 3,000 and 3,500 kg	£39.20	

*Including seatbelt installation check

METHOD OF TRAVEL TO WORK, *Great Britain* *(percentage*)*

	1997	2002
Car, van, minibus, works van	71	70
Bus, coach, private bus	8	8
Train (incl. Underground and light rail)	6	7
Walk	11	11
Other	5	5
All	100	100

* All figures are rounded

Source: DfT/The Stationery Office - *Transport Statistics Great Britain* (Crown copyright)

SHIPPING AND PORTS

Since earliest times sea trade has played a central role in Britain's economy. By the 17th-century Britain had built up a substantial merchant fleet and by the early 20th century it dominated the world shipping industry. In recent years the size and tonnage of the UK-registered trading fleet has declined; the UK-flagged merchant fleet now constitutes about 1 per cent of the world fleet. In December 1998 the Government published a document,

British Shipping: Charting a New Course, which outlined strategies to promote the long-term interests of British shipping.

Freight is carried by liner and bulk services, almost all scheduled liner services being containerised. About 95 per cent by weight of Britain's overseas trade is carried by sea; this amounts to 75 per cent of its total value. Passengers and vehicles are carried by roll-on, roll-off ferries, hovercraft, hydrofoils and high-speed catamarans. There were about 49 million ferry passengers a year in 2000, of whom 28 million travelled internationally. The leading British operators of passenger services are P&O Stena, Stena Line (which has a Swedish parent company) and P&O European Ferries.

Lloyd's of London provides the most comprehensive shipping intelligence service in the world. Lloyd's Shipping Index, published daily, lists some 25,000 ocean-going vessels and gives the latest known report of each.

PORTS

There are about 100 commercially significant ports in Great Britain, including such ports as London, Dover, Forth, Tees and Hartlepool, Grimsby and Immingham, Sullom Voe, Milford Haven, Southampton, Felixstowe and Liverpool. Belfast is the principal freight port in Northern Ireland.

Broadly speaking, ports are owned and operated by private companies, local authorities or trusts. The largest operator is Associated British Ports (formerly the British Transport Docks Board, privatised in 1981), which owns 23 ports. Total traffic through UK ports in 2001 amounted to 566 million tonnes, a decrease of 1 per cent on the previous year's figure of 573 million tonnes.

MARINE SAFETY

By 1 October 2002 all roll-on, roll-off ferries operating to and from the UK will be required to meet the new international safety standards on stability established by the Stockholm Agreement.

The Maritime and Coastguard Agency (MCA) was established on 1 April 1998 by the merger of the Coastguard Agency and the Marine Safety Agency. It is an executive agency of the Department for Transport, Local Government and the Regions. The Agency's aims are to minimise loss of life amongst seafarers and coastal users, respond to maritime emergencies 24 hours a day, develop, promote and enforce high standards of marine safety and to minimise the risk of pollution of the marine environment from ships and where pollution occurs, minimise the impact on UK interests. Each year HM Coastguard respond to around 12,000 incidents, rescuing around 5,000 people. Locations hazardous to shipping in coastal waters are marked by lighthouses and other lights and buoys. The lighthouse authorities are the Corporation of Trinity House (for England, Wales and the Channel Islands), the Northern Lighthouse Board (for Scotland and the Isle of Man), and the Commissioners of Irish Lights (for Northern Ireland and the Republic of Ireland). Trinity House maintains 73 lighthouses, 13 major floating aids to navigation and more than 429 buoys, the Northern Lighthouse Board maintains 83 lighthouses, 118 minor lights and 131 buoys; and Irish Lights 80 lighthouses and 145 buoys.

Harbour authorities are responsible for pilotage within their harbour areas; and the Ports Act 1991 provides for the transfer of lights and buoys to harbour authorities where these are used for mainly local navigation.

UK–OWNED TRADING VESSELS
OF 500 GROSS TONS AND OVER *as at end 2000*

	No.	Gross tonnage
Tankers	133	2,952,000
Bulk carriers	29	904,000
Specialised carriers	10	53,000
Container (fully cellular)	73	2,240,000
Ro-Ro	103	1,260,000
Other general cargo	139	492,000
Passenger	16	604,000
TOTAL	503	8,505,000

Source: Lloyds Register of Shipping

PASSENGER MOVEMENT BY SEA 2000

Arrivals plus departures at UK seaports by country of embarkation or landing*

All passenger movements	28,917,000
Irish Republic	4,234,000
Belgium	1,507,000
France†	19,755,000
Netherlands	1,938,000
Other EU countries	762,000
Other European countries‡	228,000
Rest of the World	27,000
Pleasure Cruises	466,000

*Passengers are included at both departure and arrival if their journeys begin and end at a UK seaport

Source: Department for Transport

Religion in the UK

There are two established, i.e. state, churches in the United Kingdom: the Church of England and the Church of Scotland. There are no established churches in Wales or Northern Ireland, though the Church in Wales, the Scottish Episcopal Church and the Church of Ireland are members of the Anglican Communion.

About 63 per cent of the population of the UK (37.5 million people) would call itself broadly Christian (in the Trinitarian sense), with 43 per cent (25.6 million) identifying with Anglican churches, 10 per cent (5.8 million) with the Roman Catholic Church, 4 per cent (2.6 million) with Presbyterian Churches, 2 per cent (1.2 million) with the Methodist Churches and 4 per cent (2.5 million) with other Christian churches; but only about 7.9 per cent of the population of Great Britain (4.60 million people) regularly attends a Christian church. Church attendance in Northern Ireland is estimated at 30–35 per cent of the population.

About 2 per cent of the population (1.3 million people) is affiliated to non-Trinitarian churches, e.g. Jehovah's Witnesses, the Church of Jesus Christ of Latter-Day Saints (Mormons), the Church of Christ, Scientist and the Unitarian churches.

A further 5 per cent of the population (3.25 million people) are adherents of other faiths, including Hinduism, Islam, Judaism and Sikhism.

About 29 per cent of the population is non-religious.

ADHERENTS TO RELIGIONS IN UK *(millions)*

	1975	1985	1995	2000
Christian (Trinitarian)	40.2	39.1	38.1	37.5
Non-Trinitarian	0.7	1.0	1.3	1.3
Hindu	0.3	0.4	0.4	0.5
Jew	0.4	0.3	0.3	0.3
Muslim	0.4	0.9	1.2	1.4
Sikh	0.2	0.3	0.6	0.6
Other	0.1	0.3	0.3	0.4
Total	42.3	42.3	42.2	42.0

PERCENTAGE OF UK POPULATION ADHERING TO RELIGIONS

	1975	1985	1995	2000
Christian (Trinitarian)	72	69	65	63
Non-Trinitarian	1	2	2	2
Non-Christian religions	3	3	5	5
All religions	76	74	72	71

Source: Christian Research – *UK Christian Handbook Religious Trends No. 3 2002–2003*

INTER-CHURCH AND INTER-FAITH CO-OPERATION

The main umbrella body for the Christian churches in the UK is the Churches Together in Britain and Ireland (formerly the Council of Churches for Britain and Ireland). There are also ecumenical bodies in each of the constituent countries of the UK: Churches Together in England, Action of Churches Together in Scotland, CYTUN (Churches Together in Wales), and the Irish Council of Churches. The Free Churches' Council comprises most of the Free Churches in England and Wales, and the Evangelical Alliance represents evangelical Christians.

The Inter Faith Network for the United Kingdom promotes co-operation between faiths, and the Council of Christians and Jews works to improve relations between the two religions. Churches Together in Britain and Ireland also has a Commission on Inter-Faith Relations.

ACTION OF CHURCHES TOGETHER IN SCOTLAND, Scottish Churches House, Kirk Street, Dunblane, Perthshire FK15 0AJ. Tel: 01786-823588; Fax: 01786-825844; Email: acts.ecum@dial.pipex.com; Web: www.acts-scotland.org. *General Secretary*, Revd Dr K. Franz

CHURCHES TOGETHER IN BRITAIN AND IRELAND, Inter-Church House, 35–41 Lower Marsh, London SE1 7SA. Tel: 020-7523 2121; Fax: 020-7928 0010; Email: gensec@ctbi.org.uk; Web: www.ctbi.org.uk. *General Secretary*, Dr D. Goodbourn

CHURCHES TOGETHER IN ENGLAND, 27 Tavistock Square, London WC1H 9HH. Tel: 020-7529 8141; Fax: 020-7529 8134; Web: www.churches-together.org.uk. *General Secretary:* The Revd Bill Snelson

COUNCIL OF CHRISTIANS AND JEWS, Camelford House, 87–89 Albert Embankment, London, SE1 7TP. Tel: 020-7820 0090; Fax: 020-7820 0504; Email: cjrelations@ccj.org.uk; Web: www.ccj.org.uk. *Director*, Sr M. Shepherd, NDS

CYTÛN (CHURCHES TOGETHER IN WALES) – Tŷ John Penri, 11 St Helen's Road, Swansea SA1 4AL. Tel: 01792-460876. Web: www.cytun.org.uk General Secretary, Revd G. Abraham-Williams

EVANGELICAL ALLIANCE, Whitefield House, 186 Kennington Park Road, London SE11 4BT. Tel: 020-7207 2100; Fax: 020-7207 2150; Email: london@eauk.org; Web: www.eauk.org. *General Director*, Revd J. Edwards

INTER FAITH NETWORK FOR THE UNITED KINGDOM, 5–7 Tavistock Place, London WC1H 9SN. Tel: 020-7388 0008; Fax: 020-7387 7968; Email: ifnet.uk@interfaith.org.uk; Web: www.interfaith.org.uk. *Director*, B. Pearce, OBE

IRISH COUNCIL OF CHURCHES, Inter-Church Centre, 48 Elmwood Avenue, Belfast BT9 6AZ. Tel: 028-9066 3145. *General Secretary*, Dr R. D. Stevens

Christianity

Christianity is a monotheistic faith based on the person and teachings of Jesus Christ and all Christian denominations claim his authority. Central to its teaching is the concept of God and his son Jesus Christ, who was crucified and resurrected in order to enable mankind to attain salvation.

The Jewish scriptures predicted the coming of a *Messiah*, an 'anointed one', who would bring salvation. To Christians, Jesus of Nazareth, a Jewish rabbi (teacher), who was born in Palestine, was the promised Messiah. Jesus' birth, teachings, crucifixion and subsequent resurrection are recorded in the *Gospels*, which, together with other scriptures that summarise Christian belief, form the *New Testament*. This, together with the Hebrew scriptures, entitled the *Old Testament* by Christians, makes up the *Bible*, the sacred texts of Christianity.

BELIEFS

Christians believe that sin distanced mankind from God, and that Jesus was the Son of God, sent to redeem mankind from that sin by his death. In addition, many believe that Jesus will return again at some future date, triumph over evil and establish a kingdom on earth, thus inaugurating a new age. The Gospel assures Christians that those who believe in Jesus and obey his teachings will be forgiven their sins and will be resurrected from the dead.

PRACTICES

Christian practices vary widely between different Christian churches, but prayer is universal to all, as is charity, giving for the maintenance of the church buildings, for the work of the church, and to the poor and needy. In addition, certain days of observance, i.e. the *Sabbath*, *Easter* and *Christmas*, are celebrated by most Christians. The Orthodox, Roman Catholic and Anglican churches celebrate many more days of observance, based on saints and significant events in the life of Jesus. The belief in sacraments, physical signs believed to have been ordained by Jesus Christ to symbolise and convey spiritual gifts, varies greatly between Christian denominations; *Baptism* and the *Eucharist* are practised by most Christians. Baptism, symbolising repentance and faith in Jesus is an act marking entry into the Christian community; the Eucharist, the ritual re-enactment of the Last Supper, Jesus' final meal with his disciples, is also practised by most denominations. Other sacraments, such as anointing the sick, the laying on of hands to symbolise the passing on of the office of priesthood or to heal the sick and speaking in tongues, where it is believed that the person is possessed by the Holy Spirit, the Spirit of God, are less common. In denominations where infant baptism is practised, confirmation is common, where the person repeats the commitments made for him or her at infancy. Matrimony and the ordination of priests are also widely believed to be sacraments. Many Protestants only view baptism and the Eucharist as sacraments; the Quakers and the Salvation Army reject the use of sacraments.

Most Christians believe that God actively guides the Church.

THE EARLY CHURCH

The apostles were Jesus' first converts and are recognised by Christians as the founders of the Christian community. The new faith spread rapidly throughout the eastern provinces of the Roman Empire. Early Christianity was subject to great persecution until 313 AD, when Emperor Constantine's Edict of Toleration confirmed its right to exist and it became established as the religion of the Roman Empire in 381 AD.

The Christian faith was slowly formulated in the first millennium of the Christian era. Between AD 325 and 787 there were seven Oecumenical Councils at which bishops from the entire Christian world assembled to resolve various doctrinal disputes. The estrangement between East and West began after Constantine moved the centre of the Roman Empire from Rome to Constantinople, and it grew after the division of the Roman Empire into eastern and western halves. Linguistic and cultural differences between Greek East and Latin West served to encourage separate ecclesiastical developments which became pronounced in the tenth and early 11th centuries.

Administration of the church was divided between five ancient patriarchates: Rome and all the West, Constantinople (the imperial city – the 'New Rome'), Jerusalem and all Palestine, Antioch and all the East, and Alexandria and all Africa. Of these, only Rome was in the Latin West and after the schism in 1054, Rome developed a structure of authority centralised on the Papacy, while the Orthodox East maintained the style of localised administration.

Papal authority over the doctrine and jurisdiction of the Church in western Europe was unrivalled after the split with the Eastern Orthodox Church until the Protestant Reformation in the 16th century.

CHRISTIANITY IN BRITAIN

An English Church already existed when Pope Gregory sent Augustine to evangelise the English in AD 596. Conflicts between Church and State during the Middle Ages culminated in the Act of Supremacy in 1534, which repudiated papal supremacy and declared King Henry VIII to be the supreme head of the Church in England. Since 1559 the English monarch has been termed the Supreme Governor of the Church of England.

In 1560 the jurisdiction of the Roman Catholic Church in Scotland was abolished and the first assembly of the Church of Scotland ratified the Confession of Faith, drawn up by a committee including John Knox. In 1592 Parliament passed an Act guaranteeing the liberties of the Church and its presbyterian government. King James VI (James I of England) and later Stuart monarchs attempted to reintroduce episcopacy, but a presbyterian church was finally restored in 1690 and secured by the Act of Settlement (1690) and the Act of Union (1707).

PORVOO DECLARATION

The Porvoo Declaration was drawn up by representatives of the British and Irish Anglican churches and the Nordic and Baltic Lutheran churches and was approved by the General Synod of the Church of England in July 1995. Churches that approve the Declaration regard baptised members of each other's churches as members of their own, and allow free interchange of episcopally ordained ministers within the rules of each church.

Non-Christian Religions

BAHÁ'Í FAITH

Mirza Husayn-'Ali, known as *Bahá'u'lláh* (Glory of God) was born in Iran in 1817 and became a follower of the *Báb*, a religious reformer and prophet who was imprisoned for his beliefs and executed on the grounds of heresy in 1850. *Bahá'u'lláh* was himself imprisoned in 1852, and in 1853 he had a vision that he was the Promised One foretold by the *Báb*. He was exiled after his release from prison and eventually was exiled to Acre, now in Israel, where he continued to compose the Bahá'í sacred scriptures. He died in 1892 and was succeeded by his son, Abdu'l-Bahá, as spiritual leader, under whose guidance the faith spread to Europe and North America. He was followed by Shoghi Effendi, his grandson, who translated many of *Bahá'u'lláh*'s works into English. Upon his death in 1957, a democratic system of leadership was brought into operation.

The Bahá'í faith recognises the unity and relativity of religious truth and teaches that there is only one God, whose will has been revealed to mankind by a series of messengers, such as Zoroaster, Abraham, Moses, Buddha, Krishna, Christ, Muhammad, the Báb and Bahá'u'lláh, who were seen as the founders of separate religions, but whose common purpose was to bring God's message to

mankind. It teaches that all races and both sexes are equal and deserving of equal opportunities and treatment, that education is a fundamental right and encourages a fair distribution of wealth. In addition, mankind is exhorted to establish a world federal system to promote peace, tolerance and the free movement of people, goods and ideas.

A Feast is held every 19 days, which consists of prayer and readings of Bahá'í scriptures, consultation on community business, and social activities. Music, food and beverages usually accompany the proceedings. There is no clergy; each local community elects a local assembly, which co-ordinates community activities, enrols new members, counsels and assists members in need, and conducts Bahá'í marriages and funerals. A national assembly is elected annually by locally elected delegates, and every five years the national spiritual assemblies meet together to elect the Universal House of Justice, the supreme international governing body of the Bahá'í Faith. World-wide there are over 13,000 local spiritual assemblies; there are around five million members residing in about 235 countries, of which 182 have national organisations.

THE BAHÁ'Í INFORMATION OFFICE, 27 Rutland Gate, London SW7 1PD. Tel: 020-7584 2566; Fax: 020-7584 9402; Email: nsa@bahai.org.uk;
Web: www.bahai.org.uk; *Secretary General:* The Hon. Barnabus Leith

BUDDHISM

Buddhism originated in northern India, in the teachings of Siddharta Gautama, who was born near Kapilavastu about 560 BC and became the *Buddha* (Enlightened One).

Fundamental to Buddhism is the concept of rebirth. Each life carries with it the consequences of the conduct of earlier lives (known as the law of *karma*). This cycle of death and rebirth is broken only when the state of *nirvana* has been reached. Buddhism steers a middle path between belief in personal immortality and belief in death as the final end.

The Four Noble Truths of Buddhism (*dukkha*, suffering; *tanha*, a thirst or desire for continued existence which causes dukkha; *nirvana*, the final liberation from desire and ignorance; and *ariya*, the path to nirvana) are all held to be universal and to sum up the *dhamma* or true nature of life. Necessary qualities to promote spiritual development are *sila* (morality), *samadhi* (meditation) and *panna* (wisdom).

There are two main schools of Buddhism: *Theravada* Buddhism, the earliest extant school, which is more traditional, and *Mahayana* Buddhism, which began to develop about 500 years after the Buddha's death and is more liberal; it teaches that all people may attain Buddhahood. Important schools that have developed within Mahayana Buddhism are *Zen* Buddhism, *Nichiren* Buddhism and Pure Land Buddhism or *Amidism*. There are also distinctive Tibetan forms of Buddhism. Buddhism began to establish itself in the West in the early 20th century.

The scripture of Theravada Buddhism is the *Pali Canon*, which dates from the first century BC. Mahayana Buddhism uses a Sanskrit version of the Pali Canon but also has many other works of scripture.

There is no set time for Buddhist worship, which may take place in a temple or in the home. Worship centres around meditation, acts of devotion centring on the image of the Buddha, and, where possible, offerings to a relic of the Buddha. Buddhist festivals vary according to local traditions and within Theravada and Mahayana

Buddhism. For religious purposes Buddhists use solar and lunar calendars, the New Year being celebrated in April. Other festivals mark events in the life of the Buddha.

There is no supreme governing authority in Buddhism. In the United Kingdom communities representing all schools of Buddhism have developed and operate independently. The Buddhist Society was established in 1924; it runs courses and lectures, and publishes books about Buddhism. It represents no one school of Buddhism.

There are estimated to be at least 300 million Buddhists world-wide, and more than 500 groups and centres, an estimated 25,000 adherents and up to 20 temples or monasteries in the UK.

THE BUDDHIST SOCIETY, 58 Eccleston Square, London SW1V 1PH. Tel: 020-7834 5858; Fax: 020-7976 5238; Email: info@thebuddhistsociety.org.uk; Web: www.thebuddhistsociety.org.uk.
General Secretary, R. C. Maddox
FRIENDS OF THE WESTERN BUDDHIST ORDER, London Buddhist Centre, 51 Roman Road, E2 0HU. Tel: 020-8981 1225
THE NETWORK OF BUDDHIST ORGANISATIONS, The Old Courthouse, 43 Renfrew Road, London SE11 4NB. Tel: 020-8682 3442; fax: 020-8767 3210; Email: secretary@nbo.org.uk; Web: www.nbo.org.uk
OFFICE OF TIBET (The Official UK Agency for HH the Dalai Lama) Tibet House, 1 Culworth Street, London NW8 7AF. Tel: 020-7722 5378
SOKA GAKKAI UK, Taplow Court, Taplow, Maidenhead, Berkshire SL6 0ER. Tel: 01628-773 163

HINDUISM

Hinduism has no historical founder but had become highly developed in India by about 1200 BC. Its adherents originally called themselves Aryans; Muslim invaders first called the Aryans 'Hindus' (derived from 'Sindhu', the name of the river Indus) in the eighth century.

Most Hindus hold that *satya* (truthfulness), *ahimsa* (non-violence), honesty, sincerity and devotion to God are essential for good living. They believe in one supreme spirit (*Brahman*), and in the transmigration of *atman* (the soul). Most Hindus accept the doctrine of *karma* (consequences of actions), the concept of *samsara* (successive lives) and the possibility of all atmans achieving *moksha* (liberation from samsara) through *jnana* (knowledge), *yoga* (meditation), *karma* (work or action) and *bhakti* (devotion).

Most Hindus offer worship to *murtis* (images of deities) representing different incarnations or aspects of Brahman, and follow their *dharma* (religious and social duty) according to the traditions of their *varna* (social class), *ashrama* (stage in life), *jati* (caste) and *kula* (family).

Hinduism's sacred texts are divided into *shruti* ('that which is heard'), including the *Vedas*; or *smriti* ('that which is remembered'), including the *Ramayana*, the *Mahabharata*, the *Puranas* (ancient myths), and sacred law books. Most Hindus recognise the authority of the *Vedas*, the oldest holy books, and accept the philosophical teachings of the *Upanishads*, the *Vedanta Sutras* and the *Bhagavad-Gita*.

Brahman is omniscient, omnipotent, limitless and all-pervading, and is usually worshipped in His deity form. Brahma, Vishnu and Shiva are the most important gods worshipped by Hindus; their respective consorts are Saraswati, Lakshmi and Durga or Parvati, also known as Shakti. There are believed to have been ten *avatars* (incar-

nations) of Vishnu, of whom the most important are Rama and Krishna. Other popular gods are Ganesha, Hanuman and Subrahmanyam. All gods are seen as aspects of the supreme God, not as competing deities. Orthodox Hindus revere all gods and goddesses equally, but there are many denominations, including the Hare-Krishna movement (ISKCon), the Arya Samaj, the Swami Narayan Hindu mission and the Satya Sai-Baba movement, in which worship is concentrated on one deity. The *guru* (spiritual teacher) is seen as the source of spiritual guidance.

Hinduism does not have a centrally-trained and ordained priesthood. The pronouncements of the *shankaracharyas* (heads of monasteries) of Shringeri, Puri, Dwarka and Badrinath are heeded by the orthodox but may be ignored by the various sects.

The commonest form of worship is a *puja*, in which offerings of water, flowers, food, fruit, incense and light are made to a deity. Puja may be done either in a home shrine or a *mandir* (temple). Many British Hindus celebrate *samskars* (purification rites) to name a baby, the sacred thread (an initiation ceremony), marriage and cremation.

The largest communities of Hindus in Britain are in Leicester, London, Birmingham and Bradford, and developed as a result of immigration from India, eastern Africa and Sri Lanka.

There are an estimated 800 million Hindus world-wide; there are about 380,000 adherents and over 150 temples in the UK.

ARYA PRATINIDHI SABHA (UK) AND ARYA SAMAJ
    LONDON, 69A Argyle Road, London W13 0LY. Tel: 020-8991 1732. *President*, Prof. S. N. Bharadwaj
BHARATIYA VIDYA BHAVAN, Institute of Indian Art and Culture, 4A Castletown Road, London W14 9HE. Tel: 020-7381 4608. *Executive Director*, Dr M. N. Nandakumara
INTERNATIONAL SOCIETY FOR KRISHNA CONSCIOUSNESS (ISKCon), Bhaktivedanta Manor, Dharam Marg, Hilfield Lane, Aldenham, Watford, Herts WD2 8EZ. Tel: 01923-857244; Email: bhaktivedanta.manor@pamho.net; Web: www.iskcon.org.uk *Temple President*, Gauri Das
NATIONAL COUNCIL OF HINDU TEMPLES (UK), Bhakrivedanta Manor, Dharam Marg, Hilfield Lane, Aldenham, Watford WD2 8EZ. Tel: 01923-856269/857244; Email: bhaktivedanta@pamho.net. *Secretary*, B. Imal Krishna Das
SWAMINARAYAN HINDU MISSION (SHREE SWAMINARAYAN MANDIR), 105–119 Brentfield Road, London NW10 8JP. Tel: 020-8965 2651; Fax: 020-8965 6313; Email: shm@swaminarayan-baps.org.uk; Web: www.swaminarayan-baps.org.uk. *Secretary*, A. Patel
VISHWA HINDU PARISHAD (UK), 48 Wharfedale Gardens, Thornton Heath, Surrey CR7 6LB. Tel: 020-8684 9716. *General Secretary*, K. Ruparelia

ISLAM

Islam (which means 'peace arising from submission to the will of Allah' in Arabic) is a monotheistic religion which was taught in Arabia by the Prophet Muhammad, who was born in Mecca (Al-Makkah) in 570 CE. Islam spread to Egypt, North Africa, Spain and the borders of China in the century following the Prophet's death, and is now the predominant religion in Indonesia, the Near and Middle East, northern and parts of western Africa, Pakistan, Bangladesh, Malaysia and some of the former Soviet republics. There are also large Muslim communities in other countries.

For Muslims (adherents of Islam), there is one God (*Allah*), who holds absolute power. His commands were revealed to mankind through the prophets, who include Abraham, Moses and Jesus, but His message was gradually corrupted until revealed finally and in perfect form to Muhammad through the angel *Jibril* (Gabriel) over a period of 23 years. This last, incorruptible message has been recorded in the *Qur'an* (Koran), which contains 114 divisions called *surahs*, each made up of *ayahs*, and is held to be the essence of all previous scriptures. The *Ahadith* are the records of the Prophet Muhammad's deeds and sayings (the *Sunnah*) as recounted by his immediate followers. A culture and a system of law and theology gradually developed to form a distinctive Islamic civilisation. Islam makes no distinction between sacred and worldly affairs and provides rules for every aspect of human life. The *Shari'ah* is the sacred law of Islam based upon prescriptions derived from the Qur'an and the *Sunnah* of the Prophet.

The 'five pillars of Islam' are *shahadah* (a declaration of faith in the oneness and supremacy of Allah and the messengership of Muhammad); *salat* (formal prayer, to be performed five times a day facing the *Ka'bah* (sacred house in the holy city of Al-Makkah); *zakat* (welfare due); *sawm* (fasting during the month of Ramadan); and *hajj* (pilgrimage to Al-Makkah); some Muslims would add *jihad* (striving for the cause of good and resistance to evil).

Two main groups developed among Muslims. *Sunni* Muslims accept the legitimacy of Muhammad's first four *caliphs* (successors as head of the Muslim community) and of the authority of the Muslim community as a whole. About 90 per cent of Muslims are Sunni Muslims. *Shi'ites* recognise only Muhammad's son-in-law Ali as his rightful successor and the *Imams* (descendants of Ali, not to be confused with *imams* (prayer leaders or religious teachers)) as the principal legitimate religious authority. The largest group within Shi'ism is *Twelver Shi'ism*, which has been the official school of law and theology in Iran since the 16th century; other subsects include the *Ismailis*, the *Druze* and the *Alawis*, the latter two differing considerably from the main body of Muslims.

The *Ibadhis* of Oman are neither Sunni nor Shi'a, deriving from the strictly observant *Khariji* (Seceeders). There is no organised priesthood, but learned men such as *ulama*, *imams* and *ayatollahs* are accorded great respect. The *Sufis* are the mystics of Islam. Mosques are centres for worship and teaching and also for social and welfare activities.

Islam was first known in western Europe in the eighth century AD when 800 years of Muslim rule began in Spain. Later, Islam spread to eastern Europe. More recently, Muslims came to Europe from Africa, the Middle East and Asia in the late 19th century. Both the Sunni and Shi'a traditions are represented in Britain, but the majority of Muslims in Britain adhere to Sunni Islam.

Efforts to establish a representative central organisation recognised by all Muslims in Britain are beginning to yield good results with the emergence of the Muslim Council of Britain. In addition, there are many other Muslim organisations in Britain.

There are about 1,000 million Muslims world-wide, with nearly two million adherents and about 1,200 mosques in Britain.

IMAMS AND MOSQUES COUNCIL, 20–22 Creffield Road, London W5 3RP. Tel: 020-8992 6636. *Director of the Council and Principal of the Muslim College,* Dr M. A. Z. Badawi

ISLAMIC CULTURAL CENTRE, 146 Park Road, London NW8 7RG. Tel: 020-7724 3363. *Director,* Dr A. Al-Dubayan

MUSLIM COUNCIL OF BRITAIN, PO Box 52, Wembley, Middx HA9 0XW. Tel: 020-8903 9024; Fax: 020-8903 9026; Email: admin@mcb.org.uk; Web: www.mcb.org.uk. *Secretary-General,* Yousuf Bhailok

MUSLIM WORLD LEAGUE, 46 Goodge Street, London W1P 1FJ. Tel: 020-7636 7568. *Deputy Director,* G. Rahman

UNION OF MUSLIM ORGANISATIONS OF THE UK AND ÉIRE, 109 Campden Hill Road, London W8 7TL. Tel: 020-7229 0538/7221 6608. *General Secretary,* Dr S. A. Pasha

JAINISM

Jainism traces its history to Vardhamana Jnatiputra, known as *Tirthankara Mahavira* (The Great Hero) whose traditional dates were 599–527 BC. He was the last of a series of 24 *Jinas* (those who overcome all passions and desires) or *Tirthankaras* (those who show a way across the ocean of life) stretching back to remote antiquity. Born to a noble family in north-eastern India, he renounced the world for the life of a wandering ascetic and after 12 years of austerity and meditation he attained enlightenment. He then preached his message until, at the age of 72, he passed away and reached *moksha*, total liberation from the cycle of death and rebirth.

Jains deny the authority of the Vedas, the Hindu sacred scriptures. They recognise some of the minor deities of the Hindu pantheon, but the supreme objects of worship are the *Tirthankaras*. The pious Jain does not ask favours from the *Tirthankaras*, but seeks to emulate their example in his or her own life.

Jains believe that the universe is eternal and self-subsisting: there is no omnipotent creator God ruling it and the destiny of the individual is in his or her own hands. *Karma,* the fruit of past actions, determines the place of every living being and rebirth may be in the heavens, on earth as a human, an animal or other lower being, or in the hells. The ultimate goal of existence is *moksha* or *nirvana,* a state of perfect knowledge and tranquility for each individual soul, which can be achieved only by gaining enlightenment.

The path to liberation is defined by the Three Jewels, *samyak darsana* (right thought), *samyak jnana* (right knowledge) and *samyak charitra* (right conduct).

There are about 25,000 Jains in Britain, sizeable communities in North America and East Africa and smaller groups in many other countries.

INSTITUTE OF JAINOLOGY, Unit 18, Silicon Business Centre, 26–28 Wadsworth Road, Greenford, Middx, UB6 7JZ Tel: 020-8997 2300; Fax: 020-8997 4964

JAIN CENTRE, 32 Oxford Street, Leicester, LE1 5XU Tel: 0116-254 3091

JUDAISM

Judaism is the oldest monotheistic faith. The primary authority of Judaism is the Hebrew Bible or *Tanakh,* which records how the descendants of Abraham were led by Moses out of their slavery in Egypt to Mount Sinai where God's law (*Torah*) was revealed to them as the

chosen people. The *Talmud,* which consists of commentaries on the *Mishnah* (the first text of rabbinical Judaism), is also held to be authoritative, and may be divided into two main categories: the *halakah* (dealing with legal and ritual matters) and the *Aggadah* (dealing with theological and ethical matters not directly concerned with the regulation of conduct). The *Midrash* comprises rabbinic writings containing biblical interpretations in the spirit of the Aggadah. The *halakah* has become a source of division; Orthodox Jews regard Jewish law as derived from God and therefore unalterable; Reform and Liberal Jews seek to interpret it in the light of contemporary considerations; and Conservative Jews aim to maintain most of the traditional rituals but to allow changes in accordance with tradition. Reconstructionist Judaism, a 20th-century movement, regards Judaism as a culture rather than a theological system and accepts all forms of Jewish practice.

The family is the basic unit of Jewish ritual, with the synagogue playing an important role as the centre for public worship and religious study. A synagogue is led by a group of laymen who are elected to office. The Rabbi is primarily a teacher and spiritual guide. The Sabbath is the central religious observance. Most British Jews are descendants of either the *Ashkenazim* of central and eastern Europe or the *Sephardim* of Spain, Portugal and the Middle East.

The Chief Rabbi of the United Hebrew Congregations of the Commonwealth is appointed by a Chief Rabbinate Conference, and is the rabbinical authority of the mainstream Orthodox sector of the Ashkenazi Jewish community, the largest body of which is the United Synagogue. His formal ecclesiastical authority is not recognised by the Reform Synagogues of Great Britain (the largest progressive group), the Union of Liberal and Progressive Synagogues, the – Sephardi community, or the Assembly of Masorti Synagogues. He is, however, generally recognised both outside the Jewish community and within it as the public religious representative of the totality of British Jewry. The Chief Rabbi is President of the London *Beth Din.*

A *Beth Din* (Court of Judgement) is a rabbinic court. The *Dayanim* (Assessors) adjudicate in disputes or on matters of Jewish law and tradition; they also oversee dietary law administration.

The Board of Deputies of British Jews, established in 1760, is the representative body of British Jewry. The basis of representation is mainly synagogal, but communal organisations are also represented. It watches over the interests of British Jewry, acts as the central voice of the community and seeks to counter anti-Jewish discrimination and antisemitic activities.

In November 1998 a Consultative Committee was established comprising representatives of the Assembly of Masorti Synagogues, Reform Synagogues of Great Britain, Union of Liberal and Progressive Synagogues and the United Synagogue. The Committee holds discussions to further communal harmony and development.

There are over 12.5 million Jews world-wide; in Great Britain and Ireland there are an estimated 285,000 adherents and about 365 synagogues. Of these, 191 congregations and about 175 rabbis and ministers are under the jurisdiction of the Chief Rabbi; 99 orthodox congregations have a more independent status; and 79 congregations are outside the jurisdiction of the Chief Rabbi.

CHIEF RABBINATE, Adler House, 735 High Road, London N12 0US. Tel: 020-8343 6301; Fax: 020-8343 6301; Email: info@chiefrabbi.org; Web: www.chiefrabbi.org. *Chief Rabbi,* Prof. Jonathan Sacks; *Executive Director,* Syma Weinberg

BETH DIN (COURT OF THE CHIEF RABBI), 735 High Road, London N12 0US. Tel: 020-8343 6270; Fax: 020-8343 6257; Email: info@londonbethdin.fsnet.co.uk.
Registrar, D. Frei; *Dayanim*, Rabbi Chanoch Ehrentreu; Ivan Binstock; Menachem Gelley; Yonason Abraham
BOARD OF DEPUTIES OF BRITISH JEWS, 6 Bloomsbury Square, London WC1A 2LP. Tel: 020-7543 5400; Fax: 020-7543 0010; Email: info@bod.org.uk; Web: www.bod.org.uk. *President*, Jo Wagerman, OBE; *Director-General*, Neville Nagler
ASSEMBLY OF MASORTI SYNAGOGUES, 1097 Finchley Road, London NW11 0PU. Tel: 020-8201 8772; Fax: 020-8201 8917; Email: office@masorti.org.uk; Web: www.masorti.org.uk. *Director*, M. Gluckman
FEDERATION OF SYNAGOGUES, 65 Watford Way, London NW4 3AQ. Tel: 020-8202 2263; Fax: 020-8203 0610. *Chief Executive*, G. D. Coleman
BETH DIN OF THE FEDERATION OF SYNAGOGUES, 65 Watford Way, London NW4 3AQ. Tel: 020-8202 2263.
Registrar, Rabbi S. Unsdorfer; *Dayanim*, Yisroel Lichtenstein; Berel Berkovits; M. D. Elzas; Z. Alony
REFORM SYNAGOGUES OF GREAT BRITAIN, The Sternberg Centre for Judaism, 80 East End Road, London N3 2SY. Tel: 020-8349 5640; Fax: 020-8349 5699; Email: admin@reformjudaism.org.uk; Web: www.reformjudaism.org.uk. *Chief Executive*, Rabbi T. Bayfield
SPANISH AND PORTUGUESE JEWS' CONGREGATION, 2 Ashworth Road, London W9 1JY. Tel: 020-7289 2573; Fax: 020-7289 2709; Email: howard@sandpsyn.demon.co.uk.
Chief Executive, Howard Miller
UNION OF LIBERAL AND PROGRESSIVE SYNAGOGUES, The Montagu Centre, 21 Maple Street, London W1T 4BE. Tel: 020-7580 1663; Fax: 020-7436 4184; Email: montagu@ulps.org; Web: www.ulps.org.
Executive Director, Rabbi Dr Charles Middleburgh
UNION OF ORTHODOX HEBREW CONGREGATIONS, 140 Stamford Hill, London N16 6QT. Tel: 020-8802 6226; Fax: 020-8809 7092. *Principal Rabbinical Authority*, Rabbi Ephraim Padwa
UNITED SYNAGOGUE HEAD OFFICE, Adler House, 735 High Road, London N12 0US. Tel: 020-8343 8989; Fax: 020-8343 6262; Web: www.unitedsynagogue.org.uk. *Chief Executive*, Rabbi Saul Zneimer

SIKHISM

The Sikh religion dates from the birth of Guru Nanak in the Punjab in 1469. 'Guru' means teacher but in Sikh tradition has come to represent the divine presence of God giving inner spiritual guidance. Nanak's role as the human vessel of the divine guru was passed on to nine successors, the last of whom (Guru Gobind Singh) died in 1708. The immortal guru is now held to reside in the sacred scripture, *Guru Granth Sahib*, and so to be present in all Sikh gatherings.

Guru Nanak taught that there is one God and that different religions are like different roads leading to the same destination. He condemned religious conflict, ritualism and caste prejudices. The fifth Guru, Guru Arjan Dev, largely compiled the Sikh Holy Book, a collection of hymns *(gurbani)* known as the *Adi Granth*. It includes the writings of the first five Gurus and the ninth Guru, and selected writings of Hindu and Muslim saints whose views are in accord with the Gurus' teachings. Guru Arjan Dev also built the Golden Temple at Amritsar, the centre of Sikhism. The tenth Guru, Guru Gobind Singh, passed on the guruship to the sacred scripture, Guru Granth Sahib. He also founded the

Khalsa, an order intended to fight against tyranny and injustice. Male initiates to the order added 'Singh' to their given names and women added 'Kaur'. Guru Gobind Singh also made five symbols obligatory: *kaccha* (a special undergarment), *kara* (a steel bangle), *kirpan* (a small sword), *kesh* (long unshorn hair, and consequently the wearing of a turban), and *kangha* (a comb). These practices are still compulsory for those Sikhs who are initiated into the Khalsa (the *Amritdharis*). Those who do not seek initiation are known as *Sehajdharis*.

There are no professional priests in Sikhism; anyone with a reasonable proficiency in the Punjabi language can conduct a service. Worship can be offered individually or communally, and in a private house or a *gurdwara* (temple). Sikhs are forbidden to eat meat prepared by ritual slaughter; they are also asked to abstain from smoking, alcohol and other intoxicants. Such abstention is compulsory for the *Amritdharis*.

There are about 20 million Sikhs world-wide and about 500,000 adherents and 250 gurdwaras in Great Britain. Every gurdwara manages its own affairs and there is no central body in the UK. The Sikh Missionary Society provides an information service.
SIKH MISSIONARY SOCIETY UK, 10 Featherstone Road, Southall, Middx UB2 5AA. Tel: 020-8574 1902. *Hon. General Secretary*, M. S. Chahal
WORLD SIKH FOUNDATION (THE SIKH COURIER INTERNATIONAL), 33 Wargrave Road, South Harrow, Middx HA2 8LL. Tel: 020-8864 9228. *Secretary*, Mrs H. B. Bharara

ZOROASTRIANISM

Zoroastrianism was founded by Zarathushtra (or Zoroaster in its hellenised form) in Persia. Linguistic analysis of the earliest extant Zoroastrian texts suggests that he lived around 1500 BC. Zarathushtra's words are recorded in five poems called the *Gathas*, which, together with other scriptures, forms the *Avesta*.

Zoroastrianism teaches that there is one God, *Ahura Mazda* (the Wise Lord), and that all creation stems ultimately from God; the Gathas teach that human beings have free will, are responsible for their own actions and can choose between good and evil: Choosing *Asha* (truth or righteousness), with the aid of Vohu Manah (good mind), leads to happiness for the individual and society, whereas choosing evil leads to unhappiness and conflict. The *Gathas* also encourage hard work, good deeds and charitable acts. Zoroastrians believe that after death, the immortal soul is judged by God, and is then sent to paradise or hell, where it will stay until the end of time. It will be resurrected for the final judgement.

In Zoroastrian places of worship, an urn containing fire is the central feature; the fire symbolises purity, light, and truth and is a visible symbol of the *Fravashi* or *Farohar*, the presence of *Ahura Mazda* in every human being.

Zoroastrians respect nature and much importance is attached to cultivating land and protecting the air, the earth and water. The practice of leaving corpses on mountain tops or towers developed to avoid pollution.

Zoroastrians were persecuted in Iran following the Arab invasion of Persia in the seventh century AD, which also brought Islam and a group migrated to India in the tenth century ad, who are known as Parsis, to avoid harassment and persecution; there are fewer than 150,000 Zoroastrians worldwide, of which 7,000 reside in Britain, mainly in London and the south east.
ZOROASTRIAN TRUST FUNDS OF EUROPE, 88 Compayne Gardens, London NW6 3RU. Tel: 020-7328 6018; Email: library@ztfe.com; website: www.ztfe.com

The Churches

The Church of England

The Church of England is the established (i.e. national) church in England and seeks to serve the nation through its dioceses and parishes. It traces its life back to the first coming of Christianity to England. Its position is defined by the ancient creeds of the Church and by the 39 Articles of Religion (1571), the Book of Common Prayer (1662) and the Ordinal. The Church of England is thus both catholic and reformed. It is the mother church of the Anglican Communion.

THE ANGLICAN COMMUNION

The Anglican Communion consists of 40 independent provincial or national Christian churches throughout the world, many of which are in Commonwealth countries and originated from missionary activity by the Church of England. Every ten years all the bishops in the Communion meet at the Lambeth Conference, convened by the Archbishop of Canterbury. The Conference has no policy-making authority but is an important forum for discussing and forming consensus around issues common concern. The Anglican Consultative Council was set up in 1968 to liaise between the member churches and provinces of the Anglican Communion. It meets every three years. Meetings of the Anglican primates have taken place every two years since 1979.

There are about 70 million Anglicans and 800 archbishops and bishops world-wide.

STRUCTURE

The Church of England is divided into the two provinces of Canterbury and York, each under an archbishop. The two provinces are subdivided into 44 dioceses.

Legislative provision for the Church of England is made by the General Synod, established in 1970. It also discusses and expresses opinion on any other matter of religious or public interest. The General Synod has 580 members in total, divided between three houses: the House of Bishops, the House of Clergy and the House of Laity. It is presided over jointly by the Archbishops of Canterbury and York and normally meets twice a year. The Synod has the power, delegated by Parliament, to frame statute law (known as a Measure) on any matter concerning the Church of England. A Measure must be laid before both Houses of Parliament, who may accept or reject it but cannot amend it. Once accepted the Measure is submitted for royal assent and then has the full force of law. In addition to the General Synod, there are Synods at diocesan level.

The Archbishops' Council was established in January 1999. Its creation was the result of changes to the Church of England's national structure proposed in 1995 and subsequently approved by the Synod and Parliament. The Council's purpose, set out in the National Institutions Measure 1998, is 'to co-ordinate, promote and further the work and mission of the Church of England'. It reports to the General Synod. The Archbishops' Council comprises the Archbishops of Canterbury and York, ex officio, the Prolocutors elected by the Convocations of Canterbury and York, the Chairman and Vice-Chairman of the House of Laity, elected by that House, two bishops, two clergy and two lay persons elected by their respective Houses of the General Synod, and up to six persons appointed jointly by the two Archbishops with the approval of the General Synod.

There are also a number of national Boards, Councils and other bodies working on matters such as social responsibility, mission, Christian unity and education which report to the General Synod through the Archbishops' Council.

GENERAL SYNOD OF THE CHURCH OF ENGLAND, Church House, Great Smith Street, London SW1P 3NZ. Tel: 020-7898 1000. *Joint Presidents*, The Archbishops of Canterbury and York.

HOUSE OF BISHOPS: *Chairman*, The Archbishop of Canterbury; *Vice-Chairman*, The Archbishop of York

HOUSE OF CLERGY: *Chairmen (alternating)*, Canon Bob Baker; Canon Glyn Webster

HOUSE OF LAITY: *Chairman*, Dr Christina Baxter; *Vice-Chairman*, Brian McHenry

ARCHBISOPS' COUNCIL, Church House, Great Smith Street, London SW1P 3NZ. Tel: 020-7898 1000. *Joint Presidents*, The Archbishops of Canterbury and York. *Secretary-General*, William Fittall.

THE ORDINATION OF WOMEN

The canon making it possible for women to be ordained to the priesthood was promulgated in the General Synod in February 1994 and the first 32 women priests were ordained on 12 March 1994.

MEMBERSHIP

In 2000, 161,000 people were baptised, the Church of England had an electoral roll membership of 1.4 million, and each week about 1.3 million people attended services. At December 2001 there were two archbishops and 105 diocesan, suffragan and (stipendiary) assistant bishops. In 2001 there were 8,052 other male and 1,194 female full-time stipendiary clergy, and over 16,000 churches and places of worship.

FULL-TIME DIOCESAN CLERGY 2002 AND CHURCH ELECTORAL ROLLS 2000

| | Clergy | | Membership |
	Male	Female	
Bath and Wells	212	29	43,500
Birmingham	167	25	19,700
Blackburn	224	13	38,900
Bradford	102	11	13,300
Bristol	116	22	20,300
Canterbury	152	20	22,700
Carlisle	133	13	25,300
Chelmsford	357	48	54,100
Chester	243	31	54,100
Chichester	328	8	60,800
Coventry	128	21	18,200
Derby	170	16	22,000
Durham	207	28	28,100

| | Clergy | | Membership |
	Male	Female	
Ely	125	27	22,000
Europe	124	3	9,500
Exeter	229	19	34,700
Gloucester	136	20	27,200
Guildford	166	36	32,800
Hereford	86	20	20,300
Leicester	137	25	17,100

Lichfield	290	51	55,400
Lincoln	182	39	31,600
Liverpool	210	36	33,200
London	464	55	62,400
Manchester	247	47	39,700
Newcastle	132	18	18,600
Norwich	184	19	26,700
Oxford	352	71	63,800
Peterborough	137	18	20,000
Portsmouth	106	10	20,300
Ripon and Leeds	114	28	19,000
Rochester	197	27	33,600
St Albans	213	51	47,500
St Edmundsbury and Ipswich	140	19	26,900
Salisbury	192	33	48,700
Sheffield	157	27	22,000
Sodor and Man	20	0	3,100
Southwark	302	68	48,900
Southwell	146	29	19,000
Truro	116	7	18,000
Wakefield	140	24	25,400
Winchester	219	18	45,200
Worcester	128	25	23,300
York	228	36	40,400
TOTAL	8,158	1,194	1,377,000

STIPENDS 2002–3

Archbishop of Canterbury	£59,050
Archbishop of York	£51,740
Bishop of London	£48,250
Other diocesan bishops	£32,050
Suffragan bishops	£26,300
Assistant Bishops (full-time)	£25,260
Deans and provosts	£26,300
Archdeacons (recommended)	£26,130
Residentiary canons	£21,430
Incumbents and clergy of similar status	£17,420*

*National Stipends Benchmark

CANTERBURY

104TH ARCHBISHOP AND PRIMATE OF ALL ENGLAND
Most Revd and Rt. Hon. Rowan Williams *cons.* 1992
apptd 2002; Lambeth Palace, London SE1 7JU. *Signs*
Rowan Cantuar

BISHOPS SUFFRAGAN

Dover, Rt. Revd Stephen Venner, *cons* 1994, *apptd* 1999;
Upway, St Martin's Hill, Canterbury, Kent CT1 1PR
Maidstone, Rt. Revd Graham Cray, *cons.* 2001, *apptd*
2001, Bishop's House, Pett Lane, Charing, Ashford,
Kent TN27 0DL
Ebbsfleet, Rt. Revd Andrew Burnham, *cons.* 2001, *apptd*
2001 (provincial episcopal visitor); Bishop's House,
Dry Sandsford, Oxon OX13 6JP
Richborough, Rt. Revd Keith Newton, *cons.* 2002, *apptd*
2002 (provincial episcopal visitor); 14 Hall Place
Gardens, St Albans, Herts AL1 3SP

DEAN

Very Revd Robert Willis, *apptd* 2001

CANONS RESIDENTIARY

Roger Symon, *apptd* 1994; Dr Michael Chandler, *apptd*
1995; Richard Marsh, *apptd* 2001
Organist, D. Flood, FRCO, *apptd* 1988

ARCHDEACONS

Canterbury, Ven. Patrick Evans, *apptd* 2002
Maidstone, Ven. Philip Dolon, *apptd* 2002

Vicar-General of Province and Diocese, Chancellor Sheila
Cameron, QC
Commissary-General, His Hon. Judge Richard Walker
Joint Registrars of the Province, F. E. Robson, OBE; B. J. T.
Hanson, CBE
Diocesan Registrar and Legal Adviser, Richard Sturt
Diocesan Secretary, David Kemp, Diocesan House, Lady
Wootton's Green, Canterbury CT1 1NQ. Tel: 01227-
459401

YORK

96TH ARCHBISHOP AND PRIMATE OF ENGLAND
Most Revd and Rt. Hon. David M. Hope, KCVO, D.Phil.,
LL D, *cons.* 1985, *trans.* 1995, *apptd* 1995;
Bishopthorpe, York YO23 2GE. *Signs* David Ebor

BISHOPS SUFFRAGAN

Hull, Rt. Revd Richard M. C. Frith, *cons.* 1998, *apptd*
1998; Hullen House, Woodfield Lane, Hessle, Hull
HU13 0ES
Selby, Rt. Revd Humphrey V. Taylor, *cons.* 1991, *apptd*
1991; 10 Precentor's Court, York YO1 7EJ
Whitby, Rt. Revd Robert S. Ladds, *cons.* 1999, *apptd*
1999; 60 West Green, Stokesley, Middlesbrough TS9
5BD
Beverley, Rt. Revd Martyn Jarrett, *cons.* 1994, *apptd* 2000
(provincial episcopal visitor); 3 North Lane,
Roundhay, Leeds LS8 2QJ

DEAN

Very Revd Raymond Furnell, *apptd* 1994

CANONS RESIDENTIARY

Glyn Webster, *apptd* 1999; Edward. R. Norman, Ph.D.,
DD, *apptd* 1999; Jonathan Draper, *apptd* 2000; Jeremy
Fletcher, *apptd* 2002

CANONS LAY

Lindsay Mackinlay, *apptd* 2000; Carol Rymer, *apptd*
2000; Dr Allen Warren, *apptd* 2000; Brig. Peter Lyddon
(as Chapter Steward), *apptd* 2000; Peter Collier, QC,
apptd 2001

Organist, Philip Moore, FRCO, *apptd* 1983

ARCHDEACONS

Cleveland, Ven. Paul Ferguson, *apptd* 2001
East Riding, Ven. Peter Harrison, *apptd* 1998
York, Ven. Richard Seed, *apptd* 1999

Official Principal and Auditor of the Chancery Court, Sir
John Owen, QC
Chancellor of the Diocese, His Hon. Judge Coningsby, QC,
apptd 1977
*Vicar-General of the Province and Official Principal of the
Consistory Court,* His Hon. Judge Coningsby, QC
Registrar and Legal Secretary, Lionel Lennox
Diocesan Secretary, Colin Sheppard, Diocesan House,
Aviator Court, Clifton Moor, York YO30 4WJ. Tel:
01904-699500

LONDON (Province of Canterbury)

132ND BISHOP
Rt. Revd and Rt. Hon Richard J. C. Chartres, *cons.* 1992, *apptd.* 1995; The Old Deanery, Dean's Court, London EC4V 5AA. *Signs* Richard Londin

AREA BISHOPS
Edmonton, Rt. Revd Peter W. Wheatley, *cons.* 1999, *apptd* 1999; 27 Thurlow Road, London NW3 5PP
Kensington, Rt. Revd Michael J. Colclough, *cons.* 1996, *apptd* 1996; 19 Campden Hill Square, London W8 7JY
Stepney, vacant
Willesden, Rt. Revd Peter Broadbent, *cons.* 2001, *apptd* 2001; 173 Willesden Lane, London NW6 7YN

BISHOP SUFFRAGAN
Fulham, Rt. Revd John C. Broadhurst, *cons.* 1996, *apptd* 1996; 26 Canonbury Park South, London N1 2FN

DEAN OF ST PAUL'S
Very Revd John H. Moses, Ph.D., *apptd* 1996

CANONS RESIDENTIARY
John Halliburton, *apptd* 1989; Stephen Oliver, *apptd* 1996; Philip Buckler, *apptd* 1999; Edmund Newall, *apptd* 2001; Peter Chapman, *apptd* 2001

Registrar and Receiver of St Paul's, Maj. Gen. John Milne

Organist, John Scott, FRCO, *apptd* 1990

ARCHDEACONS
Charing Cross, Ven. Dr William Jacob, *apptd* 1996
Hackney, Ven. Lyle Dennen, *apptd* 1999
Hampstead, Ven. Michael Lawson, *apptd* 1999
London, Ven. Peter Delaney, *apptd* 1999
Middlesex, Ven. Malcolm Colmer, *apptd* 1996
Northolt, Ven. Christopher Chessun, *apptd* 2001

Chancellor, Nigel Seed, QC, *apptd* 2002
Registrar and Legal Secretary, Paul Morris
Diocesan Secretary, Keith Robinson, London Diocesan House, 36 Causton Street, London SW1P 4AU. Tel: 020-7932 1226

DURHAM (Province of York)

70TH BISHOP
Rt. Revd A. Michael A. Turnbull, *cons.* 1988, *apptd* 1994; Auckland Castle, Bishop Auckland DL14 7NR. *Signs* Michael Dunelm

BISHOP SUFFRAGAN
Jarrow, Rt. Revd John Pritchard, *cons.* 2002, *apptd* 2002; Ivy Lane, Low Fell, Gateshead NE9 6QD

DEAN
Very Revd John Arnold, *apptd* 1989

CANONS RESIDENTIARY
Prof David Brown, *apptd* 1990; Trevor Willmott, *apptd* 1997; Martin Kitchen, *apptd* 1997; David Whittington, *apptd* 1998; David Kennedy, *apptd* 2001

Organist, James Lancelot, FRCO, *apptd* 1985

ARCHDEACONS
Auckland, Ven. Ian Jagger, *apptd* 2001
Durham, Ven. Stephen Conway, *apptd* 2002
Sunderland, Ven. Stuart Bain, *apptd* 2002

Chancellor, Revd Rupert Bursell, QC, *apptd* 1989
Registrar and Legal Secretary, A. N. Fairclough
Diocesan Secretary, Jonathan Cryer, Auckland Castle, Bishop Auckland, Co. Durham DL14 7QJ. Tel: 01388-604515

WINCHESTER (Canterbury)

96TH BISHOP
Rt. Revd Michael C. Scott-Joynt, *cons.*1987, *trans.* 1995, *apptd* 1995; Wolvesey, Winchester SO23 9ND. *Signs* Michael Winton

BISHOPS SUFFRAGAN
Basingstoke, Rt. Revd Trevor Willmott, *cons.* 2002, *apptd* 2002. Bishopswood End, Kingdwood Rise, Four Marks, Alton, Hants GU34 5BD.
Southampton, Rt. Revd Jonathan Gledhill, *cons.* 1996, *apptd* 1996; Ham House, The Crescent, Romsey SO51 7NG

DEAN
Very Revd Michael Till, *apptd* 1996

Dean of Jersey (A Peculiar), Very Revd John Seaford, *apptd* 1993
Dean of Guernsey (A Peculiar), Very Revd Marc Trickey, *apptd* 1995

CANONS RESIDENTIARY
Keith Walker, *apptd* 1987; Charles Stewart, *apptd* 1997; Ven. John Guille, *apptd* 1998

Organist, Andrew Lumsden, ARCO, *apptd* 2002

ARCHDEACONS
Bournemouth, Ven. Adrian Harbidge, *apptd* 1998
Winchester, Ven. John Guille, *apptd* 1998

Chancellor, Christopher Clark, *apptd* 1993
Registrar and Legal Secretary, Peter White
Diocesan Secretary, Ray Anderton, Church House, 9 The Close, Winchester, Hants SO23 9LS. Tel: 01962-844644

BATH AND WELLS (Canterbury)

77TH BISHOP
Rt. Revd Peter Price, *cons.* 1997, *apptd* 2002; The Palace, Wells BA5 2PD. *Signs* Peter Bath & Wells

BISHOP SUFFRAGAN
Taunton, Rt. Revd Andrew John Radford, *cons.* 1998, *apptd* 1998; The Bishop's Lodge, Monkton Heights, West Monkton, Taunton, Somerset TA2 8LU

DEAN
Very Revd Richard Lewis, *apptd* 1990

CANONS RESIDENTIARY
Richard Acworth, *apptd* 1993; Russell Bowman-Eadie, *apptd* 2002; Melvyn Matthews, *apptd* 1997; Patrick Woodhouse, *apptd* 2000

Organist, Malcolm Archer, *apptd* 1996

ARCHDEACONS
Bath, Ven. Robert Evens, *apptd* 1996
Taunton, Ven. John Reed, *apptd* 1999
Wells, Ven. Richard Acworth, *apptd* 1993
Chancellor, Timothy Briden, *apptd* 1993
Registrar and Legal Secretary, Tim Berry

Diocesan Secretary, Nicholas Denison, The Old Deanery, Wells, Somerset BA5 2UG. Tel: 01749-670777

BIRMINGHAM (Canterbury)

8TH BISHOP

Rt. Revd John Sentamu, *cons.* 1996, *apptd* 2002; Bishop's Croft, Harborne, Birmingham B17 0BG. *Signs* John Birmingham

BISHOP SUFFRAGAN

Aston, Rt. Revd John Austin, *cons.* 1992, *apptd* 1992; Strensham House, 8 Strensham Hill, Moseley, Birmingham B13 8AG

PROVOST

The Very Revd Gordon Mursell, *apptd* 2000

CANONS RESIDENTIARY

Revd David Lee, *apptd* 1996; Revd Gary O'Neill, *apptd* 1997

Organist, Marcus Huxley, FRCO, *apptd* 1986

ARCHDEACONS

Aston, Ven. John Barton, *apptd* 1990
Birmingham, Ven. Hayward Osborne, *apptd* 2001

Chancellor, Francis Aglionby, *apptd* 1970
Registrar and Legal Secretary, Hugh Carslake
Diocesan Secretary, Jim Drennan, 175 Harborne Park Road, Harborne, Birmingham B17 0BH. Tel: 0121-426 0400

BLACKBURN (York)

7TH BISHOP

Rt. Revd Alan D. Chesters, *cons.* 1989, *apptd* 1989; Bishop's House, Ribchester Road, Blackburn BB1 9EF. *Signs* Alan Blackburn

BISHOPS SUFFRAGAN

Burnley, Rt. Revd John Goddard, *cons.* 2000, *apptd* 2000; Dean House, 449 Padiham Road, Burnley BB12 6TE
Lancaster, Rt. Revd Stephen Pedley, *cons.* 1998, *apptd* 1998; The Vicarage, Shireshead, Forton, Preston PR3 0AE

DEAN

Very Revd Christopher Armstrong, *apptd* 2001

CANONS RESIDENTIARY

David Galilee, *apptd* 1995; Andrew Hindley, *apptd* 1996; Peter Ballard, *apptd* 1998; Andrew Clitherow, *apptd* 2000

Organist, Richard Tanner, *apptd* 1998

ARCHDEACONS

Blackburn, Ven. John Hawley, *apptd* 2002
Lancaster, Ven. Colin Williams, *apptd* 1999

Chancellor, John Bullimore, *apptd* 1990
Registrar and Legal Secretary, Thomas Hoyle
Diocesan Secretary, Revd Michael Wedgeworth, Diocesan Office, Cathedral Close, Blackburn BB1 5AA. Tel: 01254-54421

BRADFORD (York)

9TH BISHOP

Rt. Revd David James, *apptd* 2002; Bishopscroft, Ashwell Road, Heaton, Bradford BD9 4AU. *Signs* David Bradford

DEAN

Very Revd Dr Christopher David Hancock, *apptd* 2002

CANON RESIDENTIARY

Derek Jackson, *apptd* 2000; David Brierley, *apptd* 2002

Organist, Alan Horsey, FRCO, *apptd* 1986

ARCHDEACONS

Bradford, Ven. Guy Wilkinson, *apptd* 1999
Craven, Ven. Malcolm Grundy, *apptd* 1994

Chancellor, John de G. Walford, *apptd* 1999
Registrar and Legal Secretary, Stuart Robinson
Diocesan Secretary, Malcolm Halliday, Cathedral Hall, Stott Hill, Bradford BD1 4ET. Tel: 01274-725958

BRISTOL (Canterbury)

54TH BISHOP

Rt. Revd Barry Rogerson, *cons.* 1979, *apptd* 1985; Bishop's House, Clifton Hill, Bristol BS8 1BW. *Signs* Barry Bristol: (retires 30 November 2002)

BISHOP SUFFRAGAN

Swindon, Rt. Revd Michael Doe, *cons.* 1994, *apptd* 1994; Mark House, Field Rise, Old Town, Swindon SN1 4HP

DEAN

Very Revd Robert W. Grimley, *apptd* 1997

CANONS RESIDENTIARY

Peter Johnson, *apptd* 1990; Douglas Holt, *apptd* 1998; Brendan Clover, *apptd* 1999

Organist, Mark Lee, *apptd* 1998

ARCHDEACONS

Bristol, Ven. Tim McClure, *apptd* 1999
Malmesbury, Ven. Alan Hawker, *apptd* 1998

Chancellor, Sir David Calcutt, QC, *apptd* 1971
Registrar and Legal Secretary, Tim Berry
Diocesan Secretary, Lesley Farrall, Diocesan Church House, 23 Great George Street, Bristol, Avon BS1 5QZ. Tel: 0117-906 0100

CARLISLE (York)

66TH BISHOP

Rt. Revd Graham Dow, *cons.* 1985, *apptd* 2000; Rose Castle, Dalston, Carlisle CA5 7BZ. *Signs* Graham Carlisle

BISHOP SUFFRAGAN

Penrith, Rt. Revd James Newcome, *cons.* 2002, *apptd* 2002; Holm Croft, Castle Road, Kendal, Cumbria LA9 7AU

DEAN

Very Revd Graeme Knowles, *apptd* 1998

CANONS RESIDENTIARY

Rex Chapman, *apptd* 1978; David Weston, *apptd* 1994

Organist, Jeremy Suter, FRCO, *apptd* 1991

ARCHDEACONS

Carlisle, Ven. David Thomson, *apptd* 2002
West Cumberland, Ven. Alan Davis, *apptd* 1996
Westmorland and Furness, Ven. George Howe, *apptd* 2000

Chancellor, His Hon. Judge Francis Aglionby, *apptd* 1991
Registrar and Legal Secretary, Susan Holmes
Diocesan Secretary, Canon Colin Hill, Church House, West Walls, Carlisle CA3 8UE. Tel: 01228-522573

CHELMSFORD (Canterbury)

8TH BISHOP
Rt. Revd John F. Perry, *cons.* 1989, *apptd* 1996; Bishopscourt, Margaretting, Ingatestone CM4 0HD. *Signs* John Chelmsford

BISHOPS SUFFRAGAN
Barking, Rt. Revd David Hawkins, *apptd* 2002
Bradwell, Rt. Revd Laurence Green, *cons.* 1993, *apptd* 1993; The Vicarage, Orsett Road, Horndon-on-the-Hill, Stanford-le-Hope, Essex SS17 8NS
Colchester, Rt. Revd Christopher Morgan, 1 Fitzwalter Road, Colchester, Essex CO3 3SS

PROVOST
Very Revd Peter S. M. Judd, *apptd* 1997

CANONS RESIDENTIARY
Andrew Knowles, *apptd* 1998; Walter King, *apptd* 2001

Master of Music, Peter Nardone, *apptd* 2000

ARCHDEACONS
Colchester, Ven. Martin Wallace, *apptd* 1997
Harlow, Ven. Peter Taylor, *apptd* 1996
Southend, Ven. David Lowman, *apptd* 2001
West Ham, Ven. Michael Fox, *apptd* 1996

Chancellor, George Pulman, *apptd* 2001
Registrar and Legal Secretary, Brian Hood
Diocesan Secretary, David Phillips, 53 New Street, Chelmsford, Essex CM1 1AT. Tel: 01245-294400

CHESTER (York)

40TH BISHOP
Rt. Revd Peter R. Forster, Ph.D., *cons.* 1996, *apptd* 1996; Bishop's House, Chester CH1 2JD. *Signs* Peter Cestr

BISHOPS SUFFRAGAN
Birkenhead, Rt. Revd David A. Urquhart, *cons.* 2000, *apptd* 2000; Bishop's Lodge, 67 Bidston Road, Oxton, Birkenhead CH43 6TR
Stockport, Rt. Revd Nigel Stock, *cons.* 2000, *apptd* 2000; Bishop's Lodge, Back Lane, Dunham Town, Altrincham, Cheshire WA14 4SG

DEAN
Very Revd Dr Gordon McPhate

CANONS RESIDENTIARY
Trevor Dennis, *apptd* 1994; Christopher Burkett, *apptd* 2000; John Roff, *apptd* 2000

Organist and Director of Music, David Poulter, FRCO, *apptd* 1997

ARCHDEACONS
Chester, Revd, *apptd* 2002
Macclesfield, Ven. Richard Gillings, *apptd* 1994

Chancellor, David Turner, QC, *apptd* 1998
Registrar and Legal Secretary, Alan McAllester
Diocesan Secretary, Stephen P. A. Marriott, Church House, Lower Lane, Aldford, Chester CH3 6HP. Tel: 01244-620444

CHICHESTER (Canterbury)

102ND BISHOP
Rt. Revd John Hind, *cons.* 1991, *apptd* 2001; The Palace, Chichester PO19 1PY. *Signs* John Cicestr

BISHOPS SUFFRAGAN
Horsham, Rt. Revd Lindsay G. Urwin, *cons.* 1993, *apptd* 1993; Bishop's House, 21 Guildford Road, Horsham, W. Sussex RH12 1LU
Lewes, Rt. Revd Wallace P. Benn, *cons.* 1997, *apptd* 1997; Bishop's Lodge, 16A Prideaux Road, Eastbourne, E. Sussex BN21 2NB

DEAN
Revd Nicholas Frayling, *apptd* 2002

CANONS RESIDENTIARY
Peter Atkinson, *apptd* 1997; Michael Manktelow, *apptd* 1997; Peter Kefford, *apptd* 2001

Organist, Alan Thurlow, FRCO, *apptd* 1980

ARCHDEACONS
Chichester, Ven. Douglas McKittrick, *apptd* 2002
Horsham, Ven. William Filby, *apptd* 1983
Lewes and Hastings, Ven. Nicholas Reade, *apptd* 1997

Chancellor, Mark Hill
Registrar and Legal Secretary, Christopher Butcher
Diocesan Secretary, Jonathan. Prichard, Diocesan Church House, 211 New Church Road, Hove, E. Sussex BN3 4ED. Tel: 01273-421021

COVENTRY (Canterbury)

8TH BISHOP
Rt. Revd Colin J. Bennetts; *cons.* 1994, *apptd* 1997; The Bishop's House, 23 Davenport Road, Coventry CV5 6PW. *Signs* Colin Coventry

BISHOP SUFFRAGAN
Warwick, Rt. Revd Anthony M. Priddis, *cons.* 1996, *apptd* 1996; 139 Kenilworth Road, Coventry CV4 7AF

DEAN
Very Revd John Irvine, *apptd* 2001

CANONS RESIDENTIARY
Christopher Burch, *apptd* 1995; Andrew White, *apptd* 1998; Stuart Beake, *apptd* 2000

Director of Music, Rupert Jeffcoat, *apptd* 1997

ARCHDEACONS
Coventry, Ven. Mark Bryant, *apptd* 2001
Warwick, Ven. Michael Paget-Wilkes, *apptd* 1990

Chancellor, Sir William Gage, *apptd* 1980
Registrar and Legal Secretary, David Dumbleton

Diocesan Secretary, Isobel Chapman, Church House, Palmerston Road, Coventry CV5 6FJ. Tel: 024-7667 4328

DERBY (Canterbury)

6TH BISHOP
Rt. Revd Jonathan S. Bailey, *cons.*1992, *apptd* 1995; Derby Church House, Full Street, Derby DE1 3DR. *Signs* Jonathan Derby

BISHOP SUFFRAGAN
Repton, Rt. Revd David C. Hawtin, *cons.*1999, *apptd* 1999; Repton House, Lea, Matlock, Derbys DE4 5JP

PROVOST
Very Revd Michael F. Perham, *apptd* 1998

CANONS RESIDENTIARY
Tony Chesterman, *apptd* 1989; Geoffrey Marshall, *apptd* 1992; Barrie Gauge, *apptd* 1999; David Truby, *apptd* 1998; Nicholas Henshall, *apptd* 2002
Organist, Peter Gould, *apptd* 1982

ARCHDEACONS
Chesterfield, Ven. David Garnett, *apptd* 1996
Derby, Ven. Ian Gatford, *apptd* 1992
Chancellor, John, *apptd* 1981
Registrar and Legal Secretary, James Battie
Diocesan Secretary, Bob Carey, Derby Church House, Full Street, Derby DE1 3DR. Tel: 01332-382233

ELY (Canterbury)

68TH BISHOP
Rt. Revd Dr Anthony Russell, *cons.* 1988, *apptd* 2000; The Bishop's House, Ely, Cambs CB7 4DW *Signs* Anthony Ely

BISHOP SUFFRAGAN
Huntingdon, Rt. Revd John R. Flack, *cons.* 1997, *apptd* 1996; 14 Lynn Road, Ely, Cambs CB6 1DA

DEAN
Very Revd Michael Higgins, *apptd* 1991

CANONS RESIDENTIARY
John Inge, *apptd* 1996; Peter Sills, *apptd* 2000
Organist, Paul Trepte, FRCO, *apptd* 1991

ARCHDEACONS
Ely, Ven. Jeffrey Watson, *apptd* 1993
Huntingdon, Ven. John Beer, *apptd* 1997
Wisbech, Ven. James Rone, *apptd* 1995
Chancellor, William Gage, QC
Registrar, Peter Beesley
Diocesan Secretary, Dr Matthew Lavis, Bishop Woodford House, Barton Road, Ely, Cambs CB7 4DX. Tel: 01353-652701

EXETER (Canterbury)

70TH BISHOP
Rt. Revd Michael L. Langrish, *cons.* 1993, *apptd* 2000; The Palace, Exeter, EX1 1HY. *Signs* Michael Exon

BISHOPS SUFFRAGAN
Crediton, Rt. Revd Richard S. Hawkins, *cons.* 1988, *apptd* 1996; 10 The Close, Exeter EX1 1EZ
Plymouth, Rt. Revd John H. Garton, *cons.* 1996, *apptd* 1996; 31 Riverside Walk, Tamerton Foliot, Plymouth PL5 4AQ

DEAN
Very Revd Keith Jones, *apptd* 1996

CANONS RESIDENTIARY
David Ison, *apptd* 1997; Neil Collings, *apptd* 1999; Carl Turner, *apptd* 2001
Director of Music, Andrew Millington, *apptd* 1999

ARCHDEACONS
Barnstaple, vacant
Exeter, vacant
Plymouth, Ven. Tony Wilds, *apptd* 2001
Totnes, Ven. Richard Gilpin, *apptd* 1996
Chancellor, Sir David Calcutt, QC, *apptd* 1971
Registrar and Legal Secretary, R. K. Wheeler
Diocesan Secretary, Mark Beedell, Diocesan House, Palace Gate, Exeter, Devon EX1 1HX. Tel: 01392-272686

GIBRALTAR IN EUROPE (Canterbury)

BISHOP
Rt. Revd Geoffrey Rowell, *cons.* 1994, *apptd* 2001; 14 Tufton Street, London SW1P 3QZ

BISHOP SUFFRAGAN
In Europe, Rt. Revd Henry Scriven, *cons.* 1995, *apptd* 1994; 14 Tufton Street, London SW1P 3QZ
Dean, Cathedral Church of the Holy Trinity, Gibraltar, Very Revd Kenneth Robinson
Chancellor, Pro-Cathedral of St Paul, Valletta, Malta, Canon Alan Woods
Chancellor, Pro-Cathedral of the Holy Trinity, Brussels, Belgium, Canon Nigel Walker

ARCHDEACONS
Eastern, Rt. Revd H. Scriven (acting)
North-West Europe, Ven. Geoffrey Allen
France, Ven. Martin Draper, OBE
Gibraltar, Very Revd Kenneth Robinson
Italy, Ven. Gordon Reid
Scandinavia and Germany, Ven. David Ratcliff
Switzerland, Ven. Peter Hawker, OBE
Chancellor, Sir David Calcutt, QC
Registrar and Legal Secretary, John Underwood
Diocesan Secretary, Adrian Mumford, 14 Tufton Street, London SW1P 3QZ. Tel: 020-7898 1155

GLOUCESTER (Canterbury)

39TH BISHOP
Rt. Revd David Bentley, *cons.* 1986, *apptd* 1993; Bishopscourt, Pitt Street, Gloucester GL1 2BQ. *Signs* David Gloucestr

BISHOP SUFFRAGAN
Tewkesbury, Rt. Revd John S. Went, *cons.* 1995, *apptd* 1995; Green Acre, 166 Hempsted Lane, Hempsted, Gloucester GL2 5LG

DEAN

Very Revd Nicholas Bury, *apptd* 1997

CANONS RESIDENTIARY

Roger Grey, *apptd* 1982; Norman Chatfield, *apptd* 1992; Neil Heavisides, *apptd* 1993; Christopher Morgan, *apptd* 1996; David Hoyle, *apptd* 2002

Director of Music, Andrew Nethsinghal, *apptd* 2002

ARCHDEACONS

Cheltenham, Ven. Hedley Ringrose, *apptd* 1998
Gloucester, Ven. Geoffrey Sidaway, *apptd* 2000

Chancellor and Vicar-General, June Rodgers, *apptd* 1990
Registrar and Legal Secretary, Chris Peak
Diocesan Secretary, Michael Williams, Church House, College Green, Gloucester GL1 2LY. Tel: 01452-410022

GUILDFORD (Canterbury)

8TH BISHOP

Rt. Revd John W. Gladwin, *cons.* 1994, *apptd* 1994; Willow Grange, Woking Road, Guildford GU4 7QS. Tel: 01483-590500; Fax: 01483-590501 *Signs* John Guildford

BISHOP SUFFRAGAN

Dorking, Rt. Revd Ian Brackley, *cons.* 1996, *apptd* 1995; Dayspring, 13 Pilgrims Way, Guildford GU4 8AD

DEAN

The Very Revd Victor Stock

CANONS RESIDENTIARY

Dr Maureen Palmer, *apptd* 1996; Julian Hubbard, *apptd* 1999; Dr Nicholas Thistlethwaite, *apptd* 1999

Organist, Stephen Farr, FRCO, *apptd* 1999

ARCHDEACONS

Dorking, Ven. Mark Wilson, *apptd* 1996
Surrey, Ven. Robert Reiss, *apptd* 1996
Chancellor, The Worshipful Andrew Jordan

Registrar and Legal Secretary, Peter Beesley
Diocesan Secretary, Stephen Marriott

HEREFORD (Canterbury)

103RD BISHOP

Rt. Revd John Oliver, *cons.* 1990, *apptd* 1990; The Palace, Hereford HR4 9BN. *Signs* John Hereford

BISHOP SUFFRAGAN

Ludlow, Ven. Michael Wrenford Hooper, *cons.* 2002 *apptd* 2002; Bishop's House, Halford, Craven Arms, Shropshire SY7 9BT

DEAN

Very Revd Michael Tavinor, *apptd* 2002

CANONS RESIDENTIARY

J. Tiller, *apptd* 1984; Michael Hooper, *apptd* 2002; Val Hamer, *apptd* 2002

Organist, Geraint Bowen, FRCO, *apptd* 2001

ARCHDEACONS

Hereford, Ven. John Tiller, *apptd* 2002
Ludlow, Michael Wrenford Hooper, *apptd* 2002

Chancellor, Val Hamer
Joint Registrars and Legal Secretaries, Tom Jordan; Peter Beesley
Diocesan Secretary, Sylvia Green, The Palace, Hereford HR4 9BL. Tel: 01432-353863

LEICESTER (Canterbury)

6TH BISHOP

Rt. Revd Timothy J. Stevens, *cons.* 1995, *apptd* 1999; Bishop's Lodge, 10 Springfield Road, Leicester LE2 3BD. *Signs* Timothy Leicester

PROVOST

Very Revd Vivienne F. Faull, *apptd* 2000

CANONS RESIDENTIARY

Michael Banks, *apptd* 1988; Michael Wilson, *apptd* 1988; John Craig, *apptd* 2002

Master of Music, Jonathan Gregory, *apptd* 1994

ARCHDEACONS

Leicester, Ven. Richard Atkinson, *apptd* 2002
Loughborough, Ven. Ian Stanes, *apptd* 1992

Chancellor, James Behrens
Registrar and Legal Secretary, Trevor Kirkman
Diocesan Secretary, Andrew Howard; Church House, 3–5 St Martin's East, Leicester LE1 5FX. Tel: 0116-248 7400

LICHFIELD (Canterbury)

97TH BISHOP

Rt. Revd Keith N. Sutton, *cons.* 1978, *apptd* 1984; Bishop's House, The Close, Lichfield WS13 7LG. *Signs* Keith Lichfield

BISHOPS SUFFRAGAN

Shrewsbury, Rt. Revd Alan Smith, cons. 2001, *apptd* 2002; 68 London Road, Shrewsbury SY2 6PG
Stafford, Rt. Revd Christopher J. Hill, *cons.* 1996, *apptd* 1996; Ash Garth, Broughton Crescent, Barlaston, Staffs ST12 9DD
Wolverhampton, Rt. Revd Michael G. Bourke, *cons.* 1993, *apptd* 1993; 61 Richmond Road, Wolverhampton WV3 9JH

DEAN

Very Revd Michael Yorke, *apptd* 1999

CANONS RESIDENTIARY

A. N. Barnard, *apptd* 1977; C. W. Taylor, *apptd* 1995; Ven. Christopher Liley, *apptd* 2001

Organist, Philip Scriven, *apptd* 2002

ARCHDEACONS

Lichfield, Ven. Christopher Liley, *apptd* 2001
Salop, Ven. John Hall, *apptd* 1998
Stoke-on-Trent, Ven. Godfrey Owen Stone *apptd* 2002
Walsall, Ven. Tony Sadler, *apptd* 1997

Chancellor, His Hon. Judge John Shand
Registrar and Legal Secretary, J. P. Thorneycroft
Diocesan Secretary, D. R. Taylor, St Mary's House, The Close, Lichfield, Staffs WS13 7LD. Tel: 01543-306030

LINCOLN (Canterbury)

71ST BISHOP
Rt. Revd Dr John Saxbee, *cons.* 1994, *apptd* 2002; Bishop's House, Eastgate, Lincoln LN2 1QQ. *Signs* John Lincoln

BISHOPS SUFFRAGAN
Grantham, Rt. Revd Alastair L. J. Redfern, *cons.* 1997, *apptd* 1997; Fairacre, 234 Barrowby Road, Grantham, Lincs NG31 8NP

Grimsby, Rt. Revd David D. J. Rossdale, *cons.* 2000, *apptd* 2000; Bishop's House, Church Lane, Irby-upon-Humber, Grimsby DN37 7JR

DEAN
Very Revd Alexander Knight, *apptd* 1998

CANONS RESIDENTIARY
Rex Davis, *apptd* 1977; Andrew Stokes, *apptd* 1992

Organist, Colin Walsh, FRCO, *apptd* 1988

ARCHDEACONS
Lincoln, Ven. Arthur Hawes, *apptd* 1995
Lindsey, Ven. Dr Timothy Ellis, *apptd* 2001
Stow, Ven. Dr Timothy Ellis, *apptd* 2001

Chancellor, Peter N. Collier, QC, *apptd* 1999
Registrar and Legal Secretary, Derek Wellman
Diocesan Secretary, Philip Hamlyn Williams, The Old Palace, Lincoln LN2 1PU. Tel: 01522-529241

LIVERPOOL (York)

7TH BISHOP
Rt. Revd James Jones, *cons.* 1994, *apptd* 1998; Bishop's Lodge, Woolton Park, Liverpool L25 6DT. *Signs* James Liverpool

BISHOP SUFFRAGAN
Warrington, Rt. Revd David Jennings, *cons.* 2000, *apptd* 2000; 34 Central Avenue, Eccleston Park, Prescot, Merseyside L34 2QP

DEAN
Rt. Revd Dean Dr Rupert W. N. Hoare

CANONS RESIDENTIARY
Mark Boyling, *apptd* 1994

Organist, Prof. Ian Tracey, *apptd* 1980

ARCHDEACONS
Liverpool, vacant
Warrington, Ven. Peter Bradley, *apptd* 2001

Chancellor, His Hon. Judge Richard Hamilton
Registrar and Legal Secretary, Roger Arden
Diocesan Secretary, Mike Eastwood, Church House, 1 Hanover Street, Liverpool L1 3DW. Tel: 0151-709 9722

MANCHESTER (York)

11TH BISHOP
Rt. Revd Nigel McCulloch, cons., *apptd* 2002; Bishopscourt, Bury New Road, Manchester M7 4LE. *Signs* Nigel Manchester

BISHOPS SUFFRAGAN
Bolton, Rt. Revd David K. Gillett, *cons.* 1999, *apptd* 1999; 4 Bishop's Lodge, Bolton Road, Hawkshaw, Bury BL8 4JN

Hulme, Rt. Revd Stephen R. Lowe, *cons.* 1999, *apptd.* 1999; 14 Moorgate Avenue, Withington, Manchester M20 1HE

Middleton, Rt. Revd Michael A. O. Lewis, *cons.* 1999, *apptd* 1999; The Hollies, Manchester Road, Rochdale OL11 3QY

DEAN
Very Revd Kenneth Riley, *apptd* 1993

CANONS RESIDENTIARY
John Atherton, PH.D., *apptd* 1984; Paul Denby, *apptd* 1995

Organist, Christopher Stokes, *apptd* 1992

ARCHDEACONS
Bolton, John Applegate, *apptd* 2002
Manchester, Ven Alan Wolstencroft, *apptd* 1998
Rochdale, Ven. Andrew Ballard, *apptd* 2000

Chancellor, J. L. L. Holden
Registrar and Legal Secretary, Michael Darlington
Diocesan Secretary, Nigel Spraggins, 1st Floor, Diocesan Church House, 90 Deansgate, Manchester M3 2GH. Tel: 0161-833 9521

NEWCASTLE (York)

11TH BISHOP
Rt. Revd J. Martin Wharton, *cons.* 1992, *apptd* 1997; Bishop's House, 29 Moor Road South, Gosforth, Newcastle upon Tyne NE3 1PA. *Signs* Martin Newcastle

STIPENDIARY ASSISTANT BISHOP
Rt. Revd Paul Richardson, *cons.* 1987, *apptd* 1999

HON. ASSISTANT BISHOP
Rt. Revd K. E. Gill, *cons.* 1972, *apptd* 1998

PROVOST
Very Revd Nicholas G. Coulton, *apptd* 1990

CANONS RESIDENTIARY
Peter Strange, *apptd* 1986; Ven. Peter Elliott, *apptd* 1993; Geoffrey Miller, *apptd* 1999

Master of Music, Timothy Hone, FRCO, *apptd* 1987

ARCHDEACONS
Lindisfarne, Ven. Robert Langley, *apptd* 2001
Northumberland, Ven. Peter Elliott, *apptd* 1993

Chancellor, Prof. David McClean, *apptd* 1998
Registrar and Legal Secretary, Jane Lowdon
Diocesan Secretary, Philip Davies, Church House, St John's Terrace, North Shields, NE29 6HS. Tel: 0191-270 4100

NORWICH (Canterbury)

71ST BISHOP
Rt. Revd Graham R. James, *cons.* 1993, *apptd* 2000; Bishop's House, Norwich NR3 1SB. *Signs* Graham Norvic

BISHOPS SUFFRAGAN

Lynn, Rt. Revd Anthony C. Foottit, *cons.* 1999, *apptd* 1999; The Old Vicarage, Castle Acre, King's Lynn, Norfolk PE32 2AA.
Thetford, Rt. Revd David J. Atkinson, *cons.* 2001, *apptd* 2001; Rectory Meadow, Bramerton, Norwich NR14 7DW

DEAN

Very Revd Stephen Platten, *apptd* 1995

CANONS RESIDENTIARY

Ven. Clifford Offer, *apptd* 1994; Richard Hanmer, *apptd* 1994; Jeremy Haselock, *apptd* 1998; Michael Kitchener, *apptd* 1999

Organist, David Dunnett, *apptd* 1996

ARCHDEACONS

Lynn, Ven. Martin Gray, *apptd* 1999
Norfolk, Ven. David Hayden Michael Handley, *apptd* 2002
Norwich, Ven. Clifford Offer, *apptd* 1994

Chancellor, The Hon. Mr Justice Blofeld, *apptd* 1998
Registrar and Legal Secretary, John Herring
Diocesan Secretary, Revd Richard Bowett, Diocesan House, 109 Dereham Road, Easton, Norwich, Norfolk NR9 5ES. Tel: 01603-880853

OXFORD (Canterbury)

41ST BISHOP
Rt. Revd Richard D. Harries, *cons.* 1987, *apptd* 1987; Diocesan Church House, North Hinksey Lane, Oxford OX2 0NB. *Signs* Richard Oxon

AREA BISHOPS

Buckingham, Rt. Revd Michael A. Hill *cons.* 1998, *apptd* 1998; 28 Church Street, Great Missenden, Bucks HP16 0AZ
Dorchester, Rt. Revd Colin Fletcher, *cons.* 2000, *apptd* 2000; 12 Sandy Lane, Yarnton, Oxon OX5 1PB
Reading, Rt. Revd Dominic Walker, *cons.* 1997, *apptd* 1997; Bishop's House, Tidmarsh Lane, Tidmarsh, Reading RG8 8HA

DEAN OF CHRIST CHURCH
Very Revd John H. Drury, *apptd* 1991

CANONS RESIDENTIARY

Oliver O'Donovan, D.Phil., *apptd* 1982; Marilyn Parry, *apptd* 2001; Keith Ward, *apptd* 1991; Robert Jeffery, *apptd* 1996; Prof. John Webster, *apptd* 1996; Prof. H. M. R. E. Mayr-Harting, *apptd* 1997; Ven. John Morrison, *apptd* 1998

Organist, Stephen Darlington, FRCO, *apptd* 1985

ARCHDEACONS

Berkshire, Ven. Norman Russell, *apptd* 1998
Buckingham, Sheila Watson, *apptd* 2002
Oxford, Ven. John Morrison, *apptd* 1998

Chancellor, Dr Rupert Bursell *apptd* 2001
Registrar and Legal Secretary, Dr F. E. Robson and Revd. John Rees
Diocesan Secretary, Rosemary Pearce, Diocesan Church House, North Hinksey, Oxford OX2 0NB. Tel: 01865-208202

PETERBOROUGH (Canterbury)

37TH BISHOP
Rt. Revd Ian P. M. Cundy, *cons.* 1992, *apptd* 1996; The Palace, Peterborough PE1 1YA. *Signs* Ian Petriburg

BISHOP SUFFRAGAN

Brixworth, Rt. Revd Frank White, *cons.* 2002, *apptd* 2002; 4 The Avenue, Dallington, Northampton NN1 4RZ

DEAN

Very Revd Michael Bunker, *apptd* 1992

CANONS RESIDENTIARY

Jack Higham, *apptd* 1983; Ven. David Painter, *apptd* 2000; Bill Croft, *apptd* 2001; Stephen Cottrell, *apptd* 2001
Organist, Christopher Gower, FRCO, *apptd* 1977

ARCHDEACONS

Northampton, Ven. Michael Chapman, *apptd* 1991
Oakham, Ven. David Painter, *apptd* 2000

Chancellor, Thomas Coningsby, QC, *apptd* 1989
Registrar and Legal Secretary, Raymond Hemingray
Diocesan Secretary, Richard Pestell, The Palace, Peterborough, Cambs PE1 1YB. Tel: 01733-887000

PORTSMOUTH (Canterbury)

8TH BISHOP
Rt. Revd Dr Kenneth W. Stevenson, *cons.* 1995, *apptd* 1995; Bishopsgrove, 26 Osborn Road, Fareham, Hants PO16 7DQ. *Signs* Kenneth Portsmouth

DEAN

Very Revd D. C. Brindley, *apptd* 2002

CANONS RESIDENTIARY

David Isaac, *apptd* 1990; Gavin Kirk, *apptd* 1998;
Organist, David Price, *apptd* 1996

ARCHDEACONS

Isle of Wight, Ven. Mervyn Banting, *apptd* 1996
Portsdown, Ven. Christopher Lowson, *apptd* 1999
The Meon, Ven. Peter Hancock, *apptd* 1999

Chancellor, (*acting*), C. Clark, QC
Registrar and Legal Secretary, Hilary Tyler
Diocesan Secretary, Michael Jordan, Cathedral House, St Thomas's Street, Portsmouth, Hants PO1 2HA. Tel: 023-9282 5731

RIPON AND LEEDS (York)

12TH BISHOP
Rt. Revd John R. Packer, *cons.* 1996, *apptd* 2000; Bishop Mount, Ripon HG4 5DP. *Signs* John Ripon and Leeds

BISHOP SUFFRAGAN

Knaresborough, Rt. Revd Frank V. Weston, *cons.* 1997, *apptd* 1997; 16 Shaftesbury Avenue, Roundhay, Leeds LS8 1DT

DEAN

Very Revd John Methuen, *apptd* 1995

CANONS RESIDENTIARY

Michael Glanville-Smith, *apptd* 1990; Keith Punshon, *apptd* 1996

Organist, Kerry Beaumont, FRCO, *apptd* 1994

ARCHDEACONS

Leeds, Ven. John Oliver, *apptd* 1992
Richmond, Ven. Kenneth Good, *apptd* 1993

Chancellor, His Hon. Judge Grenfell, *apptd* 1992
Registrars and Legal Secretaries, Christopher Tunnard, Nichola Harding
Diocesan Secretary, Philip Arundel, Diocesan Office, St Mary's Street, Leeds LS9 7DP. Tel: 0113-200 0540

ROCHESTER (Canterbury)

106TH BISHOP
Rt. Revd Dr Michael Nazir-Ali, *cons.* 1984, *apptd* 1994; Bishopscourt, Rochester ME1 1TS. *Signs* Michael Roffen

BISHOP SUFFRAGAN

Tonbridge, Rt. Revd Dr Brian C. Castle, *cons.* 2002, *apptd* 2002; Bishop's Lodge, 48 St Botolph's Road, Sevenoaks TN13 3AG

DEAN

Very Revd Edward Shotter, *apptd* 1990

CANONS RESIDENTIARY

Jonathan Meyrick, *apptd* 1998; Canon Ralph Godsall, *apptd* 2001

Director of Music, Roger Sayer, FRCO, *apptd* 1995

ARCHDEACONS

Bromley, Ven. Garth Norman, *apptd* 1994
Rochester, Ven. Peter Lock, *apptd* 2000
Tonbridge, Ven. Clive Mansell, *apptd* 2002

Chancellor, His Hon. Judge Michael Goodman, *apptd* 1971
Registrar and Legal Secretary, Michael Thatcher
Diocesan Secretary, Mrs Louise Gilbert, St Nicholas Church, Boley Hill, Rochester ME1 1SL. Tel: 01634-830333

ST ALBANS (Canterbury)

9TH BISHOP
Rt. Revd Christopher W. Herbert, *cons.* 1995, *apptd* 1995; Abbey Gate House, St Albans AL3 4HD. *Signs* Christopher St Albans

BISHOPS SUFFRAGAN

Bedford, Rt. Revd Richard Inwood, *apptd* 2002
Hertford, Rt. Revd Christopher R. J. Foster, *cons.* 2001, *apptd* 2001; Hertford House, Abbey Mill Lane, St Albans AL3 4HE

DEAN

Very Revd Christopher Lewis, *apptd* 1993

CANONS RESIDENTIARY

Michael Sansom, *apptd* 1988; Iain Lane, *apptd* 2000; Richard Wheeler, *apptd* 2001; Dennis Stamps, *apptd* 2002

Organist, Andrew Lucas, *apptd* 1998

ARCHDEACONS

Bedford, Ven. Malcolm Lesiter, *apptd* 1993
Hertford, Ven. Trevor Jones, *apptd* 1997
St Albans, Ven. Richard Cheetham, *apptd* 1999

Chancellor, Roger Kaye, *apptd* 2002
Registrar and Legal Secretary, David Cheetham
Diocesan Secretary, Susan Pope, Holywell Lodge, 41 Holywell Hill, St Albans AL1 1HE. Tel: 01727-854532

ST EDMUNDSBURY AND IPSWICH
(Canterbury)

9TH BISHOP
Rt. Revd J. H. Richard Lewis, *cons.* 1992, *apptd* 1997; Bishop's House, 4 Park Road, Ipswich IP1 3ST. *Signs* Richard St Edmundsbury and Ipswich

BISHOP SUFFRAGAN

Dunwich, Rt. Revd Clive Young, *cons.* 1999, *apptd* 1999; 28 Westerfield Road, Ipswich IP4 2UJ

DEAN

Very Revd James Atwell, *apptd* 1995

CANONS RESIDENTIARY

Martin Shaw, *apptd* 1989; Marion Mingins, *apptd* 1993

Organist, James Thomas, *apptd* 1997

ARCHDEACONS

Ipswich, Ven. Terry Gibson, *apptd* 1987
Sudbury, Ven. John Cox, *apptd* 1995
Suffolk, Ven. Geoffrey Arrand, *apptd* 1994

Chancellor, The Hon. Mr Justice Blofeld, *apptd* 1974
Registrar and Legal Secretary, James Hall
Diocesan Secretary, Nicholas Edgell, Churchgates House, Cutler Street, Ipswich IP1 1QU. Tel: 01473-298500

SALISBURY (Canterbury)

77TH BISHOP
Rt. Revd David S. Stancliffe, *cons.* 1993, *apptd* 1993; South Canonry, The Close, Salisbury SP1 2ER. *Signs* David Sarum

BISHOPS SUFFRAGAN

Ramsbury, Rt. Revd Peter F. Hullah, *cons.* 1999, *apptd* 1999
Sherborne, Rt. Revd Timothy M. Thornton, *cons.* 2001, *apptd* 2001

DEAN

Very Revd Derek Watson, *apptd* 1996

CANONS RESIDENTIARY

Jeremy Davies, *apptd* 1985; D. M. K. Durston, *apptd* 1992; June Osborne, *apptd* 1995

Organist, Simon Lole, *apptd* 1997

ARCHDEACONS

Dorset, Ven. Alistair Magowan, *apptd* 2000
Sherborne, Ven. Paul Wheatley, *apptd* 1991
Sarum, Wilts, Ven. Barney Hopkinson, *apptd* 1986 (Sarum), 1998 (Wilts)

Chancellor, His Hon. Judge Samuel Wiggs, *apptd* 1997
Registrar and Legal Secretary, Andrew Johnson
Diocesan Secretary, Revd Karen Curnock, Church House, Crane Street, Salisbury SP1 2QB. Tel: 01722-411922

SHEFFIELD (York)

6TH BISHOP
Rt. Revd John (Jack) Nicholls, *cons.* 1990, *apptd* 1997; Bishopscroft, Snaithing Lane, Sheffield S10 3LG. *Signs* Jack Sheffield

BISHOP SUFFRAGAN
Doncaster, Rt. Revd Cyril Guy Ashton, *cons.* 2000, *apptd* 2000; Bishop's House, 3 Farrington Court, Wickersley, Rotherham S66 1JQ

DEAN
Very Revd Michael Sadgrove, *apptd* 1995

CANONS RESIDENTIARY
Christopher Smith, *apptd* 1991; Jane Sinclair, *apptd* 1993; Ven. Richard Blackburn, *apptd* 1999

Master of Music, Neil Taylor, *apptd* 1997

ARCHDEACONS
Doncaster, Ven. Robert Fitzharris, *apptd* 2001
Sheffield, Ven. Richard Blackburn, *apptd* 1999

Chancellor, Prof. David McClean, *apptd* 1992
Registrar and Legal Secretary, Mrs Miranda Myers
Diocesan Secretary, Tony Beck, FCIS, Diocesan Church House, 95–99 Effingham Street, Rotherham S65 1BL. Tel: 01709-309100

SODOR AND MAN (York)

79TH BISHOP
Rt. Revd Noel D. Jones, CB, *cons.* 1989, *apptd* 1989; The Bishop's House, Quarterbridge Road, Douglas, Isle of Man IM2 3RF. *Signs* Noel Sodor and Man

CANONS
Brian Kelly, *apptd* 1980; Hinton Bird, *apptd* 1993; Duncan Whitworth, *apptd* 1996; Malcolm Convery, *apptd* 1999

ARCHDEACON
Isle of Man, Ven. Brian Partington, *apptd* 1996

Vicar-General and Chancellor, Clare Faulds
Registrar and Legal Secretary, Christopher Callow
Diocesan Secretary, Christine Roberts, Holly Cottage, Ballaughton Meadows, Douglas, Isle of Man IM2 1JG. Tel: 01624-626994

SOUTHWARK (Canterbury)

9TH BISHOP
Rt. Revd Dr Tom F. Butler, *cons.* 1985, *apptd* 1998; Bishop's House, 38 Tooting Bec Gardens, London SW16 1QZ. *Signs* Thomas Southwark

AREA BISHOPS
Croydon, vacant
Kingston upon Thames, Rt. Revd Richard Cheetham, *cons* 2002, *apptd* 2002
Woolwich, Rt. Revd Dr Colin O. Buchanan, *cons.* 1985, *apptd* 1996; 37 South Road, Forest Hill, London SE23 2UJ

DEAN
Very Revd Colin B. Slee, OBE, *apptd* 1994

CANONS RESIDENTIARY
Helen Cunliffe, *apptd* 1995; Jeffrey John, *apptd* 1997; Bruce Saunders, *apptd* 1997; Andrew Nunn, *apptd* 1999; Stephen Roberts, *apptd* 2000
Organist, Peter Wright, FRCO, *apptd* 1989

ARCHDEACONS
Croydon, Ven. Tony Davies, *apptd* 1994
Lambeth, Ven. Nick Baines, *apptd* 2000
Lewisham, Ven. Christine Hardman, *apptd* 2001
Reigate, Ven. Daniel Kajumba, *apptd* 2001
Southwark, Ven. Douglas Bartles-Smith, *apptd* 1985
Wandsworth, Ven. David Gerrard, *apptd* 1989

Chancellor, Charles George, QC
Registrar and Legal Secretary, Paul Morris
Diocesan Secretary, Simon Parton, Trinity House, 4 Chapel Court, Borough High Street, London SE1 1HW. Tel: 020-7939 9400

SOUTHWELL (York)

10TH BISHOP
Rt. Revd George H. Cassidy, *cons.* 1999, *apptd* 1999; Bishop's Manor, Southwell NG25 0JR. *Signs* George Southwell

BISHOP SUFFRAGAN
Sherwood, Rt. Revd Alan W. Morgan, *cons.* 1989, *apptd* 1989; Dunham House, Westgate, Southwell, Notts NG25 0JL

DEAN
Very Revd David Leaning, *apptd* 1991

CANONS RESIDENTIARY
Graham Hendy *apptd* 1997; Richard Davey, *apptd* 1999
Organist, Paul Hale, apptd 1989

ARCHDEACONS
Newark, Ven. Nigel Peyton, *apptd* 1999
Nottingham, Ven. Gordon Ogilvie, *apptd* 1996

Chancellor, John Shand, *apptd* 1981
Registrar and Legal Secretary, Christopher Hodson
Diocesan Secretary, Peter Prentis, Dunham House, Westgate, Southwell, Notts NG25 0JL. Tel: 01636-817204

TRURO (Canterbury)

14TH BISHOP
Rt. Revd William Ind, *cons.* 1987, *apptd* 1997; Lis Escop, Truro TR3 6QQ. *Signs* William Truro

BISHOP SUFFRAGAN
St Germans, Revd Royden Screech, *cons.* 2000, *apptd* 2000

DEAN
Very Revd Michael A. Moxon, LVO, *apptd* 1998

CANONS RESIDENTIARY
Perran Gay, *apptd* 1994; Paul Mellor, *apptd* 1994; Peter Walker, *apptd* 2001

Organist, Robert Sharpe, *apptd.* 2002

ARCHDEACONS
Cornwall, Ven. Rodney Whiteman, *apptd* 2000
Bodmin, Ven. Clive Cohen, *apptd* 2000

Chancellor, Timothy Briden, *apptd* 1998
Registrar and Legal Secretary, Michael Follett
Diocesan Secretary, Ben Laite, Diocesan House, Kenwyn, Truro TR1 1UQ. Tel: 01872-274351

WAKEFIELD (York)

12TH BISHOP
vacant

BISHOP SUFFRAGAN

Pontefract, Rt. Revd David C. James, *cons.* 1998, *apptd* 1998; Pontefract House, 181A Manygates Lane, Wakefield WF2 7DR

DEAN

Very Revd George P. Nairn-Briggs, *apptd* 1997

CANONS RESIDENTIARY

Richard Capper, *apptd* 1997; Robert Gage, *apptd* 1997; Ian Gaskell, *apptd* 1998; John Holmes, *apptd* 1998

Organist, Jonathan Bielby, FRCO, *apptd* 1972

ARCHDEACONS
Halifax, vacant
Pontefract, Ven. Tony Robinson, *apptd* 1997

Chancellor, Peter Collier, QC, *apptd* 1992
Registrar and Legal Secretary, Linda Box
Diocesan Secretary, Ashley Ellis, Church House, 1 South Parade, Wakefield WF1 1LP. Tel: 01924-371802

WORCESTER (Canterbury)

112TH BISHOP
Rt. Revd Dr Peter S. M. Selby, *cons.* 1984, *apptd* 1997; The Bishop's House, Hartlebury Castle, Kidderminster DY11 7XX. *Signs* Peter Wigorn:

AREA BISHOP

Dudley, Rt. Revd Dr David S. Walker, *cons.* 2000, *apptd* 2000; The Bishop's House, Bishop's Walk, Cradley Heath B64 7JF

DEAN

Very Revd Peter J. Marshall, *apptd* 1997

CANONS RESIDENTIARY

Bruce Ruddock, *apptd.* 1999; J. D. Tetley, *apptd* 1999; Alvyn Pettersen, *apptd* 2002

Organist, Adrian Lucas, *apptd* 1996

ARCHDEACONS

Dudley, Ven. Fred Trethewey, *apptd* 2001
Worcester, Ven. Dr Joy Tetley

Chancellor, Charles Mynors, *apptd* 1999
Registrar and Legal Secretary, Michael Huskinson
Diocesan Secretary, Robert Higham, The Old Palace, Deansway, Worcester WR1 2JE. Tel: 01905-20537

ROYAL PECULIARS

WESTMINSTER

The Collegiate Church of St Peter

Dean, Very Revd Dr Wesley Carr, *apptd* 1997
Sub Dean and Archdeacon, David Hutt, *apptd* 1995
Canons of Westminster, David Hutt, *apptd* 1995; Michael

Middleton, *apptd* 1997; Robert Wright, *apptd* 1998; Dr Tom Wright, *apptd* 1999
Chapter Clerk and Receiver-General, Maj.-Gen. David Burden, CB, CBE, Chapter Office, 20 Dean's Yard, London SW1P 3PA

Organist, James O'Donnell, *apptd* 1999
Registrar, Stuart Holmes, MVO
Legal Secretary, Christopher Vyse, *apptd* 2000

WINDSOR

The Queen's Free Chapel of St George within Her Castle of Windsor

Dean, Rt. Revd David Conner, *apptd* 1998
Canons Residentiary, John White, *apptd* 1982; Laurence Gunner, *apptd* 1996; Barry Thompson, Ph.D., *apptd* 1998; John Ovenden, *apptd* 1998
Chapter Clerk, Lt.-Col. Nigel Newman, *apptd* 1990, Chapter Office, The Cloisters, Windsor Castle, Windsor, Berks SL4 1NJ

Organist, Jonathan Rees-Williams, FRCO, *apptd* 1991

Other Anglican Churches

THE CHURCH IN WALES

The Anglican Church was the established church in Wales from the 16th century until 1920, when the estrangement of the majority of Welsh people from Anglicanism resulted in disestablishment. Since then the Church in Wales has been an autonomous province consisting of six sees. The bishops are elected by an electoral college comprising elected lay and clerical members, who also elect one of the diocesan bishops as Archbishop of Wales.
  The legislative body of the Church in Wales is the Governing Body, which has 350 members divided between the three orders of bishops, clergy and laity. Its President is the Archbishop of Wales and it meets twice annually. Its decisions are binding upon all members of the Church. The Church's property and finances are the responsibility of the Representative Body. There are about 90,000 members of the Church in Wales, with about 650 stipendiary clergy and 1,071 parishes.

THE GOVERNING BODY OF THE CHURCH IN WALES, 39 Cathedral Road, Cardiff CF1 9XF. Tel: 029-2034 8200. *Provincial Secretary,* J. Shirley

ARCHBISHOP OF WALES, vacant

BISHOPS

Bangor (79th), Rt. Revd F. J. Saunders Davies, *b.* 1937, *cons.* 2000, *elected* 1999; Tŷ' r Esgob, Bangor, Gwynedd LL57 2SS. *Signs* Saunders Bangor, *Stipendiary clergy,* 70
Llandaff (102nd), Rt. Revd Dr Barry C. Morgan, *b.* 1947, *cons.* 1993, *translated* 1999; Llys Esgob, The Cathedral Green, Llandaff, Cardiff CF5 2YE. *Signs* Barry Landav. *Stipendiary clergy,* 146
Monmouth (8th), vacant; Bishopstow, Stow Hill, Newport NP20 4EA. *Stipendiary clergy,* 106
St Asaph (74th), Rt. Revd John S. Davies, *b.* 1943, *cons.* 1999, *elected* 1999; Esgobty, St Asaph, Denbighshire LL17 0TW. *Signs* John St Asaph. *Stipendiary clergy,* 116
St David's (126th), Rt. Revd Carl N. Cooper, *b.* 1960, *cons.* 2002, *elected* 2002; Llys Esgob, Abergwili, Carmarthen SA31 2JG. *Signs* Carl St Davids. *Stipendiary clergy,* 126
Swansea and Brecon (8th), Rt. Revd Anthony E. Pierce, *b.* 1941, *cons.* 1999, *elected* 1999; Ely Tower, Brecon,

Powys LD3 9DE. *Signs* Anthony Swansea & Brecon. *Stipendiary clergy,* 85

The stipend of a diocesan bishop of the Church in Wales is £30,314 a year from 2002

THE SCOTTISH EPISCOPAL CHURCH

The Scottish Episcopal Church was founded after the Act of Settlement (1690) established the presbyterian nature of the Church of Scotland. The Scottish Episcopal Church is in full communion with the Church of England but is autonomous. The governing authority is the General Synod, an elected body of approximately 170 members which meets once a year. The diocesan bishop who convenes and presides at meetings of the General Synod is called the Primus and is elected by his fellow bishops.

There are 46,237 members of the Scottish Episcopal Church, of whom 29,810 are communicants. There are seven bishops, approximately 520 serving clergy, and 327 churches and places of worship.

THE GENERAL SYNOD OF THE SCOTTISH EPISCOPAL CHURCH, 21 Grosvenor Crescent, Edinburgh EH12 5EE. Tel: 0131-225 6357.

Web: www.scottishepiscopal.com

Secretary-General, J. F. Stuart

PRIMUS OF THE SCOTTISH EPISCOPAL CHURCH, Most Revd A. Bruce Cameron (Bishop of Aberdeen and Orkney), *elected* 2000

BISHOPS

Aberdeen and Orkney, A. Bruce Cameron, *b.* 1941, *cons.* 1992, *elected* 1992. *Clergy,* 53

Argyll and the Isles, Douglas M. Cameron, *b.* 1935, *cons.* 1993, *elected* 1992. *Clergy,* 24

Brechin, Neville Chamberlain, *b.* 1939, *cons.* 1997, *elected* 1997. *Clergy,* 30

Edinburgh, Brian Smith, *b.* 1943, *cons.* 1993, *elected* 2001. *Clergy,* 143

Glasgow and Galloway, Idris Jones, *b.* 1943, *cons.* 1998, *elected* 1998. *Clergy,* 105

Moray, Ross and Caithness, John Crook, *b.* 1940, *cons.* 1999, *elected* 1999. *Clergy,* 32

St Andrews, Dunkeld and Dunblane, Michael H. G. Henley, *b.* 1938, *cons.* 1995, *elected* 1995. *Clergy,* 70

The minimum stipend of a diocesan bishop of the Scottish Episcopal Church was £24,354 in 2002 (i.e. 1.5 x the minimum clergy stipend of £16,236)

THE CHURCH OF IRELAND

The Anglican Church was the established church in Ireland from the 16th century but never secured the allegiance of a majority of the Irish and was disestablished in 1871. The Church of Ireland is divided into the provinces of Armagh and Dublin, each under an archbishop. The provinces are subdivided into 12 dioceses.

The legislative body is the General Synod, which has 660 members in total, divided between the House of Bishops and the House of Representatives. The Archbishop of Armagh is elected by the House of Bishops; other episcopal elections are made by an electoral college.

There are about 375,000 members of the Church of Ireland, with two archbishops, ten bishops, about 600 clergy and about 1,100 churches and places of worship.

CENTRAL OFFICE, Church of Ireland House, Church Avenue, Rathmines, Dublin 6. Tel: 00-353-1-4978422.

Chief Officer and Secretary of the Representative Church Body, D. C. Reardon

PROVINCE OF ARMAGH

ARCHBISHOP OF ARMAGH AND PRIMATE OF ALL IRELAND, Most Revd Robert H. A. Eames, Ph.D., *b.* 1937, *cons.* 1975, *trans.* 1986. *Clergy,* 55

BISHOPS

Clogher, Michael G. Jackson, *b.* 1956, *cons.* 2002, *apptd* 2002. *Clergy,* 32

Connor, Alan E. T. Harper, OBE, *b.* 1944, *cons.* 2002, *apptd* 2002. *Clergy,* 106

Derry and Raphoe, Kenneth R. Good, *b.* 1592, *cons.* 2002, *apptd* 2002. *Clergy,* 51

Down and Dromore, Harold C. Miller, *b.* 1950, *cons.* 1997, *apptd* 1997. *Clergy,* 116

Kilmore, Elphin and Ardagh, Kenneth H. Clarke, *b.* 1949, *cons.* 2001, *apptd* 2001. *Clergy,* 21

Tuam, Killala and Achonry, Richard C. A. Henderson, DPhil, *b.* 1957, *cons.* 1998, *apptd* 1998. *Clergy,* 13

PROVINCE OF DUBLIN

ARCHBISHOP OF DUBLIN, BISHOP OF GLENDALOUGH, AND PRIMATE OF IRELAND, Most Revd John R. W. Neill, *b.* 1945, *apptd* 2002 *Clergy,* 86

BISHOPS

Cashel and Ossory, John R. W. Neill, *b.* 1945, *cons.* 1986, *trans.* 1997. *Clergy,* 42

Cork, Cloyne and Ross, W. Paul Colton, *b.* 1960, *cons.* 1999, *apptd* 1999. *Clergy,* 30

Limerick and Killaloe, Michael H. G. Mayes, *b.* 1941, *cons.* 1993, *apptd* 2000. *Clergy,* 19

Meath and Kildare, (Most Revd) Richard L. Clarke, Ph.D., *b.* 1949, *cons.* 1996, *apptd* 1996. *Clergy,* 26

OVERSEAS

PRIMATES

PRIMATE AND PRESIDING BISHOP OF AOTEAROA, NEW ZEALAND AND POLYNESIA, Rt. Revd John Paterson (Bishop of Auckland), *cons.* 1995, *apptd* 1998

PRIMATE OF AUSTRALIA, Most Revd Peter Carnley (Archbishop of Perth), *cons.* 1981, *apptd* 2000

PRIMATE OF BRAZIL, Most Revd Glauco Soares de Lima (Bishop of São Paulo), *cons.* 1989, *apptd* 1994

ARCHBISHOP OF THE PROVINCE OF BURUNDI, Most Revd Samuel Ndayisenga (Bishop of Buye), *apptd* 1998

ARCHBISHOP AND PRIMATE OF CANADA, Most Revd Michael G. Peers, *cons.* 1977, *elected* 1986

ARCHBISHOP OF THE PROVINCE OF CENTRAL AFRICA, Most Revd Bernard A. Malango (Bishop of Northern Zambia), *elected* 2000

PRIMATE OF THE CENTRAL REGION OF AMERICA, Most Revd Cornelius J. Wilson (Bishop of Costa Rica), *cons.* 1978, *apptd* 1998

ARCHBISHOP OF THE PROVINCE OF CONGO, Most Revd Patrice Byankya Njojo (Bishop of Boga), *cons.* 1980, *apptd* 1992

PRIMATE OF THE PROVINCE OF HONG KONG SHENG KUNG HUI, Most Revd Peter Kwong (Bishop of Hong Kong Island), *cons.* 1981, *apptd* 1998

ARCHBISHOP OF THE PROVINCE OF THE INDIAN OCEAN, Most Revd Remi Rabenirina (Bishop of Antananarivo), *cons.* 1984, *apptd* 1995

PRESIDENT-BISHOP OF JERUSALEM AND THE MIDDLE EAST, Most Revd Iraj Mottahedeh, *apptd* 2000

ARCHBISHOP OF THE PROVINCE OF KENYA, Most

Revd Dr David M. Gitari (Bishop of Nairobi), *cons.*
1975, *apptd* 1996
ARCHBISHOP OF THE PROVINCE OF KOREA, Most
Revd Paul Hwan Yoon (Bishop of Taejon), *cons.* 1987,
apptd 2000
ARCHBISHOP OF THE PROVINCE OF MELANESIA,
Most Revd Ellison L. Pogo, KBE (Bishop of Central
Melanesia), *cons.* 1981, *apptd* 1994
ARCHBISHOP OF MEXICO, Most Revd Samuel Espinoza
(Bishop of Western Mexico), *cons.* 1981, *elected* 1995
ARCHBISHOP OF THE PROVINCE OF MYANMAR, Rt.
Revd Samuel San Si Htay (Bishop of Yangon), *cons.*
2001, *apptd* 2001
ARCHBISHOP OF THE PROVINCE OF NIGERIA, Most
Revd Peter Akinola (Bishop of Abuja), *cons.* 1989,
apptd 2000
PRIMATE OF NIPPON SEI KO KAI, Rt. Revd John
Jun'Ichiro Furumoto (Bishop of Kobe), *elected* 2000
ARCHBISHOP OF PAPUA NEW GUINEA, Most Revd
James Ayong (Bishop of Aipo Rongo), *cons.* 1995,
elected 1996
PRIME BISHOP OF THE PHILIPPINES, Most Revd
Ignacio C. Soliba, *cons.* 1991, *apptd* 1997
ARCHBISHOP OF THE PROVINCE OF RWANDA, Most
Revd Emmanuel Kolini Mboni (Bishop of Kigali),
cons. 1980, *apptd* 1997
PRIMATE OF THE PROVINCE OF SOUTH EAST ASIA,
Most Revd Ping Chung Yong (Bishop of Sabah), *cons.*
1990 *apptd* 1999
METROPOLITAN OF THE PROVINCE OF SOUTHERN
AFRICA, Most Revd Winston H. N. Ndungane
(Archbishop of Cape Town), *cons.* 1991, trans. 1996
PRESIDING BISHOP OF THE SOUTHERN CONE OF
AMERICA, Rt. Revd Maurice Sinclair (Bishop of
Northern Argentina), *cons.* 1990
ARCHBISHOP OF THE PROVINCE OF THE SUDAN,
Most Revd Joseph Marona (Bishop of Juba) *cons.*
1984, *apptd* 2000
ARCHBISHOP OF THE PROVINCE OF TANZANIA, Most
Revd Donald L. Mtetemela (Bishop of Ruaha), *cons.*
1982, *apptd* 1998
ARCHBISHOP OF THE PROVINCE OF UGANDA, Most
Revd Livingstone Mpalanyi-Nkoyoyo. *cons.* 1980
PRESIDING BISHOP AND PRIMATE OF THE USA, Most
Revd Frank T. Griswold III, *cons.* 1985, *apptd* 1997
ARCHBISHOP OF THE PROVINCE OF WEST AFRICA,
Most Revd Robert Okine (Bishop of Koforidua), *cons.*
1981, *apptd* 1993
ARCHBISHOP OF THE PROVINCE OF THE WEST
INDIES, Most Revd Drexel Gomez (Bishop of Nassau
and the Bahamas), *cons.* 1972, *apptd* 1998

OTHER CHURCHES
AND EXTRA-PROVINCIAL DIOCESES

ANGLICAN CHURCH OF BERMUDA, Rt. Revd Ewen
Ratteray, *apptd* 1996
CHURCH OF CEYLON: This Church comes under the
Metropolitical authority of the Archbishop of
Canterbury.
Bishop of Colombo, vacant
Bishop of Kurunagala, Rt. Revd Andrew O. Kumarage,
cons. 1984
EPISCOPAL CHURCH OF CUBA, Rt. Revd Jorge Perera
Hurtado, *apptd* 1995
LUSITANIAN CHURCH *(Portuguese Episcopal Church)*,
Rt. Revd Fernando da Luz Soares, *apptd* 1971
SPANISH REFORMED EPISCOPAL CHURCH, Rt. Revd
Carlos Lozano Lopez, *apptd* 1995
EXTRA-PROVINCIAL TO PROVINCE IX OF THE

EPISCOPAL CHURCH IN THE USA:
PUERTO RICO, Rt. Revd David Andres Alvarez-
Velazquez, *cons.* 1987
VENEZUELA, Rt. Revd Orlando Guerrero, *cons.* 1995

MODERATORS OF CHURCHES IN FULL
COMMUNION WITH THE ANGLICAN
COMMUNION

CHURCH OF NORTH INDIA, Most Revd Zechariah J.
Terom (Bishop of Chotanagpur)
CHURCH OF SOUTH INDIA, Most Revd Joseph Samuel
(Bishop of East Kerala), *cons.* 1990, *apptd* 2000
CHURCH OF PAKISTAN, Rt. Revd Samuel Azariah,
Bishop of Raiwind
CHURCH OF BANGLADESH, Rt. Revd Barnabas Mondal,
cons. 1975, *apptd* 1975

The Church of Scotland

The Church of Scotland is the established (i.e. national)
church of Scotland. The Church is Reformed in doctrine,
and presbyterian in constitution, i.e. based on a hierarchy
of councils of ministers and elders and, since 1990, of
members of a diaconate. At local level the Kirk Session
consists of the parish minister and ruling elders. At
district level the presbyteries, of which there are 47 in
Britain, consist of all the ministers in the district, one
ruling elder from each congregation, and those members
of the diaconate who qualify for membership. The
General Assembly is the supreme authority, and is
presided over by a Moderator chosen annually by the
Assembly. The Sovereign, if not present in person, is
represented by a Lord High Commissioner who is
appointed each year by the Crown.
  The Church of Scotland has about 600,000 members,
1,200 ministers and 1,600 churches. There are about 100
ministers and other personnel working overseas.
Lord High Commissioner (2002), The Rt. Hon. Viscount
Younger of Leckie
Moderator of the General Assembly (2002), The Rt. Revd
Finlay Macdonald
Principal Clerk, Revd M. A. MacLean
Procurator, P. S. Hodge
Law Agent and Solicitor of the Church, Mrs J. S. Wilson
Parliamentary Agent, I. McCulloch (London)
General Treasurer, D. F. Ross
Secretary, Church and Nation Committee, Revd Dr D.
Sinclair
CHURCH OFFICE, 121 George Street, Edinburgh
EH2 4YN. Tel: 0131-225 5722

PRESBYTERIES AND CLERKS

Edinburgh, Revd W. P. Graham
West Lothian, Revd D. Shaw
Lothian, J. D. McCulloch, DL

Melrose and Peebles, Revd J. M. Brown
Duns, Revd J. S. H. Cutler
Jedburgh, Revd A. D. Reid

Annandale and Eskdale, Revd C. B. Haston
Dumfries and Kirkcudbright, Revd G. M. A. Savage
Wigtown and Stranraer, Revd D. W. Dutton

Ayr, Revd J. Crichton
Irvine and Kilmarnock, Revd C. G. G. Brookie
Ardrossan, Revd D. Broster

Lanark, Revd G. J. Elliott
Paisley, Revd D. Kay

Greenock, Revd D. Mill
Glasgow, Revd D. W. Lunan
Hamilton, Revd J. H. Wilson
Dumbarton, Revd D. P. Munro

South Argyll, M. A. J. Gossip, OBE
Dunoon, Revd R. Samuel
Lorn and Mull, Revd J. A. McCormick

Falkirk, Revd I. W. Black
Stirling, Revd G. G. Cringles

Dunfermline, Revd W. E. Farquhar
Kirkcaldy, Revd B. L. Tomlinson
St Andrews, Revd P. Meager

Dunkeld and Meigle, Revd J. Russell
Perth, Revd D. G. Lawson
Dundee, Revd J. A. Roy
Angus, Revd M. I. G. Rooney

Aberdeen, Revd A. M. Douglas
Kincardine and Deeside, Revd J. W. S. Brown
Gordon, Revd E. Glen
Buchan, Revd A. Macgregor
Moray, Revd G. M. Wood

Abernethy, Revd J. A. I. MacEwan
Inverness, Revd A. S. Younger
Lochaber, Revd D. M. Anderson

Ross, Revd T. M. McWilliam
Sutherland, Revd J. L. Goskirk
Caithness, Mrs M. Gillies, MBE
Lochcarron/Skye, Revd A. I. MacArthur
Uist, Revd M. Smith
Lewis, Revd T. S. Sinclair

Orkney, Revd T. G. Hunt
Shetland, Revd C. H. M.Greig
England, Revd W. A. Cairns

Europe, Revd J. A. Cowie

The minimum stipend of a minister in the Church of
Scotland in 2002 was £18,737

The Roman Catholic Church

The Roman Catholic Church is one world-wide Christian
Church acknowledging as its head the Bishop of Rome,
known as the Pope (Father). He leads a communion of
followers of Christ, who believe they continue his
presence in the world as servants of faith, hope and love
to all society. The Pope is held to be the successor of St
Peter and thus invested with the power which was
entrusted to St Peter by Jesus Christ. A direct line of
succession is therefore claimed from the earliest Christian
communities. With the fall of the Roman Empire the
Pope also became an important political leader. His
territory is now limited to the 107 acres of the Vatican
City State, created to provide some indepence to the Pope
from Italy and other nations.

The Pope exercises spiritual authority over the Church
with the advice and assistance of the Sacred College of
Cardinals, the supreme council of the Church. He is also
advised by bishops in communion with him, by a group
of officers which form the Roman Curia and by his
ambassadors, called Apostolic Nuncios, who liaise with
the Bishops' Conference in each country.

Those members of the College of Cardinals who are
under the age of 80 elect a successor of the Pope following
his death. The assembly of the Cardinals called tothe
Vatican for the election of a new Pope is known as the
Conclave. In complete seclusion the Cardinals vote by a

secret ballot; a two-thirds majority is necessary before the
vote can be accepted as final. When a Cardinal receives
the necessary number of votes, the Dean of the Sacred
College formally asks him if he will accept election and
the name by which he wishes to be known. On his
acceptance of the office of Supreme Pontiff, the Conclave
is dissolved and the first Cardinal Deacon announces the
election to the assembled crowd in St Peter's Square.

The number of cardinals was fixed at 70 by Pope Sixtus
V in 1586, but has been steadily increased since the
pontificate of John XXIII and at the end of July 2001
stood at 189, plus two cardinals created 'in pectore' (their
names being kept secret by the Pope for fear of
persecution; they are thought to be Chinese).

The Pope has full legislative, judicial and adminstrative
power over the whole church. He is aided in his
administration by the Curia, which is made up of a
number of departments. The Secretariat of State is the
central office for carrying out the Pope's instructions and
is presided over by the Cardinal Secretary of State. It
maintains relations with the departments of the Curia,
with the episcopate, with the representatives of the Holy
See in various countries, governments and private
persons. The congregations and pontifical councils are
the Pope's ministries and include departments such as the
Congregation for the Doctrine of Faith, whose field of
competence concern faith and morals; the Congregation
for the Clergy and the Congregation for the
Evangelisation of Peoples, the Pontifical Council for the
Family and the Pontifical Council for the Promotion of
Christian Unity.

The Vatican State does not have diplomatic
representatives. The Holy See, composed of the Pope and
those who help him in his mission for the Church, is
recognised by the Conventions of Vienna as an
International Moral Body. The representatives of the
Holy See are known as Apostolic Nuncios. Where
representation is only to the local churches and not to the
government of a country, the Papal representative is
known as an apostolic delegate. The Roman Catholic
Church has an estimated 1,045 million adherents under
the care of 2,707 diocesan bishops world-wide.

SOVEREIGN PONTIFF

His Holiness Pope John Paul II (Karol Wojtyla), *born*
Wadowice, Poland, 18 May 1920; *ordained priest* 1946;
appointed Archbishop of Kraków 1964; *created Cardinal*
1967; *assumed pontificate* 16 October 1978

SECRETARIAT OF STATE

Secretary of State, HE Cardinal Angelo Sodano
First Section (General Affairs), Archbishop Leonardo
Sandri (Titular Archbishop of Cittanova)
Second Section (Relations with other states), Most Revd J.
L. Tauran (Titular Archbishop of Telepte)

BISHOPS' CONFERENCE

The Roman Catholic Church in England and Wales
consists of a total of 22 diocese and is governed by the
Bishops' Conference, membership of which includes the
Diocesan Bishops, the Apostolic Exarch of the
Ukrainians, the Bishop of the Forces and the Auxiliary
Bishops. The Conference is headed by the President *(HE
Cardinal Cormac Murphy-O'Connor, Archbishop of
Westminster)* and Vice-President *(The Most Revd Patrick
Kelly, Archbishop of Liverpool).* There are five
departments, each with an episcopal chairman: the
Department for Christian Life and Worship (the Bishop
of Menevia), the Department for Mission and Unity (the
Bishop of Portsmouth), the Department for Catholic
Education and Formation (the Archbishop of

Birmingham), the Department for Christian Responsibility and Citizenship (the Bishop of Cardiff), and the Department for International Affairs (the Bishop of Leeds).

The Bishops' Standing Committee, made up of all the Archbishops and the chairman of each of the above departments, has general responsibility for continuity of policy between the plenary sessions of the Conference. It prepares the Conference agenda and implements its decisions. It is serviced by a General Secretariat. There are also agencies and consultative bodies affiliated to the Conference.

The Bishops' Conference of Scotland is the permanently constituted assembly of the Bishops of Scotland. The Conference is headed by the President (The most Revd Keith P. O'Brien, Archbishop of St. Andrews and Edinburgh). To promote its work, the Conference establishes various agencies which have an advisory function in relation to the Conference. The more important of these agencies are called Commissions and each one has a Bishop President who, with the other members of the Commissions, are appointed by the Conference.

The Irish Episcopal Conference has as its president Archbishop Brady of Armagh. Its membership comprises all the Archbishops and Bishops of Ireland and it appoints various Commissions to assist it in its work. There are three types of Commissions: (a) those made up of lay and clerical members chosen for their skills and experience, and staffed by full-time expert secretariats; (b) Commissions whose members are selected from existing -institutions and whose services are supplied on a part-time basis; and (c) Commissions of Bishops only.

The Roman Catholic Church in Britain and Ireland has an estimated 8,992,000 members, 11 archbishops, 67 bishops, 11,260 priests, and 8,588 churches and chapels open to the public.

Bishops' Conferences secretariats:

ENGLAND AND WALES, 39 Eccleston Square, London SW1V 1BX. Tel: 020-7630 8220; Fax: 020 7630 5166; Email: secretariat@cbcew.org.uk; Web: www.catholic-ew.org.uk. *General Secretary*, Mgr Andrew Summersgill

SCOTLAND, 64 Aitken Street, Airdrie, Lanarkshire ML6 6LT. *General Secretary*, Mgr Henry Docherty

IRELAND, Columba Centre, Maynooth, County Kildare. *Secretary*, The Most Revd William Lee (Bishop of Waterford and Lismore) *Executive Secretarys*, Revd Aidan O'Boyle

GREAT BRITAIN

APOSTOLIC NUNCIO TO GREAT BRITAIN
The Most Revd Pablo Puente, 54 Parkside, London SW19 5NE. Tel: 020-8946 1410

ENGLAND AND WALES

THE MOST REVD ARCHBISHOPS
Westminster, H. E. Cardinal Cormac Murphy-O'Connor, *cons.* 1977, *apptd* 2000
Auxiliaries, James J. O'Brien, *cons.* 1977; Arthur Roche, *cons.* 2001; George Stack, *cons.* 2001
Clergy, 762
Archbishop's Residence, Archbishop's House, Ambrosden Avenue, London SW1P 1QJ. Tel: 020-7798 9033
Birmingham, Vincent Nichols, *cons.* 1992, *apptd* 2000
Auxiliaries, Philip Pargeter, *cons.* 1990

Clergy, 511
Diocesan Curia, Cathedral House, St Chad's Queensway, Birmingham B4 6EX. Tel: 0121-236 5535
Cardiff, Peter Smith, *cons.* 1995, *apptd* 2001
Clergy, 126
Diocesan Curia, Archbishop's House, 41–43 Cathedral Road, Cardiff CF11 9HD. Tel: 029-2022 0411
Liverpool, Patrick Kelly, *cons.* 1984, *apptd* 1996
Auxiliary, Vincent Malone, *cons.* 1989
Clergy, 522
Diocesan Curia, Archdiocese of Liverpool, Centre for Evengelisation, Croxteth Drive, Sefton Park, Liverpool L17 1AA. Tel: 0151-522 1000
Southwark, Michael Bowen, *cons.* 1970, *apptd* 1977
Auxiliaries, John Hine, *cons.* 2001; Howard Tripp, *cons.* 1980
Clergy, 518
Diocesan Curia, Archbishop's House, 150 St George's Road, London SE1 6HX. Tel: 020-7928 5592

THE RT. REVD BISHOPS
Arundel and Brighton, Kieran Conry, *cons.* 2001, *apptd* 2001. *Clergy*, 274. *Diocesan Curia*, Bishop's House, The Upper Drive, Hove, E. Sussex BN3 6NE. Tel: 01273-506387
Brentwood, Thomas McMahon, *cons.* 1980, *apptd* 1980. *Clergy*, 175. *Bishop's Office*, Cathedral House, Ingrave Road, Brentwood, Essex CM15 8AT. Tel: 01277-232266
Clifton, Declan Lang, *cons.* 2001, *apptd* 2001. *Clergy*, 254. *Diocesan Curia*, Egerton Road, Bishopston, Bristol BS7 8HU. Tel: 0117-983 3907
East Anglia, vacant. *Clergy*, 164. *Diocesan Curia*, The White House, 21 Upgate, Poringland, Norwich NR14 7SH. Tel: 01508-492202
Hallam, John Rawsthorne, *cons.* 1981, *apptd* 1997. *Clergy*, 75. *Bishop's Residence*, 'Quarters', Carsick Hill Way, Sheffield S10 3LY. Tel: 0114-230 9101
Hexham and Newcastle, Michael Ambrose Griffiths, *cons.* 1992, *apptd* 1992. *Clergy*, 261. *Diocesan Curia*, Bishop's House, East Denton Hall, 800 West Road, Newcastle upon Tyne NE5 2BJ. Tel: 0191-228 0003
Lancaster, Patrick O'Donoghue, *cons.* 2001, *apptd* 2001. *Clergy*, 248. *Bishop's Residence*, Bishop's House, Cannon Hill, Lancaster LA1 5NG. Tel: 01524-32231
Leeds, David Konstant, *cons.* 1977, *apptd* 1985. *Clergy*, 254. *Diocesan Curia*, Hinsley Hall, 62 Headingley Lane, Leeds LS6 2BU. Tel: 0113-261 8000
Menevia (Wales), Mark Jabalé, *cons.* 2001, *apptd* 2001. *Clergy*, 60. *Diocesan Curia*, 27 Convent Street, Greenhill, Swansea SA1 2BX. Tel: 01792-644017
Middlesbrough, John Crowley, *cons.* 1986, *apptd* 1992. *Clergy*, 182. *Diocesan Curia*, 50A The Avenue, Linthorpe, Middlesbrough, Cleveland TS5 6QT. Tel: 01642-850505
Northampton, Kevin McDonald, *cons.* 2001, *apptd* 2001. *Clergy*, 159. *Diocesan Curia*, Bishop's House, Marriott Street, Northampton NN2 6AW. Tel: 01604-715635
Nottingham, Malcolm McMahon, *cons.* 2000, *apptd* 2000. *Clergy*, 214. *Diocesan Curia*, Willson House, Derby Road, Nottingham NG1 5AW. Tel: 0115-953 9800
Plymouth, Christopher Budd, *cons.* 1986, *apptd* 1985. *Clergy*, 170. *Diocesan Curia*, Bishop's House, 31 Wyndham Street West, Plymouth PL1 5RZ. Tel: 01752-224414
Portsmouth, F. Crispian Hollis, *cons.* 1987, *apptd* 1989. *Clergy*, 282. *Bishop's Residence*, Bishop's House, Edinburgh Road, Portsmouth, Hants PO1 3HG. Tel: 023-9282 0894

Salford, Terence J. Brain, *cons.* 1991, *apptd* 1997. *Clergy,* 371. Diocesan Curia, Cathedral House, 250 Chapel Street, Salford M3 5LL. Tel: 0161-834 9052

Shrewsbury, Brian Noble, *cons.* 1995, *apptd* 1995. Clergy 190. Diocesan Curia, 2 Park Road South, Prenton, Wirral CH43 4UX. Tel: 0151-652 9855

Wrexham (Wales), Edwin Regan, *cons.* 1994, *apptd* 1994. *Clergy,* 83. Diocesan Curia, Bishop's House, Sontley Road, Wrexham LL13 7EW. Tel: 01978-262726

SCOTLAND

THE MOST REVD ARCHBISHOPS

St Andrews and Edinburgh, Keith Patrick O'Brien, *cons.* 1985, *apptd* 1985 *Clergy,* 188 Diocesan Curia, 113 Whitehouse Loan, Edinburgh EH9 1BD. Tel: 0131-452 8244

Glasgow, Mario Joseph Conti, *cons.* 1977, *apptd* 2002 *Clergy,* 257 Diocesan Curia, 196 Clyde Street, Glasgow G1 4JY. Tel: 0141-226 5898

THE RT. REVD BISHOPS

Aberdeen, vacant. *Clergy,* 46. Bishop's Residence, 3 Queen's Cross, Aberdeen AB15 4XU. Tel: 01224-319154

Argyll and the Isles, Ian Murray, *cons.* 1999, *apptd* 1999. *Clergy,* 26. Diocesan Curia, St Columba's Cathedral, Esplanade, Oban, Argyll PA34 5AB. Tel: 01631-571003

Dunkeld, Vincent Logan, *cons.* 1981. *Clergy,* 44. Diocesan Curia, 24–28 Lawside Road, Dundee DD3 6XY. Tel: 01382-225453

Galloway, Maurice Taylor, *cons.* 1981, *apptd* 1981. *Clergy,* 56. Diocesan Curia, 8 Corsehill Road, Ayr KA7 2ST. Tel: 01292-266750

Motherwell, Joseph Devine, *cons.* 1977, *apptd* 1983. *Clergy,* 148. Diocesan Curia, Coursington Road, Motherwell ML1 1PP. Tel: 01698-269114

Paisley, John A. Mone, *cons.* 1984, *apptd* 1988. *Clergy,* 87. Diocesan Curia, Cathedral House, 8 East Buchanan Street, Paisley, Renfrewshire PA1 1HS. Tel: 0141-889 3601

BISHOPRIC OF THE FORCES

Francis Walmsley, *cons.* 1979, *apptd* 1979. Administration: AGPDO, Middle Hill, Aldershot, Hants GU11 1PP. Tel: 01252-349004

IRELAND

There is one hierarchy for the whole of Ireland. Several of the dioceses have territory partly in the Republic of Ireland and partly in Northern Ireland.

APOSTOLIC NUNCIO TO IRELAND

Most Revd Giuseppe Lazzarotto (titular Archbishop of Numana), 183 Navan Road, Dublin 7. Tel: (00 353) (1) 838 0577 Fax: (00 353) 1 838 0276

THE MOST REVD ARCHBISHOPS

Armagh, Sean Brady, *cons.* 1995, *apptd* 1996 *Auxiliary,* Gerard Clifford, *cons.* 1991 *Clergy,* 183 Diocesan Curia, Ara Coeli, Armagh BT61 7QY. Tel: 028-3752 2045

Cashel, Dermot Clifford, *cons.* 1986, *apptd* 1988 *Clergy,* 128 Archbishop's Residence, Archbishop's House, Thurles, Co. Tipperary. Tel: (00 353) (504) 21512

Dublin, H. E. Cardinal Desmond Connell, *cons.* 1988, *apptd* 1988

Auxiliaries, James Moriarty, *cons.* 1991; Eamonn Walsh, *cons.* 1990; Fiachra O'Ceallaigh, *cons.* 1994; Martin Drennan, *cons.* 1997; Raymond Field, *cons.* 1997 *Clergy,* 994 Archbishop's Residence, Archbishop's House, Drumcondra, Dublin 9. Tel: (00 353) (1) 8373732

Tuam, Michael Neary, *cons.* 1992, *apptd* 1995 *Clergy,* 180 Archbishop's Residence, Archbishop's House, Tuam, Co. Galway. Tel: (00 353) (93) 24166

THE MOST REVD BISHOPS

Achonry, Thomas Flynn, *cons.* 1975, *apptd* 1977. *Clergy,* 62. Bishop's Residence, Bishop's House, Ballaghadaderreen, Co. Roscommon. Tel: (00 353) (907) 60021

Ardagh and Clonmacnois, Colm O'Reilly, *cons.* 1983, *apptd* 1983. *Clergy,* 70. Diocesan Office, Bishop's House, St Michael's, Longford, Co. Longford. Tel: (00 353) (43) 46432

Clogher, Joseph Duffy, *cons.* 1979, *apptd* 1979. *Clergy,* 108. Bishop's Residence, Bishop's House, Monaghan. Tel: (00 353) (47) 81019

Clonfert, John Kirby, *cons.* 1988. *Clergy,* 71. Bishop's Residence, St Brendan's, Coorheen, Loughrea, Co. Galway. Tel: (00 353) (91) 41560

Cloyne, John Magee, *cons.* 1987, *apptd* 1987. *Clergy,* 158. Diocesan Centre, Cobh, Co. Cork. Tel: (00 353) (21) 4811430

Cork and Ross, John Buckley, *cons.* 1984, *apptd* 1998. *Clergy,* 338. Diocesan Office, Bishop's House, Redemption Road, Cork. Tel: (00 353) (21) 4301717

Derry, Seamus Hegarty, *cons.* 1982, *apptd* 1994. *Clergy,* 138. Bishop's Residence, Bishop's House, St Eugene's Cathedral, Derry BT48 9AP. Tel: 028-7126 2302 *Auxiliary,* Francis Lagan, *cons.* 1988

Down and Connor, Patrick J. Walsh, *cons.* 1983, *apptd* 1991. *Clergy,* 248. Bishop's Residence, Lisbreen, 73 Somerton Road, Belfast, Co. Antrim BT15 4DE. Tel: 028-9077 6185 *Auxiliaries,* Anthony Farquhar, *cons.* 1983; Donald McKeown, *cons.* 2001

Dromore, John McAreavey, *cons.* 1999, *apptd* 1999. *Clergy,* 78. Bishop's Residence, Bishop's House, Violet Hill, Newry, Co. Down BT35 6PN. Tel: 028-3026 2444

Elphin, Christopher Jones, *cons.* 1994, *apptd* 1994. *Clergy,* 65. Bishop's Residence, St Mary's, Sligo. Tel: (00 353) (71) 626701

Ferns, Brendon Comiskey, *cons.* 1980, *apptd* 1984. *Clergy,* 161. Bishop's Office, Bishop's House, Summerhill, Wexford. Tel: (00 353) (53) 22177

Galway and Kilmacduagh, James McLoughlin, *cons.* 1993, *apptd* 1993. *Clergy,* 90. Diocesan Office, The Cathedral, Galway. Tel: (00 353) (91) 563566

Kerry, William Murphy, *cons.* 1995, *apptd* 1995. *Clergy,* 133. Bishop's Residence, Bishop's House, Killarney, Co. Kerry. Tel: (00 353) (64) 31168

Kildare and Leighlin, Laurence Ryan, *cons.* 1984. *Clergy,* 136. Bishop's Residence, Bishop's House, Carlow. Tel: (00 353) (503) 76725

Killala, John Fleming, *cons.* 2002, *apptd* 2002. *Clergy,* 62. Bishop's Residence, Bishop's House, Ballina, Co. Mayo. Tel: (00 353) (96) 21518

Killaloe, William Walsh, *cons.* 1994. *Clergy,* 149. Bishop's Residence, Westbourne, Ennis, Co. Clare. Tel: (00 353) (65) 28638

Kilmore, Leo O'Reilly, *cons.* 1997, *apptd* 1998. *Clergy,* 98. Bishop's Residence, Bishop's House, Cullies, Co. Cavan. Tel: (00 353) (49) 31496

Limerick, Donal Murray, *cons.* 1982, *apptd* 1996. *Clergy,* 136. *Diocesan Offices,* 66 O'Connell Street, Limerick. Tel: (00 353) (61) 315856

Meath, Michael Smith, *cons.* 1984, *apptd* 1990. *Clergy,* 141. *Bishop's Residence,* Bishop's House, Dublin Road, Mullingar, Co. Westmeath. Tel: (00 353) (44) 48841

Ossory, Laurence Forristal, *cons.* 1980, *apptd* 1981. *Clergy,* 95. *Bishop's Residence,* Sion House, Kilkenny. Tel: (00 353) (56) 62448

Raphoe, Philip Boyce, *cons.* 1995, *apptd* 1995. *Clergy,* 96. *Bishop's Residence,* Ard Adhamhnáin, Letterkenny, Co. Donegal. Tel: (00 353) (74) 21208

Waterford and Lismore, William Lee, *cons.* 1993. *Clergy,* 130. *Bishop's Residence,* John's Hill, Waterford. Tel: (00 353) (51) 71432

PATRIARCHS IN COMMUNION WITH THE ROMAN CATHOLIC CHURCH

Alexandria, HB Cardinal Stephanos II Ghattas (Patriarch for Catholic Copts)

Antioch, HB Ignace Pierre VIII Abdel-Ahad (Patriarch for Syrian rite Catholics); HB Gregory III Laham (Patriarch for Greek Melekite rite Catholics); HE Cardinal Nasrallah Pierre Sfeir (Patriarch for Maronite rite Catholics)

Jerusalem, HB Michel Sabbah (Patriarch for Latin rite Catholics); HB Maximos V. Hakim (Patriarch for Greek Melekite rite Catholics)

Babiloina of the Chaldeans, HB Raphael I Bidawid

Cilicia of the Armenians, HB Jean Pierre XVIII Kasparian (Patriarch for Armenian rite Catholics)

Oriental India, Archbishop Raul Nicolau Gonsalves

Lisbon, vacant

Venice, HE Archbishop Angelo Scola

Other Churches in the UK

AFRICAN AND AFRO-CARIBBEAN CHURCHES

There are more than 160 Christian churches or groups of African or Afro-Caribbean origin in the UK. These include the Apostolic Faith Church, the Cherubim and Seraphim Church, the New Testament Church Assembly, the New Testament Church of God, the Wesleyan Holiness Church and the Aladura Churches.

The Afro-West Indian United Council of Churches and the Council of African and Afro-Caribbean Churches UK (which was initiated as the Council of African and Allied Churches in 1979 to give one voice to the various Christian churches of African origin in the UK) are the media through which the member churches can work jointly to provide services they cannot easily provide individually.

There are about 70,000 adherents of African and Afro-Caribbean churches in the UK, and over 1,000 congregations. The Afro-West Indian United Council of Churches has about 30,000 individual members, 135 ministers and own over 100 places of worship. The Council of African and Afro-Caribbean Churches UK has about 17,000 members, 250 ministers and 125 congregations.

AFRO-WEST INDIAN UNITED COUNCIL OF CHURCHES, c/o New Testament Church of God, Arcadian Gardens, High Road, London N22 5AA. Tel: 020-8888 9427. *Secretary,* Bishop E. Brown

COUNCIL OF AFRICAN AND AFRO-CARIBBEAN CHURCHES UK, 31 Norton House, Sidney Road, London SW9 0UJ. Tel: 020-7274 5589; Fax: 020-7274 4726. *Chairman,* His Grace The Most Revd Father Olu A. Abiola

ASSOCIATED PRESBYTERIAN CHURCHES OF SCOTLAND

The Associated Presbyterian Churches came into being in 1989 as a result of a division within the Free Presbyterian Church of Scotland. Following two controversial disciplinary cases, the culmination of deepening differences within the Church, a presbytery was formed calling itself the Associated Presbyterian Churches (APC). The Associated Presbyterian Churches has about 1,000 members, 15 ministers and 20 churches.

Clerk of the Scottish Presbytery, Revd A. N. McPhail, Fernhill, Polvinster Road, Oban PA34 5TN. Tel: 01631-567076

THE BAPTIST CHURCH

Baptists trace their origins to John Smyth, who in 1609 in Amsterdam reinstituted the baptism of conscious believers as the basis of the fellowship of a gathered church. Members of Smyth's church established the first Baptist church in England in 1612. They came to be known as 'General' Baptists and their theology was Arminian, whereas a later group of Calvinists who adopted the baptism of believers came to be known as 'Particular' Baptists. The two sections of the Baptists were united into one body, the Baptist Union of Great Britain and Ireland, in 1891. In 1988 the title was changed to Baptist Union of Great Britain.

Baptists emphasise the complete autonomy of the local church, although individual churches are linked in various kinds of associations. There are international bodies (such as the Baptist World Alliance) and national bodies, but some Baptist churches belong to neither. However, in Great Britain the majority of churches and associations belong to the Baptist Union of Great Britain. There are also Baptist Unions in Wales, Scotland and Ireland which are much smaller than the Baptist Union of Great Britain, and there is some overlap of membership.

There are over 40 million Baptist church members world-wide; in the Baptist Union of Great Britain there are 142,636 members, 1,773 pastors and 2,122 churches. In the Baptist Union of Scotland there are 14,267 members, 156 pastors and 172 churches. In the Baptist Union of Wales (Undeb Bedyddwyr Cymru) there are 18,578 members, 107 pastors and 484 churches. In the Association of Baptist Churches (formerly the Baptist Union of Ireland) there are 8,446 members, 97 pastors and 111 churches.

President of the Baptist Union of Great Britain (2002–3), Revd Nigel Wright

General Secretary, Revd David Coffey, Baptist House, PO Box 44, 129 Broadway, Didcot, Oxon OX11 8RT. Tel: 01235-517700; Email: info@baptist.org.uk Web: www.baptist.org.uk

President of the Baptist Union of Scotland (2002–3) Dr Jim Brooks

General Secretary, Revd William Slack, 14 Aytoun Road, Glasgow G41 5RT. Tel: 0141-423 6169; Fax: 0141-424 1422; Email; admin@scottishbaptist.org.uk

President of the English Assembly of the Baptist Union of Wales (2002–3), Revd Dr Peter Baines

President of the Welsh Assembly of the Baptist Union of Wales (2002–3), Mary Wynne Jones

General Secretary of the Baptist Union of Wales, Revd P. D. Richards, 94 Stryd Mansel, Swansea SA1 5TZ. Tel: 01792-655468

General Secretary of the Association of Baptist Churches in Ireland, Revd W. Colville, 19 Ballinderry Road, Lisburn BT28 2SA. Tel: 028-9266 9366

THE CONGREGATIONAL FEDERATION

The Congregational Federation was founded by members of Congregational churches in England and Wales who did not join the United Reformed Church in 1972. There are also churches in Scotland and France affiliated to the Federation. The Federation exists to encourage congregations of believers to worship in free assembly, but it has no authority over them and emphasises their right to independence and self-government.

The Federation has 11,104 members, 71 recognised ministers and 313 churches in England, Wales and Scotland.

President of the Federation (2002–3), Mrs Felicity Cleaves

General Secretary, Revd. M. Heaney, The Congregational Centre, 8 Castle Gate, Nottingham NG1 7AS. Tel: 0115-911 1460

THE FREE CHURCH OF ENGLAND

The Free Church of England is a union of two bodies in the Anglican tradition, the Free Church of England, founded in 1844 as a protest against the Oxford Movement in the established Church, and the Reformed Episcopal Church, founded in America in 1873 but which also had congregations in England. As both Churches sought to maintain the historic faith, tradition and practice of the Anglican Church since the Reformation, they decided to unite as one body in England in 1927. The historic episcopate was conferred on the English Church in 1876 through the line of the American bishops, who had pioneered an open table Communion policy towards members of other denominations.

The Free Church of England has 1,400 members, 41 ministers and 25 churches in England. It also has three house churches and three ministers in New Zealand and one church and one minister in St Petersburg, Russia.

General Secretary, Revd R. E. Talbot, 32 Bonnywood Road, Hassocks, W. Sussex BN6 8HR. Tel: 01273-845092

THE FREE CHURCH OF SCOTLAND

The Free Church of Scotland was formed in 1843 when over 400 ministers withdrew from the Church of Scotland as a result of interference in the internal affairs of the church by the civil authorities. In 1900, all but 26 ministers joined with others to form the United Free Church (most of which rejoined the Church of Scotland in 1929). In 1904 the remaining 26 ministers were recognised by the House of Lords as continuing the Free Church of Scotland.

The Church maintains strict adherence to the Westminster Confession of Faith (1648) and accepts the Bible as the sole rule of faith and conduct. Its General Assembly meets annually. It also has links with Reformed Churches overseas. The Free Church of Scotland has 4,600 communicating members, 90 ministers and 110 churches.

General Treasurer, I. D. Gill, The Mound, Edinburgh EH1 2LS. Tel: 0131-226 5286.

Email: office@freechurchofscotland.org.uk

THE FREE PRESBYTERIAN CHURCH OF SCOTLAND

The Free Presbyterian Church of Scotland was formed in 1893 by two ministers of the Free Church of Scotland who refused to accept a Declaratory Act passed by the Free Church General Assembly in 1892. The Free Presbyterian Church of Scotland is Calvinistic in doctrine and emphasises observance of the Sabbath. It adheres strictly to the Westminster Confession of Faith of 1648.

The Church has about 3,000 members in Scotland and about 4,000 in overseas congregations. It has 19 ministers and 50 churches in the UK.

Moderator, Revd D. J. MacDonald, Free Presbyterian Manse, Evelix, Dornoch, Sutherland IV25 3RD. Tel: 01862-811 138

Clerk of Synod, Revd J. MacLeod, 16 Matheson Road, Stornoway, Isle of Lewis HS1 2LA. Tel: 01851-702755

THE HOLY APOSTOLIC CATHOLIC ASSYRIAN CHURCH OF THE EAST

The Holy Apostolic Catholic Assyrian Church of the East traces its beginnings to the middle of the first century. It spread from Upper Mesopotamia throughout the territories of the Persian Empire. The Assyrian church of the East became theologically separated from the rest of the Christian community following the Council of Ephesus in 431. The Church is headed by the Catholicos Patriarch and is episcopal in government. The liturgical language is Syriac (Aramaic). The Assyrian Church of the East and the Roman Catholic Church agreed a common Christological declaration in 1994 and a process of dialogue between the Assyrian Church of the East and the Chaldean Catholic Church, which is in communion with Rome but shares the Syriac liturgy, was instituted in 1996.

The Church numbers about 400,000 members in the Middle East, India, Europe, North America and Australasia. There are around 1,000 members in the UK

The Church in Great Britain forms part of the diocese of Europe under Mar Odisho Oraham.

Representative in Great Britain, Very Revd Younan Y. Younan, 66 Montague Road, London W7 3PQ. Tel: 020-8579 7259.

THE INDEPENDENT METHODIST CHURCHES

The Independent Methodist Churches seceded from the Wesleyan Methodist Church in 1805 and remained independent when the Methodist Church in Great Britain was formed in 1932. They are mainly concentrated in the industrial areas of the north of England.

The churches are Methodist in doctrine but their organisation is congregational. All the churches are members of the Independent Methodist Connexion of Churches. The controlling body of the Connexion is the Annual Meeting, to which churches send delegates. The Connexional President is elected annually. Between annual meetings the affairs of the Connexion are handled by departmental committees. Ministers are appointed by the churches and trained through the Connexion. The ministry is open to both men and women and is unpaid.

There are 2,552 members, 108 ministers and 96 churches in Great Britain.

Connexional President (2002–2003), C. Scholes

General Secretary, W. C. Gabb, 66 Kirkstone Drive, Loughborough LE11 3RW. Tel: 01942-223526

THE LUTHERAN CHURCH

Lutheranism is based on the teachings of Martin Luther, the German leader of the Protestant Reformation. The authority of the scriptures is held to be supreme over Church tradition and creeds, and the key doctrine is that of justification by faith alone.

Lutheranism is one of the largest Protestant denominations and it is particularly strong in northern Europe and the USA. Some Lutheran churches are episcopal, while others have a synodal form of organisation; unity is based on doctrine rather than structure. Most Lutheran churches are members of the Lutheran World Federation, based in Geneva.

Lutheran services in Great Britain are held in eighteen languages to serve members of different nationalities. Services usually follow ancient liturgies. English-language congregations are members either of the Lutheran Church in Great Britain, or of the Evangelical Lutheran Church of England. The Lutheran Church in Great Britain and other Lutheran churches in Britain are members of the Lutheran Council of Great Britain, which represents them and co-ordinates their common work.

There are over 70 million Lutherans world-wide; in Great Britain there are about 100,000 members, 50 clergy and 100 congregations.

General Secretary of the Lutheran Council of Great Britain, Revd T. Bruch, 30 Thanet Street, London WC1H 9QH. Tel: 020-7554 2900; Fax 020-7383 3081; Email: enquiries@lutheran.org.uk
Web: www.lutheran.org.uk

THE METHODIST CHURCH

The Methodist movement started in England in 1729 when the Revd John Wesley, an Anglican priest, and his brother Charles met with others in Oxford and resolved to conduct their lives and study by 'rule and method'. In 1739 the Wesleys began evangelistic preaching and the first Methodist chapel was founded in Bristol in the same year. In 1744 the first annual conference was held, at which the Articles of Religion were drawn up. Doctrinal emphases included repentance, faith, the assurance of salvation, social concern and the priesthood of all believers. After John Wesley's death in 1791 the Methodists withdrew from the established Church to form the Methodist Church. Methodists gradually drifted into many groups, but in 1932 the Wesleyan Methodist Church, the United Methodist Church and the Primitive Methodist Church united to form the Methodist Church in Great Britain as it now exists.

The governing body and supreme authority of the Methodist Church is the Conference, but there are also 33 district synods, consisting of all the ministers and selected lay people in each district, and circuit meetings of the ministers and lay people of each circuit.

There are over 60 million Methodists world-wide; in Great Britain (1998 figures) there are 353,330 members, 3,727 ministers, 10,746 lay preachers and 6,452 churches.
President of the Conference in Great Britain (2002–3), Revd I. White
Vice-President of the Conference (2002–3), Prof. P. Howdle
Secretary of the Conference, Revd Dr N. T. Collinson, Methodist Church, Conference Office, 25 Marylebone Road, London NW1 5JR. Tel: 020-7486 5502; Fax: 020-7467 5226;
Email: conferenceoffice@methodistchurch.org.uk;
Web: www.methodist.org.uk

THE METHODIST CHURCH IN IRELAND

The Methodist Church in Ireland is closely linked to British Methodism but is autonomous. It has a community roll of 55585, 16,104 members, 197 ministers, 293 lay preachers and 222 churches.
President of the Methodist Church in Ireland (2002–3), Revd W Winston Graham, 1 Green Road, Belfast BT5 6JA. Tel: 028 9065 3413
Secretary of the Methodist Church in Ireland, Revd E. T. I. Mawhinney, 1 Fountainville Avenue, Belfast BT9 6AN. Tel: 028-9032 4554

THE (EASTERN) ORTHODOX CHURCH

The Eastern (or Byzantine) Orthodox Church is a communion of self-governing Christian churches recognising the honorary primacy of the Oecumenical Patriarch of Constantinople.

The position of Orthodox Christians is that the faith was fully defined during the period of the Oecumenical Councils. In doctrine it is strongly trinitarian, and stresses the mystery and importance of the sacraments. It is episcopal in government. The structure of the Orthodox Christian year differs from that of western Churches.

Orthodox Christians throughout the world are estimated to number about 300 million.

PATRIARCHS OF THE EASTERN ORTHODOX CHURCH
Archbishop of Constantinople, New Rome and Oecumenical Patriarch, Vartholomaeos, *elected* 1991
Pope and Patriarch of Alexandria and All Africa, Petros VII, *elected* 1997
Patriarch of Antioch and All the East, Ignatios IV, *elected* 1979
Patriarch of Jerusalem and All Palestine, Irinaos *elected* 2001
Patriarch of Moscow and All Russia, Alexei II, *elected* 1990
Archbishop of Pec, Metropolitan of Belgrade and Karlovci, Patriarch of Serbia, Pavle, *elected* 1990
Archbishop of Bucharest and Patriarch of Romania, Teoctist, *elected* 1986
Metropolitan of Sofia and Patriarch of Bulgaria, Maxim, *elected* 1971
Archbishop of Tbilisi and Mtskheta, Catholicos-Patriarch of All Georgia, Ilia II, *elected* 1977

HEADS OF AUTOCEPHALOUS ORTHODOX CHURCHES
Archbishop of Cyprus, Chrysostomos, *elected* 1977
Archbishop of Athens and All Greece, Christodoulos, *elected* 1998
Metropolitan of Warsaw and All Poland, Sawa, *elected* 1998
Archbishop of Tirana and All Albania, Anastas, *elected* 1992
Archbishop of Prague and All the Czech Lands and Slovakia, Nikolaj, *elected* 2000

EASTERN ORTHODOX CHURCHES IN THE UK

THE PATRIARCHATE OF ANTIOCH

There are ten parishes served by 15 clergy. In Great Britain the Patriarchate is represented by the Revd Fr Samir Gholam, St George's Cathedral, 1A Redhill Street, London NW1 4BG. Tel: 020-7383 0403.

THE GREEK ORTHODOX CHURCH (PATRIARCHATE OF CONSTANTINOPLE)

The presence of Greek Orthodox Christians in Britain dates back at least to 1677 when Archbishop Joseph

Geogirenes of Samos fled from Turkish persecution and came to London. The present Greek cathedral in Moscow Road, Bayswater, was opened for public worship in 1879 and the Diocese of Thyateira and Great Britain was established in 1922. There are now 120 parishes and other communities (including monasteries) in the UK, served by five bishops, 113 clergy, nine cathedrals and about 93 churches.

In Great Britain the Patriarchate of Constantinople is represented by Archbishop Gregorios of Thyateira and Great Britain, Thyateira House, 5 Craven Hill, London W2 3EN. Tel: 020-7723 4787; fax: 020-7224 9301.

THE RUSSIAN ORTHODOX CHURCH (PATRIARCHATE OF MOSCOW) AND THE RUSSIAN ORTHODOX CHURCH OUTSIDE RUSSIA

The records of Russian Orthodox Church activities in Britain date from the visit to England of Tsar Peter I in the early 18th century. Clergy were sent from Russia to serve the chapel established to minister to the staff of the Imperial Russian Embassy in London.

In Great Britain the Patriarchate of Moscow is represented by Metropolitan Anthony of Sourozh, 67 Ennismore Gardens, London SW7 1NH. Fax only: 020-7584 9864. He is assisted by one assistant bishop, one vicar bishop and 30 clergy. There are 27 parishes and smaller communities.

The Russian Orthodox Church Outside Russia is represented by Archbishop Mark of Berlin, Germany and Great Britain, c/o 57 Harvard Road, London W4 4ED. Tel: 020-8742 3493. There are eight communities, including two monasteries, served by ten clergy.

THE SERBIAN ORTHODOX CHURCH (PATRIARCHATE OF SERBIA)

There are 33 parishes and smaller communities in Great Britain served by 11 clergy. The Patriarchate of Serbia is represented by the Episcopal Vicar, the Very Revd Milenko Zebić, 131 Cob Lane, Bournville, Birmingham B30 1QE. Tel: 0121-486 1220.

OTHER NATIONALITIES

Most of the Ukrainian parishes in Britain have joined the Patriarchate of Constantinople, leaving a small number of Ukrainian parishes in Britain under the care of other patriarchates (not all of which are recognised by the other Orthodox Churches). The Latvian, Polish and some Belarusian parishes are also under the care of the Patriarchate of Constantinople. The Patriarchate of Romania has one parish served by two clergy. The Patriarchate of Bulgaria has one parish served by one priest. The Belarusian Autocephalous Orthodox Church has five parishes served by two priests.

THE ORIENTAL ORTHODOX CHURCHES

The term 'Oriental Orthodox Churches' is now generally used to describe a group of six ancient eastern churches which reject the Christological definition of the Council of Chalcedon (AD 451) and use Christological terms in different ways from the Eastern Orthodox Church. There are about 34 million members of the Oriental Orthodox Churches.

PATRIARCHS OF THE ORIENTAL ORTHODOX CHURCHES

ARMENIAN ORTHODOX CHURCH – *Supreme Patriarch Catholicos of All Armenians (Etchmiadzin)*, Karekin II, *elected* 1999; *Catholicos of Cilicia*, Aram I, *elected* 1995;

Patriarch of Jerusalem, Torkom II, *elected* 1994; *Patriarch of Constantinople*, Mesrob II, *elected* 1998
COPTIC ORTHODOX CHURCH – *Pope of Alexandria and Patriarch of the See of St Mark*, Shenouda III, *elected* 1971
ERITREAN ORTHODOX CHURCH – *Patriarch of Eritrea*, Philipos I, *elected* 1998
ETHIOPIAN ORTHODOX CHURCH – *Patriarch of Ethiopia*, Paulos, *elected* 1992
MALANKARA ORTHODOX SYRIAN CHURCH – *Catholicos of the East*, Basilios Mar Thoma Mathews II, *elected* 1991
SYRIAN ORTHODOX CHURCH – *Patriarch of Antioch and All the East*, Ignatius Zakka I, *elected* 1980

ORIENTAL ORTHODOX CHURCHES IN THE UK

THE ARMENIAN ORTHODOX CHURCH (PATRIARCHATE OF ETCHMIADZIN)

The Armenian Orthodox Church is the longest-established Oriental Orthodox community in Great Britain. It is represented by the Rt. Revd Bishop Nathan Hovhannisian, Armenian Primate of Great Britain, Armenian Vicarage, Iverna Gardens, London W8 6TP. Tel: 020-7937 0152. Email: hbishopnathan@aol.com

THE COPTIC ORTHODOX CHURCH

The Coptic Orthodox Church is the largest Oriental Orthodox community in Great Britain. It has five dioceses (London; Birmingham; Scotland, Ireland and North-East England; the British Orthodox Church; and churches directly under Pope Shenouda III). The senior bishop in Great Britain is Metropolitan Seraphim, 10 Heathwood Gardens, London SE7 8EP. Tel: 020-8854 3090. Email: boc@nildram.co.uk

THE ERITREAN ORTHODOX CHURCH

In Great Britain the Eritrean Orthodox Church is represented by Bishop Markos, 11 Anfield Close, Weir Road, London SW12 0NT. Tel: 020-8675 5115.

THE ETHIOPIAN ORTHODOX CHURCH

The Ethiopian Orthodox Church in Great Britain is represented by Like Teguhan Tekle Mariam Edwards, PO Box 14738, London N15 3NJ. Tel: 020-8889 9355.

THE MALANKARA ORTHODOX SYRIAN CHURCH

The Malankara Orthodox Syrian Church is part of the Diocese of Europe under Metropolitan Thomas Mar Makarios. His representative in Great Britain is Fr M. S. Skariah, Paramula House, 44 Newbury Road, Newbury Park, Ilford, Essex IG2 7HD. Tel: 020-8599 3836.

THE SYRIAN ORTHODOX CHURCH

The Syrian Orthodox Church in Great Britain comes under the Patriarchal Vicar, whose representative is Fr Touma Hazim Dakkama, Antiochian, 5 Canning Road, Croydon CR0 6QA. Tel: 020-8654 7531. The Indian congregation under the Syrian Patriarch of Antioch is represented by Fr Eldhose Koungampillil, 1 Roslyn Court, Roslyn Avenue, East Barnet, Herts EN4 8DJ. Tel: 020-8368 2794.

THE COUNCIL OF ORIENTAL ORTHODOX CHURCHES, 34 Chertsey Road, Church Square, Shepperton, Middx TW17 9LF. Tel: 020-8368 8447; Email: nour@antaccia.u-net.coml. *Secretary*, Deacon Aziz M. A. Nour

PENTECOSTAL CHURCHES

Pentecostalism is inspired by the descent of the Holy Spirit upon the apostles at Pentecost. The movement began in Los Angeles, USA, in 1906 and is characterised by baptism with the Holy Spirit, divine healing, speaking in tongues (glossolalia), and a literal interpretation of the scriptures. The Pentecostal movement in Britain dates from 1907. Initially, groups of Pentecostalists were led by laymen and did not organise formally. However, in 1915 the Elim Foursquare Gospel Alliance (more usually called the Elim Pentecostal Church) was founded in Ireland by George Jeffreys and in 1924 about 70 independent assemblies formed a fellowship, the Assemblies of God in Great Britain and Ireland. The Apostolic Church grew out of the 1904–5 revivals in South Wales and was established in 1916, and the New Testament Church of God was established in England in 1953. In recent years many aspects of Pentecostalism have been adopted by the growing charismatic movement within the Roman Catholic, Protestant and Eastern Orthodox churches.

There are about 105 million Pentecostalists world-wide, with about 200,000 adult adherents in Great Britain and Ireland.

THE APOSTOLIC CHURCH, International Administration Offices, PO Box 389, 24–27 St Helens Road, Swansea SA1 1ZH. Tel: 01792-473992. *President*, Pastor R. W. Jones; *Administrator*, Pastor A. Saunders. The Apostolic Church has about 110 churches, 5,500 adherents and 91 ministers

THE ASSEMBLIES OF GOD IN GREAT BRITAIN AND IRELAND, General Offices, 16 Bridgford Road, West Bridgford, Nottingham NG2 6AF. Tel: 0115-981 1188. *General Superintendent*, P. C. Weaver; *General Administrator*, D. H. Gill. The Assemblies of God has 630 churches, about 75,000 adherents (including children) and 890 accredited ministers

THE ELIM PENTECOSTAL CHURCH, PO Box 38, Cheltenham, Glos GL50 3HN. Tel: 01242-519904. Email: info@elimhq.com *General Superintendent*, Revd J. J. Glass; *Administrator*, Pastor B. Hunter. The Elim Pentecostal Church has 600 churches, 68,500 adherents and 650 accredited ministers

THE NEW TESTAMENT CHURCH OF GOD, Main House, Overstone Park, Overstone, Northampton NN6 0AD. Tel: 01604-643311. *National Overseer*, Revd Dr R. O. Brown. The New Testament Church of God has 104 organised congregations, about 8,500 baptised members, about 10,000 adherents and 256 accredited ministers

PLYMOUTH BRETHREN

The Brethren was founded in Dublin in 1827–28. It rejected denominationalism and clericalism and based itself on the structures and practices of the early Church. Many groups sprang up and that at Plymouth became the best known, which resulted in the designation by others as Plymouth Brethren. Other groups are based in Ireland, USA, Burma and Guyana.

Early worship had a prescribed form but quickly assumed an unstructured, non-liturgical format. There were services devoted to worship, usually involve the Breaking of Bread, and separate preaching meetings. There was no salaried ministry.

A theological dispute led in 1848 to schism between the Open Brethren and the Closed or Exclusive Brethren, each branch later suffering further divisions.

Open Brethren churches are completely independent, but freely co-operate with each other. Churches are run by appointed elders. Exclusive Brethren churches believe in a universal fellowship between congregations. They do not have elders, but appoint respected members of their congregation to perform certain administrative functions.

The Brethren are established throughout the UK, Ireland, Europe, India, Africa and Australasia. Total membership in the UK is 80,941.

GOSPEL TRACT PUBLICATIONS, 85 Portman Street, Glasgow G41 1EJ. Tel: 0141-427 4661 *(Open Brethren)*

CHAPTER TWO, Fountain House, Conduit Mews, London SE18 7AP. Tel: 020-8316 5389 *(Exclusive Brethren)*

THE PRESBYTERIAN CHURCH IN IRELAND

The Presbyterian Church in Ireland is Calvinistic in doctrine and presbyterian in constitution. Presbyterianism was established in Ireland as a result of the Ulster plantation in the early 17th century, when English and Scottish Protestants settled in the north of Ireland.

There are 21 presbyteries and five regional synods under the chief court known as the General Assembly. The General Assembly meets annually and is presided over by a Moderator who is elected for one year. The ongoing work of the Church is undertaken by 18 boards under which there are a number of specialist committees.

There are about 279,000 Presbyterians in Ireland, mainly in the north, in 557 congregations and with 400 ministers.

Moderator (2002–3), Rt. Revd Dr R. I. Birney

Clerk of Assembly and General Secretary, Very Revd Dr S. Hutchinson, Church House, Belfast BT1 6DW. Tel: 028-9032 2284

THE PRESBYTERIAN CHURCH OF WALES

The Presbyterian Church of Wales or Calvinistic Methodist Church of Wales is Calvinistic in doctrine and presbyterian in constitution. It was formed in 1811 when Welsh Calvinists severed the relationship with the established church by ordaining their own ministers. It secured its own confession of faith in 1823 and a Constitutional Deed in 1826, and since 1864 the General Assembly has met annually, presided over by a Moderator elected for a year. The doctrine and constitutional structure of the Presbyterian Church of Wales was confirmed by Act of Parliament in 1931–2.

The Church has 43,606 members, 119 ministers and 869 churches.

Moderator (2001–2), Dr B. F. Roberts

General Secretary, Revd W. G. Edwards, 53 Richmond Road, Cardiff CF24 3WJ. Tel: 029-2049 4913

THE RELIGIOUS SOCIETY OF FRIENDS (QUAKERS)

Quakerism is a movement, not a church, which was founded in the 17th century by George Fox and others in an attempt to revive what they saw as 'primitive Christianity'.

Emphasis is placed on the experience of God in daily life rather than on sacraments or religious occasions. There is no church calendar. Worship is largely silent and there are no appointed ministers; the responsibility for conducting a meeting is shared equally among those

present. Social reform and religious tolerance have always been important to Quakers, together with a commitment to non-violence in resolving disputes.

There are 213,800 Quakers world-wide, with over 19,000 in Great Britain and Ireland.

CENTRAL OFFICES: (GREAT BRITAIN) Friends House, 173 Euston Road, London NW1 2BJ. Tel: 020-7663 1000; Fax: 020-7663 1001; Email: betha@quaker.org.uk Web: www.quaker.org.uk

THE SALVATION ARMY

The Salvation Army was founded by a Methodist minister, William Booth, in the east end of London in 1865, and has since become established in 108 countries world-wide. In 1878 it adopted a quasi-military command structure intended to inspire and regulate its endeavours and to reflect its view that the Church was engaged in spiritual warfare. Salvationists emphasise evangelism and the provision of social welfare. There are over 1.5 million members worldwide, of which 62,836 are in Great Britain and Ireland.

International Leader, Gen. John Gowans
UK Leader, Commissioner Alex Hughes
TERRITORIAL HEADQUARTERS, 101 Newington Causeway, London SE1 6BN. Tel: 020-7367 4500

THE SEVENTH-DAY ADVENTIST CHURCH

The Seventh-day Adventist Church was founded in 1863 in the USA. Its members look forward to the second coming of Christ and observe the Sabbath (the seventh day) as a day of rest, worship and ministry. The Church bases its faith and practice wholly on the Bible and has developed 27 fundamental beliefs.

In the British Isles the administrative organisation of the church is arranged in three tiers: the local churches; the regional conferences for south England, north England, Wales, Scotland and Ireland; and the national headquarters.

There are over 11 million Adventists and 46,740 churches in 205 countries world-wide. In the UK and Ireland there are 21,137 member and 246 churches.

President of the British Union Conference, Pastor C. R. Perry
BRITISH ISLES HEADQUARTERS, Stanborough Park, Watford WD25 9JZ. Tel: 01923-672251

THE (SWEDENBORGIAN) NEW CHURCH

The New Church is based on the teachings of the 18th century Swedish scientist and theologian Emanuel Swedenborg (1688–1772), who believed that Jesus Christ appeared to him and instructed him to reveal the spiritual meaning of the Bible. He claimed to have visions of the spiritual world, including heaven and hell, and conversations with angels and spirits.

The Second Coming of Jesus Christ is believed to have already taken place and is still taking place, being not an actual physical reappearance of Christ, but rather His return in spirit.

There are around 30,000 Swedenborgians world-wide, with 1,205 members, 30 Churches and 11 ministers in the UK.

THE GENERAL CONFERENCE OF THE NEW CHURCH, Swedenborg House, 20 Bloomsbury Way, London WC1A 2TH. Tel: 020-7229 9340

UNDEB YR ANNIBYNWYR CYMRAEG
The Union of Welsh Independents

The Union of Welsh Independents was formed in 1872 and is a voluntary association of Welsh Congregational Churches and personal members. It is mainly Welsh-speaking. Congregationalism in Wales dates back to 1639 when the first Welsh Congregational Church was opened in Gwent. Member churches are Calvinistic in doctrine, although a wide range of interpretations is permitted, and congregationalist in organisation.

The Union has 34,500 members, 230 ministers and 514 member churches.

President of the Union (2002 – 2003) Revd Geraint Tudur
General Secretary, Revd D. Myrddin Hughes, Tŷ ŷ John Penry, 11 Heol Sant Helen, Swansea SA1 4AL. Tel: 01792-652542; Fax: 01792-650647

THE UNITED REFORMED CHURCH

The United Reformed Church was first formed by the union of most of the Congregational churches in England and Wales with the Presbyterian Church of England in 1972. Congregationalism dates from the mid 16th century. It is Calvinistic in doctrine, and its followers form independent self-governing congregations bound under God by covenant, a principle laid down in the writings of Robert Browne (1550–1633). From the late 16th century the movement was driven underground by persecution, but the cause was defended at the Westminster Assembly in 1643 and the Savoy Declaration of 1658 laid down its principles. Congregational churches formed county associations for mutual support and in 1832 these associations merged to form the Congregational Union of England and Wales. Presbyterianism in England also dates from the mid 16th century, and was Calvinistic and evangelical in its doctrine. It was governed by a hierarchy of courts.

In the 1960s there was close co-operation locally and nationally between Congregational and Presbyterian Churches. This led to union negotiations and a Scheme of Union, supported by Act of Parliament in 1972. In 1981 a further unification took place, with the Reformed Association of Churches of Christ becoming part of the URC. In 2000 a third union took place, with the Congregational Union of Scotland. In its basis the United Reformed Church reflects local church initiative and responsibility with a conciliar pattern of oversight. The General Assembly is the central body, and is made up of equal numbers of ministers and lay members. There are 90,314 members and 1,745 local churches.

GENERAL SECRETARY, Revd Dr David C. Cornick, 86 Tavistock Place, London WC1H 9RT. Tel: 020-7916 2020; Fax: 7916 2021; Email: david.cornick@urc.org.uk

THE WESLEYAN REFORM UNION

The Wesleyan Reform Union was founded by Methodists who left or were expelled from Wesleyan Methodism in 1849 following a period of internal conflict. Its doctrine is conservative evangelical and its organisation is congregational, each church having complete independence in the government and administration of its affairs. The Union has 2,030 members and 109 churches.

President (2002–3) Revd M. Nicholls
General Secretary, Revd A. J. Williams, Wesleyan Reform Church House, 123 Queen Street, Sheffield S1 2DU. Tel: 0114-272 1938

Non-Trinitarian Churches

CHRISTADELPHIANISM

Christadelphians believe that the Bible is the literal Word of God and that it reveals both God's dealing with mankind in the past and his plans for the future. These plans centre on the work of Jesus Christ who is believed shortly to return to earth to establish God's Kingdom. Christadelphians have existed since the 1850s beginning in the USA through the work of an Englishman, Dr. John Thomas.

CHRISTADELPHIAN MAGAZINE AND PUBLISHING ASSOCIATION, 404 Shaftmoor Lane, Birmingham B28 8SZ. Tel: 0121-777 6324

THE CHURCH OF CHRIST, SCIENTIST

The Church of Christ, Scientist was founded by Mary Baker Eddy in the USA in 1879 to 'reinstate primitive Christianity and its lost element of healing'. Christian Science teaches the need for spiritual regeneration and salvation from sin, but is best known for its reliance on prayer alone in the healing of sickness. Adherents believe that such healing is a law, or Science, and is in direct line with that practised by Jesus Christ (revered, not as God, but as the Son of God) and by the early Christian Church.

The denomination consists of The First Church of Christ, Scientist, in Boston, Massachusetts, USA (the Mother Church) and its branch churches in over 60 countries world-wide. The Bible and Mary Baker Eddy's book, *Science and Health with Key to the Scriptures*, are used at services; there are no clergy.

No membership figures are available, since Mary Baker Eddy felt that numbers are no measure of spiritual vitality and ruled that such statistics should not be published. There are over 2,400 branch churches world-wide, including nearly 200 in the UK.

CHRISTIAN SCIENCE COMMITTEE ON PUBLICATION, 9 Elysium Gate, 126 New Kings Road, London SW6 4LZ. Tel: 020-7384 8600; Fax: 020-7371 9204; Email: joynesh@compub.org; *District Manager for Great Britain and Ireland*, H. Joynes

THE CHURCH OF JESUS CHRIST OF LATTER-DAY SAINTS

The Church (often referred to as 'the Mormons') was founded in New York State, USA, in 1830, and came to Britain in 1837. The oldest continuous branch in the world is to be found in Preston, Lancs. Mormons are Christians who claim to belong to the 'Restored Church' of Jesus Christ. They believe that true Christianity died when the last original apostle died, but that it was given back to the world by God and Christ through Joseph Smith, the Church's founder and first president. They accept and use the Bible as scripture, but believe in continuing revelation from God and use additional scriptures, including *The Book of Mormon: Another Testament of Jesus Christ*.

There are more than 11 million members world-wide, with about 180,000 adherents in Britain.

President of the Europe North Area (including Britain), Elder Harold G. Hillam

BRITISH HEADQUARTERS, Church Offices, 751

Warwick Road, Solihull, W. Midlands B91 3DQ. Tel: 0121-712 1202

JEHOVAH'S WITNESSES

The movement now known as Jehovah's Witnesses grew from a Bible study group formed by Charles Taze Russell in 1872 in Pennsylvania, USA. In 1896 it adopted the name of the Watch Tower Bible and Tract Society, and in 1931 its members became known as Jehovah's Witnesses. Jehovah's (God's) Witnesses believe in the Bible as the word of God, and consider it to be inspired and historically accurate. They take the scriptures literally, except where there are obvious indications that they are figurative or symbolic, and reject the doctrine of the Trinity. Witnesses also believe that the earth will remain for ever and that all those approved of by Jehovah will have eternal life on a cleansed and beautified earth; only 144,000 will go to heaven to rule with Christ. They believe that the second coming of Christ began in 1914 and his thousand-year reign on earth is imminent, and that Armageddon (a final battle in which evil will be defeated) will precede Christ's rule of peace. They refuse to take part in military service, and do not accept blood transfusions.

There are over 6 million Jehovah's Witnesses world-wide, with 130,000 Witnesses in the UK organised into over 1,400 congregations.

BRITISH ISLES HEADQUARTERS, Watch Tower House, The Ridgeway, London NW7 1RN. Tel: 020-8906 2211 Fax: 020-8371 0051 Web: www.watchtower.org

UNITARIAN AND FREE CHRISTIAN CHURCHES

Unitarianism has its historical roots in the Judaeo-Christian tradition but rejects the deity of Christ and the doctrine of the trinity. It allows the individual to embrace insights from all the world's faiths and philosophies, as there is no fixed creed. It is accepted that beliefs may evolve in the light of personal experience.

Unitarian communities first became established in Poland and Transylvania in the 16th century. The first avowedly Unitarian place of worship in the British Isles opened in London in 1774. The General Assembly of Unitarian and Free Christian Churches came into existence in 1928 as the result of the amalgamation of two earlier organisations. There are about 7,000 Unitarians in Great Britain and Ireland, and about 150 Unitarian ministers.

GENERAL ASSEMBLY OF UNITARIAN AND FREE CHRISTIAN CHURCHES, Essex Hall, 1–6 Essex Street, London WC2R 3HY. Tel: 020-7240 2384; Fax: 020-7240 3089 Web: www.unitarian.org.uk. *General Secretary*, Jeffrey J. Teagle

Communications

Postal Services

On 26 March 2001 the Post Office became a public limited company and adopted a new name, Consignia plc. Responsibility for running postal services in the UK remains with Consignia. While the company has signalled its eagerness to expand into the global market, domestic services including Royal Mail, Parcelforce and the local branches of the Post Office remain unchanged. An independent postal services regulator, The Postal Services Commission (Postcomm), has been appointed by the Government to oversee Consignia's operation. The Secretary of State for Trade and Industry has powers to suspend Consignia's letter monopoly in certain areas and to issue licences to other bodies to provide an alternative service.

As the range of postal services increases it is not possible for us to include full details and costings for each one. Below are details of a number of popular services along with costings where available at the time of going to press. For further details please contact the relevant service provider, i.e Royal Mail or Parcelforce. For a quick reference guide to the details and price of postal services visit www.royalmail.com.

INLAND POSTAL SERVICES AND REGULATIONS

INLAND LETTER POST RATES*

Not over	1st class†	2nd class†
60 g	27p	19p
100 g	41p	33p
150 g	57p	44p
200 g	72p	54p
250 g	84p	66p
300 g	96p	76p
350 g	£1.09	87p
400 g	£1.30	£1.05
450 g	£1.48	£1.19
500 g	£1.66	£1.35
600 g	£2.00	£1.60
700 g	£2.51	£1.83
750 g	£2.69	£1.94 (not
800 g	£2.91	Admissible
900 g	£3.20	over 750g)
1,000 g	£3.49	
Each extra 250 g over 1kg	85p	

UK PARCEL RATES

Parcel Force Standard Tariff

Not over	
1 kg	£3.15
2 kg	£4.35
4 kg	£6.55
6 kg	£7.15
8 kg	£8.15
10 kg	£8.75

*Postcards travel at the same rates as letter post
† First class letters are normally delivered the following day and second class post within three days

OVERSEAS POSTAL SERVICES AND REGULATIONS

Details of overseas parcel rates are available from Parcelforce Worldwide by telephoning 0800-224466.

OVERSEAS SURFACE MAIL RATES*
Letters

Not over		Not over	
20 g	37p	250 g	£1.89
60 g	61p	300 g	£2.23
100 g	87p	350 g	£2.57
150 g	£1.21	400 g	£2.91
200 g	£1.55	450 g	£3.25

500 g	£3.59	1,500 g	£10.39
750 g	£5.29	1,750 g	£12.09
1,000 g	£6.99	2,000 g	£13.79
1,250 g	£8.69		

*Postcards travel at 20 g letter rate

AIRMAIL LETTER RATES †

Europe: Letters

Not over		Not over	
20 g	37p	280 g	£2.34
40 g	52p	300 g	£2.49
60 g	68p	320 g	£2.64
80 g	84p	340 g	£2.79
100 g	99p	360 g	£2.94
120 g	£1.14	380 g	£3.09
140 g	£1.29	400 g	£3.24
160 g	£1.44	420 g	£3.39
180 g	£1.59	440 g	£3.54
200 g	£1.74	460 g	£3.69
220 g	£1.89	480 g	£3.84
240 g	£2.04	500 g	£3.99
260 g	£2.19	1,000 g	£7.74
		*2,000 g	£15.24

* Max. 2 kg
† Postcards to Europe travel at 20 g letter rate

Outside Europe: Letters

	Not over 10 g	Not over 20 g	Over 20 g
Zones 1 & 2	47p	68p	Varies

STAMPS

Postage stamps are sold in values of 1p, 2p, 4p, 5p, 8p, 10p, 19p, 20p, 27p, 33p, 41p, 42p, 45p, 50p, 65p, £1, £1.50, £2.00, £3.00 and £5.00.

Printed postage stamps cut from envelopes, postcards, newspaper wrappers, etc., may be used as stamps in payment of postage, provided that they are not imperfect or defaced.

RESTRICTIONS

Advice as to what articles may not be sent through the post is available from Royal Mail (Tel: 08457-740740) for letters and small packets; Parcelforce (Tel: 0800-224466) for parcels; or local post office counter staff.

The exportation of some goods by post is prohibited except under Department of Trade and Industry (DTI) licence. For further information, please contact the Department of Trade and Industry, 1 Victoria Street, London SW1H 0ET. Tel: 020-7215 5000.

SPECIAL DELIVERY SERVICES

DATAPOST

A guaranteed service for the delivery of documents and packages. Delivery times include 9 a.m., 10 a.m. and before noon. There is also an International Datapost Service. For full details call 0800-224466.

ROYAL MAIL SPECIAL DELIVERY

A guaranteed next working day delivery service by 12.00 p.m. to most UK destinations for first class letters and packets. Prices start at £3.65. If a package does not arrive by the next working day, postage is refunded. Compensation of up to £250 can be awarded for loss or damage, however, compensation of up to £2,500 may be awarded if an additional fee has been paid. For further information, call 08457-740740.

SWIFTAIR

An express airmail service. Items are placed on the first available flight to the destination country. Although Swiftair mail receives priority treatment, delivery times are not guaranteed. The fee is £2.85 plus normal postage.

OTHER SERVICES

BUSINESS SERVICES

A range of services are available to help businesses manage their postal needs most effectively. These include: business collection, freepost, business reply services, business packaging for special deliveries and international mailing options.

CERTIFICATE OF POSTING

Issued free on request at time of posting.

COMPENSATION (INLAND AND INTERNATIONAL)

Inland: compensation up to a maximum of £27 may be paid where it can be shown that a letter was damaged or lost in the post due to the fault of Consignia, its employees or agents. Consignia does not accept responsibility for loss or damage arising from faulty packing.

International: compensation up to a maximum of £27 may be given for loss or damage occurring in the UK. Compensation of up to £28 may be given in respect of International Recorded Delivery items. Details of other compensation levels can be obtained by telephoning 08457-740740.

PASSPORT APPLICATIONS

Around 2,000 post offices process passport applications. To find out your nearest office, and for further information, telephone 08457-223344.

POSTE RESTANTE

Poste Restante is solely for travellers. A packet may be addressed to any post office, except town sub-offices, and should state 'Poste Restante' or 'to be called for' in the address. Redirection from a Poste Restante is undertaken for up to three months.

PRIVATE BOX

Provides an alternative address (e.g. PO Box 123) and users of this service can choose to collect mail from a local delivery office or have it delivered. The fee is £42 for 6 months and £52 for one year.

RECORDED MAIL

Provides a record of posting and delivery of letters and ensures a signature on delivery. This service is recommended for items of little or no monetary value. All packets must be handed to the post office and a certificate of posting issued. Charges: 63p plus postage (inland); £2.60 plus postage (international).

REDIRECTION

By agent of addressee: mail other than parcels, business reply and freepost items may be reposted free not later than the day after delivery (not counting Sundays and public holidays) if unopened and if original addressee's name is unobscured. Parcels may be redirected free within the same time limits only if the original and substituted address are in the same local parcel delivery area (or the London postal area). Registered packets must be taken to a post office and are re-registered free up to the day after delivery.

By the Post Office: a printed form obtainable from the Post Office must be signed by the person to whom the letters are to be addressed. A fee is payable for each different surname on the application form. Charges: up to 1 calendar month, £6.30 (abroad via airmail, £12.60); up to 3 calendar months, £13.65 (£27.30); up to 12 calendar months, £31.50 (£63.00).

REGISTERED MAIL (INTERNATIONAL)

All packets must be handed to the post office and a certificate of posting obtained. Charges (plus postage):

Compensation up to	Registered fee plus postage
£500	£3.15
£2,200	£4.20

Compensation in respect of currency or other forms of monetary worth is given only if money is sent by registered letter post. Compensation is only paid for well-packed fragile articles and not for exceptionally fragile or perishable articles.

SMALL PACKETS POST AND PRINTED PAPERS (INTERNATIONAL)

Permits the transmission of goods up to 2 kg to all countries, in the same mails as printed papers. Packets can be sealed and can contain personal correspondence relating to the contents. Registration is allowed as insurance as long as the item is packed in a way complying with any insurance regulations. A customs declaration is required and the packet must be marked with 'small packet' and a return address.

Surface mail: worldwide

Not over		Not over	
100 g	60p	450 g	£1.90
150 g	80p	500 g	£2.09
200 g	£1.00	750 g	£3.04
250 g	£1.20	1,000 g	£3.99
300 g	£1.40	1,500 g	£5.89
350 g	£1.60	2,000 g	£7.79
400 g	£1.80		

U## **Airmail and IDD Codes**

U### AIRMAIL ZONES (AZ)

The table includes airmail letter zones for countries outside Europe, and destinations to which European and European Union airmail letter rates apply. (*Source:* Post Office)

1   airmail zone 1
2   airmail zone 2
e   Europe

INTERNATIONAL DIRECT DIALLING (IDD)

International dialling codes are composed of four elements which are dialled in sequence:
(i)   the international code
(ii) the country code
(iii) the area code
(iv) the telephone number

Calls to some countries must be made via the international operator.

* Can vary depending on area and/or carrier

UNDELIVERED AND UNPAID MAIL

Undelivered mail is returned to the sender provided the return address is indicated either on the outside of the envelope or inside. If the sender's address is not available, items not containing property are destroyed. If the packet contains something of value it is retained for up to three months. Undeliverable second class mail containing newspapers, magazines or commercial advertising is destroyed.

Country	AZ	IDD from UK	IDD to UK
Afghanistan	1	00 93	00 44
Albania	e	00 355	00 44
Algeria	1	00 213	00 44
Andorra	e	00 376	00 44
Angola	1	00 244	00 44
Anguilla	1	00 1 264	011 44
Antigua and Barbuda	1	00 1 268	011 44
Argentina	1	00 54	00 44
Armenia	e	00 374	810 44
Aruba	1	00 297	00 44
Ascension Island	1	00 247	00 44
Australia	2	00 61	00 11 44
Austria	e	00 43	00 44
Azerbaijan	e	00 994	810 44
Azores	e	00 351	00 44
Bahamas	1	00 1 242	011 44
Bahrain	1	00 973	0 44
Bangladesh	1	00 880	00 44
Barbados	1	00 1 246	011 44
Belarus	e	00 375	810 44
Belgium	e	00 32	00 44
Belize	1	00 501	00 44
Benin	1	00 229	00 44
Bermuda	1	00 1 441	011 44
Bhutan	1	00 975	00 44
Bolivia	1	00 591	00 44
Bosnia-Hercegovina	e		
Muslim-Croat Federation		00 387	00 44
Republika Srpska		00 381	00 44
Botswana	1	00 267	00 44
Brazil	1	00 55	00 44
British Virgin Islands	1	00 1 284	011 44
Brunei	1	00 673	00 44
Bulgaria	e	00 359	00 44
Burkina Faso	1	00 226	00 44
Burundi	1	00 257	90 44

Country	AZ	IDD from UK	IDD to UK
Cambodia	1	00 855	00 44
Cameroon	1	00 237	00 44
Canada	1	00 1	011 44
Canary Islands	e	00 34	00 44
Cape Verde	1	00 238	0 44
Cayman Islands	1	00 1 345	011 44
Central African Republic	1	00 236	19 44
Chad	1	00 235	15 44
Chile	1	00 56	00 44
China	2	00 86	00 44
Hong Kong	1	00 852	001 44
Macao	1	00 853	00 44
Colombia	1	00 57	009 44
Comoros	1	00 269	00 44
Congo, Dem. Rep. of	1	00 243	00 44
Congo, Republic of	1	00 242	00 44
Cook Islands	2	00 682	00 44
Costa Rica	1	00 506	00 44
Côte d'Ivoire	1	00 225	00 44
Croatia	e	00 385	00 44
Cuba	1	00 53	119 44
Cyprus	e	00 357	00 44
Czech Republic	e	00 420	00 44
Denmark	e	00 45	00 44
Djibouti	1	00 253	00 44
Dominica	1	00 1 767	011 44
Dominican Republic	1	00 1 809	011 44
East Timor	2	00 670	00 44
Ecuador	1	00 593	00 44
Egypt	1	00 20	00 44
Equatorial Guinea	1	00 240	00 44
Eritrea	1	00 291	00 44
Estonia	e	00 372	800 44
Ethiopia	1	00 251	00 44
Falkland Islands	1	00 500	0 44
Færøe Islands	e	00 298	009 44
Fiji	2	00 679	05 44
Finland	e	00 358	00 44*
France	e	00 33	00 44
French Guiana	1	00 594	00 44
French Polynesia	2	00 689	00 44
Gabon	1	00 241	00 44
The Gambia	1	00 220	00 44
Georgia	e	00 995	810 44
Germany	e	00 49	00 44
Ghana	1	00 233	00 44
Gibraltar	e	00 350	00 44
Greece	e	00 30	00 44
Greenland	e	00 299	009 44
Grenada	1	00 1 473	011 44
Guadeloupe	1	00 590	00 44
Guam	2	00 1 671	001 44
Guatemala	1	00 502	00 44
Guinea	1	00 224	00 44
Guinea-Bissau	1	00 245	099 44
Guyana	1	00 592	001 44
Haiti	1	00 509	00 44
Honduras	1	00 504	00 44
Hungary	e	00 36	00 44
Iceland	e	00 354	00 44

Country	AZ	IDD from UK	IDD to UK
India	1	00 91	00 44
Indonesia	1	00 62	001 44*
			008 44*
Iran	1	00 98	00 44
Iraq	1	00 964	00 44
Ireland, Republic of	e	00 353	00 44
Israel	1	00 972	00 44*
Italy	e	00 39	00 44
Jamaica	1	00 1 876	011 44
Japan	2	00 81	001 44*
			0041 44*
			0061 44*
Jordan	1	00 962	00 44*
Kazakhstan	e	00 7	810 44
Kenya	1	00 254	00 44
Kiribati	2	00 686	00 44
Korea, North	2	00 850	00 44
Korea, South	2	00 82	001 44*
			002 44*
Kuwait	1	00 965	00 44
Kyrgyzstan	e	00 996	00 44
Laos	1	00 856	00 44
Latvia	e	00 371	00 44
Lebanon	1	00 961	00 44
Lesotho	1	00 266	00 44
Liberia	1	00 231	00 44
Libya	1	00 218	00 44
Liechtenstein	e	00 423	00 44
Lithuania	e	00 370	810 44
Luxembourg	e	00 352	00 44
Macedonia	e	00 389	99 44
Madagascar	1	00 261	00 44
Madeira	e	00 351 91	00 44*
Malawi	1	00 265	101 44
Malaysia	1	00 60	00 44
Maldives	1	00 960	00 44
Mali	1	00 223	00 44
Malta	e	00 356	00 44
Mariana Islands, Northern	2	00 1 670	011 44
Marshall Islands	2	00 692	011 44
Martinique	1	00 596	00 44
Mauritania	1	00 222	00 44
Mauritius	1	00 230	00 44
Mayotte	1	00 269	10 44
Mexico	1	00 52	98 44
Micronesia, Federated States of	2	00 691	011 44
Moldova	e	00 373	810 44
Monaco	e	00 377	00 44
Mongolia	2	00 976	00 44
Montenegro	e	00 381	99 44
Montserrat	1	00 1 664	011 44
Morocco	1	00 212	00 44
Mozambique	1	00 258	00 44
Myanmar	1	00 95	00 44
Namibia	1	00 264	00 44
Nauru	2	00 674	00 44
Nepal	1	00 977	00 44
Netherlands	e	00 31	00 44
Netherlands Antilles	1	00 599	00 44
New Caledonia	2	00 687	00 44
New Zealand	2	00 64	00 44
Nicaragua	1	00 505	00 44
Niger	1	00 227	00 44
Nigeria	1	00 234	009 44
Niue	2	00 683	00 44
Norfolk Island	2	00 672	011 44
Norway	e	00 47	00 44
Oman	1	00 968	00 44
Pakistan	1	00 92	00 44
Palau	2	00 680	011 44
Panama	1	00 507	00 44
Papua New Guinea	2	00 675	05 44
Paraguay	1	00 595	00 44*
			003 44*
Peru	1	00 51	00 44
Philippines	2	00 63	00 44
Poland	e	00 48	00 44
Portugal	e	00 351	00 44
Puerto Rico	1	00 1 787	011 44
Qatar	1	00 974	00 44
Réunion	1	00 262	00 44
Romania	e	00 40	00 44
Russia	e	00 7	810 44
Rwanda	1	00 250	00 44
St Christopher and Nevis	1	00 1 869	011 44
St Helena	1	00 290	0 44
St Lucia	1	00 1 758	011 44
St Pierre and Miquelon	1	00 508	00 44
St Vincent and the Grenadines	1	00 1 784	011 44
El Salvador	1	00 503	0 44
Samoa	2	00 685	0 44
Samoa, American	2	00 684	00 44
San Marino	e	00 378	00 44
São Tomé and Príncipe	1	00 239	00 44
Saudi Arabia	1	00 966	00 44
Senegal	1	00 221	00 44
Serbia	e	00 381	99 44
Seychelles	1	00 248	00 44
Sierra Leone	1	00 232	00 44
Singapore	1	00 65	001 44
Slovak Republic	e	00 421	00 44
Slovenia	e	00 386	00 44
Solomon Islands	2	00 677	00 44
Somalia	1	00 252	16 44
South Africa	1	00 27	09 44
Spain	e	00 34	00 44
Sri Lanka	1	00 94	00 44
Sudan	1	00 249	00 44
Suriname	1	00 597	00 44
Swaziland	1	00 268	00 44
Sweden	e	00 46	00944*
Switzerland	e	00 41	00 44
Syria	1	00 963	00 44
Taiwan	2	00 886	002 44
Tajikistan	e	00 7	810 44
Tanzania	1	00 255	00 44
Thailand	1	00 66	001 44
Tibet	1	00 86	00 44
Togo	1	00 228	00 44
Tonga	2	00 676	00 44
Trinidad and Tobago	1	00 1 868	011 44
Tristan da Cunha	1	00 2 897	
Tunisia	1	00 216	00 44
Turkey	e	00 90	00 44
Turkmenistan	e	00 993	810 44
Turks and Caicos Islands	1	00 1 649	0 44
Tuvalu	2	00 688	00 44
Uganda	1	00 256	00 44
Ukraine	e	00 380	810 44

Country	AZ	IDD from UK	IDD to UK	Country	AZ	IDD from UK	IDD to UK
United Arab Emirates	1	00 971	00 44	Vatican City State	e	00 390 66982	00 44
Uruguay	1	00 598	00 44	Venezuela	1	00 58	00 44
USA	1	00 1	011 44	Vietnam	1	00 84	00 44
Alaska		00 1 907	011 44	Virgin Islands (US)	1	00 1 340	011 44
Hawaii		00 1 808	011 44	Yemen	1	00 967	00 44
Uzbekistan	e	00 998	810 44	Yugoslav Fed. Rep.	e	00 381	99 44
Vanuatu	2	00 678	00 44	Zambia	1	00 260	00 44
				Zimbabwe	1	00 263	00 44

The UK Mobile Communications Industry

CURRENT NETWORK OPERATOR MARKET SHARES

April 2002	O_2	Vodafone	T-Mobile	Orange
Current Subscriber Base	11,140,000	11,735,540	10,750,000	12,475,000
Total Market Share	24.2%	25.5%	23.3%	27.1%

5-YEAR SUBSCRIBER GROWTH

Date	Jan 1998	Jan 1999	Jan 2000	Jan 2001	Jan 2002
Subscriber Base	8,344,000	13,001,000	23,944,000	40,057,300	45,677,600
Penetration Rate	14.3%	22.3%	41%	67.2%	76.6%

GENERAL INTRODUCTION

The UK's mobile communications industry is in the midst of great change; the government sold the latest set of operating licenses at considerable profit and Network Operators are trying to recoup their expenses by developing more services. As a result, the country's mobile users are having to come to terms with a host of new acronyms – WAP, GPRS, 3G etc – and a range of services they did not know they wanted. Two of the four operators have recently undergone major rebranding. O_2 was rebranded following its demerger from BT and T-Mobile acquired its new face as part of its German parent company's global branding effort. This is in addition to new brand images for the Network Operators formerly known as BT Cellnet and One2One, now referred to as O_2 and T-Mobile respectively.

THE INDUSTRY PLAYERS

The mobile communications industry has a number of players: Network Operators who own the infrastructure and provide services; Service Providers and MVNOs who do not own infrastructure but have commercial agreements with the Network Operators; and the Regulator who is responsible for setting the controls of the mobile market and ensuring that industry players do not behave anti-competitively.

NETWORK OPERATORS

Competition was introduced to the UK's mobile market at an early stage meaning that there are now four companies actively offering mobile services: O_2, Vodafone, T-Mobile and Orange. A fifth, Hutchison 3G, has been licensed but is yet to launch. Network Operators are responsible for billing and maintaining the network infrastructure, they can set tariffs and have a direct billing relationship with the end users.

ALTERNATIVE SUPPLIERS

Service Providers were introduced to the UK market at the very beginning as a means to stimulate competition within the market. Service Providers buy airtime wholesale from the Network Operators and sell it onto the end users. This agreement means that they can set their own tariff structures and bill the end users. The incumbent operators (those who have been operating since the start), O_2 and Vodafone, have an obligation under the terms of their licenses to offer wholesale minutes of airtime to Service Providers. The next two entrants, Orange and T-Mobile, have never been subject to this condition. There are said to be around 50 Service Providers still operating in the market including One.Tel, Sainsbury's, Sony Cellular Services and Martin Dawes.

The newest players are MVNOs – Mobile Virtual Network Operators. Unlike Service Providers there is no obligation for the network operators to open their networks to MVNOs – rather it is an entirely commercial agreement – where the Network Operator allows the MVNO access to their network. This differs from the Service Provider in that a true MVNO that has its own mobile network code; issues its own SIM cards (Subscriber Identity Module card – the 'brain' of the handset); operates its own mobile switching centre; and has a pricing structure fully independent from the network operator. As these are commercial agreements, there are as yet no regulations covering MVNOs but as with mobile Internet access the Regulator is currently observing development closely and may step in as MVNOs become a more important force.

To date the most successful MVNO is Virgin Mobile which operates on the back of the T-Mobile network. As the company does not have infrastructure costs, Virgin Mobile has been able to keep costs low and attract a large number of customers in a relatively short space of time. Other emerging MVNOs include Energis and FT Mobile, a joint venture between the Financial Times and the Carphone Warehouse.

TYPES OF SERVICE

Mobile Operators, Service Providers and MVNOs offer two basic types of service; contract and pre-paid. Monthly contracts mean that the end user pays a fixed subscription fee each month that entitles them to a number of basic services and gives them a certain amount of 'free' airtime each month. Pre-paid subscribers have access to the same services but pay in advance and simply top up their account when it is running low. Initially this allowed industry players to target additional consumer segments, in particular the youth market and customers who would not normally pass the credit checks necessary for a contract. It has proved to be a very popular option as it allows customers to control their spend.

The Development of Mobile Infrastructure

Migration Path	GSM	GPRS	UMTS
Data Rate	9.6 – 14.4 kbps	>170 kbps	>2Mbps
Introduced	1992	2001	Due 2003
Services	Voice & SMS	Voice & basic data services	Voice & multimedia

Services were introduced to the UK in 1985 using an analogue technology called TACS. In 1992 Vodafone launched a new digital GSM network, referred to as second generation or 2G. BT Cellnet (now O₂) and two more entrants launched GSM services in the following two years making the UK one of Europe's most competitive markets.

The next upgrade to the infrastructure was called GPRS (General Packet Radio Service). GPRS is not a completely new network, rather an upgrade to the existing infrastructure and so has been dubbed 2.5G.

GPRS has one crucial difference from the GSM network – the ability to bill customers in packets of data rather than in simple airtime. This means that operators can charge customers for the amount of data they transfer across the network rather than the amount of time it took them to transfer it. This is a brand new concept for mobile customers and the UK's operators are still mainly targeting GPRS services at the less price conscious business segment.

The industry is waiting for the delivery of the next generation of mobile services, 3G, or, to give it its proper title UMTS (Universal Mobile Telecommunications System). Since UMTS is an entirely new network, Network Operators must hold a license to deploy it. The UK was the third European country to license 3G operators after Finland and Spain but was the first to auction its licences. Auctions are not new to the European communications industry – many of the second and third entrants to Europe's communications markets had to bid for their licenses – but what was spectacular about the UK's 3G auction was the size of the bids. While industry observers had speculated that the auction might reach £4 billion, in the event a total of £22 billion was raised from the sale of spectrum.

UK 3G Licence Winners and Total Cost

Hutchison 3G UK	Licence A	2x 15MHz paired 5MHz unpaired	€ 7 billion
Vodafone	Licence B	2x15MHz paired	€ 9.6 billion
BT Cellnet	Licence C	2x10 MHz paired 5MHz unpaired	€ 6.5 billion
One2One	Licence D	2x10 MHz paired 5MHz unpaired	€ 6.4 billion
Orange	Licence E	2x10 MHz paired 5MHz unpaired	€ 6.6 billion
Total			€ 36.1 billion

The Importance of Data Services

The transition to GSM from analogue brought clearer voice quality but a mobile customer will not receive better voice quality from a UMTS network – what they will get is the ability to increase their phone's functionality. This is important for the industry as it reaches saturation point and as Network Operators begin to move from simply trying to acquire new customers to trying to get existing customers to do more with their phones.

Competition has driven down price and revenue from basic voice services so data services offer the Network Operators the ability both to increase revenue and to differentiate themselves from their competitors. To date the most important data services offered by the mobile operators are based on SMS and WAP.

SMS (Short Messaging Services) or 'text messaging' allows consumers to send and receive text messages up to 160 characters long on their mobile phones. Due to its simplicity and popularity among young users the number of SMS messages being sent each day has increased dramatically.

Total Number of SMS Sent in the UK

Date	December '98	December '99	December '00	December '01
Number of messages	170 million	271 million	756 million	1.3 billion

SMS is a relatively simple technology, as users have become more familiar with 'texting' it has begun to evolve and services allowing users to send logos, basic pictures and ringtones are emerging. This type of messaging is referred to as EMS, Enhanced Messaging Services.

WAP, Wireless Application Protocol, is a software language that allows Internet-style data to be downloaded and viewed on a mobile phone. Given the slow data rate of a GSM network and the size of a mobile phone screen, WAP applications have, so far, been uninspiring. Consumers access content from mobile portals which, like traditional Internet portals, aggregate and display mobile Internet content in an accessible manner. As could be expected, there are a number of independent mobile Internet portals and content sites springing up for UK consumers.

WAP services will become more attractive to customers as GPRS is introduced as it will allow faster download times and additional charging options. Take up has been much slower than anticipated but it is key to Network Operators' future businesses that users accept and use more WAP and SMS based applications. These services are the basis for the migration to more data-centric 3G services which will allow Network Operators to recoup the expenses of the 3G licence.

Regulation

A draft Communications Bill was published by the UK government in May 2002 which, if enacted, will dramatically change the regulation of the mobile industry. At the moment, the two government bodies covering the regulation of the mobile industry are the Radiocommunications Agency, which is the part of the DTI responsible for radio frequency allocation, and OFTEL. The greater part of regulation is the responsibility of OFTEL which has jurisdiction over the country's telecommunications market. OFTEL was created by the 1984 Telecommunications Act and empowered competition in the UK market. It was given authority over licensing procedures, tariffing, interconnection (where one operator has access to another's infrastructure) as well as acting as an arbitrator between operators in disputes. The policies adopted and enforced by OFTEL are largely driven by the European Commission. This follows the European Court of Justice's ruling allowing the European Commission to apply the competition rules of the Treaty of Rome to telecommunications (in 1985).

In general, policy has been aimed at providing access to networks and public services and guarantee harmonised, objective, transparent and non-discriminatory conditions based on the so called 'Open Network Provision' (ONP) principles which aim to ensure fair

competition and access for new entrants. Among other things that have impacted on the mobile industry, the Commission has addressed:

Universal Service
Services must be provided to all customers irrespective of their location. New entrants often have to contribute to the cost of universal service provision.

Number Portability
This allows the customer to keep his or her telephone number even if they change service provider. Number portability was introduced to the UK's fixed line communications industry in June 1997 and to the mobile industry in January 1999.

Licensing
The provision of and requirements of the licensing process.

Incumbent's Tariffs
This provision is to stop incumbent operators abusing their positions as providers of both local, national and long distance services by cross-subsidising one with another.

The current regulation structure was created by the 1981 Telecommunications Act, which divided the General Post Office into BT and the Post Office and made provision for the introduction of competition, and the 1984 Telecommunications Act, which established BT as a public limited company and created OFTEL as the industry watchdog. However, the Communications Bill of 2002 is expected to change the regulation as new European directives are implemented. The Communications Bill will abolish OFTEL and create a new regulatory body for the whole communications industry in a move that is intended to better reflect the convergent nature of the industry and will harmonise telecommunications regulations in all EU countries.
The new regulatory body will be called OFCOM, The Office of Communications, and will replace the existing communications and broadcasting regulators: OFTEL (The Office of Telecommunications); the Independent Television Commission, ITC); the Broadcasting Standards Commission; the Radio Authority and the Radiocommunications Agency.
OFCOM will become operational in 2003. While OFTEL is currently funded by licence fees, OFCOM will levy administration charges, most likely as a percentage of relevant turnover.
From the point of view of the mobile industry, the key features of the draft bill include:

- The abolition of licensing requirements
- The provision for spectrum trading
- New enforcement provisions for dealing with anti-competitive behaviour

PMR

There is another operational national mobile network. Dolphin Telecom operates a national PMR (Private Mobile Radio) mobile network based on the TETRA standard. PMR differs from other mobile networks in its ability to allow group communication – a single user has the ability to push a button which allows him to broadcast to members of a pre-selected group. PMR networks are most often used by the emergency services but Dolphin rolled out a national network interconnecting with the fixed network and marketed primarily to business users as the UK's fifth mobile network. However the take up of Dolphin's services has been much slower than anticipated and with only

approximately 76,000 digital subscribers, Dolphin called in administrators in August 2001.
However, in January 2002, a company called Inquam applied for a licence from the DTI that would allow it to provide telecoms services within the UK. Inquam are said to be interested in acquiring the assets of Dolphin and will need a general licence to be able to hold the spectrum licence. Inquam is a joint venture between Qualcomm and Omnia, a Middle East investment fund. Should it be successful in acquiring Dolphin's assets, it is unknown whether Inquam will attempt to revive the PMR business in the UK or will try to utilise the spectrum with another technology (which would require a change to their licence).

CONTACTS

OFTEL
50 Ludgate Hill, London EC4M 7JJ
Tel: 020-7634 8700; Fax: 020-7634 8943
Web: www.oftel.co.uk

DEPARTMENT OF TRADE AND INDUSTRY (DTI)
Telecommunications Division
151 Buckingham Palace Road, London SW1W 9SS
Tel: 020-7215 5000; Fax: 020-7215 2909

O₂
260 Bath Road, Slough, Berkshire SL1 4DX
Tel: 01753-565000; Fax: 01753-565010
Web: www.O2.co.uk

DOLPHIN TELECOM
The Crescent, Jays Close, That Viables, Basingstoke
Hampshire RG22 4BS
Tel: 01256-811822; Fax: 01256-474537
Web: www.dolphin-telecom.co.uk

HUTCHINSON 3G UK
43 New Bond Street, London W1Y 9HB
Tel: 020-7499 1886; Fax: 020-7491 7266
Web: www.hutchison3G.com

ORANGE PLC
The Economist Building, 25 St James Street, London
SW1A 1HA
Tel: 020-7766 1766; Fax: 020-7766 1767
Web: www.orange.co.uk

T-MOBILE
Imperial Place, Maxwell Road, Borehamwood, UK
WD6 1EA
Tel: 020-8214 2121; Fax: 020-8214 3601
Web: www.t-mobile.co.uk

VODAFONE GROUP
The Courtyard, 2–4 London Road, Newbury, Berkshire
RG14 1JX
Tel: 01635-33251; Fax: 01635-45713
Web: www.vodafone.co.uk

Information Technology and Computer Science

ANCESTRY

The ancestors of the modern computer are the Difference Engine and Analytical Engine devised by mathematician Charles Babbage. Designed in 1820 to automatically compute mathematical tables, construction of his mechanical, clockwork-like Difference Engine was abandoned by Babbage in the 1840s for personal and financial reasons. In 1834 he began work on his Analytical Engine. Unlike the Difference Engine, the Analytical Engine was designed as a general purpose tool with a store to hold information.

Babbage's work relied heavily on mechanics and physical machinery. It was not until the twentieth century invention of the electrical vacuum tube, and then the transistor, that computers became a feasible means to solving problems.

FIRST GENERATION

War has been a significant factor in the development of the computer. In 1943, during World War II, the British and Americans developed electro mechanical computers. Colossus, a British effort, was specifically developed to crack German coding ciphers, whilst an American effort, Harvard Mark I, was developed as a more general purpose electromechanical programmable computer (partly for atom bomb research). Regarded as early first generation computers, these machines primarily comprised wired circuits and vacuum valves. Punched cards were employed as the input, output and main storage systems. ENIAC (Electronic Numerical Integrator and Computer) was completed in 1946 at the University of Pennsylvania, USA. Capable of carrying out 100,000 calculations a second, it was remarkable for its day despite weighing thirty tons.

SECOND GENERATION

Similar to light bulbs, valves were prone to failure, requiring tedious checks to resolve problems (ENIAC alone contained 18,000 vacuum valves). In 1947, the transistor was invented. Performing the same role as a vacuum valve but less prone to failure, smaller and more efficient, the transistor allowed smaller 'second generation' computers to be developed throughout the 1950s and early 1960s.

THIRD GENERATION

In 1958 Jack St Claire Kilby produced the first integrated circuit 'micro-chip'. A micro-chip is comprised of a large number of transistors and other components bonded to a wafer ('chip') of silicon, interconnected by a surface film of conductive material rather than by wires. By reducing distance between components, savings are made in both size and electricity. In 1963 the first 'third generation' computers based on micro-chip technology appeared.

FOURTH GENERATION

In 1971 Intel produced the first 'microprocessor' heralding a 'fourth generation' of computers. The Intel 4004 (capable of 60,000 instructions per second) grouped much of the processing functions onto a single micro-chip. Around the same time, Intel invented the RAM (random access memory) chip which grouped significant amounts of memory onto a single chip.

Supercomputers and mainframes, utilising scores of microprocessors, had terrific power in the order of 150 million instructions per second. Developments such as multi-layer circuits, and the use of copper instead of gold, yielded gains in size and performance through miniaturisation. The size of the transistor scaled down from thumb size to far smaller than the thickness of a human hair, allowing a greater density and thus exponentially increasing the total power of the computer.

NEXT GENERATION

Most modern computers are still regarded as 'fourth generation' as they use essentially the same technology, albeit highly miniaturised. The future of computer technology is widely thought to be dependent on the physics of light. Already used extensively in the computer industry for high-speed communications, light offers future possibilities for both calculation and storage.

PROGRAMMING LANGUAGES

A multitude of programming languages have been devised with the common purpose of devising a program of instructions for computers to follow to achieve a task. The languages are categorised by generation:

1GL or first-generation language is the machine language that the processor chips execute in raw binary form (strings of zeros and ones).

2GL or second-generation language. Assembly language is a human-understandable language insofar as it uses names as well as numbers. An assembler program takes assembly language and turns it into a machine code program. Very common on early systems where resources (speed, storage) were at a premium, it is typically only used today as an output from 3GL and higher systems.

3GL or third-generation language is a 'high-level' programming language typically more readable and concise than assembly language.

4GL or fourth generation language is designed to be closer to natural language than a 3GL language.

5GL or fifth-generation programming uses graphical development environments to create source language to be compiled with a 3GL or 4GL language compiler. Often a mix of generations is used, with a high level language (4 or 5GL) used to produce interface elements and a lower level language used to provide the processing power.

OPERATING SYSTEMS

An operating system (OS) is a set of utility programs that acts as the liaison between the computer user, the hardware (processor unit, memory) and its peripherals (disks, mouse, display, printer, network etc) and the program that the user is running (e.g. a word processor). The first computers had no operating system, and each program had to directly control the hardware on its own adding greatly to the burden of programming. Early operating systems were hardware and manufacturer-specific with assembly language or machine code as the programming language. Each computer model or series tended to have its own specific operating system. UNIX was one of the first operating systems that could be ported (converted) to a variety of system hardware. This

ability was made largely through the use of the 'C' programming language.

PERSONAL COMPUTER OPERATING SYSTEMS

Since the 1990s, the personal computer world has been dominated by Microsoft Corporation. Although not a significant manufacturer of computer equipment, the Microsoft Corporation has built on its market share secured in the 1980s with MS DOS to become the market leading operating system provider. Microsoft's MS Windows personal computer operating systems are installed on more computers than any other commercial operating system.

Microsoft's main personal computer rival is Apple. Established in the 1970s, Apple became highly successful with its Apple I, II and III range of personal computers, and is one of the few personal computer companies from that time that has continued to manufacture both its own hardware and operating system to run upon it.

THE NET

Prior to the Internet (or 'the Net' or 'the Web' as it is known colloquially) computers tended to be connected together by hardware and protocols that were specific to each particular connection. Typically, links were point-to-point (a link had to be directly and physically established between the two computers). In 1969 ARPANET was formed by the US Department of Defence, to establish a way for the computer capability of the military to be dispersed so that no one centre was critical to the operation of the network as a whole. This was achieved by interconnecting computers both directly and by way of other intermediary computers; thus if one computer was hit by a nuclear bomb, other pathways of communication could be established. The interconnections, when drawn, appeared as a mesh or net or web. ARPANET was extended to non-military users such as universities early in the 1970s, with initial international links appearing in 1972.

The introduction of domain names (e.g. whitakers-almanack.co.uk) in 1984 offered an easier means of using the Web. Prior to domain names one had to remember IP numbers (e.g.192.168.1.100) for accessing destination computers. However, before 1989 the Internet was primarily limited to government agencies, the military, academic and research organisations and some big businesses.

In 1989, what most people perceive as 'the Net' was born. It was effectively invented at CERN (the European Particle Physics Laboratory) by Tim Berners-Lee as a way for scientists to share information by placing it in a prescribed format on a server. Initially text only, development of computer capability allowed inclusion of images.

By 1993 a whole new industry of ISPs (Internet Service Providers) had begun, allowing computer users to dial up via a modem and access the Internet and to view the Web through a browser (*see* glossary). Developments through the late 1990s have allowed music, video, games, text, graphics and telephone calls to travel the Internet. The future is likely to see the majority of telephone calls, and probably video, being transmitted over the Internet for at least part of their journey. Expansion of fibre-optic cable networks to homes and businesses will underpin this. The advent of high-capacity mobile phones will also facilitate and demand expansion of the Internet.

GLOSSARY OF TERMS

The following is a selected list of modern computing terms. It is by no means exhaustive but is intended to cover those that the average computer user might encounter.

ADSL: Asymmetric Digital Subscriber Line – high speed internet connection, four or more times faster than a modem, but using the same standard cables as regular telephone. Faster at downloading than uploading (hence asymmetric).

Animated Gif: A multi-layered Gif file that allows simple animations to be created by transitions between the layers. Banner advertising on the Internet tends to utilise animated Gifs. *See also* Gif.

Bluetooth: Standard for short range (10 metre) wireless connectivity between devices such as laptops, cell phones and printers to interact without cables.

Broadband Internet: Generic term to describe high speed Internet – using technologies such as ISDN, ADSL etc. as opposed to Narrowband internet connections via modem.

Browser: Typically referring to a 'web browser' that allows a computer user to view web page content on their computer. E.g. Microsoft Explorer, Netscape Navigator, AOL etc.

Burn: To 'burn', 'toast' or 'rip' a file or files to a CD-ROM or similar media means to copy the files to the media from hard disk (or other source). Derived from the fact that CD-ROMs are burnt by a laser during the process of writing to the disk.

C: A 3GL programming language developed in the late 1960s in parallel with the UNIX operating systems. Primarily limited to UNIX until the mid-1980s when standards such as POSIX emerged, allowing C to be widely adopted on many operating systems. UNIX used C as its core programming language.

Cat-5: An electrical performance and cable quality standard prescribed to support high-speed Ethernet networks. There are higher category and capability specifications denoted by higher numbers but Cat-5 is the most commonly installed today.

CD: Compact Disc – a digital disk format capable of storing 650 megabytes of information per side. A laser head detects pits etched into the substrate of the spinning disk and interprets them as information. Widely used in an audio format for storing recorded music. The computer format CD-ROM is likely to be superseded by the higher capacity DVD in the next few years. CD-RAM/CD-RW and CD-R are modifiable versions that use lasers to alter the disk substrate to make the pits interpreted later as information. *See also* DVD.

DNS: Domain Name Server – a server that translates domain names into the IP numbers used by programs to directly access computers on the Internet. Each server has an IP number and a name. DNS is analogous to the telephone directory enquiry service, providing a means of looking up and locating a computer connected to the Internet.

Domain: A set of words, numbers and letters separated by dots used to identify an Internet server or group of servers, e.g. www.whitakers-almanack.co.uk, where 'www' denotes a web (http) server, 'whitakers-almanack' denotes the organisation name, 'co' denotes that the organisation is a company and 'uk' denotes United Kingdom (there are alternatives for every country but 'us' is typically omitted for the United States).

DVD: Digital Versatile Disc – DVD-ROM is a high capacity (read only) disk format that has the same form factor as CD-ROM but can store several Gigabytes of information on each surface and can have four readable surfaces (through laser focusing technology). DVD-RAM is a modifiable version. Various formats are available, the most common being that used to store high-quality digital video, an alternative to the laser disk or video tape. *See also* CD.

Email: Electronic mail – an email message is a document that is addressed to one or more persons from an individual address. Usually containing a message, it can also include other documents. It has superceded the telex, telegram, postcard and letter for rapidly exchanging information. The advent of the Internet has seen an explosion in the use of email in modern life. Without encryption or digital signature, an Internet email is not secure.

Ethernet: Utilising simple, standard and relatively cheap cable and connectors, Ethernet has become the standard for local area networks. Ethernet employs a system whereby each computer listens for information addressed to its own unique address. Before transmitting, each computer waits for silence on the line; if multiple computers start transmitting simultaneously, they each detect the 'collision' and wait a random period of time before trying again, thus allowing communications to proceed politely.

Extranet: An extranet is a secure and private subset of the Internet, protected by security protocols and typically used for exchanging information and services between a specific group.

File Server: A computer on a network that stores computer files that users can access from other computers on the network. Popular modern systems include Windows NT, UNIX, Novell NetWare, AppleShare IP and MacOS X Server.

Firewall: Computer or device to protect a network from security risks posed by the Internet, just as a firewall protects parts of a building from a fire raging on the other side, a network firewall stops risks posed by the Internet from egressing into a private network.

FireWire: Apple Computer's implementation of IEEE 1394. *See also* IEEE 1394.

FTP: File Transfer Protocol – an Internet protocol whereby an FTP client program can exchange files with a remote server.

Gbps: giga bits per second – denoting 1,000 million bits transmitted per second.

GIF: Graphics Interchange Format – compressed graphic format suitable for logos and non-photographic images. Invented by Unisys to allow images to be electronically sent in an efficient manner.

HTML: HyperText Mark-up Language – a small programming language used to denote or mark-up how an internet page should be presented to a user from a HTTP server via a web browser. HTTP is an evolving standard that has grown greatly from its first version to accommodate new types of web content and features provided by the different web browsers (e.g. Netscape and Internet Explorer).

HTTP: HyperText Transfer Protocol – an Internet protocol whereby a web server sends web pages, images and files to a web browser. HTTP is an evolving protocol.

IEEE 1394: High speed serial (400 mbps) connection standard for hard disks, digital video cameras and other multimedia devices. Popularised as iLink (Sony) and FireWire (Apple).

iLink: Sony's implementation of IEEE 1394. *See also* IEEE 1394.

IMAP: Internet Mail Access Protocol – an Internet protocol IMAP allows a user to review, manipulate and store email on a central server from one or more workstations without necessitating message removal from the server.

Internet: An abstract concept applied to describe the global network of INTER-connected computer NET-works of computers. *See* body of article.

Intranet: Subset of the Internet, using Internet protocols over a local area network. Common today for publishing information and services within an organisation.

IRC: Internet Relay Chat – protocol that allows users to 'chat' online with other users using their keyboards. Under IRC a user can log into various chat rooms under their own name or an alias and have a text 'conversation' in real time with other users.

ISDN: Integrated Services Digital Network – widely adopted in the United Kingdom and Europe but not North America, ISDN allows both digital computer data and voice telephony to exist simultaneously on the same cable circuits. Data can be digitally exchanged at 64 kbps per circuit. Typically used for point-to-point file transfer of large documents when first introduced, more recently it has been used for 'dial-up' Internet.

JPEG: Joint Photographic Experts Group – compressed graphic format suitable for compression of photographic images in a manner that simplifies the image, losing definition in the process. As the level of compression increases so too does the image degradation.

Kbps: Kilo bits per second – measure of transmission speed, denoting 1,000 bits transmitted per second.

MacOS: Operating system developed by Apple Computer for use on their own Macintosh computers.

Mbps: Mega bits per second – denoting 1 million bits transmitted per second.

Modem: Modulator/demodulator – a device that modulates digital signals from a computer into analogue signals for transmission over a standard telephone line and demodulates an incoming analogue signal and converts it to a digital signal for the computer.

MP3: Motion picture group 1 layer 3 – popular format for compressing audio information for transmission over the Internet for later playback on personal computers, music players and other devices.

MPEG: Motion Picture Encoding Group – popular format standard for compressing video and audio information for transmission over the Internet for later playback on personal computers and on hand-held devices.

MS-DOS: Microsoft Corporation's Disk Operating System – an early OS commercially developed but not invented by Microsoft for use on early Intel-based personal computers. *See also* Operating System.

NNTP: Network News Transfer Protocol – an Internet protocol that implements a bulletin board on a global scale. Using a NNTP browser one can subscribe and contribute to one or more news groups of a large variety of topics.

Operating System (OS): Computer software developed to provide computer programs with standard facilities to interact with users and with computer hardware (via drivers). *See also* MS-DOS, UNIX, MacOS.

PNG: An improved royalty-free graphics file replacement for GIF.

POP3: Post Office Protocol 3 – an Internet protocol whereby a workstation can collect email from a personal mailbox on an email server and move it to a user's own machine.

Print Server: A computer or device on a network that manages the sharing of one or more printers between multiple computers over a network. Many modern printers have a print server built in.

Router: Where multiple networks are joined together, a router acts like a fast sorting office, examining the destination address of each information packet and passing or routing it to the appropriate network. Routers can select the most efficient route for packets.

SMTP: Simple Mail Transfer Protocol – an Internet protocol whereby a workstation can send email to a server or whereby two servers can exchange email.

SNMP: Simple Network Management Protocol – widely used protocol for remotely monitoring and managing network device status and function.

Stuffit: Popular Apple Macintosh mechanism to compress information for transmission and later expansion without loss of information. Stuffit is a proprietary brand name of Aladdin Systems. *See also* Zip.

TCP/IP: Transmission Control Protocol/Internet Protocol – a protocol which is the lifeblood of the Internet, TCP/IP defines how information and requests generated by all other protocols are transmitted over the Internet. Information on the Internet is chopped up into small chunks or packets which are addressed with a destination and origination address. It sometimes happens that a packet gets lost and TCP/IP dictates how such a loss is handled.

UNIX: *See* body of article. Modern versions include Linux, MacOS X, Solaris, FreeBSD.

USB: Universal Serial Bus – standard for connecting serial devices such as scanners, mice, keyboards, modems and printers to computers. With USB, speeds of 10 Mbps and higher are possible.

USB 2: Universal Serial Bus 2 – a revised, higher performance version of USB.

URL: Uniform Resource Locator – address of an Internet file accessible on the Internet. E.g. http://www.whitakers-almanack.co.uk.

Virus: A computer program or script written for the express purpose of replicating itself onto as many machines as possible (much like its biological namesake) often with negative side effects to the host computer and computer network. Such effects vary from harmless screen messages to corruption of document integrity, network overload or compromising data security or privacy. Historically transmitted slowly by floppy disk and over networks within offices, the prevalence of email means viruses can spread globally within hours.

WAP: Wireless Application Protocol – a set of standards to define how portable devices connected via radio waves (such as cell phones) can access Internet services.

XML: Extensible Mark-up Language; similar to HTML but more powerful, XML allows pages of information to be encoded for later publishing on the web and for traditional paper print publishing.

Zip: Compression – a popular mechanism on PCs to compress information for transmission and later expansion without loss of information. *See also* Stuffit.

The Environment

Legislation and strategies to protect the environment in the UK are driven by the requirements of international conventions and protocols (of which there are over 50) and European Directives (of which there are over 300), as well as the desires of the UK government, the Scottish Executive and the Northern Ireland Assembly. The Environment Agency, the Scottish Environment Protection Agency and the Environment and Heritage Service for Northern Ireland are responsible for regulation.

EUROPEAN UNION MEASURES

The European Union's (EU) work is developed based on its Environmental Action Programme which began in the 1970s. The European Commission's Sixth Environmental Action Programme, *Environment 2010: Our Future, Our Choice*, was adopted in January 2001 and sets the programme to 2010. It proposes five priority areas: improving the implementation of existing legislation; integrating environmental concerns into other policies; working more closely with the market; empowering private citizens and helping them to change behaviour; and taking account of the environment in land-use planning and management decisions. The programme focuses on four topics: climate change, nature and biodiversity, environment and health, and natural resources and waste.

SUSTAINABLE DEVELOPMENT AND LOCAL AGENDA 21

The environmental agenda, both at a business and government level is moving forward to address sustainability which incorporates social, environmental and economic development. The most commonly used definition is 'development that meets the needs of the present without compromising the ability of future generations to meet their own needs'.

The 2002 world summit on sustainable development (Rio + 10) was held in Johannesburg from 26 August to 4 September. United Nations Secretary-General Kofi Annan identified five key areas for the meeting "in which progress is possible with the resources and technologies at our disposal". These are water and sanitation, energy, health, agriculture and biodiversity.

As part of the EU's preparation for the world summit, a sustainable development strategy was adopted last year. It sets out long-term objectives including: to meet the commitments under the Kyoto Protocol and then to reduce greenhouse gas emissions by an average of 1 per cent per year over 1990 levels up to 2020; limiting major threats to public health; and breaking the link between economic growth and transport growth.

The UK published its first national sustainable development strategy in 1994 and its first set of sustainable development indicators in 1996. The latest strategy, *A Better Quality of Life*, was published in May 1999. It establishes a framework for integrating social, environmental and economic policies to meet four objectives: social progress, to protect the environment, prudent use of natural resources, and to maintain high and stable levels of economic growth and employment.

The strategy contains 15 headline indicators, which are backed by a further 150, against which progress in the UK is measured. Leading businesses are beginning to use the indicators in assessing and reporting their own progress towards achieving sustainability.

In March 2002, the government published its second annual progress report on sustainable development. Ten of the 15 headline indicators showed progress in the right direction.

The Scottish Executive launched a statement on sustainable development, together with 24 initial indicators, in April 2002. Some of the indicators have targets, while others are still being developed. Full data on each indicator will be published by the end of 2002 and the indicators will be reviewed in 2003, particularly in light of discussions at the world summit on sustainable development.

Local authorities also have a role to play in sustainable development. Under Local Agenda 21, which came out of the UN Conference on Environment and Development in Rio, Brazil in 1992, local authorities have an obligation to draw up sustainable development strategies for their areas. Regional Development Agencies take Local Agenda 21 strategies into account in sustainable development frameworks for each English region.

WASTE

Waste policy in the UK follows a number of principles: the waste hierarchy of reduce, reuse, recycle, dispose; the proximity principle of disposing of waste close to its generation; and national self-sufficiency.

Directives from Europe are playing an increasingly important role in driving UK policy, particularly regarding commercial and industrial waste. For instance, the Landfill Directive, which was adopted in July 1999, sets stringent targets for reducing the amount of waste sent to landfill and the technical requirements for landfill sites. The directive should have been implemented by July 2001. However, in April 2002, regulations were laid before the UK parliament for implementation in England and Wales. The Scottish Executive and Northern Ireland Assembly will develop separate legislation.

The proposed European integrated products policy aims to internalise the environmental costs of products throughout their life-cycle through market forces, by focusing on eco-design and incentives to ensure increased demand for greener products. Greater responsibility for end-of-life products is already being addressed by: the producer responsibility directives for packaging waste, which came into force in the UK in 1997; the end-of-life-vehicle directive, which entered into force in December 2001; the proposed directives on waste from electrical and electronic equipment and the proposed directives on the restriction of the use of certain hazardous substances in such equipment.

In November 2001, the UK Government held a waste summit to start the process of looking at forward policies to implement the Waste Strategy for England and Wales, which was published in May 2000. The strategy aims to: tackle the amount of waste produced; increase recycling rates through statutory targets for local authorities; reduce the amount of waste sent to landfill; and develop markets and end-uses for secondary materials. To meet the targets, the public and local authorities will have to vastly increase their current recycling rates. The Government's Performance and Innovation Unit began a study in December 2001 into the Government's waste strategy.

Scotland also has a national waste strategy which aims to encourage more effective use of natural resources through greater efficiency, waste minimisation, recycling and increased value recovery from waste. A National Waste Plan for Scotland is expected to be published by the end of 2002. It will be based on the Area Waste Plans that are currently nearing completion.

The Northern Ireland waste strategy is a framework to help achieve the goal of sustainable waste management and meet the targets for the diversion of waste from landfill.

CLIMATE CHANGE AND AIR POLLUTION

The UK's response to climate change is driven by the Framework Convention on Climate Change. This is a binding agreement that has been signed and ratified by 186 countries. It was ratified in the UK in December 1993 and came into force in March 1994. It is intended to reduce the risks of global warming by limiting 'greenhouse' gas emissions.

Progress towards the convention's targets are assessed at regular conferences. At Kyoto in 1997, a protocol (the Kyoto Protocol) to the convention was adopted. It covers the six main greenhouse gases – carbon dioxide, methane, nitrous oxide, hydrofluorocarbons (HFCs), perfluorocarbons (PFCs) and sulphur hexafluoride. Under the protocol, industrialised countries agreed to legally binding targets for cutting emissions of greenhouse gases by 5.2 per cent below 1990 levels by 2008–2012. EU members agreed to an 8 per cent reduction and the UK's target is a 12.5 per cent cut.

The protocol set three ways (Kyoto mechanisms) for countries to increase the flexibility and reduce the cost of making emission cuts – the clean development mechanism, emissions trading and joint implementation. At the seventh Conference of the Parties in Marrakech, Morocco, in November 2001 the operational details of the Kyoto Protocol were finalised, following several years of tough negotiation. The rulebook specifies how to measure emissions and reductions, the extent to which carbon dioxide absorbed by carbon sinks (offsetting emissions by growing forests) can be counted towards Kyoto targets, how the joint implementation and emissions trading systems will work and rules for ensuring compliance.

In November 2000, a UK climate change programme was published which sets out how the UK intends to meet its Kyoto target and progress towards its domestic goal of a 20 per cent cut in carbon dioxide emissions by 2010, some of the policies mentioned are already in place. The proposed measures include: a climate change levy which came into effect in April and applies to sales of electricity, coal, natural gas and liquefied petroleum gas to the business and public sectors; agreements with energy intensive sectors to meet targets; integrated pollution prevention and control; cutting transport congestion and pollution; energy efficiency standards of performance requiring electricity and gas suppliers to help domestic consumers save energy; better countryside management; cuts in fertiliser use; new targets for improving energy management of public buildings; and emissions trading.

The voluntary greenhouse gas emissions trading scheme started in April 2002. Direct participants are required to make reductions in their emissions of greenhouse gases in exchange for an incentive payment. A total of 34 companies took on legally binding emissions reduction targets through a competitive auction held in March. Other companies that already have emission targets can also buy or sell allowances.

The European Commission European is proposing to introduce a mandatory emissions trading scheme at company level for carbon dioxide in the European Union beginning in 2006. The scheme proposes 'cap and trade', whereby governments will have to impose total carbon dioxide caps on companies, which they would then be able to trade as carbon dioxide allowances within the European Union.

Other conventions covering air pollution include the Convention on Long Range Transboundary Air Pollution which was adopted in 1979 and came into force in 1993. Protocols to this convention cover various pollutants, such as sulphur and nitrogen oxides.

The UK has also developed its own policy on air pollution. The Environmental Protection Act 1990 established two regimes: integrated pollution control (IPC) to regulate emissions to any environmental medium from certain industrial processes; and local air pollution control to regulate emissions to air from smaller processes. The European Integrated Pollution Prevention and Control (IPPC) Directive was largely based on the UK's IPC regime. This new regime came into force in the UK in August 2000 (and Scotland in September 2000) after much delay and wrangling over details. Although IPPC is very similar to the UK's IPC it covers many more installations and includes returning sites to a satisfactory state on closure, using energy efficiently and noise and vibration regulation. IPPC has been implemented in the UK through the replacement to the Environmental Protection Act – the Pollution Prevention and Control regulations 2000.

These regulations have also been used to implement the European Commission's Solvent Emissions Directive, which aims to prevent or reduce the effects of emissions of volatile organic compounds. The regulations do not cover all sectors affected by the directive and the government consulted on regulations for these in the summer of 2002.

The UK's first National Air Quality Strategy was published in 1997 and was revised in January 2000. The strategy sets air quality objectives for the main pollutants (benzene, 1-3, butadiene, carbon monoxide, lead, nitrogen dioxide, sulphur dioxide, ozone, and particulates) to be met by 2003–2008.

Under the strategy, all district and unitary authorities have a duty to review air quality, including likely future air quality, in their areas. This is accompanied by an assessment of whether air quality objectives (set in the strategy) are being, or are likely to be, met. If authorities find that any part of their area breaches the objectives, an air quality management area must be declared and an action plan drawn up for improvements.

The UK Government and the Scottish Executive has consulted on proposals to supplement the current air quality objectives for carbon monoxide and benzene taking account of new European limit values; set new long-term objectives for particulates, and introduce an objective for polycyclic aromatic hydrocarbons. The overall message from the consultation was one of support for the proposals and they are to be implemented.

WATER

Water quality targets are set at both EU and UK levels for drinking water sources, wastewater discharges, rivers, coastal water and bathing water. The EU's water framework directive, which entered into force in December 2000, has an objective to achieve 'good water status' throughout the EU by 2015. The UK published a draft Water Bill for consultation in November 2000. In May 2002, the government published its response to the

consultation. In February, a consultation paper covering the water environment section of the Water Environment and Water Services Bill for Scotland was issued.

The EC Bathing Water Directive sets standards for bathing waters. This applies to 391 coastal and nine inland bathing waters in the UK. This directive is over 25 years old and a new version is being drafted. The Environment Agency sets river quality objectives for each stretch of river. Water quality is currently protected through licensing abstraction and regulating discharges. Consents to discharge sewage and industrial effluent are regulated under the Water Resources Act 1991 and the IPPC regime. Discharge consents are based on the river quality objectives and relevant EU directives and specify the concentration and quantity permitted.

The European Urban Waste Water Treatment Directive sets minimum standards for sewage treatment before discharge into coastal waters with the levels of treatment needed depending on the sensitivity of the receiving water. In 1999 the government set more stringent UK targets for all significant coastal discharges to have a minimum of secondary treatment by 2005.

SELECTED UK TARGETS

Global atmosphere

- Reduce greenhouse gas emissions to 12.5 per cent below 1990 levels by 2010
- Reduce carbon dioxide emissions to 20 per cent below 1990 levels by 2010

Air quality

- Reduce sulphur dioxide emissions by 63 per cent based on 1990 levels by 2010
- Reduce emissions of nitrogen oxides by 41 per cent based on 1990 levels by 2010
- Reduce emissions of volatile organic compounds by 40 per cent based on 1990 levels by 2010
- Reduce ammonia emissions by 17 per cent based on 1990 levels by 2010

Fresh water and sea

- 97 per cent of bathing waters to meet European directive standards consistently by 2005
- Provide secondary treatment for all significant coastal discharges (over 2,000 population equivalent) by 2005

Waste

- Reduce industrial and commercial waste going to landfill by 85 per cent of 1998 levels by 2005
- Recover 40 per cent of municipal waste by 2005, 45 per cent by 2010 and 67 per cent by 2015
- Recycle or compost 25 per cent of household waste by 2005, 30 per cent by 2010 and 33 per cent by 2015
- Reduce biodegradable waste sent to landfill to 75 per cent of 1995 levels by 2010, 50 per cent by 2013 and 35 per cent by 2020
- Ensure 60 per cent of UK newspaper feedstock content is waste paper by end of 2001, 65 per cent by end of 2003 and 70 per cent by end of 2006
- 2002 recovery of packaging waste set at 59 per cent, and 19 per cent material-specific recycling, up from the 2000 targets of 56 per cent and 18 per cent.
- Proposed reuse and recovery of 85 per cent of the mass of end-of-life vehicles with a minimum of 80 per cent recycling by 2006, 95 per cent and 85 per cent by 2015
- EU target to reduce the amount of waste going to final disposal by 20 per cent by 2010 and 50 per cent by 2050

Land

- Ensure 60 per cent of all new housing is built on re-used sites

CONTACTS

ADVISORY COMMITTEE ON BUSINESS AND THE ENVIRONMENT, Zone 6/E8, Ashdown House, 123 Victoria Street, London SW1E 6DE. Tel: 020-7944 6278; Web: www.defra.gov.uk/environment/acbe

DEPARTMENT OF ENVIRONMENT, FOOD AND RURAL AFFAIRS, Nobel House, 17 Smith Square, London SW1P 3JR. Tel: 020-7238 6000; Web: www.defra.gov.uk

ENVIRONMENT AGENCY, Rivers House, Waterside Drive, Aztec West, Almondsbury, Bristol BS12 4UD. Tel: 01454-624400; Web: www.environment-agency.gov.uk

ENVIRONMENT AND HERITAGE SERVICE FOR NORTHERN IRELAND, Calvert House, 23 Castle Place, Belfast BT1 1FY. Tel: 028-9025 4754; Web: www.ehsni.gov.uk

ENVIROWISE, THE ENVIRONMENT AND ENERGY HELPLINE. Tel: 0800 585794; Web: www.environwise.gov.uk

EUROPEAN COMMISSION, European Commission, B-1049 Brussels, Belgium. Tel: Brussels 299 1111; Web: www.europa.eu.int

EUROPEAN ENVIRONMENT AGENCY, Kongens Nytorv 6, DK-1050 Copenhagen K, Denmark. Tel: Copenhagen 3336 7100. www.eea.eu.int

NORTHERN IRELAND ASSEMBLY, Parliament Buildings, Belfast BT4 3XX. Tel: 028-9052 1333; Web: www.ni-assembly.gov.uk/index.htm

ROYAL COMMISSION ON ENVIRONMENTAL POLLUTION, Third Floor, The Sanctuary, London SW1P 3JS. Tel: 020-7799 8970; Web: www.rcep.org.uk

SCOTTISH ENVIRONMENTAL PROTECTION AGENCY, Erskine Court, Castle Business Park, Stirling FK9 4TR. Tel: 01786-457700; Web: www.sepa.org.uk

SCOTTISH EXECUTIVE, ENVIRONMENT AND RURAL AFFAIRS DEPARTMENT, Pentland House, 47 Robb's Loan, Edinburgh EH14 1TY. Tel: 0131-556 8400; Web: www.scotland.gov.uk

SUSTAINABLE DEVELOPMENT COMMISSION, A505, Romney House, Tufton Street, London SW1P 3RA. Tel: 020-7944 4964; Web: www.sd-commission.gov.uk

SUSTAINABLE DEVELOPMENT UNIT, 5/B2 Ashdown House, 123 Victoria Street, London SW1E 6DE. Tel: 020-7944 6485; Web: www.sustainable-development.gov.uk

UN COMMISSION ON SUSTAINABLE DEVELOPMENT, Division for Sustainable Development, 2 UN Plaza, Room DC2-2220, New York, NY 10017, USA. Tel: +1212 963 0902. Web: www.un.org/esa/sustdev

Conservation and Heritage

Conservation of the Countryside

ENGLAND AND WALES

The ten National Parks of England and Wales were set up under the provisions of the National Parks and Access to the Countryside Act 1949 to conserve and protect scenic landscapes from inappropriate development and to provide access to the land for public enjoyment.

The Countryside Agency (established on 1 April 1999 from the merger of the Countryside Commission and the Rural Development Commission) is the statutory body which has the power to designate National Parks in England, and the Countryside Council for Wales is responsible for National Parks in Wales. Designations in England are confirmed by the Secretary of State for Environment, Food and Rural Affairs and those in Wales by the National Assembly for Wales. The designation of a National Park does not affect the ownership of the land or remove the rights of the local community. The majority of the land in the National Parks is owned by private landowners (74 per cent) or by bodies such as the National Trust (7 per cent) and the Forestry Commission (7 per cent). The National Park Authorities own only 2.3 per cent of the land.

The Environment Act 1995 replaced the existing National Park boards and committees with free-standing National Park Authorities (NPAs). NPAs are the sole local planning authorities for their areas and as such influence land use and development, and deal with planning applications. Their duties include conserving and enhancing the natural beauty, wildlife and cultural heritage of the National Parks; promoting opportunities for public understanding and enjoyment of the National Parks; and fostering the economic and social well-being of the communities within National Parks. The NPAs publish management plans as statements of their policies and appoint their own officers and staff.

Membership of the NPAs differs slightly between England and Wales. In England membership is split between representatives of the constituent local authorities and members appointed by the Secretary of State (of whom one half, minus one, are nominated by the parish councils in the park), with the local authority representatives in a majority of one. The Countryside Agency advises the Secretary of State on appointments not nominated by the parish councils. In Wales two-thirds of NPA members are appointed by the constituent local authorities and one-third by the National Assembly for Wales, advised by the Countryside Council for Wales.

Central government provides 75 per cent of the funding for the parks through the National Park Grant. The remaining 25 per cent is supplied by the local authorities concerned.

The National Parks (with date of designation confirmed) are:

BRECON BEACONS (1957), Powys (66 per cent)/Carmarthenshire/Rhondda, Cynon and Taff/Merthyr Tydfil/Blaenau Gwent/Monmouthshire, 1,351 sq. km/522 sq. miles – The park is centred on the Beacons, Pen y Fan, Corn Du and Cribyn, but also includes the valley of the Usk, the Black Mountains to the east and the Black Mountain to the west. There are information centres at Brecon, Craig-y-nos Country Park, Abergavenny and Llandovery, a study centre at Danywenallt and a day visitor centre near Libanus.
Information Office, 7 Glamorgan Street, Brecon, Powys LD31 7DP. Tel: 01874-624437;
Email: enquiries@breconbeacons.org
National Park Officer, C. Gledhill

DARTMOOR (1951 and 1994), Devon, 954 sq. km/368 sq. miles – The park consists of moorland and rocky granite tors, and is rich in prehistoric remains. There are information centres at Haytor, Newbridge, Princetown and Postbridge.
Information Office, Parke, Haytor Road, Bovey Tracey, Devon TQ13 9JQ. Tel: 01626-832093;
Email: hq@dartmoor-npa.gov.uk
National Park Officer, N. Atkinson

EXMOOR (1954), Somerset (71 per cent)/Devon, 693 sq. km/268 sq. miles – Exmoor is a moorland plateau inhabited by wild ponies and red deer. There are many ancient remains and burial mounds. There are information centres at Lynmouth, County Gate, Dulverton and Combe Martin.
Information Office, Exmoor House, Dulverton, Somerset TA22 9HL. Tel: 01398-323665;
Email: info@exmoor-nationalpark.gov.uk
National Park Officer, N. Stone

LAKE DISTRICT (1951), Cumbria, 2,292 sq. km/885 sq. miles – The Lake District includes England's highest mountains (Scafell Pike, Helvellyn and Skiddaw) but it is most famous for its glaciated lakes. There are information centres at Broughton, Keswick, Waterhead, Hawkshead, Seatoller, Bowness, Grasmere, Coniston, Glenridding and Pooley Bridge and a park centre at Brockhole,Windermere.
Information Office, Murley Moss, Oxenholme Road, Kendal, Cumbria, LA9 7RL. Tel: 01539-724555;
Email: hq@lake-district.gov.uk
National Park Officer, P. Tiplady

NORTHUMBERLAND (1956), Northumberland, 1,049 sq. km/405 sq. miles – The park is an area of hill country stretching from Hadrian's Wall to the Scottish Border. There are information centres at Ingram, Once Brewed and Rothbury.
Information Office, Eastburn, South Park, Hexham, Northumberland HE46 1BS. Tel: 01434-605555;
Email: admin@nnpa.org.uk
National Park Officer, G. Taylor

NORTH YORK MOORS (1952), North Yorkshire (96 per cent)/Redcar and Cleveland, 1,432 sq. km/554 sq. miles – The park consists of woodland and moorland, and includes the Hambleton Hills and the Cleveland Way. There are information centres at Danby, Sutton Bank and at The Old Coastguard Station in Robin Hood's Bay.
Information Office, The Old Vicarage, Bondgate, Helmsley, York YO6 5BP. Tel: 01439-770657;

Email: general@northyorkmoors-npa.gov.uk
National Park Officer, A. Wilson
PEAK DISTRICT (1951), Derbyshire (64 per cent)/Staffordshire/South Yorkshire/Cheshire/West Yorkshire/Greater Manchester, 1,438 sq. km/555 sq. miles – The Peak District includes the gritstone moors of the 'Dark Peak' and the limestone dales of the 'White Peak'. There are information centres at Bakewell, Edale, Castleton and Upper Derwent.
Information Office, Aldern House, Baslow Road, Bakewell, Derbyshire DE45 1AE. Tel: 01629-816200; Email: aldern@peakdistrict-npa.gov.uk
National Park Officer, C. Harrison
PEMBROKESHIRE COAST (1952 and 1995), Pembrokeshire, 620 sq. km/240 sq. miles – The park includes cliffs, moorland and a number of islands, including Skomer. There are information centres at St David's and Newport.
Information Office, Winch Lane, Haverfordwest, Pembrokeshire SA61 1PY. Tel: 01437-764636; Email: pcnp@pembrokeshirecoast.org.uk
National Park Officer, N. Wheeler
SNOWDONIA (1951), Gwynedd/Conwy, 2,142 sq. km/827 sq. miles – Snowdonia is an area of deep valleys and rugged mountains. There are information centres at Aberdyfi, Beddgelert, Betws y Coed, Blaenau Ffestiniog, Conwy, Dolgellau and Harlech.
Information Office, Penrhyndeudraeth, Gwynedd LL48 6LF. Tel: 01766-770274; Email: parc@eryri-npa.gov.uk
National Park Officer, G. I. Huws
YORKSHIRE DALES (1954), North Yorkshire (88 per cent)/Cumbria, 1,769 sq. km/683 sq. miles – The Yorkshire Dales are composed primarily of limestone overlaid in places by millstone grit. The three peaks of Ingleborough, Whernside and Pen-y-Ghent are within the park. There are information centres at Grassington, Hawes, Aysgarth Falls, Malham, Reeth and Sedbergh.
Information Office, Yorebridge House, Bainbridge, Leyburn, N. Yorks DL8 3BP. Tel: 01969-650456; Email: info@yorkshiredales.org.uk
National Park Officer, D. Butterworth

Two other areas considered to have equivalent status to the National Parks are The Broads and the New Forest. The Broads Authority, a special statutory authority, was established in 1989 to develop, conserve and manage the Norfolk and Suffolk Broads. In 1992 the Government declared its intention of giving the New Forest a status equivalent to that of a national park by declaring it an 'area of national significance'. In October 1999 the Countryside Agency began the process of designating the New Forest as a National Park. The South Downs (within the Sussex Downs and east Hampshire 'Areas of Outstanding Natural Beauty') are also being considered for designation as a National Park.

THE BROADS (1989), Norfolk, 303 sq. km/117 sq. miles – The Broads are located between Norwich and Great Yarmouth on the flood plains of the five rivers flowing through the area to the sea. The area is one of fens, winding waterways, woodland and marsh. The 40 or so broads are man-made, and are connected to the rivers by dikes, providing over 200 km of navigable waterways. There are information centres at Beccles, Hoveton, North west Tower (Yarmouth), Potterheigham, Ranworth and Toad Hole.
Broads Authority, Thomas Harvey House, 18 Colegate, Norwich NR3 1BQ. Tel: 01603 610734; Email: broads@broads-authority.gov.uk
Chief Executive, J. Packman

THE NEW FOREST Hampshire, 580 sq. km/224 sq. miles – The forest has been protected since 1079 when it was declared a royal hunting forest. The area consists of forest, ancient woodland and heathland. Much of the Forest is managed by the Forestry Commission, which provides several camp-sites. The main villages are Brockenhurst, Burley and Lyndhurst, which has a visitor centre.
The New Forest Committee, 4 High Street, Lyndhurst, Hants SO43 7BD. Tel: 023-8028 4144. *Chairman*, E. Johnson, FRICS, *Committee Officer*, M. Jago

SCOTLAND AND NORTHERN IRELAND

The National Parks and Access to the Countryside Act 1949 dealt only with England and Wales and made no provision for Scotland or Northern Ireland.

On 9 August 2000 The National Parks (Scotland) Bill received Royal Assent, providing the Parliament with the ability to create National Parks in Scotland in any area deemed to be appropriate. The first Scottish National Parks, Loch Lomond and the Trossachs, and the Cairngorms, are in the process of becoming operational.

There is power to designate National Parks in Northern Ireland under the Amenity Lands Act 1965 and the Nature Conservation and Amenity Lands Order (Northern Ireland) 1985.

AREAS OF OUTSTANDING NATURAL BEAUTY

ENGLAND AND WALES

Under the National Parks and Access to the Countryside Act 1949, provision was made for the designation of Areas of Outstanding Natural Beauty (AONBs) by the Countryside Commission. The Countryside Agency is now responsible for AONBs in England and since April 1991 the Countryside Council for Wales has been responsible for the Welsh AONBs. Designations in England are confirmed by the Secretary of State for Environment, Food and Rural Affairs and those in Wales by the National Assembly for Wales. The Countryside and Rights of Way Act 2000 provided for the creation of conservation boards for individual AONBs and placed greater responsibility on local authorities to protect them.

Although less emphasis is placed upon the provision of open-air enjoyment for the public than in the national parks, AONBs are areas which are no less beautiful and require the same degree of protection to conserve and enhance the natural beauty of the countryside. This includes protecting flora and fauna, geological and other landscape features. In AONBs planning and management responsibilities are split between county and district councils and the newly established conservation boards (where they exist). In Wales, unitary authorities have sole responsibility for the planning and management. Several AONBs cross local authority boundaries. Finance for the AONBs is provided by grant-aid.

The 41 Areas of Outstanding Natural Beauty (with date of designation confirmed) are:
ANGLESEY (1967), Anglesey, 221 sq. km/85 sq. miles
ARNSIDE AND SILVERDALE (1972), Cumbria/Lancashire, 75 sq. km/2;29 sq. miles
BLACKDOWN HILLS (1991), Devon/Somerset, 370 sq. km/143 sq. miles
CANNOCK CHASE (1958), Staffordshire, 68 sq. km/26 sq. miles
CHICHESTER HARBOUR (1964), Hampshire/West Sussex, 74 sq. km/29 sq. miles

CHILTERNS (1965; extended 1990),
Bedfordshire/Hertfordshire/Buckinghamshire/Oxford
shire, 833 sq. km/322 sq. miles
CLWYDIAN RANGE (1985), Denbighshire/Flintshire,
157 sq. km/60 sq. miles
CORNWALL (1959; Camel estuary 1983), 958 sq. km/370
sq. miles
COTSWOLDS (1966; extended 1990),
Gloucestershire/Wiltshire/Warwickshire/
Worcestershire/Somerset, 2,038 sq. km/787 sq. miles
CRANBORNE CHASE AND WEST WILSHIRE DOWNS
(1983), Dorset/Hampshire/Somerset/Wiltshire,
983 sq. km/379 sq. miles
DEDHAM VALE (1970; extended 1978, 1991),
Essex/Suffolk, 90 sq. km/35 sq. miles
DORSET (1959), 1,129 sq. km/436 sq. miles
EAST DEVON (1963), 268 sq. km/103 sq. miles
EAST HAMPSHIRE (1962), 383 sq. km/148 sq. miles
FOREST OF BOWLAND (1964), Lancashire/North
Yorkshire, 802 sq. km/310 sq. miles
GOWER (1956), Swansea, 188 sq. km/73 sq. miles
HIGH WEALD (1983), Kent/Surrey/East Sussex/West
Sussex, 1,460 sq. km/564 sq. miles
HOWARDIAN HILLS (1987), North Yorkshire, 204 sq.
km/79 sq. miles
ISLE OF WIGHT (1963), 189 sq. km/73 sq. miles
ISLES OF SCILLY (1976), 16 sq. km/6 sq. miles
KENT DOWNS(1968), 878 sq. km/339 sq. miles
LINCOLNSHIRE WOLDS (1973), 558 sq. km/215 sq.
miles
LLEYNN (1957), Gwynedd, 161 sq. km/62 sq. miles
MALVERN HILLS (1959),
Herefordshire/Worcestershire/Gloucestershire,
105 sq. km/40 sq. miles
MENDIP HILLS (1972; extended 1989), Somerset,
198 sq. km/76 sq. miles
NIDDERDALE (1994), North Yorkshire, 603 sq. km/233
sq. miles
NORFOLK COAST (1968), 451 sq. km/174 sq. miles
NORTH DEVON (1960), 171 sq. km/66 sq. miles
NORTH PENNINES (1988),
Cumbria/Durham/Northumberland, 1,983 sq.
km/766 sq. miles
NORTHUMBERLAND COAST (1958), 135 sq. km/52 sq.
miles
QUANTOCK HILLS (1957), Somerset, 99 sq. km/38 sq.
miles
SHROPSHIRE HILLS (1959), 804 sq. km/310 sq. miles
SOLWAY COAST (1964), Cumbria, 115 sq. km/44 sq.
miles
SOUTH DEVON (1960), 337 sq. km/130 sq. miles
SOUTH HAMPSHIRE COAST (1967), 77 sq. km/30 sq.
miles
SUFFOLK COASTS AND HEATHS (1970), 403 sq. km/
156 sq. miles
SURREY HILLS (1958), 419 sq. km/162 sq. miles
SUSSEX DOWNS (1966), 983 sq. km/379 sq. miles
TAMAR VALLEY (1995), Cornwall/Devon, 195 sq.
km/115 sq. miles
NORTH WESSEX DOWNS (1972),
Berkshire/Hampshire/Oxfordshire/Wiltshire,
1,730 sq. km/668 sq. miles
WYE VALLEY (1971),
Monmouthshire/Gloucestershire/Herefordshire,
326 sq. km/126 sq. miles

NORTHERN IRELAND

The Department of the Environment for Northern
Ireland, with advice from the Council for Nature
Conservation and the Countryside, designates Areas of
Outstanding Natural Beauty in Northern Ireland. At
present there are nine and these cover a total area of
approximately 284,948 hectares (704,121 acres).

ANTRIM COAST AND GLENS, Co. Antrim, 70,600 ha/
74,452 acres
CAUSEWAY COAST, Co. Antrim, 4,200 ha/10,378 acres
LAGAN VALLEY, Co. Down, 2,072 ha/5,119 acres
LECALE COAST, Co. Down, 3,108 ha/7,679 acres
MOURNE, Co. Down, 57,012 ha/140,876 acres
NORTH DERRY, Co. Londonderry, 12,950 ha/31,999
acres
RING OF GULLION, Co. Armagh, 15,353 ha/37,938 acres
SPERRIN, Co. Tyrone/Co. Londonderry, 101,006 ha/
249,585 acres
STRANGFORD LOUGH Co. Down, 18,647 ha/46,077
acres

NATIONAL SCENIC AREAS

In Scotland, National Scenic Areas have a broadly
equivalent status to AONBs. Scottish Natural Heritage
recognises areas of national scenic significance. At end
March 2002 there were 40, covering a total area of
1,001,800 hectares (2,475,448 acres).

Development within National Scenic Areas is dealt with
by local authorities, who are required to consult Scottish
Natural Heritage concerning certain categories of
development. Disagreements between Scottish Natural
Heritage and local authorities are referred to the Scottish
Executive. Land management uses can also be modified
in the interest of scenic conservation.

ASSYNT-COIGACH, Highland, 90,200 ha/222,884 acres
BEN NEVIS AND GLEN COE, Highland/Argyll and
Bute/Perth and Kinross, 101,600 ha/251,053 acres
CAIRNGORM MOUNTAINS,
Highland/Aberdeenshire/Moray, 67,200 ha/166,051
acres
CUILLIN HILLS, Highland, 21,900 ha/54,115 acres
DEESIDE AND LOCHNAGAR, Aberdeenshire/Angus,
40,000 ha/98,840 acres
DORNOCH FIRTH, Highland, 7,500 ha/18,532 acres
EAST STEWARTRY COAST, Dumfries and Galloway,
4,500 ha/11,119 acres
EILDON AND LEADERFOOT, Scottish Borders,
3,600 ha/8,896 acres
FLEET VALLEY, Dumfries and Galloway, 5,300 ha/13,096
acres
GLEN AFFRIC, Highland, 19,300 ha/47,690 acres
GLEN STRATHFARRAR, Highland, 3,800 ha/9,390 acres
HOY AND WEST MAINLAND, Orkney Islands,
14,800 ha/36,571 acres
JURA, Argyll and Bute, 21,800 ha/53,868 acres
KINTAIL, Highland, 15,500 ha/38,300 acres
KNAPDALE, Argyll and Bute, 19,800 ha/48,926 acres
KNOYDART, Highland, 39,500 ha/97,604 acres
KYLE OF TONGUE, Highland, 18,500 ha/45,713 acres
KYLES OF BUTE, Argyll and Bute, 4,400 ha/10,872 acres
LOCH NA KEAL, MULL, Argyll and Bute,
12,700 ha/31,382 acres
LOCH LOMOND, Argyll and Bute/Stirling/West
Dunbartonshire, 27,400 ha/67,705 acres
LOCH RANNOCH AND GLEN LYON, Perth and
Kinross/Stirling, 48,400 ha/119,596 acres
LOCH SHIEL, Highland, 13,400 ha/33,111 acres
LOCH TUMMEL, Perth and Kinross, 9,200 ha/22,733
acres
LYNN OF LORN, Argyll and Bute, 4,800 ha/11,861 acres
MORAR, MOIDART AND ARDNAMURCHAN, Highland,
13,500 ha/33,358 acres

NORTH-WEST SUTHERLAND, Highland, 20,500 ha/ 50,655 acres
NITH ESTUARY, Dumfries and Galloway, 9,300 ha/ 22,980 acres
NORTH ARRAN, North Ayrshire, 23,800 ha/58,810 acres
RIVER EARN, Perth and Kinross, 3,000 ha/7,413 acres
RIVER TAY, Perth and Kinross, 5,600 ha/13,838 acres
ST KILDA, Western Isles, 900 ha/2,224 acres
SCARBA, LUNGA AND THE GARVELLACHS, Argyll and Bute, 1,900 ha/4,695 acres
SHETLAND, Shetland Islands, 11,600 ha/28,664 acres
SMALL ISLES, Highland, 15,500 ha/38,300 acres
SOUTH LEWIS, HARRIS AND NORTH UIST, Western Isles, 109,600 ha/270,822 acres
SOUTH UIST MACHAIR, Western Isles, 6,100 ha/15,073 acres
THE TROSSACHS, Stirling, 4,600 ha/11,367 acres
TROTTERNISH, Highland, 5,000 ha/12,355 acres
UPPER TWEEDDALE, Scottish Borders, 10,500 ha/25,945 acres
WESTER ROSS Highland, 145,300 ha/359,036 acres

THE NATIONAL FOREST

The National Forest is being planted across 200 square miles of Derbyshire, Leicestershire and Staffordshire. About 30 million trees, of mixed species but mainly broadleaved, will be planted, and will eventually cover about one-third of the designated area. The project is funded by the Department for Environment, Food and Rural Affairs. It was developed in 1992–5 by the Countryside Commission and is now run by the National Forest Company, which was established in April 1995. Since then almost 5 million trees have been planted on 2,500 hectares of land across 480 sites. Under the National Forest Tender Scheme, anybody wishing to undertake a project can submit a competitive bid to the National Forest Company.

NATIONAL FOREST COMPANY, Enterprise Glade, Bath Lane, Moira, Swadlincote, Derbys DE12 6BD. Tel: 01283-551211. *Chief Executive*, Miss S. Bell, OBE

Nature Conservation Areas

SITES OF SPECIAL SCIENTIFIC INTEREST

Site of Special Scientific Interest (SSSI) is a legal notification applied to land in England, Scotland or Wales which English Nature (EN), Scottish Natural Heritage (SNH), or the Countryside Council for Wales (CCW) identifies as being of special interest because of its flora, fauna, geological or physiographical features. In some cases, SSSIs are managed as nature reserves.

EN, SNH and CCW must notify the designation of a SSSI to the local planning authority, every owner/occupier of the land, and the Secretary of State for Environment, Food and Rural Affairs, the First Minister in Scotland or the National Assembly for Wales. Forestry and agricultural departments and a number of other bodies are also informed of this notification.

Objections to the notification of a SSSI can be made and ultimately considered at a full meeting of the Council of EN or CCW. In Scotland an objection will be dealt with by the appropriate area board or the main board of SNH, depending on the nature of the objection. Unresolved

objections on scientific grounds must be referred to the Advisory Committee on SSSI.

The protection of these sites depends on the co-operation of individual landowners and occupiers. Owner/occupiers must consult EN, SNH or CCW and gain written consent before they can undertake certain listed activities on the site. Funds are available through management agreements and grants to assist owners and occupiers in conserving sites' interests. As a last resort a site can be purchased.

The number and area of SSSIs in Britain as at July 2002 was:

	no.	Hectares	Acres
England	4,105	1,050,876	2,596,714
Scotland	1,447	1,007,253	2,488,922
Wales	1,026	228,124	563,694

NORTHERN IRELAND

In Northern Ireland 196 Areas of Special Scientific Interest (ASSIs) have been declared by the Department of the Environment for Northern Ireland. These cover a total area of 91,600.87 hectares (226,348.23 acres).

NATIONAL NATURE RESERVES

National Nature Reserves are defined in the National Parks and Access to the Countryside Act 1949 as land designated for the study and preservation of flora and fauna, or of geological or physiographical features.

English Nature (EN), Scottish Natural Heritage (SNH) or the Countryside Council for Wales (CCW) can designate as a National Nature Reserve land which is being managed as a nature reserve under an agreement with one of the statutory nature conservation agencies; land held and managed by EN, SNH or CCW; or land held and managed as a nature reserve by another approved body. EN, SNH or CCW can make by-laws to protect reserves from undesirable activities; these are subject to confirmation by the Secretary of State for Environment, Food and Rural Affairs, the National Assembly for Wales or the Scottish Ministers in Scotland.

The number and area of National Nature Reserves in Britain as at April 2002 was:

	no.	Hectares	Acres
England	210	86,096	212,657
Scotland	73	130,904	323,459
Wales	65	18,790	46,395

NORTHERN IRELAND

National Nature Reserves are established and managed by the Department of the Environment for Northern Ireland, with advice from the Council for Nature Conservation and the Countryside. There are 48 National Nature Reserves covering 4,746.3 hectares (11,723 acres).

LOCAL NATURE RESERVES

Local Nature Reserves are defined in the National Parks and Access to the Countryside Act 1949 as land designated for the study and preservation of flora and fauna, or of geological or physiographical features. The Act gives local authorities in England, Scotland and Wales the power to acquire, declare and manage local nature reserves in consultation with English Nature, Scottish Natural Heritage and the Countryside Council for Wales. Conservation trusts can also own and manage non-statutory local nature reserves.

The number and area of designated Local Nature Reserves in Britain as at May 2002 was:

	no.	Hectares	Acres
England	720	31,392	77,569
Scotland	34	9,382	23,183
Wales	53	4,706	11,620

FOREST NATURE RESERVES

Forest Enterprise (an executive agency of the Forestry Commission) is responsible for the management of the Commission's forests. It has created 46 Forest Nature Reserves with the aim of protecting and conserving special forms of natural habitat, flora and fauna. There are about 300 SSSIs on the estates, some of which are also Nature Reserves.

Forest Nature Reserves extend in size from under 50 hectares (124 acres) to over 500 hectares (1,236 acres). The largest include the Black Wood of Rannoch, by Loch Rannoch; Cannop Valley Oakwoods, Forest of Dean; Culbin Forest, near Forres; Glen Affric, near Fort Augustus; Kylerhea, Skye; Pembrey, Carmarthen Bay; Starr Forest, in Galloway Forest Park; and Wyre Forest, near Kidderminster.

Forest Enterprise also manages 18 Caledonian Forest Reserves in Scotland. These reserves are intended to protect and expand 16,000 hectares of native oak and pine woods in the Scottish highlands.

NORTHERN IRELAND

There are 35 Forest Nature Reserves in Northern Ireland, covering 1,637 hectares (4,043 acres). They are designated and administered by the Forest Service, an agency of the Department of Agriculture and Rural Development for Northern Ireland. There are also 16 National Nature Reserves on Forest Service-owned property.

MARINE NATURE RESERVES

The Secretary of State for Environment, Food and Rural Affairs, the National Assembly for Wales and the Scottish Executive have the power to designate Marine Nature Reserves. English Nature, Scottish Natural Heritage and the Countryside Council for Wales select and manage these reserves. Marine Nature Reserves may be established in Northern Ireland under a 1985 Order.

Marine Nature Reserves provide protection for marine flora and fauna, and geological and physiographical features on land covered by tidal waters or parts of the sea in or adjacent to the UK. Reserves also provide opportunities for study and research.

The three statutory Marine Nature Reserves are:

LUNDY (1986), Bristol Channel
SKOMER (1990), Dyfed
STRANGFORD LOUGH (1995), Northern Ireland

Two other areas proposed for designation as reserves are: the Menai Strait, and Bardsey Island and part of the Llyn peninsula, both in Wales.

A number of non-statutory marine reserves have been set up by conservation groups.

EUROPEAN MARINE SITES

The 1992 EC Habitats Directive and the 1979 Birds Directive allow the UK government to establish Special Areas of Conservation (SACs) or Special Protection Areas (SPAs) for animals and birds on land and at sea. Where the designated area includes sea or seashore it is described as a European marine site. The 1998–2002 UK Marine SACs project formed a demonstration initiative, funded partly by the EU, to establish management schemes for twelve of the marine SACs in the UK.

World Heritage Sites

The Convention Concerning the Protection of the World Cultural and Natural Heritage was adopted by UNESCO in 1972 and ratified by the UK in 1984. As at 14 June 2002 the convention had been ratified by 172 states. The convention provides for the identification, protection and conservation of cultural and natural sites of outstanding universal value.

Cultural sites may be:
– monuments
– groups of buildings
– sites of historic, aesthetic, archaeological, scientific, ethnologic or anthropologic value
– historic areas of towns
– 'cultural landscapes', i.e. sites whose characteristics are marked by significant interactions between human populations and their natural environment

Natural sites may be:
– those with remarkable physical, biological or geological formations
– those with outstanding universal value from the point of view of science, conservation or natural beauty
– the habitat of threatened species and plants

Governments which are party to the convention nominate sites in their country for inclusion in the World Cultural and Natural Heritage List. Nominations are considered by the World Heritage Committee, an inter-governmental committee composed of 21 representatives of the parties to the convention. The committee is advised by the International Council on Monuments and Sites (ICOMOS), the International Centre for the Study of the Preservation and Restoration of Cultural Property (ICCROM) and the World Conservation Union (IUCN). ICOMOS evaluates and reports on proposed cultural sites, ICCROM provides expert advice and training on how to conserve the listed sites and IUCN advises on proposed natural sites. The Department for Culture, Media and Sport represents the UK government in matters relating to the convention.

A prerequisite for inclusion in the World Cultural and Natural Heritage List is the existence of an effective legal protection system in the country in which the site is situated (e.g. listing, conservation areas and planning controls in the United Kingdom) and a detailed management plan to ensure the conservation of the site. Inclusion in the list does not confer any greater degree of protection on the site than that offered by the national protection framework.

If a site is considered to be in serious danger of decay or damage the committee may add it to a complementary list, the World Heritage in Danger List. Sites on this list may benefit from particular attention or emergency measures.

Financial support for the conservation of sites on the World Cultural and Natural Heritage List is provided by the World Heritage Fund. This is administered by the World Heritage Committee, which determines the financial and technical aid to be allocated. The fund's income is derived from contributions of the parties to the convention, voluntary contributions from other States, other United Nations and intergovernmental organisations, public or private bodies and individuals, through interest due on the fund and from events organised for the benefit of the fund.

DESIGNATED SITES

As at June 2002 there were 730 sites in 125 countries on the World Cultural and Natural Heritage List. Of these, 21 are in the United Kingdom and three in British overseas territories; 18 are listed for their cultural significance (†) and six for their natural significance (*). The year in which sites were designated appears in parentheses.

United Kingdom
†Bath – the city (1987)
†Blaenavon, Wales (2000)
†Blenheim Palace and park, Oxfordshire (1987)
†Canterbury Cathedral, St Augustine's Abbey, St Martin's Church, Kent (1988)
†Castle and town walls of King Edward I, north Wales – Beaumaris, Anglesey, Caernarfon Castle, Conwy Castle, Harlech Castle (1986)
†Derwent Valley Mills, Derbyshire (2001)
*Dorset and East Devon Coast (2001)
†Durham Cathedral and Castle (1986)
†Edinburgh Old and New Towns (1995)
*Giant's Causeway and Causeway coast, Co. Antrim (1986)
†Greenwich, London – maritime Greenwich, including the Royal Naval College, Old Royal Observatory, Queen's House, town centre (1997)
†Hadrian's Wall, northern England (1987)
†Heart of Neolithic Orkney (1999)
†Ironbridge Gorge, Shropshire – the world's first iron bridge and other early industrial sites (1986)
†New Lanark, South Lanarkshire, Scotland (2001)
*St Kilda, Western Isles (1986)
†Saltaire, West Yorkshire (2001)
†Stonehenge, Avebury and related megalithic sites, Wiltshire (1986)
†Studley Royal Park, Fountains Abbey, St Mary's Church, N. Yorkshire (1986)
†Tower of London (1988)
†Westminster Abbey, Palace of Westminster, St Margaret's Church, London (1987)

British Overseas Territories
*Henderson Island, Pitcairn Islands, South Pacific Ocean (1988)
*Gough Island wildlife reserve (part of Tristan da Cunha), South Atlantic Ocean (1995)
*St George town and related fortifications, Bermuda (2000)

ARCHITECTURE AND HISTORIC ENVIRONMENT DIVISION, Department for Culture, Media and Sport, 2–4 Cockspur Street, London SW1Y 5DH. Tel: 020-7211 6000; Email: enquiries@culture.gov.uk

WORLD HERITAGE CENTRE, UNESCO, 7 place de Fontenoy, 75352 Paris, France. Tel: (00 33) (1) 4568 1876; Email: wh-info@unesco.org; Web: www.unesco.org

INTERNATIONAL CENTRE FOR THE STUDY OF THE PRESERVATION AND RESTORATION OF CULTURAL PROPERTY (ICCROM), Via di San Michele 13, I-00153 Rome, Italy. Tel: (00 39) (06) 585 531; Email: iccrom@iccrom.org; Web: www.iccrom.org

INTERNATIONAL COUNCIL ON MONUMENTS AND SITES (ICOMOS), 10 Barley Mow Passage, London W4 4PH. Tel. 020-8994 6477. Email: icomos-uk@iconos.org; Web: www.icomos.org

THE WORLD CONSERVATION UNION (IUCN), rue Mauverney 28, CH-1196 Gland, Switzerland. Tel: (00 41) (22) 999 0001; Email: mail@hq.iucn.org; Web: www.iucn.org

Conservation of wildlife and habitats

The UK is party to a number of international conventions.

RAMSAR CONVENTION

The 1971 Ramsar Convention on Wetlands of International Importance especially as Waterfowl Habitat, entered into force in the UK in May 1976. By July 2002, 133 countries were party to the convention.

The aim of the convention is the conservation and wise use of wetlands and their flora and fauna. Governments that are party to the convention must designate wetlands and include wetland conservation considerations in their land-use planning. A total of 1,179 wetland sites, totalling 102.3 million hectares have been designated for inclusion in the List of Wetlands of International Importance. The UK currently has 169 designated sites covering 854,389 hectares. The member countries meet every three years to assess the progress of the convention and the latest meeting was scheduled for November 2002.

The UK has set targets under the Ramsar Strategic Plan, 1997–2002. Progress towards these is monitored by the UK Ramsar Committee, known as the Joint Working Party. The UK and the Republic of Ireland have established a formal protocol to ensure common monitoring standards for waterbirds in the two countries. Ramsar Convention Bureau, Rue Mauverney 28, CH-1196 Gland, Switzerland. Tel: (00 41) (22) 999 0170; Web: www.ramsar.org

BIODIVERSITY

There is much synergy between the Ramsar Convention and the 1992 Convention on Biological Diversity. In 1996 the Ramsar Secretariat became a lead partner in implementing activities under the Convention on Biological Diversity with joint work plans. The UK ratified the Convention on Biological Diversity in June 1994. There are currently 183 parties to the convention.

The objectives are the conservation of biological diversity, the sustainable use of its components and the fair and equitable sharing of the benefits arising out of the use of genetic resources. There are thematic work programmes addressing marine and coastal, forest, inland waters, dry land and semi-humid land.

The UK published its own Biodiversity Action Plan in 1994. A report from the UK Biodiversity Steering Group, published in 1995, proposed monitoring a list of 1,252 species to check on biodiversity within the UK. It also produced action plans for 116 species and 14 habitats as well as making recommendations to produce further action plans, improve the quality and accessibility of data, provide initial guidance for local biodiversity action plans and over 80 proposals to increase public awareness and education in biodiversity.

A report, *Sustaining the Variety of Life: 5 years of the UK Biodiversity Action Plan*, was published in March 2001, and made a number of recommendations including to support actions for conservation of species and habitats at UK, county and local levels. There are now over 160 local biodiversity action plans at various stages of development in the UK. The England Biodiversity Group with DEFRA and the Biodiversity Policy Unit have recently prepared a Biodiversity Strategy for England. BIODIVERSITY POLICY UNIT, Zone 1/10b, Temple Quay House, 2 The Square, Temple Quay, Bristol BS1 6EB. Tel: 0117-372 6276.
Email: biodiversity.defra@gtnet.gov.uk;
Web: www.ukbap.org.uk

CITES

The 1973 Convention on International Trade in Endangered Species of Wild Fauna and Flora (CITES) came into force in the UK in July 1975. Currently 158 countries are members. The countries party to the convention ban commercial international trade in an agreed list of endangered species and regulate and monitor trade in others species that might become endangered. The convention covers around 30,000 species.

The Conference of the Parties to CITES meets every two to three years to review the convention's implementation.

The Global Wildlife Division at the Department for Environment, Food and Rural Affairs carries out the government's responsibilities under CITES and the Bonn Convention on the Conservation of Migratory Species of Wild Animals.

CITES SECRETARIAT, International Environment House, Chemin des Anémones, CH-1219 Châtelaine, Geneva, Switzerland. Tel: (00 41) (22) 917 8139/8140. Email: cites@unep.ch; Web: www.cites.org/eng

BONN CONVENTION

The 1979 Convention on Conservation of Migratory Species of Wild Animals came into force in the UK in October 1979. By February 2002, 79 parties were party to the convention.

It requires the protection of listed endangered migratory species and encourages international agreements covering these and other threatened species. International agreements can range from legally binding treaties to less formal memoranda of understanding.

Nine agreements have been concluded to date under the convention. They aim to conserve: bats in Europe; cetaceans of the Mediterranean and Black Seas; small cetaceans of the Baltic and North Seas; seals in the Wadden Sea; African-Eurasian migratory waterbirds; Siberian Crane; the Slender-billed Curlew; marine turtles; and middle-European great bustards.

Further agreements are being developed for a wide range of migratory species, including albatrosses of the southern hemisphere, plus Bukhara deer and Saiga antelope. UNEP/CMS Secretariat, Martin-Luther-King-Str. 8, D-53175, Bonn, Germany. Tel: (00 49) (228) 815 2401/2; Email: cms@unep.deweb: www.wcmc.org.uk/cms

BERN CONVENTION

The 1979 Bern Convention on the Conservation of European Wildlife and Natural Habitats came into force in the UK in June 1982. Currently there are 45 Contracting Parties and a number of other states attend meetings as observers.

The aims are to conserve wild flora and fauna and their natural habitats, especially where this requires the co-operation of several countries, and to promote such co-operation. The convention gives particular emphasis to endangered and vulnerable species.

All parties to the convention must promote national conservation policies and take account of the conservation of wild flora and fauna when setting planning and development policies.

SECRETARIAT OF THE BERN CONVENTION STANDING COMMITTEE, Council of Europe, 67075 Strasbourg-Cedex, France. Tel: (00 33) (3) 8841 3192. Web: www.nature.coe.int

EUROPEAN WILDLIFE TRADE REGULATION

The Council (EC) Regulation on the Protection of Species of Wild Fauna and Flora by Regulating Trade Therein came into force in the UK on 1 June 1997. It is intended to standardise wildlife trade regulations across Europe and to improve the application of CITES. Approximately 30,000 plant and animal species are protected under the regulation.

UK LEGISLATION

The Wildlife and Countryside Act 1981 gives legal protection to a wide range of wild animals and plants. Subject to parliamentary approval, the Secretary of State for the Environment, Food and Rural Affairs may vary the animals and plants given legal protection. The most recent variation of Schedules 5 and 8 came into effect in March and April 1998.

Under Section 9 of the Act it is an offence to kill, injure, take, possess or sell (whether alive or dead) any wild animal included in schedule 5 of the Act and to disturb its place of shelter and protection or to destroy that place.

Under Section 13 of the Act it is illegal without a licence to pick, uproot, sell or destroy any of the plants listed in schedule 8. Since January 2001, under the Countryside and Rights of way Act 2000, persons found guilty of an offence under Part 1 of the Wildlife and Countryside Act 1981 face a maximum penalty of up to £5,000 and/or up to six months custodial sentence per specimen.

The Act lays down a close season for wild birds (other than game birds) from 1 February to 31 August inclusive, each year. Exceptions to these dates are made for:

Capercaillie and (except Scotland) *Woodcock* – 1 February to 30 September
Snipe – 1 February to 11 August
Wild Duck and Wild Goose (below high water mark) – 21 February to 31 August

Birds which may be killed or taken outside the close season (except on Sundays and on Christmas Day in Scotland, and on Sundays in prescribed areas of England and Wales) are the above-named, plus coot, certain wild duck (gadwall, goldeneye, mallard, pintail, pochard, shoveler, teal, tufted duck, wigeon), certain wild geese (Canada, greylag, pink-footed, white-fronted (in England and Wales only)), moorhen, golden plover and woodcock.

Certain wild birds may be killed or taken subject to the conditions of a general licence at any time by authorised persons: crow, collared dove, gull (great and lesser black-backed or herring), jackdaw, jay, magpie, pigeon (feral or wood), rook, sparrow (house), and starling. Conditions usually apply where the birds pose a threat to agriculture, public health, air safety, other bird species and to prevent the spread of disease.

All other British birds are fully protected by law throughout the year.

Animals protected by Schedule 5

Adder (*Vipera berus*)
Allis shad (*Alosa alosa)*
Atlantic Stream Crayfish (Austropotomobias pallipes)
Anemone, Ivell's Sea (*Edwardsia ivelli)*
Anemone, Starlet Sea (*Nematosella vectensis*)
Apus, Tadpole shrimp (*Triops cancriformis*)
Bat, Horseshoe (*Rhinolophidae*, all species)
Bat, Typical (*Vespertilionidae*, all species)
Beetle (*Graphoderus zonatus*)
Beetle (*Hypebaeus flavipes*)
Beetle, Lesser Silver Water (*Hydrochara caraboides*)

Beetle, Mire Pill (*Curimopsis nigrita*)
Beetle, Rainbow Leaf (*Chrysolina cerealis*)
Beetle, Stag (*Lucanus cervus*)
Beetle, Violet Click (*Limoniscus violaceus*)
Beetle, Water (*Graphoderus zonatus*)
Burbot (*Lota lota*)
Butterfly, Adonis Blue (*Lysandra bellargus*)
Butterfly, Black Hairstreak (*Strymonidia pruni*)
Butterfly, Brown Hairstreak (*Thecla betulae*)
Butterfly, Chalkhill Blue (*Lysandra coridon*)
Butterfly, Chequered Skipper (*Carterocephalus palaemon*)
Butterfly, Duke of Burgundy Fritillary (*Hamearis lucina*)
Butterfly, Glanville Fritillary (*Melitaea cinxia*)
Butterfly, Heath Fritillary (*Mellicta athalia (or Melitaea athalia)*)
Butterfly, High Brown Fritillary (*Argynnis adippe*)
Butterfly, Large Blue (*Maculinea arion*)
Butterfly, Large Copper (*Lycaena dispar*)
Butterfly, Large Heath (*Coenonympha tullia*)
Butterfly, Large Tortoiseshell (*Nymphalis polychloros*)
Butterfly, Lulworth Skipper (*Thymelicus acteon*)
Butterfly, Marsh Fritillary (*Eurodryas aurinia*)
Butterfly, Mountain Ringlet (*Erebia epiphron*)
Butterfly, Northern Brown Argus (*Aricia artaxerxes*)
Butterfly, Pearl-bordered Fritillary (*Boloria euphrosyne*)
Butterfly, Purple Emperor (*Apatura iris*)
Butterfly, Silver Spotted Skipper (*Hesperia comma*)
Butterfly, Silver-studded Blue (*Plebejus argus*)
Butterfly, Small Blue (*Cupido minimus*)
Butterfly, Swallowtail (*Papilio machaon*)
Butterfly, White Letter Hairstreak (*Stymonida w-album*)
Butterfly, Wood White (*Leptidea sinapis*)
Cat, Wild (*Felis silvestris*)
Cicada, New Forest (*Cicadetta montana*)
Crayfish, Atlantic stream (*Austropotamobius pallipes*)
Cricket, Field (*Gryllus campestris*)
Cricket, Mole (*Gryllotalpa gryllotalpa*)
Damselfly, Southern (*Coenagrion mercuriale*)
Dolphin (*Cetacea*)
Dormouse (*Muscardinus avellanarius*)
Dragonfly, Norfolk Aeshna (*Aeshna isosceles*)
Frog, Common (*Rana temporaria*)
Goby, Couch's (*Gobius couchii*)
Goby, Giant (*Gobius cobitis*)
Grasshopper, Wart-biter (*Decticus verrucivorus*)
Hatchet Shell, Northern (*Thyasira gouldi*)
Hydroid, Marine (*Clavopsella navis*)
Lagoon Snail (*Paludinella littorina*)
Lagoon Snail, De Folin's (*Caecum armoricum*)
Lagoon Worm, Tentacled (*Alkmaria romijni*)
Leech, Medicinal (*Hirudo medicinalis*)
Lizard, Sand (*Lacerta agilis*)
Lizard, Viviparous (*Lacerta vivipara*)
Marten, Pine (*Martes martes*)
Moth, Barberry Carpet (*Pareulype berberata*)
Moth, Black-veined (*Siona lineata (or Idaea lineata)*)
Moth, Essex Emerald (*Thetidia smaragdaria*)
Moth, Fiery clearwing (*Bembecia chrysidiformis*)
Moth, Fisher's estuarine (*Gortyna borelii*)
Moth, New Forest Burnet (*Zygaena viciae*)
Moth, Reddish Buff (*Acosmetia caliginosa*)
Moth, Sussex Emerald (*Thalera fimbrialis*)
Mussel, Fan (*Atrina fragilis*)
Mussel, Freshwater Pearl (*Margaritifera margaritifera*)
Newt, Great Crested (or Warty) (*Triturus cristatus*)
Newt, Palmate (*Triturus helveticus*)
Newt, Smooth (*Triturus vulgaris*)
Otter, Common (*Lutra lutra*)
Porpoise (*Cetacea*)

Sandworm, Lagoon (*Armandia cirrhosa*)
Sea Fan, Pink (*Eunicella verrucosa*)
Sea Slug, Lagoon (*Tenellia adspersa*)
Shad, Twaite (*alosa fallax*)
Shark, Basking (*Cetorhinus maximus*)
Shrimp, Fairy (*Chirocephalus diaphanus*)
Shrimp, Lagoon Sand (*Gammarus insensibilis*)
Slow-worm (*Anguis fragilis*)
Snail, Glutinous (*Myxas glutinosa*)
Snail, Sandbowl (*Catinella arenaria*)
Snake, Grass (*Natrix natrix* (*Natrix helvetica*))
Snake, Smooth (*Coronella austriaca*)
Spider, Fen Raft (*Dolomedes plantarius*)
Spider, Ladybird (*Eresus niger*)
Squirrel, Red (*Sciurus vulgaris*)
Sturgeon (*Acipenser sturio*)
Toad, Common (*Bufo bufo*)
Toad, Natterjack (*Bufo calamita*)
Turtle, Marine (*Dermochelyidae and Cheloniidae,* all species)
Vendace (*Coregonus albula*)
Vole, Water (*Arvicola terrestris*)
Walrus (*Odobenus rosmarus*)
Whale (*Cetacea*)
Whitefish (*Coregonus lavaretus*)

Plants protected by Schedule 8

Adder's tongue, Least (*Ophioglossum lusitanicum*)
Alison, Small (*Alyssum alyssoides*)
Anomodon, Long leaved (*Anomodon longifolius)*
Beech-lichen, New Forest (*Enterographa elaborata)*
Blackwort (*Southbya nigrella)*
Bluebell (*Hyacinthoides non-scripta*)
Bolete, Royal (*Boletus regius*)
Broomrape, Bedstraw (*Orobanche caryophyllacea*)
Broomrape, Oxtongue (*Orobanche loricata*)
Broomrape, Thistle (*Orobanche reticulata*)
Cabbage, Lundy (*Rhynchosinapis wrightii*)
Calamint, Wood (*Calamintha sylvatica*)
Caloplaca, Snow (*Caloplaca nivalis*)
Catapyrenium, Tree (*Catapyrenium psoromoides*)
Catchfly, Alpine (*Lychnis alpina*)
Catillaria, Laurer's (*Catellaria laureri*)
Centaury, Slender (*Centaurium tenuiflorum*)
Cinquefoil, Rock (*Potentilla rupestris*)
Cladonia, Convoluted (*Cladonia convoluta*)
Cladonia, Upright Mountain (*Cladonia stricta*)
Clary, Meadow (*Salvia pratensis*)
Club-rush, Triangular (*Scirpus triquetrus*)
Colt's-foot, Purple (*Homogyne alpina*)
Cotoneaster, Wild (*Cotoneaster integerrimus*)
Cottongrass, Slender (*Eriophorum gracile*)
Cow-wheat, Field (*Melampyrum arvense*)
Crocus, Sand (*Romulea columnae*)
Crystalwort, Lizard (*Riccia bifurca*)
Cudweed, Broad-leaved (*Filago pyramidata*)
Cudweed, Jersey (*Gnaphalium luteoalbum*)
Cudweed, Red-tipped (*Filago lutescens*)
Cut-grass (*Leersia oryzoides*)
Deptford Pink (England and Wales only) (*Dianthus armeria*)
Diapensia (*Diapensia lapponica*)
Dock, Shore (*Rumex rupestris*)
Earwort, Marsh (*Jamesoniella undulifolia*)
Eryngo, Field (*Eryngium campestre*)
Fern, Dickie's bladder (*Cystopteris dickieana*)
Fern, Killarney (*Trichomanes speciosum*)
Flapwort, Norfolk (*Leiocolea rutheana*)
Fleabane, Alpine (*Erigeron borealis*)
Fleabane, Small (*Pulicaria vulgaris*)

Fleawort, South stack (*Tephroseris integrifolia* (*ssp maritima*))
Frostwort, Pointed (*Gymnomitrion apiculatum*)
Fungus, Hedgehog (*Hericium erinaceum*)
Galingale, Brown (*Cyperus fuscus*)
Gentian, Alpine (*Gentiana nivalis*)
Gentian, Dune (*Gentianella uliginosa*)
Gentian, Early (*Gentianella anglica*)
Gentian, Fringed (*Gentianella ciliata*)
Gentian, Spring (*Gentiana verna*)
Germander, Cut-leaved (*Teucrium botrys*)
Germander, Water (*Teucrium scordium*)
Gladiolus, Wild (*Gladiolus illyricus*)
Goosefoot, Stinking (*Chenopodium vulvaria*)
Grass-poly (*Lythrum hyssopifolia*)
Grimmia, Blunt-leaved (*Grimmia unicolor*)
Gyalecta, Elm (*Gyalecta ulmi*)
Hare's-ear, Sickle-leaved (*Bupleurum falcatum*)
Hare's-ear, Small (*Bupleurum baldense*)
Hawk's-beard, Stinking (*Crepis foetida*)
Hawkweed, Northroe (*Hieracium northroense*)
Hawkweed, Shetland (*Hieracium zetlandicum*)
Hawkweed, Weak-leaved (*Hieracium attenuatifolium*)
Heath, Blue (*Phyllodoce caerulea*)
Helleborine, Red (*Cephalanthera rubra*)
Helleborine, Young's (*Epipactis youngiana*)
Horsetail, Branched (*Equisetum ramosissimum*)
Hound's-tongue, Green (*Cynoglossum germanicum*)
Knawel, Perennial (*Scleranthus perennis*)
Knotgrass, Sea (*Polygonum maritimum*)
Lady's-slipper (*Cypripedium calceolus*)
Lecanactis, Churchyard (*Lecanactis hemisphaerica*)
Lecanora, Tarn (*Lecanora archariana*)
Lecidea, Copper (*Lecidea inops*)
Leek, Round-headed (*Allium sphaerocephalon*)
Lettuce, Least (*Lactuca saligna*)
Lichen, Arctic kidney (*Nephroma arcticum*)
Lichen, Ciliate strap (*Heterodermia leucomelos*)
Lichen, Coralloid rosette (*Heterodermia propagulifera*)
Lichen, Ear-lobed dog (*Peltigera lepidophora*)
Lichen, Forked hair (*Bryoria furcellata*)
Lichen, Golden hair (*Teloschistes flavicans*)
Lichen, Orange fruited Elm (*Caloplaca luteoalba*)
Lichen, River jelly (*Collema dichotomum*)
Lichen, Scaly breck (*Squamarina lentigera*)
Lichen, Stary breck (*Buellia asterella*)
Lily, Snowdon (*Lloydia serotina*)
Liverwort, Leafy (*Petallophyllum ralfsi*)
Liverwort, Lindenberg's (*Adelanthus lindenbergianus*)
Marsh-mallow, Rough (*Althaea hirsuta*)
Marshwort, Creeping (*Apium repens*)
Milk-parsley, Cambridge (*Selinum carvifolia*)
Moss (*Drepanocladius vernicosus*)
Moss, Alpine copper (*Mielichoferia mielichoferi*)
Moss, Baltic bog (*Sphagnum balticum*)
Moss, Blue dew (*Saelania glaucescens*)
Moss, Blunt-leaved bristle (*Orthotrichum obtusifolium*)
Moss, Bright green cave (*Cyclodictyon laetevirens*)
Moss, Cordate beard (*Barbula cordata*)
Moss, Cornish path (*Ditrichum cornubicum*)
Moss, Derbyshire feather (*Thamnobryum angustifolium*)
Moss, Dune thread (*Bryum mamillatum*)
Moss, Flamingo (*Desmatodon cernuus*)
Moss, Glaucous beard (*Barbula glauca*)
Moss, Green shield (*Buxbaumia viridis*)
Moss, Hair silk (*Plagiothecium piliferum*)
Moss, Knothole (*Zygodon forsteri*)
Moss, Large yellow feather (*Scorpidium turgescens*)
Moss, Millimetre (*Micromitrium tenerum*)
Moss, Multifruited river (*Cryphaea lamyana*)

Moss, Nowell's limestone (*Zygodon gracilis*)
Moss, Rigid apple (*Bartramia stricta*)
Moss, Round-leaved feather (*Rhyncostegium rotundifolium*)
Moss, Schleicher's thread (*Bryum schleicheri*)
Moss, Triangular pygmy (*Acaulon triquetrum*)
Moss, Vaucher's feather (*Hypnum vaucheri*)
Mudwort, Welsh (*Limosella australis*)
Naiad, Holly-leaved (*Najas marina*)
Naiad, Slender (*Najas flexilis*)
Orache, Stalked (*Halimione pedunculata*)
Orchid, Early spider (*Ophrys sphegodes*)
Orchid, Fen (*Liparis loeselii*)
Orchid, Ghost (*Epipogium aphyllum*)
Orchid, Lapland marsh (*Dactylorhiza lapponica*)
Orchid, Late spider (*Ophrys fuciflora*)
Orchid, Lizard (*Himantoglossum hircinum*)
Orchid, Military (*Orchis militaris*)
Orchid, Monkey (*Orchis simia*)
Panneria, Caledonia (*Panneria ignobilis*)
Parmelia, New Forest (*Parmelia minarum*)
Parmentaria, Oil stain (*Parmentaria chilensis*)
Pear, Plymouth (*Pyrus cordata*)
Penny-cress, Perfoliate (*Thlaspi perfoliatum*)
Pennyroyal (*Mentha pulegium*)
Pertusaria, Alpine moss (*Pertusaria bryontha*)
Physcia, Southern grey (*Physcia tribacioides*)
Pigmyweed (*Crassula aquatica*)
Pine, Ground (*Ajuga chamaepitys*)
Pink, Cheddar (*Dianthus gratianopolitanus*)
Pink, Childing (*Petroraghia nanteuilii*)
Pink, Deptford (*Dianthus armeria*) (England and Wales only)
Plantain, Floating water (*Luronium natans*)
Polypore, Oak (*Buglossoporus pulrinus*)
Pseudocyphellaria, Ragged (*Pseudocyphellaria lacerata*)
Psora, Rusty Alpine (*Psora rubiformis*)
Puffball, Sandy Stilt (*Battarraea phalloides*)
Ragwort, Fen (*Senecio paludosus*)
Ramping-fumitory, Martin's (*Fumaria martinii*)
Rampion, Spiked (*Phyteuma spicatum*)
Restharrow, Small (*Ononis reclinata*)
Rock-cress, Alpine (*Arabis alpina*)
Rock-cress, Bristol (*Arabis stricta*)

Rustwort, Western (*Marsupella profunda*)
Sandwort, Norwegian (*Arenaria norvegica*)
Sandwort, Teesdale (*Minuartia stricta*)
Saxifrage, Drooping (*Saxifraga cernua*)
Saxifrage, Marsh (*Saxifrage hirulus*)
Saxifrage, Tufted (*Saxifraga cespitosa*)
Solenopsora, Serpentine (*Solenopsora liparina*)
Solomon's-seal, Whorled (*Polygonatum verticillatum*)
Sow-thistle, Alpine (*Cicerbita alpina*)
Spearwort, Adder's-tongue (*Ranunculus ophioglossifolius*)
Speedwell, Fingered (*Veronica triphyllos*)
Speedwell, Spiked (*Veronica spicata*)
Spike rush, Dwarf (*Eleocharis parvula*)
Stack Fleawort, South (*Tephroseris integrifolia* (ssp *maritima*))
Star-of-Bethlehem, Early (*Gagea bohemica*)
Starfruit (*Damasonium alisma*)
Stonewort, Bearded (*Chara canescens*)
Stonewort, Foxtail (*Lamprothamnium papulosum*)
Strapwort (*Corrigiola litoralis*)
Sulphur-tresses, Alpine (*Alectoria ochroleuca*)
Threadmois, Long-leaved (*Bryum neoclamense*)
Turpswort (*Geocalyx graveolens*)
Violet, Fen (*Viola persicifolia*)
Viper's-grass (*Scorzonera humilis*)
Water-plantain, Ribbon-leaved (*Alisma gramineum*)
Wood-sedge, Starved (*Carex depauperata*)
Woodsia, Alpine (*Woodsia alpina*)
Woodsia, Oblong (*Woodsia ilvenis*)
Wormwood, Field (*Artemisia campestris*)
Woundwort, Downy (*Stachys germanica*)
Woundwort, Limestone (*Stachys alpina*)
Yellow-rattle, Greater (*Rhinanthus serotinus*)

MOST UNDER THREAT

The animals and birds considered to be most under threat in Great Britain by the Joint Nature Conservation Committee are the high brown fritillary butterfly; violet click beetle; new forest burnet moth; corncrake; aquatic warbler; tree sparrow; wryneck; water vole; red squirrel; allis shad; and twaite shad.

Historic Buildings and Monuments

LISTING

Under the Planning (Listed Buildings and Conservation Areas) Act 1990, the Secretary of State for Culture, Media and Sport has a statutory duty to compile lists of buildings or groups of buildings in England which are of special architectural or historic interest. Under the Ancient Monuments and Archaeological Areas Act 1979 as amended by the National Heritage Act 1983, the Secretary of State is also responsible for compiling a schedule of ancient monuments. Decisions are taken on the advice of English Heritage.

Listed buildings are classified into Grade I, Grade II* and Grade II. There are currently about 370,000 individual listed buildings in England, of which about 92 per cent are Grade II listed. Almost all pre-1700 buildings are listed, and most buildings of 1700 to 1840. English Heritage carries out thematic surveys of particular types of buildings with a view to making recommendations for listing, and members of the public may propose a building for consideration. The main purpose of listing is to ensure that care is taken in deciding the future of a building. No changes which affect the architectural or historic character of a listed building can be made without listed building consent (in addition to planning permission where relevant). Applications for listed building consent are normally dealt with by the local planning authority, although English Heritage is always consulted about proposals affecting Grade I and Grade II* properties. It is a criminal offence to demolish a listed building, or alter it in such a way as to affect its character, without consent.

There are currently about 18,300 scheduled monuments in England. English Heritage is carrying out a Monuments Protection Programme assessing archaeological sites with a view to making recommendations for scheduling, and members of the public may propose a monument for consideration. All monuments proposed for scheduling are considered to be of national importance. Where buildings are both scheduled and listed, ancient monuments legislation takes precedence. The main purpose of scheduling a monument is to preserve it for the future and to protect it from damage, destruction or any unnecessary interference. Once a monument has been scheduled, scheduled monument consent is required before any works are carried out. The scope of the control is more extensive and more detailed than that applied to listed buildings, but certain minor works, as detailed in the Ancient Monuments (Class Consents) Order 1994, may be carried out without consent. It is a criminal offence to carry out unauthorised work to scheduled monuments.

Under the Planning (Listed Buildings and Conservation Areas) Act 1990 and the Ancient Monuments and Archaeological Areas Act 1979, the Secretary of State for Wales is responsible for listing buildings and scheduling monuments in Wales on the advice of CADW, the Historic Buildings Council for Wales and the Royal Commission on the Ancient and Historical Monuments of Wales. The criteria for evaluating buildings are similar to those in England and the same listing system is used. There are approximately 26,400 listed buildings and approximately 3,500 scheduled monuments in Wales.

Under the Planning (Listed Buildings and Conservation Areas) (Scotland) Act 1997 and the Ancient Monuments and Archaeological Areas Act 1979,

Scottish Ministers are responsible for listing buildings and scheduling monuments in Scotland on the advice of Historic Scotland, the Historic Buildings Council for Scotland and the Royal Commission on the Ancient and Historical Monuments of Scotland. The criteria for evaluating buildings are similar to those in England but an A, B, C categorisation is used. There are approximately 46,000 listed buildings and 6,500 scheduled monuments in Scotland.

Under the Planning (Northern Ireland) Order 1991 and the Historic Monuments and Archaeological Objects (Northern Ireland) Order 1995, the Department of the Environment of the Northern Ireland Executive is responsible for listing buildings and scheduling monuments in Northern Ireland on the advice of the Historic Buildings Council for Northern Ireland and the Historic Monuments Council for Northern Ireland. The criteria for evaluating buildings are similar to those in England but no statutory grading system is used. In December 2001 there were 8,544 listed buildings and 1,511 scheduled monuments in Northern Ireland.

OPENING TO THE PUBLIC

The following is a selection of the many historic buildings and monuments open to the public. Admission charges and opening hours vary. Many properties are closed in winter (usually November-March) and some are also closed in the mornings. Most properties are closed on Christmas Eve, Christmas Day, Boxing Day and New Years Day, and many are closed on Good Friday. During the winter season, many English Heritage monuments are closed on Mondays and Tuesdays and monuments in the care of CADW are closed on Sunday mornings. In Northern Ireland many monuments are closed on Mondays except on bank holidays. Information about a specific property should be checked by telephone.

ENGLAND

For more information on any of the English Heritage properties listed below, the official website is: www.english-heritage.org.uk.
For more information on any of the National Trust properties listed below, the official website is: www.nationaltrust.org.uk.
EH English Heritage property
NT National Trust property

A LA RONDE (NT), Summer Lane, Exmouth, Devon. Tel: 01395-265514.
  Unique 16-sided house completed c.1796
ALNWICK CASTLE, Northumberland. Tel: 01665-510777. Seat of the Dukes of Northumberland since 1309; Italian Renaissance-style interior
ALTHORP, Northants. Tel: 0870 167 9000.
  Spencer family seat. Diana, Princess of Wales memorabilia
ANGLESEY ABBEY (NT), Cambs. Tel: 01223-811200.
  House built c.1600. Houses many paintings and a unique clock collection
APSLEY HOUSE, London W1. Tel: 020-7499 5676.
  Built by Robert Adam 1771–8, home of the Dukes of Wellington since 1817 and known as 'No. 1 London'. Collection of fine and decorative arts

ARUNDEL CASTLE, W. Sussex. Tel: 01903-883136. Castle dating from the Norman Conquest. Seat of the Dukes of Norfolk

AVEBURY (NT), Wilts. Tel: 01672-539250. Remains of stone circles constructed 4,000 years ago surrounding the later village of Avebury

BANQUETING HOUSE, Whitehall, London SW1. Tel: 020-7930 4179. Designed by Inigo Jones; ceiling paintings by Rubens. Site of the execution of Charles I

BASILDON PARK (NT), Berks. Tel: 0118-984 3040. Palladian house built in 1776–83 by John Carr

BATTLE ABBEY (EH), E. Sussex. Tel: 01424-773792. Remains of the abbey founded by William the Conqueror on the site of the Battle of Hastings

BEAULIEU, Hants. Tel: 01590-612345. House and gardens, Beaulieu Abbey and exhibition of monastic life, National Motor Museum

BEESTON CASTLE (EH), Cheshire. Tel: 01829-260464. Thirteenth-century inner ward with gatehouse and towers, and remains of outer ward

BELTON HOUSE (NT), Grantham, Lincs. Tel: 01476-566116. Fine 17th-century house in landscaped park

BELVOIR CASTLE, nr Grantham, Lincs. Tel: 01476-870262. Seat of the Dukes of Rutland; 19th-century Gothic-style castle

BERKELEY CASTLE, Glos. Tel: 01453-810332. Completed 1153; site of the murder of Edward II (1327)

BLENHEIM PALACE, Woodstock, Oxon. Tel: 01993-811325. Seat of the Dukes of Marlborough and Winston Churchill's birthplace; designed by Vanbrugh

BLICKLING HALL (NT), Norfolk. Tel: 01263-738030. Jacobean house with state rooms, temple and 18th-century orangery

BODIAM CASTLE (NT), E. Sussex. Tel: 01580-830436. Well-preserved medieval moated castle, built 1385

BOLSOVER CASTLE (EH), Derbys. Tel: 01246-823349. Notable 17th-century buildings

BOSCOBEL HOUSE (EH), Shropshire. Tel: 01902-850244. Timber-framed 17th-century hunting lodge, refuge of fugitive Charles II

BOUGHTON HOUSE, Northants. Tel: 01536-515731. A 17th-century house with French-style additions

BOWOOD HOUSE, Wilts. Tel: 01249-812102. An 18th-century house in Capability Brown park, with lake, temple and arboretum

BROADLANDS, Hants. Tel: 01794-505010. Palladian mansion in Capability Brown parkland. Mountbatten exhibition

BRONTË PARSONAGE, Haworth, W. Yorks. Tel: 01535-642323. Home of the Brontë sisters; museum and memorabilia

BUCKFAST ABBEY, Devon. Tel: 01364-642519. Benedictine monastery on medieval foundations

BUCKINGHAM PALACE, London SW1. Tel: 020-7839 1377. Purchased by George III in 1762, and the Sovereign's official London residence since 1837. Eighteen state rooms, including the Throne Room, and Picture Gallery

BUCKLAND ABBEY (NT), Devon. Tel: 01822-853607. A 13th-century Cistercian monastery. Home of Sir Francis Drake

BURGHLEY HOUSE, Stamford, Lincs. Tel: 01780-752451. Late Elizabethan house; vast state apartments

CALKE ABBEY (NT), Derbys. Tel: 01332-863822. Baroque 18th-century mansion

CARISBROOKE CASTLE (EH), Isle of Wight. Tel: 01983-522107. Norman castle; prison of Charles I 1647–8

CARLISLE CASTLE (EH), Cumbria. Tel: 01228-606000. Medieval castle, prison of Mary Queen of Scots

CARLYLE'S HOUSE (NT), Cheyne Row, London SW3. Tel: 020-7352 7087. Home of Thomas Carlyle

CASTLE ACRE PRIORY (EH), Norfolk. Tel: 01760-755394. Remains include 12th-century church and prior's lodgings

CASTLE DROGO (NT), Devon. Tel: 01647-433306. Granite castle designed by Lutyens

CASTLE HOWARD, N. Yorks. Tel: 01653-648444. Designed by Vanbrugh 1699–1726; mausoleum designed by Hawksmoor

CASTLE RISING CASTLE (EH), Norfolk. Tel: 01553-631330. A 12th-century keep in a massive earthwork with gatehouse and bridge

CHARTWELL (NT), Kent. Tel: 01732-866368. Home of Sir Winston Churchill

CHATSWORTH, Derbys. Tel: 01246-582204. Tudor mansion in magnificent parkland

CHESTERS ROMAN FORT (EH), Northumberland. Tel: 01434-681379. Roman cavalry fort

CHYSAUSTER ANCIENT VILLAGE (EH), Cornwall. Tel: 07831-757934. Romano-Cornish village, 2nd- and 3rd-century AD, on a probably late Iron Age site

CLIFFORD'S TOWER (EH), York. Tel: 01904-646940. A 13th-century tower built on a mound

CLIVEDEN (NT), Berks. Tel: 01628-605069. Former home of the Astors, now an hotel set in garden and woodland

CORBRIDGE ROMAN SITE (EH), Northumberland. Tel: 01434-632349. Excavated central area of a Roman town and successive military bases

CORFE CASTLE (NT), Dorset. Tel: 01929-481294. Ruined former royal castle dating from 11th-century

CROFT CASTLE (NT), Herefordshire. Tel: 01568-780246. Pre-Conquest border castle with Georgian-Gothic interior

DEAL CASTLE (EH), Kent. Tel: 01304-372762. Largest of the coastal defence forts built by Henry VIII

DICKENS HOUSE, Doughty Street, London WC1. Tel: 020-7405 2127. House occupied by Dickens 1837–9; manuscripts, furniture and portraits

DR JOHNSON'S HOUSE, 17 Gough Square, London EC4. Tel: 020-7353 3745. Web: www.drjh.dircon.co.uk. Home of Samuel Johnson

DOVE COTTAGE, Grasmere, Cumbria. Tel: 01539-435544. Wordsworth's home 1799–1808; museum

DOVER CASTLE (EH), Kent. Tel: 01304-201628. Castle with Roman, Saxon and Norman features; wartime operations rooms

DUNSTANBURGH CASTLE (EH), Northumberland. Tel: 01665-576231. A 14th-century castle on a cliff, with a substantial gatehouse-keep

ELTHAM PALACE (EH), Court Yard, Eltham, London SE9. Tel: 020-8294 2548. Combines a 1930s country house and remains of medieval palace set in moated gardens.

FARLEIGH HUNGERFORD CASTLE (EH), Somerset. Tel: 01225-754026. Late 14th-century castle with two courts; chapel with tomb of Sir Thomas Hungerford

FARNHAM CASTLE KEEP (EH), Surrey. Tel: 01252-713393. Large 12th-century shell-keep

FOUNTAINS ABBEY (NT), nr Ripon, N. Yorks. Tel: 01765-608888. Deer park, visitor centre and St Mary's Church. Ruined Cistercian monastery; 18th-century landscaped gardens of Studley Royal estate

FRAMLINGHAM CASTLE (EH), Suffolk. Tel: 01728-724189. Castle (c.1200) with high curtain walls enclosing an almshouse (1639)

FURNESS ABBEY (EH), Cumbria. Tel: 01229-823420. Remains of church and conventual buildings founded in 1123

GLASTONBURY ABBEY, Somerset. Tel: 01458-832267. Ruins of a 12th-century abbey rebuilt after fire. Site of an early Christian settlement

GOODRICH CASTLE (EH), Herefordshire. Tel: 01600-890538. Remains of 13th- and 14th-century castle with 12th-century keep

GREENWICH, London SE10. *Royal Observatory*. Tel: 020-8858 6575. Web: www.rof.nmm.ac.uk Former Royal Observatory (founded 1675) housing the time ball and zero meridian of longitude. *The Queen's House*. Tel: 020-8858 4422. Designed for Queen Anne, wife of James I, by Inigo Jones. *Painted Hall and Chapel* (Royal Naval College)

GRIME'S GRAVES (EH), Norfolk. Tel: 01842-810656. Neolithic flint mines. One shaft can be descended

GUILDHALL, London EC2. Tel: 020-7332 1460. Centre of civic government of the City. Built *c.*1441; facade built 1788–9

HADDON HALL, Derbys. Tel: 01629-812855. Well-preserved 12th-century manor house

HAILES ABBEY (EH), Glos. Tel: 01242-602398. Ruins of a 13th-century Cistercian monastery

HAM HOUSE (NT), Richmond, Surrey. Tel: 020-8940 1950. Stuart house with fine interiors

HAMPTON COURT PALACE, East Molesey, Surrey. Tel: 020-8781 9500. A 16th-century palace with additions by Wren. Gardens with maze; Tudor tennis court (summer only)

HARDWICK HALL (NT), Derbys. Tel: 01246-850430. Built 1591–7 for Bess of Hardwick; notable furnishings

HARDY'S COTTAGE (NT), Dorset. Tel: 01305-262366. Birthplace of Thomas Hardy

HAREWOOD HOUSE, W. Yorks. Tel: 0113-288 6331. An 18th-century house designed by John Carr and Robert Adam; park by Capability Brown

HATFIELD HOUSE, Herts. Tel: 01707-262823. Jacobean house built by Robert Cecil; surviving wing of Royal Palace of Hatfield (1497)

HELMSLEY CASTLE (EH), N. Yorks. Tel: 01439-770442. A 12th-century keep and curtain wall with 16th-century buildings. Spectacular earthwork defences

HEVER CASTLE, Kent. Tel: 01732-865224. A 13th-century double-moated castle, childhood home of Anne Boleyn

HOLKER HALL, Cumbria. Tel: 01539-558328. Former home of the Dukes of Devonshire; award-winning gardens

HOLKHAM HALL, Norfolk. Tel: 01328-710227. Fine Palladian mansion

HOUSESTEADS ROMAN FORT (EH), Northumberland. Tel: 01434-344363. Excavated infantry fort on Hadrian's Wall with extra-mural civilian settlement

HUGHENDEN MANOR (NT), High Wycombe. Tel: 01494-755565. Home of Disraeli; small formal garden

JANE AUSTEN'S HOUSE, Chawton, Hants. Tel: 01420-83262. Jane Austen's home 1809–17

KEDLESTON HALL (NT), Derby. Tel: 01332-842191. A classical Palladian mansion built 1759-65; complete Robert Adam interiors

KELMSCOTT MANOR, nr Lechlade, Oxon. Tel: 01367-252486. Summer home of William Morris, with products of Morris and Co.

KENILWORTH CASTLE (EH), Warks. Tel: 01926-852078. Largest castle ruin in England

KENSINGTON PALACE, London W8. Tel: 020-7937 7079. Built in 1605 and enlarged by Wren; bought by William and Mary in 1689. Birthplace of Queen Victoria. Royal Ceremonial Dress Collection

KENWOOD HOUSE (EH), Hampstead Lane, London NW3. Tel: 020-8348 1286. Adam villa housing the Iveagh bequest of paintings and furniture. Open-air concerts in summer

KEW, Surrey. Tel: 020-8332 5189. *Queen Charlotte's Cottage*

KINGSTON LACY HOUSE (NT), Dorset. Tel: 01202-883402. A 17th-century house with 19th-century alterations; important art collection

KNEBWORTH HOUSE, Herts. Tel: 01438-812661. Tudor manor house concealed by 19th-century Gothic decoration; Lutyens gardens

KNOLE (NT), Kent. Tel: 01732-450608. House dating from 1456 set in parkland; fine art treasures

LAMBETH PALACE, London SE1. Tel: 020-7898 1200. Web: www.archbishopofcanterbury.org. Official residence of the Archbishop of Canterbury. A 19th-century house with parts dating from the 12th-century

LANERCOST PRIORY (EH), Cumbria. Tel: 01697-73030. The nave of the Augustinian priory church, *c.*1166, is still used; remains of other claustral buildings

LANHYDROCK (NT), Cornwall. Tel: 01208-73320. House dating from the 17th-century; 45 rooms, including kitchen and nursery

LEEDS CASTLE, Kent. Tel: 01622-765400. Castle dating from 9th-century, on two islands in lake

LEVENS HALL, Cumbria. Tel: 01539-560321. Elizabethan house with unique topiary garden (1694). Steam engine collection

LINCOLN CASTLE. Tel: 01522-511068. Built by William the Conqueror in 1068

LINDISFARNE PRIORY (EH), Northumberland. Tel: 01289-389200. Bishopric of the Northumbrian kingdom destroyed by the Danes; re-established in the 11th-century as a Benedictine priory, now ruined

LITTLE MORETON HALL (NT), Cheshire. Tel: 01260-272018. Timber-framed moated manor house with knot garden

LONGLEAT HOUSE, Wilts. Tel: 01985-844400. Elizabethan house in Italian Renaissance style

LULLINGSTONE ROMAN VILLA (EH), Kent. Tel: 01322-863467. Large villa occupied for much of the Roman period; fine mosaics

MANSION HOUSE, London EC4. Tel: 020-7626 2500. The official residence of the Lord Mayor of London

MARBLE HILL HOUSE (EH), Twickenham, Middx. Tel: 020-8892 5115. English Palladian villa with Georgian paintings and furniture

MICHELHAM PRIORY, E. Sussex. Tel: 01323-844224. Tudor house built onto an Augustinian priory

MIDDLEHAM CASTLE (EH), N. Yorks. Tel: 01969-623899. A 12th-century keep within later fortifications. Childhood home of Richard III

MONTACUTE HOUSE (NT), Somerset. Tel: 01935-823289. Elizabethan house with National Portrait Gallery portraits from period

MOUNT GRACE PRIORY (EH), N. Yorks. Tel: 01609-623899. Carthusian monastery, with remains of monastic buildings

NETLEY ABBEY (EH), Hants. Tel: 023-8045 3076. Remains of Cistercian abbey, used as house in Tudor period

OLD SARUM (EH), Wilts. Tel: 01722-335398. Earthworks enclosing remains of the castle and the 11th-century cathedral

ORFORD CASTLE (EH), Suffolk. Tel: 01394-450472. Circular keep of c.1170 and remains of coastal defence castle built by Henry II

OSBORNE HOUSE (EH), Isle of Wight. Tel: 01983-200022. Queen Victoria's seaside residence

OSTERLEY PARK HOUSE (NT), Isleworth, Middx. Tel: 020-8232 5050. Elizabethan mansion set in parkland

PENDENNIS CASTLE (EH), Cornwall. Tel: 01326-316594. Well-preserved coastal defence castle

PENSHURST PLACE, Kent. Tel: 01892-870307. House with medieval Baron's Hall and gardens

PETWORTH (NT), W. Sussex. Tel: 01798-343929. Late 17th-century house set in deer park

PEVENSEY CASTLE (EH), E. Sussex. Tel: 01323-762604. Walls of a 4th-century Roman fort; remains of an 11th-century castle

PEVERIL CASTLE (EH), Derbys. Tel: 01433-620613. A 12th-century castle defended on two sides by precipitous rocks

POLESDEN LACEY (NT), Surrey. Tel: 01372-458203. Regency villa remodelled in the Edwardian era. Fine paintings and furnishings

PORTCHESTER CASTLE (EH), Hants. Tel: 023-9237 8291. Walls of a late Roman fort enclosing a Norman keep and an Augustinian priory church

POWDERHAM CASTLE, Devon. Tel: 01626-890243. Medieval castle with 18th- and 19th-century alterations

RABY CASTLE, Co. Durham. Tel: 01833-660202. A 14th-century castle with walled gardens

RAGLEY HALL, Warks. Tel: 01789-762090. A 17th-century house with gardens, park and lake

RICHBOROUGH ROMAN FORT (EH), Kent. Tel: 01304-612013. Landing-site of the Claudian invasion in AD 43

RICHMOND CASTLE (EH), N. Yorks. Tel: 01748-822493. A 12th-century keep with 11th-century curtain wall and domestic buildings

RIEVAULX ABBEY (EH), N. Yorks. Tel: 01439-798228. Remains of a Cistercian abbey founded c.1131

ROCHESTER CASTLE (EH), Kent. Tel: 01634-402276. An 11th-century castle partly on the Roman city wall, with a square keep of c.1130

ROCKINGHAM CASTLE, Northants. Tel: 01536-770240. Built by William the Conqueror

ROYAL PAVILION, Brighton. Tel: 01273-290900. Palace of George IV, in Chinese style with Indian exterior and Regency gardens

RUFFORD OLD HALL (NT), Lancs. Tel: 01704-821254. A 16th-century hall with unique screen

ST AUGUSTINE'S ABBEY (EH), Kent. Tel: 01227-767345. Remains of Benedictine monastery, with Norman church, on site of abbey founded AD 598 by St Augustine

ST MAWES CASTLE (EH), Cornwall. Tel: 01326-270526. Coastal defence castle built by Henry VIII

ST MICHAEL'S MOUNT (NT), Cornwall. Tel: 01736-710507. A 12th-century castle with later additions, off the coast at Marazion

SANDRINGHAM, Norfolk. Tel: 01553-772675. The Queen's private residence; a neo-Jacobean house built in 1870

SCARBOROUGH CASTLE (EH), N. Yorks. Tel: 01723-372451. Remains of 12th-century keep and curtain walls

SHERBORNE CASTLE, Dorset. Tel: 01935-813182. Web: www.sherbournecastle.com. Sixteenth-century castle built by Sir Walter Raleigh

SHUGBOROUGH (NT), Staffs. Tel: 01889-881388. House set in 18th-century park with monuments, temples and pavilions in the Greek Revival style

SKIPTON CASTLE, N. Yorks. Tel: 01756-792442. D-shaped castle with six round towers and beautiful inner courtyard

SMALLHYTHE PLACE (NT), Kent. Tel: 01580-762334. Half-timbered 16th-century house; home of Ellen Terry 1899-1928

STANFORD HALL, Leics. Tel: 01788-860250. William and Mary house with Stuart portraits. Motorcycle museum

STONEHENGE (EH), Wilts. Tel: 01980-624715. Prehistoric monument consisting of concentric stone circles surrounded by a ditch and bank

STONOR PARK, Oxon. Tel: 01491-638587. Medieval house with Georgian facade. Centre of Roman Catholicism after the Reformation

STOURHEAD (NT), Wilts. Tel: 01747-841152. English Palladian mansion with famous gardens

STRATFIELD SAYE HOUSE, Hants. Tel: 01256-882882. Web: www.stratfield-saye.co.uk House built 1630–40; home of the Dukes of Wellington since 1817

STRATFORD-UPON-AVON, Warks. *Shakespeare's Birthplace Trust* with Shakespeare Centre; *Anne Hathaway's Cottage*, home of Shakespeare's wife; *Mary Arden's House*, home of Shakespeare's mother; *Nash's House and New Place*, where Shakespeare died; and *Hall's Croft*, home of Shakespeare's daughter. Tel: 01789-204016. Web: www.shakespeare.org.uk. Also *Grammar School* attended by Shakespeare, *Holy Trinity Church*, where Shakespeare is buried, *Royal Shakespeare Theatre* (burnt down 1926, rebuilt 1932) and *Swan Theatre* (opened 1986)

SUDELEY CASTLE, Glos. Tel: 01242-602308. Castle built in 1442; restored in the 19th-century

SYON HOUSE, Brentford, Middx. Tel: 020-8560 0883. Built on the site of a former monastery; Adam interior

TILBURY FORT (EH), Essex. Tel: 01375-858489. A 17th-century coastal fort

TINTAGEL CASTLE (EH), Cornwall. Tel: 01840-770328. A 12th-century cliff-top castle and Dark Age settlement site

TOWER OF LONDON, London EC3N 4AB. Tel: 020-7709 0765. Web: www.hrp.org.uk. Royal palace and fortress begun by William the Conqueror in 1078. Houses the Crown Jewels

TRERICE (NT), Cornwall. Tel: 01637-875404. Elizabethan manor house

TYNEMOUTH PRIORY AND CASTLE (EH), Tyne and Wear. Tel: 0191-257 1090. Remains of a Benedictine priory, founded c.1090, on Saxon monastic site

UPPARK (NT), W. Sussex. Tel: 01730-825857. Late 17th-century house, completely restored after fire. Fetherstonhaugh art collection

WALMER CASTLE (EH), Kent. Tel: 01304-364288. One of Henry VIII's coastal defence castles, now the residence of the Lord Warden of the Cinque Ports

WALTHAM ABBEY (EH), Essex. Tel: 01992-702200. Ruined abbey including the nave of the abbey church, 'Harold's Bridge' and late 14th-century gatehouse. Traditionally the burial place of Harold II (1066)

WARKWORTH CASTLE (EH), Northumberland. Tel: 01665-711423. A 15th-century keep amidst earlier ruins, with 14th-century hermitage upstream

WARWICK CASTLE. Tel: 01926-406600. Medieval castle with Madame Tussaud's waxworks, in Capability Brown parkland

WHITBY ABBEY (EH), N. Yorks. Tel: 01947-603568. Remains of Norman church on the site of a monastery founded in AD 657

WILTON HOUSE, Wilts. Tel: 01722-746720. A 17th-century house on the site of a Tudor house and Saxon abbey

WINDSOR CASTLE, Berks. Tel: 01753-831118. Official residence of The Queen; oldest royal residence still in regular use. Also *St George's Chapel*

WOBURN ABBEY, Beds. Tel: 01525-290666. Built on the site of a Cistercian abbey; seat of the Dukes of Bedford. Important art collection; antiques centre

WROXETER ROMAN CITY (EH), Shropshire. Tel: 01743-761330. Second-century public baths and part of the forum of the Roman town of Viroconium

WALES

For more information on any of the National Trust properties listed below, the official website is: www.nationaltrust.org.uk.

For more information on any of the Cadw properties listsed below, the official website is: www.cadw.wales.gov.uk.

(C) Property of CADW: Welsh Historic Monuments
(NT) National Trust property

BEAUMARIS CASTLE (C), Anglesey. Tel: 01248-810361. Concentrically-planned castle, still almost intact

CAERLEON ROMAN BATHS AND AMPHITHEATRE (C), nr Newport. Tel: 01633-890104. Rare example of a legionary bath-house and late 1st-century arena surrounded by bank for spectators

CAERNARFON CASTLE (C). Tel: 01286-677617. Important Edwardian castle built, with the town wall, between 1283 and 1330

CAERPHILLY CASTLE (C). Tel: 029-2088 3143. Concentrically-planned castle (c.1270) notable for its scale and use of water defences

CARDIFF CASTLE. Tel: 029-2087 8100. Castle built on the site of a Roman fort; spectacular towers and rich interior

CASTELL COCH (C), nr Cardiff. Tel: 029-2081 0101. Rebuilt 1875-90 on medieval foundations

CHEPSTOW CASTLE (C). Tel: 01291-624065. Rectangular keep amid extensive fortifications

CONWY CASTLE (C). Tel: 01492-592358. Built by Edward I, 1283-7

CRICCIETH CASTLE (C). Tel: 01766-522227. Native Welsh 13th-century castle, altered by Edward I

DENBIGH CASTLE (C). Tel: 01745-813385. Remains of the castle (begun 1282), including triple-towered gatehouse

HARLECH CASTLE (C). Tel: 01766-780552. Well-preserved Edwardian castle, constructed 1283-90, on an outcrop above the former shoreline

PEMBROKE CASTLE. Tel: 01646-681510. Web: www.pembrokecastle.co.uk Castle founded in 1093; Great Tower built 1200; birthplace of King Henry VII

PENRHYN CASTLE (NT), Bangor. Tel: 01248-353084. Neo-Norman castle built in the 19th-century. Industrial railway museum

PORTMEIRION, Penrhyndeudraeth. Tel: 01766-770228. Village in Italianate style

POWIS CASTLE (NT), nr Welshpool. Tel: 01938-551920. Medieval castle with interior in variety of styles; 17th-century gardens and Clive of India museum

RAGLAN CASTLE (C). Tel: 01291-690228. Remains of 15th-century castle with moated hexagonal keep

ST DAVIDS BISHOP'S PALACE (C), St Davids. Tel: 01437-720517. Remains of residence of Bishops of St Davids built 1328–47

TINTERN ABBEY (C), nr Chepstow. Tel: 01291-689251. Remains of 13th-century church and conventual buildings of a Cistercian monastery

TRETOWER COURT AND CASTLE (C), nr Crickhowell. Tel: 01874-730279. Medieval house with remains of 12th-century castle nearby

SCOTLAND

For more information on any of the Historic Scotland properties listed below, the official website is: www.historic-scotland.gov.uk.

For more information on any of the National Trust For Scotland properties listed below, the official website is: www.nts.org.uk.

(HS) Historic Scotland property
(NTS) National Trust for Scotland property

ANTONINE WALL, between the Clyde and the Forth. Built about AD 142, consists of ditch, turf rampart and road, with forts every two miles

BALMORAL CASTLE, nr Braemar. Tel: 01339-742334. Web: www.balmoralcastle.com. Baronial-style castle built for Victoria and Albert. The Queen's private residence

BLACKHOUSE, ARNOL (HS), Lewis, Western Isles. Tel: 01851-710395. Traditional Lewis thatched house

BLAIR CASTLE, Blair Atholl. Tel: 01796-481207. Mid 18th-century mansion with 13th-century tower; seat of the Dukes of Atholl

BONAWE IRON FURNACE (HS), Argyll and Bute. Tel: 01866-822432. Charcoal-fuelled ironworks founded in 1753

BOWHILL, SELKIRK. Tel: 01750-22204. Seat of the Dukes of Buccleuch and Queensberry; fine collection of paintings, including portrait miniatures

BROUGH OF BIRSAY (HS), Orkney. Remains of Norse church and village on the tidal island of Birsay. Tel: 01856-841815.

CAERLAVEROCK CASTLE (HS), nr Dumfries. Tel: 01387-770244. Fine early classical Renaissance building

CALANAIS STANDING STONES (HS), Lewis, Western Isles. Tel: 01851-621422. Standing stones in a cross-shaped setting, dating from 3000 BC

CATHERTUNS (BROWN AND WHITE) (HS), nr Brechin. Two large Iron Age hill forts

CAWDOR CASTLE, Inverness. Tel: 01667-404615. A 14th-century keep with 15th- and 17th-century additions

CLAVA CAIRNS (HS), Highland. Tel: 01667-460232. Late Neolithic or early Bronze Age cairns

CRATHES CASTLE (NTS), nr Banchory. Tel: 01330-844525. A 16th-century baronial castle in woodland, fields and gardens

CULZEAN CASTLE (NTS), S. Ayrshire. Tel: 01655-760274. An 18th-century Adam castle with oval staircase and circular saloon

DRYBURGH ABBEY (HS), Scottish Borders. Tel: 01835-822381. A 12th-century abbey containing tomb of Sir Walter Scott

DUNVEGAN CASTLE, Skye. Tel: 01470-521206. A 13th-century castle with later additions; home of the chiefs of the Clan MacLeod; trips to seal colony

EDINBURGH CASTLE (HS). Tel: 0131-225 9846. Includes the Scottish National War Memorial, Scottish United Services Museum and historic apartments

EDZELL CASTLE (HS), nr Brechin. Tel: 01356-648631. Medieval tower house; unique walled garden
EILEAN DONAN CASTLE, Wester Ross. Tel: 01599-555202. A 13th-century castle with Jacobite relics
ELGIN CATHEDRAL (HS), Moray. Tel: 01343-547171. A 13th-century cathedral with fine chapterhouse
FLOORS CASTLE, Kelso. Tel: 01573-223333. Largest inhabited castle in Scotland; seat of the Dukes of Roxburghe
FORT GEORGE (HS), Highland. Tel: 01667-462777. An 18th-century fort
GLAMIS CASTLE, Angus. Tel: 01307-840393. Seat of the Lyon family (later Earls of Strathmore and Kinghorne) since 1372
GLASGOW CATHEDRAL (HS). Tel: 0141-552 6891. Medieval cathedral with elaborately vaulted crypt
GLENELG BROCH (HS), Highlands. Two broch towers with well-preserved structural features
HOPETOUN HOUSE, nr Edinburgh. Tel: 0131-331 2451. House designed by Sir William Bruce, enlarged by William Adam
HUNTLY CASTLE (HS). Tel: 01466-793191. Ruin of a 16th- and 17th-century house
INVERARAY CASTLE, Argyll. Tel: 01499-302203. Gothic-style 18th-century castle; seat of the Dukes of Argyll
IONA ABBEY, Inner Hebrides. Tel: 01681-700793. Monastery founded by St Columba in AD 563
JARLSHOF (HS), Shetland. Tel: 01950-460112. Remains from Stone Age
JEDBURGH ABBEY (HS), Scottish Borders. Tel: 01835-863925. Romanesque and early Gothic church founded c.1138
KELSO ABBEY (HS), Scottish Borders. Remains of great abbey church founded 1128
LINLITHGOW PALACE (HS). Tel: 01506-842896. Ruin of royal palace in park setting. Birthplace of Mary, Queen of Scots
MAES HOWE (HS), Orkney. Tel: 01856-761606. Neolithic tomb
MEIGLE SCULPTURED STONES (HS), Angus. Tel: 01828-640612. Celtic Christian stones
MELROSE ABBEY (HS), Scottish Borders. Tel: 01896-822562. Ruin of Cistercian abbey founded c.1136
MOUSA BROCH (HS), Shetland. Finest surviving Iron Age broch tower
NEW ABBEY CORN MILL (HS), nr Dumfries. Tel: 01387-850260. Water-powered mill
PALACE OF HOLYROODHOUSE, Edinburgh. Tel: 0131-556 7371. The Queen's official Scottish residence. Main part of the palace built 1671–9
RING OF BROGAR (HS), Orkney. Tel: 01865- 841815. Neolithic circle of upright stones with an enclosing ditch
RUTHWELL CROSS (HS), Dumfries and Galloway. Tel: 01387-870249. Seventh-century Anglian cross
ST ANDREWS CASTLE AND CATHEDRAL (HS), Fife. Tel: 01334-477196 (castle); 01334-472563 (cathedral). Ruins of 13th-century castle and remains of the largest cathedral in Scotland
SCONE PALACE, Perth. Tel: 01738-552300. House built 1802–13 on the site of a medieval palace
SKARA BRAE (HS), Orkney. Tel: 01856-841815. Stone-Age village with adjacent 17th-century house
SMAILHOLM TOWER (HS), Scottish Borders. Tel: 01573-460365. Well-preserved tower-house
STIRLING CASTLE (HS), Tel: 01786-450000. Great Hall and gatehouse of James IV, palace of James V, Chapel Royal remodelled by James VI
TANTALLON CASTLE (HS), E. Lothian. Tel: 01620-892727. Fortification with earthwork defences and a 14th-century curtain wall with towers

THREAVE CASTLE (HS), Dumfries and Galloway. Tel: 0831-168512. Late 14th-century tower on an island; reached by boat, long walk to castle
URQUHART CASTLE (HS), Loch Ness. Tel: 01456-450551. Castle remains with well-preserved tower

NORTHERN IRELAND

For more information on any of the National Trust properties listed below, the official website is: www.nationaltrust.org.uk.

DE Property in the care of the Northern Ireland Department of the Environment
NT National Trust property

CARRICKFERGUS CASTLE (DE), Co. Antrim. Tel: 028-9335 1273. Castle begun in 1180 and garrisoned until 1928
CASTLE COOLE (NT), Enniskillen. Tel: 028-6632 2690. An 18th-century mansion by James Wyatt in parkland
CASTLE WARD (NT), Co. Down. Tel: 028-4488 1204. An 18th-century house with Classical and Gothic facades
DEVENISH ISLAND (DE), Co. Fermanagh. Island monastery founded in the 6th-century by St Molaise
DOWNHILL CASTLE (NT), Co. Londonderry. Tel: 028-7084 8728. Ruins of palatial house in landscaped estate including Mussenden Temple
DUNLUCE CASTLE (DE), Co. Antrim. Tel: 028-9054 3037. Ruins of 16th-century stronghold of the MacDonnells
FLORENCE COURT (NT), Co. Fermanagh. Tel: 028-6634 8249. Mid-18th-century house with rococo plasterwork
GREY ABBEY (DE), Co. Down. Tel: 028-9054 3037. Substantial remains of a Cistercian abbey founded in 1193
HILLSBOROUGH FORT (DE), Co. Down. Built in 1650
MOUNT STEWART (NT), Co. Down. Tel: 028-4278 8387. An 18th-century house, childhood home of Lord Castlereagh
NENDRUM MONASTERY (DE), Mahee Island, Co. Down. Founded in the 5th-century by St Machaoi
TULLY CASTLE (DE), Co. Fermanagh. Fortified house and bawn built in 1613
WHITE ISLAND (DE), Co. Fermanagh. Tenth-century monastery and 12th-century church. Access by ferry

Museums and Galleries

There are approximately 2,500 museums and galleries in the United Kingdom. Around 1,800 are registered with Resource: The Council for Museums, Archives and Libraries, formerly the Museums and Galleries Commission, which indicates that they have an appropriate constitution, are soundly financed, have adequate collection management standards and public services, and have access to professional curatorial advice. Museums must achieve full or provisional registration status in order to be eligible for grants from Resource and from Area Museums Councils. Many of the registered museums are run by a local authority.

The national museums and galleries receive direct government grant-in-aid. These are: British Museum; Imperial War Museum; National Army Museum; National Galleries of Scotland; National Gallery; National Maritime Museum; National Museums and Galleries on Merseyside; National Museum of Wales; National Museums of Scotland; National Portrait Gallery; Natural History Museum; RAF Museum; Royal Armouries; Science Museum; Tate Gallery; Ulster Folk and Transport Museum; Ulster Museum; Victoria and Albert Museum; Wallace Collection. An online art museum (Web: www.24hourmuseum.org.uk) has also been awarded national collection status.

Local authority museums are funded by the local authority and may also receive grants from Resource. Independent museums and galleries mainly rely on their own resources but are also eligible for grants from Resource.

Area Museum Councils, which are independent charities, give advice and support to the museums in their area and may offer improvement grants. They also circulate exhibitions and assist with training and marketing. For further information *see* the Public Bodies Section.

Opening to the Public

The following is a selection of the museums and art galleries in the United Kingdom. Opening hours and admission charges vary. Most museums are closed on Christmas Eve, Christmas Day, Boxing Day and New Year's Day; many are closed on Good Friday, and some are closed on May Day Bank Holiday. Some smaller museums close at lunchtimes. Information about a specific museum or gallery should be checked by telephone. For further information about museums and galleries in the UK, including local authority status and whether a collection is designated pre-eminent, contact the Museums Association on 020-7426 6970.

ENGLAND

BARNARD CASTLE, Co. Durham – *The Bowes Museum*, Westwick Road DR12 8NP. Tel: 01833-690606; Web: www.barnard-castle.co.uk
European art from the late medieval period to the 19th-century; music and costume galleries; English period rooms from Elizabeth I to Victoria; local archaeology

BATH – *American Museum in Britain*, Claverton Manor BA2 7BD. Tel: 01225-460503;
Web: www.americanmuseum.org
American decorative arts from the 17th- to 19th-century

Museum of Costume, Bennett Street BA1 2EW. Tel: 01225-477789;
Web: www.museumofcostume.co.uk
Fashion from the 16th-century to the present day
Roman Baths Museum, Abbey Church Yard BA1 1LZ. Tel: 01225-477774; Web: www.romanbaths.co.uk
Museum adjoins the remains of a Roman baths and temple complex
Victoria Art Gallery, Bridge Street BA2 4AT. Tel: 01225-477772; Web: www.victoria.gal.org.uk
European Old Masters and British art since the 18th-century

BEAMISH, Co. Durham – *Beamish, The North of England Open Air Museum*, DH9 0RG. Tel: 0191-370 4000; Web: www.countydurham.com/beamish
Recreated northern town *c*.1900, with rebuilt and furnished local buildings, colliery village, farm, railway station, tramway, Pockerley Manor and horse-yard (set *c*.1800)

BEAULIEU, Hants – *National Motor Museum*. SO42 7ZN. Tel: 01590-612345; Web: www.beaulieu.co.uk
Displays of over 250 vehicles dating from 1895 to the present day

BIRMINGHAM – *Aston Hall*, Trinity Road, B6 6JD. Tel: 0121-327 0062.
Jacobean House containing paintings, furniture and tapestries from the 17th- to 19th-century
Barber Institute of Fine Arts, off Edgbaston Park Road, B15 2TS. Tel: 0121-472 0962; Web: www.barber.org.uk
Fine arts, including Old Masters
Birmingham Nature Centre, Edgbaston, B5 7RL. Tel: 0121-472 7775.
Indoor and outdoor enclosures displaying wildlife, especially British and European
City Museum and Art Gallery, Chamberlain Square. Tel: 0121-303 2834;
Web: www.bmag.org.uk/museum_and_art_gallery
Includes notable collection of Pre-Raphaelites
Museum of the Jewellery Quarter, Vyse Street, Hockley. Tel: 0121-554 3598;
Web: www.bmag.org.uk/jewellery_quarter
Built around a real jewellery workshop
Soho House, Soho Avenue. Tel: 0121-554 9122;
Web: www.bmag.org.uk/soho_house
Eighteenth-century home of industrialist Matthew Boulton

BOVINGTON CAMP, Dorset – *Tank Museum* BH20 6JD. Tel: 01929-405096; Web: www.tankmuseum.org.uk
Collection of 300 tanks from the earliest days of tank warfare to the present

BRADFORD – *Cartwright Hall Art Gallery*, Lister Park BD9 4NS. Tel: 01274-751212.
British 19th- and 20th-century fine art
Industrial Museum and Horses at Work, Moorside Road BD2 3HP. Tel: 01274-631756;
Web: www.bradford.gov.uk
Engineering, textiles, transport and social history exhibits, including recreated back-to-back cottages, shire horses and horse tram-rides
National Museum of Photography, Film and Television BD1 1NQ. Tel: 01274-202030; Web: www.nmpft.org.uk
Photography, film and television interactive exhibits. Features the UK's first IMAX cinema and the only public Cinerama screen in the world

BRIGHTON – Booth Museum of Natural History, Dyke Road. Tel: 01273-292777.

Zoology, botany and geology collections; British birds in recreated habitats

Brighton Museum and Art Gallery, Church Street, BN1 1UE. Tel: 01273-290900;
Web: www.royalpavilion.brighton.co.uk
Includes fine art and design, fashion, non-Western art, Brighton history

BRISTOL – *Arnolfini*, Narrow Quay BS1 4QA. Tel: 0117-929 9191; Web: www.arnolfini.demon.co.uk
Contemporary visual arts, dance, performance, music, talks and workshops

Blaise Castle House Museum, Henbury BS10 7QS. Tel: 0117-950 6789; Web: www.bristol-city.gov.uk
Agricultural and social history collections in an 18th-century mansion

Bristol Industrial Museum, Prince Street BS1 4RN. Tel: 0117-925 1470; Web: www.bristol-city.gov.uk
Industrial, maritime and transport collections

City Museum and Art Gallery, Queen's Road B58 1RL. Tel: 0117-922 3571;
Web: www.bristol-city.gov.uk/museums
Includes fine and decorative art, oriental art, Egyptology and Bristol ceramics and paintings

CAMBRIDGE – *Duxford Airfield*, Duxford CB2 4QR. Tel: 01223-835000; Web: www.lwm.org.uk
Displays of military and civil aircraft, tanks, guns and naval exhibits

Fitzwilliam Museum, Trumpington Street CB2 1RB. Tel: 01223-332900; Web: www.fitzmuseum.cam.ac.uk
Antiquities, fine and applied arts, clocks, ceramics, manuscripts, furniture, sculpture, coins and medals, temporary exhibitions

Sedgwick Museum of Geology, Downing Street, CB2 3EQ. Tel: 01223-333456;
Extensive geological collection

University Museum of Archaeology and Anthropology, Downing Street CB2 3EJ. Tel: 01223-333516; Web: www.cumaa.archanth.cam.ac.uk
Archaeology and anthropology from all parts of the world

University Museum of Zoology, Downing Street CB2 3EJ. Tel: 01223-336650; Web: www.zoo.cam.ac.uk
Extensive zoological collection

Whipple Museum of the History of Science, Free School Lane CB2 3RH. Tel: 01223-330906;
Scientific instruments from the 14th-century to the present

CARLISLE – *Tullie House Museum and Art Gallery*, Castle Street CA3 8TP. Tel: 01228-534781;
Web: www.tulliehouse.co.uk.
Prehistoric archaeology, Hadrian's Wall, Viking and medieval Cumbria, and the social history of Carlisle; also British 19th- and 20th-century art and English porcelain

CHATHAM – *World Naval Base* ME4 4TZ. Tel: 01634-823807; Web: www.worldnavalbase.org.uk
Maritime attractions including HMS *Cavalier*, the UK's last World War II destroyer

Royal Engineers Museum, Brompton Barracks ME4 4U9. Tel: 01634-406397; Web: www.royalengineers.org.uk
Regimental history, ethnography, decorative art and photography

CHELTENHAM – *Art Gallery and Museum*, Clarence Street GL50 3JT. Tel: 01242-237431;
Web: www.cheltenhammuseum.org.uk
Paintings, arts and crafts

CHESTER – *Grosvenor Museum*, Grosvenor Street CH1 2DD. Tel: 01244-402008;
Web: www.chestercc.gov.uk/heritage/museum/home.htm

Roman collections, natural history, art, Chester silver, local history and costume

CHICHESTER – *Weald and Downland Open Air Museum*, Singleton PO18 0EU. Tel: 01243-811363;
Web: www.wealddown.co.uk
Rebuilt vernacular buildings from south-east England; includes medieval houses, agricultural and rural craft buildings and a working watermill

COLCHESTER – *Colchester Castle Museum*, Castle Park CO1 1YG. Tel: 01206-282931;
Web: www.colchestercastle.co.uk
Largest Norman keep in Europe standing on foundations of roman Temple of Claudius; tours of the Roman vaults, castle walls and chapel with medieval and prison displays

COVENTRY – *Herbert Art Gallery and Museum*, Jordan Well CV1 5QP. Tel: 024-7683 2565;
Web: www.coventrymuseum.org.uk
Local history, archaeology and industry, and fine and decorative art

Museum of British Road Transport, Hales Street CV1 1PN. Tel: 024-7683 2425; Web: www.mbrt.co.uk
Hundreds of motor vehicles and bicycles

CRICH, nr Matlock, Derbys – *Crich Tramway Museum* BE4 5DP. Tel: 0870 758 7267; Web: www.tramway.co.uk
Open-air working museum with tram rides

DERBY – *Derby Museum and Art Gallery*, The Strand DE1 1BS. Tel: 01332-716659;
Web: www.derby.gov.uk/museums
Includes paintings by Joseph Wright of Derby and Derby porcelain

Industrial Museum, off Full Street DE1 3AR. Tel: 01332-255308; Web: www.derby.gov.uk/museums
Rolls-Royce aero engine collection and a railway engineering gallery

DEVIZES – *Wiltshire Heritage Museum*, Long Street SN10 1NS. Tel: 01380-727369;
Web: www.wiltshireheritage.org.uk
Natural and local history, art gallery, archaeological finds from Bronze Age, Iron Age, Roman and Saxon sites

DORCHESTER – *Dorset County Museum*, High West Street, DT1 1XA. Tel: 01305-262735;
Web: www.dorsetcountymuseum.com
Includes a collection of Thomas Hardy's manuscripts, books, notebooks and drawings

DOVER – *Dover Museum*, Market Square CT16 1PB. Tel: 01304-201066; Web: www.dovermuseum.co.uk
Contains Dover Bronze Age Boat Gallery and archaeological finds from the Bronze Age, Roman and Saxon sites.

ELLESMERE PORT – *Boat Museum*, South Pier Road CH65 4FW. Tel: 0151-355 5017;
Web: www.boatmuseum.co.uk
Craft and boating history

EXETER – *Royal Albert Memorial Museum and Art Gallery*, Queen Street EX4 3RX. Tel: 01392-165858;
Web: www.exeter.gov.uk
Natural history, archaeology, worldwide fine and decorative art including Exeter silver

GATESHEAD – *Shipley Art Gallery*, Prince Consort Road NE8 4JB. Tel: 0191-477 1495.
Contemporary crafts

The Baltic Centre for Contemporary Art, South Shore Road, Gateshead, NE8 3BA. Tel: 0191-478 1810;
Web: www.balticmill.com
Presents a constantly changing programme of contemporary art exhibitions and events.

GAYDON, Warwick – *British Motor Industry Heritage Trust*, Heritage Motor Centre, Banbury Road CB35 0BJ. Tel: 01926-641188; Web; www.heritage.org.uk
History of British motor industry from 1895 to present; classic vehicles; engineering gallery; Corgi and Lucas collections

GLOUCESTER – *National Waterways Museum*, Llanthony Warehouse, Gloucester Docks GL1 2EH.
Tel: 01452-318054; Web: www.nwm.org.uk
Two-hundred-year history of Britain's canals and inland waterways

GOSPORT, Hants – *Royal Navy Submarine Museum*, Haslar Jetty Road PO12 2AS. Tel: 023-9252 9217;
Web: www.rnsubmus.co.uk
Underwater warfare, including the submarine Alliance; historical and nuclear galleries; and first Royal Navy submarine

GRASMERE, Cumbria – *Dove Cottage* and the *Wordsworth Museum* LA22 9SH. Web: www.wordsworth.org.uk

HALIFAX – *Eureka! The Museum for Children*, Discovery Road HX1 2NE. Tel: 01426-983191;
Web: www.eureka.org.uk
Hands-on museum designed for children up to age 12

HULL – *Ferens Art Gallery*, Queen Victoria Square HU1 3RA. Tel: 01482-613902;
Web: www.hullcc.gov.uk/museums/index.htm
European art, especially Dutch 17th-century paintings, British portraits from 17th- to 20th-century, and marine paintings
Hull Maritime Museum, Queen Victoria Square HU1 3DX. Tel: 01482-613902;
Web: www.hullcc.gov.uk/museums
Whaling, fishing and navigation exhibits

HUNTINGDON – *Cromwell Museum*, Grammar School Walk P29 3LS. Tel: 01480-375830;
Web: www.cromwell.argonet.co.uk.
Portraits and memorabilia relating to Oliver Cromwell

IPSWICH – *Christchurch Mansion and Wolsey Art Gallery*, Christchurch Park IP4 2BE. Tel: 01473-253246.
Tudor house with paintings by Gainsborough, Constable and other Suffolk artists; furniture and 18th-century ceramics. Art gallery for temporary exhibitions

LEEDS – *City Art Gallery*, The Headrow LS1 3AA. Tel: 0113-247 8248.
British and European paintings including English watercolours, modern sculpture, Henry Moore gallery, print room
Leeds Industrial Museum at Armley Mills, Canal Road, Armley LS12 2QF. Tel: 0113-263 7861;
Web: www. leeds.gov.uk.
Largest woollen mill in world
Lotherton Hall, Aberford. Tel: 0113-281 3259.
Costume and oriental collections in furnished Edwardian house; deer park and bird garden
Royal Armouries Museum, Armouries Drive.
Tel: 0113-220-1940.
National collection of arms and armour from BC to present; demonstrations of foot combat in museum's five galleries; falconry and mounted combat in the tiltyard
Temple Newsam House LS15 0AE. Tel: 0113-264 7321.
Old Masters and 17th- and 18th-century decorative art in furnished Jacobean/Tudor house

LEICESTER – *Jewry Wall Museum*, St Nicholas Circle.
Tel: 0116-247 3021
Archaeology, Roman Jewry Wall and baths, and mosaics
New Walk Museum and Art Gallery, New Walk LE1 7EA.
Tel: 0116-255 4100; Web: www.leicestermuseums.ac.uk
Natural history, geology, ancient Egypt gallery, European art and decorative arts

Snibston Discovery Park, Coalville LE67 3LN.
Tel: 01530-278444.
Open-air science and industry museum on site of a coal mine; country park with nature trail

LINCOLN – *Museum of Lincolnshire Life*, Burton Road LN1 3LY. Tel: 01522-528448.
Social history and agricultural collection
Usher Gallery, Lindum Road LN2 1NN.
Tel: 01522-527980.
Watches, miniatures, porcelain, silver; collection of Peter de Wint works; Lincolnshire topography and Royal Lincs Regiment memorabilia

LIVERPOOL – *Lady Lever Art Gallery*, Wirral CH62 5EQ.
Tel: 0151-478 4136; Web: www.portsunlight.org.uk
Paintings, furniture and porcelain
Liverpool Museum, William Brown Street L3 8EN.
Tel: 0151-478 4399; Web: www.nmgm.org.uk
Includes Egyptian mummies, weapons and classical sculpture; planetarium, aquarium, vivarium and natural history centre
Merseyside Maritime Museum, Albert Dock L3 4AQ.
Tel: 0151-478 4499; Web: www.nmgm.org.uk
Floating exhibits, working displays and craft demonstrations; incorporates HM Customs and Excise National Museum
Museum of Liverpool Life, Pier Head, Albert Dock L3 4AQ. Tel: 0151-478 4499; Web: www.nmgm.org.uk
The history of Liverpool
Sudley House, Mossley Hill Road. Tel: 0151-724 3245.
Late 18th- and 19th-century British paintings in former shipowner's home
Tate Gallery Liverpool, Albert Dock L3 4BB.
Tel: 0151-702 7400; Web: www.tate.org.uk/liverpool
Twentieth-century painting and sculpture
Walker Art Gallery, William Brown Street .
Tel: 0151-478 4199.
Paintings from the 14th- to 20th-century

LONDON: GALLERIES – *Barbican Art Gallery*, Barbican Centre EC2Y 8DS. Tel: 020-7638 8891;
Web: www.barbican.org.uk
Temporary exhibitions
Courtauld Gallery, Somerset House, Strand, WC2.
Tel: 020-7848 2526.
The University of London galleries
Dulwich Picture Gallery, College Road, SE21 7AD.
Tel: 020-8693 5254;
Web: www.dulwichpicturegallery.org.uk
Built by Sir John Soane to house 17th- and 18th-century paintings
Hayward Gallery, Belvedere Road, SE1 8XZ.
Tel: 020-7928 3144; Web: www.haywardgallery.org.uk
Temporary exhibitions
National Gallery, Trafalgar Square, WC2N 5DN.
Tel: 020-7839 3321; Web: www.nationalgallery.org.uk
Western painting from the 13th- to 20th-century; early Renaissance collection in the Sainsbury wing
National Portrait Gallery, St Martin's Place, WC2H 0HE.
Tel: 020-7306 0055; Web: www.npg.org.uk
Portraits of eminent people in British history
Percival David Foundation of Chinese Art, Gordon Square, WC1H 0PD. Tel: 020-7387 3909;
Web: www.pdfmuseum.org.uk
Chinese ceramics from 10th- to 18th-century
Photographers Gallery, Great Newport Street, WC2.
Tel: 020-7831 1772; Web: www.photonet.org.uk
Temporary exhibitions
The Queen's Gallery, Buckingham Palace, SW1A 1AA.
Tel: 020-7839 1377; Web: www.royal.org.uk
Art from the Royal Collection
Royal Academy of Arts, Piccadilly, W1V 0DS.
Tel: 020-7300 8000; Web: www.royalacademy.org.uk

British art since 1750 and temporary exhibitions; annual Summer Exhibition
Saatchi Gallery, Boundary Road, NW8 0RH.
Contemporary art including paintings, photographs, sculpture and installations
Serpentine Gallery, Kensington Gardens, W2 3XA.
Tel: 020-7298 1515;
Web: www.serpentinegallery.org.uk
Temporary exhibitions of British and international contemporary art
Tate Britain, Millbank, SW1P 4RG. Tel: 020-7887 8000;
Web: www.tate.org.uk
British painting and 20th-century painting and sculpture.
Tate Modern, Bankside, SE1. Tel: 020-7887 8000;
Web: www.tate.org.uk
International modern art from 1900 to the present.
Wallace Collection, Manchester Square, W1U 3BN.
Tel: 020-7563 9500;
Web: www.wallace-collection.org.uk
Paintings and drawings, French 18th-century furniture, armour, porcelain, clocks and sculpture
Whitechapel Art Gallery, Whitechapel High Street, E1 7QZ. Tel: 020-7522 7878;
Web: www.whitechapel.org.uk
Temporary exhibitions of modern art
LONDON: MUSEUMS – *Bank of England Museum*, Threadneedle Street, EC2R 8AH. (entrance from Bartholomew Lane). Tel: 020-7601 5545;
Web: www.bankofengland.co.uk.
History of the Bank since 1694
Bethnal Green Museum of Childhood, Cambridge Heath Road, E2 1PA. Tel: 020-8983 5200;
Web: www.museumofchildhood.org.uk.
Toys, games and exhibits relating to the social history of childhood
British Museum, Great Russell Street, WC1B 3DG.
Tel: 020-7323 8000;
Web: www.thebritishmuseum.ac.uk
Antiquities, coins, medals, prints and drawings
Cabinet War Rooms, King Charles Street, SW1A 7AQ.
Tel: 020-7930 6961; Web: www.iwm.org.uk
Underground rooms used by Churchill and the Government during the Second World War
Commonwealth Experience, Kensington High Street W8 6NQ. Tel: 020-7603 4535;
Web: www.commonwealth.org.uk
Exhibitions on Commonwealth nations, visual arts and crafts; Interactive World
Cutty Sark, Greenwich, SE10 9HT. Tel: 020-8858 3445;
Web: www.cuttysark.org.uk
Restored and re-rigged tea clipper with exhibits on board.
Design Museum, Shad Thames, SE1. Tel: 020-7378 6055;
Web: www.designmuseum.org.uk
The development of design and the mass-production of consumer objects
Estorick Collection, Canonbury Square, N1 2AN.
Tel: 020-7704 9522; Web: www.estorickcollection.com
Stages the main Estorick Collection of modern Italian art together with temporary loan exhibitions
Firepower! The Royal Artillery Museum, Royal Arsenal, Woolwich, SE18 6ST. Tel: 020-8855 7755;
Web: www.firepower.org.uk
The history and development of artillery over the last 700 years including the collections of the Royal Regiment of Artillery
Geffrye Museum, Kingsland Road, E2 8EA.
Tel: 020-7739 9893;
Web: www.geffrye-museum.org.uk

English urban domestic interiors from 1600 to present day; also paintings, furniture, decorative arts, walled herb garden and period garden rooms
Gilbert Collection, The Strand WC2R 1LA.
Tel: 020-7420 9400;
Web: www.gilbert-collection.org.uk
The collection comprises some 800 works of art including European silver, gold snuff boxes and Italian mosaics
HMS Belfast, Morgans Lane, Tooley Street, SE1 2JH.
Tel: 020-7940 6300; Web: www.hmsbelfast.org.uk
Life on a World War II warship
Horniman Museum and Gardens, London Road SE23 3PQ. Tel: 020-8699 1872;
Web: www.horniman.demon.co.uk
Museum of ethnography, musical instruments, natural history and aquarium; reference library; sunken, water and flower gardens
Imperial War Museum, Lambeth Road SE1 6HZ.
Tel: 020-7416 5320; Web: www.iwm.org.uk
All aspects of the two world wars and other military operations involving Britain and the Commonwealth since 1914
Jewish Museum, Camden Town, Albert Street NW1 7NB.
Tel: 020-7284 1997; Web: www.jewishmuseum.co.uk.
Jewish life, history and religion
Jewish Museum, Finchley, East End Road N3 2SY.
Tel: 020-8349 1143; Web: www.jewishmuseum.co.uk
Jewish life in London and Holocaust education
London Transport Museum, Covent Garden WC2E 7BB.
Tel: 020-7379 6344; Web: www.ltmuseum.co.uk
Vehicles, photographs and graphic art relating to the history of transport in London
MCC Museum, Lord's NW8 8QN. Tel: 020-7289 1611;
Web: www.lords.org
Cricket museum. Conducted tours by appointment with Tours Manager.
Museum of Garden History, Lambeth Palace Road SE1 7LB. Tel: 020-7401 8865;
Web: www.museumgardenhistory.org
Exhibition of aspects of garden history and re-created 17th-century garden
Museum of London, 150 London Wall, EC2Y 5HN.
Tel: 020-7600 3699;
Web: www.museumoflondon.org.uk
History of London from prehistoric times to present day
National Army Museum, Royal Hospital Road SW3 4HT.
Tel: 020-7730 0717;
Web: www.national-army-museum.co.uk
Five-hundred-year history of the British soldier; exhibits include model of the Battle of Waterloo and Army for Today gallery
Natural History Museum, Cromwell Road SW7 5BD.
Tel: 020-7942 5000; Web: www.nhm.ac.uk
Natural history collections
National Maritime Museum, Greenwich SE10 9NF.
Tel: 020-8858 4422; Web; www.nmm.ac.uk
Comprises the main building, the Royal Observatory and the Queen's House. Maritime history of Britain; collections include globes, clocks, telescopes and paintings
Petrie Museum of Egyptian Archaeology, University College London, Malet Place WC1E 6BT.
Tel: 020-7504 2884. Egyptian archaeology collection
Royal Air Force Museum, Colindale, NW9 5LL.
Tel: 020-8205 2266; Web: www.rafmuseum.org.uk
National museum of aviation with over 70 full-size aircraft; aviation from before the Wright brothers to the present-day RAF; flight simulator

Royal Mews, Buckingham Palace SW1A 1AA.
Tel: 020-7839 1377.
Carriages, coaches, stables and horses
Science Museum, Exhibition Road, SW7 2DD.
Tel: 0870 870 4771; Web: www.sciencemuseum.org.uk
Science, technology, industry and medicine collections
Shakespeare Globe Theatre Tour and Exhibition,
Bankside SE1 9DT. Tel: 020-7902 1500;
Web: www.shakespeare-globe.org
Recreation of Elizabethan theatre using 16th-century
techniques
Sherlock Holmes Museum, Baker Street NW1 6XE.
Tel: 020-7935 8866; Web: www.sherlock-holmes.co.uk
Recreated rooms of the fictional detective
Sir John Soane's Museum, Lincoln's Inn Fields
WC2A 3BP. Tel: 020-7430 0175; Web: www.soane.org
Art and antiques
Theatre Museum, Russell Street WC2.
Tel: 020-7836 2330; Web: www.theatremuseum.org
History of the performing arts
Tower Bridge Experience, SE1. Tel: 020-7403 3761
History of the bridge and display of Victorian steam
machinery; panoramic views from walkways
Victoria and Albert Museum, Cromwell Road SW7 2RL.
Tel: 020-7942 2000; Web: www.varn.ac.uk
Includes National Art Library and Print Room. Fine
and applied art and design, including furniture, glass,
textiles, dress collections
Wellington Museum, Apsley House, W1J 7NT.
Tel: 0207-499 5676.
Wimbledon Lawn Tennis Museum, Church Road
SW19 5AE. Tel: 020-8946 6131.
Tennis trophies, fashion and memorabilia; view of
Centre Court
MANCHESTER – *Gallery of Costume*, Rusholme M14 5LL.
Tel: 0161-224 5217.
Exhibits from the 16th- to 20th-century
Imperial War Museum North, Trafford Wharf Road,
Trafford Park, Manchester M17 1TZ. Tel: 0161-836 4000;
Web: www.iwm.org.uk/north
Manchester Art Gallery, Mosley Street M2 3JL.
Tel: 0161-235 8888; Web: www.manchestergalleries.org
Manchester Museum, Oxford Road M13 9PL. Tel: 0161-
275 2634; Web: www.museum.man.ac.uk
Archaeology, archery, botany, Egyptology, entomology,
ethnography, geology, natural history, numismatics,
oriental and zoology collections
Museum of Science and Industry, Castlefield M3 4SP.
Tel: 0161-832 2244; Web: www.msim.org.uk
On site of world's oldest passenger railway station;
galleries relating to space, energy, power, transport,
aviation, textiles and social history; interactive science
centre
People's History Museum, Pump House, Left Bank
M3 3ER. Tel: 0161-839 6061;
Web: www.peopleshistorymuseum.org.uk
Political and and working life history
Whitworth Art Gallery, Oxford Road M15 6ER.
Tel: 0161-275 7450; Web: www.whitworth.man.ac.uk
Watercolours, drawings, prints, textiles, wallpapers and
20th-century British art
MONKWEARMOUTH – *Monkwearmouth Station Museum*,
North Bridge Street SR5 1AP. Tel: 0191-567 7075.
Victorian train station
NEWCASTLE UPON TYNE – *Hancock Museum*, Barras
Bridge. Tel: 0191-222 7418.
Natural history
Laing Art Gallery, Higham Place NE1 8AG.
Tel: 0191-232 7734.

British and European art, ceramics, glass, silver, textiles
and costume; Art on Tyneside display
Newcastle Discovery Museum, Blandford Square
NE1 4JA. Tel: 0191-232 6789;
Web: www.thenortheast.com/museums/news.htm
Science and industry, local history, fashion and
Tyneside's maritime history; Turbinia (first steam-
driven vessel) gallery
NEWMARKET – *National Horseracing Museum*, High
Street CB8 8JL. Tel: 01638-667333;
Web: www.nhrm.co.uk
The Essential Horse Millennium Exhibition,
horseracing exhibits and tours of local trainers' yards
and studs
NORTHAMPTON – *Central Museum and Art Gallery*,
Guildhall Road NN1 1DP. Tel: 01604-238548;
Web: www.northampton.gov.uk/museums
Boot and shoe collection
NORTH SHIELDS – *Stephenson Railway Museum*, Middle
Engine Lane. Tel: 0191-200 7144.
Locomotive engines and rolling stock
NOTTINGHAM – *Brewhouse Yard Museum*, Castle
Boulevard NG7 1FB. Tel: 0115-915 3600.
Daily life from the 17th- to 20th-century
Castle Museum and Art Gallery NG1 6EL.
Tel: 0115-915 3700.
Paintings, ceramics, silver and glass; history of
Nottingham
Industrial Museum, Wollaton Park. Tel: 0115-915 3910.
Lacemaking machinery, steam engines and transport
exhibits
Museum of Costume and Textiles, Castle Gate NG1 6AF.
Tel: 0115-915 3500.
Costume displays from 1790 to the mid-20th century
in period rooms
Natural History Museum, Wollaton Park.
Tel: 0115-915 3900.
Local natural history and wildlife dioramas
OXFORD – *Ashmolean Museum*, Beaumont Street
OX1 2PH. Tel: 01865-278000;
Web: www.ashmol.ox.ac.uk
European and Oriental fine and applied arts,
archaeology, Egyptology and numismatics
Museum of Modern Art, Pembroke Street OX1 1BP.
Tel: 01865-722733; Web: www.moma.org.uk
Temporary exhibitions
Museum of the History of Science, Broad Street OX1 3AZ.
Tel: 01865-277280; Web: www.mhs.ox.ac.uk
Displays include early scientific instruments, chemical
apparatus, clocks and watches
Oxford University Museum of Natural History, Parks
Road. Tel: 01865-272950; Web: www.oum.ox.ac.uk
Entomology, geology, mineralogy and zoology
Pitt Rivers Museum, South Parks Road OX1 3PP.
Tel: 01865-270927; Web: www.prm.ox.ac.uk
Ethnographic and archaeological artefacts
PLYMOUTH – *City Museum and Art Gallery*, Drake Circus
PL4 8AJ. Tel: 01752-304774;
Web: www.plymouth.gov.co.uk
Local and natural history, ceramics, silver, Old Masters,
temporary exhibitions
The Dome, The Hoe. Tel: 01752-603300.
Maritime history museum
PORTSMOUTH – *Charles Dickens Birthplace Museum*, Old
Commercial Road PO1 4QL. Tel: 023-9282 7261.
Dickens memorabilia
D-Day Museum, Clarence Esplanade PO5 2NT.
Tel: 023-9282 7261;
Web: www.portsmouthmuseums.co.uk
Includes the Overlord Embroidery

Flagship Portsmouth, HM Naval Base. Incorporates the *Royal Naval Museum* (Tel: 023-9272 7562), *HMS Victory* (Tel: 023-9282 2034), *HMS Warrior* (Tel: 023-9229 1379), the *Mary Rose* (Tel: 023-9275 0521) and the *Dockyard Museum*. History of the Royal Navy and of the dockyard and the trades in it

PRESTON – *Harris Museum and Art Gallery*, Market Square PR1 2PP. Tel: 01772-258248;
Web: www.visitpreston.gov
British art since the 18th-century, ceramics, glass, costume and local history; also contemporary exhibitions

READING – *Rural History Museum*, University of Reading, Whiteknights RG6 6AG. Tel: 0118-931 8660; Web: www.ruralhistory.org
History of farming and the countryside over the last 200 years

ST ALBANS – *Verulamium Museum*, St Michael's AL3 4SW. Tel: 01727-751810;
Web: www.stalbansmuseums.org.uk
Iron Age and Roman Verulamium, including wall plasters, jewellery, mosaics and room reconstructions

ST IVES, CORNWALL – *Tate Gallery St Ives*, Porthmeor Beach TR26 1TG. Tel: 01736-796226;
Web: www.tate.org.uk
Painting and sculpture by artists associated with St Ives

SALISBURY - *Salisbury and South Wiltshire Museum*, The Close SP1 2EN Tel: 01722-332151.
Archaeology collection

SHEFFIELD – *City Museum and Mappin Art Gallery*, Weston Park S10 2TP. Tel: 0114-278 2600.
Includes applied arts, natural history, Bronze Age archaeology and ethnography, 19th- and 20th-century art
Graves Art Gallery, Surrey Street. Tel: 0114-273 5158.
Twentieth-century British art, Grice Collection of Chinese ivories
Kelham Island Industrial Museum, off Alma Street. Tel: 0114-272 2106.
Local industrial and social history
Ruskin Gallery and Ruskin Craft Gallery, Norfolk Street LA21 8DU. Tel: 0114-203 9416.

SOUTHAMPTON – *City Art Gallery*, Civic Centre SO14 7LP. Tel: 023-8083 2277;
Web: www.southampton.gov.uk/leisure/arts
Fine art, especially 20th-century British
Maritime Museum, Town Quay SO14 2AR.
Tel: 023-8022 3941. Southampton maritime history
Museum of Archaeology, Town Quay SO14 2NY. Tel: 023-8063 5904.
Roman, Saxon and medieval archaeology
Tudor House Museum and Garden, Bugle Street SO14 2AD. Tel: 023-8033 2513.
Restored 16th- century garden; social history exhibitions

SOUTH SHIELDS – *Arbeia Roman Fort*, Baring Street NE33 2BB. Tel: 0191-456 1369.
Excavated ruins
South Shields Museum and Art Gallery, Ocean Road NE33 2JA. Tel: 0191-456 8740.
South Tyneside history, including reconstructed street

STOKE-ON-TRENT – *Etruria Industrial Museum*, Etruria ST4 7AF. Tel: 01782-233144.
Britain's sole surviving steam-powered potter's mill
Gladstone Pottery Museum, Longton ST3 1PQ.
Tel: 01782-319232; Web: www.stoke.gov.uk/gladstone
A working Victorian pottery
Potteries Museum and Art Gallery, Hanley ST1 3DE.
Tel: 01782-232323;
Web: www.stoke.gov.uk/citymuseum

Pottery, china and porcelain collections and a Mark XVI Spitfire. Pottery factory tours are available by arrangement, at the following: *Royal Doulton*, Burslem; *Spode*, Stoke; *Wedgwood*, Barlaston; *W. Moorcroft*, Cobridge; *H & R Johnson Tiles*, Tunstall; *Staffordshire Enamels*, Longton; *Royale Stratford China*, Fenton

STYAL, Cheshire – *Quarry Bank Mill* FK9 4LA.
Tel: 01625-527468; Web: www.quarrybankmill.org.uk
Working mill illustrating history of cotton industry; costumed guides at restored Apprentice House

SUNDERLAND – *Sunderland Art Gallery*, Sunderland SR1 1PP. Tel: 0191-553 2323.
Fine and decorative art

TELFORD – *Ironbridge Gorge Museums* TF8 7AW.
Tel: 01952-432166; Web: www.ironbridge.org.uk
Includes first iron bridge; Blists Hill (late Victorian working town); Museum of Iron; Jackfield Tile Museum; Coalport China Museum; Tar Tunnel; Broseley Pipeworks

WAKEFIELD – *Yorkshire Sculpture Park*, West Bretton WS4 4Lg. Tel: 01924-830231; Web: www.ysp.co.uk
Open-air sculpture gallery including works by Moore, Hepworth, Frink and others in 300 acres of parkland

WASHINGTON – *Washington 'F' Pit Museum*, Albany Way
Colliery-related collection

WORCESTER – *City Museum and Art Gallery*, Foregate Street WR1 1DT. Tel: 01905-25371.
Includes a military museum, River Severn Gallery and changing art exhibitions
Museum of Worcester Porcelain and Royal Worcester Visitor Centre, Severn Street WR1 2NE.
Tel: 01905-746000; Web: www.royal-worcester.co.uk

WROUGHTON, nr Swindon, Wilts – *Science Museum*, Wroughton Airfield. Tel: 01793-814466.
Aircraft displays and some of the Science Museum's transport and agricultural collection

YEOVIL, Somerset – *Fleet Air Arm Museum*, Royal Naval Air Station, Yeovilton BA22 8HT. Tel: 01935-840565;
Web: www.fleetairarm.com
History of naval aviation; historic aircraft, including Concorde 002

YORK – *Beningbrough Hall*, Shipton-by-Beningbrough YO6 1DD. Tel: 01904-470666.
Portraits from the National Portrait Gallery
Castle Museum, Castle Walk YO1 9RY.
Tel: 01904-653611.
Reconstructed streets; costume and military collections
City Art Gallery, Exhibition Square YO1 7EW.
Tel: 01904-551861; Web: www.york.gov.uk
European and British painting spanning seven centuries; modern pottery
Jorvik – The Viking City, Coppergate YO1 9WT.
Tel: 01904-643211; Web: www.vikingjorvik.com
Reconstruction of Viking York
National Railway Museum, Leeman Road YO2 4XJ.
Tel: 01904-621261; Web: www.nrm.org.uk
Includes locomotives, rolling stock and carriages
Yorkshire Museum, Museum Gardens YO1 7FR.
Tel: 01904-551800; Web: www.york.gov.uk
Yorkshire life from Roman to medieval times; geology gallery

WALES

BODELWYDDAN, Denbighshire – *Bodelwyddan Castle* LL18 5Ya. Tel: 01745-584060.
Portraits from the National Portrait Gallery, furniture from the Victoria and Albert Museum and sculptures from the Royal Academy
CAERLEON – *Roman Legionary Museum.* Tel: 01633-423134.
Material from the site of the Roman fortress of Isca and its suburbs
CARDIFF – *National Museum and Gallery Cardiff,* Cathays Park CF1 3NP. Tel: 029-2039 7951; Web: www.nmgw.ac.uk
Includes natural sciences, archaeology and Impressionist paintings
Museum of Welsh Life, St Fagans CF5 6XB.
Tel: 029-2056 9441; Web: www.nmgw.ac.uk
Open-air museum with re-erected buildings, agricultural equipment and costume
DRE-FACH FELINDRE, nr Llandysul – *Museum of the Welsh Woollen Industry* SA44 5UP. Tel: 01559-370929; Web: www.nmgw.ac.uk
Exhibitions, a working woollen mill and craft workshops
LLANBERIS, nr Caernarfon – *Welsh Slate Museum* LL55 4TY. Tel: 01286-870630; Web: www.nmgw.ac.uk.
Former slate quarry with original machinery and plant; slate crafts demonstrations
LLANDRINDOD WELLS – *National Cycle Collection,* Automobile Palace, Temple Street. Tel: 01597-825531; Web: www.cyclemuseum.org.uk. Over 200 bicycles on display, from 1818 to the present day
SWANSEA – *Glynn Vivian Art Gallery and Museum,* Alexandra Road SA1 5DZ. Tel: 01792-655006.
Paintings, ceramics, Swansea pottery and porcelain, clocks, glass and Welsh art
Swansea Maritime and Industrial Museum, Museum Square SA1 1SN. Tel: 01792-650351.
Includes a working woollen mill and historic boats afloat
Swansea Museum, Victoria Road SA1 1SN.
Tel: 01792-653763; Web: www.swansea.gov.uk
Archaeology, social history, Swansea pottery

SCOTLAND

ABERDEEN – *Aberdeen Art Gallery,* Schoolhill AB10 1FQ.
Tel: 01224-523700; Web: www.aberdeencity.gov.uk.
Art from the 18th- to 20th-century
Aberdeen Maritime Museum, Shiprow AB11 5BY.
Tel: 01224-337700; Web: www.aagm.co.uk
Maritime history, incl. shipbuilding and North Sea oil
EDINBURGH – *Britannia,* Leith docks. Tel: 0131-555 5566; Web: www.royalyachtbritannia.co.uk
Former royal yacht with royal barge and royal family picture gallery. Tickets must be pre-booked
City Art Centre, Market Street EH1 1DE.
Tel: 0131-529 3993.
Late 19th- and 20th-century art and temporary exhibitions
Museum of Childhood, High Street EH1 1TG.
Tel: 0131-529 4142; Web: www.cac.org.uk
Toys, games, clothes and exhibits relating to the social history of childhood
Museum of Edinburgh, Canongate EH8 8DD.
Tel: 0131-529 4143; Web: www.cac.org.uk
Local history, silver, glass and Scottish pottery

Museum of Flight, East Fortune Airfield, nr North Berwick. Tel: 01620-880308.
Display of aircraft
Museum of Scotland, Chambers Street EH1 1JF.
Tel: 0131-247 4422; Web: www.nms.ac.uk
Scottish history from prehistoric times to the present
National Gallery of Scotland, The Mound EH2 2EL.
Tel: 0131-624 6200; Web: www.nationalgalleries.org
Paintings, drawings and prints from the 16th- to 20th-century, and the national collection of Scottish art
The People's Story, Canongate EH8 8BN.
Tel: 0131-529 4057.
Edinburgh life since the 18th-century
Royal Museum of Scotland, Chambers Street EH1 1JF.
Tel: 0131-225 7534; Web: www.nms.ac.uk
Scottish and international collections from prehistoric times to the present
Scottish Agricultural Museum, Ingliston.
Tel: 0131-333 2674.
History of agriculture in Scotland
Scottish National Gallery of Modern Art, Belford Road EH4 3DR. Tel: 0131-624 6200;
Web: www.natgalscot.ac.uk
20th-century painting, sculpture and graphic art
Scottish National Portrait Gallery, Queen Street EH2 1JD.
Tel: 0131-624 6200; Web; www.natgalscot.ac.uk
Portraits of eminent people in Scottish history, and the national collection of photography
The Writers' Museum, Lawnmarket EH1 2PA.
Tel: 0131-529 4901; Web: www.edinburgh.gov.uk
Robert Louis Stevenson, Walter Scott and Robert Burns exhibits
FORT WILLIAM – *West Highland Museum,* Cameron Square PH33 6AJ. Tel: 01397-702169.
Includes tartan collections and exhibits relating to 1745 uprising
GLASGOW – *Burrell Collection,* Pollokshaws Road G43 1AT. Tel: 0141-287 2550.
Paintings, textiles, furniture, ceramics, stained glass and silver from classical times to the 19th-century
Gallery of Modern Art, Queen Street G1 3AZ.
Tel: 0141-229 1996.
Collection of contemporary Scottish and world art
Glasgow Art Gallery and Museum, Kelvingrove G3 8AG.
Tel: 0141-287 2699.
Includes Old Masters, 19th-century French paintings and armour collection
Hunterian Art Gallery, Hillhead Street G12 8QQ.
Tel: 0141-330 4221; Web: www.hunterian.ac.uk
Rennie Mackintosh and Whistler collections; Old Masters, Scottish paintings and modern paintings, sculpture and prints
McLellan Galleries, Sauchiehall Street G2 3EH.
Tel: 0141-331 1854.
Temporary exhibitions
Museum of Transport, Bunhouse Road G3 8DP.
Tel: 0141-287 2720;
Web: www.clyde-valley.com/glasgow/transmus.htm
Includes a reproduction of a 1938 Glasgow street, cars since the 1930s, trams and a Glasgow subway station
People's Palace Museum, Glasgow Green G40 1AT.
Tel: 0141-554 0223; Web: www.glasgow.gov.uk
History of Glasgow since 1175
St Mungo Museum of Religious Life and Art, Castle Street G4 0RH. Tel: 0141-553 2557.
Explores universal themes through objects of all the main world religions

NORTHERN IRELAND

BELFAST – *Ulster Museum*, Botanic Gardens BT9 5AB. Tel: 028-9038 3000; Web: www.ulstermuseum.org.uk
Irish antiquities, natural and local history, fine and applied arts
HOLYWOOD, CO. DOWN – *Ulster Folk and Transport Museum*, Cultra. Tel: 028-9042 8428; Web: www.nidex.com/uftm
Open-air museum with original buildings from Ulster town and rural life c.1900; indoor galleries including Irish rail and road transport and *Titanic* exhibitions

LONDONDERRY – *The Tower Museum*, Union Hall Place P248 6LU. Tel: 028-7137 2411; Web: www.derrycity.gov.uk
Tells the story of Ireland through the history of Londonderry
OMAGH, Co. Tyrone – *Ulster American Folk Park*, Castletown BT78 5QY. Tel: 028-8224 3292; Web: www.folkpark.com
Open-air museum telling the story of Ulster's emigrants to America; restored or recreated dwellings and workshops; ship and dockside gallery

Sights of London

For historic buildings and museums and galleries in London, see Museums and Galleries section.

ALEXANDRA PALACE, Alexandra Palace Way, Wood Green, London N22 7AY. Tel: 020-8365 2121. The Victorian Palace was severely damaged by fire in 1980 but was restored, and reopened in 1988. Alexandra Palace now provides modern facilities for exhibitions, conferences, banquets and leisure activities. There is an ice rink, a boating lake, the Phoenix Bar and a conservation area.

BARBICAN CENTRE, Silk Street, London EC2Y 8DS. Tel: 020-7638 4141. Web: www.barbican.org.uk. Owned, funded and managed by the Corporation of London, the Barbican Centre opened in 1982 and houses the Barbican Theatre, a studio theatre called The Pit, and Barbican Hall. There are also three cinemas, six conference rooms, two art galleries, a sculpture court, a lending library, trade and banqueting facilities, conservatory, shops, restaurants, cafés and bars.

BRIDGES. The bridges over the Thames (from east to west) are:

The Queen Elizabeth II Bridge, opened 1991, from Dartford to Thurrock

Tower Bridge, opened 1894

London Bridge, opened after rebuilding by Rennie, 1831; the new London Bridge opened 1973

Alexandra Bridge (railway bridge), built 1863–6

Southwark Bridge (Rennie), built 1814–19; rebuilt 1912-21

Millennium Bridge, opened June 2000; reopened after modification February 2002

Blackfriars Railway Bridge, completed 1864

Blackfriars Bridge, built 1760–9; rebuilt 1860–9; widened 1907–10

Waterloo Bridge (Rennie), opened 1817; rebuilt 1937–42

Hungerford Footbridge, opened 2002

Hungerford Railway Bridge (Brunel), suspension bridge built 1841–5; replaced by present railway and footbridge 1863

Westminster Bridge (width 84ft), opened 1750; rebuilt 1854–62

Lambeth Bridge, built 1862; rebuilt 1929–32

Vauxhall Bridge, built 1811–16; rebuilt 1895–1906

Grosvenor Bridge (railway bridge), built 1859–60; rebuilt 1963–7

Chelsea Bridge, built 1851–8; replaced by suspension bridge 1934; widened 1937

Albert Bridge, opened 1873; restructured (Bazalgette) 1884; strengthened 1971–3

Battersea Bridge (Holland), opened 1772; rebuilt (Bazalgette) 1890

Battersea Railway Bridge, opened 1863

Wandsworth Bridge, opened 1873; rebuilt 1940

Putney Railway Bridge, opened 1889

Putney Bridge, built 1727–9; rebuilt (Bazalgette) 1882–6; starting point of Oxford and Cambridge Boat Race

Hammersmith Bridge, built 1824–7; rebuilt (Bazalgette) 1883–7; closed in 1997 for safety work

Barnes Railway Bridge (also pedestrian), built 1846–9; restructured 1893

Chiswick Bridge, opened 1933

Kew Railway Bridge, opened 1869

Kew Bridge, built 1758–9; rebuilt and renamed King Edward VII Bridge 1903

Richmond Lock, lock, weir and footbridge opened 1894

Twickenham Bridge, opened 1933

Richmond Railway Bridge, opened 1848; restructured 1906–8

Richmond Bridge, built 1774–7; widened 1937

Teddington Lock, footbridge opened 1889; marks the end of the tidal reach of the Thames

Kingston Bridge, built 1825–8; widened 1914

Hampton Court Bridge, built 1753; replaced by iron bridge 1865; present bridge built 1933

CEMETERIES. *Abney Park*, Stamford Hill, N16 (35 acres), tomb of General Booth, founder of the Salvation Army, and memorials to many Nonconformist divines. *Brompton*, Old Brompton Road, SW10 (40 acres), graves of Sir Henry Cole, Emmeline Pankhurst, John Wisden. *City of London Cemetery and Crematorium*, Aldersbrook Road, E12 (200 acres). Golders Green Crematorium, Hoop Lane, NW11 (12 acres), with Garden of Rest and memorials to many famous men and women. *Hampstead*, Fortune Green Road, NW6 (36 acres), graves of Kate Greenaway, Lord Lister, Marie Lloyd. *Highgate*, Swains Lane, N6 (38 acres), tombs of George Eliot, Faraday and Marx; guided tours only, west side. *Kensal Green*, Harrow Road, W10 (70 acres), tombs of Thackeray, Trollope, Sydney Smith, Wilkie Collins, Tom Hood, George Cruikshank, Leigh Hunt, I. K. Brunel and Charles Kemble. *Churchyard of the former Marylebone Chapel*, Marylebone High Street, W1, Charles Wesley and his son Samuel Wesley buried; chapel demolished in 1949, now Garden of Rest. *Nunhead*, Linden Grove, SE15 (26 acres), closed in 1969, recently restored and opened for burials. *St Marylebone Cemetery and Crematorium*, East End Road, N2 (47 acres). *West Norwood Cemetery and Crematorium*, Norwood High Street, SE27 (42 acres), tombs of Sir Henry Bessemer, Sir Henry Tate and Joseph Whitaker (Whitaker's Almanack).

CENOTAPH, Whitehall, London SW1. The word 'cenotaph' means 'empty tomb'. The monument, erected 'To the Glorious Dead', is a memorial to all ranks of the sea, land and air forces who gave their lives in the service of the Empire during the First World War. Designed by Sir Edwin Lutyens and erected as a temporary memorial in 1919, it was replaced by a permanent structure unveiled by George V on Armistice Day 1920. An additional inscription was made after the Second World War to commemorate those who gave their lives in that conflict.

CHARTERHOUSE, Charterhouse Square, London EC1M 6AN. Tel: 020-7253 9503. A Carthusian monastery from 1371 to 1537, purchased in 1611 by Thomas Sutton, who endowed it as a residence for aged men 'of gentle birth' and a school for poor scholars (removed to Godalming in 1872).

CHELSEA PHYSIC GARDEN, 66 Royal Hospital Road, London SW3 4HS. Tel: 020-7352 5646; Web: www.cpgarden.demon.co.uk. A garden of general botanical research and education, maintaining a wide range of rare and unusual plants. The garden was established in 1673 by the Society of Apothecaries.

DOWNING STREET, London SW1. Number 10 Downing Street is the official town residence of the Prime Minister, No. 11 of the Chancellor of the Exchequer and No. 12 is the office of the Government Whips. The street was named after Sir George Downing, Bt., soldier and diplomatist, who was MP for Morpeth from 1660 to 1684. *Chequers*, a Tudor mansion in the Chilterns near Princes Risborough, was presented by Lord and

Lady Lee of Fareham in 1917 to serve, from 1921, as a country residence for the Prime Minister of the day.
GEORGE INN, Borough High Street, London SE1. The last galleried inn in London, built in 1677. Now run as an ordinary public house.
GREENWICH, London SE10. *The Royal Naval College*, Tel: 020-8269 4791, was until 1873 the Greenwich Hospital. It was built by Charles II, largely from designs by John Webb, and by Queen Mary II and William III, from designs by Wren. It stands on the site of an ancient abbey, a royal house and Greenwich Palace which was constructed by Henry VII. Henry VIII, Mary I and Elizabeth I were born in the royal palace and Edward VI died there. *Greenwich Park* (196.5 acres) was enclosed by Humphrey, Duke of Gloucester, and laid out by Charles II from the designs of Le Nôtre. On a hill in Greenwich Park is the Royal Observatory (founded 1675). Its buildings are now managed by the National Maritime Museum and the earliest building is named Flamsteed House, after John Flamsteed (1646–1719), the first Astronomer Royal. *The Cutty Sark*, the last of the famous tea clippers, has been preserved as a memorial to ships and men of a past era. Sir Francis Chichester's round-the-world yacht, *Gipsy Moth IV*, can also be seen.
HORSE GUARDS, Whitehall, London SW1. Archway and offices built about 1753. The mounting of the guard takes place at 11a.m. (10a.m. on Sundays) and the dismounted inspection at 4p.m. Only those with the Queen's permission may drive through the gates and archway into *Horse Guards' Parade* (230,000 sq. ft), where the Colour is 'trooped' on The Queen's official birthday.
THE HOUSE OF COMMONS, Westminster, London SW1A 2TT. Tel: 020-7219 4272. E-mail: hcinfo@parliament.uk. The royal palace of Westminster, originally built by Edward the Confessor, was the normal meeting place of Parliament from about 1340. St Stephen's Chapel was used from about 1550 for the meetings of the House of Commons, which had previously been held in the Chapter House or Refectory of Westminster Abbey. The House of Lords met in an apartment of the royal palace.
The fire of 1834 destroyed much of the palace and the present Houses of Parliament were erected on the site from the designs of Sir Charles Barry and Augustus Welby Pugin between 1840 and 1867. The chamber of the House of Commons was destroyed by bombing in 1941 and a new Chamber designed by Sir Giles Gilbert Scott was used for the first time in 1950.
Lord Chancellor's Residence, Lord Chancellor's Office, House of Lords, London, SW1A 0PW. Tel: 020-7219 3107.
Westminster Hall and the Crypt Chapel was the only part of the old palace of Westminster to survive the fire of 1834. It was built by William Rufus (1097–9) and altered by Richard II (1394–9). The hammerbeam roof of carved oak dates from 1396–8. The Hall was the scene of the trial of Charles I.
The Victoria Tower of the House of Lords is about 330 ft high, and when Parliament is sitting the Union flag flies by day from its flagstaff. *The Clock Tower* of the House of Commons is about 320 ft high and contains 'Big Ben', the hour bell said to be named after Sir Benjamin Hall, First Commissioner of Works when the original bell was cast in 1856. This bell, which weighed 16 tons 11 cwt, was found to be cracked in 1857. The present bell (13.5 tons) is a recasting of the original and was first brought into use in 1859. The

dials of the clock are 23 ft in diameter, the hands being 9 ft and 14 ft long (including balance piece). A light is displayed from the Clock Tower at night when Parliament is sitting.
For security reasons tours of the Houses of Parliament are available only to those who have made advance arrangements through an MP or peer. The Palace is open during the summer recess for line of route tours which should be booked via Ticketmaster on 020-7344 9966 or www.ticketmaster.co.uk. Tickets are also on sale at the palace.
Admission to the Strangers' Gallery of the House of Lords is arranged by a peer or by queue via St Stephen's Entrance. Admission to the Strangers' Gallery of the House of Commons is by Members' order (Members' orders should be sought several weeks in advance), or by queue via St Stephen's Entrance. The House does not always sit on Fridays. Overseas visitors may write to the Parliamentary Education Unit to obtain a permit to tour the Houses of Parliament, or obtain cards of introduction from their Embassy or High Commission to attend the public gallery.
INNS OF COURT. The *Inner* and *Middle Temple*, Fleet Street/Victoria Embankment, London EC4. Tel: 020-7797 8250. Have occupied since the early 14th-century the site of the buildings of the Order of Knights Templars. *Inner Temple Hall* is open by appointment on application to the Treasury Office. *Middle Temple Hall* (1562–70) is open when not in use. In the Temple Gardens Shakespeare (Henry VI, Part I) places the incident which led to the 'Wars of the Roses' (1455–85).
Temple Church, London EC4. Tel: 020-7353 8559. Has a nave which forms one of five remaining round churches in England. *Master of the Temple*, Revd R. Griffith-Jones.
Lincoln's Inn, Chancery Lane/Lincoln's Inn Fields, London WC2. Tel: 020-7405 1393; Email: mail@lincolninn.org.uk. Occupies the site of the palace of a former Bishop of Chichester and of a Black Friars monastery. The hall and library buildings are of 1845, although the library is first mentioned in 1474; the old hall (late 15th-century) and the chapel were rebuilt c. 1619–23. Halls open by appointment, chapel and gardens, Monday–Friday 12–2.30. Chapel services Sunday 11.30 a.m. during law terms. *Lincoln's Inn Fields* (7 acres). The square was laid out by Inigo Jones.
Gray's Inn, Holborn/Gray's Inn Road, London WC1. Tel: 020-7458 7800. Web: www.graysinn.org.uk. Founded early 14th-century; Hall 1556–8.
No other 'Inns' are active, but there are remains of *Staple Inn*, a gabled front on Holborn (opposite Gray's Inn Road). *Clement's Inn* (near St Clement Danes Church), *Clifford's Inn*, Fleet Street, and *Thavies Inn*, Holborn Circus, are all rebuilt. *Serjeants' Inn*, Fleet Street, and another (demolished 1910) of the same name in Chancery Lane, were composed of Serjeants-at-Law, the last of whom died in 1922.
LLOYD'S, Lime Street, London EC3M 7HA. Tel: 020-7327 1000; E-mail: lloyds-external-enquiries@lloyds.com. Web: www.lloydsoflondon.com; International insurance market which evolved during the 17th-century from Lloyd's Coffee House. The present building was opened for business in May 1986, and houses the Lutine Bell. Underwriting is on three floors with a total area of 114,000 sq. ft.
LONDON EYE, The Thames South Bank. Opened in February 2000 as London's millennium landmark, this 450ft observation wheel is the capital's fourth largest structure. The wheel provides a 30 minute ride offering

spectacular panoramic views of the capital. Tel: 0870 5000 600; Web: www.londoneye.com

LONDON PARKS, ETC.

Royal Parks

Bushy Park (1,099 acres), Middx. Adjoining Hampton Court, contains avenue of horse-chestnuts enclosed in a fourfold avenue of limes planted by William III. 'Chestnut Sunday' (when the trees are in full bloom with their 'candles') is usually about 1 to 15 May.

Green Park (53 acres), London W1. Between Piccadilly and St James's Park, with Constitution Hill leading to Hyde Park Corner.

Greenwich Park (183.5 acres), London SE10

Hyde Park (350 acres), London W1/W2. From Park Lane to Kensington Gardens, containing the Serpentine. Fine gateway at Hyde Park Corner, with Apsley House, the Achilles Statue, Rotten Row and the Ladies' Mile. To the north-east is the Marble Arch, originally erected by George IV at the entrance to Buckingham Palace and re-erected in the present position in 1851.

Kensington Gardens (275 acres), London W2/W8. From the western boundary of Hyde Park to Kensington Palace, containing the Albert Memorial and Peter Pan statue.

Kew, Royal Botanic Gardens

Regent's Park and Primrose Hill (472 acres), London NW1. From Marylebone Road to Primrose Hill surrounded by the Outer Circle and divided by the Broad Walk leading to the Zoological Gardens.

Richmond Park (2,500 acres), Middx

St. James's Park (93 acres), London SW1. From Whitehall to Buckingham Palace. Ornamental lake of 12 acres. The original suspension bridge built in 1857 was replaced in 1957. The Mall leads from the Admiralty Arch to Buckingham Palace, Birdcage Walk from Storey's Gate to Buckingham Palace. Maintained by the Royal Parks Agency.

Hampton Court Gardens (54 acres), Middx

Hampton Court Green (17 acres), Middx

Hampton Court Park (622 acres), Middx

CORPORATION OF LONDON OPEN SPACES

Ashtead Common (500 acres), Surrey

Burnham Beeches and Fleet Wood (540 acres), Bucks. Purchased by the Corporation for the benefit of the public in 1880, Fleet Wood (65 acres) being presented in 1921.

Coulsdon Common (133 acres), Surrey

Epping Forest (6,000 acres), Essex. Purchased by the Corporation and opened to the public in 1882. The present forest is 12 miles long by 1 to 2 miles wide, about one-tenth of its original area.

Farthing Downs (121 acres), Surrey

Hampstead Heath (789 acres), London NW3. Including Golders Hill (36 acres) and Parliament Hill (271 acres)

Highgate Wood (70 acres), London N6/N10

Kenley Common (138 acres), Surrey

Queen's Park (30 acres), London NW6

Riddlesdown (90 acres), Surrey

Spring Park (51 acres), Kent

West Ham Park (77 acres), London E15

West Wickham Common (25 acres), Kent

Woodredon and Warlies Park Estate (740 acres), Waltham Abbey.

Also many smaller open spaces within the City of London, including Finsbury Circus Gardens.

LONDON PLANETARIUM, Marylebone Road, London NW1 5LR. Tel: 0890 4003000. Star show and interactive exhibits.

LONDON ZOO, Regent's Park, London NW1. Tel: 020-7722 3333. Opened in 1826.

MADAME TUSSAUD'S, Marylebone Road, London NW1 5LR. Tel: 0870-400 3000. Web: www.madame-tussauds.com Waxwork exhibition.

MARKETS. The London markets are mostly administered by the Corporation of London. *Billingsgate* (fish), Thames Street site dating from 1875, a market site for over 1,000 years, moved to the Isle of Dogs in 1982. *Borough*, SE1 (vegetables, fruit, flowers, etc.), established on present site 1756, privately owned and run. *Covent Garden* (vegetables, fruit, flowers, etc.), established in 1661 under a charter of Charles II, moved in 1973 to Nine Elms. *Leadenhall*, EC3 (meat, poultry, fish, etc.), built 1881, part recently demolished. *London Fruit Exchange*, Brushfield Street, built by Corporation of London 1928–9 as buildings for Spitalfields market; not connected with the market since it moved in 1991. *Petticoat Lane*, Middlesex Street, E1, a market has existed on the site for over 500 years, now a Sunday morning market selling almost anything. *Portobello Road*, W11, originally for herbs and horse-trading from 1870; became famous for antiques after the closure of the Caledonian Market in 1948. *Smithfield, Central Meat, Fish, Fruit, Vegetable and Poultry Markets*, built 1851–66, the site of St Bartholomew's Fair from 12th- to 19th-century, new hall built 1963, market refurbished 1993–4. *Spitalfields*, E1 (vegetables, fruit, etc.), established 1682, modernised 1928, moved to Leyton in 1991. A much smaller market still exists on the original site on Commercial Street, selling arts, crafts, books, clothes and antiques on Sundays.

MARLBOROUGH HOUSE, Pall Mall, London SW1A 5HX. Tel: 020-7839 3411. E-mail: info@commonwealth.int. Web: www.thecommonwealth.org. Built by Wren for the first Duke of Marlborough and completed in 1711, the house reverted to the Crown in 1835. In 1863 it became the London house of the Prince of Wales and was the London home of Queen Mary until her death in 1953. In 1959 Marlborough House was given by The Queen as the headquarters for the Commonwealth Secretariat and it was opened as such in 1965. The Queen's Chapel, Marlborough Gate was begun in 1623 from the designs of Inigo Jones for the Infanta Maria of Spain, and completed for Queen Henrietta Maria.

LONDON MONUMENT (commonly called The Monument), Monument Street, London EC3. Built from designs of Wren, 1671–7, to commemorate the Great Fire of London, which broke out in Pudding Lane on 2 September 1666. The fluted Doric column is 120 ft high; the moulded cylinder above the balcony supporting a flaming vase of gilt bronze is an additional 42 ft; and the column is based on a square plinth 40 ft high (with fine carvings on the west face) making a total height of 202 ft. Splendid views of London from gallery at top of column (311 steps).

MONUMENTS (sculptor's name in parenthesis). *Albert Memorial* (Durham), Kensington Gore; *Royal Air Force* (Blomfield), Victoria Embankment; *Viscount Alanbrooke*, Whitehall; *Beaconsfield*, Parliament Square; *Beatty* (Macmillan), Trafalgar Square; *Belgian Gratitude* (setting by Blomfield, statue by Rousseau), Victoria Embankment; *Boadicea* (or Boudicca), Queen of the Iceni (Thornycroft), Westminster Bridge; *Brunel* (Marochetti), Victoria Embankment; *Burghers of Calais* (Rodin), Victoria Tower Gardens, Westminster; *Burns* (Steel), Embankment Gardens; *Canada*

Memorial (Granche), Green Park; *Carlyle* (Boehm), Chelsea Embankment; *Cavalry* (Jones), Hyde Park; *Edith Cavell* (Frampton), St Martin's Place; *Cenotaph* (Lutyens), Whitehall; *Charles I* (Le Sueur), Trafalgar Square; *Charles II* (Gibbons), South Court, Chelsea Hospital; *Churchill* (Roberts-Jones), Parliament Square; *Cleopatra's Needle* (68.5 ft high, c.1500 BC, erected on the Thames Embankment in 1877–8; the sphinxes are Victorian); *Clive* (Tweed), King Charles Street; *Captain Cook* (Brock), The Mall; *Crimean*, Broad Sanctuary; *Oliver Cromwell* (Thornycroft), outside Westminster Hall; *Cunningham* (Belsky), Trafalgar Square; *Gen. Charles de Gaulle*, Carlton Gardens; *Lord Dowding* (Faith Winter), Strand; *Duke of Cambridge* (Jones), Whitehall; *Duke of York* (124 ft), Carlton House Terrace; *Edward VII* (Mackennal), Waterloo Place; *Elizabeth I* (1586, oldest outdoor statue in London; from Ludgate), Fleet Street; *Eros* (Shaftesbury Memorial) (Gilbert), Piccadilly Circus; *Marechal Foch* (Mallisard, copy of one in Cassel, France), Grosvenor Gardens; *Charles James Fox* (Westmacott), Bloomsbury Square; *George III* (Cotes Wyatt), Cockspur Street; *George IV* (Chantrey), riding without stirrups, Trafalgar Square; *George V* (Reid Dick), Old Palace Yard; *George VI* (Macmillan), Carlton Gardens; *Gladstone* (Thornycroft), Strand; *Guards'* (Crimea) (Bell), Waterloo Place; (Great War) (Ledward, figures, Bradshaw, cenotaph), Horse Guards' Parade; *Haig* (Hardiman), Whitehall; *Sir Arthur (Bomber) Harris* (Faith Winter), Strand; *Irving* (Brock), north side of National Portrait Gallery; *James II* (Gibbons and/or pupils), Trafalgar Square; *Jellicoe* (Wheeler), Trafalgar Square; *Samuel Johnson* (Fitzgerald), opposite St Clement Danes; *Kitchener* (Tweed), Horse Guards' Parade; *Abraham Lincoln* (Saint-Gaudens, copy of one in Chicago), Parliament Square; *Milton* (Montford), St Giles, Cripplegate; *The Monument* (see above); *Mountbatten*, Foreign Office Green; *Nelson* (170 ft 2 in), Trafalgar Square, with Landseer's lions (cast from guns recovered from the wreck of the *Royal George*); *Florence Nightingale* (Walker), Waterloo Place; *Palmerston* (Woolner), Parliament Square; *Peel* (Noble), Parliament Square; *Pitt* (Chantrey), Hanover Square; *Portal* (Nemon), Embankment Gardens; *Prince Consort* (Bacon), Holborn Circus; *Queen Elizabeth Gate*, Hyde Park Corner; *Raleigh* (Macmillan), Whitehall; *Richard I (Coeur de Lion)* (Marochetti), Old Palace Yard; *Roberts* (Bates), Horse Guards' Parade; *Franklin D. Roosevelt* (Reid Dick), Grosvenor Square; *Royal Artillery* (South Africa) (Colton), The Mall; (Great War), Hyde Park Corner; *Captain Scott* (Lady Scott), Waterloo Place; *Shackleton* (Sarjeant Jagger), Kensington Gore; *Shakespeare* (Fontana, copy of one by Scheemakers in Westminster Abbey), Leicester Square; *Smuts* (Epstein), Parliament Square; *Sullivan* (Goscombe John), Victoria Embankment; *Trenchard* (Macmillan), Victoria Embankment; *Victoria Memorial*, in front of Buckingham Palace; *Raoul Wallenberg* (Phillip Jackson), Great Cumberland Place; *George Washington* (Houdon copy), Trafalgar Square; *Wellington* (Boehm), Hyde Park Corner, (Chantrey) riding without stirrups, outside Royal Exchange; *John Wesley* (Adams Acton), City Road; *William III* (Bacon), St James's Square; *Wolseley* (Goscombe John), Horse Guards' Parade.

PORT OF LONDON. Port of London Authority, Bakers' Hall, 7 Harp Lane, London EC3R 6LB. Tel: 020-7743 7900. The Port of London covers the tidal section of the River Thames from Teddington to the seaward limit (the outer Tongue buoy and the Sunk light vessel), a distance of 150km. The governing body is the Port of London Authority (PLA). Cargo is handled at privately operated riverside terminals between Fulham and Canvey Island, including the enclosed dock at Tilbury, 40km below London Bridge. Passenger vessels and cruise liners can be handled at moorings at Greenwich, Tower Bridge and Tilbury.

ROMAN REMAINS. The city wall of Roman *Londinium* was largely rebuilt during the medieval period but sections may be seen near the White Tower in the Tower of London; at Tower Hill; at Coopers' Row; at All Hallows, London Wall, its vestry being built on the remains of a semi-circular Roman bastion; at St Alphage, London Wall, showing a succession of building repairs from the Roman until the late medieval period; and at St Giles, Cripplegate. Sections of the great forum and basilica, more than 165 m^2, have been encountered during excavations in the area of Leadenhall, Gracechurch Street and Lombard Street. Traces of Roman activity along the river include a massive riverside wall built in the late Roman period, and a succession of Roman timber quays along Lower and Upper Thames Street. Finds from these sites can be seen at the Museum of London.

Other major buildings are the amphitheatre at Guildhall; remains of bath-buildings in Upper and Lower Thames Street; and the temple of Mithras in Walbrook.

ROYAL ALBERT HALL, Kensington Gore, London SW7 2AP. Tel: 020-7589 3203.
E-mail: sales@royalalberthall.com.
Web: www.royalalberthall.com. The elliptical hall, one of the largest in the world, was completed in 1871, and since 1941 has been the venue each summer for the Promenade Concerts founded in 1895 by Sir Henry Wood. Other events include pop and classical music concerts, dance, opera, sporting events, conferences and banquets.

ROYAL HOSPITAL CHELSEA, Royal Hospital Road, London SW3 4SR. Tel: 020-7881 5204. Web: www.chelseapensioner.org.uk. Founded by Charles II in 1682, and built by Wren; opened in 1692 for old and disabled soldiers. The extensive grounds include the former Ranelagh Gardens and are the venue for the Chelsea Flower Show each May. Governor, Gen. Sir Jeremy Mackenzie, GCB, OBE.

ROYAL OPERA HOUSE, Covent Garden, London WC2E 9DD. Tel: Information line and box office 020-7304 4000. Home of The Royal Ballet (1931) and The Royal Opera (1946). The Royal Opera House is the third theatre to be built on the site, opening 1858; the first was opened in 1732.

ST JAMES'S PALACE, Pall Mall, London SW1A 1BP. Tel: 020-7930 4832. Web: www.royal.gov.uk. Built by Henry VIII; the Gatehouse and Presence Chamber remain; later alterations were made by Wren and Kent. Representatives of foreign powers are still accredited 'to the Court of St James's'. *Clarence House* (1825) in the palace precinct was the home of The Queen Mother.

ST PAUL'S CATHEDRAL, St Paul's Churchyard, London EC4M 8AD. Tel: 020-7246 8348.
E-mail: chapterhouse@stpaulscathedral.org.uk.
Web: www.stpauls.co.uk Built 1675–1710, cost £747,660. The cross on the dome is 365 ft above the ground level, the inner cupola 218 ft above the floor. 'Great Paul' in the south-west tower weighs nearly 17 tons. The organ by Father Smith (enlarged by Willis and rebuilt by Mander) is in a case carved by Grinling Gibbons, who also carved the choir stalls.

SOMERSET HOUSE, Strand and Victoria Embankment, London WC2. The river façade (600 ft long) was built in 1776–86 from the designs of Sir William Chambers; the eastern extension, which houses part of King's College, was built by Smirke in 1829. Somerset House was the property of Lord Protector Somerset, at whose attainder in 1552 the palace passed to the Crown, and it was a royal residence until 1692. Somerset House has recently undergone extensive renovation and is home to the Gilbert Collection, Hermitage Rooms and the Courtauld Institute Gallery.

SOUTH BANK, London SE1. Tel: 020-7960 4242. E-mail: boxoffice@rfh.org.uk. Web: www.rfh.org.uk. The arts complex on the south bank of the River Thames which consists of the *Royal Festival Hall* (opened in 1951 for the Festival of Britain), the adjacent 1,056-seat *Queen Elizabeth Hall*, the *Purcell Room*, and the *Voice Box*.

The *National Film Theatre* (Opened 1952) Tel: 020-7928 3232. Web: www.bfi.org.uk/nft. Administered by the British Film Institute, has three auditoria showing over 2,000 films a year. The London Film Festival is held here every November. There is also an IMAX cinema with 500 seats.

The *Royal National Theatre* Tel: 020-7452 3000. Web: www.nationaltheatre.org.uk. Opened in 1976 and stages classical, modern, new and neglected plays in its three auditoria: the Olivier theatre, the Lyttelton theatre and the Cottesloe theatre.

SOUTHWARK CATHEDRAL, London SE1 9DA. Tel: 020-7367 6700. E-mail: cathedral@dswark.org.uk. Web: www.dswark.org. Mainly 13th-century, but the nave is largely rebuilt. The tomb of John Gower (1330–1408) is between the Bunyan and Chaucer memorial windows in the north aisle; Shakespeare's effigy, backed by a view of Southwark and the Globe Theatre, is in the south aisle; the tomb of Bishop Andrewes (died 1626) is near the screen. The lady chapel was the scene of the consistory courts of the reign of Mary (Gardiner and Bonner) and is still used as a consistory court. John Harvard, after whom Harvard University is named, was baptised here in 1607, and the chapel by the north choir aisle is his memorial chapel.

THAMES EMBANKMENTS. The *Victoria Embankment*, on the north side from Westminster to Blackfriars, was constructed by Sir Joseph Bazalgette (1819–91) for the Metropolitan Board of Works, 1864–70; the seats, of which the supports of some are a kneeling camel, laden with spicery, and of others a winged sphinx, were presented by the Grocers' Company and by W. H. Smith, MP, in 1874; the *Albert Embankment*, on the south side from Westminster Bridge to Vauxhall, 1866–9; the *Chelsea Embankment*, 1871–4. The total cost exceeded £2,000,000. Bazalgette also inaugurated the London main drainage system, 1858–65. A medallion (*Flumini vincula posuit*) has been placed on a pier of the Victoria Embankment to commemorate the engineer.

THAMES FLOOD BARRIER. Officially opened in May 1984, though first used in February 1983, the barrier consists of ten rising sector gates which span 570 yards from bank to bank of the Thames at Woolwich Reach. When not in use the gates lie horizontally, allowing shipping to navigate the river normally; when the barrier is closed, the gates turn through 90 degrees to stand vertically more than 50 feet above the river bed. The barrier took eight years to complete and can be raised within about 30 minutes.

THAMES TUNNELS. The *Rotherhithe Tunnel*, opened 1908, connects Commercial Road, London E14, with Lower Road, Rotherhithe SE16; it is 1 mile 332 yards long, of which 525 yards are under the river. The first *Blackwall Tunnel* (northbound vehicles only), opened 1897, connects East India Dock Road, Poplar, with Blackwall Lane, East Greenwich. The height restriction on the northbound tunnel is 13ft 4in. A second tunnel (for southbound vehicles only) opened 1967. The lengths of the tunnels measured from East India Dock Road to the Gate House on the south side are 6,215 ft (old tunnel) and 6,152 ft. *Greenwich Tunnel* (pedestrians only), opened 1902, connects the Isle of Dogs, Poplar, with Greenwich; it is 406 yards long. The *Woolwich Tunnel* (pedestrians only), opened 1912, connects North and South Woolwich below the passenger and vehicular ferry from North Woolwich Station, London E16, to High Street, Woolwich, London SE18; it is 552 yards long.

WALTHAM CROSS, Herts. At Waltham Cross is one of the crosses (partly restored) erected by Edward I to mark a resting place of the corpse of Queen Eleanor on its way to Westminster Abbey. Ten crosses were erected, but only those at Geddington, Northampton and Waltham survive; 'Charing' Cross originally stood near the spot now occupied by the statue of Charles I at Whitehall.

WESTMINSTER ABBEY, Broad Sanctuary, London, SW1P. Tel: 0207-7222 5152. E-mail: info@westminster-abbey.org. Web: www.westminster-abbey.org. Founded as a Benedictine monastery over 1,000 years ago, the Church was rebuilt by Edward the Confessor in 1065 and again by Henry III in the 13th-century. The Abbey is the resting place for monarchs including Edward I, Henry III, Henry V, Henry VII, Elizabeth I, Mary I and Mary Queen of Scots, and has been the setting of coronations since that of William the Conqueror in 1066. In Poets' Corner there are memorials to many literary figures, and many scientists and musicians are also remembered here. The grave of the Unknown Warrior is to be found in the nave.

WESTMINSTER CATHEDRAL, Ashley Place, London SW1P 1QW. Tel: 020-7798 9055.
Web: www.westminstercathedral.org.uk
Roman Catholic cathedral built 1895–1903 from the designs of J. F. Bentley. The campanile is 283 feet high.

LONDON TOURIST BOARD AND CONVENTION BUREAU, 1 Warwick Row, London, SW1E 5ER. Tel: Tourist information (60p per minute): 09068 66 33 44. Web: www.londontouristboard.com

Hallmarks

Hallmarks are the symbols stamped on gold, silver or platinum articles to indicate that they have been tested at an official Assay Office and that they conform to one of the legal standards. With certain exceptions, all gold, silver or platinum articles are required by law to be hallmarked before they are offered for sale. Hallmarking was instituted in England in 1300 under a statute of Edward I.

MODERN HALLMARKS

Since 1 January 1999, UK hallmarks have consisted of three compulsory symbols – the sponsor's mark, the fineness (standard) mark and the assay office mark. Traditional marks such as the year date letter, the Britannia for 958 silver, the lion passant for 925 silver (lion rampant in Scotland) and the orb for 950 platinum may be added voluntarily. The distinction between UK and foreign articles has been removed, and more finenesses are now legal, reflecting the more common finenesses elsewhere in Europe.

SPONSOR'S MARK

Instituted in England in 1363, the sponsor's mark was originally a device such as a bird or fleur-de-lis. Now it consists of the initial letters of the name or names of the manufacturer or firm. Where two or more sponsors have the same initials, there is a variation in the surrounding shield or style of letters.

FINENESS (STANDARD) MARK

The fineness (standard) mark indicates that the content of the precious metal in the alloy from which the article is made, is not less than the legal standard. The legal standard is the minimum content of precious metal by weight in parts per thousand, and the standards are:

Gold	999	
	990	
	916.6	(22 carat)
	750	(18 carat)
	585	(14 carat)
	375	(9 carat)
Silver	999	
	958.4	(Britannia)
	925	(sterling)
	800	
Platinum	999	
	950	
	900	
	850	

ASSAY OFFICE MARK

This mark identifies the particular assay office at which the article was tested and marked. The British assay offices are:

LONDON, Goldsmiths' Hall, London EC2V 8AQ. Tel: 020-7606 8971

BIRMINGHAM, Newhall Street, Birmingham B3 1SB. Tel: 0121-236 6951; Web: www.theassayoffice.co.uk

SHEFFIELD, 137 Portobello Street, Sheffield S1 4DS. Tel: 0114-275 5111; Web: www.assayoffice.co.uk

EDINBURGH, 24a Broughton Street, Edinburgh EH1 3RH. Tel: 0131-556 1144; Web: www.assayofficescotland.com

Assay offices formerly existed in other towns, e.g. Chester, Exeter, Glasgow, Newcastle, Norwich and York, each having its own distinguishing mark.

DATE LETTER

The date letter shows the year in which an article was assayed and hallmarked. Each alphabetical cycle has a distinctive style of lettering or shape of shield. The date letters were different at the various assay offices and the particular office must be established from the assay office mark before reference is made to tables of date letters. Date letter marks became voluntary from 1 January 1999.

The table below shows specimen shields and letters used by the London Assay Office on silver articles in each period from 1498. The same letters are found on gold articles but the surrounding shield may differ. Since 1 January 1975, each office has used the same style of date letter and shield for all articles.

OTHER MARKS

FOREIGN GOODS

Foreign goods imported into the UK are required to be hallmarked before sale, unless they already bear a convention mark (see below) or a hallmark struck by an independent assay office in the European Economic Area which is deemed to be equivalent to a UK hallmark.

The following are the assay office marks used for gold until the end of 1998. For silver and platinum the symbols remain the same but the shields differ in shape.

 London

 Birmingham

 Sheffield

 Edinburgh

CONVENTION HALLMARKS

Special marks at authorised assay offices of the signatory countries of the International Convention on Hallmarking (Austria, the Czech Republic, Denmark, Finland, Ireland, the Netherlands, Norway, Portugal, Sweden, Switzerland and the UK) are legally recognised in the United Kingdom as approved hallmarks. These consist of a sponsor's mark, a common control mark, a fineness mark (arabic numerals showing the standard in parts per thousand), and an assay office mark. There is no date letter.

The fineness marks are:

Gold	999	
	990	(22 carat)
	916	(18 carat)
	750	(14 carat)
	585	(9 carat)
	375	
Silver	999	
	925	(sterling)
	800	
Platinum	999	
	950	
	900	
	850	

The common control marks are:

Gold (18 carat)

Silver

Platinum

COMMEMORATIVE MARKS

There are three other marks to commemorate special events: the silver jubilee of King George V and Queen Mary in 1935, the coronation of Queen Elizabeth II in 1953, and her silver jubilee in 1977. During 1999 and 2000 there was a voluntary additional Millennium Mark.

A new mark to commemorate the golden jubilee of Queen Elizabeth II was available during 2002.

LONDON (GOLDSMITHS' HALL) DATE LETTERS FROM 1498

Black letter, small	1498–9	1517–8
Lombardic	1518–9	1537–8
Roman and other capitals	1538–9	1557–8
Black letter, small	1558–9	1577–8
Roman letter, capitals	1578–9	1597–8

Lombardic, external cusps	1598–9	1617–8
Italic letter, small	1618–9	1637–8
Court hand	1638–9	1657–8
Black letter, capitals	1658–9	1677–8
Black letter, small	1678–9	1696–7
Court hand	1697	1715–6
Roman letter, capitals	1716–7	1735–6
Roman letter, small	1736–7	1738–9
Roman letter, small	1739–40	1755–6
Old English, capitals	1756–7	1775–6
Roman letter, small	1776–7	1795–6
Roman letter, capitals	1796–7	1815–6
Roman letter, small	1816–7	1835–6
Old English, capitals	1836–7	1855–6
Old English, small	1856–7	1875–6
Roman letter, capitals [A to M square shield N to Z as shown]	1876–7	1895–6
Roman letter, small	1896–7	1915–6
Black letter, small	1916–7	1935–6
Roman letter, capitals	1936–7	1955–6
Italic letter, small	1956–7	1974
Italic letter, capitals	1975	

Economic Statistics

The Budget 2002

GOVERNMENT RECEIPTS *£ billion*

	Outturn 2000–2001	Outturn 2001–2002	Projection 2002–2003
Inland Revenue			
Income tax (gross of tax credits)	106.0	110.2	117.5
Corporation tax[1]	32.4	32.4	33.2
Tax credits[2]	−1.2	−2.6	−3.9
Petroleum revenue tax	1.5	1.3	1.4
Capital gains tax	3.2	2.9	1.8
Inheritance tax	2.2	2.3	2.5
Stamp duties	8.2	7.1	8.2
Customs and Excise			
Value added tax	58.5	61.1	63.9
Fuel duties	22.6	21.9	23.1
Tobacco duties	7.6	7.8	7.7
Spirits duties	1.8	1.9	2.0
Wine duties	1.8	2.0	2.2
Beer and cider duties	3.0	3.1	3.1
Betting and gaming duties	1.5	1.4	1.3
Air passenger duty	1.0	0.8	0.8
Insurance premium tax	1.7	1.9	1.9
Landfill tax	0.5	0.5	0.5
Climate change levy	0.0	0.6	0.9
Aggregates levy	0.0	0.0	0.2
Customs duties and levies	2.1	2.0	2.1
Vehicle excise duties	4.3	4.4	4.5
Oil royalties	0.6	0.6	0.5
Business rates[3]	17.3	18.2	18.5
Social security contributions	60.6	63.2	65.0
Council tax	14.2	14.9	16.1
Other taxes and royalties[4]	9.0	10.6	10.7
Net taxes and social security contributions[5]	360.4	370.3	385.6
Interest and dividends	5.8	4.2	4.2
Accrual adjustments on taxes	2.8	0.9	0.8
Less own resources contribution to EU budget	−6.3	−6.1	−5.4
Less PC corporation tax payments	−0.1	−0.1	−0.2
Tax credits[6]	1.2	1.2	1.6
Other receipts[7]	19.4	20.4	20.6
CURRENT RECEIPTS	383.0	390.8	407.2
North Sea revenues[8]	4.3	5.2	5.3

[1] National Accounts measure gross of enhanced and payable tax credits.
[2] Personal tax credits scored as negative tax under OECD rules, plus enhanced and payable company tax credits (zero in 2000-2001, £50 million in 2001-2002 and £350 million in 2002-2003).
[3] Includes district council rates in Northern Ireland paid by business.
[4] Includes money paid into the National Lottery Distribution Fund.
[5] Includes VAT and 'traditional own resources' contributions to EC budget.
[6] Tax credits scored as expenditure in the National Accounts but negative tax in net taxes and social security contributions.
[7] Includes gross operating surplus and rent; net of oil royalties.
[8] Consists of North Sea corporation tax (before ACT set-off), petroleum revenue tax and royalties.
Source: The Stationery Office – Budget 2002 (Crown Copyright).

GOVERNMENT EXPENDITURE

The Economic and Fiscal Strategy Report in June 1998 introduced changes to the public expenditure control regime. Three-year departmental expenditure limits (DELs) now apply to most government departments. Spending which cannot easily be subject to three-year planning is reviewed annually in the Budget as annually managed expenditure (AME). Current and capital expenditure are treated separately.

DEPARTMENTAL EXPENDITURE LIMITS
RESOURCE AND CAPITAL BUDGETS *£ billion*

	Outturn 2000–2001	Estimate 2001–2002	Plans 2002–2003
RESOURCE BUDGET			
Education and Skills	14.3	17.0	20.2
Health	43.6	48.8	53.4
of which NHS	42.7	47.7	51.2
Transport and the Regions	3.7	4.2	5.2
Local Government	35.3	36.9	37.4
Home Office	8.4	9.6	9.4
Lord Chancellor's Departments	2.5	2.9	2.7
Attorney General's Departments	0.4	0.4	0.4
Defence	19.2	18.9	18.9
Foreign and Commonwealth Office	1.2	1.3	1.3
International Development	2.4	2.8	2.9
Trade and Industry	3.0	3.9	3.7
Environment, Food and Rural Affairs	1.5	2.4	1.7
Culture, Media and Sport	0.9	0.9	1.2
Work and Pensions[1] (administration)	5.9	6.3	6.9
Scotland[2]	12.6	14.2	15.3
Wales[2]	6.8	7.7	8.2
Northern Ireland Executive[2]	4.4	5.2	5.2
Northern Ireland Office	0.9	1.1	1.1
Chancellor of the Exchequer's departments	3.5	3.9	4.0
Cabinet Office	1.2	1.4	1.4

Invest to Save budget	0	0	0
Capital Modernisation Fund	0	0	0
Policy Innovation Fund	0	0	0
Reserve	0	0	0.7
Allowance for shortfall	0	−2.0	0
TOTAL RESOURCE BUDGET	171.8	187.8	201.2
CAPITAL BUDGET			
Education and Skills	1.6	2.5	3.0
Health	1.3	1.9	2.4
of which NHS	*1.3*	*1.8*	*2.3*
Transport and the Regions	6.0	6.8	8.5
Local Government	0.1	0.1	0.3
Home Office	0.5	0.9	0.9
Lord Chancellor's Departments	0.1	0.1	0.1
Attorney General's Departments	0	0	0.0
Defence	5.7	5.6	5.7
Foreign and Commonwealth Office	0.1	0.1	0.1
International Development	0.2	0.3	0.4
Trade and Industry[3]	0.3	0.6	0.8
Environment, Food and Rural Affairs	0.3	0.5	0.5
Culture, Media and Sport	0.0	0	0.1
Work and Pensions (administration)[1]	0.8	0.2	0.1
Scotland[2]	2.0	2.3	2.4
Wales[2]	0.8	0.9	1.1
Northern Ireland Executive[2]	0.6	0.8	0.6
Northern Ireland Office	0.0	0.1	0.1
Chancellor of the Exchequer's departments	−0.2	0.2	0.2
Cabinet Office	0.2	0.2	0.2
Invest to Save budget	0	0	0.0
Capital Modernisation Fund	0	0	0.9
Policy Innovation Fund	0	0	0.0
Reserve	0	0	0.0
Allowance for shortfall	0	0	0.0
TOTAL CAPITAL BUDGET DEL	20.6	24.0	28.3
TOTAL DEPARTMENTAL EXPENDITURE LIMITS	192.3	211.8	229.5

[1] Includes Welfare to Work expenditure financed by the Windfall Tax.
[2] For Scotland, Wales and Northern Ireland, the split between current and capital budgets is decided by the respective executives.
[3] Includes the capital expenditure of the Export Credits Guarantee Department.
Source: The Stationery Office – *Budget 2002* (Crown Copyright).

ANNUALLY MANAGED EXPENDITURE

(FORECASTS)   *£ billion*

	2000–2001	2001–2002	2002–2003
Departmental expenditure limits	194.2	212.3	228.5
Social security benefits	99.1	104.9	108.6
Housing revenue account subsidies	3.2	4.6	4.3
Common agricultural policy	2.7	2.6	2.7
Export Credits Guarantee Department	1.1	0.8	0.4
Net payment to EC institution	3.5	2.7	2.6
Self-financing public corporations	1.4	1.1	1.2
Locally financed expenditure	17.8	19.1	20.1
Net public service pensions	5.4	5.6	5.6
National Lottery	2.0	2.3	2.2
Central government gross debt interest	26.6	23.1	24.2
Accounting and other adjustments	−12.2	−8.7	−8.8
Annually managed expenditure	174.0	181.4	189.2

Source: The Stationery Office – *Budget 2002* (Crown Copyright).

SUMMARY OF LOCAL AUTHORITY 2000/2001 BUDGETS (OUTTURN PRICES) AND 2001/02 BUDGETS (OUTTURN PRICES)   *£ billion*

	Budget Estimates 2000/01	Budget Estimates 2001/02	Change %
	£m	£m	
Total Service Expenditure	57,943	62,142	7.2
Mandatory Student Awards, Rent Allowances, Levies & Other Adjustments	7,025	6,945	(1.1)
Net Current Expenditure	64,968	69,087	6.3
Capital Financing, Interest Receipts, Dividends and Other Items	4,627	4,691	1.4
Gross Revenue Expenditure	69,595	73,778	6.0
Funded By:			
Specific Grants outside Aggregate External Finance	(8,889)	(8,577)	(3.5)
Specific Grants inside Aggregate External Finance	(3,748)	(5,527)	47.5
Net Revenue Expenditure (all services)	56,958	59,674	4.8
Met From:			
Reserves	(592)	(572)	(3.4)
Budget Requirement	56,366	59,102	4.9
SSA Reduction Grant/Council Tax Reduction Grant	(35)	(6)	(82.9)

Police Grant	(3,813)	(3,993)	4.7
Revenue Support Grant	(21,468)	(23,240)	8.3
Central Support Protection Grant	(34)	(1)	(97.1)
Council Tax Benefit Subsidy Limitation Scheme	51	83	62.7
National Non-Domestic Rates	(16,042)	(15,840)	1.3
General Greater London Authority Grant	(22)	(23)	–
Council Tax	(12,652)	(13,727)	8.5
Gross Expenditure on Council Tax Benefits and Expenditure funded by Council Tax Transitional Reduction Scheme Grant	(2,219)	(2,235)	0.7
Other Items	(132)	(120)	(9.1)

Source: CIPFA – Finance and General Statistics 2001–02.

PUBLIC SECTOR FINANCES £ billion

PUBLIC SECTOR CAPITAL EXPENDITURE

	Outturn 2000–2001	Estimate 2001–2002	Projection 2002–2003
Central government spending and local authority support in departmental expenditure limits	11.6	14.7	17.3
Locally-financed spending	0	1.9	2.0
National Lottery	1.1	0.9	1.3
Public corporations	4.6	4.7	6.2
Other capital spending in annually managed expenditure	1.0	2.4	1.7
Public sector gross investment	18.4	24.8	28.4
Proceeds from the sale of fixed assets	5.0	5.1	3.8

Source: The Stationery Office – Budget 2002 (Crown Copyright).

GROSS VALUE ADDED AT BASIC PRICES BY INDUSTRY 2000
*£ million

Agriculture, hunting, forestry and fishing	8,912
Mining and quarrying, including oil and gas extraction	24,244
Manufacturing	155,531
Electricity, gas and water supply	15,677
Construction	43,287
Wholesale and retail trade	130,782
Transport and communication	68,195
Financial intermediation	238,510
Adjustment for financial services	–37,091
Public administration, defence	42,091
Education; health; social work	102,489
Other services	42,560
ALL INDUSTRIES	831,053

* Components may not sum to totals due to rounding.
Source: The Stationery Office – Annual Abstract of Statistics 2002 (Crown copyright).

BALANCE OF PAYMENTS £ million

CURRENT ACCOUNT

Trade in goods	
Exports	187,656
Imports	218,036
Trade in goods balance	–30,380
Services balance	14,661
Investment income	5,974
Transfers balance	–8,823
CURRENT BALANCE	–18,425

Source: The Stationery Office – Annual Abstract of Statistics 2002 (Crown copyright).

UK TRADE ON A BALANCE OF PAYMENTS BASIS
£ million

	Exports	Imports	Balance
1990	102,313	121,020	–18,707
1991	103,939	114,162	–10,223
1992	107,863	120,913	–13,050
1993	122,039	135,295	–13,066
1994	135,143	146,269	–11,126
1995	153,577	165,600	–12,023
1996	167,196	180,918	–13,722
1997	171,923	184,265	–12,342
1998	164,056	185,869	–21,813
1999	166,198	193,722	–27,524
2000	187,656	218,036	–30,380

Source: The Stationery Office – Annual Abstract of Statistics 2002 (Crown copyright).

VALUE OF UK EXPORTS 2000
BY DESTINATION £ million

European Union	107,600
Other western Europe	7,486
North America	33,845
Other OECD countries	10,931
Oil exporting countries	6,056
Rest of the world	21,739

Source: The Stationery Office – Annual Abstract of Statistics 2002 (Crown copyright).

VALUE OF UK EXPORTS 2000
BY SOURCE £ million

European Union	111,188
Other western Europe	13,165
North America	33,591
Other OECD countries	18,071
Oil exporting countries	4,281
Rest of the worlds	37,740

Source: The Stationery Office – Annual Abstract of Statistics 2002 (Crown copyright).

EMPLOYMENT

UK EMPLOYMENT BY AGE AND GENDER (2001)

Age	Male	Female
16-17	319,000	320,000
18-24	1,769,000	1,531,000
25-34	3,864,000	2,998,000
35-49	5,701,000	4,802,000
50-64(m)/59(f)	3,541,000	2,409,000
65+(m)/60+(f)	265,000	547,000
All aged 16 and over	15,459,000	12,607,000

Source: The Stationery Office – Annual Abstract of Statistics 2002 (Crown copyright).

EMPLOYMENT STATUS OF PEOPLE OF WORKING AGE (UK) (2001)

	Male	Female
All in employment	15,459,000	12,607,000
Working full-time	11,880,000	6,550,000
Working part-time	1,107,000	5,124,000
Self-employed	2,325,000	817,000
Temporary employees	768,000	888,000
Unemployed	859,000	546,000
All economically active	16,318,000	13,153,000
Economically inactive	6,600,000	10,762,000

Source: The Stationery Office – Annual Abstract of Statistics 2002 (Crown copyright).

DISTRIBUTION OF THE UK WORKFORCE (2001), SEASONALLY ADJUSTED, AT JUNE

Employees	25,496,000
Self-employed	3,411,000
HM Forces	204,000
Government-supported trainee	117,000
Claimant unemployed	963,000

Source: The Stationery Office – Annual Abstract of Statistics 2002 (Crown copyright).

UK EMPLOYEE JOBS, BY MAIN SECTOR (2001)

Service industries	19,947,000
Manufacturing industries	3,821,000
Energy and water supply	188,000
Agriculture, hunting, forestry and fishing	298,000
Transport, storage and communications	1,593,000

Source: The Stationery Office – Annual Abstract of Statistics 2002 (Crown copyright).

AVERAGE GROSS WEEKLY EARNINGS OF FULL-TIME EMPLOYEES (GREAT BRITAIN) 2000

All adults	£410.60
All men	£453.30
Men, manual	£343.90
Men, non-manual	£533.90
All women	£337.60
Women, manual	£227.90
Women, non-manual	£357.50

Source: The Stationery Office – Annual Abstract of Statistics 2002 (Crown copyright).

REGIONAL UNEMPLOYMENT RATES 2001, NOT SEASONALLY ADJUSTED

United Kingdom	4.8%
England:	4.6%
East	3.6%
East Midlands	4.9%
London	5.8%
North East	7.4%
North West	5.1%
South East	3.0%
South West	3.5%
West Midlands	5.0%
Yorkshire and the Humber	4.9%
Wales	5.7%
Scotland	5.8%
Northern Ireland	6.2%

Source: The Stationery Office – Annual Abstract of Statistics 2002 (Crown copyright).

UNEMPLOYMENT RATES BY AGE AND GENDER 2001 (UK)

Age	Male	Female
16-17	69,000	46,000
18-24	216,000	130,000
25-34	192,000	139,000
35-49	227,000	174,000
50-64(m)/59(f)	147,000	50,000
65+(m)/60+(f)	–	–
All aged 16+	859,000	546,000

Source: The Stationery Office – Annual Abstract of Statistics 2002 (Crown copyright).

INDUSTRIAL STOPPAGES 2000 (UK)

Duration	
Not more than 5 days	187,000
6-10 days	14,000
11-20 days	5,000
21-30 days	1,000
31-50 days	3,000
More than 50 days	2,000
Total number of stoppages	212,000

Source: The Stationery Office – Annual Abstract of Statistics 2002 (Crown copyright).

TRADE UNIONS (UK)

Year	No. of unions at end of year	Total membership at end of year
1989	338	10,174,000
1990	327	9,960,000
1991	306	9,555,000
1992	315	9,171,000
1993	302	8,848,000
1994	281	8,297,000
1995	271	8,111,000
1996	261	7,982,000
1997	257	7,842,000
1998	243	7,894,000
1999	241	7,940,000

Source: The Stationery Office – Annual Abstract of Statistics 2002 (Crown copyright)

HOUSEHOLD INCOME AND EXPENDITURE

AVERAGE INCOME OF HOUSEHOLDS BEFORE AND AFTER TAXES AND BENEFITS, 1999–2000

Number of Households in the UK Population	25,334,000
Average per household (£ per year)	
Original income	22,004
Disposable income	20,225
Post-tax income	16,134

Source: The Stationery Office – Annual Abstract of Statistics 2002 (Crown copyright)

AVERAGE NUMBER OF PERSONS
PER HOUSEHOLD

All persons	2.3
Males	1.1
Females	1.2
Adults[1]	1.8
Persons under 65	1.4
Persons 65 and over	0.3
Children[1]	0.5
Children under 2	0.1
Children 2 and under 5	0.1
Children 5 and under 18	0.4
Persons economically active	1.1
Persons not economically active	1.2
Men 65 and over, women 60 and over	0.4
Others	0.8

[1] Adults = all persons aged 18 and over and married persons
under 18.
Children = all unmarried persons under 18.
Source: The Stationery Office – *Annual Abstract of Statistics
2002* (Crown copyright)

HOUSEHOLD EXPENDITURE ON COMMODITIES AND
SERVICES – WEEKLY AVERAGE (2000–2001)

	£	As % of total
Housing	63.90	17
Fuel and power	11.90	3
Food	61.90	16
Alcoholic drink	15.00	4
Tobacco	6.10	2
Clothing and footwear	22.00	6
Household goods	32.60	8
Household services	22.00	6
Personal goods and services	14.70	4
Motoring expenditure	55.10	14
Fares and other travel costs	9.50	2
Leisure goods	19.70	5
Leisure services	50.60	13
Miscellaneous	0.70	–
Total	385.70	100.0

Source: The Stationery Office – *Annual Abstract of Statistics
2002* (Crown copyright).

SOURCES OF HOUSEHOLD INCOME
2000–2001

AVERAGE WEEKLY INCOME BY SOURCE (£)

Wages and salaries	336.70
Self-employment	44.50
Investments	20.00
Annuities and pensions (other than social security benefits)	35.00
Social security benefits	60.10
Other sources	6.20
Total	502.50

SOURCES AS A PERCENTAGE OF TOTAL
HOUSEHOLD INCOME (%)

Wages and salaries	67.0
Self-employment	9.0
Investments	4
Annuities and pensions (other than social security benefits)	7.0
Social security benefits	12.0
Other sources	1.0
Total	100.0

Source: The Stationery Office – *Annual Abstract of Statistics
2002* (Crown copyright).

AVAILABILITY OF CERTAIN DURABLE
GOODS 2000–2001

	% of households
Car	72
One	44
Two	22
Three or more	6
Central heating, full or partial	91
Washing machine	92
Fridge/freezer or deep freezer	94
Refrigerator	53†
Television	98*
Telephone	93
Home computer	44
Internet Access	32
Video recorder	87

† 1999–2000 figure.
* 1992 figure.
Source: The Stationery Office – *Annual Abstract of Statistics
2002* (Crown copyright).

Cost of Living and Inflation Rates

The first cost of living index to be calculated took July 1914 as 100 and was based on the pattern of expenditure of working-class families in 1914. The cost of living index was superseded in 1947 by the general index of retail prices (RPI), although the older term is still popularly applied to it.

GENERAL INDEX OF RETAIL PRICES

The general index of retail prices measures the changes month by month in the average level of prices of goods and services purchased by most households in the United Kingdom. The spending pattern on which the index is based is revised each year, mainly using information from the Family Expenditure Survey. The expenditure of certain higher income households and of households mainly dependent on state pensions is excluded.

The index is compiled using a selection of over 600 goods and services, and the prices charged for these items are collected at regular intervals in about 146 locations throughout the country. For the index, the price changes are weighted in accordance with the pattern of consumption of the average family.

INFLATION RATE

The twelve-monthly percentage change in the 'all items' index of the RPI is usually referred to as the rate of inflation. The percentage change in prices between any two months/years can be obtained using the following formula:

$$\frac{\text{Later date RPI} - \text{Earlier date RPI}}{\text{Earlier date RPI}} \times 100$$

e.g. to find the rate of inflation for 1988, using the annual averages for 1987 and 1988:

$$\frac{106.9 - 101.9}{101.9} \times 100 = 4.9\%$$

PURCHASING POWER OF THE POUND

Changes in the internal purchasing power of the pound may be defined as the 'inverse' of changes in the level of prices; when prices go up, the amount which can be purchased with a given sum of money goes down. To find the purchasing power of the pound in one month or year, given that it was 100p in a previous month or year, the calculation would be:

$$100p \times \frac{\text{Ealier month/year RPI}}{\text{Later month/year RPI}}$$

Thus, if the purchasing power of the pound is taken to be 100p in 1975, the comparable purchasing power in 1997 would be:

$$100p \times \frac{34.2}{157.5} = 21.7p$$

For longer term comparisons, it has been the practice to use an index which has been constructed by linking together the RPI for the period 1962 to date; an index derived from the consumers expenditure deflator for the period from 1938 to 1962; and the prewar 'cost of living' index for the period 1914 to 1938. This long-term index enables the internal purchasing power of the pound to be calculated for any year from 1914 onwards. It should be noted that these figures can only be approximate.

	Long-term index of consumer goods and services (Jan. 1987 = 100)	Comparable purchasing power of £1 in 1998	Rate of inflation (annual average)
1914	2.8	58.18	
1915	3.5	46.54	
1920	7.0	23.27	
1925	5.0	32.58	
1930	4.5	36.20	
1935	4.0	40.72	
1938	4.4	37.02	
There are no official figures for 1939–45			
1946	7.4	22.01	
1950	9.0	18.10	
1955	11.2	14.54	
1960	12.6	12.93	
1965	14.8	11.00	
1970	18.5	8.80	
1975	34.2	4.76	
1980	66.8	2.44	18.0
1981	74.8	2.18	11.9
1982	81.2	2.01	8.6
1983	84.9	1.92	4.6
1984	89.2	1.83	5.0
1985	94.6	1.72	6.1
1986	97.8	1.67	3.4
1987	101.9	1.60	4.2
1988	106.9	1.52	4.9
1989	115.2	1.41	7.8
1990	126.1	1.29	9.5
1991	133.5	1.22	5.9
1992	138.5	1.18	3.7
1993	140.7	1.16	1.6
1994	144.1	1.13	2.4
1995	149.1	1.09	3.5
1996	152.7	1.07	2.4
1997	157.5	1.03	3.1
1998	162.9	1.00	3.4
1999	165.4	0.98	1.5
2000	170.3	0.96	3.0
2001	173.3	0.94	1.8

The RPI figures are published around the middle of each month. They are available as a recorded message which can be heard by telephoning 020-7533 5866. Each month an updated Consumer Price Indices bulletin is published by the Office of National Statistics.

OFFICE OF NATIONAL STATISTICS, 1 Drummond Gate, London SW1V 2QQ. Public Enquiries Line: 020-7533 5874 Web: www.statistics.gov.uk

Lotteries and Gaming

Gaming and lotteries in the UK are officially regulated and may only be run by licensed operators or in licensed premises. Responsibility for policy and the laws on gaming and lotteries rests with the Department for Culture, Media and Sport. The National Lottery is regulated by the National Lottery Commission. Supervision of other lottery operations and gaming is the responsibility of the Gaming Board for Great Britain.

Most betting is on horseracing and greyhound racing and may take place at racecourses and greyhound tracks, or at off-course betting offices.

Other forms of gaming and lotteries include the following:

Number of casinos operating	117
Total drop (2000–2001)	£3.3 billion
Number of Bingo clubs operating	705
Amount staked (2000-2001)	£1.12 billion
Number of gaming machines sited in Great Britain	c.250,000+
Society and local authority lottery schemes registered	657
Total ticket sales (£ million)	£107m

In 2000–2001 sales of society and local authority lottery tickets increased by 3.5 per cent to £107 million. Of this, £29 million (27 per cent) was spent on prizes, £27 million (26 per cent) on expenses and £51 million (47 per cent) went to good causes.

Source: Report of the Gaming Board for Great Britain 2000–2001

THE NATIONAL LOTTERY

The National Lottery is currently run by a private company, Camelot Group plc. The initial seven-year licence granted to Camelot expired on 30 September 2001. A new seven-year licence commenced on 27 January 2002.

The National Lottery Commission is responsible for the granting, enforcing and variation of licences to run the National Lottery. The Commission's duties are to ensure that the National Lottery is run with all due care and attention, that the interests of players are protected and, subject to these two points, to maximise the money raised for good causes.

The first National Lottery tickets draw was made on 19 November 1994, with a mid week draw introduced on Wednesday 5 February 1997. Instants (scratchcards) were introduced on 21 March 1995. Camelot has also introduced three other draws; the weekly Thunderball draw, launched on 12 June 1999, the bi-weekly Lottery Extra, introduced on 13 November 2000 and Hotpicks, launched on 7 July 2002. Since 18 May 2002, the National Lottery has been known as Lotto. Tickets for the main Lotto game cost £1 and can be bought in a shop, by telephone, online or by subscription. The highest win on a single ticket to date was £22,590,829 on 10 June 1995. By May 2002, 1,344 millionaires had been created. During the period of the first licence, over 80 per cent of the population participated in the National Lottery.

SALES 2001–2002

Average number of tickets (online and instants) sold per week	c.90m
Average number of people playing weekly	c.29
% of adult population buying tickets regularly	c.65%

Amount raised by ticket sales, 1994 to May 2002	c.£37.5 billion
Amount returned as prize money	£16.5 billion
Total ticket sales for 2000–2001	£4.9 billion

Sources: Camelot, Department for Culture, Media and Sport

DISTRIBUTION OF PROCEEDS

over the seven-year licence period

Allocated to:	%
Prize money	50
Tax	12
Retailer commission	5
Camelot (operating costs and profit)	5
Good causes	28

The 'good causes' originally benefiting from lottery funds were the arts, sport, heritage, charities and Millennium projects. In July 1998 the National Lottery Act created a sixth good cause, the New Opportunities Fund, to fund health, education and environmental initiatives. The New Opportunities Fund announced its first awards in summer 1999. The Act also created a National Endowment for Science, Technology and the Arts (NESTA), a non-departmental public body whose objectives are: to help talented individuals; to enable inventions and ideas to be commercially exploited; and to promote public knowledge of science, technology and the arts. NESTA received an initial £200 million from Lottery Funds but thereafter is to generate its own income.

The percentage of all the funds allocated to the good causes received by each cause is as follows: the arts, sport, heritage and charities 16.66 per cent each with 33.3 per cent going to the New Opportunities Fund (this includes the 20 per cent share that, prior to 21 August 2001, was allocated to the Millennium Commission).

The cumulative amount allocated to the good causes from November 1994 to April 2002 was £12.6 billion.

AWARDS 2001–2002

Most awards are conditional on partnership funding being obtained from other sources.

	Number	Total value £
Arts Council of England	2,196	157,171,880
Arts Council of Wales	627	13,368,000
Scottish Arts Council	323	10,184,925
Arts Council of Northern Ireland	109	7,688,161
Film Council*	80	27,504,348
Scottish Screen	103	5,200,000
Millennium Commission	5,464	18,503,937
Heritage Lottery Fund	2,323	332,135,306
Community Fund	7,232	301,400,000
New Opportunities Fund*	2,215	215,190,716
Sport, total	3,291	210,144,856
Sport England	4,516	220,938,490
Sports Council for Wales	1,819	9,749,049
Sportscotland	1,038	27,853,099
Sports Council for Northern Ireland	134	2,735,511
UK Sport*	356	61,542,930

*2000–2001 figures

Finance

British Currency

The unit of currency is the pound sterling (£) of 100 pence. The decimal system was introduced on 15 February 1971.

COIN

Gold Coins	‡Bi-colour Coins
*One hundred pounds £100	Two pounds £2
*Fifty pounds £50	*Nickel-Brass Coins*
*Twenty-five pounds £25	§Two pounds £2
*Ten pounds £10	One pound £1
Five pounds £5	
Two pounds £2	*Cupro-Nickel Coins*
Sovereign £1	Crown £5 (since 1990)
Half-Sovereign 50p	50 pence 50p
	Crown 25p (pre-1990)
Silver Coins	20 pence 20p
(*Britannia coins)	10 pence 10p
Two pounds £2	5 pence 5p
One pound £1	
50 pence 50p	*Bronze Coins*
Twenty pence 20p	2 pence 2p
(†*Maundy Money*)	1 penny 1p
Fourpence 4p	
Threepence 3p	*Copper-plated Steel Coins*
Twopence 2p	2 pence 2p
Penny 1p	1 penny 1p

*Britannia coins: gold bullion coins introduced 1987; silver coins introduced 1997
†Gifts of special money distributed by the Sovereign annually on Maundy Thursday to the number of aged poor men and women corresponding to the Sovereign's own age
‡Cupro-nickel centre and nickel-brass outer ring
§Commemorative coins; not intended for general circulation

GOLD COIN

Gold ceased to circulate during the First World War. Since then controls on buying, selling and holding gold coin have been imposed at various times but subsequently have been revoked. Under the Exchange Control (Gold Coins Exemption) Order 1979, gold coins may now be imported and exported without restriction, except gold coins which are more than 50 years old and valued at a sum in excess of £8,000; these cannot be exported without specific authorisation from the Department of Trade and Industry.

Value Added Taxation on the sale of gold coins was revoked in 2000.

SILVER COIN

Prior to 1920 silver coins were struck from sterling silver, an alloy of which 925 parts in 1,000 were silver. In 1920 the proportion of silver was reduced to 500 parts. From 1 January 1947 all 'silver' coins, except Maundy money, have been struck from cupro-nickel, an alloy of copper 75 parts and nickel 25 parts, except for the 20p, composed of copper 84 parts, nickel 16 parts. Maundy coins continue to be struck from sterling silver.

BRONZE COIN

Bronze, introduced in 1860 to replace copper, is an alloy of copper 97 parts, zinc 2.5 parts and tin 0.5 part. These proportions have been subject to slight variations in the past. Bronze was replaced by copper-plated steel in September 1992 with the exception of 1998 when the 2p was made in both copper plated steel and bronze.

LEGAL TENDER

Gold (dated 1838 onwards, if not below least current weight)	to any amount
£5 (Crown since 1990)	to any amount
£2	to any amount
£1	to any amount
50p	up to £10
25p (Crown pre-1990)	up to £10
20p	up to £10
10p	up to £5
5p	up to £5
2p	up to 20p
1p	up to 20p

The £1 coin was introduced in 1983 to replace the £1 note.

These coins ceased to be legal tender on the following dates:

Farthing	31 December 1960
Halfpenny ($\frac{1}{2}$d)	1 July 1969
Half-crown	1 January 1970
Threepence	31 August 1971
Penny (1d)	31 August 1971
Sixpence	30 June 1980
Halfpenny ($\frac{1}{2}$d)	31 December 1984
old 5 pence	31 December 1990
old 10 pence	30 June 1993
old 50 pence	28 February 1998

Since 1982 the word 'new' in 'new pence' displayed on decimal coins has been dropped.

The Channel Islands and the Isle of Man issue their own coinage, which are legal tender only in the island of issue.

	Metal	Standard weight (g)	Standard diameter (m)
Penny	bronze	3.564	20.3
Penny	copper-plated steel	3.564	20.3
2 pence	bronze	7.128	25.9
2 pence	copper-plated steel	7.128	25.9
5p	cupro-nickel	3.25	18.0
10p	cupro-nickel	6.5	24.5
20p	cupro-nickel	6.0	21.4
25p Crown	cupro-nickel	28.28	38.6
50p	cupro-nickel	13.5	30.0
50p	cupro-nickel	8.00	27.3
£1	nickel-brass	9.5	22.5
£2	nickel-brass	15.98	28.4
‡£2	cupro-nickel, nickel-brass	12.00	28.4
£5 Crown	cupro-nickel	28.28	38.61

The 'remedy' is the amount of variation from standard permitted in weight and fineness of coins when first issued from the Mint.

The Trial of the Pyx is the examination by a jury to ascertain that coins made by the Royal Mint, which have

been set aside in the pyx (or box), are of the proper weight, diameter and composition required by law. The trial is held annually, presided over by the Queen's Remembrancer (the Senior Master of the Supreme Court), with a jury of freemen of the Company of Goldsmiths.

BANKNOTES

Bank of England notes are currently issued in denominations of £5, £10, £20 and £50 for the amount of the fiduciary note issue, and are legal tender in England and Wales. No £1 notes have been issued since 1984 and in March 1998 the outstanding notes were written off in accordance with the provision of the Currency Act 1983.

The current E series of notes was introduced from June 1990, replacing the D series (*see* below). The historical figures portrayed in this series are:

£5	May 2002–	Elizabeth Fry
£5	June 1990–	George Stephenson
£10	November 2000–	Charles Darwin*
£20	June 1991–2001	Michael Faraday†
£20	June 1999–	Sir Edward Elgar
£50	April 1994–	Sir John Houblon

†Withrawn from circulation on 28 February 2001.
*The version of the Bank of England £10 banknote issued in April 1992, bearing a portrait of Charles Dickens, remains legal tender. No plans have been announced to remove it from circulation.

NOTE CIRCULATION

Note circulation is highest at the two peak spending periods of the year, around Christmas and during the summer holiday period. The total value of notes in circulation at 3 January 2001 was £29,360 million, compared to £25,991 million at 23 December 1998.

The value of notes in circulation at the end of February 2000 and 2001 was:

	2000	2001
£5	£1,045m	£1,041m
£10	£5,684m	£6,107m
£20	£13,197m	£14,381m
£50	£4,195m	£4,657m
Other notes †	£1,014m	£1,009m
Total	£25,135m	£27,195m

† Includes higher value notes used internally in the Bank of England, e.g. as cover for the note issues of banks in Scotland and Northern Ireland in excess of their permitted issue

LEGAL TENDER

Banknotes which are no longer legal tender are payable when presented at the head office of the Bank of England in London.

The white notes for £10, £20, £50, £100, £500 and £1,000, which were issued until April 1943, ceased to be legal tender in May 1945, and the white £5 note in March 1946.

The white £5 note issued between October 1945 and September 1956, the £5 notes issued between 1957 and 1963 (bearing a portrait of Britannia) and the first series to bear a portrait of The Queen, issued between 1963 and 1971, ceased to be legal tender in March 1961, June 1967 and September 1973 respectively.

The series of £1 notes issued during the years 1928 to 1960 and the 10 shilling notes issued from 1928 to 1961 (those without the royal portrait) ceased to be legal tender in May and October 1962 respectively. The £1 note first issued in March 1960 (bearing on the back a

representation of Britannia) and the £10 note first issued in February 1964 (bearing a lion on the back), both bearing a portrait of The Queen on the front, ceased to be legal tender in June 1979. The £1 note first issued in 1978 ceased to be legal tender on 11 March 1988. The 10 shilling note was replaced by the 50p coin in October 1969, and ceased to be legal tender on 21 November 1970.

The D series of banknotes was introduced from 1970 and ceased to be legal tender from the dates shown below. The predominant identifying feature of each note was the portrayal on the back of a prominent figure from British history:

£1	Feb. 1978–March 1988	Sir Isaac Newton
£5	Nov. 1971–Nov. 1991	The Duke of Wellington
£10	Feb. 1975–May 1994	Florence Nightingale
£20	July 1970–March 1993	William Shakespeare
£50	March 1981–Sept. 1996	Sir Christopher Wren

The £1 coin was introduced on 21 April 1983 to replace the £1 note.

OTHER BANKNOTES

SCOTLAND – Banknotes are issued by three Scottish banks. The Royal Bank of Scotland issues notes for £1, £5, £10, £20 and £100. The Bank of Scotland and the Clydesdale Bank issue notes for £5, £10, £20, £50 and £100. Scottish notes are not legal tender in Scotland but they are an authorised currency and enjoy a status comparable to that of Bank of England notes.

NORTHERN IRELAND – Banknotes are issued by four banks in Northern Ireland. The Bank of Ireland, the Northern Bank and the Ulster Bank issue notes for £5, £10, £20, £50 and £100. The First Trust Bank issues notes for £10, £20, £50 and £100. Northern Ireland notes are not legal tender in Northern Ireland but they circulate widely and enjoy a status comparable to that of Bank of England notes.

CHANNEL ISLANDS – The States of Guernsey issues its own currency notes and coinage. The notes are for £1, £5, £10, £20 and £50, and the coins are for 1p, 2p, 5p, 10p, 20p, 50p, £1, £2 and £5. The States of Jersey issues its own currency notes and coinage. The notes are for £1, £5, £10, £20 and £50, and the coins are for 1p, 2p, 5p, 10p, 20p, 50p, £1 and £2.

THE ISLE OF MAN – The Isle of Man Government issues notes for £1, £5, £10, £20 and £50. Although these notes are only legal tender in the Isle of Man, they are accepted at face value in branches of the clearing banks in the UK. The Isle of Man issues coins for 1p, 2p, 5p, 10p, 20p, 50p, £1, £2 and £5.

Although none of the series of notes specified above is legal tender in the UK, they are generally accepted by the banks irrespective of their place of issue. At one time the banks made a commission charge for handling Scottish and Irish notes but this was abolished some years ago.

Banking

There are two main types of deposit-taking institutions: banks and building societies, although National Savings and Investments also provides savings products. Banks and building societies are supervised by the Financial Services Authority although National Savings and Investments is not. As a result of the conversion of several building societies into banks in recent years, the size of the banking sector, which was already substantially greater than the non-bank deposit-taking sector, has increased further.

The main institutions within the British banking system are the Bank of England (the central bank), the retail banks, the investment banks and the overseas banks. In its role as the central bank, the Bank of England acts as banker to the Government and as a note-issuing authority; it also oversees the efficient functioning of payment and settlement systems.

Since May 1997, the Bank of England has had operational responsibility for monetary policy. At monthly meetings of its monetary policy committee the Bank sets the interest rate at which it will lend to the money markets.

OFFICIAL INTEREST RATES 2000–2002

13 January 2000	5.75%
10 February 2000	6.00%
8 February 2001	5.75%
5 April 2001	5.50%
10 May 2001	5.25%
2 August 2001	5.00%
18 September 2001	4.75%
4 October 2001	4.50%
8 November 2001	4.00%

RETAIL BANKS

The major retail banks are Abbey National, Alliance and Leicester, Barclays (including Woolwich), Bradford and Bingley, HBOS (including Halifax and Bank of Scotland), HSBC, Lloyds/TSB, Northern Rock and The Royal Bank of Scotland (including National Westminster).

Retail banks offer a wide variety of financial services to companies and individuals, including current and deposit accounts, loan and overdraft facilities, automated teller (cash dispenser) machines, cheque guarantee cards, credit cards and debit cards. Most banks also offer telephone and Internet banking facilities.

The Financial Ombudsman Service scheme provides independent and impartial arbitration in disputes between a bank and its customer.

Banking hours differ throughout the UK. Many banks now open longer hours and some at weekends, and hours vary from branch to branch. Current core opening hours are:

ENGLAND AND WALES: Monday–Friday, 9.30–4.30
SCOTLAND: Monday–Friday, 9.00–5.00
NORTHERN IRELAND: Monday–Friday, 9.30–4.30
(Wednesdays 10.00–4.30, except Ulster Bank Ltd);
Northern Bank, 10.00–3.30, Saturdays 9.30–12.30

PAYMENT CLEARINGS

The Association for Payment Clearing Services (APACS) is an umbrella organisation for payment clearings in the UK. It manages three clearing companies:
–BACS Ltd is the UK's automated clearing house for bulk clearing of electronic debits and credits (e.g. direct debits and salary credits)
–the Cheque and Credit Clearing Company Ltd operates bulk clearing systems for inter-bank cheques and paper credit items in Great Britain
–CHAPS Clearing Company Ltd provides same-day clearing for electronic funds transfers throughout the UK in sterling and globally in euro
Membership of APACS and the clearing companies is open to any appropriately regulated financial institution providing payment services and meeting the relevant membership criteria. As at June 2002, APACS had 31 members, comprising the major banks, building societies and Consignia.

ASSOCIATION FOR PAYMENT CLEARING SERVICES (APACS), Mercury House, Triton Court, 14 Finsbury Square, London EC2A 1LQ. Tel: 020-7711 6200; Web: www.apacs.org.uk.
Head of Public Affairs, R. Tyson-Davies
BACS LTD, De Havilland Road, Edgware, Middx HA8 5QA. Tel: 0870-165 0019. *Chief Executive*, G. Younger
CHEQUE AND CREDIT CLEARING COMPANY LTD, Mercury House, Triton Court, 14 Finsbury Square, London EC2A 1LQ. Tel: 020-7711 6200
CHAPS CLEARING COMPANY LTD, Mercury House, Triton Court, 14 Finsbury Square, London EC2A 1LQ. Tel: 020-7711 6200

MAJOR RETAIL BANKS: FINANCIAL RESULTS 2001

Bank Group	Profit before taxation £m	Profit after taxation £m	Total assets £m	Number of UK branches
Abbey National	1,938	1,335	214,906	756
Alliance and Leicester	396	287	37,882	310
Barclays (incorporating Woolwich)	3,608	–	356,649	2,088
HBOS (Halifax/Bank of Scotland)	3,000	2,200	312,000	over 1,000
Lloyds/TSB	3,550	2,579	236,539	2,300
HSBC	2,290	1,739	132,682	2,300
Northern Rock	2,952	2.059	31,100	76
The Royal Bank of Scotland Group (incorporating National Westminster)	4,275	2,738	368,782	2,165

Stamp Duties and Stamp Duty Reserve Tax

Stamp duty is a tax on documents; Stamp duty reserve tax is charged upon agreements for the sale of shares and securities where there is no stamped stock transfer form.

For the majority of people, contact with Stamp duty arises when they purchase a property. Stamp duty is payable by the buyer through a solicitor upon completion as a way of raising money for the government based on the purchase price of a property. Stamp duty on share dealing is levied at 0.5 per cent or, in special circumstances 1.5 per cent.

Where stamp duty is not paid or deposited with the Stamp Office within 30 days after execution, interest accrues. This applies where the instrument is executed offshore. For agreements for leases the interest commences from 30 days after the execution of the lease. A stampable instrument may be stamped without penalty if presented for stamping within 30 days after its date of first execution. Where wholly executed abroad, the period begins to run from the date of arrival in the UK.

Instruments presented after the proper time may be subject to a penalty.

Under the Finance Act 1999, a person dissatisfied with a decision of the Commissioners as to the issuing or the appropriate level of stamp duty may appeal within thirty days of their decision.

AGREEMENT FOR SALE OF PROPERTY

Charged with *ad valorem* duty as if an actual conveyance on sale, with certain exceptions, e.g. agreements for the sale of legal interests in land, stocks and shares, goods, wares or merchandise, a ship or foreign property. If *ad valorem* duty is paid on an agreement in accordance with this provision, the subsequent conveyance or transfer is not chargeable with any *ad valorem* duty and the Commissioners will, upon application, either place a denoting stamp on such conveyance or transfer or will transfer the *ad valorem* duty thereto. Further, if such an agreement is not performed the *ad valorem* duty paid will be returned.

CONVEYANCE OR TRANSFER ON SALE

'Sale' includes transfers for cash, shares and debt and in the case of land exchanges, any other property.

Value not exceeding £60,000, *nil*
Value of £60,001–£250,000, 1 per cent
Value of £250,001–£500,000, 3 per cent
Value exceeding £500,000, 4 per cent

Readers should note that when assessing how much stamp duty is payable, the entire purchase price must be taken into account. For example, on a property purchased for £300,000, 3 per cent, £9,000 is payable.

From 30 November 2001 stamp duty exemption is available for the purchase of property in certain designated disadvantaged areas of the UK, and where the consideration, or premium for a lease, does not exceed £150,000. Visit www.inlandrevenue.gov.uk/so/disadvantaged.htm for further information.

Stamp duty for shares and marketable securities is levied at a rate of 0.5 per cent.

CONVEYANCE OR TRANSFER OF ANY OTHER KIND

There is a fixed duty, however, under the Stamp Duty (Exempt Instruments) Regulations 1987, instruments which would otherwise fall under this head are exempt from stamp duty provided that the document is duly certified.

LEASES (INCLUDING AGREEMENTS FOR LEASES)

A letting agreement for any definite term less than a year of any furnished property where the rent exceeds £5,000 per annum attracts a fixed duty of £5.

Of any lands, tenements etc. in consideration of any rent, according to the following:

Term not exceeding seven years or indefinite (and rent exceeding £5,000 p.a.), 1 per cent
Term between 7 and 35 years, 2 per cent
Term between 35 and 100 years, 12 per cent
Term exceeding 100 years, 24 per cent

Where a consideration other than rent is payable e.g. a premium in cash or other property, the same rule applies where the consideration does not exceed £60,000 as under conveyance or transfer on sale (except stock or marketable securities), provided that any rent payable does not exceed £600 a year and a certificate of value is included in the conveyance or transfer and the reduced rates of 1 per cent for consideration not exceeding £250,000 and 4 per cent for consideration not exceeding £500,000 apply.

Where a lease is granted pursuant to a prior written agreement for lease, the agreement itself is liable to duty. Credit for any duty paid on the agreement will be given against the duty payable on the lease and the Commissioners will place a denoting stamp on the lease. Where there is no prior written agreement for lease, the lease must contain a certificate that it has not been made in pursuance of such an agreement.

STAMP DUTIES

UNIT TRUST INSTRUMENT

Duty was abolished in the Finance Act 1988. Transfer of property to a unit trust or agreement to transfer units is generally subject to Conveyance on Sale duty or Stamp Duty Reserve Tax. By the Finance Act 1989, the transfer of units in certain authorised unit trusts is no longer subject to duty.

VOLUNTARY DISPOSITION, *INTER VIVOS*

There is a fixed duty, however, under the Stamp Duty (Exempt Instruments) Regulations 1987, instruments which would otherwise fall under this head are exempt provided that the document is certified as falling within category L in the schedule to the Regulations.

STAMP DUTY RESERVE TAX

This is charged where there is a contract for the transfer of chargeable securities unless the charge is cancelled. The tax is payable by or on behalf of the buyer who is required to report the transaction and pay the tax on the seventh day of the month following that in which the contract is made or becomes unconditional. Penalties and interest are imposed for late payment or reporting.

For further information, the Inland Revenue Stamp Offices can be contacted. They have offices in Belfast, London, Birmingham, Bristol, Worthing, Manchester, Edinburgh and Newcastle. Visit the Inland Revenue site at www.inlandrevenue.co.uk

Mutual Societies

The term 'mutual societies' covers member-based organisations registered under the Building Societies Acts, the Friendly Societies Acts and the Industrial and Provident Societies Acts, many of which are familiar long-established names.

Until midnight on 30 November 2001 the various statutory responsibilities for the supervision and registration of mutual societies rested with the Chief Registrar of Friendly Societies (CR), the Building Societies Commission (BSC) and the Friendly Societies Commission (FSC). The office of CR and the government department of the Registry of Friendly Societies (RFS), from which the BSC and FSC were more recently supported, date back to 1875. However, the existence in one form or another of an office for the registration of friendly societies and a Registrar dates back to 1829, when its function was initially seen as bringing regulation and social control over a potentially revolutionary popular movement.

In 1997 the Government announced the creation of a single financial regulatory authority for the UK, the Financial Services Authority (FSA). The FSA initially supported the functions of the CR, BSC and FSC under contract. On the full entry into force of the Financial Services and Markets Act 2001 on 1 December 2001, the responsibilities and powers of the BSC, FSC and CR passed to the FSA.

FRIENDLY SOCIETIES IN BRITAIN

Friendly societies are voluntary mutual organisations, where the main purposes are assisting members during sickness, unemployment or retirement, and the provision of life assurance. Many of the older traditional societies complement their business activities by social activity and a general care for individual members in ways normally outside the scope of a purely commercial organisation. There are three main categories of friendly societies: societies with separately registered branches, commonly called orders; centralised societies, which conduct business directly with members (having no separately registered branches); and collecting societies which conduct industrial assurance business (commonly known as home service assurance). Collecting societies will benefit from a number of deregulatory measures included in the Financial Services and Markets Act 2000 involving relaxation for the future administration of existing contracts and by the removal of special requirements, in the industrial assurance legislation, concerning the selling of future contracts. Such business will be subject to the general conduct of business rules governing the marketing and selling of investment products.

The Friendly Societies Act 1992 created a new legislative framework for friendly societies, enabling them to provide a wider range of services to their members and allowing them to compete on more equal terms with other financial institutions. At the same time it provided for more flexible prudential supervision to safeguard members of societies.

The Act enables friendly societies to incorporate and establish subsidiaries to provide various financial and other services to their members and the public. The activities which subsidiaries are able to conduct include those to establish and manage unit trust schemes and personal equity plans; to arrange for the provision of credit, whether as agents or providers; to carry on long-

term or general insurance business; to provide insurance intermediary services; to provide fund management services for trustees of pension funds; to administer estates and execute trusts of wills; and to establish and manage sheltered housing, residential homes for the elderly, hospitals and nursing homes.

The Act established a new framework to oversee friendly societies, including a Friendly Societies Commission, whose principal functions are to regulate the activities of friendly societies, promote their financial stability and protect members' funds. All friendly societies carrying on insurance or non-insurance business require authorisation by the Commission, which has a broad range of prudential powers. Friendly societies were also to be brought within the scope of the Policyholders Protection Act 1975, the statutory investor protection scheme covering insurance policyholders.

Of the 239 societies on the register at 30 November 2001, there were 103 authorised to write new business. Societies not able to write new business nevertheless continued to have liabilities to meet. Many of these were small with a declining membership. Of the authorised societies 40 were incorporated; 37 were previously registered under the 1974 Act, with three new registrations under the 1992 legislation. Sixteen of these societies had active subsidiaries.

There were 39 Life Directive societies, i.e. those subject to the requirements of EU Life Insurance Directives, and four Incorporated Societies which were transacting long-term insurance business but not subject to the Directives. These 43 societies, with total assets in excess of £15 billion, accounted for over 97 per cent of the total funds of the movement as at 31 December 2000. Contribution income paid by their members in that year amounted to over £1.2 billion. Statistics for these societies are set out in the table below.

LIFE DIRECTIVE AND INCORPORATED SOCIETIES

	1999	2000
No. of Societies	42	43
Membership (000s)	4,736	5,512
Contribution income (£000s)	906,624	1,219,663
Investment income (£000s)	1,375,616	255,772
Benefits paid (£000s)	959,308	1,201,628
Management expenses (£000s)	332,276	327,864
Total assets	15,088,479	15,019,152

The Friendly Societies Act 1974 allowed three other main classes of society to be registered: benevolent societies, working men's clubs and specially authorised societies. Benevolent societies are established for any charitable or benevolent purpose, to provide the same type of benefits as would be permissible for a friendly society, but in contrast the benefits must be for persons who are not members instead of, or in addition to, members. Working men's clubs provide social and recreational facilities for members. Specially authorised societies are registered for any purpose authorised by the Treasury as a purpose to which some or all of the provisions of the 1974 Act ought to be extended. Examples are societies for the promotion of science, literature and the fine arts, or to enable members to pursue an interest in sports and games. No new societies of any type may now be registered under this Act.

The numbers of the various types of bodies registered under the Friendly Societies Acts at 30 November 2001 were:

FRIENDLY SOCIETIES

Orders*	13
Collecting societies	11
Other centralised societies	215
OTHER BODIES	
Benevolent societies*	55
Working men's clubs	1,842
Specially authorised societies	101
* With 612 branches	

INDUSTRIAL AND PROVIDENT SOCIETIES IN BRITAIN

The familiar 'Co-op' societies are amongst the wide variety which are registered under the Industrial and Provident Societies Act 1965. This consolidating Act, provides for the registration of societies and lays down the broad framework within which they must operate. Internal relations of societies are governed by their registered rules.

Registration under the Act confers upon a society corporate status by its registered name with perpetual succession and a common seal, and limited liability. A society qualifies for registration if it is carrying on an industry, business or trade, and it satisfies the Registrar either (a) that it is a bona fide co-operative society, or (b) that in view of the fact that its business is being, or is intended to be, conducted for the benefit of the community, there are special reasons why it should be registered under the Act rather than as a company under the Companies Act.

The Credit Unions Act 1979 added a new class of society registrable under the 1965 Act. It also made provision for the supervision of these savings and loan bodies. Unlike other classes, where the role of the Registry (and subsequently the FSA) remained solely that of a registration authority, for Credit Unions (CUs) it became also the financial advisor. On 2 July 2002 a new system of regulation by the FSA for all CUs came into effect. The key features of the new regulatory regime for CUs were:

- to meet a basic test of solvency (with additional capital requirements for the larger CUs)
- to maintain a minimum liquidity ratio
- to meet the standard in FSA's rules for approved persons
- to operate an effective complaints scheme with access to the Financial Ombudsman
- to participate in the Financial Services Compensation Scheme providing members with deposit protection for the first time

Announcing the changes, the FSA said the new standards were designed to allow the credit union movement to advance while giving greater protection to members.

Comparative figures for 2000 show that the housing sector re-established itself as the largest single class of society in terms of asset holdings, overtaking the general service sector. The assets held were £27.3 billion and £26.5 billion respectively. The clubs sector remained the largest in terms of numbers of societies, with 3,291 clubs on the register at the end of the year. The total number of industrial and provident societies on the register (excluding CUs as at 30 November 2001 was 8,304. In spite of 155 new registrations since the beginning of the year, this represented a continued reduction in numbers, mainly due to ongoing work to ensure that defunct societies were removed from the register.

Although the number of CUs again increased, there were only 39 new registrations in 2000, the lowest

number since 1996. In spite of this, the number of new credit unions has been growing steadily at the average rate of 50 registrations per year since 1991. In 2001, up to 30 November, there were a further 22 registrations.

The principal statistics for all classes of society at the end of 2000 are given below:

	No. of societies	No. of members 000s	Funds of members £000s	Total assets £000s
Retail	95	5,827	1,637,473	3,637,450
Wholesale and productive	90	286	830,557	2,660,592
Agricultural	817	1,101	229,784	601,400
Fishing	69	5	14,761	41,738
Clubs	3,291	2,224	369,792	546,547
General service	991	632	2,122,094	26,459,715
Housing	3,029	166	9,170,312	27,336,139
Credit unions	687	322	202,591	214,524
TOTAL	9,609	10,563	14,577,364	61,498,105

BUILDING SOCIETIES IN THE UK

The Building Societies Act 1997, which received royal assent on 21 March 1997, made substantive amendments to, but did not replace, the Building Societies Act 1986. It liberalised the statutory regime for building societies to enable them to compete on more level terms with other financial institutions without having to forego their mutual status.

The Building Societies Act 1986 gave building societies a completely new legal framework for the first time since the initial comprehensive building society legislation in 1874. The 1986 Act sets out detailed provisions in relation to:

- the constitution of building societies
- building societies' powers in relation to raising funds, advances, loans, other assets and the provision of services
- the powers of control of the Building Societies Commission
- protection of investors, and complaints and disputes
- management of building societies, accounts and audit
- mergers and transfers of business

The 1986 Act was prescriptive in respect of building societies' powers and the way in which they were exercised. However, it gave numerous powers to the Building Societies Commission and/or the Treasury to make statutory instruments which, subject to parliamentary approval, can amend, extend and supplement the provisions of the Act. Since it came into force on 1 January 1987 the Act had been amended and extended considerably, especially in respect of building societies' powers.

The main purposes of the Building Societies Act 1997 are:

- remove the prescriptive powers' regime relating to building societies and to replace it with a permissive regime with appropriately revised balance-sheet 'nature limits', thus increasing the commercial freedom of societies and allowing increased competition and wider choice for customers
- enhance the powers of control of the Building Societies Commission
- introduce a package of measures to enhance the accountability of building societies' boards to their members
- make changes to the provisions relating to the transfer of a building society's business to a company

The Act came fully into force on 21 October 1997. Under it a building society may pursue any activities set out in its memorandum, subject only to:

- principal purpose: its purpose or principal purpose must be that of making loans which are secured on residential properties and are funded substantially by its members
- lending limit: at least 75 per cent of its business assets must be loans fully secured on residential property
- funding limit: at least 50 per cent of its funds must be raised in the form of shares held by individual members
- restrictions: subject to certain exceptions, it must not act as a market maker in securities, commodities or currencies; trade in commodities or currencies; enter into transactions involving derivatives, except in relation to hedging; nor create a floating charge over its assets
- prudential: it must comply with the criteria of prudential management

All authorised building societies, after making the necessary changes to their memoranda and rules, are now operating under the more liberal statutory regime set out in the 1997 Act.

CONVERSIONS AND MERGERS

During the year ending 31 March 2002, there were no conversions to plc status but two societies merged with (or in statutory terms, 'transferred engagements' to) other building societies. The Gainsborough Building Society transferred to the Yorkshire on 31 December 2001. At the previous year end, the Gainsborough had assets of £34 million and over 7,000 members. At 31 December 2001 the Yorkshire's balance sheet shows assets of £12.5 billion and 1.8 million members.

On 16 November 2001 the Ilkeston Permanent Building Society transferred to the Derbyshire. At the previous year-end the Ilkeston had assets of £17 million and over 3,000 members. The Derbyshire had assets of £3.5 billion and 378,000 members at 31 December 2001.

OMBUDSMAN SCHEME

Complaints about the actions of building societies may be resolved through societies' own internal complaints procedures. All authorised building societies are, in addition, members of the Building Societies Ombudsmen scheme which provides an independent service to consider and determine complaints which are within its remit. The Financial Services and Markets Act 2000 brings together the Building Societies Ombudsman and seven others including the Banking Ombudsman and the Insurance Ombudsman, in a single Financial Ombudsman Service. This complaints-handling organisation provides consumers with a free, informal and independent service for resolving disputes with most providers of financial products and services.

From 1 April 2000 this body provided a complaints handling service on behalf of each of the existing schemes. On 1 December 2001 the Financial Ombudsman Service received powers in its own right as the new legislation was brought into force. Complainants may contact the Service at South Quay Plaza, 183 Marsh Wall, London E14 9SR. Tel: 020-8964 1000.

The principal statistics for building society activity for 2000–2001 are given in the table below:

BUILDING SOCIETIES 1999–2000

	2000	2001
Authorised societies	67	65
No. of shareholders (000s)	22,237	20,310
No. of depositors (000s)	740	568
No. of borrowers (000s)	3,107	2,750
Share balances (£m)	119,299	119,815
Deposit balances (£m)	43,579	37,985
Mortgage balances (£m)	134,100	128,322
Total assets (£m)	177,747	171,375
Advances during year		
No. (000s)	548	509
Amount (£m)	31,514	31,845

MORTGAGE AND SHARE INTEREST RATES

Prevailing interest rates on mortgages and savings or other investments vary from society to society and in relation to the type, terms and amount of the loan or investment. The intervals between payments and the compounding of interest may be critical in determining the competitiveness of specific offers. As well as a full comparison of other terms, care should be taken to ensure that quoted interest rates are exactly comparable, for example, by considering the annual percentage rate (APR).

The table below shows bank base rates and dates of change over the period from 1 January 2000 and the building society quarterly average share and mortgage rates to mid-2002.

INTEREST RATES 2000–2002

BANK BASE RATE

Date of change	Rate %
13 Jan 2000	5.75
10 Feb 2000	6.00
8 Feb 2001	5.75
5 Apr 2001	5.50
10 May 2001	5.25
2 Aug 2001	5.00
18 Sept 2001	4.75
4 Oct 2001	4.50
8 Nov 2001	4.00

BUILDING SOCIETY RATES

Year/quarter	Average gross share %	Average mortgage %
Q1 2000	5.39	6.87
Q2	5.46	6.86
Q3	5.53	6.82
Q4	5.48	6.65
Q1 2001	5.28	6.44
Q2	4.84	6.07
Q3	4.61	5.83
Q4	3.81	5.17
Q1 2002	3.73	5.05
Q2	3.73	5.05

AUTHORISED SOCIETIES AT END OF JULY 2002
BUILDING SOCIETIES

Name of Building Society(a) and principal office address	Members (b)	Total assets (c) £'000
Barnsley, Regent Street, Barnsley, S. Yorks S70 2EH	72,741	282,562
Bath, 20 Charles Street, Bath BA1 1HY	22,500	117,208
Beverley, 57 Market Place, Beverley, E. Yorks HU17 8AA	13,000	65,345
Britannia, Britannia House, Cheadle Road, Leek, Staffs ST13 5RG	2,223,553	17,405,200
Buckinghamshire, High Street, Chalfont St Giles, Bucks HP8 4QB	9,610	106,530
Cambridge, 51 Newmarket Road, Cambridge CB5 8FF	123,980	573,632
Catholic, 7 Strutton Ground, London SW1P 2HY	3,759	34,235
Century, 21 Albany Street, Edinburgh EH1 3QW	3,731	15,539
Chelsea, Thirlestaine Hall, Thirlestaine Road, Cheltenham, Glos GL53 7AL	574,000	5,915,858
Chesham, 12 Market Square, Chesham, Bucks HP5 1ER	20,824	185,952
Cheshire, Castle Street, Macclesfield, Cheshire SK11 6AF	422,000	2,928,000
Chorley and District, Key House, Foxhole Road, Chorley, Lancs PR7 1NZ	18,534	110,292
City of Derry, 31A Carlisle Road, Londonderry BT48 6JJ	2,235	16,882
Clay Cross, Eyre Street, Clay Cross, Chesterfield S45 9NS	5,216	21,144
Coventry, PO Box 9, High Street, Coventry CV1 5QN	970,000	7,192,623
Cumberland, Cumberland House, Castle Street, Carlisle CA3 8RX	180,000	888,727
Darlington, Sentinel House, Lingfield Way, Darlington, Co. Durham DL1 4PR	89,888	469,499
Derbyshire, Duffield Hall, Duffield, Derby DE56 1AG	377,561	3,459,731
Dudley, Dudley House, Stone Street, Dudley DY1 1NP	23,000	140,616
Dunfermline, Caledonia House, Carnegie Avenue, Dunfermline, Fife KY11 8PJ	345,000	1,724,833
Earl Shilton, 22 The Hollow, Earl Shilton, Leicester LE9 7NB	17,274	82,866
Ecology, 18 Station Road, Cross Hills, Keighley, W. Yorks BD20 7EH	8,388	39,696
Furness, 51–55 Duke Street, Barrow-in-Furness LA14 1RT	112,000	546,927
Hanley Economic, Granville House, Festival Park, Hanley, Stoke-on-Trent, Staffs ST1 5TB	42,000	252,193
Harpenden, 14 Station Road, Harpenden, Herts AL5 4SE	17,251	83,861
Hinckley and Rugby, Upper Bond Street, Hinckley, Leics LE10 1DG	100,000	501,489
Holmesdale, 43 Church Street, Reigate, Surrey RH2 0AE	9,169	116,317
Ipswich, 44 Upper Brook Street, Ipswich IP4 1DP	31,270	288,052
Kent Reliance, Reliance House, Sun Pier, Chatham, Kent ME4 4ET	72,000	401,054
Lambeth, 118–120 Westminster Bridge Road, London SE1 7XE	72,254	721,140
Leeds and Holbeck, 105 Albion Street, Leeds LS1 5AS	565,096	4,138,470
Leek United, 50 St Edward Street, Leek, Staffs ST13 5DH	68,098	526,053
Loughborough, 6 High Street, Loughborough, Leics LE11 2QB	22,350	173,297
Manchester, 24 Queen Street, Manchester M2 5AH	22,421	278,418
Mansfield, Regent House, Regent Street, Mansfield, Notts NG18 1SS	28,061	162,313
Market Harborough, Welland House, The Square, Market Harborough, Leics LE16 7PD	59,784	324,133
Marsden, 6–20 Russell Street, Nelson, Lancs BB9 7NJ	77,828	304,081
Melton Mowbray, 39 Nottingham Street, Melton Mowbray, Leics LE13 1NR	66,244	292,455
Mercantile, Mercantile House, Silverlink Business Park, Wallsend, Tyne and Wear NE28 9NY	37,021	209,690
Monmouthshire, John Frost Square, Newport, Gwent NP20 1PX	47,098	326,179
National Counties, National Counties House, Church Street, Epsom, Surrey KT17 4NL	40,335	703,861
Nationwide, Nationwide House, Pipers Way, Swindon SN38 1NW	10,400,000	74,454,900
Newbury, 17–20 Bartholomew Street, Newbury, Berks RG14 5LY	66,855	396,765
Newcastle, Portland House, New Bridge Street, Newcastle upon Tyne NE1 8AL	411,343	22,655,967
Norwich and Peterborough, Peterborough Business Park, Lynch Wood, Peterborough PE2 6WZ	413,078	2,458,700
Nottingham, 5–13 Upper Parliament Street, Nottingham NG1 2BX	234,632	1,734,481
Penrith, 7 King Street, Penrith, Cumbria CA11 7AR	6,879	64,099
Portman, Portman House, Richmond Hill, Bournemouth, Dorset BH2 6EP	1,249,024	9,046,331
Principality, PO Box 89, Principality Buildings, Queen Street, Cardiff CF10 1UA	370,000	2,739,699
Progressive, 33–37 Wellington Place, Belfast BT1 6HH	113,113	846,454
Saffron Walden, Herts and Essex, 1A Market Street, Saffron Walden, Essex CB10 1HX	92,000	400,889
Scarborough, Prospect House, PO Box 6, Scarborough, N. Yorks YO12 6EQ	137,574	1,187,940
Scottish, 23 Manor Place, Edinburgh EH3 7XE	28,841	172,855
Shepshed, Bull Ring, Shepshed, Loughborough, Leics LE12 9QD	10,300	51,741
Skipton, The Bailey, Skipton, N. Yorks BD23 1DN	500,000	6,216,933
Stafford Railway, 4 Market Square, Stafford ST16 2JH	11,739	78,697

Name of Building Society (a) and principal office address	Members (b)	Total assets (c) £'000
Staffordshire, Jubilee House, PO Box 66, 84 Salop Street, Wolverhampton WV3 0SA	240,000	1,635,298
Stroud and Swindon, Rowcroft, Stroud, Glos GL5 3BG	212,071	1,667,375
Swansea, 11 Cradock Street, Swansea SA1 3EW	5,169	42,844
Teachers, Allenview House, Hanham Road, Wimborne, Dorset BH21 1AG	21,030	200,450
Tipton and Coseley, 70 Owen Street, Tipton, W. Midlands DY4 8HG	36,156	187,101
Universal, Universal House, Kings Manor, Newcastle upon Tyne NE1 6PA	62,000	432,997
Vernon, 19 St Petersgate, Stockport, Cheshire SK1 1HF	40,845	172,727
West Bromwich, 374 High Street, West Bromwich, W. Midlands B70 8LR	517,206	3,734,800
Yorkshire, Yorkshire House, Yorkshire Drive, Bradford BD5 8LJ	1,821,237	12,468,163

(a) Building Society are the last words in every society's name
(b) Includes both investing and borrowing members. Some totals are estimated or the latest available
(c) From latest available balance sheet – mainly as at 31 December 2001

National Savings and Investments

National Savings and Investments (formerly National savings) is one of the largest savings organisations in the UK, and is a government department and executive agency of HM Treasury. Savings and investment products are offered to personal savers and investors and money placed with National Savings and Investments is used to manage the national debt more effectively. When people invest in national savings they are lending money to the government which pays them interest in return.

INVESTMENT AND ORDINARY ACCOUNTS

Interest is earned at 0.6 per cent per year on each ordinary account for every complete calendar month in which the balance is £500 or more. The minimum deposit is £10; maximum balance £10,000 plus interest credited.

The investment account pays a higher rate of interest depending on the account balance (the current rate can be found at any post office). The minimum deposit is £20; maximum balance £100,000 plus interest credited.

Since April 1999 Individual Savings Accounts (ISAs) have been offered by National Savings and Investments. A cash mini ISA can be opened with £10. Interest is calculated daily on balances of over £1 and is free of tax. The same regulations apply as for ISAs offered by all companies.

PREMIUM BONDS

Premium Bonds are a government security which were first introduced in 1956. Premium Bonds enable savers to enter a regular draw for tax-free prizes, while retaining the right to get their money back. A sum equivalent to interest on each bond is put into a prize fund and distributed by monthly prize draws. (The rate of interest is 2.5 per cent per year from 1 March 2002.) The prizes are drawn by ERNIE (electronic random number indicator equipment) and are free of all UK income tax and capital gains tax.

Bonds are in units of £1, with a minimum purchase of £100; above this, purchases must be in multiples of £10, up to a maximum holding limit of £20,000 per person. The scheme offers a facility to reinvest prize wins automatically. Upon completion of an automatic prize reinvestment mandate, holders receive new bonds which are immediately eligible for future prize draws. Bonds can only be held in the name of an individual and not by organisations.

Bonds become eligible for prizes once they have been held for one clear calendar month following the month of purchase. Each £1 unit can win only one prize per draw, but it will be awarded the highest for which it is drawn. Bonds remain eligible for prizes until they are repaid. When a holder dies, bonds remain eligible for prizes up to and including the twelfth monthly draw after the month in which the holder dies.

Following the June 2002 prize draw, nearly 600,000 prizes totalling £34.1 million were distributed. Between July 2001 and June 2002, some 8,200,000 prizes were awarded at a total value of around £500 million.

INCOME BONDS

National Savings and Investments Income Bonds were introduced in 1982. They are suitable for those who want to receive regular monthly payments of interest while preserving the full cash value of their capital. The bonds are sold in multiples of £500. The minimum holding is £500 and the maximum £1,000,000 (sole or joint holding).

Interest is calculated on a day-to-day basis and paid monthly. Interest is taxable but is paid without deduction of tax at source. The bonds have a guaranteed life of ten years, but may be repaid at par before maturity on giving three months' notice. Repayment is also possible without giving notice but incurs a penalty. If the sole or sole surviving holder dies, however, no fixed period of notice is required and there is no loss of interest for repayment made within the first year.

PENSIONERS GUARANTEED INCOME BONDS

Pensioners Guaranteed Income Bonds were introduced in January 1994 and are designed for people aged 60 and over who wish to receive regular monthly payments with a rate of interest that is fixed for a five-year period whilst preserving the full cash value of their investment. A two-year fixed rate term bond was introduced in May 1999. In October 2000 a new one-year fixed rate term bond was also introduced.

The minimum limit for each purchase is £500. The maximum holding is £1,000,000 (sole or joint holding); within those limits bonds can be bought for any amount in pounds and pence. The rate of interest is fixed and guaranteed for the first one, two or five years, depending on the term invested in. Interest is taxable but is paid without deduction of tax at source.

Holders can apply for repayment (or part repayment of a bond subject to the minimum holding limits) by giving 60 days' notice (if repayment is before the fifth anniversary date). No interest is earned during the notice period. If repayment is requested within two weeks of any fifth anniversary of purchase, there is no formal period of notice. Repayment is possible without giving notice but a penalty is incurred. On the death of a holder or sole surviving investor in a joint holding, repayment will be made without notice. Interest will be paid in full up to the date of repayment.

CHILDREN'S BONUS BONDS

Children's Bonus Bonds were introduced in 1991. The latest issue, Issue 3, was introduced on 22 March 2002. They can be bought for any child under 16 and will go on growing in value until he or she is 21. The bonds are sold in multiples of £25. The minimum holding is £25. The maximum holding in Issue 3 is £1,000 per child. This is in addition to holdings of earlier issues of the bond (excluding interest and bonuses). Bonds for children under 16 must be held by a parent or guardian.

Children's Bonus Bonds (Issue 3) earn 3.0 per cent a year over five years. A bonus (9.60 per cent) of the purchase price is added at the fifth anniversary. This is equal to 4.65 per cent a year compound. All returns are totally exempt from UK income tax. No interest is earned on bonds cashed in before the first anniversary of purchase. Bonuses are only payable if the bond is held until the next bonus date. Bonds over five years old continue to earn interest and bonuses until the holder is 21, when they should be cashed in. If bonds are not cashed in on the holder's 21st birthday, they earn no interest after that birthday.

FIXED RATE SAVINGS BOND

Fixed Rate Savings Bonds are lump sum investments that earn guaranteed rates of interest over set periods of time from six months to three years. Interest, from which basic rate tax is deducted at source, can be paid out or reinvested into the bond monthly, annually or at the end of the term. Holders can also choose where the interest is paid.

CAPITAL BONDS

National Savings and Investments Capital Bonds were introduced in 1989. The latest series, Series 6, was introduced on 22 March 2002. Capital Bonds offer capital growth over five years with guaranteed returns at fixed rates. The interest is taxable each year (for those who pay income tax) but is not deducted at source. The minimum purchase is £100. There is a maximum holding limit of £250,000 from Series B onwards.

Capital Bonds will be repaid in full with all interest gained at the end of five years. No interest is earned on bonds repaid in the first year. Reinvestment or extension terms may also be available.

NATIONAL SAVINGS AND INVESTMENTS TREASURER'S ACCOUNT

The Treasurer's Account, introduced in September 1996, offers attractive rates and security to non-profit making organisations such as charities, friendly societies, clubs, etc. The minimum holding is £10,000 and the maximum is £2 million. Interest is paid at the rate of 3.00 per cent a year on holdings of £10,000 to £24,999, 3.20 per cent a year on holdings of £25,000 to £99,999, and 3.60 per cent a year on holdings of £100,000 and above.

NATIONAL SAVINGS AND INVESTMENTS CERTIFICATES

RECENT ISSUES

Interest, index-linked increase, bonus or other sum payable is free of UK income tax (including investment income surcharge) and capital gains tax.

From June 1982, savings certificates of the 7th to 43rd Issues have been extended on general extension rates as they reach the end of their existing extension periods. The percentage interest rate is determined by the Treasury and any change in this general extension rate will be applicable from the first of the month following its announcement. Under the system, a certificate earns interest for each complete period of three months beyond the expiry of the previous extension terms. Within each three-month period, interest is calculated separately for each month at the rate applicable from the beginning of that month. The interest for each month is one-twelfth of the annual rate (i.e. it does not vary with the number of days in the month) and is capitalised annually on the anniversary of the date of purchase. The current rate of interest under the general extension rate is given in leaflets available at post offices. Since October 2001, the holders of other Issues have had the option to reinvest or rollover.

National Savings and Investments can be contacted on 0845-694 5000 or by email at customerenquiries@nsandi.com.
Visit the National Savings and Investments website at www.nsandi.com

Insurance

AUTHORISATION

The Insurance Companies Act 1982 empowered the Department of Trade and Industry, Insurance Division to authorise corporate bodies to transact insurance in the United Kingdom provided they comply with the financial and other regulations detailed in the Act. In January 1998 an interim transfer of this function to the Insurance Directorate of HM Treasury was completed. The Financial Services and Markets Act transferred this function to the Insurance and Friendly Societies Division of the Financial Services Authority, (FSA), 25 The North Colonnade, London E14 5HS; www.fsa.gov.uk.

At the end of 2001 there were over 820 insurance companies with authorisation from the FSA to transact one or more classes of insurance business. However, with the establishment of the single European insurance market on 1 July 1994 an insurer authorised in any of the European Union countries can now transact insurance in the UK without further formality; this creates a potential market of over 5,000 insurance companies.

REGULATION

Over 23,000 firms are authorised to conduct a wide variety of investment business in the UK. The overall regulator for investment business of any kind is the Financial Services Authority.

The FSA does not undertake all the regulatory work itself. Instead it recognises a number of specialist bodies to carry out the frontline regulation. The bulk of this work is undertaken by three Self Regulating Organisations (SROs).

The main regulator of firms advising on and arranging deals in life insurance and pensions, friendly society investments, unit trusts and investment trusts is one of the SROs, the Personal Investment Authority (PIA), 25 The North Colonnade, Canary Wharf, London E14 5HS.

Disputes between policyholders and life or general insurers can be referred to the Financial Ombudsman Service administered by the FSA. The Chief Ombudsman is Walter Merricks. Private policyholders with a complaint against their insurer must firstly take the matter to the highest level within the company. Thereafter, if it remains unresolved, they can refer their problem, free of charge, to the Ombudsman who examines the facts of a complaint and delivers a decision, which is binding on the insurer (but not the policy holder). Small businesses with a turnover of up to £1m also have access to the scheme. The Financial Ombudsman Service also covers other areas of the industry including banks, building societies and investment firms.

ASSOCIATION OF BRITISH INSURERS

Over 97 per cent of the world-wide business of UK insurance companies is transacted by the 400 members of the Association of British Insurers (ABI), 51 Gresham Street, London EC2V 7HQ; www.abi.org.uk. ABI is a trade association which represents both life and general insurers.

Chairman, Mike Ross
Chief Executive, Mary Francis

GENERAL INSURANCE STANDARDS COUNCIL

The General Insurance Standards Council, 110 Cannon Street, London EC4N 6EU; www.gisc.co.uk, is a non-statutory regulatory organisation for the general insurance industry. It was initially intended that GISC would regulate the sales, advisory and service standards of insurers, intermediaries and brokers. However, in December 2001 the Treasury announced that the selling of general insurance would be regulated by the FSA from 2003. The need for this move was not based on any perceived inadequacy in the GISC but the statutory regulation requirements of the EC Intermediaries Directive which the GISC could not achieve.

BALANCE OF PAYMENTS

The insurance industry contributes just over 2 per cent to the UK's Gross Domestic Product (GDP). In 2000 the total overseas earnings of the UK insurance sector was nearly £8 billion.

TAKEOVERS AND MERGERS

The year 2001 was considerably quieter than 2000 for take-overs and mergers. Major activity saw Liverpool Victoria acquire the Royal Pension Fund for Nurses and Churchill Insurance acquire the General Insurance business of Pearl Assurance (part of AMP).

GENERAL INSURANCE

The tragic events in New York and Washington on 11 September 2001 had repercussions that went far beyond insurance. Nevertheless, claims arising out of the damage caused to the World Trade Centre are estimated to be between $40 billion and $70 billion. This is by far the largest insurance loss ever. In the past, serious disasters have often led to large claims but these have been in a small number of classes of business. This event involved claims on many different types of insurance including life, workman's compensation, legal liability, personal accident, holiday insurance as well as the more obvious aircraft, property damage and business interruption.

The only way insurers throughout the world are able to deal with claims of this magnitude is through the reinsurance contracts they have in place to deal with catastrophes. Not surprisingly, reinsurers began looking at the cover they offer for terrorist damage shortly after 11 September 2001. First to feel the effects were aviation insurers who found that terrorism reinsurance cover was withdrawn almost immediately. Government intervention in many countries, including the UK, was required to maintain cover. Other forms of reinsurance, such as commercial property, were also under threat. This led to the Treasury announcing in December 2001 that it was reviewing, with the ABI and others, the extent of cover offered by the jointly funded Pool Re which was set up to reinsure the risks from terrorist attack posed by the IRA and others in the 1990s.

Further flooding in the UK during late 2000 and early 2001 led to calls for action by the Government on planning guidance for flood plain areas and improving coastal and river defences. Initially an agreement was made that property in areas prone to flooding should continue to be able to get insurance cover (albeit on higher terms) but there were indications by early 2002 that some insurers may not be prepared to continue with this.

General insurance fraud continued to be a problem throughout the year which led to the launch of a new database of all insured vehicles. This will be a major

factor in the battle against uninsured driving which is believed to cost honest policyholders over £400 million per year. This move was not without criticism, however, as some commentators believe that driving uninsured becomes a more attractive option as premiums increase and fines for offenders remain low.

September 11 aside, claims figures continued to show rises for commercial and domestic fire and domestic theft. Weather damage claims and commercial theft recorded small falls but these were from record levels in 2000.

At the end of 2001 the Treasury announced that to comply with the EC Intermediaries Directive, the Financial Services Authority would take over the regulation of general insurance. During 2001 the system was self-regulated by a code administered by the ABI and it was intended that this would transfer to the General Insurance Standards Council. Although GISC will continue in the short-term, the FSA will act a statutory regulator from a date to be agreed.

LONDON INSURANCE MARKET

The London Insurance Market is a distinct, separate sector of the UK insurance and reinsurance industry. It is the world's leading market for internationally traded insurance and reinsurance, its business comprising mainly overseas non-life large and high-exposure risks. The market is centred on the City of London, which provides the required international financial, banking, legal and other support services. Currently there are 86 Lloyd's syndicates, 70 insurance companies and 34 Marine Protection and Indemnity Clubs active in the market. In 2000 the market had a written gross premium income of over £15,000 million. Most of the business is brought to the market Lloyd's brokers.

The trade association for the international insurance and reinsurance companies writing primarily non-marine insurance and all classes of reinsurance business in the London Market is the International Underwriting Association (IUA) London Underwriting Centre, 3 Minster Court, Mincing Lane, London EC3R 7DD; www.iua.co.uk.

BRITISH INSURANCE COMPANIES

The following insurance company figures refer to members and certain non-members of the ABI.

CLAIMS STATISTICS (£ million)

	2000	2001
Domestic claims		
Theft	542	568
Fire	334	371
Weather	857	933
Subsidence	350	265
Business interruption	n/a	n/a
Total	2,083	2,137
Commercial claims		
Theft	198	159
Fire	521	679
Weather	438	172
Subsidence	n/a	n/a
Business interruption	215	97
Total	1,372	1,107

WORLD-WIDE GENERAL BUSINESS TRADING RESULT

	1999 £m	2000 £m
Net written premiums	34,870	36,649
Underwriting profit (loss) for one year account business	(3,519)	(4,920)
Transfer to profit and loss account for 3 year business		
Marine, Aviation, Transport	(177)	(352)
Other	(186)	(406)
Total underwriting result	(3,519)	(4,920)
Net investment income	4,414	5,880
Overall trading profit	895	960
Profit as % of premium income	2.6	2.6

WORLD-WIDE GENERAL BUSINESS UNDERWRITING RESULT

	1999					2000				
	UK	Other EU	USA	Other	Total	UK	Other EU	USA	Other	Total
Motor										
Premiums: £m	7,044	1,592	1,425	1,587	11,648	7,648	1,814	1,948	1,624	13,034
Profit (loss): £m	(1,310)	(352)	(93)	(56)	(1,811)	(916)	(275)	(347)	(74)	(1,612)
% of premiums	(18.6)	(22.1)	(6.5)	(3.5)	(15.5)	(12.0)	(15.1)	(3.8)	(4.6)	(12.4)
Non-motor										
Premiums: £m	12,794	2,549	2,114	1,627	19,084	12,334	2,869	2,841	1,744	19,788
Profit (loss): £m	(433)	(51)	(195)	(178)	(857)	(875)	(326)	(789)	(106)	(2,096)
% of premiums	(3.4)	(2)	(9.2)	(11.0)	(4.5)	(7.1)	(11.4)	(27.8)	(6.1)	(10.6)

NET PREMIUM INCOME BY TERRITORY 2000

	UK £m	Other EU £m	USA £m	Other £m	Total £m
Motor	7,648	1,814	1,948	1,624	13,034
Non-motor	12,334	2,869	2,841	1,744	19,788
Marine, Aviation and Transport	850	212	131	132	1,325
Non-MAT reinsurance	1,231	305	28	229	1,793
Other funded business	627	19	0.5	17	835.5
Total general business	22,690	5,219	4,948.5	3,746	36,603
Ordinary long-term	118,044	7,993	5,596	6,840	138,473
Industrial long-term	754	—	—	—	754
Total long-term business	118,798	7,993	5,596	6,840	139,227

LLOYD'S OF LONDON

Lloyd's of London is an international market for almost all types of general insurance. Lloyd's currently has a capacity to accept insurance premiums of over £11,000 million. Much of this business comes from outside Great Britain and makes a valuable contribution to the balance of payments.

A policy is underwritten at Lloyd's by a mixture of private and corporate members, corporate members having been admitted for the first time in 1992. Specialist underwriters accept insurance risks at Lloyd's on behalf of members (referred to as 'Names') grouped in syndicates. There are currently 108 syndicates of varying sizes, some with up to 2,000 names, each managed by an underwriting agent approved by the Council of Lloyd's.

Individual members are still in the majority at Lloyd's with a total of 2,848 individuals as opposed to 895 corporate members. In 2001 the market capacity of the corporate sector was £9,258 million while individuals represented £1,800 million of capacity.

Lloyd's is incorporated by an Act of Parliament (Lloyd's Acts 1971 onwards) and is governed by a Council comprising six working and six external members together with six nominated members whose appointment is confirmed by the Governor of the Bank of England. Market management is handled by a Market Board of 18 members (comprising three working members of the Council, three external members of the Council and three Corporation executives including the chief executive officer, eight additional market practitioners and one external member. Regulation is supervised by a Board of 15 members Chaired by John Young who is also Deputy Chairman of the Council of Lloyd's.

The Corporation is a non-profit making body chiefly financed by its members' subscriptions. It provides the premises, administrative staff and services enabling Lloyd's underwriting syndicates to conduct their business. It does not, however, assume corporate liability for the risks accepted by its members. Individual members are responsible to the full extent of their personal means for their underwriting affairs.

At present, Lloyd's syndicates have no direct contact with the public. All business is transacted through insurance brokers accredited by the Corporation of Lloyd's. In addition, non-Lloyd's brokers in the UK, when guaranteed by Lloyd's brokers, are able to deal directly with Lloyd's motor syndicates, a facility which has made the Lloyd's market more accessible to the insuring public.

On 30 November 2001 the Financial Services and Markets Act came fully into force and the Financial Services Authority took over ultimate responsibility for the regulation of the Lloyd's market. However, in situations where Lloyd's internal regulatory and compensation arrangements are more far-reaching, as for

example with the Lloyd's Central Fund, which safeguards claim payments to policyholders, the regulatory role is delegated to the Council of Lloyd's.

Lloyd's also provides the most comprehensive shipping intelligence service in the world. The shipping and other information received from Lloyd's agents, shipowners, news agencies and other sources throughout the world is collated and distributed to the media as well as to the maritime and commercial sectors in general. *Lloyd's List* is London's oldest daily newspaper and contains news of general commercial interest as well as shipping information. *Lloyd's Shipping Index*, also published daily, lists some 25,000 ocean-going vessels in alphabetical order and gives the latest known report of each.

RECENT DEVELOPMENTS

The loss for the 1999 year of account was £1,891 million, a further steep rise on the £1,065 million figure for 1998. The losses reflected the very poor rating conditions and a high level of catastrophes. It was always expected that 1999 would be the bottom of the underwriting cycle with early indications of the 2000 out-turn being slightly better but still very much on the negative side.

December 1999 saw three severe windstorms in Europe – Anatole, Lothar and Martin – which cost insurers $10 billion. The year also saw earthquakes in Taiwan and Turkey. Added to these losses, the market saw some of the softest rates over almost all classes of insurance. In marine insurance, for example, premiums had fallen by up to 75 per cent between 1994 and 1999.

There is very little that is positive in a review of 1999 results for Lloyd's and the losses are clearly not going to improve with the effects of 11 September taking their toll in the next two years of account. However, the negative publicity generated by the disputes between disaffected Names and Lloyd's in previous years look to have significantly reduced.

Chairman, Saxon Riley
Chief Executive, Nick Prettejohn

LLOYD'S MEMBERSHIP

	1999	2000	2001
Total no. of underwriting members participating			
Individuals	4,503	3,296	2,848
Corporate	668	853	895

TOTAL MARKET CAPACITY

	1999 £m	2000 £m	2001 £m
Individual	2,700	2,003	1,800
Corporate	7,170	8,062	9,258
Total	9,870	10,065	11,058

LLOYD'S PREMIUM INCOME 2000 BY CATEGORY

	MAT	Home Foreign	Non-marine Treaty	Accident & Health	Motor	Property	General liability	Pecuniary loss	Total
	£m	£m	£m	£m	£m	£m	£m	£m	£m
Gross premiums	2,465.3	3,714.8	2,285.7	171.8	1,427.3	385.7	504.9	194.2	11,149.7
Net Premiums	1,322.1	3,149.1	1,543.8	159.2	1,275.5	318.9	407.0	186.3	8,361.8

	1998 and prior years of account £m	1999 pure year results £m
Gross premiums written (net of brokerage)	7,6621	8,958
Outward reinsurance premiums	2,747	3,126
Net premiums	4,874	5,832
Reinsurance to close premiums received from earlier years of account	5,060	–
Amounts retained to meet all known and unknown outstanding liabilities brought forward	345	–
	10,279	5,832
Gross claims paid	7,929	7,246
Reinsurers' share	3,081	2,707
Net claims	4,848	4,539
Other reinsurance premiums paid to close the year of account	5,530	2,032
Amounts retained to meet all known and unknown outstanding liabilities carried forward	678	824
	11,056	7,395
Underwriting result	(777)	(1,641)
Other profit (loss) on exchange	0	(28)
Syndicate operating expenses	(497)	(545)
Balance on technical account	(1,274)	(2,214)
Investment income	478	492
Investment expenses and charges	(9)	(9)
Investment gains less losses	(42)	74
Result before personal expenses	(763)	(1,657)
Personal expenses	(302)	(234)
Result after personal expenses	(1,065)	(1,891)

LIFE AND LONG-TERM INSURANCE AND PENSIONS

Lloyd's, Life Insurance

Low interest rates and poor investment returns continued to have an effect on Life and long-term insurance in the UK. New regular premium business rose 16.7 per cent to £4,100 million. Single premium business saw an increase of 2.7 per cent to £50,400 million. Sixty per cent of both individual regular premium business and single premium business are now sold by Independent Financial Advisers (IFAs). Direct sales forces account for about a quarter with the remainder sold by tied agents, direct marketing, telesales and other sales channels.

A number of important regulatory moves occurred during 2001. During the year, evidence was gathered for a major Government review of medium and long-term savings. Policy makers, regulators, the Government and product providers all agreed that there was a serious savings gap – the difference between the amount individuals would need for a financially secure retirement and the actual amount currently being saved. In a report prepared for ABI the savings gap was estimated to be £27 billion.

One measure designed to help reduce the savings gap was launched in April 2001. Stakeholder pensions were an attempt by the Government to give more people, particularly those in the lower income groups, opportunity to save for their retirement by investing in a low-cost flexible pension. These contracts have a cap on charges. Following the launch, fifty products became available and by the end of 2001 just under 650,000 contracts had been purchased. The main question for the Government to address is whether further incentives, or maybe even compulsion, will help achieve the aim of closing the savings gap?

Low interest rates and investment returns continued to contribute to problems for holders of low-cost endowment mortgages. Following a review by the Financial Services Authority, holders of all endowments now have their contracts checked by their insurers and receive a notification of any action needed to ensure that their funds are sufficient to repay their mortgage.

In October 2001, ABI and the Government agreed the details of a five-year moratorium on the use of genetic test results by insurers. It is hoped that during the five years all stakeholders will have an opportunity to agree on the way this controversial issue will be handled for the future.

New Non-Linked Personal Pension Business

	Regular premium policies		Single premium policies	
	No. new policies	New premiums £m	No. new policies	New premiums £m
1996	307,000	391	114,000	1,865
1997	330,000	424	144,000	2,173
1998	419,000	555	125,000	1,419
1999	316,000	443	109,000	1,273
2000	213,000	431	68,000	1,520
New Linked Personal Pension Business				
1996	573,000	582	165,000	2,169
1997	693,000	768	196,000	2,913
1998	730,000	919	173,000	2,989
1999	750,000	1,000	184,000	3,241
2000	556,000	1,108	236,000	3,430

NET PREMIUM INCOME FOR WORLD-WIDE LONG-
TERM INSURANCE BUSINESS

	1999 £m	2000 £m
Ordinary Branch		
Business written in UK		
Annual premiums		
Life	13,085	13,041
Annuities	45	35
Pensions	12,646	12,173
Income Protection	795	960
Industrial Business	858	754
Single premiums		
Life	23,471	25,861
Annuities	156	237
Pensions	37,245	63,318
Income protection	85	174
Business written overseas		
Annual premiums	5,118	6,583
Single premiums	12,943	13,846
Total	*105,630*	*136,227*

PAYMENTS TO POLICYHOLDERS

	1999 £m	2000 £m
Payments to UK policyholders	60,816	82,114
Payments to overseas policyholders	10,861	12,914
Total	*71,677*	*95,028*

INVESTMENTS OF INSURANCE COMPANIES 2000

Investment of funds	Long-term business £m	General business £m
Index-linked British Government securities	23,704	1,945
Non-index-linked British Government securities	97,898	10,571
Other UK public sector debt securities	10,264	1,157
Overseas government, provincial and municipal securities	35,005	13,918
Debentures, loan shares, preference and guaranteed stocks and shares		
UK	101,206	11,275
Overseas	42,149	6,512
Ordinary stocks and shares		
UK	374,526	16,545
Overseas	136,219	9,067
Unit trusts		
Equities	72,681	918
Fixed interest	3,541	34
Loans secured on property	13,994	2,371
Real property and ground rents	58,052	3,400
Other invested assets	73,506	26,168
Total invested assets	*1,042,745*	*1,038,851*
Net investment income	*36,348*	*5,693*

The London Stock Exchange

The London Stock Exchange serves the needs of industry and investors by providing facilities for raising capital and a central market-place for securities trading. This market-place covers government stocks (called gilts), UK and overseas company shares (called equities and fixed interest stocks), and traditional options.

PRIMARY MARKETS

The Exchange enables companies to raise capital for development and growth through the issue of securities. For a company entering the market for the first time there is a choice of Exchange markets, depending upon the size, history and requirements of the company. The first is the main market, which exists for well-established companies; these must comply with stringent criteria relating to all aspects of their operations.

A company's securities are admitted to the Official List by the UK Listing Authority (UKLA), a division of the Financial Services Authority, and also admitted to trading by the Exchange. In parallel to the UKLA's listing process, the Exchange has its own set of admission and disclosure standards which are designed to sit alongside the UKLA's listing rules.

The Alternative Investment Market (AIM) began trading in June 1995. It enables small, young and growing companies to raise capital, widen their investor base and have their shares traded on a regulated market without the expense of a full Exchange listing. Many companies use AIM as a stepping-stone to a full listing.

Once admitted to the Exchange, all companies are obliged to keep their shareholders informed of their progress, making announcements of a price-sensitive nature through the Exchange's company announcement department.

At the end of 2001 there were 1,809 UK companies listed on the London Stock Exchange; their equity capital had a total market value of £1,523 billion. In addition, 453 international companies were listed, with a total equity market value of £2,580 billion. By the end of 2001 AIM had attracted 629 companies, with a total capitalisation of £11.6 million.

UK equity turnover in 2001 was £1,904,844 million with an average 127,000 bargains a day. International equity turnover in 2001 totalled £3,676,342 million.

BIG BANG

During 1986 the London Stock Exchange went through the greatest period of change in its 200-year history. In March 1986 it opened its doors for the first time to overseas and corporate membership of the Exchange, allowing banks, insurance companies and overseas securities houses to become members of the Exchange and to buy existing member firms. On 27 October 1986, three major reforms took place, changes which became known as 'Big Bang'.

- the abolition of scales of minimum commissions, allowing clients to negotiate freely with their brokers about the charge for their services
- the abolition of the separation of member firms into brokers and jobbers: firms are now broker/dealers, able to act as agents on behalf of clients; to act as principals buying and selling shares for their own account; and to become registered market makers, making continuous buying and selling prices in specific securities
- the introduction of the Stock Exchange automated quotations (SEAQ) system

Since the introduction of SEAQ in 1986, dealing in stocks and shares has taken place by telephone in the firms' own dealing rooms, rather than face to face on the floor of the Exchange. The Stock Exchange Electronic Trading Service (SETS), launched in 1997, introduced over-driven trading in which deals are executed electronically on an electronic order book. SETS runs alongside SEAQ and allows remote control access to the Exchange. The new systems also provide increased investor protection. All deals taking place via the Exchange systems are recorded on a database which can be used to resolve disputes or to carry out investigations.

Members of the London Stock Exchange buy and sell shares on behalf of the public, as well as institutions such as pension funds or insurance companies. In return for transacting the deal, the broker will charge a commission, which is usually based upon the value of the transaction. The market makers, or wholesalers, in each security do not charge a commission for their services, but will quote the broker two prices, a price at which they will buy and a price at which they will sell. It is the middle of these two prices which is published in lists of Stock Exchange prices in newspapers.

REGULATORY BODIES

The London Stock Exchange and the Securities and Futures Authority are the two main regulatory bodies. They were formed under the provisions of the Financial Services Act 1986, which requires investment businesses to be authorised and regulated by a self-regulating organisation (SRO), of which the Securities and Futures Authority is one. The Act also requires business to be conducted through a recognised investment exchange (RIE). The London Stock Exchange is an RIE, regulating three main markets: UK equities, international equities and gilts. In May 2000 the UKLA, which regulates the flotation of UK companies on public markets, transferred to the Financial Services Authority.

DEMUTUALISATION AND LISTING

On 15 March 2000, the 298 members voted to become shareholders in a demutualised London Stock Exchange, making possible the further commercialisation of the company.

At the end of May 2001 the exchange announced its intention to list on its own main market. The exchange listed on 20 July following an annual general meeting on 19 July 2001. The full listing is intended to enable the Exchange to exploit business opportunities with greater flexibility.

LONDON STOCK EXCHANGE, Old Broad Street, London EC2N 1HP. Tel: 020-7797 1000
Web: www.londonstockexchange.com
Chairman, D. Cruickshank
Chief Executive, C. Furse
Executive Directors, M. Wheatley, J. Howell
Non-Executive Directors, G. Allen, CBE; Baroness Cohen; O. Fanjul; M. Marks; P. Meinertzhagen; I. Salter; N. Stapleton; R. Webb, QC.

Financial Services Regulation

THE FINANCIAL SERVICES AUTHORITY

The FSA is the independent watchdog set up under the Financial Services and Markets Act 2000 (FSMA) to regulate financial services in the UK and protect the rights of retail customers. The FSA's aim is to maintain efficient, orderly and clean financial markets and help consumers get a fair deal.

The FSA is required to pursue four statutory objectives:
– maintaining market confidence
– raising public awareness
– protecting consumers
– reducing financial crime

The legislation also requires the FSA to carry out its general functions, whilst having regard to:
– the need to use its resources in the most efficient way
– the responsibilities of regulated firms' own management
– being proportionate in imposing burdens or restrictions on the industry.
– facilitating innovation
– the international character of financial services and the competitive position of the United Kingdom
– the need to facilitate, and not have unnecessarily adverse effect, on competition

THE FSA AS AN ORGANISATION

The FSA is a company limited by guarantee, financed by levies on the industry. It receives no funds from the public purse. It is accountable to Treasury Ministers and, through them, to Parliament. Under the new legislation the FSA must report annually on the achievement of its statutory objectives to the Treasury, which is required to lay the report before Parliament.

The FSA's governing body is a board, consisting of a chairman, three executive directors and eleven non-executives, all appointed by the Treasury. The Board sets overall FSA policy. Day-to-day operational decisions and management of the staff are the responsibility of the Executive. The Chairman is responsible for the overall strategic direction and management of the FSA. Three Managing Directors and a Chief Operating Officer report to the chairman. Together they constitute the executive management of the FSA.

The FSA currently has over 2,200 staff. Its total budget for 2002–3 is £221.1 million. The FSA regulates approximately 11,000 institutions. This total includes over 7,500 investment firms, over 650 banks, around 70 building societies, almost 1,000 insurance companies and friendly societies, about 1,000 professional firms, around 700 credit unions and the Lloyd's insurance market. In addition the FSA regulates about 180,000 approved individuals.

FSA CENTRAL REGISTER/CONSUMER HELPLINE

The FSA maintains a Central Register of all firms that are, or were, authorised to carry on investment business and authorised deposit takers. The entry for each firm gives its name, address and telephone number; a reference number; its authorisation status; and states which organisation regulates it; and whether it can handle client money.

The Consumer Helpline is available to members of the public seeking information about firms listed on the register. In addition, the Helpline explains complaints procedures and provides information on what is and is not regulated by the FSA.

Consumer Helpline: 0845-606 1234
Web: www.fsa.gov.uk

FINANCIAL SERVICES AUTHORITY, 25 the North Colonade, Canary Wharf, London E14 5HS. Tel: 020-7676 1000. Fax: 020-7676 1099. *Chairman*, Howard Davies

COMPENSATION

Under the FSMA the Financial Services Compensation Scheme (FSCS) replaced the eight previous compensation schemes. It provides compensation if an authorised firm is unable or likely to be unable to pay claims against it. This is usually when a firm stops trading or is insolvent. The FSCS covers deposits, insurance and investments.

The FSCS is independent from the FSA, with separate staff and premises. However, the FSA appoints the board of the FSCS and makes its rules. The FSCS is funded by levies on authorised firms.

THE FINANCIAL SERVICES COMPENSATION SCHEME, 7th Floor, Lloyds Chambers, 1 Portsoken Street, E1 8BN. Tel: 020-7892 7300. Fax: 020-7892 7301. Email: enquiries@fscs.org.uk Web: www.fscs.org.uk *Chairman*, Nigel Hamilton. *Chief Executive*, Suzanne McCarthy

AUTHORISED DEPOSIT-TAKING INSTITUTIONS

For deposit-taking institutions, *see* Banking

DESIGNATED PROFESSIONAL BODIES

Professional firms are exempt from requiring direct regulation by the FSA if they carry out only certain restricted activities that arise out of, or are complementary to the provision of professional services, such as arranging the sale of shares on the instructions of executors or trustees or providing services to small, private companies. These firms are, however, supervised by Designated Professional Bodies (DPBs). There are a number of safeguards to protect consumers dealing with firms that do not require direct regulation. These arrangements include:
– FSA's power to ban a specific firm from taking advantage of the exemption and to restrict the regulated activities permitted to the firms
– rules which require professional firms to ensure that their clients are aware that they are not authorised persons
– a requirement for the DPBs to supervise and regulate the firms and inform the FSA on how the professional firms carry on their regulated activities

The DPBs are:

INSTITUTE OF CHARTERED ACCOUNTANTS IN ENGLAND AND WALES, Chartered Accountants' Hall, PO Box 433, Moorgate Place, London EC2P 2BJ. Tel: 020-7920 8100

INSTITUTE OF CHARTERED ACCOUNTANTS OF SCOTLAND, CA House, 21 Haymarket Yards, Edinburgh EH12 5BH. Tel: 0131-347 0100

INSTITUTE OF CHARTERED ACCOUNTANTS IN IRELAND, 11 Donegall Square South, Belfast BT1 5JE. Tel: 028-9032 1600

ASSOCIATION OF CHARTERED CERTIFIED ACCOUNTANTS, 29 Lincoln's Inn Fields, London WC2A 3EE. Tel: 020-7396 7000

INSTITUTE OF ACTUARIES, Staple Inn Hall, High Holborn, London WC1V 7QJ. Tel: 020-7632 2100

THE LAW SOCIETY OF ENGLAND AND WALES, 113 Chancery Lane, London WC2A 1PL. Tel: 020-7242 1222

LAW SOCIETY OF NORTHERN IRELAND, Law Society House, 98 Victoria Street, Belfast BT1 3JZ. Tel: 028-9023 1614

LAW SOCIETY OF SCOTLAND, Law Society's Hall, 26 Drumsheugh Gardens, Edinburgh EH3 7YR. Tel: 0131-226 7411

RECOGNISED INVESTMENT EXCHANGES

The FSA supervises eight Recognised Investment Exchanges (RIEs). These are organised markets on which member firms can trade investments such as equities and derivatives. Examples are the London Stock Exchange and the London Metal exchange. As a regulator the FSA must also focus on the impact of changes brought about by the continued growth in electronic trading by exchanges and other organisations. Issues such as how these changes affect market quality, reliability and access are important and the FSA works with the exchanges to ensure that new systems meet regulatory requirements. The RIEs are:

COREDEAL MTS LTD, 99 Bishopsgate, London EC2M 3XD. Tel: 020-7786 6001. Fax: 020-7786 6012

INTERNATIONAL PETROLEUM EXCHANGE (IPE), International House, 1 St Katharine's Way, London E1W 1UY. Tel: 020-7481 0643. Fax: 020-7481 8485

JIWAY, Old London Exchange, 131 Finsbury Pavement, London EC2A 1NT. Tel: 020-7065 8700. Fax: 020-7065 8705. Email: info@jiway.com Web: www.jiway.com

LONDON INTERNATIONAL FINANCIAL FUTURES EXCHANGE (LIFFE), Cannon Bridge House, 1 Cousins Lane, London EC4R 3XX. Tel: 020-7623 0444

LONDON METAL EXCHANGE (LME), 56 Leadenhall Street, London EC3A 2DX. Tel: 020-7264 5555. Fax: 020-7680 0505

LONDON STOCK EXCHANGE (LSE), Old Broad Street, London EC2N 1HP. Tel: 020-7797 1000. Web: www.londonstockexchange.com

OM GROUP, 131 Finsbury Pavement, London EC2A 1NT. Tel: 020-7065 8000. Fax: 020-7065 8001

VIRT-X EXCHANGE LTD, 34th Floor, One Canada Square, London E14 5AA. Tel: 020-7074 4444. Fax: 020-7074 4433. Web: www.virt-x.com

RECOGNISED CLEARING HOUSES

The FSA is also responsible for recognising and supervising Recognised Clearing Houses. These are bodies which organise the settlement of transactions on Recognised Investment Exchanges. These are:

CREST CO LTD, 33 Cannon Street, London EC4M 5SB. Tel: 020-7849 0000. Fax: 020-7849 0130. Email: info@crestco.co.uk Web: www.crestco.co.uk

LONDON CLEARING HOUSE LTD (LCH), Aldgate House, 33 Aldgate High Street, London EC3N 1EA. Tel: 020-7426 7000. Fax: 020-7426 7001

EURO CCP, St Helen's, 1 Undershaft, London EC3A 8EE. Tel: 020-74444 0400. Fax: 020-7444 0404. Web: www.euroccp.com

OMBUDSMAN SCHEMES

The Financial Ombudsman Service has been set up by the Financial Services and Markets Act to provide consumers with a free, independent service for resolving disputes with financial firms. It brought together eight existing complaints-handling schemes within the financial sector including the Banking Ombudsman, the Insurance Ombudsman, the Investment Ombudsman and the Personal Investment Authority Ombudsman.

The Financial Ombudsman Service can help with most financial complaints about:

– Banking services
– Endowment Policies
– Financial and investment advice
– Mortgages
– Health and loan protection insurance
– Household and buildings insurance
– Investment portfolio management
– Life assurance
– Motor insurance
– Personal pension plans (mis-selling)
– Private medical insurance
– Saving plans and accounts
– Stocks and shares
– Travel insurance
– Unit trusts and income bonds

Complainants must first complain to the firm involved. They do not have to accept the ombudsman's decision and are free to go to court if they wish.

The Pensions Ombudsman is appointed and operates under the Pension Schemes Act 1993 as amended by the Pensions Act 1995; he is responsible to Parliament. He investigates and decides complaints and disputes concerning occupational and personal pension schemes, primarily alleged maladministration by the persons responsible for managing pension schemes.

FINANCIAL OMBUDSMAN SERVICE, South Quay Plaza, 183 Marsh Wall, London, E14 9SR Tel: 020-7964 1000 Fax: 020-7964 1001 Web: www.financial-ombudsman.org.uk *Chief Ombudsman*: W. Merricks *Principle Ombudsmen: Banking and Loans*: D. Thomas; *Insurance*: T. Boorman; *Investment*: J. Whittles

THE PENSIONS OMBUDSMAN, 6th Floor, 11 Belgrave Road, London SW1V 1RB. Tel: 020-7834 9144. *Pensions Ombudsman*, D. Laverick

THE TAKEOVER PANEL

The Takeover Panel was set up in 1968 in response to concern about practices unfair to shareholders in take-over bids for public and certain private companies. Its principal objective is to ensure equality of treatment, and fair opportunity for all shareholders to consider on its merits an offer that would result in the change of control of a company. It is a non-statutory body that operates the City code on take-overs and mergers.

The chairman, deputy chairmen and three lay members of the panel are appointed by the Bank of England. The remainder are representatives of the banking, insurance, investment, pension fund and accountancy professional bodies and the CBI.

THE PANEL ON TAKEOVERS AND MERGERS, PO Box 226, The Stock Exchange Building, London, EC2P 2JX. Tel: 020-7382 9026. Web: www.takeoverpanel.org.uk; *Chairman*, Peter Scott, QC

BUYING GOODS ABROAD

JOURNEYS WITHIN THE EU:

Since 30 June 1999, travellers have no longer been able to buy duty- and tax-free goods on journeys within the EU. Only food and drink for consumption on board ferries, aircraft or cruise ships will continue to be duty-and tax free. There are no limits on quantities of goods obtained in the EU provided they are for the traveller's own use. If the guidance levels below are exceeded, the traveller must satisfy a customs officer that the goods are not for commercial use.

Tobacco goods
800 cigarettes *plus* 400 cigarillos *plus* 200 cigars *plus* 1 kg of tobacco
Alcoholic drinks
90 litres of still table wine (not more than 60 litres should be sparkling wine) *plus* 10 litres over 22% vol. (e.g. spirits and strong liqueurs) *plus* 20 litres not over 22% vol. (e.g. low strength liqueurs, fortified wine or sparkling wine) *plus* 110 litres of beer
Perfume No limit *Toilet water* No limit *Other goods* No limit

JOURNEYS TO AND FROM NON-EU COUNTRIES

Duty-and tax free goods are still available to travellers to and from other countries. The quantities are set out below. Passengers under 17 are not, however, entitled to tobacco and drinks allowances.

Tobacco goods
200 cigarettes *or* 100 cigarillos *or* 50 cigars *or* 250 grammes of tobacco
Alcoholic drinks
2 litres of still table wine *plus* 1 litre over 22% vol. (e.g. spirits and strong liqueurs) *or* 2 litres not over 22% vol. (e.g. low strength liqueurs, fortified wine or sparkling wine)
Perfume
50 grammes (60 cc) *Toilet water* 250 cc (9 fl. oz) *Other goods* £145 worth

Anyone visiting the United Kingdom for less than six months is also entitled to bring in, free of duty and tax, all personal effects (except tobacco goods, alcoholic drinks and perfume) which they intend to take with them when they leave.

NOTES ON ALLOWANCES

1. The countries of the European Union are Austria, Belgium, Denmark, Finland, France, Germany, Greece, the Irish Republic, Italy, Luxembourg, the Netherlands, Portugal, Spain (but not the Canary Islands), Sweden and the United Kingdom (but not the Channel Islands)
2. The allowances apply only to goods carried by travellers at the time of their arrival
3. The allowances do not apply to goods brought in for sale or for other commercial purposes
4. The allowances of individuals travelling in a family group cannot be pooled towards an item worth more than the limit
5. If a single item is worth more than the 'other goods' allowance, charges are calculated on the full value, not just on the value above the limit
6. Whisky, gin, rum, brandy, vodka and most liqueurs normally exceed 22% vol. but advocaat, cassis, fraise, suze and aperitifs may be less. Fortified wines include port, sherry, vermouth and madeira. Sparkling wines include champagne, perelada, spumante and semi-sparkling wines. Still table wines include claret, sauterne, graves and chianti. burgundy, chablis, hock and moselle may be either sparkling or still, depending on manufacture

7. One litre is approximately 1 3/4 pints
8. A cigarillo's maximum weight is 3 grammes

PROHIBITED AND RESTRICTED GOODS

Customs officers are able to provide full information. This is a list of more frequently met items:
– Controlled drugs (such as opium, heroin, morphine, cocaine, cannabis, amphetamines, lysergide (LSD) and barbiturates)
– Firearms (including gas pistols, stun guns and similar weapons), ammunition, CS gas sprays, pepper sprays, and explosives
– Offensive weapons (including certain types of knife, swordsticks, knuckle-dusters and other martial arts equipment)
– Counterfeit currency and other counterfeit goods, such as fake watches and sports shirts; goods bearing a false indication of their place of manufacture or in breach of UK copyright
– Obscene books, magazines, films, videotapes, laser discs, computer software and other material
– Radio transmitters (walkie-talkies, Citizen's Band radios, cordless telephones, etc.) not approved for use in the UK
– Meat and poultry, and most of their products, including ham, bacon, sausage, paté, eggs, milk and cream. (Exception: 1 kg per passenger of fully cooked meat or poultrymeat products in cans or other hermetically sealed containers of glass or foil)
– Plants, parts thereof and plant produce, including trees and shrubs, soil, potatoes and certain other vegetables, fruit, bulbs and seeds
– Most animals and birds, whether alive or dead (e.g. stuffed), certain fish and fish eggs, whether live or dead, or bees
– Certain articles derived from rare species, including fur skins, ivory, reptile leather and goods made from them

NB: Cats, dogs and other mammals, including mice, rats, guinea-pigs and gerbils, must not be landed unless a British import licence (rabies) has previously been issued.

EXPORT CONTROL

The following are some of the goods subject to export control and should be declared to the customs officer. There are formalities to be completed in respect of these goods prior to arrival at the port of exportation and further information is available through any local office of Customs and Excise (address in the telephone directory).

– Controlled drugs
– Firearms and ammunition
– Photographic material over 50 years old and valued at £6,000 or more
– Portraits (including sculptures) of British historical personages which are over 50 years old and valued at £6,000 or more
– Paintings (other than of British historical personages) in water-colour, gouache or pastel which are over 50 years old and valued at £23,800 or more
– Paintings (other than of British historical personages) in oil or tempera which are over 50 years old and valued at £119,000 or more
– Antiques, collectors' items, etc. (including works of art other than paintings) over 50 years old and valued at £39,600 or more
– Certain archaeological material
– Most live animals and birds, and items made from animals occurring wild in the UK

Taxation

INCOME TAX

Income tax is charged on the taxable income of individuals for a year of assessment commencing on 6 April and ending on the following 5 April. Many changes have been introduced during recent years which affect both the calculation of income chargeable to tax and the rate or rates at which the amount of tax due must be determined. The following information is confined to the year of assessment 2002–3 ending on 5 April 2003 and has only limited application to earlier years, however, some changes affecting future years are noted where the information is available.

An individual's liability to satisfy income tax for 2002–3 is determined by establishing the level of taxable income for the year. This income must then be allocated between three different headings, namely: (a) all income excluding that arising from savings and dividends; (b) income from savings; (c) company dividends, including distributions.

Once this allocation has been completed the first calculation must be limited to taxable income excluding that arising from both savings and dividends. This income will be reduced by an individual's personal allowance and any other available allowances. The first £1,920 of taxable income remaining is assessed to income tax at the starting rate of 10 per cent. The next £27,980 is taxable at the basic rate of 22 per cent. Should any excess over £29,900 (£1,920 plus £27,980) remain, this will be taxable at the higher rate of 40 per cent.

The second calculation is limited to income from savings, if any. Liability may arise at the starting rate of 10 per cent, the lower rate of 20 per cent or the higher rate of 40 per cent. There is no liability to income tax at the basic rate of 22 per cent. The appropriate rate which must be used is determined by adding income from savings to other taxable income, excluding dividends. To the extent that the addition does not increase taxable income above £1,920, income from savings is taxed at the starting rate of 10 per cent. Should this level be exceeded but total income does not reach £29,900 any excess remains taxable at the lower rate of 20 per cent. Where the addition of savings extends total income above £29,900 the excess is taxed at the higher rate of 40 per cent.

Finally, any company dividends are taxed at either the Schedule F ordinary rate of 10 per cent or the Schedule F upper rate of 32.5 per cent. The amount of dividends (with the addition of any tax credit) must be added to taxable income comprising general income together with income from savings. If this addition does not increase total taxable income above £29,900 dividends remain taxable at the ordinary rate of 10 per cent only. However, if or to the extent that the addition discloses dividends exceeding the £29,900 level the excess is taxed at the upper rate of 32.5 per cent.

Trustees administering settled property and personal representatives dealing with the estate of a deceased person are chargeable to income tax at the basic rate of 22 per cent. Where trustees retain discretionary powers or income from settled property is accumulated, liability may be increased to 34 per cent. Companies residing in the UK are not liable to income tax but suffer corporation tax on income, profits and gains. Income arising overseas will often incur liability to foreign taxation. If that income is also chargeable to UK income tax, excessive liability could arise. The UK has concluded double taxation agreements with the governments of many overseas territories and these ensure that the same slice of income is not doubly taxed.

HUSBAND AND WIFE

A husband and wife are separately taxed, with each entitled to his or her personal allowance. A married man 'living with' his wife can only obtain a married couple's allowance if one party to the marriage was over the age of 64 years before 6 April 2000. In the absence of any claim, this allowance must be used by the husband but where any balance remains the surplus may be transferred to the wife. It is possible for a married woman to claim half the basic married couple's allowance as of right. The entire basic allowance may be claimed by the wife, if her husband so agrees. Each spouse may obtain other allowances and reliefs where the required conditions are satisfied. Income must be accurately allocated between the couple by reference to the individual beneficially entitled to that income. Where income arises from jointly-held assets, this must be apportioned equally between husband and wife. However, in those cases where the beneficial interests in jointly-held assets are not equal, a special declaration can be made to apportion income by reference to the actual interests in that income.

SELF ASSESSMENT

Self-assessment for income tax purposes affects individuals, trustees and personal representatives. Central to self-assessment is the requirement to deliver a completed tax return. This must normally be submitted by 31 January following the end of the year of assessment (the previous 5 April) to which the return relates. The taxpayer must also calculate the amount of income tax due. If a taxpayer wishes the Inland Revenue to calculate the tax due, the return must be forwarded to the Inland Revenue not later than the previous 30 September.

It is the responsibility of the taxpayer to submit payments of income tax on time. There are three different dates on which payments may fall due:

(a) an interim payment due on 31 January in the year of assessment itself
(b) second interim payment due on the following 31 July
(c) a balancing payment, or possibly a repayment, on the following 31 January

The two interim payments will be based on tax payable for the previous year of assessment but liability may be reduced where income has fallen or even avoided entirely where the amounts are not substantial.

The impact of self-assessment is largely restricted to some nine million persons receiving tax returns. These comprise self-employed individuals, those receiving income from the exploitation of land in the UK, company directors, others with investment income liable to higher rate income tax, trustees and personal representatives. Elderly persons receiving small amounts of untaxed income may be excluded from the need to complete a tax return.

Failure to submit completed tax returns by 31 January or to discharge payments of income tax on time will incur a liability to interest, surcharges and penalties.

INCOME TAXABLE

Income tax is assessed under several Schedules. Each Schedule determines the extent of liability and establishes the amount to be included in taxable income. In some instances the actual income arising in a year of assessment will be charged to income tax for that year. A different basis must be used for business profits taxable under Case I or Case II of Schedule D. This basis requires taxable profits to be those for the business accounting period ending in the year of assessment, with special adjustments for the opening and closing years of a business. Other income assessable under Schedule D will be that which arises in the actual year of assessment. Following the withdrawal of income tax liability for most commercial woodlands in the UK, Schedule B no longer applies. Schedule C has also been withdrawn as the result of further changes. The contents of the remaining schedules are shown below.

Schedule A

Tax is charged under Schedule A on the annual profits or gains arising from a business carried on for the exploitation of land in the UK. The determination of profits from a Schedule A business adopts principles identical to those used when establishing the profits or gains of a trade, profession or vocation. Rents and other income from the exploitation of land are included in the calculation, and outgoings incurred wholly and exclusively for the purposes of the Schedule A business may be deducted from income.

Schedule A does not extend to profits from farming, market gardening or woodlands, nor does it apply to mineral rents and royalties. Premiums arising on the grant of a lease for a period not exceeding 50 years in duration are treated as rents. However, the amount of the taxable premium may be reduced by 2 per cent for each complete year, after the first 12 months, of the leasing period. Income arising from the provision of certain furnished holiday accommodation attracts a number of tax advantages not otherwise available for most income chargeable under Schedule A. Receipts not exceeding £4,250 annually and accruing to an individual from letting property furnished in his or her own home are usually excluded from liability to income tax.

Schedule D

This Schedule is divided into six Cases:

Cases I and II – profits arising from trades, professions and vocations, including farming and market gardening. Profits must be calculated on an accounting basis which provides 'a true and fair view' of business results. This remains subject to any statutory adjustment which may be required. For example, only sums laid out 'wholly and exclusively' for the purposes of a business may be subtracted from receipts, notwithstanding that those outgoings may reflect a proper accounting charge. Capital expenditure incurred on assets used for business purposes will often produce an entitlement to capital allowances which reduce the profits chargeable. These profits may also be reduced by claims for loss relief and other matters.

Case III – interest on government stocks not taxed at source, interest on National Savings and Investments deposits and discounts. Interest up to £70 on ordinary National Savings and Investments deposits is exempt from income tax. The exemption applies to both husband and wife separately. Interest on National Savings and Investments special investment accounts is not exempt. Interest and other items of savings income incur liability

at the starting rate, lower rate or the higher rate depending on the level of the recipient's income.

Cases IV and V – interest from overseas securities, rents, dividends and all other income accruing outside the UK. Assessment is based on the full amount of income arising, whether remitted to the UK or retained overseas, but individuals who are either not domiciled in the UK or who are ordinarily resident overseas may be taxed on a remittance basis. Overseas pensions are taxable but the amount arising may be reduced by 10 per cent for assessment purposes. Interest received on most overseas investments is chargeable at the same rates as those which apply to interest from sources within the UK. Overseas dividends are usually taxed at 10 per cent or 32.5 per cent.

Case VI – sundry profits and annual receipts not assessed under any other Case or Schedule. These may include insurance commissions, post-cessation receipts from a discontinued business and numerous other receipts specifically charged under Case VI.

Schedule E

All earnings from an office or employment are assessable under this Schedule. There are three Cases:

Case I – applies to all earnings of an individual resident and ordinarily resident in the UK.

Case II – of application where the individual is not resident or not ordinarily resident and extends to earnings for duties undertaken in the UK.

Case III – applies in rare situations to other earnings remitted to the UK.

A 'receipts basis' applies for determining the year of assessment to which earnings must be allocated and taxed. Where earnings are assessable under Case I or Case II, the date of receipt will comprise the earlier of the date of payment, or the date entitlement arises. In the case of company directors it is the earlier of these two dates, with the addition of the following three which establish the time of receipt: the date earnings are credited in the company's books; where earnings for a period are determined after the end of that period, the date of determination; where earnings for a period are determined in that period, the last day of that period. The earnings assessable under Schedule E include all salaries, wages, director's fees and other money sums. In addition, the value of a wide range of benefits must be added to taxable earnings. These include the provision of living accommodation on advantageous terms and advantages arising from the use of vouchers.

Further taxable benefits accrue to directors and also to employees receiving earnings of £8,500 or more in the year of assessment. Such benefits include the reimbursement of expenses, the availability of motor cars for private motoring, the provision of petrol or other fuel for private motoring, the use of vans, the provision of interest-free loans, and other benefits provided at the employer's expense. The cost of providing a limited range of child care facilities and a works bus for the transportation of employees may be excluded. Mileage allowances paid to employees who provide their own motor vehicles or cycles for business travel may also be excluded unless they exceed stated limits.

In arriving at the amount to be assessed under Schedule E, all expenses incurred wholly, exclusively and necessarily in the performance of the duties, together with the cost of business travel, may be deducted. Fees and subscriptions paid to certain professional bodies and learned societies may also be deducted. Fees paid to managers by entertainers, actors and others assessable under Schedule E may be deducted, up to a maximum of 17.5 per cent of earnings.

Compensation for loss of office and other sums received on the termination of an office or employment are assessable to tax. However, the first £30,000 may be excluded with only the balance remaining chargeable, unless the compensatory payment is linked with the retirement of the recipient or the performance of their duties.

Schedule F

This Schedule is concerned with dividends and distributions received from a UK resident company.

INCOME FROM SAVINGS

Many payments of interest made by building societies and banks are received after the deduction of income tax at the lower rate of 20 per cent. However, investors not liable to income tax may arrange to receive interest gross with no tax being deducted on payment.

Interest of this nature represents 'income from savings'; an expression which also extends to interest on government securities, interest on a restricted range of National Savings and Investments products and the income element of purchased life annuities. In addition, 'income from savings' may extend to other income of a similar nature arising outside the United Kingdom. Not all forms of investment income are included in the list, notable exceptions comprising income from letting property and company dividends.

A great deal of interest arising from sources in the United Kingdom will be received after deduction of income tax at the lower rate of 20 per cent. Although this interest is not taxable at the basic rate it remains chargeable at the starting rate of 10 per cent, the lower rate of 20 per cent or the higher rate of 40 per cent. Where such interest, when added to other income, excluding dividends, falls within the starting rate band tax will be due at 10 per cent. As tax will have been suffered by deduction at the lower rate of 20 per cent a repayment of the excess may well be obtained from the Inland Revenue.

To the extent that interest from savings when added to other income exceeds £1,920 but does not exceed £29,900, liability arises at the lower rate of 20 per cent. In those situations where, or to the extent that, income from savings when added to other income produces a combined total exceeding £29,900, liability arises at the higher rate of 40 per cent. As income tax will usually have been deducted at source at the rate of 20 per cent, higher rate liability arises at a further 20 per cent (40 per cent less 20 per cent).

DIVIDENDS

Dividends and other distributions paid by a UK resident company have a tax credit attached equal to one-ninth of the sum received in 2002–3. Therefore, a recipient shareholder also residing in the UK who receives a cash dividend of £90 will have a tax credit of £10. The gross dividend or distribution (sum received plus tax credit) is regarded as having suffered income tax, equal to the tax credit, at the rate of 10 per cent. Where the shareholder is not liable, or not fully liable, to income tax it is not possible to claim a repayment of the tax credit. However, for 2002–3 dividends are taxed at the Schedule F ordinary rate of 10 per cent or the Schedule F upper rate of 32.5 per cent. Where the total income of an individual is not unduly substantial the amount of the tax credit, namely 10 per cent, will be offset against the Schedule F ordinary rate of income tax, which is also 10 per cent, leaving no further liability. Should the gross amount of dividends or distributions when added to other taxable income exceed £29,900 the excess is chargeable at the Schedule F upper

rate of 32.5 per cent. The amount of the tax credit will then reduce tax otherwise payable at the upper rate. Although the rates of 10 per cent and 32.5 per cent apply to dividends and distributions from United Kingdom companies, they also extend to income of a similar nature arising outside the UK.

INCOME NOT TAXABLE

Income which is not taxable in 2002–3 includes interest on National Savings and Investments certificates, most scholarship income, bounty payments to members of the armed services and annuities payable to the holders of certain awards. Dividend income arising from qualifying investments in personal equity plans (PEPs) and venture capital trusts is exempt from tax. Although tax credits on dividends from such trusts can no longer be recovered it is possible for PEP managers to obtain repayment of credits during a five-year period ending on 5 April 2004. Income received under maintenance agreements and court orders made following separation or divorce will not be liable to tax. Nor will payments made under many deeds of covenant be recognised for tax purposes, unless the recipient is a charity. Interest arising on a tax exempt special savings account (TESSA) opened with a building society or bank will be exempt from tax if the account is maintained throughout a five-year period.

A popular investment, the individual savings account (ISA), is available to United Kingdom residents aged 18 years and over. The ISA may have three components, namely cash, stocks and shares and life assurance. Interest on the cash component, usually comprising bank or building society deposits, is exempt from income tax. Dividends on most quoted buildings in the stocks and shares component are also immune from liability to income tax, with tax credits being repaid for years up to and including that ending on 5 April 2004. Income and gains accruing to the provider of the life assurance component will be free of all liability to taxation.

A maximum subscription of £7,000 can be made by an individual to an ISA during 2002–3. Of this sum no more than £3,000 can be allocated to the cash component and £1,000 to the life assurance component. Potential investors are provided with the choice of whether to invest in a maxi-ISA or in mini-ISAs. Should a maxi-ISA be selected, the entire £7,000 can be invested in stocks and shares, but the use of a mini-ISA limits such investment to £3,000 with the balance of £4,000 capable of being used to invest in the cash and life assurance components.

Although no new TESSA accounts can now be opened, where an existing TESSA matures at the end of a five-year period the capital (but not the income) proceeds can be separately invested in the cash component of an ISA. This is in addition to the normal limits governing investment in an ISA.

SOCIAL SECURITY BENEFITS

Many social security benefits are not liable to income tax. Benefits which are taxable include the retirement pension, widow's pension, widowed mother's allowance and jobseeker's allowance. Short-term sick pay and maternity pay payable by an employer are also chargeable to tax. Incapacity benefit is chargeable to tax but no liability arises on most short-term benefit.

A working families' tax credit and a disabled persons tax credit may be payable to many individuals.

PAY AS YOU EARN

The Pay As You Earn (PAYE) system is not an independent form of taxation but is designed to collect

income tax by deduction from most earnings. When paying earnings to employees, an employer is usually required to deduct income tax and account for that tax to the Inland Revenue. In many cases this deduction procedure will fully exhaust the individual's liability to income tax, unless there is other income. The date of 'receipt' for assessment purposes also identifies the date of 'payment' when establishing liability for PAYE. The PAYE system is used to collect tax on certain payments made 'in kind'. The system is also used when collecting tax on many pensions, jobfinders benefits, some incapacity benefits and maternity pay.

ALLOWANCES

Allowances which can be obtained for 2002–3 are shown below.

Personal allowance

Basic personal allowance	£4,615
Those over 64 on 5 April 2003	£6,100
Those over 74 on 5 April 2003	£6,370

The increased allowance for older individuals is available for those who died during the year of assessment but who would otherwise have achieved the appropriate age not later than 5 April 2003. The amount of the increased personal allowance for older taxpayers will be reduced by one-half of total income in excess of £17,900. This reduction in the allowance will continue until it has been reduced to the basic personal allowance of £4,615. The personal allowance is given as a deduction in calculating taxable income and may therefore produce relief at the rate of 10, 22 or 40 per cent, as appropriate.

Married couple's allowance

A married man who was 'living with' his wife at any time in the year ending on 5 April 2003 will be entitled to a married couple's allowance if at least one party to the marriage reached the age of 65 years before 6 April 2000. The allowance cannot be obtained where both parties were below this age on that date, nor will it be forthcoming where a husband or wife reaches 65 on some future date.

The allowance is £5,465. It may be increased to £5,535 where either party to the marriage was 75 or over on 5 April 2003. Where an individual would otherwise have reached the age of 75 by 5 April 2002 but who died earlier in the year, the increased allowance is given. The amount of the married couple's allowance will be reduced where the income of the husband (excluding the income of the wife) exceeds £17,900. The deduction will comprise:

(a) one-half of the husband's total income in excess of £17,900, less

(b) the amount of any reduction made when calculating the husband's increased personal allowance.

This reduction in the married couple's allowance cannot reduce that allowance below a basic allowance of £2,110.

If husband and wife were married during 2002–3 the married couple's allowance must be reduced by one-twelfth for each complete month commencing on 6 April 2002 and preceding the date of marriage.

Unlike the personal allowance, the married couple's allowance does not reduce taxable income. Relief is granted by reducing the tax otherwise payable by 10 per cent of the allowance. For example, where the basic allowance of £2,110 is available, the amount of tax payable may be reduced by £211. Should the amount of the reduction exceed tax otherwise payable, no tax will be due, nor will any repayment arise.

In the absence of any further action, the married couple's allowance will be given to the husband. If he is unable to utilise all or any part of that allowance due to an absence of income, the husband may transfer the unused portion to his wife. The decision whether or not to transfer remains at the discretion of the husband. However, a wife may file an election to obtain one-half of the basic married couple's allowance of £2,110 as of right, leaving the husband with the balance of that allowance. Alternatively, the couple may jointly elect that the entire basic allowance should be allocated to the wife only. Should either spouse be unable to utilise his or her share of the total married couple's allowance the unused part may be transferred to the other spouse.

Blind person's allowance

An allowance of £1,480 is available to an individual if at any time during the year ending on 5 April 2003, he or she was registered as blind on a register maintained by a local authority. If the individual is 'living with' a wife or husband, any unused part of the blind person's allowance can be transferred to the other spouse. The allowance reduces taxable income and may therefore give rise to relief at the taxpayer's highest rate of tax suffered.

CHILDREN'S TAX CREDIT

A special allowance, the children's tax credit, is available for both 2001–2 and 2002–3. The credit can be claimed by an individual who has one or more qualifying children resident with him or her during all of the tax year. The credit for 2002–3 is £5,290 and will be given at the rate of 10 per cent as a deduction from income tax otherwise payable. This may achieve a maximum deduction of £529. However, where the income of the claimant incurs liability to income tax at the higher rate of 40 per cent, the credit of £5,290 is reduced by two-thirds of the income chargeable at the higher rate.

An adjustment is necessary where a husband and wife are 'living together'; or a man and woman are 'living together' as husband and wife. In this situation the credit will be given to whichever of the two individuals has the higher taxable income. This allocation will determine whether any restriction is necessary due to income tax liability being at the higher rate. Where neither individual has sufficient income to incur liability at the higher rate the children's tax credit may be allocated between the couple.

An addition to the children's tax credit may be available for 2002–3 only. To obtain this addition it must be shown that a baby was born during the year of assessment and resides with the claimant. The amount of the 'baby rate' credit is £5,200 and will be added to the normal children's tax credit of £5,290 to produce an aggregate of £10,490. This aggregate remains subject to the restriction shown above where the claimant has sufficient income to produce liability at the higher rate of 40 per cent. Only one children's tax credit is available notwithstanding the number of qualifying children or births. After the 2003–4 tax year, children's tax credit will be replaced by a new child tax credit which combines all income-related support for children under a single system.

MAINTENANCE PAYMENTS

Relief for maintenance payments made in 2002–3 to a separated spouse or a divorced former spouse is limited to £2,110 or the amount of the payment, whichever is smaller. A further requirement before relief can be obtained is that at least one of the parties to the transaction has reached his/her 65th birthday before

6 April 2000. No relief is available to younger parties. Relief is given at the rate of 10 per cent and subtracted from the amount of tax otherwise due by the payer. The maintenance payment is exempt from liability to income tax in the hands of the recipient.

INTEREST

In some instances, interest paid by a business proprietor may be included when calculating profits chargeable to income tax under Case I or Case II of Schedule D. In addition, relief for interest paid on a loan applied to acquire or develop land and buildings for letting may be obtained by including the outlay in the calculation of income chargeable under Schedule A. However, many private individuals cannot obtain relief in this manner and must satisfy stringent requirements before relief will be forthcoming. In general terms it is a requirement that before interest can qualify for relief it must be paid for a qualifying purpose. Relief will not be available to the extent that interest exceeds a reasonable commercial rate and no relief is forthcoming for interest on an overdraft.

Interest paid in 2002–3 which can be treated as laid out for a qualifying purpose will include the following payments:

(a) Interest on a loan used to acquire an interest in a close company or in a partnership, or to advance money to such a person or body

(b) Interest on a loan to a member of a partnership to acquire machinery or plant for use in the partnership business

(c) Interest on a loan to an employed person to acquire machinery or plant for the purposes of his or her employment

(d) Interest on a loan made for the purpose of contributing capital to an industrial co-operative

(e) Interest on a loan applied for investment in an employee-controlled company

(f) Interest on a loan to personal representatives to provide funds for the payment of inheritance tax

(g) Interest on a loan made to elderly persons for the purchase of an annuity where the loan is secured on land. If the loan exceeds £30,000, relief is limited to interest on this amount. This relief is restricted to income tax at the basic rate of 22 per cent. Whilst the relief remains for existing borrowers, it cannot be obtained for interest only new loans taken out after 8 March 1999

Relief under headings (a) to (f) is given by deducting interest from taxable income. This enables the taxpayer to obtain relief at his or her top rate of tax suffered.

CHARITABLE DONATIONS

A number of charitable donations and qualify for tax relief and may involve donations of money or transferable assets. A popular arrangement is the Gift Aid scheme which requires the making of a money payment to a recognised charity. Providing that the donor receives little or no benefit in return, and certain formalities are complied with, the donation is then treated as a net sum paid after deducting income tax at the basic rate of 22 per cent. On the assumption that the donor suffers a sufficient amount of income tax at that rate, no additional income tax will be payable. However, if the donor suffers liability at the higher rate of 40 per cent, he/she may obtain relief for the outlay at the difference between the basic rate of 22 per cent and the higher rate of 40 per cent – 18 per cent – on the grossed up amount of the donation.

OTHER OUTGOINGS

Many employees pay contributions to an approved occupational pension scheme. The amount of their contributions may be deducted when calculating earnings assessable under Schedule E. Relief should also be available for any additional voluntary contributions paid. Self-employed individuals and those receiving earnings not covered by an occupational pension scheme may contribute under personal pension scheme arrangements or under stakeholder schemes. Individuals may also pay premiums under retirement annuity schemes if the arrangements were concluded before 1 July 1988. Contributions paid under all headings and which do not exceed upper limits may obtain income tax relief by deduction from taxable income.

Subject to a maximum of £150,000 in 2002–3, the cost of subscribing for shares in an unquoted trading company or companies may qualify for relief under the Enterprise Investment Scheme. Many requirements must be satisfied before this relief can be obtained, but a husband and wife may each take advantage of the £150,000 maximum. Relief is given by reducing tax payable at the rate of 20 per cent of the share subscription cost. Further relief on an outlay, up to a maximum of £100,000 and also given at the rate of 20 per cent, is available for a subscription of shares in a venture capital trust company.

CAPITAL GAINS TAX

An individual is potentially chargeable to capital gains tax on chargeable gains that accrue from disposals made by him/her during a year of assessment. The following information is largely confined to the year of assessment 2002–3, ending on 5 April 2003.

Liability extends to individuals who are either resident or ordinarily resident for the year but special rules apply where a person permanently leaves the UK or comes to this territory for the purpose of acquiring residence. Non-residents are not usually liable to capital gains tax unless they carry on a business in the UK through a branch or agency. However, individuals who left the UK after 16 March 1998 and who have been resident or ordinarily resident in at least four of the seven years preceding departure may remain liable to capital gains tax unless they reside overseas throughout a period of five complete tax years. Exceptions from this may apply where there is a disposal of assets acquired in the period of absence.

Trustees residing in the UK, together with personal representatives are chargeable to capital gains tax at the flat rate of 34 per cent but chargeable gains accruing to companies are assessable to corporation tax.

In earlier years, capital gains tax was chargeable on the net chargeable gains accruing to a person in a year of assessment after subtracting the annual exemption for that year. Net chargeable gains represented capital gains less capital losses arising from disposals carried out during the year. Unused losses brought forward from an earlier year could be offset against current net chargeable gains, but in the case of individuals were not to reduce the net gains below the annual exemption limit. It was possible to utilise trading losses against chargeable gains where those losses had not been offset against income.

TAPER RELIEF

However, the calculation of net gains chargeable to capital gains tax is now governed by the availability of taper relief. The purpose of this relief, which replaced the

former indexation allowance, is to require that only a percentage of gains become chargeable to capital gains tax. Taper relief draws a distinction between business assets and non-business assets. The expression 'business asset' broadly identifies an asset used for business purposes in addition to some holdings of shares in both trading and non-trading companies. Where the nature of an asset has changed during the period of ownership from a business asset to a non-business asset, or vice versa, the asset must be effectively broken down into two parts. This may be particularly relevant where the period overlaps 5 April 2000 or 5 April 2002 when some previously non-business assets were re-classified as business assets.

The percentage which must be used to calculate taper relief is governed by the number of complete years of ownership falling after 5 April 1998. Initially an additional 'bonus year' could be added for most assets acquired before 17 March 1998. This 'bonus year' continues to apply to non-business assets but has been withdrawn where the disposal of a business asset takes place after 5 April 2000.

The maximum percentage attributable to business assets was previously achieved after an ownership period extending throughout 10 years but this was reduced to one of four years only where the disposal takes place after 5 April 2000 and before 6 April 2002. No corresponding change was made in the percentages attributable to non-business assets. The percentages which must be used for disposals taking place after 5 April 2000 and before 6 April 2002 are as follows:

	Percentage of gain chargeable	
No. of whole years of ownership	Business assets	Non-business assets
	%	%
1	87.5	100
2	75.0	100
3	50.0	95
4	25.0	90
5	25.0	85
6	25.0	80
7	25.0	75
8	25.0	70
9	25.0	65
10	25.0	60

Where the disposal of business assets takes place on or after 6 April 2002 the ownership period has been further reduced. Once that period exceeds one year, only 50 per cent of the gain will be chargeable, falling to 25 per cent where two whole years are exceeded. No change has been made to the ownership period of non-business assets.

If only chargeable gains arise from disposals carried out in 2002–3 the taper relief, if any, must be calculated by reference to each disposal. The aggregate sum of taper relief will then be subtracted from the total chargeable gains to produce the net gains for the year. Where disposals in 2002–3 give rise to both gains and losses, the losses must be subtracted from the gains and taper relief calculated on the net sum remaining. It is necessary to allocate the losses between the gains where there are two or more disposals. Losses brought forward from an earlier year must also be subtracted when calculating the net gains qualifying for taper relief. However, the losses brought forward are not to reduce the net gains below the annual exemption limit of £7,700 which applies for 2002–3.

ANNUAL EXEMPTION

The initial slice of net gains arising in a tax year is exempt from liability to capital gains tax. This slice, comprising the annual exemption, is £7,700 for 2002–3. Should any part of the exemption remain unused, this cannot be carried forward to a future year.

RATES OF TAX

The net gains remaining, if any, calculated after subtracting the annual exemption, incur liability to capital gains tax for 2002–3. Although income tax rates are used for this purpose, liability arises only at the starting rate of 10 per cent, the lower rate of 20 per cent, the higher rate of 40 per cent, or a combination of the three rates. Unlike some income tax commitments, there is no liability at the basic rate of 22 per cent.

The first step is to calculate the amount of taxable income chargeable to income tax. This will include income from savings, company dividends and all other forms of taxable income. The second step is to add the amount of net chargeable gains to the taxable income chargeable to income tax. To the extent that this does not increase the aggregate total above £1,920, capital gains tax will be charged at the rate of 10 per cent. If the aggregate total exceeds £1,920 but does not exceed £29,900 any balance needed to reach £1,920 is chargeable at 10 per cent and the excess at 20 per cent. If, or to the extent that, any part of the chargeable gains exceed the limit of £29,900 the excess is chargeable at 40 per cent. Although some income tax rates are used, capital gains tax remains an entirely separate tax. Capital gains tax for 2002–3 falls due for payment in full on 31 January 2004. If payment is delayed, interest or surcharges may be imposed.

HUSBAND AND WIFE

Independent taxation requires that a husband and wife 'living together' are separately assessed to capital gains tax. Each spouse must independently calculate his or her gains and losses, with each entitled to the benefit of taper relief, if any, and the annual exemption of £7,700 for 2002–2003. No liability to capital gains tax arises from the transfer of assets between husband and wife 'living together'.

DISPOSAL OF ASSETS

Before chargeable gains potentially liable to capital gains tax can arise, a disposal or deemed disposal of an asset must take place. This occurs not only where assets are sold or exchanged but applies on the making of a gift. There is also a disposal of assets where any capital sum is derived from assets, e.g. where compensation is received for loss or damage to an asset. The date on which a disposal must be treated as having taken place will determine the year of assessment into which the chargeable gain or allowable loss falls. In those cases where a disposal is made under an unconditional contract, the time of disposal will be that when the contract was entered into and not the subsequent date of conveyance or transfer. A disposal under a conditional contract or option is treated as taking place when the contract becomes unconditional or the option is exercised. Disposals by way of gift are undertaken when the gift becomes effective.

VALUATION OF ASSETS

The amount received as consideration for the disposal of an asset will be the sum from which very limited outgoings must be deducted for the purpose of establishing the gain or loss. In cases where the

consideration does not accurately reflect the value of the asset, a different basis must be used. This applies, in particular, where an asset is transferred by way of gift or otherwise than by a bargain made at arm's length. Such transactions are deemed to take place for a consideration representing market value, which will determine both the disposal proceeds accruing to the transferor and the cost of acquisition to the transferee.

Market value represents the price which an asset might reasonably be expected to fetch on a sale in the open market. In the case of unquoted shares or securities, it is to be assumed that the hypothetical purchaser in the open market would have available all the information which a prudent prospective purchaser of shares or securities might reasonably require if that person were proposing to purchase them from a willing vendor by private treaty and at arm's length. The market value of unquoted shares or securities will often be established following negotiations with the Shares Valuation Division of the Capital Taxes Office. The valuation of land and interests in land in the UK will be dealt with by the District Valuer. Special rules apply to determine the market value of shares quoted on the Stock Exchange.

DEDUCTION FOR OUTGOINGS

Once the actual or notional disposal proceeds have been determined, it only remains to subtract eligible outgoings for the purpose of computing the gain or loss. There is the general rule that any outgoings deducted, or which are available to be deducted, when calculating income tax liability must be ignored. Subject to this, deductions will usually be limited to:

(a) the cost of acquiring the asset, together with incidental costs wholly and exclusively incurred in connection with the acquisition
(b) expenditure incurred wholly and exclusively on the asset in enhancing its value, being expenditure reflected in the state or nature of the asset at the time of the disposal, and any other expenditure wholly and exclusively incurred in establishing, preserving or defending title to, or a right over, the asset
(c) the incidental costs of making the disposal

Where the disposal concerns a leasehold interest having less than 50 years to run, any expenditure falling under (a) and (b) must be written off throughout the duration of the lease using a 'curved line' approach.

INDEXATION ALLOWANCE

For many years an indexation allowance could be inserted when calculating a gain on the disposal of an asset. The allowance was based on percentage increases in the retail prices index between the month of March 1982, or the month in which expenditure was incurred if later, and the month of disposal.

Taper relief has largely replaced the indexation allowance for disposals made after 5 April 1998. However, where an asset was acquired before this date, the indexation allowance will be calculated to the month of April 1998 and frozen. The frozen allowance then enters into the calculation of chargeable gain, if any, when the asset is disposed of at some later date. The adjustment for the indexation allowance must be made before calculating taper relief on the net sum remaining.

EXEMPTIONS

There is a general exemption from liability to capital gains tax where the net gains of an individual for 2002–2 do not exceed £7,700. This general exemption applies separately to a husband and wife whether or not the parties are 'living together'. The disposal of many assets will not give rise to chargeable gains or allowable losses and these assets include:

(a) private motor cars
(b) government securities
(c) loan stock and other securities (but not shares)
(d) options and contracts relating to securities within (b) and (c)
(e) National Savings and Investments Certificates, Premium Bonds, Defence Bonds and National Development Bonds
(f) currency of any description acquired for personal expenditure outside the UK
(g) decorations awarded for valour
(h) betting wins and pools, lottery or games prizes
(i) compensation or damages for any wrong or injury suffered by an individual in his or her person, profession or vocation
(j) life assurance and deferred annuity contracts where the person making the disposal is the original beneficial owner
(k) dwelling-houses and land enjoyed with the residence which is an individual's only or main residence
(l) tangible movable property, the consideration for the disposal of which does not exceed £6,000
(m) certain tangible movable property which is a wasting asset having a life not exceeding 50 years
(n) assets transferred to charities and other bodies
(o) works of art, historic buildings and similar assets
(p) assets used to provide maintenance funds for historic buildings
(q) assets transferred to trustees for the benefit of employees
(r) assets held in a Personal Equity Plan or Individual Savings Account

DWELLING-HOUSES

Exemption from capital gains tax will usually be available for any gain which accrues to an individual from the disposal of, or of an interest in, a dwelling-house or part of a dwelling-house which has been his or her only or main residence. The exemption extends to land which has been occupied and enjoyed with the residence as its garden or grounds. Some restriction may be necessary where the land exceeds half a hectare.

The gain will not be chargeable to capital gains tax if the dwelling-house, or part, has been the individual's only or main residence throughout the period of ownership, or throughout the entire period except for all or any part of the final three years. A proportionate part of the gain will be exempt in other cases if the dwelling-house has been the individual's only or main residence for part only of the period of ownership. In the case of property acquired before 31 March 1982, the period of ownership is treated as commencing on this date. Where part of the dwelling-house has been used exclusively for business purposes, that part of the gain attributable to business use will not be exempt. In those cases where part of a qualifying dwelling-house has been used to provide rented residential accommodation, this non-personal use may frequently be ignored when calculating exemption from capital gains tax, unless relatively substantial sums are involved. Dwellings occupied by dependent relatives, separated spouses or divorced former spouses, may also qualify for the exemption, but only where occupation commenced before 6 April 1988.

ROLL-OVER RELIEF

Persons carrying on business will often undertake the disposal of an asset and use the proceeds to finance the acquisition of a replacement asset. Where this situation

arises, a claim for roll-over relief may be available. The broad effect of such a claim is that all or part of the gain arising on the disposal of the old asset may be disregarded. The gain or part is then subtracted from the cost of acquiring the replacement asset. As this cost is reduced, any gain arising from the future disposal of the replacement asset will be correspondingly increased, unless a further roll-over situation then develops.

It remains a requirement that both the old and the replacement asset must be used for the purpose of the taxpayer's business or for the purpose of business carried out by a company in which the taxpayer retains an interest. Relief will only be available if the acquisition of the replacement asset takes place within a period commencing twelve months before, and ending three years after, the disposal of the old asset, although the Inland Revenue retains a discretion to extend this period where the circumstances were such that it was impossible for the taxpayer to acquire the replacement asset before the expiration of the normal time limit. Whilst many business assets qualify for roll-over relief there are exceptions.

Roll-over relief may also be available where a gain arises on the disposal of land or buildings to an authority capable of exercising compulsory purchase powers. Similar relief may be forthcoming where shares in a company are transferred to trustees administering an employees' share ownership plan for the benefit of persons employed by that company or group of companies of which the company is a member.

DEFERRAL RELIEF

A form of roll-over relief, known as 'deferral relief' enables gains arising on the disposal of an asset to be matched, in whole or in part, with a subscription for shares in a restricted range of unquoted companies, including certain companies whose shares are dealt in on the Alternative Investment Market. Where matching can be achieved any part of the gain arising on disposal, not exceeding the cost of the qualifying share subscription, may become the subject of a claim. Unlike most form of roll-over relief, this claim for deferral relief does not eliminate or reduce the chargeable gain. It has the effect of deferring that gain until the time of some future event, which will usually be identified by the disposal of the newly acquired shares or the loss of UK residential status.

A similar form of deferral relief is available for gains arising on other disposals which are matched with a qualifying share investment in a venture capital trust company. To the extent of the gain arising, which must not exceed the amount of the investment qualifying for income tax relief, that gain is deferred until the time of a future event, which will normally comprise the disposal of shares in the venture capital trust or the loss of UK residential status.

HOLD-OVER RELIEF – GIFTS

The gift of an asset is treated as a disposal made for a consideration equal to market value, with a corresponding acquisition by the transferee at an identical value. In the case of gifts made by individuals and a limited range of trusts to a transferee resident in the UK, a form of hold-over relief may be available. Relief, which must be claimed, is limited to the transfer of certain assets, including the following:

(a) assets used for the purposes of a trade or similar activity carried on by the transferor or his/her personal company

(b) shares or securities of a trading company which is not listed on a stock exchange

(c) shares or securities of a trading company which is listed but which is the transferor's personal company

(d) many interests in agricultural property qualifying for agricultural property relief for inheritance tax purposes

(e) assets involved in transactions which are lifetime transfers for inheritance tax purposes, other than potentially exempt transfers

The transfer of shares or securities to a company is now precluded from obtaining relief. The effect of a valid claim for hold-over relief is similar to that following a claim for roll-over relief on the disposal of business assets, but adjustments may be necessary where some consideration is given for the transfer, the asset has not been used for business purposes throughout the period of ownership, or not all assets of a company are used for business purposes.

RETIREMENT RELIEF

Retirement relief is available to an individual who disposes by way of sale or gift of the whole or part of a business. The isolated disposal of assets used for the purpose of a business will not necessarily represent the disposal of the whole or part of a business. The main condition for granting this relief is that throughout a period of at least one year the business has been owned either by the individual or by a trading company in which the individual retained a sufficient shareholding interest. The relief extends also to cases where an individual disposes by way of sale or gift of shares or securities of a company. It must be demonstrated that the company was a trading company, that the individual retained a sufficient shareholding interest, and that he or she was engaged as a full-time working officer or employee.

An individual who has attained the age of 50 years at the time of a disposal may obtain substantial retirement relief which shelters gains from liability to capital gains tax. No retirement relief will be forthcoming if the disposal occurs before the individual's 50th birthday, unless he/she was compelled to retire early on the grounds of ill-health.

Maximum relief was available for disposals taking place not later than 5 April 1999. The amount of relief then reduces on an annual basis before being abolished entirely for disposals taking place on and after 6 April 2003. Retirement relief must be subtracted from the net gains arising on disposal, leaving the balance, if any, chargeable to capital gains tax in the normal manner. Taper relief applies only to this balance of net gains and not to the gains eliminated by retirement relief.

DEATH

No capital gains tax is chargeable on the value of assets retained at the time of death. However, the personal representatives administering the deceased's estate are deemed to acquire those assets for a consideration representing market value on death. This ensures that any increase in value occurring before the date of death will not be chargeable to capital gains tax. If a legatee or other person acquires an asset under a will or intestacy no chargeable gain will accrue to the personal representatives, and the person taking the asset will also be treated as having acquired it at the time of death for its then market value.

INHERITANCE TAX

Liability to inheritance tax may arise on a limited range of lifetime gifts and other dispositions and also on the value of assets retained, or deemed to be retained, at the time of death. An individual's domicile at the time of any gift or on death is an important matter. Domicile will generally be determined by applying normal rules, although special considerations may be necessary where an individual was previously domiciled in the UK but subsequently acquired a domicile of choice overseas. In addition, individuals who have been resident in the UK for at least 17 of the previous 20 years at the time of an event are treated as domiciled in the UK for this purpose. Where a person was domiciled, or treated as domiciled, in the UK at the time of a disposition or on death the location of assets is immaterial and full liability to inheritance tax arises. Individuals domiciled outside the UK are, however, chargeable to inheritance tax only on transactions affecting assets located in the UK. The assets of husband and wife are not merged for inheritance tax purposes. Each spouse is treated as a separate individual entitled to receive the benefit of his or her exemptions, reliefs and rates of tax. Where husband and wife retain similar assets, e.g. shares in the same family company, special 'related property' provisions may require the merger of those assets for valuation purposes only.

Lifetime Gifts and Dispositions

Gifts and dispositions made during lifetime fall under four broad headings, namely:
(a) dispositions which are not transfers of value
(b) exempt transfers
(c) potentially exempt transfers
(d) chargeable transfers

Dispositions which are not transfers of value

Several lifetime transactions are not treated as transfers of value and may be entirely disregarded for inheritance tax purposes. These include transactions not intended to confer gratuitous benefit, the provision of family maintenance, the waiver of the right to receive remuneration or dividends, and the grant of agricultural tenancies for full consideration.

Exempt transfers

The main exempt transfers are:
Transfers between spouses – Transfers between husband and wife are usually exempt. However, if the transferor is, but the transferee spouse is not, domiciled in the UK, transfers will be exempt only to the extent that the total does not exceed £55,000. Unlike the requirement used for income tax and capital gains tax purposes, it is immaterial whether husband and wife are living together.
Annual exemption – The first £3,000 of gifts and other dispositions made in a year ending on 5 April is exempt. If the exemption is not used, or not wholly used, in any year the balance may be carried forward to the following year only. The annual exemption will only be available for a potentially exempt transfer if that transfer becomes chargeable by reason of the donor's subsequent death.
Small gifts – outright gifts of £250 or less to any person in one year ending on 5 April are exempt.
Normal expenditure – a transfer made during lifetime and comprising normal expenditure is exempt. To obtain this exemption it must be shown that:
(a) the transfer was made as part of the normal expenditure of the transferor;

(b) taking one year with another, the transfer was made out of income; and
(c) after allowing for all transfers of value forming part of normal expenditure the transferor was left with sufficient income to maintain his or her usual standard of living
Gifts in consideration of marriage – these are exempt if they satisfy certain requirements. The amount allowed will be governed by the relationship between the donor and a party to the marriage. The allowable amounts comprise:
(a) gifts by a parent, £5,000
(b) gifts by a grandparent, £2,500
(c) gifts by a party to the marriage, £2,500
(d) gifts by other persons, £1,000
Gifts to charities – these are exempt from liability.
Gifts to political parties – gifts which satisfy certain requirements are generally exempt.
Gifts for national purposes – gifts made to certain bodies are exempt from liability. These bodies include, among others, the National Gallery, the British Museum, the National Trust, the National Art Collections Fund, the National Heritage Memorial Fund, the Historic Buildings and Monuments Commission for England (English Heritage), any local authority, and any university or university college in the UK.
A number of other gifts made for the public benefit are also exempt.

Potentially exempt transfers

Lifetime gifts and dispositions which are neither to be ignored nor comprise exempt transfers incur possible liability to inheritance tax. However, relief is available for a range of potentially exempt transfers. These comprise gifts made by an individual to:
(a) a second individual
(b) trustees administering an accumulation and maintenance trust
(c) trustees administering a disabled person's trust
The accumulation and maintenance trust mentioned in (b) must provide that on reaching a specified age, not exceeding 25 years, a beneficiary will become absolutely entitled to trust assets or obtain an interest in possession in the income from those assets. Additions to the above list affect settled property administered by trustees where an individual, or individuals, retain an interest in possession. The transfer of assets to, the removal of assets from, or the rearrangement of interests in such property comprise potentially exempt transfers if the person transferring an interest and the person benefiting from the transfer are both individuals.
No immediate liability to inheritance tax will arise on the making of a potentially exempt transfer. Should the donor survive for a period of seven years, immunity from liability will be confirmed. However, the donor's death within the seven-year inter vivos period produces liability if the amounts involved are sufficiently substantial (*see* below).

Chargeable transfers

Any remaining lifetime gifts or dispositions which are neither to be ignored nor represent exempt transfers or potentially exempt transfers, incur liability to inheritance tax.

Gifts with Reservation

A lifetime gift of assets made at any time after 17 March 1986 may incur additional liability to inheritance tax if the donor retains some interest in the subject matter of

the gift. This may arise, for example, where a parent transfers a dwelling-house to a son or daughter and continues to occupy the property or to enjoy some benefit from that property. The retention of a benefit may be ignored where it is enjoyed in return for full consideration, perhaps a commercial rent, or where the benefit arises from changed circumstances which could not have been foreseen at the time of the original gift. The gift with reservation provisions will not usually apply to most exempt transfers.

There are three possibilities which may arise where the donor reserves or enjoys some benefit from the subject matter of a previous gift and subsequently dies, namely:

(a) if no benefit is enjoyed within a period of seven years before death there can be no further liability

(b) if the benefit ceased to be enjoyed within a period of seven years before the date of death, the original donor is deemed to have made a potentially exempt transfer representing the value of the asset at the time of cessation

(c) if the benefit is enjoyed at the time of death, the value of the asset must be included when arriving at the value of the deceased's estate on death

It must be emphasised that the existence of a benefit enjoyed at any time within a period of seven years before death will establish liability to tax on gifts with reservation, notwithstanding that the gift may have been made many years earlier, providing it was undertaken after 17 March 1986.

Death

Immediately before the time of death an individual is deemed to make a transfer of value. This transfer will comprise the value of assets forming part of the deceased's estate after subtracting most liabilities. Any exempt transfers may, however, be excluded. These include transfers for the benefit of a surviving spouse, a charity and a qualifying political party, together with bequests to approved bodies and for national purposes.

Death may also trigger three additional liabilities:

(a) A potentially exempt transfer made within the period of seven years ending on death loses its potential status and becomes chargeable to inheritance tax

(b) The value of gifts made with reservation may incur liability if any benefit was enjoyed within a period of seven years preceding death

(c) Additional tax may become payable for chargeable lifetime transfers made within seven years before death

Valuations

The valuation of assets establishes the value transferred for lifetime dispositions and also the value of a person's estate at the time of death. The value of property will represent the price which might reasonably be expected from a sale in the open market.

In some cases it may be necessary to incorporate the value of 'related property'. This will include property comprised in the estate of the transferor's spouse and certain property previously transferred to charities. The purpose of the related property valuation rules is not to add the value of the property to the estate of the transferor. Related property must be merged to establish the aggregate value of the respective interests and this value is then apportioned, usually on a *pro rata* basis, to the separate interests.

The value of shares and securities listed on the Stock Exchange will be determined by extracting figures from the daily list of official prices.

Where quoted shares and securities are sold or the quotation is suspended within a period of 12 months following the date of death, a claim may be made to substitute the proceeds or subsequent value for the value on death. This claim will only be beneficial if the gross proceeds realised are lower or the value has fallen below market value at the time of death. A similar claim may be available for interests in land sold within a period of four years following death.

Relief for Selected Assets

Special relief is made available for certain assets:

Woodlands

Where woodlands pass on death the value will usually be included in the deceased's estate. However, an election may be made in respect of land in the UK on which trees or underwood is growing to delete the value of those assets. Relief is confined to the value of trees or underwood and does not extend to the land on which they are growing. Liability to inheritance tax will arise if and when the trees or underwood are sold.

Agricultural property

Relief is available for the agricultural value of agricultural property. Such property must be occupied and used for agricultural purposes and relief is confined to the agricultural value only.

The value transferred, either on a lifetime gift or on death, must be determined. This value may then be reduced by a percentage. For events taking place after 9 March 1992, a 100 per cent deduction will be available if the transferor retained vacant possession or could have obtained that possession within a period of 12 months following the transfer. In other cases, notably including land let to tenants, a lower deduction of 50 per cent is usually available. However, this lower deduction may be increased to 100 per cent if the letting was made after 31 August 1995.

It remains a requirement that the agricultural property was either occupied by the transferor for the purposes of agriculture throughout a two-year period ending on the date of the transfer, or was owned by him or her throughout a period of seven years ending on that date and also occupied for agricultural purposes.

Business property

Where the value transferred is attributable to relevant business property, that value may be reduced by a percentage. The reduction in value applies to:

(a) property consisting of a business or an interest in a business (i.e. a partnership)

(b) securities of an unquoted company which, together with any unquoted shares in the same company provided the transferor with control

(c) other unquoted shares in a company

(d) shares or securities of a quoted company which provided the transferor with control

(e) any land, building, machinery or plant which, immediately before the transfer, was used wholly or mainly for the purposes of a business carried on by a company of which the transferor had control

(f) any land, building, machinery or plant which, immediately before the transfer, was used wholly or mainly for the purposes of a business carried on by a partnership of which the transferor was a partner

(g) any land, building, machinery or plant which, immediately before the transfer, was used wholly or mainly for the purposes of a business carried on by

the transferor and was then settled property in which he/she retained an interest in possession

The percentage deduction has changed from time to time but for events occurring after 5 April 1996, a deduction of 100 per cent is available for assets falling within (a), (b) and (c). A deduction of 50 per cent remains for assets within (d) to (g).

It is a general requirement that the property must have been retained for a period of two years before the transfer or death and restrictions may be necessary if the property has not been used wholly for business purposes. The same property cannot obtain both business property relief and the relief available for agricultural property.

CALCULATION OF TAX PAYABLE

The calculation of inheritance tax payable adopts the use of a cumulative total. Each chargeable lifetime transfer is added to the total with a final addition made on death. The top slice added to the total for the current event determines the rate at which inheritance tax must be paid. However, the cumulative total will only include transfers made within a period of seven years before the current event and those undertaken outside this period must be excluded.

Lifetime chargeable transfers

The value transferred by the limited range of lifetime chargeable transfers must be added to the seven-year cumulative total to calculate whether any inheritance tax is due. Should the nil rate band be exceeded, tax will be imposed on the excess at the rate of 20 per cent. However, if the donor dies within a period of seven years from the date of the chargeable lifetime transfer, additional tax may be due. This is calculated by applying tax at the full rate or 40 per cent in substitution for the rate of 20 per cent previously used. The amount of tax is then reduced to a percentage by applying tapering relief. This percentage is governed by the number of years from the date of the lifetime gift to the date of death, as follows:

Period of years before death	
Not more than 3	100%
More than 3 but not more than 4	80%
More than 4 but not more than 5	60%
More than 5 but not more than 6	40%
More than 6 but not more than 7	20%

Should this exercise produce liability greater than that previously paid at the 20 per cent rate on the lifetime transfer, additional tax, representing the difference, must be discharged. Where the calculation shows an amount falling below tax paid on the lifetime transfer, no additional liability can arise nor will the shortfall become repayable.

Tapering relief will, of course, only be available if the calculation discloses a liability to inheritance tax. There can be no liability to the extent that the lifetime transfer falls within the nil rate band.

Potentially exempt transfers

Where a potentially exempt transfer loses immunity from liability due to the donor's death within the seven-year inter vivos period, the value transferred by that transfer enters into the cumulative total. Any liability to inheritance tax will be calculated by applying the full rate of 40 per cent, reduced to the percentage governed by tapering relief if the original transfer occurred more than three years before death. Liability can only arise to the extent, if any, that the nil rate band is exceeded.

Death

The final addition to the seven-year cumulative total will comprise the value of an estate on death. Inheritance tax will be calculated by applying the full rate of 40 per cent to the extent the nil rate band is exceeded. No tapering relief can be obtained.

RATES OF TAX

In earlier times there were several rates of inheritance tax which progressively increased as the value transferred grew in size. However, since 1988 there have been only three rates, namely:
(a) a nil rate
(b) a lifetime rate of 20 per cent
(c) a full rate of 40 per cent
The nil rate band usually changes on an annual basis and for events taking place after 5 April 2002 applies to the first £250,000. Any excess over this level is taxable at 20 per cent or 40 per cent as the case may be.

PAYMENT OF TAX

Inheritance tax usually falls due for payment six months after the end of the month in which the chargeable transaction takes place. Where a transfer other than that made on death occurs after 5 April and before the following 1 October, tax falls due on the following 30 April, although there are some exceptions to this. Inheritance tax attributable to the transfer of certain land, controlling shareholding interests, unquoted shares, businesses and interests in businesses, together with agricultural property, may usually be satisfied by instalments spread over ten years. Except in the case of non-agricultural land, where interest is charged on outstanding instalments, no liability to interest arises where tax is paid on the due date. In all cases, delay in the payment of tax may incur a liability to discharge interest.

SETTLED PROPERTY

Complex rules apply to establish inheritance tax liability on settled property. Where a person is beneficially entitled to an interest in possession, that person is effectively deemed to own the property in which the interest subsists. It follows that where the interest comes to an end during the beneficiary's lifetime and some other person becomes entitled to the property or interest, the beneficiary is treated as having made a transfer of value. However, this will usually comprise a potentially exempt transfer. In addition, no liability will arise where the property vests in the absolute ownership of the beneficiary retaining the interest in possession. The death of a person entitled to an interest in possession will require the value of the underlying property to be added to the value of the deceased's estate.

In the case of other settled property where there is no interest in possession (e.g. discretionary trusts), liability to tax will arise on each ten-year anniversary of the trust. There will also be liability if property ceases to be held on discretionary trusts before the first ten-year anniversary date is reached or between anniversaries. The rate of tax suffered will be governed by several considerations, including previous dispositions made by the settlor of the trust, transactions concluded by the trustees, and the period throughout which property has been held in trust.

Accumulation and maintenance settlements which require assets to be distributed, or interests in income to be created, not later than a beneficiary's 25th birthday may be exempt from any liability to inheritance tax.

CORPORATION TAX

Profits, gains and income accruing to companies resident in the UK incur liability to corporation tax. Non-resident companies are immune from this tax unless they carry on a trade in the UK through a permanent establishment, branch or office. Companies residing outside the UK may be liable to income tax at the basic rate on other income arising in the UK, perhaps from letting property. The following comments are confined to companies resident in the UK. Liability to corporation tax is governed by the profits, gains or income for an accounting period. This is usually the period for which financial accounts are made up, and in the case of companies preparing accounts to the same accounting date annually will comprise successive periods of 12 months.

RATE OF TAX

The amount of profits or income for an accounting period must be determined on normal taxation principles. The special rules which apply to individuals where a source of income is acquired or discontinued are ignored and consideration is confined to the actual profits or income for an accounting period.

The rate of corporation tax is fixed for a financial year ending on 31 March. Where the accounting period of a company overlaps this date and there is a change in the rate of corporation tax, profits and income must be apportioned.

The full rate of corporation tax for each of the five financial years ending on the 31 March 2000 to 31 March 2004 inclusive is 30 per cent. This may be reduced to a lower level where profits fall within the small companies' rate or companies' starting rate bands. Although the full rate of tax for the year ending on 21 March 2004 is known, the small companies rate and the starting rate for the same year will not be announced until a later date.

SMALL COMPANIES' RATE

Where the profits of a company do not exceed stated limits, corporation tax becomes payable at the small companies' rate. This may be replaced by a lower starting rate where profits are very small, as discussed later. It is the amount of profits and not the size of the company which governs the application of both the small companies' rate and the starting rate.

For each of the financial years ending on 31 March 2000, 31 March 2001 and 31 March 2002 the small companies' rate remained at 20 per cent. It was then reduced to 19 per cent for the year ending March 2003. The level of profits which a company may derive without losing the benefit of the small companies' rate is £300,000 for each of the four years. However, if profits exceed £300,000 but fall below £1,500,000, marginal small companies' rate relief applies. The effect of marginal relief is that the average rate of corporation tax imposed on all profits steadily increases from the lower small companies' rate to the full rate of 30 per cent, with tax being imposed on profits in the margin at an increased rate. Where a change in the rate of tax is introduced and the accounting period of a company overlaps 31 March, profits must be apportioned to establish the appropriate rate for each part of those profits.

The lower limit of £300,000 and the upper limit of £1,500,000 apply to a period of 12 months and must be proportionately reduced for shorter periods. Some restriction in the small companies' rate and the marginal rate may be necessary if there are two or more associated companies, namely companies under common control. The small companies' rate is not available for close investment-holding companies.

COMPANIES' STARTING RATE

A new companies' starting rate was introduced for the financial year ending on 31 March 2001 and extended to later years. This rate applies where profits of a twelve-month period do not exceed £10,000, with marginal relief where profits exceed this figure but are not in excess of £50,000. The starting rate was 10 per cent for each of the financial years ending on 31 March 2001 and 31 March 2002 and zero for the financial year ending on 31 March 2003. The effect of marginal relief is to increase the average rate of tax suffered until it reaches the small companies' rate for the same financial year.

PAYMENT OF TAX

Corporation tax charged on profits for an accounting period usually falls due for payment in a single lump sum nine months after the end of that period. Most companies discharge corporation tax on this basis but other arrangements concern large companies for accounting periods ending on or after 1 July 1999. These companies must discharge their liability by four instalments. The receipt of annual profits amounting to £1,500,000 or more is sufficient to identify a large company. Where a company is a member of a group the profits of the entire group must be merged to establish whether the company is large.

CAPITAL GAINS

Chargeable gains arising to a company are calculated in a manner similar to that used for individuals. However, the withdrawal of the indexation allowance after April 1998, and the introduction of taper relief from the same date, have no application to companies. Nor are they entitled to the annual exemption of £7,700. However, many gains arising to companies from the disposal of substantial shareholdings after 31 March 2002 are non-exempt from tax. Companies do not suffer capital gains tax on chargeable gains but incur liability to corporation tax. Tax is due on the full chargeable gain of an accounting period after subtracting relief for losses, if any.

DISTRIBUTIONS

Dividends and other qualifying distributions made by a UK resident company on or after 6 April 1999 are not satisfied after deduction of income tax. Similar outgoings made by a company previously required the payment of advance corporation tax but this obligation no longer applies. The only effect which the payment of a dividend or the making of a distribution now has on a company is that the outlay cannot form an ingredient in the calculation of profits.

INTEREST

On making many payments of interest a company is required to deduct income tax at the lower rate of 20 per cent and account for the tax deducted to the Inland Revenue. The gross amount of interest paid will usually be included in the calculation of profits on which corporation tax becomes payable. The requirement to deduct tax will not usually apply where payments are being made to a company.

GROUPS OF COMPANIES

Each company within a group is separately charged to corporation tax on profits, gains and income. However, where one group member realises a loss, other than a

capital loss, a claim may be made to offset the deficiency against profits of some other member of the same group.

It is possible to avoid the deduction of income tax on most payments of interest for transactions between members of a group of companies. The transfer of capital assets from one member of a group to a fellow member will usually incur no liability to tax on chargeable gains.

COMPLIANCE

For several years a 'pay and file' system affected all companies. A feature of this system required that tax should be payable nine months following the end of the accounting period involved with accounts and returns being submitted three months later. This system has been replaced following the introduction of self-assessment which now extends to all companies for accounting periods ending after 30 June 1999.

Self-assessment requires that the corporation tax return should normally be submitted not later than 12 months following the end of the accounting period to which it relates. In addition, a copy of the financial accounts must be included. Failure to file the return within the appropriate time limit will incur a liability to penalties.

VALUE ADDED TAX

Value added tax (VAT) is charged on the value of the supplies made by a registered trader and extends to both the supply of goods and the supply of services. It is administered by Customs and Excise. Liability to account for VAT arises on the value of goods imported into the UK from sources outside the European Community. In contrast goods imported by a trader from a second trader in a member state of the European Community attract no VAT on importation. Instead there is an acquisition tax whereby a trader who acquires goods must include the acquisition in his normal VAT return and account for the tax due. A UK trader who exports goods to a member state will not be required to account for VAT on the supply, if that trader observes the requirements laid down by regulations.

REGISTRATION

All traders, including professional persons and companies, making taxable supplies of a value exceeding stated limits are required to register for VAT purposes. Taxable supplies represent the supply of goods and services potentially chargeable with VAT. The limits which govern mandatory registration are amended periodically, and from 25 April 2002 an unregistered trader must register:
(a) at any time, if there are reasonable grounds for believing that the value of taxable supplies in the next 30 days will exceed £55,000
(b) at the end of any month if the value of taxable supplies in the 12 months then ending has exceeded £55,000.
Liability to register under (b) may be avoided if it can be shown that the value of supplies in the period of 12 months then beginning will not exceed £53,000. There may, however, be liability to register immediately where a business is taken over from another trader as a 'going concern'. Other limits apply where goods are acquired from within the European Community.

Where the limits governing mandatory registration have been exceeded, the trader must notify Customs and Excise. In the event of failure to provide prompt notification, the person concerned will be required to account for VAT from the proper registration date. A trader whose taxable supplies do not reach mandatory registration limits may apply for voluntary registration. This step may be thought advisable to recover input tax or to compete with other registered traders. A registered trader may submit an application for deregistration if the value of taxable supplies subsequently falls. From 25 April 2002, an application for de-registration can be made if the value of taxable supplies for the year beginning on the application date is not expected to exceed £53,000.

INPUT TAX

A registered trader will both suffer tax (input tax) when obtaining goods or services for the purposes of his business and also become liable to account for tax (output tax) on the value of goods and services which he or she supplies. Relief can usually be obtained for input tax suffered, either by setting that tax against output tax due or by repayment. Most items of input tax can be relieved in this manner. Where a registered trader makes both exempt supplies and taxable supplies to his customers or clients, there may be some restriction in the amount of input tax which can be recovered.

OUTPUT TAX

When making a taxable supply of goods or services, a registered trader must account for output tax, if any, on the value of the supply. Usually the price charged by the registered trader will be increased by adding VAT but failure to make the required addition will not remove liability to account for output tax. The liability to account for output tax, and also relief for input tax, may be affected where a trader is using a special second-hand goods scheme.

EXEMPT SUPPLIES

No VAT is chargeable on the supply of goods or services which are treated as exempt supplies. These include the provision of burial and cremation facilities, insurance, finance and education. The granting of a lease to occupy land or the sale of land will usually comprise an exempt supply, but there are numerous exceptions. In particular, the sale of new non-domestic buildings or certain buildings used by charities cannot be treated as exempt supplies. A taxable person may elect to tax rents and other supplies relating to buildings and agricultural land not used for residential or charitable purposes. Exempt supplies do not enter into the calculation of taxable supplies which governs liability to mandatory registration. Such supplies made by a registered trader may, however, limit the amount of input tax which can be relieved. It is for this reason that the election may be useful.

RATES OF TAX

Two main rates of VAT have applied for many years, namely:
(a) a zero, or nil, rate
(b) a standard rate of 17.5 per cent
In addition, a special reduced rate of 5 per cent applies to supplies of domestic fuels, installation of energy saving materials in domestic premises and children's car seats. From 1 June 2002 the 5 per cent rate was extended to include a range of residential conversions and renovations.

ZERO-RATING

A large number of supplies are zero-rated. The following list is not exhaustive but indicates the wide range of supplies which may be included under this heading:
(a) the supply of many items of food and drink. This does not include ice cream, chocolate, sweets, potato crisps and alcoholic drinks. Nor does it extend to supplies made in the course of catering or to items supplied for consumption in a restaurant or café. Whilst the supply of cold items, e.g. sandwiches for consumption away from the supplier's premises, is zero-rated, the supply of hot food, e.g. fish and chips, is not
(b) animal feeding stuffs
(c) sewerage and water, unless for industrial purposes
(d) books, brochures, pamphlets, leaflets, newspapers, maps and charts
(e) talking books for the blind and handicapped, and wireless sets for the blind
(f) supplies of services, other than professional services, when constructing a new domestic building or a building to be used by a charity. The supply of materials for such a building is zero-rated, together with the sale or the grant of a long lease. Alterations to some protected buildings are zero-rated
(g) the transportation of persons in a vehicle, ship or aircraft designed to carry not less than 10 persons
(h) supplies of drugs, medicines and other aids for the handicapped
(i) supplies of children's clothing and footwear
(j) supplies of pedal cycle helmets
(k) exports
Although no tax is due on a zero-rated supply, this does comprise a taxable supply which must be included in the calculation governing liability to register.

COLLECTION OF TAX

Registered traders submit VAT returns for accounting periods usually of three months in duration but arrangements can be made to submit returns on a monthly basis. Very large traders must account for tax on a monthly basis but this does not affect the three-monthly return. The return will show both the output tax due for supplies made by the trader in the accounting period and also the input tax for which relief is claimed. If the output tax exceeds input tax the balance must be remitted with the VAT return. Where input tax suffered exceeds the output tax due the registered trader may claim recovery of the excess from Customs and Excise.
This basis for collecting tax explains the structure of VAT. Where supplies are made between registered traders the supplier will account for an amount of tax which will usually be identical to the tax recovered by the person to whom the supply is made. However, where the supply is made to a person who is not a registered trader there can be no recovery of input tax and it is on this person that the final burden of VAT eventually falls.
Where goods are acquired by a UK trader from a supplier within a member state of the European Community, the trader must also account for the tax due on acquisition.
An optional scheme is available for registered traders having an annual turnover of taxable supplies not exceeding £600,000. Such traders may render returns annually. Nine interim payments of VAT will be made on account, with a final balancing payment accompanying submission of the return. The number of interim payments may be reduced if turnover is small.

A further optional scheme came into operation on 25 April 2002 and is available to businesses having a tax exclusive annual taxable turnover not exceeding £100,000, a figure increased to £125,000 by including exempt and other non-taxable income. Businesses able to satisfy these requirements may discharge VAT by calculating a flat rate percentage of their total turnover. The rate used is governed by the trade sector into which the business falls.

BAD DEBTS

Many retailers operate special retail schemes for calculating the amount of VAT due. These schemes are based on the volume of consideration received in an accounting period. Should a customer fail to pay for goods or services supplied, there will be no consideration on which to calculate VAT.
To avoid the problem of bad debts incurred by traders not operating a special retail scheme, an optional system of cash accounting is available. This scheme, confined to traders with annual taxable supplies not exceeding £600,000, enables returns to be made on a cash basis, in substitution for the normal supply basis. Traders using such a scheme will not include bad debts in the calculation of cash receipts.
Where neither the cash accounting arrangements nor a special retail scheme applies, output tax falls due on the value of the supply and liability is not affected by failure to receive consideration. However, where a debt is more than six months old, relief for bad debts will be forthcoming. The calculation of the six-month period commences from the date on which payment for the supply falls due. In those cases where a supplier obtains relief for a bad debt, the person to whom the supply has been made must refund to Customs and Excise any input tax relief which may have been granted.

OTHER SPECIAL SCHEMES

In addition to the schemes for retailers, there are several special schemes applied to calculate the amount of VAT due and which also limit the ability to recover input tax.

FARMERS

Farmers may elect to apply a special flat rate scheme. This scheme is available to farmers who are not registered traders.

Legal Notes

IMPORTANT

These notes outline certain aspects of the law as they might affect the average person. They are intended only as a broad guideline and are by no means definitive. The law is constantly changing so expert advice should always be taken. In some cases, sources of further information are given in these notes.

It is always advisable to consult a solicitor without delay; timely advice will set your mind at rest but sitting on your rights can mean that you lose them. Anyone who does not have a solicitor already can contact the Citizens' Advice Bureau, the Community Legal Service (www.legalservices.gov.uk), the Law Society of England and Wales (113 Chancery Lane, London WC2A 1PL. Tel: 020-7242 1222) or the Law Society of Scotland (26 Drumsheugh Gardens, Edinburgh EH3 7YR. Tel: 0131-226 7411) for assistance in finding one.

The community legal service fund and legal aid and assistance schemes exist to make the help of a lawyer available to those who would not otherwise be able to afford one. Entitlement depends on an individual's means but a solicitor or Citizens' Advice Bureau will be able to advise about entitlement.

ADOPTION OF CHILDREN

In England and Wales the adoption of children is mainly governed by the Adoption Act 1976 and the Children Act 1989.

Anyone over 21 (or 18 if the natural birth parent wants to adopt with a partner who must be over 21) can legally adopt a child. Married couples must adopt 'jointly', unless one partner cannot be found, is incapable of making an application, or if a separation is likely to be permanent. Unmarried couples may not adopt 'jointly' although one partner in that couple may adopt. Passing through parliament, at the time of going to press, is the new Adoption and Children Bill which, if passed, will enable unmarried couples to adopt jointly. The only organisations allowed to arrange adoptions are the social services departments of local authorities or voluntary agencies which are registered with the local authorities.

Once an adoption has been arranged, a court order is necessary to make it legal. These are obtained from the High Court (Family Division) or from a magistrates', county or family proceedings court. The child's natural parents (or guardians) must consent to the adoption, unless the court dispenses with the consent, e.g. where the natural parent has neglected the child or is incapable of giving consent. Once adopted, the child has the same status as a child born to the adoptive parents and the natural parents cease to have any rights or responsibilities where the child is concerned. The adopted child will be treated as the natural child of the adoptive parents for the purposes of intestate succession, national insurance, family allowances, etc. The adopted child ceases to have any rights to the estates of his/her natural parents.

It is an offence for a person other than an adoption agency to make arrangements for the adoption of a child or place a child for adoption unless the proposed adopter is a relative or is acting according to a court order. It is also an offence to receive a child who is placed in breach of this rule and it is an offence to make or receive payments for adoption.

REGISTRATION AND CERTIFICATES

All adoptions in England and Wales are registered in the Adopted Children Register kept by the Office of National Statistics, and by the General Register Office for Scotland. Certificates from the registers can be obtained in a similar way to birth certificates.

TRACING NATURAL PARENTS OR CHILDREN WHO HAVE BEEN ADOPTED

An adult adopted person may apply to the Registrar-General for information to enable him/her to obtain a full birth certificate. For those adopted before 12 November 1975 it is obligatory to receive counselling services before this information is given; for those adopted after that date counselling services are optional. There is also an Adoption Contact Register (created after the 1989 Act) in which details of adult adopted people and of their relatives may be recorded. The BAAF can provide addresses of organisations which offer advice, information and counselling to adopted people, adoptive parents and people who have had their children adopted.

Further information can be obtained from:
BRITISH ASSOCIATION FOR ADOPTION AND
  FOSTERING (BAAF), Skyline House, 200 Union
  Street, London SE1 0LX. Tel: 020-7593 2000;
  Web: www.baaf.org.uk

SCOTLAND

The relevant legislation is the Adoption (Scotland) Act 1978 (as amended by the Children Act 1995) and the provisions are similar to those described above. In Scotland, petitions for adoption are made to the Sheriff Court or the Court of Session.

Further information can be obtained from:
BRITISH ASSOCIATION FOR ADOPTION AND
  FOSTERING (BAAF), BAAF Scottish Centre,
  40 Shandwick Place, Edinburgh EH2 4RT.
  Tel: 0131-220 4749
SCOTTISH ADOPTION ADVICE SERVICE
  16 Sandyford Place, Glasgow G3 7NB
  Tel: 0141-339 0772

BIRTHS (REGISTRATION)

The birth of a child must be registered within 42 days of birth at the register office of the district in which the baby was born. In England and Wales it is possible to give the particulars to be registered at any other register office. Responsibility for registering the birth rests with the parents, except in the case of an illegitimate child, when the mother is responsible for registration. Responsibility rests firstly with the parents (in Scotland, if the father of the child is not married to the mother and has not been married to her since the child's conception, the mother alone is responsible for registration) but if they fail, particulars may be given to the registrar by:
– a relative of either parent (in Scotland only)
– the occupier of the house in which the baby was born
– a person present at the birth
– the person who is responsible for the child
Failure to register the birth within 42 days without reasonable cause may leave the parents liable to a penalty in England and Wales and may lead to a court decree being granted by a sheriff in Scotland.

If the parents were married at the time of the birth, either parent may register the birth and details about both parents will be entered on the register. If the parents were unmarried at the time of the birth, the father's details are entered only if both parents attend or if the parents have made a statutory declaration confirming the identity of the father. Copies of the forms necessary to make such a declaration are available at the register offices. A short birth certificate is issued when the birth is registered.

RE-REGISTRATION

In certain circumstances it may be necessary to re-register a birth, e.g. where the birth of an illegitimate child is legitimated by the subsequent marriage of the parents. It is also possible to re-register the birth of an illegitimate child so that the father's name is entered on the register.

BIRTH ABROAD

Births of British subjects occurring abroad are registered with consular officers and certificates of birth are subsequently available from the Registrar-General.

SCOTLAND

In Scotland the birth of a child must be registered within 21 days at the register office of either the district in which the baby was born or the district in which the mother was resident at the time of the birth.

If the child is born, either in or out of Scotland, on a ship, aircraft or land vehicle that ends its journey at any place in Scotland, the child, in most cases, will be registered as if born in that place.

CERTIFICATES OF BIRTHS, DEATHS OR MARRIAGES

Certificates of births, deaths or marriages that have taken place in England and Wales since 1837 can be obtained from the Office of National Statistics (General Register Office) or the Family Records Centre. Applications can be made:
– by a personal visit
– by postal application (forms can be downloaded from www.statistics.gov.uk)
Certificates are also available from the Superintendent Registrar for the district in which the event took place or, in the case of marriage certificates, from the minister of the church in which the marriage took place. Any register office can advise about the best way to obtain certificates. The fees for certificates are:

From the Family Records Centre, London by personal application:
Full certificate of birth, death or marriage, £6.50
Full certificate of adoption, £6.50
Short certificate of birth, £6.50
Short certificate of adoption, £5.00

By postal application:
Full certificate of birth, marriage or death, £11.00
Full certificate of birth, marriage or death with ONS index reference supplied, £8.00
Short abbreviated certificate of birth, £11.00
Short abbreviated certificate of adoption, £9.50
Extra copies of the same birth, marriage or death certificate issued at the same time, £6.50
A Priority Service is also available with certificates despatched on the working day following receipt of your application.
Visit www.statistics.gov.uk or call 0870-243 7788 for further information.

Indexes prepared from the registers are available for searching by the public at the Family Records Centre in London or at a Superintendent Registrar's Office; indexes at the latter relate only to births, deaths and marriages which occurred in that registration district. There is no charge for searching the indexes in the Public Search Room at the Family Records Centre but a general search fee is charged for searches at a Superintendent Registrar's Office. A fee is charged for verifying index references against the records.

The Society of Genealogists has many records of baptisms, marriages and deaths prior to 1837.

SCOTLAND

Certificates of births, deaths or marriages that have taken place in Scotland since 1855 can be obtained from the General Register Office for Scotland or from the appropriate local registrar. The General Register Office for Scotland also keeps the Register of Divorces (including decrees of declaration of nullity of marriage), and holds parish registers dating from before 1855.

Fees for certificates (from 1 April 2002) are:

Certificates (full or abbreviated) of birth, death, marriage or adoption:
Personal application: £11.00
Postal or telephone ordering system: £13.00
A priority service for a response within 24 hours is available for an additional fee of £10.00

General search in the indexes to the statutory registers and parochial registers, per day or part thereof:
Full day search (i.e. 9 a.m. to 4.30 p.m.), £17.00
Afternoon (i.e. 1 p.m. to 4.30 p.m.) search £10.00
Full day (i.e. 9 a.m. to 4.30 p.m.) search with payment being made not less than 14 days in advance, £13.00 (only available for the period November 2001 to January 2002)
One week search, £65.00
Four week search, £220.00
One quarter search, £500.00
One year search, £1,500.00

Further information can be obtained from:
THE GENERAL REGISTER OFFICE, Office for National Statistics, Smedley Hydro, Trafalgar Road, Southport, Merseyside PR8 2HH. Tel: 0870-243 7788
FAMILY RECORDS CENTRE, 1 Myddelton Street, London EC1R 1UW. Opens 9 a.m. on Monday, Wednesday, Thursday, Friday, 10 a.m. Tuesday, 9.30 a.m. Saturday. Closes 5 p.m. Monday, Wednesday, Friday, Saturday, 7 p.m. Tuesday, Thursday
THE GENERAL REGISTER OFFICE FOR SCOTLAND, New Register House, Edinburgh EH1 3YT.
Tel: 0131-334 0380; Web: www.gro-scotland.gov.uk
THE SOCIETY OF GENEALOGISTS, 14 Charterhouse Buildings, Goswell Road, London EC1M 7BA.
Tel: 020-7251 8799

BRITISH CITIZENSHIP

The British Nationality Act 1981 which came into force on 1 January 1983 established three types of citizenship to replace the single form of Citizenship of the UK and Colonies created by the British Nationality Act 1948. The three forms of citizenship are: British Citizenship; British Dependent Territories Citizenship; and British Overseas Citizenship. Three residual categories were created: British Subjects; British Protected Persons; and British Nationals (Overseas).

666   Legal Notes

BRITISH CITIZENSHIP

Almost everyone who was a citizen of the UK and colonies and had a right of abode in the UK prior to the 1981 Act became British citizens when the Act came into force. British citizens have the right to live permanently in the UK and are free to leave and re-enter the UK at any time.

A person born on or after 1 January 1983 in the UK (including, for this purpose, the Channel Islands and the Isle of Man) is entitled to British citizenship if he/she falls into one of the following categories:
– he/she has a parent who is a British citizen
– he/she has a parent who is settled in the UK
– he/she is a newborn infant found abandoned in the UK
– his/her parents subsequently settle in the UK
– he/she lives in the UK for the first ten years of his/her life and is not absent for more than 90 days in each of those years
– he/she is adopted in the UK and one of the adopters is a British Citizen

A person born outside the UK may acquire British citizenship if he/she falls into one of the following categories:
– he/she has a parent who is a British citizen otherwise than by descent, e.g. a parent who was born in the UK
– he/she has a parent who is a British citizen serving the Crown overseas
– the Home Secretary consents to his/her registration while he/she is a minor
– he/she is a British Dependent Territories citizen, a British Overseas citizen, a British subject or a British protected person and has been lawfully resident in the UK for five years
– he/she is a British Dependent Territories citizen who acquired that citizenship from a connection with Gibraltar
– he/she is adopted or naturalised

Where parents are married, the status of either may confer citizenship on their child. If a child is illegitimate, the status of the mother determines the child's citizenship.

Under the 1981 Act, Commonwealth citizens and citizens of the Republic of Ireland were entitled to registration as British citizens before 1 January 1988. In 1985, citizens of the Falkland Islands were granted British citizenship.

Renunciation of British citizenship must be registered with the Home Secretary and will be revoked if no new citizenship or nationality is acquired within six months. If the renunciation was required in order to retain or acquire another citizenship or nationality, the citizenship may be reacquired once.

BRITISH DEPENDENT TERRITORIES CITIZENSHIP

Under the 1981 Act, this type of citizenship was conferred on citizens of the UK and colonies by birth, naturalisation or registration in British Dependent Territories. British Dependent Territories citizens may be entitled to registration as British citizens on completion of five years' legal residence in the UK.

On 1 July 1997 citizens of Hong Kong who did not qualify to register as British citizens under the British Nationality (Hong Kong) Act 1990 lost their British Dependent Territories citizenship on the handover of sovereignty to China; they may, however, have applied to register as British Nationals (Overseas).

Eligibility for British Dependent Territories citizenship is determined by similar rules to those for acquiring British citizenship, except that the connection is with the dependent territory rather than with the UK.

BRITISH OVERSEAS CITIZENSHIP

Under the 1981 Act, this type of citizenship was conferred on any UK and colonies citizens who did not qualify for British citizenship or citizenship of the British Dependent Territories. British Overseas citizenship may be acquired by the wife and minor children of a British Overseas citizen in certain circumstances. British Overseas citizens may be entitled to registration as British citizens on completion of five years' legal residence in the UK.

RESIDUAL CATEGORIES

British subjects, British protected persons and British Nationals (Overseas) may be entitled to registration as British citizens on completion of five years' legal residence in the UK.

Citizens of the Republic of Ireland who were also British subjects before 1 January 1949 can retain that status if they fulfil certain conditions.

EUROPEAN UNION CITIZENSHIP

British citizens (including Gibraltarians who are registered as such) are also EU citizens and are entitled to travel freely to other EU countries to work, study, reside and set up a business. EU citizens have the same rights with respect to the United Kingdom.

NATURALISATION

Naturalisation is granted at the discretion of the Home Secretary. The basic requirements are five years' residence (three years if the applicant is married to a British citizen), good character, adequate knowledge of the English, Welsh or Scottish Gaelic language, and an intention to reside permanently in the UK.

STATUS OF ALIENS

Aliens may not hold public office or vote in Britain and they may not own a British ship or aircraft. Citizens of the Republic of Ireland are not deemed to be aliens. Certain provisions of the Immigration and Asylum Act 1999 make provision about immigration and asylum and about procedures in connection with marriage by superintendent registrar's certificate.

CONSUMER LAW

SALE OF GOODS

A sale of goods contract is the most common type of contract. It is governed by the Sale of Goods Act 1979 (as amended by the Sale and Supply of Goods Act 1994). The Act provides protection for buyers by implying terms into every sale of goods contract. These terms are:
– a condition that the seller will pass good title to the buyer (unless the seller agrees to transfer only such title as he has)
– where the seller sells goods by reference to a description, a condition that the goods will match that description and, where the sale is by sample and description, a condition that the bulk of the goods will correspond with such sample and description
– where goods are sold by a business seller, a condition that the goods will be of satisfactory quality if they meet the standard that a reasonable person would regard as satisfactory taking into account any description of the goods, the price, and all other

relevant circumstances. The quality of the goods includes their state and condition, relevant aspects being whether they are suitable for their common purpose, their appearance and finish, freedom from minor defects and their safety and durability. This term will not be implied, however, if a buyer has examined the goods and should have noticed the defect or if the seller specifically drew the buyer's attention to the defect

– where goods are sold by a business seller, a condition that the goods are reasonably fit for any purpose made known to the seller by the buyer, unless the buyer does not rely on the seller's judgement, or it is not reasonable for him/her to do so

– where goods are sold by sample, conditions that the bulk of the sample will correspond with the sample in quality, that the buyer will have a reasonable opportunity of comparing the two and that the goods are free from any defect rendering them unsatisfactory which would not be obvious from the sample

Some of the above terms can be excluded from contracts by the seller. The seller's right to do this is, however, restricted by the Unfair Contract Terms Act 1977. The Act offers more protection to a buyer who 'deals as a consumer', that is where the sale is a business sale, the goods are of a type ordinarily bought for private use and the goods are bought by a buyer who is not a business buyer. In a sale by auction or competitive tender, a buyer never deals as consumer. Also, a seller can never exclude the implied term as to title mentioned above.

HIRE-PURCHASE AGREEMENTS

Terms similar to those implied in contracts of sales of goods are implied into contracts of hire-purchase, under the Supply of Goods (Implied Terms) Act 1973. The 1977 Act limits the exclusion of these implied terms as before.

SUPPLY OF GOODS AND SERVICES

Under the Supply of Goods and Services Act 1982, similar terms are also implied in other types of contract under which ownership of goods passes, e.g. a contract for 'work and materials' such as supplying new parts while servicing a car, and contracts for the hire of goods. These types of contracts have additional implied terms:

– that the supplier will use reasonable care and skill
– that the supplier will carry out the service in a reasonable time (unless the time has been agreed)
– that the supplier will make a reasonable charge (unless the charge has already been agreed)

The 1977 Act limits the exclusion of these implied terms in a similar manner as before.

UNFAIR TERMS

The Unfair Terms in Consumer Contracts Regulations 1999 apply to contracts between business sellers (or suppliers of goods and services) and consumers, where the terms have not been individually negotiated, i.e where the terms were drafted in advance so that the consumer was unable to influence those terms. An unfair term is one which operates to the detriment of the consumer. An unfair term does not bind the consumer but the contract will continue to bind the parties if it is capable of existing without the unfair term. The regulations contain a non-exhaustive list of terms which are regarded as unfair. Whether a term is regarded as fair or not will depend on many factors, including the nature of the goods or services, the surrounding circumstances (such as the bargaining strength of both parties) and the other terms in the contract.

TRADE DESCRIPTIONS

It is a criminal offence under the Trade Descriptions Act 1968 for a business seller to apply a false trade description of goods or to supply or offer to supply any goods to which a false description has been applied. A 'trade description' includes descriptions of quality, size, composition, fitness for purpose and method, and place and date of manufacture of the goods. It is also an offence to give a false indication of the price of goods.

FAIR TRADING

The Fair Trading Act 1973 is designed to protect the consumer. It provides for the appointment of a Director-General of Fair Trading, one of whose duties is to review commercial activities in the UK relating to the supply of goods and services to consumers. An example of a practice which has been prohibited by a reference made under this Act is that of business sellers posing in advertisements as private sellers.

CONSUMER PROTECTION

Under the Consumer Protection Act 1987, producers of goods are liable for any injury or for any damage exceeding £275 caused by a defect in their product (subject to certain defences).

The Consumer Protection (Cancellation of Contracts Concluded Away from Business Premises) Regulations 1987 allow consumers a seven-day period in which to cancel contracts for the supply of goods and services, where the contracts were made during an unsolicited visit to the consumer's home or workplace. This only applies to contracts where the cost exceeds £35.

Consumers are also afforded protection under the Consumer Protection (Distance Selling) Regulations 2000.

CONSUMER CREDIT

In matters relating to the provision of credit (or the supply of goods on hire or hire-purchase), consumers are also protected by the Consumer Credit Act 1974. Under this Act a licence, issued by the Director-General of Fair Trading, is required to conduct a consumer credit or consumer hire business or to deal in credit brokerage, debt adjusting, counselling or collecting. Any 'fit' person may apply to the Director-General of Fair Trading for a licence, which is normally renewable after ten years. A licence is not necessary if such types of business are only transacted occasionally, or if only exempt agreements are involved. The provisions of the Act only apply to 'regulated' agreements, i.e. those that are with individuals or partnerships, those that are not exempt (such as certain local authority and building society loans), and those where the total credit does not exceed £25,000. Provisions include:

– the terms of the regulated agreement can be altered by the creditor provided the agreement gives him/her the right to do so; in such cases the debtor must be given proper notice of this

– in order for a creditor to enforce a regulated agreement, the agreement must comply with certain formalities and must be properly executed. The debtor must also be given specified information by the creditor or his/her broker or agent during the negotiations which take place before the signing of the agreement. The agreement must state certain information such as the amount of credit, the annual interest rate, the amount and timing of repayments

– if an agreement is signed other than at the creditor's (or credit broker's or negotiator's) place of business

and oral representations were made in the debtor's presence during discussions pre-agreement, the debtor has a right to cancel the agreement. Time for cancellation expires five clear days after the debtor receives a second copy of the agreement. The agreement must inform the debtor of his right to cancel and how to cancel
– if the debtor is in arrears (or otherwise in breach of the agreement), the creditor must serve a default notice before taking any action such as repossessing the goods
– if the agreement is a hire-purchase or conditional sale agreement, the creditor cannot repossess the goods without a court order if the debtor has paid one-third of the total price of the goods
– in agreements where the debtor is required to make grossly exorbitant payments or where the agreement grossly contravenes the ordinary principles of fair trading, the debtor may request that the court alter or set aside some of the terms of the agreement. The agreement can also be reopened during enforcement proceedings by the court itself
Where a credit reference agency has been used to check the debtor's financial standing, the creditor must give the agency's name to the debtor, who is entitled to see the agency's file on him. A fee of £1 is payable to the agency.

SCOTLAND

The legislation governing the sale and supply of goods applies to Scotland as follows:
– the Sale of Goods Act 1979 applies with some modifications and it has been amended by the Sale and Supply of Goods Act 1994
– the Supply of Goods (Implied Terms) Act 1973 applies
– the Supply of Goods and Services Act 1982 does not extend to Scotland but some of its provisions were introduced by the Sale and Supply of Goods Act 1994
– only Parts II and III of the Unfair Contract Terms Act 1977 apply
– the Trade Descriptions Act 1968 applies with minor modifications
– the Consumer Credit Act 1974 applies
– the Consumer Protection Act 1987 applies
– the General Product Safety Regulations 1994 apply
– the Unfair Terms in Consumer Contracts 1999 apply
– the Consumer Protection (Distance Selling) Regulations 2000 apply
The main difference between consumer law in Scotland and England is in the court procedure to be taken. Many consumer disputes in Scotland will be dealt with under the small claims or summary cause procedure. Further information can be obtained from your local sheriff court.

PROCEEDINGS AGAINST THE CROWN

Until 1947, proceedings against the Crown were generally possible only by a procedure known as a petition of right, which put the litigant at a considerable disadvantage. The Crown Proceedings Act 1947 placed the Crown (not the Sovereign in his/her private capacity, but as the embodiment of the State) largely in the same position as a private individual. The Act did not, however, extinguish or limit the Crown's prerogative or statutory powers, and it granted immunity to HM ships and aircraft. It also left certain Crown privileges unaffected. The Act largely abolished the special procedures which previously applied to civil proceedings by and against the Crown.

Civil proceedings may be instituted against the appropriate government department or against the Attorney-General.

In Scotland proceedings against the Crown founded on breach of contract could be taken before the 1947 Act and no special procedures applied. The Crown could, however, claim certain special pleas. The 1947 Act applies in part to Scotland and brings the practice of the two countries as closely together as the different legal systems permit. As a result of the Scotland Act 1998 actions against government departments should be raised against the Lord Advocate or the Advocate General. Actions should be raised against the Lord Advocate where the department involved administers a devolved matter. Devolved matters include agriculture, education, housing, local government, health and justice. Actions should be raised against the Advocate General where the department is dealing with a reserved matter. Reserved matters include defence, foreign affairs and social security.

DEATHS

WHEN A DEATH OCCURS

If the death (including stillbirth) was expected, the doctor who attended the deceased during their final illness should be contacted. If the death was sudden or unexpected, the family doctor (if known) and police should be contacted. If the cause of death is quite clear the doctor will provide:
– a medical certificate that shows the cause of death
– a formal notice that states that the doctor has signed the medical certificate and that explains how to get the death registered
If the death was known to be caused by a natural illness but the doctor wishes to know more about the cause of death, he/she may ask the relatives for permission to carry out a post-mortem examination. This should not delay the funeral.

In England and Wales a coroner is responsible for investigating deaths occurring in the following circumstances:
– where there is no doctor who can issue a medical certificate of cause of death
– when no doctor has treated the deceased during his or her last illness or when the doctor attending the patient did not see him or her within 14 days before death, or after death; or
– when the death occurred during an operation or before recovery from the effect of an anaesthetic; or
– when the death was sudden and unexplained or attended by suspicious circumstances; or
– when the death might be due to an industrial injury or disease, or to accident, violence, neglect or abortion, or to any kind of poisoning; or
– the death occurred in prison or in police custody
The doctor will write on the formal notice that the death has been referred to the coroner; if the post mortem shows that death was due to natural causes, the coroner may issue a notification which gives the cause of death so that the death can be registered. If the cause of death was violent or unnatural, the coroner is obliged to hold an inquest.

In Scotland the office of coroner does not exist. The local procurator fiscal inquires into sudden or suspicious deaths. A fatal accident inquiry will be held before the sheriff where the death has resulted from an accident during the course of the employment of the person who

has died, or where the person who has died was in legal custody, or where the Lord Advocate deems it in the public interest that an inquiry be held.

For queries about the role of the Procurator Fiscal contact:

THE CROWN OFFICE, 25 Chambers Street, Edinburgh EH1 1LA. Tel: 0131-226 2626.

REGISTERING A DEATH

In England and Wales the death must be registered by the registrar of births and deaths for the district in which it occurred; details can be obtained from the telephone directory (under registration of births and deaths and marriages), from the doctor or local council, or at a post office or police station. From April 1997, information concerning a death can be given before any registrar of births and deaths in England and Wales. The registrar will pass the relevant details to the registrar for the district where the death occurred, who will then register the death or, if different in the registration district in which the death took place. In England and Wales the death must normally be registered within five days; in Scotland it must be registered within eight days. If the death has been referred to the coroner/local procurator fiscal it cannot be registered until the registrar has received authority from the coroner/local procurator fiscal to do so. Failure to register a death involves a penalty in England and Wales and may lead to a court decree being granted by a sheriff in Scotland.

If the death occurred at a house, the death may be registered by:
- any relative of the deceased
- any person present at the death
- the occupier or any inmate of the house or hospital if he/she knew of the occurrence of the death
- any person making the funeral arrangements
- the deceased's executor or legal representative.

The person registering the death should take the medical certificate of the cause of death with them; it is also useful, though not essential, to take the deceased's birth and marriage certificates, medical card (if possible), pension documents and life assurance details. The registrar will issue a certificate for burial or cremation and a certificate of registration of death; both are free of charge. A death certificate is a certified copy of the entry in the death register; these can be provided on payment of a fee and may be required for the following purposes:
- the will
- bank and building society accounts
- savings bank certificates and premium bonds
- insurance policies
- pension claims

If the death occurred abroad or on a foreign ship or aircraft, the death should be registered according to the local regulations of the relevant country and a death certificate should be obtained. The death can also be registered with the British Consul in that country and a record will be kept at the General Register Office. This avoids the expense of bringing the body back.

After 12 months (3 months in Scotland) of death or the finding of a dead body, no death can be registered without the consent of the Registrar-General.

BURIAL AND CREMATION

In most circumstances in England and Wales a certificate for burial or cremation must be obtained from the registrar before the burial or cremation can take place. If the death has been referred to the coroner, an order for burial or a certificate for cremation must be obtained. In Scotland a body may be buried (but not cremated) before the death is registered.

Funeral costs can normally be repaid out of the deceased's estate and will be given priority over any other claims. If the deceased has left a will it may contain directions concerning the funeral; however, these directions need not be followed by the executor.

The deceased's papers should also indicate whether a grave space had already been arranged. Most town churchyards and many suburban churchyards are no longer open for burial because they are full. Most cemeteries are non-denominational and may be owned by local authorities or private companies; fees vary.

If the body is to be cremated, an application form, two cremation certificates (for which there is a charge) or a certificate for cremation if the death was referred to the coroner, and a certificate signed by the medical referee must be completed in addition to the certificate for burial or cremation (the form is not required if the coroner has issued a certificate for cremation). All the forms are available from the funeral director or crematorium. Most crematoria are run by local authorities; the fees usually include the medical referee's fee and the use of the chapel. Ashes may be scattered, buried in a churchyard or cemetery, or kept.

The registrar must be notified of the date, place and means of disposal of the body within 96 hours (England and Wales) and three days (Scotland).

If the death occurred abroad or on a foreign ship or aircraft, a local burial or cremation may be arranged. If the body is to be brought back to England or Wales, a death certificate from the relevant country or an authorisation for the removal of the body from the country of death from the coroner or relevant authority will be required. To arrange a funeral in England or Wales, an authenticated translation of a foreign death certificate or a death certificate issued in Scotland or Northern Ireland which must show the cause of death, is needed, together with a certificate of no liability to register from the registrar in England and Wales in whose sub-district it is intended to bury or cremate the body. If it is intended to cremate the body, a cremation order will be required from the Home Office or a certificate for cremation.

Further information can be obtained from:

THE GENERAL REGISTER OFFICE, Office for National Statistics, Smedley Hydro, Trafalgar Road, Southport, Merseyside PR8 2HH. Tel: 0870-243 7788

THE GENERAL REGISTER OFFICE FOR SCOTLAND, New Register House, Edinburgh EH1 3YT. Tel: 0131-334 0380

DIVORCE AND RELATED MATTERS

ENGLAND AND WALES

There are two types of matrimonial suit: those seeking the annulment of a marriage, and those seeking a judicial separation or divorce. To obtain an annulment, judicial separation or divorce in England and Wales, one or both of the parties must have their permanent home in England and Wales when the petition is started, or have been living in England and Wales for at least a year on the day the petition is started. All cases are commenced in divorce county courts or in the Divorce Registry in London. If a suit is defended it may be transferred to the High Court.

NULLITY OF MARRIAGE

Various circumstances will render a marriage invalid including if: the marriage has not been consumated; one partner had a venereal disease at the time of the marriage and the other did not know about it; the female partner was pregnant at the time of marriage with another person's child and the male partner did not know of the pregnancy; the parties were within the prohibited degrees of consanguinity, affinity or adoption; the parties were not male and female; either of the parties was already married; either of the parties was under the age of 16; the formalities of the marriage were defective, e.g. the marriage did not take place in an authorised building, and both parties knew of the defect. Declarations of nullity are sought in very few cases.

SEPARATION

A couple may enter into an agreement to separate by consent but for the agreement to be valid it must be followed by an immediate separation; a solicitor should be contacted.

Judicial separation does not dissolve a marriage and it is not necessary to prove that the marriage has irretrievably broken down. Either party can petition for a judicial separation at any time; the grounds listed below as grounds for divorce are also grounds for judicial separation. To petition for judicial separation the parties do not have to prove that they have been married for 12 months or more. A financial settlement between spouses which accompanies a judicial separation will not bind the court after instigation of divorce proceedings.

DIVORCE

Neither party can petition for divorce until at least one year after the date of the marriage. The sole ground for divorce is the irretrievable breakdown of the marriage; this must be proved on one or more of the following grounds:

- the respondent has committed adultery and the petitioner finds it intolerable to live with him/her; however, the petitioner cannot rely on an act of adultery by the other party if they have lived together for more than six months after the discovery that adultery had been committed
- the respondent has behaved in such a way that the petitioner cannot reasonably be expected to continue living with him/her
- the respondent deserted the petitioner for two years immediately before the petition. Desertion may be defined as a voluntary withdrawal from cohabitation by the respondent without just cause and against the wishes of the petitioner; where one party is guilty of serious misconduct which forces the other party to leave, the party at fault is said to be guilty of constructive desertion
- the respondent and the petitioner have lived separately for two years immediately before the petition and the respondent consents to the decree
- the respondent and the petitioner have lived separately for five years immediately before the petition

A total period of less than six months during which the parties have resumed living together is disregarded in determining whether the prescribed period of separation or desertion has been continuous (but cannot be included as part of the period of separation).

The Matrimonial Causes Act 1973 requires the solicitor for the petitioner in certain cases to certify whether the possibility of a reconciliation has been discussed with petitioner.

THE DECREE NISI

A decree nisi does not dissolve or annul the marriage but must be obtained before a divorce or annulment can take place.

Where the suit is undefended, the evidence normally takes the form of a sworn written statement made by the petitioner which is considered by a district judge. If the judge is satisfied that the petitioner has proved the contents of the petition, he/she will set a date for the pronouncement of the decree nisi in open court; neither party need attend.

If the judge is not satisfied that the petitioner has proved the contents of the petition, or if the suit is defended, the petition will be heard in open court with the parties giving oral evidence.

THE DECREE ABSOLUTE

The decree nisi is usually made absolute after six weeks and on the application of the petitioner. If the judge thinks it may be necessary to exercise any of his/her powers under the Children Act 1989, he/she can in exceptional circumstances delay the granting of the decree absolute. The decree absolute dissolves or annuls the marriage.

CHILDREN

Neither parent is now awarded 'custody' of any children of the marriage in England and Wales. Both parents, if married, have 'parental responsibility'. Either parent can exercise this, independently of the other. However, in the case of unmarried parents, the mother has automatic parental responsibility and the father must apply to the courts for a parental responsibility order. Any dispute between the parents can be resolved by the courts. In all court cases concerning children, whether connected to a matrimonial suit or not, the welfare of the child is the paramount consideration.

MAINTENANCE, ETC.

Either party may be liable to pay maintenance to their former spouse. If there were any children of the marriage, both parents have a legal responsibility to support them financially if they can afford to do so. These so-called ancillary matters, including any property settlements, may be settled before the divorce goes through but currently can go on long after the marriage is dissolved.

The courts are responsible for assessing maintenance for the former spouse, taking into account each party's income and essential outgoings and other aspects of the case. The court also deals with any maintenance for a child that has been treated by the spouses as a 'child of the family', e.g. a stepchild, and any property settlements.

The Child Support Agency (CSA) was set up under the Child Support Act 1991 and is now responsible for assessing the maintenance that absent parents should pay for their natural or adopted children (whether or not a marriage has taken place). The CSA accepts applications only when all the people involved are habitually resident in the UK; the courts will continue to deal with cases where one of the people involved lives abroad. The CSA deals with all new cases, and is gradually taking on cases where the parent with care (or his/her new partner) was already receiving income support, family credit or disability working allowance before 5 April 1993. People with existing court orders or written maintenance agreements made before 5 April 1993 should continue to use the courts. Where it is already collecting child maintenance, the CSA has the power to offer a collection and enforcement service for certain other payments of maintenance.

A formula is used to work out how much child maintenance is payable. The formula ensures that after the payment of child maintenance the absent parent's income, and that of any second family he/she may now have, remains significantly above basic income support rates. Also, no absent parent will normally be assessed to pay more than 30 per cent of his/her net income in current child maintenance, or more than 33 per cent if he/she is also liable for any arrears. Absent parents are normally expected to pay at least a minimum amount of child maintenance.

A scheme has begun to be introduced since the end of 1996 which allows departures from the formula in certain tightly defined circumstances, e.g. the high costs of travel to maintain contact with a child, or to have a property and capital transfer ('clean break' settlement) entered into before April 1993 taken into account; there will also be some additional grounds which may result in liability being increased.

Some cases involving unusual circumstances are treated as special cases and the assessment is modified. Where there is financial need (e.g. because of disability or continuing education), maintenance may be ordered by the court for children even beyond the age of 18.

The level of maintenance is reviewed automatically every two years. Either parent can report a change of circumstances and request a review at any time. An independent complaints examiner for the CSA was appointed in early 1997.

If the absent parent does not pay the child maintenance, the CSA may make an order for payments to be deducted directly from his/her salary or wages; if all other methods fail, the CSA may take court action to enforce the payment. In cases where the parent maintaining a child has a high income an application can be made under the Children Act 1989 for top-up payments. Applications for lump sum and property adjustment orders are also made under this statute.

Court Orders

Magistrates' courts used for domestic proceedings are now called family proceedings courts. A spouse can apply to the family proceedings court for a court order on the grounds that the other spouse:
- has failed to pay reasonable maintenance for the applicant
- has failed to make a proper contribution towards the reasonable maintenance of a 'child of the family'
- has deserted the applicant
- has behaved in such a way that the applicant cannot reasonably be expected to live with the respondent

If the case is proved, the court can order:
- periodical payments for the applicant and/or a 'child of the family'
- a lump sum payment to the applicant and/or a 'child of the family'

In deciding what orders (if any) to make, the court must consider guidelines which are similar to those governing financial orders in divorce cases. There are also special provisions relating to consent orders and separation by agreement. An order may be enforceable even if the parties are living together, but in some cases it will cease to have effect if they continue to do so for six months.

Matrimonial Property

Married couples can own property in two ways. The first is according to the title deeds (joint ownership) and the second relates to contributions to the property (beneficial interest). Just because a couple jointly own a property does not mean that in the event of divorce that the proceeds of matrimonial property will be distributed evenly. When deciding on what financial orders to make the court will take into consideration the length of marriage, the parties' ages, the parties' needs, the parties' earning capacity and the needs of the children to the marriage.

Cohabiting Couples

Rights of unmarried couples are not the same as for married couples. By virtue of this it may be worth considering entering into a contract which establishes how money and property should be divided in the event of a relationship breakdown. These contracts are commonly known as 'separation deeds' or 'cohabitation contracts'.

Domestic Violence

If one spouse has been subjected to violence at the hands of the other, it is now possible to obtain a court order very quickly to restrain further violence and if necessary to have the other spouse excluded from the home. Such orders may also relate to unmarried couples and to a range of other relationships including parents and children.

SCOTLAND

Although there is separate legislation for Scotland covering nullity of marriage, judicial separation, divorce and ancillary matters, the provisions are in most respects the same as those for England and Wales. The following is confined to major points on which the law in Scotland differs.

An action for 'declarator of nullity' can be brought only in the Court of Session. Where a spouse is capable of sexual intercourse but refuses to consummate the marriage, this is not a ground of nullity in Scots law, though it could be a ground for divorce. The fact that a spouse was suffering from venereal disease at the time of marriage and the other spouse did not know this is not a ground of nullity in Scots law, neither is the fact that a wife was pregnant by another man at the time of marriage and her husband did not know this.

An action for judicial separation or divorce may be raised in the Court of Session; it may also be raised in the Sheriff Court if either party was resident in the sheriffdom for 40 days immediately before the date of the action or for 40 days ending not more than 40 days before the date of the action. The fee for starting a divorce petition in the Sheriff Court is £72.

When adultery is cited as proof that the marriage has broken down irretrievably, it is not necessary in Scotland to prove also that it is intolerable for the pursuer to live with the defender. In the case of desertion, irretrievable breakdown is not established if, after the two year desertion period has expired, the parties resume living together at any time after the end of three months from the date when they first resume living together.

Where a divorce action has been raised, it may be sisted or put on hold for a variety of reasons.

If the parties do cohabit during such postponement, no account is taken of the cohabitation if the action later proceeds.

In actions for divorce and separation, the court has the power to award a residence order in respect of any children of the marriage. The welfare of the children is of paramount importance, and the fact that a spouse has caused the breakdown of the marriage does not in itself preclude him/her from being awarded residence.

A simplified procedure for 'do-it-yourself' divorce was

introduced in 1983 for certain divorces. If the action is based on two or five years' separation and will not be opposed, and if there are no children under 16 and no financial claims, and there is no sign that the applicant's spouse is unable to manage his or her affairs through mental illness or handicap, the applicant can write directly to the local sheriff court or to the Court of Session for the appropriate forms to enable him or her to proceed. The fee is £57, unless the applicant receives income support, family credit or legal advice and assistance, in which case there is no fee.

An extract decree, which dissolves or annuls marriage, will be made available 14 days after the divorce has been granted.

Further information can be obtained from any divorce county court, solicitor or Citizens' Advice Bureau, the Lord Chancellor's Department or the Lord Advocate's Office, or the following:

THE PRINCIPAL REGISTRY, First Avenue House, 42–49 High Holborn, London WC1V 6NP.

THE COURT OF SESSION, Parliament House, Parliament Square, Edinburgh EH1 1HQ. Tel: 0131-225 2595

THE CHILD SUPPORT AGENCY, Longbenton, Newcastle upon Tyne NE98 1YX. Tel: 0191-213 5000

EMPLOYMENT LAW

PAY AND CONDITIONS

The Employment Rights Act 1996 consolidates the statutory provisions relating to employees' rights. Employers must give each employee employed for more than one month a written statement containing the following information:
- names of employer and employee
- date when employment began
- remuneration and intervals at which it will be paid
- job title or description of job
- hours and place(s) of work
- holiday entitlement and holiday pay
- entitlement to sick leave and sick pay
- details of pension scheme(s)
- length of notice period that employer and employee need to give to terminate employment, or the end date for a fixed-term contract
- details of any collective agreement which affects the terms of employment
- details of disciplinary and grievance procedures
- if the employee is to work outside the UK for more than one month, the period of such work and the currency in which payment is made

This must be given to the employee within two months of the start of their employment. The Working Time Regulation 1998, the National Minimum Wage Act 1998 and the Employment Relations Act 1999 now supplement the 1996 Act.

SICK PAY

Employees absent from work through illness or injury are entitled to receive Statutory Sick Pay (SSP) from the employer for a maximum period of 28 weeks in any three-year period. This applies to all employees, both men and women, up to the age of 65.

DEDUCTIONS FROM PAY

Employers may not make deductions from an employee's wages without the employee's prior written consent or unless authorised by statute (e.g. deductions for national insurance or tax).

SUNDAY TRADING

The Sunday Trading Act 1994 gave new rights to shop workers. They have the right not to be dismissed, selected for redundancy or to suffer any detriment (such as the denial of overtime, promotion or training) if they refuse to work on Sundays. This does not apply to those who, under their contracts, are employed to work on Sundays.

DISPUTES

Where it has not been possible to settle a dispute in the workplace, it may be possible for employees to make a complaint to an industrial tribunal. ACAS offers advice and conciliation in employment disputes.

TERMINATION OF EMPLOYMENT

An employee may be dismissed without notice if guilty of gross misconduct but in other cases a period of notice must be given by the employer. The minimum periods of notice specified in the Employment Rights Act 1996 are:
- at least one week if the employee has been continuously employed for one month or more but for less than two years
- at least two weeks if the employee has been continuously employed for two years or more. A week is added for every complete year of continuous employment up to 12 years
- at least 12 weeks for those who have been continuously employed for 12 years or more
- longer periods apply if these are specified in the contract of employment

If an employee is dismissed with less notice than he/she is entitled to, the employer is generally liable to pay wages for the period of proper notice (or for the period of the contract for those on fixed-term contracts). Generally, no notice needs to be given of the expiry of a fixed-term contract.

REDUNDANCY

An employee dismissed because of redundancy may be entitled to a lump sum. This applies if:
- the employee has at least two years' continuous service
- the employee is actually dismissed by the employer (even in cases of voluntary redundancy)
- dismissal is due to a reduction in the work force

An employee may not be entitled to a redundancy payment if offered a new job by the same employer. The amount of payment depends on the length of service, the salary and the age of the employee. The redundancy payment is guaranteed by the State in cases where the employer becomes insolvent (subject to the conditions above).

UNFAIR DISMISSAL

Complaints about unfair dismissal are dealt with by an employment tribunal. Any employee, with one years' continuous service subject to exceptions, regardless of their hours of work, can make a complaint to the tribunal. At the tribunal the employer must prove that the dismissal was due to one or more of the following reasons:
- the employee's capability for the job
- the employee's conduct
- redundancy
- a legal restriction preventing the continuation of the employee's contract
- some other substantial reason (including breaking the law)

If so, the tribunal must decide whether the employer acted reasonably in dismissing the employee for that reason. If the employee is found to have been unfairly dismissed, the tribunal can order that he/she be reinstated or compensated. Any person believing that they may have been unfairly dismissed should contact their local Citizens' Advice Bureau. A claim must be brought within 3 months of the date of termination.

The maximum award for unfair dismissal is £52,600 which relates to dismissals occurring on or after 1 February 2002.

DISCRIMINATION

Discrimination in employment on the grounds of sex, race, colour, nationality, ethnic or national origins, married status or (subject to wide exceptions) disability is unlawful. Discrimination legislation also covers sexual harassment and gender reassignment. Discrimination on the grounds of age is not unlawful. The following legislation applies to those employed in Great Britain but not to employees in Northern Ireland or (subject to EC exceptions) to those who work mainly abroad:

- The Equal Pay Act 1970 (as amended) entitles men and women to equality in matters related to their contracts of employment. Those doing like work for the same employer are entitled to the same pay and conditions regardless of their sex
- The Sex Discrimination Act 1975 (as amended by the Sex Discrimination Act 1986) makes it unlawful to discriminate on grounds of sex or marital status. This covers all aspects of employment, including advertising for recruits, terms offered, opportunities for promotion and training, and dismissal procedures
- The Race Relations Act 1976 gives individuals the right not to be discriminated against in employment matters on the grounds of race, colour, nationality, or ethnic or national origins. It applies to all aspects of employment
- The Disability Discrimination Act 1995 makes discrimination against a disabled person in all aspects of employment unlawful. Unlike sex and race discrimination, an employer may show that the treatment is justified and that the employer acted reasonably. Employers with fewer than 15 employees are exempt.

The Equal Opportunities Commission, the Commission for Racial Equality and the Disability Rights Commission have the function of eliminating such discriminations in the workplace and can provide further information and assistance.

In Northern Ireland similar provisions exist but are constituted in separate legislation which also provides protection against religious discrimination.

RECENT CHANGES

The Employment Relations Act 1999 has made a number of important changes to the existing law. The main changes are :

- a right of accompaniment. A worker attending a serious disciplinary or grievance hearing will have a right to be accompanied by a trade union representative or co-worker of their choice
- a new scheme of compulsory trade union recognition following a workplace ballot
- greater protection from dismissal for striking employees
- more 'family friendly' measures, including greater rights to maternity leave and parental leave

HUMAN RIGHTS

On 2 October 2000 the Human Rights Act 1998 came into force. This Act incorporates the European Convention on Human Rights into the law of the United Kingdom and it is expected to have a wide impact.

The main principles of the Act are as follows :-

- all legislation must be interpreted by the courts as compatible with the Convention so far as it is possible to do so
- subordinate legislation (e.g. statutory instruments) which are incompatible with the Convention can be struck down by the courts
- primary legislation (e.g. Acts of Parliament) which is incompatible with the Convention cannot be struck down by a court, but the higher courts can make a declaration of incompatibility which is a signal to Parliament to change the law
- all public authorities (including courts and tribunals) must not act in a way which is incompatible with the Convention;
- individuals whose Convention rights have been infringed by a public authority may bring proceedings against that authority, but the Act is not intended to create new rights as between individuals.

The main human rights protected by the Convention are the right to life (article 2); protection from torture and inhuman or degrading treatment (article 3); protection from slavery or forced labour (article 4); the right to liberty and security of the person (article 5); right to a fair trial (article 6); the right not to be subject to retrospective criminal offences (article 7); right to private and family life (article 8); freedom of thought, conscience and religion (article 9); freedom of expression (article 10); freedom of association and assembly (article 11); right to marry and found a family (article 12); protection from discrimination (article 14); the right to property (article 1 Protocol No.1) and the right to education (article 2 Protocol No.1). Most of the Convention rights are subject to limitations which are 'necessary in a democratic society'.

ILLEGITIMACY AND LEGITIMATION

The Children Act 1989 gives the mother parental responsibility for the child when she is not married to the father. The unmarried father can acquire parental responsibility either by agreement with her (in prescribed form) or by applying to the court. If an illegitimate child is to be adopted, the father's consent is required only where he has been awarded parental rights by the court.

Every child born to a married woman during marriage is presumed to be legitimate, unless the couple are separated under court order when the child is conceived, in which case the child is presumed not to be the husband's child. It is possible to challenge the presumption of legitimacy or illegitimacy through civil proceedings.

In Scotland, the relevant legislation is the Children (Scotland) Act 1995, which also gives the mother parental responsibility for her child when she is not married to the child's father. The Act also provides that a father has no automatic parental rights when unmarried to the mother, but can acquire parental responsibility by applying to the court or by acquiring them under a parental responsibilities and parental rights agreement made with the mother. A child's father will only have automatic rights and responsibilities if he was married to the mother at the time of conception or subsequently marries her.

LEGITIMATION

Under the Legitimacy Act 1976, an illegitimate person automatically becomes legitimate when his/her parents marry. This applies even where one of the parents was married to a third person at the time of the birth. In such cases it is necessary to re-register the birth of the child. In Scotland, the relevant legislation is the Legitimation (Scotland) Act 1968 and the Adoption (Scotland) Act 1978.

JURY SERVICE

In England and Wales a person charged with any but the most minor offences is entitled to be tried by jury (However the right to trial by jury will be restricted if the Criminal Justice (Mode of Trial) (No.2) Bill presently before Parliament becomes law). No such right exists in Scotland, although more serious offences are heard before a jury. In England and Wales there are 12 members of a jury in a criminal case and eight members in a civil case. In Scotland there are 12 members of a jury in a civil case in the Court of Session (the civil jury being confined to the Court of Session and a restricted number of actions), and 15 in a criminal trial. Jurors are normally asked to serve for ten working days, although jurors selected for longer cases are expected to sit for the duration of the trial.

Every parliamentary or local government elector between the ages of 18 and 70 who has lived in the UK (including, for this purpose, the Channel Islands and the Isle of Man) for any period of at least five years since reaching the age of 13 is qualified to serve on a jury unless he/she is ineligible or disqualified.

ENGLAND AND WALES

Those ineligible for jury service include:
- those who have at any time been judges, magistrates or senior court officials
- those who have within the previous ten years been concerned with the administration of justice
- priests of any religion and vowed members of religious communities
- certain sufferers from mental illness

Those disqualified from jury service include:
- those who have at any time been sentenced by a court in the UK (including, for this purpose, the Channel Islands and the Isle of Man) to a term of imprisonment or custody of five years or more
- those who have within the previous ten years served any part of a sentence of imprisonment, youth custody or detention, been detained in a young offenders' institution, received a suspended sentence of imprisonment or order for detention, or received a community service order
- those who have within the previous five years been placed on probation
- those who are on bail in criminal proceedings

Those who may be excused as of right from jury service include:
- persons over the age of 65
- members and officers of the Houses of Parliament
- members of the National Assembly for Wales
- representatives to the European Parliament
- full-time serving members of the armed forces
- registered and practising members of the medical, dental, nursing, veterinary and pharmaceutical professions
- those who have served on a jury in the previous two years

The court has the discretion to excuse a juror from service, or defer the date of service, if the service would be a hardship to the juror. If a person serves on a jury knowing himself/herself to be ineligible or disqualified, he/she is liable to be fined up to £5,000 if disqualified and up to £1,000 for all other offences. The defendant can object to any juror if he/she can show cause.

A juror may claim travelling expenses, a subsistence allowance and an allowance for other financial loss (e.g. loss of earnings or benefits, fees paid to carers or childminders) up to a stated limit.

It is an offence for a juror to disclose what happened in the jury room even after the trial is over. A jury's verdict must normally be unanimous, but if no verdict has been reached after two hours' consideration (or such longer period as the court deems to be reasonable) a majority verdict is acceptable if ten jurors agree to it.

SCOTLAND

Qualification criteria for jury service in Scotland are similar to those in England and Wales, except that the maximum age for a juror is 65, members of the judiciary are ineligible for ten years after ceasing to hold their post, and others concerned with the administration of justice are only eligible for service five years after ceasing to hold office. Certain persons who have the right to be excused include full-time members of the medical profession, full-time members of the armed forces, ministers of religion, persons who have served on a jury within the previous 5 years, members of the Scottish Parliament, members of the Scottish Executive and junior Scottish Ministers. If you have been convicted of a serious crime then you are automatically disqualified. Those who are incapable by reason of a mental disorder may also be excused. The maximum fine for a person serving on a jury knowing himself/herself to be ineligible is £1,000. The maximum fine for failing to attend without good cause is also £1,000.

Further information can obtained from:

THE COURT SERVICE, Southside, 105 Victoria Street, London SW1E 6QT. Tel: 020-7210 2266
THE CLERK OF JUSTICIARY, High Court of Justiciary, Lawnmarket, Edinburgh EH2 2NS. Tel: 0131-225 2595

LANDLORD AND TENANT

When a property is rented to a tenant, the rights and responsibilities of the landlord and the tenant are determined largely by the tenancy agreement but also by statutory provisions. Some of the main provisions are outlined below but it is advisable to contact the Citizens' Advice Bureau or the local authority housing department for further information.

RESIDENTIAL LETTINGS

The provisions outlined here apply only where the tenant lives in a separate dwelling from the landlord and where the dwelling is the tenant's only or main home. It does not apply to licensees such as lodgers, guests or service occupiers.

The 1996 Housing Act radically changes certain aspects of the legislation referred to below, in particular the grant of assured and assured shorthold tenancies under the Housing Act 1988.

ASSURED SHORTHOLD TENANCIES

If a tenancy was granted on or after 15 January 1989 and before 28 February 1997, the tenant may have an assured tenancy giving that tenant greater rights. The tenant could, for example, stay in possession of the dwelling for

as long as the tenant observed the terms of the tenancy. The landlord cannot obtain possession from such a tenant unless the landlord can establish a specific ground for possession (set out in the Housing Act 1988) and obtains a court order. The rent payable is that agreed with the landlord unless the rent has been fixed by the rent assessment committee of the local authority. The tenant or the landlord may request that the committee set the rent in line with open market rents for that type of property. Any rent increases that are to take place should be written into the agreement but failing that, the landlord must give advance notice of the increase.

Under the Housing Act 1996, most new lettings entered into on or after 28 February 1997 will be assured shorthold tenancies. This means that tenants are given limited rights. The landlord must obtain a court order, however, to obtain possession if the tenant refuses to vacate at the end of the tenancy. If the tenant owes two months rent or more, the landlord can serve notice proceedings and apply to the courts for an order for possession. If the tenancy is an assured shorthold tenancy, the court must grant the order.

REGULATED TENANCIES

Before the Housing Act 1988 came into force (15 January 1989) there were regulated tenancies; some are still in existence and are protected by the Rent Act 1977. Under this Act it is possible for the landlord or the tenant to apply to the local rent officer to have a 'fair' rent registered. The fair rent is then the maximum rent payable.

SECURE TENANCIES

Secure tenancies are generally given to tenants of local authorities, housing associations and certain other bodies. This gives the tenant lifelong tenure unless the terms of the agreement are broken by the tenant. In certain circumstances those with secure tenancies may have the right to buy their property. In practice this right is generally only available to council tenants.

AGRICULTURAL PROPERTY

Tenancies in agricultural properties are governed by the Agricultural Holdings Act 1986 and the Rent (Agricultural) Act 1976, which give similar protections to those described above, e.g. security of tenure, right to compensation for disturbance, etc. The Agricultural Holdings (Scotland) Act 1991 applies similar provisions to Scotland.

EVICTION

Under the Protection from Eviction Act 1977 (as amended by the Housing Act 1988), a landlord must give reasonable notice that he/she is to evict the tenant, and in most cases a possession order, granted in court, is necessary. Notice is generally to be at least four weeks and in prescribed statutory form (notices are available from law stationers). It is illegal for a landlord to evict a person by putting their belongings onto the street, by changing the locks and so on. It is also illegal for a landlord to harass a tenant in any way in order to persuade him/her to give up the tenancy.

LANDLORD RESPONSIBILITIES

Under the Landlord and Tenant Act 1985, where the term of the lease is less than seven years the landlord is responsible for maintaining the structure and exterior of the property and all installations for the supply of water, gas and electricity, for sanitation, and for heating and hot water.

LEASEHOLDERS

Legally leaseholders have bought a long lease rather than a property and in certain limited circumstances the landlord can end the tenancy. Under the Leasehold Reform Act 1967 (as amended by the Housing Acts 1969, 1974 and 1980), leaseholders of houses may have the right to buy the freehold or to take an extended lease for a term of 50 years. This applies to leases where the term of the lease is over 21 years and where the leaseholder has occupied the house as his/her main residence for the last three years, or for a total of three years over the last ten.

The Leasehold Reform, Housing and Urban Development Act came into force in 1993 and allows the leaseholders of flats in certain circumstances to buy the freehold of the building in which they live.

Responsibility for maintenance of the structure, exterior and interior of the building should be set out in the lease. Usually the upkeep of the interior of his/her part of the property is the responsibility of the leaseholder, and responsibility for the structure, exterior and common interior areas is shared between the freeholder and the leaseholder(s).

If leaseholders are in any way dissatisfied with treatment from their landlord or with charges made in respect of lease extensions, they are entitled to have their situation evaluated by the Leasehold Valuation Tribunal.

BUSINESS LETTINGS

The Landlord and Tenant Acts 1927 and 1954 (as amended) give security of tenure to the tenants of most business premises. The landlord can only evict the tenant on one of the grounds laid down in the 1954 Act, and in some cases where the landlord repossesses the property the tenant may be entitled to compensation.

SCOTLAND

In Scotland assured and short assured tenancies exist for lettings after 2 January 1989 and are similar to assured tenancies in England and Wales. The relevant legislation is the Housing (Scotland) Act 1988.

Most tenancies created before 2 January 1989 were regulated tenancies and the Rent (Scotland) Act 1984 still applies where these exist. The Act defines, among other things, the circumstances in which a landlord can increase the rent when improvements are made to the property. The provisions of the Rent Act do not apply to tenancies where the landlord is the Crown, a local authority, the development corporation of a new town or a housing corporation.

The Housing (Scotland) Act 1987 and its provisions relate to local authority responsibilities for housing, the right to buy, and local authority secured tenancies. The provisions are broadly similar to England and Wales.

In Scotland, business premises are not controlled by statute to the same extent as in England and Wales, although the Tenancy of Shops (Scotland) Act 1949 gives some security to tenants of shops. Tenants of shops can apply to the sheriff, within 21 days of being served a notice to quit, for a renewal of tenancy if threatened with eviction. This application may be dismissed on various grounds including where the landlord has offered to sell the property to the tenant at an agreed price or, in the absence of agreement as to price, at a price fixed by a single arbiter appointed by the parties or the sheriff. The Act extends to properties where the Crown or government departments are the landlords or the tenants.

Under the Leases Act 1449 the landlord's successors (either purchasers or creditors) are bound by the agreement made with any tenants so long as the following

conditions are met:
- the lease, if for more than one year, must be in writing
- there must be a rent
- there must be a term of expiry
- the tenant must have entered into possession – the subjects of the lease must be land
- the landlord, if owner, must be infeft – i.e. the title deeds are recorded in the Register of Sasines or the Land Register

Many leases contain references to term and quarter days.

LEGAL AID

The Access to Justice Act 1999 has transformed what used to known as the Legal Aid system. The Legal Aid Board has been abolished and replaced from 1 April 2000 with the Legal Services Commission (85 Gray's Inn Road, London, WC1X 8TX. Tel: 020-7759 0000). The changeover from the Legal Aid system continued until 2002 with a major change being the introduction of the Criminal Defence Service in April 2001 to replace the old system of criminal legal aid. Up-to-date information and further guidance can be obtained from the Legal Services Commission website www.legalservices.gov.uk. The Legal Services Commission administers the Community Legal Service fund under which people on low or moderate incomes may qualify for help with the costs of legal advice or representation. Further advice about entitlement to assistance should be sought from a solicitor or Citizens' Advice Bureau. A key element of the reforms has been the introduction of the Community Legal Service which is designed to increase access to legal information and advice by involving a much wider network of funders and providers in giving publicly funded legal services. In Scotland, provision of legal aid is governed by the Legal Aid (Scotland) Act 1986.

CIVIL LEGAL AID

From 1 January 2000, only organisations (solicitors or Citizens' Advice Bureau) with a contract with the Legal Services Commission have been able to give initial help in any civil matter. Moreover, from that date decisions about funding were devolved from the Legal Services Commission to contracted organisations in relation to any level of publicly funded service in family and immigration cases. For other types of case, applications for public funding are made through a solicitor (or other contracted legal services providers) in much the same way as the former Legal Aid. From 1 April 2001 the so-called civil contracting scheme will be extended to cover all levels of service for all types of cases.

Under the new civil funding scheme there are broadly seven levels of service available:
- legal help
- help at court (the first two types of service are limited to advice and assistance with preparing a case, but do not include representation)
- approved family help - either general family help or help with mediation (special levels of service for family cases)
- legal representation - either investigative help or full representation (this covers assistance with representation in court)
- support funding - either investigative support or litigation support (this is a new type of assistance which allows the costs of a privately funded case to be topped up from public funds. It is only available for

personal injury claims)
- family mediation
- such other services as are specifically authorised by the Lord Chancellor

In general, public funding is not available for the following type of cases:
- personal injury (except for the availability of support funding and clinical negligence claims)
- allegations of negligent damage to property
- conveyancing
- boundary disputes
- the making of wills
- matters of trust law
- defamation proceedings
- partnership disputes and company law
- other matters arising out of the carrying on of a business.

ELIGIBILITY

Eligibility for funding from the Community Legal Service depends broadly on five factors :
- the level of service sought (see above)
- whether the applicant qualifies financially
- the merits if the applicant's case
- a costs-benefits analysis (if the costs are likely to outweigh any benefit that might be gained from the proceedings, funding may be refused)
- whether there is any public interest in the case being litigated (i.e. whether the case has a wider public interest beyond that of the parties involved - for example, a human rights case)

The limits on capital and income above which a person is not entitled to public funding vary with the type of service sought.

CONTRIBUTIONS

Some of those who qualify for Community Legal Service funding will have to contribute towards their legal costs. Contributions must be paid by anyone who has a disposable income or disposable capital exceeding a prescribed amount. The rules relating to applicable contributions is complex and detailed information can be obtained from the Legal Services Commission. Tel: 020-7759 0000; Web: www.legalservices.gov.uk

STATUTORY CHARGE

A statutory charge is made if a person receives money or property in a case for which they have received legal aid. This means that the amount paid by the Community Legal Service fund on their behalf is deducted from the amount that the person receives. This does not apply if the court has ordered that the costs be paid by the other party (unless the amount paid by the other party does not cover all of the costs) or if the payments are for maintenance.

CONTINGENCY OR CONDITIONAL FEES

This system was introduced by the Courts and Legal Services Act 1990. It offers legal representation on a "no win, no fee" basis. It provides an alternative form of assistance, especially for those cases which are ineligible for funding by the Community Legal Service. The main area for such work is in the field of personal injuries which claims are now largely exempt from public funding (except for clinical negligence claims).

Not all solicitors offer such a scheme and different solicitors may well have different terms. The effect of the agreement is that solicitors will not make any charges until the case is concluded successfully. The merits of a case are usually assessed before the scheme is offered to

potential litigants. Should the case be accepted, then the charges will be linked to the risks involved: the higher the risks, the higher the fees. Any agreement should be in writing and set out the exact terms of the agreement and the effects of success and failure. If a case is won then the losing party will usually have to pay towards costs, with the winning party contributing around one-third.

SCOTLAND

Civil legal aid is available for cases in the following:
– the House of Lords
– the Court of Session
– the Lands Valuation Appeal Court
– the Scottish Land Court
– sheriff courts
– the Lands Tribunal for Scotland
– the Employment Appeal Tribunals
– the Restrictive Practices Court
Civil legal aid is not available for defamation actions, small claims or simplified divorce procedures.

Eligibility for civil legal aid is assessed in a similar way to that in England and Wales, though the financial limits differ in some respects and are as follows:
– a person is eligible if disposable income is £9,188 or less and disposable capital is £8,560 or less
– if disposable income is between £2,814 and £9,188, contributions are payable
– if disposable capital exceeds £3,000, contributions are payable
– those receiving income support or income related job seeker's allowance qualify automatically.

CRIMINAL LEGAL AID

Criminal legal aid is now administered by the Legal Services Commission. As part of the changes under the Access to Justice Act 1999, in April 2001 the Criminal Defence Service replaced the old system of criminal legal aid. Up-to-date information and further guidance can be obtained from the Legal Services Commission website www.legalservices.gov.uk or from a solicitor or Citizens' Advice Bureau.

The courts will grant criminal legal aid if it is desirable in the interests of justice (e.g. if there are important questions of law to be argued or the case is so serious that if found guilty the person may go to prison) and the person needs help to pay their legal costs.

Criminal legal aid covers the cost of preparing a case and legal representation (including the cost of a barrister) in criminal proceedings. It is also available for appeals against verdicts or sentences in magistrates' courts, the Crown Court or the Court of Appeal. It is not available for bringing a private prosecution in a criminal court.

If granted criminal legal aid, either the person may choose their own solicitor or the court will assign one. Contributions to the legal costs must be paid by anyone who has a disposable income or disposable capital which exceeds a prescribed amount. The rules relating to applicable contributions are complex and detailed information can be obtained from the Legal Services Commission. Tel: 020-7759 0000; Web: www.legalservices.gov.uk.

DUTY SOLICITORS

The Legal Aid Act 1988 also provides free advice and assistance to anyone questioned by the police (whether under arrest or helping the police with their enquiries). No means test or contributions are required for this. The advice or assistance can be from the duty solicitor at the police station, from a person's own solicitor or from any local solicitor (a list is available at police stations).

Duty solicitors are usually available at the magistrates' court, in criminal cases, for advice and/or representation on first appearances. This assistance is not means-tested.

SCOTLAND

Legal advice and assistance operates in a similar way in Scotland. A person is eligible:
– if disposable income does not exceed £189 a week. If disposable income is between £81 and £189 a week, contributions are payable
– if disposable capital does not exceed £1,000 (£1,335 if the person has one dependant, £1,535 if two dependants with an additional £100 for every other dependant). There are no contributions from capital. The procedure for application for criminal legal aid depends on the circumstances of each case. In solemn cases (more serious cases, such as homicide) heard before a jury, a person is automatically entitled to criminal legal aid until they are given bail or placed in custody. Thereafter, it is for the court to decide whether to grant legal aid. The court will do this if the person accused cannot meet the expenses of the case without undue hardship on him or his dependants. In less serious cases the procedure depends on whether the person is in custody:
– anyone taken into custody has the right to free legal aid from the duty solicitor up to and including the first court appearance
– if the person is not in custody and wishes to plead guilty, they are not entitled to criminal legal aid but may be entitled to legal advice and assistance, including assistance by way of representation
– if the person is not in custody and wishes to plead not guilty, they can apply for criminal legal aid. This must be done within 14 days of the first court appearance at which they made the plea
The criteria used to assess whether or not criminal legal aid should be granted is similar to the criteria for England and Wales. When meeting with your solicitor, take evidence of your financial position such as details of savings, bank statements, pay slips, pension book or benefits book.
Further information can be obtained from:
THE SCOTTISH LEGAL AID BOARD, 44 Drumsheugh Gardens, Edinburgh EH3 7SW. Tel: 0131-226 7061.

MARRIAGE

Any two persons may marry provided that:
– they are at least 16 years old on the day of the marriage (in England and Wales persons under the age of 18 must generally obtain the consent of their parents; if consent is refused an appeal may be made to the High Court, the county court or a court of summary jurisdiction)
– they are not related to one another in a way which would prevent their marrying
– they are unmarried (a person who has already been married must produce documentary evidence that the previous marriage has been ended by death, divorce or annulment)
– they are not of the same sex
– they are capable of understanding the nature of a marriage ceremony and of consenting to marriage
– the marriage would be regarded as valid in any foreign country of which either party is a citizen

Degrees of Relationship

A marriage between persons within the prohibited degrees of consanguinity, affinity or adoption is void.

A man may not marry his mother, daughter, grandmother, granddaughter, sister, aunt, niece, great-grandmother, great-granddaughter, adoptive mother, former adoptive mother, adopted daughter or former adopted daughter. In some circumstances he may now be allowed to marry his former wife's daughter, former wife's granddaughter, father's former wife or grandfather's former wife.

A woman may not marry her father, son, grandfather, grandson, brother, uncle, nephew, great-grandfather, great-grandson, adoptive father, former adoptive father, adopted son or former adopted son. In some circumstances she may now be allowed to marry her former husband's son, former husband's grandson, mother's former husband or grandmother's former husband.

ENGLAND AND WALES

Types of Marriage Ceremony

It is possible to marry by either religious or civil ceremony. A religious ceremony can take place at a church or chapel of the Church of England or the Church in Wales, or at any other place of worship which has been formally registered by the Registrar-General.

A civil ceremony can take place at a register office, a registered building or any other premises approved by the local authority.

An application for an approved premises licence must be made by the owners or trustees of the building concerned; it cannot be made by the prospective marriage couple. Approved premises must be regularly open to the public so that the marriage can be witnessed; the venue must be deemed to be a permanent and immovable structure. Open-air ceremonies are prohibited.

Non-Anglican marriages may also be solemnised following the issue of a Registrar-General's licence in unregistered premises where one of the parties is seriously ill, is not expected to recover, and cannot be moved to registered premises. Detained and housebound persons may be married at their place of residence.

Marriage in the Church of England or the Church in Wales

Marriage by banns

The marriage must take place in a parish in which one of the parties lives, or in a church in another parish if it is the usual place of worship of either or both of the parties. The banns must be called in the parish in which the marriage is to take place on three Sundays before the day of the ceremony; if either or both of the parties lives in a different parish the banns must also be called there. After three months the banns are no longer valid.

Marriage by common licence

The vicar who is to conduct the marriage will arrange for a common licence to be issued by the diocesan bishop; this dispenses with the necessity for banns. One of the parties must have lived in the parish for 15 days immediately before the issuing of the licence or must usually worship at the church. Affidavits are prepared from the personal instructions of one of the parties and the licence will be given to the applicant in person.

Marriage by special licence

A special licence is granted by the Archbishop of Canterbury in special circumstances for the marriage to take place at any place, with or without previous residence in the parish, or at any time. Application must be made to the Faculty Office of the Archbishop of Canterbury, 1 The Sanctuary, London SW1P 3JT. Tel: 020-7222 5381.

Marriage by certificate

The marriage can be conducted on the authority of the superintendent registrar's certificate, provided that the vicar's consent is obtained. One of the parties must live in the parish or must usually worship at the church.

Marriage by Other Religious Ceremony

One of the parties must normally live in the registration district where the marriage is to take place. In addition to giving notice to the superintendent registrar it may also be necessary to book a registrar to be present at the ceremony.

Civil Marriage

A marriage may be solemnised at any register office, registered building or approved premises in England and Wales. The superintendent registrar of the district should be contacted, and, if the marriage is to take place at approved premises, the necessary arrangements at the venue must also be made.

Notice of Marriage

Unless it is to take place by banns or under common or special licence in the Church of England or the Church in Wales, a notice of the marriage must be given in person to the superintendent registrar. Notice of marriage may be given in the following ways:
- by certificate. Both parties must have lived in a registration district in England or Wales for at least seven days immediately before giving notice at the local register office. If they live in different registration districts, notice must be given in both districts. The marriage can take place in any register office or other approved premises in England and Wales no sooner than 16 days after notice has been given
- by licence (often known as 'special licence'). One of the parties must have lived in a registration district in England or Wales for at least 15 days before giving notice at the register office; the other party need only be a resident of, or be physically in, England and Wales on the day notice is given. The marriage can take place one clear day (other than a Sunday, Christmas Day or Good Friday) after notice has been given

A notice of marriage is valid for 12 months. It is not therefore possible to give formal notice of a marriage more than three months before it is to take place, but it should be possible to make an advance (provisional) booking 12 months before the ceremony. In this case it is still necessary to give formal notice three months before the marriage. When giving notice of the marriage it is necessary to produce official proof, if relevant, that any previous marriage has ended in divorce or death by producing a decree absolute or death certificate; it is also useful, but not necessary, to take birth certificates or passports as proof of age and identity.

Solemnisation of the Marriage

On the day of the wedding there must be at least two other people present who are prepared to act as witnesses and sign the marriage register. A registrar of marriages must be present at a marriage in a register office or at approved premises, but an authorised person may act in the capacity of registrar in a registered building.

If the marriage takes place at approved premises, the room must be separate from any other activity on the premises at the time of the ceremony, and no food or drink can be sold or consumed in the room during the ceremony or for one hour beforehand.

The marriage must be solemnised between 8 a.m. and 6 p.m., with open doors. At some time during the ceremony the parties must make a declaration that they know of no legal impediment to the marriage and they must also say the contracting words; the declaratory and contracting words may vary according to the form of service in use but the most basic forms are:

- (*declaratory words*) 'I declare that I know of no legal reason why I, A. B., may not be joined in marriage to C. D.' Alternatively, the couple may answer 'I am' to the question 'Are you, A. B., free lawfully to marry C. D.?'
- (*contracting words*) 'I, A. B., take you, C. D., to be my wedded wife [or husband]'

A civil marriage cannot contain any religious aspects, but it may be possible for non-religious music and/or poetry readings to be included. It may also be possible to embellish the marriage vows taken by the couple.

If both parties are Jewish, they may be married in a synagogue, in a private house or elsewhere. The wedding may take place at any time of day and must be registered by the secretary of the synagogue of which the man is a member. The presence of a registrar of marriages is not necessary.

If both parties are members of the Society of Friends (Quakers), they may be married in a Friends' meeting-house. The marriage must be registered by the registering officer of the Society appointed to act for the district in which the meeting-house is situated. The presence of a registrar of marriages is not necessary.

CIVIL FEES

Marriage at a Register Office By superintendent registrar's certificate, £94.00

This includes a fee of £34.00 for the registrar's attendance on the day of the wedding

Marriage on Approved Premises

By superintendent registrar's certificate, £60.00

An additional fee will also be payable for the superintendent registrar's and registrar's attendance at the marriage. This is set locally by the local authority responsible. A further charge is likely to be made by the owners of the building for the use of the premises. For marriages taking place in a religious building other than the Church of England or Church of Wales, an additional fee of £40.00 is payable for the registrar's attendance at the marriage unless an "Authorised Person" appointed by the trustees of the building have agreed to register the marriage. Additional fees may be charged by the trustees of the building for the wedding and by the person who performs the ceremony.

A fee of £3.50 is payable to the registrar for a marriage certificate on the day of the marriage.

ECCLESIASTICAL FEES

(Church of England and Church in Wales*)
Marriage by banns
For publication of banns, £16.00
For certificate of banns issued at time of publication, £9.00
For marriage service, £152.00
Marriage by common licence
Fee for licence, £60.00
Marriage by special licence
Fee for licence, £125.00

Further fees may be payable for additional facilities at the marriage, e.g. the organist's fee.

*Some of these fees may not apply to the Church in Wales

SCOTLAND

REGULAR MARRIAGES

A regular marriage is one which is celebrated by a minister of religion or authorised registrar or other celebrant. Each of the parties must complete a marriage notice form and return it to the district registrar for the area in which they are to be married, irrespective of where they live, at least 15 days before the ceremony is due to take place. The district registrar must then enter the date of receipt and certain details in a marriage book kept for this purpose, and must also enter the names of the parties and the proposed date of marriage in a list which is displayed in a conspicuous place at the registration office until the date of the marriage has passed. All persons wishing to enter into a regular marriage in Scotland must follow the same preliminary procedure regardless of whether they intend to have a religious or civil ceremony. Before the marriage ceremony takes place any person may submit an objection in writing to the district registrar.

A marriage schedule, which is prepared by the registrar, will be issued to one or both of the parties in person up to seven days before a religious marriage; for a civil marriage the schedule will be available at the ceremony. The schedule must be handed to the celebrant before the ceremony starts; it must be signed immediately after the wedding and the marriage must be registered within three days.

The authority to conduct a religious marriage is deemed to be vested in the authorised celebrant rather than the building in which it takes place; open-air religious ceremonies are therefore permissible in Scotland.

From 10 June 2002 it has been possible, under the Marriage (Scotland) Act 2002, for venues or couples to apply to the local council for a licence to allow a civil ceremony to take place at a venue other than a registration office. To obtain further information, a venue or couple should contact the district registrar in the area they wish to marry. A list of licensed venues is also available on the General Registers of Scotland website at www.gro-scotland.gov.uk.

MARRIAGE BY COHABITATION WITH HABIT AND REPUTE

If two people live together constantly as husband and wife and are generally held to be such by the neighbourhood and among their friends and relations, there may arise a presumption from which marriage can be inferred. Before such a marriage can be registered, however, a decree of declarator of marriage must be obtained from the Court of Session.

CIVIL FEES

The fee for a religious marriage is £34.00, comprising a fee of £13.00 per person for the statutory notice of an intention to marry and an £8.00 fee for a copy of the marriage certificate. The cost of marrying in a registration office or under a local authority licence varies and it is recommended that parties confirm the costs with the district registrar in the office or area that they intend marrying.

Further information can be obtained from:
THE GENERAL REGISTER OFFICE, Office for National Statistics, Smedley Hydro, Trafalgar Road, Southport, Merseyside PR8 2HH. Tel: 0870-243 7788

The General Register Office for Scotland, New Register House, Edinburgh EH1 3YT. Tel: 0131-334 0380

TOWN AND COUNTRY PLANNING

The planning system is important in helping to protect the environment, as well as assisting individuals in assessing their land rights. There are a number of Acts governing the development of land and buildings in the UK and advice should always be sought from a Citizen's Advice Bureau or local planning authority before undertaking building works to any land or property. If building takes place which requires planning permission without permission being sought in advance, the situation may need to be rectified.

PLANNING PERMISSION

Planning permission is needed if the work involves:
- making a material change in use, such as dividing off part of the house so that it can be used as a separate home or dividing off part of the house for commercial use, e.g. for a workshop
- going against the terms of the original planning permission, e.g. there may be a restriction on fences in front gardens on an open-plan estate
- building, engineering for mining, except for the permissions below
- new or wider access to a main road
- additions or extensions to flats or maisonettes

Planning permission is not needed to carry out internal alterations or work which does not affect the external appearance of the building.

There are certain types of development for which the Secretary of State for the Environment has granted general permissions (permitted development rights). These include:
- house extensions and additions (including conservatories, loft conversions, garages and dormer windows). Up to 10 per cent or up to 50 cubic metres (whichever is the greater) can be added to the original house for terraced houses. Up to 15 per cent or 70 cubic metres (whichever is the greater) to other kinds of houses. The maximum that can be added to any house is 115 cubic metres
- buildings such as garden sheds and greenhouses so long as they are no more than 3 metres high (or 4 metres if the roof is ridged), are no nearer to a highway than the house, and at least half the ground around the house remains uncovered by buildings
- adding a porch with a ground area of less than 3 square metres and that is less than 3 metres in height
- putting up fences, walls and gates of under 1 metre in height if next to a road and under 2 metres elsewhere
- laying patios, paths or driveways for domestic use

OTHER RESTRICTIONS

It may be necessary to obtain other types of permissions before carrying out any development. These permissions are separate from planning permission and apply regardless of whether or not planning permission is needed, e.g.:
- building regulations will probably apply if a new building is to be erected, if an existing one is to be altered or extended, or if the work involves building over a drain or sewer The building control department of the local authority will advise on this
- any alterations to a listed building or the grounds of a listed building must be approved by the local authority

- local authority approval is necessary if a building (or, in some circumstances, gates, walls, fences or railings) in a conservation area is to be demolished; each local authority keeps a register of all local buildings that are in conservation areas
- many trees are protected by tree preservation orders and must not be pruned or taken down without local authority consent
- bats and other species are protected and English Nature, the Countryside Council for Wales or Scottish Natural Heritage must be notified before any work is carried out that will affect the habitat of protected species, e.g. timber treatment, renovation or extensions of lofts
- any development in areas designated as a National Park, an Area of Outstanding National Beauty, a National Scenic Area or in the Norfolk or Suffolk Broads is subject to greater restrictions. The local planning authority will advise or refer enquirers to the relevant authority

If you think you require planning permission, contact your local planning authority. They will advise you and provide the correct form for your application.

VOTERS' QUALIFICATIONS

Those entitled to vote at parliamentary, European Union (EU) and local government elections are those who are:
- on the electoral roll. Local authorities administer the roll and non-registration can lead to a fine of up to £1,000
- over 18 years old
- Commonwealth (which includes British) citizens or citizens of the Republic of Ireland

British citizens resident abroad are entitled to vote, for 20 years after leaving Britain, as overseas electors in parliamentary and EU elections in the constituency in which they were last resident. Members of the armed forces, Crown servants and employees of the British Council who are overseas and their spouses are entitled to vote regardless of how long they have been abroad.

European Union citizens resident in the UK may vote in EU and local government elections.

The main categories of people who are not entitled to vote are:
- sitting peers in the House of Lords
- patients detained under mental health legislation who have criminal convictions
- those serving prison sentences
- those convicted within the previous five years of corrupt or illegal election practices

Under the Representation of the Peoples Act 2000, several new groups of people are permitted to vote for the first time. These include: people who live on barges; unconvicted or remand prisoners; people in mental health hospitals (other than those with criminal convictions) and homeless people who have made a 'declaration of local connection'.

Registering to Vote

Voters must be entered on an electoral register, which runs from 16 February in one year to 15 February in the following year. The registration officer for each constituency is responsible for preparing and publishing the register. A registration form is sent to all households in the autumn of each year and the householder is required to provide details of all occupants who are eligible to vote, including ones who will reach their 18th birthday in the year covered by the register. Those who fail to give the required information or who give false

information are liable to be fined. A draft register is usually published at the end of November. Any person whose name has been omitted may ask to be registered and should contact the registration officer. Anyone on the register may object to the inclusion of another person's name, in which case he/she should notify the registration officer, who will investigate that person's eligibility. Supplementary electors lists are published throughout the duration of the register.

VOTING

Voting is not compulsory in the UK. Those who wish to vote must generally vote in person at the allotted polling station. Those who will be away at the time of the election, those who will not be able to attend in person due to physical incapacity or the nature of their occupation, and those who have changed address during the period for which the register is valid, may apply for a postal vote or nominate a proxy to vote for them. Overseas electors who wish to vote must do so by proxy. Further information can be obtained from the local authority's electoral registration officer in England and Wales or the electoral registration office in Scotland, or the Chief Electoral Officer in Northern Ireland (3rd Floor, St Anne's House, 15 Church Street, Belfast BT1 1ER. Tel: 028-9033 9955).

WILLS AND INTESTACY

In a will a person leaves instructions as to the disposal of their property after they die. A will is also used to appoint executors (who will administer the estate), give directions as to the disposal of the body, appoint guardians for children and, for larger estates, can operate to reduce the level of inheritance tax. It is best to have a will drawn up by a solicitor but if a solicitor is not employed, the following points must be taken into account:

– if possible the will must not be prepared on behalf of another person by someone who is to benefit from it or who is a close relative of a major beneficiary
– the language used must be clear and unambiguous and it is better to avoid the use of legal terms where the same thing can be expressed in plain language
– it is better to rewrite the whole document if a mistake is made. If necessary, alterations can be made by striking through the words with a pen, and the signature or initials of the testator and the witnesses must be put in the margin opposite the alteration. No alteration of any kind should be made after the will has been executed
– if the person later wishes to change the will or part of it, it is better to write a new will revoking the old. The use of codicils (documents written as supplements or containing modifications to the will) should be left to a solicitor
– the will should be typed or printed, or if handwritten be legible and preferably in ink. Commercial will forms can be obtained from some stationers.

The form of a will varies to suit different cases; the following is an example of how a will might be written. The notes after this example explain the terms used and procedures that need to be followed in drawing up a will.

This is the last will and testament of me [*Thomas Smith*] of [*Heather Cottage, Prospero Road, Manchester* M1 4DK] which I make this [*seventeenth*] day of [*May 2002*] and I revoke all previous wills and testamentary dispositions.
1. I appoint as my executors and trustees [*Ann Green of _____and Richard Brown of_____*]. In my

will the expression 'my Trustees' means any executors and trustees for the time being of my will and of any trust arising under it.
2. I give all my property to [*such of my children as shall survive me by 28 days and if more than one in equal shares or as the case may be*].
or
2. I give to [*Pamela Henderson of _____*] the sum of [£___] and to [*Michael Broadbent of_____*] the sum of [£___] and to [*Ruth Walker of _____*] all of my [*jewellery, books or as the case may be*]
and
3. I give everything not otherwise disposed of to [*Richard Black of _____*]
Signed by the testator in our joint presence and then by us in his.
Thomas Smith
[*Signature of the person making the will*]
Elizabeth Wall
[*Signature of witness*] of 67 Beatrice Lane, Manchester M1 4DK, journalist
William Jones
[*Signature of witness*] of 17 Paris Road, Manchester M1 4EN, tailor

SPECIFIC GIFTS AND LEGACIES

Gifts of specific items usually fail if the property is not owned by the person making the will on their death. This problem can be avoided by making a gift of any property fulfilling a particular description, e.g. a car, which is owned at the date of death. It is better in all cases where such gifts are made, to insert a clause which reads 'I give everything not otherwise disposed of to [*Richard Black of _____*], even if it seems that all property has already been disposed of in the will.

LAPSED LEGATEES

If a person who has been left property in a will dies before the person who has made the will, the gift fails and will pass to the person entitled to everything not otherwise disposed of (the residuary estate).

If the person left the residuary estate dies before the person who made the will, their share will generally pass to the closest relative(s) of the person who made the will (as in intestacy) unless the will names a beneficiary such as a charity who will take as a 'long stop' if this gift is unable to take effect for any reason.

It is always better to draw up a new will if a beneficiary predeceases the person who made the will.

EXECUTORS

It is usual to appoint two executors, although one is sufficient. No more than four persons can deal with the estate of the person who has died. The name and address of each executor should be given in full (the addresses are not essential but including them adds clarity to the document).

Executors should be 18 years of age or over. An executor may be a beneficiary of the will.

WITNESSES

A person who is a beneficiary of a will, or the spouse of a beneficiary at the time the will is signed, must not act as a witness or else he/she will be unable to take his/her gift. Husband and wife can both act as witnesses provided neither benefits from the will. It is better that a person does not act as an executor and as a witness, as he/she can take no benefit under a will to which he/she is witness. The identity of the witnesses should be made as explicit as possible.

EXECUTION OF A WILL

The person making the will should sign his/her name at the foot of the document, in the presence of the two witnesses. The witnesses must then sign their names while the person making the will looks on. If this procedure is not adhered to, the will will be considered invalid. There are certain exceptional circumstances where these rules are relaxed, e.g. where the person may be too ill to sign, and in these cases the attestation clause which normally reads 'signed by the testator in our joint presence and then by us in his/hers' should be reworded as follows:

'The will was read over to Thomas Smith in our presence when he stated that he understood it. It was then signed on his behalf by Thomas Brown in the presence of the testator and by his direction in our joint presence and then by us in his'.

CAPACITY TO MAKE A WILL

Anyone aged 18 or over can make a will. However, if there is any suspicion that the person making the will is not, through reasons of infirmity or age, fully in command of his/her faculties, it is advisable to arrange for a medical practitioner to examine the person making the will at the time it is to be executed to verify his/her mental capacity and to record that medical opinion in writing, and to ask the examining practitioner to act as a witness. If a person is not mentally able to make a will, the Court may do this for him/her by virtue of the Mental Health Act 1983.

Revocation

A will may be revoked or cancelled in a number of ways:
– a later will revokes an earlier one if it says so; otherwise the earlier will is impliedly revoked by the later one to the extent that it contradicts or repeats the earlier one
– a will is also revoked if the physical document on which it is written is destroyed by the person whose will it is. There must be an intention to revoke the will. It may not be sufficient to obliterate the will with a pen
– a will is revoked when the person marries, unless it is clear from the will that the person intended the will to stand after the marriage
– where a marriage ends in divorce or is annulled or declared void, gifts to the spouse and the appointment of the spouse as executor fail unless the will says that this is not to happen. A former spouse is treated as having predeceased the testator. A separation does not change the effect of a married person's will.

PROBATE AND LETTERS OF ADMINISTRATION

Probate is granted to the executors named in a will and once granted, the executors are obliged to carry out the instructions of the will. Letters of administration are granted where no executor is named in a will or is willing or able to act or where there is no will or no valid will; this gives a person, often the next of kin, similar powers and duties to those of an executor.

Applications for probate or for letters of administration can be made to the Principal Registry of the Family Division, to a district probate registry or to a probate sub-registry. Applicants will need the following documents: the original will (if any); a certificate of death; oath for executors or administrators; particulars of all property and assets left by the deceased; a list of debts and funeral expenses. Certain property, up to the value of £5,000, may be disposed of without a grant of probate or letters of administration.

WHERE TO FIND A PROVED WILL

Since 1858 wills which have been proved, that is wills on which probate or letters of administration have been granted, must have been proved at the Principal Registry of the Family Division or at a district probate registry. The Lord Chancellor has power to direct where the original documents are kept but most are filed where they were proved and may be inspected there and a copy obtained. The Principal Registry also holds copies of all wills proved at district probate registries and these may be inspected at First Avenue House, High Holborn. An index of all grants, both of probate and of letters of administration, is compiled by the Principal Registry and may be seen either at the Principal Registry or at a district probate registry.

It is also possible to discover when a grant of probate or letters of administration is issued by requesting a standing search. In response to a request and for a small fee, a district probate registry will supply the names and addresses of executors or administrators and the registry in which the grant was made, of any grant in the estate of a specified person made in the previous 12 months or following six months. This is useful for applicants who may be beneficiaries to a will but who have lost contact with the deceased and for creditors of the deceased.

SCOTLAND

In Scotland any person over 12 and of sound mind can make a will. The person making the will can only freely dispose of the heritage and what is known as the 'dead's part' of the estate because:
– the spouse has the right to inherit one-third of the moveable estate if there are children or other descendants, and one-half of it if there are not
– children are entitled to one-third of the moveable estate if there is a surviving spouse, and one-half of it if there is not

The remaining portion is the dead's part, and legacies and bequests are payable from this. Debts are payable out of the whole estate before any division.

From August 1995, wills no longer needed to be 'holographed' and it is now only necessary to have one witness. The person making the will still needs to sign each page. It is better that the will is not witnessed by a beneficiary although the attestation would still be sound and the beneficiary would not have to relinquish the gift.

Subsequent marriage does not revoke a will but the birth of a child who is not provided for may do so. A will may be revoked by a subsequent will, either expressly or by implication, but in so far as the two can be read together both have effect. If a subsequent will is revoked, the earlier will is revived.

Wills may be registered in the sheriff court Books of the Sheriffdom in which the deceased lived or in the Books of Council and Session at the Registers of Scotland.

CONFIRMATION

Confirmation (the Scottish equivalent of probate) is obtained in the sheriff court of the sheriffdom in which the deceased was resident at the time of death. Executives are either 'nominate' (named by the deceased in the will) or 'dative' (appointed by the court in cases where no executor is named in a will or in cases of intestacy). Applicants for confirmation must first provide an inventory of the deceased's estate and a schedule of debts, with an affidavit. In estates under £25,000 gross, confirmation can be obtained under a simplified procedure at reduced fees, with no need for a solicitor. The local sheriff clerk's office can provide assistance.

Further information can be obtained from:
PRINCIPAL REGISTRY (FAMILY DIVISION), First
Avenue House, 42–49 High Holborn, London,
WC1V 6NP.
REGISTERS OF SCOTLAND, Meadowbank House,
153 London Road, Edinburgh, EH8 7AU.
Tel: 0131-659 6111

INTESTACY

Intestacy occurs when someone dies without leaving a
will or leaves a will which is invalid or which does not take
effect for some reason. Intestacy can be partial, for
instance, if there is a will which disposes of some but not
all of the testator's property. In such cases the person's
estate (property, possessions, other assets following the
payment of debts) passes to certain members of the
family. The relevant legislation is the Administration of
Estates Act 1925, as amended by various legislation
including the Intestates Estates Act 1952, the Law Reform
(Succession) Act 1995, and the Trusts of Land and
Appointment of Trustees Act 1996 and Orders made
there under. Some of the provisions of this legislation are
described below. If a will has been written that disposes of
only part of a person's property, these rules apply to the
part which is undisposed of.

If the person (intestate) leaves a spouse who survives
for 28 days and children (legitimate, illegitimate and
adopted children and other descendants), the estate is
divided as follows:

– the spouse takes the 'personal chattels' (household
  articles, including cars, but nothing used for business
  purposes), £125,000 free of tax (with interest payable
  at 6 per cent from the time of the death until
  payment) and a life interest in half of the rest of the
  estate (which can be capitalised by the spouse if
  he/she wishes)
– the rest of the estate goes to the children*

If the person leaves a spouse who survives for 28 days
but no children:

– the spouse takes the personal chattels, £200,000 free
  of tax (interest payable as before) and full ownership
  of half of the rest of the estate
– the other half of the rest of the estate goes to the
  parents (equally, if both alive) or, if none, to the
  brothers and sisters of the whole blood*
– if there are no parents or brothers or sisters of the
  whole blood or their children, the spouse takes the
  whole estate

If there is no surviving spouse, the estate is distributed
among those who survive the intestate as follows:

– to surviving children*, but if none to
– parents (equally, if both alive), but if none to
– brothers and sisters of the whole blood*, but if none to
– brothers and sisters of the half blood*, but if none to
– grandparents (equally, if more than one), but if none to
– aunts and uncles of the whole blood*, but if none to
– aunts and uncles of the half blood*, but if none to
– the Crown, Duchy of Lancaster or the Duke of
  Cornwall (bona vacantia)

* To inherit, a member of these groups must survive the
intestate and attain 18, or marry under that age. If they die
under 18 (unless married under that age), their share goes to
others, if any, in the same group. If any member of these groups
predeceases the intestate leaving children, their share is divided
equally among their children.

In England and Wales the provisions of the Inheritance
(Provision for Family and Dependants) Act 1975 may
allow other people to claim provision from the deceased's
assets. This Act also applies to cases where a will has been
made and allows a person to apply to the Court if they
feel that the will or rules of intestacy or both do not make
adequate provision for them. The Court can order
payment from the deceased's assets or the transfer of
property from them if the applicant's claim is accepted.
The application must be made within six months of the
grant of probate or letters of administration and the
following people can make an application:

– the spouse
– a former spouse who has not remarried
– a child of the deceased
– someone treated as a child of the deceased's family
– someone maintained by the deceased
– someone who has cohabited for two years before the
  death in the same household as the deceased and as
  the husband or wife of the deceased

SCOTLAND

Under the Succession (Scotland) Act 1964, no distinction
is made between 'moveable' and 'heritable' property in
intestacy cases.

A surviving spouse is entitled to 'prior rights'. This
means that from 1 April 1999 the spouse has the right to
inherit:

– the matrimonial home up to a value of £130,000, or
  one matrimonial home if there is more than one, or,
  in certain circumstances, the value of the
  matrimonial home
– the furnishings and contents of that home, up to the
  value of £22,000
– a cash sum of £35,000 if the deceased left children or
  other descendants, or £58,000 if not

These figures are increased from time to time by
regulations.

Once prior rights have been satisfied, what remains of
the estate is generally divided between the surviving
spouse and children (legitimate and illegitimate)
according to 'legal' rights. Legal rights are:

Jus relicti(ae) – the right of a surviving spouse to one-half
of the net moveable estate, after satisfaction of prior
rights, if there are no surviving children; if there are
surviving children, the spouse is entitled to one-third of
the net moveable estate

Legitim – the right of surviving children to one-half of
the net moveable estate if there is no surviving spouse; if
there is a surviving spouse, the children are entitled to
one-third of the net moveable estate after the satisfaction
of prior rights

Where there are no surviving spouse or children, half of
the estate is taken by the parents and half by the brothers
and sisters. Failing that, the lines of succession, in general,
are:

– to descendants
– if no descendants, then to collaterals (i.e. brothers
  and sisters) and parents
– surviving spouse
– if no collaterals or parents or spouse, then to
  ascendants collaterals (i.e. aunts and uncles), and so
  on in an ascending scale
– if all lines of succession fail, the estate passes to the
  Crown

Relatives of the whole blood are preferred to relatives of
the half blood. The right of representation, i.e. the right of
the issue of a person who would have succeeded if he/she
had survived the intestate, also applies.

Intellectual Property

COPYRIGHT

Copyright protects all original literary, dramatic, musical and artistic works (including photographs, maps and plans), published editions of works, computer programs, sound recordings, films (including video), broadcasts (including satellite broadcasts) and cable programmes (including on-line information services). Under copyright the creators of these works can control the various ways in which their material may be exploited, the rights broadly covering copying, adapting, issuing (including renting and lending) copies to the public, performing in public, and broadcasting the material.

Copyright protection in the United Kingdom is automatic and there is no registration system. The main legislation is the Copyright, Designs and Patents Act 1988, which has been amended by other Acts and by Statutory Instrument to take account of EC Directives. As a result of an EC Directive effective from January 1996, the term of copyright protection for literary, dramatic, musical and artistic works lasts until 70 years after the death of the author, and for film now lasts for 70 years after the death of the last to survive of the director, author of the screenplay, author of the dialogue and composer of music specially created for the film. Sound recordings are protected for 50 years after their publication, and broadcasts and cable programmes for 50 years from the end of the year in which the first broadcast/transmission is made. Published editions remain under copyright protection for 25 years from the end of the year in which the edition was published. An EC Directive effective from January 1998 created a 15-year non-copyright called 'database right' to protect substantial investment in obtaining, verifying or presenting the contents of a database.

The main international treaties protecting copyright are the Bern Convention for the Protection of Literary and Artistic Works, the Rome Convention for the Protection of Performers, Producers of Phonograms and Broadcasting Organisations, and the Universal Copyright Convention (UCC); the UK is a signatory to these conventions. Copyright material created by UK nationals or residents is protected in each country which is a member of the conventions by the national law of that country. A list of participating countries may be obtained from the Patent Office. The World Trade Organisation Trade-Related Aspects of Intellectual Property Agreement (TRIPS) also confers reciprocal obligations on signatory states to protect copyright works.

Two treaties were agreed in December 1996. These are WIPO (World Intellectual Property Organisation) Copyright Treaty, and the WIPO Performance and Phonograms Treaty, which strengthen and update international standards of protection, particularly in relation to new technologies.

LICENSING

Use of copyright material without seeking permission in each instance may be permitted under "blanket" licences available from copyright licensing agencies. The International Federation of Reproduction Rights Organisations facilitates agreements between its member licensing agencies and on behalf of its members with organisations such as the WIPO, UNESCO, the European Union and the Council of Europe.

PATENTS

A patent is a document issued by the Patent Office relating to an invention and giving the proprietor monopoly rights, effective within the United Kingdom (including the Isle of Man). In return the patentee pays a fee to cover the costs of processing the patent and publicly discloses details of the invention.

To qualify for a patent an invention must be new, must exhibit an inventive step, and must be capable of industrial application. The patent is valid for a maximum of 20 years from the date on which the application was filed, subject to payment of annual fees from the end of the fourth year.

The Patent Office, established in 1852, is responsible for ensuring that all stages of an application comply with the Patents Act 1977, and that the invention meets the criteria for a patent.

The WIPO is responsible for administering many of the international conventions on intellectual property. The Patent Co-operation Treaty allows inventors to file a single application for patent rights in some or all of the contracting states. This application is searched by an International Searching Authority and published by the International Bureau of WIPO. It may also be the subject of an (optional) international preliminary examination. Applicants must then deal directly with the patent offices in the countries where they are seeking patent rights.

The European Patent Convention, linked to the Patent Co-operation Treaty, allows inventors to obtain patent rights in all the contracting states by filing a single European patent application which is processed by the European Patent Office (EPO). Once granted, the patent is subject to national laws in each signatory country. To comply with security requirements, an applicant resident in the UK must file a European patent application with the UK Patent Office unless the Patent Office gives permission for it to be filed directly with the EPO.

TRADE MARKS

Trade marks are a means of identification, whether a word or device or a combination of both, a logo, or the shape of goods or their packaging, which enable traders to make their goods or services readily distinguishable from those supplied by other traders. Registration prevents other traders using the same or similar trade marks for similar products or services for which the mark is registered.

In the UK trade marks are registered at the Trade Marks Registry in the Patent Office. In order to qualify for registration a mark must be capable of distinguishing its proprietor's goods or services from those of other undertakings. It should be non-deceptive and not easily confused with a mark that has already been registered for the same or similar goods or services. The relevant current legislation is the Trade Marks Act 1994.

It is possible to obtain an international trade mark registration, effective in 70 countries, under the Madrid Agreement or the Madrid Protocol, to which the UK is party. British companies can obtain international trade mark registration through a single application to WIPO in those countries party to the protocol.

EC trade mark regulation is now in force and is administered by the Office for Harmonisation in the Internal Market (Trade Marks and Designs) in Alicante,

Spain. The office registers EC trade marks, which are a unitary right valid throughout the European Union. The national registration of trade marks in member states is continuing in parallel with the EC trade mark.

DESIGN PROTECTION

Design protection covers the outward appearance of an article and takes two forms in the UK, registered design and design right, which are not mutually exclusive. Registered design protects the aesthetic appearance of an article, including shape, configuration, pattern or ornament, although artistic works such as sculptures are excluded, being generally protected by copyright. In order to qualify for protection, a design must be new and materially different from earlier UK published designs. The owner of the design must apply to the Designs Registry at the Patent Office. Initial registration lasts for five years and is extendible in five-yearly steps to a maximum of 25 years. The current legislation is the Registered Designs Act 1949 (as amended).

There is no international design registry currently available to UK applicants; in general, separate applications must be made in each country in which protection is sought. However, the EC Directive for the Legal Protection of Designs was adopted in 1998 to harmonise laws on certain aspects of design protection throughout the European Union. Member states had to amend their laws to comply with the Directive by 28 October 2001.

Design right is an automatic right which applies to the shape or configuration of articles and does not require registration. Unlike registered design, two-dimensional designs do not qualify for protection but designs of semiconductor chips (topographies) are protected by design right. Designs must be original and non-commonplace. The term of design right is ten years from first marketing of the design and the right is effective only in the UK. The current legislation is Part 3 of the Copyright, Designs and Patents Act 1988.

LEGAL DEPOSIT

Publishers are legally obliged to send one copy of every new printed publication distributed in the United Kingdom or Republic of Ireland to each of the legal deposit libraries within one month of publication. This is based on the Copyright Act of 1911 and the Irish Copyright Act 1963 (currently being replaced by similar provisions in the Copyright and Related Rights Bill of 1999). This legislation does not account for non-print publications and the British Library operates a voluntary deposit scheme for such publications.

The aim of legal deposit is to keep a complete national archive of published works as a current reference and information source. The legal deposit libraries are the British Library, the Bodleian Library in Oxford, Cambridge University Library, the National Library of Scotland, the National Library of Wales, and Trinity College Library in Dublin.

INTELLECTUAL PROPERTY ORGANISATIONS

COPYRIGHT LIBRARIES AGENCY, 100 Euston Street, London NW1 2HQ. Tel: 020-7388 5061. *Agent,* C. Allardice

CHARTERED INSTITUTE OF PATENT AGENTS, Staple Inn Buildings, High Holborn, London WC1V 7PZ. Tel: 020-7405 9450, *Secretary and Registrar:* M. Ralph
DESIGNS REGISTRY, The Patent Office, Cardiff Road, Newport NP10 8QQ. Tel: 0845-950-0505
EUROPEAN PATENT OFFICE, Headquarters, Erhardtstrasse 27, D-8000, Munich 2, Germany. Tel: 49-399 4538 *President:* I. Kober
INTERNATIONAL FEDERATION OF REPRODUCTION RIGHTS ORGANISATIONS (IFRRO), rue du Prince Royal 87, B-1050 Brussels, Belgium. Tel: 32-551 0899
LEGAL DEPOSIT OFFICE, The British Library, Boston Spa, Wetherby, W. Yorks LS23 7BY. Tel: 01937-546267
NEWSPAPER LEGAL DEPOSIT OFFICE, The British Library, Newspaper Library, Colindale Avenue, London NW9 5LF. Tel: 020-7412 7378
OFFICE FOR HARMONISATION IN THE INTERNAL MARKET (TRADE MARKS AND DESIGNS), Avenida de Europa 4, Aptdo de Correos 77, E-03080 Alicante, Spain, Tel: 34 139459
THE PATENT OFFICE, Cardiff Road, Newport NP10 8QQ. Tel: 0845-950 0505
SCIENCE REFERENCE LIBRARY, 96 Euston Road, London NW1 2DB. Tel: 020-7412 7494
STATIONERS' HALL REGISTRY LTD, The Registrar, Stationers' Hall, Ave Maria Lane, London EC4M 7DD. Tel: 020-7248 2934
TRADE MARKS REGISTRY, The Patent Office, Cardiff Road, Newport NP10 8QQ. Tel: 0845-950 0505
WORLD INTELLECTUAL PROPERTY ORGANISATION (WIPO), 34 chemin des Colombettes, 1211 Geneva 20, Switzerland. Tel: 41-338 9111

COPYRIGHT LICENSING/COLLECTING AGENCIES

AUTHORS' LICENSING AND COLLECTING SOCIETY, Marlborough Court, 14–18 Holborn, London EC1N 2LE. Tel: 020-7395 0600
CHRISTIAN COPYRIGHT LICENSING (EUROPE) LTD, PO Box 1339, Eastbourne, E. Sussex BN21 4YF. Tel: 01323-417711
COPYRIGHT LICENSING AGENCY LTD, 90 Tottenham Court Road, London W1P 0LP. Tel: 020-7631 5555. *Chief Executive:* P. Shepherd
DESIGN AND ARTISTS COPYRIGHT SOCIETY, Parchment House, 13 Northburgh Street, London EC1V 0JP. Tel: 020-7336 8811
EDUCATIONAL RECORDING AGENCY LTD, New Premier House, 150 Southampton Row, London WC1B 5AL. Tel: 020-7837 3222
INTERNATIONAL FEDERATION OF THE PHONOGRAPHIC INDUSTRIES, 54 Regent Street, London W1B 5RE. Tel: 020-7878 7900. Fax: 020-7878 7950. *Chairman and Chief Executive:* J. Berman
MCPS-PRS ALLIANCE, Copyright House, 29–33 Berners Street, London W1T 3AB.Tel: 020-7580 5544
NEWSPAPER LICENSING AGENCY, Wellington Gate, Church Road, Tunbridge Wells, Kent TN1 1NL. Tel: 01892-525274
PHONOGRAPHIC PERFORMANCE LTD, 1 Upper James Street, London W1F 9DE. Tel: 020-7534 1000. *Executive Chairman:* F. Nervkla
PUBLISHERS LICENSING SOCIETY, 5 Dryden Street, London WC2E 9NW. Tel: 020-7829 8486. *Chief Executive:* J. Bammel
VIDEO PERFORMANCE LTD, 1 Upper James Street, London W1R 3HG. Tel: 020-7534 1400

The Media

A new Communications Bill was proposed by Government in May 2002. If passed, it is expected to overhaul the rules of cross-media ownership. The Government aims to simplify and liberalise these rules to encourage dispersion of ownership and new market entry. However, there will continue to be rules preventing the most influential media in any community being controlled by too narrow a range of interests. Within individual markets this means scrapping the restriction on the ownership of more than one national TV or radio service, set out in the Broadcasting Act 1996.

Cross-media regulation will be reduced to three core rules:
– A rule limiting joint-ownership of national newspapers and ITV: no one controlling more than 20 per cent of the national newspaper market may hold any licence for ITV or hold a stake in any of its services. A company may not own more than a 20 per cent share in such a service if more than 20 per cent of its stock is in turn owned by a national newspaper proprietor with more than 20 per cent of the market
– No one owning a regional ITV licence may own more than 20 per cent of the local/regional newspaper market in the same region
– There will also be a scheme to uphold the plurality of ownership that exists in local media. This should ensure that at least 3 local commercial radio operators, and at least 3 local or regional commercial media voices (in TV, radio and newspapers), exist in most local communities.
– As a consequence, some new forms of cross-holding will be allowed:
– Joint-ownership of national TV and national radio licences.
– Joint ownership of a regional Channel 3 licence and a local radio licence in the same area (as long as there are two or more other radio stations that reach more than 50 per cent of the adult population in the radio station's area).
– Ownership of more than 20 per cent of the national newspaper market and Channel 5.
– Ownership of more than 20 per cent of the national newspaper market and national and/or local radio licences.

A single unified body, the Office of Communications (OFCOM), will be introduced where five separate regulators (*see* below) currently preside. The new chairman of OFCOM has been confirmed as Lord Currie of Marylebone.

Broadcasting

The British Broadcasting Corporation is responsible for public service broadcasting in the UK. Its constitution and finances are governed by royal charter and agreement. On 1 May 1996 a new royal charter came into force, establishing the framework for the BBC's activities until 2006.

The Independent Television Commission and the Radio Authority set up under the terms of the Broadcasting Act 1990, are due to be replaced by a single broadcasting regulator, OFCOM, in the summer of 2003. The ITC is until then the regulator and licensing authority for all commercially-funded television services, including cable and satellite services. The Radio Authority is, until summer 2003, the regulator and licensing authority for all independent radio services.

The Broadcasting Standards Commission was set up in April 1997 under the Broadcasting Act 1996 and was formed from the merger of the Broadcasting Complaints Commission and the Broadcasting Standards Council. It is due to be replaced by OFCOM in summer 2003. Currently the Commission considers and adjudicates upon complaints of unfair treatment or unwarranted infringement of privacy in all broadcast programmes and advertisements on television, radio, cable, satellite and digital services. It also monitors the portrayal of violence and sex, and matters of taste and decency.

BROADCASTING STANDARDS COMMISSION, 7 The Sanctuary, London SW1P 3JS. Tel: 020-7808 1000. *Chairman,* Lord Dubs of Battersea; *Deputy Chairman,* Lady Suzanne Warner; *Director,* Paul Bolt

---

TELEVISION

All channels are broadcast in colour on 625 lines UHF from a network of transmitting stations. The BBC's transmission network was sold to the Castle Tower Consortium (now Crown Castle International) in February 1997; ITV transmission services are owned and operated by ntl. Transmissions are available to more than 99 per cent of the population.

The total number of television licences in force in the UK at the end of 2002 was just under 23 million of which over 99 per cent were for colour televisions. Annual television licence fees until 1 April 2003 are: monochrome £37.50; colour £112.00.

No overall statistics are available for subscriptions in the UK to satellite television services; British Sky Broadcasting had 10.2 million subscribers at the end of June 2002 (6.1 million via digital and analogue satellite, 4.1 million via cable).

Digital broadcasting is increasing the number and quality of television channels. It uses digital modulation to improve reception and digital compression to make more effective use of the frequency channels available than PAL, the analogue system currently used.

The Broadcasting Act 1996 provided for the licensing of 20 or more digital terrestrial television channels (on six frequency channels or 'multiplexes'). Analogue broadcasting will eventually be discontinued, with the frequencies being sold to mobile telephone companies. A set-top digital decoder or an integrated digital television set is required to convert the digital signals into analogue sound and picture waves in order to watch the digital channels. A basic package is available for free and services are also offered by cable and satellite companies.

In June 1997 the licences to run the remaining digital multiplexes were awarded by the ITC to British Digital Broadcasting (subsequently called Ondigital and ITV Digital), a consortium led by Carlton Communications and Granada. The first digital services went on air in autumn 1998 and reached 1 million subscribers by 2001.

In 2002 ITV Digital, unable to fulfil its contract with the Football League, went into administration and was put up for sale.

ESTIMATED AUDIENCE SHARE *for 12 months to 31 December 2001*

	Percentage*
ITV companies	26.0
BBC 1	26.8
BBC 2	11.1
Cable, satellite and digital channels	17.4
Channel 4	9.6
Channel 5	5.7
S4C Wales	0.3

Source: Independent Television Commission
*rounded to one decimal point and only channels achieving a share of more than 0.1 per cent are included

BBC TELEVISION

Television Centre, Wood Lane, London W12 7RJ.
Tel: 020-8743 8000. Web: www.bbc.co.uk/info

The BBC's experiments in television broadcasting started in 1929 and in 1936 the BBC began the world's first public service of high-definition television from Alexandra Palace. The BBC broadcasts two UK-wide terrestrial television services, BBC One and BBC Two; outside England these services are designated BBC Scotland on One, BBC Scotland on Two, BBC One Northern Ireland, BBC Two Northern Ireland, BBC Wales on One and BBC Wales on Two. The BBC's digital services include BBC One, BBC Two, BBC Four, BBC Choice, BBC Knowledge, BBC News 24 and BBC Parliament. The services are funded by the licence fee.

BBC WORLDWIDE LTD
Woodlands, 80 Wood Lane, London W12 0TT
Tel 020-8433 2000; Fax: 020-8749 0538
Web: www.bbcworldwide.com

BBC Worldwide Limited is the commercial arm, and a wholly owned subsidiary, of the British Broadcasting Corporation. The company was formed in 1994 to develop a co-ordinated approach to the BBC's commercial activities: television, publishing, product licensing, Internet and interactive media. BBC Worldwide exists to maximise the value of the BBC's programme and publishing assets for the benefit of the licence payer, and re-invest in public service programming.

INDEPENDENT TELEVISION

The ITV network comprises 15 independent regional television licensees, whose licences are awarded by the Independent Television Commission (ITC) for a minimum of ten years. These companies broadcast across 14 regions of the UK (there are 2 licences for London). The ITV Network Centre commissions and schedules programmes and, as with the BBC, 25 per cent of programmes must come from independent producers. There are over 1,500 independent production companies in the UK which generate about £1bn of programming.

Channel 4 and S4C (the fourth channel in Wales) were set up to provide programmes with a distinctive character and which appeal to interests not catered for by ITV and are also funded through advertising. Channel 5 began broadcasting in 1997 and now reaches about 80 per cent of the population.

ITV NETWORK CENTRE/ITV ASSOCIATION
200 Gray's Inn Road, London WC1X 8HF.
Tel: 020-7843 8000. Web: www.itv.com

The ITV Network Centre is wholly owned by the ITV companies and undertakes commissioning and scheduling of programmes shown across the ITV network and, as with the BBC, 25 per cent of programmes must come from independent producers. In addition to the terrestrial channel ITV1, in December 1998 ITV launched its digital ITV2, aimed at a younger audience. *Chairman*, Leslie Hill

INDEPENDENT TELEVISION NETWORK COMPANIES

ANGLIA TELEVISION LTD (owned by United Broadcasting and Entertainment) *(eastern England)*, Anglia House, Norwich NR1 3JG. Tel: 01603-615151 Web: www.anglia.tv.co.uk

BORDER TELEVISION PLC *(the Borders)*, The Television Centre, Carlisle CA1 3NT. Tel: 01228-525101 Web: www.border-tv.com

CARLTON UK TELEVISION *(London (weekdays))*, 101 St Martin's Lane, London WC2N 4AZ. Tel: 020-7240 4000 Web: www.carlton.com

CENTRAL INDEPENDENT TELEVISION LTD (owned by Carlton Communications) *(the Midlands)*, Central Court, Gas Street, Birmingham B1 2JT. Tel: 0121-643 9898

CHANNEL TELEVISION LTD *(Channel Islands)*, The Television Centre, St Helier, Jersey JE1 3ZD. Tel: 01534-816816 Web: www.channeltv.co.uk

GMTV LTD *(breakfast television)*, The London Television Centre, Upper Ground, London SE1 9LT. Tel: 020-7827 7000 Web: www.gmtv.co.uk

GRAMPIAN TELEVISION PLC (owned by Scottish Media) *(northern Scotland)*, Queen's Cross, Aberdeen AB15 2XJ. Tel: 01224-846846 Web: www.grampiantv.co.uk

GRANADA TELEVISION LTD (owned by Granada Media) *(north-west England)*, Quay Street, Manchester M60 9EA. Tel: 0161-832 7211 Web: www.granadatv.co.uk

HTV GROUP PLC (owned by United Broadcasting and Entertainment) *(Wales and western England)*, HTV Wales, The Television Centre, Culverhouse Cross, Cardiff CF5 6XJ. Tel: 029-2059 0590; HTV West, The Television Centre, Bath Road, Bristol BS4 3HG. Tel: 0117-977 8366

LONDON WEEKEND TELEVISION LTD (owned by Granada Media) *(London (weekends))*, The London Television Centre, Upper Ground, London SE1 9LT. Tel: 020-7620 1620 Web: www.lwt.co.uk

MERIDIAN BROADCASTING LTD (owned by United Broadcasting and Entertainment) *(south and south-east England)*, The Television Centre, Southampton SO14 0PZ. Tel: 023-8022 2555 Web: www.meridian.co.uk

SCOTTISH TELEVISION PLC (owned by Scottish Media) *(central Scotland)*, Cowcaddens, Glasgow G2 3PR. Tel: 0141-300 3000 Web: www.scottishtv.co.uk

TYNE TEES TELEVISION LTD (owned by Granada Media) *(north-east England)*, The Television Centre, City Road, Newcastle upon Tyne NE1 2AL. Tel: 0191-261 0181

ULSTER TELEVISION PLC *(Northern Ireland)*, Havelock House, Ormeau Road, Belfast BT7 1EB. Tel: 028-9032 8122 Web: www.utvlive.com

WESTCOUNTRY TELEVISION LTD (owned by Carlton Communications) *(south-west England)*, Langage Science Park, Plymouth PL7 5BG. Tel: 01752-333333

YORKSHIRE TELEVISION LTD (owned by Granada Media) *(Yorkshire)*, The Television Centre, Kirkstall Rd, Leeds LS3 1JS. Tel: 0113-243 8283

OTHER INDEPENDENT TELEVISION COMPANIES

CHANNEL 5 BROADCASTING LTD, 22 Long Acre, London WC2E 9LY. Tel: 020-7550 5555

CHANNEL FOUR TELEVISION CORPORATION, 124 Horseferry Road, London SW1P 2TX. Tel: 020-7396 4444. Provides a service to the UK except Wales and is charged to cater for interests under-represented by the ITV network companies. Channel 4 sells its own advertising.

INDEPENDENT TELEVISION NEWS LTD, 200 Gray's Inn Road, London WC1X 8XZ. Tel: 020-7833 3000

TELETEXT LTD, 101 Farm Lane, London SW6 1QJ. Tel: 020-7386 5000. Provides teletext services for the ITV companies and Channel 4.

WELSH FOURTH CHANNEL AUTHORITY (Sianel Pedwar Cymru), Parc Ty Glas, Llanishen, Cardiff CF4 5DU. Tel: 029-2074 7444. S4C schedules Welsh language and most Channel 4 programmes.

DIRECT BROADCASTING BY SATELLITE TELEVISION

BRITISH SKY BROADCASTING LTD, 6 Centaurs Business Park, Grant Way, Isleworth, Middx TW7 5QD. Tel: 020-7705 3000.

British Sky Broadcasting is the UK's broadband entertainment company, delivering sports, movies, entertainment, news and interactive services to 15 million viewers in 6.1 million households throughout the UK and Eire. BSkyB's own channels such as Sky News, Sky One and Sky Sports are available in a further 4.1 million homes receiving cable services in the UK and Ireland.

Sky Digital, launched on 1 October 1998, offers over 200 channels, pay-per-view services and interactive entertainment, including email, on-screen shopping and voting. In 2001 BSkyB introduced the next generation integrated digital satellite set-top box/personal video recorder, Sky+. BSkyB is listed on the London and New York Stock Exchanges. For more information visit www.sky.com/corporate.

RADIO

UK domestic radio services are broadcast across three wavebands: FM (or VHF), medium wave and long wave (used by BBC Radio 4). In the UK the FM waveband extends in frequency from 87.5 MHz to 108 MHz and the medium wave band extends from 531 kHz to 1602 kHz. Some radios are still calibrated in wavelengths rather than frequency. To convert frequency to wavelength, divide 300,000 by the frequency in kHz.

DIGITAL RADIO

Digital radio allows more services to be broadcast to a higher technical quality and provides the data facility for text and pictures. It improves the robustness of high fidelity radio services, especially compared with current FM and AM radio transmissions. It was developed in a collaborative research project under the pan-European EUREKA initiative and has been adopted as a world standard for new digital radio systems. The frequencies allocated for terrestrial digital radio in the UK are 217.5 to 230 MHz.

The Broadcasting Act 1996 provided for the licensing of digital radio services (on seven frequency channels or 'multiplexes'). The BBC has been allocated a multiplex capable of broadcasting six to eight national stereo services; BBC digital broadcasts began in the London area in September 1995. A national digital multiplex has also been made available to the three independent national radio stations, and local and regional services (BBC and commercial) will use the remaining five multiplexes. The Radio Authority is responsible for awarding licences for capacity on the non-BBC multiplexes. The first national independent radio digital licence was awarded to Digital One, which began broadcasting in November 1999. The first local multiplex licence was awarded in May 1999 (to CE Digital, for Birmingham) and commenced broadcasting in May 2000.

It is necessary to buy a new digital radio set in order to receive digital radio broadcasts. Several sorts of sets are available including portable radios, hi-fi stacks, car radios and PC cards. The latter bring digital radio to the desktop and associated data to the computer screen.

Estimated Audience Share as at end June 2002

	Percentage
BBC Radio 1	8.3
BBC Radio 2	15.6
BBC Radio 3	1.1
BBC Radio 4	11.3
BBC Radio 5 Live	4.9
BBC Local/Regional	11.3
TEAMtalk 252	0.2
Classic FM	4.9
TalkSport (was Talk Radio)	1.8
Virgin Radio (AM only)	1.2
Local commercial	37.5
Other	1.9

Source: RAJAR/RSL

BBC RADIO

Broadcasting House, Portland Place, London W1A 1AA. Tel: 020-7580 4468

BBC Radio broadcasts six network services to the UK, Isle of Man and the Channel Islands. There is also a tier of national services in Wales, Scotland and Northern Ireland and 38 local radio stations in England and the Channel Islands. In Wales and Scotland there are also dedicated language services in Welsh and Gaelic respectively. The frequency allocated for digital BBC broadcasts is 225.648 MHZ.

BBC NETWORK RADIO SERVICES

RADIO 1 (Contemporary pop music, social action campaigns and entertainment news) – 24 hours a day. *Frequencies:* 97.6–99.8 FM, coverage 99%

RADIO 2 (Popular music, entertainment, comedy and the arts) – 24 hours a day. *Frequencies:* 88–90.2 FM, coverage 99%

RADIO 3 (Classical music, classic drama, documentaries and features) – 24 hours a day. *Frequencies:* 90.2–92.4 FM, coverage 99%

RADIO 4 (News, documentaries, drama, entertainment, and cricket on long wave in season) – 5.55 a.m.– 1.00 a.m. daily, with BBC World Service overnight. *Frequencies:* 92.4–94.6 FM and 198 LW, coverage 99%

RADIO 5 LIVE (News and sport) – 24 hours a day. *Frequencies:* 693 and 909 MW

RADIO 6 (Digital only) (Contemporary and classic pop and rock music) – 24 hours a day. *Frequency:* 225.648 MHZ, coverage 65%

BBC NATIONAL RADIO SERVICES

RADIO CYMRU (Welsh-language) *Frequencies:* 92.4–94.6 FM, 95.7 FM (*Llanfyllin*), 96.1 FM (*Llandinam*), 96.8 FM and 103.5–105 FM, coverage 97%

RADIO NAN GAIDHEAL (Gaelic service) *Frequencies:* 103.5–105 FM, 990 MW in Aberdeen, coverage 90%.

RADIO SCOTLAND *Frequencies:* 810 MW plus two local fillers; 92.4–94.7 FM, coverage 99%. Local programmes on FM as above: HIGHLANDS; NORTH-EAST; BORDERS; SOUTH-WEST (also 585 MW); ORKNEY; SHETLAND

RADIO ULSTER *Frequencies:* 1341 MW (873 MW Enniskillen), plus two local fillers; 92.4–95.4 FM, coverage 96%. Local programmes on RADIO FOYLE *Frequencies:* 792 AM; 93.1 MW

RADIO WALES *Frequencies:* 882 MW plus two local fillers; 95.1 FM, 95.9 FM (*Gwent*), 103.9 FM (Cardiff), 95.4 FM (Wrexham), coverage 97%

BBC LOCAL RADIO STATIONS

There are 39 local stations serving England and the Channel Islands:

BERKSHIRE, BBC Radio Berkshire, PO Box 1044, Reading RG94 8FH. Tel: 0645 311444. *Frequencies:* 94.6, 95.4, 104.1, 104.4 FM

BRISTOL/SOMERSET SOUND, PO Box 194, Bristol BS99 7QT. Tel: 0117-974 1111; *Frequencies:* 94.9, 95.5, 104.6, 1548 MW

CAMBRIDGESHIRE, PO Box 96, Hills Road, Cambridge CB2 1LD. Tel: 01223-259696. *Frequencies:* 95.7/96.0 FM, 1026/1449 MW

CLEVELAND, PO Box 95FM, Newport Road, Middlesbrough TS1 5DG. Tel: 01642-225211. *Frequencies:* 95.0/95.8 FM

CORNWALL, Phoenix Wharf, Truro, Cornwall TR1 1UA. Tel: 01872-275421. *Frequencies:* 95.2/96.0/103.9 FM, 630/657 MW

CUMBRIA, Annetwell Street, Carlisle CA3 8BB. Tel: 01228-592444. *Frequencies:* 95.2/95.6/96.1/104.1 FM, 756/837/1458 MW

DERBY, PO Box 269, Derby DE1 3HL. Tel: 01332-361111. *Frequencies:* 94.2/95.3/104.5 FM, 1116 MW

DEVON, PO Box 5, Plymouth PL1 1XT. Tel: 01752-260323. *Frequencies:* 103.4/96.0/95.8/94.8 FM, 801, 855, 990, 1458 MW

ESSEX, 198 New London Road, Chelmsford CM2 9XB. Tel: 01245-616000. *Frequencies:* 95.3/103.3 FM, 729/765/1530 MW

GLOUCESTERSHIRE, London Road, Gloucester GL1 1SW. Tel: 01452-308585. *Frequencies:* 95/95.8/104.7 FM

GLR (GREATER LONDON RADIO), 35C Marylebone High Street, London W1A 4LG. Tel: 020-7224 2424. *Frequency:* 94.9 FM

GMR (GREATER MANCHESTER RADIO), PO Box 951, Oxford Road, Manchester M60 1SD. Tel: 0161-200 2000. *Frequencies:* 95.1/104.6 FM

GUERNSEY, Commerce House, Les Banques, St Peter Port, Guernsey GY1 2HS. Tel: 01481-728977. *Frequencies:* 1116 AM, 93.2 FM

HEREFORD AND WORCESTER, Hylton Road, Worcester WR2 5WW. Tel: 01905-748485. *Frequencies:* 94.7/104.0/104.6 FM, 818/738 MW

HUMBERSIDE, 9 Chapel Street, Hull HU1 3NU. Tel: 01482-323232. *Frequency:* 95.9 FM, 1485 MW

JERSEY, 18 Parade Road, St Helier, Jersey JE2 3PL. Tel: 01534-870000. *Frequencies:* 1026 AM, 88.8 FM

KENT, Sun Pier, Chatham, Kent ME4 4EZ. Tel: 01634-830505. *Frequencies:* 96.7/97.6/104.2 FM, 774/1602 MW

LANCASHIRE, 26 Darwen Street, Blackburn BB2 2EA. Tel: 01254-262411. *Frequencies:* 95.5/103.9/104.5 FM, 855/1557 MW

LEEDS, Broadcasting House, Woodhouse Lane, Leeds LS2 9PN. Tel: 0113-244 2131. *Frequencies:* 774 AM, 92.4/95.3/103.9 FM, 774 MW

LEICESTER/ASIAN NETWORK, Epic House, Charles Street, Leicester LE1 3SH. Tel: 0116-251 6688. *Frequency:* 104.9 FM

LINCOLNSHIRE, PO Box 219, Newport, Lincoln LN1 3XY. Tel: 01522-511411. *Frequencies:* 94.9 FM, 1368 MW

LONDON, BBC London Live, 35C Marylebone High Street, London W1A 4LG. Tel: 020-7224 2424. *Frequency:* 94.9 FM

MERSEYSIDE, 55 Paradise Street, Liverpool L1 3BP. Tel: 0151-708 5500. *Frequency:* 95.8 FM, 1485 MW

NEWCASTLE, Broadcasting Centre, Barrack Road, Newcastle upon Tyne NE99 1RN. Tel: 0191-232 4141. *Frequencies:* 95.4/96.0/103.7/104.4 FM, 206 MW

NORFOLK, Norfolk Tower, Surrey Street, Norwich NR1 3PA. Tel: 01603-617411. *Frequencies:* 95.1/104.4 FM, 855/873 MW

NORTHAMPTON, Broadcasting House, Abington Street, Northampton NN1 2BH. Tel: 01604-239100. *Frequencies:* 103.6/104.2 FM, 1107 MW

NOTTINGHAM, York House, Mansfield Road, Nottingham NG1 3JB. Tel: 0115-955 0500. *Frequencies:* 95.5/103.8 FM, 1584 MW

OXFORD, BBC Radio Oxford, 269 Banbury Road, Oxford OX2 7DW. Tel: 01865-311444. *Frequency:* 95.2 FM

SHEFFIELD, Ashdell Grove, 60 Westbourne Road, Sheffield S10 2QU. Tel: 0114-268 6185. *Frequencies:* 88.6/94.7/104.1 FM

SHROPSHIRE, 2–4 Boscobel Drive, Shrewsbury SY1 3TT. Tel: 01743-248484. *Frequencies:* 95.0/96.0 FM, 1584 MW

SOLENT, Broadcasting House, Havelock Road, Southampton SO14 7PW. Tel: 023-8063 1311. *Frequencies:* 96.1/ FM, 999 MW

SOUTHERN COUNTIES, Broadcasting Centre, Guildford GU2 5AP. Tel: 01483-306306. *Frequencies:* 95–95.3/104–104.8 FM

STOKE, Cheapside, Hanley, Stoke-on-Trent ST1 1JJ. Tel: 01782-208080. *Frequencies:* 94.6/104.1 FM, 1503 MW

SUFFOLK, Broadcasting House, St Matthew's Street, Ipswich IP1 3EP. Tel: 01473-250000. *Frequencies:* 95.5/103.9/104.6 FM

THREE COUNTIES RADIO, PO Box 3CR, Luton, Beds LU1 5XL. Tel: 01582-637400. *Frequencies:* 95.5/103.8/104.5 FM, 630/1161 MW

WILTSHIRE SOUND, Broadcasting House, Prospect Place, Swindon SN1 3RW. Tel: 01793-513626. *Frequencies:* 103.5/103.6/104.3/104.9 FM, 1332/1368 MW

WM (COVENTRY AND WARWICKSHIRE), Holt Court, 1 Greyfriars Road, Coventry CV1 2WR. Tel: 024-7623 1231. *Frequencies:* 94.8/103.7/104.0 FM

WM (WEST MIDLANDS), Pebble Mill Road, Birmingham B5 7SD. Tel: 0121-432 8484 *Frequency:* 95.6 FM.

YORK, 20 Bootham Row, York YO3 7BR. Tel: 01904-641351. *Frequencies:* 95.5/103.7/104.3 FM, 666/1260 MW

BBC WORLD SERVICE
Bush House, Strand, London WC2B 4PH.
Tel 020-7240 3456

The BBC World Service broadcasts over 1,280 hours of programmes a week in 43 languages including English. It has a weekly audience of 150 million globally, of whom 42 million listen to English language services. Many services are also available by satellite and on the Internet. *UK frequencies:* 648 MW in Southern England and on BBC Radio 4 at night.

The World Service is organised into five world regions, each responsible for programmes in English as well as regional languages.

AFRICA AND THE MIDDLE EAST, Arabic, French, Hausa, Kinyarwanda/Kirundi, Portuguese, Somali and Swahili; English programmes including *Network Africa* and *Focus on Africa*

ASIA AND THE PACIFIC, Bengali, Burmese, Cantonese, Hindi, Indonesian, Mandarin, Nepali, Sinhala, Tamil, Thai, Urdu and Vietnamese; English programmes including *East Asia Today*

EUROPE, Albanian, Bulgarian, Croatian, Czech, Greek, Hungarian, Macedonian, Polish, Romanian, Serbian, Slovak and Slovene; English programmes including *The World Today*

FORMER SOVIET UNION AND SOUTH-WEST ASIA, Azeri, Kazakh, Kyrgyz, Pashto, Persian, Russian, Turkish, Ukrainian and Uzbek

THE AMERICAS, Portuguese for Brazil, Spanish; English programmes including *The World* (a global news magazine for American listeners), *Caribbean Report* and *Calling the Falklands*

BBC ENGLISH teaches English world-wide through radio, television and a wide range of published courses

BBC MARKET INTELLIGENCE carries out audience research and sells printed publications and data

BBC MONITORING supplies news and information from the output of overseas radio and television stations and news agency sources

BBC WORLD SERVICE TRAINING runs journalism, management and skills training courses for overseas broadcasters

BBC WORLD SERVICE TRUST is a registered charity established in 1999 by BBC World Service. It promotes development through the innovative use of the media in the developing world. The trust presently works in 23 countries worldwide, tackling health, education and good governance.

INDEPENDENT RADIO

The Radio Authority began advertising new licences for the development of independent radio in January 1991. Since then it has awarded three national licences and 153 new local radio licences (including sixteen regional licences). The Authority has also licensed one 'additional service' licence (to use the spare capacity in an existing channel which is not used by the programme service), and around 3,472 short-term restricted service licences (for temporary low-powered radio services). It licenses satellite and cable services, and long-term restricted service licences for stations serving non-commercial establishments such as hospitals and universities. The first (and only) national commercial digital multiplex licence was awarded in October 1998. Since then the Authority has awarded 36 local digital multiplex licences and continues to advertise new local multiplex licences. The Commercial Radio Companies Association is the trade body for commercial radio companies in the United Kingdom. It is a voluntary, non profit making body, funded by the subscriptions of its member radio companies, who share the cost of CRCA in proportion to their shares of the industry's broadcasting revenue, and was formed by the first radio companies when Independent Radio began in 1973.

THE RADIO AUTHORITY, Holbrook House, 14 Great Queen Street, London WC2B 5DG. Tel: 020-7430 2724. Fax: 020 7405 7062. Web: www.radioauthority.org.uk

COMMERCIAL RADIO COMPANIES ASSOCIATION, 77 Shaftesbury Avenue, London W1V 7AD. Tel: 020-7306 2603. Email: info@crca.co.uk. Web: www.crca.co.uk. *Chief Executive*, P. Brown

INDEPENDENT NATIONAL RADIO STATIONS

CLASSIC FM, 7 Swallow Place, London W1R 7AA. Tel: 020-7343 9000. 24 hours a day. *Frequencies:* 99.9/101.9 FM

TALK SPORT, 18 Hatfields, London SE1 8DJ. Tel: 020-7959 7900. 24 hours a day. *Frequencies:* 1053/1089 AM

VIRGIN RADIO, 1 Golden Square, London W1R 4DJ. Tel: 020-7434 1215. 24 hours a day. *Frequencies:* 1215/1197/1233/1242/1260 AM

INDEPENDENT REGIONAL LOCAL RADIO STATIONS

100.7 HEART FM *(west Midlands)*, 1 The Square, 111 Broad Street, Birmingham B15 1AS. Tel: 0121-626 1007. *Frequency:* 100.7 FM

CENTURY 105 *(north-west)*, Century House, Waterfront Quay, Salford Quays, Manchester M5 2XW. Tel: 0161-400 0105. *Frequency:* 105.4 FM

CENTURY 106 *(east Midlands)*, City Link, Nottingham NG2 4NG. Tel: 0115-910 6100. *Frequency:* 106.0 FM

CENTURY RADIO (north-east), Century House, PO Box 100, Gateshead NE8 2YX. Tel: 0191-477 6666. Frequencies: 100.7/101.8/96.2/96.4 FM

GALAXY 101 *(Severn estuary)*, Millennium House, 26 Baldwin Street, Bristol BS1 1SE. Tel: 0117-901 0101. *Frequencies:* 101.0/97.2 FM (Bristol)

GALAXY 105 *(Yorkshire)*, Joseph's Well, Westgate, Leeds LS3 1AB. Tel: 0113-213 0105. *Frequencies:* 105.1 FM (Leeds); 105.6 FM (Bradford and Sheffield); 105.8 FM (Hull)

GALAXY 105-106 *(north-east)*, Kingfisher Way, Silverlink Business Park, Tyne and Wear NE28 9ND. Tel: 0191-206 8000. *Frequencies:* 105.3/105.6/106.4 FM

JAZZ FM 100.4 *(north-west)*, The World Trade Centre, Exchange Quay, Manchester M5 3EJ. Tel: 0161-877 1004. *Frequency:* 100.4 FM

SCOT FM *(central Scotland)*, 1 Albert Quay, Leith EH6 7DN. Tel: 0131-554 6677. *Frequencies:* 100.3/101.1 FM

VIBE FM *(east)*, Reflection House, The Anderson Centre, Olding Road, Bury St Edmunds, Suffolk IP33 3TA. Tel: 01284-718800. *Frequencies:* 107.7 FM (Peterborough); 105.6 FM (Cambridge); 106.1 FM (Norwich); 106.4 FM (Ipswich)

WAVE 105 FM *(Solent)*, 5 Manor Court, Barnes Wallis Road, Segensworth East, Fareham, Hants PO15 5TH. Tel: 01489-481050. *Frequencies:* 105.2 FM (Solent); 105.8 FM (Poole)

INDEPENDENT LOCAL RADIO STATIONS

England

2-TEN FM, PO Box 2020, Reading RG31 7FG. Tel: 0118-945 4400. *Frequencies:* 97.0/102.9/103.4 FM

2BR FM, Imex Lomeshaye Business Village, Nelson, Lancs BB9 7DR. Tel: 01282-690000. *Frequency:* 99.8 FM

2CR FM, 5 Southcote Road, Bournemouth BH1 3LR. Tel: 01202-259259. *Frequency:* 102.3 FM

96 TRENT FM 29–31 Castle Gate, Nottingham NG1 7AP. Tel: 0115-952 7000. *Frequencies:* 96.2/96.5 FM

96.3 AIRE FM, 51 Burley Road, Leeds LS3 1LR. Tel: 0113-283 5500. *Frequency:* 96.3 FM

96.4 FM BRMB, Nine Brindley Place, 4 Oozells Square, Birmingham B1 2DJ. Tel: 0121-245 5000. *Frequency:* 96.4 FM

96.4 THE EAGLE, Dolphin House, North Street, Guildford, Surrey GU1 4AA. Tel: 01483-300964. *Frequency:* 96.4 FM

96.9 VIKING FM, Commercial Road, Hull HU1 2SG. Tel: 01482-325141. *Frequency:* 96.9 FM

97.2 STRAY FM, PO Box 972, Station Parade, Harrogate HG1 5YF. Tel: 01423-522972. *Frequency:* 97.2 FM

97.4 VALE FM, Longmead, Shaftesbury, Dorset SP7 8QQ. Tel: 01747-855711. *Frequency:* 97.4 FM

102.4 WISH FM, Orrell Lodge, Orrell Road, Orrell, Wigan WN5 8HJ. Tel: 01942-761024. *Frequency:* 102.4 FM

102.7 HEREWARD FM, PO Box 225, Queensgate Centre, Peterborough PE1 1XJ. Tel: 01733-460460. *Frequency:* 102.7 FM

103.2 POWER FM, Radio House, Whittle Avenue, Segensworth West, Fareham, Hants PO15 5SH. Tel: 01489-589911. *Frequency:* 103.2 FM

103.4 THE BEACH, PO Box 103.4, Lowestoft, Suffolk NR32 2TL. Tel: 07000-001035. *Frequency:* 103.4 FM

105.4 CENTURY FM , Laser House, Waterfront Quay, Salford Quays, Manchester M5 2XW. Tel: 0161-400 0105. *Frequency:* 105.4 FM

106 CTFM RADIO, 16 Lower Bridge Street, Canterbury, Kent CT1 2HQ. Tel: 01227-789106. *Frequency:* 106.0 FM

106.9 SILK FM, Radio House, Bridge Street, Macclesfield, Cheshire SK11 6DJ. Tel: 01625-268000. *Frequency:* 106.9 FM

107 OAK FM, 7 Waldron Court, Prince William Road, Loughborough, Leics LE11 5GD. Tel: 01509-211711. *Frequency:* 107.0 FM

107.2 WIRE FM, Warrington Business Park, Long Lane, Warrington WA2 8TX. Tel: 01925-445545. *Frequency:* 107.2 FM

107.3 THE EAGLE, Bristol Evening Post Building, Temple Way, Bristol BS99 7HD. Tel: 0117-910 6600. *Frequency:* 107.3 FM

107.4 TELFORD FM, PO Box 1074, Telford TF3 3WG. Tel: 01952-280011. *Frequency:*107.4 FM

107.5 CAT FM, Regent Arcade, Cheltenham, Glos GL50 1JZ. Tel: 01242-699555. *Frequency:* 107.5 FM

107.6 KESTREL FM, 2nd Floor, Paddington House, The Walks Shopping Centre, Basingstoke, Hants RG21 7LJ. Tel: 01256-694000. *Frequency:* 107.6 FM

107.7 CHELMER FM, Cater House, High Street, Chelmsford, Essex CM1 1AL. Tel: 01245-259400. *Frequency:* 107.7 FM

107.7 THE WOLF, 10th Floor, Mander House, Wolverhampton WV1 3NB. Tel: 01902-571070. *Frequency:* 107.7 FM

107.7 WFM, 11 Beaconsfield Road, Weston-super-Mare, Somerset BS23 1YE. Tel: 01934-624455. *Frequency:* 107.7FM

107.8 ARROW FM, Priory Meadow Centre, Hastings, E. Sussex TN34 1PJ. Tel: 01424-461177. *Frequency:* 107.8 FM

107.8 FM THAMES RADIO, Brentham House, 45C High Street, Hampton Wick, Kingston upon Thames KT1 4DG. Tel: 020-8288 1300. *Frequency:* 107.8 FM

107.9 THE EAGLE, Radio House, Sturton Street, Cambridge CB1 2QF. Tel: 01223-722300. *Frequency:* 107.9 FM

963/972 LIBERTY RADIO, 7th Floor, Trevor House, 100 Brompton Road, London SW3 1ER. Tel: 020-7893 8966. *Frequency:* 963/972 AM

1458 LITE AM, PO Box 1458, Quay West, Trafford Park, Manchester M17 1FL. Tel: 0161-872 1458. *Frequency:* 1458 AM

ACTIVE 107.5 FM, Lambourne House, 7 Western Road, Romford, Essex RM1 3LD. Tel: 01708-731643. *Frequency:* 107.5 FM

ALPHA 103.2, Radio House, 11 Woodland Road, Darlington DL3 7BJ. Tel: 01325-255552. *Frequency:* 103.2 FM

ASIAN SOUND RADIO, Globe House, Southall Street, Manchester M3 1LG. Tel: 0161-288 1000. *Frequencies:* 1377/963 AM

B97 CHILTERN FM, 55 Goldington Road, Bedford MK40 3LT. Tel: 01234-272400. *Frequency:* 96.9 FM

BATH FM, Station House, Ashley Avenue, Lower Weston, Bath BA1 3DS. Tel: 01225-471571. *Frequency:* 107.9 FM

THE BAY, PO Box 969, St George's Quay, Lancaster LA1 3LD. Tel: 01524-848747. *Frequencies:* 96.9/102.3/103.2 FM

BCR FM, 33 Manor Road, Bridgwater, Somerset TA6 4RJ. Tel: 01278 444211. *Frequencies:* 107.4 FM

BEACON FM, 267 Tettenhall Road, Wolverhampton WV6 0DQ. Tel: 01902-461300. *Frequencies:* 97.2 FM (Wolverhampton and Black Country); 103.1 FM (Shrewsbury and Telford)

BIG AM, Forster Square, Bradford, Yorks BD1 5NE. Tel: 01274 203040. *Frequencies:* 1278/1530 AM

BIG 1170, Stoke Road, Stoke-on-Trent ST4 2SR. Tel: 01782-747047. *Frequency:* 1170 AM

BIG 1458 AM, 4th Floor, Quay West, Trafford Park, Manchester M17 1FL. Tel: 0161-607 0420. *Frequency:* 1458 AM

THE BREEZE, Radio House, Clifftown Road, Southend-on-Sea, Essex SS1 1SX. Tel: 01702-333711. *Frequencies:* 1359 AM (Chelmsford); 1431 AM (Southend)

BREEZE 1521, The Stanley Centre, Kelvin Way, Crawley, W. Sussex RH10 2SE. Tel: 01293-519161. *Frequency:* 1521 AM

BRIGHT 106.4, The Market Place Shopping Centre, Burgess Hill, West Sussex RH15 9NP. Tel: 01444-239822. *Frequency:* 106.4 FM

BROADLAND 102, St George's Plain, 47–49 Colegate, Norwich NR3 1DB. Tel: 01603-630621. *Frequency:* 102.4 FM

THE BUZZ 97.1, Media House, Claughton Road, Birkenhead CH41 6EY. Tel: 0151-650 1700. *Frequency:* 97.1 FM

CAPITAL FM, 30 Leicester Square, London WC2H 7LA. Tel: 020-7766 6000. *Frequency:* 95.8 FM

CAPITAL GOLD (1152), Nine Brindleyplace, 4 Oozells Square, Birmingham B1 2DJ. Tel: 0121-245 5000. *Frequency:* 1152 AM

CAPITAL GOLD (1170 AND 1557), Radio House, Whittle Avenue, Segensworth West, Fareham, Hants PO15 5SH. Tel: 01489-589911. *Frequencies:* 1170/1557 AM

CAPITAL GOLD (1242 AND 603), Radio House, John Wilson Business Park, Whitstable, Kent CT5 3QX. Tel: 01227-772004. *Frequencies:* 603 AM (East Kent); 1242 AM (Maidstone and Medway)

CAPITAL GOLD (1323 AND 945), Radio House, PO Box 2000, Brighton BN41 2SS. Tel: 01273-430111. *Frequencies:* 945/1323 AM

CAPITAL GOLD (1548), 30 Leicester Square, London WC2H 7LA. Tel: 020-7766 6000. *Frequency:* 1548 AM

CENTRE FM, 5–6 Aldergate, Tamworth, Staffs B79 7DJ. Tel: 01827-318000. *Frequencies:* 101.6/102.4 FM

CENTURY (106), City Link, Nottingham NG2 4NG. Tel: 0115-910 6100. *Frequency:* 106 FM

CENTURY FM, Century House, PO Box 100, Gateshead NE8 2YY. Tel: 0191-477 6666. *Frequencies:* 96.2/96.4/100.7/101.8 FM

CFM, PO Box 964, Carlisle, Cumbria CA1 3NG. Tel: 01228-818964. *Frequencies:* 96.4 FM (Penrith); 102.5 FM (Carlisle); 102.2 FM (Workington); 103.4 FM (Whitehaven)

CHANNEL 103 FM, 6 Tunnell Street, St Helier, Jersey JE2 4LU. Tel: 01534-888103. *Frequency:* 103.7 FM

CHELMER FM (107.7), Cater House, High Street, Chelmsford CM1 1AL. Tel: 01245-259400. *Frequency:* 107.7FM

CHILTERN FM (96.9), 55 Goldington Road, Bedford, Beds MK40 3LT. Tel: 01234-272400. *Frequency:* 96.9 FM

CHILTERN FM (97.6), Chiltern Road, Dunstable, Beds LU6 1HQ. Tel: 01582-676200. *Frequency:* 97.6 FM

CHOICE FM, 291–299 Borough High Street, London SE1 1JG. Tel: 020-7378 3969. *Frequency:* 96.9 FM

CHOICE (107.1), 291-299 Borough High Street, London SE1 1JG. Tel: 020-8348 1033. *Frequency:* 107.1 FM

CLASSIC GOLD 666/954, Hawthorn House, Exeter Business Park, Exeter EX1 3QS. Tel: 01392-444444. *Frequencies:* 666/954 AM

CLASSIC GOLD 774, Bridge Studios, Eastgate Centre, Gloucester GL1 1SS. Tel: 01452-313200. *Frequency:* 774 AM

CLASSIC GOLD 792/828, Chiltern Road, Dunstable, Beds LU6 1HQ. Tel: 01582-676200. *Frequencies:* 792 AM (Bedford); 828 AM (Luton)

CLASSIC GOLD 828, 5 Southcote Road, Bournemouth, Dorset BH1 3LR. Tel: 01202-259259. *Frequency:* 828 AM

CLASSIC GOLD 936/1161 AM, PO Box 2000, Swindon SN4 7EX. Tel: 01793-842600. *Frequencies:* 936 AM (West Wilts); 1161 AM (Swindon)

CLASSIC GOLD RADIO 954/1530, The Old Smithy, Post Office Lane, Kempsey, Worcs WR5 3NS. Tel: 01905-820659. *Frequencies:* 954 AM (Hereford); 1530 AM (Worcester)

CLASSIC GOLD 1260, PO Box 2020, Watershed, Canons Road, Bristol BS99 7SN. Tel: 0117-984 3200. *Frequency:* 1260 AM

CLASSIC GOLD 1332 AM, PO Box 2020, Queensgate Centre, Peterborough PE1 1LL. Tel: 01733-460460. *Frequency:* 1332 AM

CLASSIC GOLD 1359, Hertford Place, Coventry CV1 3TT. Tel: 024-7686 8200. *Frequency:* 1359 AM

CLASSIC GOLD 1431/1485, PO Box 2020, Reading RG31 7FG. Tel: 0118-945 4400. *Frequencies:* 1431/1485 AM

CLASSIC GOLD 1557, 19–21 St Edmunds Road, Northampton NN1 5DY. Tel: 01604-795600. *Frequency:* 1557 AM

CLASSIC GOLD AMBER, St George's Plain, 47–49 Colegate, Norwich NR3 1DB. Tel: 01603-630621. *Frequency:* 1152 AM

CLASSIC GOLD AMBER (SUFFOLK), Alpha Business Park, 6–12 White House Road, Ipswich IP1 5LT. Tel: 01473-461000. *Frequency:* 1170 AM (Ipswich); 1251 AM (Bury St Edmunds)

CLASSIC GOLD GEM, 29–31 Castle Gate, Nottingham NG1 7AP. Tel: 0115-952 7000. *Frequencies:* 945/999 AM

CLASSIC GOLD WABC, 267 Tettenhall Road, Wolverhampton WV6 0DQ. Tel: 01902-461300. *Frequencies:* 990 AM (Wolverhampton); 1017 AM (Shrewsbury and Telford)

COMPASS FM, 26 Wellowgate, Grimsby DN32 0RA. Tel: 01472-346666. *Frequency:* 96.4 FM

CONNECT FM, Unit 1, Centre 2000, Kettering, Northants, NN16 8PU. Tel: 01536-412413. *Frequency:* 97.2 FM/107.4 FM

COUNTY SOUND RADIO 1566 MW, Dolphin House, North Street, Guildford GU1 4AA. Tel: 01483-300964. *Frequency:* 1566 MW

DELTA FM 97.1, 65 Weyhill, Haslemere, Surrey GU27 1HN. Tel: 01428-651971. *Frequency:* 97.1/101.6/102 FM

DREAM 100 FM, Northgate House, St Peter's Street, Colchester, CO1 1HT. Tel: 01206-764466. *Frequency:* 100.2 FM

DUNE FM, The Power Station, Victoria Way, Southport PR8 1RR. Tel: 01704-502500. *Frequency:* 107.9 FM

ESSEX FM, Radio House, Clifftown Road, Southend-on-Sea, Essex SS1 1SX. Tel: 01702-333711. *Frequencies:* 96.3 FM (Southend); 97.5 FM (Southend Centre); 102.6 FM (Chelmsford)

FLR 107.3, Astra House, Arklow Road, London SE14 6EB. Tel: 020-8691 9202. *Frequency:* 107.3 FM

FM 102 – THE BEAR, The Guard House Studios, Banbury Road, Stratford-upon-Avon, Warks CV37 7HX. Tel: 01789-262636. *Frequency:* 102.0 FM

FM 103 HORIZON, The Broadcast Centre, Vincent Avenue, Crownhill, Milton Keynes MK8 0AB. Tel: 01908-269111. *Frequency:* 103.3 FM

FM 107 THE FALCON, Brunel Mall, London Road, Stroud, Glos GL5 2BP. Tel: 01453-767369. *Frequency:* 107.2/107.9 FM

FM 107.6 THE FIRE, PO Box 1234, Bournemouth BH5 2AD. Tel: 01202-318100. *Frequency:* 107.6 FM

FOSSEWAY RADIO, PO Box 107, Hinckley, Leics LE10 1WR. Tel: 01455-614151. *Frequency:* 107.9 FM

FOX FM, Brush House, Pony Road, Oxford OX4 2XR. Tel: 01865-871000. *Frequencies:* 102.6/97.4 FM

FRESH AM, Gargrave Road, Skipton, N. Yorks BD23 1YD. Tel: 01756-799991. *Frequencies:* 936 MW (Hawes); 1413 MW (Skipton)

FUSION 107.3 FM, Astra House, Arklow Road, London SE14 6EB. Tel: 020-8691 9202. *Frequency:* 107.3 FM

FUSION 107.9 FM, Suite 41, Westgate Centre, Oxford OX1 1PD. Tel: 01865-724442. *Frequency:* 107.9 FM

GALAXY 101, Millennium House, 26 Baldwin Street, Bristol BS1 1SE. Tel: 0117-901 0101. *Frequencies:* 97.2 FM (Bristol); 101 FM (Severn Estuary)

GALAXY 102, 127–129 Portland Street, Manchester M1 6ED. Tel: 0161-228 0102. *Frequency:* 102.0 FM

GALAXY 102.2, 1 The Square, 111 Broad Street, Birmingham B15 1AS. Tel: 0121-695 0000. *Frequency:* 102.2 FM

GALAXY 105, Joseph's Well, Westgate, Leeds LS3 1AB. Tel: 0113-213 0105. *Frequencies:* 105.1 FM (Leeds); 105.6 FM (Bradford and Sheffield); 105.8 FM (Hull)

GALAXY 105-106, Kingfisher Way, Silverlink Business Park, Tyne and Wear NE28 9ND. Tel: 0191-206 8000. *Frequencies:* 105.3/105.6/106.4 FM

GEMINI FM, Hawthorn House, Exeter Business Park, Exeter EX1 3QS. Tel: 01392-444444. *Frequencies:* 96.4/97.0/103.0 FM

GWR FM (BRISTOL AND BATH), PO Box 2000, Watershed, Canon's Road, Bristol BS99 7SN. Tel: 0117-984 3200. *Frequencies:* 96.3 FM (Bristol); 103.0 FM (Bath)

GWR FM (SWINDON AND WEST WILTSHIRE), PO Box 2000, Swindon SN4 7EX. Tel: 01793-842600. *Frequencies:* 97.2 FM (Swindon); 102.2 FM (West Wilts); 96.5 FM (Marlborough)

HALLAM FM, Radio House, 900 Herries Road, Sheffield S6 1RH. Tel: 0114-285 3333. *Frequencies:* 97.4 FM (Sheffield); 102.9 FM (Barnsley); 103.4 FM (Doncaster)

HEART 106.2 The Chrysalis Building, Bramley Road, London W10 6SP. Tel: 020-7468 1062. *Frequency:* 106.2 FM

HEART FM, 1 The Square, 111 Broad Street, Birmingham B15 1AS. Tel: 0121-695 0000. *Frequency:* 100.7 FM

HERTBEAT 106.9 FM, PO Box 299, Herts, Hertfordshire SG14 3XN. Tel: 01992-505362. *Frequencies:* 106.7/106.9 FM

HOME 107.9, The Old Stableblock, Lockwood Park, Huddersfield HD1 3UR. Tel: 01484-321107. *Frequency:* 107.9 FM

IMAGINE FM, Regent House, Heaton Lane, Stockport SK4 1BX. Tel: 0161-285 4545. *Frequencies:* 96.4 FM (Cheshire); 104.9 FM (Stockport)

INVICTA FM, Radio House, John Wilson Business Park, Whitstable, Kent CT5 3QX. Tel: 01227-772004. *Frequencies:* 103.1 FM (Maidstone and Medway); 102.8 FM (Canterbury); 95.9 FM (Thanet); 97.0 FM (Dover); 96.1 FM (Ashford)

ISLAND FM, 12 Westerbrook, St Sampsons, Guernsey GY2 4QQ. Tel: 01481-242000. *Frequencies:* 93.7 FM (Alderney); 104.7 FM (Guernsey)

ISLE OF WIGHT RADIO, Dodnor Park, Newport, Isle of Wight PO30 5XE. Tel: 01983-822557. *Frequencies:* 102.0/107.0 FM

ITN NEWS DIRECT 97.3 FM, 200 Gray's Inn Road, London WC1X 8XZ. Tel: 020-7973 1152. *Frequency:* 97.3 FM

JAZZ FM 102.2, 26–27 Castlereagh Street, London W1H 6DJ. Tel: 020-7706 4100. *Frequency:* 102.2 FM

JAZZ FM 100.4, The World Trade Centre, Exchange Quay, Manchester M5 3EJ. Tel: 0161-877 1004. *Frequency:* 100.4 FM

JUICE 107, PO Box 107, Brighton BN1 1QG. Tel: 01273-386107. *Frequency:* 107.2 FM

JUICE 107.6, 27 Fleet Street, Liverpool L1 4AR. Tel: 0151-707 3107. *Frequency:* 107.6 FM

KCR, PO Box 106, Prescot, Merseyside L35 0RN. Tel: 0151-290 1501. *Frequency:* 106.7 FM

KEY 103, Castle Quay, Castlefield, Manchester M15 4PR. Tel: 0161-288 5000. *Frequency:* 103 FM

KICK FM, The Studios, 42 Bone Lane, Newbury, Berks RG14 5SD. Tel: 01635-841600. *Frequencies:* 105.6/107.4 FM

KISS 100 FM, Kiss House, 80 Holloway Road, London N7 8JG. Tel: 020-7700 6100. *Frequency:* 100.0 FM

KIX 96, Watch Close, Spon Street, Coventry CV1 3LN. Tel: 024-7652 5656. *Frequency:* 96.2 FM

KL.FM 96.7, PO Box 77, 18 Blackfriars Street, King's Lynn, Norfolk PE30 1NN. Tel: 01553-772777. *Frequency:* 96.7 FM

LANTERN FM, 2B Lauder Lane, Roundswell Business Park, Barnstaple EX31 3TA. Tel: 01271-340340. *Frequency:* 96.2 FM

LBC 1152 AM, 200 Gray's Inn Road, London WC1X 8XZ. Tel: 020-7973 1152. *Frequency:* 1152 AM

LEICESTER SOUND, Granville House, Granville Road, Leicester LE1 7RW. Tel: 0116-256 1300. *Frequency:* 105.4 FM

LINCS FM, Witham Park, Waterside South, Lincoln LN5 7JN. Tel: 01522-549900. *Frequencies:* 102.2/96.7 FM (Grantham Relay)/97.6 FM (Scunthorpe Relay)

LITE FM, 5 Church Street, Peterborough PE1 1XJ. Tel: 01733-898106. *Frequency:* 106.8 FM

LONDON GREEK RADIO, Florentia Village, Vale Road, London N4 1TD. Tel: 020-8800 8001. *Frequency:* 103.3 FM

LONDON TURKISH RADIO LTR, 185B High Road, Wood Green, London N22 6BA. Tel: 020-8881 0606. *Frequency:* 1584 AM

MAGIC 105.4 FM, The Network Building, 97 Tottenham Court Road, London W1P 9HF. Tel: 020-7504 7000. *Frequency:* 105.4 FM

MAGIC 828, 51 Burley Road, Leeds LS3 1LR. Tel: 0113-283 5500. *Frequency:* 828 AM

MAGIC 999, PO Box 999, Preston, Lancs PR1 1XR. Tel: 01772-556301. *Frequency:* 999 AM

MAGIC 1152, Castle Quay, Castlefield, Manchester M15 4PR. Tel: 0161-288 5000. *Frequency:* 1152 AM

MAGIC 1152 AM, Newcastle upon Tyne NE99 1BB. Tel: 0191-420 3040. *Frequency:* 1152 AM

MAGIC 1161 AM, Commercial Road, Hull HU1 2SG. Tel: 01482-325141. *Frequency:* 1161 AM

MAGIC 1170, Radio House, Yales Crescent, Thornaby, Stockton-on-Tees, Cleveland TS17 6AA. Tel: 01642-888222. *Frequency:* 1170 AM

MAGIC 1548, 8–10 Stanley Street, Liverpool L1 6AF. Tel: 0151-227 5100. *Frequency:* 1548 AM

MAGIC AM, Radio House, 900 Herries Road, Sheffield S6 1RH. Tel: 0114-285 2121. *Frequencies:* 990/1305/1548 AM

MANCHESTER'S MAGIC (1152), Castle Quay, Castlefield, Manchester M15 4PR. Tel: 0161-288 5000. *Frequency:* 1152 AM

MANSFIELD 103.2, The Media Suite, Brunts Business Centre, Samuel Brunts Way, Mansfield, Notts NG18 2AH. Tel: 01623-646666. *Frequency:* 103.2 FM

MARCHER GOLD, The Studios, Mold Road, Wrexham LL11 4AF. Tel: 01978-752202. *Frequency:* 1260 AM

MEDWAY FM, Berkeley House, 186 High Street, Rochester ME1 1EY. Tel: 01634-841111. *Frequencies:* 107.9/100.4 FM

MERCIA FM, Hertford Place, Coventry CV1 3TT. Tel: 024-7686 8200. *Frequencies:* 97.0/102.9 FM

MERCURY 96.2 FM, 1 East Street, Tonbridge, Kent TN9 1AR. Tel: 01732-369200. *Frequencies:* 96.2 FM (South); 101.6 FM (North)

MERCURY 96.6 FM, 9 Christopher Place, Shopping Centre, St Albans, Herts AL3 5DQ. Tel: 01727-831966. *Frequency:* 96.6 FM

MERCURY 102.7 FM, The Stanley Centre, Kelvin Way, Crawley, W. Sussex RH10 2SE. Tel: 01293-519161. *Frequencies:* 97.5/102.7 FM

MERCURY 107.9 FM, Berkeley House, 186 High Street, Rochester ME1 1EY. Tel: 01634-841111. *Frequencies:* 100.4/107.9 FM

METRO RADIO, Newcastle upon Tyne NE99 1BB. Tel: 0191-420 0971. *Frequencies:* 97.1 FM (Northumberland, Tyne and Wear, Durham); 103.0 FM (Tyne Valley); 102.6 FM (Alnwick); 103.2 FM (Hexham)

MFM 103.4, The Studios, Mold Road, Gwersyllt, Nr Wrexham LL11 4AF. Tel: 01978-752202. *Frequency:* 103.4 FM

MILLENNIUM RADIO, Harrow Manor Way, Thamesmead, London SE2 9XH. Tel: 020-8311 3112. *Frequency:* 106.8 FM

MINSTER FM, PO Box 123, Dunnington, York YO1 5ZX. Tel: 01904-488888. *Frequencies:* 104.7 FM (York); 102.3 FM (Thirsk)

MIX 96, Friars Square Studios, 11 Bourbon Street, Aylesbury, Bucks HP20 2PZ. Tel: 01296-399396. *Frequency:* 96.2 FM

NEPTUNE RADIO, PO Box 1068, Dover CT16 1GB; PO Box 964, Folkestone CT18 8GG. Tel: 01304-202505. *Frequencies:* 96.4 FM (Folkestone); 106.8 FM (Dover)

NORTHANTS 96, 19–21 St Edmunds Road, Northampton NN1 5DY. Tel: 01604-795601. *Frequency:* 96.6 FM

THE NRG, PO Box 1234, Bournemouth BH1 3YH. Tel: 01202-318100. *Frequency:* 107.6 FM

OCEAN FM, Radio House, Whittle Avenue, Segensworth West, Fareham, Hants PO15 5SH. Tel: 01489-589911. *Frequencies:* 96.7/97.5 FM

ORCHARD FM, Haygrove House, Taunton, Somerset TA3 7BT. Tel: 01823-338448. *Frequencies:* 96.5 FM (Taunton); 97.1 FM (Yeovil); 102.6 FM (Somerset)

OXYGEN 107.9 FM, Suite 41, Westgate Centre, Oxford OX1 1PD. Tel: 01865-724442. *Frequency:* 107.9 FM

PEAK 107 FM, Radio House, Foxwood Road, Chesterfield, Derbys S41 9RF. Tel: 01246-269107. *Frequencies:* 107.4 FM (Chesterfield and NE Derbyshire); 102.0 FM (Matlock and Bakewell)

PICCADILLY KEY, Castle Quay, Castlefield, Manchester M15 4PR. Tel: 0161-288 5000. *Frequency:* 103 FM

PIRATE FM 102, Carn Brea Studios, Wilson Way, Redruth, Cornwall TR15 3XX. Tel: 01209-314400. *Frequencies:* 102.2 FM (East Cornwall and West Devon); 102.8 FM (West Cornwall and Isles of Scilly)

PLYMOUTH SOUND FM, Earl's Acre, Plymouth PL3 4HX. Tel: 01752-227272. *Frequencies:* 96.6/97.0 FM

PREMIER CHRISTIAN RADIO, Glen House, Stag Place, London SW1E 5Ag. Tel: 020-7316 1300. *Frequencies:* 1305/1332/1413 AM

PRIDE FM, 8 East Street, Warminster, Wiltshire BA12 9BN. Tel: 01722-416644. *Frequencies:* to be arranged

THE PULSE, Pennine House, Forster Square, Bradford BD1 5NE. Tel: 01274-203040. *Frequencies:* 97.5 FM (Bradford); 102.5 FM (Huddersfield and Halifax)

Q103 FM, Enterprise House, The Vision Park, Chivers Way, Histon, Cambridge CB4 4WW. Tel: 01223-235255. *Frequencies:* 103.0 FM (Cambridge); 97.4 FM (Newmarket)

QUAY WEST RADIO, Harbour Studios, The Esplanade, Watchet, Somerset TA23 0AJ. Tel: 01984-634900. *Frequency:* 102.4 FM

RADIO CITY 96.7, 8–10 Stanley Street, Liverpool L1 6AF. Tel: 0151-227 5100. *Frequency:* 96.7 FM

RADIO XL 1296 AM, KMS House, Bradford Street, Birmingham B12 0JD. Tel: 0121-753 5353. *Frequency:* 1296 AM

RAM FM, 35-36 Irongate, Derby DE1 3GA. Tel: 01332-205599. *Frequency:* 102.8 FM

REVOLUTION, PO Box 962, Oldham OL1 1FE. Tel: 0161-628 8787. *Frequency:* 96.2 FM

RIDINGS FM, 2 Thornes Office Park, Monckton Road, Wakefield WF2 7AN. Tel: 01924-367177. *Frequency:* 106.8 FM

RITZ 1035 AM, 33–35 Wembley Hill Road, London HA9 8RT. Tel: 020-8733 1300. *Frequency:* 1035 AM

ROCK FM, PO Box 974, Preston PR1 1XS. Tel: 01772-556301. *Frequency:* 97.4 FM

RUTLAND RADIO, Rutland Business Centre, Gaol Street, Oakham, Rutland LE15 6AY. Tel: 01572-757868. *Frequency:* 107.2 FM (Rutland); 97.4 FM (Stamford)

SABRAS RADIO, Radio House, 63 Melton Road, Leicester LE4 6PN. Tel: 0116-261 0666. *Frequency:* 1260 AM

SAGA RADIO, The Saga Building, Enbrook Park, Folkestone, Kent CT20 3SE. Tel: 01303-771003. *Frequency:* 105.7 FM

SEVERN SOUND FM, Bridge Studios, Eastgate Centre, Gloucester GL1 1SS. Tel: 01452-313200. *Frequencies:* 103.0/102.4 FM

SGR COLCHESTER, Abbeygate Two, 9 Whitewell Road, Colchester CO2 7DE. Tel: 01206-575859. *Frequency:* 96.1 FM

SGR-FM, Radio House, Alpha Business Park, White House Road, Ipswich IP1 5LT. Tel: 01473-461000. *Frequencies:* 97.1 FM (Ipswich); 96.4 FM (Bury St Edmunds)

SIGNAL 1 FM, Stoke Road, Stoke-on-Trent ST4 2SR. Tel: 01782-747047. *Frequencies:* 96.9/102.6 FM

SIGNAL'S BIG AM, Stoke Road, Stoke-on-Trent ST4 2SR. Tel: 01782-747047. *Frequency:* 1170 AM

SOUTHCITY FM, City Studios, Marsh Lane, Southampton, SO14 3ST. Tel: 023-8022 0020. *Frequency:* 107.8 FM

SOUTHERN FM, Radio House, PO Box 2000, Brighton BN41 2SS. Tel: 01273-430111. *Frequencies:* 102.0 FM (Hastings); 102.4 FM (Eastbourne); 96.9 FM (Newhaven); 103.5 FM (Brighton)

SOUTH HAMS RADIO, Unit 9, South Hams Business Park, Churchstow, Knightsbridge, Devon TQ7 3QR. Tel: 01548-854595. *Frequency:* 100.5 FM (Totnes); 100.8 FM (Dartmouth); 101.2 FM (South Hams); 101.9 FM (Ivybridge)

SOVEREIGN RADIO, 14 St Mary's Walk, Hailsham, E. Sussex BN27 1AF. Tel: 01323-442700. *Frequency:* 107.5 FM

SPECTRUM INTERNATIONAL RADIO, International Radio Centre, 204–206 Queenstown Road, London SW8 3NR. Tel: 020-7627 4433. *Frequency:* 558 AM

SPIRE FM, City Hall Studios, Malthouse Lane, Salisbury, Wilts SP2 7QQ. Tel: 01722-416644. *Frequency:* 102.0 FM

SPIRIT FM, Dukes Court, Bognor Road, Chichester, W. Sussex PO19 2FX. Tel: 01243-773600. *Frequencies:* 96.6/102.3 FM

STAR FM, The Observatory Shopping Centre, Slough, Berks SL1 1LH. Tel: 01753-551066. *Frequency:* 106.6 FM

STAR 107.3, Bristol Evening Post Building, Temple Way, Bristol BS99 7HD. Tel: 0117-910 6600. *Frequency:* 107.3 FM

STAR 107.9, Radio House, Sturton Street, Cambridge CB1 1QF. Tel: 01223-722300. *Frequency:* 107.9 FM

SUN FM, PO Box 1034, Sunderland SR5 2YL. Tel: 0191-548 1034. *Frequency:* 103.4 FM

SUNRISE FM, Sunrise House, 30 Chapel Street, Little Germany, Bradford BD1 5DN. Tel: 01274-735043. *Frequency:* 103.2 FM

SUNRISE RADIO, Sunrise House, Sunrise Road, Southall, Middx UB2 4AU. Tel: 020-8574 6666. *Frequency:* 1458 AM

SUNSHINE 855, Sunshine House, Waterside, Ludlow, Shropshire SY8 1PE. Tel: 01584-873795. *Frequency:* 855 AM

SWAN FM, PO Box 1170, High Wycombe, Bucks HP13 6YT. Tel: 01494-446611. *Frequency:* 1170 FM

TEN 17, Latton Bush Centre, Southern Way, Harlow, Essex CM18 7BU. Tel: 01279-431017. *Frequency:* 101.7 FM

TFM, Radio House, Yale Crescent, Thornaby, Stockton-on-Tees TS17 6AA. Tel: 01642-888222. *Frequency:* 96.6 FM

TLR, Imperial House, 2–14 High Street, Margate, Kent CT9 1DH. Tel: 01843-220222. *Frequency:* 107.2 FM

TOWER FM, The Mill, Brownlow Way, Bolton BL1 2RA. Tel: 01204-387000. *Frequency:* 107.4 FM

TRAX FM, PO Box 444, Worksop, Notts S81 9YW. Tel: 01909-500611. *Frequency:* 107.9 FM

TRAX FM, PO Box 444, Doncaster DN3 3GB. Tel: 01302-341166. *Frequency:* 107.1 FM

VIBE FM, Reflection House, The Anderson Centre, Olding Road, Bury, St Edmunds IP33 3TA. Tel: 01284-718800. *Frequencies:* 105.6 FM (Cambridge); 106.1 FM (Norwich); 106.4 FM (Ipswich); 107.7 FM (Peterborough)

VICTORY 107.4, Media House, Tipner Wharf, Twyford Avenue, Portsmouth PO2 8PE. Tel: 023-9263 9922. *Frequency:* 107.4 FM

VIRGIN 105.8, 1 Golden Square, London W1R 4DJ. Tel: 020-7434 1215. *Frequency:* 105.8 FM

THE WAVE 96.5, 965 Mowbray Drive, Blackpool FY3 7JR. Tel: 01253-304965. *Frequency:* 96.5 FM

WAVE 105 FM, 5 Manor Court, Barnes Wallis Road, Segensworth East, Fareham, Hampshire PO15 5TH. Tel: 01489-481050. *Frequencies:* 105.2 FM (Solent); 105.8 FM (Poole)

WESSEX FM, Radio House, Trinity Street, Dorchester DT1 1DJ. Tel: 01305-250333. *Frequencies:* 97.2/96.0 FM

WESTMORELAND RADIO (LAKELAND RADIO), c/o Rayrigg Rover, Mintsfeet Road Kendal LA9 6DE. Tel: 01539-738464. *Frequencies:* 100.8/100.1 FM

WIN 107.2, PO Box 1072, The Brooks, Winchester SO23 8FT. Tel: 01962-841071. *Frequency:* 107.2 FM

WYVERN FM, 5—6 Barbourne Terrace, Worcester WR1 3JZ. Tel: 01905-612212. *Frequencies:* 97.6 FM (Hereford); 102.8 FM (Worcester); 96.7 FM (Kidderminster)

X-CEL FM, 46 Camel Road, Littleport, Cambs CB6 1EW. Tel: 01353-865102. *Frequencies:* 107.1/107.5 FM

XFM, 30 Leicester Square, London WC2H 7LA. Tel: 020-7766 6600. *Frequency:* 104.9 FM

YORKSHIRE COAST RADIO, PO Box 962, Scarborough, N. Yorks YO12 5YX. Tel: 01723-500962. *Frequencies:* 96.2/103.1 FM

YORKSHIRE COAST RADIO BRIDLINGTON'S BEST, Old Harbour Master's Office, Harbour Road, Bridlington, E. Yorks YO15 5NR. Tel: 01262-404400. *Frequency:* 102.4 FM

Wales

106.3 BRIDGE FM, 25 Wyndham Street, Bridgend CF31 1EB. Tel: 01656-647777. *Frequency:* 106.3 FM

CAPITAL GOLD, West Canal Wharf, Cardiff CF10 5XL. Tel: 029-2023 7878. *Frequencies:* 1359 AM (Cardiff); 1305 AM (Newport)

CHAMPION FM, Llys y Dderwen, Parc Menai, Bangor LL57 4BN. Tel: 01248-671888. *Frequency:* 103.0 FM

COAST FM, 41 Conwy Road, Colwyn Bay LL28 5AB. Tel: 01492-533733. *Frequency:* 96.3 FM

RADIO CEREDIGION, Yr Hen Ysgol Gymraeg, Ffordd Alexandra, Aberystwyth SY23 1LF. Tel: 01970-627999. *Frequencies:* 96.6/97.4/103.3/FM

RADIO MALDWYN, The Studios, The Park, Newtown, Powys SY16 2NZ. Tel: 01686-623555. *Frequency:* 756 AM

REAL RADIO, PO Box 6105, Ty-Nant Court, Cardiff CF15 8YF. Tel: 029-2023 1863. *Frequency:* 105/106 FM.

RED DRAGON FM, Radio House, West Canal Wharf, Cardiff CF10 5XL. Tel: 029-2038 4041. *Frequencies:* 103.2 FM (Cardiff); 97.4 FM (Newport)

SWANSEA SOUND, PO Box 1170, Victoria Road, Gowerton, Swansea SA4 3AB. Tel: 01792-511170. *Frequency:* 1170 AM

VALLEYS RADIO, Festival Park, Victoria, Ebbw Vale NP3 6XW. Tel: 01495-301116. *Frequencies:* 999/1116 AM

THE WAVE 96.4 FM, PO Box 964, Victoria Road, Gowerton, Swansea SA4 3AB. Tel: 01792-511964. *Frequency:* 96.4 FM

Scotland

96.3 QFM, 26 Lady Lane, Paisley PA1 2LG. Tel: 0141-887 9630. *Frequency:* 96.3 FM

ARGYLL FM, 27—29 Longrow, Campbeltown, Argyll PA28 6ER. Tel: 01586-551800. *Frequency:* 107.1/107.7/106.5 FM

BEAT 106, Four Winds Pavilion, Pacific Quay, Glasgow G51 1EB. Tel: 0141-566 6106. *Frequencies:* 105.7/106.1 FM

CASTLE ROCK FM, Pioneer Park Studios, Unit 3, 80 Castlegreen Street, Dumbarton G82 1JB. Tel: 01389-734411. *Frequency:* 103 FM

CENTRAL FM, 201 High Street, Falkirk FK1 1DU. Tel: 01324-611164. *Frequency:* 103.1 FM

CLAN FM, Radio House, Rowantree Avenue, Newhouse Industrial Estate, Newhouse ML1 5RX. Tel: 01689-733107. *Frequency:* 107.5/107.9 FM

CLYDE 1 (FM) AND 2 (AM), Clydebank Business Park, Clydebank, Glasgow G81 2RX. Tel: 0141-565 2200. *Frequencies:* 102.5 FM; 103.3 FM (Firth of Clyde); 97.0 FM (Vale of Leven); 1152 AM

FORTH AM AND FM, Forth House, Forth Street, Edinburgh EH1 3LF. Tel: 0131-556 9255. *Frequencies:* 1548 AM, 97.3/97.6/102.2 FM

HEARTLAND FM, Atholl Curling Rink, Lower Oakfield, Pitlochry, Perthshire PH16 5HQ. Tel: 01796-474040. *Frequency:* 97.5 FM

ISLES FM, PO Box 333, Stornoway, Isle of Lewis HS1 2PU. Tel: 01851-703333. *Frequency:* 103.0 FM

KINGDOM FM, Haig House, Haig Business Park, Markinch, Fife KY7 6AQ. Tel: 01592-753753. *Frequencies:* 95.2/96.1 FM

LOCHBROOM FM, Radio House, Mill Street, Ullapool, Wester Ross IV26 2UN. Tel: 01854-613131. *Frequency:* 102.2 FM

MORAY FIRTH RADIO, Scorguie Place, Inverness IV3 8UJ. Tel: 01463-224433. *Frequencies:* 97.4 FM, 1107 AM; *local opt-outs:* MFR Speysound 96.6 FM, MFR Keith Community Radio 102.8 FM; MFR Kinnaird Radio 96.7 FM; MFR Caithness 102.5 FM

NECR (NORTH-EAST COMMUNITY RADIO), Town House, Kintore, Inverurie, AB51 0US. Tel: 01467-632909. *Frequencies:* 97.1 FM (Braemar); 102.1 FM (Meldrum and Inverurie); 102.6 FM (Kildrummy); 103.2 FM (Colpy)

NEVIS RADIO, Inverlochy, Fort William, Inverness-shire PH33 6LU. Tel: 01397-700007. *Frequencies:* 96.6 FM (Fort William); 97.0 FM (Glencoe); 102.3 FM (Skye); 102.4 FM (Loch Leven)

NORTHSOUND ONE (FM) AND TWO (AM), 45 Kings Gate, Aberdeen AB15 4EL. Tel: 01224-337000. *Frequencies:* 1035 AM, 96.9/97.6/103.0 FM

OBAN FM, 132 George Street, Oban, Argyll PA34 5NT. Tel: 01631-570057. *Frequency:* 103.3 FM

RADIO BORDERS, Tweedside Park, Galashiels TD1 3TD. Tel: 01896-759444. *Frequencies:* 96.8/97.5/103.1/103.4 FM

RADIO TAY AM AND TAY FM, 6 North Isla Street, Dundee DD3 7JQ. Tel: 01382-200800. *Frequencies:* 1161 AM, 102.8 FM (Dundee); 1584 AM, 96.4 FM (Perth)

RNA FM, Arbroath Infirmary, Rosemount Road, Arbroath, Angus DD11 2AT. Tel: 01241-879660. *Frequency:* 96.6 FM

SCOT FM, 1 Albert Quay, Leith EH6 7DN. Tel: 0131-625 8400. *Frequencies:* 100.3 FM (West); 101.1 FM (East)

SIBC, Market Street, Lerwick, Shetland ZE1 0JN. Tel: 01595-695299. *Frequencies:* 96.2/102.2 FM

SOUTH WEST SOUND, Campbell House, Bankend Road, Dumfries DG1 4TH. Tel: 01387-250999. *Frequencies:* 96.5/97.0/103.0 FMWave 102, 8 South Tay Street, Dundee DD1 1PA. Tel: 01382-901000. *Frequency:* 102 FM

WAVE 102,8 South Tay Street, Dundee DD1 1PA. Tel: 01382-901000. *Frequency:* 102 FM

WAVES RADIO PETERHEAD, Unit 2, Blackhouse Industrial Estate, Peterhead AB42 1BW. Tel: 01779-491012. *Frequency:* 101.2 FM

WEST SOUND AM AND WEST FM, Radio House, 54a Holmston Road, Ayr KA7 3BE. Tel: 01292-283662. *Frequencies:* 1035 AM, 96.7 FM (Ayr); 97.5 FM (Girvan)

CITY BEAT 96.7, Lamont Buildings, Stranmillis Embankment, Belfast BT9 5FN. Tel: 028-9020 5967. *Frequency:* 96.7 FM

COOL FM, PO Box 974, Belfast BT1 1RT. Tel: 028-9081 7181. *Frequency:* 97.4 FM

DOWNTOWN RADIO, Newtownards, Co. Down BT23 4ES. Tel: 028-9181 5555. *Frequencies:* 1026 AM (Belfast); 96.4 FM (Limavady); 96.6 FM (Enniskillen); 97.1 FM (Larne); 102.3 FM (Ballymena); 102.4 FM (Londonderry); 103.1 FM (Newry); 103.4 FM (Newcastle); 102.6 AM (Belfast)

Q97.2 FM, 24 Clafin Road, Coleraine BT52 2NU. Tel: 028-7035 9100. *Frequency:* 97.2 FM

Q102.9 FM The Riverside Suite, Old Waterside Railway Station, Duke Street, Londonderry BT47 6DH. Tel: 028-7134 4449. *Frequency:* 102.9 FM

Channel Islands

104.7 ISLAND FM, 12 Westerbrook, St Sampsons, Guernsey GY2 4QQ. Tel: 01481-242000. *Frequencies:* 104.7 FM (Guernsey); 93.7 FM (Alderney)

CHANNEL 103 FM, 6 Tunnell Street, St Helier, Jersey JE2 4LU. Tel: 01534-888103. *Frequency:* 103.7 FM

DIGITAL MULTIPLEXES

DIGITAL ONE, 20 Southampton Street, London WC2E 7QH. Tel: 020-7288 4600. Programme services: Classic FM; Virgin Radio; talkSPORT; Planet Rock; Core; Life; Oneword; PrimeTimeRadio; Bloomberg Radio; ITN. *Frequencies:* 11D (England and Wales); 12A (Scotland)

CAPITAL RADIO DIGITAL, 30 Leicester Square, London WC2H 7LA. Tel: 020-7766 6000. Programme services: Red Dragon FM; Capital Gold; The Storm; MTV Dance; Adult Contemporary; Xfm; BBC Radio Wales; BBC Radio Cymru. *Frequency:* 11C

CE DIGITAL LTD, 30 Leicester Square, London WC2H 7LA. Tel: 020-7766 6000.

Birmingham, Programme services: BRMB; Capital Gold; Xfm; Magic; Radio XL; Kiss; BBC Radio WM. *Frequency:* 11C

London, Programme services: Capital FM; Capital Gold; Kiss; Xfm, Magic; News Direct; Sunrise Radio; LBC; Century London. *Frequency:* 12C

Manchester, Programme services: Key 103; Magic; Kiss; Big Am; Xfm; Asian Sound Radio; BBC GMR. *Frequency:* 11C

EMAP DIGITAL RADIO LTD, Emap Performance, Mappin House, 4 Winsley Street, London W1W 8HF. Tel: 020-7436 1515.

Leeds, Programme services: 96.3 Aire FM; Classic Gold; Kiss; Magic 828; Ridings FM; Xfm, Real Radio; BBC Radio Leeds. *Frequency:* 12D

Liverpool, Programme services: Radio City 96.7; Magic 1548; Kiss; Classic Gold; Real Radio; Ritz; BBC Radio Merseyside. *Frequency:* 12D

South Yorkshire, Programme services: Hallam FM; Magic; Kiss; Trax FM; Classic Gold; Xfm; Real Radio; BBC Radio Sheffield. *Frequency:* 11C

Teesside, Programme services: Classic Gold; Real Radio; Hot AC Service (tbc); Kiss; Magic 1170; 96.6 TFM; Xfm; BBC Radio Cleveland. *Frequency:* 11B

Humberside, Programme services: Viking FM; Magic 1161; Links FM; Classic Gold; Xfm; Real Radio; Kiss; BBC Radio Humberside. *Frequency:* 11B

Tyne and Wear, Programme services: Metro FM; Magic 1152; Kiss; Real Radio; 3C Continuous Cool Country; Classic Gold; Xfm; BBC Radio Newcastle. *Frequency:* 11C

Central Lancashire, Emap Performance, Mappin House, 4 Winsley Street, London W1W 8HF. Tel: 020-7436 1515. Programme services: 97.4 Rock FM; Kiss; Magic 999; Real Radio; Xfm; BBC Radio Lancashire. *Frequency:* 12A

MXR The Chrysalis Building, 13 Bramley Road, London W10 6SP. Tel: 020-7221 2213.

North West England, Programme services: Cube; Urban Flava; Heart; The Arrow; Smooth; Digital News Network; Galaxy 102; Jazz FM 100.4; 105.4 Century FM. *Frequency:* 12C

North East England, Programme services: Cube; Heart; The Arrow; Smooth; Digital News Network; Jazz FM; Galaxy 105–106; Century 100–102; Urban Flava. *Frequency:* 12C

West Midlands, Programme services: Cube; Heart FM; The Arrow; Smooth; Digital News Network; Galaxy 102.2; Jazz FM; Saga Radio; BBC Asian Network. *Frequency:* 12A

South Wales/Severn Estuary, Programme services: Cube; Urban Flava; Heart; The Arrow; Smooth; Digital News Network; Galaxy 101; Jazz FM; Real Radio; *Frequency:* 12C

NOW DIGITAL LTD, PO Box 2269, London W1A 5UQ. Tel: 020-7911 7300. Web: www.now-digital.com

Wolverhampton, Shrewsbury and Telford. Programme services: Beacon FM; Classic Gold WABC; The Storm; The Rhythm; Xfm; Sunrise radio; Student service (tba); BBC Radio WM; BBC Radio Shropshire. *Frequency:* 11B

Bristol/Bath, Programme services: GWR FM; Classic Gold 1359; Kix 96; The Storm; Vibe; Xfm; The Rhythm; The Lounge; @Bristol; BBC Radio Bristol. *Frequency:* 11B

Coventry, Programme services: Mercia FM; Classic Gold 1359; Kix 96; The Storm; The Rhythm; Vibe; Flix; Sunrise radio; BBC Radio Coventry and Warwickshire. *Frequency:* 12B

Southend and Chelmsford, Programme services: Essex FM; Breeze; The Rhythm; Dance service; Easy Listening Service; Ritz; Flix; BBC Radio Essex. *Frequency:* 12D

SCORE DIGITAL, 3 South Ave, Clydebank Business Park, Glasgow G81 2RX. Tel: 0141 565 2347. Web: www.scoredigital.co.uk

Edinburgh. Programme services: Forth One, Forth 2; 3C; Sunrise Radio; Xfm; Saga Radio; BBC Radio Scotland. *Frequency:* 12D

Glasgow, Clyde 1; Clyde 2; 3C; Sunrise radio; 96.3 Qfm Ltd; Xfm; Kiss; Saga Radio; BBC Radio Scotland. *Frequency:* 11C

Northern Ireland, Programme services: Downtown; Cool FM; City Beat; Q102.9; Classic FM; Virgin; talkSPORT; PrimeTime; 3C; BBC Radio Ulster. *Frequency:* 12D

SWITCHDIGITAL LTD, 18 Hatfields, London SE1 8DJ. Tel: 020-7959 7869. Web: www.switchdigital.com

Greater London, Programme services: Ministry of Sound Radio; WLON The Mix; Big London; The Lounge; The Groove; Travel Now; Heart 106.2 FM; Jazz FM; BBC London Live. *Frequency:* 12A

Aberdeen, Programme services: Ministry of Sound Radio; The Rhythm; Ritz Country; The Lounge; The Groove; Travel Now; Heart 106.2.FM; Jazz FM; BBC London Live. *Frequency:* 11C

Central Scotland, Programme services: Ministry of Sound Radio; The Rhythm; WSCO; The Mix; Big-Scotland; The Lounge; Jazz FM; Scot FM; Beat 106; BBC Radio Nan Galdheal. *Frequency:* 11D

The Press

The newspaper and periodical press in the UK is large and diverse, catering for a wide variety of views and interests. There is no state control or censorship of the press, though it is subject to the laws on publication and the Press Complaints Commission was set up by the industry as a means of self-regulation.

The press is not state-subsidised and receives few tax concessions. The income of most newspapers and periodicals is derived largely from sales and from advertising; the press is the largest advertising medium in Britain.

SELF-REGULATION

The Press Complaints Commission was founded by the newspaper and magazine industry in January 1991 to replace the Press Council (established in 1953). It is a voluntary, non-statutory body set up to operate the press's self-regulation system following the Calcutt report in 1990 on privacy and related matters, when the industry feared that failure to regulate itself might lead to statutory regulation of the press. The performance of the Press Complaints Commission was reviewed after 18 months of operation (the *Calcutt Review of Press Self-Regulation*, presented to Parliament in January 1993) to determine whether statutory measures were required. No proposals for replacing the self-regulation system have been made to date. The Commission is funded by the industry through the Press Standards Board of Finance.

COMPLAINTS

The Press Complaints Commission's aims are to consider, adjudicate, conciliate, and resolve complaints of unfair treatment by the press; and to ensure that the press maintains the highest professional standards with respect for generally recognised freedoms, including freedom of expression, the public's right to know, and the right of the press to operate free from improper pressure. The Commission judges newspaper and magazine conduct by a code of practice drafted by editors, agreed by the industry and ratified by the Commission.

Seven of the Commission's members are editors of national, regional and local newspapers and magazines, and nine, including the chairman, are drawn from other fields. One member has been appointed Privacy Commissioner with special powers to investigate complaints about invasion of privacy.

PRESS COMPLAINTS COMMISSION, 1 Salisbury Square, London EC4Y Tel: 020-7353 1248. Fax: 020-7353 8355. Email: complaints@pcc.org.uk; Web: www.pcc.org.uk; *Chairman*, Sir Christopher Meyer, *Director*, G. Black

---

NEWSPAPERS

Newspapers are usually financially independent of any political party, though most adopt a political stance in their editorial comments, usually reflecting proprietorial influence. Ownership of the national and regional daily newspapers is concentrated in the hands of large corporations whose interests cover publishing and communications. The rules on cross-media ownership, as amended by the Broadcasting Act 1996, limit the extent to which newspaper organisations (with over 20 per cent of national circulation) may become involved in broadcasting.

There are about 14 daily and 14 Sunday national papers

and several hundred local papers that are published weekly or twice-weekly. Scotland, Wales and Northern Ireland all have at least one daily and one Sunday national paper.

Newspapers are usually published in either broadsheet or tabloid format. The 'quality' daily papers, e.g. those providing detailed coverage of a wide range of public matters, have a broadsheet format. The tabloid papers take a more popular approach and are more illustrated.

CIRCULATION (*net average for May 2002*)

National Daily Newspapers

Daily Express	939,417
Daily Mail	2,405,694
Daily Mirror	2,128,755
Daily Record	558,343
Daily Star	680,040
Daily Telegraph	1,001,692
Financial Times	479,832
Racing Post	84,024
The Guardian	400,452
The Independent	227,175
The Scotsman	78,666
The Star – Republic of Ireland	105,585
The Sun	3,459,026
The Times	706,930

National Sunday Newspapers

Independent on Sunday	233,521
Mail on Sunday	2,298,338
News of the World	3,864,915
Sunday Express	883,106
Sunday People	1,319,219
Scotland on Sunday	83,120
Sunday Mail	664,804
Sport First	54,051
Sunday Mirror	1,749,985
Sunday Sport	195,512
Sunday Telegraph	781,617
Sunday Times	1,399,754
The Business	93,652
The Observer	460,709

Source: Audit Bureau of Circulations Ltd, May 2002. For further information please see www.abc.org.uk

NATIONAL DAILY NEWSPAPERS

Please note: Circulation figures given in this list have been provided directly by the publication concerned and have been rounded to the nearest hundred.

DAILY EXPRESS, Ludgate House, 245 Blackfriars Road, London, SE1 9UX. Tel: 020-7928 8000. Fax: 020-7633 0244. Web: www.express.co.uk. Editor: Chris Williams. Circulation: 908,000

DAILY MAIL, Northcliffe House, 2 Derry Street, London W8 5TT. Tel: 020-7938 6000. Fax: 020-7937 3251. Web: www.dailymail.co.uk. Editor: Paul Dacre Circulation: 2,446,000

DAILY MIRROR, 1 Canada Square, Canary Wharf, London E14 5AP. Tel: 020-7293 3000. Fax: 020-7293 3405. Web: www.mirror.co.uk. Editor: Piers Morgan. Circulation: 2,109,000

DAILY STAR, Ludgate House, 245 Blackfriars, Road London SE1 9UX. Tel: 020-7928 8000. Fax: 020-7633 0244. Web: www.megastar.co.uk. Editor: Peter Hill. Circulation: 667,000.

DAILY TELEGRAPH, 1 Canada Square, Canary Wharf, London E14 5DT. Tel: 020-7538 5000. Fax: 020-7513 2506. Web: www.telegraph.co.uk. Editor: Charles Moore. Circulation: 1,006,000

FINANCIAL TIMES, 1 Southwark Bridge, London SE1 9HL. Tel: 020-7873 3000. Fax: 020-7873 3072. Web: www.ft.com. Editor: Andrew Gowers. Circulation: 494,000

MORNING STAR, Cape House, 787 Commercial Road, London E14 7HG. Tel: 020-7538 5181. Fax: 020-7538 5125. Web: www.poptel.org.uk/morning-star/. Editor: J. Haylett. Circulation: 5,000

RACING POST, 1 Canada Square, Canary Wharf, London E14 5AP. Tel: 020-7293 3000. Fax: 020-7293 3758. Web: www.racingpost.co.uk. Editor: Chris Smith. Circulation: 86,000

THE GUARDIAN, 119 Farringdon Road, London EC1R 3ER. Tel: 020-7278 2332. Fax: 020-7837 2114. Web: www.guardian.co.uk. Editor: A. Rusbridger. Circulation: 405,000

THE INDEPENDENT, Independent House, 191 Marsh Wall, London E14 9RS. Tel: 020-7005 2000 Fax: 020-7005 2999. Web: www.independent.co.uk. Editor-in-Chief: S. Kelner. Circulation: 227,000.

THE SCOTSMAN, Barclay House, 108 Holyrood Road, Edinburgh EH8 8AS. Tel: 0131-620 8620. Fax: 0131-620 8615/6. Web: www.scotsman.com. Editor: Iain Martin. Circulation: 79,000

THE SUN, 1 Virginia Street, London E1 9XR. Tel: 020-7782 4000. Fax: 020-7782 5605. Web: www.the-sun.co.uk. Editor: David Yelland. Circulation: 3,352,000

THE TIMES, The Times House, 1 Pennington Street, London E98 1TT. Tel: 020-7782 5000. Fax: 020-7782 5988. Web: www.thetimes.co.uk. Editor: R. Thomson. Circulation: 717,000

REGIONAL DAILY NEWSPAPERS

BERKSHIRE

READING EVENING POST, 8 Tessa Road, Reading RG1 8NS. Tel: 0118-918 3000. Fax: 0118-959 9363. Web: www.getreading.co.uk. Editor: A. Murrill. Circulation: 25,000

CAMBRIDGESHIRE

CAMBRIDGE EVENING NEWS, Winship, Road Milton, Cambridge CB4 6PP. Tel: 01223-434434. Fax: 01223-434415. Web: www.cambridge-news.co.uk Editor: C. Grant. Circulation: 40,800

PETERBOROUGH EVENING TELEGRAPH, New Priestgate House, 57 Priestgate, Peterborough PE1 1JW. Tel: 01733-555111. Fax: 01733-555188. Editor: K. Booth.

COUNTY DURHAM, CLEVELAND AND NORTH YORKSHIRE

NORTHERN ECHO, PO Box 14, Priestgate, Darlington DL1 1NF. Tel: 01325-381313. Fax: 01325-380539. Web: www.thisisthenortheast.co.uk. Editor: Peter Baron. Circulation: 62,800

CUMBRIA

NEWS AND STAR NEWSPAPER, House Dalston Road, Carlisle CA2 5UA. Tel: 01228-612600. Fax: 01228-612601. Web: www.newsandstar.co.uk. Editor: K. Sutton.

NORTH-WEST EVENING MAIL NEWSPAPER, House Abbey Road, Barrow-in-Furness LA14 5QS. Tel: 01229-821835. Fax: 01229-840164. Editor: S. Brauner. Circulation: 21,000

DERBYSHIRE

DERBY EVENING TELEGRAPH, Northcliffe House, Meadow Road, Derby DE1 2DW. Tel: 01332-291111. Fax: 01332-253011. Web: www.thisisderbyshire.co.uk. Editor: M. Norton.

DEVON

EVENING HERALD, 17 Brest Road, Derriford Business Park, Plymouth PL6 5AA. Tel: 01752-765500. Fax: 01752-765515. Web: www.thisisplymouth.co.uk. Editor: A. Qualtrough. Circulation: 48,000

EXPRESS AND ECHO, Heron Road, Sowton, Exeter EX2 7NF. Tel: 01392-442211. Fax: 01392-442294. Web: www.thisisexeter.co.uk. Editor: S. Hall.

HERALD EXPRESS, Harmsworth House, Barton Hill Road, Torquay TQ2 8JN. Tel: 01803-676000. Fax: 01803-676228. Web: www.thisissouthdevon.co.uk. Editor: B. Hanrahan. Circulation: 28,000

MORNING NEWS, 17 Brest Road, Derriford Business Park, Plymouth PL6 5AA. Tel: 01752-765500. Fax: 01752-765535. Editor: B. Williams. Circulation: 50,000

DORSET

DORSET ECHO, Fleet House, Hampshire Road, Granby Industrial Estate, Weymouth, Dorset DT4 9XD. Tel: 01305-830930. Fax: 01305-830802. Web: www.dorsetecho.co.uk. Editor: D. Murdock. Circulation: 20,700

THE DAILY ECHO, Richmond Hill, Bournemouth BH2 6HH. Tel: 01202-554601. Fax: 01202-297543. Web: www.thisisdorset.net. Editor: N. Butterworth. Circulation: 45,000

DURHAM, CLEVELAND AND NORTH YORKSHIRE

DARLINGTON AND STOCKTON TIMES, PO Box 14, Priestgate, Darlington DL1 1NF. Tel: 01325-381313. Web: www.thisisthenortheast.co.uk. Editor: Malcolm Warne. Circulation: 32,900

EAST SUSSEX, WEST SUSSEX, MID SUSSEX

THE ARGUS, Argus House, Crowhurst Road, Hollingury, Brighton BN1 8AR. Tel: 01273-544544. Fax: 01273-566114. Web: www.thisisbrightonandhove.co.uk. Editor: Simon Bradshaw. Circulation: 50,000

ESSEX

EVENING GAZETTE, Oriel House 43-44 North Hill, Colchester CO1 1TZ. Tel: 01206-506000. Fax: 01206-508274. Editor: Ms I. Kettle. Circulation: 28,200

GLOUCESTERSHIRE

GLOUCESTERSHIRE ECHO, 1 Clarence Parade, Cheltenham GL50 3NY. Tel: 01242-271900. Fax: 01242-271792. Web: www.thisisgloucestershire.co.uk. Editor: Ms A. Syvret. Circulation: 25,000

THE CITIZEN, St John's Lane, Gloucester GL1 2AY. Tel: 01452-424442. Fax: 01452-420664. Web: www.thisisgloucestershire.co.uk. Editor: Spencer Feeney. Circulation: 35,000

GREATER MANCHESTER

MANCHESTER EVENING NEWS, 164 Deansgate,
Manchester M3 3RN. Tel: 0161-832 7200.
Fax: 0161-832 5351.
Web: www.manchesteronline.co.uk.
Editor: P. Horrocks. Circulation: 168,000

HAMPSHIRE

THE NEWS, The News Centre, Hilsea, Portsmouth
PO2 9SX. Tel: 023-9266 4488. Fax: 023-9267 3363
Web: www.portsmouth.co.uk. Editor: M. Gilson.
Circulation: 68,000

KENT

MEDWAY TODAY, 395 High Street, Chatham, Kent
ME4 4PQ. Tel: 01634-830600. Fax: 01634-829484.
Web: www.kent-online.co.uk. Editor: Bob Dimond.

LANCASHIRE

BOLTON EVENING NEWS, Newspaper House,
Churchgate, Bolton BL1 1DE. Tel: 01204-522345.
Fax: 01204-365068. Web: www.thisisbolton.co.uk.
Editor: Steve Hughes. Circulation: 42,000
LANCASHIRE EVENING POST, Oliver's Place, Fulwood,
Preston PR2 9ZA. Tel: 01772-254841.
Fax: 01772-880173. Editor: S. Reynolds.
LANCASHIRE EVENING TELEGRAPH, Newspaper House,
High Street, Blackburn BB1 1HT. Tel: 01254-678678.
Fax: 01254-682185. Editor: K. Young.
WIGAN EVENING POST, Mart Land Mill, Mart Land
Mill Lane, Wigan WN5 0LX. Tel: 01942-227131.
Fax: 01942-226110. Editor: Ms G. Gray.
Circulation: 12,500

LEICESTERSHIRE

LEICESTER MERCURY, St George Street, Leicester LE1
9FQ. Tel: 0116-251 2512. Fax: 0116-262 4687.
Editor: N. Carter.

LINCOLNSHIRE

GRIMSBY EVENING TELEGRAPH, 80 Cleethorpe Road,
Grimsby DN31 3EH. Tel: 01472-360360.
Fax: 01472-352272. Editor: P. Moore.

LONDON

THE EVENING STANDARD, Northcliffe House, 2 Derry
Street, London W8 5TT. Tel: 020-7938 6000.
Fax: 020-7937 3745. Editor: V. Wadley.

MERSEYSIDE

DAILY POST, AND LIVERPOOL ECHO, PO Box 48, Old
Hall Street, Liverpool L69 3EB. Tel: 0151-227 2000.
Fax: 0151-236 4682. Web: www.icliverpool.co.uk.
Editor: Mark Dickinson. Circulation: 150,900

NORTH LINCOLNSHIRE

SCUNTHORPE TELEGRAPH, 4–5 Park Square, Scunthorpe
North, Lincolnshire DN15 6JH. Tel: 01724-273273.
Fax: 01724-273101. Editor: Michelle Lalor.
Circulation: 23,500

NORTHAMPTONSHIRE

Chronicle and Echo, Upper Mounts, Northampton NN1
3HR. Tel: 01604-467000. Fax: 01604-467190. Editor:
Mark Edwards. Circulation: 27,800

NOTTINGHAMSHIRE

NOTTINGHAM EVENING POST, Castle Wharf House,
Nottingham NG1 7EU. Tel: 0115-948 2000.
Fax: 0115-964 4032.
Web: www.thisisnottingham.co.uk.
Editor: G. Glen. Circulation: 95,000

OXFORDSHIRE

THE OXFORD MAIL, Newspaper House, Osney Mead,
Oxford OX2 0EJ. Tel: 01865-425262.
Fax: 01865-425554. Editor: James Mc Clure.

SHROPSHIRE

SHROPSHIRE STAR, Ketley, Telford TF1 5HU.
Tel: 01952-242424. Fax: 01952-254605.
Editor: A. Faber.

SOMERSET

BRISTOL EVENING POST, AND WESTERN DAILY PRESS,
Temple Way, Bristol BS99 7HD. Tel: 0117-934 3000.
Fax: 0117-934 3571. Web: www.epost.co.uk.

STAFFORDSHIRE

BURTON MAIL, 65–68 High Street, Burton on Trent,
DE14 1LE. Tel: 01283-512345. Fax: 01283-510075.
Editor-in-Chief: Paul Hazeldine.
THE SENTINEL, Sentinel House, Etruria,
Stoke-on-Trent, ST1 5SS.
Tel: 01782-602525. Fax: 01782-280781.
Web: www.thisisstaffordshire.co.uk.
Editor: Sean Dooley. Circulation: 81,500

SUFFOLK AND NORTH ESSEX

EAST ANGLIAN DAILY TIMES, AND EVENING STAR,
30 Lower Brook Street, Ipswich IP4 1AN.
Tel: 01473-230023. Fax: 01473-211391.
Web: www.archant.co.uk.
Editor: T. Hunt and N. Pickover. Circulation: 44,000

TYNE AND WEAR

SUNDERLAND ECHO, Echo House, Pennywell,
Sunderland SR4 9ER. Tel: 0191-5015800.
Fax: 0191-5345975.
Web: www.sunderlandtoday.co.uk. Editor: A. Smith.
Circulation: 52,400

WARWICKSHIRE

HEARTLAND EVENING NEWS, Newspaper House, 11–15
Newtown Road, Nuneaton CV11 4HP.
Tel: 02476-353534. Fax: 02476-353481.
Editor: Tony Parratt. Circulation: 8,000

WEST MIDLANDS

EXPRESS AND STAR, 51–53 Queen Street,
Wolverhampton WV1 1ES. Tel: 01902-313131.
Fax: 01902-710106. Web: www.westmidlands.com.
Editor: A. Faber.
THE BIRMINGHAM POST, AND BIRMINGHAM EVENING
MAIL, 28 Colmore Circus, Queensway, Birmingham
B4 6AX. Tel: 0121-236 3366. Fax: 0121-233 0271.
Web: www.icbirmingham.co.uk. Editor: D. Mason
(Post) R. Borrell (Mail).

WILTSHIRE

SWINDON EVENING ADVERTISER, Newspaper House,
100 Victoria Road, Swindon SN1 3BE.
Tel: 01793-528144. Fax: 01793-542434.
Web: www.thisiswiltshire.co.uk.

WORCESTERSHIRE

WORCESTER EVENING, NEWS Hylton Road, Worcester
WR2 5JX. Tel: 01905-748200. Fax: 01905-748009.
Web: www.thisisworcester.co.uk. Editor: S. Gilbert.
Circulation: 23,200

YORKSHIRE

EVENING PRESS, PO Box 29, 76–86 Walmgate, York

YO1 9YN. Tel: 01904-653051. Fax: 01904-612853.
Web: www.thisisyork.co.uk. Editor: Ms L. Page.
Circulation: 42,200
HALIFAX EVENING COURIER, PO Box 19, Courier
Buildings, King Cross Street, Halifax HX1 2SF.
Tel: 01422-260200. Fax: 01422-260341.
Web: www.halifaxtoday.co.uk. Editor: E. Riley.
Circulation: 26,000
HUDDERSFIELD DAILY EXAMINER, PO Box A26, Queen
Street South, Huddersfield, HD1 2TD.
Tel: 01484-430000. Fax: 01484-437789.
Web: www.examiner.co.uk. Editor: R. Wright.
Circulation: 36,000
HULL DAILY MAIL, Blundell's Corner, Beverley Road,
Hull HU3 1XS. Tel: 01482-327111.
Fax: 01482-584353. Web: www.thisishull.co.uk.
Editor: J. Meehan. Circulation: 84,800
SCARBOROUGH EVENING NEWS, 17–23 Aberdeen Walk,
Scarborough YO11 1BB. Tel: 01723-363636.
Fax: 01723-354092.
Web: www.scarborougheveningnews.co.uk.
Editor: D. Penman. Circulation: 17,200
SHEFFIELD STAR, York Street, Sheffield S1 1PU.
Tel: 0114-276 7676. Fax: 0114-272 5978.
Web: www.thisissheffield.net. Editor: P. Charlton.
YORKSHIRE EVENING POST, PO Box 168, Wellington
Street, Leeds LS1 1RF. Tel: 0113-243 2701.
Fax: 0113-244 3430.
Web: www.yorkshire-evening-post.co.uk.
YORKSHIRE POST, PO Box 168, Wellington Street, Leeds
LS1 1RF. Tel: 0113-243 2701. Fax: 0113-238 8537.
Web: www.yorkshirepost.co.uk. Editor: T. Watson.

WALES

EVENING LEADER, Mold Business Park, Wrexham Road,
Mold CH7 1XY. Tel: 01352-707707.
Fax: 01352-700048. Web: www.nwn.co.uk.
Editor: Mark Rossiter.
SOUTH WALES ARGUS, Cardiff Road, Maesglas,
Newport NP20 3QN. Tel: 01633-810000.
Fax: 01633-777002. Editor: Gerry Keighley.
SOUTH WALES ECHO, Thomson House, Havelock
Street, Cardiff CF10 1XR. Tel: 029-2058 3622.
Fax: 029-2058 3624. Editor: Alistair Milburn.
Circulation: 70,900
WESTERN MAIL, Thomson House, Havelock Street,
Cardiff CF10 1XR. Tel: 029-2058 2022.
Fax: 029-2058 3652. Web: www.icwalls.co.uk.
Editor: N. Fowler.

SCOTLAND

COURIER AND ADVERTISER, 80 Kingsway, East Dundee
DD4 8SL. Tel: 01382-223131. Fax: 01382-454590.
Web: www.thecourier.co.uk. Editor: A. Arthur.
Circulation: 88,560
DAILY RECORD, 1 Central Quay, Glasgow G3 8DA.
Tel: 0141-248 7000. Fax: 0141-242 7802.
Web: www.record-mail.co.uk.
Editor-in-Chief: Peter Cox. Circulation: 650,000
EDINBURGH EVENING NEWS, Barclay House,
108 Holyrood Road, Edinburgh EH8 8AS.
Tel: 0131-620 8620. Fax: 0131-620 8616.
Web: www.scotsman.com. Editor: J. McLellan.
Circulation: 75,000
EVENING EXPRESS, PO Box 43, Lang Stracht, Mastrick,
Aberdeen AB15 6DF. Tel: 01224-690222.
Fax: 01224-344106.
Web: www.thisisnorthscotland.co.uk.
Editor: D. Martin. Circulation: 65,600

EVENING TELEGRAPH AND POST, 80 Kingsway east,
Dundee DD4 8SL. Tel: 01382-223131.
Fax: 01382-454590.
Web: www.eveningtelegraph.co.uk.
Editor: A. Proctor. Circulation: 29,200
EVENING TIMES, 200 Renfield Street, Glasgow G2 3PR.
Tel: 0141-302700. Fax: 0141-302660.
Web: www.eveningtimes.co.uk. Editor: C. McGhee.
Circulation: 110,600
PRESS AND JOURNAL, PO Box 43, Lang Stracht,
Mastrick, Aberdeen AB15 6DF. Tel: 01224-690222.
Fax: 01224-663575.
Web: www.thisisnorthscotland.co.uk.
Editor: D. Tucker. Circulation: 100,400

NORTHERN IRELAND

BELFAST TELEGRAPH, 124–144 Royal Avenue, Belfast
BT1 1EB. Tel: 028-9026 4000. Fax: 028-9055 4506.
Web: www.belfasttelegraph.co.uk. Editor: E. Curran.
Circulation: 111,600

CHANNEL ISLANDS

GUERNSEY PRESS AND STAR, PO Box 57, Guernsey
GY1 3BW. Tel: 01481-240240. Fax: 01481-240235.
Web: www.guernsey-press.com. Editor: R. Digard.
Circulation: 16,100.
JERSEY EVENING POST, PO Box 582, Five Oaks, St
Saviour, Jersey JE4 8XQ. Tel: 01534-611611.
Fax: 01534-611622. Web: www.thisisjersey.com. Editor:
Chris Bright. Circulation: 23,000

WEEKLY NEWSPAPERS

THE BUSINESS, The Business PA News Centre, 4th
Floor, 292 Vauxhall Bridge Road, London SW1V 1SS.
Tel: 020-7961 0000. Fax: 020-7961 0101.
Editor: Ian Watson.
COMMUNITY TELEGRAPH, 124–144 Royal Avenue,
Belfast BT1 1EB. Editor: Robin Young.
Circulation: 142,100
INDEPENDENT ON SUNDAY, Independent House, 191
Marsh Wall, London E14 9RS. Tel: 020-7005 2000.
Fax: 020-7005 2047. Web: www.independent.co.uk.
Editor: Tristan Davies. Circulation: 232,000
MAIL ON SUNDAY, Northcliffe House, 2 Derry Street,
London W8 5TS. Tel: 020-7938 6000.
Fax: 020-7937 7896. Web: www.mailonsunday.co.uk.
Editor: Peter Wright. Circulation: 2,349,000
NEWS OF THE WORLD, 1 Virginia Street, London
E98 1NW. Tel: 020-7782 4000. Fax: 020-7583 9504.
Web: www.newsoftheworld.co.uk.
Editor: Ms R. Wade. Circulation: 3,922,000
THE OBSERVER, 119 Farringdon Road, London
EC1R 3ER. Tel: 020-7278 2332. Fax: 020-7713 4250.
Web: www.observer.co.uk. Editor: Roger Alton.
Circulation: 460,000
SCOTLAND ON SUNDAY, 108 Holyrood Road, Edinburgh
EH8 8AS. Tel: 0131-620 8620. Fax: 0131-523 0313.
Web: www.scotlandonsunday.com.
Editor: Margot Wilson. Circulation: 86,000
SUNDAY EXPRESS, Ludgate House, 245 Blackfriars Road,
London SE1 9UX. Tel: 020-7928 8000.
Fax: 020-7633 0244. Web: www.express.co.uk.
Editor: Martin Townsend. Circulation: 902,000
SUNDAY LIFE, 122–144 Royal Avenue, Belfast BT1 1EB.
Editor: Martin Lindsay. Circulation: 94,700
SUNDAY MAIL, 1 Central Quay, Glasgow G3 8DA.
Tel: 0141-309 3000. Fax: 0141-309 3587.
Web: www.sundaymail.co.uk. Editor: Allan Rennie.
Circulation: 2,422,000

SUNDAY MIRROR, 1 Canada Square, Canary Wharf, London E14 5AP. Tel: 020-7293 3000. Fax: 020-7293 3405. Web: www.sundaymirror.co.uk. Editor: Tina Weaver. Circulation: 1,762,000

SUNDAY PEOPLE, 1 Canada Square, Canary Wharf, London E14 5AP. Tel: 020-7293 3000. Fax: 020-7293 3405. Web: www.mirror.co.uk. Editor: Neil Wallis. Circulation: 1,340,000

SUNDAY SPORT, 840B Melton Road, Thurmaston, Leicester LE4 8BJ. Tel: 0116-269 4892. Fax: 0116-264 0948. Web: www.sundaysport.com. Editor: Tony Livesey. Circulation: 196,000

THE SUNDAY POST, Courier Place, Dundee DD1 9QJ. Tel: 01382-223131. Fax: 01382-201064. Web: www.sundaypost.com. Editor: D. Pollington. Circulation: 692,000

THE SUNDAY TELEGRAPH, 1 Canada Square, Canary Wharf, London E14 5DT. Tel: 020-7538 5000. Fax: 020-7512 2504. Web: www.telegraph.co.uk. Editor: Dominic Lawson. Circulation: 779,000

THE SUNDAY TIMES, 1 Pennington Street, London E98 1ST. Tel: 020-7782 5000. Fax: 020-7782 5046. Web: www.sunday-times.co.uk. Editor: John Witherow. Circulation: 1,426,000

WALES ON SUNDAY, Thomson, House, Havelock Street, Cardiff CF1 1XR. Tel: 029-2058 3733. Fax: 029-2058 3725. Web: www.icwales.co.uk. Editor: A. Edmunds. Circulation: 65,000

WEEKLY NEWS, Courier Place, Dundee DD1 9QJ. Tel: 01382-223131. Fax: 01382-201390. Web: www.dcthomson.co.uk. Editor: David Burness. Circulation: 140,000

RELIGIOUS PAPERS

BAPTIST TIMES, PO Box 54, 129 The Broadway, Didcot, Oxon OX11 8XB. Tel: 01235-517670. Fax: 01235-517678. Editor: John Capon. Circulation: 8,750

CATHOLIC HERALD, Herald House, Lambs Passage, Bunhill Row, London EC1Y 8TQ. Tel: 020-7588 3101. Fax: 020-7256 9728. Web: www.catholicherald.co.uk. Editor: Dr William Oddie. Circulation: 43,000

THE CHURCH OF ENGLAND NEWSPAPER, 20-26 Brunswick Place, London N1 6DZ. Tel: 020-7417 5800. Fax: 020-7216 6410. Web: www.churchnewspaper.com. Editor: C. Blakely. Circulation: 8,500

CHURCH OF IRELAND GAZETTE, 3 Wallace Avenue, Lisburn, Co. Antrim BT27 4AA. Tel: 028-9267 5743. Fax: 028-9267 5743. Web: www.gazette.ireland.anglican.org. Editor: Canon Ian Ellis. Circulation: 5,000

CHURCH TIMES, 33 Upper Street, London N1 0PN. Tel: 020-7359 4570. Fax: 020-7226 3073. Web: www.churchtimes.co.uk. Editor: Paul Handley. Circulation: 37,000

ENGLISH CHURCHMAN, 22 Fitch drive, Brighton BN2 4HX. Tel: 01273-818555. Fax: 01273-386362. Editor: Dr. N. Malcolm.

THE FRIEND, New Premier House, 150 Southampton Row, London WC1B 5BQ. Tel: 020-7387 7549. Fax: 020-7387 9382. Web: www.thefriend.org. Editor: H. Albright. Circulation: 5,000

GOOD NEWS PAPER, 50 Loxwood Avenue, Worthing, West Sussex BN14 7RA. Tel: 01903-824174. Fax: 01903-824174. Editor: D. Banks. Circulation: 24,000

JEWISH TELEGRAPH, Telegraph House, 11 Park Hill, Bury Old Road, Prestwich, Manchester M25 0HH. Tel: 0161-740 9321. Fax: 0161-740 9325. Web: www.jewishtelegraph.com. Editor: P. Harris. Circulation: 80,000

LIFE AND WORK, Church of Scotland, 121 George Street, Edinburgh EH2 4YN. Tel: 0131-225 5722. Fax: 0131-240 2207. Web: www.lifeandwork.org. Editor: Ms. M. Armstrong. Circulation: 44,100

METHODIST RECORDER, 122 Golden Lane, London EC1Y 0TL. Tel: 020-7251 8414. Fax: 020-7608 3490. Web: www.methodistrecorder.co.uk. Editor: Ms M. Sleight. Circulation: 21,000

ORTHODOX OUTLOOK, 42 Withens Lane, Wallasey, Wirral CH45 7NN. Tel: 0151-639 6509. Fax: 0151-200 6359. Editor: Fr P. Sanders. Circulation: 3,500

PRESBYTERIAN HERALD, Church House, Fisherwick Place, Belfast BT1 6DW. Tel: 028-9032 2284. Fax: 028-9024 8377. Web: www.presbyterianireland.org. Editor: Revd A. Clarke. Circulation: 15,000

QUAKER MONTHLY, Friends House, Euston Road, London NW1 2BJ. Tel: 020-7663 1000. Fax: 020-7663 1001. Editor: Trish Carn. Circulation: 2,000

REFORM, United Reformed Church, 86 Tavistock Place, London WC1H 9RT. Tel: 020-7916 8630. Fax: 020-7916 2021. Web: www.urc.org.uk. Editor: D. Lawrence. Circulation: 13,000

SCOTTISH CATHOLIC OBSERVER, 19 Waterloo Street, Glasgow G2 6BT. Tel: 0141-221 4956. Fax: 0141-221 4546. Web: www.scottishcatholicobserver.com. Editor: Harry Conroy. Circulation: 41,200

THE SIKH COURIER INTERNATIONAL, World Sikh Foundation, 33 Wargrave Road, Harrow, Middx HA2 8LL. Tel: 020-8864 9228. Editor: Mrs H. Bharara. Circulation: 1,000

THE SIKH MESSENGER, 43 Dorset Road, London SW19 3EZ. Tel: 020-8540 4148. Editor: I. Singh, OBE. Circulation: 3,000

THE TABLET, 1 King Street Cloisters, Clifton Walk, London W6 0QZ. Tel: 020-8748 8484. Fax: 020-8748 1550. Web: www.thetablet.co.uk. Editor: J. Wilkins. Circulation: 20,300

THE WAR CRY, 101 Newington Causeway, London SE1 6BN. Tel: 020-7367 4900. Fax: 020-7367 4710. Web: www.salvationarmy.org.uk/warcry. Editor: Maj. N. Bovey. Circulation: 66,000

PERIODICALS

CONSUMER PERIODICALS

AMATEUR GARDENING, Westover House, West Quay Road, Poole, Dorset BH15 1JG. Tel: 01202-440840. Fax: 01202-440860. Editor: Tim Rumball. Circulation: 63,000

AMATEUR PHOTOGRAPHER, King's Reach Tower, Stamford Street, London SE1 9LS. Tel: 020-7261 5100. Fax: 020-7261 5404. Web: www.amateurphotographer.com. Editor: G. Coward-Williams. Circulation: 30,000

ANGLING TIMES, Bushfield House, Orton Centre, Peterborough PE2 5UW. Tel: 01733-232600. Fax: 01733-465844. Circulation: 70,000

ARENA, 3rd Floor, Block A, Exmouth House, Pine Street, London EC1R 0JL. Tel: 020-7689 7500. Fax: 020-7689 7514. Editor: Anthony Noguera. Circulation: 50,000

ART MONTHLY, 4th Floor, 28 Charing Cross Road, London WC2H 0DB. Tel: 020-7240 0389. Fax: 020-7240 0389. Web: www.artmonthly.co.uk. Editor: Ms P. Bickers. Circulation: 6,000

ATHLETICS WEEKLY, Descartes Publishing Ltd, 83 Park Road, Peterborough PE1 2TN. Tel: 01733-898440.

Fax: 01733-898441. Web: www.athleticsweekly.com.
Editor: Jason Henderson.

BBC GARDENERS' MAGAZINE, Woodlands, Room
AG185, 80 Wood Lane, London W12 0TT.
Tel: 020-8433 3959. Fax: 020-8433 3986.
Web: www.gardenersworld.co.uk. Editor: A. Pasco.

BBC GOOD FOOD MAGAZINE, Woodlands,
80 Wood Lane, London W12 0TT. Tel: 020-8433 2000.
Fax: 020-8433 3931. Editor: O. Murrin.
Circulation: 322,600

BBC HOMES AND ANTIQUES, BBC Worldwide,
Woodlands, 80 Wood Lane, London W12 0TT.
Tel: 020-8433 3490. Fax: 020-8433 3867.
Editor: Ms J. Hall. Circulation: 175,000

BBC WILDLIFE MAGAZINE, Broadcasting House,
Whiteladies Road, Bristol, BS8 2LR.
Tel: 0117-973 8402. Fax: 0117-946 7075.
Editor: Ms R. Kidman Cox. Circulation: 50,800

BEST, 33 Broadwick Street, London W1.
Tel: 020-7519 5500. Fax: 020-7519 5508.
Editor: L. Court.

BIKE, Media House, Lynch Wood, Peterborough
PE2 6EA. Tel: 01733-468000. Fax: 01733-468196.
Editor: Tim Thompson. Circulation: 95,300

BIRD WATCHING, Emap Active, Bretton Court, Bretton,
Peterborough PE3 8DZ. Tel: 01733-264666.
Fax: 01733-282654. Editor: David Cromack.

BIRDS, RSPB, The Lodge, Sandy, Beds SG19 2DL.
Tel: 01767-680551. Fax: 01767-683262.
Web: www.rspb.org.uk. Editor: R. A. Hume.
Circulation: 596,800

BOXING MONTHLY, 40 Morpeth Road, London E9 7LD.
Tel: 020-8986 4141. Fax: 020-8986 4145.
Web: www.boxing-monthly.co.uk. Editor: G. Leach.
Circulation: 30,000

BRIDES, Vogue House, Hanover Square, London
W1S 1JU. Tel: 020-7499 9080. Fax: 020-7460 6369.
Web: www.bridesuk.net. Editor: Sandra Boler.
Circulation: 61,500

BRITISH PHILATELIC BULLETIN, Royal Mail, 2–14
Bunhill Row, London EC1Y 8HQ. Fax: 020-7847 3359.
Web: www.royalmail.com. Editor: J. Holman.
Circulation: 23,000

CAMPING AND CARAVANNING, Greenfields House,
Westwood Way, Coventry CV4 8JH.
Tel: 024-7669 4995. Fax: 024-7685 6722.
Web: www.campingandcaravanningclub.co.uk.
Editor: N. Harding. Circulation: 157,700

CAR MAGAZINE, 3rd Floor, Priory Court,
30–32 Farringdon Lane, London EC1R 3AU.
Tel: 020-7017 3542. Fax: 020-7017 3530.
Editor: G. Fountain. Circulation: 122,800

CHAT, King's Reach Tower, Stamford Street, London
SE1 9LS. Tel: 020-7261 6565. Fax: 020-7261 6534.
Web: www.ipcmedia.com. Editor: Paul Merrill.
Circulation: 495,000

CLASSIC & SPORTS CAR, Somerset House, Somerset
Road, Teddington, Middx TW11 8RT.
Tel: 020-8267 5399. Fax: 020-8267 5318.
Editor: J. Elliott. Circulation: 91,200

COARSE FISHERMAN, 67 Tyrrell Street, Leicester LE3 5SB.
Tel: 0116-251 1277. Fax: 0116-251 1335.
Editor: S. Dexter.

COMPANY, National Magazine House, 72 Broadwick
Street, London W1V 2BP. Tel: 020-7439 5000.
Fax: 020-7439 5117. Web: www.company.co.uk.
Editor: S. Baker. Circulation: 260,000

COMPUTER SHOPPER, Neach Hill, Long Lane, Cosford,
Nr Shifnal TF11 8PJ. Tel: 01902 372999.
Fax: 01902 374001. Web: www.shopperlabs.com.
Editor: J. Spencer.

COSMOPOLITAN, National Magazine House,
72 Broadwick Street, London W1V 2BP.
Tel: 020-7439 5000. Fax: 020-7439 5016.
Web: www.natmags.co.uk. Editor: Lorraine Candy.
Circulation: 463,000

COUNTRY HOMES & INTERIORS, King's Reach Tower,
Stamford Street, London SE1 9LS. Tel: 020-7261 6451.
Fax: 020-7261 6895. Editor: Mrs D. Barker.

COUNTRY LIFE, King's Reach Tower, Stamford Street,
London SE1 9LS. Tel: 020-7261 7058. Fax: 020-7261
5139. Web: www.countrylife.co.uk. Editor: C. Aslet.
Circulation: 46,000

COUNTRY LIVING MAGAZINE, National Magazine
House, 72 Broadwick Street, London W1F 9EP.
Tel: 020-7439 5000. Fax: 020-7439 5093.
Web: www.natmags.co.uk. Editor: Ms S. Smith.
Circulation: 150,000

CYCLING WEEKLY, Focus House, Dingwall Avenue,
Croydon CR9 2TA. Tel: 020-8774 0811.
Fax: 020-8774 0952. Editor: R. Garbutt.
Circulation: 31,000

DALESMAN, Stable Courtyard, Broughton Hall,
Skipton, N. Yorks BD23 3AE. Tel: 01756-701381.
Fax: 01756-701326. Web: www.dalesman.co.uk.
Editor: T. Fletcher. Circulation: 50,600

DANCE THEATRE JOURNAL, Laban Centre London,
Laurie Grove, London SE14 6NH.
Tel: 020-8692 4070. Fax: 020-8694 8749.
Web: www.dancetheatrejournal.co.uk.
Editor: I. Bramley. Circulation: 2,000

DANCE TODAY, 45–47 Clerkenwell Green, London
EC1R 0EB. Tel: 020-7250 3006. Fax: 020-7253 6679.
Editor: Bronya Seifert. Circulation: 3,000

DANCING TIMES, 45–47 Clerkenwell Green, London
EC1R 0EB. Tel: 020-7250 3006 Fax: 020-7253 6679.
Web: www.dancing-times.co.uk
Editor: Ms Mary Clarke.

DAZED AND CONFUSED, 112–116 Old Street, London
EC1V 9BG. Web: www.confused.co.uk.
Editor: Rachel Newsome.

DOG WORLD, Somerfield House, Wotton Road,
Ashford, Kent TN23 6LW. Tel: 01233-621877.
Fax: 01233-645669. Web: www.dogworld.co.uk.
Editor: S. Parsons.

ELLE, Endeavour House, 189 Shaftesbury Avenue,
London WC2H 8JG. Tel: 020-7437 9011.
Fax: 020-7208 3599. Editor: Sarah Bailey.
Circulation: 210,000

ELLE DECORATION, Endeavour House, 189 Shaftesbury
Avenue, London WC2H 8JG.

EMPIRE, Endeavour House, 189 Shaftesbury Avenue,
London WC2H 8JG. Tel: 020-7437 9011.
Fax: 020-7859 8613. Web: www.empireonline.co.uk.
Editor: Ms E. Cochrane. Circulation: 519,000

ESQUIRE, National Magazine House, 72 Broadwick
Street, London W1V 2BP. Tel: 020-7439 5000.
Fax: 020-7312 3920. Web: www.esquire.co.uk.
Editor: P. Howarth.

EXCHANGE AND MART, Link House, 25 West Street,
Poole, Dorset BH15 1LL. Tel: 01202-445000.
Fax: 01202-445245. Web: www.ixm.co.uk.

FAMILY CIRCLE, King's Reach Tower, Stamford Street,
London SE1 9LS. Tel: 020-7261 6195.
Fax: 020-7261 5929. Editor: Ms G. Carter.
Circulation: 230,000

FHM, Happin House, 4 Winsley Street, London
W1W 8HF. Tel: 020-7436 1515. Fax: 020-7343 3000.
Web: www.fhm.com. Editor: David Davies.

FILM REVIEW, 9 Blades Court, Deodar Road, London
SW15 2NU. Tel: 020-8875 1520. Fax: 020-8875 1588.
Web: www.visimag.com. Editor: N. Corry.
Circulation: 45,000

GARDEN NEWS, Bretton Court, Bretton, Peterborough
PE3 8DZ. Tel: 01733-264666. Fax: 01733-282695.
Editor: Sarah Page. Circulation: 62,000
GAY TIMES, Ground Floor, Worldwide House,
116–134 Bayham Street, London NW1 0BA.
Tel: 020-7482 2576. Fax: 020-7284 0329.
Web: www.gaytimes.co.uk. Editor: V. Powell.
GEOGRAPHICAL JOURNAL, Royal Geographical Society,
1 Kensington Gore, London SW7 2AR. Tel: 020-7591
3026. Fax: 020-7591 3001. Web: www.rgs.org.
Editor: Prof. A. Millington. Circulation: 8,500
GOLF WORLD, Bushfield House, Orton Centre,
Peterborough PE3 8DZ. Tel: 01733-237111.
Fax: 01733-288025. Editor: Neil Pope.
Circulation: 70,000
GQ, Vogue House, Hanover Square, London W1S 1JU.
Tel: 20-7499 9080. Fax: 020-7495 1679.
Editor: D. Jones. Circulation: 150,000
GRAMOPHONE, Haymarket Magazines Ltd,
38–42 Hampton Road, Teddington, Middx TW11 0JE.
Tel: 020-8267 5000. Fax: 020-8267 5844.
Web: www.gramophone.co.uk. Editor: J. Jolly.
Circulation: 50,320
GRANTA, 2–3 Hanover, Yard, Noel Road, London N1
8BE. Tel: 020-7704 9776. Fax: 020-7704 0474.
Web: www.granta.com. Editor: Ian Jack.
GUIDING MAGAZINE, 17–19 Buckingham Palace Road,
London SW1W 0PT. Tel: 020-7592 821.
Fax: 020-7828 5791. Web: www.guides.org.uk.
Acting Editor: Ms V. Wheater. Circulation: 80,000
HARPERS AND QUEEN, National Magazine House,
72 Broadwick Street, London W1V 2BP.
Tel: 020-7439 5000. Fax: 020-7439 5482.
Editor: Lucy Yeomans.
HEAT, Endeavour House, 189 Shaftesbury Avenue,
London WC2H 8JG. Tel: 020-7437 9011.
Fax: 020-7208 3709.
HELLO!, 69–71 Upper Ground, London SE1 9PQ.
Tel: 020-7667 8700. Fax: 020-7667 8716.
Web: www.hellomagazine.com. Editor: Phil Hall.
Circulation: 527,000
HISTORY TODAY, 20 Old Compton Street, London
W1D 4TW. Tel: 020-7534 8000.
Web: www.historytoday.com. Editor: P. Furtado.
Circulation: 29,500
HORSE AND HOUND, Room 2018, King's Reach Tower,
Stamford Street, London SE1 9LS.
Tel: 020-7261 6315. Fax: 020-7261 5429.
Web: www.horseandhound.co.uk.
Editor: Mark Hedges. Circulation: 69,000
HOUSE BEAUTIFUL, National Magazine House,
72 Broadwick Street, London W1F 9EP.
Tel: 020-7439 5000. Fax: 020-7439 5625.
Web: www.housebeautiful.co.uk.
Editor: Sarah Whelan. Circulation: 192,400
I-D MAGAZINE, 124 Tabernacle Street, London EC2A
4SA. Tel: 020-7490 9710. Fax: 020-7251 2225.
Editor: Avril Mair.
IDEAL HOME, King's Reach Tower, Stamford Street,
London SE1 9LS. Tel: 020-7261 6474.
Fax: 020-7261 6697.
IN BRITAIN, Glen House, Stag Place, Victoria, London
SW1E 5AQ. Tel: 020-7233 9191. Fax: 020-7630 8084.
Web: www.inbritain.co.uk. Editor: Andrea Spain.
Circulation: 44,000
IRISH POST, Cambridge House, Cambridge Grove,
London W6 0LE. Tel: 020-8741 0649.
Fax: 020-8741 3382. Web: www.irishpost.co.uk.
Editor: Frank Murphy. Circulation: 40,000

JAZZ JOURNAL INTERNATIONAL, 3 & 3A Forest Road,
Loughton, Essex IG10 1DR. Tel: 020-8532 0456.
Fax: 020-8532 0440. Editor: Eddie Cook.
Circulation: 9,000
LABOUR RESEARCH, 78 Blackfriars Road, London SE1
8HF. Tel: 020-7928 3649. Fax: 020-7928 0621.
Web: www.lrd.org.uk. Editor: Ms C. Ruhemann.
Circulation: 6,000
LAND AND LIBERTY, Suite 427, London Fruit Exchange,
Brushfield Street, London E1 6EL.
Tel: 020-7377 8885. Fax: 020-7377 8686.
Web: www.henrygeorge.org.uk. Editor: Tony Vickers.
Circulation: 2,050
LITERARY REVIEW, 44 Lexington Street, London W1F
0LW. Tel: 020-7437 9392. Fax: 020-7734 1844.
Editor: Ms N. Sladek. Circulation: 12,000
LOADED, King's Reach Tower, Stamford Street, London
SE1 9LS. Tel: 020-7261 5000. Fax: 020-7261 5640.
Web: www.uploaded.com.
LONDON REVIEW OF BOOKS, 28 Little Russell Street,
London WC1A 2HN. Tel: 020-7209 1101.
Fax: 020-7209 1102. Web: www.lrb.co.uk.
Editor: Ms Mary-Kay Wilmers. Circulation: 38,600
MARIE CLAIRE, 2 Hatfields, London SE1 9PG.
Tel: 020-7261 5240. Fax: 020-7261 5277.
Web: www.jpcmedia.com.
Editor: Ms Marie O'Riordan.
MIZZ, 27th Floor, King's Reach Tower, Stamford Street,
London SE1 9LS. Tel: 020-7261 6319. Fax: 020-7261
6032. Editor: Sharon Christal. Circulation: 164,000
MONEYWISE, 11 Westferry Circus, Canary Wharf,
London E14 4HE. Tel: 020-7715 8000.
Fax: 020-7715 8181. Web: www.moneywise.co.uk.
Editor: David Ellis. Circulation: 92,700
MORE!, Endeavour House, 189 Shaftesbury Avenue,
London WC2H 8JG. Tel: 020-7208 3122.
Fax: 020-7208 3569. Editor: Marianne Jones.
MOTHER AND BABY, Greater London House,
Hampstead Road, London NW1 7EJ.
Tel: 020-7347 1869. Fax: 020-7347 1888.
Editor: D. Zur. Circulation: 796,000
MY WEEKLY, 80 Kingsway East, Dundee DD4 8SL.
Tel: 01382-223131. Fax: 01382-452491.
Editor: H. Watson. Circulation: 350,000
NATURE, The Macmillan Building, Porters South,
4 Crinan Street, London N1 9XQ. Tel: 020-7843 4960.
Fax: 020-7843 4998. Editor: P. Cambell.
NEEDLECRAFT, Future Publishing, 30 Monmouth Street,
Bath BA1 2BW. Tel: 01225-442244.
Fax: 01225-732398. Web: www.futurenet.co.uk.
Editor Ms D. Bradle. Circulation: 23,500
NEW INTERNATIONALIST, 55 Rectory Road, Oxford
OX4 1BW. Tel: 01865-728181. Fax: 01865-793152.
Web: www.newint.org. Editors: D. Ransom;
Ms V. Baird; K. Ainger. Circulation: 65,000
NEW MUSICAL EXPRESS (NME), King's Reach Tower,
Stamford Street, London SE1 9LS. Tel: 020-7261 6472.
Fax: 020-7261 5185.
NEW SCIENTIST, 151 Wardour Street, London W1F 8WE.
Tel: 020-7331 2702. Fax: 020-7331 2777.
Web: www.newscientist.com. Editor: Jeremy Webb.
Circulation: 135,000
NEW STATESMAN, 7th Floor, Victoria Station House,
191 Victoria Street, London SW1E 5NE. Tel: 020-7828
1232. Fax: 020-7828 1881.
Web: www.newstatesman.co.uk.
Editor: P. Wilby.
NEW WOMAN, Endeavour House, 189 Shaftesbury
Avenue, London WC2H 8JG. Tel: 020-7208 3456
Fax: 020-7208 3585 Editor: Ms S. Cremer.
Circulation: 305,000

NEWSWEEK, 18 Park Street, London W1K 2HQ.
Tel: 020-7629 8361. Fax: 020-7408 1403.
Web: www.newsweek.msnbc.com.
Editor: S. McGuire.

OK!, Ludgate House, 245 Blackfriars Road, London SE1
9UX. Tel: 020-7928 8000. Fax: 020-7579 4607.
Editor: N. McCarthy.

OPERA, 36 Black Lion Lane, London W6 9BE.
Tel: 020-8563 8893. Fax: 020-8563 8635.
Web: www.opera.co.uk. Editor: J. Allison.
Circulation: 11,000

OPERA NOW, 241 Shaftesbury Avenue, London WC2H
8TF. Tel: 020-7333 1740. Fax: 020-7333 1769.
Web: www.rhinegold.co.uk. Editor: A. Khandekar.
Circulation: 17,000

OUR DOGS, 5 Oxford Road, Station Approach,
Manchester M60 1SX. Tel: 0161-236 2660.
Fax: 0161-236 5534. Web: www.ourdogs.co.uk.
Editor: William Moores.

PEOPLE'S FRIEND, 80 Kingsway East, Dundee DD4 8SL.
Tel: 01382-223131. Fax: 01382-452491.
Editor: Ms Margaret McCoy.

PHILOSOPHY NOW, 43A Jerningham Rd, London SE14
5NQ. Tel: 020-7639 7314. Fax: 020-7639 7314.
Web: www.philosophynow.org.
Editor: Richard Lewis. Circulation: 11,000

POETRY REVIEW, 22 Betterton Street, London WC2H
9BX. Tel: 020-7420 9880. Fax: 020-7240 4818.
Web: www.poetrysoc.com. Editors: Robert Potts and
David Herd. Circulation: 4,500

PONY MAGAZINE, Haslemere House, Lower Street,
Haslemere, Surrey GU27 2PE. Tel: 01428-651551.
Fax: 01428-653888. Web: www.ponymag.com.
Editor: Ms J. Rising. Circulation: 32,000

PRACTICAL BOAT OWNER, Westover House, West Quay
Road, Poole, Dorset BH15 1JG. Tel: 01202-440820.
Fax: 01202-440860. Web: www.pbo.co.uk.
Editor: R. Witt. Circulation: 54,000

PRACTICAL HOUSEHOLDER, 53–79 Highgate Road,
London NW5 1TW. Tel: 020-7331 1000.
Fax: 020-7331 1269. Editor: J. Gowan.

PRACTICAL PHOTOGRAPHY, Bretton Court, Bretton,
Peterborough PE3 8DZ. Tel: 01733-264666.
Fax: 01733-465246. Editor: William Cheung.
Circulation: 72,000

PRIMA, 72 Broadwick Street, London W1F 9EP.
Tel: 020-7439 5000. Fax: 020-7312 4100.
Editor: Maire Fahey. Circulation: 380,000

PRIVATE EYE, 6 Carlisle Street, London W1D 3BN.
Tel: 020-7437 4017. Fax: 020-7437 0705.
Web: www.private-eye.co.uk. Editor: I. Hislop.
Circulation: 188,000

Q, Mappin House, 4 Winsley Street, London W1W 8HF.
Tel: 020-7312 8182. Fax: 020-7312 8247.
Web: www.q4music.com. Editor: D. Eccleston.
Circulation: 210,000

RAILWAY MODELLER, 33-39 Bowling Green, London
EC1V 7QP. Tel: 020-7505 8000. Fax: 020-7505 8185.
Web: www.4retail.net. Editor: Neill Denny.
Circulation: 15,000

RUGBY WORLD, King's Reach Tower, Stamford Street,
London SE1 9LS. Tel: 020-7261 6810.
Fax: 020-7261 5419. Web: www.rugbyworld.com.
Editor: P. Morgan. Circulation: 40,000

SCOTTISH FIELD, Royston House, Caroline Park,
Edinburgh EH5 1QJ. Tel: 0131-551 2942.
Fax: 0131-551 2938. Web: www.scottishfield.co.uk.
Editor: Archie Mackenzie. Circulation: 12,700

SCOUTING MAGAZINE, Gilwell House, Gilwell Park,
Chingford, London E4 7QW. Fax: 020-8433 7103.
Web: www.scouts.org.uk. Editor: Ms A. Sorensen
Thomson. Circulation: 20,000

SEA ANGLER, Emap Active, Bushfield House, Orton
Centre, Peterborough PE2 5UW. Tel: 01733-237111.
Fax: 01733-465658. Web: www.seaangler.8m.com.
Editor: Mel Russ. Circulation: 50.000

SHE, National Magazine House, 72 Broadwick Street,
London W1F 9EP. Tel: 020-7439 5000.
Fax: 020-7312 3981. Web: www.natmags.co.uk.
Editor: Ms Eve Cameron. Circulation: 176,100

SHOOTING TIMES AND COUNTRY MAGAZINE, King's
Reach Tower, Stamford Street, London SE1 9LS.
Tel: 020-7261 6180. Fax: 020-7261 7179.
Editor: Robert Gray.

SIGHT AND SOUND, Tower House, Sovereign Park,
Market Harborough, Leicester LE16 9EF.
Tel: 01858-438848

SMASH HITS, Mappin House, 4 Winsley Street, London
W1W 8HF. Tel: 020-7436 1515. Fax: 020-7636 5792.
Web: www.smashhits.net. Editor: Ms E. Jones.
Circulation: 200,200

TATLER, Vogue House, Hanover Square, London W1R
0AD. Tel: 020-7499 9080. Fax: 020-7495 0451.
Web: www.tatler.co.uk. Editor: G. Greig.

THE BIG ISSUE, 1/5 Wandsworth Road, London SW8
2LN. Tel: 020-7526 3200. Fax: 020-7526 3201.
www.thebigissue.com. Editor: M. Collins.
Circulation: 127,100

THE COUNTRYMAN, Sheep Street, Burford, Oxfordshire,
OX18 4LS. Tel: 01993-824424. Fax: 01993-822012.
Editor: David Horan. Circulation: 27,700

THE CRICKETER INTERNATIONAL, Ridge Farm,
Lamberhurst, Tunbridge Wells, Kent TN3 8ER.
Tel: 01892-893000. Fax: 01892-893023.
Web: www.cricketer.com. Editor: P. Perchard.

THE ECOLOGIST, Unit 18, Chelsea Wharf, 15 Lots Road,
London SW10 0QJ. Tel: 020-7351 3578.
Fax: 020-7351 3617. Web: www.theecologist.org.
Editor: Z. Goldsmith. Circulation: 25,000

THE ECONOMIST, 25 St James's Street, London SW1A
1HG. Tel: 020-7830 7000. Fax: 020-7839 2968.
Web: www.economist.com. Editor: B. Emmott.

THE FACE, 2nd Floor, Block A, Exmouth House, Pine
Street, London EC1R 0JL. Tel: 020-7689 9999.
Fax: 020-7689 0300. Editor: Neil Stevenson.
Circulation: 80,000

THE FIELD, King's Reach Tower, Stamford Street,
London SE1 9LS. Tel: 020-7261 5198. Fax: 020-7261
5358. Web: www.thefield.co.uk. Editor: J. Young.
Circulation: 33,700

THE GOOD SKI GUIDE, Profile Media Group, The
Interchange, Oval Road, London NW1 7DZ.
Tel: 020-7267 5000. Fax: 020-7267 1500.
Web: www.goodskiguide.com. Editor: Owain Jones.
Circulation: 40,000

THE LADY, 39–40 Bedford Street, London WC2E 9ER.
Tel: 020-7379 4717. Fax: 020-7836 4620.
Web: www.lady.co.uk. Editor: Ms A. Usden.
Circulation: 42,500

THE OLDIE, 65 Newman Street, London
Tel: 020-7436 8801. Fax: 020-7436 8804.
Web: www.theoldie.co.uk. Editor: R. Ingrams.

THE RACING CALENDAR, British Horseracing Board
Publications, c/o Weatherbys Group Ltd, Sanders
Road, Wellingborough, Northants NN8 4BX.
Tel: 01933-440077. Fax: 01933-270300.
Web: www.weatherbys-group.com.
Editor: G. Lingley. Circulation: 2,500

THE RAILWAY MAGAZINE, King's Reach Tower, Stamford Street, London SE1 9LS. Tel: 020-7261 5821. Fax: 020-7261 5269. Editor: N. Pigott. Circulation: 33,200

THE SPECTATOR, 56 Doughty Street, London WC1N 2LL. Tel: 020-7405 1706. Fax: 020-7242 0603. Web: www.spectator.co.uk. Editor: B. Johnson. Circulation: 58,400

THE STRAD, SMG Orpheus Publications, 3 Waterhouse Square, 138-142 Holbron, London EC1N 2NY. Tel: 020-7882 1040. Fax: 020 7882 1020. Web: www.thestrad.com. Editor: Ms J. Pieters. Circulation: 17,500

THE TIMES EDUCATIONAL SUPPLEMENT, Admiral House, 66–68 East Smithfield, London E1W 1BX. Tel: 020-7782 3000. Fax: 020-7782 3202. Web: www.tes.co.uk. Editor: Robert Doe. Circulation: 115,500

THE TIMES HIGHER EDUCATION SUPPLEMENT, Admiral House, 66–68 East Smithfield, London E1 9XY. Tel: 020-7782 3375. Fax: 020-7782 3300. Web: www.thes.co.uk.

THE TIMES LITERARY SUPPLEMENT, Admiral House, 66–68 East Smithfield, London E1W 1BX. Tel: 020-7782 3000. Fax: 020-7782 3100. Web: www.the-tls.co.uk. Editor: F. Mount. Circulation: 35,000

THE VOICE, 234-244 Blue Star House, Stockwell Road, London SW9 9UG. Tel: 020-7737 7377. Fax: 020-7274 8994. Web: www.voice-online.co.uk. Editor: M. Best.

THE WEEKLY TELEGRAPH, 1 Canada Square, Canary Wharf, London E14 5DT. Tel: 020-7538 5000. Fax: 020-7513 2509. Web: www.globalnetwork.co.uk. Editor: K. Jenkins. Circulation: 100,000

THE WORLD OF INTERIORS, Vogue House, Hanover Square, London W1S 1JU. Tel: 020-7499 9080. Fax: 020-7493 4013. Editor: R. Thomas. Circulation: 65,000

THIS ENGLAND, Alma House, 73 Rodney Road, Cheltenham, Glos GL50 1HT. Tel: 01242-537900. Fax: 01242-537901. Web: www.thisengland.co.uk. Editor: R. Faiers. Circulation: 175,000

TIME MAGAZINE, Brettenham House, Lancaster Place, London WC2E 7TL. Tel: 020-7490 4080. Fax: 020-7322 1230. Web: www.timeinc.com. Editors: Don and Ann Morrison. Circulation: 137,400

TIME OUT, Universal House, 251 Tottenham Court Road, London W1T 7AB. Tel: 020-7813 3000. Fax: 020-7813 6001. Web: www.timeout.com. Editor: Laura Lee Davies. Circulation: 94,100

TRIBUNE, 9 Arkwright Road, London NW3 6AN. Tel: 020-7433 6410. Web: www.tribuneuk.co.uk. Editor: Mark Seddon. Circulation: 10,000

TROUT AND SALMON, Bushfield House, Orton Centre, Peterborough PE2 5UW. Tel: 01733-237111. Fax: 01733-465820. Editor: S. Leventon. Circulation: 40,500

TV TIMES, King's Reach Tower, Stamford Street, London SE1 9LS. Tel: 020-7261 7000. Fax: 020-7261 7888. Web: www.unmissabletv.com. Editor: P. Genower.

VANITY FAIR, Vogue House, 1 Hanover Square, London W1S 1JU. Tel: 020-7499 9080. Fax: 020-7493 1962.

VIZ MAGAZINE, 9 Dallington Street, London EC1V 0BQ. Tel: 020-7687 7000. Web: www.viz.co.uk. Editors: S. Donald, G. Dury and S. Thorp.

VOGUE, Vogue House, Hanover Square, London W1S 1JU. Tel: 020-7499 9080. Fax: 020-7408 0559.

Web: www.vogue.co.uk. Editor: Ms A. Shulman.

WEATHER, Royal Meteorological Society, 104 Oxford Road, Reading RG1 7LL. Tel: 0118-956 8500. Fax: 0118-956 8571. Web: www.royal-met-soc.org.uk. Editor: Dr G. R. Bigg. Circulation: 5,000

WHAT CAR?, 60 Waldegrave Road, Teddington, Middx TW11 8LG. Tel: 020-8267 5688. Fax: 020-8267 5750. Web: www.whatcar.co.uk. Editor: Rob Aherne. Circulation: 143,000

WHICH?, 2 Marylebone Road, London NW1 4DF. Tel: 020-7770 7000. Fax: 020-7770 7485. Web: www.which.net. Editor: Helen Parker.

WOMAN, Low Rise, King's Reach Tower, Stamford Street, London SE1 9LS. Tel: 020-7261-7023. Fax: 020-7261 5997. Web: www.ipcmedia.com. Editor: Ms C. Russell. Circulation: 670,200

WOMAN'S OWN, King's Reach Tower, Stamford Street, London SE1 9LS. Tel: 020-7261 5500. Fax: 020-7261 5346. Editor: E. McAlonan. Circulation: 600,000

WOMAN'S WEEKLY, King's Reach Tower, Stamford Street, London SE1 9LS. Tel: 0870 444 5000. Fax: 020-7261 5322. Editor: Ms G. Sinclair.

YACHTING MONTHLY, King's Reach Tower, Stamford Street, London SE1 9LS. Tel: 020-7261 6040. Fax: 020-7261 7555. Web: www.yachtingmonthly.com. Editor: Ms Sarah Norbury. Circulation: 40,500

ZEST, National Magazine House, 72 Broadwick Street, London W1F 9EP. Tel: 020-7439 5000. Fax: 020-7312 3750. Web: www.zest.co.uk. Editor: Mrs Alison Plykkanen. Circulation: 110,100

TRADE, PROFESSIONAL AND ACADEMIC PERIODICALS

ACCOUNTANCY, King's Reach Tower, Stamford Street, London, SE1 9LS. Tel: 020-7833 3291. Fax: 020-7833 2085. Web: www.accountancymagazine.com.

ACCOUNTANCY AGE, VNU House, 32–34 Broadwick Street, London, W1A 2HG. Tel: 020-7316 9000. Fax: 020-7316 9250. Web: www.accountancyage.com. Editor: D. Wild. Circulation: 79,000

ANTIQUARIAN BOOK REVIEW (ABR), PO Box 97, High Wycombe, Bucks, HP14 4GH. Tel: 01494-562266. Fax: 01494-565533. Web: www.abmr.co.uk. Editor: E. Lewis.

ANTIQUES TRADE GAZETTE, 115 Shaftesbury Avenue, London, WC2H 8AD. Tel: 020-7420 6600. Fax: 020-7420 6605. Web: www.antiquestradegazette.com. Editor: I. Macquisten. Circulation: 19,400

APOLLO, 1 Castle Lane, London, SW1E 6DR. Tel: 020-7233 6640. Fax: 020-7630 7791. Web: www.apollomag.com. Editor: D. Ekserdjian.

BIOLOGIST, Institute of Biology, 20–22 Queensberry Place, London, SW7 2DZ. Tel: 020-7581 8333. Fax: 020-7823 9409. Web: www.iob.org. Editor: Mrs A. Bailey. Circulation: 17,000

BRAIN: A JOURNAL OF NEUROLOGY, Oxford University Press, Journals Division, Great Clarendon Street, Oxford, OX2 6DP. Tel: 01865-556767. Fax: 01865-353835. Web: www.brain.oupjournals.org. Editor: Prof. J. Newsom-Davis.

BREWING AND DISTILLING INTERNATIONAL, 52 Glenhouse Road, London, SE9 1JQ. Tel: 020-8859 4300. Fax: 020-8859 5813. Web: www.bdinews.com. Editor: B. Stevens. Circulation: 3,000

BRITISH BAKER, Quantum House, 19 Scarbrook Road, Croydon, CR9 1LX. Tel: 020-8565 4285. Fax: 020-8565 4303. Web: www.britishbaker.net. Editor: Sylvia Macdonald. Circulation: 6,500

BRITISH DENTAL JOURNAL, 64 Wimpole Street,, London, W1G 8YS. Tel: 020-7535 5830. Fax: 020-7535 5843. Web: www.bdj.co.uk. Editor: M. Grace.

BRITISH FOOD JOURNAL, 60–62 Toller Lane, Bradford, W. Yorks, BD8 9BY. Tel: 01274-777700. Fax: 01274-785200. Web: www.mcb.co.uk. Editor: Prof. Leo Pyle. Circulation: 1,500

BRITISH JOURNAL OF PHOTOGRAPHY, 39 Earlham Street, London, WC2H 9LT. Tel: 020-7306 7000. Fax: 020-7306 7017. Web: www.bjphoto.co.uk. Editor: J. Tarrant.

BRITISH JOURNAL OF PSYCHIATRY, Royal College of Psychiatrists, 17 Belgrave Square, London, SW1X 8PG. Tel: 020-7235 2351. Fax: 020-7259 6507. Web: www.rcpsych.ac.uk. Editor: Prof. G. Wilkinson.

BRITISH JOURNAL OF PSYCHOLOGY, British Psychological Society, St Andrews House, 48 Princess Road East, Leicester, LE1 7DR. Tel: 0116-252 9580. Fax: 0116-247 0787. Web: www.bps.org.uk. Editor: Prof. G. Underwood. Circulation: 2,800

BRITISH MEDICAL JOURNAL, British Medical Association, BMA House, Tavistock Square, London, WC1H 9JR. Tel: 020-7387 4499. Fax: 020-7383 6418. Web: www.bmj.com. Editor: Dr R. Smith. Circulation: 115,000

BRITISH TAX REVIEW, 100 Avenue Road, London, NW3 3PF. Tel: 020-7393 7000. Fax: 020-7393 7020. Editor: Erica Stary.

BUILDING, Exchange Tower, 2 Harbour Exchange Square, London, E14 9GE. Tel: 020-7560 4000. Fax: 020-7560 4014. Editor: Adrian Barrick.

BUILDING TRADE AND INDUSTRY, Forum Place, Hatfield, Herts, AL10 0RN. Tel: 01707-276 6400.

CA MAGAZINE, Institute of Chartered Accountants of Scotland, 1A St Bernards Row, Stockbridge, Edinburgh, EH4 1HW. Tel: 0131-3437500. Fax: 0131-3437505. Web: www.icas.org.uk. Editor: Robert Outram. Circulation: 22,600

CABINET MAKER, Ludgate House, 245 Blackfriars Road, London, SE1 9UR. Tel: 020-7579 4315. Fax: 020-7579 4347. Web: www.corridor.com. Consultant Editor: Audrey Dixon.

CAMPAIGN, 174 Hammersmith Road, London, W6 7JP. Tel: 020-8267 4656. Fax: 020-8267 4915. Web: www.campaignlive.com. Editor: Caroline Marshall.

CARPET FLOORING RETAIL, Ludgate House, 245 Blackfriars Road, Tonbridge, SE1 9UR. Tel: 020-7579 4323. Fax: 020-7579 4347. Editor: Alison Gay. Circulation: 3,800

CATERER AND HOTELKEEPER, Quadrant House, The Quadrant, Sutton, Surrey, SM2 5AS. Tel: 020-8652 8680. Fax: 020-8652 8973. Editor: F. Mutch.

CHEMICAL COMMUNICATIONS, Royal Society of Chemistry, Thomas Graham House, Science Park, Milton Road, Cambridge, CB4 0WF. Tel: 01223-432360. Fax: 01223-426017. Web: www.rsc.org.

CHEMIST AND DRUGGIST, Sovereign House, Sovereign Way, Tonbridge, Kent, TN9 1RW. Tel: 01732-377487. Fax: 01732-367065. Web: www.dotpharmacy.com. Editor: P. Grice. Circulation: 15,000

CHEMISTRY AND INDUSTRY, 15 Belgrave Square, London, SW1X 8PS. Tel: 020-7235 3681. Fax: 020-7235 9410. Web: www.chemind.org. Editor: S. Robinson. Circulation: 9,000

CHEMISTRY IN BRITAIN, Royal Society of Chemistry, Burlington House, Piccadilly, London, W1J 0BA. Tel: 020-7440 3360. Fax: 020-7494 1134. Web: www.chemsoc.org. Editor: R. Stevenson. Circulation: 46,000

CHILD EDUCATION, Villiers House, Clarendon Avenue, Leamington Spa, Warks, CV32 5PR. Tel: 01926-887799. Fax: 01926-883331. Web: www.scholastic.co.uk. Editor: J. Sugden. Circulation: 35,000

CLASSICAL MUSIC, 241 Shaftesbury Avenue, London, WC2H 8TF. Tel: 020-7333 1742. Fax: 020-7333 1769. Web: www.rhinegold.co.uk. Editor: K. Clarke. Circulation: 10,000

COMMUNITY CARE, Quadrant House, The Quadrant, Sutton, Surrey, SM2 5AS. Tel: 020-8652 3500. Fax: 020-8652 4739. Web: www.community-care.co.uk. Editor: Ms P. Neate. Circulation: 57,000

COMPUTER WEEKLY, Quadrant House, The Quadrant, Sutton, Surrey, SM2 5AS. Tel: 020-8652 3095. Fax: 020-8652 8979. Web: www.cw360.com. Editor: K. Schneider.

COMPUTING, VNU House, 32–34 Broadwick Street, London, W1A 2HG. Tel: 020-7316 9000. Fax: 020-7316 9160. Web: www.vnunet.com. Editor: Colin Barker. Circulation: 135,000

CONSTRUCTION NEWS, 151 Rosebery Avenue, London, EC1R 4GB. Tel: 020-7505 6868. Fax: 020-7505 6867. Web: www.onplus.co.uk. Editor: A. Morby.

CONTAINER MANAGEMENT, Suite 3, The Sanctuary, 23 Oakhill Grove, Surbiton, Surrey, KT6 6DU. Tel: 020-8390 8073. Fax: 020-8399 4807. Web: www.containermanagement.net. Editor: Ms J. Nunan. Circulation: 6,000

CONTRACT JOURNAL, Quadrant House, The Quadrant, Sutton, Surrey, SM2 5AS. Tel: 020-8652 4642. Fax: 020-8652 8958. Web: www.contractjournal.com. Editor: R. Willock. Circulation: 31,000

COUNTRYSIDE FOCUS, The Countryside Agency, John Dower House, Crescent Place, Cheltenham, Glos, GL50 3RA. Tel: 01242-521381. Fax: 01242-584270. Web: www.countryside.gov.uk. Editor: Suzanne Bennett. Circulation: 17,000

CRAFTS MAGAZINE, Crafts Council, 44A Pentonville Road, London, N1 9BY. Tel: 020-7806 2538. Fax: 020-7837 6891. Web: www.craftscouncil.org.uk. Editor: Ms G. Rudge. Circulation: 16,000

DAIRY INDUSTRIES INTERNATIONAL, Wilmington House, Maidstone Road, Foots Cray, Sidcup, DA14 5HZ. Tel: 020-8269 7700. Fax: 020-8269 7802. Web: www.connectingdairy.com. Editor: R. Clarke. Circulation: 6,500

DESIGN WEEK, St Giles House, 49–50 Poland Street, London, W1F 7AX. Tel: 020-7970 6666. Fax: 020-7970 6430. Web: www.design-week.co.uk. Editor: Linda Relph Knight.

DRAPERS RECORD, Greater London House, Hampstead Road, London, NW1 7EJ. Tel: 020-7391 3300.

EDUCATION TODAY, Datateam Publishing Ltd, London Road, Maidstone, Kent, ME16 8LY. Tel: 01622-687031. Fax: 01622-757646. Web: www.datateam.co.uk. Editor: Roger Hooper. Circulation: 18,000

ELECTRICAL AND RADIO TRADING, Queensway House, 2 Queensway, Redhill, Surrey, RH1 1QS. Tel: 01737-855450. Fax: 01737-855460. Web: www.dmg.co.uk. Editor: C. Ward. Circulation: 91,000

ENGINEERING, 355 Station Road, Dorridge, Solihull, B93 8EY. Tel: 01564-771772. Fax: 01564-774776. Web: www.engineeringnet.co.uk. Editor: Dr J. Ward. Circulation: 22,000

ENGLISH TODAY, Cambridge University Press, The Edinburgh Building, Shaftesbury Road, Cambridge, CB2 2RU. Tel: 01223-325757. Fax: 01223-315052. Editor: Tom McArthur.

EQUITY JOURNAL, Guild House, Upper St Martin's Lane, London, WC2H 9EG. Tel: 020-7379 6000. Fax: 020-7379 6074. Web: www.equity.org.uk. Editor: M. Brown. Circulation: 40,000

FARMERS WEEKLY, Quadrant House, The Quadrant, Sutton, Surrey, SM2 5AS. Tel: 020-8652 4911. Fax: 020-8652 4005. Web: www.fwi.co.uk. Editor: S. Howe. Circulation: 90,000

FINANCIAL MANAGEMENT, Chartered Institute of Management Accountants, 26 Chapter Street, London, SW1P 4NP. Tel: 020-7663 5441. Fax: 020-7580 6916. Editor: Ms G. Townley. Circulation: 120,000

FINANCIAL WORLD, IFS House, 4–9 Burgate Lane, Canterbury, Kent, CT1 2XJ. Tel: 01227-818602. Fax: 01227-763788. Web: www.ifslearning.com. Editor: Lawrie Holmes. Circulation: 400,000

FIRE, Queensway House, 2 Queensway, Redhill, Surrey, RH1 1QS. Tel: 01737-855431. Fax: 01737-855418. Editor: Andrew Lynch. Circulation: 3,500

FIRE PREVENTION, Fire Protection Association, Bastille Court, 2 Paris Garden, London, SE1 8ND. Tel: 020-7902 5308. Fax: 020-7902 5301. Web: www.thefpa.co.uk. Editor: Ms A. Hayes. Circulation: 16,000

FISHING NEWS INTERNATIONAL, Telephone House, 69–77 Paul Street, London, EC2A 4LQ. Tel: 020-7017 4509. Fax: 020-7017 4536. Editor: Ian Strutt.

FLIGHT INTERNATIONAL, Quadrant House, The Quadrant, Sutton, Surrey, SM2 5AS. Tel: 020-8652 3842. Fax: 020-8652 3840. Web: times. Editor: Ms C. Reed.

FOOD TRADE REVIEW, Station House, Hortons Way, Westerham, Kent, TN16 1BZ. Tel: 01959-563944. Fax: 01959-561285. Editor: A. Binsted. Circulation: 5,200

GEOGRAPHY, Geographical Association, 160 Solly Street, Sheffield, S1 4BF. Tel: 0114-296 0088. Fax: 0114-296 7176. Web: www.geography.org.uk. Editor: Dr K. Lynch. Circulation: 4,500

GEOLOGICAL MAGAZINE, Cambridge University Press, The Edinburgh Building, Shaftesbury Road, Cambridge, CB2 2RU. Tel: 01223-325757. Fax: 01223-315052.

HEATING, Ventilating and Plumbing, Hereford House, Bridle Path, Croydon, Surrey, CR9 4NL. Tel: 020-8680 4200. Fax: 020-8681 5049. Web: www.hvpmag.co.uk. Editor: Ms B. Field. Circulation: 32,500

INDEX ON CENSORSHIP, Writers and Scholars International Ltd, 33 Islington High Street, London, N1 9LH. Tel: 020-7278 2313. Fax: 020-7278 1878. Web: www.indexoncensorship.org. Editor: Ms J. Vidal-Hall. Circulation: 13,000

INDUSTRIAL EXCHANGE AND MART, Link House, 25 West Street, Poole, Dorset, BH15 1LL. Tel: 01202-445184. Fax: 01202-445189. Web: www.iem-net.co.uk. Circulation: 30,000

INTERNATIONAL AFFAIRS, RIIA, 10 St. James's Square, London, SW1Y 4LE. Tel: 020-7957 5700. Fax: 020-7957 5710. Web: www.riia.org. Editor: Caroline Soper. Circulation: 6,000

JANE'S DEFENCE WEEKLY, Sentinel House, 163 Brighton Road, Coulsdon, Surrey, CR5 2YH. Tel: 020-8700 3700. Fax: 020-8763 1007. Web: www.jdw.janes.com. Editor: C. Beal. Circulation: 26,000

JOURNAL OF ALTERNATIVE AND COMPLEMENTARY MEDICINE, The White House, Roxby Place, London, SW6 1RS. Tel: 020-7385 9848. Editor: E. Millar.

JOURNAL OF FAMILY HEALTH CARE, PO Box 100,, Chichester, West Sussex, PO18 8HD. Tel: 01243-576444. Fax: 01243-576456. Web: www.pmn.uk.com. Editor: P. Scowen. Circulation: 5,500

JOURNAL OF THE BRITISH ASTRONOMICAL ASSOCIATION, Burlington House, Piccadilly, London, W1J 0DU. Tel: 020-7734 4145. Fax: 020-7439 4629. Web: www.star.ucl.ac.uk. Editor: Mrs H McGee.

JUSTICE OF THE PEACE REPORTS, Butterworth Tolley, Halsbury House, 35 Chancery Lane, London, WC2A 1EL. Tel: 020-7400 2828. Fax: 020-7400 2805. Editor: Dr R. Munday.

LAW QUARTERLY REVIEW, The Hatchery, Hall Bank Lane, Mytholmroyd, Hebden Bridge, West Yorkshire, HX7 5HQ. Tel: 01422-888000. Fax: 01422-888001. Web: www.sweetandmaxwell.co.uk. Editor: Prof. Francis Reynolds.

LEATHER INTERNATIONAL, Tubs Hill House, London Road, Sevenoaks, TN13 1BY. Tel: 01732-470024. Fax: 01732-470045. Editor: Ms S. Davy. Circulation: 5,000

LEISURE AND HOSPITALITY BUSINESS, St Giles House, 49–50 Poland Street, London, WIF 7AX. Tel: 020-7970 4588. Fax: 020-7970 4891. Web: www.leisureandhospitalitybusiness.co.uk. Editor: Ms Melanie Swift.

LIBRARY AND INFORMATION UPDATE, 7 Ridgmount Street, London, WC1E 7AE. Tel: 020-7255 0500. Fax: 020-7255 0581. Web: www.cilip.org.uk/update. Editor: Ms E. Hyams. Circulation: 26,000

LLOYD'S LOADING LIST, 69-77 Paul Street, London, EC2A 4LQ. Tel: 01206-772277. Fax: 01206-772771.

LLOYD'S SHIPPING INDEX, 69-77 Paul Street, London, EC2A 4LQ. Tel: 01206-772277. Fax: 01206-772771.

LLOYD'S REGISTER - FAIRPLAY, 3rd Floor, Lombard House, 3 Princess Way, Redhill, Surrey, RH1 1UP. Tel: 01737 379000. Fax: 01737 379001. Web: www.fairplay.co.uk. Editor: P. Gunton. Circulation: 4,800

LOCAL GOVERNMENT CHRONICLE, Greater London House, Hampstead Rd, London, NW1 7EJ. Tel: 020-7347 1837. Fax: 020-7347 1831. Web: www.lgcnet.com. Editor: R. Vize. Circulation: 8,000

MACHINERY MARKET, Wadham House, 6 Blyth Road, Bromley, Kent, BR1 3RX. Tel: 020-8460 4224. Fax: 020-8290 1668. Web: www.machinery_market.co.uk. Editor: C. Granger. Circulation: 8,600

MANAGEMENT TODAY, 174 Hammersmith Road, London, W6 7JP. Tel: 020-8267 4610. Fax: 020-8267 4966. Web: www.clickmt.com. Editor: Matthew Gwyther. Circulation: 93,400

MANAGING INFORMATION, Aslib-IMI, Staple Hall, Stone House Court, London, EC3A 7PB. Tel: 020-7903 0000. Fax: 020-7903 0011. Web: www.managinginformation.com. Editor: G. Coult. Circulation: 10,000

MANUFACTURING CHEMIST, Tubs Hill House, London Road, Sevenoaks, Kent, TN13 1BY. Tel: 01732-470028. Fax: 01732-470070. Editor: Hilary Ayshford. Circulation: 5,000

MARKETING WEEK, 12-26 Lexington Street, London, W1R 4HQ. Tel: 020-7970 4000. Fax: 020-7970 6721. Web: www.marketing-week.co.uk. Editor: S. Smith.

MATERIALS RECYCLING WEEK, 19th Floor, Leon House, 233 High Street, Croydon, Surrey, CR0 9XT. Tel: 020-8277 5000. Fax: 020-8277 5650. Editor: Ms J. Rayner. Circulation: 5,000

MATERIALS WORLD, Institute of Materials, 1 Carlton House Terrace, London, SW1Y 5DB. Tel: 020-7451 7321. Fax: 020-7451 7406. Web: www.materials.org.uk. Editor: Dr S. Hill. Circulation: 19,000

MEAT TRADES JOURNAL, Quantum House, 19 Scarbrook Road, Croydon, Surrey, CR9 1LX. Tel: 020-8565 4255. Fax: 020-8565 4250. Web: www.mtj.co.uk. Editor: F. A'Court. Circulation: 5,900

MEDIA WEEK, Quantum House, 19 Scarbrook Road, Croydon, Surrey, CR9 1LX. Tel: 020-8565 4323. Fax: 020-8565 4394. Web: www.mediaweek.co.uk. Editor: P. Barrett. Circulation: 22,000

MUNICIPAL JOURNAL, 32 Vauxhall Bridge Road, London, SW1V 2SS. Tel: 020-7973 6400. Fax: 020-7233 5053. Editor: Michael Burton.

MUSIC JOURNAL, Incorporated Society of Musicians, 10 Stratford Place, London, W1C 1AA. Tel: 020-7629 4413. Fax: 020-7408 1538. Web: www.ism.org. Editor: N. Hoyle. Circulation: 5,100

MUSICIAN, 241 Shaftesbury Avenue, London, WC2H 8TF. Tel: 020-7333 1733. Fax: 020-7333 1736. Web: www.musiciansunion.org.uk. Editor: B. Blain. Circulation: 35,000

NURSING TIMES, Greater London House, Hampstead Road, London, NW1 7EJ. Tel: 020-7874 0505. Fax: 020-7874 0505. Web: www.nursingtimes.net. Editor: Tricia Reid. Circulation: 56,800

OPTICIAN, Quadrant House, The Quadrant, Sutton, Surrey, SM2 5AS. Tel: 020-8652 8243. Fax: 020-8652 8993. Web: www.optometryonline.net. Editor: C. Bennett. Circulation: 7,400

PARLIAMENTARY DEBATES (COMMONS) (HANSARD), The Stationery Office, PO Box 29, Norwich NR3 1GN. Tel: 0870-600 5522. Fax: 0870-600 5533.

PARLIAMENTARY DEBATES (LORDS) (HANSARD), The Stationery Office, PO Box 29, Norwich NR3 1GN. Tel: 0870-600 5522. Fax: 0870-600 5533.

PEOPLE MANAGEMENT, 17 Britton Street, London, EC1M 5TP. Tel: 020-7880 6200. Fax: 020-7336 7635. Web: www.peoplemanagement.co.uk. Editor: S. Crabb. Circulation: 107,000

PERSONAL COMPUTER WORLD, VNU House, 32–34 Broadwick Street, London, W1A 2HG. Tel: 020-7316 9000. Fax: 020-7316 9313. Web: www.pcw.co.uk. Editor: D. Armbrust. Circulation: 110,000

PHARMACEUTICAL JOURNAL, Royal Pharmaceutical Society of Great Britain, 1 Lambeth High Street, London, SE1 7JN. Tel: 020-7735 9141. Fax: 020-7582 7327. Web: www.pharmj.com. Editor: Ms O. Timbs. Circulation: 47,000

PHILOSOPHY (JOURNAL OF THE ROYAL INSTITUTE OF PHILOSOPHY), The Royal Institute of Philosophy, 14 Gordon Square, London, WC1H 0AG. Tel: 020-7387 4130. Fax: 020-7383 4061. Web: www.royalinstitutephilosophy.org. Editor: A. O'Hear.

POLICE REVIEW, JANE'S INFORMATION GROUP, 180 Wardour Street, London, W1F 8FS. Tel: 020-7851 9700. Editor: Katrina Marchant.

PRESS GAZETTE, Quantum House, 19 Scarbrook Road, Croydon, Surrey, CR9 1LX. Tel: 020-8565 4200. Fax: 020-8565 4395. Web: www.pressgazette.co.uk. Editor: Philippa Kennedy.

PRIMARY GEOGRAPHER, Geographical Association, 160 Solly Street, Sheffield, S1 4BF. Tel: 0114-296 6088. Fax: 0114-296 7176. Web: www.geography.org.uk. Editor: Dr Margaret Mackintosh. Circulation: 5,000

PRINTING WORLD, Sovereign House, Sovereign Way, Tonbridge, Kent, TN9 1RW. Tel: 01732-377391. Fax: 01732-377552. Web: www.dotprint.com. Editor: Garth Ward. Circulation: 15,000

PROBATION JOURNAL, 217A Balham High Road, London, SW17 7BP. Tel: 020-8671 0640. Fax: 020-8671 0640. Editor: H. Singh Bhui. Circulation: 8,000

QUARRY MANAGEMENT, 7 Regent Street, Nottingham, NG1 5BS. Tel: 0115-941 1315. Fax: 0115-948 4035. Web: www.qmj.co.uk. Editor: S. Adam. Circulation: 6,500

RAILWAY GAZETTE INTERNATIONAL, Quadrant House, The Quadrant, Sutton, Surrey, SM2 5AS. Tel: 020-8652 8608. Fax: 020-8652 3738. Web: www.railwaygazette.com. Editor: Murray Hughes. Circulation: 9,700

RETAIL NEWSAGENT, Robert Taylor House, 11 Angel Gate, City Road, London, EC1V 2SD. Tel: 020-7689 0600. Fax: 020-7689 0500. Editor: Alexander Desforges. Circulation: 17,000

RETAIL WEEK, 33-39 Bowling Green Lane, London, EC1V 7QP. Tel: 020-7505 8000. Fax: 020-7505 8185. Web: www.4retail.net. Editor: Neill Denny. Circulation: 15,000

RUSI JOURNAL, Royal United Services Institute for Defence Studies, Whitehall, London, SW1A 2ET. Tel: 020-7930 5854. Fax: 020-7321 0943. Web: www.rusi.org/journal. Editor: T. MacNamee.

SCREEN INTERNATIONAL, 33–39 Bowling Green Lane, London, EC1R 0DA. Tel: 020-7505 8080. Fax: 020-7505 8116. Web: www.screendaily.com. Editor-in-Chief: C. Brown. Circulation: 9,300

SHIPPING WORLD AND SHIPBUILDER, 1 Sutton Court Road, Sutton, Surrey, SM1 1HW. Tel: 020-8661 1160. Fax: 020-8661 1173.

SOLICITORS JOURNAL, 100 Avenue Road, London, NW3 3PG. Tel: 020-7393 7000. Fax: 020-7393 7880. Web: www.sweetandmaxwell.co.uk. Editor: Ms L. Hickman.

STRUCTURAL ENGINEER (INSTITUTION OF STRUCTURAL ENGINEERS), 11 Upper Belgrave Street, London, SW1X 8BH. Tel: 020-7201 9120. Fax: 020-7201 9109. Web: www.thestructuralengineer.org.uk. Editor: Ms K. Stansfield. Circulation: 19,500

SURVEYOR, 32 Vauxhall Bridge Road, London, SW1V 2SS. Tel: 020-7973 6402. Fax: 020-7973 6677. Web: www.hemming-group.co.uk. Editor: M. Hobley. Circulation: 5,200

TAX ADVISER, The Chartered Institute of Taxation, 12 Upper Belgrave Street, London, SW1X 8BB. Tel: 020-7235 9381. Fax: 020-7235 2562. Web: www.tax.org.uk. Editor: Lesley Stephenson. Circulation: 22,000

TAXI, Taxi House, 7–11 Woodfield Road, London, W9 2BA. Tel: 020-7432 1429. Fax: 020-7266 2297. Editor: S. Pessok. Circulation: 12,000

TEACHING GEOGRAPHY, Geographical Association, 160 Solly Street, Sheffield, S1 4BF. Tel: 0114-296 6088. Fax: 0114-296 7176. Web: www.geography.org.uk. Editor: Ms E. Barratt Hacking. Circulation: 5,000

TEACHING HISTORY, The Historical Association, 59a Kennington Park Road, London, SE11 4JH. Tel: 020-7735 3901. Fax: 020-7582 4989. Web: www.history.org.uk. Circulation: 3,000

TELEVISION, Royal Television Society, Holborn Hall, 100 Gray's Inn Road, London, WC1X 8AL. Tel: 020-7430 1000. Fax: 020-7430 0924. Web: www.rts.org.uk. Editor: Steve Clarke. Circulation: 4,000

TEXTILE MONTH, Perkin House, 1 Longlands Street, Bradford, W. Yorks, BD1 2TP. Tel: 01274-378800. Fax: 01274-378811. Web: www.world-textile.com. Editor: A. Wilson. Circulation: 10,000

THE ARCHITECTS' JOURNAL, 151 Rosebery Avenue, London, EC1R 4GB. Tel: 020-7505 6700. Fax: 020-7505 6701. Web: www.ajplus.co.uk. Editor: I. Allen. Circulation: 164,400

THE ARCHITECTURAL REVIEW, 151 Rosebery Avenue, London, EC1R 4GB. Tel: 020-7505 6725. Fax: 020-7505 6701. Web: www.arplus.com. Editor: P. Davey. Circulation: 23,200

THE AUTHOR, Society of Authors, 84 Drayton Gardens, London, SW10 9SB. Tel: 020-7373 6642. Fax: 020-7373 5768. Web: www.societyofauthors.org. Editor: D. Parker.

THE BIOCHEMIST, The Biochemical Society, 59 Portland Place, London, W1N 3AJ. Tel: 020-7580 5530. Fax: 020-7323 1136. Web: www.biochemistry.org. Editor: Dr Richard Reece. Circulation: 74,000

THE BOOKSELLER, 5th Floor, Endeavour House, 189 Shaftesbury Avenue, London, WC2H 8TJ. Tel: 020-7420 6006. Fax: 020-7420 6103. Web: www.thebookseller.com. Editor: N. Clee. Circulation: 12,500

THE DENTIST, Unit 2, Riverview Business Park, Walnut Tree Close, Guildford, Surrey, GU1 4QT. Tel: 01483-304944. Fax: 01483-303191. Editor: Jenny Dyer.

THE DIRECTOR, (Magazine of the Institute of Directors), 116 Pall Mall, London, SW1Y 5ED. Tel: 020-7766 8950. Fax: 020-7766 8840. Web: www.iod.com. Editor: Ms J. Higgins. Circulation: 53,100

THE ENGINEER, St Giles House, 50 Poland Street, London, W1F 7AX. Tel: 020-7970 4100. Fax: 020-7970 4189. Web: www.e4engineering.com. Editor: Sean Brierley. Circulation: 36,000

THE GROCER, Broadfield Park, Crawley, W. Sussex, RH11 9RT. Tel: 01293-613400. Fax: 01293-610333. Web: www.william-reed.co.uk. Editor: C. Beddall. Circulation: 45,000

THE HEALTH SERVICE JOURNAL, Greater London House, Hampstead Road, London, NW1 7EJ. Tel: 020-7874 0200. Fax: 020-7874 0254. Web: www.hsj.co.uk. Editor: Alastair McLellan. Circulation: 21,500

THE JOURNALIST, National Union of Journalists, Headland House, 308-312 Gray's Inn Road, London, WC1X 8DP. Tel: 020-7278 7916. Fax: 020-7278 1812. Editor: T. Gopsill.

THE LANCET, 32 Jamestown Road, London, NW1 7BY. Tel: 020-7424 4910. Web: www.thelancet.com. Editor: Dr R. Horton.

THE LAW REPORTS, Megarry House, 119 Chancery Lane, London, WC2A 1PP. Tel: 020-7242 6741. Fax: 020-7831 5247. Web: www.lawreports.co.uk. Editor: R. Williams.

THE PHOTOGRAPHER, British Institute of Professional Photography, Fox Talbot House, Amwell End, Ware, Herts, SG12 9HN. Tel: 01920-464011. Fax: 01920-487056. Web: www.bipp.com. Editor: S. Bavister.

THE PRACTITIONER, City Reach, 5 Greenwich View Place, Millharbour, London, E14 9NN. Tel: 020-7861 6478. Fax: 020-7861 6544. Editor: Gavin Atkin.

THE PSYCHOLOGIST, British Psychological Society, St Andrews House, 48 Princess Road East, Leicester, LE1 7DR. Tel: 0116-254 9568. Fax: 0116-247 0787. Web: www.bps.org.uk. Editor: Dr J. Sutton. Circulation: 35,000

THE PUBLICAN NEWSPAPER, Quantum House, 19 Scarbrook Road, Croydon, Surrey, CR9 1LX. Tel: 020-8565 4200. Fax: 020-8565 4202. Web: www.thepublican.com. Editor: Ms L. Harrison. Circulation: 33,000

THE SOCIOLOGICAL REVIEW, 108 Cowley Road, Oxford, OX4 1JF. Tel: 01865-791100. Fax: 01865-791347. Web: www.blackwellpublishers.co.uk/journals/SOCREV. Editors: Ms R. Deem and Ms S. MacDonald.

THE STAGE, 47 Bermondsey Street, London, SE1 3XT. Tel: 020-7403 1818. Fax: 020-7357 9287. Web: www.thestage.co.uk. Editor: B. Attwood. Circulation: 41,800

THE TEACHER, National Union of Teachers, Hamilton House, Mabledon Place, London, WC1H 9BD. Tel: 020-7380 4708. Fax: 020-7383 7230. Web: www.teachers.org.uk. Editor: Mitch Howard. Circulation: 280,000

THE TRADER, Link House, 25 West Street, Poole, Dorset, BH15 1LL. Tel: 01202-445320. Fax: 01202-445309. Web: www.the-trader.co.uk. Publishing Manager: Ms A. Boyer. Circulation: 25,000

THE WEEKLY LAW REPORTS, Megarry House, 119 Chancery Lane, London, WC2A 1PP. Tel: 020-7242 6471.

Fax: 020-7831 5247. Web: www.lawreports.co.uk. Editor: R. Williams.

TOWN AND COUNTRY PLANNING, Town and Country Planning Association, 17 Carlton House Terrace, London, SW1Y 5AS. Tel: 020-7930 8903. Fax: 020-7930 3280. Web: www.tcpa.org.uk. Editor: N. Matthews.

TOWN PLANNING REVIEW, 4 Cambridge Street, Liverpool, L69 7ZU. Tel: 0151-794 2237. Fax: 0151-794 2235. Web: www.liverpool-unipress.co.uk. Editors: Prof. P. Batey, Dr David Massey and Prof. Cecilia Wong.

TRADE MARKS JOURNAL, Patent Office, Cardiff Road, Newport, Gwent, NP9 1RH. Tel: 01633-811063. Fax: 01633-811415. Web: www.patent.gov.uk. Editor: Ms A. Newman.

TRAVEL TRADE GAZETTE (UK AND IRELAND), 1st Floor, City Reach, 5 Greenwich View Place, Millharbour, London, E14 9NN. Tel: 020-7861 6096. Fax: 020-7861 6227. Editor: P. Davies. Circulation: 250,000

VETERINARY RECORD, 7 Mansfield Street, London, W1M 0AT. Tel: 020-7636 6541. Editor: Martin Alder.

WORLD'S FAIR, PO Box 57, Holinwood Business Centre, Oldham, Lancs, OL8 3WF. Tel: 0161-683 8000. Fax: 0161-683 8001. Web: www.worldsfair.co.uk. Editor: Michael Mellor. Circulation: 15,000

Book Publishers

There are over 28,000 active publishers in the UK, but many of those publish very few or very specialised titles. The following list comprises publishers whose names are most familiar to the general public. Entries include name, contact details and a letter code indicating the type of books published. (The full list of publishers can be found in Whitaker's Books in Print, published by J. Whitaker and Sons)

A	Fiction
B	Education
C	Religious
D	Technical and Scientific
E	Legal and Parliamentary
F	Medical
G	Commercial and Professional
H	Naval and Military
I	Dictionaries
J	Reference Books
K	Maps and Atlases
L	Directories and Guides
M	Music and Dance
N	Poetry, Film and Drama
O	Illustrated
P	Art and Architecture
Q	History, Archaeology, Biography
R	Politics, Sociology, Political Economy
S	Philosophy
T	Other Academic
U	Children's Books
V	Sports, Games and Pastimes
W	Foreign language
X	General Literature, e.g. Travel, Essays, Humour

AA PUBLISHING
Fanum House, Basingstoke, Hants RG21 4EA.
Tel: 01256-491524; Fax: 01256-322575.
Web: www.theaa.com. K, L, O

IAN ALLAN
Riverdene Business Park, Molesey Road, Hersham KT12 4RG. Tel: 01932-266600; Fax: 01932-266601.
Web: www.ianallanpub.co.uk. H, O, Q, V

ALLEN & UNWIN
PO Box 30474, London NW6 7FQ.
Tel: 020-8537 1531; Fax: 020-8621 3701.
Web: www.allen-unwin.com.au. U

ALLISON & BUSBY
Suite 111, Bon Marche Centre, 241–251 Ferndale Rd, London SW9 8BJ.
Tel: 020-7738 7888; Fax: 020-7733 4244.
Web: www.allisonandbusby.ltd.uk.

APPLE PRESS
4th Floor, 112–116 Western Road, Hove, BN3 1DD.
Tel: 01273-716012; Fax: 01273-716269. J, O

HODDER ARNOLD
338 Euston Road, London NW1 3BH.
Tel: 020-7873 6000; Fax: 020-7873 6325.
Web: www.hodderheadline.com.
B, D, E, F, G, I, J, K, Q, R, S, T, U, V, W

ARROW BOOKS
The Random House Group, 20 Vauxhall Bridge Road, London SW1V 2SA.
Tel: 020-7840 8400; Fax: 020-7233 6127.
Web: www.randomhouse.co.uk. A

ASHGATE
Gower House, Croft Road, Aldershot GU11 3HR.
Tel: 01252-331551; Fax: 01252-344405.
Web: www.ashgate.com.
C, D, E, F, G, H, J, M, P, Q, R, S, T

AURUM PRESS
25 Bedford Avenue, London WC1B 3AT.
Tel: 020-7637 3225; Fax: 020-7580 2469.
Web: www.aurumpress.co.uk.
H, N, P, Q, V, X

BANTAM BOOKS
61–63 Uxbridge Road, London W5 5SA.
Tel: 020-8579 2652; Fax: 020-8231 6612.
Web: www.booksattransworld.co.uk.
A, O, Q, R, V, X

B. T. BATSFORD
64 Brewery Road, London N7 9NY.
Tel: 020-7697 3000; Fax: 020-7697 3001.
N, P, Q, V

BERLITZ PUBLISHING CO.
58 Borough High Street, London SE1 1XF.
Tel: 020-7569 3160.
Web: www.berlitz.co.uk.

A&C BLACK
37 Soho Square, London W1D 3QZ.
Tel: 020-7758 0200; Fax: 020-7758 0222.
Web: www.acblack.com
B, I, J, L, M, N, O, P, Q, U, V

BLACKWELL
108 Cowley Road, Oxford OX4 1JF.
Tel: 01865-791100; Fax: 01865-791347.
Web: www.blackwellpublishers.co.uk.
C, D, F, O, Q, R, S, T, W

BLOOMSBURY PUBLISHING
38 Soho Square, London W1D 3HB.
Tel: 020-7494 2111; Fax: 020-7434 0151.
Web: www.bloomsbury.com. A, I, J, U

BOWKER
Windsor Court, East Grinstead House, East Grinstead RH19 1XA. Tel: 01342-336149; Fax: 01342-336192.
Web: www.bowker.co.uk. J, L

BOXTREE
20 New Wharf Road, London N1 9RR.
Tel: 020-7014 6000; Fax: 020-7014 6001.
Web: www.panmacmillan. M, N, O, V

BUTTERWORTH TOLLEY
Halsbury House, 35 Chancery Lane, London WC2A 1EL. Tel: 020-7400 2500; Fax: 020-7400 2842.
Web: www.butterworths.co.uk. E, G

CADOGAN GUIDES
Network House, 1 Ariel Way, London W12 7SL.
Tel: 020-8600 3550; Fax: 020-8600 3599.
Web: www.cadoganguides.com. L, X

CAMBRIDGE UNIVERSITY PRESS
The Edinburgh Building, Shaftesbury Road, Cambridge CB2 2RU. Tel: 01223-325566.
Web: www.uk.cambridge.org.
B, C, G, Q, R, S, T

CANONGATE BOOKS
14 High Street, Edinburgh EH1 1TE.
Tel: 0131-557 5111; Fax: 0131-557 5211.
Web: www.canongate.net.
A, C, M, N, V, X

JONATHAN CAPE
20 Vauxhall Bridge Road, London SW1V 2SA.
Tel: 020-7840 8400; Fax: 020-7233 6117.
Web: www.randomhouse.co.uk. A, N, Q

CASSELL & CO
Wellington House, 125 Strand, London WC2R 0BB.
Tel: 020-7420 5555; Fax: 020-7240 7261.

FRANK CASS
47 Chase Side, London N14 5BP.
Tel: 020-8920 2100; Fax: 020-8447 8548.
Web: www.frankcass.com. H, Q, R

CAVENDISH PUBLISHING
The Glass House, Wharton Street, London WC1X 9PX.
Tel: 020-7278 8000; Fax: 020-7278 8080.
Web: www.cavendishpublishing.com. E, F, G, J

CENTURY
20 Vauxhall Bridge Road, London SW1V 2SA.
Tel: 020-7840 8400; Fax: 020-7233 6127.
Web: www.randomhouse.co.uk. A, Q, X

CHAMBERS HARRAP PUBLISHERS LTD
7 Hopetoun Crescent, Edinburgh EH7 4AY.
Tel: 0131-556 5929; Fax: 0131-556 5313.
Web: www.chambersharrap.com. I, J, W

CHATTO & WINDUS
20 Vauxhall Bridge Road, London SW1V 2SA.
Tel: 020-7840 8400; Fax: 020-7233 6117.
Web: www.randomhouse.co.uk. A, Q, R

CHIVERS PRESS
Windsor Bridge Road, Bath BA2 3AX.
Tel: 01225-335336; Fax: 01225-310771.
Web: www.chivers.co.uk.

CHRYSALIS BOOKS
8-10 Blenheim Court, Brewery Road, London N7 9NY.
Tel: 020-7697 3000; Fax: 020-7697 3001.
Web: www.chrysalisbooks.co.uk. O, P, Q, V, X

CHURCH HOUSE PUBLISHING
Church House, Great Smith Street, London SW1P
3NZ. Tel: 020-7898 1451; Fax: 020-7898 1449.
Web: www.chpublishing.co.uk. C

T. & T. CLARK
59 George Street, Edinburgh EH2 2LQ.
Tel: 0131-225 4703; Fax: 0131-220 4260.
Web: www.tandtclark.co.uk. C

CMP INFORMATION
Riverbank House, Angel Lane Tonbridge Kent TN9
1SE. Tel: 01732-377695; Fax: 01732-377479.
Web: www.cmpdata.com. D, F, G, L

CONSTABLE & ROBINSON
3 The Lanchesters, 162 Fulham Palace Road, London
W6 9ER. Tel: 020-8741 3663; Fax: 020-8748 7562.
Web: www.constable.robinson.com. A, H, J, P, Q, U, X

CORGI BOOKS
61–63 Uxbridge Road, London W5 5SA.
Tel: 020-8579 2652; Fax: 020-8231 6612.
Web: www.booksattransworld.co.uk. A, Q, X

CREATION BOOKS
4th Floor, 72/80 Leather Lane, London EC1N 7TR.
Tel: 020-7430 9878; Fax: 020-7242 5527.
Web: www.creationbooks.com. N, P, Q, X

DARTON, LONGMAN & TODD
1 Spencer Court, 140–142 Wandsworth High Street,
London SW18 4 JJ.
Tel: 020-8875 0155; Fax: 020-8875 0133.
B, C, Q, R, S, T

DAVID & CHARLES
Brunel House, Newton Abbot, Devon TQ1 4PU.
Tel: 01626-323200. Web: www.davidandcharles.co.uk. O

DEBRETT'S PEERAGE LTD
Kings Court, 2–16 Goodge Street, London W1T 2QA.
Tel: 020-7753 4213; Fax: 020-7753 4212.
Web: www.debretts.co.uk. J

ANDRE DEUTSCH
Carlton Publishing Group, 20 Mortimer Street,
London W1T 3JW.
Tel: 020-7612 0400; Fax: 020-7612 0401.
C, H, J, M, N, O, P, Q, U, V, X

DORLING KINDERSLEY
80 Strand, London WC2R 0RL.
Tel: 020-7010 3000.Web: www.dk.com.
All categories

DOUBLEDAY
61–63 Uxbridge Road, London W5 5SA.
Tel: 020-8579 2652; Fax: 020-8579 5479.
Web: www.booksattransworld.co.uk.
A, O, Q, R, X

DUCKWORTH & CO.
61 Frith Street, London W1D 3JL.
Tel: 020-7434 4242; Fax: 020-7434 4420.
Web: www.ducknet.co.uk. H, Q, T

EBURY PRESS
20 Vauxhall Bridge Road, London SW1V 2SA.
Tel: 020-7840 8400.
Web: www.randomhouse.co.uk. C, F, J, M, M, O, Q, V, X

ELSEVIER SCIENCE AND TECHNOLOGY BOOKS
The Boulevard, Langford Lane, Kidlington, Oxon OX5
1GB. Tel: 01865-843000.
Web: www.elsevier.co.uk. B, D, G, P, T

ENCYCLOPAEDIA BRITANNICA (UK)
2nd Floor, Unity Wharf, 13 Mill Street, London SE1
2BH. Tel: 020-7500 7800; Fax: 020-7500 7878.
Web: www.britannica.co.uk. J, K, U

EPWORTH PRESS
c/o SCM Press, 9–17 St Albans Place, London N1 0NX.
Tel: 020-7359 8033; Fax: 020-7359 0049. C

EVANS BROS
2A Portman Mansions, Chiltern Street, London W1U
6NR. Tel: 020-7487 0920; Fax: 020-7487 0921.
Web: www.evansbooks.co.uk. B, J, N, U

EVERYMAN
4th Floor, Gloucester Mansions, 140A Shaftesbury
Avenue, London WC2H 8HD.
Tel: 020-7539 7600; Fax: 020-7379 4060.
Web: www.everyman.uk.com. A, L, O, X

FABER & FABER
3 Queen Square London WC1N 3AU.
Tel: 020-7465 0045; Fax: 020-7465 0034.
Web: www.faber.co.uk. A, N, Q, U, X

G. T. FOULIS
Sparkford, Nr Yeovil, Somerset BA22 7JJ.
Tel: 01963-440635; Fax: 01963-440001.
Web: www.haynes.com. D, J, Q, V

FOURTH ESTATE
77–85 Fulham Palace Road, London W6 8JB.
Tel: 020-8741 4414; Fax: 020-8307 4466.
Web: www.4thestate.co.uk. A, Q, X

SAMUEL FRENCH LTD
52 Fitzroy Street, London W1T 5JR.
Tel: 020-7387 9373; Fax: 020-7387 2161.
Web: www.samuelfrench-london.co.uk. N

GALE RESEARCH INTERNATIONAL
High Holborn House, 50–51 Bedford Row, London
WC1R 4LR. Tel: 020-7067 2500; Fax: 020-7067 2600.
Web: www.gale.com/world. G

GOWER PUBLISHING LTD
Gower House, Croft Road, Aldershot, Hants GU11
3HR. Tel: 01252-331551; Fax: 01252-344405.
Web: www.gowerpub.com. G

GRANTA BOOKS
2–3 Hanover Yard, Noel Road, London N1 8BE.
Tel: 020-7704 9776; Fax: 020-7354 3469.
Web: www.granta.com. A, Q, R, X

ROBERT HALE
45 Clerkenwell Green, London EC1R 0HT.
Tel: 020-7251 2661; Fax: 020-7490 4958.
Web: www.halebooks.com. A, H, Q, V, X

HAMISH HAMILTON
27 Wrights Lane, London W8 5TZ.
Tel: 020-7416 3000; Fax: 020-7416 3099.
Web: www.penguin.co.uk. A

HAMLYN
2–4 Heron Quays, London E14 4JP.
Tel: 020-7531 8400; Fax: 020-7531 8650.
Web: www.hamlyn.co.uk. J, M, O, P, V

HARCOURT BRACE
32 Jamestown Rd, London NW1 7BY.
Tel: 020-7424 4200.

HARLEQUIN MILLS & BOON LTD
Eton House, 18–24 Paradise Road, Richmond Surrey
TW9 1SR. Tel: 020-8288 2800; Fax: 020-8288 2899.
Web: www.millsandboon.co.uk. A

HARPERCOLLINS PUBLISHERS
77–85 Fulham Palace Road, London W6 8JB.
Tel: 020-8741 7070; Fax: 020-8307 4440.
Web: www.fireandwater.com.
A, B, H, I, J, K, L, O, Q, R, U, V, X

J. H. HAYNES & CO. LTD
Sparkford, Yeovil, Somerset BA22 7JJ.
Tel: 01963-440635; Fax: 01963-440001.
Web: www.haynes.com. D, I, J, K, L

R. HAZELL & CO
PO Box 39, Henley on Thames, Oxfordshire RG9 5UA.
Tel: 01491-641018. E, J, L

WILLIAM HEINEMANN
20 Vauxhall Bridge Road, London SW1V 2SA.
Tel: 020-7840 8400; Fax: 020-7233 6127.
Web: www.randomhouse.co.uk. A, X

HODDER HEADLINE
338 Euston Road, London NW1 3BH.
Tel: 020-7873 6000; Fax: 020-7873 6024.
Web: www.madaboutbooks.com.
A, B, C, D, F, G, H, J, M, O, R, U, V, X

THOMSON CORPORATION
High Holborn House, 50/51 Bedford Row London
WC1R 4LR. Tel: 020-7497 1422.

JANE'S INFORMATION GROUP
Sentinel House, 163 Brighton Road, Coulsdon,
Surrey CR5 2YH.
Tel: 020-8700 3700; Fax: 020-8763 1006.
Web: www.james.com. H

JARROLD PUBLISHING
Whitefriars, Norwich NR3 1TR.
Tel: 01603-763300; Fax: 01603-662748.
Web: www.jarrold-publishing.co.uk. L, Q

JORDAN PUBLISHING
21 St Thomas Street, Bristol BS1 6JS.
Tel: 0117-923 0600; Fax: 0117-925 0486.
Web: www.jordanpublishing.co.uk. E

MICHAEL JOSEPH
80 Strand, London WC2R 0RL.
Tel: 020-7010 3000; Fax: 020-7010 6710. A, Q, V, X

KEGAN PAUL
PO Box 256, London WC1B 3SW.
Tel: 020-7580 5511; Fax: 020-7436 0899.
Web: www.keganpaul.com.
A, C, F, H, I, J, K, L, O, P, Q, R, S, X

KINGFISHER PUBLICATIONS PLC
New Penderel House, 283–288 High Holborn,
London WC1V 7HZ.
Tel: 020-7903 9999; Fax: 020-7242 4979.
Web: www.kingfisherpub.com. C, D, J, Q, X

JESSICA KINGSLEY PUBLISHERS
116 Pentonville Road, London N1 9JB.
Tel: 020-7833 2307; Fax: 020-7837 2917.
Web: www.jkp.com. B, C, D, F, G, R, S, T

KLUWER ACADEMIC
241 Borough High Street, London, SE1 1GB.
Tel: 020-7940 7490; Fax: 020-7940 7495.
Web: www.wkap.nl. D, F, S, T

KOGAN PAGE
120 Pentonville Road, London N1 9JN.
Tel: 020-7278 0433; Fax: 020-7837 6348.
Web: www.kogan-page.co.uk. B, D, G, I, J, L

LADYBIRD BOOKS
80 Strand, London WC2R 0RL.
Tel: 020-7010 3000. Web: www.ladybird.co.uk. U

LETTS EDUCATIONAL
The Chiswick Centre, 414 Chiswick Group, London
W4 5TF. Tel: 020-8996 3333; Fax: 020-8742 8390.
Web: www.letts-education.com.B

FRANCES LINCOLN
4 Torriano Mews, Torriano Avenue, London NW5 2RZ.
Tel: 020-7284 4009; Fax: 020-7485 0490.
Web: www.franceslincoln.com. O, P, U

LION PUBLISHING
Mayfield House, 256 Banbury Road, Summertown,
Oxford OX2 7DH.
Tel: 01865-302750; Fax: 01865-302757.
Web: www.lion-publishing.co.uk. C, J, U

LONELY PLANET
10A Spring Place, London NW5 3BH.
Tel: 020-7428 4800; Fax: 020-7428 4828.
Web: www.lonelyplanet.co.uk. K, L, W

LUTTERWORTH PRESS
PO Box 60 , Cambridge CB1 2NT.
Tel: 01223-350865; Fax: 01223-366951.
Web: www.lutterworth.com. B, C, O, P, Q, T, U, V

PAN MACMILLAN
20 New Wharf Road, London N1 9RR.
Tel: 020-7014 6000; Fax: 020-7014 6001.
Web: www.macmillan.com.
A, H, N, O, Q, U, V, X

MAINSTREAM PUBLISHING CO.
7 Albany Street, Edinburgh EH1 3UG.
Tel: 0131-557 2959; Fax: 0131-556 8720.
Web: www.mainstreampublishing.com.
A, F, H, L, M, P, Q, R, V, X

MANCHESTER UNIVERSITY PRESS
Oxford Road, Manchester M13 9NR.
Tel: 0161-275 2310; Fax: 0161-274 3346.
Web: www.manchesteruniversitypress.co.uk.
N, P, Q, R, W

MCGRAW-HILL EDUCATION
Shoppenhangers Road, Maidenhead, Berks SL6 2QL.
Tel: 01628-502500; Fax: 01628-770224.
Web: www.mcgraw-hill.co.uk.
B, D, F, G, H, I, J, M, N, P, Q, R, S, T, U, W

METHUEN PUBLISHING LTD
215 Vauxhall Bridge Road, London SW1V 1EJ.
Tel: 020-7798 1600; Fax: 020-7828 2098.
Web: www.methuen.co.uk. A, N, Q, V, X

JOHN MURRAY
50 Albemarle Street, London W1S 4BD.
Tel: 020-7493 4361; Fax: 020-7499 1792.
Web: www.johnmurray.co.uk. B, H, Q, R

NEW HOLLAND PUBLISHERS
Garfield House, 86 Edgware Road, London W2 2EA.
Tel: 020-7724 7773; Fax: 020-7724 6184. K, L, O, V

W. W. NORTON AND COMPANY
Castle House, 75/76 Wells Street, London W1T 3QT.
Tel: 020-7323 1579; Fax: 020-7436 4553.
Web: www.wwnorton.co.uk.
H, M, N, P, Q, R, S, T, W, X

OCTOPUS PUBLISHING GROUP
2–4 Heron Quays London E14 4JP.
Tel: 020-7531 8400; Fax: 020-7531 8650.
Web: www.octopus-publishing.co.uk.
B, C, J, K, L, O, P, U, V

MICHAEL O'MARA BOOKS LTD
9 Lion Yard, Tremadoc Road, London SW4 7NQ.
Tel: 020-7720 8643; Fax: 020-7627 8953.
Web: www.mombooks.com. O, Q, U, V, X

OPEN UNIVERSITY PRESS
Celtic Court, 22 Ballmoor Buckingham MK18 1XW.
Tel: 01280-823388. B, F, R, T

ORION PUBLISHING GROUP
5 Upper St Martin's Lane, London WC2H 9EA.
Tel: 020-7240 3444.

OSPREY PUBLISHING
1st Floor, Elms Court, Chapel Way, Botley, Oxford
OX2 9LP. Tel: 01865-727022; Fax: 01865-242009.
Web: www.ospreypublishing.com.H, Q

OXFORD UNIVERSITY PRESS
Great Clarendon Street, Oxford OX2 6DP.
Tel: 01865-556767; Fax: 01865-556646.
Web: www.oup.co.uk.
B, C, D, E, F, G, I, J, K, P, Q, R, S, T, W, X

PEARSON EDUCATION
Edinburgh Gate, Harlow CM20 2JE.
Tel: 01279-623928.
Web: www.pearsoned-ema.com. B, J

THE PENGUIN GROUP UK
80 Strand, London WC2R 0RL.
Tel: 020-7010 3000; Fax: 020-7010 6060.
Web: www.penguin.co.uk.
A, B, I, J, K, L, N, O, Q, T, U, V, X

PHAIDON PRESS
Regent's Wharf, All Saints Street, London N1 9PA.
Tel: 020-7843 1234; Fax: 020-7843 1111.
All categories

PIATKUS BOOKS
5 Windmill Street, London W1T 2JA.
Tel: 020-7631 0710; Fax: 020-7436 7137.
Web: www.piatkus.co.uk. A, C, F, G, H, M, Q, X

PLUTO PRESS
345 Archway Road, London N6 5AA.
Tel: 020-8348 2724; Fax: 020-8348 9133.
Web: www.plutobooks.com. R, T

PRENTICE HALL
Pearson Education, Edinburgh Gate, Harlow,
Essex CM20 2JE. Tel: 01279-623623.

PROQUEST
The Quorum, Barnwell Road, Cambridge, CB5 8SW.
Tel: 01223-215512; Fax: 01223-215513.
Web: www.proquest.co.uk. B, D, E, F, G, H, P, Q

PUFFIN BOOKS
80 Strand, London, WC2R 0RL.
Tel: 020-7010 3000; Fax: 020-7010 6060.
Web: www.puffin.co.uk. U

QUARTET BOOKS
27 Goodge Street, London W1T 2LD.
Tel: 020-7636 3992; Fax: 020-7637 1866. A, M, Q, X

RANDOM HOUSE UK
20 Vauxhall Bridge Road, London SW1V 2SA.
Tel: 020-7840 8400. A, B, C, G, Q, R, S, T, X

READER'S DIGEST ASSOCIATION
11 West Ferry Circus, London E14 4HE.
Tel: 020-7715 8000; Fax: 020-7715 8181.
Web: www.readersdigest.co.uk. A, J, X

REED BUSINESS INFORMATION
Quadrant House, The Quadrant, Sutton, Surrey SM2
5AS. Tel: 020-8652 3500; Fax: 020-8652 8932.
Web: www.reedbusiness.co.uk.

ROUGH GUIDES
62–70 Shorts Gardens, London WC2H 9AH.
Tel: 020-7556 5000; Fax: 020-7556 5050.
Web: www.roughguides.com. J, K, X

ROUTLEDGE
11 New Fetter Lane, London EC4P 4EE.
Tel: 020-7583 9855; Fax: 020-7842 2298.
Web: www.tandf.co.uk.
C, G, H, I, J, K, L, M, N, P, Q, R, S, T, W

SAGE PUBLICATIONS
6 Bonhill Street, London EC2A 4PU.
Tel: 020-7374 0645. Web: www.sagepub.co.uk.
B, D, J, L, R, S, T

SAINT ANDREW PRESS
121 George Street, Edinburgh EH2 4YN.
Tel: 0131-225 5722; Fax: 0131-220 3113.
Web: www.standrewpress.com. A, C, N, U

SCHOLASTIC CHILDREN'S BOOKS
Commonwealth House, 1–19 New Oxford Street,
London WC1A 1NU.
Tel: 020-7421 9000; Fax: 020-7421 9001.
Web: www.scholastic.co.uk. U

SERPENT'S TAIL
4 Blackstock Mews, London N4 2BT.
Tel: 020-7354 1949; Fax: 020-7704 6467.
Web: www.serpentstail.com. A

SEVERN HOUSE
9-15 Sutton High Street, Sutton, Surrey SM1 1DF.
Tel: 020-8770 3930; Fax: 020-8770 3850.
Web: www.severnhouse.com. A

SIMON AND SCHUSTER
Africa House, 64-78 Kingsway,
London WC2B 6AH. A, J, M, X

SPCK
Holy Trinity Church, Marylebone Road, London
NW1 4DU. Tel: 020-7643 0382; Fax: 020-7643 0391.
Web: www.spck.org.uk. C

THE STATIONERY OFFICE LTD
PO Box 29 , Norwich NR3 1GN.
Tel: 0870-600 5522.
Web: www.tso.co.uk. E, G, J, L

PATRICK STEPHENS LTD
Sparkford, Yeovil BA22 7JJ.
Tel: 01963-440635; Fax: 01963-440001.
Web: www.haynes.com. H, Q, V

SUTTON PUBLISHING
Phoenix Mill, London Road, Stroud GL5 2BU.
Tel: 01453-731114; Fax: 01453-731117.
Web: www.suttonpublishing.co.uk. H, Q

SWEET & MAXWELL
100 Avenue Road, London NW3 3PF.
Tel: 020-7393 7000; Fax: 020-7393 7010.
Web: www.sweetandmaxwell.co.uk. E

TAYLOR & FRANCIS
11 New Fetter Lane, London EC4P 4EE.
Tel: 020-7583 9855; Fax: 020-7842 2298.
Web: www.tandf.co.uk. D, G, T

THAMES & HUDSON
181A High Holborn, London WC1V 7QX.
Tel: 020-7845 5000; Fax: 020-7845 5050.
Web: www.thamesandhudson.com.
C, D, I, J, K, L, M, O, P, Q

TIME WARNER BOOKS UK
Brettenham House, Lancaster Place London WC2E
7EN. Tel: 020-7911 8000; Fax: 020-7911 8100.
Web: www.timewarnerbooks.com.
A, J, O, Q, R, V, X

TRANSWORLD PUBLISHERS
61-63 Uxbridge Road, London W5 5SA.
Tel: 020-8579 2652; Fax: 020-8579 5479.
Web: www.booksattransworld.co.uk.
A, D, H, J, Q, U, V, X

USBORNE PUBLISHING
  Usborne House, 83-85 Saffron Hill, London EC1N
  8RT. Tel: 020-7430 2800; Fax: 020-7430 1562.
  Web: www.usborne.com. U
VIKING
  27 Wrights Lane, London W8 5TZ.
  Tel: 020-7416 3000; Fax: 020-7416 3290.
  Web: www.penguin.co.uk. A, Q
VIRAGO PRESS
  Brettenham House, Lancaster Place, London WC2E
  7EN. Tel: 020-7911 8000; Fax: 020-7911 8100.
  Web: www.virago.co.uk. A, Q
VIRGIN PUBLISHING
  Units 5 and 6, Thames Wharf, Rainville Road,
  London W6 9HA. Tel: 020-7386 3300.
  Web: www.virgin-books.com. M, N, X
WARD LOCK EDUCATIONAL CO.
  BIC Ling Kee House, 1 Christopher Road, East
  Grinstead, W. Sussex RH19 3BT.
  Tel: 01342-318980; Fax: 01342-410980.
  Web: www.wardlockeducational.com. B
WATTS PUBLISHING GROUP
  96 Leonard Street, London EC2A 4XD.
  Tel: 020-7739 2929; Fax: 020-7739 2318.
  Web: www.wattspub.co.uk. U
WHICH? BOOKS
  Consumers' Association, 2 Marylebone Road,
  London NW1 4DF.
  Tel: 020-7770 7000; Fax: 020-7770 7660.
  Web: www.which.net. E, F, J, L, T, X
WHITAKER INFORMATION SERVICES
  VNU Entertainment Media UK Ltd, Woolmead
  House West, Bear Lane, Farnham GU9 7LG.
  Tel: 01252-742500; Fax: 01252-742501. L
WILEY EUROPE
  The Atrium, Southern Gate, Chichester PO19 8SQ.
  Tel: 01243-779777; Fax: 01234-775878.
  Web: www.wileyeurope.co.uk.
  B, D, F, G, I, J, P, Q, R, S, T, W
THE WOMEN'S PRESS
  34 Great Sutton Street, London EC1V 0LQ.
  Tel: 020-7251 3007; Fax: 020-7608 1938.
  Web: www.the-womens-press.com. A, R, T, U
YALE UNIVERSITY PRESS
  23 Pond Street, London NW3 2PN.
  Tel: 020-7431 4422; Fax: 020-7431 3755.
  Web: www.yaleup.co.uk. P, Q, R, S, T

Annual Reference Books

This list comprises a selection of popular reference books and their price. If the address of the editorial office differs from the address to which orders should be sent, the address given is usually the one for orders.

A.S.K. HOLLIS – THE DIRECTORY OF UK ASSOCIATIONS (£180)
Harlequin House, 7 High Street, Teddington, TW11 8EL. Tel: 020-8977 7711; Fax: 020-8977 1133.
Web: www.hollis–pr.com

ADVERTISER'S ANNUAL (£260)
Harlequin House, 7 High Street, Teddington TW11 8EL. Tel: 020-8977 7711; Fax: 020-8977 1133.
Web: www.hollis–pr.co.uk

ALMANACH DE GOTHA (£60)
Boydell & Brewer Ltd, PO Box 9, Woodbridge Suffolk IP12 3DF. Tel: 01394-411320.

ANNUAL ABSTRACT OF STATISTICS (£39.50)
PO Box 29, Norwich NR3 1GN. Tel: 0870-600 5522.

ANNUAL REGISTER: A RECORD OF WORLD EVENTS (£123). Keesings Worldwide, 28A Hills Road, Cambridge CB2 1LA. Tel: 01223-508050;
Fax: 01223-508049.

ANTHONY AND BERRYMAN MAGISTRATES' COURT GUIDE (£35)
2 Addiscombe Road, Croydon, Surrey, CR9 5AF.
Tel: 020-8662 2000.

ANTIQUE SHOPS OF BRITAIN, GUIDE TO THE (£14.95)
The Book Service Ltd, Distribution Centre, Colchester Road, Frating Green, Colchester CO7 7DW. Tel: 01206-256000; Fax: 01206-255715.

ART WORLD DIRECTORY (£20)
Art Review Ltd., 23–24 Smithfield Street, London EC1A 9LF. Tel: 020-7246 4880; Fax: 020-7246 3371.
Web: www.art-review.co.uk

ARTISTS AND AGENTS (£34.95)
Douglas House, 3 Richmond Buildings, London, W1D 3HE. Tel: 020-7437 9556; Fax: 020-7287 3463.
Web: www.rhpco.co.uk

ASLIB DIRECTORY OF INFORMATION SOURCES IN THE UNITED KINGDOM (£335)
Aslib Publications, Staple Hall, Stone House Court, London EC3A 7PB. Tel: 020-7903 0000.

ASSOCIATION OF CONSULTING ENGINEERS DIRECTORY OF MEMBERS FIRMS (£35)
Alliance House, 12 Caxton Street, London SW1H 0QL.
Tel: 020-7222 6557; Fax: 020-7222 0750.
Web: www.acenet.co.uk

ASTRONOMICAL ALMANAC (£32.50)
PO Box 29, Norwich NR3 1GN. Tel: 0870-600 5522.

ATHLETICS ASSOCIATION OF TRACK AND FIELD STATISTICIANS YEAR BOOK
Vine House Distribution Ltd, Waldenbury, North Chailey, Lewes, E. Sussex BN8 4DR.
Tel: 01825-723398; Fax: 01825-724188.

AUTOMOBILE YEAR (£33)
Waldenbury, North Common, North Chailey, Lewes, E. Sussex BN8 4DR.
Tel: 01825-723398; Fax: 01825-724188.

BANKERS' ALMANAC, THE (£550)
Windsor Court, East Grinstead House, East Grinstead, W. Sussex RH19 1XA.
Tel: 01342-335946; Fax: 01342-335969.
Web: www.bankersalmanac.com

BENEDICTINE AND CISTERCIAN MONASTIC YEAR BOOK
Ampleforth Abbey, York YO62 4EN.
Tel: 01439-766466; Fax: 01439-766467.
Web: www.benedictines.org.uk

BENN'S MEDIA: UNITED KINGDOM (£170)
Riverbank House, Angel Lane, Tonbridge Kent TN9 1SE. Web: www.cmpdata.co.uk

BRITISH AND INTERNATIONAL MUSIC YEAR BOOK (£27.95)
Rhinegold Publishing, 241 Shaftesbury Avenue, London WC2H 8TF.
Tel: 020-7333 1721; Fax: 020-7333 1769.

BRITISH DESIGN AND ART DIRECTION ANNUAL (£69)
71 Great Russell Street, London WC1B 3BP.
Tel: 020-7430 8850.

BRITISH EXPORTS (£185)
Windsor Court, East Grinstead House, East Grinstead, W. Sussex RH19 1XA.
Tel: 01342-335876; Fax: 01342-335998.
Web: www.icompass.co.uk

BRITISH PERFORMING ARTS YEAR BOOK (£26.95)
Rhinegold Publishing, 241 Shaftesbury Avenue, London WC1H 8TF.
Tel: 020-7333 1721; Fax: 020-7333 1769.

BRITISH PLASTICS AND RUBBER DIRECTORY (£18)
MCM Publishing, 37 Nelson Road, Caterham, Surrey CR3 5PP. Tel: 01883-347059.

BRITISH THEATRE DIRECTORY (£42.95)
Douglas House, 3 Richmond Buildings, London W1D 3HE. Tel: 020-7437 9556; Fax: 020-7287 3463.
Web: www.rhpco.co.uk

BROWN'S NAUTICAL ALMANAC DAILY TIDE TABLES (£45) 4–10 Darnley Street, Glasgow G41 2SD.
Tel: 0141-429 1234; Fax: 0141-420 1694.
Web: www.skipper.co.uk

BUILDING SOCIETIES YEAR BOOK (£52.25)
Arnold House, 36–41 Holywell Lane, London EC2A 3SF. Tel: 020-7827 5454; Fax: 020-7827 0567.

BUSES YEAR BOOK (£13.99)
Ian Allen Publishing, Riverdene Business Park, Molesey Road, Hersham Surrey
Tel: 01932-2666600.

BUTTERWORTHS LAW DIRECTORY AND LEGAL SERVICES DIRECTORY (£64.29)
Martindale Hubbell, Holden House, 57 Rathbone Place, London WC2A 1EL. Tel: 020-7868 4890.

CASSELL DIRECTORY OF PUBLISHING (£75)
Orca, Stanley House, 3 Fleets Lane, Poole, Dorset BH15 3AJ. Tel: 01202-665432.

CHARITIES CHOICE (£69.95)
Paulton House, 8 Shepherdess Walk, London N1 7LB.
Tel: 020-7490 0049.

CHEMIST AND DRUGGIST DIRECTORY (£129)
Riverbank House, Angel Lane, Tonbridge, Kent TN9 1SE.

CHRISTIES' REVIEW OF THE YEAR (£45)
1 Langley Lane, London SW8 1TH.
Tel: 020-7389 2242; Fax: 020-7820 9659.
Web: www.christies.com

CHURCH OF ENGLAND YEARBOOK (£27.50)
Church House Publishing, Church House, Great Smith Street, London SW1P 3NZ.
Tel: 020-7898 1578; Fax: 020-7898 1449.
Web: www.chpublishing.co.uk

CHURCH OF SCOTLAND YEAR BOOK (£12)
121 George Street, Edinburgh EH2 4YN.
Tel: 0131-343 6039; Fax: 0131-220 3113.

CITY OF LONDON DIRECTORY AND LIVERY
COMPANIES GUIDE (£21.50)
Seatrade House, 42–48 North Station Road,
Colchester CO1 1RB.
Tel: 01206-545121; Fax: 01206-545190.

CIVIL SERVICE YEAR BOOK (£42.50)
PO Box 29, Norwich NR3 1GN.
Tel: 0870-600 5522.

COMMONWEALTH YEAR BOOK (£50)
PO Box 29, Norwich NE3 1GN.
Tel: 0870-600 5522.

CONCRETE YEAR BOOK (£75)
151 Rosebery Avenue, London EC1R 4GB.
Tel: 020-7505 6600; Fax: 020-7505 3813.
Web: www.nceplus.co.uk

CURRENT LAW YEAR BOOK (£325)
Cheriton House, North Way, Andover, Hants SP10 5BE.

DEBRETT'S PEOPLE OF TODAY (£140)
Kings Court, 2–16 Goodge Street, London W1T 2QA.
Tel: 020-7915 9633.

DIMENSIONS OF THE VOLUNTARY SECTOR (£75)
Charities Aid Foundation, Kings Hill, West Malling,
Kent ME19 4TA. Tel: 01732-520125.
Web: www.cafonline.org

DIPLOMATIC SERVICE LIST (£27.50)
PO Box 29, Norwich NR3 1GN.
Tel: 0870-600 5522.
Web: www.clicktso.com

DIRECTORY OF DIRECTORS (£285)
Windsor Court, East Grinstead House,
East Grinstead, W. Sussex RH19 1XA.
Tel: 01342-332042; Fax: 01342-332072.
Web: www.reedinfo.co.uk

DIRECTORY OF FURTHER EDUCATION (£76.50)
Plymbridge Distributors, Plymbridge House, Estover,
Plymouth PL6 7PY. Tel: 01752-202300.

DIRECTORY TO THE FURNITURE AND FURNISHINGS
INDUSTRY (£120)
Riverbank House, Angel Lane, Tonbridge, Kent TN9 1SE.

DOD'S PARLIAMENTARY COMPANION (£130)
1 Douglas Street, London SW1P 4PA.
Tel: 020-7828 7256; Fax: 020-7828 7269.
Web: www.dodonline.co.uk

EDUCATION AUTHORITIES' DIRECTORY AND
ANNUAL (£75)
Darby House, Bletchingley Road, Merstham, Redhill,
Surrey RH1 3DN.
Tel: 01737-642223; Fax: 01737-644283.
Web: w.schoolgovernment.co.uk/pages/pub/ead.htm

EDUCATION YEAR BOOK (£92)
128 Long Acre, London WC2E 9AN.
Tel: 020–7447 2000.

ELECTRONICS AND ELECTRICAL BUYER'S GUIDE
(£99) CMP Information Ltd, Data and Information
Services Division, Riverbank House, Angel Lane,
Tonbridge, Kent TN9 1SE.
Tel: 01732–377556; Fax: 01732–377454.
Web: www.electronics-electrical.co.uk

ENGINEERING BUYERS GUIDE (£90)
CMP Information Ltd, Data and Information
Services Division, Riverbank House, Angel Lane,
Tonbridge, Kent TN9 1SE.
Tel: 01732-377591; Fax: 01732-377454.
Web: www.cmpinformation.co.uk

EUROPA DIRECTORY OF INTERNATIONAL
ORGANISATIONS (£150)
11 New Fetter Lane, London EC4P 4EE.
Tel: 020-7842 2110; Fax: 020-7842 2249.
Web: www.europapublications.co.uk

EUROPA WORLD YEAR BOOK (£535)
11 New Fetter Lane, London EC4P 4EE.
Tel: 020-7842 2110; Fax: 020-842 2249.

FILM REVIEW (£19.95)
61A Priory Road, Kew Gardens, Richmond, Surrey
TW9 3DH. Tel: 020-8940 5198.

FOOD TRADES DIRECTORY OF THE UK AND
EUROPE (£165)
32 Vauxhall Bridge Road, London SW1V 2SS.
Tel: 020-7973 4601; Fax: 020-7973 4798.
Web: www.foodtrades.co.uk

FREELANCE PHOTOGRAPHER'S MARKET HANDBOOK
(£15.95)
Focus House, 497 Green Lanes, London N13 4BP.
Tel: 020-8882 3315; Fax: 020-8886 5174.
Web: www.thebfp.com

GAS INDUSTRY DIRECTORY (£112)
Riverbank House, Angel Lane, Tonbridge,
Kent TN9 1SE.

GLOBAL CIVIL SOCIETY (£15.99)
OUP Distribution Services, Saxon Way West, Corby,
Northants NN18 9ES.
Tel: 01536-741519; Fax: 01536-746337.
Web: www.oup.com

GOOD BRITAIN GUIDE (£14.99)
The Book Service Ltd, Colchester Road, Frating
Green, Colchester CO7 7DW.
Tel: 01206-256000; Fax: 01206-255715.

GOOD FOOD GUIDE (£15.99)
PO Box 44, Hertford, SG12 1SH.
Tel: 0800-252 1000.

GOOD GARDENS GUIDE (£14.99)
Macmillan Distribution, Houndmills, Basingstoke,
London RG21 6XS. Tel: 01256-302692.

GUARDIAN MEDIA GUIDE (£15.99)
3–7 Ray Street, London, EC1R 3DR.
Tel: 020-7239 9857; Fax: 020-7713 4471.

GUIDE TO ART EXHIBITIONS (£7.95)
Lund Humphries, Gower House, Croft Road,
Aldershot Hants GU11 3HR.
Tel: 01252-331551; Fax: 01252-344405.
Web: www.lundhumphries.com

GUINNESS WORLD RECORDS (£18)
Macmillan Distribution, Brunel Road, Houndsmills,
Basingstoke, Hants RG21 2XS.
Tel: 01256-302692.

HOLLIS SPONSORSHIP AND DONATIONS YEARBOOK
(£115)
Harlequin House, 7 High Street, Teddington
TW11 8EL. Tel: 020-8977 7711; Fax: 020-8977 1133.
Web: www.hollis-pr.com

HOLLIS UK PRESS AND PUBLIC RELATIONS ANNUAL
(£137.50)
Harlequin House, 7 High Street, Teddington
TW11 8EL. Tel: 020-8977 7711; Fax: 020-8977 1133.
Web: www.hollis-pr.com

HOUSING AND PLANNING YEAR BOOK (£110)
128 Long Acre, London WC2E 9AN.
Tel: 020-7447 2000.

INDEPENDENT SCHOOLS YEAR BOOK (£30)
17 Popes Grove, Twickenham, Middlesex TW2 5TA.
Tel: 020-8894 3066; Fax: 020-8893 3957.
Web: www.isyb.co.uk

INSURANCE DIRECTORY (£280)
39 Earlham Street, London WC2H 9LT.
Tel: 020-7306 7000; Fax: 020-7306 7141.
INTERNATIONAL SHOWCASE: THE MUSIC BUSINESS
GUIDE (£50)
Harlequin House, 7 High Street, Teddington TW11
8EL. Tel: 020-8977 7711.
Web: www.hollis-pr.com
INTERNATIONAL WHO'S WHO (£275)
11 New Fetter Lane, London EC4P 4EE.
Tel: 020-7822 4300; Fax: 020-7842 2249.
Web: www.europapublications.co.uk
JANE'S ALL THE WORLD'S AIRCRAFT (£380)
Sentinel House, 163 Brighton Road, Coulsdon,
Surrey CR5 2YH.
Tel: 020-8700 3700; Fax: 020-8700 3715.
JANE'S ARMOUR AND ARTILLERY (£380)
Sentinel House, 163 Brighton Road, Coulsdon, Surrey
CR5 2YH. Tel: 020-8700 3803; Fax: 020-8700 3715.
Web: www.janes.com
JANE'S FIGHTING SHIPS (£380)
Sentinel House, 163 Brighton Road, Coulsdon,
Surrey CR5 2NH.
Tel: 020-8700 3700; Fax: 020-8700 3715.
JANE'S HIGH SPEED MARINE TRANSPORTATION
(£365)
Sentinel House, 163 Brighton Road, Coulsdon, Surrey
CR5 2NH. Tel: 020-8700 3700; Fax: 020-8700 3715.
JANE'S INFANTRY WEAPONS (£345)
Sentinel House, 163 Brighton Road, Coulsdon, Surrey
CR5 2NH. Tel: 020-8700 3700.
Web: www.janes.com
JANE'S NAVAL WEAPON SYSTEMS (£570)
Sentinel House, 163 Brighton Road, Coulsdon, Surrey
CR5 2NH. Tel: 020-8700 3700; Fax: 020-8700 3715.
Web: www.janes.com
JANE'S WORLD RAILWAYS (£395)
Sentinel House, 163 Brighton Road, Coulsdon,
Surrey CR5 2NH.
JEWISH YEAR BOOK (£28)
Vallentine Mitchell & Co Ltd, Crown House,
47 Chase Side, Southgate, London N14 5BP.
Web: www.vmbooks.com
KELLY'S INDUSTRIAL DIRECTORY (£299)
East Grinstead House, Windsor Court,
East Grinstead, W. Sussex RH19 1XA.
Tel: 01342-326972; Fax: 01342-335747.
Web: www.kellysarch.com
KEMPE'S ENGINEERS YEAR BOOK (£128)
Riverbank House, Angel Lane, Tonbridge,
Kent TN9 1SE. Tel: 01732-377591; Fax: 01732-377479.
Web: www.cmpdata.co.uk
LAW SOCIETY'S DIRECTORY OF SOLICITORS AND
BARRISTERS, THE (£95)
Marston Book Services, PO Box 312,
Abingdon, Oxon OX14 4YN.
Tel: 01235-465656; Fax: 01235-465660.
LAXTON'S BUILDING PRICE BOOK (£99)
Linacre House, Jordan Hill, Oxford, Oxon OX2 8DP.
Web: www.bti.com
LIBRARY AND INFORMATION PROFESSIONALS
YEARBOOK, THE CHARTERED INSTITUTE OF
(£37.50)
Bookpoint Ltd, 130 Milton Park, Abingdon Oxon
OX14 4TD. Tel: 01235-827794; Fax: 01235-400454.
LLOYD'S LIST OF SHIPOWNERS (£180)
Lombard House, 3 Princess Way, Redhill, Surrey RH1
1UP. Tel: 01737-379700; Fax: 01737-379701.

LLOYD'S MARITIME DIRECTORY (£275)
Sheepen Place, Colchester CO3 3LP.
Tel: 01206-772222; Fax: 01206-772092.
Web: www.informamaritime.com
LLOYD'S PORTS OF THE WORLD (£250)
Lombard House, 3 Princess Way, Redhill, RH1 1UP.
Tel: 01737-379700; Fax: 01737-379701.
LLOYD'S REGISTER OF SHIPS (£665)
Lombard House, 3 Princess Way, Redhill, Surrey RH1
1UP. Tel: 01737–379700; Fax: 01737-379701.
LYLE OFFICIAL ANTIQUES PRICE GUIDE (£18.99)
The Book Service Limited, Distribution Centre,
Colchester Road, Frating Green, Colchester CO7 7DW.
Tel: 01206-256000; Fax: 01206-255715.
MACMILLAN REED NAUTICAL ALMANAC (£31.95)
The Book Barn, White Chimney Row, Westbourne,
Hampshire PO10 8RS.
Tel: 01243-377977; Fax: 01243-379136.
Web: www.nauticaldata.com
MARKETING HANDBOOK (£70)
Harlequin House, 7 High Street, Teddington TW11
8EL. Tel: 020-8977 7711; Fax: 020-8977 1133.
Web: www.hollis-pr.com
MEDAL YEARBOOK (£16.95)
Orchard House, Duchy Road, Heathpark, Honiton
Devon EX14 1YD. Tel: 01404-46972.
MILLER'S ANTIQUES PRICE GUIDE (£24.99)
Littlehampton Book Services, Faraday Close,
Durrington, Worthing BN13 3RB.
Tel: 01903-828911.
MINING ANNUAL REVIEW AND METALS AND
MINERALS ANNUAL REVIEW (£85)
PO Box 10, Edenbridge, Kent TN8 5NE.
Web: www.mining-journal.com
MOTOR INDUSTRY OF GREAT BRITAIN WORLD
AUTOMOTIVE STATISTICS (£155)
Forbes House, Halkin Street, London SW1X 7DS.
Tel: 020-7235 7000; Fax: 020-7235 7112.
Web: www.smmt.co.uk
MUNICIPAL YEAR BOOK, 32 Vauxhall Bridge Road,
London SW1V 2SS.
Tel: 020-7973 6402; Fax: 020-7973 4794.
Web: www.localgov.co.uk
NATURE YEARBOOK OF SCIENCE AND TECHNOLOGY
(£150)
Macmillan Distribution Ltd, Brunel Road,
Houndmills, Basingstoke, Hampshire RG21 2XS.
Tel: 01256-302692.
OFFICIAL FORMULA ONE ANNUAL OF THE SEASON
(£35)
8-16 Great New Street, London EC4A 3BN.
Tel: 020 7583 9797.
OFFSHORE OIL AND BANK DIRECTORY (£99)
CMP Information Ltd, Data and Information
Services Division, Riverbank House, Angel Lane,
Tonbridge, Kent TN9 1SE.
Tel: 01732-377591; Fax: 01732-377454.
Web: www.cmpdata.co.uk
PACKAGING INDUSTRY DIRECTORY (£99)
CMP Informations Ltd, Data and Information
Services Division, Riverbank House, Angel Lane,
Tonbridge, Kent TN9 1SE.
Tel: 01732-377591; Fax: 01732-377454.
Web: www.cmpdata.co.uk
PEARS CYCLOPEDIA (£16.99)
Penguin Direct, Bath Road, Harmondsworth, Middx
UB7 0DA. Tel: 020-8757 4030.
PHILLIPS' INTERNATIONAL PAPER DIRECTORY (£150)
Riverbank House, Angel Lane, Tonbridge, Kent TN9 1SE.
PHOTOGRAPHY YEAR BOOK (£25)
10 Hillside, London SW19 4NH.
Tel: 020-8971 2094; Fax: 020-8971 2094.

POLITICAL COMPANION (£95)
PO Box 29, Norwich NR3 1GN.
Tel: 0870-600 5522.
Web: www.clicktso.com

PRINTING TRADES DIRECTORY (£115)
Riverbank House, Angel Lane, Tonbridge Kent TN1
1SE. Tel: 01732-377591; Fax: 01732-377479.
Web: www.cmpdata.co.uk

RAILWAY DIRECTORY (£199)
PO Box 935, Finchingfield, Braintree, Essex CM7 4LN.
Tel: 01371-810433; Fax: 01371-811065.

REGIONAL TRENDS (£39.50)
PO Box 29, Norwich NR3 1GN.
Tel: 0870-600 5522.

RETAIL DIRECTORY OF THE UK (£170)
32 Vauxhall Bridge Road, London SW1V 2SS.

RIBA DIRECTORY OF PRACTICES (£50)
Construction House, 56-64 Leonard Street, London
EC2A 4LT. Tel: 020-7251 0791; Fax: 020-7608 2375.
Web: www.ribabookshop.com

ROYAL AND ANCIENT GOLFER'S HANDBOOK (£20)
Pan Macmillan Ltd, 20 New Wharf Road, London N1
9RR. Tel: 020-7014 6000; Fax: 020-7014 6001.
Web: www.panmacmillan.com

ROYAL SOCIETY YEAR BOOK (£23)
6-9 Carlton House Terrace, London SW1Y 5AG.
Tel: 020-7451 2500; Fax: 020-7930 2170.
Web: www.royalsoc.ac.uk

SOCIAL SERVICES YEAR BOOK (£125)
128 Long Acre, London WC2E 9AN.
Tel: 020-7447 2000.

SOCIAL TRENDS (£39.50)
PO Box 29, Norwich NR3 1GN.
Tel: 0870-600 5522.

SPECIAL EDUCATION DIRECTORY (£50)
Darby House, Bletchingley Road, Merstham, Redhill
RH1 3DN. Tel: 01737-642223; Fax: 01737-644283.
Web: www.schoolgovernment.co.uk/pages/sped.htm

SPON'S ARCHITECTS' AND BUILDERS' PRICE BOOK
(£115)
Spon Press, New Fetter Lane, London EC4B 4FH.
Tel: 08700-768858; Fax: 020-7842 2300.

SPON'S MECHANICAL AND ELECTRICAL SERVICES
PRICE BOOK (£115)
Spon Press, New Fetter Lane, London EC4B 4FH.
Tel: 08700-768858; Fax: 020-7842 2300.

STATESMAN'S YEARBOOK (£65)
Macmillan Building, Crinan Street, London N1 9XW.
Tel: 020-7843 4665; Fax: 020-7843 4650.
Web: www.palgrave.com

STOCK EXCHANGE YEARBOOK (£270)
Caritas Data, Paulton House, 8 Shepherdess Walk,
London N1 7LB. Tel: 020-7566 8210.

STONE'S JUSTICES' MANUAL (£325)
Halsbury House, 35 Chancery Lane, London WC2A
1EL. Tel: 020-7400 2500; Fax: 020-7400 2842.

TANKER REGISTER (£180)
12 Camomile Street, London EC3A 7BP.
Tel: 020-7334 3134; Fax: 020-7522 0330.

TRAVEL TRADE GAZETTE DIRECTORY (£66)
Riverbank House, Angel Lane, Tonbridge,
Kent TN9 1SE.

UK KOMPASS REGISTER (£470)
East Grinstead, Windsor Court, East Grinstead,
W. Sussex RH19 1XA.
Tel: 0800-018 5882; Fax: 01342-335998.
Web: www.kompass.co.uk

UK: THE OFFICIAL YEARBOOK OF THE UNITED
KINGDOM AND NORTHERN IRELAND (£37.50)
PO Box 29, Norwich NR3 1GN.
Tel: 0870-600 5522.

UNITED KINGDOM MINERALS YEARBOOK (£35)
Onshore Mineral and Energy Resources, British
Geological Survey, Keyworth, Notts NG12 5GG.
Tel: 0115-936 3100; Fax: 0115-936 3200.
Web: www.mineralsuk.com

VOLUNTARY AGENCIES DIRECTORY (£30)
NCVO Publications, Earlstrees Court, Earlstrees
Road, Corby, Northants NN17 4HH.
Tel: 01536-399016.

WHITAKER'S BOOKS IN PRINT (£550)
Woolmead House West, Bear Lane, Farnham,
Surrey GU9 7LG.
Tel: 01252-742500; Fax: 01252-742501.
Web: www.whitaker.co.uk

WHITAKER'S RED BOOK - THE DIRECTORY OF
PUBLISHERS (£15)
Woolmead House West, Bear Lane, Farnham,
Surrey GU9 7LG.
Tel: 01252-742500; Fax: 01252-742501.
Web: www.whitaker.co.uk

WHO OWNS WHOM? (£1,700)
Business Reference, Holmers Farm Way,
High Wycombe, Bucks HP12 4UL.
Tel: 01494-422000.

WHO'S WHO (£130)
37 Soho Square, London W1D 3QZ.
Tel: 020-7287 5366; Fax: 020-7734 6856.
Web: www.acblack.com

WILLING'S PRESS GUIDE (£265)
Chess House, 34 Germain Street, Chesham, Bucks
HP5 1ST. Tel: 0870-736 0010; Fax: 0870-736 0011.
Web: www.willingspress.com

WISDEN CRICKETERS' ALMANACK (£35)
13 Old Aylesfield, Froyle Road, Golden Pot, Nr. Alton
Hants GU34 4BY. Tel: 01420-83415.
Web: www.wisden.com

WOLRDWIDE GOVERNMENT DIRECTORY (£236)
Keesings Worldwide, 28A Hills Road, Cambridge,
CB2 1LA. Tel: 01223-508050; Fax: 01223-508049.

WORLD HOTEL DIRECTORY (£140)
128 Long Acre, London WC2E 9AN.
Tel: 020-7447 2000.

WORLD OF LEARNING (£335)
Europa Publications, 11 New Fetter Lane, London
EC4P 4EE. Tel: 020-7822 4300; Fax: 020-7842 4329.
Web: www.europapublications.co.uk

WORLD PRESS PHOTO YEARBOOK (£12.95)
Thames and Hudson, 181A High Holborn, London
WC1V 7QX. Tel: 020-7845 5000; Fax: 020-7845 5050.

WORLD RADIO TV HANDBOOK (£19.95)
WRTH Publications Ltd, PO Box 290, Oxford, OX2
7FT. Fax: 01865-516717.
Web: www.wrth.com

WORLD SHIPPING DIRECTORY (£220)
Lombard House, 3 Princess Way, Redhill, Surrey RH1.
1UP. Tel: 01737-379700; Fax: 01737-379001.

WRITERS' AND ARTISTS' YEARBOOK
37 Soho Square, London, W1D 3QZ.
Tel: 020-7287 5338; Fax: 020-7734 6856.
Web: www.acblack.com

YEARBOOK OF ASTRONOMY (£14.99)
25 Eccleston Place, London SW1W 9NF.
Tel: 020-7014 6000.

ZURICH INVESTMENT AND SAVINGS HANDBOOK
(£28.99)
128 Long Acre, London WC2E 9AN.
Tel: 020-7447 2000.
Web: www.pearsomed-ema.com

Employers' and Trade Associations

Most national employers' associations are members of the Confederation of British Industry (CBI).

CBI (CONFEDERATION OF BRITISH INDUSTRY)
Centre Point, 103 New Oxford Street, London WC1A 1DU.
Tel: 020-7379 7400

The CBI was founded in 1965 and is an independent non-party political body financed by industry and commerce. It exists primarily to ensure that the Government understands the intentions, needs and problems of British business. It is the recognised spokesman for the business viewpoint and is consulted as such by the Government.

The CBI represents, directly and indirectly, some 250,000 companies, large and small, from all sectors.

The governing body of the CBI is the 200-strong Council, which meets four times a year in London under the chairmanship of the President. It is assisted by 17 expert standing committees which advise on the main aspects of policy. There are 13 regional councils and offices, covering the administrative regions of England, Wales, Scotland and Northern Ireland. There is also an office in Brussels.
President, Sir Iain Vallance
Director-General, Digby Jones
Secretary, P. Forder

WALES: Ground Floor Unit 3, Columbus Walk, Brigantine Place, Atlantic Wharf, Cardiff CF10 4WW. Tel: 029–2045 3710.
Regional Director, David Rosser
SCOTLAND: 16 Robertson Street, Glasgow G2 8DS. Tel: 0141–222 2184.
Regional Director, I. McMillan
NORTHERN IRELAND: Scottish Amicable Building, 11 Donegall Square, Belfast BT1 5SE. Tel: 028–9032 6658.
Regional Director, N. Smyth

ASSOCIATIONS

ADVERTISING ASSOCIATION, Abford House, 15 Wilton Road London. Tel: 020-7828 2771; Fax: 020-7931; 0376; Web: www.adassoc.org.uk
ASSOCIATION OF BRITISH INSURERS, 51 Gresham Street, London EC2V 7HQ. Tel: 020-7600 3333; Fax: 020-7696 8999; Web: www.abi.org.uk
ASSOCIATION OF PRIVATE MARKET OPERATORS, 4 Worrygoose Lane, Rotherham, S. Yorks S60 4AD. Tel: 01709-700072; Fax: 01709-703648.
BLC LEATHER TECHNOLOGY CENTRE LTD, Leather Trade House, Kings Park Road, Moulton Park, Northampton NN3 6JD. Tel: 01604-679999; Fax: 01604-679998; Web: www.blcleathertech.com
BOSS FEDERATION, 6 Wimpole Street, London W1G 9SL. Tel: 020-7637 7692; Fax: 020-7436 3137; Web: www.bossfed.co.uk
BRITISH APPAREL AND TEXTILE CONFEDERATION, 5 Portland Place, London W1B 1PW. Tel: 020-7636 7788; Fax: 020-7636 7515.;Web: www.batc.co.uk
BRITISH BANKERS' ASSOCIATION, Pinners Hall, 105–108 Old Broad Street, London EC2N 1EX. Tel: 020-7216 8800; Fax: 020-7216 8811; Web: www.bba.org.uk

BRITISH BEER AND PUB ASSOCIATION, Market Towers, 1 Nine Elms Lane, London SW8 5NQ. Tel: 020-7627 9191; Fax: 020-7627 9123; Web: www.blra.co.uk
BRITISH CLOTHING INDUSTRY ASSOCIATION LTD, 5 Portland Place, London W1B 1PW. Tel: 020-7636 7788; Fax: 020-7636 7515.
BRITISH MARINE FEDERATION, Marine House, Thorpe Lea Road, Egham, Surrey TW20 8BF. Tel: 01784-223600; Fax: 01784-439678.
BRITISH PLASTICS FEDERATION, 6 Bath Place, Rivington Street, London EC2A 3JE. Tel: 020-7457 5000; Fax: 020-7457 5045; Web: www.bpf.co.uk
BRITISH PORTS ASSOCIATION, Africa House, 64–78 Kingsway, London WC2B 6AH. Tel: 020-7242 1200; Fax: 020-7405 1069; Web: www.britishports.org.uk
BRITISH PRINTING INDUSTRIES FEDERATION, Farringdon Point, 29-35 Farringdon Road, London EC1M 3JF. Tel: 020-7915 8300; Fax: 020-7405 7784; Web: www.bpif.org.uk
BRITISH PROPERTY FEDERATION, 7th Floor, 1 Warwick Row, London SW1E 5ER. Tel: 020-7828 0111; Fax: 020-7834 3442; Web: www.bpf.org.uk
BRITISH RETAIL CONSORTIUM, 2nd Floor, 21 Dartmouth Street, London SW1H 9BP. Tel: 020-7854 8900; Fax: 020-7854 8901.
BRITISH RUBBER MANUFACTURERS' ASSOCIATION LTD, 6 Bath Place, Rivington Street, London EC2A 3JE. Tel: 020-7457 5040; Fax: 020-7972 9008.
THE CHAMBER OF SHIPPING LTD, Carthusian Court, 12 Carthusian Street, London EC1M 6EZ. Tel: 020-7417 2800; Fax: 020-7726 2080; Web: www.british-shipping.org
CHEMICAL INDUSTRIES ASSOCIATION LTD, Kings Buildings, Smith Square, London SW1P 3JJ. Tel: 020-7963 6701; Fax: 020-7834 4470; Web: www.cia.irg.uk
COMMERCIAL RADIO COMPANIES ASSOCIATION (CRCA), 77 Shaftesbury Avenue, London W1D 5DU. Tel: 020-7306 2603; Fax: 020-7470 0062; Web: www.crca.co.uk
CONFEDERATION OF PASSENGER TRANSPORT UK, Imperial House, 15-19 Kingsway, London WC2B 6UN. Tel: 020-7240 3131; Fax: 020-7240 6565; Web: www.cpt-uk.org/cpt
CONSTRUCTION CONFEDERATION, Construction House, 56-64 Leonard Street, London EC2A 4JX. Tel: 020-7608 5004; Fax: 020-7608 5003; Web: www.constructionconfederation.co.uk
CONSTRUCTION PRODUCTS ASSOCIATION, 26 Store Street, London WC1E 7BT. Tel: 020-7323 3770; Fax: 020-7323 0307; Web: www.constprod.org.uk
DAIRY INDUSTRY FEDERATION, 19 Cornwall Terrace, London NW1 4QP. Tel: 020-7486 7244; Fax: 020-7935 3920.
ENGINEERING EMPLOYERS' FEDERATION, Broadway House, Tothill Street, London SW1H 9NQ. Tel: 020-7222 7777; Fax: 020-7222 0792; Web: www.eef.org.uk
FEDERATION OF BRITISH ELECTROTECHNICAL AND ALLIED MANUFACTURERS' ASSOCIATIONS (BEAMA), Westminster Tower, 3 Albert Embankment, London SE1 7SL. Tel: 020-7793 3000; Fax: 020-7793 3003; Web: www.beama.org.uk
FEDERATION OF MASTER BUILDERS, Gordon Fisher House, 14–15 Great James Street, London WC1N 3DP. Tel: 020-7242 7583; Fax: 020-7404-0296; Web: www.fmb.org.uk

THE FEDERATION OF BAKERS, 6 Catherine Street, London C2B 5JW. Tel: 020-7420 7190; Fax: 020-7379 0542; Web: www.bakersfederation.org.uk

FINANCE AND LEASING ASSOCIATION, 15–19 Imperial House, Kingsway, London WC2B 6UN. Tel: 020-7836 6511; Fax: 020-7420 9600; Web: www.fla.org.uk

FOOD AND DRINK FEDERATION, 6 Catherine Street, London WC2B 5JJ. Tel: 020-7836 2460; Fax: 020-7836 0580; Web: www.fdf.org.uk

FREIGHT TRANSPORT ASSOCIATION LTD, Hermes House, St John's Road, Tunbridge Wells, Kent N4 9UZ. Tel: 01892-526171; Fax: 01892-534989; Web: www.fta.co.uk

INSTITUTE OF CHARTERED FORESTERS, 7A St. Colme Street, Edinburgh EH3 6AA. Tel: 0131-225 2705. Web: www.charteredforesters.org

KNITTING INDUSTRIES' FEDERATION LTD, 12 Beaumanor Road, Leicester LE4 5QA. Tel: 0116-266 3332; Fax: 0116-266 3335.

MANAGEMENT CONSULTANCIES ASSOCIATION, 49 Whitehall, London SW1A 2BX. Tel: 020-7321 3990; Fax: 020-7321 3991; Web: www.mca.org.uk

THE NATIONAL FARMERS' UNION (NFU), Agriculture House, 164 Shaftesbury Avenue, London WC2H 8HL. Tel: 020-7331 7200; Fax: 020-7331 7313; Web: www.nfu.org.uk

NATIONAL FEDERATION OF RETAIL NEWSAGENTS, Yeoman House, Sekforde Street, London EC1R 0HD. Tel: 020-7253 4225; Fax: 020-7250 0927; Web: www.nfrn.org.uk

NATIONAL MARKET TRADERS' FEDERATION, Hampton House, Hawshaw Lane, Hoyland, Barnsley S74 0HA. Tel: 01226-749021; Fax: 01226-740329; Web: www.nmtf.co.uk

NEWSPAPER PUBLISHERS ASSOCIATION LTD, 34 Southwark Bridge Road, London SE1 9EU. Tel: 020-7207 2200; Fax: 020-7928 2067.

NEWSPAPER SOCIETY, Bloomsbury House, 74–77 Great Russell Street, London WC1B 3DA. Tel: 020-7636 7014; Fax: 020-7580 1972; Web: www.newspapersoc.org.uk

THE PAPER FEDERATION OF GREAT BRITAIN, Papermakers House, Rivenhall Road, Swindon SN5 7BD. Tel: 01793-889600; Fax: 01793-878700; Web: www.paper.org.uk

THE PUBLISHERS ASSOCIATION, 29B Montague Street, London WC1B 5BH. Tel: 020-7691 9191; Fax: 020-7691 9199; Web: www.publishers.org.uk

THE ROAD HAULAGE ASSOCIATION LTD, Roadway House, 35 Monument Hill, Weybridge Surrey KT13 8RN. Tel: 01932-841515; Fax: 01932-852516; Web: www.rha.net

SOCIETY OF BRITISH AEROSPACE COMPANIES LTD, Duxbury House, 60 Petty France, London SW1H 9EU. Tel: 020-7227 1000; Fax: 020-7227 1067; Web: www.sbac.co.uk

SOCIETY OF MOTOR MANUFACTURERS AND TRADERS LTD, Forbes House, Halkin Street, London SW1X 7DS. Tel: 020-7235 7000; Fax: 020-7235 7112; Web: www.smmt.co.uk

THE SPORT INDUSTRIES FEDERATION, Federation House, National Agricultural Centre, Stoneleigh Park, Kenilworth, Warks CV8 2RF. Tel: 02476-414999. Fax: 02476-414990; Web: www.sports-life.com

THE TIMBER TRADE FEDERATION, Clareville House, 26-27 Oxendon Street, London SW1Y 4EL. Tel: 020-7839 1891; Fax: 020-7930 0094; Web: www.ttf.co.uk

UK OFFSHORE OPERATORS ASSOCIATION LTD, Second Floor, 232-242 Vauxhall Bridge Road, London SW1V 1AY. Tel: 020-7802 2400; Fax: 020-7802 2401; Web: www.oilandgas.org.uk

UK PETROLEUM INDUSTRY ASSOCIATION LTD, 9 Kingsway, London WC2B 6XF. Tel: 020-7240 0289; Fax: 020-7379 3102; Web: www.ukpia.com

ULSTER FARMERS' UNION, 475 Antrim Road, Belfast BT15 3DA. Tel: 028-9037 0222; Fax: 028-9037 1231; Web: www.ufuni.org.

Trade Unions

Nearly 80 per cent of trade union members belong to unions affiliated to the TUC.

The Central Arbitration Committee arbitrates on trade disputes, adjudicates on disclosure of information complaints, determines claims for statutory recognition under the Employment Relations Act 1999 and certain issues relating to the implementation of the European Works Council Directive.

THE CENTRAL ARBITRATION COMMITTEE, 3rd Floor, Discovery House, 28–42 Banner Street, London EC1Y 8QE. Tel: 020-7251 9747; Fax: 020-7251 3114; Web: www.cac.gov.uk
Chairman, Sir Michael Burton; *Secretary and Chief Executive*, Katharine Elliott

TUC-AFFILIATED TRADE UNIONS

TRADES UNION CONGRESS (TUC)

Congress House, 23–28 Great Russell Street, London WC1B 3LS. Tel 020-7636 4030; Fax 020-7636 0632; Web: www.tuc.org.uk

The Trades Union Congress, founded in 1868, is an independent association of trade unions. The TUC promotes the rights and welfare of those in work and helps the unemployed. It helps its member unions promote membership in new areas and industries, and campaigns for rights at work for all employees, including part-time and temporary workers, whether union members or not. TUC representatives sit on many public bodies at national and international level. It makes representations to government, political parties, employers and international bodies such as the European Union.

The governing body of the TUC is the annual Congress. Between Congresses, business is conducted by a General Council, which meets five times a year, and an Executive Committee, which meets monthly. The full-time staff is headed by the General Secretary who is elected by Congress and is a permanent member of the General Council.

There are some 71 affiliated unions with a membership of nearly 6,800,000.
President (2002–2003), Nigel de Gruchy
General Secretary, J. Monks, elected 1993

SCOTTISH TRADES UNION CONGRESS

333 Woodlands Road, Glasgow G3 6NG
Tel 0141-337 8100; fax 0141-337 8101
Email: info@stuc.org.uk

The Congress was formed in 1897 and acts as a national centre for the trade union movement in Scotland. The STUC promotes the rights and welfare of those in work and helps the unemployed. It helps its member unions to promote membership in new areas and industries, and campaigns for rights at work for all employees, including part-time and temporary workers, whether union members or not. It makes representations to government and employers. In July 2002 it consisted of 47 unions with a total membership of 626,816 and 30 directly affiliated Trade Councils.

The Annual Congress in April elects a 39-member General Council on the basis of six industrial sections.
Chairperson, Pauline Frazer
General Secretary, Bill Speirs

AFFILIATED UNIONS AS AT JULY 2002

ABBEY NATIONAL GROUP UNION (ANGU), 2nd Floor, 16-17 High Street, Tring, Herts HP23 5AH. Tel: 01442-891122; Fax: 01442-891133; Web: www.angu.org.uk

ACCORD, Simmons House, 46 Old Bath Road, Charvil, Reading RG10 9QR. Tel: 0118-934 1808; Fax: 0118-932 0208; Web: www.accord-myunion.org

AMICUS (FORMERLY AEEU), Hayes Court, West Common Road, Bromley, Kent BR2 7AU. Tel: 020-8462 7755; Fax: 020-8315 8215; Web: www.aeeu.org.uk

AMICUS (FORMERLY MSF), MSF Centre, 33-37 Moreland Street, London EC1V 8BB. Tel: 020-7505 3000; Fax: 020-7505 3020; Web: www.msf.org.uk

ALLIANCE AND LEICESTER GROUP UNION OF STAFF (ALGUS), 22 Upper King Street, Leicester LE1 6XE. Tel: 0116-285 6585; Fax: 0116-285 4996.

ASSOCIATED SOCIETY OF LOCOMOTIVE ENGINEERS AND FIREMEN (ASLEF), 9 Arkwright Road, London NW3 6AB. Tel: 020-7317 8600; Fax: 020-7794 6406; Web: www.aslef.org.uk

ASSOCIATION OF EDUCATIONAL PSYCHOLOGISTS (AEP), 26 The Avenue, Durham DH1 4ED. Tel: 0191-384 9512; Fax: 0191-386 5287; Web: www.aep.org.uk

ASSOCIATION OF FIRST DIVISION CIVIL SERVANTS (FDA), 2 Caxton Street, London SW1H 0QH. Tel: 020-7343 1111; Fax: 020-7343 1105; Web: www.fda.org.uk

ASSOCIATION OF FLIGHT ATTENDANTS (AFA), United Airlines Cargo Centre, FA Council 07, Shoreham Road East, Heathrow Airport Hounslow TW6 3UA. Tel: 020-8276 6723; Fax: 020-8276 6706; Web: www.unitedafa.org/councils/7-london.html

ASSOCIATION OF MAGISTERIAL OFFICERS (AMO), 1 Fellmongers Path, Tower Bridge Road, London SE1 3LY. Tel: 020-7403 2244; Fax: 020-7403 2274; Web: www.amo-online.org.uk

ASSOCIATION OF UNIVERSITY TEACHERS (AUT), Egmont House, 25-31 Tavistock Place, London WC1H 9UT. Tel: 020-7670 9700; Fax: 020-7670 9799; Web: www.aut.org.uk

ASSOCIATION OF TEACHERS AND LECTURERS (ATL), 7 Northumberland Street, London WC2N 5RD. Tel: 020-7930 6441; Fax: 020-7930 1359; Web: www.askatl.org.uk

BAKERS, FOOD AND ALLIED WORKERS' UNION (BFAWU), Stanborough House, Great North Road, Stanborough, Welwyn Garden City Herts AL8 7TA. Tel: 01707-260150; Fax: 01707-261570.

BRITANNIA STAFF UNION (BSU), Court Lodge, Leonard Street, Leek, Staffordshire ST13 5JP. Tel: 01538-399627; Fax: 01538-371342; Web: www.britanniasu.org.uk

BRITISH AIR LINE PILOTS ASSOCIATION (BALPA), 81 New Road, Harlington, Hayes, Middx UB3 5BG. Tel: 020-8476 4000; Fax: 020-8476 4077; Web: www.balpa.org

BRITISH ASSOCIATION OF COLLIERY MANAGEMENT - TECHNICAL, ENERGY AND ADMINISTRATIVE MANAGEMENT (BACM-TEAM), 17 South Parade, Doncaster S. Yorks DN1 2DR. Tel: 01302-815551; Fax: 01302-815552; Web: www.bacmteam.org.uk

BRITISH ORTHOPTIC SOCIETY (BOS), Tavistock
House North, Tavistock Square, London WC1H 9HX.
Tel: 020-7387 7992; Fax: 020-7383 2584;
Web: www.orthoptics.org.uk

BROADCASTING, ENTERTAINMENT, CINEMATOGRAPH
AND THEATRE UNION (BECTU), Clapham Road,
London, SW9 9BT. Tel: 020-7346 0900; Fax: 020-7373-
377 Web: www.bectu.org.uk

CARD SETTING MACHINE TENTERS' SOCIETY
(CSMTS), 48 Scar End Lane, Staincliffe, Dewsbury
W. Yorks WF13 4NY. Tel: 01924-400206; Fax: 01924-
400206.

CERAMIC AND ALLIED TRADES UNION (CATU),
Hillcrest House, Garth Street, Hanley, Stoke-on-Trent
ST1 2AB. Tel: 01782-272755; Fax: 01782-284902.

THE CHARTERED SOCIETY OF PHYSIOTHERAPY
(CSP), 14 Bedford Row, London WC1R 4ED. Tel: 020-
7306 6666; Fax: 020-7306 6611;
Web: www.csp.org.uk

COMMUNICATION WORKERS UNION (CWU), 150
The Broadway, Wimbledon, London SW19 1RX. Tel:
020-8971 7200; Fax: 020-8971 7300;
Web: www.cwu.org

COMMUNITY AND DISTRICT NURSING ASSOCIATION
(CDNA), Thames Valley University, 32–38 Uxbridge
Road, Ealing, London W5 2BS. Tel: 020-8280 5342;
Fax: 020-8280 5341; Web: www.cdna.tvu.ac.uk

COMMUNITY AND YOUTH WORKERS UNION
(CYWU), Unit 302, The Argent Centre, 60 Frederick
Street, Birmingham B1 3HS. Tel: 0121-244 3344;
Fax: 0121-244 3345.

CONNECT, THE UNION FOR PROFESSIONALS IN
COMMUNICATIONS, 30 St George's Road, London
SW19 4BD. Tel: 020-8971 6000; Fax: 020-8971 6002;
Web: www.connectuk.org

EDUCATIONAL INSTITUTE OF SCOTLAND (EIS), 46
Moray Place, Edinburgh EH3 6BH. Tel: 0131-225 6244;
Fax: 0131-220 3151; Web: www.eis.org.uk

ENGINEERING AND FASTENER TRADE UNION
(EFTU), 22 Willow Way, Edgbaston, Warley, West
Midlands B17 8HD.

EQUITY, Guild House, Upper St Martin's Lane, London
WC2H 9EG. Tel: 020-7379 6000; Fax: 020-7379 7001;
Web: www.equity.org.uk

THE FIRE BRIGADES UNION (FBU), Bradley House,
68 Coombe Road, Kingston upon Thames, Surrey
KT2 7AE. Tel: 020-8541 1765; Fax: 020-8546 5187;
Web: www.fbu.org.uk

GENERAL UNION OF LOOM OVERLOOKERS (GULO),
9 Wellington Street, St Johns, Blackburn Lancs BB1
8AF. Tel: 01254-51760; Fax: 01254-51760.

GMB, 22–24 Worple Road, London SW19 4DD.
Tel: 020-8947 3131; Fax: 020-8944 6552;
Web: www.gmb.org.uk

GRAPHICAL, PAPER AND MEDIA UNION (GPMU),
Keys House, 63–67 Bromham Road, Bedford MK40
2AG. Tel: 01234-351521; Fax: 01234-270580;
Web: www.gpmu.org.uk

GUINNESS STAFF ASSOCIATION (GSA), Sun Works
Cottage, Park Royal Brewery, London NW10 7RR.
Tel: 020-8965 7700; Fax: 020-8963 5184.

HOSPITAL CONSULTANTS AND SPECIALISTS
ASSOCIATION (HCSA), 1 Kingsclere Road, Overton,
Basingstoke, Hants RG25 3JA. Tel: 01256-771777;
Fax: 01256-770999; Web: www.hcsa.com

INDEPENDENT UNION OF HALIFAX STAFF (IUHS),
Simmons House, 46 Old Bath Road, Charvil,
Reading RG10 9QR. Tel: 0118-934 1808;
Fax: 0118-932 0208.

ISTC, Swinton House, 324 Gray's Inn Road, London
WC1X 8DD. Tel: 020-7239 1200; Fax: 020-7278 8378;
Web: www.istc-tu.org

MUSICIANS' UNION (MU), 60–62 Clapham Road,
London SW9 0JJ. Tel: 020-7582 5566; Fax: 020-7582
9805; Web: www.musiciansunion.org.uk

NASUWT (NATIONAL ASSOCIATION OF
SCHOOLMASTERS/UNION OF WOMEN TEACHERS),
Hillscourt Education Centre, Rednal, Birmingham
B45 8RS. Tel: 0121-453 6150; Fax: 0121-457 6208;
Web: www.teachersunion.org.uk

NATFHE (THE UNIVERSITY AND COLLEGE
LECTURERS' UNION), 27 Britannia Street, London
WC1X 9JP. Tel: 020-7837 3636; Fax: 020-7837 4403;
Web: www.natfhe.org.uk

NATIONAL ASSOCIATION OF COLLIERY OVERMEN,
DEPUTIES AND SHOTFIRERS (NACODS), 37
Church Street, Barnsley S70 2AR. Tel: 01226-203743;
Fax: 01226-295563; Web: www.nacods.co.uk

NATIONAL ASSOCIATION OF CO-OPERATIVE
OFFICIALS (NACO), 6A Clarendon Place, Hyde,
Cheshire, SK14 2QZ. Tel: 0161-351 7900; Fax: 0161-
366 6800.

NATIONAL ASSOCIATION OF PROBATION OFFICERS
(NAPO), 4 Chivalry Road, London SW11 1HT.
Tel: 020-7223 4887; Fax: 020-7223 3503.

NATIONAL UNION OF DOMESTIC APPLIANCES AND
GENERAL OPERATIVES (NUDAGO), 1st Floor, 7–8
Imperial Buildings, Corporation Street, Rotherham,
S. Yorks S60 1PB. Tel: 01709-382820; Fax: 01709-
382129.

NATIONAL UNION OF JOURNALISTS (NUJ), Headland
House, 308–312 Gray's Inn Road, London WC1X 8DP.
Tel: 020-7278 7916; Fax: 020-7837 8143;
Web: www.nuj.org.uk

NATIONAL UNION OF KNITWEAR, FOOTWEAR AND
APPAREL TRADES (KFAT), 55 New Walk, Leicester
LE1 7EA. Tel: 0116-255 6703; Fax: 0116-254 4406;
Web: www.kfat.org.uk

NATIONAL UNION OF LOCK AND METAL WORKERS
(NULMW), Bellamy House, Wilkes Street, Willenhall
W. Midlands WV13 2BS. Tel: 01902-366651;
Fax: 01902-368035.

NATIONAL UNION OF MARINE, AVIATION AND
SHIPPING TRANSPORT OFFICERS (NUMAST),
Oceanair House, 750–760 High Road, London E11
3BB. Tel: 020-8989 6677; Fax: 020-8530 1015;
Web: www.numast.org

NATIONAL UNION OF MINEWORKERS (NUM),
Miners' Offices, 2 Huddersfield Road, Barnsley S.
Yorks S70 2LS. Tel: 01226-215555; Fax: 01226-215561.

NATIONAL UNION OF RAIL, MARITIME AND
TRANSPORT WORKERS (RMT), Unity House, 39
Chalton Street, London NW1 1JD. Tel: 020-7387 4771;
Fax: 020-7387 4123; Web: www.rmt.org.uk

NATIONAL UNION OF TEACHERS (NUT), Hamilton
House, Mabledon Place, London WC1H 9BD.
Tel: 020-7388 6191; Fax: 020-7387 8458;
Web: www.teachers.org.uk

PRISON OFFICERS' ASSOCIATION (POA), Cronin
House, 245 Church Street, London N9 9HW.
Tel: 020-8803 0255; Fax: 020-8803 1761.

PROFESSIONAL FOOTBALLERS ASSOCIATION (PFA),
20 Oxford Court, Bishopsgate, Manchester M2 3WQ.
Tel: 0161-236 0575; Fax: 0161-228 7229;
Web: www.givemefootball.com

PROSPECT, Prospect House, 75–79 York Road, London
SE1 7AQ. Tel: 020-7902 6600; Fax: 020-7902 6667;
Web: www.prospect.org.uk

PUBLIC AND COMMERCIAL SERVICES UNION (PCS), 160 Falcon Road, London SW11 2LN. Tel: 020-7801 2820; Fax: 020-7924 1847; Web: www.pcs.org.uk

SHEFFIELD WOOL SHEAR WORKERS' UNION (SWSWU), 17 Galsworthy Road, Sheffield S5 8QX. Tel: 07718-559 439.

THE SOCIETY OF CHIROPODISTS AND PODIATRISTS (SCP), 1 Fellmongers Path, Tower Bridge Road, London SE1 3LY. Tel: 020-7234 8620; Fax: 020-7234 8621; Web: www.feetforlife.org

THE SOCIETY OF RADIOGRAPHERS (SoR), 207 Providence Square, Mill Street, London SE1 2EW. Tel: 020-7740 7200; Fax: 020-7740 7204; Web: www.sor.org

TRANSPORT AND GENERAL WORKERS' UNION (T&G), Transport House, 128 Theobalds Road, London WC1X 8TN. Tel: 020-7611 2500; Fax: 020-7611 2555; Web: www.tgwu.org.uk

TRANSPORT SALARIED STAFFS' ASSOCIATION (TSSA), Walkden House, 10 Melton Street, London NW1 2EJ. Tel: 020-7387 2101; Fax: 020-7383 0656; Web: www.tssa.org.uk

UNDEB CENEDLAETHOL ATHRAWON CYMRU (NATIONAL ASSOCIATION OF TEACHERS OF WALES), Pen Roc, Rhodfa'r Môr, Aberystwyth Ceredigion SY23 2AZ. Tel: 01970-615577; Fax: 01970-626765; Web: www.athrawon.com

UBAC (Representing staff in the Bradford and Bingley Group and AllTel Mortgage Solutions), 18D Market Place, Malton N. Yorks YO17 7LX. Tel: 01653-697634; Fax: 01653-695222.

UNIFI, Sheffield House, 1b Amity Grove, London SW20 0LG. Tel: 020-8946 9151; Fax: 020-8879 7916; Web: www.unifi.org.uk

UNION OF CONSTRUCTION, ALLIED TRADES AND TECHNICIANS (UCATT), UCATT House, 177 Abbeville Road, London SW4 9RL. Tel: 020-7622 2442; Fax: 020-7720 4081; Web: www.ucatt.org.uk

UNION OF SHOP, DISTRIBUTIVE AND ALLIED WORKERS (USDAW), Oakley, 188 Wilmslow Road, Fallowfield, Manchester M14 6LJ. Tel: 0161-224 2804; Fax: 0161-257 2566; Web: www.usdaw.org.uk

UNION OF TEXTILE WORKERS (UTW), 18 West Street, Leek, Staffs ST13 8AA. Tel: 01538-382068; Fax: 01538-384270.

UNISON, 1 Mabledon Place, London WC1H 9AJ. Tel: 020-7388 2366; Fax: 020-7387 6692; Web: www.unison.org.uk

WRITERS' GUILD OF GREAT BRITAIN (WGGB), 430 Edgware Road, London W2 1EH. Tel: 020-7723 8074; Fax: 020-7706 2413; Web: www.writersguild.org.uk

YORKSHIRE INDEPENDENT STAFF ASSOCIATION (YISA), c/o Yorkshire Building Society, 26 Church Street, Dewsbury, West Yorkshire WF13 1JU.

WISA – THE UNION FOR WOOLWICH STAFF, 40 High Street, Swanley, Kent, BR8 8BQ. Tel: 01322-614957; Fax: 01322-614947.

NATIONWIDE GROUP STAFF UNION (NGSU), Middleton Farmhouse, 37 Main Road, Middleton Cheney, Banbury, Oxfordshire OX17 2QT. Tel: 01295-710767; Fax: 01295-712580; Web: www.ngsu.org.uk

NON-AFFILIATED UNIONS AS AT JULY 2002

BRITISH DENTAL ASSOCIATION 64 Wimpole Street, London, W1G 8YS. Tel: 020-7935 0875 Fax: 020-7487 5232 Web: www.bda-dentistry.org.uk

CHARTERED INSTITUTE OF JOURNALISTS 2 Dock Offices, Surrey Quays Road, London, SE16 2XU. Tel: 020-7252 1187 Fax: 020-7232 2302 Web: www.ioj.co.uk

NATIONAL ASSOCIATION OF HEAD TEACHERS (NAHT) 1 Heath Square, Boltro Road, Haywards Heath, W. Sussex, RH16 1BL. Tel: 01444-472472 Fax: 01444-472473

NATIONAL SOCIETY FOR EDUCATION IN ART AND DESIGN The Gatehouse, Corsham Court, Corsham Wilts, SN13 0BZ Tel: 01249-714825 Fax: 01249-716138 Web: www.nsead.org

PRISON GOVERNORS ASSOCIATION Room 718, Horseferry House, Dean Ryle Street, London, SW1P 2AW. Tel: 020-7217 8591, Fax: 020-7217 8923 Web: www.wavespace.waverider.co.uk/~prisgvuk/

RETAIL BOOK, STATIONERY AND ALLIED TRADES EMPLOYEES' ASSOCIATION 8–9 Commercial Road, Swindon, SN1 5RB. Tel: 01793-615811; Fax: 01793-421319

ROYAL COLLEGE OF MIDWIVES 15 Mansfield Street, London, W1G 9NH. Tel: 020-7312 3535; Fax: 020-7312 3536; Web: www.rcm.org.uk

SECONDARY HEADS ASSOCIATION 130 Regent Road, Leicester, LE1 7PG. Tel: 0116-299 1122; Fax: 0116-299 1123; Web: www.sha.org.uk

SOCIETY OF AUTHORS 84 Drayton Gardens, London, SW10 9SB. Tel: 020-7373 6642; Fax: 020-7373 5768; Web: www.societyofauthors.org

UNITED ROAD TRANSPORT UNION 6 High Lane, Chorlton, Manchester, M21 9EF. Tel: 0800-526639 Fax: 0161-861 0976; Web: www.urtu.com

National Academies of Scholarship

THE BRITISH ACADEMY (1901)
10 Carlton House Terrace, London SW1Y 5AH
Tel: 020-7969 5200
Web: www.britac.ac.uk

The British Academy is an independent, self-governing learned society for the promotion of the humanities and social sciences. It supports advanced academic research and is a channel for the Government's support of research in those disciplines.

The Fellows are scholars who have attained distinction in one of the branches of study that the Academy exists to promote. Candidates must be nominated by existing Fellows. At 1 June 2002 there were 729 Fellows, 13 Honorary Fellows and 317 Corresponding Fellows overseas.

President, The Viscount Runciman, PBA
Treasurer, Prof. R. J. P. Kain, FBA
Foreign Secretary, Prof. C. N. J. Mann, FBA
Publications Secretary, Dr D. J. McKitterick, FBA
Secretary, P. W. H. Brown, CBE

ROYAL ACADEMY OF ARTS (1768)
Burlington House, Piccadilly, London W1J OBD
Tel: 020-7300 8000; Fax: 020-7300 8001
Web: www.royalacademy.org.uk

The Royal Academy of Arts is an independent, self-governing society devoted to the encouragement and promotion of the fine arts.

Membership of the Academy is limited to 80 Royal Academicians, all being painters, engravers, sculptors or architects. Candidates are nominated and elected by the existing Academicians. There is also a limited class of honorary membership and there were 17 honorary members in 2002.

President, Prof. P. King, CBE, PRA
Treasurer, Prof. P. Huxley, RA
Keeper, Prof. B. Neiland, RA
Secretary, Miss L. Fitt

THE ROYAL ACADEMY OF ENGINEERING (1976)
29 Great Peter Street, London SW1P 3LW
Tel: 020-7222 2688
Web: www.raeng.org.uk

The Royal Academy of Engineering was established as the Fellowship of Engineering in 1976. It was granted a royal charter in 1983 and its present title in 1992. It is an independent, self-governing body whose object is the pursuit, encouragement and maintenance of excellence in the whole field of engineering, in order to promote the advancement of the science, art and practice of engineering for the benefit of the public.

Election to the Fellowship is by invitation only from nominations supported by the body of Fellows. Fellows are chosen from engineers of all disciplines. At July 2002 there were 1,210 Fellows, 23 Honorary Fellows and 86 Foreign Members. The Duke of Edinburgh is the Senior Fellow and the Duke of Kent is a Royal Fellow.

President, Sir Alec Broers, FRS, FREng
Senior Vice-President, Sir Duncan Michael, FREng
Vice-Presidents, G. A. Campbell, FREng; Prof. P. J. Dowling, CBE, FREng, FRS; Dr S. E. Ion, OBE, FREng; P. C. Ruffles, CBE, FRS, FREng; Prof. R. W. E. Shannon, FREng; Sir Peter Williams, CBE, FRS, FREng
Hon. Treasurer, J. W. Herbert, FREng
Hon. Secretaries, Prof. R. W. E. Shannon, FREng (*International Activities*); Prof. G. F. Hewitt, FREng, FRS (*Education and Training*)
Executive Secretary, J. Burch

THE ROYAL SCOTTISH ACADEMY (1838)
17 Waterloo Place, The Mound, Edinburgh EH1 3BG
Tel: 0131-558 7097; Fax: 0131-557 6417
Web: www.royalscottishacademy.org

The Scottish Academy was founded in 1826 to arrange exhibitions of contemporary paintings and to establish a society of fine art in Scotland. The Academy was granted a royal charter in 1838.

Members are elected from the disciplines of painting, sculpture, architecture and printmaking. Elections are from nominations put forward by the existing membership. At mid-2002 there were 3 Senior Academicians, 6 Senior Associates, 36 Academicians, 39 Associates, 4 non-resident Associates and 28 Honorary Members.

The administrative offices are temporarily located at 17 Waterloo Place while the R. S. A. building undergoes major refurbishment, scheduled for completion in Summer 2003.

President, I. McKenzie Smith, OBE, PRSA
Secretary, W. Scott, RSA
Treasurer, I. Metzstein, RSA
Librarian, P. Collins, RSA
Administrative Secretary, B. Laidlaw, ACIS

ROYAL SOCIETY (1660)
6-9 Carlton House Terrace, London SW1Y 5AG
Tel: 020-7839 5561; Fax: 020-7451 2615
Web: www.royalsoc.ac.uk

The Royal Society is an independent academy promoting the natural and applied sciences. Founded in 1660, the Society has three roles, as the UK academy of science, as a learned Society, and as a funding agency. It is an independent, self-governing body under a royal charter, promoting and advancing all fields of physical and biological sciences, of mathematics and engineering, medical and agricultural sciences and their application.

Fellows are elected for their contributions to science, both in fundamental research resulting in greater understanding, and also in leading and directing scientific and technological progress in industry and research establishments. A maximum of 42 new Fellows, who must be citizens or residents of the British Commonwealth countries or Ireland, may be elected annually.

Up to 6 Foreign Members, who are selected from those not eligible to become Fellows because of citizenship or residency, are elected annually for their contributions to science.

One Honorary Fellow may be elected each year from those not eligible for election as Fellows or Foreign members.

President, Lord May of Oxford, Kt, AC
Treasurer, Sir Eric Ash, Kt, CBE, FREng, FRS
Biological Secretary, Prof. P. Bateson, FRS
Physical Secretary, Prof. J. Enderby, CBE, FRS
Foreign Secretary, Prof. J. Higgins, DBE, FRS
Executive Secretary, S. Cox, CVO

THE ROYAL SOCIETY OF EDINBURGH
(1783)
22-26 George Street, Edinburgh EH2 2PQ
Tel: 0131-240 5000
Web: www.royalsoced.org.uk

The Royal Society of Edinburgh (RSE) is Scotland's National Academy. A wholly independent, non party-political body with charitable status, the RSE provides a forum for broadly-based interdisciplinary activity in Scotland. This includes organising conferences and lectures both for the specialist and for the general public; providing independent, expert advice to key decision making bodies, including Government and Parliament; strengthening links between academia and industry and boosting wealth generation at home. The Society's Research Awards programme annually awards nearly half a million pounds to exceptionally talented young academics and potential entrepreneurs in Scotland.

Fellows are elected by ballot after being nominated by at least four existing Fellows. At June 2002 there were 1,227 Ordinary Fellows, 69 Honorary Fellows and 14 Corresponding Fellows.

President, Prof. Sir William Stewart, FRS, FRSE
Vice-Presidents, Sir David Carter, FRSE; Prof. A. C. Walker, FRSE; The Rt. Hon. Lord Ross, PC, FRSE
Treasurer, Prof. Sir Laurence Hunter, CBE, FRSE
General Secretary, Prof. A. Miller, CBE, FRSE
Executive Secretary, Dr W. Duncan

The Research Councils

The Government funds basic and applied civil science research, mostly through the seven research councils, which are supported by the Department of Trade and Industry. The councils support research and training in universities and other higher education establishments. They also receive income for research commissioned by Government departments and the private sector. A total of £356 million is being added to the science budget over three years from 2002 to increase basic research. Of this, £252 million, (including £12 million of capital) is to be directed to cross-councils research programmes in genomics, e-science and basic technology. The remaining £104 million of resource is to be added to the science budget, mainly to provide an uplift to existing council programmes. In July 2000, the Chancellor announced a £1 billion of investment in science infrastructure for the years 2002–4, comprising £755 million from Government and £225 million from the Wellcome Trust.

The Government science budget for 2001–2 was £1,792,877 million and included the following allocations:

	2002–3 £m	2003–4 £m
BBSRC	232.603	250.151
ESRC	82.763	91.533
EPSRC	461.540	489.911
MRC	371.930	387.151
NERC	205.414	216.750
PPARC	220.383	232.208
*CCLRC	8.113	9.952
Pensions	28.450	29.740
Royal Society	28.745	29.245
Royal Academy of Engineering	4.770	5.270
DIAMOND	20.000	20.000
OST Administrative Costs	11.192	11.192
OST initiatives	3.100	3.350
Foresight Challenge	3.000	5.000
Joint Research Equipment Initiative	10.000	10.000
University Challenge	5.000	–
Higher Education Innovation Fund	20.000	40.000
Joint Infrastructure Fund	–	–
Science Enterprise Challenge	5.000	10.000
Science Research Investment Fund	125.000	250.000
Cambridge/MIT	14.000	14.000
Exchange Rate and Contingency Reserve	15.464	16.014
Exploitation of Discoveries at PSREs	–	–
Capital not yet allocated	34.000	34.000

*partially funded by the European Union

BIOTECHNOLOGY AND BIOLOGICAL SCIENCES RESEARCH COUNCIL (BBSRC)
Polaris House, North Star Avenue, Swindon SN2 1UH
Tel: 01793-413200

The BBSRC promotes and supports research and postgraduate training relating to the understanding and exploitation of biological systems; advances knowledge and technology; provides trained scientists to meet the needs of biotechnological-related industries; and provides advice, disseminates knowledge, and promotes public understanding of biotechnology and the biological sciences.
Chairman, Dr P. Doyle, CBE, FRSE
Chief Executive, Prof. J. Goodfellow, CBE

INSTITUTES

BABRAHAM INSTITUTE
Babraham Hall, Babraham, Cambridge CB2 4AT. Tel: 01223-496000. *Director*, Dr R. G. Dyer,

INSTITUTE FOR ANIMAL HEALTH
COMPTON LABORATORY, Compton, Newbury, Berks RG20 7NN. Tel: 01635-578411. *Director*, Dr C. J. Bostock
BBSRC/MRC NEUROPATHOGENESIS UNIT, Ogston Building, West Mains Road, Edinburgh EH9 3JF. Tel: 0131-667 5204.
PIRBRIGHT LABORATORY, Ash Road, Pirbright, Woking, Surrey GU24 0NF. Tel: 01483-232441. *Director*, Dr A. I. Donaldson

INSTITUTE OF ARABLE CROPS RESEARCH (IACR)
Rothamsted, Harpenden, Herts AL5 2JQ. Tel: 01582-763133. *Director*, Prof. I. R. Crute
BROOM'S BARN, Higham, Bury St Edmunds, Suffolk IP28 6NP. Tel: 01284-812200. *Director*, Dr J. D. Pidgeon
LONG ASHTON RESEARCH STATION, Long Ashton, Bristol BS18 9AF. Tel: 01275-392181. *Director*, Prof. P. R. Shewry

INSTITUTE OF FOOD RESEARCH
Norwich Research Park, Colney Lane, Norwich nr4 7ua. Tel: 01603-255000. Director, Prof. A. Robertson
INSTITUTE OF GRASSLAND AND ENVIRONMENTAL RESEARCH Aberystwyth Research Centre, Plas Gogerddan, Aberystwyth, SY23 3EB. Tel: 01970-823000. *Director*, Prof. C. Pollock, CBE
NORTH WYKE RESEARCH STATION, Okehampton, Devon EX20 2SB. *Head*, Prof. S. Jarvis

JOHN INNES CENTRE
Norwich Research Park, Colney, Norwich NR4 7UH. Tel: 01603-452571. *Director*, Prof. C. Lamb

ROSLIN INSTITUTE
Roslin, Midlothian EH25 9PS. Tel: 0131-527 4200. *Director*, Prof. G. Bulfield, FRSE

SILSOE RESEARCH INSTITUTE
Wrest Park, Silsoe, Bedford MK45 4HS. Tel: 01525-860000. *Director*, Prof. B. Day

SCOTTISH AGRICULTURAL AND BIOLOGICAL RESEARCH INSTITUTES

BIOMATHEMATICS AND STATISTICS SCOTLAND (BioSS) (administered by SCRI), University of Edinburgh, James Clerk Maxwell Building, The King's Buildings, Mayfield Road, Edinburgh EH9 3JZ. Tel: 0131-650 4901. *Director*, R. A. Kempton
HANNAH RESEARCH INSTITUTE, Mauchlin Road, Ayr KA6 5HL.Tel: 01292-674000. *Director*, Prof. M. Peaker, FRS

MACAULAY LAND USE RESEARCH INSTITUTE, Craigiebuckler, Aberdeen AB15 8QH. Tel: 01224-318611. *Director*, Prof. E. M. Gill
MOREDUN RESEARCH INSTITUTE, Pentlands Science Park, Bush Loan, Penicuik, Midlothian EH26 0PZ. Tel: 0131-445 5111. *Director*, Prof. Q. A. McKellar
ROWETT RESEARCH INSTITUTE, Greenburn Road, Bucksburn, Aberdeen AB21 9SB. Tel: 01224-712751. *Director*, Prof. P. J. Morgan
SCOTTISH CROP RESEARCH INSTITUTE (SCRI), Invergowrie, Dundee DD2 5DA. Tel: 01382-562731. *Director*, Prof. J. Hillman, FRSE

CENTRAL LABORATORY OF THE RESEARCH COUNCILS (CLRC)

Chilton, Didcot, Oxon OX11 0QX
Tel: 01235-445789; Fax: 01235-446665
Web: www.clrc.ac.uk

The CLRC was formed in April 1995. CLRC comprises Daresbury, Chilbolton and Rutherford Appleton Laboratories, which provide advanced facilities and specialist expertise to support academic and industrial research in the physical and life sciences. It is operated by the Council for the Central Laboratory of the Research Councils (CCLRC), an independent, non-departmental public body of the Office of Science and Technology, which is itself part of the Department of Trade and Industry.
Chairman, Prof. Sir Graeme Davies
Chief Executive, Prof. J. Wood

CHILBOLTON OBSERVATORY, Stockbridge, Hampshire SO20 6BJ. Tel: 01264 860391
DARESBURY LABORATORY, Daresbury, Warrington, Cheshire WA4 4AD. Tel: 01925-603000
RUTHERFORD APPLETON LABORATORY, Chilton, Didcot, Oxon OX11 0QX. Tel: 01235-821900

ECONOMIC AND SOCIAL RESEARCH COUNCIL (ESRC)

Polaris House, North Star Avenue, Swindon SN2 1UJ
Tel: 01793-413000

The purpose of the ESRC is to promote and support research and postgraduate training in the social sciences; to advance knowledge and provide trained social scientists; to provide advice on, and disseminate knowledge and promote public understanding of the social sciences.
Chairman, F. Cairncross, CBE
Chief Executive, Dr G. Marshall, FBA

RESEARCH CENTRES

CENTRE FOR THE ANALYSIS OF SOCIAL EXCLUSION, London School of Economics, Houghton Street, London WC2A 2AE. Tel: 020-7955 7419. *Director*, Prof. J. Hills
CENTRE FOR BUSINESS RESEARCH, Department of Applied Economics, University of Cambridge, Sidgwick Avenue, Cambridge CB3 9DE. Tel: 01223-335248. *Director*, Prof. A. Hughes
CENTRE FOR ECONOMIC LEARNING AND SOCIAL EVOLUTION, Department of Economics, University College London, Gower Street, London WC1E 6BT. Tel: 020-7387 7050. *Research Director (Acting)*, Prof. T. Börgers

CENTRE FOR ECONOMIC PERFORMANCE, London School of Economics, Houghton Street, London WC2A 2AE. Tel: 020-7955 7048. *Directors*, Prof. R. Layard; Prof. R. Freeman
CENTRE FOR MICROECONOMIC ANALYSIS OF PUBLIC POLICY (CMAPP), Institute for Fiscal Studies, 7 Ridgmount Street, London WC1E 7AE. Tel: 020-7636 3784. *Director*, Prof. R. Blundell
CENTRE FOR ORGANISATION AND INNOVATION, Institute of Work Psychology, University of Sheffield, Sheffield S10 2TN. Tel: 0114-222 3287. *Director*, Prof. T. Wall
CENTRE FOR RESEARCH IN DEVELOPMENT, INSTRUCTION AND TRAINING, Department of Psychology, University of Nottingham, Nottingham NG7 2RD. Tel: 0115-951 5312. *Director*, Prof. D. Wood
CENTRE FOR RESEARCH INTO ELECTIONS AND SOCIAL TRENDS, SOCIAL AND COMMUNITY PLANNING RESEARCH, 35 Northampton Square, London EC1V 0AX. Tel: 020-7250 1866. *Director*, Prof. R. Jowell
CENTRE FOR RESEARCH ON INNOVATION AND COMPETITION, Faculty of Economic and Social Studies, University of Manchester M13 9PL. Tel: 0161-275 2000. *Directors*, Prof. S. Metcalfe; Prof. R. Coombs
CENTRE FOR SKILLS, KNOWLEDGE AND ORGANISATIONAL PERFORMANCE (SKOPE), University of Oxford, Department of Economics, Manor Road, Oxford, OX1 3UP. Tel: 01865-271087. *Director*, K. Mayhews
CENTRE FOR SOCIAL AND ECONOMIC RESEARCH ON THE GLOBAL ENVIRONMENT, School of Environmental Sciences, University of East Anglia, Norwich NR4 7TJ. Tel: 01603-593176. *Director*, Prof. R. K. Turner
CENTRE FOR THE STUDY OF GLOBALISATION AND REGIONALISATION, Department of Political Science, University of Warwick, Coventry CV4 7AL. Tel: 024-7652 3916. *Directors*, Prof. R. Higgott; J. Whalley
CENTRE ON MICRO-SOCIAL CHANGE, University of Essex, Wivenhoe Park, Colchester, Essex CO4 3SQ. Tel: 01206-872957. *Director*, Prof. J. Ermisch
CENTRIM, University of Brighton, Brighton BN1 9PH. Tel: 01273-642188. *Director*, Prof. H. Rush
COMPLEX PRODUCT SYSTEMS INNOVATION CENTRE, SPRU, Mantell Building, University of Sussex, Brighton BN1 9RF. Tel: 01273-686758. *Director*, Prof. M. Hobday
FINANCIAL MARKETS CENTRE, London School of Economics, Houghton Street, London WC2A 2AE. Tel: 020-7955 7002. *Director*, Prof. D. Webb
TRANSPORT STUDIES UNIT, Centre for Transport Studies, University College London, Gower Street, London WC1E 6BT. Tel: 020-7380 7009. *Director*, Prof. P. Goodwin

RESOURCE CENTRES

BUSINESS PROCESS RESOURCE CENTRE, Warwick Manufacturing Group, University of Warwick, Coventry CV4 7AL. Tel: 024-7652 4173. *Director*, Prof. K. Bhattacharrya
CENTRE FOR ECONOMIC POLICY RESEARCH, 90–98 Goswell Road, London EC1V 7DB. Tel: 020-7878 2900. *Director*, Prof. R. Portes
ESRC DATA ARCHIVE, University of Essex, Wivenhoe Park, Colchester, Essex CO4 3SQ. Tel: 01206-872001. *Director*, K. Schurer
ESRC UK CENTRE FOR EVIDENCE BASED POLICY, Queen Mary and Westfield College, Department of Politics, Mile End Road, London E1 4NS. *Director*, Prof. K. Young

INTERNATIONAL BIBLIOGRAPHY OF THE SOCIAL SCIENCES, British Library of Political and Economic Science, London School of Economics, Houghton Street, London WC2A 2AE. Tel: 020-7955 7000. *Director*, Ms J. Sykes

INTERNATIONAL BIBLIOGRAPHY OF THE SOCIAL SCIENCES: ON-LINE RESOURCE CENTRE, LSE, 10 Portugal Street, London WC2A 2HD. Tel: 020-7955 7455. *Director*, Ms. L. Brindley

QUALITATIVE DATA ARCHIVAL RESOURCE CENTRE, DEPARTMENT OF SOCIOLOGY, University of Essex, Colchester, Essex CO4 3SQ. Tel: 01206-873058. *Director*, Prof. P. Thompson

RESOURCE CENTRE FOR ACCESS TO DATA IN EUROPE, Department of Geography, University of Durham, Durham DH1 3HP. Tel: 0191-374 7350. *Director*, Prof. R. Hudson

ENGINEERING AND PHYSICAL SCIENCES RESEARCH COUNCIL (EPSRC)

Polaris House, North Star Avenue, Swindon SN2 1ET
Tel: 01793-444000

The EPSRC promotes and supports basic, strategic and applied research and training in UK higher education institutions in the physical sciences and engineering.
Chairman, Prof. A. Ledwith, CBE, FRS
Chief Executive, Prof. J. O'Reilly, FREng, CEng

MEDICAL RESEARCH COUNCIL (MRC)

20 Park Crescent, London W1B 1AL
Tel: 020-7636 5422; Fax: 020-7436 2663;
Web: www.mrc.ac.uk

The purpose of the MRC is to promote medical and related biological research. The council employs its own research staff and funds research by other institutions and individuals, complementing the research resources of the universities and hospitals.
Chairman, Sir Anthony Cleaver
Chief Executive, Prof. G. K. Radda, CBE, D.Phil., FRS
Chairman, Neurosciences and Mental Health Board, Prof. E. Johnstone, MD, FRCP, FRCPsych
Chairman, Molecular and Cellular Medicine Board, Prof. I. C. MacLennan
Chairman, Physiological Medicine and Infections Board, Prof. N. J. Rothwell
Chairman, Health Services and Public Health Research Board, Prof. R. Fitzpatrick

LABORATORY OF MOLECULAR BIOLOGY, Hills Road, Cambridge CB2 2QH. Tel: 01223-248011. *Director*, Dr R. Henderson, FRS

RESEARCH UNITS

BIOCHEMICAL AND CLINICAL MAGNETIC RESONANCE UNIT, Magnetic Resonance Spectroscopy, John Radcliffe Hospital, Headington, Oxford OX3 9DU. Tel: 01865-221111. *Hon. Director*, P. Styles, D.Phil.

CENTRE FOR BRAIN REPAIR (MRC CAMBRIDGE), Ed Brian Building, University Forvie Site, Robinson Way, Cambridge CB2 2PY. Tel: 01223-331160. *Chairman*, Prof. D. A. S. Compston, MD, FRCP

CENTRE FOR COGNITIVE NEURO-SCIENCE (MRC IRC), Department of Experimental Psychology, University of Oxford, Oxford OX1 3UD. Tel: 01865-271144. *Director*, Prof. C. Blakemore, FRS

CENTRE FOR MECHANISMS OF HUMAN TOXICITY, Hodgkin Building, University of Leicester, PO Box 138, Lancaster Road, Leicester LE1 9HN. Tel: 0116-252 5600. *Director*, Prof. G. C. K. Roberts

CENTRE FOR PROTEIN ENGINEERING, MRC Centre, Hills Road, Cambridge CB2 2QH. Tel: 01223-248011. *Director*, Prof. A. Fersht, FRS

HUMAN GENOME MAPPING PROJECT RESOURCE CENTRE, Hinxton Hall, Hinxton, Cambridge CB10 1RQ. Tel: 01223-494500. *Director*, Dr D. Campbell

INTERDISCIPLINARY RESEARCH CENTRE IN CELL BIOLOGY, MRC Laboratory for Molecular Cell Biology, University College London, Gower Street, London WC1E 6BT. Tel: 020-7380 7806. *Director*, Dr J. Cope

MAMMALIAN GENETICS UNIT, Harwell Site, Chilton, Didcot, Oxon OX11 0RD. Tel: 01235-834393. *Director*, Prof. S. Brown

MRC ANATOMICAL NEUROPHARMACOLOGY UNIT, Mansfield Road, Oxford OX1 3TH. Tel: 01865-271865. *Director*, Prof. P. Somogyi

MRC BIOSTATISTICS UNIT, Institute of Public Health, University Forvie Site, Robinson Way, Cambridge CB2 2SR. Tel: 01223-330366. *Hon. Director*, Prof. N. E. Day

MRC CANCER CELL UNIT, HUTCHINSON/MRC RESEARCH CENTRE, Hills Road, Cambridge CB2 2XZ. Tel 01223-248011. *Director*, Prof. R. Laskey

MRC CELL BIOLOGY UNIT, University College London, Gower Street, London, WC1E 6BT. *Director*, Prof. A. Hall

MRC CENTRE, Oxford, Manor House, John Radcliffe Hospital, Headington, Oxford OX3 9DU. Tel: 01865-222124. *Head of Centre*, Dr A.-M. Coriat

MRC CLINICAL SCIENCES CENTRE, Imperial College of Medicine, Hammersmith Hospital, Du Cane Road, London, W12 0NN. *Director*, Prof. C. Higgins

MRC CLINICAL TRIALS UNIT, 222 Euston Road, London NW1 2DA. Tel: 020-7380 9991. *Director*, Prof. J. H. Darbyshire

MRC COGNITION AND BRAIN SCIENCES UNIT, 15 Chaucer Road, Cambridge CB2 2EF. Tel: 01223-355294. *Director*, Prof. W. Marslen-Wilson, FBA

MRC DUNN HUMAN NUTRITION UNIT, The Wellcome Trust, MRC Building, Addenbrooks Site, Hill Road, Cambridge CB2 2XY. Tel: 01223-415695. *Director*, Prof. Sir John Walker, D.Phil., FRS

MRC ENVIRONMENTAL EPIDEMIOLOGY UNIT, Southampton General Hospital, Southampton SO16 6YD. Tel: 023-8077 7624. *Director*, Prof. D. J. P. Barker, MD, FRCP, FRCOG

MRC FUNCTIONAL GENETICS UNIT, The Department of Human Anatomy, South Parks Road, Oxford OX1 3QX. *Director*, K. E. Davies

MRC HEALTH SERVICES RESEARCH COLLABORATION, University of Bristol, Canynge Hall, Whiteladies Road, Bristol BS8 2PR. Tel: 0117-928 9000. *Director*, Prof. P. Dieppe

MRC HUMAN GENETICS UNIT, Western General Hospital, Crewe Road, Edinburgh EH4 2XU. Tel: 0131-322 2471. *Director*, Prof. N. D. Hastie, FRSE

MRC HUMAN IMMUNOLOGY UNIT, Weatherall Institute of Molecular Science, John Radcliffe Hospital, Headington, Oxford OX1 9DS. Tel: 01865-222443. *Director*, Prof. A. McMichael

MRC HUMAN REPRODUCTIVE SCIENCES UNIT, Centre for Reproductive Biology, 37 Chalmers Street, Edinburgh EH3 9EW. Tel: 0131-229 2575. *Director*, Prof. R. P. Millar, FRCPath.

MRC IMMUNOCHEMISTRY UNIT, University Department of Biochemistry, South Parks Road, Oxford OX1 3QU. Tel: 01865-275354. *Director*, Prof. K. B. M. Reid

MRC INSTITUTE FOR ENVIRONMENT AND HEALTH, University of Leicester, 94 Regent Road, Leicester LE1 7DD. Tel: 0116-223 1600. *Director*, Dr P. Harrison

MRC INSTITUTE OF HEARING RESEARCH, University of Nottingham, Nottingham NG7 2RD. Tel: 0115-922 3431. *Director*, Prof. D. Moore

MRC LABORATORIES, THE GAMBIA, Atlantic Road, Fajara, Near Banjul, The Gambia, W. Africa. *Director*, Prof. K. McAdam, FRCP

MRC MOLECULAR HAEMATOLOGY UNIT, Weatherall Institute of Molecular Medicine, John Radcliffe Hospital, Headington, Oxford OX3 9DU. Tel: 01865-222359. *Hon. Director*, Prof. D. Higgs

MRC MOUSE GENOME CENTRE, MRC Mammalian Genetics Unit, Harwell, Didcot, Oxon OX11 0RD. Tel: 01235-834393. *Director*, Prof. S. Brown

MRC NATIONAL INSTITUTE FOR MEDICAL RESEARCH, The Ridgeway, Mill Hill, London NW7 1AA. Tel: 020-8959 3666. *Director*, Sir John Skehel

MRC PRION UNIT, Imperial College School of Medicine at St Mary's, Norfolk Place, London W2 1PG. Tel: 020-7594 3760. *Director*, Prof. J. Collinge

MRC PROTEIN PHOSPHORYLATION UNIT, Department of Biochemistry, Medical Sciences Institute, University of Dundee, Dundee DD1 5EH. Tel: 01382-344241. *Hon. Director*, Prof. Sir Philip Cohen, FRS, FRSE

MRC RADIATION AND GENOME STABILITY UNIT, Harwell Site, Chilton, Didcot, Oxon OX11 0RD. Tel: 01235-834393. *Director*, Prof. D. Goodhead, OBE, D.Phil.

MRC RESOURCE CENTRE FOR HUMAN NUTRITION RESEARCH, Elsie Widdowson Laboratory, Fulbourn Road, Cambridge CB1 9LR. Tel: 01223-426356. *Director*, Dr A. Prentice

MRC SOCIAL AND PUBLIC HEALTH SCIENCES UNIT, 6 Lilybank Gardens, Glasgow G12 8QQ. Tel: 0141-357 3949. *Director*, Prof. S. Macintyre, OBE, FRSE

MRC TOXICOLOGY UNIT, Hodgkin Building, University of Leicester, PO Box 138, Lancaster Road, Leicester LE1 9HN. Tel: 0116-252 5600. *Acting Director*, Prof. P. Nicotera

MRC VIROLOGY UNIT, INSTITUTE OF VIROLOGY, Church Street, Glasgow G11 5JR. Tel: 0141-330 4017. *Director*, Prof. D. J. McGeoch

SOCIAL, GENETIC AND DEVELOPMENTAL PSYCHIATRY RESEARCH CENTRE, Institute of Psychiatry, De Crespigny Park, Denmark Hill, London SE5 8AF. Tel: 020-7919 3873. *Director*, Prof. P. McGuffin

SYNAPATIC PLASTICITY CENTRE, School of Medical Sciences, University of Bristol, University Walk, Bristol BS8 1TD. Tel: 0117-928 7420. *Director*, Prof. G. L. Collingridge

WEATHERALL INSTITUTE OF MOLECULAR MEDICINE, John Radcliffe Hospital, Headington, Oxford OX3 9DU. Tel: 01865-222359. *Director*, Prof. A. McMichael, FRCP, FRS

NATURAL ENVIRONMENT RESEARCH COUNCIL (NERC)

Polaris House, North Star Avenue, Swindon SN2 1EU
Tel: 01793-411500; Fax: 01793-411510;
Web:www.nerc.ac.uk

The UK's Natural Environment Research Council (NERC) funds and carries out impartial scientific research in the sciences of the environment. Its work covers the full range of atmospheric, earth, terrestrial and aquatic sciences, from the depth of the oceans to the upper atmosphere. Its mission is to gather and apply knowledge, create understanding and predict the behaviour of the natural environment and its resources. *Chairman*, R. Margetts, CBE, FREng *Chief Executive*, Prof. J. Lawton, CBE, FRS

RESEARCH CENTRES

BRITISH ANTARCTIC SURVEY, High Cross, Madingley Road, Cambridge, CB3 0ET. Tel: 01233-221400. *Director*, Prof. C. Rapley

BRITISH GEOLOGICAL SURVEY, Kingsley Dunham Centre, Keyworth, Nottingham, NG12 5GG. Tel: 0115-936 3100. *Director*, Dr D. Fawley

CENTRE FOR ECOLOGY AND HYDROLOGY (CEH), Corporate Planning Office, Polaris House, North Star Avenue, Swindon, SN2 1EU. Tel: 01793-442524. *Director*, Prof. P. Nuttall, OBE

COLLABORATIVE CENTRES

CENTRE FOR OBSERVATION AND MODELLING OF EARTHQUAKES AND TECTONICS, COMET Centre of Excellence, Department of Earth Sciences, University of Oxford, Parks Road, Oxford OX1 3PR. Tel: 01865-272000. *Head of Department*, Prof. J. Woodhouse

CENTRE FOR POLAR OBSERVATION AND MODELLING, Department of Space and Climate Physics, Pearson Building, University College London, Gower Street, London WC1E 6BT. Tel: 020-7679 3031. *Director*, Dr B. Parson

CENTRE FOR POPULATION BIOLOGY, Imperial College, Silwood Park, Ascot, SL5 7PY. Tel: 0200-7594 2474. *Director*, Prof. J. Godfray

DATA ASSIMILATION RESEARCH CENTRE, Department of Meteorology, University of Reading, Reading RG6 6BB. Tel: 0118-931 6981. *Director*, Prof. R. O'Neill

ENVIRONMENTAL SYSTEMS SCIENCE CENTRE, University of Reading, PO Box 238, Reading, RG6 6AL. Tel: 0118- 931 8741. *Director*, Prof. R. Gurney

NERC CENTRE FOR ATMOSPHERIC SCIENCE, University of Reading, Earley Gate, PO Box 243, Reading RG6 6BB. Tel: 0118-931 6979

NERC CENTRE FOR TERRESTRIAL CARBON DYNAMICS, University of Sheffield, Hicks Building, Hounsfield Road, Sheffield S3 7RH. Tel: 0114-222 3803

PLYMOUTH MARINE LABORATORY, Prospect Place, West Hoe, Plymouth, PL1 3DH. Tel: 01752-633100. *Director*, Prof. N. Owens

PROUDMAN OCEANOGRAPHIC LABORATORY, Bidston Observatory, Birkenhead, Merseyside L43 7RA. Tel: 0151-653 8633. *Director*, Dr E. Hill

SCOTTISH ASSOCIATION FOR MARINE SCIENCE, Dunstaffnage Marine Laboratory, by Dunbeg, Oban, Argyll, PA37 1QA. Tel: 01631-559000. *Director*, Prof. G. Shimmield

SEA MAMMAL RESEARCH UNIT, Gatty Marine Laboratory, University of St Andrews, Fife, KY16 8LB. Tel: 01334-462630, *Director*, Prof. I. Boyd

SOUTHAMPTON OCEANOGRAPHY CENTRE, University of Southampton, European Way, Southampton, SO14 3ZH. Tel: 023-8059 6666. *Director*, Prof. H. Roe

TYNDALL CENTRE, School of Environmental Sciences, University of East Anglia, Norwich, Norfolk NR4 7TJ. Tel: 01603-593900. *Director*, Dr M. Hulme

PARTICLE PHYSICS AND ASTRONOMY RESEARCH COUNCIL (PPARC)

Polaris House, North Star Avenue, Swindon SN2 1SZ
Tel: 01793-442000; Fax: 01793-442002;
Email: pr.pus@pparc.ac.uk

The Particle Physics and Astronomy Research Centre (PPARC) is the UK's strategic science investment agency. It funds research, education and public understanding in four broad areas of science – particle physics, astronomy, cosmology and space sciences.

PPARC is government funded and provides research grants and studentships to scientists in British universities, gives researchers access to world-class facilities and funds the UK membership of international bodies such as the European Laboratory for Particle Physics (CERN), the European Space Agency (ESA) and The European Southern Observatory (ESO). It also contributes money to the UK telescopes overseas on La Palma, Hawaii, Australia and in Chile, the UK Astronomy Technology Centre at the Royal Observatory, Edinburgh and the MERLIN/VLBI National Facility.
Chairman, P. Warry
Chief Executive, Prof. I. Halliday, FRSE, FINSTP

ISAAC NEWTON GROUP OF TELESCOPES, Apartado de Coreos 321, Santa Cruz de la Palma, Tenerife 38780, Canary Islands. Tel: 00 3422-411048. *Director*, R. Rutten

JOINT ASTRONOMY CENTRE, 660 N A'ohoku Place, University Park, Hilo, Hawaii 96720. Tel: Hawaii 961 3756. *Head*, Prof. G. Davies

UK ASTRONOMY TECHNOLOGY CENTRE, Blackford Hill, Edinburgh EH9 3HJ. Tel: 0131-668 8100. *Director*, Dr A. Russell

Research and Technology Organisations

The following industrial and technological research bodies are members of the Applied Industrial Research Trading Organisations (AIRTO). Members' activities span a wide range of disciplines from life sciences to engineering. Their work includes basic research, development and design of innovative products or processes, instrumentation testing and certification, and technology and management consultancy. AIRTO publishes a directory to help clients identify the organisations that might be able to assist them.

AIRTO, PO Box 85, Leatherhead, Surrey KT22 7RY. Tel: 01372- 374153. *President*, Dr B. Blunden, OBE

ADVANCED MANUFACTURING TECHNOLOGY RESEARCH INSTITUTE, Hulley Road, Macclesfield, Cheshire SK10 2NE. Tel: 01625-425421. *Managing Director*, D. Palethorpe

AIRCRAFT RESEARCH ASSOCIATION LTD, Manton Lane, Bedford MK41 7PF. Tel: 01234-350681. *Chief Executive*, B. Timmins

BLC (THE LEATHER TECHNOLOGY CENTRE), Leather Trade House, Kings Park Road, Moulton Park, Northants NN3 6JD. Tel: 01604-679999. *Chief Executive*, Dr K. Alexander

BRE (BUILDING RESEARCH ESTABLISHMENT), Gartson, Watford, Hertfordshire, WD2 7JR. Tel: 01923-664000. *Chief Executive*, Dr M. Wyatt

BREWING RESEARCH INTERNATIONAL (*Alcoholic beverages*), Lyttel Hall, Coopers Hill Road, Nutfield, Surrey RH1 4HY. Tel: 01737-822272. *Director-General*, Dr M. Kierstan

BRITISH MARITIME TECHNOLOGY LTD, Orlando House, 1 Waldegrave Road, Teddington, Middx TW11 8LZ. Tel: 01923-664000. *Chief Executive*, D. Goodrich.

BRITISH TEXTILE TECHNOLOGY GROUP, Wira House, West Park Ring Road, Leeds LS16 6QL. Tel: 0113-259 1999; Shirley House, Wilmslow Road, Didsbury, Manchester M20 2RB. Tel: 0161-445 8141. *Chief Executive*, A. King

BUILDING SERVICES RESEARCH AND INFORMATION ASSOCIATION, Old Bracknell Lane West, Bracknell, Berks RG12 7AH. Tel: 01344-426511. *Chief Executive*, A. Eastwell

CAMPDEN AND CHORLEYWOOD FOOD RESEARCH ASSOCIATION, Chipping Campden, Glos GL55 6LD. Tel: 01386-842000. *Director-General*, Prof. C. Dennis

CENTRAL LABORATORY OF THE RESEARCH COUNCILS, Chilton, Didcot, Oxfordshire, OX11 0QX. Tel: 01235-821900. *Chairman*, Prof. B. Eyre

CERAM RESEARCH (BRITISH CERAMIC RESEARCH LTD), Queen's Road, Penkhull, Stoke-on-Trent ST4 7LQ. Tel: 01782-764444. *Chief Executive*, Dr N. E. Sanderson

CIRIA (CONSTRUCTION INDUSTRY RESEARCH AND INFORMATION ASSOCIATION), 6 Storey's Gate, London SW1P 3AU.
Tel: 020-7222 8891. *Director-General*, Dr P. L. Bransby

CRL (*Specialist products, technology licences, research and development*), Dawley Road, Hayes, Middx UB3 1HH. Tel: 020-8848 9779. *Managing Director*, Dr J. White

ERA TECHNOLOGY LTD (*Electronic, electrical, materials and structural engineering*), Cleeve Road, Leatherhead, Surrey KT22 7SA. Tel: 01372-367000. *Financial and Commercial Director*, C. Perks

FIRA INTERNATIONAL LTD (FURNITURE INDUSTRY RESEARCH ASSOCIATION), Maxwell Road, Stevenage, Herts SG1 2EW. Tel: 01438-313433. *Managing Director*, H. Davies

HR WALLINGFORD GROUP LTD (*Hydroinformatics and engineering*), Howbery Park, Wallingford, Oxon OX10 8BA. Tel: 01491-835381. *Chief Executive*, Dr S. W. Huntington

ITRI LIMITED, (*Tin and chemicals*), Kingston Lane, Uxbridge, Middlesex UB8 3PJ. Tel: 01895-272 406. *Company Secretary*, G. W. Noyes

LABORATORY OF THE GOVERNMENT CHEMIST, Queens Road, Teddington, Middx TW11 0LY. Tel: 020-8943 7300. *Chief Executive and Government Chemist*, Dr R. Worswick

LEATHERHEAD FOOD RESEARCH ASSOCIATION, Randalls Road, Leatherhead, Surrey KT22 7RY. Tel: 01372-376761. *Director*, Dr R. Pugh

MATERIALS ENGINEERING RESEARCH LABORATORY LTD, Tamworth Road, Hertford SG13 7DG. Tel: 01992-500120. *Managing Director*, Dr. R. H. Martin

MINERAL INDUSTRY RESEARCH ORGANISATION, Expert House, Sandford Street, Lichfield, Staffs WS13 6QA. Tel: 01543-262957. *Director*, N. Roberts

MOTOR INDUSTRY RESEARCH ASSOCIATION, Watling Street, Nuneaton, Warks CV10 0TU. Tel: 024-7635 5000. *Managing Director*, J. R. Wood

MOTOR INSURANCE REPAIR RESEARCH CENTRE, Colthorp Lane, Thatcham, Berks, RG19 4NP. Tel: 01635-868855. *Chief Executive*, P. Roberts

THE NATIONAL COMPUTING CENTRE LTD, Oxford
House, Oxford Road, Manchester M1 7ED. Tel: 0161-
228 6333. *Chief Executive*, M. Gough
NATIONAL PHYSICAL LABORATORY, Queens Road,
Teddington, Middx TW11 0LW. Tel: 020-8977 3222.
Deputy Director, Dr A. Wallard
NCIMB LIMITED (*Microbiological supply and bacterial
culture collection*), 23 St Machar Drive, Aberdeen, AB24
3RY. Tel: 01224-273332. *Chief Executive*, Dr A. Syms
PAINT RESEARCH ASSOCIATION, 8 Waldegrave Road,
Teddington, Middx TW11 8LD. Tel: 020-8977 4427.
*Acting Managing Director, Company Secretary and
Finance Director*, J. Marshall
PERA GROUP (*Multi-disciplinary research, design,
development and consultancy*), Middle Aston House,
Middle Aston, Oxon OX6 3PT. Tel: 01869-347755. *Chief
Executive*, Dr P. Davies
PIRA INTERNATIONAL (*Paper and board, printing,
publishing and packaging*), Randalls Road,
Leatherhead, Surrey KT22 7RU. Tel: 01372-802000.
Managing Director, M. Hancock
QINETIQ, (*Science Consultancy*), Cody Building, Ively
Road, Farnborough, Hants GU14 0LX. Tel: 01252-
394555. *Chief Executive*, Sir John Chisholm, FEng
RAPRA TECHNOLOGY LTD (*Rubber and plastics*),
Shawbury, Shrewsbury SY4 4NR. Tel: 01939-250383;
North East Centre, 18 Belasis Court, Belasis
Technology Park, Billingham TS23 4AZ. Tel: 01642-
370406. *Managing Director*, A. Ward
SATRA TECHNOLOGY CENTRE (*Footwear, apparel,
safety products and furniture*), Satra House,
Rockingham Road, Kettering, Northants NN16 9JH.
Tel: 01536-410000. *Chief Executive*, Dr R. E. Whittaker
SCOTCH WHISKY RESEARCH INSTITUTE, The
Robertson Trust Building, Research Park North,
Riccarton, Edinburgh, EH14 4AP. Tel: 0131 449-8900.
Director, Dr G. M. Steele
SIRA LTD (*Measurement, instrumentation, control and
optical systems technology*), South Hill, Chislehurst,
Kent BR7 5EH. Tel: 020-8467 2636. *Managing Director*,
Prof. R. A. Brook
SMITH INSTITUTE (*Mathematics and computing*), PO
Box 183, Guildford, Surrey GU2 5GG. Tel: 01483-
579108. *Chairman of the Council*, Dr B. Smith
SPORTS TURF RESEARCH INSTITUTE, St Ives Estate,
Bingley, W. Yorks BD16 1AU. Tel: 01274-565131. *Chief
Executive*, Dr G. McKillop
STEEL CONSTRUCTION INSTITUTE, Silwood Park,
Ascot, Berks SL5 7QN. Tel: 01344-623345. *Director*, Dr
G. Owens
TNO BIBRA INTERNATIONAL LTD, Woodmansterne
Road, Carshalton, Surrey SM5 4DS. Tel: 020-8652 1000,
Director, Dr G. van der Veek
TRADA TECHNOLOGY LTD (*Timber and wood-based
products*), Chiltern House, Stocking Lane, Hughenden
Valley, High Wycombe, Bucks HP14 4ND. Tel: 01494-
563091. *Managing Director*, A. Abbott
TRANSPORT RESEARCH LABORATORY, Old
Wokingham Road, Crowthorne, Berks RG45 6AU.
Tel: 01344-773131. *Chief Executive*, G. Clarke
TWI ABINGTON HALL, Abington, Cambridge CB1 6AL.
Tel: 01223-891162. *Chief Executive*, A. B. M.
Braithwaite, OBE

Sports Bodies

CENTRAL COUNCIL OF PHYSICAL RECREATION,
Francis House, Francis Street, London SW1P 1DE.
Tel: 020-7828 3163; Fax: 020-7630 8820; *General
Secretary,* M. Denton
SPORT ENGLAND, 16 Upper Woburn Place, London
WC1H 0QP. Tel: 020-7273 1500; Fax: 020-7383 5740;
Web: www.sportengland.org; *Chief Executive,* D.
Moffett. *Chairman,* T. Brooking
SPORTSCOTLAND, Caledonia House, South Gyle,
Edinburgh EH12 9DQ. Tel: 0131-317 7200;
Fax: 0131-317 7202; Web: www.sportscotland.org.uk;
Chief Executive, I. Robson. *Chairman,* A. Dempster
SPORTS COUNCIL FOR NORTHERN IRELAND, House
of Sport, Upper Malone Road, Belfast BT9 5LA.
Tel: 028-9038 1222; Fax: 028-9068 2757;
Web: www.sportni.net; *Chief Executive,* E. McCartan.
Chairman, Prof. E. Saunders
SPORTS COUNCIL FOR WALES, Sophia Gardens,
Cardiff CF11 9SW. Tel: 029-2030 0500; Fax: 029-2030
0600; Web: www.sports-council-wales.co.uk; *Chief
Executive,* Dr H. Jones. *Chairman,* G. Davies
UK SPORT, 40 Bernard Street, London WC1N 1ST.
Tel: 020-7841 9500; Fax: 020-7841 8850;
Web: www.uksport.gov.uk; *Chief Executive,* R.
Callicott. *Chairman,* Sir Rodney Walker

Angling
NATIONAL FEDERATION OF ANGLERS, Halliday
House, Egginton Junction, Derbys DE65 6GU.
Tel: 01283-734735; Fax: 01283-734799;
Web: www.nfadirect.com; *Administration Manager,*
Mrs J. A. Price. *President,* K. W. Ball

Archery
GRAND NATIONAL ARCHERY SOCIETY, Lilleshall
National Sports Centre, Newport, Shropshire TF10
9AT. Tel: 01952-677888; Fax: 01952-606019;
Web: www.gnas.org; *Chief Executive,* D. Sherratt.
Chairman, D. V. Whiteman. *President,* A. Davies

Association Football
FOOTBALL ASSOCIATION, 25 Soho Square, London
W1D 4FA. Tel: 020-7745 4545; Fax: 020-7745 4546;
Web: www.thefa.org; *Chairman,* G. Thompson, *Chief
Executive,* A. Crozier
FOOTBALL ASSOCIATION OF WALES, Plymouth
Chambers, 3 Westgate Street, Cardiff CF10 1DP.
Tel: 029-2037 2325; Fax: 029-2034 3961;
Web: www.faw.org.uk; *Secretary-General,* D. G.
Collins. *President,* D. W. Shantlin
FOOTBALL LEAGUE, 11 Connaught Place,
London W2 2ET. Tel: 0870-4420 1888;
Web: www.football-league.co.uk; *Chairman,* Keith
Harris.
IRISH FOOTBALL LEAGUE, 96 University Street, Belfast
BT7 1HE. Tel: 028-9024 2888; Fax: 028-9033 0773;
Web: www.irish-league.co.uk; *Secretary,* H. Wallace.
President, J. Semple
SCOTTISH FOOTBALL ASSOCIATION, Hampden Park,
Glasgow G42 9AY. Tel: 0141-616 6000; Fax: 0141-616
6001; Web: www.scottishfa.co.uk; *Chief Executive,* D.
Taylor. *President,* J. McGinn
SCOTTISH FOOTBALL LEAGUE, The National Stadium,
Hampden Park, Glasgow G42 9EB.
Tel: 0141-620 4160; Fax: 0141-620 4161;
Web: www.scottishfootball.com; *Secretary,* Peter
Donald

Athletics
ATHLETICS ASSOCIATION OF WALES, The Manor,
Coldra Woods, Newport NP18 1WA. Tel: 01633-
416633; Fax: 01633-416699;
Web: www.welshathletics.org; *President,* Dr Hedydd
Davies; *Hon Secretary,* Jan Evans
NORTHERN IRELAND ATHLETIC FEDERATION,
Athletics House, Old Coach Road, Belfast BT9 5PR.
Tel: 028-9060 2707; Fax: 028-9030 9939;
Web: www.niathletics.org; *Secretary,* J. Allen.
Chairman, Robert Rea. *President,* E H Wilson
SCOTTISH ATHLETICS FEDERATION, Caledonia House,
South Gyle, Edinburgh EH12 9DQ. Tel: 0131-317
7320; Fax: 0131-317 7321; Web: www.saf.org.uk;
President, Mr Frank Clement. *Chief Executive,* D. Joy
UK ATHLETICS, Athletics House, 10 Harborne Road,
Edgbaston, Birmingham B15 3AA. Tel: 0121-456 5098;
Fax: 0121-456 8752; Web: www.ukathletics.org; *Chief
Executive,* D. Moorcroft, OBE. *Information Officer,* W.
Adcocks

Badminton
BADMINTON ASSOCIATION OF ENGLAND LTD,
National Badminton Centre, Bradwell Road,
Loughton Lodge, Milton Keynes MK8 9LA.
Tel: 01908-268400; Fax: 01908-268412;
Web: www.baofe.co.uk; *Chief Executive,* S. Baddeley.
Chairman, J. Havers. *President,* W. Andrew
SCOTTISH BADMINTON UNION, Cockburn Centre,
40 Bogmoor Place, Glasgow G51 4TQ.
Tel: 0141-445 1218; Fax: 0141-425 1218;
Web: www.scotbadminton.demon.co.uk; *Chief
Executive,* Miss A. Smillie. Hon. *Secretary,* I. E. Brown
WELSH BADMINTON UNION, Fourth Floor, 3 Westgate
Street, Cardiff CF10 1DP. Tel: 029-2022 2082;
Fax: 029-2039 4282; Web: www.welshbadminton.net;
Director of Badminton, L. Williams

Baseball
SOFTBALL UK, Ariel House, 74A Charlotte Street,
London W1P 1LR. Tel: 020-7453 7055; Fax: 020-7453
7007; Web: www.baseballsoftballuk.com; *Chief
Executive,* B. Fromer

Basketball
BASKETBALL SCOTLAND, Caledonia House, South
Gyle, Edinburgh EH12 9DQ. Tel: 0131-317 7260; Fax:
0131-317 7489; Web: www.scottish-basketball.com;
Administration Officer, Kevin Pringle.
ENGLISH BASKETBALL ASSOCIATION, 48 Bradford
Road, Stanningley, Leeds LS28 6DF.
Tel: 0113-236 1166; Fax: 0113-236 1022;
Web: www.englandbasketball.co.uk; *Chief Executive,*
S. Kirkland. *President,* K. Mitchell, OBE

Billiards
WORLD LADIES BILLIARDS AND SNOOKER
ASSOCIATION, The Ground Floor, Albert House,
111–117 Victoria Street, Bristol BS1 6AX.
Tel: 0117-317 8200. *Chairman* J. Ferguson
WORLD PROFESSIONAL BILLIARDS AND SNOOKER
ASSOCIATION, Ground Floor, Albert House,
111–117 Victoria Street, Bristol BS1 6AX. Tel: 0117-
317 8200; Fax: 0117-317 8300; Web:
www.worldsnooker.com; *Chairman,* J. Ferguson

Bobsleigh

BRITISH BOBSLEIGH ASSOCIATION, Department of Sports Development and Recreation, University of Bath, Claverton Down, Bath BA2 7AY. Tel: 01225-826826; Fax: 01225-32369; Web: www.british-bobsleigh.com; *Chairman*, R. B. B. Ropner. *Administrator*, G. C. Fraser

Bowls

BRITISH ISLES BOWLS COUNCIL, 23 Leysland Avenue, Countesthorpe, Leics LE8 5XX. Tel: 0116-277 3234; Fax: 0116-277 3234; *Hon. Secretary*, Mr Swatland

BRITISH ISLES WOMEN'S BOWLING COUNCIL, EWBA Office, Victoria Park, Archery Road, Leamington Spa, Devon EX12 2AP. Tel: 01296-43068; Fax: 01296-332024; *Hon. Secretary*, Mrs N. Colling, MBE

BRITISH ISLES WOMEN'S INDOOR BOWLS COUNCIL, 101 Skyline Drive, Lambeg Lisburn BT27 4HW. *Secretary*, Mrs Doreen Miskelly

ENGLISH BOWLING ASSOCIATION, Lyndhurst Road, Worthing, W. Sussex BN11 2AZ. Tel: 01903-820222; Fax: 01903-820444; Web: www.bowlsengland.com; *Chief Executive*, G. D. Shaw

ENGLISH INDOOR BOWLING ASSOCIATION, David Cornwell House, Bowling Green, Leicester Road, Melton Mowbray, Leics LE13 0FA. Tel: 01664-481900; Fax: 01664-428888; Web: www.eiba.co.uk; *Secretary*, D. N. Brown. *President*, D. R. Murley

ENGLISH WOMEN'S BOWLING ASSOCIATION, EWBA Office, Victoria Park, Archery Road, Leamington Spa, Warks CV31 3PT. Tel: 01296-430686; Fax: 01296-332024; *Hon. Secretary*, Mrs N. Colling, MBE. *President*, Mrs B. Morley

ENGLISH WOMEN'S INDOOR BOWLING ASSOCIATION, 3 Scirocco Close, Moulton Park, Northampton NN3 6AP. Tel: 01604-494163; Fax: 01604-494434; *Secretary*, Mrs M. E. Ruff. *President*, J. Mason

Boxing

THE AMATEUR BOXING ASSOCIATION OF ENGLAND LTD, Crystal Palace National Sports Centre, London SE19 2BB. Tel: 020-8778 0251; Fax: 020-8778 9324; *Chairman*, J. Smart

BRITISH BOXING BOARD OF CONTROL LTD, Jack Petersen House, 52A Borough High Street, London SE1 1XN. Tel: 020-7403 5879; Fax: 020-7378 6670; Web: www.bbbofc.com; *General Secretary*, S. J. Block. *President*, L. Read, QPM. *Chairman*, Lord Brooks of Tremorfa, DL

Canoeing

BRITISH CANOE UNION, John Dudderidge House, Adbolton Lane, West Bridgford, Nottingham NG2 5AS. Tel: 0115-982 1100; Fax: 0115-982 1797; Web: www.bcu.org.uk; *Chief Executive*, P. Owen. *Chairman*, A. Laws

Chess

BRITISH CHESS FEDERATION, The Watch Oak, Chain Lane, Battle, E. Sussex TN33 0YD. Tel: 01424-775222; Fax: 01424-775904; Web: www.bcf.ndirect.co.uk; *President*, Gerry Walsh. *Chief Executive*, Susan Richards

Cricket

ENGLAND AND WALES CRICKET BOARD, Lord's Cricket Ground, London NW8 8QN. Tel: 020-7432 1200; Fax: 020-7289 5619; Web: www.ecb.co.uk; *Chief Executive*, T. Lamb

MCC, Lord's Cricket Ground, London NW8 8QN. Tel: 020-7289 1611; Fax: 020-7289 9100; Web: www.mcc.org.uk; *Secretary and Chief Executive*, R. D. V. Knight. *President*, E. R. Dexter, CBE

Croquet

CROQUET ASSOCIATION, c/o The Hurlingham Club, Ranelagh Gardens, London SW6 3PR. Tel: 020-7736 314; Fax: 020-7736 3148; Web: www.croquet.org.uk; *Secretary*, N. R. Graves. *Chairman*, R. Q. Barrett. *President*, J. W. Solomon

Cycling

BRITISH CYCLING FEDERATION, National Cycling Centre, Stuart Street, Manchester M11 4DQ. Tel: 0870-871 2000; Fax: 0870-871 2001; Web: www.britishcycling.org.uk; *Chief Executive*, P. King. *President*, B. Cookson

CYCLING TIME TRIALS, 77 Arlington Drive, Pennington, Leigh, Lancs WN7 3QP. Tel: 01942-603976; Fax: 01942-262326; Web: www.ctt.org.uk; *National Secretary*, P. Heaton. *Chairman*, P. McGrath

Darts

BRITISH DARTS ORGANISATION, 2 Pages Lane, Muswell Hill, London N10 1PS. Tel: 020-8883 5544; Fax: 020-8883 0109; Web: www.bdodarts.com; *Director*, O. A. Croft

Equestrianism

BRITISH EQUESTRIAN FEDERATION, National Agricultural Centre, Stoneleigh Park, Kenilworth, Warks CV8 2RH. Tel: 024-7669 8871; Fax: 024-7669 6484; Web: www.bef.co.uk; *Chief Executive*, A. Finding. *Chairman and President*, P. Billington

BRITISH EVENTING, National Agricultural Centre, Stoneleigh Park, Kenilworth, Warks CV8 2RN. Tel: 024-7669 8856; Fax: 024-7669 7235; Web: www.britisheventing.com; *Chief Executive*, P. Durrant

Eton Fives

ETON FIVES ASSOCIATION, 3 Bourchier Close, Sevenoaks, Kent TN13 1PD. Tel: 01732-458775; Fax: 01732-743112; Web: www.etonfives.co.uk; *Secretary*, M. R. Fenn. *Chairman*, M. D. Constantinidi. *President*, J. D. C. Vargas

Fencing

BRITISH FENCING ASSOCIATION, 1 Baron's Gate, 33–35 Rothschild Road, London W4 5HT. Tel: 020-8742 3032; Fax: 020-8742 3033; Web: www.britishfencing.com; *President*, Keith Smith

Gliding

BRITISH GLIDING ASSOCIATION, Kimberley House, Vaughan Way, Leicester LE1 4SE. Tel: 0116-253 105; Fax: 0116-251 5939; Web: www.gliding.co.uk; *Secretary*, B. Rolfe

Golf

LADIES' GOLF UNION, The Scores, St Andrews, Fife KY16 9AT. Tel: 01334-475811; Fax: 01334-472818; Web: www.lgu.org; *Secretary/CEO*, Andy Salmon

THE ROYAL AND ANCIENT GOLF CLUB OF ST ANDREWS, St Andrews, Fife KY16 9JD. Tel: 01334-460000; Fax: 01334-460001; Web: www.randa.org; *Secretary*, P. Dawson

Greyhound Racing

NATIONAL GREYHOUND RACING CLUB LTD, Twyman House, 16 Bonny Street, London NW1 9QD. Te: 020-7267 9256; Fax: 020-7482 1023; *Chief Executive*, F. Melville. *Senior Steward*, J. H. C. Nicholson

Gymnastics

BRITISH GYMNASTICS, Ford Hall, Lilleshall National Sports Centre, Newport, Shropshire TF10 9NB. Tel: 01952-820300; Fax: 01952-820306; Web: www.baga.co.uk; *Chief Executive*, Alan Sommerville

Hockey

ENGLISH HOCKEY UNION, National Hockey Stadium, Silbury Boulevard, Milton Keynes MK9 1HA. Tel: 01908-544644; Fax: 01908-241106; Web: www.hockeyonline.co.uk; *President,* Martin Tolliday

SCOTTISH HOCKEY UNION, 589 Lanark Road, Edinburgh, EH14 5DA. Tel: 0131-453 9070; Fax: 0131-453 9079; Web: www.scottish-hockey.org.uk; *Chairman,* G. Ralph

WELSH HOCKEY UNION, 80 Woodville Road, Cardiff CF24 4ED. Tel: 029-2023 3257; Fax: 029-2023 3258; Web: www.welsh-hockey.co.uk; *Chairman,* A. J. Rookes

Horse-racing

BRITISH HORSERACING BOARD, 42 Portman Square, London W1H 0EN, Tel: 020-7396 0011, Fax: 020-7935 3626; Web: www.bhb.co.uk; *Chairman,* P. Savill. *Chief Executive,* G. Nichols. *Secretary-General,* T. Ricketts

THE JOCKEY CLUB, 42 Portman Square, London W1H 6EN. Tel: 020-7486 4921; Fax: 020-7935 8703; Web: www.thejockeyclub.co.uk; *Senior Steward,* C. Spence

Ice Hockey

ICE HOCKEY UK, 47 Westminster Buildings, Theatre Square, Nottingham NG1 6LG. Tel: 0115-924 1441; Fax: 0115-924 3443; Web: www.icehockeyuk.co.uk; *Directors,* J. Anderson; A. Moutrey; N. Moralee; S. Robertson; G. Stefan; R. Stirling; R. Zeller

Ice Skating

NATIONAL ICE SKATING ASSOCIATION OF THE UK LTD, National Ice Centre, Lower Parliament Street, Nottingham NG1 1LA. Tel: 0115-853 3100; Fax: 0115-853 3101; Web: www.nisa-org.uk; *Chairman,* Haig Oundjian; *General Secretary,* Keith Horton

Judo

BRITISH JUDO ASSOCIATION, 7A Rutland Street, Leicester LE1 1RB. Tel: 0116-255 9669; Fax: 0116-255 9660; Web: www.britishjudo.org.uk; *Head of Corporate Affairs,* Donald Steel

Lacrosse

ENGLISH LACROSSE ASSOCIATION, 26 Wood Street, Manchester, Tel: 0161-834 4582; Fax: 0161-834 4582; Web: www.englishlacrosse.co.uk; *Co-Presidents,* Sue Redfern, David Walkden; *Chair of Executive Committee,* Prof. A. Dyer

Lawn Tennis

LAWN TENNIS ASSOCIATION, The Queen's Club, London W14 9EG. Tel: 020-7381 7000; Fax: 020-7381 3773; *Secretary,* J. C. U. James

Martial Arts

MARTIAL ARTS DEVELOPMENT COMMISSION, PO Box 416, Wembley, Middlesex HA0 3WD. Tel: 0870-770 0461; Fax: 0870-770 0462; Web: www.madec.org; *Administration Manager,* Dawn Howe. *Chairman,* R. Thomas

Motor Sports

MOTORCYCLE GREAT BRITAIN, AUTO-CYCLE UNION, ACU House, Wood Street, Rugby, Warks CV21 2YX Tel: 01788-566400; Fax: 01788-573585; Web: www.acu.org.uk; www.motorcyclinggb.com; *General Secretary,* P. Miller; *Chairman,* E. P. Bartlett

THE MOTOR SPORTS ASSOCIATION, Motor Sports House, Riverside Park, Colnbrook, Berks SL3 0HG. Tel: 01753-765000; Fax: 01753-682938; Web: www.msauk.org; *Chief Executive,* Colin Hilton

SCOTTISH AUTO CYCLE UNION LTD, 28 West Main Street, Uphall, W. Lothian EH52 5DW. Tel: 01506-858354; Fax: 01506-855792; Web: www.sacu.co.uk

Mountaineering

BRITISH MOUNTAINEERING COUNCIL, 177–179 Burton Road, West Didsbury, Manchester, M20 2BB. Tel: 0870-010 4878; Fax: 0161-445 4500; Web: www.thebmc.co.uk; *Chief Officer,* D. Turnbull

Multi-Sport Bodies

BRITISH OLYMPIC ASSOCIATION, 1 Wandsworth Plain, London SW18 1EH. Tel: 020-8871 2677; Fax: 020-8871 9104; Web: www.olympics.org.uk; *Chief Executive,* Simon Clegg

BRITISH UNIVERSITIES SPORTS ASSOCIATION, 8 Union Street, London SE1 1SZ. Tel: 020-7357 8555; Fax: 020-7403 0127; Web: www.busaresults.org.uk; *Chief Executive,* G. Gregory-Jones; *Chairman,* L. Barry

COMMONWEALTH GAMES FEDERATION, 4th Floor, 26 Upper Brook Street, London W1K 7QE. Tel: 020-7491 8801; Fax: 020-7409 7803; Web: www.thecgf.com; *Chief Executive Officer,* Michael Cooper

Netball

ALL ENGLAND NETBALL ASSOCIATION LTD, Netball House, 9 Paynes Park, Hitchin, Herts SG5 1EH, Tel: 01462-442344; Fax: 01462-442343; Web: www.england-netball.co.uk; *Chief Executive,* Mrs P. Harrison; *President,* Mrs J. Jack

NETBALL SCOTLAND, 24 Ainslie Road, Hillington Business Park, Hillington, Glasgow G52 4RU. Tel: 0141-570 4016; Fax: 0141-570 4017; Web: www.netballscotland.freeserve.co.uk;

NORTHERN IRELAND NETBALL ASSOCIATION, House of Sport, Upper Malone Road, Belfast BT9 5LA. Tel: 028-9038 1222

WELSH NETBALL ASSOCIATION, 2nd Floor, 33–35 Cathedral Rd, Cardiff CF11 9HB. Tel: 029-2023 7048; Fax: 029-2022 6430; Web: www.welshnetball.co.uk; *Chief Executive Officer,* Mrs S. J. Holvey; *President,* Miss P. Nicholas

Orienteering

BRITISH ORIENTEERING FEDERATION, Riversdale, Dale Road North, Darley Dale, Matlock, Derbys, DE4 2HX. Tel: 01629-734042; Fax: 01629-733769; Web: www.britishorienteering.org.uk; *Secretary-General,* D. Locke

Polo

THE HURLINGHAM POLO ASSOCIATION, Manor Farm, Little Coxwell Faringdon, Oxfordshire SN7 7LW. Tel: 01367-242828; Fax: 01367-242829; Web: www.hpa-polo.co.uk; *Chief Executive,* D. J. B. Woodd

Rackets and Real Tennis

TENNIS AND RACKETS ASSOCIATION, c/o The Queen's Club, Palliser Road, London W14 9EQ. Tel: 020-7386 3447/8; Fax: 020-7385 7424; Web: www.rackets.co.uk; www.real-tennis.com; *Chief Executive and Secretary,* James D. Wyatt. *Chairman,* C. J. Swallow. *President,* The Rt. Hon. Lord Aberdare, KBE, DL

Rifle Shooting

NATIONAL RIFLE ASSOCIATION, Bisley Camp, Brookwood, Woking, Surrey GU24 0PB. Tel: 01483-797777; Fax: 01483-797285; Web: www.nra.org.uk; *Chief Executive,* Col. C. C. C. Cheshire, OBE. *Chairman,* J. F. Jackman

NATIONAL SMALL-BORE RIFLE ASSOCIATION, Lord Roberts Centre, Bisley Camp, Brookwood, Woking, Surrey GU24 0NP. Tel: 0845-130 6772; Fax: 01483-476392; Web: www.nsra.co.uk; *Secretary*, Lt.-Col. J. D. Hoare. *Chairman*, G. D. Pound

Rowing

AMATEUR ROWING ASSOCIATION LTD, The Priory, 6 Lower Mall, London W6 9DJ. Tel: 020-8237 6700; Fax: 020-8237 6749; Web: www.ara-rowing.org; *National Manager*, Mrs R. Napp

HENLEY ROYAL REGATTA, Regatta Headquarters, Henley-on-Thames, Oxon RG9 2LY. Tel: 01491-572153; Fax: 01491-575509; Web: www.hrr.co.uk; *Secretary*, R. S. Goddard

Rugby Fives

RUGBY FIVES ASSOCIATION, The Old Forge, Sutton Valence, Maidstone, Kent ME17 3AW. Tel: 01622-842278; Web: www.rfa.org.uk; *General Secretary*, M. F. Beaman. *President*, D. J. Hebden

Rugby League

BRITISH AMATEUR RUGBY LEAGUE ASSOCIATION, West Yorkshire House, 4 New North Parade, Huddersfield HD1 5JP. Tel: 01484-544131; Fax: 01484-519985; Web: www.barla.org.uk; *Chief Executive*, I. Cooper. *Chairman*, M. F. Oldroyd

THE RUGBY FOOTBALL LEAGUE, Red Hall, Red Hall Lane, Leeds LS17 8NB. Tel: 0113-232 9111; Fax: 0113-232 3666; Web: www.rfl.uk.com

Rugby Union

IRISH RUGBY FOOTBALL UNION, 62 Lansdowne Road, Ballsbridge, Dublin 4. Tel: 00 353-1-647 3800; Fax: 00 353-1-647 3801; Web: www.irfu.ie; *Chief Executive*, P. R. Browne. *President*, D. M. Crowley

RUGBY FOOTBALL UNION, Rugby House, Rugby Road, Twickenham TW1 1DS. Tel: 020-8892 2000; Fax: 020-8892 9816; Web: www.rfu.com; *Chief Executive*, F. Baron. *Chairman of the Management Board*, G. Cattermole

RUGBY FOOTBALL UNION FOR WOMEN, Rugby House, Rugby Road, Twickenham, Middlesex TW1 1DS. Tel: 020-8831 7996; Fax: 020-8892 9816; Web: www.rfu-women.co.uk; *Secretary*, Ms Helen Ives

SCOTTISH RUGBY UNION, Murrayfield, Roseburn Street, Edinburgh EH12 5PJ. Tel: 0131-346 5000; Fax: 0131-346 5001; Web: www.sru.org.uk; *Chief Executive*, W. S. Watson. *Secretary*, I. A. L. Hogg

SCOTTISH WOMEN'S RUGBY UNION, Scottish Rugby Union, Roseburn Terrace, Murrayfield, Edinburgh EH12 5PJ. Tel: 0131-346 5163; Fax: 0131-346 5001; Web: www.sru.org.uk; *Chairwoman*, Sandra Kinnear

WELSH RUGBY UNION, Custom House, Custom House Street, Cardiff CF10 1RF. Tel: 029-2078 1700; Fax: 029-2022 5601; Web: www.wru.co.uk; *Secretary* D. Gethin. *Chairman*, G. S. Griffiths. *President*, Sir Tasker Watkins, VC, GBE, DL

Shooting

CLAY PIGEON SHOOTING ASSOCIATION LTD, Bisley Camp, Brookwood, Woking, Surrey GU24 0NP. Tel: 01483-485400; Fax: 01483-485410; Web: www.cpsa.co.uk; *Director*, E. G. Orduna

Skiing

BRITISH SKI AND SNOWBOARD FEDERATION, Hillend, Biggar Road, Midlothian EH10 7EF. Tel: 0131-445 7676; Fax: 0131-445 7722; Web: www.bssf.co.uk; *Operations Director*, Mrs F. McNeilly

Snooker

WORLD LADIES BILLIARDS AND SNOOKER ASSOCIATION, PO Box 16, Wisbech PE13 2ZX. Tel: 01945-588598; Fax: 01945-588598; Web: www.worldsnooker.com; *Chairman and Administrator*, Mandy Fisher

WORLD PROFESSIONAL BILLIARDS AND SNOOKER ASSOCIATION, Ground Floor, Albert House, 111–117 Victoria Street, Bristol BS1 6AX. Tel: 0117-317 8200; Fax: 0117-317 8300; Web: www.worldsnooker.com;

Speedway

SPEEDWAY CONTROL BOARD LTD, ACU Headquarters, Wood Street, Rugby Warks CV21 2YX. Tel: 01788-565603; Fax: 01788-552308; *Chairman*, J. Quenby

Squash Rackets

SCOTTISH SQUASH, Caledonia House, South Gyle, Edinburgh EH12 9DQ. Tel: 0131-317; Fax 7343 0131-317 7734; Web: www.scottishsquash.org; *Administration Manager*, Derek Welch

SQUASH RACKETS ASSOCIATION, Ground Floor, Bellevue Athletics Centre, Pink Bank Lane, Manchester M12 5GL. Tel: 0161-231 4499; Fax: 0161-231 4231; Web: www.englandsquash.com; *Chief Executive*, Jeremy Lister. *President*, M. Corby

SQUASH WALES, St Mellons Country Club, St Mellons, Cardiff CF3 2XR. Tel: 01633-682108; Fax: 01633-680998; Web: www.squashwales.co.uk; *Administrator*, Ms D. Selley. *Chairman*, D. Jenkins. *President*, A. James

Swimming

AMATEUR SWIMMING ASSOCIATION, Harold Fern House, Derby Square, Loughborough, Leics LE11 5AL. Tel: 01509-618700; Fax: 01509-618701; Web: www.britishswimming.org; *Chief Executive*, D. Sparkes

SCOTTISH SWIMMING, National Swimming Academy, University of Stirling, Stirling, FK9 4LA. Tel: 01786-466520; Fax: 01786-466521; Web: www.scottishswimming.com; *Chief Executive*, P. Bush

WELSH AMATEUR SWIMMING ASSOCIATION, Roath Park House, Ninian Road, Cardiff CF23 5ER. Tel: 029-2048 8820; Fax: 029-2048 8820; Web: www.welshasa.co.uk; *Director of Swimming Development*, B. Williams. *Head of Administration*, Julie Tyler

Table Tennis

ENGLISH TABLE TENNIS ASSOCIATION, Queensbury House, Havelock Road, Hastings, E. Sussex TN34 1HF. Tel: 01424-722525; Fax: 01424-422103; Web: www.etta.co.uk; *Chief Executive*, R. Yule. *Chairman*, A. E. Ransome, OBE

Volleyball

ENGLISH VOLLEYBALL ASSOCIATION, 27 South Road, West Bridgford, Nottingham NG2 7AG. Tel: 0115-981 6324; Fax: 0115-945 5429; Web: www.volleyballengland.org; *Chief Executive Officer*, T. Ojasoo

SCOTTISH VOLLEYBALL ASSOCIATION, 48 The Pleasance, Edinburgh EH8 9TJ. Tel: 0131-556 4633; Fax: 0131-557 4314; Web: www.scottishvolleyball.org; *Director*, N. S. Moody

Walking

RACE WALKING ASSOCIATION, Hufflers, Heard's Lane, Shenfield, Brentwood, Essex CM15 0SF. Tel: 01277-220687; Fax: 01277-212380; Web: www.racewalkingassociation.btinternet.co.uk; *Hon. General Secretary*, P. J. Cassidy. *President*, R. W. Dobson

Water Skiing

BRITISH WATER SKI FEDERATION, 390 City Road, London EC1V 2QA. Tel: 020-7833 2855; Fax: 020-7837 2855; Web: www.britishwaterski.co.uk; *Executive Officer*, Ms G. Hill

Weightlifting

BRITISH WEIGHTLIFTERS ASSOCIATION, (BWLA) 131 Hurst Street Oxford OX4 1HE. Tel: 01865-200339; Fax: 01865-790096; Web: www.bawla.com; *Chief Executive*, S. Cannon. *President*, H. Binder *Chairman*, B. Barton

Wrestling

BRITISH WRESTLING ASSOCIATION, 12 Westwood Lane, Brimington, Chesterfield, Derbyshire S43 1PA. Tel: 01246-236443; Fax: 01246-236443; Web: www.britishwrestling.org; *Chairman*, M. Morley. *Treasurer*, S. McNeil

Yachting

ROYAL YACHTING ASSOCIATION, RYA House, Romsey Road, Eastleigh, Hants SO50 9YA. Tel: 023-8062 7400; Fax: 023-8062 9924; Web: www.rya.org.uk; *Chief Executive*, R. P. Carr. *Chairman*, G. L. Clark

Clubs

ALPINE CLUB (1857), 55 Charlotte Road, London EC2A 3QF. Tel: 020-7613 0755; Fax: 020-7613 0755; Web: www.alpine-club.org.uk

AMERICAN WOMEN'S CLUB (1899), 68 Old Brompton Road, London SW7 3LQ. Tel: 020-7589 8292; Fax: 020-7283 9006; Web: www.london.fawco.org *Women Only*

ANGLO-BELGIAN CLUB (1955), 60 Knightsbridge, London SW1X 7LF. Tel: 020-7235 2121; Fax: 020-7245 9470

ARMY AND NAVY CLUB (1837), 36 Pall Mall, London SW1Y 5JN. Tel: 020-7930 9721; Fax: 020-7930 9720; Web: www.armynavyclub.co.uk

ARTS CLUB (1863), 40 Dover Street, London W1S 4NP. Tel: 020-7499 8581; Fax: 020-7409 0913; Web: www.theatresclub.co.uk

THE ATHENAEUM (1824), 107 Pall Mall, London SW1Y 5ER. Tel: 020-7930 4843; Fax: 020-7839 4114

AUTHORS' CLUB (1892), 40 Dover Street, London W1S 4NP. Tel: 020-7499 8581; Fax: 020-7409 0913

BEEFSTEAK CLUB (1876), 9 Irving Street, London WC2H 7AH. Tel: 020-7930 5722; Fax: 020-7925 2325 *Men Only*

BROOKS'S (1764), St James's Street, London SW1A 1LN. Tel: 020-7493 4411; Fax: 020-7499 3736 *Men Only*

BUCK'S CLUB (1919), 18 Clifford Street, London W1S 3RF. Tel: 020-7734 6896; Fax: 020-7287 2097 *Men Only*

CALEDONIAN CLUB (1891), 9 Halkin Street, London SW1X 7DR. Tel: 020-7235 5162; Fax: 020-7235 4635; Web: www.caledonian-club.org.uk

CANNING CLUB (1910), 4 St James's Square, London SW1Y 4JU. Tel: 020-7827 5757; Fax: 020-7827 5758

CARLTON CLUB (1832), 69 St James's Street, London SW1A 1PJ. Tel: 020-7493 1164; Fax: 020-7495 4090; Web: www.carltonclub.co.uk

CAVALRY AND GUARDS CLUB (1893), 127 Piccadilly, London W1J 7PX. Tel: 020-7499 1261; Fax: 020-7495 5956

CHELSEA ARTS CLUB (1891), 143 Old Church Street, London SW3 6EB. Tel: 020-7376 3311; Fax: 020-7351 5986; Web: chelseaartsclub.com

CITY LIVERY CLUB (1914), 20 Aldermanbury, London EC2V 7HP. Tel: 020-7814 0200; Fax: 020-7814 0201; Web: www.cityliveryclub.com

CITY OF LONDON CLUB (1832), 19 Old Broad Street, London EC2N 1DS. Tel: 020-7588 7991; Fax: 020-7374 2020; Web: www.cityclub.uk.com *Men Only*

CITY UNIVERSITY CLUB (1895), 50 Cornhill, London EC3V 3PD. Tel: 020-7626 8571; Fax: 020-7626 8572; Web: www.city-university-club.demon.co.uk

THE CRUISING ASSOCIATION (1908), CA House, 1 Northey Street, Limehouse Basin, London E14 8BT. Tel: 020-7537 2828; Fax: 020-7537 2266; Web: www.cruising.org.uk

DEN NORSKE KLUB LTD (1887), In & Out, 4 St James's Square, London SW1Y 4JU. Tel: 020-7839 6242; Fax: 020-7930 7946; Web: www.dennorskeklub.co.uk

EAST INDIA CLUB (1849), 16 St James's Square, London SW1Y 4LH. Tel: 020-7930 1000; Fax: 020-7321 0217 *Men Only*

FARMERS CLUB (1842), 3 Whitehall Court, London SW1A 2EL. Tel: 020-7930 3751; Fax: 020-7839 7864; Web: www.thefarmersclub.com

FLYFISHERS' CLUB (1884), 69 Brook Street, London W1K 4ER. Tel: 020-7629 5958 *Men Only*

GARRICK CLUB (1831), 15 Garrick Street, London WC2E 9AY. Tel: 020-7379 6478; Fax: 020-7379 5966; Web: www.garrickclub.co.uk *Men Only*

THE GROUCHO CLUB (1985), 45 Dean Street, London W1D 4QB. Tel: 020-7439 4685; Fax: 020-7437 0373

HURLINGHAM CLUB (1869), Ranelagh Gardens, London SW6 3PR. Tel: 020-7736 8411; Fax: 020-7731 1289

LANSDOWNE CLUB (1934), 9 Fitzmaurice Place, London W1J 5JD. Tel: 020-7629 7200; Fax: 020-7408 0246; Web: www.lansdowneclub.com

LONDON ROWING CLUB (1856), Embankment, Putney, London SW15 1LB. Tel: 020-8788 1400; Fax: 020-8874 9056; Web: www.londonrc.org.uk

THE KENNEL CLUB (1873), 1–5 Clarges Street, London W1J 8AB. Tel: 0870-606 6750; Fax: 020-7518 1058; Web: www.the-kennel-club.org.uk

MCC (MARYLEBONE CRICKET CLUB) (1787), Lord's Cricket Ground, London NW8 8QN. Tel: 020-7289 1611; Fax: 020-7289 9100; Web: www.lords.org

THE NATIONAL CLUB (1845), c/o Carlton Club, 69 St James's Street, London SW1A 1PJ. Tel: 020-8579 0874; Fax: 020-8363 2269 *Men Only*

NATIONAL LIBERAL CLUB (1882), Whitehall Place, London SW1A 2HE. Tel: 020-7930 9871; Fax: 020-7839 4768; Web: www.nlc.org.uk

NAVAL AND MILITARY CLUB (1862), 4 St James's Square, London SW1Y 4JU. Tel: 020-7827 5757; Fax: 020-7827 5758; Web: www.navalandmilitaryclub.co.uk

NAVAL CLUB (1946), 38 Hill Street, London W1J 5NS. Tel: 020-7493 7672; Fax: 020-7629 7995; Web: www.navalclub.co.uk

NEW CAVENDISH CLUB (1920), 44 Great Cumberland Place, London W1H 7BS. Tel: 020-7723 0391; Fax: 020-7262 8411

ORIENTAL CLUB (1824), Stratford House, Stratford Place, London W1C 1ES. Tel: 020-7629 5126; Fax: 020-7629 0494

OXFORD AND CAMBRIDGE CLUB (1972), 71 Pall Mall, London SW1Y 5HD. Tel: 020-7930 5151; Fax: 020-7930 9490; Web: www.oxfordandcambridgeclub.co.uk

PORTLAND CLUB (1816), 69 Brook Street, London W1Y 2ER. Tel: 020-7499 1523

PRATT'S CLUB (1841), 14 Park Place, London SW1A 1LP. Tel: 020-7493 0397; Fax: 020-7499 3736 *Men Only*

THE QUEEN'S CLUB (1886), Palliser Road, London W14 9EQ. Tel: 020-7385 3421; Fax: 020-7386 8295; Web: www.queensclub.co.uk

RAILWAY CLUB (1899), Room 208, 25 Marylebone Road, London NW1 5JS

REFORM CLUB (1836), 104–105 Pall Mall, London SW1Y 5EW. Tel: 020-7930 9374; Fax: 020-7930 1857; Web: www.reformclub.com

ROEHAMPTON CLUB (1901), Roehampton Lane, London SW15 5LR. Tel: 020-8480 4200; Fax: 020-8480 4265; Web: www.roehamptonclub.co.uk

ROYAL AIR FORCE CLUB (1918), 128 Piccadilly, London W1J 7PY. Tel: 020-7399 1000; Fax: 020-7355 1516; Web: www.rafclub.org.uk

ROYAL AUTOMOBILE CLUB (1897), 89–91 Pall Mall, London SW1Y 5HS. Tel: 020-7930 2345; Fax: 020-7976 1086; Web: www.royalautomobileclub.co.uk

ROYAL OCEAN RACING CLUB (1925), 20 St James's Place, London SW1A 1NN. Tel: 020-7493 2248; Fax: 020-7493 5252; Web: www.rorc.org

ROYAL OVER-SEAS LEAGUE (1910), Over-Seas House, Park Place, St James's Street, London SW1A 1LR. Tel: 020-7408 0214; Fax: 020-7499 6738; Web: www.rosl.org.uk

ROYAL THAMES YACHT CLUB (1775), 60 Knightsbridge, London SW1X 7LF. Tel: 020-7235 2121; Fax: 020-7245 9470; Web: www.royalthames.com

SAVAGE CLUB (1857), 1 Whitehall Place, London SW1A 2HD. Tel: 020-7930 8118; Web: www.savageclub.com *Men Only*

SAVILE CLUB (1868), 69 Brook Street, London W1K 4ER. Tel: 020-7629 5462; Fax: 020-7499 7087; Web: www.savileclub.co.uk *Men Only*

ST STEPHEN'S CONSTITUTIONAL CLUB (1870), 34 Queen Anne's Gate, London SW1H 9AB. Tel: 020-7222 1382; Fax: 020-7222 8740; Web: www.ststephensclub.co.uk

THAMES ROWING CLUB (1860), Embankment, Putney, London SW15 1LB. Tel: 020-8788 0798; Fax: 020-8788 0798; Web: www.thamesrc.demon.co.uk

TRAVELLERS CLUB (1819), 106 Pall Mall, London SW1Y 5EP. Tel: 020-7930 8688; Fax: 020-7930 2019; Web: www.csma.org.uk *Men Only*

TURF CLUB (1868), 5 Carlton House Terrace, London SW1Y 5AQ. Tel: 020-7930 8555; Fax: 020-7930 7206

VICTORY SERVICES CLUB (1907), 63–79 Seymour Street, London W2 2HF. Tel: 020-7723 4474; Fax: 020-7402 9496; Web: www.vsc.co.uk

WHITE'S (1693), 37–38 St James's Street, London SW1A 1JG. Tel: 020-7493 6671; Fax: 020-7495 6674 *Men Only*

CLUBS OUTSIDE LONDON AND YACHT CLUBS

THE ATHENAEUM (1797), Church Alley, Liverpool, L1 3DD. Tel: 0151-709 7770; Fax: 0151-709 0418

BATH AND COUNTY CLUB (1858), Queen's Parade, Bath, BA1 2NJ. Tel: 01225-423732; Fax: 01225-423997; Web: www.bathandcountyclub.com

BEMBRIDGE SAILING CLUB (1886), Embankment Road, Bembridge, Isle of Wight PO35 5NR. Tel: 01983-872237; Fax: 01983-874950; Web: www.bembridgesailingclub.org

CARDIFF AND COUNTY CLUB (1866), Westgate Street, Cardiff, CF10 1DA. Tel: 029-2022 0846; Fax: 029-2037 3393; *Men Only*

CHICHESTER YACHT CLUB (1967), Chichester Marina, Birdham, Chichester, W. Sussex PO20 7EJ. Tel: 01243-512918; Fax: 01243-512627; Web: www.cyc.co.uk

CLIFTON CLUB (1882), 22 The Mall, Clifton, Bristol, BS8 4DS. Tel: 0117-974 5039; Fax: 0117-974 3910; *Men Only*

DISTRICT AND UNION CLUB (1849) Northwood, 1 West Park Road, Blackburn BB2 6DE. Tel: 01254-51474 *Men Only*

ESSEX YACHT CLUB (1890) HQS Bembridge, Foreshore, Leigh-on-Sea, Essex SS9 1HQ. Tel: 01702-478404; Web: www.sailinginleigh.com

FREWEN CLUB (1869), 98 St Aldate's, Oxford, OX1 1BT. Tel: 01865-243816 *Men Only*

HOVE CLUB (1882), 28 Fourth Avenue, Hove, E. Sussex BN3 2PJ. Tel: 01273-730872; Fax: 01273-732481 *Men Only*

KENT AND CANTERBURY CLUB (1873) The Elms, 17 Old Dover Road, Canterbury, CT1 3JB. Tel: 01227-462181; Web: www.kcgc.org.uk *Men Only*

THE KINGSWAY CLUB (1868) Lightfoot Institute, Kingsway, Bishop Auckland, Co. Durham DL14 7JN. Tel: 01388-603219 *Men Only*

THE LEAMINGTON TENNIS COURT CLUB (1846), 50 Bedford Street, Leamington Spa, Warks CV32 5DT. Tel: 01926-424977; Fax: 01926 435724 *Men Only*

LEANDER CLUB (1818), Henley-on-Thames, Oxon RG9 2LP. Tel: 01491-575782; Fax: 01491-410291; Web: www.leander.co.uk

THE LEEDS CLUB (1849), 3 Albion Place, Leeds LS1 6JL. Tel: 0113-242 1591; Fax: 0113-245 0755; Web: www.leedsclub.org.uk

NEW CLUB (1874), 2 Montpellier Parade, Cheltenham, GL50 1UD. Tel: 01242-541121; Fax: 01242-541154; Web: www.newclub.org.uk

THE NORFOLK CLUB (1770), 17 Upper King Street, Norwich NR3 1RB. Tel: 01603-610652

NORTH BAILEY CLUB (1842), 24 North Bailey, Durham, DH1 3EW. Tel: 0191-384 3724; Fax: 0191-384 7060; Web: www.dur.ac.uk/DUS

NORTHAMPTON AND COUNTY CLUB (1873), George Row, Northampton, NN1 1DF. Tel: 01604-632962

NORTHERN CONSTITUTIONAL CLUB (1882), 37 Pilgrim Street, Newcastle upon Tyne, NE1 6QE. Tel: 0191-232 0884

THE NOTTINGHAM CLUB (1920) Newdigate House, Castle Gate, Nottingham NG1 6AF. Tel: 0115-912 6220; Fax: 0115-912 6220

OLD BOYS' AND PARK GREEN CLUB (1771), 7 Churchside, Macclesfield, Cheshire SK10 1HG. Tel: 01625-423292 *Men Only*

PAIGNTON CLUB (1882), The Esplanade, Paignton, Devon TQ4 6ED. Tel: 01803-559682; Fax: 01803-559043

PARKSTONE YACHT CLUB (1895), Pearce Avenue, Poole, Dorset BH14 8EH. Tel: 01202-743610; Fax: 01202-716394; Web: www.parkstoneyc.co.uk

PENARTH YACHT CLUB (1880), The Esplanade, Penarth, Vale of Glamorgan CF64 3AU. Tel: 029-2070 8196

PHYLLIS COURT CLUB (1906), Marlow Road, Henley-on-Thames, Oxon RG9 2HT. Tel: 01491-570500; Fax: 01491-570528; Web: www.phylliscourt.co.uk

POOLE HARBOUR YACHT CLUB (1949), 38 Salterns Way, Lilliput, Poole, Dorset BH14 8JR. Tel: 01202-707321; Fax: 01202-700398; Web: www.salterns.co.uk

THE POOLE YACHT CLUB (1865), New Harbour Road West, Hamworthy, Poole, Dorset BH15 4AQ. Tel: 01202-672687; Fax: 01202-661174; Web: www.pooleyc.co.uk

ROYAL ANGLESEY YACHT CLUB (1802), 5–6 Green Edge, Beaumaris, Anglesey LL58 8BY. Tel: 01248-810295; Fax: 01248-811788; Web: www.royalanglesey.mariner.co.uk

ROYAL CANOE CLUB (1866), Trowlock Island, Teddington, Middx TW11 9QZ. Tel: 020-8977 5269; Fax: 020-8977 5269; Web: www.royalcanoeclub.org.uk

ROYAL CHANNEL ISLANDS YACHT CLUB (1862) Le
Mont du Boulevard, St Aubin, Jersey, JE3 8AD.
Tel: 01534-745783; Fax: 01534-490042;

ROYAL CINQUE PORTS YACHT CLUB (1872), 5
Waterloo Crescent, Dover, Kent CT16 1LA.
Tel: 01304-206262; Fax: 01304-206262

ROYAL CORINTHIAN YACHT CLUB (1872), The Quay,
Burnham-on-Crouch, Essex CM0 8AX.
Tel: 01621-782105; Fax: 01621-784965;
Web: www.royalcorinthian.co.uk

ROYAL DART YACHT CLUB (1866), Priory Street,
Kingswear, Dartmouth, Devon TQ6 0AB.
Tel: 01803-752496; Fax: 01803-752496;
Web: www.royaldart.co.uk

ROYAL DORSET YACHT CLUB (1875), 11 Custom
House Quay, Weymouth, Dorset DT4 8BG.
Tel: 01305-786258; Fax: 01305-786258;
Web: www.rdyc.freeuk.com

ROYAL FOWEY YACHT CLUB (1881) Whitford Yard,
Fowey, Cornwall PL23 1BH. Tel: 01726-833573;
Fax: 01726-833573; Web: www.rfyc.fowey.org.uk

ROYAL HARWICH YACHT CLUB (1843), Woolverstone,
Ipswich IP9 1AT. Tel: 01473-780319;
Fax: 01473-780919; Web: www.rhyc.demon.co.uk

ROYAL LYMINGTON YACHT CLUB (1922), Bath Road,
Lymington, Hants SO41 3SE. Tel: 01590-672677;
Fax: 01590-671642; Web: www.rlymyc.org.uk

ROYAL MERSEY YACHT CLUB (1844), Bedford Road
East, Rock Ferry, Birkenhead, Merseyside CH42 1LS.
Tel: 0151-645 3204

ROYAL NAVAL CLUB AND ROYAL ALBERT YACHT
CLUB (1867), 17 Pembroke Road, Portsmouth PO1
2NT. Tel: 023-9282 5924; Fax: 023-9282 4491;
Web: rnc-raye.co.uk

ROYAL NORFOLK AND SUFFOLK YACHT CLUB (1859),
Royal Plain, Lowestoft, Suffolk NR33 0AQ.
Tel: 01502-566726; Fax: 01502-517981

ROYAL PLYMOUTH CORINTHIAN YACHT CLUB
(1877), Madeira Road, Plymouth PL1 2NY.
Tel: 01752-664327; Fax: 01752-256140;
Web: www.rpcyc.com

ROYAL SOLENT YACHT CLUB (1878), Yarmouth, Isle of
Wight PO41 0NS. Tel: 01983-760256;
Fax: 01983-761172; Web: www.royalsolentyc.org.uk

ROYAL SOUTHAMPTON YACHT CLUB, 1 Channel Way,
Ocean Village, Southampton, SO14 3QF.
Tel: 023-8022 3352; Fax: 023-8033 0613;
Web: www.rsyc.org.uk

ROYAL SOUTHERN YACHT CLUB (1837), Rope Walk,
Hamble, Southampton, SO31 4HB.
Tel: 023-8045 0300; Fax: 023-8045 0310;
Web: www.royal-southern.co.uk

ROYAL TEMPLE YACHT CLUB (1857), 6 Westcliff
Mansions, Ramsgate, Kent CT11 9HY.
Tel: 01843-591766; Fax: 01843-583211;
Web: www.rtyc.com

ROYAL TORBAY YACHT CLUB (1863), 12 Beacon
Terrace, Torquay, Devon TQ1 2BH. Tel: 01803-292006;
Fax: 01803-200297; Web: www.royaltorbay.org

ROYAL ULSTER YACHT CLUB (1866), 101 Clifton Road,
Bangor, Co. Down BT20 5HY.
Tel: 028-9127 0568; Fax: 028-9127 3525;
Web: www.royalulsteryachtclub.org

ROYAL WESTERN YACHT CLUB OF ENGLAND (1827)
Queen Anne's Battery, Plymouth, PL4 0TW.
Tel: 01752-660077; Fax: 01752-224299;
Web: www.rwyc.org

ROYAL WINDERMERE YACHT CLUB (1860), Fallbarrow
Road, Bowness-on-Windermere, Windermere,
Cumbria LA23 3DJ. Tel: 015394-43106

ROYAL YACHT SQUADRON (1815) The Castle, Cowes,
IOW PO31 7QT. Tel: 01983-292191;
Fax: 01983-200253; Web: www.rys.org.uk

ROYAL YORKSHIRE YACHT CLUB (1847), 1 Windsor
Crescent, Bridlington, E. Yorks YO15 3HX.
Tel: 01262-672041; Fax: 01262-678319;
Web: www.ryyc.org.uk

STOURBRIDGE OLD EDWARDIAN CLUB (1898), Drury
Lane, Stourbridge, W. Midlands DY8 1BL.
Tel: 01384-395635 *Men Only*

THAMES ESTUARY YACHT CLUB (1895), 3 The Leas,
Westcliff-on-Sea, Essex SS0 7ST. Tel: 01702-345967;
Web: www.dowden.demon.co.uk/teyc/

ULSTER REFORM CLUB (1885), 4 Royal Avenue, Belfast,
BT1 1DA. Tel: 028-9032 3411; Fax: 028-9031 2833;
Web: www.ulsterreformclub.com

UNITED CLUB (1870), Pier Steps, St Peter Port,
Guernsey, GY1 2LF. Tel: 01481-725722 *Men Only*

VICTORIA CLUB (1853), Beresford Street, St Helier,
Jersey JE2 4WN. Tel: 01534-723381; Fax: 01534-874700

Societies and Institutions

Although this section is arranged in alphabetical order, organisations are usually listed by the key word in their title. The date in parenthesis after the organisation's title is the year of its foundation.

2CARE (1929), 11 Harwood Road, London SW6 4QP. Tel: 020-7371 0118; Fax: 020-7371 7519. *Chief Executive*, Miss E. C. R. O'Sullivan

ABBEYFIELD SOCIETY (1956), Abbeyfield House, 53 Victoria Street, St Albans, Herts AL1 3UW. Tel: 01727-857536; Fax: 01727-846166; Web: www.abbeyfield.com. *Chief Executive*, B. House

ABOLITION OF VIVISECTION, BRITISH UNION FOR THE (1898), 16A Crane Grove, London N7 8NN. Tel: 020-7700 4888; Fax: 020-7700 0252; Web: www.buav.org. *Chief Executive*, Ms M. Thew

ACCOUNTANTS IN ENGLAND AND WALES, INSTITUTE OF CHARTERED (1880), Chartered Accountants' Hall, PO Box 433, Moorgate Place, London EC2P 2BJ. Tel: 020-7920 8100; Fax: 020-7920 0547; Web: www.icaew.co.uk/library. *Secretary-General*, J. S. Collier

ACCOUNTANTS, ASSOCIATION OF CHARTERED CERTIFIED (1904), 29 Lincoln's Inn Fields, London WC2A 3EE. Tel: 020-7242 6855; Fax: 020-7396 7070; Web: www.accaglobal.org.uk. *Chief Executive*, Mrs A. L. Rose

ACCOUNTANTS, INSTITUTE OF COMPANY (1928), 40 Tyndalls Park Road, Bristol BS8 1PL. Tel: 0117-973 8261; Fax: 0117-923 8292; *Director General*, B. T. Banks

ACCOUNTANTS, INSTITUTE OF FINANCIAL (1916), Burford House, 44 London Road, Sevenoaks, Kent TN13 1AS. Tel: 01732-458080; Fax: 01732-455848; Web: www.ifa.org.uk. *Chief Executive*, J. M. Dean

ACCOUNTING TECHNICIANS, ASSOCIATION OF (1980), 154 Clerkenwell Road, London EC1R 5AD. Tel: 020-7837 8600; Fax: 020-7837 6970; Web: www.aat.co.uk. *Chief Executive*, Ms J. Scott Paul

ACOUSTICS, INSTITUTE OF, 77A St Peter's Street, St Albans, Herts AL1 3BN. Tel: 01727 848195; Fax: 01727 850553; Web: www.ioa.org.uk. *Chief Executive*, Roy D Bratby

ACTION FOR BLIND PEOPLE (1857), 14–16 Verney Road, London SE16 3DZ. Tel: 020-7635 4800; Fax: 020-7635 4900; Web: www.afbp.org. *Chief Executive*, S. Remington

ACTION RESEARCH (1952), Vincent House, Horsham, W. Sussex RH12 2DP. Tel: 01403-210406; Fax: 01403-210541; Web: www.actionresearch.co.uk. *Chief Executive*, Simon Moore

ACTORS' BENEVOLENT FUND (1882), 6 Adam Street, London WC2N 6AD. Tel: 020-7836 6378; Fax: 020-7836 8978; Web: www.actorsbenevolentfund.co.uk. *General Secretary*, Mrs Jane Skerrett

ACTORS' CHARITABLE TRUST, THE (1896), 255–256 Africa House, 64–78 Kingsway, London WC2B 6BD. Tel: 020-7242 0111; Fax: 020-7242 0234; Web: www.tactactors.org. *General Secretary*, R. Ashby

ACTUARIES IN SCOTLAND, FACULTY OF (1856), 18 Dublin Street, Edinburgh EH1 3PP. Tel: 0131-240 1300; Fax: 0131-240 1313. Web: www.actuaries.org.uk

ACTUARIES, INSTITUTE OF (1848), Staple Inn Hall, High Holborn, London WC1V 7QJ. Tel: 020-7632 2100; Fax: 020-7632 2111; Web: www.actuaries.org.uk. *President*, J. Goford, FIA

ADAM SMITH INSTITUTE (1977), 23 Great Smith Street, London SW1P 3BL. Tel: 020-7222 4995; Fax: 020-7222 7544; Web: www.adamsmith.org.uk. *President*, Dr M. Pirie; *Director*, Dr E. Butler

ADMINISTRATIVE MANAGEMENT, INSTITUTE OF (1915), 12 Park Crescent, London W1B 1BA. Tel: 020-7612 7099; Fax: 020-7612 7094; Web: www.instam.org. *Chief Executive*, David Woodgate

ADULT SCHOOL ORGANISATION, NATIONAL (1899), Riverton, 370 Humberstone Road, Leicester LE5 0SA. Tel: 0116-253 8333; Fax: 0116-251 3626; Web: www.naso.org.uk. *General Secretary*, Mrs P. C. Dean

ADVERTISING STANDARDS AUTHORITY (1962), 2 Torrington Place, London WC1E 7HW. Tel: 020-7580 5555; Fax: 020-7631 3051; Web: www.asa.org.uk. *Director-General*, C. Graham

AFRICAN INSTITUTE, INTERNATIONAL (1926), SOAS, Thornhaugh Street, Russell Square, London WC1H 0XG. Tel: 020-7898 4420; Fax: 020-7898 4419; Web: www.iaionthe.net. *Hon. Director*, Prof. P. Spencer

AFRICAN MEDICAL AND RESEARCH FOUNDATION, UK (1961), 4 Grosvenor Place, London SW1X 7HJ. Tel: 020-7201 6070; Fax: 020-7201 6170; Web: www.amref.org. *Executive Director*, A. Heroys

AGE CONCERN CYMRU, 4th Floor, 1 Cathedral Road, Cardiff CF11 9SD. Tel: 029-2037 1566; Fax: 029-2039 9562. *Director*, R. W. Taylor

AGE CONCERN ENGLAND (1940), Astral House, 1268 London Road, London SW16 4ER. Tel: 020-8765 7200; Helpline: 0800-009966; Fax: 020-8765 7211; Web: www.ageconcern.org.uk/. *Director-General*, G. Lishman, OBE

AGE CONCERN SCOTLAND (1943), 113 Rose Street, Edinburgh EH2 3DT. Tel: 0131-220 3345; Fax: 0131-220 2779; Web: www.ageconcernscotland.org.uk. *Director*, Ms M. O'Neill

AGRICULTURAL ENGINEERS ASSOCIATION (1875), Samuelson House, Paxton Road, Orton Centre, Peterborough PE2 5LT. Tel: 01733-362925; Fax: 01733-370664; Web: www.aea.uk.com. *Director-General*, J. Vowles

AIDS TRUST, NATIONAL (1987), New City Cloisters, 196 Old Street, London EC1V 9FR. Tel: 020-7216 0111; Fax: 020-7814 6767; Web: www.nat.org.uk. *Chief Executive*, Derek Bodell

ALCOHOLICS ANONYMOUS (1947), PO Box 1, Stonebow House, Stonebow, York YO1 2NJ. Tel: 01904-644026. National Helpline: 0845-769 7555; Fax: 01904-629091; Web: www.alcoholics-anonymous.org.uk. *General-Secretary*, J. Keeney

ALEXANDRA ROSE DAY (1912), 2A Ferry Road, London SW13 9RX. Tel: 020-8748 4824; Fax: 020-8748 3188. *National Director*, Alan Leng

ALMSHOUSES, NATIONAL ASSOCIATION OF (1951), Billingbear Lodge, Carter's Hill, Workingham, Berks RG40 5RU. Tel: 01344-452922; Fax: 01344-862062; Web: www.almshouses.org. *Director*, Maj.-Gen. A. deC. L. Leask

ALZHEIMER'S SOCIETY (1979), Gordon House, 10 Greencoat Place, London SW1P 1PH. Tel: 020-7306 0606. Helpline: 0845-300 0336; Fax: 020-7306 0808; Web: www.alzheimers.org.uk. *Chief Executive*, H. Cayton

AMNESTY INTERNATIONAL UNITED KINGDOM (1961), 99–119 Rosebery Avenue, London EC1R 4RE. Tel: 020-7814 6200; Fax: 020-7833 1510; Web: www.amnesty.org.uk. *Director*, Ms K. Allen

ANAESTHETISTS OF GREAT BRITAIN AND IRELAND, ASSOCIATION OF (1932), 9 Bedford Square, London WC1B 3RE. Tel: 020-7631 1650; Fax: 020-7631 4352; Web: www.aagbi.org. *General Manager*, Lesley Turpin

ANCIENT MONUMENTS SOCIETY (1924), St Ann's Vestry Hall, 2 Church Entry, London EC4V 5HB. Tel: 020-7236 3934; Fax: 020-7329 3677; Web: www.ancientmonumentssociety.org.uk. *Secretary*, M. J. Saunders, MBE

ANGLO-BELGIAN SOCIETY (1982), 5 Hartley Close, Bickley, Kent BR1 2TP. Tel: 020-8467 8442; Fax: 020-8467 8442. *Hon. Secretary*, P. R. Bresnan

ANGLO-BRAZILIAN SOCIETY (1943), 32 Green Street, London W1K 7AU. Tel: 020-7493 8493; Fax: 020-7493 8493; Web: www.anglobraziliansociety.org. *Secretary*, E. Dell'Aglio

ANGLO-DANISH SOCIETY (1924), Hillgate House, 26 Old Bailey, London EC4M 7HW. Tel: 01753-883510. *Chairman*, Mr P. J. Willoughby, JP, FCA

ANGLO-NORSE SOCIETY (1918), 25 Belgrave Square, London SW1X 8QD. Tel: 020-7235 9529; Fax: 020-7235 9529; *Chairman*, Sir John Robson, KCMG

ANIMAL HEALTH TRUST (1942), Lanwades Park, Kentford, Newmarket, Suffolk CB8 7UU. Tel: 01638-751000; Fax: 01638-750410; Web: www.aht.org.uk. *Executive Chairman*, E. Chandler, FRCVS

ANTHROPOSOPHICAL SOCIETY IN GREAT BRITAIN (1923), Rudolf Steiner House), 35 Park Road, London NW1 6XT. Tel: 020-7723 4400; Fax: 020-7724 4364; Web: www.anth.org.uk. *General Secretary*, N. C. Thomas

ANTI-SLAVERY INTERNATIONAL (1839), Thomas Clarkson House, The Stableyard, Broomgrove Road, London SW9 9TL. Tel: 020-7501 8920; Fax: 020-7738 4110; Web: www.antislavery.org. *Director*, H. Cunneen

ANTIQUARIES OF LONDON, SOCIETY OF (1707), Burlington House, Piccadilly, London W1J 0BE; Fax: 020-7287 6967; Web: www.sal.org.uk. *General-Secretary*, D. Morgan Evans, FSA

ANTIQUARIES OF SCOTLAND, Society of (1780), Royal Museum, Chambers Street, Edinburgh EH1 1JF. Tel: 0131-247 4115/4133; Fax: 0131-247 4163; Web: www.socantscot.org. *Director*, Mrs F. Ashmore, FSA

ANTIQUE DEALERS' ASSOCIATION, BRITISH (1918), 20 Rutland Gate, London SW7 1BD. Tel: 020-7589 4128; Fax: 020-7581 9083; Web: www.bada.org; *Secretary-General*, Mrs E. J. Dean. *Deputy Secretary-General*, M. N. Dodgson

APOTHECARIES OF LONDON, SOCIETY OF (1617), 14 Black Friars Lane, London EC4V 6EJ. Tel: 020-7236 1189; Fax: 020-7329 3177; Web: www.apothecaries.org. *Clerk*, R. J. Stringer

ARBITRATORS, CHARTERED INSTITUTE OF (1915), 12 Bloomsbury Square, London WC1A 2LP. Tel: 020-7421 7444; Fax: 020-7404 4023; Web: www.arbitrators.org. *Secretary-General*, D. Farrar-Hockley

ARCHAEOLOGY, COUNCIL FOR BRITISH (1944), Bowes Morrell House, 111 Walmgate, York YO1 9WA. Tel: 01904-671417; Fax: 01904-671384; Web: www.britarch.ac.uk. *Director*, G. Lambrick

ARCHITECTS BENEVOLENT SOCIETY (1850), 43 Portland Place, London W1B 1QH. Tel: 020-7580 2823; Fax: 020-7580 7075. *Secretary*, K. Robinson

ARCHITECTURAL ASSOCIATION INC. (1847), 34–36 Bedford Square, London WC1B 3ES. Tel: 020-7887 4000; Fax: 020-7414 0782; Web: www.aaschool.ac.uk. *Chief Executive*, Mohsen Mostafavi

ARCHITECTURAL HERITAGE FUND (1976), Clareville House, 26–27 Oxendon Street, London SW1Y 4EL. Tel: 020-7925 0199; Fax: 020-7930 0295; Web: www.ahfund.org.uk. *Director*, J. Thompson

ARCHITECTURE AND SURVEYING INSTITUTE (1926), St Mary House, 15 St Mary Street, Chippenham, Wilts SN15 3WD. Tel: 01249-444505; Fax: 01249-443602; Web: www.asi.org.uk. *Chief Executive*, I. N. Norris

ARCHIVISTS, SOCIETY OF (1947), 40 Northampton Road, London EC1R 0HB. Tel: 020-7278 8630; Fax: 020-7278 2107; Web: www.archives.org.uk. *Executive Secretary*, P. S. Cleary

ARLIS (ART LIBRARIES SOCIETY UK AND IRELAND) (1969), 18 College Road, Bromsgrove, Worcs B60 2NE. Tel: 01527-579298; Fax: 01527-579298; Web: www.arlis.nal.vam.ac.uk. *Administrator*, Ms S. French

ARMY CADET FORCE ASSOCIATION (1930), E Block, Duke of York's HQ, London SW3 4RR. Tel: 020-7730 9733; Fax: 020-7730 8264; Web: www.armycadets.com. *General Secretary*, Brig. J. E. Neeve; *Deputy General Secretary*, Lt-Col. A. G. C. Horridge

ART COLLECTIONS FUND, NATIONAL (1903), Mallais House, 7 Cromwell Place, London SW7 2JN. Tel: 020-7225 4800; Fax: 020-7225 4848; Web: www.art-fund.org. *Director*, D. Barrie

ARTISTS, FEDERATION OF BRITISH (1961), 17 Carlton House Terrace, London SW1Y 5BD. Tel: 020-7930 6844; Fax: 020-7839 7830; Web: www.mallgalleries.org.uk. *Chairman*, J. R. S. Boas

ARTS LTD, NATIONAL CAMPAIGN FOR THE (1985), Pegasus House, 37–43 Sackville Street, London W1S 3EH. Tel: 020-7333 0375; Fax: 020-7333 0660; Web: www.artscampaign.org.uk. *Director*, Ms V. Todd

ARTS, CONTEMPORARY APPLIED (1948), 2 Percy Street, London W1T 1DD. Tel: 020-7436 2344; Fax: 020-7436 2446; Web: www.caa.org.uk. *Director*, Ms M. La Trobe-Bateman

ASIAN AFFAIRS, THE ROYAL SOCIETY FOR (1901), 2 Belgrave Square, London SW1X 8PJ. Tel: 020-7235 5122; Fax: 020-7259 6771; Web: www.rsaa.org.uk. *Chairman*, Sir Harold Walker, KCMG

ASIAN FAMILY COUNSELLING SERVICE (1985), Suite 51, The Lodge, Windmill Place, 2–4 Windmill Lane, Southall UB2 4NJ. Tel: 020-8571 3933; Fax: 020-8571 3933. *Director*, R. Atma

ASLIB (THE ASSOCIATION FOR INFORMATION MANAGEMENT) (1924), Staple Hall, Stone House Court, London EC3A 7PB. Tel: 020-7903 0000; Fax: 020-7903 0011; Web: www.aslib.com. *Chief Executive*, R. Bowes

ASTHMA CAMPAIGN, NATIONAL (1990), Providence House, Providence Place, London N1 0NT. Tel: 020-7226 2260; Fax: 020-7704 0740; Web: www.asthma.org.uk. *Chief Executive*, Donna Covey

ASTRONOMICAL ASSOCIATION, BRITISH (1890), Burlington House, Piccadilly, London W1J 0DU. Web: www.britastro.org. *Assistant Secretary*, Miss P. M. Barber

ATS AND WRAC ASSOCIATION BENEVOLENT FUND (1944), AGC Centre, Worthy Down, Winchester, Hants SO21 2RG. Tel: 01962-887612; Fax: 01962-887612. *Secretary*, Maj. D. M. McElligott

AUTHORS, SOCIETY OF, 84 Drayton Gardens, London SW10 9SB. Tel: 020-7373 6642; Fax: 020-7373 5768; Web: www.societyofauthors.org. *General Secretary*, M. Le Fanu, OBE

AUTOMOBILE ASSOCIATION (1905), Norfolk House, Priestley Road, Basingstoke, Hants RG24 9NY. Tel: 0990-500600; Fax: 01256-493389; Web: www.theaa.com. *Managing Director*, Roger Wood

AYRSHIRE ARCHAEOLOGICAL AND NATURAL HISTORY SOCIETY (1947), 17 Bellrock Avenue, Prestwick KA9 1SQ. Tel: 01292-282109; Web: www.ayrshirearchaeologicalandnaturalhistory society.org.uk. *Hon. Secretary*, Mrs Sheena Andrew

BACKCARE, 16 Elmtree Road, Teddington, Middx TW11 8ST. Tel: 020-8977 5474; Fax: 020-8943 5318; Web: www.backpain.org. *Chief Executive*, Ms Alison Mills

BALTIC AIR CHARTER ASSOCIATION (1949), The Baltic Exchange, St Mary Axe, London EC3A 8BH. Tel: 020-7623 5501; Fax: 020-7369 1623; Web: www.baca.org.uk. *Chairman*, John Ellis

BALTIC EXCHANGE (1744), St Mary Axe, London EC3A 8BH. Tel: 020-7623 5501; Fax: 020-7369 1622; Web: www.balticexchange.com. *Chief Executive*, J. Buckley

BALTIC EXCHANGE CHARITABLE SOCIETY (1978), 13 Norton Folgate, Bishopsgate, London E1 6DB. Tel: 020-7247 6863; Fax: 020-7247 6758. *Secretary*, D. A. Painter

BANKERS IN SCOTLAND, CHARTERED INSTITUTE OF (1875), Drumsheugh House, 38B Drumsheugh Gardens, Edinburgh EH3 7SW. Tel: 0131-473 7777; Fax: 0131-473 7788; Web: www.ciobs.org.uk. *Chief Executive*, Prof. C. W. Munn

BAR ASSOCIATION FOR LOCAL GOVERNMENT AND THE PUBLIC SERVICE (1945), c/o Birmingham City Council, Ingleby House, 11–14 Cannon Street, Birmingham B2 5EN. Tel: 0121-303 9991; Fax: 0121-303 1312; Web: www.balgps.freeserve.co.uk. *Chairman*, M. F. N. Ahmad

BARNARDO'S (1866), Tanners Lane, Barkingside, Ilford, Essex IG6 1QG. Tel: 020-8550 8822; Fax: 020-8551 6870; Web: www.barnardos.org.uk. *Chief Executive*, R. Singleton

BARONETAGE, STANDING COUNCIL OF THE (1903), 3 Eastcroft Road, West Ewell, Epsom, Surrey KT19 9TX. Tel: 020-8393 6620; Fax: 020-8393 6620; *Chairman*, Sir Geoffrey Errington, Bt., OBE

BARRISTERS' BENEVOLENT ASSOCIATION (1873), 14 Gray's Inn Square, London WC1R 5JP. Tel: 020-7242 4761; Fax: 020-7831 5366; *Secretary*, Mrs L. C. Carlier

BCCB (1965), One Westminster Palace Gardens, 1–7 Artillery Row, London SW1P 1RJ. Tel: 020-7222 3651; Fax: 020-7222 3664; Web: www.bccb.org.uk. *Director*, C. Adams, CBE

BEE-KEEPERS' ASSOCIATION, BRITISH, National Beekeeping Centre, Stoneleigh Park, Kenilworth, Warks CV8 2LG. Tel: 0247-669 6679; Fax: 0247-669 0682; Web: www.bbka.demon.co.uk; *General Secretary*, P. B. Spencer

BERKSHIRE ARCHAEOLOGICAL SOCIETY (1871), 43 Laburnham Road, Maidenhead, Berks SL6 4DE. Tel: 01628-631225; *Hon. Secretary*, L. J. Over

BEVIN BOYS ASSOCIATION (1989), School Cottage, 49A Hogshill Street, Beaminster, Dorset DT8 3AG. Tel: 01308-861488; Fax: 01308-861488. *Vice President and Public Relations*, W. H. Taylor, MBE

BIBLE SOCIETY, BRITISH AND FOREIGN (1804), Stonehill Green, Westlea, Swindon SN5 7DG. Tel: 01793-418100; Fax: 01793-418118; Web: www.biblesociety.org.uk. *Chief Executive*, James Catford

BIBLIOGRAPHICAL SOCIETY (1892), c/o The Wellcome Library, 183 Euston Road, London NW1 2BE. Tel: 020-7611 7244; Fax: 020-7611 8703. *Hon. Secretary*, D. Pearson

BIOCHEMICAL SOCIETY (1911), 59 Portland Place, London W1B 1QW. Tel: 020-7580 5530; Fax: 020-7637 3626; Web: www.biochemistry.org. *Executive Secretary*, G. D. Jones

BIOLOGY, INSTITUTE OF (1950), 20–22 Queensberry Place, London SW7 2DZ. Tel: 020-7581 8333; Fax: 020-7823 9409; Web: www.iob.org. *Chief Executive*, Prof. A. D. B. Malcolm

BIRMINGHAM AND WARWICKSHIRE ARCHAEOLOGICAL SOCIETY (1870), c/o Birmingham and Midland Institute, Margaret Street, Birmingham B3 3BS. Web: www.bwas.swinternet.co.uk. *Hon. Secretary*, Miss S. Middleton

BLIND, NATIONAL LIBRARY FOR THE (1828), Far Cromwell Road, Bredbury, Stockport, Cheshire SK6 2SG. Tel: 0161-355 2000; Fax: 0161-355 2098; Web: www.nlbuk.org. *Acting Chief Executive*, Helen Brazier

BLOOD SERVICE, NATIONAL, Oak House, Reeds Crescent, Watford, Herts WD1 1QH. Tel: 01923-486800; Fax: 01923-486801; Web: www.blood.co.uk. *Chairman*, M. Fogden, CB. *Chief Executive*, Martin Graham

BLUE CROSS (1897), Shilton Road, Burford, Oxon OX18 4PF. Tel: 01993-822651; Fax: 01993-823083; Web: www.bluecross.org.uk. *Chief Executive*, John Rutter, MBE

BODLEIAN, FRIENDS OF THE (1925), Bodleian Library, Oxford OX1 3BG. Tel: 01865-277022/277234; Fax: 01865-277182/277187; Web: www.bodley.ox.ac.uk/friends. *Secretary*, G. Groom

BOOK AID INTERNATIONAL (1954), 39–41 Coldharbour Lane, London SE5 9NR. Tel: 020-7733 3577; Fax: 020-7978 8006; Web: www.bookaid.org. *Director*, Mrs S. Harrity, MBE

BOOKSELLERS ASSOCIATION OF THE UK & IRELAND LTD (1895), Minster House, 272 Vauxhall Bridge Road, London SW1V 1BA. Tel: 020-7834 5477; Fax: 020-7834 8812; Web: www.booksellers.org.uk. *Chief Executive*, T. E. Godfray

BOOKTRUST (1926), Book House, 45 East Hill, London SW18 2QZ. Tel: 020-8516 2977; Fax: 020-8516 2978; Web: www.booktrust.org.uk. *Executive Director*, C. Meade

BOTANICAL SOCIETY OF SCOTLAND (1836), c/o Royal Botanic Garden, Inverleith Row, Edinburgh EH3 5LR. Tel: 0131-552 7171; Fax: 0131-248 2901. *Hon. General Secretary*, R. Galt

BOTANICAL SOCIETY OF THE BRITISH ISLES (1836), c/o Department of Botany, The Natural History Museum, Cromwell Road, London SW7 5BD. Tel: 020-7942 5002; Web: www.members.aol.com/bsbihgs. *Hon. General Secretary*, Miss A. Burns

BOYS' BRIGADE (1883), Felden Lodge, Hemel Hempstead, Herts HP3 0BL. Tel: 01442-231681; Fax: 01442-235391; Web: www.boys-brigade.org.uk. *Chief Executive*, Don McLaren

BREWING, INSTITUTE AND GUILD OF (1886), 33 Clarges Street, London W1J 7EE. Tel: 020-7499 8144; Fax: 020-7499 1156; Web: www.igb.org.uk. *Chief Executive*, B. E. A. Pegnall

BRISTOL AND GLOUCESTERSHIRE ARCHAEOLOGICAL SOCIETY (1876), 22 Beaumont Road, Gloucester GL2 0EJ. Tel: 01452-302610; Web: www.bgas.org.uk. *Hon. Secretary*, D. J. H. Smith, FSA

BRITAIN-NEPAL SOCIETY (1960), 3C Gunnersbury Avenue, London W5 3NH. Tel: 020-8992 0173. *Hon. Secretary*, Mrs P. Mellor

BRITAIN-RUSSIA CENTRE - BRITISH EAST-WEST CENTRE (1959), 1 Nine Elms Lane, London SW8 5NQ. Tel: 020-7498 6640; Fax: 020-7498 4660. *Director*, G. Cromwell

BRITISH AND FOREIGN SCHOOL SOCIETY (1808), Croudace House, Godstone Road, Caterham, Surrey CR3 6RE. Tel: 01883-331177. *Director*, J. Kidd

BRITISH EXECUTIVE SERVICE OVERSEAS (1972), 164 Vauxhall Bridge Road, London SW1V 4RB. Tel: 020-7630 0644; Fax: 020-7630 0624; Web: www.beso.org. *Chief Executive*, G. Ramsey, CBE

BRITISH INSTITUTE IN EASTERN AFRICA (1959), 10 Carlton House Terrace, London SW1Y 5AH. Tel: 020-7969 5201; Fax: 020-7969 5401; Web: www.britac.ac.uk/institutes/eafrica. *London Secretary*, Mrs J. Moyo; *President*, Prof. David W. Phillipson

BRITISH INTERPLANETARY SOCIETY (1933), 27–29 South Lambeth Road, London SW8 1SZ. Tel: 020-7735 3160; Fax: 020-7820 1504; Web: www.bis-spaceflight.com. *Executive Secretary*, Ms S. A. Jones

BRITISH ISRAEL WORLD FEDERATION (1919), 8 Blades Court, Deodar Road, London SW15 2NU. Tel: 020-8877 9010; Fax: 020-8871 4770; Web: www.britishisrael.co.uk. *Hon. Secretary*, M. A. Clark

BRITISH MEDICAL ASSOCIATION (1832), BMA House, Tavistock Square, London WC1H 9JP. Tel: 020-7387 4499; Fax: 020-7383 6400; Web: www.bma.org.uk. *Secretary*, J. Strachan

BTBS THE BOOK TRADE CHARITY (1837), The Foyle Centre, The Retreat, Kings Langley, Herts WD4 8LT. Tel: 01923-263128; Fax: 01923-270732; Web: www.booktradecharity.demon.co.uk. *Chief Executive*, David Hicks

BUCKINGHAMSHIRE ARCHAEOLOGICAL SOCIETY (1847), County Museum, Church Street, Aylesbury, Bucks HP20 2QP. Tel: 01296-678114. *Hon. Secretary*, Mrs L. T. James

BUDGERIGAR SOCIETY (1925), Spring Gardens, Northampton NN1 1DR. Tel: 01604-624549; Fax: 01604-627108; Web: www.budgerigarsociety.com. *General Secretary*, D. Whittaker

BUILDING ENGINEERS, ASSOCIATION OF (1925), Lutyens House, Billing Brook Road, Weston Favell, Northampton NN3 8NW. Tel: 01604-404121; Fax: 01604-784200; Web: www.abe.org.uk. *Chief Executive*, D. Gibson

BUILDING SERVICES ENGINEERS, CHARTERED INSTITUTION OF (1898), Delta House, 222 Balham High Road, London SW12 9BS. Tel: 020-8675 5211; Fax: 020-8675 5449. *Chief Executive*, J. Amey

BUILDING SOCIETIES ASSOCIATION (1869), 3 Savile Row, London W1S 3PB. Tel: 020-7437 0655; Fax: 020-7734 6416; Web: www.bsa.org.uk. *Director-General*, A. Coles

BUILDING, CHARTERED INSTITUTE OF (1834), Englemere), King's Ride, Ascot, Berks SL5 7TB. Tel: 01344-630700; Fax: 01344-630777; Web: www.ciob.org.uk. *Chief Executive*, Chris Blythe

BUSINESS AND PROFESSIONAL WOMEN UK LTD (1938), PO Box 214, 24 Knifesmithgate, Chesterfield S40 1XW. Tel: 01246-211988; Fax: 01246-211988; Web: www.bpwuk.org.uk

BUSINESS RECOVERY PROFESSIONALS, ASSOCIATION OF (1990), Halton House, 20–23 Holborn, London EC1N 2JE. Tel: 020-7831 6563; Fax: 020-7405 7047; Web: www.r3.org.uk. *Chief Operating Officer*, R. M. Stancombe

CAFOD (CATHOLIC FUND FOR OVERSEAS DEVELOPMENT) (1962), Romero Close, Stockwell Road, London SW9 9TY. Tel: 020-7733 7900; Fax: 020-7274 9630; Web: www.cafod.org.uk. *Director*, J. Filochowski

CALOUSTE GULBENKIAN FOUNDATION (1956), 98 Portland Place, London W1B 1ET. Tel: 020-7636 5313; Fax: 020-7908 7580; Web: www.gulbenkian.org.uk. *Director*, Ms P. Ridley

CAMBRIAN ARCHAEOLOGICAL ASSOCIATION (1847), Halfway House, Pont y Pandy, Bangor, Gwynedd LL57 3DG. Tel: 01248-364865. *General Secretary*, P. Llewellyn

CAMBRIDGE ANTIQUARIAN SOCIETY (1849), 99 Cambridge Road, Girton, Cambridge CB3 0PN. *Hon. Secretary*, Ms E. Allan

CAMBRIDGE PRESERVATION SOCIETY (1928), Wandlebury Ring, Gog Magog Hills, Babraham, Cambridge CB2 4AE. Tel: 01223-243830; Fax: 01223-243830; Web: www.cpswandlebury.org. *Director*, B. Pearce

CAMERON FUND, Tavistock House North, Tavistock Square, London WC1H 9HR. Tel: 020-7388 0796; Fax: 020-7554 6334. *Secretary* Mrs L. Dluska-Miziura

CAMPAIGN FOR FREEDOM OF INFORMATION (1984), Suite 102, 16 Baldwin Gardens, London EC1N 7RJ. Tel: 020-7831 7477; Fax: 020-7831 7461; Web: www.cfoi.org.uk. *Director*, M. Frankel

CAMPAIGN FOR NUCLEAR DISARMAMENT (CND) (1958), 162 Holloway Road, London N7 8DQ. Tel: 020-7700 2393; Fax: 020-7700 2357; Web: www.cnduk.org. *Chair*, Carol Naughton

CANCER RESEARCH UK (2002), PO Box 123, London WC2A 3PX. Tel: 020-7242 0200; Fax: 020-7269 3100; Web: www.cancerresearchuk.org. *Director General (Fundraising and Communications)*, Prof. J. G. McVie; *Director General (Science)*, Sir Paul Nurse

CANCER RESEARCH: ROYAL CANCER HOSPITAL, THE INSTITUTE OF (1909), 123 Old Brompton Road, London SW7 3RP. Tel: 020-7352 8133; Fax: 020-7370 5261; Web: www.icr.ac.uk. *Chief Executive*, Prof. P. W. J. Rigby

CARERS UK (1988), Ruth Pitter House, 20–25 Glasshouse Yard, London EC1A 4JT. Tel: 020-7490 8818; Fax: 020-7490 8824; Web: www.carersonline.org.uk. *Chief Executive*, Ms D. Whitworth

CARNEGIE DUNFERMLINE TRUST (1903), Abbey Park House, Dunfermline, Fife KY12 7PB. Tel: 01383-723638; Fax: 01383-721862. *Secretary and Treasurer*, W. C. Runciman

CARNEGIE HERO FUND TRUST (1908), Abbey Park House, Dunfermline, Fife KY12 7PB. Tel: 01383-723638; Fax: 01383-721862. *Secretary and Treasurer*, W. C. Runciman

CARNEGIE UNITED KINGDOM TRUST (1913), Comely Park House, Dunfermline, Fife KY12 7EJ. Tel: 01383-721445; Fax: 01383-620682; Web: www.carnegieuktrust.org.uk. *Chief Executive*, C. John Naylor, OBE

CAST METAL ENGINEERS, INSTITUTE OF, Bordesley Hall, The Holloway, Alvechurch, Birmingham B48 7QA. Tel: 01527-596100; Fax: 01527-596102; Web: www.icme.org.uk. *Secretary*, A. M. Turner

CATHEDRALS FABRIC COMMISSION FOR ENGLAND (1991), Church House, Great Smith Street, London SW1P 3NZ. Tel: 020-7898 1863; Fax: 020-7898 1881. *Secretary*, Dr R. Gem

CATHOLIC UNION OF GREAT BRITAIN (1872), St Maxmilian Kolbe House, 63 Jeddo Road, London W12 9EE. Tel: 020-8749 1321; Fax: 020-8735 0816; Web: www.catholicunion.org. *Secretary*, P. H. Higgs

CATTLE ASSOCIATION (DAIRY), NATIONAL, Brick House), Ribbury, Leominster, Herefordshire HR6 0NQ. Tel: 01568-760632; Fax: 01568-760523. *Executive Secretary*, Tim Brigstoke

CATTLE BREEDERS' CLUB, BRITISH (1950), c/o SDHBS, Westpoint, Clyst St Mary, Exeter EX5 1DJ. Tel: 01392-447494; Fax: 01392-447495. *Secretary*, Mrs L. Lewin

CENTRAL AND CECIL HOUSING TRUST (1926), 2 Priory Road, Kew, Richmond, Surrey TW9 3DG. Tel: 020-8940 9828; Fax: 020-8332 1044. *Chief Executive*, G. Brighton

CENTREPOINT, Neil House, 7 Whitechapel Road, London E1 1DU. Tel: 020-7426 5300; Fax: 020-7426 5301; Web: www.centrepoint.org.uk. *Chief Executive*, Anthony Lawton

CEREDIGION ANTIQUARIAN SOCIETY, Henllys, Lûn Tyllwyd, Llanfarian, Aberystwyth SY23 4UH. Tel: 01970-625818. *Hon. Secretary,* T. G. Davies

CHAMBERS OF COMMERCE, BRITISH, Manning House, 22 Carlisle Place, London SW1P 1JA. Tel: 020-7565 2000; Fax: 020-7565 2049; Web: www.britishchambers.org.uk. *Director-General,* David Lennan

CHAMBERS OF COMMERCE, SCOTTISH (1948), 12 Broughton Place, Edinburgh EH1 3RX. Tel: 0131-557 9500; Fax: 0131-558 3257; Web: www.scottishchambers.org.uk. *Director,* L. Gold, CBE

CHARITIES AID FOUNDATION (1924), Kings Hill, West Malling, Kent ME19 4TA. Tel: 01732-520000; Fax: 01732-520001; Web: www.cafonline.org. *Chief Executive,* M. Brophy

CHEMICAL ENGINEERS, INSTITUTION OF (1922), Davis Building, 165–189 Railway Terrace, Rugby, Warks CV21 3HQ. Tel: 01788-578214; Fax: 01788-560833; Web: www.icheme.org. *Chief Executive,* Dr T. J. Evans

CHESS FEDERATION, BRITISH (1904), The Watch Oak, Chain Lane, Battle, E. Sussex TN33 0YD. Tel: 01424-775222; Fax: 01424-775904; Web: www.bcf.mdirect.co.uk. *President,* Gerry Walsh

CHESTER ARCHAEOLOGICAL SOCIETY (1849), Ochr Cottage, Porch Lane, Hope Mountain, Caergwrle, Flintshire LL12 9HG. Tel: 01978-760834; Web: www.chesterarchaeolsoc.org.uk. *Secretary,* Dr D. J. P. Mason, FSA

CHILDBIRTH TRUST, NATIONAL (1956), Alexandra House, Oldham Terrace, Acton, London W3 6NH. Tel: Administration 0870-770 3236. Enquiries: 0870 444 8707; Fax: 0870-770 3237; Web: www.nctpregnancyandbabycare.com. *Chief Executive,* Ms B. Phipps

CHILDREN 1ST (ROYAL SCOTTISH SOCIETY FOR PREVENTION OF CRUELTY TO CHILDREN) (1884), 41 Polwarth Terrace, Edinburgh EH11 1NU. Tel: 0131-337 8539; Fax: 0131-346 8284; Web: www.children1st.org.uk. *Chief Executive,* Margaret McKay

CHILDREN'S SOCIETY (1881), Edward Rudolf House, Margery Street, London WC1X 0JL. Tel: 020-7841 4000; Fax: 020-7841 4500; Web: www.childrenssociety.org.uk. *Chief Executive,* Bob Reitermeier

CHIROPODISTS AND PODIATRISTS, The Society of (1912), 1 Fellmongers Path, Tower Bridge Road, London SE1 3LY. Tel: 020-7234 8620; Fax: 020-7234 8621; Web: www.feetforlife.org. *Chief Executive,* Hilary de Lyon

CHOIRS SCHOOLS ASSOCIATION, The Minster School, Deangate, York YO1 7JA. Tel: 01904-624900; Fax: 01904-557232; Web: www.choirschools.org.uk. *Administrator,* Mrs W. Jackson

CHRISTIAN AID SCOTLAND, 41 George IV Bridge, Edinburgh EH1 1EL. Tel: 0131-220 1254; Fax: 0131-225 8861; Web: www.christian-aid.org.uk. *National Secretary,* Revd J. Wylie

CHRISTIAN EDUCATION (1965), Royal Buildings, Victoria Street, Derby DE1 1GW. Tel: 01332-296655; Fax: 01332-343253; Web: www.cem.org.uk. *Director,* Peter Fishpool

CHRISTIAN EDUCATION (1803), 1020 Bristol Road, Selly Oak, Birmingham B29 6LB. Tel: 0121-472 4242; Fax: 0121-472 7575; Web: www.christianeducation.org.uk. *Director,* Peter Fishpool

CHRISTIAN KNOWLEDGE, SOCIETY FOR PROMOTING (SPCK) (1698), Holy Trinity Church, Marylebone Road, London NW1 4DU. Tel: 020-7643 0382; Fax: 020-7643 0391; Web: www.spck.org.uk. *General Secretary,* G. C. King

CHRISTIANS AND JEWS, COUNCIL OF (1942), 5th Floor, Camelford House, 87–89 Albert Embankment, London SE1 7TP. Tel: 020-7820 0090; Fax: 020-7820 0504; Web: www.ccj.org.uk. *Director,* Sr M. Shepherd

CHURCH ARMY (1882), Marlow House, 109 Station Road, Sidcup DA15 7AD. Tel: 020-8309 3991; Fax: 020-8309 3500; Web: www.churcharmy.org.uk. *Chief Secretary,* Capt. P. Johanson

CHURCH BELL RINGERS, CENTRAL COUNCIL OF (1891), The Cottage, School Hill, Warnham, Horsham RH12 3QN. Tel: 01403-269743; Web: www.cccbr.org.uk. *Secretary,* Mr I. H. Oram

CHURCH HISTORY SOCIETY, SCOTTISH (1927), Crown Manse, 39 Southside Road, Inverness IV2 4XA. Tel: 01463-231140; Fax: 01463-230537. *Hon. Secretary,* Revd Dr P. H. Donald

CHURCH HOUSE, CORPORATION OF (1888), Church House, Dean's Yard, London SW1P 3NZ. Tel: 020-7898 1310; Fax: 020-7898 1321. *Secretary,* C. D. L. Menzies

CHURCH LADS' AND CHURCH GIRLS' BRIGADE (1891), 2 Barnsley Road, Wath upon Dearne, Rotherham, S. Yorks S63 6PY. Tel: 01709-876535; Fax: 01709-878089; Web: www.clagb.org.uk. *General Secretary,* A. J. Reed Screen

CHURCH MISSION SOCIETY, Partnership House, 157 Waterloo Road, London SE1 8UU. Tel: 020-7928 8681; Fax: 020-7401 3215; Web: www.cms-uk.org. *General Secretary,* Revd Canon T. Dakin

CHURCH MONUMENTS SOCIETY (1979), c/o Society of Antiquaries, Burlington House, Piccadilly, London W1J 0BE. Tel: 020-7734 0193; Fax: 020-7287 6967; Web: www.churchmonumentssociety.org. *Hon. Secretary,* Dr Sophie Oosterwijk

CHURCH UNION (1859), Faith House, 7 Tufton Street, London SW1P 3QN. Tel: 020-7222 6952; Fax: 020-7976 7180; Web: www.churchunion.care4free.net. *House Manager,* Mrs J. Miller

CHURCH'S MINISTRY AMONG JEWISH PEOPLE (1809), 30C Clarence Road, St Albans, Herts AL1 4JJ. Tel: 01727-833114; Fax: 01727-848312; Web: www.cmj.org.uk. *General Director,* Revd T. Higton

CHURCHES, COUNCIL FOR THE CARE OF (1921), Church House, Great Smith Street, London SW1P 3NZ. Tel: 020-7898 1866; Fax: 020-7898 1881.
Acting Secretary, Stephen Bowler

CHURCHES, FRIENDS OF FRIENDLESS (1957), St Ann's Vestry Hall, 2 Church Entry, London EC4V 5HB. Tel: 020-7236 3934; Fax: 020-7329 3677; Web: www.friendsoffrriendlesschurches.org.uk. *Hon. Director,* M. Saunders, MBE

CHURCHILL SOCIETY - LONDON (1990), c/o 18 Grove Lane, Ipswich, Suffolk IP4 1NR. Tel: 01473-413533; Fax: 01473-413533; Web: www.churchill-society-london.org.uk/index.htm. *General Secretary,* N. H. Rogers

CHURCHILL SOCIETY, INTERNATIONAL (1968), PO Box 1257, Melksham, Wilts SN12 6GQ. Tel: 01380-828609; Fax: 01380-828609; Web: www.winstonchurchill.org. *Chairman,* N. B. Knocker, OBE

CITIZENS ADVICE BUREAUX, NATIONAL ASSOCIATION OF (1939), Myddelton House, 115–123 Pentonville Road, London N1 9LZ. Tel: 020-7833 2181; Fax: 020-7833 4371; Web: www.nacab.org.uk. *Chief Executive,* D. Harker

CITY PAROCHIAL FOUNDATION (1891), 6 Middle Street, London EC1A 7PH. Tel: 020-7606 6145; Fax: 020-7600 1866; Web: www.cityparochial.org.uk. *Clerk,* B. Mehta, OBE

CIVIC TRUST (1957), 17 Carlton House Terrace, London SW1Y 5AW. Tel: 020-7930 0914; Fax: 020-7321 0180; Web: www.civictrust.org.uk. *Chief Executive,* Martin Bacon

CIVIL ENGINEERS, INSTITUTION OF (1818), 1 Great George Street, London SW1P 3AA. Tel: 020-7222 7722; Fax: 020-7222 7500; Web: www.ice.org.uk. *Chief Executive,* Amar Bhogell

CLASSICAL ASSOCIATION (1903), Senate House, Malet Street, London WC1E 7HU. Tel: 020-7862 8706; Fax: 020-7862 8729; Web: www.sas.ac.uk/icls/classass. *Administrator,* C. L. Roberts

CLEAN AIR AND ENVIRONMENTAL PROTECTION, NATIONAL SOCIETY FOR, 44 Grand Parade, Brighton BN2 9QA. Tel: 01273-878770; Fax: 01273-606626; Web: www.nsca.org.uk. *Secretary-General,* R. Mills

CLUBS FOR YOUNG PEOPLE, NATIONAL ASSOCIATION OF (1925), 371 Kennington Lane, London SE11 5QY. Tel: 020-7793 0787; Fax: 020-7820 9815; Web: www.nacyp.org.uk. *National Director,* C. Groves

CO-OPERATIVE GROUP (CWS) LTD. (1863), PO Box 53, New Century House, Manchester M60 4ES. Tel: 0161-834 1212; Fax: 0161-834 4507; Web: www.co-op.co.uk. *Chief Executive,* Sir Graham Melmoth

CO-OPERATIVE PARTY, 72 Weston Street, London SE1 3SD. Tel: 020-7357 0230; Fax: 020-7407 4476; Web: www.co-op-party.org.uk. *Secretary,* P. Hunt

CO-OPERATIVE UNION LTD (1869), Holyoake House, Hanover Street, Manchester M60 0AS. Tel: 0161-246 2900; Fax: 0161-831 7684; Web: www.co-opunion.co.uk. *Chief Executive,* Ms P. Green

COLITIS AND CROHN'S DISEASE, NATIONAL ASSOCIATION FOR (1979), 4 Beaumont House, Sutton Road, St Albans, Herts AL1 5HH. Tel: 01727-830038; Fax: 01727-862550; Web: www.nacc.org.uk. *Director,* R. Driscoll

COMMONWEALTH EX-SERVICES LEAGUE, BRITISH (1921), 48 Pall Mall, London SW1Y 5JG. Tel: 020-7973 7263; Fax: 020-7973 7308; Web: www.bcel.org.uk. *Secretary-General,* Colonel B. G. G. Nicholson, OBE

COMMONWEALTH, ENGLISH-SPEAKING UNION OF THE (1918), Dartmouth House, 37 Charles Street, London W1J 5ED. Tel: 020-7529 1550; Fax: 020-7495 6108; Web: www.esu.org. *Director-General,* Mrs V. Mitchell, OBE

COMMUNICATORS IN BUSINESS, BRITISH ASSOCIATION FOR (1949), 42 Borough High Street, London SE1 1XW. Tel: 020-7378 7139; Fax: 020-7378 7140; Web: www.bacb.org. *Secretary-General,* Mrs K. Jones

COMPUTER SOCIETY, BRITISH (1957), 1 Sanford Street, Swindon SN1 1HJ. Tel: 01793-417417; Fax: 01793-480270; Web: www.bcs.org.uk. *Chief Executive,* David Clarke

CONSERVATION OF HISTORIC AND ARTISTIC WORKS, INTERNATIONAL INSTITUTE FOR (1950), 6 Buckingham Street, London WC2N 6BA. Tel: 020-7839 5975; Fax: 020-7976 1564; Web: www.iiconservation.org. *Secretary-General,* D. Bomford

CONSULTING ENGINEERS, ASSOCIATION OF (1913), Alliance House, 12 Caxton Street, London SW1H 0QL. Tel: 020-7222 6557; Fax: 020-7222 0750; Web: www.acenet.co.uk. *Chief Executive,* N. Bennett

CONSULTING SCIENTISTS, ASSOCIATION OF (1958), PO Box 4040, Thorpe-le-Soken, Clacton-on-Sea CO16 0EL. Tel: 01255-862526; Fax: 01255-862526. *Secretary,* D. Simpson

CONSUMERS' ASSOCIATION (1957), 2 Marylebone Road, London NW1 4DF. Tel: 020-7770 7000; Fax: 020-7770 7600; Web: www.which.net. *Director,* Ms S. McKechnie, OBE

CONVENIENCE STORES, ASSOCIATION OF (1995), Federation House, 17 Farnborough Street, Farnborough, Hants GU14 8AG. Tel: 01252-515001; Fax: 01252-515002; Web: www.thelocalshop.com. *Chief Executive,* David Rae

COPYRIGHT COUNCIL, BRITISH (1965), 29–33 Berners Street, London W1T 3AB. Tel: 01986-788122; Fax: 01986-788847. *Secretary,* Ms J. Ibbotson

CORAM FAMILY (1739), 49 Mecklenburgh Square, London WC1N 2QA. Tel: 020-7520 0300; Fax: 020-7520 0301; Web: www.coram.org.uk. *Chief Executive,* Dr G. Pugh, OBE

CORONER'S SOCIETY OF ENGLAND AND WALES (1846), 44 Ormond Avenue, Hampton, Middx TW12 2RX. Tel: 020-8979 6805; Fax: 020-8979 6805. *Hon. Secretary*, M. J. C. Burgess

CORPORATE TREASURERS, ASSOCIATION OF (1979), Ocean House, 10–12 Little Trinity Lane, London EC4V 2DJ. Tel: 020-7213 9728; Fax: 020-7248 2591; Web: www.treasurers.org. *Chief Executive*, Dr D. Creed

CORRESPONDENCE COLLEGES, ASSOCIATION OF BRITISH (1955), PO Box 17926, London SW19 3WB. Tel: 020-8544 9559; Fax: 020-8540 7657; Web: www.homestudy.org.uk. *Secretary*, Mrs H. Owen

COUNCIL SECRETARIES AND SOLICITORS, ASSOCIATION OF (1974, merged 1996), Trafalgar Wharf, 150 Mountbatten Close, Ashton on Ribble, Preston PR2 2XE. Tel: 01772-739073; Fax: 01772-739073; Web: www.acses.org.uk. *Executive Officer*, N. Yates

COUNSEL AND CARE (1954), Twyman House, 16 Bonny Street, London NW1 9PG. Tel: 020-7241 8555; Fax: 020-7267 6877; Web: www.counselandcare.org.uk. *Chief Executive*, M. Green

COUNSELLING AND PSYCHOTHERAPY, BRITISH ASSOCIATION FOR (1977), 1 Regent Place, Rugby, Warks CV21 2PJ. Tel: 0870-443 5252; Fax: 0870-443 5160; Web: www.bacp.co.uk

COUNTRY HOUSES ASSOCIATION (1955), Suite 10, Aynhoe Park, Aynhoe, Banbury, Oxon OX17 3BQ. Tel: 01869-812800; Fax: 01869-812819; Web: www.cha.org.uk. *Chief Executive*, Brigadier C. K. Price, CBE

COUNTRY LAND & BUSINESS ASSOCIATION (1907), 16 Belgrave Square, London SW1X 8PQ. Tel: 020-7235 0511; Fax: 020-7235 4696; Web: www.cla.org.uk. *President*, Sir Edward Greenwell

COUNTRYSIDE ALLIANCE (1998), Old Town Hall, 367 Kennington Road, London SE11 4PT. Tel: 020-7582 5432; Fax: 020-7793 8484; Web: www.countryside-alliance.org. *Chairman*, J. Jackson; *Chief Executive*, R. Burge

COUNTY CHIEF EXECUTIVES, ASSOCIATION OF (1974), Office of the Chief Executive, County Hall, Trowbridge, Wiltshire BA14 8JF. Tel: 01225-713101; Fax: 01225-713092. *Hon. Secretary*, K. Robinson

COUNTY TREASURERS, SOCIETY OF, Derbyshire County Council, County Hall, Matlock, Derbyshire DE4 3AH. Tel: 01629-585068; Fax: 01629-585985; Web: www.sctnet.org.uk. *Hon. Secretary*, Peter Swaby

COVENTRY AND DISTRICT ARCHAEOLOGICAL SOCIETY (1965), 1 Holloway Field, Coventry CV6 2DA. Tel: 024-7659 1078. *Hon. Secretary*, Mrs J. Smith

CPRE (COUNCIL FOR THE PROTECTION OF RURAL ENGLAND) (1926), 128 Southwark Street, London SE1 0SW. Tel: 020-7976 6433; Fax: 020-7976 6373; Web: www.cpre.org.uk. *Director*, Ms K. Parminter

CRAFTS COUNCIL (1971), 44A Pentonville Road, London N1 9BY. Tel: 020-7278 7700; Fax: 020-7837 6891; Web: www.craftscouncil.org.uk. *Director*, Ms J. Barnes

CRISIS UK (1967), Warwick House, 25/27 Buckingham Palace Road, London SW1E 0PP. Tel: 0870-011 3335; Fax: 0870-011 3336; Web: www.crisis.org.uk. *Chief Executive*, S. Ghosh

CRUELTY TO ANIMALS, SCOTTISH SOCIETY FOR THE PREVENTION OF (1839), Braehead Mains, 603 Queensferry Road, Edinburgh EH4 6EA. Tel: 0131-339 0222; Fax: 0131-339 4777; Web: www.scottishspca.org. *Chief Executive*, I. R. Gardiner

CRUSE BEREAVEMENT CARE (1959), 126 Sheen Road, Richmond, Surrey TW9 1UR. Tel: 020-8939 9530. Helpline: 0870-167 1677; Fax: 020-8940 7638; Web: www.crusebereavementcare.org.uk. *Executive Director*, Anne Viney

CTC (CYCLISTS' TOURING CLUB), 69 Meadrow, Godalming, Surrey GU7 3HS. Tel: 0870-873 0060; Fax: 01483-426994; Web: www.ctc.org.uk. *Director*, K. Mayne

CUMBERLAND AND WESTMORLAND ANTIQUARIAN AND ARCHAEOLOGICAL SOCIETY (1866), 2 High Tenterfell, Kendal, Cumbria LA9 4PG. Tel: 01539-773542; Fax: 01539-773538; Web: www.cwaas.org.uk. *Hon. Secretary*, R. Hall

CYMMRODORION, HONOURABLE SOCIETY OF (1751), 30 Eastcastle Street, London W1W 7DJ. Tel: 020-7631 0502; Web: www.cymmrodorion1751.org.uk. *Hon. Secretary*, J. Samuel

CYSTIC FIBROSIS TRUST (1964), 11 London Road, Bromley, Kent BR1 1BY. Tel: 020-8464 7211; Fax: 020-8313 0472; Web: www.cftrust.org.uk. *Chief Executive*, Mrs R. Barnes

DATA (DESIGN AND TECHNOLOGY ASSOCIATION) (1989), 16 Wellesbourne House, Walton Road, Wellesbourne, Warks CV35 9JB. Tel: 01789-470007; Fax: 01789-841955; Web: www.data.org.uk. *Chairman*, Dr R.V. Peacock, OBE; *Chief Executive*, A. Breckon

DEAF 'SOUND SEEKERS', COMMONWEALTH SOCIETY FOR THE (1959), 34 Buckingham Palace Road, London SW1W 0RE. Tel: 020-7233 5700; Fax: 020-7233 5800; Web: www.sound-seekers.org.uk. *Chief Executive*, Brig. J. A. Davis

DEAF ASSOCIATION, BRITISH (1890), 1 Worship Street, London EC2A 2AB. Tel: 0870-770 3300 Textphone: 0800 6522 965; Fax: 020-7588 3527; Web: www.bda.org.uk. *Chief Executive*, J. McWhinney

DENTAL ASSOCIATION, BRITISH (1880), 64 Wimpole Street, London W1G 8YS. Tel: 020-7563 4563; Fax: 020-7487 4563; Web: www.bda-dentistry.org.uk. *Chief Executive*, Ian Wylie

DENTAL COUNCIL, GENERAL (1956), 37 Wimpole Street, London W1G 8DQ. Tel: 020-7887 3800; Fax: 020-7224 3294; Web: www.gdc-uk.org. *Chief Executive & Registrar*, Antony Townsend

DESIGN AND INDUSTRIES ASSOCIATION (1915), 22 Ambra Vale East, Cliftonwood, Bristol BS8 4RE; Fax: 0117-946 7461; Web: www.dia.org.uk. *Chairman*, Paul Williams

DESIGNERS FOR INDUSTRY, Faculty of Royal, RSA, 8 John Adam Street, London WC2N 6EZ. Tel: 020-7451 6801; Fax: 020-7839 5805; Web: www.rsa.org.uk

DEVON ARCHAEOLOGICAL SOCIETY (1929), RAM Museum, Queen Street, Exeter EX4 3RX. Tel: 01392-265858. *Hon. Secretary*, Mrs J. Cannell

DIABETES UK (1934), 10 Parkway, London NW1 7AA. Tel: 020-7424 1000; Fax: 020-7424 1001; Web: www.diabetes.org.uk. *Chief Executive*, P. Streets

DIANA, PRINCESS OF WALES MEMORIAL FUND (1997), County Hall, Westminster Bridge Road, London SE1 7PB. Tel: 020-7902 5500; Fax: 020-7902 5511; Web: www.theworkcontinues.org.uk. *Chief Executive*, Dr A. Purkis

DIRECTORS, INSTITUTE OF (1903), 116 Pall Mall, London SW1Y 5ED. Tel: 020-7839 1233; Fax: 020-7930 1949; Web: www.iod.com. *Chief Executive*, A. Main Wilson

DIRECTORY & DATABASE PUBLISHERS ASSOCIATION (1970), PO Box 23034, London W6 0RJ. Tel: 020-8846 9707; Fax: 0870 168 0552; Web: www.directory-publisher.co.uk. *Secretary*, Ms R. Pettit

DISPENSING OPTICIANS, ASSOCIATION OF BRITISH (1925), 199 Gloucester Terrace, London W2 6HX. *Registrar*, D. G. Baker

DITCHLEY FOUNDATION (1958), Ditchley Park, Enstone, Chipping Norton, Oxon OX7 4ER. Tel: 01608-677346; Fax: 01608-677399; Web: www.ditchley.co.uk. *Director*, Sir Nigel Broomfield, KCMG

DORSET NATURAL HISTORY AND ARCHAEOLOGICAL SOCIETY, Dorset County Museum, Dorchester, Dorset DT1 1XA. Tel: 01305-262735; Fax: 01305-257180; Web: www.dorsetcountymuseum.com. *Secretary*, R. M. de Peyer

DOWNS SYNDROME ASSOCIATION (1970), 155 Mitcham Road, London SW17 9PG. Tel: 020-8682 4001; Fax: 020-8682 4012; Web: www.downs-syndrome.org.uk. *Director*, Ms C. Boys

DOWSERS, BRITISH SOCIETY OF (1933), Sycamore Barn, Hastingleigh, Ashford, Kent TN25 5HW. Tel: 01233-750253; Fax: 01233-750253; Web: www.britishdowsers.org. *General Secretary*, M. D. Rust

DRAINAGE AUTHORITIES, ASSOCIATION OF (1937), The Mews, 3 Royal Oak Passage, High Street, Huntingdon, Cambs PE29 3EA. Tel: 01480-411123; Fax: 01480-431167; Web: www.ada.org.uk. *Chief Executive*, D. Noble

DRIVING SOCIETY, BRITISH (1957), 27 Dugard Place, Barford, Warwick CV35 8DX. Tel: 01926-624420; Fax: 01926-624633; Web: www.britishdrivingsociety.co.uk. *Secretary*, Mrs J. M. Dillon

DRUGSCOPE (2000), 32–36 Loman Street, London SE1 0EE. Tel: 020-7928 1211; Fax: 020-7928 1771; Web: www.drugscope.org.uk. *Chief Executive*, R. Howard

DUKE OF EDINBURGH'S AWARD, Gulliver House, Madeira Walk, Windsor, Berks SL4 1EU. Tel: 01753-727400; Fax: 01753-810666; Web: www.theaward.org. *Director*, M. P. Gretton, CB

DYERS AND COLOURISTS, SOCIETY OF (1884), PO Box 244, Perkin House, 82 Grattan Road, Bradford BD1 2JB. Tel: 01274-725138; Fax: 01274-392888; Web: www.sde.org.uk. *General Secretary*, K. M. McGhee

DYSLEXIA INSTITUTE (1972), 133 Gresham Road, Staines, Middx TW18 2AJ. Tel: 01784-463851; Fax: 01784-460747; Web: www.dyslexia-inst.org.uk. *Chief Executive*, Shirley Cramer

EAST HERTFORDSHIRE ARCHAEOLOGICAL SOCIETY (1898), 1 Marsh Lane, Stanstead Abbots, Ware, Herts SG12 8HH. Tel: 01920-870664. *Hon. Secretary*, Mrs M. C. Readman

EAST OF ENGLAND AGRICULTURAL SOCIETY (1797), East of England Showground, Peterborough PE2 6XE. Tel: 01733-234451; Fax: 01733-370038; Web: www.eastofengland.org.uk. *Chief Executive*, Andrew Mercer

EATING DISORDERS ASSOCIATION, First Floor, Wensum House, 103 Prince of Wales Road, Norwich NR1 1DW. Helpline: 01603-621414. Youthline: 01603-765050; Fax: 01603-664915; Web: www.edauk.com. *Chief Executive*, Mrs N. Bryant

ECCLESIASTICAL HISTORY SOCIETY, 21 Aytoun Road, Pollokshields, Glasgow G41 5HW. Tel: 0141-423 0901. *President*, Prof. Henry Mayr-Harting. *Secretary*, Michael Kennedy

ECCLESIOLOGICAL SOCIETY (1839), c/o Society of Antiquaries of London, Burlington House, London W1V 0HS. Tel: 020-8492 2111; Web: www.ecclsoc.org. *Hon. Secretary*, Kenneth V. Richardson

ECOLOGICAL SOCIETY, BRITISH, 26 Blades Court, Deodar Road, Putney, London SW15 2NU. Tel: 020-8871 9797; Fax: 020-8871 9779; Web: www.britishecologicalsociety.org

ECONOMIC AFFAIRS, INSTITUTE OF (1955), 2 Lord North Street, London SW1P 3LB. Tel: 020-7799 8900; Fax: 020-7799 2137; Web: www.iea.org.uk. *General Director*, J. Blundell

EDINBURGH CHAMBER OF COMMERCE AND ENTERPRISE (1786), 27 Melville Street, Edinburgh EH3 7JF. Tel: 0131-477 7000; Fax: 0131-477 7002; Web: www.ecce.org. *Chief Executive*, W. Furness

EDITH CAVELL AND NATION'S FUND FOR NURSES (1920), Flints, Petersfield Road, Winchester, Hants SO23 0JD. Tel: 01962-860900; Fax: 01962-860900. *Administrator*, Mrs A. Rich

EDITORS, SOCIETY OF (1999), University Centre, Granta Place, Cambridge CB2 1RU. Tel: 01223-304080; Fax: 01223-304090; Web: www.societyofeditors.org. *Executive Director*, R. Satchwell

EDUCATION OFFICERS, SOCIETY OF (1972), Manchester House, 84–86 Princess Street, Manchester M1 6NG. Tel: 0161-236 5766; Fax: 0161-236 6742. *General Secretary*, Chris Waterman

EDUCATIONAL RESEARCH IN ENGLAND AND WALES, NATIONAL FOUNDATION FOR (1946), The Mere, Upton Park, Slough SL1 2DQ. Tel: 01753-574123; Fax: 01753-691632; Web: www.nfer.ac.uk. *Director*, Dr S. Hegarty

EGYPT EXPLORATION SOCIETY, 3 Doughty Mews, London WC1N 2PG. Tel: 020-7242 1880; Fax: 020-7404 6118; Web: www.ees.ac.uk. *Secretary-General*, Dr P. A. Spencer

ELECTORAL REFORM SOCIETY (1884), 6 Chancel Street, London SE1 0UU. Tel: 020-7928 1622; Fax: 020-7401 7789; Web: www.electoral-reform.org.uk. *President*, Rt Hon. Prof. The Earl Russell, FBA

ELECTRICAL ENGINEERS, INSTITUTION OF, Savoy Place, London WC2R 0BL. Tel: 020-7240 1871; Fax: 020-7240 7735; Web: www.iee.org.uk. *Secretary*, Dr A. Roberts

ELGAR FOUNDATION, The Elgar Birthplace Museum, Lower Broadheath, Worcester WR2 6RH. Tel: 01905-333224; Fax: 01905-333426; Web: www.elgar.org. *Museum Director*, Cathy Sloan

ELGAR SOCIETY (1951), c/o 29 Van Diemens Close, Chinnor, Oxon OX39 4QE. Tel: 01844-354096; Fax: 01844-354459; Web: www.elgar.org. *Hon. Secretary*, Ms W. Hillary

EMERGENCY PLANNING SOCIETY (1993), Northumberland House, 11 The Pavement, Popes Lane, London W5 4NG. Tel: 020-8579 7971; Fax: 020-8579 7972; Web: www.emergplansoc.org.uk. *Hon. Secretary*, I. Hoult

ENABLE (SCOTTISH SOCIETY FOR THE MENTALLY HANDICAPPED) (1954), 7 Buchanan Street, Glasgow G1 3HL. Tel: 0141-226 4541; Fax: 0141-204 4398; Web: www.enable.org.uk. *Director*, N. Dunning

ENERGY WATCH (2000), 4th Floor), Artillery House, Artillery Row, London SW1P 1RT. Tel: 020-7799 8340; Fax: 020-7799 8341; Web: www.energywatch.org.uk. *Director*, P. Hamer

ENERGY, INSTITUTE OF (1927), 18 Devonshire Street, London W1G 7AU. Tel: 020-7580 7124; Fax: 020-7580 4420; Web: www.instenergy.org.uk. *Chief Executive and Secretary*, Mrs L. Kingham

ENGINEERING COUNCIL (UK), THE (2002), 10 Maltravers Street, London WC2R 3ER. Tel: 020-7240 7891; Fax: 020-7379 5586; Web: www.engc.org.uk. *Executive Director*, A. V. Ramsay

ENGINEERING DESIGNERS, INSTITUTION OF (1945), Courtleigh, Westbury Leigh, Westbury, Wilts BA13 3TA. Tel: 01373-822801; Fax: 01373-858085; Web: www.ied.org.uk. *Secretary*, E. Brodhurst

ENGINEERS, INSTITUTION OF BRITISH (1928), Clifford Hill Court, Clifford Chambers, Stratford-upon-Avon CV37 8AA. Tel: 01789-298739; Fax: 01789-294442. *Secretary*, Ms J. Busby

ENGINEERS, INSTITUTION OF ROYAL (1875), Brompton Barracks, Chatham, Kent ME4 4UG. Tel: 01634-842669. *Secretary*, Lt. Col. D. N. Hamilton, MBE

ENGINEERS, SOCIETY OF (1854), Guinea Wiggs, Nayland, Colchester, Essex CO6 7NF. Tel: 01206-263332; Fax: 01206-262624; Web: www.society-of-engineers.org.uk. *Secretary*, Mrs L. C. A. Wright; *President*, D. W. Purnell, FSE

ENGLISH ASSOCIATION, THE (1906), University of Leicester, University Road, Leicester LE1 7RH. Tel: 0116-252 3982; Fax: 0116-252 2301; Web: www.le.ac.uk/engassoc/. *Chief Executive*, Ms H. Lucas

ENVIRONMENT COUNCIL, THE, 212 High Holborn, London WC1V 7BF. Tel: 020-7836 2626; Fax: 020-7242 1180; Web: www.the-environment-council.org.uk. *Chief Executive*, S. Robinson

ENVIRONMENTAL HEALTH, CHARTERED INSTITUTE OF (1883), Chadwick Court, 15 Hatfields, London SE1 8DJ. Tel: 020-7928 6006; Fax: 020-7827 5866; Web: www.cieh.org.uk. *Chief Executive*, G. Jukes

EPILEPSY ACTION (1950), New Anstey House, Gate Way Drive, Yeadon, Leeds LS19 7XY. Tel: 0113-210 8800. Helpline: 0808-800 5050; Fax: 0113-391 0300; Web: www.epilepsy.org.uk. *Chief Executive*, P. Lee

EPILEPSY, NATIONAL SOCIETY FOR (1892), Chesham Lane, Chalfont St Peter, Bucks SL9 0RJ. Tel: 01494-601300; Fax: 01494-871927; Web: www.epilepsynse.org.uk. *Chief Executive*, Graham Faulkner

EQUESTRIAN FEDERATION, BRITISH, National Agricultural Centre, Stoneleigh Park, Kenilworth, Warks CV8 2RH. Tel: 0247-669 8871; Fax: 0247-669 6484; Web: www.bef.co.uk. *Secretary-General*, A. Finding

ESPERANTO ASSOCIATION OF BRITAIN, Wedgwood Memorial College, Barlaston, Stoke-on-Trent ST12 9DG. Tel: 01782-372141; Fax: 01782-372393; Web: www.esperanto.demon.co.uk. *Director of Development*, David Kelso

ESTATE AGENTS, NATIONAL ASSOCIATION OF (1962), Arbon House, 21 Jury Street, Warwick CV34 4EH. Tel: 01926-496800; Fax: 01926-400953; Web: www.naea.co.uk. *Chief Executive*, H. Dunsmore-Hardy

ESTATE AGENTS, OMBUDSMAN FOR (1998), Beckett House, 4 Bridge Street, Salisbury, Wilts SP1 2LX. Tel: 01722-333306; Fax: 01722-332296; Web: www.oea.co.uk. *Ombudsman*, S. R. Carr-Smith

EVANGELICAL LIBRARY, 78A Chiltern Street, London W1U 5HB. Tel: 020-7935 6997; Web: www.elib.org.uk. *Librarian*, S. J. Taylor

EX-SERVICES MENTAL WELFARE SOCIETY (1919), Hollybush House, Hollybush, nr Ayr KA6 7EA. Tel: 01292-560214; Fax: 01292-560871; Web: www.combatstress.com. *Regional Director Scotland and Ireland,* Wg Cdr D. Devine

EXPORT, INSTITUTE OF (1935), Minerva Business Park, Lynchwood, Peterborough PE2 6FT. Tel: 01733-404400; Fax: 01733-404444; Web: www.export.org.uk. *Chief Executive,* Hugh Allen

FABIAN SOCIETY (1884), 11 Dartmouth Street, London SW1H 9BN. Tel: 020-7227 4900; Fax: 020-7976 7153; Web: www.fabian-society.org.uk. *General Secretary,* M. Jacobs

FAIR ISLE BIRD OBSERVATORY TRUST (1948), Fair Isle Bird Observatory, Fair Isle, Shetland ZE2 9JU. Tel: 01595-760258; Fax: 01595-760258; Web: www.fairislebirdobs.co.uk. *Administrator,* H. Shaw

FALSE MEMORY SOCIETY, BRITISH (1993), Bradford on Avon, Wilts BA15 1NF. Tel: 01225-868682; Fax: 01225-862251; Web: www.bfms.org.uk. *Director,* M. Greenhalgh

FAMILY HISTORY SOCIETIES, FEDERATION OF (1974), PO Box 2425, Coventry CV5 6YX. Tel: 07041-492032; Fax: 07041-492032; Web: www.ffhs.org.uk. *Administrator,* Maggie Loughran

FAMILY MEDIATION, NATIONAL, 9 Tavistock Place, London WC1H 9SN. Tel: 020-7383 5993; Fax: 020-7383 5994; Web: www.nfm.u-net.com. *Chief Executive,* Matthew Devlin

FAMILY WELFARE ASSOCIATION (1869), 501–505 Kingsland Road, London E8 4AU. Tel: 020-7254 6251; Fax: 020-7245 5443. *Chief Executive,* Ms H. Dent

FAUNA AND FLORA INTERNATIONAL (1903), Great Eastern House, Tenison Road, Cambridge CB1 2TT. Tel: 01223-571000; Fax: 01223-461481; Web: www.fauna-flora.org. *Executive Director,* M. Rose

FIELD ARCHAEOLOGISTS, INSTITUTE OF (1982), University of Reading, 2 Earley Gate, PO Box 239, Reading RG6 6AU. Tel: 0118-931 6446; Fax: 0118-931 6448; Web: www.archaeologists.net; *Director,* P. Hinton

FIELD STUDIES COUNCIL (1943), Preston Montford, Montford Bridge, Shrewsbury SY4 1HW. Tel: 01743-852100; Fax: 01743-852101; Web: www.field-studies-council.org. *Chief Executive,* A. D. Thomas

FILM CLASSIFICATION, BRITISH BOARD OF (1912), 3 Soho Square, London W1D 3HD. Tel: 020-7440 1570; Fax: 020-7287 0141; Web: www.bbfc.co.uk. *Director,* R. Duval

FIRE ENGINEERS, INSTITUTION OF, 148 New Walk, Leicester LE1 7QB. Tel: 0116-255 3654; Fax: 0116-247 1231; Web: www.ife.org.uk. *Chief Executive Officer,* Ellen Jessett

FIRE PROTECTION ASSOCIATION (1946), Bastille Court, 2 Paris Garden, London SE1 8ND. Tel: 020-7902 5300; Fax: 020-7902 5301; Web: www.thefpa.co.uk. *Managing Director,* Jonathan O'Neill; *Deputy Managing Director,* Chris Mounsey

FIRE SERVICES NATIONAL BENEVOLENT FUND (1943), Fund Headquarters, Marine Court, Fitzalan Road, Littlehampton, W. Sussex BN17 5NF. Tel: 01903-736062; Fax: 01903-731095; Web: www.fsnbf.org.uk. *Chief Executive,* R. Lawrenson

FLEET AIR ARM OFFICERS' ASSOCIATION (1957), 4 St James's Square, London SW1Y 4JU. Tel: 020-7930 7722; Fax: 020-7930 7728; Web: www.fleetairarmoa.org. *Administration Director,* Cdr J. D. O. Macdonald, RN

FOLK DANCE AND SONG SOCIETY, English (1932), Cecil Sharp House, 2 Regent's Park Road, London NW1 7AY. Tel: 020-7485 2206; Fax: 020-7284 0534; Web: www.efdss.org.com. *Chief Executive,* T. Walker

FOOD FROM BRITAIN, 123 Buckingham Palace Road, London SW1W 9SA. Tel: 020-7233 5111; Fax: 020-7233 9515; Web: www.foodfrombritain.com. *Chief Executive,* D. McNair

FOOD SCIENCE AND TECHNOLOGY, INSTITUTE OF (1964), 5 Cambridge Court, 210 Shepherd's Bush Road, London W6 7NJ. Tel: 020-7603 6316; Fax: 020-7602 9936; Web: www.ifst.org. *Chief Executive,* Ms H. G. Wild

FOOTBALLERS' ASSOCIATION, PROFESSIONAL (1907), 20 Oxford Court, Bishopsgate, Manchester M2 3WQ. Tel: 0161-236 0575; Fax: 0161-228 7229; Web: www.givemefootball.com. *Chief Executive,* G. Taylor

FORCES PENSION SOCIETY (1946), 68 South Lambeth Road, London SW8 1RL. Tel: 020-7820 9988; Fax: 020-7820 7583; Web: www.forpen.co.uk. *General Secretary,* Maj.-Gen. J. C. M. Gordon, CBE

FOREIGN PRESS ASSOCIATION IN LONDON (1888), 11 Carlton House Terrace, London SW1Y 5AJ. Tel: 020-7930 0445; Fax: 020-7925 0469; Web: www.foreign-press.org.uk. *General Secretary,* B. Jenner

FORENSIC SCIENCE SOCIETY (1959), Clarke House, 18A Mount Parade, Harrogate, N. Yorks HG1 1BX. Tel: 01423-506068; Fax: 01423-566391; Web: forensic-science-society.org.uk. *Hon. Secretary,* P. Lamb

FORENSIC SCIENCES, British Academy of, Anaesthetic Unit, The Royal London Hospital, Whitechapel, London E1 1BB. Tel: 020-7377 9201; Fax: 020-7377 7126. *Secretary-General,* Dr P. J. Flynn

FORESTRY ASSOCIATION, Commonwealth, c/o Oxford Forestry Institute, South Parks Road, Oxford OX1 3RB. Tel: 01865-271037; Fax: 01865-275074. *Chairman,* Prof. Julian Evans

FOUNDATION FOR THE STUDY OF INFANT DEATHS (1971), 11–19 Artillery Row, London SW1P 1RT. Tel: 020-7222 8001. Helpline: 020-7233 2090; Fax: 020-7222 8002; Web: www.sids.org.uk/fsid/. *Director,* Mrs J. Epstein

FPA (FAMILY PLANNING ASSOCIATION) (1930), 2–12 Pentonville Road, London N1 9FP. Tel: 020-7837 5432; Fax: 020-7837 3042; Web: www.fpa.org.uk. *Chief Executive,* Ms A. Weyman

FRANCO-BRITISH SOCIETY (1904), Room 623, Linen
Hall, 162–168 Regent Street, London W1R 5TB.
Tel: 020-7734 0815; Fax: 020-7734 0815.
Executive Secretary, Mrs K. Brayn

FREEMASONS, GRAND LODGE OF ANTIENT FREE AND
ACCEPTED MASONS OF SCOTLAND (1736),
Freemasons' Hall, 96 George Street, Edinburgh EH2
3DH. Tel: 0131-225 5304; Fax: 0131-225 3953;
Web: www.grandlodgescotland.com.
Grand Secretary, A. D. Orr Ewing

FREEMEN OF ENGLAND AND WALES (1966),
Nunlands, 23 Stanmore Hill, Stanmore, Middlesex
HA7 3DS. Tel: 020-8954 2206.
Deputy President, M. E. Pickering

FREEMEN OF THE CITY OF LONDON, GUILD OF
(1908), 4 Dowgate Hill, London EC4R 2SH.
Tel: 020-8541 1435; Fax: 020-8541 1455.
Clerk, Brigadier M. I. Keun

FREEMEN OF THE CITY OF YORK, GUILD OF (1953), 29
Albermarle Road, York YO23 1EW. Tel: 01904-653698;
Fax: 0870-052 9911; Web: www.bedern.demon.co.uk.
Hon. Clerk, R. Lee

FREEMEN'S GUILD, CITY OF COVENTRY (1946), 47
Brownshill Green Road, Coventry CV6 2AP.
Tel: 024-7627 4321;
Web: www.coventryfreemensguild.co.uk.
Hon. Clerk, K. Talbot

FRIENDLY SOCIETIES, ASSOCIATION OF (1995), 10–13
Lovat Lane, London EC3R 8DT. Tel: 020-7397 9550;
Fax: 020-7397 9551; Web: www.afs.org.uk.
General Secretary, Miss M. Poole

FRIENDS OF CATHEDRAL MUSIC (1956), Aeron House,
Llangeitho, Tregaron, Ceredigion SY25 6SU.
Web: www.fcm.org.uk. *Secretary,* M. J. Cooke

FRIENDS OF THE EARTH SCOTLAND (1978), 72
Newhaven Road, Edinburgh EH6 5QG.
Tel: 0131-554 9977; Fax: 0131-554 8656;
Web: www.foe-scotland.org.uk.
Director, K. Dunion, OBE

FRIENDS OF THE NATIONAL LIBRARIES (1931), c/o
Department of Manuscripts, The British Library, 96
Euston Road, London NW1 2DB. Tel: 020-7412 7559;
Fax: 020-8374 5585. *Chairman,* Lord Egremont

FURNITURE HISTORY SOCIETY (1964), 1 Mercedes
Cottages, St John's Road, Haywards Heath, W. Sussex
RH16 4EH. Tel: 01444-413845; Fax: 01444-413845.
Membership Secretary, Dr B. Austen

GALLIPOLI ASSOCIATION (1969), Earleydene Orchard,
Earleydene, Ascot, Berks SL5 9JY. Tel: 01344-626523;
Web: www.gallipoli-association.org.
Hon. Secretary, J. C. Watson Smith

GAME CONSERVANCY TRUST, Fordingbridge, Hants
SP6 1EF. Tel: 01425-652381; Fax: 01425-655848;
Web: www.gct.org.uk. *Chief Executive,* Teresa Dent

GARDEN HISTORY SOCIETY (1965), 70 Cowcross
Street, London EC1M 6EJ. Tel: 020-7608 2409;
Fax: 020-7490 2974. *Director,* Andrew Plumridge

GARDENERS' ASSOCIATION, THE GOOD (1966), 4 Lisle
Place, Wotton-under-Edge, Glos GL12 7AZ.
Tel: 01453-520322; Web: www.goodgardeners.org.uk.
Secretary, Matthew Adams

GARDENERS' ROYAL BENEVOLENT SOCIETY (1839),
Bridge House, 139 Kingston Road, Leatherhead,
Surrey KT22 7NT. Tel: 01372-373962;
Fax: 01372-384055; Web: www.gardeners-grbs.org.uk.
Chief Executive, R. T. Capewell

GARDENS SCHEME CHARITABLE TRUST, NATIONAL
(1927), Hatchlands Park, East Clandon, Guildford,
Surrey GU4 7RT. Tel: 01483-211535; Fax: 01483-
211537; Web: www.ngs.org.uk.
Chief Executive, Beryl Evans

GAS ENGINEERS, INSTITUTION OF, 21 Portland Place,
London W1B 1PY. Tel: 020-7636 6603;
Fax: 020-7636 6602; Web: www.igem.org.uk.
Chief Executive, C. J. Bleach

GEMMOLOGICAL ASSOCIATION AND GEM TESTING
LABORATORY OF GREAT BRITAIN (1931), 27
Greville Street (Saffron Hill entrance), London EC1N
8TN. Tel: 020-7404 3334; Fax: 020-7404 8843;
Web: www.gagtl.com. *Director,* Dr R. R. Harding

GENEALOGISTS AND RECORD AGENTS, ASSOCIATION
OF (1968), 29 Badgers Close, Horsham, W. Sussex
RH12 5RU. *Company Secretary,* David R. Young

GENEALOGISTS AND RESEARCHERS IN ARCHIVES,
ASSOCIATION OF (1968), 29 Badgers Close,
Horsham, W. Sussex RH12 5RU. Web: www.agra.org.uk

GENEALOGISTS ENTERPRISES LTD, SOCIETY OF (1911
and 1999), 14 Charterhouse Buildings, Goswell Road,
London EC1M 7BA. Tel: 020-7251 8799;
Fax: 020-7250 1800; Web: www.sog.org.uk.
Acting Chief Executive, June Perrin

GENEALOGY SOCIETY, SCOTTISH (1953), Library and
Family History Centre, 15 Victoria Terrace,
Edinburgh EH1 2JL. Tel: 0131-220 3677;
Fax: 0131-220 3677; Web: www.scots gy.com.
Hon. Secretary, Miss J. P. S. Ferguson

GENTLEPEOPLE, GUILD OF AID FOR (1921), 10 St
Christopher's Place, London W1U 1HZ.
Tel: 020-7935 0641. *Secretary,* Miss N. E. Inkson

GEOGRAPHICAL ASSOCIATION (1893), 160 Solly Street,
Sheffield S1 4BF. Tel: 0114-296 0088;
Fax: 0114-296 7176; Web: www.geography.org.uk

GEOLOGICAL SOCIETY (1807), Burlington House,
Piccadilly, London W1J 0BJ. Tel: 020-7434 9944;
Fax: 020-7439 8975; Web: www.geolsoc.org.uk.
Executive Secretary, E. Nickless

GEOLOGISTS' ASSOCIATION (1858), Burlington House,
Piccadilly, London W1V 9AG. Tel: 020-7434 9296;
Fax: 020-7287 0280;
Web: www.geologist.demon.co.uk.
Executive Secretary, Mrs S. Stafford

GEORGIAN GROUP (1937), 6 Fitzroy Square, London
W1T 5DX. Tel: 020-7387 1720; Fax: 020-7387 1721.
Secretary, Robert Bargery

GIFTED CHILDREN, NATIONAL ASSOCIATION FOR
(1967), Suite 14, Challenge House, Bletchley, Milton
Keynes MK3 6DP. Tel: 01908-673677;
Fax: 0870-770 3219; Web: www.nagcbritain.org.uk.
Director, K. Bore

GILBERT AND SULLIVAN SOCIETY (1924), 7–20
Hampden Gurney Street, London W1H 5AX.
Hon. Secretary, Miss V. C. Colin-Russ

GINGERBREAD (1970), 7 Sovereign Close, London E1W 3HW. Tel: 020-7488 9300. Helpline: 0800-018 4318; Fax: 020-7488 9333; Web: www.gingerbread.org.uk. *Chief Executive*, Ms A. L. Ball

GIRLS' BRIGADE ENGLAND AND WALES, Girls' Brigade House, 62 Foxhall Road, Didcot, Oxon OX11 7BQ. Tel: 01235-510425; Fax: 01235-510429; Web: www.girlsbrigadeew.org.uk. *National Director*, Ruth Gilson

GIRLS' FRIENDLY SOCIETY IN ENGLAND AND WALES (1875), 126 Queens Gate, London SW7 5LQ. Tel: 020-7589 9628; Fax: 020-7225 1458; Web: www.gfyplatform.org.uk. *Chief Executive*, Mrs H. Crompton

GLASGOW CHAMBER OF COMMERCE AND MANUFACTURES (1783), 30 George Square, Glasgow G2 1EQ. Tel: 0141-204 2121; Fax: 0141-221 2336; Web: www.glasgowchamber.org. *Chief Executive*, Duncan Tannahill

GLASS ENGRAVERS, GUILD OF (1975), 87 Nether Street, Finchley, London N12 7NP. Tel: 020-8446 4050; Web: www.gge.org.uk. *Secretary*, Ms C. Reyland

GLASS TECHNOLOGY, SOCIETY OF (1916), Don Valley House, Savile Street East, Sheffield S4 7UQ. Tel: 0114-263 4455; Fax: 0114-263 4411; Web: www.sgt.org. *Managing Editor*, D. Moore

GLIDING ASSOCIATION, BRITISH (1929), Kimberley House, Vaughan Way, Leicester LE1 4SE. Tel: 0116-253 1051; Fax: 0116-251 5939; Web: www.gliding.co.uk. *Secretary*, B. Rolfe

GOSPEL, UNITED SOCIETY FOR THE PROPAGATION OF THE (1701), Partnership House, 157 Waterloo Road, London SE1 8XA. Tel: 020-7928 8681; Fax: 020-7928 2371; Web: www.uspg.org.uk. *Secretary*, Rt Revd M. Rumalshah

GRAPHOLOGISTS, BRITISH INSTITUTE OF, 24–26 High Street, Hampton Hill, Hampton, Middx TW12 1PD. Tel: 01753-891241; Web: www.britishgraphology.org. *Chairman*, Elaine Quigley

GREEK INSTITUTE, 34 Bush Hill Road, London N21 2DS. Tel: 020-8360 7968. *Director*, Dr K. Tofallis

GREENPEACE UK, Canonbury Villas, London N1 2PN. Tel: 020-7865 8100; Fax: 020-7865 8200; Web: www.greenpeace.org.uk. *Executive Director*, Stephen Tindale

GUIDE ASSOCIATION, THE (1910), 17–19 Buckingham Palace Road, London SW1W 0PT. Tel: 020-7834 6242; Fax: 020-7828 8317; Web: www.guides.org.uk. *Chief Executive*, Miss Denise King

GUIDE DOGS FOR THE BLIND ASSOCIATION, THE (1934), Hillfields, Burghfield Common, Reading, Berks RG7 3YG. Tel: 0118-983 5555; Fax: 0118-983 5433; Web: www.gdba.org.uk. *Chief Executive*, Mrs G. Peacock

GURKHA WELFARE TRUST (1969), 2nd Floor, 1 Old Street, London EC1V 9XB. Tel: 020-7251 5234; Fax: 020-7251 5248; Web: www.gwt.org.uk. *Director*, E. D. Powell-Jones

HAEMOPHILIA SOCIETY (1950), Chesterfield House, 385 Euston Road, London NW1 3AU. Tel: 020-7380 0600; Fax: 020-7387 8220; Web: www.haemophilia.org.uk. *Chief Executive*, Ms K. Pappenheim

HAIG HOMES (1929), Alban Dobson House, Green Lane, Morden, Surrey SM4 5NS. Tel: 020-8685 5777; Fax: 020-8685 5778; Web: www.haighomes.org.uk

HAKLUYT SOCIETY (1846), c/o Map Library, The British Library, 96 Euston Road, London NW1 2DB. Tel: 01428-641850; Web: www.hakluyt.com. *Hon. Secretary*, Dr A. Cook

HALIFAX ANTIQUARIAN SOCIETY (1900), 66 Drub Lane, Gomersal, Cleckheaton, W. Yorks BD19 4BU. Tel: 01274-865418. *Editor*, Dr J. A. Hargreaves

HANSARD SOCIETY FOR PARLIAMENTARY GOVERNMENT, THE (1944), St Philips Building North, Sheffield Street, London WC2A 2EX. Tel: 020-7955 7459; Fax: 020-7955 7492; Web: www.hansardsociety.org.uk. *Director*, Mrs S. Diplock

HARVEIAN SOCIETY OF LONDON (1831), Lettsom House, 11 Chandos Street, London W1G 9EB. Tel: 020-7580 1043; Fax: 020-7580 5793. *Executive Secretary*, Col. R. Kinsella-Bevan

HAWICK ARCHAEOLOGICAL SOCIETY (1856), Orrock House, Stirches Road, Hawick, Roxburghshire TD9 7HF. Tel: 01450-375546. *Hon. Secretary*, I. W. Landles

HEALTH CARE ASSOCIATION, BRITISH (1930), 24A Main Street, Garforth, Leeds LS25 1AA. Tel: 0113-232 0903; Fax: 0113-232 0904; Web: www.bhca.org.uk. *Chief Executive*, Mrs C. Bell

HEALTH PROFESSIONS WALES (2002), 2nd Floor, Golate House, 101 St Mary Street, Cardiff CF10 1DX. Tel: 029-2026 1400; Fax: 029-2026 1499. *Chief Executive*, D. A. Ravey

HEALTH PROMOTION AND EDUCATION, INSTITUTE OF, Department of Oral Health and Development, University Dental Hospital, Higher Cambridge Street, Manchester M15 6FH. Tel: 0161-275 6610; Fax: 0161-275 6299; Web: www.ihpe.org.uk. *Hon. Secretary*, Prof. A. S. Blinkhorn

HEALTH, GUILD OF (1904), PO Box 227, Epsom KT19 9WQ. Tel: 020-8786 0517; Fax: 020-8786 0517; Web: www.gohealth.org.uk. *General Secretary and Chaplain*, Revd A. Lynn

HEALTHCARE MANAGEMENT, INSTITUTE OF, PO Box 33239, London SW1W 0WN. Tel: 020-7881 9235; Fax: 020-7881 9236; Web: www.ihm.org.uk. *Chief Executive*, S. Marples

HEARING CONCERN (BRITISH ASSOCIATION FOR THE HARD OF HEARING) (1947), 7–11 Armstrong Road, London W3 7JL. Tel: 020-8743 1110. Helpline: 0845-0744600; Fax: 020-8742 9043; Web: www.hearingconcern.org.uk. *Director*, Fiona Robertson

HEART FOUNDATION, BRITISH (1961), 14 Fitzhardinge Street, London W1H 6DH. Tel: 020-7487 7186; Fax: 020-7486 5820; Web: www.bhf.org.uk. *Director General*, Maj.-Gen. L. F. H. Busk, CB

HEDGEHOG PRESERVATION SOCIETY, BRITISH (1982),
Hedgehog House, Dhustone, Ludlow, Shropshire SY8
3LQ. Tel: 01584-890801; Fax: 01584-891313;
Web: www.software-technics.com/bhps.
Chief Admin. Officer, Fay Vass

HELLENIC STUDIES, SOCIETY FOR THE PROMOTION
OF (1879), Senate House, Malet Street, London WC1E
7HU. Tel: 020-7862 8730; Fax: 020-7862 8731;
Web: www.sas.ac.uk/icls/hellenic/.
Executive Secretary, R. W. Shone

HELP THE AGED (1961), 207-221 Pentonville Road,
London N2 9UZ. Tel: 020-7278 1114;
Fax: 020-7278 1116; Web: www.helptheaged.org.uk.
Director General, C. M. Lake, CBE

HERALDIC AND GENEALOGICAL STUDIES, INSTITUTE
OF (1961), 79–82 Northgate, Canterbury, Kent CT1
1BA. Tel: 01227-768664; Fax: 01227-765617;
Web: www.ihgs.ac.uk.
Registrar, J. Palmer; *Principal*, C. R. Humphery-Smith

HERALDRY SOCIETY, THE (1947), PO Box 32,
Maidenhead, Berks SL6 3FD. Tel: 0118-932 0210;
Fax: 0118-932 0210. *Secretary*, Mrs M. Miles, MBE, RD

HERPETOLOGICAL SOCIETY, BRITISH, c/o Zoological
Society of London, Regent's Park, London NW1 4RY.
Tel: 020-8452 9578; Fax: 01908-370112.
Secretary, Mrs M. Green

HISTORIC HOUSES ASSOCIATION (1973), 2 Chester
Street, London SW1X 7BB. Tel: 020-7259 5688;
Fax: 020-7259 5590; Web: www.hha.org.uk.
Director General, R. C. Wilkin, LVO, MBE

HISTORICAL ASSOCIATION, THE (1906), 59A
Kennington Park Road, London SE11 4JH.
Tel: 020-7735 3901; Fax: 020-7582 4989;
Web: www.history.org.uk.
Chief Executive, Mrs M. Stiles

HOME FARM TRUST (1962), Merchants House,
Wapping Road, Bristol BS1 4RW. Tel: 0117-927 3746;
Fax: 0117-930 2678; Web: www.hft.org.uk.
Chief Executive, Brian Perowne, CB

HONG KONG ASSOCIATION, Swire House, 59
Buckingham Gate, London SW1E 6AJ.
Tel: 020-7963 9445/47; Fax: 020-7630 0353.
Executive Director, R. L. Guy

HOROLOGICAL INSTITUTE, BRITISH (1858), Upton
Hall, Upton, Newark, Notts NG23 5TE.
Tel: 01636-813795; Fax: 01636-812258;
Web: www.bhi.co.uk. *General Manager*, Martin Taylor

HORSE SOCIETY, BRITISH (1947), Stoneleigh Deer
Park, Kenilworth, Warks CV8 2XZ. Tel: 08701-202244;
Fax: 01926-707800; Web: www.bhs.org.uk.
Chief Executive, Mrs Kay Driver

HOSPITAL FEDERATION, INTERNATIONAL (1947), 46
Grosvenor Gardens, London SW1W 0EB.
Tel: 020-7881 9222; Fax: 020-7881 9223;
Web: www.hospitalmanagement.net and
www.ihf.co.uk. *Director General*, Dr E. N. Pickering

HOSPITAL SATURDAY FUND (1873), 24 Upper Ground,
London SE1 9PD. Tel: 020-7928 6662;
Fax: 020-7928 0446; Web: www.hsf.eu.com.
Chief Executive, K. R. Bradley

HOSPITAL SAVING ASSOCIATION (1922), Hambleden
House, Andover, Hants SP10 1LQ. Tel: 01264-353211;
Fax: 01264-333650; Web: www.has.co.uk.
Chief Executive, Des Benjamin

HOSPITALITY ASSOCIATION, BRITISH (1907), Queens
House, 55–56 Lincoln's Inn Fields, London WC2A 3BH.
Tel: 020-7404 7744; Fax: 020-7404 7799;
Web: www.bha-online.org.uk.
Chief Executive, Bob Cotton, OBE

HOSTELLING INTERNATIONAL NORTHERN IRELAND,
22–32 Donegall Road, Belfast BT12 5JN.
Tel: 028-9032 4733; Fax: 028-9043 9699;
Web: www.hini.org.uk. *Hon. Secretary*, D. Forsythe

HOWARD LEAGUE FOR PENAL REFORM, THE (1866),
1 Ardleigh Road, London N1 4HS. Tel: 020-7249 7373;
Fax: 020-7249 7789; Web: www.howardleague.org.
Director, Ms F. Crook

HUGUENOT SOCIETY OF GREAT BRITAIN AND
IRELAND (1885), The Huguenot Library, University
College, Gower Street, London WC1E 6BT.
Tel: 020-7679 7094; Web: www.ucl.ac.uk/ucl-
info/divisions/library/huguenot.htm.
Hon. Secretary, Mrs M. Bayliss

HUMANE RESEARCH TRUST (1962), Brook House, 29
Bramhall Lane South, Bramhall, Stockport, Cheshire
SK7 2DN. Tel: 0161-439 8041; Fax: 0161-439 3713;
Web: www.btinternet.com/~shawweb/hrt/.
Chairman, K. Cholerton

HUMANIST ASSOCIATION, BRITISH (1896), 47
Theobald's Road, London WC1X 8SP. Tel: 020-7430
0908; Fax: 020-7430 1271;
Web: www.humanism.org.uk.
Executive Director, Hanne Stinson

HYDROGRAPHIC SOCIETY, THE (1972), PO Box 103,
Plymouth PL4 7YP. Tel: 91752-223512;
Web: www.hydrographicsociety.org.
Hon. Secretary, P. J. H. Warden

HYMN SOCIETY OF GREAT BRITAIN AND IRELAND
(1936), 7 Paganel Road, Minehead, Somerset TA24 5ET.
Tel: 01643-703530; Fax: 01643-703530.
Secretary, Revd G. Wrayford

ICAN (THE NATIONAL EDUCATIONAL CHARITY FOR
CHILDREN WITH SPEECH AND LANGUAGE
DIFFICULTIES), 4 Dyers Buildings, Holborn, London
EC1N 2QP. Tel: 0870-010 4066; Fax: 0870-010 4067;
Web: www.ican.org.uk.
Chief Executive, Ms G. Edelman

IMMIGRATION ADVISORY SERVICE (1970), County
House), 190 Great Dover Street, London SE1 4YB.
Tel: 020-7357 7511; Fax: 020-7403 5875;
Web: www.iasuk.org. *Chief Executive*, Keith Best

INDEPENDENT SCHOOLS CAREERS ORGANISATION
(1973), 12A Princess Way, Camberley, Surrey GU15
3SP. Tel: 01276-21188; Fax: 01276-691833;
Web: www.isco.org.uk. *National Director*, J. D. Stuart

INDEPENDENT SCHOOLS COUNCIL (1986), Grosvenor
Gardens House, 35–37 Grosvenor Gardens, London
SW1W 0BS. Tel: 020-7798 1590; Fax: 020-7798 1591;
Web: www.iscis.uk.net.
General Secretary, Dr A. B. Cooke, OBE

INDEPENDENT SCHOOLS' BURSARS ASSOCIATION (1932), 5 Chapel Close, Old Basing, Basingstoke, Hants RG24 7BZ. Tel: 01256-330369; Fax: 01256-330376; Web: www.isba.uk.com. *General Secretary*, M. J. Sant

INDEXERS, SOCIETY OF (1957), Globe Centre, Penistone Road, Sheffield S6 3AE. Tel: 0114-281 3060; Fax: 0114-281 3061; Web: www.socind.demon.co.uk. *Secretary*, Mrs Ann Kingdom

INDUSTRIAL SOCIETY, Robert Hyde House, 48 Bryanston Square, London W1H 2EA. Tel: 020-7479 2000; Fax: 020-7479 2222; Web: www.indsoc.co.uk. *Chief Executive*, W. Hutton

INDUSTRY AND PARLIAMENT TRUST (1977), 1 Buckingham Place, London SW1E 6HR. Tel: 020-7630 3700; Fax: 020-7630 3701; Web: www.ipt.org.uk. *Director*, F. R. Hyde-Chambers

INDUSTRY TRAINING ORGANISATIONS, NATIONAL COUNCIL OF, 10 Meadowcourt, Amos Road, Sheffield S9 1BX. Tel: 0114-261 9926. *Chief Executive*, Dr A. Powell

INSURANCE BROKERS' ASSOCIATION, BRITISH (1978), BIBA House, 14 Bevis Marks, London EC3A 7NT. Tel: 020-7623 9043; Fax: 020-7626 9676; Web: www.biba.org.uk. *Chief Executive*, R. M. Williams

INSURANCE INSTITUTE, CHARTERED (1897), 20 Aldermanbury, London EC2V 7HY. Tel: 020-8989 8464; Fax: 020-7726 0131; Web: www.cii.co.uk. *Director-General*, Dr A. Scott, MRCP, FRSA

INSURERS, ASSOCIATION OF BRITISH (1985), 51 Gresham Street, London EC2V 7HQ. Tel: 020-7600 3333; Fax: 020-7696 8999; Web: www.abi.org.uk. *Director-General*, Mrs M. Francis

INTERCONTINENTAL CHURCH SOCIETY (1823), 1 Athena Drive, Tachbrook Park, Warwick CV34 6NL. Tel: 01926-430347; Fax: 01926-888092; Web: www.ics-uk.org. *Chief Executive*, The Revd Ian Watson

INTERNATIONAL FRIENDSHIP LEAGUE, 3 Creswick Road, Acton, London W3 9HE. Tel: 020-8752 0055; Fax: 020-8752 0066; Web: www.itl-peacehaven.co.uk. *Chairman*, Mrs B. Macdolnald

INTERNATIONAL PEN (1921), 9–10 Charterhouse Buildings, Goswell Road, London EC1M 7AT. Tel: 020-7253 4308; Fax: 020-7253 5711; Web: www.oneworld.org/internatpen. *International Secretary*, T. Carlbom

INTERNATIONAL POLICE ASSOCIATION (BRITISH SECTION) (1950), 1 Fox Road, West Bridgford, Nottingham NG2 6AJ. Tel: 0115-981 3638; Web: www.ipa-uk.org. *Executive Officer*, Mrs E. Jones

INTERNATIONAL STUDENTS HOUSE (1922), 1 Park Crescent, London W1B 1SH. Tel: 020-7631 8300; Fax: 020-7631 8315; Web: www.ish.org.uk. *Executive Director*, P. Rapson

INTERSERVE (1852), 325 Kennington Road, London SE11 4QH. Tel: 020-7735 8227; Fax: 020-7587 5362; Web: www.interserveonline.org.uk. *National Director*, R. Clark

INVALIDS-AT-HOME (1965), Bamford Cottage, South Hill Avenue, Harrow, Middx HA1 3PA. Tel: 020-8864 3818. *Executive Officer*, Mrs Mary Rose

IRAN SOCIETY, 2 Belgrave Square, London SW1X 8PJ. Tel: 020-7235 5122; Fax: 020-7259 6771; Web: www.iransoc.dircon.co.uk. *Chairman*, M. Noïl-Clarke; *Hon. Secretary*, A. D. Ashmole

IRISH GENEALOGICAL RESEARCH SOCIETY (1936), c/o The Irish Club, 82 Eaton Square, London SW1W 9AJ. Tel: 020-7235 4164. *Hon. Librarian*, T. G. Chartres

ISLE OF WIGHT NATURAL HISTORY AND ARCHAEOLOGICAL SOCIETY (1919), Salisbury Gardens, Dudley Road, Ventnor, Isle of Wight PO38 1EJ. Tel: 01983-855385. *Hon. Secretary*, Dr M. Jackson

JACQUELINE DU PRÈ MUSIC BUILDING LTD (1995), St Hilda's College, Oxford OX4 1DY. Tel: 01865-276821; Fax: 01865-286674; Web: www.sthildas.ox.ac.uk/jdp. *Manager*, Ms M. A. Frappat

JAPAN SOCIETY (1891), Swire House, 59 Buckingham Gate, London SW1E 6AJ. Tel: 020-7828 6330; Fax: 020-7828 6331; Web: www.japansociety.org.uk. *Executive Director*, Capt. Robert Guy

JERUSALEM AND THE MIDDLE EAST CHURCH ASSOCIATION, 1 Hart House, The Hart, Farnham, Surrey GU9 7HJ. Tel: 01252-726994; Fax: 01252-735558. *Secretary*, Mrs V. Wells

JEWISH HISTORICAL SOCIETY OF ENGLAND (1893), 33 Seymour Place, London W1H 5AP. Tel: 020-7723 5852; Fax: 020-7723 5852; Web: www.jhse.org. *Hon. Secretary*, Dr Gerry Black

JOHN CURWEN SOCIETY, 5 Bigbury Close, Styvechale, Coventry CV3 5AJ. Tel: 02476-413010; Fax: 02476-413564. *Chairman*, J. Dowding

JOHN STUART MILL INSTITUTE (1992), 1 Whitehall Place, London SW1A 2HE. Tel: 01582-615067; Fax: 01582-896452; Web: www.jsminstitute.org.uk. *Hon. Secretary*, J. Wates

JOURNALISTS, CHARTERED INSTITUTE OF (1884), 2 Dock Offices, Surrey Quays Road, London SE16 2XU. Tel: 020-7252 1187; Fax: 020-7232 2302. *General Secretary*, C. J. Underwood

JUSTICE (1957), 59 Carter Lane, London EC4V 5AQ. Tel: 020-7329 5100; Fax: 020-7329 5055; Web: www.justice.org.uk. *Director*, Roger Smith

JUSTICES' CLERKS' SOCIETY, 2nd Floor, Port of Liverpool Building, Pier Head, Liverpool L3 1BY. Tel: 0151-255 0790; Fax: 0151-236 4458; Web: www.jc-society.co.uk. *Chief Executive*, Sid Brighton

KENT ARCHAEOLOGICAL SOCIETY (1857), Three Elms, Woodlands Lane, Shorne, Gravesend, Kent DA12 3HH; Web: www.kentarchaeology.org. *Hon. General Secretary*, A. I. Moffat

KING'S FUND (1897), 11–13 Cavendish Square, London W1G 0AN. Tel: 020-7307 2400; Fax: 020-7307 2801; Web: www.kingsfund.org.uk. *Chief Executive*, Rabbi Julia Neuberger

KIPLING SOCIETY, THE (1927), 6 Clifton Road, London W9 1SS. Tel: 020-7286 0194; Fax: 020-7286 0194; Web: www.kipling.org.uk. *Hon. Secretary,* Jane S. Keskar

LANDOWNERS' FEDERATION, SCOTTISH, Stuart House, Eskmills Business Park, Musselburgh EH21 7PB. Tel: 0131-653 5400; Fax: 0131-653 5401; Web: www.slf.org.uk. *Director,* Dr M. S. Hankey

LANGUAGE LEARNING, ASSOCIATION FOR (1990), 150 Railway Terrace, Rugby CV21 3HN. Tel: 01788-546443; Fax: 01788-544149; Web: www.all-languages.co.uk. *President,* T. Lamb

LAW REPORTING FOR ENGLAND AND WALES, INCORPORATED COUNCIL OF (1865), Megarry House, 119 Chancery Lane, London WC2A 1PP. Tel: 020-7242 6471; Fax: 020-7831 5247; Web: www.lawreports.co.uk. *Secretary,* J. Cobbett

LEAGUE OF THE HELPING HAND, Petersham Hollow, 226 Petersham Road, Petersham, Richmond, Surrey TW10 7AL. Tel: 020-8940 7303; Fax: 020-8940 7303. *Secretary,* Mrs I. Goodlad

LEGAL EXECUTIVES, INSTITUTE OF (1963), Kempston Manor, Kempston, Bedford MK42 7AB. Tel: 01234-841000; Fax: 01234-840373; Web: www.ilex.org.uk. *Secretary General,* Mrs D. Burleigh

LEGAL SCHOLARS, SOCIETY OF (1908), Law Faculty, Southampton University, Southampton WC2R 2LS. Tel: 023-8059 3416; Fax: 023-8059 3024; Web: www.law.warwick.ac.uk/sls/. *Hon. Secretary,* Prof. N. J. Wikeley

LEPROSY MISSION (ENGLAND AND WALES) (1874), Goldhay Way, Orton Goldhay, Peterborough PE2 5GZ. Tel: 01733-370505; Fax: 01733-404880; Web: www.leprosymission.org.uk. *National Director,* Warren Lancaster

LEUKAEMIA RESEARCH FUND (1960), 43 Great Ormond Street, London WC1N 3JJ. Tel: 020-7405 0101; Fax: 020-7405 3139; Web: www.lrf.org.uk. *Chief Executive,* D. L. Osborne

LIBRARIES ASSOCIATION, PRIVATE (1956), Ravelston, South View Road, Pinner, Middx HA5 3YD. Web: www.the-old-school.demon.co.uk/pla.htm. *Hon. Secretary,* F. Broomhead

LIBRARY AND INFORMATION PROFESSIONALS, THE CHARTERED INSTITUTE OF (2002), 7 Ridgmount Street, London WC1E 7AE. Tel: 020-7255 0500; Textphone 020-7255 0505; Fax: 020-7255 0501; Web: www.cilip.org.uk. *Chief Executive,* Dr R. A. McKee, FRSA, MCLIP

LIBRARY, CITY BUSINESS (1970), Corporation of London, 1 Brewers' Hall Garden, London EC2V 5BX. Tel: 020-7332 1812; Fax: 020-7332 1847; Web: www.cityoflondon.gov.uk. *Business Librarian,* G. P. Humphreys, ALA, FRSA

LIBRARY, SCOTTISH NATURAL HISTORY (1970), Foremount House, Kilbarchan, Renfrewshire PA10 2EZ. Tel: 01505-702419. *Director,* Dr J. A. Gibson

LIFE SAVING SOCIETY UK, THE ROYAL (1891), River House, High Street, Broom, Warks B50 4HN. Tel: 01789-773994; Fax: 01789-773995; Web: www.lifesavers.org.uk. *Chief Executive,* D. Stanley

LINCOLNSHIRE HISTORY AND ARCHAEOLOGY, SOCIETY FOR, Jew's Court, Steep Hill, Lincoln LN2 1LS. Tel: 01522-521337; Fax: 01522-521337. *Chairman,* Miss P. Wheatley

LINGUISTS, INSTITUTE OF (1910), Saxon House, 48 Southwark Street, London SE1 1UN. Tel: 020-7940 3100; Fax: 020-7940 3101; Web: www.iol.org.uk. *Director,* H. Pavlovich

LINNEAN SOCIETY OF LONDON (1788), Burlington House, Piccadilly, London W1J 0BF. Tel: 020-7434 4479; Fax: 020-7287 9364; Web: www.linnean.org. *President,* Sir David Smith, FRS, FRSE

LIONS CLUBS INTERNATIONAL (BRITISH ISLES AND IRELAND) (1950), 257 Alcester Road South, Kings Heath, Birmingham B14 6DT. Tel: 0121-441 4544; Fax: 0121-441 4510. *Office Manager,* Mrs J. Davis

LISTENING BOOKS, 12 Lant Street, London SE1 1QH. Tel: 020-7407 9417; Fax: 020-7403 1377; Web: www.listening-books.org.uk. *Director,* Bill Dee

LIVING STREETS (1929), 31–33 Bondway, London SW8 1SJ. Tel: 020-7820 1010; Fax: 020-7820 8208; Web: www.livingstreets.org.uk. *Director,* B. Plowden

LLOYD'S OF LONDON, 1 Lime Street, London EC3M 7HA. Tel: 020-7327 1000; Fax: 020-7327 6512; Web: www.lloyds.com. *Chief Executive Officer,* N. E. Prettejohn

LOCAL AUTHORITY CHIEF EXECUTIVES AND SENIOR MANAGERS, SOCIETY OF, Hope House, 45 Great Peter Street, London SW1P 3LT. Tel: 0845-601 0649; Fax: 01977-707070; Web: www.solace.org.uk. *Director-General,* David Clark

LOCAL GOVERNMENT ASSOCIATION (1997), Local Government House, Smith Square, London SW1P 3HZ. Tel: 020-7664 3000; Fax: 020-7664 3030; Web: www.lga.gov.uk. *Chief Executive,* B. Briscoe

LOCAL HISTORY, BRITISH ASSOCIATION FOR (1952), PO Box 1576, Salisbury, Wilts SP2 8SY. Tel: 01722-322158; Fax: 01722-413242; Web: www.balh.co.uk. *General Secretary,* M. Cowan

LOGISTICS AND TRANSPORT, INSTITUTE OF (1926), 11–12 Buckingham Gate, London SW1E 6LB. Web: www.iolt.org.uk

LONDON AND MIDDLESEX ARCHAEOLOGICAL SOCIETY, c/o Museum of London, 150 London Wall, London EC2Y 5HN. Tel: 020-8879 7109; Web: www.lamas.org.uk. *Hon. Secretary,* M. Curtis

LONDON APPRECIATION SOCIETY (1932), 45 Friars Avenue, Friern Barnet, London N20 0XG. *Chairman,* Anthea H. Gray

LONDON CHAMBER OF COMMERCE AND INDUSTRY, 33 Queen Street, London EC4R 1AP. Tel: 020-7248 4444; Fax: 020-7203 1570; Web: www.londonchamber.co.uk. *Acting Chief Executive,* P. E. Bishop

LONDON CITY MISSION (1835), 175 Tower Bridge Road, London SE1 2AH. Tel: 020-7407 7585; Fax: 020-7403 6711; Web: www.lcm.org.uk. *General Secretary*, Revd J. McAllen

LONDON DISTRICT SURVEYORS ASSOCIATION (1845), London Borough of Harrow, PO Box 37, Civic Centre, Harrow, Middx HA1 2UY. *President*, Alan Phillips

LONDON FLOTILLA & PRESIDENT RETIRED OFFICERS ASSOCIATION (PRDA) (1937), 40 Endlesham Road, London SW12 8JL. Tel: 020-8673 1879; Fax: 020-8673 1879. *Hon. Membership Recruitment Secretary*, Lt.-Cdr. H. C. R. Upton, RD, RNR

LONDON GOVERNMENT, ASSOCIATION OF (2000), 59S Southwark Street, London SE1 0AL. Tel: 020-7934 9999. *Chief Executive*, M. Pilgrim

LONDON LIBRARY, THE (1841), 14 St James's Square, London SW1Y 4LG. Tel: 020-7930 7705; Fax: 020-7766 4766; Web: www.londonlibrary.co.uk. *Librarian*, Inez T. P. A Lynn

LONDON PLAYING FIELDS SOCIETY (1890), Fraser House, 29 Albermarle Street, London W1S 4JB. Tel: 020-7493 3211; Fax: 020-7409 3405; Web: www.lpfs.org.uk. *Chief Executive*, Dr C. Goodson-Wickes, DL

LONDON SOCIETY, THE (1912), Mortimer Wheeler House, 46 Eagle Wharf Road, London N1 7ED. Tel: 020-7253 9400; Web: www.lonsoc.org.uk/lonsoc/. *Hon. Secretary*, Mrs B. Jones

LORD'S DAY OBSERVANCE SOCIETY (1831), 3 Epsom Business Park, Kiln Lane, Epsom, Surrey KT17 1JF. Tel: 01372-728300; Fax: 01372-722400; Web: www.lordsday.co.uk. *General Secretary*, J. G. Roberts

LOTTERIES COUNCIL, THE (1979), 2 Regan Road, Moira Ashby-de-la-Zouch DE12 6DS. Tel: 01283-229811; Fax: 01283-229810; Web: www.lotteriescouncil.co.uk. *Chairman*, Mr A. Austin

LUNG FOUNDATION, BRITISH (1984), 78 Hatton Garden, London EC1N 8LD. Tel: 020-7831 5831; Fax: 020-7831 5832; Web: www.lunguk.org. *Chief Executive*, Dame Helena Shovelton

MAGISTRATES' ASSOCIATION (1920), 28 Fitzroy Square, London W1T 6DD. Tel: 020-7387 2353; Fax: 020-7383 4020; Web: www.magistrates-association.org.uk/mags.assn/. *Chief Executive*, Ms S. Dickinson

MAIL USERS' ASSOCIATION (1976), 70 Main Road, Hermitage, Near Emsworth, W. Sussex PO10 8AX. Tel: 07976-710315; Fax: 01243-370840. *Chairman*, John Ivens

MAILING PREFERENCE SERVICE (1983), 3rd Floor, DMA House, 70 Margaret Street, London W1W 8SS. Tel: 020-7291 3310; Fax: 020-7323 4226; Web: www.mpsonline.org.uk. *Director of Compliance Operations*, Ms T. Kelly

MANAGEMENT INSTITUTE, CHARTERED (1947), Management House, Cottingham Road, Corby, Northants NN17 1TT. Tel: 01536-204222; Fax: 01536-201651; Web: www.managers.org.uk. *Director-General*, Ms M. Chapman

MANIC DEPRESSION FELLOWSHIP (1983), Castle Works, 21 St George's Road, London SE1 6ES. Tel: 020-7793 2600; Fax: 020-7793 2639; Web: www.mdf.org.uk. *Acting Chief Executive*, Michelle Rowett

MANORIAL SOCIETY OF GREAT BRITAIN (1906), 104 Kennington Road, London SE11 6RE. Tel: 020-7735 6633; Fax: 020-7582 7022; Web: www.msgb.co.uk. *Hon. Chairman*, R. A. Smith

MANPOWER SOCIETY LTD (1970), 34 Downview Road, Felpham, Bognor Regis, W. Sussex PO22 8HH. Tel: 01243-837355; Fax: 01243-837355; Web: www.mansoc.demon.co.uk. *President*, Dr Clive Purkis

MARIE CURIE CANCER CARE (1948), 89 Albert Embankment, London SE1 7TP. Tel: 020-7599 7777; Fax: 020-7599 7788; Web: www.mariecurie.org.uk. *Chief Executive*, Thomas Hughes-Hallett

MARINE BIOLOGICAL ASSOCIATION OF THE UK (1884), Citadel Hill, Plymouth PL1 2PB. Tel: 01752-633100; Fax: 01752-633102; Web: www.mbaac.uk. *Director*, Prof. S. J. Hawkins

MARINE ENGINEERING, SCIENCE AND TECHNOLOGY, INSTITUTE OF (1889), 80 Coleman Street, London EC2R 5BJ. Tel: 020-7382 2600; Fax: 020-7382 2670; Web: www.imarest.org. *Director General*, K. F. Read

MARINE SCIENCE, SCOTTISH ASSOCIATION FOR (1884), Dunstaffnage Marine Laboratory, Oban, Argyll PA37 1QA. Tel: 01631-559000; Fax: 01631-559001; Web: www.sams.ac.uk. *Director*, Prof. G. B. Shimmield, FIBiol, FRSE

MARINE SOCIETY, THE (1756), 202 Lambeth Road, London SE1 7JW. Tel: 020-7261 9535; Fax: 020-7401 2537; Web: www.marine-society.org. *Director*, Capt. J. J. Howard

MARIO LANZA EDUCATIONAL FOUNDATION (1976), 7 Lionfields Avenue, Allesley Village, Coventry CV5 9GN. *Hon. Secretary*, Miss Patricia Barron

MARKET AUTHORITIES, NATIONAL ASSOCIATION OF BRITISH (1919), 13 Moor Road, Orrell Post, Wigan WN5 8ND. Tel: 01942-203797; Fax: 01942-205885; Web: www.nabma.com. *General Secretary*, J. Edwards

MARRIAGE CARE (1946), Clitherow House, 1 Blythe Mews, Blythe Road, London W14 0NW. Tel: 020-7371 1341; Fax: 020-7371 4921; Web: www.marriagecare.org.uk. *Chief Executive*, Terry Prendergast

MASONIC TRUST FOR GIRLS AND BOYS (1982), 31 Great Queen Street, London WC2B 5AG. Tel: 020-7405 2644; Fax: 020-7831 4094; Web: www.mtgb.org. *Secretary*, Lt.-Col. J. C. Chambers

MASONS, GRAND LODGE OF MARK MASTER, Mark Masons' Hall, 86 St James's Street, London SW1A 1PL. Tel: 020-7839 5274; Fax: 020-7930 9750. *Grand Secretary*, T. J. Lewis

MATERIALS, INSTITUTE OF (1993), 1 Carlton House Terrace, London SW1Y 5DB. Tel: 020-7451 7300; Fax: 020-7839 1702; Web: www.materials.org.uk. *Chief Executive*, Dr B. A. Rickinson

MATERNITY ALLIANCE (1980), 45 Beech Street, London EC2P 2LX. Tel: 020-7588 8583. Information line: 020-7588 8582; Fax: 020-7588 8584; Web: www.maternityalliance.org.uk. *Director*, Ms C. Gowdridge

MATHEMATICAL ASSOCIATION (1871), 259 London Road, Leicester LE2 3BE. Tel: 0116-221 0013; Fax: 0116-212 2835; Web: www.m-a.org.uk. *Office Manager*, Ms M. Murray

MATHEMATICAL ASSOCIATION, 4 Corringham Road, Stanford-le-Hope, Essex SS17 0AH. Tel: 01375-642466; Fax: 01375-360256; Web: www.meassociation.org.uk. *Chief Executive*, Ms V. Hockey

MATHEMATICS AND ITS APPLICATIONS, INSTITUTE OF (1964), Catherine Richards House, 16 Nelson Street, Southend-on-Sea, Essex SS1 1EF. Tel: 01702-354020; Fax: 01702-354111; Web: www.ima.org.uk

MEASUREMENT AND CONTROL, INSTITUTE OF (1944), 87 Gower Street, London WC1E 6AF. Tel: 020-7387 4949; Fax: 020-7388 8431; Web: www.instmc.org.uk. *Secretary*, M. J. Yates

MECHANICAL ENGINEERS, INSTITUTION OF (1847), 1 Birdcage Walk, London SW1H 9JJ. Tel: 020-7222 7899; Fax: 020-7222 7899; Web: www.imeche.org.uk. *Director-General*, Sir Michael Moore, KBE, LVO

MEDIAWATCH-UK (1965), 3 Willow House, Kennington Road, Ashford, Kent TN24 0NR. Tel: 01233-633936; Fax: 01233-633836; Web: www.mediawatchuk.org. *Director*, J. C. Beyer

MEDICAL COUNCIL, GENERAL (1858), 178 Great Portland Street, London W1W 5JE. Tel: 020-7580 7642; Fax: 020-7915 3641; Web: www.gmc-uk.org. *Chief Executive*, F. M. Scott, TD

MEDICAL SOCIETY FOR THE STUDY OF VENEREAL DISEASES, 1 Wimpole Street, London W1G 0AE. Tel: 020-7290 2968; Fax: 020-7290 2989; Web: www.rsm.ac.uk. *Hon. Secretary*, Dr Keith Radcliffe

MEDICAL SOCIETY OF LONDON (1773), Lettsom House, 11 Chandos Street, London W1G 9EB. Tel: 020-7580 1043; Fax: 020-7580 5793. *Registrar*, Col. R. Kinsella-Bevan

MEDICAL WOMEN'S FEDERATION (1917), Tavistock House North, Tavistock Square, London WC1H 9HX. Tel: 020-7387 7765; Fax: 020-7387 7765; Web: www.mwfonline.org.uk. *President*, Prof. Llora Finlay

MEDICINE, INSTITUTE OF COMPLEMENTARY (1982), PO Box 194, London SE16 7QZ. Tel: 020-7237 5165; Fax: 020-7237 5175; Web: www.icmedicine.co.uk. *Director*, H. Endacott

MENCAP (ROYAL MENCAP SOCIETY) (1946), 123 Golden Lane, London EC1Y 0RT. Tel: 020-7454 0454; Fax: 020-7608 3254; Web: www.mencap.co.uk. *Chief Executive*, F. Heddell, CBE

MENSA LTD, BRITISH (1946), St John's House, St Johns Square, Wolverhampton WV2 4AH. Tel: 01902-772771; Fax: 01902-392500; Web: www.mensa.org.uk. *General Manager*, J. Stevenage

MENTAL HEALTH FOUNDATION, 7th Floor, 83 Victoria Street, London SW1H 0HN. Tel: 020-7802 0300; Fax: 020-7802 0301; Web: www.mentalhealth.org.uk. *Chair*, C. Martin

MENTAL HEALTH, SCOTTISH ASSOCIATION FOR (1923), Cumbrae House, 15 Carlton Court, Glasgow G5 9JP. Tel: 0141-568 7000; Fax: 0141-568 7001; Web: www.samh.org.uk. *Chief Executive*, Ms S. M. Barcus

METROPOLITAN HOSPITAL-SUNDAY FUND (1873), 45 Westminster Bridge Road, London SE1 7JB. Tel: 020-7620 1826; Fax: 020-7401 3641; Web: www.mhsf.org.uk. *Secretary*, H. F. Doe

MIDDLE EAST ASSOCIATION, THE (1961), Bury House, 33 Bury Street, London SW1Y 6AX. Tel: 020-7839 2137; Fax: 020-7839 6121; Web: www.the-mea.co.uk. *Director General*, B. P. Constant, CBE

MIGRAINE ACTION ASSOCIATION (1958), Unit 6, Oakley Hay Lodge Business Park, Great Oakley, Northants NN18 9AS. Tel: 01536-461338; Fax: 01536-461444; Web: www.migraine.org.uk. *Director*, Mrs A. Turner

MIGRAINE TRUST, THE (1965), 45 Great Ormond Street, London WC1N 3HZ. Tel: 020-7831 4818; Fax: 020-7831 5174; Web: www.migrainetrust.org. *Director*, Ms A. Rush

MILITARY HISTORICAL SOCIETY (1948), National Army Museum, Royal Hospital Road, London SW3 4HT. Tel: 01322-446649. *Secretary*, Mr P. Jobson

MIND (NATIONAL ASSOCIATION FOR MENTAL HEALTH) (1946), Granta House, 15–19 Broadway, London E15 4BQ. Tel: 020-8519 2122; Fax: 020-8215 2468; Web: www.mind.org.uk. *Chief Executive*, Richard Brook

MINERALOGICAL SOCIETY (1876), 41 Queen's Gate, London SW7 5HR. Tel: 020-7584 7516; Fax: 020-7823 8021; Web: www.minersoc.org. *General Secretary*, Dr F. Wall

MINING AND METALLURGY, INSTITUTION OF (1892), Danum House, 6A South Parade, Doncaster, S. Yorks DN1 2DY. Tel: 01302-320486; Fax: 01302-340554; Web: www.imm.org.uk. *Secretary*, Dr G. J. M. Woodrow

MISSING PERSONS HELPLINE, NATIONAL (1992), Roebuck House, 284-286 Upper Richmond Road West, London SW14 7JE. Tel: 020-8392 4590; Helpline: 0500-700700; Fax: 020-8878 7752; Web: www.missingpersons.org. *Co-Founders*, Mrs M. Asprey, OBE; Mrs J. Newman, OBE

MOTHERS' UNION, THE (1876), Mary Sumner House, 24 Tufton Street, London SW1P 3RB. Tel: 020-7222 5533; Fax: 020-7222 1591; Web: www.themothersunion.org. *Chief Executive*, R. Bailey

MOTOR INDUSTRY, INSTITUTE OF THE, Fanshaws, Brickendon, Hertford SG13 8PQ. Tel: 01992-511521; Fax: 01992-511548. *Chief Executive*, Sarah Sillars

MULTIPLE SCLEROSIS SOCIETY (1953), MS National Centre, 372 Edgware Road, Staples Corner, London NW2 6ND. Tel: 020-8438 0700; Fax: 020-8438 0701; Web: www.mssociety.org.uk.
Chief Executive, Mike O'Donovan

MUSEUMS ASSOCIATION, 24 Calvin Street, London E1 6NW. Tel: 020-7426 6970; Fax: 020-7426 6961; Web: www.museumsassociation.org.
Director, M. Taylor

MUSIC HALL SOCIETY, BRITISH, 82 Fernlea Road, London SW12 9RW. Tel: 020-8673 2175.
Hon. Secretary, Mrs D. Masterton

MUSIC INFORMATION CENTRE, BRITISH, 10 Stratford Place, London W1C 1BA. Tel: 020-7499 8567; Fax: 020-7499 4795; Web: www.bmic.co.uk.
Director, M. Greenall

MUSIC SOCIETIES, NATIONAL FEDERATION OF (1935), 7–15 Rosebery Avenue, London EC1R 4SP. Tel: 0870-872 3300; Fax: 0870-872 3400; Web: www.makingmusic.org.uk.
Chief Executive, R. Osterley

MUSICIANS BENEVOLENT FUND (1921), 16 Ogle Street, London W1W 6JA. Tel: 020-7636 4481; Fax: 020-7637 4307; Web: www.mbf.org.uk.
Secretary, Ms H. Faulkner

MUSICIANS, INCORPORATED SOCIETY OF (1882), 10 Stratford Place, London W1C 1AA. Tel: 020-7629 4413; Fax: 020-7408 1538; Web: www.ism.org.
Chief Executive, N. Hoyle

NABS, 32 Wigmore Street, London W1U 2RP. Tel: 020-7299 2888; Fax: 020-7299 2887; Web: www.nabs.org.uk.
Chief Executive, Miss K. Harris

NACRO, THE CRIME REDUCTION CHARITY (1966), 169 Clapham Road, London SW9 0PU. Tel: 020-7582 6500; Fax: 020-7735 4666; Web: www.narco.org.uk. *Chief Executive*, P. Cavadino

NATIONAL BENEVOLENT INSTITUTION (1812), 61 Bayswater Road, London W2 3PG. Tel: 020-7723 0021; Fax: 020-7706 7035; Web: www.nbicharity.com.
Secretary, Gp Capt. D. St J. Homer, MVO

NATIONAL EXTENSION COLLEGE (1963), Michael Young Centre, Purbeck Road, Cambridge CB2 2HN. Tel: 01223-400200; Fax: 01223-400399; Web: www.nec.ac.uk. *Director*, Dr R. Morpeth

NATIONAL SOCIETY, THE (1811), Church House, Great Smith Street, London SW1P 3NZ. Tel: 020-7898 1518; Fax: 020-7898 1493; Web: www.natsoc.org.uk.
General Secretary, Canon J. Hall

NATURALISTS' ASSOCIATION, BRITISH (1905), 1 Bracken Mews, London E4 7UT. Web: www.bna-naturalists.org.
Hon. Membership Secretary, Mrs Y. H. Griffiths

NAUTICAL RESEARCH, SOCIETY OF (1910), c/o National Maritime Museum, Greenwich, London SE10 9NF. Tel: 020-8312 6712; Fax: 020-8312 6722; Web: www.snr.org.uk. *Hon. Secretary*, Liza Verity

NAVY RECORDS SOCIETY (1893), c/o Department of War Studies, King's College, The Strand, London WC2R 2LS. Web: www.navyrecordssociety.com.
Hon. Secretary, Dr A. D. Lambert

NCH (1869), 85 Highbury Park, London N5 1UD. Tel: 020-7704 7000; Fax: 020-7226 2537; Web: www.nch.org.uk. *Chief Executive*, D. Mead

NEWCASTLE UPON TYNE, SOCIETY OF ANTIQUARIES OF (1813), Black Gate, Castle Garth, Newcastle upon Tyne NE1 1RQ. Tel: 0191-261 5390; Web: www.museums.ncl.ac.uk/socantiqs.
Secretary, N. Hodgson

NEWCOMEN SOCIETY (1920), The Science Museum, London SW7 2DD. Tel: 020-7371 4445; Fax: 020-7371 4445; Web: www.newcomen.com.
President, Sir Neil Cossons

NEWSPAPER PRESS FUND (1864), Dickens House, 35 Wathen Road, Dorking, Surrey RH4 1JY. Tel: 01306-887511; Fax: 01306-888212.
Director, D. Ilott

NHS CONFEDERATION, THE, 1 Warwick Row, London SW1E 5ER. Tel: 020-7959 7272; Fax: 020-7959 7273; Web: www.nhsconfed.net.
Chief Executive, Dr Gill Morgan

NOISE ABATEMENT SOCIETY, 44 Grande Parade, Brighton BN2 9QA. Helpline: 01273-878782; Fax: 01695-50219;.*Chairman*, Gloria Elliott

NORFOLK AND NORWICH ARCHAEOLOGICAL SOCIETY (1846), 30 Brettingham Avenue, Norwich NR4 6XG. Tel: 01603-455913. *Secretary*, R. Bellinger

NORWOOD RAVENSWOOD (1996), Broadway House, 80–82 The Broadway, Stanmore, Middx HA7 4HB. Tel: 020-8954 4555; Fax: 020-8420 6800.
Chief Executive, Ms N. Brier

NOTARIES SOCIETY, THE (1882), 23 New Street, Woodbridge, Suffolk IP12 1DN. Tel: 01394-384134; Fax: 01394-382906; Web: www.thenotariessociety.org.uk.
Secretary, A. G. Dunford

NUCLEAR ENERGY SOCIETY, BRITISH, 1–7 Great George Street, London SW1P 3AA. Tel: 020-7665 2241; Fax: 020-7799 1325; Web: www.bnes.org.uk.
Secretary, I. M. Andrews

NUFFIELD FOUNDATION, THE (1943), 28 Bedford Square, London WC1B 3JS. Tel: 020-7631 0566; Fax: 020-7323 4877; Web: www.nuffieldfoundation.org.
Director, A. Tomei

NUFFIELD TRUST (1940), 59 New Cavendish Street, London W1G 7LP. Tel: 020-7631 8450; Fax: 020-7631 8451; Web: www.nuffieldtrust.org.uk.
Secretary, J. Wyn Owen, CB

NURSING AND MIDWIFERY COUNCIL (2002), 23 Portland Place, London W1B 1PZ. Tel: 020-7637 7181; Fax: 020-7436 2924; Web: www.nmc-uk.org.
President, Jonathan Asbridge

NUTRITION FOUNDATION, BRITISH (1967), High Holborn House, 52–54 High Holborn, London WC1V 6RQ. Tel: 020-7404 6504; Fax: 020-7404 6747; Web: www.nutrition.org.uk.
Director-General, Prof. R. S. Pickard, PhD, CBiol

760 Societies and Institutions

NUTRITION SOCIETY (1941), 10 Cambridge Court, 210 Shepherds Bush Road, London W6 7NJ. Tel: 020-7602 0228; Fax: 020-7602 1756; Web: www.nutsoc.org.uk. *President*, Prof John Mathers

OCCUPATIONAL SAFETY AND HEALTH, INSTITUTION OF (1945), The Grange, Highfield Drive, Wigston, Leics LE18 1NN. Tel: 0116-257 3100; Fax: 0116-257 3101; Web: www.iosh.co.uk. *Chief Executive*, R. W. H. Strange

OFFICERS' ASSOCIATION, THE, 48 Pall Mall, London SW1Y 5JY. Tel: 020-7930 0125; Fax: 020-7930 9053; Web: www.officersassociation.org.uk. *General Secretary*, Maj.-Gen. A. I. Ramsay, CBE, DSO

OPAS (THE PENSIONS ADVISORY SERVICE) (1983), 11 Belgrave Road, London SW1V 1RB. Tel: 0845-601 2923; Fax: 020-7233 8016; Web: www.opas.org.uk. *Chief Executive*, M. McLean, OBE

OPEN SPACES SOCIETY (1865), 25a Bell Street, Henley-on-Thames, Oxon RG9 2BA. Tel: 01491-573535; Fax: 01491-573051; Web: www.oss.org.uk. *General Secretary*, Miss K. Ashbrook

OPERATIC AND DRAMATIC ASSOCIATION, NATIONAL (1899), NODA House, 1 Crestfield Street, London WC1H 8AU. Tel: 0870-770 2480; Fax: 0870-770 2490; Web: www.noda.org.uyk. *Chief Executive*, M. Pemberton

OPERATIONS ENGINEERS, THE SOCIETY FOR (2000), 22 Greencoat Place, London SW1P 1PR. Tel: 020-7630 1111; Fax: 020-7630 6677; Web: www.soe.org.uk. *Chief Executive*, T. Fischer, MBA, IEng

OPSIS (1992), c/o Queen Alexandra College, Court Oak Road, Birmingham B17 9TG. Tel: 0121-428 5037; Fax: 0121-428 5048; Web: www.opsis.org.uk. *Executive Manager*, C. Gregory; *Chairman*, Sir Geoffrey Holland, KCB

OPTICAL COUNCIL, GENERAL (1959), 41 Harley Street, London W1G 8DJ. Tel: 020-7580 3898; Fax: 020-7436 3525; Web: www.optical.org. *Chief Executive and Registrar*, P. C. Coe

OPTOMETRISTS, COLLEGE OF (1980), 42 Craven Street, London WC2N 5NG. Tel: 020-7839 6000; Fax: 020-7839 6800; Web: www.college-optometrists.org. *Secretary*, P. D. Leigh

ORDERS AND MEDALS RESEARCH SOCIETY (1942), PO Box 1904, Southam CV47 2ZX. Tel: 01295-690009; Web: www.omrs.org.uk. *General Secretary*, P. M. R. Helmore

ORIENTAL CERAMIC SOCIETY (1921), 30B Torrington Square, London WC1E 7LJ. Tel: 020-7636 7985; Fax: 020-7580 6749; Web: www.ocs-london.com. *President*, Ross Kerr

ORNITHOLOGISTS' UNION, BRITISH (1858), c/o The Natural History Museum, Akeman Street, Tring, Herts HP23 6AP. Tel: 01442-890080; Fax: 01442-870693; Web: www.bou.org.uk. *Administrator*, S. P. Dudley

ORNITHOLOGY, BRITISH TRUST FOR, The Nunnery, Thetford, Norfolk IP24 2PU. Tel: 01842-750050; Fax: 01842-750030; Web: www.bto.org. *Director*, Dr J. J. D. Greenwood

OSTEOPATHIC COUNCIL, GENERAL (1993), Osteopathy House, 176 Tower Bridge Road, London SE1 3LU. Tel: 020-7357 6655; Fax: 020-7357 0011; Web: www.osteopathy.org.uk. *Chief Executive & Registrar*, Miss M. J. Craggs

OSTEOPATHIC MEDICINE, LONDON COLLEGE OF, 8–10 Boston Place, London NW1 6QH. Tel: 020-7262 1128; Fax: 020-7723 7492. *Clinic Manager*, Mrs A. Dalby

OSTEOPOROSIS SOCIETY, NATIONAL (1986), Manor Farm, Skinners Hill, Camerton, Bath BA2 0PJ. Tel: 01761-471771; Fax: 01761-471104; Web: www.nos.org.uk. *Communications Manager*, Trevor Reid

OUTWARD BOUND SCOTLAND (1941), Loch Eil Centre, Achdalieu, Corpach, Fort William, Inverness-shire PH33 7NN. Tel: 01397-772866; Fax: 01397-773905; Web: www.outwardbound-uk.org. *Director*, Sir Michael Hobbs, KCVO, CBE

OVERSEAS DEVELOPMENT INSTITUTE, 111 Westminster Bridge Road, London SE1 7JD. Tel: 020-7922 0300; Fax: 020-7922 0399; Web: www.odi.org.uk. *Director*, S. Maxwell

OVERSEAS SERVICE PENSIONERS' ASSOCIATION (1960), 138 High Street, Tonbridge, Kent TN9 1AX. Tel: 01732-363836. *Secretary*, D. F. B. Le Breton, CBE

OXFAM GREAT BRITAIN (1942), 274 Banbury Road, Oxford OX2 7DZ. Tel: 01865-311311; Web: www.oxfam.org.uk. *Director*, B. Stocking, CMG

OXFORD PRESERVATION TRUST (1927), 10 Turn Again Lane, St Ebbes, Oxford OX1 1QL. Tel: 01865-242918; Fax: 01865-251022. *Secretary*, Mrs D. Dance

OXFORD UNIVERSITY SOCIETY, Oxenford House, Magdalen Street, Oxford OX1 3AB. Tel: 01865-288088; Fax: 01865-288086; Web: www.alumni.ox.ac.uk. *Secretary*, A. I. Lack

OXFORDSHIRE ARCHITECTURAL AND HISTORICAL SOCIETY (1839), 53 Radley Road, Abingdon, Oxon OX14 3PN. Tel: 01235-525960; Fax: 0870-056 0773; Web: www.oahs.org.uk. *Hon. Secretary*, Dr A. J. Dodd

PALAEONTOLOGICAL ASSOCIATION (1957), c/o Department of Geological Sciences, The University, South Road, Durham DH1 3LE. Tel: 0121-414 4173; Fax: 0191-374 2510; Web: www.palass.org. *Secretary*, Dr H. A. Armstrong

PARENTS AT WORK, 45 Beech Street, London EC2Y 8AD. Tel: 020-7628 3565; Fax: 020-7628 3591; Web: www.parentsatwork.org.uk. *Joint Chief Executives*, Ms S. Jackson; Ms S. Monk

PARLIAMENTARY AND SCIENTIFIC COMMITTEE (1939), 48 Westminster Palace Gardens, 1–7 Artillery Row, London SW1P 1RR. Tel: 020-7222 7085; Fax: 020-7222 5355;. *Administrative Secretary*, Dr A. Whitehouse

PASTORAL PSYCHOLOGY, GUILD OF (1937), PO Box 1107, London W3 6ZP. Tel: 020-8993 8366; Fax: 020-8993 3148; Web: www.guildofpastoralpsychology.org.uk. *Chairman,* Revd Lyn Phillips

PATIENTS ASSOCIATION, PO Box 935, Harrow, Middx HA1 3YJ. Tel: 020-8423 9111. Helpline: 0845-608 4455; Fax: 020-8423 9119; Web: www.patients-association.com. *Director,* M. Stone

PETROLEUM, INSTITUTE OF (1913), 61 New Cavendish Street, London W1G 7AR. Tel: 020-7467 7100; Fax: 020-7255 1472; Web: www.petroleum.co.uk. *Director General,* J. Pym

PHARMACOLOGICAL SOCIETY, BRITISH (1931), 16 Angel Gate, City Road, London EC1V 2SG. Tel: 020-7417 0110; Fax: 020-7417 0114; Web: www.bps.ac.uk. *President,* Prof. R. J. Flower

PHILOLOGICAL SOCIETY (1842), School of Oriental and African Studies, University of London, Thornhaugh Street, London WC1H 0XG; Web: lings.ln.man.ac.uk/html/philsoc. *Hon. Secretary,* Dr Andrew Simpson

PHOTOGRAPHY, BRITISH INSTITUTE OF PROFESSIONAL (1901), Fox Talbot House, Amwell End, Ware, Herts SG12 9HN. Tel: 01920-464011; Fax: 01920-487056; Web: www.bipp.com. *Executive Secretary,* A. Mair

PHYSICS AND ENGINEERING IN MEDICINE, INSTITUTE OF, Fairmount House, 230 Tadcaster Road, York YO24 1ES. Tel: 01904-610821; Fax: 01904-612279; Web: www.ipem.org.uk. *General Secretary,* R. W. Neilson

PHYSIOLOGICAL SOCIETY, THE (1876), PO Box 11319, London WC1E 7JF. Tel: 020-7631 1458; Fax: 020-7631 1462; Web: www.physoc.org. *Chief Executive,* Esther Williams

PIG ASSOCIATION, BRITISH, Scotsbridge House, Scots Hill, Rickmansworth, Herts WD3 3BB. Tel: 01923-695295; Fax: 01923-695347; Web: www.britishpigs.org. *Chief Executive,* M. Bates

PILGRIM TRUST, THE (1930), Cowley House, 9 Little College Street, London SW1P 3XS. Tel: 020-7222 4723; Fax: 020-7976 0461; Web: www.thepilgrimtrust.org.uk. *Director,* Miss G. Nayler

PILGRIMS OF GREAT BRITAIN, THE (1902), Allington Castle, Maidstone, Kent ME16 0NB. Tel: 01622-606404; Fax: 01622-606402; *Chairman,* R. M. Worcester; *Hon. Secretary,* M. P. S. Barton

PLAIN ENGLISH CAMPAIGN (1979), PO Box 3, New Mills, High Peak SK22 4QP. Tel: 01663-744409; Fax: 01663-747038; Web: www.plainenglish.co.uk. *Director,* Ms C. Maher

PLAYING FIELDS ASSOCIATION, NATIONAL (1925), Stanley House, St Chads Place, London WC1X 9HH. Tel: 020-7833 5360; Fax: 020-7833 5365; Web: www.npfa.co.uk. *Director,* Ms E. Davies

PLUNKETT FOUNDATION (1919), 23 Hanborough Business Park, Long Hanborough, Oxford OX29 8SG. Tel: 01993-883636; Fax: 01993-883576; Web: www.plunkett.co.uk. *Director,* R. Moreton

POETRY SOCIETY, THE (1919), 22 Betterton Street, London WC2H 9BX. Tel: 020-7420 9880; Fax: 020-7240 4818; Web: www.poetrysoc.com. *Director,* Ms C. Patterson

POLICE REHABILITATION AND RETRAINING TRUST (1999), Maryfield Complex, 100 Belfast Road, Holywood, Co. Down, N. Ireland BT18 9QY. Tel: 028-9042 7788; Fax: 028-9042 3566; Web: www.prrt.org

POLIO FELLOWSHIP, BRITISH (1939), Ground Floor, Unit A, Eagle Office Centre, The Runway, South Ruislip, Middx HA4 6SE. Tel: 0800-018 0586; Fax: 020-8842 0555; Web: www.britishpolio.org. *Chief Executive,* A. Kemp, CQSW

POLITE SOCIETY AND CAMPAIGN FOR COURTESY, THE (1986), 18 The Avenue, Basford, Newcastle-under-Lyme, Staffs ST5 0LY. Tel: 01782-614407. *Founder/Secretary,* The Revd Ian Gregory

POLITICS NETWORK, NEW, 6 Cynthia Street, London N1 9JF. Tel: 020-7278 4443; Fax: 020-7278 4425; Web: www.new-politics.net. *Director,* Peter Facey

PONY CLUB, THE (1929), National Agricultural Centre, Stoneleigh Park, Kenilworth, Warks CV8 2RW. Tel: 024-7669 8300; Fax: 024-7669 6836; Web: www.pcuk.org. *Chief Executive,* Mr D. Robb

POPES SOCIETY, THE, c/o Greyfriars Hall, Iffley Road, Oxford Road OX4 1SB. Tel: 07092-261683; Web: www.popes.cjb.net

POSTWATCH, 28-30 Grosvenor Gardens, London SW1W 0TT. Tel: 020-7259 1200; Fax: 020-7730 3044; Web: www.postwatch.co.uk. *Chairman,* Peter Carr

POWYSLAND CLUB (1867), Llgyad y Dyffryn, Llanidloes, Powys SY18 6JD. Tel: 01686-412277; Web: www.powyslandclub.co.uk. *Hon. Secretary,* Miss P. M. Davies

PRAYER BOOK SOCIETY, THE (1975), St James Garlickhythe, Garlick Hill, London EC4V 2AF. Tel: 01243-784832; Web: www.prayerbookuk.com. *Chairman,* Roger Evans

PRE-SCHOOL LEARNING ALLIANCE (1961), 69 Kings Cross Road, London WC1X 9LL. Tel: 020-7833 0991; Fax: 020-7837 4942; Web: www.pre-school.org.uk. *Chief Executive,* Ms M. Lochrie

PRINCESS ROYAL TRUST FOR CARERS (1991), 142 Minories, London EC3N 1LB. Tel: 020-7480 7788; Fax: 020-7481 4729; Web: www.carers.org. *Chief Executive,* Ms A. Ryan

PRINTERS' CHARITABLE CORPORATION (1827), 7 Cantelupe Mews, Cantelupe Road, East Grinstead, W. Sussex RH19 3BG. Tel: 01342-318882; Fax: 01342-318887; Web: www.printerscharitablecorporation.co.uk. *Director,* Ms T. Searle

PRINTING HISTORICAL SOCIETY (1965), St Bride Institute, Bride Lane, London EC4Y 8EE. *Hon. Secretary*, Philip Wickens

PRINTING, INSTITUTE OF (1980), The Mews, Hill House, Clanricarde Road, Tunbridge Wells, Kent TN1 1PJ. Tel: 01892-538118; Fax: 01892-518028; Web: www.institute of printing.org. *Secretary-General*, D. Freeland

PRISON VISITORS, NATIONAL ASSOCIATION OF, 32 Newnham Avenue, Bedford ME41 9PT. *General Secretary*, Mrs A. G. McKenna

PRISONERS ABROAD (1978), 89–93 Fonthill Road, London N4 3JH. Tel: 020-7561 6820; Fax: 020-7561 6821; Web: www.prisonersabroad.org.uk. *Director*, I. Acheson

PROFESSIONAL CLASSES AID COUNCIL, 10 St Christopher's Place, London W1U 1HZ. Tel: 020-7935 0641. *Secretary*, Miss N. E. Inkson

PROTECTION OF ANCIENT BUILDINGS, SOCIETY FOR THE (1877), 37 Spital Square, London E1 6DY. Tel: 020-7377 1644; Fax: 020-7247 5296; Web: www.spab.org.uk. *Secretary*, P. Venning, FSA

PROTECTION OF RURAL SCOTLAND, ASSOCIATION FOR (1926), 3rd Floor, Gladstone's Land, 483 Lawnmarket, Edinburgh EH1 2NT. Tel: 0131-225 7012/3; Fax: 0131-225 6592; Web: www.aprs.org.uk. *Director*, Mrs J. Geddes

PROTECTION OF UNBORN CHILDREN, SOCIETY FOR THE (1967), 5–6 St Matthew Street, London SW1P 2JT. Tel: 020-7222 5845; Fax: 020-7222 0630; Web: www.spuc.org.uk. *National Director*, J. Smeaton

PROTECTION OF WILD BIRDS, SCOTTISH SOCIETY FOR THE (1928), Foremount House, Kilbarchan, Renfrewshire PA10 2EZ. Tel: 01505-702419. *Secretary*, Dr J. A. Gibson

PROTESTANT ALLIANCE (1845), 77 Ampthill Road, Flitwick, Bedford MK45 1BD. Tel: 01525-712348; Fax: 01525-712348. *General Secretary*, Dr S. J. Scott-Pearson

PSORIASIS ASSOCIATION (1968), 7 Milton Street, Northampton NN2 7JG. Tel: 01604-711129; Fax: 01604-792894. *Chief Executive*, Gladys Edwards

PSYCHICAL RESEARCH, SOCIETY FOR (1882), 49 Marloes Road, London W8 6LA. Tel: 020-7937 8984; Fax: 020-7937 8984; Web: www.spr.ac.uk. *Secretary*, P. M. Johnson

PSYCHOLOGICAL SOCIETY, BRITISH (1901), St Andrews House, 48 Princess Road East, Leicester LE1 7DR. Tel: 0116-254 9568; Fax: 0116-247 0787; Web: www.bps.org.uk. *Chief Executive*, B. A. Brooking

PUBLIC POLICY RESEARCH, INSTITUTE FOR (1988), 30–32 Southampton Street, London WC2E 7RA. Tel: 020-7470 6100; Fax: 020-7470 6111; Web: www.ippr.org.uk. *Director*, M. Taylor

PUBLIC POLICY, THE SCHOOL OF, University College London, 29 Tavistock Square, London WC1H 9QU. Tel: 020-7679 4999; Fax: 020-7679 4969; Web: www.ucl.ac.uk/spp/. *Director*, Professor Helen Margetts

PURCHASING AND SUPPLY, CHARTERED INSTITUTE OF (1932), Easton House, Easton on the Hill, Stamford, Lincs PE9 3NZ. Tel: 01780-756777; Fax: 01780-751610; Web: www.cips.org. *Chief Executive*, K. James

QUAKER PEACE AND SOCIAL WITNESS, Friends House, 173–177 Euston Road, London NW1 2BJ. Tel: 020-7663 1000; Fax: 020-7663 1001; Web: www.quaker.org.uk. *General Secretary*, Ms L. Fielding

QUALITY ASSURANCE, INSTITUTE OF, 12 Grosvenor Crescent, London SW1X 7EE. Tel: 020-7245 6722; Fax: 020-7245 6788; Web: www.iqa.org. *Director General*, F. R. Steer, MBE

QUARRYING, INSTITUTE OF (1917), 7 Regent Street, Nottingham NG1 5BS. Tel: 0115-941 1315; Fax: 0115-948 4035; Web: www.inst-of-quarrying.org/iq/. *General Manager*, Dr M. R. Smith

QUEEN ELIZABETH'S FOUNDATION FOR DISABLED PEOPLE (1934), Leatherhead Court, Leatherhead, Surrey KT22 0BN. Tel: 01372-841100; Fax: 01372-844072; Web: www.qefd.org. *Director*, Cynthia Robinson

QUEEN VICTORIA CLERGY FUND (1897), Church House, Dean's Yard, London SW1P 3NZ. Tel: 020-7898 1310; Fax: 020-7898 1321. *Secretary*, C. D. L. Menzies

QUEEN VICTORIA SCHOOL (1908), Dunblane, Perthshire FK15 0JY. Tel: 01786-822288; Fax: 0131-310 2955; Web: www.qvs.pkc.org.uk. *Headmaster*, B. Raine

QUEEN'S ENGLISH SOCIETY, THE (1973), 20 Jessica Road, London SW18 2QN. Tel: 020-8874 2200; Web: www.queens-english-society.com. *Hon. Secretary*, Miss P. Raper

QUEEN'S NURSING INSTITUTE (1887), 3 Albemarle Way, London EC1V 4RQ. Tel: 020-7490 4227; Fax: 020-7490 1269; Web: www.qni.org.uk. *Director*, Mrs J. Hesketh

QUIT, Ground Floor, 211 Old Street, London EC1V 9NR. Tel: 020-7251 1551; Fax: 020-7251 1661. *Chief Executive*, P. McCabe

RADAR (ROYAL ASSOCIATION FOR DISABILITY AND REHABILITATION) (1977), 12 City Forum, 250 City Road, London EC1V 8AF. Tel: 020-7250 3222; Fax: 020-7250 0212; Web: www.radar.org.uk. *Director*, Kate Nash

RAIL PASSENGERS COUNCIL (1949), Whittles House, 14 Pentonville Road, London N1 9HF. Tel: 020-7713 2700. *Chairman*, S. Francis

RAILWAY AND CANAL HISTORICAL SOCIETY (1954), 3 West Court, West Street, Oxford OX2 0NP. Tel: 01865-240514; Web: www.bodley.ox.ac.uk/external/rchs/index.html. *Hon. Secretary*, M. Searle

RAILWAY BENEVOLENT INSTITUTION (1858), Elcetra Way, Crewe Business Park, Crewe, Cheshire CW1 6HS. Tel: 01270-251316; Fax: 01270-503966. *Director*, B. R. Whitnall

RAMBLERS' ASSOCIATION (1935), 2nd Floor, Camelford House, 87–90 Albert Embankment, London SE1 7TW. Tel: 020-7339 8500; Fax: 020-7339 8501; Web: www.ramblers.org.uk. *Chief Executive*, Nick Barrett

RARE BREEDS SURVIVAL TRUST (1973), National Agricultural Centre, Stoneleigh Park, Kenilworth, Warks CV8 2LG. Tel: 024-7669 6551; Fax: 024-7669 6706; Web: www.rare-breeds.com. *Chief Executive*, Ms R. Mansbridge

RED CROSS, BRITISH (1870), 9 Grosvenor Crescent, London SW1X 7EJ. Tel: 020-7235 5454; Fax: 020-7245 6315; Web: www.redcross.org.uk and www.redcrossdonations.org.uk. *Chief Executive*, Sir Nicholas Young

REGIONAL STUDIES ASSOCIATION (1965), PO Box 2058, Seaford BN25 4QU. Tel: 01323-899698; Fax: 01323-899798; Web: www.regional-studies-assoc.ac.uk. *Chief Executive*, Mrs S. Hardy

REGULAR FORCES EMPLOYMENT ASSOCIATION LTD (1885), 49 Pall Mall, London SW1Y 5JG. Tel: 020-7321 2011; Fax: 020-7839 0970; Web: www.rfea.org.uk. *Chief Executive*, Air Cdre. Peter G. Johnson, OBE

RELATE (1938), Herbert Gray College, Little Church Street, Rugby, Warks CV21 3AP. Tel: 01788-753241; Fax: 01788-535007; Web: www.relate.org.uk. *Chief Executive*, Ms A. Sibson

RESEARCH DEFENCE SOCIETY (1908), 58 Great Marlborough Street, London W1V 1DD. Tel: 020-7287 2818; Fax: 020-7287 2627; Web: www.rds-online.org.uk. *Executive Director*, Dr M. Matfield

RESERVE FORCES ASSOCIATION (1972), Duke of York's HQ, London SW3 4SG. Tel: 020-7414 5588; Fax: 020-7414 5589; *Secretary-General*, Air Vice-Marshal A. J. Stables, CB

RETHINK (1972), 30 Tabernacle Street, London EC2A 4DD. Tel: 020-7330 9100; Fax: 020-7330 9102; Web: www.rethink.org. *Chief Executive*, Cliff Prior

RETIRED NURSES' NATIONAL HOME, Riverside Avenue, Bournemouth BH7 7EE. Tel: 01202-396418; Fax: 01202-302530. *Chairman*, Ms J. Deacon

RETIREMENT PENSIONS ASSOCIATIONS, NATIONAL FEDERATION OF (1940), Thwaites House, Railway Road, Blackburn BB1 5AX. Tel: 01254-52606; Fax: 01254-52606. *General Secretary*, R. Stansfield

REVENUES, RATINGS AND VALUATION (1882), 41 Doughty Street, London WC1N 2LF. Tel: 020-7831 3505; Fax: 020-7831 2048. *Director*, D. Magor, IRRV, OBE

RICHARD III SOCIETY (1924), 4 Oakley Street, London SW3 5NN; Web: www.richardiii.net. *Secretary*, Miss E. M. Nokes

ROAD SAFETY OFFICERS (1971), Pin Point, 1–2 Rosslyn Crescent, Harrow HA1 2SB. Tel: 0870-010 4442; Fax: 0870-333 7772; Web: www.irsoweb.org. *Chairman*, R. Doherty

ROMAN STUDIES, SOCIETY FOR THE PROMOTION OF (1910), Senate House, Malet Street, London WC1E 7HU. Tel: 020-7862 8727; Fax: 020-7862 8728; Web: www.sas.ac.uk/icls/roman/. *Secretary*, Dr H. M. Cockle

ROOM: THE NATIONAL COUNCIL FOR HOUSING AND PLANNING (1900), 14–18 Old Street, London EC1V 9BH. Tel: 020-7251 2363; Fax: 020-7608 2830; Web: www.room.org.uk. *Director*, Prof. K. MacDonald

ROTARY INTERNATIONAL IN GREAT BRITAIN AND IRELAND (1905), Kinwarton Road, Alcester, Warks B49 6BP. Tel: 01789-765411; Fax: 01789-765570; Web: www.rotary-ribi.org. *Secretary*, R. Freeman

ROUND TABLES OF GREAT BRITAIN AND IRELAND, NATIONAL ASSOCIATION OF (1927), Marchesi House, 4 Embassy Drive, Egbaston, Birmingham B15 1TP. Tel: 0121-456 4402; Fax: 0121-456 4185; Web: www.roundtable.org.uk. *General Secretary*, J. Handley

ROYAL AERONAUTICAL SOCIETY, 4 Hamilton Place, London W1J 7BQ. Tel: 020-7670 4302; Fax: 020-7499 6230. *Director*, K. Mans

ROYAL AGRICULTURAL BENEVOLENT INSTITUTION (1860), Shaw House, 27 West Way, Oxford OX2 0QH. Tel: 01865-724931; Fax: 01865-202025; Web: www.rabi.org.uk. *Chief Executive*, W. A. McMahon, CVO, AFC

ROYAL AGRICULTURAL SOCIETY OF ENGLAND (1840), National Agricultural Centre, Stoneleigh Park, Warks CV8 2LZ. Tel: 024-7669 6969; Fax: 024-7669 6900. *Chief Executive*, M. Calvert

ROYAL AGRICULTURAL SOCIETY OF THE COMMONWEALTH (1957), 2 Grosvenor Gardens, London SW1W 0DH. Tel: 020-7259 9678; Fax: 020-7259 9675; Web: www.commagshow.org. *Hon. Secretary*, C. Runge

ROYAL AIR FORCE BENEVOLENT FUND (1919), 67 Portland Place, London W1B 1AR. Tel: 020-7580 8343; Fax: 020-7307 3374; Web: www.raf-benfund.org.uk. *Controller*, Air Chief Marshal Sir David Cousins, KCB, AFC, BA

ROYAL AIR FORCES ASSOCIATION, 43 Grove Park Road, London W4 3RX. Tel: 020-8994 8504; Fax: 020-8742 1927; Web: www.rafa.org.uk. *Secretary-General*, John Hartley

ROYAL ARCHAEOLOGICAL INSTITUTE (1844), c/o Society of Antiquaries of London, Burlington House, Piccadilly, London W1J 0BE. Tel: 020-7479 7092. *Secretary*, J. G. Coad, FSA

ROYAL ARMOURED CORPS WAR MEMORIAL BENEVOLENT FUND, c/o RHQ RTR, Bovington Camp, Wareham, Dorset BH20 6JA. Tel: 01929-403331; Fax: 01929-403488. *Secretary*, Maj. A. Henzie, MBE

ROYAL ARTILLERY ASSOCIATION, Artillery House, Front Parade, Royal Artillery Barracks, Woolwich, London SE18 4BH. Tel: 020-8781 3003; Fax: 020-8854 3617; Web: www.raa.uk.com

ROYAL ASIATIC SOCIETY, 60 Queen's Gardens, London W2 3AF. Tel: 020-7724 4742; Fax: 020-7706 4008; Web: www.royalasiaticsociety.co.uk. *Publications Officer*, A. P. A. Belloli

ROYAL ASSOCIATION FOR DEAF PEOPLE, Centre for Deaf People, Walsingham Road, Colchester, Essex CO2 7BP. Tel: 01206-509509. Text: 01206 577090; Fax: 01206-769755; Web: www.royaldeaf.org.uk/royaldeaf/. *Chief Executive*, Tom Fenton

ROYAL ASSOCIATION OF BRITISH DAIRY FARMERS, Dairy House, 60 Kenilworth Road, Leamington Spa, Warks CV32 6JX. Tel: 01926-887477; Fax: 01926-887585. *Chairman*, T. D. A. Brigstocke

ROYAL BIRMINGHAM SOCIETY OF ARTISTS, 4 Brook Street, Birmingham B3 1SA. Tel: 0121-236 4353; Fax: 0121-236 4555; Web: www.rbsa.org.uk

ROYAL BRITISH LEGION (1921), 48 Pall Mall, London SW1Y 5JY. Tel: 0845-772 5725; Fax: 020-7973 7399; Web: www.britishlegion.org.uk. *Secretary-General*, Brig. I. G. Townsend

ROYAL BRITISH LEGION SCOTLAND (1921), New Haig House, Logie Green Road, Edinburgh EH7 4HR. *General Secretary*, Wing Cdre. R. J. Woodroffe, MBE

ROYAL CALEDONIAN SCHOOLS TRUST (1815), 80A High Street, Bushey, Watford, Herts WD2 3DE. Tel: 020-8421 8845; Fax: 020-8421 8845; Web: www.royalcaledonianschools.org.uk. *Chief Executive*, J. Horsfield

ROYAL CAMBRIAN ACADEMY OF ARTS (1882), Crown Lane, Conwy LL32 8AN. Tel: 01492-593413; Fax: 01492-593413; Web: www.rcaconwy.co.uk. *President*, Sir Kyffin Williams

ROYAL CELTIC SOCIETY (1820), 23 Rutland Street, Edinburgh EH1 2RN. Tel: 0131-228 6449; Fax: 0131-229 6987. *Secretary*, J. G. Camerson, WS

ROYAL CHORAL SOCIETY (1872), Studio 9, 92 Lots Road, London SW10 0QD. Tel: 020-7376 3718; Fax: 020-7376 3719; Web: www.royalchoralsociety.co.uk. *Administrator*, Helen Body

ROYAL COLLEGE OF GENERAL PRACTITIONERS (1952), 14 Princes Gate, London SW7 1PU. Tel: 020-7581 3232; Fax: 020-7225 3047; Web: www.rcgp.org.uk. *Chairman of Council*, David Hasborn

ROYAL COLLEGE OF NURSING (1916), 20 Cavendish Square, London W1G 0RN. Tel: 020-7409 3333; Fax: 020-7647 3434; Web: www.rcn.org.uk. *General Secretary*, Dr Beverly Malone

ROYAL COLLEGE OF OBSTETRICIANS AND GYNAECOLOGISTS (1929), 27 Sussex Place, Regent's Park, London NW1 4RG. Tel: 020-7772 6200; Fax: 020-7723 0575; Web: www.rcog.org.uk. *College Secretary*, P. A. Barnett

ROYAL COLLEGE OF PAEDIATRICS AND CHILD HEALTH, 50 Hallam Street, London W1W 6DE. Tel: 020-7307 5600; Fax: 020-7307 5601; Web: www.rcpch.ac.uk. *Secretary*, Len Tyler

ROYAL COLLEGE OF PATHOLOGISTS, 2 Carlton House Terrace, London SW1Y 5AF. Tel: 020-7451 6700; Fax: 020-7451 6701; Web: www.rcpath.org. *Chief Executive*, Daniel Ross

ROYAL COLLEGE OF PHYSICIANS (1518), 11 St Andrews Place, Regent's Park, London NW1 4LE. Tel: 020-7935 1174; Fax: 020-7487 5218; Web: www.rcplondon.ac.uk. *Chief Executive*, A. P. Masterton-Smith

ROYAL COLLEGE OF PSYCHIATRISTS (1841), 17 Belgrave Square, London SW1X 8PG. Tel: 020-7235 2351; Fax: 020-7245 1231; Web: www.rcpsych.ac.uk. *Chief Executive*, Dr M. Shooter; *President*, Prof. J. Cox

ROYAL COLLEGE OF RADIOLOGISTS (1975), 38 Portland Place, London W1N 4JQ. Tel: 020-7636 4432; Fax: 020-7323 3100; Web: www.rcr.ac.uk. *General Secretary*, A. J. Cowles

ROYAL COLLEGE OF SURGEONS OF ENGLAND, 35–43 Lincoln's Inn Fields, London WC2A 3PN. Tel: 020-7405 3474; Fax: 020-7869 6165; Web: www.rcseng.ac.uk. *Secretary*, C. Duncan

ROYAL COLLEGE OF VETERINARY SURGEONS (1844), Belgravia House, 62–64 Horseferry Road, London SW1P 2AF. Tel: 020-7222 2001; Fax: 020-7222 2004; Web: www.rcvs.org.uk. *Registrar*, Miss J. C. Hern

ROYAL ENGINEERS ASSOCIATION (1869), RHQ Royal Engineers), Brompton Barracks, Chatham, Kent ME4 4UG. Tel: 01634-847005; Fax: 01634-822394; Web: www.reahq.org.uk. *Controller*, Lt.-Col. J. McLennan (Retd)

ROYAL FACULTY OF PROCURATORS IN GLASGOW, 12 Nelson Mandela Place, Glasgow G2 1BT. Tel: 0141-331 0533; Fax: 0141-332 9401; Web: www.rfpg.org. *General Manager*, I. C. Pearson

ROYAL FORESTRY SOCIETY OF ENGLAND, WALES AND NORTHERN IRELAND (1882), 102 High Street, Tring, Herts HP23 4AF. Tel: 01442-822028; Fax: 01442-890395; Web: www.rfs.org.uk. *Director*, Dr J. E. Jackson

ROYAL GEOGRAPHICAL SOCIETY (WITH THE INSTITUTE OF BRITISH GEOGRAPHERS) (1830), 1 Kensington Gore, London SW7 2AR. Tel: 020-7591 3000; Fax: 020-7591 3001; Web: www.rgs.org. *Director*, Dr R. Gardner

ROYAL HIGHLAND AND AGRICULTURAL SOCIETY OF SCOTLAND (1784), Royal Highland Centre, Ingliston, Edinburgh EH28 8NF. Tel: 0131-335 6200; Fax: 0131-333 5236; Web: www.rhass.org.uk. *Chief Executive*, R. Jones

ROYAL HISTORICAL SOCIETY (1868), University College London, Gower Street, London WC1E 6BT. Tel: 020-7387 7532; Fax: 020-7387 7532; Web: www.rhs.ac.uk. *Executive Secretary*, Mrs J. N. McCarthy

ROYAL HORTICULTURAL SOCIETY (1804), 80 Vincent Square, London SW1P 2PE. Tel: 020-7834 4333; Fax: 020-7630 6060; Web: www.rhs.org.uk. *Director-General*, Dr A. Colquhoun

ROYAL HOSPITAL FOR NEURO-DISABILITY (1854), West Hill, Putney, London SW15 3SW. Tel: 020-8780 4500; Fax: 020-8780 4501; Web: www.neuro-disability.org.uk. *Chief Executive*, Peter Franklyn

ROYAL HUMANE SOCIETY (1774), Brettenham House, Lancaster Place, London WC2E 7EP. Tel: 020-7836 8155; Fax: 020-7836 8155; *Secretary*, Maj.-Gen. C. Tyler, CB

ROYAL INCORPORATION OF ARCHITECTS IN SCOTLAND (1916), 15 Rutland Square, Edinburgh EH1 2BE. Tel: 0131-229 7545; Fax: 0131-228-2188; Web: www.rias.org.uk. *Secretary and Treasurer*, S. Tombs

ROYAL INSTITUTE OF BRITISH ARCHITECTS, 66 Portland Place, London W1B 1AD. Tel: 020-7580 5533. Information: 0906-302 0400; Fax: 020-7255 1541; Web: www.architecture.com. *Chief Executive*, Richard Hastilow

ROYAL INSTITUTE OF INTERNATIONAL AFFAIRS (1920), Chatham House, 10 St James's Square, London SW1Y 4LE. Tel: 020-7957 5700; Fax: 020-7957 5710; Web: www.riia.org. *Director*, Victor Bulmer-Thomas

ROYAL INSTITUTE OF NAVIGATION (1947), 1 Kensington Gore, London SW7 2AT. Tel: 020-7591 3130; Fax: 020-7591 3131; Web: www.rin.org.uk. *Director*, Gp Capt. D. W. Broughton, MBE

ROYAL INSTITUTE OF OIL PAINTERS (1882), 17 Carlton House Terrace, London SW1Y 5BD. Tel: 020-7930 6844; Fax: 020-7839 7830; Web: www.mallgalleries.org.uk. *Secretary*, Brian Roxby

ROYAL INSTITUTE OF PAINTERS IN WATER COLOURS (1831), 17 Carlton House Terrace, London SW1Y 5BD. Tel: 020-7930 6844; Fax: 020-7839 7830; Web: www.mallgalleries.org.uk. *Secretary*, T. Hunt

ROYAL INSTITUTE OF PHILOSOPHY, THE (1925), 14 Gordon Square, London WC1H 0AR. Tel: 020-7387 4130; Fax: 020-7383 4061; Web: www.royalinstitutephilosophy.org. *Director*, Prof. A. O'Hear

ROYAL INSTITUTION OF CHARTERED SURVEYORS (1868), 12 Great George Street, Parliamentary Square, London SW1P 3AD. Tel: 020-7222 7000; Fax: 020-7222 9430; Web: www.rics.org. *Chief Executive*, J. H. A. J. Armstrong

ROYAL INSTITUTION OF NAVAL ARCHITECTS (1860), 10 Upper Belgrave Street, London SW1X 8BQ. Tel: 020-7235 4622; Fax: 020-7259 5912; Web: www.rina.org.uk. *Chief Executive*, T. Blakeley

ROYAL LITERARY FUND, 3 Johnson's Court, off Fleet Street, London EC4A 3EA. Tel: 020-7353 7150; Fax: 020-7353 1350. *General Secretary*, Ms E. M. Gunn

ROYAL LONDON SOCIETY FOR THE BLIND (1838), Dorton House, Seal, Sevenoaks, Kent TN15 0ED. Tel: 01732-592500; Fax: 01732-592506; Web: www.rlsb.org.uk. *Chief Executive*, Brian J. Cooney

ROYAL MASONIC BENEVOLENT INSTITUTION (1842), 20 Great Queen Street, London WC2B 5BG. Tel: 020-7596 2400; Fax: 020-7404 0724; Web: www.rmbi.org.uk. *Chief Executive*, Peter J. Gray

ROYAL MEDICAL BENEVOLENT FUND (1836), 24 King's Road, London SW19 8QN. Tel: 020-8540 9194; Fax: 020-8542 0494; Web: www.rmbf.org. *Chief Executive*, M. Baber

ROYAL METAL TRADES BENEVOLENT SOCIETY, Brooke House, 4 The Lakes, Bedford Road, Northampton NN4 7YD. Tel: 01604-622023; Fax: 01604-631252. *General Secretary*, Mrs D. Webb

ROYAL MICROSCOPICAL SOCIETY (1839), 37–38 St Clements, Oxford OX4 1AJ. Tel: 01865-248768; Fax: 01865-791237; Web: www.rms.org.uk. *Administrator*, P. B. Hirst

ROYAL MUSICAL ASSOCIATION (1874), Royal Academy of Music, Marylebone Road, London NW1 5HT. *President*, C. Price

ROYAL NATIONAL COLLEGE FOR THE BLIND (1872), College Road, Hereford HR1 1EB. Tel: 01432-265725; Fax: 01432-353478; Web: www.rncb.ac.uk. *Principal*, Mrs R. Burge

ROYAL NATIONAL INSTITUTE FOR DEAF PEOPLE, 19–23 Featherstone Street, London EC1Y 8SL. Tel: 020-7296 8000; Fax: 020-7296 8199; Web: www.rnid.org.uk. *Chief Executive*, J. Strachan

ROYAL NATIONAL LIFEBOAT INSTITUTION (1824), West Quay Road, Poole, Dorset BT15 1HZ. Tel: 01202-663000; Fax: 01202-663167; Web: www.rnli.org.uk. *Chief Executive*, A. Freemantle, MBE

ROYAL NAVAL ASSOCIATION, 82 Chelsea Manor Street, London SW3 5QJ. Tel: 020-7352 6764; Fax: 020-7351 0610. *General Secretary*, Capt. R. McQueen, CBE, RN

ROYAL NAVAL BENEVOLENT SOCIETY FOR OFFICERS (1739), 1 Fleet Street, London EC4Y 1BD. Tel: 020-7427 7471; Fax: 020-7427 7471. *Secretary*, Commander W. K. Ridley, OBE, RN

ROYAL NAVAL BENEVOLENT TRUST (1922), Castaway House, 311 Twyford Avenue, Portsmouth PO2 8PE. Tel: 023-9269 0112/9266 0296; Fax: 023-9266 0852; Web: www.rnbt.org.uk. *Chief Executive*, Cdr. J. Owens

ROYAL NAVY OFFICERS, ASSOCIATION OF (1920), 70 Porchester Terrace, London W2 3TP. Tel: 020-7402 5231; Fax: 020-7402 5533; Web: www.eurosurf.com/arno. *Secretary*, Lt.-Cdr. I. M. P. Coombes

ROYAL OVER-SEAS LEAGUE (1910), Over-Seas House, Park Place, St James's Street, London SW1A 1LR. Tel: 020-7408 0214; Fax: 020-7499 6738; Web: www.rosl.org.uk. *Director General*, R. F. Newell, LVO

ROYAL PATRIOTIC FUND CORPORATION (1854), 40 Queen Anne's Gate, London SW1H 9AP. Tel: 020-7233 1894; Fax: 020-7233 1799. *Secretary*, Brig. T. G. Williams, CBE

ROYAL PHARMACEUTICAL SOCIETY OF GREAT
BRITAIN (1841), 1 Lambeth High Street, London SE1
7JN. Tel: 020-7735 9141; Fax: 020-7735 7629;
Web: www.rpsgb.org.uk.
Secretary and Registrar, Ms A. M. Lewis, OBE

ROYAL PHILATELIC SOCIETY LONDON (1869), 41
Devonshire Place, London W1G 6JY. Tel: 020-7486
1044; Fax: 020-7486 0803; Web: www.rpsl.org.uk.
Hon. Secretary, K. B. Fitton

ROYAL PHOTOGRAPHIC SOCIETY (1853), The Octagon,
Milsom Street, Bath BA1 1DN. Tel: 01225-462841;
Fax: 01225-448688; Web: www.rps.org.
President, John R. Page, FRPS

ROYAL SCHOOL OF CHURCH MUSIC (1927),
Cleveland Lodge, Westhumble, Dorking, Surrey RH5
6BW. Tel: 01306-872800; Fax: 01306-887260;
Web: www.rscm.com.
Director-General, Prof. J. Harper

ROYAL SCHOOL OF DEAF CHILDREN MARGATE
(1792), Victoria Road, Margate, Kent CT9 1NB.
Tel: 01843-227561; Fax: 01843-227637;
Web: www.royalschoolfordeaf.kent.sch.uk.
Secretary, J. Gibson

ROYAL SCHOOL OF NEEDLEWORK (1872), Apartment
12A, Hampton Court Palace, Surrey KT8 9AU.
Tel: 020-8943 1432; Fax: 020-8943 4910;
Web: www.royal-needlework.co.uk.
Principal, Mrs E. Elvin

ROYAL SCOTTISH AGRICULTURAL BENEVOLENT
INSTITUTION (1897), South Bungalow, Ingliston,
Edinburgh EH28 8NB. Tel: 0131-333 1023;
Fax: 0131-333 1027; Web: www.rsabi.org.uk.
Director, I. C. Purves-Hume

ROYAL SOCIETY FOR THE ENCOURAGEMENT OF
ARTS, MANUFACTURES AND COMMERCE (RSA)
(1754), 8 John Adam Street, London WC2N 6EZ.
Tel: 020-7930 5115; Fax: 020-7839 5805;
Web: www.rsa.org.uk. *Director*, Penny Egan

ROYAL SOCIETY FOR THE PREVENTION OF
ACCIDENTS (1917), ROSPA House, Edgbaston Park,
353 Bristol Road, Birmingham B5 7ST. Tel: 0121-248
2000; Fax: 0121-248 2001; Web: www.rospa.co.uk.
Chief Executive, Dr J. Hooper

ROYAL SOCIETY FOR THE PREVENTION OF CRUELTY
TO ANIMALS (1824), Wilberforce Way, Horsham, W.
Sussex RH13 9RS. Tel: 0870-010 1181;
Fax: 0870-753 0048; Web: www.rspca.org.uk.
Director-General, P. R. Davies, CB

ROYAL SOCIETY FOR THE PROMOTION OF HEALTH,
THE (1876), 38A St George's Drive, London SW1V
4BH. Tel: 020-7630 0121; Fax: 020-7976 6847;
Web: www.rsph.org. *Chief Executive*, H. Lowson

ROYAL SOCIETY FOR THE PROTECTION OF BIRDS
(RSPB) (1889), The Lodge, Sandy, Beds SG19 2DL.
Tel: 01767-680551; Fax: 01767-692365;
Web: www.rspb.org.uk. *Chief Executive*, G. R. Wynne

ROYAL SOCIETY OF CHEMISTRY (1841), Burlington
House, Piccadilly, London W1V 0BN. Tel: 020-7437
8656; Fax: 020-7437 8883;
Web: www.rsc.org and www.chemsoc.org.
Secretary-General and Chief Executive, Dr D.
Giachardi

ROYAL SOCIETY OF LITERATURE (1820), Somerset
House, Strand, London WC2R 1LA. Tel: 020-7845 4676;
Fax: 020-7845 4679; Web: www.rslit.org.
Chairman, Ronald Harwood, CBE

ROYAL SOCIETY OF MARINE ARTISTS (1945),
17 Carlton House Terrace, London SW1Y 5BD.
Tel: 020-7930 6844; Fax: 020-7839 7830;
Web: www.mallgalleries.org.uk. *Secretary*, D. Howell

THE ROYAL SOCIETY OF MEDICINE (1805),
1 Wimpole Street, London W1G 0AE. Tel: 020-7290
2900; Fax: 020-7290 2992; Web: www.rsm.ac.uk.
Executive Director, Dr A. Grocock

ROYAL SOCIETY OF MINIATURE PAINTERS,
SCULPTORS AND GRAVERS (1895), 1 Knapp
Cottages, Wyke, Gillingham, Dorset SP8 4NQ.
Tel: 01747-825718; Fax: 01747-826835;
Web: www.royal-miniature-society.org.uk.
Executive Secretary, Mrs P. Henderson

THE ROYAL SOCIETY OF MUSICIANS OF GREAT
BRITAIN (1738), 10 Stratford Place, London W1C 1BA.
Tel: 020-7629 6137; Fax: 020-7629 6137;
Secretary, Mrs M. Gibb

ROYAL SOCIETY OF PAINTER-PRINTMAKERS (1880),
Bankside Gallery, 48 Hopton Street, London SE1 9JH.
Tel: 020-7928 7521; Fax: 020-7928 2820.
President, Prof. D. Carpanini

ROYAL SOCIETY OF PORTRAIT PAINTERS (1891),
17 Carlton House Terrace, London SW1Y 5BD.
Tel: 020-7930 6844; Fax: 020-7839 7830;
Web: wwwbanksidegallery.com. *Secretary*, D. Cobley

ROYAL SOCIETY OF ST GEORGE (1894), 127 Sandgate
Road, Folkstone, Kent CT20 2BH. Tel: 01303-241795;
Fax: 01303-211710;
Web: www.royalsocietyofstgeorge.com.
Chairman, Vice-Adm. Sir James Weatherall, KCVO,
KBE

ROYAL SOCIETY OF TROPICAL MEDICINE AND
HYGIENE (1907), Manson House, 26 Portland Place,
London W1B 1EY. Tel: 020-7580 2127; Fax: 020-7436
1389; Web: www.rstmh.org.
Hon. Secretary, Prof. R. D. Ward

THE ROYAL STAR AND GARTER HOME FOR
DISABLED EX-SERVICE MEN AND WOMEN (1916),
Richmond Hill, Richmond, Surrey TW10 6RR.
Tel: 020-8940 3314; Fax: 020-8940 1953;
Web: www.starandgarter.org.
Chief Executive, Lynn McDougall

ROYAL THEATRICAL FUND (1839), 11 Garrick Street,
London WC2E 9AR. Tel: 020-7836 3322;
Fax: 020-7379 8273; Web: www.trtf.com.
Secretary, Mrs R. M. Foster

ROYAL TOWN PLANNING INSTITUTE, 41 Botolph
Lane, London EC3R 8DL. Tel: 020-7929 9494;
Fax: 020-7929 9490; Web: www.rtpi.org.uk.
Secretary-General, R. Upton

ROYAL ULSTER AGRICULTURAL SOCIETY, The King's
Hall, Balmoral, Belfast BT9 6GW. Tel: 028-9066 5225;
Fax: 028-9066 1264; Web: www.balmoralshow.co.uk.
Chief Executive, W. H. Yarr, OBE

ROYAL UNITED KINGDOM BENEFICENT
ASSOCIATION (1863), 6 Avonmore Road, London
W14 8RL. Tel: 020-7605 4200; Fax: 020-7605 4201;
Web: www.rukba.org.uk.
Chief Executive, Jonathan Powell

ROYAL UNITED SERVICES INSTITUTE FOR DEFENCE
STUDIES (1831), Whitehall, London SW1A 2ET.
Tel: 020-7930 5854; Fax: 020-7321 0943;
Web: www.rusi.org.
Director, Rear-Adm. R. Cobbold, CB

ROYAL WATERCOLOUR SOCIETY (1804), Bankside
Gallery, 48 Hopton Street, London SE1 9JH.
Tel: 020-7928 7521; Fax: 020-7928 2820;
Web: www.banksidegallery.com.
President, F. Bowyer

ROYAL ZOOLOGICAL SOCIETY OF SCOTLAND (1909),
Scottish National Zoological Park, Edinburgh Zoo,
134 Corstorphine Road, Edinburgh EH12 6TS.
Tel: 0131-334 9171; Fax: 0131-316 4050;
Web: www.edinburghzoo.org.uk.
Interim Chief Executive, Henry Elliott

RURAL WALES, CAMPAIGN FOR THE PROTECTION OF
(1928), Ty Gwyn, 31 High Street, Welshpool, Powys
SY21 7YD. Tel: 01938-552525; Fax: 01938-552741;
Web: www.cprw.org.uk. *Director*, M. Williams

SALMON AND TROUT ASSOCIATION (1903),
Fishmongers' Hall, London Bridge, London EC4R 9EL.
Tel: 020-7283 5838; Fax: 020-7626 5137;
Web: www.salmon-trout.org. *Director*, P. R. J. Knight

SALTIRE SOCIETY (1936), 9 Fountain Close, 22 High
Street, Edinburgh EH1 1TF. Tel: 0131-556 1836;
Fax: 0131-557 1675;
Web: www.saltire-society.demon.co.uk.
Administrator, Mrs K. Munro

SAMARITANS, THE (1953), The Upper Mill, Kingston
Road, Ewell, Surrey KT17 2AF. Tel: 020-8394 8300;
Fax: 020-8394 8301; Web: www.samaritans.org.uk.
Chief Executive, S. Armson

SANE (1986), 1st Floor, Cityside House, 40 Adler
Street, London E1 1EE. Tel: 020-7375 1002.
Helpline: 0845-767 8000; Fax: 020-7375 2162;
Web: www.sane.org.uk.
Chief Executive, Ms M. Wallace, MBE

SAVE BRITAIN'S HERITAGE (1975), 70 Cowcross Street,
London EC1M 6EJ. Tel: 020-7253 3500;
Fax: 020-7253 3400;
Web: www.savebritainsheritage.org.
President, M. Binney, OBE

SAVE THE CHILDREN UK (1919), 17 Grove Lane,
London SE5 8RD. Tel: 020-7703 5400;
Fax: 020-7703 2278;
Web: www.savethechildren.org.uk.
Director General, M. Aaronson

SCHOOL LIBRARY ASSOCIATION (1937), Unit 2,
Lotmead Business Village, Lotmead Farm,
Wanborough, nr Swindon SN4 0UY.
Tel: 01793-791787; Fax: 01793-791786;
Web: www.sla.org.uk.
Chief Executive, Ms K. Lemaire

SCHOOLMASTERS AND SCHOOLMISTRESSES, SOCIETY
OF (1798), The King's School, Canterbury, Kent CT1

2ES. Tel: 01227-595546; Fax: 01227-595589.
Hon. Secretary, Dr R. B. Mallion

SCHOOLMISTRESSES AND GOVERNESSES BENEVOLENT
INSTITUTION (1848), Queen Mary House, Manor
Park Road, Chislehurst, Kent BR7 5PY.
Tel: 020-8468 7997. *Director*, L. I. Baggott

SCIENCE EDUCATION, ASSOCIATION FOR (1901),
College Lane, Hatfield, Herts AL10 9AA.
Tel: 01707-283000; Fax: 01707-266532;
Web: www.ase.org.uk. *Chief Executive*, Dr D. Bell

SCIENCE, BRITISH ASSOCIATION FOR THE
ADVANCEMENT OF (1831), 23 Savile Row, London
W1S 2EZ. Tel: 020-7973 3500; Fax: 020-7973 3063;
Web: www.the-ba.net. *Chief Executive*, Dr P. Briggs

SCOPE (1952), 6 Market Road, London N7 9PW.
Tel: 0808-800 3333; Fax: 01908-321051;
Web: www.scope.org.uk/.
Chief Executive, R. P. Brewster

SCOTTISH CHIEFS, STANDING COUNCIL OF, Hope
Chambers, 52 Leith Walk, Edinburgh EH6 5HW.
Tel: 0131-554 6321; Fax: 0131-553 5319.
General Secretary, George Way of Plean

SCOTTISH NATIONAL WAR MEMORIAL, The Castle,
Edinburgh EH1 2YT. Tel: 0131-226 7393;
Fax: 0131-225 8920; Web: www.snwm.org.
Secretary to the Trustees, Lt.-Col. I. Shepherd

SCOUT ASSOCIATION, THE (1907), Gilwell Park,
Chingford, London E4 7QW. Tel: 020-8443 7100;
Fax: 020-8443 7103; Web: www.scoutbase.org.uk/.
Chief Executive, D. M. Twine;

SCRIBES AND ILLUMINATORS, SOCIETY OF (1921), 6
Queen Square, London WC1N 3AT. Tel: 01524-251534;
Fax: 01524-251534; Web: www.calligraphyonline.org.
Hon. Secretary, Mrs G. Hazeldine

SCRIPTURE UNION (1867), 207–209 Queensway,
Bletchley, Milton Keynes MK2 2EB. Tel: 01908-856000;
Fax: 01908-856111; Web: www.scriptureunion.org.uk.
Chief Executive, Keith Civval

SEA CADET ASSOCIATION, THE, 202 Lambeth Road,
London SE1 7JF. Tel: 020-7928 8978; Fax: 020-7928
8914; Web: www.sea-cadets.org.
Chief Executive, Cdre. R. M. Parker, RN

SECRETARIES AND ADMINISTRATORS, INSTITUTE OF
CHARTERED (1891), 16 Park Crescent, London W1B
1AH. Tel: 020-7580 4741; Fax: 020-7323 1132;
Web: www.icsa.org.uk.
Chief Executive, M. J. Ainsworth

SECULAR SOCIETY, NATIONAL (1866), 25 Red Lion
Square, London WC1R 4RL. Tel: 020-7404 3126;
Fax: 020-7404 3126; Web: www.secularism.org.uk.
Executive Director, K. P. Wood

SEEABILITY (1799), SeeAbility House, Hook Road,
Epsom, Surrey KT19 8SQ. Tel: 01372-755000;
Fax: 01372-755001. *Chief Executive*, R. M. Perkins

SELDEN SOCIETY (1887), Faculty of Laws, Queen Mary
and Westfield College, Mile End Road, London E1
4NS. Tel: 020-7882 5136; Fax: 020-8981 8733;
Web: www.selden-society.qmw.ac.uk.
Secretary, V. Tunkel

SENSE (THE NATIONAL DEAFBLIND AND RUBELLA ASSOCIATION), 11–13 Clifton Terrace, London N4 3SR. Tel: 020-7272 7774; Fax: 020-7272 6012; Web: www.sense.org.uk. *Chief Executive*, A. Best

SHAFTESBURY HOMES AND ARETHUSA (1843), The Chapel, Royal Victoria Patriotic Building, Trinity Road, London SW18 3SX. Tel: 020-8875 1555; Fax: 020-8875 1954. *Chief Executive*, Ms A. Chesney

SHAFTESBURY SOCIETY, THE (1844), 16 Kingston Road, London SW19 1JZ. Tel: 020-8239 5555; Fax: 020-8239 5580; Web: www.shaftesburysoc.org.uk. *Chief Executive*, Ms F. Beckett

SHELLFISH ASSOCIATION OF GREAT BRITAIN (1903), Fishmongers' Hall, London Bridge, London EC4R 9EL. Tel: 020-7283 8305; Fax: 020-7929 1389; Web: www.shellfish.org.uk. *Director*, Dr P. Hunt

SHELTER (NATIONAL CAMPAIGN FOR HOMELESS PEOPLE), 88 Old Street, London EC1V 9HU. Tel: 020-7505 2000. Shelterline: 0808-800 4444; Fax: 020-8505 2169; Web: www.shelter.org.uk. *Director*, C. Holmes, CBE

SHERLOCK HOLMES SOCIETY OF LONDON (1934), 13 Crofton Avenue, Orpington, Kent BR6 8DU. Tel: 01689-811314; Web: www.sherlock-holmes.org.uk. *Membership Secretary*, R. J. Ellis

SHIPBROKERS, INSTITUTE OF CHARTERED, 3 St Helen's Place, London EC3A 6EJ. Tel: 020-7628 5559; Fax: 020-7628 5445; Web: www.ics.org.uk. *Director-General*, D. A. Phillips

SHIRE HORSE SOCIETY (1878), East of England Showground, Peterborough PE2 6XE. Tel: 01733-234451; Fax: 01733-370038; Web: www.shire-horse.org.uk. *Secretary*, A. Mercer

SHRIEVALTY ASSOCIATION, 20-21 Took's Court, London EC4A 1LB. Tel: 020-7025 2599; Fax: 020-7025 2551. *Secretary*, Mrs C. L. Sandbrook

SHROPSHIRE ARCHAEOLOGICAL AND HISTORICAL SOCIETY (1877), Westcott Farm, Pontesbury, Shrewsbury SY5 0SQ. Tel: 01743-790531; Web: www.shropshirearchaeology.com. *Chairman*, J. B. Lawson

SIGHT SAVERS INTERNATIONAL (ROYAL COMMONWEALTH SOCIETY FOR THE BLIND) (1950), Grosvenor Hall, Bolnore Road, Haywards Heath, W. Sussex RH16 4BX. Tel: 01444-446600; Fax: 01444-446688; Web: www.sightsavers.org.uk. *Executive Director*, R. Porter

SIMPLIFIED SPELLING SOCIETY (1908), 4 Valette Way, Wellesbourne, Warwick CV35 9TB. Web: www.spellingsociety.org. *Membership Secretary*, John Gledhill

SIR OSWALD STOLL FOUNDATION (1917), 446 Fulham Road, London SW6 1DT. Tel: 020-7385 2110; Fax: 020-7381 7485; Web: www.oswaldstoll.org.uk. *Chief Executive*, R. C. Brunwin

SOCIAL WORKERS, BRITISH ASSOCIATION OF (1970), 16 Kent Street, Birmingham B5 6RD. Tel: 0121-622 3911; Fax: 0121-622 4860; Web: www.basw.co.uk. *Director*, I. Johnston

SOCIÉTÉ JERSIAISE, Archaeological Section (1873), 7 Pier Road, St Helier, Jersey JE2 4XW,

SOIL ASSOCIATION (1946), Bristol House, 40–56 Victoria Street, Bristol BS1 6BY. Tel: 0117-929 0661; Fax: 0117-925 2504; Web: www.soilassociation.org. *Director*, P. Holden

SOLICITORS IN THE SUPREME COURT OF SCOTLAND, SOCIETY OF (1784), SSC Library, Parliament House, 11 Parliament Square, Edinburgh EH1 1RF. Tel: 0131-225 6268; Fax: 0131-225 2270; Web: www.ssclibrary.co.uk. *Secretary*, I. L. S. Balfour

SOMERSET ARCHAEOLOGICAL AND NATURAL HISTORY SOCIETY (1849), Taunton Castle, Taunton, Somerset TA1 4AA. Tel: 01823-272429; Fax: 01823-272429. *Hon. Secretary*, Alex Maxwell-Findlater

SOUTH AMERICAN MISSION SOCIETY (1844), Allen Gardiner Cottage, Pembury Road, Tunbridge Wells, Kent TN2 3QU. Tel: 01892-538647; Fax: 01892-525797; Web: www.samsgb.org. *General Secretary*, Rt. Revd D. R. J. Evans

SOUTH WALES INSTITUTE OF ENGINEERS, THE, 2nd Floor, Empire House, Mount Stuart Square, Cardiff CF10 5FN. Tel: 029-2048 1726; Fax: 029-2045 1953; Web: www.celtic.co.uk/swie. *Hon. Secretary*, T. H. Rhodes

SPEAKERS CLUBS, ASSOCIATION OF (1971), Beanlands Chase, 20 Rivermead Drive, Garstang, Preston, Lancashire PR3 1JJ. Tel: 01995-602560; Fax: 01995-602560; Web: www.the-asc.org.uk. *National Secretary*, Mrs D. M. Dickinson

SPINA BIFIDA AND HYDROCEPHALUS, ASSOCIATION FOR (1966), ASBAH House, 42 Park Road, Peterborough PE1 2UQ. Tel: 01733-555988; Fax: 01733-555985; Web: www.asbah.demon.co.uk. *Executive Director*, A. Russell

SPORT AND THE ARTS, FOUNDATION FOR (1991), PO Box 20, Liverpool L13 1HB. Tel: 0151-259 5505; Fax: 0151-230 0664. *Secretary*, G. Endicott, OBE

SPORT HORSE BREEDING OF GREAT BRITAIN (1886), 96 High Street, Edenbridge, Kent TN8 5AR. Tel: 01732-866277; Fax: 01732-867464; Web: www.sporthorsegb.co.uk. *General Secretary*, Mrs K. P. Hall

SPORTS MEDICINE, INSTITUTE OF (1965), Department of Surgery, Royal Free and University College Medical School, 67–73 Riding House Street, London W1W 7 EJ. Tel: 020-7813 2832; Fax: 020-7813 2832. *Hon. Secretary*, Dr W. T. Orton

SPURGEON'S CHILD CARE (1867), 74 Wellingborough Road, Rushden, Northants NN10 9TY. Tel: 01933-412412; Fax: 01933-412010; Web: www.spurgeonschildcare.org. *Chief Executive*, D. C. Culwick

SSAFA FORCES HELP (1885), 19 Queen Elizabeth Street, London SE1 2LP. Tel: 020-7403 8783; Fax: 020-7403 8815; Web: www.ssafa.org.uk. *Controller*, Maj.-Gen. P. Sheppard, CB, CBE

ST ALBANS AND HERTFORDSHIRE ARCHITECTURAL AND ARCHAEOLOGICAL SOCIETY (1845), 24 Rose Walk, St Albans, Herts AL4 9AF. Tel: 01727-853204. *Hon. Secretary*, B. E. Moody

St Deiniol's Residential Library (1894), Hawarden, Deeside, Flintshire CH5 3DF. Tel: 01244-532350; Fax: 01244-520643; Web: www.stdeiniolschester.ac.uk. *Warden and Chief Librarian*, Revd P. B. Francis

St Dunstan's (Caring for Blind Ex-Service Men and Women) (1915), 12-14 Harcourt Street, London W1H 4HD. Tel: 020-7723 5021; Fax: 020-7262 6199; Web: www.st-dunstans.org.uk. *Chief Executive*, Robert Leader

Stewart Society, The (1899), 53 George Street, Edinburgh EH2 2HT. Tel: 0131-220 4512; Fax: 0131-220 4512; Web: www.stewartsociety.org. *Secretary*, Mrs C. Larkins, MVO

Stoke-on-Trent, Museum Archaeological Society, City of (1959), The Potteries Museum and Art Gallery, Hanley, Stoke-on-Trent ST1 3DW. Tel: 01782-232323. *Chairman*, E. E. Royle, MBE

Strategic Planning Society, The (1967), 17 Portland Place, London W1B 1PU. Tel: 020-7636 7737; Fax: 020-7323 1692; Web: www.sps.org.uk

Strategic Studies, The International Institute for (1958), Arundel House, 13–15 Arundel Street, Temple Place, London WC2R 3DX. Tel: 020-7379 7676; Fax: 020-7836 3108; Web: www.iiss.org. *Director*, Dr J. Chipman

Structural Engineers, Institution of (1908), 11 Upper Belgrave Street, London SW1X 8BH. Tel: 020-7235 4535; Fax: 020-7235 4294; Web: www.istructe.org.uk. *Chief Executive*, Dr K. J. Eaton

Students, National Union of (1922), Nelson Mandela House, 461 Holloway Road, London N7 6LJ. Tel: 020-7272 8900; Fax: 020-7263 5713; Web: www.nusonline.co.uk

Suffolk Horse Society, The Market Hill, Woodbridge, Suffolk IP12 4LU. Tel: 01394-380643; Fax: 01394-610058; Web: www.suffolkhorsesociety.org.uk. *Secretary*, Mrs A. V. Hillier

Suffolk Institute of Archaeology and History (1848), Roots, Church Lane, Playford, Ipswich IP6 9DS. Web: www.suffolkarch.org.uk. *Hon. Secretary*, B. J. Seward

Sunderland Antiquarian Society (1900), Simonburn, 7 Crow Lane, Mid Herrington, Sunderland SR3 3TF. Tel: 0191-522 0517. *President*, D. W. Smith

Surrey Archaeological Society (1854), Castle Arch, Guildford, Surrey GU1 3SX. Tel: 01483-532454; Fax: 01483-532454. *Hon. Secretary*, Mrs R. Hunter

Survival International (1969), 6 Charterhouse Buildings, London EC1M 7ET. Tel: 020-7687 8700; Fax: 020-7687 8701; Web: www.survival-international.org. *Director*, S. Corry

Sussex Archaeological Society (1846), Bull House, 92 High Street, Lewes, E. Sussex BN7 1XH. Tel: 01273-486260; Fax: 01273-486990; Web: www.sussexpast.co.uk. *Chief Executive*, J. Manley

Suzy Lamplugh Trust (1986), 14 East Sheen Avenue, London SW14 8AS. Tel: 020-8392 1839; Fax: 020-8392 1830; Web: www.suzylamplugh.org. *Hon.Trust Director*, David Lamplugh, OBE

Swedenborg Society (1810), 20–21 Bloomsbury Way, London WC1A 2TH. Tel: 020-7405 7986; Fax: 020-7831 5848; Web: www.swedenborg.org.uk. *Secretary*, Richard Lines

Tavistock Institute, The (1947), 30 Tabernacle Street, London EC2A 4UE. Tel: 020-7417 0407; Fax: 020-7417 0566; Web: www.tavistockinstitute.org. *Principal*, John Kelleher

Taxation, Chartered Institute of (1930), 12 Upper Belgrave Street, London SW1X 8BB. Tel: 020-7235 9381; Fax: 020-7235 2562. *Secretary-General*, R. A. Dommett

Teachers of Mathematics, Association of (1952), 7 Shaftesbury Street, Derby DE23 8YB. Tel: 01332-346599; Fax: 01332-204357; Web: www.atm.org.uk. *Hon. Secretary*, S. Welford

Teachers, College of, Third Floor, 33 John Street, London WC1N 2AT. Tel: 01992-812727; Fax: 01992-814690; Web: www.collegeofteachers.ac.uk. *Chief Executive Officer*, R. Page

Telecommunications Users' Association (1965), Woodgate Studios, 2–8 Games Road, Cockfosters, Barnet, Herts EN4 9HN. Tel: 020-8449 8844; Fax: 020-8447 4901; Web: www.tua.co.uk. *Executive Chairman*, W. E. Mieran

Temperance League, British National (1834), Westbrook Court, 2 Sharrow Vale Road, Sheffield S11 8YZ. Tel: 0114-267 9976; Fax: 0114-267 9976; Web: www.bntl.org. *Manager*, Mrs B. Briggs

Terrence Higgins Trust, 52–54 Grays Inn Road, London WC1X 8JU. Tel: 020-7831 0330; Fax: 020-7242 0121; Web: www.tht.org.uk. *Chief Executive*, N. Partridge

Textile Institute (1925), 1st Floor, St James's Building, Oxford Street, Manchester M1 6FQ. Tel: 0161-237 1188; Fax: 0161-236 1991; Web: www.texi.org. *Director-General*, T. Hennessey

Theatre Research, Society for (1948), c/o The Theatre Museum, 1E Tavistock Street, London WC2E 7PR; Web: www.str.org.uk. *Joint Hon. Secretaries*, Ms E. Cottis; Ms F. Dann

Theatres Trust (1976), 22 Charing Cross Road, London WC2H 0QL. Tel: 020-7836 8591; Fax: 020-7836 3302; Web: www.theatrestrust.org.uk. *Director*, P. Longman

Theosophical Society in England (1875), 50 Gloucester Place, London W1U 8EA. Tel: 020-7935 9261; Fax: 020-7935 9543; Web: www.theosophical-society.org.uk. *National President*, C. Price

Thoresby Society (1889), Claremont, 23 Clarendon Road, Leeds LS2 9NZ. Tel: 0113-245 7910; Web: www.thoresby.org.uk. *President*, Mr P. S. Morrish

TIN TECHNOLOGY LTD, Kingston Lane, Uxbridge, Middx UB8 3PJ. Tel: 01895-272406; Fax: 01895-251841; Web: www.tintechnology.com. *Director*, D. Bishop

TOURISM COUNCIL, ENGLISH, Thames Tower, Black's Road, London W6 9EL. Tel: 020-8563 3000; Fax: 020-8563 0302; Web: www.englishtourism.org.uk. *Chief Executive*, Ms M. Lynch

TOURIST BOARD, NORTHERN IRELAND, St Anne's Court, 59 North Street, Belfast BT1 1NB. Tel: 028-9023 1221; Fax: 018-9024 0960; Web: www.nitb.com. *Chief Executive*, A. Clarke

TOWNSWOMEN'S GUILDS, Chamber of Commerce House, 75 Harborne Road, Birmingham B15 3DA. Tel: 0121-456 3435; Fax: 0121-452 1890; Web: www.townswomen.org.uk. *National Secretary*, Mrs D. Calvert

TRADE MARK ATTORNEYS, INSTITUTE OF (1934), Canterbury House, 2–6 Sydenham Road, Croydon CR0 9XE. Tel: 020-8686 2052; Fax: 020-8680 5723; Web: www.itma.org.uk. *Secretary*, Mrs M. J. Tyler

TRADING STANDARDS INSTITUTE (1881), 3-5 Hadleigh Business Centre, 351 London Road, Hadleigh, Essex SS7 2BT. Tel: 0870-872 9000; Fax: 0870-872 9025; Web: www.tradingstandards.gov.uk. *Chief Executive*, Ron Gainsford

TRANSLATION AND INTERPRETING, INSTITUTE OF (1986), Exchange House, 494 Midsummer Blv., Milton Keynes MK9 2EA. Tel: 01908-255905; Fax: 01908-255700; Web: www.iti.org.uk. *Chairman*, Dr C. Greensmith

TRANSPORT ADMINISTRATION, INSTITUTE OF (1944), Mill House, 11 Nightingale Road, Horsham, West Sussex RH12 2NN. Tel: 01403-242412; Fax: 01403-242413. *Director*, J. K. Millar

TRAVEL AGENTS, ASSOCIATION OF BRITISH (1950), 68–71 Newman Street, London W1T 3AH. Tel: 020-7637 2444; Fax: 020-7637 0713; Web: www.abtanet.com. *Chief Executive*, I. Reynolds

TREE COUNCIL, THE (1974), 51 Catherine Place, London SW1E 6DY. Tel: 020-7828 9928; Fax: 020-7828 9060; Web: www.treecouncil.org.uk. *Director-General*, Pauline Buchanan Black

TURNER SOCIETY (1975), BCM Box Turner, London WC1N 3XX. Web: www.turnersociety.org.uk. *Chairman*, Eric Shanes

UFAW (1926), The Old School, Brewhouse Hill, Wheathampstead, Herts AL4 8AN. Tel: 01582-831818; Fax: 01582-831414; Web: www.ufaw3.dircon.co.uk. *Scientific Director*, Dr J. K. Kirkwood

UK YOUTH (1911), 2nd Floor, Kirby House, 20–24 Kirby Street, London EC1N 8TS. Tel: 020-7242 4045; Fax: 020-7242 4125; Web: www.ukyouth.org.uk. *Chief Executive*, J. Bateman

ULSTER TEACHERS' UNION (1919), 94 Malone Road, Belfast BT9 5HP. Tel: 028 9066 2216; Fax: 028-9066 3055; Web: www.utu.edu/home.html. *General Secretary*, R. Calvin

UNITED GRAND LODGE OF ENGLAND (1717), Freemasons' Hall, Great Queen Street, London WC2B 5AZ. Tel: 020-7831 9811; Fax: 020-7831 6021; Web: www.grandlodge-england.org. *Grand Master*, HRH The Duke of Kent, KG, GCMG, GCVO

UNITED KINGDOM ALLIANCE (1853), 176 Blackfriars Road, London SE1 8ET. Tel: 020-7928 1538. *General Secretary*, D. Sinclair

UNITED NATIONS ASSOCIATION OF GREAT BRITAIN AND NORTHERN IRELAND, 3 Whitehall Court, London SW1A 2EL. Tel: 020-7930 2931; Fax: 020-7930 5893; Web: www.oneworld.org./una_uk. *Director*, M. C. Harper

UNITED REFORMED CHURCH HISTORY SOCIETY (1972), Westminster College, Madingley Road, Cambridge CB3 0AA. Tel: 01223-741300. *Hon. Secretary*, Revd E. J. Brown

UNIVERSITIES UK, Woburn House, 20 Tavistock Square, London WC1H 9HQ. Tel: 020-7419 4111; Web: www.universitiesuk.ac.uk. *Chief Executive*, Baroness Warwick

URDD GOBAITH CYMRU (1922), Swyddfa'r Urdd, Aberystwyth, Sir Ceredigion SY23 1EY. Tel: 01970-613100; Fax: 01970-626120; Web: www.urdd.org. *Chief Executive*, J. O'Rourke

VEGAN SOCIETY, THE (1944), Donald Watson House, 7 Battle Road, St Leonards-on-Sea, E. Sussex TN37 7AA. Tel: 0845-458 8244; Fax: 01424-717064; Web: www.vegansociety.com. *Chief Executive*, Rick Savage

VEGETARIAN SOCIETY OF THE UNITED KINGDOM LTD (1847), Parkdale, Dunham Road, Altrincham, Cheshire WA14 4QG. Tel: 0161-925 2000; Fax: 0161-926 9182; Web: www.vegsoc.org. *Chief Executive*, Ms T. Fox

VERNACULAR ARCHITECTURE GROUP, THE (1952), 'Ashley', Willows Green, Chelmsford, Essex CM3 1QD. Tel: 01245-361408; Web: www.vag.org.uk. *Hon. Secretary*, Mrs B. A. Watkin

VETERINARY ASSOCIATION, BRITISH (1883), 7 Mansfield Street, London W1G 9NQ. Tel: 020-7636 6541; Fax: 020-7436 2970; Web: www.bva.co.uk and www.vetrecord.co.uk. *Chief Executive*, J. H. Baird

VICTIM SUPPORT (NATIONAL ASSOCIATION OF VICTIMS SUPPORT SCHEMES) (1979), National Office, Cranmer House, 39 Brixton Road, London SW9 6DZ. Tel: 020-7735 9166. Helpline: 0845-3030 900; Fax: 020-7582 5712. *Chief Executive*, Dame Helen Reeves, DBE

VICTIM SUPPORT SCOTLAND (1985), 15–23 Hardwell Close, Edinburgh EH8 9RX. Tel: 0131-668 4486; Fax: 0131-662 5400; Web: www.victimsupportsco.demon.co.uk. *Chief Executive*, David McKenna

VICTORIA CROSS AND GEORGE CROSS ASSOCIATION (1956), Horse Guards, Whitehall, London SW1A 2AX. Tel: 020-7930 3506; Fax: 020-7930 4303. *Secretary*, Mrs D. Grahame, MVO

VICTORIA INSTITUTE, THE (PHILOSOPHICAL SOCIETY OF GREAT BRITAIN) (1865), 41 Marne Avenue, Welling, Kent DA16 2EY. Tel: 020-8303 0465; Fax: 020-8303 0465.
Chairman of Council, T. C. Mitchell

VICTORIAN SOCIETY, THE (1958), 1 Priory Gardens, Bedford Park, London W4 1TT. Tel: 020-8994 1019; Fax: 020-8747 5899; Web: www.victorian-society.org.uk.
Director, Dr Ian Dungavell

VIKING SOCIETY FOR NORTHERN RESEARCH (1892), DEPARTMENT OF SCANDINAVIAN STUDIES), University College, Gower Street, London WC1E 6BT. Tel: 020-7679 7176; Fax: 020-7679 7750; *Hon. Secretaries,* Prof. M. P. Barnes; Dr J. Jesh

VISITSCOTLAND (1969), 23 Ravelston Terrace, Edinburgh EH4 3TP. Tel: 0131-332 2433; Fax: 0131-332 4441. *Chief Executive,* Philip Riddle

VOLUNTARY ORGANISATIONS, SCOTTISH COUNCIL FOR, Mansfield Traquair Centre, 15 Mansfield Place, Edinburgh EH3 6BB. Tel: 0131-556 3882; Fax: 0131-556 0279; Web: www.scvo.org.uk. *Chief Executive,* M. Sime

VSO (VOLUNTARY SERVICE OVERSEAS) (1958), 317 Putney Bridge Road, London SW15 2PN. Tel: 020-8780 7200; Fax: 020-8780 7300; Web: www.vso.org.uk. *Chief Executive,* M. Goldring

WALES TOURIST BOARD (1969), Brunel House, 2 Fitzalan Road, Cardiff CF24 0UY. Tel: 029-2049 9909; Fax: 029-2048 5031; Web: www.visitwales.com. *Chief Executive,* J. Jones

WAR WIDOWS ASSOCIATION OF GREAT BRITAIN (1971), 44 Victory Road, Stubbington, Fareham, Hampshire PO14 2SG. Tel: 01246-590302. *Chairman,* I. K. Evans

WASTES MANAGEMENT, INSTITUTE OF, 9 Saxon Court, St Peter's Gardens, Northampton NN1 1SX. Tel: 01604-620426; Fax: 01604-621339; Web: www.iwm.co.uk. *Chief Executive,* M. J. Philpott

WATER AND ENVIRONMENTAL MANAGEMENT, CHARTERED INSTITUTION OF (1895), 15 John Street, London WC1N 2EB. Tel: 020-7831 3110; Fax: 020-7405 4967; Web: www.ciwem.org.uk. *Executive Director,* N. Reeves

WELLBEING – HEALTH RESEARCH CHARITY FOR WOMEN AND BABIES (1965), 27 Sussex Place, Regent's Park, London NW1 4SP. Tel: 020-7772 6400; Fax: 020-7724 7725; Web: www.wellbeing.org.uk. *Director,* Mrs J. Arnell

WES WORLD-WIDE EDUCATION SERVICE LTD, Canada House, 272 Field End Road, Eastcote, Ruislip, Middx HA4 9NA. Tel: 020-8582 0317; Fax: 020-8429 4838; Web: www.wesworldwide.com. *Director,* Mrs T. Mulder-Reynolds

WESLEY HISTORICAL SOCIETY, 34 Spiceland Road, Northfield, Birmingham B31 1NJ. Tel: 0121-475 4914; *General Secretary,* Dr E. D. Graham

WEST LONDON MISSION (1893), 19 Thayer Street, London W1U 2QJ. Tel: 020-7935 6179; Fax: 020-7487 3965; Web: www.methodist.org.uk/west.london.mission. *Superintendent,* Revd Geoff Cornell

WESTMINSTER FOUNDATION FOR DEMOCRACY (1992), 2nd Floor, 125 Pall Mall, London SW1Y 5EA. Tel: 020-7930 0408; Fax: 020-7930 0449; Web: www.wfd.org.
Chief Officer, Trevor Williams, OBE

WILDFOWL AND WETLANDS TRUST, THE (1947), The New Grounds, Slimbridge, Glos GL2 7BT. Tel: 01453-890333; Fax: 01453-890827; Web: www.wwt.org.uk.
Managing Director, A. E. Richardson

WILDLIFE TRUST, SCOTTISH (1964), Cramond House, Kirk Cramond, Cramond Glebe Road, Edinburgh EH4 6NS. Tel: 0131-312 7765; Fax: 0131-312 8705; Web: www.swt.org.uk. *Chief Executive,* S. Sankey

WILLIAM MORRIS SOCIETY AND KELMSCOTT FELLOWSHIP, Kelmscott House, 26 Upper Mall, London W6 9TA. Tel: 020-8741 3735; Fax: 020-8748 5207; Web: www.morrissociety.org. *Hon. Secretary,* P. Faulkner

WILTSHIRE ARCHAEOLOGICAL AND NATURAL HISTORY SOCIETY (1853), Wiltshire Heritage Museum, 41 Long Street, Devizes, Wilts SN10 1NS. Tel: 01380-727369; Fax: 01380-722150; Web: www.wiltshireheritage.org.uk. *Chief Executive,* Dr G. Chancellor

WINE AND SPIRIT ASSOCIATION, THE (1824), Five Kings House, 1 Queen Street Place, London EC4R 1XX. Tel: 020-7248 5377; Fax: 020-7489 0322; Web: www.wsa.org.uk. *Director,* Q. Rappoport

WINE, INSTITUTE OF MASTERS OF (1955), Five Kings House, 1 Queen Street Place, London EC4R 1QS. Tel: 020-7236 4426; Fax: 020-7213 0499; Web: www.masters-of-wine.org.
Executive Director, Jane Carr

WOMEN ARTISTS, THE SOCIETY OF (1855), 1 Knapp Cottages, Wyke, Gillingham, Dorset SP8 4NQ. Tel: 01747-825718; Fax: 01747-826835; Web: www.society-women-artists.org.uk. *Executive Secretary,* Mrs P. Henderson

WOMEN GRADUATES, BRITISH FEDERATION OF (1907), 4 Mandeville Courtyard, 142 Battersea Park Road, London SW11 4NB. Tel: 020-7498 8037; Fax: 020-7498 5213; *Secretary,* Mrs A. B. Stein

WOMEN OF GREAT BRITAIN, NATIONAL COUNCIL OF, 36 Danbury Street, London N1 8JU. Tel: 020-7354 2395; Fax: 020-7354 9214; Web: www.ncwgb.org.
President, Ms Marie Birkenhead

WOMEN'S ENGINEERING SOCIETY (1919), 2 Queen Anne's Gate Buildings, Dartmouth Street, London SW1H 9BP. Tel: 020-7233 1974; Web: www.wes.org.uk. *Secretary,* Mrs C. MacGillivray

WOMEN'S INSTITUTES OF NORTHERN IRELAND, FEDERATION OF (1932), 209–211 Upper Lisburn Road, Belfast BT10 0LL. Tel: 028-9030 1506/9060-1781; Fax: 020-9043 1127.
General Secretary, Mrs I. A. Sproule

WOMEN'S INSTITUTES, NATIONAL FEDERATION OF, 104 New Kings Road, London SW6 4LY. Tel: 020-7371 9300; Fax: 020-7736 3652; Web: www.womens-insitute.co.uk. *General Secretary,* Mrs J. Osborne

WOMEN'S REGISTER, NATIONAL, 3A Vulcan House, Vulcan Road North, Norwich NR6 6AQ. Tel: 01603-406767; Fax: 01603-407003; Web: www.nwr.og; *Marketing and Membership Co-ordinators*, Mrs M. Dodkins; Mrs E. Thorn

WOMEN'S ROYAL NAVAL SERVICE BENEVOLENT TRUST (1941), 311 Twyford Avenue, Portsmouth PO2 8PE. Tel: 023-9265 5301; Fax: 023-9267 9040. *General Secretary*, Mrs S. Tarabella

WOMEN'S ROYAL VOLUNTARY SERVICE (1938), Milton Hill House, Milton Hill, Abingdon, Oxfordshire OX13 6AF. Tel: 01235-442900; Fax: 01235-861166; *Chairman*, Ms T. Tietjen.

WOMEN'S RURAL INSTITUTES, SCOTTISH (1917), 42 Heriot Row, Edinburgh EH3 6ES. Tel: 0131-225 1724; Fax: 0131-225 8129; Web: www.swri.org.uk. *General Secretary*, Mrs A. Peacock

WOOD PRESERVING AND DAMP-PROOFING ASSOCIATION, BRITISH (1930), 1 Gleneagle House, Vernon Gate, Derby DE1 1UP. Tel: 01332-225100; Fax: 01332-225101; Web: www.bwpda.co.uk. *Director*, Dr C. R. Coggins

WOODLAND TRUST (1972), Autumn Park, Dysart Road, Grantham, Lincs NG31 6LL. Tel: 01476-581111; Fax: 01476-590808; Web: www.woodland-trust.org.uk. *Deputy Chief Executive*, J. Purvis

WOOLHOPE NATURALISTS' FIELD CLUB (1851), Chy an Whyloryon, Wigmore, Leominster, Herefordshire HR6 9UD. Tel: 01568-770356. *Hon. Assistant Secretary*, Mrs M. Tonkin

WORCESTERSHIRE ARCHAEOLOGICAL SOCIETY (1854), 26 Albert Road, Malvern WR14 1HN. Tel: 01299-250416; Fax: 01299-251890; Web: www.worcestershire.gov.uk/museum; *Hon. Secretary*, Mrs J. W. Funlavy

WORLD MISSION, COUNCIL FOR (1977), Ipalo House, 32–34 Great Peter Street, London SW1P 2DB. Tel: 020-7222 4214; Fax: 020-7233 1747; Web: www.cwmission.org.uk. *General Secretary*, Revd Dr D. van der Water

WORLD SHIP SOCIETY (1947), 101 The Everglades, Hempstead, Gillingham, Kent ME7 3PZ. Tel: 01634-372015; Web: www.worldshipsociety.org. *Secretary*, J. Poole

WRITERS TO HM SIGNET, SOCIETY OF (1594), Signet Library, Parliament Square, Edinburgh EH1 1RF. Tel: 0131-220 3426; Fax: 0131-220 4016; Web: www.signetlibrary.co.uk. *General Manager*, M. R. McVittie

YORKSHIRE AGRICULTURAL SOCIETY (1837), Great Yorkshire Showground, Harrogate, N. Yorks HG2 8PW. Tel: 01423-541000; Fax: 01423-541414; Web: www.yas.co.uk

YORKSHIRE SOCIETY, THE (1812), 35 Waldorf Heights, Camberley, Surrey. Tel: 01276-516484. *Secretary*, G. G. Prince, FCIS, TD

YOUNG MEN'S CHRISTIAN ASSOCIATION (YMCA), National Council of YMCAs, 640 Forest Road, London E17 3DZ. Tel: 020-8520 5599; Fax: 020-8509 3190; Web: www.ymca.org.uk. *Acting National Secretary*, Graeme A. Rogie Angus

YOUTH HOSTELS ASSOCIATION (ENGLAND & WALES) (1930), Trevelyan House, Dimple Road, Matlock DE4 3YH. Tel: 01629-592600; Fax: 01629-592702; Web: www.yha.org.uk. *Chief Executive*, R. Clarke

YOUTH HOSTELS ASSOCIATION, SCOTTISH (1931), 7 Glebe Crescent, Stirling FK8 2JA. Tel: 01786-891400; Fax: 01786-891333; Web: www.syha.org.uk. *Chief Executive*, Lorna MacDonald

YOUTHACTION NORTHERN IRELAND (1944), Hampton, Glenmachan Park, Belfast BT4 2PJ. Tel: 028-9076 0067; Fax: 028-9076 8799; Web: www.youthaction.org. *Director*, Ms J. Trimble

YWCA OF ENGLAND AND WALES (1855), Clarendon House, 52 Cornmarket Street, Oxford OX1 3EJ. Tel: 01865-304200; Fax: 01865-204805; Web: www.ywca-gb.org.uk. *Chief Executive*, Ms G. Tishler

ZOOLOGICAL SOCIETY OF LONDON (1826), Regent's Park, London NW1 4RY. Tel: 020-7722 3333; Fax: 020-7586 5743; Web: www.zsl.org. *Director-General*, Dr Michael Dixon

ZOOLOGICAL SOCIETY, NORTH OF ENGLAND (1934), Chester Zoo, Upton by Chester, Chester CH2 1LH. Tel: 01244-380280; Fax: 01244-371273; Web: www.chesterzoo.co.uk. *Zoo Director*, Prof. G. McGregor Reid

The World

World Geographical Statistics

Populations, Currencies and Exchange Rates

Time Zones

European Union

International Organisations

Countries of the World A-Z

World Geographical Statistics

THE EARTH

The shape of the Earth is that of an oblate spheroid or solid of revolution whose meridian sections are ellipses, whilst the sections at right angles are circles.

DIMENSIONS

Equatorial diameter = 12,756.27 km (7,926.38 miles)
Polar diameter = 12,713.50 km (7,899.80 miles)
Equatorial circumference = 40,075.01 km (24,901.46 miles)
Polar circumference = 40,007.86 km (24,859.73 miles)
Mass = 5,974,000,000,000,000,000,000 tonnes
(5.879×10^{21} tons)

The equatorial circumference is divided into 360 degrees of longitude, which is measured in degrees, minutes and seconds east or west of the Greenwich meridian (0°) to 180°, the meridian 180° E. coinciding with 180° W. This dateline was internationally ratified on 13 October 1884.

Distance north and south of the Equator is measured in degrees, minutes and seconds of latitude. The Equator is 0°, the North Pole is 90° N. and the South Pole is 90° S. The Tropics lie at 23° 27′ N. (Tropic of Cancer) and 23° 27′ S. (Tropic of Capricorn). The Arctic Circle lies at 66° 33′ N. and the Antarctic Circle at 66° 33′ S. (NB The Tropics and the Arctic and Antarctic circles are affected by the slow decrease in obliquity of the ecliptic, of about 0.47 arcseconds per year. The effect of this is that the Arctic and Antarctic circles are currently moving towards their respective poles by about 14 metres per annum, while the Tropics move towards the Equator by the same amount.

AREA, ETC

The surface area of the Earth is 510,069,120 km²; (196,938,800 miles²), of which the water area is 70.92 per cent and the land area is 29.08 per cent.

The radial velocity on the Earth's surface at the Equator is 1,669.79 km per hour (1,037.56 m.p.h.). The Earth's mean velocity in its orbit around the Sun is 107,229 km per hour (66,629 m.p.h.). The Earth's mean distance from the Sun is 149,597,870 km (92,955,807 miles).

OCEANS

AREA

	km²	miles²
Pacific	155,557,000	59,270,000
Atlantic	76,762,000	29,638,000
Indian	68,556,000	26,467,000
Southern	20,327,000	7,848,300
Arctic	14,056,000	5,427,000

The division by the Equator of the Pacific into the North and South Pacific and the Atlantic into the North and South Atlantic makes a total of six oceans. In 2000 the International Hydrographic Organisation approved the description of the 20, 327, 000 km² (7,848,300 miles²) of circum-Antarctic waters up to 60° S. as the Southern Ocean – a seventh ocean.

GREATEST OCEAN DEPTHS

Greatest depth	location	metres	feet
Mariana Trench	Pacific	10,924	35,840
Puerto Rico Trench	Atlantic	8,605	28,232
South Sandwich Trench	Southern	7,235	23,737
Java (Sunda) Trench	Indian	7,125	23,376
Molloy Deep	Arctic	5,680	18,400

SEAS

AREA

	km²	miles²
South China	2,974,600	1,148,500
Caribbean	2,515,900	971,400
Mediterranean	2,509,900	969,100
Bering	2,261,000	873,000
Gulf of Mexico	1,507,600	582,100
Okhotsk	1,392,000	537,500
Japan	1,012,900	391,100
Hudson Bay	730,100	281,900
East China	664,600	256,600
Andaman	564,880	218,100
Black Sea	507,900	196,100
Red Sea	453,000	174,900
North Sea	427,100	164,900
Baltic Sea	382,000	147,500
Yellow Sea	294,000	113,500
Persian/Arabian Gulf	230,000	88,800

GREATEST SEA DEPTHS

	Maximum depth metres	feet
Caribbean	8,605	28,232
East China (Ryu Kyu Trench)	7,507	24,629
South China	7,258	23,812
South Sandwich Trench	7,235	23,737
Mediterranean (Ionian Basin)	5,150	16,896
Andaman	4,267	14,000
Bering	3,936	12,913
Gulf of Mexico	3,504	11,496
Okhotsk	3,365	11,040
Japan	3,053	10,016
Red Sea	2,266	7,434
Black Sea	2,212	7,257
North Sea	439	1,440
Hudson Bay	111	364
Baltic Sea	90	295
Persian Gulf	73	240
Yellow Sea	58	190

THE CONTINENTS

There are six geographic continents, although America is often divided politically into North and Central America, and South America, so making seven.

AFRICA is surrounded by sea except for the narrow isthmus of Suez in the north-east, through which was cut

the Suez Canal (1869). Its extreme longitudes are 17° 20' W. at Cape Verde, Senegal, and 51° 24' E. at Ras Hafun, Somalia. The extreme latitudes are 37° 20' N. at Cape Blanc, Tunisia, and 34° 50' S. at Cape Agulhas, South Africa, about 4,400 miles apart. The Equator passes through the middle of the continent.

NORTH AMERICA, including Mexico, is surrounded by ocean except in the south, where the isthmian states of CENTRAL AMERICA link North America with South America. Its extreme longitudes are 168° 5' W. at Cape Prince of Wales, Alaska, and 55° 40' W. at Cape Charles, Newfoundland. The extreme continental latitudes are the tip of the Boothia peninsula, NW Territories, Canada (71° 51' N.) and 14° 22' N. at Ocós in the south of Mexico.

SOUTH AMERICA lies mostly in the southern hemisphere; the Equator passing through the north of the continent. It is surrounded by ocean except where it is joined to Central America in the north by the narrow isthmus through which was cut the Panama Canal (1914). Its extreme longitudes are 34° 47' W. at Cape Branco in Brazil and 81° 20' W. at Punta Pariña, Peru. The extreme continental latitudes are 12° 25' N. at Punta Gallinas, Colombia, and 53° 54' S. at the southernmost tip of the Brunswick peninsula, Chile. Cape Horn, on Cape Island, Chile, lies at 55° 59' S.

ANTARCTICA lies almost entirely within the Antarctic Circle (66° 33' S.) and is the largest of the world's glaciated areas. Ninety-nine per cent of the continent is permanently ice-covered. The ice amounts to some 7.2 million cubic miles and represents more than 90 per cent of the world's fresh water. The environment is too hostile for unsupported human habitation.

ASIA is the largest continent and occupies 29.6 per cent of the world's land surface. The extreme longitudes are 26° 05' E. at Baba Buran, Turkey and 169° 40' W. at Mys Dezhneva (East Cape), Russia, a distance of about 6,000 miles. Its extreme northern latitude is 77° 45' N. at Cape Celjuskin, Russia, and it extends over 5,000 miles south to about 1° 15' N. of the Equator.

AUSTRALIA is the smallest of the continents and lies in the southern hemisphere. It is entirely surrounded by ocean. Its extreme longitudes are 113° 11' E. at Steep Point and 153° 11' E. at Cape Byron. The extreme latitudes are 10° 42' S. at Cape York and 39° S. at South East Point, Tasmania. Australia, together with New Zealand (Australasia), Papua New Guinea and Pacific Islands, comprises Oceania.

EUROPE, including European Russia, is the smallest continent in the northern hemisphere. Its extreme latitudes are 71° 11' N. at North Cape in Norway, and 36° 23' N. at Cape Matapan in southern Greece, a distance of about 2,400 miles. Its breadth from Cabo Carvoeiro in Portugal (9° 34' W.) in the west to the Kara River, north of the Urals (66° 30' E.) in the east is about 3,300 miles. The division between Europe and Asia is generally regarded as the watershed of the Ural Mountains; down the Ural river to Gur'yev, Kazakhstan; across the Caspian Sea to Apsheronskiy Poluostrov, near Baku; along the watershed of the Caucasus Mountains to Anapa and thence across the Black Sea to the Bosporus in Turkey; across the Sea of Marmara to Çanakkale Boğazi (Dardanelles).

| | Area | |
	km²	miles²
Asia	43,998,000	16,988,000
*America	41,918,000	16,185,000
Africa	29,800,000	11,506,000
Antarctica	13,209,000	5,100,000
†Europe	9,699,000	3,745,000
Australia	7,618,493	2,941,526

*North and Central America has an area of 24,255,000 km² (9,365,000 miles²)

†Includes 5,571,000 km² (2,151,000 miles²) of former USSR territory, including the Baltic states, Belarus, Moldova, Ukraine and the part of Russia west of the Ural Mountains and Kazakhstan west of the Ural river.

European Turkey (24,378 km²/9,412 miles²) comprises territory to the west and north of the Bosporus and the Dardanelles

GLACIATED AREAS

It is estimated that 15,915,000 km² (6,145,000 miles²) or 10.73 per cent of the world's land surface is permanently covered with ice.

| | Area | |
	km²	miles²
South Polar regions	13,830,000	5,340,000
North Polar regions (incl. Greenland or Kalaallit Nunaat)	1,965,000	758,500
Alaska-Canada	58,800	22,700
Asia	37,800	14,600
South America	11,900	4,600
Europe	10,700	4,128
New Zealand	1,015	391
Africa	238	92

The largest glacier is the 515 km/320 mile-long Lambert-Fisher Ice Passage, Antarctica.

PENINSULAS

| | Area | |
	km²	miles²
Arabian	3,250,000	1,250,000
Southern Indian	2,072,000	800,000
Alaskan	1,500,000	580,000
Labradorian	1,300,000	500,000
Scandinavian	800,300	309,000
Iberian	584,000	225,500

LARGEST ISLANDS

| Island, and Ocean | Area | |
	km²	miles²
Greenland (Kalaallit Nunaat), Arctic	2,175,500	840,000
New Guinea, Pacific	792,500	306,000
Borneo, Pacific	725,450	280,100
Madagascar, Indian	587,040	226,658
Baffin Island, Arctic	507,451	195,928

Sumatra, Indian	427,350	165,000
Honshu, Pacific	227,413	87,805
*Great Britain, Atlantic	218,077	84,200
Victoria Island, Arctic	217,292	83,897
Ellesmere Island, Arctic	196,236	75,767
Sulawesi (Celebes), Indian	189,036	72,987
South Island, NZ, Pacific	151,213	58,384
Java, Indian	126,650	48,900
North Island, NZ, Pacific	114,487	44,204
Cuba, Atlantic	110,862	42,804
Newfoundland, Atlantic	108,855	42,030
Luzon, Pacific	105,360	40,680
Iceland, Atlantic	102,820	39,700
Mindanao, Pacific	95,247	36,775
Ireland, Atlantic	82,462	31,839

*Mainland only

Península Valdés, Chubut, Argentina	40	131
Lake Eyre, South Australia	16	52

The world's largest exposed depression is the Prikaspiyskaya Nizmennost' covering the hinterland of the northern third of the Caspian Sea, which is itself 28 m (92 ft) below sea-level.

Western Antarctica and Central Greenland largely comprise crypto-depressions under ice burdens. The Antarctic Bentley subglacial trench has a bedrock 2,538 m (8,326 ft) below sea-level. In Greenland (lat. 73° N., long. 39° W.) the bedrock is 365 m (1,197 ft) below sea-level.

Nearly one quarter of the area of The Netherlands lies marginally below sea-level, an area of more than 10,000 km³/3,860 miles².

LARGEST DESERTS

	Area (approx.)	
	km²	miles²
The Sahara, N. Africa	9,000,000	3,500,000
Australian Desert (Great Sandy, Gibson and Great Victoria)	1,350,000	520,000
The Gobi, Mongolia/China	1,300,000	500,000
Arabian Desert	1,000,000	385,000
Kalahari Desert, Botswana/ Namibia/S. Africa	570,000	220,000
Taklimakan Shamo, Mongolia/China	320,000	125,000
*Kara Kum, Turkmenistan	310,000	120,000
Thar Desert, India/Pakistan	260,000	100,000
Somali Desert, Somalia	260,000	100,000
Atacama Desert, Chile	180,000	70,000
Sonoran Desert, USA/Mexico	180,000	70,000
Dasht-e Lut, Iran	52,000	20,000
Mojave Desert, USA	38,850	15,000

*Together with the Kyzyl Kum known as the Turkestan Desert
Antarctica is described as a Polar Desert.

DEEPEST DEPRESSIONS

	Maximum depth below sea level	
	metres	feet
Dead Sea, Jordan/Israel	408	1,338
Lake Assal, Djibouti	156	511
Turfan Depression, Sinkiang, China	153	505
Qattara Depression, Egypt	132	436
Mangyshlak peninsula, Kazakhstan	131	433
Danakil Depression, Ethiopia	116	383
Death Valley, California, USA	86	282
Salton Sink, California, USA	71	235
W. of Ustyurt plateau, Kazakhstan	70	230
Prikaspiyskaya Nizmennost', Russia/Kazakhstan	67	220
Lake Sarykamysh, Uzbekistan/Turkmenistan	45	148
El Faiyûm, Egypt	44	147

LONGEST MOUNTAIN RANGES

Range, and location	Length	
	km	miles
Cordillera de Los Andes, W. South America	7,200	4,500
Rocky Mountains, W. North America	4,800	3,000
Himalaya-Karakoram-Hindu Kush, S. Central Asia	3,800	2,400
Great Dividing Range, E. Australia	3,600	2,250
Trans-Antarctic Mts, Antarctica	3,500	2,200
Atlantic Coast Range, E. Brazil	3,000	1,900
West Sumatran-Javan Range, Indonesia	2,900	1,800
Aleutian Range, Alaska and NW Pacific	2,650	1,650
Tien Shan, S. Central Asia	2,250	1,400
Central New Guinea Range, Irian Jaya/Papua New Guinea	2,000	1,250

HIGHEST MOUNTAINS

The world's 8,000-metre (26,246 ft) mountains (with six subsidiary peaks) are all in the Himalaya-Karakoram-Hindu Kush ranges.

Mountain	Height	
	metres	feet
Mt Everest*	8,850	29,035
K2 (Qogir)†	8,611	28,251
Kangchenjunga	8,597	28,208
Lhotse	8,510	27,923
Makalu I	8,480	27,824
Lhotse Shar (II)	8,400	27,560
Dhaulagiri I	8,171	26,810
Manaslu I (Kutang I)	8,156	26,760
Cho Oyu	8,153	26,750
Nanga Parbat (Diamir)	8,125	26,660
Annapurna I	8,078	26,504
Gasherbrum I (Hidden Peak)	8,068	26,470
Broad Peak I	8,046	26,400
Shisham Pangma (Gosainthan)	8,013	26,287
Gasherbrum II	8,034	26,360
Makalu South-East	8,010	26,280
Broad Peak Central	8,000	26,246

*Named after Sir George Everest (1790–1866), Surveyor-General of India 1830–43, in 1863. He pronounced his name Eve-rest
†Formerly named after Col. H. H. Godwin-Austen (1834–1923)

The culminating summits in the other major mountain ranges are:

Mountain, by range or country	Height metres	feet
Pik Pobedy, Tien Shan	7,439	24,406
Cerro Aconcagua, Cordillera de Los Andes	6,960	22,834
Mt McKinley (*S. Peak*), Alaska Range	6,194	20,320
Kilimanjaro (*Kibo*), Tanzania	5,894	19,340
Hkakabo Razi, Myanmar	5,881	19,296
El'brus, (W. Peak), Caucasus	5,642	18,510
Citlaltépetl (Orizaba), Sierra Madre Oriental, Mexico	5,610	18,405
Vinson Massif, E. Antarctica	4,897	16,066
Puncak Jaya, Central New Guinea Range	4,884	16,023
Mt Blanc, Alps	4,807	15,771
Klyuchevskaya Sopka, Kamchatka peninsula, Russia	4,750	15,584
Ras Dashan, Ethiopian Highlands	4,620	15,158
Zard Kuh, Zagros Mts, Iran	4,547	14,921
Mt Kirkpatrick, Trans Antarctic	4,527	14,855
Mt Belukha, Altai Mts, Russia/Kazakhstan	4,505	14,783
Mt Elbert, Rocky Mountains	4,400	14,433
Mt Rainier, Cascade Range, N. America	4,392	14,410
Nevado de Colima, Sierra Madre Occidental, Mexico	4,268	14,003
Jebel Toubkal, Atlas Mts, N. Africa	4,165	13,665
Kinabalu, Crocker Range, Borneo	4,101	13,455
Kerinci, West Sumatran-Javan Range, Indonesia	3,800	12,467
Jabal an NabiShu'ayb, N. Tihamat, Yemen	3,760	12,336
Mt Cook (Aorangi), Southern Alps, New Zealand	3,754	12,315
Teotepec, Sierra Madre del Sur, Mexico	3,703	12,149
Thaban Ntlenyana, Drakensberg, South Africa	3,482	11,425
Pico de Bandeira, Atlantic Coast Range	2,890	9,482
Shishaldin, Aleutian Range	2,861	9,387
Kosciusko, Great Dividing Range	2,228	7,310

HIGHEST VOLCANOES

Volcano (last major eruption), and location	Height metres	feet
Ojos del Salado (1981), Andes, Argentina/Chile	6,880	22,572
Llullaillaco (1877), Andes, Argentina/Chile	6,723	22,057
San Pedro (1960), Andes, Chile	6,199	20,325
Guallatiri (1960, 1993), Andes, Chile	6,071	19,918
Cotopaxi (1940, 1975), Andes, Ecuador	5,897	19,347
Tupungatito (1986), Andes, Chile	5,640	18,504
Láscar (2000), Andes, Chile	5,591	18,346
Popocatépetl (1999–2001), Mexico	5,465	17,930
Nevado del Ruiz (1985, 1991), Colombia	5,321	17,457
Sangay (1998), Andes, Ecuador	5,188	17,021
Irruputancu (1995), Chile	5,163	16,939
Klyuchevskaya Sopka (1999, 2001), Kamchatka peninsula, Russia	4,835	15,863
Guagua Pichincha (2000), Andes, Ecuador	4,784	15,696
Puracé (1977), Colombia	4,756	15,601

Wrangel (1907), Alaska, USA	4,316	14,163
Shasta (1786), California, USA	4,316	14,162
Galeras (2000), Colombia	4,275	14,028
Mauna Loa (1984, 1987), Hawaii Is.	4,170	13,680
Cameroon (2000), Cameroon	4,095	13,435

OTHER NOTABLE VOLCANOES

	Height metres	feet
Erebus (1998), Ross Island, Antarctica	3,794	12,450
Fuji (1708), Honshu, Japan	3,775	12,388
Santa Maria (2000), Guatemala	3,772	12,375
Semeru (since 1967), Java, Indonesia	3,675	12,060
Nyiragongo (2002), Dem Rep. of Congo	3,474	11,400
Mt Etna (1169, 1669, 1993, 1996-9, 2000–1), Sicily, Italy	3,368	11,053
Raung (2000), Java, Indonesia	3,322	10,932
Sheveluch (1997, 1999, 2000–1), Kamchatka, Russia	3,283	10,771
Llaima (1998), Chile	3,125	10,253
Mt St Helens (1980, 1986, 1991, 1998), Washington State, USA	2,549	8,363
Beerenberg (1985), Jan Mayen Island	2,277	7,470
Pinatubo (1991, 1995), Luzon, Philippines	1,598	5,249
Hekla (1981, 1991, 2000), Iceland	1,491	4,892
Mt Unzen (1792, 1991, 1996, 2000), Kyushu, Japan	1,360	4,462
Vesuvius (AD 79, 1631, 1944), Italy	1,281	4,203
Kilauea (1996, 1997, 2000–1), Hawaii, USA	1,249	4,009
Soufrière (1979, 1997), St Vincent	1,178	3,865
Soufrière Hills (1997–2001), Montserrat	914	3,001
Stromboli (1996, 1998, 2000), Lipari Is., Italy	926	3,038
Krakatau (1883, 1995, 1999, 2001), Sunda Strait, Indonesia	813	2,667
Santoríni (Thíra) (1628 BC, 1950), Aegean Sea, Greece	564	1,850
Tristan da Cunha (1961), South Atlantic	243	800
Surtsey (1963–7), off Iceland	173	568

LARGEST LAKES

The areas of some of the lakes listed are subject to seasonal variation.

	Area km²	miles²	Length km	miles
Caspian Sea, Iran/ Azerbaijan/Russia/ Turkmenistan/ Kazakhstan	371,000	143,000	1,171	728
*Michigan–Huron, USA/Canada	117,610	45,300	1,010	627
Superior, Canada/USA	82,100	31,700	563	350
Victoria, Uganda/ Tanzania/Kenya	69,500	26,828	362	225
Tanganyika, Dem. Rep. of Congo/ Tanzania/Zambia/ Burundi	32,900	12,665	725	450
Great Bear, Canada	31,328	12,096	309	192
‡Aral Sea, Kazakhstan/ Uzbekistan	30,700	11,850	320	200

	Area		Length	
	km²	miles²	km	miles
†Baykal (*Baikal*), Russia	30,500	11,776	620	385
Malawi (Nyasa), Tanzania/				
Malawi/Mozambique	28,900	11,150	580	360
Great Slave, Canada	28,570	11,031	480	298
Erie, Canada/USA	25,670	9,910	388	241
Winnipeg, Canada	24,390	9,417	428	266
Ontario, Canada/USA	19,010	7,340	310	193
Balkhash, Kazakhstan	18,427	7,115	605	376
Ladozhskoye (*Ladoga*),				
Russia	17,700	6,835	193	120

*Lakes Michigan and Huron may be regarded as lobes of the same lake. The Michigan lobe has an area of 57,750 km² (22,300 miles²) and the Huron lobe an area of 59,570 km² (23,000 miles²)
†World's deepest lake (1,940 m/6,365 ft)
‡ Northern part (Little Aral Sea) dammed off in 1997
The most voluminous lakes are the Caspian Sea (saline) with 78,700 km³ (18, 880 miles³) and Baikal (fresh water) with 23,000 km³ (5,518 miles³).

UNITED KINGDOM BY COUNTRY

Lough Neagh,				
Northern Ireland	381.73	147.39	28.90	18.00
Loch Lomond, Scotland	71.12	27.46	36.44	22.64
Windermere, England	14.74	5.69	16.90	10.50
Lake Vyrnwy, Wales				
(artificial)	4.53	1.75	7.56	4.70
Llyn Tegid (*Bala*), Wales				
(natural)	4.38	1.69	5.80	3.65

LONGEST RIVERS

River, source and outflow	Length	
	km	miles
Nile (*Bahr-el-Nil*), R. Luvironza,		
Burundi – E. Mediterranean Sea	6,725	4,180
Amazon (*Amazonas*), Lago Villafro,		
Peru – S. Atlantic Ocean	6,448	4,007
Yangtze-Kiang (*Chang Jiang*),		
Kunlun Mts, W. China – Yellow Sea	6,380	3,964
Mississippi-Missouri-Red Rock,		
Montana – Gulf of Mexico	5,970	3,710
Yenisey-Angara, W. Mongolia – Kara Sea	5,536	3,440
Huang He (*Yellow River*), Bayan Har		
Shan range, central China – Yellow Sea	5,463	3,395
Ob'-Irtysh, W. Mongolia – Kara Sea	5,410	3,362
Zaïre (*Congo*), R. Lualaba, Dem. Rep.		
of Congo-Zambia – S. Atlantic Ocean	4,665	2,900
Amur-Argun, R. Argun, Khingan Mts,		
N. China – Sea of Okhotsk	4,416	2,744
Lena-Kirenga, R. Kirenga, W. of Lake		
Baykal – Laptev Sea, Arctic Ocean	4,400	2,734
Mekong, Lants'ang, Tibet – South		
China Sea	4,345	2,700
Mackenzie-Peace, Tatlatui Lake,		
British Columbia – Beaufort Sea	4,240	2,635
Paraná-Río de la Plata, R. Paranáiba,		
central Brazil – S. Atlantic Ocean	4,240	2,635
Niger, Loma Mts, Guinea – Gulf of		
Guinea, E. Atlantic Ocean	4,170	2,590
Murray-Darling, SE Queensland – Lake		
Alexandrina, S. Australia	3,717	2,310
Volga, Valdai plateau – Caspian Sea	3,685	2,290

OTHER NOTABLE RIVERS

Rio Grande, USA – Mexican border	3,057	1,900
Ganges-Brahmaputra, R. Matsang,		
SW Tibet – Bay of Bengal	2,900	1,800
Indus, R. Sengge,		
SW Tibet – N. Arabian Sea	2,897	1,800
Danube (*Donau*), Black Forest,		
SW Germany – Black Sea	2,856	1,775
Tigris-Euphrates, R. Murat, E.		
Turkey – Persian Gulf	2,800	1,740
Zambezi, NW Zambia – S. Indian		
Ocean	2,735	1,700
Irrawaddy, R. Mali Hka,		
Myanmar – Andaman Sea	2,151	1,337
Don, SE of Novomoskovsk –		
Sea of Azov	1,969	1,224

BRITISH ISLES

Shannon, Co. Cavan, Rep. of Ireland –		
Atlantic Ocean	386	240
Severn, Powys, Wales – Bristol Channel	354	220
Thames, Gloucestershire, England –		
North Sea	346	215
Tay, Perthshire, Scotland – North Sea	188	117
Clyde, Lanarkshire, Scotland –		
Firth of Clyde	158	98.5
Tweed, Peeblesshire, Scotland – North Sea	155	96.5
Bann (Upper and Lower), Co. Down,		
N. Ireland – Atlantic Ocean	122	76

GREATEST WATERFALLS – BY HEIGHT

Waterfall, river and location	Total drop		Greatest single leap	
	metres	feet	metres	feet
Saltó Angel, Carrao				
Auyán Tepuí, Venezuela	979	3,212	807	2,648
Utigård, Jostedal Glacier,				
Norway	800	2,625	600	1,970
Mongefossen, Monge,				
Norway	774	2,540	–	–
Yosemite, Yosemite Creek,				
USA	739	2,425	435	1,430
*Østre Mardøla Foss,				
Mardals, Norway	655	2,149	296	974
*Tyssestrengene, Tysso,				
Norway	646	2,120	289	948
Tugela, Tugela, Natal,				
S. Africa	613	2,014	410	1,350
Cuquenán, Arabopó,				
Venezuela	610	2,000	–	–
Sutherland, Arthur, NZ	580	1,904	248	815

*Volume much affected by hydroelectric harnessing

BRITISH ISLES, BY COUNTRY

Waterfall, river and location	Total drop	
	metres	feet
Eas a' Chuàl Aluinn,		
Glas Bheinn,		
Sutherland, Scotland	200	658
Powerscourt Falls,		
Dargle, Co. Wicklow,		
Rep. of Ireland	106	350
Pistyll-y-Llyn, Powys/		
Dyfed border, Wales	c.72	c.235 (cascades)

Pistyll Rhyadr, Clwyd/		
Powys border, Wales	71.5	235 (single leap)
Caldron Snout, R. Tees,		
Cumbria/Durham,		
England	61	200 (cascades)

GREATEST WATERFALLS – BY VOLUME

Waterfall, river and location	Mean annual flow	
	m³/sec	galls/sec
Inga (Congo dam site), Dem.		
Rep. of Congo	43,000	9,460,000
Khône, Mekong, Laos	42,500	9,350,000
Boyoma (Stanley), R. Lualaba,		
Dem. Rep. of Congo	c.17,000	c.3,750,000
Guayra (Sete Quedas), Brazil	13,000	2,860,000
Rio Paraná, Argentina/Paraguay	11,900	2,619,000
Niagara (Horseshoe), R. Niagara/		
Lake Erie–Lake Ontario	6,000	1,320,000
Paulo Afonso, R. São Francisco,		
Brazil	2,830	622,500
Urubupunga, Alto Paraná, Brazil	2,745	604,000
Cataratas del Iguazú, R. Iguaçu,		
Brazil/Argentina	1,743	380,000
Patos-Maribando, Rio Grande,		
Brazil	1,500	330,000
Churchill, R. Churchill, Canada	1,132	249,000
Victoria (Mosi-oa-tunya),		
R. Zambezi, Zambia/Zimbabwe	1,087	242,000

TALLEST DAMS

	metres	feet
*Rogun, R. Vakhsh, Tajikistan	335	1,098
Nurek, R. Vakhsh, Tajikistan	300	984
Grande Dixence, Switzerland	285	935
*Longtan, R. Hangshui, China	285	935
Inguri, Georgia	272	892
Borucu, Costa Rica	267	876
Vaiont, Italy	262	859
Manuel M. Torres, Chicoasén,		
Mexico	261	856
Tehri, R. Bhagivathi, India	261	856

*Under construction

The world's most massive dam is the Syncrude Tailings dam in Alberta, Canada, which will have a volume of 540 million cubic metres/706 million cubic yards.

The Three Gorges Chang Jiang (Yangtze) Dam, China, with a crest length of 1,983 m/6,505 ft, is due for completion in 2009 (stage 3).

The Yacyretá-Apipe dam across the River Paraná, Argentina-Paraguay, is being completed to a length of 69,600 m/43.24 miles.

TALLEST INHABITED BUILDINGS

Building and city	Height	
	metres	feet
Petronas Towers I and II, Kuala Lumpur,		
Malaysia (1998)	451.9	1,482
Sears Tower, Chicago[1] (1974, 110 stories)	443	1,454
Jin Mao, Shanghai, China (1998)	420	1,378

Xianmen Fairwell International Centre,		
China (2002)	397	1,302
CITIC Plaza, Guangzhou, China (1996)	391	1,283
Shun Hing Square, Shenzhen, China (1996)	384	1,260
Empire State Building, New York[2] (1931)	381	1,250
Central Plaza, Hong Kong (1992)	373	1,227
Bank of China Tower, Hong Kong (1989)	368	1,209
Emirates Tower One, Dubai (2000)	355	1,165
The Centre, Hong Kong (1998)	350	1,148
Tuntex & Chein-Tai Tower, Taiwan (1998)	347	1,140
Aon Center, Chicago (1973)	346	1,136
Kingdom Centre, Riadh, Saudi Arabia (2001)	345	1,132
John Hancock Center, Chicago (1969	343	1,127
Baurj al Arab Hotel, Dubai (1999)	321	1,053
Baiyoke Tower II, Bangkok, Thailand (1998)	320	1,050

1. With TV antennae, 520 m/1,707 ft
2. With TV tower (added 1950–1), 430.9 m/1,414 ft
Note: The Two World Trade Centre towers, One/North (1972) 110 stories, 415m/1,368ft or 521,m/1,716ft with TV antennae; and Two/South (1973) 110 stories, 415m/1,362ft, were destroyed by two terrorist hijacked aircraft on 11 September 2001.

TALLEST STRUCTURES

Structure and location	Height	
	metres	feet
*Warszawa Radio Mast,		
Konstantynow, Poland (1974)	646	2,120
KVLY (formerly KTHI)-TV Mast,		
Blanchard, North Dakota (guyed) (1963)	629	2,063
Indosat Telkom Tower, Jakarta, Indonesia	558	1,831
CN Tower, Metro Centre, Toronto,		
Canada (1975)	555	1,822
Ostankino Tower, Moscow (1967)	540	1,772

*Collapsed during renovation, August 1991. New structure planned on site at Solkajawski. The USA has 8 other guyed TV towers above 555m (1,822 ft).

LONGEST BRIDGES – BY SPAN

Bridge and location	Length	
	metres	feet
SUSPENSION SPANS		
Akashi-Kaikyo, Shikoku, Japan (1998)	1,990	6,529
Storebaelt East Bridge, Denmark (1998)	1,624	5,328
Humber Estuary, Humberside,		
England (1981)	1,410	4,626
Jiangyin (Yangtze), China (1999)	1,385	4,544
Tsing Ma, Hong Kong, China (1997)	1,377	4,518
Verrazano Narrows, Brooklyn–Staten I,		
USA (1964)	1,298	4,260
Golden Gate, San Francisco Bay,		
USA (1937)	1,280	4,200
Hoga Kusten, Sweden (1997)	1,210	3,970
Chesapeake Bay No.2, Virginia, USA (1999)	1,158	3,800
Mackinac Straits, Michigan, USA (1957)	1,158	3,800
Minami Bisan-Seto, Japan (1988)	1,118	3,668
Bosporus II, Istanbul, Turkey (1992)	1,090	3,576
Bosporus I, Istanbul, Turkey (1973)	1,074	3,524
George Washington, Hudson River,		
New York City, USA (1931)	1,067	3,500
Kurushima III, Japan (1998)	1,030	3,379
Kurushima II, Japan (1998)	1,020	3,346
Ponte 25 de Abril (Tagus), Lisbon,		
Portugal (1966)	1,013	3,323

Firth of Forth (road), nr Edinburgh,
Scotland (1964)   1,006   3,300
Kita Bisan-Seto, Japan (1988)   1,006   3,330
*Severn River, Severn Estuary,
England (1966)   988   3,240

*The main span of the 5.15 km/3.2 mile long Second Severn bridging, opened in 1996, is 456 m/1,496 ft.

CANTILEVER SPANS

Pont de Québec (rail-road), St Lawrence,
Canada (1917)   548.6   1,800
Ravenswood, W. Virginia, USA   525.1   1,723
Firth of Forth (rail), nr Edinburgh, Scotland
(two spans of 1,170ft each) (1890)   521.2   1,710
Minato, Osaka, Japan (1975)   510.0   1,673
Commodore Barry, Chester, Pennsylvania,
USA (1975)   494.3   1,622
Greater New Orleans, Louisiana,
USA (I 1958, II 1988)   480.0   1,575
Howrah (rail-road), Calcutta, India
(1936-43)   457.2   1,500

STEEL ARCH SPANS

New River Gorge, Fayetteville, W. Virginia,
USA (1977)   518.0   1,700
Bayonne (Kill van Kull), Bayonne,
NJ – Staten I., USA (1931)   503.5   1,652
Sydney Harbour, Sydney, Australia (1932)   502.9   1,650

The 'floating' bridging at Evergreen Point, Seattle, Washington State, USA (1963), is 3,839 m/12,596 ft long, of which 2,310 m/7,578 ft floats.

The longest stretch of bridgings of any kind is that carrying the Interstate 55 and Interstate 10 highways at Manchac, Louisiana (1979), on twin concrete trestles over 55.21 km/34.31 miles.

LONGEST VEHICULAR TUNNELS

Tunnel and location	Length km	miles
*Seikan (rail), Tsugaru Channel, Japan (1988)	53.90	33.49
*Channel Tunnel, (rail) Cheriton, Kent – Sangatte, Calais (1994)	49.94	31.03
Moscow metro, Belyaevo – Bittsevsky, Moscow, Russia (1979)	37.90	23.50
Northern line tube, East Finchley – Morden, London (1939)	27.84	17.30
Laerdal – Aurland Road Link (2000)	24.51	15.22
*Oshimizu (rail), Honsh, Japan (1982)	22.17	13.78
Simplon II (rail), Brigue, Switzerland – Iselle, Italy (1922)	19.82	12.31
Simplon I (rail), Brigue, Switzerland – Iselle, Italy (1906)	19.80	12.30
Vereina, Switzerland (1999)	19.06	11.84
*Shin-Kanmon (rail), Kanmon Strait, Japan (1975)	18.68	11.61
Appennino (rail), Vernio, Italy (1934)	18.49	11.49
St Gotthard (road), Göschenen – Airolo, Switzerland (1980, re-opened 2001)	16.91	10.51

*Sub-aqueous

The longest non-vehicular tunnelling in the world is the Delaware Aqueduct in New York State, USA, constructed in 1937–44 to a length of 168.9 km/105 miles. St Gotthard (rail) tunnel (2010) will be 56.9 km/33.6 miles.

BRITAIN – RAIL TUNNELS

	miles	yards
Severn, Bristol – Newport (1873 – 86)	4	484
Totley, Manchester – Sheffield	3	950
Standedge, Manchester – Huddersfield	3	66
Sodbury, Swindon – Bristol	2	924
Strood, Medway, Kent	2	426
Disley, Stockport – Sheffield	2	346
Ffestiniog, Llandudno – Blaenau Ffestiniog	2	338
Bramhope, Leeds – Harrogate	2	241
Cowburn, Manchester – Sheffield	2	182

The longest road tunnel in Britain is the Mersey Road Tunnel (1934), 3.42 km/2 miles 228 yards long. The longest canal tunnel, at Standedge, W. Yorks, is 5.12 km/3 miles 417 yards long; it was completed in 1811, closed in 1944 and reopened in 2001.

LONGEST SHIP CANALS

Canal (opening date)	Length km	miles	Min. depth metres	feet
White Sea-Baltic (formerly Stalin) (1933), of which Canalised river 51.5 km/32 miles	235	146.02	5.0	16.5
*Suez (1869) Links Red and Mediterranean Seas	162	100.60	12.9	42.3
V. I. Lenin Volga-Don (1952) Links Black and Caspian Seas	100	62.20	n/a	n/a
Kiel (or North Sea) (1895) Links North and Baltic Seas	98	60.90	13.7	45.0
*Houston (1940) Links inland city with sea	91	56.70	10.4	34.0
Alphonse XIII (1926) Gives Seville access to sea	85	53.00	7.6	25.0
Panama (1914) Links Pacific Ocean and Caribbean Sea; lake chain, 78.9 km/49 miles dug	82	50.71	12.5	41.0
Manchester Ship (1894) Links city with Irish Channel	64	39.70	8.5	28.0
Welland (1932) Circumvents Niagara Falls and Rapids	43.5	27.00	8.8	29.0
Brussels (Rupel Sea) (1922) Renders Brussels an inland port	32	19.80	6.4	21.0

*Has no locks

The first section of China's Grand Canal, running 1,782 km/1,107 miles from Beijing to Hangzhou, was opened AD 610 and completed in 1283. Today it is limited to 2,000 tonne vessels.

The St Lawrence Seaway comprises the Beauharnois, Welland and Welland Bypass and Seaway 54–59 canals, and allows access to Duluth, Minnesota, USA via the Great Lakes from the Atlantic end of Canada's Gulf of St Lawrence, a distance of 3,769 km/2,342 miles. The St Lawrence Canal, completed in 1959, is 293 km/182 miles long.

Distances from London by Air

This list details the distances in miles from London, Heathrow, to various cities (airports) abroad.

To	Miles
Abidjan	3,197
Abu Dhabi (International)	3,425
Addis Ababa	3,675
Adelaide (International)	10,111
Aden	3,670
Algiers	1,035
'Ammān (Queen Alia)	2,287
Amsterdam (Schiphol)	230
Ankara (Esenboga)	1,770
Athens	1,500
Atlanta	4,198
Auckland	11,404
Baghdād (Saddam)	2,551
Bahrain	3,163
Baku	2,485
Bangkok	5,928
Barbados (Grantley Adams)	4,193
Barcelona (Muntadas)	712
Basel-Mulhouse	447
Beijing (Capital)	5,063
Beirut	2,161
Belfast (Aldergrove)	325
Belgrade	1,056
Berlin (Tegel)	588
Bermuda	3,428
Bern	476
Bogotá	5,262
Bombay (Mumbai)	4,478
Boston	3,255
Brasília	5,452
Bratislava	817
Brisbane (Eagle Farm)	10,273
Brussels	217
Bucharest (Otopeni)	1,307
Budapest (Ferihegy)	923
Buenos Aires	6,915
Cairo (International)	2,194
Calcutta	4,958
Calgary	4,357
Canberra	10,563
Cape Town	6,011
Caracas	4,639
Casablanca (Mohamed V)	1,300
Chicago (O'Hare)	3,941
Cologne	331
Colombo (Katunayake)	5,411
Copenhagen	608
Dakar	2,706
Dallas (Fort Worth)	4,736
Dallas (Lovefield)	4,732
Damascus (International)	2,223
Dar-es-Salaam	4,662
Darwin	8,613
Delhi	4,180
Denver	4,655
Detroit (Metropolitan)	3,754
Dhahran	3,143
Dhaka	4,976
Doha	3,253
Dubai	3,414

Dublin	279
Durban	5,937
Düsseldorf	310
Entebbe	4,033
Frankfurt (Main)	406
Freetown	3,046
Geneva	468
Gibraltar	1,084
Gothenburg (Landvetter)	664
Hamburg (Fuhlsbüttel)	463
Harare	5,156
Havana	4,647
Helsinki (Vantaa)	1,148
Hobart	10,826
Ho Chi Minh City	6,345
Hong Kong	5,990
Honolulu	7,220
Houston (Intercontinental)	4,821
Houston (William P. Hobby)	4,837
Islamabad	3,767
Istanbul (Atatürk)	1,560
Jakarta (Halim Perdanakusuma)	7,295
Jeddah	2,947
Johannesburg	5,634
Kabul	3,558
Karachi	3,935
Kathmandu	4,570
Khartoum	3,071
Kiev (Borispol)	1,357
Kiev (Julyany)	1,337
Kingston, Jamaica	4,668
Kuala Lumpur (Subang)	6,557
Kuwait	2,903
Lagos	3,107
Larnaca	2,036
Lima (Callao)	6,303
Lisbon	972
Lomé	3,129
Los Angeles (International)	5,439
Madras	5,113
Madrid (Barajas)	773
Malta	1,305
Manila (Ninoy Aquino)	6,685
Marseille (Provence)	614
Mauritius	6,075
Melbourne (Essendon)	10,504
Melbourne (Tullamarine)	10,499
Mexico City	5,529
Miami	4,414
Milan (Linate)	609
Minsk	1,176
Montego Bay	4,687
Montevideo	6,841
Montreal (Dorval)	3,241
Moscow (Sheremetievo)	1,557
Munich (Franz Josef Strauss)	584
Muscat	3,621
Nairobi (Jomo Kenyatta)	4,248
Naples	1,011
Nassau	4,333
New York (J. F. Kennedy)	3,440
Nice (Côte d'Azur)	645
Oporto	806

Oslo (Gardermoen)	722
Ottawa	3,321
Palma, Majorca (Son San Juan)	836
Paris (Charles de Gaulle)	215
Paris (Le Bourget)	215
Paris (Orly)	227
Perth, Australia	9,008
Port of Spain	4,404
Prague (Ruzine)	649
Pretoria	5,602
Reykjavík (Domestic)	1,167
Reykjavík (Keflavík)	1,177
Rhodes	1,743
Rio de Janeiro (Galeão)	5,745
Riyadh (King Khaled) International	3,067
Rome (Leonardo da Vinci)	895
St John's, Newfoundland	2,308
St Petersburg	1,314
Salzburg (Mozart)	651
San Francisco	5,351
São Paulo (Guarulhos)	5,892
Sarajevo	1,017
Seoul (Kimpo)	5,507
Shanghai	5,725
Shannon	369
Singapore (Changi)	6,756
Sofia	1,266
Stockholm (Arlanda)	908
Suva	10,119
Sydney (Kingsford Smith)	10,568
Tangier	1,120
Tehran	2,741
Tel Aviv	2,227
Tokyo (Narita)	5,956
Toronto	3,544
Tripoli (International)	1,468
Tunis	1,137
Turin (Caselle)	570
Ulaanbaatar	4,340
Valencia	826
Vancouver	4,707
Venice (Marco Polo)	715
Vienna (Schwechat)	790
Vladivostok	5,298
Warsaw (Okecie)	912
Washington (Dulles)	3,665
Wellington	11,692
Yangon/Rangoon	5,582
Yokohama (Aomori)	5,647
Zagreb	848
Zürich	490

THE ANTARCTIC

The Antarctic is generally defined as the area lying within the Antarctic Convergence, the zone where cold northward-flowing Antarctic sea water sinks below warmer southward-flowing water. This zone is at about latitude 50° S. in the Atlantic Ocean and latitude 55°–62° S. in the Pacific Ocean. The continent itself lies almost entirely within the Antarctic Circle, an area of about 13.66 million sq. km (5.3 million sq. miles), 99.67 per cent of which is permanently ice-covered. The average thickness of the ice is 2,450 m (7,100 ft) but in places exceeds 4,500 m (14,500 ft). Some mountains protrude, the highest being Vinson Massif, 4,897 m (16,067 ft). The lowest point has been recorded as the Bentley Subglacial Trench at –2,540 metres. The ice amounts to some 30 million cubic km (7.2 million cubic miles) and represents more than 90 per cent of the world's fresh water. Much of the sea freezes in winter, forming fast ice which breaks up in summer and drifts north as pack ice.

The most conspicuous physical features of the continent are its high inland plateau (much of it over 3,000 m (10,000 ft)), the Transantarctic Mountains and the mountainous Antarctic Peninsula and off-lying islands which extend northwards towards South America.

CLIMATE

On land, summer temperatures range from just above freezing around the coast to –34° C (about –30° F) on the plateau, and in winter from –20° C (about –4° F) on the coast to –65° C (about –85° F) inland. Over a large area the maxima do not exceed –15° C (+5° F).

Precipitation is scant over the plateau but amounts to 25–76 cm (10–30 in) (water equivalent) along the coast and some scientific stations are permanently buried by snow. Some rain falls over the more northerly areas in summer. Gravity winds on the plateau slopes and cyclonic storms further north can both exceed 160 km/h (100 m.p.h.) and visibility can be reduced to zero in blizzards.

FLORA AND FAUNA

Although a small number of flowering plants, ferns and clubmosses occur on the sub-Antarctic islands, only two (a grass and a pearlwort) extend south of 60° S. Antarctic vegetation is dominated by lichens and mosses, with a few liverworts, algae and fungi. Most of these occur around the coast or on islands.

The only land animals are tiny insects and mites with nematodes, rotifers, and tardigrades in the mosses, but large numbers of seals, penguins and other sea-birds go ashore to breed in the summer. The emperor penguin is the only species which breeds ashore throughout the winter. By contrast, the Antarctic seas abound with life, a wide variety of invertebrates (including krill) and fish providing food for the seals, penguins and other birds, and a residual population of whales.

In 1994 the International Whaling Commission agreed to establish a whale sanctuary around Antarctica in which commercial whaling will be banned for ten years.

POTENTIAL RESOURCES

Minerals may be present in great variety but not in commercially exploitable concentrations in accessible localities. There are indications that off-shore hydrocarbons may be present but mostly below great depths of stormy, ice-infested seas. A 50-year ban on Antarctic mineral exploitation came into effect in January 1998.

Currently, the chief interest is in marine protein, including the shrimp-like krill already fished commercially by Japan and Poland. It is estimated that these could sustain a yield equal to the present total annual world fish catch.

THE ANTARTIC TREATY

The co-operative 12 nations (Argentina, Australia, Belgium, Chile, France, Japan, New Zealand, Norway, South Africa, the Soviet Union, the UK and the USA) pledged themselves to promote scientific and technical co-operation unhampered by politics, and the Antarctic Treaty was signed by the 12 states in 1959. The signatories agreed to establish free use of the Antarctic continent for peaceful scientific purposes; to freeze all territorial claims and disputes in the Antarctic; to ban all military activities in the area; and to prohibit nuclear explosions and disposal of radioactive waste. Since then additional agreements have been reached to promote conservation and regulate tourism, waste disposal and pollution.

The Antarctic Treaty was defined as covering areas south of latitude 60° S., excluding the high seas but including the ice shelves, and came into force in 1961. It has since been signed by a further 31 states, 14 of which are active in the Antarctic and have therefore been accorded consultative status, bringing the number of consultative parties to 26. In 1998 an extension to the treaty came into effect, placing a 50-year ban on mining, oil exploration and mineral extraction in Antarctica. Furthermore, all tourists, explorers and expeditions will now need permission to enter the Antarctic.

TERRITORIAL CLAIMS

Under the provisions of the Antarctic Treaty all territorial claims and disputes were frozen without the acceptance or denial of the claims of the various claimants. The US and Soviet governments also made it clear that although they had not made any specific territorial claims, they did not relinquish the right to make such claims.

Seven states have made claims in the Antarctic: Argentina claims the part of Antarctica between 74° W. and 25° W.; Chile that part between 90° W. and 53° W.; Britain claims the British Antarctic Territory, an area of 1,709,340 sq. km (660,000 sq. miles) between 20° and 80° W. longitude; France claims Terre Adélie, 432,000 sq. km (166,800 sq. miles) between 136° and 142° E.; Australia claims the Australian Antarctic Territory, 6,120,000 sq. km (2,320,000 sq. miles) between 160° and 45° E. longitude excluding Terre Adélie; Norway claims Queen Maud Land between 20° W. and 45° E.; and New Zealand claims the Ross Dependency, 450,000 sq. km (175,000 sq. miles) between 160° E. and 150° W. longitude. The Argentinian, British and Chilean claims overlap; the part of the continent between 90° W. and 150° W. is unclaimed by any state.

SCIENTIFIC RESEARCH

There were 37 permanently occupied stations in 2001–2 operated by the following nations: Argentina (6), Australia (3), Brazil (1), Chile (2), China (2), France (2), Germany (2), India (1), Japan (2), New Zealand (1), Poland (1), Russia (4), South Africa (1), UK (2), Ukraine (1), Uruguay (2), USA (3, including one at the South Pole) and one operated by the environmental organisation Greenpeace.

The staff of these stations and summer field-workers are the only people present on the continent and off-lying islands. There are no indigenous inhabitants.

Countries of the World

WORLD AREA AND POPULATION

The total population of the world in mid-1990 was estimated at 5,292 million, compared with 3.019 million in 1960 and 2.070 million in 1930.

Continent, etc.	Area sq. miles '000	sq. km '000	Estimated population mid-1990
Africa	11,704	30,313	642,000,000
North America[1]	8,311	21,525	276,000,000
Latin America[2]	7,933	20,547	448,000,000
Asia[3]	10,637	27,549	3,113,000,000
Europe[4]	1,915	4,961	498,000,000
Former USSR	8,649	22,402	289,000,000
Oceania[5]	3,286	8,510	26,500,000
TOTAL	52,435	135,807	5,292,000,000

[1] Includes Greenland and Hawaii
[2] Mexico and the remainder of the Americas south of the USA
[3] Includes European Turkey, excludes former USSR
[4] Excludes European Turkey and former USSR
[5] Includes Australia, New Zealand and the islands inhabited by Micronesian, Melanesian and Polynesian peoples.
Source: UN Demographic Yearbook 1990 (pub. 1992)

A United Nations report *The Sex and Age Distribution of the World Populations* puts the world's population in the late 20th and the 21st centuries at the following levels (medium variant data):

1995	5,176.4m	2030	8,670.6m
2000	6,158.0m	2040	9,318.2m
2010	7,032.3m	2050	9,833.2m
2020	7,887.8m		

The population forecast for the years 2000 and 2050 is:

Continent, etc.	Estimated population (million) 2000	2050
Africa	831.596	2,140.844
North America[1]	306.280	388.997
Latin America[2]	523.875	838.527
Asia	3,753.846	5,741.005
Europe	729.803	677.764
Oceania	30,651	46,070
TOTAL	6,158.051	9,833.207

[1] Includes Bermuda, Greenland, and St Pierre and Miquelon
[2] Mexico and the remainder of the Americas south of the USA

AREA AND POPULATION BY CONTINENT

No complete survey of many countries has yet been achieved and consequently accurate area figures are not always available. Similarly, may countries have not recently, or have never, taken a census. The areas of countries given below are derived from estimate figures published by the United Nations or other selected sources. The conversion factors used are:
(i) to convert square miles to square km, multiply by 2.589988
(ii) to convert square km to square miles, multiply by 0.3861022
Population figures for countries are derived from the most recent estimates available. Accurate and up-to-date data for the populations of capital cities are scarce, and definitions of cities' extent differ. The figures given below are the latest estimates available.

Ψ seaport. This symbol is used throughout Countries of the World A-Z

AFRICA

COUNTRY/TERRITORY	AREA Sq. miles	Sq. Km	POPULATION	CAPITAL	POPULATION OF CAPITAL
Algeria	919,595	2,381,741	29,272,344	Ψ Algiers	1,507,241
Angola	481,354	1,246,700	11,569,000	Ψ Luanda	475,328
Benin	43,484	112,622	5,828,000	Ψ Porto Novo	179,138
Botswana	224,607	581,730	1,533,000	Gaborone	286,779
Burkina Faso	105,792	274,000	11,087,000	Ouagadougou	c.1,000,000
Burundi	10,747	27,834	6,194,000	Bujumbura	235,440
Cameroon	183,569	475,442	13,937,000	Yaoundé	653,670
Cape Verde	1,557	4,033	406,000	Ψ Praia	61,644
Central African Republic	240,535	622,984	3,245,000	Bangui	473,817
Chad	495,755	1,284,000	6,702,000	N'Djaména	179,000
Comoros	863	2,235	651,000	Moroni	17,267
Congo, Democratic Republic Of	905,355	2,344,858	48,040,000	Kinshasa	2,664,309
Congo-Brazzaville, Rep. Of	132,047	342,000	2,745,000	Brazzaville	596,200
Côte d'Ivoire	124,504	322,463	14,300,000	Yamoussoukro	126,191
Djibouti	8,958	23,200	634,000	Ψ Djibouti	62,000
Egypt	386,662	1,001,449	69,536,644	Cairo	6,800,000
Equatorial Guinea	10,831	28,051	486,060	Ψ Malabo	30,418
Eritrea	45,406	117,600	4,298,269	Asmara	450,000
Ethiopia	426,373	1,104,300	65,891,874	Addis Ababa	2,495,000
Gabon	103,347	267,668	1,221,175	Ψ Libreville	251,000
Gambia	4,361	11,295	1,411,205	Ψ Banjul	109,986

COUNTRY/TERRITORY	AREA Sq. miles	Sq. Km	POPULATION	CAPITAL	POPULATION OF CAPITAL
Ghana	92,098	238,533	19,894,014	Ψ Accra	1,445,515
Guinea	94,926	245,857	7,613,870	Ψ Conakry	763,000
Guinea–Bissau	13,948	36,125	1,315,822	Ψ Bissau	109,214
Kenya	224,081	580,367	30,765,916	Nairobi	c.2,000,000
Lesotho	11,720	30,355	2,177,062	Maseru	367,000
Liberia	43,000	111,369	3,225,837	Ψ Monrovia	421,053
Libya	679,362	1,759,540	5,240,599	Ψ Tripoli	1,000,000
Madagascar	226,658	587,041	15,982,563	Antananarivo	2,000,000
Malaŵi	45,747	118,484	10,548,250	Lilongwe	505,200
Mali	478,841	1,240,192	11,008,518	Bamako	809,552
Mauritania	395,956	1,025,520	2,747,312	Nouakchott	850,000
Mauritius	788	2,040	1,199,881	Ψ Port Louis	146,499
Mayotte *(Fr.)*	144	372	94,410	Mamoudzou	12,000
Morocco	172,414	446,550	30,645,305	Ψ Rabat	1,220,000
Western Sahara	102,703	266,000	244,943	El-Aaiün	20,010
Mozambique	309,494	801,590	19,371,057	Ψ Maputo	1,039,700
Namibia	318,261	824,292	1,797,677	Windhoek	147,056
Niger	489,191	1,267,000	10,335,156	Niamey	500,000
Nigeria	356,669	923,768	126,635,626	Abuja	378,671
Réunion *(Fr.)*	969	2,510	673,000	St Denis	121,999
Rwanda	10,169	26,338	7,312,756	Kigali	116,227
Saint Helena *(UK)*	47	122	5,157	Ψ Jamestown	884
Ascension *(UK)*	34	88	1,051	Ψ Georgetown	—
Tristan Da Cunha *(UK)*	38	98	284	Ψ Edinburgh of the Seven Seas	—
São Tomé and Príncipe	372	964	165,034	Ψ São Tomé	43,420
Senegal	75,955	196,722	10,284,929	Ψ Dakar	1,641,358
Seychelles	176	455	79,725	Ψ Victoria	24,324
Sierra Leone	27,699	71,740	5,426,618	Ψ Freetown	469,776
Somalia	246,201	637,657	7,488,773	Ψ Mogadishu	230,000
South Africa	471,445	1,221,037	43,686,000	{ Pretoria / Ψ Cape Town / Bloemfontein	1,800,000 / 3,088,028 / 467,400
Sudan	967,500	2,505,813	30,080,373	Khartoum	947,483
Swaziland	6,704	17,364	1,104,343	Mbabane	38,290
Tanzania	341,216	883,749	36,232,074	Dodoma	1,502,344
Togo	21,925	56,785	5,153,088	Ψ Lomé	366,476
Tunisia	63,170	163,610	9,660,000	Ψ Tunis	929,500
Uganda	93,065	241,038	23,985,712	Kampala	750,000
Zambia	290,587	752,618	9,770,199	Lusaka	982,362
Zimbabwe	150,872	390,757	11,365,366	Harare	1,189,103

AMERICA

North America

Canada	3,849,674	9,970,610	30,491,294	Ottawa	1,010,498
Greenland *(Den.)*	840,004	2,175,600	56,000	Ψ Godthåb (Nuuk)	12,483
Mexico	756,066	1,958,201	97,483,412	Mexico City	16,674,160
Saint Pierre and Miquelon *(Fr.)*	93	242	6,316	Ψ St Pierre	5,416
United States of America	3,536,382	9,156,119	281,421,906	Washington DC	4,923,153

Central America and the West Indies

Anguilla *(UK)*	37	96	12,394	The Valley	2,400
Antigua and Barbuda	171	442	70,000	Ψ St John's	22,342
Aruba *(Neth.)*	75	193	87,000	Ψ Oranjestad	25,000
Bahamas	5,358	13,878	289,000	Ψ Nassau	172,196
Barbados	166	430	262,000	Ψ Bridgetown	108,000
Belize	8,763	22,696	230,000	Belmopan	44,087
Bermuda *(UK)*	20	53	60,000	Ψ Hamilton	2,277
Cayman Islands *(UK)*	102	264	40,900	Ψ George Town	20,626
Costa Rica	19,730	51,100	3,943,204	San José	1,220,412
Cuba	42,804	110,861	11,059,000	Ψ Havana	2,184,990
Dominica	290	751	71,200	Ψ Roseau	16,243

Country/Territory	Area Sq. miles	Sq. Km	Population	Capital	Population of Capital
Dominican Republic	18,730	48,511	8,097,000	Ψ Santo Domingo	2,134,779
El Salvador	8,124	21,041	6,237,662	San Salvador	1,200,000
Grenada	133	344	89,227	Ψ St George's	4,788
Guadeloupe *(Fr.)*	658	1,705	437,000	Ψ Basse Terre	29,522
Guatemala	42,042	08,889	12,974,361	Guatemala City	1,675,589
Haïti	10,714	27,750	6,964,549	Ψ Port-au-Prince	884,472
Honduras	43,277	112,088	6,406,052	Tegucigalpa	670,100
Jamaica	4,243	10,990	2,665,636	Ψ Kingston	524,638
Martinique *(Fr.)*	425	1,102	388,000	Ψ Fort de France	133,920
Montserrat *(UK)*	39	102	4,500	Ψ Plymouth	1,478
Netherlands Antilles *(Neth.)*	309	800	207,333	Ψ Willemstad	50,000
Nicaragua	50,193	130,000	4,918,393	Managua	864,201
Panama	29,157	75,517	2,815,644	Ψ Panama City	464,928
Puerto Rico *(USA)*	3,427	8,875	3,817,633	Ψ San Juan	1,222,316
Saint Kitts – Nevis	101	261	38,756	Ψ Basseterre	12,200
Saint Lucia	240	622	158,178	Ψ Castries	51,994
Saint Vincent and The Grenadines	150	388	109,022	Ψ Kingstown	15,466
Trinidad and Tobago	1,981	5,130	1,169,682	Ψ Port of Spain	43,396
Turks and Caicos Islands *(UK)*	166	430	23,000	Ψ Grand Turk	3,691
Virgin Islands, British *(UK)*	58	151	20,000	Ψ Road Town	3,983
Virgin Islands, US *(USA)*	134	347	114,483	Ψ Charlotte Amalie	11,842
South America					
Argentina	1,073,518	2,780,400	35,672,000	Ψ Buenos Aires	11,298,030
Bolivia	424,165	1,098,581	8,140,000	La Paz	739,453
Brazil	3,300,171	8,547,403	159,884,000	Brasília	1,737,813
Chile	292,135	756,626	14,622,000	Santiago	4,640,635
Colombia	439,737	1,138,914	41,539,000	Bogotá	5,398,998
Ecuador	109,484	283,561	13,839,978	Quito	1,153,458
Falkland Islands *(UK)*	4,700	12,173	2,564	Ψ Stanley	1,989
French Guiana *(Fr.)*	34,749	90,000	159,000	Ψ Cayenne	41,164
Guyana	83,000	214,969	697,181	Ψ Georgetown	250,000
Paraguay	157,048	406,752	5,734,139	Asunción	550,060
Peru	496,225	1,285,216	27,483,864	Lima	6,321,173
South Georgia *(UK)*	1,580	4,092	—	—	—
Suriname	63,037	163,265	433,998	Ψ Paramaribo	265,000
Uruguay	67,574	175,016	3,360,105	Ψ Montevideo	1,303,182
Venezuela	352,145	912,050	25,160,000	Caracas	3,435,795

ASIA

	Area Sq. miles	Sq. Km	Population	Capital	Population of Capital
Afghanistan	251,773	652,090	22,132,000	Kabul	1,424,400
Bahrain	268	694	620,000	Ψ Manama	140,401
Bangladesh	55,598	143,998	123,100,000	Dhaka	9,912,908
Bhutan	18,147	47,000	1,862,000	Thimphu	15,000
Brunei Darussalam	2,226	5,765	307,000	Bandar Seri Begawan	49,902
Cambodia	69,898	181,035	11,437,656	Ψ Phnom Penh	832,000
China[1]	3,705,408	9,596,961	1,248,100,000	Beijing	7,362,426
Hong Kong *(China)*	415	1,075	6,724,900	—	—
Macao *(China)*	7	18	440,000	Ψ Macao	241,413
East Timor	5,743	14,874	839,719	Ψ Dili	62,000
India	1,269,213	3,287,263	1,027,015,247	New Delhi	301,297
Indonesia	735,358	1,904,569	228,437,870	Ψ Jakarta	9,160,500
Iran	630,574	1,633,188	66,128,965	Tehran	6,750,043
Iraq	169,235	438,317	23,331,985	Baghdād	3,841,268
Israel[2]	8,130	21,056	6,100,000	Tel Aviv	1,919,700
West Bank and Gaza Strip	2,406	6,231	2,920,454	Gaza City	120,000
Japan	145,880	377,829	126,771,612	Tokyo	11,880,000
Jordan	37,738	97,740	5,153,378	'Ammān	1,270,000
Kazakhstan	1,052,085	2,724,900	15,049,100	Astana	320,000
Korea, Democratic People's Republic	46,540	120,538	21,968,228	Pyongyang	2,741,260
Korea, Republic of	38,327	99,268	47,904,370	Seoul	10,321,000

COUNTRY/TERRITORY	AREA Sq. miles	Sq. Km	POPULATION	CAPITAL	POPULATION OF CAPITAL
Kuwait	6,880	17,818	2,041,961	Ψ Kuwait City	388,663
Kyrgyzstan	77,181	199,900	4,753,003	Bishkek	589,400
Laos	91,429	236,800	5,635,967	Vientiane	555,100
Lebanon	4,015	10,400	3,627,774	Ψ Beirut	1,500,000
Malaysia	127,320	329,758	22,229,040	Kuala Lumpur; Putrajaya	1,297,526
Maldives	115	298	310,764	Ψ Malé	74,069
Mongolia	604,829	1,566,500	2,654,999	Ulaanbaatar	515,100
Myanmar	261,228	676,578	41,994,678	Ψ Yangon (Rangoon)	2,513,023
Nepal	56,827	147,181	25,284,463	Kathmandu	535,000
Oman	82,030	212,457	2,400,000	Ψ Muscat (Masqat)	600,000
Pakistan	307,374	796,095	144,616,639	Islamabad	350,000
Philippines	115,831	300,000	82,841,518	Ψ Manila	8,594,150
Qatar	4,247	11,000	769,152	Ψ Doha	217,294
Saudi Arabia	830,000	2,149,690	22,757,092	Riyadh	3,100,000
Singapore	239	618	4,017,733	—	—
Sri Lanka	25,332	65,610	19,408,635	Ψ Colombo	615,000
Syria	71,498	185,180	16,728,808	Damascus	1,549,000
Taiwan	13,800	35,742	22,350,000	Taipei	2,646,474
Tajikistan	55,251	143,100	6,578,681	Dushanbe	528,600
Thailand	198,115	513,115	61,797,751	Ψ Bangkok	5,882,000
Turkey[3]	314,508	814,578	66,493,970	Ankara	3,258,026
Turkmenistan	188,456	488,100	5,500,000	Ashgabat	407,000
United Arab Emirates	32,278	83,600	2,407,460	Abu Dhabi	450,000
Uzbekistan	172,742	447,400	25,000,000	Tashkent	2,200,000
Vietnam	128,066	331,689	79,939,014	Hanoi	1,073,760
Yemen	203,850	527,968	18,078,035	Sana'a'	926,595

[1] Including Tibet
[2] Including East Jerusalem, the Golan Heights and Israeli citizens on the West Bank
[3] Including Turkey in Europe

EUROPE

Albania	11,099	28,748	3,731,000	Tirana	244,153
Andorra	181	468	65,971	Andorra la Vella	21,189
Armenia	11,506	29,800	3,800,00	Yerevan	1,254,400
Austria	32,378	83,859	8,110,244	Vienna	1,608,656
Azerbaijan	33,436	86,600	8,100,000	Ψ Baku	1,149,000
Belarus	80,155	207,600	10,000,000	Minsk	1,708,308
Belgium	11,787	30,528	10,188,000	Brussels	953,175
Bosnia-Hercegovina	19,767	51,197	3,784,000	Sarajevo	529,021
Bulgaria	42,823	110,912	8,306,000	Sofia	1,192,735
Croatia	21,824	56,538	4,498,000	Zagreb	867,717
Cyprus	3,572	9,251	766,000	Nicosia	193,000
Czech Republic	30,450	78,866	10,304,000	Prague	1,202,552
Denmark	16,639	43,094	5,284,000	Ψ Copenhagen	1,362,264
Færøe Islands	540	1,399	48,000	Ψ Tórshavn	16,218
Estonia	17,413	45,100	1,423,316	Tallinn	415,299
Finland	130,559	338,145	5,175,783	Ψ Helsinki	905,555
France	212,935	551,500	59,551,227	Paris	9,319,367
Georgia	26,911	69,700	4,989,285	Tbilisi	1,268,000
Germany	137,846	357,022	83,029,536	Berlin	3,472,009
Gibraltar (UK)	2.3	6.0	27,649	Ψ Gibraltar	—
Greece	50,949	131,957	10,623,855	Athens	3,072,922
Hungary	35,920	93,032	10,106,017	Budapest	1,896,507
Iceland	39,769	103,000	277,906	Ψ Reykjavík	111,345
Ireland, Republic of	27,132	70,273	3,626,087	Ψ Dublin	952,692
Italy	116,339	301,318	57,523,000	Rome	2,648,843
Latvia	24,942	64,600	2,385,231	Riga	796,732
Liechtenstein	62	160	32,528	Vaduz	5,106
Lithuania	25,174	65,200	3,483,972	Vilnius	542,287
Luxembourg	998	2,586	442,972	Luxembourg	77,400
Macedonia	9,928	25,713	2,046,209	Skopje	429,964
Malta	122	316	382,525	Ψ Valletta	7,048

788 Countries of the World

Country/Territory	Area Sq. miles	Sq. Km	Population	Capital	Population of Capital
Moldova	13,012	33,700	4,335,000	Chişinău	655,940
Monaco	0.4	1	31,842	Monaco	27,063
Netherlands	16,033	41,526	15,981,472	Ψ Amsterdam	1,102,323
Norway[1]	125,050	323,877	4,504,000	Ψ Oslo	499,693
Poland	124,808	323,250	38,633,912	Warsaw	1,700,000
Portugal[2]	35,514	91,982	9,920,760	Ψ Lisbon	2,561,225
Romania	92,043	238,391	22,430,457	Bucharest	2,066,723
Russia[3]	6,592,850	17,075,400	144,200,000	Moscow	8,598,896
San Marino	24	61	26,336	San Marino	4,357
Slovakia	18,923	49,012	5,414,937	Bratislava	452,278
Slovenia	7,821	20,256	1,987,000	Ljubljana	273,000
Spain[4]	195,365	505,992	40,037,995	Madrid	3,084,673
Sweden	173,732	449,964	8,875,053	Ψ Stockholm	1,148,953
Switzerland	15,940	41,284	7,283,274	Bern	321,932
Ukraine	233,090	603,700	48,900,000	Kiev (Kyiv)	2,630,000
United Kingdom[5]	93,784	242,900	59,647,790	Ψ London	7,074,265
England	50,351	130,410	48,903,000	—	
Northern Ireland	5,467	14,160	1,649,000	Ψ Belfast	297,300
Scotland	30,420	78,789	5,137,000	Ψ Edinburgh	448,850
Wales	8,015	20,758	2,917,000	Ψ Cardiff	315,040
Vatican City State	0.2	0.44	890	Vatican City	766
Yugoslavia	39,449	102,173	10,766,290	Belgrade	1,338,856

[1]Excludes Svalbard and Jan Mayen Islands (approx. 24,101 sq. miles (62,422 sq. km) and 3,000 population)
[2]Includes Madeira (314 sq. miles) and the Azores (922 sq. miles)
[3]Includes Russia in Asia
[4]Includes Balearic Islands, Canary Islands, Ceuta and Melilla
[5]Excludes Isle of Man (221 sq. miles (572 sq. km), 69,788 population), and Channel Islands (75 sq. miles (194 sq. km), 142,949 population)

OCEANIA

American Samoa (USA)	77	199	58,000	Ψ Pago Pago	3,519
Australia	2,988,902	7,741,220	19,603,500	Canberra	313,900
Norfolk Island	14	36	1,772	Ψ Kingston	
Fiji	7,056	18,274	844,330	Ψ Suva	141,273
French Polynesia (Fr.)	1,544	4,000	227,000	Ψ Papeete	36,784
Guam (USA)	212	549	145,780	Agana	1,139
Kiribati	280	726	94,149	Tarawa	17,921
Marshall Islands	70	181	70,822	Dalap-Uliga-Darrit	20,000
Micronesia, Federated States Of	271	702	134,597	Palikir	—
Nauru	8	21	12,088	Ψ Nauru	—
New Caledonia (Fr.)	7,172	18,575	193,000	Ψ Noumea	97,581
New Zealand	104,454	270,534	3,864,129	Ψ Wellington	346,500
Cook Islands	91	236	20,000	Rarotonga	9,281
Niue	100	260	2,000	Alofi	—
Ross Dependency[1]	175,000	453,248	—	—	—
Tokelau	5	12	2,000	—	—
Northern Mariana Islands (USA)	179	464	49,000	Saipan	52,706
Palau	177	459	19,092	Koror	10,493
Papua New Guinea	178,704	462,840	5,049,055	Ψ Port Moresby	173,500
Pitcairn Islands (UK)	2	5	54	—	—
Samoa	1,093	2,831	168,000	Ψ Apia	36,000
Solomon Islands	11,157	28,896	480,442	Ψ Honiara	40,000
Tonga	288	747	104,227	Ψ Nuku'alofa	34,000
Tuvalu	10	26	10,991	Ψ Fongafale	2,856
Vanuatu	4,706	12,189	192,910	Ψ Port Vila	26,100
Wallis and Futuna Islands (Fr.)	77	200	15,000	Ψ Mata–Utu	—

[1]Includes permanent ice shelf

Currencies of the World

AND EXCHANGE RATES AGAINST £ STERLING

Country/Territory	Monetary Unit	Average Rate to £1 19 September 2001	Average Rate to £1 30 August 2002
Afghanistan	Afghani (Af) of 100 puls	Af 6945.45	Af 7270.11
Albania	Lek (Lk) of 100 qindraka	Lk 207.486	Lk 214.208
Algeria	Algerian dinar (DA) of 100 centimes	DA 109.808	DA 121.133
American Samoa	Currency is that of the USA	US$ 1.4622	US$ 1.53060
Andorra	Euro (€) of 100 cents	Francs – 10.6435	
		Peseta – 269.976	€ 1.56200
Angola	Readjusted kwanza (Krzl) of 100 lwei	Krzl 34.3712	Krzl 70.6112
Anguilla	East Caribbean dollar (EC$) of 100 cents	EC$ 3.9480	EC$ 4.13250
Antigua and Barbuda	East Caribbean dollar (EC$) of 100 cents	EC$ 3.9480	EC$ 4.13250
Argentina	Peso of 10,000 australes	Pesos 1.4617	Pesos 5.56360
Armenia	Dram of 100 louma	Dram 809.898	Dram 855.577
Aruba	Aruban florin	Florins 2.6174	Florins 2.73970
Ascension Island	Currency is that of St Helena	at parity with £ sterling	
Australia	Australian dollar ($A) of 100 cents	$A 2.9507	$A 2.76750
Norfolk Island	Currency is that of Australia	$A 2.9507	$A 2.76750
Austria	Euro (€) of 100 cents	€ 1.5864/Schilling 21.8284	€ 1.56200
Azerbaijan	Manat of 100 gopik	Manat 6862.10	Manat 7490.51
The Bahamas	Bahamian dollar (B$) of 100 cents	B$ 1.4622	B$ 1.53060
Bahrain	Bahraini dinar (BD) of 1,000 fils	BD 0.5513	BD 0.57710
Bangladesh	Taka (Tk) of 100 poisha	Tk 83.2724	Tk 88.2363
Barbados	Barbados dollar (BD$) of 100 cents	BD$2.9098	BD$3.04580
Belarus	Belarusian rouble of 100 kopeks	BYR 2152.36	BYR 2839.17
Belgium	Euro (€) of 100 cents	€ 1.5864/Francs 63.9924	€ 1.56200
Belize	Belize dollar (BZ$) of 100 cents	BZ$ 2.8952	BZ$ 3.01520
Benin	Franc FCA	Francs 1040.57	Francs 1024.57
Bermuda	Bermuda dollar of 100 cents	$ 1.4622	$ 1.53060
Bhutan	Ngultrum of 100 chetrum (Indian currency is also legal tender)	Ngultrum 70.1417	Ngultrum 74.2011
Bolivia	Boliviano ($b) of 100 centavos	$b 9.8260	$b 11.1570
Bosnia-Hercegovina	Convertible marka	Marka 3.1026	Marka 3.06980
Botswana	Pula (P) of 100 thebe	P 8.5609	P 9.69940
Brazil	Real of 100 centavos	Real 3.9136	Real 4.70570
Brunei	Brunei dollar (B$) of 100 sen (fully interchangeable with Singapore currency)	$ 2.5386	$ 2.67290
Bulgaria	Lev of 100 stotinki	Leva 3.0878	Leva 3.04190
Burkina Faso	Franc CFA	Francs 1040.57	Francs 1024.57
Burundi	Burundi franc of 100 centimes	Francs 1230.44	Francs 1336.61
Cambodia	Riel of 100 sen	Riel 5607.54	Riel 5869.66
Cameroon	Franc CFA	Francs 1040.57	Francs 1024.57
Canada	Canadian dollar (C$) 100 cents	C$ 2.2974	C$ 2.37660
Cape Verde	Escudo Caboverdiano of 100 centavos	Esc 175.099	Esc 183.360
Cayman Islands	Cayman Islands dollar (CI$) of 100 cents	CI$ 1.1990	CI$ 1.25510
Central African Republic	Franc CFA	Francs 1040.57	Francs 1024.57
Chad	Franc CFA	Francs 1040.57	Francs 1024.57
Chile	Chilean peso of 100 centavos	Pesos 1009.65	Pesos 1081.41
China	Renminbi Yuan of 10 jiao or 100 fen	Yuan 12.1024	Yuan 12.6679
Hong Kong	Hong Kong (HK$) of 100 cents	HK$ 11.4051	HK$ 11.9383
Macao	Pataca of 100 avos	Pataca 11.7459	Pataca 12.2949
Colombia	Colombian peso of 100 centavos	Pesos 3419.65	Pesos 4092.61
The Comoros	Comorian franc (KMF) of 100 centimes	Francs 804.423	Francs 777.111
Congo, Rep. of	Franc CFA	Francs 1040.57	Francs 1024.57
Congo, Dem. Rep. of	Congolese franc	CFr 6.57980	CFr 535.692
Costa Rica	Costa Rican colón (₡) of 100 céntimos	₡ 485.845	₡ 558.788

Côte d'Ivoire	Franc CFA	Francs 1040.57	Francs 1024.57
Croatia	Kuna of 100 lipa	Kuna 11.9834	Kuna 11.5007
Cuba	Cuban peso of 100 centavos	Pesos 30.7062	Pesos 32.1416
Cyprus	Cyprus pound (C£) of 100 cents	C£ 0.9085	C£ 0.89520
Czech Republic	Koruna (Kčs) of 100 haléřu	Kčs 54.3953	Kčs 47.9088
Denmark	Danish krone of 100 øre	Kroner 11.8059	Kroner 11.5978
Færøe Islands	Currency is that of Denmark	Kroner 11.8059	Kroner 11.5978
Dijbouti	Dijbouti franc of 100 centimes	Francs 250.767	Francs 252.388
Dominica	East Caribbean dollar (EC$) of 100 cents	EC$ 3.9480	EC$ 4.13250
Dominican Republic	Dominican Republic peso (RD$) of 100 centavos	RD$ 23.8339	RD$ 26.1724
East Timor	Currency is that of the USA	US$ 1.4622	US$ 1.53060
Ecuador	Currency is that of the USA (formerly sucre of 100 centavos)	US$ 1.4622	US$ 1.53060
Egypt	Egyptian pound (£E) of 100 piastres or 1,000 millièmes	£E 6.2144	£E 7.09030
El Salvador	El Salvador colón (₡) of 100 centavos	₡ 12.7972	₡ 13.3877
Equatorial Guinea	Franc CFA	Francs 1040.57	Francs 1024.57
Eritrea	Nakfa	—	—
Estonia	Kroon of 100 sents	Kroons 24.8343	Kroons 24.4405
Ethiopia	Ethiopian birr (EB) of 100 cents	EB 12.2869	EB 12.7036
Falkland Islands	Falkland pound of 100 pence	at parity with £ sterling	
Fiji	Fiji dollar (F$) of 100 cents	F$ 33.3461	F$ 3.29800
Finland	Euro (€) of 100 cents	€ 1.5864/Mk 9.4319	€ 1.56200
France	Euro (€) of 100 cents	€ 1.5864/Francs 10.4057	€ 1.56200
French Guiana	Euro (€) of 100 cents	€ 1.5864/Francs 10.4057	€ 1.56200
French Polynesia	Franc CFP	Francs 191.038	Francs 184.618
Gabon	Franc CFA	Francs 1040.57	Francs 1024.57
The Gambia	Dalasi (D) of 100 butut	D 24.8940	D 30.6493
Georgia	Laria of 100 tetri	Laria 3.0412	Laria 3.33660
Germany	Euro (€) of 100 cents	€ 1.5864/DM 3.1026	€ 1.56200
Ghana	Cedi of 100 pesewas	Cedi 10367.0	Cedi 12761.0
Gibraltar	Gibraltar pound of 100 pence	at parity with £ sterling	
Greece	Euro (€) of 100 cents	€ 1.5864/Drachmae 540.542	€ 1.56200
Greenland	Currency is that of Denmark	Kroner 11.8059	Kroner 11.5978
Grenada	East Caribbean dollar (EC$) of 100 cents	EC$ 3.9480	EC$ 4.13250
Guadeloupe	Euro (€) of 100 cents	€ 1.5864/Francs 10.4057	€ 1.56200
Guam	Currency is that of the USA	US$ 1.4622	US$ 1.53060
Guatemala	Quetzal (Q) of 100 centavos	Q 11.5390	Q 12.0707
Guinea	Guinea franc of 100 centimes	Francs 2865.92	Francs 3025.13
Guinea-Bissau	Franc CFA	Francs 1040.57	Francs 1024.57
Guyana	Guyana dollar (G$) of 100 cents	G$ 263.196	G$ 276.264
Haiti	Gourde of 100 centimes	Gourdes 34.7273	Gourdes 42.8554
Honduras	Lempira of 100 centavos	Lempiras 22.7665	Lempiras 25.1010
Hungary	Forint of 100 fillér	Forints 408.005	Forints 384.038
Iceland	Icelandic króna (Kr) of 100 aurar	Kr 146.220	Kr 133.418
India	Indian rupee (Rs) of 100 paisa	Rs 70.1417	Rs 74.2011
Indonesia	Rupiah (Rp) of 100 sen	Rp 14000.6	Rp 13602.8
Iran	Rial	Rials 2558.85	Rials 2678.46
Iraq	Iraqi dinar (ID) of 1,000 fils	ID 0.4548	ID 0.47600
Ireland, Republic of	Euro (€) of 100 cents	€ 1.5864/IR£1.2494	€ 1.56200
Israel	Shekel of 100 agora	Shekels 6.3767	Shekels 7.13700
Italy	Euro (€) of 100 cents	€ 1.5864/Lire 3071.56	€ 1.56200
Jamaica	Jamaican dollar (J$) of 100 cents	J$ 66.6032	J$ 73.8490
Japan	Yen	Yen 171.699	Yen 180.888
Jordan	Jordanian dinar (JD) of 1,000 fils	JD 1.0393	JD 1.07900
Kazakhstan	Tenge	Tenge 215.989	Tenge 236.738
Kenya	Kenya shilling (Ksh) of 100 cents	Ksh 115.368	Ksh 120.294
Kiribati	Australian dollar ($A) of 100 cents	$A 2.9507	$A 2.76750
Korea, Dem. People's Rep. of	Won of 100 chon	Won 3.2169	Won 3.36720
Korea, Republic of	Won	Won 1896.47	Won 1836.43
Kuwait	Kuwaiti dinar (KD) of 1,000 fils	KD 0.4458	KD 0.46220
Kyrgyzstan	Som	Som 69.7818	Som 70.4058
Laos	Kip (K) of 100 at	K11112.7	K11632.2
Latvia	Lats of 100 santims	Lats 0.9031	Lats 0.92300
Lebanon	Lebanese pound (L£) of of 100 piastres	L£ 2214.14	L£ 2314.57

Lesotho	Loti (M) of 100 lisente	M 12.6772	M 16.1452
Liberia	Liberian dollar (L$) of 100 cents	L$ 1.4622	L$ 1.53060
Libya	Libyan dinar (LD) of 1,000 dirhams	LD 0.9411	LD 1.91470
Liechtenstein	Swiss franc of 100 rappen (or centimes)	Francs 2.3486	Francs 2.29360
Lithuania	Litas of 100 centas	Litas 5.84745	Litas 5.39250
Luxembourg	Euro (€) of 100 cents	€ 1.5864/LF 63.9924	€ 1.56200
Macedonia	Denar of 100 deni	Den 96.2675	Den 95.4881
Madagascar	Franc malgache(FMG) of 100 centimes	FMG 9011.54	FMG 10178.2
Malawi	Kwacha (K) of 100 tambala	MK 90.0204	MK 116.460
Malaysia	Malaysian dollar (ringgit) (M$) of 100 sen	M$ 5.5564	M$ 5.81610
Maldives	Rufiyaa of 100 laaris	Rufiyaa 17.2101	Rufiyaa 18.0146
Mali	Franc CFA	Francs 1040.57	Francs 1024.57
Malta	Maltese lira (LM) of 100 cents of 1,000 mils	LM 0.6461	LM 0.64690
Marshall Islands	Currency is that of the USA	US$ 1.4622	US$ 1.53060
Martinique	Currency is that of France	€ 1.5864/Francs 10.4057	€ 1.56200
Mauritania	Ouguiya (UM) of 5 khoums	UM 374.353	UM 419.218
Mauritius	Mauritius rupee of 100 cents	Rs 43.2446	Rs 45.5645
Mayotte	Euro (€) of 100 cents	€ 1.5864/Francs 10.4057	€ 1.56200
Mexico	Peso of 100 centavos	Pesos 13.8105	Pesos 15.0851
Micronesia, Federated States of	Currency is that of the USA	US$ 1.4622	US$ 1.53060
Moldova	Moldovan leu of 100 bani	MDL 18.8258	MDL 20.8155
Monaco	Euro (€) of 100 cents	€ 1.5864/Francs 10.4057	€ 1.56200
Mongolia	Tugrik of 100 möngö	Tugriks 1608.42	Tugriks 1694.32
Montserrat	East Caribbean dollar (EC$) of 100 cents	EC$ 3.9480	EC$ 4.13250
Morocco	Dirham (DH) of 100 centimes	DH 16.3950	DH 16.3758
Mozambique	Metical (MT) of 100 centavos	MT 31645.7	MT 35605.2
Myanmar	Kyat (K) of 100 pyas	K 9.66380	K 9.78740
Namibia	Namibian dollar of 100 cents	at parity with SA Rand	
Nauru	Australian dollar ($A) of 100 cents	$A 2.9507	$A 2.76750
Nepal	Nepalese rupee of 100 paisa	Rs 111.595	Rs 117.857
The Netherlands	Euro (€) of 100 cents	€ 1.5864/Guilders 3.4959	€ 1.56200
Netherlands Antilles	Netherlands Antilles guilder of 100 cents	Guilders 2.6027	Guilders 2.72440
New Caledonia	Franc CFP	Francs 191.038	Francs 191.038
New Zealand	New Zealand dollar (NZ$) of 100 cents	NZ$ 3.5703	NZ$ 3.24450
Cook Islands	Currency is that of New Zealand	NZ$ 3.5703	NZ$ 3.24450
Niue	Currency is that of New Zealand	NZ$ 3.5703	NZ$ 3.24450
Tokelau	Currency is that of New Zealand	NZ$ 3.5703	NZ$ 3.24450
Nicaragua	Córdoba (C$) of 100 centavos	C$ 19.9152	C$ 21.9634
Niger	Franc CFA	Francs 1040.57	Francs 1024.57
Nigeria	Naira (N) of 100 kobo	N 164.732	N 194.763
Northern Mariana Islands	Currency is that of the USA	US$ 1.4622	US$ 1.53060
Norway	Krone of 100 øre	Kroner 12.6693	Kroner 11.5452
Oman	Rial Omani (OR) of 1,000 baisas	OR 0.5630	OR 0.58930
Pakistan	Pakistan rupee of 100 paisa	Rs 93.9829	Rs 91.1061
Palau	Currency is that of the USA	US$ 1.4622	US$ 1.53060
Panama	Balboa of 100 centésimos (US notes are also in circulation)	Balboa 1.4622	Balboa 1.53060
Papua New Guinea	Kina (K) of 100 toea	K 5.0640	K 6.11160
Paraguay	Guarani (Gs) of 100 céntimos	Gs 6465.12	Gs 9542.98
Peru	New Sol of 100 cénts	New Sol 5.1155	New Sol 5.50390
The Philippines	Philippine peso (P) of 100 centavos	P 75.2302	P 79.7799
Pitcairn Islands	Currency is that of New Zealand	NZ$ 3.5703	NZ$ 3.24450
Poland	Złoty of 100 groszy	Złotych 6.1832	Złotych 6.38470
Portugal	Euro (€) of 100 cents	€ 1.5864/Esc 318.031	€ 1.56200
Puerto Rico	Currency is that of the USA	US$ 1.4622	US$ 1.53060
Qatar	Qatar riyal of 100 dirhams	Riyals 5.3234	Riyals 5.57240
Réunion	Euro (€) of 100 cents	€ 1.5864/Francs 10.4057	€ 1.56200
Romania	Leu of 100 bani	Lei 44238.9	Lei 50844.9
Russia	Rouble of 100 kopeks	Rbl 43.0764	Rbl 48.3440
Rwanda	Rwanda franc of 100 centimes	Francs 638.981	Francs 713.236
St Christopher and Nevis	East Caribbean dollar (EC$) of 100 cents	EC$ 3.9480	EC$ 4.13250
St Helena	St Helena pound (£) of 100 pence	at parity with £ sterling	
St Lucia	East Caribbean dollar (EC$) of 100 cents	EC$ 3.9480	EC$ 4.13250

St Pierre and Miquelon	Euro (€) of 100 cents	€ 1.5864/Francs 10.4057	€ 1.56200
St Vincent and the Grenadines	East Caribbean dollar (EC$) of 100 cents	EC$ 3.9480	EC$ 4.13250
Samoa	Tala (S$) of 100 sene	S$ 5.0507	S$ 5.03480
San Marino	Euro (€) of 100 cents	€ 1.5864/Lire 3071.56	€ 3024.35
São Tomé and Príncipe	Dobra of 100 centavos	Dobra 13068.0	Dobra 13805.1
Saudi Arabia	Saudi riyal (SR) of 20 qursh or 100 halala	SR 5.4842	SR 5.73990
Senegal	Franc CFA	Francs 1040.57	Francs 1024.57
Seychelles	Seychelles rupee of 100 cents	Rs 8.0531	Rs 8.59860
Sierra Leone	Leone (Le) of 100 cents	Le 2846.90	Le 3114.67
Singapore	Singapore dollar (S$) of 100 cents	S$ 2.5386	S$ 2.67290
Slovakia	Koruna (Sk) of 100 halierov	Kčs 69.3560	Kčs 68.2321
Slovenia	Tolar (SIT) of 100 stotin	Tolars 348.749	Tolars 354.162
Solomon Islands	Solomon Islands dollar (SI$) of 100 cents	SI$ 7.8402	SI$ 11.4220
Somalia	Somali shilling of 100 cents	Shillings 3830.96	Shillings 4010.04
South Africa	Rand (R) of 100 cents	R 12.6772	R 16.1452
Spain	Euro (€) of 100 cents	€ 1.5864/Pesetas 263.943	€ 1.56200
Sri Lanka	Sri Lankan rupee of 100 cents	Rs 131.795	Rs 147.415
Sudan	Sudanese dinar (SD) of 100 piastres	SD 378.271	SD 395.953
Suriname	Surinamese guilder of 100 cents	Guilders 1434.42	Guilders 3334.30
Swaziland	Lilangeni (E) of 100 cents (South African currency is also in circulation)	at parity with SA Rand	
Sweden	Swedish krona of 100 öre	Kronor 15.4366	Kronor 14.2699
Switzerland	Swiss franc of 100 rappen (or centimes)	Francs 2.3486	Francs 2.29360
Syria	Syrian pound (S£) of 100 piastres	S£ 75.8151	S£ 74.7674
Taiwan	New Taiwan dollar (NT$) of 100 cents	NT$ 50.5483	NT$ 52.3908
Tajikistan	Somoni (TJS) of 100 dirams	TJS 3.5341	TJS 1473.92
Tanzania	Tanzanian shilling of 100 cents	Shillings 1302.82	Shillings 1473.92
Thailand	Baht of 100 satang	Baht 64.5854	Baht 64.5586
Togo	Franc CFA	Francs 1040.57	Francs 1024.57
Tonga	Pa'anga (T$) of 100 seniti	T$ 2.9507	T$ 2.76750
Trinidad and Tobago	Trinidad and Tobago dollar (TT$) of 100 cents	TT$ 8.8463	TT$ 9.15270
Tristan da Cunha	Currency is that of the UK	—	—
Tunisia	Tunisian dinar of 1,000 millimes	Dinars 2.0712	Dinars 2.11780
Turkey	Turkish lira (TL) of 100 kurus	TL 2186722	TL 2505511
Turkmenistan	Manat of 100 tenge	—	—
Turks and Caicos Islands	US dollar (US$)	US$ 1,4622	US$ 1.53060
Tuvalu	Australian dollar ($A) of 100 cents	$A 2.9507	$A 2.76750
Uganda	Uganda shilling of 100 cents	Shillings 2554.46	Shillings 2764.17
Ukraine	Hryvna of 100 kopiykas	UAH 7.8115	UAH 8.15560
United Arab Emirates	UAE dirham (Dh) of 100 fils	Dirham 5.3705	Dirham 5.62180
United Kingdom	Pound sterling (£) of 100 pence		
United States of America	US dollar (US$) of 100 cents	US$ 1.4622	US$ 1.53060
Uruguay	Uruguayan peso of 100 centésimos	Pesos 20.0066	Pesos 41.0570
Uzbekistan	Sum of 100 tiyin	Sum 617.341	Sum 1169.51
Vanuatu	Vatu of 100 centimes	Vatu 213.335	Vatu 211.599
Vatican City State	Euro (€) of 100 cents	€ 1.5864/Lire 3071.56	€ 1.56200
Venezuela	Bolívar (Bs) of 100 céntimos	Bs 1088.61	Bs 2130.15
Vietnam	Dông of 10 hào or 100 xu	Dông 21928.6	Dông 23471.0
Virgin Islands, British	US dollar (US$) (£ sterling and EC$ also circulate)	US$ 1.4622	US$ 1.53060
Virgin Islands, US	Currency is that of the USA	US$ 1.4622	US$ 1.53060
Wallis and Futuna Islands	Franc CFP	Francs 191.038	Francs 191.038
Yemen	Riyal of 100 fils	Riyals 247.594	Riyals 269.974
Yugoslavia†	New dinar of 100 paras	New Dinars 98.4090	New Dinars 96.2603
Zambia	Kwacha (K) of 100 ngwee	K 5468.64	K 6887.48
Zimbabwe	Zimbabwe dollar (Z$) of 100 cents	Z$ 80.8963	Z$ 84.8691

†The euro is also legal tender in Kosovo and Montenegro

Time Zones

Standard time differences from the Greenwich meridian

+	hours ahead of GMT
–	hours behind GMT
*	may vary from standard time at some part of the year (Summer Time or Daylight Saving Time)
‡	some areas may keep another time zone
h	hours
m	minutes

	h	m
Afghanistan	+ 4	30
*Albania	+ 1	
Algeria	+ 1	
*Andorra	+ 1	
Angola	+ 1	
Anguilla	– 4	
Antigua and Barbuda	– 4	
Argentina	– 3	
*Armenia	+ 4	
Aruba	– 4	
Ascension Island	0	
*Australia		
ACT, NSW (except Broken Hill area) Qld, Tas., Vic, Whitsunday Islands	+10	
*Broken Hill area (NSW)	+ 9	30
*Lord Howe Island	+10	30
Northern Territory	+ 9	30
*South Australia	+ 9	30
Western Australia	+ 8	
*Austria	+ 1	
*Azerbaijan	+ 4	
*Bahamas	– 5	
Bahrain	+ 3	
Bangladesh	+ 6	
Barbados	– 4	
*Belarus	+ 2	
*Belgium	+ 1	
Belize	– 6	
Benin	+ 1	
*Bermuda	– 4	
Bhutan	+ 6	
Bolivia	– 4	
*Bosnia–Hercegovina	+ 1	
Botswana	+ 2	
Brazil		
western states	– 5	
central states	– 4	
N. and NE coastal states	– 3	
*S. and E. coastal states, including Brasília	– 3	
Fernando de Noronha Island	– 2	
British Antarctic Territory	– 3	
British Indian Ocean Territory	+ 5	
Diego Garcia	+ 6	
British Virgin Islands	– 4	
Brunei	+ 8	
*Bulgaria	+ 2	
Burkina Faso	0	
Burundi	+ 2	
Cambodia	+ 7	
Cameroon	+ 1	

	h	m
Canada		
*Alberta	– 7	
*‡British Columbia	– 8	
*‡Labrador	– 4	
*Manitoba	– 6	
*New Brunswick	– 4	
*Newfoundland	– 3	30
*Northwest Territories		
east of 85° W.	– 5	
85° W.–102° W.	– 6	
*Nunavut	– 7	
*Nova Scotia	– 4	
Ontario		
*east of 90° W.	– 5	
west of 90° W.	– 5	
*Prince Edward Island	– 4	
Québec		
east of 63° W.	– 4	
*west of 63° W.	– 5	
‡Saskatchewan	– 6	
*Yukon	– 8	
Cape Verde	– 1	
Cayman Islands	– 5	
Central African Republic	+ 1	
Chad	+ 1	
*Chatham Islands	+12	45
*Chile	– 4	
China (inc. Hong Kong and Macao)	+ 8	
Christmas Island (Indian Ocean)	+ 7	
Cocos (Keeling) Islands	+ 6	30
Colombia	– 5	
Comoros	+ 3	
Congo (Dem. Rep.)		
Haut–Zaïre, Kasai, Kivu, Shaba	+ 2	
Kinshasa, Mbandaka	+ 1	
Congo–Brazzaville	+ 1	
Costa Rica	– 6	
Côte d'Ivoire	0	
*Croatia	+ 1	
*Cuba	– 5	
*Cyprus	+ 2	
*Czech Republic	+ 1	
*Denmark	+ 1	
*Færøe Islands	0	
*Greenland	– 3	
Danmarkshavn Mesters Vig	0	
*Scoresby Sound	– 1	
*Thule area	– 4	
Djibouti	+ 3	
Dominica	– 4	
Dominican Republic	– 5	
East Timor	+ 9	
Ecuador	– 5	
Galápagos Islands	– 6	
*Egypt	+ 2	
El Salvador	– 6	
Equatorial Guinea	+ 1	
Eritrea	+ 3	
Estonia	+ 2	
Ethiopia	+ 3	
*Falkland Islands	– 4	
Fiji	+12	

	h	m
*Finland	+ 2	
*France	+ 1	
French Guiana	– 3	
French Polynesia	–10	
Guadeloupe	– 4	
Martinique	– 4	
Réunion	+ 4	
Marquesas Islands	– 9	30
Gabon	+ 1	
The Gambia	0	
*Georgia	+ 3	
*Germany	+ 1	
Ghana	0	
*Gibraltar	+ 1	
*Greece	+ 2	
Grenada	– 4	
Guam	+10	
Guatemala	– 6	
Guinea	0	
Guinea–Bissau	0	
Guyana	– 4	
Haïti	– 5	
Honduras	– 6	
*Hungary	+ 1	
Iceland	0	
India	+ 5	30
Indonesia		
Java, Kalimantan (west and central), Madura, Sumatra	+ 7	
Bali, Flores, Kalimantan (south and east), Lombok, Sulawesi, Sumbawa, West Timor	+ 8	
Irian Jaya, Maluku,	+ 9	
*Iran	+ 3	30
*Iraq	+ 3	
*Ireland, Republic of	0	
*Israel	+ 2	
*Italy	+ 1	
Jamaica	– 5	
Japan	+ 9	
*Jordan	+ 2	
*Kazakhstan		
western	+ 4	
central	+ 5	
eastern	+ 6	
Kenya	+ 3	
Kiribati	+12	
Line Islands	+14	
Phoenix Islands	+13	
Korea, North	+ 9	
Korea, South	+ 9	
Kuwait	+ 3	
*Kyrgyzstan	+ 5	
Laos	+ 7	
Latvia	+ 2	
*Lebanon	+ 2	
Lesotho	+ 2	
Liberia	0	
Libya	+ 2	
*Liechtenstein	+ 1	
Line Islands, not part of Kiribai	–10	
Lithuania	+ 1	
*Luxembourg	+ 1	

	h m		h m		h m
*Macedonia	+ 1	Zone 9	+10	Vietnam	+ 7
Madagascar	+ 3	Zone 10	+11	Virgin Islands (US)	− 4
Malaŵi	+ 2	Zone 11	+12	Yemen	+ 3
Malaysia	+ 8	Rwanda	+ 2	*Yugoslavia (Fed. Rep. of)	+ 1
Maldives	+ 5	St Helena	0	Zambia	+ 2
Mali	0	St Christopher and Nevis	− 4	Zimbabwe	+ 2
*Malta	+ 1	St Lucia	− 4		
Marshall Islands	+12	*St Pierre and Miquelon	− 3		
Ebon Atoll	−12	St Vincent and the			
Mauritania	0	Grenadines	− 4		
Mauritius	+ 4	Samoa	−11		
*Mexico	− 6	Samoa, American	−11		
*Nayarit, Sinaloa, S. Baja		*San Marino	+ 1		
California, Sonora	− 7	São Tomé and Princípe	0		
N. Baja California	− 8	Saudi Arabia	+ 3		
Micronesia		Senegal	0		
Caroline Islands	+10	Seychelles	+ 4		
Kosrae, Pingelap,		Sierra Leone			
Pohnpei	+11	Singapore	+ 8		
*Moldova	+ 2	*Slovakia	+ 1		
*Monaco	+ 1	*Slovenia	+ 1		
Mongolia	+ 8	Solomon Islands	+11		
Montserrat	− 4	Somalia	+ 3		
Morocco	0	South Africa	+ 2		
Mozambique	+ 2	South Georgia	− 2		
Myanmar	+ 6 30	*Spain	+ 1		
*Namibia	+ 1	*Canary Islands	0		
Nauru	+12	Sri Lanka	+ 6		
Nepal	+ 5 45	Sudan	+ 3		
*Netherlands	+ 1	Suriname	− 3		
Netherlands Antilles	− 4	Swaziland	+ 2		
New Caledonia	+11	*Sweden	+ 1		
*New Zealand	+12	*Switzerland	+ 1		
*Cook Islands	−10	*Syria	+ 2		
Nicaragua	− 6	Taiwan	+ 8		
Niger	+ 1	Tajikistan	+ 5		
Nigeria	+ 1	Tanzania	+ 3		
Niue	−11	Thailand	+ 7		
Norfolk Island	+11 30	Togo	0		
Northern Mariana Islands	+10	*Tonga	+13		
*Norway	+ 1	Trinidad and Tobago	− 4		
Oman	+ 4	Tristan da Cunha	0		
Pakistan	+ 5	Tunisia	+ 1		
Palau	+ 9	*Turkey	+ 2		
Panama	− 5	Turkmenistan	+ 5		
Papua New Guinea	+10	*Turks and Caicos Islands	− 5		
*Paraguay	− 4	Tuvalu	+12		
Peru	− 5	Uganda	+ 3		
Philippines	+ 8	*Ukraine	+ 2		
*Poland	+ 1	United Arab Emirates	+ 4		
*Portugal	0	*United Kingdom	0		
*Azores	− 1	*United States of America			
*Madeira	0	Alaska	− 9		
Puerto Rico	− 4	Aleutian Islands, east of			
Qatar	+ 3	169° 30' W.	− 9		
Réunion	+ 4	Aleutian Islands, west of			
*Romania	+ 2	169° 30' W.	−10		
*Russia		eastern time	− 5		
Zone 1	+ 2	central time	− 6		
Zone 2	+ 3	Hawaii	−10		
Zone 3	+ 4	mountain time	− 7		
Zone 4	+ 5	Pacific time	− 8		
Zone 5	+ 6	Uruguay	− 3		
Zone 6	+ 7	Uzbekistan	+ 5		
Zone 7	+ 8	Vanuatu	+11		
Zone 8	+ 9	*Vatican City State	+ 1		
		Venezuela	− 4		

Source: reproduced with permission from data produced by HM Nautical Almanac Office

The European Union

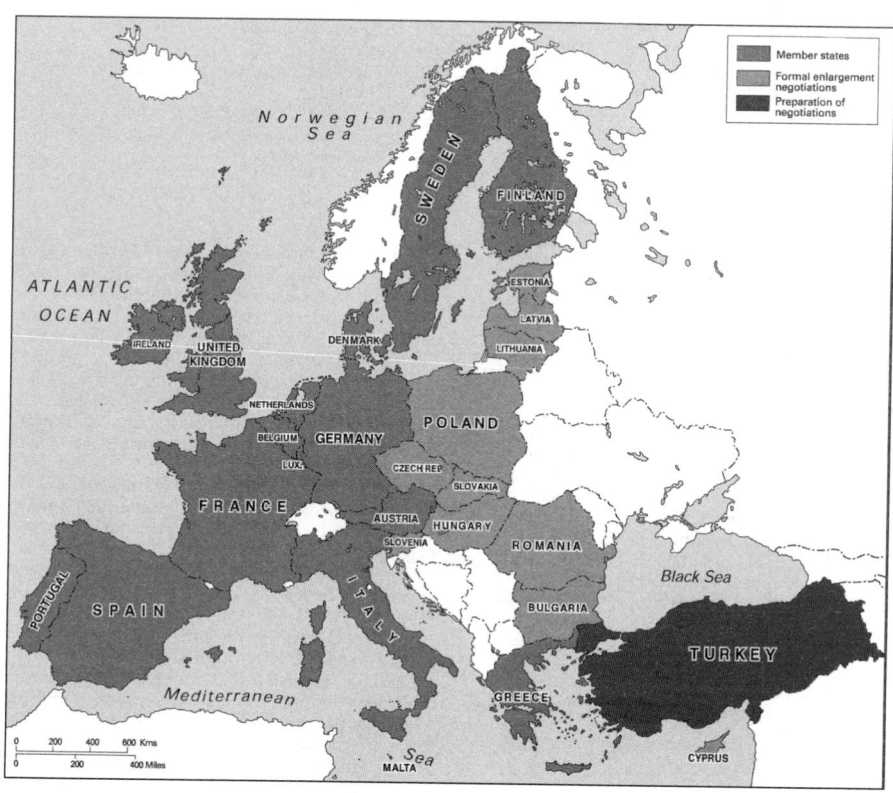

			Member states
			Formal enlargement negotiations
			Preparation of negotiations

MEMBERS

STATE	ACCESSION DATE	POPULATION (million) (2000)	GNP (US$ million) (2000)	GDP PER HEAD IN PPS (ECU) (1999	COUNCIL VOTES	EP SEATS
Austria	1 January 1995	8.10	204,250	23,484	4	21
Belgium	1 January 1958*	10.24	252,461	23,446	5	25
Denmark	1 January 1973	5.33	170,995	25,026	3	16
Finland	1 January 1995	5.17	128,999	21,442	3	16
France	1 January 1958*	59.30	1,429,390	20,861	10	87
Germany	1 January 1958*†	82.16	2,057,633	22,712	10	99
Greece	1 January 1981	10.55	126,245	14,198	5	25
Ireland	1 January 1973	3.78	87,108	24,133	3	15
Italy	1 January 1958*	57.68	1,154,271	21,158	10	87
Luxembourg	1 January 1958*	0.44	19,420	38,773	2	6
Netherlands	1 January 1958*	15.86	400,280	23,838	5	31
Portugal	1 January 1986	10.00	110,674	16,065	5	25
Spain	1 January 1986	39.44	590,150	17,319	8	64
Sweden	1 January 1995	8.86	237,473	21,620	4	22
UK	1 January 1973	59.62	1,463,474	21,598	10	87
TOTAL		376.53	8,432,823		87	626

Sources: Eurostat Yearbook 2001, World Bank World Development Indicators database
* Acceded to the European Coal and Steel Community (ECSC) on its formation in 1952
† Federal Republic of Germany (West) 1952/1958; German Democratic Republic (East) acceded on German reunification (3 October 1990)
EP European Parliament PPS - purchasing power standards

DEVELOPMENT

1950 Robert Schuman (French foreign minister) proposes that France and West Germany pool their coal and steel industries under a supranational authority (Schuman Plan)

1951 Paris Treaty signed by France, West Germany, Belgium, Italy, Luxembourg and the Netherlands establishes the European Coal and Steel Community (ECSC)

1952 ECSC Treaty enters into force

1957 25 March: Treaty of Rome signed by the six ECSC member countries, establishes the European Economic Community (EEC) and the European Atomic Energy Authority (EURATOM). Treaty aims to create a customs union; remove obstacles to free movement of capital, goods, people and services; establish common external trade policy and common agricultural and fisheries policies; co-ordinate economic policies; harmonise social policies; promote co-operation in nuclear research

1958 1 January: EEC and EURATOM begin operation. Joint Parliament and Court of Justice established for all three communities, and the Commission, Council of Ministers, Economic and Social Committee and Investment Bank for the EEC established

1962 Common Agricultural Policy (CAP) agreed

1967 EEC, ECSC and EURATOM merge to form the European Communities (EC), with a single Council of Ministers and Commission

1968 EEC customs union completed
Implementation of CAP completed

1974 Regular heads of governments summits begin

1975 'Own resources' funding of EC budget introduced
UK renegotiates its terms of accession
European Regional Development Fund created

1979 European Monetary System (EMS) comes into operation
First direct elections to European Parliament (June)

1984 Fontainebleau summit settles UK annual budget rebate and agrees first major CAP reform

1986 Single European Act (SEA) signed
European Political Co-operation (EPC) established

1988 Second major CAP reform

1991 Maastricht Treaty agreed

1992 31 December: Single internal market programme completed

1993 September: the exchange rate mechanism (ERM) of the EMS effectively suspended
1 November: The Maastricht Treaty enters into force, establishing the European Union (EU)

1994 1 January: European Economic Area (EEA) agreement comes into operation. Norway rejects EU membership in referendum

1997 Amsterdam Treaty agreed

1998 11 states chosen to enter first round of European Monetary Union (EMU)
European Central Bank replaces European Monetary Institute

1999 1 January: Euro launched

March: 'Agenda 2000' financial and policy reform agreed
1 May: The Amsterdam Treaty enters into force

2000 9 December: Treaty of Nice agreed

2001 7 June: Ireland rejects Treaty of Nice in referendum

2002 1 January: Euro coins and banknotes enter circulation
23 July: ECSC Treaty expires following transfer of coal and steel sectors to the Treaty of Rome

ENLARGEMENT AND EXTERNAL RELATIONS

The procedure for accession to the EU is laid down in the Treaty of Rome; states must be stable European democracies governed by the rule of law with free market economies. A membership application is studied by the Commission, which produces an Opinion. If the Opinion is positive, negotiations may be opened leading to an Accession Treaty which must be approved by all member state governments and parliaments, the European Parliament, and the applicant state's government and parliament.

Applicants: Morocco (applied 1987/rejected 1987), Turkey (applied 1987/negative Opinion 1989/offered accession partnership 1999), Cyprus (applied 1990/ negotiations begun 1998), Malta (applied 1990/reapplied following a change of government 1998/negotiations begun 2000), Switzerland (applied 1992/application put on hold 1994), Hungary (applied 1994/negotiations begun 1998), Poland (applied 1994/negotiations begun 1998), Bulgaria (applied 1995/offered partnership 1998/negotiations begun 2000), Estonia (applied 1995/negotiations begun 1998), Latvia (applied 1995/offered partnership 1998/negotiations begun 2000), Lithuania (applied 1995/offered partnership 1998/negotiations begun 2000), Romania (applied 1995/offered partnership 1998/negotiations begun 2000), Slovakia (applied 1995/offered partnership 1998/negotiations begun 2000), the Czech Republic (applied 1996/negotiations begun 1998), Slovenia (applied 1996/negotiations begun 1998).

Apart from the EEA Agreement, the EU has three types of agreements with other European and CIS states. 'Europe' agreements commit the EU and signatory states to long-term political and economic integration, a free trade zone (apart from agriculture and labour-movement) and eventual EU membership. Government representatives from the signatory states are entitled to attend one summit and two finance and foreign council meetings a year. Agreements have been signed with Bulgaria (1993), the Czech Republic (1993), Estonia (1995), Hungary (1991), Latvia (1995), Lithuania (1995), Poland (1991), Romania (1993), Slovakia (1993) and Slovenia (1996). Association agreements include a commitment to EU financial aid and to eventual membership; agreements have been signed with Malta (1970), Cyprus (1972) and Turkey (1963). Partnership and co-operation agreements are based on regulating and improving political and economic relations and mutual trade concessions but exclude any possibility of membership. Agreements have been implemented with Russia (1997), Ukraine (1998) and Georgia, Kazakhstan, Kyrgyzstan,

Moldova and Uzbekistan (1999). Agreements have been signed with Belarus (1995) and Turkmenistan (1998) but are not yet in force.

Agenda 2000, a document issued by the Commission in 1997, addressed both the challenges posed by further enlargement of the Union, the institutional reforms that would be required to enable the Union to function effectively with additional members, and also evaluated each applicant in relation to the accession criteria, establishing a new financial framework for the period 2000–2006.

In March 1998, formal accession negotiations were begun with Hungary, Poland, Estonia, the Czech Republic, Slovenia and Cyprus; they were begun with Bulgaria, Romania, Latvia, Lithuania, Malta and Slovakia in 2000, following the Helsinki summit in December 1999, when it was also agreed that an accession partnership should be offered to Turkey.

The Göteborg summit in June 2001 agreed on a timetable for accession for the first group of countries to complete negotiations.

THE COUNCIL OF THE EUROPEAN UNION
Wetstraat 175, B-1048 Brussels, Belgium

The Council of the European Union (Council of Ministers) formally comprises the foreign ministers of the member states but in practice the ministers attending depend on the subject under discussion. Council decisions are taken by qualified majority vote (in which members' votes are weighted), by a simple majority, or by unanimity. The Council is assisted by a General Secretariat, whose head has since 1999 been the High Representative for the Common Foreign and Security Policy.

Unanimity votes are taken on sensitive issues such as taxation and constitutional matters; in preparation for an expanded Union, the Amsterdam Treaty extended areas where qualified majority votes may be taken, to areas such as Single Market laws and harmonisation, environment policy, health and safety, transport policy, overseas aid, research and development, culture, consumer protection, education and training, the development of a single currency and some aspects of social policy. Member states have weighted votes in the Council loosely proportional to their relative population sizes (see introductory table), with a total of 87 votes. For a proposal from the Commission to be passed, it must receive 62 votes; 26 votes are necessary to block a proposal, and 23 votes constitute a temporary blocking minority. For other proposals to be passed they must receive 62 votes cast by at least ten member states.

The Treaty of Nice, which was agreed on 7–9 December 2000 and signed on 26 February 2001, agreed amendments to the treaties in relation to the size and composition of the European Commission, the weighting of votes and the extension of qualified majority voting in the Council of Ministers and other issues relating to the Treaty of Amsterdam. The extension of qualified majority voting to external border controls, the EU budget, the composition of the European Courts and certain committees, visa rules and, by 2007, structural funds, was also agreed.

The European Council, comprising the heads of state or government of the member states and the President of the European Commission, meets twice a year to provide overall policy direction. The presidency of the EC is held in rotation for six-month periods, setting the agenda for and chairing all Council meetings. The European Council holds a summit in the country holding the presidency at the end of its period in office. The holders of the presidency for the years 2002–2004 are:

2002 Spain, Denmark
2003 Greece, Italy
2004 Ireland, Netherlands

GENERAL SECRETARIAT OF THE COUNCIL OF THE EUROPEAN UNION
Wetstraat 175, B-1048 Brussels, Belgium
E-mail: public.info@consilium.eu.int
Secretary-General of the Council of the European Union and High Representative for the Common Foreign and Security Policy, Javier Solana Madariaga (Spain)
Deputy Secretary-General of the Council of the European Union, Pierre de Boissieu (France)

OFFICE OF THE UNITED KINGDOM PERMANENT REPRESENTATIVE TO THE EUROPEAN UNION
Oudergemselaan 10, B-1040 Brussels, Belgium
Ambassador and UK Permanent Representative, HE Sir Nigel Sheinwald, KCMG, *apptd* 2000
Deputy Permanent Representative, W. Stow

THE EUROPEAN COMMISSION
Wetstraat 200, B-1049 Brussels, Belgium

The Commission consists of 20 Commissioners, two each from France, Germany, Italy, Spain and the UK, and one each from the remaining member states. The members of the Commission are appointed for five-year renewable terms by the agreement of the member states; the terms run concurrently with the terms of the European Parliament. The President and the other Commissioners are nominated by the governments of the member states, and, under the terms of the Amsterdam Treaty, the appointments are approved by the European Parliament. The Commissioners pledge sole allegiance to the EC. The Commission initiates and implements EC legislation and is the guardian of the EC treaties. It is the exponent of Community-wide interests rather than the national preoccupations of the Council. Each Commissioner is supported by advisers and oversees whichever of the departments, known as Directorates-General (DGs), is assigned to him. Each Directorate-General is headed by a Director-General.

President Romano Prodi was nominated by the governments of the member states on 24 March 1999, and under the terms of the Amsterdam Treaty, his appointment was approved by the European Parliament on 15 September 1999, having already announced his new Commission in June. The previous Commission had resigned en masse after a committee of experts appointed by the European Parliament had concluded that lax management had allowed fraud and nepotism in the Commission's services. The new Commission has restructured the Directorates-General to reflect the priorities of the new administration.

The Commission has a total staff of around 16,000 permanent civil servants.

COMMISSIONERS *as at March 2002*
President, Romano Prodi (Italy)
Vice-President for Administrative Reform; Personnel and Administration; Linguistic Services, Neil Kinnock (UK)
Vice-President for Relations with the European Parliament, and for Transport and Energy, Loyola de Palacio (Spain)

Members
Agriculture, Rural Development and Fisheries, Franz Fischler (Austria)
Budget, Financial Control, European Anti-Fraud Office, Michaele Schreyer (Germany)
Competition, Mario Monti (Italy)
Development, Humanitarian Aid, Chief Executive of EuropeAid, Poul Nielson (Denmark)
Economic and Monetary Affairs, Pedro Solbes Mira (Spain)
Education and Culture, Viviane Reding (Luxembourg)
Employment and Social Affairs, Anna Diamantopoulou (Greece)
Enlargement, Günter Verheugen (Germany)
Enterprise and Information Society, Erkki Liikanen (Finland)
Environment, Margot Wallström (Sweden)
External Relations, Chairman of EuropeAid, Chris Patten (UK)
Internal Market, Taxation and Customs Union, Frits Bolkestein (Netherlands)
Justice and Home Affairs, António Vitorino (Portugal)
Public Health, Consumer Protection, David Byrne (Ireland)
Regional Policy and Institutional Reform, Inter-Governmental Conference, Michel Barnier (France)
Research, Philippe Busquin (Belgium)
Trade, Pascal Lamy (France)

THE EUROPEAN PARLIAMENT

Email: civis@europarl.eu.int
Web: www.europarl.eu.int

The European Parliament (EP) originated as the Common Assembly of the ECSC; it acquired its present name in 1962. Members (MEPs) were initially appointed from the membership of national parliaments; direct elections to the Parliament were first held in 1979 and take place at five-year intervals. Elections to the Parliament are held on differing bases throughout the EC; in June 1999, British MEPs were elected for the first time by a 'regional list' system of proportional representation. The Parliament comprises 626 seats. The most recent elections were held in June 1999. For total number of seats per member and political groupings, *see* table below. MEPs serve on committees which scrutinise draft EC legislation and the activities of the Commission. A minimum of 12 plenary sessions a year are held in Strasbourg and Brussels, committees meet in Brussels, and the Secretariat's headquarters is in Luxembourg.

The EP has gradually expanded its influence within the EU through the Single European Act, which introduced the co-operation procedure, the Maastricht Treaty, which extended the co-operation procedure and introduced the co-decision procedure

(*see* Legislative Process), and the Amsterdam Treaty, which effectively extended co-decision to all areas except economic and monetary union. It has general powers of supervision over the Commission, and consultation and co-decision with the Council; it votes to approve a newly appointed Commission and can dismiss it at any time by a two-thirds majority (as it threatened to do in January 1999). Under the Maastricht Treaty it has the right to be consulted on the appointment of the new Commission and can veto its appointment. It can reject the EU budget as a whole, alter non-compulsory expenditure not specified in the EU primary legislation, and can question the Commission's management of the budget and call in the Court of Auditors. Although the EP cannot directly initiate legislation, its reports can spur the Commission into action. In accordance with the Maastricht Treaty the EP appointed an ombudsman in October 1995, to provide citizens with redress against maladministration by EU institutions.

The Parliament's organisation is deliberately biased in favour of multinational political groupings, recognition of a political grouping in the parliament entitling it to offices, funding, representation on committees and influence in debates and legislation. A political grouping with members from only one country needs a minimum of 29 members for recognition, whereas one with members from two countries needs 23 members, a grouping with members from three countries needs 18 members, and a grouping with members from four or more countries needs only 14 members.

PARLIAMENT, Palais de l'Europe, Allée du Printemps, BP 1024/F, F-67070 Strasbourg Cedex, France. Tel: (00 33) (3) 8817 4001; Fax: (00 33) (3) 8825 6501; Wiertzstraat, Postbus 1047, B-1047 Brussels, Belgium. Tel: (00 32) (2) 284 2111; Fax: (00 32) (2) 284 9075/9077

SECRETARIAT, Centre Européen, Plateau du Kirchberg, BP 1601, L-2929 Luxembourg. Tel: (00 352) 43001; Fax: (00 352) 4300 29393/29292
President, Patrick Cox (Ireland)
Ombudsman, Jacob Söderman (Finland), 1 avenue du Président Robert Schuman, BP 403, F-67001, Strasbourg, France.
Email: euro-ombudsman@europarl.eu.int
Web: www.euro-ombudsman.eu.int

THE LEGISLATIVE PROCESS

The core of the EU policymaking process is a dialogue between the Commission, which initiates and implements policy, and the Council of Ministers, which takes policy decisions. An increasing degree of democratic control is exercised by the European Parliament.

The original legislative process is known as the consultative procedure. The Commission drafts a proposal which it submits to the Council and to the Parliament. The Council then consults the Economic and Social Committee (ESC), the Parliament and the Committee of the Regions; the Parliament may request that amendments are made. With or without these amendments, the proposal is then adopted by the Council and becomes law.

Under the Single European Act (SEA), the role of the Parliament was strengthened by the introduction of the co-operation procedure. The Parliament now has a second reading of proposals in some fields, and

after the second reading its rejection of a proposal can only be overturned by a unanimous decision of the Council. The Maastricht Treaty extended the scope of the co-operation procedure, which was applied to Single Market laws and harmonisation, trans-European networks, development policy, the social fund, and some aspects of transport, environment, research, social policy and competition policy.

The SEA introduced the assent procedure, whereby an absolute majority of the Parliament must vote to approve laws in certain fields before they are passed. Issues covered by the assent procedure include foreign treaties, accession treaties, international agreements with budgetary implications, citizenship, residence rights, the CAP, and regional and structural funds.

The Maastricht Treaty introduced the co-decision procedure; if, after the Parliament's second reading of a proposal, the Council and Parliament fail to agree, a conciliation committee of the two will reach a compromise. If a compromise is not reached, the Parliament can reject the legislation by the vote of an absolute majority of its members. The Amsterdam Treaty extended co-decision to all areas covered by qualified majority voting, with the exception of measures related to European Monetary Union (EMU).

The Council issues the following legislation:
–Regulations, which are binding in their entirety and directly applicable to all member states; they do not need to be incorporated into national law to come into effect
–Directives, which are less specific, binding as to the result to be achieved but leaving the method of implementation open to member states; a directive thus has no force until it is incorporated into national law
–Decisions, which are also binding but are addressed solely to one or more member states or individuals in a member state
–Recommendations
–Opinions, which are merely persuasive

The Council also has certain budgetary powers, including the power to reject the budget as a whole and to increase expenditure or redistribute money within sectors. However, the final decision on whether the budget should be adopted or rejected lies with the Parliament.

The Council may delegate legislative powers to the Commission. These consist of implementing powers and technical updating of existing legislation. The European Central Bank has legislative powers within its field of competence. The Commission also has limited legislative powers, where it has been delegated the power to implement or revise legislation by the Council.

THE COMMUNITY BUDGET

The principles of funding the European Community budget were established by the Treaty of Rome and remain with modifications to this day. There is a legally binding limit on the overall level of resources (known as 'own resources') that the Community can raise from its member states; this limit is defined as a percentage of gross national product (GNP). Budget revenue and expenditure must balance and there is therefore no deficit financing. The own resources decision, which came into effect in 1975

and has been regularly updated, states that there are four sources of Community funding under which each member state makes contributions: levies charged on agricultural imports into the Community from non-member states; customs duties on imports from non-member states; contributions based on member states' shares of a notional Community harmonised VAT base; and contributions based on member states' shares of Community GNP. The latter is the budget-balancing item and covers the difference between total expenditure and the revenue from the other three sources. Since 1984 the UK has had an annual rebate equivalent to 66 per cent of the difference between what the UK contributes to the budget and what it receives. This was introduced to compensate the UK for disproportionate contributions caused by its high proportion of agricultural and non-agricultural imports from non-member states and its relatively small receipts from the Common Agricultural Policy, the most important portion of Community expenditure.

BUDGET 2002

	Billion euro*	As % of total
Agriculture	44.3	44.9
Regional and Social	33.8	34.3
External Action	4.8	4.9
Pre-accession Aid	3.3	3.3
Internal policies	6.6	6.6
Administration	5.2	5.3
Reserves	0.7	0.7
TOTAL		100.0

Source: General Budget of the European Union for the Financial Year 2002

* 1 euro = £0.646 as at 11 June 2002

Under the Edinburgh summit agreement (December 1992) the EC budget rose to a maximum of 1.27 per cent of the EU's GNP in 1999. The agreed budget for 2000–2006 will keep the 1.27 per cent ceiling, but resources devoted to the existing member states will fall to 0.98 per cent, with the remaining resources devoted to enlargement.

THE COMMON AGRICULTURAL POLICY

The Common Agricultural Policy (CAP) was established to increase agricultural production, provide a fair standard of living for farmers and ensure the availability of food at reasonable prices. This aim was achieved by a number of mechanisms:
–import levies
–intervention purchase
–export subsidies

These measures stimulated production but also placed increasing demands on the EC budget which were exacerbated by the increase in EC members and yields enlarged by technological innovation; CAP now accounts for over 40 per cent of EC expenditure. To surmount these problems reforms were agreed in 1984, 1988, 1992, 1997 and 1999.

REFORMS

The 1984 reforms created the system of co-responsibility levies: farm payments to the EC by

volume of product sold. This system was supplemented by national quotas for particular products, such as milk. The 1988 reforms emphasised 'set-aside', whereby farmers are given direct grants to take land out of production as a means of reducing surpluses. The set-aside reforms were extended in 1993 for another five years and to every farm in the EC. The 1999 reforms will further reduce surpluses of cereals, beef and milk by cutting the intervention prices by up to 20 per cent and compensating producers by making area payments. Under the reforms, CAP rules will also be simplified, eliminating inconsistencies between policies.

Under the Uruguay round agreement of GATT concluded in 1993, the EU must, over a six-year period from 1 January 1995, reduce its import levies by 36 per cent, reduce its domestic subsidies by 20 per cent, reduce its export subsidies by 36 per cent in value, and reduce its subsidised exports by 21 per cent in volume. Agenda 2000, the programme to overhaul the policies of the EU and prepare it for the accession of new member states, will temporarily increase the cost of the CAP by €1,000 million a year in compensation payments, but leave it broadly stable by the end of the current planning period in 2006.

THE SINGLE MARKET

Even after the removal of tariffs and quotas between member states in the 1970s and 1980s, the EC was still separated into a number of national markets by a series of non-tariff barriers. It was to overcome these internal barriers to trade that the concept of the Single Market was developed. The measures to be undertaken were codified in the Commission's 1985 White Paper on completing the internal market.

The White Paper included articles removing obstacles that distorted the internal market: the elimination of frontier controls; the mutual recognition of professional qualifications; the harmonisation of product specifications, largely by the mutual recognition of national standards; open tendering for public procurement contracts; the free movement of capital; the harmonisation of VAT and excise duties; and the reduction of state aid to particular industries. The target date for the completion of this process was 31 December 1992. The Single European Act aided the completion of the Single Market by changing the legislative process within the EC, particularly with the introduction of qualified majority voting in the Council of Ministers for some policy areas, and the introduction of the assent procedure in the European Parliament. The SEA also extends EC competence into the fields of technology, the environment, regional policy, monetary policy and external policy. The Single Market came into effect on 1 January 1993. The full implementation of the elimination of frontier controls and the harmonisation of taxes have, however, been repeatedly delayed.

THE EUROPEAN ECONOMIC AREA (see also EFTA)

The EC Single Market programme spurred European non-member states to open negotiations with the EC on preferential access for their goods, services, labour and capital to the Single Market. Principal among these states were European Free Trade Association (EFTA) members who opened negotiations on extending the Single Market to EFTA

by the formation of the European Economic Area (EEA) encompassing all 19 EC and EFTA states. Agreement was reached in May 1992 but the operation of the EEA was delayed by its rejection in a Swiss referendum, necessitating an additional protocol agreed by the remaining 18 states. The EEA came into effect on 1 January 1994 after ratification by 17 member states (Liechtenstein joined on 1 May 1995 after adapting its customs union with Switzerland).

Austria, Finland and Sweden joined the EU itself on 1 January 1995, leaving only Norway, Iceland and Liechtenstein as the non-EU EEA members. Under the EEA agreement, the three states are to adopt the EU's *acquis communautaire*, apart from in the fields of agriculture, fisheries, and coal and steel.

The EEA is controlled by regular ministerial meetings and by a joint EU-EFTA committee which extends relevant EU legislation to EEA states. Apart from single market measures, there is co-operation in education, research and development, consumer policy and tourism. An EFTA Court of Justice has been established in Luxembourg and an EFTA Surveillance Authority in Brussels to supervise the implementation of the EEA Agreement.

THE EUROPEAN MONETARY SYSTEM AND THE SINGLE CURRENCY

The European monetary system (EMS) began operation in March 1979 with three main purposes. The first was to establish monetary stability in Europe, initially in exchange rates between EC member state currencies through the exchange rate mechanism (ERM), and in the longer term to be part of a wider stabilisation process, overcoming inflation and budget and trade deficits. The second purpose was to overcome the constraints resulting from the interdependence of EC economies, and the third was to aid the long-term process of European monetary integration.

The Maastricht Treaty set in motion timetables for achieving economic and monetary union (EMU) and a single currency (the euro). At the Brussels summit in May 1998, 11 member states were judged to fulfil or be close to fulfilling the necessary convergence criteria for participation in the first stage of EMU: Austria, Belgium, Finland, France, Germany, Ireland, Italy, Luxembourg, the Netherlands, Portugal and Spain.

The criteria were that:
–the budget deficit should be 3 per cent or less of gross domestic product (GDP)
–total national debt must not exceed 60 per cent of GDP
–inflation should be no more than 1.5 per cent above the average rate of the three best performing economies in the EU
–long-term interest rates should be no more than 2 per cent above the average of the three best performing economies in the EU in the previous 12 months
–applicants must have been members of the ERM for two years without having realigned or devalued their currency

Under the terms of a stability and growth pact agreed in Dublin in December 1996, penalties may be imposed on EMU members with high budget deficits. Governments with deficits exceeding 3 per cent of GDP will receive a warning and will be obliged to pay up to 0.5 per cent of their GDP into a

fund after ten months. This will become a fine if the budget deficit is not rectified within two years. A member state with negative growth will be allowed to apply for an exemption from the fine in 'exceptional circumstances', e.g. a recession whereby GDP had fallen by 0.75 per cent or more during one year.

On 1 January 1999, the qualifying member states adopted the euro at irrevocably fixed exchange rates (*see* table below), the European Central Bank (ECB) took charge of the single monetary policy, and the euro replaced the ECU on a one-for-one basis.

On 19 June 2000, Greece was judged to have fulfilled the criteria for participation and adopted the euro on 1 January 2001. A referendum on the adoption of the euro was held in Denmark on 28 September 2000, but participation was rejected by the electorate.

The euro is now the legal currency in the participating states. Euro notes and coins were introduced on 1 January 2002 and circulated alongside national currencies for a period of up to two months, after which time national notes and coins ceased to be legal tender. The Swedish government announced in January 2002 that a referendum on adopting the euro would be held in 2003 and the Danish government was considering holding a second referendum on the issue.

The conversion rates between the euro and the currencies of the Member States adopting the euro were:

€1 =   13.7603 Austrian Schilling
        40.3399 Belgian Francs
        2.20371 Dutch Gulden
        5.94573 Finnish Markka
        6.55957 French Francs
        1.95583 German Deutsche Mark
        340.750 Greek Drachmae
        0.787564 Irish Punts
        1,936.27 Italian Lire
        40.3399 Luxembourg Francs
        200.482 Portuguese Escudos
        166.386 Spanish Pesetas

Source: The Official Journal of the European Communities

The ECB meets every two weeks to set interest rates for the countries participating in the euro. Its governing council has 17 members, being the six members of the ECB's executive board and the 11 governors of the national central banks of the participating states.

With the advent of EMU, the ERM was revised and Denmark became a member of ERM II, which requires it to maintain its currencies within set margins of the euro. Membership of ERM II is voluntary, although all member states outside the euro zone are encouraged to take part. Sweden and the UK are currently not members.

THE MAASTRICHT TREATY

The Treaty on European Union was agreed at a meeting of the European Council in Maastricht, the Netherlands, in December 1991. It came into effect in November 1993 following ratification by the member states.

Three 'pillars' formed the basis of the new treaty:
–the European Community with its established institutions and decision-making processes
–a Common Foreign and Security Policy (*see* below) with the Western European Union as the potential defence component of the EU
–co-operation in justice and home affairs, with the Council of Ministers to co-ordinate policies on asylum, immigration, conditions of entry, cross-border crime, drug trafficking and terrorism

The Treaty established a common European citizenship for nationals of all member states and introduced the principle of subsidiarity whereby decisions are taken at the most appropriate level: national, regional or local. It extended EC competency into the areas of environmental and industrial policies, consumer affairs, health, and education and training, and extended qualified majority voting in the Council of Ministers to some areas which had previously required a unanimous vote. The powers of the European Parliament over the budget and over the Commission were also enhanced and a co-decision procedure enabled the Parliament to override decisions made by the Council of Ministers in certain policy areas. A separate protocol to the Maastricht Treaty on social policy was agreed by 11 states and was incorporated into the Amsterdam Treaty in 1997 following adoption by the UK.

THE AMSTERDAM TREATY

The treaties of Rome and Maastricht were again amended through the Treaty of Amsterdam, which was signed in October 1997 and which came into effect on 1 May 1999. It extends the scope of qualified majority voting and the powers of the European Parliament. It also includes a formal commitment to fundamental human rights, gives additional powers to the European Court of Justice and provides for the appointment of a High Representative for EU Common Foreign and Security Policy.

COMMON FOREIGN AND SECURITY POLICY

The Common Foreign and Security Policy (CFSP) was created as a pillar of the EU by the Maastricht Treaty (*see* above). It adopted the machinery of the European Political Co-operation (EPC) framework which it replaced and was charged with providing a forum for member states and EU institutions to consult on foreign affairs.

The CFSP system is headed by the Council of the European Union, which provides general lines of policy. Specific policy decisions are taken by the Council of Foreign Ministers, which meets at least four times a year to determine areas for joint action. The High Representative of the CFSP initiates action, manages the CFSP and represents it abroad. The Council of Ministers is supported by the Political Committee which meets monthly, or within 48 hours if there is a crisis, to prepare for ministerial discussions. A group of correspondents, designated diplomats in each member's foreign ministry, provides day-to-day contact.

The Amsterdam Treaty introduced qualified majority voting for foreign affairs and created a high representative on CFSP to act as a spokesperson. It also established a new policy planning and early warning unit to monitor international

developments. The unit is to consist of specialists from the member states, the Council and the Commission, as well as from the Western European Union (WEU).

The member states agreed at the Helsinki summit in December 1999 to establish a capability for military crisis-management operations, known as the rapid reaction force, which would be able to undertake peacemaking missions independently of NATO. The force was declared operational at the Laeken summit on 14–15 December 2001.

THE SCHENGEN AGREEMENT

The Schengen Agreement was signed by France, Germany, Belgium, Luxembourg and the Netherlands in 1985. The Agreement committed the five states to abolishing internal border controls and erecting external frontiers against illegal immigrants, drug traffickers, terrorists and organised crime.

Subsequently signed by Spain and Portugal, the Agreement was ratified by the seven signatory states and entered into force in March 1995 with the removal of internal frontier, passport, customs and immigration controls. Italy and Austria became full members in April 1998 and Greece achieved full membership on 1 January 2000. Provisional agreement was reached in June 1995 between the signatory states and the Nordic Union on a merger of the two frontier-free zones, but Denmark, Finland, Sweden, Iceland and Norway are not yet full members, although all five have signed the Schengen Agreement. The UK and the Republic of Ireland have not signed the Agreement, but have expressed their intention to join in some aspects of its work.

The Schengen Agreement originated as an intergovernmental agreement but became part of the EU following the signing of the Amsterdam Treaty.

THE TREATY OF NICE

The Treaty of Nice aims to enable the EU to accommodate up to 13 new member states. It extends qualified majority voting to 30 further articles of the treaties that previously required unanimity. The weighting of votes in the EU Council is to be altered from 1 January 2005 in preparation for the new member states, whose numbers of votes have been set. To obtain a qualified majority, a decision will require a specified number of votes (to be reviewed following each accession); the decision will have to be approved by a majority of member states and represent at least 62 per cent of the total population of the EU. The Treaty also sets the number of MEPs that both existing and new member states will have following enlargement.

The Treaty of Maastricht had established the right of groups of member states to work together without requiring the participation of all (enhanced co-operation); the Treaty of Nice removes the right of individual member states to veto the launch of enhanced co-operation and establishes a minimum number of eight member states for establishing enhanced co-operation in the field of common foreign and security policy (CFSP).

The European Commission will be limited to one member per member state from 2005, with a maximum of 27 commissioners; a rotation system is to be introduced once EU membership exceeds 27 states.

The Treaty also adds to the powers of the President of the Commission and amends the rules of the operation of the Court of Justice.

The Treaty was rejected by 54 per cent of voters in a referendum in Ireland, the only country to put the issue to its electorate.

THE LAEKEN SUMMIT

At the European Council held in Laeken, Belgium on 14–15 December 2001, a declaration was agreed which established a convention to prepare for treaty reforms at the intergovernmental conference due to be held in 2004. The convention, composed of representatives of national governments (15 members), national parliaments (30), the European Parliament (16), the European Commission (2) and the applicant states (39), started work on 28 February 2002, under the chairmanship of former French president Valérie Giscard d'Estaing.

The convention, established to discuss fundamental issues such as the consolidation and simplification of the European treaties, the division of powers between the EU and member states, and how the EU's institutions can be made more relevant to the citizens of the Union, is due to report its recommendations in March 2003. The Laeken European Council also agreed a common definition of terrorism, decided to institute an EU-wide arrest warrant, creating a single security area and thereby making it no longer necessary to extradite those accused of serious crimes, and established Eurojust to co-ordinate cross-border co-operation in crime investigation.

COURT OF JUSTICE OF THE EUROPEAN COMMUNITIES

Palais de la Cour de justice, Boulevard Konrad Adenauer, Kirchberg, L–2925 Luxembourg
Email: info@curia.eu.int;
Web: www.curia.eu.int

The Court of Justice is common to the three European Communities. It exists to safeguard the law in the interpretation and application of the Community treaties, to decide on the legality of decisions of the Council of Ministers or the Commission, and to determine infringements of the treaties. Cases may be brought to it by the member states, the Community institutions, firms or individuals. Its decisions are directly binding in the member countries, and the Maastricht Treaty enhanced the Court's powers by permitting it to impose fines on member states. The 15 judges and eight advocates-general of the Court are appointed for renewable six-year terms by the member governments in concert. During 2000, 503 new cases were lodged at the court and 526 cases were concluded.

Composition of the Court, in order of precedence, as at July 2002:

G. C. Rodríguez Iglesias (*President*); F. G. Jacobs (*Advocate-General*); C. G. Gulmann (*Judge*); D. A. O. Edward (*Judge*); A. M. La Pergola (*Judge*); J.-P. Puissochet (*Judge*); P. Léger (*Advocate-General*); P. Jann (*Judge*); D. Ruíz-Jarabo Colomer (*Advocate-General*); M. Wathelet (*Judge*); R. Schintgen (*Judge*); S. Alber (*Advocate-General*); J. Mischo (*Advocate-General*); V. Skouris (*Judge*); F. Macken (*Judge*); N.

Colneric (*Judge*); S. von Bahr (*Judge*); A. Tizzano (*Advocate-General*); J. N. da Cunha Rodrigues (*Judge*); C. W. A. Timmermans (*Judge*); L. A. Geelhoed (*Advocate-General*); C. Stix-Hackl (*Advocate-General*); A. Rosas (*Judge*); R. Grass (*Registrar*)

COURT OF FIRST INSTANCE

Palais de la Cour de justice, Boulevard Konrad Adenauer, Kirchberg, L-2925 Luxembourg

Established under powers conferred by the Single European Act, the Court of First Instance has jurisdiction to hear and determine all actions brought by natural or legal persons. It is composed of 15 judges, appointed for renewable six-year terms by the governments of the member states. During 2000, 398 new cases were lodged at the court and 344 cases were concluded.

Composition of the Court, as at July 2002:
B. Vesterdorf (*President of the Court of First Instance*); P. Lindh (*Judge*); J. Azizi (*Judge*); P. Mengozzi (*Judge*); A. Meij (*Judge*); R. García-Valdecasas y Fernández (*Judge*); K. Lenaerts (*Judge*); V. Tiili (*Judge*); H. Legal (*Judge*); R. Moura Ramos (*Judge*); J. Cooke (*Judge*); M. Jaeger (*Judge*); J. Pirrung (*Judge*); M. Vilaras (*Judge*); N. Forwood (*Judge*); H. Jung (*Registrar*)

THE COMMITTEE OF THE REGIONS
Montoyerstraat 92/102, B-1000
Brussels, Belgium
Email: info@cor.eu.int
Web: www.cor.eu.int

The Committee of the Regions (COR) is an advisory and consultative body established to redress the lack of a role for regional and local authorities in the EU democratic system. The COR is composed of 222 appointed and indirectly elected members, of whom half are from large regions and half are from small local authorities, who meet five times each year for two days. The COR has eight commissions which deliver opinions on policies affecting regions, such as trans-border transport links, economic and social cohesion, education and training, social policy, culture and regional policy.
President, Jos Chabert (Belgium)

THE EUROPEAN ECONOMIC AND SOCIAL COMMITTEE
Ravensteinstraat 2, B-1000 Brussels, Belgium
Web: www.esc.eu.int

The European Economic and Social Committee (EESC) is an advisory and consultative body. It has 222 members, nominated by member states, and is divided into three groups: employers, workers, and other interest groups such as consumers, farmers and the self-employed. It issues opinions on draft EC legislation and can bring matters to the attention of the Commission, Council and Parliament. The EESC's competencies have increased as a result of revisions to the Treaty of Rome, and the Amsterdam Treaty. The Treaty of Nice formally recognised the importance of the opinions of the EU's economic and social partners.
President, Göke Daniel Frerichs (Germany)

THE EUROPEAN CENTRAL BANK
29 Kaiserstrasse, D-60311 Frankfurt-am-Main,
Germany
E-mail: info@ecb.int
Web: www.ecb.int

The European Central Bank (ECB), which superseded the European Monetary Institute, was established on 1 July 1998. Its governing bodies are the Executive Board, the Governing Council and the General Council. The Executive Board consists of the President, the Vice-President and four other members, who are appointed by the governments of the states participating in the single currency, from people with recognised standing and professional experience; the Governing Council comprises the six members of the Executive Board and the 12 governors of the national central banks of the participating states; the General Council comprises the President and Vice-President and the 15 governors of the national central banks, the other members of the Executive Board being entitled to participate but not to vote. The ECB is independent of national governments and of all other EU institutions. It became fully operational on 1 January 1999, and defines and implements the single monetary policy necessary for EMU. It operates as part of the European System of Central Banks (ESCB), which consists of the ECB and the national central banks of the EU member states.
President, Willem Duisenberg (Netherlands)
Vice-President, Christian Noyer (France)

THE EUROPEAN COURT OF AUDITORS
12 rue A. De Gasperi, L-1615 Luxembourg
Email: euraud@eca.eu.int
Web: www.eca.eu.int

The European Court of Auditors, established in 1977, examines the accounts of all revenue and expenditure of the European Communities and Community bodies and evaluates whether all revenue has been received and all expenditure incurred in a lawful and regular manner and in accordance with the principles of sound financial management. The Court issues an annual report and a statement of assurance as to the reliability of the accounts and the legality and regularity of the underlying transactions. It also publishes special reports on specific topics and delivers opinions on financial matters. The Court has 15 members appointed for six-year terms by the Council of Ministers following consultation with the European Parliament.
President, Juan M. Fabra Vallés (Spain)

THE EUROPEAN INVESTMENT BANK
100 Boulevard Konrad Adenauer, L-2950
Luxembourg
Email: info@eib.org
Web: www.eib.orgeu.int

The European Investment Bank (EIB) was set up in 1958 under the terms of the Treaty of Rome to finance capital investment projects promoting the balanced development of the European Community

by providing loans for capital investment projects furthering EU policy objectives, in fields such as regional development, transport and communications, security of energy supplies, the environment, international competitiveness, support for small and medium-sized enterprises, health and education investment, and investment to encourage a knowledge-based economy.

Outside the EU, the EIB participates in the implementation of the EU's development policy, through long-term loans from own resources or subordinated loans and risk capital from EU or member states' budgetary funds, in some 150 non-EU countries: in pre-accession countries and, under the terms of different association or co-operation agreements, with countries in the Mediterranean region, in the Balkans, in Latin America, Asia and South Africa, in Africa, the Caribbean and the Pacific.

The Bank's total financing operations in 2001 amounted to €36.8 billion, of which €31.2 billion was for investment within the EU.

In June 2000, the EIB launched the Innovation 2000 Initiative, under which €12,000–15,000 million would be available over a three-year period to invest in the provision of new technologies in education, co-finance research and development, finance information and communications technology networks, make use of information technology to increase access to public services and assist SMEs to acquire and use information technologies.

The members of the EIB are the 15 member states of the EU, who have all subscribed to the Bank's capital of €100,000 million. The bulk of the funds required by the Bank to carry out its tasks are borrowed on the capital markets of the EU and non-member countries, and on the international market.

As it operates on a non-profit-making basis, the interest rates charged by the EIB reflect the cost of the Bank's borrowings and closely follow conditions on world capital markets.

The Board of Governors of the EIB consists of one government minister nominated by each of the member countries, usually the finance, economic affairs or treasury minister, who lay down general directives on the credit policy of the Bank and appoint members to the Board of Directors (24 nominated by the member states, one by the European Commission), which takes decisions on the granting and raising of loans and the fixing of interest rates. A Management Committee, composed of the Bank's President and seven Vice-Presidents, also appointed by the Board of Governors, is responsible for the day-to-day operations of the Bank. The President and Vice-Presidents also preside as Chairman and Vice-Chairmen at meetings of the Board of Directors.

President, Philippe Maystadt (Belgium)

Vice-Presidents, Wolfgang Roth; Massimo Ponzellini; Ewald Nowotny; Francis Mayer; Peter Sedgwick; Isabel Martín Castellá; Michael G. Tutty

---

THE EUROPEAN POLICE OFFICE

PO Box 90850, NL-2509 LW The Hague, The Netherlands
Email: info@europol.eu.int
Web: www.europol.eu.int

The European Police Office (Europol) came into being on 1 October 1998 and assumed its full powers on 1 July 1999. It superseded the Europol Drugs Unit and exists to improve police co-operation between member states and to combat terrorism, illicit traffic in drugs and other serious forms of international crime. It is ultimately responsible to the Council. Each member state has set up a national unit to liaise with Europol, and the units send at least one liaison officer to represent its interests at Europol headquarters. Europol maintains a computerised information system, designed to facilitate the exchange of information between member states; the system is maintained by the national units and may be consulted by Europol agents. The computerised database may contain both personal and non-personal data; individuals are entitled to request access to data concerning themselves. Europol has a Management Board comprising one senior police representative from each member state. All Europol activities are monitored by an independent joint supervisory body, to ensure the rights of the individual are upheld.

Director, Jürgen Storbeck (Germany)

Deputy Directors, Willy Bruggeman (Belgium); Gilles Leclair (France); Emanuele Marotta (Italy); Georges Rauchs (Luxembourg); David Valls-Russell (UK)

Other bodies:

THE EUROPEAN MEDICINE EVALUATION AGENCY (EMEA), 7 Westferry Circus, London E14 4HB; Email: mail@emea.eudra.org

THE EUROPEAN ENVIRONMENT AGENCY (EEA), Kongens Nytorv 6, DK- 1050, København, Denmark; Email: eea@eea.eu.int

THE EUROPEAN TRAINING FOUNDATION, Villa Gualino, Viale Settimio Severo 65, I-10133 Torn, Italy; Email: info@etf.eu.int

THE EUROPEAN CENTRE FOR THE DEVELOPMENT OF VOCATIONAL TRAINING (CEDEFOP), PO Box 22427, GR-55102 Thessaloniki (Finikas), Greece; Email: webmaster@cedefop.gr

THE EUROPEAN MONITORING CENTRE FOR DRUGS AND DRUG ADDICTION, Rua da Cruz de Santa Apolónia 23–25, P-1149-045 Lisboa, Portugal; Email: info@emcdda.org

THE EUROPEAN FOUNDATION FOR THE IMPROVEMENT OF LIVING AND WORKING CONDITIONS, Wyattville Road, Loughlinstown, Co. Dublin, Ireland; Email: postmaster@eurofound.ie

THE OFFICE FOR HARMONISATION IN THE INTERNAL MARKET (OHIM), Avenida de Europa 4, AC 77, E-03080 Alicante, Spain; Email: information@oami.eu.int

THE COMMUNITY PLANT VARIETY RIGHTS OFFICE (CPVO), BP 2141, F- 49021 Angers Cédex 02, France; Email: cpvo@cpvo.eu.int

THE EUROPEAN AGENCY FOR RECONSTRUCTION (EAR), PO Box 10177, GR-54626 Thessaloniki, Greece; Email: huges.mingarelli@ear.eu.int

THE EUROPEAN AGENCY FOR SAFETY AND HEALTH AT WORK, Gran Vía 33, E-48009 Bilbao, Spain; Email: information@osha.eu.int

THE TRANSLATION CENTRE FOR BODIES IN THE EUROPEAN UNION, Bâtiment Nouvel Hémicycle, niveau 4, 1 rue du Fort Thüngen, L-1499 Luxembourg; Email: cdt@eu.int

THE EUROPEAN MONITORING CENTRE ON RACISM AND XENOPHOBIA, Rahlgasse 3, A-1060 Wien, Austria; Email: office@eumc.eu.int

EUROPEAN COMMUNITY INFORMATION

EUROPEAN COMMISSION REPRESENTATION OFFICES
ENGLAND, 8 Storey's Gate, London SW1P 3AT. Tel:
020-7973 1992
WALES, 4 Cathedral Road, Cardiff CF11 9SG. Tel:
029-2037 1631
SCOTLAND, 9 Alva Street, Edinburgh EH2 4HP. Tel:
0131-225 2058
NORTHERN IRELAND, Windsor House, 9–15 Bedford
Street, Belfast BT2 7EG. Tel: 028-9024 0708
REPUBLIC OF IRELAND, 18 Dawson Street, Dublin 2

EUROPEAN COMMISSION DELEGATIONS
AUSTRALIA, 18 Arkana Street, Yarralumla, ACT 2600,
and a number of other cities
CANADA, Inn of the Provinces, Office Tower (Suite
1110), 350 Sparks Street, Ottawa, Ontario K1R 7SA
USA, 2300 M Street NW (Suite 707), Washington
DC 20037; 1 Dag Hammarskjöld Plaza, 254 East
47th Street, New York, NY 10017
UK OFFICE OF THE EUROPEAN PARLIAMENT 2 Queen
Anne's Gate, London SW1H 9AA.
Tel: 020-7227 4300

There are European Information Centres, set up to
give information and advice to small and medium-
sized businesses, in 25 British towns and cities. A
number of universities maintain European
Documentation Centres. Many local authorities also
maintain European Public Information Centres,
which provide information to the general public.

EUROPEAN PARLIAMENT

POLITICAL GROUPINGS

	PES	EPP-ED	UEN	ELDR	EUL/NGL	Green/EFA	EDD	Ind.	Total
Austria	7	7	–	–	–	2	–	5	21
Belgium	5	6	–	5	–	7	–	2	25
Denmark	2	1	1	6	2	–	4	–	16
Finland	3	5	–	5	1	2	–	–	16
France	22	19	3	1	11	9	9	12	86*
Germany	35	53	–	–	7	4	–	–	99
Greece	9	9	–	–	7	–	–	–	25
Ireland	1	5	6	1	–	2	–	–	15
Italy	16	35	10	8	6	2	–	10	87
Luxembourg	2	2	–	1	–	1	–	–	6
Netherlands	6	9	–	8	1	4	3	–	31
Portugal	12	9	2	–	2	–	–	–	25
Spain	24	28	–	3	4	4	–	1	64
Sweden	6	7	–	4	3	2	–	–	22
UK	29	37	–	11	–	6	2	2	87
TOTAL	179	232	22	53	44	45	18	32	625*

*one seat is currently vacant

PES   Party of European Socialists (including the British, Irish and Dutch Labour Parties, Northern Ireland Social Democratic and Labour Party, Austrian, Danish, Finnish, German, Italian and Swedish Social Democrats, Belgian, French, Greek, Portuguese, and Spanish Socialists, Italian Democratic Left Party, Luxembourg Socialist Workers' Party), Socialist, Social Democratic and Labour parties

EPP-ED   European People's Party and European Democrats (including British and Danish Conservative Parties, Spanish Popular Party, French Nouvelle UDF, RPR and DL, Irish Fine Gael, Swedish Moderate Party, Finnish National Coalition Party, Austrian People's Party, Greek New Democracy, Belgian Christian Socialists, Italian Christian Democrats, Pensioners' Party and People's Party, Luxembourg Christian Socialists, Portuguese Social Democrats), Christian Democrats, Christian Socialists and Conservatives

UEN   Union for a Europe of Nations

ELDR   European Liberal, Democrat and Reform Party (including British Liberal Democrats, Danish Left and Radical Left Parties, Dutch Democrats '66 and People's Party for Freedom and Democracy, Belgian Liberals, Italian and Luxembourg Democrats, Swedish Liberal People's Party, Finnish Swedish People's Party and Centre Party), centre and liberal parties

EUL/NGL   Confederal Group of the European United Left/Nordic Green Left (French, Greek, Italian and Portuguese Communist Parties, Italian Refounded Communist Party, Danish, Dutch, Swedish, Finnish, Greek and Spanish Socialist/Left parties)

Green/EFA   Greens/European Free Alliance Group (Austrian, British, Danish, Finnish, French, German, Greek, Irish, Italian, Luxembourgish, Portuguese, Spanish and Swedish Green Parties, Dutch Green Left Party, Belgian Ecological Parties, Plaid Cymru and Scottish National Parties), green and nationalist parties

International Organisations

ANDEAN COMMUNITY
General Secretariat, Paseo de la República 3895, esq. Aramburú, San Isidro, Lima 27, Peru
Tel: (00 51) (1) 411 1400; Fax: (00 51) (1) 221 3329
Email: contacto@comunidadandina.org
Web: www.comunidadandina.org

The Andean Community came into being on 1 August 1997. It facilitates the development of the member countries through economic and social integration and co-operation, acceleration of the economic growth of the Andean countries, the promotion of job creation, furthering the aim of creating a Latin American common market, strengthening the position of the member states in the international economic context, and reducing the differences in development that exist between the member states.

It aims to achieve its objectives by a programme of complete trade liberalisation, a common external tariff, the reduction of border controls, the progressive harmonisation of economic and social policies, the co-ordination of national legislation in relevant fields, promoting industrialisation and agricultural development, and supporting technological development programmes.

It comprises the five member states, Bolivia, Colombia, Ecuador, Peru and Venezuela, and the bodies of the Andean Integration System (AIS). The General Secretariat of the Andean Community is its executive body, which is responsible for administration, ensuring that member states comply with their obligations, and resolving disputes. The General Secretariat is under the direction of the Secretary-General, who is elected by the Andean Council of Foreign Ministers (ACFM). The General Secretariat can propose decisions or suggestions to the ACFM and to the Commission. It also manages the integration process, ensures that Community commitments are fulfilled, and maintains relations with the member countries and the executive bodies of other international bodies.

The Andean Presidential Council is the highest-level body of the AIS and comprises the presidents of the member states; it meets at least once a year and decides on new policies, evaluates the integration process and makes decisions on reports and suggestions from other bodies. The chairmanship is rotated among the members of the council on a calendar year basis. The ACFM co-ordinates the positions of the member states in international issues, signs international agreements on behalf of its member states and can issue decisions that are legally binding in the member states. The Commission of the Andean Community is composed of a plenipotentiary representative from each member state and makes, implements and evaluates policies in the field of trade and investment in the region. The Court of Justice of the Andean Community comprises one judge from each member state. It ensures the uniform implementation of decisions and settles disputes. The Andean Development Corporation aims to support the sustainable development of the member states by promoting trade and investment. The Andean Parliament is presently composed of representatives of the national legislatures of the member states, but is due to become directly elected in 2003. It submits proposals to other bodies and promotes the harmonisation of legislation.

Secretary-General, Sebastián Alegrett

ARAB MAGHREB UNION
27 Avenue Okba, Rabat, Morocco
Tel: (00 212) (7) 777 2668; Fax: (00 212) (7) 777 2693
Email: sg.uma@maghrebarabe.org
Web: www.maghrebarabe.org

The treaty establishing the Arab Maghreb Union (AMU) was signed on 17 February 1989 by the heads of state of the five member states, Algeria, Libya, Mauritania, Morocco and Tunisia. The AMU aims to strengthen ties between the member states, who share strong historical, cultural and linguistic affinities, by developing agriculture and commerce, introducing the free circulation of goods and services, and establishing joint projects and economic co-operation programmes.

Decisions are made by the Council of Heads of State, which meets annually, and must be unanimous. A Council of Foreign Affairs Ministers meets regularly to prepare for the sessions of the Council of Heads of State. The Secretariat is based in Rabat and there is a Consultative Assembly, which consists of 30 representatives from each member state, based in Algiers, and a Court of Justice, with two judges from each country, based in Nouakchott, Mauritania.

Secretary-General, Mohamed Habib Boularès (Tunisia)

ASIAN DEVELOPMENT BANK
PO Box 789, 0980 Manila, Philippines
Tel: (632) 632 444; Fax: (632) 636 2444
Email:information@adb.org
Web: www.adb.org

The Asian Development Bank (ADB) was founded in 1966 and is a multilateral financial institution dedicated to reducing poverty in Asia and the Pacific. The ADB extends loans, equity investments and technical assistance to governments and public and private enterprises in its developing member countries, promotes investment of public and private capital for development and assists in co-ordinating development policies and plans in the developing member countries. The bank's projects and programmes prioritise economic growth, human development, gender and development, good governance, environmental protection, private sector development and regional co-operation. The ADB raises funds through members' contributions and bond issues on the world's capital markets. In 2000, the ADB provided loans totalling US$5.8 billion and technical assistance costing US$172 million. There are 59 member countries in the Asian and Pacific region and in Western Europe and North America. The Board of Governors comprises one representative from each member country and meets annually. It elects the 12 members of the Board of Directors and the ADB president, who is also the chairperson of the Board of Directors.

The ADB's headquarters is in the Philippines and there are 22 offices around the world.

ASIA-PACIFIC ECONOMIC CO-OPERATION
438 Alexandra Road, #14–00 Alexandra Point,
Singapore 119958
Tel: (00 65) 6276 1880; Fax: (00 65) 6276 1775
Email: info@mail.apecsec.org.sg
Web: www.apecsec.org.sg

Asia-Pacific Economic Co-operation (APEC) was founded in 1989 in response to the growing interdependence among Asia-Pacific economies. The 1994 Declaration of Common Resolve envisaged a free trade zone, to be established by 2010 by the industrialised countries and by 2020 by the developing member states. There are three pillars of APEC activities: trade and investment liberalisation, business facilitation, and economic and technical co-operation. Members define and fund work programmes for APEC's three committees, one sub-committee, 11 working groups and other APEC fora.

The members are: Australia, Brunei, Canada, Chile, China (People's Republic), China (Hong Kong), Indonesia, Japan, Republic of Korea, Malaysia, Mexico, New Zealand, Papua New Guinea, Peru, the Philippines, Russia, Singapore, Taiwan, Thailand, the USA and Vietnam.

The APEC chairman is responsible for hosting the annual ministerial meeting of foreign and economic ministers. The chairmanship rotates annually among member states. Senior officials of the organisation make recommendations to the ministers and carry out their decisions. They oversee and co-ordinate budgets and work programmes. In addition, there are many advisory groups.

There is a permanent secretariat based in Singapore.

ASSOCIATION OF SOUTH EAST ASIAN NATIONS
70 A. Jalan Sisingamangaraja, Jakarta 12110, Indonesia
Tel: (00 62) (21) 726 2991; Fax: (00 62) (21) 739 8234
Email: public@asean.or.id
Web: www.asean.or.id

The Association of South East Asian Nations (ASEAN) was formed in 1967 with the aims of accelerating economic growth, social progress and cultural development, and ensuring regional stability. The founding members are Indonesia, Malaysia, the Philippines, Singapore and Thailand. Brunei and Vietnam joined in 1984 and 1995 respectively. Laos and Myanmar were admitted in July 1997. Cambodia was admitted on 30 April 1999.

The ASEAN Summit, a meeting of the heads of government, which convenes every three years, is ASEAN's highest authority, but informal summits are held annually. The ASEAN Ministerial Meeting (AMM) is an annual meeting of ASEAN foreign ministers and is responsible for the formulation of policy guidelines and the co-ordination of activities, although other relevant ministers are included in the AMM depending on the subject under discussion. The ASEAN Economic Ministers (AEM) meet annually to co-ordinate economic policy. The AMM and AEM usually hold a joint ministerial meeting before an ASEAN summit.

The 1992 Summit agreed to set up the ASEAN Free Trade Area (AFTA), which is due to be fully implemented by 2003. A common preferential tariff was introduced in 1993. At the annual summit in 1995, a South East Asia nuclear weapon-free zone was declared.

The Secretary-General of ASEAN is appointed on merit by the heads of government and can initiate, advise on, co-ordinate and implement ASEAN activities. In addition to the ASEAN Secretariat based in Jakarta, each member state has a national secretariat in its foreign ministry which organises and implements activities at national level.

Secretary-General, Rodolfo C. Severino (Philippines)
ASEAN COMMITEE IN THE UK, Indonesian Embassy,
38 Grosvenor Square, London W1X 9AD
Tel 020-7499 7661; Fax 020-7491 4993
Chairman, H.E. Nana S. Sutresna

BALTIC ASSEMBLY
Basteja bulvaris 12, LV-1050 Riga, Latvia
Tel: (00 371) 770 1795; Fax: (00 371) 770 1796
Email: baltasam@parks.lv
Web: www.baltasam.org

The Baltic Assembly (BA) is an international organisation for co-operation between the parliaments of Estonia, Latvia and Lithuania, established in November 1991.

The legislature of each member state appoints 20 parliamentarians to the BA, including a head and deputy head of the national delegation. The BA holds two sessions per year, which are held in each of the member states in rotation.

The Presidium of the BA comprises the head and deputy head of each national delegation. It selects a Chairman, who is the head of the delegation of the member state which will host the following session, and the heads of the two other delegations become Deputy Chairmen. The Presidium is responsible for co-ordinating the activities of BA institutions, organises the sessions, supervises the budget and maintains relations with international organisations and the member states' national legislatures. In addition, there are permanent and ad-hoc committees.

The Baltic Assembly meets once a year with the Baltic Council of Ministers, which comprises the heads of government and ministers of the Baltic states and which carries out intergovernmental and regional co-operation between the Baltic States; the joint sessions are known as the Baltic Council.

Chairperson of the Presidium, Giedrè Purvaneckienè (Lithuania)
Deputy Chairmen, Romualds Ražuks (Latvia); Trivimi Velliste (Estonia); Audrius Klišonis (Lithuania); Arnis Razminovičs (Latvia)

BANK FOR INTERNATIONAL SETTLEMENTS
Centralbahnplatz 2, CH-4002 Basel, Switzerland
Tel: (00 41) (61) 280 8080;
Fax: (00 41) (61) 280 9100/8100
Email: email@bis.org
Web: www.bis.org

The Bank for International Settlements (BIS), which was founded in 1930, fosters international monetary and financial co-operation by acting as a forum to promote discussion and facilitate decision-making processes among central banks and within the international financial community. It also acts as a centre for economic and monetary research and an agent in connection with international financial operations.

The statutory organs of the BIS are the General Meeting and the Board of Directors. Forty-nine central banks have rights of voting and representation at General Meetings. Administrative control is vested in the

Board of Directors which comprises 17 members including the Governor of the Bank of England.
Chairman of the Board of Directors and President of the Bank for International Settlements, Nout Wellink (Netherlands)

CAB INTERNATIONAL
Wallingford, Oxon OX10 8DE
Tel: 01491-832111; Fax: 01491-833508
Email: cabi@cabi.org
Web: www.cabi.org

CAB International (formerly the Commonwealth Agricultural Bureau) was founded in 1929. It generates, disseminates and applies scientific knowledge in support of sustainable development, with an emphasis on agriculture, forestry and natural resources and the needs of developing countries. The organisation is owned and governed by its 41 member governments, each represented on an Executive Council. A Governing Board provides guidance to management on policy issues.

CABI has two divisions: bioscience and publishing. These undertake research and consultancy aimed at raising agricultural productivity, conserving biological resources, protecting the environment and controlling disease. The organisation publishes books, journals and newsletters and produces bibliographic databases on agriculture, health and allied disciplines. It also undertakes contracted scientific research and provides consultancy services and information support to developing countries.
Director-General, Dr Denis Blight

CARIBBEAN COMMUNITY AND COMMON MARKET
PO Box 10827, Georgetown, Guyana
Tel: (00 592) (226 9281/9; Fax: (00 592) (226 7816
Email: carisec2@caricom.org
Web: www.caricom.org

The Caribbean Community and Common Market (CARICOM) was established in 1973 with the signing of the Treaty of Chaguaramas, which was revised in 2001. The objectives of Caricom are to improve working and living standards, to aim for full employment, to promote economic development and convergence, to expand economic relations with third states, to enhance economic competitiveness and productivity, to co-ordinate member states' foreign and economic policies and enhance functional co-operation in the delivery of common services, including the promotion of activities in the fields of health, education, transport and telecommunications.

The supreme organ is the Conference of Heads of Government, which determines policy, takes strategic decisions and is responsible for resolving conflicts and all matters relating to the founding treaty. The Community Council of Ministers consists of ministers of government responsible for CARICOM affairs and any other ministers designated by member states, and is responsible for strategic planning in the areas of economic integration, functional co-operation and external relations. The principal administrative arm is the Secretariat, based in Guyana. The Bureau of the Conference of Heads of Government is the executive body. It comprises the Chairman of the Conference, the outgoing Chairman and the Secretary-General, who are authorised to initiate proposals and to secure the implementation of CARICOM decisions. In addition, there are four ministers' councils dealing with trade and economic development, foreign and community relations, human and social development, and finance and planning.

The 14 member states are Antigua and Barbuda, the Bahamas (which is not a member of the Common Market), Barbados, Belize, Dominica, Grenada, Guyana, Jamaica, Montserrat, St Christopher and Nevis, St Lucia, St Vincent and the Grenadines, Suriname and Trinidad and Tobago. Anguilla, the British Virgin Islands and the Turks and Caicos Islands are associate members. Aruba, Bermuda, the Cayman Islands, Colombia, the Dominican Republic, Mexico, the Netherlands' Antilles, Puerto Rico and Venezuela have observer status. Following a successful application for membership, Haiti is to be admitted as a full member of the Caribbean Community upon depositing an instrument of accession.
Secretary-General, Edwin W. Carrington

THE COMMONWEALTH

The Commonwealth is a voluntary association of 54 sovereign independent states together with their associated states and dependencies. All of the states were formerly parts of the British Empire or League of Nations (later UN) mandated territories, except for Mozambique which was admitted as a unique case because of its history of co-operation with neighbouring Commonwealth nations.

The status and relationship of member nations were first defined by the Inter-Imperial Relations Committee of the 1926 Imperial Conference, when the six existing dominions (Australia, Canada, the Irish Free State, Newfoundland, New Zealand and South Africa) were described as 'autonomous Communities within the British Empire, equal in status, in no way subordinate one to another in any aspect of their domestic or external affairs, though united by a common allegiance to the Crown and freely associated as Members of the British Commonwealth of Nations'. This formula was given legal substance by the Statute of Westminster 1931.

This concept of a group of countries owing allegiance to a single Crown changed in 1949 when India decided to become a republic. Her continued membership of the Commonwealth was agreed by the other members on the basis of her 'acceptance of The King as the symbol of the free association of its independent member nations and as such the head of the Commonwealth'. This paved the way for other republics to join the association in due course. Member nations agreed at the time of the accession of Queen Elizabeth II to recognise Her Majesty as the new Head of the Commonwealth. However, the position is not vested in the British Crown.

THE MODERN COMMONWEALTH

As the UK's former colonies joined, initially with India and Pakistan in 1947, the Commonwealth was transformed from a grouping of all-white dominions into a multiracial association of equal, sovereign nations. It increasingly focused on promoting development and racial equality and effectively expelled South Africa in 1961 over its policy of apartheid.

The new goals of advocating democracy, the rule of law, good government and social justice were enshrined in the Harare Commonwealth Declaration (1991), which formed the basis of new membership guidelines agreed in Cyprus in 1993. Following the adoption of

measures at the New Zealand summit in 1995 against serious or persistent violations of these principles, Nigeria was suspended in 1995 and Sierra Leone was suspended in 1997 for anti-democratic behaviour. Sierra Leone's suspension was revoked in March 1998 when the legitimate government was returned to power. Similarly, Nigeria's suspension was lifted on 29 May 1999, the day a newly elected civilian president took office. The heads of government meeting in Edinburgh in 1997 established a set of economic principles for the Commonwealth, promoting economic growth whilst protecting smaller member states from the negative effects of globalisation.

MEMBERSHIP

Membership of the Commonwealth involves acceptance of the association's basic principles and is subject to the approval of existing members. There are 54 members at present. (The date of joining the Commonwealth is shown in parentheses.)

*Antigua and Barbuda (1981)	Guyana (1966)
*Australia (1931)	India (1947)
*The Bahamas (1973)	*Jamaica (1962)
Bangladesh (1972)	Kenya (1963)
*Barbados (1966)	Kiribati
*Belize (1981)	Lesotho (1966)
Botswana (1966)	Malawi (1964)
Brunei (1984)	Malaysia (1957)
Cameroon (1995)	The Maldives (1982)
*Canada (1931)	Malta (1964)
Cyprus (1961)	Mauritius (1968)
Dominica (1978)	Mozambique (1995)
‡Fiji (1970, 1997)	Namibia(1990)
The Gambia (1965)	Nauru (1968)
Ghana (1957)	*New Zealand (1931)
*Grenada (1974)	Nigeria (1960
†Pakistan (1947)	Sri Lanka (1948)
*Papua New Guinea (1975)	Swaziland (1968)
*St Christopher and	Tanzania (1961)
Nevis (1983)	Tonga (1970)
*St Lucia (1979)	Trinidad and
*St Vincent and the	Tobago (1962)
Grenadines (1979)	*Tuvalu (1978)
Samoa (1976)	Uganda (1962)
Seychelles (1976)	*United Kingdom
Sierra Leone (1961)	Vanuatu (1980)
Singapore (1965)	Zambia (1964)
*Solomon Islands (1978)	§ Zimbabwe (1980)
South Africa (1931)	

*Realms of Queen Elizabeth II; †Suspended 18 October 1999; ‡ Suspended 6 June 2000, readmitted 21 December 2001 § Suspended 20 March 2002

Tuvalu became a full member on 1 September 2000. Pakistan's membership was suspended on 18 October 1999, following a military coup. Fiji's membership was suspended on 6 June 2000 following the overthrow of its democratically elected government.

Countries which have left the Commonwealth
Fiji (1987, rejoined 1997, suspended 2000, rejoined 2001)
Republic of Ireland (1949)
Pakistan (1972, rejoined 1989, suspended 1999)
South Africa (1961, rejoined 1994)

Of the 54 member states, 16 have Queen Elizabeth II as head of state, 33 are republics, and five have national monarchies.

In each of the realms where Queen Elizabeth II is head of state (except for the UK), she is personally represented by a Governor-General, who holds in all essential respects the same position in relation to the administration of public affairs in the realm as is held by Her Majesty in Britain. The Governor-General is appointed by The Queen on the advice of the government of the state concerned.

INTERGOVERNMENTAL AND OTHER LINKS

The main forum for consultation is the Commonwealth heads of government meetings held biennially to discuss international developments and to consider co-operation among members. Decisions are reached by consensus, and the views of the meeting are set out in a communiqué. There are also annual meetings of finance ministers and frequent meetings of ministers and officials in other fields, such as education, health, women's affairs, agriculture, and science. Intergovernmental links are complemented by the activities of some 300 Commonwealth non-governmental organisations linking professionals, sportsmen and sportswomen, and interest groups, forming a 'people's Commonwealth'. The Commonwealth Games take place every four years.

Assistance to other Commonwealth countries normally has priority in the bilateral aid programmes of the association's developed members (Australia, Britain, Canada and New Zealand), who direct about 30 per cent of their aid to other member countries. Developing Commonwealth nations also assist their poorer partners, and many Commonwealth voluntary organisations promote development.

COMMONWEALTH SECRETARIAT

The Commonwealth has a secretariat, established in 1965 in London, which is funded by all member governments. This is the main agency for multilateral communication between member governments on issues relating to the Commonwealth as a whole. It promotes consultation and co-operation, disseminates information on matters of common concern, organises meetings including the biennial summits, co-ordinates Commonwealth activities, and provides technical assistance for economic and social development through the Commonwealth Fund for Technical Co-operation.

The Commonwealth Foundation was established by Commonwealth governments in 1966 as an autonomous body with a board of governors representing Commonwealth governments that fund the Foundation. It promotes and funds exchanges and other activities aimed at strengthening the skills and effectiveness of professionals and non-governmental organisations. It also promotes culture, rural development, social welfare and the role of women.

COMMONWEALTH SECRETARIAT, Marlborough House, Pall Mall, London SW1Y 5HX. Tel: 020-7839 3411; Fax: 020-7839 9081 Email: info@commonwealth.int Web: www.thecommonwealth.org
Secretary-General, Rt. Hon. Don McKinnon (New Zealand)

COMMONWEALTH FOUNDATION, Marlborough House, Pall Mall, London SW1Y 5HY. Tel: 020-7930 3783.
Director, Colin Ball (UK)

COMMONWEALTH INSTITUTE, Kensington High Street, London W8 6NQ. Tel: 020-7603 4535. *Director-General*, David French

COMMONWEALTH OF INDEPENDENT STATES

Ul. Kirava 17, Minsk, Belarus
Tel: (00 375) (17) 222 3517; Fax: (00 375) (17) 227 2339
Email: webmaster@www.cis.minsk.by
Web: www.cis.minsk.by

The Commonwealth of Independent States (CIS) is a multilateral grouping of 12 sovereign states that were formerly constituent republics of the USSR (Armenia, Azerbaijan, Belarus, Georgia, Kazakhstan, Kyrgyzstan, Moldova, Russia, Tajikistan, Turkmenistan, Ukraine and Uzbekistan). It was formed in 1991. Georgia joined in 1993. The CIS charter, signed in 1993 by seven states (Armenia, Belarus, Kazakhstan, Kyrgyzstan, Russia, Tajikistan, Uzbekistan) and open for signing by the other states, formally established the functions of the organisation and the obligations of its member states.

The CIS acts as a co-ordinating mechanism for foreign, defence and economic policies and is a forum for addressing problems which have arisen from the break-up of the USSR. These matters are addressed in more than 70 inter-state, intergovernmental co-ordinating and consultative statutory bodies. However, member states have criticised the CIS for operating ineffectively and for failing to carry through decisions made by CIS organs.

STRUCTURE

The two supreme CIS bodies are the Council of Heads of State and the Council of Heads of Government. The Council of Heads of State is the highest organ of the CIS and there are various ministerial, parliamentary, banking, economic and security councils. The Executive Committee, based in Minsk and Moscow, provides administrative support.

DEFENCE CO-OPERATION

On becoming member states of the CIS, the member states agreed to recognise their existing borders, respect one another's territorial integrity and reject the use of military force or other forms of coercion to settle disputes between them.

A Treaty on Collective Security was signed in 1992 by six states and a joint peacemaking force, to intervene in CIS conflicts, was agreed upon by nine states. Russia concluded bilateral and multilateral agreements with other CIS states under the supervision of the Council of Heads of Collective Security (established 1993). These were gradually upgraded into CIS agreements under the umbrella of the Treaty on Collective Security, enabling Russia to station troops in eight of the other 11 CIS states (not Moldova, Turkmenistan or Ukraine), and giving Russian forces de facto control of virtually all of the former USSR's external borders. Only Ukraine and Moldova remained outside the defence co-operation framework and did not sign the Treaty on Collective Security, from which Azerbaijan, Georgia and Uzbekistan withdrew in 1999, forming a new defensive grouping with Moldova and Ukraine. Russian border guards were also withdrawn from Georgia, Kyrgyzstan and Turkmenistan in 1999.

ECONOMIC CO-OPERATION

In 1991, 11 republics signed a treaty forming an economic community. The principles of the treaty were embodied within the CIS and formed the basis of its economic co-operation. Members agreed to refrain from economic actions that would damage each other and to co-ordinate economic and monetary policies. A Co-ordinating Consultative Committee, an economic arbitration court and an inter-state bank were established. A single monetary unit, the rouble, was originally agreed upon by all member states, and the members recognised that the basis of recovery for their economies was private ownership, free enterprise and competition.

The 11 CIS members who signed the Treaty on the Establishment of an Economic Union in September 1993 (Ukraine is an associate member of the economic union) committed themselves to a common economic space with free movement of goods, services, capital and labour. Belarus, Kazakhstan, Kyrgyzstan and Russia signed the Treaty on the Establishment of a Customs Union in March 1996; the treaty was later signed by Tajikistan and on 10 October 2000, the presidents of the five countries approved a treaty establishing the Eurasian Economic Community.

Executive Secretary, Yuri Yarov

CONFERENCE ON INTERACTION AND CONFIDENCE-BUILDING MEASURES IN ASIA

The Conference on Interaction and Confidence-Building Measures in Asia (CICA) aims to create a security framework for Asia along the same lines as the OSCE in Europe. The foreign ministers of the member states signed the Declaration on the Principles Guiding Relations on 14 September 1999, in which the signatories confirmed their determination to uphold the principles of sovereignty, territorial integrity, peaceful settlement of disputes, non-intervention in internal affairs, economic, social and cultural co-operation, and human rights and fundamental freedoms.

The founder members of CICA are Afghanistan, Azerbaijan, China, Egypt, India, Iran, Israel, Kazakhstan, Kyrgyzstan, Pakistan, the Palestinian National Authority, Russia, Tajikistan, Turkey and Uzbekistan. Mongolia joined in June 2001. Observers are Indonesia, Japan, Lebanon, Malaysia, South Korea, Thailand, Ukraine, the USA and Vietnam.

There is at present no permanent secretariat.

CO-OPERATION COUNCIL FOR THE ARAB STATES OF THE GULF

PO Box 7153, Riyadh 11 462, Saudi Arabia
Tel: (00 966) (01) 482 7777; Fax (00 966) (01) 482 9109
Web: www.gcc-sg.org

The Co-operation Council for the Arab States of the Gulf, or Gulf Co-operation Council (GCC), as it is informally known, was established on 25 May 1981 with the objectives of increasing co-ordination and integration between its member states, harmonising economic, commercial, educational and social policies and promoting scientific and technical innovation in key economic areas.

The GCC has six members: Bahrain, Kuwait, Oman, Qatar, Saudi Arabia and the United Arab Emirates.

The highest authority of the GCC is the Supreme Council, whose presidency rotates among members' heads of states based on the (Arabic) alphabetical order of their names. It holds one regular session every year, but extraordinary sessions may be convened if necessary. The meeting of the Supreme Council is considered valid

812 International Organisations

if attended by two-thirds of the member states.
The Ministerial Council, which ordinarily meets every
three months, consists of the Foreign Ministers of the
member states or other delegated ministers. The
presidency of the Ministerial Council is held by the state
which last presided over the Supreme Council or, if
necessary, the state which is next to preside over the
Supreme Council. Disputes at either commission can be
referred to an *ad hoc* commission.

Administrative functions are dealt with by a General
Secretariat, which is composed of a Secretary-General,
Assistant Secretaries-General and a number of staff.

COUNCIL OF THE BALTIC SEA STATES
Secretariat, Strömsborg, PO Box 2010, S-103
11 Stockholm, Sweden
Tel: (00 46) (8) 440 1920; Fax: (00 46) (8) 440 1944
Email: cbss@cbss.st
Web: www.cbss.st

The Council of the Baltic Sea States (CBSS) was founded
in March 1992 with the aim of creating a regional forum
to increase co-operation and co-ordination among the
states which border on the Baltic Sea in assisting new
democratic institutions, economic and technical
development, humanitarian aid and health, energy and
environmental issues, cultural programmes, education,
tourism, transportation and communication.

There are 12 members: Denmark, Estonia, Finland,
Germany, Iceland, Latvia, Lithuania, Norway, Poland,
Russia, Sweden and the European Commission.

The Council consists of the foreign ministers of each
member state and a member of the European
Commission. Chairmanship of the Council rotates on
an annual basis, and the annual session is held in the
country currently in the chair. The foreign minister of
the presiding country is responsible for co-ordinating
activities between the sessions.
Chairmanship July 2002-June 2003, Finland, *July 2003-
June 2004*, Estonia

THE COUNCIL OF EUROPE
F-67075 Strasbourg, France
Tel: (00 33) (3) 8841 2033; Fax: (00 33) (3) 8841 2745
Email: point_i@coe.int
Web: www.coe.int

The Council of Europe was founded in 1949. Its aim is
to achieve greater unity between its members, to
safeguard their European heritage and to facilitate their
progress in economic, social, cultural, educational,
scientific, legal and administrative matters, and in the
furtherance of pluralist democracy, human rights and
fundamental freedoms.

The 44 members are Albania, Andorra, Armenia,
Austria, Azerbaijan, Belgium, Bosnia-Hercegovina,
Bulgaria, Croatia, Cyprus, Czech Republic, Denmark,
Estonia, Finland, France, Georgia, Germany, Greece,
Hungary, Iceland, Republic of Ireland, Italy, Latvia,
Liechtenstein, Lithuania, Luxembourg, Macedonia,
Malta, Moldova, the Netherlands, Norway, Poland,
Portugal, Romania, Russia, San Marino, Slovakia,
Slovenia, Spain, Sweden, Switzerland, Turkey, the UK
and Ukraine. 'Special guest status' has been granted to
Yugoslavia, Canada, Japan, Mexico, the USA, and the
Vatican City State has observer status.

The organs are the Committee of Ministers,
consisting of the foreign ministers of member countries,

who meet twice yearly, and the Parliamentary Assembly
of 301 members, elected or chosen by the national
parliaments of member countries in proportion to the
relative strength of political parties. There is also a Joint
Committee of Ministers and Representatives of the
Parliamentary Assembly.

The Committee of Ministers is the executive organ.
The majority of its conclusions take the form of
international agreements (known as European
Conventions) or recommendations to governments.
Decisions of the Ministers may also be embodied in
partial agreements to which a limited number of
member governments are party. Member governments
accredit Permanent Representatives to the Council in
Strasbourg, who are also the Ministers' Deputies. The
Committee of Deputies meets every month to transact
business and to take decisions on behalf of Ministers.

The Parliamentary Assembly holds three week-long
sessions a year. Its 13 permanent committees meet once
or twice between each public plenary session of the
Assembly. The Congress of Local and Regional
Authorities of Europe each year brings together mayors
and municipal councillors in the same numbers as the
members of the Parliamentary Assembly.

One of the principal achievements of the Council of
Europe is the European Convention on Human Rights
(1950) under which was established the European
Commission and the European Court of Human Rights,
which were merged in 1993. The reorganised European
Court of Human Rights sits in chambers of seven judges
or exceptionally as a grand chamber of 17 judges.
Litigants must exhaust legal processes in their own
country before bringing cases before the court.

Among other conventions and agreements are the
European Social Charter, the European Cultural
Convention, the European Code of Social Security, the
European Convention on the Protection of National
Minorities, and conventions on extradition, the legal
status of migrant workers, torture prevention,
conservation and the transfer of sentenced prisoners.
Most recently, the specialised bodies of the Venice
Commission and Demosthenes have been set up to assist
in developing legislative, administrative and
constitutional reforms in central and eastern Europe.

Non-member states take part in certain Council of
Europe activities on a regular or *ad hoc* basis; thus the
Holy See participates in all the educational, cultural and
sports activities. The European Youth Centre is an
educational residential centre for young people. The
European Youth Foundation provides youth
organisations with funds for their international
activities.
Secretary-General, Walter Schwimmer (Austria)
Permanent UK Representative, HE Andrew Carter, CMG,
apptd 1997

THE ECONOMIC COMMUNITY OF WEST AFRICAN STATES
Secretariat Building, 60 Yakubu Gowon Crescent, PMB
401, Abuja, Nigeria
Tel: (00 234) (9) 314 7647 9; Fax: (00 234) (9) 314 3005/6
Email: info@ecowasmail.net
Web: www.ecowas.int

The Economic Community of West African States
(ECOWAS) was founded in 1975 and came into
operation in 1977. It aims to promote the cultural,
economic and social development of West Africa
through mutual co-operation. A revised ECOWAS

Treaty was signed in 1993 and came into effect in July 1995. It makes the prevention and control of regional conflicts an aim of ECOWAS and provides for the imposition of a community tax and for the establishment of a regional parliament, an economic and social council and a court of justice.

The supreme authority of ECOWAS is vested in the annual summit of heads of government of all 15 member states. A Council of Ministers, two from each member state, meets biannually to monitor the organisation and make recommendations to the summit. ECOWAS operates through a Secretariat, headed by the Executive Secretary. In addition there are four Deputy Executive Secretaries.

The ECOWAS Parliament was inaugurated in November 2000 and justices for the Court of Justice were sworn in in January 2001.

The Fund for Co-operation, Compensation and Development, situated at Lomé, Togo, has been restructured into three funds: the ECOWAS Regional Development Fund, the ECOWAS Bank for Investment and Development and the ECOWAS Regional Investment Bank. The funds finance development projects and provide compensation to member states who have suffered losses as a result of ECOWAS's policies, particularly trade liberalisation.

The members of ECOWAS are: Benin, Burkina Faso, Cape Verde, Côte d'Ivoire, Gambia, Ghana, Guinea, Guinea-Bissau, Liberia, Mali, Niger, Nigeria, Senegal, Sierra Leone and Togo. Mauritania left the organisation in December 2000.

An ECOWAS Monitoring Group (ECOMOG) peacekeeping force has been involved in attempts to restore peace in Liberia (1990–6), in Guinea-Bissau (1998–9) and in Sierra Leone since 1997.

Executive Secretary, Dr Mohammed Ibn Chambas (Ghana)

THE EUROPEAN BANK FOR RECONSTRUCTION AND DEVELOPMENT

One Exchange Square, London EC2A 2JN
Tel: 020-7338 6000; Fax: 020-7338 6100
Web: www.ebrd.com

The European Bank for Reconstruction and Development (EBRD), established in 1991, is an international institution with 62 members (60 countries, the European Community and the European Investment Bank).

The aim of the EBRD is to build market economies and democracies in 27 countries in central and eastern Europe and central Asia.

The EBRD finances projects in both the private and public sectors, providing direct funding for financial institutions, infrastructure and other key sectors. The main forms of EBRD financing are loans, equity investments and guarantees. No more than 40 per cent of the EBRD's investment can be made in state-owned concerns. EBRD is the largest foreign investor in the region's private sector and in addition to its own lending, facilitates significant foreign direct investment. EBRD pays particular attention to strengthening the financial sector and to promoting small and medium-sized enterprises. It works in co-operation with national governments, private companies, and international organisations such as the OECD, the IMF, the World Bank and the UN specialised agencies.

The EBRD has a subscribed capital of €20 billion. The EBRD is also able to borrow on world capital markets. Its major subscribers are the USA, 10 per cent; Britain, France, Germany, Italy and Japan, 8.5 per cent each. As of 31 December 2001, the EBRD had signed 807 projects with a total net value of €20.2 billion.

The highest authority is the Board of Governors; each member appoints one Governor and one Alternate. The Governors delegate most powers to a 23-member Board of Directors; the Directors are responsible for the EBRD's operations and budget, and are elected by the Governors for three-year terms. The Governors also elect the President of the Board of Directors, who acts as the Bank's president for a four-year term.

President of the Board of Directors, Jean Lemierre (France)

Chairman of the Board of Governors, Guilhermo d'Oliveira Martins (Portugal)

EUROPEAN FREE TRADE ASSOCIATION

Headquarters: 9–11 rue de Varembé, CH-1211 Geneva 20, Switzerland
Tel: (00 41) (22) 749 1111; Fax: (00 41) (22) 733 9291
Web: www.secretariat.efta.int
EEA matters: Trierstraat 74, B-1040 Brussels, Belgium
Tel: (00 32) (2) 286 1711; Fax: (00 32) (2) 286 1750
Email: efta-mailbox@efta.int

The European Free Trade Association (EFTA) was established in 1960 by Austria, Denmark, Norway, Portugal, Sweden, Switzerland and the UK, and was subsequently joined by Finland (associate member 1961, full member 1986), Iceland (1970) and Liechtenstein (1991). Six members have left to join the European Union: Denmark and the UK (1972), Portugal (1985), Austria, Finland and Sweden (1995). The existing members are Iceland, Liechtenstein, Norway and Switzerland.

The first objective of EFTA was to establish free trade in industrial products between members; this was achieved in 1966. Its second objective was the creation of a single market in western Europe and in 1972 EFTA signed free trade agreements with the EC covering trade in industrial goods; the remaining tariffs on industrial products were abolished in 1977 and the Luxembourg Declaration on broader co-operation between EFTA and the European Community was signed in 1984.

An agreement on the creation of the European Economic Area (EEA), an extension of the EC single market to the EFTA states, was signed in 1992 and entered into force on 1 January 1994. Switzerland rejected EEA membership in a referendum in 1992 and Liechtenstein joined on 1 May 1995 after adapting its customs union with Switzerland. The implementation of the agreement is supervised by the EEA Council, composed of EFTA and EU ministers, and the EFTA Surveillance Authority. The three EFTA EEA members also participate in a wide range of other EC programmes including research and development, environmental matters, and education and training.

EFTA has signed free trade agreements with Turkey (1991), Israel, Poland and Romania (1992), Bulgaria, the Czech Republic, Hungary and Slovakia (1993), Estonia, Latvia, Lithuania and Slovenia (1995), Morocco (1997), the PLO (1998), Macedonia and Mexico (2000), Croatia and Jordan (2001) and Singapore (2002). In addition, EFTA has signed declarations of economic co-operation with Albania (1992), Egypt and Tunisia (1995), Lebanon (1997), the GCC, Mercosur (2000), Ukraine, and Yugoslavia.

The EFTA Council is the principal organ of the Association. It meets regularly at the level of ambassadors to the EFTA Secretariat in Geneva.
Secretary-General, William Rossier (Switzerland)
Deputy Secretary-General (Geneva), Grétar Már Sigurdsson (Iceland)
Deputy Secretary-General (Brussels), Per Mannes (Norway)

EUROPEAN ORGANISATION FOR NUCLEAR RESEARCH (CERN)
CH-1211 Geneva 23, Switzerland
Tel: (00 41) (22) 767 4101; Fax: (00 41) (22) 785 0247
Web: www.cern.ch

The Convention establishing the European Organisation for Nuclear Research (CERN) came into force in 1954. CERN promotes European collaboration in high energy physics of a scientific, rather than a military nature.
    The member countries are Austria, Belgium, Bulgaria, the Czech Republic, Denmark, Finland, France, Germany, Greece, Hungary, Italy, the Netherlands, Norway, Poland, Portugal, Slovakia, Spain, Sweden, Switzerland and the UK. Israel, Japan, Russia, Turkey, the USA, the EU Commission and UNESCO have observer status.
    The Council is the highest policy-making body and comprises two delegates from each member state. There is also a Committee of the Council comprising a single delegate from each member state (who is also a Council member) and the chairmen of the scientific policy and finance advisory committees. The Council is chaired by the President who is elected by the Council in Session. The Council also elects the Director-General, who is responsible for the internal organisation of CERN. The Director-General heads a workforce of approximately 3,000, including physicists, craftsmen, technicians and administrative staff. At present over 6,500 physicists use CERN's facilities.
    The member countries contribute to the budget in proportion to their net national revenue. The 2001 budget was SFr 1,050 million.
President of the Council, Maurice Bourquin (Switzerland)
Director-General (1999–2004), Prof. Luciano Maiani (Italy)

EUROPEAN SPACE AGENCY
8–10 rue Mario Nikis, F-75738 Paris Cedex 15, France
Tel: (00 33) (1) 5369 7654; Fax: (00 33) (1) 5369 7560
Web: www.esa.int

The European Space Agency (ESA) was created in 1975 by the merger of the European Space Research Organisation (ESRO) and the European Launcher Development Organisation (ELDO). Its aims include the advancement of space research and technology and the implementation of a long-term European space policy.
    The member countries are Austria, Belgium, Denmark, Finland, France, Germany, Republic of Ireland, Italy, the Netherlands, Norway, Portugal, Spain, Sweden, Switzerland and the UK. Canada is a co-operating state.
    The agency is directed by a Council composed of the representatives of the member states; its chief officer is the Director-General.
Director-General, Antonio Rodotà, *apptd* 1997

FOOD AND AGRICULTURE ORGANISATION OF THE UNITED NATIONS
Viale delle Terme di Caracalla, I-00100 Rome, Italy
Tel: (00 39) (6) 57051; Fax: (00 39) (6) 5705 3152
Email: fao-hq@fao.org
Web: www.fao.org

The Food and Agriculture Organisation (FAO) is a specialised UN agency, established in 1945. It assists rural populations by raising levels of nutrition and living standards, and by encouraging greater efficiency in food production and distribution. It analyses and disseminates information on agriculture and natural resources. The FAO also advises governments on national agricultural policy and planning; its Investment Centre, together with the World Bank and other financial institutions, helps to prepare development projects. The FAO's field programme covers a range of activities, including strengthening crop production, rural and livestock development, and conservation.
    The FAO's top priorities are sustainable agriculture, rural development and food security. The Organisation attempts to ensure the availability of adequate food supplies, stability in the flow of supplies and the securing of access to food by the poor. The FAO monitors potential famine areas. The Special Relief Operations Service channels emergency aid from governments and other agencies, and assists in rehabilitation. The Technical Co-operation Programme responds to urgent or unforeseen requests for technical assistance.
    The FAO had 184 members (183 states plus the EU) as at November 2001. It is governed by a biennial conference of its members which sets a programme and budget. The November 2001 budget for 2000–1 was US$650million, funded by member countries in proportion to their gross national products. The FAO is also funded by the UN Development Programme, donor governments and other institutions.
    The Conference elects a Director-General and a 49-member Council which governs between conferences. The Regular and Field Programmes are administered by a Secretariat, headed by the Director-General. Five regional, five sub-regional and 80 national offices help administer the Field Programme.
Director-General, Jacques Diouf (Senegal)

GUUAM

GUUAM (Georgia, Ukraine, Uzbekistan, Azerbaijan and Moldova) was founded as a political, economic and strategic alliance designed to strengthen the independence and sovereignty of its members.
    GUUAM seeks to promote trade, economic growth, and co-operation between its members primarily through the establishment of a Eurasian-Transcaucasian transportation corridor (TRACECA); GUUAM is also a forum for the discussion of security problems, promoting conflict resolution and a common position in international organisations.
    Following growing co-operation between their countries, on 10 October 1997, the presidents of Azerbaijan, Georgia, Moldova and Ukraine declared their mutual interest in promoting co-operation, and security, political and economic contacts. Uzbekistan joined the group in April 1999.

It was decided in September 2000 to convene summits of the Heads of State at least once a year, and meetings at the level of Ministers for Foreign Affairs at least twice a year. A Committee of National Co-ordinators meets Quarterly.

An information office is to be established in Kyiv, Ukraine.

INTERNATIONAL ATOMIC ENERGY AGENCY

Vienna International Centre, Wagramerstrasse 5, PO Box 100, A-1400 Vienna, Austria
Tel: (00 43) (1) 26000; Fax: (00 43) (1) 26007
Email: Official.Mail@iaea.org
Web: www.iaea.org/worldatom

The International Atomic Energy Agency (IAEA) was established in 1957. It is an intergovernmental organisation that reports to, but is not a specialised agency of, the UN.

The IAEA aims to enhance the contribution of atomic energy to peace, health and prosperity and to ensure that any assistance that it provides is not used for military purposes. It establishes atomic energy safety standards and offers services to its member states for the safe operation of their nuclear facilities and for radiation protection. It is the focal point for international conventions on the early notification of a nuclear accident, assistance in the case of such an accident, civil liability for nuclear damage, physical protection of nuclear material, nuclear safety and the safety of spent fuel and radioactive waste management. The IAEA also encourages research and training in nuclear power. It is additionally charged with drawing up safeguards and verifying their use in accordance with the Nuclear Non-Proliferation Treaty (NPT) 1968, the Treaty for the Prohibition of Nuclear Weapons in Latin America (Tlatelolco Treaty) 1968, the Treaty on a South Pacific Nuclear Free Zone (Rarotonga Treaty), the South East Asia Nuclear Weapon-Free Zone Treaty (Bangkok Treaty) and the African Nuclear Weapon-Free Zone Treaty (Pelindaba Treaty) 1996. Together with the Food and Agriculture Organisation and the World Health Organisation, the IAEA established an International Consultative Group on Food Irradiation in 1983.

The IAEA concluded a safeguards agreement with North Korea in April 1992 and began inspections to verify that its nuclear programme was for peaceful purposes only. In 1993 the IAEA informed the UN Security Council that North Korea had violated its NPT obligations and all technical aid to North Korea was suspended. North Korea resigned from the IAEA in 1994, but permitted IAEA inspections under the terms of an agreement with the USA which enabled the IAEA to resume safeguards inspections.

The IAEA had 134 members as at April 2002. A General Conference of all its members meets annually to decide policy, a programme and a budget (2001, US$225 million), as well as electing a Director-General and a 35-member Board of Governors. The Board meets four times a year to formulate policy which is implemented by the Secretariat under a Director-General.

Director-General, Mohamed El Baradei (Egypt)
Permanent UK Representative, Dr John Freeman, Jaurèsgasse 12, A-1030 Vienna, Austria

INTERNATIONAL CIVIL AVIATION ORGANISATION

999 University Street, Montréal, Québec, Canada H3C 5H7
Tel: (00 1) (514) 954 8219; Fax: (00 1) (514) 954 6077
Email: icaohq@icao.int
Web: www.icao.int

The International Civil Aviation Organisation (ICAO) was founded with the signing of the Chicago Convention on International Civil Aviation in 1944, and became a specialised agency of the United Nations in 1947. It sets international technical standards and recommended practices for all areas of civil aviation, including airworthiness, air navigation, air traffic control and pilot licensing. It encourages uniformity and simplicity in ground regulations and operations at international airports, including immigration and customs control. The ICAO also promotes regional air navigation, plans for ground facilities and collects and distributes air transport statistics world-wide. It is dedicated to improving safety and to the orderly development of civil aviation throughout the world.

The ICAO had 188 members as at June 2002. It is governed by an assembly of its members which meets at least once every three years. A Council of 33 members is elected, which represents leading air transport nations as well as less developed countries. The Council elects the President, appoints the Secretary-General and supervises the organisation through subsidiary committees, serviced by a Secretariat.

President of the Council, Dr Assad Kotaite (Lebanon)
Secretary-General, R. C. Costa Pereira (Brazil)
UK Representative, D. S. Evans, CMG

INTERNATIONAL CONFEDERATION OF FREE TRADE UNIONS

Koning Albert II laan 5, Bus 1, B-1210 Brussels, Belgium
Tel: (00 32) (2) 224 0211; Fax: (00 32) (2) 201 5815
Email: internetpo@icftu.org
Web: www.icftu.org

The International Confederation of Free Trade Unions (ICFTU) was created in 1949. It aims to establish, maintain and promote free trade unions, and to promote peace with economic security and social justice.

Affiliated to the ICFTU are 225 individual unions and representative bodies in 148 countries and territories. There were 157 million members as at July 2002.

The Congress, the supreme authority of the ICFTU, convenes at least every four years. It is composed of delegates from the affiliated trade union organisations. The Congress elects an Executive Board of 53 members, including five nominated by the Women's Committee and one representing young workers, which meets not less than once a year. The Board establishes the budget and receives suggestions and proposals from affiliates as well as acting on behalf of the Confederation. The Congress also elects the General Secretary.

General Secretary, Guy Ryder (UK)
UK Affiliate, TUC, Congress House, 23–28 Great Russell Street, London WC1B 3LS. Tel: 020-7636 4030

INTERNATIONAL CRIMINAL POLICE ORGANISATION (INTERPOL)
200 Quai Charles de Gaulle, F-69006 Lyon, France
Tel: (00 33) (4) 7244 7000; Fax: (00 33) (4) 7244 7163
Email: compr@interpol.int
Web: www.interpol.int

Interpol was set up in 1923 to establish an international criminal records office and to harmonise extradition procedures. As of July 2002, the organisation comprised 179 member states.

Interpol's aims are to promote co-operation between criminal police authorities, and to support government agencies concerned with combating crime, whilst respecting national sovereignty. It is financed by annual contributions from the governments of member states.

Interpol's policy is decided by the General Assembly which meets annually; it is composed of delegates appointed by the member states. The 13-member Executive Committee is elected by the General Assembly from among the member states' delegates, and is chaired by the President, who has a four-year term of office. The permanent administrative organ is the General Secretariat, headed by the Secretary-General, who is appointed by the General Assembly.

Secretary-General, Ronald Noble (USA)
UK OFFICE, NCIS Interpol, PO Box 8000, London SE11 5EN. Tel: 020-7238 8000.
UK Representative, J. M. Abbott, CBE, QPM

INTERNATIONAL ENERGY AGENCY
9 rue de la Fédération, F-75739 Paris Cedex 15, France
Tel: (00 33) (1) 4057 6551; Fax: (00 33) (1) 4057 6559
Email: info@iea.org
Web: www.iea.org

The International Energy Agency (IEA), founded in 1974, is an autonomous agency within the framework of the Organisation for Economic Co-operation and Development (OECD). The IEA had 26 member countries as at July 2002.

The IEA's objectives include improvement of energy co-operation world-wide, increased efficiency, development of alternative energy sources and the promotion of relations between oil producing and oil consuming countries. The IEA also maintains an emergency system to alleviate the effects of severe oil supply disruptions.

The main decision-making body is the Governing Board, composed of senior energy officials from member countries. Various standing groups and special committees exist to facilitate the work of the Board. The IEA Secretariat, with a staff of energy experts, carries out the work of the Governing Board and its subordinate bodies. The Executive Director is appointed by the Board.

Executive Director, Robert Priddle (UK)

INTERNATIONAL FRANCOPHONE ORGANISATION
Cabinet du Secrétaire général, 28 rue de Bourgogne, F-75007 Paris, France
Tel: (00 33) (1) 44111250; Fax: (00 33) (1) 441112 76
Email: webmaitre@francophonie.org
Web: www.francophonie.org

The International Francophone Organisation (known as La Francophonie) is an intergovernmental organisation founded in 1970 by 21 French-speaking countries. It aims to prevent conflict and promote development and co-operation between the Francophone countries, to represent its member states internationally and to promote French culture and the use of the French language.

The Conference of Heads of State and Heads of Government of Countries using French as a Common Language, also known as the Francophone Summit, takes place biennially. Other institutions include the Ministerial Conference of La Francophonie, the Permanent Council of La Francophonie and the Secretariat.

The Ministerial Conference of La Francophonie, which consists of the foreign minister or the minister responsible for Francophone affairs of each member state, implements decisions made at the summits and makes preparations for the following summit. It also puts forward prospective new members.

The Permanent Council of La Francophonie, which is chaired by the Secretary-General and consists of representatives of the member states, oversees the execution of decisions made by the Ministerial Conference, allocates funds, and reviews and approves projects. It has 18 members, chosen in advance of each summit, in rotation from among the member states.

La Francophonie has a current membership of 55 member states and regional governments (Albania (observer), Belgium, the Francophone Community of Belgium, Benin, Bulgaria, Burkina Faso, Burundi, Cambodia, Cameroon, Canada, Canada (New Brunswick), Canada (Québec), Cape Verde, Central African Republic, Chad, the Comoros, Czech Republic (observer), Democratic Republic of Congo, Republic of Congo-Brazzaville, Côte d'Ivoire, Djibouti, Dominica, Egypt, Equatorial Guinea, France, Gabon, Guinea, Guinea-Bissau, Haiti, Laos, Lebanon, Lithuania (observer), Luxembourg, Macedonia (observer), Madagascar, Mali, Mauritania, Mauritius, Moldova, Monaco, Morocco, Niger, Poland (observer), Romania, Rwanda, St Lucia, São Tomé e Princípe, Senegal, Seychelles, Slovenia (observer), Switzerland, Togo, Tunisia, Vanuatu and Vietnam).

Secretary-General, Boutros Boutros-Ghali

INTERNATIONAL FUND FOR AGRICULTURAL DEVELOPMENT
107 Via del Serafico, I-00142 Rome, Italy
Tel: (00 39) (6) 54591; Fax: (00 39) (6) 5459 2143
Email: ifad@ifad.org
Web: www.ifad.org

The establishment of the International Fund for Agricultural Development (IFAD) was proposed by the 1974 World Food Conference and IFAD began operations as a UN specialised agency in 1977. Its purpose is to mobilise additional funds for agricultural and rural development projects in developing countries that benefit the poorest

rural populations; provide employment and additional income for poor farmers; reduce malnutrition; and improve food distribution systems.

IFAD had 162 members as at July 2002. Membership is divided into three lists: List A (OECD countries), List B (OPEC countries), and List C (developing countries) which is subdivided into C1 (Africa), C2 (Africa, Asia and the Pacific) and C3 (Latin America and the Caribbean). All powers are vested in a Governing Council of all member countries. It elects an 18-member Executive Board (with 18 alternate members) responsible for IFAD's operations. The Council meets annually and elects a President who is also chairman of the Board. The President serves a four-year term that is renewable once and is assisted by a Vice-President and three Assistant Presidents.

Since its establishment, IFAD has committed a total of US$7.7 billion in loans and grants for 603 approved projects in 115 countries and territories.

President, Lennart Båge (Sweden), *apptd* 2001

INTERNATIONAL LABOUR ORGANISATION

4 route des Morillons, CH-1211 Geneva 22, Switzerland
Tel: (00 41) (22) 799 6111; Fax: (00 41) (22) 798 8685
Web: www.ilo.org

The International Labour Organisation (ILO) was established in 1919 as an autonomous body of the League of Nations and became the UN's first specialised agency in 1946. The ILO aims to increase employment, improve working conditions, raise living standards and encourage democratic development. It sets minimum international labour standards through the drafting of international conventions. Member countries are obliged to submit these to their domestic authorities for ratification, and thus undertake to bring their domestic legislation in line with the conventions. Members must report to the ILO periodically on how these regulations are being implemented. The ILO plays a major role in helping developing countries achieve economic stability and job expansion through its wide-ranging programme of technical co-operation. The ILO is also the world's principal resource centre for information, analysis and guidance on labour and employment. The organisation aims to improve working and living conditions throughout the world and to support the transition to democracy and market economies under way in many states.

The ILO had 175 members as at January 2002. It is composed of the International Labour Conference, the Governing Body and the International Labour Office. The Conference of members meets annually, and is attended by national delegations comprising two government delegates, one worker delegate and one employer delegate. It formulates international labour conventions and recommendations, provides a forum for discussion of world employment and social issues, and approves the ILO's programme and budget. The programme and budget set out four strategic objectives for the ILO: the promotion of fundamental principles and rights at work; the creation of greater employment and earning opportunities; the enhancement of social protection; and the strengthening of social dialogue. The 56-member Governing Body, composed of 28 government, 14 worker and 14 employer members, acts as the ILO's executive council. Ten governments, including the UK, hold permanent seats on the Governing Body because of their industrial importance. There are also various regional conferences and advisory committees. The International Labour Office acts as a secretariat and as a centre for operations, publishing and research.

Director-General, Juan Somavia (Chile)
UK OFFICE, Millbank Tower, 21-24 Millbank, London SW1P 4QP. Tel: 020-7828 6401; Fax: 020-7233 5925. Email: ipu@ilo-london.org.uk

INTERNATIONAL MARITIME ORGANISATION

4 Albert Embankment, London SE1 7SR
Tel: 020-7753 7611; Fax: 020-7587 3210
Email: info@imo.org
Web: www.imo.org

The International Maritime Organisation (IMO) was established as a UN specialised agency in 1948. Owing to delays in treaty ratification it did not commence operations until 1958. Originally it was called the Inter-Governmental Maritime Consultative Organisation (IMCO) but changed its name in 1982.

The IMO fosters intergovernmental co-operation in technical matters relating to international shipping, especially with regard to safety at sea, efficiency in navigation and protecting the marine environment by preventing and controlling marine pollution caused by shipping. The IMO is responsible for convening maritime conferences and drafting marine conventions. It also provides technical aid to countries wishing to develop their activities at sea.

The IMO had 162 members and two associate members as at April 2002. It is governed by an Assembly comprising delegates of all its members. It meets biennially to formulate policy, set a budget (2002–3, £39.5 million), vote on specific recommendations on pollution and maritime safety and elect the Council. The Council, which meets twice a year, fulfils the functions of the Assembly between sessions and appoints the Secretary-General. It consists of 40 members: ten from the world's largest shipping nations, ten from the nations most dependent on seaborne trade, and 20 other members to ensure a fair geographical representation. The Maritime Safety, Marine Environment Protection, Legal, Technical Co-operation and Facilitation Committees make reports and recommendations to the Council and the Assembly. There are a number of other specialist subsidiary committees.

The IMO acts as the secretariat for the London Convention (1972) which regulates the disposal of land-generated waste at sea.

Secretary-General, William A. O'Neil (Canada)

INTERNATIONAL MONETARY FUND

700 19th Street NW, Washington DC 20431, USA
Tel: (00 1) (202) 623 7300; Fax: (00 1) (202) 623 6278
Email: publicaffairs@imf.org
Web: www.imf.org

The International Monetary Fund (IMF) was established in 1944, at the UN Monetary and Financial Conference held at Bretton Woods, New Hampshire. Its Articles of Agreement entered into force in 1945 and it began operations in 1947.

The IMF exists to promote international monetary co-operation, the expansion of world trade, and exchange stability. It advises members on their economic and financial policies; promotes policy co-ordination among the major industrial countries; and gives

technical assistance in central banking, balance of payments accounting, taxation, and other financial matters. The IMF serves as a forum for members to discuss important financial and monetary issues and seeks the balanced growth of international trade and, through this, high levels of employment, income and productive capacity. In June 2002 the IMF had 183 members.

Upon joining the IMF, a member is assigned a 'quota', based on the member's relative standing in the world economy and its balance of payments position, that determines its capital subscription to the Fund, its access to IMF resources, its voting power, and its share in the allocation of Special Drawing Rights (SDRs). Quotas are reviewed every five years and adjusted accordingly. Since the 11th General Review of quotas in 1999, total Fund quotas stand at SDR 212 billion. The SDR, an international reserve asset issued by the IMF, is calculated daily on a basket of usable currencies and is the IMF's unit of account; on 22 June 2001, SDR 1 equalled US$1.24877. SDRs are allocated at intervals to supplement members' reserves and thereby improve international financial liquidity.

IMF financial resources derive primarily from members' capital subscriptions, which are equivalent to their quotas. In addition, the IMF is authorised to borrow from official lenders. It may also draw on a line of credit of SDR 18.5 billion from various countries under the so-called General Arrangements to Borrow (GAB). Periodic charges are also levied on financial assistance. At the end of May 2001, total outstanding IMF credits amounted to SDR 51.5 billion.

The IMF is not a bank and does not lend money; it provides temporary financial assistance by selling a member's SDRs or other members' currencies in exchange for the member's own currency. The member can then use the purchased currency to alleviate its balance of payments difficulties. The IMF's credit under its regular facilities is made available to members in tranches or segments of 25 per cent of quota. For first credit tranche purchases, members are required to demonstrate reasonable efforts to overcome their balance of payments difficulties. There are no performance criteria. Upper credit tranche purchases are normally associated with stand-by arrangements and are aimed at overcoming balance of payment difficulties and are required to meet certain performance criteria. Repurchases are made in three and a quarter to five years.

The IMF supports long-term efforts at economic reform and transformation as well as medium-term programmes under the extended Fund facility, which runs for three to four years and is aimed at overcoming balance of payments difficulties stemming from macroeconomic and structural problems. Members experiencing a temporary balance of payments shortfall have access to the compensatory and contingency financing facility.

The IMF is headed by a Board of Governors, comprising representatives of all members, which meets annually. The Governors delegate powers to 24 Executive Directors, who are appointed or elected by member countries. The Executive Directors operate the Fund on a daily basis under a Managing Director, whom they elect.

Managing Director, Horst Köhler (Germany)
UK Executive Director, Tom Scholar, Room 11-120, IMF, 700 19th Street NW, Washington DC 20431, USA

INTERNATIONAL RED CROSS AND RED CRESCENT MOVEMENT
17 avenue de la Paix, CH-1211 Geneva, Switzerland
Web: www.icrc.org

The International Red Cross and Red Crescent Movement is composed of three elements – the International Committee of the Red Cross, the International Federation of Red Cross and Red Crescent Societies and the national Red Cross and Red Crescent societies.

The International Committee of the Red Cross (ICRC), the organisation's founding body, was formed in 1863. It aims to negotiate between warring factions and to protect and assist victims of armed conflict. It also seeks to ensure the application of the Geneva Conventions with regard to prisoners of war and detainees.

The International Federation of Red Cross and Red Crescent Societies was founded in 1919 to contribute to the development of the humanitarian activities of national societies, to co-ordinate their relief operations for victims of natural disasters, and to care for refugees outside areas of conflict. There are Red Cross and Red Crescent societies in 175 countries, with a total membership of 250 million.

The International Conference of the Red Cross and Red Crescent meets every four years, bringing together delegates of the ICRC, the International Federation and the national societies, as well as representatives of nations bound by the Geneva Conventions.
President of the ICRC, Jakob Kellenberger
BRITISH RED CROSS, 9 Grosvenor Crescent, London SW1X 7EJ. Tel: 020-7235 5454; Fax: 020-7245 6315.
Email: information@redcross.org.uk
Web: www.redcross.org.uk.
Director-General, Sir Nicholas Young

INTERNATIONAL TELECOMMUNICATION UNION
Place des Nations, CH-1211 Geneva 20, Switzerland
Tel: (00 41) (22) 730 5111; Fax: (00 41) (22) 733 7256
Email: itumail@itu.int
Web: www.itu.int

The International Telecommunication Union (ITU) was founded in Paris in 1865 as the International Telegraph Union and became a UN specialised agency in 1947.

ITU is an intergovernmental organisation for the development of telecommunications and the harmonisation of national telecommunication policies. ITU comprises 189 member states and some 700 members who represent public and private organisations involved in telecommunications. ITU's mission is to promote the development of telecommunications and information and communication technologies; to promote and offer technical assistance to developing countries; and to promote at international level the adoption of a broader approach to the issues of telecommunications.

ITU fulfils its mission through initiatives aimed at promoting the growth and expansion of electronic commerce; a programme of strategic workshops; the adoption of international regulations and treaties governing uses of the frequency spectrum; the adoption of technical standards that foster global interconnectivity and interoperability; and the provision of policy advice and technical assistance to developing countries.

ITU also organises world-wide and regional exhibitions and forums to exchange ideas, knowledge and technology.

Secretary-General, Yoshio Utsumi (Japan)

LEAGUE OF ARAB STATES

Maidane Al-Tahrir, Cairo, Egypt
Tel: (00 20) (2) 575 0511; Fax: (00 20) (2) 574 0331
Web: www.leagueofarabstates.org

The purpose of the League of Arab States, founded in 1945, is to ensure co-operation among member states and protect their independence and sovereignty, to supervise the affairs and interests of Arab countries, to control the execution of agreements concluded among the member states, and to promote the process of integration among them. The League considers itself a regional organisation and has observer status at the United Nations.

Member states are Algeria, Bahrain, the Comoros, Djibouti, Egypt, Iraq, Jordan, Kuwait, Lebanon, Libya, Mauritania, Morocco, Oman, Palestine, Qatar, Saudi Arabia, Somalia, Sudan, Syria, Tunisia, the UAE and Yemen.

Member states participate in various specialised agencies of the League whose role is to develop specific areas of co-operation between Arab states. These include: the Arab Organisation for Mineral Resources; the Arab Monetary Fund; the Arab Satellite Communications Organisation; the Arab Academy of Maritime Transport; the Arab Bank for Economic Development in Africa; the Arab League Educational, Cultural and Scientific Organisation and the Council of Arab Economic Unity.

Secretary-General, Amre Moussa (Egypt)
UK OFFICE, 52 Green Street, London W1Y 3RH. Tel: 020-7629 0044; Fax: 020-7493 7943

MERCOSUR

Dr. Luis Piera 1992, piso 1, 11200-Montevideo, Uruguay
Tel: (00 598) (2) 402 9024; Fax: (00 598) (2) 400 0958
Email: webmaster@mercosur.org
Web: www.mercosur.org

Brazil and Argentina signed a Treaty for Integration, Co-operation and Development in 1988 which aimed to create a common market between the two countries within ten years, with the elimination of all tariff barriers and harmonisation of macroeconomic policies; the agreement was to be open to other Latin American countries. Paraguay and Uruguay expressed their interest and MERCOSUR (the Southern Common Market) was created by the Treaty of Asunción, which was signed by the four countries on 26 March 1991. Chile became an associate member in 1996 and Bolivia in 1997.

The Common Market Council (CMC) is the highest-level agency of MERCOSUR, with authority to conduct its policy, and responsibility for compliance with the objects and time frames set forth in the Asunción Treaty. It comprises the ministers of foreign affairs and the economy of the member states. Each country presides over the council for a period of six months, in rotating alphabetical order. The CMC meets at least once a year. The presidents of the member states can take part whenever possible.

The Common Market Group (CMG) is the executive body of MERCOSUR and is co-ordinated by the foreign ministries of the member states. Its function is to ensure compliance with the Asunción Treaty and to implement decisions made by the CMC, and where necessary, to help resolve disputes. It can establish work subgroups to work on particular issues. It is composed of four permanent members and four substitutes from each country. It normally meets at least four times a year.

Other bodies include a Joint Parliamentary Committee, a Trade Commission and a Socio-economic Advisory Forum.

NON-ALIGNED MOVEMENT

Permanent Representative to the UN, New York
10 016, USA
Tel: (00 1)(212) 213 5583; Fax: (00 1) (212) 592 2498

The Non-Aligned Movement (NAM) was created following a conference of non-aligned states held in Belgrade, Yugoslavia in September 1961. Members must be committed to the coexistence of states with different political and social systems, they must not be members of multinational military alliances allied to the great powers, and they should support national liberation movements.

NAM was set up to campaign for an end to colonialism, neo-colonialism, racism and occupation, the dissolution of military blocs, national self-determination for all countries and non-interference in internal affairs, north-south dialogue and political-economic co-operation in the third world (south-south relations) and a new world economic mechanism involving military disarmament and the use of the thereby freed means for development projects.

There are 115 members and 17 observers and about 30 further countries have guest status.

The chairmanship of NAM is held by the head of state of the country due to hold the following summit. The chairman is responsible for the promotion of the principles and activities of the movement and the country's ambassador to the UN represents the organisation at UN level.

THE NORDIC COUNCIL

The Nordic Council was established in March 1952 as an advisory body on economic and social co-operation, comprising parliamentary delegates from Denmark, Iceland, Norway and Sweden. It was subsequently joined by Finland (1956), and representatives from the Færøes (1970), the Åland Islands (1970), and Greenland (1984).

Co-operation is regulated by the Treaty of Helsinki signed in 1962. This was amended in 1971 to create the Nordic Council of Ministers, which discusses all matters except defence and foreign affairs. Matters are given preparatory consideration by a Committee of Co-operation Ministers' Deputies and joint committees of officials. Decisions of the Council of Ministers, which are taken by consensus, are binding, although if ratification by member parliaments is required, decisions only become effective following parliamentary approval. The Council of Ministers is advised by the Nordic Council, to which it reports annually. There are Ministers for Nordic Co-operation in every member government.

The Nordic Council, comprising 87 voting delegates nominated from member parliaments and about 80 non-voting government representatives, meets at least once a year in plenary sessions. The full Council chooses

a 13-member Praesidium, which conducts business between sessions. A Secretariat, headed by a Secretary-General, liaises with the Council of Ministers and provides administrative support. The Council of Ministers has a separate Secretariat.

SECRETARIAT OF THE NORDIC COUNCIL, PO Box 3043, DK-1021 Copenhagen K, Denmark. Tel: (00 45) 3396 0400; Fax: (00 45) 3311 1870
Email: nordisk-rad@nordisk-rad.dk;
Web: www.norden.org
Secretary-General, Frida Nokken (Norway)
SECRETARIAT OF THE NORDIC COUNCIL OF MINISTERS, Store Strandstræde 18, DK-1255 Copenhagen K, Denmark. Tel: (00 45) 3396 0200; Fax: (00 45) 3311 1870 Web: www.norden.org
Secretary-General, Søren Christensen (Denmark)

NORTH AMERICAN FREE TRADE AGREEMENT

NAFTA Secretariat, Canadian Section, 90 Sparks Street, Suite 705, Ottawa, Ontario K1P 5B4, Canada Tel: (00 1) (613) 992 9388; Fax: (00 1) (613) 992 9392
NAFTA Secretariat, Mexican Section, Blvd. Adolfo López Mateos 3025, 2° Piso, Col. Héroes de Padierna, C.P. 10700, Mexico, D.F. Tel: (00 52) (5) 629 9630; Fax: (00 52) (5) 629 9637
NAFTA Secretariat, US Section, 14th Street and Constitution Avenue, NW, Room 2061, Washington DC, 20230, USA Tel: (00 1) (202) 482 5438; Fax: (00 1) (202) 482 014
Email: webmaster@nafta-sec-alena.org
Web: www.nafta-sec-alena.org

The leaders of Canada, Mexico and the USA signed the North American Free Trade Agreement (NAFTA) on 17 December 1992 in their respective capitals; it came into force on 1 January 1994 after being ratified by the legislatures of the three member states.

NAFTA aims to eliminate barriers to trade in goods and services, promote fair competition within the free trade area, protect and enforce intellectual property rights and create a framework for further co-operation. To achieve these aims, import tariffs and quotas are being removed, with the aim of achieving a free trade zone by 2008 at the latest.

The NAFTA Secretariat is composed of Canadian, Mexican and US sections. It is responsible for the administration of the dispute settlement provisions of the agreement, provides assistance to the Free Trade Commission and support for various committees and working groups, and facilitates the operation of the agreement.

NORTH ATLANTIC TREATY ORGANISATION

Leopold III laan, Brussels B-1110, Belgium
Tel: (00 32) (2) 707 4111; Fax: (00 32) (2) 707 4579
Email: natodoc@hq.nato.int
Web: www.nato.int

The North Atlantic Treaty (Treaty of Washington) was signed in 1949 by Belgium, Canada, Denmark, France, Iceland, Italy, Luxembourg, the Netherlands, Norway, Portugal, the UK and the USA. Greece and Turkey acceded to the Treaty in 1952, the Federal Republic of Germany in 1955 (the reunited Germany acceded in October 1990), Spain in 1982, and the Czech Republic, Hungary and Poland in 1999.

The North Atlantic Treaty Organisation (NATO) is the structural framework for a defensive political and military alliance designed to provide common security for its members through co-operation and consultation in political, military and economic as well as scientific and other non-military fields.

STRUCTURE

The North Atlantic Council (NAC), chaired by the Secretary-General, is the highest authority of the Alliance and is composed of permanent representatives of the 19 member countries. It meets at ministerial level (foreign and/or defence ministers) at least twice a year. The permanent representatives (ambassadors) head national delegations of advisers and experts. The Defence Planning Committee (DPC) and the Nuclear Planning Group (NPG) are composed of representatives of all member countries except France (which does not participate in the integrated military structure). Both the DPC and the NPG also meet at ministerial level (defence ministers) at least twice a year. The NATO Secretary-General chairs the Council, the DPC and the NPG.

The senior military authority in NATO, under the Council and DPC, is the Military Committee composed of the Chief of Defence Staffs of each member country except Iceland, which has no military and is represented by a civilian. The Military Committee, which is assisted by an integrated international military staff, also meets in permanent session with permanent military representatives and is responsible for making recommendations to the Council and DPC on measures considered necessary for the common defence of the NATO area and for supplying guidance on military matters to the major NATO commanders. The Chairman of the Military Committee, elected for a period of two to three years, represents the committee on the Council.

The strategic area covered by the North Atlantic Treaty is divided between two major NATO commands (MNCs), European and Atlantic; and three major subordinate commands (MSCs) within Allied Command Europe, South, Central and North-West. There is also a Regional Planning Group (Canada and the United States).

The major NATO commanders are responsible for the development of defence plans for their respective areas, for the determination of force requirements and for the deployment and exercise of the forces under their command. The major NATO commanders report to the Military Committee. The integrated military structure of the Alliance has been reorganised. The new structure, based on reduced numbers of permanent headquarters and more flexible and mobile forces, is expected to be fully in place by 2003.

POST-COLD WAR DEVELOPMENTS

In response to the new security environment arising from the demise of the Warsaw Pact and the end of the Cold War in 1990, NATO issued a Declaration on Peace and Co-operation in 1991, and published new strategic concepts in 1991 and 1999.

The Euro-Atlantic Partnership Council (EAPC) was established in 1997 to develop closer security links with eastern European and former Soviet states. It focuses on defence planning, defence industry conversion, defence management and force structuring, and the democratic concepts of civilian-military relations. Its membership comprises the 19 NATO members and Albania, Armenia, Austria, Azerbaijan, Belarus, Bulgaria, Croatia, Estonia, Finland, Georgia, Ireland, Kazakhstan, Kyrgyzstan, Latvia, Lithuania, Macedonia, Moldova,

Romania, Russia, Slovakia, Slovenia, Sweden, Switzerland, Tajikistan, Turkmenistan, Ukraine and Uzbekistan. Partnership for Peace (PfP) is the basis for practical security co-operation between NATO and individual partner countries in the fields of defence planning and budgeting, military exercises and civil emergency operations. Most of the 27 PfP partners send liaison officers to NATO and participate in joint military exercises co-ordinated by NATO. All EAPC members are members of PfP. EAPC meets monthly at ambassadorial level in Brussels and twice a year at foreign minister and defence minister level.

In 1994, NATO announced that it would consider admitting new members, and in March 1999, Poland, the Czech Republic and Hungary acceded to the Treaty. In 1997 NATO and Ukraine signed a charter establishing a programme of co-operation and consultation between them. NATO and Russia committed themselves to help build a stable, secure and undivided continent on the basis of partnership and mutual interest, when they signed the 1997 Founding Act on Mutual Relations, Co-operation and Security, which provided for the creation of a Permanent Joint Council, which meets at foreign minister level at least twice a year. The Mediterranean Dialogue, launched in 1994, aims to promote security and stability in the Mediterranean region and involves the NATO members, Algeria, Egypt, Israel, Jordan, Mauritania, Morocco and Tunisia.

The development of a European Security and Defence Identity (ESDI), which would strengthen NATO's European pillar, was agreed at the 1999 Washington summit.

At the Washington summit a Defence Capabilities Initiative (DCI) was launched, which aims to improve defence capabilities and interoperability among Alliance forces to ensure the effectiveness of future multinational operations. A temporary High Level Steering Group (HLSG) was established to oversee the implementation of the DCI.

NATO AND THE FORMER YUGOSLAVIA

With the signing of the Bosnian peace agreement in 1995, a NATO-led multinational Implementation Force (IFOR) was formed, which was replaced by the Sustaining Force (SFOR) in December 1996.

In March 1999, NATO began air operations against military and industrial targets in Yugoslavia following the repression and ethnic cleansing of ethnic Albanians in Kosovo. Yugoslavia accepted a peace plan drawn up by NATO and Russia on 3 June 1999 and the withdrawal of Yugoslav forces from Kosovo took place between 10–20 June. On 12 June 1999, the NATO-led security force (KFOR) entered Kosovo to oversee the demilitarisation of the Kosovo Liberation Army, facilitate the return of over 850,000 refugees and provide humanitarian support.

Following the brokering of a cease-fire to end fighting between ethnic Albanians and the Macedonian armed forces, NATO launched 'Operation Essential Harvest' on 22 August 2001 at the request of the Macedonian government. The mission, whose job it was to disarm the Albanian groups, was replaced in September 2001 by a new mission, 'Operation Amber Fox', to protect international monitors overseeing the implementation of a peace plan.

THE 11 SEPTEMBER TERRORIST ATTACKS

Following the terrorist attacks on the USA on 11 September 2001, the NATO members immediately declared their solidarity with the USA and on 12 September formally invoked Article 5 of the Washington Treaty (which stipulates that an armed attack against one or more NATO members is to be considered an attack against all), declaring that the terrorist attack on the USA was an attack on the NATO alliance. The EAPC countries also condemned the atrocities and pledged to undertake efforts to combat terrorism.

Whilst NATO did not lead the campaign against the al-Qa'eda terrorist network in Afghanistan, it provided intelligence support, blanket overflight rights for US and other allied aircraft, and access to ports and airfields. European capabilities were also deployed in the Balkans to replace US assets.

Secretary-General and Chairman of the North Atlantic Council, of the DPC and of the NPG, Lord Robertson (UK)

UK Permanent Representative on the North Atlantic Council, Dr Emyr Jones Parry

Chairman of the Military Committee, Gen. Harald Kujat (Germany)

Supreme Allied Commander, Europe, Gen. Joseph Ralston (USA)

Supreme Allied Commander, Atlantic, Lt. Gen. William. F. Kernan (USA)

ORGANISATION FOR ECONOMIC CO-OPERATION AND DEVELOPMENT

2 rue André-Pascal, F-75116 Paris
Tel: (00 33) (1) 4524 8200; Fax: (00 33) (1) 4524 8500
Email: webmaster@oecd.org
Web: www.oecd.org

The Organisation for Economic Co-operation and Development (OECD) was formed in 1961 to replace the Organisation for European Economic Co-operation. It is the instrument for international co-operation among industrialised member countries on economic and social policies. Its objectives are to assist its member governments in the formulation and co-ordination of policies designed to achieve high, sustained economic growth while maintaining financial stability, to contribute to world trade on a multilateral basis and to stimulate members' aid to developing countries.

The members are Australia, Austria, Belgium, Canada, Czech Republic, Denmark, Finland, France, Germany, Greece, Hungary, Iceland, Republic of Ireland, Italy, Japan, Republic of Korea, Luxembourg, Mexico, the Netherlands, New Zealand, Norway, Poland, Portugal, Slovakia, Spain, Sweden, Switzerland, Turkey, the UK and the USA.

The Council is the supreme body of the organisation. It is composed of one representative for each member country and meets at permanent representative level under the chairmanship of the Secretary-General, and at ministerial level (usually once a year) under the chairmanship of a minister elected annually. Decisions and recommendations are adopted by the unanimous agreement of all members. Most of the OECD's work is undertaken in over 200 specialised committees and working parties. Five autonomous or semi-autonomous bodies are associated in varying degrees to the Organisation: the Nuclear Energy Agency, the International Energy Agency, the Development Centre, the Centre for Educational Research and Innovation, and the European Conference of Ministers of Transport. These bodies, the committees and the Council are serviced by an international Secretariat headed by the Secretary-General.

Secretary-General, Donald J. Johnston (Canada)
UK Permanent Representative, HE Christopher Crabbie, 19 rue de Franqueville, Paris F-75116

ORGANISATION FOR SECURITY AND CO-OPERATION IN EUROPE

Kärntner Ring 5–7, A-1010 Vienna, Austria
Tel: (00 43) (1) 514 36 180; Fax: (00 43) (1) 514 36 105
Email: info@osce.org
Web: www.osce.org

The Organisation for Security and Co-operation in Europe (OSCE) was launched in 1975 (as the Conference on Security and Co-operation in Europe (CSCE)) under the Helsinki Final Act. This established agreements between NATO members, Warsaw Pact members, and neutral and non-aligned European countries covering security, co-operation and human rights.

The Charter of Paris for a New Europe, signed on 21 November 1990, committed members to support multiparty democracy, free-market economics, the rule of law, and human rights. The signatories also agreed to regular meetings of heads of government, ministers and officials. The first institutionalised heads of state and government summit was held in Helsinki in December 1992, at which the Helsinki Document was adopted. This declared the CSCE to be a regional organisation and defined the structures of the organisation. The summit also appointed a High Commissioner on National Minorities. At its December 1994 summit the CSCE was renamed the Organisation for Security and Co-operation in Europe.

Three structures have been established: the Ministerial Council, which comprises the foreign ministers of participating states and is the central decision-making and governing body, and which meets at least once a year; the Senior Council, which prepares work for the Ministerial Council, carries out its decisions and is responsible for the overview, management and co-ordination of OSCE activities and meets at least three times a year; and the Permanent Council, which is responsible for the day-to-day operational tasks of the OSCE and is the regular body for political consultation, meeting weekly. The chairmanship of the Ministerial Council, Senior Council and Permanent Council rotates among participating states with the Senior Council meeting in Prague and the Permanent Council in Vienna.

The OSCE is also underpinned by five permanent institutions: a Secretariat (Vienna); a Forum for Security Co-operation (Vienna), which meets weekly to discuss arms control, disarmament and security-building measures; an Office for Democratic Institutions and Human Rights (Warsaw), which is charged with furthering human rights, democracy and the rule of law; an office of the High Commissioner on National Minorities (The Hague), which identifies ethnic tensions that might endanger peace and promotes their resolution; and a Representative on Freedom of the Media (Vienna), which is responsible for assisting governments in the furthering of free, independent and pluralistic media. There is also a documentation and conference centre in Prague, an OSCE Parliamentary Assembly with a secretariat based in Copenhagen, and a Court of Conciliation and Arbitration in Geneva.

The OSCE has monitoring missions in 19 OSCE countries. OSCE has sent an assistance group to Chechnya. The OSCE supervised all elections in Bosnia-Hercegovina between 1996 and 2000 and in Kosovo since 2000. A Joint Consultative Group of the OSCE promotes the objectives and implementation of the Conventional Armed Forces in Europe (CFE) Treaty (1990) which limits conventional ground and air forces. In November 1999, the Charter on European Security committed the OSCE to co-operate with other organisations and institutions concerned with the promotion of security within the OSCE area.

The OSCE has 55 participating states: Albania, Andorra, Armenia, Austria, Azerbaijan, Belarus, Belgium, Bosnia-Hercegovina, Bulgaria, Canada, Croatia, Cyprus, Czech Republic, Denmark, Estonia, Finland, France, Georgia, Germany, Greece, Hungary, Iceland, Republic of Ireland, Italy, Kazakhstan, Kyrgyzstan, Latvia, Liechtenstein, Lithuania, Luxembourg, Macedonia, Malta, Moldova, Monaco, the Netherlands, Norway, Poland, Portugal, Romania, Russia, San Marino, Slovakia, Slovenia, Spain, Sweden, Switzerland, Tajikistan, Turkey, Turkmenistan, the UK, Ukraine, the USA, Uzbekistan, the Vatican and Yugoslavia.

Chair of the OSCE, Portugal (2002); Netherlands (2003)
Secretary-General of the OSCE, Ján Kubi (Slovakia)
Director of the Office for Democratic Institutions and Human Rights, Gérard Stoudmann (Switzerland)
OSCE High Commissioner on National Minorities, Max van der Stoel (Netherlands)
Representative on Freedom of the Media, Freimut Duve (Germany)

ORGANISATION OF AFRICAN UNITY/AFRICAN UNION

PO Box 3243, Addis Ababa, Ethiopia
Tel: (00 251) (1) 517700; Fax: (00 251) (1) 513036

The Organisation of African Unity (OAU) was established in 1963 and has 53 members; Morocco suspended its participation in 1985 in protest at the Polisario-proclaimed Saharan Arab Democratic Republic (SADR), representing Western Sahara, being admitted as a member. The OAU aims to further African unity and solidarity, to co-ordinate political, economic, social and defence policies, and to eliminate colonialism in Africa.

The chief organs are the Assembly of heads of state or government, which is the supreme organ of the OAU and meets once a year to consider matters of common African concern and to co-ordinate the Organisation's policies; the Council of foreign ministers, which is the Organisation's executive body responsible for the implementation of the Assembly's policies, and which meets twice a year; and the Commission of Mediation, Conciliation and Arbitration which promotes the peaceful settlement of disputes between member countries. The main administrative body is the General Secretariat, based in Addis Ababa, headed by a Secretary-General who is elected by the Assembly for a four-year term.

Substantial budgetary arrears due to delays in the payment of national contributions has meant that the OAU continually faces difficulties in furthering its aims. Its budget for 2001 was about US$31 million. In June 1991 the Assembly adopted an African Economic Community Treaty which envisages establishment of the Economic Community after ratification by two-thirds of the OAU's membership. In June 1993 a mechanism was created for conflict prevention, management and resolution, and a peace fund was established.

Following an initiative put forward by Libyan leader Col. Muammar al-Gadhafi at a special conference in Sirte, Libya, in September 1999, it was agreed at the 36th

summit of the OAU in July 2000 in Lomé, Togo, to establish an African Union.

The creation of the African Union, which is to have its own parliament, central bank and court of justice, was declared at an extraordinary summit meeting in Sirte on 1-2 March 2001, and legally began operations on 26 May 2001 when two-thirds of the member states had ratified the constituent act.

Secretary-General, Amara Essy (Côte d'Ivoire)

ORGANISATION OF AMERICAN STATES
17th Street and Constitution Avenue NW, Washington DC 20006, USA
Tel: (00 1) (202) 458 3000; Fax: (00 1) (202) 458 6421
Email: pi@oas.org
Web: www.oas.org

Originally founded in 1890 for largely commercial purposes, the Organisation of American States (OAS) adopted its present name and charter in 1948. The charter entered into force in 1951 and was amended in 1967, 1985 and 1996; the 1992 Protocol of Washington will enter into force upon ratification by two-thirds of member states.

The OAS aims to strengthen the peace and security of the continent; to promote and consolidate representative democracy with due respect for the principle of non-intervention; to prevent possible causes of difficulties and to ensure the peaceful resolution of disputes arising among its member states; to provide for common action on the part of those states in the event of aggression; to seek the resolution of political, judicial and economic problems that may arise among them; to promote, by co-operative action, their economic, social and cultural development; and to achieve an effective limitation of conventional weapons so that resources can be devoted to economic and social development.

The Declaration of Principles and the Plan of Action resulting from the 1994 Miami summit and signed by all the members except Cuba, envisage the establishment of a free trade area, in which barriers to trade and investment will be progressively eliminated.

Policy is determined by the annual General Assembly, which is the supreme authority and elects the Secretary-General for a five-year term. The Meeting of Consultation of ministers of foreign affairs considers urgent problems on an *ad hoc* basis. The Permanent Council, comprising one representative from each member state, promotes friendly inter-state relations, acts as an intermediary in case of disputes arising between states and oversees the General Secretariat, the main administrative body. The Inter-American Council for Integral Development was created in 1996 by the ratification of the Protocol of Managua to promote sustainable development.

The 35 member states are Antigua and Barbuda, Argentina, the Bahamas, Barbados, Belize, Bolivia, Brazil, Canada, Chile, Colombia, Costa Rica, Cuba, Dominica, Dominican Republic, Ecuador, El Salvador, Grenada, Guatemala, Guyana, Haiti, Honduras, Jamaica, Mexico, Nicaragua, Panama, Paraguay, Peru, St Christopher and Nevis, St Lucia, St Vincent and the Grenadines, Suriname, Trinidad and Tobago, Uruguay, the USA and Venezuela. The European Union and 39 non-American states have permanent observer status.

Secretary-General, Dr César Gaviria Trujillo (Colombia)

ORGANISATION OF ARAB PETROLEUM EXPORTING COUNTRIES
PO Box 20501, Safat 13066, Kuwait
Tel: (00 965) 484 4500; Fax: (00 965) 481 5747
Email: oapec@qualitynet.net
Web: www.oapecorg.org

The Organisation of Arab Petroleum Exporting Countries (OAPEC) was founded in 1968. Its objectives are to promote co-operation in economic activities, to safeguard members' interests, to unite efforts to ensure the flow of oil to consumer markets, and to create a favourable climate for the investment of capital and expertise.

The Ministerial Council is composed of oil ministers from the member countries and meets twice a year to determine policy and to approve the budgets and accounts of the General Secretariat and the Judicial Tribunal. The Judicial Tribunal is composed of seven part-time judges who rule on disputes between member countries and disputes between countries and oil companies. The executive organ of OAPEC is the General Secretariat.

The members are Algeria, Bahrain, Egypt, Iraq, Kuwait, Libya, Qatar, Saudi Arabia, Syria and the United Arab Emirates. Tunisia's membership has been inactive since 1987.

Secretary-General, Abdel-Aziz A. Al-Turki

ORGANISATION OF THE BLACK SEA ECONOMIC CO-OPERATION
Permanent International Secretariat, Istinye Caddesi, Müsir Fuad Pasa Yalisi, Eski Tersane, 80860 I stinye-Istanbul, Turkey
Tel: (00 90) (212) 229 6330/6335;
Fax: (00 90) (212) 229 6336
Email: bsec@turk.net
Web: www.bsec-organization.org

The Black Sea Economic Co-operation (BSEC) resulted from the Istanbul Summit Declaration and the adoption of the Bosporus Statement on 25 June 1992. BSEC acquired a permanent secretariat in 1994. Following the Yalta Summit of the Heads of State or Government in June 1998, a charter was drawn up to found the Organisation of the Black Sea Economic Co-operation, which was inaugurated on 1 May 1999.

The organisation aims to promote closer political and economic co-operation in the context of the European integration process between the countries in the Black Sea region and to foster security, regional initiatives, social justice, economic liberty and respect for human rights.

The Council of the Ministers of Foreign Affairs, the highest decision-making authority, meets twice yearly. The meetings rotate among the member states and the chairman is the foreign minister of the state in which the meeting is held. There is also a Committee of Senior Officials and 15 working groups, which deal with specific areas of co-operation.

There are 11 member states: Albania, Armenia, Azerbaijan, Bulgaria, Georgia, Greece, Moldova, Romania, Russia, Turkey and Ukraine.

ORGANISATION OF THE ISLAMIC CONFERENCE
PO Box 178, Jeddah 21411, Saudi Arabia
Tel: (00 966) (2) 680 0800; Fax: (00 966) (2) 687 3568
Email: oiccabinet@oic-un.org
Web: www.oic-oci.org

The Organisation of the Islamic Conference (OIC) was established in 1969 with the purpose of promoting solidarity and co-operation between Islamic countries. It also has the specific aims of co-ordinating efforts to safeguard the Muslim holy places, supporting the formation of a Palestinian state, assisting member states to maintain their independence, co-ordinating the views of member states in international forums such as the UN, and improving co-operation in the economic, cultural and scientific fields.

The OIC has three central organs, supreme among them the Conference of the Heads of State which meets once every three years to discuss issues of importance to Islamic states. The Conference of Foreign Ministers meets annually to prepare reports for the Conference of Heads of State. The General Secretariat carries out administrative tasks. It is headed by a Secretary-General who is elected by the Conference of Foreign Ministers for a non-renewable four-year term.

In addition to this structure, the OIC has several subsidiary bodies, specialised institutions, affiliated bodies and standing committees. These include the Islamic Solidarity Fund, to aid Islamic institutions in member countries, the Islamic Development Bank, to finance development projects in poorer member states and the Islamic Educational, Scientific and Cultural Organisation. The OIC runs various offices to organise the economic boycott of Israel.

The achievement of the OIC's aims has often been prevented by political rivalry and conflicts between member states, such as the Iran-Iraq war and the Iraqi invasion of Kuwait. Egypt's membership was suspended from 1979 to 1984 because of its peace treaty with Israel. Saudi Arabia, the main source of funding, exercises great influence within the OIC. Since 1991 the OIC has become more united and has spoken out against violence against Muslims in India, the Occupied Territories and Bosnia-Hercegovina. From 1993 to 1995 the OIC co-ordinated the offering of troops to the UN by Muslim states to protect Muslim areas of Bosnia-Hercegovina.

The Organisation has 56 members (55 sovereign Muslim states in Africa, the Middle East, central and south-east Asia and Europe, plus the Palestine Liberation Organisation) and three observers, the Central African Republic, Turkish Northern Cyprus and Côte d'Ivoire. It has an annual budget of US$11 million.
Secretary-General, Dr Abdelouahed Belkeziz (Morocco)

ORGANISATION OF THE PETROLEUM EXPORTING COUNTRIES
Obere Donaustrasse 93, A-1020 Vienna, Austria
Tel: (00 43) (1) 21112 279; Fax: (00 43) (1) 214 9827
Email: prid@opec.org
Web: www.opec.org

The Organisation of the Petroleum Exporting Countries (OPEC) was created in 1960 as a permanent intergovernmental organisation with the principal aims of unifying and co-ordinating the petroleum policies of its members, determining ways of protecting their interests individually and collectively, and ensuring the stabilisation of prices in international oil markets with a view to eliminating unnecessary fluctuations. Since 1982 OPEC has attempted (only partially successfully) to impose overall production limits and production quotas in an attempt to maintain stable oil prices.

The supreme authority is the Conference of Ministers of oil, mines and energy of member countries, which meets at least twice a year to formulate policy. The Board of Governors, nominated by member countries, directs the management of OPEC and implements conference resolutions. The Secretariat carries out executive functions under the direction of the Board of Governors.

The member states are Algeria, Indonesia, Iran, Iraq, Kuwait, Libya, Nigeria, Qatar, Saudi Arabia, the UAE and Venezuela. Ecuador withdrew in 1992 and Gabon in 1995.

OPEC member countries account for about 41 per cent of global crude oil production and 55 per cent of internationally traded crude oil, and have 77.8 per cent of the world's proven oil reserves. The value of OPEC oil exports in 2001 was US$180 billion.
Secretary-General, HE Dr Alí Rodríguez-Araque (Venezuela)

PACIFIC ISLANDS FORUM
Secretariat, Private Mail Bag, Suva, Fiji
Tel: 679 331 2600; Fax: 679 330 5573
Email: info@forumsec.org.fj
Web: www.forumsec.org.fj

The Pacific Islands Forum (PIF) was established in 1971 and represents heads of governments of all the independent and self-governing Pacific Island countries. It aims to foster co-operation between its governments and to represent the interests of the region in international organisations. The PIF meets annually, following which a dialogue is conducted at ministerial level with a variety of surrounding nations and regional powers.

The members are Australia, the Cook Islands, Micronesia, Fiji, Kiribati, Nauru, New Zealand, Niue, Palau, Papua New Guinea, the Marshall Islands, Samoa, the Solomon Islands, Tonga, Tuvalu and Vanuatu.

The PIF Secretariat comprises divisions dealing with development and economic policy, trade and investment, political and international affairs, and corporate services.
Secretary-General, W. Noel Levi, CBE (Papua New Guinea)

THE SECRETARIAT OF THE PACIFIC COMMUNITY
BP D5, 98848 Nouméa Cedex, New Caledonia
Tel: (00 687) 262000; Fax: (00 687) 263818
Email: spc@spc.int
Web: www.spc.int

The Secretariat of the Pacific Community (formerly the South Pacific Commission) was established in 1947 by Australia, France, the Netherlands, New Zealand, the UK and the USA with the aim of promoting the economic and social stability of the islands in the region. The Community now numbers 27 member states and territories: the five remaining founder states (the Netherlands has withdrawn), in which no programmes are run, and the other 22 states and territories of

Melanesia, Micronesia and Polynesia.

The Secretariat of the Pacific Community (SPC) is a technical assistance agency with programmes in marine resources (coastal and oceanic fisheries; maritime programme), land resources (agriculture, animal health and plant protection; forestry) and social resources (community health; socio-economic and statistical services; community education services).

The governing body is the Conference of the Pacific Community, which meets every two years. The Director-General is the chief executive.

Director-General, Lourdes Pangelinan (Guam)

Deputy Directors-General, Dr Jimmie Rodgers (Solomon Islands); Yves Corbel (France)

SHANGHAI CO-OPERATION ORGANISATION

The treaty establishing the Shanghai Co-operation Organisation was signed by China, Kazakhstan, Kyrgyzstan, the Russian Federation, Tajikistan and Uzbekistan on 15 June 2001 in Shanghai. The organisation was set up following five years of co-operation between the signatories (with the exception of Uzbekistan); who had been informally called the Shanghai Five. The Shanghai Co-operation Organisation has been established on the basis of the agreements on confidence-building in the military field and on the mutual reduction of armed forces in the border area signed in Shanghai and Moscow in 1996 and 1997 respectively.

The organisation aims to strengthen mutual trust, friendship and good-neighbourliness between the member states; to encourage effective co-operation between them in the political, trade and economic, scientific and technical, cultural, educational, energy, transport, environmental, and other spheres; and to undertake joint efforts for the maintenance of peace, security and stability in the region, and the building of a new, democratic, just and rational international political and economic order. Co-operation within the organisation's framework is already under way in political, trade and economic, cultural, scientific and technical, and other spheres.

The heads of state hold annual official meetings and there are regular meetings of the heads of government, held alternately in each of the member states. There is no permanent secretariat.

SOUTH ASIAN ASSOCIATION FOR REGIONAL CO-OPERATION

PO Box 4222, Kathmandu, Nepal
Tel: (00 977) (1) 221794/221785; Fax: (00 977) (1) 227033/223991
Email: saarc@saarc-sec.org
Web: www.saarc-sec.org

The South Asian Association for Regional Co-operation (SAARC) was established in 1985 by Bangladesh, Bhutan, India, the Maldives, Nepal, Pakistan and Sri Lanka. Its primary objective is the acceleration of the process of economic and social development in member states through collective action in agreed areas of co-operation. These include agriculture and rural development, human resource development, environment, meteorology and forestry, science and technology, transport and communications, energy, and social development.

A SAARC preferential trading arrangement (SAPTA), which is designed to reduce tariffs on trade between SAARC member states, was signed in 1993 and entered into force in December 1995. A committee of experts was established in 1998 to draft a comprehensive treaty to create a free trade area. The text of the treaty was due to be finalised by the end of 2002. Agreement was reached in January 2002 to work towards the establishment of a South Asian economic union.

The highest authority rests with the heads of state or government of each member state. The Council of Ministers, which meets twice a year, is made up of the foreign ministers of the member states; it is responsible for formulating policy and considering new projects. The Standing Committee is composed of the foreign secretaries of the member states and monitors and co-ordinates SAARC programmes; it meets twice a year. Technical committees are responsible for individual areas of SAARC's activities. The Secretariat co-ordinates, monitors, facilitates and promotes SAARC's activities and serves as a channel of communication between the association and other regional and intergovernmental institutions.

Secretary-General, Q. A. M. A. Rahim (Bangladesh)

SOUTHERN AFRICAN DEVELOPMENT COMMUNITY

Private Bag 0095, Gaborone, Botswana
Tel: (00 267) 351 863; Fax: (00 267) 372 848
Email: sadcsec@sadc.int
Web: www.sadc.int

The Southern African Development Community (SADC) was formed in August 1992 by the members of its predecessor, the Southern African Development Co-ordination Conference, founded in 1980 to harmonise economic development among the countries in Southern Africa and reduce their dependence on South Africa. The SADC now comprises 14 countries, including South Africa, and works on a regional basis to increase economic integration and regional security.

It aims to evolve common political values, systems and institutions, to promote development and economic growth, regional security, self-sustaining development and the interdependence of member states, and to maximise production and strengthen and consolidate the historical, social and cultural links among the peoples of the region.

The original ten members, Angola, Botswana, Lesotho, Malawi, Mozambique, Namibia, Swaziland, Tanzania, Zambia and Zimbabwe, were joined by South Africa in 1994, Mauritius in 1995 and the Democratic Republic of Congo and the Seychelles in 1997.

The headquarters of the SADC is in Gaborone, Botswana, but member states each have a responsibility for an area of economic activity.

Executive Secretary, Dr Prega Ramsamy

Chairman, Bakili Muluzi (Malawi)

THE UNITED NATIONS

UN Plaza, New York, NY 10017, USA
Tel: (00 1) (212) 963 1234
Web: www.un.org

The United Nations (UN) is an intergovernmental organisation of member states, dedicated through signature of the UN Charter to the maintenance of international peace and security and the solution of

economic, social and political problems through international co-operation.

The UN was founded as a successor to the League of Nations and inherited many of its procedures and institutions. The name 'United Nations' was first used in the Washington Declaration 1942 to describe the 26 states that had allied to fight the Axis powers. The UN Charter developed from discussions at the Moscow Conference of the foreign ministers of China, the UK, the USA and the Soviet Union in 1943. Further progress was made at Dumbarton Oaks, Washington, in 1944 during talks involving the same states. The role of the Security Council was formulated at the Yalta Conference in 1945. The Charter was formally drawn up by 50 allied nations at the San Francisco Conference between April and 26 June 1945, when it was signed. Following ratification the UN came into effect on 24 October 1945, which is celebrated annually as United Nations Day. The UN flag is light blue with the UN emblem centred in white.

The principal organs of the UN are the General Assembly, the Security Council, the Economic and Social Council, the Trusteeship Council, the Secretariat and the International Court of Justice. The Economic and Social Council and the Trusteeship Council are auxiliaries, charged with assisting and advising the General Assembly and Security Council. The official languages used are Arabic, Chinese, English, French, Russian and Spanish. Deliberations at the International Court of Justice are in English and French only.

A Millennium summit was held in New York on 6–8 September 2000 at which the reform of the UN was debated and an attempt was made to redefine its role.

MEMBERSHIP

Membership is open to all countries which accept the Charter and its principle of peaceful co-existence. New members are admitted by the General Assembly on the recommendation of the Security Council. The original membership of 51 states has grown to 190.

Afghanistan; Albania; Algeria; Andorra; Angola; Antigua and Barbuda; Argentina*; Armenia; Australia*; Austria; Azerbaijan; Bahamas; Bahrain; Bangladesh; Barbados; Belarus*; Belgium; Belize; Benin; Bhutan; Bolivia*; Bosnia-Herzegovina; Botswana; Brazil*; Brunei Darussalam; Bulgaria; Burkina Faso; Burundi; Cambodia; Cameroon; Canada*; Cape Verde; Central African Republic; Chad; Chile; China*; Colombia*; Comoros; Congo; Costa Rica*; Côte d'Ivoire; Croatia; Cuba*; Cyprus; Czech Republic; Democratic People's Republic of Korea; Democratic Republic of the Congo; Denmark*; Djibouti; Dominica; Dominican Republic*; Ecuador*; Egypt*; El Salvador*; Equatorial Guinea; Eritrea; Estonia; Ethiopia*; Fiji; Finland; France*; Gabon; Gambia; Georgia; Germany; Ghana; Greece*; Grenada; Guatemala*; Guinea; Guinea-Bissau; Guyana; Haiti*; Honduras*; Hungary; Iceland; India*; Indonesia; Iran*; Iraq*; Ireland; Israel; Italy; Jamaica; Japan; Jordan; Kazakhstan; Kenya; Kiribati; Korea; Kuwait; Kyrgyzstan; Laos; Latvia; Lebanon*; Lesotho; Liberia*; Libya; Liechtenstein; Lithuania; Luxembourg*; Macedonia; Madagascar; Malawi; Malaysia; Maldives; Mali; Malta; Marshall Islands; Mauritania; Mauritius; Mexico*; Micronesia (Federated States of); Moldova; Monaco; Mongolia; Morocco; Mozambique; Myanmar; Namibia; Nauru; Nepal; Netherlands*; New Zealand*; Nicaragua*; Niger; Nigeria; Norway*; Oman; Pakistan; Palau; Panama*; Papua New Guinea; Paraguay*; Peru*; Philippines*; Poland*; Portugal; Qatar; Romania;

Russian Federation*; Rwanda; Saint Christopher and Nevis; Saint Lucia; Saint Vincent and the Grenadines; Samoa; San Marino; São Tomé and Príncipe; Saudi Arabia*; Senegal; Seychelles; Sierra Leone; Singapore; Slovakia; Slovenia; Solomon Islands; Somalia; South Africa*; Spain; Sri Lanka; Sudan; Suriname; Swaziland; Sweden; Syrian Arab Republic*;Tajikistan; Tanzania*; Thailand; Togo; Tonga; Trinidad and Tobago; Tunisia; Turkey*; Turkmenistan; Tuvalu; Uganda; Ukraine*; United Arab Emirates; United Kingdom*; United States of America*; Uruguay*; Uzbekistan; Vanuatu; Venezuela*; Vietnam; Yemen; Yugoslavia; Zambia; Zimbabwe.

*Original member (i.e. from 1945)

OBSERVERS

Permanent observer status is held by the Holy See. The Palestine Liberation Organisation has special observer status.

NON-MEMBERS

A number of countries are not members, including Taiwan, which was replaced by the People's Republic of China in 1971, East Timor and the Holy See.

THE GENERAL ASSEMBLY
UN Plaza, New York, NY 10017, USA

The General Assembly is the main deliberative organ of the UN. It consists of all members, each entitled to five representatives but having only one vote. The annual session begins on the third Tuesday of September, when the President is elected, and usually continues until mid-December. Special sessions are held on specific issues and emergency special sessions can be called within 24 hours.

The Assembly is empowered to discuss any matter within the scope of the Charter, except when it is under consideration by the Security Council, and to make recommendations. Under the 'uniting for peace' resolution, adopted in 1950, the Assembly may also take action to maintain international peace and security when the Security Council fails to do so because of a lack of unanimity of its permanent members. Important decisions, such as those on peace and security, the election of officers, the budget, etc., need a two-thirds majority. Others need a simple majority. The Assembly has effective power only over the internal operations of the UN itself; external recommendations are not legally binding.

The work of the General Assembly is divided among six main committees, on each of which every member has the right to be represented: disarmament and international security; economic and financial; social, humanitarian and cultural; special political issues and decolonisation (including non-self governing territories); administrative and budgetary; and legal. In addition, the General Assembly appoints ad hoc committees to consider special issues, such as human rights, peacekeeping, disarmament and international law. All committees consider items referred to them by the Assembly and recommend draft resolutions to its plenary meeting.

The Assembly is assisted by a number of functional committees. The General Committee co-ordinates its proceedings and operations, while the Credentials Committee verifies the credentials of representatives. There are also two standing committees, the Advisory Committee on Administration and Budgetary

Questions and the Committee on Contributions, which suggests the scale of members' payments to the UN.
President of the General Assembly (2002), Han Seung-Soo (Republic of Korea)

The Assembly has created a large number of specialised bodies over the years, which are supervised jointly with the Economic and Social Council. They are supported by UN and voluntary contributions from governments, non-governmental organisations and individuals. These organisations include:

THE CONFERENCE ON DISARMAMENT (CD)

Palais des Nations, CH-1211 Geneva 10, Switzerland
Established by the UN as the Committee on Disarmament in 1962, the CD is the single multilateral disarmament negotiating forum. The present title of the organisation was adopted in 1984. There are 66 members.

A Chemical Weapons Convention was agreed in Paris in 1993 and came into force in April 1997 after being ratified by 87 countries. It bans the use, production, stockpiling and transfer of all chemical weapons. All US and Russian weapons must be destroyed within 15 years of the Convention entering into force and all other states' weapons must be destroyed within ten years.
Secretary-General, Vladimir Petrovsky (Russia)
UK Representative, I. Soutar, 37–39 rue de Vermont, CH-1211 Geneva 20, Switzerland

THE UNITED NATIONS CHILDREN'S FUND (UNICEF)

3 UN Plaza, New York, NY 10017, USA

Established in 1947 to assist children and mothers in the immediate post-war period, UNICEF now concentrates on developing countries. It provides primary healthcare and health education. In particular, it conducts programmes in oral hydration, immunisation against leading diseases, child growth monitoring and the encouragement of breast-feeding. Its operations are often conducted in co-operation with the World Health Organisation (WHO).
Executive Director, Carol Bellamy (USA)

THE UNITED NATIONS DEVELOPMENT PROGRAMME

1 UN Plaza, New York, NY 10017, USA

Established in 1966 from the merger of the UN Expanded Programme of Technical Assistance and the UN Special Fund, UNDP is the central funding agency for economic and social development projects around the world. Much of its annual expenditure is channelled through UN specialised agencies, governments and non-governmental organisations.
Administrator, Mark Maloch-Brown

THE UNITED NATIONS HIGH COMMISSIONER FOR REFUGEES (UNHCR)

94 rue Montbrillant, PO Box 2500, CH-1211 Geneva 2, Switzerland

Established in 1951 to protect the rights and interests of refugees, UNHCR organises emergency relief and longer-term solutions, such as voluntary repatriation, local integration or resettlement.
High Commissioner, Ruud Lubbers (Netherlands)
UK OFFICE, 21st Floor, Millbank Tower, 21–24 Millbank, London SW1P 4QH. Tel: 020-7828 9191

THE UN RELIEF AND WORKS AGENCY FOR PALESTINE REFUGEES IN THE NEAR EAST (UNRWA)

Vienna International Centre, Wagramerstrasse 5, PO Box 700, A-1400 Vienna, Austria
Established in 1949 to bring relief to the Palestinians displaced by the Arab-Israeli conflict.
Commissioner-General, Peter Hansen (Denmark)

THE UNITED NATIONS HIGH COMMISSIONER FOR HUMAN RIGHTS

Established in 1993 to secure respect for, and prevent violations of human rights by engaging in dialogue with governments and international organisations. Responsible for the co-ordination of all UN human rights activities.
High Commissioner, Mary Robinson (Ireland)

Other bodies include:

THE UN CENTRE FOR HUMAN SETTLEMENTS (Habitat), PO Box 30030, Nairobi, Kenya
THE UN CONFERENCE ON TRADE AND DEVELOPMENT (UNCTAD), Palais des Nations, CH-1211 Geneva 10, Switzerland
OFFICE FOR THE CO-ORDINATION OF HUMANITARIAN AFFAIRS (DHA), Palais des Nations, Avenue de la Paix 8–14, CH-1211 Geneva 10, Switzerland
THE INTERNATIONAL SEABED AUTHORITY, 14–20 Port Royal Street, Kingston, Jamaica
THE UN ENVIRONMENT PROGRAMME (UNEP), PO Box 30552, Nairobi, Kenya
THE UN POPULATION FUND (UNFPA), 220 East 42nd Street, New York, NY 10017, USA
THE UN INSTITUTE FOR THE ADVANCEMENT OF WOMEN (INSTRAW), PO Box 21747, Santo Domingo, Dominican Republic
THE UN UNIVERSITY (UNU), 53–70, Jingumae, 5-Chome, Shibuya-ku, Tokyo 150, Japan
THE WORLD FOOD PROGRAMME (WFP), Via Cesare Giulio Viola 68, Parco de Medici, I-00148 Rome, Italy

BUDGET OF THE UNITED NATIONS

The budget adopted for the biennium 2001–2 was US$2,535 million. The scale of assessment contributions is set at the minimum 0.01 per cent. The ten largest assessments are: USA, 22 per cent; Japan, 19.268; Germany, 9.493; Russia, 6.283; France, 6.283; UK, 5.380; Italy, 4.992; Canada, 2.573; Spain, 2.448; Australia, 1.604.

THE SECURITY COUNCIL
UN Plaza, New York, NY 10017, USA

The Security Council is the senior arm of the UN and has the primary responsibility for maintaining world peace and security. It consists of 15 members, each with one representative and one vote. There are five permanent members, China, France, Russia, the UK and the USA, and ten non-permanent members. Each of the non-permanent members is elected for a two-year term by a two-thirds majority of the General Assembly and is ineligible for immediate re-election. Five of the elective seats are allocated to Africa and Asia, one to eastern Europe, two to Latin America and two to western Europe and remaining countries. Procedural questions are determined by a majority vote. Other matters require a majority inclusive of the votes of the permanent members; they thus have a right of veto. The abstention

of a permanent member does not constitute a veto. The presidency rotates each month by state in (English) alphabetical order. Parties to a dispute, other non-members and individuals can be invited to participate in Security Council debates but are not permitted to vote.

The Security Council is empowered to settle or adjudicate in disputes or situations which threaten international peace and security. It can adopt political, economic and military measures to achieve this end. Any matter considered to be a threat to or breach of the peace or an act of aggression can be brought to the Security Council's attention by any member state or by the Secretary-General. The Charter envisaged members placing at the disposal of the Security Council armed forces and other facilities which would be co-ordinated by the Military Staff Committee, composed of military representatives of the five permanent members. The Security Council is also supported by a Committee of Experts, to advise on procedural and technical matters, and a Committee on Admission of New Members.

Owing to superpower disunity, the Security Council rarely played the decisive role set out in the Charter; the Military Staff Committee was effectively suspended from 1948 until 1990, when a meeting was convened during the Gulf Crisis on the formation and control of UN-supervised armed forces. However, at an extraordinary meeting of the Security Council in January 1992, heads of government laid plans to transform the UN in light of the changed post-Cold War world. The Secretary-General was asked to draw up a report on enhancing the UN's preventive diplomacy, peacemaking and peacekeeping ability. The report, *An Agenda for Peace*, was produced in June 1992 and centred on the establishment of a UN army composed of national contingents on permanent standby, as envisaged at the time of the UN's formation.

PEACEKEEPING FORCES

The Security Council has established a number of peacekeeping forces since its foundation, comprising contingents provided mainly by neutral and non-aligned UN members. Current forces include: the UN Truce Supervision Organisation (UNTSO), Israel, 1948; the UN Military Observer Group in India and Pakistan (UNMOGIP), 1949; the UN Peacekeeping Force in Cyprus (UNFICYP), 1964; the UN Disengagement Observer Force (UNDOF), Golan Heights, Syria, 1974; the UN Interim Force in Lebanon (UNIFIL), 1978; the UN Iraq-Kuwait Observation Mission (UNIKOM), 1991; the UN Mission for the Referendum in Western Sahara (MINURSO), 1991; the UN Observer Mission in Georgia (UNOMIG), 1993; the United Nations Mission in Bosnia and Herzegovina (UNMIBH), 1995; the United Nations Mission of Observers in Prevlaka (UNMOP), 1996; the United Nations Interim Administration Mission in Kosova (UNMIK), 1999; the United Nations Mission in Sierra Leone (UNAMSIL), 1999; the United Nations Organisation Mission in the Democratic Republic of the Congo (MONUC), 1999; the United Nations Mission in Ethiopia and Eritrea (UNMEE), 20000; the United Nations of Support in East Timor (UNMISET), 2002.

THE ECONOMIC AND SOCIAL COUNCIL
UN Plaza, New York, NY 10017, USA

The Economic and Social Council is responsible under the General Assembly for the economic and social work of the UN and for the co-ordination of the activities of the 15 specialised agencies and other UN bodies. It makes reports and recommendations on economic, social, cultural, educational, health and related matters, often in consultation with non-governmental organisations, passing the reports to the General Assembly and other UN bodies. It also drafts conventions for submission to the Assembly and calls conferences on matters within its remit.

The Council consists of 54 members, 18 of whom are elected annually by the General Assembly for a three-year term. Each has one vote and can be immediately re-elected on retirement. A President is elected annually and is also eligible for re-election. One substantive session is held annually and decisions are reached by simple majority vote of those present.

The Council has established a number of standing committees on particular issues and several commissions. Commissions include: Statistical, Human Rights, Social Development, Sustainable Development, Status of Women, Crime Prevention and Criminal Justice, Narcotic Drugs, Science and Technology for Development, and Population; and Regional Economic Commissions for Europe, Asia and the Pacific, Western Asia, Latin America and Africa.

THE TRUSTEESHIP COUNCIL
UN Plaza, New York, NY10017, USA

The Trusteeship Council supervised the administration of territories within the UN Trusteeship system inherited from the League of Nations. It consists of the five permanent members of the Security Council. With the independence of the Republic of Palau in October 1994, all eleven trusteeships have now progressed to independence or merged with neighbouring states and the Trusteeship Council suspended its operations on 1 November 1994.

THE SECRETARIAT
UN Plaza, New York, NY 10017, USA

The Secretariat services the other UN organs and is headed by a Secretary-General elected by a majority vote of the General Assembly on the recommendation of the Security Council. He is assisted by an international staff, chosen to represent the international character of the organisation. The Secretary-General is charged with bringing to the attention of the Security Council any matter which he considers poses a threat to international peace and security. He may also bring other matters to the attention of the General Assembly and other UN bodies and may be entrusted by them with additional duties. As chief administrator to the UN, the Secretary-General is present in person or via representatives at all meetings of the other five main organs of the UN. He may also act as an impartial mediator in disputes between member states.

The power and influence of the Secretary-General has been determined largely by the character of the office-holder and by the state of relations between the superpowers. The thaw in these relations since the mid-1980s has increased the effectiveness of the UN, particularly in its attempts to intervene in international disputes. It helped to end the Iran-Iraq war and sponsored peace in Central America. Following Iraq's invasion of Kuwait in 1990 the UN took its first collective security action since the Korean War. UN action to protect the Kurds in northern Iraq has widened its legal authority by breaching the prohibition on its intervention in the essentially domestic affairs of states. Currently the UN is involved in peacekeeping, aid

distribution and negotiations in the former Yugoslavia; and is addressing the global problems of AIDS and environmental destruction.

Secretary-General, Kofi Annan, apptd 1996 (Ghana)
Deputy Secretary-General, Louise Frechette, *apptd* 1998 (Canada)

UNDER-SECRETARIES-GENERAL

Administration and Management, Joseph Connor (USA)
Economic and Social Affairs, Nitin Desai (India)
Executive Office of the Secretary-General, Iqbal Riza (Pakistan)
General Assembly Affairs and Conference Services, Jin Yongjian (China)
Humanitarian Affairs, Kenzo Oshima (Japan)
Legal Affairs and UN Legal Counsel, Hans Corell (Sweden)
Peacekeeping Operations, Jean-Marie Guehenno (France)
Political Affairs, Sir Kieran Prendergast (UK)

FORMER SECRETARIES-GENERAL

1946–53	Trygve Lie (Norway)
1953–61	Dag Hammarskjöld (Sweden)
1961–71	U Thant (Burma)
1971–81	Kurt Waldheim (Austria)
1981–91	Javier Pérez de Cuéllar (Peru)
1991–96	Boutros Boutros-Ghali (Egypt)

INTERNATIONAL COURT OF JUSTICE
The Peace Palace, NL-2517 KJ
The Hague, The Netherlands

The International Court of Justice is the principal judicial organ of the UN. The Statute of the Court is an integral part of the Charter and all members of the UN are *ipso facto* parties to it. The Court is composed of 15 judges, elected by both the General Assembly and the Security Council for nine-year terms which are renewable. Judges may deliberate over cases in which their country is involved. If no judge on the bench is from a country which is a party to a dispute under consideration, that party may designate a judge to participate ad hoc in that particular deliberation. If any party to a case fails to adhere to the judgement of the Court, the other party may have recourse to the Security Council.

President, Gilbert Guillaume (France) (2006)
Vice-President, Stephen M. Schwebel (USA) (2006)
Judges, Carl-August Fleischhauer (Germany) (2003); Géza Herczegh (Hungary) (2003); Rosalyn Higgins (UK) (2009); Shi Jiuyong (China) (2003); Pieter H. Kooijmans (Netherlands) (2006); Abdul G. Koroma (Sierra Leone) (2003); Shigeru Oda (Japan) (2003); Gonzalo Parra-Aranguren (Venezuela) (2009); Raymond Ranjeva (Madagascar) (2009); José Francisco Rezek (Brazil) (2006); Vladlen S. Vereshchetin (Russia) (2006); Mohammed Bedjaoui (Algeria) (2006); Akin Shawkat Al-Khasawneh (Jordan) (2009); Thomas Buergenthal (USA) (2009)

INTERNATIONAL CRIMINAL TRIBUNAL FOR THE FORMER YUGOSLAVIA
Churchill Plein 1, PO Box 13888, NL-2501 EW The Hague, The Netherlands

In February 1993, the Security Council voted to establish a war crimes tribunal for the former Yugoslavia to hear cases covering grave breaches of the Geneva Conventions and crimes against humanity. The Court

was inaugurated in November 1993 in The Hague with 11 judges elected by the UN General Assembly from 11 states, divided into two trial chambers of three judges each and an appeal chamber of five judges. The court is unable to force suspects to stand trial but is empowered to pass verdicts in the absence of suspects and can put suspects under an 'act of accusation' which prevents them from leaving their own country.

In October 1995, the tribunal formally charged the Bosnian Serb leaders Radovan Karadžić and Gen. Ratko Mladić, and the Croatian Serb President Milan Martić and 21 others with genocide and crimes against humanity. As at January 1997 only one of the 75 suspected war criminals to be indicted has been imprisoned. In May 1999, the tribunal formally charged the Yugoslav president Slobodan Milošević the Serbian president Milan Milutinović, two other Serb politicians and the Yugoslav armed forces chief of staff Dragoljub Ojdanić.

President, Antonio Cassese (Italy)
Chief Prosecutor, Louise Arbour (Canada)

INTERNATIONAL CRIMINAL TRIBUNAL FOR RWANDA

In November 1994, the UN Security Council voted to establish a tribunal to try those responsible for genocide and other violations of international humanitarian law in Rwanda between 1 January and 31 December 1994. The tribunal, based in Arusha, Tanzania, is empowered to try the most senior people responsible for the massacre. It formally opened in November 1995 to consider 463 indictments.

Chief Prosecutor, Carla del Ponte (Switzerland)

UNITED NATIONS MONITORING, VERIFICATION AND INSPECTION COMMISSION

Room S-3120, New York, NY 10017, USA
Tel: (00 1) (212) 963 3017; Fax: (00 1) (212) 963 3922
Web: www.unmovic.org

The United Nations Monitoring, Verification and Inspection Commission (UNMOVIC), was created by UN Security Council Resolution 1284, adopted in December 1999. It replaced the former United Nations Special Commission for the Elimination of Iraq's Weapons of Mass Destruction (UNSCOM).

UNMOVIC is mandated to verify Iraq's compliance with its obligation not to possess or acquire weapons of mass destruction (biological or chemical weapons of mass destruction, together with ballistic missiles with a target distance of more than 150 km), to destroy all research, development and production facilities and to desist from the future development or acquisition of such weapons and operate a monitoring and verification programme to ensure that prohibited items and programmes are not reactivated.

The lifting of sanctions on the export of goods to Iraq was linked to its co-operation with UNMOVIC. To date, UNMOVIC has not been permitted to enter Iraq and fulfil its mandate.

Executive Chairman, Dr Hans Blix (Sweden)

SPECIALISED AGENCIES

Fifteen independent international organisations, each with its own membership, budget and headquarters, carry out their responsibilities in co-ordination with the UN under agreements made with the Economic and Social Council. An entry for each appears elsewhere in the International Organisations section. They are: the Food and Agriculture Organisation of the UN;

International Civil Aviation Organisation; International Fund for Agricultural Development; International Labour Organisation; International Maritime Organisation; the International Monetary Fund; International Telecommunications Union; UN Educational, Scientific and Cultural Organisation; UN Industrial Development Organisation; Universal Postal Union; World Bank (International Bank for Reconstruction and Development, International Development Agency, International Finance Corporation); World Health Organisation; World Intellectual Property Organisation; and World Meteorological Organisation. The International Atomic Energy Agency and the World Trade Organisation are linked to the UN but are not specialised agencies.

UK MISSION TO THE UNITED NATIONS

1 Dag Hammarskjöld Plaza, 885 Second Avenue, New York, NY 10017, USA
Tel: (00 1) (212) 745 9250; Fax: (00 1) (212) 745 9316
Web: www.ukun.org
Permanent Representative to the United Nations and Representative on the Security Council, Sir Jeremy Greenstock, KCMG, *apptd* 1998
Deputy Permanent Representative, S. G. Eldon, CMG, OBE

UK MISSION TO THE OFFICE OF THE UN AND OTHER INTERNATIONAL ORGANISATIONS IN GENEVA

37–39 rue de Vermont, CH-1211 Geneva 20, Switzerland
Tel: (00 41) (22) 918 2300; Fax: (00 41) (22) 918 2333
Email: mission.uk@ties.itu.int
Permanent UK Representative, S. W. J. Fuller, CMG, *apptd* 2000
Deputy Permanent Representative, N. M. McMillan, CMG

UK MISSION TO THE UN IN VIENNA

Jaurèsgasse 12, A-1030 Vienna, Austria
UK Permanent Representative, P. R Jenkins, *apptd* 2001
Deputy Permanent Representative, M. R. Etherton

UN OFFICE AND INFORMATION CENTRE

21st Floor, Millbank Tower, 21–24 Millbank, London, SW1P 4QH
Tel: 020-7630 1981; Fax: 020-7976 6478

UNITED NATIONS EDUCATIONAL, SCIENTIFIC AND CULTURAL ORGANISATION

7 place de Fontenoy, F-75352 Paris 07 SP, France
Tel: (00 33) (1) 4568 1000; Fax: (00 33) (1) 4567 1690
Email: clearing-house@unesco.org
Web: www.unesco.org

The United Nations Educational, Scientific and Cultural Organisation (UNESCO) was established in 1946. It promotes collaboration among its member states in education, science, culture and communication. It aims to further a universal respect for human rights, justice and the rule of law, without distinction of race, sex, language or religion, in accordance with the UN Charter.

UNESCO runs a number of programmes to improve education and extend access to it. It provides assistance to ensure the free flow of information and its wider and better balanced dissemination without any obstacle to freedom of expression, and to maintain cultural heritage in the face of development. It fosters research and study in all areas of the social and environmental sciences.

UNESCO had 188 member states as at May 2002. The General Conference, consisting of representatives of all the members, meets biennially to decide the programme and the budget (2000–1, US$544,400,000). It elects the 58-member Executive Board, which supervises operations, and appoints a Director-General who heads a Secretariat responsible for carrying out the organisation's programmes. In most member states national commissions liaise with UNESCO to execute its programme.

The UK withdrew from UNESCO in 1985; it rejoined on 1 July 1997.

Director-General, Koichiro Matsuura (Japan)

UNITED NATIONS INDUSTRIAL DEVELOPMENT ORGANISATION

Vienna International Centre, Wagramerstrasse 5, PO Box 300, A-1400 Vienna, Austria
Tel: (00 43) (1) 260 260; Fax: (00 43) (1) 269 2669
Email: unido@unido.org
Web: www.unido.org

The United Nations Industrial Development Organisation (UNIDO) was established in 1966 by the UN General Assembly to act as the central co-ordinating body for industrial activities within the UN. It became a UN specialised agency in 1985. UNIDO aims to help developing countries and those with economies in transition to develop sustainable industrialisation by concentrating on economic competitiveness, environmental awareness and employment issues both in the public and private sectors. UNIDO designs and implements programmes to support industrial development in individual member states and offers specialised support for programme development.

UNIDO had 169 members as at July 2002. It is funded by regular and operational budgets, together with contributions for technical co-operation activities. The regular budget is derived from member states' contributions. Technical co-operation is funded mainly through voluntary contributions from donor countries and institutions and by intergovernmental and non-governmental organisations. A General Conference of all the members meets biennially to discuss strategy and policy, approve the budget (2002–3, €133.7 million) and elect the Director-General. The Industrial Development Board is composed of members from 53 member states and reviews the work programme and the budget, which is prepared by the Programme and Budget Committee.

Director-General, Carlos Magariños (Argentina)
Permanent UK Representative, Peter Jenkins, British Embassy, Vienna

UNIVERSAL POSTAL UNION

Weltpoststrasse 4, CH-3000 Bern 15, Switzerland
Tel: (00 41) (31) 350 3111; Fax: (00 41) (31) 350 3110
Email: info@upu.int
Web: www.upu.int

The Universal Postal Union (UPU) was established by the Treaty of Bern 1874, taking effect from 1875, and became a UN specialised agency in 1948. The UPU is an intergovernmental organisation that exists to form and regulate a single postal territory of all member countries for the reciprocal exchange of correspondence without discrimination. It also assists and advises on the improvement of postal services.

The UPU had 189 members as at July 2002. A

Universal Postal Congress of all its members is the UPU's supreme authority and meets every five years to review the Treaty. A Council of Administration composed of 41 members was established by the 1999 Congress. It meets annually to ensure continuity between congresses, study regulatory developments and broad policies, approve the budget and examine proposed Treaty changes. A Postal Operations Council, which is also elected by the Congress, meets annually to deal with specific technical and operational issues. The three UPU bodies are served by the International Bureau, a secretariat headed by a Director-General.

Funding is provided by members according to a scale of contributions drawn up by the Congress. The Council sets the biennial budget (2001–2, SFr71,400,000) within a five-year figure decided by the Congress.

Director-General, Thomas E. Leavey (USA)

UNREPRESENTED NATIONS AND PEOPLES ORGANISATION
Eisenhowerlaan 136, NL-2517 KN,
The Hague, The Netherlands
Tel: (00 31) (70) 360 3318; Fax: (00 31) (70) 360 3346
Email: unponl@unpo.org
Web: www.unpo.org

The Unrepresented Nations and Peoples Organisation (UNPO) was founded in 1991 to offer an international forum for occupied nations, indigenous peoples and national minorities who are not represented in other international organisations.

UNPO does not aim to represent these nations and peoples, but rather to assist and empower them to represent themselves more effectively, and provides professional services and facilities as well as education and training in the fields of diplomacy, international and human rights law, democratic processes, institution building, conflict management and resolution, and environmental protection.

Participation is open to all nations and peoples who are inadequately represented at the United Nations and who declare allegiance to five principles relating to the right of self-determination of all peoples, human rights, democracy, non-violence and the rejection of terrorism, and protection of the natural environment. Applicants must show that they constitute a 'nation or people' and that the organisation applying for membership is representative of that nation or people.

As at July 2002, there were 53 full members and five former members, who have achieved full independence.

Director-General, Karl von Habsburg (Austria)

WESTERN EUROPEAN UNION
Verenigingstraat 15, B-1000 Brussels, Belgium
Tel: (00 32) (2) 500 4412; Fax: (00 32) (2) 500 4470
Email: ueo.secretariatgeneral@skynet.be
Web: www.weu.int

The Western European Union (WEU) originated as the Brussels Treaty Organisation (BTO) established under the Treaty of Brussels, signed in 1948 by Belgium, France, Luxembourg, the Netherlands and the UK, to provide collective self-defence and economic and social collaboration amongst its signatories. The BTO was modified to become the WEU in 1954 with the admission of West Germany and Italy.

From the late 1970s onwards efforts were made to add a security dimension to the EC's European Political Co-operation. Opposition to these efforts from Denmark, Greece and Ireland led the remaining EC countries, all WEU members, to decide to reactivate the Union in 1984. Members committed themselves to harmonising their views on defence and security and developing a European security identity, while bearing in mind the importance of transatlantic relations. Portugal and Spain joined the WEU in 1988, and Greece became a full member in 1995.

In 1991, the EU Maastricht Treaty committed the European Community to the establishment of a Common Foreign and Security Policy (CFSP). The WEU was designated as the future defence component of the European Union and member states of the EU who were not already members of the WEU were invited to join or become observers. In November 1992 the WEU's role as the common security dimension of the EU was enhanced when WEU ministers signed a declaration with remaining European NATO members to give them various forms of WEU membership. Iceland, Norway and Turkey became associate members; the Republic of Ireland, Denmark, Austria, Finland and Sweden became observers. In 1994 the WEU reached agreements with Estonia, Latvia, Lithuania, Poland, the Czech Republic, Slovakia, Hungary, Romania and Bulgaria, under which they all became associate partners; Slovenia became an associate partner in 1996. The Czech Republic, Hungary and Poland, who had been associate partners, became associate members in 1999, following their accession to NATO.

The WEU has worked in close co-operation with the Atlantic Alliance, and relations between the WEU and NATO were developed on the basis of transparency and complementarity. The 1993 Luxembourg Declaration states that the WEU is ready to participate in the future work of the NATO Alliance as its European pillar, and at the Atlantic Alliance summit in January 1994, NATO expressed its readiness to make Alliance assets and capabilities available for WEU operations. In June 1996, NATO foreign and defence ministers approved the Combined Joint Task Force (CJTF) concept and the elaboration of multinational European command arrangements for WEU-led operations.

A Council of Ministers (foreign and defence) has met biannually in the capital of the presiding country; the presidency rotates biannually, and from 1999 the sequence of WEU presidencies has been harmonised with those of the EU Council of Ministers. A Permanent Council of the member states' permanent representatives meets in Brussels. The Permanent Council is chaired by the Secretary-General and serviced by the Secretariat.

In 1999, NATO and the EU decided to establish a direct relationship; the EU committed itself to ensuring that it was able to take decisions on conflict prevention and crisis management and NATO agreed to give the EU access to its collective assets and capabilities for operations in which NATO as a whole was not engaged. The WEU's crisis management functions were transferred to the EU in June 2001.

The Assembly of the WEU is composed of 115 parliamentarians of member states and meets twice annually in Paris to debate matters within the scope of the revised Brussels Treaty.

Presidency (2002) Spain, Portugal; (2003) Greece, Italy
Secretary-General, Javier Solana Madariaga (Spain)
UK Representative on the Permanent Council, David Richmond

ASSEMBLY, 43 avenue du Président Wilson, F-75775 Paris Cedex 16, France

THE WORLD BANK GROUP
1818 H Street NW, Washington 20433, USA
Tel: (00 1) (202) DC 477 1000; Fax: (00 1) (202) 477 6391
Email: feedback@worldbank.org
Web: www.worldbank.org

The World Bank Group was founded in 1944 and is one of the world's largest sources of development assistance. The Bank has 183 members.

Originally directed towards post-war reconstruction in Europe, the Bank subsequently turned towards assisting less-developed countries and is currently working in more than 100 developing countries. The Bank, which provided US$17.3 billion in loans to its client countries in the 2001 financial year, works with government agencies, non-governmental organisations and the private sector to formulate assistance strategies. Its local offices implement the Bank's programme in each country. It has offices in more than 100 countries.

The Bank is owned by the governments of member countries and its capital is subscribed by its members. It finances its lending primarily from borrowing in world capital markets, and derives a substantial contribution to its resources from its retained earnings and the repayment of loans. The interest rate on its loans is calculated in relation to its cost of borrowing. Loans generally have a grace period of five years and are repayable within 20 years.

The World Bank Group consists of five institutions. The International Bank for Reconstruction and Development (IBRD) provides loans and development assistance to middle-income countries and creditworthy poorer countries. The International Finance Corporation (IFC) promotes private sector investment in developing member countries by mobilising domestic and foreign capital. The International Development Association (IDA) performs the same function as the World Bank but primarily to less-developed countries and on terms that bear less heavily on their balance of payments than IBRD loans. The Multilateral Investment Guarantee Agency (MIGA) promotes foreign direct investment in developing states by providing guarantees to potential investors and advisory services to developing member countries. MIGA has a membership of 154 countries. The International Centre for Settlement of Investment Disputes (ICSID) provides facilities for the settlement by conciliation or arbitration of investment disputes between foreign investors and their host countries. ICSID has a membership of 150 countries.

The IBRD and its affiliates are financially and legally distinct but share headquarters. The IBRD is headed by a Board of Governors, consisting of one Governor and one alternate Governor appointed by each member country. Twenty-four Executive Directors exercise all powers of the Bank except those reserved to the Board of Governors. The President, elected by the Executive Directors, conducts the business of the Bank, assisted by an international staff. Membership in both the IFC (175 members) and the IDA (162 members) is open to all IBRD countries. The IDA is administered by the same staff as the Bank; the IFC has its own personnel but draws on the IBRD for administrative and other support. All share the same President.

President, James D. Wolfensohn (USA)

UK Executive Director, Stephen Tickford, Room 11-120, IMF, 700 19th Street NW, Washington DC 20431

UK OFFICE, New Zealand House, 15th Floor, Haymarket, London SW1Y 4TQ. Tel: 020-7930 8511; Fax: 020-7930 8515

WORLD HEALTH ORGANISATION
20 avenue Appia, CH-1211 Geneva 27, Switzerland
Tel: (00 41) (22) 791 2111; Fax: (00 41) (22) 791 0746
Email: info@who.ch
Web: www.who.ch

The UN International Health Conference, held in 1946, established the World Health Organisation (WHO) as a UN specialised agency, with effect from 1948. It is dedicated to attaining the highest possible level of health for all. It collaborates with member governments, UN agencies and other bodies to improve health standards, control communicable diseases and promote all aspects of family and environmental health. It seeks to raise the standards of health teaching and training, and promotes research through collaborating research centres worldwide. Its other services include the *International Pharmacopoeia*, epidemiological surveillance, and the collation and publication of statistics. WHO activities are orientated to achieving 'Health for All'.

WHO had 191 members as at July 2002. It is governed by the annual World Health Assembly of members which meets to set policy, approve the budget (2002–3, US$2,223 million), appoint a Director-General, and adopt health conventions and regulations. It also elects 32 members who designate one expert to serve on the Executive Board. The Board effects the programme, suggests initiatives and is empowered to deal with emergencies. A Secretariat, headed by the Director-General, supervises the activities of six regional offices.

Director-General, Gro Harlem Bruntland (Norway)

WORLD INTELLECTUAL PROPERTY ORGANISATION
34 chemin des Colombettes, CH-1211 Geneva 20, Switzerland
Tel: (00 41) (22) 338 9111; Fax: (00 41) (22) 733 5428
Email: wipo@wipo.int
Web: www.wipo.int

The World Intellectual Property Organisation (WIPO) was established in 1967 by the Stockholm Convention, which entered into force in 1970. In addition to that Convention, WIPO administers 23 treaties, the principal ones being the Paris Convention for the Protection of Industrial Property and the Bern Convention for the Protection of Literary and Artistic Works. WIPO became a UN specialised agency in 1974.

WIPO promotes the protection of intellectual property throughout the world through co-operation among states, and the administration of various 'Unions', each founded on a multilateral treaty and dealing with the legal and administrative aspects of intellectual property.

Intellectual property comprises two main branches: industrial property (inventions, trademarks, industrial designs and appellations of origin); and copyright (literary, musical, photographic, audiovisual and artistic works, etc.). WIPO also assists creative intellectual activity and facilitates technology transfer, particularly to developing countries.

WIPO had 179 members as at May 2002. The biennial session of all its governing bodies sets policy, a programme and a budget (2000–1, SFr410 million). WIPO has three governing bodies: the General Assembly, composed of WIPO members who are also

members of the Paris or Bern conventions; the Conference, composed of all WIPO members; and the Co-ordination Committee, composed of member states elected by members of WIPO and the Paris and Bern conventions. The General Assembly elects a Director-General, who heads the International Bureau (secretariat).

A separate International Union for the Protection of New Varieties of Plants (UPOV), established by convention in 1961, is linked to WIPO. It has 50 members.

Director-General, Dr Kamil Idris (Sudan)

WORLD METEOROLOGICAL ORGANISATION

7 bis, avenue de la Paix, PO Box 2300,
CH-1211 Geneva 2, Switzerland
Tel: (00 41) (22) 730 8111; Fax: (00 41) (22) 730 8181
Email: wmo@gateway.wmo.ch
Web: www.wmo.ch

The World Meteorological Organisation (WMO) was established in 1950 and became a UN specialised agency in 1951, succeeding the International Meteorological Organisation founded in 1873. It facilitates co-operation in the establishment of networks for making meteorological, climatological, hydrological and geophysical observations, as well as their exchange, processing and standardisation, and assists technology transfer, training and research. It also fosters collaboration between meteorological and hydrological services, and furthers the application of meteorology to aviation, shipping, environment, water problems, agriculture and the mitigation of natural disasters.

The WMO had 179 member states and six member territories as at April 2001. Six regional associations are responsible for the co-ordination of activities within their own regions, There are also eight technical commissions, which study meteorological and hydrological problems, establish methodology and procedures, and make recommendations to the Executive Council and the Congress. The supreme authority is the World Meteorological Congress of member states and member territories, which meets every four years to determine general policy, make recommendations and set a budget (2000–3, SFr252.3 million). It also elects 26 members of the 36-member Executive Council, the other members being the President and three Vice-Presidents of the WMO, and the Presidents of the six regional associations, who are ex-officio members. The Council supervises the implementation of Congress decisions, initiates studies and makes recommendations on matters needing international action. The Secretariat is headed by a Secretary-General, appointed by the Congress.

Secretary-General, G. O. P. Obasi (Nigeria)

WORLD TRADE ORGANISATION

Centre William Rappard, 154 rue de Lausanne, 1211
CH-Geneva 21, Switzerland
Tel: (00 41) (22) 739 5111; Fax: (00 41) (22) 739 5458
Email: enquiries@wto.org
Web: www.wto.org

The World Trade Organisation was established on 1 January 1995 as the successor to the General Agreement on Tariffs and Trade (GATT). GATT was established in 1948 as an interim agreement until the charter of a new international trade organisation could be drafted by a committee of the UN Economic and Social Council and ratified by member states. The charter was never ratified and GATT became the only regime for the regulation of world trade, evolving its own rules and procedures.

GATT was dedicated to the expansion of non-discriminatory international trade and progressively extended free trade via 'rounds' of multilateral negotiations. Eight rounds were concluded: Geneva (1947), Annecy (1948), Torquay (1950), Geneva (1956), Dillon (1960–1), Kennedy (1964–7), Tokyo (1973–9) and Uruguay (1986–94). By the time the measures of the Uruguay Round are fully implemented in 2002, the average duties on manufactured goods will have been reduced from 40 per cent in the 1940s to 3 per cent. The Final Act of the Uruguay Round was signed by trade ministers from the 128 GATT negotiating states and the EU in Marrakesh, Morocco, on 15 April 1994. It established the World Trade Organisation (WTO) to supersede GATT and implement the Uruguay Round agreements. A summit held in Seattle, USA, in December 1999 was unable to reach agreement on further integration of the international trading system.

The WTO is the legal and institutional foundation of the multilateral trading system. It provides the contractual obligations determining how governments frame and implement trade policy and provides the forum for the debate, negotiation and adjudication of trade problems. The WTO's principal aims are to liberalise world trade and place it on a secure basis, and it seeks to achieve this partly by an agreed set of trade rules and market access agreements and partly through further trade liberalisation negotiations. The WTO also administers and implements a further 29 multilateral agreements in fields such as agriculture, textiles and clothing, services, government procurement, rules of origin and intellectual property.

The highest authority of the WTO is the Ministerial Conference composed of all members, which meets at least once every two years. The General Council meets as required and acts on behalf of the Ministerial Conference in regard to the regular working of the WTO. Composed of all members, the General Council also convenes in two particular forms: as the Dispute Settlement Body, dealing with disputes between members arising from the Uruguay Round Final Act; and as the Trade Policy Review Body, conducting regular reviews of the trade policies of members. A secretariat of 500 staff headed by a Director-General services WTO bodies and provides trade performance and trade policy analysis.

As at April 2002 there were 144 WTO members, and a further 30 governments had applied to join. The WTO budget for 2001 was SFr131 million, with members' contributions calculated on the basis of their share of the total trade conducted by WTO members. The official languages of the WTO are English, French and Spanish.

Acting Director-General, Mike Moore
Permanent UK Representative, Simon Fuller, 37–39 rue de Vermont, CH-1211 Geneva 20

Countries of the World: A-Z

AFGHANISTAN
Afğānistān (Pushtu)/
Afqânestân (Dari)
Afghanistan

AREA – 251,773 sq. miles (652,090 sq. km). Neighbours:
Iran (west), Pakistan (south), Tajikistan, Uzbekistan
and Turkmenistan (north), Pakistan and China (east)

POPULATION – 22,132,000: Pushtuns (38 per cent)
predominate in the south and west; Tajiks (25 per
cent); Hazaras (19 per cent) in the centre; Uzbeks (6
per cent) in the north; Aimaqs (4 per cent); Baluchis
(0.5 per cent). The principal languages are Dari (a
form of Persian) and Pushtu

CAPITAL – Kābol (Kabul) (population, 1,424,400, 1988)

MAJOR CITIES – Herāt (177,300); Jalālābād (55,000);
Qandahār (225,500); Māzār-e-Sharif (130,600) (1988
UN estimates)

CURRENCY – Afghani (Af) of 100 puls

NATIONAL ANTHEM – Sorūd-e-Melli

NATIONAL DAY – 19 August

NATIONAL FLAG – Three vertical stripes of black, red
and green with the royal arms and Arabic device
'There is no God but Allah and Muhammad is His
Messenger' in the centre

LIFE EXPECTANCY (years) – male 43.0; female 43.5

POPULATION GROWTH RATE – 2.7 per cent (1999)

POPULATION DENSITY – 34 per sq. km (1999)

Mountains, chief among which are the Hindu Kush,
cover three-quarters of the country. There are three great
river basins, the Oxus, Helmand, and Kābol. The climate
is dry, with extreme temperatures.

HISTORY AND POLITICS

In December 1979 Soviet troops invaded Afghanistan and
installed a pro-Soviet government. Armed Islamic
resistance groups, the mujahidin, fought against Soviet
and Afghan forces until the government collapsed in
April 1992. Mujahidin forces overran Kābol and declared
an Islamic state.

Fighting between factions of the mujahidin resumed in
December 1992. Between 1994–98, divided mujahidin
forces suffered heavy defeats at the hands of the Talibān
(armed Islamic students), which extended its power
across more than 90 per cent of the country. The forces of
the former government were forced northwards. The
United Islamic Front for the Salvation of Afghanistan
(UIFSA) or Northern Alliance was formed by the four
main mujahidin factions. The Talibān, thought to be
backed by Pakistan and Saudi Arabia, imposed strict
Shari'ah law.

The United Nations imposed limited sanctions on
Afghanistan on 19 December 2000 for refusing to
extradite Osama bin Laden, an Islamic terrorist.

Following the 11 September 2001 terrorist attacks on
the USA, which had been carried out by bin Laden's al-
Qa'eda (the base) organisation, and Afghanistan's
subsequent refusal to surrender bin Laden and the al-
Qa'eda leadership to the US authorities, US and UK
forces began military operations against al-Qa'eda and
Talibān targets in Afghanistan on 7 October 2001.
Surrounding countries offered their facilities to the US
forces and intensive US air bombardment conducted

from air bases in Uzbekistan, Tajikistan and Pakistan,
together with material and intelligence assistance by US
and UK special services ground troops to Northern
Alliance forces, swiftly caused the Talibān regime to
collapse in the north of the country, which led to
defections from the Talibān in the south and successes for
anti-Talibān Pashtun militias. Māzār-e-Sharif fell to the
Northern Alliance forces on 9 November, Herāt on 12
November, Kābol on 18 November, and Qandahār
surrendered to opposition forces on 6 December.

Moves to form an alternative government from among
the numerous anti-Talibān factions had begun in
September 2001 and leaders met near Bonn, Germany,
where on 5 December 2001 a multiethnic interim
government was named, which was formed of supporters
of the Northern Alliance, Royalists and other opposition
groups. On 15 December, the interim government, by
now in power in Kābol, thanked the USA for ridding the
country of the Talibān. However, attempts to locate and
capture bin Laden and Mullah Omar, the Talibān leader,
were unsuccessful and pockets of al-Qa'eda and Talibān
forces remained in the mountains in the centre of the
country and along its frontier with Pakistan. Sporadic
outbreaks of violence between rival militias have
continued and the authority of the interim government
has failed to reach all corners of the country. Forces from
the UK and US continued to carry out military
operations against the pockets of al-Qa'eda and Talibān
troops. On 8 April 2002, an assassination attempt was
made upon the Defence Minister and Vice-Chairman of
the interim government, Mohammad Fahim, increasing
tension across the country.

POLITICAL SYSTEM

The National Assembly was abolished in 1992 and no
new legislature has been established.

Following the collapse of Talibān rule in December
2001, an interim government was agreed, which was to
hold office for six months pending the holding of a *Loya
Jirga* (tribal council), which would appoint a transitional
government, to be followed by a general election within
two years. On 13 June 2002, following the *Loya Jirga*, the
interim leader, Hamid Karzai, was voted in as president of
the country.

HEAD OF STATE

President, Hamid Karzai, *elected* 13 June 2002
Vice-Presidents, Gen. Mohammad Qasim Fahim Khan;
Haji Qadir; Karim Khalili; Nematullah Shahrani.

TRANSITIONAL GOVERNMENT *as at July 2002*
Agriculture and Livestock, Hussein Anwari
Border Affairs, Aref Khan Nurzai
Civil Aviation and Tourism, Sadeq Mir Wais
Commerce, Mustafa Kazemi
Communications, Masum Stanakzai
Education, Yunus Qanuni
Endowment and Religious Affairs, Mohammad Amin
  Naserya
Finance, Ashraf Ghani Ahmadzai
Foreign Affairs, Abdullah Abdullah
Health, Suhaila Seddiqi
Higher Education, Sharif Faez
Housing and Town Planning, Mohammad Yusof Pashton
Information, Culture, Rahin Makhdoom
Interior, Taj Mohammad Wardak
Irrigation and Environment, Ahmad Yusof Nurestani
Justice, Abdul Rahmi Karimi
Labour and Social Affairs, Nur Mohammad Farqin
Light Industries, Mohammad Alem Razm
Martyrs and Disabled, Abdullah Wardak
Mines and Industries, Joma Mohammad Mohammad
Planning, Ustad Mohammad Mohaqqeq
Public Works, Abdul Qadir
Reconstruction, Mohammad Amin Farhang
Return of Refugees, Enayatullah Nazeri
Rural Development, Hanef Atmal
Transport, Mohammad Ali Jawid
Water and Electricity, Shaker Kargar
Women's Affairs, Habiba Sorabi

EMBASSY OF AFGHANISTAN
31 Princes Gate, London SW7 1QQ
Tel: 020-7589 8891
Ambassador Extraordinary and Plenipotentiary, HE Ron
  Nash
Minister-Counsellor and Chargé d'Affaires, Ahmad Wali
  Masoud

BRITISH EMBASSY
Karte Parwan, Kābol
Staff were withdrawn from post in February 1989.

ECONOMY

The economy has been devastated by the political
upheavals of the last 20 years. Traditional industries have
diminished as the narcotics trade has grown. In 2000
around 3,200 tonnes of opium were produced, which
accounted for three-quarters of total world production.

By the end of 2000 one million people were thought to
be close to starvation due to continuing fighting and crop
failures caused by three successive years of drought. Food
shortages, together with the on-going civil war resulted in
the flight of more than two million refugees to Iran and
Pakistan, and several hundred thousand internal refugees.
Food aid has begun to reach the country since the
collapse of the Taliban.

Agriculture and sheep raising were traditionally the
principal industries. Silk, woollen and hair cloths and
carpets were manufactured. Salt, silver, copper, coal, iron,
lead, rubies, lapis lazuli, gold, chrome, barite, uranium,
and talc are found.

There are thought to be considerable fuel reserves.
GDP – US$11,166 million (1998); US$178 per capita
(1999)
ANNUAL AVERAGE GROWTH OF GDP – 6.0 per cent
(1998)
INFLATION RATE – 56.7 per cent (1991); estimated to
be 400 per cent in 1996

TRADE

In the past, exports have been Persian lambskins
(Karakul), dried fruits, nuts, cotton, raw wool, carpets,
spice and natural gas, while the imports are chiefly oil,
cotton yarn and piece goods, tea, sugar, machinery and
transport equipment.

In 1995 imports totalled US$50 million and exports
US$26 million.

Trade with UK	2000	2001
Imports from UK	£3,251,000	£3,812,000
Exports to UK	8,493,000	564,000

COMMUNICATIONS

Main roads run from Kābol to Qandahār, Herāt,
Meymaneh via Mazār-e-Sharīf and Feyzābād. Roads
cross the border with Pakistan at Chaman and via the
Khyber Pass, and there are roads from Herāt to the
borders of Turkmenistan and Iran. Much of the country's
road system has been damaged during the fighting.

There are about 21,000 km of roads, of which 2,793 km
are surfaced. There are two international airports at
Kābol and Qandahār and about 1,200 km of inland
waterways.

EDUCATION

Education is free and nominally compulsory, elementary
schools having been established in most centres; there are
secondary schools in large urban areas and four
universities, in Kābol (established 1932), Jalālābād
(established 1962), Balkh and Herāt (both established
1988). During the period of Talibān rule, schooling for
girls was only permitted for those under the age of 12.

ILLITERACY RATE – 63.7 per cent (2000)
ENROLMENT (percentage of age group) – primary 29
per cent (1993); secondary 14 per cent (1993);
tertiary 1.8 per cent (1990)

ALBANIA
Republika e Shqipërisë – Republic of Albania

AREA – 11,099 sq. miles (28,748 sq. km). Neighbours:
Montenegro (north), Kosovo and Macedonia (east),
Greece (south)
POPULATION – 3,731,000 (1997 UN estimate). Muslim
(70 per cent), Greek Orthodox (20 per cent), Roman
Catholic (10 per cent). The language is Albanian
CAPITAL – Tirana (population, 244,153, 1990)
CURRENCY – Lek (Lk) of 100 qindarka
NATIONAL ANTHEM - Rreth Flamurit Të Për Bashkuar
(The Flag That United Us In The Struggle)
NATIONAL DAY – 28 November
NATIONAL FLAG – Black two-headed eagle on a red
field
LIFE EXPECTANCY (years) – male 70.9; female 76.7
POPULATION GROWTH RATE – 3.7 per cent (1999)
POPULATION DENSITY – 108 per sq. km (1999)
ENROLMENT (percentage of age group) – primary 100
per cent (1997); tertiary 12 per cent (1997)

HISTORY AND POLITICS

Albania was under Turkish suzerainty from 1468 until 1912, when independence was declared. After a period of unrest, a republic was declared in 1925, and in 1928 a monarchy. The King went into exile in 1939 when the country was occupied by the Italians; Albania was liberated in November 1944. Elections in 1945 resulted in a Communist-controlled Assembly; the King was deposed in absentia and a republic declared in January 1946.

From 1946 to 1991 Albania was a one-party, Communist state. In March 1991 multiparty elections took place. Rioting broke out in January 1997 following the collapse of several pyramid investment schemes. Anti-government protests, taking the form of armed rebellion, spread throughout the country.

Following the abandonment of the Rambouillet peace talks on the future of Kosovo, NATO commenced air operations against Yugoslavia in March 1999. Yugoslavia responded by actively expelling hundreds of thousands of Kosovar Albanians, with the majority fleeing to Albania. In April 1999, Albania granted NATO unrestricted access to Albania's airspace, ports and military infrastructure. There were several incursions into Albanian territory by Serb troops. By mid-May 1999, over 400,000 Kosovar Albanians had taken refuge in Albania and over 10,000 NATO troops were stationed there. In June 1999 the refugees began returning home following the end of air operations and the entry of NATO forces into Kosovo. By the end of 1999, nearly all of the refugees had left Albania and the number of NATO troops stationed in the country had fallen to 2,000.

The most recent general election took place on 24 June and 8, 22 and 29 July 2001; resulted in the Socialist Party of Albania (SP) winning 70 seats and the Democratic Alliance Party (DAP) winning 36 seats in the 140-member People's Assembly.

HEAD OF STATE

President, Rexhep Mejdani, *elected by parliament* 24 July 1997

COUNCIL OF MINISTERS *as at July 2002*

Prime Minister, Pandeli Majko (SP)
Deputy PM, Labour and Social Affairs, Skender Gjinushi (SDP)
Agriculture and Food, Agron Duka (SP)
Culture, Youth and Sport, Agron Tato (SP)
Defence, Luan Rama (SP)
Economic Co-operation and Trade, Ermelinda Meksi (SP)
Environment, Lufter Xhuveli (SP)
Education and Science, Luan Memushi (SP)
Finance, Kastriot Islami (SP)
Foreign Affairs, Arta Dade (SP)
Health, Mustafa Xhani (SP)
Interior, Stefan Cipa (SP)
Justice, Spiro Peci (HRUP)
Local Government and Decentralisation, Ethem Ruka (SP)
Ministers of State, Viktor Doda (SP) (*Industry and Energy*); Marko Bello (DAP) (*Integration*); Ndri Legisi (SP) (*Prevention of Corruption*)
Public Works and Tourism, Fatmir Xhafa
Transport, Maqo Lakori (SP)

AP Agrarian Party; DAP Democratic Alliance Party; HRUP Human Rights Union Party; SP Socialist Party; SDP Social Democratic Party

EMBASSY OF THE REPUBLIC OF ALBANIA
2nd Floor, 24 Buckingham Gate, London SW1E 6LB
Tel: 020-7828 8897
Ambassador Extraordinary and Plenipotentiary, HE Agim Besim Fagu, apptd 1997

BRITISH EMBASSY
Rruga Skenderbeu 12, Tirana
Tel: (00 355) (42) 40856/7
Ambassador Extraordinary and Plenipotentiary, HE Dr Peter January, apptd 1999

BRITISH COUNCIL DIRECTOR, Michael Moore, MBE
c/o The British Embassy;
Email: Elsona.Agolli@britishcouncil.org.al

DEFENCE

The Army has 400 main battle tanks and 103 armoured personnel carriers. The Navy has 20 patrol and coastal combatant vessels at four bases. The Air Force has 98 combat aircraft.
MILITARY EXPENDITURE – 3.0 per cent of GDP (2000)
MILITARY PERSONNEL – 27,000: Army 20,000, Navy 2,500, Air Force 4,500

ECONOMY

Much of the country is mountainous and nearly a half is covered by forest. The main crops are wheat, maize, sugar beet, potatoes and fruit. There are large chromium deposits. The principal industries are agricultural product processing, textiles, oil products and cement.

Since April 1992, the government has imposed austerity measures in an attempt to reduce the budget deficit and to cut inflation. Up to US$1,200 million worth of personal savings were lost in the collapse of several fraudulent pyramid savings schemes in January 1997, and the value of the lek fell heavily.

Remittances from 500,000 overseas workers remain an important source of revenue.
GNP – US$3,757 million (2000); US$930 per capita (1999)
GDP – US$3,032 million (1998); US$1,174 per capita (1999)
ANNUAL AVERAGE GROWTH OF GDP – 8.0 per cent (1998)
INFLATION RATE – 0.1 per cent (2000)
TOTAL EXTERNAL DEBT – US$975 million (1999)

TRADE

Exports include crude oil, minerals (bitumen, chrome, nickel, copper), tobacco, fruit and vegetables. In 2000 imports totalled US$1,092 million and exports US$263 million. In 2000 Albania had a trade deficit of US$814 million and a current account deficit of US$156 million.

Trade with UK	2000	2001
Imports from UK	£6,994,000	£21,732,000
Exports to UK	2,915,000	1,204,000

ALGERIA
Al-Jumhūriyya al-Jazā'iriyya ad-Dimuqratiyya ash-Sha'biyya - People's Democratic Republic of Algeria

AREA – 919,595 sq. miles (2,381,741 sq. km).
Neighbours: Morocco and Western Sahara (west), Mauritania and Mali (south-west), Niger (south-east), Libya and Tunisia (east)
POPULATION – 31,040,000 (2000 estimate). Arabic is the official language although French and Berber languages are also spoken. The state religion is Sunni Islam

CAPITAL – ΨAlgiers (El Djazaïr, Al-Jazā'ir) (population, 1,507,241, 1987). It is one of the principal ports of the Mediterranean
MAJOR CITIES – Ψ Annaba; Ψ Bejaia; Blida (El Boulaida); Constantine (Qacentina); Ψ Mostaganem; Ψ Oran (Wahran); Setif; Sidi-Bel-Abbès; Ψ Skikda; Tizi Ouzou; Tlemcen
CURRENCY – Algerian dinar (DA) of 100 centimes
NATIONAL ANTHEM – Qassaman Bin Nazilat Il-Mahiqat (We Swear By The Lightning That Destroys)
NATIONAL DAY – 1 November
NATIONAL FLAG – Divided vertically green and white with a red crescent and star over all in the centre
LIFE EXPECTANCY (years) – male 68.7; female 71.8
POPULATION GROWTH RATE –1.43 per cent (2000)
POPULATION DENSITY – 13 per sq. km (1999)
ILLITERACY RATE – 31.1 per cent (2002)
ENROLMENT (percentage of age group) – primary 100 per cent (1997); secondary 63 per cent (1997); tertiary 12.0 per cent (1997)

HISTORY AND POLITICS

Algeria was annexed to France from 1830 until gaining its independence in 1962 following an eight-year armed liberation struggle by the Front de Libération Nationale (FLN). Ben Bella was elected president in 1963, but was deposed in 1965 by Col. Houari Boumediène, who was formally elected president in 1976. Boumediène died in 1978 and was succeeded by Chadli Bendjedid.

A new constitution agreed by referendum in 1988 moved Algeria towards pluralism. However, the 1991 legislative elections were abandoned in anticipation of the success of the opposition Islamic Salvation Front (FIS), which had campaigned on a radical 'Islamist' platform. President Bendjedid resigned and a Higher Committee of State (HCS), headed by former FLN veteran Mohammed Boudiaf, took power. Gen. Liamine Zeroual was elected president for a five-year term in November 1995, but announced his intention to stand down from office in September 1998. Abdelaziz Bouteflika was elected president on 15 April 1999. The other candidates decided to boycott the election some days before it took place, saying that the military had intervened to rig the vote in his favour.

The most recent elections to the National Assembly took place on 30 May 2002 and were won by the FLN, with Ali Benflis as Prime Minister, securing 199 of the 389 seats. The last National Council elections were held on 30 December 2000.

INSURGENCY

Since the abortive elections in 1992, the FIS-backed Islamic Salvation Army (AIS) and the more extreme Armed Islamic Group (GIA) have waged an armed campaign against the regime in favour of an Islamic state. The two groups have targeted the military and security forces, their secular supporters in the population, and foreign expatriates, resulting in up to 100,000 deaths since 1992. The AIS announced in June 1999 that it was renouncing the armed struggle following negotiations with the government; the resulting peace plan was approved by 98 per cent of the electorate in a referendum which was held on 16 September 1999. On 5 January 2000, the AIS announced that it had agreed to disband, however, attacks have continued.

Rioting broke out in the Berber-populated Kabyle region in April and May 2001, resulting in about 80 deaths. A joint session of the National People's assembly (the bicameral legislature) on 8 April, backed reform to give the Berber language, Tamazight, equal status with Arabic.

POLITICAL SYSTEM

The legislature is bicameral. The National Assembly (the lower chamber) has 389 members, directly elected for a five-year term. The *Majlis el-Umma* (Council of the Nation) is the upper chamber, with a third of its 144 members appointed by the president; two-thirds are indirectly elected for six-year terms, of which half are re-elected every three years.

HEAD OF STATE

President, Abdelaziz Bouteflika, *elected* April 1999

COUNCIL OF MINISTERS *as at July 2002*
Prime Minister, Ali Benflis
Agriculture and Rural Development, Said Barkat
Communications and Culture, Khalida Toumi
Defence, The President
Employment and Solidarity, Tayeb Belaiz
Energy and Mines, Chakib Khelil
Finance, Mohamed Terbeche
Fishing and Marine Resources, Smaïl Mimoun
Health and Population, Abdelhamid Aberkane
Higher Education, Rachid Hraoubia
Housing, Nadir Ahmimid
Industry, Hachemi Djaaboub
Labour and Social Security, Tayeb Louh
Ministers Delegate, Abdelkader Messahel (*African Affairs*); Fatma Zahra Bouchemla (*National Community Abroad*); Dahou Ould Kablia (*Local Authorities*); Bouthaina Chriet (*Family Affairs and Women's Issues*); Abdelkader Sellat (*Prison Reform*); Rachid Benaissa (*Rural Development*); Leila Hamou Boutlelis (*Scientific Research*); Fatiha Mentouri (*Financial Reform*)
Ministers of State, Abdelaziz Belkhadem (*Foreign Affairs*); Noureddine Zerhouni (*Interior and Local Government*); Mohammed Cherfi (*Justice*); Ahmed Ouyahia (*Personal Spokesperson for the President*)
National Education, Boubeker Benbouzid
Parliamentary Relations, Noureddine Taleb
Participation and Investment Promotion, Hamid Temmar
Participation and Co-ordination of Reforms, Noureddine Boukrouh
Post, Postal Services, Information Technology and Telecommunications, Zineddine Youbi
Public Works, Omar Ghoul
Relations with Parliament, Abdelwahab Derbal
Religious Affairs and Endowments, Bouabdellah Ghalamallah
Secretary-General, Ahmed Noui
Small and Medium-sized Enterprises and Craft, Mostafa Benbada
Tourism and Traditional Industries, Lakhdar Dorbani
Transport, Abdelmalek Sellal
Urban Planning and the Environment, Cherif Rahmani
Vocational Training, Abdelhamid Abbad
War Veterans, Mohamed Cherif Abbas
Water Resources, Adelmadjid Attar
Youth and Sports, Boubekeur Benbouzid

ALGERIAN EMBASSY
54 Holland Park, London W11 3RS
Tel: 020-7221 7800
Ambassador Extraordinary and Plenipotentiary, HE Ahmed Attaf, apptd 2001

BRITISH EMBASSY
6 Avenue Souidani Boudejemaa
BP08 Alger-Gare 16000, Algiers
Tel: (00 213) (21) 230068
Ambassador Extraordinary and Plenipotentiary, HE Richard Smale, apptd 2001

BRITISH COUNCIL, c/o The British Embassy,
Email: rachida.benyahia@fco.gov.uk

DEFENCE

The Army has 1,089 main battle tanks and 530 armoured personnel carriers. The Navy has two submarines, three frigates and 17 patrol and coastal vessels. The Air Force has 176 combat aircraft and 63 armed helicopters.
MILITARY EXPENDITURE – 6.8 per cent of GDP (2000)
MILITARY PERSONNEL – 124,000: Army 107,000, Navy 7,000, Air Force 10,000; Paramilitaries 181,200
CONSCRIPTION DURATION – 18 months

ECONOMY

The main industry is the hydrocarbons industry. Oil and natural gas are pumped from the Sahara to terminals on the coast before being exported; the gas is first liquefied at liquefaction plants at Skikda and Arzew, although pipelines serve Libya and Italy direct. In November 1996 a 750-mile gas pipeline to Spain was opened, enabling Algeria to double its gas exports to Morocco, Spain, Germany and France.

Other major industries include a steel industry, motor vehicles, building materials, paper making, chemical products and metal manufactures. Most major industrial enterprises are still under state control.

Prior to 1989 the economy was centrally planned and state-controlled in most sectors. Economic reform, begun in 1987, was speeded up in 1988 and now includes industrial and financial sectors. In 1994 the government finally accepted full economic reform and liberalisation under a reform programme agreed with the IMF. The government has cut the budget deficit, devalued the currency and freed price controls. An extensive privatisation programme began in 1997 and there are plans to liberalise the energy, mining and electricity sectors.
GNP – US$48,325 million (2000); US$1,550 per capita (1999)
GDP – US$50,816 million (1998); US$1,726 per capita (1999)
ANNUAL AVERAGE GROWTH OF GDP – 3.8 per cent (1998)
INLFLATION RATE – 2.6 per cent (1999)
UNEMPLOYMENT – 28.7 per cent (1997)
TOTAL EXTERNAL DEBT – US$28,015 million (1999)

TRADE

Export earnings come mainly from crude oil and liquefied natural gas sales. Algeria's main trading partners are France, Italy, USA, Spain and Germany.

In 1996 imports totalled US$8,840 million and exports US$12,620 million. In the first quarter of 2000, Algeria recorded a US$1.98 billion surplus in its trade balance.

Trade with UK	2000	2001
Imports from UK	£105,025,000	£118,467,000
Exports to UK	442,343,000	235,294,000

ANDORRA

Principat d'Andorra - Principality of Andorra

AREA – 181 sq. miles (468 sq. km). Neighbours: Spain and France
POPULATION – 65,971 (1999); less than one-quarter of the population are native Andorrans. The official language is Catalan, but French and Spanish (Castilian) are also spoken. The established religion is Roman Catholicism
CAPITAL　– Andorra la Vella (population, 21,189, 1999)

CURRENCY – Euro (€) of 100 cents
NATIONAL ANTHEM - El Gran Carlemany, Mon Pare (Great Charlemagne, My Father)
NATIONAL DAY – 8 September
NATIONAL FLAG – Three vertical bands, blue, yellow, red; Andorran coat of arms frequently imposed on central (yellow) band but not essential
POPULATION GROWTH RATE 3.9 per cent (1999)
POPULATION DENSITY – 160 per sq. km (1999)
URBAN POPULATION – 93.0 per cent (2000 estimate)

HISTORY AND POLITICS

Andorra is a small, neutral principality formed by a treaty in 1278. The first elections under the new constitution were held in December 1993, and on 20 January 1994 the first sovereign government of Andorra took office.

POLITICAL SYSTEM

Under a new constitution promulgated in May 1993, Andorra became an independent, democratic parliamentary co-principality, with sovereignty vested in the people rather than in the two co-princes, as had previously been the case. The constitution enables Andorra to establish an independent judiciary and to carry out its own foreign policy, whilst its people may now join trade unions and political parties. The two co-princes, the President of the French Republic and the Spanish Bishop of Urgel, remain heads of state but now only have the power to veto treaties with France and Spain which affect the state's borders and security. The co-princes are represented by Permanent Delegates of whom one is the French Prefect of the Pyrénées Orientales department at Perpignan and the other is the Spanish Vicar-General of the diocese of Urgel.

Andorra has a unicameral legislature of 28 members known as the *Consell General de las Valls d'Andorra* (Valleys of Andorra General Council). Fourteen members are elected on a national list basis and 14 in seven dual-member constituencies based on Andorra's seven parishes. The Council appoints the head of the executive government, who designates the members of his government.
Permanent French Delegate, Frederic de Saint-Sernin
Permanent Episcopal Delegate, Nemesi Marqués Oste

EXECUTIVE COUNCIL *as at July 2002*

President, Marc Forné Molné
Agriculture and the Environment, Olga Adellach Coma
Chef de Cabinet, Jordi Guillamet Anton
Economy, Miquel Àlvarez Marfany
Education, Youth and Sports, Pere Cervós Cardona
Finance, Mireia Maestre Cortadella
Foreign Affairs, Juli Minoves Triquell
Health and Welfare, Mònica Codina Tort
Justice and Interior, Jordi Visent Guitart
Secretary-General, Joaquima Sol Ordis
Territorial Planning, Jordi Serra Malleu
Tourism and Culture, Enric Pujal Areny

ANDORRAN DELEGATION, 63 Westover Road, London SW18 2RF. Tel: 020-8874 4806
Ambassador Extraordinary and Plenipotentiary, HE Albert Pintat, apptd 2002
BRITISH AMBASSADOR – HE Peter Torry, resident at Madrid, apptd 1998

ECONOMY

Potatoes are produced in the highlands and tobacco in the valleys. The economy is largely based on tourism, banking, commerce, tobacco, construction and forestry; a

third of the country is classified as forest. Andorra has negotiated a customs union with the European Union which came into force in 1991. The economy is now diversifying rapidly into offshore financial services.
GDP – US$1,062 million (1998); US$14,939 per capita (1999)
ANNUAL AVERAGE GROWTH OF GDP - 4.0 per cent (1998)

Trade with UK	2000	2001
Imports from UK	£10,584,000	£17,185,000
Exports to UK	93,000	86,000

COMMUNICATIONS

A road into the valleys from Spain is open all year round, and that from France is closed only occasionally in winter. There are two radio stations in Andorra, one privately owned and Radio Andorra, operated by the government, as well as a state-owned television station.

ANGORA
República de Angola – Republic of Angola

AREA – 481,354 sq. miles (1,246,700 sq. km).
Neighbours: Democratic Republic of Congo (north and east), Zambia (east), Namibia (south). The enclave of Cabinda is separated from the rest of Angola by the Democratic Republic of Congo and also borders on the Republic of Congo–Brazzaville
POPULATION – 11,569,000. Main ethnic groups are Ovimbundu (37 per cent); Kimbundu (25 per cent); Bakongo (13 per cent). The official language is Portuguese
CAPITAL – ΨLuanda (population, 475,328, 1970; now estimated at 3,000,000)
CURRENCY – Readjusted kwanza (Kzrl) of 100 lwei
NATIONAL ANTHEM – Angola Avante (Advance Angola)
NATIONAL DAY – 11 November (Independence Day)
NATIONAL FLAG – Red and black with a yellow star, machete and cog-wheel
LIFE EXPECTANCY (years) – male 44.5; female 47.1
POPULATION GROWTH RATE - 3.2 per cent (1999)
POPULATION DENSITY – 10 per sq. km (1999)
ENROLMENT (percentage of age group) – tertiary 0.7 per cent (1991)

HISTORY AND POLITICS

After a Portuguese presence of five centuries, and an anti-colonial war since 1961, Angola became independent on 11 November 1975 in the midst of civil war. The Popular Movement for the Liberation of Angola (MPLA) took control early in 1976, but remained under pressure from the National Union for the Total Independence of Angola (UNITA). A peace agreement was signed between the government and UNITA in 1991 and multiparty legislative and presidential elections took place in 1992, which were won by the MPLA and its leader, José Eduardo dos Santos. UNITA refused to accept the results and the civil war resumed in 1993.
    UNITA and the MPLA government signed a peace agreement (the Lusaka Protocol) in 1994. A government of national reconciliation was formed in April 1997 and 70 UNITA legislators took up their seats in parliament, although UNITA's leader, Dr Jonas Savimbi, rejected an offer of the vice-presidency. UNITA also refused to allow central state administration to be restored in key areas and fighting resumed in May 1997.

On 31 October 1997 the UN Security Council ordered sanctions against UNITA for failing to meet its obligations under the Lusaka Protocol. UNITA returned much of its territory to government control in December, and in March 1998 UNITA became a legitimate political party. Three of its representatives were appointed governors of provinces of Angola.
    Fighting continued and the UN Security Council adopted a resolution in September 1998 which urged the rejection of military force by all parties and named UNITA as 'the primary cause of the crisis in Angola'. In February 1999 the UN Security Council voted to withdraw the UN Observer Mission in Angola, the UN Secretary-General Kofi Annan having declared that the country was on the verge of a catastrophic breakdown and that there was no more peace to keep. In December 1999 Namibia allowed the Angolan government to use its territory and armed forces for a joint operation against the UNITA rebels. The UN Security Council adopted a further resolution on 13 April 2000, which called for an investigation into allegations that several countries had violated sanctions imposed on UNITA. Government forces succeeded in capturing large tracts of UNITA-controlled territory in late 2000. UNITA and the government signed a formal ceasefire agreement in Luanda on 4 April 2002 and pledged to adhere to the 1994 peace agreement, the Lusaka protocol. In addition, provision was made for the demobilisation of around 50,000 UNITA fighters, to be monitored by the UN, and the provision of state aid for some 300,000 family members of these soldiers.

SECESSION

In the northern enclave of Cabinda, the Front for the Liberation of the Cabinda Enclave (FLEC) fought a 20-year war of independence until the signing of a cease-fire with the government in September 1995, which was followed by the initialling of a peace agreement in April 1996.

POLITICAL SYSTEM

The MPLA, formerly a Marxist-Leninist party, was the sole legal party until early 1991 when a multiparty system was adopted. The constitution declares Angola to be a democratic state and provides for a president, who appoints a Council of Ministers to assist him, and a 223-member National Assembly. In November 1996 the National Assembly adopted a constitutional amendment extending its mandate for between two and four years.

HEAD OF STATE

President and Prime Minister, José Eduardo dos Santos, re-elected 30 September 1992

COUNCIL OF MINISTERS *as at July 2002*

Agriculture and Rural Development, Gilberto Buta Lutukuta (MPLA)
Assistance and Social Reintegration, João Baptista Kussumua (MPLA)
Commerce, Victorino Domingos Hossi (UNITA)
Defence, Gen. Kundi Paihama (MPLA)
Education and Culture, Antonio Burity da Silva Neto (MPLA)
Energy and Water, Luis Felipe da Silva (MPLA)
Ex-Servicemen and War Veterans, Pedro José van Dúnem (MPLA)
Family and Women's Advancement, Candida Celeste da Silva (MPLA)

Finance, Julio Bessa (MPLA)
Fisheries and Environment, Maria de Fatima Monteiro Jardim (MPLA)
Foreign Affairs, João Bernardo de Miranda (MPLA)
Geology and Mines, Manuel Antonio Africano (MPLA)
Governor of the National Bank, Aguinaldo Jaime (MPLA)
Health, Albertina Julia Hamukuya (UNITA)
Hotel Industry and Tourism, Jorge Alicerces Valentim (UNITA)
Industry, Joaquim David (MPLA)
Information, Pedro Hendrik vaal Neto (MPLA)
Interior, Fernando da Piedade Dias dos Santos (MPLA)
Justice, Paulo Tjipilica (FDA)
Oil, José Maria Botelho de Vasconcelos (MPLA)
Planning, Ana Dias Lourenáo (MPLA)
Posts and Telecommunications, Licinio Tavares Ribeiro (MPLA)
Public Administration, Employment and Social Welfare, Antonio Pitra Costra Neto (MPLA)
Public Works and Town Planning, António Henriques da Silva (MPLA)
Science and Technology, João Baptista Ngandagina (MPLA)
Territorial Administration, Fernando Faustino Muteka (MPLA)
Transport, André Luis Brandão (MPLA)
Youth and Sports, José Marcos Barrica (MPLA)

FDA Angolan Democratic Forum; MPLA Popular Movement for the Liberation of Angola; UNITA National Union for the Total Independence of Angola

EMBASSY OF THE REPUBLIC OF ANGOLA
22 Dorset Street, London W1U 3QY
Tel: 020-7299 9850
Ambassador Extraordinary and Plenipotentiary, HE Antonio DaCosta Fernandes, apptd 1993

BRITISH EMBASSY
Rua Diogo Cao 4 (Caixa Postal 1244), Luanda
Tel: (00 244) (2) 334582
Ambassador Extraordinary and Plenipotentiary, HE John Thompson, apptd 2002

DEFENCE

The Army has 400 main battle tanks and 170 armoured personnel carriers. The Navy has seven patrol vessels. The Air Force has 104 combat aircraft and 40 armed helicopters.
MILITARY EXPENDITURE – 19.2 per cent of GDP (2000)
MILITARY PERSONNEL – 130,500: Army 120,000, Navy 2,500, Air Force 8,000; Paramilitaries 15,000

ECONOMY

Angola has valuable oil and diamond deposits and exports of these two commodities account for over 90 per cent of total exports. Principal agricultural crops are cassava, maize, bananas, coffee, palm oil and kernels, cotton and sisal. Coffee, sisal, maize and palm oil are exported; exports also include mahogany and other hardwoods from the tropical rain forests in the north of the country.
The government is attempting to restructure the socialist economy by free market reforms but is making little progress, with high inflation and a collapsing economy.

The government raised fuel prices by 1,600 per cent in February 2000 in response to IMF demands to remove state subsidies on petroleum products.
GNP – US$3,079 million (2000); US$270 per capita (1999)
GDP – US$6,382 million (1998); US$588 per capita (1999)
ANNUAL AVERAGE GROWTH OF GDP - 1.0 per cent (1998)
INFLATION RATE – 325.0 per cent (2000)
TOTAL EXTERNAL DEBT – US$10,871 million (1999)

Trade with UK	2000	2001
Imports from UK	£76,252,000	£92,898,000
Exports to UK	5,556,000	72,195,000

ANTIGUA AND BARBUDA
State of Antigua and Barbuda

AREA -- 171 sq. miles (442 sq. km); Antigua 108 sq. miles (279 sq. km); Barbuda 62 sq.miles (160 sq. km); Redonda $^1/_2$ sq. mile (1.2 sq. km)
POPULATION – 70,000 (2001 estimate); 65,962, Antigua 64,562, Barbuda 1,400 (official census 1991); the official language is English
CAPITAL – Ψ St John's (population, 22,342, 1991)
MAJOR TOWNS – The town of Barbuda is Codrington
CURRENCY – East Caribbean dollar (EC$) of 100 cents
NATIONAL ANTHEM – Fair Antigua and Barbuda
NATIONAL DAY – 1 November (Independence Day)
NATIONAL FLAG – Red with an inverted triangle divided black over blue over white, with a rising gold sun on the white band
LIFE EXPECTANCY (years) – male 68.45; female 73.14
POPULATION GROWTH RATE – 0.7 per cent (2001)
POPULATION DENSITY – 152 per sq. km (1999)
MILITARY EXPENDITURE – 0.6 per cent of GDP (2000)
MILITARY PERSONNEL – 170: Army 125, Navy 45

Antigua is part of the Leeward Islands in the eastern Caribbean. It is distinguished from the rest of the Leeward group by its absence of high hills and forest, and a drier climate than most of the West Indies. Barbuda is very flat with a large lagoon.

HISTORY AND POLITICS

Antigua was first settled by the English in 1632, and was granted to Lord Willoughby by Charles II. It became internally self-governing in 1967 and fully independent on 1 November 1981.
The Antigua Labour party won the general election of 9 March 1999 and a sixth successive term of office with 12 seats in the House of Representatives compared to four seats for the United Progressive Party.

POLITICAL SYSTEM

Antigua and Barbuda is a constitutional monarchy with Queen Elizabeth II as Head of State, represented by the Governor-General. There is a Senate of 17 appointed members and a House of Representatives of 17 members elected every five years. The Attorney-General may be appointed.
Governor-General, HE Sir James Carlisle, GCMG

CABINET *as at July 2002*

Prime Minister, Finance, Foreign Affairs, Justice and Legal Affairs, National Security, Economic Development, Trade, Industry and Commerce, Lester Bird
Agriculture, Land and Fisheries, Vere Bird Jr
Attorney-General, Gertel Thom
Education, Culture and Technology, Rodney Williams
Health and Social Improvement, Home Affairs, Urban Renewal and Rural Development, John St Luce
Information, Broadcasting, Sports, Carnivals, Guy Yearwood
Labour and Co-operatives, Public Safety, Steadroy Benjamin
Ministers of State, Jeremy Longford (*Economic Development*); George B. Walker (*Information, Broadcasting and Public Works*); Asot Michael (*Finance*)
Planning, Implementation and Public Service Affairs; Trade, Gaston Browne
Public Utilities, Housing, Transportation and Aviation, Robin Yearwood
Tourism and Environment, Molwyn Joseph

HIGH COMMISSON FOR ANTIGUA AND BARBUDA
15 Thayer Street, London W1U 3JT
Tel: 020-7486 7073
High Commissioner, HE Sir Ronald M. Sanders, KCN, CMG, apptd 1995

BRITISH HIGH COMMISSION
PO Box 483, 11 Old Parham Road, St John's
Tel: (00 1 268) 462 0008/9
High Commissioner, HE John White, apptd 2001, resident at Bridgetown, Barbados

ECONOMY

The economy is largely based on tourism and related services, and offshore financial services. Agricultural production includes livestock, sea island cotton, mixed market gardening and fishing.

In 1999 Antigua and Barbuda had a trade deficit of US$292 million and in 2000, a current account deficit of US$28 million. In 1999 imports totalled US$330 million and exports US$38 million.
GNP – US$625 million (2000); US$8,990 per capita (1999)
GDP – US$626 million (1998); US$9,979 per capita (1999)
ANNUAL AVERAGE GROWTH OF GDP – 3.7 per cent (1999)
INFLATION RATE – 1.6 per cent (1999)

Trade with UK	2000	2001
Imports from UK	£24,419,000	£17,282,000
Exports to UK	2,601,000	3,362,000

ARGENTINA
República Argentina - Argentine Republic

AREA – 1,073,518 sq. miles (2,780,400 sq. km).
　Neighbours: Bolivia (north), Paraguay, Brazil and Uruguay (north-east), Chile (west) from which it is separated by the Cordillera de los Andes
POPULATION – 35,672,000; The language is Spanish
CAPITAL – Ψ Buenos Aires (population, 11,298,030, 1991; metropolitan area 2,965,403)
MAJOR CITIES – Córdoba (1,208,554); Ψ La Plata (642,979); Ψ Mar del Plata (512,880); Mendoza (773,113); Ψ Rosario (1,118,905); San Miguel de Tucumán (622,324)
CURRENCY – Peso of 10,000 australes
NATIONAL ANTHEM – Oid Mortales! (Hear, Oh Mortals!)
NATIONAL DAY – 25 May
NATIONAL FLAG – Horizontal bands of blue, white, blue; gold sun in centre of white band
LIFE EXPECTANCY (years) – male 70.6; female 77.7
POPULATION GROWTH RATE – 1.3 per cent (1999)
POPULATION DENSITY – 13 per sq. km (1999)
URBAN POPULATION – 88.9 per cent (1997)

Argentina occupies the greater portion of the southern part of the South American continent, and extends from Bolivia to Cape Horn.

HISTORY AND POLITICS

The estuary of La Plata was discovered in 1515 by Juan Díaz de Solís and the region was subsequently colonised by the Spanish. Spain ruled the territory from the 16th century until 1810. In 1816, after a long campaign of liberation conducted by General José de San Martín, independence was declared by the Congress of Tucumán. The country's constitution was adopted in 1853 followed by a period of national organisation.

President Juan Domingo Perón was overthrown in 1955, and there followed 18 years of instability until 1973 when he was recalled from exile. Perón died within a year and was succeeded by his widow, Vice-President María Estela Martínez de Perón. A coup led to the establishment of a military junta in 1976. Following the Falkland Islands/Malvinas defeat in 1982, the President, Gen. Galtieri, resigned and the Army appointed Gen. Bignone. A civilian president was elected in 1983. In the October 1999 general election the Radical Civic Union-National Solidarity Front (UCR-Frepaso) Alliance became the largest party in the Chamber of Deputies and took office on 10 December 1999.

Vice-President Carlos Alvárez resigned in October 2000 in protest at the president's decision not to dismiss two senior officials involved in a bribery allegation. President Fernando de la Rúa resigned on 20 December 2001 in the face of serious unrest caused by the collapsing economy. Adolfo Rodriguez Saa was elected his interim successor by Congress on 23 December but resigned on 31 September. Eduardo Alberto Duhalde was appointed president by Congress on 1 January 2002, to serve for the rest of the la Rúa's term, which is due to end in October 2003.

POLITICAL SYSTEM

The 1853 constitution was amended in 1994. Power is vested in the president who appoints the Cabinet and is directly elected for a once-renewable four-year term. A presidential candidate must win at least 45 per cent of the

vote, or 40 per cent with a 10 per cent lead over the nearest challenger, to gain victory in the first round of voting; if no candidate meets these criteria, a second round must be held. The legislature consists of a 72-member (three for each province) Senate and a 257-member Chamber of Deputies. A half of the Chamber of Deputies is elected every two years. Deputies serve for a four-year term. Senators have served for a nine-year term, with a third being elected every three years, but the terms of all sitting senators ended in December 2001. In October 2001 the Senate was directly elected by the provinces for a six-year term, with one-third renewable every two years.

FEDERAL STRUCTURE

The republic is divided into 23 provinces, each with an elected Governor and legislature, and one federal district (Buenos Aires), with an elected mayor and autonomous government.

Province	Area (sq. km)	Population (1991 census)	Capital
Buenos Aires	307,571	12,594,974	La Plata
Catamarca	102,602	264,234	Catamarca
Chaco	99,633	839,677	Resistencia
Chubut	224,686	357,189	Rawson
Córdoba	165,321	2,766,683	Córdoba
Corrientes	88,199	795,594	Corrientes
Entre Ríos	78,781	1,020,257	Paraná
Federal Capital	200	2,965,403	Buenos Aires
Formosa	72,066	398,413	Formosa
Jujuy	53,219	512,329	San Salvador de Jujuy
La Pampa	143,440	259,996	Santa Rosa
La Rioja	89,680	229,729	La Rioja
Mendoza	148,827	1,412,481	Mendoza
Misiones	29,801	788,915	Posadas
Neuquén	94,078	388,833	Neuquén
Rio Negro	203,013	506,772	Viedma
Salta	155,488	866,153	Salta
San Juan	89,651	528,715	San Juan
San Luis	76,748	286,458	San Luis
Santa Cruz	243,943	159,839	Rio Gallegos
Santa Fé	133,007	2,798,422	Santa Fé
Santiago del Estero	136,351	671,988	Santiago del Estero
Tierra del Fuego	21,571	69,369	Ushuaia
Tucumán	22,524	1,142,105	San Miguel de Tucumán

HEAD OF STATE

President, Eduardo Alberto Duhalde, appointed by Congress 1 January 2002
Vice-President, vacant

CABINET *as at July 2002*

Cabinet Chief, Alfredo Atanasof
Defence, José Horacio Jaunarena
Economy, Roberto Lavagna
Education, Graciela María Giannetasio
Foreign Relations, International Trade and Worship, Carlos Federico Ruckauf
Health, Ginés Gonzalez Garcia
Infrastructure and Housing, vacant
Interior, Jorge Matzkin
Justice and Human Rights, Jorge Reinaldo Vanossi
Labour, Employment and Human Resources, Graciela Camaño
Secretary-General of the Presidency, Anibal Domingo Fernandez

Secretary-General of Domestic Security, Juan Jose Alvarez
Secretary of State Intelligence, Carlos Ernesto Soria
Social Development (acting), Hilda Gonzalez de Ouhalde
Treasury Counsel, Ruben Miguel Citara

EMBASSY OF THE ARGENTINE REPUBLIC
65 Brook Street, London W1K 4AH
Tel: 020-7318 1300
Ambassador Extraordinary and Plenipotentiary, HE Vicente Berasategui, apptd 2000
Defence and Naval Attaché, Capt. Luis A. de Vincenti
Counsellor (Economic and Commercial Affairs), Gustavo Martino
Cultural Attaché, Secretary, Marcos Bednarski

BRITISH EMBASSY
Dr Luis Agote 2412/52, 1425 Buenos Aires
Tel: (00 54) (11) 4576 2222
Ambassador Extraordinary and Plenipotentiary, HE Sir Robin Christopher, KBE, CMG, apptd 2000
Deputy Head of Mission and Minister, Steve Williams
Air Attaché, Gp Capt. T. Brewer, OBE
Defence, Naval and Military Attaché, Col. P. A. Reynolds
First Secretary (Commercial), H. Deas
Cultural Attaché and British Council Director, P. Dick, Marcelo T. de Alvear 590, C1058AAF Buenos Aires; Email: info@britishcouncil.org.ar

DEFENCE

The Army has 200 main battle tanks, 764 armoured infantry fighting vehicles, 449 armoured personnel carriers and 38 helicopters. The Navy has three submarines, six destroyers, seven frigates, 15 patrol and coastal vessels, 21 combat aircraft and 14 armed helicopters. The Air Force has 133 combat aircraft and 27 armed helicopters.
MILITARY EXPENDITURE – 1.7 per cent of GDP (2000)
MILITARY PERSONNEL – 70,100: Army 41,400, Navy 16,200, Air Force 12,500; Paramilitaries 31,240

ECONOMY

The principal crops are wheat, maize, oats, barley, rye, linseed, sunflower seed, alfalfa, sugar, fruit and cotton. Argentina is pre-eminent in the production of beef, mutton and wool. There is an oil refinery in San Lorenzo (Santa Fé province). Natural gas is also produced. Coal, lead, zinc, tungsten, iron ore, sulphur, mica and salt are the other chief minerals being exploited. There are small worked deposits of beryllium, manganese, bismuth, uranium, antimony, copper, kaolin, arsenate, gold, silver and tin. Coal is produced at the Rio Turbio mine in the province of Santa Cruz.

Meat-packing is one of the principal industries; flour-milling, sugar-refining, and the wine industry are also important. In recent years progress has been made by the textile, plastic and machine tool industries and engineering, especially in the production of motor vehicles and steel manufactures.

Since late 1998 Argentina has been in a recession. A bill passed in October 2000 declared an economic state of emergency and in December 2000 a package of economic austerity measures was introduced in an attempt to tackle the budget deficit, low growth and high unemployment. In April 2001, measures to reassure international investors that the country would not default on its debt repayments were introduced. In November 2001, the President announced several economy-boosting measures but defaulted on part of its large public debt in December 2001. The peso has lost 70 per cent of its value against the dollar since it was floated in early 2002. A wave of protests took place across the country in the wake of continued economic instability.

GNP – US$275,547 million (2000); US$7,550 per capita (1999)
GDP – US$298,180 million (1998); US$7,735 per capita (1999)
ANNUAL AVERAGE GROWTH OF GDP – 3.9 per cent (1998)
INFLATION RATE – 0.9 per cent (2000)
UNEMPLOYMENT – 12.8 per cent (1998)
TOTAL EXTERNAL DEBT – US$147,881 million (1999)

TRADE

The chief imports are machinery, industrial and transport equipment, chemicals, metals and plastics. The chief exports are vegetable products, processed foods, minerals, live animals and oils. Argentina's main trading partners are Brazil and the USA.

In 2000 Argentina had a trade surplus of US$2,558 million and a current account deficit of US$8,903 million. Imports totalled US$25,149 million and exports US$26,298 million.

Trade with UK	2000	2001
Imports from UK	£286,270,000	£266,382,000
Exports to UK	185,184,000	214,033,000

COMMUNICATIONS

The 25,386 miles of railway are state-owned. The combined national and provincial road network totals approximately 137,000 miles of which 23,180 miles are surfaced.

CULTURE AND EDUCATION

The literature of Spain is part of Argentine culture. There is little indigenous literature before the break from Spain, but all branches have flourished since the latter half of the 19th century. About 450 daily newspapers are published in Argentina, including seven major ones in the city of Buenos Aires.

Education is compulsory for the seven grades of primary school (six to 13). Secondary schools (14 to 17+) are available in and around Buenos Aires and in most of the important towns. Most secondary schools are administered by the Central Ministry of Education in Buenos Aires, while primary schools are administered by the Central Ministry or by Provincial Ministries of Education. Private schools, of which there are many, are also loosely controlled by the Central Ministry. The total number of universities is over 50 with 24 national, 25 private and a small number of provincial universities.
ILLITERACY RATE – 3.0 per cent (2002)
ENROLMENT (percentage of age group) – primary 100 per cent (1997); secondary 73 per cent (1997); tertiary 36 per cent (1997)

ARMENIA
Hayastani Hanrapetut'yun - Republic of Armenia

AREA – 11,506 sq. miles (29,800 sq. km). Neighbours: Azerbaijan (east and south-west), Georgia (north), Iran (south), Turkey (west)
POPULATION – 3,800,000 (2002 estimate). Armenians 93.8 per cent, Kurds 1.7 per cent and Russians 1.6 per cent. Azeris formed 2.6 per cent of the population, but most fled or were expelled after the outbreak of war with Azerbaijan. There are also Ukrainians, Greeks and Assyrians. The Armenian diaspora numbers some 5,300,000. Armenian is the official language, though Russian is widely spoken and understood. The main religion is Armenian Orthodox Christian (Armenian Church centred in

Etchmiadzin). Armenia adopted Christianity as its official religion in AD 301, the first state in the world to do so.
CAPITAL – Yerevan (population, 1,254,400, 1996 estimate)
CURRENCY – Dram of 100 louma
NATIONAL ANTHEM - Mer Hayrenik Azat, Ankakh (Land Of Our Fathers)
NATIONAL DAY – 21 September (Independence Day)
NATIONAL FLAG – Three horizontal stripes of red, blue and orange
LIFE EXPECTANCY (years) – male 70.3; female 76.2
POPULATION GROWTH RATE – 0.2 per cent (1999)
POPULATION DENSITY – 127 per sq. km (1999)

Armenia lies between the Black and Caspian Seas, occupying the south-western part of the Caucasus region of the former Soviet Union. It is very mountainous, consisting of several vast tablelands surrounded by ridges. The climate is continental, dry and cold, but the Ararat valley has a long, hot and dry summer.

HISTORY AND POLITICS

Armenia was first unified in 95 BC but was divided between the Persian and Byzantine Empires in AD 387 and then conquered in the 11th century by the Seljuk Turks and the Mongols. In the 16th century most of Armenia was incorporated into the Ottoman Empire. In 1639 the country was divided again, the easternmost portions, now the republic of Armenia, becoming part of the Persian Empire. In 1828 eastern Armenia became part of the Russian Empire while western Armenia remained under Ottoman rule. The Ottomans launched pogroms against the Armenians from 1894 onwards, and in 1915 to 1918 massacred 1,500,000 Armenians.

Armenia declared its independence on 28 May 1918, but was crushed and divided between Turkish and Soviet forces in 1920, with the area under Soviet control proclaimed a Soviet Socialist Republic on 29 November 1920. The Soviet government was overthrown by a nationalist revolt in 1921 but reinstated by the Red Army a few months later. In early 1922 Armenia acceded to the USSR.

An Armenian nationalist movement swept to power in national elections in mid-1990. In a referendum in 1991, 99 per cent of the electorate voted for independence, which was declared on 21 September 1991.

Prime Minister Vazgen Sarkissian and six other politicians were shot dead in the National Assembly during an attempted coup on 27 October 1999; Aram Sarkissian, the younger brother of Vazgen Sarkissian, was appointed prime minister on 5 November 1999, but was replaced by Andranik Markarian in May 2000.

FOREIGN RELATIONS

The dispute between the (ethnic Armenian) Nagorno-Karabakh forces supported by Armenia and the Azeri government over Nagorny-Karabakh erupted into all-out war in May 1992, when Nagorno-Karabakh forces breached Azerbaijan's defences to form a land bridge to Armenia. By the end of summer 1992 all of Nagorny-Karabakh was under Armenian control, and by the end of 1993 all Azeri territory that separated Nagorny-Karabakh from Armenia and all mountainous Azeri territory around Nagorny-Karabakh was under the control of Nagorno-Karabakh Armenians. Armenia claims this territory as historically Armenian land arbitrarily given to Azerbaijan by Stalin in 1921–2. A cease-fire agreement between Armenia, Azerbaijan and Nagorny-Karabakh was reached in May 1994, and talks mediated by the

OSCE continue to seek a peaceful resolution to the dispute.

In August 1997 Armenia and Russia renewed a Treaty of Friendship, Co-operation and Mutual Assistance in effect since 1991.

POLITICAL SYSTEM

There is a 131-member unicameral National Assembly (Azgayin Joghov), directly elected every four years. A new constitution was approved by a referendum in July 1995. Armenia is divided into 11 Administrative Regions.

Since the 1999 election, Unity, an alliance of the Republican Party and the People's Party, has been the dominant grouping in the National Assembly.

HEAD OF STATE

President, Robert Kocharian, elected 30 March 1998, sworn in 9 April 1998

CABINET *as at July 2002*

Prime Minister, Andranik Markarian
Agriculture, David Zadoyan
Culture, Youth and Sport, Roland Sharoian
Defence, Serge Sarkissian
Ecology, Vardan Ayvazyan
Education and Science, Levon Mkrtchian
Energy, Armen Movsisian
Finance and Economy, Vardan Khachatryan
Foreign Affairs, Vardan Oskanian
Head of the Government Executive, Manuk Topuzyan
Health, Ararat Mkrtchian
Internal Affairs, Haik Haroutiounian
Justice, David Haroutiounian
National Security, Karlos Petrosian
Prime Minister's Chief of Staff, Karine Kirakosian
Social Security, Razmik Martirosian
State Income, Yervand Zakaryan
State Property, David Vardanian
Territorial Administration and Production Infrastructures, Ovik Abramyan
Trade and Economic Development, Karen Chshmaritian
Transport and Communications, Andranik Manukian
Urban Development, David Lokian

EMBASSY OF THE REPUBLIC OF ARMENIA
25A Cheniston Gardens, London W8 6TG
Tel: 020-7938 5435
Ambassador Extraordinary and Plenipotentiary, HE Dr Vahram Abadjian, apptd 2001

BRITISH EMBASSY
28 Charents Street, Yerevan
Tel: (00 374) (1) 151 841
Ambassador Extraordinary and Plenipotentiary, HE Timothy A. Jones, apptd 1999

DEFENCE

The Army has 110 main battle tanks, 80 armoured infantry fighting vehicles and 11 armoured personnel carriers, eight combat aircraft and 12 armed helicopters.

Russia maintains 2,900 army personnel in Armenia. An agreement on military co-operation with Russia was signed in 1996 which paved the way for joint military exercises. A protocol was also signed on the establishment of coalition troops in Transcaucasia and the planned use of Russian and Armenian armed forces as part of coalition troops in cases of mutual interest. On 19 December 2001, Russian President Vladimir Putin signed a federal law "On Ratifying the Agreement between the Russian Federation and the Republic of Armenia on the

Joint Planning of the Use of Troops (Forces) in the Interests of Joint Security Provision". This stipulates measures to prevent the use by third countries of the territory of Armenia for purposes that may inflict damage on Russian national interests.

MILITARY EXPENDITURE – 8.0 per cent of GDP (2000)
MILITARY PERSONNEL – 42,060: Army 38,900, Air Force 3,160; Paramilitaries 1,000
CONSCRIPTION DURATION – Two years

ECONOMY

The Armenian economy has been badly affected by the Azeri and Turkish economic embargoes which have been in place since 1988. The main trade and transportation routes now lie via Georgia and Iran.

Armenia has a strong agricultural sector in low-lying areas, where industrial and fruit crops are grown. Grain is grown in the hills and the country is also noted for its wine and brandy. There are large copper ore and molybdenum deposits and other minerals. The country also has developed chemicals, industrial vehicles and textiles industries.

The government introduced a programme of economic reforms in November 1994 with IMF support, including the liberalisation of prices, stabilisation of the currency and privatisation.

In 1999 Armenia had a trade deficit of US$474 million and a current account deficit of US$319 million. In 2000, imports totalled US$882 million and exports US$294 million.

GNP – US$1,990 million (2000); US$490 per capita (1999)
GDP – US$1,885 million (1998); US$491 per capita (1999)
ANNUAL AVERAGE GROWTH OF GDP – 3.3 per cent (1999)
INFLATION RATE – 0.8 per cent (2000)
UNEMPLOYMENT – 9.3 per cent (1998)
TOTAL EXTERNAL DEBT – US$932 million (1999)

Trade with UK	2000	2001
Imports from UK	£3,870,000	£7,678,000
Exports to UK	547,000	567,000

CULTURE AND EDUCATION

The Armenian alphabet was established in AD 405. Major cultural figures include the poets Narekatsi (10th century), Frick (13th century), Nahapet Kuchak (16th century) and Sayat-Nova (18th century), the composer Aram Khachaturian (1903–78), the film director Sergei Parajanov and the long-standing world chess grandmaster Gary Kasparov.

ENROLMENT (percentage of age group) – tertiary 12.0 per cent (1996)

AUSTRALIA
The Commonwealth of Australia

AREA – 2,988,902 sq. miles (7,741,220 sq. km)
POPULATION – 19,603,500 (2001 estimate): 410,000 of Aboriginal and Torres Strait Islander origin (2001 estimate). The language is English
CAPITAL – Canberra, in the Australian Capital Territory (population, 313,900, 2001 estimate). It has been the seat of government since 1927
MAJOR CITIES – Ψ Adelaide (1,100,100); Ψ Brisbane (1,656,700); Ψ Hobart (194,400); Ψ Melbourne (3,522,000); Ψ Perth, including Fremantle (1,400,500); Ψ Sydney (4,140,800), 2001 estimates
CURRENCY – Australian dollar ($A) of 100 cents
NATIONAL ANTHEM – Advance Australia Fair
NATIONAL DAY – 26 January (Australia Day)
NATIONAL FLAG – The British Blue Ensign with five stars of the Southern Cross in the fly and the white Commonwealth Star of seven points beneath the Union Flag
LIFE EXPECTANCY (years) – male 76.6; female 82.0
POPULATION GROWTH RATE – 1.3 per cent (2001)
POPULATION DENSITY – 2.5 per sq. km (2001)
URBAN POPULATION – 84.7 per cent (2000 estimate)

Australia is a continent in the southern hemisphere. The highest point is Mt. Kosciusko (2,228 m) and the lowest, Lake Eyre (–15 m). Climatic conditions range from the alpine to the tropical. Two-thirds of the continent is arid or semi-arid although good rainfalls (over 800 mm annually) occur in the northern monsoonal belt and along the eastern and southern highland regions.

HISTORY AND POLITICS

Australia was discovered by Europeans in the 17th century. Its eastern coast was claimed by Capt. James Cook on behalf of Britain in 1770 and became a penal colony; Tasmania, Western Australia, South Australia, Victoria and Queensland were established as colonies between 1825 and 1859. The colonies were federated as the Commonwealth of Australia on 1 January 1901, at which time Australia gained dominion status within the British Empire. Australia became independent within the

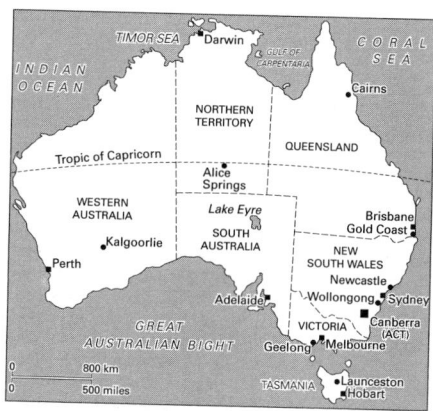

British Commonwealth by the 1931 Statute of Westminster. Following a referendum in 1967, the Aboriginal population was granted full political rights. In 1986, the Australia Act was passed, which abolished the remaining legislative, executive and judicial links to the UK, while retaining the British monarch as head of state.

On 13 February 1998, the Constitutional Convention voted by 89 votes to 52 to sever constitutional links with the United Kingdom monarchy. A national referendum was held on the issue on 6 November 1999; the proposition to make Australia a republic was defeated, with 45.3 per cent voting in favour and 54.7 per cent against.

The general election on 10 November 2001 was won by the ruling Liberal Party-National Party Coalition.

POLITICAL SYSTEM

The government is that of a federal commonwealth within the Commonwealth, the executive power being vested in the Sovereign (through the Governor-General), assisted by a federal government. Under the constitution the powers of the federal government are defined, and residuary legislative power remains with the states. The right of a state to legislate on any matter is not abrogated except in connection with matters exclusively under

STATES AND TERRITORIES

	Area (sq. km)	Resident Population 31 December 2001	Capital	Governor	Premier
Australian Capital Territory (ACT)	2,349	322,600	Canberra	—	Jon Stanhope (Lab)‡
New South Wales (NSW)	801,352	6,642,900	Sydney	HE Prof. Marie Bashir, AO	Robert Carr (Lab)
Northern Territory (NT)	1,352,212	199,900	Darwin*	John Anictomatis, OAM†	Clare Martin (Lab)‡
Queensland (Qld)	1,734,190	3,670,500	Brisbane	HE Maj.-Gen. Peter Arnison, AO	Peter Beattie (Lab)
South Australia (SA)	985,324	1,518,900	Adelaide	Marjorie Jackson-Nelson, AC, MBE	Mike Rann (Lab)
Tasmania (Tas.)	67,914	473,300	Hobart	HE Sir Guy Green, AC, KBE, CVO	Jim Bacon (Lab)
Victoria (Vic.)	227,590	4,854,100	Melbourne	HE John Landy, AC, MBE	Steve Bracks (Lab)
Western Australia (WA)	2,532,422	1,918,800	Perth	HE Lt.-Gen. John M. Sanderson, AC	Dr Geoff Gallop, MLA (Lab)

* Seat of administration
† Administrator
‡ Chief Minister

federal control, but where a state law is inconsistent with a law of the Commonwealth the latter prevails to the extent of the inconsistency.

Parliament consists of Queen Elizabeth II, the Senate and the House of Representatives. The constitution provides that the number of members of the House of Representatives shall be, as nearly as practicable, twice the number of senators. Members of the Senate are elected for six years by universal suffrage, half the members retiring every third year, except in the Australian Capital Territory and the Northern Territory, where members are elected for a three-year term. Each of the six states returns 12 senators, and the Australian Capital Territory and the Northern Territory two each. The House of Representatives, similarly elected for a maximum of three years, contains members proportionate to the population, with a minimum of five members for each state. There are now 150 members in the House of Representatives, including one member for the Northern Territory and two for the Australian Capital Territory.

The High Court exercises jurisdiction over all matters arising under the constitution, all matters arising between the states and between residents of different states, matters to which the Commonwealth of Australia is a party, matters arising under any treaty, and matters affecting foreign representatives in Australia. The High Court also hears appeals from the Federal Court and from the Supreme Courts of states and territories.

The Federal Court of Australia has jurisdiction over important industrial, trade practices, intellectual property, administrative law, admiralty law and bankruptcy matters. It also acts as a court of appeal for decisions from the Australian Capital Territory Supreme Court and certain decisions of state Supreme Courts exercising federal jurisdiction. Each state has its own judicature of supreme, superior and minor courts for criminal and civil cases.

FEDERAL STRUCTURE

In the states, executive authority is vested in a Governor (appointed by the Crown), assisted by a Council of Ministers or Executive Council. Each state has a legislature comprising a Legislative Council and a Legislative Assembly or House of Assembly which are elected for four-year terms, except Queensland, which has a Legislative Assembly only.

The Northern Territory and Australian Capital Territory have a Legislative Assembly only.

GOVERNOR-GENERAL

Governor-General, HE The Rt. Revd Dr Peter Hollingworth, AC, OBE, assumed office 29 June 2001

CABINET *as at July 2002*

Prime Minister, John Howard (LP)
Deputy Prime Minister, Transport and Regional Services, John Anderson (NP)
Agriculture, Fisheries and Forestry, Warren Truss (NP)
Attorney-General, Daryl Williams (LP)
Communications, Information Technology and the Arts, Sen. Richard Alston (LP)
Defence, Robert Hill (LP)
Education, Science and Training, Brendan Nelson (LP)
Employment, Workplace Relations and Small Business, Leader of the House, Tony Abbott (LP)
Environment and Heritage, Leader of the Government in the Senate, David Kemp (LP)
Family and Community Services, Amanda Vanstone (LP)
Finance and Administration, Nick Minchin (LP)
Foreign Affairs, Alexander Downer (LP)

Health and Aged Care, Kay Patterson (LP)
Immigration and Multicultural Affairs, Aboriginal and Torres Strait Islander Affairs, Philip Ruddock (LP)
Industry, Tourism and Resources, Ian MacFarlane (LP)
Trade, Mark Vaile (NP)
Treasurer, Peter Costello (LP)
President of the Senate, Sen. Margaret Reid (LP)
Speaker, House of Representatives, Neil Andrew (LP)

LP Liberal Party; NP National Party

AUSTRALIAN HIGH COMMISSION
Australia House, Strand, London WC2B 4LA
Tel: 020-7379 4334
High Commissioner, HE Michael L'Estrange, apptd 2000
Deputy High Commissioner, B. Twidell
Minister-Counsellor, F. Buffinton (Marketing)
Head of Defence Staff, Cdre Geoffrey Geraghty
NEW SOUTH WALES GOVERNMENT OFFICE, The Australia Centre, Strand, London WC2B 4LG.
Tel: 020-7887 5871. Director, Gary Offner
AGENT-GENERAL FOR QUEENSLAND, 392 Strand, London WC2R 0LZ. Tel: 020-7836 1333. Agent-General, John Dawson
AGENT-GENERAL FOR SOUTH AUSTRALIA, Australia Centre, Strand, London WC2B 4LG. Tel: 020-7836 3455. Agent-General, Maurice de Rohan
AGENT-GENERAL FOR VICTORIA, Victoria House, Melbourne Place, Strand, London WC2B 4LG.
Tel: 020-7836 2656. Agent-General, Peter A. Hansen
AGENT-GENERAL FOR WESTERN AUSTRALIA, Australia Centre, Strand, London WC2B 4LG.
Tel: 020-7240 2881. Agent-General, Robert Fisher

BRITISH HIGH COMMISSION
Commonwealth Avenue, Yarralumla, Canberra, ACT 2600 Tel: (00 61) (2) 6270 6666
High Commissioner, HE Sir Alistair Goodlad, KCMG, apptd 1999
Deputy High Commissioner, R. Court
Consuls-General, S. J. Hiscock (Brisbane); P. M. Innes (Melbourne); H. Dunnachie (Perth); P. Beckingham (Sydney)
Cultural Adviser and British Council Director, Simon Gammell, Suite 401, Edgecliff Centre, 203–233 New South Head Road (PO Box 88), Edgecliff, Sydney, NSW 2027; Email: enquiries@britishcouncil.org.au

DEFENCE

The Army has 71 main battle tanks, 463 armoured personnel carriers, 111 light assault vehicles, six aircraft and 123 armed helicopters. The Navy has four submarines, one destroyer, nine frigates, 15 patrol and coastal vessels and 16 armed helicopters. There are bases at Sydney, Stirling, Cairns and Darwin. The Air Force has 141 combat aircraft.

MILITARY EXPENDITURE – 1.9 per cent of GDP (2000)
MILITARY PERSONNEL – 50,700: Army 24,150, Navy 12,500, Air Force 14,050

ECONOMY

The wide range of climatic and soil conditions has resulted in a diversity of crops. Generally, cereal crops (excluding rice and sorghum) are widely grown, while other crops are confined to specific locations in a few states. However, scant or erratic rainfall, limited potential for irrigation and unsuitable soils or topography have restricted intensive agriculture.

Livestock ranching is widespread, primarily cattle and sheep; meat, meat derivatives, wool and dairy products are significant agricultural products.

Significant mineral resources include bauxite, coal, copper, crude petroleum, gems, gold, ilmenite, iron ore, lead, limestone, manganese, nickel, rutile, salt, silver, tin, tungsten, uranium, zinc and zircon. In 1999 298,464,000 tonnes of coal, 30,306,000 tonnes of crude oil, 30,352,000 cubic metres of natural gas, 162,224,000 tonnes of iron ore, 927,000 tonnes of lead, and 310,378 kilograms of gold were produced.

GNP – US$652,799 million (2001); US$20,950 per capita (1999)

GDP – US$620,963 million (1999-2000); US$21,319 per capita (1999)

ANNUAL AVERAGE GROWTH OF GDP – 4.2 per cent (2000)

INFLATION RATE – 2.9 per cent (2002)

UNEMPLOYMENT – 6.2 per cent (2002)

TRADE

In 2000–2001 the main exports were metalliferous ores and metal scrap (12.3 per cent); coal, coke and briquettes (9.1 per cent); non-ferrous metals (7.9 per cent); gold (4.3 per cent); and cereals and cereal preparations (4.5 per cent). The major imports were manufactured articles (11.9 per cent); motor vehicles and parts (12.1 per cent); computer technology (7.0 per cent); petroleum and related products (8.7 per cent); telecommunications equipment (6.7 per cent); electrical machinery (5.7 per cent); and general industrial machinery and parts (4.8 per cent).

Australia's main trading partners are Japan, the USA, New Zealand, China, Korea, Germany, Taiwan, Singapore and the UK.

In 2000 Australia had a trade deficit of US$4,712 million and a current account deficit of US$15,520 million. Imports totalled US$71,531 million and exports US$63,870 million.

Trade with UK	2000	2001
Imports from UK	£2,682,828,000	£2,321,828,000
Exports to UK	1,587,084,000	1,837,977,000

COMMUNICATIONS

There are six government-owned railway systems, operated by the State Rail Authority of NSW, VicRail, Queensland Government Railways, Western Australian Government Railways, the State Transport Authority of Southern Australia, and the National Rail Corporation (NRC). The NRC incorporates the former Commonwealth Railways system, and the Tasmanian and non-metropolitan South Australian railways (urban rail services in Southern Australia remain the responsibility of the State Transport Authority). In 1999 there was a total of 39,930 km of railway track.

The Northern Territory has three main ports: Darwin, and the private mining ports of Gove and Groote Eylandt. Most freight in the Territory is moved by road trains. These are massive trucks hauling two or three trailers, having a net capacity of about 100 tonnes and measuring up to 45 metres in length.

EDUCATION

Education is administered by the state governments and is compulsory between the ages of five or six and 15 years. It is available at government schools controlled by the state education department and at private or independent schools, some of which are denominational. Tertiary education is available through universities, and technical and further education colleges. There are 39 universities in Australia; the Australian Capital Territory

has two universities, New South Wales 11, Queensland eight, Northern Territory one, South Australia three, Tasmania two, Victoria nine and Western Australia five.

ENROLMENT (percentage of age group) – primary 100 per cent (1997); secondary 100 per cent (1997); tertiary 80 per cent (1997)

EXTERNAL TERRITORIES

ASHMORE AND CARTIER ISLANDS

Ashmore Islands (known as Middle, East and West Islands) and Cartier Island are situated in the Indian Ocean 850 km and 790 km west of Darwin respectively. The islands are uninhabited. The territory has been administered by the Australian Government since 1933.

THE AUSTRALIAN ANTARCTIC TERRITORY

The Australian Antarctic Territory was established in 1933 and comprises all the islands and territories, other than Adélie Land, which are situated south of the latitude 60° S. and lying between 160° E. longitude and 45° E. longitude. The territory is administered by the Antarctic Division of the Department of the Environment and Heritage.

CHRISTMAS ISLAND

AREA – 52 sq. miles (135 sq. km)

POPULATION – 1,928 (2001)

Christmas Island is situated in the Indian Ocean about 1,408 km NW of North West Cape in Western Australia. The island became an Australian territory in 1958 and is managed by the Department of Transport and Regional Services. The Shire of Christmas Island (SOCI) has nine elected members. SOCI is responsible for municipal functions and services on the island.

Administrator, W. Taylor

COCOS (KEELING) ISLANDS

AREA – 5.4 sq. miles (14 sq. km)

POPULATION – 600 (2001)

The Cocos (Keeling) Islands are two separate atolls (North Keeling Island and, 24 km to the south, the main atoll) comprising some 27 small coral islands, situated in the Indian Ocean. The main islands of the southern atoll are West Island (about 9 km in length); Home Island, where the Cocos Malay community lives; Direction Island, Horsburgh and South Island.

The islands were declared a British possession in 1857. All land in the islands was granted to George Clunies-Ross and his heirs by Queen Victoria in 1886. In 1978 the Australian Government purchased all Clunies-Ross land and property interests except for the family home and grounds; the last of the remaining grounds were purchased in 1993. Between 1979 and 1984 most of the land was transferred to trusts with the Cocos (Keeling) Islands Council as trustee, the local government body established in 1979 which was replaced by the Shire of the Cocos (Keeling) Islands in July 1992.

On 6 April 1984 the Cocos community, in a UN-supervised Act of Self-Determination, chose to integrate with Australia. The islands are managed by the Australian Government through the Department of Transport and Regional Services.

Administrator, W. Taylor

CORAL SEA ISLANDS TERRITORY

The Coral Sea Islands Territory lies east of Queensland between the Great Barrier Reef and longitude 156° 06'E.,

and between latitudes 12° and 24° S. It comprises scattered islands, spread over a sea area of 780,000 sq. km. The islands are formed mainly of coral and sand, and most are extremely small. There is a manned meteorological station in the Willis Group but the remaining islands are uninhabited.

The territory is managed by the Department of Transport and Regional Services.

HEARD ISLAND AND McDONALD ISLANDS

The Territory of the Heard and McDonald Islands, about 4,100 km south-west of Perth, comprises all the islands and rocks lying between 52° 30'; and 53° 30'; S. latitude and 72° and 74° 30'; E. longitude. The islands are administered by the Antarctic Division of the Department of the Environment and Heritage.

NORFOLK ISLAND

AREA – 13.3 sq. miles (34.5 sq. km)
POPULATION – 2,037 (2001)
SEAT OF GOVERNMENT – Kingston

Norfolk Island is situated in the South Pacific Ocean. It is about 8 km long by 5 km wide. The climate is mild and subtropical.

The island, discovered by Captain Cook in 1774, served as a penal colony from 1788 to 1814 and 1825 to 1855. In 1856, 194 descendants of the Bounty mutineers accepted an invitation to leave Pitcairn and settle on Norfolk Island. Norfolk Island is an Australian external territory.

In 1979 Norfolk Island gained a substantial degree of self-government. Wide powers are exercised by a nine-member Legislative Assembly. The Administrator is responsible to the Australian Minister for Regional Services, Territories and Local Government.

Administrator, A. J. Messner

AUSTRIA
Republik österreich - Republic of Austria

AREA – 32,378 sq. miles (83,859 sq. km). Neighbours: the Czech Republic and Slovakia (north), Italy and Slovenia (south), Hungary (east), Germany (north-west), Switzerland and Liechtenstein (west)
POPULATION – 8,110,244 (2000 census). The language is German, but the rights of the Slovene, Croat, Hungarian, Czech, Slovak, Roma and Sinti minorities are protected. The predominant religion is Roman Catholicism
CAPITAL – Vienna, on the Danube (population, 1,608,656, 2000 census)
MAJOR CITIES – Graz (240,967); Innsbruck (111,752); Klagenfurt (91,149); Linz (188,022); Salzburg (144,247)
CURRENCY – Euro (€) of 100 cents
NATIONAL ANTHEM – Land Der Berge, Land Am Strome (Land Of Mountains, Land On The River)
NATIONAL DAY – 26 October
NATIONAL FLAG – Three equal horizontal stripes of red, white, red
LIFE EXPECTANCY (years) – male 75.4; female 81.5
POPULATION GROWTH RATE – 0.4 per cent (1999)
POPULATION DENSITY – 98 per sq. km (1999)

HISTORY AND POLITICS
The Austrian state dates back to the eighth century AD when Emperor Charlemagne conquered the territory and founded the *Ostmark*, the eastern march of the Holy Roman Empire, which had been settled from the sixth century AD onwards by Bavarian Germans. The Habsburg dynasty established an empire which included much of central Europe, including present-day Austria and Hungary. The Republic of Austria was established in 1918 on the break-up of the Austro-Hungarian Empire. In March 1938 Austria was incorporated into Nazi Germany under the name *Ostmark*. After the liberation of Vienna in 1945, the Republic of Austria was reconstituted within the 1937 frontiers and a freely-elected government took office in December 1945. The country was divided into four zones occupied respectively by the UK, USA, USSR and France, while Vienna was jointly occupied by the four Powers. In 1955 the Austrian State Treaty was signed by the foreign ministers of the four Powers and of Austria. This treaty recognised the re-establishment of Austria as a sovereign, independent and democratic state, having the same frontiers as on 1 January 1938. Austria acceded to the European Union on 1 January 1995.

After the general election of 17 December 1995 the Social Democrats and the People's Party formed a coalition government. In the general election of 3 October 1999, the Social Democrats won 65 seats and the People's Party and the Freedom Party won 52 seats each. Attempts to form a coalition between the Social Democrats and the People's Party were unsuccessful. A coalition government between the People's Party and the Freedom Party, which had stood on an anti-immigration platform and whose leader, Jörg Haider, had expressed support for some aspects of the wartime Nazi regime, was sworn in on 5 February 2000 after the signing by both parties of a document expressing the commitment of the new government to the European Union and condemning discrimination and intolerance. International opposition to the inclusion of the Freedom Party in the government resulted in the suspension of bilateral relations between the governments of the other EU members and Austria. On 1 May, Jörg Haider resigned as leader of the Freedom Party in an attempt to calm the situation. The suspension of relations between the EU members and Austria was lifted in September 2000 following an investigation into the Austrian government which cleared it of any wrongdoing.

POLITICAL SYSTEM

There is a bicameral national assembly; the lower house (*Nationalrat*) has 183 members and the upper house (*Bundesrat*) has 64 members. There is a 4 per cent qualification for parliamentary representation.

FEDERAL STRUCTURE

There are nine provinces:

Provinces	Area (sq. km)	Population	Capital
Burgenland	3,965	277,962	Eisenstadt
Carinthia	9,533	563,207	Klagenfurt
Lower Austria	19,174	1,542,393	St Pölten
Salzburg	7,154	517,096	Salzburg
Styria	16,388	1,202,275	Graz
Tirol	12,648	669,710	Innsbruck
Upper Austria	11,980	1,379,524	Linz
Vienna	415	1,608,656	Vienna
Vorarlberg	2,601	349,421	Bregenz

HEAD OF STATE

President of the Republic of Austria, Thomas Klestil, *took office* 8 July 1992, *re-elected* 19 April 1998

CABINET *as at July 2002*

Chancellor, Wolfgang Schüssel (ÖVP)
Vice-Chancellor, Public Services and Sports, Susanne Riess-Passer (FPÖ)
Agriculture and Forestry; Environment and Water Management, Wilhelm Molterer (ÖVP)
Economic Affairs and Labour, Martin Bartenstein (ÖVP)
Education, Science and Cultural Affairs, Elisabeth Gehrer (ÖVP)
Finance, Karl-Heinz Grasser (FPÖ)
Foreign Affairs, Benita Ferrero-Waldner (ÖVP)
Interior, Ernst Strasser (ÖVP)
Justice, Dieter Böhmdorfer (Ind.)
National Defence, Herbert Scheibner (FPÖ)
Social Security and Generations, Herbert Haupt (FPÖ)
Transport, Innovation and Technology, Matthias Reichhold (FPÖ)
ÖVP People's Party; FPÖ Freedom Party; Ind Independent

AUSTRIAN EMBASSY
18 Belgrave Mews West, London SW1X 8HU
Tel: 020-7235 3731
Ambassador Extraordinary and Plenipotentiary, HE Alexander Christiani, apptd 2000
Minister, I. Rauscher
Defence Attaché, Brig.-Gen. W. Plasche
Consul-General, S. Bagyura
Commercial Counsellor and Trade Commissioner, G. Müller

BRITISH EMBASSY
Jaurésgasse 12, 1030 Vienna
Tel: (00 43) (1) 716130
Ambassador Extraordinary and Plenipotentiary, HE Anthony Ford, CMG, apptd 2000
Deputy Head of Mission, Counsellor and Consul-General, P. Baker
Defence Attaché, Lt.-Col. J. A. Bourne
First Secretaries, H. D. Marcelin; J. Hall

BRITISH CONSULAR OFFICES – There is a consular office at Vienna, and Honorary Consulates at Bregenz, Graz, Innsbruck and Salzburg.

BRITISH COUNCIL DIRECTOR, Dr Simon Cole, Schenkenstrasse 4, A–1010 Vienna; Email: bc.vienna@britishcouncil.at

DEFENCE

The Army has 277 main battle tanks and 488 armoured personnel carriers. The Air Force has 52 combat aircraft and 11 armed helicopters.

Women were permitted to join the army for the first time in February 1998.

MILITARY EXPENDITURE – 0.8 per cent of GDP (2000)
MILITARY PERSONNEL – Army 34,600, of which Air Force 6,500
CONSCRIPTION DURATION – Eight months, or seven months plus refresher training

ECONOMY

Major industries include iron and steel production, chemicals, electrical goods, mechanical engineering, textiles and paper production. Agricultural products include wheat, rye, barley, oats, maize, potatoes, sugar beet and turnips. Timber forms a valuable source of Austria's indigenous wealth, about 47 per cent of the total land area consisting of forest areas. Strict regulations have preserved Austria's environment. Foreign exchange receipts from tourism are a major contribution to the balance of payments.

GNP – US$204,250 million (2000); US$25,430 per capita (1999)
GDP – US$210,913 million (1998); US$25,748 per capita (1999)
ANNUAL AVERAGE GROWTH OF GDP – 3.3 per cent (2000)
INFLATION RATE – 2.4 per cent (2000)
UNEMPLOYMENT – 3.8 per cent (1999)

TRADE

Main exports are processed goods (iron and steel, other metal goods, textiles, paper and cardboard products), machinery and transport equipment, other finished goods (including clothing), raw materials, chemical products and foodstuffs. Main imports are machinery and transport equipment, processed goods, chemical products, foodstuffs, fuel and energy. Austria's main trading partners are Germany, Italy, France and Switzerland.

In 2000, Austria had a trade deficit of US$2,732 million and a current account deficit of US$5,205 million. Imports totalled US$68,972 million and exports US$64,155 million.

Trade with UK	2000	2001
Imports from UK	£1,081,500,000	£1,158,500,000
Exports to UK	1,341,200,000	1,767,000,000

COMMUNICATIONS

There is a network of 1,567 km of *Autobahn* between major cities which also links up with the German and Italian networks. The railways are state-owned. Of the 425 km of waterways, 350 km are navigable and there is considerable trade through the Danube ports by both local and foreign shipping. There are six commercial airports.

CULTURE AND EDUCATION

In the late 18th and 19th centuries, Vienna became the centre of classical music and the city attracted composers from many countries. Austrian composers include Joseph Haydn, Wolfgang Amadeus Mozart, Franz Peter Schubert, Johann Strauss II, Gustav Mahler and Arnold Schönberg. Important artists include Gustav Klimt, Egon Schiele and Oskar Kokoschka. Austrian literary figures include the novelists Arthur Schnitzler, Stefan Zweig and Franz Kafka, the poet and novelist Rainer Maria Rilke, and the dramatists Franz Grillparzer and Johann Nestroy.

Education is free and compulsory between the ages of six and 15 and there are good facilities for secondary, technical and professional education. There are 19 university-level institutions and six colleges of art.

ENROLMENT (percentage of age group) – primary 100 per cent (1997); secondary 100 per cent (1997); tertiary 48 per cent (1997)

AZERBAIJAN
Azərbaycan Respublıkası - Azerbaijani Republic

AREA – 33,436 sq. miles (86,600 sq. km). Neighbours: Iran (south), Armenia (west), Georgia and Russia (north)
POPULATION – 8,100,000 (2002 estimate): 83 per cent Azeri, 6 per cent Russian and 6 per cent Armenian. There are also Kurds, Jews, Georgians and Turks. There are more Azeris in Iran than in Azerbaijan. The population is predominantly Shia Muslim although it was heavily secularised during the Soviet era. The language is Azeri
CAPITAL – Ψ Baki (Baku) (population, 1,149,000)
MAJOR CITIES – Gäncä (293,300); Sumqayit (274,200), 1997 estimates
CURRENCY – Manat of 100 gopik
NATIONAL ANTHEM – Azerbaijan! Azerbaijan!
NATIONAL DAY – 28 May (Independence Day)
NATIONAL FLAG – Three horizontal stripes of blue, red and green with a white crescent and eight-pointed star in the centre
LIFE EXPECTANCY (years) – male 68.7; female 75.5
POPULATION GROWTH RATE – 1.0 per cent (1999)
POPULATION DENSITY – 92 per sq. km (1999)
URBAN POPULATION – 53.0 per cent (1995)
ILLITERACY RATE – 0.4 per cent

Azerbaijan occupies the eastern part of the Caucasus region of the former Soviet Union, on the shore of the Caspian Sea. The north-eastern part of the republic is taken up by the south-eastern end of the main Caucasus ridge, its south-western part by the smaller Caucasus hills, and its south-eastern corner by the spurs of the Talysh Ridge. Its central part is a depression irrigated by the River Kura and the lower reaches of its tributary the Araks. Azerbaijan has a continental climate.

Azerbaijan has 64 administrative districts and also includes the Nakhchevan Autonomous Republic, which is geographically separated from the rest of Azerbaijan by Armenia and borders on Iran and Turkey, and the Nagorno-Karabakh Autonomous Province.

HISTORY AND POLITICS

The Turkic Azeri people formed an independent state in the first century BC. Invading Arabs introduced Islam in the seventh century. In the 16th century Azerbaijan was again invaded by Persia and became a Persian province. The country was divided during the Russo-Persian wars of the early 19th century, the northern portion (the present-day Azerbaijan) becoming part of the Russian Empire and the southern portion remaining Persian and subsequently Iranian.

In 1918 the Azerbaijan Democratic Republic was established. It was overthrown by Communists in 1918 and Azerbaijan acceded to the USSR in 1922.

In January 1990, the Azeri Popular Front took power from the local Communist Party and declared independence from the Soviet Union. Soviet troops overthrew the Popular Front and restored the Communist regime, which declared Azerbaijan's independence in August 1991. At the presidential election in June 1992 the Popular Front leader Abulfaz Elchibey was elected.

Popular discontent at military defeats caused Elchibey to flee Baku in June 1993 and the former Azeri Communist Party First Secretary Heydar Aliyev took over the presidency. The new regime was confirmed in office in a referendum in August and Aliyev won the presidential election in October 1993.

The Milli Majlis (parliament) has 125 seats, of which 100 are directly elected and 25 are allocated by proportional representation.

Presidential elections were held on 11 October 1998. The incumbent President Aliyev won 76.1 per cent of the vote, but the elections were criticised by the OSCE and other international monitoring groups. A general election was held on 5 November 2000. The New Azerbaijan party, founded by Aliyev, won 62.5 per cent of the vote and 78 seats. The election was boycotted by several parties, who alleged that electoral fraud had been committed; their claims were supported by OSCE observers. Repeat elections were held on 7 January 2001 in 11 districts.

SECESSION

In 1988 fighting broke out in the predominantly Armenian-populated region of Nagorny-Karabakh between Soviet Azeri forces and ethnic Armenians demanding unification with Armenia. In late 1993 Nagorno-Karabakh forces captured all of the region, together with all Azeri territory separating the region from Armenia (20 per cent of Azeri territory). Azeri forces pushed back the Nagorno-Karabakh forces in early 1994 before a cease-fire agreement was signed in May 1994. Between 500,000 and one million Azeris have been displaced by the fighting, which briefly flared up again along the Azeri-Armenian border in April and May 1997. Peace talks, held under the auspices of the OSCE, have yet to yield any significant results, although both sides reaffirmed their commitment to finding a peaceful solution at a meeting in October 1997, in which both sides rejected the idea of full independence for Nagorny-Karabakh as 'unrealistic'. President Aliyev held talks with President Kocharian of Armenia in March and April 2001, but the leaders failed to reach an agreement on the future of Nagorny-Karabakh.

POLITICAL SYSTEM

A new constitution was approved by a referendum in November 1995, which created a presidential republic with executive power to be exercised by the president and with legislative power vested in the unicameral Milli Majlis (National Assembly). The president appoints the prime minister and the Cabinet. Both the president and the National Assembly are directly elected for five-year terms.

HEAD OF STATE

President, Heydar Alirza oglu Aliyev, assumed office 18 June 1993, elected 3 October 1993, re-elected 11 October 1998

GOVERNMENT *as at July 2002*
Prime Minister, Artur Rasi-Zade
First Deputy PM, Abbas Abbasov
Deputy Prime Ministers, Abid Shazifov; Ali Gasanov (*Chair of State Refugee Committee*); Yagub Abdulla Eyyubov; Elehin Efendiyev
Agriculture, Irshad Aliyev
Communications, Nadir Akhmedov
Culture, Polad Bulbuloglu
Defence, Lt.-Gen. Safar Abiyev
Ecology and Natural Resources, Huseyn Bagirov
Economic Development, Farhad Aliyev
Education, Misir Mardanov
Finance, Avaz Alekperov
Foreign Affairs, Vilayat Mukhtar oglu Guliyev

Fuel and Energy, Mejid Kerimov
Health, Ali Insanov
Interior, Lt.-Gen. Ramil Usubov
Justice, Fikrat Farrukh Mammadov
Labour and Social Security, Ali Nagiyev
National Security, Namiq Abbasov
Taxation, Fazil Mamedov
Youth and Sports, Abdulfaz Karayev

EMBASSY OF THE AZERBAIJAN REPUBLIC
4 Kensington Court, London W8 5DL
Tel: 020-7938 5482/3412
Ambassador Extraordinary and Plenipotentiary,
HE Rafael Ibrahimov, apptd 2001

BRITISH EMBASSY
2 Izmir Street, Baku 370065
Tel: (00 994) (12) 975188
Email: office@britemb.baku.az
Ambassador Extraordinary and Plenipotentiary, HE
Andrew Tucker, apptd 2000

BRITISH COUNCIL DIRECTOR, Margaret Jack, 1 Vali
Mammadov Street, AZ-370004 Baku;
Email: enquiries@britishcouncil.az

DEFENCE

The Army has 262 main battle tanks, 253 armoured
infantry fighting vehicles and 381 armoured personnel
carriers. The Navy is based at Baku, with a share of the
former Soviet Caspian Fleet Flotilla, comprising six patrol
and coastal vessels. The Air Force has 35 combat aircraft
and 36 attack helicopters.
MILITARY EXPENDITURE – 4.5 per cent of GDP (2000)
MILITARY PERSONNEL – 72,100: Army 62,000, Navy
2,200, Air Force 7,900; Paramilitaries 15,000
CONSCRIPTON DURATION – 17 months

ECONOMY

Azerbaijan was heavily industrialised as part of the
Russian Empire. Industry is dominated by oil and natural
gas extraction and related industries centred on Baku and
Sumgait and the large oil deposits in the Caspian Sea,
estimated at more than 6,000 million barrels. Natural gas
reserves are estimated to be more than 1,200,000 million
cubic metres. Five contracts to explore and exploit
oilfields in the Caspian Sea have been signed since 1994.
  The republic is also rich in mineral resources, with
iron, copper, aluminium, lead and zinc, and is important
as a cotton-growing area and a silkworm-breeding area.
  Around 90 per cent of agricultural land has been
privatised. Grapes, cereals (primarily wheat, barley, maize
and rice), cotton, vegetables and fruit are the major
agricultural products.
  The Azeri economy was devastated by the war although
it is now showing signs of recovery.
  In 2000 Azerbaijan had a trade surplus of US$319
million and a current account deficit of US$168 million.
In 1999 imports totalled US$1,036 million and exports
US$929 million.
GNP – US$4,881 million (2000); US$460 per capita
(1999)
GDP – US$4,117 million (1998); US$513 per capita
(1999)
ANNUAL AVERAGE GROWTH GDP – 11.0 per cent
(1998)
INFLATION RATE – 1.8 per cent (2000)
UNEMPLOYMENT– 1.2 per cent (1999)
TOTAL EXTERNAL DEBT – US$1.036 million (1999)

Trade with UK	2000	2001
Imports from UK	£35,544,000	£36,856,000
Exports to UK	9,908,000	9,806,000

COMMUNICATIONS

There are 2,200 km of railway track, much of it
electrified, and over 25,000 km of roads. There are ferry
links to Turkmenistan. Oil pipelines link the Azeri
oilfields to the Russian Black Sea port of Novorossiysk
and the Georgian port of Supsa. Moscow has agreed to
grant $300 million for the construction of the Azeri part
of the north-south transport highway linking northern
and central Europe with the Gulf countries across
Azerbaijan.

CULTURE AND EDUCATION

Azerbaijan was the birthplace of the prophet Zoroaster,
who founded one of the first monotheistic religions in
the world. The country has witnessed a succession of
three religions: Zoroastrianism, Christianity and Islam.
  Azeri is one of the Turkic languages. Previously written
in the Russian script, Azeri in the Latin script was adopted
as the official language in December 1992. In the 18th and
19th centuries Azerbaijani literature produced the poets
and dramatists Vagif, Vazekhi, Zakir, Akhundov and
Vezirov.
  Education up to university level is free. There are
several universities and colleges of higher education.

THE BAHAMAS
The Commonwealth of The Bahamas

AREA – 5,358 sq. miles (13,878 sq. km)
POPULATION – 289,000 (2001 estimate). The language
is English
CAPITAL – Ψ Nassau (population, 172,196, 1996
estimate)
CURRENCY – Bahamian dollar (B$) of 100 cents
NATIONAL ANTHEM – March On, Bahamaland
NATIONAL DAY – 10 July (Independence Day)
NATIONAL FLAG – Horizontal stripes of aquamarine,
gold and aquamarine, with a black equilateral
triangle on the hoist
LIFE EXPECTANCY (years) – male 65.2; female 73.9
POPULATION GROWTH RATE – 1.9 per cent (1999)
POPULATION DENSITY – 22 per sq. km (1999)

The Bahamas extend from the coast of Florida on the
north-west almost to Hispaniola on the south-east. The
group consists of more than 4,000 islands, islets and cays.
The 14 major islands are inhabited, as are a few of the
smaller islands. The principal islands include: Abaco,
Acklins, Andros, Berry Islands, Bimini, Cat Island,
Crooked Island, Eleuthera, Exuma, Grand Bahama,
Harbour Island, Inagua, Long Island, Mayaguana, New
Providence (on which is located the capital, Nassau),
Ragged Island, Rum Cay, San Salvador and Spanish Wells.
San Salvador was the first landfall in the New World of
Christopher Columbus on 12 October 1492.

HISTORY AND POLITICS

The Bahamas were settled by the British and became a
Crown colony in 1717. Taken over in 1782 by the Spanish,
the Treaty of Versailles in 1783 restored them to the British.
The Bahamas gained independence on 10 July 1973.
  A general election held in May 2002 was won by the
Progressive Liberal Party which defeated the Free National
Movement Party. The Progressive Liberal Party holds 29

seats in the House of Assembly, the Free National Movement seven seats and Independents four seats.

POLITICAL SYSTEM

The head of state is Queen Elizabeth II who is represented in the islands by a Governor-General. There is an appointed Senate of 16 members and an elected House of Assembly of 40 members.

Governor-General, Dame Ivy Dumont

CABINET *as at July 2002*

Prime Minister, Finance, Perry Christie
Deputy Prime Minister, National Security, Cynthia Pratt
Agriculture, Fisheries and Local Government, V. Alfred Grey
Attorney-General, Education, Alfred Sears
Economic Development, Zhivargo Laing
Financial Services and Investments, Allyson Maynard-Gibson
Foreign Affairs, Public Service, Fred Mitchell
Health and Environment, Marcus Bethel
Housing and National Insurance, Shane Gibson
Labour and Immigration, Vincent Peet
Minister of State for Finance, James Smith
Social Services and Community Development, Melanie Griffin
Tourism, Obie Wilchcombe
Trade and Industry, Leslie Miller
Transport and Aviation, Glenys Hanna-Martin
Works and Utilities, Bradley Roberts
Youth, Sports and Culture, Neville Wisdom

BAHAMAS HIGH COMMISSION
Bahamas House, 10 Chesterfield Street, London W1J 5JL
Tel: 020-7408 4488
High Commissioner, HE Basil O'Brien, CMG, apptd 1999

BRITISH HIGH COMMISSION
Ansbacher House (3rd Floor), East Street
PO Box N-7516, Nassau
Tel: (00 1 242) 325 7471
High Commissioner, HE P. Heigl, apptd 2000

DEFENCE
The Navy has seven patrol and coastal vessels, four harbour patrol units and four light aircraft.
MILITARY EXPENDITURE – 0.6 per cent of GDP (2000)
MILITARY PERSONNEL – Navy 860

ECONOMY
Tourism employs about 40 per cent of the labour force and provides about half of the country's GDP. International banking and finance are also important, accounting for about 15 per cent of GDP. The absence of direct taxation coupled with internal stability have enabled the country to become one of the world's leading offshore financial centres. A securities exchange was opened in May 2000.

Manufacturing and agriculture account for less than 10 per cent of GDP. Agricultural production is mainly of fresh vegetables, fruit, meat and eggs. Crawfish, other seafood, vegetables, fruit and salt are exported. Reserves of aragonite and limestone are being commercially exploited. Freeport is the country's leading industrial centre, with a pharmaceutical and chemicals plant, an oil trans-shipment and storage terminal, and port and bunkering facilities. There are also a brewery and a rum distillery on New Providence.
GNP – US$4,533 million (2000); US$11,940 per capita (1995)
GDP – US$3,374 million (1998); US$13,302 per capita (1999)

ANNUAL AVERAGE GROWTH OF GDP – 2.2 per cent (1998)
INFLATION RATE – 1.6 per cent (2000)
UNEMPLOYMENT – 7.7 per cent (1998)

TRADE
The imports are chiefly vehicles, manufactured articles, chemicals and petroleum. The chief exports are machinery and transport equipment, foodstuffs and livestock, raw materials, chemicals, manufactured goods, and beverages and tobacco.

In 2000 the Bahamas had a trade deficit of US$1,355 million and a current account deficit of US$438 million. Imports totalled US$1,421 million and exports US$400 million.

Trade with UK	2000	2001
Imports from UK	£25,264,000	£15,166,000
Exports to UK	45,983,000	7,108,000

COMMUNICATIONS
The main ports are Nassau (New Providence), Freeport (Grand Bahama) and Matthew Town (Inagua). International air services are operated from Abaco, Bimini, Eleuthera, Exuma, Grand Bahama and New Providence. More than 60 smaller airports and landing strips facilitate services between the islands, the services being mainly provided by Bahamasair, the national carrier. In 1997 there were 2,693 km of roads. There are no railways.

EDUCATION
Education is compulsory between the ages of five and 16. More than 66,000 students are enrolled in Ministry of Education and independent schools in New Providence and the Family Islands.
ILLITERACY RATE – 4.5 per cent (2002)
ENROLMENT (percentage of age group) – primary 98 per cent (1993); secondary 86 per cent (1993); tertiary 17.7 per cent (1985)

BAHRAIN
Dawlat al-Bahrayn - The Kingdom of Bahrain

AREA – 268 sq. miles (694 sq. km)
POPULATION – 620,000 (1997 UN estimate); about 70 per cent are Bahraini; about 40 per cent of the Bahrainis are Sunni Muslims, the remaining 60 per cent being Shias; the ruling family and many of the most prominent merchants are Sunnis. The official language is Arabic; English is often used for business, and Farsi, Hindi and Urdu are also spoken
CAPITAL – Ψ Manama (Al-Manámah) (population, 140,401, 1991 census)
CURRENCY – Bahraini dinar (BD) of 1,000 fils
NATIONAL ANTHEM - Bahrayn Ona, Baladolaman (Our Bahrain, Secure)
NATIONAL DAY – 16 December
NATIONAL FLAG – Red, with vertical serrated white bar next to staff
LIFE EXPECTANCY (years) – male 72.1; female 76.3
POPULATION GROWTH RATE – 3.6 per cent (1999)
POPULATION DENSITY – 960 per sq. km (1999)
ILLITERACY RATE – 11.5 per cent (2002)
ENROLMENT (percentage of age group) – primary 98 per cent (1996); secondary 83 per cent (1996); tertiary 20.2 per cent (1993)

Bahrain consists of a group of low-lying islands situated about half-way down the Gulf, some 20 miles off the east coast of Saudi Arabia. The largest of these, Bahrain Island, is about 30 miles long and 10 miles wide at its broadest, with the capital, Manama, situated on the north shore. The second largest, Al-Muharraq, with the town and Bahrain International Airport, is connected to Manama by a causeway 1.5 miles long.

INSURGENCIES

Since 1994 Shi'ite protestors demanding the re-establishment of the National Assembly have regularly clashed with security forces and Shi'ite leaders have been detained. Opponents of the government have engaged in a sustained bombing campaign.

POLITICAL SYSTEM

Bahrain is a constitutional monarchy and has been fully independent since 1971, when British protectorate status was ended. The 1973 constitution provides for a National Assembly but this was dissolved in 1975. A 40-member Consultative Council, the Majlis al-Shura, was appointed in September 1996; it is an advisory body with no legislative powers.

In February 2001, a referendum on constitutional change was held, in which over 98 per cent of the electorate approved plans for the introduction of elections for some of the members of the Consultative Council, the establishment of an independent judiciary and a constitutional monarchy. Women were able to vote for the first time in the referendum. The new constitution was given the royal assent on 14 February 2002.

HEAD OF STATE

HH The Amir of Bahrain, C.–in–C., Bahrain Defence Force, Shaikh Hamad bin Isa al-Khalifa, KCMG *succeeded* 6 March 1999, *proclaimed king* 14 Feburary 2002

CABINET *as at July 2002*

Prime Minister, HH Shaikh Khalifa bin Sulmin al-Khalifa
Commerce and Industry, Ali Saleh Abdullah al-Saleh
Communications, Shaikh Ali bin Khalifa bin Sulman al-Khalifa
Defence, Maj.-Gen. Shaikh Khalifa bin Ahmed al-Khalifa
Education, Mohammad Jassem al-Ghatam
Electricity and Water, Shaikh Abdullah bin Sulman al-Khalifa
Finance and National Economy, Abdullah Hassan Seif
Foreign Affairs, Shaikh Mohammed bin Mubarak al-Khalifa
Health, Faisal Radhi al-Mousawi
Housing and Agriculture, Shaikh Khalid bin Abdullah al-Khalifa
Information, Nabil Yacub al-Hamar
Interior, Shaikh Mohammed bin Khalifa al-Khalifa
Justice and Islamic Affairs, Shaikh Abdullah bin Khalid al-Khalifa
Labour and Social Affairs, Abdul-Nabi Abdullah al-Shula
Ministers of State, Mohammed Ibrahim al-Mutawa
(*Cabinet Affairs*); Brig.-Gen. Abdul-Aziz Mohammed al-Fadhil (*Consultative Council Affairs*); Mohammad Abdul Ghaffar Abdullah (*Foreign Affairs*); Jawad Salim al-Arrayed (*Municipal and Environmental Affairs*); Majed Jawad al-Jeshi (*PM's Office*); Mohammad Hassan Kamaledin (*Without Portfolio*)
Oil, Shaikh Isa bin Ali bin Hamad al-Khalifa
Public Works, Fahmi Ali al-Jouder

EMBASSY OF THE KINGDOM OF BAHRAIN
98 Gloucester Road, London SW7 4AU
Tel: 020-7370 5132/3
Ambassador Extraordinary and Plenipotentiary, HE Shaikh Khalid bin Ahmed al Khalifa, apptd 2001

BRITISH EMBASSY
21 Government Avenue, Manama 306, PO Box 114
Tel: (00 973) 534404
Email: britemb@batelco.com.bh
Ambassador Extraordinary and Plenipotentiary, HE Peter Ford, apptd 1999

BRITISH COUNCIL DIRECTOR, Amanda Burrell, AMA Centre, 146 Shaikh Salman Highway, PO Box 452, Manama 356; Email: bc.enquiries@britishcouncil.org.bh

DEFENCE

The Army has 106 main battle tanks and 235 armoured personnel carriers. The Navy, based at Mina Sulman, has one frigate and 10 patrol and coastal vessels. The Air Force has 34 combat aircraft and 40 armed helicopters.
MILITARY EXPENDITURE – 6.4 per cent of GDP (2000)
MILITARY PERSONNEL – 11,000: Army 8,500, Navy 1,000, Air Force 1,500; Paramilitaries 10,160

ECONOMY

The largest sources of revenue are oil production and refining. The Bahrain field, discovered in 1932, is wholly owned by the Bahrain National Oil Co. The Sitra refinery derives about 70 per cent of its crude oil by submarine pipeline from Saudi Arabia. Bahrain also has a half share with Saudi Arabia in the profits of the offshore Abu Sa'afa field. A reservoir of unassociated gas has recently been developed on Bahrain Island.

There is some heavy industry on the islands and a number of small to medium-sized industrial units.

The state has developed as a financial centre. Apart from several commercial banks, many international banks have been licensed as offshore banking units; there are also money brokers and merchant banks.
GNP – US$4,909 million (1998); US$7,640 per capita (1998)
GDP – US$5,757 million (1998); US$9,369 per capita (1999)
ANNUAL AVERAGE GROWTH OF GDP – 4.0 per cent (1999)
INFLATION RATE – 0.4 per cent (1998)

TRADE

In 2000 the government had a trade surplus of US$1,327 million and a current account surplus of US$113 million. Imports totalled US$4,612 million and exports US$5,701 million.

Trade with UK	2000	2001
Imports from UK	£124,882,000	£155,920,000
Exports to UK	83,401,000	101,653,000

COMMUNICATIONS

Bahrain International airport is one of the main air traffic centres of the Gulf; it is the headquarters of Gulf Air, and a stopping point on routes between Europe and Australia and the Far East for other airlines. A causeway links Bahrain to Saudi Arabia.

BANGLADESH
Gan Prajātantri Bamlādeś – People's Republic of Bangladesh

AREA – 56,977 sq. miles (147,570 sq.km). Neighbours: India (west, north and east), Myanmar (east)
POPULATION – 123,100,000 (2001 census). The state language is Bengali. Use of Bengali is compulsory in all government departments. English is understood and is used widely as an unofficial second language. The faith of 88 per cent of the population is Islam and 10.5 per cent Hinduism. Islam has been declared the state religion
CAPITAL – Dhaka (population, 9,912,908, 2001 census)
CURRENCY – Taka (Tk) of 100 paisa
NATIONAL ANTHEM – Amar Sonar Bangla (My Golden Bengal)
NATIONAL DAY – 26 March (Independence Day)
NATIONAL FLAG – Red circle on a bottle-green ground
LIFE EXPECTANCY (years) – male 60.6; female 60.8
POPULATION GROWTH RATE – 1.5 per cent (2001)
POPULATION DENSITY – 834 per sq. km (2001)
URBAN POPULATION – 23.4 per cent (2001)

The country is crossed by a network of rivers, including the eastern arms of the Ganges (Padma), the Jamuna (Brahmaputra) and the Meghna, flowing into the Bay of Bengal. The climate is tropical and monsoon; hot and extremely humid during the summer, and mild and dry during the short winter.

HISTORY AND POLITICS

Prior to becoming the eastern province of Pakistan, Bangladesh had been the region of East Bengal and the Sylhet district of Assam of British India. The territory acceded to Pakistan in August 1947, which became a republic on 23 March 1956. Bangladesh achieved its independence from Pakistan on 16 December 1971, following a civil war. Pakistan and Bangladesh accorded one another mutual recognition in 1974.

In 1975 a one-party presidential system was introduced by the ruling Awami League, but this was replaced by a multiparty presidential system of government in 1978 by President Zia Rahman. After President Zia's assassination in 1981, Justice Abdus Sattar became president and was overthrown in a coup led by Army Chief Gen. Ershad in 1982. Following parliamentary elections in 1986, Gen. Ershad was elected president. Popular unrest forced his resignation in December 1990; the Bangladesh Nationalist Party (BNP) won the subsequent parliamentary elections. In August 1991 a constitutional amendment returned Bangladesh to parliamentary rule.

In December 1994, the opposition parties resigned from parliament, demanding fresh elections. Public disorder persisted despite a general election in February 1996 which was won by the BNP, although turnout was a mere five per cent. In March 1996, Prime Minister Zia agreed to new elections; these elections in June 1996 produced a majority for the Awami League under Prime Minister Sheikh Hasina Wajed. In November 1997, the BNP walked out of parliament, accusing the government of repression. They returned in March 1998 after signing a memorandum of understanding with the government.

Border clashes occurred between Bangladeshi and Indian troops on the northern border in April 2001.

In the elections held under a caretaker government on 1 October 2001, the BNP led four party alliance won more than two-thirds of the seats in Parliament. On 10 October 2001, Khaleda Zia was sworn in as prime

minister for a fourth time. In November 2001 Badruddoza Chowdhury was elected president, however, following his resignation on 21 June 2002, Jamiruddin Sircar was appointed as acting president.

POLITICAL SYSTEM

There is a unicameral parliament (Jatiya Sangsad) of 300 directly elected members who can amend the constitution by a two-thirds majority. The country is divided into six administrative divisions, sub-divided into 64 districts.

HEAD OF STATE

President (acting), Jamiruddin Sircar, appointed 21 June 2002

CABINET *as at July 2002*

Prime Minister, Armed Forces Division, Cabinet Division, Defence, Establishment, Energy and Minerals, Hill Tracts Affairs, Primary and Mass Education, Khaleda Zia
Agriculture, Motiur Rahman Nizami
Commerce, Khosru Mahmud Chowdhury
Communications, Nazmul Huda
Disaster Management and Relief, Chowdhury Kamal Ibne Yousuf
Education, Osman Faruque
Environment and Forest, Shajahan Siraj
Finance and Planning, Saifur Rahman
Fisheries and Livestock, Sadek Hossain Khoka
Food, Tariqul Islam
Foreign Affairs, Morshed Khan
Health and Family Welfare, Khondoker Mosharraf Hossain
Home Affairs, Altaf Hossain Chowdhury
Housing and Public Works, Mirza Abbas
Industries, M. K.Anwar
Information, Moyeen Khan
Jute, Hafiz Uddin Ahmad
Labour and Employment, Abdullah Al Noman
Land, M. Shamsul Islam
Law, Justice and Parliamentary Affairs, Moudud Ahmed
Local Government, Rural Development and Co-operatives, Abdul Mannan Bhuiyan
Post and Telecommunications, Mohammad Aminul Hoque
Shipping, Lt-Col. Akbar Hossain
Social Welfare, Ali Ahsan Mujahid

Textiles, Abdul Matin Chowdhury
Water Resources, L. K. Siddique
Without Portfolio, Hurunar Rashid Khan Monno
Women and Children's Affairs, Khurshid Jahan Hoque

BANGLADESH HIGH COMMISSION
28 Queen's Gate, London SW7 5JA
Tel: 020-7584 0081
High Commissioner, HE Sheikh Razzak Ali, apptd 2002
First Secretary (Commerce), Mohammed Mahmud Reza Khan

BRITISH HIGH COMMISSION
United Nations Road, Baridhara, Dhaka
PO Box 6079, Dhaka-1212
Tel: (00 880) (2) 882 2705
Email: dhaka.press@fco.gov.uk
High Commissioner, HE Dr David Carter, CVO
Deputy High Commissioner, S. E. Turner
Defence Adviser, Brig. S. M. A. Lee, OBE

BRITISH COUNCIL DIRECTOR,
Carl Reuter, 5 Fuller Road, PO Box 161, Dhaka 1000; Email: Dhaka.Enquiries@bd.britishcouncil.org. There is a regional director in Chittagong.

DEFENCE

The army has 200 main battle tanks and 130 armoured personnel carriers. The Navy has four frigates and 33 patrol and coastal vessels. The Air Force has 83 combat aircraft.
MILITARY EXPENDITURE – 1.8 per cent of GDP (2000)
MILITARY PERSONNEL – 137,000: Army 120,000, Navy 10,500, Air Force 6,500; Paramilitaries 63,200

ECONOMY

Bangladesh is self-sufficient in food production. Agricultural products include rice, wheat, tobacco, tea, oil seeds, pulses and sugar cane. The chief industries are jute, cotton, tea, leather, pharmaceuticals, fertiliser, sugar, prawn fishing and natural gas. Garment manufacturing is the main export. Remittances sent home by Bangladeshis abroad are of considerable significance to the economy.

Heavy flooding during the summer of 1998 left 23 million people homeless and killed 1,500; two-thirds of the country was under water and 800,000 hectares of farmland was destroyed.

International donors agreed in April 2000 to provide around US$2,000 million in additional aid over a 20-year period dependent on the introduction of free-market economic reforms.
GNP – US$49,930 million (2000); US$370 per capita (1999)
GDP – US$37,288 million (1998); US$291 per capita (1999)
ANNUAL AVERAGE GROWTH GDP – 5.5 per cent (2000)
INFLATION RATE – 2.3 per cent (2000)
UNEMPLOYMENT – 2.5 per cent (1996)
TOTAL EXTERNAL DEBT – US$17,534 million (1999)

TRADE

In 2000 Bangladesh had a current account deficit of US$306 million and a trade deficit of US$1,654 million. Imports totalled US$8,360 million and exports US$4,692 million.

Trade with UK	2000	2001
Imports from UK	£74,494,000	£67,952,000
Exports to UK	381,937,000	455,184,000

COMMUNICATIONS

Principal seaports are Chittagong and Mongla. The Bangladesh Shipping Corporation was set up by the Government to operate the Bangladesh merchant fleet. The principal airports are Dhaka (Zia International) and Chittagong. The international airline, Bangladesh Biman, serves Europe, the Middle East, South and South-East Asia, and an internal network. A railway line links the Bangladeshi town of Benapol with Petrapol in India.

EDUCATION

Primary education is compulsory and free. There are 16 public universities and 29 private universities.
ILLITERACY RATE – 57.4 per cent (2002)
ENROLMENT (percentage of age group) – primary 96.6 per cent (2000); secondary 42.8 per cent (2000); tertiary 4.4 per cent (1990)

BARBADOS

AREA – 166 sq. miles (430 sq. km); nearly 21 miles long by 14 miles broad
POPULATION – 262,000 (1997 UN estimate). The official language is English
CAPITAL – Ψ Bridgetown in the parish of St Michael (population, 108,000, 1990)
MAJOR TOWNS – Holetown in St James, Oistins in Christ Church and Speightstown in St Peter
CURRENCY– Barbados dollar (BD$) of 100 cents
NATIONAL ANTHEM – In Plenty And In Time Of Need
NATIONAL DAY – 30 November (Independence Day)
NATIONAL FLAG– Three vertical stripes, aquamarine, gold and aquamarine, with a trident head on gold stripe
LIFE EXPECTANCY (years) – male 74.5; female 79.5
POPULATION GROWTH RATE – 0.3 per cent (1999)
POPULATION DENSITY – 621 per sq. km (1999)
MILITARY EXPENDITURE – 0.5 per cent of GDP (2000)
MILITARY PERSONNEL – 610: Army 500, Navy 110
Barbados is the most easterly of the Caribbean islands. The land rises in a series of terraced tablelands to the highest point, Mt Hillaby (1,116 ft).

HISTORY AND POLITICS

The first inhabitants of Barbados were Arawak Indians but the island was uninhabited when first settled by the British in 1627. It was a Crown Colony from 1652 until it became an independent state within the Commonwealth on 30 November 1966.

The last general election took place on 20 January 1999 and seats in the House of Assembly were distributed as follows: Barbados Labour Party 26, Democratic Labour Party 2.

POLITICAL SYSTEM

The head of state is the British sovereign whose local representative is the Governor-General. The legislature consists of a Senate and a House of Assembly. The Senate comprises 21 Senators appointed by the Governor-General for a five-year term, of whom 12 are appointed on the advice of the prime minister, two on the advice of the Leader of the Opposition and seven by the Governor-General at his/her discretion to represent religious, economic or social interests. The House of Assembly comprises 28 members elected every five years by adult suffrage.

There are 11 administrative areas (parishes): St Michael, Christ Church, St Andrew, St George, St James, St John, St Joseph, St Lucy, St Peter, St Philip and St Thomas.

Governor-General, HE Sir Clifford Husbands, GCMG, KA, apptd 1996

CABINET *as at July 2002*

Prime Minister, Defence and Security, Finance, Owen Arthur
Deputy Prime Minister, Foreign Affairs, Foreign Trade, Billie Miller
Agriculture and Rural Development, Anthony Wood
Attorney-General and Home Affairs, Mia Mottley
Commerce, Consumer Affairs and Business Development, Ronald Toppin
Education, Youth Affairs and Sports, Rudolph Greenidge
Environment and Physical Development, Elizabeth Thompson
Health, Jerome Walcott
Housing and Lands, Gline Clarke
Industry, International Business and Economic Development, Reginald Farley
Labour and Social Security, Rawle Eastmond
Minister of State, Education, Cynthia Forde
Minister of State, Prime Minister's Office, Glyne Murray
Public Works and Transport, Rommell Marshall
Social Transformation, Hamilton Lashley
Tourism and International Transport, Noel Anderson Lynch

BARBADOS HIGH COMMISSION
1 Great Russell Street, London WC1B 3ND Tel: 020-7631 4975 High Commissioner, HE Peter Simmons, apptd 1995
Deputy High Commissioner, Herbert Yearwood
First Secretary (Commercial), Janette Babb

BRITISH HIGH COMMISSION
Lower Collymore Rock, PO Box 676, Bridgetown
Tel: (00 1 246) 430 7800
Email: britishhc@sunbeach.net
High Commissioner, HE John White, apptd 2001
Deputy High Commissioner, M. J. E. Mayhew
Defence Adviser, Capt. S. C. Ramm
First Secretary (Chancery), P. Curwen

ECONOMY

The economy is based on tourism, sugar and light manufacturing. In 1998, 472,000 tourists visited Barbados. Chief exports are sugar, chemicals, electronic components and clothing.
GNP – US$2,487 million (2000); US$8,600 per capita (1999)
GDP – US$2,337 million (1998); US$9,380 per capita (1999)
ANNUAL AVERAGE GROWTH OF GDP – 2.5 per cent (1999)
INFLATION RATE – 2.4 per cent (2000)
UNEMPLOYMENT – 14.5 per cent (1997)
TOTAL EXTERNAL DEBT – US$589 million (1999)

TRADE

In 1998 Barbados had a current account deficit of US$57 million and a trade deficit of US$644 million. In 2000 exports totalled US$272 million and imports US$1,156 million.

Trade with UK	2000	2001
Imports from UK	£51,191,000	£55,734,000
Exports to UK	24,496,000	40,238,000

COMMUNICATIONS

Barbados has some 965 miles of roads, of which about 917 miles are asphalted. The Grantley Adams International airport is situated at Seawell, 12 miles from Bridgetown. Bridgetown, the only port of entry, has a deep-water harbour with berths for eight ships; oil is pumped ashore at Spring Garden and at an Esso installation on the West Coast.

EDUCATION

Education is free in government schools at primary and secondary levels. There are 105 primary schools, 22 government secondary schools and 10 private secondary schools.
ENROLMENT (percentage of age group) – primary 78 per cent (1991); secondary 75 per cent (1989); tertiary 29.4 per cent (1995)

BELARUS
Respublika Belarus – Republic of Belarus

AREA – 80,155 sq. miles (207,600 sq. km). Neighbours: Latvia and Lithuania (north), Russia (east), Ukraine (south), Poland (west)
POPULATION – 10,000,000 (2002 estimate): 78 per cent Belarusian, 13 per cent Russian, 4 per cent Polish and 3 per cent Ukrainian, with smaller numbers of Jews and Lithuanians. Belarusian and Russian have equal official language status. Most of the population are Belarusian Orthodox with a minority of Roman Catholics
CAPITAL – Minsk (population, 1,708,308) the administrative centre of the CIS
MAJOR CITIES – Brest (297,235); Homyel' (501,926); Hrodna (306,296); Mahilyow (368,886); Vitsyebsk (355,829), 1998 estimates
CURRENCY – Belarusian rouble
NATIONAL ANTHEM – The former Soviet national anthem but with the words omitted
NATIONAL DAY – 3 July (Independence Day)
NATIONAL FLAG – Red with a green strip along the lower edge, and in the hoist a vertical red and white ornamental pattern
LIFE EXPECTANCY (years)– male 62.8; female 74.4
POPULATION GROWTH RATE – 0.3 per cent (1999)
POPULATION DENSITY – 49 per sq. km (1999)
URBAN POPULATION – 69.1 per cent (1996)

Belarus is situated in the western part of the European area of the former USSR. The main rivers are the upper reaches of the Dnieper and of the Niemen and of the Western Dvina. Much of the land is a plain, with many lakes, swamps and marshy areas. The climate is continental with mild, humid winters and relatively cool and rainy summers.

HISTORY AND POLITICS

After being absorbed into Lithuania in the 13th and 14th centuries, the Belarusian nationality, language and culture flourished until Belarus came under Polish rule in the mid-16th century. Two hundred years of Polish rule followed until Belarus was re-absorbed into the Russian Empire.
Belarus was devastated by the German invasion in the Second World War; 25 per cent of the population was killed and thousands deported.
Belarus issued a Declaration of State Sovereignty on 27 July 1990 and declared its independence from the Soviet Union after the failed coup in Moscow in August 1991. Stanislav Shuskevich became Belarusian leader at the

head of a coalition of Communists and democrats, but he was forced to resign in January 1994 and was replaced by Gen. Mecheslav Grib who pursued closer political, economic and trade relations with Russia. The presidential election in June 1994 was won by Alyaksandr Lukashenka.

The legislative election held on 15 October 2000, with a second round on 29 October, was condemned as neither free nor fair by opposition groups and international observers from OSCE, the European Parliament and the Council of Europe. Most opposition parties boycotted the election and many opposition candidates were prevented from standing or intimidated into withdrawing by the authorities. Repeat elections were held in 13 of the 110 constituencies of the House of Representatives on 13–18 March 2001, with a second round on 1 April. In the presidential elections held on 9 September 2001 Lukashenka was re-elected with more than 75 per cent of the vote. Observers from the CIS stated that the election was legitimate but observers from the OSCE announced that the election did not comply with OSCE standards.

FOREIGN RELATIONS

An agreement was signed with Russia in April 1996 to form a Commonwealth of Independent States (CIS). In April 1997 a treaty of union was signed with Russia. The presidents of Belarus and Russia signed documents in December 1998 which called for the adoption of a common budget and single currency and for joint defence and security policies. On 8 December 1999, they signed the Treaty on the Creation of a Union State, which committed the two countries to eventually becoming a confederal state. In April 2001, the National Assembly ratified an agreement to introduce the Russian rouble as the currency of the Russia-Belarus Union State from 2005, with a new union currency from 2008.

POLITICAL SYSTEM

The president's term of office is five years, although two referendums in 1996 and 1997 extended Lukashenka's term until 2002; the legitimacy of these extensions was contested by the opposition and a fresh presidential election was held in September 2001. The president has authority to appoint half the members of the constitutional court and the electoral commission. The legislature is the bicameral National Assembly, comprising a 110-member House of Representatives (lower chamber) and a 64-member Council of the Republic (upper chamber). Eight members of the upper chamber are appointed by the president, the rest are indirectly elected by members of the local soviets in each region.

The republic is divided into six regions (*oblasts*): Brest, Homyel', Hrodna, Minsk, Mahilow and Vitsyebsk.

HEAD OF STATE

President, Alyaksandr Lukashenka, *elected* 10 July 1994, re-elected 9 September 2001

COUNCIL OF MINISTERS *as at July 2002*

Prime Minister, Gennady Novitsky
First Deputy Prime Minister, Andrei Kabyakov
Deputy Prime Ministers, Alexander Popkov (*Agroindustrial Complex*); Sergei Sidorsky (*Industry and Construction*), Vladimir Drazhin (*Social Affairs, Science and Trade*)
Agriculture and Food, Mikhail Rusy
Architecture and Construction, Gennady Kurochkin
Communications, Vladimir Goncharenko
Culture, Leonid Gulyako

Defence, Lt.-Gen. Leonid Maltsev
Economy, Vladimir Shimov
Education, Pyotr Brigadin
Emergency Situations, Valery Astapov
Energy, Vladimir Semashko
Finance, Nikolai Korbut
Foreign Affairs, Mikhail Khvostov
Health, vacant
Housing and Communal Services, Aleksandr Milkota
Industry, Anatoly Kharlap
Information, Mikhail Podgainy
Internal Affairs, Maj.-Gen. Vladimir Naumov
Justice, Viktor Golovanov
Labour and Social Security, Antonina Morova
Natural Resources and Environmental Protection, Leonty Khoruzhik
Revenues, Konstantin Sumar
Sport and Tourism, Yevgeny Vorsin
Statistics and Analysis, Vladimir Zinovsky
Trade, Aleksandr Kulichkov
Transport and Communications, Mikhail Borovoy

EMBASSY OF THE REPUBLIC OF BELARUS
6 Kensington Court, London W8 5DL
Tel: 020-7937 3288
Ambassador Extraordinary and Plenipotentiary, HE Dr Valery Sadokho, apptd 2000

BRITISH EMBASSY
37 Karl Marx Street, 220030 Minsk
Tel: (00 375) (172) 105920
Email: pia@bepost.belpak.minsk.by
Ambassador Extraordinary and Plenipotentiary, HE Iain Kelly, apptd 1999

DEFENCE

The Army has 1,683 main battle tanks, 1,577 armoured infantry fighting vehicles and 919 armoured personnel carriers. The Air Force has 177 combat aircraft and 58 armed helicopters.
MILITARY EXPENDITURE – 4.0 per cent of GDP (2000)
MILITARY PERSONNEL – 82,900: Army 43,600, Air Force 12,000, Air Defence Force 10,200, Central Units 17,100; Paramilitaries 110,000
CONSCRIPTION DURATION – 18 months

ECONOMY

As a result of the collapse of the Soviet centrally planned economic system, the country lost cheap supplies of energy and raw materials. Energy from Russia is still the largest import.

In May 1995 a customs union agreement with Russia took effect. A treaty was signed with Kazakhstan, Kyrgyzstan and Russia in March 1996 aimed at the establishment of a single customs territory. In December 1997 the first Russia-Belarus joint budget was endorsed, with projects estimated to cost US$100 billion. Industrial output increased by 9.7 per cent in 1999.

A Russian Belarus Union State budget was endorsed on 12 April 2002, amounting to 2.6 billion roubles. Russia will contribute 65 per cent of this and Belarus 35 per cent. Of this amount, 57 per cent will go to production, 24.7 per cent to military and technical co-operation and state security provision and 10.3 per cent to education, culture, social policy, healthcare and mass media. Equal prices for natural gas, electricity and railroad shipments were agreed and Belarus agreed that local markets would be opened for Russian investment and that it would share access to its gas pipelines with Russia.

In 2000 Belarus had a trade deficit of US$838 million and a current account deficit of US$162 million. Imports totalled US$8,477 million and exports US$7,380 million. GNP – US$29,959 million (2000); US$2,620 per capita (1999)
GDP – US$14,024 million (1998); US$877 per capita (1999)
ANNUAL AVERAGE GROWTH OF GDP– 5.9 per cent (2000)
INFLATION RATE – 168.6 per cent (2000)
UNEMPLOYMENT – 2.0 per cent (1999)
TOTAL EXTERNAL DEBT – US$1,136 million (1999)

Trade with UK	2000	2001
Imports from UK	£36,251,000	£32,543,000
Exports to UK	34,158,000	18,003,000

CULTURE AND EDUCATION

Belarusian is an Eastern Slavonic language, closely related to Russian and Ukrainian and written in the Cyrillic script. Important cultural figures include the poet Yanka Kupala (1882-1942), the writer Yakub Kolas (1882-1956) and the painter Marc Chagall (1887-1985).

The national education system comprises pre-school, general secondary, out-of-school, vocational training and trade schools, secondary specialised and higher education. General secondary education begins at the age of six. There are also 22 private educational institutions.
ILLITERACY RATE – 0.4 per cent (2002)
ENROLMENT (percentage of age group) – primary 98 per cent (1997); tertiary 44.0 per cent (1997)

BELGIUM
Koninkrijk België/Royaume de Belgique/Königreich Belgien - Kingdom of Belgium

AREA – 11,787 sq. miles (30,528 sq. km). Neighbours: the Netherlands (north), France (south), Germany and Luxembourg (east)
POPULATION – 10,239,085 (2000 estimate). Greater Brussels 959,318; Flanders 5,940,251; Wallonia 3,339,516. Roman Catholicism is the religion of 86 per cent of the population. The official languages are Flemish, French and German
CAPITAL – Brussels (population, 959,318, 2000 estimate)
MAJOR CITIES – Ψ Antwerp, the chief port (931,718); Bruges (269,158); Charleroi (424,515); Ψ Ghent (493,329); Liège (588,312); Leuven (453,772); Mons (250,748); Namur (279,675), 1998 estimates
CURRENCY – Euro (€) of 100 cents
NATIONAL ANTHEM – O Vaderland, O Edel Land Der Belgen (Oh Fatherland, Oh Noble Land Of The Belgians)
NATIONAL DAY – 21 July (Accession of King Leopold I, 1831)
NATIONAL FLAG – Three vertical bands, black, yellow, red
LIFE EXPECTANCY (years) – male 75.7; female 81.9
POPULATION GROWTH RATE – 0.3 per cent (1997)
POPULATION DENSITY – 333 per sq. km (1999)
URBAN POPULATON – 97.3 per cent (2000)

The Maas and its tributary, the Sambre, divide Belgium into two distinct regions, that in the west being generally level and fertile, while the tableland of the Ardennes, in the east, has mostly poor soil. The polders near the coast, which are protected by dykes against floods, cover an area of 193 sq. miles. The principal rivers are the Schelde and the Maas.

Belgium is divided between those who speak Dutch (the Flemings) and those who speak French (the Walloons). Dutch is recognised as the official language in the northern areas and French in the southern (Walloon) area and there are guarantees for the respective linguistic minorities. Brussels is officially bilingual. There is a small German-speaking area (Eupen and Malmédy) along the German border, east of Liège.

HISTORY AND POLITICS

The kingdom formed part of the Low Countries (Netherlands) from 1815 until 14 October 1830, when a National Congress proclaimed its independence. Belgium was invaded by Germany in 1914 and Eupen and Malmédy were ceded to Belgium by Germany under the Versailles Treaty of 1919. The kingdom was again invaded by Germany in 1940 and was occupied by Nazi troops until liberated by the Allies in September 1944. In 1977 Belgium was divided into three administrative regions: Flanders, Wallonia and Brussels.

The last general election was held on 13 June 1999. The results were as follows (seats):

Chamber of Deputies: Christian Social Party (CVP) (Flemish) 22; Socialist Party (PS) (Francophone) 19; Flemish Liberals and Democrats (VLD) 23; Socialist Party (SP) (Flemish) 14; Liberal Reform Party-Democratic Front (PRL-FDF) (Francophone) 18; Christian Social Party (PSC) (Francophone) 10; Vlaams Blok (Flemish Nationalist Party) 15; Ecolo (Francophone Ecology Party) 11; Agalev (Flemish Environmental Party) 9; Flemish People's Union (VU) 8; Front National (FN) 1.

Senate: of the 40 seats directly elected, CVP 6; SP 4; VLD 6; PRL-FDF 5; PS 4; PSC 3; Vlaams Blok 4; VU 2; Ecolo 3; Agalev 3. A further 31 Senators are indirectly elected or co-opted. The next elections are planned for June 2003.

POLITICAL SYSTEM

Belgium is a constitutional representative and hereditary monarchy with a bicameral legislature, consisting of the King, the Senate and the Chamber of Deputies. The parliamentary term is four years. Amendments to the constitution enacted since 1968 have devolved power to the regions. The national government retains competence only in foreign and defence policies, the national budget and monetary policy, social security, and the judicial, legal and penal systems. The Senate has 71 seats, of which 40 are directly elected, 21 indirectly elected and ten co-opted by the Flemish and Francophone Communities. The Chamber of Deputies has 150 seats. There are four levels of sub-national government: community, regional, provincial, and communal.

FEDERAL STRUCTURE

There are three communities: Flemish, Francophone, Germanophone. Each community has its own assembly, which elects the community government. At this level, Flanders is covered by the Flemish Community Assembly; most of Wallonia is covered by the Francophone Community Assembly, and the areas of Wallonia in the German-speaking communities of Eupen and Malmédy are covered by the Germanophone Community Assembly; Brussels is covered by a Joint Community Commission of the Flemish and Francophone Community Assemblies.

At regional level, Belgium is divided into the three regions of Wallonia, Brussels and Flanders. Each region has its own assembly and government.

There are ten provinces; five French-speaking in Wallonia (Hainaut, Liège, Luxembourg, Namur and

French Brabant); and five Dutch-speaking in Flanders (Antwerp, East Flanders, West Flanders, Limburg and Flemish Brabant). In addition, Belgium has 589 communes as the lowest level of local government.

Minister-President of the Flemish Government, Patrick Dewael (VLD)
Minister-President of the Walloon Regional Government, Jean-Claude Van Cauwenberghe (PS)
Minister-President of the French Community, Hervé Hasquin (PRL)
Minister-President of the German-Speaking Community, Karl-Heinz Lambertz (SP)
Head of City Government in Brussels, François-Xavier de Donnéa

HEAD OF STATE

HM The King of the Belgians, King Albert II, *born* 6 June 1934; *succeeded* 9 August 1993; *married* 2 July 1959, Donna Paola Ruffo di Calabria, and has *issue* Prince Philippe; Princess Astrid, *b.* 5 June 1962; Prince Laurent, *b.* 19 October 1963
Heir, HRH Prince Philippe Léopold Louis Marie, *born* 15 April 1960; *married* 4 December 1999, Mathilde d'Udekem d'Acoz; has *issue* Princess Elisabeth Thérèse Marie Hélène, *b.* 25 October 2001

CABINET *as at July 2002*

Prime Minister, Guy Verhofstadt (VLD)
Deputy Prime Minister, Budget, Social Integration and Social Economy, Johan Vande Lanotte (SP)
Deputy Prime Minister, Foreign Affairs, Louis Michel (PRL)
Deputy Prime Minister, Labour and Equal Opportunities, Laurette Onkelinx (PS)
Deputy Prime Minister, Mobility and Transport, Isabelle Durant (Ecolo)
Civil Service and Modernisation of Public Administration, Luc Van Den Bossche (SP)
Consumer Protection, Public Health and Environment, Magda Aelvoet (Agalev)
Defence, André Flahaut (PS)
Economic Affairs and Scientific Research, Charles Picqué (PS)
Finance, Didier Reynders (PRL)
Interior, Antoine Duquesne (PRL)
Justice, Mark Verwilghen (VLD)
Minister attached to the Ministry of Foreign Affairs and in charge of Agriculture, Annemie Neyts
Social Affairs and Pensions, Frank Vandenbroucke (SP)
Telecommunications, Public Enterprises and Participation, Rik Daems (VLD)

Agalev Green Party (Flemish); Ecolo Green Party (Francophone); PS Socialist Party (Francophone); SP Socialist Party (Flemish); PRL Liberal Reform Party (Francophone); VLD Liberal Democrats (Flemish)

BELGIAN EMBASSY
103 Eaton Square, London SW1W 9AB
Tel: 020-7470 3700
Ambassador Extraordinary and Plenipotentiary, HE Thierry de Grüben, apptd 2002
Minister-Counsellors, P. Roland (*Political*); F. De Sutter (*Economic*)
Defence Attaché, Col. D. De Cock

BRITISH EMBASSY
Aarlenstraat 85, B-1040 Brussels
Tel: (00 32) (2) 287 6211
Ambassador Extraordinary and Plenipotentiary, HE Gavin Hewitt CMG, apptd 2001
Deputy Head of Mission, Counsellor (Commercial and Economic) and Consul-General, J. Smith
Defence Attaché, Gp Capt. J. D. Bullen, CBE
There are British Consular Offices at Brussels, Antwerp and Liège.

BRITISH COUNCIL DIRECTOR FOR BELGIUM AND LUXEMBOURG – Martin Rose, Leopold Plaza, Troonstraat 108, B-1050 Brussels; Email: bc.brussels@britishcouncil.be

DEFENCE
The Army has 132 main battle tanks, 491 armoured personnel carriers, 274 armoured infantry fighting vehicles and 74 helicopters. The Navy is based at Ostend and Zeebrugge and has three frigates. The Air Force has 90 combat aircraft.
The headquarters of NATO, SHAPE and the Western European Union Military Planning Cell are in Belgium; 1,425 US personnel are stationed in the country.
MILITARY EXPENDITURE – 1.4 per cent of GDP (2000)
MILITARY PERSONNEL – 39,420: Army 26,400, Navy 2,560, Air Force 8,600, Medical Service 1,860

ECONOMY
The service sector accounts for more than half of Belgium's GDP. With no natural resources except coal, production of which has now ceased, industry is based largely on the processing for re-export of imported raw materials. Principal industries are steel and metal products, chemicals and petrochemicals, textiles, glass, and foodstuffs.
Belgium has participated in the European Single Currency since 1 January 1999.

Province	Area (sq. km)	Population (2000)	Main Town	Population (1998)
FLANDERS				
Antwerp	2,867	1,643,972	Antwerp	931,718
East Flanders	2,982	1,361,623	Ghent	493,329
Flemish Brabant	2,106	1,014,704	Leuven	453,772
Limburg	2,422	791,178	Hasselt	67,456
West Flanders	3,144	1,128,774	Bruges	269,158
WALLONIA				
Hainaut	3,786	1,279,467	Mons	92,260
Liège	3,862	1,019,442	Liège	588,312
Luxembourg	4,440	246,820	Arlon	215,000
Namur	3,666	443,903	Namur	279,675
Walloon Brabant	1,091	349,884	Wavre	27,000

In 1999 there was a budget deficit of 0.9 per cent of GDP and public debt was 112.5 per cent of GDP. By the end of 2001, the debt ratio had been reduced to 103.3 per cent of GDP.
GNP – US$252,461 million (2000); US$24,650 per capita (1999)
GDP – US$250,392 million (1998); US$24,277 per capita (1999)
ANNUAL AVERAGE GROWTH OF GDP – 4.0 per cent (2000)
INFLATION RATE – 2.5 per cent (2000)
UNEMPLOYMENT – 8.6 per cent (1999)

TRADE

External trade figures relate to Luxembourg as well as Belgium since the two countries formed an economic union in 1921. The main trading partners are Germany, France, the Netherlands and the UK .
In 2000 Belgium and Luxembourg had a trade surplus of US$5,335 million and a current account surplus of US$11,851 million. Exports from Belgium totalled US$186,227 million and imports US$173,388 million.

Trade with UK	2000	2001
Imports from UK	£9,570,300,000	9,181,600,000
Exports to UK	9,688,400,000	10,862,800,000

COMMUNICATIONS

The railways are operated by the Belgian National Railways. Major ports include Antwerp, Zeebrugge, Ghent and Ostend. There are 1,586 km of inland waterways; ship canals link Ghent with Terneuzen in the Netherlands, Willebroek Rupel with Brussels, Zeebrugge with Bruges, Liège with Antwerp and Charleroi with Brussels. The rivers Maas, Sambre and Schelde form an integral part of the network.
There are 14,421 km of trunk road, of which 1,631 km are motorways.

CULTURE AND EDUCATION

The literature of France and the Netherlands is supplemented by an indigenous Belgian literary activity in both French and Dutch. Flemish literary figures include Guido Gezelle (1830-1899) and Karel van de Woestijne (1878-1929). Francophone authors include Maurice Maeterlinck (1862 –1949), who was awarded the Nobel Prize for Literature in 1911, the poet Émile Verhaeren (1855–1916) and Georges Simenon (1903–1989).
Nursery schools provide free education for children from two and a half to six years. There are over 4,000 primary schools (6 to 12 years), more than 1,000 secondary schools offering a general academic education slightly over half of which are free institutions (predominantly Roman Catholic but subsidised by the state) and the remainder official institutions. The official school-leaving age is 18.
ENROLMENT (percentage of age group) – primary 100 per cent (1997); secondary 100 per cent (1997); tertiary 56 per cent (1997)

BELIZE

AREA – 8,763 sq. miles (22,696 sq. km). Neighbours: Mexico (north and north-west), Guatemala (west and south)
POPULATION – 230,000 (1997 UN estimate): 44 per cent Mestizo (Maya-Spanish); 26 per cent Creole; 11 per cent Maya; plus a number of East Indian and Spanish descent. The races are now inter-mixed. The majority of the population is Christian, about 58 per cent Catholic and 34 per cent Protestant. The official language and language of instruction is English. Spanish is also widely spoken and English Creole is the vernacular. There are also Garifuna and Maya speakers
CAPITAL – Belmopan (population, 44,087, 1991)
MAJOR CITIES – Ψ Belize City (1993 census 46,342), the former capital; Corozal (7,420); Dangriga (6,761); Orange Walk (11,573); San Ignacio (9,417)
CURRENCY – Belize dollar (BZ$) of 100 cents. The Belize dollar is tied to the US dollar
NATIONAL ANTHEM – Land Of The Free
NATIONAL DAY – 21 September (Independence Day)
NATIONAL FLAG – Blue ground with red band along top and bottom edges, and in centre a white disc containing the coat of arms surrounded by a green garland
LIFE EXPECTANCY (years) – male 73.0; female 75.9
POPULATION GROWTH RATE – 2.0 per cent (1999)
POPULATION DENSITY – 10 per sq. km (1999)
URBAN POPULATION – 50.4 per cent (1997)
MILITARY EXPENDITURE – 2.4 per cent of GDP (2000)
MILITARY PERSONNEL – Army 1,050

The coastal areas are mostly flat and swampy with many islets but the country rises gradually towards the interior, which is mainly forest. The northern and western districts are hilly, and in the south the Maya Mountains and the Cockscombs form the backbone of the country, reaching a height of 3,700 feet at Victoria Peak. The climate is sub-tropical.

HISTORY AND POLITICS

Numerous ruins in the area indicate that Belize was heavily populated by the Maya Indians. The first British settlement was established in 1638 but was subject to repeated attacks by the Spanish, who claimed sovereignty until defeated by the Royal Navy and settlers in 1798. In 1871 the area was recognised by Britain as a colony and called British Honduras. The colony became self-governing in 1964, with the UK retaining control of foreign policy, internal security and defence. In 1973 the colony was renamed Belize, and was granted independence on 21 September 1981.
The 1998 elections were won by the People's United Party, who took 26 out of the 29 seats in the House of Representatives.

FOREIGN RELATIONS

A long-standing territorial dispute with Guatemala was provisionally resolved in 1992 when the Guatemalan Congress and Supreme Court voted to recognise Belize and establish diplomatic relations. Guatemala still retains its claim, subject to arbitration by the International Court of Justice.

POLITICAL SYSTEM

Queen Elizabeth II is head of state, represented in Belize by a Governor-General. There is a National Assembly, comprising a House of Representatives (29 members elected for five years) and a Senate (eight members appointed by the Governor-General on the advice of the prime minister and the leader of the opposition). Executive power is vested in the Cabinet, which is responsible to the National Assembly.

Governor-General, HE Sir Colville Norbert Young, GCMG, apptd 17 November 1993

CABINET as at July 2002

Prime Minister, Finance, Foreign Trade and Economic Development, Said Musa
Deputy PM, Natural Resources, Environment, Commerce and Industry, John Briceño
Agriculture, Fisheries and Co-operatives, Daniel Silva
Attorney-General, Information, Godfrey Smith
Budget Management, Investment and Public Utilities, Ralph Fonseca
Defence and National Emergency Management, Senior Minister, George Price
Education, Youth and Sports, Cordel Hyde
Health and Public Services, José Coye
Home Affairs, Maxwell Samuels
Housing and Urban Renewal, Richard Bradley
Human Development, Women and Civil Society, Dolores Balderamos García
Rural Development, Marcial Mes
Sugar Industry, Local Government and Labour, Valdemar Castillo
Tourism and Culture, Mark Espat
Works, Communications and Transport, Citrus and Banana Industries, Henry Canton

BELIZE HIGH COMMISSION
22 Harcourt House, 19 Cavendish Square, London W1M 9AD. Tel: 020-7499 9728
High Commissioner, HE Alexis Rosado, apptd 2002

BRITISH HIGH COMMISSION
PO Box 91, Belmopan
Tel: (00 501) (8) 22146/7
Email: brithicom@btl.net
High Commissioner, HE Philip Priestley, apptd 2001

ECONOMY

About 30 per cent of the population is engaged in agriculture. The country is more or less self-sufficient in fresh beef, pork and poultry, but processed meat and dairy products are imported. About 25 per cent of timber production (mostly mahogany) is exported, and there is a large US market for lobster, conch and scale fish. Tourism is also a valuable source of income.

In 2000 Belize had a trade deficit of US$191 million and a current account deficit of US$139 million. Imports totalled US$6450 million and exports US$194 million.
GNP – US$751 million (2000); US$2,730 per capita (1999)
GDP – US$630 million (1998); US$3,045 per capita (1999)
ANNUAL AVERAGE GROWTH OF GDP – 8.9 per cent (2000)
INFLATION RATE – 0.6 per cent (2000)
UNEMPLOYMENT – 12.7 per cent (1997)
TOTAL EXTERNAL DEBT – US$351 million (1999)

Trade with UK	2000	2001
Imports from UK	£11,460,000	£13,789,000
Exports to UK	39,565,000	34,939,000

COMMUNICATIONS

There is a government-operated radio service and six privately-owned radio stations but no official television service in the country. An automatic telephone service, operated by Belize Telecommunications Ltd, covers the whole country.

The principal airport is at Belize City and various airlines operate international flights to the USA and other Central American states. The main port is also Belize City, which has deep water quays. Several inland waterways are also navigable. There are 1,865 miles of road, including four main highways, but there is no railway system.

EDUCATION

Education is compulsory from six to 14 years of age.
ILLITERACY RATE – 6.3 per cent (2002)
ENROLMENT (percentage of age group) – primary 99 per cent (1994); secondary 36 per cent (1992)

BENIN
République du Benin - Republic of Benin

AREA – 43,484 sq. miles (112,622 sq. km). Neighbours: Togo (west), Burkina Faso and Niger (north), Nigeria (east)
POPULATION – 5,828,000. The official language is French
CAPITAL – Porto Novo (population, 179,138, 1992)
MAJOR TOWNS – Ψ Cotonou (487,020, 1992) is the principal commercial town and port
CURRENCY – Franc CFA of 100 centimes
NATIONAL ANTHEM - L'aube nouvelle (The New Dawn)
NATIONAL DAY – 30 November
NATIONAL FLAG – Two horizontal stripes of yellow over red with a vertical green band in the hoist
LIFE EXPECTANCY (years) – male 52.5; female 55.7
POPULATION GROWTH RATE – 2.8 per cent (1999)
POPULATION DENSITY – 54 per sq. km (1999)
URBAN POPULATION - 37.5 per cent (1996)
MILITARY EXPENDITURE – 1.4 per cent of GDP (2000)
MILITARY PERSONNEL – 4,750: Army 4,500, Navy 100, Air Force 150; Paramilitaries 2,500
CONSCRIPTION DURATION – 18 months (selective)

ILLITERACY RATE – 60.2 per cent (2002)
ENROLMENT (percentage of age group) – primary 78 per cent (1997); tertiary 3 per cent (1997)

Benin (formerly known as Dahomey) has a short coastline of 78 miles on the Gulf of Guinea but extends northwards inland for 437 miles. The four main regions, running horizontally, are a narrow sandy coastal strip, a succession of inter-communicating lagoons, a clay belt and a sandy plateau in the north.

HISTORY AND POLITICS

Benin was placed under French administration in 1892 and became an independent republic within the French Community in December 1958; full independence outside the Community was proclaimed on 1 August 1960. Between 1963 and 1972 successive governments were overthrown by the military until a coup d'état in 1972 brought to power a Marxist-Leninist military government headed by Lt.-Col. Kérékou.

A pluralistic constitution was adopted in December 1990 and legislative and presidential elections were held in 1991. Nicéphore Soglo was sworn in as president and appointed a Benin Renaissance Party (PRB)-dominated provisional government. He was defeated by Gen. Kérékou in a presidential election in March 1996. Legislative elections to the 83-seat National Assembly in March 1999 gave the PRB and allies 27 seats and opposition parties 42 seats. Gen. Kérékou won a second term of office in presidential elections held on 4 and 22 March 2001.

POLITICAL SYSTEM

The president is head of government as well as head of state, and is directly elected for a five-year term, renewable once only. The president appoints and presides over the Council of Ministers. The National Assembly has 83 members, directly elected for a maximum of four years.

HEAD OF STATE

President and Head of the Armed Forces, HE Gen. Mathieu Kérékou, elected 1996, re-elected 22 March 2001, sworn in 3 April 2001

CABINET as at July 2002

State Minister in charge of Co-ordination of Government Action, Planning, Job Creation and Expansion, Bruno Amoussou
Minister Delegate to the Presidency, Defence, Pierre Osho
Agriculture, Husbandry and Fishery, Théophile Nata
Civil Service, Administrative Reform, Ousmane Batoko
Commerce, Industry, Community Development and Employment Promotion, Lazare Sehoueto
Culture, Handicrafts, Tourism, Amos Elegbe
Communications and the Promotion of New Information Technologies, Gaston Zossou
Environment, Housing and Town Planning, Luc-Marie Constant Gnancadja
Family Affairs, Social Welfare and Solidarity, Claire Hougan Ayemona
Finance and Economy, Abdoulaye Bio Tchane
Foreign Affairs and African Integration, Antoine Kolawole Idji
Higher Education and Scientific Research, Dorothée Sossa
Interior, Security and Territorial Administration, Daniel Tawema
Justice, Legislation and Human Rights, Joseph Gnonlonfou
Mines, Energy and Water Resources, Kamarou Fassassi

Primary and Secondary Education, Jean Bio Tchabi Orou
Public Health, Céline Seignon Kandissounon
Public Works and Transport, Joseph Attin
Relations with Institutions, Civilian Society and Benin Nationals Abroad, Sylvain Adekpedjou Akindes
Vocational Training, Dominique Sohounhloue
Youth, Sports and Leisure, Valentin Aditi House

EMBASSY OF THE REPUBLIC OF BENIN
87 Avenue Victor Hugo, F-75116 Paris, France
Tel: (00 33) (1) 4500 9882
Ambassador Extraordinary and Plenipotentiary, HE André-Guy Ologoudou, apptd 1998

HONORARY CONSULATE, Dolphin House, 16 The Broadway, Stanmore, Middx HA7 4DW. Tel: 020-8954 8800. Honorary Consul, Lawrence Landau

BRITISH AMBASSADOR, HE Philip Thomas, resident at Lagos, Nigeria

ECONOMY

The principal exports are cotton, palm products, groundnuts, shea-nuts, and coffee. Small deposits of gold, iron and chrome have been found. Oil production started in 1983.

In July 2000 the IMF and the International Development Association agreed to a US$460 million debt reduction package for Benin.

In 1997 Benin had a trade deficit of US$153 million and a current account deficit of US$154 million. In 2000 imports totalled US$602 million and exports US$376 million.

GNP – US$2,398 million (2000); US$380 per capita (1999)
GDP – US$2,306 million (1998); US$386 per capita (1999)
ANNUAL AVERAGE GROWTH OF GDP – 5.0 per cent (2000)
INFLATION RATE – 4.2 per cent (2000)
TOTAL EXTERNAL DEBT – US$1,686 million (1999)

Trade with UK	2000	2001
Imports from UK	£43,430,000	£33,301,000
Exxports to UK	1,049,000	746,000

BHUTAN
Druk Gyal Khab - Kingdom of Bhutan

AREA – 18,147 sq. miles (47,000 sq. km). Neighbours: Tibet (north), India (west, south and east)
POPULATION – 1,862,000: about 80 per cent are Buddhists, the remainder (mostly the Nepali Bhutanese) are Hindu. The official language, for administrative and religious purposes, is Dzongkha, a variant of Tibetan, which functions as a lingua franca amongst a variety of languages and dialects. Nepali remains a recognised language and English remains the medium of instruction and the working language of the administration
CAPITAL – Thimphu (population, 15,000, 1987 estimate)
CURRENCY – Ngultrum of 100 chetrum (Indian currency is also legal tender)
NATIONAL ANTHEM - Druk Tsendhen Koipi Gyelknap Na (In The Thunder Dragon Kingdom)
NATIONAL DAY – 17 December
NATIONAL FLAG – Saffron yellow and orange-red divided diagonally, with dragon device in centre
LIFE EXPECTANCY (years) – male 62.0; female 64.5
POPULATION GROWTH RATE – 2.8 per cent (1999)

POPULATION DENSITY – 44 per sq. km (1999)
MILITARY EXPENDITURE – 5.6 per cent of GDP (2000)
ILLITERACY RATE – 52.7 per cent (2000)

There is a mountainous northern region which is infertile and sparsely populated, a central zone of upland valleys where most of the population and cultivated land is found, and in the south the densely forested foothills of the Himalayas, which are mainly inhabited by Nepalese settlers and indigenous tribespeople.

INSURGENCIES

In January 1989 the King introduced a code of national etiquette designed to protect the national culture and language from Nepali encroachment. These measures, together with the granting of citizenship only to Nepalis settled in Bhutan before 1958, led to an exodus of ethnic Nepalis to Nepal, where about 96,000 live in camps. A low-level insurgency has been waged in the south of the country against the King's policies by ethnic Nepalis since 1990. Talks between the Nepali and Bhutanese governments continue in an attempt to resolve the fate of the refugees.

FOREIGN RELATIONS

Under a 1949 treaty Bhutan is guided by the advice of India in regard to its external relations. It retains its own diplomatic representatives and is a member of the UN. It also receives from India an annual payment of Rs500,000 as compensation for portions of its territory annexed by the British Government in India in 1864.

POLITICAL SYSTEM

Bhutan has a 154-member unicameral Tshogdu (National Assembly), 105 of whom are directly elected and serve three-year terms, 12 are representatives of religious bodies and 37 are nominated by the government. The National Assembly meets twice a year. The ten-member Royal Advisory Council, nominated by the King and the National Assembly, acts as a consultative body when the National Assembly is not in session. The King is also assisted by the *Lhengyal Shungtshog* (Cabinet). There are no political parties.

In July 1998 the King introduced reforms giving the legislature the right to dismiss the King and to nominate the members of the cabinet, although the King retains the right to assign their portfolios. On 30 November 2001, the process of democratisation was taken further with the inauguration by royal decree of a committee to draft a written constitution.

HEAD OF STATE

HM The King of Bhutan, Jigme Singye Wangchuk, *born* 11 November 1955; *succeeded his father* July 1972; *crowned* 2 June 1974
Heir, Crown Prince Jigme Gesar Namgyal Wangchuk, *designated* 31 October 1988

CABINET *as at July 2002*

Cabinet Chairman, Trade and Industry, Khandu Wangchuk
Chair of the Royal Advisory Council, Kungang Tsangbi
Chair of the Third Committee (Social, Humanitarian, Cultural), Ugyen Tsering
Agriculture, Kinzang Dorji
Education and Health, Sangay Ngedup
Finance, Yeshey Zimba
Foreign Affairs, Jigme Thinley
Home Affairs, Thinley Gyamtsho
Law, Sonam Tobgye

ECONOMY

The economy is based on industry, which in 1998 accounted for 35 per cent of GDP, and agriculture (37 per cent of GDP). Agriculture and animal husbandry engage around 94 per cent of the workforce in what is largely a self-sufficient rural society. The principal food crops are rice, wheat, maize and barley. Vegetables and fruit are also produced. Bhutan is the world's largest producer of cardamom, which forms its principal export to countries other than India. Agriculture is, however, limited by the country's mountainous topography and 60 per cent forest cover.

The mountains contain rich deposits of limestone, gypsum, dolomite and graphite and small amounts of coal, which are exported to India. A distillery and cement, chemicals and food-processing plants are in production; a forestry industries complex is being expanded. Tourism and postage stamps are increasingly important sources of foreign exchange.

In 1997 imports totalled US$137 million and exports US$118 million.

GNP – US$441 million (2000); US$510 per capita (1999)
GDP – US$398 million (1998); US$214 per capita (1999)
ANNUAL AVERAGE GROWTH OF GDP – 5.8 per cent (1998)
INFLATION RATE – 6.8 per cent (1999)
TOTAL EXTERNAL DEBT – US$184 million (1999)

TRADE

Trade with India accounted for 71 per cent of imports and 95 per cent of exports in 1997. Principal exports are electricity, calcium carbide and timber; main imports are rice, machinery and diesel oil. Bhutan's airline, Druk Air, flies between Paro, New Delhi and Calcutta.

Trade with UK	2000	2001
Imports from UK	£1,208,000	£1,644,000
Exports to UK	1,662,000	2,342,000

BOLIVIA
República de Bolivia – Republic of Bolivia

AREA – 424,165 sq. miles (1,098,581 sq. km).
  Neighbours: Brazil (north and east), Paraguay and Argentina (south), Chile and Peru (west)
POPULATION – 8,140,000 (1999 estimate): 12 per cent is of white European descent, 30 per cent Mestizo (mixed European-Indian), 25 per cent Quechua Indian and 17 per cent Aymará Indian. The official language is Spanish; Quechua and Aymará are also spoken. Roman Catholicism was the state religion until disestablishment in 1961
CAPITAL – La Paz, the seat of government (population, 940,281, 1998 estimate)
MAJOR CITIES – Cochabamba (565,395); El Alto (534,466); Oruro (223,553); Potosí (140,642); Santa Cruz (935,361); Sucre, the legal capital and seat of the judiciary (178,426)
CURRENCY – Boliviano ($b) of 100 centavos
NATIONAL ANTHEM – Bolivianos, El Hado Propicio (Oh Bolivia, Our Long-Felt Desires)
NATIONAL DAY – 6 August (Independence Day)
NATIONAL FLAG – Three horizontal bands, red, yellow, green
LIFE EXPECTANCY (years) – male 61.9; female 65.3
POPULATION GROWTH RATE – 2.3 per cent (1999)
POPULATION DENSITY – 7 per sq. km (1999)
URBAN POPULATION – 61.1 per cent (1997)

The chief topographical feature is the great central

plateau over 500 miles in length, at an average altitude of 12,500 feet above sea level, between the two great chains of the Andes, which traverse the country from south to north. The total length of the navigable rivers is about 12,000 miles, the principal rivers being the Itenez, Beni, Mamore and Madre de Dios.

HISTORY AND POLITICS

Bolivia won its independence from Spain in 1825 after a war of liberation led by Simon Bolivar (1783–1830), from whom the country derives its name. From 1964 to 1982 Bolivia was ruled by military juntas until civilian rule was restored.

Congressional and presidential elections were held in June 1997. No party won an outright majority in Ccongress and a multiparty government was formed. Following a period of protests and strikes which had been prompted by proposed increases in water rates, a state of emergency was declared between 8–20 April 2000. The Cabinet resigned on 24 April 2000; a new Cabinet, was appointed the following day.

A new wave of protests and strikes took place in September and October 2000, but ended after the government made concessions to public sector workers and promised investment in areas where coca was produced. In April 2001 the protestors claimed that the government had failed to deliver the promised concessions and recommenced the campaign of demonstrations and strikes. Presidential and legislative elections were held on 30 June 2002, but were inconclusive. Following a second round of voting, Gonzalo Sánchez de Lozada was elected president.

POLITICAL SYSTEM

The constitution provides for a directly elected executive president who appoints the Cabinet. The legislature (Congress) consists of a 27-member Senate and a 130-member Chamber of Deputies; both chambers are elected for five-year terms, and the president also for five years.

HEAD OF STATE

President, Gonzalo Sánchez de Lozada
Vice-President, Carlos D. Mesa Gisbert

CABINET *as at July 2002*

Agriculture, Livestock and Rural Development, Arturo Baldiviezo
Economic Development, Oscar Mealla
Education, Culture and Sport, Issac Gisbert
Foreign Affairs and Worship, Carlos Bruno
Foreign Trade and Investment, Juan Carlos Virreira Méndez
Government, Alberto Vargas
Health and Social Prevention, Javier Tórrez Goitia Caballero
Home and Basic Services, Carlos Lándivar
Justice and Human Rights, Gina Luz Méndez Hurtado
Minister of Sustainable Development and Planning, José Justiniano
Minister of Treasury, Javier Salinas
National Defence, Freddy Ortiz
Presidency, Carlos Berzaín
Without Portfolio, Hermán Muñóz; Franciscao Suárez Ramirez; Silvia Amparo Velarde Olmos
Work and Micro-enterprise, Jaime Navarro Tordío

BOLIVIAN EMBASSY

106 Eaton Square, London SW1W 9AD
Tel: 020-7235 3357/4248/4255
Ambassador Extraordinary and Plenipotentiary, HE Marcelo Perez-Monasterios, apptd 2001

BRITISH EMBASSY

Avenida Arce 2732, (Casilla 694) La Paz
Tel: (00 591) (2) 433424
Email: ppa@mail.megalink.com
Ambassador Extraordinary and Plenipotentiary, HE William Sinton, apptd 2001
Deputy Head of Mission and Consul, P. Hogarth

BRITISH COUNCIL DIRECTOR, Eric Lawrie, Avenida Arce 2708 (esq. Campos), Casilla 15047, La Paz; Email: information@britishcouncil.org.bo

DEFENCE

The Army has 72 armoured personnel carriers. The Navy has 18 patrol vessels. The Air Force has 37 combat aircraft and 16 armed helicopters.

MILITARY EXPENDITURE – 1.4 per cent of GDP (2000)
MILITARY PERSONNEL – 31,500: Army 25,000, Navy 3,500, Air Force 3,000; Paramilitaries 37,100
CONSCRIPTION DURATION – 12 months (selective)

ECONOMY

Mining, natural gas, petroleum and agriculture are the principal industries. The ancient silver mines of Potosí are now worked chiefly for tin, but gold is obtained on the Eastern Cordillera of the Andes. Tin output, together with other minerals (copper, tungsten, antimony, lead, zinc, asbestos, wolfram, bismuth salt and sulphur), provides over one-third of exports. Following a decline in the price of tin, many workers have taken to growing coca, which has become a significant export. A government plan to reduce coca production by offering growers alternative means of support has been of limited success. New incentives to coca growers to abandon its production were announced in October 2000. Small quantities of oil are produced for internal consumption, and gas (currently providing about a quarter of export income) is piped to Argentina; in December 1997 the World Bank approved financing for the 3,150 km Bolivia-Brazil gas pipeline, which is now in operation. Gas reserves were estimated in 2000 at nearly 40 trillion cubic feet.

The economy deteriorated badly in the late 1970s and early 1980s; in the mid-1980s economic reforms were introduced with privatisation of some state-owned firms and the encouragement of foreign investment. The peso was replaced in 1987 with the Boliviano of 1,000,000 old pesos in a successful effort to stem hyperinflation. The economy and currency have stabilised.

In 1996 the government signed an agreement with the South American Common Market (Mercosur) to create a free trade zone within 18 years.

GNP – US$8,305 million (2000); US$990 per capita (1999)
GDP – US$8,571 million (1998); US$1,032 per capita (1999)
ANNUAL AVERAGE GROWTH OF GDP – 4.7 per cent (1998)
INFLATION RATE – 4.6 per cent (2000)
UNEMPLOYMENT – 4.2 per cent (1996)
TOTAL EXTERNAL DEBT – US$6,157 million (1999)

TRADE

Mineral exports represent about 40 per cent of total trade. Bolivia has now developed its own smelters and is exporting metals. The chief imports are wheat and flour, iron and steel products, machinery, vehicles and textiles.

In 2000 Bolivia had a trade deficit of US$381 million and a current account deficit of US$464 million. In 1999 imports totalled US$1,227 million and exports US$1,033 million.

Trade with UK	2000	2001
Imports from UK	£7,660,000	£10,220,000
Exports to UK	14,693,000	12,574,000

COMMUNICATIONS

There are 4,300 km of railways in operation. There are about 52,000 km of roads, of which about 20 per cent are paved. In 1993 Bolivia and Peru signed an agreement granting Bolivia a concession of 162 hectares at the southern Peruvian port of Ilo for 98 years to construct a free trade zone.

Commercial aviation is conducted by the national airline, Lloyd Aereo Boliviano and Transporte Aereo Militar between the major towns; Lloyd Aereo Boliviano and a number of foreign airlines provide international flights to the USA, South and Central America and Europe.

EDUCATION

Elementary education is compulsory and free and there are secondary schools in urban centres. Provision is also made for higher education; in addition to St Francisco Xavier's University at Sucre, founded in 1624, there are seven other universities, the largest being the University of San Andrés at La Paz, and ten private universities.

ILLITERACY RATE – 13.3 per cent (2002)

ENROLMENT (percentage of age group) – primary 91 per cent (1990); secondary 29 per cent (1990); tertiary 22 per cent (1991)

BOSNIA-HERCEGOVINA

Republika Bosna i Hercegovina – Republic of Bosnia and Hercegovina

AREA – 19,767 sq. miles (51,197 sq. km). Neighbours: Serbia (east), Montenegro (south-east), Croatia (north and west)

POPULATION – 3,784,000; 4.4 million (1991 census): 44 per cent Bosniac, 33 per cent Serbs and 17 per cent Croats. The languages are Bosnian (spoken by Bosniacs and written in the Latin script), Serbian (spoken by Serbs and written in the Cyrillic alphabet) and Croatian (spoken by Croats and written in the Latin script)

CAPITAL – Sarajevo (population, 529,021, 1991 estimate)

MAJOR CITIES – Banja Luka (195,994); Mostar (127,034); Tuzla (131,866); Zenica (145,837)

CURRENCY – Convertible marka

NATIONAL ANTHEM – Jedna Si Jedina (You Are Unique)

NATIONAL DAY – 1 March (anniversary of 1992 declaration of independence)

NATIONAL FLAG – Blue, bearing a yellow triangle above a line of white stars

LIFE EXPECTANCY (years) – male 71.3; female 76.7

POPULATION GROWTH RATE – 2.1 per cent (1999)

POPULATION DENSITY – 75 per sq. km (1999)

MILITARY EXPENDITURE – 3.7 per cent of GDP (2000)

MILITARY PERSONNEL – Bosniac Army (VF-B): 16,800; Croat Defence Council (VF-H): 7,200; Bosnian Serb Army (VRS): 14,000

GNP – US$4,930 million (2000); US$1,210 per capita (1999)

GDP – US$3,900 million (1998); US$1,094 per capita (1999)

ANNUAL AVERAGE GROWTH OF GDP – 20.0 per cent (1998)

TOTAL EXTERNAL DEBT – US$1,962 million (1999)

HISTORY AND POLITICS

The country was settled by Slavs in the seventh century and conquered by the Ottoman Turks in 1463. Ruled by the Turks for over 400 years, the country came under Austro-Hungarian control in 1878. The assassination of the heir to the Austro-Hungarian throne in Sarajevo by an ethnic Serb precipitated the First World War, after which Bosnia-Hercegovina became part of the 'Kingdom of Serbs, Croats and Slovenes' (renamed Yugoslavia in 1929). It was occupied by German and Axis forces between 1941 and 1945. At the end of the war Bosnia-Hercegovina became part of the Socialist Federal Republic of Yugoslavia, which eventually collapsed with the secession of Slovenia and Croatia in 1991.

The Bosnia-Hercegovina government issued a declaration of sovereignty in October 1991 against the wishes of the ethnic Serb Democratic Party. Independence was declared on 1 March 1992 following a referendum which was boycotted by the Bosnian Serbs. Bosnia-Hercegovina was recognised as an independent state by the EC and USA in April 1992 and admitted to UN membership in May 1992.

THE WAR

Fighting broke out in March 1992 between the pro-independence Muslims and Bosnian Serbs who wanted to merge with the Serbian republic to form a Greater Serbia. The Bosnian Serbs, assisted by the Federal Yugoslav Army (JNA), gained control of 70 per cent of Bosnia and in August 1992 declared their own 'Republika Srpska' with its capital at Pale.

The Bosnian government (Muslim) forces formed an alliance with Bosnian Croat and Croat forces in early 1992 which collapsed in 1993. The Muslims then came under fire from both Bosnian Serb and Bosnian Croat forces.

In August 1993 the Bosnian Croats declared a 'Republic of Herceg-Bosna', with its capital in Mostar, and following a cease-fire in February 1994 joined the government forces in a Muslim-Croat Federation.

NATO galvanised the USA, Britain, France, Germany and Russia to form the Contact Group (CG) to co-ordinate peace efforts. The CG brought about a cease-fire in June 1994 and presented a peace plan, which was rejected by the Bosnian Serbs.

Fighting intensified in 1995, climaxing in a land-grab during the final months of the war. Bosnian Serb forces overran the UN safe areas of Zepa and Srebrenica in July, allegedly massacring thousands of fleeing Muslims, and then laid siege to the Bihać 'safe area' together with Croatian Serbs and rebel Muslims. Bosnian government and Croatian forces lifted the siege of Bihać in August, enabling a joint attack on Serb-held central Bosnia.

The foreign ministers of Bosnia, Croatia and Serbia (rump Yugoslavia) met in Geneva in September 1995 and agreed to a US-sponsored peace accord. A ceasefire agreement was signed on 5 October and observed from 22 October, delayed by a Federation advance in the west and north-west, and Bosnian Serbs overrunning Tuzla.

THE PEACE AGREEMENT

The Dayton Peace Treaty was signed in Paris on 14 December 1995. It was agreed to preserve Bosnia as a single state with a 51:49 division of territory between the Bosnian and Croat Federation and the Republika Srpska (Bosnian Serbs). A Republican (national) government, presidency and democratically elected institutions, based in Federation-controlled Sarajevo, were provided for.

The Dayton agreement provided for the deployment of a NATO-led Peace Implementation Force (IFOR) which took over from UNPROFOR on 20 December 1995 and

was mandated until December 1996. IFOR was replaced by a NATO-led Stabilisation Force (SFOR).

Mostar, which had been divided during the war between the Muslims and Croats of the Federation and administered by the EU, held elections in June 1996. The EU withdrew in December 1996, when the Bosnian Croat state of Herceg-Bosna ceased to exist. Following a decision by international arbitrators, the northern town of Brčko, which had been under Bosnian Serb control, was merged into a self-governing neutral district in March 1999.

Elections were held for the presidency of the Republika Srpska, the House of Representatives and the legislative assemblies of the Bosnian-Croat Federation and the Republika Srpska on 11 November 2000. The non-nationalist Alliance for Change coalition became the largest grouping in the House of Representatives.

On 3 March 2001 the Croat National Congress, a grouping of Croatian parties, resolved to boycott the government and set up parallel institutions in mainly Croat areas, a decision which led to violent clashes between Croats and SFOR troops determined to preserve the unity of the Federation.

POLITICAL SYSTEM

Under the Dayton peace agreement, the Bosnian republican (national) government was made responsible for foreign affairs, currency, citizenship and immigration. Executive authority was vested in a democratically elected rotating presidential triumvirate comprising a representative from each community, but in March 2001 the Assembly of Bosnia-Hercegovina nominated two members of a multi-ethnic party.

Legislative authority is vested in a bicameral parliament, the Assembly of Bosnia-Hercegovina, comprising a House of Peoples and a House of Representatives. Both houses have two-year terms. The House of Peoples has 15 members, 10 from the Bosniac-Croat Federation and 5 from the Republika Srpska, who are selected by the House of Representatives. The House of Representatives has 42 members who are directly elected to the two constituent chambers, the Chamber of Deputies of the Federation, which has 28 members, and the Chamber of Deputies of the Republika Srpska, which has 14 members. Within the Bosniac-Croat Federation there is a 140-member House of Representatives and ten cantonal assemblies; in the Republika Srpska there is an 83-member People's Assembly.

Legislative elections and elections for the collective presidency and the presidency of the Republika Srpska were scheduled for 5 October 2002.

The Dayton peace agreement uses the term 'Bosniac' to refer to Bosnian Muslims.

HEADS OF STATE (FOR ALL BOSNIA)

Current President, Beriz Belkić
Presidency Members, Jozo Krizanović, Zivko Radišić

HEAD OF THE FEDERATION
President, Safet Halilović
Vice-President, Karlo Filipović

HEAD OF REPUBLIKA SRPSKA
President, Mirko Sarović
Vice-President, Dragan Cavić

COUNCIL OF MINISTERS (FOR ALL BOSNIA) *as at July 2002*

Prime Minister, European Integration, Dragan Mikerević
Civil Works and Communications, Svetozar Mihajlović
Foreign Affairs, Zlatko Lagumdzija

Foreign Trade and Economic Relations, Azra Hadziahmetović
Human Rights and Refugees, Kresimir Zubak
Treasury, Ante Domazet

FEDERATION CABINET *as at July 2002*

Prime Minister, Alija Behmen
Agriculture, Water Power and Forestry, Behija Hadžihajdarević
Defence, Mijo Anić
Education, Science, Culture and Sport, Mujo Demirović
Health, Željko Mišanović
Industry, Energy and Mining, Hasan Becirović
Interior, Ramo Maslesa
Justice, Zvonko Mijan
Labour, Social Affairs, Displaced People and Refugees, Gen. Sefer Halilović
Trade, Andrija Jurković
Transport and Communications, Besim Mehmedić
Urban Planning and Environment, Ramiz Mehmedović
Veterans and Disabled from the War of Freedom, Suada Hadžović
Without Portfolio, Mladen Ivanković; Gavrilo Grahovac

REPUBLIKA SRPSKA GOVERNMENT *as at July 2002*

Prime Minister, Mladen Ivanić
Deputy Prime Minister, Local Administration, Petar Kunić
Agriculture, Forestry and Water Management, Rodoljub Trkulja
Defence, Slobodan Bilić
Education, Gojko Savanović
External Economic Affairs, Fuad Turalić
Finance, vacant
Health and Social Care, Milorad Balaban
Industry, Pero Bukejlović
Interior, Dragomir Jovicić
Justice, Biljana Marić
Mining and Energy, Bosko Lemez
Refugees and Displaced Persons, Mico Micić
Religion, Dušan Antelj
Science, Mitar Novaković
Sport, Zoran Tesanović
Town Planning, Nedjo Djurić
Trade and Tourism, Boro Babić
Transport and Communications, Branko Dokić
War Veterans, Dragan Solaja

EMBASSY OF BOSNIA-HERCEGOVINA
4th Floor, Morley House, 320 Regent Street, London W1B 3BF
Tel: 020-7255 3758
Ambassador Extraordinary and Plenipotentiary, HE Elvira Begović, apptd 2001

BRITISH EMBASSY
8 Tina Ujevica, Sarajevo
Tel: (00 387) (33) 444429
Email: britemb@bih.net.ba
Ambassador Extraordinary and Plenipotentiary, HE Ian Cliff, apptd 2001

BRITISH COUNCIL DIRECTOR, Clare Newton, 2nd Floor, Obala Kulina Bana 4, Sarajevo 71000;
Email: british.council@britishcouncil.ba

ECONOMY

Wheat, maize, potatoes and cabbage are among the major crops; crude steel and lignite are among the principal mineral products.

Trade with UK	2000	2001
Imports from UK	£20,654,000	£14,713,000
Exports to UK	2,936,000	2,601,000

BOTSWANA
The Republic of Botswana

AREA – 224,607 sq. miles (581,730 sq. km). Neighbours: South Africa (south and east), Zimbabwe (north and north-east), Namibia (west), Zambia (north)
POPULATION – 1,533,000 (1997 UN estimate): Batswana (95 per cent); the remainder are Bakalanga, Basarwa, Bakgalagadi, Basubya, Baherero, Bayei, Bambukushu and Europeans. The national language is Setswana and the official language is English
CAPITAL – Gaborone (population, 286,779, 1997 UN estimate)
MAJOR CITIES – Francistown (55,244); Lobatse (26,052); Selebi-Phikwe (39,772)
CURRENCY – Pula (P) of 100 thebe
NATIONAL ANTHEM – Fatshe La Rona (Blessed Be This Noble Land)
NATIONAL DAY –30 September
NATIONAL FLAG –Light blue with a horizontal black stripe fimbriated in white across the centre
LIFE EXPECTANCY (years) – male 36.5; female 35.6
POPULATION GROWTH RATE – 2.5 per cent (1999)
POPULATION DENSITY – 3 per sq. km (1999)
URBAN POPULATION – 48.2 per cent (1996)

A plateau at a height of about 4,000 feet divides Botswana into two main topographical regions. To the east of the plateau streams flow into the Marico, Notwani and Limpopo rivers; to the west lies a flat region comprising the Bakgalagadi Desert, the Okavango Swamps and the Northern State Lands area. The climate is generally sub-tropical.

HISTORY AND POLITICS

The Tswana people were dominant in the area now known as Botswana from the 17th century. In 1885, at the request of indigenous chiefs fearing invasion by the Boers, Britain formally took control of Bechuanaland, and the northern part of the territory was formally declared a British protectorate, while land to the south of the Molopo river became British Bechuanaland, which was later incorporated into the Cape Colony. On 30 September 1966 the British Protectorate of Bechuanaland became a republic within the Commonwealth under the name Botswana.

The last general election on 16 October 1999 was won by the Botswana Democratic Party with 33 seats to the Botswana National Front's 7 seats.

POLITICAL SYSTEM

The president is head of state and is elected by an absolute majority in the National Assembly. He appoints as vice-president a member of the National Assembly who is leader of government business in the National Assembly. The Assembly consists of the president, 40 members elected on a basis of universal adult suffrage, four co-opted members, and the Attorney-General (non-voting). Presidential and legislative elections are held every five years. There is also a 15-member House of Chiefs which considers legislation affecting the constitution and chieftaincy matters. In August 1997 the minimum voting age was lowered from 21 to 18.

HEAD OF STATE
President, HE Festus Mogae, sworn in 2 April 1998
Vice-President, Lt.-Gen. Ian Khama

CABINET as at July 2002

Agriculture, Johnnie Swartz
Assistant Ministers, Pelokgale Seloma (Agriculture); Boyce Sebetela (Finance and Development Planning); Gladys Kokorwe (Local Government, Lands and Housing)
Education, George Kgoroba
Finance and Development Planning, Baledzi Gaolathe
Foreign Affairs, Lt.-Gen. Mompati Merafhe
Health, Joy Phumaphi
Labour and Home Affairs, Thebe Mogami
Lands and Housing, Jacob Nkate
Local Government, Margaret Nasha
Mineral Resources, Energy and Water Affairs, Boometswe Mokgothu
Presidential Affairs and Public Administration, Daniel Kwelaobe
Trade, Industry, Tourism and Wildlife, Pelonomi Venson
Works, Transport and Communications, Tebelelo Seretse

BOTSWANA HIGH COMMISSION
6 Stratford Place, London W1C 1AY
Tel: 020-7499 0031
High Commissioner, HE Roy Warren Blackbeard, apptd 1998

BRITISH HIGH COMMISSION
Private Bag 0023, Gaborone
Tel: (00 267) 352841/2/3
Email: british@britishcouncil.org.bw
High Commissioner, HE David Merry, apptd 1998

BRITISH COUNCIL DIRECTOR, David Knox, British High Commission Building, Queen's Road, The Mall, PO Box 439, Gaborone;
Email: general.enquiries@british council.org.bw

DEFENCE
The Army has 44 armoured personnel carriers. The Air Wing has 30 combat aircraft.
MILITARY EXPENDITURE – 5.5 per cent of GDP (2000)
MILITARY PERSONNEL – 9,000: Army 8,500, Air Wing 500; Paramilitaries 1,000

ECONOMY
Agriculture is predominantly pastoral and accounts for around 3 per cent of GDP. The national herd is around 2.2 million cattle and one million sheep and goats. Cattle rearing accounts for about 85 per cent of agricultural output.

Mineral extraction and processing is now the major source of income following the opening of large mines for diamonds, copper and nickel. Botswana is one of the largest producers of diamonds in the world, with diamonds accounting for 74 per cent of export revenue. Large deposits of coal have been discovered and are now being mined.

Service industries account for nearly half of GDP. Tourism is the third largest industry, generating about 7 per cent of GDP. Main imports are motor vehicles, machinery and electrical equipment and foodstuffs; main exports are diamonds, motor vehicles, cupro-nickel and beef.

In 1998 Botswana had a trade surplus of US$77 million and a current account surplus of US$170 million. Imports totalled US$2,387 million and exports US$1,948 million.
GNP – US$5,280 million (2000); US$3,240 per capita (1999)
GDP – US$4,819 million (1998); US$3,625 per capita (1999)

ANNUAL AVERAGE GROWTH OF GDP – 7.7 per cent (2000)
INFLATION RATE – 8.6 per cent (2000)
UNEMPLOYMENT – 21.5 per cent (1995)
TOTAL EXTERNAL DEBT – US$462 million (1999)

Trade with UK	2000	2001
Imports from UK	£19,944,000	£24,248,000
Exports to UK	353,250,000	1,076,865,000

COMMUNICATIONS

The railway from Cape Town to Zimbabwe passes through eastern Botswana. The main roads are the north-south road, which closely follows the railway, and the road running east-west that links Francistown and Maun. Air services are provided on a scheduled basis between the main towns.

EDUCATION

There are 657 primary schools, 163 community junior secondary schools and 23 government and government-aided senior secondary schools.
ILLITERACY RATE – 21.1 per cent (2002)
ENROLMENT (percentage of age group) – primary 100 per cent (1997); secondary 65 per cent (1997); tertiary 6 per cent (1997)

BRAZIL
República Federativa do Brasil – Federative Republic of Brazil

AREA – 3,300,171 sq. miles (8,547,403 sq. km).
  Neighbours: Guyana, Suriname, French Guiana, Colombia and Venezuela (north), Peru, Bolivia, Paraguay and Argentina (west), Uruguay (south)
POPULATION – 159,884,000 (2000 census). Portuguese is the national language. Spanish and English are widely spoken
CAPITAL – Brasília (population, 1,737,813, 2000 census)
MAJOR CITIES – Belo Horizonte (2,232,747);
  Ψ Fortaleza (2,138,234); Ψ Porto Alegre (1,360,033);
  Ψ Recife (1,421,993); Ψ Rio de Janeiro (5,851,914), the former capital; Ψ Salvador (2,440,828); São Paulo (10,405,867)
CURRENCY – Real of 100 centavos
NATIONAL ANTHEM – Ouviram Do Ipiranga Às Margens Plácidas (From Peaceful Ypiranga's Banks)
NATIONAL DAY – 7 September (Independence Day)
NATIONAL FLAG – Green with a yellow lozenge containing a blue sphere studded with white stars, and crossed by a white band with the motto Ordem e Progresso
LIFE EXPECTANCY (years) – male 64.7; female 72.6
POPULATION GROWTH RATE – 1.5 per cent (1999)
POPULATION DENSITY – 19 per sq. km (1999)

The north is mainly wide, low-lying, forest-clad plains. The central areas are principally plateau land and the east and south are traversed by successive mountain ranges interspersed with fertile valleys. The principal ranges are the Serra do Mar, the Serra da Mantiqueira and the Serra do Espinhaco along the east coast. The River Amazon flows from the Peruvian Andes to the Atlantic.

HISTORY AND POLITICS

Brazil was discovered by the Portuguese navigator Pedro Álvares Cabral in 1500 and colonised by Portugal in the early 16th century. In 1822 it became independent under Dom Pedro I, son of King João VI of Portugal, who had been forced to flee to Brazil during the Napoleonic Wars.

In 1889, Dom Pedro II was dethroned and a republic was proclaimed. In 1985 Brazil returned to democratic rule after two decades of military government.

Fernando Henrique Cardoso of the Social Democratic Party won the presidential election of October 1994 and was returned for a second term on 4 October 1998. In simultaneous legislative elections, the five-party coalition which supported him won 377 seats in the Chamber of Deputies and 21 state governorships. The coalition ceased to be the largest block in the legislature when the Brazilian Labour Party left the coalition in August 2000 but remained in power.

Legislative and presidential elections were due in October 2002.

POLITICAL SYSTEM

The Federative Republic of Brazil is composed of the federal district and 26 states. Under the 1988 constitution the president, who heads the executive, is directly elected for a four-year term; in June 1997 the constitution was amended to allow the president to stand for a second term. The Congress consists of an 81-member Senate (three senators per state elected for an eight-year term) and a 513-member Chamber of Deputies which is elected every four years; the number of deputies per state depends upon the state's population. Each state has a Governor, and a Legislative Assembly with a four-year term.

FEDERAL STRUCTURE

Federal Unit	Area (sq. km)	Population (2000 census)	Capital
Central west		11,616,745	
Distrito Federal	5,822	2,043,169	Brasília
Goiás	341,290	4,996,439	Goiânia
Mato Grosso	906,807	2,502,260	Cuiabá
Mato Grosso do Sul	358,159	2,074,877	Campo Grande
North		12,841,299	
Acre	153,150	557,226	Rio Branco
Amapá	143,454	423,581	Macapá
Amazonas	1,577,820	2,813,085	Manaus
Pará	1,253,165	6,189,550	Belém
Rondônia	238,513	1,377,792	Pôrto Velho
Roraima	225,116	324,152	Boa Vista
Tocantins	278,421	1,155,913	Palmas
North-east		47,693,254	
Alagoas	27,933	2,819,172	Maceió
Bahia	567,295	13,066,910	Salvador
Ceará	146,348	7,418,476	Fortaleza
Maranhão	333,366	5,642,960	São Luís
Paraíba	56,585	3,439,344	João Pessoa
Pernambuco	98,938	7,911,937	Recife
Piauí	252,378	2,841,202	Teresina
Rio Grande do Norte	53,307	2,771,538	Natal
Sergipe	22,050	1,781,714	Aracajú
South		25,089,783	
Paraná	199,709	9,558,454	Curitiba
Rio Grande do Sul	282,062	10,181,749	Pôrto Alegre
Santa Catarina	95,443	5,349,580	Florianópolis
South-east		72,297,351	
Espírito Santo	46,184	3,094,390	Vitória
Minas Gerais	588,384	17,866,402	Belo Horizonte
Rio de Janeiro	43,910	14,367,083	Rio de Janeiro
São Paulo	248,809	36,969,476	São Paulo

HEAD OF STATE

President, Fernando Henrique Cardoso, *sworn in* 1 January 1995
Vice-President, Marco Maciel

CABINET *as at July 2002*

Agrarian Development, José Abrão
Agriculture, Livestock and Supply, Marcus Vinícius Pratini de Moraes
Civilian Household of the Presidency, Pedro Parente
Communications, Juarez Martinho Quadros do Nascimento
Culture, Francisco Corrêa Weffort
Defence, Geraldo Magela da Cruz Quintão
Development, Industry and Foreign Trade, Sérgio Amaral
Education, Paulo Renato Souza
Energy and Mines, Francisco Gomide
Environment, José Carlos Carvalho
External Relations, Celso Lafer
Finance, Pedro Sampaio Malan
Foreign Affairs, Celso Lafer
Health, Barjas Negri
Justice, Miguel Reale
Labour and Employment, Paulo Jobim Filho
Military Household of the Presidency, Gen. Alberto Cardoso
National Integration, Mary Dayse Kinzo
Planning, Budget and Management, Gulherme Gomes Dias
Presidential Spokesman, Georges Lamazière
Science and Technology, Ronaldo Mota Sardenberg
Secretariat of the Presidency, Arthur Virgilio
Social Security and Welfare, José Cechin
Sport and Tourism, Caio Luiz de Carvalho
Transport, Joyão Henrique de Almeida Sousa

BRAZILIAN EMBASSY
32 Green Street, London W1Y 4AT
Tel: 020-7499 0877
Ambassador Extraordinary and Plenipotentiary, HE Celso Luiz Nunes Amorim, apptd 2001
Military Attachés, Col. Eduardo da Cunha (*Army*), Capt. Paulo Cezar de Quadros Kuster (*Defence and Navy*), Gp. Capt. Antonio Biasus (*Air Force*)
Counsellor (Commercial Affairs), Eduardo Botelho Barbosa
There is also a Brazilian Consulate-General in London and honorary consular offices at Cardiff and Glasgow.

BRITISH EMBASSY
Setor de Embaixadas Sul, Quadra 801, Conjunto K, CEP 70.408–900, Brasília DF
Tel: (00 55) (61) 225 2710
Email: britemb@zaz.com.br
Ambassador Extraordinary and Plenipotentiary, HE Roger Bone, KCMG, apptd 1999
Deputy Head of Mission, Consul-General, A. Soper
Defence Attaché, Col. J. M. Bowles, MBE
There are British Consulates-General at Rio de Janeiro and São Paulo.

BRITISH COUNCIL DIRECTOR, Dave Cooke, Edificio Centro Empresarial Varig, SCN Quadra 04, Bloco B, Torre Oeste Conjunto 202, 70710-926- Brasília DF; Email: brasilia@britishcouncil.org.br. Regional directors in Curitiba, Recife, Rio de Janeiro and São Paulo

DEFENCE

The Army has 178 main battle tanks, 803 armoured personnel carriers and 70 helicopters. The Navy has bases

at Rio de Janeiro, Salvador, Recife, Belém, Florianópolis and Ladario. It is equipped with four submarines, one aircraft carrier, 14 frigates and 50 patrol and coastal vessels. Naval aviation has 24 combat aircraft and 54 armed helicopters; the Marines have 33 armoured personnel carriers. The Air Force has 281 combat aircraft and 29 armed helicopters.

MILITARY EXPENDITURE – 2.8 per cent of GDP (2000)
MILITARY PERSONNEL – 287,600: Army 189,000, Navy 48,600, Air Force 50,000; Paramilitaries 385,600
CONSCRIPTION DURATION – 12 months (can be extended to 18)

ECONOMY

There are large mineral deposits including iron ore (hematite), manganese, bauxite, beryllium, chrome, nickel, tungsten, cassiterite, lead, gold, monazite (containing rare earths and thorium) and zirconium. Diamonds and precious and semi-precious stones are also found. Brazil is the world's largest producer of coffee; the other main agricultural products are cassava, maize, soya, rice, wheat, sugar, potatoes, cotton, cocoa, tobacco and peanuts. Tourism is a growing industry; Brazil attracted 5.1 million visitors in 2000.

In 1994 the government introduced the Real Plan. The plan introduced a new currency, the real, doubled interest rates, increased taxes and cut budgets, and succeeded in bringing inflation under control and stabilising the economy.

GNP – US$606,775 million (2000); US$4,350 per capita (1999)
GDP – US$775,022 million (1998); US$3,525 per capita (1999)
ANNUAL AVERAGE GROWTH OF GDP – 0.8 per cent (1999)
INFLATION RATE – 7.0 per cent (2000)
UNEMPLOYMENT – 9.0 per cent (1998)
TOTAL EXTERNAL DEBT – US$244,673 million (1999)

TRADE

Principal imports are machinery, fuel and lubricants, mineral products, transport equipment and chemicals. Principal exports are industrial goods, coffee, iron ore and soya.

In 2000 Brazil had a trade deficit of US$696 million and a current account deficit of US$24,632 million. Imports totalled US$58,532 million and exports US$55,086.

Trade with UK	2000	2001
Imports from UK	£774,953,000	£813,401,000
Exports to UK	1,158,389,000	1,327,651,000

COMMUNICATIONS

There are 1,670,148 km of highways, of which 161,503 km are paved, and the route-length of railways is 30,129 km, of which 2,150 km are electrified. There are ten international airports and internal air services are highly developed. There are some 50,000 km of navigable inland waterways. Rio de Janeiro and Santos are the two leading ports. A 3,415 km gas pipeline running from Santa Cruz, Bolivia, to São Paolo, was opened in 2000.

EDUCATION

The education system includes both public and private institutions. Public education is free at all levels.
ILLITERACY RATE – 14.0 per cent (2002)
ENROLMENT (percentage of age group) – primary 100 per cent (1997); secondary 62 per cent (1997); tertiary 15 per cent (1997)

BRUNEI
Negara Brunei Darussalam - State of Brunei Darussalam

AREA – 2,226 sq. miles (5,765 sq. km). Neighbour: Malaysia

POPULATION – 307,000: 66.9 per cent Malay, 15.2 per cent Chinese, 5.9 per cent indigenous races and 12 per cent European, Indian and other races. The majority are Sunni Muslims. The official language is Malay; English and dialects of Chinese are also spoken

CAPITAL – Bandar Seri Begawan (population, 49,902, 1994 estimate)

CURRENCY – Brunei dollar (B$) of 100 sen (fully interchangeable with Singapore currency)

NATIONAL ANTHEM – Allah Peliharakan Sultan (God Bless His Majesty)

NATIONAL DAY – 23 February

NATIONAL FLAG – Yellow with diagonal stripes of white over black and the arms in red all over the centre

LIFE EXPECTANCY (years) – male 74.2; female 78.9

POPULATION GROWTH RATE – 2.8 per cent (1999)

POPULATION DENSITY – 57 per sq. km (1999)

ILLITERACY RATE – 8.5 per cent (2002)

ENROLMENT (percentage of age group) – primary 91 per cent (1994); secondary 68 per cent (1994); tertiary 6.6 per cent (1996)

Brunei is situated on the north-west coast of the island of Borneo. It has a humid tropical climate.

HISTORY AND POLITICS

Formerly a powerful Muslim sultanate, Brunei was reduced to its present size by the mid-19th century and became a British Protectorate in 1888. In 1959 the Sultan promulgated the first written constitution and on 1 January 1984 Brunei resumed full independence from Britain.

POLITICAL SYSTEM

Supreme executive authority rests with the Sultan, who presides over and is advised by the Privy Council, the Religious Council and the Council of Ministers. The Sultan effectively rules by decree as a state of emergency has been in effect since a revolt in 1962; there are no political parties and no elections.

HEAD OF STATE

HM The Sultan of Brunei, HM Sultan Haji Hassanal Bolkiah Mu'izzaddin Waddaullah, Sultan and Yang Di-Pertuan, GCB, *acceded* 1967, *crowned* 1 August 1968
Crown Prince, Prince Al-Muhtadee Billah

COUNCIL OF MINISTERS *as at July 2002*

Prime Minister, Defence, Finance, HM The Sultan
Communications, Pehin Dato Zakaria
Development, Dato Haji Ahmad
Education, Pehin Dato Haji Abdul Aziz
Foreign Affairs, Prince Mohamed Bolkiah
Home Affairs, Special Adviser in the Prime Minister's Office, Pehin Dato Haji Isa Utama
Industry and Primary Resources, Pehin Dato Haji Abdul Rahman
Religious Affairs, Pehin Dato Haji Mohammad Zain
Youth, Sports and Culture, Pehin Dato Haji Awang Hussein

BRUNEI DARUSSALAM HIGH COMMISSION
19–20 Belgrave Square, London SW1X 8PG
Tel: 020-7581 0521
High Commissioner, HE Pengiran Haji Yunus, apptd 2001

BRITISH HIGH COMMISSION
PO Box 2197, Bandar Seri Begawan 8674
Email: brithc@brunet.bn
Tel: (00 673) (2) 222231
High Commissioner, Andrew Caie, apptd 2002

BRITISH COUNCIL DIRECTOR, Amanda Griffiths, Level 2, Block D, Yayasan Sultan Hj Hassanal Bolkia JI Pretty, PO Box 3049, Bandar Seri Begawan BS8675. Email: all.enquiries@bn.britishcouncil.org

DEFENCE

The Army has 39 armoured personnel carriers. The Navy, based in Muara, has six patrol and coastal vessels. The Air Force has five armed helicopters.

MILITARY EXPENDITURE – 5.8 per cent of GDP (2000)

MILITARY PERSONNEL – 5,900: Army 3,900, Navy 900, Air Force 1,100; Paramilitaries 3,750

ECONOMY

The economy is based on the production of oil and natural gas, which accounted for about 36 per cent of GDP in 1996 and 90 per cent of exports. Royalties and taxes from these operations form the bulk of government revenue and have enabled the construction of free health, education and welfare services.

The country has eight hospitals, 350 schools and one university. Royal Brunei Airlines operates scheduled flights to the UK, Australia and throughout the Far East. Radio Television Brunei broadcasts one television and three radio channels from the capital.

In 1998 Brunei produced 7,800,000 tonnes of crude petroleum and 10,700 million cubic metres of natural gas. In 1994 imports totalled US$1,634 million and exports US$2,215 million.

GNP – US$7,754 million (1998); US$14,240 per capita (1994)

GDP – US$4,323 million (1998); US$15,055 per capita (1999)

ANNUAL AVERAGE GROWTH OF GDP – 1.0 per cent (1998)

Trade with UK	2000	2001
Imports from UK	£97,206,000	£59,666,000
Exports to UK	102,256,000	34,090,000

COMMUNICATIONS

There are two main ports, at Muara and Kuala Belait, and an international airport at Bandar Seri Begawan.

BULGARIA
Republika Bălgarija – Republic of Bulgaria

AREA – 42,823 sq. miles (110,912 sq. km). Neighbours: Romania (north), Serbia and the Former Yugoslav Republic of Macedonia (west), Greece and Turkey (south)

POPULATION – 8,306,000 (1997 estimate): 85.7 per cent Bulgarian, 9.4 per cent Turkish, 3.7 per cent Roma, 1.2 per cent others. The language is Bulgarian, a Southern Slavonic tongue closely allied to Serbo-Croat and Russian with local admixtures of modern Greek, Albanian and Turkish words. The alphabet is

Cyrillic. The predominant religion is the Bulgarian Orthodox Church (85.7 per cent of the population); Islam is the second largest religion (13.1 per cent).

CAPITAL – Sofia (population, 1,192,735, 1997 estimate)
MAJOR CITIES – Ψ Burgas (212,369); Plovdiv (340,142); Ψ Varna (305,516), 1997 estimates
CURRENCY – Lev of 100 stotinki
NATIONAL ANTHEM – Gorda Stara Planina (Proud And Ancient Mountains)
NATIONAL DAY – 3 March
NATIONAL FLAG – Three horizontal bands, white, green, red
LIFE EXPECTANCY (years) – male 67.1; female 74.8
POPULATION GROWTH RATE – 0.6 per cent (1999)
POPULATION DENSITY – 74 per sq. km (1999)
URBAN POPULATION – 67.7 per cent (1994)

HISTORY AND POLITICS

A principality of Bulgaria was created by the Treaty of Berlin in 1878, and in 1908 the country was declared an independent kingdom. A coup d'état in September 1944 gave power to the Fatherland Front, a coalition of Communists, Agrarians and Social Democrats. In August 1945, the main body of Agrarians and Social Democrats left the government. A referendum in September 1946 led to the abolition of the monarchy and the establishment of a republic.

The post-war period was dominated by the Communist Party (BCP), led by Todor Zhivkov. In January 1990 the National Assembly voted to abolish the BCP's constitutional guarantee of power and establish a multiparty democracy.

In November 2001 the Bulgarian Socialist Party's (BSP) candidate, Georgi Parvanov, became president. The general election held on 17 June 2001 was won by the National Movement for Simeon II, a movement founded in April 2001 by the former king, which won 43.74 per cent of the vote and 120 of the 240 seats in the legislature.

POLITICAL SYSTEM

A new constitution was adopted in 1991. It provides for a directly-elected president who serves for no more than two five-year terms. The chief executive is the prime minister, who is appointed by the president, and is usually the leader of the largest party in the legislature. There is a unicameral National Assembly of 240 members who are directly elected by proportional representation for four-year terms.

HEAD OF STATE

President, Georgi Parvanov (BSP), *elected* 2002 , *elected* 18 November 2001, *took office* 19 January 2002
Vice President, Angel Marin (BSP)

COUNCIL OF MINISTERS *as at July 2002*

Prime Minister, Simeon Saxecoburggotski,
Deputy PM, Economy, Nikolay Vassilev
Deputy PM, Labour and Social Policy, Lydia Shouleva
Deputy PM, Regional Development and Public Works, Kostadin Paskalev
Agriculture and Forestry, Mekhmed Dikme
Civil Service, Dimitar Kalchev
Culture, Bujidar Abrashev
Defence, Nikolay Svinarov
Education and Science, Vladimir Atanassov
Energy and Energy Resources, Milko Kovachev
Environment and Water, Dolores Arsenova
European Affairs, Meglena Kuneva

Finance, Milen Velchev
Foreign Affairs, Solomon Passy
Health, Bojidar Finkov
Internal Affairs, Georgi Petkanov
Justice, Anton Stankov
Transport and Communications, Plamen Petrov
Without Portfolio, Nezhdet Mollor

EMBASSY OF THE REPUBLIC OF BULGARIA
186–188 Queen's Gate, London SW7 5HL
Tel: 020-7584 9400/9433
Ambassador Extraordinary and Plenipotentiary, HE Valentin Dobrev, apptd 1998
First Secretary (Commercial/Economic Affairs), Martin Dimitrov

BRITISH EMBASSY
38 Boulevard Vassil Levski, Sofia
Tel: (00 359) (2) 2980 1220
Email: britembsof@mbox.cit.bg
Ambassador Extraordinary and Plenipotentiary, HE Ian Soutar, apptd 2001

BRITISH COUNCIL DIRECTOR, Kevin Lewis, 7 Tulovo Street, BG-1504, Sofia.
Email: bc.sofia@britishcouncil.bg

DEFENCE

The Army has 1,475 main battle tanks, 214 armoured infantry fighting vehicles and 1,750 armoured personnel carriers. The Navy has one submarine, one frigate, 23 patrol and coastal vessels, and nine armed helicopters. The Air Force has 181 combat aircraft and 43 armed helicopters.

MILITARY EXPENDITURE – 2.8 per cent of GDP (2000)
MILITARY PERSONNEL – 77,260: Army 42,400, Navy 5,260, Air Force 18,300; Paramilitaries 34,000
CONSCRIPTION DURATION – Nine months

ECONOMY

The principal crops are wheat, maize, beet, tomatoes, tobacco, oleaginous seeds, fruit, vegetables and cotton. Around 24 per cent of the population is engaged in agriculture, which accounted for 19 per cent of GDP in 1998. Cadmium, coal, copper, pig iron, kaolin, lead, silver and zinc are produced.

The government adopted a radical reform package in 1997 in order to stimulate the economy and bring inflation under control. The package included pegging the lev to the Deutsche Mark.

GNP – US$12,355 million (2000); US$1,410 per capita (1999)
GDP – US$12,257 million (1998); US$1,543 per capita (1999)
ANNUAL AVERAGE GROWTH OF GDP – 3.5 per cent (1998)
INFLATION RATE – 10.3 per cent (2000)
UNEMPLOYMENT – 14.4 per cent (1997)
TOTAL EXTERNAL DEBT – US$9,872 million (1999)

TRADE

The principal imports are fuels, industrial equipment, chemicals, textiles and clothing, and foodstuffs and beverages. The principal exports are textiles and clothing, iron and steel products, foodstuffs, beverages, industrial equipment, oil derivatives and non-ferrous metals.

In 1993 Bulgaria signed an Association Agreement with the EU, and EU duties on many Bulgarian industrial

goods were abolished by 1995 and levies on agricultural goods significantly lowered.

In 2000 Bulgaria had a trade deficit of US$1,175 million and a current account deficit of US$701 million. Imports totalled US$6,492 million and exports US$4,810 million. The principal trading partners are Russia, Germany and Italy.

Trade with UK	2000	2001
Imports from UK	£86,313,000	£121,130,000
Exports to UK	88,215,000	100,706,000

EDUCATION

Education is free and compulsory for children from six to 16 years inclusive. There are three universities (at Sofia, Plovdiv and Veliko Turnovo), an American University and 21 higher education establishments.
ILLITERACY RATE – 1.4 per cent (2002)
ENROLMENT (percentage of age group) – primary 99 per cent (1997); secondary 77 per cent (1997); tertiary 41.2 per cent (1996)

BURKINA FASO
République Démocratique du Burkina Faso – Democratic Republic of Burkina Faso

---

AREA – 105,792 sq. miles (274,000 sq. km). Neighbours: Mali (west), Niger and Benin (east), Togo, Ghana and Côte d'Ivoire (south)
POPULATION – 11,087,000. The official language is French. Mossi, More, Dioula and Gourmantché are indigenous languages
CAPITAL – Ouagadougou (population, 1,000,000 2000 estimate)
MAJOR CITIES – Bobo-Dioulasso (228,668); Koudougou (30,000)
CURRENCY – Franc CFA of 100 centimes
NATIONAL ANTHEM – Ditanyé (Hymn of Victory)
NATIONAL DAY – 11 December
NATIONAL FLAG – Equal bands of red over green, with a yellow star in centre
LIFE EXPECTANCY (years) – male 47.0; female 49.0
POPULATION GROWTH RATE – 3.0 per cent (1997)
POPULATION DENSITY – 42 per sq. km (1999)
URBAN POPULATION – 15.0 per cent (1995)
MILITARY EXPENDITURE – 1.8 per cent of GDP (2000)
MILITARY PERSONNEL – 10,000: Army 5,600, Air Force 200, Paramilitaries 4,200
ILLITERACY RATE – 74.3 per cent (2002)
ENROLMENT (percentage of age group) – primary 40 per cent (1997); tertiary 1 per cent (1997)
Burkina Faso (formerly Upper Volta) is an inland savannah state in West Africa. The largest tribe is the Mossi whose king, the Moro Naba, still wields a certain moral influence.

HISTORY AND POLITICS

Burkina Faso was annexed by France in 1896 and between 1932 and 1947 was administered as part of the Colony of the Ivory Coast. It decided on 11 December 1958 to remain an autonomous republic within the French Community; full independence outside the Community was proclaimed on 5 August 1960.

Following a number of military coups, Capt. Blaise Compaoré seized power in 1987. A new constitution was adopted in 1991. A general election was held in May 2002 and won by the Congress for Democracy and Progress group (CDP); since October 1999 the government has included members of the Burkina Greens and the

Movement for Tolerance and Progress. Presidential elections were held in November 1998 and won by Compaoré, the CDP candidate, in the face of a boycott by the opposition parties.

HEAD OF STATE
President, Capt. Blaise Compaoré, *assumed office* October 1987, *elected* December 1991, *re-elected* November 1998

COUNCIL OF MINISTERS *as at July 2002*
Prime Minister, Paramanga Ernest Yonli
Agriculture, and Water Resources, Salif Diallo
Animal Resources, Alphonse Bonou
Basic Education and Literacy, Mathieu Ouédraogo
Civil Service and Administrative Reform, Lassane Savadogo
Culture and Arts, Mahmadou Ouédrago
Defence, Kouamé Lougué
Economy and Development, Seydou Bouda
Employment, Labour and Youth, Alain Ludovic Tou
Energy, Mines and Quarries, Abdoulayé Abdul Kader Cissé
Environment, Dakar Djibrill
Finance and Budget, Jean-Baptiste Marie Compaoré
Foreign Affairs and Regional Co-operation, Youssouf Ouédraogo
Health, Bedouma Alain Yoda
Human Rights Promotion, Monique Ilbondo
Information, Raymond Edouard Ouédraogo
Infrastructure, Housing and Transport, Hyppolite Lingani
Justice, Keeper of the Seals and Promotion of Human Rights, Boureima Badini
Post and Telecommunications, Justin Tièba Thombiano
Regional Administration and Decentralisation, Moumouni Fabré
Relations with Parliament, Adama Fofana
Secondary and Higher Education, Scientific Research, Laya Sawadogo
Security, Djibril Yipéné Bassole
Social Affairs and National Solidarity, Mariam Lamizana
Sports and Leisure, Tioundoum Sessouma
Women's Promotion, Gisèle Guigma

EMBASSY OF THE REPUBLIC OF BURKINA FASO
16 Place Guy d'Arezzo, 1180 Brussels, Belgium
Tel: (00 32) (2) 345 9912
Ambassador Extraordinary and Plenipotentiary, Kadré Désiré Ouédraogo, apptd 2001

HONORARY CONSULATE, 5 Cinnamon Row, Plantation Wharf, London SW11 3TW. Tel: 020-7738 1800.
Honorary Consul, S. G. Singer

BRITISH AMBASSADOR, HE Jean Francis Gordon, resident at Abidjan, Côte d'Ivoire

ECONOMY

The principal industry is cattle and sheep rearing. Agriculture employs over 90 per cent of the workforce and contributes 33 per cent of GDP. The chief exports are cotton, livestock and animal feed, and gold. The chief imports are capital goods, foodstuffs and fuel oils.

In 2000 imports totalled US$491 million and exports US$166 million.
GNP – US$2,640 million (2000); US$240 per capita (1999)
GDP – US$2,495 million (1998); US$234 per capita (1999)
ANNUAL AVERAGE GROWTH OF GDP – 2.2 per cent

(2000)

INFLATION RATE – 0.3 per cent (2000)
TOTAL EXTERNAL DEBT – US$1,518 million (1999)

Trade with UK	2000	2001
Imports from UK	£5,702,000	£7,631,000
Exports to UK	1,364,000	3,165,000

COMMUNICATIONS

There are 12,349 km of roads, of which 1,988 km are bituminised, and 617 km of railway track in operation. There are two main airports, Ouagadougou and Bobo-Dioulasso.

BURUNDI
République du Burundi – Republic of Burundi

AREA – 10,747 sq. miles (27,834 sq. km). Neighbours: Rwanda (north), Tanzania (east and south), Democratic Republic of Congo (west)
POPULATION – 6,194,000: 83 per cent Hutu, 15 per cent Tutsi. The official languages are Kirundi, a Bantu language, and French. Kiswahili is also used
CAPITAL – Bujumbura (formerly Usumbura) (population, 235,440, 1990)
MAJOR CITIES – Kitega (18,000)
CURRENCY – Burundi franc of 100 centimes
NATIONAL DAY – 1 July
NATIONAL FLAG – Divided diagonally by a white saltire into red and green triangles; on a white disc in the centre three red six-pointed stars edged in green
NATIONAL ANTHEM – Burundi Bwacu (Dear Burundi)
LIFE EXPECTANCY (years) – male 39.8; female 41.4
POPULATION GROWTH RATE – 2.0 per cent (1999)
POPULATION DENSITY – 233 per sq. km (1999)
MILITARY EXPENDITURE – 5.6 per cent of GDP (2000)
MILITARY PERSONNEL – 45,500: Army 40,000; Paramilitaries 5,500
ILLITERACY RATE – 49.6 per cent (2002)
ENROLMENT (percentage of age group) – primary 51 per cent (1997); secondary 7 per cent (1997); tertiary 0.9 per cent (1995)

HISTORY AND POLITICS

Formerly a Belgian trusteeship under the United Nations, Burundi became independent as a constitutional monarchy on 1 July 1962. However, the monarchy was overthrown in 1966 and the country became a republic.

Although most of the population is Hutu, political and military power has traditionally rested with the Tutsi minority. Since the 1960s, Hutu attempts to overthrow Tutsi rule have resulted in ethnic massacres. The Tutsi-dominated army attempted a coup in 1993 in which President Melchior Ndadaye was killed. The government regained control in December but two months of inter-racial fighting left more than 50,000 dead and 500,000 refugees.

The Front for Democracy in Burundi (FRODEBU) and the National Unity and Progress Party (UPRONA) agreed to form a coalition government in 1994 with a Tutsi prime minister and Hutu president. However, the government was unable to halt attacks by the Tutsi-dominated army and Hutu militias on each other's communities. The fighting claimed 200,000 lives in 1993–5.

In July 1996 the army again seized power and installed Maj. Buyoya as president. Political parties were banned and the National Assembly was suspended until October 1996 when fewer than half its deputies attended. A multi-ethnic government of national unity was formed in

August 1996. More than 300,000 refugees remain in camps in Tanzania and the Democratic Republic of Congo. In April 2000, President Buyoya promised to dismantle the 'regroupment camps' into which over 800,000 Hutus had been placed to stabilise the security situation.

A transitional constitution, designed to provide for a political partnership between Hutus and Tutsis, came into being in June 1998 and a 117-member Transitional National Assembly was inaugurated in July 1998. An additional 53 members of the National Assembly were elected on 1 January 2002, in accordance with the Arusha peace deal.

A partial peace accord was formally signed in Nairobi on 20 September 2000 by President Buyoya, the Tutsi political parties and the moderate Hutu parties, but the two main Hutu rebel groups refused to sign the accord. On 18 April 2001 an attempted coup by Tutsi soldiers opposed to the peace agreement was ended peaceably. Clashes between the army and Hutu militias, and massacres of civilians have continued.

In July 2001, Burundi's 19 political parties agreed a peace accord at talks hosted by former South African president, Nelson Mandela. Under the agreement, provision was made for a three-year transitional government to be headed by President Buyoya, a Tutsi, with a Hutu as vice-president – the two switching roles midway through the three-year term.

HEAD OF STATE

President, Maj. Pierre Buyoya, *appointed* 25 July 1996, *sworn in* 11 June 1998
Vice-President, Domitien Ndayizeye

COUNCIL OF MINISTERS *as at July 2002*

Agriculture and Livestock, Pierre Ndikumagenge
Civil Service, Festus Ntanyungu
Commerce and Industry, Charles Karikurubu
Communications and Government Spokesman, Albert Mbonerane
Community Development, Casimir Ngendanganya
Defence, Maj.-Gen. Cyrille Ndayirukiye
Development Planning and Reconstruction, André Nkundikije
Energy and Mines, Mathias Hitimana
External Relations and Co-operation, Thérence Sinunguruza
Finance, Edouard Kadigiri
Good Governance and Privatisation, Didace Kiganahe
Handicrafts, Vocational Training and Adult Literacy, Godefroy Hakizimana
Institutional Reforms, Human Rights and Relations with Parliament, Alphonse Barancira
Internal Affairs and Public Security, Salvator Ntihabose
Justice, Keeper of the Seals, Fulgence Dwima-Bakana
Labour and Social Security, Dismas Nditabiriye
Minister in the Prime Minister's Office in charge of AIDS Control, Geneviève Sindabizera
Mobilisation for Peace and National Reconciliation, Luc Rukingama
National Education, Prosper Mpawenayo
Public Health, Jean Kamana
Public Works and Equipment, Balthazar Bigimana
Reintegration and Resettlement of Displaced Persons and Repatriates, Françoise Ngendahayo
Social Action and Women's Promotion, Marie Goreth Nduwimana

Territorial Development, Environment and Tourism,
Gaetan Nikobamye
Transport, Posts and Telecommunications, Severin
Ndikumugongo
Youth, Culture and Sports, Barnabé Muteragiranwa

EMBASSY OF THE REPUBLIC OF BURUNDI
46 Sq. Marie Louise, 1000 Brussels, Belgium
Tel: (00 32) (2) 2304535
Ambassador Extraordinary and Plenipotentiary, HE
Jonathas Niyungeko, apptd 1999

BRITISH AMBASSADOR, HE Susan Hogwood, apptd
2001, resident at Kigali, Rwanda

ECONOMY

The chief crops are coffee and tea, accounting for around
98 per cent of export earnings. Mineral, hide and skin
exports are also important. Agriculture accounted for 54
per cent of GDP and employed over 90 per cent of the
workforce in 1998.

In 1999 there was a trade deficit of US$42 million and
a current account deficit of US$27 million. In 2000
imports totalled US$148 million and exports US$49
million.

GNP – US$732 million (2000); US$120 per capita
(1999)
GDP – US$667 million (1998); US$128 per capita
(1999)
ANNUAL AVERAGE GROWTH OF GDP – 4.5 per cent
(1998)
INFLATION RATE – 24.3 per cent (2000)
TOTAL EXTERNAL DEBT – US$1,131 million (1999)

Trade with UK	2000	2001
Imports from UK	£1,968,000	2,205,000
Exports to UK	1,252,000	954,000

CAMBODIA
*Preăh Réachéanachâkr Kâmpuchéa - The Kingdom of
Cambodia*

AREA – 69,898 sq. miles (181,035 sq. km). Neighbours:
Laos (north), Thailand (north and west), Vietnam
(east)
POPULATION – 11,437,656 (1998 census). The official
language is Khmer. Chinese, Vietnamese and French
are also spoken
CAPITAL – ΨPhnom Penh (population, 832,000, 1998
census)
CURRENCY – Riel of 100 sen
NATIONAL ANTHEM – Nokoreach
NATIONAL DAY – 9 November (Independence Day)
NATIONAL FLAG – Three horizontal stripes of blue, red,
blue, with the blue of double width and containing a
representation of the temple of Angkor in white
LIFE EXPECTANCY (years) – male 53.6; female 58.6
POPULATION GROWTH RATE – 2.7 per cent (1999)
POPULATION DENSITY – 60 per sq. km (1999)
URBAN POPULATION – 14.4 per cent (1996)
ILLITERACY RATE – 30.8 per cent (2002)
ENROLMENT (percentage of age group) – primary 100
per cent (1997); tertiary 24 per cent (1997)

HISTORY AND POLITICS

Cambodia became a French protectorate in 1863 and was
granted independence within the French Union as an
Associate State in 1949. Full independence was
proclaimed in 1953, and Prince Norodom Sihanouk

became head of state. In 1970 Prince Sihanouk was
deposed and a Khmer Republic was declared.

In 1975, Phnom Penh fell to the North Vietnamese-
backed Khmer Rouge. During Khmer Rouge rule
hundreds of thousands of Cambodians fled into exile and
an estimated two million were killed.

In 1978, Vietnamese troops invaded Cambodia and the
state was renamed. The People's Republic of Kampuchea
(PRK); in 1989 it became the State of Cambodia (SOC).
Following the Vietnamese withdrawal in 1989, the
resistance forces regained ground.

In September 1990, the government and the resistance
forces established a Supreme National Council and peace
agreements were signed in October 1991. In March 1992
the United Nations Transitional Authority for Cambodia
(UNTAC) assumed authority from the government in the
run-up to the multiparty elections, which were held in
May 1993. In September 1993 a new constitution was
adopted under which Cambodia became a pluralist
liberal democracy with a constitutional monarchy. Prince
Sihanouk was elected king and he appointed a new
government.

In November 1998 a coalition government was formed
with Hun Sen as prime minister and Prince Ranariddh as
chairman of the National Assembly.

INSURGENCIES

In July 1994 the Royal Government outlawed the Khmer
Rouge, which responded by declaring a provisional
government. Large numbers of Khmer Rouge defected to
the Royal Government. Khmer Rouge leader Pol Pot was
captured by a group of defectors in June 1997 and died in
captivity on 15 April 1998. The remaining 4,332 Khmer
Rouge soldiers surrendered on 9 February 1999.

On 15 January 2001 the Royal Government approved
legislation creating an international tribunal composed of
Cambodians and UN appointees to prosecute former
leaders of the Khmer Rouge regime for atrocities
committed during its rule.

POLITICAL SYSTEM

Legislative power is vested in the National Assembly,
which has 122 members elected for five-year terms, and
the Senate, which has 61 appointed members and was
formed on 25 March 1999, following an amendment to
the constitution by the National Assembly. Executive
power rests in the Royal Government, with the King
having the power only to make appointments and declare
a state of emergency, in consultation with the
government.

HEAD OF STATE

HM The King of Cambodia, Norodom Sihanouk, *elected
by the Council of the Throne* 24 September 1993
Chair of the National Assembly, Norodom Ranariddh

ROYAL GOVERNMENT OF CAMBODIA *as at July 2002*

Prime Minister, Hun Sen (CPP)
Deputy Prime Minister, Co-Minister of Interior, Sar
Kheng (CPP)
Deputy Prime Minister, Education, Youth and Sports, Tol
Loah (F)
*Agriculture, Forestry and Fishing, Personal Advisor to the
Prime Minister,* Chan Sarun (CCP)
Co-Minister of National Defence, Prince Sisowath
Sereiroat (F)
Commerce, Cham Prasit (CPP)
Culture and Fine Arts, Princess Norodom Bophadevi (F)
Environment, Mok Maret (CPP)

Foreign Affairs and International Co-operation, Hor Namhong (CPP)
Health, Hong Sun-huot (F)
Industry, Mines and Energy, Suy Sem (CPP)
Information and Press, Loe Laysreng (F)
Justice, Neav Sithong (F)
Landscaping, Urbanism and Construction, Im Chhunlim (CPP)
Planning, Chhay Than (CPP)
Post and Telecommunications, So Khun (CPP)
Public Works and Transport, Khi Tanglim (F)
Relations with National Assembly and Inspection, Khun Hang (F)
Religious Affairs, Chea Savoeun (F)
Rural Development, Li Thuch (F)
Social Affairs, Labour, Vocational Training and Youth Rehabilitation, It Sam-heng (CPP)
State Minister, Co-Minister of Interior, Yu Hokkri (F)
State Minister, Co-Minister of National Defence, Gen. Tie Banh (CPP)
State Minister, Economy and Finance, Keat Chon (CPP)
State Minister, Office of the Council of Ministers, Sok An (CPP)
State Ministers, Loe Laysreng (F); Hor Namhong (F)
Tourism, Veng Sereivut (F)
Water Resources, Lim Kean-hao (CPP)
Women's and Veterans' Affairs, Mu Sok-huo (F)

CPP Cambodian People's Party; F United National Front for an Independent, Neutral, Peaceful and Co-operative Cambodia (FUNCINPEC)

ROYAL EMBASSY OF CAMBODIA
4 rue Adolph Yvon, F-75116 Paris, France
Tel: (00 33) (1) 45 03 47 20
Ambassador Extraordinary and Plenipotentiary, HE Prak Sokhonn, apptd 1999

BRITISH EMBASSY
29 Street 75, Phnom Penh
Tel: (00 855) (23) 427124
Ambassador Extraordinary and Plenipotentiary, HE Stephen Bridges, apptd 2001

DEFENCE

The Army has 150 main battle tanks and 190 armoured personnel carriers. The Navy has 4 patrol and coastal vessels. The Air Force has 24 combat aircraft.
MILITARY EXPENDITURE – 6.1 per cent of GDP (2000)
MILITARY PERSONNEL – 140,000: Army 90,000, Navy 3,000, Air Force 2,000, Provincial Forces 45,000; Paramilitaries 67,000

ECONOMY

The economy is largely based on agriculture, fishing and forestry. Agriculture employs over 70 per cent of the workforce and produced 32 per cent of GDP in 2001. In addition to rice, which is the staple crop, the major products are rubber, livestock, maize, timber, pepper, palm sugar, fresh and dried fish, kapok, beans, soya and tobacco. Textiles, leather goods, furnishings, timber and rubber are the main exports; the main imports are cigarettes, gold, diesel and oil.

Under the Khmer Rouge, the urban population was forced to work on the land, and re-establish plantations producing such crops as cotton, rubber and bananas. Following the Vietnamese invasion of 1978 the towns were repopulated and factories, in particular textile mills, iron smelting works and cement works, were put back in production.

In 2000 there was a trade deficit of US$198 million and a current account deficit of US$19 million.

GNP – US$3,144 million (2000); US$260 per capita (1999)
GDP – US$2,736 million (1998); US$238 per capita (1999)
ANNUAL AVERAGE GROWTH OF GDP – 1.3 per cent (1998)
INFLATION RATE – 0.8 per cent (2000)
TOTAL EXTERNAL DEBT – US$2,262 million (1999)

Trade with UK	2000	2001
Imports from UK	£4,099,000	£3,309,000
Exports to UK	54,510,000	85,164,000

COMMUNICATIONS

The country has about 34,100 kilometres of roads, although most are now in a state of disrepair. There are two railways, one from Phnom Penh to the Thai border, the other from Phnom Penh to Kampot and Sihanoukville (Kompong Som). Phnom Penh is on a river capable of receiving ships of up to 2,500 tons all the year round. The deep water port at Sihanoukville (Kompong Som) on the Gulf of Thailand can receive ships of up to 10,000 tons. The port is linked to Phnom Penh by a modern highway.

CAMEROON
République du Cameroun – Republic of Cameroon

AREA – 183,569 sq. miles (475,442 sq. km). Neighbours: Nigeria (north and west), Chad and Central African Republic (east), Republic of Congo-Brazzaville, Gabon and Equatorial Guinea (south)
POPULATION – 13,937,000 French and English are both official languages and enjoy equal status
CAPITAL – Yaoundé (population, 653,670, 1986 estimate)
MAJOR CITIES – Ψ Douala (1,029,731) is the commercial centre
CURRENCY – Franc CFA of 100 centimes
NATIONAL ANTHEM – O Cameroun, Berceau De Nos Ancêtres (O Cameroon, Thou Cradle Of Our Forefathers)
NATIONAL DAY – 20 May
NATIONAL FLAG – Vertical stripes of green, red and yellow with single five-pointed yellow star in centre of red stripe
LIFE EXPECTANCY (years) – male 49.3; female 50.6
POPULATION GROWTH RATE – 2.5 per cent (1999)
POPULATION DENSITY – 31 per sq. km (1999)
MILITARY EXPENDITURE – 1.4 per cent of GDP (2000)
MILITARY PERSONNEL – 22,100: Army 11,500, Navy 1,300, Air Force 300; Paramilitaries 9,000
ILLITERACY RATE – 22.1 per cent (2002)
ENROLMENT (percentage of age group) – secondary 85 per cent (1997); tertiary 3.3 per cent (1990)

HISTORY AND POLITICS

The German colony of the Cameroons, established in 1884, was captured by British and French forces in 1916 and divided into the League of Nations-mandated territories (later UN trusteeships) of East (French) and West (British) Cameroon. On 1 January 1960 East Cameroon became independent as the Republic of Cameroon. This was joined on 1 October 1961 by the southern part of West Cameroon after a plebiscite held under United Nations auspices; the northern part joined Nigeria. Cameroon became a federal republic with

separate East and West Cameroon state governments. After a plebiscite held in 1972, Cameroon became a unitary republic and a one-party state.

After extensive unrest, multiparty elections were held in March 1992. The ruling People's Democratic Movement formed a coalition government with a small opposition party, the Movement for the Defence of the Republic.

A legislative election held on 30 June 2002 was dominated by the ruling Cameroon People's Democratic Movement (CPDM) which increased its majority. However, observers reported widespread fraud and members of the opposition party called for the election results to be annulled.

INTERNATIONAL RELATIONS

There have been armed clashes with Nigeria over the disputed Bakassi peninsula. The dispute is under consideration at the International Court of Justice.

POLITICAL SYSTEM

The president is directly elected for a seven-year term, and appoints the prime minister and Cabinet. The National Assembly comprises 180 members, directly elected for a five-year term. Under the 1995 constitutional amendments a Senate is to be created.

HEAD OF STATE

President and Commander-in-Chief of the Armed Forces, Paul Biya, *acceded* 6 November 1982, *elected* 14 January 1984, *re-elected* 24 April 1988, 10 October 1992, 12 October 1997

CABINET *as at July 2002*

Prime Minister, Peter Mafany Musonge
Agriculture, Zacharie Perevet
City Affairs, Claude Joseph Mbafou
Civil Service and Administrative Reform, René Ze Nguele
Communication, Jacques Famé Ndongo
Culture, Ferdinand Leopold Oyono
Delegate at the Presidency in charge of Defence, Laurent Esso
Economy and Finance, Michel Meva'a Meboutou
Employment, Labour and Social Causes, Pius Ondoua
Environment and Forests, Sylvester Naah Ondoua
Foreign Affairs, François-Xavier Goubeyou
Higher Education, Jean-Marie Atangana Mebara
Industrial and Commercial Development, Bello Bouba Maigari
Justice, Keeper of the Seals, Ali Amadou
Livestock, Fisheries and Animal Industries, Ajoudji Hamadjoda
Mines, Water Resources and Energy, Yves Mbelle
National Education, Joseph Owona
Post and Telecommunications, Maximin Koué Kongo
Public Health, Urbain Olanguena Awono
Public Investments and Regional Planning, Martin Okouda
Public Works, Jérome Etah
Scientific and Technical Research, Henri Hogbe Nlend
Secretary-General of the Presidency, Territorial Administration (acting), Marafa Hamiduo Yaya
Social Affairs, Marie Madeleine Fouda
Tourism, Pierre Hele
Town Planning and Housing, Boubakary Yerima Halilou
Transport, Christopher Nsalai
Women's Affairs, Catherine Bakang Mbock
Youth and Sports, Bidoung Mkpatt

HIGH COMMISSION FOR THE REPUBLIC OF CAMEROON

84 Holland Park, London W11 3SB
Tel: 020-7727 0771
Ambassador Extraordinary and Plenipotentiary, HE Samuel Libock-Mbei, apptd 1995

BRITISH HIGH COMMISSION

Avenue Winston Churchill, BP 547 Yaoundé
Tel: (00 237) 220545
High Commissioner, HE Peter Boon, MBE, apptd 1998

BRITISH COUNCIL DIRECTOR, June Rollinson, Avenue Charles de Gaulle, BP 818, Yaoundé.
Email: bc.yaounde@britishcouncil.cm

ECONOMY

Principal products are cocoa, coffee, bananas, cotton, timber, groundnuts, aluminium, rubber and palm products. Crude petroleum is also one of Cameroon's principal products.

France, Italy and other European Union states are Cameroon's main trading partners. In 1995 there was a trade surplus of US$627 million and a current account surplus of US$90 million. In 1999 exports totalled US$1,601 million and imports US$1,318 million.

GNP – US$8,564 million (2000); US$600 per capita (1999)
GDP – US$10,047 million (1998); US$686 per capita (1999)
ANNUAL AVERAGE GROWTH OF GDP – 5.2 per cent (1998)
INFLATION RATE – 5.3 per cent (1999)
TOTAL EXTERNAL DEBT – US$9,443 million (1999)

Trade with UK	2000	2001
Imports from UK	£23,534,000	£35,901,000
Exports to UK	47,364,000	40,397,000

CANADA

AREA – 3,849,674 sq. miles (9,970,610 sq. km).
Neighbours: USA (south), Alaska (USA) (west)
POPULATION – 30,871,957 (2001 estimate). The languages are English and French
CAPITAL – Ottawa (population, 1,010,498, 1997 estimate).
MAJOR CITIES – Calgary (885,130); Edmonton (899,466); Hamilton (663,587); Montréal (3,384,233); Québec (700,197); Toronto (4,511,966); Vancouver (1,927,998); Winnipeg (677,291), 1997 estimates
CURRENCY – Canadian dollar (C$) of 100 cents
NATIONAL ANTHEM – O Canada
NATIONAL DAY – 1 July (Canada Day)
NATIONAL FLAG – Red maple leaf with 11 points on white square, flanked by vertical red bars one-half the width of the square
LIFE EXPECTANCY (years) – male 76.2; female 81.8
POPULATION GROWTH RATE – 1.0 per cent (1999)
POPULATION DENSITY – 3 per sq. km (1999)
URBAN POPULATION – 76.7 per cent (1995)

Canada occupies the whole of the northern part of the North American continent, with the exception of Alaska. In eastern Canada, the southernmost point is Middle Island in Lake Erie. Canada has six main physiographic divisions: the Appalachian-Acadian region, the Canadian shield, which comprises more than half the country, the St Lawrence-Great Lakes lowland, the interior plains, the

Cordilleran region and the Arctic archipelago.

The climate of the eastern and central portions presents greater extremes than in corresponding latitudes in Europe, but in the south-western portion of the prairie region and the southern portions of the Pacific slope the climate is milder.

HISTORY AND POLITICS

Canada was originally discovered by Cabot in 1497 and the French took possession of the country in 1534. The first permanent settlement at Port Royal (now Annapolis), Nova Scotia, was founded in 1605, and Québec was founded in 1608. In 1759 Québec was captured by British forces under General Wolfe and in 1763 the whole territory of Canada became a possession of Great Britain by the Treaty of Paris 1763. Nova Scotia was ceded in 1713 by the Treaty of Utrecht, the provinces of New Brunswick and Prince Edward Island being subsequently formed out of it. British Columbia was formed into a Crown colony in 1858, having previously been a part of the Hudson Bay Territory, and was united to Vancouver Island in 1866.

The constitution of Canada has its source in the British North America Act of 1867 which formed a Dominion, under the name of Canada, of the four provinces of Ontario, Québec, New Brunswick and Nova Scotia. To this federation the other provinces and territories have subsequently been admitted: Manitoba and Northwest Territories (1870), British Columbia (1871), Prince Edward Island (1873), Yukon (1898), Alberta and Saskatchewan (1905) and Newfoundland (1949). In 1982, the constitution was patriated (severed from the British parliament) with the approval of all provinces except Québec. In 1985, the federal prime minister and the provincial premiers concluded the Meech Lake Accord which provided for Québec to be recognised as a distinct society within Canada. However, two provincial legislatures withheld approval and the accord did not come into force. In Québec, a referendum calling for sovereignty and a new political and economic partnership was defeated in October 1995. In September 1997 Québec was recognised as having a 'unique character' by leaders of the other provinces and territories. A new territory, Nunavut, which means 'our land' in the Inuit language of Inuktitut, was created on 1 April 1999 by partitioning the Northwest Territories.

In the federal election on 27 November 2000 the Liberal Party won a third consecutive term of office. The state of parties in the House of Commons following the election was Liberals 172, Canadian Alliance 66, Bloc Québécois 38, New Democrats 13, and Progressive Conservatives 12.

POLITICAL SYSTEM

Executive power is vested in a Governor General appointed by the Sovereign on the advice of the prime minister.

Parliament consists of a Senate and a House of Commons. The Senate consists of 105 members, nominated by the Governor General on the advice of the prime minister, the seats being distributed between the various provinces. The House of Commons has 301 members directly elected for a five-year term. Representation is proportional to the population of each province.

The judicature is administered by judges following the civil law in Québec province and common law in other provinces. Each province has a Court of Appeal. All superior, county and district court judges are appointed by the Governor General, the others by the Lieutenant-Governors of the provinces.

The highest federal court is the Supreme Court of Canada, which exercises general appellate jurisdiction throughout Canada in civil and criminal cases. There is one other federally constituted court, the Federal Court of Canada, which has jurisdiction on appeals from its trial division, from federal tribunals and reviews of decisions and references by federal boards and commissions.

GOVERNOR GENERAL

Governor General and Commander-in-Chief, HE Adrienne Clarkson

FEDERAL CABINET *as at July 2002*

Prime Minister, Jean Chrétien
Deputy Prime Minister, Finance and Infrastructure, John Manley
Agriculture and Agri-Food, Lyle Vanclief
Citizenship and Immigration, Denis Coderre
Environment, David Anderson
Fisheries and Oceans, Robert Thibault
Foreign Affairs, William Graham
Health, Anne McLellan
Heritage, Sheila Copps
Human Resources Development, Jane Stewart
Indian Affairs and Northern Development, Robert Nault
Industry, Allan Rock
Intergovernmental Affairs, President of the Privy Council, Stéphane Dion
International Co-operation, Susan Whelan
International Trade, Pierre Pettigrew
Justice and Attorney-General, Martin Cauchon
Labour, Claudette Bradshaw
Leader of the Government in the House of Commons, Ralph Goodale
Leader of the Government in the Senate, Sharon Carstairs
Canadian Wheat Board, Public Works and Government Services, Ralph Goodale
Leader of the Government in the Senate, Sharon Carstairs
National Defence, John McCallum
National Revenue, Elinor Caplan
Natural Resources, Herb Dhaliwal
President of the Treasury Board, Lucienne Robillard
Public Works and Government Services, Don Boudria
Solicitor-General, Lawrence MacAulay
Transport, David Collenette
Veterans' Affairs, Secretary of State for Science, Research and Development, Rey Pagtakhan

CANADIAN HIGH COMMISSION

Macdonald House, 1 Grosvenor Square, London W1K 4AB. Tel: 020-7258 6600
Canada House, Pall Mall East, London SW1Y 5BJ
High Commissioner, HE Jeremy Kinsman, apptd 2000
Deputy High Commissioner, R. Rochon
Minister, D. Plunkett

BRITISH HIGH COMMISSION

80 Elgin Street, Ottawa K1P 5K7
Tel: (00 1) (613) 237 1530
High Commissioner, HE Sir Andrew Burns, KCMG, apptd 2000
Deputy High Commissioner, R. Codrington
Defence and Military Adviser, Brig. C. J. R. Day

CONSULATES-GENERAL – Montréal, Toronto, Vancouver
CONSULATES – Halifax/Dartmouth, Québec City, St John's, Winnipeg

FEDERAL STRUCTURE

Provinces or Territories (with official contractions)	Area (sq.kilometres)	Population, 1 January 2001	Capital	Lieutenant-Governor	Premier
Alberta (AB)	661,848	3,022,861	Edmonton	Lois Hole	Ralph Klein
British Columbia (BC)	944,735	4,077,369	ΨVictoria	Iona Campagnolo	Gordon Campbell
Manitoba (MB)	647,797	1,149,220	Winnipeg	Peter Liba	Gary Doer
New Brunswick (NB)	72,908	757,26	Fredericton	Marilyn Trenholme Counsell	Bernard Lord
Newfoundland and Labrador (NF)	405,212	537,797	ΨSt John's	Arthur House	Roger Grimes
Northwest Territories (NT)	1,346,106	42,105	Yellowknife	†Glenna Hansen	Stephen Kakfwi
Nova Scotia (NS)	55,284	942,322	ΨHalifax	Myra Freeman	John Hamm
§Nunavut (NT)	2,093,190	27,978	Iqaluit	†Peter Irniq	Paul Okalik
Ontario (ON)	1,076,395	11,741,793	ΨToronto	James Bartleman	Ernie Eves
Prince Edward Island (PE)	5,660	139,078	ΨCharlottetown	J. Léonce Bernard	Patrick Binns
Québec (QC)	1,542,056	7,383,300	ΨQuébec	Lise Thibeault	Bernard Landry
Saskatchewan (SK)	651,036	1,020,650	Regina	Lynda Haverstock	Lorne Calvert
Yukon Territory (YT)	482,443	30,194	Whitehorse	†Jack Cable	Pat Duncan

Area figures include land and water area
† Commissioner
§ Nunavut was created in 1999 from the Northwest Territories

BRITISH COUNCIL DIRECTOR, Peter Chenery, c/o British High Commission. Email: ottawa.enquiries@ca.britishcouncil.org
BRITISH COUNCIL DIRECTOR IN QUÉBEC, Sarah Dawbarn, 1000 ouest rue de La Gauchetière, Montréal, Québec H3B 4W5; Email: montreal.enquiries@ca.britishcouncil.org

DEFENCE

The Canadian armed forces are unified and organised into three functional commands: Land Force Command; Maritime Command; Air Command.

The Army (Land Forces) has 114 main battle tanks and 1,275 armoured personnel carriers. The Navy (Maritime Forces) has one submarine, four destroyers, 12 frigates and 14 patrol and coastal vessels. The Air Force has 140 combat aircraft.

MILITARY EXPENDITURE – 1.2 per cent of GDP (2000)
MILITARY PERSONNEL – 56,800: Army 18,600, Navy 9,000, Air Force 13,500, Paramilitaries 9,350

ECONOMY

About 68 million hectares of land is farmed, around 7.3 per cent of the total land area. Over 60 per cent of this is under cultivation, the remainder being predominantly classified as unimproved pasture. More than 80 per cent of the cultivated land is in the prairie region of western Canada. The farm sector accounts for about 3 per cent of GDP and employs about 3.7 per cent of the labour force.

Almost half of Canada's land area is forest, making it the world's largest exporter of timber, pulp and newsprint.

The fishing industry contributed C$1,657 million in 1998.

Canada is one of the world's largest producers of potash and uranium, nickel, asbestos, cadmium, zinc and elemental sulphur. The country is also rich in gold, copper, lead, molybdenum, platinum group metals, gypsum, cobalt, titanium concentrates, and aluminium. The total value of mineral production in 2000 was C$83,854 million.

Production of gold in 2002 was 4.8 million ounces (estimate) and production of silver in 2000 was 37.7 million ounces. Uranium production in 2001 was 14,743 tonnes.

There were 18.8 million foreign tourists in 1998, who accounted for receipts of C$11.2 billion.

GNP – US$647,126 million (2000); US$20,140 per capita (1999)

GDP – US$594,106 million (1998); US$20,822 per capita (1999)

ANNUAL AVERAGE GROWTH OF GDP – 4.4 per cent (2000)

INFLATION RATE – 2.7 per cent (2000)

UNEMPLOYMENT – 7.6 per cent (1999)

TRADE

The main exports are automotive products, including cars, trucks and parts, machinery and equipment, industrial products and raw materials, forestry products, including wood, wood pulp and paper products, agricultural products (chiefly wheat and meat products), fishery products, and energy products, including crude petroleum and natural gas.

Trade with the USA accounts for about 84 per cent of Canada's exports and 77 per cent of its imports.

In 2000 imports totalled US$244,786 million and exports US$276,635 million. There was a trade surplus of US$36,609 million and a current account surplus of US$12,666 million.

Trade with UK	2000	2001
Imports from UK	£3,507,718,000	£3,251,220,000
Exports to UK	4,057,600,000	3,787,129,000

COMMUNICATIONS

In 1999 there were 901,902 km of roads, of which 318,371 km were paved, and 36,114 km of railway track in operation.

The bulk of canal shipping in Canada is handled through the two sections of the St Lawrence Seaway, which provide access to the Great Lakes for ocean-going ships.

EDUCATION

Education is under the control of the provincial governments, the cost of the publicly controlled schools being met by local taxation, aided by provincial grants. Education is compulsory between the ages of five or six and 15 or 16.

ENROLMENT (percentage of age group) – primary 100 per cent (1997); secondary 100 per cent (1997); tertiary 88 per cent (1997)

CAPE VERDE
República de Cabo Verde – Republic of Cape Verde

AREA – 1,557 sq. miles (4,033 sq. km). Comprising the Windward Islands (Santo Antão, São Vicente, Santa Luzia, São Nicolau, Bôa Vista and Sal) and Leeward Islands (Maio, São Tiago, Fogo and Brava)

POPULATION – 406,000, the majority of whom are Roman Catholic. The official language is Portuguese; a creole is spoken by most of the population

CAPITAL – Ψ Praia (population, 61,644, 1995 estimate)

CURRENCY – Escudo Caboverdiano of 100 centavos

NATIONAL ANTHEM - É Patria Amada (This Is Our Beloved Country)

NATIONAL DAY – 5 July (Independence Day)

NATIONAL FLAG – Blue with three horizontal stripes of white, red, white near the bottom; over all on these near the hoist a ring of ten yellow stars

LIFE EXPECTANCY (years) – male 67.0; female 72.8

POPULATION GROWTH RATE – 2.0 per cent (1999)

POPULATION DENSITY – 104 per sq. km (1999)

MILITARY EXPENDITURE – 2.7 per cent of GDP (2000)

MILITARY PERSONNEL – 1,200: Army 1,000, Air Force 100, Coast Guard 100

CONSCRIPTION DURATION – Selective conscription

ILLITERACY RATE – 24.2 per cent (2002)

ENROLMENT (percentage of age group) – primary 100 per cent (1989); secondary 48 per cent (1997)

HISTORY AND POLITICS

The islands, colonised c.1460, achieved independence from Portugal on 5 July 1975 under the Partido Africano da Independência da Guiné e Cabo Verde (PAIGC). A federation of the islands with Guinea Bissau was planned but this was dropped following the 1980 coup in Guinea Bissau.

The republic was a one-party state under the African Party for the Independence of Cape Verde (PAICV) until the constitution was amended in 1990. Multiparty elections, held in January 1991, were won by the opposition Movement for Democracy (MPD), which was re-elected in December 1995. President António Mascarenhas Monteiro of the MPD was elected in February 1991 and re-elected unopposed in February 1996. The general election held on 14 January 2001 returned the PAICV to power with 40 of the 72 seats in the National Assembly. The MPD won 30 seats and the Democratic Alliance for Change won two seats. Pedro Pires of the PAICV narrowly won the second round of the presidential election held on 25 February 2001 by 164 votes. The MPD candidate, Carlos Veiga, appealed to the Supreme Court, citing irregularities in the conduct of the elections; the court upheld some of the appeals, which reduced Pires's winning margin to just 12 votes.

HEAD OF STATE

President, Pedro Pires, elected 25 February 2001, *assumed office* 22 March 2001

COUNCIL OF MINISTERS *as at July 2002*

Prime Minister, Defence, José Maria Neves
Agriculture and Fisheries, Mario Anselmo Couto de Matos
Education, Culture and Sport, Victor Borges
Finance, Carlos Augusto Duarte Burgo
Foreign Affairs and Communities, Manuel Inocencio Sousa
Health, Employment and Solidarity, Dario Laval Rezende Dantas Dos Reis
Infrastructure and Transport, Jorge Lima Delgado Lopes
Justice and Interior, Cristina Fontes
Secretary of State for Foreign Affairs, Fatima Lima Veiga
Secretary of State for Parliamentary Affairs and Defence, Armindo Cipriano Mauricio
Secretary of State for State Reforms, Public Administration and Local Government, Edeltrudes Pires Neves
Secretary of State for Youth Affairs, Maria de Jesus Veiga Miranda Mascarenhas
Tourism, Industry and Trade, José Armando Duarte

EMBASSY OF THE REPUBLIC OF CAPE VERDE
Burgemeester Patijnlaan 1930, 2585 CB, The Hague, Netherlands (00 31) (70) 355 3651
Ambassador Extraordinary and Plenipotentiary, vacant

BRITISH AMBASSADOR, HE Alan Burner, resident at Dakar, Senegal
There is a British Consulate on São Vicente.

ECONOMY

The islands have little rain and agriculture is mostly confined to irrigated inland valleys. The chief products are bananas and coffee (for export), maize, sugar cane and nuts. Fish and shellfish are important exports. Salt is obtained on Sal, Bôa Vista and Maio; volcanic rock is also mined for export.

In 1998 there was a trade deficit of US$186 million and a current account deficit of US$58 million. In 1995 imports totalled US$252 million and exports US$9 million.

The main ports are Praia and Mindelo, and there is an international airport on Sal.

GNP – US$587 million (2000); US$1,330 per capita (1999)

GDP – US$443 million (1998); US$1,400 per capita (1999)

ANNUAL AVERAGE GROWTH OF GDP – 3.0 per cent (1998)

INFLATION RATE – 4.4 per cent (1998)

TOTAL EXTERNAL DEBT – US$284 million (1999)

Trade with UK	2000	2001
Imports from UK	£4,077,000	£4,080,000
Exports to UK	1,684,000	2,877,000

CENTRAL AFRICAN REPUBLIC
République Centrafricaine/Ködrö tî Bê-Afrîka – Central African Republic

AREA – 240,535 sq. miles (622,984 sq. km). Neighbours: Chad (north), Sudan (east), Democratic Republic of Congo and Congo-Brazzaville (south), Cameroon (west)

POPULATION – 3,245,000. French is the official language; the national language is Sangho.

CAPITAL – Bangui (population, 473,817, 1984 estimate)

CURRENCY – Franc CFA of 100 centimes

NATIONAL ANTHEM – La Renaissance (The Revival)

NATIONAL DAY – 1 December

NATIONAL FLAG – Four horizontal stripes, blue, white, green, yellow, crossed by central vertical red stripe with a yellow five-pointed star in top left-hand corner

LIFE EXPECTANCY (years) – male 42.7; female 46.0

POPULATION GROWTH RATE – 1.9 per cent (1999)

POPULATION DENSITY – 6 per sq. km (1999)

MILITARY EXPENDITURE – 3.7 per cent of GDP (2000)

MILITARY PERSONNEL – 4,150: Army 3,000, Air Force 150, Paramilitaries 1,000

CONSCRIPTION DURATION – Two years (selective)

ILLITERACY RATE – 50.4 per cent (2002)

ENROLMENT (percentage of age group) – primary 53 per cent (1990); tertiary 1.4 per cent (1991)

HISTORY AND POLITICS

In December 1958 the French colony of Ubanghi Shari elected to remain within the French Community and adopted the title of the Central African Republic. It became fully independent on 17 August 1960. The first president, David Dacko, was overthrown in 1966 by the then Col. Bokassa, who in 1976 proclaimed himself Emperor and renamed the country the Central African Empire. In 1979 Bokassa was deposed by Dacko in a bloodless coup and the country reverted to a republic. President Dacko surrendered power in 1981 to Gen. André Kolingba, who instituted military rule until 1985, when a civilian-dominated Cabinet was appointed. In November 1986 a referendum was held which approved a new constitution and the establishment of a one-party state.

President Kolingba formed a coalition government in February 1993. Presidential elections held in 1993 were won by Ange-Félix Patasse of the Central African People's Liberation Party (MLPC); he was re-elected in September 1999. Legislative elections were held on 22 November and 13 December 1998. The MLPC emerged as the largest party with 47 of 109 seats and formed a multiparty coalition government The next legislative elections are due to take place in 2003.

POLITICAL SYSTEM

Constitutional reforms were passed in a national referendum in December 1994 which created a constitutional court, introduced elected local assemblies, extended the presidential mandate to a maximum of two six-year terms and subordinated the government to the president.

INSURGENCY

The army is divided between southerners loyal to former President Gen. Kolingba and northerners loyal to President Patasse. The 1,100 French troops stationed near Bangui have been called upon to quell frequent mutinies by Gen. Kolingba's supporters; in March 1998 the French troops were replaced by the UN MINURCA peacekeeping force, which withdrew on 15 February 2000.

HEAD OF STATE

President, Ange-Félix Patasse, *elected* 19 September 1993, *re-elected* 19 September 1999

COUNCIL OF MINISTERS *as at July 2002*

Prime Minister, Martin Ziguele (MLPC)

Civil Service, Employment and Social Security, Laurent Ngon Baba (ADP)

Economy, Planning and International Co-operation, Alexis N'gomba (PLD)

Energy, Mines and Waterworks, André Nalke Dorogo (MLPC)

Foreign Affairs, Agba Otikpo Mezode (Ind.)

Interior and Territorial Administration, Joseph Mouzoule

Justice, Keeper of the Seals, Marcel Metefara (MLPC)

Minister of State, Communications, Posts and Telecommunications, Gabriel Jean-Édouard Koyambounou (MLPC)

Minister of State, Finance and Budget, Eric Sorongope (MLPC)

National Defence, Pierre Angoua

National Education and Scientific Research, Timoléon M'baikoua (MLPC)

Promotion of Rural Life, Salomon Namkoserena (MLPC)

Public Health and Population, Joseph Kalite (MLPC)

Public Works, Transport and Settlement, André Toby Kotazo

Relations with Parliament, Michel Doko (PLD)

Social Affairs, Promotion of Women, Children and the Disabled, Françoise Ibrahim N'doma (CN)

Trade, Industry and Private Sector Promotion, Jacob M'baitadjim (MLPC)

Water Resources, Forestry, Fisheries, Environment and Tourism, Constance Nathalie Gounebana (PLD)

Youth and Sports, Jean Dominique N'darata (UDR/FK)

CN National Convention; MLPC Central African People's Liberation Party; ADP Alliance for Democracy and Progress; PLD Liberal Democratic Party; UDR/FK Democratic Union for Renewal - Fini Ködrö; Ind. Independent

EMBASSY OF THE CENTRAL AFRICAN REPUBLIC
30 rue des Perchamps, F-75016, Paris
Tel: (00 33) (1) 4224 4256
BRITISH AMBASSADOR, HE Peter Boon, resident at
Yaoundé, Cameroon

ECONOMY

Cotton, diamonds, coffee and timber are the major
exports. Industrial goods, machinery and transport
equipment, foodstuffs and fuels are the main imports.
  In 1994 there was a trade surplus of US$15 million and
a current account deficit of US$25 million. In 1997
exports totalled US$154 million and imports US$145
million.

GNP – US$1,053 million (2000); US$290 per capita
  (1999)
GDP – US$1,032 million (1998); US$277 per capita
  (1999)
ANNUAL AVERAGE GROWTH OF GDP – 5.5 per cent
  (1998)
INFLATION RATE – 1.5 per cent (1999)
TOTAL EXTERNAL DEBT – US$913 million (1999)

Trade with UK	2000	2001
Imports from UK	£550,000	£2,095,000
Exports to UK	215,000	228,000

CHAD
République du Tchad – Republic of Chad

AREA – 495,755 sq. miles (1,284,000 sq. km).
  Neighbours: Niger, Nigeria and Cameroon (west),
  Libya (north), Sudan (east), Central African Republic
  (south)
POPULATION – 6,702,000; French and Arabic are the
  official languages; there are more than 50 indigenous
  languages, of which the most widely spoken is Sara
CAPITAL – N'Djaména (population, 179,000, 1972
  estimate)
CURRENCY – Franc CFA of 100 centimes
NATIONAL ANTHEM – Peuple Tchadien, Debout Et À
  L'ouvrage (People Of Chad, Arise And To Work)
NATIONAL DAY – 1 December
NATIONAL FLAG – Vertical stripes, blue, yellow and red
LIFE EXPECTANCY (years) – male 45.1; female 47.5
POPULATION GROWTH RATE – 2.7 per cent (1999)
POPULATION DENSITY – 6 per sq. km (1999)
MILITARY EXPENDITURE – 2.8 per cent of GDP (2000)
MILITARY PERSONNEL – 30,350: Army 25,000, Air
  Force 350, Republican Guard 5,000; Paramilitaries
  4,500
ILLITERACY RATE – 54.2 per cent (2002)
ENROLMENT (percentage of age group) – primary 58
  per cent (1997); secondary 10 per cent (1997);
  tertiary 1 per cent (1997)

HISTORY AND POLITICS

Chad became a member state of the French Community
in 1958, and was proclaimed fully independent on 11
August 1960. The constitution was suspended in 1975
when President Tombalbaye was killed in a coup by Gen.
Félix Malloum; following a succession of further coups,
Idriss Déby came to power in 1990 and announced the
adoption of a multiparty system, allowing the legalisation
of political parties in 1991 and 1992. A Higher
Transitional Council (CST) was elected in 1993 to serve
as the transitional legislature and appointed a transitional
government in conjunction with President Déby. The

CST has twice extended the transitional period by one
year to allow sufficient time to organise elections. In
March 1996, the government concluded the Franceville
agreement with opposition parties which provided for a
national ceasefire and an independent commission to
oversee the election. A new constitution, establishing a
unified, democratic state, was confirmed by a
referendum. Déby won the first multiparty presidential
elections in 1996 and was re-elected in the presidential
elections held in May 2001. Elections to the 155-member
National Assembly on 21 April 2002 were won by the pro-
Déby Patriotic Salvation Movement (MPS).

INSURGENCIES

Three rebel movements, the Movement for Unity and the
Republic (MUR), the Movement for Democracy and
Justice in Chad (MDJT), and the Democratic
Revolutionary Council (DRC), announced that they had
formed an alliance in February 2000.
  In July 2000, the government came to an agreement
with the Armed Resistance against Anti-Democratic
Forces (RAFAD) movement and agreed to integrate its
members into the armed forces.

HEAD OF STATE

President, Idriss Déby, *took power* December 1990, *elected*
  3 *July* 1996, *re-elected* 20 May 2001

GOVERNMENT *as at July 2002*

Prime Minister, Haroun Kabadi
Agriculture, David Houdeingar Ngarimaden
Civil Service, Labour and Employment, Abakaka
  Moustapha Lopa
Communications, Government Spokesman, Moktar Wawa
  Dahab
Culture, Youth and Sport, Mahamat Zene Bada
Education, Yokabdjim Mandigui
Environment and Water, Oumar Kadjalami Boukar
Finance and Economy, Idriss Ahmed Idriss
Foreign Affairs and African Integration, Mahamat Saleh
  Annadif
*Higher Education, Scientific Research and Professional
  Training,* Adoum Guemessou
Industry, Commerce and Handicrafts, Mahamat
  Abdoulaye
Justice, Keeper of the Seals, Djimnaye Gaou
Livestock, Mahamat Alahou Taher
Mines and Energy, Laoual Adjigrema
National Defence, Veterans and Victims of War, Mahamat
  Nouri
Oil, Ousmane Mahamat Nour Elimi
Planning, Development and Co-operation, Djimrangar
  Dadnaji
Posts and Telecommunications, Routouang Yoma Golom
Public Health, Maïna Touka Sahanaye
Public Security and Immigration, Mahamat Ali Abdallah
Public Works and Transport, Moussa Faki Mahamat
Regional Administration, Abderrahmane Moussa
Social Action and Family, Agnes Alafi Maimouna
Tourism Development, Akia Abouna

EMBASSY OF THE REPUBLIC OF CHAD
Lambermont 52, 1030 Brussels, Belgium
Tel: (00 32) (2) 215 1975
Ambassador Extraordinary and Plenipotentiary, HE
  Abderahim Yacoub Ndiaye, apptd 2000
BRITISH AMBASSADOR, HE Peter Boon, resident at
  Yaoundé, Cameroon

HONORARY CONSULATE, BP877, Avenue Charles de Gaulle, N'Djaména

ECONOMY

About 90 per cent of the workforce is occupied in agriculture, fishing and forestry. There is an oilfield in Kanem and salt is mined around Lake Chad, but the most important activities are cotton growing and animal husbandry. Raw cotton, meat and groundnuts are the main exports. Chad's main trading partners are France and Cameroon.

On 7 January 2000 the IMF approved a loan facility of about US$26.5 million to support the government's 1999–2002 economic programme.

In 1994 Chad had a trade deficit of US$77 million and a current account deficit of US$38 million. In 2000 imports totalled US$290 million and exports US$183 million.

GNP – US$1,504 million (2000); US$210 per capita (1999)

GDP – US$1,091 million (1998); US$128 per capita (1999)

ANNUAL AVERAGE GROWTH OF GDP – 6.0 per cent (1998)

INFLATION RATE – 3.8 per cent (2000)

TOTAL EXTERNAL DEBT – US$1,142 million (1999)

Trade with UK	2000	2001
Imports from UK	£2,452,000	£3,664,000
Exports to UK	62,000	39,000

CHILE
República de Chile – Republic of Chile

AREA – 292,135 sq. miles (756,626 sq. km). Neighbours: Peru (north), Bolivia and Argentina (east)

POPULATION – 14,622,000. The main groups are: indigenous Araucanian Indians, Fuegians, Rapanui and Changos; Spanish settlers and their descendants; mixed Spanish Indians; and European immigrants. Because of extensive intermarriage only a few indigenous Indians are racially separate. The language is Spanish, with admixtures of local words of Indian origin. The main religion is Roman Catholicism

CAPITAL – Santiago (population, 4,690,684, 1998 UN estimate)

MAJOR CITIES – Ψ Antofagasta (246,023); Concepción (368,428); Puente Alto (384,016); Ψ Valparaíso (284,086); Ψ Punta Arenas (121,533), on the Straits of Magellan, is the southernmost city in the world (1998 UN estimates)

CURRENCY – Chilean peso of 100 centavos

NATIONAL ANTHEM – Canción Nacional De Chile (National Anthem Of Chile)

NATIONAL DAY – 18 September (National Anniversary)

NATIONAL FLAG – Two horizontal bands, white, red; in top sixth a white star on blue square, next staff

LIFE EXPECTANCY (years) – male 73.0; female 79.0

POPULATION GROWTH RATE – 1.4 per cent (1999)

POPULATION DENSITY – 20 per sq. km (1999)

URBAN POPULATION – 84.9 per cent (1997)

Chile lies between the Andes (5,000 to 15,000 feet above sea level) and the shores of the South Pacific, extending coastwise from the arid north around Arica to Cape Horn. The extreme length of the country is about 2,800 miles, with an average breadth, north of 41°, of 100 miles. Island possessions include the Juan Fernández group (three islands) about 360 miles from Valparaíso; one of these islands is the reputed scene of Alexander Selkirk's (Robinson Crusoe) shipwreck. Easter Island, about 2,000 miles away in the South Pacific Ocean, contains stone platforms and hundreds of stone figures.

HISTORY AND POLITICS

Chile was discovered by Spanish adventurers in the 16th century and remained under Spanish rule until 1810, when the first autonomous government was established. Full independence was consolidated in 1818 after a revolutionary war.

A Marxist, Salvador Allende, was elected president in 1970, but was overthrown in a military coup in 1973. Gen. Pinochet, who led the coup, assumed the presidency until presidential and congressional elections were held in 1989, beginning the transition to full democracy.

Gen. Pinochet was arrested in London on 16 October 1998 following a request by the Spanish government for his extradition, but extradition proceedings were dropped on the grounds of poor health on 2 March 2000, and he was freed and allowed to return to Chile. The Chilean Supreme Court lifted his immunity from prosecution in August 2000 and on 1 December he was put under house arrest pending trial on charges relating to the kidnapping and murder of more than 70 political opponents. The charges were dismissed by the Court of Appeals, but formally reinstated on 31 January 2001 after it had been determined that Gen. Pinochet was fit to stand trial. On 8 March the charges were reduced to conspiracy to conceal the actions of military death squads.

Presidential and legislative elections were held in 1993. Eduardo Frei won the presidential election and his ruling Coalition for Democracy (CPD) (centre and centre-left parties) won 70 seats in the Chamber of Deputies and 22 in the Senate. In the legislative elections held on 16 December 2001, the CPD remained the largest group in the Chamber of Deputies but lost its majority in elections to the senate.

POLITICAL SYSTEM

Executive power is held by the president. Legislative power is exercised by a Congress which comprises a Senate of 47 Senators (38 elected and nine appointed) and a Chamber of Deputies of 118 elected members. Senators serve eight-year terms and deputies serve four-year terms. The presidential term is six years with no possibility of re-election.

HEAD OF STATE

President of the Republic, Ricardo Lagos Escobar, *elected* 16 January 2000, *sworn* in 11 March 2000

CABINET *as at July 2002*

Agriculture, Jaime Campos
Defence, Michelle Bachelet
Economy and Energy, Jorge Rodríguez Grossi
Education, Mariana Aylwin
Finance, Nicolás Eyzaguirre
Foreign Affairs, María Soledad Alvear
Health, Osvaldo Artaza
Housing, Town Planning and Public Land, Jaime Ravinet
Interior, José Miguel Insulza
Justice, José Antonio Gómez
Labour and Social Security, Ricardo Solari
Mining, Alfonso Dulanto
National Women's Secretariat, Adriana del Piano
Planning, Cecilia Pérez
Public Works, Transport and Communications, Javier Etcheverry
Secretary-General of the Government, Heraldo Muñoz
Secretary-General of the Presidency, Mario Fernández

EMBASSY OF CHILE
12 Devonshire Street, London W1G 7DS
Tel: 020-7580 6392
Ambassador Extraordinary and Plenipotentiary, vacant
Chargé d'Affairs, Luis Palma

BRITISH EMBASSY
Avenida El Bosque 0125, Casilla 72-D, Santiago
Tel: (00 56) (2) 370 4100
Email: consulate@santiago.mail.fco.gov.uk
Ambassador Extraordinary and Plenipotentiary, HE Greg
  Faulkner, apptd 2000
Deputy Head of Mission, Counsellor and Consul-
  General, P. Whiteway
Defence Attaché, Col. R. Rollo-Walker
First Secretary (Commercial), P.Taylor
CONSULAR OFFICES – Punta Arenas, Valparaíso.

BRITISH COUNCIL DIRECTOR, John Knagg, OBE,
  Eliodoro Yáñez 832, Providencia, Santiago;
  Email: info@british council.cl

DEFENCE
The Army has 290 main battle tanks, 20 armoured infantry
fighting vehicles and 552 armoured personnel carriers. The
Navy has three submarines, three destroyers, three frigates,
27 patrol and coastal vessels, five combat aircraft and 20
armed helicopters. The Air Force has 77 combat aircraft.
MILITARY EXPENDITURE – 3.4 per cent of GDP (2000)
MILITARY PERSONNEL – 87,500: Army 51,000, Navy
24,000, Air Force 12,500; Paramilitaries 34,700
CONSCRIPTION DURATION – 12–22 months (voluntary
from 2002)

ECONOMY
Economic reforms during the late 1970s and the 1980s,
with large-scale privatisation and deregulation, have
made Chile one of the most successful economies in Latin
America. Cereals, vegetables, fruit, tobacco, hemp and
vines are grown extensively and livestock accounts for
nearly 40 per cent of agricultural production. Sheep
farming predominates in the extreme south. There are
large timber tracts in the central and southern zones
which produce timber, cellulose and wood for export.
Fishing is also a major industry.
  Chile is rich in copper-ore, iron-ore and nitrates, and
has the only commercial production of nitrate of soda
(Chile saltpetre) from natural resources in the world.
There are large deposits of high grade sulphur. Oil and
natural gas are produced in the Magallanes area, but
domestic production is now declining.
  In 2000 there was a trade surplus of US$1,438 million
and a current account deficit of US$991 million.
GNP – US$69,936 million (2000); US$4,630 per capita
(1999)
GDP – US$72,949 million (1998); US$4,505 per capita
(1999)
ANNUAL AVERAGE GROWTH OF GDP – 5.4 per cent
(2000)
INFLATION RATE – 3.8 per cent (2000)
UNEMPLOYMENT – 7.2 per cent (1998)
TOTAL EXTERNAL DEBT – US$37,762 million (1999)

TRADE
The principal exports are minerals, timber and metal
products, fish products and vegetables. The principal
imports are food products, industrial raw materials,
machinery, and equipment and spares. The main trade
partners are Japan and the USA; in 1996 Chile joined the
Mercosur Free Trade Zone, and in March 1998 signed an
extension to a free trade agreement with Mexico. In 2000
imports totalled US$18,107 million and exports

US$18,158 million.

Trade with UK	2000	2001
Imports from UK	£115,230,000	£131,178,000
Exports to UK	469,708,000	481,785,000

COMMUNICATIONS
With the improvement of the roads an increasing share of
internal transportation is moving by road and rail,
although shipping is still important. The road system is
about 80,000 km in length, of which around 11,000 km is
paved.
  There are 6,782 km of railway track. A railway line runs
from Valparaíso through La Calera and Santiago to
Puerto Montt. With the completion of a section of 435
miles from Corumba, Brazil, to Santa Cruz, Bolivia, the
Trans-Continental Line will link the Chilean Pacific port
of Arica with Rio de Janeiro on the Atlantic. A line runs
from Antofagasta to Salta (Argentina).
  Domestic air traffic is carried by Línea Aérea Nacional
(LAN) and LADECO, which also operate internationally,
and smaller regional carriers.

CULTURE AND EDUCATION
Chilean Nobel Prize winners include the writers Gabriela
Mistral (1945) and Pablo Neruda (1971).
  Elementary education is free and compulsory. There are
eight state universities (three in Santiago, two in
Valparaíso, one each in Antofagasta, Concepción and
Valdivia), and many private universities.
ILLITERACY RATE – 3.9 per cent (2002)
ENROLMENT (percentage of age group) – primary 100
per cent (1997); secondary 75 per cent (1997);
tertiary 32 per cent (1997)

CHINA
Zhonghua Renmin Gongheguo –
The People's Republic of China

AREA – 3,705,408 sq. miles (9,596,961 sq. km).
Neighbours: Russia and Mongolia (north), North
Korea (east), Vietnam, Laos, Myanmar, India, Bhutan
and Nepal (south), India, Pakistan, Afghanistan,
Tajikistan, Kyrgyzstan and Kazakhstan (west)
POPULATION – 1,248,100,000. Han Chinese make up
91.9 per cent of the population and the remainder of
the population belongs to around 55 ethnic
minorities. Among the largest are the Zhuang of
Guangxi, the Hui of Ningxia, the Miao of southern
China, the Manchu of Heilongjiang, the Uygurs and
Kazakhs of Xinjiang, the Tibetans and the Mongols.
The indigenous religions are Confucianism, Taoism
and Buddhism. There are also Muslims (officially
estimated at about 12 million) and Christians
(unofficially estimated at about 50 million). The
official language is Mandarin Chinese; of the many
local dialects the largest are Cantonese, Fukienese,
Xiamenhua and Hakka. The autonomous regions of
Mongolia, Tibet and Xinjiang have their own
languages
CAPITAL – Beijing (population, 7,362,426, 1990
estimate)
MAJOR CITIES – Chengdu (2,954,872); Chongqing
(3,172,178); Dalian (2,483,776); Guangzhou
(Canton) (3,935,193); Harbin (2,990,921); Qingdo
(2,101,808); Ψ Shanghai (8,214,384); Shenyang
(4,669,737); Tianjin (5,855,044); Wuhan (4,040,113);
Wuxi (1,013,606); Yantai (847,285); Zaozhuang
(1,793,103)
CURRENCY – Renminbi Yuan of 10 jiao or 100 fen
NATIONAL ANTHEM – Yiyongjun Jinxingqu (March Of

The Volunteers)
NATIONAL DAY – 1 October (Founding of People's Republic)
NATIONAL FLAG – Red, with large gold five-point star and four small gold stars in crescent, all in upper quarter next staff
LIFE EXPECTANCY (years) – male 69.1; female 73.5
POPULATION GROWTH RATE – 0.9 per cent (1999)
POPULATION DENSITY – 132 per sq. km (1999)

HISTORY AND POLITICS

China was ruled by imperial dynasties for over 20 centuries until revolutionaries led by Sun Yat-sen forced the Emperor to abdicate on 10 October 1911. Neither the new Nationalist Party (Kuomintang (KMT)) government nor the emergent Chinese Communist Party (CCP) were able to unify China, or to agree on the basis for further reform. Warlord infighting rendered China weak, enabling Japan to occupy Manchuria and all the important northern and coastal areas of China by 1939. Japan's occupation was ended by its defeat by the allies in 1945.

The Communists established control over large areas of China in the early 1940s, seizing the territory abandoned by Japan in 1945. Civil war lasted until 1949 when the CCP, led by Mao Zedong (Mao Tse-tung), inaugurated the People's Republic of China (PRC), and the KMT under Chiang Kai-shek went into exile in Taiwan. The USA continued to recognise the Chiang Kai-shek regime as the rightful government of China until 1971, when the PRC took over China's membership of the United Nations from Taiwan.

Under Mao Zedong China was ruled on the basis of four 'cardinal principles': Marxist–Leninist–Maoist thought, the Socialist Road, the dictatorship of the proletariat, and the leadership of the CCP. Mao's 'Great Leap Forward' (1958–61) was an attempt to industrialise rural areas which resulted in a famine in which 30–40 million people died. China was plunged into chaos during the Cultural Revolution (1966–70) when the Red Guards were used to rid the country of 'rightist elements'.

Following the death of Mao Zedong in 1976, the disgraced Deng Xiaoping was recalled. In 1977 he was elected Vice-Chairman of the CCP, becoming the dominant force within the party by eliminating leftist influence, rehabilitating fallen leaders and promoting an 'open door' policy of economic liberalisation. The Congresses of 1982 and 1987 reaffirmed Deng's policies, and in 1987 most of the revolutionary generation were replaced in the top posts by younger, more liberal supporters of reform.

Student-led pro-democracy demonstrations in April and May 1989, centred on Tiananmen Square in Beijing, ended on 3–4 June when the army took control of Beijing, killing thousands of protesters. This strengthened the position of hardliners within the leadership, who re-adopted policies of centralisation based on Marxist ideology. Deng retired from his last official post in November 1989 but retained effective control until late 1994.

At Deng's instigation during 1992 the emphasis switched back to economic reform and the power of the hardliners waned. The 14th Party Congress in 1992 endorsed Deng's calls for faster, bolder economic reforms and his 'socialist market economy'. Deng died on 19 February 1997 and Jiang Zemin assumed the mantle of leader.

In addition to continuing economic reforms, Jiang has sought to improve China's standing in the international community.

The plenary session of the Central Committee of the Communist Party declared in September 1999 that the reform of the state sector was the country's most pressing task. A ten-year restructuring programme is due to be completed by 2010.

INSURGENCIES

Separatists from the Uygur Muslim minority group in Xinjiang Autonomous Region have demonstrated against Han rule. They have claimed responsibility for bomb attacks in the provincial capital, Ürümqi, and in Beijing. Two Muslim separatists were executed in January 1999 as part of an effort to tighten control of the region and in February 2001, the death sentence was passed on the founder of an underground Islamic party.

The government banned the Falun gong cult on 22 July 1999, which had claimed to have 70 million followers; the government had become worried after it was revealed that a large number of Chinese Communist Party officials and senior officers in the People's Liberation Army had joined the cult.

POLITICAL SYSTEM

Under the 1982 constitution, the National People's Congress is the highest organ of state power. It is elected for a term of five years and is supposed to hold one session a year. It is empowered to amend the constitution, make laws, select the president and vice-president and other leading officials of the state, approve the national economic plan, the state budget and the final state accounts, and to decide on questions of war and peace. The State Council is the highest organ of the state administration. It is composed of the Premier, the Vice-Premiers, the State Councillors, heads of Ministries and Commissions, the Auditor-General and the Secretary-General. Command over the armed forces is vested in the Central Military Commission.

Deputies to Congresses at the primary level are 'directly elected' by the voters 'through a secret ballot after democratic consultation'. This is now extended to county level. These Congresses elect the deputies to the Congress at the next higher level. Deputies to the National People's Congress are elected by the People's Congresses of the provinces, autonomous regions and municipalities directly under the central government, and by the armed forces.

Local government is conducted through People's Governments at provincial, municipal and county levels. Autonomous regions, prefectures and counties exist for national minorities and are described as self-governing.

HEAD OF STATE

President of the People's Republic of China, Jiang Zemin, *elected* March 1993, *re-elected* 16 March 1998
Vice-President, Hu Jintao
Chairman of the Standing Committee of the National People's Congress, Li Peng
Chairman of the Central Military Committee, Jiang Zemin
Deputy Chairmen of the Central Military Committee, Chi Haotian; Hu Jintao; Zhang Wannian

STATE COUNCIL *as at July 2002*

Premier, Zhu Rongji
Vice-Premiers, Qian Qichen; Li Lanqing; Wen Jiabao; Wu Bangguo
State Councillors, Gen. Chi Haotian; Ismail Amat; Luo Gan; Wu Yi; Wang Zhongyu

MINISTERS

Agriculture, Du Qinglin
Civil Affairs, Doje Cering
Communications, Huang Zhendong
Construction, Wang Guangtao
Culture, Sun Jiazheng
Defence, Gen. Chi Haotian
Education, Chen Zhili
Finance, Xiang Huaicheng
Foreign Affairs, Tang Jiaxuan
Foreign Trade and Economic Co-operation, Shi
  Guansheng
Health, Zhang Wenkang
Information Industry, Wu Jichuan
Justice, Zhang Fusen
Labour and Social Security, Zhang Zuoji
Land and Natural Resources, Tian Fengshan
Personnel, Zhang Xuezhong
Public Security, Jia Chunwang
Railways, Fu Zhihuan
Science and Technology, Zhu Lilian
State Security, Xu Yongyue
Supervision, He Yong
Water Resources, Wang Shucheng

MINISTERS IN CHARGE OF STATE COMMISSIONS

Development Planning, Zeng Peiyan
Economics and Trade, Li Rongrong
Ethnic Affairs, Li Dezhu
Family Planning, Zhang Weiqing
Science, Technology and Industry for National Defence,
  Liu Jibin

Auditor-General, Li Jinhua
Governor of the People's Bank of China, Dai Xianglong

CHINESE PEOPLE'S POLITICAL CONSULTATIVE
CONFERENCE

Chair, Li Ruihuan

THE CHINESE COMMUNIST PARTY

General Secretary, Jiang Zemin
Politburo Standing Committee, Jiang Zemin; Li Peng;
  Zhu Rongji; Li Ruihuan; Hu Jintao; Wei Jiangxing; Li
  Lanqing
Politburo of the Central Committee, Tian Jiyun; Li
  Tieying; Ding Guangen; Qian Qichen; Wu Bangguo;
  Huang Ju; Wen Jiabao; Li Changchun; Wu
  Guanzheng; Chi Haotian; Zhang Wannian; Luo Gan;
  Jia Qinglin; Jiang Chunyun *(full members)*; Zeng
  Qinghong; Wu Yi *(alternate members)*
Secretariat of the Central Committee, Zeng Qinghong;
  Ding Guangen; Hu Jintao; Wei Jianxing; Wen Jiabao;
  Luo Gan
Membership, 52,000,000 (1993)

EMBASSY OF THE PEOPLE'S REPUBLIC OF CHINA

49-51 Portland Place, London WI8 1JL
Tel: 020–7299 4049
Ambassador Extraordinary and Plenipotentiary, HE Ma
  Zhengang, apptd 1997
Minister Counsellor, Li Ruiyu
Defence Attaché, Maj.- Gen. Miao Pengsheng

BRITISH EMBASSY
11 Guang Hua Lu, Jian Guo Men Wai, Beijing 100600
Tel: (00 86) (10) 6532 1961/2/3/4
Email: beinfo@public.bta.net.cn
Ambassador, HE Christopher Hum, CMG, apptd 2002
Minister, Consul-General and Deputy Head of Mission, N. J. Cox
Counsellors, C. Nettleton (Political and Economic); C. Haswell (Commercial); Defence, Military and Air Attaché, Brig. J. G. Kerr, OBE, QGM
BRITISH CONSULATES-GENERAL – Chongqing, Shanghai and Guangzhou

BRITISH COUNCIL DIRECTOR – Michael O'Sullivan *(Cultural Counsellor),* Cultural and Education Section, British Embassy, Landmark Building, 8 North Dongsanhuan Road, Chaoyang District, Beijing 100004;
Email: enquiry@britishcouncil.org.cn
Regional directors in Chongqing, Guangzhou and Shanghai

DEFENCE

All three military arms are parts of the People's Liberation Army (PLA). China has at least 20 intercontinental and 130 intermediate range land-based, and 13 submarine-launched nuclear ballistic missiles. The Army has about 8,000 main battle tanks and 5,000 armoured personnel carriers and armoured infantry fighting vehicles.

The Navy has 69 submarines, 21 destroyers, 41 frigates, 368 patrol and coastal vessels, 471 combat aircraft and 37 armed helicopters. The Air Force has about 2,900 combat aircraft and some armed helicopters.

MILITARY EXPENDITURE – 5.3 per cent of GDP (2000)
MILITARY PERSONNEL – 2,310,000: Army 1,600,000; Navy 250,000; Air Force 420,000; Strategic Missile Forces 100,000; Paramilitaries 1,500,000
CONSCRIPTION DURATION – Two years (selective)

ECONOMY

Economic liberalisation in the early 1980s reduced central planning and broadened the role of the market, which led to an explosion in manufacturing, concentrated in China's coastal regions. Foreign direct investment, especially from Hong Kong and Taiwan, has enabled the construction of a significant industrial base and transport infrastructure. In the coastal regions the economy has become a free market in all but name, with several stock markets and Shanghai's emergence as a financial centre. Since 1980, special economic zones have been established in Guangdong, Fujian and Hainan provinces. In addition, there are free trade and development zones throughout the country, designed to stimulate both foreign trade and internal economic development. The reforms have enabled the economy to grow more than five-fold since 1980. China has become the third-largest beneficiary of foreign investment in the world, primarily into its export industries.

Agriculture remains of great importance, employing nearly half the working population and accounting for about 18 per cent of GDP. Cereals, with peas and beans, are grown in the northern provinces, and rice, tea and sugar in the south. Rice is the staple food of the inhabitants. Cotton (mostly in valleys of the Yangtze and Yellow Rivers), tea (in the west and south), with hemp, jute and flax, are the most important crops. Livestock is raised in large numbers. Sericulture is one of the oldest industries. Cottons, woollens and silks are manufactured in large quantities.

Coal, iron ore, tin, antimony, wolfram, bismuth and molybdenum are abundant. Oil is produced in several northern provinces, particularly in Heilongjiang and Shandong, and off-shore deposits are being sought in co-operation with western and Japanese companies. In November 1997, a deal was reached with Russia over the construction of a US$12 billion liquefied natural gas (LNG) pipeline to take LNG from Siberia to China's Pacific coast. In March 1998, China announced the construction of a US$2.3 billion 1,875-mile oil pipeline along the Silk Route to Kazakhstan.

Overcapacity in some of the traditional industries is being tackled, with the closure of 26,000 coal mines and 2,500 steel smelters. The more successful state-owned enterprises are being prepared for listing on the stockmarket, others are being prepared for sale, and failing companies are being wound up.

Tourism has become a major industry, with 7.11 million foreign visitors in 1998.

GNP – US$1,064,537 million (2000); US$780 per capita (1999)
GDP – US$959,001 million (1998); US$798 per capita (1999)
ANNUAL AVERAGE GROWTH OF GDP – 8.0 per cent (2000)9.2 per cent (2000)
INFLATION RATE – 1.4 per cent (2001)1.4 per cent (2001)
UNEMPLOYMENT – 3.1 per cent (1999)
TOTAL EXTERNAL DEBT – US$154,223 million (1999)

TRADE

Foreign trade and external economic relations have grown enormously since 1978. In 1995, import tariffs were cut to an average 23 per cent in line with China's attempts to join the World Trade Organisation. The principal exports are clothing, electronics, machine plant, yarns and fabrics, chemicals, footwear, travel goods, and iron and steel. The principal imports are machinery, electronics, raw materials, yarns and fabrics, plastics and motor vehicles. The main trading partners are Japan, the USA, Hong Kong, South Korea, Taiwan and Germany.

In 2000 China had a trade surplus of US$34,474 million and a current account surplus of US$20,518 million. Imports totalled US$206,132 million and exports US$249,297 million.

Trade with UK	2000	2001
Imports from UK	£1,468,692,000	£1,722,272,000
Exports to UK	5,005,763,000	5,964,414,000

COMMUNICATIONS

There are approximately 57,600 km of railway lines, of which 13,022 km are electrified, and approximately 1,278,000 km of highway, of which 6,258 km are motorways. In addition, internal civil aviation has been developed, with routes totalling more than 1,506,000 km.

In the past the principal means of communication east to west was by the rivers, the most important of which are the Yangtze (Changjiang) (3,400 miles), the Yellow River (Huanghe) (2,600 miles) and the West River (Xihe) (1,650 miles). These, together with the network of canals connecting them, are still much used but their overall importance has declined. Coastal port facilities are being improved and the merchant fleet expanded.

Postal services and telecommunications have developed in recent years and it is claimed that 95 per cent of all rural townships are on the telephone and that postal routes reach practically every production brigade headquarters.

EDUCATION

Primary education lasts six years and secondary education lasts six years (three years in junior middle school and three years in senior middle school). In 1998 there were 1,022 universities and colleges.
ILLITERACY RATE – 14.6 per cent (2002)
ENROLMENT (percentage of age group) – primary 100 per cent (1997); tertiary 6 per cent (1997)

CULTURE

The Chinese language has many dialects, notably Cantonese, Hakka, Amoy, Foochow, Changsha, Nanchang, Wu (Shanghai) and the northern dialect. The Common Speech or putonghua (often referred to as Mandarin) is based on the northern dialect. The Communists have promoted it as the national language and it is taught throughout the country. As putonghua encourages the use of the spoken language in writing, the old literary style and ideographic form of writing has fallen into disuse. Since 1956 simplified characters have been introduced to make reading and writing easier. In 1958 the National People's Congress adopted a system of romanisation known as pinyin.

Chinese literature is one of the richest in the world. Paper has been employed for writing and printing for nearly 2,000 years. The Confucian classics which formed the basis of traditional Chinese culture date from the Warring States period (fourth to third centuries BC), as do the earliest texts of Taoism. Histories, philosophical and scientific works, poetry, literary and art criticism, novels and romances survive from most periods.

TIBET

AREA – 463,000 sq. miles (1,199,164 sq. km)
POPULATION – 2,260,000 (1993)
CAPITAL – Lhasa
Tibet is a plateau seldom lower than 10,000 feet, which forms the northern frontier of India (boundary imperfectly demarcated), from Kashmir to Myanmar, but is separated therefrom by the Himalayas.

From 1911 to 1950, Tibet was virtually an independent country though its status was never officially recognised. In 1950 Chinese Communist forces invaded eastern Tibet. In 1951 an agreement was reached whereby the Chinese army was allowed entry into Tibet, and a Communist military and administrative headquarters was set up. A series of revolts against Chinese rule culminated in 1959 in a rising in Lhasa, the capital. Fighting continued for several days before the rebellion was crushed and military rule was imposed. The Dalai Lama fled to India where he and his followers were granted political asylum and established a government in exile.

In 1964 the Dalai Lama and the Panchen Lama were dismissed, marking the end of co-operation between the Chinese government and the traditional religious authorities. Tibet became an Autonomous Region of China in 1965. Martial law was declared in Tibet in 1989 after serious unrest, and sporadic outbursts of unrest continue.

The Panchen Lama died in 1989. China rejected the Dalai Lama's choice of successor, who is believed to have been executed, and enthroned its own candidate.

In December 1997, the International Commission of Jurists issued a report declaring that Tibet was 'under alien subjugation' and called for a UN-managed referendum to decide its future status. China contested that the report failed to acknowledge its historical claims to the region.

The 17th Karmapa Lama, the first reincarnation of a living Buddha to be recognised by both China and the Dalai Lama, defected from Tibet in late December 1999 and fled to India, where he appealed for political asylum. On 16 January 2000, the 7th Reting Lama was ordained in Tibet; the Dalai Lama had refused to recognise him as the reincarnation of the previous Reting Lama.

In May 2001 the government published details of a modernisation programme for Tibet which aimed to improve the low standard of living by promoting market reforms and extensive public construction projects.

SPECIAL ADMINISTRATIVE REGIONS

HONG KONG

AREA – 417 sq. miles (1,080 sq. km)
POPULATION – 6,724,900 (2001)
CURRENCY – Hong Kong dollar (HK$) of 100 cents
FLAG – Red, with a white bauhinia flower of five petals each containing a red star
LIFE EXPECTANCY (years) – male 78.2; female 84.1
POPULATION GROWTH RATE – 0.9 per cent (2001)
POPULATION DENSITY – 6,250 per sq. km (2001)
URBAN POPULATION – 93.1 per cent (2000 estimate)

Hong Kong, consisting of more than 230 islands and of a portion of the mainland (Kowloon and the New Territories) on the south-east coast of China, is situated at the eastern side of the mouth of the Pearl River. Hong Kong Island is about 11 miles (18 km) long and from two to five miles (three to eight km) broad. It is separated from the mainland by a narrow strait.

The climate is sub-tropical, tending towards temperate for nearly half the year. The mean monthly temperature ranges from 16° C to 29° C. The average annual rainfall is 2,214 mm, of which nearly 80 per cent falls between May and September. Tropical cyclones occur between May and November, causing high winds and heavy rain.

HISTORY AND POLITICS

Hong Kong Island was first occupied by Great Britain in 1841 and formally ceded by the Treaty of Nanking in 1842. Kowloon was acquired by the Beijing Convention of 1860 and the New Territories, consisting of a peninsula in the southern part of the Guangdong province together with adjacent islands, by a 99-year lease signed on 9 June 1898.

On 19 December 1984 the UK and China signed a Joint Declaration in which it was agreed that China would resume sovereignty over Hong Kong on 1 July 1997. In the run-up to the 1997 handover, the Chinese government's insistence on a greater say in the running of the colony and Governor Patten's plan for an extension of democracy prompted acrimonious disputes. The Chinese government refused to accept the reforms and replaced the Legislative Council.

Hong Kong became, with effect from 1 July 1997, a Special Administrative Region (SAR) of the People's Republic of China.

The Joint Declaration which took effect in May 1985 guarantees: the free movement of goods and capital; the retention of Hong Kong's free port status, separate customs territory and freely convertible currency; the protection of property rights and foreign investment; the right of free movement to and from Hong Kong; Hong Kong's autonomy in the conduct of its external commercial relations and its own monetary and financial policies; and judicial independence. Hong Kong's constitution is the Basic Law, which was passed by China's

Countries of the World

National People's Congress in 1990 and guarantees that the SAR's social and economic systems will remain unchanged for 50 years.

A Legislative Council election was held on 10 September 2000. The Democratic Party, a pro-democracy opposition party, remained the largest in the legislature with 12 seats and the pro-China Democratic Alliance for the Betterment of Hong Kong won 11 seats; 20 seats were won by independent candidates.

POLITICAL SYSTEM

Hong Kong is administered by the Hong Kong SAR government, headed by the Chief Executive, who is aided by an Executive Council and a Legislative Council. The Executive Council consists of 14 Principal Officials and five non-officials.

The Legislative Council consists of 60 members, of whom 24 are directly elected. Thirty members are elected by functional constituencies composed of professional and business groups and six more are elected by an election committee.

Chief Executive, Tung Chee-hwa, *sworn in* 1 July 1997

EXECUTIVE COUNCIL *as at July 2002*

Non-official Members, Leung Chun-ying (Convenor); Dr Raymond Ch'ien Kuo-fung; Chung Shui-ming; Nellie Fong Wong; Lee Yeh-kwong; Tam Yiu-chung; Henry Tang; Rosanna Wong; Yang Ti-liangLeung Chun-ying); James Tien Pei-chun; Jasper Tsang; Cheng Yiu-tong; Andrew Liao Cheung-sing
Ex-officio Members, Tung Chee-hwa, Anthony Leung; Donald Tsang; Elsie Leung

GOVERNMENT SECRETARIAT *as at July 2002*
Chief Secretary for Administration, Donald Tsang
Financial Secretary, Antony Leung
Justice, Elsie Leung
Civil Service, Joseph Wong
Commerce, Technology and Industry, Henry Tang
Constitutional Affairs, Stephen Lam
Economic Development and Labour, Stephen Ip
Education and Manpower, Arthur Li
Environment, Transport and Works, Sarah Liao
Financial Services and the Treasury, Frederick Ma
Health, Welfare and Food, Dr E. Yeoh
Home Affairs, Patrick Ho
Housing, Planning and Lands, Michael Suen
Security, Regina Ip

CONSUL-GENERAL, Sir James Hodge, KCVO, CMG, 1 Supreme Court Road, Central, (PO Box 528), Hong Kong. Tel: (00 852) 2901 3000
BRITISH COUNCIL DIRECTOR, Desmond Lauder, 3 Supreme Court Road, Admiralty, Hong Kong
Email: info@britishcouncil.org.hk
HONG KONG ECONOMIC AND TRADE OFFICE, 6 Grafton Street, London W1X 3LB.
Tel: 020-7499 9821.
Commissioner, Andrew Yeung, *apptd* 2001

ECONOMY

The main economic sector is the services industry, especially financial services. It employed 85 per cent of the workforce and contributed 84.7 per cent of GDP in 1998. Principal exports are clothing, electrical machinery and apparatus, and textiles.

Diversification in terms of products and markets continues to be the main feature of recent industrial development, as are industrial partnerships with overseas companies. The economy is based on export rather than

the domestic market. Tourism is very important to the economy; 13.7 million people visited Hong Kong in 2001.
GNP – US$166,502 million (2001); US$24,759 per capita (2001)
GDP – US$161,869 million (2001); US$24,070 per capita (2001)
ANNUAL AVERAGE GROWTH OF GDP – 10.5 per cent (2000)
INFLATION RATE – 3.7 per cent (2000)

TRADE

In 2000 Hong Kong had a trade deficit of US$8,218 million and a current account surplus of US$8,826 million. In 2001 imports totalled US$201,050 million and exports US$189,870 million. Hong Kong's principal customers for its domestic products, in order of value of trade, were China, USA and the United Kingdom. China was its principal supplier. About 40 per cent of China's foreign trade passes through Hong Kong.

Trade with UK	2000	2001
Imports from UK	£2,673,859,000	£2,699,380,000
Exports to UK	6,138,486,000	5,977,696,000

COMMUNICATIONS

Hong Kong has one of the world's finest natural harbours, and it is the busiest container port in the world, with eight terminals, as well as large modern cargo and liner terminals. Dockyard facilities include eight floating drydocks, the largest being capable of docking vessels up to 150,000 tonnes deadweight. A new 17-berth container port will open in stages between 1997 and 2003.

An international airport built on reclaimed land at Chek Lap Kok opened in July 1998.

EDUCATION

Free education for children up to the age of 15 is compulsory. Post-secondary education is provided by six universities and one college. The Open Learning Institute of Hong Kong provides university education. There are also seven technical institutes and the Hong Kong Institute of Education.
ILLITERACY RATE – 6.2 per cent (2002)
ENROLMENT (percentage of age group) – primary 98.7 per cent (2001); secondary 91 per cent (2001); tertiary 31.8 per cent (2001)

MACAO (AOMEN)

AREA – 7 sq. miles (18 sq. km)
POPULATION – 469,000 (1997)
CURRENCY – Pataca of 100 avos
FLAG – Green, with a white lotus flower above a white stylised bridge and water, under a large gold five-point star and four gold stars in crescent

Macao, situated at the mouth of the Pearl River, comprises a peninsula and the islands of Coloane and Taipa.

Macao became a Portuguese colony in 1557; in a Sino-Portuguese treaty of 1887 China recognised Portugal's sovereignty over Macao. An agreement to transfer the administration of Macao to the Chinese authorities was signed on 13 April 1987. Macao became the Macao Special Administrative Region (MSAR) of China when power was transferred by the outgoing Portuguese governor Vasco Rocha Vieira to the new chief executive on 19 December 1999. The final session of the Macao SAR Basic Law Drafting Committee had been held in Beijing in January 1993 and had approved the Basic Law which was to serve as Macao's constitution after 1999.

On 10 April 1999, a 200-member committee of Macao residents was established to determine the composition of the first government of the Macao SAR. They elected Edmund Ho Hao Wah to be its first chief executive. The Chief Executive announced in September 1999 that he had appointed the 10 members of his Executive Council, a body intended to assist the chief executive in policy-making. In addition, he appointed seven legislators to the 23-member MSAR First Legislative Council, which included 15 members of the previous 16-member Legislative Assembly; a replacement was chosen for the member who had not wished to continue.

Chief Executive, Edmund Ho Hao Wah

EXECUTIVE COUNCIL SECRETARIAT *as at July 2002*

Administration and Justice, Florinda da Rosa Silva Chan
Economy and Finance, Francis Tam Pak Yuen
Security, Cheong Kuoc Va
Social Affairs and Culture, Fernando Chui Sai On
Transport and Public Works, Ao Man Long

CONSUL-GENERAL, Sir James Hodge, KCVO, CMG, resident at Hong Kong

ECONOMY

Service industries comprise the greatest part of the economy, providing 71.2 per cent of employment in 1997. In 1998, gambling provided 43 per cent of GNP and there were 6.9 million foreign visitors. Gaming taxes account for about 60 per cent of government revenues. In 2000 imports totalled US$2,255 million and exports US$2,537 million.

The main trading partners are the EU, the USA, China, Hong Kong and Japan.

Trade with UK	2000	2001
Imports from UK	£39,337,000	£19,647,000
Exports to UK	41,134,000	39,416,000

COLOMBIA
República de Colombia – Republic of Colombia

AREA – 439,737 sq. miles (1,138,914 sq. km).
  Neighbours: Venezuela (north and east), Brazil (south-east), Peru (south), Ecuador (south-west), Panama (north-west)
POPULATION – 41,539,000 (1997 UN estimate): 58 per cent mestizo, 20 per cent white, 14 per cent mulatto, 4 per cent black, 3 per cent mixed black-Amerindian, 1 per cent Amerindian. The language is Spanish. Roman Catholicism is the established religion
CAPITAL – Bogotá (population, 5,398,998, 1993)
MAJOR CITIES – Ψ Barranquilla (1,328,833), the major port on the Caribbean; Bucaramanga (759,651); Ψ Buenaventura (227,478), the major port on the Pacific; Cali (2,063,867); Ψ Cartagena (656,632); Medellín (2,556,357)
CURRENCY – Colombian peso of 100 centavos
NATIONAL ANTHEM – Oh Gloria Inmarcesible (Oh Glory Unfading!)
NATIONAL DAY – 20 July (National Independence Day)
NATIONAL FLAG – Broad yellow band in upper half, surmounting equal bands of blue and red
LIFE EXPECTANCY (years) – male 69.2; female 75.3
POPULATION GROWTH RATE – 1.9 per cent (1999)
POPULATION DENSITY – 37 per sq. km (1999)
URBAN POPULATION – 73.9 per cent (2000 estimate)

Colombia lies in the extreme north-west of South America, having a coastline on both the Caribbean Sea and Pacific Ocean.

The country is divided by the Cordillera de los Andes into a coastal region in the north and west and extensive plains in the east. The eastern range of the Colombian Andes is a series of vast tablelands. This temperate region is the most densely peopled portion of the country. The principal rivers are the Magdalena, Guaviare, Cauca, Atrato, Caquetá, Putumayo and Patia.

HISTORY AND POLITICS

The Colombian coast was visited in 1502 by Columbus, and in 1536 a Spanish expedition penetrated the interior and established a government. The country remained under Spanish rule until 1819 when Simón Bolivar established the Republic of Colombia, consisting of the territories now known as Colombia, Panama, Venezuela and Ecuador. In 1829–30 Venezuela and Ecuador withdrew, and in 1831 the remaining territories formed the Republic of New Granada. The name was changed to the Granadine Confederation in 1858, to the United States of Colombia in 1861 and to the Republic of Colombia in 1866. Panama seceded in 1903.

From 1957 to 1974 the country was governed under the 'National Front' agreement with an alternating presidency and equal numbers of ministerial posts. The alternation of the presidency ended in 1974 and parity in appointments in 1978.

The elections to the legislature took place, on 10 March 2002. In the House of Representatives, the Liberal Party (LP) secured 54 seats, while the Social Conservative Party (PSC) won 21, leaving the balance of power in the hands of minor parties. In the Senate the Liberal Party won 28 seats while some 38 minor parties collectively secured 49 seats. The 2002 presidential election was held on 26 May and was won by Alvaro Uribe Velez.

INSURGENCIES

Colombia is dogged by insurgency from left-wing guerrillas. The main active guerrilla factions are the Revolutionary Armed Forces of Colombia (FARC) and the National Liberation Army (ELN). Formal peace talks began on 9 November 1998, but fighting has continued.

In December 2000, the United Self-Defence Forces of Colombia (AUC), a right-wing paramilitary organisation, began to attack civilians in towns and villages which were suspected of being pro-FARC. ELN and FARC were also reported to have carried out joint actions against the AUC. In response, the peace process with FARC was terminated on 20 February 2002 by President Pastrana-Arango. He subsequently suspended the peace process with the ELN.

POLITICAL SYSTEM

The Congress is a bicameral legislature. The lower house (the House of Representatives) has 165 members directly elected for a four-year term. The upper house (the Senate) has 102 members, directly elected for four years; two seats are reserved for representatives of indigenous people. The president, who appoints the Cabinet, is directly elected for a single four-year term.

HEAD OF STATE

President, Alvaro Uribe Velez, *elected* 26 May 2002
Vice-President, Defence, Gustavo Bell Lemus

CABINET *as at August 2002*
Agriculture and Rural Development, Carlos Gustavo Cano
Communications, Martha Pinto
Culture, Maria Consuelo Araujo
Economic Development and Foreign Trade, Jorge Humberto Botero
Education, Cecilia Maria Velez
Environment, Cecilia Rodriguez
Finance and Public Credit, Roberto Junguito
Foreign Affairs, Carolina Barco
Foreign Trade, Angela Maria Orozco
Health Labour and Social Security, Juan Luis Londoño
Interior and Justice, Fernando Londoño
Justice, Rómulo González Trujillo
Labour and Social Security, Angelino Garzon
Mines and Energy, Luis Ernesto Mejia(PSC)
Transport, Andres Uriel Gallego

EMBASSY OF COLOMBIA
Flat 3A, 3 Hans Crescent, London SW1X 0LN
Tel: 020-7589 9177/5037
Ambassador Extraordinary and Plenipotentiary, HE Victor G. Ricardo-Piñeros, apptd 2000

BRITISH EMBASSY
Edificio Ing Barings, Carrera 9 No 76-49 Piso 9, Bogotá
Tel: (00 57) (1) 317 6690/6310/6321
Email: britain@cable.net.co
Ambassador Extraordinary and Plenipotentiary, HE Tom Duggin, apptd 2001

BRITISH CONSULAR OFFICES – Cali and Medellín

BRITISH COUNCIL DIRECTOR, Joe Docherty, Calle 87 No. 12–79, Bogotá;
Email: info@britishcouncil.org.co

DEFENCE
The Army has 12 light tanks and 180 armoured personnel carriers. The Navy has four submarines, four corvettes, 27 patrol and coastal vessels, six aircraft and four helicopters at ten naval bases. The Air Force has 58 combat aircraft and 55 armed helicopters.
MILITARY EXPENDITURE – 2.4 per cent of GDP (2000)
MILITARY PERSONNEL – 158,000: Army 136,000, Navy 15,000, Air Force 7,000; Paramilitaries 104,600
CONSCRIPTION DURATION – 12–18 months

ECONOMY
Coal, natural gas and hydroelectricity resources are largely unexploited, although development of coal is being given priority. The hydrocarbon sector accounts for over half of the mining output, precious metals (gold, platinum and silver) and iron ore accounting for the remainder. Other mineral deposits include nickel, bauxite, copper, gypsum, limestone, phosphates, sulphur and uranium. Colombia is also the world's largest producer of emeralds.
Major cash crops are coffee, sugar, bananas, cut flowers and cotton. Cattle are raised in large numbers, and meat and cured skins and hides are also exported.
The government has encouraged diversification to reduce dependence on coffee as the major export and this has led to the growth of new export-orientated industries, particularly textiles, paper products and leather goods. Stimulus to the economy has been provided by loans from the World Bank and IADB for project development.
Since the late 1980s the government has introduced trade liberalisation and privatisation measures which have effectively freed foreign exchange transactions, increased foreign competition, ended protectionism and reduced inflation.
In 2000 there was a trade surplus of US$2,543 million and a current account surplus of US$41 million. In 1996 and 1997 Colombia was blacklisted by the USA for failing to curb levels of drug production sufficiently. These sanctions were ended in March 1998.
GNP – US$88,047 million (2000); US$2,170 per capita (1999)
GDP – US$102,932 million (1998); US$2,093 per capita (1999)
ANNUAL AVERAGE GROWTH OF GDP – 2.8 per cent (2000)
INFLATION RATE – 9.5 per cent (2000)
UNEMPLOYMENT – 20.1 per cent (1999)
TOTAL EXTERNAL DEBT – US$34,538 million (1999)

TRADE
Principal exports are petroleum and derivatives, coffee, bananas, cut flowers, clothing and textiles, ferro-nickel and coal. Principal trading partners are the USA, the EU and Latin America.
In 2000 imports totalled US$11,539 million and exports US$13,040 million.

Trade with UK	2000	2001
Imports from UK	£102,243,000	£104,929,000
Exports to UK	241,555,000	320,394,000

COMMUNICATIONS
The Andes make surface transport difficult so air transport is used extensively. There are daily air services between Bogotá and all the principal towns, as well as frequent services to other countries. The road network consists of 106,600 km of roads of all types, of which 21,800 km are classified as main trunk and transversal roads. A canal to link the Pacific Ocean and the Caribbean Sea has been planned.

CULTURE AND EDUCATION
There is a flourishing press in urban areas and a national literature supplements the rich inheritance from the time of Spanish colonial rule. Gabriel García Márquez was awarded the Nobel prize for Literature in 1982. State education is free.
ILLITERACY RATE – 7.8 per cent (2002)
ENROLMENT (percentage of age group) – primary 100 per cent (1997); secondary 67 per cent (1997); tertiary 17 per cent (1997)

THE COMOROS
L'Union des Comores – Union of Comoros

AREA – 863 sq. miles (2,235 sq. km). The Comoro archipelago includes the islands of Ngazidja (formerly Grand Comore), Anjouan, Mayotte and Moheli and certain islets in the Indian Ocean
POPULATION – 651,000, mostly Muslim. French and Arabic are the official languages; the majority of the population speak Comoran, a blend of Arabic and Swahili
CAPITAL – Moroni (population, 17,267, 1980 estimate), on Great Comoro
CURRENCY – Comorian franc (KMF) of 100 centimes. The Franc CFA of 100 centimes is also used
NATIONAL ANTHEM – Udzima Wa Ya Masiwa (The Union Of The Islands)

NATIONAL DAY – 6 July (Independence Day)
NATIONAL FLAG - Four horizontal stripes – gold, white, red, blue; a green triangle based on the hoist containing a white crescent and four white stars, horns towards the fly
LIFE EXPECTANCY (years) – male 59.4; female 62.2
POPULATION GROWTH RATE – 2.7 per cent (1999)
POPULATION DENSITY – 302 per sq. km (1999)
ILLITERACY RATE – 43.7 per cent (2002)
ENROLMENT (percentage of age group) – primary 52 per cent (1993); tertiary 0.6 per cent (1995)

HISTORY AND POLITICS

The islanders voted for independence from France in December 1974 and three islands became independent on 6 July 1975. The island of Mayotte opposed independence and has remained under French administration.

An election in 1993 brought President Djohar's National Rally for Development party (RND) to power. Djohar was temporarily ousted in a coup in 1995 which was thwarted by French troops. While Djohar was abroad for medical attention, Prime Minister Caabiel Yachroutou declared himself interim president and refused to acknowledge Djohar's authority, resulting in the formation of a rival government. Djohar returned to the Comoros in January 1996 but was prohibited from contesting the March 1996 presidential election, which was won by Mohammad Taki Abdoulkarim of the National Union for Democracy in the Comoros. Taki dissolved the National Assembly and legislative elections were held in December 1996 although boycotted by the opposition Forum for National Recovery party (FRN).

President Taki died in office on 6 November 1998 and Tajiddine Ben Said Massonde took over as interim president. His government was deposed in a coup on 30 April 1999 by Col. Assoumani Azzali, who was sworn in as president on 6 May. On 2 September 1999, an unsuccessful coup was launched while Col. Azzali was overseas. He announced that he would retain power until a presidential election was held, which was due to take place by 14 April 2000. The election did not take place and Col. Azzali declared that he would not restore civilian rule due to the issue of Anjouan separatism. However, in March 2001, he announced that the country would be restored to civilian rule in 2002 and that he would not contest the presidential election. The presidential elections were held in 2002 on March 17 and April 14 (Union President); March 31 (local presidents on Anjouan and Moheli); May 12 and 19 (local president for Ngazidja).

INSURGENCIES

In August 1997 separatists on the islands of Anjouan and Moheli demanded independence from the Comoros and a return to French rule. Following a failed attempt to resolve the situation by force, President Taki assumed absolute power and established a State Transition Commission to function as a Cabinet. In a referendum in October 1997, the inhabitants of Anjouan voted overwhelmingly for independence. Talks mediated by the OAU began in December 1997 and an agreement drawn up with OAU support, which would have given each island considerable autonomy, was signed by Grand Comore and Moheli, but was rejected by Anjouan. Anjouan citizens voted by a large majority against reincorporation into the Comoros in a referendum held on 23 January 2000.

In March 1998, Anjouan's self-proclaimed President Abdallah Ibrahim appointed a prime minister and

Cabinet, though their legitimacy has not been recognised internationally. Fighting broke out between President Ibrahim's forces and those of a previous Anjouan prime minister, Chamassi Said Omar, on 5 December 1998. On 1 August 1999, President Ibrahim resigned and transferred most of his powers to Col. Said Abeid. A general election was held in Anjouan in August 1999.

President Assoumani and the leader of Anjouan, Lt.-Col. Abderemane, signed an agreement on national reconciliation on 17 February 2001, which would have given Anjouan considerable autonomy. The Anjouan government withdrew from the reconciliation process on 15 April, alleging that the conditions of the agreement had not been met.

POLITICAL SYSTEM

A new constitution which will create a federal structure for Ngazidja, Anjouan and Moheli and give greater autonomy for the islands was approved, in outline, by referendum no 23 December 2001. The final version was accepted by referendum on 17 March 2002 on Moheli and Anjouan but was rejected by the voters of Ngazidja.

HEAD OF STATE

President Col. Assoumani Azzali

COUNCIL OF MINISTERS *as at July 2002*

Vice President, Finance, Budget, Economy, External Trade, Investment and Privatisation, Caabi El-Yachroutu
Vice President, Justice, Territorial Security, Information, Religious Affairs, Human Rights, and Relations with the Houses of Parliament, Rachid Ben Massoundi
Minister of State, Foreign Relations and Co-operation, Francophone Affairs, Environment, Comorans Abroad, Mohamed El-Amine Souef
Minister-Delegate at the Ministry of External Relations, in charge of Co-operation, Government Spokesperson, Ali Moumini
Minister of State, Social Affairs, Welfare, Decentralisation, Posts and Telecommunications, International Transport, Ali Mohamed Soilih
President of Moheli, Mohamed Said Fazul
President of Anjouan, Mohammed Bacar
President of Ngazidja, Abdou Soule Elbak

EMBASSY OF THE FEDERAL ISLAMIC REPUBLIC OF THE COMOROS
20 rue Marbeau, F-75016 Paris, France
Tel: (00 33) (1) 4067 9054

BRITISH AMBASSADOR, HE C. F. Mochan, resident at Antananarivo, Madagascar

ECONOMY

The most important products are vanilla, copra, cloves and essential oils, which are the principal exports; cacao, sisal and coffee are also cultivated. Great Comoro is well forested and produces some timber.
GNP – US$213 million (2000); US$350 per capita (1999)
GDP – US$201 million (1998); US$281 per capita (1999)
ANNUAL AVERAGE GROWTH OF GDP – 1.1 per cent (1998)
TOTAL EXTERNAL DEBT – US$201 million (1999)

Trade with UK	2000	2001
Imports from UK	£877,000	£1,019,000
Exports to UK	460,000	3,603,000

DEMOCRATIC REPUBLIC OF CONGO

République Démocratique du Congo – Democratic Republic of Congo

AREA – 905,355 sq. miles (2,344,858 sq. km). Neighbours: Central African Republic (north), Sudan (north-east), Uganda, Rwanda, Burundi and Tanzania (east), Zambia (south), Angola (south-west), Republic of Congo-Brazzaville (north-west)

POPULATION – 48,040,000 (1997 UN estimate). The population was 34,671,607 at the 1985 census, composed of Bantu, Hamitic, Nilotic, Sudanese and Pygmoid groups, divided into more than 200 semi-autonomous tribes. More than 400 languages are spoken. Swahili, a Bantu language with an admixture of Arabic, is the nearest approach to a common language in the east and south, while Lingala is the language of a large area along the river and in the north, and Kikongo of the region between Kinshasa and the sea. French is the language of administration. Roman Catholicism is the predominant religion; there are also Protestants, Muslims and Kimbanguists

CAPITAL – Kinshasa (population, 2,664,309, 1984)

MAJOR CITIES – Kananga (298,693); Kisangani (317,581); Likasi (213,862); Lubumbashi (564,830); Ψ Matadi (138,798); Mbandaka (137,291)

CURRENCY – Congolese franc

NATIONAL ANTHEM – Debout Congolais (Stand Up, Congolese)

NATIONAL DAY - 30 June (Independence Day)

NATIONAL FLAG – Blue with a large yellow five-pointed star in the centre and five small yellow five-pointed stars in a vertical line down the hoist

LIFE EXPECTANCY (years) – male 51.0; female 53.5

POPULATION GROWTH RATE – 2.6 per cent (1999)

POPULATION DENSITY – 21 per sq. km (1999)

MILITARY EXPENDITURE – 8.4 per cent of GDP (2000)

MILITARY PERSONNEL – 81,400: Army 79,000, Navy 900, Air Force 1,500

ILLITERACY RATE – 12.6 per cent (2002)

ENROLMENT (percentage of age group) – primary 72 per cent (1997); secondary 26 per cent (1997); tertiary 2 per cent (1997)

The Democratic Republic of Congo (formerly Zaïre) is Africa's third largest state. Apart from the coastal district in the west which is fairly dry, the rainfall averages between 60 and 80 inches a year. The average temperature is about 27°C, but in the south the winter temperature can fall nearly to freezing point. Extensive forest covers the central districts.

HISTORY AND POLITICS

The state of the Congo, founded in 1885, became a Belgian colony in 1908 and gained its independence in 1960. Mobutu Sésé Seko came to power in a coup in 1965 and was elected president in 1970. Legislative power was vested in a unicameral National Legislative Council, with candidates proposed by the sole legal political party, Mouvement Populaire de la Révolution (MPR).

Political reforms were announced in April 1990 and President Mobutu accepted an opposition-dominated government under Prime Minister Etienne Tshisekedi in October 1991.

In January 1994 President Mobutu dissolved the government and in April promulgated a Transitional Constitutional Act which regulated a period of transition to democracy.

In October 1996 fighting broke out between Zaïrean Tutsis (Banyamulenge) and the Zaïrean army in North and South Kivu provinces which had received an influx of Hutu refugees from Rwanda. The pro-Hutu army attempted to expel the Tutsis from the region but found themselves outgunned by the rebels, under the leadership of Laurent Kabila, who were backed by the Rwandan and Ugandan governments. Kabila's Alliance of Democratic Forces for the Liberation of Congo-Zaïre (AFDL) captured Kinshasa in May 1997 and President Mobutu fled. Zaïre was renamed the Democratic Republic of Congo.

A rebellion against the government of Laurent Kabila began in Kivu on 2 August 1998 and by the end of the month the rebels had seized large areas in the east and west of the country. Angola, Chad, Kenya, Namibia and Zimbabwe promised President Kabila military support. The Angolan army quickly recaptured several towns in the south-west, but the rebels maintained their grip on the eastern regions. The rebel movement, the Congolese Democratic Rally (RCD), was supported by Uganda and Rwanda. On 17 May 1999, Ernest Wamba dia Wamba, the RCD leader, was ousted, splitting the movement into two distinct factions, that led by Wamba dia Wamba being called the Congolese Democratic Rally – Liberation Movement (RCD-LM). A cease-fire signed on 31 August 1999 between the government and the two rebel groups has remained largely intact, although localised clashes have been frequent. The main rebel groups, the RCD, the RCD-LM and the Congolese Liberation Movement (MLC) reached agreement on 20 December 1999 to form an umbrella organisation to defeat the government. A new rebel group, the Congolese Democratic Rally-National (RCD-N), was founded in October 2000 and in January 2001, the RCD and the RCD-LM were reunited as the Congolese Liberation Front.

On 6 December 2000, the government and the rebel groups signed an agreement to withdraw troops from the front line in preparation for the arrival of the United Nations Organisation Monitoring Mission in the Democratic Republic of Congo (MONUC). Foreign governments who had troops in the country agreed to withdraw their forces.

President Laurent Désiré Kabila died on 18 January 2001, having been shot by his bodyguard two days previously. His son, Maj.-Gen. Joseph Kabila, was sworn in as president on 26 January. No elections have been held since.

All the parties to the civil war had withdrawn their troops 15 km from their frontline positions by 26 March 2001, as had been stipulated in the agreement signed in December 2000.

Kabila's Cabinet was dismissed on April 4 2001 and a new one was appointed on April 14.

POLITICAL SYSTEM

A 300-member Constituent and Legislative Council was established on 21 August 2000 to draft a new constitution, which is to be put to a referendum.

There are 11 regions, each under a Governor and provincial administration: Bas-Zaïre (provincial capital, Matadi); Bandundu (Bandundu); Equateur (Mbandaka); Haut-Zaïre (Kisangani); Kinshasa (Kinshasa); Maniema (Kindu); North Kivu (Goma); South Kivu (Bukavu); Shaba (Katanga) (Lubumbashi); East Kasai (Mbuji-Mayi); West Kasai (Kananga).

HEAD OF STATE

President and Minister of Defence, Maj.-Gen. Joseph Kabila, *sworn* in 26 January 2001

CABINET *as at July 2002*
Agriculture, Fisheries and Animal Husbandry, André
Philip Futa
Civil Service, Benjamin Mukulungu
Communication and Press, Kikaya bin Karubi
Culture and the Arts, Marthe Ngalula Wakuana
Delegate for National Defence, Irong Awan
Economy, Finance and Budget, Matungulu Nguyamu
Education, Kutumisa Tshioka
Energy, George Buse Talai
Foreign Affairs and International Co-operation, Leonard
She Okitundu
Health, Masako Mamba
Human Rights, Ntumba Luaba
Industry, Commerce and SMEs, Helen Mateibo
Interior, Mira Ndjoku
Justice and Keeper of the Seals, Ngele Masudi
Labour and Social Security, Marie-Ange Lukiana
Land Affairs, Environment and Tourism, Salomo
Banamuwere
Mines and Hydrocarbons, Simon Bawangamio
Tumawako
Minister at the Presidency, Augustin Katumba Mwanke
National Security and Public Order, Mwenze Kongolo
Planning and National Reconstruction, Maj. Denis
Kalume Nunbi
Post and Telecommunications, Philippe Kohotama
Mawuoko
*Public Works, Territorial Administration, Urban
Development and Housing*, Nkodi Mbaki
Social Affairs, Jeanne Ebamba Boboto
Transport, Dakahu Dino Wakale Minada
Youth and Sports, Timote Moleka Ngulama

EMBASSY OF THE DEMOCRATIC REPUBLIC OF
CONGO
38 Holne Chase, London N2 0QQ
Tel: 020-8458 0254
Ambassador Extraordinary and Plenipotentiary, vacant
Chargé d'Affaires, Henri N'Swana

BRITISH EMBASSY
83 Avenue du Roi Baudouin, Kinshasa
Tel: (00 243) 88 46102
Ambassador Extraordinary and Plenipotentiary, HE
James Atkinson, apptd 2000

ECONOMY

Palm oil is the most important agricultural cash product
though it is no longer exported. Coffee, rubber, cocoa and
timber are the most important agricultural exports. The
production of cotton, pyrethrum and copal is increasing.
Copper is widely exploited, and industrial diamonds and
cobalt are also produced. Oil deposits are exploited off
the Zaïre estuary and reef-gold is mined in the north-east
of the country.
    The main industrial products are foodstuffs, beverages,
tobacco, textiles, leather, wood products, cement and
building materials, metallurgy, small river craft and
bicycles. There are reserves of hydroelectric power and
the Inga dam on the river Zaïre supplies electricity to
Matadi, Kinshasa and Shaba.
    Whilst the country has many natural resources, civil
war has led to the collapse of the economy, with total debt
amounting to more than twice the GNP.
GNP – US$5,024 million (1998); US$110 per capita
(1998)
GDP – US$4,836 million (1998); US$116 per capita
(1999)
ANNUAL AVERAGE GROWTH OF GDP – (-5.7 per
cent) (1998)

INFLATION RATE – 175.5 per cent (1997)
TOTAL EXTERNAL DEBT – US$11,906 million (1999)
TRADE
The chief exports are copper, crude oil, coffee, diamonds,
rubber, cobalt, gold, zinc and other metals.
    In 1996 imports totalled US$424 million and exports
US$592 million.

Trade with UK	2000	2001
Imports from UK	£4,146,000	£9,593,000
Exports to UK	911,000	568,000

COMMUNICATIONS

There are approximately 145,000 km of roads, of which
20,500 km are earth-surfaced, and 6,000 km of railways.
The country has four international and 40 principal
airports.

REPUBLIC OF CONGO-BRAZZAVILLE
*République du Congo-Brazzaville – Republic of Congo-
Brazzaville*

AREA – 132,047 sq. miles (342,000 sq. km). Neighbours:
Gabon (west), Cameroon and Central African
Republic (north), Angola (Cabinda) (south-west), the
Democratic Republic of Congo (east and south)
POPULATION – 2,745,000. The official language is
French; Lingala, Monokutuba and Kikongo are
widely spoken
CAPITAL – Brazzaville (population, 596,200, 1984)
MAJOR CITIES – Ψ Pointe Noire (298,014), the main
commercial centre
CURRENCY – Franc CFA of 100 centimes
NATIONAL ANTHEM – La Congolaise
NATIONAL DAY – 15 August
NATIONAL FLAG – Divided diagonally into green,
yellow and red bands
LIFE EXPECTANCY (years) – male 49.6; female 53.7
POPULATION GROWTH RATE – 2.8 per cent (1999)
POPULATION DENSITY – 8 per sq. km (1999)
MILITARY EXPENDITURE – 2.5 per cent of GDP (2000)
MILITARY PERSONNEL – 10,000: Army 8,000, Navy 800,
Air Force 1,200; Paramilitaries 2,000
ILLITERACY RATE – 17.2 per cent (2002)
ENROLMENT (percentage of age group) – primary 100
per cent (1997); tertiary 7 per cent (1992)

HISTORY AND POLITICS

Formerly the French colony of Middle Congo, Congo-
Brazzaville became a member state of the French
Community on 28 November 1958 and fully independent
on 17 August 1960.
    In 1968, a National Council of army officers took power
and created the Parti Congolais du Travail (PCT) and the
People's Republic of the Congo. After popular pressure,
the PCT abandoned its monopoly of power and
renounced Marxism in 1990. In 1992 the country
adopted a new multi-party constitution with a directly
elected president and a bicameral parliament.
    The lack of a parliamentary majority forced President
Lissouba to call fresh elections in 1993. These were won
by the Pan-African Union for Social Democracy
(UPADS) but the results were disputed by opposition
groups and violence broke out between rival parties. A
new UPADS-dominated government was appointed in
January 1995. In June 1997, fighting broke out between
forces of President Lissouba and followers of former
president Sassou-Nguesso, who was reinstalled as
president in October 1997. Elections scheduled for July

1997 were called off and a National Forum for Unity and Democracy was set up to schedule legislative elections. It declared a three-year transition period after which democratic elections will be held. A constitutional committee was inaugurated on 19 November 1998, charged with drafting a constitution to be approved by referendum in 1999.

In April 1999, supporters of former prime minister Bernard Kolelas formed themselves into a political party, the Patriotic Union of Ninja Forces. Following a period of intense fighting, negotiations between the government and the rebels began on 13 November 1999; an accord was reached in which the two sides agreed to an unconditional end to hostilities and the demilitarisation of political parties. President Omar Bongo of Gabon was appointed as mediator on 29 December.

A 'non-exclusive national dialogue' was held between 17 March and 14 April 2001. Rebel leaders and the government adopted a draft constitution, which aimed to establish a directly elected executive presidency and bicameral legislature. The new constitution was approved in a referendum on 20 January 2002. Presidential elections held in March 2002 were won by Denis Sassou-Nguesso who secured nearly 90 per cent of the vote.

HEAD OF STATE

President, Defence, Denis Sassou-Nguesso, *sworn in* 25 October 1997, *elected* 10 March 2002

CABINET *as at July 2002*

Minister in the President's Office in charge of Defence, Itihi Lekounzou Ossetouma
Agriculture and Livestock, Nkoua Celestin Gongara
Civil Service, Administrative Reform, Women's Affairs, Jeanne Dambenze
Commerce, Small and Medium Sized Enterprises, Pierre Damien Boussoukou Boumba
Communication and Government Spokesman, François Ibovi
Culture and Tourism, Mambou Eli Niamy
Energy and Water Resources, Jean-Marie Tassoua
Finance and Budget, Mathias Dzon
Foreign Affairs and Co-operation, Rodolphe Adada
Forestry, Henri Djombo
Health and National Solidarity, Leon Alfred Opimba
Industrial Development, Alphonse Mbamba
Industry and Mines, Michel Mampoya
Interior Security and Territorial Administration, Col. Pierre Oba
Justice and Keeper of the Seals, Jean-Martin M'bemba
Labour and Social Security, Lambert Ndouane
Petroleum Affairs, Jean-Baptiste Taty-Loutard
Posts and Telecommunications, Jean-Felix Demba Dello
Primary and Secondary Education, Pierre Tsiba
Social Amenities and Public Works; Reconstruction and Urban Development, Col. Florent Tsiba
Technical Education and Vocational Training, Andre Okombi Salissan
Territorial and Regional Development, Pierre Moussa
Transport, Civil Aviation and Merchant Navy, Isidore Mvouba

EMBASSY OF THE REPUBLIC OF CONGO BRAZZAVILLE 37 bis rue Paul Valéry, F-75116 Paris, France
Tel: (00 33) (1) 4500 6057
Ambassador Extraordinary and Plenipotentiary, HE Henri Marie Joseph Lopes, apptd 1999

HONORARY CONSULATE, 4 Wendle Court, 131–137 Wandsworth Road, London SW8 2LH.
Tel: 020-7622 0419.

Honorary Consul, L. Muzzu

BRITISH AMBASSADOR, HE James Atkinson, resident at Kinshasa, Democratic Republic of Congo

ECONOMY

Congo-Brazzaville has its own oil deposits, producing about 9 million tonnes annually. It also produces lead, zinc and gold. The principal agricultural products are timber, cassava and yams. Imports are mainly of machinery.

In 1997 Congo-Brazzaville had a trade surplus of US$941 million and a current account deficit of US$252 million. Imports in 1998 totalled US$680 million and exports US$1,476 million.

GNP – US$1,847 million (2000); US$550 per capita (1999)
GDP – US$1,925 million (1998); US$766 per capita (1999)
ANNUAL AVERAGE GROWTH OF GDP – 1.3 per cent (1998)
INFLATION RATE – 0.9 per cent (2000)
TOTAL EXTERNAL DEBT – US$5,031 million (1999)

Trade with UK	2000	2001
Imports from UK	£18,991,000	£16,461,000
Exports to UK	5,272,000	3,421,000

COSTA RICA
República de Costa Rica – Republic of Costa Rica

AREA – 19,730 sq. miles (51,100 sq. km). Neighbours: Nicaragua, Panama
POPULATION – 3,943,204 (2000 estimate), mainly of European origin. The language is Spanish
CAPITAL – San José (population, 1,220,412, 1998 estimate)
MAJOR CITIES – Alajuela (183,232); Cartago (125,799), 1998 UN estimates
CURRENCY – Costa Rican colón of 100 céntimos
NATIONAL ANTHEM – Noble Patria, Tu Hermosa Bandera (Noble Fatherland, Your Beautiful Flag)
NATIONAL DAY – 15 September
NATIONAL FLAG – Five horizontal bands, blue, white, red, white, blue (the red band twice the width of the others with emblem near staff)
LIFE EXPECTANCY (years) – male 75.0; female 79.7
POPULATION GROWTH RATE – 1.8 per cent (1999)
POPULATION DENSITY – 70 per sq. km (1999)
MILITARY EXPENDITURE – 0.8 per cent of GDP (2000)
MILITARY PERSONNEL – 8,400
ILLITERACY RATE – 4.4 per cent (2002)
ENROLMENT (percentage of age group) – primary 100 per cent (1997); secondary 48 per cent (1997); tertiary 30 per cent (1997)

The coastal lowlands have a tropical climate but the interior plateau, with a mean elevation of 4,000 feet, enjoys a temperate climate.

HISTORY AND POLITICS
For nearly three centuries (1530–1821) Costa Rica was under Spanish rule. In 1821 the country obtained its independence, although from 1824 to 1839 it was one of the United States of Central America.

In 1948 the Army was abolished, the President declaring it unnecessary. The main political parties are the Social Christian Unity Party (PUSC) and the National Liberation Party (PLN). In the legislative elections held on 3 February 2002, the PUSC won 19 seats in the Legislative Assembly, the PLN won 17 seats and the Citizens' Action Party won 14 seats. The presidential

elections on 3 February and 7 April 2002 were won by the PUSC candidate, Abel Pacheco.

POLITICAL SYSTEM

Executive power is vested in the president, who is head of state and government, with legislative power vested in the 57-member Legislative Assembly. Under the constitution both the president and the members of the Legislative Assembly are elected for a single four-year term and may not be re-elected.

HEAD OF STATE

President, Abel Pacheco, elected 7 April 2002
First Vice-President, Lineth Saborio
Second Vice-President, Luis Fishman

CABINET *as at July 2002*

Agriculture and Livestock, Rodolfo Coto
Culture, Youth and Sport, Guido Saenz Gonzalez
Economy and Industry, Vilmo Villabos
Environment and Energy, Carlos Manuel Rodriguez
Finance, Jorge Bolaños
Foreign Affairs, Roberto Tovar Faja
Foreign Trade, Alberto Trejos
Health, Maria del Rocio Saenz
Housing, Helio Fallas Venegas
Interior, Police and Public Security, Rogelio Vicente
Justice, Jose Miguel Villalobos
Labour and Social Security, Ovidio Pacheco Salazar
Planning, Danilo Chaverri Soto
Presidency, Rina Contreras Lopez
President of the Central Bank, Eduardo Lizano Fait
Public Education, Astrid Fischel Volio
Public Works and Transport, Javier Chaves Bolanos
Science and Technology, Rogelio Pardo Evans
Tourism, Ruben Pacheco
Women's Affairs, Gloria Valerín
Without Portfolio (National Council on Childhood), Rosalia Gil

COSTA RICAN EMBASSY
Flat 1, 14 Lancaster Gate, London W2 3LH
Tel: 020-7706 8844
Ambassador Extraordinary and Plenipotentiary, HE Rodolfo Gutiérrez, apptd 1998

BRITISH EMBASSY
Apartado 815, Edificio Centro Colón (Eleventh Floor), San José 1007
Tel: (00 506) 258 2025
Email: britemb@sol.racsa.co.cr
Ambassador Extraordinary and Plenipotentiary and Consul-General, G. S. Butler, apptd 2002

ECONOMY

Tourism is the largest single industry, with ecotourism a growing area; one third of the country is national parkland or nature reserve. In 1999, there were more than one million foreign visitors. Industrial activity is principally in the manufacturing sector and manufactured goods include computer components, foodstuffs, textiles and clothing, plastic goods and pharmaceuticals. The principal agricultural products are coffee, bananas, sugar and cattle (for meat).
GNP – US$14,448 million (2000); US$3,570 per capita (1999)
GDP – US$10,731 million (1998); US$2,942 per capita (1999)
ANNUAL AVERAGE GROWTH OF GDP – 1.7 per cent (2000)

INFLATION RATE – 11.0 per cent (2000)
UNEMPLOYMENT – 6.0 per cent (1999)
TOTAL EXTERNAL DEBT – US$4,182 million (1999)

TRADE

The chief exports are manufactured goods, bananas, coffee, fish and shellfish, machinery and tropical fruits. The chief imports are raw materials for industry, consumer goods, capital equipment, and fuel and mineral oils. The USA accounts for around 40 per cent of imports and exports. Other major trading partners are Japan, Germany, Mexico and the UK. In 1998 there was a trade deficit of US$245 million and a current account deficit of US$460 million. In 2000 imports totalled US$6,372 million and exports US$5,865 million.

Trade with UK	2000	2001
Imports from UK	£33,829,000	£42,964,000
Exports to UK	544,453,000	135,376,000

COMMUNICATIONS

The chief ports are Limón on the Atlantic coast, through which passes most of the coffee exported, and Caldera on the Pacific coast. LACSA is the national airline, operating flights throughout Central and South America, the Caribbean and the USA, besides internal flights to local airports by SANSA.

CÔTE D'IVOIRE
République de la Côte d'Ivoire – Republic of Côte d'Ivoire

AREA – 124,504 sq. miles (322,463 sq. km). Neighbours: Guinea and Liberia (west), Mali and Burkina Faso (north), Ghana (east)
POPULATION – 14,300,000: 39 per cent Muslim, 28 per cent Christian (mainly Roman Catholic) and 17 per cent maintain traditional beliefs. The official language is French, but Agni, Baoulé, Dioula, Senoufo and Yacouba are spoken
CAPITAL – Yamoussoukro (population, 126,191, 1988), the political and administrative capital since 1983
MAJOR CITIES – Ψ Abidjan (1,929,079), the economic and financial centre
CURRENCY – Franc CFA of 100 centimes
NATIONAL ANTHEM – L'Abidjanaise
NATIONAL DAY – 7 August
NATIONAL FLAG – Three vertical stripes, orange, white and green
LIFE EXPECTANCY (years) – male 47.7; female 48.1
POPULATION GROWTH RATE – 3.9 per cent (1996)
POPULATION DENSITY – 45 per sq. km (1999)
MILITARY EXPENDITURE – 0.9 per cent of GDP (2000)
MILITARY PERSONNEL – 13,900: Army 6,800, Navy 900, Air Force 700; Paramilitaries 5,500
CONSCRIPTION DURATION – Six months (selective)
ILLITERACY RATE – 50.4 per cent (2002)
ENROLMENT (percentage of age group) – primary 71 per cent (1997); tertiary 6 per cent (1997)
The climate is equatorial in the south and west, which are mainly forested; tropical in the centre and east, which are savannah regions with trees; dry and tropical in the north, which is a grassy savannah region.

HISTORY AND POLITICS

Although French contact was made in the first half of the 19th century, Côte d'Ivoire became a colony only in 1893 and was finally pacified in 1912. It decided on 5 December 1958 to remain an autonomous republic

within the French Community; full independence outside the Community was proclaimed on 7 August 1960.

After having been president since independence in 1960, President Houphouët-Boigny died in December 1993 and was replaced by the parliamentary speaker Henri Konan-Bédié. The President was deposed by Gen. Robert Guëi in a military coup on 24–25 December 1999, who announced a transitional government on 4 January 2000. A referendum on a new constitution was held on 23–24 July 2000, which was approved by 86.58 per cent of those who voted.

On 22 October 2000 a presidential election was held. President Guëi dissolved the electoral commission following early results which indicated that Laurent Gbagbo of the Ivorian Popular Front (FPI) was leading, and it was announced that Guëi had won. Demonstrations and mounting violence led to Guëi fleeing the country on 26 October and Gbagbo was inaugurated as president.

A general election held in 196 of the 225 constituencies on 10 December 2000 resulted in the FPI becoming the largest party. Following polling on 14 January 2001 in 28 of the remaining 29 seats, the FPI had won 96 seats and the Democratic Party of Côte d'Ivoire (PDCI) had won 94 seats. The election was boycotted by the Rally of Republicans (RDR), the strongest party in the north of the country.

POLITICAL SYSTEM

The Côte d'Ivoire has a presidential system of government and a single-chamber National Assembly of 225 members, directly elected for a five-year term. It has been a multiparty system since 1990. The president's term of office is five years, renewable once only.

HEAD OF STATE

President, Laurent Gbagbo, *elected* 22 October 2000, *sworn in* 26 October 2000

CABINET AS AT JULY 2002

Prime Minister, Planning and Development, Pascal Affi N'Guessan (FPI)
Agriculture and Animal Resources, Alphonse Douatiy (FPI)
Commerce, Eric Victor Kahe Kplohourou (Ind.)
Communication and New Technologies, Lia Bi Douayoua (FPI)
Construction and Urbanism, Assoa Adou (FPI)
Culture and Francophone Affairs, Kone Dramane (FPI)
Economic Infrastructure and Government Spokesman, Patrick Achi (PDCI)
Economy and Finance, Bohoun Bouabre (FPI)
Education, Michel Amani N'Guessan (FPI)
Environment and Living, Gilbert Bleu-Laine (Ind.)
Family, Women and Children, Henriette Lagou (PDCI)
Health, Raymond Abouo N'dori (FPI)
Higher Education and Scientific Research, Sery Bally (FPI)
Industry and Promotion of the Private Sector, Alain Cocauthrey (PDCI)
Justice and Civil Rights, Oulai Siéné (FPI)
Mining and Energy, Léon Emmanuel Monnet (FPI)
Minister in the PM's Office charged with the Fight against HIV/AIDS and other Pandemics, Assana Sangare (PDCI)
Ministers of State, Kouassi Moïse Lida (FPI) (*Defence and Civil Protection*); Sangare Abou Dramane (FPI) (*Foreign Affairs*); Émile Boga Doudou (FPI) (*Interior and Decentralisation*)

Relations with Parliament and other Institutions, Sébastien Dano Djedje (FPI)
Social Security and National Solidarity, Clothilde Ohouochi (PDCI)
Sport and Leisure, Geneviève Bro Grébé (PDCI)
Tourism and Crafts, Odette Likikouet Sauyet (FPI)
Transport, Aimé Kabran Appiah (PIT)
Water and Forestry, Angèle Boka (PIT)
Works, Civil Service and Administrative Reform, Hubert Oulaye (FPI)
Youth, Employment and Professional Training, Lazare Koffi Koffi (FPI)
FPI Ivorian Popular Front; PDCI Democratic Party of Côte d'Ivoire; PIT Ivorian Labour Party; Ind. Independent

EMBASSY OF THE REPUBLIC OF CÔTE D'IVOIRE
2 Upper Belgrave Street, London SW1X 8BJ
Tel: 020-7201 9601
Ambassador Extraordinary and Plenipotentiary, HE Youssoufou Bamba, apptd 2001

BRITISH EMBASSY
Immeuble 'Les Harmonies', Abidjan
Tel: (00 225) (20) 226850
Email: britemb.a@aviso.co.
Ambassador Extraordinary and Plenipotentiary, HE J. François Gordon, CMG, apptd 2001

ECONOMY

Côte d'Ivoire became wealthy in the 1970s because of the high prices of its two principal export earners, coffee and cocoa. In the late 1980s the economy contracted considerably as its exports deteriorated in competitiveness and its rivals devalued their currencies while the franc CFA remained pegged to the French franc. An economic reform and stabilisation programme began in 1989 under IMF auspices and has brought down inflation, increased investment and led to GDP growth. The devaluation of the CFA franc in January 1994 has increased exports considerably and restored a trade surplus. In February 1998 a further economic reform programme began.

The principal exports are coffee, cocoa, timber, palm oil, sugar, rubber, pineapples, bananas, and cotton. There are a few deposits of diamonds and minerals including manganese and iron. Oil and gas deposits began to be exploited in 1995.

There was a trade surplus of US$1,870 million in 1998 and a current account deficit of US$313 million. In 2000 imports totalled US$3,084 million and exports US$3,973 million.

GNP – US$10,527 million (2000); US$670 per capita (1999)
GDP – US$12,702 million (1998); US$808 per capita (1999)
ANNUAL AVERAGE GROWTH OF GDP – 5.5 per cent (1998)
INFLATION RATE – 2.5 per cent (2000)
TOTAL EXTERNAL DEBT – US$13.170 million (1999)

Trade with UK	2000	2001
Imports from UK	£53,147,000	£61,044,000
Exports to UK	78,549,000	84,838,000

CROATIA
Republika Hrvatska – Republic of Croatia

AREA – 21,824 sq. miles (56,538 sq. km). Neighbours: Slovenia, Hungary (north), the rump Federal Yugoslav state (east), Bosnia-Hercegovina (south, and east of Adriatic coastal strip)
POPULATION – 4,498,000; 78 per cent Croat, 12 per cent Serb, 2 per cent Yugoslav; also Hungarians, Italians, Albanians, Czechs, Ukrainians and Jews. Roman Catholic 76.5 per cent, Eastern Orthodox 11.1 per cent, Protestant 1.4 per cent, Muslim 1.2 per cent. The language is Croatian in the Latin script
CAPITAL – Zagreb (population, 867,717, 1991)
MAJOR CITIES – Osijek (129,792); Rijeka (167,964); Split (200,459), 1991
CURRENCY – Kuna of 100 lipa
NATIONAL ANTHEM – Lijepa Naša Domovina (Our Beautiful Homeland)
NATIONAL DAY – 30 May (Statehood Day)
NATIONAL FLAG – Three horizontal stripes of red, white, blue, with the national arms over all in the centre
LIFE EXPECTANCY (years) – male 70.3; female 78.1
POPULATION GROWTH RATE – 0.6 per cent (1999)
POPULATION DENSITY – 81 per sq. km (1999)
ILLITERACY RATE – 1.5 per cent (2002)
ENROLMENT (percentage of age group) – primary 87 per cent (1997); secondary 82 per cent (1997); tertiary 28 per cent (1997)

Croatia is divided into three major geographic regions: the Pannonian region in the north, the central mountain belt, and the Adriatic coast region of Istria and Dalmatia which has 1,185 islands and islets and 1,104 miles (1,778 km) of coastline.

HISTORY AND POLITICS

Croatia was part of the Austro-Hungarian Empire from 1526 to 1918. On 29 October 1918 the Croatian parliament declared Croatia independent and soon after Croatia joined with Slovenia, Bosnia-Hercegovina, Serbia and Montenegro to form the 'Kingdom of Serbs, Croats and Slovenes' (renamed Yugoslavia in 1929). From 1941 to 1945 Yugoslavia was occupied by the Axis powers, with Italy and Hungary annexing parts of Croatia and a pro-Nazi Croat puppet state being established in the remainder of Croatia and Bosnia-Hercegovina. The armed extremists of this state (Ustaše) engaged in fierce fighting with Serbian royalists, Communist partisans and pro-Allied Croat partisans.

At the end of the war Yugoslavia was re-established as a federal republic under Communist rule but gradually disintegrated following the death of the wartime partisan leader Josep Tito in 1980.

In April and May 1990 Croatia's first free, democratic elections were won by the Croatian Democratic Union (HDZ) of Dr Franjo Tudjman. A referendum in May 1991 backed independence from Yugoslavia, which was declared on 30 May 1991. Croatia's ethnic Serb minority, which rejected Croatia's independence, began fighting with the Croat defence forces and by September 1991 this had escalated into war between Croatia and Serbia. The war in Croatia continued until January 1992 when a cease-fire was declared. The Federal Yugoslav Army (JNA) and Serb forces had secured control of virtually all ethnic Serb areas in Croatia.

President Tudjman was re-elected in June 1997, but was temporarily replaced by Vlatko Pavletić on 26 November 1999 after he fell ill; he died on 10 December. Stipe Mesić was elected in presidential elections held on 7 February 2000. In the general election held on 3 January 2000, the opposition coalition of the Social Democratic Party of Croatia (SPH) and the Croatian Social Liberal Party (HSLS) scored a decisive victory, winning a total of 68 seats.

SECESSION

Croatia's ethnic Serbs voted to establish a Republic of Serbian Krajina (RSK) in 1993.

The Croatian government seized Western Slavonia in May 1995 and the whole of Krajina in August 1995 prompting the withdrawal of 10,000 UNCRO peacekeepers and the flight of 150,000 Serbs. The last Croatian Serb-held area of Eastern Slavonia agreed in November 1995 to its eventual reintegration into Croatia, which was achieved on 15 January 1998.

FOREIGN RELATIONS

An agreement to normalise relations with Yugoslavia was signed in August 1996. Croatia was sworn in as a member of the Council of Europe in November 1996.

POLITICAL SYSTEM

Executive power is vested in a president and government. The president is directly elected for a five-year term. Legislative power is vested in the 151-member Chamber of Representatives, whose members are directly elected for a four-year term.

The constitution was amended in November 2000 to reduce the powers of the presidency. A further amendment was agreed in March 2001, when the Chamber of Representatives voted to abolish the Chamber of Counties, the upper house of the legislature.

Croatia is divided into 21 counties. Counties are composed of groups of districts and function both as units of local government and as regional offices for central administration. There are 102 districts.

HEAD OF STATE

President, Stipe Mesić, *elected* 7 February 2000

CABINET *as at July 2002*

Prime Minister, Ivica Racan (SDP)
First Deputy Prime Minister, Drazen Budisa (HSLS)
Second Deputy Prime Minister, Goran Granić (HSLS)
Deputy PMs, Slavko Linić (SDP) (*Economy*); Željka Antunović (SDP) (*Social Affairs*)
Agriculture, Forestry and Fishing, Božidar Pankretić (HSS)
Crafts, Small and Medium Businesses, Željko Pecek (HSS)
Croatian Homeland War Defenders, Ivica Pančić
Culture, Anton Vujić (SDP)
Defence, Jozo Radoš(HSLS)
Economy, Hrvoje Vojković (HSLS)
Education and Sport, Vladimir Strugar (HSS)
Environmental Protection and Zoning, Božo Kovačević (LS)
European Integration, Neven Mimica
Finance, Mato Crkvenać (SPH)
Foreign Affairs, Tonino Picula (SDP)
Government Secretary, Jagola Premužić
Health, Andro Vlahusić (HSLS)
Interior, Šime Lučin (SDP)
Justice, Administration and Local Self-Government, Ingrid Antićvić-Marinović (SDP)
Labour and Social Welfare, Davorko Vidović (SDP)

Maritime Affairs, Transport and Telecommunications,
Mario Kovac (HSLS)
Public Works, Reconstruction and Construction, Radimir
Cačić (HNS)
Science and Technology, Hrvoje Kraljević (HSLS)
Tourism, Pave Župan Rusković
HNS Croatian People's Party; HSLS Croatian Social
Liberal Party; HSS Croatian Peasants' Party; LS Liberal
Party; SPH Social Democratic Party of Croatia

EMBASSY OF THE REPUBLIC OF CROATIA
21 Conway Street, London W1T 6BN
Tel: 020-7387 2022
Ambassador Extraordinary and Plenipotentiary, HE
Andrija Kojaković, apptd 1997

BRITISH EMBASSY
Vlaska 121/III Floor, PO Box 454, 10001 Zagreb
Tel: (00 385) (1) 455 5310
Email: british-embassy@zg.tel.hr
Ambassador Extraordinary and Plenipotentiary, HE
Nicholas Jarrold, apptd 2000

BRITISH CONSULATES – Split and Dubrovnik

BRITISH COUNCIL DIRECTOR, Roy Cross, Illica 12,
PO Box 55, 10001 Zagreb;
Email: zagreb.info@britishcouncil.hr

DEFENCE

The Army has 301 main battle tanks, 55 armoured
personnel carriers and 106 armoured infantry fighting
vehicles. The Air Force has 44 combat aircraft and 22
armed helicopters. The Navy has one submarine and 8
patrol and coastal combatants at five bases.
MILITARY EXPENDITURE – 2.7 per cent of GDP (2000)
MILITARY PERSONNEL – 58,300: Army 50,700, Navy
    3,000, Air Force 4,600; Paramilitaries 10,000
CONSCRIPTION DURATION – Six months

ECONOMY

Production was severely hampered during the conflict in
1991–5; the material damage was estimated by the
government to be US$27 billion, with the loss of 13,583
lives. Large areas of farmland were destroyed and the
tourist industry, which provided one third of total foreign
exchange earnings in 1990, was decimated.
    Shipbuilding and fishing are major industries on the
Adriatic coast. Inland there is a light manufacturing
sector, food-processing industries, bauxite deposits,
thermal mineral springs, hydroelectric potential, and
agriculture based on grain, horticulture, livestock and
tobacco. Textiles is one of the most important industries
employing more than 17 per cent of the population. In
April 1996, Croatia agreed to pay 29.5 per cent of
Yugoslavia's debt, totalling US$1.45 billion.
    In 2000 Croatia had a trade deficit of US$3,204 million
and a current account deficit of US$399 million. Imports
totalled US$7,887 million and exports US$4,432 million.
GNP – US$20,124 million (2000); US$4,530 per capita
    (1999)
GDP – US$21,321 million (1998); US$4,242 per capita
    (1999)
ANNUAL AVERAGE GROWTH OF GDP – 2.7 per cent
    (1998)
INFLATION RATE – 6.4 per cent (1998)
UNEMPLOYMENT – 11.4 per cent (1998)
TOTAL EXTERNAL DEBT – US$9,443 million (1999)

TRADE

Trade with UK	2000	2001
Imports from UK	£74,650,000	£88,103,000
Exports to UK	42,183,000	52,822,000

CUBA
República de Cuba – Republic of Cuba

AREA – 42,804 sq. miles (110,861 sq. km)
POPULATION – 11,059,000. The language is Spanish
CAPITAL –Ψ Havana (population, 2,184,990, 1996 UN
    estimate)
MAJOR CITIES – Camagüey (298,726); Guantánamo
    (205,078); Holguín (249,492); Santa Clara (207,350);
    Ψ Santiago (433,180), 1996 UN estimates
CURRENCY – Cuban peso of 100 centavos
NATIONAL ANTHEM – Al Combate, Corred Bayameses
    (To Battle, Men Of Bayamo)
NATIONAL DAY – 1 January (Day of Liberation)
NATIONAL FLAG – Five horizontal bands, blue and
    white (blue at top and bottom) with red triangle,
    close to staff, charged with five-point star
LIFE EXPECTANCY (years) – male 74.8; female 78.7
POPULATION GROWTH RATE – 0.4 per cent (1999)
POPULATION DENSITY – 101 per sq. km (1999)
URBAN POPULATION – 74.5 per cent (1995)

HISTORY AND POLITICS

The island was visited by Columbus in 1492. Early in the
16th century the island was conquered by the Spanish,
and for almost four centuries remained under Spanish
rule. Separatist agitation culminated in the closing years
of the 19th century in open warfare. In 1898 the USA
intervened and demanded the evacuation of Cuba by
Spanish forces. The Spanish–American war led to the
abandonment of the island, which came under American
military rule from 1899 until 1902, when an autonomous
government was inaugurated with an elected president,
and bicameral legislature.
    A revolution led by Dr Fidel Castro overthrew the
government of Gen. Batista in 1959. In 1965 the
Communist Party of Cuba (PCC) was formed to succeed
the United Party of the Socialist Revolution; it is the only
authorised political party. A new Socialist constitution
came into force in 1976 and indirect elections to the
National Assembly of People's Power were subsequently
held. The first direct elections to the National Assembly
were held in February 1993; all candidates were officially
approved by the Communist Party and ran for election
unopposed. The 14 provincial assemblies were elected in
the same manner. The fifth congress of the PCC was held
in October 1997. At the election of deputies to the
National Assembly in January 1998, all 601 PCC
candidates received the required 50 per cent of the vote,
and in February the National Assembly confirmed Dr
Castro as president for a further five-year term.

HEAD OF STATE

President of Council of State and Council of Ministers,
    Dr Fidel Castro Ruz, *appointed* 2 November 1976,
    re-elected 15 March 1993, 24 February 1998

COUNCIL OF STATE *as at July 2002*

President, Dr Fidel Castro Ruz
First Vice-President, Gen. Raúl Castro Ruz
Vice-Presidents, Carlos Lage Dávila; Juan Almeida
    Bosque; Abelardo Colomé Ibarra; Esteban Lazo
    Hernández; José Ramón Machado Ventura
Secretary, José Miyar Barrueco

COUNCIL OF MINISTERS *as at July 2002*

President, Dr Fidel Castro Ruz
First Vice-President, Revolutionary Armed Forces,
    Gen. Raúl Castro Ruz
Vice-Presidents, Osmany Cienfuegos Gorriaran; Pedro

Miret Prieto; José Ramón Fernández Alvárez; Adolfo Diaz Suárez
Secretary, Carlos Lage Dávila
Government Minister, Ricardo Cabrisas Ruiz
Ministers, Alfredo Jordán Morales (*Agriculture*); Lina Pedraza Rodríguez (*Auditing and Control*); Roberto Ignacio González Planas (*Information Science and Communications*); Juan Mario Junco del Pino (*Construction*); Abel Prieto Jiménez (*Culture*); Barbara Castillo Cuesta (*Domestic Trade*); José Luis Rodríguez García (*Economy and Planning*); Luis Ignacio Gómez Gutiérrez (*Education*); Manuel Millares Rodríguez (*Finance and Prices*); Alfredo López Valdez (*Fishing Industry*); Alejandro Rocas Iglesias (*Food Industry*); Marta Lomas Morales (*Foreign Investment and Economic Co-operation*); Felipe Pérez Roque (*Foreign Relations*); Raúl de la Nuez Ramírez (*Foreign Trade*); Marcos J. Portal León (*Heavy Industries*); Fernando Vecino Alegret (*Higher Education*); Gen. Abelardo Colomé Ibarra (*Interior*); Roberto Díaz Sotolongo (*Justice*); Alfredo Morales Cartaya (*Labour and Social Security*); Jesús Pérez Othon (*Light Industry*); Fernando Acosta Santana (*Metalworking and Electronics Industries*); Gen. Rogelio Acevedo Gonzalez (*President of the Cuban Institute of Civil Aeronautics*); Ernesto Lopez Rodriguez (*President of the Cuban Institute of Radio and Television*); Jorge Luis Aspiolea Roig (*President of the National Institute of Hydrography*); Humberto Rodriguez Gonzalez (*President of the National Institute of Sports*); Carlos Dotres Martínez (*Public Health*); Rosa Eleana Simeón Negrin (*Science, Technology and Environment*); Div.-Gen. Ulises Rosales del Toro (*Sugar Industry*); Ibrahim Ferradaz García (*Tourism*); Alvaro Pérez Morales (*Transport*); Wilfredo López Rodríguez; (*Without Portfolio*)

EMBASSY OF THE REPUBLIC OF CUBA
167 High Holborn, London WC1V 6PA
Tel: 020-7240 2488
Ambassador Extraordinary and Plenipotentiary, HE Dr José Fernández de Cossío, apptd 2000

BRITISH EMBASSY
Calle 34 No. 702/4, entre 7ma Avenida y 17, Miramar, Havana.
Tel: (00 53) (7) 241 771
Ambassador Extraordinary and Plenipotentiary, HE Paul Hare, apptd 2001

BRITISH COUNCIL DIRECTOR, Michael White, Calle 34 No 702, 7ma Avenida, Miramar, Havana
Email: information@cu.britishcouncil.org

DEFENCE

The Army has about 900 main battle tanks and 700 armoured personnel carriers. The Navy has five patrol and coastal vessels at six bases. The Air Force has 130 combat aircraft and 45 armed helicopters.

The last former Soviet combat personnel left Cuba in 1993, but 810 Russian military advisers remain to operate military intelligence facilities. The United States has 790 naval personnel at Guantánamo Bay Naval Base, which has been leased since before the 1959 revolution.

MILITARY EXPENDITURE – 4.5 per cent of GDP (2000)
MILITARY PERSONNEL – 46,000: Army 35,000, Navy 3,000, Air Force 8,000; Paramilitaries 26,500
CONSCRIPTION DURATION – Two years

ECONOMY

After the revolution virtually all land and industrial and commercial enterprises were nationalised. Following the curtailing of Cuba's privileged trading relationships with the Soviet bloc in 1989, the economy deteriorated sharply. GDP fell by 75 per cent between 1989 and 1994, and the government was forced to introduce reforms. Since 1993, the government has legalised the holding of US dollars by private individuals, permitted private enterprise, cut subsidies to loss-making state industries, allowed prices for some goods and services to rise, and introduced income tax. State farms have been transformed into co-operatives run by private individuals and permitted to sell 20 per cent of produce on the open market, but remain relatively unproductive. In 1995, foreign investors were permitted to buy property and own Cuban-based companies, with British and Canadian firms becoming involved in the oil and mining industries.

Following austerity measures imposed in 1993, the economy has slowly started to grow; output has risen by 15 per cent since 1994. Sugar is still the mainstay of the economy and the principal source of foreign exchange; production dropped from 8.04 million tons in 1989–90 to 4.4 million tons in 1996–7. Domestic oil production is rising and reached 1,680,000 tonnes in 1998. Lack of external finance has been a major obstacle to economic recovery, as has the long-standing trade and economic embargo imposed by the USA, which has been criticised repeatedly by the UN and was condemned by the European Parliament in November 1998.

The tourism industry has expanded since 1986 to become the country's largest foreign exchange earner. In 1999 1.6 million tourists visited Cuba, generating some US$1,900 million.

GDP – US$23,901 million (1998); US$2,208 per capita (1999)

ANNUAL AVERAGE GROWTH OF GDP – 1.2 per cent (1999)

TRADE

Cuba's exports dropped from US$8.1 billion in 1989 to US$1.7 billion in 1993 while imports declined by 73 per cent. Trade between Cuba and the former socialist economies of Europe is now less than 10 per cent of pre-1989 levels. A trade deal was signed with Russia in 1995 providing for the exchange of sugar for oil. The US trade and economic embargo remains in force, in spite of it having been repeatedly condemned by the UN General Assembly, though it was relaxed in March 1998 to allow food and medicine into the country. Principal exports are sugar, nickel, seafood, citrus fruits, tobacco and rum.

Trade with UK	2000	2001
Imports from UK	£21,657,000	£12,965,000
Exports to UK	9,644,000	11,672,000

COMMUNICATIONS

There are 12,700 km of railway track, of which 5,000 km are in public service. In 1986 there were 13,247 km of road. Scheduled international air services run to Central and South American countries and Europe. In March 1998 the ban on direct flights between Cuba and the USA was lifted. Direct telephone links between Cuba and the USA were suspended in December 2000.

CULTURE AND EDUCATION

The press and broadcasting are under the control of the government. Education is compulsory and free. In 1964 illiteracy was officially declared to be eliminated.

ILLITERACY RATE – 3.1 per cent (2002)
ENROLMENT (percentage of age group) – primary 100 per cent (1997); secondary 81 per cent (1997); tertiary 12 per cent (1997)

CYPRUS
Kypriaki Dimokratia/Kıbrıs Çumhuriyeti – Republic of Cyprus

AREA – 3,572 sq. miles (9,251 sq. km)
POPULATION – 766,000: 85 per cent Greek, 12 per cent Turkish. Greek and Turkish are official languages
CAPITAL – Nicosia, (195,300, 2000 estimate)
MAJOR CITIES – Ψ Famagusta (34,300); ΨLarnaca (110,900); Ψ Limassol (191,500); Paphos (57,400), 1998 estimates
CURRENCY – Cyprus pound (C£) of 100 cents
NATIONAL ANTHEM – Ymnos Eis Tin Eleftherian (Ode To Freedom)
NATIONAL DAY – 1 October (Independence Day)
NATIONAL FLAG – White with a gold map of Cyprus above a wreath of olive
LIFE EXPECTANCY (years) – male 76.0; female 80.5
POPULATION GROWTH RATE – 0.7 per cent (1999)
POPULATION DENSITY – 81 per sq. km (1999)
ENROLMENT (percentage of age group) – primary 96 per cent (1995); secondary 93 per cent (1995); tertiary 23 per cent (1996)

HISTORY AND POLITICS
Cyprus came under British administration from 1878, and was formally annexed to Britain in 1914 on the outbreak of war with Turkey. From 1925 to 1960 it was a Crown Colony. Following the launching in 1955 of an armed campaign by EOKA in support of union with Greece, a state of emergency was declared which lasted for four years. An agreement was signed on 19 February 1959 between the United Kingdom, Greece, Turkey, and the Greek and Turkish Cypriots which provided that Cyprus would be an independent republic.

The island became independent on 16 August 1960. The constitution provided for a Greek Cypriot president and a Turkish Cypriot vice-president. The constitution proved unworkable and led to intercommunal trouble. The UN Peacekeeping Force in Cyprus (UNFICYP) was set up in 1964.

In February 1998, Glafcos Clerides of the Democratic Rally-Liberal Party was re-elected president with 51 per cent of the vote. On 30 March 1998, formal accession talks with the EU began. A general election was held for the House of Representatives (56 Greek Cypriot and 24 vacant Turkish Cypriot seats) on 27 May 2001, resulting in the parties gaining the following seats: AKEL (Left-wing) 20; DISY (Liberal) 19; Democratic Party (DIKO) 9; KISOS (Social Democrats) 4; others 4.

HEAD OF STATE
President, Glafcos Clerides, *elected* 14 February 1993, *re-elected* 15 February 1998

COUNCIL OF MINISTERS *as at July 2002*

Agriculture, Environment and Natural Resources, Konstantinos Themistokleous
Commerce, Industry and Tourism, Nikolaos Rolandis
Communications and Works, Averof Neophytou
Defence, Socrates Hassikos
Education and Culture, Ouranios Ioannides
Finance, Takis Klerides
Foreign Affairs, Ioannis Kasoulides
Health, Frixos Savvides
Interior, Andreas Panayiotou
Justice and Public Order, Nikolaos Kosis
Labour and Social Insurance, Andreas Mousiouttas

CYPRUS HIGH COMMISSION
93 Park Street, London W1K 7ET
Tel: 020-7499 8272
High Commissioner, HE Myrna Kleopas, apptd 2000
Deputy High Commissioner, P. Kestoras
First Counsellor, Consul-General, Yannis Iacovou
Counsellors, K. Pillas (*Cultural Affairs*); A. Georgiades (*Commerce*), S. Georgiallis (*Press Counsellor*)

BRITISH HIGH COMMISSION
Alexander Pallis Street (PO Box 1978), CY-1587 Nicosia
Tel: (00 357) (2) 2-861125
High Commissioner, HE Lyn Parker, apptd 2001
Counsellor and Deputy High Commissioner, P. R. Barton
Defence Adviser, Col. J. Anderson
First Secretary (Commercial), L. Ross

BRITISH COUNCIL DIRECTOR, Peter Skelton,
3 Museum Street, CY-1097 Nicosia;
Email: enquiries@britishcouncil.org.cy

BRITISH SOVEREIGN AREAS
The UK retained full sovereignty and jurisdiction over two areas of 99 square miles in all: Akrotiri–Episkopi–Paramali and Dhekelia–Pergamos-Ayios Nicolaos–Xylophagou. The British Administrator of these areas is appointed by The Queen and is responsible to the Secretary of State for Defence. The combined total of army and RAF personnel stationed in the areas is 3,250.
Administrator of the British Sovereign Areas, Air Vice-Marshal T. W. Rimmer, OBE

DEFENCE
The National Guard has 145 main battle tanks, 70 armoured infantry fighting vehicles and 402 armoured personnel carriers. Turkey has about 36,000 troops in northern Cyprus.

In January 1998, a military airfield in Paphos was completed. It is intended to provide a base for Greek military aircraft, as Cyprus does not possess its own air force.
MILITARY EXPENDITURE – 4.8 per cent of GDP (2000)
MILITARY PERSONNEL – National Guard 10,000, Paramilitaries 750; Northern Cyprus Army 5,000, Paramilitaries 150
CONSCRIPTION DURATION – 26 months

ECONOMY
In 1997, 9.9 per cent of the workforce were employed in agriculture, 23.5 per cent in industry and 66.6 per cent in the services sector. Main products are citrus fruits, grapes and vine products, meat, milk, potatoes and other vegetables. Manufacturing, construction, distribution and other service industries are other major employers. Tourism is the main growth industry with over two million tourists producing C£878 million in foreign exchange earnings in 1998, accounting for 18.9 per cent of GDP. 1,055 foreign firms were registered as offshore companies in Cyprus in 1998, and 20 per cent of the world's ships are Cypriot registered.
GNP – US$9,086 million (1999); US$11,950 per capita (1999)
GDP – US$8,970 million (1998); US$11,715 per capita (1999)
ANNUAL AVERAGE GROWTH OF GDP – 4.5 per cent (1999)
INFLATION RATE – 4.1 per cent (2000)
UNEMPLOYMENT – 3.6 per cent (1999)

TRADE

The UK is the main trading partner, taking 15 per cent of exports in 1998 and supplying 11 per cent of imports. In 2000 there was a trade deficit of US$2,606 million and a current account deficit of US$456 million. Imports totalled US$3,846 million and exports US$953 million.

Trade with UK	2000	2001
Imports from UK	£320,153,000	£291,494,000
Exports to UK	213,853,000	250,115,000

TURKISH REPUBLIC OF NORTHERN CYPRUS

In 1974, mainland Greek officers under instructions from the military junta in Athens launched a coup and installed a former EOKA member, Nikos Sampson, as president. Turkey invaded northern Cyprus and occupied over a third of the island. In 1975 a 'Turkish Federated State of Cyprus' under Rauf Denktaş was declared in this area and in 1983 a 'Declaration of Statehood' was issued which purported to establish the 'Turkish Republic of Northern Cyprus'. The declaration was condemned by the UN Security Council and only Turkey has recognised the new 'state'. In 1985, Denktaş was elected president and a general election was held. Denktaş was re-elected in 1990, 1995 and on 15 April 2000. A UN plan for the reunification of the island was formally rejected by him on 31 August 1998. On 6 December 1998, elections to the 50-seat Republican Assembly resulted in a coalition government between the National Unity Party, who gained 24 seats, and the Democrat Party, who gained 13 seats. UN-sponsored proximity talks were held on 3–14 December 1999 between representatives of the Greek and Turkish communities, but no agreement was reached; a further round was planned.

DE FACTO HEAD OF STATE
President, Rauf Denktash, *elected* 1985, *re-elected* 1990, 1995, 15 April 2000
Prime Minister, Dervis Eroglu

CZECH REPUBLIC
Česká Republika – Czech Republic

AREA – 30,450 sq. miles (78,866 sq. km). Neighbours: Poland (north-east), Germany (west and north-west), Austria (south), Slovakia (east)
POPULATION – 10,304,000, (1997 estimate) 95 per cent Czech, 3 per cent Slovak. Czech is the official language. The majority of the population is Roman Catholic, with a small Protestant minority
CAPITAL – Prague (Praha) on the Vltava (Moldau) (population, 1,202,552, 1998 UN estimate)
MAJOR CITIES – Brno (Brünn) (386,566); Ostrava (323,539); Plzeň (Pilsen); (169,946),1998 UN estimates
CURRENCY – Koruna (Kcs) of 100 haléru
NATIONAL ANTHEM – Kde Domov Můj (Where Is My Motherland)
NATIONAL DAY – 28 October
NATIONAL FLAG – White over red horizontally with a blue triangle extending from the hoist to the centre of the flag
LIFE EXPECTANCY (years) – male 72.1; female 78.7
POPULATION GROWTH RATE – 0.1 per cent (1999)
POPULATION DENSITY – 130 per sq. km (1999)
URBAN POPULATION – 74.7 per cent (1996)

The Czech Republic is composed of Bohemia and Moravia. Bohemia is surrounded by mountain ranges while Moravian land stretches to the Danubian basin.

HISTORY AND POLITICS

The area which is now the Czech Republic came under the rule of the Habsburg dynasty in 1526 and remained part of the Austro-Hungarian Empire until 1918. The rise of Czech nationalism in the late 19th century led to the proclamation of the independence of Czechoslovakia on 28 October 1918 following an amalgamation of Bohemia, Moravia, Slovakia and Ruthenia and was confirmed by the Versailles Peace Conference in 1919.

Czechoslovakia was forced to cede the ethnic German Sudetenland to Nazi Germany in 1938 after the Munich Agreement. German forces invaded the Czech Republic in March 1939 and incorporated it into Germany while Slovakia became a puppet state. The Czech Republic was liberated by Soviet and American forces in May 1945. The pre-war democratic Czechoslovak state was re-established in 1945, having ceded Ruthenia to the Soviet Union. The Communists took power in a coup in 1948 and remained in power until 1989.

In 1968 the Communist Party under Alexander Dubček embarked on a political and economic reform programme (the Prague Spring). The reforms were suppressed following an invasion by Warsaw Pact troops on the night of 20 August 1968, and were abandoned when Gustáv Husák became leader of the Communist Party in 1969.

Mass protests in November 1989 led to the resignation of the Communist Party Central Committee. The Party was forced to concede its monopoly of power and on 10 December a new government was appointed in which only half the ministers were Communists. Husák resigned as president and was replaced by the dissident writer Václav Havel. Free elections were held in June 1990 in which the Communist Party was defeated.

In late 1992 the leaders of the Czech and Slovak republics agreed to dissolve the federation and form two sovereign states; this took effect on 1 January 1993.

The general election in June 2002 produced no outright winner. Vladimír Spidla, leader of the Czech Social Democratic Party (ČSSD), formed a coalition government. As of July 2002, the ČSSD had 70 seats, the Civic Democratic Party (ODS) 58 seats, the Communists 41 seats and the Christian Democratic Union-Czech People's Party (KDU-ČSL) 31 seats.

Following the election for 27 of the 81 seats in the Senate held in November 2000, the (KDU-ČSL) had 21 seats and its ally the Freedom Union/Civic Democratic Alliance (US-DEU) group had 18 seats. The ODS had 22 seats and the ČSSD had 15 seats. .

POLITICAL SYSTEM

The constitution vests legislative power in the bicameral parliament, comprising a 200-member Chamber of Deputies elected for a four-year term and an 81-member Senate elected for a six-year term, one-third being renewed every two years. The president is elected by parliament for a five-year term. Executive power is held by the prime minister and Council of Ministers. A two-thirds majority in parliament is necessary to amend the constitution, and federal laws remain in place unless superseded by Czech ones. A Constitutional Court has been established comprising 15 judges nominated by the president for ten-year terms with Senate approval.

HEAD OF STATE
President, Václav Havel, *elected* 26 January 1993, *re-elected* 20 January 1998

COUNCIL OF MINISTERS *as at July 2002*
Prime Minister, Vladimír Spidla (ČSSD)
Deputy Prime Minister, Commerce and Industry, Miroslav Grégr (ČSSD)

Deputy Prime Minister, Foreign Affairs, Cyril Svoboda (KDU-ČSL)
Deputy Prime Minister, Interior, Stanislav Gross (ČSSD)
Deputy Prime Minister, Justice, Pavel Rychetsky (ČSSD)
Deputy Prime Minister, Science, Research and Human Resources, Petr Mares
Agriculture, Jaroslav Palas (ČSSD)
Culture, Pavel Dostál (ČSSD)
Defence, Jaroslav Tvrdík (ČSSD)
Education, Petra Buzková (ČSSD)
Environment, Libor Ambrozek (KDU-ČSL)
Finance, Bohuslav Sobotka (ČSSD)
Health, Marie Soucková
Industry and Trade, Jiří Rusnok
Information Technology, Vladimir Mlynář (US)
Labour and Social Affairs, Zdenek Škromach (ČSSD)
Regional Development, Pavel Nemec
Transport, Milan Simonovsky (KDU-ČSL)

EMBASSY OF THE CZECH REPUBLIC
26 Kensington Palace Gardens, London W8 4QY
Tel: 020-7243 1115
Ambassador Extraordinary and Plenipotentiary, HE Anne Pringle, apptd 2002
Minister-Counsellor, Milan Čoupek
Military Attaché, Col. Pavel Zuna

BRITISH EMBASSY
Thunovská 14, CZ-11800 Prague 1
Tel: (00 420) (2) 5732 0278
Email: info@britain.cz
Ambassador Extraordinary and Plenipotentiary, HE Anne Pringle, apptd 2001
Counsellor and Deputy Head of Mission, D. E. P. P. Keefe
Defence Attaché, Col. D. A. Wynne Davies,

BRITISH COUNCIL DIRECTOR, Paul Docherty (*Cultural Counsellor*), Národní 10, CZ-11000 Prague 1
Email: info@britishcouncil.cz

DEFENCE

The army has 652 main battle tanks, 801 armoured infantry fighting vehicles and 403 armoured personnel carriers. The Air Force has 75 combat aircraft and 34 attack helicopters. The Czech Republic became a member of NATO on 12 March 1999.

MILITARY EXPENDITURE – 2.2 per cent of GDP (2000)
MILITARY PERSONNEL – 53,600: Army 23,800, Air Force 11,600, Others 18,200; Paramilitaries 5,600
CONSCRIPTION DURATION – 12 months

ECONOMY

Under Communist rule industry and most agricultural land was state-owned. An economic reform programme began in 1990 to produce a free-market economy. This has necessitated a restrictive monetary policy to stem inflation and a restructuring of industry to be competitive, and these were major reasons for the break with Slovakia. As a result, foreign investment (about US$4,500 million in 2000) and private enterprises have grown, over 90 per cent of the economy has been privatised, and reliance on trade with the former Soviet bloc countries has ended. Foreign-owned firms accounted for nearly half of all exports in 2000.

A trade-liberalising association agreement with the EU is in operation, and formal EU accession talks began in March 1998.

A customs union between the Czech and Slovak Republics is in place but separate currencies were introduced in February 1993 following speculation. The Koruna was made fully convertible in October 1995.

Principal agricultural products are sugar beet, potatoes and cereal crops; the timber industry is also very important. Having been the major industrial area of the Austro-Hungarian Empire, the country has long been industrialised, and machinery, industrial consumer goods and raw materials are major exports.

In 2000 there was a trade deficit of US$3,248 million and a current account deficit of US$2,335 million. Imports totalled US$33,852 million and exports US$28,998 million.

GNP – US$50,593 million (2000); US$5,020 per capita (1999)
GDP – US$56,402 million (1998); US$5,229 per capita (1999)
ANNUAL AVERAGE GROWTH OF GDP – 2.9 per cent (2000)
INFLATION RATE – 4.1 per cent (2001)
UNEMPLOYMENT – 8.6 per cent (2000)
TOTAL EXTERNAL DEBT – US$22,583 million (1999)

Trade with UK	2000	2001
Imports from UK	£930,940,000	£1,078,576,000
Exports to UK	824,113,000	1,124,786,000

EDUCATION

Education is compulsory and free for all children from the ages of six to 15. There are nine universities of which the oldest and most famous is Charles University in Prague (founded 1348).

ENROLMENT (percentage of age group) – primary 100 per cent (1997); secondary 99 per cent (1997); tertiary 24 per cent (1997)

CULTURE

The Reformation gave a widespread impetus to Czech literature, the writings of Jan Hus (martyred in 1415 as a religious and social reformer) familiarising the people with Wyclif's teaching. This lasted until the close of the 17th century when Jan Amos Komenský or Comenius (1592–1670) was expelled from the country. There was a period of stagnation until the national revival in the 19th century. Authors of international reputation include Jaroslav Hašek (1883–1923), Jaroslav Seifert (1901–86, Nobel Prize for Literature, 1985), Václav Havel (b. 1936) and Milan Kundera (b. 1929).

DENMARK
Kongeriget Danmark/Kingdom of Denmark

AREA – 16,639 sq. miles (43,094 sq. km). Neighbour: Germany (south)
POPULATION – 5,284,000. The majority of the population is Lutheran. The language is Danish
CAPITAL – Ψ Copenhagen (population, 1,362,264, 1998 projection)
MAJOR CITIES – Ψ Ålborg (160,937); Ψ Århus (283,673); Ψ Odense (183,584), 1997 UN estimates
CURRENCY – Danish krone of 100 øre
NATIONAL ANTHEMS – Kong Kristian stod ved højen mast (King Christian Stood By The Lofty Mast); Det er et yndigt land (There Is A Lovely Land)
NATIONAL DAY – 5 June (Constitution Day)
NATIONAL FLAG – Red, with white cross
LIFE EXPECTANCY (years) – male 74.2; female 79.1
POPULATION GROWTH RATE – 0.5 per cent (1999)
POPULATION DENSITY – 124 per sq. km (1999)
Denmark is a kingdom, consisting of the islands of Zealand (Sjælland), Funen (Fyn), Lolland, etc., the peninsula of Jutland (Jylland), the outlying island of Bornholm in the Baltic, and the Færøes and Greenland.

HISTORY AND POLITICS

The Danes were at the forefront of Viking expansionism and briefly united England and Scandinavia under Knut (Canute) (995–1035).

The Union of Kalmar (1397) brought Norway and Sweden (including Finland) under Danish rule. Danish power waned during the 16th century, however, enabling Sweden to re-establish its independence in 1523. In the 19th century Norway was ceded to Sweden under the Treaty of Kiel (1814) and both Schleswig and Holstein, which had been subsumed in 1460, were surrendered to Germany.

Denmark remained neutral during the First World War, and in a plebiscite held in accordance with the Versailles Treaty (1919), northern Schleswig voted to return to Danish sovereignty. In 1939 Denmark signed a non-aggression pact with Germany but was invaded on 9 April 1940 and coerced into contributing to the German war effort. Iceland declared its independence from Denmark in 1944 and the Færøe Islands were granted home rule in 1948. Greenland, which had had the status of a colony, was integrated into Denmark in 1953 and granted home rule in 1979. Social Democrat-led coalitions dominated the post-war era until 1982 when a right-wing government was elected. Denmark joined the European Community in 1973.

A referendum was held on 28 September 2000 on membership of   the European single currency. Membership was rejected by 53.1 per cent of those who voted.

The most recent legislative elections were held on 20 November 2001 and the Liberal Party became the largest party in Parliament. A coalition government was formed on 27 November 2001 by Anders Fogh Rasmussen between the Liberal Party and the Conservative People's Party.

POLITICAL SYSTEM

The legislature consists of one chamber, the *Folketing*, of 179 members, including two for the Færøes and two for Greenland, which is elected for a four-year term. The voting age is 18 with voting based on a proportional representation system with a 2 per cent threshold for parliamentary representation.

HEAD OF STATE

HM *The Queen of Denmark*, Queen Margrethe II, KG, *born* 16 April 1940, *succeeded* 14 January 1972, *married* 10 June 1967, Count Henri de Monpezat (Prince Henrik of Denmark), and *has issue* Crown Prince Frederik (*see below*); Prince Joachim, *born* 7 June 1969, *married* 18 November 1995, Miss Alexandra Manley (Princess Alexandra of Denmark)
Heir, HRH Crown Prince Frederik, *born* 26 May 1968

CABINET *as at May 2002*

Prime Minister, Anders Fogh Rasmussen (V)
Culture, Brian Mikkelsen (KF)
Defence, Svend Aage Jensby (V)
Ecclesiastical Affairs, Tove Fergo
Economy, Industry, Trade and Nordic Co-operation, Bendt Bendtson (KF)
Education, Ulla Toernaes (V)
Employment, Claus Hjort Frederiksen (V)
Environment and Energy, Hans Christian Schmidt (V)
Finance, Thor Pedersen (V)
Food, Agriculture and Fisheries, Mariann Fischer Boel (V)
Foreign Affairs, Per Stig Moeller (KF)
Interior and Health, Lars Loekke Rasmussen (V)
Justice, Lene Espersen (KF)

Refugees, Immigrants and Integration; Minister without portfolio responsible for European Affairs, Bertel Haarder (V)
Science, Technology and Development, Helge Saner (V)
Social Affairs and Equality, Henriette Kjaer (KF)
Taxation, Svend Erik Hovmand (KF)
Transport, Flemming Hansen (KF)
V Liberal Party; KF Conservative People's Party

ROYAL DANISH EMBASSY

55 Sloane Street, London SW1X 9SR
Tel: 020-7333 0200
Ambassador Extraordinary and Plenipotentiary, HE Tom Risdahl Jensen, apptd 2001
Counsellor (Commercial), Eric Ovesen
Defence Attaché, Capt. Uffe Haagen Olsen, CBE

BRITISH EMBASSY

36–40 Kastelsvej, DK-2100 Copenhagen Ø
Tel: (00 45) 3544 5200
Email: www.brit-emb@post6.tele.dk
Ambassador Extraordinary and Plenipotentiary, HE Philip Astley, LVO, apptd 1999
Counsellor and Deputy Head of Mission, P. B. Yaghmourian
Defence Attaché, Cmdr. R. P. B. Ayers
First Secretary (Commercial), F. J. Martin

BRITISH CONSULATES – Åbenraa, Ålborg, Århus, Esbjerg, Fredericia, Herning, Odense, Tórshavn (Færøe Islands)

BRITISH COUNCIL DIRECTOR, Dr Michael Sørensen-Jones, Gammel Mønt 12.3, DK-1117 Copenhagen K
Email: british.council@britishcouncil.dk

DEFENCE

The Army has 238 main battle tanks, 274 armoured personnel carriers and 12 attack helicopters. The Navy has four submarines, three offshore patrol frigates and 30 patrol and coastal vessels at two bases. The Air Force has 68 combat aircraft.

MILITARY EXPENDITURE – 1.5 per cent of GDP (2000)
MILITARY PERSONNEL – 21,400: Army 12,900, Navy 4,000, Air Force 4,500
CONSCRIPTION DURATION – Four to 12 months

ECONOMY

The largest sectors of employment are professional services and administration; commerce; manufacturing and agriculture. The chief agricultural products are pigs, dairy products, poultry and eggs, seeds and cereals; manufactures are mostly based on imported raw materials but there are also considerable imports of finished goods. Denmark is self-sufficient in oil and natural gas.

GNP – US$170,995 million (2000); US$32,050 per capita (1999)
GDP – US$174,348 million (1998); US$32,853 per capita (1999)
ANNUAL AVERAGE GROWTH OF GDP – 2.9 per cent (2000)
INFLATION RATE – 2.4 per cent (2001)
UNEMPLOYMENT – 4.7 per cent (2001)

TRADE

The principal imports are industrial raw materials, consumer goods, construction inputs, machinery, raw materials, vehicles and textile products. The chief exports are manufactured articles, and agricultural and dairy products. Germany and Sweden are Denmark's main trading partners.

In 2000 Denmark had a trade surplus of US$7,199

million and a current account surplus of US$3,353 million. Imports totalled US$43,704 million and exports US$49,534 million.

Trade with UK	2000	2001
Imports from UK	£2,181,900,000	£2,156,500,000
Exports to UK	2,276,700,000	2,513,200,000

COMMUNICATIONS

In 1996, the Danish mercantile fleet numbered 584 ships of more than 100 gross tonnage. There were 3,000 km of railway, 85 per cent of which belonged to the state and 15 per cent to privately-owned companies. A rail tunnel and bridge linking the islands of Sjælland and Fyn was opened in 1997, and a road and rail tunnel and bridge across the Øresund, linking Copenhagen with the Swedish city of Malmö, was opened on 1 July 2000.

CULTURE AND EDUCATION

The Danish language is akin to Swedish and Norwegian. Danish literature, ancient and modern, embraces all forms of expression, familiar names being Hans Christian Andersen (1805–75), Søren Kierkegaard (1813–55), Karen Blixen (1885–1962) and Peter Høeg (b. 1957). Some 38 newspapers are published in Denmark; eight daily papers are published in Copenhagen.

Education is free and compulsory. Special schools are numerous, commercial, technical and agricultural predominating. There are universities at Copenhagen (founded in 1479), Århus (1928), Odense (1966), Roskilde (1972) and Ålborg (1974).

ENROLMENT (percentage of age group) – primary 100 per cent (1997); secondary 100 per cent (1997); tertiary 48 per cent (1997)

THE FÆRØE ISLANDS

AREA – 540 sq. miles (1,399 sq. km)
POPULATION – 48,000 (1997 UN estimate)
CAPITAL – Tórshavn (population, 16,218, 1992)

Since 1948 the Færøes or Sheep Islands have had a degree of home rule. The islands are governed by a *Løgting* of between 27 and 32 members and a *Landsstýri* of three to six members which deals with special Færøes affairs, and send two representatives to the *Folketing* at Copenhagen. The Færøes are not part of the EU.

Prime Minister, Anfinn Kallsberg

Trade with UK	2000	2001
Imports from UK	£7,094,000	£27,935,000
Exports to UK	76,213,000	108,873,000

GREENLAND

AREA – 840,004 sq. miles (2,175,600 sq. km) of which about 16 per cent is ice-free
POPULATION – 56,000 (1997)
CAPITAL – Godthåb (Nuuk) (population, 12,483, 1997 estimate)

Greenland attained a status of internal autonomy in May 1979 and a government (*Landsstyret*) was established. It has a Landsting (*parliament*) of 31 members and sends two representatives to the *Folketing* at Copenhagen. Greenland negotiated its withdrawal from the EU, without discontinuing relations with Denmark, and left on 1 February 1985.

The USA has acquired certain rights to maintain air bases in Greenland.

Prime Minister, Jonathan Motzfeldt

Trade with UK	2000	2001
Imports from UK	£3,108,000	£2,994,000
Exports to UK	351,000	3,220,000

DJIBOUTI
Jumhūriyya Jibūt/République Djibouti – Republic of Djibouti

AREA – 8,958 sq. miles (23,200 sq. km). Neighbours: Eritrea (north), Ethiopia (west and south), Somalia (south-east)
POPULATION – 634,000, 520,000 (1991 census), mostly Afar or Issas. The official languages are Arabic and French; Afar and Somali are also spoken
CAPITAL – Ψ Djibouti (population, 62,000, 1991)
CURRENCY – Djibouti franc of 100 centimes
NATIONAL ANTHEM – Hinjinne u sara kaca (Arise With Strength)
NATIONAL DAY – 27 June (Independence Day)
NATIONAL FLAG – Blue over green with white triangle in the hoist containing a red star
LIFE EXPECTANCY (years) – male 39.4; female 41.6
POPULATION GROWTH RATE – 1.2 per cent (1999)
POPULATION DENSITY – 27 per sq. km (1999)
MILITARY EXPENDITURE – 5.0 per cent of GDP (2000)
MILITARY PERSONNEL – Army 8,000, Navy 200, Air Force 200, Paramilitaries 3,000
GNP – US$556 million (2000); US$790 per capita (1999)
GDP – US$498 million (1998); US$835 per capita (1999)
ANNUAL AVERAGE GROWTH OF GDP – 2.1 per cent (1998)
TOTAL EXTERNAL DEBT – US$280 million (1999)
ILLITERACY RATE – 33.5 per cent (2002)
ENROLMENT (percentage of age group) – primary 32 per cent (1996); secondary 12 per cent (1996); tertiary 0.3 per cent (1996)

HISTORY AND POLITICS

Formerly French Somaliland and then the French Territory of the Afars and the Issas, the Republic of Djibouti became independent on 27 June 1977. A multiparty constitution was adopted by referendum in 1992 and subsequent multiparty elections held in December 1992 were won by the Rassemblement Populaire pour le Progrès (RPP, the Popular Rally for Progress). President Aptidon was re-elected for a fourth six-year term in 1993. In December 1997, in the first elections since the 1994 peace accord, the RPP and the FRUD formed an alliance and won all 65 seats in the Chamber of Deputies. On 9 April 1999, President Ismael Omar Guelleh was elected, gaining approximately three-quarters of the votes cast; about 60 per cent of the electorate were estimated to have voted. On 7 February 2000, the government signed a peace agreement with a breakaway faction of the FRUD, which had continued its armed opposition to the government after the 1994 peace accord.

On 7 December 2000, an attempted coup by a group of police officers was quickly put down by the armed forces. The next legislative elections are due to take place in December 2002.

HEAD OF STATE

President, Ismael Omar Guelleh, *elected* 9 April 1999

COUNCIL OF MINISTERS *as at July 2002*

Prime Minister, National and Regional Development, Dilleita Mohamed Dilleita
Agriculture, Livestock and Marine Affairs, Ali Muhammad Daoud
Communication and Culture, Posts and Telecommunications, Government Spokesman,

Rifki Abdoulkader Bamakhrama
Defence, Ougoure Kifle Ahmed
Economy, Finance and Privatisation, Yacin Elmi Bouh
Energy and Natural Resources, Muhammad Ali Muhammad
Foreign Affairs and International Co-operation, Relations with Parliament, Ali Abdi Farah
Housing, Town Planning, Environment and Regional Development, Saleiban Omar Oudine
Interior, Abdallah Abdillahi Miguil
Justice, Human Rights, Islamic Affairs and Prisons, Ibrahim Idriss Djibril
Labour and Vocational Training, Mohamed Barkat Abdillahi
Ministers-Delegate, Ahmed Guirreh Waberi
(Decentralisation); Cheikh Mogueh Dirir Samatar *(Religious Affairs and Islamic Affairs);* Hawa Ahmad Yousouf *(Women, Families and Social Welfare);*
National Education, Abdi Ibrahim Absieh
Presidential Affairs and Promotion of Investments, Osman Ahmad Moussa
Public Health, Mohamed Dini Farah
Trade, Industry and Handicrafts, Elmi Obsieh Waiss
Transport and Equipment, Osman Idriss Djama
Youth, Sport, Leisure and Tourism, Dini Abdallah Bililis

EMBASSY OF THE REPUBLIC OF DJIBOUTI
26 rue Emile Ménier, F-75116 Paris, France
Tel: (00 33) (1) 4727 4922
Ambassador Extraordinary and Plenipotentiary, HE Mohamed Goumaneh Guirrah, apptd 2002

BRITISH AMBASSADOR, HE M. A. Wickstead, apptd 2000, resident at Addis Ababa, Ethiopia

BRITISH CONSULATE
PO Box 169, Rue de Djibouti, Djibouti
Honorary Consul, A. Martinet

ECONOMY AND TRADE

The economy depends mainly on the operation of the free port, which accounts for about three-quarters of Djibouti's GDP. Agriculture accounts for less than 4 per cent of GDP, but employs three-quarters of the workforce. The main imports are foodstuffs, machinery, clothing, and oil and oil derivatives. The main exports are foodstuffs and livestock. Djibouti's primary trading partners are Ethiopia, Somalia, Yemen and France.

Trade with UK	2000	2001
Imports from UK	£18,330,000	£11,609,000
Exports to UK	109,000	123,000

DOMINICA
The Commonwealth of Dominica

AREA – 290 sq. miles (751 sq. km)
POPULATION – 71,200 (2001 census). English is the official language although Creole French is more commonly used
CAPITAL – Ψ Roseau (population, 16,243, 1991)
CURRENCY – East Caribbean dollar (EC$) of 100 cents
NATIONAL ANTHEM – Isle Of Beauty
NATIONAL DAY – 3 November (Independence Day)
NATIONAL FLAG – Green ground with a cross overall of yellow, black and white stripes, and in the centre a red disc charged with a Sisserou parrot in natural colours within a ring of ten green stars
POPULATION GROWTH RATE – 0.1 per cent (1999)
POPULATION DENSITY – 95 per sq. km (1999)

Dominica, in the Lesser Antilles, lies in the Windward Islands group 95 miles south of Antigua. It is about 29 miles long and 16 miles wide. The island is of volcanic origin and very mountainous, and the soil is very fertile.

HISTORY AND POLITICS

The island was discovered by Columbus in 1493, when it was a stronghold of the Caribs, who remained virtually the sole inhabitants until the French established settlements in the 18th century. It was captured by the British in 1759 but passed back and forth between France and Britain until 1805, after which British possession was not challenged. From 1871 to 1939 Dominica was part of the Leeward Islands Colony, then from 1940 the island was a unit of the Windward Islands group. Internal self-government from 1967 was followed on 3 November 1978 by independence as a republic.

The most recent general election was held on 31 January 2000 and won by the Dominica Labour Party, which captured 10 seats, with nine seats going to the United Workers' Party and two seats to the Dominica Freedom Party.

Pierre Charles was appointed as prime minister following the sudden death of his predecessor, Roosevelt Douglas, on 1 October 2000.

POLITICAL SYSTEM

Executive authority is vested in the president, who is elected by the House of Assembly for not more than two terms of five years. Parliament consists of the president and the House of Assembly (21 representatives elected by universal adult suffrage for a five-year term) and nine senators, five of whom are appointed on the advice of the prime minister and the other four on the advice of the Leader of the Opposition.

HEAD OF STATE

President, HE Vernon Shaw, *elected* 2 October 1998, *took office* 6 October 1998

CABINET *as at July 2002*

Prime Minister, Banana Industry, Finance and Caribbean Affairs, Pierre Charles
Agriculture, Planning and the Environment, Lloyd Pascal
Attorney-General, Legal Affairs, David Bruney
Communications and Works, Reginald Austrie
Community Development and Women's Affairs, Matthew Walters
Education, Science and Technology, Herbert Sabaroche
Foreign Affairs, Trade and Marketing, Osborne Riviere
Health and Social Security, John Toussaint
Housing, Vince Henderson
Industry, Enterprise Development and Physical Planning, Ambrose George
Minister of State, Agriculture and Environment, in charge of Fishing, Urban Baron
Minister of State, Education, Loreen Bannis-Robert
Tourism, Ports and Employment, Charles Savarin
Youth and Sports, Roosevelt Skerrit

HIGH COMMISSION FOR THE COMMONWEALTH OF DOMINICA
1 Collingham Gardens, London SW5 0HW
Tel: 020-7370 5194/5
High Commissioner, vacant

BRITISH HIGH COMMISSIONER, HE John White, resident at Bridgetown, Barbados

BRITISH CONSULATE
PO Box 2269, Roseau
Honorary Consul, P. Fletcher

ECONOMY

Agriculture is the principal occupation, with tropical and citrus fruits the main crops. Products for export are bananas, fruit juices, lime oil, bay oil, copra and rum. Forestry, fisheries and agro-processing are being encouraged. The only commercially exploitable mineral is pumice, used chiefly for building purposes. Manufacturing consists largely of the processing of agricultural products although there have been attempts to diversify into light industry. In 1998 Dominica had a trade deficit of US$37 million and a current account deficit of US$18 million. In 2000 imports totalled US$147 million and exports US$53 million.

GNP – US$238 million (2000); US$3,260 per capita (1999)
GDP – US$257 million (1998); US$3,778 per capita (1999)
ANNUAL AVERAGE GROWTH OF GDP – 2.6 per cent (1998)
INFLATION RATE – 0.8 per cent (2000)
UNEMPLOYMENT – 23.1 per cent (1997)
TOTAL EXTERNAL DEBT – US$108 million (1999)

Trade with UK	2000	2001
Imports from UK	£9,357,000	£10,075,000
Exports to UK	13,928,000	12,048,000

DOMINICAN REPUBLIC
República Dominicana – Dominican Republic

AREA – 18,730 sq. miles (48,511 sq. km). Neighbour: Haiti (west)
POPULATION – 8,097,000. The language is Spanish
CAPITAL – Ψ Santo Domingo (population, 2,134,779, 1993)
MAJOR CITIES – Duarte (272,227); La Vega (335,140); Puerto Plata (255,061); San Cristóbal (409,381); San Juan (247,029); Santiago de los Caballeros (690,458), 1993 UN estimates
CURRENCY – Dominican Republic peso (RD$) of 100 centavos
NATIONAL FLAG – Divided into blue and red quarters by a white cross
NATIONAL ANTHEM – Quisqueyanos Valientes, Alcemos (Brave Men Of Quisqueya, Let's Raise Our Song)
NATIONAL DAY – 27 February (Independence Day 1844)
LIFE EXPECTANCY (years) – male 64.4; female 70.1
POPULATION GROWTH RATE – 1.9 per cent (1999)
POPULATION DENSITY – 172 per sq. km (1999)
URBAN POPULATION – 61.7 per cent (1995)
MILITARY EXPENDITURE – 0.8 per cent of GDP (2000)
MILITARY PERSONNEL – 24,500: Army 15,000, Navy 4,000, Air Force 5,500, Paramilitaries 15,000
ILLITERACY RATE – 15.9 per cent (2002)
ENROLMENT (percentage of age group) – primary 94 per cent (1997); secondary 54 per cent (1997); tertiary 23 per cent (1997)

The Dominican Republic, the eastern part of the island of Hispaniola (Haiti is the western part), is the oldest European settlement in America.

HISTORY AND POLITICS

Santo Domingo was discovered by Columbus in 1492, and was a Spanish colony until 1797, when it passed to France. It was restored to Spanish rule in 1809. Independence was proclaimed in 1821, but in 1822 it was subjugated by the neighbouring Haitians who remained in control until 1844, when the Dominican Republic was proclaimed. The country was occupied by American marines from 1916 until 1924, and ruled by Gen. Rafael

Trujillo from 1930 until 1961.
The presidential election on 16 May 2000 was won by Hipólito Mejía, the PRD candidate. The general election on 16 May 2002 resulted in the Dominican Revolutionary Party (PRD) winning 73 seats in the Chamber of Deputies and 29 seats in the Senate.

POLITICAL SYSTEM

Executive power is vested in the president, who is directly elected for a single four-year term and appoints the Cabinet. Legislative power is exercised by the Congress, which has a term of four years. The Congress comprises the Senate of 32 senators, one for each province and one for Santo Domingo, and the 150-member Chamber of Deputies.

HEAD OF STATE

President, Rafael Hipólito Mejía Domingues, *elected* 16 May 2000, *sworn* in 16 August 2000
Vice-President, Minister of Education, Fine Arts and Public Worship, Milagros Ortiz Bosch

CABINET *as at July 2002*

Agriculture, Eligio Jaquez
Attorney-General, Virgilio Bello Rosa
Culture, Tony Raful
Defence, José Miguel Soto Jiménez
Environment, Frank Moya Pons
Finance, José Malkum
Foreign Affairs, Hugo Tolentino Dipp
Health, José Rodríguez Soldevilla
Industry and Commerce, Sonia Gomez
Interior and Police, Pedro Franco Badia
Labour, Milton Ray Guevara
Presidency, Sergio Grullón
Public Works and Communications, Miguel Vargas
Sports, Physical Education and Recreation, César Cedeño
Tourism, Rafael Suberví Bonilla
Women, Yadira Henríquez
Youth, Antonio Pena Guaba

EMBASSY OF THE DOMINICAN REPUBLIC
139 Inverness Terrace, London, W2 6JF
Tel: 020-7727 6285
Ambassador Extraordinary and Plenipotentiary, HE Rafael Ludovino Fernández, apptd 2000

BRITISH EMBASSY
Edificio Corominas Pepin, Ave 27 de Febrero No 233, Santo Domingo
Tel: (00 1 809) 472 7111
Ambassador Extraordinary and Plenipotentiary, HE Andrew Ashcroft, apptd 2002

BRITISH CONSULAR OFFICE – Puerto Plata

ECONOMY

Since 1990 the government has successfully reduced inflation and increased output. Large amounts of foreign debt have been paid off but unemployment remains high.
Sugar, cocoa, coffee, bananas, rice and tobacco are the most important crops. Other products are maize, molasses, beans, tomatoes, cement, ferro-nickel, gold, silver and cattle. Light industry produces beer, tinned foodstuffs, glass products, textiles, soap, cigarettes, construction materials, plastic articles, paint, rum, matches and peanut oil. Tourism is an important part of the economy, with 2.3 million foreign visitors to the Dominican Republic in 1998.

GNP – US$17,959 million (2000); US$1,920 per capita (1999)
GDP – US$15,845 million (1998); US$2,091 per capita (1999)

ANNUAL AVERAGE GROWTH OF GDP – 6.5 per cent (2000)
INFLATION RATE – 6.5 per cent (1999)
UNEMPLOYMENT – 15.9 per cent (1997)
TOTAL EXTERNAL DEBT – US$4,771 million (1999)

TRADE

The chief imports are fuel oils, foodstuffs, motor vehicles, pharmaceuticals and machinery components. The chief exports are minerals, sugar and sugar by-products, coffee and cocoa. The USA is the main trading partner.

In 2000 there was a trade deficit of US$3,742 million and a current account deficit of US$1,027 million. Imports totalled US$7,379 million and exports US$966 million.

Trade with UK	2000	2001
Imports from UK	£48,343,000	£45,159,000
Exports to UK	29,669,000	32,137,000

COMMUNICATIONS

There are over 4,000 miles of roads and a direct road from Santo Domingo to Port-au-Prince, the capital of Haiti, but that part of it in the border area has fallen into disuse. The frontier has been closed since 1967, except for the section crossed by the main road linking the two capitals. A telephone system connects all the principal towns. There are more than 90 commercial broadcasting stations and six television stations.

EAST TIMOR

República Democrática de Timor-Leste/Republik Demokratis Timor Leste/Repúblika Demokrátika Timór-Leste – Democratic Republic of East Timor

---

AREA – 5,743 sq. miles (14,874 sq. km). Neighbour: Indonesia (west). The enclave of Oekussi is separated from the rest of East Timor by the Indonesian province of West Timor
POPULATION – 839,719 (1995 Intercensal census): 78 per cent Timorese, 20 per cent Indonesian, 2 per cent Chinese. Tetum is the national language and is spoken by about 60 per cent of the population, although Mambai, Tokodede, Kemak, Galoli, Idate, Waima'a, Naueti, Bunak, Makasae and Fataluku are also spoken. Portuguese and Bahasa Indonesian are widely understood. The population is predominantly Roman Catholic
CAPITAL – Ψ Dili (population, 62,000, 1996 estimate)
MAJOR CITY – Lautem (17,850, 1996 estimate)
CURRENCY – US dollar of 100 cents
NATIONAL ANTHEM – Funu Nain Falintil
NATIONAL FLAG – Red with a yellow triangle based on the hoist and surmounted by a black triangle containing a white star
LIFE EXPECTANCY (years) – male 49.2; female 50.9
POPULATION GROWTH RATE – 1.7 per cent (1999)
POPULATION DENSITY – 59 per sq. km (1999)

East Timor comprises the eastern half of the island of Timor and the Oekussi enclave in the western half. Parallel mountain ranges cross Timor. Tata Mailau (9,679 ft/2,950 m) is the highest mountain.

HISTORY AND POLITICS

East Timor was a Portuguese colony from 1702 until Portuguese control collapsed following the 1974 coup in Portugal. Local elections were held in early 1975, in which the left-wing, pro-independence Fretilin (Revolutionary Front for an Independent East Timor) emerged as the strongest party. Indonesia had supported Apodeti

(Popular Democratic Association of Timor), which urged the integration of the territory into Indonesia. Following its failure to gain a substantial proportion of the vote, Indonesia encouraged the pro-autonomy Democratic Union of Timor (UDT) to attempt a coup in August 1975, but this was convincingly suppressed by the better equipped and disciplined Fretilin. The Portuguese administration withdrew without formally handing over power. Indonesia began to infiltrate the border and attack villages in the frontier regions to create the illusion that the civil war was still continuing in order to justify an invasion. Fretilin proclaimed the Democratic Republic of East Timor on 28 November 1975, which was recognised by Portugal. The following day the leaders of Apodeti and UDT, who had fled to Indonesia following the failed coup, were coerced into signing a request for Indonesian assistance to restore order in East Timor. Indonesian forces began to invade East Timor on 7 December 1975 and declared East Timor Indonesia's 27th province on 17 July 1976 following their establishment of a provisional East Timorese government consisting of Apodeti ministers, which signed a petition requesting integration with Indonesia. Fretilin forces resisted strongly, but by 1979 most of East Timor was under Indonesian control. Resistance and atrocities committed by Indonesian troops left at least 200,000 East Timorese dead, predominantly civilians. About 150,000 Muslims were settled in East Timor alongside the predominantly Roman Catholic population (80 per cent in 1975). The UN did not recognise the annexation.

Following negotiations between Indonesia and Portugal, an agreement was reached to conduct a plebiscite on 30 August 1999, which would offer East Timor autonomy within Indonesia or independence. The plebiscite resulted in a turnout of 98.6 per cent of the electorate, with 78.5 per cent voting for independence for East Timor.

After extensive violence and intimidation by pro-Indonesian militias and Indonesian troops against the civilian population, and the forcible evacuation of many towns and villages, the UN voted to send in peacekeeping troops after having gained the agreement of the Indonesian government; the first UN peacekeepers arrived on 20 September 1999 and Indonesian troops began to withdraw. On 19 October, the Indonesian Consultative Assembly unanimously ratified the result of the referendum on the independence of East Timor. By early October, the UN-established International Force for East Timor (INTERFET) had managed to install its forces on the border with West Timor with the aim of preventing cross-border attacks by pro-Indonesia militias. INTERFET also managed to land troops in the East Timorese enclave of Oekussi. The commander of Indonesian forces in West Timor signed an agreement with INTERFET on the repatriation of refugees on 22 November 1999. In December 2000, it was estimated that about 120,000 East Timorese remained in Indonesian refugee camps.

The UN Security Council voted unanimously on 25 October 1999 to replace INTERFET with a UN force of up to 8,950 troops and 1,600 police to support the establishment of a UN Transitional Administration in East Timor (UNTAET). On 27 November, the pro-independence activist José Xanana Gusmão visited Jakarta to establish relations with the Indonesian government. The East Timor National Council (ETNC), which was established to make policy recommendations to UNTAET, held its first meeting on 11 December.

In December 1999, international donors pledged US$520 million in aid for the reconstruction of East Timor.

Two reports which were published on 31 January 2000 concluded that the Indonesian authorities had co-operated with the pro-Indonesian militias in wide-ranging human rights abuses and called for the establishment of an international war crimes tribunal. The ETNC adopted the US dollar as the country's transitional currency on 24 January 2000.

President Wahid signed a memorandum of understanding with UNTAET on 29 February 2000, to allow the resumption of cross-border trade and transport between East Timor and Indonesia.

In December 2000, UN prosecutors began issuing indictments for crimes against humanity against those responsible for the violence that had accompanied the referendum; the first trials began soon after. José Xanana Gusmão resigned as president of the ETNC on 28 March 2001 and was replaced by Manuel Carrascalão.

On 1 November 2001 the UN Security Council agreed that East Timor would assume full independence on 20 May 2002.

East Timor's first presidential elections were held on 14 April 2002 and were won by José Xanana Gusmão with 82.7 per cent of the vote.

Independence was achieved on 20 May 2002 and UNTAET was succeeded by the UN Mission of Support in East Timor (UNMISET) which is due to remain in place until May 2003.

POLITICAL SYSTEM

In October 2000 a 36-member transitional legislative body, the East Timor National Council, was established. It was replaced by an 88-member elected Constituent Assembly which was elected on 30 August 2001.

East Timor is divided into 13 administrative districts.

HEAD OF STATE

President, José Xanana Gusmão, *elected* 14 April 2002, took office May 20 2002

CABINET *as at July 2002*
Prime Minister, Economy and Development, Mari bin Hamud Alkatiri
Agriculture, Fisheries and Forestry, Estanislau Alexio da Silva
Education, Culture, Youth Affairs and Sport, Armindo Maia
Finance, María Madalena Brites Boavida
Foreign Affairs, José Ramos-Hurta
Health, Rui María De Araujo
Interior, Rogerio Lobato
Justice, Ana María Pessoa Pereira da Silva Pinto
Transport, Communications and Employment, Ovidio de Jesus Amaral

BRITISH REPRESENTATION OFFICE
PO Box 194, The Post Office, Dili
Tel: (00 61) 408 101 991; Email: dili.fco@gtnet.gov.uk

ECONOMY

The main commercially grown crops include coffee, coconuts, cloves and cocoa. Rice, maize and candlenuts are also widely cultivated. There is some commercial forestry. The main exports are coffee, copra, rubber, wax and sandalwood.

COMMUNICATIONS

There is only one major road, which links the main townships along the northern coast to the east of Dili.

ECUADOR
República del Ecuador – Republic of Ecuador

AREA – 109,484 sq. miles (283,561 sq. km). Neighbours: Colombia (north), Peru (east and south)
POPULATION – 13,183,978 (2001 estimate), descendants of the Spanish, Amerindians, and mestizos. Spanish is the principal language but Quechua is also a recognised language and is spoken by most Indians
CAPITAL – Quito (population, 1,573,458, 1998 estimate)
MAJOR CITIES – Cuenca (270,353); Ψ Guayaquil (2,070,040), the chief port (1998 UN estimates)
CURRENCY – Currency is that of the USA
NATIONAL ANTHEM – Salve, Oh Patria, Mil Veces, Oh Patria (Hail, Oh Fatherland, A Thousand Times, Oh Fatherland)
NATIONAL DAY – 10 August (Independence Day)
NATIONAL FLAG – Three horizontal bands, yellow, blue and red (the yellow band twice the width of the others); emblem in centre
LIFE EXPECTANCY (years) – male 68.3; female 73.5
POPULATION GROWTH RATE – 2.0 per cent (1999)
POPULATION DENSITY – 44 per sq. km (1999)
URBAN POPULATION – 65.3 per cent (2000 estimate)
MILITARY EXPENDITURE – 1.6 per cent of GDP (2000)
MILITARY PERSONNEL – 59,500: Army 50,000, Navy 5,500, Air Force 4,000; Paramilitaries 270
CONSCRIPTION DURATION – 12 months (selective)
Ecuador is an equatorial state of South America. It extends across the Western Andes, the highest peaks being Chimborazo (20,408 ft) and Ilinza (17,405 ft) in the Western Cordillera; and Cotopaxi (19,612 ft) and Cayambe (19,160 ft) in the Eastern Cordillera. Ecuador is watered by the Upper Amazon, and by the rivers Guayas, Mira, Santiago, Chone and Esmeraldas on the Pacific coast. There are extensive forests.

HISTORY AND POLITICS

The former kingdom of Quito was conquered by the Incas of Peru in the 15th century. Early in the 16th century Pizarro's conquests led to the inclusion of the present territory of Ecuador in the Spanish viceroyalty of Quito. Independence was achieved in a revolutionary war which culminated in the battle of Mount Pichincha (1822).

After seven years of military rule, Ecuador returned to democracy in 1979. In the July 1996 elections the ruling Social Christian Party (PSC) won a majority of seats. Abdala Bucaram was elected president in July 1996, and appointed a coalition government. Bucaram was ousted by the legislature on the grounds of insanity and replaced firstly by Vice-President Arteaga and then by the Speaker of the National Congress Fabián Alarcón. In the May 1998 election the Popular Democracy Party (DP) replaced the PSC as the largest party in the National Congress. The presidential elections in July 1998 were won by Jamil Mahaud, the former Mayor of Quito, who gained 51 per cent of the vote.

Presidential elections were scheduled for October 2002. A series of strikes and protests caused disruption throughout July 1999 and led to mass demonstrations calling for the removal of the president. Proposed tax increases led to another wave of protest in November, which again called for the removal of the president. On 18 January 2000, Quito and most provincial capitals were occupied by thousands of Indians. President Mahaud was deposed in a coup by a military junta on 21 January 2000, which was dissolved by the military just five hours after taking office and Vice-President Noboa was elevated to the presidency.

A tax reform bill to reduce the budget deficit, which would have increased value added tax and fuel costs, provoked widespread demonstrations and strikes by an alliance of indigenous farmers and public sector workers and students in January 2001. The government and the protestors reached a compromise agreement on 7 February, but on 8 May the National Congress refused to pass the bill.

FOREIGN RELATIONS

The border with Peru was demarcated by a 1942 treaty that was partly revoked by Ecuador in 1960 in relation to a disputed 50-mile stretch. An inconclusive four-week border war was fought with Peru in February 1995 until a cease-fire was signed on 1 March 1995. A 54-mile demilitarised zone was agreed in July 1995. An agreement was signed on 26 October 1998 by the presidents of the two countries formally ending the territorial dispute after mediation by Argentina, Brazil, Chile and the USA.

POLITICAL SYSTEM

The 1998 constitution provides for an elected president and vice-president who serve for a single four-year term. There is a unicameral National Congress which meets for two months a year and has 121 members, 20 of whom are elected on a national basis and 101 on a provincial basis, all for four-year terms. Voting is compulsory for all literate and voluntary for all illiterate citizens over the age of 18. The republic is divided into 21 provinces.

HEAD OF STATE

President, Gustavo Noboa Bejarano, *sworn* in 22 January 2000
Vice-President, Pedro Pinto Rubianes

CABINET *as at July 2002*

Agriculture and Livestock, Galo Plaza Pallares
Education, Juan Cordero
Energy and Mines, Pablo Terán
Environment, Maria Lourdes Luque
Finance and Economy, Francisco Arosemena Robles
Foreign Relations, Heinz Moeller
Foreign Trade, Industry, Fisheries, Richard Moss
Government, Rudolfo Barniol
Interior, Marcelo Merlo Jaramillo
Labour and Human Resources, Martin Insua Chang
National Defence, Adm. Hugo Unda
Presidency, Marcelo Pérez Monasterios
Public Health, Patricio Jamriska
Public Works, José Machiavello Almeida
Secretary General of the Administration, Marcelo Santos
Social Welfare, Luis Maldonado Ruiz
Tourism, Rocio Vasquez
Urban Development and Housing, Nelson Murgueytio Penaherrera

EMBASSY OF ECUADOR

Flat 3B, 3 Hans Crescent, London SW1X 0LS
Tel: 020-7584 1367/2648/8084
Ambassador Extraordinary and Plenipotentiary, HE Sixto A. Durán-Ballén, apptd 2001

BRITISH EMBASSY

Citiplaza Building, Av. Naciones Unidas and República de El Salvador, 14th Floor, PO Box 17-17-830, Quito
Tel: (00 593) (2) 970 800/1
Email: britembq@interactive.net.ec
Ambassador Extraordinary and Plenipotentiary, HE Ian Gerken, LVO, apptd 2000

BRITISH CONSULAR OFFICES – Cuenca, Galápagos and Guayaquil

ECONOMY

Agriculture is the most important sector of the economy. The main products for export are fish, bananas, which provide a third of agricultural exports, cocoa and coffee. Other important crops are sugar, soya, rice, cotton, African palm, vegetables, fruit and timber. The main imports are manufactured goods and machinery.

The economy was transformed by the discovery in 1972 of major oil fields in the Oriente area.

The US dollar was adopted in 1999 in order to stabilise the economy.

In 1999 there was a trade surplus of US$1,665 million and a current account surplus of US$955 million. In 2000 imports totalled US$3,484 million and exports US$4,853 million.

GNP – US$15,261 million (2000); US$1,360 per capita (1999)
GDP – US$19,723 million (1998); US$1,109 per capita (1999)
ANNUAL AVERAGE GROWTH OF GDP – 2.3 per cent (2000)
INFLATION RATE – 96.1 per cent (2000)
UNEMPLOYMENT – 8.4 per cent (1998)
TOTAL EXTERNAL DEBT – US$14,506 million (1999)

Trade with UK	2000	2001
Imports from UK	£26,619,000	£34,210,000
Exports to UK	30,599,000	32,998,000

COMMUNICATIONS

There are 23,256 km of permanent roads and 5,044 km of roads which are only open during the dry season. Ten commercial airlines operate international flights and there are internal services between all important towns. Two daily newspapers are published at Quito and four at Guayaquil.

EDUCATION

Elementary education is free and compulsory. There are ten universities (three at Quito, three at Guayaquil, and one each at Cuenca, Machala, Loja and Portoviejo), polytechnic schools at Quito and Guayaquil and eight technical colleges in other provincial capitals.
ILLITERACY RATE – 7.8 per cent (2002)
ENROLMENT (percentage of age group) – primary 100 per cent (1997); tertiary 20.0 per cent (1990)

GALÁPAGOS ISLANDS

The Galápagos (Giant Tortoise) Islands, forming the province of the Archipelago de Colón, were annexed by Ecuador in 1832. The archipelago lies in the Pacific, about 500 miles from the mainland. There are 12 large and several hundred smaller islands with a total area of about 3,000 sq. miles and an estimated population (1982) of 6,119. The capital is Puerto Baquerizo Moreno, on San Cristóbal Island. Although the archipelago lies on the equator, the temperature of the surrounding water is well below equatorial average owing to the Humboldt current. The province consists for the most part of National Park Territory, where unique marine birds, iguanas, and the giant tortoises are conserved. There is some local subsistence farming; the main industry, apart from tourism, is tuna and lobster fishing.

EGYPT

Al-Jumhūriyya al-Miṣriyya al-'Arabiyya – Arab Republic of Egypt

AREA – 386,662 sq. miles (1,001,449 sq. km).
Neighbours: Sudan (south), Libya (west), Gaza Strip and Israel (east)
POPULATION – 69,536,644 (2001 estimate). The largest, or 'Egyptian' element, is a Hamito-Semite race. A second element is the *Bedouin*, or nomadic Arabs of the Western and Eastern deserts, who are now mainly semi-sedentary tent-dwellers. The third element is the *Nubian* of the Nile Valley of mixed Arab and Negro blood. Over 90 per cent of the population are Muslims of the Sunni denomination, and most of the rest are Coptic Christians. Arabic is the official language
CAPITAL – Cairo (Al-Qāhirah) (population, 6,800,000, 1996 estimate) stands on the Nile about 14 miles from the head of the delta
MAJOR CITIES – Ψ Alexandria (Al-Iskandarīya) (3,328,196, 1997 estimate), founded 332 BC by Alexander the Great, was the capital for over 1,000 years; Asyūt (2,802,185); Faiyūm (1,989,881); Ismailia (715,009); Ψ Port Said (Būr Sa'īd) (469,533); Ψ Suez (As-Suways) (417,610)
CURRENCY – Egyptian pound (£E) of 100 piastres or 1,000 millièmes
NATIONAL ANTHEM – Biladi (My Homeland)
NATIONAL DAY – 23 July (Anniversary of Revolution in 1952)
NATIONAL FLAG – Horizontal bands of red, white and black, with an eagle in the centre of the white band
LIFE EXPECTANCY (years) – male 66.7; female 69.9
POPULATION GROWTH RATE – 1.8 per cent (1999)
POPULATION DENSITY – 67 per sq. km (1999)
URBAN POPULATION – 44.0 per cent (1997)
ILLITERACY RATE – 43.1 per cent (2002)
ENROLMENT (percentage of age group) – primary 100 per cent (1997); secondary 78 per cent (1997); tertiary 20 per cent (1997)

Egypt comprises Egypt proper, the peninsula of Sinai and a number of islands in the Gulf of Suez and Red Sea, of which the principal are Jubal, Shadwan, Gafatin and Zeberged (or St John's Island).

The country is mainly flat but there are mountainous areas in the south-west, along the Red Sea coast and in the south of the Sinai peninsula; the highest peak is Mt Catherina (8,668 ft). Most of the land is desert and the Nile valley and delta were the only fertile areas until the opening of the Aswan Dam allowed areas of desert to be reclaimed. West of the Nile Valley is the Western Desert, containing some depressions whose springs irrigate oases. The Eastern Desert between the Nile and the mountains along the Red Sea coast is mostly plateaux dissected by wadis (dry water-courses).

HISTORY AND POLITICS

The unification of the kingdoms of Lower and Upper Egypt under the Pharaohs c.3100 BC marked the establishment of the Egyptian state, with Memphis as its capital. Egypt was ruled for nearly 2,800 years by a succession of 31 Pharaonic dynasties which built the pyramids at Gizeh. A period of Hellenic rule began in 332 BC, followed by a period of rule by Rome (30 BC to AD 324) and then by the Byzantine Empire. In AD 640 Egypt was subjugated by Arab Muslim invaders. In 1517 the country was incorporated in the Ottoman Empire, under which it remained until the early 19th century. A British Protectorate over Egypt lasted from 1914 to 1922, when Sultan Ahmed Fuad was proclaimed King of Egypt. In 1953 the monarchy was deposed and Egypt became a republic.

In 1956 President Nasser seized the assets of the Suez Canal Company. Egyptian occupation of the Canal Zone was used as a pretext for military action by Britain and France in support of their Suez Canal Company interests. A cease-fire and Anglo-French withdrawal were negotiated by the UN.

The Israeli invasion of 1956 overran the Sinai peninsula but six months later Israel withdrew. However, mounting tension culminated in a second invasion of Sinai (the Six Day War in June 1967) and occupation of the peninsula by Israel. Sinai was returned to Egypt in 1982 under the treaty of 1979 which resulted from the Camp David talks and formally terminated a 31-year-old state of war between the two countries.

President Mubarak was nominated by the legislature to run unopposed for a fourth six-year term in June 1999, and was endorsed by a national referendum held on 26 September.

A general election was held in three rounds between 18 October and 15 November 2000. The ruling National Democratic Party (NDP) won 388 of the 444 elective seats, which included some 218 independent candidates who joined the party immediately after the election.

INSURGENCY

Militant Islamist fundamentalists re-emerged in 1992, carrying out attacks on tourists, Coptic Christians, government ministers, civil servants and the security forces. On 27 March 1999, the largest fundamentalist organisation, Gamaat-i-Islamiya, announced that it had given up its violent campaign to overthrow the government.

POLITICAL SYSTEM

The constitution of 1971 provides for an executive president who appoints the Council of Ministers and determines government policy. The president is elected by the legislature every six years. The legislature is the People's Assembly which has 454 members, 444 of whom are elected, the remaining ten nominated by the president. The Shura Council or Consultative Assembly (210 members) has an advisory role. A state of emergency, which was first introduced following the assassination of President Sadat in 1981, remains in force.

HEAD OF STATE

President, Mohammed Hosni Mubarak, *elected* 1981, *re-elected* 1987, 1993, 2 June 1999, *confirmed by national referendum* 26 September 1999

COUNCIL OF MINISTERS *as at July 2002*

Prime Minister, Economy, Atef Mohammad Obeid
Deputy PM, Agriculture and Land Reclamation, Yousef Amin Wali
Communications and Information Technology, Ahmed Muhammad Nazif
Culture, Farouk Hosni Abdel Aziz
Defence and Military Production, Field Marshal Mohammad Hussein Tantawi
Education, Hussein Kamel Bahaeddin
Electricity and Energy, Hassan Ahmed Yunes
Finance, Mohammed Midhat Hasanayn
Foreign Affairs, Ahmed Maher
Foreign Trade, Yussef Boutros Ghali
Health and Population, Mohamed Awad Afifi Tag el-Din
Higher Education and Scientific Research, Mufid Shehab
Information, Muhammad Safwat El-Sherif

Interior, Maj.-Gen. Habib al-Adli
Justice, Farouk Seif El-Nasr
Labour and Emigration, Ahmed al-Amawi
Ministers of State, Mahmoud Zaki Abu Amer
(*Administrative Development*); Ahmed Mohamed
Shafiq Zaki (*Civil Aviation*); Mamduh Ryad Tadros
(*Environment*); Fayza abu al-Nagaa (*Foreign Affairs*);
Gen. Sayyid Abduh Mustafa Mash'al (*Military
Production*); Kamal Mohammed Al Shazli (*People's
National Assembly and Consultative Council Affairs*);
Mustafa Abdel Qader (*Rural Development*); Hamdi
Abdel-Salaam Mohamed al-Shaib (*Transport*)
Oil and Mineral Resources, Amin Sameh Fahmi
Planning and International Co-operation, Osman
Mohamed Osman
Public Enterprise, Mukhtar Khattab
Public Works and Irrigation, Mahmoud Abdul Halim
Abu Zaid
Reconstruction, New Urban Zones and Environment,
Mohammed Ibrahim Soliman
Religious Affairs and Waqfs (Endowments), Mahmoud
Hamdi Zakzou
Social Insurance and Social Affairs, Amina Hamzah
al-Jundi
Supply and Internal Trade, Hassan Ali Khedr
Technological Development and Industry, Ali Fahmi
Ibrahim al-Saidi
Tourism, Mamdouh Ahmed Al-Beltagui
Youth, Ali al-Din Hilal al-Dasuqi

EMBASSY OF THE ARAB REPUBLIC OF EGYPT
26 South Street, London W1K 1DW
Tel: 020-7499 2401/3304
Ambassador Extraordinary and Plenipotentiary,
HE Abdel El-Gazzar, apptd 1997
Consul-General, M. Ebeid
Minister Plenipotentiary and Deputy Chief of Mission,
E. Elessawi
Defence Attaché, Brig. Mohamed Gaballa *Minister
Plenipotentiary (Commercial)*, M. Zidan

BRITISH EMBASSY
Ahmed Ragheb Street, Garden City, Cairo
Tel: (00 20) (2) 794 0852
Email: information@cairo.mail.fco.gov.uk
Ambassador Extraordinary and Plenipotentiary,
HE Graham Boyce, KCMG, apptd 1999
Counsellor and Deputy Head of Mission, G. D. Adams
Defence and Military Attaché, Col. P. Dennison, OBE
First Secretaries, P. Byrde (*Consul*); D. G. Reader
(*Commercial*)
BRITISH CONSULAR OFFICES – *Consulate-General*,
Alexandria; *Consulates*, Luxor, Suez

BRITISH COUNCIL DIRECTOR, Dr John Grote, OBE
(*Cultural Counsellor*), 192 Sharia el Nil, Agouza,
Cairo; Email: british.council@britishcouncil.org.eg
Regional directors in Alexandria and Heliopolis

DEFENCE

The Army has 3,860 main battle tanks, 795 armoured
infantry fighting vehicles and 4,095 armoured personnel
carriers. The Navy has one destroyer, ten frigates, four
submarines, 38 patrol and coastal vessels and 24 armed
helicopters at six bases. The Air Force has 580 combat
aircraft and 129 armed helicopters.
MILITARY EXPENDITURE – 3.2 per cent of GDP (2000)
MILITARY PERSONNEL – 443,000: Army 320,000, Navy
19,000, Air Force 29,000, Air Defence Command
75,000; Paramilitaries 325,000
CONSCRIPTION DURATION – 18 months to three years
(selective)

ECONOMY

Despite increasing industrialisation, agriculture remains
the most important economic activity, employing 35 per
cent of the labour force and producing 17 per cent of
GDP in 1998. Egypt is still a net importer of foodstuffs,
especially grain, and a food security programme has been
set up with the aim of achieving self-sufficiency. The
main cash crop is cotton, of which Egypt is one of the
world's main producers. Other important crops are
maize, rice, sugar cane, wheat and potatoes. Other fruits
and vegetables are also grown.

With its considerable reserves of petroleum and natural
gas, and the hydroelectric power produced by the Aswan
and High Dams, Egypt is self-sufficient in energy. The
major manufacturing industries are food processing,
motor cars, electrical goods, steel, chemical products,
yarns and textiles. In 1998 3.5 million foreign tourists
visited Egypt, generating US$4,063 million in revenue.

The government transferred control over exchange
rates to the central bank in January 2001.

In 2001 the government had a trade deficit of US$8,321
million and a current account deficit of US$971 million.

GNP – US$95,244 million (2000); US$1,380 per capita
(1999)
GDP – US$79,867 million (1998); US$1,307 per capita
(1999)
ANNUAL AVERAGE GROWTH OF GDP – 6.4 per cent
(2000)
INFLATION RATE – 2.7 per cent (2000)
UNEMPLOYMENT – 8.2 per cent (1998)
TOTAL EXTERNAL DEBT – US$30,404 million (1999)

TRADE

The main imports are wheat, maize, chemicals and motor
vehicles and parts. The main exports are crude
petroleum, cotton, cotton yarn, oranges, rice and cotton
textiles.

In 2000 Egypt's imports totalled US$14,010 million and
exports US$4,689 million.

Trade with UK	2000	2001
Imports from UK	£499,990,000	£454,844,000
Exports to UK	426,511,000	420,801,000

COMMUNICATIONS

There are international airports at Cairo and Luxor. The
road and rail networks link the Nile valley and delta with
the main development areas east and west of the river.
The Suez Canal was reopened in 1975 and a two-stage
development project begun to widen and deepen the
canal to allow the passage of larger shipping and to
permit two-way traffic. Port Said and Suez have been
reconstructed and the port of Alexandria is being
improved. There are two nationwide terrestrial television
channels and five regional channels and 11 satellite
channels.

EL SALVADOR

República de El Salvador – Republic of El Salvador

AREA – 8,124 sq. miles (21,041 sq. km). Neighbours:
Guatemala (north-west), Honduras (north-east and
east)
POPULATION – 6,237,662 (2001 estimate): 94 per cent
mestizo, 5 per cent Amerindian, 1 per cent European.
The language is Spanish
CAPITAL – San Salvador (population, 1,200,000, 1998)
MAJOR CITIES – San Miguel (127,696); Santa Ana
(139,389)

CURRENCY – US dollar (US$) of 100 cents/El Salvador colón (₡) of 100 centavos
NATIONAL ANTHEM – Saludemos La Patria Orgullosos (Let Us Proudly Hail The Fatherland)
NATIONAL DAY – 15 September
NATIONAL FLAG – Three horizontal bands, sky blue, white, sky blue; coat of arms on white band
LIFE EXPECTANCY (years) – male 66.7; female 69.9
POPULATION GROWTH RATE – 1.8 per cent (1999)
POPULATION DENSITY – 292 per sq. km (1999)
URBAN POPULATION – 44.0 per cent (1997)
MILITARY EXPENDITURE – 1.6 per cent of GDP (2000)
MILITARY PERSONNEL – 16,800: Army 15,000, Navy 700, Air Force 1,100; Paramilitaries 12,000
CONSCRIPTION DURATION – 12 months (selective)

El Salvador extends along the Pacific coast of Central America for 160 miles. The surface of the country is very mountainous, many of the peaks being extinct volcanoes. Much of the interior has an average altitude of 2,000 feet. The climate varies from tropical to temperate. There is a wet season from May to October, and a dry season from November to April. Earthquakes are frequent.

HISTORY AND POLITICS

El Salvador was conquered in 1526 by Pedro de Alvarado, and formed part of the Spanish viceroyalty of Guatemala until 1821. It is divided into 14 Departments.

Decades of military rule ended in October 1979; a Constituent Assembly was elected in 1982. Subsequent presidential and parliamentary elections were boycotted by the FMLN (Farabundo Martí National Liberation Front) guerrilla movement. Conflict between the guerrillas and the government continued throughout the 1980s until negotiations culminated in a peace plan signed in January 1992. In December 1992 the FMLN disarmed and became a political party.

On 7 March 1999, Francisco Flores of the ruling right-wing National Republican Alliance (ARENA) party won the presidential election; he took office on 1 June. ARENA won 29 of the Legislative Assembly's 84 seats and formed a government with other right-wing parties in legislative elections on 12 March 2000; the FMLN became the largest party, winning 31 seats.

HEAD OF STATE

President, Francisco Flores Pérez, elected 7 March 1999, took office 1 June 1999
Vice-President, Minister of the Presidency, Carlos Quintanilla

COUNCIL OF STATE as at July 2002

Agriculture and Livestock, Salvador Urrutia Loucel
Defence, Gen. Juan Antonio Martínez Varela
Director of the Salvadorean Institute of Tourism, Arturo Morales
Economy, Miguel Lacayo
Education, Ana Evelyn Jacir de Lovo
Environment and Natural Resources, Ana María Majano Guerrero
Foreign Affairs, María Eugenia Brizuela de Avila
Interior, Mario Acosta Oertel
Labour and Social Security, Jorge Nieto Menéndez
Public Health, José López Beltrán
Public Security, Justice, Francisco Bertrand Galindo
Public Works, José Angel Quiroz
Treasury, Juan José Daboub

EMBASSY OF EL SALVADOR
Mayfair House, 39 Great Portland Street,
London W1W 7JZ
Tel: 020-7436 8282
Ambassador Extraordinary and Plenipotentiary, vacant
Chargé d'Affaires, Margarita Aragón-Pineda

BRITISH EMBASSY
Edificio Inter-Inversiones, Paseo General Escalón 4828,
PO Box 1591, San Salvador
Tel: (00 503) 263 6520/7/9
Email: britemb@sal.gbm.net
Ambassador Extraordinary and Plenipotentiary,
HE Patrick Morgan, apptd 1999

ECONOMY

The principal agricultural products are coffee, cotton, sugar cane, maize, shrimps and balsam. In the lower altitudes towards the east, sisal is produced and used in the manufacture of coffee and cereal bags.

Existing factories make textiles, clothing, constructional steel, furniture, cement and household items.

The US dollar was adopted on 1 January 2001; the colón remained in use for a transitional period.

Nearly one million people were made homeless and around 20 per cent of the nation's housing was damaged in two major earthquakes in January and February 2001.
GNP – US$12,507 million (2000); US$1,920 per capita (1999)
GDP – US$11,707 million (1998); US$2,007 per capita (1999)
ANNUAL AVERAGE GROWTH OF GDP – 2.0 per cent (2000)
INFLATION RATE – 2.3 per cent (2000)
UNEMPLOYMENT – 7.3 per cent (1998)
TOTAL EXTERNAL DEBT – US$4,014 million (1999)

TRADE

Chief exports are coffee, cotton, sugar, shrimps, sisal, balsam, meat, towels, hides and skins. The chief imports are chemicals, petroleum, manufactured goods, industrial and electronic machinery, pharmaceutical goods, vehicles and consumer goods.

In 2000 there was a trade deficit of US$196 million and a current account deficit of US$48 million. In 2000 imports totalled US$3,796 million and exports US$1,342 million.

Trade with UK	2000	2001
Imports from UK	£16,258,000	£17,177,000
Exports to UK	14,581,000	7,653,000

COMMUNICATIONS

The principal ports are Cutuco, La Unión and Acajutla. There are more than 12,000 km of roads and 600 km of railways. The Pan-American Highway from the Guatemalan frontier passes through San Salvador and Santa Ana, and continues to the Honduran frontier. Comalapa international airport has daily flights to other Central American capitals, Mexico and the USA. There are 100 broadcasting stations and nine television stations. Five daily newspapers are published in San Salvador.

EDUCATION

Primary education is free and compulsory. There are 38 universities.
ILLITERACY RATE – 21.3 per cent (2002)
ENROLMENT (percentage of age group) – primary 97 per cent (1997); secondary 37 per cent (1997); tertiary 18 per cent (1997)

EQUATORIAL GUINEA
República de Guinea Ecuatorial – Republic of Equatorial Guinea

AREA – 10,831 sq. miles (28,051 sq. km). Neighbours: Cameroon (north), Gabon (east and south)
POPULATION – 486,060 (2001 estimate). The official languages are Spanish and French; Bubi, Fang, Ibo and pidgin English are also spoken
CAPITAL – Ψ Malabo on the island of Bioko (population, 30,418, 1983 estimate)
MAJOR TOWN – Ψ Bata is the principal town and port of Rio Muni
CURRENCY – Franc CFA of 100 centimes
NATIONAL ANTHEM – Caminemos Pisando La Senda De Nuestra Inmensa Felicidad (Let's Walk Down The Path Of Our Immense Happiness)
NATIONAL DAY – 12 October
NATIONAL FLAG – Three horizontal bands, green over white over red; blue triangle next staff; coat of arms in centre of white band
LIFE EXPECTANCY (years) – male 50.4; female 53.6
POPULATION GROWTH RATE – 2.5 per cent (1999)
POPULATION DENSITY – 16 per sq. km (1999)
MILITARY EXPENDITURE – 1.7 per cent of GDP (2000)
MILITARY PERSONNEL – 1,320: Army 1,100, Navy 120, Air Force 100
ILLITERACY RATE – 15.2 per cent (2002)
Equatorial Guinea consists of the island of Bioko, in the Bight of Biafra about 20 miles from the west coast of Africa, Annonbón Island in the Gulf of Guinea, the Corisco Islands (Corisco, Elobey Grande and Elobey Chico), and Rio Muni, a mainland area between Cameroon and Gabon.

HISTORY AND POLITICS

Formerly colonies of Spain, the territories now forming Equatorial Guinea were constituted as two provinces of Metropolitan Spain in 1959, became autonomous in 1963 and fully independent in 1968.

In 1979 President Macias was deposed by a revolutionary military council headed by Col. Obiang Nguema. Constitutional amendments in 1982 provided for legislative elections, which were held in 1983 and 1988, but all candidates were chosen by the president.

A multiparty political system under a new constitution was approved by a referendum in 1991 and ten opposition parties have been legalised, operating alongside the ruling Equatorial Guinea Democratic Party (PDGE). A National Pact was agreed and signed in March 1993 but legislative elections in November, which were won by the PDGE, were boycotted by most of the electorate and opposition parties. In the February 1996 election, the president claimed to have won more than 99 per cent of the vote. Most opposition parties boycotted the ballot. In June 1997 the Progress Party, the largest opposition party, was banned by the government, and in February 1998 opposition party coalitions were deemed illegal. The PDGE won 75 of the 80 seats in the National Assembly elections on 7 March 1999 amid allegations of electoral malpractice.

Prime Minister Angel Serafin Seriche Dougan resigned on 23 February 2001 due to his growing unpopularity. He was replaced by Cándido Muatetema Rivas on 26 February.

HEAD OF STATE

President of the Supreme Military Council and Minister of Defence, Brig.-Gen. Teodoro Obiang Nguema Mbasogo, *took office* August 1979, *re-elected* June 1989, 25 February 1996

COUNCIL OF MINISTERS *as at July 2002*

Prime Minister, Cándido Muatetema Rivas
Deputy PM, Civil Service and Administrative Reforms, Ignacio Milam Tang
Minister of State, Agriculture, Fishing and Animal Husbandry, Gregorio Boho Camo
Minister of State, Education and Science, Government Spokesman, Antonio Fernando Nve Ngu
Minister of State, Forestry, Fisheries and Environment, Teodoro Nguema Obiang
Minister of State, Health and Social Welfare, Marcelino Nguema Onguene
Minister of State, Information, Tourism and Culture, Lucas Nguema Esono
Minister of State, Labour and Social Security, Ricardo Mangue Obama Nfube
Minister of State, Presidency, Special Duties, Alejandro Evuna Owono Asangono
Minister of State, Presidency, Relations with Assemblies and Legal Matters, vacant
Minister of State, Secretary-General of the Government, Francisco Pascual Eyegue Obama
Minister of State, Transport and Communications, Marcelino Oyono Ntutumu
Economic Affairs and Finance, Baltasar Engonga Edjo
Foreign Affairs, International Co-operation, Francophone Affairs, Santiago Nsobeya Efuman
Industry, Commerce, Small Enterprises, Constantino Ekong Nsue
Interior and Local Corporations, Clemente Engonga Nguema Onguene
Justice and Religion, Rubén Maye Nsue
Mines and Energy, Cristóbal Menana Ela
Planning and Economic Development, Fortunato Ofa Mbo
Public Works, Housing and Urban Affairs, Florentino Nkogo Ndong
Social Affairs, Women's Development, Teresa Efua Asangono
Youth and Sports, Juan Antonio Bibang Ntutumu

EMBASSY OF THE REPUBLIC OF EQUATORIAL GUINEA
6 rue Alfred de Vigny, F-75008 Paris
Tel: (00 33) (1) 4766 4433
Ambassador Extraordinary and Plenipotentiary, vacant
BRITISH AMBASSADOR, HE Peter Boon, resident at Yaoundé, Cameroon

ECONOMY

The chief products are cocoa, coffee and wood. Production has declined and except for cocoa there is little commercial agriculture. The economy is heavily dependent on outside aid, principally from Spain. Oil and gas production is increasing. Equatorial Guinea entered the 'franc zone' in 1985.

In 1996, there was a trade deficit of US$117 million and a current account deficit of US$344 million. In 1998 imports totalled US$32 million and exports US$423 million.

GNP – US$516 million (1999); US$1,170 per capita (1999)
GDP – US$162 million (1998); US$1,907 per capita (1999)
ANNUAL AVERAGE GROWTH OF GDP – 1.4 per cent (1998)

TOTAL EXTERNAL DEBT – US$271 million (1999)

Trade with UK	2000	2001
Imports from UK	£28,075,000	£24,852,000
Exports to UK	1,074,000	5,696,0000

ERITREA

Hagere Eretra/al-Dawla al-Iritra – State of Eritrea

AREA – 45,406 sq. miles (117,600 sq. km). Neighbours: Sudan (north and north-west), Ethiopia (south and south-west), Djibouti (south-east)
POPULATION – 4,298,269 (2001 estimate), roughly half Coptic Christian (mainly highlanders) and half Muslim (mainly lowlanders). Arabic, Tigrinya and English are the main working languages. Italian is also widely spoken. There are nine indigenous language groups: Afar; Bilen; Hadareb; Kunama; Nara; Rashida; Saho; Tigre; Tigrinya
CAPITAL – Asmara (population, 450,000, 2001 estimate)
MAJOR TOWNS – Ψ Assab; Ψ Massawa
CURRENCY – Nakfa
NATIONAL DAY – 24 May (Independence Day)
NATIONAL FLAG – Divided into three triangles; the one based on the hoist is red and bears a gold olive wreath; the upper triangle is green and the lower one light blue
LIFE EXPECTANCY (years) – male 51.1; female 53.7
POPULATION GROWTH RATE – 3.9 per cent (1999)
POPULATION DENSITY – 32 per sq. km (1999)
URBAN POPULATION – 20.0 per cent
ILLITERACY RATE – 42.4 per cent (2002)
ENROLMENT (percentage of age group) – primary 53 per cent (1997); secondary 20 per cent (1997); tertiary 1 per cent (1997)

HISTORY AND POLITICS

Eritrea was colonised by Italy in the late 19th century and was the base for the 1936 Italian invasion of Abyssinia (Ethiopia). After the Italian defeat in East Africa in 1941 by British and Commonwealth forces, Eritrea became a British protectorate. This lasted until 15 September 1952 when Eritrea was federated with Ethiopia. The Ethiopian Emperor Haile Selassie incorporated Eritrea as a province of Ethiopia in 1962. An armed campaign for independence began in 1961, first against Emperor Haile Selassie's forces and from 1974 against the Mengistu regime.

In 1991 the Mengistu government was overthrown by the Eritrean People's Liberation Front (EPLF) and the Ethiopian People's Revolutionary Democratic Front (EPRDF). The new EPRDF-led government in Ethiopia agreed to an Eritrean referendum on independence which was held in April 1993 and recorded a 99.89 per cent vote in favour. Independence was declared on 24 May 1993.

On February 7 2002, the European Parliament adopted a resolution that expressed concern at increasing authoritarian tendencies in the country.

FOREIGN RELATIONS

Eritrea had claimed the Hanish and Mohabaka Islands in the Red Sea, which they seized from Yemen in December 1995; however, on 9 October 1998, the International Court of Justice ruled that the Hanish Islands belonged to Yemen and Eritrea formally handed them over to Yemen on 1 November 1998. The land border with Djibouti is also disputed.

In May 1998 sporadic fighting flared up on the border with Ethiopia, with both countries accusing the other of sending troops across the border. Proposals for a resolution of the conflict drawn up by the Organisation for African Unity (OAU) in November 1998, which called on Eritrea to hand back the disputed town of Badme pending adjudication, were rejected by Eritrea. Full-scale fighting broke out on 6 February 1999 and Ethiopia had captured the town by 28 February. Eritrea accepted the OAU's proposals on 9 March, but fighting continued. A further proposal to end the fighting was brokered by the OAU in July 1999, which envisaged a return to the original borders and was provisionally accepted by both sides, but Ethiopia later rejected some of the provisions. Fighting resumed on 23 February 2000. On 12 May, Ethiopia launched a full-scale invasion, which ended in early June after Ethiopian forces had captured much of Eritrea's western lowlands. An interim peace plan was signed by both countries on 18 June.

UN observers began to deploy on 15 September 2000. Direct talks between Eritrea and Ethiopia opened on 23 October and on 12 December a comprehensive peace agreement was signed in Algeria; UN peacekeeping troops moved into the buffer zone in April 2001 and on 21 May Eritrea and Ethiopia agreed to set up regional military commissions to solve local security issues.

POLITICAL SYSTEM

Under the 1997 constitution, the head of state is the president, elected for a five-year term by the National Assembly, of which he is chair. The 150-member unicameral legislature (the *Hagerawi Baito*) is directly elected for four years. The president is head of government and presides over a State Council, which includes six regional administrators.

HEAD OF STATE

President, Chairman of the National Assembly, Issaias Afewerki, *elected* by National Assembly 22 May 1993

STATE COUNCIL *as at July 2002*

Agriculture, Arefaine Berhe
Defence, Gen. Sehat Efrem
Education, Osman Saleh
Energy and Mines, Tesfai Ghebresselassie
Eritrean Relief, Refugee Commission, Hiwot Zemichael
Finance and Development, Berhane Abrehe
Fisheries, Ahmed Hajj Ali
Foreign Affairs, Ali Said Abdellah
Health, Saleh Meki
Industry and Trade, Gergish Teklemikael
Information, Naizghi Kiflu
Justice, Fawzia Hashim
Labour and Human Welfare, Askalu Menkerios
Land, Water and Environment, Weldenkiel Ghebremariam
Local Government, vacant
Public Works, Abraha Asfaha
Tourism, Amna Nur Husayn
Transport and Communications, Amdemikael Kahsay

EMBASSY OF THE STATE OF ERITREA
96 White Lion Street, London N1 9PF
Tel: 020-7713 0096.
Ambassador Extraordinary and Plenipotentiary,
  HE Ghirmai Ghebremariam, apptd 2000
BRITISH AMBASSADOR, HE Michael Murray, resident at Addis Ababa, Ethiopia

BRITISH EMBASSY
Emperor Yohannes Avenue, House no 24, PO Box 5584, Asmara
Tel: (00 291) (1) 120145
Email: alembca@gemel.com.er

BRITISH COUNCIL DIRECTOR, Dr Negusse Araya, PO Box 997, Asmara; Email: britcoun@aol.com.er

DEFENCE

The Army has 100 main battle tanks and 50 armoured infantry fighting vehicles and armoured personnel carriers. The Navy has eight patrol and coastal combatants. The Air Force has 17 combat aircraft.
MILITARY EXPENDITURE – 31.5 per cent of GDP (2000)
MILITARY PERSONNEL – Army 170,000, Navy 1,400, Air Force 800
CONSCRIPTION DURATION – 16 months

ECONOMY

Since 1991 the government has attempted to rebuild industry, agriculture and infrastructure which were devastated by the war of independence. The rebuilding programme has focused on the ports of Massawa and Assab, the roads from the ports to Ethiopia, and the railway from Massawa to Sudan via Asmara. The government hopes to base the rebuilding of the economy on the return of well-educated exiles, international aid and investment, the development of tourism along the coast, and the diversification of the economy away from agriculture.
GNP – US$699 million (2000); US$200 per capita (1999)
GDP – US$751 million (1998); US$221 per capita (1999)
ANNUAL AVERAGE GROWTH OF GDP – 3.0 per cent (1998)
TOTAL EXTERNAL DEBT – US$254 million (1999)

Trade with UK	2000	2001
Imports from UK	£4,707,000	£4,895,000
Exports to UK	187,000	154,000

ESTONIA
Eesti Vabariik – Republic of Estonia

AREA – 17,413 sq. miles (45,100 sq. km). Neighbours: Russia (east), Latvia (south)
POPULATION – 1,423,316 (2001 estimate): 65.3 per cent Estonian, 28.1 per cent Russian, 1.5 per cent Ukrainian, 0.9 per cent Belarusian, 0.9 per cent Finnish. The majority religion is Lutheran, with Russian Orthodox and Baptist minorities. Estonian is the first language of 64.2 per cent and Russian of 28.7 per cent
CAPITAL – Tallinn (population, 415,299, 1998 estimate)
MAJOR TOWNS AND CITIES – Kohtla-Järve (65,566); Narva (73,295); Pärnu (50,966); Tartu (101,744)
CURRENCY – Kroon of 100 sents
NATIONAL ANTHEM – Mu Isamaa, Mu Õnn Ja Rõõm (My Native Land, My Joy, Delight)
NATIONAL DAY – 24 February (Independence Day)
NATIONAL FLAG – Three horizontal stripes of blue, black, white
LIFE EXPECTANCY (years) – male 65.8; female 76.4
POPULATION GROWTH RATE – 1.2 per cent (1999)
POPULATION DENSITY – 31 per sq. km (1999)
URBAN POPULATION – 69.6 per cent (1996) 2000 estimate
MILITARY EXPENDITURE – 1.4 per cent of GDP (2000)
MILITARY PERSONNEL – 4,450: Army 4,040, Navy 300, Air Force 110; Paramilitaries 2,800
CONSCRIPTION DURATION – Eight to 11 months

Estonia includes 1,500 islands in the Baltic Sea and the Gulf of Riga. Forests cover roughly 45 per cent of the country, which also has many lakes.

HISTORY AND POLITICS

Estonia, a former province of the Russian Empire, declared its independence on 24 February 1918. A war of independence was fought against the German army until November 1918, and then against Soviet forces until the peace treaty of Tartu was signed in 1920. By this treaty Soviet Union recognised Estonia's independence.

The Soviet Union annexed Estonia in 1940 under the terms of the Molotov-Ribbentrop pact with Germany. Estonia was occupied when Germany invaded the Soviet Union during the Second World War. In 1944 the Soviet Union recaptured the country from Germany and confirmed its annexation.

The Estonian Supreme Soviet in November 1989 declared the republic to be sovereign and its 1940 annexation by the Soviet Union to be illegal. In February 1990 the leading role of the Communist Party was abolished, and following multiparty elections in March 1990 a period of transition to independence was inaugurated. Independence was declared on 20 August 1991.

After legislative elections held on 7 March 1999, a centre-right coalition government of the Pro Patria Union, the Mõõdukad Party and the Reform Party was formed. Following the resignation on 8 January 2002 of Mart Laar of Pro Patria as prime minister, Siim Kallas, leader of the Reform Party became prime minister on 28 January with a new coalition government of the RP and Centrist Party (KP). Presidential elections held on 27 and 28 August and 21 September 2001 were won by Arnold Rüütel.

POLITICAL SYSTEM

Legislative power is exercised by the unicameral Riigikogu of 101 members elected by proportional representation every four years. The president is elected for a five-year term by the Riigikogu by a two-thirds majority or, if no candidate receives this majority after three rounds of voting, by an electoral assembly composed of Riigikogu members and local government officials. Executive authority is vested in a prime minister who is nominated by the president and who forms a government. Members of the government need not be members of the Riigikogu.

HEAD OF STATE

President, Arnold Rüütel, *elected by electoral* 21 September 2001, *sworn in* 8 October 2001.

GOVERNMENT *as at July 2002*

Prime Minister, Siim Kallas (RP)
Agriculture, Jaanus Marrandi (KP)
Culture, Signe Kivi (RP)
Defence, Sven Mikser (KP)
Economic Affairs, Transport and Communications, Liina Tõnisson (KP)
Education, Mailis Rand (KP)
Environment, Heiki Kranich (RP)
Ethnic Affairs, Eldar Efendijev (KP)
Finance, Harri Õunapuu (KP)
Foreign Affairs, Kristiina Ojuland (RP)
Interior, Ain Seppik (KP)
Justice, Märt Rask (RP)
Regional Affairs, Toivo Asmer (RP)
Social Affairs, Siiri Oviir (KP)
Without Portfolio, Toivo Asmer
KP Centrist Party; RP Reform Party

EMBASSY OF THE REPUBLIC OF ESTONIA
16 Hyde Park Gate, London SW7 5DG
Tel: 020-7589 3428
Ambassador Extraordinary and Plenipotentiary, HE Kaja
Tael, apptd 2001

BRITISH EMBASSY
Wismari 6, EE-10136 Tallinn
Tel: (00 372) 667 4700
Ambassador Extraordinary and Plenipotentiary, HE Sarah
Squire, apptd 2000
BRITISH COUNCIL DIRECTOR, Kyllike Tohver, Resource
Centre, Vana Posti 7, EE-10146 Tallinn;
Email: british.council@britishcouncil.ee

ECONOMY

Since 1992 the government has introduced free-market
reforms, privatisation and restructuring. Estonia is still
dependent on Russian natural gas supplies.

Eleven per cent of the workforce is engaged in
agriculture, which accounts for 6 per cent of GDP, the
main products being rye, oats, barley, flax, potatoes, meat,
milk, butter and eggs.

Industry accounts for 20 per cent of employment and
20 per cent of GDP, concentrating on textiles, clothing
and footwear, forestry, wood and paper products, and
food and fish processing. Some heavy industry exists,
mostly chemicals and the manufacture of power
equipment.

The kroon is pegged to the euro.
GNP – US$4,894 million (2000); US$3,400 per capita
(1999)
GDP – US$5,210 million (1998); US$3,591 per capita
(1999)
ANNUAL AVERAGE GROWTH OF GDP – 6.4 per cent
(2000)
INFLATION RATE – 4.0 per cent (2000)
UNEMPLOYMENT – 11.7 per cent (1999)
TOTAL EXTERNAL DEBT – US$2,879 million (1999)

TRADE

Estonia's main trading partners are Finland, Sweden,
Germany, Japan and Latvia. The main imports are
machinery and equipment, chemicals, clothing and
footwear, foodstuffs and vehicles. Exports consist mainly
of machinery and equipment, timber and wood
products, textiles and clothing, foodstuffs, metals and
furniture. Free trade and association agreements with the
EU came into effect in 1995 and formal accession
negotiations were begun in March 1998.

In 1999 there was a trade deficit of US$878 million and
a current account deficit of US$295million. In 2000
imports totalled US$4,241 million and exports US$3,133
million.

Trade with UK	2000	2001
Imports from UK	£65,890,000	£82,239,000
Exports to UK	318,822,000	288,422,000

COMMUNICATIONS

Freedom of the press is guaranteed in the constitution,
and the state monopoly on television and radio ended
soon after independence. All newspapers have been
privatised and broadcasting channels are in the process of
being privatised. Russian-language news and
programmes are provided on Estonian Television.

EDUCATION

Estonia has a three-tier education system, consisting of
primary level (four years), secondary level (six years) and
university level (four to six years). Primary and

secondary-level education is compulsory from the age of
seven to 17, which is due to be extended to 18.
ILLITERACY RATE – 0.2 per cent
ENROLMENT (percentage of age group) – primary 94
per cent (1997); secondary 100 per cent (1997);
tertiary 42 per cent (1997)

ETHIOPIA

*Ya'Ityopya Federalawi Dimokrasyawi Repeblik – Federal
Democratic Republic of Ethiopia*

AREA – 426,373 sq. miles (1,104,300 sq. km).
Neighbours: Sudan (west), Kenya (south), Djibouti
and Somalia (east), Eritrea (north)
POPULATION – 63,495,000 (2000 estimate). About one-
third are of Semitic origin (Amharas and Tigreans)
and the remainder mainly Oromos (40 per cent),
Somalis (6 per cent) and Afar (4 per cent). Amharas,
Tigreans and many Oromos are Ethiopian Orthodox
Christians. The Afar people in the north and the
Somalis in the south-east, as well as some Oromos,
are Muslim. Amharic is the most widely used of the
70 languages
CAPITAL – Addis Ababa (population, 2,495,000, 2000
estimate)
MAJOR CITY – Dire Dawa (population, 229,000, 2000
estimate)
CURRENCY – Ethiopian birr (EB) of 100 cents
NATIONAL ANTHEM – Yezeginet Kibir
NATIONAL DAY – 28 May
NATIONAL FLAG – Three horizontal bands: green,
yellow, red; in the centre a blue disc, containing a
yellow pentagram
LIFE EXPECTANCY (years) – male 42.8; female 43.8
POPULATION GROWTH RATE – 3.0 per cent (1999)
POPULATION DENSITY – 56 per sq. km (1999)
URBAN POPULATION – 15.7 per cent (1996)

HISTORY AND POLITICS

The Hamitic culture was heavily influenced by Semitic
immigration from Arabia at about the time of Christ.
Christianity was introduced in the fourth century. The
empire attained its zenith in the sixth century under the
Axum rulers but was checked by Islamic expansion from
the east. Modern Ethiopia dates from 1855 when
Theodros established supremacy over the various tribes.
The last emperor was Haile Selassie who reigned from
1930 until 1974, when he was deposed by the armed
forces. After ten years of military rule, a Workers' Party on
the Soviet model was formed with Lt.-Col. Mengistu
Haile Mariam as General Secretary. The People's
Democratic Republic of Ethiopia was established under a
new constitution in 1987 with Lt.-Col. Mengistu as
president. Armed insurgencies by the Eritrean People's
Liberation Front (EPLF) and the Ethiopian People's
Revolutionary Democratic Front (EPRDF), originating
in Tigre, brought down Mengistu's government in May
1991.

A transitional administration comprising the EPRDF
and other opposition groups formed a Council of
Representatives which governed until 1995 under
President Meles Zenawi. In 1994, the Council agreed on a
draft federal constitution, which was adopted by an
elected Constituent Assembly on 8 December 1994.
Multiparty elections in May and June 1995 were won by
the EPRDF. The Federal Democratic Republic of Ethiopia
was proclaimed on 22 August 1995.

In the general election held on 14 May 2000, the
EPRDF won 472 seats. The elections held on 8 October
2001 were won by Lt. Girma Wolde Giorgis.

FOREIGN RELATIONS

Eritrea, which since 1962 had been a province of
Ethiopia, seceded and became independent on 24 May
1993. Relations between the two countries had been good
until fighting broke out along the border in June 1998,
with each side accusing the other of sending troops across
the border. Ethiopia launched an attack on Eritrea in May
2000, capturing much of the west of the country. An
interim peace plan was signed in June, and a
comprehensive peace agreement was signed in December
(see Eritrea).

POLITICAL SYSTEM

The constitution provides for a federal government
responsible for foreign affairs, defence and economic
policy. The president is elected by both houses of the
legislature. The House of People's Representatives *(Yehizb
Tewokayoch Mekir Bet)* has 548 directly elected members
who serve a five-year term. The House of Federation
(Yefedereshn Mekir Bet) has 108 members, indirectly
elected for a five-year term by the nine regional
administrations (Tigre, Afar, Amara, Oromia, Somali,
Benshangui, Gambela, Harer and Southern), who have
considerable autonomy and the right to secede.

HEAD OF STATE

President, Lt Girma Wolde Giorgis, *elected* 8 October 2001

COUNCIL OF MINISTERS *as at July 2002*

Prime Minister, Meles Zenawi
Deputy Prime Minister, Rural Development, Addisu
   Legesse
Agriculture, Mulatu Teshome
Commerce and Industry, Girma Birru
Education, Genet Zewde
Federal Affairs, Abbay Tsehaye
Finance and Economic Development, Sofian Ahmed
Foreign Affairs, Seyoum Mesfin
Health, Kebede Tadesse
Human Resources Development, Tefera Walua
Information, Bereket Simon
Infrastructural Development, Kassu Ilala
Justice, Harka Haroye
Labour and Social Affairs, Hassan Abdella
Mines and Energy, Mohamed Dirir
National Defence, Abbadula Gemeda
Revenue Collection, Getachew Belay
Water Resources, Shiferaw Jarso
Youth, Culture and Sport, Teshome Toga

EMBASSY OF THE FEDERAL DEMOCRATIC REPUBLIC
OF ETHIOPIA
17 Prince's Gate, London SW7 1PZ
Tel: 020-7589 7212
Ambassador Extraordinary and Plenipotentiary,
   HE Fisseha Adugna, apptd 2000

BRITISH EMBASSY
Fikre Mariam Abatechan Street (PO Box 858),
Addis Ababa
Tel: (00 251) (1) 612354

BRITISH COUNCIL DIRECTOR, Rosemary Arnott, OBE,
   PO Box 1043, Artistic Building, Adwa Avenue, Addis
   Ababa; Email: bc.addisababa@bc-addis.bcouncil.org

DEFENCE

The Army has 300 main battle tanks and 200 armoured
infantry fighting vehicles and armoured personnel

carriers. The Air Force has 51 combat aircraft and 26
armed helicopters.
MILITARY EXPENDITURE – 6.8 per cent of GDP (2000)
MILITARY PERSONNEL – 252,500: Army 250,000, Air
   Force 2,500

ECONOMY

The post-Mengistu government implemented a
programme of free-market economic reform which
reduced government spending and inflation.
   Agriculture accounts for approximately 50 per cent of
GDP and employs around 80 per cent of the workforce.
The major food crops are teff, maize, barley, sorghum,
wheat, pulses and oil seeds. Famine conditions in 1984–5
recurred to a lesser extent in 1992, 1997 and 2000.
However, agricultural liberalisation has led to dramatic
progress in food production.
   The economy deteriorated sharply in 1999 and 2000 as
a result of drought, a worsening balance of trade, and war
with Eritrea. In April 2001 Ethiopia was permitted to
reschedule some two-thirds of its US$430 million debt
until 2004.
   Manufacturing industry accounts for less than 9 per
cent of GDP and is heavily dependent on agriculture.
Ethiopia's largely unexploited, natural resources include
gold, platinum, copper and potash. Traces of oil and
natural gas have been found.
   In 2000 there was a trade deficit of US$645 million and
a current account deficit of US$16 million.
GNP – US$6,660 million (2000); US$100 per capita
   (1999)
GDP – US$6,383 million (1998); US$101 per capita
   (1999)
ANNUAL AVERAGE GROWTH OF GDP – 0.5 per cent
   (1998)
INFLATION RATE – 5.9 per cent (1999)
TOTAL EXTERNAL DEBT – US$5,551 million (1999)

TRADE

The chief imports by value are machinery and transport
equipment, manufactured goods and chemicals; the
principal exports by value are coffee, oil seeds, hides and

skins, and pulses. In 1999 imports totalled US$1,317 million and in 1998 exports totalled US$561 million.

Trade with UK	2000	2001
Imports from UK	£32,943,000	£29,349,000
Exports to UK	14,001,000	15,262,000

COMMUNICATIONS

A network of roads in rural areas links the major cities with each other, with the Sudanese and Kenyan borders and through Eritrea to the Red Sea coast.

There is a railway link from Addis Ababa to Djibouti. Ethiopian Airlines maintains regular services throughout Africa and to Europe.

EDUCATION

Elementary and secondary education are provided by government schools in the main centres of population; there are also mission schools. The National University (founded 1961) co-ordinates the institutions of higher education. There are also universities at Alemaya (agricultural), Debub, Mekele, Bashir Dar and Jimma.

Illiteracy Rate – 58.5 per cent (2002)

Enrolment (percentage of age group) – primary 43 per cent (1997); tertiary 1 per cent (1997)

FIJI

Matanitu ko Viti – Republic of the Fiji Islands

Area – 7,056 sq. miles (18,274 sq. km)

Population – 844,330 (2001 estimate),
715,373 (1986 census): 48.6 per cent Indians, 46.2 per cent Fijians, and 5.2 per cent other races. Since the 1987 coup many ethnic Indians have left and by 1994 Melanesian Fijians formed the largest population group. The main languages are Fijian and Hindi

Capital – Ψ Suva (population, 141,273, 1986), on the island of Viti Levu

Currency – Fiji dollar (F$) of 100 cents

National Anthem – God Bless Fiji

National Day – 10 October (Fiji Day)

National Flag – Light blue ground with Union flag in top left quarter and the shield of Fiji in the fly

Life Expectancy (years) – male 68.1; female 71.5

Population Growth Rate – 0.3 per cent (1999)

Population Density – 44 per sq. km (1999)

Military Expenditure – 2.1 per cent of GDP (2000)

Military Personnel – 3,500: Army 3,200, Navy 300

Illiteracy Rate – 6.5 per cent (2002)

Enrolment (percentage of age group) – primary 99 per cent (1992); tertiary 11.9 per cent (1991)

Fiji is composed of roughly 332 islands (about 100 permanently inhabited) and over 500 islets in the South Pacific, about 1,100 miles north of New Zealand. The group extends 300 miles from east to west and 300 miles north to south. The International Date Line has been diverted to the east of the island group. The largest islands are Viti Levu and Vanua Levu. The main groups of islands are Lomaiviti, Lau and Yasawas. The climate is tropical without extremes of heat.

HISTORY AND POLITICS

Fiji was a British colony from 1874 until 10 October 1970 when it became an independent state and a member of the Commonwealth. In the general election on 8–15 May 1999, the Fijian Political Party was swept from power by a coalition of parties led by the Fiji Labour Party. Its leader, Mahendra Chaudhry, became Fiji's first ethnic Indian prime minister.

On 19 May 2000 a group of indigenous Fijian rebels stormed parliament and took the Prime Minister and most of the Cabinet hostage. The army declared martial law on 29 May following the resignation of President Ratu Sir Kamisese Mara. An interim administration was set up on 28 June, following unsuccessful negotiations between the military government and the rebels. The military named an all-indigenous government to replace the multiracial coalition of the deposed premier. The interim government was to rule for two years and prepare for fresh elections. Following the release of the last hostages on 13 July, the Great Council of Chiefs announced the appointment of Ratu Josefa Iloilo as president.

The Fijian High Court ruled on 15 November 2000 that the 1997 Constitution remained in force. Following an appeal by the interim government, the Court of Appeal ruled on 1 March 2001 that the 1997 Constitution was still in force, that the parliament had been suspended rather than dissolved, and that the interim government was not legitimate, but accepted that the then Vice-President Iloilo had the right to exercise presidential powers after the resignation of President Ratu Sir Kamisese Mara. On 7 March the interim government led by Laisenia Qarase offered its collective resignation and Mahendra Chaudhry was reappointed as prime minister, but was dismissed by President Iloilo on 14 March. Qarase was reappointed as interim prime minister the following day. On 8 March 2001 the Great Council of Chiefs rejected the judgement of the Appeal Court and reaffirmed its support for the interim government and again nominated Iloilo as president.

Fiji's membership of the Commonwealth was suspended following the coup but the suspension was revoked in December 2001.

Following legislative elections held in August and September 2001, the United Fiji Party (SDL) became the largest party in the house of representatives with 32 seats.

Head of State

President, Ratu Josefa Iloilo, *appointed* 13 July 2000; *reappointed* 13 March 2001; *sworn in* 15 March 2001
Vice-President, Ratu Jope Naucabalavu Seniloii

Cabinet *as at July 2002*

Prime Minister, Fijian Affairs, Laisenia Qarase (SDL)
Agriculture, Sugar and Land Resettlement, Jonetani Galuinadi (SDL)
Attorney-General, Justice, Qoriniasi Bale
Commerce, Business Development and Investment, Tomasi Vuetilovoni (SDL)
Education, Ro Teimumu Kepa (SDL)
Finance and National Planning, Ratu Jone Kubuabola (SDL)
Fisheries and Forests, Solomone Naivalu (SDL)
Foreign Affairs and External Trade, Kaliopate Tavola (SDL)
Health, Pita Nacuva (SDL)
Home Affairs and Immigration, Joketani Cokanasiga (SDL)
Labour, Industrial Relations and Productivity, Kenneth Zinck (NLUP)
Lands and Mineral Resources, Ratu Naiqama Lalabalavu (MV)
Local Government, Housing and Squatter Settlement and Environment, Mataiasi Ragigia (SDL)
Multi-Ethnic Affairs, George Shiu Raj (SDL)
National Reconciliation, Information and Media Relations, Josefa Vosanibola (SDL)
Public Enterprises and Public Sector Reform, Irami Matiaravula (SDL)

Public Works, Telecommunications, Energy, Road Transport and Shipping, Savenaca Draunidaldo (Ind)
Regional Development, Ilaitia Tuisese (SDL)
Tourism, Culture, Heritage and Civil Aviation, Konisi Yabaki (SDL)
Women, Social Welfare and Poverty Alleviation, Asenaca Caucau (SDL)
Youth, Sports and Employment Opportunities, Isireli Leweniqila (MV)

MV Conservative Alliance; NLUP Labour Unity Party; SDL Fijian People's Party; Ind. Independent

HIGH COMMISSION OF THE REPUBLIC OF FIJI
34 Hyde Park Gate, London SW7 5DN
Tel: 020-7584 3661
High Commissioner, vacant

BRITISH HIGH COMMISSION
Victoria House, 47 Gladstone Road, PO Box 1355, Suva
Tel: (00 679) 311033
Email: ukconsular@bhc.org.fj
Ambassador Extraordinary and Plenipotentiary,
HE Michael Price, apptd 2000

ECONOMY

Agriculture accounts for 18 per cent of GDP and employs 44 per cent of the workforce. The principal cash crop is sugar cane, which is the main export, followed by coconuts, ginger and copra. A variety of other fruit, vegetables and root crops are also grown, and self-sufficiency in rice is a major aim. Forestry, fishing and beef production are being encouraged in order to diversify the economy. The processing of agricultural, marine and timber products are the main industries, along with gold mining and textiles. Tourism is second only to sugar as a money-earner, but visitor numbers have fallen as a result of the coup, causing widespread job losses.
GNP – US$1,480 million (2000); US$2,310 per capita (1999)
GDP – US$1.578 million (1998); US$2,275 per capita (1999)
ANNUAL AVERAGE GROWTH OF GDP – 1.8 per cent (1997)
INFLATION RATE – 1.1 per cent (2000)
UNEMPLOYMENT – 5.4 per cent (1995)
TOTAL EXTERNAL DEBT – US$163 million (1999)

TRADE

The chief imports are foodstuffs, machinery, mineral fuels, chemicals, beverages, tobacco and manufactured articles. Chief exports are sugar, coconut oil, fish, lumber, molasses and ginger.
  In 1998 there was a trade deficit of US$218 million and a current account deficit of US$55 million. Imports totalled US$721 million and exports US$510 million.

Trade with UK	2000	2001
Imports from UK	£4,216,000	£3,427,000
Exports to UK	66,726,000	51,240,000

COMMUNICATIONS

Fiji is one of the main aerial crossroads in the Pacific, providing services to New Zealand, Australia, Tonga, Samoa, Vanuatu, the Solomon Islands, Kiribati, Tuvalu, New Caledonia and American Samoa. Fiji has three ports of entry, at Suva, Lautoka and Levuka. There are 5,100 km of roads.

FINLAND
Suomen Tasavalta/Republiken Finland – Republic of Finland

AREA – 130,559 sq. miles (338,145 sq. km). Neighbours: Norway (north-west and north), Russia (east), Sweden (west)
POPULATION – 5,175,783 (2001 estimate). Finnish and Swedish are both official languages, 93 per cent speaking Finnish as their first language and 5.6 per cent Swedish. Sami is spoken by 1,700 of the 6,500-strong Sami population who live in the far north. The population is predominantly Lutheran
CAPITAL – Ψ Helsinki (Helsingfors) (population, 905,555, 1997 estimate)
MAJOR CITIES – Espoo (Esbo) (213,271); Ψ Oulu (Uleåborg) (120,753); Tampere (Tammerfors) (195,468); Ψ Turku (Åbo) (172,561); Vantaa (Vanda) (178,471), 2000 estimates
CURRENCY – Euro (€) of 100 cents
NATIONAL ANTHEM – Maamme/Vårt Land (Our Land)
NATIONAL DAY – 6 December (Independence Day)
NATIONAL FLAG – White with blue cross
LIFE EXPECTANCY (years) – male 74.4; female 81.5
POPULATION GROWTH RATE – 0.3 per cent (1999)
POPULATION DENSITY – 15 per sq. km (1999)
URBAN POPULATION – 64.8 per cent (1996)

The Åland archipelago (Ahvenanmaa), a group of small islands at the entrance to the Gulf of Bothnia, covers about 1,552 square km, with a population (2000) of 25,776 (95.2 per cent Swedish-speaking). The Åland islands are an autonomous province of Finland.

HISTORY AND POLITICS

Finland was part of the Swedish Empire from the Middle Ages until it was ceded to Russia in 1809 and became an autonomous grand duchy of the Russian Empire. Finland became independent after the Russian revolution of 1917, but was forced to cede around one-tenth of its land to the Soviet Union and to resettle 10 per cent of its population under the Treaty of Paris (1947). A Soviet-Finnish Co-operation Treaty forced Finland to demilitarise its Soviet border, to enter into a barter trade agreement and to adopt a stance of neutrality. These terms lasted until the demise of the Soviet Union in 1991.
  Finland joined the European Union on 1 January 1995 following a referendum in October 1994.
  The present government took office in April 1999. The five parties in the ruling coalition were the Social Democratic Party, the National Coalition Party (conservative), the Left-wing Alliance, the Swedish People's Party, and the Greens, with a total of 139 out of 200 seats. Presidential elections held on 16 January and February 2000 were won by Tarja Halonen of the Social Democratic Party.

POLITICAL SYSTEM

Under the constitution there is a unicameral legislature, the *Eduskunta,* composed of 200 members elected by universal suffrage for a four-year term. The highest executive power is held by the president who is directly elected for a period of six years. The first direct elections for the presidency were held in 1994.

HEAD OF STATE

President, Tarja Kaarina Halonen, *elected* 6 February 2000, *inaugurated* 1 March 2000

CABINET *as at July 2002*

Prime Minister, Paavo Lipponen (SDP)
Deputy Prime Minister, Interior, Ville Itälä (NCP
Agriculture and Forestry, Jari Koskinen (NCP)
Culture, Kaarina Dromberg (NCP)
Defence, Jan-Erik Enestam (SPP)
Education, Maija Rask (NCP)
Environment, Jouni Backman (SDP)
Finance, Sauli Niinistoe (NCP)
Foreign Affairs, Erkki Tuomioja (SDP)
Foreign Trade, Jari Vilen (NCP)
Health and Social Services, Eva Biaudet (SPP)
Justice, Johannes Koskinen (SDP)
Labour, Tarja Filatov (SDP)
Local Communities and Regional Policies, Martti
    Korhonen (LA)
*Minister at the Ministry of Finance, responsible for
    Taxation,* Suvi-Anne Siimes (LA)
Social Affairs and Health, Maija Perho (NCP)
Trade and Industry, Sinikka Mönkäre (SDP)
Transport and Communications, Kimmo Sasi (NCP)

SDP Social Democratic Party; NCP National Coalition
Party; LA Left-wing Alliance; SPP Swedish People's Party;
Ind. Independent

EMBASSY OF FINLAND
38 Chesham Place, London SW1X 8HW
Tel: 020-7838 6200
Ambassador Extraordinary and Plenipotentiary, HE Pertti
    Salolainen, apptd 1996
Minister, C. Hartman
Counsellor (Commercial), J. Hietala
Defence Attaché, Lt.-Col. J. Tammikivi

BRITISH EMBASSY
Itäinen Puistotie 17, FIN-00140 Helsinki
Tel: (00 358) (9) 2286 5100
Ambassador Extraordinary and Plenipotentiary, HE
    Alyson J. K. Bailes, CMG, apptd 2000

BRITISH CONSULAR OFFICES – Helsinki, Jyväskylä,
Kotka, Kuopio, Oulu, Pori, Tampere, Turku, Vaasa,
Mariehamn

BRITISH COUNCIL DIRECTOR, Tuija Talvitie,
Hakaniemenkatu 2, FIN-00530 Helsinki;
Email: office@britishcouncil.fi

DEFENCE

The Army has 230 main battle tanks, 266 armoured
infantry fighting vehicles and 840 armoured personnel
carriers. The Navy has 10 patrol and coastal vessels. The
Air Force has 64 combat aircraft.
MILITARY EXPENDITURE – 1.3 per cent of GDP (2000)
MILITARY PERSONNEL – 32,250: Army 24,550, Navy
    5,000, Air Force 2,700; Paramilitaries 3,100
CONSCRIPTION DURATION – Six to 12 months

ECONOMY

Important industries are mobile phones, rubber, plastics,
chemicals and pharmaceuticals, glass, ceramics, furniture,
footwear, foodstuffs and shipbuilding.
    The markka joined the ERM in August 1996, and has
participated in the European Single Currency since
January 1999.
    In 1997 the budget deficit was equivalent to 4.5 per cent
of GDP, and public debt was 67.7 per cent of GDP.
GNP – US$128,999 million (2000); US$24,730 per
    capita (1999)

GDP – US$128,505 million (1998); US$25,112 per
    capita (1999)
ANNUAL AVERAGE GROWTH OF GDP – 5.9 per cent
    (2000)
INFLATION RATE – 3.4 per cent (2000)
UNEMPLOYMENT – 10.1 per cent (1999)

TRADE

The principal imports are raw materials, machinery and
manufactured goods. The main exports are electronic
and electrical goods, paper and wood pulp, machinery,
and metal products. Trade with EU countries accounts
for more than half of Finland's total trade.
    In 2000 there was a trade surplus of US$13,684 million
and a current account surplus of US$8,890 million.
Imports totalled US$32,604 million and exports
US$44,524 million.

Trade with UK	2000	2001
Imports from UK	£1,392,100,000	£1,544,400,000
Exports to UK	2,654,600,000	2,834,800,000

COMMUNICATIONS

There are 5,859 km of railroad, railway connections with
Russia, and passenger boat connections with Sweden,
Germany and Estonia. There are also passenger/cargo
services between Finland and Britain

CULTURE AND EDUCATION

Newspapers, books, plays and films appear in both
Finnish and Swedish. There is a vigorous modern
literature.
    Primary education (co-educational comprehensive
school) is free and compulsory for children from seven to
16 years.
ENROLMENT (percentage of age group) – primary 99
    per cent (1997); secondary 100 per cent (1997);
    tertiary 74 per cent (1997)

FRANCE
La République française – The French Republic

AREA – 212,935 sq. miles (551,500 sq. km). Neighbours:
Belgium and Luxembourg (north-east), Germany,
Switzerland and Italy (east), Monaco (south), Spain
and Andorra (south-west)
POPULATION – 59,551,227 (2001 estimate); 57,218,000
(Metropolitan France), and 58,745,000 including
overseas departments (1992 official estimate): 72 per
cent Catholic, 8 per cent Muslim, 2 per cent Jewish.
The language is French; there are several regional
languages including Basque, Breton, Catalan,
Corsican, Dutch, German and Occitan
CAPITAL – Paris (population, 9,319,367, 1990), on the
Seine
MAJOR CITIES – Ψ Bordeaux (696,819); Grenoble
(404,837); Lille (959,433); Lyon (1,262,342);
Ψ Marseille (1,230,871); Nantes (495,229); Nice
(517,291); Strasbourg (388,466); Toulon (437,825);
Toulouse (650,311). The chief towns of Corsica are
Ψ Ajaccio (58,315) and Ψ Bastia (52,446)
CURRENCY – Euro (€) of 100 cents
NATIONAL ANTHEM – La Marseillaise
NATIONAL DAY – 14 July (Bastille Day 1789)
NATIONAL FLAG – The tricolour, three vertical bands,
blue, white, red (blue next to flagstaff)
LIFE EXPECTANCY (years) – male 75.2; female 82.8
POPULATION GROWTH RATE – 0.4 per cent (1999)
POPULATION DENSITY – 107 per sq. km (1999)

HISTORY AND POLITICS

Gaul, the area which is now France, was conquered by Julius Caesar in the 1st century bc and remained a part of the Roman Empire until the Frankish invasions in the 5th and 6th centuries. The Treaty of Verdun (AD 843) divided the Frankish Empire into three parts, of which the western part, *Francia Occidentalis*, became the basis for modern France.

As a result of the French Revolution, a republic was declared in 1792 and the king, Louis XVI, was executed. The republic was overthrown by Napoléon Bonaparte, who established the first French Empire, which ended in 1815. The ensuing Congress of Vienna restored the monarchy, but in 1848 the Second Republic was declared, which lasted only until 1852, when the Second Empire was proclaimed under Napoléon III. He was forced to abdicate after the defeat of France in the Franco-Prussian war (1870–1871) and the Third Republic was established.

In 1940, Germany invaded France, occupying most of the country and establishing a pro-German government in the south. France was liberated in 1944, a provisional government was established under Gen. Charles de Gaulle, and the Fourth Republic was declared in 1946. In 1958, the threat of a military coup following a rebellion in Algeria resulted in the assembly inviting Gen. de Gaulle to return as premier; a new constitution which strengthened the powers of the president was adopted, the Fifth Republic was proclaimed, and Gen. De Gaulle was elected president. France granted its colonies independence between 1954 and 1962.

President Jacques Chirac, the candidate of the Rally for the Republic (RPR), was elected in May 1995. The state of the parties in the Senate at September 2001 was: RPR 83; Socialist Party (PS) 68; Centrist Union (UDC) 37; Republican and Independent Union (RI) 35; Democratic and European Rally (RDE) 16; Communists (PCF) 16; Independents 5; Others 60.

The last election to the National Assembly took place in June 2002 and resulted in a government formed of a coalition of the Rally for the Republic (RPR), Union for French Democracy (UDF), Liberal Demcracy (DL) and allies.

In the first round of the presidential elections on 21 April 2002, National Front leader Jean-Marie Le Pen gained just under 200,000 more than Prime Minister Lionel Jospin. Jacques Chirac won the second round on 5 May with 82.2 per cent of the vote.

INSURGENCIES

A desire for greater autonomy and recognition of Corsica's distinctive culture and language led to a campaign of separatist bombings and shootings which began in the mid-1970s. In November 1999, Prime Minister Jospin invited all political groups on the island to engage in dialogue with the French government on the constitutional future of the island. Following discussions, Jospin presented proposals to combine the island's two departments, and give the regional parliament powers over cultural, educational, structural and planning affairs and limited legislative autonomy by 2004 in return for a permanent end to terrorism. The proposals, which were accepted by the Corsican regional parliament on 28 July 2000 and narrowly passed by the National Assembly on 19 December 2001, suffered a setback on 17 January 2002 when the Constitutional Council rejected the legislation as unconstitutional, but allowed provisions permitting the Corsican language to become part of the primary school curriculum.

POLITICAL SYSTEM

The head of state is a directly elected president, whose term of office has hitherto been seven years, but will be five years with effect from the presidential election held in April 2002. The legislature consists of the National Assembly of 577 deputies (555 for Metropolitan France and 22 for the overseas departments and territories) and the Senate of 321 Senators (296 for Metropolitan France, 13 for the overseas departments and territories and 12 for French citizens abroad). Deputies in the National Assembly are directly elected for a five-year term. One-third of the Senate is indirectly elected every three years.

The prime minister is appointed by the president, as is the Council of Ministers on the prime minister's recommendation. They are responsible to the legislature, but as the executive is constitutionally separate from the legislature, ministers may not sit in the legislature and must hand over their seats to a substitute.

France is divided into 22 metropolitan regions and 96 metropolitan and four overseas departments, which are also regions. There are also four overseas territories and two territorial collectivities.

HEAD OF STATE

President of the French Republic, Jacques Chirac, *elected* 7 May 1995, *re-elected* 5 May 2002

COUNCIL OF MINISTERS *as at July 2002*

Prime Minister, Jean-Pierre Raffarin (RPR)
Agriculture, Food, Fisheries and Rural Affairs, Hervé Gaymard (RPR)
Capital Works, Transport, Housing, Tourism and the Sea, Gilles de Robien (UDF)
Civil Service, Administrative Reform and Town and Country Planning, Jean-Paul Delevoye (RPR)
Culture and Communications, Jean-Jacques Aillagon (RPR)
Defence, War Veterans, Michèle Alliot-Marie (RPR)
Ecology and Sustainable Development, Roselyne Bachelot-Narquin (RPR)
Economy, Finance and Industry, Francis Mer
Employment and Solidarity, François Fillon (RPR)
Foreign Affairs Co-operation and Francophony, Dominique de Villepin
Health, the Family and the Disabled, Jean-François Mattéi (DL)
Interior, Internal Security and Local Freedoms, Nicolas Sarkozy (RPR)*Justice, Keeper of the Seals,* Dominique Perben (RPR)
Overseas France, Brigitte Girardin
Sport, Jean-François Lamour
Youth, National Education and Research, Luc Ferry

FRENCH EMBASSY

58 Knightsbridge, London SW1X 7JT
Tel: 020-7073 1000
Ambassador Extraordinary and Plenipotentiary,
HE Daniel Bernard, CMG, CBE, apptd 1998
Minister-Counsellor, S. Gompertz
Defence Attaché, Contre-Amiral J.-P. Tiffou
Cultural Counsellor, N. Chapuis
Minister-Counsellor (Economic and Commercial Affairs),
J.-P. Landau

BRITISH EMBASSY

35 rue du Faubourg St Honoré, F-75383 Paris Cedex 08
Tel: (00 33) (1) 4451 3100
Ambassador Extraordinary and Plenipotentiary, HE Sir John Eaton Holmes KBE, CVO, CMG , Minister, S. F. Howarth

Defence and Air Attaché, Air Cdre C. Blencowe RAF
Counsellor, D. Frost *(Finance and Economic)*
First Secretary and Consul-General, S. Gregson

BRITISH CONSULAR OFFICES – Amiens, Biarritz,
Bordeaux, Boulogne, Calais, Cherbourg, Dunkerque,
Le Havre, Lille, Lorient, Lyon, Marseille, Montpellier,
Nantes, Nice, Paris, Perpignan, St Malo-Dinard,
Saumur, Toulouse, Tours; overseas in Cayenne
(French Guiana), Noumea (New Caledonia), Papeete
(French Polynesia), Fort de France (Martinique) and
Pointe à Pitre (Guadeloupe)

BRITISH COUNCIL DIRECTOR, John Tod, OBE, 9 rue de
Constantine, F-75340 Paris Cédex 07;
Email: information@britishcouncil.fr.
Regional office in Bordeaux

DEFENCE

The Army has 809 main battle tanks, 3,900 armoured
personnel carriers, 599 armoured infantry fighting
vehicles and 410 helicopters.

The Navy has ten submarines, one aircraft carrier, one
cruiser, three destroyers, 30 frigates and 39 patrol and
coastal vessels, 51 combat aircraft and 29 armed
helicopters. The Navy has four domestic and five overseas
bases.

The Air Force has 473 combat aircraft.

France deploys 35,392 armed forces personnel abroad;
2,700 in Germany (including members of Eurocorps);
17,450 in French Overseas Departments and Territories;
6,700 in former French colonies in Africa; and 8,542 on
UN and peacekeeping duties.

MILITARY EXPENDITURE – 2.6 per cent of GDP (2000)
MILITARY PERSONNEL – 273,740: Army 150,000,
Strategic Nuclear Forces 8,400, Navy 45,600, Air Force
63,000; Paramilitaries (Gendarmerie) 100,700

ECONOMY

Viniculture is extensive, regions famous for their wines
including Bordeaux, Burgundy and Champagne.
Production of wine in 2000 was 59 million hectolitres.
Cognac, liqueurs and cider are also produced. Other
important agricultural products include sugar beet, dairy
products, cereals and oilseeds. Nearly 55 per cent of the
land area of metropolitan France is utilised for
agricultural production and a further quarter is
accounted for by forests.

Oil is produced from fields in the Landes area, but
France is a net importer of crude oil, for processing by its
important oil-refining industry. Natural gas is produced
in the foothills of the Pyrenees.

Heavy industries include oil-refining and the
production of iron and steel, and aluminium. In 2000
production of pig iron was 13.9 million tonnes and steel
21 million tonnes. Other important industries are
construction and civil engineering, chemicals, rubber and
plastics, pharmaceuticals, vehicle production and
telecommunications services.

The Banque de France was made independent in 1994
with the formation of a nine-member monetary policy
council to define and implement monetary policy
independent of the government.

France has participated in the European Single
Currency since January 1999.

GNP – US$1,429,390 million (2000); US$24,170 per
capita (1999)
GDP – US$1,451,763 million (1998); US$25,112 per
capita (1999)

ANNUAL AVERAGE GROWTH OF GDP – 3.3 per cent
(2000)
INFLATION RATE – 1.7 per cent (2000)
UNEMPLOYMENT – 11.9 per cent (1999)

TRADE

The principal imports are raw materials for the heavy and
manufacturing industries (e.g. oil, minerals, chemicals),
machinery and precision instruments, agricultural
products, chemicals and vehicles. Agricultural products,
chemicals, pharmaceuticals and vehicles are also the
principal exports. Most of France's trade is done with
other EU countries. There are around 45 million hectares
of farmland.

In 1999 there was a trade surplus of US$20,065 million
and a current account surplus of US$37,231 million. In
2000 imports totalled US$301,021 million and exports
US$295,023 million.

Trade with UK	2000	2001
Imports from UK	£17,587,500,000	£18,394,500,000
Exports to UK	17,155,800,000	18,222,100,000

COMMUNICATIONS

The length of roads in 1998 was 965,916 km, of which
9,011 km were motorways.

The railroad system is extensive. The length of lines
open for traffic in 1998 was 31,852 km.

The French mercantile marine consisted in 1998 of 210
ships of a total of 4,100,000 tonnes which transported
91,500,000 tonnes of freight.

CULTURE AND EDUCATION

French is the official language. The work of the French
Academy, founded in 1635, has established *le bon usage,*
equivalent to 'The Queen's English' in Britain. French
authors have been awarded the Nobel Prize for Literature
on 12 occasions and they include R. F. A. Sully-Prudhomme
(1901), Anatole France (1921), André Gide (1947),
François Mauriac (1952), Albert Camus (1957), Jean-Paul
Sartre (1964) and Claude Simon (1985).

Education is compulsory, free and secular from six to
16. Schools may be single-sex or co-educational. Primary
education is given in nursery schools, primary schools
and *collèges d'enseignement général* (four-year secondary
modern course); secondary education in *collèges
d'enseignement technique, collèges d'enseignement
secondaire* and *lycées* (seven-year course leading to one of
the five *baccalauréats*). Special schools are numerous.

There are many *grandes écoles* in France which award
diplomas in many subjects not taught at university,
especially applied science and engineering. Most of these
are state institutions but have a competitive system of
entry, unlike universities. There are universities in 24
towns including 13 in Paris and the immediate area.

In 1993 the government gave German official parity
with French in Alsace schools.

ENROLMENT (percentage of age group) – primary 100
per cent (1997); secondary 100 per cent (1997);
tertiary 51 per cent (1997)

OVERSEAS DEPARTMENTS

Greater powers of self-government were granted to
French Guiana, Guadeloupe, Martinique and Réunion in
1982. These former colonies had enjoyed departmental
status since 1946. Their directly elected Assemblies
operate in parallel with the existing, indirectly constituted
Regional Councils. The French government is
represented by a Prefect in each.

FRENCH GUIANA

AREA – 34,749 sq. miles (90,000 sq. km)
POPULATION – 177,562 (2001 estimate)
CAPITAL – Ψ Cayenne (41,659, 1990 census)

Situated on the north-eastern coast of South America, French Guiana is flanked by Suriname on the west and by Brazil on the south and east. Under the administration of French Guiana is a group of islands (St Joseph, Île Royal and Île du Diable), known as Îles du Salut.

Prefect, Henri Masse

GUADELOUPE

AREA – 658 sq. miles (1,705 sq. km)
POPULATION – 431,170 (2001 census)
CAPITAL – Ψ Basse-Terre (29,522) on Guadeloupe

A number of islands in the Leeward Islands group of the West Indies, consisting of the two main islands of Guadeloupe (or Basse-Terre) and Grande-Terre, with the adjacent islands of Marie-Galante, La Désirade and Îles des Saintes, and islands of St-Barthélemy and the part of St-Martin under French administration, which lie over 150 miles to the north-west. The main towns are Ψ Les Abymes (62,605); Ψ St-Martin (28,518); Ψ Pointe-à-Pitre (26,029) in Grande-Terre and Ψ Grand Bourg (6,611) in Marie-Galante.

Prefect, Jean-François Carenco

MARTINIQUE

AREA – 425 sq. miles (1,102 sq. km)
POPULATION – 418,454 (2001 estimate)
CAPITAL – Ψ Fort-de-France (133,920)

An island situated in the Windward Islands group of the West Indies, between Dominica in the north and St Lucia in the south. The main towns are Ψ Le Lamentin (30,026) and Ψ Schoelcher (19,813).

Prefect, Michel Cadot

RÉUNION

AREA – 969 sq. miles (2,510 sq. km)
POPULATION – 732,570 (2001 estimate)
CAPITAL – St-Denis (121,999, 1990 census)

Réunion, which became a French possession in 1638, lies in the Indian Ocean, about 569 miles east of Madagascar and 110 miles south-west of Mauritius. Other towns are Saint-Paul (71,669) and Saint-Pierre (58,846). The smaller, uninhabited islands of Bassas da India, Europa, Îles Glorieuses, Juan de Nova and Tromelin are administered from Réunion.

Prefect, Gonthier Friederici

TERRITORIAL COLLECTIVITIES

MAYOTTE

AREA – 144 sq. miles (372 sq. km)
POPULATION – 163,366 (2001 estimate)
CAPITAL – Mamoudzou (20,450)

Part of the Comoros Islands group, Mayotte remained a French dependency when the other three islands became independent as the Comoros Republic in 1975. Since 1976 the island has been a *collectivité territoriale*, an intermediate status between Overseas Department and Overseas Territory.

Prefect, Philippe de Mester

Trade with UK	2000	2001
Imports from UK	£1,358,000	£968,000
Exports to UK	643,000	536,000

ST PIERRE AND MIQUELON

AREA – 93 sq. miles (242 sq. km)
POPULATION – 6,928 (2001 estimate)
CAPITAL – Ψ St-Pierre (5,416)

These two small groups of islands off the coast of Newfoundland became a *collectivité territoriale* in 1985.

Prefect, Jean-François Tallec

Trade with UK	2000	2001
Imports from UK	£345,000	£2,578,000
Exports to UK	20,000	75,000

OVERSEAS TERRITORIES

FRENCH POLYNESIA

AREA – 1,544 sq. miles (4,000 sq. km)
POPULATION – 253,506 (2001 estimate)
CAPITAL – Ψ Papeete (36,784), in Tahiti

Five archipelagos in the south Pacific, comprising the Society Islands (Windward Islands group includes Tahiti, Moorea, Makatea, Mehetia, Tetiaroa, Tubuai Manu; Leeward Islands group includes Huahine, Raiatea, Tahaa, Bora-Bora, Maupiti), the Tuamotu Islands (Rangiroa, Hao, Turéia, etc.), the Gambier Islands (Mangareva, etc.), the Tubuai Islands (Rimatara, Rurutu, Tubuai, Raivavae, Rapa, etc.) and the Marquesas Islands (Nuku-Hiva, Hiva-Oa, Fatu-Hiva, Tahuata, Ua Huka, etc.).

High Commissioner, Michel Mathieu

Trade with UK	2000	2001
Imports from UK	£3,511,000	£5,928,000
Exports to UK	308,000	365,000

NEW CALEDONIA

AREA – 7,172 sq. miles (18,575 sq. km)
POPULATION – 204,863 (2001 estimate)
CAPITAL – Ψ Nouméa (97,581)

New Caledonia is a large island in the western Pacific, 700 miles east of Queensland. Dependencies are the Isles of Pines, the Loyalty Islands (Mahé, Lifou, Urea, etc.), the Bélep Archipelago, the Chesterfield Islands, the Huon Islands and Walpole.

New Caledonia was discovered in 1774 and annexed by France in 1854; from 1871 to 1896 it was a convict settlement. In 1995, the territory was divided into three provinces, each with a provincial assembly which combined to form the Territorial Assembly. In elections in July 1995, Kanaks won majorities in North province and the Loyalty Islands, whereas pro-French settlers won a majority in the South province.

A referendum in 1987 on the question of independence was boycotted by the indigenous Kanaks, and New Caledonia therefore voted to remain French. In April 1998 an agreement was reached between the pro-independence Kanak Socialist National Liberation Front, the anti-independence Rally for Caledonia in the Republic and the French government to hold a referendum on independence in 15–20 years' time, and for greater autonomy for the indigenous people in the intervening period. A referendum on the agreement, the Nouméa Accord, was held on 8 November 1998. It was

supported by 71.9 per cent of voters; more than 74 per cent of registered voters took part.

High Commissioner, Thierry Lataste

Trade with UK	2000	2001
Imports from UK	£9,942,000	£9,231,000
Exports to UK	199,000	136,000

SOUTHERN AND ANTARCTIC TERRITORIES

Created in 1955 from former Réunion dependencies, the territory comprises the islands of Amsterdam (25 sq. miles) and St Paul (2.7 sq. miles), the Kerguelen Islands (2,700 sq. miles) and Crozet Islands (116 sq. miles) archipelagos and Adélie Land (116,800 sq. miles) in the Antarctic continent. The only population are members of staff of the scientific stations.

Administrator, François Garde

WALLIS AND FUTUNA ISLANDS

AREA – 77 sq. miles (200 sq. km)
POPULATION – 15,435(2001 estimate)
CAPITAL – Ψ Mata-Utu on Uvea, the main island of the Wallis group

Two groups of islands (the Wallis Archipelago and the Îles de Hoorn) in the central Pacific, north-east of Fiji.

Administrator, Alain Waquet

Trade with UK	2000	2001
Imports from UK	£44,000	£47,000
Exports to UK	–	1,000

THE FRENCH COMMUNITY

The constitution of the Fifth French Republic, promulgated in 1958, envisaged the establishment of a French Community of States. A number of the former French states in Africa have seceded from the Community but for all practical purposes continue to enjoy the same close links with France as those that remain formally members. Most former French African colonies are closely linked to France by financial, technical and economic agreements.

GABON
République Gabonaise – Gabonese Republic

AREA – 103,347 sq. miles (267,668 sq. km). Neighbours: Equatorial Guinea and Cameroon (north), Republic of Congo-Brazzaville (east and south)
POPULATION – 1,221,175 (2001 estimate). The official language is French; Fang is widely spoken
CAPITAL – Ψ Libreville (population, 251,000)
CURRENCY – Franc CFA of 100 centimes
NATIONAL ANTHEM – La Concorde
NATIONAL DAY – 17 August
NATIONAL FLAG – Horizontal bands, green, yellow and blue
LIFE EXPECTANCY (years) – male 51.8; female 54.0
POPULATION GROWTH RATE – 6.3 per cent (1999)
POPULATION DENSITY – 5 per sq. km (1999)
MILITARY EXPENDITURE – 2.2 per cent of GDP (2000)
MILITARY PERSONNEL – 4,700: Army 3,200, Navy 500, Air Force 1,000; Paramilitaries 2,000
ILLITERACY RATE – 29.2 per cent (2002)

HISTORY AND POLITICS

The first Europeans to visit the region were the Portuguese in the 15th century, and Dutch, French and English traders arrived over the following decades. In 1849 a slave ship was captured by the French, and the freed slaves formed a settlement which they called Libreville, the current capital. The territory was annexed to French Congo in 1888.

Gabon elected on 28 November 1958 to remain an autonomous republic within the French Community and gained full independence on 17 August 1960.

Multiparty elections held in autumn 1990 were won by the ruling Parti Démocratique Gabonais (PDG), amid allegations of fraud. The PDG formed a coalition government, although the other parties left the government in 1991 in protest at PDG domination. In September 1994, the government and opposition parties signed the Paris Agreement, which provided for a new coalition government and parliamentary elections. The elections, held in December 1996, returned the PDG to power. President Bongo of the PDG, who first took office in 1967, was re-elected for a fifth term of office in December 1998. The latest elections to the National Assembly took place on 9 and 23 December 2001. The government is dominated by the PDG but includes opposition party members from the National Rally of Woodcutters (RNB-RPG) and the Social Democrat Party (PSD).

POLITICAL SYSTEM

The constitution provides for an executive president, directly elected for a seven-year term, who appoints the Council of Ministers. There is a 120-member National Assembly, directly elected for a five-year term, and a 91-member Senate, elected by municipal and regional councillors for a six-year term.

HEAD OF STATE

President, El Hadj Omar Bongo, *assumed office* December 1967, *re-elected* 1973, 1979, 1986, 1993 and 6 December 1998
Vice-President, Didjob Divungi-di-Ndinge

COUNCIL OF MINISTERS *as at July 2002*

Prime Minister, Jean-François Ntoutoume-Emane
Deputy Prime Minister, Town and Country Planning, Emmanuel Ondo Metgoho
Deputy Prime Minister, Urban Affairs, Antoine de Padoue Mboumbou Miyakou
Agriculture, Livestock and Rural Development, Pierre Claver Maganga Moussavou
Civil Service, Administrative Reform, Pascal Désiré Missong
Commerce and Industrial Development, Regional Integration, Jean-Remy Pendy Bouyiki
Communication, Post and Information Technology, Andre Dieudonne Berre
Culture and Arts, Pierre Amoughe Mba
Defence, Ali Ben Bongo
Family and the Advancement of Women, Angélique Ngoma
Finance, Economy, Budget and Privatisation, Paul Toungui
Foreign Affairs, Co-operation and Francophone Affairs, Jean Ping
Higher Education, Scientific Research and Technology, Vincent Moulengui Boukoss
Housing, Urban Affairs, Land Survey, Jacques Adiahenot
Human Rights, Paul Mba Abessole

Interior, Public Security, Decentralisation, Gen. Idriss
Ngari
Justice, Keeper of the Seals, Honorine Dossou Naki
Labour and Employment, Clotaire Christian Ivala
Merchant Navy, Felix Siby
Mines, Energy, Oil and Hydraulic Resources, Richard
Onouviet
National Education, Government Spokesperson, Daniel
Ona-Ondo
National Solidarity, Social Affairs and Welfare, Andre
Mba Obame
Planning and Development Programmes, Casimir Oye
Mba
Professional Training and Social Rehabilitation, Barnabé
Ndaki
Public Health, Faustin Boukoubi
Public Works, Equipment and Construction, Egide
Boundono-Simangoye
Relations With Parliament, Government Spokesperson,
Rene Ndemzo Obiang
Small and Medium Sized Enterprises and Industries, Paul
Biyighe-Mba
Tourism and Handicrafts, Jean Massima
Transport and Civil Aviation, Paulette Missambo
Water, Forests, Fishing, Environment Protection, Emile
Doumba
Youth and Sport, Alfred Mabicka

EMBASSY OF THE REPUBLIC OF GABON
27 Elvaston Place, London SW7 5NL
Tel: 020-7823 9986
Ambassador Extraordinary and Plenipotentiary, vacant

BRITISH AMBASSADOR, HE Peter Boon, OBE, resident at
Yaoundé, Cameroon

ECONOMY

The economy is heavily dependent on oil and, to a lesser
extent, other mineral resources, including manganese and
uranium. Gabon has considerable timber reserves with 80
per cent of the country still forested, although production
has stagnated in recent years.

France and the USA are the main trading partners. In
1997 imports totalled US$1,104 million and exports
US$3,024 million.

GNP – US$3,928 million (2000); US$3,300 per capita
(1999)
GDP – US$3,756 per capita (1999)
ANNUAL AVERAGE GROWTH OF GDP – 4.6 per cent
(1997)
INFLATION RATE – 4.0 per cent (1997)
TOTAL EXTERNAL DEBT – US$3,978 million (1999)

Trade with UK	2000	2001
Imports from UK	£17,099,000	£34,923,000
Exports to UK	4,557,000	4,325,000

THE GAMBIA
The Republic of the Gambia

AREA – 4,361 sq. miles (11,295 sq. km). Neighbour:
Senegal, which surrounds the Gambia except at the
coast
POPULATION – 1,411,205 (2001 estimate), mainly
Wollof, Mandinka and Fula peoples who originally
migrated from the north and east. The official
language is English; Fula, Jola, Mandinka, Serahule
and Wollof are indigenous languages

CAPITAL – Ψ Banjul (population, 109,986, 1980
estimate)
CURRENCY – Dalasi (D) of 100 butut
NATIONAL ANTHEM – For The Gambia, Our
Homeland
NATIONAL DAY – 18 February (Independence Day)
NATIONAL FLAG – Horizontal stripes of red, blue and
green, separated by narrow white stripes
LIFE EXPECTANCY (years) – male 45.7; female 48.5
POPULATION GROWTH RATE – 3.3 per cent (1999)
POPULATION DENSITY – 112 per sq. km (1999)
MILITARY EXPENDITURE – 3.2 per cent of GDP (2000)
MILITARY PERSONNEL – 800: Army

The Gambia is named after the Gambia River, which it
straddles for over 200 miles inland from the west coast of
Africa. There is a dry season between October and May
and heavy rainfall in July and August.

HISTORY AND POLITICS

The Gambia River basin was part of the region
dominated in the tenth to 16th centuries by the Songhai
and Mali kingdoms centred on the upper Niger. The
Portuguese reached the Gambia River in 1447; English
merchants began to trade along the river from 1588.
Merchants from France, Courland (now Latvia) and the
Netherlands also established trading posts. In 1816 the
British stationed a garrison on an island at the river
mouth which became the capital of a small British-
administered colony. In 1889 France agreed that the
British rights along the upper river should extend to 10
km from the river on either bank. British administration
was extended from the Colony to this Protectorate. The
Gambia became independent within the Commonwealth
on 18 February 1965, and a republic on 24 April 1970.

In July 1994 junior army officers launched a coup
which ousted the president and the government, and a
military council was formed. The coup leader, Lt. (later
Capt.) Jammeh, assumed the presidency, the constitution
was suspended and a civilian-military government was
formed to rule in conjunction with the Ruling Military
Council. A referendum approved a new constitution in
August 1996, Jammeh was elected president the following
month and the Ruling Military Council was dissolved. The
latest presidential elections were held on 18 October
2001 when Jammeh secured his presidency wit 53 per
cent of the vote. The most recent legislative elections were
held on 17 January 2002 were won by The Alliance for
Patriotic Reorientation and Construction (APRC).

FOREIGN RELATIONS

The relationship with Senegal remains an important
factor in political and economic policy. Moves towards a
closer association were accelerated after an abortive coup
in 1981 was put down with the help of Senegalese troops.
In 1982 the Senegambia Confederation was instituted but
following disagreements it was dissolved in 1989. A treaty
of friendship and co-operation was signed with Senegal
in 1991.

POLITICAL SYSTEM

The constitution gives enhanced powers to the president
who is elected for an indefinite term. The National
Assembly has 53 members, of whom 48 are directly
elected, and five appointed by the president, for a five-
year term.

HEAD OF STATE

President, Defence, Capt. Yahya Jammeh, *took power* 23
July 1994, *elected* 26 September 1996

Vice-President, Women and Social Affairs, Isatou Njie-Saidy

CABINET *as at July 2002*

Agriculture, Hassan Sallah
Education, Thérèse Ndong-Jatta
External Affairs, Baboucarr Blaise Jagne
Finance and Economic Affairs, Famara Jatta
Fisheries and Natural Resources, Susan Waffa-Ogooh
Health, Yankuba Gassama
Interior, Ousman Badjie
Justice, Attorney-General, Joseph Joof
Local Government and Lands, Momodou Nai Ceesay
Public Works, Communications and Information, Presidential Affairs, Capt. Edward Singhateh
Tourism and Culture, Yankuba Touray
Trade, Industry and Employment, Musa Sillah
Youth and Sports, Sarjo Jallow

GAMBIA HIGH COMMISSION
57 Kensington Court, London W8 5DG
Tel: 020-7937 6316/7/8
High Commissioner, HE Gibril Seman Joof, apptd 2000

BRITISH HIGH COMMISSION
48 Atlantic Road, Fajara (PO Box 507), Banjul
Tel: (00 220) 495133/4
Email: bhcbanjul@gamtel.gm
High Commissioner, HE John Perrott, apptd 2000

ECONOMY

Agriculture accounts for 79.9 per cent of employment and contributes 29.1 per cent of GDP. The chief product, groundnuts, forms over 80 per cent of exports. Other crops are cotton, rice, millet, sorghum and maize.

Manufactures are limited to groundnut processing, minor metal fabrications, paints, furniture, soap and bottling. Tourism is developing quickly with more than 80,000 visitors in 1996–7. Trade through the Gambia, re-exporting imported goods to neighbouring countries, is an important element in the economy. The main exports are groundnuts, cotton, and fish and fish products. The main imports are foodstuffs and live animals, industrial goods, machinery and transport equipment, and fuels. In 1997 there was a trade deficit of US$85 million and a current account deficit of US$23 million. Imports in 1999 totalled US$192 million and exports US$7 million.

GNP – US$422 million (2000); US$330 per capita (1999)
GDP – US$436 million (1998); US$342 per capita (1999)
ANNUAL AVERAGE GROWTH OF GDP – 5.4 per cent (1997)
INFLATION RATE – 0.8 per cent (2000)
TOTAL EXTERNAL DEBT – US$459 million (1999)

Trade with UK	2000	2001
Imports from UK	£14,434,000	£18,503,000
Exports to UK	3,506,000	7,726,000

COMMUNICATIONS

There is an international airport at Yundum, 17 miles from Banjul, with scheduled services flying to other West African states and to the UK and Belgium. Internal communication is by road and river.

EDUCATION

There are 24 secondary schools (eight high and 16 technical). Two high schools provide A-level education. Gambia College provides post-secondary courses in education, agriculture, public health and nursing. There

are seven vocational training institutions. Higher education and advanced training courses are taken outside The Gambia, currently by over 200 students.
ILLITERACY RATE – 61.1 per cent (2002)
ENROLMENT (percentage of age group) – primary 77 per cent (1997); secondary 25 per cent (1997); tertiary 2 per cent (1997)

GEORGIA
Sak'art'velos Respublikis – Georgia

AREA – 26,911 sq. miles (69,700 sq. km). Neighbours: Russia (north), Azerbaijan (south-east), Armenia (south), Turkey (south-west)
POPULATION – 4,989,285 (2001 estimate): 70 per cent Georgian, 8 per cent Armenian, 6 per cent Russian, 6 per cent Azerbaijani, 3 per cent Ossetian and 2 per cent Abkhazian, with smaller groups of Greeks, Ukrainians, Jews and Kurds. Georgian is the sole official language, except in Abkhazia where Abkhazian is also officially recognised. Russian and Armenian are commonly spoken. About 65 per cent of the population are adherents of the Georgian Orthodox Church, 11 per cent are Muslims, 10 per cent are Russian Orthodox and 8 per cent are Armenian Orthodox.
CAPITAL – Tbilisi (population, 1,268,000, 1990 estimate)
MAJOR CITIES – Batumi (137,000); Kutaisi (236,000); Rustavi (160,000); Sukhumi (capital of Abkhazia) (122,000), 1990 UN estimates
CURRENCY – Lari of 100 tetri
NATIONAL ANTHEM – Dideba Zetsit Kurtheuls (Praise Be To The Heavenly Bestower Of Blessings)
NATIONAL DAY – 26 May (Independence Day)
NATIONAL FLAG – Cherry red with a canton in the upper hoist divided black over white
LIFE EXPECTANCY (years) – male 69.5; female 77.6
POPULATION GROWTH RATE – 0.1 per cent (1997)
POPULATION DENSITY – 77 per sq. km (1999)
URBAN POPULATION – 55.6 per cent (1995)
MILITARY EXPENDITURE – 2.6 per cent of GDP (2000)
MILITARY PERSONNEL – 16,790: Army 8,620, Navy 1,040, Air Force 1,330; Paramilitaries 11,700
CONSCRIPTION DURATION – 18 months
ILLITERACY RATE – 0.5 per cent
ENROLMENT (percentage of age group) – primary 88 per cent (1997); secondary 77 per cent (1997); tertiary 42 per cent (1997)

Georgia occupies the north-western part of the Caucasus region of the former Soviet Union. It contains the two autonomous republics of Abkhazia and Adjaria and the disputed region of South Ossetia (Tskhinvali). Georgia is mountainous, with the Greater Caucasus in the north and the Lesser Caucasus in the south. Western Georgia has a mild and damp climate, eastern Georgia is more continental and dry. The Black Sea shore and the Rioni lowland are subtropical.

HISTORY AND POLITICS

The Georgians formed two states, Colchis and Iberia, on the edge of the Black Sea around 1000 BC. After centuries of invasions by Arabs, Turks and Khazars, Georgia entered its 'Golden Age' in the 12th century AD when trade, irrigation and communications were developed. Invasions by the Khazars and Mongols led to the division of Georgia into several states. These struggled against the Turkish and the Persian empires from the 16th to the 18th centuries, gradually turning to the Russian Empire for

protection and support. Eastern Georgia signed a treaty of alliance with Russia which recognised Russian supremacy in 1783 and joined the Russian Empire in 1801, followed soon after by Western Georgia.

In the late 19th century, nationalist and Marxist movements competed for limited political influence under autocratic Russian rule. One of the most prominent Marxist activists was Iosif Dzhugashvili (Josef Stalin). After the Russian revolution of 1917, a nationalist government came to power in Georgia supported by allied intervention forces. In 1921 Soviet forces occupied Tbilisi, and in 1922 Georgia joined the Soviet Union as part of the Transcaucasian Soviet Socialist Republic.

In March 1990 the Georgian Supreme Soviet declared illegal the treaties of 1921–2 by which Georgia had joined the Soviet Union. The Communist Party's monopoly on power was abolished and in multiparty elections held in October and November 1990 the nationalist leader Zviad Gamsakhurdia was elected president. Georgia declared its independence from the Soviet Union in May 1991 and was admitted to UN membership on 31 July 1992.

Gamsakhurdia's government faced armed opposition from 1991 onwards. Defeat in the ensuing civil war in Tbilisi led to Gamsakhurdia's overthrow in January 1992, and in March 1992 a state council was appointed with the former Soviet foreign minister Eduard Shevardnadze as chairman. Fighting continued throughout 1992 and 1993. In October 1992 Shevardnadze was elected head of state and Chairman of the Parliament, and a loose alliance of pro-Shevardnadze parties formed a government.

Gamsakhurdia returned to western Georgia in September 1993. President Shevardnadze failed to prevent the advance of Gamsakhurdia's rebels as most government forces were engaged in Abkhazia. Shevardnadze was forced to accept Russian armaments and troops to defeat the rebellion and in return agreed to join the CIS. Georgia rescinded its participation in the CIS Collective Security treaty in February 1999 and Russian troops, who had been guarding Georgia's frontier with Turkey, began to withdraw. The legislative election held on 31 October and 14 November 1999 was won by the Union of the Citizens of Georgia which gained 130 of the 235 seats. In the presidential election held on 9 April 2000, President Shevardnadze was re-elected, gaining 79.8 per cent of the vote.

SECESSION

In late 1990 the South Ossetians took up arms against Georgian rule in an attempt to join North Ossetia, itself part of Russia. The South Ossetian provincial parliament voted in November 1992 to secede from Georgia and join Russia. Fighting ceased in June 1992 and a joint Russian-Georgian-Ossetian peacekeeping force was dispatched. Representatives of the South Ossetian and Georgian governments met in April 1996 to agree security and confidence-building measures. Presidential elections in South Ossetia were won by Ludvig Chibirov, the chair of the Supreme Council, in November 1996. Legislative elections were held in May 1999.

In July 1992 the Abkhazian republican parliament declared Abkhazia independent. Fighting broke out between Georgian forces and Abkhazian separatists supported by Russian arms and irregulars; Georgian forces were defeated and were forced to withdraw in September 1993. Negotiations under Russian auspices led to an Abkhaz-Georgian cease-fire and separation of forces agreement being signed in May 1994 and the deployment of 2,500 Russian UN peacekeepers on the Abkhaz-Georgian border. In November 1994 the Abkhaz

Supreme Soviet declared Abkhazia's independence again and elected Vladislav Ardzinba as president. Abkhazia was given autonomous republic status under the 1995 constitution; this was rejected by the republican parliament. Elections to the self-declared Abkhaz People's Assembly were held in November 1996. Following a guarantee of security from President Ardzinba, ethnic Georgians who had fled Abkhazia during the fighting began returning in March 1999. A referendum held in Abkhazia in October 1999 approved a new constitution which held Abkhazia to be a sovereign state. On 11 July 2000, Georgia and Abkhazia signed a UN-sponsored protocol on stabilisation measures, agreeing to refrain from the use of force and to establish groups to combat cross-border crime.

FOREIGN RELATIONS

Georgia has signed a Partnership and Co-operation Agreement with the European Union.

In May 2002, US military instructors arrived in Tbilisi. They will stay for over a year to train up to 2,000 troops of elite units. A written commitment had been issued promising that the troops would not be used against Abkhazia.

POLITICAL SYSTEM

The 1995 constitution provides for a federal republic with a unicameral legislature, to become bicameral 'following the creation of appropriate conditions'; and a popularly elected president who serves a maximum of two five-year terms. The present parliament has 235 members, directly elected for a four-year term.

HEAD OF STATE

President, Eduard Shevardnadze, *elected* 11 October 1992, *re-elected* 1995, 9 April 2000

CABINET *as at July 2002*

Minister of State, Avtandil Djordenadze
Agriculture, David Kirtvalidze
Culture, Sesili Gogiberidze
Defence, Maj.-Gen. Davit Tevzadze
Economy, Industry and Trade, Giorgio Gachechiladze
Education, Alexandre Kartozia
Environment, Nino Chkhobadze
Finance and Tax Revenue, Mirian Gogiashvili
Foreign Affairs, Irakli Menagarishvili
Fuel and Energy, David Mirtskhulava
Interior, Koba Narchemashvili
Justice, Roland Giligashvili
Labour, Health Care and Social Welfare, Amiran Gamkrelidze
Refugees, Valeri Vashakidze
Security, Valeri Khaburzania
State Property, Solomon Pavliashvili
Transport and Communications, Merab Adeishvili
Urban Planning and Construction, Merab Chkhenkeli
Without Portfolio, Malkhaz Kakabadze

EMBASSY OF GEORGIA
4 Russell Gardens, London W14 8EZ
Tel: 020-7603 7799
Ambassador Extraordinary and Plenipotentiary,
HE Teimuraz Mamatsashvili, apptd 1995

BRITISH EMBASSY
Sheraton Metechi Palace Hotel, GE-380003 Tbilisi
Tel: (00 995) (32) 955497
Email: british.embassy@caucasus.net

Ambassador Extraordinary and Plenipotentiary,
HE Deborah Barnes-Jones, apptd 2001

BRITISH COUNCIL DIRECTOR, Jo Bakowski,
13 Chavchavadze Avenue, GE-380079 Tbilisi;
Email: office@britishcouncil.org.ge

ECONOMY

The economy was brought to the brink of collapse by civil and secessionist wars and the ending of former Soviet trading relationships. Although Georgia has deposits of coal, they have not been exploited and it is desperately short of energy supplies. . The only productive sector of the economy is agriculture, which employs 30 per cent of the workforce and generates 38 per cent of GDP, with a concentration on viniculture, tea and tobacco-growing and citrus fruits. The main exports are iron alloys, wine, nuts, chemical fertilisers, and oil and oil products. The main imports are oil and oil products, gas, automobiles, pharmaceuticals and wheat. In January 2001 the IMF approved a three-year loan to Georgia, amounting to some US$141 million. In 1998 exports totalled US$192 million and imports US$887 million.

GNP – US$3,243 million (2000); US$620 per capita (1999)
GDP – US$4,927 million (1998); US$765 per capita (1999)
ANNUAL AVERAGE GROWTH OF GDP – 11.3 per cent (1997)
INFLATION RATE – 19.1 per cent (1999)
UNEMPLOYMENT – 13.8 per cent (1999)
TOTAL EXTERNAL DEBT – US$1,652 million (1999)

Trade with UK	2000	2001
Imports from UK	£12,204,000	£19,342,000
Exports to UK	14,220,000	5,891,000

CULTURE

Famous Georgians include the 12th-century writer Shota Rustaveli, who composed the epic poem *Knight in a Tiger's Skin*, and the film director Tengiz Abuladze (b. 1924), who directed the film *Repentance*.

GERMANY
Bundesrepublik Deutschland – Federal Republic of Germany

AREA – 137,846 sq. miles (357,022 sq. km). Neighbours: Denmark (north), Poland (east), Czech Republic (east and south-east), Austria (south-east and south), Switzerland (south), France, Luxembourg, Belgium and the Netherlands (west)
POPULATION – 83,029,536 (2001 estimate). Approximately 80 per cent of the population live in the former West Germany. In 1994 there were 28,197,000 Protestants, 27,909,797 Roman Catholics, 2,700,000 Muslims and 53,797 Jews. The language is German; there are Danish- and Frisian-speaking minorities in Schleswig-Holstein and a Sorbian-speaking minority in Saxony
CAPITAL – Berlin (population, 3,472,009, 1997 estimate). The seat of government and parliament was transferred from Bonn to Berlin in 2000
MAJOR CITIES – Bremen (546,968); Cologne (964,311); Dortmund (594,866); Dresden (459,222); Duisburg (529,062); Düsseldorf (570,969); Essen (608,732); Frankfurt am Main (643,469); Hamburg (1,704,731); Hannover (520,670); Leipzig (446,491); Munich (1,205,923); Nuremberg (489,758); Stuttgart (585,274), 1998 estimates
CURRENCY – Euro (€) of 100 cents

NATIONAL ANTHEM – Einigkeit Und Recht Und Freiheit (Unity And Right And Freedom)
NATIONAL DAY – 3 October (Anniversary of 1990 Unification)
NATIONAL FLAG – Horizontal bars of black, red and gold
LIFE EXPECTANCY (years) – male 75.0; female 81.1
POPULATION GROWTH RATE – 0.1 per cent (1999)
POPULATION DENSITY – 230 per sq. km (1999)

HISTORY AND POLITICS

The first German realm was the Holy Roman Empire, established in AD 962 when Otto I of Saxony was crowned Emperor. The Empire endured until 1806, but the achievement of a national state was prevented by fragmentation into small principalities and dukedoms.

The Empire was replaced by a loose association of sovereign states known as the German Confederation, which was dissolved in 1866 and replaced by the Prussian-dominated North German Federation. The south German principalities united with the northern federation to form a second German Empire in 1871 and the King of Prussia was proclaimed Emperor.

Defeat in the First World War led to the abdication of the Emperor, and the country became a republic. The Treaty of Versailles (1919) ceded Alsace-Lorraine to France, and large areas in the east were lost to Poland. The world economic crisis of 1929 contributed to the collapse of the Weimar Republic and the subsequent rise to power of the National Socialist movement of Adolf Hitler, who became Chancellor in 1933.

After concluding a Treaty of Non-Aggression with the Soviet Union in August 1939, Germany invaded Poland (1 September 1939), precipitating the Second World War, which lasted until 1945. Hitler committed suicide on 30 April 1945. On 8 May 1945, Germany unconditionally surrendered.

THE POST-WAR PERIOD

Germany was divided into American, French, British and Soviet zones of occupation. The territories to the east of the Oder and Neisse rivers were placed under Polish and Russian administration and some 7.75 million Germans were deported.

The Federal Republic of Germany (FRG) was created out of the three western zones in 1949. A Communist government was established in the Soviet zone (henceforth the German Democratic Republic (GDR)). In 1961 the Soviet zone of Berlin was sealed off, and the Berlin Wall was built along the zonal boundary, partitioning the western sectors of the city from the eastern.

Soviet-initiated reform in eastern Europe during the late 1980s led to unrest in the GDR, culminating in the opening of the Berlin Wall in November 1989 and the collapse of Communist government. The 'Treaty on the Final Settlement with Respect to Germany', concluded between the FRG, GDR and the four former occupying powers in September 1990, unified Germany with effect from 3 October 1990 as a fully sovereign state. Economic and monetary union preceded formal union on 1 July 1990. Unification is constitutionally the accession of Berlin and the five reformed Länder of the GDR to the FRG, which remains in being. Berlin was declared to be the capital of the unified Germany and parliament and government departments were transferred from Bonn.

The distribution of seats following the last election for the Bundestag on 27 September 1998 was: Social Democrats (SPD), 298; Christian Democratic Union (CDU), 198; Christian Social Union (CSU), 47; Greens, 47; Free Democrats, 44; Democratic Socialists, 35. A

coalition of Social Democrats and Greens forms the present government,The latest presidential elections took place on May 24 1999 in which Johannes Rau was elected and the most recent legislative elections were held on September 27 1998 in which the SPD gained power. Legislative elections took place on September 22 2002. See Stop Press.

POLITICAL SYSTEM

The Basic Law provides for a president, elected by a Federal Convention (electoral college) for a five-year term, a lower house *(Bundestag)* of 669 members elected by direct universal suffrage for a four-year term of office, and an upper house *(Bundesrat)* composed of 69 members appointed by the governments of the *Länder* in proportion to *Länder* populations, without a fixed term of office.

Judicial authority is exercised by the Federal Constitutional Court, the federal courts provided for in the Basic Law and the courts of the *Länder*.

FEDERAL STRUCTURE

Germany is a federal republic composed of 16 states *(Länder)* (ten from the former West, five from the former East and Berlin). Each *Land* has its own directly elected legislature and government led by Minister-Presidents (prime ministers) or equivalents. The 1949 Basic Law vests executive power in the *Länder* governments except in those areas reserved for the federal government.

HEAD OF STATE

Federal President, Johannes Rau, *elected* 24 May 1999

CABINET *as at July 2002*

Federal Chancellor, Gerhard Schröder (SPD)
Federal Vice-Chancellor, Foreign Affairs, Joschka Fischer (Greens)
Consumer Protection, Nutrition and Agriculture, Renate Künast (Greens)
Defence, Rudolf Scharping (SPD)
Economic Co-operation and Development, Heidemarie Wieczorek-Zeul (SPD)
Economics and Technology, Werner Müller (Ind.)
Education and Research, Edelgard Bulmahn (SPD)
Environment, Nature Conservation and Reactor Safety, Jürgen Trittin (Greens)
Family, Pensioners, Women and Youth, Christine Bergmann (SPD)
Finance, Hans Eichel (SPD)
Head of Chancellory, Frank-Walter Steinmeier (SPD)
Health, Ulla Schmidt (SPD)
Interior, Otto Schily (SPD)
Justice, Herta Däubler-Gmelin (SPD)
Labour and Social Affairs, Walter Riester (SPD)
Ministers of State, Christoph Zöpel (SPD); Ludger Volmer (SPD); Hans Martin Bury (SPD); Rolf Schwanitz (SPD); Julian Nida-Ruemelin (SPD)
Transport, Construction and Housing, Kurt Bodewig (SPD)

SPD Social Democratic Party Ind. Independent

EMBASSY OF THE FEDERAL REPUBLIC OF GERMANY
23 Belgrave Square/Chesham Place, London SW1X 8PZ
Tel: 020-7824 1300
Ambassador Extraordinary and Plenipotentiary, HE Dr Hans-Friedrich von Ploetz, apptd 1999
Minister and Co-ordinator of EU Affairs, Dr. W. Kischlat
Defence Attaché, Rear-Adm. Hubert Hass

Counsellors, T. Hanckel *(Cultural Affairs)*; A. Herkes *(Economic Affairs)*

BRITISH EMBASSY
Wilhelmstrasse 70, D-10117 Berlin
Tel: (00 49) (30) 204570
Ambassador Extraordinary and Plenipotentiary, HE Sir Paul Lever, KCMG, apptd 1997
Deputy Head of Mission and Head of Political and Public Affairs, J. Cresswell
Defence and Military Attaché, Brig. B. R. Isbell, MBE
Counsellor (Economic), R. L. Turner

BRITISH EMBASSY BONN OFFICE
Argelanderstrasse 108a, D-53115 Bonn
Tel: (00 49) (228) 91670

BRITISH CONSULATES-GENERAL – Düsseldorf, Frankfurt, Hamburg, Munich, Stuttgart

BRITISH CONSULATES – Bremen, Hannover, Kiel and Nuremberg

BRITISH COUNCIL DIRECTOR, Tony Andrews, Hackescher Markt 1, D-10178 Berlin; Email: bc.berlin@britcoun.de

DEFENCE

The Army has 2,521 main battle tanks, 2,666 armoured personnel carriers, 2,243 armoured infantry fighting vehicles, and 204 attack helicopters. The Navy has 14 submarines, two destroyers, 12 frigates, 28 patrol and coastal vessels, 67 combat aircraft and 40 armed helicopters. The Air Force has 434 combat aircraft.
There remain 82,480 NATO personnel in Germany (USA 58,080; UK 17,100; Belgium 2,000; France 2,700; Netherlands 2,600).
MILITARY EXPENDITURE – 1.6 per cent of GDP (2000)
MILITARY PERSONNEL – 308,400: Army 211,800, Navy 26,050, Air Force 70,550. Under the terms of the Treaty of Unification, the German armed forces have been limited to 370,000 active personnel since the end of 1994
CONSCRIPTION DURATION – Ten months

ECONOMY

Germany has a predominantly industrial economy. Principal industries are coal mining, iron and steel production, machine construction, the electrical industry, the manufacture of steel and metal products, chemicals, automobile production, electronics, textiles and the processing of foodstuffs.
In 1998, Germany produced 207,642,000 tonnes of coal and 2,895,446 tonnes of crude petroleum. The government announced in June 2000 that it was to abolish all 19 of Germany's nuclear power stations over a 32-year period, which currently supplied over 30 per cent of the energy generated in the country.
After a mini-boom generated by new East German demand in 1990 and 1991, Germany entered its most severe recession since the war induced by the costs of reunification. In 1993 a 'Solidarity Pact' was agreed, which lays down the basis of future funding transfers to the East based on a 5.5 per cent rise in income taxes, wage restraint in the West, more private investment in the East, and the distribution of the funding burden between the federal and *Länder* governments. The government was forced to make spending cuts in order to meet the criteria for European monetary union. An austerity package was approved in August 1999, which cut DM30,000 million from public spending in 2000, and in December 1999 it

was announced that the basic rate of company tax would fall from 40 per cent to 25 per cent from 1 January 2001. The rate of economic growth increased in 1999 and 2000, aided by the weakness of the euro, but began to slow in the first quarter of 2001.

In 1999 there was a trade surplus of US$70,503 million and a current account deficit of US$20,901 million. In 2000 imports totalled US$497,803 million and exports US$549,578 million.

GNP – US$2,057,633 million (2000); US$25,620 per capita (1999)
GDP – US$2,150,480 million (1998); US$25,749 per capita (1999)
ANNUAL AVERAGE GROWTH OF GDP – 3.1 per cent (2000)
INFLATION RATE – 1.9 per cent (2000)
UNEMPLOYMENT – 7.8 per cent (2001)

Trade with UK	2000	2001
Imports from UK	£21,456,600,000	£22,589,100,000
Exports to UK	26,700,400,000	27,140,300,000

COMMUNICATIONS

In 1999 the privatised railways measured 41,841 km of which 19,325 km were electrified. Classified roads measured 230,700 km in 2000, of which motorways total 11,500 km. Merchant shipping under the German flag in 1999 amounted to 7,968,000 tonnes gross. Inland waterways are 6,929 km long.

EDUCATION

School attendance is compulsory between the ages of six and 18 and comprises nine years of full-time education at primary and main schools and three years of vocational education on a part-time basis. The secondary school leaving examination (Abitur) entitles the holder to a place of study at a university or another institution of higher education.

Children below the age of 18 who are not attending a general secondary or a full-time vocational school have compulsory day-release at a vocational school.

The largest universities are in Munich, Berlin, Hamburg, Bonn, Frankfurt and Cologne.
ENROLMENT (percentage of age group) – primary 100 per cent (1997); secondary 100 per cent (1997); tertiary 47 per cent (1997)

CULTURE

Modern (or New High) German has developed from the time of the Reformation to the present day, with differences of dialect in Austria, Alsace, Luxembourg, Liechtenstein and the German-speaking cantons of Switzerland.

The literary language is usually regarded as having become fixed by Luther and Zwingli at the Reformation, since which time many great names occur in all branches, notably philosophy, from Leibnitz to Kant, Schelling and Hegel; drama, from Goethe and Schiller to Gerhart Hauptmann; and poetry, Heinrich Heine. Eight German authors have received the Nobel Prize for Literature: Theodor Mommsen, R. Eucken, P. Heyse, Gerhart Hauptmann, Thomas Mann, N. Sachs, Heinrich Böll and Gunther Grass.

Land	Area (sq. km)	Population (1998)	Capital	Minister-President (July 2002)
Baden-Württemberg	35,752	10.4m	Stuttgart	Erwin Teufel (CDU)
Bavaria	70,548	12.1m	Munich	Dr Edmund Stoiber (CSU)
Berlin	891	3.4m	–	Klaus Wowereit (SPD)*
Brandenburg	29,476	2.6m	Potsdam	Matthias Platzeck (SPD)
Bremen	404	0.7m	–	Dr Henning Scherf (SPD)*
Hamburg	755	1.7m	–	Ole von Beust (CDU)*
Hesse	21,115	6.0m	Wiesbaden	Roland Koch (CDU)
Lower Saxony	47,613	7.9m	Hannover	Sigmar Gabriel (SPD)
Mecklenburg-Western Pomerania	23,170	1.8m	Schwerin	Dr Harald Ringstorff (SPD)
North Rhine-Westphalia	34,079	18.0m	Düsseldorf	Wolfgang Clement (SPD)
Rhineland-Palatinate	19,847	4.0m	Mainz	Kurt Beck (SPD)
Saarland	2,570	1.1m	Saarbrücken	Peter Müller (SPD)
Saxony	18,412	4.5m	Dresden	Dr Georg Milbradt (CDU)
Saxony-Anhalt	20,447	2.7m	Magdeburg	Wolfgang Böhmer (CDU)
Schleswig-Holstein	15,770	2.8m	Kiel	Heide Simonis (SPD)
Thuringia	16,172	2.5m	Erfurt	Dr Bernhard Vogel (CDU)

*Berlin, Governing Mayor; Bremen, Mayor; Hamburg, First Mayor

GHANA
The Republic of Ghana

AREA – 92,098 sq. miles (238,533 sq. km). Neighbours: Burkina Faso (north), Côte d'Ivoire (west), Togo (east)

POPULATION – 19,894,014 (2001 estimate); most are Sudanese Negroes, although Hamitic strains are common in the north. The official language is English. The principal indigenous language group is Akan, of which Twi and Fanti are the most commonly used. Ga, Ewe and languages of the Mole-Dagbani group are common in certain regions. Most Ghanaians are Christians, although there is a substantial Muslim minority in the north

CAPITAL – Ψ Accra (population, 1,445,515, 1998), Greater Accra Region (including Tema) 2,384,753 (1998 estimate)

MAJOR CITIES – Koforidua (81,378); Kumasi (577,878); Ψ Takoradi (96,897); Tamale (228,827)

CURRENCY – Cedi of 100 pesewas

NATIONAL FLAG – Equal horizontal bands of red over gold over green; five-point black star on gold stripe

NATIONAL ANTHEM – God Bless Our Homeland Ghana

NATIONAL DAY – 6 March (Independence Day)

LIFE EXPECTANCY (YEARS) – male 56.0; female 58.5

POPULATION GROWTH RATE – 2.7 per cent (1999)

POPULATION DENSITY – 82 per sq. km (1999)

MILITARY EXPENDITURE – 0.9 per cent of GDP (2000)

MILITARY PERSONNEL – 7,000: Army 5,000, Navy 1,000, Air Force 1,000

ILLITERACY RATE – 26.3 per cent (2002)

ENROLMENT (percentage of age group) – primary 79 per cent (1997)

HISTORY AND POLITICS

First reached by Europeans in the 15th century, the constituent parts of Ghana came under British administration at various times, the original Gold Coast Colony being constituted in 1874, and Ashanti and the Northern Territories Protectorate in 1901. Trans-Volta-Togoland, part of the former German colony of Togo, was mandated to Britain by the League of Nations after the First World War and was integrated with the Gold Coast Colony in 1956 following a plebiscite. The former Gold Coast Colony and associated territories became the independent state of Ghana on 6 March 1957 and became a republic in 1960.

Since 1966, Ghana has experienced long periods of military rule interspersed with short-lived civilian governments. A coup in 1979 led to the formation of an Armed Forces Revolutionary Council chaired by Flt. Lt. Jerry Rawlings. Civilian rule was restored in 1979 but another coup in December 1981 brought Rawlings back to power.

A referendum in 1992 approved a new multiparty constitution and the legalisation of political parties. The National Democratic Congress (NDC) was established as a political party from the ruling Provisional National Defence Council. The presidential and parliamentary elections in late 1992 were won by Rawlings and the NDC.

The NDC lost power in the general election held on 7 December 2000, which was won by the New Patriotic Party (NPP), which obtained 98 seats; the NDC won 93 seats. The presidential election held on 7 and 28 December 2000 was won by John Kufuor of the NPP. A new cabinet was nominated by Kufour in January 2001

and the ministers were approved by Parliament by early February. On 12 October, there was a reshuffle and on 29 March 2002 two ministers resigned after ethnic fighting broke out in northern Ghana.

POLITICAL SYSTEM

The head of state is an executive president elected for a four-year term, renewable only once. The president appoints the Council of Ministers. The unicameral legislature, the Parliament, has 200 members directly elected for a four-year term.

For political and administrative purposes Ghana is divided into ten regions, each headed by a Regional Minister who is the representative of the central government.

HEAD OF STATE

President, John Kufuor, *elected* 28 December 2000, *sworn in* 7 January 2001
Vice-President, Aliju Mahama

COUNCIL OF MINISTERS *as at July 2002*

Communications and Technology, Felix Owusu Agyepong
Defence; Interior (acting), Kwame Addo-Kufuor
Education, Christopher Ameyaw-Akumfi
Environment, Science and Technology, Dominic Fobih
Finance, Yaw Osafo Maado
Food and Agriculture, Maj. Courage Quarshigah
Foreign Affairs, Hackman Owusu-Agyemang
Health, Kwaku Afriyie
Information and Presidential Affairs, Jake Obetsebi Lamptey
Justice and Attorney-General, Nana Akufo Addo
Lands and Forestry, Kasim Kasanga
Local Government and Rural Development, Kwadwo Baah-Wiredu
Manpower Development and Employment, Cecilia Bannerman
Mines and Energy, Kwadwo Agyei-Darko
Minister of State in the Office of the Economic Team, Charles O. Nyanor
National Development Planning Commission, Ben Boukari Salifu
Parliamentary Affairs, Papa Owusu-Ankomah
Planning and Regional Economic Co-operation and Integration, Chair of the National Development Planning Commission, Paa Kwesi Nduom
Presidency, Elizabeth Akna Ohene
Roads and Transport, Richard Anane
Senior Minister, Chair of the Government Economic Team, J. H. Mensah
Tourism, Hawa Yakubu
Trade and Industry, Kofi Apraku
Women's Affairs, Gladys Asmah
Works and Housing, Yaw Barimah
Youth and Sports, Edqard Osei Kwaku

OFFICE OF THE HIGH COMMISSION OF GHANA
13 Belgrave Square, London SW1X 8PN
Tel: 020-7235 4142
High Commissioner, HE Isaac Osei, apptd 2001
Deputy High Commissioner, K. Baah-Duodu
Defence Adviser, Cdre C. B. Pupulampu

BRITISH HIGH COMMISSION
PO Box 296, Osu Link, Accra
Tel: (00 233) (21) 221665
Email: High.Commission@accra.mail.fco.gov.uk
High Commissioner, HE Rod Pullen, apptd 2000
Defence Adviser, Lt. Col. Steen Clarke, OBE

BRITISH COUNCIL DIRECTOR, Terence Humphreys,
11 Liberia Road, PO Box 771, Accra;
Email: bcaccra@britishcouncil.org.gh.
There is also an office in Kumasi.

ECONOMY

Agriculture is the basis of the economy, employing 57.4
per cent of the workforce in 1998. Crops include cocoa,
the largest single source of revenue, rice, cassava,
plantains, oranges and pineapples, groundnuts, corn,
millet, oil palms, yams, maize and vegetables. Livestock is
raised in uncultivated areas. Fishing is important in
coastal areas and in the Volta lake and river system.

Manganese production ranks among the world's
largest, with 384,173 tonnes of ore being produced in
1998. Gold is the main export; production amounted to
74,315 kg in 1998. Diamonds and bauxite are also
produced.

Since 1966 the Volta Dams at Akosombo and Kpong
have generated hydroelectric power for the processing of
bauxite and fed a power transmission network for most
of Ghana, Togo and Benin. There is considerable foreign
investment in Ghana, and its economy has grown
consistently. In 2000 there was a trade deficit of US$843
million and a current account deficit of US$413 million.
Imports in 1998 totalled US$2,563 million and exports
US$1,795 million.

GNP – US$6,785 million (2000); US$400 per capita
(1999)
GDP – US$6,639 million (1998); US$400 per capita
(1999)
ANNUAL AVERAGE GROWTH OF GDP – 3.8 per cent
(1998)
INFLATION RATE – 25.2 per cent (2000)
TOTAL EXTERNAL DEBT – US$6,928 million (1999)

TRADE

Principal exports are gold, cocoa, and timber. Principal
imports are capital goods, semi-manufactures,
consumables and energy.

Trade with UK	2000	2001
Imports from UK	£169,365,000	£144,409,000
Exports to UK	99,994,000	134,021,000

GREECE
Elliniki Dimokratia – Hellenic Republic

AREA – 50,949 sq. miles (131,957 sq. km). Neighbours:
Albania, Bulgaria and Macedonia (north), Turkey
(east)
POPULATION – 10,623,835 (2001 estimate): 98 per cent
Greek Orthodox, 1 per cent Catholic, 1 per cent
Muslim. The language is Greek
CAPITAL – Athens (population 3,072,922, 1991);
including Ψ Piraeus and suburbs, 3,096,775 (1991
census)
MAJOR CITIES – Ψ Iráklion (Heraklion) (132,117);
Lárisa (113,090); Ψ Pátrai (Patras) (170,452);
Ψ Thessaloníki (Salonika) (749,048); Ψ Vólos
(116,031), 1991
CURRENCY – Euro (€) of 100 cents
NATIONAL ANTHEM – Imnos Eis Tin Eleftherian
(Hymn To Freedom)
NATIONAL DAY – 25 March (Independence Day)
NATIONAL FLAG – Blue and white stripes with a white
cross on a blue field in the canton
LIFE EXPECTANCY (years) – male 75.9; female 81.2
POPULATION GROWTH RATE – 0.4 per cent (1999)

POPULATION DENSITY – 81 per sq. km (1999)
URBAN POPULATION – 60.1 per cent (2000)

The main areas are: Macedonia, Thrace, Epirus, Thessaly,
Continental Greece, Crete and the Peloponnese. The
main island groups are the Sporades, the Dodecanese or
Southern Sporades, the Cyclades, the Ionian Islands, and
the Aegean Islands (Chios, Lesbos, Limnos and Samos).
In Crete from about 3000 to 1400 BC a civilisation
flourished which spread its influence throughout the
Aegean, and the ruins of the palace of Minos at Knossos
afford evidence of astonishing comfort and luxury.

HISTORY AND POLITICS

Greece was under Turkish rule from the mid-15th
century until a war of independence (1821–7) led to the
establishment of a Greek kingdom in the Peloponnese in
1829. The remainder of Greece gradually became
independent until the Dodecanese were returned by Italy
in 1947. After the Nazi German occupation of 1941–4, a
civil war between monarchist and Communist groups
lasted from 1946 to 1949, and tension between right-wing
and radical groups continued after 1949. In 1967 right-
wing elements in the army seized power and established a
military regime (the 'Greek Colonels'). The King went
into voluntary exile in 1967. Unrest in Athens in 1973–4
intensified after the government was involved in the
overthrow of President Makarios of Cyprus in July 1974,
and led the Colonels to surrender power. Konstantinos
Karamanlis (prime minister 1955–63) returned from
exile to form a provisional government, and the first
elections for ten years were held in 1974. The restoration
of the monarchy was rejected by referendum on 8
December 1974 and Greece became a republic.

The most recent general election was held on 9 April
2000 with the Panhellenic Socialist Party (PASOK)
winning 158 seats, the New Democracy Party (Christian
Democrats) 125 seats, the Communist Party 11 seats, and
the Coalition of the Left and Progress six seats.

POLITICAL SYSTEM

In 1986 most executive power was transferred from the
president to the government. The unicameral 300-
member Parliament (Vouli) is elected for a four-year
term by universal adult suffrage under a system of
proportional representation, with a three per cent
threshold for parliamentary representation. The head of
state is a president, elected by parliament for a five-year
term, renewable once only.

HEAD OF STATE

President of the Hellenic Republic, Constantine
Stephanopoulos, *elected by parliament* 1995,
re-elected 10 March 2000

CABINET *as at July 2002*

Prime Minister, Costas Simitis
Aegean, Nicos Sifounakis
Agriculture, Georgios Drys
Alternate Foreign Minister, Anastassios Giannitsis
Culture, Evangelos Venizelos
Development, Apostolos-Athanassios Tsohatzopoulos
Education and Religious Affairs, Petros Ephthimiou
Environment, Town Planning and Public Works, Vasso
  Papandreou
Foreign Affairs, George Papandreou
Health and Welfare, Constantine Stefanis
Interior, Public Administration and Decentralisation,
  Costas Skandalidis

Justice, Philippos Petsalnikos
Labour and Social Affairs, Dimitrios Reppas
Macedonia and Thrace, George Pashalidis
Merchant Marine, Georgios Anomeritis
Minister of State, Office of the Prime Minister, Stefanos Manikas
National Defence, Yiannos Papantoniou
National Economy and Finance, Nikolaos Christodoulakis
Press and Media, Government Spokesman, Christos Protopapas
Public Order, Michalis Chrysohoidis
Transport and Communications, Christos Verelis

EMBASSY OF GREECE

1A Holland Park, London W11 3TP
Tel: 020-7229 3850
Ambassador Extraordinary and Plenipotentiary, HE Alexandros Sandis, apptd 2000
Defence Attaché, Capt. N. Louloudis
Minister Counsellor, C. Bitsios

BRITISH EMBASSY

1 Ploutarcou Street, GR-106 75 Athens
Tel: (00 30) (1) 727 2600
Email: britania@hol.gr
Ambassador Extraordinary and Plenipotentiary, HE David C. A. Madden, CMG, apptd 1999
Deputy Head of Mission, Counsellor and Consul-General, P. J. Millett
Defence, Naval and Air Attaché, Cdre J . L. Milnes
First Secretary (Commercial), G. G. Thomas

BRITISH CONSULAR OFFICES – Athens, Corfu, Heraklion (Crete), Kos, Patras, Rhodes, Thessaloníki, Syros and Zakynthos

BRITISH COUNCIL DIRECTOR, Chris Hickey, 17 Plateia Philikis Etairias, Athens GR-10673;
Email: british.council@britishcouncil.gr.

DEFENCE

The Army has 1,733 main battle tanks, 1,977 armoured personnel carriers and 500 armoured infantry fighting vehicles. The Navy has eight submarines, four destroyers, 12 frigates, 40 patrol and coastal vessels and 18 armed helicopters. The Air Force has a total of 458 combat aircraft.

Greece maintains 1,250 army personnel in Cyprus. There are 480 US military personnel stationed in Greece.
MILITARY EXPENDITURE – 4.9 per cent of GDP (2000)
MILITARY PERSONNEL – Army 110,000, Navy 19,000, Air Force 30,170; Paramilitaries 4,000
CONSCRIPTION DURATION – Up to 21 months

ECONOMY

The principal minerals are nickel, bauxite, iron ore, iron pyrites, manganese magnesite, chrome, lead, zinc and emery. The chief industries are textiles (cotton, woollen and synthetics), chemicals, cement, glass, metallurgy, shipbuilding, domestic electrical equipment and footwear, the production of aluminium, nickel, iron and steel products, tyres, chemicals, fertilisers and sugar (from locally-grown beet). Food processing and ancillary industries are also growing.

The development of the country's electric power resources, irrigation and land reclamation schemes, and the exploitation of lignite resources for fuel and industrial purposes are continuing. Tourism is also a major industry, with nearly 11 million visitors in 1998.

Though there has been substantial industrialisation, agriculture still employs nearly a fifth of the working population and contributes 8.1 per cent of GDP. The most important agricultural products are tobacco, wheat, cotton, sugar, rice, fruit (olives, peaches, vines, oranges, lemons, figs, almonds and currant-vines). Exports of fresh fruit, currants and vegetables are an important contributor to the economy.

In March 1998 the drachma was admitted to the ERM; Greece became a member of EMU on 1 January 2001 since when it has participated in the European Single Currency.

In 1997 there was a trade deficit of US$15,375 million and a current account deficit of US$4,860 million. In 1999 imports totalled US$25,433 million and exports US$9,815 million.
GNP – US$126,245 million (2000); US$12,110 per capita (1999)
GDP – US$121,513 million (1998); US$11,811 per capita (1999)
ANNUAL AVERAGE GROWTH OF GDP – 4.1 per cent (2000)
INFLATION RATE – 3.5 per cent (2001)
UNEMPLOYMENT – 11.3 per cent (2000)

Trade with UK	2000	2001
Imports from UK	£1,164,000,000	£1,061,900,000
Exports to UK	416,200,000	433,100,000

COMMUNICATIONS

Railways are state-owned, with the exception of the Athens–Piraeus Electric Railway. Roads total over 130,000 km. Athens has direct airline links with Australasia, North America, most countries in Europe, Africa and the Middle East.

EDUCATION

Education is free and compulsory from the age of six to 15 and is maintained by state grants. There are eighteen universities and several other institutes of higher learning.
ILLITERACY RATE – 2.6 per cent (2002)
ENROLMENT (percentage of age group) – primary 93 per cent (1997); secondary 95 per cent (1997); tertiary 47 per cent (1997)

CULTURE

Greek civilisation emerged *c*.1300 BC and the poems of Homer, which were probably current *c*.800 BC, record the struggle between the Achaeans of Greece and the Phrygians of Troy (1194 to 1184 BC).

The spoken language of modern Greece is descended from the Common Greek of Alexander the Great's empire. *Katharevousa*, a conservative literary dialect evolved by Adamantios Corais (Diamant Coray) (1748–1833) and used for official and technical matters, has been phased out. Novels and poetry are mostly in Dimotiki, a progressive literary dialect which owes much to John Psycharis (1854–1919). The poets Solomos, Palamas, Cavafy and Sikelianos have won a European reputation. George Seferis (1963) and Odysseus Elytis (1979) have won the Nobel Prize for Literature.

GRENADA
The State of Grenada

AREA – 133 sq. miles (344 sq. km)
POPULATION – 89,227 (2001 estimate), 95,000 (1992 census), of which about 75 per cent are of African descent; there are minorities of Europeans and Indians. The language is English

CAPITAL – Ψ St George's (population, 4,788, 1981)
CURRENCY – East Caribbean dollar (EC$) of 100 cents
NATIONAL ANTHEM – Hail Grenada, Land Of Ours
NATIONAL DAY – 7 February (Independence Day)
NATIONAL FLAG – Divided diagonally into yellow and green triangles within a red border containing six yellow stars, a yellow star on a red disc in the centre and a nutmeg on the green triangle in the hoist
LIFE EXPECTANCY (years) – male 62.7; female 66.3
POPULATION GROWTH RATE – 0.2 per cent (1999)
POPULATION DENSITY – 270 per sq. km (1999)

The island is about 21 miles long and 12 miles wide. Also a part of Grenada are some of the Grenadines islets, the largest of which is Carriacou, 13 square miles in area.

HISTORY AND POLITICS

Discovered by Columbus in 1498, and named Concepción, Grenada was originally colonised by France and was ceded to Great Britain by the Treaty of Versailles in 1783. It became a Crown colony in 1877, an Associated State in 1967 and an independent nation within the Commonwealth on 7 February 1974.

The government was overthrown in 1979 by the New Jewel Movement and a People's Revolutionary Government was set up. In October 1983 disagreements within the PRG led to the death of Prime Minister Maurice Bishop, whose government was replaced by a Revolutionary Military Council. These events prompted the intervention of Caribbean and US forces. The Governor-General installed an advisory council to act as an interim government until a general election was held in December 1984. A phased withdrawal of US forces was completed by June 1985.

The general election held on 18 January 1999 was won by the New National Party led by Dr Keith Mitchell. They won all 15 seats in the House of Representatives.

POLITICAL SYSTEM

Queen Elizabeth II is head of state and is represented by a Governor-General. Legislative power is vested in a bicameral parliament consisting of an elected 15-member House of Representatives and a 13-member Senate appointed by the Governor-General.

Governor-General, HE Sir Daniel Williams, GCMG, QC, apptd 1996

CABINET *as at July 2002*

Prime Minister, National Security and Information, Keith Mitchell
Agriculture, Lands, Forestry and Fisheries, Claris Charles
Attorney-General, Raymond Anthony
Communications, Works and Public Utilities, Gregory Bowen
Co-operatives, Housing and Social Services, Cuthbert McQueen
Education, Augustine John
Finance, Trade, Industry and Planning, Anthony Boatswain
Foreign Affairs and International Trade, Legal Affairs, Carriacou and Petit Martinique Affairs, Elvin Nimrod
Health and Environment, Clarice Modeste-Curwen
Implementation, Joslyn Whiteman
Labour and Local Government, Lawrence Joseph
Ministers of State, Laurina Waldron (*Health and Environment*); Mark Isaac (*Information*)
Parliamentary Secretaries, Einstein Louison (*Agriculture, Forestry, Lands and Fisheries*); Eleuthan Noel (*Carriacou and Petit Martinique Affairs*); Richard McPhail (*Communications, Works and Public Utilities*); Yolande Joseph (*Gender and Family Affairs*)

Tourism, Civil Aviation, Culture, Social Security and Gender and Family Affairs, Brenda Hood
Youth, Sports, Community Development, Adrian Mitchell

HIGH COMMISSION FOR GRENADA
Lauderdale House, 8 Queen Street, London W1X 7PH
Tel: 020-7290 2275
Email: grenada@high-commission.freeserve.co.uk
High Commissioner, HE Ruth Elizabeth Rouse, apptd 1999

BRITISH HIGH COMMISSION
14 Church Street, St George's
Tel: (00 1 473) 440 3536/440 3222
Email: bhcgrenada@caribsurf.com
High Commissioner, Mr J White, resident at Bridgetown, Barbados

ECONOMY

Services account for 61 per cent of employment and 71 per cent of GDP. The economy was principally agrarian, but agriculture now employs only 17 per cent of the workforce and produces 10 per cent of GDP. Grenada accounts for about a quarter of world nutmeg production. Cocoa and bananas are also major crops. Manufacturing consists of processing agricultural products and the production of textiles, concrete, aluminium and handicrafts. Tourism is the main foreign exchange earner. In 1998 there were 381,669 tourists.
GNP – US$345 million (2000); US$3,440 per capita (1999)
GDP – US$279 million (1998); US$3,295 per capita (1999)
ANNUAL AVERAGE GROWTH OF GDP – 3.6 per cent (1998)
INFLATION RATE – 2.2 per cent (2000)
UNEMPLOYMENT – 11.0 per cent (2000)
TOTAL EXTERNAL DEBT – US$162 million (1999)

TRADE

The most important exports are nutmegs and cocoa. Imports include machinery and transport equipment, livestock, foodstuffs and beverages, manufactured goods, and fuels. The main trading partners are the USA, the UK and Trinidad and Tobago.

In 1996 there was a trade deficit of US$123 million and there was a current account deficit of US$58 million. In 1998, imports totalled US$200 million and exports US$27 million.

Trade with UK	2000	2001
Imports from UK	£9,174,000	£6,955,000
Exports to UK	1,235,000	829,000

GUATEMALA
República de Guatemala – Republic of Guatemala

AREA – 42,042 sq. miles (108,889 sq. km). Neighbours: Mexico (north and west), El Salvador, Honduras and Belize (east)
POPULATION – 12,974,361 (2001 estimate): 56 per cent mestizo, 44 per cent Amerindian. The language is Spanish, but 40 per cent of the population speak an Indian language
CAPITAL – Guatemala City (population, 1,675,589, 1990 estimate)
MAJOR CITIES – Antigua (30,000); Mazatenango (21,000); Ψ Puerto Barrios (23,000); Quezaltenango (100,000)
CURRENCY – Quetzal (Q) of 100 centavos

NATIONAL ANTHEM – Guatemala Feliz (Guatemala Be Praised)
NATIONAL DAY – 15 September
NATIONAL FLAG – Three vertical bands, blue, white, blue; coat of arms on white stripe
LIFE EXPECTANCY (years) – male 63.0; female 68.9
POPULATION GROWTH RATE – 2.7 per cent (1999)
POPULATION DENSITY – 102 per sq. km (1999)
URBAN POPULATION – 38.7 per cent (1995)
MILITARY EXPENDITURE – 0.8 per cent of GDP (2000)
MILITARY PERSONNEL – 31,400: Army 29,200, Navy 1,500, Air Force 700; Paramilitaries 19,000
CONSCRIPTION DURATION – 30 months (selective)
ILLITERACY RATE – 30.0 per cent (2002)
ENROLMENT (percentage of age group) – primary 88 per cent (1997); secondary 26 per cent (1997); tertiary 9 per cent (1997)

Guatemala is traversed from west to east by mountains containing volcanic summits rising to 13,000 feet above sea level; earthquakes are frequent. There are numerous rivers. The climate is hot and malarial near the coast, temperate in the higher regions.

HISTORY AND POLITICS

Guatemala was under Spanish rule from 1524 until gaining independence in 1821. It formed part of the Confederation of Central America from 1823 to 1839.
  After a series of military coups, civilian rule was restored with the election of a Constituent Assembly in 1984 and the promulgation of a new constitution in 1985. In May 1993 President Serrano partially suspended the constitution and attempted to rule by decree but was effectively ousted by the army on 1 June. Ramiro de León Carpio was elected president by Congress to serve out Serrano's term to January 1996.
  The legislative election to the National Congress on 7 November 1999 was won by the Guatemalan Republican Front (FRG) which obtained 63 seats; the National Advancement Party (PAN) won 37 seats. The presidential election on 26 December 1999 was won by Alfonso Portillo of the FRG.

INSURGENCY

Since 1960 the armed forces had been fighting insurgency by the left-wing, mainly Mayan Indian, guerrillas of the Guatemalan Revolutionary National Unity Movement (URNG). Some 200,000 were killed in the fighting. Government–URNG negotiations began in 1991, leading to a reduction in fighting and agreements in 1993. In March 1994 a human rights accord was reached under which a 300-strong UN Observer Mission (MINUGUA) was established in November 1994 to supervise the implementation of government–URNG accords. An accord recognising the rights of the indigenous population was signed in March 1995, but in a referendum held on 16 May 1999, constitutional reforms which would have amended the constitution to allow for the implementation of peace accords were rejected. Representatives of the four rebel groups comprising the URNG signed a peace treaty with the government in December 1996; an independent commission into the 36-year civil war, set up under the 1996 peace treaty, published a report on 25 February 1999 which concluded that the army had committed acts of genocide against the indigenous Mayan population. In August 2000 President Portillo admitted the state's responsibility for atrocities committed during the civil war and vowed that those responsible would be prosecuted.

POLITICAL SYSTEM

Executive power is vested in the president, who is directly elected for a single four-year term. He appoints the Cabinet. Legislative authority is vested in the National Congress, whose 113 members are directly elected for a four-year term.
  The republic is divided into 22 departments.

HEAD OF STATE

President, Alfonso Portillo Cabrera, *elected* 26 December 1999, *sworn in* 14 January 2000
Vice-President, Juan Francisco Reyes López

GOVERNMENT *as at July 2002*

Agriculture, Livestock and Food, Edin Barrientos
Communications, Transport and Public Works, Flora de Ramos
Culture and Sport, Otilia Lux de Coti
Defence, Gen. Leonel Mendez Estrada
Economy, Patricia Ramirez
Education, Mario Torres
Energy and Mines, Raúl Archila
Environment and Natural Resources, Sergio Lavarreda
Foreign Affairs, Gabriel Orellana Rojas
Interior, José Adolfo Reyes
Labour and Social Security, Victor Hugo Godoy
Public Finance, Eduardo Weymann
Public Health and Social Welfare, Mario Bolaños

EMBASSY OF GUATEMALA
13 Fawcett Street, London SW10 9HN
Tel: 020-7351 3042
Ambassador Extraordinary and Plenipotentiary, HE Gladys Marithza Ruiz de Vielman, apptd 2000

BRITISH EMBASSY
Avenida La Reforma 16–00, Zona 10, Edificio Torre Internacional, Nivel 11, Guatemala City
Tel: (00 502) 367 5425/6/7/8/9
Ambassador Extraordinary and Plenipotentiary, Richard D. Lavers

ECONOMY

Agriculture provides 23 per cent of GDP and employs nearly half of the workforce. The principal export is coffee, other articles being manufactured goods, sugar, bananas and cardamom. The chief imports are raw materials and semi-manufactures, capital goods, consumer goods, and fuel oils. The USA, El Salvador and Mexico are the main trading partners.
  On 5 April 2002, the IMF announced that a one-year standby credit of US$67 million had been approved in order to underpin the government's economic policies and the implementation of the 1996 peace accords.
  In 1999 there was a trade deficit of US$1,445 million and a current account deficit of US$1,026 million. In 2000 imports totalled US$4,791 million and exports US$2,696 million.
GNP – US$19,224 million (2000); US$1,680 per capita (1999)
GDP – US$19,008 million (1998); US$1,637 per capita (1999)
ANNUAL AVERAGE GROWTH OF GDP – 3.3 per cent (2000)
INFLATION RATE – 6.0 per cent (2000)
TOTAL EXTERNAL DEBT – US$4,660 million (1999)

Trade with UK	2000	2001
Imports from UK	£27,835,000	£35,393,000
Exports to UK	21,093,000	12,892,000

GUINEA–BISSAU
República da Guiné-Bissau – Republic of Guinea-Bissau

AREA – 13,948 sq. miles (36,125 sq. km). Neighbours: Senegal (north), Guinea (east and south)
POPULATION – 1,315,822 (2001 estimate). The main ethnic groups are the Balante, Malinké, Fulani, Mandjako and Pepel. The official language is Portuguese; most of the population speak Guinean Creole
CAPITAL – Ψ Bissau (population, 109,214, 1979)
CURRENCY – Franc CFA
NATIONAL ANTHEM – É Patria Amada (This Is Our Beloved Country)
NATIONAL DAY – 24 September (Independence Day)
NATIONAL FLAG – Horizontal bands of yellow over green with vertical red band in the hoist charged with a black star
LIFE EXPECTANCY (years) – male 44.0; female 46.9
POPULATION GROWTH RATE – 2.2 per cent (1999)
POPULATION DENSITY – 33 per sq. km (1999)
MILITARY EXPENDITURE – 1.7 per cent of GDP (2000)
MILITARY PERSONNEL – 9,250: Army 6,800, Navy 350, Air Force 100; Paramilitaries 2,000
CONSCRIPTION DURATION – Selective conscription
ILLITERACY RATE – 59.0 per cent (2002)
ENROLMENT (percentage of age group) – primary 62 per cent (1997)

HISTORY AND POLITICS

Guinea-Bissau, formerly Portuguese Guinea, achieved independence on 24 September 1974. Following a coup led by Maj. (now Brig.-Gen.) Vieira in 1980, a Revolutionary Council was established. The ruling African Party for the Independence of Guinea and Cape Verde (PAIGC) introduced a multiparty system in January 1991. The PAIGC won the election held in June 1994 and Brig.-Gen. Vieira was elected president in August 1994.

In June 1998, fighting broke out in Bissau between troops loyal to President Vieira and supporters of the sacked army chief Ansumane Mane. Guinea and Senegal sent in troops to support Vieira, and a peace agreement was signed on 1 November, which promised legislative and presidential elections in March 1999. A government of national unity was formed in February 1999 and Guinean and Senegalese troops withdrew in March in accordance with the peace agreement, but no elections took place. Fighting resumed in May 1999, and the government was overthrown on 7 May by rebels loyal to Gen. Mane, who appointed the Speaker of the National Assembly as acting president. Legislative elections held on 28 November 1999 resulted in the Social Renewal Party (PRS) gaining 38 seats in the 102-seat National Assembly. The PRS's ally, the Guinea-Bissau Resistance-Batafa Movement (RGB-Batafa), gained 28 seats. In presidential elections, the founder of the PRS, Kumba Yalla, was elected on 16 January 2000. He resigned his chairmanship of the PRS on 11 May 2000. Gen. Ansumane Mane led an attempted coup in November 2000, during which he was killed. The ruling coalition collapsed on 23 January 2001; on 19 March, President Yalla appointed Faustino Imbali to form a new government which was sworn in on 27 March. Imbali was dismissed by President Yalla on 8 December 2001 and replaced by Alamara Nhasse.

POLITICAL SYSTEM

A new constitution, which limited the tenure of the presidency to two terms, was adopted in July 1999. Under the constitution, the president is the head of government and appoints the Council of Ministers. There is a unicameral legislature, the Assembleia Nacional Popular (National People's Assembly), composed of 102 members elected by universal suffrage for a four-year term.

HEAD OF STATE
President, C.-in-C. of the Armed Forces, Kumba Yalla, elected 16 January 2000, took office 17 February 2000

COUNCIL OF MINISTERS as at July 2002
Prime Minister, Alamara Nhasse (PRS)
Agriculture, Forestry and Livestock, Luis Olundo Mendes (PRS)
Defence, Brum Sith Namone (PRS)
Economy and Finance, Rui Duarte de Baros (Ind.)
Education, Youth, Sport and Culture, Geraldo Martins (PCD)
Fisheries and Marine Affairs, Antonio Artur Sanha
Foreign Affairs, Filomena Mascarenhas Tipote (PRS)
Internal Administration, Rui Sanha (PRS)
Justice, Dionisio Cabi (PRS)
Media and Parliamentary Affairs, José de Pina (PRS)
Natural Resources and Energy, Carlito Barai (PRS)
Public Health, Antonio Cherif Embalo (Ind.)
Public Service and Labour, Carlos Pinto Perreira (PCD)
Social Infrastructure, Braima Djassy (PRS)
Social Security and Employment, Fatumata Djau Balde (PCD)

PCD Democratic Convergence Party; PRS Social Renewal Party;

EMBASSY OF THE REPUBLIC OF GUINEA-BISSAU
94 rue St Lazare, Paris F-75009, France
Tel: (00 33) (1) 4526 1851
Ambassador Extraordinary and Plenipotentiary, vacant
Chargé d'Affaires, Fali Embalo

HONORARY CONSULATE
Pine Ridge Cottage, Little London Road, Heathfield, East Sussex TN21 0LT. Tel: 01435 866433
Honorary Consul, Mabel Figueiredo da Fonseca Smith

BRITISH CONSULATE
Mavegro Int., CP100, Bissau
British Ambassador, HE Alan Burner, resident at Dakar, Senegal

ECONOMY

Guinea-Bissau produces rice, coconuts, groundnuts and plantains. Cattle are raised, and there are bauxite and phosphate deposits. In May 1997 Guinea-Bissau joined the French Franc Zone, and the CFA Franc replaced the peso as currency. In December 2000 an international debt reduction package worth US$790 million for Guinea-Bissau was agreed.

In 1997 there was a trade deficit of US$14 million and a current account deficit of US$30 million. In 1999 imports totalled US$69 million and exports US$51 million.
GNP – US$221 million (2000); US$160 per capita (1999)
GDP – US$116 million (1998); US$106 per capita (1999)
ANNUAL AVERAGE GROWTH OF GDP – 2.4 per cent (1998)

INFLATION RATE – 8.6 per cent (2000)
TOTAL EXTERNAL DEBT – US$931 million (1999)

Trade with UK	2000	2001
Imports from UK	£1,111,000	£1,532,000
Exports to UK	1,000	–

GUINEA
République de Guinée – Republic of Guinea

AREA – 94,926 sq. miles (245,857 sq. km). Neighbours: Guinea-Bissau (west), Senegal and Mali (north), Côte d'Ivoire (east), Sierra Leone and Liberia (south)
POPULATION – 7,613,870 (2001 estimate); the official language is French; Fullah, Malinké and Soussou are indigenous languages
CAPITAL – Ψ Conakry (population, 763,000)
MAJOR CITIES – Kankan; Kindia; Labé; Mamou; N'Zérékoré; Siguiri
CURRENCY – Guinea franc of 100 centimes
NATIONAL ANTHEM – Liberté
NATIONAL DAY – 2 October (Anniversary of the Proclamation of Independence)
NATIONAL FLAG – Three vertical stripes of red, yellow and green
LIFE EXPECTANCY (years) – male 48.0; female 49.0
POPULATION GROWTH RATE – 6.0 per cent (2000)
POPULATION DENSITY – 30 per sq. km (1999)
MILITARY EXPENDITURE – 1.5 per cent of GDP (2000)
MILITARY PERSONNEL – 9,700: Army 8,500, Navy 400, Air Force 800, Paramilitaries 2,600
CONSCRIPTION DURATION – Two years
ILLITERACY RATE – 58.9 per cent (2002)
ENROLMENT (percentage of age group) – primary 54 per cent (1997); secondary 14 per cent (1997); tertiary 1 per cent (1997)

HISTORY AND POLITICS

Guinea was separated from Senegal in 1891 and administered by France as a separate colony. On 2 October 1958 Guinea became an independent republic.

Ahmed Sékou Touré assumed office as head of the new government, and was elected president in 1961. His death in 1984 was followed by a military coup. Guinea was ruled by a military government directed by a Military Committee for National Recovery (CMRN). A new constitution, providing for the end of military rule, was approved by referendum in 1990.

In January 1991 the CMRN was dissolved and a mixed civilian-military Transitional Committee for National Recovery (CTRN) was established which appointed a new government. Civil disturbances in 1991 caused the government to introduce a full multiparty system in April 1992, since when 40 opposition parties have been legalised. A presidential election held on 14 December 1998 was won by the incumbent President Conté with 54 per cent of the vote. Legislative elections took place on 30 June 2002 and were won by President Conté's Party of Unity (PUP), which gained 85 of the 114 National Assembly seats.

INSURGENCIES

In September 2000, anti-government rebels, believed to be members of the Guinea Liberation Movement (GLM), began a series of incursions into Guinea from Liberia and Sierra Leone. In January 2001 more fighting broke out after armed groups from Liberia had attacked across the border.

HEAD OF STATE
President, Maj.-Gen. Lansana Conté, *took power* 3 April 1984, *elected* 19 December 1993, *re-elected* 14 December 1998

COUNCIL OF MINISTERS *as at July 2002*

Prime Minister, Lamine Sidimé
Agriculture and Animal Husbandry, Jean-Paul Sarr
Commerce, Industry and Small and Medium-sized Enterprises, Mariama Dewo Baldé
Communication, Mamady Condé
Defence, Minister at the Presidency, Col. Cande Toure
Economic Affairs, Finance, Sheik Amadou Kamara
Employment and Civil Service, Lamine Camara
Fishing and Aquaculture, Mansa Moussa Sidibé
Foreign Affairs, Minister at the Presidency, François Lonseny Fall
Higher Education and Scientific Research, Eugène Camara
Justice, Keeper of the Seals, Abou Camara
Mines, Geology and Environment, Ibrahima Souma
Pre-University Teaching and Civil Education, Germain Doualamou
Public Health, Mamadou Saliou Diallo
Public Works, Transport, Cellou Dalen Diallo
Secretary-General to the Government, Ousmane Sanoko
Secretary-General to the President, El Hadj Fodé Bangoura
Social Affairs, Promotion of Women and Children, Mariama Aribot
Technical Education and Professional Training, Almamya Fodé Sylla
Territorial Administration and Decentralisation, Moussa Solana
Tourism, Hotels and Handicrafts, Sylla Koumba Diakité
Urbanisation and Housing, Blaise Ono Foromo
Water Resources and Energy, Fassou Niankoye
Youth, Sports and Culture, Abdel Kader Sangaré

EMBASSY OF THE REPUBLIC OF GUINEA
51 rue de la Faisanderie, F-75016 Paris, France
Tel: (00 33) (1) 4704 8148
Ambassador Extraordinary and Plenipotentiary, vacant

BRITISH CONSULATE
BP 834 Conakry, Guinea
Tel: (00 224) 461 680/446 982/403 523
British Ambassador, HE David Alan Jones, resident at Freetown, Sierra Leone

ECONOMY

The principal products are bauxite, alumina, palm kernels, millet, cassava, bananas, plantains and rubber. Deposits of iron ore, gold, diamonds and uranium have been discovered. Principal imports are cotton goods, petroleum products, sugar, flour and salt; exports, bauxite, alumina, iron ore, diamonds, coffee, bananas, palm kernels and pineapples.

In 1999 there was a trade surplus of US$94 million and a current account deficit of US$152 million.
GNP – US$3,345 million (2000); US$490 per capita (1999)
GDP – US$3,779 million (1998); US$453 per capita (1999)
ANNUAL AVERAGE GROWTH OF GDP – 5.0 per cent (1998)
TOTAL EXTERNAL DEBT – US$3,518 million (1999)

Trade with UK	2000	2001
Imports from UK	£22,726,000	£21,924,000
Exports to UK	579,000	157,000

GUYANA
The Co-operative Republic of Guyana

AREA – 83,000 sq. miles (214,969 sq. km). Neighbours: Venezuela (west), Brazil (west and south), Suriname (east)

POPULATION – 697,181 (2001 estimate): 51 per cent East Indian (mainly rural), 30 per cent African (mainly urban), Amerindians, Europeans, Chinese and people of mixed descent; 50 per cent Christian, 35 per cent Hindu, less than 10 per cent Muslim. Guyana is the only English-speaking country in South America

CAPITAL – Ψ Georgetown (population, 250,000)

MAJOR TOWNS – Corriverton (24,000); Linden (35,000); Ψ New Amsterdam (25,000)

CURRENCY – Guyana dollar (G$) of 100 cents

NATIONAL ANTHEM – Dear Land Of Guyana

NATIONAL DAYS – 26 May (Independence Day); 23 February (Republic Day)

NATIONAL FLAG – Green with a yellow, white-bordered triangle based on the hoist and surmounted by a red, black-bordered triangle

LIFE EXPECTANCY (years) – male 58.0; female 66.9

POPULATION GROWTH RATE – 0.8 per cent (2001)

POPULATION DENSITY – 4 per sq. km (1999)

URBAN POPULATION – 38.0 per cent (2001)

MILITARY EXPENDITURE – 0.8 per cent of GDP (2000)

MILITARY PERSONNEL – 1,600: Army 1,400, Navy 100, Air Force 100; Paramilitaries 1,500

HISTORY AND POLITICS

Guyana (formerly British Guiana) became independent on 26 May 1966, with a Governor-General appointed by Queen Elizabeth II. It became a republic on 23 February 1970.

In the October 1992 presidential election Dr Cheddi Jagan was elected and his People's Progressive Party (PPP) defeated the People's National Congress (PNC) which had governed since independence. Jagan died in March 1997 and was replaced by former Prime Minister Samuel Hinds. In the December 1997 election, Janet Jagan (who had previously served as prime minister and was the widow of the late president) was elected president and the PPP returned to power. The PNC claimed the result was fixed (in January 2001 a judicial ruling was to declare that the entire election had been null and void). President Janet Jagan resigned on 11 August 1999 on the grounds of ill health and was succeeded by Bharrat Jagdeo, who had previously been the finance minister, but was appointed prime minister just prior to her resignation, the constitution stipulating that if a president left office during his or her term, the prime minister succeeded to the presidency. The general election which was due to be held on 17 January 2001 took place on 19 March 2001; the delay was due to the failure of the National Assembly to pass a bill amending the electoral law. The PPP secured a third consecutive term of office, obtaining 34 seats; the PNC won 27 seats.

POLITICAL SYSTEM

The 1980 constitution provides for an executive president who serves a five-year term, and a National Assembly of 65 members, of which 53 are elected nationally by proportional representation and 12 are regional representatives.

HEAD OF STATE

President, Bharrat Jagdeo, *succeeded* 11 August 1999, *elected* 19 March 2001

First Vice-President, vacant
Second Vice-Masters, Parliamentary Affairs, Reepu Daman Persaud

CABINET *as at July 2002*

Prime Minister, Public Works, Sam Hinds
Agriculture, Navin Chandarpal
Amerindian Affairs, Carolyn Rodrigues
Attorney-General, Legal Affairs, Doodnauth Singh
Culture, Youth and Sports, Gail Teixeira
Economic Planning, vacant
Education, Henry Jeffrey
Finance, Saisnarine Kowlessar
Fisheries, Forestry and Livestock, Satyadeow Sawh
Foreign Affairs, Samuel Rudy Insanally
Foreign Trade and International Co-operation, Clement Rohee
Health, Leslie Ramsammy
Home Affairs, Ronald Gajraj
Housing and Water, Shaik Baksh
Human Services, Social Security and Labour, Dale Bisnauth
Local Government, Harripersaud Nokta
Minister in the Ministry of Human Services, Social Security and Labour, Bibi Shadick
Minister in the Ministry of Local Government, Clinton Collymore
Minister in the Office of President (Public Service Management), George Fung-on
Public Service Management, Jennifer Westford
Tourism, Industry and Trade, Manzoor Nadir
Transport and Hydraulics, Carl Anthony Xavier

HIGH COMMISSION GUYANA
3 Palace Court, Bayswater Road, London W2 4LP
Tel: 020-7229 7684
Email: ghc.1@ic24.net
High Commissioner, HE Laleshwar Singh, apptd 1993

BRITISH HIGH COMMISSION
44 Main Street (PO Box 10849), Georgetown
Tel: (00 592) (2) 65881/2/3/4
High Commissioner, HE Edward Glover, MVO, apptd 1998

ECONOMY

Agriculture is the principal economic activity, accounting for 39 per cent of GDP and employing 19 per cent of the workforce. Main export items include Demerara sugar, gold, rice and bauxite. Diamonds are also mined. There is some cattle ranching in the savanna country, and oil deposits have been found there. Industry is fairly small-scale. Much emphasis is now being placed on eco-tourism. Foreign aid covers much of the government deficit.

In 1997 exports totalled US$644 million and imports US$630 million.

GNP – US$667 million (2000); US$760 per capita (1999)

GDP – US$719 million (1998); US$854 per capita (1999)

ANNUAL AVERAGE GROWTH OF GDP – -3.0 per cent (1998)

INFLATION RATE – 6.1 per cent (2000)

TOTAL EXTERNAL DEBT – US$1,527 million (1999)

Trade with UK	2000	2001
Imports from UK	£19,698,000	£22,728,000
Exports to UK	64,754,000	60,600,000

COMMUNICATIONS

Georgetown and New Amsterdam are the principal ports, though bauxite ships also sail to Linden, on the Demerara, and Everton, on the Berbice. The few roads are confined mainly to the coastal areas. Paved roads total about 571 km out of a total network of 7,820 km. Air transport is the easiest form of communication between the coast and the interior. The national airline, Guyana Airways 2000, has been privatised.

There is a state-owned radio broadcasting station which operates two channels and a fledgling television service.

EDUCATION

Education is compulsory between the ages of six and 14; nursery, primary and secondary schooling are free. The government assumed total control of the education system in 1976 and made education free, but instituted fees for study at the University of Guyana in 1994.

There are several technical and vocational institutions, as well as some 30 adult education schools. There are also a number of technical and vocational institutions not under the aegis of the Ministry of Education.

ILLITERACY RATE – 1.3 per cent (2002)

ENROLMENT (percentage of age group) – primary 87 per cent (1995); secondary 66 per cent (1995); tertiary 11 per cent (1996)

HAÏTI
République d'Haïti – Republic of Haïti

AREA – 10,714 sq. miles (27,750 sq. km). Neighbour: Dominican Republic (east)

POPULATION – 6,964,549 (2001 estimate) of which 90 per cent are black and 10 per cent mulatto (mixed race). Both French and Creole are regarded as official languages. French is the language of government and the press but it is only spoken by the educated mulatto minority. The usual language is Creole

CAPITAL – Ψ Port-au-Prince (population, 884,472, 1996 estimate)

MAJOR CITIES – Ψ Cap Haïtien (102,233); Carrefour (290,204); Delmas (240,429); 1996 UN estimates

CURRENCY – Gourde of 100 centimes

NATIONAL ANTHEM – La Dessalinienne

NATIONAL DAY – 1 January

NATIONAL FLAG – Horizontally blue over red

LIFE EXPECTANCY (years) – male 50.2; female 56.5

POPULATION GROWTH RATE – 2.1 per cent (1999)

POPULATION DENSITY – 281 per sq. km (1999)

URBAN POPULATION – 35.7 per cent (2000)

MILITARY EXPENDITURE – 1.5 per cent of GDP (2000)

ILLITERACY RATE – 48.1 per cent (2002)

ENROLMENT (percentage of age group) – primary 22 per cent (1990)

The Republic of Haïti occupies the western third of the Caribbean island of Hispaniola. The climate is tropical with high humidity and an almost constant temperature.

HISTORY AND POLITICS

Haïti was a French slave colony under the name of Saint-Domingue from 1697 until 1791, when French rule was overthrown in a revolt led by Toussaint L'Ouverture. French rule was restored by Napoleon in 1802 but in 1803 French forces surrendered to a British naval blockade and on 1 January 1804 the colony was declared independent as Haïti by Jean Jacques Dessalines. Dessalines became Emperor of Haïti but was assassinated in 1806.

Haïti was under US military occupation from 1915 to 1934. Dr François 'Papa Doc' Duvalier was elected in 1957 and became life president in 1964. He was succeeded in 1971 by his son Jean-Claude 'Baby Doc' Duvalier who fled to France in 1986 in the face of sustained popular unrest. Five years of military government followed until Father Jean-Bertrand Aristide, leader of the National Front for Change and Democracy, won a free presidential election in 1990.

Aristide fled to the USA following a military coup in September 1991. The international community imposed sanctions and in September 1994, an agreement was reached on President Aristide's return and the flight of the military junta members abroad. Aristide returned on 15 October 1994 to appoint a new government.

The presidential election in December 1995 was won by Lavalas Family (FL) candidate René Préval. Following the resignation of Prime Minister Rosny Smarth in October 1997, the President and the legislature were unable to agree on a successor and Haïti had no prime minister until 12 January 1999, when the appointment of Jacques Édouard Alexis was confirmed by a presidential decree, after the Senate but not the Chamber of Deputies had approved the appointment. Elections to the 27-member Senate and 83-member Chamber of Deputies held between 21 May and 30 July 2000 were won by the pro-Aristide FL, winning 18 and 72 seats respectively; there was much international criticism of the manner in which the elections had been conducted.

The presidential election on 26 November 2000 was won by Jean-Bertrand Aristide, who obtained 92 per cent of the vote; the main opposition parties had refused to contest the election, citing irregularities in the earlier legislative election; in response, Aristide promised to hold a fresh legislative election in November 2002.

POLITICAL SYSTEM

The head of state is a president, directly elected for a five-year term that may not be renewed immediately. The National Assembly is the bicameral legislature; the lower house, the Chamber of Deputies, has 83 members directly elected for four years. The upper house or Senate has 27 members elected for six years; one third of the senators are elected every two years. The president appoints the prime minister, who must be approved by the National Assembly. The prime minister chooses the Cabinet.

HEAD OF STATE
President, Jean-Bertrand Aristide, *elected* 26 November 2000, *sworn in* 7 February 2001

CABINET *as at July 2002*

Prime Minister, Interior, Territorial Communities, Yvon Neptune
Agriculture, Natural Resources and Rural Development, Sébastien Hilaire
Commerce and Industry, Leslie Gouthier
Culture and Communication, Lilas Desquiron
Economy and Finance, Faubert Gustave
Environment, Webster Pierre
Foreign Affairs, Religious Affairs, Joseph Philippe Antonio
Haïtians Living Abroad, Leslie Voltaire
Interior, Jocelerme Privert
Justice and Public Security, Jean-Baptiste Boisrond
Labour and Social Affairs, Eudes Saint-Preux
National Education, Youth and Sport, Myrtho Celestin Saurel
Planning and External Co-operation, Pierre Duret
Public Health and Population, Henri-Claude Voltaire

Public Works, Transport and Communications, Harry Clinton
Tourism, Martine Deverson
Women's Affairs, Ginette Lubin

BRITISH AMBASSADOR, HE David Ward, resident at Santo Domingo, Dominican Republic

BRITISH CONSULATE, Hotel Montana (PO Box 1302), Port-au-Prince
Tel: (00 509) 257 3969

ECONOMY

Light industrial products account for over 80 per cent of total exports. Coffee is the second largest export earner. Corn, sorghum and rice are also grown. Increased production of tropical fruits and vegetables is being encouraged. Leather goods, textiles, electronic components and sports equipment are manufactured, using imported raw materials, for re-export. Principal imports are foodstuffs, machinery and transport equipment and fuels. In 1998 Haïti had a trade deficit of US$341 million and a current account deficit of US$38 million. In 2000 imports totalled US$1,036 million and exports US$164 million.

GNP – US$4,034 million (2000); US$460 per capita (1999)
GDP – US$3,522 million (1998); US$496 per capita (1999)
ANNUAL AVERAGE GROWTH OF GDP – 1.1 per cent (2000)
INFLATION RATE – 13.7 per cent (2000)
TOTAL EXTERNAL DEBT – US$1,191 million (1999)

Trade with UK	2000	2001
Imports from UK	£6,982,000	£10,509,000
Exports to UK	840,000	391,000

COMMUNICATIONS

There are more than 4,000 km of roads. Air services are maintained between the capital and the principal provincial towns and to the USA and Caribbean and South American countries. The principal towns and villages are connected by telephone and/or telegraph. There are several commercial radio stations and two television stations at Port-au-Prince.

HONDURAS
República de Honduras – Republic of Honduras

AREA – 43,277 sq. miles (112,088 sq. km). Neighbours: Guatemala (north-west), El Salvador (south-west), Nicaragua (south)
POPULATION – 6,406,052 (2001 estimate) of mixed Spanish and Indian blood. The Garifunas in the north are of West Indian origin. The language is Spanish, although English is spoken on the Bay Islands
CAPITAL – Tegucigalpa (population, 670,100, 1991 estimate)
MAJOR CITIES – Choluteca (63,200); Ψ La Ceiba (77,100); Ψ Puerto Cortés (32,500); San Pedro Sula (325,900); Ψ Tela (24,000)
CURRENCY – Lempira of 100 centavos
NATIONAL ANTHEM – Tu Bandera Es Un Lampo De Cielo (Your Flag Is A Heavenly Light)
NATIONAL DAY – 15 September
NATIONAL FLAG – Three horizontal bands, blue, white, blue (with five blue stars on white band)
LIFE EXPECTANCY (years) – male 63.2; female 69.1
POPULATION GROWTH RATE – 3.3 per cent (1999)

POPULATION DENSITY – 57 per sq. km (1999)
URBAN POPULATION – 49.1 per cent (1997)
MILITARY EXPENDITURE – 1.6 per cent of GDP (2000)
MILITARY PERSONNEL – 8,300: Army 5,500, Navy 1,000, Air Force 1,800; Paramilitaries 6,000
The country is mountainous, being traversed by the Cordilleras, with peaks rising to 1,500 and 2,400 metres above sea level.

HISTORY AND POLITICS

Discovered and settled by the Spanish in the 16th century, Honduras formed part of the Spanish American dominions until 1821 when independence was proclaimed. Under military government from 1972, Honduras returned to civilian rule in 1981 with an executive presidency, a 128-seat unicameral Congress, and a multi-party system. In October 1997, Congress approved a constitutional amendment reducing the legislature to 80 members. The amendment must also be ratified by the current session of Congress before it becomes law. Legislative elections held on 25 November 2001 were won by the National Party (PN) who gained 61 seats, with the Liberal Party (PLH) gaining 55 seats. The presidential election held on the same day was won by Ricardo Maduro of the PN.
The country is divided into 18 departments.

HEAD OF STATE

President of the Republic, C-in-C of the Armed Forces, Ricardo Maduro, *elected* 25 November 2001, *took office* 27 January 2002
Vice-Presidents,Vicente Williams; Armida De Lopez; Alberto Diaz

CABINET *as at July 2002*

Agriculture and Livestock, Mariano Jiménez
Culture, Arts and Sports, Mireya Batres
Defence, Federico Breve
Education, Carlos Avila
Finance, Arturo Alvarado
Foreign Relations, Guillermo Pérez
Industry and Commerce, Juliette Handal
Interior and Justice, Jorge Ramón Hernández Alcerro
Labour, Germán Leitzelar
Ministers Without Portfolio, Carlos Vargas (*Health*); Johnny Kafati (*Housing*); Camilo Atala (*Investment Promotion*); Eduardo Kafati (*Public Service*); Ramón Median (*Strategic Affairs*)
Natural Resources and Environment, Patricia Panting
Presidency, Luis Cosenza
Public Employees' Retirement and Pension, Antonio Rivera Callejas
Public Health, Elias Lizardo
Public Works, Transport and Housing, Jorge Carranza
Security, Juan Angel Arias
Tourism, Thierry De Pierrefeu

EMBASSY OF HONDURAS
115 Gloucester Place, London W1H 3PJ
Tel: 020-7486 4880
Ambassador Extraordinary and Plenipotentiary, HE Hernán Antonio Bermúdez-Aguilar, apptd 1999

BRITISH EMBASSY
Edifico Financiero Banexpo, 3er Piso, Boulevard San Juan Bosco, Colonia Payaqui, Apartado Postal 290, Tegucigalpa
Tel: (00 504) 232 0612
Ambassador Extraordinary and Plenipotentiary, HE Kay Coombs, apptd 2002
BRITISH CONSULATE – San Pedro Sula

ECONOMY

Three-quarters of the country is covered by pine forests. Agriculture and cattle raising is mainly confined to the fertile coastal plain on the Caribbean and the extensive valleys in the Comayagua and Olancho regions of the interior. The Mosquitia tropical forest covers the area from the coast to the border with Nicaragua and provides valuable reserves of timber. Lead, zinc and silver are mined on a small scale.

The chief exports are coffee, bananas, frozen meat, shrimps, lobsters and timber, the most important woods being pine, mahogany and cedar. The main imports are machinery and electrical equipment, industrial chemicals and lubricants.

In October 1998 Hurricane Mitch devastated Honduras, killing an estimated 6,500 people and wrecking Tegucigalpa. The cost of repairing the damage was estimated at US$4 billion.

In July 2000, the IMF and the World Bank granted Honduras a debt reduction package worth about US$556 million.

In 1998 Honduras had a trade deficit of US$323 million and a current account deficit of US$333 million. In 2000 imports totalled US$2,885 million and exports US$1,322 million.

GNP – US$5,517 million (2000); US$760 per capita (1999)

GDP – US$5,348 million (1998); US$856 per capita (1999)

ANNUAL AVERAGE GROWTH OF GDP – 4.8 per cent (2000)

INFLATION RATE – 11.1 per cent (2000)

UNEMPLOYMENT – 3.7 per cent (1999)

TOTAL EXTERNAL DEBT – US$5,333 million (1999)

Trade with UK	2000	2001
Imports from UK	£11,008,000	£11,415,000
Exports to UK	28,104,000	31,425,000

COMMUNICATIONS

There are about 595 km of railway in operation, chiefly to serve the banana plantations and the Caribbean ports. There are 15,100 km of roads, of which 3,050 km are paved. There are over 80 smaller airstrips and four international airports, Tegucigalpa, San Pedro Sula, La Ceiba and Roatún (Bay Island).

The chief ports are Puerto Cortés, Tela and Puerto Castilla on the north coast, through which passes the bulk of the trade with the USA and Europe. Puerto Castilla is being developed as a deep-water container port, and San Lorenzo is also experiencing rapid growth.

EDUCATION

Primary and secondary education is free, primary education being compulsory from the age of seven to 12, and the government has launched a campaign to eradicate illiteracy.

ILLITERACY RATE – 24.3 per cent (2002)

ENROLMENT (percentage of age group) – primary 100 per cent (1997); secondary 21 per cent (1991); tertiary 10.0 per cent (1997)

HUNGARY

Magyar Köztársaság – Republic of Hungary

AREA – 35,920 sq. miles (93,032 sq. km). Neighbours: Slovakia (north), Ukraine and Romania (east), the rump Yugoslav Federal state and Croatia (south), Slovenia and Austria (west)

POPULATION – 10,106,017 (2001 estimate). There are minorities of Romanies (4 per cent), ethnic Germans (3 per cent), Serbs (2 per cent), Romanians (1 per cent) and Slovaks (1 per cent). About two-thirds of the population are Roman Catholic and the remainder mostly Calvinist. The language is Hungarian (Magyar)

CAPITAL – Budapest, (population, 1,896,507, 1997 estimate)

MAJOR CITIES – Debrecen (207,666); Miskolc (176,845); Pécs (160,325); Szeged (160,579), 1997 UN estimates

CURRENCY – Forint of 100 fillér

NATIONAL ANTHEM – Isten Aldd Meg A Magyart (God Bless The Hungarians)

NATIONAL DAYS – 15 March, 20 August, 23 October

NATIONAL FLAG – Red, white, green (horizontally)

LIFE EXPECTANCY (years) – male 67.8; female 76.1

POPULATION GROWTH RATE – 0.4 per cent (1999)

POPULATION DENSITY – 108 per sq. km (1999)

URBAN POPULATION – 63.2 per cent (1996)

HISTORY AND POLITICS

The Hungarians settled the Danube basin in 896 AD and in 1000, King Istvan (Stephen) adopted Roman Catholicism and received a crown from the Pope. The Turks invaded Hungary in 1526; the Austrians finally succeeded in expelling them in 1699. Following nationalist unrest, the *Ausgleich* (compromise) of 1867 created the Dual Monarchy of Austria-Hungary, giving Hungary internal autonomy. The defeat of Austria-Hungary in the First World War led to the declaration of Hungarian independence in November 1918.

Hungary joined the Anti-Comintern Pact in February 1939 and entered the Second World War on the side of Germany in 1941. On 20 January 1945 a Hungarian provisional government of liberation signed an armistice under the terms of which the frontiers of Hungary were withdrawn to the 1937 limits.

After the liberation, a coalition of parties carried out land reform and nationalisation. By 1949 the Communists had succeeded in gaining a monopoly of power and by 1952 practically the entire economy had been 'socialised'.

Divisions within the Communist Party and popular demand for free elections and Soviet troop withdrawals grew. An uprising on 23 October 1956 was quelled by Soviet forces the following morning. But a reformist all-party coalition government under Imre Nagy was formed which declared Hungary's withdrawal from the Warsaw pact. This government was suppressed by a renewed attack by Soviet forces on Budapest on 4 November and a new Communist government under János Kádár was announced the same day.

From 1968 the government gradually introduced economic reforms and some political liberalisation. Kádár was forced to resign in May 1989. In October 1989 the National Assembly (*Országgyülés*) approved an amended constitution which described Hungary as an independent, democratic state. The 386-seat National Assembly is elected on a mixed first past the post and proportional representation basis with a 5 per cent threshold for representation. The first free multiparty elections took place in March and April 1990 and were won by the (conservative) Hungarian Democratic Forum. On 6 June 2000, Ferenc Mádl, an independent candidate was elected as president.

In the legislative elections in April 2002, no party won an overall majority. The Federation of Young Democrats-Hungarian Civic Party (Fidesz-MPP) won the largest

number of seats but Péter Medgyessy of the Hungarian Socialist Party (MszP), formed a coalition government with the Alliance of Free Democrats (SzDSz). The composition of the National Assembly in May 2002 was: Fidesz-MPP 188, MSzP 178, SzDSz 20.

HEAD OF STATE

President, Ferenc Mádl, *elected* 6 June 2000, *sworn in* 4 August 2000

CABINET *as at July 2002*

Prime Minister, Péter Medgyessy (MszP)
Prime Minister's Office, in charge of Regional Development, Religious Affairs, Ethnic Hungarians Abroad and Tourism, Elemér Kiss (MszP)
Agriculture and Rural Development, Imre Németh (MszP)
Defence, Ferenc Juhász (MszP)
Economy and Transport, István Csillag (SzDSz)
Education, Bálint Magyar (SzDSz)
Environment and Water Management, Mária Koródi (SzDSz)
Finance, Csaba László (MszP)
Foreign Affairs, László Kovács (MszP)
Health, Social and Family Affairs, Judit Csehák (MszP)
Information Science and Telecommunications, Kálmán Kovács (SzDSz)
Interior, Mónika Lamperth (MszP)
Justice, Péter Bárándy (MszP)
Labour and Employment, Péter Kiss (MszP)
National Cultural Heritage, Gábor Görgey (MszP)
Youth and Sports, György Jánosi (MszP)

MszP Hungarian Socialist Party; SzDSz Alliance of Free Democrats

EMBASSY OF THE REPUBLIC OF HUNGARY
35 Eaton Place, London SW1X 8BY
Tel: 020-7235 5218
Ambassador Extraordinary and Plenipotentiary, HE Gábor Szentiványi, GCVO, apptd 1997
Counsellor, Deputy Head of Mission, Zsolt Pataki
Counsellor and Consul-General, Dr László Takács
Commercial Counsellor, András Hirschler

BRITISH EMBASSY
Harmincad Utca 6, H-1051 Budapest
Tel: (00 36) (1) 266 2888
Email: info@britemb.hu
Ambassador Extraordinary and Plenipotentiary, HE Nigel Thorpe, CVO, RCDS, apptd 1998
Counsellor and Deputy Head of Mission, G. B. Reid
Defence Attaché, Col. Jonathan B Frere, MBE

BRITISH COUNCIL DIRECTOR, Dr John Richards, OBE, Benczúr Utca 26, H-1068 Budapest;
Email: information@britishcouncil.hu. Offices at Debrecen, Miskolc, Pécs, Szombathely and Veszprém

DEFENCE

The Army has 753 main battle tanks, 680 armoured infantry fighting vehicles and 799 armoured personnel carriers. The Air Force has 46 combat aircraft and 51 attack helicopters. Hungary became a member of NATO in March 1999.
MILITARY EXPENDITURE – 1.7 per cent of GDP (2000)
MILITARY PERSONNEL – Army 13,160, Army Maritime Wing 270, Air Force 7,500; Paramilitaries 14,000
CONSCRIPTION DURATION – Nine months

ECONOMY

Agriculture accounts for around 6 per cent of GDP and employs 7.5 per cent of the workforce. Production is concentrated on maize, wheat, sugar beet, barley, rye and oats.

Industry is mainly based on imported raw materials but Hungary has its own coal, bauxite, considerable deposits of natural gas, some iron ore and oil. Output figures in 1998 were: coal 14,494,299 tonnes; aluminium 33,700 tonnes; crude steel 1,939,784 tonnes; crude petroleum 1,257,830 tonnes. Natural gas production totalled 4,345 million cubic metres.

The economy suffered from the loss of export markets in the Soviet Union and the former Yugoslavia, and the transition to a market economy, but now exports the majority of its goods to the countries of the EU. The country has benefited from a strong inflow of foreign direct investment.

The main exports are machinery and equipment, manufactures, foodstuffs, beverages and tobacco products, raw materials and energy transmission equipment.

In 2000 Hungary had a trade deficit of US$2,106 million and a current account deficit of US$1,494 million. Imports totalled US$31,955 million and exports US$28,007 million.
GNP – US$47,462 million (2000); US$4,640 per capita (1999)
GDP – US$46,977 million (1998); US$4,813 per capita (1999)
ANNUAL AVERAGE GROWTH OF GDP – 4.4 per cent (1999)
INFLATION RATE – 9.8 per cent (2000)
UNEMPLOYMENT – 6.3 per cent (2000)
TOTAL EXTERNAL DEBT – US$29,042 million (1999)

Trade with UK	2000	2001
Imports from UK	£610,093,000	£614,505,000
Exports to UK	703,309,000	724,445,000

EDUCATION

There are five types of schools under the Ministry of Education: kindergartens for age three to six, general schools for age six to 14 (compulsory), vocational schools (15–18), secondary schools (15–18), universities and adult training schools (over 18).
ILLITERACY RATE – 0.6 per cent (2002)
ENROLMENT (percentage of age group) – primary 100 per cent (1997); secondary 98 per cent (1997); tertiary 24 per cent (1997)

CULTURE

Magyar, or Hungarian, is one of the Finno-Ugrian languages. Hungarian literature began to flourish in the second half of the 16th century. Among the greatest writers of the 19th and 20th centuries are Mihály Vörösmarty (1800–55), Sándor Petöfi (1823–49), János Arany (1817–82), Imre Madách (1823–64), Kálmán Mikszáth (1847–1910), Endre Ady (1877–1918), Attila József (1905–37), Mihály Babits (1883–1941), Dezsö Kosztolányi (1885–1936), Gyula Illyes (1902–83), János Pilinszky (1921–81) and Sándor Weöres (1913–89). Among Hungary's most celebrated musicians are composers Franz Liszt, Bela Bartok, Zoltan Kodaly, Georgy Ligeti and the conductor Sir Georg Solti.

ICELAND
Lýðveldið Ísland – Republic of Iceland

AREA – 39,769 sq. miles (103,000 sq. km)
POPULATION – 277,906 (2001 estimate). Some 87.8 per cent of the population are members of the (Lutheran) Church of Iceland. The language is Icelandic
CAPITAL – Ψ Reykjavík (population, 111,345, 2000)
MAJOR CITIES – Akranes; Ψ Akureyri; Egilsstaðir; Ψ Hafnarfjörður; Ψ Ísafjörður; Kópavogur; Reykjanesbær; Ψ Siglufjörður
CURRENCY – Icelandic króna (Kr) of 100 aurar
NATIONAL ANTHEM – Lofsöngur (Song Of Praise)
NATIONAL DAY – 17 June
NATIONAL FLAG – Blue, with white-bordered red cross
LIFE EXPECTANCY (years) – male 77.6; female 81.4
POPULATION GROWTH RATE – 0.5 per cent (2001)
POPULATION DENSITY – 3 per sq. km (1999)
URBAN POPULATION – 92.5 per cent (2000)
MILITARY PERSONNEL – Paramilitaries: 120

HISTORY AND POLITICS
Iceland was uninhabited before the ninth century, when settlers came from Norway. For several centuries a form of republican government prevailed, with an annual assembly of leading men called the *Alþingi (Althingi)*, but in 1262 Iceland became subject to Norway, and later to Denmark. During the colonial period, Iceland maintained its cultural integrity but a deterioration in the climate, together with frequent volcanic eruptions and outbreaks of disease, led to a serious drop in living standards and to a decline in the population to little more than 40,000. In the 19th century a struggle for independence led to home rule in 1918 and to independence as a republic in 1944.

The parliamentary (*Althingi*) elections on 8 May 1999 gave the Independence Party 26 seats, Unified Left 17, Progressives 12, Left-Green Alliance 6 and Liberals 2. A coalition government of the Independence Party and the Progressive Party was formed after the election. On 1 August 2000, President Ólafur Ragnar Grímsson, first elected in June 1996, was re-installed as president for a second term without an election as no other candidate was nominated.

HEAD OF STATE
President, Ólafur Ragnar Grímsson, *elected* 29 June 1996, *re-installed* 1 August 2000

CABINET *as at July 2002*

Prime Minister, Statistical Bureau of Iceland, Davið Oddsson (IP)
Agriculture, Gudni Ágústsson (PP)
Education, Culture and Science, Tomas Ingi Olrich (IP)
Environment, Siv Fridleifsdóttir (PP)
Finance, Geir Haarde (IP)
Fisheries, Árni Mathiesen (IP)
Foreign Affairs, Halldór Ásgrímsson (PP)
Health and Social Security, Jón Kristjánsson (PP)
Justice and Ecclesiastical Affairs, Sólveig Pétursdóttir (IP)
Social Affairs, Páll Pétursson (PP)
Trade and Industry, Valgerdur Sverrisdóttir (PP)
Transport, Sturla Bödvarsson (IP)

IP Independence Party; PP Progressive Party

EMBASSY OF ICELAND
2A Hans Street, London SW1X 0JE
Tel: 020-7259 3999
Ambassador Extraordinary and Plenipotentiary, HE Thorsteinn Pálsson, apptd 1999

BRITISH EMBASSY
Laufásvegur 31, IS-101 Reykjavík
Tel: (00 354) 550 5100/1/2
Email: britemb@centrum.is
Ambassador Extraordinary and Plenipotentiary and Consul-General, HE J. Culver, apptd 2000

ECONOMY
Iceland has considerable resources of hydroelectric and geothermal energy. Heavy industry includes an aluminium smelter, a nitrogen fertiliser factory, a cement factory, a diatomite plant and a ferro-silicon plant.

The major sectors of the economy are fishing and fish processing, manufacturing, agriculture, energy production and tourism, which is of growing importance with 302,913 visitors in 2000.

As a member of the European Free Trade Association (EFTA), Iceland has become a member of the European Economic Area (EEA) which extends most of the provisions of the EU's single market to EFTA states.

In 2000 Iceland had a trade deficit of US$476 million and a current account deficit of US$851 million. Imports totalled US$2,591 million and exports US$2,005 million.
GNP – US$8,736 million (2000); US$29,540 per capita (1999)
GDP – US$8,266 million (1998); US$30,597 per capita (2000)
ANNUAL AVERAGE GROWTH OF GDP – 3.6 per cent (2000)
INFLATION RATE – 5.2 per cent (2000)
UNEMPLOYMENT – 1.4 per cent (2001)

TRADE
The principal exports are fish and fish products, which account for nearly three-quarters of exports, ferro-silicon and aluminium; the chief imports are consumer durables, petroleum products, transport equipment, textiles, foodstuffs, animal feeds and timber.

Trade with UK	2000	2001
Imports from UK	£198,448,000	£157,763,000
Exports to UK	337,701,000	299,302,000

COMMUNICATIONS
At 1 January 2000, the mercantile marine consisted of 1,067 registered vessels (222,827 gross tons). There are regular shipping services between Reykjavík and Felixstowe, the Humber ports, Europe and the USA.

A regular air service is maintained by Icelandair between Glasgow and London and Reykjavík. There are also air services to Scandinavia, the USA, Germany, France, the Netherlands and Canada.

Road communications are adequate in summer but greatly restricted by snow in winter. Only roads in town centres and key highways are metalled, the rest being of gravel, mud and lava dust. The climate and terrain make first-class surfaces for highways out of the question. There are no railways.

CULTURE
The ancient Norræna (or Northern tongue) has close affinities to Anglo-Saxon and as spoken and written in Iceland today differs little from that introduced into the island in the ninth century. There is a rich literature with two distinct periods of development, from the mid-11th to the late 13th century and from the early 19th century to the present.
ENROLMENT (percentage of age group) – primary 98 per cent (1996); secondary 87 per cent (1995); tertiary 37 per cent (1996)

INDIA
The Republic of India/Bhāratīya Ganarājya

AREA – 1,269,213 sq. miles (3,287,263 sq. km).
Neighbours: Pakistan (north-west), China, Tibet, Nepal and Bhutan (north), Myanmar (east), Bangladesh
POPULATION – 1,027,015,247 (2001 census): Hindu (82.41 per cent), the rest being Muslim (11.67 per cent), Christian (2.32 per cent), Sikh (1.99 per cent), Buddhist (0.77 per cent) and Jain (0.41 per cent). The official languages are Hindi in the Devanagari script and English, though 17 regional languages also are recognised for adoption as official state languages
CAPITAL – New Delhi (population, 301,297; 8,419,084 including Delhi/Dilli), 1991
MAJOR CITIES – Ahmedabad (3,312,216); Bangalore (4,130,288); Ψ Bombay/Mumbai (12,596,243); Ψ Calcutta/Kolkata (11,021,918); Hyderabad (4,344,437); Kanpur (2,029,889); Lucknow (1,669,204); Ψ Madras/Chennai (5,421,985); Pune (2,493,987) (1991 figures)
CURRENCY – Indian rupee (Rs) of 100 paise
NATIONAL ANTHEM – Jana-Gana-Mana (Thou Art The Ruler Of The Minds Of All People)
NATIONAL DAY – 26 January (Republic Day)
NATIONAL FLAG – A horizontal tricolour with bands of deep saffron, white and dark green in equal proportions. In the centre of the white band appears an Asoka wheel in navy blue
LIFE EXPECTANCY (years) – male 63.6; female 64.9
POPULATION GROWTH RATE – 1.7 per cent (1999)
POPULATION DENSITY – 324 per sq. km (2001)
URBAN POPULATION – 28.4 per cent (2000)
ILLITERACY RATE – 41.2 per cent (2002)
ENROLMENT (percentage of age group) – tertiary 7 per cent (1997)

India has three well-defined regions: the mountain range of the Himalayas, the Indo–Gangetic plain, and the southern peninsula. The main mountain ranges are the Himalayas (over 29,000 feet) and the Western and Eastern Ghats (over 8,000 feet). Major rivers include the Ganges, Indus, Krishna, Godavari and Mahanadi.
Temperatures vary over the country between averages of about 10°C and 33°C, reaching over 38°C in some parts during the hot season. There are similar variations in rainfall, from only a few inches a year falling in the western Thar Desert to over 400 inches in Meghalaya.

HISTORY AND POLITICS
The Indus civilisation was fully developed by *c.*2500 BC but collapsed *c.*1750 BC, and was replaced by an Aryan civilisation from the west. Arab invasions of the north-west began in the seventh century and Muslim, Hindu and Buddhist states developed until the establishment of the Mughal dynasty in 1526. The British East India Company established settlements throughout the 17th century; clashes with the French and native princes led to the British government taking control of the company in 1784 and gradually extending sovereignty over the whole subcontinent. The separate dominions of India and Pakistan became independent within the Commonwealth on 15 August 1947 and India became a republic in 1950.
Between 1947 and 1996, India was ruled by Congress (I) Party for all but four years (March 1977–January 1980, November 1989–June 1991). Congress (I) has been led by members of the Nehru-Gandhi dynasty for most of the post-independence

period: Prime Ministers Jawaharlal Nehru (1947–64), Indira Gandhi (1966–1977, 1980–84) and Rajiv Gandhi (1984–89). Indira Gandhi was assassinated by Sikh extremists seeking an independent Sikh state in Punjab; her son Rajiv was assassinated by Sri Lankan Tamils.
In November 1997, the United Front government (a coalition of Communist and low-caste parties) collapsed after Congress (I) withdrew its support. The parliamentary elections in February 1998 produced no outright winner; in March 1998, the BJP formed a coalition government under Atal Bihari Vajpayee, which collapsed following the loss of a confidence motion on 17 April 1999. The opposition parties were unable to form a majority government and parliament was dissolved on 26 April 1999 by President Narayanan. The BJP-led 24-party National Democratic Alliance won elections on 3 October 1999 with a majority of 296 seats. In the presidential election held on 15 July 2002, A. P. J. Abdul Kalam was elected as India's 11th president.

SECESSION
The Hindu Maharaja of Kashmir signed his state's instrument of accession to India in October 1947, two months after India and Pakistan became independent. This was disputed by Pakistan, on the basis that the majority of the state's population was Muslim. After three Indian-Pakistani wars, a line of control was agreed under the 1972 Simla agreement (China has also occupied some of Kashmir since the 1962 Sino-Indian war). Kashmir was placed under direct rule in 1990. The Islamic militant groups Hizbul Mujahidin, Harakat-ul-Mujahidin and Lashkar-e-Tayyeba continued to launch attacks on Hindu civilians, government officials and security forces. The Indian government announced a unilateral cease-fire during the month of Ramadan, which began on 28 November 2000 and the cease-fire was extended until 24 May 2001. In response, Pakistan announced that its forces would show restraint, but attacks by Islamic militants continued unabated and repeated government offers of talks with the militants were rejected.

FOREIGN RELATIONS
In addition to the territory it won as a result of the Sino-Indian war in 1962, China claims Arunachal Pradesh and does not recognise Indian sovereignty over Sikkim.
India and Pakistan have fought three major wars since independence, in 1947–8, 1965 and 1971. Since 1985 they have continued a low-level war at altitude for control of the Siachen glacier in Kashmir.
In May 1998, India confirmed its nuclear status with five underground nuclear tests and within three weeks, Pakistan had followed suit. Both countries' tests sparked international condemnation.
In May 1999 India launched air attacks on Muslim insurgents who had occupied mountainous areas within Indian-controlled Kashmir. Small-scale incidents between the Indian and Pakistani troops stationed along the line of control dividing Kashmir continue to occur on a regular basis. The presidents of India and Pakistan held a summit in Agra in July 2001, but failed to agree a joint declaration. A terrorist attack on the federal parliament in New Delhi on 13 December left 14 people dead. India held the Islamic separatist organisations Jaish-e-Mohammed (JeM) and Lashkar-e-Tayyeba (LeT) responsible. The Kashmir crisis continued into 2002, amid international fear that the situation could escalate into a nuclear exchange between the two countries. In May, the killing of 34 people at an Indian army camp in Kashmir exacerbated the tensions. There was high-level international diplomatic activity and in June, although

the situation was still serious, the threat of war seemed less likely.

POLITICAL SYSTEM

Executive power is vested in the president, elected for a five-year term by an electoral college consisting of the elected members of the Union and State legislatures. The president appoints the prime minister and, on the latter's advice, the ministers, and can dismiss them. The Council of Ministers is collectively responsible to the *Lok Sabha* (lower house). The vice-president is ex-officio chairman of the *Rajya Sabha* (upper house).

Legislative power rests with the president, the Rajya Sabha (245 members serving six-year terms) and the Lok Sabha (545 members). Twelve members of the Rajya Sabha are presidential nominees, the rest are indirectly elected representatives of the State and Union Territories. The 543 members of the Lok Sabha representing the States and Union Territories are directly elected by universal adult franchise, and two representatives of the Anglo-Indian community are chosen, for a maximum term of five years.

FEDERAL STRUCTURE

There are 28 States and seven Union Territories. Each state is headed by a Governor, who is appointed by the president and holds office for five years, and by a Council of Ministers. All states have a Legislative Assembly, and some have also a Legislative Council, elected directly by adult suffrage for a maximum period of five years.

The Union Territories are administered, except where otherwise provided by Parliament, by the president acting through an Administrator or Lieutenant-Governor, or other authority appointed by him.

	Area (sq.km)	Population (2001 census)	Capital
STATES			
Andhra Pradesh	275,069	75,727,541	Hyderabad
Arunachal Pradesh	83,743	1,091,117	Itanagar
Assam	78,438	26,638,407	Dispur
Bihar	94,163	82,878,796	Patna
Chhattisgarh	135,191	20,795,956	Raipur
Goa	3,702	1,343,998	Panaji
Gujarat	196,022	50,596,992	Gandhinagar
Haryana	44,212	21,082,989	Chandigarh
Himachal Pradesh	55,673	6,077,248	Shimla
Jammu and Kashmir	101,387	10,069,917	Srinagar/ Jammu
Jharkhand	79,714	26,909,428	Ranchi
Karnataka	191,791	52,733,958	Bangalore
Kerala	38,863	31,838,619	Trivandrum (Thiruvanan-thapuram)
Madhya Pradesh	308,245	60,385,118	Bhopal Raipur
Maharashtra	307,713	96,752,247	Bombay (Mumbai)
Manipur	22,327	2,388,634	Imphal
Meghalaya	22,429	2,306,069	Shillong
Mizoram	21,081	891,058	Aizawl
Nagaland	16,579	1,988,636	Kohima
Orissa	155,707	36,706,920	Bhubaneswar
Punjab	50,362	24,289,296	Chandigarh
Rajasthan	342,239	56,473,122	Jaipur
Sikkim	7,096	540,493	Gangtok
Tamil Nadu	130,058	62,110,839	Madras (Chennai)
Tripura	10,486	3,191,168	Agartala
Uttar Pradesh	240,928	166,052,859	Lucknow

	Area (sq.km)	Population (1998 estimate)	Capital
Uttaranchal	53,483	8,479,562	Dehra Dun
West Bengal	88,752	80,221,171	Calcutta (Kolkata)
UNION TERRITORIES			
Andaman and Nicobar Is.	8,249	356,265	Port Blair
Chandigarh	114	900,914	
Dadra and Nagar Haveli	491	220,451	Silvassa
Daman and Diu	112	158,059	
Delhi/Dilli	1,483	13,782,976	
Lakshadweep	32	60,595	Kavaratti
Pondicherry	480	973,829	

HEAD OF STATE

President of the Republic of India, A. P. J. Abdul Kalam, elected 15 July 2002, took office 25 July 2002
Vice-President, vacant

CABINET *as at July 2002*

Prime Minister, Atomic Energy, Personnel, Planning, Public Grievances and Pensions, Space, Atal Bihari Vajpayee (BJP)
Deputy Prime Minister, Home Affairs, Coal and Mines, Lal Krishna Advani (BJP)
Agriculture, Ajit Singh (RLD)
Agro and Rural Industries, Kariya Munda (BJP)
Chemicals and Fertilisers, Sukhdev Singh Dhindsa (SAD)
Civil Aviation, Shahnawaz Hussain (BJP)
Commerce and Industry, Murasoli Maran (DMK)
Consumer Affairs and Public Distribution, Sharad Yadav (JD(U))
Culture and Tourism, Jagmohan Malhotra (BJP)
Defence, George Fernandes (SP)
Disinvestment and Development of North Eastern Region, Arun Shourie (BJP)
Environment and Forests, T. R. Baalu (DMK)
Foreign Affairs, Yashwant Sinha (BJP)
Finance and Company Affairs, Jaswant Singh (BJP)
Health and Family Welfare, Shatrughan Sinha (BJP)
Heavy Industries and Public Enterprises, Balasaheb Vikhe Patil (SS)
Human Resource Development, Science and Technology, Ocean Development, Murli Manohar Joshi (BJP)
Information and Broadcasting, Sushma Swaraj (BJP)
Labour, Sahib Singh Verma (BJP)
Law and Justice, Jana Krishnamurthi (BJP)
Parliamentary Affairs, Information Technology, Communications, Pramod Mahajan (BJP)
Petroleum and Natural Gas, Ram Naik (BJP)
Power, Suresh Prabhakar Prabhu (BJP)
Railways, Nitish Kumar (SP)
Rural Development, Shanta Kumar (BJP)
Shipping, Ved Prakash Goyal (BJP)
Social Justice and Empowerment, Satyanarain Jatiya (BJP)
Textiles, Kashiram Rana (BJP)
Tribal Affairs, Jual Oram (BJP)
Urban Development and Poverty Alleviation, Ananth Kumar (BJP)
Water Resources, Arjun Charan Sethi (BJD)
Youth Affairs and Sports, Uma Bharati (BJP)

BJP Bharatiya Janata Party; DMK Dravida Munnetra Kazhagam; JD(U) Janata Dal (United); RLD Rashtriya Lok Dal; SAD Shiromani Akali Dal; SP Samata Party; SS Shiv Sena

INDIAN HIGH COMMISSION
India House, Aldwych, London WC2B 4NA
Tel: 020-7836 8484
High Commissioner, HE Ranendra Sen, apptd 2002
Deputy High Commissioner, S. Pal
Ministers, Shri Debabrata Saha (*Political*); G. Singh
 (*Consular*); G. R. Karnad (*Culture*)
Counsellor (*Economic*), R. Pandey
Military Adviser, Brig. S. Sharma
Consulates-General – Birmingham, Edinburgh

BRITISH HIGH COMMISSION
Chanakyapuri, New Delhi 1100021
Tel: (00 91) (11) 687 2161
High Commissioner, HE Sir Rob Young, KCMG, apptd
 1998
Deputy High Commissioner and Minister, T. T. Macan
Deputy High Commissioners, H. Parkinson, OBE
 (*Bombay/Mumbai*); J. Mitchiner (*Calcutta/Kolkata*);
 M. E. J. Herridge (*Madras/Chennai*)
Defence and Military Adviser, Brig. S. M. A. Lee, OBE
Counsellor (*Economic and Commercial*), G. C. Gillham

BRITISH COUNCIL MINISTER – Edmund Marsden,
 17 Kasturba Gandhi Marg, New Delhi 110 001;
 Email: delhi.enquiry@in.britishcouncil.org. Offices at
 Bombay/Mumbai, Calcutta/Kolkata and
 Madras/Chennai. British Council libraries at these
 four centres and British libraries at Ahmedabad,
 Bangalore, Bhopal, Chandigarh, Hyderabad, Pune
 and Trivandrum/Triruvananthapuram

DEFENCE

The Army has 3,414 main battle tanks, 1,350 armoured
infantry fighting vehicles and 317 armoured personnel
carriers. The Navy has 16 submarines, one aircraft carrier,
eight destroyers, 11 frigates, 39 patrol and coastal vessels,
37 combat aircraft and 72 armed helicopters. It has nine
bases including one under construction. The Air Force
has 774 combat aircraft and 22 armed helicopters.
 India exploded its first nuclear weapon in 1974 and is
since believed to have acquired a stockpile of nuclear
arms. It conducted further nuclear tests in May 1998. In
1993–4 India successfully test-fired its intermediate-
range 'Agni' and 'Prithvi' ballistic missiles, and the latter
went into production in September 1997.
MILITARY EXPENDITURE – 3.1 per cent of GDP (2000)
MILITARY PERSONNEL – 1,263,000: Army 1,100,000,
 Navy 53,000, Air Force 110,000; Paramilitaries
 1,089,700

ECONOMY

Agriculture supports about 64 per cent of the population,
and contributes 26 per cent of GDP. Production has
grown by 2.67 per cent each year since 1951, remaining
slightly ahead of the 2 per cent increase necessary to keep
pace with the rising population. Food crops occupy three-
quarters of the total cultivated area. The main food crops
are rice, cereals (principally wheat) and pulses. The major
cash crops include sugar cane, jute, cotton and tea. Other
products include oil seeds, spices, groundnuts, soya bean,
tobacco, rubber and coffee. Livestock is raised, principally
for dairy purposes or for the hides.
 Industry is based on the exploitation and processing of
mineral resources, principally coal, oil and iron, and on
the production of textiles. The coal industry reached an
output in 1998 of 316,574,000 tonnes; production of
crude petroleum was 32,893,000 tonnes. Steel production
is mainly in the hands of the public sector, with five

public and one private sector integrated steel plants
producing 23,863,000 tonnes of ingot steel in 1998. The
engineering industry, heavy and light, is increasingly
being privatised.
 The manufacture of paper, cement, pharmaceuticals,
chemicals, fertilisers, petrochemicals, motor vehicles and
commercial vehicles has been expanded. Other principal
manufactures are those derived from agricultural products, textiles, jute goods, sugar and leather, which along
with tea, tobacco, rubber, fish and iron ore are major
exports.
 Tourism is a major industry, with 167 million domestic
tourists in 1998 and 2,641,157 overseas visitors in 2000,
employing 15.5 million people between 1999 and 2001.
 The main exports are textiles, gemstones and jewellery,
chemical products, agricultural produce, engineering
products, leather goods, marine products and ores and
minerals.
 GNP has been rising by about 6 per cent per annum,
but growth has been concentrated in the more
prosperous western and southern states, increasing
regional inequalities.
 Orissa was devastated by a cyclone on 29 October 1999,
which left at least 1.5 million people homeless and caused
widespread destruction of crops.
 In 2000 there was a trade deficit of US$12,193 million
and a current account deficit of US$4,198 million.
Imports totalled US$51,633 million and exports
US$42,101 million.
GNP – US$471,156 million (2000); US$440 per capita
 (1999)
GDP – US$414,010 million (1998); US$453 per capita
 (1999)
ANNUAL AVERAGE GROWTH OF GDP – 7.2 per cent
 (1999)
INFLATION RATE – 4.0 per cent (2000)
TOTAL EXTERNAL DEBT – US$94,393 million (1999)

Trade with UK	2000	2001
Imports from UK	£2,055,698,000	£1,782,058,000
Exports to UK	1,712,157,000	1,884,054,000

COMMUNICATIONS

The International Airports Authority manages five
international airports: Indira Gandhi (Delhi/Dilli), Sahar
(Bombay/Mumbai), Dum Dum (Calcutta/Kolkata),
Meenambakkam (Madras/Chennai) and
Triruvananthapuram. The other 88 aerodromes are
controlled and operated by the Civil Aviation
Department of the government. The national airlines are
Indian Airlines (internal) and Air India (international).
 The railways are grouped into nine administrative
zones, Southern, Central, Western, Northern, North-
Eastern, North-East Frontier, Eastern, South-Eastern and
South-Central; there is also the Konkan Railway which
links Bombay/Mumbai and Mangalore. The total track
length is 62,759 km, of which 13,490 km is electrified.
The total length of the road network is about 3,319,644
km of which 1,334,078 km is surfaced. The national
highway system comprises 51,966 km of roads.
 The chief seaports are Bombay/Mumbai, Jawahar Lal
Nehru, Calcutta/Kolkata, Haldia, Madras/Chennai,
Mormugao, Cochin, Visakhapatnam, Kandla, Paradip,
Mangalore, Ennore and Tuticorin. There are 139 minor
working ports with varying capacity.

INDONESIA

Republik Indonesia – Republic of Indonesia

AREA – 735,358 sq. miles (1,904,569 sq. km). Indonesia shares borders with Malaysia (on Borneo) and Papua New Guinea (on New Guinea)

POPULATION – 228,437,870 (2001 estimate): 87 per cent Muslim, with Christian, Buddhist, Hindu and Animist minorities. Bahasa Indonesian, a variant of Malay, is the national language, although more than 250 dialects are spoken

CAPITAL – Ψ Jakarta (population, 9,160,500, 1995 estimate)

MAJOR CITIES – (Java) Bandung (2,356,120), Ψ Semarang (1,104,405), Ψ Surabaya (2,663,820); (Kalimantan) Banjarmasin (482,931), Ψ Pontianak (409,632); (Maluku) Ambon (249,312); (Sulawesi) Ψ Ujung Pandang (1,060,257); (Sumatra) Medan (1,843,919), Palembang (1,222,764), 1995 estimates

CURRENCY – Rupiah (Rp) of 100 sen

NATIONAL ANTHEM – Indonesia Raya (Great Indonesia)

NATIONAL DAY – 17 August (Anniversary of Proclamation of Independence)

NATIONAL FLAG – Equal bands of red over white

LIFE EXPECTANCY (years) – male 65.3; female 69.3

POPULATION GROWTH RATE – 1.6 per cent (1999)

POPULATION DENSITY – 109 per sq. km (1999)

URBAN POPULATION – 37.7 per cent (1997)

ILLITERACY RATE – 12.1 per cent (2002)

ENROLMENT (percentage of age group) – primary 100 per cent (1997); secondary 56 per cent (1997); tertiary 11 per cent (1997)

Indonesia comprises the islands of Java, Madura, Sumatra, the Riouw-Lingga archipelago, Bangka and Billiton, part of the island of Borneo (Kalimantan), Sulawesi (formerly Celebes), Maluku (formerly Moluccas), the islands of Bali, Lombok, Sumbawa, Sumba, Flores and others comprising the provinces of East and West Nusa Tenggara and the western half of the islands of New Guinea (Irian Jaya) and Timor.

HISTORY AND POLITICS

From the early part of the 17th century much of the Indonesian archipelago was under Dutch rule. Following the Second World War, during which the archipelago was occupied by the Japanese, a strong nationalistic movement formed and, after sporadic fighting, all the former Dutch East Indies except western New Guinea became independent as Indonesia on 27 December 1949. Western New Guinea became part of Indonesia in 1963 under the name West Irian (now Irian Jaya), this interpretation being confirmed in an 'Act of Free Choice' in July 1969.

Rampant inflation and high food and fuel prices provoked civil unrest during 1997, and by April 1998 riots and protests calling for Gen. Suharto's resignation as president were frequent. On 21 May 1998, he announced he would step down. He was replaced by his deputy B. J. Habibie.

The Golkar party was defeated in the general election of 7 June 1999, in which the Indonesian Democratic Struggle Party (DSP) led by Megawati Sukarnoputri, daughter of Indonesia's first president, gained 37.4 per cent of the vote and won the greatest number of seats. The new government elected Abdurrahman Wahid, the leader of the National Awakening Party (NAP), as president and Megawati Sukarnoputri was voted vice-

president. A coalition government was formed, consisting of the DSP, NAP, and the National Mandate Party.

President Wahid was formally censured by the House of Representatives on 1 February 2001 and again on 30 April following a report which had implicated him in two financial scandals. Although he was cleared on 28 May of involvement in the scandals, relations between the president and the legislature had become untenable. On 30 May, the House of Representatives voted overwhelmingly to convene a special session of the People's Consultative Assembly to begin impeachment proceedings against President Wahid; the proceedings began on 20 July and resulted in his dismissal from office on 23 July. Megawati Sukarnoputri, who had been the vice-president, was immediately sworn in as his successor.

FEDERAL STRUCTURE

There are 24 provinces, two special regions and a special capital region.

PROVINCES	Area (sq.km)	Population (2000 census)	Capital
Aceh*	55,392	3,930,905	Banda Aceh
Sumatera Utara	70,787	11,649,655	Medan
Sumatera Barat	49,778	4,248,931	Padang
Riau	94,561	4,957,627	Pakanbaru
Jambi	44,800	2,413,846	Jambi
Sumatera Selatan	103,688	6,899,675	Palembang
Bengkulu	21,168	1,567,432	Bengkulu
Lampung	33,307	6,6741,439	Tanjungkarang
Jakarta Raya†	661	8,389,443	Jakarta
Jawa Barat	46,229	35,729,537	Bandung
Jawa Tengah	34,206	31,228,940	Semarang
Yogyakarta*	3,169	3,122,268	Yogyakarta
Jawa Timur	47,921	34,783,640	Surabaya
Bali	5,561	3,151,162	Denpasar
Nusa Tenggara Barat	20,177	4,009,261	Mataram
Nusa Tenggara Timur	47,876	3,952,279	Kupang
Kalimantan Barat	146,760	4,034,198	Pontianak
Kalimantan Tengah	152,600	1,857,000	Palangkaraya
Kalimantan Selatan	37,660	2,985,240	Banjarmasin
Kalimantan Timur	210,985	2,455,120	Samarinda
Sulawesi Utara	19,023	2,012,098	Menado
Sulawesi Tengah	69,726	2,218,435	Palu
Sulawesi Selatan	72,781	8,059,627	Ujung Padang
Sulawesi Tenggara	27,686	1,821,284	Kendari
Maluku	74,505	1,205,539	Amboina
Irian Jaya	421,981	2,220,934	Jayapura

* Special Region
† Special Capital City Region

INSURGENCIES

There are two armed secessionist movements based on ethnic and nationalist groups, which are fighting perceived Javanese domination. In Irian Jaya government forces are fighting the Papua Independent Organisation (OPM) guerrillas who claim the 1969 referendum was rigged and oppose Indonesian settlement. In northern Sumatra the Free Aceh Movement (GAM) is active. On 7–8 November 1999, a crowd of at least 500,000 people demonstrated in the provincial capital Banda Aceh calling for independence for Aceh. Following a series of violent incidents between separatists and the armed forces, a cease-fire began on 2 June 2000, which lasted until 15 February 2001.

Periodic outbursts of violence between Christians and Muslims in Maluku province occurred in 1999 and 2000. The violence intensified in May 2000, following the

arrival in Maluku of Laskar Jihad, a group of over 2,000 militant Islamic fighters from other parts of Indonesia.

In Central Kalimantan province, which had suffered violence between indigenous Dayaks and immigrants from the island of Madura in 1999, a renewed outbreak of attacks on immigrants in February 2001 led to about 42,000 Madurese fleeing the province; another 35,000 were living in refugee camps in Central Kalimantan.

On 12 February 2002, Christian and Muslim leaders from the eastern Molucca islands (the provinces of Maluku and North Maluku) signed a peace agreement to end three years of sectarian fighting in which 5,000 people had been killed since January 1999.

HEAD OF STATE

President, Megawati Sukarnoputri, *sworn in* 23 July 2001
Vice-President, Hamzah Haz

CABINET *as at July 2002*

Co-ordinating Minister for the Economy, Dorodjatun Kuntjoro Jakti
Co-ordinating Minister for People's Welfare, Yusuf Kalla
Co-ordinating Minister for Political, Social and Security Affairs, Susilo Bambang Yudhoyono
Agriculture, Bungaran Saragih
Culture and Tourism, I Gde Ardhika
Defence, Mathori Abdul Djalil
Energy and Mineral Resources, Puronomo Yusgiantoro
Finance, Budiono
Foreign Affairs, Hasan Wirayuda
Forestry, M. Prakosa
Health, Ahmad Sujudi
Home Affairs, Hari Sabarno
Housing and Regional Infrastructure, Soenarno
Industry and Trade, Rini Suwandi
Justice and Human Rights, Yusril Ihza Mahendra
Manpower and Transmigration, Jacob Nuwawea
Maritime Affairs and Fisheries, Rokhmin Dahuri
National Education, Malik Fajar
Religious Affairs, Said Agil Munawar
Social Affairs, Bachtiar Chamsyah
Transport and Telecommunications, Gen. Agum Gumelar

INDONESIAN EMBASSY

38 Grosvenor Square, London W1K 2HW
Tel: 020-7499 7661
Ambassador Extraordinary and Plenipotentiary, vacant
Chargé d'Affaires, N. T. Dammen

BRITISH EMBASSY

Jalan M. H. Thamrin 75, Jakarta 10310
Tel: (00 62) (21) 315 6264
Ambassador Extraordinary and Plenipotentiary, HE Richard Gozney, CMG, apptd 2000
Defence Attaché, Col. A. J. Roberts
British Consular Offices – Bali, Jakarta, Medan, Surabaya

BRITISH COUNCIL DIRECTOR, Dr Richard Phillips, S. Widjojo Centre, Jalan Jenderal Sudirman Kav 71, Jakarta 12190;
Email: information@britishcouncil.org.id.
Offices in Surabaya

DEFENCE

The Army has 481 armoured personnel carriers, 11 armoured infantry fighting vehicles and 33 aircraft. The Navy has two submarines, 17 frigates, 36 patrol and coastal vessels and 18 armed helicopters. There are five principal naval bases. The Air Force has 108 combat aircraft.

MILITARY EXPENDITURE – 1.0 per cent of GDP (2000)
MILITARY PERSONNEL – 297,000: Army 230,000, Navy 40,000, Air Force 27,000; Paramilitaries 195,000
CONSCRIPTION DURATION – Two years (selective)

ECONOMY

About 41 per cent of the population is engaged in agriculture and related production. Copra, nutmeg, pepper, palm oil, sugar, fibres, rubber, tea, coffee and tobacco are produced. Rice is a staple food and Java, Sulawesi and Sumatra are important producers.

Oil and liquefied natural gas are the most important assets. Timber is the second largest foreign exchange earner after oil. Indonesia is rich in minerals, particularly tin, of which the country is the world's third biggest producer; coal, nickel and bauxite are the other principal mineral products. There are also considerable deposits of gold, silver, manganese phosphates and sulphur.

Principal exports are petroleum, textiles and clothing, timber, natural gas and rubber. Principal imports are machinery and transport equipment, electrical equipment and chemicals.

Indonesia was one of the countries worst affected by the Asian economic crisis, which began in the latter half of 1997; the ensuing high unemployment and inflation have led to widespread political and inter-ethnic unrest.

In 1999 there was a trade surplus of US$20,644 million and a current account surplus of US$5,785 million. In 2000 imports totalled US$33,515 million and exports US$62,124 million.

GNP – US$119,871 million (2000); US$600 per capita (1999)
GDP – US$98,638 million (1998); US$674 per capita (1999)
ANNUAL AVERAGE GROWTH OF GDP – 4.8 per cent (2000)
INFLATION RATE – 3.7 per cent (2000)
UNEMPLOYMENT – 5.5 per cent (1998)
TOTAL EXTERNAL DEBT – US$150,096 million (1999)

Trade with UK	2000	2001
Imports from UK	£412,332,000	£311,721,000
Exports to UK	1,169,450,000	1,189,763,000

COMMUNICATIONS

There are railway systems in Java and Sumatra linking the main towns. There are about 137,060 km of roads.

Sea communications are maintained by the state-run shipping companies Jakarta-Lloyd (ocean-going) and PELNI (coastal and inter-island) and other small concerns. Transport by small craft on the rivers of the larger islands plays an important part in trade.

Air services are operated by Garuda Indonesian Airways and other local airlines, and Jakarta is served by various international services.

IRAN

Jomhûri-ye-Eslâmi-ye-Îrân – Islamic Republic of Iran

AREA – 630,574 sq. miles (1,648,195 sq. km).
Neighbours: Armenia, Azerbaijan, Turkmenistan (north), Afghanistan (north-east), Pakistan (south-east), Iraq (south-west), Turkey (north-west)
POPULATION – 66,128,965 (2001 estimate): 99 per cent Muslims (Shia 91 per cent and Sunni 8 per cent) with small minorities of Zoroastrians, Jews, and Armenian and Assyrian Christians. The official language is Persian (Farsi). Minority languages are Turkic (26 per cent), Kurdish (9 per cent), Luri (2 per cent), Arabic, Baluchi and Turkish (1 per cent each)

CAPITAL – Tehran (population 6,750,043, 1996 census)
MAJOR CITIES – Ahwaz (804,980); Esfahan (1,266,072);
   Mashhad (1,887,405); Qom (777,677); Shiraz
   (1,053,025); Tabriz (1,191,043), 1996 census
CURRENCY – Rial
NATIONAL ANTHEM – Sorûd-E Jomhûri-Ye Eslâmi
   (Anthem Of The Islamic Republic Of Iran)
NATIONAL DAY – 11 February
NATIONAL FLAG – Three horizontal stripes of green,
   white, red, with the slogan *Allahu Akbar* repeated 22
   times along the edges of the green and red stripes,
   and the national emblem in the centre
LIFE EXPECTANCY (years) – male 68.8; female 70.8
POPULATION GROWTH RATE – 1.5 per cent (1999)
POPULATION DENSITY – 38 per sq. km (1999)
URBAN POPULATION – 58.1 per cent (1994)

Iran is mostly an arid tableland, encircled, except in the
east, by mountains, the highest in the north rising to
18,934 ft. The central and eastern portion is a vast salt
desert.

HISTORY AND POLITICS

Iran was ruled from the end of the 18th century by Shahs
of the Qajar dynasty. In 1925 the last of the dynasty,
Sultan Ahmed Shah, was deposed in his absence by the
National Assembly, which handed executive power to
Prime Minister Reza Khan. Reza Khan was elected Shah
as Reza Shah Pahlavi by the Constituent Assembly in
December 1925. In 1941 Reza Shah abdicated in favour of
the Crown Prince, who ascended the throne as
Mohammed Reza Shah Pahlavi.

In January 1979, the Shah left Iran, handing over power
to the Prime Minister, who was ousted by Ayatollah
Khomeini, the spiritual leader of the Shia Muslims, on his
return from exile. Following a national referendum, an
Islamic Republic was declared on 1 April 1979. A new
constitution, providing for a president, prime minister,
Consultative Assembly, and leadership by Ayatollah
Khomeini, was approved by referendum in December
1979. In June 1989 Khomeini died and President
Khamenei was appointed Leader of the Islamic Republic.
Rafsanjani was elected president in July 1989, and the
post of prime minister was abolished. The 1997
presidential election was won by Mohammad Khatami,
leader of a centre-left coalition. He was seen as a
moderate, and since his election has attempted to pursue
reformist policies, although these have often been
blocked by the conservative clerical establishment. Iran
and the UK re-established full diplomatic relations in
May 1999. The three rounds of elections to the Majlis
held on 18 February, 5 May and 30 May 2000 gave a large
majority to reformist candidates. The presidential
election on 8 June 2001 resulted in the re-election of
Mohammad Khatami, who obtained over 76 per cent of
the vote; there were nine other candidates.

FOREIGN RELATIONS

Iran was at war with Iraq following the Iraqi invasion of
Iran in September 1980. International efforts to end the
fighting resulted in a cease-fire in August 1988. In August
1990 Iraq accepted Iran's conditions for settling the
conflict, including a return to the 1975 border, but a
formal peace treaty has not been signed.

Following the murder of nine Iranian diplomats in
August 1998 by Taliban militia forces in Afghanistan, Iran
held large-scale military manoeuvres on the Afghan
frontier. There were border skirmishes on 8 October
1998.

POLITICAL SYSTEM

The leader of the republic is elected by the Council of
Experts whose 83 members are popularly elected every
eight years. The president, who is the chief executive, is
directly elected for a four-year term, renewable once.
Ministers are nominated by the president and must
obtain a vote of confidence in the Majlis. The Majlis
comprises 290 representatives who are directly elected for
a four-year term. Laws passed by the Majlis must be
approved by the 12-member Guardian Council. In
November 1997, President Khatami announced the
establishment of the Committee for the Implementation
and Supervision of the Constitution, a five-member body
to ensure the constitution was abided by and that people's
rights were respected.

Leader of the Islamic Republic, Ayatollah Seyed Ali
   Khamenei, *appointed* June 1989
President, Seyed Mohammad Khatami, *elected* 23 May
   1997, *re-elected* 8 June 2001
First Vice-President, Mohammad Reza Aref

COUNCIL OF MINISTERS *as at July 2002*

Vice-Presidents, Mohammad Baqerian; Mohammed Ali
   Najafi (*Advisers to the President*); Gholamreza
   Aqazadeh (*Atomic Energy*); Abdollah Nouri
   (*Development and Social Affairs*); Masoumeh Ebtekar
   (*Environmental Protection*); Mohammad Ali Abtahi
   (*Legal and Parliamentary Affairs*); Mohsen Mehrali-
   Zadeh (*Physical Education*)
Administration and Planning, Mohammad Sattarifar
Agricultural Jihad, Mahmoud Hojjati
Commerce, Mohammad Shariatmadari
Co-operatives, Ali Sufi
Culture and Islamic Guidance, Ahmad Masjed-Jame'i
Defence and Logistics, Adm. Ali Shamkhani
Economic Affairs and Finance, Tahmasb Mazaheri
Education, Morteza Haji
Energy, Habibollah Bitaraf
Foreign Affairs, Kamal Kharrazi
Health, Massoud Pezeshkian
Higher Education, Science and Research, Mostafa Moin
Housing and Urban Development, Ali Abdol-Alizadeh
Industries and Mines, Eshaq Jahangiri
Information, Ali Yunesi
Information and Communications Technology, Ahmad
   Mo'tamedi
Interior, Chair of State Security Council, Abdulvahed
   Mouissavi-Lari
Justice, Hojjatolislam Ismail Shostari
Labour and Social Affairs, Safdar Hoseyni
Oil, Bijan Namdar Zanganeh
Roads and Transport, Ahmad Khorram

EMBASSY OF THE ISLAMIC REPUBLIC OF IRAN
16 Prince's Gate, London SW7 1PT
Tel: 020-7225 3000
Ambassador Extraordinary and Plenipotentiary, HE
   Morteza Sarmadi, apptd 2000

BRITISH EMBASSY
143 Ferdowsi Avenue, PO Box 11365–4474, Tehran
   11344
Tel: (00 98) (21) 670 5011
Ambassador Extraordinary and Plenipotentiary, HE
   Nicholas W. Browne, CMG
First Secretary (Commercial), E. Jenkinson

DEFENCE

The Army has around 1,565 main battle tanks, 590 armoured personnel carriers, 750 armoured infantry fighting vehicles and 85 attack helicopters. The Navy has six submarines, three frigates, 53 patrol and coastal vessels, five combat aircraft and 19 armed helicopters. There are six naval bases. The Air Force has some 283 combat aircraft, of which about 60–80 per cent are serviceable.

MILITARY EXPENDITURE – 7.5 per cent of GDP (2000)
MILITARY PERSONNEL – 513,000: Army 325,000, Revolutionary Guard Corps 125,000, Navy 18,000, Air Force 45,000; Paramilitaries 40,000
CONSCRIPTION DURATION – 21 months

ECONOMY

Iran's alleged support for international terrorism and its suspected nuclear weapons programme prompted the USA to impose a full trade and investment embargo in June 1995. On 17 March 2000, the USA announced that it would lift sanctions on the importation of certain goods, including carpets, caviar and pistachio nuts.

Wheat is the principal agricultural crop; other important crops are barley, rice, cotton, sugar beet, fruit, nuts and vegetables. Wool is also a major product.

The oilfields, which lie in south-western Iran, were nationalised in 1951. In 1979, the National Iranian Oil Company assumed control of the production, refining and sale of oil. Oil production was 187,700,000 tonnes in 1998.

Apart from oil, the principal industrial products are carpets, textiles, sugar, cement and other construction materials, ginned cotton, vegetable oil and other food products, leather and shoes, metal manufactures, pharmaceuticals, motor vehicles, fertilisers and plastics. Privatisation began in 1991.

It was announced in April 2000 that reserves of gas had been found in the Gavband region with an estimated value of US$16,500 million. Natural gas production was 50,000 million cubic metres in 1998.

In 1998 there was a trade deficit of US$626 million and a current account deficit of US$1,897 million. In 1997 imports totalled US$14,165 million and exports US$18,381 million.

GNP – US$104,572 million (2000); US$1,810 per capita (1999)
GDP – US$187,423 million (1998); US$3,445 per capita (1999)
ANNUAL AVERAGE GROWTH OF GDP – 2.1 per cent (1998)
INFLATION RATE – 14.5 per cent (2000)
TOTAL EXTERNAL DEBT – US$10,357 million (1999)

TRADE

Imports are mainly industrial and agricultural machinery, motor vehicles and components for assembly, iron and steel, electrical machinery and goods, foodstuffs and certain textile fabrics and yarns. The principal exports, apart from oil and gas, are carpets and fruit. Japan, Germany, France, the UAE and Italy are Iran's main trading partners.

Trade with UK	2000	2001
Imports from UK	£296,052,000	£430,841,000
Exports to UK	33,200,000	29,553,000

COMMUNICATIONS

Tehran is the centre of a network of highways linking the major towns, ports, the Caspian Sea and the national frontiers; there are 156,507 km of roads.

The Trans-Iranian Railway runs from Bandar Turcoman, on the Caspian Sea, via Tehran to Bandar Khomeini, on the Persian Gulf. Other lines link Tehran with Tabriz and Mashhad; Tabriz to Julfa; Zahedan to Quetta; Ahvaz to Khorramshahr; Qom to Kerman; and Bandar Turcoman to Gorgan. The rail system is linked to the Turkish system via Van. A track between Mashhad and Tedzhen in Turkmenistan, opened in May 1996, has re-established the ancient Silk Route between China and the Mediterranean; there are 5,612 km of railway track.

EDUCATION AND CULTURE

Since 1943 primary education has been compulsory and free. There are 74 universities in Iran. The educational system has been reformed following the revolution.

Persian or Farsi is an Indo-European language with many Arabic elements added; the alphabet is mainly Arabic, with writing from right to left. Among the great names in Persian literature are those of Abu'l Kásim Mansúr, or Firdausi (AD 939–1020), Omar Khayyám, the astronomer-poet (died AD 1122), Muslihu'd-Din, known as Sa'di (born AD 1184), and Shems-ed-Din Muhammad, or Hafiz (died AD 1389).

ILLITERACY RATE – 21.6 per cent (2002)
ENROLMENT (percentage of age group) – primary 98 per cent (1997); secondary 77 per cent (1997); tertiary 18 per cent (1997)

IRAQ
Al-Jumhūriyya al-'Iraqiyya – Republic of Iraq

AREA – 169,235 sq. miles (438,317 sq. km). Neighbours: Iran (east), Saudi Arabia, Kuwait (south), Jordan (west), Syria (north-west), Turkey (north)
POPULATION – 23,331,985 (2001 estimate), 16,278,316 (1987 census). The official language is Arabic. Minority languages include Kurdish (about 15 per cent), Turkic and Aramaic
CAPITAL – Baghdad (population, 3,841,268, 1987)
MAJOR CITIES – Ψ Al-Basra (406,296); Kirkūk (418,624); Al-Mawsil (664,221)
CURRENCY – Iraqi dinar (ID) of 1,000 fils
NATIONAL ANTHEM – Land Of Two Rivers
NATIONAL DAY – 17 July (Revolution Day)
NATIONAL FLAG – Three horizontal stripes of red, white, black; on the white stripe three stars and the slogan Allahu Akbar all in green
LIFE EXPECTANCY (years) – male 63.5; female 66.5
POPULATION GROWTH RATE – 2.8 per cent (1999)
POPULATION DENSITY – 51 per sq. km (1999)
ILLITERACY RATE – 60.0 per cent (2002)
ENROLMENT (percentage of age group) – primary 85 per cent (1997); secondary 42 per cent (1997); tertiary 11.2 per cent (1995)

In 1993 the border between Iraq and Kuwait was formally demarcated, moving a few hundred metres northwards and giving part of the port of Umm Qasr to Kuwait. The rivers Euphrates (1,700 miles) and Tigris (1,150 miles) rise in Turkey and traverse Iraq to their junction at Qurna, from where the Euphrates flows the 70 miles to the Gulf.

HISTORY AND POLITICS

Iraq is the site of the remains of several ancient civilisations: one site at Tel Hassuna, near Shura, dates back to 5000 BC; Tel Abu Shahrain near 'Ur of the Chaldees' is the site of the Sumerian city of Eridu; the ancient city of Hillah, 70 miles south of Baghdád, is near the site of Babylon and the Tower of Babel. Al-Mawsil

governorate covers a great part of the ancient kingdom of Assyria, the ruins of Nineveh, the Assyrian capital, being visible on the banks of the Tigris, opposite Al-Mawsil. Qurna, at the junction of the Tigris and Euphrates, is traditionally supposed to be the site of the Garden of Eden.

Iraq was part of the Ottoman empire from 1534 until it was captured by British forces in 1916. A provisional government was set up in 1920, and in 1921 the Emir Faisal was elected King of Iraq. The country was a monarchy until July 1958, when King Faisal II was assassinated. From 1958 Iraq has been under the rule of the Ba'ath Party.

The Arab Ba'ath Socialist Party held 165 of the 250 Assembly seats following the most recent election, held on 27 March 2000; the remaining seats were held by independents.

FOREIGN RELATIONS

Iraq invaded Iran in September 1980 and was at war until the August 1988 cease-fire. A formal peace treaty has not been signed.

Iraq invaded Kuwait on 2 August 1990 and declared Kuwait a province of Iraq. The UN Security Council declared the annexation void and in January 1991, an alliance of NATO and Middle East countries launched an offensive and liberated Kuwait in February 1991.

A United Nations Special Committee (UNSCOM), charged with securing Iraq's full nuclear, biological and chemical disarmament, was frequently hindered in its task by Iraqi officials.

In December 1999, the UN Security Council created a new weapons inspection body, the UN Monitoring, Verification and Inspection Commission (UNMOVIC), to replace UNSCOM. UNMOVIC was to monitor the elimination of Iraq's nuclear, chemical and biological weapons arsenal and was empowered to suspend all sanctions for four-month renewable phases if the Iraqi authorities co-operated fully with UNMOVIC and the IAEA within a whole 120-day period.

On 18 April 2001, Iran launched surface-to-surface missiles against military camps inside Iraq belonging to the main Iranian opposition group, the Mujahidin-i-Khalq and Iraqi aircraft shot down an unmanned Iranian reconnaissance aircraft the following day.

INSURGENCIES

Following the allied victory in Kuwait in February 1991, rebellion broke out in the Kurdish north and the Shi'ite south. A UN safe haven in northern Iraq to protect the Kurdish population and air exclusion zones north of the 36th parallel and south of the 33rd parallel were also established.

Iraqi aircraft have frequently violated the air exclusion zones; allied forces have responded by attacking Iraqi air defence installations. At the time of publication the diplomatic situation deteriorated significantly with the US preparing for military action unless Baghdad allowed the UN to inspect its weapons of mass destruction. For updates see Stop Press.

POLITICAL SYSTEM

According to the provisional constitution, the highest state authority is the Revolutionary Command Council (RCC), which elects the president from among its members. A constitutional amendment approved in September 1995 provided for the confirmation of the RCC's choice of president by the National Assembly and by a popular referendum. The president appoints the Council of Ministers. Legislative authority is shared by

the RCC and the 250-member National Assembly, which is elected every four years by universal adult suffrage. Following the amendment to the constitution, a referendum on a further seven-year term for President Saddam was approved by a claimed 99.96 per cent of voters on 15 October 1995.

HEAD OF STATE

President, Saddam Hussein, *assumed office* 16 July 1979, *reappointed* 17 October 1995
Vice-President, Deputy Prime Minister, Taha Yassin Ramadan
Vice-President, Taha Mohieddin Maarouf

REVOLUTIONARY COMMAND COUNCIL

Chairman, The President
Vice-Chairman, Izzat Ibrahim
Secretary-General, Khaled Abdel-Moneim Rasheed
Members, Taha Yassin Ramadan; Sa'adoun Shaker; Tariq Aziz; Taha Mohieddin Maarouf; Mizban Khader Hadi

COUNCIL OF MINISTERS *as at July 2002*

Deputy Prime Ministers, Tariq Aziz; Hikmat Mizban Ibrahim al-Azzawi (*Finance*); Abd al-Tawwab al-Mulla Huwaysh (*Military Industrialisation*); Ahmad Hussein Khudeir (*Presidential Office*)
Agriculture, Abd al-Ilah Hamid Muhammad Salih
Culture, Hamid Yusuf Hammadi
Defence, Lt.-Gen. Sultan Hashim Ahmad al-Jabburi Tai
Education, Fahd Salem al-Shaqra
Foreign Affairs, Naji Sabri Ahmed al-Hadithi
Health, Umid Midhat Mubarak
Higher Education and Scientific Research, Humam Abdel Khaliq abd al-Ghafur
Housing and Reconstruction, Ma'n Abdullah al-Sarsam
Industry, Minerals, Muyassar Raja Shalah
Information, Muhammad Said Kazim al-Sahhaf
Irrigation, Rasul Abd-al-Husayn al-Swadi
Interior, Mahmud Dhiyab al-Ahmad
Justice, Mondher Ibrahim al-Shawi
Labour and Social Affairs, vacant
Oil, Lt.-Gen. Amir Muhammad Rashid al-Ubaydi
Religious Endowments (Waqfs) and Religious Affairs, Abd al-Munim Ahmad Salih
Trade, Mohammad Mehdi Salih
Transport and Communications, Ahmad Murtada Khalil

IRAQI DIPLOMATIC MISSION IN LONDON

Since Iraq's breach of diplomatic relations with Britain in February 1991, the Jordanian Embassy has handled Iraqi interests in the UK.
Minister/Head of Interests Section, Dr Mudhafar Amin

BRITISH DIPLOMATIC REPRESENTATION

The British Embassy was closed in January 1991. The Russian Embassy has since handled British interests in Iraq.

DEFENCE

The Army has roughly 2,200 main battle tanks, 2,400 armoured personnel carriers, 900 armoured infantry fighting vehicles and 100 armed helicopters. The Navy has six patrol and coastal vessels at three bases. The Air Force has some 316 combat aircraft, of which about 55 per cent are serviceable.

In 1991, the UN demanded the destruction of all weapons of mass destruction and their means of production as a prerequisite for the lifting of sanctions.

MILITARY EXPENDITURE – 9.7 per cent of GDP (2000)
MILITARY PERSONNEL – 424,000: Army 375,000, Navy
2,000, Air Force 30,000, Air Defence Command 17,000;
Paramilitaries 44,000
CONSCRIPTION DURATION 18–24 months

ECONOMY

Iraq's major industry is oil production which was
nationalised in 1972. Production was 105,300,000 tonnes
in 1998.

Agricultural production is important, with two harvests
usually gathered in a year, depending on rainfall. Salinity
and soil erosion limit productivity.

The UN imposed economic sanctions and a world-
wide ban on Iraqi oil exports in August 1990. In May
1996, Iraq agreed to a UN-proposed 'oil-for-food' deal,
permitting the sale of oil to buy food and medicine.
Limited oil exports resumed in December 1996. On 14
May 2002, the UN revised the oil-for-food programme,
allowing Iraq to import all humanitarian goods apart
from those deemed to be of military use.

GDP – US$73,848 million (1998); US$3,144 per capita
(1999)

ANNUAL AVERAGE GROWTH OF GDP – 15.0 per cent
(1998)

TRADE

The principal imports are normally iron and steel,
military equipment, building materials, mechanical and
electrical machinery, motor vehicles, textiles and
clothing, essential foodstuffs and raw industrial materials.
The chief exports are normally crude petroleum, dates,
raw wool, raw hides and skins and raw cotton.

Free trade agreements have been signed with Egypt,
Syria and Tunisia, which are to be put into effect when
UN sanctions are lifted.

Trade with UK	2000	2001
Imports from UK	£50,990,000	£60,596,000
Exports to UK	62,000	865,000

COMMUNICATIONS

The port of Al-Basra has not been used since the outbreak
of hostilities with Iran in 1980. Continuous dredging of
the Shatt-al-Arab has also been suspended by hostilities
and the channel has seriously silted. The port of Umm
Qasr on the Kuwaiti border, which was developed for
freight and sulphur handling and includes a container
terminal, was opened in late 1993.

Iraqi Republican Railways provided regular passenger
and goods services between Al-Basra, Baghdad and Al-
Mawsil. There is also a metre gauge rail line connecting
Baghdad with Khanaqin, Kirkūk and Arbil.

Iraqi communications were greatly affected by the Gulf
War; large numbers of bridges were destroyed and the
railway system extensively disrupted.

Irregular flights primarily from Islamic countries began
to fly into Baghdād International Airport in October 2000
in defiance of the sanctions. In November, Iraqi Airlines
resumed its internal flights linking Baghdād with Al-
Basra and Al-Mawsil.

IRELAND
Éire/Ireland

AREA – 27,132 sq. miles (70,273 sq. km). Neighbour:
Northern Ireland (north)
POPULATION – 3,626,087 (2001 estimate). At the 1991
census religious adherence was: Roman Catholic,
3,228,327; Church of Ireland, 89,187; Presbyterians,

13,199; Methodists, 5,037; others, 189,969. Irish is the
first official language; English is recognised as a
second official language, but is more commonly used
CAPITAL – Ψ Dublin (Baile Átha Cliath) (population,
952,692, 1999 estimate)
MAJOR CITIES – Ψ Cork (*Corcaigh*) (180,000);
Ψ Galway (*Gaillimh*) (57,000); Ψ Limerick
(*Luimheach*) (79,000); Waterford (Port Láirge)
(44,000), 1999 estimates
CURRENCY – Euro (€) of 100 cents
NATIONAL ANTHEM – Amhrán na bhFiann (The
Soldier's Song)
NATIONAL DAY – 17 March (St Patrick's Day)
NATIONAL FLAG – Equal vertical stripes of green, white
and orange
LIFE EXPECTANCY (years) – male 74.4; female 79.6
POPULATION GROWTH RATE – 1.0 per cent (1999)
POPULATION DENSITY – 53 per sq. km (1999)
URBAN POPULATION – 58.1 per cent (1996)
MILITARY EXPENDITURE – 0.7 per cent of GDP (2000)
MILITARY PERSONNEL – 10,460: Army 8,500, Navy
1,100, Air Force 860

Ireland is separated from Scotland by the North Channel
and from England and Wales by the Irish Sea and St
George's Channel. The greatest length of the island, from
north-east to south-west (Torr Head to Mizen Head), is
302 miles, and the greatest breadth, from east to west
(Dundrum Bay to Annagh Head), is 174 miles. On the
north coast of Achill Island (Co. Mayo) are the highest
cliffs in the British Isles, 2,000 feet sheer above the sea.

The highest point is Carrantuohill (3,414 ft). The
principal river is the Shannon (240 miles), which drains
the central plain. The Slaney flows into Wexford Harbour,
the Liffey to Dublin Bay, the Boyne to Drogheda, the Lee
to Cork Harbour, the Blackwater to Youghal Harbour,
and the Suir, Barrow and Nore to Waterford Harbour.

The principal hydrographic feature is the loughs; the
Shannon chain of Allen, Boderg, Forbes, Ree and Derg,
and the Erne chain of Gowna, Oughter, Lower Erne, and
Erne; Melvin, Gill, Gara and Conn in the north-west; and
Corrib and Mask (joined by a hidden channel) in the
west.

The Republic of Ireland is divided into four provinces of 26 counties: Leinster (Carlow, Dublin, Kildare, Kilkenny, Laoighis, Longford, Louth, Meath, Offaly, Westmeath, Wexford and Wicklow); Munster (Clare, Cork, Kerry, Limerick, Tippe-rary and Waterford); Connacht (Galway, Leitrim, Mayo, Roscommon and Sligo); and part of Ulster (Cavan, Donegal and Monaghan).

HISTORY AND POLITICS

The first inhabitants of Ireland crossed from Scandinavia to Britain at around 6,000 BC. The settlers were joined by Celts from central Europe from the sixth century BC until about the time of Christ. The introduction of Christianity in the fifth century is traditionally associated with St Patrick and inspired 300 years of rich cultural achievements. The Vikings, who established most of the major towns, including Dublin and Cork, invaded around AD 800 and controlled Ireland until their defeat at the Battle of Clontarf (1014) by Brian Boru, who had become king of all Ireland in 1002.

In the 12th century the Norman English invaded at the invitation of Dermod MacMurrough, the deposed king of Leinster, and established feudal control over most of the island; this lasted for 300 years. King Henry VIII of England reconquered Ireland and in 1541 declared himself king of Ireland, the first English monarch to do so. Protestantism was introduced but failed to take root, except in Ulster where English and Scottish Presbyterians settled during the reign of James I (1603–25). A rebellion initiated by Ulster Catholics in 1641 was ruthlessly crushed by Oliver Cromwell's army. Catholicism was repressed and further Protestant colonisation encouraged. Following the abdication of the Catholic King James II in 1688, Irish Protestants supported William of Orange's accession to the throne. James II was defeated in Ireland, most famously at the Battle of the Boyne (1690), and Protestant ascendancy was restored, enduring throughout the 18th century.

The Irish parliament was granted independence in 1782, although the Dublin administration was still appointed by the king. The parliament was abolished by the Act of Union in 1801 following a rebellion by the Society of the United Irishmen in 1798, and subsequently Irish MPs sat at Westminster. Demands for the restoration of the Irish parliament and home rule for Ireland were successful in 1914, but were delayed when World War I broke out. A rebellion, the Easter Rising of 1916, was suppressed by the British, fuelling support for the Sinn Féin party, which won the 1918 election in Ireland and formed a legislature in Dublin under the leadership of Eamon de Valera. The resulting two-year war of independence between the Irish Republican Army and British forces ended in a truce, followed by negotiations leading to the signing of the Anglo-Irish Treaty in December 1921. The island was partitioned, the 26 counties of the Irish Free State accepting dominion status within the British Empire, while six of the nine counties of Ulster, where the majority Protestant population opposed home rule, remained part of the United Kingdom, governed by a Northern Ireland parliament.

Civil war broke out between the new Irish government and opponents of the treaty until a truce was reached in May 1923. Constitutional links between the Irish Free State and the UK were gradually removed by the Irish parliament and a new constitution enacted in 1937 declared that 'Ireland is a sovereign, independent, democratic state'. However, it continued in association with the states of the British Commonwealth until 1949, when constitutional links with Britain were severed.

Following the Good Friday Agreement of 10 April 1998, a referendum was held, in which 94 per cent of voters in the Irish Republic and 71 per cent of voters in Northern Ireland approved the agreement. The agreement recognises that Northern Ireland remains part of the United Kingdom and shall not cease to be so without the consent of a majority of the people of Northern Ireland. Additionally, a North-South Ministerial Council, comprising officials from both countries, would meet to regulate areas of common interest.

The presidential election in October 1997 was won by Mary McAleese with almost 59 per cent of second-round votes. In the elections to the Dáil Eireann held on 17 May 2002, Fianna Fáil (FF) remained the largest party but without an overall majority. The coalition government, led by Bertie Ahern of FF, includes members of the Progressive Democrats (PD). The composition of the Dáil Eireann as at June 2002 was: FF 80; Fine Gael 31; Labour 21; PD 8; Green Party 6; Sinn Fein 5; Socialist Party 1; Independents 1.

POLITICAL SYSTEM

The president (*Uachtarán na hÉireann*) is directly elected for a term of seven years, and is eligible for a second term. The president is aided and advised by a Council of State.

The National Parliament (*Oireachtas*) consists of the president, House of Representatives (*Dáil Éireann*) and Senate (*Seanad Éireann*). Dáil Éireann is composed of 166 members elected for a five-year term on a basis of proportional representation by means of the single transferable vote. Seanad Éireann is composed of 60 members, of whom 11 are nominated by the prime minister (*Taoiseach*) and 49 are elected, six by institutions of higher education and 43 from panels of candidates established on a vocational basis.

Executive power is vested in the government subject to the constitution. The government is responsible to the Dáil. The taoiseach is appointed by the president on the nomination of the Dáil. The other members of the government are appointed by the president on the nomination of the taoiseach with the previous approval of the Dáil. The taoiseach appoints a member of the government to be his deputy (the *tánaiste*).

The judicial system comprises courts of first instance and a court of final appeal called the Supreme Court (*Cúirt Uachtarach*). The courts of first instance include a High Court (*Ard-Chúirt*) and courts of local and limited juris-diction, with a right of appeal as determined by law. The High Court alone has original jurisdiction to consider the question of the validity of any law having regard to the provisions of the constitution. The Supreme Court has appellate jurisdiction from decisions of the High Court.

HEAD OF STATE

President, Mary McAleese, *elected* 30 October 1997, *sworn in* 11 November 1997

CABINET *as at July 2002*

Taoiseach (*Prime Minister*), Bertie Ahern
Tánaiste (*Deputy PM*), Enterprise, Trade and Employment, Mary Harney
Agriculture and Food, Joe Walsh
Arts, Sports and Tourism, John O'Donoghue
Communications, Marine and Natural Resources, Dermot Aherne
Community, Rural and Gaeltacht Affairs, Éamon Ó Cuív
Defence, Michael Smith
Education and Science, Noel Dempsey
Enterprise, Trade and Employment, Mary Harney
Environment and Local Government, Martin Cullen

Finance, Charlie McCreevy
Foreign Affairs, Brian Cowen
Health and Children, Michael Martin
Justice and Law Reform, Michael Mcdowell
Office of Public Works, Tom Parlon
Social and Family Affairs, Mary Coughlan
Transport, Seamus Brennan

IRISH EMBASSY
17 Grosvenor Place, London SW1X 7HR
Tel: 020-7235 2171
Ambassador Extraordinary and Plenipotentiary, HE
Dáithí O'Ceallaigh, apptd 2001
Counsellor, S. Murray *(Economic)*

BRITISH EMBASSY
29 Merrion Road, IE-Dublin 4
Tel: (00 353) (1) 205 3700
Email: bembassy@internet-ireland.ie
Ambassador Extraordinary and Plenipotentiary, HE Sir
Ivor Roberts, KCMG, apptd 1998
Counsellor and Deputy Head of Mission, J. Rankin
Defence Attaché, Col. P. Cummings

BRITISH COUNCIL DIRECTOR, Ann Malamah-Thomas,
mbe, Newmount House, 22/24 Lower Mount Street,
IE-Dublin 2; Email: helen.jones@ie.britishcouncil.org

ECONOMY

Although industry has expanded greatly since Ireland's entry into the European Community in 1973, agriculture remains important; in 2000, 7.8 per cent of the workforce was employed in agriculture, forestry and fisheries. The main crops are wheat, barley, oats, potatoes and sugar beet. Agriculture has benefited considerably from the EU Common Agricultural Policy and support funds but has suffered from the drift of the rural population to urban areas and abroad.

Industry accounted for about 38 per cent of GDP and about 28.3 per cent of employment in 1999. The traditional brewing, spirits and food-processing sectors have expanded and have been joined by the manufacture of textiles, chemicals, pharmaceuticals, electronics, office machinery and transportation equipment. The services sector is currently the fastest-growing sector of the economy and accounted for 57 per cent of GDP and 63.1 per cent of employment in 1999. Tourism is the most important part of the service sector and in recent years has provided substantial revenue, with 6,416,000 visitors in 2000.

The Kinsale gas field off the south coast provided 28 per cent of Ireland's gas needs in 2000, with 72 per cent coming via an undersea pipeline from Moffat, Scotland. There are five government-funded milled peat power-generating stations. Hydroelectric power from the Shannon barrage and other schemes is also important but Ireland still imports 47 per cent of oil and coal for power generation. Metal content of ores raised (2000) was lead, 86,896 tonnes; zinc, 431,426 tonnes.

Computer equipment and organic chemicals are the main exports. The UK, USA, Germany, France and the Netherlands are Ireland's main trading partners.

Following GDP growth of around 9 per cent in 2000, the government proposed a budget for 2001 which aimed to increase spending and reduce taxes. In February 2001 EU finance ministers issued the Irish Finance Minister, Charlie McCreevy, to amend the budget, claiming that it would raise Ireland's already high inflation rate. He refused, citing statistics showing that the rate of inflation was falling.

Having satisfied the Maastricht convergence criteria,

Ireland participates in the European Single Currency.

In 2000 Ireland had a trade surplus of US$25,416 million and a current account deficit of US$593 million. Imports totalled US$50,547 million and exports US$76,859 million.

GNP – US$87,108 million (2000); US$21,470 per capita (1999)
GDP – US$85,024 million (1998); US$24,825 per capita (1999)
ANNUAL AVERAGE GROWTH OF GDP – 8.9 per cent (1998)
INFLATION RATE – 5.6 per cent (2000)
UNEMPLOYMENT – 3.8 per cent (2001)

Trade with UK	2000	2001
Imports from UK	£11,644,200,000	£13,133,800,000
Exports to UK	9,165,000,000	8,923,600,000

COMMUNICATIONS

In 2000 there were 3,314 km of railway operated by *Iarnród Eirann*. In 1999 the number of ships with cargo which arrived at Irish ports was 17,645 (190,818,000 net registered tons), with a total weight of goods handled of 43,928 million tonnes.

Shannon Airport, Co. Clare, is on the main trans-atlantic air route. In 2000 the airport handled 2.41 million passengers. Dublin Airport serves the cross-channel and European services operated by the Irish national airline Aer Lingus and other airlines. In 2000 the airport handled 13.83 million passengers. In 2000 Cork Airport handled 1.68 million passengers.

EDUCATION

Primary education is directed by the state, with the exception of 37 private primary schools. There were 3,181 state-aided primary schools in 1998–9.

In 1998–9 there were 432 recognised secondary schools under private management (mainly religious orders), and 245 vocational schools. There were 16 state comprehensive schools and 66 community schools.

Third-level education is catered for by seven university colleges, 13 Institutes of Technology, seven teacher training colleges and a number of other third-level institutions.

ENROLMENT (percentage of age group) – primary 100 per cent (1997); secondary 100 per cent (1997); tertiary 41 per cent (1997)

ISRAEL

Medinat Yisra'el/Dawlat Isrā'īl – State of Israel

AREA – 8,130 sq. miles (21,056 sq. km). Neighbours: Lebanon (north), Syria (north-east), Jordan and the West Bank (east), the Gaza Strip and the Egyptian province of Sinai (south-west)
POPULATION – 6,100,000 (2001 estimate): roughly 82 per cent Jewish, 14 per cent Arab Muslims, 2.5 per cent Christians of which 90 per cent are Arab, and 2 per cent Druze. Since independence Israel has had a policy of granting an immigration visa to every Jew who expresses a desire to settle in Israel. Between 1948 and 1992, 2.3 million immigrants had entered Israel from over 100 different countries. Hebrew and Arabic are the official languages. Arabs are entitled to transact all official business with government departments in Arabic
CAPITAL – Most of the government departments are in Jerusalem, population 758,000 (2001 estimate). A resolution proclaiming Jerusalem as the capital of Israel was adopted by the Knesset in 1950. It is not,

HISTORY AND POLITICS

The Ottoman Empire province of Palestine was captured by British forces in 1917, the same year that the British Government issued the Balfour Declaration which was the first significant declaration in favour of a Jewish 'national home' in Palestine. The Balfour Declaration's terms were enshrined in Britain's League of Nations mandate over Palestine, leading to steady Jewish immigration in the inter-war years and a post-1945 flood by Nazi concentration camp survivors. The Arab Palestinian population revolted against Jewish immigration from 1936 onwards, while Jewish groups conducted a terrorist campaign against the British administration from 1945 onwards.

In 1947 Britain announced its withdrawal from Palestine with effect from May 1948, handing over to the UN responsibility for resolving the conflict between Arabs and Jews. Both sides ignored the UN partition plan; on the withdrawal of British forces on 14 May 1948 the State of Israel was proclaimed and the first Arab-Israeli war began. By the time of the January 1949 cease-fire Israeli forces controlled all of the former mandate territory apart from the West Bank (and East Jerusalem) and the Gaza Strip, which had come under Jordanian and Egyptian control respectively.

During the 1967 Six-Day War Israel captured the West Bank and the Gaza Strip, together with Sinai from Egypt and the Golan Heights from Syria, and annexed East Jerusalem. Israel held on to its gains in the 1973 Yom Kippur War. The Golan Heights were annexed in 1981; Sinai was returned to Egypt in 1982 in accordance with the 1979 Israeli–Egyptian peace treaty, and the South Lebanon Security Zone was established after the 1982–5 invasion of Lebanon, but vacated in June 2000. The annexations of East Jerusalem and the Golan Heights remain unrecognised internationally.

A general election on 29 May 1996, the first to have separate ballots for the prime minister and legislature, was won by Likud leader Binyamin Netanyahu. Ehud Barak, leader of the Labour Party and the One Israel electoral alliance of the Labour, Gesher and Meymad parties, was elected prime minister on 17 May 1999 and formed a six-party coalition government. President Weizman announced that he would resign from office on 10 July 2000 following allegations of fraud. On 31 July, Moshe Katsav was elected president. Ehud Barak resigned as prime minister on 9 December 2000 and called a prime ministerial election, which was held on 6 February 2001; it was won by Likud leader Ariel Sharon, who formed a broad-based eight-party coalition which commanded the support of 72 of the 120 members of the Knesset. Saleh Tarif became the first Israeli Arab to be appointed to the cabinet. On 19 August 2001 the Centre Party agreed to join the coalition, bringing its support in the Knesset to 83 members.

FOREIGN RELATIONS

A peace process, started in October 1991 in Madrid, led to agreements with the Palestine Liberation Organisation, and with Jordan on 14 September 1993. A full peace agreement with Jordan was signed on 26 October 1994.

POLITICAL SYSTEM

Israel is a sovereign democratic republic with executive power vested in a prime minister and Cabinet, and legislative power in a unicameral legislature (*Knesset*) of 120 members elected by proportional representation for a maximum term of four years. The prime minister is elected separately from the legislature. The president is head of state and is elected by the Knesset. Previous

however, recognised as the capital by the UN because East Jerusalem is part of the Occupied Territories captured in 1967. The UN and international law continues to reject the Israeli annexation of East Jerusalem and considers the pre-1950 capital Tel Aviv (population, 1,919,700) to be the capital

MAJOR CITIES – Beersheba (and district 158,400); Ψ Haifa (and district 821,200); Rishon Le'Zion (173,800), 1997 estimates

CURRENCY – Shekel of 100 agora

NATIONAL ANTHEM – Hatikvah (The Hope)

NATIONAL FLAG – White, with two horizontal blue stripes, the Shield of David in the centre

LIFE EXPECTANCY (years) – male 77.1; female 81.0

POPULATION GROWTH RATE – 2.5 per cent (1999)

POPULATION DENSITY – 291 per sq. km (1999)

URBAN POPULATION – 91.0 per cent (2001)

Israel comprises the hill country of Galilee and parts of Judea and Samaria, rising to heights of nearly 4,000 ft; the coastal plain from the Gaza strip to north of Acre, including the plain of Esdraelon running from Haifa Bay to the south-east which divides the hill region; the Negev, a semi-desert triangular-shaped region, extending from a base south of Beersheba, to an apex at the head of the Gulf of Aqaba; and parts of the Jordan valley, including the Hula region, Tiberias and the south-western extremity of the Dead Sea.

The principal river is the Jordan, which rises from three main sources in Israel, the Lebanon and Syria, and flows through the Hula valley, Lake Tiberias/Kinneret (Sea of Galilee) and the Jordan Valley into the Dead Sea, falling 1,517 ft from Hulata to the Dead Sea. The other principal rivers are the Yarkon and Kishon. The Dead Sea is a lake (shared between Israel, the West Bank and Jordan) 1,286 ft below sea-level; it has no outlet, the surplus being carried off by evaporation.

presidents have been elected for a maximum of two five-year terms, but under a bill approved by the Knesset in December 1998, the president is to be elected for a seven-year non-renewable term.

HEAD OF STATE

President of Israel, Moshe Katsav, *elected* 31 July 2000, *sworn in* 1 August 2000

CABINET *as at August 2002*

Prime Minister, Immigrant Absorption, Ariel Sharon (L)
Deputy Prime Minister, Finance, Silvan Shalom (L)
Deputy Prime Minister, Foreign Affairs, Shimon Peres (Lab)
Deputy Prime Minister, Housing and Construction, Natan Sharansky (YBA)
Deputy Prime Minister, Interior, Eli Yishai (S)
Agriculture and Rural Development, Shalom Simhon (L)
Communications, Reuven Rivlin (L)
Defence, Benjamin Ben-Eliezer (Lab)
Education, Limor Livnat (L)
Environment, Tzachi Hanegbi (L)
Health, Nissim Dahan (S)
Industry and Trade, Dalia Itzik (Lab)
Justice, Meir Sheetrit (L)
Labour and Social Affairs, Shlomo Benizri (S)
Public Security, Uzi Landau (L)
Regional Co-operation, Roni Milo (C)
Religious Affairs, Asher Ohana (S)
Science, Culture and Sport, Matan Vilnai (Lab)
Transport, Ephraim Sneh (Lab)
Without Portfolio, Tzipi Livni (L); Dan Naveh (L) (*Co-ordination between the Government and the Knesset*); Eli Suissa (S) (*Jerusalem Affairs*); Shmuel Avital (ON) (*Social Affairs*); Efraim Eitam (NRP); Yitzhak Levy (NRP); Dan Meridor (C)
C Centre; Lab Labour; L Likud; NRP National Religious Party; NU National Union–Yisrael Beytenu; ON One Nation; S Shas; YBA Yisrael B'Aliya

EMBASSY OF ISRAEL
2 Palace Green, Kensington, London W8 4QB
Tel: 020-7957 9500
Ambassador Extraordinary and Plenipotentiary, HE Zvi Shtauber, apptd 2001
Minister Plenipotentiary, Z. Rav-Ner
Defence and Armed Forces Attaché, Col. Y. Sahar

BRITISH EMBASSY
192 Hayarkon Street, Tel Aviv 63405
Tel: (00 972) (3) 725 1222
Ambassador Extraordinary and Plenipotentiary, HE Sherard Cowper-Coles, CMG, LVO, apptd 2001
Counsellor, Consul-General and Deputy Head of Mission, P. L. Carter
Defence and Military Attaché, Col. T. M. Fitzalan-Howard, OBE
First Secretary (*Commercial*), I. Morrison
Consulates – Tel Aviv, Eilat

BRITISH COUNCIL DIRECTOR, David Elliott, 140 Hayarkon Street, PO Box 3302, Tel Aviv 61032; Email: bc.telaviv@britishcouncil.org.il. Regional offices in Jerusalem and Nazareth

DEFENCE

Israel is believed to have a nuclear capacity of around 100 warheads which could be delivered by aircraft or Jericho I and II missiles.

The Army has 3,930 main battle tanks and around 9,900 armoured personnel carriers. The Navy has three submarines and 47 patrol and coastal vessels at three bases. The Air Force has 446 combat aircraft and 133 armed helicopters.

MILITARY EXPENDITURE – 8.9 per cent of GDP (2000)
MILITARY PERSONNEL – 163,500: Army 120,000, Navy 6,500, Air Force 37,000; Paramilitaries 8,050
CONSCRIPTION DURATION – 21–48 months (Jews and Druze only)

ECONOMY

The country is generally fertile although water supply for irrigation restricts production. Agriculture accounts for 4 per cent of GDP.

The 'Jaffa' orange is produced in large quantities for export, along with other summer fruits, seasonal vegetables, flowers and glasshouse crops. Olives are cultivated, mainly for the production of oil. The main winter crops are wheat, barley and various kinds of pulses, while in summer sorghum, millet, maize, sesame and summer pulses are grown. Beef, cattle and poultry farming have been developed. Tobacco and cotton are now grown.

Polished diamonds account for about 27.5 per cent of total exports. Amongst the most important industries are textiles, foodstuffs and chemicals (mainly fertilisers and pharmaceuticals). Metal-working and science-based industries are sophisticated and technologically advanced and include the aircraft and military industries. Other important manufacturing industries include plastics, rubber, cement, glass, paper and oil refining. Industry accounts for 38 per cent and services for 58 per cent of GDP.

GNP – US$99,574 million (1999); US$16,310 per capita (1999)
GDP – US$101,972 million (1998); US$17,564 per capita (1999)
ANNUAL AVERAGE GROWTH OF GDP – 5.7 per cent (2000)
INFLATION RATE – 1.1 per cent (2000)
UNEMPLOYMENT – 8.9 per cent (1999)

TRADE

The principal imports are machinery and transport equipment, semi-manufactures, uncut diamonds, chemicals and chemical products, crude oil, and foodstuffs. The principal exports are semi-manufactures, machinery, polished diamonds, chemicals and chemical products and foodstuffs.

In 2000 Israel had a trade deficit of US$3,350 million and a current account deficit of US$1,416 million. Imports totalled US$37,686 million and exports totalled US$31,338 million.

Trade with UK	2000	2001
Imports from UK	£1,518,754,000	£1,365,802,000
Exports to UK	1,061,695,000	975,348,000

COMMUNICATIONS

Israel State Railways serves Haifa, Tel Aviv, Jerusalem, Lod, Nahariya, Beersheba, Dimona, Ashdod and intermediate stations with a network of 647 km. There were 15,965 km of paved road in 2000. A major road building programme has been underway in the West Bank since 1992.

The chief ports are Haifa and Ashdod on the Mediterranean, and Eilat on the Red Sea; Acre has an anchorage for small vessels. The chief international airport is Ben Gurion between Tel Aviv and Jerusalem.

EDUCATION

Education from five to 16 years is free and compulsory. The law also provides for working youth aged 16–18, who for some reason have not completed their education, to be exempted from work in order to do so. There are seven universities including two engineering and technological institutes.

ILLITERACY RATE – 1.9 per cent (2002)

ENROLMENT (percentage of age group) – tertiary 41.1 per cent (1997)

CULTURE

Important historic sites in Israel include: *Jerusalem* – the Church of the Holy Sepulchre, the Al Aqsa Mosque and Dome of the Rock standing on the remains of the Temple Mount of Herod the Great of which the Western (wailing) Wall is a fragment, the Church of the Dormition and the Coenaculum on Mount Zion, Ein Karem, Church of the Visitation, Church of St John the Baptist; *Galilee* – the Sea, Church and Mount of the Beatitudes, ruins of Capernaum and other sites connected with the life of Christ; *Mount Tabor* – Church of the Transfiguration; *Nazareth* – Church of the Annunciation, and other Christian shrines associated with the childhood of Christ; there are also numerous sites dating from biblical and medieval days, such as Ascalon, Caesarea, Atlit, Massada, Megiddo and Hazor.

PALESTINIAN AUTONOMOUS AREAS

AREA – The total area is 2,406 sq. miles (6,231 sq. km). The area which is fully autonomous is 159 sq. miles (412 sq. km), of which the Gaza Strip is 136 sq. miles (352 sq. km) and the Jericho enclave 23 sq. miles (60 sq. km). The partially autonomous area is the remainder of the West Bank, some 2,247 sq. miles (5,819 sq. km). The UN and the international community also recognise East Jerusalem as part of the Occupied Territories

POPULATION – 2,920,454 (2001 estimate), of whom 210,209 live in East Jerusalem. In addition there are 176,000 Jewish settlers in the West Bank and 6,900 in the Gaza Strip (2000 estimate) who remain under Israeli administration and jurisdiction. Some 90 per cent of Palestinians are Muslim (the vast majority Sunni) and 10 per cent are Christians

CAPITAL – Although Palestinians claim East Jerusalem as their capital, the administrative capital has been established in Gaza City (population 120,000)

MAJOR TOWNS – Khan Yunis, Rafah in the Gaza Strip; Nablus, Hebron, Jericho, Ramallah and Bethlehem on the West Bank

FLAG – Three horizontal stripes of black, white, green with a red triangle based on the hoist (the PLO flag)

NATIONAL ANTHEM – Fidai, Fidai (Freedom Fighter, Freedom Fighter)

HISTORY AND POLITICS

Israel captured the Gaza Strip, East Jerusalem and the West Bank during the 1967 Six-Day War and annexed East Jerusalem. After the war the Israeli government began to establish settlements in the Occupied Territories. Palestinian resistance to Israeli rule was led by the Palestine Liberation Organisation (PLO) which was established in 1964. Frustration at continued Israeli occupation led to the start of the *intifada*, a campaign of sustained unrest, in 1987. When the 1991 Madrid peace process stalled, Israeli and PLO officials engaged in secret negotiations in Norway which led to the signing of the 'Declaration of Principles on Interim Self-Government Arrangements' on 13 September 1993. Under this agreement the PLO renounced terrorism and recognised Israel's right to exist in secure borders, while Israel recognised the PLO as the legitimate representative of the Palestinian people.

The Declaration of Principles established a timetable for progress towards a final settlement: negotiations leading to an Israeli military withdrawal from the Gaza Strip and Jericho by 13 April 1994, when power was to be transferred to a nominated Palestinian National Authority (PNA); elections to a new Palestinian Council, which would also exercise control over six policy areas in the rest of the West Bank (culture, tourism, health, education, social welfare, direct taxation), and the Israeli military administration dissolved by 13 July 1994; negotiations on a permanent settlement, including Jewish settlers and East Jerusalem, to begin by 13 April 1996; and a permanent settlement to be in place by 13 April 1999.

The 'Oslo B' or Taba Accord was signed on 28 September 1995 and provided for Israeli withdrawal from six towns and 85 per cent of Hebron; the extension of self-rule to most of the West Bank by 1998; the release of 5,300 Palestinian prisoners; and the striking out of the demand for Israel's destruction from the PLO's charter. On 29 December 1995 an agreement was reached on the transfer of 17 areas of civilian power to the PNA in Hebron.

Israeli troops left Ramallah, the last of the six West Bank towns, on 27 December 1995 and the inaugural Palestinian National Council meeting on 23 April 1996 voted to amend the PLO charter. The final element of the Declaration of Principles, the 'final status talks' opened in Taba, Egypt, on 5 May 1996 to decide the final status of the West Bank, Gaza and Jerusalem. The election of a Likud-led government opposed to the establishment of a Palestinian state resulted in a deadlock in negotiations in 1997 and delays in the withdrawal of Israeli troops from Hebron.

Legislative elections on 20 January 1996 were won by the mainstream al-Fatah faction of the PLO, with its leader Yasser Arafat winning 88.1 per cent of the vote to become the president of the Palestinian National Authority. Legislative elections were scheduled for 10–20 January 2003.

Yasser Arafat had planned to declare an independent Palestinian state on 4 May 1999, the end of the five-year transitional period which had been agreed in the 1993 Oslo peace accords, but the announcement was postponed in the hope that talks with the new Israeli government would lead to a negotiated settlement.

On 15 May 2000, widespread violence erupted during protests marking *al-Nakba* (the Catastrophe), the anniversary of the founding of the state of Israel in 1948, including exchanges of fire between Palestinian police and Israeli troops. In July, President Clinton hosted talks between Yasser Arafat and Ehud Barak, which aimed to resolve issues which had thwarted a comprehensive peace settlement, but no agreement was reached.

Following a controversial visit in late September 2000 by Likud leader Ariel Sharon to the Temple Mount, a holy site for both Jews and Muslims, a new intifada broke out. Relations between the Israeli government and the PNA deteriorated further after two Israeli soldiers were lynched by Palestinians; on 12 October Israeli forces launched rocket attacks on the residence and offices of Arafat and declared the peace process to be at an end. A summit was held in Sharm el-Shaikh on 17 October and an agreement was reached to end violence and restart negotiations. However, serious clashes resumed in late October. An agreement was reached on 1 November to call a new cease-fire the following day, but it had broken

down by the middle of the month. A new round of talks began on 14 December and a US draft accord was discussed, which envisaged a Palestinian state on 95 per cent of the West Bank and the entire Gaza Strip. Agreement could not be reached and the talks broke down on 27 January 2001. Following the election of Ariel Sharon as Israeli prime minister on 6 February, hopes of a peace agreement faded. Relations remained volatile throughout 2001 and 2002 with Palestinian suicide bombings and Israeli retaliation amid cease-fires and intense diplomatic intervention.

POLITICAL SYSTEM

The Oslo B accord laid down the political structure of the nascent Palestinian state. Executive authority is vested in the Palestinian National Authority which is headed by a popularly elected leader *(rais)*. Legislative authority is vested in the 88-member Palestinian Council which is directly elected by means of a first-past-the-post system, and itself elects the four-fifths of the PNA not appointed by the leader.

PALESTINIAN NATIONAL AUTHORITY *as at July 2002*
Leader, Yasser Arafat
Agriculture, Rafiq al-Natsheh
Civil Affairs, Jamil al-Tarifi
Economy, Trade and Industry, Mahir al-Masri
Education, Naim Abdul Hummus
Finance, Salam Fayad
Health, Riyad al-Za'nun
Housing and Public Works, Azzam al-Ahmad
Information and Culture, Yassir abed Rabbo
Interior, Abdel Razzek al-Yehiye
Justice, Ibrahim Dughmeh
Labour, Ghassan al-Khatib
Local Government, Dr Sa'ib Urayqat
Natural Resources, Abd al-Rahman Hamad
Planning, International Co-operation, Dr Nabil Sha'ath
Post and Telecommunications, Imad al-Faluji
Religious Affairs and Waqf, vacant
Social Affairs, Intisar al-Wazir
Supply, Abdel Aziz Shahin
Tourism and Antiquities, Nabil Qasies
Transport, Mitri Abu Ayta
Youth and Sport, Ali al-Qawasmi

PALESTINIAN GENERAL DELEGATION
5 Galena Road, London W6 0LT
Tel: 020-8563 0008
General Delegate, Afif Safieh
Deputy Head of Mission, Naim Samara

BRITISH CONSULATE-GENERAL
19 Nashashibi Street, PO Box 19690, East Jerusalem 97200
Consul-General, R. A. Kealy, CMG

BRITISH COUNCIL DIRECTOR, David Martin *(Cultural Attaché)*, 31 Nablus Road, PO Box 19136, East Jerusalem. Email: britishcouncil@ej.britishcouncil.org
Regional offices in Gaza, Nablus and Ramallah

Trade with UK	2000	2001
Imports from UK	£140,000	£240,000
Exports to UK	–	121,000

ITALY
Repubblica Italiana – Italian Republic

AREA – 116,339 sq. miles (301,318 sq. km). Neighbours: Switzerland and Austria (north), Slovenia (east), France (west)
POPULATION – 57,523,000 (2001 estimate): 83 per cent Catholic. The language is Italian, a Romance language derived from Latin. There are several regional languages including Sardinian and Catalan in Sardinia, Friulian in Friuli, German and Ladin in the South Tyrol, French in the Valle d'Aosta, and Slovene in parts of Gorizia
CAPITAL – Rome (population, 2,648,843, 1995 estimate). The Eternal City was founded, according to legend, by Romulus in 753 BC. It was the centre of Latin civilisation and capital of the Roman Republic and Roman Empire
MAJOR CITIES – Bologna (385,813); Florence (381,762); Ψ Genoa (655,704); Milan (1,305,591); Ψ Naples (1,046,987); Turin (921,485); *Sicily*, Ψ Palermo (689,349); *Sardinia*, Ψ Cagliari (173,564), 1995 estimates
CURRENCY – Euro (€) of 100 cents
NATIONAL ANTHEM – Inno Di Mameli (Hymn Of Mameli)
NATIONAL DAY – 2 June
NATIONAL FLAG – Vertical stripes of green, white and red
LIFE EXPECTANCY (years) – male 75.5; female 81.9
POPULATION GROWTH RATE – 0.1 per cent (1999)
POPULATION DENSITY – 190 per sq. km (1999)

Italy consists of a peninsula, the islands of Sicily, Sardinia, Elba and about 70 other small islands. The peninsula is for the most part mountainous, but between the Apennines, which form its spine, and the eastern coastline are two large fertile plains: Emilia-Romagna in the north and Apulia in the south. The Alps divide Italy from France, Switzerland, Austria and Slovenia. Partly within the Italian borders are Monte Rosa (15,217 ft), Matterhorn (14,780 ft) and several peaks from 12,000 to 14,000 ft. The chief rivers are the Po (405 miles), flowing through Piedmont, Lombardy and the Veneto; the Adige (Trentino and Veneto); the Arno (Florentine plain); and the Tiber (flowing through Rome to Ostia).

HISTORY AND POLITICS

Italian unity was accomplished under the House of Savoy after a struggle from 1848 to 1870 in which Mazzini (1805–72), Garibaldi (1807–82) and Cavour (1810–61) were the principal figures. It was completed when Lombardy was ceded by Austria in 1859 and Venice in 1866, and through the evacuation of Rome by the French in 1870. In 1871 the King of Italy entered Rome, and that city was declared to be the capital.

A fascist regime came to power in 1922 under Benito Mussolini, known as *Il Duce* (The Leader), who was prime minister from 1922 until 25 July 1943, when the regime was abolished. Mussolini was captured by Italian partisans while attempting to escape across the Swiss frontier and killed on 28 April 1945.

Italy became a republic following a referendum on the future of the monarchy in June 1946.

Political instability and corruption led to public disenchantment with the major political parties, whose support collapsed in the 1992 general election. The so-called 'clean hands' investigation into corruption and Mafia links that began in 1992 has led to the arrest by

magistrates of thousands of politicians and businessmen. The general election on 21 April 1996 was won by the left-wing Olive Tree alliance led by the Democratic Party of the Left, whose leader, Romano Prodi, became prime minister. The government collapsed on 9 October 1998 after the Communist Refoundation party, on whose support it had been dependent, refused to vote for the 1999 budget. Massimo D'Alema was invited by the president to form a new government on 20 October. On 19 December 1999, the government collapsed, but Massimo D'Alema was asked to form a new government the following day; he resigned as prime minister on 17 April 2000 following the defeat of his centre-left coalition in regional elections on 16 April. President Ciampi invited Giuliano Amato to form a new government and Amato was sworn in as prime minister on 26 April 2000. The general election held on 13 May 2001 was won by the centre-right House of Freedoms alliance, which obtained 368 seats. The alliance was led by Forza Italia and also comprised the Christian Democratic Centre, the Christian Democratic Union, the National Alliance, the New Italian Socialist Party and the Northern League. Silvio Berlusconi, the Forza Italia leader, was sworn in as prime minister.

POLITICAL SYSTEM

The constitution provides for the election of the president for a seven-year term by an electoral college which consists of the two houses of the parliament (the Chamber of Deputies and the Senate) sitting in joint session, together with three delegates from each region (one in the case of the Valle d'Aosta). The president, who must be over 50 years of age, has the right to dissolve one or both houses after consultation with the Speakers. Members of both houses were elected wholly by proportional representation until 1993. Now 75 per cent (232) of the 315 elected seats in the Senate are elected on a first-past-the-post basis and the remaining elected seats are filled by proportional representation. There is a variable number of life senators, who are past presidents and senators appointed by incumbent presidents. In the Chamber of Deputies 75 per cent (472) of seats are elected on a first-past-the-post basis, and 25 per cent (158) by proportional representation, with a 4 per cent threshold for parliamentary representation. A referendum on 18 April 1999 on abolishing the seats

elected by proportional representation foundered when less than the required 50 per cent of the electorate participated.

HEAD OF STATE

President, Carlo Azeglio Ciampi, *elected by electoral college* 13 May 1999

COUNCIL OF MINISTERS *as at July 2002*

Prime Minister, Foreign Affairs, Silvio Berlusconi (FI)
Deputy Prime Minister, Gianfranco Fini (AN)
Agriculture and Forestry, Giovanni Alemanno (AN)
Culture, Giuliano Urbani (FI)
Defence, Antonio Martino (FI)
Economy and Finance, Giulio Tremonti (FI)
Education, Higher Education and Scientific Research,
    Letizia Moratti (Ind.)
Employment and Social Welfare, Roberto Maroni (LN)
Environment, Altero Matteoli (AN)
Health, Gerolamo Sirchia (Ind.)
Industry, Antonio Marzano (FI)
Infrastructure and Transport, Pietro Lunardi (Ind.)
Interior, Giuseppe Pisanu (FI)
Justice, Roberto Castelli (LN)
Telecommunications, Maurizio Gasparri (AN)

AN National Alliance; FI Forza Italia; LN Northern League; Ind. Independent

ITALIAN EMBASSY
14 Three Kings Yard, Davies Street, London W1K 4EH
Tel: 020-7312 2200
Ambassador Extraordinary and Plenipotentiary, HE Luigi
    Amaduzzi, GCVO, apptd 1999
Defence and Naval Attaché, Rear-Adm.C. Bettini
Cultural Attaché, C. Panetta

BRITISH EMBASSY
Via XX Settembre 80A, I-00187 Rome
Tel: (00 39) (6) 4220 0001
Ambassador Extraordinary and Plenipotentiary,
HE Sir John Shepherd, KCVO, CMG, apptd 2000
Deputy Head of Mission, A. Leslie
Defence and Military Attaché, Brig. A. Mallinson
Counsellor (Economic and Commercial), M. Hatfull

CONSULATE-GENERAL – Milan
CONSULATES – Rome, Bari, Brindisi, Cagliari, Catania,
    Florence, Genoa, Messina, Naples, Palermo, Trieste,
    Turin, Venice

BRITISH COUNCIL DIRECTOR, Richard Alford, OBE, Via
    Quattro Fontane 20, I-00184 Rome;
    Email: info.italy@britishcouncil.it
There are British Council Offices at Milan, Bologna and
    Naples

DEFENCE

The Army has 1,349 main battle tanks and 2,777 armoured personnel carriers. The Navy has seven submarines, one aircraft carrier, one cruiser, four destroyers, 16 frigates, 15 patrol and coastal vessels, 18 combat aircraft and 80 armed helicopters. There are four naval bases. The Air Force has 329 combat aircraft and six armed helicopters.
MILITARY EXPENDITURE – 1.9 per cent of GDP (2000)
MILITARY PERSONNEL – 230,350: Army 137,000, Navy
    38,000, Air Force 55,350, Paramilitaries 252,200
CONSCRIPTION DURATION – Ten months

ECONOMY

Deposits of natural methane gas and oil have been discovered, mainly south of Sicily, and have been rapidly exploited. Production of lignite has also increased. Other minerals include iron ores and pyrites, mercury (over one-quarter of the world production), lead, zinc and aluminium. Rich gold veins were discovered in Sardinia in 1996. Marble is a traditional product of the Massa Carrara district.

Agricultural production is concentrated in Tuscany, Emilia-Romagna, Sicily and the whole of the southern third of the country. The principal products are wine, tobacco, citrus fruits, tomatoes, almonds, sugar beet, wheat and maize.

Tourism is a major contributor to the economy; in 1997, around 57 million people visited Italy. The commercial and banking services are concentrated in Rome and in Milan, where the stock market is located.

The state-owned sector of Italian industry is still important, dominated by the holding companies IRI (mechanical, steel, airlines), ENI (petrochemicals), and ENEL (electricity), although in November 1999, the government sold 34.5 per cent of ENEL, and announced in December 2000 that a further tranche of government holdings in ENEL, ENI and Telecom Italia would be sold during 2001. In July 2001, ENEL announced that it was to sell its generation business for 2.6 billion. Industry is centred around Milan (steel, machine tools, motor cars), Turin (motor cars, steel, roller bearings, textiles), Rome (light industries), Venice (shipbuilding, paper, mechanical equipment, electrical goods, woollens), Bologna/Florence (food industry, footwear and textiles, reproduction furniture, glassware, pottery, ceramics), Naples, Bari (valves, vehicle bodies, tyres), Taranto (steel, oil refining), Trieste (shipbuilding) and Cagliari (aluminium production, petrochemicals).

Following a programme of severe austerity measures, Italy satisfied the convergence criteria and participated in the European Single Currency from 1 January 1999.

In 2000 there was a trade surplus of US$10,717 million and a current account deficit of US$5,670 million. Imports totalled US$236,624 million and exports US$238,262 million.

Italy's chief exports are industrial and agricultural machinery, textiles and clothing, electrical equipment and chemicals. Chief imports are chemicals, motor vehicles and metals. Italy's main trading partners are Germany, France, the UK and the USA.

GNP – US$1,154,271 million (2000); US$20,170 per capita (1999)
GDP – US$1,185,192 million (1998); US$20,659 per capita (1998)
ANNUAL AVERAGE GROWTH OF GDP – 2.9 per cent (2000)
INFLATION RATE – 2.5 per cent (2000)
UNEMPLOYMENT – 11.4 per cent (1999)

Trade with UK	2000	2001
Imports from UK	£7,973,500,000	£8,044,800,000
Exports to UK	9,047,000,000	9,333,200,000

COMMUNICATIONS

The main railway system is state-run by the *Ferrovia dello Stato*. There are 19,660 km of railway track. A network of motorways (autostrade) covers the country, built and operated mainly by the IRI state holding company and ANAS, the state highway authority. There are 654,676 km of roads. Alitalia, the principal international and domestic airline, is also state-controlled by the IRI group. Other smaller companies, including ATI (an Alitalia subsidiary) and Air Mediterranea, operate on domestic

routes. Genoa is the major port, handling about one-third of Italy's foreign trade.

In January 2001, the Italian and French Presidents agreed plans to build a 52-km rail tunnel through the Alps as part of a high-speed rail link between Turin and Lyons.

EDUCATION

Education is free and compulsory between the ages of six and 14; this comprises five years at primary school and three in 'middle school'. Pupils who obtain the middle school certificate may seek admission to any 'senior secondary school', which may be a lyceum with a classical or scientific or artistic bias, or an institute directed at technology (of which there are eight different types), trade or industry (including vocational schools), or teacher-training. Courses at the lyceums and technical institutes usually last for five years and success in the final examination qualifies for admission to university.

There are 62 universities, some of ancient foundation; those at Bologna, Modena, Parma and Padua were started in the 12th century. University education is not free, but entrants with higher qualifications are charged reduced fees according to a sliding scale.

In general, schools, lyceums and universities are financed by local taxation and central government grants.
ILLITERACY RATE – 1.4 per cent (2002)
ENROLMENT (PERCENTAGE OF AGE GROUP) – primary 100 per cent (1997); tertiary 47 per cent (1997)

CULTURE

Florence, the capital of Tuscany, was one of the greatest cities in Europe from the 11th to the 16th centuries, and the cradle of the Renaissance. Under the Medici family in the 15th century flourished many of the greatest names in Italian art, including Filippo Lippi, Botticelli, Donatello and Brunelleschi, and in the 16th century Michelangelo and Leonardo da Vinci.

Italian literature (in addition to Latin literature, which is the common inheritance of western Europe) is one of the richest in Europe, particularly in its golden age (Dante, 1265–1321; Petrarch, 1304–74; Boccaccio, 1313–75) and in the Renaissance (Ariosto, 1474–1533; Machiavelli, 1469–1527; Tasso, 1544–95). Notable in modern Italian literature are Manzoni (1785–1873), Carducci (1835–1907) and Gabriele d'Annunzio (1864–1938). The Nobel Prize for Literature has been awarded to Italian authors on six occasions: G. Cariducci (1906), Signora G. Deledda (1926), Luigi Pirandello (1934), Salvatore Quasimodo (1959), Eugenio Montale (1975) and Dario Fo (1997).

ISLANDS

CAPRI, in the Bay of Naples; area 4 sq. miles (10 sq. km); population 12,000
EOLIAN ISLANDS, including Lipari; area 45 sq. miles (116 sq. km); popu-lation 18,636
FLEGREAN ISLANDS, including Ischia; area 23 sq. miles (60 sq. km); population 51,883
PANTELLERIA ISLAND (part of Trapani Province) in the Sicilian Narrows; area 31 sq. miles (80 sq. km); population 9,601
THE PELAGIAN ISLANDS (Lampedusa, Linosa and Lampione) are part of the province of Agrigento; area 8 sq. miles (21 sq. km); population 4,811
PONTINE ARCHIPELAGO, including Ponza; area 4 sq. miles (10 sq. km); population 2,515
TREMITI ISLANDS; area 1 sq. mile (3 sq. km); population 426
THE TUSCAN ARCHIPELAGO (including Elba); area 113 sq. miles (293 sq. km); population 31,861

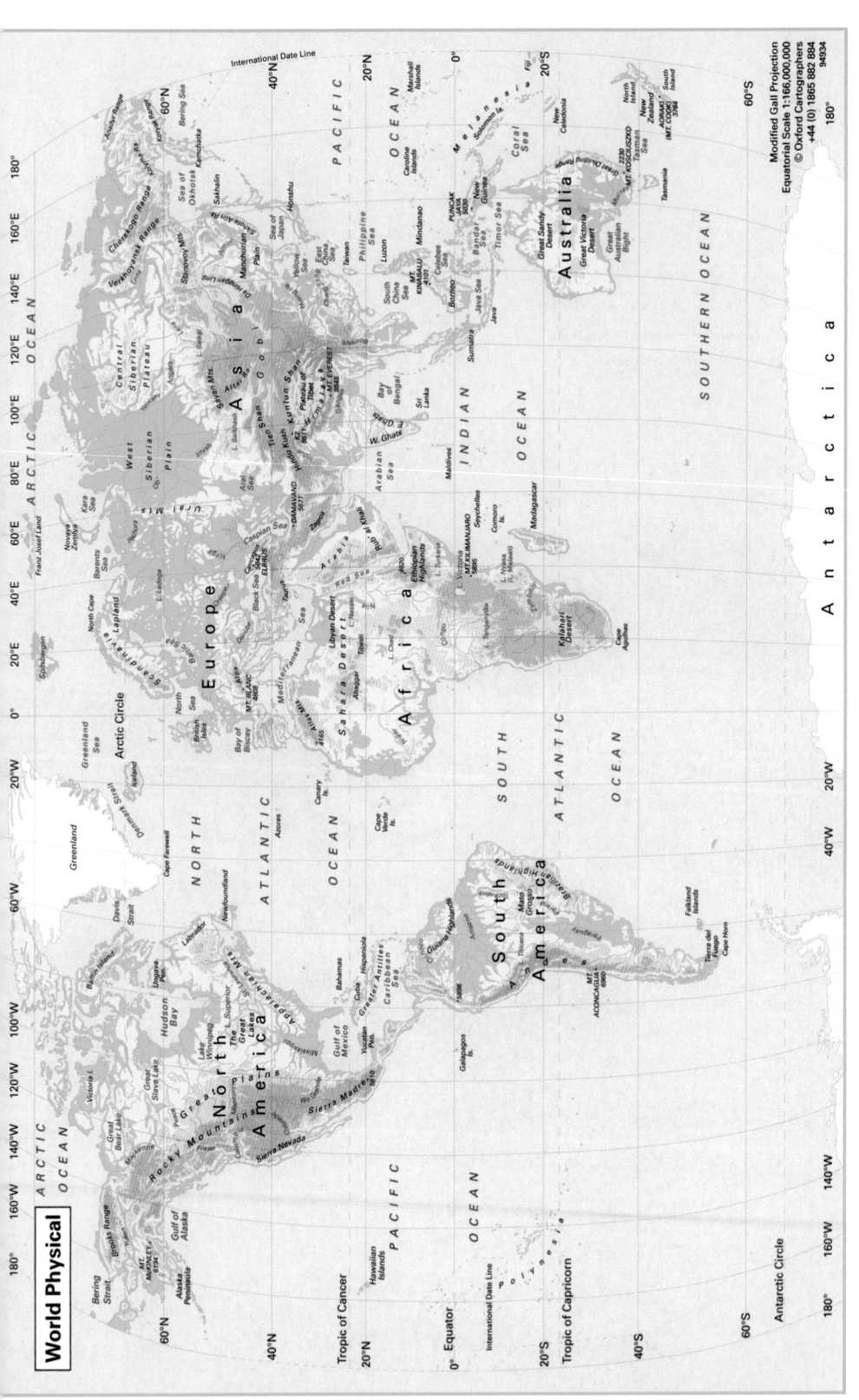

World Physical

Modified Gall Projection
Equatorial Scale 1:166,000,000
© Oxford Cartographers
+44 (0) 1865 882 884
94934

40°W 30°W 20°W 70°N 10°W 0° 10°E

Arctic Circle

Reykjavik

ICELAND

60°N

Norwegian

Sea

Bodø

N O R W E S

0 100 200 300 400 Miles
0 100 200 300 400 500 600 Kms

Conical Orthomorphic Projection

© Oxford Cartographers
+44 (0) 1865 882 884

Faroe Is.
(Denmark)

Trondheim

Shetland Is.

Bergen

Oslo

Västerå

Örebro

N

50°N

Hebrides

Orkney Is.

Stavanger

Kristiansand

Jönkö

Gothenburg

North

Skagerrak

Ålborg

Inverness

Aberdeen

Dundee

Glasgow

Edinburgh

Londonderry

Belfast

UNITED

Newcastle
upon Tyne

Sea

Århus

Helsingborg

Copenhagen

DENMARK

Malmö

Galway

Dublin

REP OF
IRELAND

Cork

KINGDOM

Liverpool

Manchester

Leeds

Sheffield

Stoke-
on-Trent

Odense

Kiel

Rostock

Bo
(D

Norwich

Hamburg

Elbe

Szc

Swansea

Cardiff

Birmingham

Bristol

London

Amsterdam

NETHERLANDS

Rotterdam

Bremen

Osnabrück

Hanover

Berlin

Plymouth

Southampton

Antwerp

Brussels

Münster

Essen

Düsseldorf

Cologne

Leipzig

Dresden

Chemnitz

English Channel

Lille

BELGIUM

GERMANY

Cherbourg

Le Havre

Amiens

Frankfurt

Plzeň

Prag

Brest

Caen

Rouen

Seine

LUX.

Luxembourg

CZECH

Reims

Metz

Mannheim

Nuremberg

Regensburg

Rennes

Paris

Strasbourg

Nancy

Rhine

Stuttgart

Danube

Nantes

Loire

Orléans

Dijon

Munich

Salzburg

Vie

Tours

FRANCE

Zurich

Bern

SWITZERLAND

LIECH.

Innsbruck

AUSTRI

Graz

Bay of

Limoges

Geneva

Lyon

Mt. Blanc
4808

Grenoble

Trento

SLOV.

Ljubljana

Trieste

Rijeka

Biscay

Bordeaux

Clermont-
Ferrand

Milan

Po

Verona

Venice

CROA

La Coruña

Gijón

Turin

Parma

Bologne

SAN
MARINO

Vigo

Bilbao

Pamplona

San Sebastian

Montpellier

Nîmes

Genoa

La Spezia

Adr

León

Oporto

Douro

Burgos

Valladolid

Zaragoza

Toulouse

Rhône

Nice

MONACO

Livorno

Florence

Ancona

Coimbra

Salamanca

ANDORRA

Marseille

Apennines

Pescara

Lerida

Corsica
(Fr.)

Rome

ITALY

Lisbon

PORTUGAL

Tagus

Madrid

Ajaccio

Setúbal

Badajoz

S P A I N

Barcelona

Valencia

Balearic Is.
(Sp.)

Naples

Sa

Huelva

Córdoba

Palma

Sardinia
(It.)

Sassari

Faro

Seville

Granada

Murcia

Mallorca

M e d i t e r r a n e a

Cadiz

Málaga

Almeria

Cartagena

Cagliari

Palermo

Messin

Tangier

Gibraltar(U.K.)

Ceuta(Sp.)

Sicily

Rabat

Tétouan

Melilla(Sp.)

Oran

Algiers

Blida

Skikda

Annaba

Tunis

Casablanca

Fès

Meknès

Oujda

Sidi Bel Abbès

Constantine

Valletta

MALTA

M O R O C C O

Mountains

A L G E R I A

TUNISIA

10°W

Atlas

0°

10°E

Sfax

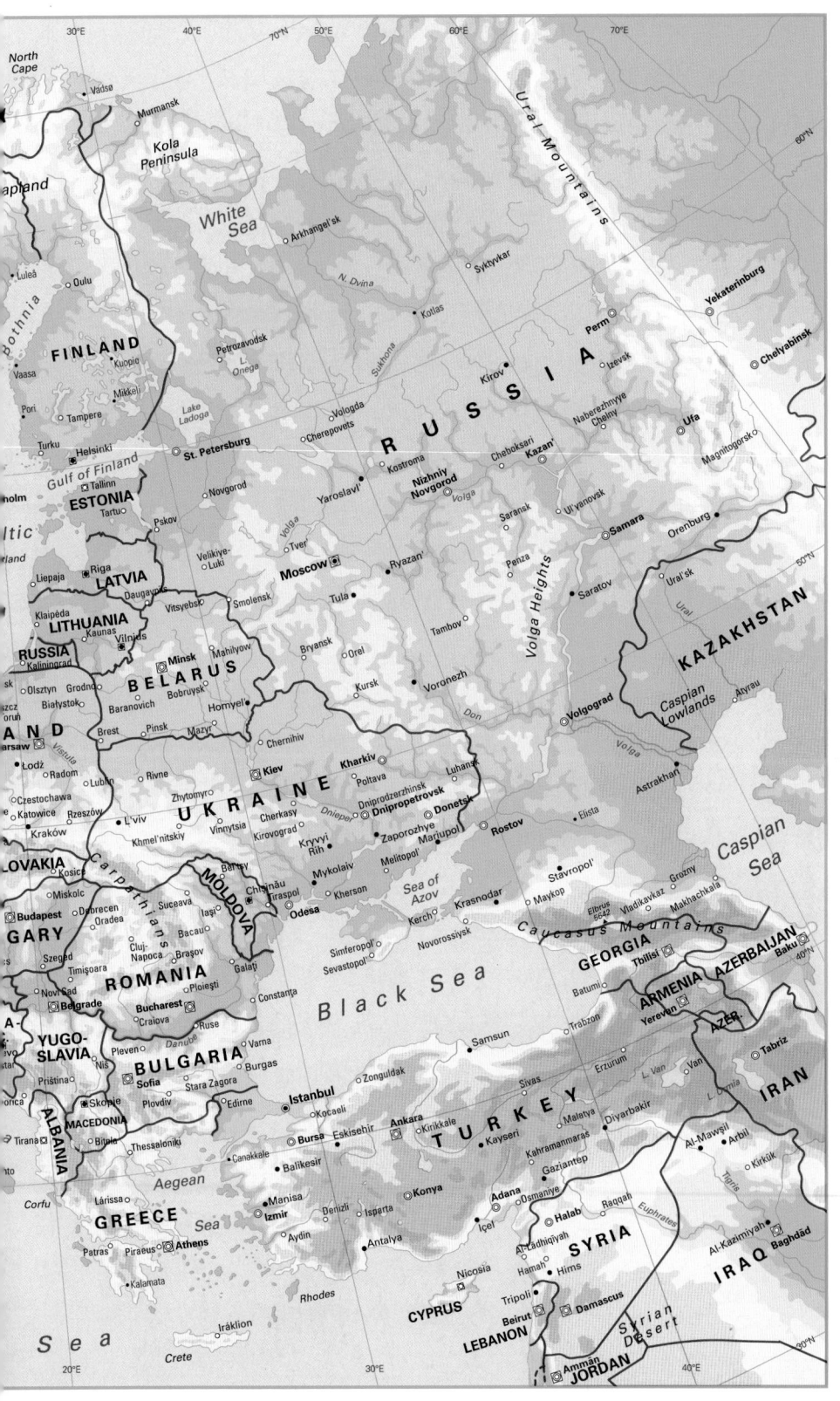

North
Cape

30°E   40°E   70°N   50°E   60°E   70°E

•Vadsø
•Vardø

Murmansk

Kola
Peninsula

60°N

apland

Lapland

White
Sea   •Arkhangel'sk

Yekaterinburg

•Luleå

•Oulu

N. Dvina
Syktyvkar

Bothnia

Kotlas

Perm
Izevsk   •Chelyabinsk

FINLAND   Petrozavodsk   Kirov   Ufa

•Vaasa   •Kuopio   L.
Onega   Naberezhnyye
Chelny

•Pori   Lake
Ladoga   •Vologda   R   U   S   S   I   A   Magnitogorsk•

•Tampere   Mikkeli   Cherepovets

•Turku   Helsinki   St. Petersburg   Kostroma   Cheboksari   Kazan'   Ufa

holm   Gulf of Finland   Novgorod   Yaroslavl'   Nizhniy
Novgorod   Saransk   Ulyanovsk   Orenburg

ltic   ESTONIA   Tallinn   Tartu   Pskov   Tver   Volga   Saransk   Samara   50°N

land   Velikiye-
Luki   Ryazan'   Penza   Saratov

rland   •Riga   LATVIA   Vitsyebsk   Smolensk   Moscow   Tula   Ural'sk

•Liepaja   Daugavpils   Volga   KAZAKHSTAN
Klaipeda   LITHUANIA   Bryansk   •Orel   Voronezh   Ural

sk   •Olsztyn Grodno   Kaunas   Vilnius   Mahilyow   Kursk   Volga Heights   Astrakhan

szcz   •Białystok   RUSSIA   Minsk   Bobruysk   Caspian
Lowlands   Atyrau
orun   Kaliningrad   BELARUS   Hornyel'   Voronezh   Volgograd

AND   •Brest   Pinsk   Mazyr   Don   Volga

arsaw   •Lodz   Vistula   Chernihiv   Elista

•Radom   •Rivne   Zhytomyr   Kiev   Kharkiv   Caspian
Sea

Czestochowa   L'viv   UKRAINE   Poltava   Luhansk

Katowice   Rzeszów   Khmel'nitskiy   Vinnytsia   Cherkasy   Dnipropetrovsk   Donets'k

•Kraków   Kirovograd   Dnieper   Zaporozhye   Mariupol   Rostov

LOVAKIA   Carpathians   Kryvyi   Melitopol'   Stavropol'

•Kosice   Barsay   Mykolaiv   Sea of   Krasnodar   Grozny

•Miskolc   MOLDOVA   Chisinau   Kherson   Azov   Maykop   Makhachkala
Budapest   Debrecen   Suceava   Tiraspol'   Kerch   Caucasus Mountains   Elbrus
5642   Vladikavkaz

GARY   Oradea   Iasi   Bacau   Odesa   Novorossiysk   GEORGIA   AZERBAIJAN
•Szeged   Cluj-
Napoca   Brasov   Galati   Simferopol   Tbilisi   Baku   40°N
•Timisoara   ROMANIA   Sevastopol'   Batumi   ARMENIA AZERBAIJAN
•Novi Sad   Ploiesti   Black Sea   Trabzon   Yerevan   AZER.
A—   Belgrade   Bucharest   Ruse   Constanta

ÃYO   YUGO-
SLAVIA   Craiova   Danube   Pleven   Varna   Samsun   IRAN
•Priština   Niš   BULGARIA   Burgas   Erzurum   L. Van •Van   •Tabriz

onica   •Skopje   Sofia   Stara Zagora   Zonguldak   Sivas   L. Urmia

ALBANIA   Plovdiv   Edirne   Istanbul   Ankara   T U R K E Y   Al-Mawsil   •Arbil

•Tirana   MACEDONIA   Bitola   Kocaeli   Kirikkale   Malatya   Diyarbakir   Kirkuk

Thessaloniki   Canakkale   Bursa   Eskisehir   Kahramanmaras   Gaziantep   Tigris

Aegean   Balikesir   Kayseri   Adana   Euphrates

Corfu   •Lárissa   GREECE   Manisa   Konya   Osmaniye   Halab   Raqqah   IRAQ   Baghdad
Sea   Izmir   Denizli Isparta   Içel   SYRIA   Al-Kazimiyah

Patras Piraeus Athens   Aydin   Antalya   Al-Ladhiqiyah

•Kalamata   Nicosia   Hamah Hims   Al-Kazimiyah
S e a   Rhodes   CYPRUS   Tripoli   Damascus   Syrian
Desert   30°N

Iráklion   Beirut   LEBANON   Amman
Crete   JORDAN

20°E   30°E   40°E

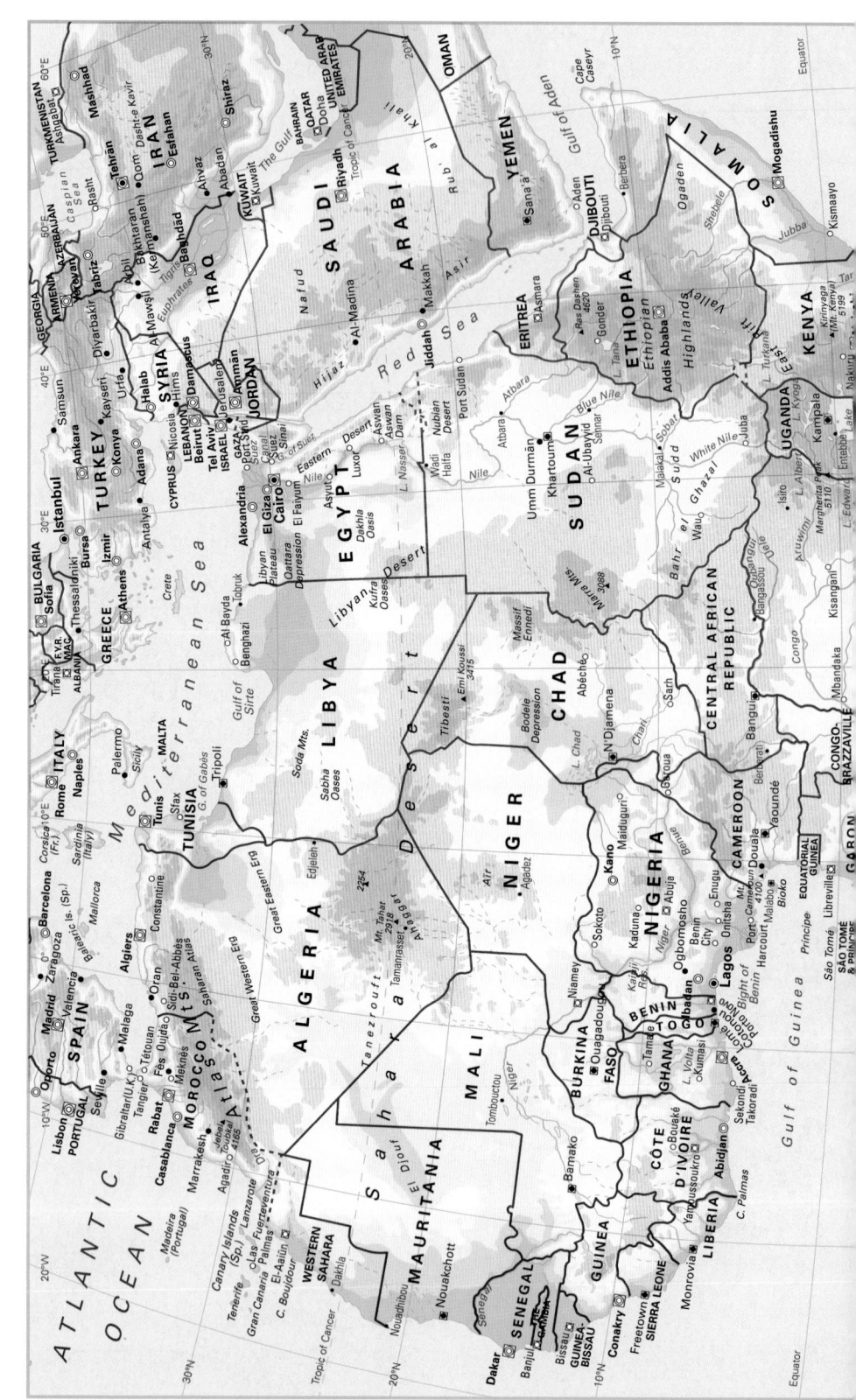

ATLANTIC OCEAN

INDIAN OCEAN

TANZANIA
Dar es Salaam
Zanzibar
Tanga
Dodoma
Tabora
Mbeya
Great Rift Valley
Tanganyika
L. Mweru

MADAGASCAR
Antsiranana
Toamasina
Mahajanga
Antananarivo
Fianarantsoa
Tolanaro
Toliara
Morondava
Ankaratra Mts
Tropic of Capricorn

COMOROS
Mayotte (France)

MOZAMBIQUE
Mozambique Channel
Mtwara
Cape Delgado
Pemba
Nacala
Nampula
Quelimane
Beira
Inhambane
Maputo
Ruvuma
Rufiji

MALAWI
L. Nyasa
(L. Malawi)
Lilongwe
Blantyre
Zambezi

ZAMBIA
Lusaka
Kitwe
Ndola
Kabwe
Lukumbashi
Bangweulu
Mweru
Likasi
Kolwezi
Kamina
Kananga
M'buji Mayi
Kalemie

ZIMBABWE
Harare
Bulawayo
Gweru
Francistown
L. Kariba
Cabora Bassa
Muchinga Mts
Livingstone
Victoria Falls

BOTSWANA
Gaborone
Makgadikgadi Salt Pan
Kalahari Desert
Okavango Delta
Molopo

NAMIBIA
Windhoek
Etosha Pan
Namib Desert
Tsumeb
Swakopmund
Walvis Bay
Lüderitz
Keetmanshoop
Cubango
Cunene

ANGOLA
Luanda
Huambo
Bié Plateau
Lobito
Benguela
Lubango
Namibe
Malanje
Cuango
Cuanza
Matadi
CABINDA (Angola)
Pointe Noire

Kinshasa
Kikwit
Kasai
Kwango

SOUTH AFRICA
Pretoria
Johannesburg
Soweto
Klerksdorp
Kimberley
Bloemfontein
Cape Town
Cape of Good Hope
Cape Agulhas
Worcester
Great Karoo
Beaufort West
Port Elizabeth
East London
Durban
Pietermaritzburg
Umtata
Drakensberg
Orange
Vaal
Port Nolloth

SWAZILAND
Mbabane

LESOTHO
Maseru
Thabana Ntlenyana 3482

Messina

St. Helena (U.K.)
Ascension I. (U.K.)
Tropic of Capricorn

0   200   400   600   800 Miles
0   200 400 600 800 1000 1200 Kms

Zenithal Equal Area Projection

© Oxford Cartographers
+44 (0) 1865 882 884

Arctic Circle

ICELAND
Reykjavík

Arctic Circle

60°N

70°N

Denmark Strait

Nunap Isua
(Cape Farewell)

K a l a a l l i t   N u n a a t
(Greenland)
(Denmark)

80°N

Nuuk
(Godthåb)

30°W

60°W

90°W

120°W

150°W

Davis Strait

B a f f i n
B a y

Ellesmere Island

Devon I.

Qikiqtaluk
(Baffin Island)

Foxe
Basin

Iqaluit

Resolution
Island

Hudson Strait

Ungava
Bay

Kuujjuaq
(Fort Chimo)

Ungava
Peninsula

Schefferville

Labrador

NEWFOUNDLAND

Gander

St. John's

St. Pierre &
Miquelon (Fr.)

Newfoundland

Sydney

Cape
Breton I.

Île
d'Anticosti

Gulf of Saint
Lawrence

Gaspé
Peninsula

NEW
BRUNSWICK
Fredericton

PRINCE
EDWARD
ISLAND

ARCTIC

OCEAN

80°N

Banks
Island

Queen Elizabeth Islands

Parry Islands

Viscount Melville
Sound

Prince of
Wales I.

Somerset
Island

Boothia
Penin.

Melville
Penin.

Southampton
Island

Coats I.

Mansel I.

Iglulligaarjuk
(Chesterfield Inlet)

H u d s o n

B a y

Belcher
Is.

James
Bay

Moosonee

Moose
Factory

Lac
Mistassini

QUÉBEC

Chicoutimi

Québec

Rouyn-
Noranda

Sudbury

Victoria
Island

Beaufort
Sea

Barrow

Inuvik

N O R T H W E S T

Norman
Wells

Mackenzie

Great Bear
Lake

T E R R I T O R I E S

Yellowknife

Great Slave
Lake

Hay
River

N U N A V U T

Uranium
City

Churchill

Reindeer
Lake

Lake
Athabasca

MANITOBA

Lake
Winnipeg

Flin Flon

Sept-Îles

Fort George

Timmins

Sault Ste
Marie

ONTARIO

Lake
Nipigon

Albany

Thunder
Bay

Lake
Superior

Duluth

MINNESOTA

70°N

RUSSIA

Bering Strait

Seward
Peninsula

Nome

Brooks Range

Arctic Circle

Fort Yukon

ALASKA
(U.S.A.)

Fairbanks

Yukon

Mackenzie Mts.

Dawson

YUKON
TERRITORY

Whitehorse

Fort Nelson

Dawson
Creek

Peace
River

Peace
River

ALBERTA

Edmonton

Red Deer

C A N A D A

Saskatoon

SASKATCHEWAN

Moose
Jaw

Regina

Brandon

Lake
Manitoba

Winnipeg

Kenora

NORTH
DAKOTA

Fargo

Grand
Forks

Bismarck

SOUTH
MINN
DAKOTA

Mt. McKinley
6194

Alaska Range

Anchorage

Cordova

Seward

Kodiak I.

Gulf of
Alaska

Juneau

Mt. Logan
5959

Coast
Mountains

Prince
George

BRITISH
COLUMBIA

R o c k y

Kamloops

Columbia

Fraser

Mt. Robson
3945

Calgary

G r e a t

Medicine
Hat

Lethbridge

M o u n t a i n s

MONTANA

Great Falls

Billings

Yellowstone

Butte

Missouri

P l a

Casper

WYO

Bethel

Bristol
Bay

Alaska Peninsula

B e r i n g

S e a

60°N

Aleutian Islands

50°N

Vancouver I.

Mt. Waddington 3394

Prince Rupert

Queen
Charlotte
Islands

Alexander
Archipelago

Victoria

Vancouver

Seattle

Tacoma

Mt. Rainier
4392

WASHINGTON

Portland

Spokane

Blue Mts.

IDAHO

Boise

OREGON

Snake

Great
Basin

Idaho Falls

Pocatello

Great
Salt
Lake

Mt. Shasta
4317

Eureka

Sierra Nev.

Reno

NEV

Coast

Range

C a s c a d e

Range

Sacramento

San Francisco

San Jose

N O R T H

P A C I F I C

O C E A N

40°N

60°N

40°W

CUBA
80°W
Camagüey
Turks & Caicos
Islands (U.K.)
70°W
60°W
50°W
40°W
20°N
20°N
Greater
Santiago
de Cuba
Guantanamo
Cayman Is.
(U.K.)
Port-au-Prince
HAITI
DOMINICAN REP.
Kingston
JAMAICA
San Juan
Leeward Is.
ANTIGUA &
BARBUDA
Santo
Domingo
Puerto
Rico
(U.S.A.)
Guadeloupe (Fr.)

N O R T H

HONDURAS
Caribbean Sea
Lesser
Antilles
DOMINICA
Martinique (Fr.)

A T L A N T I C
10°N

NICARAGUA
Lake
Nicaragua
Neth.
Antilles
ST. LUCIA
BARBADOS
10°N
Limón
Barranquilla
Maracaibo
Caracas
GRENADA
TRINIDAD
& TOBAGO
Port of Spain

O C E A N
COSTA
RICA
Colón
Cartagena
L. Maracaibo
Barquisimeto
Panama
PANAMA
City
Bucaramanga
Cúcuta
Mérida
Orinoco
Ciudad Guayana
Ciudad Bolívar
Gulf of Panama
Llanos
Manizales
Medellín
VENEZUELA
Georgetown
Paramaribo
Buenaventura
Bogotá
GUYANA
SURINAME
Cayenne
French
Guiana
Cali
Magdalena
Guaviare
Guiana
Equator
Tumaco
COLOMBIA
Boa Vista
Highlands
Equator
Quito
Cotopaxi
5896
ECUADOR
Japurá
Marajó I.
Belém
Guayaquil
Chimborazo
6310
Negro
Amazon
São Luís
Cuenca
Iquitos
Leticia
Manaus
Santarém
Fernando de
Noronha
(Brazil)
Sullana
Marañón
Amazon
Madeira
Bacabal
Teresina
Fortaleza
Chiclayo
Cajamarca
Juruá
Purús
Tapajós
Xingu
Floriano
Juàzeiro
do Norte
Mossoró
Natal
Trujillo
Cruzeiro do Sul
Selvas
B R A Z I L
Parnaíba
Campina
Grande
João Pessoa
Chimbote
Pucallpa
Pôrto
Velho
Rio Branco
Tocantins
Juazeiro
Paulo
Afonso
Recife
Callao
Huánuco
Serra dos Parecis
Maceió
Lima
Huancayo
PERU
Mamoré
São Francisco
Feira de
Santana
Aracajú
10°S
Cuzco
Trinidad
Mato Grosso
Barreiras
Salvador
10°S
Puno
Titicaca
BOLIVIA
B r a z i l i a n
Arequipa
La Paz
Cochabamba
Plateau
Cuiabá
Brasília
Ilhéus
Mollendo
Oruro
Santa Cruz
Goiânia
H i g h l a n d s
Montes Claros
Arica
Potosí
Sucre
Corumbá
Uberlândia
Governador
Iquique
Tarija
Campo Grande
Uberaba
Belo Horizonte
Valadares
Ribeirão
Prêto
Caratinga
Vitória
20°S
Tropic of Capricorn
Antofagasta
San Salvador
de Jujuy
PARAGUAY
Concepción
Marília
Londrina
Campinas
São
Paulo
Campos
Rio de Janeiro
Sorocaba
20°S
San Miguel
de Tucumán
Asunción
Paraná
Santos
Tropic of Capricorn
Salta
Gran Chaco
Formosa
Cascavel
Curitiba
San Félix
(Chile)
San
Ambrosio
(Chile)
Copiapó
Santiago
del Estero
Resistencia
Corrientes
Plateau
Passo
Fundo
Florianópolis
Catamarca
Posadas
Santa
Maria
La Serena
La Rioja
Uruguay
Jacuarembó
Porto Alegre
30°S
Cerro
Aconcagua
6960
San Juan
Santa Fé
Paraná
Pélotas
Paysandú
30°S
Juan
Fernández Is.
(Chile)
Valparaíso
Mendoza
Córdoba
Rosario
Durazno
Rocha
Santiago
San Luis
Buenos
Aires
URUGUAY
Montevideo
Rancagua
Talca
Pampas
La
Plata
Río de la Plata
P A C I F I C
S O U T H
Concepción
Chillán
Colorado
Bahía
Blanca
Mar del Plata
A T L A N T I C
Valdivia
Negro
Viedma
Osorno
A R G E N T I N A
Puerto Montt
Chiloé
Island
Valdés
Peninsula
O C E A N
Trelew
O C E A N
40°S
40°S
Comodoro Rivadavia
G. of S.
George
Coihaique
Taitao
Peninsula
Deseado
L. Buenos
Aires
Patagonia
Rio Gallegos
Stanley
Falkland
Islands
(U.K.)
Punta Arenas
Magellan Strait
Tierra del
Fuego
Ushuaia
Cape
Horn
Oblique Mercator Projection
© Oxford Cartographers
+44 (0) 1865 882 884
0   200   400   600 Miles
0   200 400 600 800 1000 Kms
South
Georgia
(U.K.)
South
Shetland
Islands
(U.K.)
South
Orkney
Islands
(U.K.)
South
Sandwich
Islands
(U.K.)
50°S
50°S
100°W
90°W
80°W
70°W
60°W
60°S
50°W
40°W
60°S
30°W
20°W
10°W

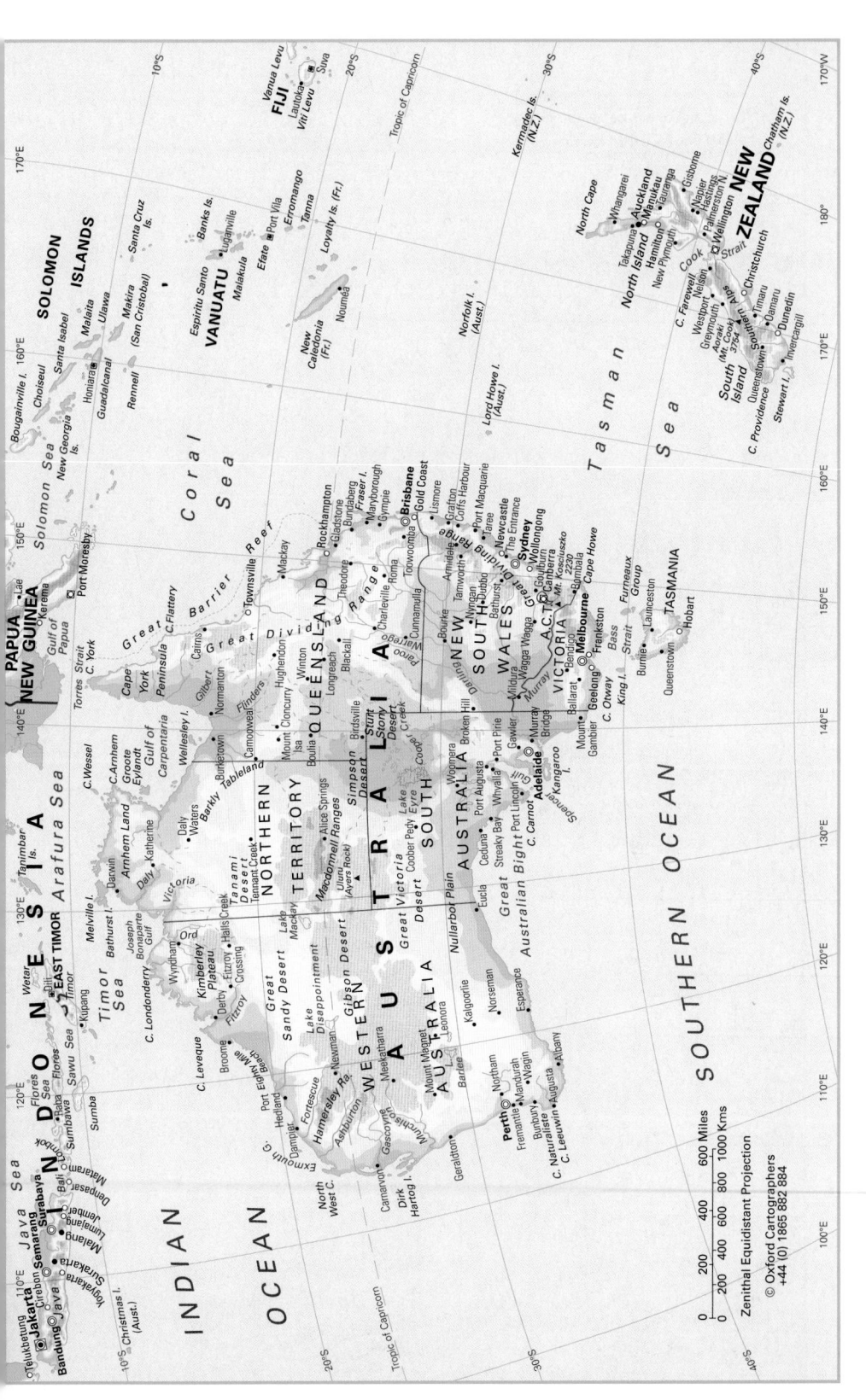

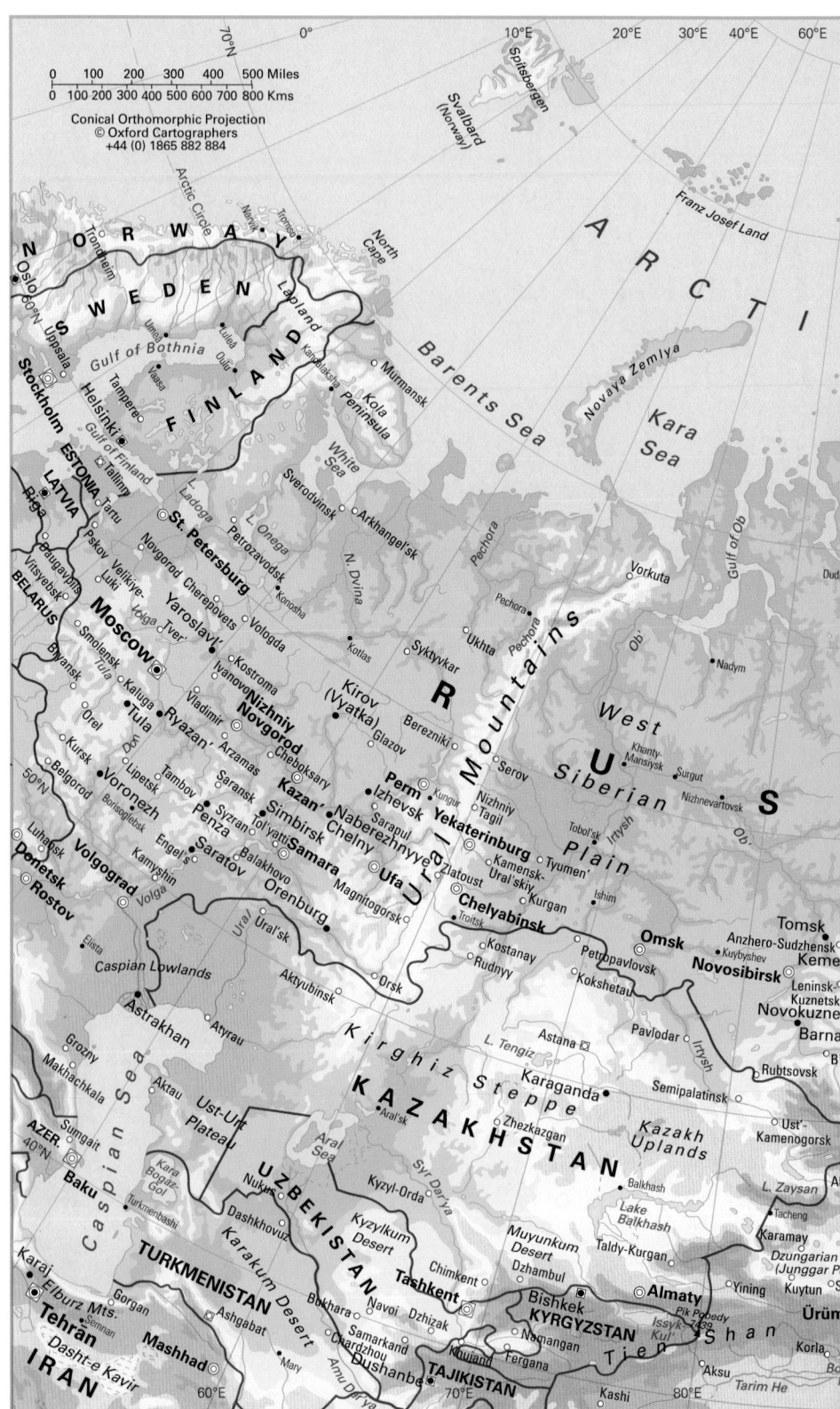

0°   10°E   20°E   30°E   40°E   60°E
70°N

0   100   200   300   400   500 Miles
0 100 200 300 400 500 600 700 800 Kms

Conical Orthomorphic Projection
© Oxford Cartographers
+44 (0) 1865 882 884

Spitsbergen

Svalbard
(Norway)

A R C T I

Franz Josef Land

Arctic Circle

Narvik   Tromsø

N O R W A Y

Trondheim

North
Cape

Barents Sea

Novaya Zemlya

Kara
Sea

S W E D E N

Lapland

Oslo Trondheim
60°N

Umeå

Uppsala

Luleå   Kandalaksha
Oulu

Murmansk

Kola
Peninsula

Gulf of Bothnia

Stockholm   Tampere   Vaasa

Helsinki

F I N L A N D

White
Sea

Sverodvinsk   Arkhangel'sk

ESTONIA   Tallinn
Gulf of Finland

LATVIA   Tartu

Riga   L. Ladoga

St. Petersburg

L. Onega
Petrozavodsk

N. Dvina

Kotlas

Vorkuta

Gulf of Ob

Dudi

Psków   Velikiye-
Luki   Novgorod   Cherepovets   Vologda

Pechora

BELARUS   Vitsyebsk
Daugavpils

Moscow   Yaroslavl'
Tver'
Volga

Pechora

Ukhta   Pechora

Ob'

Nadym

Smolensk
Bryansk   Tula   Kaluga

Ivanovo
Kostroma

Vladimir

Kirov
(Vyatka)   Glazov

Berezniki

M o u n t a i n s

West

Syktyvkar

Serov   Khanty-
Mansiysk   Surgut

Siberian

R U S S

Orel   Tula   Ryazan'   Nizhniy
Novgorod   Cheboksary

Kursk   Lipetsk   Tambov   Arzamas

Perm'   Kungur   Nizhniy
Tagil

Kazan'   Izhevsk   Yekaterinburg   Tyumen'   Nizhnevartovsk

Belgorod   Voronezh   Saransk   Naberezhnyye   Sarapul

Borisoglebsk   Penza   Syzran'   Simbirsk   Tol'yatti   Chelny
Saratov   Balakhovo   Samara   Ufa

Tobol'sk   Irtysh
Kamensk-
Ural'skiy

Plain

Ob'

50°N

Luhansk   Volgograd
Donetsk   Engels

Kamyshin   Orenburg

Magnitogorsk

Zlatoust

Chelyabinsk   Kurgan

Ishim

Tomsk   Anzhero-Sudzhensk
Kuybyshev   Keme

Rostov   Volga

Troitsk

Omsk   Novosibirsk

Ural   Ural'sk

Kostanay   Petropavlovsk
Rudnyy   Kokshetau

Leninsk-
Kuznetsk
Novokuzne

Elista

Caspian Lowlands

Aktyubinsk

Orsk

Pavlodar   Irtysh   Barna

Astrakhan

Atyrau

K i r g h i z   S t e p p e

Astana

Semipalatinsk   Rubtsovsk

Grozny
Makhachkala   Aktau

Ust-Urt
Plateau

L. Tengiz

Karaganda

Ust'-
Kamenogorsk

Sumgait

AZER.
40°N   Baku

Kara
Bogaz-
Gol'   Turkmenbashi

K A Z A K H S T A N

Aral'sk

Zhezkazgan

Kazakh
Uplands

L. Zaysan

Aral
Sea

Kyzyl-Orda

Balkhash

Tacheng

C a s p i a n   S e a

U Z B E K I S T A N

Nukus

Kyzylkum
Desert

Syr Dar'ya

Lake
Balkhash

Karamay

Dzungarian
(Junggar Pe

Karaj
Elburz Mts.   Gorgan

Dashkhovuz

Karakum Desert

Kyzyl
Desert

Muyunkum
Desert   Taldy-Kurgan

Yining   Kuytun

Ürüm

TURKMENISTAN   Bukhara   Navoi

Chimkent

Dzhambul

Almaty

Pik Pobedy
7439   S h a n

Korla   Ba

Tehrän   Semnan
Mashhad   Ashgabat

Dashkhovuz   Chardzhou

Tashkent

Samarkand
Koujand

Bishkek
KYRGYZSTAN
Namangan

Issyk-
Kul

Tien

Aksu   Tarim He

80°E

IRAN   Dasht-e Kavir

60°E   Mary   Amu Dar'ya

TAJIKISTAN   70°E   Dushanbe

Fergana

Kashi

°E 120°E 140°E 150°E 160°E 170°E 70°N 180°

Severnaya Zemlya

O C E A N

New Siberia Is.

Laptev Sea

Lyakhov Is.

Tiksi

Olenek

Taymyr Pen.

L. Taymyr

East Siberian Sea

Wrangel I.

Tevek Anadyr Range

Anadyr

Indigirka

Kolyma

Cherskogo Range

Yana

Koryak Range

60°N

Kolyma Mts.

Okhotsk Magadan

Sea of Okhotsk

sk

Central

Siberian

Plateau

S I A

S

Verkhoyansk Range

Lena

Vilyuy

Yakutsk

Aldan

Dzhugdzhur Range

Sakhalin

50°N

Lensk

Olekminsk

Nyurungri

Stanovoy Mts.

Tynda

Skovorodino

Amur

Skovorodino

Belogorsk

Blagoveshchensk

Komsomol'sk na-Amure

Amur

Tunguska

Angara

Ust'
Ilimsk

Ust'-Kut

Severobaikal'sk

Chita

Sretensk

Yablonovyy Mts.

Da Hinggan Ling

Bei'an

Birobidzhan

Khabarovsk

Achinsk Kansk Tayshek

Krasnoyarsk

Bratsk

Tulun

Lake Baikal

Hailar

Yichun

Shuangyashan

Abakan

Sayan Mts.

Usol'ye-
Sibirskoye
Angarsk

Ulan-
Ude

Manzhouli

Hegang

Quitaihe
Jixi

Jiamusi

Kyzyl

Irkutsk

Daihan

Ondorhaan

Ulanhot

Qiqihar

Daqing

Harbin

Mudanjiang

Ussuriysk

Hövsgöl
Nuur

Ulaanbaatar

Baicheng

Jilin

Yanji

Vladivostok

Uvs Nuur

Hangayan Mts.

Changchun

Siping Liaoyuan

Chongjin

DEM. PEOPLE'S
REP. OF KOREA

Hovd

Saynshand

Tongliao

Fushun

40°N

Altay

M O N G O L I A

INNER MONGOLIA

Chifeng

Shenyang

Anshan

Pyongyang

Itai Range

Gobi Desert

Fuxin
Jinzhou

Chengde

Korea
Bay

Seoul

Hami

Zhang-
jiakou

Jining

Beijing

Tangshan

Dalian

Inchon

Yantai

REP. OF
KOREA

Depression

Baotou

Hohhot

(Peking)

Tianjin

Weihai

Linhe

He (Yellow) Datong

Baoding

Cangzhou

Zibo

Bo Hai

Lop Nur

Wuhai

Huang

Shizuishan

Taiyuan

Yuci

Shijiazhuang

Dezhou

Handan Jinan

Weifang

Qingdao

Yellow
Sea

C   H   I   N

100°E

110°E

120°E

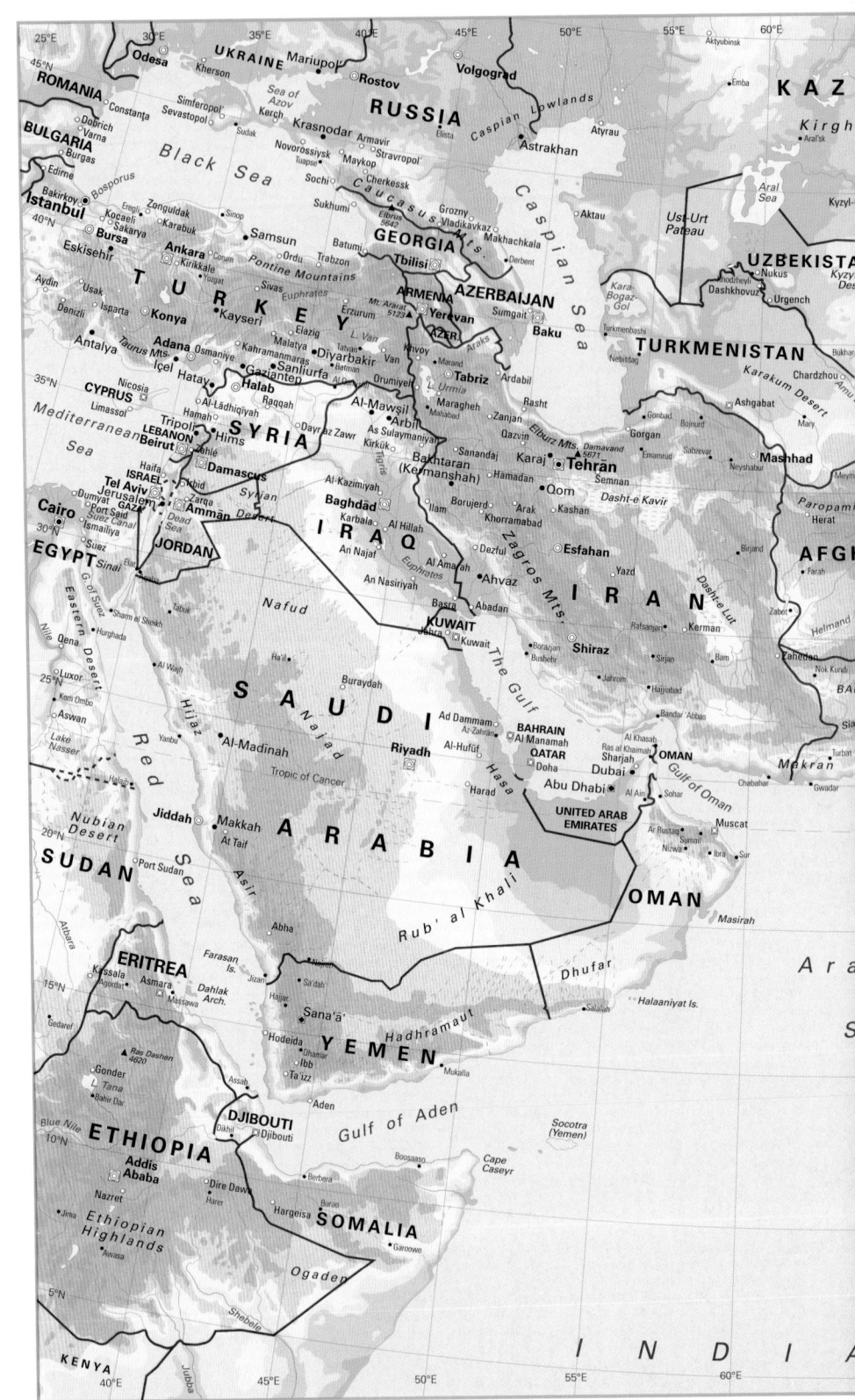

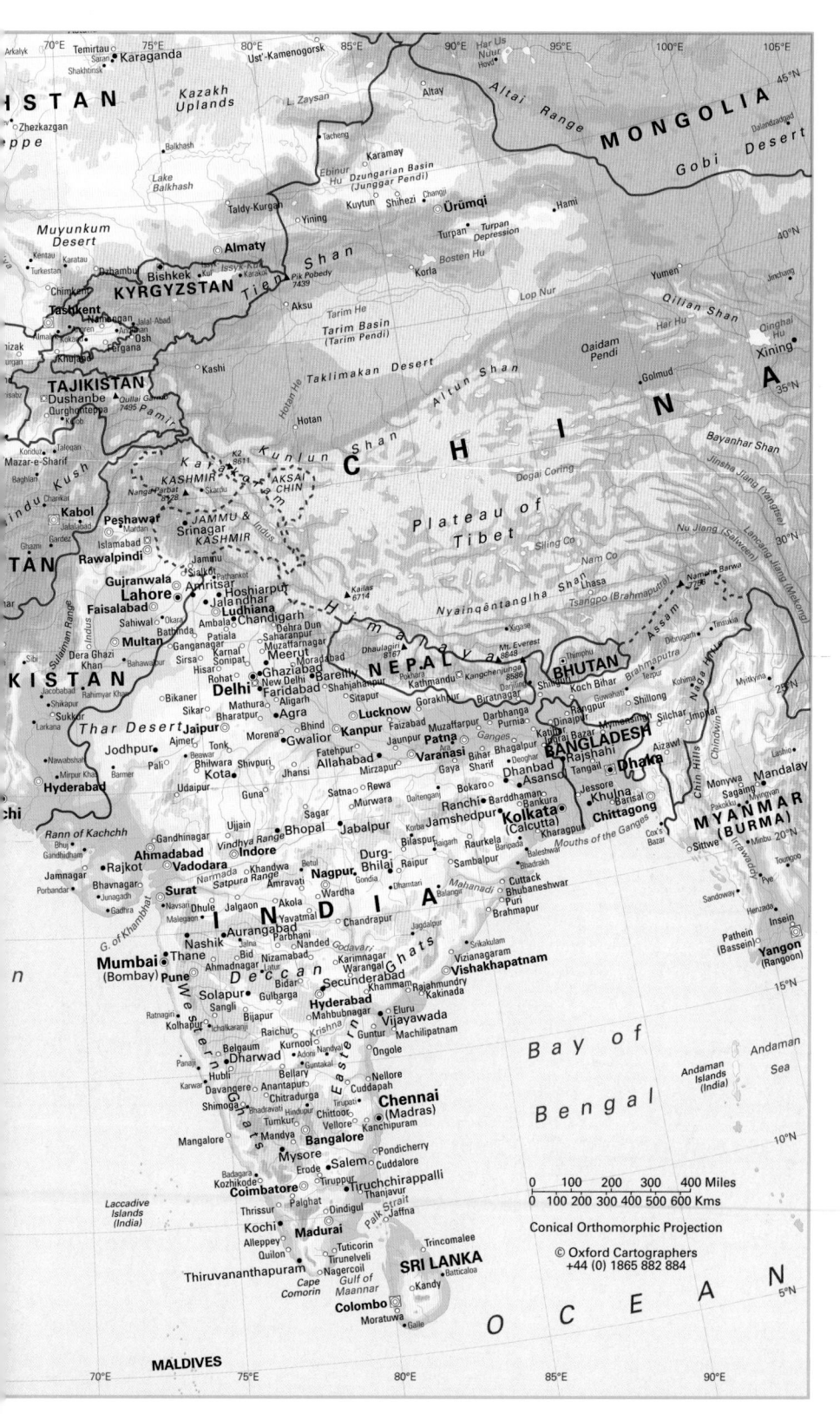

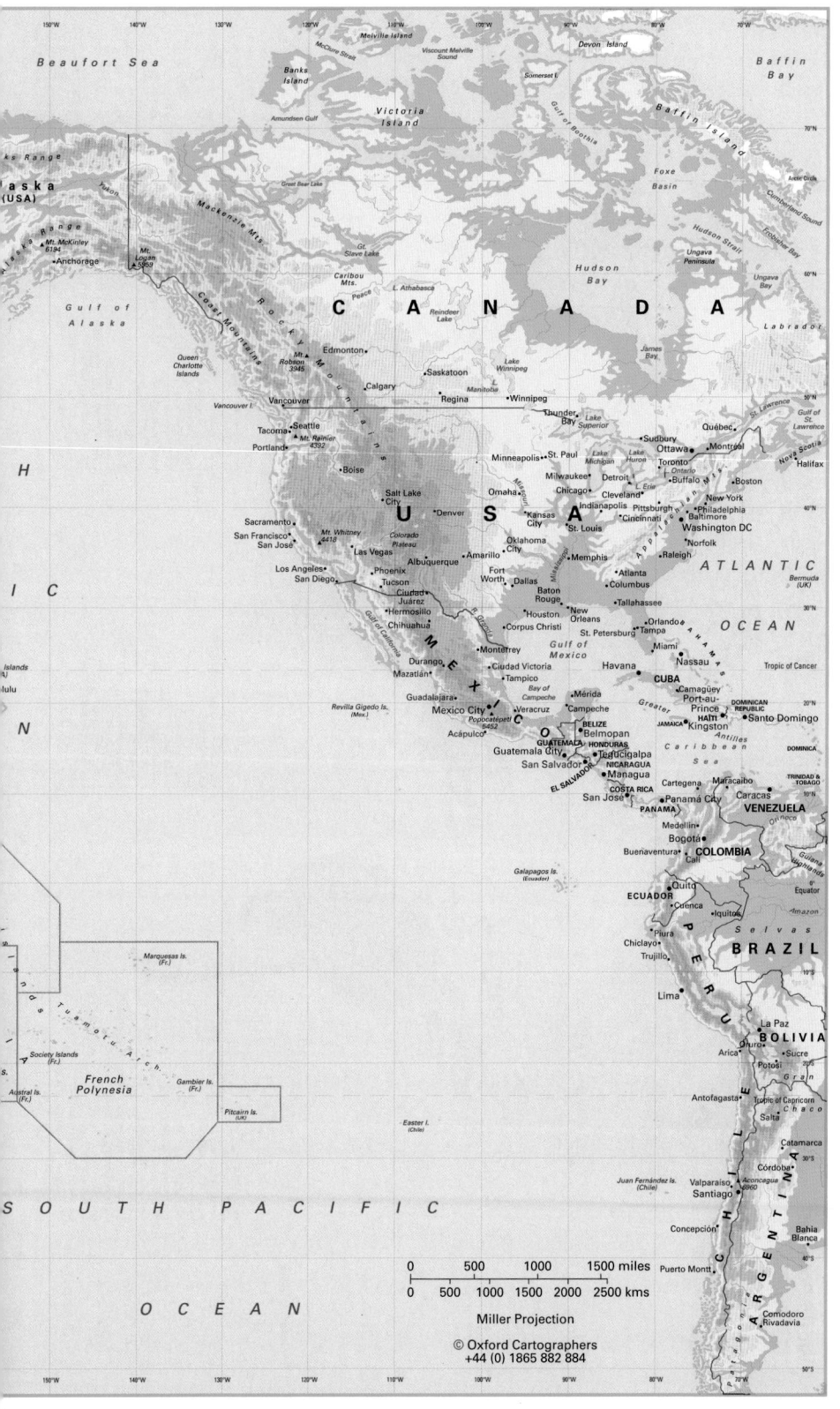

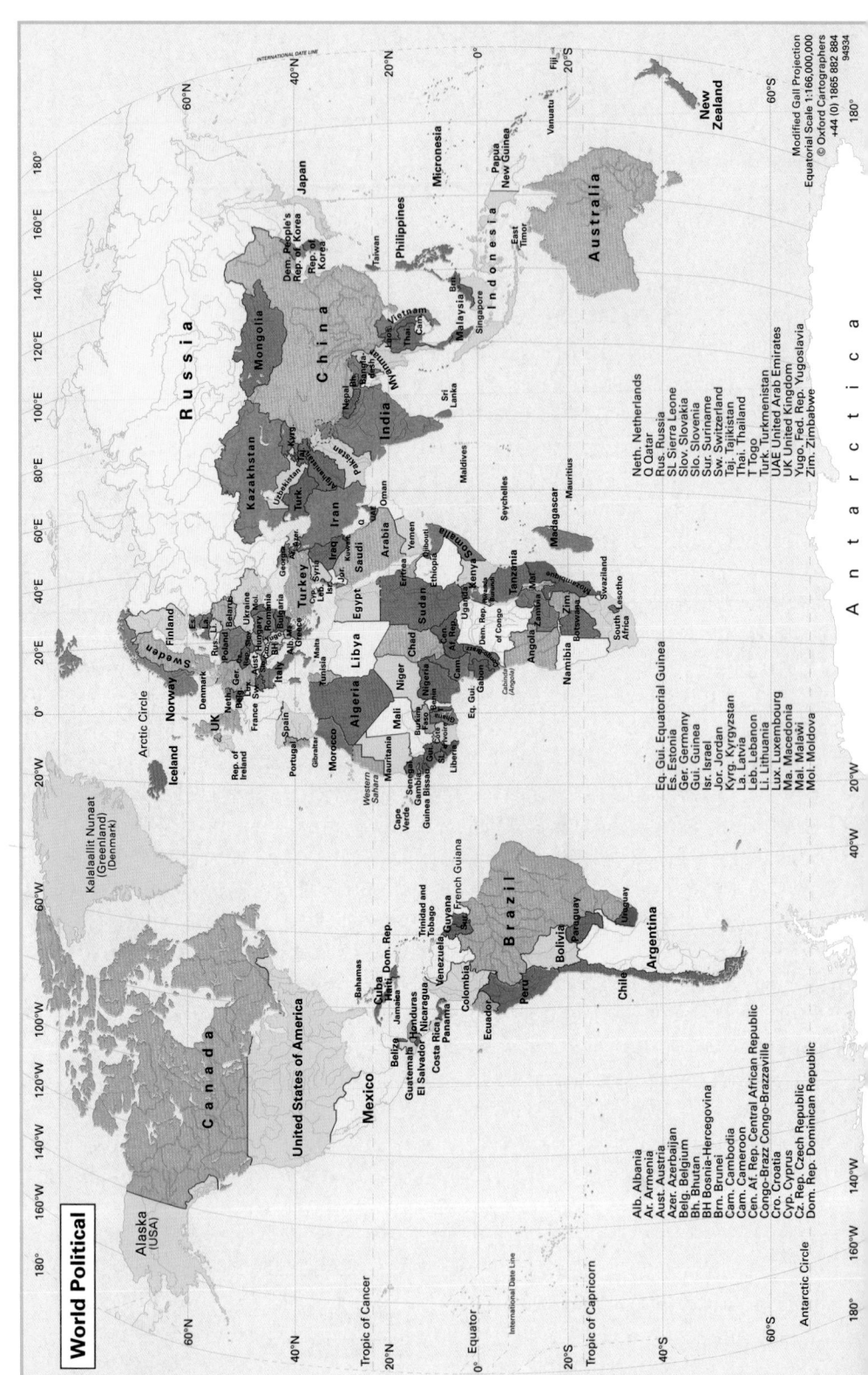

World Political

Tropic of Cancer
Arctic Circle
Tropic of Capricorn
Equator
International Date Line
Antarctic Circle

180°   160°W   140°W   120°W   100°W   80°W   60°W   40°W   20°W   0°   20°E   40°E   60°E   80°E   100°E   120°E   140°E   160°E   180°

60°N   40°N   20°N   0°   20°S   40°S   60°S

40°N   20°N   0°   20°S   40°S   60°S

INTERNATIONAL DATE LINE

Alaska (USA)

Kalaallit Nunaat (Greenland) (Denmark)

Canada

United States of America

Mexico

Bahamas
Cuba
Haiti   Dom. Rep.
Jamaica
Belize
Guatemala   Honduras
El Salvador   Nicaragua
Costa Rica   Panama
Trinidad and Tobago
Venezuela   Guyana
Colombia   Sur.   French Guiana
Ecuador
Peru
Brazil
Bolivia
Paraguay
Chile
Argentina
Uruguay

Iceland
Rep. of Ireland
UK
Norway
Sweden
Finland
Denmark
Neth.
France
Spain
Portugal
Gibraltar
Morocco
Western Sahara
Mauritania
Mali
Senegal
Cape Verde
Gambia
Guinea-Bissau
Guinea
Sierra Leone
Liberia
Côte d'Ivoire
Burkina Faso
Ghana
Togo
Benin
Niger
Nigeria
Cameroon
Eq. Gui.
Gabon
Cabinda (Angola)
Congo-Brazzaville
Dem. Rep. of Congo
Angola
Namibia
Botswana
South Africa
Lesotho
Swaziland
Zimbabwe
Zambia
Mozambique
Malawi
Tanzania
Madagascar
Mauritius
Seychelles
Comoros
Kenya
Uganda
Rwanda
Burundi
Somalia
Ethiopia
Eritrea
Djibouti
Sudan
Chad
Libya
Egypt
Tunisia
Algeria

Alb. Albania
Aus. Austria
Bel. Belgium
BH Bosnia-Hercegovina
Bulg. Bulgaria
Cro. Croatia
Cze. Czech Republic
Est. Estonia
Ger. Germany
Hung. Hungary
Lat. Latvia
Lith. Lithuania
Lux. Luxembourg
Mac. Macedonia
Mol. Moldova
Neth. Netherlands
Pol. Poland
Rom. Romania
Slo. Slovenia
Svk. Slovakia
Switz. Switzerland
Yugo. Yugoslavia

Russia
Kazakhstan
Uzbekistan
Turkmenistan
Kyrg.
Tajikistan
Afghanistan
Pakistan
Iran
Iraq
Kuwait
Saudi Arabia
Yemen
Oman
UAE
Qatar
Bahrain
Turkey
Greece
Cyprus
Syria
Lebanon
Israel
Jordan
Georgia
Armenia
Azerbaijan

Mongolia
China
Nepal
Bhutan
Bangladesh
India
Sri Lanka
Maldives
Myanmar
Laos
Thailand
Vietnam
Cambodia
Malaysia
Singapore
Indonesia
Brunei
Philippines
Taiwan
Dem. People's Rep. of Korea
Rep. of Korea
Japan

Micronesia
Papua New Guinea
East Timor
Australia
New Zealand
Fiji
Vanuatu

Antarctica

Alb. Albania
Ar. Armenia
Aust. Austria
Azer. Azerbaijan
Belg. Belgium
Bh. Bhutan
BH Bosnia-Hercegovina
Brn. Brunei
Cam. Cambodia
Cam. Cameroon
Cen. Af. Rep. Central African Republic
Congo-Brazz Congo-Brazzaville
Cro. Croatia
Cyp. Cyprus
Cz. Rep. Czech Republic
Dom. Rep. Dominican Republic

Eq. Gui. Equatorial Guinea
Es. Estonia
Ger. Germany
Gui. Guinea
Isr. Israel
Jor. Jordan
Kyrg. Kyrgyzstan
La. Latvia
Leb. Lebanon
Li. Lithuania
Lux. Luxembourg
Ma. Macedonia
Mal. Malawi
Mol. Moldova

Neth. Netherlands
Q Qatar
Rus. Russia
SL. Sierra Leone
Slov. Slovakia
Slo. Slovenia
Sur. Suriname
Sw. Switzerland
Taj. Tajikistan
Thai. Thailand
T Togo
Turk. Turkmenistan
UAE United Arab Emirates
UK United Kingdom
Yugo. Fed. Rep. Yugoslavia
Zim. Zimbabwe

Modified Gall Projection
Equatorial Scale 1:166,000,000
© Oxford Cartographers
+44 (0) 1865 882 884
94934

JAMAICA

AREA – 4,243 sq. miles (10,990 sq. km)
POPULATION – 2,665,636 (2001 estimate). The official language is English; a local patois is also spoken
CAPITAL – Ψ Kingston (population, 524,638, 1991)
MAJOR CITIES – Mandeville; May Pen; Ψ Montego Bay; Ocho Rios; Spanish Town
CURRENCY – Jamaican dollar (J$) of 100 cents
NATIONAL ANTHEM – Jamaica, Land We Love
NATIONAL DAY – 6 August (Independence Day)
NATIONAL FLAG – Gold diagonal cross forming triangles of green at top and bottom, triangles of black at hoist and in fly
LIFE EXPECTANCY (years) – male 73.7; female 77.8
POPULATION GROWTH RATE – 0.9 per cent (1999)
POPULATION DENSITY – 236 per sq. km (1999)
URBAN POPULATION – 43.3 per cent (1999)
MILITARY EXPENDITURE – 0.7 per cent of GDP (2000)
MILITARY PERSONNEL – 2,830: Army 2,500, Coast Guard 190, Air Wing 140
ILLITERACY RATE – 12.4 per cent (2002)
ENROLMENT (percentage of age group) – primary 100 per cent (1999); secondary 69 per cent (1999); tertiary 13 per cent (1999)

Jamaica is divided into three counties (Surrey, Middlesex and Cornwall) and 14 parishes. The island consists mainly of coastal plains, divided by the Blue Mountain range in the east and the hills and limestone plateaux in the central and western areas of the interior. The central chain of the Blue Mountains is over 6,000 feet above sea level, and the Blue Mountain Peak is 7,402 feet.

HISTORY AND POLITICS

The island was discovered by Columbus in 1494, and occupied by Spain from 1509 until 1655 when an English expedition under Admiral Penn and General Venables captured the island. In 1670 it was formally ceded to England by the Treaty of Madrid. Jamaica became an independent state within the Commonwealth on 6 August 1962.

At the general election of 18 December 1997, the People's National Party won 50 out of a total of 60 seats, securing a third term for the party and a second term for Prime Minister Percival Patterson. Elections were due to be held in December 2002.

POLITICAL SYSTEM

Queen Elizabeth II is the head of state, represented by the Governor-General. The legislature consists of a Senate of 21 nominated members and a House of Representatives consisting of 60 members elected by universal adult suffrage for a five-year term. The prime minister is the leader of the majority party in the House.
Governor-General, HE Sir Howard Felix Hanlon Cooke, GCMG, GCVO, apptd 1991

CABINET as at July 2002

Prime Minister, Defence, Percival J. Patterson, QC
Agriculture, Roger Clarke
Attorney-General, Legal Affairs and Justice, Arnold Nicholson
Education and Culture, Burchell Whiteman
Finance and Planning, Omar Davies
Foreign Affairs and Foreign Trade, Keith Desmond Knight
Health, John Junor
Industry, Commerce and Technology, Phillip Paulwell

Information (in the Office of the Prime Minister), Colin Campbell
Labour and Social Security, Donald Buchanan
Land and Environment, Horace Dalley
Local Government, Youth and Community Development, Arnold Bertram
Mining and Energy, Anthony Hylton
National Security, Peter Phillips
Tourism and Sports, Gender Affairs, Portia Simpson Miller
Transportation and Works, Robert Pickersgill
Water and Housing, Enoch Carl Blythe

JAMAICAN HIGH COMMISSION
1–2 Prince Consort Road, London SW7 2BZ
Tel: 020-7823 9911
High Commissioner, HE David Muirhead, apptd 1999

BRITISH HIGH COMMISSION
PO Box 575, Trafalgar Road, Kingston 10
Tel: (00 1 876) 926 9050
Email: bhckingston@cw.com
High Commissioner, HE A. F. Smith, apptd 1999

BRITISH COUNCIL MANAGER, Nicola Johnson, British High Commission, 28 Trafalgar Road, Kingston 10; Email: bcjamaica@britishcouncil.org.jm

ECONOMY

Alumina, bananas, bauxite and sugar are the main exports. Other exports include garments, processed food products, limestone and horticultural products. A task force was established in January 2001 to foster an increase in sugar production. The country's first gold mine became operational in March 2001.

Since 1989 the PNP government has abolished price subsidies, removed foreign exchange controls and introduced a 10 per cent consumption tax. Jamaica is a popular tourist resort, attracting 2,012,738 visitors in 1999. The economy has faced many problems, including interest repayments on debt which accounted for 41 per cent of government revenue in 1999, low market prices for many of Jamaica's exports and interest rates of over 30 per cent.

In 1999 Jamaica had a trade deficit of US$1,140 million and a current account deficit of US$273 million. In 2000 imports totalled US$3,216 million and exports US$1,296 million.
GNP – US$6,382 million (2000); US$2,430 per capita (1999)
GDP – US$4,280 million (1999); US$1,487 per capita (1999)
ANNUAL AVERAGE GROWTH OF GDP – 0.8 per cent (2000)
INFLATION RATE – 8.2 per cent (2000)
UNEMPLOYMENT – 15.8 per cent (1999)
TOTAL EXTERNAL DEBT – US$3,913 million (1999)

Trade with UK	2000	2001
Imports from UK	£60,306,000	£70,674,000
Exports to UK	124,884,000	117,910,000

COMMUNICATIONS

There are several excellent harbours, Kingston being the principal port. The island has 2,944 miles of main roads and 7,264 miles of subsidiary roads.

There are two international airports, the Norman Manley International Airport on the south coast serving Kingston, and Sangster Airport on the north coast serving the major tourist areas.

JAPAN
Nihon-koku – State of Japan

AREA – 145,880 sq. miles (377,829 sq. km)
POPULATION – 126,771,662 (2001 estimate). The
principal religions are Mahayana Buddhism and
Shinto. About 1 per cent of Japanese are Christians.
The language is Japanese
CAPITAL – Tokyo (population, 11,880,000, 1998
estimate)
MAJOR CITIES – Ψ Fukuoka (1,308,379); Ψ Kōbe
(1,425,139); Kyōto, the ancient capital (1,461,974);
Ψ Nagoya (2,154,376); Ψ Ōsaka (2,595,674); Sapporo
(1,790,886); Ψ Yokohama (3,339,594), 1997 estimates
CURRENCY – Yen
NATIONAL ANTHEM – Kimigayo (His Majesty's Reign)
NATIONAL FLAG – White, charged with sun (red)
LIFE EXPECTANCY (years) – male 77.8; female 85.0
POPULATION GROWTH RATE – 0.3 per cent (1999)
POPULATION DENSITY – 335 per sq. km (1999)
URBAN POPULATION – 78.1 per cent (1995)

Japan consists of four large islands: *Honshū* (or
Mainland) 88,839 sq. miles (230,448 sq. km), *Shikoku*,
7,231 sq. miles (18,757 sq. km), *Kyūshū*, 16,170 sq. miles
(42,079 sq. km), *Hokkaidō*, 30,265 sq. miles (78,508 sq.
km), and many small islands (including *Okinawa*).
The interior is very mountainous, and crossing the
mainland from the Sea of Japan to the Pacific is a group
of volcanoes, mainly extinct or dormant. Mount Fuji, the
most sacred mountain of Japan, is 12,370 ft high and has
been dormant since 1707, but volcanoes which are active
include Mount Aso in Kyūshū. There are frequent
earthquakes, mainly along the Pacific coast near the Bay
of Tōkyō. The climate varies from sub-tropical in the
south to cool temperate in the north.

HISTORY AND POLITICS

According to tradition, Jimmu, the first Emperor of
Japan, ascended the throne on 11 February 660 BC. Under
the *Meiji* constitution (1889), the monarchy is hereditary
in the male heirs of the Imperial house.

After the unconditional surrender to the Allied nations
(14 August 1945), Japan was occupied by Allied forces
under General MacArthur. A Japanese peace treaty
became effective on 28 April 1952. Japan then resumed
her status as an independent power.

The (conservative) Liberal Democratic Party (LDP)
governed Japan almost without interruption from the
Second World War until 1993.

Following the general election held on 25 June 2000, the
Liberal Democratic Party remained the largest party but
failed to retain its overall majority, winning 233 seats. The
LDP formed a coalition with its previous partners, New
Komeito and the New Conservative Party, which
accounted for 271 of the 480 seats in the Diet. Prime
Minister Yoshiro Mori resigned on 7 April 2001 following
mounting criticism of his performance and was replaced
by Junichiro Koizumi on 26 April.

POLITICAL SYSTEM

Legislative authority rests with the bicameral Diet
(Kokkai), which comprises a 480-member House of
Representatives, and a 247-member House of
Councillors. The House of Representatives chooses the
prime minister from among its ranks, ratifies treaties and
passes budget bills. Since January 2000, 180 of its
members are elected by proportional representation in 11
regional blocks and 300 in single-member, first-past-the-

post constituencies. All members serve four-year terms.
The House of Councillors elects half its members every
three years for six-year terms. Unlike the lower House it
cannot be dissolved by the prime minister. Executive
authority is vested in the Cabinet which is responsible to
the legislature.

HEAD OF STATE

His Imperial Majesty The Emperor of Japan, Emperor
Akihito, born 23 December 1933; *succeeded* 8 January
1989; *enthroned* 12 November 1990; *married* 10 April
1959, Miss Michiko Shoda, and has *issue*: the Crown
Prince, Prince Fumihito, *born* 30 November 1965; and
Princess Sayako, *born* 18 April 1969
Heir, HRH Crown Prince Naruhito Hironomiya, *born* 23
February 1960, *married* 9 June 1993, Miss Masako Owada

CABINET *as at July 2002*

Prime Minister, Junichiro Koizumi (LDP)
Agriculture, Forestry and Fisheries, Tsutomu Takebe
(LDP)
Economy, Trade and Industry, Takeo Hiranuma (LDP)
Education, Culture, Sports, Science and Technology,
Atsuko Toyama (Ind.)
Environment, Hiroshi Oki (Ind.)
Finance, Masajuro Shiokawa (LDP)
Foreign Affairs, Yoriko Kawaguchi (Ind)
Health, Labour and Welfare, Chikara Sakaguchi (NK)
Justice, Mayumi Moriyama (LDP)
Land, Infrastructure and Transport, Chikage Ogi (NCP)
*Public Management, Home Affairs, Posts and
Telecommunications*, Toranosuke Katayama (LDP)

LDP Liberal Democratic Party; NCP New Conservative
Party; NK New Komeito; Ind. Independent

EMBASSY OF JAPAN
101–104 Piccadilly, London W1J 7JT
Tel: 020-7465 6500
Ambassador Extraordinary and Plenipotentiary, HE
Masaki Orita, apptd 2001

BRITISH EMBASSY
No. 1 Ichiban-cho, Chiyoda-ku, Tokyo 102-8381
Tel: (00 81) (3) 5211-1100
Email: embassy@tokyo.mail.fco.gov.uk
Ambassador Extraordinary and Plenipotentiary, HE Sir
Stephen Gomersall, KCMG, apptd 1999

CONSULATES-GENERAL – Tokyo, Osaka
Honorary Consulates – Fukuoka, Hiroshima, Nagoya,
Sapporo

BRITISH COUNCIL DIRECTOR, Terry Toney, 1-2
Kagurazaka, Shinjuku-ku, Tokyo 162-0825;
Email: bctokyo@britishcouncil.or.jp. Regional offices
in Fukuoka, Kyoto, Nagoya and Osaka

DEFENCE

The constitution prohibits the maintenance of armed
forces, although internal security forces were created in
the 1950s and their mission was extended in 1954 to
include the defence of Japan against aggression. In the
1990s legislation was passed permitting the armed forces
limited participation in UN peacekeeping missions and
allowing them to enter foreign conflicts in order to rescue
Japanese nationals. A revision to the USA–Japan defence
co-operation guidelines agreed in 1997 permits Japan to
play a supporting role in US military operations in areas
surrounding Japan.

The Ground Self-Defence Force (GSDF) has 1,050 main battle tanks, around 750 armoured personnel carriers, 60 infantry fighting vehicles, 10 aircraft and 90 attack helicopters. The Maritime Self-Defence Force (MSDF) has 16 submarines, 42 destroyers, 12 frigates, three patrol and coastal vessels, 80 combat aircraft and 90 armed helicopters at five bases. The Air Self-Defence Force (ASDF) has 297 combat aircraft.

The USA has 38,330 personnel stationed in Japan.

MILITARY EXPENDITURE – 1.0 per cent of GDP (2000)
MILITARY PERSONNEL – 239,800: Army 148,700, Navy 44,200, Air Force 45,400; Paramilitaries 12,250

ECONOMY

Owing to the mountainous nature of the country less than 20 per cent of its area can be cultivated and only 14 per cent is used for agriculture; 67 per cent is wooded. The soil is only moderately fertile but intensive cultivation secures good crops. Tobacco, tea, potatoes, rice, maize, wheat and other cereals are all cultivated. Rice is the staple food of the people.

Mineral resources include gold, silver, copper, lead, zinc, iron chromite, white arsenic, coal, sulphur, petroleum, salt and uranium. However, iron ore, coal and crude oil are among the principal imports.

Japan is one of the most highly industrialised nations in the world, with the whole range of modern light and heavy industries, including steel, aerospace, computers, office machinery, motor vehicles, electronics, metals, machinery, chemicals, textiles (cotton, silk, wool and synthetics), cement, pottery, glass, rubber, lumber, paper, oil refining and shipbuilding.

Japan's economy was severely affected by the financial crisis in Asia during the late 1990s. Its banks had made loans totalling some US$200 billion to tiger economies, and following widespread economic collapse in the region, Japan's financial institutions have suffered. Emergency measures announced by the government were perceived by the markets as inadequate. Japan's economy contracted in 1998; GDP fell by 2.8 per cent. Unemployment reached 4.8 per cent, the highest level since the Second World War.

On 21 September 2000 the government unveiled a Yen 4,000 billion economic stimulus package. A package of economic reforms was announced on 5 April 2001, which focused on the structural reform of the financial industry.

GNP – US$4,337,268 million (2000); US$32,030 per capita (1999)
GDP – US$3,782,834 million (1998); US$34,276 per capita (1999)
ANNUAL AVERAGE GROWTH OF GDP – 0.5 per cent (2000)
INFLATION RATE – 0.1 per cent (2001)
UNEMPLOYMENT – 4.7 per cent (2001)

TRADE

Being deficient in natural resources, Japan has had to develop a complex foreign trade. Principal imports include mineral fuels, food, raw materials and metal ores. Principal exports include machinery, transport equipment, chemicals, metal products and textiles.

In 1999 Japan had a trade surplus of US$123,325 million and a current account surplus of US$106,865 million. In 2000 imports totalled US$379,511 million and exports US$479,249 million. The USA, China, Australia, Hong Kong, South Korea, Taiwan and Singapore are Japan's main trading partners.

Trade with UK	2000	2001
Imports from UK	£3,666,672,000	£3,712,360,000
Exports to UK	10,511,063,000	9,375,907,000

COMMUNICATIONS

There are 23,654 km of railway track and 1,152,207 km of roads. Shinkansen (bullet train) tracks are currently being expanded. The opening in 1988 of the Seikan rail tunnel and the Seto Ohashi rail bridge means that the four major islands are now linked for the first time. There are six international airports.

EDUCATION

Education at elementary (six-year course) and lower secondary (three-year course) schools is free, compulsory and co-educational. The (three-year) upper secondary schools are attended by 96.7 per cent of the age group.

There are two or three-year colleges and four-year universities. Some of the universities have graduate schools. In 1999 there were 622 universities and colleges, most of which are privately maintained. The most prominent universities are the seven state universities of Tōkyō, Kyōto, Tohoku (Sendai), Hokkaidō (Sapporo), Kyūshū (Fukuoka), Ōsaka and Nagoya, and the two private universities of Keio and Waseda.

ENROLMENT (percentage of age group) – primary 100 per cent (1997); secondary 100 per cent (1997); tertiary 41 per cent (1997)

CULTURE

Japanese is said to be one of the Ural-Altaic group of languages and remained a spoken tongue until the fifth to seventh centuries AD, when Chinese characters came into use. Modern Japanese is written in a mixture of Chinese characters (about 1,800) and also the syllabary characters called Kana.

JORDAN

Al-Mamlaka al-Urdunniyya al-Hashimiyya – Hashemite Kingdom of Jordan

AREA – 37,738 sq. miles (97,740 sq. km). Neighbours: Syria (north), Israel and the West Bank (west), Saudi Arabia (south and east), Iraq (east)
POPULATION – 5,153,378 (2001 estimate); 4,095,579 (1994 census). The majority are Sunni Muslims and Islam is the religion of the state; however, freedom of belief is guaranteed by the constitution
CAPITAL – 'Ammān (population, 1,270,000, 1997 estimate)
MAJOR CITIES – Irbid (231,511); Az-Zarqā' (389,815), 1997 estimates
CURRENCY – Jordanian dinar (JD) of 1,000 fils
NATIONAL ANTHEM – Asha Al Malik (Long Live The King)
NATIONAL DAY – 25 May (Independence Day)
NATIONAL FLAG – Three horizontal stripes of black, white, green and a red triangle based on the hoist, containing a seven-pointed white star
LIFE EXPECTANCY (years) – male 69.7; female 72.5
POPULATION GROWTH RATE – 3.1 per cent (1999)
POPULATION DENSITY – 66 per sq. km (1999)
ILLITERACY RATE – 9.2 per cent (2002)
ENROLMENT (percentage of age group) – primary 71 per cent (1997); secondary 57 per cent (1997); tertiary 18 per cent (1997)

HISTORY AND POLITICS

After the defeat of Turkey in the First World War, the Amirate of Transjordan was established in the area east of the River Jordan as a state under British mandate. The mandate was terminated after the Second World War and the Amirate, still ruled by its founder the Amir Abdullah, became the Hashemite Kingdom of Jordan. Following the 1948–9 war between Israel and the Arab states, that part of Palestine remaining in Arab hands (the West Bank and East Jerusalem, but excluding Gaza) was, with Palestinian agreement, incorporated into the Hashemite Kingdom. King Abdullah was assassinated in 1951; his son Talal ruled briefly but abdicated in favour of King Hussein in 1952.

Israel captured the West Bank from Jordan in the 1967 war and annexed East Jerusalem. In 1988 Jordan severed its legal and administrative ties with the occupied West Bank, but did not formally renounce sovereignty over the area. As a result of the wars of 1948–9 and 1967 there are about one million Palestinian refugees and displaced persons living in East Jordan, about 200,000 of whom live in refugee and displaced persons camps established by the UN Relief and Works Agency (UNRWA). In addition there are 300,000 self-supporting Palestinians in East Jordan. In 1993, multiparty parliamentary elections were held for the first time since 1956. In elections held on 4 November 1997, pro-government candidates won 62 out of 80 seats; the main opposition parties boycotted the elections. Elections were scheduled for early 2003.

FOREIGN RELATIONS

The Middle East peace process begun in 1991, led to Jordan signing an agreement on a 'common agenda' for peace with Israel in 1993. On 25 July 1994 King Hussein and the Israeli Prime Minister signed a framework agreement for peace which ended the state of war existing since 1948. The first Israeli–Jordanian border crossing was opened between Eilat and Aqaba in August 1994. A full peace treaty was signed on 26 October 1994 which established full diplomatic and economic relations between the two states. It included agreements on sharing water from the Jordan and Yarmouk rivers; co-operating in the fields of commerce, transport, tourism,

communications, energy and agriculture; and granted King Hussein custodianship of Islamic holy sites in Jerusalem. Israeli forces completed their withdrawal from Jordanian land in the Arava valley on 9 February 1995.

On 25 January 1999, King Hussein signed a decree naming his eldest son, Abdullah ibn al-Hussein, as his new heir, in place of his youngest brother, Prince Hassan; Prince Abdullah became King following the death of King Hussein on 7 February 1999.

Jordan and Kuwait re-established full diplomatic relations on 3 March 1999, which had been broken off following the 1990 Gulf War.

POLITICAL SYSTEM

The constitution provides for a Senate of 40 members (all appointed by the King for a four-year term) and an elected House of Representatives which has 104 members, directly elected for a four-year term.

The King appoints the members of the Council of Ministers. In 1991 a new national charter was formulated which lifted the ban on political parties, imposed in 1957.

HEAD OF STATE

His Majesty The King of the Jordan, Abdullah II, *born* 30 January 1962, *succeeded* 7 February 1999

Crown Prince, Hamzeh ibn al-Hussein, *born* 29 March 1982, son of King Hussein of Jordan

Chief of the Royal Court, Fayez Tarawneh

COUNCIL OF MINISTERS *as at July 2002*

Prime Minister, Defence, Ali Abu Ragheb
Deputy Prime Minister, Economic Affairs, Muhammad Halaiqa
Deputy Prime Minister and, Justice and Legal Affairs, Faris Nabulsi
Agriculture, Mahmoud Ayid al-Duwayri
Culture, Haidar Mahmoud
Education, Khalid Tuqan
Energy and Mineral Resources, Muhammad Ali al-Batayinah
Finance, Michel Martu
Foreign Affairs, Marwan Muasher
Health, Salih al-Nasir
Higher Education and Scientific Research, Walid Maani
Industry and Trade, Salah Bashir
Interior, Qaftan Majali
Labour, Muzahem al-Muheisin
Ministers of State, Muhammad Thneibat (*Administrative Development and Culture*); Shaher Bak (*Foreign Affairs*); Mohammad Adwan (*Political Affairs and Information*); Mustafa Qaisi (*Prime Ministry Affairs*)
Municipal, Rural, and Environmental Affairs, Abdul Razzaq Tbeishat
Planning, Bassem Awadallah
Post and Telecommunications, Fawaz Hatim al-Zu'bi
Public Works and Housing, Hosni Abu Gheida
Religious Endowments (Waqfs), Islamic Affairs and Holy Places, Ahmad Hulayyil
Social Development, Tamam Ghul
Tourism and Antiquities, Taleb al-Rifai
Transport, Nadir al-Dhahabi
Water and Irrigation, Hazim al-Nasir

EMBASSY OF THE HASHEMITE KINGDOM OF JORDAN
6 Upper Phillimore Gardens, London W8 7HA
Tel: 020-7937 3685
Ambassador Extraordinary and Plenipotentiary, HE Timoor Daghistani, apptd 1999
Counsellor, Z. S. Rifai

BRITISH EMBASSY
Abdoun (PO Box 87), 'Ammān
Tel: (00 962) (6) 592 3100/6592
Ambassador Extraordinary and Plenipotentiary, HE
Edward Graham Mellish Chaplin, OBE, apptd 2000

BRITISH COUNCIL DIRECTOR, Azza Hammoudi
(acting), Rainbow Street, PO Box 634, 'Ammān
11118; Email: bcamman@britishcouncil.org.jo

DEFENCE

The Army has 1,058 main battle tanks, 1,130 armoured personnel carriers and 26 armoured infantry fighting vehicles. The Navy has three patrol and coastal vessels at its base at Aqaba. The Air Force has 101 combat aircraft and 20 armed helicopters.
MILITARY EXPENDITURE – 6.9 per cent of GDP (2000)
MILITARY PERSONNEL – 100,240: Army 84,700, Navy 540, Air Force 15,000; Paramilitaries 10,000

ECONOMY

The main agricultural areas are the Jordan valley, the hills overlooking the valley, and the flatter country to the south of 'Ammān and around Madaba and Irbid. However, several large farms, which depend for irrigation on water pumped from deep aquifers, have been established in the southern desert area. The rest of the country is desert and semi-desert. The principal crops are wheat, barley, vegetables, olives and fruit. Agricultural production has increased considerably in recent years due to improvements in production and irrigation techniques.

Important industrial products are raw phosphates (1998, 5,925,000 tonnes) and potash (1998, 916,169 tonnes), most of which is exported, together with fertilisers and pharmaceuticals. The Trans-Arabian oil pipeline (Tapline) runs through north Jordan from Saudi Arabia to the Lebanese port of Sidon. A branch pipeline, together with oil trucked by road from Iraq, feeds a refinery at Zerqa, which meets most of Jordan's requirements for refined petroleum products. Sufficient reserves of natural gas have been discovered in the north-east to produce electricity for the national grid since 1989.

In 1998 there was a trade deficit of US$1,602 million and a current account surplus of US$14 million. In 2000 imports totalled US$4,539 million and exports US$1,897 million.
GNP – US$8,224 million (2000); US$1,630 per capita (1999)
GDP – US$8,069 million (1998); US$1,576 per capita (1999)
ANNUAL AVERAGE GROWTH OF GDP – 2.2 per cent (1998)
INFLATION RATE – 0.7 per cent (2000)
TOTAL EXTERNAL DEBT – US$8,947 million (1999)

Trade with UK	2000	2001
Imports from UK	£130,953,000	£168,910,000
Exports to UK	23,433,000	16,681,000

COMMUNICATIONS

'Ammān is linked to Aqaba, Damascus, Baghdād and Jiddah by roads which are of considerable importance in the overland trade of the Middle East.

The former Hejaz Railway runs from Syria through Jordan, and is used mainly for freight between 'Ammān and Damascus. The Aqaba railway carries phosphate rock from the mines of al-Hasa and al-Abiad to Aqaba.

KAZAKHSTAN
Qazaqstan Respūblīkasy - Republic of Kazakhstan

AREA – 1,049,155 sq. miles (2,717,300 sq. km).
Neighbours: Russia (north and west), Turkmenistan, Uzbekistan and Kyrgyzstan (south), China (east)
POPULATION – 15,049,100 (1999 census): Kazakhs (44 per cent), Russians (36 per cent), Ukrainians (5 per cent) and ethnic Germans (4 per cent), with smaller numbers of Tatars, Uzbeks, Koreans and Belarusians. The Russian population is concentrated in the north of the country, where it forms a significant majority, and in Almaty. The majority of ethnic Kazakhs are Sunni Muslims, and this is the main religion of the republic. Kazakh (one of the Turkic languages) became the official language in 1993; a law passed in July 1997 decreed Kazakh as the language of state administration; Russian has a special status as the 'social language between peoples'. Otherwise each ethnic group uses its own language
CAPITAL – Astana (population, 320,000, 2000 estimate. Known as Akmola until May 1998). The capital was moved from Alma-Ata (Almaty) in December 1997
MAJOR CITIES – Almaty (1,061,400); Pavlodar (341,500); Qaraghandy (449,200); Shymkent (439,900), 1998 estimates
CURRENCY – Tenge
NATIONAL DAY – 25 October (Republic Day)
NATIONAL FLAG – Dark blue with a sun and a soaring eagle in the centre all in gold, and a red vertical ornamentation stripe near the hoist
LIFE EXPECTANCY (years) – male 59.6; female 70.7
POPULATION GROWTH RATE – 0.4 per cent (1997)
POPULATION DENSITY – 5 per sq. km (1999)
URBAN POPULATION – 55.2 per cent (1996)
ILLITERACY RATE – 2.5 per cent
ENROLMENT (percentage of age group) – tertiary 33 per cent (1997)

Kazakhstan occupies the northern part of what was Soviet Central Asia. It stretches from the Volga and the Caspian Sea in the west to the Altai and Tienshan mountains in the east. The country consists of arid steppes and semi-deserts, flat in the west, hilly in the east and mountainous in the south-east (Southern Altai and Tienshan mountains). The main rivers are the Irtysh, the Ural, the Syr-Darya and the Ili.

HISTORY AND POLITICS

Kazakhstan was inhabited by nomadic tribes before being invaded by Ghenghiz Khan and incorporated into his empire in 1218. After his empire disintegrated, feudal towns emerged based on large oases. These towns affiliated and established a Kazakh state in the late 15th century which engaged in almost continuous warfare with the marauding Khanates on its southern border. After appealing to Russia for aid and protection, in 1731 Kazakhstan acceded to the Russian Empire under a voluntary act of accession.

After the 1917 Russian revolution, Kazakhstan came under the control of White Russian forces until 1919. On 26 August 1920 a constitution was signed under which Kazakhstan became a Soviet Socialist Republic. Under Soviet rule in the 1920s and 1930s there was rapid industrial development and the traditional nomadic way of life disappeared. The Kazakhs suffered greatly in the Stalinist purges, the merchant and religious classes being murdered and thousands dying in the desert on collective farms. Other nationalities, such as Tatars and Germans, were forcibly transported to Kazakhstan by Stalin.

Kazakhstan declared its independence on 16 December 1991.

The Communist-derived Congress of People's Unity of Kazakhstan (SNEK) won the March 1994 legislative elections which were ruled invalid by the Constitutional Court. The President responded by dissolving parliament in March 1995. Elections to the new legislature were held in December 1995; the requirement for candidates to achieve an absolute majority made run-offs necessary. A referendum on 29 April 1995 extended President Nazarbayev's term until 2000, but constitutional changes unanimously agreed by parliament brought forward presidential elections to 10 January 1999. Elections to the upper chamber of the legislature were held on 17 September 1999 and to the lower house on 10 and 24 October 1999 and were won by the Fatherland Republican Party. On 12 November 2001, a number of government ministers and officials resigned following a joint statement issued on November 16 claiming that 'democratic reforms in Kazakhstan have stopped'. On 28 January 2002, Prime Minister Kasymzhomart Tokaev resigned and was replaced by Imangali Tasmagambetov.

POLITICAL SYSTEM

Executive power is vested in the president and government. The president must be a Kazakh speaker and has the power to appoint the prime minister, other senior ministers and all ambassadors.

A new constitution approved by referendum on 30 August 1995 granted the president the power to dissolve the legislature and to rule by decree. It also nominated Kazakh as the sole official language; prohibited dual citizenship; and created a new bicameral legislature composed of a 39-member Senate, of whom 32 are indirectly elected and seven appointed, and a 77-member directly elected Majlis (lower house of the legislature). The Constitutional Court, which opposed the new constitution, was replaced by a Constitutional Council which was made subject to presidential veto.

HEAD OF STATE

President, Commander-in-Chief of the Armed Forces,
Nursultan Nazarbayev, *elected* 1 December 1991, *confirmed in office by referendum* 29 April 1995, *re-elected* 10 January 1999

GOVERNMENT *as at July 2002*

Prime Minister, Imangali Tasmagambetov
Deputy Prime Ministers, Baurzhan Mukhamedzhanov; Akhmetzhan Yesimov (*Agriculture*); Alexander Pavlov (*Finance*); Karim Kazhimkanovich (*Transport and Communications*) (*acting*)
State Secretary, Foreign Affairs, Kasymzhomart Tokayev
Culture, Information and Social Harmony, Mukhtar Kul-Mukhammbed
Defence, Mukhtar Yesenbayev
Economy and Trade, Mazhit Altynbayev
Energy and Mineral Resources, Vladimir Shkolnik
Head of Prime Minister's Office, Altay Tleuberdin
Interior, Kairbek Suleimenov
Justice, Georgi Kim
Labour and Social Security, Gulzhana Karagusova
Natural Resources and the Environment, Andar Shukputov
Public Health, Zhaksylyk Akmurzayevich Doskaliyev
Science and Education, Shamsha Berkimbayeva
State Revenues, Zeynulla Kakimzhanov
Transport and Communications, Kazhmurat Nagmanov
Without Portfolio, Aitkul Samakova

EMBASSY OF THE REPUBLIC OF KAZAKHSTAN
33 Thurloe Square, London SW7 2SD
Tel: 020-7581 4646
Ambassador Extraordinary and Plenipotentiary,
Y. Idrissov, apptd 2002

BRITISH EMBASSY
Ul. Furmanova 173, Almaty
Tel: (00 7) (3272) 506191/2
Email: british-embassy@kaznet.kz
Ambassador Extraordinary and Plenipotentiary,
HE Richard Lewington, apptd 1999

BRITISH COUNCIL DIRECTOR, James Kennedy,
Republic Square 13, KZ-480013 Almaty;
Email: general@kz.britishcouncil.org

DEFENCE

An agreement signed with Russia in January 1995 provides for eventual reunification of the two states' armed forces. The CIS mutual defence treaty of 1993, to which Kazakhstan is a signatory, retains a common air defence force, while Kazakh forces also take part in the CIS peacekeeping force along the Tajikistan–Afghanistan border. By 1996, all nuclear warheads had been returned to Russia although Kazakhstan retained 48 SS-18 intercontinental ballistic missiles. Kazakhstan participates in the NATO Partnership for Peace programme. The Army has 930 main battle tanks and 1,343 armoured combat vehicles. The Caspian Sea Flotilla, which Kazakhstan shares with Russia and Turkmenistan, operates under Russian command. The Air Force has 164 combat aircraft.
MILITARY EXPENDITURE – 2.0 per cent of GDP (2000)
MILITARY PERSONNEL – 64,000: Army 45,000, Air Force 19,000; Paramilitaries 34,500
CONSCRIPTION DURATION – 31 months

ECONOMY

Kazakhstan is rich in minerals, with copper, lead, gold, uranium, chromium, silver, zinc, iron ore, coal, oil and natural gas. In 1998 production of coal was 68,700,000 tonnes and of iron ore was 18,000,000 tonnes. The oil and gas industry, concentrated in the west of the country, has been expanded by foreign investment, which is also being used to explore the Karachaganak (gas) and Tengiz (oil) fields in the Caspian Sea. Initial exploration of the Kashagan offshore oilfield in 2000 indicated extensive reserves.

Pipelines to Turkey and Russia are in operation and on 27 November 2001, a new pipeline connecting Tengiz to Russia's Novorossiisk was put into operation. Oil production in 1998 was 25.9 million tonnes and gas output was 8.3 billion cubic metres. Industry is dominated by food processing and mining and metals production; textiles, steel and tractors are also produced. The main centres of the metal industry are in the Altai mountains, in Shimkent, north of Lake Balqash and in central Kazakhstan.

Agriculture, including stock-raising, is highly developed, particularly in the central and south-west of the republic. Grain is grown in the north and north-east, and cotton and wool produced in the south and south-east. 12.5 million tonnes of wheat and 3.5 million tonnes of barley were grown in 1999.

A treaty of economic co-operation for 1998–2007 was signed with Russia in October 1998. The tenge was floated on 5 April 1999 in a bid to reduce the trade deficit. Annual trade between Russia and Kazakhstan was maintained at a stable level of $US2.5 billion for several

years. In April 2002, this was reported to have exceeded US$4 billion with Kazakhstan being the third main CIS trading partner of Russia.

In 2000 the trade surplus was US$2,766 million and the current account surplus US$1,074 million. Imports totalled US$5,052 million and exports US$9,140 million.

GNP – US$17,640 million (2000); US$1,250 per capita (1999)

GDP – US$22,324 million (1998); US$982 per capita (1999)

ANNUAL AVERAGE GROWTH OF GDP – 2.5 per cent (1998)

INFLATION RATE – 13.2 per cent (2000)

UNEMPLOYMENT – 3.9 per cent (1999)

TOTAL EXTERNAL DEBT – US$6,182 million (1999)

Trade with UK	2000	2001
Imports from UK	£65,908,000	£92,168,000
Exports to UK	92,088,000	71,052,000

KENYA
Jamhuri ya Kenya - Republic of Kenya

AREA – 224,081 sq. miles (580,367 sq. km). Neighbours: Somalia (east), Ethiopia (north), Sudan (north-west), Uganda (west), Tanzania (south)

POPULATION – 30,765,916 (2001 estimate). The main tribal groups are the Kikuyu, Luhya, Luo, Kalenjin, Kamba and Masai. The official languages are Swahili, which is generally understood throughout Kenya, and English; numerous indigenous languages are also spoken

CAPITAL – Nairobi (population, 2,000,000, 1991 estimate)

MAJOR CITIES – Ψ Kisumu (201,100); Ψ Mombasa (600,000); Nakuru (124,200), 1991 estimates

CURRENCY – Kenya shilling (Ksh) of 100 cents

NATIONAL ANTHEM – Ee Mungu Nguvu Yetu (Oh God Of All Creation)

NATIONAL DAY – 12 December (Independence Day)

NATIONAL FLAG – Horizontally black, red and green with the red fimbriated in white, and with a shield and crossed spears all over in the centre

LIFE EXPECTANCY (years) – male 48.7; female 49.9

POPULATION GROWTH RATE – 1.3 per cent (2001 estimate)

POPULATION DENSITY – 51 per sq. km (1999)

MILITARY EXPENDITURE – 2.9 per cent of GDP (2000)

MILITARY PERSONNEL – 24,400: Army 20,000, Navy 1,400, Air Force 3,000; Paramilitary 5,000

ILLITERACY RATE – 15.7 per cent (2002)

ENROLMENT (percentage of age group) – primary 85 per cent (1997)

HISTORY AND POLITICS
Kenya became an independent state and a member of the British Commonwealth on 12 December 1963 and a republic in 1964. In 1982 the government introduced amendments to the constitution making the country a one-party state, with the Kenya African National Union (KANU) as the ruling party. In December 1991, the government yielded to internal and international pressure and introduced a multiparty democracy.

On 29 December 1997, in elections hampered by heavy flooding and marred by allegations of electoral malpractice, KANU won 109 out of 210 seats in the National Assembly, and President Daniel arap Moi won just over 40 per cent of the vote to win a fifth term in office. Elections are due to be held by early 2003.

POLITICAL SYSTEM
The head of state is a president, directly elected for a five-year term, who is head of government and appoints the Cabinet. The unicameral legislature, the *Bunge* (National Assembly), has 224 members, of whom 210 are directly elected for a five-year term, 12 appointed by the president, and two ex-officio members, the attorney-general and the speaker. In November 1999, an amendment to the constitution was passed which limited the powers of the president over the National Assembly and affirmed the Bunge's supremacy.

HEAD OF STATE
President and C.-in-C. Armed Forces, Daniel T. arap Moi (KANU), *took office* 14 October 1978, *re-elected* 1979, 1983, 1988, 1992 and 29 December 1997
Vice-President, Home Affairs, George Saitoti

CABINET *as at July 2002*

Agriculture, Bonaya Godana
Attorney-General, Amos Wako
Education, Science and Technology, Henry Kiprono Kosgey
Energy, Raila Odinga, Chrysanthus Okemo
Environment, Joseph Kamotho
Finance, Chris Mogere Obure
Foreign Affairs and International Co-operation, Maj. Marsden Madoka
Heritage and Sport, Francis Nyenze
Labour, Joseph Kimen Ngutu
Lands and Settlement, Noah Katana Ngala
Local Government, Uhuru Kenyatta
Medical Services, Hussein Maalim Mohamed
Mineral Exploration, Jackson Kalweo
Ministers of State in the President's Office, Shariff Nassir Taib; William ole Ntimama; Julius Sunkuli; Joseph Nyagah
Planning, Paul Adhu Awiti
Public Health, Samson Ongeri
Roads and Public Works, William Cheruiyot Morogo
Rural Development, Cyrus Jirongo
Science and Technology, Gideon Ndambuki
Tourism and Information, Stephen Kalonzo Musyoka
Trade and Industry, Kipyator Nicholas Biwott
Transport and Communications, Wycliffe Musalia Mudavadi
Vocational Training, Isaac Ruto
Water Resources, Kipng'eno arap Ng'eny

KENYA HIGH COMMISSION
45 Portland Place, London W1N 4AS
Tel: 020-7636 2371/5
High Commissioner, HE Nancy Kirui, apptd 2000
Defence Adviser, Col. B. Y. Haji

BRITISH HIGH COMMISSION
Upper Hill Road, PO Box 30465 Nairobi
Tel: (00 254) (2) 714699
Email: consular@nairobi.fco.gov.uk
High Commissioner, HE E. Clay, CMG,

BRITISH COUNCIL DIRECTOR, Peter Elborn, ICEA Building, Kenyatta Avenue, PO Box 40751, Nairobi; Email: information@britishcouncil.or.ke.

ECONOMY
Agriculture provides about a quarter of GDP and employs around three-quarters of the workforce. The great variation in altitude and ecology provides conditions under which a wide range of crops can be

grown. These include wheat, barley, pyrethrum, coffee, tea, sisal, coconuts, cashew nuts, cotton, maize and a wide variety of tropical and temperate fruits and vegetables.

Mineral production consists of soda ash, salt and limestone. Hydroelectric power has been developed, particularly on the Upper Tana River, and Kenya is now almost self-sufficient in electric power generation.

There has been considerable industrial development over the last 15 years and Kenya has a variety of industries processing agricultural produce and manufacturing products from local and imported raw materials. New industries are steel, textile mills, dehydrated vegetable processing and motor tyre manufacture. Smaller schemes have added to the country's consumer goods manufacturing base. There is an oil refinery in Mombasa supplying both Kenya and Uganda, and a fuel pipeline now connects Mombasa and Nairobi.

In June 2000 the government announced that the state-owned telecommunications company was to be privatised. The government also increased VAT and announced reductions in the number of state employees. Tourism generates some US$400 million per year.

GNP – US$10,715 million (2000); US$360 per capita (1999)

GDP – US$10,809 million (1998); US$355 per capita (1999)

ANNUAL AVERAGE GROWTH OF GDP – 2.7 per cent (1998)

INFLATION RATE – 5.9 per cent (2000)

TOTAL EXTERNAL DEBT – US$6,562 million (1999)

TRADE

Principal exports are coffee and tea, which account for roughly a third of total export earnings. Also exported are fruit, vegetables, and crude animal and vegetable material. Industrial machinery is the largest single import; other imports are transport equipment, petroleum and petroleum products, metals, pharmaceuticals and chemicals.

In 1998 Kenya had a trade deficit of US$1,016 million and a current account deficit of US$363 million. In 2000 imports totalled US$3,105 million and exports US$1,734 million.

Trade with UK	2000	2001
Imports from UK	£165,641,000	£172,887,000
Exports to UK	190,267,000	211,814,000

COMMUNICATIONS

The Kenya Railways Corporation has 2,778 km of railway open to traffic. There are also 67,000 km of road, of which 8,900 km are bitumen surfaced.

The principal port is Mombasa, operated by the Kenya Ports Authority. International air services operate from airports at Nairobi and Mombasa.

KIRIBATI

Ribaberikin Kiribati – Republic of Kiribati

AREA – 280 sq. miles (726 sq. km)

POPULATION – 94,149 (2001 estimate): predominantly Christian. The languages are I-Kiribati and English

CAPITAL – Tarawa (population, 17,921, 1978)

CURRENCY – Australian dollar ($A) of 100 cents

NATIONAL ANTHEM – Teirake Kain Kiribati (Stand Kiribati)

NATIONAL DAY – 12 July (Independence Day)

NATIONAL FLAG – Red, with blue and white wavy lines in base, and in the centre a gold rising sun and a flying frigate bird

LIFE EXPECTANCY (years) – male 58.0; female 63.0

POPULATION GROWTH RATE – 1.4 per cent (1999)

POPULATION DENSITY – 113 per sq. km (1999)

URBAN POPULATION – 39.2 per cent (2000 estimate)

Kiribati (pronounced Kiribas) comprises 36 islands: the Gilberts Group (17) including Banaba (formerly Ocean Island), the Phoenix Islands (8), and the Line Islands (11), which are situated in the south-west central Pacific around the point at which the International Date Line cuts the Equator. The total land area is spread over some 2 million square miles of ocean. Few of the atolls are more than half a mile in width or more than 12 feet high. The vegetation consists mainly of coconut palms, breadfruit trees and pandanus.

HISTORY AND POLITICS

The Gilbert and Ellice Islands were proclaimed a British protectorate in 1892 and annexed as the Gilbert and Ellice Islands Colony on 10 November 1915 (taking effect 12 January 1916). The Gilbert Islands were occupied by the Japanese army during World War II. Nuclear tests were carried out by the British off Kiritimati (Christmas Island) in 1957. In October 1975 the Ellice Islands seceded to become the independent state of Tuvalu. The Gilbert Islands achieved independence on 12 July 1979 as the Republic of Kiribati.

Legislative elections were held on 23 September 1998 and presidential elections held on 27 November 1998 were won by Teburoro Tito. Legislative and presidential elections were to take place by November 2002.

POLITICAL SYSTEM

The president is head of state as well as head of government and is directly elected. There is a House of Assembly of 41 members (39 elected members, the Attorney-General and a representative of the Banaban community from Rabi Island). Executive authority is vested in the Cabinet.

HEAD OF STATE

President, Foreign Affairs, Teburoro Tito, *sworn in* 1 October 1994, *re-elected* 27 November 1998

Vice-President, Finance and Economic Planning, Bniamina Tinga

CABINET *as at July 2002*

Commerce, Industry and Tourism, Moteti Kakoroa

Education, Training and Technology, Teambo Keariki

Environment, Social Development, Kataotika Tekee

Health and Family Planning, Baraniko Mooa

Home Affairs and Rural Development, Natanaera Kirata

Labour, Employment and Co-operatives, Teiraoi Tetabea

Line and Phoenix Islands, Manraoi Kaiea

Natural Resources Development, Tim Taekiti

Transport, Communications and Information, Willie Tokataake

Works and Energy, Teaiwa Tenieu

KIRIBATI HIGH COMMISSION

c/o Office of the President, P.O Box 68, Bairiki, Tarawa, Kiribati

High Commissioner, vacant

Acting High Commissioner, Peter Timeon

BRITISH HIGH COMMISSIONER, HE Michael Price, LVO, resident at Suva, Fiji

ECONOMY

Many people still practise a semi-subsistence economy, the main staples of their diet being coconuts and fish.

The principal imports are foodstuffs, consumer goods, machinery and transport equipment. The principal exports are copra and fish.

In May 2000, Japanese-funded improved port facilities at Betio were opened.

GNP – US$86 million (2000); US$910 per capita (1999)
GDP – US$48 million (1998); US$627 per capita (1999)
ANNUAL AVERAGE GROWTH OF GDP – 2.0 per cent (1998)

Trade with UK	2000	2001
Imports from UK	£338,000	£74,000
Exports to UK	1,000	111,000

COMMUNICATIONS

Air communication exists between most of the islands and is operated by Air Kiribati, a statutory corporation. Air Marshall Islands operates a weekly service between Majuro, Tarawa, Funafuti and Nadi, and Air Nauru between Tarawa, Nauru and Nadi. Inter-island shipping is operated by a statutory corporation, the Shipping Corporation of Kiribati.

EDUCATION

There are 104 primary schools, eight secondary schools and one high school. There is a teacher training college, a technical institute and a marine training centre.

KOREA

Korea's southern and western coasts are fringed with innumerable islands, of which the largest, forming a province of its own, is Cheju. The Korean language is of the Ural-Altaic Group. Its script, Hangul, was invented in the 15th century; prior to this Chinese characters alone were used. Despite the great cultural influence of the Chinese, Koreans have developed and preserved their own cultural heritage.

HISTORY

The Korean peninsula was first unified in AD 668 when Shilla, having emerged as the dominant tribal state, conquered Koguryo and Paekche. The Koryo dynasty ruled from 912 until 1392 and was succeeded by the Choson dynasty, who ruled from 1392 until 1910 when Japan formally annexed Korea. The country remained part of the Japanese Empire until the defeat of Japan in 1945, when it was occupied by troops of the USA and the USSR, the 38th parallel being fixed as the boundary between the two zones of occupation.

The UN in November 1947 resolved that elections should be held for a National Assembly which, when elected, should set up a government. The Soviet government refused to comply and a UN commission was only allowed to operate south of the 38th parallel. A general election was held on 10 May 1948, and the first National Assembly met in Seoul on 31 May. The Assembly passed a constitution on 12 July and on 15 August 1948 the republic was formally inaugurated and American military government came to an end. Meanwhile, in the Soviet-occupied zone north of the 38th parallel the Democratic People's Republic had been established with its capital at Pyongyang. A Supreme People's Soviet was elected in September 1948, and a Soviet-style constitution adopted.

THE KOREAN WAR

Korea remained divided along the 38th parallel until June 1950, when North Korean forces invaded South Korea. In response to Security Council recommendations, 16

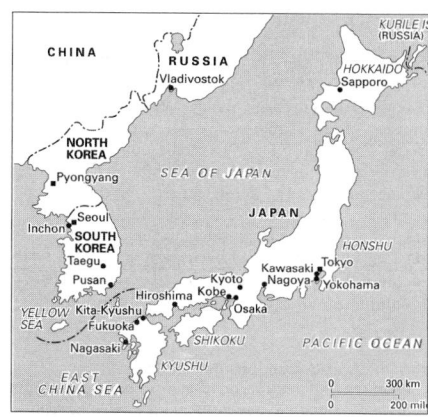

nations, including the USA and the UK, came to the aid of the Republic of Korea. China entered the war on the side of North Korea in November 1950. The fighting was ended by an armistice agreement signed on 27 July 1953. By this agreement (which was not signed by the Republic of Korea), the line of division between North and South Korea remained close to the 38th parallel.

Talks between North and South Korea on the reunification of the country have taken place intermittently. A non-aggression accord was signed between the North and South in 1991 and an agreement on the denuclearisation of the Korean peninsula was reached in 1992. A summit meeting between the presidents of North and South Korea took place on 13–15 June 2000 at which a communiqué was signed agreeing to promote economic co-operation, achieve reconciliation and eventually reunify the two countries.

DEMOCRATIC PEOPLE'S REPUBLIC OF KOREA

Chosun Minchu-chui Inmin Kongwa-guk – Democratic People's Republic of Korea

AREA – 46,540 sq. miles (120,538 sq. km). Neighbours: China, Russia (north), Republic of Korea (south)
POPULATION – 21,968,228 (2001 estimate). The language is Korean
CAPITAL – Pyongyang (approximate population, 2,741,260)
CURRENCY – Won of 100 chon
NATIONAL ANTHEM – Aegug-ga (Patriotic Hymn)
NATIONAL DAY – 16 February (Kim Jong-il's birthday)
NATIONAL FLAG – Red with white fimbriations and blue borders at top and bottom; a large red star on a white disc near the hoist
LIFE EXPECTANCY (years) – male 62.5; female 68.0
POPULATION GROWTH RATE – 1.6 per cent (1999)
POPULATION DENSITY – 197 per sq. km (1999)
URBAN POPULATION – 60.2 per cent (2000)

POLITICAL SYSTEM

The constitution of the Democratic People's Republic of Korea provides for a Supreme People's Assembly, presently consisting of 687 deputies, which is elected every five years by universal suffrage. The Assembly elects a president for a five-year term, and the Central People's Committee. In turn, the Central People's Committee directs the Administrative Council which implements the policy formulated by the Committee.

The Administrative Council (36 members), the government of North Korea, includes the prime minister and various ministers. In practice, however, the country is ruled by the Korean Workers' Party which elects a Central Committee; this in turn appoints a Politburo. The senior ministers of the Administrative Council are all members of the Communist Party Central Committee and the majority are also members of the Politburo. Kim Il-sung, who had been head of the state, party and military since the country's inception in 1948, died on 8 July 1994, but was declared the eternal president in September 1998. His son Kim Jong-il, who had been party general secretary since October 1997, became chair of the National Defence Committee, which is now de facto the highest office.

HEAD OF STATE

Eternal President, Kim Il-sung (deceased)
Chair of the National Defence Commission, Kim Jong-il
Chair of the Standing Committee of the Supreme People's Assembly, Kim Yong-nam

SPA STANDING COMMITTEE

Chairman, Kim Yong-nam
Vice-Chairmen, Yang Hyong-sop; Im Yong-tae
Secretary-General, Kim Yun-hyok
Honorary Vice-Chairmen, Pak Song-chol; Kim Yong-chu; Yi Chong-ok; Chon Mun-sop
Members, Yu Mi-yong; Kang Yong-sop; Yi Kil-song; Yi Chol-pong; Yi Il-hwan; Song Sam-sop

ADMINISTRATIVE COUNCIL *as at July 2002*

Premier, Hong Song-nam
Deputy Premiers, Kwak Pon-ki; Cho Chang-tok; Sin Il-nam
Foreign Affairs, Paek Nam-sun

MINISTERS

Agriculture, Kim Chang-sik
Chair, Physical Culture and Sports Guidance Committee, Pak Myong-chol
Chair, State Planning Committee, Pak Nam-ki
Chemical Industry, Pak Pong-chu
City Management, Choe Chong-kon
Commerce, Yi Yong-son
Construction and Building Materials Industry, Cho Yun-hui
Culture, Kang Nung-su
Director of the Central Statistics Bureau, Kim Chang-su
Director of the Secretariat and State Administration Council, Chong Mun-sang
Education, Choe Ki-chong
Finance, Mun Il-bong
Fisheries, Yi Song-un
Foreign Trade, Ri Kwang-gun
Forestry, Yi Sang-mu
Labour, Yi Won-il
Land and Maritime Transport, Kim Yong-il
Land Environmental Protection, Chang Il-son
Light Industry, Yi Yong-su
Metal and Machine Industry, Chon Sung-hun
Mining Industry, Son Chong-o
People's Armed Forces, Vice-Marshall Kim Il-chol
Posts and Telecommunications, Yi Kun-pom
Power and Coal Industry, Sin Tae-nok
President of the Academy of Sciences, Yi Kwang-ho
President of the Central Bank, Kim Wan-su
Procurement and Food Administration, Paek Chang-yong
Public Health, Kim Su-hak
Public Security, Lt.-Gen. Paek Hak-nim

Railways, Kim Yong-san
State Construction Commission, Pae Tal-chun
State Inspection, Kim Ui-sun

DEFENCE

The Army has about 3,500 main battle tanks and 2,500 armoured personnel carriers. The Navy has 26 submarines, three frigates and about 310 patrol and coastal vessels at 15 bases. The Air Force has 621 combat aircraft and 24 armed helicopters.

Between 1992 and 1994 North Korea embarked on a clandestine nuclear weapons programme despite being a signatory of the Nuclear Non-Proliferation Treaty (NPT), but halted the programme in November 1994.

MILITARY EXPENDITURE – 13.9 per cent of GDP (2000)

MILITARY PERSONNEL – 1,082,000: Army 950,000, Navy 46,000, Air Force 86,000; Paramilitaries 189,000

CONSCRIPTION DURATION – Three to ten years

ECONOMY

North Korea is rich in minerals and industry was developed, but the economy has stagnated owing to poor planning and a shortage of foreign exchange. The current economic crisis was precipitated by the curtailment of barter trade with the Soviet Union after 1991, and the end of subsidised oil and grain from China. Industrial output has collapsed, with industry operating at one-third of capacity. The economy has been sustained by foreign exchange sent by ethnic Koreans in Japan. In April 1998, South Korea lifted its ban on investment in North Korea, allowing South Koreans to send money to their relatives in the north.

A North Korean survey quoted by South Korean security services stated that up to three million people had died as a result of famine between 1995 and 1998. In January 1998, the UN World Food Programme launched a food aid operation to provide 658,000 tonnes of food to North Korea. The USA increased food aid to North Korea in May 1999.

GDP – US$10,273 million (1998); US$469 per capita (1999)

ANNUAL AVERAGE GROWTH OF GDP – 1.1 per cent (1998)

Trade with UK	2000	2001
Imports from UK	£16,798,000	£28,236,000
Exports to UK	2,981,000	1,423,000

REPUBLIC OF KOREA

Taehan Min'guk – Republic of Korea

AREA – 38,327 sq. miles (99,268 sq. km). Neighbour: Democratic People's Republic of Korea (north)

POPULATION – 47,904,370 (2001 estimate). The largest religions are Buddhism (10.3 million) and Christianity (8.8 million Protestants, 2.9 million Roman Catholics). The language is Korean

CAPITAL – Seoul (population, 10,321,000, 1999 estimate)

MAJOR CITIES – Ψ Inchon (2,524,000); Ψ Pusan (3,831,000); Taegu (2,517,000)

CURRENCY – Won

NATIONAL ANTHEM – Aegug-ga (Patriotic Hymn)

NATIONAL DAY – 15 August (Liberation Day)

NATIONAL FLAG – White with a red and blue yin-yang symbol in the centre, surrounded by four black trigrams

LIFE EXPECTANCY (years) – male 71.8; female 79.1

POPULATION GROWTH RATE – 1.0 per cent (1999)
POPULATION DENSITY – 472 per sq. km (1999)
URBAN POPULATION – 91.0 per cent (1999)

HISTORY AND POLITICS

The most recent elections to the National Assembly in April 2000 produced no outright majority. The Millennium Democratic Party won 115 seats and formed a coalition with the United Liberal Democrats, who won 17 seats; the opposition Grand National Party won 133 seats. Lee Han-dong was appointed prime minister on 22 May 2000. In the most recent presidential election of 18 December 1997, Kim Dae-jung of the National Congress for New Politics was elected president with just over 40 per cent of the vote. Presidential elections are scheduled for 12 December 2002.

POLITICAL SYSTEM

A new constitution was adopted in 1988 following a year of political unrest. The president, who is head of state, chief of the executive and commander-in-chief of the armed forces, is directly elected for a single term of five years. He appoints the prime minister with the consent of the National Assembly, and members of the State Council (Cabinet) on the recommendation of the prime minister. The president is also empowered to take wide-ranging measures in an emergency, including the declaration of martial law, but must obtain the agreement of the National Assembly. The National Assembly of 273 members is directly elected for a four-year term.

HEAD OF STATE

President, Kim Dae-jung, *elected* 18 December 1997, *sworn in* 25 February 1998

CABINET *as at July 2002*

Prime Minister, Lee Han-dong
Deputy Prime Minister, Education and Human Resources, Lee Sang-joo
Deputy Prime Minister, Finance and Economy, Jeon Yun-churl
Agriculture and Forestry, Kim Dong-tae
Chairman of Civil Service Commission, Kim Kwang-woong
Chairman of Financial Supervisory Commission, Lee Keung-young
Commerce, Industry and Energy, Shin kook-hwan
Construction and Transportation, Lim In-taik
Culture and Tourism, Namkung Jin
Defence, Kim Dong-shin
Environment, Kim Myung-ja
Foreign Affairs and Trade, Choi Sung-hong
Gender Equality, Han Myung-sook
Government Administration and Home Affairs, Lee Keun-sik
Government Information Agency, Shin Jung-sik
Government Policy Co-ordinator, Kim Ho-shik
Health and Welfare, Lee Tae-bok
Information and Communications, Yang Seung-taik
Justice, Song Jeong-ho
Labour, Bang Young-seuk
Legislation, Bahk Chan-ju
Maritime Affairs and Fisheries, Yu Sam-nam
Planning and Budget, Chang Seung-woo
Science and Technology, Chae Yung-bok
Unification, Jeong Se-hyun

EMBASSY OF THE REPUBLIC OF KOREA
60 Buckingham Gate, London SW1E 6AJ
Tel: 020-7227 5500/2

Ambassador Extraordinary and Plenipotentiary, HE Ra Jong-yil, apptd 2001

BRITISH EMBASSY
No. 4, Chung-dong, Chung-Ku, Seoul 100-120
Tel: (00 82) (2) 3210 5500
Email: bembassy@britain.or.kr
Ambassador Extraordinary and Plenipotentiary, HE Charles Humfrey, CMG, apptd 2000

BRITISH COUNCIL DIRECTOR, Shoba Ponnappa, Joongwhoo Building, 61–21 Taepyungro1-Ka, Choong-ku, Seoul 100–101; Email: info@britishcouncil.or.kr

DEFENCE

The Army has 2,330 main battle tanks, 2,480 armoured personnel carriers and 117 armed helicopters. The Navy has 19 submarines, six destroyers, nine frigates, 84 patrol and coastal vessels, 16 combat aircraft, 36 armed helicopters, 102 main battle tanks and 63 armoured personnel carriers. There are eight naval bases. The Air Force has 555 combat aircraft.

The USA maintains 36,520 personnel in the country.
MILITARY EXPENDITURE – 2.8 per cent of GDP (2000)
MILITARY PERSONNEL – 683,000: Army 560,000, Navy 60,000, Air Force 63,000; Paramilitaries 4,500
CONSCRIPTION DURATION – 26–30 months

ECONOMY

Major industries include shipbuilding, construction, iron and steel, textiles, electrical and electronic goods, semiconductors, passenger vehicles and petrochemicals.

The soil is fertile but arable land is limited by the mountainous nature of the country. Staple agricultural products are rice, barley and other cereals, beans and potatoes. Fruit-growing, sericulture and the growing of the medicinal root ginseng are also practised. The fishing industry is a major contributor to both food supply and exports.

Korea is deficient in mineral resources, except for deposits of coal on the east coast and tungsten. There are some prospects of discovering oil in the sea between Korea and Japan.

Tourism is a growing industry, with 5,320,000 foreign visitors in 2000.

In 1999 there was a trade surplus of US$23,933 million and a current account surplus of US$25,000 million. In 2000 imports totalled US$160,481 million and exports US$172,268 million. The USA, Japan, the EU and China are the main trading partners. Electronic products, machinery, metal goods, passenger vehicles, chemical products and fabric and clothing are the main exports. Electronic products, petroleum, machinery and chemical products are the main imports.

GNP – US$421,091 million (2000); US$8,490 per capita (1999)
GDP – US$320,748 million (1998); US$8,871 per capita (1999)
ANNUAL AVERAGE GROWTH OF GDP – 8.8 per cent (2000)
INFLATION RATE – 4.4 per cent (2001)
UNEMPLOYMENT – 4.2 per cent (2001)
TOTAL EXTERNAL DEBT – US$ 129,784 million (1999)

Trade with UK	2000	2001
Imports from UK	£1,350,591,000	£1,285,087,000
Exports to UK	3,515,312,000	2,844,898,000

COMMUNICATIONS

In 2000, there were 3,124 km of railway in commercial operation, of which 661 km were electrified. A high-speed railway line is being constructed between Seoul and Pusan and there are plans to build high-speed rail links between Seoul and Mokp'o and Seoul and Kangnŭng. There were 88,775 km of roads, of which 2,131 km were motorways. There are international airports in Seoul (Kimpo), Kimhae (near Pusan), Taegu and Cheju city. An international airport was opened at Inch'ŏn in March 2001. Korean Air and Asiana Airlines operate regular flights to Europe, the USA, the Middle East and southeast Asia. In 1999, 29 foreign airlines operated services to Seoul. Pusan and Inch'ŏn are the major ports with Pusan serving the industrial areas of the south-east. The port of Kwangyang is being expanded and a new container terminal is being constructed at Kadŏkto. Inch'ŏn, 28 miles from Seoul, serves the capital, but development and operation at Inch'ŏn are hampered by a tidal variation of 9-10 metres.

EDUCATION

Primary education is compulsory for six years from the age of six. Secondary and higher education is extensive with the option of middle school to age 15 and high school to age 18. In 1997 there were 150 universities and colleges of higher education. There were 888 hospitals. Some 108 daily newspapers are published.

ILLITERACY RATE – 2.0 per cent (2002)

ENROLMENT (percentage of age group) – primary 94 per cent (1997); secondary 100 per cent (1997); tertiary 68 per cent (1997)

KUWAIT

Dawlat al-Kuwayt – State of Kuwait

AREA – 6,880 sq. miles (17,818 sq. km). Neighbours: Iraq (north and west); Saudi Arabia (south and south-west)

POPULATION – 2,041,961 (2001 estimate): 41.6 per cent were Kuwaiti citizens, the remainder being other Arabs, Iranians, Indians, Pakistanis and Westerners. Islam is the official religion, though religious freedom is constitutionally guaranteed. The official language is Arabic, and English is widely spoken as a second language

CAPITAL – Ψ Kuwait City (Al-Kuwayt) (population, 388,663, 1998)

CURRENCY – Kuwaiti dinar (KD) of 1,000 fils

NATIONAL ANTHEM –Al-Nashīd Al-Watani (National Anthem)

NATIONAL DAY – 25 February

NATIONAL FLAG – Three horizontal stripes of green, white and red, with black trapezoid next to staff

LIFE EXPECTANCY (years) – male 74.9; female 79.0

POPULATION GROWTH RATE – 3.9 per cent (1999)

POPULATION DENSITY – 118 per sq. km (1999)

In 1993 the UN settled the dispute between Kuwait and Iraq, moving the border some few hundred metres northwards. Kuwait has since completed a 130-mile ditch, sand wall and barbed wire system along its border.

HISTORY AND POLITICS

Although Kuwait had been independent for some years, the 'exclusive agreement' of 1899 between the Sheikh of Kuwait and the British government was formally abrogated by an exchange of letters dated 19 June 1961.

Iraq invaded Kuwait on 2 August 1990 and it was liberated on 26 February 1991 by an alliance of Western and Arab forces. Iraq built up its armed forces on Kuwait's border in October 1994, until it was deterred by the arrival of US and British forces. Iraq formally recognised the sovereignty and territorial integrity of Kuwait as well as the UN-demarcated border in November 1994. Roughly 600 Kuwaitis are still held in Iraq.

The Amir dissolved the National Assembly on 4 May 1999; elections were held on 3 July 1999. Opposition Liberals won 16 and Islamists won 20 of the 50 seats. The government resigned on 28 January 2001 and a new Cabinet was appointed on 14 February, which included most of the members of the previous Cabinet.

POLITICAL SYSTEM

Under the constitution legislative power is vested in the Amir and the 50-member National Assembly, and executive power in the Amir and the Cabinet. Following popular pressure after the liberation, elections for the National Assembly were held in October 1992. The electorate consists of all Kuwaiti male nationals over 21 whose families have lived in the Emirate since before 1921. There are no political parties.

There are six governorates: Capital, Hawallī, Ahmadī, Al-Jahrah, Al-Farwaniya and Al-Asimah.

HEAD OF STATE

HH The Amir of Kuwait, Shaikh Jabir al-Ahmad al-Jabir al-Sabah, *born* 1928, *acceded* 31 December 1977
Crown Prince, HH Shaikh Saad al-Abdullah al-Salim al-Sabah

CABINET *as at July 2002*

Prime Minister, HH The Crown Prince
First Deputy Prime Minister, Foreign Affairs, Shaikh Sabah al-Ahmed al-Jabir al-Sabah
Deputy Prime Minister, Cabinet Affairs, National Assembly Affairs, Mohammed Dhaifallah Sharar
Deputy Prime Minister, Defence, Shaikh Jabir Mubarak al-Sabah
Deputy Prime Minister, Interior, Shaikh Mohammad Khaled al-Hamad al-Sabah
Commerce and Industry, Salah Abdel Redha Khorsheed
Communications, Shaikh Ahmad al-Abdullah al-Ahmed al-Sabah
Education and Higher Education, Musaed Rashed al-Haroun
Electricity and Water, Labour and Social Affairs, Talal Mubarak al-Ayyar
Finance and Planning, Youssef Hamad al-Ibrahim
Foreign Affairs, Shaikh Mohammad Sabah al-Salem al-Sabah
Health, Dr Mohammad Ahmad al-Jarallah
Information, Oil (acting), Shaikh Ahmad Fahad al-Ahmad al-Sabah
Justice, Waqfs and Islamic Affairs, Ahmad Yaqoub Baqer al-Abdullah
Public Works and State Minister for Housing Affairs, Dhaissan Zaban al-Lamee

EMBASSY OF THE STATE OF KUWAIT
2 Albert Gate, London SW1X 7JU
Tel: 020-7590 3400
Ambassador Extraordinary and Plenipotentiary, HE Khaled al-Duwaisan, GCVO, apptd 1993

BRITISH EMBASSY
PO Box 2, Safat, 13001 Kuwait
Tel: (00 965) 240 3334/5/6

Ambassador Extraordinary and Plenipotentiary, HE
Christopher Wilton, apptd 2002

BRITISH COUNCIL DIRECTOR, John Gildea, 2 Al Arabi
Street, Block 2, PO Box 345, 13004 Safat, Mansouriya,
Kuwait City; Email: bc.kuwait@kw.britishcouncil.org

DEFENCE

The Army has 385 main battle tanks, 151 armoured
personnel carriers and 355 armoured infantry fighting
vehicles. The Navy has ten patrol and coastal vessels,
based at Ras al-Qalaya. The Air Force has 82 combat
aircraft and 20 armed helicopters.

The USA and UK station aircraft and support units in
the country to patrol the air exclusion zone in southern
Iraq.

MILITARY EXPENDITURE – 9.8 per cent of GDP (2000)
MILITARY PERSONNEL – 15,500: Army 11,000, Navy
2,000, Air Force 2,500; Paramilitaries 5,000
CONSCRIPTION DURATION - Two years

ECONOMY

Despite the desert terrain, 8.4 per cent of land is under
cultivation; tomatoes, onions, melons and dates are the
main crops.

The oil industry is run by the Kuwait Petroleum
Corporation. Oil installations were extensively damaged
when Iraqi forces set light to oil wells prior to their
retreat. Oil production was 107,600,000 tonnes in 1998.

There are four power stations capable of generating
almost 7,000 MW of electricity. The country depends on
desalination plants for its water supply.

The economy is heavily dependent on foreign labour. In
1998 the workforce comprised 211,559 Kuwaitis and
1,040,437 non-Kuwaitis.

GDP – US$25,306 million (1998); US$16,244 per capita
(1999)
ANNUAL AVERAGE GROWTH OF GDP – 13.0 per cent
(1998)
INFLATION RATE – 1.8 per cent (2000)

TRADE

Oil is the major export. Non-oil exports, mainly to Asian
countries and the Indian sub-continent, have included
chemical fertilisers, ammonia and other chemicals, metal
pipes and building materials. Re-exports to neighbouring
states traditionally accounted for a major proportion of
non-oil exports but were brought to a halt by the Iraqi
invasion. Major trading partners are Japan, the USA, the
UAE, Saudi Arabia and Western Europe.

In 2000 Kuwait had a trade surplus of US$12,730
million and a current account surplus of US$14,865
million. In 1999 imports totalled US$7,617 million and
exports US$12,218 million.

Trade with UK	2000	2001
Imports from UK	£346,934,000	£357,391,000
Exports to UK	341,093,000	312,498,000

COMMUNICATIONS

There are some 4,741 km of roads. Telecommunications
and postal services are conducted by the government.

SOCIAL WELFARE

The government invested its considerable oil revenues in
comprehensive social services. Medical services are free to
all residents. In 1998 there were 15 hospitals and 70
clinics. Education is free and compulsory from six to 14
years. In 1999 there were 969 schools (608 government-
run, 322 private and 39 vocational) and one university.

ILLITERACY RATE – 17.0 per cent (2002)
ENROLMENT (percentage of age group) – primary 77
per cent (1997); secondary 65 per cent (1997);
tertiary 19 per cent (1997)

KYRGYZSTAN

Kyrgyz Respublikasy – Kyrgyz Republic

AREA – 77,181 sq. miles (199,900 sq. km). Neighbours:
Kazakhstan (north), China (east), Tajikistan (south
and south-west), Uzbekistan (west)
POPULATION – 4,753,003 (2001 estimate): 52.4 per cent
Kyrgyz (Turkic origin), 21.5 per cent Russian and
12.9 per cent Uzbek, with smaller numbers of
Ukrainians, Germans, Tatars and Kazakhs. Islam is
the main religion. Kyrgyz, the official language since
independence, is a Turkic language, written in the
Roman alphabet since 1992. Russian is an official
language having equal rights with Kyrgyz
CAPITAL – Bishkek (population, 589,400, 1997 estimate;
616,000, 1989 census)
CURRENCY – Som of 100 tyin (introduced on 10 May
1993 at rate of 1:200 against the rouble)
NATIONAL ANTHEM – Mamlekettik Gimni (National
Anthem)
NATIONAL DAY – 31 August (Independence Day)
NATIONAL FLAG – Red with a rayed sun containing a
representation of a yurt, all in gold
LIFE EXPECTANCY (years) – male 64.8; female 72.3
POPULATION GROWTH RATE – 1.5 per cent (1999)
POPULATION DENSITY – 24 per sq. km (1999)
URBAN POPULATION – 33.3 per cent (2000)
MILITARY EXPENDITURE – 2.4 per cent of GDP (2000)
MILITARY PERSONNEL – 9,000: Army 6,600, Air Force
2,400; Paramilitaries 5,000
CONSCRIPTION DURATION – 18 months

Kyrgyzstan (formerly Kyrgyzia) is mountainous, the
major part being covered by the ridge of the Central
Tienshan, while the Pamir-Altai system occupies its
southern part. There are a number of spacious mountain
valleys, the Alai, Susamyr and others.

HISTORY AND POLITICS

The Kyrgyz people were first mentioned in Chinese
chronicles in the second millennium BC. They are a
merger of two ethnic groups, a Turkic-speaking people
driven into the area by the Mongols from the River
Yenisei area of Central Asia, and indigenous peoples.
After a long period under Mongol, Chinese and Persian
rule, the Kyrgyz became part of the Russian Empire in the
1860s and 1870s. Kyrgyzstan became part of the Soviet
Union in 1920 and underwent some industrialisation.
Kyrgyzstan declared independence just after the failed
Moscow coup on 31 August 1991.

Ethnic tensions between the rural nomadic Kyrgyz, the
urban Russians and the wealthy Uzbeks who own many
businesses and form the majority in the second largest
town of Osh, are never far from the surface.

A referendum on amendments to the constitution was
held on 17 October 1998, which introduced private
ownership of land.

Legislative elections were held on 20 February and 12
March 2000. The largest opposition parties were not
allowed to take part on the grounds of supposed minor
infractions of the electoral procedures, a decision which
was criticised by observers from the Organisation for
Security and Co-operation in Europe; their leaders were
allowed to stand as independent candidates. The

Communist party and the pro-government Union of Democratic Forces emerged as the largest parties. The results were widely condemned by opposition groups amid allegations of widespread electoral fraud.

The presidential election held on 29 October 2000 was won by the incumbent President Askar Akayev, who obtained 74.3 per cent of the votes cast, but the conduct of the poll was criticised by OSCE observers at the time of the election and later by the EU and the USA.

POLITICAL SYSTEM

The head of state is a president directly elected for a five-year term. There is a bicameral legislature composed of a 60-member Legislative Assembly and a 45-member People's Assembly, both of which serve for five-year terms. The president appoints the prime minister and the other members of the government. The Assembly of the People of Kyrgyzstan, which comprises the leaders of the republic's ethnic communities, was designated a consultative body in January 1997.

HEAD OF STATE

President, Askar Akayev, *elected* 12 October 1991, *re-elected* 24 December 1995, 29 October 2000

CABINET *as at July 2002*

Prime Minister, Nikolay Tanayev
First Deputy Prime Minister, Kurmanbek Osmonov
Deputy Prime Minister, Economic Development, Trade and Investments, Dzhoomart Otorbayev
Agriculture and Water Resources, Aleksandr Kostyuk
Chair of the National Security Service, Kalyk Imankulov
Chair of the State Commission for Procurement and Material Reserves, Tashkul Kereksizev
Chair of the State Committee for Management of State Property and Attraction of Direct Investment, Ravshan Dzheyenbekov
Chair of the State Committee for Tourism, Sport and Youth Policy, Okmotbek Almakuchukov
Chief of Staff, Bekbolot Talgarbekov
Defence, Lt.-Gen. Esen Topoyev
Director of the State Agency for Science and Copyright, Roman Umorev
Director of the State Communications Agency, Andrei Titev
Ecology and Emergencies, Satyvaldy Chrymashev
Education, Science and Culture, Ishengul Boldjurova
Finance, Bolot Abildayev
Foreign Affairs, Askar Aitmatov
Health, Mitalip Mamytov
Interior, Bakirdin Subanbekov
Justice, Daniyar Naymbaev
Labour and Social Welfare, Roza Aknazarova
Local Government and Regional Development, Director of the State Agency for Registration of Real Estate Rights, Tolebek Umaraliyev
Trade and Industry, Sadriddin Djienbekov
Transport and Communications, Kubanychbek Dzhumaliyev

EMBASSY OF THE KYRGYZ REPUBLIC
Ascot House, 119 Crawford Street, London W1U 1BJ
Tel: 020-7935 1462
Ambassador Extraordinary and Plenipotentiary, vacant

BRITISH AMBASSADOR, HE Richard Lewington, resident at Almaty, Kazakhstan

BRITISH COUNCIL, 237 Panfilov Street, KS-720000 Bishkek; Email: bc@britcoun.elcat.kg

ECONOMY

Agriculture is the main sector of the economy, with sugar beet, grain and sheep the main products. Private ownership of land was legalised in 1997. Industry is concentrated in the food-processing, textiles, timber and mining fields. Since 1992, some 60 per cent of state-owned enterprises have been privatised. Hydroelectric power is abundant and Kyrgyzstan has reserves of gold, coal, mercury and uranium, although only gold has so far been exploited and is the country's largest export.

The president and government have made the Central Bank independent of government and parliamentary control. In March 1996, a treaty was signed with Belarus, Kazakhstan and Russia enhancing economic co-operation and working towards a single customs territory and in December 2000 an agreement was signed with Russia on the joint production of uranium and non-ferrous and precious metals.

In 1998 there was a trade deficit of US$221 million and a current account deficit of US$371 million. In 1999 imports totalled US$600 million and exports US$454 million.

GNP – US$1,330 million (2000); US$300 per capita (1999)
GDP – US$1,701 million (1998); US$1,048 per capita (1999)
ANNUAL AVERAGE GROWTH OF GDP – 3.6 per cent (1999)
INFLATION RATE – 18.7 per cent (2000)
TOTAL EXTERNAL DEBT – US$1,669 million (1999)

Trade with UK	2000	2001
Imports from UK	£4,297,000	£2,559,000
Exports to UK	112,000	163,000

CULTURE AND EDUCATION

Until the 1930s the Kyrgyz language had an oral tradition of literature which included the epic poem *Manas*, which tells the history of the Kyrgyz people. Internationally, one of the best-known writers of the former Soviet Union is the Kyrgyz writer Chingiz Aitmatov (1928–).
ILLITERACY RATE – 3.0 per cent
ENROLMENT (percentage of age group) – primary 100 per cent (1997); tertiary 12 per cent (1997)

LAOS
Satharanarath Pasathipatai Pasason Lao – Lao People's Democratic Republic

AREA – 91,429 sq. miles (236,800 sq. km). Neighbours: China (north), Vietnam (north-east and east), Cambodia (south), Thailand (west), Myanmar (north-west)
POPULATION – 5,635,967 (2001 estimate): 68 per cent Lao Loum (lowland Lao), 22 per cent Lao Theung (upland Lao), 9 per cent Lao Soung (highland Lao, including Hmong and Yau). Lao is the official language; French and English are spoken
CAPITAL – Vientiane (population, 555,100, 1997 estimate)
CURRENCY – Kip (K) of 100 at
NATIONAL ANTHEM – Pheng Xat Lao (Hymn Of The Lao People)
NATIONAL DAY – 2 December
NATIONAL FLAG – Blue background with a central white circle, framed by two horizontal red stripes
LIFE EXPECTANCY (years) – male 53.3; female 55.8
POPULATION GROWTH RATE – 2.6 per cent (1999)
POPULATION DENSITY – 22 per sq. km (1999)
MILITARY EXPENDITURE – 1.1 per cent of GDP (2000)
MILITARY PERSONNEL – 29,100: Army 25,600, Navy 600, Air Force 3,500; Paramilitaries 100,000
CONSCRIPTION DURATION – 18 months minimum
ILLITERACY RATE – 48.6 per cent (2002)
ENROLMENT (percentage of age group) – primary 100 per cent (1997); secondary 29 per cent (1997); tertiary 3 per cent (1997)

HISTORY AND POLITICS
The kingdom of Lane Xang, the Land of a Million Elephants, was founded in the 14th century but broke up at the beginning of the 16th century into the separate kingdoms of Luang Prabang and Vientiane and the principality of Champassac, which together came under French protection in 1893. In 1945 the Japanese staged a coup and suppressed the French administration. In 1947 Laos became a constitutional monarchy under King Sisvang Vong, and an independent sovereign state in 1953.

The Lao People's Democratic Republic was proclaimed in December 1975 following victory by the Pathet Lao and the abdication of the King. A president and Council of Ministers were installed, and a 45-member Supreme People's Council was appointed to draft a constitution, which was approved in 1991. The Lao People's Revolutionary Party (LPRP) is the sole legal political organisation. A general election to the enlarged 109-member National Assembly was held on 24 February 2002; all the candidates were approved by the LPRP, which won 108 seats with the remaining seat being won by an approved non-partisan candidate. The president, prime minister and Council of Ministers were confirmed in their posts by the National Assembly on 9 March 2002.

HEAD OF STATE
President, Gen. Khamtay Siphandone, *elected by the National Assembly* 24 February 1998, *re-elected* 9 April 2002
Vice-President, Choummali Saignason

COUNCIL OF MINISTERS *as at July 2002*

Prime Minister, Bounnyang Vorachit
Deputy Prime Ministers, Somsavat Lengsavad *(Foreign Affairs);* Thongloun Sisoulit *(State Planning Committee);* Maj-Gen. Asang Laoly
Agriculture and Forestry, Siene Saphangthong
Commerce and Tourism, Phoumy Thipphavone
Communications, Transport, Posts and Construction, Bouathong Vonglokham
Defence, Maj.-Gen. Douangchay Phichit
Education, Phimmasone Leuangkhamma
Finance, Soukhan Mahalat
Industry and Handicrafts, Soulivong Daravong
Information and Culture, Phandouangchit Vongsa
Interior, Security, Maj.-Gen. Soutchay Thammasith
Justice, Khamouane Boupha
Labour and Social Welfare, Somphan Phengkhammy
Ministers attached to Prime Minister, Somphavan Inthavong; Somphong Mongkhonvilai; Souly Nanthavong; Bountiam Phitsamai; Saisenglee Tengbliavue
Permanent Secretary of the President's Office, Souban Salitthilat
Public Health, Ponemek Daraloy

EMBASSY OF THE LAO PEOPLE'S DEMOCRATIC REPUBLIC
74 Avenue Raymond-Poincaré F-75116 Paris
Tel: (00 33) (1) 4553 0298
Ambassador Extraordinary and Plenipotentiary, HE Soutsakhone Pathammavong, apptd 2002

ECONOMY
A 'new economic mechanism' programme was introduced in 1986 which began the liberalisation of the economy. These reforms have produced a market-orientated economic system which has increased growth and reduced inflation. The economy is dominated by the agricultural sector, which employs about three-quarters of the workforce. The seventh congress of the LPRP held in March 2001 defined the principal economic goal to be

agricultural development. Although Laos is one of the poorest states in the world, there is potential for increased hydroelectric power exports to Thailand and there are deposits of coal, tin, iron ore, gold, bauxite and lignite. Foreign capital investment in infrastructure began with the 1994 opening of the Friendship Bridge over the Mekong river border with Thailand which links road routes from Singapore to China.

In 1998 Laos had a trade deficit of US$165 million and a current account deficit of US$150 million. In 1999 imports totalled US$525 million and exports US$311 million.

GNP – US$1,493 million (2000); US$290 per capita (1999)

GDP – US$1,292 million (1998); US$285 per capita (1999)

ANNUAL AVERAGE GROWTH OF GDP – 5.7 per cent (2000)

INFLATION RATE – 25.1 per cent (2000)

TOTAL EXTERNAL DEBT – US$2,527 million (1999)

Trade with UK	2000	2001
Imports from UK	£3,517,000	£2,316,000
Exports to UK	5,145,000	7,095,000

LATVIA
Latvijas Republika – Republic of Latvia

AREA – 24,942 sq. miles (64,600 sq. km). Neighbours: Estonia (north), Lithuania and Belarus (south), the Russian Federation (east)

POPULATION – 2,385,231 (2001 estimate): 55.3 per cent Latvian, 32.5 per cent Russian, 4.0 per cent Belarusian, with small Ukrainian and Polish minorities. The main religions are Lutheran, Roman Catholic and Russian Orthodox. The official language is Latvian; Russian is also spoken. Education is in Latvian and Russian. Public sector employees must pass language tests in Latvian to a level commensurate with the nature of their employment. The right of minorities to use their mother tongue has been acknowledged

CAPITAL – Riga (population, 796,732, 1999 estimate)

MAJOR CITIES – Daugavpils (117,502); Jelgava (70,962); Jūrmala (58,977); Liepāja (97,278); Ventspils (46,564), 1998 estimates

CURRENCY – Lats of 100 santims

NATIONAL ANTHEM – Dievs, Svētī Latviju (God Bless Latvia)

NATIONAL DAY – 18 November (Independence Day 1918)

NATIONAL FLAG – Crimson, with a white horizontal stripe across the centre

LIFE EXPECTANCY (years) – male 65.7; female 76.2

POPULATION GROWTH RATE – -0.8 per cent (1999)

POPULATION DENSITY – 38 per sq. km (1999)

URBAN POPULATION – 69.0 per cent (2000)

HISTORY AND POLITICS

Latvia came under the control of the German Teutonic Knights at the end of the 13th century. During the next few centuries the country endured sporadic invasions by the Swedes, Poles and Russians. By 1795 Latvia was entirely under Russian control. On 18 November 1918, Latvia declared its independence, but was annexed by the Soviet Union in 1940 under the terms of the Molotov–Ribbentrop pact with Germany. Latvia was invaded and occupied when Germany invaded the Soviet Union during the Second World War but recaptured by the Soviet Union in 1944.

In 1989 the Popular Front of Latvia won the elections to the Supreme Council in 1989, and on 4 May 1990 the Supreme Council declared the independent republic of Latvia to be, *de jure*, still in existence. A national referendum was held in March 1991 in which 73 per cent voted in favour of independence, and this was declared on 21 August 1991. The State Council of the Soviet Union recognised the independence of Latvia on 10 September 1991.

The general election of 3 October 1998 resulted in the People's Party gaining the most seats, but a coalition of Latvia's Way, the Union for Fatherland and Freedom and the New Party formed a government on 26 November. The Latvian Social Democratic Union joined the coalition on 4 February 1999 and the New Party left the government on 5 February 2001. Parliamentary elections were scheduled to be held in October 2002.

POLITICAL SYSTEM

Executive authority is vested in a prime minister and Cabinet of Ministers. Legislative power is exercised by the unicameral parliament *(Saeima)*, which comprises 100 deputies elected for four-year terms by proportional representation, with a 5 per cent threshold for parliamentary representation. The deputies elect a president of state, serving for four years, who in turn appoints the prime minister. The prime minister appoints, and the Saeima approves, the Cabinet of Ministers.

The electorate and citizenship had been restricted to descendants of Latvian citizens before the 1940 Soviet occupation and to those who could pass the required Latvian language tests, until 1994 when a law was passed enabling naturalisation of long-term residents. In October 1998 a referendum to amend the citizenship law was passed which granted citizenship to those children born in Latvia after Latvian independence if their parents requested it and provided for simpler language tests for older residents.

HEAD OF STATE

President, Vaira Vīķe-Freiberga, *elected* 17 June 1999, *sworn in* 8 July 1999

CABINET *as at July 2002*

Prime Minister, Andris Berzins (LC)

Agriculture, Atis Slakteris (TP)

Culture, Karīna Pētersone (LC)

Defence, Ģirts Valdis Kristovskis (TB)

Economy, Aigars Kalvitis (TP)

Education and Science, Karlis Greiskalns (TP)

Environmental Protection and Regional Development, Vladimir Makarov (TB)

Finance, Gundars Bērziņš (TP)

Foreign Affairs, Indulis Bērziņš (LC)

Interior, Mareks Segliņš (TP)

Justice, Ingrida Labucka

Special Tasks Minister for Co-operation with International Financial Institutions, Roberts Zīle (TB)

Special Tasks Minister for State Administration and Local Government, Janis Krumins (LC)

Transport, Anatolijs Gorbunovs (LC)

Welfare, Viktors Jaksons (TB)

TB Union For Fatherland and Freedom; LC Latvia's Way; TP People's Party

EMBASSY OF THE REPUBLIC OF LATVIA
45 Nottingham Place, London W1U 5LR
Tel: 020-7312 0040
Ambassador Extraordinary and Plenipotentiary, vacant

BRITISH EMBASSY
5, J. Alunana Street, Riga LV-1010
Tel: (00 371) (7) 33 8126-30
Email: british.embassy@apollo.lv
Ambassador Extraordinary and Plenipotentiary, HE
Andrew Tesoriere, apptd 2002

BRITISH COUNCIL DIRECTOR, Chris Edwards, 5A
Blaumana iela, Riga LV-1011;
Email: mail@britishcouncil.lv

DEFENCE

The Army has three main battle tanks, 13 armoured personnel carriers, the Navy has four patrol and coastal vessels and ten defence patrol craft at three bases and the Air Force has 19 aircraft and five helicopters. Russian forces withdrew from Latvia in 1994.
MILITARY EXPENDITURE – 1.0 per cent of GDP (2000)
MILITARY PERSONNEL – 6,500: Army 3,100, Navy 840, Air Force 210; National Guard, 2,350 Paramilitaries 3,500
CONSCRIPTION DURATION – 12 months

ECONOMY

By 2001, 97 per cent of previously state-owned enterprises had either been privatised or were assigned for privatisation, and privatised companies accounted for 66 per cent of GDP.

Latvia is an agricultural exporter, specialising in cattle and pig breeding, dairy farming and crops, including sugar beet, flax, cereals and potatoes. In 2001, 13.5 per cent of the population were employed in agriculture, which accounted for 4.1 per cent of GDP. Natural resources include limestone, gypsum, peat and timber.

Industry is specialised in certain areas including the production of food and beverages, motor vehicles, textiles and timber and paper products. Transit, services and banking are also large sectors with services contributing 70.6 per cent of GDP in 2001.
GNP – US$6,921 million (2000); US$2,430 per capita (1999)
GDP – US$6,397 million (1998); US$2,519 per capita (1999)
ANNUAL AVERAGE GROWTH OF GDP – 6.6 per cent (2000)
INFLATION RATE – 2.7 per cent (2000)
UNEMPLOYMENT – 14.5 per cent (1999)
TOTAL EXTERNAL DEBT – US$2,657 million (1999)

TRADE

In 1996, a free trade regime was agreed with the EU and EFTA. The main imports are machinery, chemical goods and transport vehicles, and the main exports are wood and wood products, textiles and base metals and metallic products. The most important import partners are Germany, Russia, Lithuania, Finland and Sweden. The most important export partners are Germany, the UK, Sweden, Lithuania and Russia.

In 2000 there was a trade deficit of US$1,058 million and a current account deficit of US$485 million. Imports totalled US$3,184 million and exports US$1,865 million.

Trade with UK	2000	2001
Imports from UK	£84,313,000	£86,143,000
Exports to UK	403,396,000	424,775,000

COMMUNICATIONS

Latvia has 2,413 km of railways and some 20,400 km of roads. Many of the exports from former CIS states are transported to Western Europe via Latvia. Latvia is also

being developed as a transportation route from Scandinavia to central and southern Europe. Several warm-water ports exist, of which three, Riga, Ventspils and Liepāja, are developed for commercial transport.

CULTURE AND EDUCATION

The Latvian language belongs to the Baltic branch of the Indo-European languages. The Latin alphabet is used. Latvian literature appeared in the 19th century and played a role in the fight for independence in 1918.

There are 27 higher education institutions, of which five are universities.
ILLITERACY RATE – 0.2 per cent (2002)
ENROLMENT (percentage of age group) – primary 96 per cent (1997); secondary 84 per cent (1997); tertiary 33 per cent (1997)

LEBANON
Al-Jumhūriyya al-Lubnāniyya – Republic of Lebanon

AREA – 4,015 sq. miles (10,400 sq. km). Neighbours: Syria (north and east), Israel (south)
POPULATION – 3,627,774 (2001 estimate): 32 per cent Shi'ite Muslim; 21 per cent Sunni Muslim, 40 per cent Christian, 7 per cent Druze. Arabic is the official language, and French and English are also widely used
CAPITAL – Ψ Beirut (Bayrūt) (population, 1,500,000, 1991)
MAJOR CITIES – Ψ Sayda (Sidon) (100,000); Ψ Tarābulus (Tripoli) (200,000); Ψ Sūr (Tyre) (70,000)
CURRENCY – Lebanese pound (L£) of 100 piastres
NATIONAL ANTHEM – Kulluna Lil Watan Lil'Ula Lil'alam (We All Belong To The Homeland)
NATIONAL DAY – 22 November
NATIONAL FLAG – Horizontal bands of red, white and red with a green cedar of Lebanon in the centre of the white band
LIFE EXPECTANCY (years) – male 71.9; female 75.1
POPULATION GROWTH RATE – 1.8 per cent (1999)
POPULATION DENSITY – 311 per sq. km (1999)

HISTORY AND POLITICS

Lebanon became an independent state in 1920, administered under French mandate until 22 November 1943. Powers were transferred to the Lebanese government from January 1944 and French troops were withdrawn in 1946. In 1975, fighting broke out in Beirut between Maronite, Sunni and Shia factions, the latter supported by Palestinian guerrillas based in Lebanon; fighting continued until the end of the civil war in 1990. In 1982 Israeli forces invaded and in 1985 established a buffer zone along the Israeli–Lebanon border controlled by the South Lebanon Army (SLA), a Christian militia. Since 1993 the Lebanese Army has deployed in southern villages alongside UNIFIL forces but has not disarmed Hezbollah forces, who are financed, armed and trained by Syria and Iran.

The Israeli Prime Minister Ehud Barak had committed himself to the withdrawal of Israeli forces from the buffer zone during his election campaign in May 1999 and Israel began its withdrawal in mid-May 2000, initially handing over their positions to the SLA, but a mass movement of exiled civilians, led by Hezbollah forces, effectively routed the SLA. The last Israeli troops left on 24 May 2000 and the SLA troops surrendered to the Lebanese authorities or fled to Israel. Syrian forces remain in west Beirut and in the north and the east of the country.

Parliamentary elections were held in 1992 and local elections were held in 1998. The general election held on 27 August and 3 September 2000 was won by supporters of Rafik Hariri, who had previously been prime minister between 1992 and 1998. Hariri was appointed prime minister by President Lahoud on 23 October 2000 and named his Cabinet, composed equally of Christians and Muslims, on 26 October.

FOREIGN RELATIONS

Resentment has been growing among Christians at the continuing presence of Syrian troops. There has also been tension on the border between Lebanon and Israel over the disputed Shebaa Farms, a 25-sq. km region located between Lebanon, Israel and the Israeli-occupied Golan Heights, which remained under Israeli control following the Israeli withdrawal from southern Lebanon. There was an upsurge of fighting in early 2002 between Israel and Hezbollah in southern Lebanon.

POLITICAL SYSTEM

The National Covenant (1943) is characterised by the division of power between the religious communities. The executive comprises the president, prime minister and Cabinet. The president is elected by the National Assembly for a non-renewable term of six years and must be a Maronite Christian. The prime minister is appointed following consultation between the president and National Assembly and must be a Sunni Muslim. The 128-member unicameral National Assembly comprises equal numbers of Christians and Muslims although the speaker must be a Shia Muslim. Political parties are banned.

The constitution was amended on 15 October 1998 to allow the election of Gen. Lahoud as president. Serving state officials had previously been prohibited from standing for the presidency.

HEAD OF STATE

President of the Republic of Lebanon, Gen. Émile Lahoud, *elected* 15 October 1998, *sworn in* 24 November 1998

CABINET *as at July 2002*

Prime Minister, Rafiq Hariri
Deputy PM, Issam Fares
Agriculture, Ali Abdallah
Culture, Ghassan Salameh
Displaced Persons, Marwan Hamadeh
Economy and Trade, Basil Fleihan
Education and Higher Education, Abdel Rahim Mrad
Energy and Water Resources, Mohammad Abdel Hamid Baydoun
Environment, Michel Musa
Finance, Fouad Siniora
Foreign Affairs and Emigrants, Mahmoud Hammud
Industry, Georges Frem
Information, Ghazi el-Aridi
Interior and Municipal Affairs, Elias Murr
Justice, Samir Jisr
Labour, Ali Kanso
Ministers of State, Talal Arslan; Nazih Baydoun; Pierre Helou; Beshara Merhej; Michel Pharaon; Fouad Saad (*Administrative Development*); Bahij Tabbarah
National Defence, Khalil Hrawi
Post and Telecommunications, Jean-Louis Qordahi
Public Health, Soleiman Franjieh
Public Works and Transport, Najib Miqati
Social Affairs, Assaad Diab
Tourism, Karam Karam
Youth and Sports, Sebouh Hovnanian

LEBANESE EMBASSY
15–21 Palace Gardens Mews, London W8 4QN
Tel: 020-7229 7265/7727 6696
Ambassador Extraordinary and Plenipotentiary, HE Jihad Mortada, apptd 1999

BRITISH EMBASSY
Autostrade Jal El Dib, Coolrite Building (PO Box 60180), Beirut
Tel: (00 961) (4) 715 900–03
Email: britemb@cyberia.net.lb
Ambassador Extraordinary and Plenipotentiary,
HE Richard Kinchen, apptd 2001

BRITISH COUNCIL DIRECTOR, Dr Ken Churchill, OBE, Sidani Street, Azar Building, Beirut;
Email: general.enquiries@lb.britishcouncil.org

DEFENCE

The Army has 327 main battle tanks and 1,338 armoured personnel carriers. The Navy has seven patrol and coastal vessels at two bases.

There are a 5,496-strong UN peacekeeping force, 18,000 Syrian troops and 150 Iranian Revolutionary Guards operating in Lebanon.
MILITARY EXPENDITURE – 3.5 per cent of GDP (2000)
MILITARY PERSONNEL – 71,830: Army 70,000, Navy 830, Air Force 1,000; Paramilitaries 13,000
CONSCRIPTION DURATION – 12 months

ECONOMY

Fruits are the most important products. There is some light industry, mostly for the production of consumer goods, but most factories are still in need of reconstruction because of the civil war.

A ten-year plan (1993–2002)was initiated to repair war damage and to restore Lebanon's position as a regional financial services and light industrial centre, concentrating on rebuilding housing, transport, services, education and health services, and aiding industry and agriculture.
GNP – US$16,219 million (2000); US$3,700 per capita (1999)
GDP – US$5,323 million (1998); US$1,585 per capita (1999)
ANNUAL AVERAGE GROWTH OF GDP – 5.0 per cent (1998)
INFLATION RATE – 6.8 per cent (1994)
TOTAL EXTERNAL DEBT – US$8,441 million (1999)

TRADE

Principal imports are foodstuffs, machinery and electrical equipment, vehicles, chemical products, mineral ores, and metals and metal products. There is a free trade agreement with Syria. Principal exports include foodstuffs, chemical products, jewellery, machinery and electrical goods, textiles, metals and metal products, paper and paper products, and vehicles. Lebanon is the terminal for two oil pipelines, one formerly belonging to the Iraq Petroleum Company, debouching at Tripoli, the other belonging to the Trans Arabian Pipeline Company, at Sidon. These lines have not functioned for some years.

In 2000 imports totalled US$6,230 million and exports US$715 million.

Trade with UK	2000	2001
Imports from UK	£140,852,000	£181,435,000
Exports to UK	16,540,000	15,996,000

COMMUNICATIONS

There are 7,370 km of roads, of which 6,265 km are paved; there is 222 km of railway track. There is an international airport at Beirut, served by the national carrier Middle East Airlines and other airlines. An internal service operates from Beirut to Tripoli.

EDUCATION

There are 13 universities in Lebanon, among them American and French universities, and the Lebanese National University, the Beirut University College, the Kaslik Saint Esprit University and the Arab University in Beirut, and the University of Balamand situated near Tripoli. There is a good provision throughout the country of primary and secondary schools, among which are a great number of private schools.

ILLITERACY RATE – 13.1 per cent (2002)

ENROLMENT (percentage of age group) – primary 100 per cent (1997); tertiary 27 per cent (1997)

LESOTHO

Mmuso wa Lesotho - Kingdom of Lesotho

AREA – 11,720 sq. miles (30,355 sq. km). Neighbour: South Africa, which completely surrounds Lesotho

POPULATION – 2,177,062 (2001 estimate). The languages are Sesotho and English

CAPITAL – Maseru (population, 367,000, 1992 estimate)

CURRENCY – Loti (M) of 100 lisente. The South African rand is also legal tender

NATIONAL ANTHEM – Pina Ea Sechaba

NATIONAL DAY – 4 October (Independence Day)

NATIONAL FLAG – Diagonally white over blue over green with the white of double width, and an assegai and knobkerrie on a Basotho shield in brown in the upper hoist

LIFE EXPECTANCY (years) – male 40.9; female 39.6

POPULATION GROWTH RATE – 2.3 per cent (1999)

POPULATION DENSITY – 69 per sq. km (1999)

MILITARY EXPENDITURE – 4.0 per cent of GDP (2000)

MILITARY PERSONNEL – Army: 2,000

HISTORY AND POLITICS

Lesotho (formerly Basutoland) became a constitutional monarchy within the Commonwealth on 4 October 1966. The constitution was suspended in 1970 and the country was governed by a Council of Ministers until the establishment of a National Assembly in 1974.

Leabua Jonathan's government was overthrown in 1986, and executive and legislative powers were conferred on the King. Elections were held in March 1993 and the Basotho Congress Party (BCP) won all 65 seats in the new National Assembly. A BCP government led by Ntsu Mokhele was formed and King Letsie III swore allegiance to a new multiparty democratic constitution.

On 17 August 1994 King Letsie III and sections of the military mounted a coup attempt, but after mediation, the government, which had refused to leave office, was restored by the King. King Letsie also announced his intention to abdicate in favour of his father, Moshoeshoe II, who was restored on 25 January 1995. When King Moshoeshoe II died in a car crash on 15 January 1996, King Letsie III again ascended to the throne.

At legislative elections held in May 1998, the Lesotho Congress for Democracy won 78 of the 80 seats in the National Assembly. Allegations of electoral fraud, later confirmed by an investigation which said that the election had been marred by irregularities, but that there were insufficient grounds to annul the poll, led to violent protests. There were also reports of an alleged army mutiny. The deteriorating situation led to the intervention of South African and Botswanan military forces on 22 September to restore order after a request by the prime minister, Bethuel Pakalitha Mosisili; they withdrew in May 1999.

The general election that had been due in April 2000, was postponed to 25 May 2002, when the Lesotho Congress for Democracy (LCD) retained its overall majority in the National Assembly.

POLITICAL SYSTEM

In September 1999 it was announced that the first-past-the-post electoral system would be replaced by a new system incorporating a degree of proportional representation and that the number of seats in the National Assembly would be increased by 40 to 120.

HEAD OF STATE

HM The King of Lesotho, King Letsie III, *acceded* February 1996, *crowned* 31 October 1997

COUNCIL OF MINISTERS *as at August 2002*

Prime Minister, Defence, Public Service, Bethuel Pakalitha Mosisili

Deputy Prime Minister, Education, Lesao Lehohla

Agriculture, Co-operatives and Land Reclamation, Vova Bulane

Communications, Mamphone Khaketla

Environment and Tourism, Mathabiso Lepono

Finance and Development Planning, Timothy Thahane

Foreign Affairs, Mohlabi Kenneth Tsekoa

Health and Social Welfare, Motloheloa Phooko

Home Affairs, Motsoahae Thomas Thabane

Industry, Trade and Marketing, Mpho Malie

Justice, Human Rights, Law and Constitutional Affairs, Rehabilitation, Shakane Robong Mokhehle

Labour and Employment, Sello Machakela

Local Government, Pontso Susan Matimelo Sekatle

Natural Resources, Monyane Moleleki

Prime Minister's Office, Sephiri Motanyane

Public Works and Transport, Mofelehetsi Moerane

Tourism, Gender and Youth, Mlalele Motaung

Works and Transport, Mofelehetsi Moerane

HIGH COMMISSION FOR THE KINGDOM OF LESOTHO

7 Chesham Place, London SW1X 8HN

Tel: 020-7235 5686

Email: lhc@lesotholondon.org.uk

High Commissioner, HE Lebohang Ramohlanka, apptd 2000

BRITISH HIGH COMMISSION

PO Box Ms 521, Maseru 100

Tel: (00 266) 313961

Email: hcmaseru@lesoff.co.za

High Commissioner, HE Kaye Oliver, CMG, OBE, apptd 1999

ECONOMY

The economy is based on agriculture and animal husbandry, and the adverse balance of trade (mainly consumer and capital goods) is offset by the earnings of the large numbers of the population who work in South Africa. Apart from some diamonds, Lesotho has few natural resources. Agriculture contributes 11 per cent of GDP and the main crops are maize, sorghum and vegetables. Industry contributes some 42 per cent and services around 47 per cent of GDP. The Lesotho National Development Corporation was set up to promote the development of industry, mining, trade and tourism.

In 2000 Lesotho had a trade deficit of US$516 million and a current account deficit of US$151 million. In 1998 imports totalled US$863 million and exports US$194 million.

GNP – US$1,169 million (2000); US$550 per capita (1999)
GDP – US$877 million (1998); US$460 per capita (1999)
ANNUAL AVERAGE GROWTH OF GDP – 5.5 per cent (1998)
INFLATION RATE – 6.1 per cent (2000)
TOTAL EXTERNAL DEBT – US$686 million (1999)

Trade with UK	2000	2001
Imports from UK	£313,000	£1,941,000
Exports to UK	828,000	1,883,000

COMMUNICATIONS

A tarred road links Maseru to several of the main lowland towns. The mountainous areas are linked by tarred, gravelled and earth roads and tracks. Roads link border towns in South Africa with the main towns in Lesotho. Maseru is also connected by rail with the main Bloemfontein–Natal line of the South African Railways. Scheduled international air services are operated daily between Maseru and Johannesburg, and other scheduled international flights are to Gaborone, Harare, Manzini and Maputo. Internal scheduled services are operated by the Lesotho Airways Corporation. The telephone network is fully automated in all urban centres. Radio telephone communication is used extensively in the remote rural areas.

EDUCATION

There are over 1,200 primary and over 180 secondary schools, with emphasis being laid on agricultural and vocational education. The National University of Lesotho at Roma was established as a university in 1975.
ILLITERACY RATE – 15.7 per cent (2002)
ENROLMENT (percentage of age group) – primary 100 per cent (1997); secondary 31 per cent (1997); tertiary 2 per cent (1997)

LIBERIA
Republic of Liberia

AREA – 43,000 sq. miles (111,369 sq. km). Neighbours: Guinea (north), Côte d'Ivoire (east), Sierra Leone (north-west)
POPULATION – 3,225,837 (2001 estimate). The official language is English. The main African languages are Bassa, Kpelle and Kru, though some 16 ethnic languages are spoken
CAPITAL – Ψ Monrovia (population, 421,000, 2000 estimate
MAJOR CITIES – Ψ Buchanan (Grand Bassa);
Ψ Greenville (Sinoe); Ψ Harper (Cape Palmas)
CURRENCY – Liberian dollar (L$) of 100 cents
NATIONAL ANTHEM – All Hail, Liberia, Hail
NATIONAL DAY – 26 July
NATIONAL FLAG – Alternate horizontal stripes (five white, six red), with five-pointed white star on blue field in upper corner next to flagstaff
LIFE EXPECTANCY (years) – male 54.6; female 56.7
POPULATION GROWTH RATE – 1.5 per cent (1999)
POPULATION DENSITY – 26 per sq. km (1999)
URBAN POPULATION – 44.9 per cent (2000)
MILITARY EXPENDITURE – 5.6 per cent of GDP (2000)
MILITARY PERSONNEL – 15,000 (including militias supporting government forces)
ILLITERACY RATE – 43.6 per cent (2002)

HISTORY AND POLITICS

Liberia was founded by the American Colonisation Society in 1822 as a colony for freed American slaves, and has been recognised since 1847 as an independent state.

William V. S. Tubman, President since 1944, died in 1971 and was succeeded by Dr Tolbert. The constitution was suspended following a military coup in 1980 during which Tolbert was killed. M/Sgt. Samuel Doe assumed power as chairman of a military council. A new constitution was endorsed by a referendum in 1984. Doe and his party, the National Democratic Party of Liberia (NDPL) won the elections held in 1985. Doe was killed in 1990 and civil war ensued. A cease-fire was declared in August 1993 and a council of state governed the country until a general election was held in July 1997, which was won by the National Patriotic Party (NPP), and Charles Taylor was elected president with 75 per cent of the vote in an election deemed free and fair by international observers.

CIVIL WAR

A rebel incursion in 1989 by the National Patriotic Front of Liberia (NPFL) led by Charles Taylor developed into a full-scale civil war in 1990. A five-nation Economic Community of West African States (ECOWAS) peacekeeping force (known as ECOMOG) landed in Monrovia in an effort to end the conflict but in September 1990 President Doe was killed, having refused to step down. The Interim Government of National Unity (IGNU) was formed in August 1990. A peace agreement was signed by the IGNU, NPFL and another rebel group, ULIMO, on 25 July 1993, which brought about a cease-fire on 1 August. In August 1999, President Taylor ordered a state of emergency after rebels from the Joint Forces for the Liberation of Liberia crossed the border from Guinea and briefly seized several towns.

In July 2000, the USA threatened Liberia with international sanctions if it continued to support insurgency in Sierra Leone.

Liberia accused Guinea of supporting an attack by Liberians United for Reconciliation and Democracy (LURD) rebels on border towns and villages in February 2001 and claimed that Guinea was threatening to invade.

On 7 March 2001 the UN Security Council imposed a diamond embargo on Liberia and accused the country of supporting the Revolutionary United Front, a Sierra Leonean rebel movement.

A state of emergency was declared on 8 February 2002 after LURD rebels carried out attacks close to the capital. On 29 April 2002 political activity was banned amid a renewed upsurge in fighting. In May 2002, the UN

Security Council renewed its sanctions on Liberia, saying the country has not yet severed ties with the rebels. Liberia argued that the arms embargo is preventing the military from fending off rebels in Liberia's north.

POLITICAL SYSTEM

The head of state is an executive president, directly elected for a six-year term, who appoints the Cabinet. There is a bicameral legislature consisting of a 64-member lower chamber, the House of Representatives, which is directly elected for a six-year term, and a 26-member Senate, elected for a nine-year term.

HEAD OF STATE

President, Charles Taylor, *elected* 19 July 1997, *inaugurated* 3 August 1997
Vice-President, Moses Z. Blah

CABINET *as at July 2002*

Commerce, Cora Peabody
Defence, Daniel Chea
Education, Evelyne Kandakai
Finance, Nathaniel Barnes
Foreign Affairs, Monie Captan
Gender Development, Musuleng Cooper
Health and Social Welfare, Peter Coleman
Information, Culture and Tourism, Reginald Goodridge
Internal Affairs, Richard Flomo
Justice, Eddington Varmah
Labour, Christian Herbert
Lands, Mines and Energy, Jenkins Dunbar
Ministers of State, Sam Jackson (*Planning and Economic Affairs*) (*acting*); Jonathan Taylor (*Presidential Affairs*); Augustine Zayzay (*Without Portfolio*)
National Security, Philip Kamah
Planning and Economic Affairs, Amelia Ward
Post and Telecommunications, Mewaseh Paye-Baye
Public Works, Emmet Taylor
Rural Development, Hezekiah Bowen
Transport, Joe W. Mulbah (acting)
Youth and Sports, vacant

EMBASSY OF THE REPUBLIC OF LIBERIA
2 Pembridge Place, London W2 4XB
Tel: 020-7221 1036
Ambassador Extraordinary and Plenipotentiary, vacant

BRITISH AMBASSADOR, HE Jean Gordon, CMG, resident at Abidjan, Côte d'Ivoire

ECONOMY

Before the civil war began principal exports were iron ore, crude rubber, timber, uncut diamonds, palm kernels, cocoa and coffee, but the civil war has resulted in the suspension of most economic activity.
GDP – US$759 million (1998); US$258 per capita (1999)
ANNUAL AVERAGE GROWTH OF GDP – 2.7 per cent (1998)
TOTAL EXTERNAL DEBT – US$2,077 million (1999)

Trade with UK	2000	2001
Imports from UK	£16,375,000	£10,410,000
Exports to UK	1,712,000	12,015,000

COMMUNICATIONS

The artificial harbour and free port of Monrovia was opened in 1948. There are 10,300 km of roads, of which 628 km are paved, and 490 km of railway track. There are nine ports of entry, including three river ports. Robertsfield International Airport and Spriggs Payne airfield are currently being used for flights to other West African countries.

LIBYA
Al-Jamāhīriyya Al-'Arabiyya
Al-Lībiyya Ash-Sha'biyya Al-Ishtirākiyya - Great Socialist People's Libyan Arab Jamahiriya

AREA – 679,362 sq. miles (1,759,540 sq. km).
   Neighbours: Egypt and Sudan (east), Chad and Niger (south), Algeria and Tunisia (west)
POPULATION – 5,240,599 (2001 estimate). The people of Libya are principally Arab with some Berbers in the west and some Tuareg tribesmen in the Fezzan. Islam is the official religion but other religions are tolerated. The official language is Arabic
CAPITAL – Ψ Tripoli (Tarabulus) (population, 1,000,000, 1991 estimate)
MAJOR CITIES – Ψ Bangāzī (500,000); Ψ Misrātah (200,000); Sirte (100,000)
CURRENCY – Libyan dinar (LD) of 1,000 dirhams
NATIONAL ANTHEM – Allahu Akbar (God Is Great)
NATIONAL DAY – 1 September
NATIONAL FLAG – Libya uses a plain emerald green flag
LIFE EXPECTANCY (years) – male 69.2; female 73.3
POPULATION GROWTH RATE – 2.4 per cent (1999)
POPULATION DENSITY – 3 per sq. km (1999)
ILLITERACY RATE – 18.3 per cent (2002)

Vast sand and rock deserts, almost completely barren, occupy the greater part of Libya. The southern part of the country lies within the Sahara Desert. There are few rivers and as rainfall is irregular outside parts of Cyrenaica and Tripolitania, good harvests are rare.

The ancient ruins in Cyrenaica, at Cyrene, Ptolemais (Tolmeta) and Apollonia, are outstanding, as are those at Leptis Magna, 70 miles east, and at Sabratha, 40 miles west of Tripoli. An Italian expedition found in the south-west of the Fezzan a series of rock-paintings more than 5,000 years old.

HISTORY AND POLITICS

From the 16th century Libya was dominated by the Ottoman Empire, until occupied by Italy in 1911–12 in the course of the Italo-Turkish War. Under the 1912 Treaty of Ouchy, sovereignty over the province was transferred by Turkey to Italy, and in 1939 the four provinces of Libya (Tripoli, Misurata, Bangāzī and Derna) were incorporated in the national territory of Italy as *Libia Italiana*. After the Second World War Tripolitania and Cyrenaica were placed provisionally under British and the Fezzan under French administration, and in conformity with a resolution of the UN General Assembly in 1949, Libya became on 24 December 1951 the first independent state to be created by the UN. The monarchy was overthrown by a revolution in 1969 and the country was declared a republic. It was ruled by the Revolutionary Command Council (RCC) under the leadership of Col. Muammar al-Gadhafi.

In 1977, a new form of direct democracy, the 'Jamahiriyya' (state of the masses) was promulgated and the official name of the country was changed to Great

Socialist People's Libyan Arab Jamahiriyya. Since a reorganisation in 1979, neither Col. Gadhafi nor his former RCC colleagues have held formal posts in the administration. Gadhafi continues to hold the ceremonial title 'Leader of the Revolution'.

POLITICAL SYSTEM

At local level authority is vested in about 1,500 Basic and 14 Municipal People's Congresses which appoint Popular Committees to execute policy. Officials of these congresses and committees, together with representatives from unions and other organisations, form the 750-member General People's Congress, which normally meets twice each year. In addition, a number of extraordinary sessions are held throughout the year. This is the highest policy-making body in the country.

The General People's Congress appoints its own General Secretariat and the General People's Committee, whose members head the government departments which execute policy at national level. The Secretary of the General People's Committee has functions similar to those of a prime minister.

On 1 March 2000 it was announced that 12 of the ministries run by the General People's Committee had been abolished and that their powers had been devolved to provincial committees.

Leader of the Revolution and Supreme Commander of the Armed Forces, Col. Muammar al-Gadhafi

GENERAL PEOPLE'S COMMITTEE *as at July 2002*

Secretary-General, Mubarak al-Shamikh
Assistant Secretary-General, Abdullah al-Badri
Deputy Secretary for Production, Al-Baghdadi Ali al-Mahmudi
Deputy Secretary for Services, Ammar Mabruk al-Lutayyif
Secretary, African Unity, Ali Abdel Salam Turayki
Secretary, Economy and Trade, Shukri Muhammad Ghanim
Secretary, Finance, Al-Ujayli Abd-al-Salam Burayni
Secretary, Foreign Liaison and International Co-operation, Abdel Rahman Muhammad Shalgam
Secretary, Justice and Public Security, Mohammad Ali al-Masirati
Co-ordinator of the General Provisional Committee for Defence, Abu Bakr Jaber Yunes
Speaker of the General People's Congress, Mohammad al-Zenati

LIBYAN PEOPLE'S BUREAU
61–62 Ennismore Gardens, London SW7 1NH
Tel 020-7589 6120
Ambassador Extraordinary and Plenipotentiary, HE Mohamed Abu Al-Qassim Azwai, apptd 2001
Political Counsellor, Taher Ettoumi

BRITISH EMBASSY
Sharia Uahran 1, PO Box 4206, Tripoli
Tel (00 218) (21) 333 1191/2/3
Ambassador Extraordinary and Plenipotentiary, HE Richard Dalton, CMG, apptd 1999

BRITISH COUNCIL DIRECTOR, Antony Jones, British Embassy, 24th Floor, Burj al Fatah, Tripoli; Email: info.libya@britishcouncil-ly.org

DEFENCE

The Army has about 2,025 main battle tanks, 1,000 armoured infantry fighting vehicles and 945 armoured personnel carriers. The Navy has one submarine, two frigates, 16 patrol and coastal vessels, and seven armed helicopters at seven bases. The Air Force has 372 combat aircraft and 41 armed helicopters.

As part of the UN economic sanctions imposed in April 1992, there is a total embargo on arms sales to Libya.
MILITARY EXPENDITURE – 3.2 per cent of GDP (2000)
MILITARY PERSONNEL – 76,000: Army 45,000, Navy 8,000, Air Force 23,000
CONSCRIPTION DURATION – One to two years (selective)

ECONOMY

Economic sanctions were imposed on Libya in April 1992 by the UN Security Council following Libya's failure to hand over two suspects in the bombing of Pan-Am flight 103 over Lockerbie, Scotland, in 1988, in which 270 people were killed. The UN imposed additional sanctions in December 1993, including freezing assets abroad and restricting imports of spare parts and equipment for the oil and aviation sectors. Some sanctions were suspended in April 1999, following mediation by President Mandela of South Africa in March 1999, which led to the extradition in April of the two Libyan suspects to the Netherlands to stand trial. Following the conviction of one of the two suspects, former Libyan intelligence agent Abdel Baset al-Megrahi, on 31 January 2001, the lifting of the remaining sanctions has been made dependent on Libya accepting responsibility for the Lockerbie bombing and agreeing to pay compensation to the families of the victims. In May 2002 compensation negotiations took place with Libyan officials declaring that compensation would only be made if international sanctions were lifted.

Agriculture is confined mainly to the coastal areas of Tripolitania and Cyrenaica, where barley, wheat, olives, citrus fruits and livestock are produced, and to the areas of the oases.

The main industry is oil and gas production. There are pipelines from Zaltan to the terminal at al-Burayqah, from Dahra to as-Sidrah, from Amal to Ras Lanuf, and from the Intisar field to az-Zuwaytīnah. In 1998, 69.2 million tonnes of crude oil was produced. Cement, construction materials and textiles are also produced. Economic constraints have delayed some projects, particularly since Libya decided in 1983 to go ahead with a major irrigation scheme, the 'Great Man-Made River'. The government is now seeking foreign direct investment for the oil and gas industries and to finance improvements to the country's infrastructure.
GDP – US$31,661 million (1998); US$5,244 per capita (1999)
ANNUAL AVERAGE GROWTH OF GDP – 0.6 per cent (1998)

TRADE

Exports are dominated by crude oil, but some wool, cattle, sheep and horses, olive oil, and hides and skins are also exported. Principal imports are machinery and transport equipment, foodstuffs, livestock, and most construction materials and consumer goods.

Trade with UK	2000	2001
Imports from UK	£186,546,000	£184,424,000
Exports to UK	200,824,000	189,816,000

COMMUNICATIONS

There are 25,675 km of roads; the coastal road running from the Tunisian frontier through Tripoli to Bangāzī, Tubruq and the Egyptian border serves the main population centres. Main roads also link the provincial centres, and the oil-producing areas of the south with the coastal towns.

There are airports at Tripoli and Bangāzī (Benina), Kufra, Labrag, Misrātah and Tubruk. Since April 1992 a UN embargo on air links with Libya has been in force.

LIECHTENSTEIN
Fürstentum Liechtenstein – Principality of Liechtenstein

AREA – 62 sq. miles (160 sq. km). Neighbours: Austria, Switzerland
POPULATION – 32,528 (2001 estimate). The language of the principality is Standard German. An Alemannic dialect is in general use. About 65.4 per cent of the population are Liechtensteiners, the remainder being mainly Swiss, Austrians and Germans. Roman Catholicism is the religion of 80.4 per cent of the population; there is a Protestant minority
CAPITAL – Vaduz (population, 5,106, 1998)
CURRENCY – Swiss franc of 100 rappen (or centimes)
NATIONAL ANTHEM – Oben Am Jungen Rhein (Up On The Young Rhine)
NATIONAL DAY – 15 August
NATIONAL FLAG – Equal horizontal bands of blue over red; gold crown on blue band near staff
LIFE EXPECTANCY (years) – male 66.1; female 72.9
POPULATION GROWTH RATE – 1.0 per cent (1999)
POPULATION DENSITY – 200 per sq. km (1999)

HISTORY AND POLITICS

The region was settled in the fifth century AD by the West Germanic Alemanni. The Principality of Liechtenstein was established by Emperor Charles VI in 1719. Following the First World War, Liechtenstein severed its ties with Austria and began its association with Switzerland, taking up the Swiss currency in 1921.

In November 1999, the European Court of Human Rights fined Prince Hans Adam II for abusing his subjects' freedom of speech, a development which prompted a constitutional crisis in the principality.

In February 2000, Prince Hans Adam announced that he wished to hold a referendum on constitutional reform, and threatened to abdicate if his proposals were rejected by the electorate.

The Patriotic Union (VU) and the Progressive Citizens' Party (FBP) governed the country in coalition from 1938 until March 1997. The 1997 general election was won by the VU, which lost power to the FBP, who won 13 seats in the general election held on 9 and 11 February 2001. The new government took office on 5 April.

POLITICAL SYSTEM

Liechtenstein is a constitutional monarchy. The Cabinet is appointed by the Prince on the advice of parliament and consists of a head of government and four ministers. The 25-member *Landtag*, the unicameral parliament, has a four-year term. There is a threshold of 8 per cent for parties to gain representation.

HEAD OF STATE

HSH The Prince of Liechtenstein, Hans Adam II, *born* 14 February 1945; *succeeded* 13 November 1989; *married* 30 July 1967, Countess Marie Kinsky; and has *issue*: Prince Alois; Prince Maximilian, *b.* 16 May 1969; Prince Constantin, *b.* 15 March 1972; Princess Tatjana, *b.* 10 April 1973
Heir, HSH Prince Alois, *b.* 11 June 1968, *married* 1993 Duchess Sophie of Bavaria; and has *issue*: Prince Wenzel, *b.* 24 May 1995; Princess Marie, *b.* 17 October 1996; Prince Georg, *b.* 20 April 1999

CABINET *as at July 2002*

Head of Government, Construction, Family Affairs and Equal Rights, Finance, General Government Affairs, Otmar Hasler
Deputy Head of Government, Education, Justice, Transport, Rita Kieber-Beck
Culture and Sports, Environment, Interior, Alois Ospelt
Economy, Health, Social Matters, Hansjörg Frick
Foreign Affairs, Ernst Walch

DIPLOMATIC REPRESENTATION

Liechtenstein is represented in diplomatic and consular matters in the United Kingdom by the Swiss Embassy.

BRITISH AMBASSADOR, Basil Eastwood, CMG, resident at Bern, Switzerland

ECONOMY

The main industries are high and ultra-high vacuum engineering, the semiconductor industry, roller bearings, artificial teeth, heating equipment, synthetic fibres, woollen and homespun fabrics. Following international accusations that Liechtenstein was a haven for money-laundering, the country banned anonymous bank accounts in September 2000.

In 1991 Liechtenstein became a member of the European Free Trade Association, and joined the European Economic Area on 1 May 1995.
GDP – US$1,150 million (1998); US$35,376 per capita (1999)
ANNUAL AVERAGE GROWTH OF GDP – 2.1 per cent (1998)

Trade with UK	2000	2001
Imports from UK	£7,287,000	£6,020,000
Exports to UK	21,484,000	25,010,000

LITHUANIA
Lietuvos Respublika – Republic of Lithuania

AREA – 25,174 sq. miles (65,200 sq. km). Neighbours: Latvia (north), Belarus (east and south), Poland and the Kaliningrad region of the Russian Federation (south-west)
POPULATION – 3,483,972 (2001 estimate): 85.5 per cent Lithuanian, 6.7 per cent Polish, 6.3 per cent Russian, 1.2 per cent Belarusian, 0.7 per cent Ukrainian. The majority are Roman Catholic (79 per cent), with Russian Orthodox (4.1 per cent) and Lutheran minorities. Lithuanian is the state language
CAPITAL – Vilnius (population, 542,287, 2001 estimate)
MAJOR CITIES – Kaunas (378,943); Klaipėda (192,954), 2001
CURRENCY – Litas of 100 centas, pegged to the euro, €1= 3.45 litas
NATIONAL ANTHEM – Tautiška Giesme (The National Song)
NATIONAL DAY – 16 February (Independence Day)
NATIONAL FLAG – Three horizontal stripes of yellow, green, red
LIFE EXPECTANCY (years) – male 67.6; female 77.7
POPULATION GROWTH RATE – 0.0 per cent (2001)
POPULATION DENSITY – 53 per sq. km (2001)
URBAN POPULATION – 66.9 per cent (2001)

Lithuania lies in the middle and lower basin of the river Nemunas. Along the coast is a lowland plain which rises inland to form uplands in east and central Lithuania. These uplands, the Middle Lowlands, give way to the Baltic Highlands in east and south-east Lithuania; the

highest point is 294 m (965 ft). There is a network of rivers and over 2,800 lakes, which mainly lie in the east of the country.

HISTORY AND POLITICS

The first independent Lithuanian state emerged as the Kingdom of Lithuania in 1251. After forming a joint Commonwealth and Kingdom with Poland in 1569, Lithuania was taken over by the Russian Empire in 1795.

Lithuania declared its independence from the Russian Empire on 16 February 1918 and signed a peace treaty with the Soviet Union on 12 July 1920. The Soviet Union annexed Lithuania in 1940 under the terms of the Molotov–Ribbentrop pact with Germany. Lithuania was invaded and occupied when Germany invaded the Soviet Union during the Second World War. In 1944, the Soviet Union recaptured the country and confirmed its annexation.

Over 90 per cent of the population voted for independence in a referendum in February 1991. The Soviet Union recognised the independence of Lithuania on 10 September 1991.

In the general election held on 8 October 2000, the Social Democratic Coalition won 52 seats, the Lithuanian Liberal Union (LLS) won 34 seats, the New Union (Social Liberals) NS (SL) won 29 seats, and the Homeland Union, which had formed the previous government, won only nine seats. A coalition government was formed, which comprised the LLS, the NS (SL), the Modern Christian Democrats and the Centre Union, with 71 of the 141 seats in the legislature. The governing coalition collapsed in June 2001 and President Adamkus nominated Social Democratic (SD) party leader Algirdas Brazauskas as prime minister. Brazauskas formed a coalition government comprising the SD and the NS(SL), with 81 of the 141 seats in the legislature. The new government was appointed by the new president on 5 July 2001.

FOREIGN RELATIONS

Lithuania applied for membership of the EU in December 1995; a treaty of association with the EU entered into force on 1 February 1998 and formal accession negotiations began in 2000.

POLITICAL SYSTEM

Under the 1992 constitution, the head of state is a directly elected president, whose five-year term of office is renewable once only. Executive authority is vested in the government, consisting of the prime minister, who is appointed by the president with the approval of the *Seimas*, and ministers appointed upon the recommendation of the prime minister

Legislative power is exercised by the Seimas, a unicameral parliament of 141 members directly elected for four-year terms. Seventy-one members are elected in first-past-the-post constituencies and 70 by proportional representation, with a 5 per cent threshold for representation. The constitution bans an alignment of Lithuania with any post-Soviet eastern alliance.

HEAD OF STATE

President, Valdas Adamkus, *elected* 4 February 1998; *took office* 25 February 1998

GOVERNMENT *as at July 2002*

Prime Minister, Algirdas Brazauskas (SD)
Agriculture and Forestry, Jeronimas Kraujelis (NS(SL))
Culture, Roma Dovydieniene (SD)
Defence, Linas Linkevičius (Ind.)

Economy, Petras Cesna (Ind.)
Education and Science, Algirdas Monkevičius (NS(SL))
Environment, Arunas Kundrotas (Ind.)
Finance, Dalia Grybauskaite (Ind.)
Foreign Affairs, Antanas Valionis (Ind.)
Health, Konstantinas Romualdas Dobrovolskis (Ind.)
Interior, Juozas Bernatonis (SD)
Justice, Vytautas Markevicius (Ind.)
Social Affairs and Labour, Vilija Blinkevičiūtė (Ind.)
Transport, Zigmantas Balcytis (SD)

LLS Lithuanian Liberal Union; NS (SL) New Union (Social Liberals); SD Social Democratic Party; Ind. Independent

EMBASSY OF THE REPUBLIC OF LITHUANIA
84 Gloucester Place, London W1U 6AU
Tel: 020-7486 6401/2
Email: chancery@lithuanianembassy.co.uk
Ambassador Extraordinary and Plenipotentiary, HE Aurimas Taurantas, apptd 2002

BRITISH EMBASSY
2 Antakalnio, LT-2055 Vilnius
Tel: (00 370) (5) 212 2070/1
Ambassador Extraordinary and Plenipotentiary, HE Jeremy Hill, apptd 2001

BRITISH COUNCIL DIRECTOR, Lina Balenaite, Vilnius 39, LT 2001 Vilnius;
Email: lina.balenaite@britishcouncil.lt

DEFENCE

The Army has 81 armoured personnel carriers; the Navy has two frigates and five patrol and coastal vessels based at Klaipėda; the Air Force has eight helicopters. The last Russian troops withdrew in 1993.

MILITARY EXPENDITURE – 1.8 per cent of GDP (2000)
MILITARY PERSONNEL – 12,190: Army 7,500, Navy 580, Air Force 800; Paramilitaries 12,450
CONSCRIPTION DURATION – 12 months

ECONOMY

The economy was largely agricultural prior to rapid industrialisation during the Soviet era. A privatisation programme began in 1991 and progress in the sale of small enterprises has been quick and successful. In 1997, the privatisation of communication, energy and transport companies was begun.

In 1999, agriculture and forestry accounted for 8.8 per cent of GDP, mining and manufacturing industry 23.3 per cent, construction 8 per cent and transport and communications 11 per cent. The main industries are chemicals and petrochemicals, food processing, wood products, textiles, leather goods, machinery, machine tools and household appliances.

GNP – US$10,741 million (2000); US$2,640 per capita (1999)
GDP – US$10,692 million (1998); US$2,867 per capita (1999)
ANNUAL AVERAGE GROWTH OF GDP – 5.9 per cent (2001)
INFLATION RATE – 1.3 per cent (2001)
UNEMPLOYMENT – 12.5 per cent (2001)
TOTAL EXTERNAL DEBT – US$3,584 million (1999)

TRADE

Lithuania's main trading partners are Germany, Latvia, Russia, Denmark and Belarus. In January 2001, total foreign investment in Lithuania reached US$2.3 billion.

In 2000 there was a trade deficit of US$1,104 million and a current account deficit of US$675 million. Imports totalled US$5,457 million and exports US$3,810 million.

Trade with UK	2000	2001
Imports from UK	£133,629,000	£137,257,000
Exports to UK	254,778,000	240,897,000

COMMUNICATIONS

There are 45,340 km of surfaced roads; there is a relatively well-developed railway system of 2,898 km running east-west and north-south and linking the major towns with Vilnius and Klaipèda, the main international port. Vilnius has an international airport.

CULTURE AND EDUCATION

Lithuanian culture and literature are closely linked to the national liberation movements of the 19th and early 20th centuries, and the literature of Lithuanians who went into exile during the Soviet era.

Lithuania re-established a national education system in 1990. Education is free and compulsory from seven to 16 years, with the system comprising elementary schools (four years), nine-year schools (five years), and secondary schools (three years). The language of instruction is predominantly Lithuanian, but there are also Russian and Polish schools. There are 105 vocational schools and 65 colleges. Lithuania has eight universities and seven other institutes of higher education. Vilnius University, founded in 1579, is one of the oldest universities in eastern Europe.

ILLITERACY RATE – 0.4 per cent (2002)

ENROLMENT (percentage of age group) – secondary 98 per cent (1997); tertiary 31 per cent (1997)

LUXEMBOURG

Groussherzogtom Lëtzebuerg/Grand-Duché de Luxembourg/Großherzogtum Luxembourg – Grand Duchy of Luxembourg

AREA – 998 sq. miles (2,586 sq. km). Neighbours: Germany (east), Belgium (west and north), France (south)

POPULATION – 442,972 (2001 estimate), nearly all Roman Catholic. The officially designated 'national language' is Lëtzebuergesch (Luxembourgish), the mainly spoken language. French and German are the official languages for written purposes, and French is the language of administration

CAPITAL – Luxembourg (population, 77,400, 1996)

CURRENCY – Euro (€) of 100 cents

NATIONAL ANTHEM – Ons Hémécht (Our Homeland)

NATIONAL DAY – 23 June

NATIONAL FLAG – Three horizontal bands, red, white and blue

LIFE EXPECTANCY (years) – male 74.6; female 80.9

POPULATION GROWTH RATE – 1.2 per cent (1999)

POPULATION DENSITY – 166 per sq. km (1999)

ENROLMENT (percentage of age group) – primary 81 per cent (1985); secondary 64 per cent (1994); tertiary 10 per cent (1996)

HISTORY AND POLITICS

Established as an independent state under the sovereignty of the King of the Netherlands as Grand Duke by the Congress of Vienna in 1815, Luxembourg formed part of the Germanic Confederation from 1815 to 1866, becoming neutral in 1867.

The territory was invaded by Germany in 1914 but was liberated in 1918. By the Treaty of Versailles (1919), Germany renounced its former agreements with Luxembourg and in 1921 an economic union was formed with Belgium. The Grand Duchy was again invaded and occupied by Germany in 1940, and liberated in 1944. The constitution was modified in 1948 and the stipulation of permanent neutrality was abandoned.

POLITICAL SYSTEM

There is a Chamber of 60 deputies, elected by universal suffrage for five years. Legislation is submitted to the Council of State. The last general election was held on 13 June 1999 and a coalition government was installed. In March 1998, Grand Duke Jean passed certain constitutional powers on to his son and heir, Prince Henri, and announced on 25 December 1999 that he would abdicate in favour of Prince Henri in September 2000.

HEAD OF STATE

HRH The Grand Duke of Luxembourg, HRH Grand Duke Henri, born 16 April 1955; succeeded (on abdication of his father) 7 October 2000; married 14 February 1981, Maria Teresa Mestre, and has issue, Prince Guillaume; Prince Felix, b. 3 June 1984; Prince Louis, b. 3 August 1986; Princess Alexandra, b. 2 February 1991; Prince Sébastien, b. 16 April 1992, Princess Gabriella, b. 26 March 1994

Heir, HRH Prince Guillaume, born 11 November 1981

CABINET as at July 2002

Prime Minister, Finance, Jean-Claude Juncker (CSP)

Deputy PM, Foreign Affairs, Trade, Civil Service and Administrative Reform, Lydie Polfer (DP)

Agriculture, Viticulture, Rural Development, Small Businesses, Housing and Tourism, Fernand Boden (CSP)

Culture, Higher Education and Research, Public Works, Erna Hennicot-Schoepges (CSP)

Development Aid and Defence, Environment, Charles Goerens (DP)

Economy, Transport, Henri Grethen (DP)

Employment, Religion, Parliamentary Relations, François Biltgen (CSP)

Family, Social Solidarity and Youth, Advancement of Women, Marie-Josée Jacobs (CSP)

Health and Social Security, Carlo Wagner (DP)

Home Affairs, Michel Wolter (CSP)

National Education, Vocational Training and Sport, Anne Brasseur (DP)

Secretaries of State, Joseph Schaack (DP) (Civil Service and Administrative Reform); Eugène Berger (DP) (Environment)

Treasury and Budget, Justice, Luc Frieden (CSP)

CSP Christian Social Party; DP Democratic Party

EMBASSY OF LUXEMBOURG
27 Wilton Crescent, London SW1X 8SD
Tel: 020-7235 6961
Ambassador Extraordinary and Plenipotentiary, HE Joseph Weyland, apptd 1993

BRITISH EMBASSY
14 Boulevard Roosevelt, L-2450 Luxembourg
Tel: (00 352) 229864/5/6
Ambassador Extraordinary and Plenipotentiary, HE Gordon Wetherell, apptd 2000

DEFENCE

For legal reasons, NATO's squadron of E-3A Sentry airborne early warning aircraft is registered in Luxembourg.

MILITARY EXPENDITURE – 0.8 per cent of GDP (2000)

MILITARY PERSONNEL – Army: 900; Paramilitaries 612

ECONOMY

Luxembourg is a member of the Belgium-Netherlands-Luxembourg Customs Union (Benelux 1960). The country has an important iron and steel industry and is an important financial centre. In 1998, 727,000 tourists visited Luxembourg.

The chief exports are metal goods, manufactures, machinery, chemicals, transport equipment, and foodstuffs and livestock. The chief imports are machinery, transport equipment, metal goods, manufactures, chemicals, and foodstuffs and livestock.

In 2000 imports totalled US$10,315 million and exports US$7,876 million.

GNP – US$19,420 million (2000) ; US$42,930 per capita (1999)

GDP – US$18,340 million (1998); US$44,797 per capita (1999)

ANNUAL AVERAGE GROWTH OF GDP – 7.5 per cent (1999)

INFLATION RATE – 3.1 per cent (2000)

UNEMPLOYMENT – 2.9 per cent (1999)

Trade with UK	2000	2001
Imports from UK	£216,700,000	£260,900,000
Exports to UK	121,700,000	271,600,000

MACEDONIA
Republika Makedonija – Republic of Macedonia

AREA – 9,928 sq. miles (25,713 sq. km). Neighbours: Federal Republic of Yugoslavia (north), Bulgaria (east), Greece (south), Albania (west)

POPULATION – 2,046,209 (2001 estimate); 1,936,877 (1994 census): 66.5 per cent Macedonian, 22.9 per cent Albanian, 4.0 per cent ethnic Turks, 2.3 per cent Romanies, 2.0 per cent Serbs and 0.4 per cent Vlachs. The census results are disputed by the ethnic Albanians and Serbs. Macedonian Orthodox Christianity is the majority religion, with a Muslim minority. The main language is Macedonian (a south Slavic language), which is written in the Cyrillic script

CAPITAL – Skopje (population, 429,964, 1994)

MAJOR CITIES – Bitola (84,002); Kumanovo (69,231); Prilep (70,152)

CURRENCY – Denar of 100 deni

NATIONAL ANTHEM – Denes Nad Makedonija Se Radja Novo Sonce Na Slobodata (Today A New Sun Of Liberty Appears Over Macedonia)

NATIONAL FLAG – Red with an eight-rayed sun displayed over the whole field

LIFE EXPECTANCY (years) – male 71.4; female 75.8

POPULATION GROWTH RATE – 0.6 per cent (1999)

POPULATION DENSITY – 78 per sq. km (1999)

URBAN POPULATION – 62.0 per cent (2000)

MILITARY EXPENDITURE – 2.1 per cent of GDP (2000)

MILITARY PERSONNEL – Army 15,000; Paramilitaries 10,000

CONSCRIPTION DURATION – Nine months

ENROLMENT (percentage of age group) – primary 99 per cent (1997); secondary 63 per cent (1997); tertiary 20 per cent (1997)

HISTORY AND POLITICS

From the ninth to the 14th centuries AD Macedonia was ruled alternately by the Bulgars and the Byzantine Empire. In the middle of the 14th century the area was conquered by the Turks and remained under the Ottoman Empire for over 500 years. After the defeat of Turkey in the two Balkan wars of 1912–13 the geographical area of Macedonia was divided, the major gpart becoming Serbian (the areas of the present-day Macedonia) and the remainder given to Greece and Bulgaria. In 1918 Serbian Macedonia was incorporated into Serbia as South Serbia. When Yugoslavia was reconstituted in 1944 as a Communist federal republic under President Tito, Macedonia became a constituent republic.

Multiparty elections for the 120-seat assembly held in November and December 1990 produced the first non-Communist government since the Second World War. The electorate overwhelmingly approved Macedonian sovereignty and independence in a referendum and independence was declared on 8 September 1991.

In elections to the Sobranī (National Assembly) held on 18 October and 1 November 1998, the coalition of the Internal Macedonian Revolutionary Organisation-Democratic Party for Macedonian National Unity (VMRO-DMPNE) and the Democratic Alternative (DA) won 62 of the 120 seats. It invited the Democratic Party of Albanians (DPA), an ethnic Albanian party, to join the coalition. Presidential elections on 14 November and 5 December 1999 were won by Boris Trajkovski of the VMRO-DMPNE. A new government of national unity was elected by the Assembly on 13 May 2001, which included the VMRO-DMPNE, the Democratic Party of Albanians (DPA), the Liberal Party (LP), the Social Democratic Alliance of Macedonia (SDSM) and the (ethnic Albanian) Party for Democratic Prosperity (PDP). In November 2001, the SDSM and the LDP left the coalition and New Democracy (ND) joined it. The new cabinet was approved on 30 November. The most recent elections took place on 15 September 2002.

INSURGENCY

Fighting between ethnic Albanian guerrillas belonging to the National Liberation Army (NLA) and Macedonian security forces began on 26 February 2001 in the village of Tanusevci near the border with Kosovo and by mid-March had spread to Tetovo, the largest ethnic Albanian town. The Macedonian government, which included ethnic Albanians, promised to implement reforms to increase minority rights for ethnic Albanians and moderate Albanian parties called on the guerrillas to surrender their arms. The insurgency was condemned by the UN Security Council on 21 March 2001. On 10 April, President Trajkovski announced the establishment of a commission to investigate discrimination against the Albanian minority.

On 23 May 2001, the two main Albanian parties, the DPA and the PDP, signed an agreement with the NLA, in which the rebels agreed to withdraw in return for an amnesty and NLA participation in discussions with the government. The Macedonian government and international organisations immediately condemned the agreement. President Trajkovski urged the Albanian parties to renounce the agreement, which they refused to do, but it was agreed that discussions should continue in order to preserve the coalition government.

By early June, fighting had become widespread across the north of the country. On 14 June, President Trajkovski made an official request for NATO assistance to disarm the NLA. A cease-fire declared on 12 June ended after only 11 days when Macedonian forces

launched an attack on the village of Aracinovo, but halted their offensive when the NLA agreed to withdraw its forces from the village. On 25 June, Macedonian Slavic nationalists stormed parliament in protest against the government's co-operation with NATO in escorting the besieged NLA rebels from Aracinovo to safety.

On 13 August, the leaders of the Macedonian and Albanian parties signed a peace agreement that allowed for increased recruitment of ethnic Albanians into the police force; made Albanian an official language along with Macedonian; gave Christianity and Islam equal status; removed from the constitution any reference to the ethnic background of Macedonian citizens; allowed for a limited amount of devolution; promised human rights, civil liberties, social justice and peaceful co-existence; and cleared the way for the deployment of a NATO disarmament force. Amendments to the constitution were approved by parliament on 15 and 16 November 2001. By August 2002, no further serious fighting had occurred but relations between the country's Macedonian and Albanian populations remained tense.

FOREIGN RELATIONS

A new constitution was adopted in November 1991 and then amended at the EC's request to make it clear that Macedonia had no territorial claim on its neighbours. Macedonia applied for EC recognition in December 1991 but was refused because of Greece's objections to the state's name, flag and currency which, according to the Greek government, amounted to a territorial claim on the Greek province of Macedonia. Macedonia gained UN membership on 8 April 1993 following a compromise agreement by which it is referred to formally as the 'Former Yugoslav Republic of Macedonia' (FYROM). A border demarcation agreement was signed with Yugoslavia on 23 February 2001.

HEAD OF STATE

President, Boris Trajkovski, *elected* 5 December 1999

CABINET *as at July 2002*

Prime Minister, Ljubčo Georgievski (VMRO-DPMNE)
Deputy Prime Minister, Labour and Social Policy,
  Bedredin Ibrahami (DPA)
Agriculture, Forestry and Water Resources Management,
  Marjan Gjorcev (VMRO-DPMNE)
Culture, Ganka Samoilovask-Cvetanov (VMRO-DPMNE)
Defence, Vlado Popovski (LP)
Economy, Besnik Fetai (DPA)
Education and Science, Nenad Novkovski (VMRO-DPMNE)
Environment and Urban Planning, Vladimir Dzabirski (VMRO-DPMNE)
Finance, Nikola Grujevski (VMRO-DPMNE)
Foreign Affairs, Slobodan Casule (NDP)
Health, Georgi Orovcanec (NDP)
Interior, Ljube Boskovski (VMRO-DPMNE)
Justice, Idzet Memeti (PDP)
Local Self-government, Faik Aslani (PDP)
Transport and Communications, Ljupco Balkovski (VMRO-DPMNE)
Without Portfolio, Zoran Krstevski (LP); Kemal Musliu (PDP); Xhevdet Nasufi (DPA)

DPA Democratic Party of Albanians; LP Liberal Party; NDP New Democracy; PDP Party for Democratic Prosperity; VMRO-DPMNE Internal Macedonian Revolutionary Organisation-Democratic Party for Macedonian National Unity

EMBASSY OF THE REPUBLIC OF MACEDONIA
5th Floor, 25 James Street, London W1U 1DU.
Tel: 020-7935 2823
Ambassador Extraordinary and Plenipotentiary, HE Stevo Crvenkovski, apptd 1997

BRITISH EMBASSY
Dimitrija Chupovski 26, 4th Floor, MK-9100 Skopje
Tel: (00 389) (91) 116772/109941
Ambassador Extraordinary and Plenipotentiary, HE George Edgar, apptd 2001

BRITISH COUNCIL DIRECTOR, Andrew Hadley, Bulevar Goce Delcev 6, PO Box 562, MK-1000 Skopje; Email: info@britishcouncil.org.mk

ECONOMY

The economy was decimated by the UN trade sanctions against the rump Yugoslavia (from May 1992 until November 1995), and the Greek economic blockade (from February 1994 until October 1995). Macedonia is attempting to transform its economy to a market-orientated one and to introduce privatisation; by 1997, 45 per cent of the economy was in private hands. In April 2000, the government sold 65 per cent of Macedonia's largest bank, the Stopanska bank, and parliament voted to return property expropriated during the period under Communist rule. An economic co-operation agreement was signed by Macedonia and Albania in July 1999, covering energy, mining and trade.

In 2000 63 per cent of GDP was produced by service industries, 25 per cent by industry, and 12 per cent by agriculture.

The main exports are textiles, tobacco, zinc, wine, iron ore and iron products. The main imports are oil, energy, telecommunications equipment, metal manufactures, foodstuffs and medicines.

In 2000 there was a trade deficit of US$558 million and a current account deficit of US$107 million. In 1999 imports totalled US$1,796 million and exports US$1,192 million.

GNP – US$3,481 million (2000); US$1,660 per capita (1999)
GDP – US$3,504 million (1998); US$1,697 per capita (1999)
ANNUAL AVERAGE GROWTH OF GDP – 2.9 per cent (1998)
INFLATION RATE – 1.3 per cent (1999)
UNEMPLOYMENT – 38.8 per cent (1996)
TOTAL EXTERNAL DEBT – US$1,433 million (1999)

Trade with UK	2000	2001
Imports from UK	£23,029,000	£24,560,000
Exports to UK	19,847,000	17,773,000

MADAGASCAR

Repoblikan'i Madagasikara/République de Madagascar – Republic of Madagascar

AREA – 226,658 sq. miles (587,041 sq. km)
POPULATION – 15,982,563 (2001 estimate). The people are of mixed Malayo-Polynesian, Arab and African origin. There are sizeable French, Chinese and Indian communities. The official languages are Malagasy and French
CAPITAL – Antananarivo (population, 2,000,000, 1998 estimate)
MAJOR CITIES – Ψ Antsiranana (942,410); Fianarantsoa (2,671,150); Ψ Mahajanga (100,807); Ψ Toamasina (127,441), the chief port

CURRENCY – Franc malgache (FMG) of 100 centimes
NATIONAL ANTHEM – Ry Tanindrazanay Malala O (O, Our Beloved Country)
NATIONAL DAY – 26 June (Independence Day)
NATIONAL FLAG – Equal horizontal bands of red (above) and green, with vertical white band by staff
LIFE EXPECTANCY (years) – male 52.5; female 54.8
POPULATION GROWTH RATE – 3.0 per cent (1999)
POPULATION DENSITY – 26 per sq. km (1999)
MILITARY EXPENDITURE – 0.8 per cent of GDP (2000)
MILITARY PERSONNEL – 13,500: Army 12,500, Navy 500, Air Force 500; Paramilitaries 8,100
CONSCRIPTION DURATION – 18 months
ILLITERACY RATE – 31.9 per cent (2002)
ENROLMENT (percentage of age group – primary 92 per cent (1997); tertiary 2 per cent (1997)

Madagascar lies 240 miles off the east coast of Africa and is the fourth largest island in the world.

HISTORY AND POLITICS

Madagascar (known from 1958 to 1975 as the Malagasy Republic) became a French protectorate in 1895, and a French colony in 1896 when the former queen was exiled. Republican status was adopted on 14 October 1958, and independence was proclaimed on 26 June 1960.

The post-independence civilian government was replaced by a military government in 1975 and martial law was declared. A Supreme Council of the Revolution under Didier Ratsiraka was established.

In November 1991, President Ratsiraka relinquished executive power to a new prime minister, Guy Razanamasy. However, the president retained his official position and the main opposition grouping, the *Forces Vives*, established a rival government led by Albert Zafy. In December 1991 a transitional government including Forces Vives and Razanamasy supporters was formed to draft a new constitution, approved by referendum in August 1992. In the presidential election held in November 1992 and February 1993, Albert Zafy became the first president of the Third Republic, which came into being at the same time.

President Zafy was defeated in 1996 by former president Ratsiraka. Following legislative elections held in May 1998, Ratsiraka's *Action de Renouveau de Madagascar* (AREMA) party became the largest party in the National Assembly. Following the senatorial election on 18 March 2001, AREMA held 49 of the 60 elected seats. The inconclusive presidential elections held on 16 December 2001 were followed by violent clashes between supporters of the two main candidates, President Ratsiraka and Marc Ravalomanana, and protests demanding that Ravalomanana be declared president. On 17 April 2002, Madagascar's High Constitutional Court annulled the December election results and ordered a recount. The results of the recount showed that Ravalomanana was the clear winner with 51.5 per cent of the vote against 35.9 per cent for Ratsiraka. Ravalomanana's presidency was legitimised on 6 May when he was sworn into office. Ratsiraka refused to acknowledge this result and fighting between supporters of the two contenders continued into mid-June.

POLITICAL SYSTEM

The president is directly elected and serves a five-year term. The legislature is bicameral. The National Assembly is directly elected and comprises 150 members. The Senate comprises 90 members, of whom two-thirds are elected by an electoral college and one-third are nominated by the president.

HEAD OF STATE

President, *elected* 29 April 2002, *sworn in* 6 May 2002, *accepted* 5 July 2002.

COUNCIL OF MINISTERS *as at July 2002*

Prime Minister, Jacques Sylla
Deputy PM, Finance and Economy, Narisoa Rajaonarivony
Agriculture, Livestock, Water and Forests, Yvon Randriasandratriniony
Basic and Secondary Education, Dieudonne Michel Razafindrandriatsimaniry
Civil Service, Vola Dieudonne Razafindralambo
Culture, Odette Rahaingosoa
Defence, Maj.-Gen. Jules Mamizara
Economy and Planning, Andriamparany Radavidson
Energy and Mines, Elisée Razaka
Environment, Gen. Charles Rabotoarison
Foreign Affairs, Gen. Marcel Ranjeva
Foreign Trade, Henri Rakotonirainy
Health, Andry Rasamindrakotroka
Higher Education, Jean Theodore Ranjivason
Industry and Development of the Private Sector, David Rajaona
Information and Communications, Mamy Rakotoarivelo
Interior and Administrative Reforms, Jean Seth Rambeloarijaona
Justice, Keeper of the Seals, Alice Rajaonah
Labour and Social Affairs, Maharavo Rodelys
Population, Jacob Andriampanjava
Posts and Telecommunications, Hajanirina Razafinjatovo
Public Works, Jean Lahiniriako
Public Security, Gen. Augustin Amady
Regional and Town Planning, Julien Reboza
Scientific Research, Edouard Alidina
Secretaries of State, Eric Beantanana (*External Trade*); Monique Andreas Esoavelomandroso (*Decentralisation and Development of Autonomous Provinces*); Victorine Rahelivololona (*Women's and Children's Condition*); Rear-Adml. Hippolyte Raharison (*Agriculture, Livestock, Fisheries and Ocean Resources*)
Technical Education and Vocational Training, Blaise Johana
Tourism, Christian Ntsay
Trade and Consumer Affairs, Alphonse Ralison
Transport, Environment and Meteorology, Olivier Rakotovazaha
Waters and Forests, Alibay Oneste
Youth and Sports, Rene Ndalana

EMBASSY OF THE REPUBLIC OF MADAGASCAR
4 avenue Raphael, F- 75016 Paris, France
Tel: (00 33) (1) 4504 6211
Ambassador Plenipotentiary and Extraordinary, HE Malala Zo Raolison, apptd 1998

BRITISH EMBASSY
Lot II, I Ter Alarobia Ambonilioha,
BP 167, Antananarivo
Tel: (00 261) (20) 2249378/9
Ambassador Extraordinary and Plenipotentiary, HE Charles Francis Mochan, apptd 1999

ECONOMY

The economy is still largely based on agriculture, which employs more than 80 per cent of the workforce. The main products are rice, cassava, sugar cane, coffee, fish, tropical fruits and sweet potatoes. Development plans have placed emphasis on improving communications, the

exploitation of mineral deposits and the creation of small industries. Madagascar was hit by three cyclones in February and April 2000, which caused widespread flooding, resulting in the destruction of much of the rice crop.

In 1998 there was a trade deficit of US$154 million and a current account deficit of US$301 million. Imports totalled US$514 million and exports US$243 million.
GNP – US$3,959 million (2000); US$250 per capita (1999)
GDP – US$3,136 million (1998); US$239 per capita (1999)
ANNUAL AVERAGE GROWTH OF GDP – 4.8 per cent (2000)
INFLATION RATE – 12.0 per cent (2000)
TOTAL EXTERNAL DEBT – US$4,409 million (1999)

Trade with UK	2000	2001
Imports from UK	£6,787,000	£6,651,000
Exports to UK	20,623,000	24,979,000

MALAŴI
Mfuko la Malaŵi/Republic of Malaŵi

AREA – 45,747 sq. miles (118,484 sq. km). Neighbours: Tanzania (north-east), Zambia (west), Mozambique (south)
POPULATION – 10,548,250 (2001 estimate). The official languages are Chichewa and English
CAPITAL – Lilongwe (population, 505,200, 2000 estimate)
MAJOR CITIES – Blantyre (502,053), incorporating Blantyre and Limbe, the major commercial and industrial centre; Mzuzu (86,980); Zomba (65,915), the former capital, 1998
CURRENCY – Kwacha (K) of 100 tambala
NATIONAL ANTHEM – O God Bless Our Land Of Malaŵi
NATIONAL DAY – 6 July (Independence Day)
NATIONAL FLAG – Horizontal stripes of black, red and green, with rising sun in the centre of the black stripe
LIFE EXPECTANCY (years) – male 39.6; female 39.0
POPULATION GROWTH RATE – 1.5 per cent (2001)
POPULATION DENSITY – 90 per sq. km (1999)
URBAN POPULATION – 19.6 per cent (1996)
MILITARY EXPENDITURE – 1.8 per cent of GDP (2000)
MILITARY PERSONNEL – Army, 5,300; Paramilitaries 1,500
Malaŵi lies in south-eastern Africa. Much of the eastern border of Malaŵi is formed by Lake Malaŵi (formerly Lake Nyasa), which covers nearly half of the north of the country. The valley of the River Shire runs south from the lake, its watershed with the Zambezi lying on the western border with Mozambique and its tributary, the Ruo, with lakes Chiuta and Chirwa, lying on the eastern border with Mozambique. The north and centre are plateaus, and the south highlands.

HISTORY AND POLITICS
Malaŵi (formerly Nyasaland) assumed internal self-government on 1 February 1963, and became independent on 6 July 1964. It became a republic on 6 July 1966.

In 1991–2 Life President Hastings Banda, who had ruled since independence, came under increasing pressure to introduce a multiparty democratic system of government. In May 1992 aid donors tied new loans to improvements in the human rights record and moves to multiparty democracy. A referendum was held on the adoption of a multiparty democracy in June 1993 and approved by 63 per cent of voters. President Banda and the Malaŵi Congress Party refused to resign but parliament passed a law to amend the constitution to allow multiparty politics and Banda announced a political amnesty to allow exiles to return. Multiparty presidential and legislative elections held in May 1994 were won by Bakili Muluzi and the United Democratic Front (UDF) respectively. Foreign and multilateral aid has since been restored. Former President Banda died on 25 November 1997. Presidential and legislative elections were due to be held on 25 May 1999, but were delayed until 15 June; they were won by the UDF, who won 93 seats. President Muluzi was also re-elected.

POLITICAL SYSTEM
There is a Cabinet consisting of the president and ministers. The unicameral National Assembly, which usually meets three times a year, consists of 193 members elected by universal suffrage for a five-year term of office.

HEAD OF STATE
President, Commander-in-Chief, Bakili Muluzi, *elected* 17 May 1994, *sworn in* 21 May 1994, *re-elected* 15 June 1999
Vice-President, Privatisation, Justin Malewezi

CABINET *as at July 2002*
The President
The Vice-President
Agriculture and Irrigation Development, Aleke Banda
Attorney-General, Justice, Henry Ptoya
Commerce and Industry, Peter Kaleso
Defence, Rodwell Munyenyembe
Education, Science and Technology, George Nga Mtafu
Finance and Economic Planning, Friday Jumbe
Foreign Affairs and International Co-operation, Lilian Patel
Gender, Youth and Community Services, Mary Banda
Health and Population, Yusufu Mwawa
Home Affairs and Internal Security, Mangeza Maluza
Information, Clement Stambuli
Labour and Vocational Training, Alice Sumani
Lands, Physical Planning and Services, Thengo Maloya
Natural Resources and Environmental Affairs, Harry Thomson
Sports and Culture, Moses Dossi
Tourism, National Parks and Wildlife, Ken Lipenga
Transport and Public Works, Samuel Kaliyoma Phumisa
Water Development, Lee Mulanga
Without Portfolio, Uladi B. Mussa

MALAŴI HIGH COMMISSION
33 Grosvenor Street, London WIK 4OT
Tel: 020-7491 4172
High Commissioner, HE Bright Msaka, apptd 1998

BRITISH HIGH COMMISSION
PO Box 30042, Lilongwe 3
Tel: (00 265) 772 400
Email: bhc@wiss.co.mw
High Commissioner, Norman Ling, apptd 2001

BRITISH COUNCIL DIRECTOR, Richard Weyers, Plot No. 13/20 City Centre, PO Box 30222, Lilongwe 3; Email: info@britishcouncil.org.mw

ECONOMY
The economy is largely agricultural, providing 90 per cent of export earnings; maize is the main subsistence crop, and tobacco, cassava, millet and rice are the main cash

990   Countries of the World

crops and principal exports. There are two sugar mills. A number of light manufacturing industries have been established, mainly in agricultural processing, clothing/textiles and building materials.

In 1999 imports totalled US$698 million and exports US$442 million.

GNP – US$1,884 million (2000); US$180 per capita (1999)

GDP – US$1,615 million (1998); US$174 per capita (1999)

ANNUAL AVERAGE GROWTH OF GDP – 2.3 per cent (2000)

INFLATION RATE – 29.5 per cent (2000)

TOTAL EXTERNAL DEBT – US$2,751 million (1999)

Trade with UK	2000	2001
Imports from UK	£10,878,000	£8,183,000
Exports to UK	11,067,000	14,994,000

COMMUNICATIONS

A single-track railway runs from Mchinji on the Zambian border, through Lilongwe and Salima on Lake Malaŵi (itself served by two passenger and a number of cargo boats) through to Blantyre. The route south to the Mozambique port of Beira was severed by the Mozambican civil war, but the route to Nacala in Mozambique is open again; there are 797 km of railway track. There are 16,451 km of roads in Malaŵi of which 3,126 km are bituminised.

EDUCATION

The Ministry of Education and Culture is responsible for secondary schools, technical education and primary teacher training. The University of Malaŵi was opened in 1965; there are also four colleges and one polytechnic.

ILLITERACY RATE – 38.2 per cent (2002)

ENROLMENT (percentage of age group) – primary 100 per cent (1997); secondary 17 per cent (1997); tertiary 1 per cent (1997)

MALAYSIA

AREA – 127,320 sq. miles (329,758 sq. km). Thailand borders the Malay peninsula to the north. On Borneo, Malaysia (Sarawak and Sabah) borders Indonesia to the south, and surrounds Brunei to the north

POPULATION – 22,229,040 (2001 estimate); 16,921,300 (1988 census): Malays (58 per cent), Chinese (27 per cent), and those of Indian and Sri Lankan origin, as well as the indigenous races of Sarawak and Sabah. Bahasa Malaysia (Malay) is the official language, but English, various dialects of Chinese, and Tamil are also widely spoken. There are a few indigenous languages widely spoken in Sabah and Sarawak. Islam is the official religion of Malaysia, each ruler being the head of religion in his state (except in Sabah and Sarawak). The Yang di-Pertuan Agong is the head of religion in Melaka and Penang. The constitution guarantees religious freedom.

CAPITAL – Kuala Lumpur (population, 1,297,526, 2000 census); Putrajaya (Administrative Capital) (population 3,000, 1999 estimate)

MAJOR CITIES – Ipoh (566,211); Johore Bharu (384,613); Petaling Jaya (438,084), 2000

CURRENCY – Malaysian dollar (ringgit) (M$) of 100 sen

NATIONAL ANTHEM – Negara-Ku (My Country)

NATIONAL DAY – 31 August (Hari Kebangsaan)

NATIONAL FLAG – Equal horizontal stripes of red

(seven) and white (seven); 14-point yellow star and crescent in blue canton

LIFE EXPECTANCY (years) – male 70.6; female 75.5

POPULATION GROWTH RATE – 2.3 per cent (1999)

POPULATION DENSITY – 69 per sq. km (1999)

URBAN POPULATION – 54.7 per cent (1995)

ILLITERACY RATE – 11.6 per cent (2002)

ENROLMENT (percentage of age group) – primary 100 per cent (1997); tertiary 12 per cent (1997)

Malaysia comprises the 11 states of peninsular Malaya plus Sabah and Sarawak. It occupies two distinct regions, the Malay peninsula which extends from the isthmus of Kra to the Singapore Strait, and the north-western coastal area of the island of Borneo. Each is separated from the other by the South China Sea.

HISTORY AND POLITICS

The Federation of Malaya became an independent country within the Commonwealth on 31 August 1957. On 16 September 1963 the federation was enlarged by the accession of the states of Singapore, Sabah (formerly British North Borneo) and Sarawak, and the name of Malaysia was adopted from that date. On 9 August 1965 Singapore seceded from the federation.

The National Front (Barisan Nasional) Coalition led by Dr Mahathir Mohamed won a fifth term in office in a general election held on 29 November 1999, winning 148 of the 193 seats.

POLITICAL SYSTEM

The constitution provides for a strong federal government and a degree of autonomy for the state governments. It created a constitutional Supreme Head of the Federation (HM the Yang di-Pertuan Agong) and a Deputy Supreme Head (HRH Timbalan Yang di-Pertuan Agong) to be elected for a term of five years by the rulers from among their number. The Malay rulers are either chosen or succeed to their position in accordance with the custom of the particular state. In other states of Malaysia, choice of the head of state is at the discretion of the Yang di-Pertuan Agong after consultation with the Chief Minister of the state.

The Federal Parliament consists of two houses, the Senate and the House of Representatives. The Senate (Dewan Negara) consists of 69 members who serve a six-year term, 26 being elected by the Legislative Assemblies of the states (two from each) and 43 appointed by the Yang di-Pertuan Agong. The House of Representatives (Dewan Rakyat) consists of 193 members elected for a five-year term by universal adult suffrage with a common electoral roll.

FEDERAL STRUCTURE

According to the constitution, each state shall have its own constitution not inconsistent with the federal constitution, with the ruler or governor acting on the advice of an Executive Council appointed on the advice of the Chief Minister and a single-chamber Legislative Assembly. The Legislative Assemblies are fully elected on the same basis as the federal parliament.

State	Area (sq. km)	Population (2000 census)	Main Town
Johor	18,987	2,565,701	ΨJohor Baharu
Kedah	9,425	1,572,107	Alor Setar
Kelantan	15,024	1,289,199	Kota Baharu
Melaka	1,652	602,867	ΨMelaka
Negeri Sembilan	6,644	830,080	Seremban

State	Area (sq. km)	Population (2000 census)	Main Town
Pahang	35,965	1,231,176	Ψ Kuantan
Penang	1,031	1,225,501	Ψ Georgetown
Perak	21,005	2,030,382	Ipoh
Perlis	795	198,335	Kangar
Sabah	73,619	2,449,389	Ψ Kota Kinabalu
Sarawak	124,450	2,012,616	Ψ Kuching
Selangor	7,960	3,947,527	Ψ Shah Alam
Terengganu	12,955	879,691	Ψ Kuala Terengganu

Federal Territories

Kuala Lumpur   1,297,526
Labuan   70,517

HEAD OF STATE

Supreme Head of State, HM Tuanku Syed Sirajuddin Putra Jamalullail (Yang di-Pertuan Agong of Perlis), *sworn in* 13 December 2001

CABINET *as at July 2002*

Prime Minister, Finance and Special Functions, Dr Mahathir Mohamed
Deputy Prime Minister, Home Affairs, Abdullah Ahmad Badawi
Agriculture, Mohamed Effendi Norwani
Culture, Arts and Tourism, Abdul Kadir Sheikh Fadzir
Defence, Mohamed Najib Tun Razak
Domestic Trade and Consumer Affairs, Muhyiddin Yasin
Education, Musa Mohamad
Energy, Telecommunications and Posts, Leo Moggie Anak Irok
Entrepreneurial Development, Mohamed Nazri Abdul Aziz
Foreign Affairs, Hamid Albar
Health, Chua Jui Meng
Housing and Local Government, Ong Ka Ting
Human Resources, Fong Chan Ong
Information, Mohamad Khalil Yaakob
International Trade and Industry, Rafidah Aziz
Lands and Co-operative Development, Kasitah Gaddam
National Unity and Social Development, Zaharah binti Sulaiman
Primary Industries, Dr Lim Keng Yaik
Prime Minister's Office, Bernard Dompok; Pandikar Amin Musa; Abdul Hamid Zainal Abidin; Rais Yatim
Public Works, S. Samy Vellu
Rural Development, Azmi Khalid
Science, Technology and Environment, Law Hieng Ding
Transport, Dr Ling Liong Sik
Women's Affairs, Shahrizat Abdul Jalil
Youth and Sports, Hishamuddin Tun Hussein

MALAYSIAN HIGH COMMISSION

45 Belgrave Square, London SW1X 8QT
Tel: 020-7235 8033
Email: mwlondon@btinternet.com
High Commissioner, HE Dato Salim bin Hashim, *apptd* 2001

BRITISH HIGH COMMISSION

185 Jalan Ampang (PO Box 11030), 50732 Kuala Lumpur
Tel: (00 60) (3) 2170 2200
High Commissioner, HE Bruce Cleghorn, CMG, *apptd* 2001

BRITISH COUNCIL DIRECTOR, Dr Tom Cameron, Jalan Bukit Aman, PO Box 10539, 50916 Kuala Lumpur; Email: kualalumpur@britishcouncil.org.my.

DEFENCE

The Army has 816 armoured personnel carriers. The Royal Malaysian Navy has four frigates, 41 patrol and coastal vessels and nine armed helicopters at three bases. The Royal Malaysian Air Force has 71 combat aircraft.

Australia maintains an infantry company and an air force detachment in Malaysia.

MILITARY EXPENDITURE – 3.1 per cent of GDP (2000)
MILITARY PERSONNEL – 100,500: Army 80,000, Navy 12,500, Air Force 8,000; Paramilitaries 20,100

ECONOMY

From being an agriculturally-based economy reliant on raw materials exports at independence, Malaysia has undergone an industrialisation programme and now produces clothing, textiles, rubber goods, electronics, office equipment, cars, household appliances, semiconductors, food processing and chemicals. The National Development Policy 1990–2000 is seen as the second stage in making Malaysia a fully-developed industrial state by 2020; it aims for GDP growth of 8 per cent per year. There are extensive privatisation programmes involving telecommunications, railways, airports, electricity and shipping. In 2000 42 per cent of GDP was produced by services, 44 per cent by manufacturing and 14 per cent by agriculture.

In October 2000 and March 2001, the government announced measures to stimulate the economy, which included increased spending on schools, agricultural subsidies and incentives to increase spending.

GNP – US$78,529 million (2000); US$3,390 per capita (1999)
GDP – US$71,023 million (1998); US$3,613 per capita (1999)
ANNUAL AVERAGE GROWTH OF GDP – 8.5 per cent (2000)
INFLATION RATE – 1.5 per cent (2000)
UNEMPLOYMENT – 3.4 per cent (1999)
TOTAL EXTERNAL DEBT – US$45,939 million (1999)

TRADE

Malaysia is the largest exporter of natural rubber, tin, palm oil and tropical hardwoods. Other major export commodities are manufactured and processed products, petroleum, oil and other minerals, palm kernel oil, tea and pepper. Imports consist mainly of machinery and transport equipment, manufactured goods, foods, consumer durables and metal products. Japan, the USA and Singapore are the main trading partners.

In 1997 Malaysia had a trade surplus of US$3,876 million and a current account deficit of US$4,792 million. In 2000 imports totalled US$82,199 million and exports US$98,135 million.

Trade with UK	2000	2001
Imports from UK	£911,966,000	£1,033,178,000
Exports to UK	2,374,441,000	2,012,187,000

MALDIVES

Divehi Rājjē Jumhūriyyā – Republic of the Maldives

AREA – 115 sq. miles (298 sq. km)
POPULATION – 310,764 (2001 estimate). The people are Sunni Muslims and the Maldivian (Dhivehi) language is akin to Elu or old Sinhalese
CAPITAL – Ψ Malé (population, 74,069, 2000)
CURRENCY – Rufiyaa of 100 laaris
NATIONAL ANTHEM – Gavmī Mi Ekuverikan Matī Tibegen Kurīme Salām (In National Unity We Salute Our Nation)

NATIONAL DAY – 26 July
NATIONAL FLAG – Green field bearing a white crescent, with wide red border
LIFE EXPECTANCY (years) – male 68.3; female 67.0
POPULATION GROWTH RATE – 2.7 per cent (1999)
POPULATION DENSITY – 931 per sq. km (1999)
MILITARY EXPENDITURE – 9.5 per cent of GDP (2000)
ILLITERACY RATE – 3.0 per cent (2002)

The Maldives are a chain of coral atolls 400 miles to the south-west of Sri Lanka, stretching north for about 600 miles from just south of the Equator. There are about 19 coral atolls comprising over 1,200 islands, 198 of which are inhabited. No point in the entire chain of islands is more than eight feet above sea-level.

HISTORY AND POLITICS

Until 1952 the islands were a sultanate under the protection of the British Crown. Internal self-government was achieved in 1948 and full independence in 1965. The Maldives became a special member of the Commonwealth in 1982 and a full member in 1985. The Maldives form a republic which is elective. The legislature, the Citizens' Assembly *(Majlis)*, has 42 representatives elected from all the atolls, and eight appointed by the president, for a five-year term. The government consists of a Cabinet, which is responsible to the Majlis. There are no political parties. Under the 1998 constitution, the president is elected by the Majlis and confirmed by a referendum. The most recent legislative election took place on 19 November 1999.

HEAD OF STATE

President, Defence, National Security, Finance and Treasury, HE Maumoon Abdul Gayoom, *elected* 1978, re-elected 1983, 1989, 1993, 16 October 1998

CABINET *as at July 2002*

The President
Atolls Administration, Speaker of the Majlis, Abdullah Hameed
Attorney-General, Mohamed Munnawwar
Chief Justice, President of the Supreme Council on Islamic Affairs, Mohamed Rashid Ibrahim
Construction and Public Works, Umar Zahir
Education, Dr Mohamed Latheef
Fisheries and Agriculture, Abdul Rasheed Hussain
Foreign Affairs, Fathullah Jameel
Health, Ahmed Abdulla
Home Affairs, Housing and Environment, Ismail Shafeeu
Human Resources, Employment and Labour, Abdullah Kamaaludheen
Information, Arts and Culture, Ibrahim Manik
Justice, Ahmed Zahir
Minister at the President's Office, Abdullah Jameel
Ministers of State, Maj.-Gen. Anbaree Abdul Sattar *(Defence and National Security);* Mohamed Jaleel *(Finance and Treasury);* Muhamed Hussein *(Presidential Affairs);* Ismail Fathy *(Without Portfolio)*
Mustashaaru of the Supreme Council on Islamic Affairs, Moosa Fathuhy
Planning and National Development, Ibrahim Hussain Zaki
Tourism, Hassan Sobir
Trade and Industry, Abdulla Yameen
Transport and Civil Aviation, Ilyas Ibrahim
Women's Affairs and Social Welfare, Rashida Yoosuf
Youth and Sports, Mohamed Zahir Hussain

HIGH COMMISSION OF THE REPUBLIC OF MALDIVES
22 Nottingham Place, London W1U 5NJ
Tel: 020-7224 2135
High Commissioner, vacant
Acting High Commissioner, Adam Hassan

BRITISH HIGH COMMISSIONER, HE Linda Duffield, resident at Colombo, Sri Lanka

ECONOMY

The vegetation of the islands is coconut palms with some scrub. Hardly any cultivation of crops is possible and nearly all food to supplement the basic fish diet has to be imported. Tourism is expanding rapidly (461,063 visitors in 2001). The principal industry is fishing, which together with tourism accounts for about 30 per cent of GDP. The Maldives National Ship Management Ltd (MNSML) has a fleet of nine merchant ships. There is an international airport at Malé.

In 1999 the Maldives had a trade deficit of US$266 million and a current account deficit of US$60 million. In 2000 imports totalled US$389 million and exports US$76 million.
GNP – US$403 million (2000); US$1,200 per capita (1999)
GDP – US$366 million (1998); US$1,382 per capita (1999)
ANNUAL AVERAGE GROWTH OF GDP – 4.8 per cent (2000)
INFLATION RATE – 1.1 per cent (2000)
TOTAL EXTERNAL DEBT – US$217 million (1999)

Trade with UK	2000	2001
Imports from UK	£5,092,000	£5,027,000
Exports to UK	6,814,000	6,447,000

MALI
République du Mali – Republic of Mali

AREA – 478,841 sq. miles (1,240,192 sq. km).
Neighbours: Senegal (west), Mauritania (north-west), Algeria (north-east), Niger (east), Burkina Faso and Côte d'Ivoire (south), Guinea (south-west)
POPULATION – 11,008,518 (2001 estimate): 50 per cent Mande (Bambara, Malinke, Sarakole), 17 per cent Peul, 12 per cent Voltaic, 6 per cent Songhai, 10 per cent Tuareg and Moor. The official language is French; Bambara is the largest local language
CAPITAL – Bamako (population, 809,552, 1996 UN estimate)
MAJOR CITIES – Gao; Kayes; Mopti; Ségou; Sikasso; Timbuktu (all regional capitals)
CURRENCY – Franc CFA of 100 centimes
NATIONAL ANTHEM – A Ton Appel, Mali (At Your Call, Mali)
NATIONAL DAY – 22 September
NATIONAL FLAG – Vertical stripes of green (by staff), yellow and red
LIFE EXPECTANCY (years) – male 51.1; female 53.0
POPULATION GROWTH RATE – 2.4 per cent (1999)
POPULATION DENSITY – 9 per sq. km (1999)
MILITARY EXPENDITURE – 1.0 per cent of GDP (2000)
MILITARY PERSONNEL – 7,350: Army; Paramilitaries 4,800
CONSCRIPTION DURATION – Two years (selective)
ILLITERACY RATE – 55.2 per cent (2002)
ENROLMENT (percentage of age group) – primary 49 per cent (1997); secondary 13 per cent (1997); tertiary 1 per cent (1997)

HISTORY AND POLITICS

Formerly the French colony of Soudan, the territory elected on 24 November 1958 to remain an autonomous republic within the French Community. It associated with Senegal in the Federation of Mali, which was granted full independence on 20 June 1960. The Federation was effectively dissolved in August 1960 by the secession of Senegal. The title of the Republic of Mali was adopted in September 1960.

A new constitution establishing a multiparty political system was approved by referendum in January 1992. Alpha Konaré, the Alliance for Democracy in Mali (ADEMA) leader, won the presidential elections in April 1992 and was re-elected in May 1997. In legislative elections in July and August 1997, ADEMA won 129 out of 147 seats in the National Assembly. On 14 February 2000, the government resigned and a new prime minister and government was formed the following day, comprising members of ADEMA and opposition parties. Former military leader and independent candidate Amadou Toumani Touré won the presidential elections held on 12 May 2002. Legislative elections were scheduled for 14 July 2002.

HEAD OF STATE

President, Amadou Toumani Touré, *elected* 12 May 2002; *took office* 8 June 2002

CABINET as at June 2002

Prime Minister, African Integration, Mohamed Ag Hamani
Armed Forces and Veterans, Mahamane Maïga
Communications, Mamadou Malle Cissé
Cottage Industry and Tourism, Bah N'diaye
Culture, André Traoré
Economy and Finance, Ousmane Issoufi Maiga
Education, Mamadou Lamine Traoré
Employment and Professional Training, Younous Hammey Dicko
Foreign Affairs, Malians Abroad, Lassine Traoré
Health, Traoré Fatoumata Nafo
Industry, Commerce, Transport, Mamadou Dalo Maïga
Infrastructure, Town Planning and Housing, Lanceni Keita
Justice and Keeper of the Seals, Abdoulaye Ogotembely Poudiougou
Mines, Energy and Water Resources, Ahmed Semega
Rural Development and Environment, Seydou Traoré
Security and Civil Protection, Souleymane Sidibé
Social Development, Solidarity and the Elderly, N'diayé Fatoumata Coulibaly
State, Properties and Land, Aboubacar Sidiki Touré
Territorial Administration and Local Communities, Gen. Kafougouna Koné
Women, Children and the Family, Bah Odette Yattara
Youth and Sports, Djibril Tangara

EMBASSY OF THE REPUBLIC OF MALI

Avenue Molière 487, B-1050 Brussels, Belgium
Tel: (00 32) (2) 345 7432
Ambassador Extraordinary and Plenipotentiary, Ahmed Mohamed Ag Hamani, *apptd* 2001

BRITISH EMBASSY

Rue 132, Porte 902, Badalabougou-Ouest, BP 2069 Bamako
Tel: (00 223) 223 3412 Email: info@britembmali.org
Ambassador Extraordinary and plenipotentiary, HE Graeme Loten

ECONOMY

Mali's principal exports are cotton and gold. Principal imports include machinery and vehicles, petroleum, and foodstuffs. Mali rejoined the CFA Franc Zone in 1984. The IMF and the International Development Association agreed in September 2000 to provide Mali with US$870 million under the Heavily Indebted Poor Countries initiative.

In 1997 Mali had a trade surplus of US$10 million and a current account deficit of US$178 million. In 2000 imports totalled US$688 million and exports US$377 million.

GNP – US$2,568 million (2000); US$240 per capita (1999)
GDP – US$2,716 million (1998); US$254 per capita (1999)
ANNUAL AVERAGE GROWTH OF GDP – 5.7 per cent (1998)
INFLATION RATE – 0.7 per cent (2000)
TOTAL EXTERNAL DEBT – US$3,183 million (1999)

Trade with UK	2000	2001
Imports from UK	£17,903,000	£17,039,000
Exports to UK	6,851,000	1,487,000

MALTA

Repubblika ta' Malta/Republic of Malta

AREA – 122 sq. miles (316 sq. km)
POPULATION – 382,525 (2000). The Maltese are mainly Roman Catholic. The Maltese language is of Semitic origin and held by some to be derived from the Carthaginian and Phoenician tongues. Maltese and English are the official languages
CAPITAL – ΨValletta (population, 7,048, 2000)
CURRENCY – Maltese lira (LM) of 100 cents or 1,000 mils
NATIONAL ANTHEM – L-Innu Malti (Hymn Of Malta)
NATIONAL DAYS – 31 March (Freedom Day); 7 June (Sette Giugno Riots); 8 September (Our Lady of Victories); 21 September (Independence Day); 13 December (Republic Day)
NATIONAL FLAG – Two equal vertical stripes, white at the hoist and red at the fly. A representation of the George Cross is carried edged with red in the canton of the white stripe
LIFE EXPECTANCY (years) – male 75.9; female 81.0
POPULATION GROWTH RATE – 1.0 per cent (1999)
POPULATION DENSITY – 1,222 per sq. km (1999)
MILITARY EXPENDITURE – 0.7 per cent of GDP (2000)
MILITARY PERSONNEL – 2,140: Armed Forces of Malta

Malta lies in the Mediterranean Sea, 93 km (58 miles) from Sicily and about 288 km (180 miles) from the African coast. It is about 27 km (17 miles) in length and 14.5 km (9 miles) in breadth. Malta also includes the islands of Gozo (area 67 sq. km (25.9 sq. miles)), Comino and minor islets.

HISTORY AND POLITICS

Malta was in turn held by the Phoenicians, Carthaginians, Romans and Arabs. In 1090 it was conquered by Count Roger of Normandy and in 1530 handed over to the Knights of St John. In 1565 it sustained the famous siege, when the Turks were successfully withstood by Grandmaster La Valette. The Knights fortified the islands and built Valletta before being expelled by Napoleon in 1798. The Maltese rose against the French garrison soon afterwards and the island was subsequently blockaded by

the British fleet. The Maltese people requested the protection of the British Crown in 1802 on condition that their rights would be respected. The islands were finally annexed to the British Crown by the Treaty of Paris in 1814.

Malta was again besieged during the Second World War. From June 1940 to the end of the war, 432 members of the garrison and 1,540 civilians were killed by enemy aircraft. The island was awarded the George Cross for gallantry on 15 April 1942.

On 21 September 1964 Malta became an independent state within the Commonwealth, and on 13 December 1974 a republic within the Commonwealth.

Elections to the unicameral parliament of 65 members are held every five years by a system of proportional representation; to ensure that a party receiving more than 50 per cent of the votes cast obtains a parliamentary majority, extra seats may be allocated to that party. Elections held in September 1998 were won by the Nationalist Party, who gained 35 seats; Eddie Fenech-Adami, a strong supporter of Malta's accession to the European Union, was appointed prime minister.

FOREIGN RELATIONS

Malta applied for EC membership in 1990, but in October 1996 the Labour government announced its intention to withdraw Malta's EU application and its participation in NATO's Partnership for Peace programme. Following the election in 1998, the new Nationalist government immediately re-activated Malta's application for EU membership. Accession negotiations commenced in February 2000.

HEAD OF STATE

President, Guido de Marco, *took office* 4 April 1999

CABINET *as at July 2002*

Prime Minister, Edward Fenech-Adami
Deputy Prime Minister, Social Policy, Lawrence Gonzi
Agriculture and Fisheries, Ninu Zammit
Economic Services, Josef Bonnici
Education, Louis Galea
Environment, Francis Zammit Dimech
Finance, John Dalli
Foreign Affairs, Joe Borg
Gozo, Giovanna Debono
Health, Louis Deguara
Home Affairs, Tonio Borg
Justice and Local Government, Austin Gatt
Tourism, Michael Refalo
Transport and Communications, Censu Galea

MALTA HIGH COMMISSION
Malta House, 36–38 Piccadilly, London W1J 0LE. Tel: 020-7292 4800
High Commissioner, HE George Bonello DuPuis, *apptd* 1999

BRITISH HIGH COMMISSION
7 St Anne Street, Floriana (PO Box 506), Malta GC
Tel: (00 356) 233134/7
Email: bhc@vol.net.mt
High Commissioner, HE Howard John Pearce, CVO, *apptd* 1999
British Council Director, Ronnie Micallef, c/o British High Commission;
Email: veronica.attard@britcouncil.org.mt

ECONOMY

Tourism has assumed primary importance, with 1,180,145 tourists visiting the island in 1999. In 1999 3 million passengers passed through Malta International Airport.

In 2001 manufacturing employed 21.8 per cent of the workforce and accounted for 22.9 per cent of GDP. Industry is orientated primarily towards exports.

Industries include communications equipment, food processing, textiles, footwear and clothing, printing and publishing, plastics and chemical products, electrical machinery, medical equipment and furniture. Value Added Tax was re-introduced in January 1999. Financial services are a growing part of Malta's economy.

In 2001 there was a trade deficit of US$769 million and a current account deficit of US$180 million. Imports totalled US$2,726 million and exports US$1,957 million.

GNP – US$3,447 million (2000); US$8,838 per capita (2000)
GDP – US$3,571 million (2000); US$9,156 per capita (2000)
ANNUAL AVERAGE GROWTH OF GDP – 4.7 per cent (2000)
INFLATION RATE – 2.4 per cent (2000)
UNEMPLOYMENT – 5.0 per cent (2000)
TOTAL EXTERNAL DEBT – US$10,600 million (1999)

TRADE

The principal imports are foodstuffs (mainly wheat, livestock and meats, milk and fruit), fodder, beverages and tobacco, fuels, chemicals, textiles and machinery (industrial, agricultural and transport). The chief exports are processed food, electronics, textiles, and other manufactures.

Trade with UK	2000	2001
Imports from UK	£213,843,000	£217,418,000
Exports to UK	129,683,000	148,010,000

EDUCATION

Education is compulsory between the ages of five and 16 and is free at all levels. Secondary education in state schools is provided in secondary schools and junior lyceums. There are ten junior lyceums, 18 secondary schools and five centres catering for low achievers. A Junior College, administered by the University of Malta, prepares students specifically for a university course. Tertiary education is available at the University of Malta. The Malta College of Arts, Science and Technology provides technical and vocational courses at post-secondary level. There are also schools administered by the Catholic Church and other private schools.

ILLITERACY RATE – 7.3 per cent (2002)
ENROLMENT (percentage of age group) – primary 100 per cent (1999); secondary 100 per cent (1999); tertiary 21 per cent (1999)

MARSHALL ISLANDS
Republic of the Marshall Islands

AREA – 70 sq. miles (181 sq. km)
POPULATION – 70,822 (2001 estimate): 99 per cent are Micronesian. Almost half the population is under 15. About 60 per cent of the population is concentrated on the two atolls of Majuro and Kwajalein. The population is Christian, primarily Protestant but with a substantial Catholic minority. Marshallese and English are the official languages

CAPITAL – Dalap-Uliga-Darrit, on Majuro Atoll
(population, 20,000)
MAJOR TOWN – Ebeye (9,200)
CURRENCY – Currency is that of the USA
NATIONAL ANTHEM – Forever Marshall Islands
NATIONAL DAY – 1 May (Independence Day)
NATIONAL FLAG – Blue with a diagonal ray divided
white over orange running from the lower hoist to
the upper fly; in the canton a white sun
LIFE EXPECTANCY (years) – male 59.1; female 63.0
POPULATION GROWTH RATE – 2.7 per cent (1999)
POPULATION DENSITY – 343 per sq. km (1999)

The Republic of the Marshall Islands consists of 29 atolls
and five islands in the central Pacific. The islands and
atolls form two parallel chains running north-west to
south-east: the Ratak (Sunrise) chain and the Ralik
(Sunset) chain. The largest atoll is Kwajalein in the Ralik
chain. The atolls are coral and the islands are volcanic.
None of the islands rises more than a few metres above
sea level.

HISTORY AND POLITICS

The Marshall Islands were claimed by Spain in 1592 but
were left undisturbed by the Spanish Empire for 300
years. In 1886 the Marshall Islands formally became a
German protectorate. On the outbreak of the First World
War in 1914, Japan took control of the islands on behalf
of the Allied powers, and after the war administered the
territory as a League of Nations mandate. During the
Second World War US armed forces seized the islands
from the Japanese after intense fighting. In 1947 the USA
entered into agreement with the UN Security Council to
administer the Micronesia area, of which the Marshall
Islands are a part, as the UN Trust Territory of the Pacific
Islands.

The islands became internally self-governing in 1979,
and the US Trusteeship administration came to an end on
21 October 1986, when a Compact of Free Association
between the USA and the Republic of the Marshall
Islands came into effect. By this agreement the USA
recognised the Republic of the Marshall Islands as a fully
sovereign and independent state. The UN Security
Council terminated the UN Trust Territory of the Pacific
in relation to the Marshall Islands and recognised its
independence in December 1990.

FOREIGN RELATIONS

The Republic of the Marshall Islands has no defence
forces. The Compact of Free Association places full
responsibility for defence of the Marshall Islands on the
USA. The US Department of Defense retains control of
islands within Kwajalein Atoll where it has a missile test
range. In 2000 the government of the Marshall Islands
petitioned the USA for US$2.7 billion to fund medical
care for victims of radiation from US nuclear tests in the
islands in the 1940s and 1950s and to rectify
environmental damage.

POLITICAL SYSTEM

The republic is a democracy based on a parliamentary
system of government. The executive is headed by the
president, who is elected by the Nitijela from among its
members. The president serves for a four-year term. The
legislature has two chambers, the Council of Chiefs (Iroij)
of 12 members and the Nitijela of 33 members. The
Nitijela is the law-making chamber, to which the
president and government are accountable. The Iroij has
an advisory role.

In the general election which took place on 15 November
1999, the United Democratic Party won 18 seats.

HEAD OF STATE
President, Kessai Note, elected 3 January 2000

GOVERNMENT as at July 2002
The President
Education, Wilfred Kendall
Finance, Michael Konelious
Foreign Affairs, Gerald Zackios
Health and Environment, Alvin Jacklick
Internal Affairs and Welfare, Nidel Lorak
Justice, Witten Philippo
Minister in Assistance to the President, Tadashi Lometo
Public Works, Rien Morris
Resources and Development, John Silk
Transportation and Communications, Brenson Wase

BRITISH AMBASSADOR, HE Michael Price, LVO, resident
at Suva, Fiji

ECONOMY

The economy is a mixture of subsistence and a service-
based sector. About half the working population is
engaged in agriculture and fishing, with coconut oil and
copra production comprising 90 per cent of total exports.
Imports include oil, food and machinery. The service
sector is based in Majuro and Ebeye and concentrated in
banking and insurance, construction, transportation and
tourism. Direct US aid under the Compact accounts for
two-thirds of the islands' budget. The islands charge
foreign fishing fleets licences for fishing tuna in the waters
around the islands. The USA, Japan and Australia are the
main trading partners.
GNP – US$102 million (2000); US$1,950 per capita
(1999)
GDP – US$91 million (1998); US$1,920 per capita
(1999)
ANNUAL AVERAGE GROWTH OF GDP – -2.8 per cent
(1998)

Trade with UK	2000	2001
Imports from UK	£7,414,000	£933,000
Exports to UK	633,000	234,000

COMMUNICATIONS

Air Marshall Islands provides air services within the
islands and to Hawaii. Continental Air Micronesia serves
Majuro and Kwajalein with flights to Hawaii and Guam.
Majuro also has shipping links to Hawaii, Australia, Japan
and throughout the Pacific.

SOCIAL WELFARE

Majuro and Ebeye have hospitals run by the government
with aid from the US Public Health Service. Each outer
island community has a health assistant. The state school
system provides education up to age 18, but only 25 per
cent of students proceed beyond elementary level because
of inadequate resources.

MAURITANIA
Al-Jumhūriyya al-Islāmiyya al-Mawrītāniyya – Islamic
Republic of Mauritania

AREA – 395,956 sq. miles (1,025,520 sq. km).
Neighbours: Senegal (south-west), Mali (east and
south), Algeria and Western Sahara (north)
POPULATION – 2,747,312 (2001 estimate). The official
language is Arabic. Pulaar, Soninke, Wolof and
French are also spoken
CAPITAL – Nouakchott (population, 850,000)
CURRENCY – Ouguiya (UM) of 5 khoums

NATIONAL DAY – 28 November
NATIONAL FLAG – Yellow star and crescent on green
ground
LIFE EXPECTANCY (years) – male 50.9; female 54.1
POPULATION GROWTH RATE – 3.2 per cent (1999)
POPULATION DENSITY – 3 per sq. km (1999)
MILITARY EXPENDITURE – 2.8 per cent of GDP (2000)
MILITARY PERSONNEL – 15,650: Army 15,000, Navy
500, Air Force 150; Paramilitaries 5,000
CONSCRIPTION DURATION – Two years
ILLITERACY RATE – 58.8 per cent (2002)
ENROLMENT (percentage of age group) – primary 79
per cent (1997); tertiary 4 per cent (1997)

HISTORY AND POLITICS

Mauritania elected on 28 November 1958 to remain
within the French Community as an autonomous
republic. It became fully independent on 28 November
1960. In 1972 Mauritania left the Franc Zone.

Mauritania and Morocco occupied the Western Sahara
territory in February 1976 when Spain formally
relinquished it and in April 1976 agreed on a new frontier
dividing the territory between them. In August 1979,
Mauritania relinquished all claim to the southern sector
of the Western Sahara after a three-year war against
Polisario Front guerrillas.

After a military coup in 1978, Mauritania was ruled by
a Military Committee for National Salvation. In April
1991 President ould Taya announced a political amnesty,
followed by multiparty elections for a reconvened Senate
and National Assembly. The constitution was approved
by referendum in July 1991. Multiparty legislative
elections were held in March 1992 and won by the
Republican Democratic and Social Party (PRDS) led by
President ould Taya. In the presidential election in
December 1997, President ould Taya was re-elected
following a boycott by opposition parties. The legislative
election held in October 2001 was won by the PRDS who
gained 64 of the 81 seats in the National Assembly.

HEAD OF STATE

President, Col. Moaouia ould Sidi Mohammed Taya
(PRDS), *took power* 12 December 1984, *elected* 17
January 1992, *re-elected* 12 December 1997

COUNCIL OF MINISTERS *as at July 2002*

Prime Minister, Cheik El-Avia ould Mohamed Khouna
Civil Service, Labour, Youth, Sports, Baba ould Sidi
Communications and Relations with Parliament, Cheyakh
ould Ely
Culture, Islamic Orientation, Isselmou ould Sidi
Moustapha
Defence, Kaba ould Elewa
Economic and Development Affairs, Mohamed ould Nani
Equipment and Transport, Diabira Bakary
Finance, Biodiel ould Houmeid
Fisheries and Marine Economy, Ahmedou ould Ahmedou
Foreign Affairs and Co-operation, Dah ould Abdi
Health and Social Affairs, Diop Abdoul Hamet
Interior, Post and Telecommunications, Lemrabet Sidi
Mahmoud ould Cheikh Ahmed
Justice, Seghaier ould Mbarek
Mines and Industry, Zidane ould Hamida
National Education, Aboubekrine ould Ahmed
Rural Development and Environment, Moustapha ould
Maouloud
Trade, Handicrafts and Tourism, Isselmou ould
Abdelkader
Water Power, Energy, Kane Moustapha

EMBASSY OF THE ISLAMIC REPUBLIC OF MAURITANIA
1 Chessington Avenue, London N3 3DS
Tel: 020-8343 2829
Ambassador Extraordinary and Plenipotentiary, HE Dr
Youssouf Diagana, apptd 1999

BRITISH AMBASSADOR, HE Anthony M. Layden,
resident at Rabat, Morocco

ECONOMY

The main source of potential wealth lies in rich deposits
of iron ore around Zouérate, in the north of the country,
and rich fishing grounds off the coast.

In 1998 Mauritania had a trade surplus of US$40
million and a current account surplus of US$77 million.
GNP – US$978 million (2000); US$390 per capita
(1999)
GDP – US$830 million (1998); US$313 per capita
(1999)
ANNUAL AVERAGE GROWTH OF GDP – 3.0 per cent
(1998)
INFLATION RATE – 3.3 per cent (2000)
TOTAL EXTERNAL DEBT – US$2,528 million (1999)

Trade with UK	2000	2001
Imports from UK	£8,983,000	£8,006,000
Exports to UK	5,397,000	5,809,000

MAURITIUS
Republic of Mauritius

AREA – 788 sq. miles (2,040 sq. km)
POPULATION – 1,199,881 (2001 estimate): Asiatic races
(Hindus 51.8 per cent, Muslims 16.5 per cent,
Chinese 2.8 per cent), and persons of European
(mainly French) extraction, mixed and African
descent (28.6 per cent). English is the official
language but French may be used in the National
Assembly and lower law courts. Creole is the most
commonly used language and several Asian languages
are also used
CAPITAL – ΨPort Louis (population, 146,499, 2000
estimate)
MAJOR TOWNS – Beau Bassin-Rose Hill (102,770);
Curepipe (81,233); Quatre Bornes (78,384); Vacoas-
Phoenix (101,000), 2000 estimates
CURRENCY – Mauritius rupee of 100 cents
NATIONAL ANTHEM – Glory To Thee, Motherland
NATIONAL DAY – 12 March
NATIONAL FLAG – Red, blue, yellow and green
horizontal stripes
LIFE EXPECTANCY (years) – male 68.4; female 75.8
POPULATION GROWTH RATE – 1.0 per cent (2001)
POPULATION DENSITY – 576 per sq. km (1999)
URBAN POPULATION – 43.6 per cent (1995)
MILITARY EXPENDITURE – 1.8 per cent of GDP (2000)
MILITARY PERSONNEL – Paramilitaries: 1,600

Mauritius is an island group lying in the Indian Ocean,
550 miles east of Madagascar. The climate is sub-tropical
and maritime, with a wide range of rainfall and
temperature resulting from the mountainous nature of
the island. Humidity is high throughout the year.

HISTORY AND POLITICS

Mauritius was discovered in 1511 by the Portuguese; the
Dutch visited it in 1598 and named it Mauritius after
Prince Maurice of Nassau. From 1638 to 1710 it was held
as a Dutch colony; the French took possession in 1715 but
did not settle it until 1721. Mauritius was taken by a

British force in 1810 and became a Crown Colony. It became an independent state within the Commonwealth on 12 March 1968 and a republic on 12 March 1992.

The general election held on 11 September 2000 resulted in a victory for the coalition of the Mauritian Socialist Movement and the Mauritian Militant Movement, who won 54 of the 62 directly elected seats. On 15 February 2002 President Cassam Uteem resigned after refusing to sign a controversial anti-terrorism bill. His successor, acting president Angidi Chettiar also refused to sign the bill and resigned on 18 February. On 19 February the bill was signed into law by interim president Arianga Pillay and a presidential election was held on 25 February and won by Karl Offman.

POLITICAL SYSTEM

The president is head of state and is elected by the National Assembly. The prime minister, appointed by the president, is the member of the National Assembly who appears to the president best able to command support of the majority of members of the Assembly. Other ministers are appointed by the president acting on the advice of the prime minister.

The National Assembly has a five-year term and consists of 62 elected members (the island of Mauritius is divided into 20 three-member constituencies and Rodrigues returns two members), and eight specially elected members. Of the latter, four seats go to the 'best loser' of whichever communities in the island are under-represented in the Assembly after the general election and the four remaining seats are allocated on the basis of both party and community. In November 2001 the National Assembly approved amendments to the constitution giving a considerate degree of autonomy to the island of Rodrigues, including the establishment of an 18-member regional assembly.

HEAD OF STATE

President, Karl Offmann, *elected* 25 February 2002
Vice-President, Raouf Bundhun

COUNCIL OF MINISTERS *as at July 2002*

Prime Minister, Defence and Home Affairs, Sir Anerood Jugnauth
Deputy Prime Minister, Finance, Paul Bérenger
Agriculture, Pravind Jugnauth
Arts and Culture, Motee Ramdass
Attorney-General, Justice and Human Rights, Emmanuel Leung Shing
Civil Service Affairs and Administrative Reform, Ahmad Sulliman Jeewah
Commerce, Industry and International Trade, Jayen Cuttaree
Co-operatives, Premdut Koonjoo
Education, Louis Steven Obeegadoo
Environment, Rajesh Anand Bhagwan
Financial Services and Corporate Affairs, Sushil Kushiram
Fisheries, Sylvio Michel
Foreign Affairs, Anil Gayan
Health, Ashok Jugnauth
Housing and Lands, Mookhesswur Choonee
Labour and Industrial Relations, Showkutally Soodhun
Public Infrastructure and Internal Transport, Anil Kumar Bachoo
Public Utilities, Alan Ganoo
Regional Administration of Rodrigues, Urban and Rural Development, Joe Lesjongard
Social Security and Reform Institutions, Samioullah Lauthan
Telecommunications and Information Technology, Pradeep Jeeha

Tourism, Nando Bodha
Training, Skills Development and Productivity, Sangeet Fowdar
Women's Rights and Family Welfare, Marie-Arianne Navarre
Youth and Sports, Ravi Yerrigadoo

MAURITIUS HIGH COMMISSION
32–33 Elvaston Place, London SW7 5NW
Tel: 020-7581 0294/5
High Commissioner, HE Mohunlall Goburdhun, apptd 2001

BRITISH HIGH COMMISSION
Les Cascades Building, Edith Cavell Street, Port Louis (PO Box 1063)
Tel: (00 230) 202 9400
Email: bhc@intnet.mu
High Commissioner, HE David Snoxell, apptd 2000

BRITISH COUNCIL DIRECTOR, Rosalind Burford, Royal Road, PO Box 111, Rose Hill.
Email: general.enquiries@mu.britishcouncil.org

ECONOMY

The major cash crop is sugar cane. Tea and tobacco are grown commercially on a smaller scale. Production in 2001 was: sugar, 645,598 tonnes; tea (manufactured), 1,517 tonnes; in 1999 production of tobacco (leaves) was, air cured 60,238 kg and Virginia flue-cured 662,457 kg. In 1998 production of molasses, mainly for export, was 168,891 tonnes. Other products include alcohol, rum, denatured spirits, perfumed spirits and vinegar.

The bulk of the island's requirements in manufactured products still has to be imported. However, the Mauritius Export Processing Zone (MEPZ) Scheme has attracted investment from overseas and the number of export-orientated enterprises had risen from ten in 1971 to 522 in 2001. The biggest firms are in clothing manufacture, particularly woollen knitwear, but the range of goods produced includes toys, plastic products, leather goods, diamond cutting and polishing, watches, television sets and telephones.

Tourism is a major source of income, with an estimated 685,000 tourists in 2002. France is the most important source of tourists, followed closely by the neighbouring French island of Réunion.

GNP – US$4,512 million (2000); US$3,540 per capita (1999)
GDP – US$4,253 million (1998); US$3,638 per capita (1999)
ANNUAL AVERAGE GROWTH OF GDP – 3.4 per cent (1999)
INFLATION RATE – 5.4 per cent (2001)
UNEMPLOYMENT – 9.8 per cent (1995)
TOTAL EXTERNAL DEBT – US$2,464 million (1999)

TRADE

Most foodstuffs and raw materials have to be imported from abroad. Apart from local consumption (about 36,500 tonnes a year), the sugar produced is exported, mainly to Britain.

In 2000 Mauritius had a trade deficit of US$495 million and a current account deficit of US$33 million. In 2001 imports totalled US$1,999 million and exports US$1,595 million.

Trade with UK	2000	2001
Imports from UK	£55,434,000	£52,293,000
Exports to UK	290,444,000	337,840,000

COMMUNICATIONS

Port Louis, on the north-west coast, handles the bulk of the island's external trade. A bulk sugar terminal capable of handling the total crop began operating in 1980. The international airport is located at Plaisance, about five miles from Mahébourg.

EDUCATION

Primary and secondary education are free and primary education is compulsory. There are a number of training facilities offering vocational training. The Institute of Education is responsible for training primary and secondary school teachers and for curriculum development. The University of Mauritius had about 6,000 students in 2000–2001.

ILLITERACY RATE – 14.7 per cent (2002)
ENROLMENT (percentage of age group) – primary 106 per cent (1997); tertiary 6 per cent (1997)

RODRIGUES AND DEPENDENCIES

Rodrigues, formerly a dependency but now part of Mauritius, is about 350 miles east of Mauritius, with an area of 40 square miles. Population (2000) 35,776. Cattle, salt fish, sheep, goats, pigs, maize and onions are the principal exports. The island is administered by an interim Island Secretary pending the establishment of the devolved Regional Assembly.

Interim Island Secretary, J.-C. Pierre Louis

The islands of Agalega and St Brandon are dependencies of Mauritius. Total population (2000) 170.

MEXICO
Estados Unidos Mexicanos – United Mexican States

AREA – 756,066 sq. miles (1,958,201 sq. km).
Neighbours: USA (north), Guatemala and Belize (south-east)
POPULATION – 97,483,412 (2000 census). Spanish is the official language and is spoken by about 95 per cent of the population. There are five main groups of Indian languages (Náhuatl, Maya, Zapotec, Otomí, Mixtec) and 59 dialects derived from them
CAPITAL – Mexico City (population, 16,674,160, 1995)
MAJOR CITIES – Ciudad Juárez (1,011,786); Guadalajara (3,461,819); León (1,174,180); Monterrey (3,022,268); Puebla (1,561,558); Tijuana (991,592); Toluca (1,080,081); Torreón (870,651), 1995
CURRENCY – Peso of 100 centavos
NATIONAL ANTHEM – Mexicanos, Al Grito De Guerra (Mexicans, To The War Cry)
NATIONAL DAY – 16 September (Proclamation of Independence)
NATIONAL FLAG – Three vertical bands in green, white, red, with the Mexican emblem (an eagle on a cactus devouring a snake) in the centre
LIFE EXPECTANCY (years) – male 70.4; female 76.4
POPULATION GROWTH RATE – 1.9 per cent (2000)
POPULATION DENSITY – 50 per sq. km (1999)
URBAN POPULATION – 73.5 per cent (1995)
ILLITERACY RATE – 8.1 per cent (2002)
ENROLMENT (percentage of age group) – primary 100 per cent (1997); secondary 64 per cent (1997); tertiary 16 per cent (1997)

The Sierra Nevada, known in Mexico as the Sierra Madre, and Rocky Mountains continue south from the northern border with the USA, running parallel to the west and east

coasts. The interior consists of an elevated plateau between the two ranges. In the west is the peninsula of Lower California (Baja California), separated from the mainland by the Gulf of California (Mar de Cortez). The main rivers are the Rio Grande (Rio Bravo), which forms part of the northern boundary and is navigable for about 70 miles from its mouth in the Gulf of Mexico, and the Rio Grande de Santiago, the Rio Balsas and Rio Papaloapan.

HISTORY AND POLITICS

Present-day Mexico and Guatemala were once the centre of a civilisation which flowered in the periods from AD 500 to 1100 and 1300 to 1500 and collapsed before the Spanish army in the years following 1519. Pre-Columbian Mexico was divided between different Indian cultures, most notably the Mayan, Teotihuacáno, Zapotec, Totonac and Toltec cultures. The last and most famous Indian culture, the Aztec, suffered more than the others at the hands of the Spanish and very few Aztec monuments remain.

After the conquest, the country was largely converted to Christianity and a distinctive colonial civilisation emerged. In 1810 a revolt began against Spanish rule. This was finally successful in 1821, when independence was proclaimed.

Friction with the USA led to the war of 1846–8, at the end of which Mexico was forced to cede the northern provinces of Texas, California and New Mexico. In 1910 began the Mexican Revolution which reformed the social structure and the land system, curbed the power of foreign companies and ushered in the independent industrial Mexico of today.

There are 11 registered political parties; the Partido Revolucionario Institucional (PRI) which constituted the governing party for more than 60 years, until its defeat in July 2000, the Partido de Acción Nacional (PAN) and the Partido de la Revolución Democrática (PRD) are the largest.

In presidential and legislative elections on 2 July 2000, Vicente Fox, the PAN candidate, was elected as president and the PAN-led alliance gained 224 seats, the PRI 209 seats and the PRD 67 seats in the Chamber of Deputies.

INSURGENCIES

Two armed revolts of Zapatista peasant Indians in the southern state of Chiapas in January-August 1994 and December 1994-February 1995 caused a political and economic crisis. Negotiations with the Zapatistas produced a preliminary agreement on indigenous rights in February 1996, but talks broke down and were suspended in September 1996. Further talks took place in November 1998.

Following the inauguration of President Fox on 1 December 2000, the Zapatistas announced that peace talks could be resumed on condition that troops were withdrawn from the Chiapas, a bill of indigenous rights was enacted by Congress and an amnesty was declared for Zapatista rebels held by the authorities. On 24 February 2001, the General Staff, the ruling body of the Zapatistas, began a 3,360-km march from Chiapas to Mexico City in support of the bill. They arrived on 11 March, accompanied by hundreds of supporters, and their leaders addressed parliament on 28 March. Congress enacted a bill of indigenous rights on 1 May, but the Zapatistas broke off negotiations with the government, claiming that the provisions of the bill had been watered down.

POLITICAL SYSTEM

Congress consists of a Senate *(Cámara de Senadores)* of 128 members, elected for six years, and of a Chamber of

Deputies (*Cámara de Diputados*), at present numbering 500, elected for three years. The chief executive of the government is the president, who is elected for a six-year term and may not be re-elected.

FEDERAL STRUCTURE

State	Area (sq. km)	Population (2000 census)	Capital
Federal District	1,499	8,605,239	Mexico City
Aguascalientes	5,589	944,285	Aguascalientes
Baja California	70,113	2,487,367	Mexicali
Baja California Sur	73,677	424,041	La Paz
Campeche	51,833	690,689	Campeche
Coahuila	151,571	2,298,070	Saltillo
Colima	5,455	542,627	Colima
Chiapas	73,887	3,920,892	Tuxtla Gutiérrez
Chihuahua	247,087	3,052,907	Chihuahua
Durango	119,648	1,448,661	Victoria de Durango
Guanajuato	30,589	4,663,032	Guanajuato
Guerrero	63,794	3,079,649	Chilpancingo
Hidalgo	20,987	2,235,591	Pachuca de Soto
Jalisco	80,137	6,322,002	Guadalajara
México	21,461	13,096,686	Toluca de Lerdo
Michoacán	59,864	3,985,667	Morelia
Morelos	4,941	1,555,296	Cuernavaca
Nayarit	27,621	920,185	Tepic
Nuevo León	64,555	3,834,141	Monterrey
Oaxaca	95,364	3,438,765	Oaxaca de Juárez
Puebla	33,919	5,076,686	Puebla de Zaragoza
Querétaro	11,769	1,404,306	Querétaro
Quintana Roo	50,350	721,538	Chetumal
San Luis Potosí	62,848	2,299,360	San Luis Potosí
Sinaloa	58,092	2,536,844	Culiacán Rosales
Sonora	184,934	2,216,969	Hermosillo
Tabasco	24,661	1,891,829	Villahermosa
Tamaulipas	79,829	2,753,222	Ciudad Victoria
Tlaxcala	3,914	962,646	Tlaxcala
Veracruz	72,815	6,908,975	Jalapa Enríquez
Yucatán	39,340	1,658,210	Mérida
Zacatecas	75,040	1,353,610	Zacatecas

HEAD OF STATE

President, Vicente Fox, *elected* 2 July 2000, *sworn in* 1 December 2000

CABINET *as at July 2002*

Agrarian Reform, María Teresa Herrera Tello
Agriculture, Livestock, Rural Development, Fisheries and Food, Javier Usabiaga
Attorney-General, Gen. Rafael Macedo de la Concha
Communications and Transport, Pedro Cerisola
Comptroller-General, Francisco Barrio Terrazas
Defence, Gen. Gerardo Clemente Ricardo Vega
Economy, Luís Ernesto Derbez
Education, Reyes Tamez Guerra
Energy, Ernesto Martens
Environment, Natural Resources, Victor Lichtinger
Finance and Public Credit, Francisco Gil Diaz
Foreign Affairs, Jorge Castaneda
Health, Julio José Frenk Mora
Interior, Santiago Creel Miranda
Labour and Social Welfare, Carlos Abascal
Naval Affairs, Adm. Marco Antonio Peyrot
Public Safety, Alejandro Gertz Manero
Social Development, Josefina Vázquez Mota
Tourism, Leticia Navarro

MEXICAN EMBASSY
42 Hertford Street, London W1J 7JR
Tel: 020-7499 8586
Ambassador Extraordinary and Plenipotentiary, HE Alma Rosa Moreno Razo, apptd 2001

BRITISH EMBASSY
Calle Río Lerma 71, Colonia Cuauhtémoc, 06500 Mexico City
Tel: (00 52) (5) 242 8500
Email: infogen@mail.embajadabritanica.com.mx
Ambassador Extraordinary and Plenipotentiary, HE Denise Holt, CMG, apptd 2002

CONSULAR OFFICES – Mexico City, Acapulco, Cancún, Ciudad Juárez, Guadalajara, Monterrey, Oaxaca, Tijuana, Veracruz

BRITISH COUNCIL DIRECTOR, Alan Curry, Lope de Vega 316, Col. Chapultepec Morales, 11570 Mexico DF; Email: bc.mexico@britishcouncil.org.mx

DEFENCE

The Army has 862 armoured personnel carriers. The Navy has three destroyers, eight frigates, 109 patrol and coastal vessels, and eight combat aircraft. There are 20 naval bases. The Air Force has 107 combat aircraft and 71 armed helicopters.
MILITARY EXPENDITURE – 1.0 per cent of GDP (2000)
MILITARY PERSONNEL – 192,770: Army 144,000, Navy 37,000, Air Force 11,770; Paramilitaries 11,000
CONSCRIPTION DURATION – 12 months (four hours per week) by lottery

ECONOMY

The principal crops are maize, beans, sorghum, rice, wheat, barley, sugar cane, coffee, cotton, tomatoes, chillies, tobacco, chick-peas, groundnuts, cocoa and many kinds of fruit. The maguey, or Mexican cactus, yields several fermented drinks, mezcal and tequila (distilled) and pulque (undistilled). Another species of the plant supplies sisal-hemp (henequen). The forests contain mahogany, rosewood, ebony and chicle trees. Agriculture employs an estimated 20 per cent of the working population.

Until recently, the principal industries were mining and petroleum, but there has been considerable expansion of both light and heavy industries; exports of manufactured goods now average almost 90 per cent of total exports. The steel industry expanded steadily until recently and current production is around 5.8 million tons.

The mineral wealth is great, and principal minerals are gold, silver, copper, fluorspar, lead, zinc, quicksilver, iron and sulphur. Substantial reserves of uranium have been found. The oil industry is state-owned.

Tariffs on trade between Mexico and the USA and Canada are being reduced and are due to be abolished in 2004 under the North American Free Trade Area agreement.

There is great social inequality; a poverty-alleviation programme guarantees money and food to 2.6 million of the poorest families if they send their children to school.

Mexico joined GATT in 1986 and the OECD in 1994.
GNP – US$498,018 million (2000); US$4,440 per capita (1999)
GDP – US$414,350 million (1998); US$5,036 per capita (1999)
ANNUAL AVERAGE GROWTH OF GDP – 6.9 per cent (2000)
INFLATION RATE – 9.5 per cent (2000)
UNEMPLOYMENT – 1.7 per cent (1999)
TOTAL EXTERNAL DEBT – US$166,960 million (1999)

TRADE

Major imports include computers, auto assembly material, electrical parts, auto and truck parts, powdered milk, corn and sorghum, transport, sound-recording and power-generating equipment, chemicals, industrial machinery, pharmaceuticals and specialised appliances. Principal exports include oil, automobiles, auto engines, fruits and vegetables, shrimps, coffee, computers, cattle, glass, iron and steel pipes, and copper. The main trading partners are the USA, EU, Latin America and Japan. The North American Free Trade Agreement, to which Mexico is a signatory, came into effect on 1 January 1994; trade between Mexico, Canada and the USA rose by 17 per cent per year. Mexico has free trade agreements with EFTA, the EU, Bolivia, Chile, Colombia, Costa Rica, El Salvador, Guatemala, Honduras, Israel, Nicaragua and Venezuela.

In 2000 Mexico had a trade deficit of US$8,049 million and a current account deficit of US$17,768 million. In 1999 imports totalled US$148,648 million and exports US$136,391 million.

Trade with UK	2000	2001
Imports from UK	£674,683,000	£686,723,000
Exports to UK	632,867,000	702,499,000

COMMUNICATIONS

Veracruz, Tampico and Coatzacoalcos are the chief ports on the Atlantic, and Guaymas, Mazatlán, Puerto Lázaro Cárdenas and Salina Cruz on the Pacific. Work is proceeding on the reorganisation and re-equipment of the whole rail system. There were 329,532 km of roads in 1999; total track length of the railways was 26,622 km. Mexico City may be reached by at least three highways from the USA, and from the south from Yucatán as well as on two principal highways from the Guatemalan border.

There are 50 international airports and 33 national airports in Mexico. There are many airline companies, including two major, now private, national airlines, Mexicana de Aviación and Aeroméxico.

FEDERATED STATES OF MICRONESIA

AREA – 271 sq. miles (702 sq. km)
POPULATION – 134,597 (2001 estimate). The population is Micronesian and predominantly Christian. English (official) and eight other languages are used in different parts of the Federated States: Yapese, Ulithian, Woleaian, Pohnpeian, Nukuoran, Kapingamarangi, Chuukese and Kosraean
FEDERAL CAPITAL – Palikir, on Pohnpei
CURRENCY – Currency is that of the USA
NATIONAL ANTHEM – Patriots Of Micronesia
NATIONAL FLAG – United Nations blue with four white stars in the centre
LIFE EXPECTANCY (years) – male 64.4; female 68.8
POPULATION GROWTH RATE – 3.7 per cent (1997)
POPULATION DENSITY – 165 per sq. km (1999)

The Federated States of Micronesia comprise more than 600 islands extending 2,900 km (1,800 miles) across the archipelago of the Caroline Islands in the western Pacific Ocean. The islands vary geologically from mountainous islands to low coral atolls.

HISTORY AND POLITICS

The Spanish Empire claimed sovereignty over the Caroline Islands until 1899, when Spain withdrew from her Pacific territories and sold her possessions in the Caroline Islands to Germany. The Caroline Islands became a German protectorate until the outbreak of the First World War in 1914, when Japan took control of the islands and was given a League of Nations mandate to administer the territory in 1920. During the Second World War, US armed forces took control of the islands from the Japanese. In 1947 the USA entered into agreement with the UN Security Council to administer the Micronesia area, of which the Federated States of Micronesia were a part, as the UN Trust Territory of the Pacific Islands.

The US Trusteeship administration came to an end on 3 November 1986, when a Compact of Free Association between the USA and the Federated States of Micronesia came into effect. By this agreement the USA recognised the Federated States of Micronesia as a fully sovereign and independent state. The independence of the Federated States of Micronesia was recognised by the UN in December 1990.

POLITICAL SYSTEM

The constitution separates the executive, legislative and judicial branches. There is a bill of rights and provision for traditional rights. The executive comprises a federal president and vice-president, both of whom must be chosen from amongst the four nationally elected senators. There is a single-chamber Congress of 14 members, four members elected on a state-wide basis and ten members elected from congressional districts apportioned by population.

The Compact of Free Association places full responsibility for the defence of the Federated States of Micronesia on the USA.

The judiciary is headed by the Supreme Court, which is divided into trial and appellate divisions. Below this, each state has its own judicial system.

FEDERAL STRUCTURE

The Federated States of Micronesia is a federal republic of four constituent states: Chuuk, Kosrae, Pohnpei and Yap. Each of the constituent states has its own government and legislative system.

State	Area (sq. km)	Population (1994)	Capital
Chuuk	127	52,870	Weno
Kosrae	109	7,354	Lelu
Pohnpei	344	33,372	Kolonia
Yap	119	11,128	Colonia

HEAD OF STATE

President, Leo Falcam
Vice-President, Redley Killion

CABINET *as at July 2002*

Economic Affairs, Sebastian Anefal
Finance and Administration, John Ehsa
Foreign Affairs, Ieske Iehsi
Health, Education and Social Services, Eliuel Pretrick
Justice, Paul McIlraith
Public Defender, Beauleen Worswick
Transportation, Communications and Infrastructure, Lambert Lokopwe

BRITISH AMBASSADOR, HE Michael Price, LVO, resident at Suva, Fiji

ECONOMY

The economy is dependent mainly on subsistence agriculture, which employs almost half the population, and foreign aid. Copra and fish are the two main exports.

The majority of the working population is engaged in government administration, subsistence farming, fishing, copra production and the tourist industry. Pepper is produced for export on Pohnpei and citrus fruits are commercially grown on Kosrae. The government derives a significant income from licensing fees paid by foreign vessels fishing for tuna and tuna processing plants are being constructed in Pohnpei and Kosrae.
GNP – US$250 million (2000); US$1,830 per capita (1999)
GDP – US$210 million (1998); US$1,922 per capita (1999)

Trade with UK	2000	2001
Imports from UK	£33,000	£7,000
Exports to UK	2,000	28,000

MOLDOVA
Republica Moldova – Republic of Moldova

AREA – 13,012 sq. miles (33,851 sq. km) Neighbours: Ukraine (north, east and south-east), Romania (west)
POPULATION – 4,335,000 (2001 estimate): 65 per cent are Moldovan, 14.2 per cent Ukrainian and 13 per cent Russian, together with smaller numbers of Gagauz (ethnic Turks), Jews and Bulgarians. Most of the population are adherents of the Moldovan Orthodox Church. Moldovan was made the official language (written in the Latin script) in 1989 but the use of Russian in official business is permitted
CAPITAL – Chişinău (population, 655,940, 1997 estimate)
CURRENCY – Moldovan leu of 100 bani (plural lei)
NATIONAL ANTHEM – Lîmbă Noastră (Our Language)
NATIONAL DAY – 27 August (Independence Day)
NATIONAL FLAG – Vertical stripes of blue, yellow, red, with the national arms in the centre
LIFE EXPECTANCY (years) – male 62.8; female 70.3
POPULATION GROWTH RATE – -0.2 per cent (1997)
POPULATION DENSITY – 129 per sq. km (1999)
URBAN POPULATION – 46.4 per cent (1995)
MILITARY EXPENDITURE – 1.7 per cent of GDP (2000)
MILITARY PERSONNEL – Army 7,120, Air Force 800; Paramilitaries 3,400
CONSCRIPTION DURATION – Up to 18 months
ILLITERACY RATE – 1.0 per cent (2002)
ENROLMENT (percentage of age group) – tertiary 27 per cent (1997)

HISTORY AND POLITICS
In the 15th century a Moldovan principality was formed which was absorbed into the Turkish Empire in the 16th century. Moldova became the site of many Russo-Turkish battles and skirmishes in the 18th century before the area between the Dniester and Prut rivers (later known as Bessarabia) was annexed to the Russian Empire by the Bucharest Peace Treaty of 1812.
After the Russian Revolution in 1917, an independent Moldovan state was proclaimed in Bessarabia, which came under the control of White Russian forces and was annexed to Romania under the Versailles Peace Treaty (1919). In 1924 the Moldavian Autonomous Soviet Socialist Republic (ASSR) was established on the east bank of the Dniester river as part of Soviet Ukraine. In August 1940 the Soviet Union forced Romania to cede Bessarabia and the Moldavian Soviet Socialist Republic was formed from the majority of Bessarabia (the southernmost parts were incorporated into the Ukraine) and the Moldavian ASSR.
Moldova (formerly Moldavia) declared its independence from the USSR in August 1991.

Reunification with Romania was rejected in a referendum on 6 March 1994, following which the Moldovan parliament voted to join the CIS. Following the adoption in September 2000 of constitutional changes giving parliament the power to elect the president, a series of parliamentary votes was held in December 2000, in which none of the candidates were able to obtain the support of the required 61 members. In accordance with the constitutional changes, parliament was dissolved on 12 January 2001 and a general election was held on 25 February, which was won by the Communist Party of Moldova (PCM), who obtained 71 seats. The new parliament elected the PCM leader, Vladimir Voronin, as president on 4 April 2001 and approved a new Cabinet, led by Vasile Tarlev, an independent MP.

INSURGENCIES
After independence was declared, the majority ethnic Romanian (Moldovan) population expressed a wish to rejoin Romania. This alienated the ethnic Ukrainian and Russian populations, who formed a majority east of the Dniester, and they declared their independence from Moldova as the Transdniester republic in December 1991. The Moldovan government refused to recognise this and in 1992 a war was waged between government forces and Transdniester forces, who were supported by local Russian soldiers and volunteers.
A mainly Russian CIS peacekeeping force (later changed to a joint Russian-Moldovan-Transdniester force) was deployed in July 1992 and a cease-fire has held since August 1992. The Moldovan government in February 1994 agreed to an OSCE plan for the Transdniester area to have a high degree of autonomy within Moldova but no independent or federal status. A memorandum of understanding on the normalisation of relations between the two sides was signed in May 1997, which committed both parties to hold further talks within 'the framework of a single state'.
A referendum in Transdniester on 24 December 1995 approved independence. President Igor Smirnov was re-elected in presidential elections in Transdniester in December 1996.
A legislative election was held in Transdniester on 10 December 2000 in which the majority of candidates elected were independents.
President Voronin and the leader of Transdniester, Igor Smirnov, agreed on 16 May 2001 to co-ordinate their policies on taxation and remove customs posts along the mutual border. In July 2001, a draft treaty on the status of Transdniestria was published in the Moldovan state press. According to this draft, which was prepared with international mediators from Russia, Ukraine and the Organisation for Security and Co-operation in Europe, Moldova is to become a federal state, with each part of the federation having its own constitution.

POLITICAL SYSTEM
In July 1994 the Moldovan parliament adopted a new constitution which established a presidential parliamentary republic and provided for autonomous status for the Gagauz region, which was given its own elected National Assembly.
Parliament is elected by proportional representation for a four-year term.
On 22 September 2000, the legislature passed a law transforming Moldova into a parliamentary republic. The president is elected by parliament and must obtain the support of at least 61 of the 101 deputies. If no candidate achieves this, parliament must be dissolved and a general election held.

HEAD OF STATE

President, Vladimir Voronin, *elected* by parliament 4
April 2001

GOVERNMENT *as at July 2002*

Prime Minister, Vasile Tarlev
First Deputy Prime Minister, Vasilie Iovv
Deputy Prime Ministers, Dmitrii Todoroglo *(Agriculture
and Food Industry)*; Stefan Odagiu *(Economy)*;
Valerian Cristea *(Without Portfolio)*
Culture, Ion Pacuraru
Defence, Victor Gaiciuc
Education and Science, Gheorghe Sima
Energy, Iacob Timciuc
Environment, Construction and Territorial Development,
Gheorghe Duca
Finance, Zinaida Greceanii
Foreign Affairs, Nicolae Dudau
Health, Andrei Gherman
Industry, Mihail Garstea
Interior, Col. George Papuc
Justice, Ion Morei
Labour, Social Protection and Family Affairs, Valerian
Revenco
Transport and Communications, Victor Topa

EMBASSY OF THE REPUBLIC OF MOLDOVA
Rue Tenbosch 54, Brussels 1050, Belgium
Tel: (00 32) (2) 732 5847
Ambassador Extraordinary and Plenipotentiary, HE Ion
Capatina, apptd 1999

BRITISH AMBASSADOR, HE Bernard Whiteside, CVO,
CMG

ECONOMY

The main sector is agriculture, especially viniculture,
fruit-growing and market gardening. Industry is small
and concentrated east of the Dniester. Severe drought in
1992, the severance of most trading ties with former
Soviet republics, war damage and reductions in Russian
fuel deliveries paralysed the economy from 1992 to 1994.
An economic reform programme aiming to attract
foreign investment began in 1993; a privatisation
programme was completed in 1995. Moldova is
dependent on Russia for energy supplies and owes
roughly US$6,000 million.

In 1999 there was a trade deficit of US$123 million and
a current account deficit of US$33 million. In 1998
imports totalled US$1,018 million and exports US$644
million.

GNP – US$1,413 million (2000); US$410 per capita
(1999)
GDP – US$1,639 million (1998); US$270 per capita
(1999)
ANNUAL AVERAGE GROWTH OF GDP – -8.6 per cent
(1998)
INFLATION RATE – 31.3 per cent (2000)
UNEMPLOYMENT – 11.1 per cent (1999)
TOTAL EXTERNAL DEBT – US$943 million (1999)

Trade with UK	2000	2001
Imports from UK	£5,062,000	£9,915,000
Exports to UK	3,942,000	4,667,000

MONACO
Principauté de Monaco – Principality of Monaco

AREA – 0.4 sq. miles (1 sq. km). Neighbour: France
POPULATION – 31,842 (2001 estimate). Only 7,175
residents have full Monégasque citizenship and thus

the right to vote. The official language is French.
Monégasque, a mixture of Provençal and Ligurian, is
also spoken
CAPITAL – Monaco
CURRENCY – Euro (€) of 100 cents
NATIONAL ANTHEM – Hymne Monégasque
(Monegasque Anthem)
NATIONAL DAY – 19 November
NATIONAL FLAG – Two equal horizontal stripes, red
over white
LIFE EXPECTANCY (years) – male 74.7; female 83.6
POPULATION GROWTH RATE – 1.1 per cent (1999)

A small principality on the Mediterranean, with land
frontiers joining France at every point, Monaco is divided
into the districts of Monaco-Ville, La Condamine,
Fontvieille and Monte Carlo.

HISTORY AND POLITICS
The principality, ruled by the Grimaldi family since 1297,
was abolished during the French Revolution and re-
established in 1815 under the protection of the kingdom
of Sardinia. In 1861 Monaco came under French
protection.

The 1962 constitution, which can be modified only
with the approval of the National Council, maintains the
traditional hereditary monarchy and guarantees freedom
of association, trade union freedom and the right to
strike. Legislative power is held jointly by the Prince and
a unicameral, 18-member National Council elected by
universal suffrage. In the legislative election on 1 and 8
February 1998, all 18 seats were won by the National and
Democratic Union. Executive power is exercised by the
Prince and a four-member Council of Government,
headed by a Minister of State, who is nominated by the
Prince from a list of three French diplomats submitted by
the French government. The judicial code is based on that
of France. The next election is due to be held in February
2003.

HEAD OF STATE

HSH The Prince of Monaco, Prince Rainier III Louis-
Henri-Maxence Bertrand, born 31 May 1923,
succeeded 9 May 1949; *married* 19 April 1956, Miss
Grace Patricia Kelly (died 14 September 1982) and
has issue Prince Albert; Princess Caroline Louise
Marguerite, *born* 23 January 1957; and Princess
Stephanie Marie Elisabeth, *born* 1 February 1965
Heir, HRH Prince Albert Alexandre Louis Pierre, *born*
14 March 1958
President of the Crown Council, Charles Ballerio
President of the National Council, Dr Jean-Louis
Campora
Minister of State, Patrick Leclercq
Finance and Economy, Franck Biancheri
Interior, Philippe Deslandes
Public Works and Social Affairs, José Badia

CONSULATE-GENERAL OF MONACO
4 Cromwell Place, London SW7 2JE
Tel: 020-7225 2679
Consul-General, I. B. Ivanovic

BRITISH CONSULATE-GENERAL
33 Boulevard Princesse Charlotte, BP 265, MC-98005
Monaco CEDEX
Tel: (00 377) 93 50 99 66
Consul-General, Simon Jeffrey Lever, apptd 2002

ECONOMY

The whole available ground is built over so that there is no cultivation, though there are some notable public and private gardens. The economy is based on real estate revenues, the financial sector and tourism. There is a small harbour (30 ft alongside quay). Monaco has been in a customs union with the European Union since 1984.

GDP – US$814 million (1998); US$24,267 per capita (1999)

ANNUAL AVERAGE GROWTH OF GDP – 3.3 per cent (1998)

MONGOLIA
Mongol Uls – Mongol State

AREA – 604,829 sq. miles (1,566,500 sq. km).
Neighbours: Russia (north), China (south)

POPULATION – 2,654,999 (2001 estimate). Mongolians also live in China and in the neighbouring regions of Russia, especially the Mongolian Buryat-Autonomous Region. The official language is Khalkha Mongolian

CAPITAL – Ulaanbaatar (population, 515,100, 1998 estimate)

CURRENCY – Tugrik of 100 möngö

NATIONAL ANTHEM – Mongol Ulsiin Teriin Duulal (Mongol National Anthem)

NATIONAL DAY – 11 July

NATIONAL FLAG – Vertical tricolour red, blue, red and in the hoist the traditional Soyombo symbol in gold

LIFE EXPECTANCY (years) – male 61.9; female 65.9

POPULATION GROWTH RATE – 3.3 per cent (1999)

POPULATION DENSITY – 2 per sq. km (1999)

MILITARY EXPENDITURE – 2.0 per cent of GDP (2000)

MILITARY PERSONNEL – 9,100: Army 7,500, Air Defence 800; Paramilitaries 7,200

CONSCRIPTION DURATION – 12 months

ILLITERACY RATE – 1.0 per cent (2002)

ENROLMENT (percentage of age group) – primary 88 per cent (1997); secondary 56 per cent (1997); tertiary 17.0 per cent (1997)

Mongolia, which is almost entirely at least 1,000 metres above sea level, forms part of the central Asiatic plateau and rises towards the west in the mountains of the Mongolian Altai and Hangai ranges. The Hentai range, situated to the north-east of the capital Ulaanbaatar, is lower. The Gobi region covers much of the southern half of the country and contains sand deserts interspersed with semi-desert. There are several long rivers and many lakes but good water is scarce as much of the lake water is salty.

HISTORY AND POLITICS

Mongolia, under Genghis Khan the conqueror of China and much of Asia, was for many years a buffer state between Tsarist Russia and China, although it was under general Chinese suzerainty. The Mongolian People's Republic was formally established in 1924. Under the Yalta Agreement, President Chiang Kai-shek of China agreed to a plebiscite, held in 1945, in which the Mongolians declared their desire for independence and this was formally recognised by China.

The Mongolian People's Revolutionary Party (MPRP) was the sole political party from 1924 to 1990. Demonstrations in favour of political and economic reform began in December 1989 and led to changes in the MPRP leadership in March 1990. The MPRP's constitutionally guaranteed monopoly of power was subsequently relinquished, and the introduction of a

multiparty system was approved by the Great People's Hural (parliament). The MPRP won the first multiparty elections, held in July 1990. The country's first direct presidential election was held in 1993 and won by the incumbent Punsalmaagiyn Ochirbat, who stood as an opposition candidate after the MPRP refused to endorse him as its candidate; he was ousted in May 1997 by the leader of the MPRP, Natsagyn Bagabandi, who won a second term of office on 20 May 2001, obtaining 58.13 per cent of the votes cast. The June 1996 election was won by the Democratic Union Coalition (Mongolian National Democratic Party and Mongolian Social Democratic Party). The legislative election held on 2 July 2000 resulted in a victory for the MPRP, who gained 72 seats.

The country and three city districts (Ulanbaatar, Darkhan and Erdenet) are divided into 21 *aimaks* (provinces) and beneath these into 258 *somons* (districts), and these form the basis of the state organisation of the country. The last remaining former Soviet armed forces personnel were withdrawn in late 1992.

POLITICAL SYSTEM

A new constitution was approved in January 1992 which established a democratic parliamentary system of government. The president is directly elected for a term of four years and the unicameral legislature is the State Great Hural *(Ulsyn Ikh Khural)*, which has 76 members, elected for four-year terms by a simple majority amounting to at least 25 per cent of the votes cast. In July 2000 a constitutional amendment came into force, which gives the president the right to dissolve the Great State Hural if it is unable to reach agreement on appointing a prime minister.

HEAD OF STATE

President, Natsagyn Bagabandi, *elected* 18 May 1997, *re-elected* 20 May 2001

CABINET *as at July 2002*

Prime Minister, Nambariyn Enkhbayar
Government Secretariat, Ulziysaihany Enkhtuvshin
Defence, Jugderdemidyn Gurragchaa
Education, Culture and Science, Ayurzanyn Tsanjid
Environment, Ulambaryn Barsbold
Finance and Economy, Chultemiyn Ulaan
Food and Agriculture, Darjaagyn Nasanjargal
Foreign Affairs, Luvsangyn Erdenechuluun
Health, Pagvajavyn Nyamdavaa
Industry and Commerce, Chimidzorigyn Ganzorig
Infrastructure, Byambyn Jigjid
Justice and Internal Affairs, Tsendyn Nyamdorj
Social Welfare and Labour, Shiylegiyn Batbayar

EMBASSY OF MONGOLIA
7 Kensington Court, London W8 5DL
Tel: 020-7937 0150
Ambassador Extraordinary and Plenipotentiary, HE Davaasambuu Dalrain, apptd 2001

BRITISH EMBASSY
30 Enkh Taivny Gudamzh (PO Box 703), Ulaanbaatar 13.
Tel: (00 976) (1) 458133
Email: britemb@magicnet.mn
Ambassador Extraordinary and Plenipotentiary, HE Philip Rouse, MBE, apptd 2001

ECONOMY

Traditionally the Mongolians led a nomadic life tending flocks of sheep, goats, horses, cows and camels. Collectivisation at the end of the 1950s into huge *negdels*

(co-operatives) and state farms hastened the process of settlement, but within these the herdsmen and their families still move with their traditional *gers* (circular tents) from pasture to pasture as the seasons change.

The semi-desert areas of the Gobi region provide pasture for sheep, goats, camels, horses and cattle. In the steppe areas to the north of the Gobi pasturage is better and livestock more abundant. Even further north, in the better-watered provinces, grain, fodder and vegetable crops are grown.

Although the economy remains predominantly pastoral, factories have started up, coal, copper and molybdenum are mined and the electricity industry has been developed. Ulaanbaatar and Darkhan are the main seats of industry, which includes lime, cement and building materials, a flour mill and a power station. Choibalsan is also being developed industrially.

All trade barriers were abolished in May 1997.

A prolonged drought and an exceptionally severe winter in 1999–2000 resulted in the deaths of an estimated two million livestock, affecting 800,000 herders. At least a further 1.3 million livestock were estimated to have died in another severe winter in 2000–2001. In May 2001, international donors promised US$330 million in aid.

GNP – US$926 million (2000); US$390 per capita (1999)

GDP – US$992 million (1998); US$348 per capita (1999)

ANNUAL AVERAGE GROWTH OF GDP – 3.5 per cent (1998)

INFLATION RATE – 7.6 per cent (1999)

UNEMPLOYMENT – 5.7 per cent (1998)

TOTAL EXTERNAL DEBT – US$891 million (1999)

TRADE

Foreign trade was formerly dominated by the Soviet Union and other Eastern bloc countries, but trade with Western countries, Japan and South Korea is now increasing. Since January 1991, trade has been in hard currency, causing particular strain. The principal exports are animal by-products (especially wool, hides and furs) and cattle.

In 1999 there was a trade deficit of US$56 million and a current account deficit of US$112 million. Imports totalled US$426 million and exports US$233 million.

Trade with UK	2000	2001
Imports from UK	£2,117,000	£2,405,000
Exports to UK	9,296,000	8,923,000

COMMUNICATIONS

Communication is still difficult as there are only 1,563 km of surfaced roads and horses are still the characteristic means of transport for the rural population. The trans-Mongolian railway links Mongolia with both China and Russia; total track length is 1,815 km.

MOROCCO

Al-Mamlaka Al-Maghribiyya – *Kingdom of Morocco*

AREA – 172,414 sq. miles (446,550 sq. km). Neighbours: Algeria (east and south-east), Western Sahara (south-west)

POPULATION – 30,645,305 (2001 estimate). Standard Arabic is the official language. Maghrebi Arabic and various Berber languages (Tachelhit, Tamazight and Tarafit) are the vernacular. French and Spanish are also spoken, mainly in the towns. Islam is the state religion

CAPITAL – ΨRabat (population, 1,220,000, 1993 estimate)

MAJOR CITIES – ΨAgadir (923,000); ΨCasablanca (Ad-Dar-el-Beida) (3,100,000); Fez (554,000); Marrakesh (878,000); Meknès (614,000); Oujda (430,000), 1997 estimates

CURRENCY – Dirham (DH) of 100 centimes

NATIONAL ANTHEM – Hymne Cherifien

NATIONAL DAY – 30 July (Anniversary of the Throne)

NATIONAL FLAG – Red, with green pentagram

LIFE EXPECTANCY (years) – male 66.8; female 70.5

POPULATION GROWTH RATE – 1.7 per cent (1999)

POPULATION DENSITY – 63 per sq. km (1999)

URBAN POPULATION – 50.3 per cent (1996)

Morocco is traversed in the north by the Rif mountains and, in a south-west to north-east direction, by the Middle Atlas, the High Atlas, the Anti-Atlas and the Sarrho ranges. The north-westerly point of Morocco is the peninsula of Tangier dominated by the Jebel Mousa which, with the rocky eminence of Gibraltar, was known to the ancients as the Pillars of Hercules, the western gateway of the Mediterranean.

HISTORY AND POLITICS

Morocco became an independent sovereign state in 1956, following joint declarations made with France on 2 March 1956 and with Spain on 7 April 1956. The Sultan of Morocco, Sidi Mohammad ben Youssef, adopted the title of King Mohammad V.

Elections were held on 14 November 1997 to the new House of Representatives; no party won an overall majority, but Abderrahmane El Youssoufi was appointed prime minister as the leader of the Socialist Union of Popular Forces, the largest party in the House of Representatives. On 15 September 2000, elections to the Chamber of Councillors were held. Elections to the House of Representatives were due in November 2002.

POLITICAL SYSTEM

The King nominates the prime minister and, on the latter's recommendation, appoints the members of the Council of Ministers. The government is responsible both to parliament and to the King. There is a bicameral legislature. The House of Representatives *(Majlis an-Nuwab)* has 325 members elected for a five-year term by universal suffrage using a first-past-the-post system. The Chamber of Councillors *(Majlis al-Mustashareen)* has 270 members, 60 per cent of whom are elected by local councils, 20 per cent by employers' associations and 20 per cent by trade unions. One third of its members are elected every three years.

HEAD OF STATE

HM The King of Morocco, King Mohammed VI (Sidi Mohammed Ben Hassan), *born* 21 August 1963, *acceded* 23 July 1999

COUNCIL OF MINISTERS *as at July 2002*

Prime Minister, Abderrahmane El Youssoufi
Agriculture and Rural Development, Ismail Alaoui
Culture and Communications, Mohamed Achaari
Economic Estimates and Planning, Abdelhamid Aouad
Economy, Finance and Tourism, Fathallah Oualalou
Employment, Vocational Training, Social Development and Solidarity, Abbas Fassi
Energy and Mining, Industry and Commerce, Mustapha Mansouri
Equipment, Bouamar Tighouane
Foreign Affairs and Co-operation, Mohamed Ben Aissa
General Secretary of the Government, Abdessadek Rabii
Health, Thami Khiari
Higher Education and Scientific Research, Najib Zerouali

Human Rights, Mohamed Aoujar
Interior Affairs, Driss Jettou
Justice, Omar Azziman
Marine Fisheries, Said Chbaatou
National Education, Abdallah Saaf
Public Sector and Privatisation, Mohamed Khalifa
Relations with Parliament, Mohamed Bouzoubaa
Social Economy, Small and Medium Enterprises and
   Handicrafts, General Government Affairs, Ahmed
   Halimi Alami
Town and Country Planning, Environment, Housing,
   Mohamed el Yazghi
Transport and Merchant Navy, Abdeslam Zenined
Waqf and Islamic Affairs, Abdelkebir M'Daghri Alaoui
Youth and Sports, Ahmed Moussaoui

EMBASSY OF THE KINGDOM OF MOROCCO
49 Queen's Gate Gardens, London SW7 5NE
Tel: 020-7581 5001/4
Ambassador Extraordinary and Plenipotentiary, HE
   Mohammed Belmahi, apptd 1999

BRITISH EMBASSY
17 Boulevard de la Tour Hassan (BP 45), Rabat
Tel: (00 212) (37) 238600
Email: britemb@mtds.com
Ambassador Extraordinary and Plenipotentiary, HE
   Haydon Warren-Gash, apptd 2002
CONSULATE-GENERAL – Casablanca
CONSULATES – Agadir, Marrakesh, Tangier

BRITISH COUNCIL DIRECTOR, Graham McCulloch,
   MBE, BP 427, 36 rue de Tanger, Rabat;
   Email: britcoun.morocco@britishcouncil.org.ma

DEFENCE

The Army has 744 main battle tanks, 115 armoured
infantry fighting vehicles, and 785 armoured personnel
carriers. The Navy has one frigate and 27 patrol and
coastal combatant vessels at five bases. The Air Force has
95 combat aircraft and 24 armed helicopters.

MILITARY EXPENDITURE – 5.1 per cent of GDP (2000)
MILITARY PERSONNEL – 198,500: Army 175,000, Navy
   10,000, Air Force 13,500; Paramilitaries 48,000
CONSCRIPTION DURATION – 18 months

ECONOMY

Morocco's main sources of wealth are agricultural and
mineral. A large-scale privatisation programme has
attracted substantial foreign investment.

Agriculture contributes 17 per cent of GDP and
employs 38.5 per cent of the workforce. The main
agricultural exports are fruit and vegetables, with cereals
and sugar beet produced and sheep reared for domestic
consumption. Cork and wood pulp are the most
important commercial forest products. There is a fishing
industry and substantial quantities of canned fish are
exported.

For a developing country Morocco has a large
industrial sector. The main sectors are chemicals, textiles
and leather goods, food processing and cement
production. Manufacturing industries are centred in
Casablanca, Fez, Tangier and Safi.

Morocco's mineral exports are phosphates, fluorite,
barite, manganese, iron ore, lead, zinc, cobalt, copper and
antimony. Morocco possesses nearly three-quarters of the
world's estimated reserves of phosphates.

Morocco has a high proportion of public employees;
the salaries of its 750,000 civil servants consume about 12
per cent of the country's GDP.

Tourism is of great importance to the economy, with
development concentrated in Agadir and Marrakesh.

GNP – US$33,820 million (2000); US$1,190 per capita
   (1999)
GDP – US$35,651 million (1998); US$1,263 per capita
   (1999)
ANNUAL AVERAGE GROWTH OF GDP – 0.9 per cent
   (2000)
INFLATION RATE – 1.9 per cent (2000)
UNEMPLOYMENT – 22.0 per cent (1999)
TOTAL EXTERNAL DEBT – US$19,060 million (1999)

TRADE

The main imports are petroleum products, machinery,
chemical products, iron and steel, grain and textiles. The
EU, with which an association agreement was signed in
November 1995, is Morocco's largest trading partner and
in May 1998 awarded Morocco grants totalling US$98
million. The main exports are phosphates and
phosphoric acid, textiles and leather, and fish and
agricultural products.

In 1998 Morocco had a trade deficit of US$2,319
million and a current account deficit of US$236 million.
In 2000 imports totalled US$11,484 million and exports
US$7,417 million.

Trade with UK	2000	2001
Imports from UK	£409,271,000	£370,602,000
Exports to UK	470,675,000	456,682,000

COMMUNICATIONS

Railroads cover 1,907 km, linking the major towns. There
are 60,449 km of roads; an extensive network of 30,374
km of surfaced roads covers all the main towns.

EDUCATION

Education is compulsory between the ages of seven and
16. There are government primary, secondary and
technical schools. In 1991 there were 4,890 government
schools. At Fez there is a theological university of great
repute in the Muslim world. There is a secular university
at Rabat. Schools for special denominations, Jewish and
Catholic, are permitted and may receive government
grants. American schools operate in Rabat and
Casablanca. There is an English-language university in
Ifrane.

ILLITERACY RATE – 49.2 per cent (2002)
ENROLMENT (percentage of age group) – primary 86
   per cent (1997); secondary 39 per cent (1977);
   tertiary 11 per cent (1997)

WESTERN SAHARA

Al-Jumhūriyya al-'Arabiyya as-Ṣahrāwiyya ad-
Dimuqrāiyya – Sahrawi Arab Democratic Republic

AREA – 97,344 sq. miles (252,120 sq. km) Neighbours:
   Morocco (north), Algeria (north-east), Mauritania
   (east and south)
POPULATION – 244,943 (2000 estimate). Arabic is the
   official language. Hassaniya and Moroccan Arabic are
   the main spoken languages; Spanish is widely spoken
   in the towns. Almost all the population is Sunni
   Muslim
CAPITAL – El-Aaiūn (population, 139,000 1990
   estimate)
NATIONAL FLAG – Three horizontal stripes of black,
   white and green with a red crescent and five-pointed
   star in the centre and red triangle based on the hoist
LIFE EXPECTANCY (years) – male 62.3; female 65.6
POPULATION GROWTH RATE – 3.4 per cent (1999) per
   cent (1999)
POPULATION DENSITY – 1 per sq. km (1999)

Formerly the Spanish Sahara, the territory was split between Morocco and Mauritania in 1976 after Spain withdrew in December 1975. In 1976 the Polisario Front (Frente Popular para la Liberación de Saguia y Río de Oro) declared Western Sahara to be an independent state, the Sahrawi Arab Democratic Republic, and formed a government which remains in exile. The Polisario Front has been recognised as the legitimate government of Western Sahara by over 70 states and the Organisation of African Unity. In 1979 Mauritania renounced its claim to its share of the territory, which was added by Morocco to its area.

About 167,000 Sahrawis are in exile in Algeria and 15,000 in Mauritania.

In 1988, Morocco and the Polisario Front accepted a UN peace plan under which a cease-fire came into effect in September 1991. A referendum to determine the future of the area was to have been held in January 1992 but has not yet taken place because the Moroccan government and Polisario have not agreed on the referendum terms or voter eligibility. Voter identification began in August 1994 but the failure to agree on eligibility prompted the UN to threaten the suspension of the UN Mission for the Referendum in Western Sahara (MINURSO), which had been deployed since 1991.

In September 2000, representatives of the Moroccan government and the Polisario Front held negotiations to discuss differences that prevented the implementation of the UN-mediated referendum on the future of the Western Sahara. The talks failed when the Polisario refused to discuss a Moroccan proposal that the territory accept autonomy status within Morocco.

In September 2001, Polisario rejected a UN peace plan which proposed replacing a referendum by a political arrangement whereby Western Sahara would operate for the following five years as a semi-autonomous territory with Morocco maintaining sovereignty. Legislative elections to the National Assembly were held in 1995; President Mohamed Abdelaziz, who had been elected president since 1982 by the party congress of the Polisario Front, was re-elected by the National Assembly in 1995. Following a vote of no confidence in the previous incumbent, Bouchraya Hamoudi Bayoun was named Prime Minister on 10 February 1999.

The UN has some 231 personnel in Western Sahara pending the referendum (*see* above). The Polisario Front deploys 3,000–6,000 troops in Western Sahara with Algerian-supplied and captured Moroccan tanks, armoured personnel carriers, anti-tank and anti-aircraft weapons.

POLISARIO FRONT OFFICE
138 Tachbrook Street, London SW1V 2ND
Tel: 020-7834 6618
Representative, Ibrahim Mokhtar

MOZAMBIQUE
República de Moçambique - Republic of Mozambique

AREA – 309,494 sq. miles (801,590 sq. km). Neighbours: Swaziland (south), South Africa (south and west), Zimbabwe (west), Zambia and Malawi (north-west), Tanzania (north)
POPULATION – 19,371,057 (2001 estimate). The official language is Portuguese
CAPITAL – ΨMaputo (population, 1,039,700, 1998 census)
MAJOR CITIES – ΨBeira (264,202); ΨNacala (182,505), 1986 estimates

CURRENCY – Metical (MT) of 100 centavos
NATIONAL ANTHEM – Hino Nacional (National Anthem)
NATIONAL DAY – 25 June (Independence Day)
NATIONAL FLAG – Horizontally green, black, yellow with white fimbriations; a red triangle based on the hoist containing the national emblem
LIFE EXPECTANCY (years) – male 37.3; female 38.6
POPULATION GROWTH RATE – 3.6 per cent (1997)
POPULATION DENSITY – 22 per sq. km (1999)
MILITARY EXPENDITURE – 3.6 per cent of GDP (2000)
MILITARY PERSONNEL – 11,600: Army 10,000, Navy 600, Air Force 1,000
CONSCRIPTION DURATION – Two to three years
ILLITERACY RATE – 53.5 per cent (2002)
ENROLMENT (percentage of age group) – primary 60 per cent (1997); secondary 7 per cent (1997); tertiary 1 per cent (1997)

HISTORY AND POLITICS

Mozambique, discovered by Vasco da Gama in 1498 and colonised by Portugal, achieved independence on 25 June 1975. It was a Marxist one-party (Frelimo) state until a multiparty system was adopted in 1990.

The Frelimo government and the rebel Mozambican National Resistance (Renamo) signed a peace agreement in October 1992 which ended 16 years of civil war. Demobilisation of government and Renamo troops took place in 1994.

Presidential and legislative elections were held on 3–5 December 1999. The incumbent, Joaquim Chissano of Frelimo, won the presidential election with 52.3 per cent of the vote. Frelimo also won the legislative election, gaining 133 seats to Renamo's 117, amid allegations by Renamo of vote-rigging. No other parties were able to secure the 5 per cent of the total vote necessary to obtain representation.

Mozambique was admitted to the Commonwealth on 12 November 1995 as a special case, because of its close links with Commonwealth countries.

POLITICAL SYSTEM

The president is directly elected and serves a term of five years, which is renewable no more than twice consecutively. The unicameral legislature, the Assembly of the Republic (*Assembleia Da Republica*), is directly elected for a five-year term and comprises 250 members.

HEAD OF STATE

President, Joaquim Alberto Chissano, *sworn in* November 1986, *elected* 29 October 1994, *re-elected* 5 December 1999

COUNCIL OF MINISTERS *as at July 2002*

Prime Minister, Pascoal Mocumbi
Agriculture and Rural Development, Helder Monteiro
Culture, Miguel Costa Mkaima
Education, Alcido Nguenha
Environmental Action Co-ordination, John Katchamila
Fisheries, Cadmiel Muthemba
Foreign Affairs and Co-operation, Leonardo Simão
Health, Francisco Songane
Higher Education, Science and Technology, Lidia Brito
Independence War Veterans, Gen. (retd) António Hama Thay
Industry and Commerce, Carlos Morgado
Justice, José Abudo
Labour, Mario Sevene
Mineral Resources and Energy, Castigo Langa

Ministers in the President's Office, Almirinho da Cruz Manhenje *(Defence, Security Affairs and Interior);* Francisco Madeira *(Parliamentary and Diplomatic Affairs)*
National Defence, Tobias Dai
Planning and Finance, Luisa Diogo
Public Works and Housing, Roberto White
Tourism, Fernando Sumbane Junior
Transport and Communications, Tomas Salomão
Women's Affairs and Social Welfare Action Co-ordination, Virginia Matabele
Youth and Sports, Joel Libombo

HIGH COMMISSION FOR THE REPUBLIC OF MOZAMBIQUE
21 Fitzroy Square, London W1T 6EL
Tel: 020-7383 3800
High Commissioner, HE Antonio Gumende, apptd 2002

BRITISH HIGH COMMISSION
Av. Vladimir I Lenine 310, CP 55, Maputo
Tel: (00 258) (1) 320111/2/5/6/7
Email: bhc@virconn.com
High Commissioner, HE Robert Dewar, apptd 2000

BRITISH COUNCIL DIRECTOR, Simon Ingram-Hill, Rua John Issa 226, PO Box 4178, Maputo;
Email: general.enquiries@britishcouncil.org.mz

ECONOMY

The basis of the economy is subsistence agriculture, but there is an industrial sector based mainly in Beira and Maputo. There are substantial coal deposits in Tete province and an offshore gas field at Pande. Economic subsidies have been removed and an IMF reform programme is being implemented. The economy is still heavily dependent on aid. A five-year plan has been launched with the priorities of rural development, education, health and land reform.

Severe flooding in February 2000 caused widespread devastation, killing 700 people, destroying a third of the maize crop and up to one million homes. Further flooding in January and February 2001 resulted in some 700,000 people becoming homeless and 35,000 hectares of crops lost. In 2002, a severe drought occurred in many central and southern parts of the country, including previously flood-stricken areas.

GNP – US$3,734 million (2000); US$220 per capita (1999)
GDP – US$1,737 million (1998); US$134 per capita (1999)
ANNUAL AVERAGE GROWTH OF GDP – 9.0 per cent (1999)
INFLATION RATE – 2.0 per cent (1999)
TOTAL EXTERNAL DEBT – US$6,959 million (1999)

TRADE

The main exports are shellfish, cotton, sugar, cashew nuts, copra, tea and sisal. Mozambique's main trading partners are South Africa, Portugal, Spain and Japan. The tourism industry is growing.

In 1998 Mozambique had a trade deficit of US$491 million and a current account deficit of US$429 million. In 2000 imports totalled US$1,158 million and exports US$364 million.

Trade with UK	2000	2001
Imports from UK	£18,487,000	£12,625,000
Exports to UK	5,067,000	7,549,000

MYANMAR

Pyidaungsu Myanmar Naingngandaw – Union of Myanmar

AREA – 261,228 sq. miles (676,578 sq. km). Neighbours: Bangladesh (west), India (north-west), China (north-east), Laos and Thailand (east)
POPULATION – 41,994,678 (2001 estimate). The indigenous inhabitants are of similar racial types and speak languages of the Tibeto-Burman, Mon-Khmer and Thai groups. The three significant non-indigenous elements are Indians, Chinese and Bangladeshis. Burmese is the official language, but minority languages include Bamar, Chin, Kachin, Kayah, Kayin (Karen), Mon, Rakhine and Shan. English is spoken in educated circles. Buddhism is the religion of 89.3 per cent of the people, with 5.6 per cent Christians, 3.8 per cent Muslims, 0.2 per cent Animists and 0.5 per cent Hindus
CAPITAL – ΨYangon (Rangoon) (population, 2,513,023, 1983)
MAJOR CITIES – Mandalay (532,949); Mawlamyine/Moulmein (219,961); Pathein/Bassein (144,096)
CURRENCY – Kyat (K) of 100 pyas
NATIONAL ANTHEM – Gba Majay Myanmar (We Shall Love Myanmar For Ever)
NATIONAL DAY – 4 January
NATIONAL FLAG – Red, with a canton of dark blue, inside which are a cogwheel and two rice ears surrounded by 14 white stars
LIFE EXPECTANCY (years) – male 53.8; female 58.8
POPULATION GROWTH RATE – 1.2 per cent (1999)
POPULATION DENSITY – 67 per sq. km (1999)

HISTORY AND POLITICS

The Union of Burma (the name was officially changed to the Union of Myanmar in 1989) became an independent republic outside the British Commonwealth on 4 January 1948 and remained a parliamentary democracy for 14 years. In 1962 the army took power, suspended the parliamentary constitution and instituted a socialist state.

After months of popular demonstrations and a series of presidents during 1988, Gen. Saw Maung, leader of the armed forces, assumed power in September 1988. The People's Assembly, the Council of State and the Council of Ministers were abolished and replaced by the State Law and Order Restoration Council (SLORC). The constitution was effectively abrogated.

A People's Assembly Election Law was published in 1989 and multiparty elections were held on 27 May 1990, resulting in a majority for the National League for Democracy (NLD) even though its leader Aung San Suu Kyi had been under house arrest since July 1989. The SLORC refused to transfer power to a civilian government and large numbers of NLD MPs and supporters were detained or fled to Thailand where an exile government was set up. The SLORC released Aung San Suu Kyi (who won the Nobel Peace Prize in 1991) on 10 July 1995, although on several occasions subsequently she has been forcibly prevented from attending political meetings by government troops. Many other opposition figures remain in detention or under house arrest. In November 1997, the SLORC was renamed the State Peace and Development Council (SPDC).

The SPDC detained several hundred NLD members in September 1998 to thwart the NLD's plan to convene a 'People's Parliament' representing the assembly which would have resulted from the 1990 general election; most

1008 Countries of the World

were released in October and November. Instead, the NLD set up an interim representation committee to act on behalf of the 'People's Parliament', which declared all laws and orders issued by the military government since the general election to be invalid. In January 2001, 84 NLD activists were released and during the course of the year, this number reached around 200. In May 2002, Aung San Kyi was released from house arrest. San Kyi demanded freedom for all the country's dissidents. More than 400 have been released since talks began almost two years ago and the remaining NLD activists are expected to be freed in the coming months.

Myanmar is comprised of seven states (Chin, Kachin, Kayin (Karen), Kayah, Mon, Rakhine, Shan) and seven divisions (Ayeyarwady (Irrawaddy), Magway (Magwe), Mandalay, Bago (Pegu), Yangon (Rangoon), Sagaing, Tanintharyi (Tenasserim)).

INSURGENCIES

Since independence in 1948 the government has fought various armed insurgent groups, the largest of which were derived from the Kachin, Kayin (Karen), Karenni, and Wa ethnic groups but the Shan, Mon, Arakan and Chin ethnic minorities have also formed armed groups.

Since 1992, as a result of government offensives, 15 ethnic groups have signed cease-fire agreements with the government. In November 1999, the government launched a military offensive against Kayin (Karen) National Union (KNU) guerrillas and their allies in Karen state.

STATE PEACE AND DEVELOPMENT COUNCIL *as at July 2002*

Chairman, Senior Gen. Than Shwe
Vice-Chairman, Gen. Maung Aye
Members, Rear-Adml Nyunt Thein; Maj.-Gen. Kyaw Than; Maj.-Gen. Aung Htwe; Maj.-Gen. Ye Myint; Maj.-Gen. Khin Maung Than; Maj.-Gen. Kyaw Win; Maj.-Gen. Thein Sein; Maj.-Gen. Thura Thiha Thura Sit Maung; Brig.-Gen. Thura Shwe Mahn; Brig.-Gen. Myint Aung; Brig.-Gen. Maung Bo; Brig.-Gen. Thiha Thura Tin Aung Myint Oo; Brig.-Gen. Soe Win; Brig.-Gen. Tin Aye
Secretary, Lt.-Gen. Khin Nyunt

CABINET *as at July 2002*

Prime Minister, Defence, Senior Gen. Than Shwe
Agriculture and Irrigation, Maj.-Gen. Nyunt Tin
Commander in Chief of the Navy, Minister in charge of Political, Economic and Social Tasks within his Command, Vice-Adm. Kyi Min
Commander of Coastal Military Command, Minister in charge of Political, Economic and Social Tasks within his Command, Maj.-Gen. Aye Kywe
Commerce, Brig.-Gen. Pyi Sone
Construction, Maj.-Gen. Saw Tun
Co-operatives, Lt-Gen. Tin Ngwe
Culture and Labour, U Tin Win
Education, U Than Aung
Electric Power, Maj.-Gen. Tin Htut
Energy, Brig.-Gen. Lun Thi
Finance and Revenue, U Khin Maung Thein
First Minister for Industry, U Aung Thaung
Foreign Affairs, U Win Aung
Forestry, U Aung Phone
Health, Maj.-Gen. Ket Sein
Home Affairs, Col. Tin Hlaing
Immigration and Population, Social Welfare, Relief and Resettlement, Maj.-Gen. Sein Htwa
Information, Maj.-Gen. Kyi Aung

Livestock Breeding and Fisheries, Brig.-Gen. Maung Maung Thein
Mines, Brig.-Gen. Ohn Myint
Ministers in the Office of the SPDC Chairman, Lt.-Gen. Min Thein; Brig.-Gen. David Abel
National Planning and Economic Development, U Soe Tha
Prime Minister's Office, U Than Shwe; Maj.-Gen Tin Ngwe
Progress of Border Areas and National Races, Development Affairs, Col. Thein Nyunt
Rail Transport, U Pan Aung
Religious Affairs, U Aung Khin
Second Minister for Industry, Hotels and Tourism, Maj.-Gen. Saw Lin
Science and Technology, U Thaung
Sports, Brig.-Gen. Thura Aye Myint
Telecommunications, Posts and Telegraphs, Brig.-Gen. Thein Zaw
Transport, Maj.-Gen. Hla Myint Swe

EMBASSY OF THE UNION OF MYANMAR
19A Charles Street, Berkeley Square, London W1J 5DX
Tel: 020-7499 8841
Ambassador Extraordinary and Plenipotentiary, HE Dr Kyaw Win, apptd 1999

BRITISH EMBASSY
80 Strand Road (Box No. 638), Yangon
Tel: (00 95) (1) 295300
Ambassador Extraordinary and Plenipotentiary, HE Dr John Jenkins, LVO, apptd 1999

BRITISH COUNCIL DIRECTOR, Graham Millington *(Cultural Attaché),* 78 Kanna Road, PO Box 638, Yangon; Email: enquiries@britishcouncil.org.mm

DEFENCE

The Army has some 100 main battle tanks and 270 armoured personnel carriers. The Navy has 68 patrol and coastal vessels at six bases. The Air Force has 113 combat aircraft and 29 armed helicopters.
MILITARY EXPENDITURE – 0.6 per cent of GDP (2000)
MILITARY PERSONNEL – 344,000: Army 325,000, Navy 10,000, Air Force 9,000, Paramilitaries 100,000

ECONOMY

Myanmar is rich in minerals, including petroleum, zinc, nickel, lead, silver, tungsten, wolfram and gemstones. Production of crude petroleum in 1998 totalled 1,177,000 tonnes. There are refineries at Chauk, the main oilfield, Syriam and Mann. Major reserves of natural gas have been discovered in the Martaban Gulf.

Since 1988, Myanmar has moved from a centrally planned economy to a market-oriented economy and has liberalised domestic and external trade, promoted the development of the private sector and encouraged foreign investment.

Myanmar is thought to be the world's leading producer of opium with an estimated annual output of 2,600 tons, although the government claimed to have destroyed 3,800 hectares of opium poppies between November 1998 and March 1999.

The principal exports are agricultural, forestry and fish products, minerals and precious stones. The principal imports are capital goods, chiefly transport equipment, machinery and plant, consumer goods and semi-manufactures.

In July 1997, Myanmar became a member of ASEAN. In 1997 the EU stripped Myanmar of trading privileges and the USA imposed economic sanctions.

In 2000 there was a trade deficit of US$843 million and a current account deficit of US$293 million. Imports totalled US$2,371 million and exports US$1,402 million.
GDP – US$12,557 million (1998); US$730 per capita (1999)
ANNUAL AVERAGE GROWTH OF GDP – 6.2 per cent (2000)
INFLATION RATE – 0.1 per cent (2000)
TOTAL EXTERNAL DEBT – US$5,999 million (1999)

Trade with UK	2000	2001
Imports from UK	£8,646,000	£9,452,000
Exports to UK	49,270,000	66,634,000

COMMUNICATIONS

The Irrawaddy and its chief tributary, the Chindwin, are important waterways, the main stream being navigable 900 miles from its mouth and carrying much traffic. The chief seaports are Yangon (Rangoon), Mawlamyine (Moulmein), Akyab (Sittwe) and Pathein (Bassein).
The railway network covers 3,955 km, extending to Myitkyina on the Upper Irrawaddy. There are 2,452 miles of highways and 14,318 miles of other main roads. The airport at Mingaladon, about 13 miles north of Yangon (Rangoon), handles limited international air traffic.

EDUCATION

Most children attend primary school, and nearly five million are currently enrolled; in middle and high schools, enrolment is over two million. In 1999 there were 37,627 primary schools, 3,695 middle schools and 1,572 high schools. There are 16 universities, nine degree-awarding colleges and 87 other higher education institutions.
Vocational training is provided at 17 teachers' training institutes and schools, 11 technical institutes, 17 technical high schools, 17 agricultural institutes and schools, and 41 vocational schools.
ILLITERACY RATE – 14.7 per cent (2002)
ENROLMENT (percentage of age group) – tertiary 5 per cent (1997)

NAMIBIA
The Republic of Namibia

AREA – 318,261 sq. miles (824,292 sq. km). Neighbours: Angola (north), South Africa (south), Botswana (east), Zambia and Zimbabwe (north-east)
POPULATION – 1,797,677 (2001 estimate). The main population groups are: Ovambo (587,000), Kavango (110,000), Damara (89,000), Herero (89,000), whites (78,000), Nama (57,000), coloured (48,000), Caprivians (44,000), Bushmen (34,000), Rehoboth Baster (29,000), Tswana (7,000). English is the official language, with Afrikaans, German and local languages also in use
CAPITAL – Windhoek (population, 147,056, 1995)
MAJOR TOWNS – Ondangwa (33,000); Oshakati (37,000); Rehoboth (21,500); Swakopmund (18,000); Walvis Bay (50,000), 1995
CURRENCY – Namibian dollar of 100 cents at parity to South African rand
NATIONAL ANTHEM – Namibia, Land Of The Brave
NATIONAL DAY – 21 March (Independence Day)
NATIONAL FLAG – Divided diagonally blue, red and green with the red fimbriated in white; a gold twelve-rayed sun in the upper hoist
LIFE EXPECTANCY (years) – male 44.3; female 44.1
POPULATION GROWTH RATE – 2.3 per cent (1999)
POPULATION DENSITY – 2 per sq. km (1999)

MILITARY EXPENDITURE – 3.6 per cent of GDP (2000)
MILITARY PERSONNEL – 9,200: Army 9,000, Coast Guard 200; Paramilitaries 6,000
ILLITERACY RATE – 16.7 per cent (2002)
ENROLMENT (percentage of age group) – primary 100 per cent (1997); secondary 62 per cent (1997); tertiary 8 per cent (1997)

HISTORY AND POLITICS

The German protectorate of South West Africa from 1884 to 1915, the territory was entrusted to South Africa by the 1919 Treaty of Versailles. The UN terminated South Africa's mandate in 1967.
An administrator-general was appointed in 1977 to govern the territory until independence and a transitional government was installed in 1985. Elections for Namibia's National Assembly took place under UN supervision on 7–11 November 1989 and independence was declared on 21 March 1990. Namibia joined the Commonwealth on independence.
Previously a British and South African colony separate from German South West Africa/Namibia, Walvis Bay was governed from August 1992 by the joint South African-Namibian Walvis Bay Administrative Body until 28 February 1994, when South Africa renounced its claim to sovereignty over the enclave and it became part of Namibia.
Presidential and legislative elections were held on 30 November–1 December 1999 and were won by the incumbent, Sam Nujoma, and by the South West Africa People's Organisation of Namibia (SWAPO) respectively. In the 72-seat National Assembly SWAPO has 55 seats, the Congress of Democrats and the Democratic Turnhalle Alliance 7 seats each, and other parties three seats. On 28 August 2002, Prime Minister Hage Geingob was replaced by Theo-Ben Gurirab.

INSURGENCIES

Government officials claimed to have uncovered a plot by Mishake Muyongo, a former leader of the opposition Democratic Turnhalle Alliance, and Mishake Boniface Mamili, a Mafwe chief, to launch a secessionist rebellion in the Caprivi strip in November 1998. An attempted uprising on 9 August 1999, believed to have been led by the Caprivi Liberation Army, was quickly quashed by government forces and 125 of the leaders of the uprising were put on trial for treason.

POLITICAL SYSTEM

Namibia has an executive president as head of state who exercises the functions of government with the assistance of a Cabinet headed by a prime minister. The president is directly elected for a maximum of two five-year terms. On 19 November 1998, parliament approved an amendment to the constitution allowing President Nujoma to stand for a third term of office in the 1999 elections. There is a bicameral legislature consisting of the 72-member National Assembly, elected for a five-year term, and the National Council, whose 26 members are indirectly elected by the regional councils from among their own members. The National Council is elected for a six-year term, and its main function is to review and consider legislation from the National Assembly. The constitution can only be changed by a two-thirds majority in the National Assembly.

HEAD OF STATE

President, Dr Sam Nujoma, *elected* 16 February 1990, *re-elected* 8 December 1994, 1 December 1999

CABINET *as at August 2002*

Prime Minister, Theo-Ben Guirab
Agriculture, Water and Rural Development, Helmut Angula
Basic Education, Culture and Sport, John Mutorwa
Defence, Erikki Nghimtina
Environment and Tourism, Philemon Malima
Finance, Nangolo Mbumba
Fisheries and Marine Resources, Abraham Iyambo
Foreign Affairs, Hidipo Hamutenya
Health and Social Services, Dr Libertina Amathila
Higher Education, Training and Employment Creation, Nahas Angula
Home Affairs, Jerry Ekandjo
Justice, Attorney-General, Ngarikutuke Tjiriange
Labour, Marco Hausiku
Lands, Resettlement, Rehabilitation, Hifikepunye Pohamba
Mines and Energy, Dr Nickey Iyambo
Prisons and Correctional Services, Andimba Toivo ya Toivo
Regional and Local Government and Housing, vacant
Trade and Industry, Jesaya Nyamu
Women's Affairs and Child Welfare, Netumbo Nandi-Ndaitwah
Works, Transport and Communication, Moses Amweelo

HIGH COMMISSION OF THE REPUBLIC OF NAMIBIA
6 Chandos Street, London W1G 9LU
Tel: 020-7636 6244
Email: namibia-highcomm@btconnect.com
High Commissioner, HE Monica Ndiliawike Nashandi, apptd 1999

BRITISH HIGH COMMISSION
116 Robert Mugabe Avenue, PO Box 22202, Windhoek
Tel: (00 264) (61) 274800
Email: bhc@mweb.com.na
High Commissioner, HE Alasdair MacDermott, apptd 2002

BRITISH COUNCIL OFFICER IN CHARGE, Patience Mahlalela, 1-5 Fidel Castro Street, Windhoek
Email: general.enquiries@britishcouncil.org.na

ECONOMY

Manufacturing contributes around 31 per cent of GDP, with food production, metals and wooden products the most important areas. Around 44 per cent of the population are engaged in agriculture, primarily livestock. Guano is also exported. Deposits of diamonds along the coast and offshore along the sea bed are estimated at between 1,500 and 3,000 million carats; Namibia accounts for roughly 8 per cent of world diamond production. Walvis Bay and Lüderitz are the main ports. There are 62,258 km of roads, of which 5,250 km are surfaced; there are 2,382 km of railway track.

The principal imports are machinery and transport equipment, foodstuffs, beverages and tobacco, and mineral fuels. The principal exports are diamonds and agricultural products.

In 1998 there was a trade deficit of US$173 million and a current account surplus of US$162 million.

GNP – US$3,569 million (2000); US$1,890 per capita (1999)
GDP – US$3,044 million (1998); US$1,734 per capita (1999)
ANNUAL AVERAGE GROWTH OF GDP – 2.4 per cent (1998)
INFLATION RATE – 8.6 per cent (1999)

Trade with UK	2000	2001
Imports from UK	£12,554,000	£12,658,000
Exports to UK	59,665,000	316,005,000

NAURU
The Republic of Nauru/Naoero

AREA – 8 sq. miles (21 sq. km)
POPULATION – 12,088 (2001 estimate); 8,042 (1983 census): Nauruans 4,964; other Pacific Islanders 2,134; Asians 682; Caucasians 262. About 43 per cent of Nauruans are adherents of the Nauruan Protestant Church and there is a Roman Catholic mission on the island. The main languages are English and Nauruan
CAPITAL – ΨNauru
CURRENCY – Australian dollar ($A) of 100 cents
NATIONAL ANTHEM – Nauru Bwiema (Nauru, Our Homeland)
NATIONAL DAY – 31 January (Independence Day)
NATIONAL FLAG – Twelve-point star (representing the 12 original Nauruan tribes) below a gold bar (representing the Equator), all on a blue background
LIFE EXPECTANCY (years) – male 57.7; female 64.9 (2001 estimate)
POPULATION GROWTH RATE – 0.5 per cent (1999)
POPULATION DENSITY – 524 per sq. km (1999)

HISTORY AND POLITICS

From 1888 until the First World War Nauru was administered by Germany. In 1920 it became a British Empire-mandated territory under the League of Nations, administered by Australia. A trusteeship superseding the mandate was approved in 1947 by the UN and Nauru continued to be administered by Australia until it became independent on 31 January 1968. Rene Harris was elected president in April 1999 after his predecessor, Bernard Dowiyogo, lost a vote of confidence. Harris resigned on 20 April 2000 and Dowiyogo was re-elected president on 24 April 2000, but lost a vote of confidence on 30 March 2001. Rene Harris was immediately re-elected. Nauru became a full member of the Commonwealth on 1 May 1999; it had been an associate member since 1968.

POLITICAL SYSTEM

Parliament has 18 members including the Cabinet and Speaker. Voting is compulsory for all Nauruans over 20 years of age, except in certain specified instances. Elections are held every three years. The Cabinet is chosen by the president, who is elected by the parliament from amongst its members, and comprises not fewer than five nor more than six members including the president.

HEAD OF STATE

President, Civil Aviation, Foreign Affairs, Home Affairs, Industry and Investment, Public Service, Works, Rene Harris, *elected by parliament* 29 March 2001

CABINET *as at July 2002*

The President
Finance, Good Governance, Aloyisius Amwano
Health, Sports, Nimrod Botelanga
Justice, Marine Resources, Godfrey Thoma
Minister assisting the President, Economic Development, Education, Telecommunications, Transport, Remy Namaduk

HONORARY CONSULATE, Romshed Courtyard, Underriver, Nr. Sevenoaks, Kent TN15 0SD. Tel: 01732-746061; Email: nauru@weald.co.uk. *Honorary Consul*, M. Weston

BRITISH HIGH COMMISSIONER, HE Michael Price, LVO, resident at Suva, Fiji

ECONOMY

The only fertile areas are in the narrow coastal belt and local requirements of fruit and vegetables are mostly met by imports. The economy is heavily dependent on the extraction of phosphate, of which the island has one of the world's richest deposits. Considerable investments have been made abroad with the royalties on phosphate exports to provide for a time when production declines. A 20-year package of health and education programmes was agreed with Australia in 1993 as part of a compensation package for environmental damage caused by phosphate mining prior to independence. Recent low world phosphate prices have adversely affected the economy.

Air Nauru operates air services throughout the Pacific region and to Australia, New Zealand, Japan, Singapore and the Philippines.

GDP – US$32 million (1998); US$2,830 per capita (1999)

ANNUAL AVERAGE GROWTH OF GDP – -1.9 per cent (1998)

Trade with UK	2000	2001
Imports from UK	£2,139,000	£799,000
Exports to UK	128,000	4,000

EDUCATION

Education is compulsory between the ages of six and 17. There are 10 infant and primary and two secondary schools on the island with a total enrolment of about 2,707 pupils.

NEPAL
Nepāl Adhirājya/Kingdom of Nepal

AREA – 56,827 sq. miles (147,181 sq. km). Neighbours: China (north), India (south, west and east)
POPULATION – 25,284,463 (2001 estimate). The inhabitants are of mixed stock, with Tibetan characteristics prevailing in the north and Indian in the south. The official religion is Hinduism; 87 per cent of the population are Hindus, 8 per cent Buddhist and 3 per cent Muslim. Gautama Buddha was born in Nepal. The official language is Nepali
CAPITAL – Kathmandu (population, 535,000, 1993)
MAJOR CITIES – Bhadgaon (61,122); Biratnagar (130,129); Patan (117,023), 1991
CURRENCY – Nepalese rupee of 100 paisa
NATIONAL ANTHEM – Sri Man Gumbhira Nepali Prachanda Pratapi Bhupati (May Glory Crown Our Illustrious Sovereign, The Gallant Nepalese)
NATIONAL DAYS – 18 February (National Democracy Day); 28 December (The King's Birthday)
NATIONAL FLAG – Double pennant of crimson with blue border on peaks; white moon with rays in centre of top peak; white quarter sun, recumbent in centre of bottom peak
LIFE EXPECTANCY (years) – male 60.1; female 59.6
POPULATION GROWTH RATE – 2.4 per cent (1999)
POPULATION DENSITY – 152 per sq. km (1999)
MILITARY EXPENDITURE – 0.9 per cent of GDP (2000)

MILITARY PERSONNEL – 46,000: Army; Paramilitaries 40,000
ILLITERACY RATE – 55.9 per cent (2002)
ENROLMENT (percentage of age group) – tertiary 5 per cent (1997)

Nepal lies between India and the Tibet Autonomous Region of China on the slopes of the Himalayas, and includes Mount Everest.

The southern region, the Terai, was covered with jungle but has been more widely cultivated recently. It forms about 23 per cent of the total land area and nearly 44 per cent of the population live there. The central belt is hilly, but with many fertile valleys, leading up to the snowline at about 16,000 feet. The hills account for 42 per cent of the area and about 48 per cent of the population. The remainder of the country, the Himalayan region, consists of high mountains which are sparsely inhabited. The country is drained by three great river systems rising within and beyond the Himalayan mountain ranges and eventually flowing into the Ganges in India.

HISTORY AND POLITICS

Nepal was originally divided into numerous hill clans and petty principalities but emerged as a nation in the middle of the 18th century when it was unified by the warrior Raja of Gorkha, Prithvi Narayan Shah, who founded the present Nepalese dynasty. In 1846 power was seized by Jung Bahadur Rana after a massacre of nobles, and he was the first of a line of hereditary Rana prime ministers who ruled Nepal for 104 years. During this time the role of the monarchs was mainly ceremonial.

In 1950–1 a revolutionary movement broke the hereditary power of the Ranas and restored the monarchy to its former position. King Mahendra proscribed all political parties and assumed direct powers in 1960. In 1962 introduced a new constitution embodying a tiered, partyless system of *panchyat* (council) democracy. Mass agitation for political reform led in April 1990 to the abolition of the panchyat system. A new constitution was promulgated in November 1990 establishing a multiparty, parliament-ary system of government and a constitutional monarchy. Elections in May 1991 were won by the Nepali Congress Party.

In October 1997 the government was brought down by a vote of no confidence and several coalition governments ruled until a general election held on 3 and 17 May 1999 gave an absolute majority to the Nepali Congress Party (NCP) who won 110 seats.

Prime Minister Krishna Prasad Bhattarai resigned on 16 March 2000, after a motion of no confidence in him was signed by 58 NCP members; he was replaced on 20 March by Girija Prasad Koirala. Koirala effectively lost control of the NCP on 28 December 2000 when 56 of the party's 113 MPs signed a no-confidence motion against him, accusing him of having failed to control the Maoist insurgency and administrative corruption. On 5 February 2001, opposition parties called on him to resign over allegations of government corruption and launched a campaign of disruption. In response, King Birendra prorogued both houses of parliament on 5 April 2001.

On 1 June 2001, King Birendra and Queen Aishwara were shot dead by their son, Crown Prince Dipendra, who then shot himself, but survived long enough to be proclaimed king the following day. King Dipendra was declared dead on 4 June, having never regained consciousness, and Prince Gyanendra, the brother of the late King Birendra, was crowned as king.

Prime Minister Girija Prasad Koirala resigned on 19 July 2001; he was replaced by former prime minister Sher

Bahadur Deuba on 22 July 2001. On 22 May 2002, King Gyanendra dissolved parliament on the recommendation of Prime Minister Deuba and called an early election to the House of Representatives to take place on 13 November 2002.

INSURGENCIES

Maoist guerrillas from the Communist Party of Nepal, who are opposed to the monarchy, began an armed rebellion in 1996; they organised a campaign to boycott the general election in May 1999 which involved strikes and attacks on government and industrial targets. In November 1999, the government offered an amnesty to the guerrillas if they agreed to abandon violence and enter into dialogue with the government. The guerrillas and the government announced a cease-fire on 23 July 2001 and agreed to hold talks. A state of emergency was declared on 26 November 2001 after guerrillas of the Communist Party of Nepal launched a series of attacks. Deployment of the Royal Nepalese Army was authorised and during the night of 16–17 February 2002, heavy casualties occurred on both sides. On 28 August 2002, the state of emergency was lifted ahead of the parliamentary elections scheduled for November.

POLITICAL SYSTEM

The King retains joint executive power with the Council of Ministers. The bicameral legislature consists of a 205-member House of Representatives, directly elected for a five-year term, and a 60-member National Council, 50 of whom are indirectly elected for a six-year term and ten royal nominees.

HEAD OF STATE

HM The King of Nepal, King Gyanendra Bir Bikram Shah Dev, crowned 4 June 2001

CABINET as at July 2002

Prime Minister, Royal Palace Affairs, Defence, Forest and Soil Conservation, Sher Bahadur Deuba
Agriculture and Co-operatives, vacant
Culture, Tourism and Civil Aviation, Bal Bahadur
Education and Sports, vacant
Finance, vacant
Foreign Affairs, Madhuraman Acharya
General Administration, Khemraj Bhatta Mayalu
Health, Sarat Singh Bhandari
Home Affairs, Local Development, Khum Badahar Khadka
Industry, Commerce and Supplies, Purna Bahadur Khadka
Information and Communication, Jaya Prakash Prasad Gupta
Labour and Transport Management, Palten Gurung
Law, Justice and Parliamentary Affairs, Narendra Bikram Nemwang
Physical Planning and Public Works, Chiranjibi Wagle
Population and Environment, Prem Lal Singh
Water Resources, Bijaya Kumar Gachchadar
Without Portfolio in the Prime Minister's Office, Rishikesh Gautam
Women, Children and Social Welfare, vacant

ROYAL NEPALESE EMBASSY

12A Kensington Palace Gardens, London W8 4QU
Tel: 020-7229 1594/6231/5352
Email: rnelondon@btconnect.com
Ambassador Extraordinary and Plenipotentiary, HE Dr Singha Bahadur Basnyat, apptd 1997

BRITISH EMBASSY

Lainchaur Kathmandu, PO Box 106
Tel: (00 977) (1) 410583/411281/414588/411590
Email: britemb@wlink.com.np
Ambassador Extraordinary and Plenipotentiary, HE Keith Bloomfield, apptd 2002

BRITISH COUNCIL DIRECTOR, Barbara Wickham, PO Box 640, Lainchaur, Kathmandu
Email: general.enquiry@britishcouncil.org.np

ECONOMY

The main imports are machinery and transport equipment, and chemical and pharmaceutical products. Tourism is the single largest commercial earner of foreign exchange. Nepal's main trading partners are India, Germany and the USA.

In 1999 Nepal had a trade deficit of US$861 million and a current account deficit of US$57 million. In 2000 imports totalled US$1,573 million and exports US$804 million.

GNP – US$5,324 million (2000); US$220 per capita (1999)
GDP – US$4,495 million (1998); US$218 per capita (1999)
ANNUAL AVERAGE GROWTH OF GDP – 6.0 per cent (2000)
INFLATION RATE – 1.5 per cent (2000)
TOTAL EXTERNAL DEBT – US$2,970 million (1999)

Trade with UK	2000	2001
Imports from UK	£7,900,000	£5,932,000
Exports to UK	11,797,000	9,869,000

COMMUNICATIONS

The total length of roads is 13,223 km, of which 4,073 km are paved. Kathmandu is connected by road with India and Tibet. Internally, the road network links Kathmandu to Kodari and Pokhara, and Pokhara to Sunauli. There are 155 km of railway track.
Royal Nepal Airlines operates an extensive network of domestic flights, and there are international flights to Europe, the Middle East and throughout Asia. There is an international airport at Kathmandu.

THE NETHERLANDS
Koninkrijk der Nederlanden – Kingdom of the Netherlands

AREA – 16,033 sq. miles (41,526 sq. km). Neighbours: Belgium (south), Germany (east)
POPULATION – 15,981,472 (2000 estimate): 36 per cent Catholic, 27 per cent Reformed Church, 8 per cent Muslim. The language is Dutch, a West Germanic language of Low Franconian origin closely akin to Old English and Low German. It is spoken in the Netherlands and the northern part of Belgium (Flanders). Frisian is spoken in Friesland. Dutch is the official language in the Netherlands Antilles and Aruba; Papiamento, a mixture of Dutch and Spanish, is the vernacular
CAPITAL – ΨAmsterdam (population, 1,102,323, 1996 estimate)
SEAT OF GOVERNMENT – The Hague (Den Haag or, in full, 's-Gravenhage), population 695,815, 1996 estimate
MAJOR CITIES – Eindhoven (399,756); Groningen (209,051); Haarlem (211,124); ΨRotterdam (1,077,818); Tilburg (239,057); Utrecht (549,773), 1996 estimates
CURRENCY – Euro (€) of 100 cents

NATIONAL ANTHEM – Wilhelmus van Nassouwe (William of Nassau)
NATIONAL FLAG – Three horizontal bands of red, white and blue
LIFE EXPECTANCY (years) – male 75.6; female 81.0
POPULATION GROWTH RATE – 0.6 per cent (1999)
POPULATION DENSITY – 381 per sq. km (1999)
URBAN POPULATION – 61.0 per cent (1996)

The Kingdom of the Netherlands is a maritime country of western Europe, situated on the North Sea, consisting of 12 provinces (Eastern and Southern Flevoland being amalgamated to form the twelfth province). The land is generally flat and low, intersected by numerous canals and connecting rivers. The principal rivers are the Rhine, Maas, IJssel and Schelde.

HISTORY AND POLITICS

Following a revolt against Spanish rule under the leadership of William of Orange, the northern provinces were united by the Union of Utrecht (1579) and in 1581 independence was declared. Dutch economic and military power flourished in the 17th and 18th centuries.

The Netherlands were overrun by France in the late 18th century, becoming part of the French Empire until 1814, when the northern and southern Netherlands were united into one kingdom. In 1830 the southern provinces seceded to form Belgium. The Duchy of Luxembourg was made an independent state in 1867.

The Netherlands remained neutral during the First World War but were invaded by Germany during the Second World War and occupied until the war ended. The Netherlands joined the Benelux economic union with Belgium and Luxembourg in 1948 and became a member of NATO in 1949. The Dutch East Indies gained independence as Indonesia in 1949.

In 2001, the Netherlands became the first country in the world to legalise euthanasia and to allow same sex marriages.

On 6 May 2002, right-wing politician Pim Fortuyn, leader of the List Pim Fortuyn (LPF) party, was assassinated, nine days before the general elections on 15 May in which the Christian Democratic Appeal (CDA) gained 43 of the 150 seats in the second chamber. The state of the parties as at May 2002 was: CDA 43; LPF 26; People's Party for Freedom and Democracy 66 7; others 8. A coalition government headed by CDA leader Jan Peter Balkenende and comprising the CDA, LPF and VVD was sworn in on 22 July.

POLITICAL SYSTEM

The States-General consists of the *Eerste Kamer* (First Chamber) of 75 members, elected for four years by the Provincial Council; and the *Tweede Kamer* (Second Chamber) of 150 members, elected for four years by voters of 18 years and upwards. Members of the *Tweede Kamer* are paid.

HEAD OF STATE

HM The Queen of the Netherlands, Queen Beatrix Wilhelmina Armgard, KG, GCVO, born 31 January 1938; *succeeded* 30 April 1980, upon the abdication of her mother Queen Juliana; *married* 10 March 1966, HRH Prince Claus George Willem Otto Frederik Geert of the Netherlands, Jonkheer van Amsberg; and *has issue*, Prince Willem; Prince Johan Friso, *b.* 25 September 1968; Prince Constantijn Christof, *b.* 11 October 1969

Heir, HRH Prince Willem Alexander, *b.* 27 April 1967; *married* 2 February 2002, Máxima Zorreguieta

CABINET *as at August 2002*

Prime Minister, General Affairs, Jan Peter Balkenende (CDA)
Deputy Prime Minister, Health, Welfare and Sport, Eduard Bomhoff (LPF)
Deputy Prime Minister, Interior and Kingdom Relations, Johan Remkes (VVD)
Agriculture, Nature Management and Fisheries, Kees Veerman (CDA)
Defence, Benk Korthals
Economic Affairs, Herman Heinsbroek (LPF)
Education, Cultural Affairs and Science, Maria van der Hoeven (CDA)
Finance, Hans Hoogervorst (VVD)
Foreign Affairs, Jaap de Hoop Scheffer (CDA)
Housing, Spatial Planning and Environment, Henk Kamp (VVD)
Immigration and Integration, Hilbrand Nawijn (LPF)
Justice, Piet Hein Donner (CDA)
Social Affairs and Employment, Aart Jan de Geus (CDA)
Transport and Public Works and Water Management, Roelf de Boer (LPF)

CDA Christian Democratic Appeal
LPF List Pim Fortuyn
VVD People's Party for Freedom and Democracy

ROYAL NETHERLANDS EMBASSY
38 Hyde Park Gate, London SW7 5DP
Tel: 020-7590 3200
Ambassador Extraordinary and Plenipotentiary, HE Baron Willem Oswald Bentinck van Schoonheten, apptd 1999

BRITISH EMBASSY
Lange Voorhout 10, The Hague, NL-2514 ED
Tel: (00 31) (70) 427 0427
Ambassador Extraordinary and Plenipotentiary, HE Colin R. Budd, CMG, apptd 2001

CONSULATE-GENERAL – Amsterdam
CONSULATE – Willemstad (Curaçao); Vice-Consulate – Philipsburg (St Maarten) (both Netherlands Antilles)
BRITISH COUNCIL DIRECTOR, David Alderdice, Weteringschans 85A, NL-1017 RZ Amsterdam
Email: david.alderdice@britcoun.nl

DEFENCE

The Army has 320 main battle tanks, 361 armoured infantry fighting vehicles and 345 armoured personnel carriers. The Navy has four submarines, two destroyers, ten frigates, ten combat aircraft and 21 armed helicopters. The Air Force has 157 combat aircraft and 19 armed helicopters.
MILITARY EXPENDITURE – 1.9 per cent of GDP (2000)
MILITARY PERSONNEL – 50,430: Army 23,100, Navy 12,130, Air Force 10,000, Paramilitaries 5,200

ECONOMY

The chief agricultural products are potatoes, wheat, rye, barley, sugar beet, cattle, poultry, pigs, dairy products, vegetables, fruit, flower bulbs, plants and cut flowers and there is an important fishing industry.

Among the principal industries are engineering, electronics, nuclear energy, petrochemicals and plastics, road vehicles, aircraft and defence equipment, shipbuilding repair, steel, textiles of all types, electrical appliances, metal ware, furniture, paper, cigars, sugar, liqueurs, beer and clothing.

The majority of the workforce, 71.8 per cent, are engaged in service industries.

GNP – US$400,280 million (2000); US$25,140 per capita (1999)
GDP – US$391,269 million (1998); US$24,929 per capita (1999)
ANNUAL AVERAGE GROWTH OF GDP – 3.8 per cent (2000)
INFLATION RATE – 2.5 per cent (2000)
UNEMPLOYMENT – 4.4 per cent (1998)

TRADE

The Dutch are traditionally a trading nation. Trade, banking and shipping are of particular importance to the economy. The Netherlands is the sixth largest exporter and third largest agricultural exporter in the world. The geographical position of the Netherlands, at the mouths of the Rhine, Maas and Schelde, brings a large volume of transit trade to and from the interior of Europe to Dutch ports. Principal trading partners are Germany, Belgium/Luxembourg, the UK and France.

In 2000 the Netherlands had a trade surplus of US$19,022 million and a current account surplus of US$16,307 million. Imports totalled US$197,251 million and exports US$208,813 million.

Trade with UK	2000	2001
Imports from UK	£14,188,100,000	£13,916,200,000
Exports to UK	14,355,200,000	14,294,000,000

COMMUNICATIONS

There are 58,133 km of inter-urban roads, of which 2,207 km are motorways. The total extent of navigable rivers including canals is 5,046 km. The total length of the railway system is 2,808 km, of which 2,061 km are electrified. The mercantile marine in 1996 consisted of 379 ships with a total of total 2,795,000 gross registered tons.

EDUCATION

Primary and secondary education is given in both denominational and state schools and is compulsory.

The principal universities are at Leiden, Utrecht, Groningen, Amsterdam (two), Nijmegen, Maastricht and Rotterdam, and there are technical universities at Delft, Eindhoven, Enschede and Wageningen (agriculture).

ENROLMENT (percentage of age group) – primary 100 per cent (1997); secondary 100 per cent (1997); tertiary 47 per cent (1997)

OVERSEAS TERRITORIES

ARUBA

AREA – 75 sq. miles (193 sq. km)
POPULATION – 70,007 (2001 estimate)
CAPITAL – ΨOranjestad (population 25,000); and Sint Nicolaas (17,000)
CURRENCY – Aruban florin

The island of Aruba was from 1828 part of the Dutch West Indies and from 1845 part of the Netherlands Antilles. On 1 January 1986 it became a separate territory within the Kingdom of the Netherlands. The 1983 Constitutional Conference agreed that Aruba's separate status would last for ten years from 1986, after which the island would become fully independent. In 1994 this decision was changed and it was decided that Aruba will retain its separate status within the Kingdom of the Netherlands.

Governor, Olindo Koolman
Prime Minister, Nelson O. Oduber

Trade with UK	2000	2001
Imports from UK	£27,709,000	£32,429,000
Exports to UK	22,508,000	13,778,000

NETHERLANDS ANTILLES

AREA – 309 sq. miles (800 sq. km)
POPULATION – 202,782 (1999), Curaçao 143,387, Bonaire 13,724, St Maarten 41,718, St Eustatius 2,249, Saba 1,704, 1999
CAPITAL – ΨWillemstad (on Curaçao) (pop. 50,000)
CURRENCY – Netherlands Antilles guilder of 100 cents

The Netherlands Antilles comprise the islands of Curaçao, Bonaire, part of St Maarten, St Eustatius, and Saba in the West Indies. The Netherlands Antilles, which have a 22-member federal parliament, are largely self-governing under the terms of the Realm Statute which took effect in 1954. The part of St Maarten belonging to the Netherlands voted in a non-binding referendum held on 23 June 2000 to secede from the Netherlands Antilles and become an independent state within the Kingdom of the Netherlands. This was rejected by the government of the Netherlands, which did not believe that St Maarten was large enough to be a viable state, but discussions on its future status continue.

Governor, Frits Goedgedrag
Prime Minister, Etienne Ys

Trade with UK	2000	2001
Imports from UK	£33,299,000	£35,167,000
Exports to UK	8,045,000	6,862,000

NEW ZEALAND

AREA – 104,454 sq. miles (270,534 sq. km)
POPULATION – 3,864,129 (2001 estimate): 79 per cent European stock, 13 per cent Māori, 5 per cent other Pacific islanders. The main religion is Christianity. In 1991 the principal denominations were Anglican 22.1 per cent, Presbyterian 16.3 per cent, Roman Catholic 15 per cent, Methodist 4.2 per cent, Baptist 2.1 per cent. The official languages are English and Māori

Islands	Area (sq. miles)	Population (census 1996)
North Island	44,281	2,749,788
South Island	58,093	930,824
Other islands	1,362	934
Total	103,736	3,681,546

Territories		
Tokelau	5	1,487
Niue	100	1,708 (a)
Cook Islands	93	18,008
Ross Dependency	175,000	—

(a)1997 census

CAPITAL – ΨWellington (population, 346,500, 2000 estimate)
MAJOR CITIES – ΨAuckland (1,105,700); ΨChristchurch (342,100); ΨDunedin (111,700); Hamilton (170,900); ΨNapier-Hastings (114,500), 2000 estimates
CURRENCY – New Zealand dollar (NZ$) of 100 cents

NATIONAL ANTHEM – God Save The Queen/God Defend New Zealand
NATIONAL DAY – 6 February (Waitangi Day)
NATIONAL FLAG – Blue ground, with Union Flag in top left quarter, four five-pointed red stars with white borders on the fly
LIFE EXPECTANCY (years) – male 75.3; female 80.7
POPULATION GROWTH RATE – 1.0 per cent (1999)
POPULATION DENSITY – 14 per sq. km (1999)
URBAN POPULATION – 85.4 per cent (1996)

New Zealand consists of a number of islands in the South Pacific Ocean, and also has administrative responsibility for the Ross Dependency in Antarctica. The two larger islands, North Island and South Island, are separated by a relatively narrow strait. The remaining islands are much smaller and widely dispersed.

Much of the North and South Islands is mountainous. The principal range is the Southern Alps, extending the entire length of the South Island and having its culminating point in Mount Cook/Mount Aoraki (3,754 m/ 12,349 ft). The North Island mountains include several volcanoes, two of which are active. Of the numerous glaciers in the South Island, the Tasman (18 miles long by 1¼ wide), the Franz Josef and the Fox are the best known. The more important rivers include the Waikato (425 km/270 miles in length), Wanganui (180 miles), and Clutha (210 miles) and lakes include Taupo, 234 sq. miles in area; Wakatipu, 113; and Te Anau, 133.

New Zealand includes, in addition to North and South Islands: Chatham Islands (Chatham, Pitt, South East Islands and some rocky islets, combined area, 965 sq. km (373 sq. miles), largely uninhabited); Stewart Island (area 1,746 sq. km (674 sq. miles), largely uninhabited); the Kermadec Group (Raoul or Sunday, Macaulay, Curtis Islands, L'Esperance, and some islets; population 9–10, all government employees at a meteorological station); Campbell Island, used as a weather station; the Three Kings (discovered by Tasman on the Feast of the Epiphany); Auckland Islands; Antipodes Group; Bounty Islands; Snares Islands and Solander.

HISTORY AND POLITICS

The discoverers and first colonists of New Zealand were Polynesians, ancestors of the modern-day Māori, who settled the islands between the ninth and 14th centuries. The Dutch navigator, Abel Tasman, sighted the coast in 1642 but did not land, but the British explorer James Cook circumnavigated New Zealand and landed in 1769. Largely as a result of increased British emigration, the country was annexed by the British government in 1840. The British Lieutenant-Governor, William Hobson, proclaimed sovereignty over the North Island by virtue of the Treaty of Waitangi, signed by him and many Māori chiefs, and over the South Island and Stewart Island by right of discovery. In 1841 New Zealand was created a separate colony distinct from New South Wales. In 1907 the designation was changed to 'The Dominion of New Zealand'.

Following the general election of 27 July 2002, the state of the parties in the House of Representatives was: Labour Party (LP) 52 seats, National Party 27, New Zealand First 13, ACT New Zealand 9; Green Party 9; United Future 8; Jim Anderton's Progressive Coalition (PC) 2. The Labour Party and the Progressive Coalition formed a minority administration.

POLITICAL SYSTEM

The executive authority is entrusted to a Governor-General appointed by the Crown and aided by an Executive Council, within a unicameral legislature, the House of Representatives. A non-binding referendum, held simultaneously with the general election in November 1999, approved a reduction in the number of members to 100 in future parliaments. There is no written constitution. The judicial system comprises a High Court, a Court of Appeal and district courts having both civil and criminal jurisdiction.

GOVERNOR-GENERAL

Governor-General and Commander-in-Chief, HE Dame Silvia Cartwright, *sworn* in April 2001

THE CABINET *as at August 2002*

The Governor-General
Prime Minister, Arts, Culture and Heritage, Helen Clark (LP)
Deputy Prime Minister, Finance and Revenue, Dr Michael Cullen (LP)
Agriculture, Biosecurity, Forestry and Trade Negotiations, Jim Sutton (LP)
Attorney-General, Courts, Labour, Treaty of Waitangi Negotiations, Margaret Wilson (LP)
Commerce, Lianne Dalziel
Conservation, Local Government, Chris Carter (LP)
Corrections, Housing, Pacific Island Affairs, Racing, Mark Gosche (LP)
Defence, State-owned Enterprises, Tourism, Mark Burton (LP)
Economic Development, Industry and Regional Development, Jim Anderton (PC)
Education, State Services, Sport and Recreation, Trevor Mallard (LP)
Energy, Fisheries, Research, Science and Technology, Crown Research Institutes, Pete Hodgson (LP)
Environment, Disarmament and Arms Control, Marian Hobbs (LP)
Foreign Affairs and Trade, Justice, Phil Goff (LP)
Health and Food Safety, Annette King (LP)
Māori Affairs, Parekura Horomia (LP)
Police, Civil Defence, Internal Affairs, Veteran's Affairs, George Hawkins (LP)
Social Services, Employment, Broadcasting, Steve Maharey (LP)
Transport, Communications and Information Technology, Paul Swain (LP)
Women's Affairs, Ruth Dyson (LP)
Youth Affairs, Land Information and Statistics, John Tamihere (LP)

NEW ZEALAND HIGH COMMISSION

New Zealand House, 80 The Haymarket, London SW1Y 4TQ. Tel: 020-7930 8422
High Commissioner, HE Russell Marshall, apptd 2002
Deputy High Commissioner, Suzanne Blumhardt
Minister, J. Waugh (Commercial)
Head, Defence Staff, Cdre A. Peck

BRITISH HIGH COMMISSION

44 Hill Street (PO Box 1812), Wellington 1
Tel: (00 64) (4) 924 2888
Email: ppa.mailbox@fco.gov.uk
High Commissioner, HE Richard Fell, CVO, apptd 2001
CONSULATE-GENERAL – Auckland
CONSULATES – Christchurch; Rarotonga (Cook Islands)

BRITISH COUNCIL DIRECTOR, Paul Atkins, 44 Hill Street, PO Box 1812, Wellington 1
Email: enquiries@britishcouncil.org.nz.
Regional office in Auckland

DEFENCE

The Army has 77 armoured personnel carriers. The Navy has three frigates, four patrol and coastal vessels and three armed helicopters. The Air Force has 40 combat aircraft.
MILITARY EXPENDITURE – 1.5 per cent of GDP (2000)
MILITARY PERSONNEL – 9,230: Army 4,450, Navy 1,980, Air Force 2,800

ECONOMY

A far-reaching programme of privatisation was carried out in the 1980s and early 1990s, which resulted in only modest economic growth but increased social inequality, and since December 1999 the government has ruled out further privatisation, increased the powers of trade unions, renationalised accident insurance and raised the top rate of income tax. Agricultural production is dominated by cattle- and sheep-rearing, for meat, wool, dairy products and other by-products, such as skins, leather, etc. Timber and wood pulp are also important. Non-metallic minerals such as coal, clay, limestone and dolomite are more important than metallic ones. Of the metals, the most important are gold and ironsand. Natural gas deposits in the offshore Taranaki Maui field and onshore fields are increasingly being exploited and used for electricity generation and as a premium fuel. Manufacturing is based on food processing, machinery production, motor vehicle assembly, chemicals, electrical and electronic goods, and paper and printing. Tourism is the fastest growing sector of the economy, with 1,539,230 visitors in 1999.

In 2000 New Zealand had a trade surplus of US$615 million and a current account deficit of US$2,756 million.
GNP – US$50,120 million (2000); US$13,990 per capita (1999)
GDP – US$53,087 million (1998); US$14,754 per capita (1999)
ANNUAL AVERAGE GROWTH OF GDP – 2.0 per cent (2000)
INFLATION RATE – 2.6 per cent (2000)
UNEMPLOYMENT – 6.8 per cent (1999)

TRADE

New Zealand's largest trading partners are Australia, the USA, Japan, and the UK. Main exports include dairy products, meat, timber, fish, fruits and nuts, machinery and aluminium products. Imports include machinery, vehicles, petroleum and petroleum products, textiles, plastics and aircraft. In 2001 imports totalled US$13,842 million and exports US$13,345 million.

Trade with UK	2000*	2001*
Imports from UK	£304,054,000	£311,539,000
Exports to UK	558,934,000	560,459,000

*Includes Niue, Tokelau and Cook Islands

COMMUNICATIONS

The national railway system is owned and operated by the privately-owned Tranz Rail Ltd. There are 4,439 km of railway track. In December 1995 there were 2,977 ships registered in New Zealand (gross tonnage 482,180).
There are international airports at Auckland, Christchurch and Wellington. Air New Zealand is the national carrier.
There are 91,864 km of maintained roads.

EDUCATION

Schools are free and attendance is compulsory between the ages of six and 15. There are 2,226 state and 56 private primary schools and 320 state and 23 private secondary schools. There are seven universities and 25 polytechnics.
ENROLMENT (percentage of age group) – primary 100 per cent (1997); secondary 100 per cent (1997); tertiary 63 per cent (1997)

TERRITORIES

TOKELAU (OR UNION ISLANDS)

Tokelau is a group of atolls, Fakaofo, Nukunonu and Atafu. It was proclaimed part of New Zealand as from 1 January 1949. A Council of Faipule, composed of one elected representative from each atoll, was established in August 1992 to govern Tokelau when the council of elders (General Fono) was not in session. The position of Ulu-o-Tokelau (leader) was also established in 1992 and is rotated among the three Faipule members annually. Administrative responsibility for Tokelau lies with the Administrator but in January 1994 his powers were delegated to the General Fono and Council of Faipule. The Tokelau Amendment Act, passed by the New Zealand Parliament in 1996, conferred legislative power on the General Fono. New Zealand provides substantial aid (NZ$8.5 million in year ended 30 June 2001).
Administrator, Lindsay Watt
Ulu-o-Tokelau (2002), Pio Tuia

THE ROSS DEPENDENCY

The Ross Dependency, placed under the jurisdiction of New Zealand in 1923, is defined as all the Antarctic islands and territories between 160° E. and 150° W. longitude which are situated south of the 60° S. parallel, including Edward VII Land and portions of Victoria Land. Since 1957 a number of research stations have been established in the Dependency.

ASSOCIATED STATES

COOK ISLANDS

Included in the realm of New Zealand since June 1901, the Cook Islands group consists of the islands of Rarotonga, Aitutaki, Mangaia, Atiu, Mauke, Mitiaro, Manuae, Takutea, Palmerston, Penrhyn or Tongareva, Manihiki, Rakahanga, Suwarrow, Pukapuka or Danger, and Nassau. The population is mainly Māori; English and Cook Island Māori are the principle languages spoken.
Queen Elizabeth II has a representative on the islands, and there is a New Zealand High Commissioner. Since 1965 the islands have been in free association with New Zealand and enjoyed complete internal self-government, executive power being in the hands of a Cabinet consisting of a prime minister and five other ministers. There is a 25-member Legislative Assembly. New Zealand has an obligation to assist with foreign affairs and defence if requested. The Cook Islanders are constitutionally guaranteed citizenship both of the Cook Islands and of New Zealand.
Agriculture accounts for 7 per cent of GDP, tourism accounts for 30 per cent and offshore banking and trade are of increasing importance to the economy.
HM Representative, Frederick Goodwin
Prime Minister, Dr. Robert Woonton
New Zealand High Commissioner, Kurt Meyer

NIUE

A New Zealand High Commissioner is stationed at Niue, which since 1974 has been self-governing in free association with New Zealand. New Zealand is responsible for external affairs and defence, and

continues to give financial aid. Executive power is in the hands of a premier and a Cabinet of three drawn from the Assembly of 20 members. The Assembly is the supreme legislative body.

New Zealand High Commissioner, John Bryan

NICARAGUA
República de Nicaragua – Republic of Nicaragua

AREA – 50,193 sq. miles (130,000 sq. km). Neighbours: Honduras (north), Costa Rica (south)
POPULATION – 4,918,393 (2001 estimate): three-quarters are of mixed blood, another 15 per cent are white, mostly of pure Spanish descent, and the remaining 10 per cent are West Indians or Indians. The latter group includes the Misquitos, who live on the Atlantic coast. The official language is Spanish and the majority are Roman Catholic, although the English language and the Moravian Church are widespread on the Atlantic coast
CAPITAL – Managua (population, 864,201, 1995 estimate)
MAJOR CITIES – Chinandega (144,291); Granada (72,640); León (158,577); Masaya (78,308)
CURRENCY – Córdoba (C$) of 100 centavos
NATIONAL ANTHEM – Salve A Tí Nicaragua (Hail, Nicaragua)
NATIONAL DAY – 15 September
NATIONAL FLAG – Horizontal stripes of blue, white and blue, with the Nicaraguan coat of arms in the centre of the white stripe
LIFE EXPECTANCY (years) – male 67.2; female 71.9
POPULATION GROWTH RATE – 2.7 per cent (1999)
POPULATION DENSITY – 38 per sq. km (1999)
URBAN POPULATION – 63.3 per cent (1995)
ILLITERACY RATE – 32.8 per cent (2002)
ENROLMENT (percentage of age group) – primary 100 per cent (1997); secondary 55 per cent (1997); tertiary 12 per cent (1997)

HISTORY AND POLITICS
Spanish colonisation of Nicaragua began in 1523. Independence was secured in 1838. Guerrillas of the Sandinista National Liberation Front (FSLN) overthrew the government in 1979, but after ten years in power and a civil war against US-backed Contra guerrillas, the Sandinistas lost their parliamentary majority in elections held in February 1990. A coalition of former opposition parties, the Unión Nacional de Opositora (UNO), formed a government. With the defeat of the Sandinistas, the civil war came to an end. In presidential and legislative elections held on 4 November 2001, Enrique Bolaños Geyer of the Liberal Constitutional Party (PLC) was elected president and the PLC gained 47 seats in the National Assembly with the FSLN winning 43 seats. The government is formed by a coalition led by the PLC.

FOREIGN RELATIONS
Following a long-running dispute between Nicaragua and Honduras concerning their maritime boundaries, the two countries signed a border accord on 7 March 2000, in which they agreed to conduct joint patrols in the Caribbean and the Gulf of Fonseca, and to withdraw all military forces from their mutual frontier. In February 2001 the Nicaraguan government accused Honduras of failing to withdraw its forces from the mutual border. An agreement was reached on 7 June 2001 which permitted observers from the Organisation of American States to monitor the deployment of land and maritime forces on both sides of the frontier.

POLITICAL SYSTEM
The head of government is the president, elected for a five-year term, not immediately renewable. The president appoints the Cabinet. There is a unicameral legislature, the National Assembly, with 90 members elected for a six-year term.

HEAD OF STATE
President, Enrique Bolaños Geyer, *elected* 4 November 2001, *sworn in* 10 January 2002
Vice-President, José Rízo

CABINET *as at August 2002*
Agriculture and Forests, José Augusto Navarro
Defence, José Adán Guerra
Education, Culture and Sports, Silvio de Franco
Environment and Natural Resources, Jorge Salazar
Family Affairs, Natalia Barillas
Finance and Public Credit, Eduardo Montealegre
Foreign Co-operation, Norman Caldera
Health, Lucía Salvo
Industry and Commerce, Mario Arana
Interior, Arturo Harding Lacayo
Labour, Virgilio José Gurdián
Presidential Secretary, Julio Vega
Transport and Infrastructure, Pedro Solórzano

EMBASSY OF NICARAGUA
Suite 31, Vicarage House, 58–60 Kensington Church Street, London W8 4DP
Tel: 020-7938 2373
Ambassador Extraordinary and Plenipotentiary, HE Juan B. Sacasa, apptd 2001

BRITISH EMBASSY
Apartado A-169, Plaza Churchill, Reparto 'Los Robles', Managua
Tel: (00 505) (2) 780014/7800887/674050
Ambassador and Consul-General, HE Hal Wiles, apptd 2001

DEFENCE
The Army has 127 main battle tanks and 166 armoured personnel carriers. The Navy has 5 patrol and coastal vessels at three bases. The Air Force has 15 armed helicopters. Full military relations with the USA were restored after 21 years in May 2000.
MILITARY EXPENDITURE – 0.8 per cent of GDP (2000)
MILITARY PERSONNEL – 16,000: Army 14,000, Navy 800, Air Force 1,200
CONSCRIPTION DURATION – 18–36 months

ECONOMY
The country is mainly agricultural. The major crops are maize, sugar cane, rice, sorghum, beans, bananas and coffee; livestock and timber production are also important. Nicaragua possesses deposits of gold and silver. In December 2000, the IMF and the World Bank announced a debt relief package worth US$4.5 billion to be made available to Nicaragua during 2001–2; the country's total foreign debt amounted to US$6.5 billion. In 2000 there was a trade deficit of US$995 million and a current account deficit of US$505 million. Imports totalled US$1,759 million and exports US$631 million.
GNP – US$2,126 million (2000); US$410 per capita (1999)
GDP – US$2,125 million (1998); US$459 per capita (1999)

ANNUAL AVERAGE GROWTH OF GDP – 5.0 per cent (1999)
INFLATION RATE – 11.2 per cent (1999)
UNEMPLOYMENT – 13.3 per cent (1998)
TOTAL EXTERNAL DEBT – US$6,986 million (1999)

TRADE

Considerable quantities of foodstuffs are imported as well as cotton goods, jute, iron and steel, machinery and petroleum products. The chief exports are cotton, coffee, beef and sugar.

Trade with UK	2000	2001
Imports from UK	£6,553,000	£2,807,000
Exports to UK	7,180,000	9,469,000

COMMUNICATIONS

The Inter-American Highway runs between the Honduras and the Costa Rican borders; the inter-oceanic highway runs from Corinto on the Pacific coast via Managua to Rama, where there is a natural waterway to Bluefields on the Atlantic; there are 15,478 km of roads. The main airport is at Managua. The chief port is Corinto on the Pacific. There are 252 miles of railway, all on the Pacific side of the country. There are 51 radio stations and five television stations in Managua.

NIGER
République du Niger – Republic of Niger

AREA – 489,191 sq. miles (1,267,000 sq. km).
Neighbours: Algeria and Libya (north), Chad (east), Nigeria and Benin (south), Mali and Burkina Faso (west). Apart from a small region along the Niger Valley in the south-west near the capital, the country is entirely savannah or desert
POPULATION – 10,355,156 (2001 estimate): Hausa (54 per cent) in the south, Songhai and Djerma in the south-west, Fulani, Beriberi–Manga, and nomadic Tuareg in the north. 95 per cent of the population are Muslims, with Christian and Animist minorities. The official language is French. Hausa, Djerma and Fulani are also spoken
CAPITAL – Niamey (population, 500,000, 1994 estimate)
CURRENCY – Franc CFA of 100 centimes
NATIONAL ANTHEM – Auprès Du Grand Niger Puissant (By The Banks Of The Mighty Great Niger)
NATIONAL DAY – 18 December
NATIONAL FLAG – Three horizontal stripes, orange, white and green with an orange disc in the middle of the white stripe
LIFE EXPECTANCY (years) – male 45.9; female 46.5
POPULATION GROWTH RATE – 3.2 per cent (1999)
POPULATION DENSITY – 8 per sq. km (1999)
MILITARY EXPENDITURE – 1.5 per cent of GDP (2000)
MILITARY PERSONNEL – 5,300: Army 5,200, Air Force 100; Paramilitaries 5,400
CONSCRIPTION DURATION – Two years (selective)
ILLITERACY RATE – 83.0 per cent (2002)
ENROLMENT (percentage of age group) – primary 29 per cent (1997); secondary 7 per cent (1997); tertiary 0.7 per cent (1991)

HISTORY AND POLITICS

The first French expedition arrived in 1891 and the country was fully occupied by 1914. It decided on 18 December 1958 to remain an autonomous republic within the French Community; full independence outside the Community was proclaimed on 3 August 1960. The president and government were overthrown in a military coup led by Col. Ibrahim Barre Mainassara on 27 January 1996, who was elected president on 8 July 1996. The pro-Mainassara National Union of Independents for Democratic Renewal won the largest number of seats in legislative elections in November 1996, though these were boycotted by main opposition groups. On 24 November 1997, President Mainassara dismissed the government led by Prime Minister Amadou Boubacar Cissé on grounds of incompetence, and appointed a new government under Ibrahim Hassane Mayaki.

President Mainassara was assassinated on 9 April 1999. On 11 April Major Daouda Mallam Wanke, head of the presidential guard unit responsible for the assassination, was named as the country's new president. In May, President Wanke established a Consultative Council which drafted a new constitution; it was approved by representatives of political groups in June and approved following a national referendum in July. Presidential elections were held in November 1999 and won by Mamadou Tandja of the National Movement for Society in Development (MNSD), who took power on 6 December 1999 and was sworn in as president on 22 December. In the simultaneous legislative elections the MNSD won an overall majority in the National Assembly.

INSURGENCY

An ethnic Tuareg-based insurgency began in the north of Niger in November 1991; a peace accord was signed with the main group, the Front for the Liberation of Aïr and Azawad (FLAA), in 1995 and two splinter groups agreed to a cease-fire in 1997. All rebel groups had been disarmed by June 1998.

HEAD OF STATE

President, Mamadou Tandja, *elected* 24 November 1999, *sworn in* 22 December 1999

COUNCIL OF MINISTERS *as at July 2002*

Prime Minister, Hama Amadou
Agricultural Development, Wassalké Boukari
Animal Resources, Koroné Maoudé
Basic Education, Ari Ibrahim
Civil Service, Labour and Government Spokesman, Moussa Saïbou Kassaï
Commerce and Promotion of the Private Sector, Seïni Oumarou
Equipment, Housing and Territorial Development, Abdou Labo
Finance and Economy, Ali Badjo Gamatié
Foreign Affairs, Co-operation and African Integration, Aïssatou Mindaoudou
Interior and Territorial Administration, Lawal Amadou
Justice, Keeper of the Seals, Relations with Parliament, Mati Moussa
Mines and Energy, Tamponé Ibrahim
National Defence, Sabiou Dadi Gao
Privatisation and Restructuring of Enterprises, Fatima Trapsida
Public Health and the Fight against Endemic Diseases, Ibrahim Komma
Secondary and Higher Education, Research and Technology, Sala Habi Salissou
Secretary of State for Economic Reforms, Hamida Arzaki
Secretary of State for Endemic Diseases, Abdoul Wahid Halimatou Ousseyni
Social Development, Population, Women and Children's Protection, Nana Aïchatou Foumakoye
Sport and Culture, Issa Lamine
Tourism and Cottage Industry, Rissa ag Boula

Transport and Communication, Mamane Sani Mallam Mahamane
Water Resources, Environment and the Fight against Desert Encroachment, Adamou Namata
Youth and Professional Integration of Youths, Souley Hassane 'Bonto'

EMBASSY OF THE REPUBLIC OF NIGER
154 rue de Longchamp, F-75116, Paris
Tel: (00 33) (1) 4504 8060
Ambassador Extraordinary and Plenipotentiary, HE Mariama Hima, apptd 1999

BRITISH AMBASSADOR, HE J. François Gordon, CMG, resident at Abidjan, Côte d'Ivoire

ECONOMY

The cultivation of groundnuts and the production of livestock are the main industries and provide two of the main exports. Other agricultural products include millet, cassava and sugar cane. There are large uranium deposits at Arlit and Akouta, and this is the main export. Gold deposits exist north-west of Niamey. France and Nigeria are the main trading partners.

In 1995 Niger had a trade deficit of US$18 million and a current account deficit of US$152 million. In 2000 imports totalled US$360 million and exports US$260 million.

GNP – US$1,988 million (2000); US$190 per capita (1999)
GDP – US$1,602 million (1998); US$200 per capita (1999)
ANNUAL AVERAGE GROWTH OF GDP – 3.4 per cent (1998)
INFLATION RATE – 2.9 per cent (2000)
TOTAL EXTERNAL DEBT – US$1,621 million (1999)

Trade with UK	2000	2001
Imports from UK	£4,196,000	£5,788,000
Exports to UK	585,000	10,228,000

NIGERIA
Federal Republic of Nigeria

AREA – 356,669 sq. miles (923,768 sq. km). Neighbours: Benin (west), Niger (north), Chad (north-east), Cameroon (east)
POPULATION – 126,635,626 (2001 estimate); 88,514,501 (1991 census). The main ethnic groups are Hausa/Fulani, Yoruba and Ibo, and the principal languages are English, Hausa, Yoruba and Ibo. There are some 373 ethnic groups, who speak over 500 different languages. The main religions are Islam (45 per cent, mainly in the north and west) and Christianity (49 per cent, mainly in the south, the remainder being Animists
CAPITAL – Abuja (population, 378,671), declared the federal capital in 1991
MAJOR CITIES – Ibadan (1,295,000); Kaduna (309,600); Kano (699,900); Lagos, the former capital (1,347,000); Ogbomosho (660,600); ΨPort Harcourt (371,000)
CURRENCY – Naira (N) of 100 kobo
NATIONAL ANTHEM – Arise, O Compatriots
NATIONAL DAY – 1 October (Independence Day)
NATIONAL FLAG – Three equal vertical bands, green, white and green
LIFE EXPECTANCY (years) – male 52.0; female 52.2
POPULATION GROWTH RATE – 2.4 per cent (1999)

POPULATION DENSITY – 118 per sq. km (1999)
ILLITERACY RATE – 33.3 per cent (2002)
ENROLMENT (percentage of age group) – tertiary 4.1 per cent (1993)

A belt of mangrove swamp forest lies along the entire coastline. North of this there is a zone of tropical rain forest and oil-palms. North of the rain forest, the land rises and the vegetation changes to open woodland and savannah. In the extreme north the country is semi-desert. The Niger and Benue are the main rivers. The climate is tropical.

HISTORY AND POLITICS

The Federation of Nigeria attained independence as a member of the Commonwealth on 1 October 1960 and became a republic in 1963. Originally comprising three regions, the Federation is now divided into 36 states and the Federal Capital Territory. In 1966 the military took power; in 1979 civil rule was restored after elections at national and state level. The administration was overthrown by the military in December 1983, this regime itself being overthrown in August 1985. An Armed Forces Ruling Council (AFRC) was sworn in and governed until January 1993, when it was replaced by a National Defence and Security Council (NDSC) and a civilian Transitional Council. Full power was handed over to the Transitional Council in August 1993. Continued instability led Defence Minister Gen. Sanni Abacha to launch a military coup on 17 November 1993 and install himself as head of state.

The military regime vowed to hand over power to an elected government in October 1998. In June 1998 Gen. Abacha died of a heart attack and was replaced by Gen. Abdulsalami Abubakar, who promised to continue with the handover to civilian rule and began the release of political prisoners.

A general election was held on 20 February 1999 in which the People's Democratic Party (PDP) won a majority in both houses of parliament; a presidential election was held on 27 February, in which Gen. Olusegun Obasanjo, the PDP candidate, was elected president. President Obasanjo and the civilian administration took office on 29 May 1999. Several predominantly Muslim northern states introduced the Islamic *Shari'ah* legal system during 2000 (Zamfara, Niger, Kano, Jigawa, Yobe and Borno), which President Obasanjo had declared unconstitutional on 1 November 1999. Bauchi adopted Shari'ah law in June 2001.

In June 2002, the Independent National Electoral Commission (INEC), announced that only three of the 24 parties that had applied for registration would be officially recognised. These were the All Progressive Grand Alliance (APGA), the National Democratic Party (NDP) and the United Nigeria People's Party (UNPP). Together with the three existing parties, the All People's Party (APP), the Alliance for Democracy (AD) and the People's Democratic Party (PDP), this brings the number of officially recognised parties in the country to six.

INSURGENCIES

Clashes between Muslim Hausas and Christian Yorubas have occurred in various parts of the country. The debate on Shari'ah law has exacerbated the divisions between Muslims and Christians and there have been sporadic clashes in which hundreds have been killed. A Yoruba separatist organisation, the Odua People's Congress, was banned on 19 October 2000 following clashes between its members and Hausas in Lagos. Fighting has also occurred between Ijaw and Ilaje tribesmen in the Niger Delta

region and the Isoko and Oleh tribes in Olomoro.

Fighting between Tivs and Hausas in Nassarawa state broke out in June 2001. In early February 2002, serious fighting occurred in Lagos between Muslim Hausas from the north of the country and mainly Christian Yorubas from the south.

FEDERAL STRUCTURE

State	Population (1991)	Capital
Sokoto	4,392,391	Sokoto
*Zamfara		Gusau
Kebbi	2,062,226	Birnin-Kebbi
Niger	2,482,367	Minna
Kwara	1,566,469	Ilorin
Kogi	2,099,046	Lokoja
Benue	2,780,398	Makurdi
Plateau	3,283,704	Jos
*Nassarawa		Lafia
Taraba	1,480,590	Jalingo
Adamawa	2,124,049	Yola
Borno	2,596,589	Maiduguri
Yobe	1,411,481	Damaturu
Bauchi	4,294,413	Bauchi
*Gombe		Gombe
Jigawa	2,829,929	Dutse
Kano	5,632,040	Kano
Katsina	3,878,344	Katsina
Kaduna	3,969,252	Kaduna
Federal Capital Territory	378,671	Abuja
Oyo	3,488,789	Ibadan
Osun	2,203,016	Oshogbo
Ogun	2,338,570	Abeokuta
Lagos	5,685,781	Ikeja
Ondo	3,884,485	Akure
*Ekiti		Ado Ekiti
Edo	2,159,848	Benin City
Delta	2,570,181	Asaba
Rivers	3,983,857	Port-Harcourt
*Bayelsa		Yenagoa
Abia	2,297,978	Umuahia
Imo	2,485,499	Owerri
*Ebonyi		Abakaliki
Anambra	2,767,903	Awka
Enugu	3,161,295	Enugu
Cross River	1,865,604	Calabar
Akwa Ibom	2,359,736	Uyo

*State, created on 1 October 1996 by dividing state immediately preceding it in list

HEAD OF STATE

President, Olusegun Obasanjo, *elected* 27 February 1999, sworn in 29 May 1999
Vice-President, Atiku Abubakar

FEDERAL EXECUTIVE COUNCIL *as at August 2002*

Agriculture and Rural Development, Mallam Adamu Bello
Aviation, Kema Chikwe
Commerce in Africa, Mustapha Bello
Communications, Bello Haliru Mohammed
Culture and Tourism, Boma Bromillow-Jack
Defence, Lt.-Gen. Yakubu Theophilus Danjuma
Education, Babalola Borishade
Environment, Mohammed Kabir Said
Federal Capital Territory, Mohammed Abba-Gana
Finance, Mallam Adamu Ciroma
Foreign Affairs, Sule Lamido
Health, Alphonsus Bosa Nwosu
Industry, Chief Kolawole Babalola Jamodu

Information, Jerry Gana
Internal Affairs, Chief Sunday Afolabi
Justice, Attorney-General, Kanu Godwin Agabi
Labour, Employment and Productivity, Musa Gwadabe
Ministers in the Presidency, Chief Bimbola Ogunkelu (*Co-operation and Integration in Africa*); Prince Vincent Ogbuleafor (*Economic Matters*); Ibrahim Umar Kida (*Inter-governmental Affairs*); Yomi Edu (*Special Duties*)
Police Affairs, Steven Akiga
Power and Steel, Olusegun Agagu
Science and Technology, Turner Isoun
Solid Mineral Resources, Dupe Adelja
Sports and Social Development, Steven Ibn Akiga
Transport, Chief Ojo Maduekwe
Water Resources, Muktari Shagari
Women and Youth, Aishat Ismail
Works and Housing, Chief Tony Anenih

NIGERIA HIGH COMMISSION

Nigeria House, 9 Northumberland Avenue, London WC2N 5BX
Tel: 020-7839 1244
High Commissioner, HE Dr Christopher Kolade, apptd 2002
Deputy High Commissioner, M. Sanusi
Minister, A. A. Ella

BRITISH HIGH COMMISSION

Shehu Shangari Way (North), Maitama, Abuja
Tel: (00 234) (9) 413 2010/2011/2796/2880
Email: consular@abuja.mail.fco.gov.uk
11 Walter Carrington Crescent, Victoria Island, Lagos
Tel: (00 234) (1) 261 9531/9537/9541/9543
High Commissioner, HE Philip Thomas, CMG, apptd 2001
LIAISON OFFICES – Ibadan, Kaduna, Kano, Port Harcourt

BRITISH COUNCIL DIRECTOR, Cathy Stephens, Plot 2935, IBB Way, Maitama, P.M.B. 550, Garki, Abuja
Email: info.abuja@ng.britishcouncil.org. Branch offices at Kano, Lagos and Port Harcourt.

DEFENCE

The Army has 200 main battle tanks and 330 armoured personnel carriers. The Navy has one frigate, eight patrol and coastal vessels and two helicopters at three bases. The Air Force has 86 combat aircraft and ten armed helicopters.
MILITARY EXPENDITURE – 4.5 per cent of GDP (2000)
MILITARY PERSONNEL – 78,500: Army 62,000, Navy 7,000, Air Force 9,500; Paramilitaries 82,000

ECONOMY

Nigeria was a predominantly agricultural country until the early 1970s when oil became the principal source of export revenue (over 90 per cent). Recent governments have attempted to stimulate greater self-reliance by encouraging non-oil exports and the use of local rather than imported raw materials. Much of Nigeria's oil revenue has been squandered on major projects which have failed to generate the predicted returns. Nigeria has also suffered from endemic corruption, especially under Gen. Sani Abacha. Many state and local governments have not published audited accounts for many years. President Obasanjo has attempted to tackle the problem by retiring many army officers suspected of corruption and suspending government contracts signed during the last three months of the previous administration, pending investigations.

Agricultural production has fallen since 1970, largely as a result of a system of marketing boards, which fixed prices for agricultural commodities, often setting prices at levels which were too high or low.

Petrol prices are fixed at a level below market rates. These act as a disincentive to producers to refine their oil, which has resulted in widespread fuel shortages. Three oil refineries are in operation at Port Harcourt, Warri and Kaduna, and steel plants at Warri and Ajaokuta (non-operational). Other projects include natural gas lique-faction, petrochemicals, fertilisers, power stations and irrigation schemes. Tin and calumbite mining on the Jos plateau, textiles and coal mining are also important.

GNP – US$32,814 million (2000); US$260 per capita (1999)

GDP – US$77,023 million (1998); US$473 per capita (1999)

ANNUAL AVERAGE GROWTH OF GDP – 2.4 per cent (1998)

INFLATION RATE – 6.9 per cent (2000)

TOTAL EXTERNAL DEBT – US$29,358 million (1999)

TRADE

The principal exports are oil, groundnuts, tin, cocoa, rubber, fish and timber. In 1999 there was a trade surplus of US$4,288 million and a current account surplus of US$506 million. In 1998, imports totalled US$10,002 million and exports US$9,729 million.

Trade with UK	2000	2001
Imports from UK	£534,725,000	£684,132,000
Exports to UK	95,357,000	68,249,000

COMMUNICATIONS

There are 194,394 km of roads. The Nigerian railway system, which is controlled by the Nigerian Railway Corporation, has 3,557 route km of lines. The principal international airlines operate from Lagos, Kano and Port Harcourt. A network of internal air services connects the main centres. The principal seaports are served by a number of shipping lines, including the Nigerian National Line.

NORWAY
Kongeriket Norge – Kingdom of Norway

AREA – 125,050 sq. miles (323,877 sq. km) of which Svalbard and Jan Mayen have a combined area of 24,355 sq. miles (63,080 sq. km). Neighbours: Sweden, Finland, Russia (east)

POPULATION – 4,504,000 (2001 estimate). The language is Norwegian and has two forms: Bokmål and Nynorsk. Sami is spoken in the north of the country. The state religion is Evangelical Lutheran

CAPITAL – ΨOslo (population, 508,726, 2001)

MAJOR CITIES – ΨBergen (230,948); ΨKristiansand (73,087); ΨStavanger (108,848); ΨTrondheim (150,166), 2001

CURRENCY – Krone of 100 øre

NATIONAL ANTHEM – Ja, Vi Elsker Dette Landet (Yes, We Love This Country)

NATIONAL DAY – 17 May (Constitution Day)

NATIONAL FLAG – Red, with white-bordered blue cross

LIFE EXPECTANCY (years) – male 76.0; female 81.9

POPULATION GROWTH RATE – 0.6 per cent (1999)

POPULATION DENSITY – 14 per sq. km (1999)

The coastline is deeply indented with numerous fjords and fringed with rocky islands. The surface is mountainous, consisting of elevated and barren tablelands separated by deep and narrow valleys. At the North Cape the sun does not appear to set from about 14 May to 29 July, causing the phenomenon known as the Midnight Sun; conversely, there is no apparent sunrise from about 18 November to 24 January. During the long winter nights are seen the Northern Lights or Aurora Borealis.

HISTORY AND POLITICS

Norway was unified under Harald I Fairhair c.AD 900 and participated in the Viking expansion from the ninth to the 11th centuries. The accession of Magnus VII (1319) unified the Norwegian and Swedish crowns until his son became King Håkon VI of Norway in 1343. The Norwegian and Danish crowns were united in 1380 and confirmed by the Union of Kalmar (1397) which also brought Sweden under the rule of Queen Margrethe of Denmark. Norway remained a Danish province until transferred to Sweden under the Treaty of Kiel (1814). The union with Sweden was dissolved on 7 June 1905 when Norway regained complete independence.

Norway remained neutral during the First World War and on the outbreak of the Second World War but was invaded by Germany in 1940. Neutrality was abandoned when Norway joined NATO in 1949. Norway became a founder member of EFTA in 1960. The Labour Party governed from 1945 to 1965 when the extensive welfare state system was built. A referendum in 1972 rejected membership of the EC.

The ruling centre-right coalition collapsed in October 1990 over the question of EC membership and was replaced by a minority Labour government. This was returned to power in the general election held on 13 September 1993. A general election was held on 10 September 2001, in which no party won an outright majority. The Labour Party has the largest number of seats (43) but, following a month of talks, three parties, the Conservative Party (H), the Christian People's Party (KrF) and the Liberal Party (V), agreed to form a coalition government. On 17 October Labour Prime Minister Jens Stoltenberg handed in his government's resignation and on 19 October Kjell Magne Bondevik of the KrF was appointed prime minister.

FOREIGN RELATIONS

The Storting voted in November 1992 to apply to join the European Community. Negotiations with the EU concluded on 1 March 1994 with a proposed accession date of 1 January 1995, subject to parliamentary and national referendum ratifications. However, in a national referendum on 28 November 1994 the electorate voted against joining the EU by 52.4 per cent to 47.6 per cent.

POLITICAL SYSTEM

Under the 1814 constitution, the 165-member unicameral legislature, the *Storting*, elects one-quarter of its members to constitute the *Lagting* (Upper Chamber), the other three-quarters forming the *Odelsting* (Lower Chamber), dividing when legislative matters are under discussion.

HEAD OF STATE

HM The King of Norway, King Harald V, GCVO, *born* 21 February 1937; *succeeded* 17 January 1991, on the death of his father King Olav V; *married* 29 August 1968, Sonja Haraldsen, and has *issue*, Prince Håkon Magnus, and Princess Martha Louise, *born* 22 September 1971

Heir, HRH Crown Prince Håkon Magnus, *born* 20 July 1973, *married* Mette-Marit Tjessem Hoiby

CABINET *as at July 2002*

Prime Minister, Kjell Magne Bondevik (KrF)
Agriculture, Lars Sponheim (V)
Children and Family Affairs, Laila Dåvøy (KrF)
Church and Cultural Affairs, Valgerd Svarstad Haugland (KrF)
Defence, Kristin Krohn Devold (H)
Education and Research, Kristin Clemet (H)
Environment, Børge Brende (H)
Finance, Per-Kristian Foss (H)
Fisheries, Svein Ludvigsen (H)
Foreign Affairs, Jan Petersen (H)
Health, Dagfinn Høybråten (KrF)
Industry and Trade, Ansgar Gabrielsen (H)
International Development, Hilde Frafjord Johnson (KrF)
Justice and Police, Odd Einar Dørum (V) *Labour and Government Administration,* Victor Danielsen Norman (H)
Local Government and Regional Development, Erna Solberg (H)
Petroleum and Energy, Einar Steensnaes (KrF)
Social Affairs, Ingierd Schou (H)
Transport and Communications, Torild Skogsholm (V)

ROYAL NORWEGIAN EMBASSY

25 Belgrave Square, London SW1X 8QD
Tel: 020-7591 5500
Ambassador Extraordinary and Plenipotentiary, HE Tarald Osnes Brautaset, apptd 2000

BRITISH EMBASSY

Thomas Heftyesgate 8, N-0244 Oslo
Tel: (00 47) 2313 2700
Ambassador Extraordinary and Plenipotentiary, HE Sir Richard Dales, KCVO, CMG, apptd 1998

BRITISH CONSULAR OFFICES – Oslo; Honorary Consulates at Ålesund, Bergen, Harstad, Kristiansand (South), Kristiansund (North), Stavanger, Tromsø, Trondheim

BRITISH COUNCIL DIRECTOR, Sarah Prosser, Fridtjof Nansens Plass 5, N-0160 Oslo;
Email: british.council@britishcouncil.no

DEFENCE

Norway is a member of NATO. The Army has 170 main battle tanks, 157 armoured infantry fighting vehicles and 189 armoured personnel carriers. The Navy has six submarines, three frigates and 14 patrol and coastal vessels at three bases. The Air Force has 61 combat aircraft.
MILITARY EXPENDITURE – 1.8 per cent of GDP (2000)
MILITARY PERSONNEL – 26,700: Army 14,700, Navy 6,100, Air Force 5,000
CONSCRIPTION DURATION – 12 months plus refresher training

ECONOMY

The cultivated area is about 10,703 sq. km, 3.5 per cent of the total surface area. Forests cover 23 per cent; the rest consists of highland pastures or uninhabitable mountains. The chief agricultural products are grain, vegetables, milk, furs and timber.
   The Gulf Stream causes the sea temperature to be higher than the average for the latitude, which brings shoals of herring and cod into the fishing grounds. In 1997 the catch totalled more than 9 million tonnes. In

1998, dried cod worth €352 million/US$400 million was produced.
   The chief industries are oil production and transport, construction, electricity supply, manufactures, agriculture and forestry, fisheries, mining, metal and ferro-alloy production and shipping. Industries providing both manufactured products and services for the development of North Sea energy resources have become increasingly important. In 1998 150,006,000 tonnes of crude oil were produced. Norway produces large amounts of hydroelectric power.
GNP – US$151,153 million (2000); US$33,470 per capita (1999)
GDP – US$146,729 million (1998); US$34,377 per capita (1999)
ANNUAL AVERAGE GROWTH OF GDP – 2.7 per cent (2000)
INFLATION RATE – 3.1 per cent (2000)
UNEMPLOYMENT – 3.2 per cent (1999)

TRADE

The chief imports are motor vehicles, ships and machinery, clothing, foods and textiles. Exports consist chiefly of crude oil and gas, machinery and transport equipment and manufactured goods.
   In 2000 Norway had a trade surplus of US$25,500 million and a current account surplus of US$22,986 million. Imports totalled US$32,655 million and exports US$57,514 million.

Trade with UK	2000	2001
Imports from UK	£2,101,072,000	£1,897,826,000
Exports to UK	5,858,714,000	5,896,996,000

COMMUNICATIONS

The total length of railways open at the end of 1999 was 4,021 km, excluding private lines. There are 90,880 km of public roads in Norway (including urban streets). Scheduled internal air services are operated by Scandinavian Airlines System (SAS) on behalf of Det Norske Luftfartselskap (DNL), by Braathens South American and Far East Airtransport (SAFE), and by Widerøes Flyveselskap AS. There are international airports at Oslo, Bergen and Stavanger.

CULTURE AND EDUCATION

The Norwegian language in both its present forms is closely related to other Scandinavian languages. Independence from Denmark (1814) and resurgent nationalism led to the development of 'new Norwegian' based on dialects, which now has equal official standing with 'bokmål', in which Danish influence is more obvious. Ludvig Holberg (1684–1754) is regarded as the father of Norwegian literature, though the modern period begins with the writings of Henrik Wergeland (1808–45). Some of the famous names are Henrik Ibsen (1828–1906), Bjørnstjerne Bjørnson (1832–1910), Nobel Prizewinner in 1903, and the novelists Jonas Lie (1833–1908), Alexander Kielland (1849–1906), Knut Hamsun (1859–1952) and Sigrid Undset (1882–1949), the latter two also Nobel Prizewinners. Old Norse literature is among the most ancient and richest in Europe.
   Education from six to 16 is free and compulsory in the 'basic schools', and free from 16 to 19 years. The majority of the pupils receive post-compulsory schooling at 'upper secondary' schools, regional colleges akin to polytechnics, and 11 universities and other university-level specialist colleges.

ENROLMENT (percentage of age group) – primary 100 per cent (1997); secondary 100 per cent (1997); tertiary 62 per cent (1997)

TERRITORIES

SVALBARD, area 24,295 sq. miles (62,923 sq. km); population 2,332 (2001 estimate); inhabitants mainly engaged in coal-mining. The Svalbard archipelago consists of the main island, Spitsbergen (15,200 sq. miles), North East Land, the Wiche Islands, Barents and Edge Islands, Prince Charles Foreland, Hope Island, Bear Island and many islands in the neighbourhood of the main group. Glaciers cover 60 per cent of the land area. The sovereignty of Norway over the archipelago was recognised by other nations in 1920 and in 1925 Norway assumed sovereignty

JAN MAYEN ISLAND was joined to Norway by law in 1930

NORWEGIAN ANTARCTIC TERRITORIES

BOUVET ISLAND was declared a dependency of Norway in 1930

PETER THE FIRST ISLAND was declared a dependency of Norway in 1931

PRINCESS RAGNHILD LAND has been claimed as Norwegian since 1931

QUEEN MAUD LAND was declared Norwegian territory by the Norwegian government in 1939

OMAN
Saltanat 'Umān – Sultanate of Oman

AREA – 119,499 sq. miles (309,500 sq. km). Neighbours: Yemen, Saudi Arabia and the UAE (west)

POPULATION – 2,400,000 (2000 estimate). The official language is Arabic. Islam is the official religion. The majority of the population are Ibadhi Muslims; there is a large Sunni and a small Shia minority. Other religions are tolerated

CAPITAL – ΨMuscat (Masqat) (population, 600,000)

MAJOR CITIES – ΨBarka; ΨMutrah and Ruwi (the commercial centres); ΨSalālah (the main town of Dhofar); ΨSuhār; ΨSūr

CURRENCY – Rial Omani (OR) of 1,000 baisas

NATIONAL ANTHEM – Ya Rabbana Ifadh Lana Jalalat Al Sultan (O Lord, Protect For Us His Majesty The Sultan)

NATIONAL DAY – 18 November

NATIONAL FLAG – Red with a white panel in the upper fly and a green one in the lower fly; in the canton the national emblem in white

LIFE EXPECTANCY (years) – male 70.2; female 73.2

POPULATION GROWTH RATE – 2.5 per cent (2000)

POPULATION DENSITY – 11 per sq. km (2000)

Oman lies at the eastern corner of the Arabian peninsula. Sharjah and Fujairah (UAE) separate the main part of Oman from the northernmost part of the state, a peninsula extending into the Strait of Hormuz. The north and the south of Oman are divided by nearly 400 miles of desert. The Batinah, the coastal plain, is fertile. The Hajjar is a mountain spine running from north-west to south-east and for the most part barren, but valleys penetrate the central massif which are irrigated by wells or a system of underground canals called *aflaj* which tap the water table. The two plateaus leading from the western slopes of the mountains descend to the Empty Quarter of the Arabian Desert. Dhofar, the southern province, is the only part of the

Arabian peninsula to be touched by the south-west monsoon.

HISTORY AND POLITICS

Oman became part of the Islamic empire in the seventh century. From the ninth to 16th centuries the area was governed by a succession of religious leaders, or imams of the Ibadhi branch of Islam. The Portuguese established trading posts on the coast in 1507 but were expelled in 1649.

In 1744 Ahmad bin Said Al bu Said established the current ruling dynasty of sultans. The country was divided between the sultan's stronghold in the coastal Muscat-Matrah region and the imam in the interior. The sultan cultivated close relations with Britain and the Sultanate of Muscat and Oman became a British protectorate in 1798. In the late 19th century Dhofar was annexed.

In the 1950s the imam proclaimed an independent state in a revolt which was put down with British assistance. A seven-year-long Marxist uprising was crushed in 1975. The current sultan ousted his father in a palace coup in 1970 and changed the state's name to the Sultanate of Oman. Dhofar is still governed as a separate province and Muscat has special status.

POLITICAL SYSTEM

A State Consultative Council established in 1981 was replaced by royal decree in 1991 by a *Majlis ash Shura*, or State Advisory Council. This body, meeting twice a year, consists of representatives from each of the 59 wilayats, or governorates, of the Sultanate. The Council has the right to review legislation, question ministers and make policy proposals. Effective political power remains with the sultan, who rules by decree and is advised by the Cabinet of Ministers, which he appoints. On 16 December 1997 the sultan appointed 41 members to the new *Majlis al-Dawlah* (Council of State). On 15 September 2000 the first direct election to the *Majlis ash-Shura* (Consultative Council) took place.

In November 1996 the sultan issued the Basic Statute of the State which decreed Oman to be a hereditary absolute monarchy. The Sultan is advised by the Council of State, whose 41 members are appointed by the Sultan. The 82-member Consultative Council has been directly elected since September 2000. The electorate comprises 175,000 men and women 'of good standing'.

HEAD OF STATE

HM The Sultan of Oman, Sultan Qaboos bin Said al-Said, *succeeded* on deposition of Sultan Said bin Taimur, 23 July 1970

COUNCIL OF MINISTERS *as at July 2002*

Prime Minister, The Sultan

Personal Representative of HM The Sultan, HH Sayyid Thuwaini bin Shehab al-Said

Deputy Prime Minister for Cabinet Affairs, HH Sayyid Fahd bin Mamud al-Said

Agriculture and Fisheries, Shaikh Salim bin Halil al-Khalili

Civil Service, Shaikh Abdel Aziz bin Matar bin Salim al-Azizi

Commerce, Industry and Minerals, Maqbul bin Ali bin Sultan

Defence, Badr bin Saud bin Hareb al-Busaidi

Education and Teaching, Yahia bin Saud Al-Sallimi

Foreign Affairs, Yusuf bin Alawi bin Abdullah

Health, Dr Ali bin Mohammed bin Mousa

Higher Education, Yahya bin Mahfudh al-Mantheri

Housing, Electricity and Water, Shaikh Suhail bin Mustahail bin Salim al-Shamas
Information, Hamad bin Muhammad bin Muhsin al-Rashidi
Interior, Sayyid bin Ibrahim al-Busaidi
Justice, Shaikh Mohammed bin Abdullah bin Zahir al-Hinai
Labour and Training, Jomaa bin Ali bin Jomaa
Minister of State and Governor of Dhofar, Shaikh Mohammad bin Ali al-Qatabi
Minister of State and Governor of Muscat, Mutasim bin Hamud al-Busaidi
Minister of State for Legal Affairs, Mohammed bin Ali bin Nasir al-Alawi
Municipalities, Environment and Water Resources, Khamis bin Mubarak bin Isa al-Alawi
National Economy and Finance, Ahmed bin Abdulnabi Makki
National Heritage and Culture, Haytham bin Tareq al-Said
Palace Affairs, Ali bin Hamud al-Bussaidi
Palace Security, Gen. Ali bin Majed al-Mamari
Personal Representative of the Sultan, Thuwaini bin Shehab al-Said
Petroleum and Gas, Dr Mohammed bin Hamad bin Saif al-Romhi
Religious Property and Affairs, Shaikh Abdallah bin Mahammed al-Salimi
Social Affairs, Shaikh Amer bin Shuwain al-Hosni
Special Advisers to the Sultan, Faisal bin Ali bin Faisal al-Said *(Cultural Affairs)*; Shahib ibn Taymur al-Said *(Environment)*
Transport and Telecommunications, Col. Malik bin Sulaiman al-Ma'amari

EMBASSY OF THE SULTANATE OF OMAN

167 Queen's Gate, London SW7 5HE
Tel: 020-7225 0001
Ambassador Extraordinary and Plenipotentiary, HE Hussain Ali Abdullatif, apptd 1995

BRITISH EMBASSY

PO Box 300, Muscat, Postal Code 113
Tel: (00 968) 693077
Email: becomu@omantel.net.om
Ambassador Extraordinary and Plenipotentiary, HE Stuart Laing, apptd 2002

BRITISH COUNCIL DIRECTOR, Colin Hepburn, Road One, Madinat al Sultan, Qaboos West, PO Box 73, Muscat; Email: bc.muscat@om.britishcouncil.org. There is also an office in Seeb

DEFENCE

The Army has 117 main battle tanks and 189 armoured personnel carriers. The Navy has 13 patrol and coastal vessels at five bases. The Air Force has 40 combat aircraft.
MILITARY EXPENDITURE – 10.0 per cent of GDP (2000)
MILITARY PERSONNEL – 43,400: Army 25,000, Navy 4,200, Air Force 4,100, Royal Household 6,400; Paramilitaries 4,400

ECONOMY

Although there is considerable cultivation in the fertile areas and cattle are raised in the mountains, the backbone of the economy is the oil industry, accounting for about 40 per cent of GDP. Petroleum Development (Oman) (PDO) (owned 60 per cent by the Oman Government) began exporting oil in 1967. Concessions (off and on shore) are held by several major international companies. Oil production in 1998 was 44,788,000 tonnes and

natural gas production was 5,200 million cubic metres. The government is actively encouraging the diversification of the economy and private sector development. Tourism is also an expanding area.

In 1998 there was a trade surplus of US$291 million and a current account deficit of US$2,970 million.
GDP – US$14,162 million (1998); US$6,386 per capita (1999)
ANNUAL AVERAGE GROWTH OF GDP – -1.0 per cent (1999)
INFLATION RATE – -1.1 per cent (2000)
TOTAL EXTERNAL DEBT – US$3,603 million (1999)

TRADE

Trade is mainly with the UAE, UK, Japan, South Korea and China. Chief imports are machinery and transport equipment, industrial goods and foodstuffs. Oil accounts for 82.9 per cent of exports.

In 2000 imports totalled US$5,040 million. In 1998 exports US$5,508 million.

Trade with UK	2000	2001
Imports from UK	£278,280,000	£302,053,000
Exports to UK	97,445,000	68,455,000

COMMUNICATIONS

Port Qaboos at Mutrah has eight deep-water berths which have been constructed as part of the harbour facilities; a new port is due for completion at Suhār in December 2002. There are some 34,000 km of roads, of which 9,000 km are paved, linking most main population centres of the country with the coast and with the towns of the UAE, though only a trunk road links the north and south of Oman. There are airports at Seeb, Salālah, Sūr, Masirah, Khasab and Diba. Five daily newspapers are published, three in Arabic and two in English.

SOCIAL WELFARE AND EDUCATION

For many years the Sultanate was a poor country but the advent of oil revenues and the change of regime in 1970 led to the initiation of a wide-ranging development programme, especially concerned with health, education and communications. There are now 55 hospitals and 118 health centres. Mass immunisation programmes have eradicated poliomyelitis and diphtheria. In 2000 there were 1,008 state schools. There is one state university and several private universities.
ILLITERACY RATE – 25.6 per cent (2002)
ENROLMENT (percentage of age group) – primary 76 per cent (1997); secondary 67 per cent (1997); tertiary 8 per cent (1997)

PAKISTAN

Islāmī Jamhūriya-e-Pākistān – Islamic Republic of Pakistan

AREA – 307,374 sq. miles (796,095 sq. km). Neighbours: Iran (west), Afghanistan (north and north-west), China (north-east), the disputed territory of Kashmir, India (east)
POPULATION – 144,616,639 (2001 estimate); 95 per cent Muslim, 3.5 per cent Christian, about 1 per cent Hindu, and 0.5 per cent Buddhist. Urdu is the national language, but is only spoken by a small minority of the population. The most widely used language is Punjabi, followed by Sindi and Pushto. English is used in business, government and higher education

CAPITAL – Islamabad (population, 350,000, 1998 census)

MAJOR CITIES – Faisalabad (1,977,246); ΨKarachi (9,269,265); Lahore (5,063,499); Rawalpindi (1,406,214), 1998 census

CURRENCY – Pakistan rupee of 100 paisa

NATIONAL ANTHEM – Pak Sarzamin Shad Bad (Blessed Be The Sacred Land)

NATIONAL DAYS – 23 March (Pakistan Day), 14 August (Independence Day)

NATIONAL FLAG – Green with a white crescent and star, and a white vertical strip in the hoist

LIFE EXPECTANCY (years) – male 61.2; female 60.9

POPULATION GROWTH RATE – 2.9 per cent (1997)

POPULATION DENSITY – 169 per sq. km (1999)

URBAN POPULATION – 32.2 per cent (1995)

Running through Pakistan are five great rivers, the Indus, Jhelum, Chenab, Ravi and Sutlej. The upper reaches of these rivers are in Kashmir, and their sources are in the Himalayas.

HISTORY AND POLITICS

Pakistan was constituted as a Dominion under the Indian Independence Act 1947, becoming a republic on 23 March 1956. Until 1972 Pakistan consisted of two geographical units, West and East Pakistan, separated by about 1,100 miles of Indian territory. East Pakistan's insistence on complete autonomy led to civil war, which broke out on 25 March 1971 and continued until December 1971 when a cease-fire was arranged. The independence of East Pakistan as Bangladesh was proclaimed in April 1972. Under the 1972 Simla Agreement with India, a line of control was established in Kashmir; Pakistan controls an area of 33,653 sq. miles (87,159 sq. km) to the north and west of the line.

Elections held in February 1997 were won by the Pakistan Muslim League with 134 seats. President Farooq Leghari resigned on 2 December 1997 following a dispute with Prime Minister Sharwaz. Muhammad Rafiq Tarar was subsequently elected president.

The government was overthrown by the military under Gen. Pervez Musharraf on 12 October 1999 after the Prime Minister, Nawaz Sharif, had tried to sack him. Gen. Musharraf declared himself chief executive and dissolved the legislature, but left the president in office. Gen. Musharraf established the National Security Council to run the country, comprising the military chiefs of staff and civilian technocrats.

Pakistan's membership of the Commonwealth was suspended on 18 October 1999.

A coalition of 17 of the main political parties, was formed in November 2000 to campaign for the restoration of democracy.

On 20 June 2001, Gen. Musharraf dismissed the elected president, Muhammad Rafiq Tarar, and assumed the presidency himself. The extension of Musharraf's presidency for a further five years was approved by referendum on 30 April 2002. In August 2002 President Musharraf granted himself new powers, including the right to dismiss an elected parliament.

Legislative elections were scheduled to take place on 10 October 2002.

INSURGENCY

Since early 1994 there has been civil disorder in Sind province, especially in Karachi, in two conflicts: armed militants of the Mohajir Qaumi Movement (MQM) Party, which represents Urdu-speaking Indian Muslims who fled from India at partition and their descendants, are fighting for an autonomous Karachi province; and

there is an armed conflict between Shia and Sunni fundamentalists. During 2002 a series of attacks occurred against Christian and Western groups in the country, one of which was a suicide bomb attack in Karachi on 8 May which killed 15 people, including 12 French nationals. The attacks were thought to be the work of Islamic militants opposed to Pakistan's support for the US-led war on terrorism that followed the 11 September 2001 terrorist attacks on New York and Washington DC.

FOREIGN RELATIONS

The conflict with India over Kashmir flared up in May 1999 when India launched air attacks on Muslim insurgents who had occupied mountainous regions inside India–controlled Kashmir. Small-scale conflicts continued but in December 2001, India and Pakistan assembled troops along the common border and during May and June 2002 there was concern that the conflict could spiral into a nuclear exchange. Following intense international diplomatic activity, the threat of war receded in July but the situation remains tense.

POLITICAL SYSTEM

The legislature is bicameral, but was suspended following the coup in October 1999. Under the constitution, the Majlis as-Shoora (National Assembly) has a five-year term and comprises 237 members, of whom 207 are directly elected, 10 represent religious minorities and 20 are co-opted women. The Senate has 87 members, with a six-year term; half of the seats are renewed every three years. In January 1997 the interim government set up a Council for Defence and National Security including members of the Cabinet and armed forces to advise on foreign, defence and economic policies. The four provinces each have a provincial assembly and are represented in both legislative chambers.

The National Assembly amended the constitution in April 1997 to remove from the president the power to dismiss the government and dissolve parliament.

FEDERAL STRUCTURE

Province	Area (sq. km)	Population (1998 census)	Capital
Baluchistan	347,190	6,511,000	Quetta
Federal Capital Territory Islamabad	906	805,000	–
Federally Administered Tribal Areas	27,220	3,138,000	–
North-West Frontier Province	74,521	17,555,000	Peshawar
Punjab	205,344	72,585,000	Lahore
Sind	140,914	29,991,000	Karachi

HEAD OF STATE

President, Chief Executive, Chief of Army Staff, Gen. Pervez Musharraf, *assumed office* 20 June 2001, *confirmed in office by referendum* 30 April 2002

NATIONAL SECURITY COUNCIL *as at July 2002*

Chief of Air Staff, Air Chief Marshal Mushaf Ali Mir
Chief of Naval Staff, Adm. Abdul Aziz Mirza
Commerce, Industry and Production, Abdul Razzak Daud
Finance, Revenue, Economic Affairs, Planning, Development and Statistics, Shaukat Aziz
Foreign Affairs, Inam ul-Haq
Interior and Narcotics Control, Capital Administration and Development Divisions, Lt.-Gen. (retd) Moeenuddin Haider
Vice-Chief of Army Staff, Gen. Mohammad Yousuf

1026 Countries of the World

FEDERAL MINISTERS *as at July 2002*
Adviser to the Chief Executive for Food, Agriculture and Livestock, Shafi Nafiz
Adviser to the Chief Executive for Foreign Affairs, Law, Justice and Human Rights, Sharifuddin Pirzada
Chair of the Federal Land Commission, Imtiaz Ahmad Ghazi
Communications and Railways, Lt.-Gen. Javed Asharaf
Education, Science and Technology, Zubaida Jalal
Food and Agriculture, Khair Mohammad Junejo
Health, Abdul Malik Kasi
Information, Nisar Memon
Kashmir Affairs, Northern Areas, States and Frontier Regions, Housing and Works, Abbass Sarfaraz Khan
Law, Justice, Human Rights and Parliamentary Affairs, Shahida Jamil
Local Government and Rural Development, Labour, Environment, Overseas Pakistanis, Owais Ahmad Ghani
Minister of State, Deputy Chair of Planning Commission, Shahid Amjad Chaudhry
Petroleum and Natural Resources, Usman Aminuddin
Privatisation, Altaf M. Saleem
Religious Affairs, Mahmood Ahmed Ghazi
Science and Technology, Ataur Rahman
Sports, Culture, Tourism and Minorities Affairs, Col. S. K. Trassler
Women's Development, Social Welfare and Special Education, Population Welfare, Attiya Inayatullah

HIGH COMMISSION FOR THE ISLAMIC REPUBLIC OF PAKISTAN
35–36 Lowndes Square, London SW1X 9JN
Tel: 020-7664 9200
High Commissioner, HE Abdul Kader Jaffer, apptd 2000

BRITISH HIGH COMMISSION
Diplomatic Enclave, Ramna 5, PO Box 1122, Islamabad
Tel: (00 92) (51) 2206071/5
Email: bhctrade@isb.comsats.net.pk
High Commissioner, HE Hilary Synnott, CMG, apptd 2000
BRITISH COUNCIL DIRECTOR, Peter Ellwood, House 1, Street 61, F-6/3, PO Box 1135, Islamabad; Email: bc.islamabad@britishcouncil.org.pk. There are offices at Karachi, Lahore and Peshawar

DEFENCE

On 28 and 30 May 1998, Pakistan carried out six underground nuclear tests, less than a month after India had carried out its own nuclear tests. In doing so, it became the world's seventh declared nuclear power.
The Army has some 2,300 main battle tanks, 1,150 armoured personnel carriers and 20 attack helicopters. The Navy has ten submarines, eight frigates, nine patrol and coastal vessels, five combat aircraft and nine armed helicopters based at Karachi. The Air Force has 353 combat aircraft.
MILITARY EXPENDITURE – 5.8 per cent of GDP (2000)
MILITARY PERSONNEL – 620,000: Army 550,000, Navy 25,000, Air Force 45,000; Paramilitaries 288,000

ECONOMY

Agriculture employs half the workforce and contributes a quarter of GDP. The principal crops are cotton, rice, wheat and sugar cane. Pakistan has one of the longest irrigation systems in the world, irrigating 42.5 million acres. There are large deposits of rock salt.
Pakistan also produces hides and skins, leather, wool, fertilisers, paints and varnishes, soda ash, paper, cement,

fish, carpets, sports goods, surgical appliances and engineering goods, including switchgear, transformers, cables and wires.
In July 2001, the World Bank commended the efforts of the government to stabilise and deregulate the economy and to alleviate poverty.
In 1997 there was a trade deficit of US$2,399 million and a current account deficit of US$1,712 million.
GNP – US$64,550 million (2000); US$470 per capita (1999)
GDP – US$67,917 million (1998); US$487 per capita (1999)
ANNUAL AVERAGE GROWTH OF GDP – 5.6 per cent (2000)
INFLATION RATE – 4.4 per cent (2000)
UNEMPLOYMENT – 6.1 per cent (1997)
TOTAL EXTERNAL DEBT – US$34,423 million (1999)

TRADE

Principal imports are petroleum products, machinery, fertilisers, transport equipment, edible oils, chemicals and ferrous metals. Principal exports are cotton yarn and cloth, carpets, rice, petroleum products, textiles, leather and fish.
In 2000 imports totalled US$11,048 million and exports US$9,173 million.

Trade with UK	2000	2001
Imports from UK	£205,922,000	£229,613,000
Exports to UK	378,142,000	437,863,000

COMMUNICATIONS

There are major seaports at Karachi and Port Qasim. The main airports are at Karachi, Islamabad, Lahore, Peshawar and Quetta. Pakistan International Airlines operates air services between the principal cities as well as abroad. There are 86,597 km of roads and 7,344 km of rail track.

EDUCATION

Education consists of five years of primary education (five to nine years), three years of middle or lower secondary (general or vocational), two years of upper secondary, two years of higher secondary (intermediate) and two to five years of higher education in colleges and universities. Education is free to upper secondary level.
ILLITERACY RATE – 55.1 per cent (2002)
ENROLMENT (percentage of age group) – tertiary 3.0 per cent (1991)

PALAU

Belu'u era Belau/Republic of Palau

AREA – 177 sq. miles (459 sq. km)
POPULATION – 19,092 (2001 estimate); 13,900 live on Koror and Babelthaup. The population is Micronesian, and predominantly Roman Catholic with a Protestant minority. Palauan and English are official languages
CAPITAL – Koror (population, 10,493, 1994)
CURRENCY – Currency is that of the USA
NATIONAL FLAG – Light blue with a yellow disc set near the hoist
LIFE EXPECTANCY (years) – male 65.0; female 69.0
POPULATION GROWTH RATE – 1.8 per cent (1997)
POPULATION DENSITY – 37 per sq. km (1997)

The Republic of Palau consists of 340 islands and islets in the western Pacific Ocean, of which eight are inhabited. Part of the Caroline Islands group, the Palau archipelago

stretches over 400 miles (644 km) between 2° and 8°N., and 131° and 138°E. Koror island is about 810 miles (1,300 km) south-west of Guam and about 530 miles (852 km) south-east of Manila.

HISTORY AND POLITICS

Spain acquired sovereignty over the Caroline Islands, of which the Palau archipelago is part, in 1886. After defeat in the Spanish-American war of 1898, Spain sold its remaining Pacific possessions, including Palau, to Germany in 1899. On the outbreak of the First World War in 1914, Japan took control of Palau on behalf of the Allied powers, and Japanese administration was confirmed in a League of Nations mandate in 1921. During the Second World War, Allied forces gained control of the archipelago after intense fighting. In 1947 the USA entered into agreement with the UN Security Council to administer the Micronesia area, including Palau, as the UN Trust Territory of the Pacific Islands.

In July 1978, the Palau electorate voted in a referendum not to join the new Federated States of Micronesia and instead became a separate part of the UN Trust Territory. A Compact of Free Association was signed with the USA in 1982 and implemented on 1 October 1994. Under this agreement the USA recognised the Republic of Palau as a fully sovereign and independent state and assumed responsibility for its defence for 50 years.

The last presidential and legislative elections were held on 7 November 2000.

POLITICAL SYSTEM

Executive power is vested in the president and vice-president, who are elected for four-year terms; the president appoints the Cabinet. There is a bicameral legislature *(Olbiil era Kelulau)* composed of the 16-member House of Delegates (one member elected from each of the 16 constituent states) and the 14-member Senate. There is also a Council of Chiefs to advise the president on matters concerning traditional law and customs. Each of the 16 component states have their own elected governors and legislatures.

HEAD OF STATE

President, Tommy Remengesau, *elected* 7 November 2000, *took office* 19 January 2001
Vice-President, Administration, Sandra Pierantozzi

CABINET *as at July 2002*

Commerce and Trade, George Ngirarsaol
Community and Cultural Affairs, Riosang Salvador
Education, Billy Kuartei
Health, Masao Ueda
Justice, Salvador Ingereklii
Minister of State, Sabias Anastacio
Resources and Development, Marcelino Melairei

BRITISH AMBASSADOR, HE Michael Price, LVO, resident at Suva, Fiji

ECONOMY

The economy remains heavily dependent on US financial support, which the USA is committed to giving under the Compact. Fisheries, tourism, subsistence agriculture and government service are the main areas of employment. Agricultural products include coconuts and copra, and Palau earns significant revenue from the sale of fishing licences to foreign fleets fishing for tuna. The chief exports are fish, mussels, coconuts and copra. Tourism is being developed; there were 75,139 visitors in 1997. There are three airports on Koror, Peleliu and Angaur which

have daily flights from Guam operated by Continental Micronesia. There are 61 km of roads, of which 36 km are paved. There is a privately owned television station and a government-operated radio station.

GDP – US$119 million (1998); US$6,722 per capita (1999)
ANNUAL AVERAGE GROWTH OF GDP – -4.0 per cent (1998)

Trade with UK	2000	2001
Imports from UK	£78,000	£39,000
Exports to UK	1,000	–

EDUCATION AND SOCIAL WELFARE

There is a free public school system which, together with independent missionary schools, provides primary and secondary education. A tertiary technical school has been established on Koror since 1969. General medical and dental care is provided by a public hospital.

PANAMA
República de Panamá – Republic of Panama

AREA – 29,157 sq. miles (75,517 sq. km). Neighbours: Colombia (east), Costa Rica (west)
POPULATION – 2,815,644 (2000 census): 70 per cent mestizo, 14 per cent mixed Amerindian and black, 10 per cent European, 6 per cent Amerindian. Spanish is the official language
CAPITAL – ΨPanama City (population, 464,928, 2000 census)
CURRENCY – Balboa of 100 centésimos (US notes are also in circulation)
NATIONAL ANTHEM – Alcanzamos Por Fin La Victoria (Victory Is Ours At Last)
NATIONAL DAY – 3 November
NATIONAL FLAG – Four quarters; white with blue star (top, next staff), red (in fly), blue (below, next staff) and white with red star
LIFE EXPECTANCY (years) – male 72.6; female 77.3
POPULATION GROWTH RATE – 1.6 per cent (1999)
POPULATION DENSITY – 37 per sq. km (1999)
URBAN POPULATION – 55.5 per cent (1997)
MILITARY EXPENDITURE – 1.3 per cent of GDP (2000)
MILITARY PERSONNEL – Paramilitaries: 11,800
ILLITERACY RATE – 7.7 per cent (2002)
ENROLMENT (percentage of age group) – primary 100 per cent (1997); secondary 69 per cent (1997); tertiary 32 per cent (1997)

HISTORY AND POLITICS

After a revolt in 1903, Panama declared its independence from Colombia and established a separate government.

On 25 February 1998, President Delvalle was removed by the National Assembly. Presidential elections were held in May 1989 but Gen. Noriega, the Commander of the Defence Forces, annulled the results and on 15 December he assumed power formally as head of state. On 20 December US troops invaded Panama to oust Noriega. Guillermo Endara, believed to have won the May elections, was installed as president. In December 1991 the Legislative Assembly approved a change to the constitution which abolished the armed forces. The most recent presidential election, on 2 May 1999, was won by Mireya Elisa Moscoso de Gruber of the Union for Panama coalition. Simultaneous legislative elections were won by the New Nation coalition with 46 of the 71 contested seats.

POLITICAL SYSTEM

Legislative power is vested in a unicameral Legislative Assembly of 71 members; executive power is held by the president, assisted by two elected vice-presidents and an appointed Cabinet. Elections are held every five years under a system of universal and compulsory adult suffrage.

HEAD OF STATE

President, Mireya Elisa Moscoso de Gruber, *elected* 2 May 1999, *sworn in* 1 September 1999
First Vice-President, Arturo Vallarino
Second Vice-President, Dominador Kaiser Bazán

CABINET *as at July 2002*

Agricultural Development, Pedro Adán Gordón
Canal Affairs, Ricardo Martinelli Berrocal
Commerce and Industry, Joaquín Jácome Diez
Education, Doris Rosas de Mata
Finance and Economy, Norberto Delgado
Foreign Relations, José Miguel Alemán
Health, Fernando Gracia García
Housing, Miguel Cárdenas
Interior and Justice, Anibal Raul Salas
Labour and Social Welfare, Joaquín José Vallarino III
Presidency, Ivonne Young Valdez
Public Works, Victor Juliao
Women, Youth, Family and Children, Alba Ester Tejada de Rolla

EMBASSY OF THE REPUBLIC OF PANAMA

40 Hertford Street, London W1J 7SH
Tel: 020-7493 4646
Ambassador Extraordinary and Plenipotentiary, HE Ariadne Singares Robinson, apptd 2000
Counsellor (Financial and Commercial), S. Kheireddine

BRITISH EMBASSY

Torre Swiss Bank, Calle 53 (Apartado 889) Zona 1, Panama City
Tel: (00 507) 269 0866
Ambassador Extraordinary and Plenipotentiary, HE Jim Malcolm, OBE, *apptd* 2002

ECONOMY

The soil is moderately fertile, but nearly one-half of the land is uncultivated. The chief crops are bananas, sugar, coconuts, coffee and cereals. Over 13,000 foreign ships are registered in Panama. The shrimping industry plays an important role in the economy. Tourism is the principal foreign currency earner. There are 547 km of railway track and 10,792 km of roads.

GNP – US$9,316 million (2000); US$3,080 per capita (1999)
GDP – US$9,097 million (1998); US$3,397 per capita (1999)
ANNUAL AVERAGE GROWTH OF GDP – 2.7 per cent (2000)
INFLATION RATE – 1.4 per cent (2000)
UNEMPLOYMENT – 11.8 per cent (1999)
TOTAL EXTERNAL DEBT – US$7,313 million (1999)

TRADE

Imports are mostly manufactured goods, machinery, lubricants, chemicals and foodstuffs. Exports are bananas, petroleum products, shrimps, sugar, meat, coffee and fishmeal.

In 2000 Panama had a trade deficit of US$1,291 million and a current account deficit of US$927 million. Imports totalled US$3,379 million and exports US$859 million.

Trade with UK†	2000	2001
Imports from UK	£48,171,000	£64,523,000
Exports to UK	8,153,000	10,029,000

†Including Colón Free Zone

THE PANAMA CANAL ZONE

The Panama Canal Zone was created in 1903 by a contract between Panama and the USA, under which the USA was given the right to build and operate the canal and administer the adjacent territory. With effect from 1 October 1979 the Canal Zone (1,142 sq. km/647 sq. miles) was disestablished, with all areas of land and water within the Zone reverting to Panama. By the 1977 treaty with the USA, the USA was allowed the use of operating bases for the Panama Canal, together with several military bases, but the Republic of Panama was sovereign in all such areas. Control of the Canal reverted to Panama at noon on 31 December 1999.

In the fiscal year 2000, the total number of transits by ocean-going commercial traffic was 12,303; canal net tons totalled 229,459,659; cargo tons totalled 193,714,277.

PAPUA NEW GUINEA

Independent State of Papua New Guinea/Gau Hedinarai ai Papua-Matamata Guinea

AREA – 178,704 sq. miles (462,840 sq. km). Neighbour: Indonesia (west, on New Guinea)
POPULATION – 5,049,055 (2001 estimate). English is the official language; Hiri Motu and Neo-Melanesian are widely used
CAPITAL – ΨPort Moresby (population, 173,500, 1990)
MAJOR CITIES – Goroka; Lae; Madang; Mount Hagen; Rabaul; Wewak
CURRENCY – Kina (K) of 100 toea
NATIONAL ANTHEM – Arise All You Sons
NATIONAL DAY – 16 September (Independence Day)
NATIONAL FLAG – Divided diagonally red (fly) and black (hoist); on the red a soaring Bird of Paradise in yellow and on the black five white stars of the Southern Cross
LIFE EXPECTANCY (years) – male 56.8; female 58.7
POPULATION GROWTH RATE – 3.6 per cent (1999)
POPULATION DENSITY – 10 per sq. km (1999)
MILITARY EXPENDITURE – 1.2 per cent of GDP (2000)
MILITARY PERSONNEL – 4,400: Army 3,800, Navy 400, Air Force 200
ILLITERACY RATE – 34.7 per cent (2002)
ENROLMENT (percentage of age group) – tertiary 3 per cent (1997)

The country has many island groups, principally the Bismarck Archipelago, a portion of the Solomon Islands, the Trobriands, the D'Entrecasteaux Islands and the Louisade Archipelago. The main islands of the Bismarck Archipelago are New Britain, New Ireland and Manus. Bougainville is the largest of the Solomon Islands within Papua New Guinea.

HISTORY AND POLITICS

In 1884 a British protectorate, British New Guinea, was proclaimed over the southern coast of New Guinea (Papua) and the adjacent islands, which were annexed outright in 1888. In 1906 the territory was placed under the authority of Australia. The northern areas were under German administration between 1884 and 1914, when they were occupied by Australian troops and in 1921 became a League of Nations mandate administered by

Australia. The territories were occupied by Japan between 1942 and 1945.

From 1970 there was a gradual assumption of powers by the Papua New Guinea government, culminating in formal self-government in December 1973. Papua New Guinea achieved full independence within the Commonwealth on 16 September 1975.

On 14 March 2001 there was a mutiny by disaffected troops angry at defence cuts and poor equipment and living conditions, who demanded the resignation of the government. The mutineers were granted an amnesty after they peacefully surrendered their weapons on 26 March.

Following elections in June 2002, a coalition government was formed, which was led by the National Alliance Party (NAP).

INSURGENCIES

Following a 1989 insurrection, the Bougainville Revolutionary Army (BRA) declared an independent republic in May 1990. Government forces returned to the island in October 1992, subsequently capturing 90 per cent of rebel-held territory.

A permanent cease-fire came into effect on 30 April 1998, bringing to an end the nine-year civil war. A small group of rebels led by Francis Ona vowed to continue the armed campaign for an independent Bougainville. An interim Bougainville Reconciliation Government was established on 1 January 1999, which renamed itself the Bougainville People's Congress in April. Elections were held in early May. Joseph Kabui, a former rebel leader, was elected president. Agreement was reached on 26 January 2001 that a referendum on the future of Bougainville should be held within 15 years. The BRA surrendered its weapons during May and a final agreement was reached on 24 June 2001, which granted Bougainville its own system of criminal law, and a separate police force and limited the role of the military.

POLITICAL SYSTEM

Elections are held every five years. The National Parliament comprises 109 elected members, 20 from regional electorates, the remainder from open electorates. The Governor-General is appointed by parliament for a six-year term. Provincial governments were abolished in August 1995, and replaced with councils combining local and national politicians and headed by an appointed governor.

GOVERNOR-GENERAL, HE Sir Silas Atopare, GCMG, *appointed* 14 November 1997

NATIONAL EXECUTIVE COUNCIL *as at August 2002*

Prime Minister, Sir Michael Somare
Deputy Prime Minister, Trade and Industry, Allan Marat
Agriculture and Livestock, Moses Maladina
Attorney-General, Michael Gene
Communications and Information, Ben Semri
Correctional Institution Services, Peter Oresi
Culture and Tourism, Alois King
Defence, Yarka Kappa
Education, Michael Laimo
Environment and Conservation, Sasa Zibe
Finance and Treasury, Bart Philemon
Fisheries, Andrew Baing
Foreign Affairs and Trade, Sir Rabbie Namaliu
Forestry, Patrick Pruaitch
Health, Melchior Pep
Housing, Yuntuvi Bao
Inter-government Relations, Sir Peter Barter

Internal Security, Yawa Silupa
Justice, Mark Maipakai
Labour and Industrial Relations, Peter O'Neill
Lands and Physical Planning, Robert Koopaol
Mining, Sam Akoitai
National Planning and Monitoring, Sinai Brown
Petroleum and Energy, Sir Moi Avei
Public Service, Puka Temu
Science and Technology, Alphonse Moroi
Transport and Civil Aviation, Don Polye
Welfare and Social Development, Lady Carol Kidu
Works, Gabriel Karpis

PAPUA NEW GUINEA HIGH COMMISSION
3rd Floor, 14 Waterloo Place, London SW1R 4AR
Tel: 020-7930 0922/7
High Commissioner, HE Jean L. Kekedo, OBE, apptd 2002

BRITISH HIGH COMMISSION
PO Box 212, Waigani NCD 131, Port Moresby
Tel: (00 675) 325 1643/1645
Email: bhcpng@datec.com.pg
High Commissioner, HE Simon Mansfield Scadden, apptd 2000

ECONOMY

A variety of commercial agricultural developments co-exist with the traditional rural economy. In 1995, the government initiated an austerity programme intended to reduce the budget deficit, privatise state assets and eliminate trade tariffs. Following prolonged drought and the financial crisis in south-east Asia, the country is facing its worst financial crisis since independence, with debt servicing amounting to a quarter of government spending.

There are extensive mineral deposits throughout Papua New Guinea, including copper, gold, silver, nickel, bauxite and commercial deposits of oil. The Bougainville copper mine, run by the Anglo-Australian consortium Rio Tinto, closed indefinitely in 1989 because of the unrest on the island. It had provided more than 15 per cent of the country's annual revenue. On 7 September 2000, landowners on Bougainville filed a damages claim against Rio Tinto, alleging that the company had caused environmental, social and health damage in its running of the mine and that the company had effectively controlled the Papuan military in its operations on Bougainville, which, it was claimed, had resulted in 15,000 civilian deaths. Industry includes processing of primary products, and brewing, packaging, paint, plywood, and metal manufacturing and the construction industries.

In 1999 there was a trade surplus of US$856 million and a current account surplus of US$95 million. In 2000 imports totalled US$1,142 million and exports US$2,021 million.

GNP – US$3,665 million (2000); US$810 per capita (1999)
GDP – US$3,480 million (1998); US$759 per capita (1999)
ANNUAL AVERAGE GROWTH OF GDP – 3.9 per cent (1999)
INFLATION RATE – 15.6 per cent (2000)
TOTAL EXTERNAL DEBT – US$2,847 million (1999)

Trade with UK	2000	2001
Imports from UK	£5,374,000	£4,319,000
Exports to UK	56,144,000	41,438,000

COMMUNICATIONS

Air Niugini operates regular air services to other countries in the region, as well as internal air services.

Several shipping companies operate cargo services to Australia, Europe, the Far East and USA. There are very limited cargo and passenger services between Papua New Guinea main ports, outports, plantations and missions. There are 21,433 km of roads, the most important road being that linking Lae with the populous highlands. Papua New Guinea is linked by international cable to Australia, Guam, Hong Kong, the Far East and the USA.

PARAGUAY
República del Paraguay – Republic of Paraguay

AREA – 157,048 sq. miles (406,752 sq. km). Neighbours: Bolivia (north-west), Brazil (north-east and east), Argentina (south)

POPULATION – 5,734,139 (2001 estimate): 95 per cent mestizo. Spanish is the official language of the country but outside the larger towns Guaraní, the language of the largest single group of Amerindian inhabitants, is widely spoken, and is also an official language

CAPITAL – Asunción (population, 550,060 1997)

MAJOR CITIES – Ciudad del Este (133,881); San Lorenzo (133,395)

CURRENCY – Guaraní (Gs) of 100 céntimos

NATIONAL ANTHEM – Paraguayos, República O Muerte (Paraguayans, Republic Or Death)

NATIONAL DAY – 15 May

NATIONAL FLAG – Three horizontal bands, red, white, blue with the National seal on the obverse white band and the Treasury seal on the reverse white band

LIFE EXPECTANCY (years) – male 68.6; female 73.1

POPULATION GROWTH RATE – 2.6 per cent (1999)

POPULATION DENSITY – 13 per sq. km (1999)

MILITARY EXPENDITURE – 1.3 per cent of GDP (2000)

MILITARY PERSONNEL – 18,600: Army 14,900, Navy 2,000, Air Force 1,700; Paramilitaries 14,800

CONSCRIPTION DURATION – One to two years

Paraguay is an inland subtropical state of South America, situated between Argentina, Bolivia and Brazil. It is a country of grassy plains and forested hills. In the angle formed by the Paraná-Paraguay confluence are extensive marshes, one of which, known as Neembucú (or endless) is drained by Lake Ypoa, a large lagoon south-east of the capital. The Chaco, lying between the rivers Paraguay and Pilcomayo and bounded on the north by Bolivia, is a flat plain, rising uniformly towards its western boundary to a height of 1,140 feet; it suffers from floods and drought, but the building of dams and reservoirs has converted part of it into good pasture for cattle.

HISTORY AND POLITICS

Paraguay was settled as a Spanish possession in 1537 and became independent in 1811.

Gen. Alfredo Stroessner, dictator from 1954, was overthrown in February 1989 by Gen. Andrés Rodríguez, who was elected president in May 1989. Elections to the parliament were held in December 1991. Amendments to the constitution came into effect in June 1992. The last presidential and legislative elections were held on 10 May 1998. The presidential election was won by Raúl Cubas Grau of the Colorado Party, after its original candidate Gen. Lino Oviedo was banned from standing in elections for his part in a failed coup in 1996. In the legislative election, the distribution of seats in the Senate was: Colorado Party (CP) 24; Democratic Alliance (DA) 20; Blanco Party 1. In the Chamber of Deputies, the CP won 45 seats and the DA 35.

Vice-President Luis María Argaña was assassinated on 23 March 1999, following a power struggle between his supporters and those of President Cubas Grau and Gen. Oviedo. Supporters of Argaña demanded the resignation of the president and an indefinite general strike was called. The Chamber of Deputies voted to initiate impeachment proceedings against President Cubas Grau. He resigned on 28 March and was granted asylum in Brazil. The president of the Senate, Luis González Macchi, was immediately sworn in as the new president. Gen. Oviedo fled to Argentina, where he was granted asylum, but in December fled to Brazil. An attempted coup, thought to be by supporters of Gen. Oviedo, was foiled by government forces on 18 May 2000. Gen. Oviedo was arrested in Brazil on 11 June 2000 pending extradition proceedings.

A vice-presidential election was held on 13 August 2000 and was won by Julio César Franco of the Authentic Radical Liberal Party. Legislative and presidential elections were scheduled for 27 April 2003.

POLITICAL SYSTEM

The constitution provides for a two-chamber legislature consisting of a 45-member Senate and an 80-member Chamber of Deputies, both elected for five-year terms. Deputies are elected on a regional basis, the number of seats allocated to each regional department being directly proportional to the department's population. Voting is compulsory for all citizens over 18. The president is elected for a five-year term and may not be re-elected. The vice-president may only contest the presidency if he resigns his post six months before the election. The president appoints the Cabinet, which exercises all the functions of government.

HEAD OF STATE
President, Luis González Macchi, *sworn in* 28 March 1999
Vice-President, Julio César Franco

CABINET *as at July 2002*

Agriculture and Livestock, Pedro Lino Morel
Defence, Adm. Miguel Angel Candia
Education and Culture, Dario Zárate Arellano
Executive Secretary of the Technical Secretariat of Planning and Economic and Social Development of the Republic, Luis Alberto Meyer
Finance and Economy, James Spalding
Foreign Affairs, José Antonio Moreno Ruffinelli
Industry and Commerce, Euclides Acevedo
Interior, Francisco Oviedo
Justice and Labour, Silvio Ferreira
Public Health and Social Welfare, Martín Chiola
Public Works, Communications, Alcides Jiménez
Secretary for Women's Affairs, Cristina Muñoz

EMBASSY OF PARAGUAY
344 High Street Kensington, 3rd Floor, London W14 8NS
Tel: 020-7937 1253/6629
Ambassador Extraordinary and Plenipotentiary, Raúl Dos Santos, apptd 1998

BRITISH EMBASSY
Avda. Boggiani 5848, C/R 16 Boquerón, Asunción
Tel: (00 595) (21) 612611
Email: brembasu@rieder.net.py
Ambassador Extraordinary and Plenipotentiary and Consul-General, HE Anthony Cantor, apptd 2001

ECONOMY

President Rodríguez introduced an economic liberalisation programme which has been continued by subsequent governments. In November 2000, Congress approved a privatisation programme. This has reduced foreign debt and attracted foreign investment, notably from Brazil. About half of the population are engaged in agriculture and cattle raising. Cassava, sugar cane, soya, cotton and wheat are the main agricultural products. The forests contain many varieties of timber which find a good market abroad. Paraguay's rivers give it considerable hydroelectric capacity. There is a hydroelectric power station at Acaray which exports surplus power to Argentina and Brazil. Joint projects have been undertaken with Brazil, on a hydroelectric dam at Itaipú (the largest in the world), and with Argentina, at Yacyretá.

GNP – US$7,991 million (2000); US$1,560 per capita (1999)

GDP – US$8,505 million (1998); US$1,445 per capita (1999)

ANNUAL AVERAGE GROWTH OF GDP – -0.4 per cent (2000)

INFLATION RATE – 9.0 per cent (2000)

UNEMPLOYMENT – 8.2 per cent (1996)

TOTAL EXTERNAL DEBT – US$2,514 million (1999)

TRADE

The chief imports are machinery, fuels and lubricants, vehicles, drinks and tobacco. The chief exports are soya, cotton fibres, meat, timber and coffee. The main trading partners are Brazil, Argentina and the USA.

In 2000 Paraguay had a trade deficit of US$532 million and a current account deficit of US$137 million. In 1999 imports totalled US$1,725 million and exports US$741 million.

Trade with UK	2000	2001
Imports from UK	£24,144,000	£22,047,000
Exports to UK	1,265,000	2,176,000

COMMUNICATIONS

There are direct shipping services from Asunción to Europe and the USA, and river steamer services for internal transport. Eight airlines operate services from Asunción. There are 28,900 km of roads in Paraguay, connecting Asunción with São Paulo via the Bridge of Friendship and Foz de Yguazú, and with Buenos Aires via Puerto Pilcomayo. Many earth roads are liable to be closed or to become impassable in wet weather. There are 971 km of railway track. Rail services, with train ferries, provide internal and international links.

EDUCATION

Education is free and compulsory. There are 11 universities and one institute of education.

ILLITERACY RATE – 6.3 per cent (2002)

ENROLMENT (percentage of age group) – primary 100 per cent (1997); secondary 47 per cent (1997); tertiary 10 per cent (1997)

PERU

República del Perú – Republic of Peru

AREA – 496,225 sq. miles (1,285,216 sq. km).
Neighbours: Ecuador and Colombia (north), Brazil and Bolivia (east), Chile (south)

POPULATION – 27,483,864 (2001 estimate): 50 per cent Amerindian, 40 per cent mestizo, 7 per cent European, also Africans, Chinese and Japanese. The official languages are Spanish and Quechua. Aymara is also widely spoken

CAPITAL – Lima (including ΨCallao, population, 6,321,173, 1993 census)

MAJOR CITIES – Arequipa (624,500); Chiclayo (448,400); Chimbote (314,700); Trujillo (521,200)

CURRENCY – New Sol of 100 cénts

NATIONAL ANTHEM – Somos Libres, Seámoslo Siempre (We Are Free, Let Us Remain So Forever)

NATIONAL DAY – 28 July (Anniversary of Independence)

NATIONAL FLAG – Three vertical stripes of red, white, red

LIFE EXPECTANCY (years) – male 67.3; female 72.4

POPULATION GROWTH RATE – 1.7 per cent (1999)

POPULATION DENSITY – 20 per sq. km (1999)

MILITARY EXPENDITURE – 1.3 per cent of GDP (2000)

MILITARY PERSONNEL – 100,000: Army 60,000, Navy 25,000, Air Force 15,000; Paramilitaries 77,000

CONSCRIPTION DURATION – Two years (selective)

The country is traversed throughout its length by the Andes, running parallel to the Pacific coast. There are three main regions, the Costa, west of the Andes, the Sierra or mountain ranges of the Andes, which include the Punas or mountainous wastes below the region of perpetual snow, and the Montaña or Selva, which is the vast area of jungle stretching from the eastern foothills of the Andes to the eastern frontiers of Peru. The coastal area, lying upon and near the Pacific, is not tropical though close to the Equator, being cooled by the Humboldt Current.

HISTORY AND POLITICS

Peru was conquered in the early 16th century by Francisco Pizarro (1478–1541). He subjugated the Incas (the ruling caste of the Quechua Indians), who had started their rise to power some 500 years earlier, and for nearly three centuries Peru remained under Spanish rule. A revolutionary war of 1821–4 established its independence, declared on 28 July 1821. A military junta ruled Peru from 1968 until 1980 when civilian government was restored.

In April 1992 President Fujimori, faced with increasing terrorist violence, suspended the constitution, dissolved Congress and began to govern by decree. In November 1992 a legislative election was held to an 80-seat Democratic Constituent Congress (CCD) which was installed as an interim legislature and constituent assembly to write a new constitution. Parties supporting Fujimori's suspension of the constitution gained a majority in the CCD. In January 1993, the 1979 constitution was re-established and the CCD declared Fujimori constitutional head of state. The CCD produced a new constitution which was endorsed in a national referendum in October 1993.

Parliamentary and presidential elections were held on 9 April 1995, with President Fujimori winning the first round of the presidential election outright and his Cambio 90-Nueva Mayoría Party winning 67 out of 120 seats in the new *Congreso de la República* (Congress of the Republic).

President Fujimori announced in December 1999 that he would run for a third term of office. Following objections by the opposition, the National Elections Board ruled that Fujimori had been elected president only once since the introduction of the 1993 constitution and was therefore eligible to stand again. President Fujimori was unable to win the first round of the presidential election on 9 April 2000 outright, but polled

the most votes. In the simultaneous legislative election, his Peru 2000 alliance won 51 seats, losing its absolute majority. The Peru Possible party won 28 seats and the Moralising Independent Front won nine seats. In the second round of the presidential election on 28 May, President Fujimori was re-elected with 51.2 per cent of the vote after his opponent, Alejandro Toledo of the Peru Possible party refused to campaign, following accusations of widespread ballot rigging in the first round. Although voting was compulsory, Toledo asked his supporters to spoil their ballot papers; he gained 17.7 per cent of the votes and 31.1 per cent of ballot papers were spoiled. The chief of the Organisation of American States observer mission concluded that the entire electoral process had been irregular.

President Fujimori announced on 16 September 2000 that he intended to step down and call a presidential election in which he would not stand. Following his attendance at an APEC summit in Brunei, Fujimori fled to Japan and announced his resignation on 17 November. Congress voted on 21 November to reject Fujimori's resignation and instead dismissed him on the grounds of moral incapacity, and Valentín Paniagua of the Popular Action party was sworn in as interim president the following day.

A general election was held on 8 April 2001 in which the Peru Possible (PP) party won 43 seats and the Peruvian Aprista Party (APRA) won 28 seats. The presidential election was held in two rounds on 8 April and 3 June and was won by the PP candidate, Alejandro Toledo, who was sworn in as president on 28 July, becoming the first Amerindian to hold the position.

FOREIGN RELATIONS

A 78-km stretch of the border with Ecuador has been in dispute since 1960. In 1995 an inconclusive border war was fought between the two countries, and in July 1995 a demilitarised zone was established around the disputed area. Four guarantor countries (Argentina, Brazil, Chile and the USA) adjudicated the claims of both countries and produced an agreement which was signed on 26 October 1998 by the presidents of Ecuador and Peru, formally ending the dispute.

INSURGENCIES

Since the late 1970s the government has faced violence from drug organisations and insurgencies from two leftist guerrilla movements, the Maoist Sendero Luminoso (Shining Path) and the Movimiento Revolucionario Túpac Amaru (MRTA), with fighting having left 30,000 dead.

Security forces captured the leader of the MRTA in November 1998 and the leader of Shining Path in December 1998.

On 20 March 2002 two bombs exploded in Lima ahead of the visit to the country of US President George W. Bush on 23 March. Nine people were killed in one of the bomb attacks, which were believed to be the work of a faction of the Shining Path guerrilla movement.

POLITICAL SYSTEM

The constitution, promulgated in December 1993, provides for the president to be able to serve two terms rather than one, as previously; the introduction of the death penalty for treason; and the formation of a new 120-member unicameral Congress. A constitutional panel approved a Bill in August 1996, allowing President Fujimori to stand for a third term in office.

HEAD OF STATE
President of the Republic, Alejandro Toledo Manrique, elected 3 June 2001, sworn in 28 July 2001
First Vice-President, Diez Canseco
Second Vice-President, David Waisman

CABINET as at August 2002
President of the Council of Ministers, Roberto Dañino
Advancement of Women, Human Development, Cecilia Blondet
Agriculture, Alvaro Quijandria
Defence, Aurelio Loret de Mola
Economy and Finance, Pedro Pablo Kuczynski
Education, Nicolás Lynch
Energy and Mines, Jaime Quijandria
Fisheries, Javier Reategui Rosello
Foreign Affairs, Diego García Sayan
Health, Fernando Carbone Campoverde
Industry, Tourism, Integration and International Commerce, Raúl Diez Canseco
Interior, Gino Costa
Justice, Fernando Olivera
Labour and Social Promotion, Fernando Villarán
Presidency, Carlos Ricardo Bruce
Transport, Communications and Housing, Luis Vicente Chang Reyes

EMBASSY OF PERU
52 Sloane Street, London SW1X 9SP
Tel: 020-7235 1917/2545/8302
Ambassador Extraordinary and Plenipotentiary, HE Armando Lecaros-de-Cossío, apptd 2002

BRITISH EMBASSY
Torre Parque Mar (Piso 22), Avenida José Larco 1301, Miraflores, Lima 18 Tel: (00 51) (1) 617 3000
Email: britemb@terra.com.pe
Ambassador Extraordinary and Plenipotentiary, HE Roger Dudley Hart, CMG, apptd 1999

CONSULAR OFFICE – Lima

HONORARY CONSULATES – Arequipa, Cusco, Iquitos, Piura, Trujillo

BRITISH COUNCIL DIRECTOR, Gail Liesching, c/o British Embassy, Lima
Email: bc.lima@britishcouncil.org.pe

ECONOMY

The chief products of the coastal belt are cotton, sugar and petroleum. There are large tracts of land suitable for cultivation and stock-raising (cattle, sheep, llamas, alpacas and vicuñas) on the eastern slopes of the Andes, and in the mountain valleys maize, potatoes and wheat are grown. The jungle area is a source of timber and petroleum. Other major crops are fruit, vegetables, rice, barley, grapes and coffee. The mountains contain rich mineral deposits and mineral exports include lead, zinc, copper, iron ore and silver. Peru is normally the world's largest exporter of fishmeal.

Since 1990 the government has launched a radical free-market restructuring programme which has rebuilt foreign exchange reserves, reduced inflation from 7,600 per cent a year in 1990 to four per cent in 1999, cut subsidies and import tariffs, freed interest rates and privatised most state firms. Foreign investment has been encouraged and has grown dramatically. The economic recovery has increased the gap between rich and poor.

Following a slowdown in economic growth, falling output, rising unemployment and a decline in the

popularity of the government, further privatisation has been halted.

GNP – US$53,898 million (2000); US$2,130 per capita (1999)
GDP – US$62,518 million (1998); US$2,060 per capita (1999)
ANNUAL AVERAGE GROWTH OF GDP – 3.1 per cent (2000)
INFLATION RATE – 3.8 per cent (2000)
UNEMPLOYMENT – 8.0 per cent (1999)
TOTAL EXTERNAL DEBT – US$32,284 million (1999)

TRADE

The principal imports are machinery, chemicals and pharmaceutical products. The chief exports are minerals and metals, fishmeal, sugar, cotton and coffee.

In 2000 Peru had a trade deficit of US$323 million and a current account deficit of US$1,628 million. Imports totalled US$8,797 million and exports US$7,028 million.

Trade with UK	2000	2001
Imports from UK	£45,975,000	£41,209,000
Exports to UK	142,472,000	166,553,000

COMMUNICATIONS

There are 73,766 km of roads, of which 16,876 km are unsurfaced. The Andean Highway forms a link between the Pacific, the Amazon and the Atlantic. The Pan-American Highway runs along the Peruvian coast connecting it with Ecuador and Chile.

The railway is administered by the government. There are 1,992 km of railway track. There is also steam navigation on the Ucayali and Huallaga, and in the south on Lake Titicaca. Air services are maintained throughout Peru, and there is an international airport at Lima.

EDUCATION

Education is compulsory and free between seven and 16. There are 51 universities.

ILLITERACY RATE – 9.4 per cent (2002)
ENROLMENT (percentage of age group) – primary 100 per cent (1997); secondary 73 per cent (1997); tertiary 26 per cent (1997)

THE PHILIPPINES
Repúblika ng Pilipinas – Republic of the Philippines

AREA – 115,831 sq. miles (300,000 sq. km)
POPULATION – 82,841,518 (2001 estimate). The inhabitants are of Malay stock, with admixtures of Spanish and Chinese blood in many localities. The Chinese minority is estimated at 500,000, with smaller numbers of Spanish, American and Indian. About 90 per cent are Christian, predominantly Roman Catholics. Most of the remainder are Muslims or indigenous animists. The official languages are Filipino and English. Filipino is based on Tagalog, one of the Malay–Polynesian languages. English, the language of government, is spoken by at least 44 per cent of the population. Spanish is now spoken by a very small minority

CAPITAL – ΨManila (population, 8,594,150, 1994)
MAJOR CITIES – Bacolod (402,345); ΨCebu (662,299); ΨDavao (1,008,640); ΨIloilo (334,539); ΨZamboanga (511,139), 1995 UN estimates
CURRENCY – Philippine peso (P) of 100 centavos
NATIONAL ANTHEM – Lupang Hinirang (Beloved Land)
NATIONAL DAY – 12 June (Independence Day 1898)
NATIONAL FLAG – Equal horizontal bands of blue

(above) and red; gold sun with three stars on a white triangle next to staff
LIFE EXPECTANCY (years) – male 68.0; female 72.0
POPULATION GROWTH RATE – 1.5 per cent (1999)
POPULATION DENSITY – 249 per sq. km (1999)

There are 11 larger islands and 7,079 other islands. The principal islands (area in sq. km) are: Luzon (104,688); Mindanao (94,630); Samar (13,080); Negros (12,710); Palawan (11,785); Panay (11,515); Mindoro (9,735); Leyte (7,214); Cebu (4,422); Bohol (3,865); Masbate (3,269). Other groups are the Sulu islands (capital, Jolo), Babuyanes and Batanes; the Calamian islands; and Kalayaan Islands.

HISTORY AND POLITICS

The Philippines were conquered by Spain in 1565 and named Filipinas after Philip II of Spain. Independence was declared on 12 June 1898. In the Spanish–American War of 1898, Manila was captured by American troops and remained under US control until 1946. The Republic of the Philippines came into existence on 4 July 1946.

Ferdinand Marcos was president from 1965 to 1986, when he was forced from power by Corazón Aquino, who took over as president and survived seven coup attempts. Fidel Ramos was elected president in May 1992 and was succeeded by Joseph Estrada, the former Vice-President, in May 1998.

The House of Representatives voted on 13 November 2000 to initiate impeachment proceedings against President Estrada, accusing him of corruption. The trial began on 7 December 2000 in the Senate, but foundered on 16 January 2001 after senators refused to consider evidence which allegedly proved Estrada's guilt, and the trial was indefinitely adjourned on the following day. Up to 500,000 demonstrators, led by Vice-President Gloria Macapagal-Arroyo and supported by former presidents Corazón Aquino and Fidel Ramos, gathered in Manila and called on Estrada to resign. On 19 January, the armed forces announced that they had withdrawn their support from the president and on 20 January the Supreme Court ruled that the presidency was vacant, thus allowing Macapagal-Arroyo to be sworn in. Her legitimacy as president was confirmed by the Supreme Court on 2 March.

Elections were held for the House of Representatives and 13 of the 24 Senate seats on 14 May 2001.

INSURGENCIES

On 2 September 1996, the government signed an agreement with the Moro National Liberation Front (MNLF) on the creation of an autonomous Muslim region in Mindanao, Palawan, Sulu and Basilan, ending a 24-year rebellion which had left more than 120,000 people dead. The Moro Islamic Liberation Front (MILF), a radical breakaway group, threatened to disrupt the agreement. The Communist New People's Army (NPA) maintains a presence in eastern Mindanao, Negros, Samar, Bicol, the mountains of northern Luzon and Bataan. The NPA signed a cease-fire agreement with the government in December 1993; peace talks were suspended in February 1999.

On 23 April 2000, 21 people, including ten foreign tourists, were kidnapped on the Malaysian island of Sipadan and taken to the Philippine island of Jolo by Abu Sayyaf, an Islamic rebel group.

The army captured the MILF military headquarters on 9 July 2000, following which MILF withdrew from peace talks scheduled for August. After military action against MILF was formally ended on 6 February 2001, MILF

declared a cease-fire on 3 April and negotiations with the government led to a comprehensive peace deal which came into effect on 22 June. Further peace agreements were signed on 6 and 7 May 2002, which dealt with the MILF's co-operation with the armed forces and the police in the areas it controlled and entrusted government funds to the MILF as reparation for areas of Mindanao devastated by the government's military offensives in 2000.

POLITICAL SYSTEM

A new constitution came into force in July 1987. Legislative authority is vested in a bicameral Congress. The House of Representatives has 250 members, of whom 204 are directly elected and 46 appointed by the President for a three-year term. The Senate has 24 members, of whom 12 are re-elected every three years.

The Autonomous Region of Mindanao consists of four provinces: Sulu, Tawitawi, Lanao del Sur and Maguinadanao. There is a 24-member regional assembly and a governor.

HEAD OF STATE

President, Foreign Affairs, Gloria Macapagal Arroyo, assumed office 20 January 2001
Vice-President, Teofisto Guingona

CABINET *as at July 2002*

Agrarian Reform, Hernani Braganza
Agriculture, Leonardo Montemayor
Budget and Management, Emilia Boncodin
Defence, Gen. Angelo Reyes
Education, Culture and Sport, Raúl Roco
Energy, Vicente Perez
Environment and Natural Resources, Heherson Álvarez
Executive Secretary, Alberto Romulo
Finance, José Isidro Camacho
Health, Manuel Dayrit
Housing, Michael Defensor
Interior and Local Government, José Lina
Justice, Hernando Perez
Labour and Employment, Patricia Santo Tomás
Presidential Advisor for Special Concerns, Norberto Gonzales
Public Works and Highways, Simeon Datumanong
Science and Technology, Estrella Alabastro
Social Welfare and Development, Corazón Solimon
Socio-economic Planning, Dante Canlas
Tourism, Richard Gordon
Trade and Industry, Manuel Roxas
Transportation and Communications, Gen. Leandro Mendoza

EMBASSY OF THE REPUBLIC OF THE PHILIPPINES
9A Palace Green, London W8 4QE
Tel: 020-7937 1600
Ambassador Extraordinary and Plenipotentiary, HE César Bautista, apptd 1999

BRITISH EMBASSY
Floors 15–17, LV Locsin Building, 6752 Ayala Avenue, Corner Makati Avenue, 1226 Makati, Metro Manila (PO Box 2927 MCPO)
Tel: (00 63) (2) 816 7116
Email: uk@info.com.ph
Ambassador Extraordinary and Plenipotentiary, HE Paul Dimond, apptd 2002

BRITISH COUNCIL DIRECTOR, Gill Westaway, 10th Floor, Taipan Place, Emerald Avenue, Ortigas Centre, Pasig City 1605, Metro Manila
Email: britishcouncil@britishcouncil.org.ph

DEFENCE

The Army has 85 armoured infantry fighting vehicles and 370 armoured personnel carriers. The Navy has one frigate and 58 patrol and coastal vessels at three bases. The Air Force has 44 combat aircraft and 97 armed helicopters.
MILITARY EXPENDITURE – 1.9 per cent of GDP (2000)
MILITARY PERSONNEL – 107,000: Army 67,000, Navy 24,000, Air Force 16,000; Paramilitaries 44,000

ECONOMY

In 1998, 39.8 per cent of the workforce were engaged in agriculture. The chief products are rice, coconuts, sugar cane, bananas, maize and pineapples. There is an increasing number of manufacturing industries and it is the policy of the government to diversify the economy. There are also deposits of copper, coal, gold, silver, chromium, iron and nickel.

The Philippines has been bypassed by the economic growth of most of the rest of south-east Asia since the 1960s, mainly because of the incompetence and corruption of the Marcos regime. Recently, however, an economic reform programme of liberalisation, privatisation and deregulation has been put in place and has led to increased exports, increased foreign investment, and a reduction in inflation. In July 1998, the Bank of the Philippines effectively devalued the peso following attacks from speculators, prompted by the devaluation of the Thai baht. Prompt and firm measures from the government are credited with limiting the damage caused by the regional economic crisis.
GNP – US$78,705 million (2000); US$1,050 per capita (1999)
GDP – US$65,221 million (1998); US$1,032 per capita (1999)
ANNUAL AVERAGE GROWTH OF GDP – 4.0 per cent (2000)
INFLATION RATE – 4.4 per cent (2000)
UNEMPLOYMENT – 9.4 per cent (1999)
TOTAL EXTERNAL DEBT – US$52,022 million (1999)

TRADE

Principal exports are electronic products, machinery and transport equipment, clothing, coconut oil and products, and minerals. Principal imports are fuelstuffs and oils, electronic goods and components, machinery, base metals, transport equipment, textiles and yarns, and cereals. The major trading partners are the USA, Japan, Singapore and Hong Kong. In 2000 the Philippines had a trade surplus of US$6,917 million and a current account surplus of US$9,081 million. Imports totalled US$33,808 million and exports US$39,783 million.

Trade with UK	2000	2001
Imports from UK	£274,282,000	£393,308,000
Exports to UK	1,194,163,000	1,198,584,000

COMMUNICATIONS

The highway system covers about 187,000 km. The Philippine National Railway operates 429 km of track. There are 415 ports. There are 82 national airports and 137 privately operated airports. Philippine Airlines has regular flights throughout the Far East, to the USA and Europe, in addition to inter-island services.

EDUCATION

Secondary and higher education is extensive and there are 21 public and 53 private universities recognised by the government, including the Dominican University of Santo Tomás (founded in 1611). There are also 530 other institutions of higher education.

ILLITERACY RATE – 4.3 per cent (2002)
ENROLMENT (percentage of age group) – primary 100 per cent (1997); secondary 78 per cent (1997); tertiary 29 per cent (1997)

POLAND
Rzeczpospolita Polska – Republic of Poland

AREA – 124,808 sq. miles (323,250 sq. km). Neighbours: the Russian Federation (Kaliningrad) (north), Germany (west), the Czech Republic and Slovakia (south), Belarus, Ukraine and Lithuania (east)
POPULATION – 38,633,912 (2001 estimate). Roman Catholicism is the religion of 95 per cent of the inhabitants. The language is Polish; there are German, Ukrainian and Belarusian minorities
CAPITAL – Warsaw (population, 1,618,468, 1999), on the Vistula
MAJOR CITIES – Bydgoszcz (386,855); ΨGdańsk (Danzig) (458,988); Katowice (345,934); Kraków (740,666); Łódź (806,728); Poznań (578,235); ΨSzczecin (Stettin) (416,988); Wrocław (Breslau) (637,877), 1999
CURRENCY – Zloty of 100 groszy
NATIONAL ANTHEM – Jeszcze Polska Nie Zginęla (Poland Has Not Yet Perished)
NATIONAL DAY – 3 May
NATIONAL FLAG – Equal horizontal stripes of white (above) and red
LIFE EXPECTANCY (years) – male 69.8; female 78.0
POPULATION GROWTH RATE – 0.2 per cent (1997)
POPULATION DENSITY – 120 per sq. km (1999)
URBAN POPULATION – 62.0 per cent (1997)

HISTORY AND POLITICS

The Polish Commonwealth ceased to exist in 1795 after three successive partitions in 1772, 1793 and 1795 in which Prussia, Russia and Austria shared. The Republic of Poland was proclaimed at Warsaw in November 1918, and its independence guaranteed by the signatories of the Treaty of Versailles.

German forces invaded Poland on 1 September 1939; on 17 September, Russian forces invaded eastern Poland, and on 21 September 1939 Poland was declared by Germany and Russia to have ceased to exist. At the end of the war, its frontiers were redrawn; eastern Poland was ceded to the Soviet Union in return for the German territory east of the rivers Oder and Neisse. A coalition government was formed in which the Polish Workers' Party played a large part. In December 1948, the Polish Workers' Party and the Polish Socialist Party merged to form the Polish United Workers' Party (PUWP). A new constitution modelled on the Soviet constitution was adopted in 1952, and was modified in 1976.

Steep price rises in 1980 prompted strikes which forced the government to allow independent trade unions, including 'Solidarity' led by Lech Wałęsa. The unions agitated for further reforms although their activities were suspended when martial law was in force from December 1981 until July 1983.

A wave of strikes resulted in talks between Wałęsa and the PUWP early in 1989. Multiparty parliamentary elections were held in the summer of 1989, following which the PUWP ceased to be the ruling party. The post-Communist governments have introduced a market economy but economic difficulties and a fragmented parliament have led to a succession of short-lived governments.

President Kwaśniewski was re-elected for a second term in the first round of the presidential election on 8 October 2000, gaining 53.92 per cent of the vote. Elections held on 23 September 2001 were won by an electoral alliance of the Democratic Left Alliance (SLD) and the Labour Union (UP), which won 216 seats in the *Sejm* and 75 in the senate. A coalition government comprising the SLP, UP and the Polish Peasant Party (PSL) took office on 19 October.

FOREIGN RELATIONS

In July 1997, Poland was invited to join NATO. It has also been approved by the European Commission for membership of the EU, and formal accession talks began in March 1998.

POLITICAL SYSTEM

A new constitution came into effect on 16 October 1997. The President, directly elected for a maximum of two five-year terms, appoints the Prime Minister and has the right to be consulted over the appointment of the foreign, defence and interior ministers. The National Assembly is the bicameral legislature, comprising a 460-member *Sejm* (Diet) and a Senate of 100 members. Both houses have a four-year term. The Senate is elected on a provincial basis.

HEAD OF STATE
President, Aleksander Kwaśniewski, *elected* 19 November 1995, *sworn in* 23 December 1995, *re-elected* 8 October 2000

COUNCIL OF MINISTERS *as at July 2002*
Prime Minister, Leszek Miller (SLD)
Deputy Prime Minister, Agriculture and Rural Development, Jarosław Kalinowski (PSL)
Deputy Prime Minister, Finance, Marek Belka (SLD)
Deputy Prime Minister, Infrastructure, Marek Pol (UP)
Culture, Andrzej Celiński (SLD)
Defence, Jerzy Szmajdziński (SLD)
Economy, Jacek Piechota (SLD)
Education, Krystyna Łybacka (SLD)
Environment, Stanisław Żelichowski (PSL)
Foreign Affairs, Włodzimierz Cimoszewicz (SLD)
Health, Mariusz Łapiński (SLD)
Internal Affairs and Administration, Krzysztof Janik (SLD)
Justice, Barbara Piwnik (Ind.)
Labour, Jerzy Hausner (SLD)
Science, Michał Kleiber (SLD)
Treasury, Wiesław Kaczmarek (SLD)

PSL Polish Peasant Party; SLD Democratic Left Alliance; UP Labour Union; Ind. Independent

EMBASSY OF THE REPUBLIC OF POLAND
47 Portland Place, London W1B 1JH
Tel: 0870-774 2700
Ambassador Extraordinary and Plenipotentiary, HE Stanisław Komorowski, apptd 1999

BRITISH EMBASSY
Aleje Róz No. 1, PL00-556 Warsaw
Tel: (00 48) (22) 628 1001/5
Email: britemb@it.com.pl
Ambassador Extraordinary and Plenipotentiary, HE Michael Pakenham, CMG, apptd 2001

CONSULATES – Gdańsk, Katowice, Kraków, Lublin, Poznań, Szczecin, Wrocław (Breslau)

BRITISH COUNCIL DIRECTOR, Dr Jeremy Eyres, OBE, Al. Jerozolimskie 59, PL-00–697 Warsaw; Email: bc.warsaw@britishcouncil.pl. There is an office in

Kraków and libraries in Białystok, Gdańsk, Katowice, Łódź, Lublin, Poznań, Szczecin, Torun and Wrocław

DEFENCE

The Army has 1,677 main battle tanks, 1,404 armoured infantry fighting vehicles and 33 armoured personnel carriers. The Navy has three submarines, one destroyer, two frigates, 23 patrol and coastal vessels, 26 combat aircraft and 11 armed helicopters at five bases. The Air Force has 212.
MILITARY EXPENDITURE – 2.0 per cent of GDP (2000)
MILITARY PERSONNEL – 206,045: Army 120,300, Navy 16,760, Air Force 43,735; Paramilitaries 22,000
CONSCRIPTION DURATION – 12 months

ECONOMY

Poland is well endowed with mineral resources; there are large reserves of brown coal in central and south-western Poland and hard coal in Upper Silesia and the Wałbrzych and Lublin regions; sulphur, copper, zinc, lead, natural gas and salt are also produced.

In 1990, the government embarked upon a series of measures designed to introduce a free-market economy. The transition to a market economy has been painful, with unemployment doubling between 1990 and 1995 and remaining high. Industrial output has improved and the rate of growth of GDP has increased although inflation remains high.

A programme is underway to modernise the agricultural sector and adapt it to the EU's common agricultural policy.

Poland's major imports are machinery and vehicles, chemical products, leather and textiles, livestock, foodstuffs, luxury goods and metal products. Its major exports are machinery and vehicles, leather and textiles, metal goods, livestock, foodstuffs, luxury goods and chemical products. Germany is Poland's main trading partner.

In 1998 there was a trade deficit of US$12,836 million and a current account deficit of US$6,901 million. In 2000 imports totalled US$48,940 million and exports US$31,651 million.
GNP – US$162,169 million (2000); US$4,070 per capita (1999)
GDP – US$158,574 million (1998); US$4.567 per capita (2001)
ANNUAL AVERAGE GROWTH OF GDP – 4.1 per cent (2000)
INFLATION RATE – 10.1 per cent (2000)
UNEMPLOYMENT – 17.8 per cent (2002)
TOTAL EXTERNAL DEBT – US$54,268 million (1999)

Trade with UK	2000	2001
Imports from UK	£1,307,364,000	£1,299,320,000
Exports to UK	930,677,000	1,192,724,000

EDUCATION

Elementary education (ages seven to 15) is compulsory and free. Secondary education is optional and free. There are 179 institutions of higher education, including universities at Kraków, Warsaw, Poznań, Łódź, Wrocław, Lublin and Toruń and a number of other towns.
ILLITERACY RATE – 0.3 per cent (2002)
ENROLMENT (percentage of age group) – primary 96 per cent (1997); secondary 98 per cent (1997); tertiary 25 per cent (1997)

CULTURE

Polish is a western Slavonic tongue, the Latin alphabet being used. Major writers include Henryk Sienkiewicz

(1846–1916), Nobel Prize winner for Literature in 1905; Bolesław Prus (1847–1912); Stanisław Reymont (1867–1925), Nobel Prize winner in 1924; Czesław Miłosz, Nobel Prize winner in 1980; and Wisława Szymborska, Nobel Prize winner in 1996.

PORTUGAL
República Portuguesa – Portuguese Republic

AREA – 35,514 sq. miles (91,982 sq. km). Neighbour: Spain (north and east)
POPULATION – 10,066,253 (2001 estimate); 9,833,014 (excluding the Azores and Madeira, 1995). 94 per cent of the population are Catholic. The language is Portuguese
CAPITAL – ΨLisbon (population, 2,561,225, 1991)
MAJOR CITIES – ΨOporto (1,683,000)
CURRENCY – Euro (€) of 100 cents
NATIONAL ANTHEM – A Portuguesa
NATIONAL DAY – 10 June
NATIONAL FLAG – Divided vertically into unequal parts of green and red with the national emblem over all on the line of division
LIFE EXPECTANCY (years) – male 72.6; female 79.6
POPULATION GROWTH RATE – 0.2 per cent (1999)
POPULATION DENSITY – 109 per sq. km (1999)

HISTORY AND POLITICS

Portugal was a monarchy from the 12th century until 1910, when an armed rising in Lisbon drove King Manuel II into exile and a republic was set up. A period of political instability ensued until the military stepped in and abolished political parties in 1926. The constitution of 1933 gave formal expression to the corporative 'Estado Novo' (New State) which was personified by Dr Antonio Salazar, Prime Minister 1932–68. Dr Caetano succeeded Salazar as Prime Minister in 1968 but his failure to liberalise the regime or to conclude the wars in the African colonies resulted in his government's overthrow by a military coup on 25 April 1974. There was great political turmoil between April 1974 and July 1976, a period in which most of the colonies gained their independence, but with the failure of an attempted coup by the extreme left in November 1975 the situation stabilised. Full civilian government was restored in 1982.

Macao, which had been a Portuguese colony since 1557, was transferred to Chinese sovereignty on 19 December 1999.

In the presidential election held on 14 January 2001, Jorge Sampaio of the Socialist Party was re-elected, gaining 55.8 per cent of the votes cast. In the general election held on 17 March 2002, the Social Democratic Party (PSD) became the largest party in the Assembly winning 102 seats. José Manuel Durão Barroso of the PSD was sworn in as prime minister on 6 April, leading a coalition government of the PSD and the People's Party (PP).

POLITICAL SYSTEM

Under the 1976 constitution, amended in 1982 and 1989, the President is elected for a five-year term by universal adult suffrage. The Prime Minister is designated by the largest party in the legislature. Legislative authority is vested in the 230-member Assembly of the Republic, elected by a system of proportional representation every four years. The President retains certain limited powers to dismiss the government, dissolve the Assembly or veto laws.

HEAD OF STATE
President of the Republic, Jorge Sampaio, *elected* 14 January 1996, *inaugurated* 9 March 1996, *re-elected* 14 January 2001

COUNCIL OF MINISTERS *as at July 2002*

Prime Minister, José Manuel Durão Barroso
Agriculture, Rural Development and Fisheries, Armando José Cordeiro Sevinate Pinto
Assistant to the Prime Minister, José Luis Fazenda Arnaut Duarte
Culture, Pedro Manuel da Cruz Roseta
Economy, Carlos Manuel Tavaras da Silva
Education, José David Gomes Justino
Foreign Affairs and Portuguese Communities Abroad, António Manuel de Mendonça Martins da Cruz
Health, Luis Filipe da Conceição Pereira
Internal Administration, António Jorge de Figueiredo Lopes
Justice, Maria Celeste Ferreira Lopes Cardona
Minister of State for Finance, Maria Manuela Dias Ferreira Leite
Minister of State for National Defence, Paulo Sacadura Cabral Portas
Parliamentary Affairs, Luís Manuel Gonçalves Marques Mendes
Presidency, Nuno Albuquerque Morais Sarmento
Public Works, Transport and Housing, Luís Francisco Valente de Oliveira
Science and Higher Education, Pedro Augusto Lynce de Faria
Social Security and Work, António José de Castro Bagão Félix
Towns, Territorial Planning and Environment, Isaltino Afonso de Morais

PORTUGUESE EMBASSY
11 Belgrave Square, London SW1X 8PP
Tel: 020-7235 5331
Ambassador Extraordinary and Plenipotentiary, José Gregório Faria, apptd 1997

BRITISH EMBASSY
Rua de São Bernardo 33, P-1249-082 Lisbon
Tel: (00 351) (21) 392 4000
Email: consular@lisbon.mail.fco.gov.uk
Ambassador Extraordinary and Plenipotentiary, HE Dame Glynne Evans, CMG, DBE, apptd 2001

CONSULATES – Oporto, Portimão
HONORARY CONSULATES – Portimão, Funchal (Madeira), Ribeira Grande (Azores)

BRITISH COUNCIL DIRECTOR, Robert Ness, Rua de São Marçal 174, P-1249-062 Lisbon; Email: lisbon.enquiries@britcounpt.org. There are also offices at Coimbra, Oporto and Parede

DEFENCE

The Army has 187 main battle tanks and 370 armoured personnel carriers. The Navy has two submarines, six frigates and 31 patrol and coastal vessels at four bases. The Air Force has 51 combat aircraft.

Lisbon is the base of the NATO Iberian Atlantic Command and the USA maintains 990 personnel in mainland Portugal and on the Azores.

MILITARY EXPENDITURE – 2.2 per cent of GDP (2000)
MILITARY PERSONNEL – 43,600: Army 25,400, Navy 10,800, Air Force 7,400; Paramilitaries 46,400
CONSCRIPTION DURATION – Four to 12 months

ECONOMY

The chief agricultural products are wines, dairy products, potatoes, tomatoes, maize, meat, fruits, olives, wheat, fish, cork and rice. There are extensive forests of pine, cork, eucalyptus and chestnut covering about 38 per cent of the country. Around 13 per cent of the workforce are engaged in agriculture, the highest percentage in the EU. The principal mineral products are limestone, granite, marble, copper, coal, kaolin and wolframite.

The country is moderately industrialised. The principal manufactures are motor vehicle components, clothing and footwear, textiles, machinery, pulp and paper, pharmaceuticals, foodstuffs, chemicals, fertilisers, wood, cork, furniture, cement, glassware and pottery. There are a modern steelworks and large shipbuilding and repair yards at Lisbon and Setúbal, working mainly for foreign shipowners. There are several hydroelectric power stations and two thermal power stations.

Portugal has experienced rapid economic growth since joining the EU in 1986.

Portugal was one of 11 states to adopt the European single currency on 1 January 1999.

GNP – US$110,674 million (2000); US$11,030 per capita (1999)
GDP – US$109,344 million (1998); US$11,229 per capita (1999)
ANNUAL AVERAGE GROWTH OF GDP – 3.3 per cent (2000)
INFLATION RATE – 2.9 per cent (2000)
UNEMPLOYMENT – 5.0 per cent (1998)

TRADE

The principal imports are machinery, vehicles, textiles, agricultural products, chemicals, oil and base metals. The principal exports are textiles, clothing and shoes, machinery, automobile parts, wood, pulp, paper and cork, and minerals.

In 2000 Portugal had a trade deficit of US$14,143 million and a current account deficit of US$10,632 million. Imports totalled US$38,249 million and exports US$23,310 million.

Trade with UK	2000	2001
Imports from UK	£1,570,400,000	£1,505,000,000
Exports to UK	1,655,400,000	1,493,500,000

COMMUNICATIONS

There are 3,072 km of railway track, of which 461 km are electrified. There are international airports at Lisbon, Oporto, Faro and Santa Maria and Lages (Azores) and Funchal (Madeira).

EDUCATION

Education is free and compulsory for nine years from the age of six. Secondary education is mainly conducted in state general unified schools, lyceums, technical and professional schools, but there are also private schools. There are also military, naval, polytechnic and other special schools. There are 17 public and private universities including those at Coimbra (founded in 1290), Oporto, Lisbon, Braga, Aveiro, Vila Real, Faro, Evora and in the Azores.

ILLITERACY RATE – 7.0 per cent (2002)

ENROLMENT (percentage of age group) – primary 100 per cent (1997); secondary 100 per cent (1997); tertiary 39 per cent (1997)

AUTONOMOUS REGIONS

Madeira and The Azores are two administratively autonomous regions of Portugal, having locally elected assemblies and governments.

MADEIRA is a group of islands in the Atlantic Ocean about 520 miles south-west of Lisbon, and consists of Madeira, Porto, Santo and three uninhabited islands (Desertas). Total area is 300 sq. miles (779 sq. km); population, 257,290 (1995). ΨFunchal in Madeira, the largest island (270 sq. miles), is the capital (population 44,111)

THE AZORES are a group of nine islands (Flores, Corvo, Terceira, São Jorge, Pico, Faial, Graciosa, São Miguel and Santa Maria) in the Atlantic Ocean; area 895 sq. miles (2,330 sq. km); population, 241,490 (1995). ΨPonta Delgada, on São Miguel, is the capital (population, 137,700). Other ports are ΨAngra, in Terceira (55,900) and ΨHorta (16,300)

QATAR
Dawlat Qatar – State of Qatar

AREA – 4,247 sq. miles (11,000 sq. km). Neighbours: United Arab Emirates (south), Saudi Arabia (south-west)

POPULATION – 769,152 (2001 estimate). Most of the population is concentrated in the urban district of Doha. Arabic is the official language. Islam is the religion of 95 per cent of the population

CAPITAL – ΨDoha (Ad-Dawhah) (population, 392,384, 1995 estimate)

MAJOR CITIES – Ar-Rayyān; Dukhān; ΨMusay'īd; Al-Wakrah

CURRENCY – Qatar riyal of 100 dirhams

NATIONAL DAY – 3 September

NATIONAL FLAG – White and maroon, white portion nearer the mast; vertical indented line comprising 17 angles divides the colours

LIFE EXPECTANCY (years) – male 69.4; female 72.1

POPULATION GROWTH RATE – 1.8 per cent (1999)

POPULATION DENSITY – 54 per sq. km (1999)

MILITARY EXPENDITURE – 11.7 per cent of GDP (2000)

MILITARY PERSONNEL – 12,330: Army 8,500, Navy 1,730, Air Force 2,100

ILLITERACY RATE – 17.9 per cent (2002)

ENROLMENT (percentage of age group) – primary 80 per cent (1993); secondary 69 per cent (1993); tertiary 27 per cent (1996)

The state of Qatar covers the peninsula of Qatar in the Gulf from approximately the northern shore of Khor al Odaid to the eastern shore of Khor al Salwa.

HISTORY AND POLITICS

Qatar was one of nine independent emirates in the Gulf in special treaty relations with the UK until 1971. On 2 April 1970, a provisional constitution for Qatar was proclaimed, providing for the establishment of a Council of Ministers and for the formation of a Consultative Council to assist the Council of Ministers in running the affairs of the state. There are no political parties or legislature; ministers are chosen by the Amir.

The Amir, who had ruled since 22 February 1972, was overthrown on 27 June 1995 by his son and heir, who assumed power as Amir the same day. A coup attempt was thwarted in February 1996.

The Amir announced in November 1998 that a committee of experts would be formed to draft a new constitution and that an elected National Assembly would be established. Municipal elections were held on 8 March 1999, the first in which women were allowed to vote and contest seats.

FOREIGN RELATIONS

A territorial dispute between Qatar and Bahrain was settled on 16 March 2001 when the International Court of Justice awarded the Hawar islands to Bahrain and the town of Zubarah to Qatar.

HEAD OF STATE

HH Amir of Qatar, Minister of Defence and Commander-in-Chief of Armed Forces, Sheikh Hamad bin Khalifa al-Thani, KCMG, *assumed power* 27 June 1995

Crown Prince, HH Sheikh Jassem bin Hamad al-Thani

COUNCIL OF MINISTERS *as at August 2002*

Prime Minister, HH Shaikh Abdulla bin Khalifa al-Thani

Deputy Prime Minister, Shaikh Mohammed bin Khalifa al-Thani

Awqaf (Religious Endowments) and Islamic Affairs, Ahmed Abdulla al-Marri

Civil Service Affairs and Housing, Shaikh Falah bin Jassim al-Thani

Communications and Transport, Shaikh Ahmed bin Nasser al-Thani

Education, Higher Education and Culture, Dr Mohammed Abdulrahim Kafoud

Energy and Industry, Abdulla bin Hamad al-Attiyah

Finance, Economy and Trade, Shaikh Hamad bin Faysal al-Thani

Foreign Affairs, Shaikh Hamad bin Jassem bin Jabr al-Thani

Internal Affairs, Shaikh Abdulla bin Khalid al-Thani

Justice, Hassan bin Abdulla al-Ghanem

Municipal Affairs, Agriculture, Ali Mohammed al-Khater

Public Health, Dr Hajr bin Ahmed Hajr

EMBASSY OF THE STATE OF QATAR
1 South Audley Street, London W1K 1NB
Tel: 020-7493 2200
Ambassador Extraordinary and Plenipotentiary, HE Nasser bin Hamid M. Al-Khalifa, apptd 2000

BRITISH EMBASSY
PO Box 3, Doha
Tel: (00 974) 4421991
Email: bembcomm@qatar.net.qa
Ambassador Extraordinary and Plenipotentiary, HE David MacLennan, apptd 1997

BRITISH COUNCIL DIRECTOR, Alan Smart, 93 Al Sadd Street, PO Box 2992, Doha; Email: alan.smart@qa.britishcouncil.org

ECONOMY

Although Qatar is a desert country, there are gardens and smallholdings near Doha and to the north, and agriculture is being developed with the aim of self-sufficiency.

The Qatar General Petroleum Corporation is the state-owned company controlling Qatar's interests in oil, gas and petrochemicals. The corporation is responsible for Qatar's oil production onshore and offshore. The large reserves of natural gas in the North Field came into production in September 1991.

Current industries include a steel mill, a fertiliser plant, a cement factory, a petrochemical complex and two natural gas liquids plants. With the exception of the cement works at Umm Bāb, all these industries are at Musay'īd, about 30 miles south of Doha. Qatar is also expanding its infrastructure, including electrical generation and water distillation, roads, houses, and government buildings. The recent drop in demand for crude oil has slowed the economy considerably.

The chief imports are machinery and equipment, manufactures, foodstuffs and livestock, and chemicals. In 1999 imports totalled US$2,500 million.

GDP – US$10,460 million (1998); US$21,220 per capita (1999)

ANNUAL AVERAGE GROWTH OF GDP – 4.0 per cent (1998)

INFLATION RATE – -1.0 per cent (2000)

Trade with UK	2000	2001
Imports from UK	£183,994,000	£174,811,000
Exports to UK	30,268,000	32,062,000

COMMUNICATIONS

There are 1,210 km of roads, of which 1,089 km are surfaced. Regular air services provided by Gulf Air and Qatar Airways connect Qatar with the other Gulf states, the Middle East, the Indian sub-continent, Africa and Europe. The Qatar Broadcasting Service transmits on medium wave, shortwave and VHF.

ROMANIA

România – Romania

AREA – 92,043 sq. miles (238,391 sq. km). Neighbours: Ukraine (north and east), Moldova (east), Bulgaria (south), Yugoslavia (south-west), Hungary (north-west)

POPULATION – 22,430,457 (2001 estimate); 22,810,035 (1992 census): 89.4 per cent Romanian, 7.1 per cent Hungarian, 1.7 per cent Roma, 0.5 per cent German, 0.3 per cent Ukrainian, 0.04 per cent Jews and others. Religious affiliation: Orthodox 86.8 per cent, Roman Catholic 5 per cent, Reformed 3.5 per cent, Greek Catholic 1 per cent. Romanian is a Romance language with many archaic forms and with admixtures of Slavonic, Turkish, Magyar and French words

CAPITAL – Bucharest (population, 2,066,723, 2001 estimate)

MAJOR CITIES – Ψ Brasov (324,104); Constanta (348,985); Cluj-Napoca (321,850); Craiova (303,033); Ψ Galati (324,234); Iasi (337,643); Oradea (221,559); Ploiesti (254,304); Timisoara (325,359), 2001 estimates

CURRENCY – Leu (Lei) of 100 bani

NATIONAL ANTHEM – Desteaptâte, Române, Din Somnul Cel De Moarte (Awake Ye, Romanians, From Your Deadly Slumber)

NATIONAL DAY – 1 December

NATIONAL FLAG – Three vertical bands, blue, yellow, red

LIFE EXPECTANCY (years) – male 66.5; female 73.3

POPULATION GROWTH RATE – 0.2 per cent (1999)

POPULATION DENSITY – 94 per sq. km (1999)

URBAN POPULATION – 54.9 per cent (1996)

HISTORY AND POLITICS

Romania has its origin in the union of the Danubian principalities of Wallachia and Moldavia in 1859. In 1918 Bessarabia, Bukovina, Transylvania and Banat were united with Romania.

In 1947 Romania became 'The Romanian People's Republic' under the leadership of the Romanian Communist Party. A revolution in December 1989 led to the overthrow of Nicolae Ceauşescu, president since 1965. A provisional government abolished the leading role of the Communist Party and held free elections in May 1990.

In the elections held on 26 November 2000 the Social Democratic Party of Romania (SDPR) gained 155 seats in the Chamber of Deputies and 65 seats in the Senate, becoming the largest party in both houses. The SDPR presidential candidate, Ion Iliescu, obtained 36.35 per cent of the vote in the first round of the presidential election. He won the second round, held on 10 December, obtaining 66.83 per cent of the vote. On 27 December, the SDPR reached an agreement with other centre-right parties to enable it to form a workable minority government.

POLITICAL SYSTEM

The constitution of 1991 formally makes Romania a multiparty democracy and endorses human rights and a market economy. The parliament comprises the Chamber of Deputies with 345 seats, of which 18 are reserved for ethnic minorities, and the Senate with 140 seats. Both houses are elected for four-year terms.

HEAD OF STATE

President of the Republic, Ion Iliescu, *elected* 10 December 2000

CABINET *as at August 2002*

Prime Minister, Adrian Năstase
Agriculture, Food and Forestry, Ilie Sârbu
Communications and Information Technology, Dan Nica
Culture and Religious Affairs, Răzvan Theodorescu
Defence, Ioan Mircea Paşcu
Development and Forecasts, Gheorghe Cazan
Education and Research, Ecaterina Andronescu
European Integration, Hildegard Puwak
Finance, Mihai Tănăcescu
Foreign Affairs, Mircea Geoană
Health and Family, Daniela Bartoş
Industry and Resources, Dan Ioan Popescu
Interior, Ioan Rus
Justice, Rodica Mihaela Stănoiu
Labour, Social Solidarity, Marian Sârbu
Minister-Delegate, Ministry for Education and Research, Şerban Constantin Valeca
Minister-Delegate to the Prime Minister, Chief EU Negotiator, Vasile Puşcaş
Parliamentary Relations, Acsinte Gaspar
Privatisation, Ovidiu Muşetescu
Public Administration, Octav Cozmâncă

Public Information, Vasile Dâncu
Public Works, Transport and Housing, Miron Mitrea
Secretary-General of the Government, Petru Şerban Mihăilescu
Small and Medium Enterprises and Co-operatives, Silvia Ciornei
Tourism, Matei Agathon Dan
Water and Environment, Petru Lificiu
Youth and Sports, Georgiu Gingăraş

EMBASSY OF ROMANIA
Arundel House, 4 Palace Green, London W8 4QD
Tel: 020-7937 9666
Ambassador Extraordinary and Plenipotentiary, HE Dan Ghibernea, apptd 2002
Minister-Counsellor, G. Molosaga (*Economic*)

BRITISH EMBASSY
24 Strada Jules Michelet, RO-70154 Bucharest
Tel: (00 40) (2) 201 7200
Ambassador Extraordinary and Plenipotentiary, HE Richard Ralph, CVO, CMG, apptd 1999

BRITISH COUNCIL DIRECTOR, Stephan Roman, Calea Dorobantilor 14, RO-71132 Bucharest;
Email: bc.romania@britishcouncil.ro. There are libraries in Cluj-Napoca, Constanta, Iasi, Sibiu and Timisoara

DEFENCE
The Army has 1,373 main battle tanks, 1,316 armoured personnel carriers and 177 armoured infantry fighting vehicles. The Navy has one submarine, one destroyer, six frigates, 61 patrol and coastal vessels, seven helicopters and 120 main battle tanks at six bases. The Air Force has 307 combat aircraft and 18 attack helicopters.
MILITARY EXPENDITURE – 2.2 per cent of GDP (2000)
MILITARY PERSONNEL – Army 52,900, Navy 10,200, Air Force 18,900; Paramilitaries 75,900
CONSCRIPTION DURATION – 12 months

ECONOMY
Agriculture employed 40.8 per cent of the workforce in 2000 and contributed 12.8 per cent of GDP. The principal crops are cereals, vegetables, flax and hemp. Vines and fruits are also grown. The forests of the mountainous regions are extensive, and the timber industry is important.

There are plentiful supplies of natural gas, together with various mineral deposits including coal, iron ore, bauxite, chromium and uranium in quantities which allow a substantial part of the requirements of industry to be met from local resources. Production of crude oil was 12 million tonnes in 1999.

The economy, which was characterised by state-owned and co-operative ownership, excessive centralisation, rigid planning and low efficiency, has been slowly reformed. Since 1996 the pace of privatisation and restructuring has quickened, subsidies have been reduced and prices liberalised. An extensive programme of privatisation was announced in March 2002.
GNP – US$37,370 million (2000); US$1,470 per capita (1999)
GDP – US$38,157 million (1998); US$1,392 per capita (1999)
ANNUAL AVERAGE GROWTH OF GDP – 5.3 per cent (2001)
INFLATION RATE – 31.4 per cent (2001)
UNEMPLOYMENT – 8.6 per cent (2001)
TOTAL EXTERNAL DEBT – US$6,482 million (2000)

TRADE
The main imports are machines and equipment, minerals, textiles, chemicals and metallurgical products. The main exports are textiles, metallurgical products, machinery components, minerals, chemicals, shoes and transport equipment. Italy, Germany, Russia, France and the UK are Romania's most important trading partners.

In 2000 Romania had a trade deficit of US$1,684 million and a current account deficit of US$1,359 million. Imports totalled US$13,055 million and exports US$10,367.

Trade with UK	2000	2001
Imports from UK	£383,053,000	£341,709,000
Exports to UK	30,268,000	458,381,000

COMMUNICATIONS
In 1999 there were 11,376 km of railway track, over a third of which was electrified, and 153,358 km of roads, of which 78,213 km are paved. The main national roads largely follow the railway lines and almost all lead to the capital. The principal ports are Constanta and Mangalia (on the Black Sea), Sulina (on the Danube Estuary), Galati, Brăila, Giurgiu and Drobeta-Turnu Severin. The Danube and the Black Sea are linked by a canal completed in 1984.

EDUCATION
Education is free and primary and secondary education are compulsory. There are state universities in seven cities, 66 private universities, six polytechnics, two commercial academies, and five agricultural colleges.
ILLITERACY RATE – 1.7 per cent (2002)
ENROLMENT (percentage of age group) – primary 100 per cent (1997); secondary 78 per cent (1997); tertiary 23 per cent (1997)

RUSSIA
Rossiiskaya Federatsiya – Russian Federation

AREA – 6,592,850 sq. miles (17,075,400 sq. km).
Neighbours: Norway, Finland, Estonia, Latvia, Belarus and Ukraine (west), Georgia, Azerbaijan, Kazakhstan, China, Mongolia and North Korea (south). The Kaliningrad enclave borders Lithuania and Poland
POPULATION – 144,200,000 (2001 estimate): 87.5 per cent Russian, 3.5 per cent Tatar, 2.7 per cent Ukrainian, 1.3 per cent ethnic German, 1.1 per cent Chuvash, 0.9 per cent Bashkir, 0.7 per cent Belarusian and 0.7 per cent Mordovian. There are another six minorities with populations of over half a million and more than 130 nationalities in total. The Russian Orthodox Church is the predominant religion, though the Tatars and many in the north Caucasus are Muslims and there are Jewish communities in Moscow and St Petersburg. The language is Russian
CAPITAL – Moscow (population, 8,539,000, 2001 estimate), founded about 1147, became the centre of the rising Moscow principality and in the 15th century the capital of the whole of Russia (Muscovy). In 1325 it became the seat of the Metropolitan of Russia. In 1703 Peter the Great transferred the capital to St Petersburg, but on 14 March 1918 Moscow was again designated as the capital
MAJOR CITIES – Ψ St Petersburg (4,660,800, 2001), from 1914 to 1924 Petrograd and from 1924 to 1991 Leningrad. Other cities: Chelyabinsk (1,111,000); Kazan (1,077,750); Nizhny-Novgorod/Gorky (1,380,100); Novosibirsk/Novonikolayevsk

(1,398,350); Omsk (1,785,000); Perm/Molotov (1,050,950); Rostov-on-Don (1,013,635); Samara/Kuibyshev (1,215,050); Ufa (1.098,150); Yekaterinburg/Sverdlovsk (1,275,000), 1997 estimates
CURRENCY – Rouble of 100 kopeks
NATIONAL ANTHEM – Russia, Sacred Our Empire (the former Soviet national anthem, with new lyrics)
NATIONAL DAY – 12 June (Independence Day)
NATIONAL FLAG – Three horizontal stripes of white, blue, red
LIFE EXPECTANCY (years) – male 60.0; female 72.5
POPULATION GROWTH RATE – 0.4 per cent (1999)
POPULATION DENSITY – 9 per sq. km (1999)
ILLITERACY RATE – 0.4 per cent (2002)

Russia occupies three-quarters of the land area of the former Soviet Union.

The Russian Federation comprises 89 members: 49 regions (*oblast*) – Amur, Arkhangelsk, Astrakhan, Belgorod, Bryansk, Chelyabinsk, Chita, Irkutsk, Ivanovo, Kaliningrad, Kaluga, Kamchatka, Kemerovo, Kirov, Kostroma, Kurgan, Kursk, Leningrad, Lipetsk, Magadan, Moscow, Murmansk, Nizhniy-Novgorod, Novgorod, Novosibirsk, Omsk, Orel, Orenburg, Penza, Perm, Pskov, Rostov, Ryazan, Sakhalin, Samara, Saratov, Smolensk, Sverdlovsk, Tambov, Tomsk, Tula, Tver, Tyumen, Ulyanovsk, Vladimir, Volgograd, Vologda, Voronezh, Yaroslavl; six autonomous territories (krai) – Altai, Khabarovsk, Krasnodar, Krasnoyarsk, Primorye, Stavropol; 21 republics – Adygeia, Altai, Bashkortostan, Buryatia, Chechnya, Chuvash, Daghestan, Ingush, Kabardino-Balkar, Kalmykia, Karachai-Cherkessia, Karelia, Khakassia, Komi, Mari-El, Mordovia, North Ossetia (Alania), Sakha, Tatarstan, Tyva, Udmurt; ten autonomous areas – Aga-Buryat, Chuckchi, Evenki, Khanty-Mansi, Komi-Permyak, Koryak, Nenets, Taimyr, Ust-Orda-Buryat, Yamal-Nenets; two cities of federal status – Moscow, St Petersburg; and one autonomous Jewish region, Birobijan.

There are three principal geographic areas: a low-lying flat western area stretching eastwards up to the Yenisei and divided in two by the Ural ridge; the eastern area between the Yenisei and the Pacific, consisting of a number of tablelands and ridges; and a southern mountainous area. Russia has a very long coastline, including the longest Arctic coastline in the world (about 17,000 miles).

The most important rivers are the Volga, the Northern Dvina and the Pechora, the Neva, the Don and the Kuban in the European part, and in the Asiatic part, the Ob, the Irtysh, the Yenisei, the Lena and the Amur, and, further north, Khatanga, Olenek, Yana, Indigirka, Kolyma and Anadyr. Lake Baikal in eastern Siberia is the deepest lake in the world.

HISTORY AND POLITICS

Russia was formally created from the principality of Muscovy and its territories by Tsar Peter I (The Great) (1682-1725), who initiated its territorial expansion, introduced Western ideas of government and founded St Petersburg.

Discontent caused by autocratic rule, the poor conduct of the military in the First World War and wartime privation led to a revolution which broke out in March 1917. A power struggle ensued between the provisional government and the Bolshevik Party. This led to a second revolution in November 1917 in which the Bolsheviks, led by Lenin, seized power.

Civil war between 'red' Bolshevik forces and 'white' monarchist and anti-Communist forces lasted until the

end of 1922. During the civil war, Russia had been declared a Soviet Republic and other Soviet republics had been formed in Ukraine, Belorussia and Transcaucasia. These four republics merged to form the Union of Soviet Socialist Republics (USSR) on 30 December 1922.

Joseph Stalin introduced a policy of rapid industrialisation under a series of five-year plans, brought all sectors of industry under government control, abolished private ownership and enforced the collectivisation of agriculture.

In the Second World War, the USSR lost 27 million combatants and civilians.

Mikhail Gorbachev became Soviet leader in March 1985 and introduced the policies of *perestroika* (complete restructuring) and *glasnost* (openness) in order to revamp the economy, which had stagnated since the 1970s, to root out corruption and inefficiency, and to end the Cold War. The retreat from total control by the Communist Party unleashed ethnic and nationalist tensions.

Following the defeat of an attempted coup by hardline Communists in August 1991, effective political power was now in the hands of the republican leaders, especially Russian President Yeltsin, and the Soviet Union began to break up as the constituent republics declared their independence. Gorbachev resigned as Soviet President on 25 December 1991 and on 26 December 1991 the USSR formally ceased to exist.

Russia was recognised as an independent state by the EC and USA in January 1992; it took over the Soviet Union's seat at the UN in December 1991.

A new Russian Federal Treaty was signed on 13 March 1992 between the central government and the autonomous republics. Tatarstan and Bashkortostan signed the treaty in 1994 after securing considerable legislative and economic autonomy.

The state of the parties in the State *Duma* following the general election on 19 December 1999 was: Communist Party 113 seats; Unity 72; Fatherland-All Russia 67; Union of Rightist Forces 29; Yabloko 21; Zhirinovski's Bloc 17; Our Home is Russia 7; DPA 2; Russian All People Unity 2; others 5.

In the presidential election held on 26 March 2000, Vladimir Putin won 52.94 per cent of the vote, in which the turnout was 68.88 per cent, and was formally inaugurated on 7 May 2000.

POLITICAL SYSTEM

The 1993 constitution enshrines the right to private ownership and the freedoms of press, speech, association, worship and travel, and states that Russia is a multiparty democracy. The President is directly elected for a maximum of two four-year terms. The Prime Minister takes over from the President in the event that he is unable to fulfil his duties.

Legislative power is vested in the Federal Assembly, comprising the Federation Council (upper house) of 178 members, two elected by each of the 89 members of the Russian Federation; the State *Duma* (lower house) of 450 members, of which 225 are elected by constituencies on a first-past-the-post basis and 225 by proportional representation, with a five per cent threshold for representation.

The judicial system consists of a Constitutional Court of 19 members appointed for a 12-year term which protects and interprets the constitution and decides if laws are compatible with it. The Supreme Court adjudicates in criminal and civil laws cases. The Arbitration Court deals with commercial disputes between companies.

INSURGENCIES

The Chechen republic declared its independence in November 1991 after a nationalist coup in the republic and refused to sign the Russian Federal Treaty in March 1992. Civil war began in early 1994 between the Chechen government and armed opposition forces tacitly supported by the Russian government. The Russian military launched an invasion of Chechnya in December 1994 and captured Grozny in February 1995.

Russian troops were withdrawn in January 1997 when presidential and legislative elections were also held in Chechnya. A treaty renouncing the use of force to resolve Chechnya's status was signed between Presidents Maskhadov and Yeltsin in May 1997.

Following an incursion by Islamic militants into Dagestan on 10 August 1999, Russian forces launched airstrikes and Russian ground troops entered the territory. Russian forces captured the Chechen capital, Grozny, on 6 February 2000 and captured the last Chechen-held town on 29 February, but Chechen guerrilla attacks on Russian targets continued. On 8 June 2000, President Putin imposed temporary direct presidential rule on Chechnya.

FOREIGN RELATIONS

A union treaty was signed by the presidents of Russia and Belarus in April 1997. Both countries will retain sovereignty and territorial integrity although citizens of the two countries will also be citizens of the Union. The presidents of the two countries decided in December 1998 to effect a currency union.

A Founding Act was signed by Russia and NATO in May 1997 which lays down the principles of post-Cold War co-operation. A joint permanent council has since been set up.

HEAD OF STATE

President, Vladimir Putin, elected 26 March 2000, inaugurated 7 May 2000

GOVERNMENT as at August 2002

Chair, Atomic Energy, Property Relations, Science, Industry and Technology, Customs, Mikhail Kasyanov
Deputy Chairs, Aleksey Gordeyev (Agriculture and Food, Fisheries, Cartography and Land Survey); Aleksey Kudrin (Finance, Economic Development and Trade); Viktor Khristenko (Energy, Natural Resources, Communications, Railways, Housing and Construction); Valentina Matviyenko (Labour, Health, Education, Culture and Media, Sport)
Anti-Monopoly and Entrepreneurial Affairs, Ilya Yuzhanov
Atomic Energy, Aleksandr Rumyantsev
Culture, Mikhail Shvydkoi
Defence, Sergey Ivanov
Director of the Federal Security Services, Nikolai Patrushev
Economic Development and Trade, German Gref
Education, Vladimir Filippov
Emergencies, Civil Defence, Natural Disasters, Sergei Shoigu
Employment and Social Development, Aleksandr Pochinok
Energy, Igor Yusufov
Foreign Affairs, Igor Ivanov
Head of Government Administration, Igor Shuvalov
Health, Yuri Shevchenko
Interior, Boris Gryzlov
Justice, Yuri Chaika
Nationalities Policy, Vladimir Zorin

Natural Resources, Vitaly Artyukhov
Press, Broadcasting and Mass Communications, Mikhail Lesin
Privatisation, Farid Gazizullin
Railways, Gennady Fadeyev
Secretary of the Security Council, Vladimir Rushailo
Social and Economic Development of Chechnya, Vladimir Yelagin
Tax and Levy Collection, Gennady Bukayev
Telecommunications and Information, Leonid Reyman
Transport, Sergei Frank

EMBASSY OF THE RUSSIAN FEDERATION
13 Kensington Palace Gardens, London W8 4QX
Tel: 020-7229 2666/3628/6412
Ambassador Extraordinary and Plenipotentiary, HE Grigory B. Karasin, apptd 2000

BRITISH EMBASSY
Smolenskaya Naberezhnaya 10, RUS-121099 Moscow
Tel: (00 7) (095) 956 7200
Email: moscow@britishembassy.ru
Ambassador Extraordinary and Plenipotentiary, HE Sir Roderic Lyne, KBE, CMG, apptd 1999
CONSULATES-GENERAL – Ekaterinburg, St Petersburg,

BRITISH COUNCIL DIRECTOR, Adrian Greer, Ulitsa Nikoloyamskaya 1, RUS-109189 Moscow; Email: bc.moscow@britishcouncil.ru. There are also offices at Ekaterinburg, Nizhniy-Novgorod, Sochi, St Petersburg and Tomsk

DEFENCE

Since the demise of the Soviet Union the Russian armed forces have been considerably reduced. In November 2000 it was announced that the armed forces would be reduced to 850,000 personnel by 2005. Major army reform is planned for the period 2004–10, including the transition from conscription to voluntary service.

A joint CIS air defence system covers Russia, Armenia, Belarus, Kazakhstan, Kyrgyzstan and Uzbekistan.

The Strategic Nuclear Forces have 17 nuclear-powered ballistic missile submarines with 280 missiles, 740 intercontinental ballistic missiles and 100 anti-ballistic missiles.

The Army has about 21,820 main battle tanks, 25,975 armoured personnel carriers and armoured infantry fighting vehicles, and 1,700 helicopters. The Navy has 56 submarines, one aircraft carrier, seven cruisers, 17 destroyers, ten frigates, 108 patrol and coastal vessels, 217 combat aircraft and 80 armed helicopters. The Air Force has 2,636 combat aircraft.

Russia deploys forces in Armenia (2,900), Georgia (4,000), Moldova (1,500) and Tajikistan (8,000). Russia is the world's third largest contributor to peacekeeping operations. An agreement with Ukraine on the division on the Black Sea Fleet was signed in May 1997.

MILITARY EXPENDITURE – 5.0 per cent of GDP (2000)
MILITARY PERSONNEL – 977,100: Strategic Nuclear Forces 149,000, Army 321,000, Navy 171,500, Air Force 184,600, Paramilitaries 409,100
CONSCRIPTION DURATION – 18-24 months

ECONOMY

Under the Soviet regime, an essentially agrarian economy in 1917 was transformed by the early 1960s into the second strongest industrial power in the world. However, by the early 1970s the concentration of resources on the military-industrial complex was causing the civilian economy to stagnate. Free market reforms were introduced by President Gorbachev, including the

legalisation of small private businesses, the reduction of state control over the economy, and denationalisation and privatisation. The first stage of mass privatisation of state industries began in October 1992 and the central distribution system was abolished with effect from 1 January 1993. By February 1996, 80 per cent of the economy had been privatised.

From 1994 to 1996, the economy began to stabilise with economic reforms judged to have become irreversible.

The devaluation of the rouble in 1998 caused the return of growth in the Russian economy in 1999. However, low productivity, overstaffing, and a lack of investment and entrepreneurship remained a problem.

In 2001, industrial production grew by more than 5 per cent and investments in basic capital from all sources of financing grew by 8 per cent. GDP rose by 5.1 per cent in 2001 with about 60 per cent of the growth arising from increased consumer demand.

Russia has some of the richest mineral deposits in the world. Coal is mined in the Kuznetsk area, in the Urals, south of Moscow, in the Donets basin and in the Pechora area in the north. Oil is produced in the northern Caucasus, between the Volga and the Urals, and in western Siberia, which also has large deposits of natural gas. A pipeline to bring Caspian oil into Russia via Dagestan and North Ossetia is under construction. Oil production in 2000 was 323.3 million tonnes. Coal and gas deposits in Siberia and the far east (especially Yakutia) are being developed. In November 2001, an oil pipeline between Novorossiisk and Tengiz in Kazakhstan for transporting oil for export came into operation. It is expected that 20 million tons of oil will be transported via the pipeline by the end of 2002. The Ural mountains contain high-quality iron ore, manganese, copper, aluminium, platinum, precious stones, salt, asbestos, pyrites, coal, oil, etc. Iron ore is also mined near Kursk, Tula, Lipetsk, in several areas in Siberia and in the Kola Peninsula. Non-ferrous metals are found in the Altai, in eastern Siberia, in the northern Caucasus, in the Kuznetsk basin, in the far east and in the far north. 106 tonnes of gold were produced in 1997.

The vast area and the great variety in climatic conditions are reflected in the structure of agriculture. In the far north reindeer breeding, hunting and fishing are predominant. Further south, timber industry is combined with grain growing. In the southern half of the forest zone and in the adjacent forest-steppe zone, the acreage under grain crops is larger and the structure of agriculture more complex. Between the Volga and the Urals cericulture is predominant (particularly summer wheat), followed by cattle breeding. Beyond the Urals is another important grain-growing and stock-breeding area in the southern part of the western Siberian plain. The southern steppe zone is the main wheat granary of Russia, containing also large acreages under barley, maize and sunflowers. In 2001 85 million tons of grain was harvested, an increase of 20 million tons on 2000. In the extreme south cotton is cultivated. Vine, tobacco and other southern crops are grown on the Black Sea shore of the Caucasus.

Moscow and St Petersburg are still the two largest industrial centres in the country, but new industrial areas have been developed in the Urals, the Kuznetsk basin, in Siberia and the far east.

GNP – US$241,110 million (2000); US$2,250 per capita (1999)

GDP – US$285,464 million (1998); US$1,257 per capita (1999)

ANNUAL AVERAGE GROWTH OF GDP – 4.6 per cent (1998)

INFLATION RATE – 20.8 per cent (2000)
UNEMPLOYMENT – 13.4 per cent (1999)
TOTAL EXTERNAL DEBT – US$173,940 million (1999)

TRADE

Russia's main trading partners are Germany, the USA, Italy, China and the former Soviet states. In 2000 there was a trade surplus of US$460,703 million and a current account surplus of US$46,317 million. Imports totalled US$49,125 million and exports US$104,836 million.

Trade with UK	2000	2001
Imports from UK	£668,956,000	£898,259,000
Exports to UK	1,532,019,000	2,110,905,000

COMMUNICATIONS

The European area of Russia is well served by railways, but there are still large areas, notably in the far north and Siberia, with few or no railways. In 2001 there were 149,000 km of railways, of which 86,000 km were used for passenger transport.

The most important ports (Taganrog, Rostov and Novorossiisk) lie around the Black Sea and the Sea of Azov. The northern ports (St Petersburg, Murmansk and Arkhangelsk) are, with the exception of Murmansk, icebound during winter. Several ports have been built along the Arctic Sea route between Murmansk and Vladivostok and are in regular use every summer. The far eastern port of Vladivostok, the Pacific naval base of Russia, is kept open by icebreakers all the year round.

There are 95,900 km of waterways. The great rivers of European Russia flow outwards from the centre, linking all parts of the plain with the chief ports. They are supplemented by a system of canals which provide a through traffic between the White, Baltic, Black and Caspian Seas. The most notable are the White Sea-Baltic Canal, the Moscow-Volga Canal and the Volga-Don Canal linking the Baltic and the White Seas in the north to the Caspian Sea, the Black Sea and the Sea of Azov in the south.

CULTURE

Russian is a branch of the Slavonic family of languages and is written in the Cyrillic script.

Before the westernisation of Russia under Peter the Great (1682–1725), Russian literature consisted mainly of folk ballads (byliny), epic songs, chronicles and works of moral theology. The 18th and 19th centuries saw the development of poetry and fiction. Poetry reached its zenith with Alexander Pushkin (1799–1837), Mikhail Lermontov (1814–41), Alexander Blok (1880–1921), the 1958 Nobel Prize laureate Boris Pasternak (1890–1960), Vladimir Mayakovsky (1893–1930) and Anna Akhmatova (1888–1966). Fiction is associated with the names of Nikolai Gogol (1809–52), Ivan Turgenev (1818–83), Fyodor Dostoevsky (1821–81), Leo Tolstoy (1828–1910), Anton Chekhov (1860–1904), Maxim Gorky (1868–1936), Ivan Bunin (1870-1953), Mikhail Bulgakov (1891–1940), Mikhail Sholokhov (1905–84) and Alexander Solzhenitsyn (b. 1918).

Great names in music include Glinka (1804–57), Borodin (1833–87), Mussorgsky (1839–81), Rimsky-Korsakov (1844–1908), Rubinstein (1829–94), Tchaikovsky (1840–93), Rachmaninov (1873–1943), Skriabin (1872–1915), Prokofiev (1891–1953), Stravinsky (1882–1971), Shostakovich (1906–75) and Alfred Schnittke (1934–98).

RWANDA
Republika y'u Rwanda/République Rwandaise – Republic of Rwanda

AREA – 10,169 sq. miles (26,338 sq. km). Neighbours: Burundi (south), Democratic Republic of Congo (west), Uganda (north), Tanzania (east)
POPULATION – 7,312,756 (2001 estimate): Hutus 90 per cent, Tutsis 9 per cent, Twa (pygmy) 1 per cent. Kinyarwanda, French and English are the official languages. Swahili is also spoken
CAPITAL – Kigali (population, 116,227)
CURRENCY – Rwanda franc of 100 centimes
NATIONAL ANTHEM – Rwanda Rwacu, Rwanda Gihugu Cyambyage (My Rwanda, Rwanda Who Gave Me Birth)
NATIONAL DAY – 1 July
NATIONAL FLAG – Broad blue band in upper half, with a sun next fly surmounting equal bands of yellow and green
LIFE EXPECTANCY (years) – male 40.2; female 41.7
POPULATION GROWTH RATE – 8.0 per cent (1999)
POPULATION DENSITY – 275 per sq. km (1999)
MILITARY EXPENDITURE – 4.7 per cent of GDP (2000)
MILITARY PERSONNEL – 71,000: Army 64,000, Air Force 1,000, Paramilitaries 6,000
ILLITERACY RATE – 30.8 per cent (2002)
ENROLMENT (percentage of age group) – primary 75 per cent (1991); secondary 8 per cent (1991); tertiary 0.5 per cent (1990)

HISTORY AND POLITICS
The majority Hutu population rebelled against Tutsi feudal rule (under the Belgian colonial authority) in 1959–61, leading to the massacre of thousands of Tutsis. Large numbers fled into exile in Uganda. Rwanda became an independent republic on 1 July 1962.

Armed Tutsi exiles repeatedly attempted to invade Rwanda in the 1960s and 1970s but were defeated by the predominantly Hutu army. Continued Hutu-Tutsi conflict left thousands dead over a period of 30 years. In October 1990 Rwanda was invaded by the Rwandan Patriotic Front (RPF) of exiled Tutsis and moderate Hutus, who forced the one-party MRND (National Revolutionary Movement for Development) government to introduce a multiparty constitution in 1991. After the government reneged on a 1992 peace agreement, the RPF advanced on Kigali and forced the government to restart negotiations, which led to the August 1993 Arusha peace accord. The accord provided for a transitional period under a broad-based government including the RPF until the 1995 elections, with UN forces in the country throughout the period.

President Habyarimana, who had retained the interim presidency, died on 6 April 1994 in a plane crash widely believed to have been caused by a rocket attack by extremist sections of the Hutu army. The Hutu army and armed militia, the *interahamwe*, then carried out a preplanned act of genocide against the Tutsi minority and moderate Hutus; 800,000 people were massacred in three months. The civil war restarted and the RPF gradually re-established its control over the country, forcing the defeated government forces and two million Hutu refugees into exile. A government report issued in February 2002 revealed that 1,074,017 people, more than 93 per cent of them Tutsis, were killed between 1990 and 1994. On 18 July 1994 the RPF declared victory and established a broad-based government of national unity in which moderate Hutus were given the presidency and premiership and the RPF took eight of the 22 seats.

The 70-member Transitional National Assembly provided for by the Arusha agreement began operation on 12 December 1994 with the extremist Hutu MRND excluded.

Killings by both Hutu militia and government forces continued, and Hutu attacks in central and western Rwanda were frequent in the first half of 1998 and recurred in May and June 2001 in the north west of the country.

At the ICTR in May 1998, former Prime Minister Jean Kambanda pleaded guilty to charges of genocide, the first admission by a senior Hutu official that genocide had taken place. The ICTR announced in December 2000 that it would investigate revenge atrocities committed by the RPF in the wake of the 1994 genocide. The RPF promised its full co-operation. Rwanda has supported a rebellion in the Democratic Republic of Congo led by the Congolese Democratic Rally, a Congolese Tutsi group. Rwandan troops have also been deployed in the Democratic Republic of Congo.

The Transitional National Assembly was extended for four further years on 9 June 1999. Elections scheduled for June 1999 were postponed to 2003.

POLITICAL SYSTEM
The President is head of state and is elected by the Transitional National Assembly. The President appoints the Council of Ministers.

The Transitional National Assembly was appointed in 1994 for a five-year term, since extended for a further four years. The number of seats in the Assembly was increased from 70 to 74 in September 2000.

HEAD OF STATE
President, Maj-Gen. Paul Kagame, *appointed* 17 April 2000, *sworn in* 22 April 2000

GOVERNMENT *as at August 2002*

The President (FPR)
Prime Minister, Bernard Makusa (MDR)
Agriculture, Livestock, Environment and Rural Development, Ephraim Kabayija
Civil Service and Labour, Sylvie Zainab Kayitesi
Commerce, Industry and Tourism, Alexandre Byambabaje
Defence and National Security, Col. Emmanuel Habyarimana
Education, Science and Technology, Romain Murenzi
Energy, Water and Natural Resources, Bonaventure Niyibizi
Finance and Economic Planning, Donat Kaberuka
Foreign Affairs and Regional Co-operation, André Bumaya
Gender and Women's Promotion, Angeline Muganza
Health, Ezechias Rwabuhihi
Internal Affairs, Jean de Dieu Ntiruhungwa
Justice and Institutional Relations, Jean de Dieu Mucyo
Lands, Resettlement and Environmental Protection, Laurent Nkusi
Local Government and Social Affairs, Désiré Nyandwi
Public Works, Transport and Communications, Kalinganire Silas
Youth, Culture and Sports, François Ngarambe

FPR Rwandan Patriotic Front; MDR Republican Democratic Movement

EMBASSY OF THE REPUBLIC OF RWANDA
Uganda House, 58-59 Trafalgar Square, London
WC2N 5DX.
Tel: 020-7930 2570
Ambassador Extraordinary and Plenipotentiary, HE
Rosemary K. Museminali, apptd 2000

BRITISH EMBASSY
Parcelle No. 1131, Blvd de l'Umuganda, Kacyira-Sud, BP
576 Kigali
Tel: (00 250) 84098/85771/85773
Ambassador Extraordinary and Plenipotentiary, HE
Susan Elizabeth Hogwood, MBE, apptd 2001

ECONOMY

Coffee, tea and sugar are grown. Tin, hides, bark of
quinine and extract of pyrethrum flowers are also
exported.

In 2000 there was a trade deficit of US$153 million and
a current account deficit of US$7 million. Imports
totalled US$213 million and exports US$53 million.
GNP – US$1,984 million (2000); US$250 per capita
(1999)
GDP – US$1,484 million (1998); US$217 per capita
(1999)
ANNUAL AVERAGE GROWTH OF GDP – 6.0 per cent
(2000)
INFLATION RATE – 4.3 per cent (2000)
TOTAL EXTERNAL DEBT – US$1,292 million (1999)

Trade with UK	2000	2001
Imports from UK	£3,630,000	£5,028,000
Exports to UK	103,000	481,000

ST KITTS AND NEVIS
The Federation of St Christopher and Nevis

AREA – 101 sq. miles (261 sq. km)
POPULATION – 38,756 (2001 estimate). The language is
English
CAPITAL – ΨBasseterre (population, 12,200, 1994
estimate)
MAJOR TOWNS – ΨCharlestown (1,700, 1994 estimate),
the chief town of Nevis
CURRENCY – East Caribbean dollar (EC$) of 100 cents
NATIONAL ANTHEM – Oh Land Of Beauty
NATIONAL DAY – 19 September (Independence Day)
NATIONAL FLAG – Three diagonal bands, green, black
and red; each colour separated by a stripe of yellow.
Two white stars on the black band
LIFE EXPECTANCY (years) male 68.2; female 71.6
POPULATION GROWTH RATE – 2.7 per cent (1999)
POPULATION DENSITY – 149 per sq. km (1999)

The state of St Christopher and Nevis is located at the
northern end of the eastern Caribbean. It comprises the
islands of St Christopher (St Kitts) (68 sq. miles) and
Nevis (36 sq. miles). The central area of St Christopher is
forest-clad and mountainous, rising to the 3,792 ft Mount
Liamuiga. Nevis is separated from the southern tip of St
Christopher by a strait two miles wide and is dominated
by Nevis Peak, 3,232 ft.

HISTORY AND POLITICS

St Christopher was the first island in the British West
Indies to be colonised (1623). The Territory of St
Christopher and Nevis became a State in Association with
Britain in 1967. The State of St Christopher and Nevis
became an independent nation on 19 September 1983.

On 10 August 1998 a referendum was held in Nevis on
the question of independence from St Christopher;

although 61.8 per cent voted in favour of secession, it fell
short of the two-thirds majority needed for
independence.

In the legislative election held on 6 March 2000, the
Labour Party won all eight of the seats on St Christopher.
On Nevis, the Concerned Citizens' Movement won two
seats and the Nevis Reformation Party one seat.

POLITICAL SYSTEM

Under the constitution, Queen Elizabeth II is Head of
State, represented in the islands by the Governor-General.
There is a central government with a ministerial system,
the head of which is the Prime Minister of St Christopher
and Nevis, and a National Assembly located on St
Christopher. The National Assembly is composed of the
Speaker, three senators (nominated by the Prime Minister
and the Leader of the Opposition) and 11 directly elected
representatives, who serve a five-year term. On Nevis
there is a Nevis Island Administration, the head being
styled Premier of Nevis, and a Nevis Island Assembly of
five elected and three nominated members.

Governor-General, HE Sir Cuthbert Montraville
Sebastian, GCMG, OBE, apptd 1996

CABINET *as at August 2002*

*Prime Minister, Finance, National Security, Planning,
Development*, Denzil Douglas
*Deputy Prime Minister, Labour, Social Security,
International Trade and Caricom Affairs,
Telecommunications and Technology*, Sam Condor
Agriculture, Fisheries, Co-operatives, Lands and Housing,
Cedric Liburd
Attorney-General, Justice and Legal Affairs, Delano Bart
Foreign Affairs, Education, Timothy Harris
Health, Environment, Earl Asim Martin
Information, Culture, Youth Affairs and Sports, Jacinth
Henry-Martin
Public Works, Utilities, Transport and Posts, Halva
Hendrickson
Social Development, Community and Gender Affairs,
Rupert Herbert
Tourism Commerce, Consumer Affairs, Dwyer Astaphan

HIGH COMMISSION FOR ST CHRISTOPHER AND
NEVIS
2nd Floor, 10 Kensington Court, London W8 5DL
Tel: 020-7460 6500
High Commissioner for St Christopher and Nevis, HE
James Ernest Williams, apptd 2001

BRITISH HIGH COMMISSIONER, HE John White,
resident at Bridgetown, Barbados

ECONOMY

The economy of the islands has been based on sugar for
over three centuries. Tourism and light industry,
concentrating on distilling, food processing, clothing and
electronics, are now being developed. The economy of
Nevis centres on small peasant farmers, but a sea-island
cotton industry is being developed for export.

The main exports are sugar, lobsters, beverages and
electrical equipment. Foodstuffs, energy, machinery and
transport equipment are the main imports.

About 70 per cent of homes on St Christopher were
damaged by Hurricane Georges in September 1998.

In 1996 imports totalled US$149 million and exports
US$22 million.
GNP – US$273 million (2000); US$6,330 per capita
(1999)
GDP – US$290 million (1998); US$7,974 per capita
(1999)

ANNUAL AVERAGE GROWTH OF GDP – 2.8 per cent (1999)
INFLATION RATE – 3.9 per cent (1999)
TOTAL EXTERNAL DEBT – US$136 million (1999)

Trade with UK	2000	2001
Imports from UK	£11,284,000	£7,469,000
Exports to UK	7,227,000	7,118

COMMUNICATIONS

Basseterre is a port of registry and has deep water harbour facilities. Golden Rock airport, on St Kitts, can take most large jet aircraft; Newcastle airstrip on Nevis can take small aircraft and has night landing facilities. The sea ferry route from Basseterre to Charlestown is 11 miles.

ST LUCIA

AREA – 208 sq. miles (539 sq. km)
POPULATION – 158,178 (2001 estimate). The official language is English. A French creole is spoken by most of the population
CAPITAL – ΨCastries (population, 51,994, 1997 estimate)
CURRENCY – East Caribbean dollar (EC$) of 100 cents
NATIONAL ANTHEM – Sons And Daughters Of Saint Lucia
NATIONAL DAY – 22 February (Independence Day)
NATIONAL FLAG – Blue, bearing in centre a device of yellow over black over white triangles having a common base
LIFE EXPECTANCY (years) – male 71.1; female 76.4
POPULATION GROWTH RATE – 1.1 per cent (1999)
POPULATION DENSITY – 282 per sq. km (1999)

St Lucia, the second largest of the Windward group, is 27 miles in length, with an extreme breadth of 14 miles. It is mountainous, its highest point being Mt Gimie (3,145 ft) and for the most part it is covered with forest and tropical vegetation.

HISTORY AND POLITICS

Possession of St Lucia was fiercely disputed and it constantly changed hands between the British and the French until 1814 when it was ceded to Britain by the Treaty of Paris. It became independent within the Commonwealth on 22 February 1979.

The St Lucia Labour Party maintained its majority in the House of Assembly in a general election on 3 December 2001, winning 14 seats.

POLITICAL SYSTEM

The Head of State is Queen Elizabeth II, represented on the island by a St Lucian Governor-General, and there is a bicameral legislature. The Senate has 11 members, six appointed by the ruling party, three by the Opposition and two by the Governor-General. The House of Assembly, which has a life of five years, has 17 elected members and a Speaker, who may be appointed from outside the House.

Governor-General, HE Dame Pearlette Louisy, apptd 1997

CABINET as at August 2002

Prime Minister, Finance, Economic Affairs, Information, Kenny Anthony
Agriculture, Forestry and Fisheries, Calixte George
Commerce, Tourism, Investment and Consumer Affairs, Phillip J. Pierre
Communications, Works, Transport and Public Utilities, Felix Finisterre
Development, Planning, Environment and Housing, Walter François
Education, Human Resources Development, Youth and Sport, Mario Michel
Foreign Affairs, International Trade and Civil Aviation, Julian Hunte
Health, Human Services, Family Affairs, Damian Greaves
Home Affairs and Gender Relations, Sarah Flood-Beaubrun
Labour Relations, Public Service and Co-operatives, Velon John
Social Transformation, Culture and Local Government, Menissa Rambally

HIGH COMMISSION FOR ST LUCIA
1 Collingham Gardens, London SW5 0HW
Tel: 020-7370 7123
High Commissioner for St Lucia, HE Emmanuel Cotter, MBE, apptd 1998

OFFICE OF THE BRITISH HIGH COMMISSION
Francis Compton, 2nd Floor (PO Box 227), Waterfront, Castries
Tel: (00 1 758) 452 2484/5
Email: britishhc@candw.lc
High Commissioner, HE John White, resident at Bridgetown, Barbados

ECONOMY

The economy is mainly agrarian, with manufacturing based on the processing of agricultural products. Principal crops are bananas, coconuts, cocoa, mangoes, breadfruit, yams and citrus fruit. Attempts are being made to increase industrialisation. The currency is tied to the US dollar at a rate of EC$2.70=US$1.00. There were 414,000 visitors to the island in 1998.

GNP – US$634 million (2000); US$3,820 per capita (1999)
GDP – US$613 million (1998); US$4,505 per capita (1999)
ANNUAL AVERAGE GROWTH OF GDP – 2.8 per cent (1998)
INFLATION RATE – 5.4 per cent (1999)
UNEMPLOYMENT – 20.5 per cent (1997)
TOTAL EXTERNAL DEBT – US$181 million (1999)

TRADE

The principal exports are bananas, coconut products (copra, edible oils, soap), cardboard boxes, beer, and textile manufactures. The chief imports are flour, meat, machinery, building materials, motor vehicles, manufactured goods, petroleum and fertilisers.

In 1996 St Lucia had a trade deficit of US$184 million and a current account deficit of US$80 million. In 1997 imports totalled US$332 million and exports US$66 million.

Trade with UK	2000	2001
Imports from UK	£13,771,000	£17,004,000
Exports to UK	33,429,000	16,501,000

ST VINCENT AND THE GRENADINES

AREA – 150 sq. miles (388 sq. km)
POPULATION – 109,022 (2002 estimate). The language is English
CAPITAL – ΨKingstown (population, 13,857, 2000)
CURRENCY – East Caribbean dollar (EC$) of 100 cents

NATIONAL ANTHEM – St Vincent, Land So Beautiful
NATIONAL DAY – 27 October (Independence Day)
NATIONAL FLAG – Three vertical bands, of blue, yellow and green, with three green diamonds in the shape of a 'V' mounted on the yellow band
LIFE EXPECTANCY (years) – male; 71.5; female 74.5
POPULATION GROWTH RATE – 0.3 per cent (1999)
POPULATION DENSITY – 289 per sq. km (1999)

The territory of St Vincent includes certain of the Grenadines, a chain of small islands stretching 40 miles across the Caribbean Sea between Grenada and St Vincent, some of the larger of which are Bequia, Canouan, Mayreau, Mustique, Union Island, Petit St Vincent and Prune Island.

HISTORY AND POLITICS

St Vincent was discovered by Christopher Columbus in 1498. It was granted by Charles I to the Earl of Carlisle in 1627 and after subsequent grants and a series of occupations alternately by the French and English, it was finally restored to Britain in 1783. St Vincent achieved full independence within the Commonwealth as St Vincent and the Grenadines on 27 October 1979.

The governing New Democratic Party (NDP) won eight seats and the United Labour Party (ULP) seven seats at the election held on 15 June 1998. As a consequence of opposition groups and trade unions pressing for the resignation of the government after the government had approved increased benefits for members of the legislature, the government and opposition agreed that the next general election should be held before 31 March 2001. The election took place on 28 March 2001 and was decisively won by the ULP, who obtained 12 seats. The NDP, who had been in power since 1984, won the remaining three seats.

POLITICAL SYSTEM

Queen Elizabeth II is Head of State, represented by a Governor-General. The House of Assembly consists of 15 elected members and four Senators appointed by the government and two by the Opposition. It is presided over by a Speaker elected by the House from within or without it.
Governor-General, Monica Deacon (*acting*), *sworn in* 5 October 2001

CABINET *as at August 2002*

Prime Minister, Finance, Planning, Economic Development, Labour, Information, Grenadine Affairs, Legal Affairs, Ralph Gonsalves
Deputy Prime Minister, Foreign Affairs, Commerce and Trade, Louis Straker
Agriculture, Lands and Fisheries, Selmon Walters
Education, Youth Affairs, Sport, Mike Browne
Health and the Environment, Douglas Slater
Ministers of State, Montgomery Daniel (*Agriculture, Lands and Fisheries*); Clayton Burgin (*Education, Youth Affairs, Sport*); Conrad Sayers (*Foreign Affairs, Commerce and Trade*)
National Security, Public Service, Airport Development, Vincent Beache
Social Development, Family, Gender Affairs, Ecclesiastical Affairs, Girlyn Miguel
Telecommunications, Science, Technology, Industry, Jerrol Thompson
Tourism and Culture, Rene Baptiste
Transport, Works, Housing, Julian Francis

HIGH COMMISSION FOR ST VINCENT AND THE GRENADINES
10 Kensington Court, London W8 5DL
Tel: 020-7565 2874; Email: svghighcom@clara.co.uk
High Commissioner for St Vincent and the Grenadines, HE Cenio E. Lewis, apptd 2001

BRITISH HIGH COMMISSION
Granby Street (PO Box 132), Kingstown
Tel: (00 1 784) 457 1701
Email: bhcvg@caribsurf.com
High Commissioner, HE John White, resident at Bridgetown, Barbados

ECONOMY

This is based mainly on agriculture but tourism (254,091 visitors in 2001) and manufacturing industries have been expanding. The main products are bananas, arrowroot, coconuts, cocoa, spices and various kinds of food crops. The main imports are foodstuffs, textiles, lumber, chemicals, motor vehicles and fuel. Bananas accounted for 36 per cent of exports in 2000.

In 1996 St Vincent and the Grenadines had a trade deficit of US$75 million and a current account deficit of US$35 million. In 2000 imports totalled US$163 million and exports US$47 million.
GNP – US$309 million (2000); US$2,640 per capita (1999)
GDP – US$316 million (1998); US$3,018 per capita (1999)
ANNUAL AVERAGE GROWTH OF GDP – 5.2 per cent (1998)
INFLATION RATE – 0.2 per cent (2000)
TOTAL EXTERNAL DEBT – US$192 million (1999)

Trade with UK	2000	2001
Imports from UK	£6,151,000	£9,223,000
Exports to UK	18,797,000	13,666,000

SAMOA
Ole Malo Tutoatasi o Samoa – Independent State of Samoa

AREA – 1,093 sq. miles (2,831 sq. km)
POPULATION – 179,058 (2001 estimate); 162,000 (1989 census), the largest numbers being on Upolu (114,980) and Savai'i (43,150). The Samoans are a Polynesian people, though the population also includes other Pacific Islanders, Euronesians, Chinese and Europeans. The main languages are Samoan and English. The islanders are Christians of different denominations
CAPITAL – ΨApia (population, 36,000, 1989), on Upolu. Robert Louis Stevenson died and was buried at Apia in 1894
CURRENCY – Tala (S$) of 100 sene
NATIONAL ANTHEM – The Banner Of Freedom
NATIONAL DAY – 11 June (Independence Day)
NATIONAL FLAG – Red with a blue canton bearing five white stars of the Southern Cross
LIFE EXPECTANCY (years) – male 66.9; female 73.5
POPULATION GROWTH RATE – 0.3 per cent (1999)
POPULATION DENSITY – 160 per sq. km (1999)
ILLITERACY RATE – 10.4 per cent (2002)
ENROLMENT (percentage of age group) – primary 96 per cent (1996); secondary 45 per cent (1995)

Samoa consists of the islands of Savai'i, Upolu, Apolima, Manono, Fanuatapu, Namua, Nuutele, Nuulua and Nuusafee. All the islands are mountainous. Upolu, the

most fertile, contains the harbours of Apia and Mulifanua, and Savai'i the harbour of Salelologa.

HISTORY AND POLITICS

Formerly administered by New Zealand (latterly with internal self-government), Western Samoa became fully independent on 1 January 1962. The state was treated as a member country of the Commonwealth until its formal admission on 28 August 1970. A constitutional amendment came into effect on 4 July 1997 changing the state's name to the Independent State of Samoa.

Suffrage was made universal following a referendum held in 1990.

In the general election held on 4 March 2001, the Human Rights Protection Party won 23 seats, the Samoan National Development Party won 13 seats and 13 seats were won by independents.

POLITICAL SYSTEM

The 1962 constitution provides for a head of state to be elected by the 49-member legislative assembly, the *Fono*, for a five-year term. Initially two of the four Paramount chiefs jointly held the office of head of state for life. When one of the chiefs died in April 1963, Susuga Malietoa Tanumafili II became head of state for life. The Head of State's functions are analogous to those of a constitutional monarch. Executive government is carried out by a Cabinet of Ministers.

HEAD OF STATE

Head of State for Life, HH Susuga Malietoa Tanumafili II, GCMG, CBE, since 15 April 1963

CABINET *as at August 2002*

Prime Minister, Foreign Affairs, Attorney-General, Police and Prisons, Immigration, Public Service Commission, Tuilaepa Sailele Malielegaoi
Deputy Prime Minister, Finance, Misa Telefoni Retzlaff
Agriculture, Forests and Fisheries, Tuisugaletaua Sofara Aveau
Revenue, Audit, Ombudsman, Gaiga Tino
Education, Fiame Naomi Mata'afa
Health, Labour, Mulitalo Siafausa
Justice, Seumanu Aita Ah Wa
Public Works, Faumuina Liuga
Tourism, Lands, Survey and Environment, Tuala Sale Tagaloa
Trade and Industry, Hans Joachim Keil
Transport and Shipping, Palusalue Faapo II
Women's Affairs, Internal Affairs, Broadcasting, Tuala Ainiu Iusitino
Youth, Sports and Culture, Ulu Vaomalo Ulu Kini

HIGH COMMISSION FOR THE INDEPENDENT STATE OF SAMOA
Franklin D. Rooseveltlaan 123, B-1050 Brussels
Tel: (00 32) (2) 660 8454

High Commissioner for the Independent State of Samoa, HE Tau'ili'ili'u'ili Meredith, apptd 1998
BRITISH HIGH COMMISSIONER, HE Richard Fell, CVO, apptd 2002, resident at Wellington, New Zealand
HONORARY CONSULATE – PO Box 2029, Apia

ECONOMY

Agriculture is the basis of the economy, employing about two-thirds of the labour force and supplying about 40 per cent of GDP and 90 per cent of exports, the principal cash crops (and exports) being coconuts (copra, oil and cream), cocoa and bananas. Efforts are being made to develop fishing on a commercial scale. Manufacturing is

very small in scope and concerned largely with processing agricultural products, but is being encouraged by the government.

Samoa and American Samoa signed a memorandum of understanding on trade, education, health, agriculture and law enforcement in January 2000.

In 1998 Samoa had a trade deficit of US$77 million and a current account surplus of US$20 million. In 2000 imports totalled US$106 million and exports US$14 million.

GNP – US$246 million (2000); US$1,070 per capita (1999)
GDP – US$219 million (1998); US$1,505 per capita (1999)
ANNUAL AVERAGE GROWTH OF GDP – 1.1 per cent (1998)
INFLATION RATE – 1.0 per cent (2000)
TOTAL EXTERNAL DEBT – US$192 million (1999)

Trade with UK	2000	2001
Imports from UK	£377,000	£4,768,000
Exports to UK	34,000	13,000

SAN MARINO
Repubblica di San Marino – Republic of San Marino

AREA – 24 sq. miles (61 sq. km). Neighbour: Italy
POPULATION – 27,336 (2001 estimate). The official language is Italian and the religion is Roman Catholic
CAPITAL – San Marino (population, 4,357, 1994), on the slope of Monte Titano
CURRENCY – Euro (€) of 100 cents
NATIONAL ANTHEM – Inno Nazionale (National Anthem)
NATIONAL DAY – 3 September
NATIONAL FLAG – Two horizontal bands, white, blue (with coat of arms of the republic in centre)
LIFE EXPECTANCY (years) – male 73.2; female 79.1
POPULATION GROWTH RATE – 1.0 per cent (1999)
POPULATION DENSITY – 426 per sq. km (1999)
URBAN POPULATION – 89.4 per cent (1995)
GDP – US$535 million (1998); US$20,421 per capita (1999)
ANNUAL AVERAGE GROWTH OF GDP – 1.3 per cent (1998)
UNEMPLOYMENT – 4.1 per cent (1998)

HISTORY AND POLITICS

San Marino is a small republic in the hills near Rimini, on the Adriatic, founded, it is said, by a pious stonecutter of Dalmatia in the fourth century. The republic resisted Papal claims and those of neighbouring dukedoms during the 15th to 18th centuries, and its integrity and sovereignty is recognised and respected by Italy.

The principal products are wine, cereals and fruits, and the main industries are tourism, metals, machinery, textiles and food.

San Marino is in a customs union with the European Union.

Following the general election held on 10 June 2001, the number of seats held in the Grand and General Council was as follows: Christian Democratic Party (PDCS) 25, the Socialist Party (PSS) 15, the Progressive Democratic Party (PPDS) 12, others 8.

POLITICAL SYSTEM

Executive power is vested in the Congress of State composed of ten ministries under the presidency of the two heads of state, who are elected at six-monthly intervals (every April and October). Legislative power is

exercised by the 60-member Great and General Council which is elected for a term of five years. A Council of Twelve forms in certain cases a Supreme Court of Justice.

HEADS OF STATE

Regents, Two 'Capitani Reggenti'

CONGRESS OF STATE *as at August 2002*

Education, University, Cultural Institutes, Fausta Morganti
Finance, Budget, Economic Planning, Relations with State Corporations, Transport, Fiorenzo Stolfi
Foreign and Political Affairs, Augusto Casali
Health and Social Security, Maurizio Rattini
Industry, Handicrafts, Economic Co-operation, Claudio Felici
Internal Affairs, Post and Telecommunications, Civil Protection, Emma Rossi
Justice, Information, Relations with the Castles Councils, Tito Masi
Labour and Co-operation, Fernando Bindi
Territory, Environment, Agriculture, Fabio Berardi
Tourism, Commerce and Sport, Paride Andreoli

EMBASSY OF THE REPUBLIC OF SAN MARINO
c/o Consulate of the Republic of San Marino,
Flat 51, 162 Sloane Street, London SW1X 9BS
Tel: 020-7823 4762
Ambassador Extraordinary and Plenipotentiary, HE Countess Marina Meneghetti de Camillo, apptd 2002, resident at Rome, Italy

BRITISH AMBASSADOR, HE Sir John Shepherd, KCVO, CMG, resident at Rome, Italy
BRITISH CONSULATE-GENERAL FOR SAN MARINO
Lungarno Corsini 2, I-50123 Florence, Italy.
Tel: (00 39) (55) 284133
Consul-General, R. J. Griffiths, OBE

Trade with UK	2000	2001
Imports from UK	£8,694,000	£7,943,000
Exports to UK	7,595,000	5,377,000

SÃO TOMÉ AND PRÍNCIPE
República Democrática de São Tomé e Príncipe –
Democratic Republic of São Tomé and Príncipe

AREA – 372 sq. miles (964 sq. km)
POPULATION – 165,034 (2001 estimate). The official language is Portuguese
CAPITAL – ΨSão Tomé (population, 43,420, 1995 estimate)
CURRENCY – Dobra of 100 centavos
NATIONAL ANTHEM – Independência Total (Total Independence)
NATIONAL DAY – 12 July (Independence Day)
NATIONAL FLAG – Horizontal stripes of green, yellow, green, the yellow of double width and bearing two black stars; and a red triangle in the hoist
LIFE EXPECTANCY (years) – male 64.15; female 67.07 (2001 estimate)
POPULATION GROWTH RATE – 3.1 per cent (1999)
POPULATION DENSITY – 149 per sq. km (1999)

The islands of São Tomé and Príncipe are situated in the Gulf of Guinea, off the west coast of Africa.

HISTORY AND POLITICS
The islands were first settled by the Portuguese in 1493. In 1951 they became an overseas province of Portugal, and gained full independence on 12 July 1975. A multiparty constitution was approved by referendum in August 1990. The Movement for the Liberation of São Tomé and Príncipe-Social Democratic Party (MLSTP-PSD), which had been the sole legal party since independence, was defeated by the opposition Democratic Convergence Party (PCD) in legislative elections held on 20 January 1991. Miguel Trovoada, an independent, was elected president on 3 March 1991.

A government of national unity incorporating opposition party members was appointed on 5 January 1996. President Trovoada was re-elected in July 1996.

In the presidential election which took place on 29 July 2001, Fradique de Menezes of the Independent Democratic Alliance was elected with 56.31 per cent of the vote. Legislative elections were held on 3 March 2002, in which the MLSTP-PSD won 24 of the 55 seats in the National Assembly. The Force for Change Democratic Movement-Democratic Convergence Party (MDFM-PCD) won 23 seats and the Ue Kedadji coalition (UK) won 8 seats. Gabriel Costa of the MLSTP-PSD was appointed Prime Minister on 26 March and a government of national unity comprising members of all three parties and Independents was sworn in on 8 April.

HEAD OF STATE

President and Commander-in-Chief of the Armed Forces, Fradique de Menezes, *elected* 29 July 2001, *sworn in* 3 September 2001

CABINET *as at August 2002*

Prime Minister, Gabriel Costa (MLSTP-PSD)
Agriculture, Rural Development and Fisheries, Julio Lopes Silva (UK)
Commerce, Industry and Tourism, Maria das Neves de Sousa (MLSTP-PSD)
Defence, Interior, Victor Taveres Monteiro (Ind.)
Foreign Affairs and Co-operation, Communities, Alda Bandeira (MDFM-PCD)
Health, Edgar Neves (MDFM-PCD)
Infrastructure and Public Works, Rafael Branco (MLSTP-PSD)
Justice, State and Administrative Reform, Alda Meol Santos (Ind.)
Labour, Employment and Solidarity, Damiano Vaz d'Almeida (MLSTP-PSD)
Planning and Finance, Maria Santos Tebus (MDFM-PCD)
Secretary of State for Environment, Territorial Integrity and Conservation, Arlindo Carvalho (UK)
Secretary of State for State and Administrative Reform, Carlos Edmundo Lito (Ind.)
MDFM-PCD Force for Change Democratic Movement-Democratic Convergence Party; MLS TP-PSD Movement for the Liberation of São Tomé and Príncipe-Social Democratic Party; UK Ue Kedadji; Ind. Independent

EMBASSY OF THE DEMOCRATIC REPUBLIC OF SÃO TOMÉ AND PRÍNCIPE
Square Montgomery, 175 Avenue de Tervuren, B-1150 Brussels
Tel: (00 32) (2) 734 8966
Chargé d'Affaires, Antonio de Lima Veigas

BRITISH CONSULATE
Residencial Avenida, Av. Da Independencia CP 257, São Tomé
Tel: (00 239) (12) 21026/7
British Ambassador, HE John Thompson, MBE

ECONOMY

Agriculture accounts for nearly a quarter of GDP and employs nearly 40 per cent of the workforce, with cocoa accounting for 86 per cent of exports in 1997. Drought and mismanagement have led to declining cocoa production, which has resulted in balance of payments deficits.

On 28 April 2000, the IMF approved a three-year credit of US$8.7 million to support the government's 2000-2 economic programme. A further debt reduction package worth about US$200 million was agreed by the IMF and the World Bank on 20 December 2000.

In 1997 imports totalled US$16 million and exports US$5 million.

GNP – US$43 million (2000); US$270 per capita (1999)
GDP – US$30 million (1998); US$257 per capita (1999)
ANNUAL AVERAGE GROWTH OF GDP – 2.6 per cent (1998)
TOTAL EXTERNAL DEBT – US$254 million (1999)

Trade with UK	2000	2001
Imports from UK	£1,941,000	£3,353,000
Exports to UK	8,000	132,000

SAUDI ARABIA

Al-Mamlaka al-'Arabiyya as-Sa'ūdiyya – Kingdom of Saudi Arabia

AREA – 830,000 sq. miles (2,149,690 sq. km).
　　Neighbours: UAE and Qatar (east), Jordan, Iraq and Kuwait (north), Yemen and Oman (south)
POPULATION – 22,757,092 (2001 estimate); 16,929,294 (1992 census). Islam is the only permitted religion. The language is Arabic
CAPITAL – Riyadh (Ar-Riyad) (population, 3,100,000, 1998 estimate)
MAJOR CITIES – Jiddah (1.5 million); Buraydah; Ad-Dammām; Al-Hofūf; Makkah (Mecca); Al-Madīnah; Tabūk
CURRENCY – Saudi riyal (SR) of 20 qursh or 100 halala
NATIONAL ANTHEM – Āsh Al-Malīk (Long Live Our Beloved King)
NATIONAL DAY – 23 September (proclamation and unification of the Kingdom, 1932)
NATIONAL FLAG – Green oblong, white Arabic device in centre: 'There is no God but God and Muhammad is the Prophet of God', and a white scimitar beneath the lettering
LIFE EXPECTANCY (years) – male 71.1; female 73.7
POPULATION GROWTH RATE – – 2.2 per cent (1999)
POPULATION DENSITY – 9 per sq. km (1999)

Saudi Arabia comprises most of the Arabian peninsula. The Nejd ('plateau') extends over the centre of the peninsula, including the Nafud and Dahna deserts. The Hejaz ('the boundary') extends along the Red Sea coast to Asir and contains the holy towns of Mecca (Al-Makkah) and Medina (Al-Madīnah). Asir ('inaccessible') is so named for its mountainous terrain, and, with the coastal plain of the Tihama, lies along the southern Red Sea coast from the Hejaz to the border with Yemen. It is the only region to enjoy substantial rainfall. The east and south-east of the country are lower-lying and largely desert.

Mecca (Al-Makkah), about 60 km east of Jeddah, is the birthplace of the Prophet Muhammad, and contains the Great Mosque, within which is the Kaaba (*Ka'abah*) or sacred shrine of the Muslim religion. This is the focus of the annual Hajj ('pilgrimage'). Medina (Al-Madīnah) Al Munawwarah ('The City of Light'), some 300 km north

of Al-Makkah, is celebrated as the first city to embrace Islam and as the Prophet Muhammad's burial place.

HISTORY AND POLITICS

In the 18th century Nejd was an independent state governed from Diriya. It subsequently fell under Turkish rule; in 1913 Abdul Aziz ibn Saud threw off Turkish rule and captured the Turkish province of Al Hasa. In 1920 he captured the Asir and in 1921 the Jebel Shammar territory of the Rashid family. In 1925 he completed the conquest of the Hejaz. Great Britain recognised Abdul Aziz ibn Saud as an independent ruler, King of the Hejaz and of Nejd and its Dependencies, in 1927. The name was changed to the Kingdom of Saudi Arabia in September 1932.

POLITICAL SYSTEM

Saudi Arabia is a hereditary monarchy, ruled by the sons and grandsons of Abdul Aziz ibn Saud, in accordance with the Islamic Shari'ah law. The line of succession passes from brother to brother according to age, although several sons of ibn Saud renounced their right to the throne. All sons and grandsons of ibn Saud must be consulted before a new king accedes to the throne.

In 1992 King Fahd announced a new Basic Law for the system of government based on Shari'ah law and including rules to protect personal freedoms. The constitution is defined as the Holy Koran (*Qur'an*) and the *Sunnah* (the teachings and sayings of the Prophet Muhammad). The King and the Council of Ministers (established in 1953) retain executive power. A consultative council (*Majlis-ash-Shūra*) of a chairman and 120 members appointed by the King was set up to share power with, and question, the government and to make recommendations to the King. The Majlis-ash-Shūra debates government policy in the areas of the budget, defence, foreign and social affairs. Members of the ruling al-Saud family are excluded from membership of the Council, which has a four-year term and takes decisions by majority vote. Cabinet ministers have terms of four years, with the possibility of a two-year extension.

In 1993 the country was reorganised into 13 provinces: Riyadh; Makkah; Al-Madīnah; Al Qasim; Eastern; Asir; Tabūk; Hā'il; Northern Border; Jīzān; Najrān; Baha; Al-Jawf. Each province has a governor appointed by the King and a council of prominent local citizens to advise the governor on local government, budgetary and planning issues.

HEAD OF STATE

Custodian of the Two Holy Mosques and HM The King of Saudi Arabia, King Fahd ibn Abdul Aziz al-Saud, *born 1923, ascended the throne* 1 June 1982
HRH Crown Prince, Prince Abdullah ibn Abdul Aziz al-Saud

COUNCIL *of Ministers as at August 2002*

Prime Minister, HM The King
First Deputy Prime Minister, Commander of the National Guard, HRH The Crown Prince
Second Deputy Prime Minister, Defence and Civil Aviation, HRH Prince Sultan ibn Abdul Aziz al-Saud
Agriculture and Water Resources, Abdullah ibn Abdul Aziz ibn Muammar
Civil Service, Mohammad ibn Ali al-Fayez
Commerce, Osama ibn Jaafar ibn Ibrahim al-Faqih
Education, Mohammad ibn Ahmad al-Rashid
Finance and National Economy, Ibrahim ibn Abdel Aziz al-Assaf

Foreign Affairs, HRH Prince Saud al-Faisal ibn Abdul Aziz al-Saud
Health, Osama ibn Abdul-Majid Shabakshi
Higher Education, Khalid ibn Muhammad al-Anqari
Industry and Electricity, Hashem ibn Abdullah ibn Hashem Yamani
Information, Fouad ibn Abdul-Salam Mohammad Farisi
Interior, HRH Prince Nayef ibn Abdul Aziz al-Saud
Islamic Affairs, Shaikh Salah ibn Abdul-Aziz al-Shaikh
Justice, Abdullah ibn Muhammed ibn Ibrahim al-Shaikh
Labour and Social Affairs, Ali ibn Ibrahim al-Nemla
Minister of State, Ali ibn Talal al-Jehani
Municipal and Rural Affairs, Mohammad ibn Ibrahim al-Jarallah
Oil and Mineral Resources, Ali Ibrahim al-Naimi
Pilgrimage Affairs, Ayad ibn Amin Madani
Planning, Posts, Telegraphs and Telecommunications, Khaled ibn Mohammad al-Qussaibi
Public Works and Housing, HRH Prince Miteb ibn Abdul Aziz al-Saud
Transport, Nasir ibn Muhammad al-Sallum

ROYAL EMBASSY OF SAUDI ARABIA
30 Charles Street, London W1X 7PM
Tel: 020-7917 3000
Ambassador Extraordinary and Plenipotentiary, HE Dr Ghazi Algosaibi, apptd 1992

BRITISH EMBASSY
PO Box 94351, Riyadh 11693
Tel: (00 966) (1) 488 0077
Ambassador Extraordinary and Plenipotentiary, HE Sir Derek J. Plumbly, KCMG, apptd 2000

CONSULATE-GENERAL – PO Box 393, Jiddah 21411.
Consul-General, A. Henderson

BRITISH COUNCIL DIRECTOR, Dr David Burton, OBE, Tower B, 2nd Floor, Al-Mousa Centre, Olaya Street, PO Box 58012, Riyadh 11594; Email: enquiry.riyadh@sa.britishcouncil.org. There are also offices in Jeddah and Ad-Dammām

DEFENCE

The Army has 1,055 main battle tanks, 1,900 armoured personnel carriers, 970 armoured infantry fighting vehicles and 12 attack helicopters. The Navy has four frigates, 26 patrol and coastal vessels and 21 armed helicopters at six bases. The Air Force has 348 combat aircraft.

Saudi Arabia is base to the Gulf Co-operational Council Peninsula Shield Force of 7,000 troops. The USA, UK and France station aircraft and support units in the country to patrol the air exclusion zone in southern Iraq.

MILITARY EXPENDITURE – 10.1 per cent of GDP (2000)
MILITARY PERSONNEL – 126,500: Army 75,000; Navy 15,500; Air Force 20,000; Air Defence Force 16,000; National Guard 75,000; Paramilitaries 15,500

ECONOMY

Saudi Arabia's revenue fell when world oil prices dropped from the mid-1980s onwards, and financial reserves had to be used up to meet budget deficits. However, the sharp rise in world oil prices in 2000 has improved the country's economic prospects.

Agriculture accounted for 6.1 per cent of GDP and engaged 12.2 per cent of the workforce in 1997. The productivity of traditional dryland farming is supplemented by extensive irrigation, desalination and use of aquifers.

The principal industry is oil extraction and processing; 405,200,000 tonnes were produced in 1998. Oil was first found in commercial quantities in 1938. Proven oil reserves of 259 billion barrels account for more than one-quarter of the world's proven reserves. The country is the world's largest oil exporter. Recoverable gas reserves of 204.5 trillion cubic feet, in fields associated with crude oil and those separate from it, are beginning to be exploited; production in 1998 was 46,820 million cubic metres. Mineral exploitation of gold, silver, copper and other minerals is also beginning, with gold production of 5.1 tonnes in 1998.

The government, in a series of five-year development plans begun in 1970, has actively encouraged the establishment of manufacturing industry. Industries have developed in the fields of construction materials, metal fabrication, simple machinery and electrical equipment, food and beverages, textiles, chemicals and plastics. The seventh development plan, covering 2000–5, was approved in September 2000. It aimed to eliminate the budget and current account deficits, promote economic growth and diversity and introduce legislation to increase the proportion of Saudi Arabian citizens in the workforce.

GNP – US$139,365 million (1999); US$6,900 per capita (1999)
GDP – US$146,494 million (1998); US$7,095 per capita (1999)
ANNUAL AVERAGE GROWTH OF GDP – 4.5 per cent (2000)
INFLATION RATE – -0.8 per cent (2000)

TRADE

Oil remains the main source of receipts in the balance of payments. The leading suppliers of imports are the USA, the UK, Germany and Japan, and the chief customers for exports are Japan, the USA, South Korea and Singapore. There is a total ban on the importation of alcohol, pork products, firearms, and items regarded as non-Islamic or pornographic.

In 2000 there was a trade surplus of US$51,176 million and a current account surplus of US$15,567 million. In 1999 imports totalled US$28,011 million and exports totalled US$50,761 million.

Trade with UK	2000	2001
Imports from UK	£1,598,179,000	£1,516,348,000
Exports to UK	1,054,304,000	991,316,000

COMMUNICATIONS

There is one railway line from Ad-Dammām to Riyadh, which was opened in 1951 and is operated by the Saudi Government Railway Organisation. The line is being extended to the port of Al-Jubail on the Gulf. A network of 139,200 km of roads (of which 45,200 km are paved), including an expressway system, connects all the cities and main towns. There are 21 ports, of which the major ones are Ad-Dammām and Al-Jubayl (Gulf) and Jiddah, Yanbu and Jizan (Red Sea). The 15.5 mile-long King Fahd Causeway completed in 1986 connects the Eastern Province to the state of Bahrain and is the world's second longest causeway.

There are international airports at Az-Zahrān (King Fahd), Jiddah (King Abdul Aziz), and Riyadh (King Khalid).

Telecommunications are being rapidly expanded with 3.1 million telephone lines in 1998 and seven earth stations linked to the Intelsat system, allowing direct dialling to 185 countries.

EDUCATION

With the exception of a few schools for expatriate children, all schools are government-supervised and are segregated for boys and girls. There are universities in Jiddah, Al-Makkah, Riyadh (branches in Abha and Qassim), Ad-Dammām (branch at Al-Hufūf) and Az-Zahrān, and there are Islamic universities in Al-Madīnah and Riyadh together with 83 tertiary colleges. There is great emphasis on vocational training, provided at literacy and artisan skill training centres and more advanced industrial, commercial and agricultural education institutes.

ILLITERACY RATE – 22.0 per cent (2002)

ENROLMENT (percentage of age group) – primary 76 per cent (1997); secondary 61 per cent (1997); tertiary 16.3 per cent (19967)

SENEGAL

République du Sénégal – Republic of Senegal

AREA – 75,955 sq. miles (196,722 sq. km). Neighbours: Mauritania (north), Mali (east), Guinea-Bissau and Guinea (south), the Gambia

POPULATION – 10,284,929 (2001 estimate), 94 per cent Muslim, 4 per cent Christian, 1 per cent Animist. The official language is French; the principal local language is Wolof. Fulani, Serer, Mandinka, Jola and Sarakole are also spoken

CAPITAL – ΨDakar (population, 1,641,358, 1998 UN estimate)

MAJOR CITIES – Rufisque (150,000); Thiés (248,000); ΨZiguinchor (192,000), 1998 UN estimates

CURRENCY – Franc CFA of 100 centimes

NATIONAL ANTHEM – Pincez Tous Vos Koras, Frappez Les Balafons (All Pluck Your Koras, Strike The Balafons)

NATIONAL DAY – 4 April

NATIONAL FLAG – Three vertical bands, green, yellow and red; a green star on the yellow band

LIFE EXPECTANCY (years) – male 52.5; female 56.2

POPULATION GROWTH RATE – 2.6 per cent (1999)

POPULATION DENSITY – 47 per sq. km (1999)

MILITARY EXPENDITURE – 1.2 per cent of GDP (2000)

MILITARY PERSONNEL – 10,000: Army 8,000, Navy 600, Air Force 800; Paramilitaries 5,800

CONSCRIPTION DURATION – Two years (selective)

ILLITERACY RATE – 60.8 per cent (2002)

ENROLMENT (percentage of age group) – primary 60 per cent (1997); tertiary 3.4 per cent (1994)

HISTORY AND POLITICS

Formerly a French colony, Senegal elected in 1958 to remain within the French Community as an autonomous republic. It became independent as part of the Federation of Mali in June 1960 and seceded to form the Republic of Senegal in September 1960.

Abdoulaye Wade, the leader of the Senegalese Democratic Party, was elected in the second round of the presidential election on 19 March 2000 with 58.49 per cent of the vote, thus becoming the first president not to belong to the Socialist Party. The legislative election on 29 April 2001 was won by an alliance of 40 parties, the Sopi (Change) coalition, led by the Senegalese Democratic Party (PDS). Sopi won 89 seats, the Socialist Party (PS), which had been in government, secured only ten seats, and the Alliance of Progress Forces won 11 seats.

INSURGENCY

A separatist civil war has been fought in the southern Casamance region for the past 17 years. The government

and the Casamance Movement of Democratic Forces (MFDC) agreed a cease-fire on 26 December 1999. A meeting between the two sides in January 2000 agreed to establish a joint body to monitor progress, to withdraw army and rebel forces from occupied villages, and to co-operate on mine clearance and the refugee problem. The government and the MFDC signed a peace agreement on 16 March 2001, but violence in the region increased during the election campaign in April 2001.

POLITICAL SYSTEM

A referendum to approve a new constitution took place on 7 January 2001. The constitution, which was approved by 96 per cent of those voting, dissolved the Senate, reduced the number of MPs in the National Assembly from 140 to 120, shortened the presidential term of office to five years, and guaranteed the right to form political parties. A general election for the National Assembly is held every five years.

HEAD OF STATE

President, Abdoulayé Wade, *elected* 19 March 2000, *sworn in* 1 April 2000

COUNCIL OF MINISTERS *as at August 2002*

Prime Minister, Mamé Madior Boyé
Agriculture and Livestock, Pape Diouf
Armed Forces, Youba Sambou
Civil Service, Labour and Employment, Yero Deh
Culture, Tourism and Leisure, Mamadou Makalou
Economy and Finance, Abdoulayé Diop
Education, Moustapha Sourang
Equipment and Transport, Youssouf Sakho
Family and Children, Awa Gueye Kebe
Fisheries, Cheikh Saadibou Fall
Foreign Affairs, African Union and Senegalese Abroad, Cheikh Tidiane Gadio
Handicrafts and Industry, Landing Savane
Health and Prevention, Awa Marie Coll Seck
Interior, Maj.-Gen. Mamadou Niang
Justice and Keeper of the Seals, Basile Senghor
Mines, Energy and Water Resources, Macky Sall
Ministers-Delegate, Cheikh Hadjibou Soumare (*Budget*); Thiéwo Cisse Ducoure (*Local Constituencies*)
Relations with Assemblies, Mamadou Diop
Small and Medium Enterprises and Commerce, Aïcha Agne Pouye
Social Development and National Solidarity, Aminata Tall
Sport, Joseph Ndong
Technical and Vocational Training, Basic Education and National Languages, Bécaye Diop
Town and Country Planning, Seydou Sall
Youth, Environment and Public Hygiene, Modou Fada Diagne

EMBASSY OF THE REPUBLIC OF SENEGAL
39 Marloes Road, London W8 6LA
Tel: 020-7938 4048/7937 7237
Ambassador Extraordinary and Plenipotentiary, HE El Hadj Amadou Niang, apptd 2001

BRITISH EMBASSY
20 rue du Docteur Guillet (BP 6025), Dakar
Tel: (00 221) 823 7392/9971
Email: britemb@telecomplus.sn
Ambassador Extraordinary and Plenipotentiary, HE E. Alan Burner, apptd 1997

BRITISH COUNCIL DIRECTOR, Steve McNulty, 34–36 Blvd de la République, BP 6232, Dakar; Email: steve.mcnulty@britishcouncil.sn

ECONOMY

Around 60 per cent of the workforce are employed in agriculture. Senegal's principal exports are fish, groundnuts (raw and processed) and phosphates. Tourism is also of growing importance as a revenue earner; in 1999 there were some 400,000 overseas visitors. Principal imports are food, machinery, fuel oils and transport equipment. Senegal exports fish, furniture, oilseeds and fruit, rubber, fertilisers and animal fodder to the UK, and imports foodstuffs, cigarettes, chemicals, machinery and transport equipment, vegetable fats and oils, and manufactured goods from the UK.

In 1996 there were 14,576 km of roads, of which 4,271 km were paved. There are 1,225 km of railway track.

In 1997 there was a trade deficit of US$271 million and a current account deficit of US$185 million. In 2000 imports totalled US$1,365 million and exports US$997 million.

GNP – US$4,726 million (2000); US$500 per capita (1999)

GDP – US$4,666 million (1998); US$522 per capita (1999)

ANNUAL AVERAGE GROWTH OF GDP – 5.6 per cent (1998)

INFLATION RATE – 0.7 per cent (2000)

TOTAL EXTERNAL DEBT – US$3,705 million (1999)

Trade with UK	2000	2001
Imports from UK	£32,253,000	£41,168,000
Exports to UK	12,663,000	10,827,000

SEYCHELLES

The Republic of Seychelles/République des Seychelles/Repiblik Sesel

AREA – 176 sq. miles (455 sq. km)

POPULATION – 79,715 (2001 estimate). The languages are English, French and Créole

CAPITAL – ΨVictoria (population, 24,324, 1987), on Mahé

CURRENCY – Seychelles rupee of 100 cents

NATIONAL ANTHEM – Koste Seselwa (Seychellois Unite)

NATIONAL DAY – 18 June

NATIONAL FLAG – Five rays extending from the lower hoist over the whole field, coloured blue, yellow, green, white and red

LIFE EXPECTANCY (years) – male 65.3; female 74.1

POPULATION GROWTH RATE – 1.6 per cent (1999)

POPULATION DENSITY – 177 per sq. km (1999)

MILITARY EXPENDITURE – 1.8 per cent of GDP (2000)

MILITARY PERSONNEL – 450: Army 200, Paramilitaries 250

Seychelles, in the Indian Ocean, consists of 115 islands spread over 400,000 sq. miles of ocean. There is a relatively compact granitic group, 32 islands in all, with high hills and mountains (highest point about 2,972 ft), of which Mahé is the largest and most populated (90 per cent of the population live on Mahé); and the outlying coralline group, for the most part only a little above sea-level. Although only 4° S. of the Equator, the climate is pleasant though tropical.

HISTORY AND POLITICS

Proclaimed French territory in 1756, the Mahé group was settled as a dependency of Mauritius from 1770, was captured by a British ship in 1794, and changed hands several times between 1803 and 1814, when it was finally

assigned to Great Britain. In 1903 these islands, together with the coralline group, were formed into a separate colony. On 29 June 1976, the islands became an independent republic within the Commonwealth. A coup d'état took place in 1977. Seychelles was a one-party state from 1979 until 1991, when a multiparty democratic system was proposed by President René.

In legislative elections held in March 1998, the Seychelles People's Progressive Front formed a government after winning 30 seats in the National Assembly. In presidential elections held from 31 August – 2 September 2001, President René was re-elected with 54 per cent of the vote.

POLITICAL SYSTEM

Under the constitution adopted in 1993, multiparty politics was institutionalised, a National Assembly of up to 34 members (23 elected by constituencies, up to 11 by proportional representation) was established and the presidential mandate was set at five years, renewable three times.

HEAD OF STATE

President, Head of Government, Defence, Interior and Legal Affairs, France-Albert René, assumed office 5 June 1977; elected 1979; re-elected 1984, 1989, 1993, 22 March 1998, 2 September 2001

Vice-President, Finance, Economic Planning, Information Technology and Communications, James Michel

COUNCIL OF MINISTERS as at August 2002

The President
The Vice-President
Administration and Manpower Development, Noellie Alexander
Agriculture and Marine Resources, William Herminie
Education and Youth, Danny Faure
Employment and Social Affairs, Dolor Ernesta
Environment, Ronald Jumeau
Foreign Affairs, Jérémie Bonnelame
Health, Patrick Pillay
Industry and International Business, Jacquelin Dugasse
Land Use and Habitat, Joseph Belmont
Local Government, Sports and Culture, Sylvette Pool
Tourism and Transport, Simone de Commarmond

SEYCHELLES HIGH COMMISSION
2nd Floor, Eros House, 111 Baker Street, London
W1U 6RR.
Tel: 020-7224 1660
Email:seyhclon@aol.com
High Commissioner, HE Bertrand Rassool, apptd 1999

BRITISH HIGH COMMISSION
Oliaji Trade Centre, PO Box 161 Victoria, Mahé
Tel: (00 248) 225225/225356
Email: bhcsey@seychelles.net
High Commissioner, HE Fraser Wilson, MBE, apptd 2002

ECONOMY

The economy is based on tourism, fishing, small-scale agriculture and manufacturing, and the re-export of fuel for aircraft and ships. Deep sea tuna fishing by foreign fleets under licence, improved port facilities at Victoria and exports from a tuna canning factory attract growing revenues. The government is attempting to reduce the reliance on tourism, which generates the majority of foreign exchange earnings, by promoting the country as an offshore haven for financial services. There were 128,258 foreign visitors in 1998.

GNP – US$593 million (2000); US$6,500 per capita (1999)
GDP – US$559 million (1998); US$7,804 per capita (1999)
ANNUAL AVERAGE GROWTH OF GDP – 2.9 per cent (1999)
INFLATION RATE – 6.3 per cent (2000)
TOTAL EXTERNAL DEBT – US$172 million (1999)

TRADE

Principal exports in 1998 were canned tuna, frozen prawns, fish and cinnamon bark. The principal imports were machinery and transport equipment, manufactures, foodstuffs and tobacco, fuel oils and chemicals.

In 1997 there was a trade deficit of US$188 million and a current account deficit of US$63 million. In 1999 imports totalled US$434 million and exports US$145 million.

Trade with UK	2000	2001
Imports from UK	£14,026,000	£13,374,000
Exports to UK	38,647,000	47,857,000

SIERRA LEONE
The Republic of Sierra Leone

AREA – 7,699 sq. miles (71,740 sq. km). Neighbours: Guinea (north, north-east), Liberia (south-east)
POPULATION – 5,426,618 (2001 estimate). The south is inhabited by peoples whose languages fall into the Mende group; the north by the Temne and smaller groups such as the Limba, Loko, Koranko and Susu
CAPITAL – Ψ Freetown (population, 469,776, 1985)
CURRENCY – Leone (Le) of 100 cents
NATIONAL ANTHEM – High We Exalt Thee, Realm of the Free
NATIONAL DAY – 27 April (Independence Day)
NATIONAL FLAG – Three horizontal stripes of leaf green, white and cobalt blue
LIFE EXPECTANCY (years) – male 39.2; female 41.8
POPULATION GROWTH RATE – 3.0 per cent (1999)
POPULATION DENSITY – 66 per sq. km (1999)
MILITARY EXPENDITURE – 1.2 per cent of GDP (2000)
MILITARY PERSONNEL – Navy 200 (Army is being reformed and willhave a strength of c.8,000)

HISTORY AND POLITICS

In the late 18th century a project was begun to settle destitute Africans from England on Freetown peninsula. In 1808 the settlement was declared a Crown colony and became the main base in West Africa for enforcing the 1807 Act outlawing the slave trade. Africans from North America and the West Indies, and Africans rescued from slave ships also settled there. In 1896 a Protectorate was declared over the hinterland.

In 1951 the colony of Freetown and the Protectorate were united and on 27 April 1961 Sierra Leone became a fully independent state within the Commonwealth. In 1971 a republican constitution was adopted and Dr Siaka Stevens became the first executive president. In 1978 Sierra Leone became a one-party state, following approval by Parliament and a referendum.

In September 1991 a new multiparty constitution was adopted and an interim government formed, which was overthrown by a military coup on 29 April 1992. The military government surrendered power to a civilian government on 29 March 1996.

The Sierra Leone People's Party (SLPP) won 27 seats in

the 68-member National Assembly and formed a government with the support of the People's Democratic Party and the Democratic Centre Party. The SLPP's candidate, Ahmad Tejan Kabbah, won the presidential contest, attracting 59.4 per cent of the vote.

In May 1997 army officers led by Major Johnny Koroma seized power. President Kabbah fled and a 20-member Armed Forces Revolutionary Council was set up with Koroma as chairman and Revolutionary United Front (RUF) leader Foday Sankoh as Vice-Chairman. In July 1997, a Nigerian-led ECOMOG force was sent to oust Koroma and restore the legitimate government. On 24 October 1997, a peace agreement was reached which provided for Kabbah to return to power within six months and granted immunity from prosecution to Koroma. ECOMOG troops gained control of Freetown on 12 February 1998, and ousted the Koroma regime. President Kabbah returned to Freetown on 10 March 1998.

In the presidential elections held on 14 May 2002, President Kabbah was re-elected with 70 per cent of the vote and the SLPP won 83 of the 112 seats in the parliament. A new cabinet, composed of members of the SLPP and independents, was appointed in 21 May.

INSURGENCY

Since May 1991 government forces have been fighting the RUF whose aim is to force all foreigners out of the country and to nationalise the mining sector. Attacks by the RUF intensified in December 1998 and on 6 January 1999 the RUF attacked Freetown. ECOMOG troops launched a counter-attack on 9–10 January, recapturing the city.

President Kabbah and Foday Sankoh signed a cease-fire agreement on 18 May 1999 and it was agreed in July 1999 that Sankoh would be appointed Vice-President and head the Mineral Resources Commission and that the RUF would be given four cabinet posts. A government of national unity was announced on 2 November 1999. Violence continued, despite the efforts of a UN peacekeeping force, the UN Mission to Sierra Leone (UNAMSIL), which officially took over from ECOMOG on 29 April 2000. The cease-fire agreement collapsed when the RUF abducted 500 UNAMSIL peacekeepers between 30 April–6 May, and on 6 May the RUF used captured UNAMSIL weaponry to launch an advance on Freetown. A temporary British military deployment was despatched to evacuate British, EU and Commonwealth nationals from Freetown. UNAMSIL troops, along with Sierra Leonean Army (SLA) and Nigerian Army troops, went on the offensive and drove the RUF back. RUF leader Foday Sankoh, who had been the Vice-President since November 1999, was arrested on 17 May 2000. Following the withdrawal of British forces on 14 June 2000, the British government sent an army team to begin a three-year training programme to assist the SLA.

A cease-fire brokered by ECOWAS was signed by the government and the RUF on 11 November 2000, but was never fully implemented. An agreement to end all hostilities was signed by the RUF and the pro-government Civil Defence Forces on 16 May 2001. The state of emergency imposed in 1998 was lifted in March 2002.

HEAD OF STATE
President, Defence, Ahmad Tejan Kabbah, *elected* 15 March 1996, *re-elected* 14 May 2002
Vice-President, Solomon Berewa

CABINET *as at August 2002*

The President
The Vice-President
Agriculture, Forestry and Marine Resources, Sama
   Mondeh
Attorney-General, Justice, Eke Halloway
Development and Economic Planning, Mohamed Daramy
Education, Science and Technology, Alpha Wurie
Energy and Power, Emmanuel Grant
Finance, Joseph Bandaba Dauda
Foreign Affairs and International Co-operation, Momodu
   Koroma
Health and Sanitation, Agnes Taylor-Lewis
Information and Broadcasting, Septimus Kaikai
Internal Affairs, Chief Sam Hinga Norman
Labour, Industrial Relations and Social Security, Alpha
   Timbo
Lands, Country Planning, Forestry and Environment,
   Alfred Bobson Sesay
Marine Resources, Okere Adams
Mineral Resources, Alhaji Mohamed Deen
Ministers of State, Sahr Randolph Fillie-Faboe (*East*);
   Dennis Sankoh (*North*); Foday Yumkella (*Presidential
   Affairs*); S.U.M. Jah (*South*)
Political and Parliamentary Affairs, George Banda
   Thomas
Rural Development and Local Government, Sidikie Brima
Social Welfare, Gender, Children's Affairs, Shirley
   Gbujama
Trade and Industry, Kadi Sesay
Transport and Communications, Prince A. Harding
Works, Housing and Technical Maintenance, Caiser
   Boima
Youth and Sports, Dennis Bright

SIERRA LEONE HIGH COMMISSION
1st and 3rd Floors Oxford Circus House, 245 Oxford
   Street, London W1D 2LX
Tel: 020-7287 9884
High Commissioner, HE Sulaiman Tejan-Jalloh, apptd
   2000

BRITISH HIGH COMMISSION
Spur Road, Freetown
Tel: (00 232) (22) 232563/4/5
Email: bhc@sierratel.sl
High Commissioner, HE David Alan Jones, apptd 2000

BRITISH COUNCIL DIRECTOR, Rajive Bendre, PO Box
   124, Tower Hill, Freetown; Email: bcouncil@sierratel.sl

ECONOMY
On the Freetown peninsula, farming is largely confined to
the production of cassava and crops such as maize and
vegetables for local consumption. In the hinterland the
principal agricultural product is rice, which is the staple
food of the country, and cash crops such as cocoa, coffee,
palm kernels and ginger. Cattle production is also
important.
   The economy depends largely on mineral exports,
mainly diamonds, gold and bauxite, although mineral
production has been disrupted by the insurgency.
   In December 1999, the IMF approved US$21.31 million
to assist the government's reconstruction and economic
recovery programme.
   In 2000 imports totalled US$141 million and exports
US$13 million.
GNP – US$633 million (2000); US$130 per capita
   (1999)
GDP –US$703 million (1998); US$159 per capita (1999)

ANNUAL AVERAGE GROWTH OF GDP – 3.8 per cent
   (2000)
INFLATION RATE – 0.8 per cent (2000)
TOTAL EXTERNAL DEBT – US$1,249 million (1999)

Trade with UK	2000	2001
Imports from UK	£77,752,000	£62,051,000
Exports to UK	1,676,000	3,046,000

COMMUNICATIONS
Since the phasing out of the railway system in 1974 the
road network has been developed considerably; there are
now 7,000 miles of roads in the country. A bridge has
been constructed over the Mano River linking Sierra
Leone and Liberia.
   The Freetown international airport is situated at Lungi.
The main port is Freetown, which has one of the largest
natural harbours in the world. There are smaller ports at
Pepel, Bonthe and Niti.

EDUCATION
Technical education is provided in the two government
technical institutes, situated in Freetown and Kenema, in
two trade centres and in the technical training
establishments of the mining companies. Teacher
training is carried out at the University of Sierra Leone,
six colleges in the provinces and in the Milton Margai
Training College near Freetown.
ILLITERACY RATE – 63.7 per cent (2000)
ENROLMENT (percentage of age group) – tertiary 1.3
   per cent (1990)

SINGAPORE
*Repablik Singapura/Xinjiapo Gongheguo/Singapur
Kuṭiyarāśu/Republic of Singapore*

AREA – 239 sq. miles (618 sq. km)
POPULATION – 4,017,733 (2001): Chinese 76.8 per
   cent, Malays 13.9 per cent, Indians (including those
   of Pakistani, Bangladeshi and Sri Lankan origin) 7.9
   per cent and 1.4 per cent from other ethnic groups.
   Malay, Mandarin, Tamil and English are the official
   languages. At least eight Chinese dialects are used.
   Malay is the national language and English is the
   language of administration. The religions are
   Buddhism 42.5 per cent, Islam 14.9 per cent,
   Christianity 14.6 per cent, Taoism 8.5 per cent,
   Hinduism 4.0 per cent
CURRENCY – Singapore dollar (S$) of 100 cents
NATIONAL ANTHEM – Majullah Singapura (May
   Singapore Progress)
NATIONAL DAY – 9 August
NATIONAL FLAG – Horizontal bands of red over white;
   crescent with five five-point stars on red band near
   staff
LIFE EXPECTANCY (years) – male 76.4; female 80.4
POPULATION GROWTH RATE – 2.8 per cent (2001)
POPULATION DENSITY – 6,055 per sq. km (2001)
MILITARY EXPENDITURE – 4.9 per cent of GDP (2000)
MILITARY PERSONNEL – 60,500: Army 50,000, Navy
   4,500, Air Force 6,000; Paramilitaries 94,000
CONSCRIPTION DURATION – 24–30 months
ILLITERACY RATE – 7.1 per cent (2002)
ENROLMENT (percentage of age group) – primary 94 per
   cent (1997); tertiary 39 per cent (1997)

Singapore consists of the island of Singapore and 63
islets. Singapore island is 26 miles long and 14 miles in
breadth and is situated just north of the Equator off the
southern extremity of the Malay peninsula, from which it

is separated by the Straits of Johore. A causeway crosses the three-quarters of a mile to the mainland. The climate is hot and humid.

HISTORY AND POLITICS

Singapore, where Sir Stamford Raffles first established a trading post under the East India Company in 1819, was incorporated with Penang and Malacca to form the Straits Settlements in 1826. The Straits Settlements became a Crown colony in 1867. Singapore fell into Japanese hands in 1942 and civil government was not restored until 1946, when it became a separate colony. Internal self-government was introduced in 1959. Singapore became a state of Malaysia in September 1963, but left Malaysia and became an independent sovereign state within the Commonwealth on 9 August 1965. Singapore adopted a republican constitution from that date.

S. R. Nathan became President of Singapore on 1 September 1999; no election was held as he was the sole candidate. After the general election of 3 November 2001 the People's Action Party (PAP) had 82 seats in Parliament.

POLITICAL SYSTEM

The president is directly elected for a six-year term, and can veto government decisions relating to internal security, the budget, financial reserves and the appointment of senior civil servants. The President appoints the Prime Minister and, on his advice, the members of the Cabinet. There is a Parliament of 84 directly elected members, with up to six further non-constituency members from opposition parties (NCMPs), dependent on their share of the vote, directly elected for a five year term. Up to nine members can also be nominated by the government for a two-year term (NMPs). In the present parliament, there are two NCMPs and six NMPs.

HEAD OF STATE

President, Sellapan Rama Nathan, took office 1 September 1999

CABINET as at August 2002

Prime Minister, Goh Chok Tong
Senior Minister, Prime Minister's Office, Lee Kuan Yew
Deputy Prime Minister, Defence, Tony Tan Kheng Yam
Deputy Prime Minister, Finance, Lee Hsien Loong
Community Development and Sports, Muslim Affairs, Abdullah Tarmugi
Education, Second Minister for Defence, Rear-Adm. Teo Chee Hean
Environment, Lim Swee Say
Foreign Affairs and Law, Shanmugam Jayakumar
Health, Second Minister for Finance, Lim Hng Kiang
Home Affairs, Wong Kan Seng
Information, Communications and the Arts (acting) and Senior Minister of State in the Ministry of Defence, David Lim Tik En
Labour, Lee Boon Yang
National Development, Mah Bow Tan
Prime Minister's Office, Second Minister for Foreign Affairs, Lee Yock Suan
Trade and Industry, Brig.-Gen. George Yong Boon Yeo
Transport, Cheow Tong Yeo
Without Portfolio, Prime Minister's Office, Lim Boon Heng

HIGH COMMISSION FOR THE REPUBLIC OF SINGAPORE
9 Wilton Crescent, London SW1X 8SP

Tel: 020-7235 8315
High Commissioner, HE Michael Eng Cheng Teo, apptd 2002

BRITISH HIGH COMMISSION
Tanglin Road, Singapore 247919
Tel: (00 65) 424 4200
Email: commercial.singapore@fco.gov.uk
High Commissioner, HE Sir Stephen Brown, KCVO, apptd 2001

BRITISH COUNCIL DIRECTOR, Les Dangerfield, 30 Napier Road, Singapore 258509; Email: britcoun@britishcouncil.org.sg

ECONOMY

Historically Singapore's economy was based on the sale and distribution of raw materials from surrounding countries and on entrepôt trade in finished products. An industrialisation programme launched in 1968 has established a wide range of manufacturing industries, including shipbuilding, iron and steel, micro-electronics, electrical goods, telecommunications equipment, office machinery, scientific instruments, pharmaceuticals, etc. Singapore has also become an important financial services centre with significant insurance and foreign exchange markets, a stock exchange, 149 commercial banks and 79 merchant banks and an oil-refining centre. In February 1998 the government announced substantial liberalising reforms of the financial sector, aimed at allowing the country to compete more competitively with other financial sectors in the region. Singapore has not been as badly affected as its neighbours by the economic crisis in south-east Asia, due in part to currency reserves estimated at US$118 billion; it was praised by the IMF for its adroit response to the crisis, which included wage cuts.

There were 7,690,000 foreign visitors in 2000.

Singapore's major trading partners are the USA, Malaysia, the EU, Hong Kong and Japan.

In 2000 Singapore had a trade surplus of US$11,400 million and a current account surplus of US$21,797 million. Imports totalled US$134,545 million and exports US$137,875 million.

GNP – US$99,404 million (2000); US$24,150 per capita (1999)
GDP – US$85,425 million (1998); US$22,072 per capita (1999)
ANNUAL AVERAGE GROWTH OF GDP – 9.9 per cent (2000)
INFLATION RATE – 1.4 per cent (2000)
UNEMPLOYMENT – 4.6 per cent (1999)

Trade with UK	2000	2001
Imports from UK	£1,627,314,000	£1,603,512,000
Exports to UK	2,485,372,000	2,146,369,000

COMMUNICATIONS

Singapore is one of the largest and busiest seaports in the world, with six terminals, deep water wharves and ship repairing facilities. Ships also anchor in the roads, unloading into lighters. In 2000, the total volume of cargo handled was 325,591,100 tonnes. There were 145,383 ship arrivals in 2000.

The international airport is at Changi, in the east of the island, with 64 airlines operating flights to 50 countries and 28,618,200 passengers using the airport in 2000. There are 25.8 km of railway connected to the Malaysian rail system by the causeway across the Straits of Johore, and 3,122 km of roads.

Singapore's government has prioritised information technology and telecommunications in its programme to

transform the country into a knowledge-based economy by 2010. As at December 2000, there were 59.3 fixed line telephones, 74.8 mobile phones and 25.7 pagers per cent of population; access to the internet amounted to 59.5 per cent.

SLOVAKIA
Slovenská Republika – Slovak Republic

AREA – 18,923 sq. miles (49,012 sq. km). Neighbours: Poland (north), Ukraine (east), Hungary (south), Austria (west), the Czech Republic (north-west)
POPULATION – 5,414,937 (2001 estimate): 87.7 per cent are ethnic Slovaks, 10.6 per cent ethnic Hungarians, 1.4 per cent Romany, 1 per cent Czech, with smaller numbers of Ruthenians, Ukrainians and Germans. The population is mainly Christian, some 60 per cent Roman Catholic and 8 per cent Protestant. Slovak is the official language, while Hungarian and Czech are also spoken
CAPITAL – Bratislava (population, 452,278, 1996 estimate), on the Danube
MAJOR CITIES – Košice (241,163), 1996 estimate
CURRENCY – Koruna (Sk) of 100 halierov
NATIONAL ANTHEM – Nad Tatrou Sa Blýska (Storm Over The Tatras)
NATIONAL DAYS – 1 January (Establishment of Slovak Republic); 5 July (Day of the Slav Missionaries); 29 August (Slovak National Uprising); 1 September (Constitution Day)
NATIONAL FLAG – Three horizontal stripes of white, blue, red with the arms all over near the hoist
LIFE EXPECTANCY (years) – male 69.8; female 77.6
POPULATION GROWTH RATE – 0.1 per cent (1999)
POPULATION DENSITY – 110 per sq. km (1999)
URBAN POPULATION – 57.0 per cent (1995)
ENROLMENT (percentage of age group) – tertiary 22 per cent (1997)

The Tatry (Tatras) mountains in the centre and north of Slovakia reach heights of 2,655 m. The major river is the Váh which flows from the Tatry mountains to join the Danube at the Hungarian border.

HISTORY AND POLITICS

At the end of the 11th century Slovakia became part of the Hungarian state when the Magyars gained control of the area. Following the dissolution of the Austro-Hungarian Empire, Slovakia was amalgamated into Czechoslovakia on 28 October 1918, but became independent in March 1939 as a Nazi puppet state when Germany invaded the Czech lands. Slovakia was liberated by Soviet forces in 1945 and returned to Czechoslovakia. The formation of a federal republic between the Czech lands and Slovakia was the only Prague Spring reform to survive the Soviet invasion of 1968. Following the collapse of Communist rule in 1989, the Czech and Slovak republics began to negotiate the dissolution of the federation into two sovereign states in 1992. Dissolution took effect on 1 January 1993.

A coalition government led by the Movement for a Democratic Slovakia (HZDS) was sworn in on 12 January 1993 but was brought down by a no-confidence vote in March 1994. Legislative elections on 30 September and 1 October 1994 returned the HZDS to power at the head of a three-party coalition which took office on 13 December 1994.

Following the legislative elections on 25–26 September 1998, the HZDS remained the largest party, but a four-party coalition government led by the Slovak Democratic Coalition (SDK) was formed.

The number of seats held by each of the parties in the National Council following the 1998 election was: HZDS 43; SDK 42; Party of the Democratic Left (SDL) 23; Hungarian Coalition Party (SMK) 15; Slovak National Party (SNS) 14; Party of Civic Understanding (SOP) 13. President Kováč's term of office ended on 2 March 1998. The presidential elections were not contested by the ruling HZDS, who were accused by opposition parties of trying to create a constitutional vacuum; since no president was elected by the end of Kováč's term, certain presidential powers were transferred to the prime minister. After the 1998 legislative elections, the National Council voted on 14 January 1999 for direct presidential elections, which were held on 29 May 1999 and won by Rudolf Schuster of the SOP.

On 11 November 2000, a referendum which had been called by the opposition HZDS to demand an early general election failed to obtain the necessary 50 per cent voter turnout; the government had urged voters not to take part. Legislative elections were scheduled for 20–21 September 2002.

POLITICAL SYSTEM

The constitution vests legislative power in the National Council of 150 members directly elected for a four-year term by proportional representation with a five per cent threshold for parliamentary representation. The president is elected for a five-year term, renewable only once, by direct election; executive power is held by the prime minister and Cabinet.

HEAD OF STATE

President, Rudolf Schuster, *elected* 29 May 1999, *sworn in* 15 June 1999

CABINET *as at August 2002*

Prime Minister, Mikuláč Dzurinda (SDK)
Deputy Prime Ministers, Ivan Mikloš (SDK) (*Economy, Transport, Post and Telecommunications*); Mária Kadlečíková (SOP) (*European Integration*); Pál Csáky (SMK) (*Human and Minority Rights and Regional Development*); L'ubomír Fogaš (SDL) (*Legislation*)
Agriculture, Pavel Koncoš (SDL)
Construction and Public Works, István Harna (SMK)
Culture, Milan Knažko (SDK)
Defence, Jozef Stank (SDL)
Economy, L'ubomír Harach (SDK)
Education, Peter Ponický (SDL)
Environment, László Miklós (SMK)
Finance, František Hajnovič (SDL)
Foreign Affairs, Eduard Kukan (SDK)
Health, Roman Kováč (SDL)
Interior, Ivan Šimko (SDK)
Justice, Ján Čarnogurský (SDK)
Labour, Social Affairs and the Family, Peter Magvaši (SDL)
Privatisation, Mária Machová (SOP)

EMBASSY OF THE SLOVAK REPUBLIC
25 Kensington Palace Gardens, London W8 4QY
Tel: 020-7313 6470
Ambassador Extraordinary and Plenipotentiary, HE František Dlhopolček, apptd 2000

BRITISH EMBASSY
Panská 16, SK-811 01 Bratislava
Tel: (00 421) (2) 5441 9632/3
Email: bebra@internet.sk

Ambassador Extraordinary and Plenipotentiary, HE
Roderic Todd, apptd 2002

BRITISH COUNCIL DIRECTOR, Jim Mcgrath, PO Box
68, Panská 17, SK-814 99 Bratislava;
Email: information.centre@britishcouncil.sk. There
are also offices at Banská Bystríca and Košice

DEFENCE

The Army has 272 main battle tanks, 175 armoured
personnel carriers and 476 armoured infantry fighting
vehicles. The Air Force has 56 combat aircraft and 19
attack helicopters.
MILITARY EXPENDITURE – 1.8 per cent of GDP (2000)
MILITARY PERSONNEL – 33,000: Army 19,800, Air
Force 10,200; Paramilitaries 4,700
CONSCRIPTION DURATION – Nine months

ECONOMY

From independence until mid-1994 Slovakia faced
economic difficulties because of the structure of its
centrally-planned and inefficiently managed economy,
reliant on state-subsidised heavy industries with low
productivity, and because of the ambivalent attitude to
reform of the HZDS government. In mid-1994 the
economic situation stabilised as the Moravčik
government implemented a second round of
privatisation. The election of an HZDS-led government
in October 1994 slowed the pace of reform. Following
severe depreciation of the Koruna and the failure of the
economy to achieve the anticipated growth targets, the
SDK-led government introduced a package of austerity
measures on 20 May 1999; the basic rate of VAT was
raised, there were increases in energy, water,
telecommunications and housing prices, and import
taxes were reintroduced.

The EU suspended aid to Slovakia in April 2001
following allegations of the misuse of funds.

Natural resources include brown coal, natural gas, iron
ore, antimony, lead, zinc and magnesite.

In 2000 Slovakia had a trade deficit of US$895 million
and a current account deficit of US$694 million. Imports
totalled US$13,316 million and exports US$11,803
million.
GNP – US$19,995 million (2000); US$3,770 per capita
(1999)
GDP – US$20,362 million (1998); US$3,492 per capita
(1999)
ANNUAL AVERAGE GROWTH OF GDP – 2.2 per cent
(2000)
INFLATION RATE – 12.0 per cent (2000)
UNEMPLOYMENT – 16.2 per cent (1999)
TOTAL EXTERNAL DEBT – US$9,150 million (1999)

Trade with UK	2000	2001
Imports from UK	£157,125,000	£192,446,000
Exports to UK	139,797,000	180,559,000

SLOVENIA
Republika Slovenija – Republic of Slovenia

AREA – 7,821 sq. miles (20,256 sq. km). Neighbours:
Austria (north), Hungary (north-east), Croatia (east
and south), Italy (west)
POPULATION – 1,987,000 (2001 estimate). The
population is mostly Slovenian. There are small
Hungarian (0.5 per cent) and Italian (0.1 per cent)
minorities, together with a Romany population. The
main religion is Roman Catholicism. Slovene is the
official language, together with Hungarian and Italian
in ethnically mixed regions

CAPITAL – Ljubljana (population, 273,000, 1996
estimate)
MAJOR CITIES – Maribor (100,000), 1996 estimate
CURRENCY – Tolar (SIT) of 100 stotin
NATIONAL ANTHEM – Zdravljica (A Toast)
NATIONAL DAY – 25 June (Statehood Day)
NATIONAL FLAG – Three horizontal stripes of white,
blue, red, with the arms in the upper hoist
LIFE EXPECTANCY (years) – male 72.3; female 79.6
POPULATION GROWTH RATE – 0.1 per cent (1997)
POPULATION DENSITY – 98 per sq. km (1999)
URBAN POPULATION – 70.0 per cent (1999)
MILITARY EXPENDITURE – 1.2 per cent of GDP (2000)
MILITARY PERSONNEL – 7,600: Army; Paramilitaries
4,500
CONSCRIPTION DURATION – Seven months

Slovenia is a small mountainous state which is the most
northerly of the former Yugoslav republics. The two
major rivers are the Sava and the Drava. There is a short
coastline in the south-west 29 miles (46 km) in length on
the Adriatic.

HISTORY AND POLITICS

The area that is now Slovenia came under the control of
the Habsburg Empire in the 13th and 14th centuries and
remained so until the defeat of the Austro-Hungarian
Empire in 1918. On 27 October 1918 Slovenia became
part of Yugoslavia. In 1941 German forces invaded
Yugoslavia and Slovenia was divided between Germany,
Italy and Hungary. Slovenia was reformed as a constituent
republic of the federal Yugoslav state in May 1945. After a
dispute with Italy and nine years of international
administration, the Adriatic coast and hinterland were
returned to Slovenia in 1954 and Italy retained Trieste.

Slovenian fears of Serbian dominance led the Slovene
Assembly in 1989 to amend the republican constitution
to lay the basis of a sovereign state. The first democratic
elections, held in April 1990, were won by the pro-
independence 'Demos' coalition. In a referendum in
December 1990, 88 per cent of the electorate voted for
independence, which was declared on 25 June 1991. A
ten-day war with the Yugoslav National Army followed
before the Army called off hostilities and withdrew under
the mediation of the EU.

A coalition led by Liberal Democracy of Slovenia (LDS)
formed a government following the 1996 legislative
election. President Kučan was re-elected on 23 November
1997.

In the general election which took place on 15 October
2000, the LDS won 34 seats, the Social Democratic Party
(SDS) won 14 seats, the United List of Social Democrats
(ZLSD) won 11 seats, the Slovene People's Party-Slovene
Christian Democrats (SLS-SKD) won 9 seats, New
Slovenia won 8 seats, the Democratic Party of Pensioners
(DeSUS) won 4 seats and other parties won 10 seats. A
coalition government was formed by the LDS, the ZLSD,
the SLS-SKD and the DeSUS. Presidential elections were
scheduled for 10 November 2002.

FOREIGN RELATIONS

Slovenia signed an association agreement and applied for
membership of the EU in June 1996. The EU began
formal accession negotiations with Slovenia on 10
November 1998.

POLITICAL SYSTEM

The head of state is the president, elected for a five-year
term. Executive power is vested in the prime minister and
Cabinet of Ministers. The lower house of the legislature,

the National Assembly, has 90 members directly elected for a four-year term. The upper house, the 40-member National Council, has an advisory role. The National Assembly is elected on a proportional representation basis, with one seat each reserved for the Italian and Hungarian minorities.

HEAD OF STATE

President, Milan Kučan, *elected* April 1990, *re-elected* December 1992, 23 November 1997

EXECUTIVE COUNCIL *as at August 2002*

President of the Executive Council (*Prime Minister*), Janez Drnovšek (LDS)
Agriculture, Forestry and Food, Franc But (SLS-SKD)
Culture, Andreja Rihter (ZLSD)
Defence, Anton Grizold (LDS)
Economic Affairs, Tea Petrin (LDS)
Education and Science, Lucija Čok (LDS)
Environment and Physical Planning, Janez Kopač (LDS)
Finance, Anton Rop (LDS)
Foreign Affairs, Dimitrij Rupel (LDS)
Health, Dušan Keber (LDS)
Information Society, Pavel Gantar (LDS)
Internal Affairs, Rado Bohinc (ZLSD)
Justice, Ivo Bizjak (SLS-SKD)
Labour, Family and Social Affairs, Vlado Dimovski (ZLSD)
Transport, Jakob Presečnik (SLS-SKD)
Without Portfolio, European Affairs, Janez Potočnik

LDS Liberal Democracy of Slovenia; SLS-SKD Slovene People's Party-Slovene Christian Democrats; ZLSD United List of Social Democrats

EMBASSY OF THE REPUBLIC OF SLOVENIA
10 Little College Street, London SW1P 3SH
Tel: 020-7222 5400
Ambassador Extraordinary and Plenipotentiary, HE vacant

BRITISH EMBASSY
4th Floor, Trg Republike 3, SI-1000 Ljubljana
Tel: (00 386) (1) 200 3910
Email: info@british-embassy.si
Ambassador Extraordinary and Plenipotentiary, HE Hugh Mortimer, LVO, apptd 2000

BRITISH COUNCIL DIRECTOR, Steve Green, Cankarjevo nabrezje 27, SI-1000 Ljubljana; Email: info@britishcouncil.si

ECONOMY

Slovenia's economy has emerged as the most stable of the former Yugoslav economies. It has successfully re-orientated its exports towards Western markets, its main trading partners being Germany, Italy, France, Austria and Croatia. The privatisation process was completed in 1998.

In 1999 agriculture contributed 4 per cent to the total value of GDP, industry 38.5 per cent and services 59.9 per cent. The main agricultural products are potatoes, wheat, corn, sugar beet and wine. The major manufacturing sectors are metalworking, electronics, textiles, automotive parts, chemicals, glass products and food-processing. Tourism and transport are major export earners, with 1,957,000 tourists visiting in 2000.

In 2000 Slovenia had a trade deficit of US$1,081 million and a current account deficit of US$594 million. In 2000 imports totalled US$10,107 million and exports US$8,733 million.

GNP – US$20,022 million (2000); US$10,000 per capita (1999)
GDP – US$19,524 million (1998); US$10,052 per capita (1999) Annual Average Growth of GDP – 4.8 per cent (2000)
INFLATION RATE – 10.8 per cent (2000)
UNEMPLOYMENT – 7.4 per cent (1999)
TOTAL EXTERNAL DEBT – US$4,762 million (1997); US$5,491 million (1999 estimate)

Trade with UK	2000	2001
Imports from UK	£157,911,000	£157,552,000
Exports to UK	126,105,000	153,370,000

COMMUNICATIONS

There are 20,128 km of roads and 1,201 km of rail track, of which 499 km is electrified. Important road and rail communications cross the country from west to east (Milan–Ljubljana–Budapest), and north to south (Munich–Ljubljana–Zagreb–Belgrade–Athens). There are international airports at Ljubljana, Maribor and Portorož (Adriatic Coast). Koper is an important shipment point for goods from Austria, Hungary, the Czech Republic and Slovakia.

EDUCATION

Education is compulsory and free between the ages of six and 14. There are 816 primary schools (age six–14), 147 secondary or middle schools (age 14–19), 44 colleges and two universities (Ljubljana and Maribor).
ILLITERACY RATE – 0.3 per cent (2002)
ENROLMENT (percentage of age group) – primary 98 per cent (1997); tertiary 36 per cent (1997)

SOLOMON ISLANDS

AREA – 11,157 sq. miles (28,896 sq. km)
POPULATION – 480,442 (2001 estimate). English is the official language; there are over 80 local languages
CAPITAL – ΨHoniara (population, 40,000, 1991)
CURRENCY – Solomon Islands dollar (SI$) of 100 cents
NATIONAL ANTHEM – God Bless Our Solomon Islands
NATIONAL DAY – 7 July (Independence Day)
NATIONAL FLAG – Blue over green divided by a diagonal yellow band, with five white stars in the top left quarter
LIFE EXPECTANCY (years) – male 67.9; female 70.7
POPULATION GROWTH RATE – 3.1 per cent (1999)
POPULATION DENSITY – 15 per sq. km (1999)

Forming a scattered archipelago of mountainous islands and low-lying coral atolls, the Solomon Islands stretches about 900 miles in a south-easterly direction from the Shortland Islands to the Santa Cruz islands. The six biggest islands are Choiseul, New Georgia, Santa Isabel, Guadalcanal, Malaita and Makira.

HISTORY AND POLITICS

The origin of the present Melanesian inhabitants is uncertain. European interest in the islands began in the mid-16th century and continued intermittently for about 300 years, when the inauguration of sugar plantations in Queensland and Fiji (which created a need for labour) and the arrival of missionaries and traders led to increased European interest in the region. Great Britain declared a Protectorate in 1893 over the Southern Solomons, adding the Santa Cruz group in 1898 and 1899. The islands of the Shortland groups were transferred from Germany to Great Britain by treaty in 1900. The Solomon Islands achieved internal self-

government in 1976, and became independent in July 1978.

In November 2000, a conference of provincial governmental heads called for the introduction of a federal system of government; some of the islands had earlier threatened secession. Legislative elections were held on 5 December 2001 in which the People's Alliance Party gained 20 of the 50 seats in the National Parliament. The party's parliamentary leader, Sir Allan Kemakeza was elected prime minister on 17 December and the new Cabinet was sworn in on 19 December.

INSURGENCY

Following tension between indigenous inhabitants and settlers from other parts of the country, on 28 June 1999, a peace agreement was signed by representatives of the national and provincial governments and the Isatabu Freedom Fighters (IFF), a local militant group, following mediation by the Commonwealth special envoy Sitiveni Rabuka. Following further tension, on 28 February 2000 the government banned the IFF and their rivals the Malaita Eagles Force (MEF), but lifted the ban on 15 May to facilitate peace talks. MEF guerrillas took Prime Minister Ulufa'alu hostage on 5 June 2000 and took over the capital. The prime minister was freed on 10 June and the MEF and the IMF agreed to a two-week truce to allow mediation by a Commonwealth delegation. A peace deal was signed by the IFF and the MEF on 15 October 2000, agreeing to disarm within 30 days. In response, the National Assembly passed a bill granting an amnesty for those involved in the conflict. A peace deal was signed by the IFF and the Marau Eagles Force, a smaller Malaitan militia, on 7 February 2001. Fighting resumed on 18 March on Guadalcanal.

POLITICAL SYSTEM

The Solomon Islands is a constitutional monarchy. Queen Elizabeth II is represented locally by the Governor-General. Executive authority is exercised by the Cabinet. Legislative power is vested in a unicameral National Parliament of 50 members, elected for a four-year term.

Governor-General, HE John Lapli, GCMG, apptd 1999

CABINET *as at August 2002*

Prime Minister, Sir Allan Kemakesa
Deputy Prime Minister, National Planning, Snyder Rini
Agriculture and Livestock, Edward Huniehu
Commerce Employment and Trade, Trevor Olavae
Economic Reform and Structural Adjustment, Daniel Fa'afunua
Education and Training, Mathias Taro
Finance, Lori Hok Si Chan
Fisheries and Marine Resources, Nelson Kile
Foreign Affairs, Nollen Leni
Forests, Environment and Conservation, David Holosivi
Health and Medical Services, Benjamin Una
Home Affairs, Clement Rojumana
Lands and Surveys, Siriako Usa
Mines and Energy, Stephen Paeni
National Unity, Reconciliation and Peace, Nathaniel Waena
Police, National Security, Justice, Augustine Taneko
Provincial Government and Rural Development, Walton Naezon
Tourism and Aviation, Alex Bartlett
Transport, Works and Communication, David Giro
Youth, Sports and Women's Affairs, vacant

HIGH COMMISSION OF THE SOLOMON ISLANDS
Avenue Edourd Lacomble 17, B-1040 Brussels.
Tel: (00 32) (2) 2732 7285
Email: siembassy@compuserve.com
High Commissioner, HE Robert Sisilo, apptd 1996

BRITISH HIGH COMMISSION
Telekom House, Mendana Avenue, Honiara.
Tel: (00 677) 21705/6
Email: bhc@solomon.com.sb
High Commissioner, HE Brian Baldwin, apptd 2001

ECONOMY

The main imports are foodstuffs, consumer goods, machinery and transport materials. Principal exports are timber, fish, palm oil, copra and cocoa.

In 1998 there was a trade deficit of US$18 million and a current account surplus of US$8 million. In 1996 imports totalled US$151 million and exports totalled US$162 million.

GNP – US$278 million (2000); US$750 per capita (1999)
GDP – US$297 million (1998); US$801 per capita (1999)
ANNUAL AVERAGE GROWTH OF GDP – 2.2 per cent (1998)
INFLATION RATE – 8.3 per cent (1999)
TOTAL EXTERNAL DEBT – US$160 million (1999)

Trade with UK	2000	2001
Imports from UK	£ 481,000	£272,000
Exports to UK	4,844,000	477,000

COMMUNICATIONS

Solomon Airlines operates international services to other Pacific states and Australia. Air Niugini flies from Port Moresby to Honiara.

SOMALIA
Jamhuuriyadda Dimoqraadiya Soomaaliya – Somali Democratic Republic

AREA – 246,201 sq. miles (637,657 sq. km). Neighbours: Djibouti, Ethiopia and Kenya (west)
POPULATION – 7,488,773 (2001 estimate). Somali and Arabic are the official languages. English and Italian are also spoken
CAPITAL – ΨMogadishu (Muqdisho) (population, 900,000, 1990 estimate)
MAJOR CITIES – ΨBerbera (15,000); Boroma (65,000); Burao (15,000); Hargeysa (20,000); ΨKisimaayo (60,000)
CURRENCY – Somali shilling of 100 cents
NATIONAL DAY – under review
NATIONAL FLAG – Five-pointed white star on blue ground
LIFE EXPECTANCY (years) – male 47.4; female 50.5
POPULATION GROWTH RATE – 4.1 per cent (1999)
POPULATION DENSITY – 15 per sq. km (1999)

HISTORY AND POLITICS

The British protectorate of Somaliland and the Italian trust territory of Somalia were joined and became independent on 1 July 1960. In 1969, the armed forces seized power and established a ruling Revolutionary Council under Siad Barre's leadership. Siad Barre was overthrown by rebels in January 1991, sparking civil war between rival clan-based movements. The United Somali Congress (USC) seized control in Mogadishu, while the Somali National Movement formed a rival

administration in the north. Fighting between the USC and supporters of the Somali National Alliance (SNA) of Gen. Mohammed Aideed devastated Mogadishu and large parts of the south, exacerbating famine conditions. The UN Operation in Somalia proved ineffective in securing aid distribution routes and was replaced on 9 December 1992 by a UN-approved, US-led, United Task Force (UNITAF).

On 4 May 1993, UNITAF handed over to UNOSOM. The UN withdrew its troops in March 1995. On 12 June 1995, Gen. Aideed was ousted as SNA leader by a joint USC-SNA congress which nominated Osman Ali Ato as its leader. Gen. Aideed responded by declaring himself president on 15 June 1995, but was shot dead in July 1996 and was replaced as president by his son, Hussein Aideed.

A peace plan proposed by Djibouti was overwhelmingly supported on 16 November 1999 by representatives of civil society and the armed factions at a forum in Nairobi. A Somali National Reconciliation Conference in Djibouti opened on 2 May 2000, which aimed to lay the foundations of the transitional institutions of the Somali state, but was opposed by the Rahawein Resistance Army, the Somali Patriotic Movement and the leaders of Puntland. The National Reconciliation Conference appointed a transitional national assembly on 13 August, which on 26 August appointed Abdiqassim Salad Hassan as president. President Hassan appointed Ali Khalif Galayadh as prime minister on 3 October 2000. .

Fighting between pro- and anti-government militias broke out in the south of the country in July 2001. Prime Minister Galayadh resigned on 28 October 2001 following a vote of no confidence. Hassan Abshir Farah was appointed prime minister on 12 November and a reshuffled cabinet was named on 16 February 2002 and accepted by the Transitional National Assembly on 6 March.

Further factional fighting in Mogadishu on 28 May 2002 resulted in the deaths of over 60 people. Fighting had continued into July.

INSURGENCIES

With the downfall of Siad Barre, the SNM took control of the north-west (the former British Somaliland Protectorate) and in May 1991 declared unilateral independence as the 'Somaliland Republic'. A government and legislature was formed which elected Mohammed Ibrahim Egal as president in May 1993; he was re-elected in February 1997. A referendum on a new constitution, which confirmed the independence of Somaliland, was held on 31 May 2001 and was approved by 97.09 per cent of those who voted. Egal died on 3 May 2002 and was succeeded by Vice-President Dahir Riyale Kahin.

An autonomous administration was proclaimed in north-eastern Somalia on 23 July 1998. Col. Ahmed Abdullahi Yusuf was named as president of the region, calling itself Puntland. A Cabinet was appointed. On 15 September 1998, a 69-member parliament was inaugurated. On 30 June 2001 Abdullahi was replaced by Yusuf Haji Nur as interim president pending elections held on 14 November in which Jama Ali Jama was elected president. Abdullahi has refused to relinquish his claim to the presidency and by May 2002 his supporters had taken control of the whole of the territory.

HEAD OF STATE

Interim President, Abdiqassim Salad Hassan, sworn in 27 August 2000

INTERIM CABINET as at August 2002

Prime Minister, Hasan Abshir Farah
Consitution and Federalism, vacant
Culture and Heritage, Ali Mursal Muhammad
Defence, Abdiwahab Muhammad Husayn
Disabled and Rehabilitation, Andiqadir Muhammad Abdulle
Disapora and Refugee Affairs, Ahmad Abdullahi Jama
Education and Training, Husayn Muhammad Usman Jumbur
Energy, vacant
Environment, Abubakar Abdi Usman
Finance, Husayn Mahmud Shaykh Husayn
Foreign Affairs, Yusuf Hassan Ibrahim
Health, Muhammad Nurani Bakar
Higher Education, Zakariya Mahmud Haji Abdi
Industry, Yusuf Ma'alin Amin 'Badiow'
Information, Abdirahman Adan Ibrahim Ibbi
Internal Affairs, Dahir Sheikh Muhammad Nur
International Co-operation, Husayn Eelaabe Fahiye
Justice and Religious Affairs, Mahmud Umar Farah
Labour, Abdullahi Muhammad Shirwa
Livestock, Sayid Ahmad Shakh Dahir
Local Government, Muhammad Nur Jiley
Monetary Affairs, Umar Hashi Adan
Ports and Shipping, Abdiweli Jama' Warsameh
Public Works, Muhammad Warsame Ali
Reconciliation and Conflict Resolution, Muhammad Meydane Burale
Reconstruction and Resettlement, Abdiqadir Aw Yusuf Muhammad
Science and Technology, Abdi'aziz Shaykh Muqtar
Sports and Youth Affairs, Abdi'aziz Muqtar Qaridi
Tourism and Wildlife, Hasan Farah Hujaleh
Trade, Muhammad Warsameh Ali
Transport, Abdi Guled Muhammad
Water and Minerals, Ahmad Muhammad Handulle
Women's Affairs, Saynab Aweys Husayn

ECONOMY

Livestock raising is the main occupation and there is a modest export trade in livestock, skins and hides. Italy, the Gulf States and Saudi Arabia import the bulk of the banana crop, the biggest export, which accounts for approximately 40 per cent of exports. The principal imports are machinery and transport equipment, industrial goods and foodstuffs.

GDP – US$1,631 million (1998); US$240 per capita (1999)
ANNUAL AVERAGE GROWTH OF GDP – 2.5 per cent (1998)
TOTAL EXTERNAL DEBT – US$2,606million (1999)

Trade with UK	2000	2001
Imports from UK	£11,486,000	£5,960,000
Exports to UK	8,000	213,000

SOUTH AFRICA
Republic of South Africa

AREA – 471,445 sq. miles (1,221,037 sq. km).
  Neighbours: Namibia (north-west), Botswana and Zimbabwe (north), Mozambique and Swaziland (north-east), Lesotho, which is completely surrounded by South Africa
POPULATION – 43,686,000 (2000 estimate); 40,583,573 (1996 census): 76.7 per cent African, 10.9 per cent White, 8.9 per cent mixed white, Malayan and black descent, 2.6 per cent Indian/Asian. The constitution

designates 11 official languages: Afrikaans (spoken by 14.4 per cent as a first language); English (8.6 per cent); IsiNdebele (1.5 per cent); IsiXosa (17.9 per cent), IsiZulu (22.9 per cent); Sepedi (9.2 per cent); Sosetho (7.7 per cent); SiSwati (2.5 per cent); Setswana (8.2 per cent); Tshivenda (2.2 per cent); Xitsonga (4.4 per cent). Afrikaans and English are to remain the languages of record although any citizen may correspond official business in his own language. The majority (77 per cent) of the population is Christian. There are also Hindus (1.7 per cent), Muslims (1.1 per cent) and Jews (0.4 per cent)

CAPITAL – The seat of the government is Pretoria (population 1,800,000, 1999 estimate); the seat of the legislature is Cape Town (population, 3,088,028, 1999 estimate); the seat of the judiciary is Bloemfontein (467,400, 1999 estimate)

MAJOR CITIES – ΨDurban (2,589,977); ΨEast London (520,008); Johannesburg (3,800,652); Pietermaritzburg (397,086); ΨPort Elizabeth (1,011,378), 1999 estimates

CURRENCY – Rand (R) of 100 cents

NATIONAL ANTHEMS – Nkosi Sikelel' iAfrika (God Bless Africa); Die Stem Van Suid-Afrika (The Call Of South Africa)

NATIONAL DAY – 27 April (Freedom Day)

NATIONAL FLAG – Divided red over blue by a horizontal white-fimbriated green Y; in the hoist a black triangle fimbriated in yellow

LIFE EXPECTANCY (years) – male 46.5; female 48.3

POPULATION GROWTH RATE – 2.2 per cent (1999)

POPULATION DENSITY – 35 per sq. km (1999)

URBAN POPULATION – 50.4 per cent (2000 estimate)

South Africa occupies the southernmost part of the African continent from the courses of the Limpopo, Marico, Molopo, Nosop and Orange Rivers to the Cape of Good Hope, with the exception of Lesotho, Swaziland and the extreme south of Mozambique. To the west, east and south lie the south Atlantic and southern Indian Oceans. Some 1,192 miles (1,920 km) to the south-east of Cape Town lie Prince Edward and Marion Islands, part of South Africa since 1947.

The Orange, with its tributary the Vaal, is the principal river, rising in the Drakensberg and flowing into the Atlantic near the border with Namibia. The Limpopo, or Crocodile River, in the north, rises in North-West Province and flows into the Indian Ocean through Mozambique.

HISTORY AND POLITICS

Hunter-gatherers, the San (Bushmen) and Khoikhoi (Hottentots) inhabited southern Africa from c.8,000 bc. By the eighth century ad, Bantu-speaking peoples had settled the north of the country.

The Portuguese navigator Bartolomeu Días charted the coast in 1488 and the Dutch founded the colony of the Cape of Good Hope in 1652, which was taken by Britain in 1806. The Orange Free State and Transvaal republics were founded by the Boers (the descendants of Dutch settlers) and were recognised by Britain in 1853–4. Natal was annexed to Cape Colony by the British in 1844 and then formed as a separate colony in 1856, to which Zululand was added in 1897 after the British victory in the Zulu wars. Transvaal and the Orange Free State became British colonies after the Boer defeat in the Second Boer War 1899–1902. The self-governing colonies became united in 1910 under the name of the Union of South Africa. Independence within the Commonwealth was gained in 1931 under the Statute of Westminster.

From 1948, when the Afrikaner National Party came to power, South Africa's social and political structure was based on apartheid, a policy of racial segregation. Opposition protests culminated in the Sharpeville massacre in 1960, following which the African National Congress (ANC) and other opposition groups were banned. South Africa left the Commonwealth and became a republic on 31 May 1961, largely as a result of international condemnation.

MOVES TO DEMOCRACY

The first moves to reform apartheid came in 1984, when a new constitution extended the franchise to the Coloured and Indian populations. In 1989, F. W. de Klerk became president of South Africa and lifted the ban on the ANC and restrictions on other anti-apartheid groups and freed Nelson Mandela, the main ANC political detainee. In 1991 the laws implementing apartheid were effectively abolished. In 1992 a referendum amongst the white electorate on continued political reform and a new constitution reached by negotiation was approved.

In 1991 the government, ANC, Inkatha Freedom Party and other civic groups reached agreement on the establishment of an inter-racial administration and the formation of a five-year coalition government following a multiracial election.

In the country's first multiracial general election held on 26–29 April 1994 the ANC gained 252 seats in the 400-seat National Assembly and 60 seats in the 90-seat Senate. The parliament has passed two significant pieces of legislation to settle the legacy of the apartheid era. In November 1994 parliament passed legislation to restore the rights of those dispossessed of their land. In June 1995 the Truth Commission was established to assess confessions, grant amnesties for political crimes and set compensation for victims.

Following legislative and provincial elections held on 2 June 1999, the ANC gained 266 seats in the National Assembly and, being one seat short of the two-thirds majority required to amend the constitution, entered into a coalition with the Minority Front, which held just one seat in the National Assembly.

On 14 June 1999 the National Assembly met to select a new president. Thabo Mbeki was elected unopposed and was formally sworn in on 16 June 1999.

POLITICAL SYSTEM

The final constitution came into effect in 1997. Executive power is vested in a president and Cabinet, with the

president elected by the National Assembly. Legislative power is vested in a bicameral parliament, a directly elected 400-member National Assembly elected by proportional representation for a five-year term, and an indirectly elected 90-member National Council of Provinces composed of ten members elected by each of the nine regional legislatures for a five-year term. South Africa is divided into nine regions (Western Cape, Northern Cape, Eastern Cape, Free State, North-West, KwaZulu/Natal, Gauteng, Limpopo, Mpumalanga). Each region has its own premier, a legislature of between 30 and 100 seats elected by proportional representation, and its own constitution.

HEAD OF STATE

President, Commander-in-Chief of the Armed Forces, Thabo Mbeki (ANC), *elected* by parliament 14 June 1999, *sworn in* 16 June 1999
Executive Deputy President, Jacob Zuma (ANC)

CABINET *as at August 2002*

Agriculture and Land Affairs, Angela Didiza (ANC)
Arts, Culture, Science and Technology, Ben Ngubane (IFP)
Communications, Ivy Matsepe-Casaburri (ANC)
Correctional Services, Ben Skosana (IFP)
Defence, Patrick Lekota (ANC)
Education, Kader Asmal (ANC)
Environmental Affairs and Tourism, Mohammed Valli Moosa (ANC)
Finance, Trevor Manuel (ANC)
Foreign Affairs, Nkosazana Dlamini-Zuma (ANC)
Health, Mantombazana Tshabala-Msimang (ANC)
Home Affairs, Chief Mangosuthu Buthelezi (IFP)
Housing, Sankie Mthembi-Mahanyele (ANC)
Intelligence Service, Lindiwe Sisulu-Guma (ANC)
Justice and Constitutional Development, Penuell Maduna (ANC)
Labour, Membathisi Mdladlana (ANC)
Mineral and Energy Affairs, Phumzile Mlambo-Ngcuka (ANC)
Office of the President, Essop Pahad (ANC)
Provincial and Local Government, Sydney Mufamadi (ANC)
Public Enterprises, Jeffrey Radebe (ANC)
Public Service and Administration, Geraldine Fraser-Moleketi (ANC)
Public Works, Stella Sigcau (ANC)
Safety and Security, Charles Nqakula (SACP)
Sports and Recreation, Ngconde Balfour (ANC)
Trade and Industry, Alec Erwin (ANC)
Transport, Dullah Omar (ANC)
Water Affairs and Forestry, Ronnie Kasrils (ANC)
Welfare and Population Development, Zola Skweyiya (ANC)
ANC African National Congress; IFP Inkatha Freedom Party; SACP South African Communist Party

HIGH COMMISSION FOR THE REPUBLIC OF SOUTH AFRICA
South Africa House, Trafalgar Square, London WC2N 5DP. Tel: 020-7451 7299
High Commissioner, HE Dr Lindiwe Mabuza, apptd 2001

BRITISH HIGH COMMISSION
255 Hill Street, Arcadia 0002 Pretoria
Tel: (00 27) (12) 483 1200
91 Parliament Street, Cape Town, 8001
Tel: (00 27) (21) 405 2400
Email: britain@icon.co.za

High Commissioner (Cape Town), HE Ann Grant, apptd 2001
CONSULATES-GENERAL – Cape Town, Johannesburg
CONSULATES – Durban, Port Elizabeth

BRITISH COUNCIL DIRECTOR, Clive Gobby, Ground Floor, Forum 1, Braampark, 33 Hoofd Street, Braamfontein, Johannesburg 2001; Email:information@british council.org.za. There are also offices in Cape Town, Durban and Pretoria

DEFENCE

The new South African National Defence Force (SANDF) was created from the merger of the South African Defence Forces (SADF), the Umkhonto we Sizwe (MK) armed wing of the ANC, the Azanian People's Liberation Army (APLA) of the PAC, and the defence forces of the four former independent homelands.
The Army has 168 main battle tanks, 967 armoured personnel carriers and 1,200 armoured infantry fighting vehicles. The Navy has two submarines and 11 patrol and coastal vessels at two bases. The Air Force has 86 combat aircraft and 7 armed helicopters.
MILITARY EXPENDITURE – 1.6 per cent of GDP (2000)
MILITARY PERSONNEL – Army 41,750, Navy 5,000, Air Force 9,250

ECONOMY

Mining is of great importance, employing more than 400,000 people in 2000. It is the largest source of foreign exchange. The principal minerals produced are gold, coal, diamonds, copper, iron ore, manganese, lime and limestone, uranium, platinum, fluorspar, andalusite, zinc, zirconium, vanadium, titanium and chrome. South Africa is the world's largest producer of gold, platinum, diamonds, manganese, chrome and vanadium, and has the world's largest reserves of chrome ore, manganese, vanadium and andalusite. In 2000 420 tonnes of gold were produced.
Agriculture, forestry and fishing accounted for 3.2 per cent of GDP in 2000. Over 70 per cent of land is pasture so livestock farming is widespread. Principal crops are maize, sugar cane, fruits and vegetables, wheat, sorghum, sunflower seeds and groundnuts. Cotton is widely grown, and viticulture is also widespread.
Industries, concentrated most heavily around Johannesburg, Pretoria and the major ports, process foodstuffs, metals and non-metallic mineral products, produce oil from coal, and also produce beverages and tobacco, motor vehicles, chemicals and chemical products, machinery, textiles and clothing, and paper and paper products. Industry contributed 30.9 per cent of GDP in 2000.
Energy production is based upon coal and natural gas and the production of synthetic liquid fuel from coal. One nuclear power station is in operation and others are planned. South Africa exports electricity through its electric grid connections to all states in southern Africa.
Tourism accounts for 3.4 per cent of GDP. In 2000 5.9 million foreign tourists visited South Africa.
In 2000 there was a trade surplus of US$4,231 million and a current account deficit of US$469 million. Imports totalled US$29,695 million and exports US$29,983 million.
GNP – US$129,171 million (2000); US$3,170 per capita (1999)
GDP – US$133,962 million (1998); US$3,067 per capita (1999)
ANNUAL AVERAGE GROWTH OF GDP – 3.1 per cent (2000)

INFLATION RATE – 5.3 per cent (2000)
UNEMPLOYMENT – 5.3 per cent (1998)
TOTAL EXTERNAL DEBT – US$24,158 million (1999)

TRADE

Principal exports are gold, base metals and metal products, coal, diamonds, food (especially fruit) and wool. Principal imports are machinery, chemicals, motor vehicles, metals and metal products, food, inedible raw materials and textiles. South Africa's main trading partners are Germany, the USA, the UK, Italy and Japan.

Trade with UK	2000	2001
Imports from UK	£1,411,856,000	£1,547,363,000
Exports to UK	2,651,501,000	2,953,369,000

COMMUNICATIONS

There are international airports at Johannesburg, Durban and Cape Town. South African Airways operates international services to Europe, South America, the Far East, Africa, Australia and the USA, and it is the principal operator of domestic flights. Durban is the largest seaport. Other major ports are Cape Town, Port Elizabeth, East London, Saldanha Mossel Bay and Richards Bay.

CULTURE AND EDUCATION

Higher education is provided at 21 universities and 15 other tertiary-level colleges.
ILLITERACY RATE – 14.0 per cent (2002)
ENROLMENT (percentage of age group) – primary 100 per cent (1997); secondary 95 per cent (1997); tertiary 19 per cent (1997)

SPAIN
Reino de España – Kingdom of Spain

AREA – 195,365 sq. miles (505,992 sq. km). Neighbours: Portugal (west), France (north)
POPULATION – 40,037,995 (2001 estimate): 96 per cent Catholic, 1 per cent Muslim. Castilian Spanish is the official language, although Basque, Catalan, Galician and Valencian, a dialect of Catalan, are spoken and have official status in the autonomous regions where they are spoken
CAPITAL – Madrid (population, 3,084,673, 1996)
MAJOR CITIES – ΨBarcelona (4,748,236); ΨValencia (2,200,319); Málaga (1,224,959); Sevilla (1,719,446); Zaragoza (852,332), 1995
CURRENCY – Euro (€) of 100 cents
NATIONAL ANTHEM – Marcha Real Española (Spanish Royal March)
NATIONAL DAY – 12 October
NATIONAL FLAG – Three horizontal stripes of red, yellow, red, with the yellow of double width
LIFE EXPECTANCY (years) – male 75.4; female 82.3
POPULATION GROWTH RATE – 0.1 per cent (1999)
POPULATION DENSITY – 78 per sq. km (1999)

The interior of the Iberian peninsula consists of an elevated tableland surrounded and traversed by mountain ranges: the Pyrenees, the Cantabrian Mountains, the Sierra de Guadarrama, Sierra Morena, Sierra Nevada, Montes de Toledo, etc. The principal rivers are the Duero, the Tajo, the Guadiana, the Guadalquivir, the Ebro and the Miño.

HISTORY AND POLITICS

The kingdoms of Castile and Aragón were united in 1479; they captured Granada, the last region of Spain under Moorish rule, in 1492 and conquered Navarra in 1512. In 1492 Columbus reached the Americas on behalf of Spain and began the process of colonisation which led to most of central and south America coming under Spanish rule until their independence in the 19th century. A republic was proclaimed in 1931 and in February 1936 the Popular Front, a left-wing coalition, was elected. In July 1936 a counter-revolution broke out in military garrisons in Spanish Morocco and spread throughout Spain. Civil war ensued until March 1939, when the Popular Front governments in Madrid and Barcelona surrendered to the Nationalists (as Gen. Franco's followers were then named). Gen. Franco became president and ruled the country until his death in 1975, when, according to his wishes, he was succeeded as head of state by Prince Juan Carlos of Bourbon (grandson of Alfonso XIII) and Spain again became a monarchy. The first free election was held on 15 June 1977. The general election of 12 March 2000 was won by the Popular Party (PP), which won 183 seats in the Congress of Deputies.

INSURGENCIES

The Basque separatist organisation ETA (*Euzkadi ta Azkatasuna* – Basque Nation and Liberty) has since its formation in 1959 carried out a terrorist campaign of bombings, shootings and kidnappings against the Spanish state and its security forces in an attempt to gain independence for the Basque country. ETA rejected regional autonomy for the Basque country in 1979 as insufficient and continued its campaign, but increased co-operation between French and Spanish security forces had greatly weakened ETA by the early 1990s. On 23 January 2000, over a million people demonstrated in Madrid against ETA terrorist attacks following a car bomb explosion in Madrid on 21 January. On 22 March 2002, a local politician from the Socialist Worker's Party was shot and killed in the Basque town of Orio in what was thought to be an ETA attack. In August 2002, Spanish MPs voted to outlaw the Basque political party, Batsuna, because of its links with ETA.

POLITICAL SYSTEM

Under the 1978 constitution there is a bicameral *Cortes Generales* comprising a 350-member Congress of Deputies (*Congreso de los Diputados*) elected for a maximum term of four years, which elects the prime minister; and a Senate (*Senado*) consisting of 208 directly elected representatives and 51 representatives appointed by the assemblies of the autonomous regions. Since the promulgation of the 1978 constitution, 19 autonomous regions have been established, with their own parliaments and governments. These are Andalucía, Aragón, Asturias, Balearics, the Basque country, Canaries, Cantabria, Castilla-La Mancha, Castilla y León, Catalunya, Ceuta, Extremadura, Galicia, Madrid, Melilla, Murcia, Navarra, La Rioja and Valencia.

HEAD OF STATE

HM The King of Spain, King Juan Carlos I de Borbón, KG, GCVO, *born* 5 January 1938, *acceded to the throne* 22 November 1975, *married* 14 May 1962, Princess Sophie of Greece *and has issue* Príncipe Felipe; Infanta Elena Maria Isabel Dominga, *born* 20 December 1963; and Infanta Cristina Federica Victoria Antonia, *born* 13 June 1965
Heir, HRH The Prince of the Asturias (Príncipe Felipe Juan Pablo Alfonso y Todos los Santos), *born* 30 January 1968

CABINET *as at August 2002*

Prime Minister, José María Aznar López
First Deputy Prime Minister, Cabinet Office, Interior,
  Mariano Rajoy Brey
Second Deputy Prime Minister, Economy, Rodrigo de
  Rato y Figaredo
Agriculture, Food and Fisheries, Miguel Arias Cañete
Defence, Federico Trillo-Figueroa y Martínez Conde
Development, Francisco Alvárez-Cascos Fernández
Education, Culture and Sport, Pilar del Castillo Vera
Environment, Jaime Matas Palou
Foreign Affairs, Ana Palacio
Government Spokesman, Presidency, Mariano Rajoy Brey
Health and Consumer Affairs, Ana María Pastor
Interior, Ángel Acebes
Justice, José María Michavila
Labour and Social Affairs, Eduardo Zaplana
Public Administration, Javier Arenas
Science and Technology, Josep Piqué i Camps
Treasury, Cristóbal Montoro Romero

SPANISH EMBASSY
39 Chesham Place, London SW1X 8SB
Tel: 020-7235 5555
Ambassador Extraordinary and Plenipotentiary, HE The
  Marqués de Tamarón, apptd 1999

BRITISH EMBASSY
Calle de Fernando el Santo 16, E-28010 Madrid
Tel: (00 34) (91) 700 8200
Ambassador Extraordinary and Plenipotentiary, HE Peter
  Torry, apptd 1998

CONSULATES-GENERAL – Madrid, Barcelona, Bilbao
CONSULATES – Alicante (Alacant), Granada, Málaga,
  Palma de Mallorca, Las Palmas, Santander, Seville,
  Tenerife, Vigo

BRITISH COUNCIL DIRECTOR, Peter Sandiford, OBE,
Paseo del General Martínez, Campos 31, E-28010
Madrid; Email:madrid@britishcouncil.es. There are
offices in Barcelona, Segovia, Terrassa and Valencia

DEFENCE

The Army has 688 main battle tanks, 2,023 armoured
personnel carriers and 28 attack helicopters. The Navy
has eight submarines, one aircraft carrier, 15 frigates, 37
patrol and coastal vessels, 17 combat aircraft and 37
armed helicopters at seven bases. The Air Force has 211
combat aircraft. The USA maintains 1,760 naval and 360
air force personnel in Spain.
MILITARY EXPENDITURE – 1.3 per cent of GDP (2000)
MILITARY PERSONNEL – 143,450: Army 92,000, Navy
  26,950, Air Force 24,500; Paramilitaries 71,260
CONSCRIPTION DURATION – Conscription ended 31
  December 2001

ECONOMY

The expansion of the economy and accession to the EU
have led to reforms in Spanish agriculture, extensive
industrial modernisation and widespread privatisation.
The country is generally fertile, and olives, oranges,
lemons, almonds, pomegranates, bananas, apricots,
tomatoes, peppers, cucumbers and grapes are cultivated.
Other agricultural products include wheat, barley, oats,
rice, hemp and flax. The vine is cultivated widely; in the
south-west, around Jerez, sherry and tent wines are
produced. Spain has one of Europe's largest fishing
industries.
  Spain's mineral resources of coal, iron, wolfram, copper,
zinc, lead and iron ores are exploited. The principal

industrial goods are cars, steel, ships, manufactured
goods, textiles, chemical products, footwear and other
leather goods. Tourism is a major industry with
58,588,944 tourists in 1999, of whom 26,799,261 were
from overseas.
  Spain successfully met the convergence criteria laid
down for EU economic and monetary union and was a
participant in the European single currency, the euro, on
1 January 1999. The centre-right government has
withdrawn subsidies from uncompetitive industries,
privatised the steel industry and reduced income tax. The
economy has been performing well and unemployment
has been falling steadily.
  In 2000 Spain had a trade deficit of US$32,755 million
and a current account deficit of US$17,257 million.
Imports totalled US$152,870 million and exports
US$113,325 million.
GNP – US$590,150 million (2000); US$14,800 per
  capita (1999)
GDP – US$582,138 million (1998); US$14,939 per
  capita (1999)
ANNUAL AVERAGE GROWTH OF GDP – 4.9 per cent
  (2000)
INFLATION RATE – 3.4 per cent (2000)
UNEMPLOYMENT – 13.7 per cent (2001)

TRADE

The principal imports are manufactures, military
hardware, semimanufactures, vehicles, consumer goods,
foodstuffs and energy. The principal exports include
manufactures,   military   hardware,   vehicles,
semimanufactures, foodstuffs, consumer goods and
energy.

Trade with UK	2000	2001
Imports from UK	£7,863,700,000	£7,953,300,000
Exports to UK	5,757,100,000	6,488,500,000

EDUCATION

Education is free for those aged six to 18, and compulsory
up to the age of 16. Private schools (30 per cent of
primary and 60 per cent of secondary schools) have to
fulfil certain criteria to receive government maintenance
grants. There are 33 public sector universities, the oldest
of which, Salamanca, was founded in 1218. Other ancient
foundations are Valladolid (1346), Barcelona (1430),
Zaragoza (1474), Santiago (1495), Valencia (1500), Seville
(1505), Madrid (1508), Granada (1531), Oviedo (1604).
Private universities are Deusto in Bilbao, Navarra in
Pamplona, Carlos III in Madrid and one in Salamanca.
ILLITERACY RATE – 2.2 per cent (2002)
ENROLMENT (percentage of age group) – primary 100
  per cent (1997); secondary 100 per cent (1997);
  tertiary 51 per cent (1997)

CULTURE

Castilian is the language of more than three-quarters of
the population of Spain. Basque, said to have been the
original language of Iberia, is spoken in Vizcaya,
Guipúzcoa and Álava. Catalan is spoken in Provençal
Spain, and Galician, spoken in the north-western
provinces, is akin to Portuguese. The governments of
these regions actively encourage use of their local
languages.
  The literature of Spain is one of the oldest and richest
in the world, the *Poem of the Cid,* the earliest of the heroic
songs of Spain, having been written about 1140. The
outstanding writings of its golden age are those of Miguel
de Cervantes Saavedra (1547–1616), Lope Felix de Vega
Carpio (1562–1635) and Pedro Calderón de la Barca

(1600–81). The Nobel Prize for Literature has five times been awarded to Spanish authors: J. Echegaray, J. Benavente, Juan Ramón Jiménez , Vicente Aleixandre and Camilo José Cela.

ISLANDS AND ENCLAVES

THE BALEARIC ISLES form an archipelago off the east coast of Spain. There are four large islands (Majorca, Minorca, Ibiza and Formentera), and seven smaller (Aire, Aucanada, Botafoch, Cabrera, Dragonera, Pinto and El Rey). Area 1,935 sq. miles (5,011 sq. km); population 685,088. The archipelago forms a province of Spain, the capital is ΨPalma in Majorca, population 323,138

THE CANARY ISLANDS are an archipelago in the Atlantic, off the African coast, consisting of seven islands and six islets. Area 2,807 sq. miles (7,270 sq. km); population 1,444,626. The Canary Islands form two provinces of Spain: Las Palmas, comprising Gran Canaria, Lanzarote (38,500), Fuerteventura (19,500) and the islets of Alegranza, Roque del Este, Roque del Oeste, Graciosa, Montaña Clara and Lobos, with seat of administration at ΨLas Palmas (373,772) in Gran Canaria; and Santa Cruz de Tenerife, comprising Tenerife, La Palma (76,000), Gomera (31,829), and Hierro (10,000), with seat of administration at ΨSanta Cruz in Tenerife, population estimate 204,948

ISLA DE FAISANES is an uninhabited Franco-Spanish condominium, at the mouth of the Bidassoa in La Higuera bay

ΨCEUTA is a fortified post on the Moroccan coast, opposite Gibraltar. Area 5 sq. miles (13 sq. km); population 70,864

ΨMELILLA is a town on a rocky promontory of the Rif coast, connected with the mainland by a narrow isthmus. Population 58,449. Ceuta and Melilla are autonomous regions of Spain

OVERSEAS TERRITORIES

The following territories are Spanish settlements on the Moroccan seaboard: Peñón de Alhucemas is a bay including six islands, population 366; Peñón de la Gomera (or Peñón de Velez) is a fortified rocky islet, population 450; The Chaffarinas (or Zaffarines) is a group of three islands near the Algerian frontier, population 610

SRI LANKA

S,ri Laṅkā Prajātāntrika Samājavādi Janarajaya/Ilaṅkaiś Śaṅanāyaka Ṣośaliśak Kuṭiyaraśa
– Democratic Socialist Republic of Sri Lanka

AREA – 25,332 sq. miles (65,610 sq. km)
POPULATION – 19,408,635 (2001 estimate): 74 per cent Sinhalese, 12.6 per cent Sri Lankan Tamils, 5.6 per cent Indian Tamils, 7.1 per cent Sri Lankan Moors, 0.7 per cent Burghers, Malays and others. The religion of the majority is Buddhism (69.3 per cent), then Hinduism (15.5 per cent), Islam (7.6 per cent), and Christianity (7.5 per cent). The national languages are Sinhala and Tamil
CAPITAL – ΨColombo (population, 615,000, 1993)
MAJOR CITIES – ΨGalle (971,000); ΨJaffna (879,000); Kandy (1,269,000); ΨTrincomalee (323,000)
CURRENCY – Sri Lankan rupee of 100 cents
NATIONAL ANTHEM – Namo Namo Matha (We All Stand Together)
NATIONAL DAY – 4 February (Independence Day)

NATIONAL FLAG – On a dark red field, within a golden border, a golden lion passant holding a sword in its right paw, and a representation of a bo-leaf, issuing from each corner; and to its right, two vertical stripes of saffron and green also placed within a golden border, to represent the minorities of the country
LIFE EXPECTANCY (years) – male 69.9; female 75.9
POPULATION GROWTH RATE – 1.2 per cent (1999)
POPULATION DENSITY – 290 per sq. km (1999)
ILLITERACY RATE – 7.9 per cent (2002)

Sri Lanka (formerly Ceylon) is an island in the Indian Ocean, off the southern tip of India and separated from it by the narrow Palk Strait. Forests, jungle and scrub cover the greater part of the island. In areas over 2,000 ft above sea level grasslands (*patanas* or *talawas*) are found. One of the highest peaks in the central massif is Adam's Peak (7,360 ft), a place of pilgrimage for Buddhists, Hindus and Muslims.

HISTORY AND POLITICS

The Portuguese landed in Ceylon in the early 16th century and founded settlements. The Dutch East India Company controlled the country from 1658 until 1796. The maritime provinces of Ceylon were ceded by the Dutch to the British in 1798, becoming a British Crown Colony in 1802. With the annexation of the Kingdom of Kandy in 1815, all Ceylon came under British rule. Ceylon became a self-governing state and a member of the British Commonwealth on 4 February 1948. A republican constitution was adopted in 1972 and the country was renamed Sri Lanka (meaning 'Resplendent Island').

Eight provincial councils were set up in 1988 under the Indo-Sri Lankan peace accord in an attempt to diffuse ethnic tension. Since then, except for the temporarily merged North-East province, all provinces have had elected provincial councils.

In the presidential election held on 21 December 1999, President Kumaratunga was elected for a second term, gaining 51.37 per cent of the vote. Prime Minister Sirimavo Bandaranaike resigned on 10 August 2000 and was replaced by Ratnasiri Wickremanayake. In the general election of 5 December 2001, the United National Party (UNP) won 109 seats and the People's Alliance (PA), which had formed the government prior to the election in coalition with other parties, won 77 seats. Ranil Wickremasinghe of the UNP was sworn in as prime minister on 9 December and the new Cabinet was appointed on 12 December.

INSURGENCIES

The Liberation Tigers of Tamil Eelam (LTTE) guerrilla group has been fighting Sri Lankan forces for control of the Tamil majority areas in the north and east of the country since 1983. On 22 April 2000, LTTE forces captured the Elephant Pass, the only land link to the Jaffna peninsula. On 3 May 2000, President Kumaratunga imposed a state of war, invoked an ordinance that gave the police wide powers of arrest and confiscation, banned strikes and political rallies and imposed censorship of military, political and economic reporting. All non-essential development projects were suspended and the defence levy sales tax was raised to make more funds available to the military.

The LTTE declared a month-long unilateral cease-fire on 21 December 2000, to facilitate peace talks. The government rejected the cease-fire and troops launched a fresh offensive in the Jaffna peninsula. The LTTE extended the cease-fire in January 2001, and again in

February and March, but the government refused to reciprocate, launching a series of attacks on the Jaffna peninsula. Tensions continued and violence broke out between Hindu and Muslim Tamils in June 2002. Peace talks began in Thailand in September 2002, between delegates from the Sri Lankan Government and the Tamil Tiger rebels. These talks were the first formal negotiations in seven years.

POLITICAL SYSTEM

The 1978 constitution introduced a system of proportional representation. Legislative power is vested in the parliament, whose 225 members are directly elected for a six-year term. Executive power is exercised by the president, elected for six years, and the Cabinet.

HEAD OF STATE

President, Media, Welfare, Chandrika Bandaranaike Kumaratunga, *elected* 9 November 1994, *re-elected* 21 December 1999, *sworn in* 22 December 1999

CABINET *as at August 2002*

The President
Prime Minister, Policy Development, Implementation and Poverty Alleviation, Ranil Wickremasinghe
Agriculture and Livestock, Social Welfare, S. B. Dissanayake
Central Region Development, Tissa Attanayake
Co-operatives, Abdul Rahim Mohideen Cader
Defence, Transport, Highways and Aviation, Tilak Marapone
Eastern Development and Muslim Religious Affairs, Ports, Development and Shipping, Rauf Hakeem
Enterprise Development, Industrial Policy, Investment Promotion, Constitutional Affairs, G. L. Peiris
Environment and Natural Resources, Rukman Senanayake
Finance, K. N. Choksy
Fisheries and Ocean Resources , Mahinda Wijesekara
Foreign Affairs, Tyronne Fernando
Health, P. Dayaratne
Home Affairs and Local Government, Alik Aluvihare
Housing and Plantation Infrastructure, Arumugam Thondaman
Interior, John Amaratunga
Irrigation and Water Management, Gamini Jayawickrema Perera
Justice, Law Reform and National Reconciliation, W. J. M. Lokubandara
Plantation Industries, Lakshman Kiriella
Power and Energy, Karu Jayasuriya
Rural Economy, Bandula Gunawardena
Southern Region Development, Ananda Kularatne
Tourism, Gamini Kulawansa Lokuge
Western Region Development, Mohamed Hanifa Mohamad
Women's Affairs, Amara Piyasiri Ratnayake

HIGH COMMISSION FOR THE DEMOCRATIC SOCIALIST REPUBLIC OF SRI LANKA
13 Hyde Park Gardens, London W2 2LU
Tel: 020-7262 1841/7
Email: mail@slhc.globalnet.co.uk
High Commissioner, HE Faisz Musthapha, apptd 2002

BRITISH HIGH COMMISSION
190 Galle Road, Kollupitiya, PO Box 1433, Colombo 3
Tel: (00 94) (1) 437336/437343
Email: bhc@eureka.lk
High Commissioner, HE Linda Duffield, CMG, apptd 1999

BRITISH COUNCIL DIRECTOR, Susan Maingay, 49 Alfred House Gardens, PO Box 753, Colombo 3; Email: enquiries@britishcouncil.lk. There is a regional office in Kandy

DEFENCE

The Army has 65 main battle tanks, 152 armoured personnel carriers and 52 armoured infantry fighting vehicles. The Navy has 40 patrol and coastal vessels at seven bases. The Air Force has 29 combat aircraft and 20 armed helicopters.
MILITARY EXPENDITURE – 5.3 per cent of GDP (2000)
MILITARY PERSONNEL – 123,000: Army 95,000, Navy 18,000, Air Force 10,000; Paramilitaries 88,600

ECONOMY

The staple products are tea, rubber, copra, spices and gems. There is increasing emphasis on local production of food, especially rice, and plans for the large-scale production of sugar cane, cotton and citrus fruits.
The prinicipal exports are industrial goods, agricultural products (especially tea), and oil derivatives. Principal imports are manufactures, textiles and clothing, capital goods, consumer goods and oil. Tourism is an important industry, with 400,414 foreign visitors in 2000. In 1998 there was a trade deficit of US$567 million and a current account deficit of US$288 million. In 2000 imports totalled US$7,177 million and exports US$5,430 million.
GNP – US$16,632 million (2000); US$820 per capita (1999)
GDP – US$15,711 million (1998); US$836 per capita (1999)
ANNUAL AVERAGE GROWTH OF GDP – 6.0 per cent (2000)
INFLATION RATE – 6.2 per cent (2000)
UNEMPLOYMENT – 10.6 per cent (1998)
TOTAL EXTERNAL DEBT – US$9,473 million (1999)

Trade with UK	2000	2001
Imports from UK	£164,308,000	£142,372,000
Exports to UK	426,063,000	400,811,000

COMMUNICATIONS

There are 25,952 km of roads in Sri Lanka, of which 11,077 km are surfaced, and a government-run railway system with 1,459 km of lines. The principal airport is at Katunayake, north of Colombo.

SUDAN
Al-Jumhūriyya as-Sūdān – Republic of the Sudan

AREA – 967,500 sq. miles (2,505,813 sq. km). Neighbours: Egypt (north), Eritrea and Ethiopia (east), Kenya, Uganda and the Democratic Republic of Congo (south), Central African Republic, Chad and Libya (west)
POPULATION – 36,080,373 (2001 estimate). Arab and Nubian peoples populate the north and centre, Nilotic and Negro peoples the south. Arabic is the official language and Islam the state religion, although the Nilotics of the Bahr el Ghazal and Upper Nile valleys are generally Animists or Christians
CAPITAL – Khartoum (Al-Khartum) (population, 947,483, 1993 census). The combined population of Khartoum, Khartoum North and Umm Durmān (excluding refugees and displaced people) is estimated at 3,000,000

MAJOR CITIES – Al-Ubayyid (229,425); Nyala (227,183); ΨPort Sudan (Būr Sūdān) (308,195), 1993 census
CURRENCY – Sudanese dinar (SD) of 100 piastres
NATIONAL ANTHEM – Nahnu Djundullah (We Are The Army Of God)
NATIONAL DAY – 1 January (Independence Day)
NATIONAL FLAG – Three horizontal stripes of red, white and black with a green triangle next to the hoist
LIFE EXPECTANCY (years) – male 55.6; female 58.4
POPULATION GROWTH RATE – 2.8 per cent (2001)
POPULATION DENSITY – 12 per sq. km (1999)
MILITARY EXPENDITURE – 6.1 per cent of GDP (2000)
MILITARY PERSONNEL – 117,000: Army 112,500, Navy 1,500, Air Force 3,000; Paramilitaries 7,000
CONSCRIPTION DURATION – Three years

The White Nile, as the Bahr el Jebel, flows through Sudan from Nimule to Wadi Halfa. The Blue Nile flows from Lake Tana on the Ethiopian plateau through Sudan to join the White Nile at Khartoum. The next confluence of importance is at Atbara where the main Nile is joined by the River Atbara. Between Khartoum and Wadi Halfa lie five of the six cataracts.

HISTORY AND POLITICS

The Anglo-Egyptian Condominium over Sudan was established in 1899 and ended when the Sudan House of Representatives, on 19 December 1955, declared Sudan a fully independent sovereign state. A republic was proclaimed on 1 January 1956, and was recognised by Great Britain and Egypt. Sudan was under military rule from 1958 to 1964, from 1969 to 1986, and from 1989 until presidential and legislative elections were held in March 1996. President al-Bashir was elected with 75.7 per cent of the vote having faced no serious contender. The founding of political parties was legalised on 1 January 1999. In early January 1999, the voting age was lowered to 17 and a new dress code was imposed on women, requiring them to wear headscarves. In December 1999, President al-Bashir suspended the National Assembly and declared a three-month state of emergency, shortly before a vote on constitutional changes, which included the reduction of the powers of the president, was due to be debated. The state of emergency has been repeatedly extended and in December 2001 was extended indefinitely.

Presidential and legislative elections were held on 13–23 December 2000, but were boycotted by most opposition parties. President al-Bashir was re-elected, winning 86.5 per cent of votes cast, and the National Congress won 355 of the 360 seats which were up for election. The civil war prevented balloting in three provinces.

INSURGENCIES

Nearly 17 years of insurrection in the southern provinces ended in 1972 with the signing of an agreement recognising southern regional autonomy within the Sudanese state. However, insurrection resumed in 1983 and since then there has been civil war in the south of the country between government forces and the Christian and Animist majority in the area, organised into the Sudan People's Liberation Army (SPLA). A peace process begun in September 2000 continued through 2001 and a cease-fire was agreed in January 2002. However in March 2002 the SPLA warned that its attacks on oil installations would continue. The warfare has left an estimated 1.4 million dead, including 300,000 who died in the war-induced famine in 1988 and thousands in a similar situation in 1994. Some three million refugees have fled the fighting, either to the north, to neighbouring states or to the far south near the Ugandan border. The fighting has left large areas of the south desolate and uninhabitable. In July 2002 the government and SPLA signed a framework deal aimed at ending the civil war. The terms of the agreement state that southern Sudan will be able to hold an independence referendum after a six-year power-sharing transition period.

FOREIGN RELATIONS

In 1995 Sudan's relations with its neighbours, notably Egypt, Eritrea and Uganda, deteriorated as they considered that Sudan was arming Islamic and insurgent groups in their states. On 2 May 1999 a peace agreement was signed with Eritrea. Sudan and the UK agreed to resume full diplomatic representation in June 1999. On 8 December 1999, Sudan and Uganda signed an agreement under which they agreed to cease supporting rebel groups in each other's countries, to disarm and disband such groups and to re-establish full diplomatic links. On 24 December, Sudan and Egypt agreed to normalise their relations and seek a solution to their dispute over the Hala'ib region.

HEAD OF STATE

President, Prime Minister, Lt.-Gen. Omar Hassan Ahmad al-Bashir, *appointed* 16 October 1993, *elected* 17 March 1996, *re-elected* 20 December 2000.
First Vice-President, Maj.-Gen. Ali Osman Mohamad Taha
Vice-President, Moses Machar Kashol

CABINET *as at August 2002*

The President
Agriculture and Forestry, Majdhub al-Khalifah Ahmad
Animal Resources, Riek Gai
Aviation, Joseph Malwal
Cabinet Affairs, Martin Malwal Arop
Culture and Tourism, Abd al-Basit Abd al-Majid
Defence, Maj.-Gen. Bakri Hassan Salih
Education, Ali Tamim Fartak
Energy and Mining, Awad Ahmad al-Jaz
Environment and Construction Development, Maj.-Gen. al-Tijani Adam al-Tahir
Finance and National Economy, Ahmad Hasan al-Zubayr
Foreign Affairs, Mustapha Osman Ismail
Foreign Trade, Abdel Hamid Mussa Kasha
Guidance and Awqaf, Isam Ahmad al-Bashir
Health, Ahmad Bilal Uthman
Higher Education, Mubarak Muhammad Ali al-Majdhub
Industry and Investment, Jalal Yusuf Muhammad al-Dugayr
Information and Communications, Mahdi Ibrahim
Internal Affairs, Maj.-Gen. Abd al-Rahim Muhammad Husayn
International Co-operation, Karam-al-din Abd-al-Mawla
Irrigation and Water Resources, Kamal Ali Muhammad
Justice, Ali Mohammad Uthman Yassin
Labour and Administrative Reform, Maj.-Gen Allison Manani Magaya
Minister in the Federal Administration Office, Nafi Ali Nafi
Presidency, Lt.-Gen. Salah Muhammad Muhammad Salih
Relations with the National Assembly, Abd al-Basit Salih Sabdarat
Roads and Bridges, Muhammad Tahir Ila
Social Development, Samiyah Ahmad Muhammad
Science and Technology, Zubayr Bashir Taha

Transport, Lam Akol Ajawin
Youth and Sport, Hasan Uthman Rizq

EMBASSY OF THE REPUBLIC OF THE SUDAN
3 Cleveland Row, London SW1A 1DD
Tel: 020-7839 8080
Ambassador Extraordinary and Plenipotentiary, HE Dr
Hasan Abdin, apptd 2000

BRITISH EMBASSY
PO Box 801, Khartoum East
Tel: (00 249) (11) 777105
Email: information.khartoum@fco.gov.uk
Ambassador Extraordinary and Plenipotentiary, HE
Richard Makepeace, apptd 1999

BRITISH COUNCIL DIRECTOR, Paul Doubleday, 14 Abu
Sin Street (PO Box 1253), Khartoum;
Email: bc.khartoum@bc-khartoum.bcouncil.org

ECONOMY

Agriculture provides employment for over half the labour force and contributes nearly half of GDP. It is based on large and medium-sized public sector irrigation projects. Mechanised and traditional agriculture is practised in areas of sufficient rainfall. The principal grain crops are *dura* (great millet) and wheat, the staple food of the population. Sesame and groundnuts are other important food crops, which also yield an exportable surplus, and a promising start has been made with castor seed. Sudan still has to achieve self-sufficiency in its production.

In 2000 Sudan had a trade surplus of US$440 million and a current account deficit of US$557 million. In 1998 imports totalled US$1,915 million and exports US$596 million.

GNP – US$9,596 million (2000); US$330 per capita (1999)
GDP – US$8,642 million (1998); US$315 per capita (1999)
ANNUAL AVERAGE GROWTH OF GDP – 6.0 per cent (1998)
INFLATION RATE – 16.0 per cent (1999)
TOTAL EXTERNAL DEBT – US$16,132 million (1999)

Trade with UK	2000	2001
Imports from UK	£58,198,000	£80,018,000
Exports to UK	6,741,000	10,098,000

COMMUNICATIONS

The railway system, adversely affected by the civil war, has a route length of about 5,516 km. There are 11,610 km of roads, of which 4,203 km are paved. Nile river services between Khartoum and Juba have been interrupted by the southern insurrection. Port Sudan is the country's main seaport. Sudan Airways flies services from Khartoum to other parts of Sudan and to other African states, Europe and the Middle East.

EDUCATION

School education is free for most children but not compulsory, beginning with six years of primary education, followed by three years of secondary education at general secondary schools, the more academic higher secondary schools or vocational schools. The medium of instruction is Arabic. English has not been taught in schools since new Arabisation legislation came into effect in 1991.

In addition to 20 universities there are various technical post-secondary institutes as well as professional and vocational training establishments.

ILLITERACY RATE – 40.0 per cent (2002)

SURINAME
Republiek Suriname – Republic of Suriname

AREA – 63,037 sq. miles (163,265 sq. km). Neighbours: French Guiana (east), Brazil (south), Guyana (west)
POPULATION – 33,998 (2001 estimate): 37 per cent Indians, 31 per cent creoles, 15 per cent Javanese, 10 per cent Africans, small numbers of Amerindians, Chinese and Europeans. The official language is Dutch, the native language is Sranang Tongo, and other widely-used languages are Hindustani and Javanese
CAPITAL – ΨParamaribo (population, 265,000, 1993)
CURRENCY – Suriname guilder of 100 cents
NATIONAL ANTHEM – God Zij Met Ons Suriname (God Be With Our Suriname)
NATIONAL DAY – 5 November
NATIONAL FLAG – Horizontal stripes of green, white, red, white, green, with a five-pointed yellow star in the centre
LIFE EXPECTANCY (years) – male 68.5; female 73.7
POPULATION GROWTH RATE – 0.4 per cent (1999)
POPULATION DENSITY – 3 per sq. km (1999)
URBAN POPULATION – 69.9 per cent (1996)
MILITARY EXPENDITURE – 2.7 per cent of GDP (2000)
MILITARY PERSONNEL – 2,040: Army 1,600, Navy 240, Air Force 200
ILLITERACY RATE – 8 per cent (2000)

HISTORY AND POLITICS

Formerly known as Dutch Guiana, Suriname remained part of the Netherlands West Indies until 25 November 1975, when it achieved complete independence. The civilian government was ousted in 1980 by the military who appointed a predominantly civilian government in 1982.

The New Front for Democracy, a four-party bloc consisting of the National Party of Suriname (NPS), The Progressive Reform Party, Pertjajah Luhur and the Suriname Labour Party, won 32 of the 51 seats in the elections to the National Assembly on 25 May 2000 and appointed Ronald Venetiaan of the NPS as president on 4 August 2000.

POLITICAL SYSTEM

The unicameral legislature, the National Assembly, has 51 members, directly elected for a five-year term. The president is elected by a two-thirds majority in the National Assembly, or if the required majority cannot be achieved, by a specially convened United Peoples' Conference, including district and local council representatives, for a five-year term of office.

HEAD OF STATE

President, Ronald Venetiaan, *inaugurated* 4 August 2000
Vice-President, Prime Minister, Jules Ajodhia

COUNCIL OF MINISTERS *as at August 2002*

Agriculture, Animal Husbandry and Fisheries, Geeta Gangaram Panday
Defence, Ronald Assen
Education and Community Development, Walter Sandriman
Finance, Natural Resources, Humphrey Hildenberg
Foreign Affairs, Marie Levens
Health, Rakieb Khudabux
Internal Affairs, Trade and Industry, Urmila Joella-Sewnundum
Justice and Police, Siegfried Gilds

Labour and Technological Sciences, Clifford Marica
Natural Resources, Rudi Demon
Planning and Development Co-operation, Stanley Raghoebarsingh
Public Works, Dewanand Balesar
Regional Development, Romeo van Russel
Social Affairs and Housing, Paul Salam Somohardjo
Trade and Industry, John Tjon Tjin Joe
Transport, Communication and Tourism, Guno Castelen

EMBASSY OF THE REPUBLIC OF SURINAME Alexander Gogelweg 2, NL-2517 JH The Hague, The Netherlands
Tel: (00 31) (070) 361 7445
Ambassador Extraordinary and Plenipotentiary, vacant
Chargé d'Affaires, N. Stadwijk Kappel

BRITISH AMBASSADOR, HE Edward Glover, MVO, resident at Georgetown, Guyana
BRITISH CONSULATE, c/o VSH United Buildings, Van't Hogerhuystraat, PO Box 1860, Paramaribo.

ECONOMY

Suriname has large timber resources. Rice and sugar cane are the main crops. Bauxite is mined, and is the principal export. Principal trading partners are the Netherlands, the USA and Norway. In 2000 Suriname had a trade surplus of US$153 million and a current account surplus of US$32 million. Imports totalled US$246 million and exports US$399 million.

GNP – US$684 million (1998); US$1,660 per capita (1998)
GDP – US$1,015 million (1998); US$1,657 per capita (1999)
ANNUAL AVERAGE GROWTH OF GDP – 0.6 per cent (1998)
INFLATION RATE – 64.3 per cent (2000)

Trade with UK	2000	2001
Imports from UK	£10,035,000	£8,020,000
Exports to UK	25,917,000	19,102,000

SWAZILAND
Umbuso we Swatini/Kingdom of Swaziland

AREA – 6,704 sq. miles (17,364 sq. km). Neighbours: South Africa (north, west and south), Mozambique (east)
POPULATION – 1,104,343 (2001 estimate). The languages are English and Swazi
CAPITAL – Mbabane (population, 38,290, 1986)
MAJOR TOWNS – Manzini (30,000); Hlatikulu; Mhlume; Nhlangano; Pigg's Peak; Siteki
CURRENCY – Lilangeni (E) of 100 cents (South African currency is also in circulation). Swaziland is a member of the Common Monetary Area and its unit of currency *Emalangeni* (singular *Lilangeni*) has a par value with the South African rand
NATIONAL ANTHEM – Ingoma Yesive
NATIONAL DAY – 6 September (Independence Day)
NATIONAL FLAG – Blue with a wide crimson horizontal band bordered in yellow across the centre, bearing a shield and two spears horizontally
LIFE EXPECTANCY (years) – male 38.1; female 38.1
POPULATION GROWTH RATE – 1.9 per cent (1999)
POPULATION DENSITY – 56 per sq. km (1999)
URBAN POPULATION – 25.3 per cent (1996)
ILLITERACY RATE – 19.1 per cent (2002)
ENROLMENT (percentage of age group) – primary 91 per cent (1996); secondary 37 per cent (1996); tertiary 6 per cent (1996)

The broken mountainous Highveld along the western border, with an average altitude of 4,000 ft, is densely forested, mainly with conifers and eucalyptus; the Middleveld, averaging about 2,000 ft, is a mixed farming area including cotton and pineapples; and the Lowveld in the east was mainly scrubland until the introduction of large sugar-cane plantations. Four rivers, the Komati, Usutu, Mbuluzi and Ngwavuma, flow from west to east.

HISTORY AND POLITICS

The Kingdom of Swaziland came into being on 25 April 1967 under a self-government constitution and became an independent kingdom, headed by HM Sobhuza II, in membership of the Commonwealth on 6 September 1968.

An illegal general strike was held on 13–14 November 2000 to support a petition demanding the legalisation of political parties, the revocation of restrictive labour laws and the abolition of the right of traditional chiefs to force people to work without pay. The petition had been drawn up by the Swaziland Federation of Trade Unions and a group of illegal political parties. Several trade union and opposition leaders were arrested shortly before the strike took place and during the demonstrations. The findings of a Constitutional Review Commission, published in August 2001, demonstrated that a majority of the population wanted to extend the already wide powers of the King, were opposed by pro-democracy groups.

POLITICAL SYSTEM

The King, assisted by his appointed Cabinet, holds considerable executive, legislative and judicial authority. There is a bicameral legislative body comprising a Senate and a House of Assembly. Each of the 55 *Tinkhundla* (administrative districts) directly elects one member to the House of Assembly. The King appoints ten members to the House of Assembly, making 65 in all, who then elect ten members of their own number to the Senate. To these are added 20 senators appointed by the King, bringing the full membership of the Senate to 30. In addition, the King appoints Commissions, who assess public opinion. There are also public gatherings, where any citizen can express an opinion. All political parties are banned.

Legislative elections to the House of Assembly were held on 16–24 October 1998. The members of the Senate were elected and appointed in November 1998.

HEAD OF STATE

King of Swaziland, HM King Mswati III, *inaugurated* 25 April 1986

CABINET *as at August 2002*

Prime Minister, Dr Barnabas Sibusiso Dlamini
Deputy Prime Minister, Arthur Khoza
Agriculture and Co-operatives, Roy Fernoukis
Economic Planning and Development, Prince Guduza Dhalamini
Education, John Carmichael
Enterprise and Employment, Lufto Dlamini
Finance, Majozi Sithole
Foreign Affairs and Trade, Abedenigo Ntshangase
Health and Social Welfare, Dr Phetsile Dlamini
Home Affairs, Prince Sobandla Dlamini
Housing and Urban Development, Albert Shabangu
Justice and Constitutional Development, Chief Maweni Simelane
Natural Resources and Energy, Ephraim Magwagwa Mdluli

Public Service and Information, Mntonzima Dlamini
Public Works and Transport, Titus Mlangeni
Tourism, Environment and Communications, Stella Lukhele

KINGDOM OF SWAZILAND HIGH COMMISSION
20 Buckingham Gate, London SW1E 6LB
Tel: 020-7630 6611
High Commissioner, HE Revd Percy Mngomezulu, apptd 1994

BRITISH HIGH COMMISSION
2nd Floor, Lilunga House, Gilfillan Street, Mbabane
Tel: (00 268) 404 2581/2/3
Email: mbabane@fco.gov.uk
High Commissioner, HE David Reader, apptd 2001

ECONOMY

Manufacturing has replaced agriculture as the dominant sector, with timber, textiles and footwear the main products. Agricultural products include sugar cane and fruit. GDP growth rates have declined in the 1990s, partly as a result of lower growth rates in South Africa, on which the Swazi economy is strongly dependent. South Africa accounts for around 60 per cent of exports from Swaziland and about 85 per cent of imports.

In 1999 Swaziland had a trade deficit of US$111 million and a current account surplus of US$17 million. In 1996 imports totalled US$1,174 million and exports US$893 million.

GNP – US$1,350 million (2000); US$1,350 per capita (1999)
GDP – US$1,218 million (1998); US$1,304 per capita (1999)
ANNUAL AVERAGE GROWTH OF GDP – 3.5 per cent (1999)
INFLATION RATE – 16.7 per cent (2000)
TOTAL EXTERNAL DEBT – US$258 million (1999)

Trade with UK	2000	2001
Imports from UK	£4,932,000	£4,314,000
Exports to UK	33,877,000	33,561,000

COMMUNICATIONS

Swaziland's railway is 297 km long and connects with the Mozambique port of Maputo and the South African railway network to Richards Bay. A rail line to the north-west border provides a link to Komatipoort. There are 2,896 km of roads, of which 828 km are paved. Most passenger and goods traffic is carried by privately-owned motor transport services. There is an international airport at Manzini. Royal Swazi National Airways provides scheduled air services to southern and eastern Africa. International telecommunications and television services are provided through a satellite earth station.

SWEDEN
Konungariket Sverige - Kingdom of Sweden

AREA – 173,732 sq. miles (449,964 sq. km). Neighbours: Norway (west), Finland (east)
POPULATION – 8,875,053 (2001 estimate); 8,745,109 (1993 census). The state religion is Lutheran Protestant, to which over 95 per cent officially adhere. The language is Swedish; in the north there are both Finnish- and Lapp-speaking communities
CAPITAL – ΨStockholm (population, 1,148,953, 1995)
MAJOR CITIES – ΨGothenburg (Göteborg) (454,016); ΨMalmö (248,007); Uppsala (184,507), 1996 estimates

CURRENCY – Swedish krona of 100 öre
NATIONAL ANTHEM – Du Gamla, Du Fria (Thou Ancient, Thou Freeborn)
NATIONAL DAY – 6 June (Day of the Swedish Flag)
NATIONAL FLAG – Yellow cross on a blue ground
LIFE EXPECTANCY (years) – male 77.6; female 82.6
POPULATION DENSITY – 20 per sq. km (1999)

HISTORY AND POLITICS

Sweden takes its name from the Svear people who inhabited the region during the seventh century AD. The Swedes participated in the Viking expansion during the ninth to 11th centuries and established sovereignty over Finland in the 13th century. The Union of Kalmar (1397) brought Sweden and Norway under Danish rule. Northern Sweden regained its independence following a rebellion by noblemen in 1521 which resulted in the election to the Swedish throne of Gustav I of the house of Vasa.

Sweden's power climaxed in the 17th century under Gustavus II Adolf. The Danes were driven out of southern Sweden, the Baltic coast of Russia was seized and the Swedish army pushed into Germany after vanquishing the Catholic League. Swedish power waned in the 17th and 18th centuries. Finland was lost to Russia in 1809; Norway was ceded to Sweden under the Congress of Vienna (1814–15) but seceded in 1905.

Sweden remained neutral during both World Wars. Post-war party politics was dominated by Social Democrat-led coalitions which established a mixed economy and a generous welfare state. Right-wing and centrist parties held power from 1976–82 and 1991–4. Sweden applied for EU membership in July 1991 and acceded to the EU on 1 January 1995.

In the general election held on 15 September 2002 the Social Democrats remained the largest party in the legislature.

POLITICAL SYSTEM

Sweden is a constitutional monarchy, with the monarch retaining purely ceremonial functions as head of state. Under the Act of Succession 1810 (with amendments) the throne is hereditary in the House of Bernadotte. The constitution is based upon the Instrument of Government 1974, which amended the 1810 Act and removed from the monarch the roles of appointing the prime minister and signing parliamentary bills into law. A 1979 amendment vested the succession in the monarch's eldest child irrespective of sex.

Executive power is vested in the prime minister and Council of Ministers. There is a unicameral legislature (*Riksdag*) of 349 members elected by universal suffrage on a proportional representation basis (with a 4 per cent threshold for representation) for four years. The Council of Ministers (*Statsråd*) is responsible to the *Riksdag*. Sweden is divided into 24 counties (*län*) and 288 municipalities (*kommun*).

HEAD OF STATE

HM The King of Sweden, Carl XVI Gustaf, KG, born 30 April 1946, *succeeded* 15 September 1973, *married* 19 June 1976 Fräulein Silvia Renate Sommerlath and has *issue*, Crown Princess Victoria; Prince Carl Philip Edmund Bertil, Duke of Värmland, *born* 13 May 1979; Princess Madeleine Thérèse Amelie Josephine, Duchess of Hälsingland and Gästrikland, *born* 10 June 1982

Heir, HRH Crown Princess Victoria Ingrid Alice Désirée, Duchess of Västergötland, *born* 14 July 1977

CABINET *as at August 2002*
Prime Minister, Göran Persson
Deputy Prime Minister, Lena Hjelm-Wallén
Agriculture, Food and Fisheries, Gender Equality Affairs,
   Margareta Winberg
Culture, Marita Ulvskog
Defence, Björn von Sydow
Education and Science, Schools and Adult Education,
   Thomas Östros
Environment (acting), Lena Sommestad
Finance, Bosse Ringholm
Foreign Affairs, Anna Lindh
Health and Social Affairs, Lars Engqvist
Industry, Employment and Communications, Björn
   Rosengren
Justice, Thomas Bodström
Ministers Delegate, Jan Karlsson (*Development Co-
   operation, Migration and Asylum Policy*); Ingela
   Thalen (*Social Security*); Leif Pagrotsky (*Trade*)

EMBASSY OF SWEDEN
11 Montagu Place, London W1H 2AL
Tel: 020-7917 6400
Ambassador Extraordinary and Plenipotentiary, HE Mats
   Bergquist, CMG, apptd 1997

BRITISH EMBASSY
Skarpögatan 6–8, Box 27819, S-115 93 Stockholm
Tel: (00 46) (8) 671 3000
Ambassador Extraordinary and Plenipotentiary, HE John
   Grant, CMG, apptd 1999
CONSULATE-GENERAL – Gothenburg
CONSULATES – Malmö, Sundsvall

BRITISH COUNCIL DIRECTOR, Jim Potts, PO Box
   27819,
   S-115 93 Stockholm; Email: info@britishcouncil.se

DEFENCE

The Army has 368 main battle tanks, 570 armoured
personnel carriers and 1,080 armoured infantry fighting
vehicles. The Navy has seven submarines and 45 patrol
and coastal vessels at four bases. The Air Force has 250
combat aircraft.

Sweden has a policy of non-alignment in peace and
neutrality in war, and it maintains a 'total defence' which
includes peacetime organisations for civil, economic and
psychological defence.

It was announced in March 1999 that the size of the
armed forces was to be reduced by about 50 per cent in
line with budget cuts and the perceived diminished threat
to Sweden's security.
MILITARY EXPENDITURE – 2.2 per cent of GDP (2000)
MILITARY PERSONNEL – 33,900: Army 19,100, Navy
   7,100, Air Force 7,700; Paramilitaries 600
CONSCRIPTION DURATION – Seven to 15 months

ECONOMY

Less than 10 per cent of the land area is farmland and less
than 3 per cent of the labour force is employed in
farming, although Sweden is more than 80 per cent self-
sufficient in food.

Industrial prosperity is based on natural resources:
forests, mineral deposits and water power. The forests
cover about half the total land surface and sustain timber,
finished wood products, pulp and paper milling
industries. The mineral resources include iron ore, lead,
zinc, sulphur, granite, marble, precious and heavy metals
(the latter not exploited) and extensive deposits of low-
grade uranium ore. Industries based on mining are

important but it is the general engineering industry that
provides 80 per cent of Sweden's exports, especially
specialised machinery and systems, motor vehicles,
aircraft, electrical and electronic equipment,
pharmaceuticals, plastics and chemical industries.

Hydroelectricity supplies 15 per cent of energy needs.
Sweden has no significant indigenous resources of
conventional hydrocarbon fuels and relies for 50 per cent
of its energy needs upon imported oil and coal.

Sweden experienced a deep recession between 1992 and
1994. The centre-right government, elected in 1991,
introduced austerity measures and free market economic
reforms. In October 1997 Sweden decided not to join
European economic and monetary union (EMU) at the
first stage; however, a referendum on EMU membership
is to be held after the general election in September 2002.
Unemployment has been falling steadily since 1997.

In 2000 there was a trade surplus of US$15,215 million
and a current account surplus of US$6,617 million.
Imports totalled US$72,634 million and exports
US$86,908 million.
GNP – US$237,473 million (2000); US$26,750 per
   capita (1999)
GDP – US$237,764 million (1998); US$26,968 per
   capita (1999)
ANNUAL AVERAGE GROWTH OF GDP – 4.6 per cent
   (2000)
INFLATION RATE – 1.0 per cent (2000)
UNEMPLOYMENT – 5.6 per cent (1999)

TRADE

About 45 per cent of industrial output is exported,
mainly in the form of cars, trucks, machinery, and
electrical and communications equipment. Sweden
conducts 70 per cent of its trade with EFTA and the rest
of the EU.

Trade with UK	2000	2001
Imports from UK	£3,987,700,000	£3,783,600,000
Exports to UK	4,740,800,000	4,425,100,000

COMMUNICATIONS

The total length of railroads is 12,821 km. The road
network is about 210,000 km in length. The mercantile
marine amounted in 1996 to 2,950,000 gross tonnage.
Regular domestic air traffic is maintained by the
Scandinavian Airlines System and by Malmö Aviation.
Regular European and intercontinental air traffic is
maintained by the Scandinavian Airlines System.

EDUCATION

The state system provides nine years' free and compulsory
schooling from the age of seven to 16 in the
comprehensive elementary schools. 95 per cent continue
into further education of two to four years' duration in
the upper secondary schools and a unified higher
education system administered in six regional areas
containing one of the universities: Uppsala (founded
1477); Lund (1668); Stockholm (1878); Gothenburg
(1887); Umeå (1963) and Linköping (1967). There are 40
institutions of higher education including three technical
universities in Stockholm, Gothenburg and Luleå.
Enrolment (percentage of age group) – primary 100 per
   cent (1997); secondary 100 per cent (1997); tertiary
   50 per cent (1997)

CULTURE

Swedish belongs, with Danish and Norwegian, to the
North Germanic language group. Swedish literature dates

back to King Magnus Eriksson, who codified the old Swedish provincial laws in 1350. With his translation of the Bible, Olaus Petri (1493–1552) formed the basis for the modern Swedish language. Literature flourished during the reign of Gustavus III, who founded the Swedish Academy in 1786. Notable Swedish writers include Almquist (1795–1866), Strindberg (1849–1912) and Lagerlöf (1858–1940), Nobel Prizewinner in 1909. Contemporary authors include Lagerquist (1891–1974), Nobel Laureate in 1951, Martinson (1904–78) and Johnson (1900–76), Nobel Laureates jointly in 1974. The Swedish scientist Alfred Nobel (1833–96) founded the Nobel Prizes for literature, science and peace.

SWITZERLAND
Schweizerische Eidgenossenschaft/Confédération Suisse/Confederazione Svizzera/Confederaziun Svizra – Swiss Confederation

AREA – 15,940 sq. miles (41,284 sq. km). Neighbours: France (west and north-west), Germany (north), Austria and Liechtenstein (east), Italy (south)
POPULATION – 7,283,274 (2001 estimate): 46.1 per cent Roman Catholic, 40 per cent Protestant, 5 per cent other religions and 8.9 per cent without religion. The official languages are German (the first language of 63.7 per cent), French (19.2 per cent), Italian (7.6 per cent) and Romansch (0.6 per cent). German is the dominant language in 19 of the 26 cantons; French in Fribourg, Jura, Geneva, Neuchâtel, Valais and Vaud; Italian in Ticino; and Romansch in parts of Graubünden
CAPITAL – Bern (population, 321,932, 1999 estimate)
MAJOR CITIES – Basel (404,418); Geneva (446,217); Lausanne (284,707); Lucerne (181,015); Winterthur (117,328); Zürich (929,070), 1996 estimates
CURRENCY – Swiss franc of 100 rappen (or centimes)
NATIONAL ANTHEM – Schweizerpsalm (Swiss Psalm)
NATIONAL DAY – 1 August
NATIONAL FLAG – Square and red, bearing a couped white cross
LIFE EXPECTANCY (years) – male 75.9; female 82.3
POPULATION GROWTH RATE – 0.4 per cent (1999)
POPULATION DENSITY – 173 per sq. km (1999)
URBAN POPULATION – 67.6 per cent (1996)

Switzerland is the most mountainous country in Europe. The Alps, from 1,700 to 4,634 m (5,000 to 15,217 ft) in height, occupy its southern and eastern frontiers and the chief part of its interior; the Jura mountains rise in the north-west. The Alps occupy 60 per cent, and the Jura mountains 12 per cent of the country. The highest peak, Mont Blanc, Pennine Alps (4,807 m/15,782 ft) is partly in France and partly in Italy; Monte Rosa (4,634 m/15,217 ft) and Matterhorn (4,478 m/14,780 ft) are partly in Switzerland and partly in Italy. The highest wholly Swiss peaks are Finsteraarhorn (4,274 m/14,026 ft), Aletschhorn (4,195/13,711), Jungfrau (4,158/13,671), Mönch (4,099/13,456), Eiger (3,970/13,040), Schreckhorn (4,078/13,385), and Wetterhorn (3,701/12,150) in the Bernese Alps, and Dom (4,545/14,918), Weisshorn (4,506/14,803) and Breithorn (4,165/13,685). The Swiss lakes include Lakes Maggiore, Zürich, Lucerne, Neuchâtel, Geneva, Constance, Thun, Zug, Lugano, Brienz and the Walensee.

HISTORY AND POLITICS

The Swiss confederation was formed as an alliance of three cantons in 1291 and achieved full independence under the Peace of Westphalia (1648), having been a province of the Holy Roman Empire since 1033. French Revolutionary forces seized Switzerland in 1789 and named it the Helvetic Republic. Independence was not restored until the Congress of Vienna (1815), which also joined Geneva, Neuchâtel and Valais to the confederation and instituted perpetual neutrality in foreign affairs. In 1847 a war broke out between the Protestant and Roman Catholic cantons, the latter being defeated. A new constitution was adopted in 1848 which enhanced the powers of the central government.

Proportional representation was introduced in 1919 and has ensured coalition governments throughout the 20th century. Women were given the vote in 1971.

On 24 October 1999, the ruling coalition, comprising the Social Democrats, the Swiss People's Party, the Radical Democrats and the Christian Democrats, in power since 1959, was re-elected with 173 of the 200 seats in the National Council.

FOREIGN RELATIONS

The Federal Council voted in 1992 to apply for European Community membership. The European Economic Area (EEA) Treaty between the EC and EFTA, which extends the provisions of the EC single internal market to EFTA states, was rejected in a national referendum on 6 December 1992. Switzerland is consequently the only EFTA state outside the EEA. On 21 May 2000, a referendum on seven bilateral agreements with the EU, which would progressively reduce trade barriers and allow the free movement of people between Switzerland and the EU, was passed, with 67.2 per cent of voters in favour.

Switzerland has had observer status at the UN. In a national referendum held on 3 March 2002 the electorate voted by a narrow majority to support the government's proposal for full UN membership.

POLITICAL SYSTEM

The federal government consists of the Federal Assembly of two chambers, a National Council (*Nationalrat*) of 200 members, and a States Council (*Ständerat*) of 46 members (two from each canton and one from each demi-canton). Members of the National Council are elected for four years, elections taking place in October. The executive power is in the hands of a Federal Council (*Bundesrat*) of seven members, elected for four years by the Federal Assembly and presided over by the president of the Confederation. Each year the Federal Assembly elects from the Federal Council the president and the vice-president. Not more than one person from the same canton may be elected a member of the Federal Council; however, there is a tradition that Italian- and French-speaking areas should between them be represented on the Federal Council by at least two members.

CONFEDERAL STRUCTURE

There are 23 cantons, three of which are subdivided, making 26 in all. Each canton has its own government. The main language in 19 of the cantons is German; in the others it is French (*) or Italian (†).

Canton	Area (sq. km)	Population (1999)
Aargau	1,404	540,600
Appenzell-Ausserrhoden	243	53,700
Appenzell-Innerrhoden	173	14,900
Basel-Country (Basel-Landschaft)	517	258,600
Basel-Town (Basel-Stadt)	37	188,500
Bern	5,959	943,400
*Fribourg	1,671	234,300
*Geneva	282	403,100
Glarus	685	38,700
Graubünden/Grischun	7,105	186,000
*Jura	838	68,800
Lucerne (Luzern)	1,493	345,400
*Neuchâtel	803	165,600
Nidwalden	276	37,700
Obwalden	491	32,200
St Gallen	2,026	447,600
Schaffhausen	299	73,600
Schwyz	908	128,200
Solothurn	791	243,900
Thurgau	991	227,300
†Ticino	2,812	308,500
Uri	1,077	35,500
*Valais	5,225	275,600
*Vaud	3,212	616,300
Zürich	1,729	1,198,600
Zug	239	97,800

FEDERAL COUNCIL *as at August 2002*

President of the Swiss Confederation (2002), *Finance,* Kaspar Villiger (FDP)
Vice-President (2002), *Public Economy,* Pascal Couchepin (FDP)
Federal Chancellor, Annemarie Huber-Hotz (FDP)
Defence, Civil Protection and Sport, Samuel Schmid (SVP)
Foreign Affairs, Joseph Deiss (CVP)
Interior, Ruth Dreifuss (SPS)
Justice and Police, Ruth Metzler-Arnold (CVP)*Transport, Communications and Energy,* Moritz Leuenberger (SPS)

CVP Christian Democratic People's Party; SPS Social Democratic Party; FDP Radical Democratic Party; SVP Swiss People's Party

EMBASSY OF SWITZERLAND
16–18 Montagu Place, London W1H 2BQ
Tel: 020-7616 6000
Ambassador Extraordinary and Plenipotentiary, HE Bruno Max Spinner, apptd 2000

BRITISH EMBASSY
Thunstrasse 50, CH-3005 Bern
Tel: (00 41) (31) 359 7700
Email: info@britain-in-switzerland.ch
Ambassador Extraordinary and Plenipotentiary, HE Basil Eastwood, CMG, apptd 2001
CONSULATE-GENERAL – Geneva
CONSULAR OFFICES – Basel, Bern (at Embassy), Lugano, Montreux, Valais, Zürich

BRITISH COUNCIL DIRECTOR, Caroline Morrissey, Sennweg 2, PO Box 532, CH-3000 Bern 9; Email: britishcouncil@britishcouncil.ch

DEFENCE

The Army has 556 main battle tanks, 1,180 armoured personnel carriers, 435 armoured infantry fighting vehicles and 60 helicopters. The Air Force has 138 combat aircraft.
MILITARY EXPENDITURE – 1.2 per cent of GDP (2000)
MILITARY PERSONNEL – 3,600 active (351,200 to be mobilised: Army 320,600, Air Force 30,600); Paramilitaries 280,000
CONSCRIPTION DURATION – 15 weeks, then ten refresher courses

ECONOMY

Agriculture is followed chiefly in the valleys and the central plateau, where cereals, flax, hemp, wine and tobacco are produced, and fruits and vegetables are grown. Dairying and stock-raising are the principal industries; there are 293,949 hectares of open arable land, 115,933 hectares of cultivated grassland and 626,799 hectares of natural grassland and pasture. The forests cover about 30 per cent of the whole surface. The chief manufacturing industries comprise engineering and electrical engineering, metalworking, chemicals and pharmaceuticals, textiles, watchmaking, woodworking, foodstuffs, publishing and footwear. Banking, insurance and tourism are major industries.
GNP – US$273,690 million (2000); US$38,380 per capita (1999)
GDP – US$262,113 million (1998); US$36,031 per capita (1999)
ANNUAL AVERAGE GROWTH OF GDP – 3.4 per cent (2000)
INFLATION RATE – 1.6 per cent (2000)
UNEMPLOYMENT – 3.1 per cent (1999)

TRADE

The principal imports are machinery, chemicals, vehicles, metals, textiles, precision instruments, watches and jewellery. The principal exports are machinery, chemicals, precision instruments, watches and jewellery, and metals.
In 1998 Switzerland had a trade surplus of US$988 million and a current account surplus of US$24,547 million. In 2000 imports totalled US$76,070 million and exports US$74,865 million.

Trade with UK	2000	2001
Imports from UK	£3,155,615,000	£3,761,730,000
Exports to UK	5,745,145,000	4,830,993,000

COMMUNICATIONS

There were in 1996, 5,041 km of railway tracks and in 1997, 71,086 km of roads, of which 1,613 km were national highways. Goods handled at Basel Rhine ports amounted to 11 million tonnes in 1998.

EDUCATION

Education is controlled by cantonal and communal authorities. Primary education is free and compulsory. School age varies, generally seven to 14, with secondary education from age 12 to 15. Special schools make a feature of commercial and technical instruction. Universities are Basel (founded 1460), Bern (1834), Fribourg (1889), Geneva (1873), Lausanne (1890), Zürich (1832), and Neuchâtel (1909), the technical universities of Lausanne and Zürich and the economics university of St Gall.
ENROLMENT (percentage of age group) – primary 97 per cent (1997); secondary 100 per cent (1997); tertiary 33 per cent (1997)

SYRIA
Al-Jumhūriyya Al-'Arabiyya as-Sūriyya – Syrian Arab Republic

AREA – 71,498 sq. miles (185,180 sq. km). Neighbours: Lebanon (west), Israel and Jordan (south-west), Iraq (east), Turkey (north)
POPULATION – 6,728,808 (2001 estimate): mostly Muslim. Arabic is the principal language, but Kurdish, Turkish and Armenian are spoken among significant minorities and a few villages still speak Aramaic, the language spoken by Christ and the Apostles. English has taken over from French as the main foreign language
CAPITAL – Damascus (Dimashq) (population, 1,549,000, 1994)
MAJOR CITIES – Halab (Aleppo) (1,542,000); Hamāh (273,000); Hims (558,000); Ψ̄Al-Lādhiqīyah, the principal port (303,000), 1994 estimates
CURRENCY – Syrian pound (S$) of 100 piastres
NATIONAL ANTHEM – Humata Al-Diyari Alaykum Salaam (Defenders Of The Realm On You Be Peace)
NATIONAL DAY – 17 April
NATIONAL FLAG – Red over white over black horizontal bands, with two green stars on central white band
LIFE EXPECTANCY (years) – male 70.6; female 73.1
POPULATION GROWTH RATE – 3.2 per cent (1999)
POPULATION DENSITY – 87 per sq. km (1999)
URBAN POPULATION – 51.4 per cent (1995)

The Orontes flows northwards from the Lebanon range across the northern boundary to Antakya (Antioch, Turkey). The Euphrates crosses the northern boundary near Jerablus and flows through north-eastern Syria to the boundary of Iraq.

The region is rich in historical remains. Damascus (Dimishq ash-Sham) is said to be the oldest continuously inhabited city in the world (although Halab disputes this claim), having existed as a city for many 4,000 years. The city contains the Omayed Mosque, the Tomb of Saladin, and the 'street which is called Straight' (Acts 9:11), while to the north-east is the Roman outpost of Dmeir and further east is Palmyra. On the Mediterranean coast at Amrit are ruins of the Phoenician town of Marath, and of Crusaders' fortresses at Markab, Sahyoun, and Krak des Chevaliers. One of the oldest alphabets in the world has been discovered at Ugarit (Ras Shamra), a Phoenician village near Al-Lādhiqīyah. Hittite cities dating from 2000 to 1500 BC, have been explored on the west bank of the Euphrates at Jerablus and Kadesh.

HISTORY AND POLITICS
Once part of the Ottoman Empire, Syria came under French mandate after the First World War. Syria became an independent republic during the Second World War; the first independently elected parliament met in August 1943, but foreign troops were in occupation until April 1946. Syria remained an independent republic until 1958, when it became part, with Egypt, of the United Arab Republic. It seceded from the United Arab Republic in September 1961.

Elections to the 250-seat People's Council in November 1998 resulted in the National Progressive Front retaining all of its 167 seats unchallenged. This seven-party bloc is dominated by the Ba'ath Party, its allies being the Arab Socialist Union, Socialist Unionist Party, Arab Socialist Movement, Syrian Communist Party and Socialist

Unionist Democratic Party. Independents won 83 seats. Mahmoud Zubi, who had been prime minister since 1987, resigned on 7 March 2000 and was replaced by Mustafa Mohamad Miro on 13 March. Zubi committed suicide on 21 May following his expulsion from the Ba'ath Party amid allegations of corruption.

President Hafez al-Assad, who had seized power in a military coup in 1970 and been elected president in 1971 and re-elected in 1978, 1985, 1992 and 1999, died on 10 June 2000. On 18 June, his son, Bashar al-Assad, was unanimously elected as leader by the Ba'ath Party, on 27 June the legislature nominated him for the presidency, and on 10 July he was elected president, gaining 97.29 per cent of the votes cast. Legislative elections were due in November 2002.

POLITICAL SYSTEM
The constitution promulgated in 1973 declares that Syria is a democratic, popular socialist state, and that the Arab Socialist Renaissance (Ba'ath) Party, which has been the ruling party since 1963, is the leading party in the state and society. The president is head of state and is elected by parliament for a seven-year term. The legislature, the *Majlis al-Chaab* (People's Council) has 250 members directly elected for a four-year term.

HEAD OF STATE
President, Bashar al-Assad, *elected by parliament* 27 June 2000, *approved by referendum* 10 July 2000
Vice-Presidents, Abdel Halim Khaddam; Zuheir Masharqa

CABINET *as at August 2002*

Prime Minister, Mohamad Mustafa Miro
Deputy Prime Minister, Defence, First Lt.-Gen. Mustafa Tlass
Deputy Prime Minister, Economic Affairs, Mohammad al-Husayn
Deputy Prime Minister, Foreign Affairs, Farouk al-Shara
Deputy Prime Minister, Service Affairs, Mohammad Naji Otri
Agriculture and Agrarian Reform, Nur-al-Din Muna
Awqaf (Religious Endowments), Mohammad Abd ar-Ra'uf Ziyadah
Construction and Building, Husam al-Aswad
Culture, Najwa Qassab Hasan
Economy and Foreign Trade, Ghassan al Rifa'I
Education, Mahmud al-Sayyed
Electricity, Mounib bin Assaad Saem al-Daher
Finance, Mohammad al-Atrash
Health, Mohammad Iyad al-Shatti
Higher Education, Hassan Risheh
Housing and Public Services, Ayman Wanli
Industry, Issam al-Zaim
Information, Adnan Omran
Interior, Maj-Gen. Ali Hammud
Irrigation, Mohammad Radwan Martini
Justice, Nabil al-Khatib
Labour and Social Affairs, Ghadah al-Jabi
Local Administration, Hilal al-Atrash
Petroleum and Mineral Resources, Ibrahim Haddad
Presidential Affairs, Haitham Duahi
Supply and Internal Trade, Bassam Mohammad Rustum
Telecommunications, Bashir al-Munajjid
Tourism, Sa'dallah Agha al-Qal'ah
Transport, Makram Obeid

EMBASSY OF THE SYRIAN ARAB REPUBLIC
8 Belgrave Square, London SW1X 8PH
Tel: 020-7245 9012
Ambassador Extraordinary and Plenipotentiary, vacant

BRITISH EMBASSY
Kotob Building, 11 Mohammad Kurd Ali Street, Malki,
Damascus (PO Box 37)
Tel: (00 963) (11) 373 9241/2/3/7
Ambassador Extraordinary and Plenipotentiary, HE
Henry Hogger, apptd 2000

BRITISH COUNCIL DIRECTOR, Patrick Brazier,
Maysaloun Street, Shalaan, PO Box 33105, Damascus
Email: britcoun@bc-damascus.bcouncil.org.

DEFENCE

The Army has 4,700 main battle tanks, 1,600 armoured
personnel carriers and 2,250 armoured infantry fighting
vehicles. The Navy has two frigates, 18 patrol and coastal
vessels and 16 armed helicopters at three bases. The Air
Force has 589 combat aircraft and 87 armed helicopters.
Syria maintains a force of some 18,000 men in Lebanon;
1,035 UN troops are deployed on the Golan Heights.
MILITARY EXPENDITURE – 5.6 per cent of GDP (2000)
MILITARY PERSONNEL – 321,000: Army 215,000, Navy
6,000, Air Force 40,000, Air Defence Command
60,000; Paramilitaries 108,000
CONSCRIPTION DURATION – 30 months

ECONOMY

Large areas are under cultivation in the north-east of the
country as a result of irrigation from the Thawra dam.
There are an increasing number of light assembly plants
as Syria's industrialisation programme develops. Leather
goods, wool and silk, textiles, vegetable oil, soap, sugar,
plastics and metal utensils are produced. Oil production
is proceeding in the region of Deir ez Zor. A pipeline has
been built to the Mediterranean port of Banias, via Hims.
Two oil refineries are in production at Hims and Banias.
Oil production in 1998 was 29,300,000 tonnes. Syria also
has gas reserves, deposits of phosphate and rock salt, and
produces asphalt.
GNP – US$16,014 million (2000); US$970 per capita
(1999)
GDP – US$38,473 million (1998); US$2,525 per capita
(1999)
ANNUAL AVERAGE GROWTH OF GDP – 1.8 per cent
(1999)
INFLATION RATE – 10.4 per cent (2000)
TOTAL EXTERNAL DEBT – US$22,369 million (1999)

TRADE

The principal imports are manufactures, metals and
metal goods, machinery, foodstuffs and transport
equipment. Principal exports include oil and oil
derivatives, agricultural products (chiefly fruit and
vegetables, cotton and wheat) and textiles.
In 1998 Syria had a trade deficit of US$172 million and
a current account surplus of US$59 million. In 2000
imports totalled US$16,706 million and exports
US$19,260 million.

Trade with UK	2000	2001
Imports from UK	£71,410,000	£66,695,000
Exports to UK	56,794,000	88,087,000

COMMUNICATIONS

A railway track connects Hims with Damascus and a
track links Hims, Hamāh, Halab, Deir ez Zor and

Qamishliye to the Iraqi frontier. All the principal towns in
the country are connected by roads which vary from
modern dual carriageways to narrow country lanes. An
internal air service operates between all major towns. The
main international airport is at Damascus.

EDUCATION

Education is under state control. Elementary education is
free at state schools and is compulsory from the age of
seven. Secondary education is not compulsory and is free
only at the state schools. There are universities at
Damascus, Halab, Tishrin, Al-Lādhiqīyah and the Ba'ath
University, Hims.
ILLITERACY RATE – 23.9 per cent (2002)
ENROLMENT (percentage of age group) – primary 100
per cent (1997); secondary 43 per cent (1997);
tertiary 16 per cent (1997)

TAIWAN
Chung-hua Min-kuo – Republic of China

AREA – 3,800 sq. miles (35,742 sq. km)
POPULATION – 22,350,000 (2001 estimate). Mandarin
Chinese has been the official language since 1949.
Now Taiwanese, spoken by 85 per cent of the
population, is growing in importance
CAPITAL – Taipei (population, 2,646,474, 2001 estimate)
MAJOR CITIES – ΨKaohsiung (1,490,560); ΨKeelung
(381,695); Taichung (965,790); Tainan (734,650), 1998
CURRENCY – New Taiwan dollar (NT$) of 100 cents
NATIONAL ANTHEM – an Min Chu I (Our Aim Shall Be
To Found A Free Land)
NATIONAL DAY – 10 October
NATIONAL FLAG – Red, with blue quarter at top next
staff, bearing a 12-point white sun

An island in the China Sea, Taiwan, formerly Formosa,
lies 90 miles east of the Chinese mainland. The eastern
part of the main island is mountainous and forested. Mt
Morrison (Yu Shan) (13,035 ft) and Mt Sylvia
(Tz'ukaoshan) (12,972 ft) are the highest peaks.
Territories include the Pescadores Islands (50 sq. miles),
some 35 miles west of Taiwan, as well as Kinmen
(Quemoy) (68 sq. miles) and Matsu (11 sq. miles) which
are only a few miles from mainland China.

HISTORY AND POLITICS

Settled for centuries by the Chinese, the island was ceded
by China to Japan in 1895 and remained part of the
Japanese empire until Japan's defeat in 1945. Nationalist
Kuomintang (KMT) leader Gen. Chiang Kai-shek
withdrew to Taiwan in 1949, towards the end of the war
against the Communist regime in mainland China, after
which the territory continued under his presidency until
his death in 1975. He was succeeded as president by his
son Gen. Chiang Ching-kuo who ruled until his death in
1988, when Vice-President Lee Teng-hui was appointed
president. Martial law was lifted in 1987 after 38 years.
In 1991, President Lee announced that the 'period of
Communist rebellion' on the Chinese mainland was over,
recognising de facto the People's Republic of China. The
announcement also ended emergency measures which
had frozen political life on Taiwan since 1949. In 1991–2
power shifted away from mainlanders to native Taiwanese
with the forcible retirement of the 'Senior
Parliamentarians' who had retained their seats since
being elected on the mainland in 1948. The new
parliament, the Legislative Yuan, gained control of the

budget, of law-making and of the appointment of the prime minister.

President Chen Shui-bian of the Democratic Progressive Party won the presidential election on 18 March 2000 with 39 per cent of the vote, ahead of two KMT candidates, and took office on 20 May. In the general election to the Legislative Yuan on 1 December 2001, the Democratic Progressive Party (DPP) won 87 of the 225 seats; the KMT won 68 seats; the People First Party won 46 seats; the Taiwan Solidarity Union won 13 seats; independents and minor parties won 11 seats.

President Chen Shui-bian named Yu Shyi Kun and he took office on 1 February 2002. Efforts to create a coalition government were rebuffed by the KMT and the Executive Yuan comprises members of the DPP and independents.

FOREIGN RELATIONS

Taiwan (Republic of China) held China's seat on the UN Security Council until 25 October 1971 when it was replaced by the People's Republic of China. The Republic of China is recognised by less than 30 states.

Direct tourism, trade and communications links between mainland China and the Taiwanese islands of Kinmen and Matsu were inaugurated on 2 January 2001, the first direct links between Taiwan and the People's Republic of China since 1949.

POLITICAL SYSTEM

The legislature is bicameral. The Legislative Yuan has 225 members, 176 elected and 49 appointed proportionally by party, and serves a three-year term. Constitutional reforms passed by the Legislative Yuan in 1994 provide for the president and vice-president to be directly elected for four-year terms (previously the president was elected by parliament). The National Assembly, which had previously been an elected upper chamber, voted on 24 April 2000 to transform itself into a largely ceremonial body, to be convened when necessary to consider constitutional amendments, the impeachment of a president, or territorial changes. Members will be appointed proportionally by the parties in the Legislative Yuan.

HEAD OF STATE

President, Chen Shui-bian, *elected* 18 March 2000, *sworn in* 20 May 2000
Vice-President, Annette Lu

EXECUTIVE YUAN *as at August 2002*

Prime Minister, Yu Shyi-kun
Deputy Prime Minister, Chair of Council for Economic Planning and Development, Lin Hsin-yi
Administrator, Environmental Protection Administration, Hao Lung-pin
Chairs of Commissions, Chen Chien-nien (*Aboriginal Affairs*), Ouyang Min-shen (*Atomic Energy Commission*); Hsu Chih-hsiung (*Mongolian and Tibetan Affairs*), Lin Feng-mei (*National Youth Commission*); Chang Fu-mei (*Overseas Chinese Affairs*); Lin Chia-cheng (*Research, Development and Evaluation*); Gen. Yang Teh-chih (*Veterans' Affairs*)
Chairs of Councils, Fan Chen-tsung (*Agriculture*); Chen Yu-hsiu (*Cultural Affairs*); Yeh Chu-lan (*Hakka Affairs*); Chen Chu (*Labour Affairs*); Tsai Ying-wen (*Mainland Affairs*); Wei Che-ho (*National Science Council*); Lin Te-fu (*Physical Fitness and Sports*)
Directors, Wang Chun (*Coast Guard Administration*); Tu Cheng-sheng (*National Palace Museum*)

Directors-General, Lin Chuan (*Budget, Accounting and Statistics*); Lee Yi-yang (*Central Personnel Administration*); Lee Ming-liang (*Department of Health*); Arthur Iap (*Government Information Office*)
Economic Affairs, Lin Yi-fu
Education, Huang Jung-tsun
Finance, Lee Yung-shan
Foreign Affairs, Eugene Chien
Health, Lee Ming-liang
Interior, Yu Cheng-hsien
Justice, Chen Ding-nan
National Defence, Tang Yao-ming
Secretary-General of the Executive Yuan, Lee Ying-yuan
Spokesperson for the Executive Yuan, Chuang Suo-hang
Transport and Communications, Lin Lin-san

BRITISH COUNCIL DIRECTOR, Geoff Evans, 7-F-1, British Trade and Cultural Office, Education and Cultural Section, 99 Jen Ai Road, Section 2, Taipei 100; Email: inquiries@britishcouncil.org.tw. There is a regional office in Kaohsiung

DEFENCE

The Army has 926 main battle tanks, 950 armoured personnel carriers, 225 armoured infantry fighting vehicles and 20 aircraft. The Navy has four submarines, 11 destroyers, 20 frigates, 59 patrol and coastal vessels, 32 combat aircraft and 21 armed helicopters at four bases. The Air Force has 482 combat aircraft.

MILITARY EXPENDITURE – 5.6 per cent of GDP (2000)
MILITARY PERSONNEL – 370,000: Army 240,000, Navy 62,000, Air Force 68,000; Paramilitaries 26,650
CONSCRIPTION DURATION – 22 months

ECONOMY

Taiwan has transformed itself from a mainly agricultural country to a highly developed industrial economy. The industrial base has expanded to include steel, shipbuilding, chemicals, cement, machinery, electrical equipment and services. In 1997 agriculture contributed 3.5 per cent of GDP, manufacturing 36.3 per cent and services 60.2 per cent. The soil is very fertile, producing sugar, rice, sweet potatoes, tea, fruit and tobacco. Livestock provided a third of the value of Taiwan's agricultural produce in 1996. Taiwan produces one-tenth of its coal needs and some natural gas. The principal seaports are Keelung and Kaohsiung.

TRADE

The principal exports are electronic goods, machinery, metal goods, textiles, plastic products, and toys and games. The main imports are oil, chemicals, machinery and natural resources. The main trading partners are the USA, Japan, Hong Kong, Germany, and the Republic of Korea.

In 2000 imports totalled US$140,01 million and exports US$148.3 million.

Trade with UK	2000	2001
Imports from UK	£1,014,207,000	£881,251,000
Exports to UK	3,691,710,000	2,891,871,000

TAJIKISTAN
Çumhurii Toçikiston – Republic of Tajikistan

AREA – 55,251 sq. miles (143,100 sq. km). Neighbours: Uzbekistan (north-west), Kyrgyzstan (north-east), China (east), Afghanistan (south)
POPULATION – 6,578,681 (2001 estimate): 62 per cent Tajik, 23 per cent Uzbek and 8 per cent Russian, with smaller numbers of Tatars, Kyrgyz, Germans and Ukrainians. The people are predominantly Sunni Muslim. The main languages are Tajik, Uzbek and Russian. Tajik is close to the Farsi spoken in Iran
CAPITAL – Dushanbe (population, 528,600, 1993 estimate)
CURRENCY – Somoni of 100 dirams
NATIONAL DAY – 9 September (Independence Day)
NATIONAL FLAG – Three horizontal stripes of red, white and green with the white of double width and charged with a crown and seven stars, all in gold
LIFE EXPECTANCY (years) – male 65.2; female 70.8
POPULATION GROWTH RATE – 1.7 per cent (1999)
POPULATION DENSITY – 44 per sq. km (1999)
MILITARY EXPENDITURE – 6.5 per cent of GDP (2000)
MILITARY PERSONNEL – 6,000: Army 6,000; Paramilitaries 1,200
CONSCRIPTION DURATION – Two years
ILLITERACY RATE – 0.7 per cent (2002)
ENROLMENT (percentage of age group) – tertiary 20 per cent (1997)

The republic includes the Gorno-Badakhstan Autonomous Province and the Kulyab, Kurgan-Tyubinsk and Khodzhent Provinces. The country is mountainous with the Pamir highlands in the east and the high ridges of the Pamir-Altai system in the centre. Plains are formed by wide stretches of the Syr-Darya valley in the north and of the Amu-Darya in the south.

HISTORY AND POLITICS
The area that is now Tajikistan was conquered by Alexander the Great in the fourth century BC and remained under Greek and Greco-Persian rule for 200 years, until the Kingdom of Kusha was established, based on Bacharia (Bukhara). Tajikistan was invaded by both the Arabs and the Samanid Persians between the seventh and ninth centuries AD. The cities of Bukhara and Samarkand were two of the most important cultural and educational centres in the Islamic world. The Tajiks lived under the control of various feudal emirates until the area was subsumed within the Russian Empire in 1868. At the time of the Russian revolution in 1917 the central Asian emirates attempted to re-establish their independence. Soviet power was re-established in northern Tajikistan by 1 April 1918, when the Turkestan Soviet Socialist Republic was formed, and the Bukhara emirate was overthrown by Soviet forces in 1920. In 1924 the Tajikistan Autonomous Soviet Socialist Republic was formed as part of the Uzbek Republic before Tajikistan was given full republican status within the Soviet Union in 1929.
Tajikistan declared independence from the Soviet Union on 9 September 1991. The Islamic-Democratic alliance formed a government in September 1992 but civil war broke out as forces loyal to the former Communist regime rebelled against the new government. By early November, pro-Communist forces controlled virtually all the country and the Supreme Soviet installed Emomaly Rakhmonov as its Speaker and head of state.
A cease-fire in October 1994 allowed presidential and parliamentary elections to be held, which were won by

Emomaly Rakhmonov and the ruling (former Communist) People's Democratic Party of Tajikistan (HDKT), although the elections were boycotted by most opposition groups. Fighting restarted in early 1995. A peace agreement was signed in December 1996 which provided for the formation of a National Reconciliation Commission (NRC), a general amnesty and an exchange of prisoners. The agreement has held, although there have been sporadic outbreaks of violence since it was signed. A referendum was held on constitutional amendments demanded by the opposition on 26 September 1999 and was approved by the electorate. It amended the 1994 constitution to create a bicameral legislature, extended the president's term of office from five to seven years and allowed the formation of religious political parties. Legislation to allow the formation of a bicameral legislature was passed in December 1999.
Presidential elections which took place on 6 November 1999 resulted in a landslide victory for the incumbent President Rakhmonov, who gained over 96 per cent of the vote. Oqil Oqilov was named as prime minister on 20 December when President Rakhmonov announced a new government. Following an election to the Assembly of Representatives on 27 February and 12 March 2000, the HDKT won 30 of the 63 seats, gaining 64.5 per cent of the vote; the Communist Party won 13 seats, the Islamic Renaissance Party won 2 and independent candidates won 15 seats, with three seats remaining vacant.

POLITICAL SYSTEM
Under the new constitutional arrangements, the president serves a single seven-year term. The new bicameral legislature consists of a 63-seat *Majlisi Mamoyandogan* (Assembly of Representatives), which is directly elected and serves a five-year term, and the *Majlisi Milli* (National Assembly), which has 33 members, 25 of which are elected for a five-year term by five regional assemblies and eight are appointed by the president. Administratively Tajikistan is divided into two regions and one autonomous region.

HEAD OF STATE
President, Emomaly Sharifovich Rakhmonov, *elected by Supreme Soviet* 19 November 1992, *elected* 6 November 1994, *re-elected* 6 November 1999

COUNCIL OF MINISTERS *as at August 2002*
Prime Minister, Oqil Oqilov
First Deputy Prime Minister, Relations with CIS States, Haji Akbar Turajonzoda
Deputy Prime Ministers, Kozidavlat Koimdodov; Nigina Sharapova; Zokir Vazirov; Maj.-Gen. Saidamir Zuhurov
Agriculture, Tursun Rahmatov
Chairs of State Committees, Matlubkhon Davlatov (*Administration of Affairs of State*); Ismat Eshmirzoyev (*Construction and Architecture*); Khayrulloyev Sadullo (*Land Resources and Reclamation*); Salomsho Muhabbatov (*Oil and Gas*); Rahimov Sayfullo (*Radio and Television*)
Culture, Karomatullo Olimov
Defence, Lt.-Gen. Sherali Khayrulloyev
Economics and Trade, Hakim Soliyev
Education, Safarali Radzhabov
Emergency Situations and Civil Defence, Maj.-Gen. Mirzo Ahmadovich Zieyev
Energy, Abdullo Yorov
Environmental Protection and Water Resources, Ismail Davlatov
Finance, Anvarsho Muzaffurov

Foreign Affairs, Talbak Nazarov
Grain, Bekmurod Urokov
Health, Alamkhon Ahmedov
Industry, Zayd Sherovich Saidov
Interior, Mahmadnazar Solehov
Justice, Halifabobo Hamidov
Labour, Employment and Social Welfare, Rafiqa
   Ghaniyevna Musoyeva
Security, Khayruddin Abdurahimov
State Revenue and Tax Collection, Ghulomjon Boboyev
Transport and Roads, Abdujalol Salimov
HONORARY CONSULATE
33 Ovington Square, London SW3 1LJ
Honorary Consul, Benjamin Brahms

ECONOMY

In January 1994 Tajikistan entered into a monetary union
with Russia. The Tajik rouble replaced the Russian rouble
in May 1995. The economy is being reformed and
privatisation undertaken in order to attract foreign
investment. In 1997 GDP grew by 1.7 per cent and
industry grew by 9 per cent. Agriculture is the major
sector of the economy, concentrating on cotton-growing
and cattle-breeding. Tajikistan also has rich mineral
deposits of mercury, lead, zinc, oil, gold and uranium.
Industry specialises in the production of clothing and
textiles.

A new currency, the somoni, was introduced on 30
October 2000, replacing the Tajik rouble.

GNP – US$1,107 million (2000); US$280 per capita
   (1999)
GDP – US$1,320 million (1998); US$159 per capita
   (1999)
Annual Average Growth of GDP – 8.3 per cent (2000)
Total External Debt – US$889 million (1999)

Trade with UK	2000	2001
Imports from UK	£1,035,000	£619,000
Exports to UK	2,602,000	1,226,000

TANZANIA
*Jamhuri ya Muungano wa Tanzania – United Republic of
Tanzania*

AREA – 341,216 sq. miles (883,749 sq. km). Neighbours:
Kenya and Uganda (north), Mozambique (south),
Malawi and Zambia (south-west), Rwanda, Burundi
and the Democratic Republic of Congo (west)
POPULATION – 6,232,074 (2001 estimate). Africans
form a large majority, with European, Asian, and
other non-African minorities. The African
population consists mostly of tribes of mixed Bantu
race. The official languages are Swahili and English
CAPITAL – Dodoma (population, 1,502,344, 1995)
MAJOR CITIES – ΨDar es Salaam (1,096,000), the
economic and administrative centre; Mbeya
(194,000); Mwanza (252,000); ΨTanga (172,000),
1985 estimates
CURRENCY – Tanzanian shilling of 100 cents
NATIONAL ANTHEM – Mungu Ibariki Afrika (God Bless
Africa)
NATIONAL DAY – 26 April (Union Day)
NATIONAL FLAG – Green (above) and blue; divided by
diagonal black stripe bordered by gold, running from
bottom (next staff) to top (in fly)
LIFE EXPECTANCY (years) – male 50.1; female 52.0
POPULATION GROWTH RATE – 3.7 per cent (1999)
POPULATION DENSITY – 37 per sq. km (1999)

MILITARY EXPENDITURE – 1.8 per cent of GDP (2000)
MILITARY PERSONNEL – 27,000: Army 23,000, Navy
   1,000, Air Force 3,000; Paramilitaries 1,400
CONSCRIPTION DURATION – Two years

Tanzania comprises Tanganyika, on the mainland of east
Africa, and the island of Zanzibar. The greater part of the
country is occupied by the central African plateau from
which rise, among others, Mt Kilimanjaro (19,340 ft), the
highest point on the continent of Africa, and Mt Meru
(14,974 ft). The Serengeti National Park covers an area of
6,000 sq. miles in the Arusha, Mwanza and Mara Regions.

HISTORY AND POLITICS

Tanganyika became an independent state and a member
of the British Commonwealth on 9 December 1961, and
a republic within the Commonwealth on 9 December
1962. Zanzibar, comprising the islands of Zanzibar,
Pemba and Mafia, was formerly ruled by the Sultan of
Zanzibar and was a British Protectorate until 10
December 1963 when it became an independent state
within the Commonwealth. On 26 April 1964 Tanganyika
united with Zanzibar to form the United Republic of
Tanzania.

The sole legal political party from 1977 to 1992 was the
Chama Cha Mapinduzi – the Revolutionary Party of
Tanzania (CCM). The constitution was amended in 1992
to allow multiparty politics, with the stipulation that all
parties must be active in both the mainland and in
Zanzibar and that parties must not be formed on
regional, religious, tribal or racial grounds.

The first multiparty presidential and parliamentary
elections were held in October and November 1995 and
were won by the CCM.

Presidential and general elections were held on 29
October 2000. President Mkapa was re-elected, winning
71.7 per cent of the vote, and the CCM won an
overwhelming majority in the National Assembly.

In Zanzibar, Amani Abeid Karume, the CCM candidate,
was elected president and the CCM won a majority, but
the results were disputed following violent protests and
the annulment of the results in 16 of the 50 constituencies
by the National Electoral Commission because of
irregularities. A rerun was held in the 16 constituencies
on 5 November. All 16 seats were won by the CCM. A
series of demonstrations in protest at the conduct of the
elections was organised by the main opposition party, the
Civic United Front, in January 2001.

POLITICAL SYSTEM

The president is directly elected and may serve two five-
year terms. The National Assembly contains up to 296
members, of whom 280 are directly elected, five are
chosen by the Zanzibar House of Representatives, up to
ten members are appointed by the president and one seat
is reserved for the Attorney-General. Constituency
members are elected at a general election held at a
maximum of five-yearly intervals. Although Zanzibar has
its own president, government and 60-member House of
Representatives, Tanganyika is governed by the
government of the Union. The president of Zanzibar is
also a member of the Union Cabinet.

HEAD OF STATE

President of the United Republic, Benjamin Mkapa,
elected 29 October 1995, *re-elected* 5 November 2000
Vice-President, Ali Mohamed Sheni
President of Zanzibar, Amani Abeid Karume

1080　Countries of the World

CABINET *as at August 2002*

The President
The Vice-President
Prime Minister, Frederick Sumaye
Agriculture and Food, Charles Keenja
Attorney-General, Andrew Cheng
Communications and Transport, Mark Mwandosya
Community Development, Women's Affairs and Children,
　Asha-Rose Migiro
Co-operatives and Marketing, George Kahama
Defence, Philemon Sarungi
Education, James Mungai
Energy and Mineral Resources, Daniel Yona Ndhiwa
Finance, Basil Mramba
Foreign Affairs and International Co-operation, Jakaya
　Kikwete
Health, Anna Abdallah
Home Affairs, Mohammed Seif Khatib
Justice and Constitutional Affairs, Harith Bakari
　Mwapachu
Labour, Youth Development and Sport, Juma Athumani
　Kapuya
Land, Housing and Urban Development, Gideon Cheyo
Ministers of State in the President's Office, Mary Nagu
　(*Civil Service*); Abdallah Kigoda (*Planning and
　Privatisation*); Brig.-Gen. Hassan Ngwiliza (*Regional
　Administration and Local Government*); Wilson
　Masilingi (*Security*)
Ministers of State in the Prime Minister's Office, William
　Lukuvi (*Information and Policy*); Ramadhani Mapuri
Ministers of State in the Vice-President's Office, Edgar
　Maokola Majogo (*Poverty*); Arcado Ntagwiza
Natural Resources, Tourism and Environment, Zakia
　Meghji
Science, Technology and Higher Education, Pius
　Ng'wandu
Trade and Industry, Juma Ngasongwa
Water and Livestock Development, Edward Lowassa
Works, John Magufuli

HIGH COMMISSION FOR THE UNITED REPUBLIC OF
TANZANIA
43 Hertford Street, London W1Y 8DB
Tel: 020-7499 8951/4
High Commissioner, HE Hassan Omar Gumbo Kibelloh,
apptd 2002

BRITISH HIGH COMMISSION
78 Haile Selaisse (PO Box 9200), Dar es Salaam
Tel: (00 255) (22) 2666355
High Commissioner, HE R. Clarke, apptd 2001

BRITISH COUNCIL DIRECTOR, Tom Cowin, Samora
Avenue/Ohio Street, PO Box 9100, Dar es Salaam
Email: info@britishcouncil.or.tz

ECONOMY

The islands of Zanzibar and Pemba produce a large part
of the world's supply of cloves and clove oil; coconuts,
coconut oil and copra are also produced. Tanzania's chief
exports are coffee, cotton and cashew nuts. The chief
imports are capital equipment, oil and oil derivatives, and
consumer goods. Industry is largely concerned with the
processing of raw material for export or local
consumption.

In 2000 Tanzania had a trade deficit of US$671 million
and a current account deficit of US$517 million.

Imports totalled US$1,524 million and exports
US$663 million.

GNP – US$9,266 million (2000); US$260 per capita
(1999)

GDP – US$6,827 million (1998); US$245 per capita
(1999)
ANNUAL AVERAGE GROWTH of GDP – 3.8 per cent (1998)
INFLATION RATE – 5.9 per cent (2000)
TOTAL EXTERNAL DEBT – US$7,968 million (1999)

Trade with UK	2000	2001
Imports from UK	£56,664,000	£6,679,000
Exports to UK	30,223,000	35,249,000

COMMUNICATIONS

The main ports are Dar es Salaam, Tanga, Mtwara,
Zanzibar, Mkoani and Wete, in addition to Mwanza,
Musoma and Bukoba on Lake Victoria and Kigoma on
Lake Tanganyika. Coastal shipping services connect the
mainland to Zanzibar and lake services are operated on
Lake Tanganyika and Lake Malawi. The principal
international airports are Dar es Salaam, Kilimanjaro and
Zanzibar. There are two railway systems; one connecting
Dar es Salaam to Zambia, and the second having two
main lines running from Dar es Salaam, one to northern
Tanzania and Kenya and the other to Lakes Tanganyika
and Victoria.

EDUCATION

The school system is administered in Swahili but the
government is making efforts to improve English
standards for the purposes of secondary and higher
education. There are three institutes of higher education.
ILLITERACY RATE – 22.9 per cent (2002)
ENROLMENT (percentage of age group) – primary 67
per cent (1997); tertiary 1 per cent (1997)

THAILAND
Prathes Thai – Kingdom of Thailand

AREA – 198,115 sq. miles (513,115 sq. km). Neighbours:
Malaysia (south), Myanmar (west), Laos and
Cambodia (east)
POPULATION – 61,797,751 (2001 estimate). The
principal language is Thai, a monosyllabic, tonal
language of the Indo-Chinese linguistic family, with a
vocabulary strongly influenced by Sanskrit and Pali.
It is written in an alphabetic script derived from
ancient Indian scripts. Significant minorities speak
Chinese (in urban areas), Lao (in the north-east),
Khmer (in the east) and Malay (in the far south). The
principal religion is Buddhism (94.37 per cent), with
Muslim and Christian minorities
CAPITAL – ΨBangkok (population, 5,882,000, 1998
estimate)
MAJOR CITIES – Chiang Mai (159,000); Chon Buri
(229,400); Nakhon Ratchasima (260,500);
Nanthanburi (476,300); Songkhla (288,000), 1998
estimates
CURRENCY – Baht of 100 satang
NATIONAL ANTHEM – Pleng Chart (National Anthem)
NATIONAL DAY – 5 December (The King's Birthday)
NATIONAL FLAG – Five horizontal bands, red, white,
dark blue, white, red (the blue band twice the width
of the others)
LIFE EXPECTANCY (years) – male 67.9; female 73.8
POPULATION GROWTH RATE – 1.0 per cent (1999)
POPULATION DENSITY – 120 per sq. km (1999)

Thailand, formerly known as Siam, is divided
geographically into four: the centre is a plain; to the
north-east there is a plateau area and to the north-west
mountains. The south of Thailand consists of a narrow

mountainous peninsula. The principal rivers are the Chao Phraya in the central plains, and the Mekong on the northern and north-eastern borders.

HISTORY AND POLITICS

The Thai nation was founded in the 13th century. Although occupied by Burma in the 18th century, Thailand is the only country in the region not to have been colonised by a European power.

Following a revolution in 1932, Thailand became a constitutional monarchy. After a military coup in February 1991, a new constitution was approved under which the military would have significant political power. Parties aligned with the military won the general election in March 1992, but mass demonstrations held in Bangkok, with the help of the King, forced the government from power. Military power was curbed, the 1978 constitution was restored and the interim government sacked military chiefs.

Parliamentary elections in September 1992 resulted in a majority for those parties not allied with the military. The first election to the Senate was held on 4 March 2000. A rerun was held in 78 seats on 29 April following evidence of fraud. Further reruns were necessary for some seats.

A general election took place on 6 January 2001. The Thai Rak Thai (TRT) party won 248 seats and formed a coaltion with the Chart Thai party and the New Aspiration party.

FOREIGN RELATIONS

Laos occupied two Thai islands in the Mekong river on 19 August 2000 and evicted the inhabitants, claiming that it had jurisdiction over all the islands in the Mekong under a 1926 treaty. On 9–11 February 2001, fighting occurred between the Thai army and Myanmarese troops who had crossed the border in pursuit of rebels in Chiang Rai province. The two countries agreed on 19–20 June to resolve the border tension and co-operate on fighting drug production and smuggling.

POLITICAL SYSTEM

The constitution provides for a National Assembly consisting of a 200-member Senate, directly elected on a non-party basis for a six-year term, and a 500-member House of Representatives elected by universal adult suffrage, 400 elected in single-member constituencies and 100 from party lists, for a term of four years.

HEAD OF STATE

HM The King of Thailand, King Bhumibol Adulyadej, born 5 December 1927; succeeded his brother 9 June 1946; married 28 April 1950 Mom Rajawongse Sirikit Kitiyakara; crowned 5 May 1950; and has issue, Princess Ubol Ratana, born 6 April 1951; Crown Prince Maha Vajiralongkorn; Princess Maha Chakri Sirindhorn, born 2 April 1955; Princess Chulabhorn, born 4 July 1957

Heir, HRH Crown Prince Maha Vajiralongkorn, born 28 July 1952; married 3 January 1977 Soamsawali Kitiyakara

CABINET as at August 2002

Prime Minister, Thaksin Shinawatra (TRT)
Deputy Prime Ministers, Gen. Chawalit Yongchaiyudh (TRT) (Defence); Somkit Chatusipitak (TRT) (Economic Affairs, Minister of Finance) Daj Boonlong (TRT) (Labour and Social Welfare); Pongpol Adireksan (TRT); Pitak Intravitayanant (TRT); Kon Thappharansi
Ministers attached to the Prime Minister's Office, Krasae Chanawong (TRT); Gen. Thammarak Isarakuan na Ayuthaya (TRT); Somsak Thepsutin (TRT); Pongthep Thepkanjana (CT); Suwat Liptapanlop (University Affairs)
Agriculture and Co-operatives, Chuchief Harnsawad (TRT)
Commerce, Adisai Bodharamik (TRT)
Education, Suwit Khunkitti (TRT)
Foreign Affairs, Surakiet Sathirathai (TRT)
Industry, Suriya Rungruangkit (TRT)
Interior, Purachai Piumsombun (TRT)
Justice, Jaturon Chaisang (TRT)
Public Health, Sudarat Keyuraphan (TRT)
Science, Technology and Environment, Sontaya Kunplome (CT)
Transport and Communications, Wanmuhadnoor Matha (NAP)

CT Chart Thai; NAP New Aspiration Party; TRT Thai Rak Thai

ROYAL THAI EMBASSY

29–30 Queen's Gate, London SW7 5JB
Tel: 020-7589 2944
Ambassador Extraordinary and Plenipotentiary, HE Sir Vidhya Rayananonda, KCVO, apptd 1994

BRITISH EMBASSY

1031 Wireless Road, Bangkok 10330
Tel: (00 66) (2) 305 8333
Ambassador Extraordinary and Plenipotentiary, HE Lloyd Barnaby Smith, apptd 2000

BRITISH COUNCIL DIRECTOR, Bhaskar Chakravarti, 254 Chulalongkorn Soi 64, Siam Square, Phayathai Road, Pathumwan, Bangkok 10330

DEFENCE

The Army has 333 main battle tanks, 970 armoured personnel carriers and five attack helicopters. The Navy has one aircraft carrier, 12 frigates, 88 patrol and coastal vessels, 44 combat aircraft and five armed helicopters at five bases. The Air Force has 153 combat aircraft.

MILITARY EXPENDITURE – 2.0 per cent of GDP (2000)
MILITARY PERSONNEL – 306,000: Army 190,000, Navy 68,000, Air Force 48,000; Paramilitaries 104,000

ECONOMY

Thailand was one of the countries worst affected by the economic crisis in south-east Asia. In May 1997 the stock market fell to an eight-year low. In July 1997 the government allowed the currency to float freely, resulting in a de facto devaluation of 20 per cent and triggering a currency crisis throughout south-east Asia. On 5 August 1997, an IMF loan of US$16.7 billion was announced, in return for emergency financial reforms. However, these reforms were only implemented after a delay and were seen by the markets as inadequate, further damaging economic confidence. The government resigned on 3 November 1997, and was replaced by an eight-party coalition. The Thai economy contracted by about 8 per cent in 1998. In March 1999, the government announced a package of tax cuts and increased spending designed to stimulate the economy.

The agricultural sector employs around half of the labour force. In 1999 it contributed 13 per cent of GDP. Rice remains the most important crop; other main crops are sugar, maize, sorghum, cassava, rubber, tobacco, kenaf and jute. In recent years fishing and livestock production have gained importance. There are reserves of oil, natural gas and lignite; mineral resources include tin, tungsten, lead and iron.

Important industrial sectors include textiles, transportation vehicles and equipment, construction materials, brewing, petroleum refining, electrical appliances, plastics, computers and parts, and integrated circuits. In 1999, industry contributed 40 per cent of GDP. Since 1982 tourism has been the main foreign exchange earner. In 1998, there were 7.8 million foreign visitors.
GNP – US$121,760 million (2000); US$2,010 per capita (1999)
GDP – US$113,990 million (1998); US$2,000 per capita (1999)
ANNUAL AVERAGE GROWTH OF GDP – 4.4 per cent (2000)
INFLATION RATE – 1.5 per cent (2000)
UNEMPLOYMENT – 3.0 per cent (1999)
TOTAL EXTERNAL DEBT – US$96,335 million (1999)

TRADE

Thailand's main exports are computers and parts, cars, integrated circuit boards, precious stones, rice, maize, canned sea food, fabrics, sugar and tin. Main imports are crude oil, chemicals, electrical goods, industrial machinery, iron, steel and transport equipment.

In 2000 Thailand had a trade surplus of US$11,757 million and a current account surplus of US$9,195 million. Imports totalled US$61,924 million and exports US$69,057 million.

Trade with UK	2000	2001
Imports from UK	£580,796,000	£595,702,000
Exports to UK	1,661,419,000	1,669,135,000

COMMUNICATIONS

Navigable waterways have a length of about 1,100 km in the dry season and 1,600 km in the wet season. There are 4,071 km of railways. Bangkok is the international airport, though airports at Chiang Mai, Phuket and Hat Yai also receive international flights. There are two important ports in the country, Bangkok and Sattahip. There are 3,999 km of principal waterways. In September 1999, the government approved a plan to build a 350-km gas pipeline from the Gulf of Thailand to Songkhla province to link with the Malaysian network.

EDUCATION

Primary education is compulsory and free, and secondary education in government schools is free. Private universities and colleges are playing an increasing role in higher education. Out of 43 universities and other similar higher institutes of learning, 21 are private.
ILLITERACY RATE – 4.2 per cent (2002)
ENROLMENT (percentage of age group) – tertiary 22 per cent (1997)

TOGO
République Togolaise – Togolese Republic

AREA – 21,925 sq. miles (56,785 sq. km). Neighbours: Ghana (west), Burkina Faso (north), Benin (east)
POPULATION – 5,153,088 (2001 estimate). The official language is French; Ewe, Watchi and Kabiyé are the main indigenous languages
CAPITAL – ΨLomé (population, 366,476, 1983)
CURRENCY – Franc CFA of 100 centimes
NATIONAL ANTHEM – Écartons Tous Mauvais Esprit Qui Gêne L'unité Nationale (Let Us Discard All Ill Feelings Which Harm National Unity)
NATIONAL DAY – 27 April
NATIONAL FLAG – Five alternating green and yellow horizontal stripes; a quarter in red at top next staff bearing a white star
LIFE EXPECTANCY (years) – male 51.1; female 53.3
POPULATION GROWTH RATE – 2.6 per cent (1999)
POPULATION DENSITY – 79 per sq. km (1999)
MILITARY EXPENDITURE – 2.0 per cent of GDP (2000)
MILITARY PERSONNEL – 9,450: Army 9,000, Navy 200, Air Force 250; Paramilitaries 750
CONSCRIPTION DURATION – Two years (selective)
ILLITERACY RATE – 40.7 per cent (2002)
ENROLMENT (percentage of age group) – primary 100 per cent (1997); secondary 27 per cent (1997); tertiary 4 per cent (1997)

HISTORY AND POLITICS

The first president of Togo, Sylvanus Olympio, was assassinated in 1963. In 1967, there was an army coup d'état and the army commander Lt.-Col. (later Gen.) Eyadéma named himself president. In April 1990, following increasing popular pressure, the government was forced to concede a political amnesty, the introduction of a multiparty constitution and a national conference. In August 1991 the national conference stripped President Eyadéma of all powers, banned the *Rassemblement du peuple togolais* (RPT), which had been the sole legal party, and elected Kokou Koffigoh as prime minister of an interim government. Troops loyal to President Eyadéma three times attempted to overthrow Koffigoh (in October, November and December 1991) but were frustrated by pro-democracy supporters. A new multiparty constitution was approved by referendum in September 1992. In November, Eyadéma, who had regained the position of head of state in August 1992, ordered the Army to crush civil unrest and a general strike against his rule. In February 1993, as violence continued, Koffigoh and Eyadéma agreed on the formation of a crisis government, which the national conference and the Collective Democratic Opposition-2 (COD-2) declared illegal.

The presidential election of 21 June 1998 was won by Gen. Eyadéma. Legislative elections to the 81-seat National Assembly were held on 21 March 1999. Opposition parties, who had refused to accept the results of the presidential election in 1998, boycotted the

election, with the result that the ruling RPT gained 79 seats, the remaining two seats being won by independents. Eugene Koffi Adoboli was appointed prime minister on 22 May 1999 and a new Cabinet was appointed on 18 June. The government and opposition parties reached an agreement in July 1999 that a fresh election would be held in March 2000 and President Eyadéma agreed not to run in the 2003 presidential elections. The general election was repeatedly postponed and re-scheduled and on 3 March 2002 was postponed indefinitely.

HEAD OF STATE

President, Gen. Gnassingbé Eyadéma, *assumed office* 14 April 1967 *re-elected* 1986, 1993, 21 June 1998

GOVERNMENT *as at August 2002*

Prime Minister, Koffi Sama
Agriculture, Livestock and Fisheries, Komikpime Bamnante
Civil Service, Labour and Employment, Kokou Tozoun
Commerce, Industry, Transport and Development of the Free Zone, Dama Dramani
Communication and Civic Education, Pitang Tchalla
Culture, Youth and Sport, Komi Klassou
Economic Affairs, Finance and Privatisation, Kossi Assimaidou
Environment and Forest Resources, Rodolphe Osseyi
Equipment, Mines, Energy, Post and Telecommunications, Tchamga Andjo
Interior, Security and Decentralisation, Col. Sising Akawilou Walla
Justice and Keeper of the Seals, Brig.-Gen. Déyi Méméne
Minister-Delegate at the Prime Minister's Office, in charge of the Private Sector, Angèle Aguigah
Minister of State, Foreign Affairs and Co-operation, Koffi Panou
National Defence and Veterans, Brig.-Gen. Assani Tidjani
National Education and Research, Charles Kondi Agba
Public Health, Social Affairs and Promotion of Women, Suzanne Aho
Regional Integration, Parliamentary Relations, Joseph Kokou Koffigoh
Secretary of State at the Ministry of Enonomy, Finance and Privatisation, in charge of the Budget, Legzim M'ba
Technical Education and Professional Training, Edo Kodjo Maurille Agbobli
Tourism, Handicrafts and Leisure, Tankpadja Lalle

EMBASSY OF THE REPUBLIC OF TOGO
8 rue Alfred-Roll, F-75017 Paris, France
Tel: (00 33) (1) 4380 1213
Ambassador Extraordinary and Plenipotentiary, vacant
BRITISH AMBASSADOR, HE Rod Pullen, resident at Accra, Ghana

ECONOMY

Although the economy remains largely agricultural, exports of phosphates have superseded agricultural products as the main source of export earnings. Other exports include palm kernels, copra and manioc.

In December 1998 the EU announced that it would not resume developmental aid to Togo following irregularities in the country's election process.

In 1998 Togo had a trade deficit of US$133 million and a current account deficit of US$140 million. In 2000 imports totalled US$542 million and exports US$330 million.

GNP – US$1,385 million (2000); US$310 per capita (1999)
GDP – US$1,511 million (1998); US$342 per capita (1999)

ANNUAL AVERAGE GROWTH OF GDP – 6.0 per cent (1998)
INFLATION RATE – 1.9 per cent (2000)
TOTAL EXTERNAL DEBT – US$1,500 million (1999)

Trade with UK	2000	2001
Imports from UK	£20,515,000	£33,871,000
Exports to UK	1,504,000	1,072,000

TONGA
Pule'anga Tonga – Kingdom of Tonga

AREA – 50 sq. miles (650 sq. km)
POPULATION – 104,227 (2001 estimate). The languages are Tongan and English
CAPITAL – ΨNuku'alofa (population, 34,000, 1990), on Tongatapu
CURRENCY – Pa'anga (T$) of 100 seniti
NATIONAL ANTHEM – E, 'Otua Mafimafi (Oh, Almighty God Above)
NATIONAL DAY – 4 June (Emancipation Day)
NATIONAL FLAG – Red with a white canton containing a couped red cross
LIFE EXPECTANCY (years) – male 68.3; female 69.4
POPULATION GROWTH RATE – 0.1 per cent (1999)
POPULATION DENSITY – 151 per sq. km (1999)

Tonga, or the Friendly Islands, comprises a group of islands situated in the southern Pacific some 450 miles east-south-east of Fiji. The largest island, Tongatapu, was discovered by Tasman in 1643. Most of the islands are of coral formation, but some are volcanic (Tofua, Kao and Niuafoou or 'Tin Can' Island).

HISTORY AND POLITICS

The Kingdom of Tonga is an independent constitutional monarchy within the Commonwealth. Prior to 4 June 1970 it had been a British-protected state for 70 years. The constitution provides for a government consisting of the Sovereign, an appointed privy council which functions as a Cabinet, a legislative assembly and a judiciary. The 30-member legislative assembly comprises the King, the 11-member privy council, nine hereditary nobles elected by their peers, and nine popularly elected representatives who hold office for three years. The most recent election took place on 7 March 2002 when the Human Rights and Democracy Movement won seven of the popularly elected seats in the Legislative Assembly.

HEAD OF STATE

King of Tonga, HM King Taufa'ahau Tupou IV, GCMG, GCVO, KBE, *born* 4 July 1918, *acceded* 16 December 1965
Heir, HRH Crown Prince Tupouto'a

CABINET *as at August 2002*

Prime Minister, Agriculture and Fisheries, Civil Aviation and Communications, Foreign Affairs and Defence, HRH Prince 'Ulukalala Lavaka Ata
Deputy Prime Minister (acting), Works, Marines and Ports, Environment and Natural Disaster and Relief, Cecil Cocker
Education (acting), Paul Bloomfield
Finance, Siosiua Utoikamanu
Governor of Ha'apai, Malupo
Governor of Vava'u, Capt. S. M. Tuita
Health, Viliami Tangi
Justice and Attorney-General, Osiua Tuopiau

Labour, Commerce and Industries, Tourism, Paunga
Massaso
Lands, Survey, and Natural Resources, Fielakepa
Police, Prisons and Fire Services, Immigration, Clive
Edwards

TONGA HIGH COMMISSION
36 Molyneux Street, London W1H 5BQ
Tel: 020-7724 5828
High Commissioner, HE Col. Fetu'utolu Tupou, apptd
2000

BRITISH HIGH COMMISSION
PO Box 56, Nuku'alofa
Tel: (00 676) 24285/24395
Email: britcomt@kalianet.to
High Commissioner, HE Paul Nessling, apptd 2002

ECONOMY

The economy is primarily agricultural; the main crops are
coconuts, vanilla, yams, taro, cassava, groundnuts, squash
pumpkins and other fruits. Fish is an important staple
food, though recent shortfalls have led to canned fish
being imported. Industry is based on the processing of
agricultural produce, and the manufacture of foodstuffs,
clothing and sports equipment.
GNP – US$166 million (2000); US$1,730 per capita
(1999)
GDP – US$158 million (1998); US$1,574 per capita
(1999)
ANNUAL AVERAGE GROWTH OF GDP – 0.3 per cent
(1998)
INFLATION RATE – 5.9 per cent (2000)
TOTAL EXTERNAL DEBT – US$64 million (1999)

TRADE

The principal exports are fish and vanilla. The principal
imports are manufactures, foodstuffs, machinery and
transport equipment and combustible fuels. In 1999
imports totalled US$73 million and exports US$12
million.

Trade with UK	2000	2001
Imports from UK	£1,883,000	£1,281,000
Exports to UK	470,000	253,000

TRINIDAD AND TOBAGO
The Republic of Trinidad and Tobago

AREA – 1,981 sq. miles (5,130 sq. km)
POPULATION – 1,169,682 (2001 estimate). The language
is English. The main religions are Roman Catholicism
(29.4 per cent of the population), Hinduism (23.8 per
cent); Anglicanism (10.9 per cent); Islam (5.8 per
cent) and Presbyterianism (3.4 per cent)
CAPITAL – ΨPort of Spain (population, 43,396, 1994)
MAJOR CITIES – San Fernando (55,784);
ΨScarborough, the main town of Tobago
CURRENCY – Trinidad and Tobago dollar (TT$) of 100
cents
NATIONAL ANTHEM – Forged From The Love Of
Liberty
NATIONAL DAY – 31 August (Independence Day)
NATIONAL FLAG – Black diagonal stripe bordered with
white stripes, running from top by staff, all on a red
field
LIFE EXPECTANCY (years) – male 72.5; female 77.2
POPULATION GROWTH RATE – 0.6 per cent (1999)
POPULATION DENSITY – 251 per sq. km (1999)

MILITARY EXPENDITURE – 0.5 per cent of GDP (2000)
MILITARY PERSONNEL – 2,700: Army 2,000, Coast
Guard 700

Trinidad, the most southerly of the West Indian islands,
lies seven miles off the north coast of Venezuela. The
island is about 50 miles in length by 37 miles in width.
Two mountain systems, the Northern and Southern
Ranges, stretch across almost its entire width and a third,
the Central Range, lies diagonally across its middle
portion; otherwise the island is mostly flat. Tobago lies 19
miles north-east of Trinidad. The island is 32 miles long
at its widest point, and 11 miles wide. Corozal Point and
Icacos Point, the north-west and south-west extremities
of Trinidad, enclose the Gulf of Paria. West of Corozal
Point lie several islands, of which Chacachacare, Huevos,
Monos and Gaspar Grande are the most important.

HISTORY AND POLITICS

Trinidad was discovered by Columbus in 1498, was
colonised in 1532 by the Spaniards, capitulated to the
British in 1797, and was ceded to Britain under the Treaty
of Amiens (1802). Tobago was discovered by Columbus
in 1498. Dutch colonists arrived in 1632; Tobago
subsequently changed hands numerous times until it was
ceded to Britain by France in 1814 and amalgamated with
Trinidad in 1888. The Territory of Trinidad and Tobago
became an independent state and a member of the
British Commonwealth on 31 August 1962, and a
republic in 1976.
  In the general election held on 10 December 2001 the
ruling United National Congress (UNC) and the
opposition People's National Movement (PNM) each
won 18 of the 36 seats in the House of Representatives.
On 24 December President Robinson chose Patrick
Manning, leader of PNM, as prime minister. The UNC
condemned the president's choice and called for fresh
elections. A new Cabinet was sworn into office on 27
December. On 6 April 2002 President Robinson
suspended parliament because no speaker had been
elected. Elections were expected to be held by the end
of 2002.

POLITICAL SYSTEM

The president is elected for five years by all members of
the Senate and the House of Representatives. The House
of Representatives has 36 members, directly elected for a
five-year term, and the Senate has 31, of whom 16 are
appointed on the advice of the prime minister, six on the
advice of the Leader of the Opposition and nine at the
discretion of the president. Legislation was passed in
September 1980 which afforded Tobago a degree of self-
administration through the 15-member Tobago House of
Assembly, of whom 12 are directly elected and three
chosen by the House for a four-year term.

HEAD OF STATE

President, HE Arthur N. Robinson, *elected* 14 February
1997

CABINET *as at August 2002*

Prime Minister, Finance, Patrick Manning
Agriculture, Land and Marine Resources, John Rahael
Attorney-General, Glenda Morean
Community Development and Gender Affairs, Joan Yuille
  Williams
Culture and Tourism, Eudine Job-Davis
Ecclesiastical Affairs, Donna Carter
Education, Hazel Anne Marie Manning
Energy and Energy Industries, Eric Williams

Foreign Affairs, Knowlson Gift
Health, Colm Imbert
Housing, Danny Montano
Labour, Small and Micro Enterprises, Lawrence Achong
Legal Affairs, Camille Robinson-Regis
Local Government, Jarrette Narine
Ministers of State, Eulalie James; Edward Hart; Stanford Callender; Fitzgerald Hinds; Mustapha Abdul-Hamid; Rennie Dumas
National Security, Howard Chin Lee
Planning and Development, Keith Rowley
Public Administration and Information, Lenny Saith
Public Utilities and Environment, Martin Joseph
Science, Technology and Tertiary Education, Hedwige Bereaux
Social Development, Penelope Beckles
Sports and Youth Affairs, Roger Boynes
Trade, Industry and Consumer Affairs, Minister in the Ministry of Finance, Kenneth Valley
Minister in the Ministry of Finance, Conrad Enill
Works and Transport, Arnold Piggot

HIGH COMMISSION OF THE REPUBLIC OF TRINIDAD AND TOBAGO
42 Belgrave Square, London SW1X 8NT
Tel: 020-7245 9351
High Commissioner, vacant

BRITISH HIGH COMMISSION
19 St Clair Ave, St Clair, Port of Spain
Tel: (00 1 868) 622 2748/8960
Email: csbhc@opus.co.tt
High Commissioner, HE Peter. Harborne, apptd 1999

ECONOMY

Trinidad and Tobago's main source of revenue is from oil. Trinidad has large reserves of natural gas, and in March 2000, an agreement was signed to expand significantly the production of liquefied natural gas. In May 2000, it was announced that an additional natural gas deposit of some 56,600 million cubic metres had been discovered and the discovery of a further deposit of some three trillion cubic feet was announced in September. Fertilisers, tyres, clothing, soap, furniture and foodstuffs are manufactured locally while motor vehicles, radios, TV sets, and electro-domestic equipment are assembled from parts, mainly from Japan. The main agricultural products are sugar, cocoa, coffee, horticultural products and teak.

In 1998 Trinidad and Tobago had a trade deficit of US$741 million and a current account deficit of US$644 million. in 1999 imports totalled US$2,741 million and exports US$2,804 million.
GNP – US$6,477 million (2000); US$4,750 per capita (1999)
GDP – US$5,930 million (1998); US$5,119 per capita (1999)
ANNUAL AVERAGE GROWTH of GDP – 3.3 per cent (1998)
INFLATION RATE – 3.6 per cent (2000)
UNEMPLOYMENT – 14.2 per cent (1998)
TOTAL EXTERNAL DEBT – US$2,462 million (1999)

Trade with UK	2000	2001
Imports from UK	£76,031,000	£91,611,000
Exports to UK	49,710,000	53,927,000

COMMUNICATIONS

The three main ports are Scarborough (Tobago), Port of Spain and Point Lisas where new industries powered by local natural gas are located. The international airport, Piarco, is at Port of Spain.

EDUCATION

Attendance is compulsory for children aged six to 12 years, after which attendance at free secondary schools is determined by success in the secondary school entrance examination at 11 years. There are three technical institutes, two teachers-training colleges, and one of the three branches of the University of the West Indies is located in Trinidad. A medical teaching complex at Mt Hope operates in collaboration with the University of the West Indies.
ILLITERACY RATE – 1.5 per cent (2002)
ENROLMENT (percentage of age group) – primary 99 per cent (1997); secondary 74 per cent (1997); tertiary 8 per cent (1997)

TUNISIA
Al-Jumhūriyya at-Tūnisiyya – Republic of Tunisia

AREA – 63,170 sq. miles (163,610 sq. km). Neighbours: Algeria (west), Libya (south)
POPULATION – 9,660,000 (2001 estimate). Arabic is the official language
CAPITAL – ΨTunis (population, 929,500, 2001 estimate)
MAJOR CITIES – ΨBizerte (518,500); ΨSfax (808,700); ΨSousse (492,500), 2001 estimates
CURRENCY – Tunisian dinar of 1,000 millimes
NATIONAL ANTHEM – Himat Al Hima (Defenders Of The Homeland)
NATIONAL DAY – 20 March
NATIONAL FLAG – Red with a white disc containing a red crescent and star
LIFE EXPECTANCY (years) – male 69.6; female 72.2
POPULATION GROWTH RATE – 1.1 per cent (2001)
POPULATION DENSITY – 62 per sq. km (2001)
URBAN POPULATION – 62.6 per cent (2001)
MILITARY EXPENDITURE – 1.7 per cent of GDP (2000)
MILITARY PERSONNEL – 35,000: Army 27,000, Navy 4,500, Air Force 3,500; Paramilitaries 12,000
CONSCRIPTION DURATION – 12 months (selective)

HISTORY AND POLITICS

A French Protectorate from 1881 to 1956, Tunisia became an independent sovereign state on 20 March 1956. In 1957 the Constituent Assembly abolished the monarchy and elected M. Bourguiba president of the Republic. In March 1975 the National Assembly proclaimed M. Bourguiba as president for life. He was deposed on 7 November 1987 and succeeded by President Zine el-Abidine Ben Ali, who was subsequently elected in 1989 and re-elected in 1994.

President Ben Ali was elected for a third term of office on 24 October 1999, gaining 99.4 per cent of the vote; there were two other candidates. A parallel legislative election was won by the Democratic Constitutional Rally (RCD), who gained 91.6 per cent of the vote, winning 148 of the 182 seats in the National Assembly (*Majlis al-Nuwaab*). The Movement of Social Democrats (MDS) won 13 seats, the Unionist Democratic Union (UDU) and the Party of People's Unity (PUP) won 7 seats each, the Movement for Renewal (MR) won 5 seats and the Social-Liberal Party won 2 seats.

HEAD OF STATE

President, Gen. Zine el-Abidine Ben Ali, *took office* 7 November 1987, *elected* 2 April 1989, *re-elected* 20 March 1994, 24 October 1999

CABINET *as at August 2002*
Prime Minister, Mohammed Ghannouchi
Agriculture, Sadok Rabah
Communication Technologies, Ahmed Friaa
Culture, Abdelbaki Hermassi
Director of the Presidential Office, Ahmed Eyadh
   Ouederni
Economic Development, Abdellatif Saddam
Education, Moncer Rouissi
Environment and Land Development, Mohamed Nabli
Finance, Taoufik Baccar
Foreign Affairs, Habib Ben Yahia
Higher Education, Sadok Chaâbane
Industry, Moncef Ben Abdallah
Interior, Hedi M'henni
International Co-operation and Foreign Investment, Fethi
   Merdassi
Justice, Bechir Takali
*Minister-Delegate to the Prime Minister in charge of
   Human Rights, Communications and Relations with
   the Parliament,* Slaheddine Maaoui
*Minister-Delegate to the Prime Minister, in charge of
   Scientific Research and Technology,* Abdelkrim Zbidi
*Minister Delegate to the Prime Minister, in charge of
   Women and the Family,* Neziha Ben Yedder
Minister of State, Special Adviser to the President,
   Abdelaziz Ben Dhia
National Defence, Dali Jazi
Public Health, Habib Mbarek
Public Works and Housing, Slaheddine Belaid
Religious Affairs, Jelloul Jeribi
Secretary-General of the Government, Mohamed Rachid
   Kechiche
Social Affairs, Hedi M'henni
State Property, Real Estate Affairs, Ridha Grira
Tourism, Entertainment and Handicrafts, Mondher
   Zenaidi
Trade, Taher Sioud
Transport, Houcine Chouk
Vocational Training and Employment, Neziha Zarrouk
Youth, Childhood and Sport, Abderrahim Zouari

TUNISIAN EMBASSY
29 Prince's Gate, London SW7 1QG
Tel: 020-7584 8117
Ambassador Extraordinary and Plenipotentiary, HE
Khémaies Jhinaoui, apptd 1999

BRITISH EMBASSY
5 Place de la Victoire, Tunis 1000
Tel: (00 216) (7) 341444
Email: british.emb@planet.tn
Ambassador Extraordinary and Plenipotentiary, HE
Robin Kealy, CMG, apptd 2002

ECONOMY

Agriculture and fisheries employed 22 per cent of the
workforce in 1999 and accounted for 13 per cent of GDP.
The valleys of the northern region support large flocks
and herds and contain rich agricultural areas in which
cereal crops, citrus fruits, dates, melons, potatoes, peppers
and tomatoes are grown. Vines and olives are extensively
cultivated. Crude oil production in 1998 was 3.9 million
tonnes. Gas has also been discovered off the east coast but
is only exploited in small quantities. Tourism is the main
foreign exchange earner and there were 5.6 million
visitors in 2001.
   In 1999 Tunisia had a trade deficit of US$2,141 million
and a current account deficit of US$503 million. In 2000
imports totalled US$8,560 million and exports US$5,850
million.

GNP – US$20,057 million (2000); US$2,090 per capita
(1999)
GDP – US$19,956 million (1998); US$2,247 per capita
(1999)
ANNUAL AVERAGE GROWTH OF GDP – 5.0 per cent
(2000)
INFLATION RATE – 2.9 per cent (2000)
UNEMPLOYMENT – 13.5 per cent (2001)
TOTAL EXTERNAL DEBT – US$11,872 million (1999)

TRADE

The chief exports are manufactures, textiles and leather
goods, phosphates, mechanical and electronic products,
agricultural products and energy. The chief imports are
manufactures, raw materials and semi-manufactures,
consumer goods, capital goods, and foodstuffs. France
remains the main trading partner. Tunisia became an
associate of the EC in 1969. In July 1995 an EU-Tunisian
partnership agreement was signed which aims to
modernise Tunisia's economy and improve its
competitiveness with a view to creating a free trade zone
with the EU by 2008.

Trade with UK	2000	2001
Imports from UK	£133,290,000	£141,433,000
Exports to UK	109,727,000	120,062,000

EDUCATION

There are 90 centres of higher education, of which six are
universities (four in Tunis, one each in Sousse and Sfax).
There are plans to establish two new universities in
Jendouba and Gafsa.
ILLITERACY RATE – 26.8 per cent (2002)
ENROLMENT (percentage of age group) – primary 100
per cent (1997); secondary 64 per cent (1997);
tertiary 14 per cent (1997)

TURKEY
Türkiye Cumhuriyeti – Republic of Turkey

AREA – 314,508 sq. miles (774,815 sq. km). Neighbours:
Greece (west), Bulgaria (north), Georgia, Armenia,
Naxçivan (Azerbaijan) and Iran (east), Syria and Iraq
(south)
POPULATION – 66,493,970 (2001 estimate). Islam ceased
to be the state religion in 1928 but 98.99 per cent of
the population are Muslim. The main religious
minorities, which are concentrated in Istanbul and on
the Syrian frontier, are Greek Orthodox, Armenian,
Syrian Christian, and Jewish. The language is Turkish;
Kurdish is widely spoken in the south-east of the
country
CAPITAL – Ankara (Angora), in Asia (population,
3,258,026, 1997 estimate). Ankara (or Ancyra) was
the capital of the Roman Province of *Galatia Prima*,
and a marble temple (now in ruins), dedicated to
Augustus, contains the *Monumentum (Marmor)
Ancyranum*, inscribed with a record of the reign of
Augustus Caesar
MAJOR CITIES – Adana (1,682,483); Bursa (1,958,529);
Gaziantep (1,127,686); ΨIstanbul (9,198,809);
ΨIzmir (3,114,859); Konya (1,931,773), 2000
estimates. Istanbul, in Europe, is the former capital.
The Roman city of Byzantium, it was selected by
Constantine the Great as the capital of the Roman
Empire about AD 328 and renamed Constantinople.
Istanbul contains the celebrated church of St Sophia,
which, after becoming a mosque, was made a

museum in 1934. It also contains Topkapi, former palace of the Ottoman Sultans, which is also a museum
CURRENCY – Turkish lira (TL) of 100 kurus
NATIONAL ANTHEM – Istiklal Marsi (The Independence March)
NATIONAL DAY – 29 October (Republic Day)
NATIONAL FLAG – Red, with white crescent and star
LIFE EXPECTANCY (years) – male 68.0; female 73.2
POPULATION GROWTH RATE – 1.5 per cent (1999)
POPULATION DENSITY – 83 per sq. km (1999)
URBAN POPULATION – 73.1 per cent (2001)

Turkey in Europe consists of Eastern Thrace, including the cities of Istanbul and Edirne, and is separated from Asia by the Bosporus at Istanbul and by the Dardanelles (about 40 miles in length with a width varying from one to four miles). Turkey in Asia comprises the whole of Asia Minor or Anatolia.

HISTORY AND POLITICS

On 29 October 1923 the National Assembly declared Turkey a republic and elected Gazi Mustafa Kemal (later known as Kemal Atatürk) president. In 1945 a multiparty system was introduced but in 1960 the government was overthrown by the armed forces. A new constitution was adopted in 1961 and a civilian government took office. Civilian governments remained in power until September 1980 when mounting problems with the economy and terrorism led to a military takeover. Following the general election in November 1983 the military leadership handed over power to a civilian government. Following elections on 18 April 1999, the Democratic Left Party (DSP) won the most seats and formed a coalition with the Nationalist Action Party (MHP) and the Motherland Party (ANAP). Hadep, the pro-Kurdish People's Democracy Party, won control of several towns in south-eastern Turkey in simultaneous local elections.

INSURGENCIES

Since 1984 Turkey has been fighting armed guerrillas of the Marxist–Leninist Kurdistan Workers' Party (PKK) in the south-east of the country where Kurds are the majority population. The leader of the PKK, Abdullah Öcalan was captured by Turkish authorities in February 1999 in Kenya and returned to Turkey to stand trial, where he was found guilty of treason on 31 May and sentenced to death on 29 June 1999. The Turkish government announced on 12 January 2000 that it would suspend the execution, pending an appeal. The PKK announced on 8 February 2000 that it had renounced violence and removed the word 'Kurdistan', which is illegal in Turkey, from its title.

POLITICAL SYSTEM

A new constitution, extending the powers of the president, was approved in 1982. It provided for the separation of powers between the legislature, executive and judiciary, and the holding of free elections to the unicameral Grand National Assembly, which now has 550 members elected every five years.

HEAD OF STATE

President, Ahmet Necdet Sezer, elected by parliament for a seven-year term 5 May 2000, took office 16 May 2000

CABINET as at September 2002

Prime Minister, Bülent Ecevit (DSP)

Deputy Prime Minister, EU Relations, Mesut Yilmaz
Deputy Prime Minister, Foreign Affairs, Sükrü Sina Gürel
Deputy Prime Minister, Minister of State, Devlet Bahçeli
Agriculture and Rural Affairs, Hüsnü Yusuf Gökalp
Culture, Burhan Suat Çaglayan
Education, Necdet Tekin
Energy and Natural Resources, Zeki Çakan
Environment, Fevzi Aytekin
Finance, Sümer Oral
Forestry, Nami Çağan
Health, Osman Durmuş
Interior, Muzaffer Ecemiş
Justice, Aysel Çelikel
Labour and Social Security, Nejat Arseven
National Defence, Sabahattin Çakmakoğlu
Public Works and Housing, Abdülkadir Akcan
Tourism, Mustafa Taşar
Trade and Industry, Ahmet Kenan Tanrikulu
Transport, Naci Kinacioglu

TURKISH EMBASSY
43 Belgrave Square, London SW1X 8PA
Tel: 020-7393 0202
Ambassador Extraordinary and Plenipotentiary, HE Korkmaz Haktanir, apptd 2000

BRITISH EMBASSY
Şehit Ersan Caddesi 46/A, Çankaya, Ankara
Tel: (00 90) (312) 455 3344
Email: britembank@fco.gov.uk
Ambassador Extraordinary and Plenipotentiary, HE Peter Westmacott, CMQ, LVO apptd 2002

BRITISH COUNCIL DIRECTOR, Ray Thomas, Esat Caddesi No: 41, Kucukesat, TR-06660 Ankara
Email: bc.ankara@britishcouncil.org.tr.

DEFENCE

The Army has 4,205 main battle tanks, 3,643 armoured personnel carriers, 650 armoured infantry fighting vehicles and 37 attack helicopters. The Navy has 13 submarines, 23 frigates, 49 patrol and coastal vessels and 16 armed helicopters at eight bases. The Air Force has 505 combat aircraft. Between 150,000 and 200,000 troops are stationed in the south-east of the country to prevent Kurdish insurgency. Since its invasion of Cyprus in 1974, Turkey has maintained forces in the north of the island and at present has about 36,000 men stationed there.

As a member of NATO, Turkey is host to the Headquarters Allied Land Forces South-Eastern Europe and the Sixth Allied Tactical Air Force Headquarters. US (2,040 personnel) and UK (160 personnel) air force detachments are based at Incirlik air base in southern Turkey to patrol the air exclusion zone over northern Iraq.
MILITARY EXPENDITURE – 5.2 per cent of GDP (2000)
MILITARY PERSONNEL – 515,100: Army 402,000, Navy 53,000, Air Force 60,100; Paramilitaries 152,200
CONSCRIPTION DURATION – 18 months

ECONOMY

Agricultural production accounted for 14.4 per cent of GDP in 2000. About 40 per cent of the working population is employed in agriculture. The principal crops are wheat, barley, rice, tobacco, sugar beet, tea, olives, grapes, figs and hazelnuts. Tobacco, sultana and fig cultivation is centred around Izmir, where substantial quantities of cotton are also grown. The main cotton area is in the Cukurova plain around Adana. The main export minerals are chromite and boron. Tourism is a major industry, with over 7.5 million visitors in 1999.

The bulk of the country's requirements in sugar, cotton, woollen and silk textiles, and cement, is produced locally.

Other industries include vehicle assembly, paper, glass and glassware, iron and steel, leather and leather goods, sulphur refining, canning and rubber goods, soaps and cosmetics, pharmaceutical products, and prepared foodstuffs.

A customs union with the EU came into force on 1 January 1996 which was expected to boost the economy, although Greece has managed to suspend EU aid packages. A gas deal worth £14,800 million was signed with Iran in August 1996 which provided for a 20-year supply of Iranian gas.

Turkey was accepted as a candidate for EU membership in December 1999.

Following a banking crisis in December 2000, the IMF authorised US$7,500 million in new loans to Turkey in 2001, in addition to the US$2,900 million already agreed.

A public row between the president and the prime minister concerning allegations of corruption within the Cabinet led to a financial crisis on 22–23 February 2001, in which interest rates rose and the lira fell by 36 per cent against the US dollar. An economic recovery plan was unveiled in March 2001, which envisaged restructuring the country's banking system and privatising indebted state industries, beginning with Türk Telekom and Turkish Airlines. In May, the IMF authorised US$15,700 million of loans to Turkey.

GNP – US$201,497 million (2000); US$2,900 per capita (1999)

GDP – US$183,314 million (1999); US$2,813 per capita (1999)

ANNUAL AVERAGE GROWTH OF GDP – 7.5 per cent (2000)

INFLATION RATE – 54.9 per cent (2000)

UNEMPLOYMENT – 7.3 per cent (1999)

TOTAL EXTERNAL DEBT – US$101,796 million (1999)

TRADE

The main imports are machinery, crude oil and petroleum products, iron and steel, vehicles, medicines, chemicals and electrical appliances. Agricultural commodities represented 13.9 per cent of total exports in 2000. Other exports are minerals, textiles, glass and cement. In 2000 Turkey had a trade deficit of US$22,341 million and a current account deficit of US$9,765 million. Imports totalled US$53,499 million and exports US$26,572 million.

Trade with UK	2000	2001
Imports from UK	£1,858,018,000	£1,202,014,000
Exports to UK	1,519,103,000	1,775,821,000

EDUCATION

Education is free and secular, and since August 1997, compulsory from the ages of six to 14. There are elementary, secondary and vocational schools. There are 73 universities in Turkey.

ILLITERACY RATE – 13.9 per cent (2002)

ENROLMENT (percentage of age group) – primary 107 per cent (1997); secondary 58 per cent (1997); tertiary 21 per cent (1997)

CULTURE

Turkish is a Ural-Altaic language. Turkish was written in Arabic script until 1928 when a version of the Roman alphabet reflecting Turkish phonetics was adopted.

TURKMENISTAN
Turkmenostan Respublikasy – Republic of Turkmenistan

AREA – 188,456 sq. miles (488,100 sq. km). Neighbours: Iran and Afghanistan (south), Uzbekistan (east and north), Kazakhstan (north-west)

POPULATION – 4,500,000 (2002 estimate); 4,483,000 (1996 census): 77 per cent Turkmen, 9.2 per cent Uzbek, 6.7 per cent Russian, together with smaller numbers of Kazakhs, Tatars, Ukrainians and Armenians. Most of the population are Sunni Muslims. The main languages are Turkmen (72 per cent), Russian (9 per cent), Uzbek (9 per cent). Turkmen is one of the Turkic languages

CAPITAL – Ashgabat (population, 407,000, 1990)

MAJOR CITIES – Charjou (164,000); Tashauz (114,000), 1990

CURRENCY – Manat of 100 tenge

NATIONAL ANTHEM – Garashciiz Bitarap Turkmenistaniin Devlet Gimni (Independent, Neutral Turkmenistan State Anthem)

NATIONAL DAY – 27–28 October (Independence Day)

NATIONAL FLAG – Green with a vertical carpet pattern near the hoist in black, white, green and wine-red; and in the lower part of the carpet design two laurel branches; in the upper hoist a crescent and five stars, all in white

LIFE EXPECTANCY (years) – male 63.9; female 70.4

POPULATION GROWTH RATE – 0.7 per cent (1999)

POPULATION DENSITY – 9 per sq. km (1999)

MILITARY EXPENDITURE – 4.0 per cent of GDP (2000)

MILITARY PERSONNEL – 17,500: Army 14,500, Air Force 3,000

CONSCRIPTION DURATION – 24 months

The republic comprises five regions: Ashgabat; Charjou; Krasnovodsk; Mary; and Tashauz. Ninety per cent of the country is taken up by the Obe Kara-Kum (Black Sands) desert.

HISTORY AND POLITICS

Turkmenistan has been invaded and occupied by many empires: Persian; Greek under Alexander the Great; Parthian; Mongol. From the early 19th century until 1886 Turkmenistan was gradually incorporated into the Russian Empire. Soviet control over Turkmenistan was established on 30 April 1918 when it became an Autonomous Soviet Socialist Republic. Turkmenistan became a full republic of the Soviet Union in February 1925. Turkmenistan declared its independence from the Soviet Union on 27 October 1991 and gained UN membership on 2 March 1992.

The autocratic government of President Niyazov has prevented any effective political opposition or free press through harassment and authoritarianism. The political leadership has rejected political pluralism and instead a cult of personality has developed around President Niyazov. The Supreme Soviet voted on 30 December 1993 to extend the term of President Niyazov to 2002 and this was confirmed by a 99.99 per cent vote in a referendum on 15 January 1994. On 28 December 1999, the legislature removed the limit on his term of office, effectively making him life president. The Communist Party, renamed the Democratic Party (DP), remains in power. Legislative elections to the Khalk Maslakhaty held on 5 April 1998 were won by the Democratic Party. General elections were held on 12 December 1999, in

which all 50 seats in the Majlis were won by candidates of the DP, the sole legal party.

FOREIGN RELATIONS

In late 1993 Turkmen–Russian agreements were signed allowing Russian troops to protect the borders with Iran and Afghanistan, Russian citizens to undergo military training in Turkmenistan, Turkmen officers to train in Russia, and Turkmenistan to bear the cost of Russian forces in the country. Agreement on dual citizenship for ethnic Russians in Turkmenistan was also reached. In December 1993 Turkmenistan signed the CIS charter to become a full CIS member and in January 1994 became a member of the CIS economic union.

POLITICAL SYSTEM

The 1992 constitution declares the president head of state and government. The legislature is the 50-member Majlis (formerly the Supreme Soviet). The Khalk Maslakhaty (People's Council) is a supervisory body with no legislative powers. The Majlis approved an amendment to the constitution on 28 December 1999, allowing President Niyazov to remain in power indefinitely.

HEAD OF STATE

President, Saparmurad Niyazov, *elected* 27 October 1990, *re-elected* 21 June 1992, *appointed head of government* 18 May 1992, *elected by referendum for an eight-year term* 15 January 1994, *term extended indefinitely* 28 December 1999

COUNCIL OF MINISTERS *as at August 2002*

Prime Minister, The President
Deputy Prime Ministers, Rejep Saparov (*Agriculture*); Muhammetnazar Hudaygulyyev (*Construction and Construction Materials Industry*); Rejepbay Arazow (*Defence*); Gurbanguli Berdyhamedov (*Health and the Pharmaceutical Industry*); Yolly Gurbanmuradov; Seitbay Gandimov (*Interbank Council*); Djamal Geklenova (*Textile Industry*)
Chairmen, Maj.-Gen. Poran Berdiev (*Committee for National Security*); Arslan Sakoyevich Nepesov (*Committee for Tourism and Sports*); Tirkish Tyrmyev (*State Border Service*); Seyitguly Chareyev (*State Committee for Land Use and Land Reform*); Ilyas Mahtumovich Chariyev (*State Commodity and Raw Materials Exchange*); Ovezgeldy Atayev (*Supreme Court*)
Communications and Transport, Resulberdi Khodzhagurbanov
Culture, Orazgeldi Aydogdiyev
Economy and Finance, Geldyyevna Atayeva
Education, Annagurban Ashirov
Energy and Industry, Annaguly Jumagylyjow
Foreign Affairs, Rashid Meredov
General Public Prosecutor, Kurbanbibi Atadjanova
Interior, Col. Annaberdy Kakabaev
Justice, Gen. Gurbanmuhamed Kasimov
Natural Resources and Environmental Protection, Matkarim Rajapov
Oil and Gas Industry and Mineral Resources, Gurban Nazarov
Social Security, Enebay Ataeva
Trade and Foreign Economic Relations, Dortguly Aidogdyev
Water Resources, Gurbangeldi Velmyradov

EMBASSY OF TURKMENISTAN

2nd Floor South, St George's House, 14/17 Wells Street, London W1P 3FP. Tel: 020-7255 1071
Ambassador Extraordinary and Plenipotentiary, HE Chary Babaev, apptd 1999

BRITISH EMBASSY

301–308, Office Building, Four Points Ak Altin Hotel, Ashgabat. Tel: (00 993) (12) 363462
Ambassador Extraordinary and Plenipotentiary, HE Paul Brummell, apptd 2001

ECONOMY

Revenue from natural gas reserves make the country economically viable and have enabled the government to maintain low stable prices for basic commodities and utilities. The principal industries are cotton cultivation, stock-raising and mineral extraction, together with natural gas production and the silk industry. Arable land is irrigated by the Niyazov canal, which cuts through the Kara Kum desert. There are estimated reserves of some 700 million tonnes of oil and 8,000,000 million cubic metres of natural gas. Natural gas is exported by pipeline to Ukraine and western Europe. An agreement to build further pipelines under the Caspian Sea, through Azerbaijan and Georgia, to supply gas to Turkey was reached in November 1999. In 1997 there was a trade deficit of US$231 million and a current account deficit of US$580 million.

GNP – US$4,049 million (2000); US$670 per capita (1999)
GDP – US$2,509 million (1998); US$705 per capita (1999)
ANNUAL AVERAGE GROWTH OF GDP – 5.0 per cent (1998)
TOTAL EXTERNAL DEBT – US$2,015 million (1999)

Trade with UK	2000	2001
Imports from UK	£9,335,000	£6,679,000
Exports to UK	2,807,000	2,035,000

TUVALU – *Fakavae Aliki-Moloi Tuvalu/Constitutional Monarchy of Tuvalu*

AREA – 10 sq. miles (26 sq. km)
POPULATION – 10,991 (2001 estimate). About 1,500 Tuvaluans work overseas, mostly in Nauru, or as seamen. The people are almost entirely Polynesian. The principal languages are Tuvaluan and English. A large majority of the population is Christian, predominantly Protestant
CAPITAL – Ψ Fongafale (population, 2,856)
CURRENCY – The Australian dollar ($A) of 100 cents is legal tender. In addition there are Tuvalu dollar and cent coins in circulation
NATIONAL ANTHEM – Tuvalu Mo Te Atua (Tuvalu For The Almighty)
NATIONAL DAY – 1 October (Independence Day)
NATIONAL FLAG – Light blue ground with Union flag in top left quarter and nine five-pointed gold stars in the fly
POPULATION GROWTH RATE – 1.8 per cent (1999)
POPULATION DENSITY – 423 per sq. km (1999)

Tuvalu comprises nine coral atolls situated in the south-west Pacific around the point at which the International Date Line cuts the Equator. Few of the atolls are more than 12 ft above sea level.

HISTORY AND POLITICS

Tuvalu, formerly the Ellice Islands, formed part of the Gilbert and Ellice Islands Colony until 1 October 1975, when separate constitutions came into force. Separation from the Gilbert Islands was implemented on 1 January 1976. On 1 October 1978 Tuvalu became a fully independent state within the Commonwealth.

1090   Countries of the World

Following the death of Prime Minister Ionatana Ionatana on 8 December 2000, Faimalaga Luka was chosen to replace him on 23 February 2001. Luka's government lost a vote of no confidence on 7 December 2001 and Koloa Talake was elected prime minister on 13 December. In parliamentary elections held on 25 July 2002 Prime Minister Talake lost his seat. Saufatu Sopanga was elected prime minister by parliament on 2 August.

Tuvalu became a full member of the UN on 17 February 2000.

POLITICAL SYSTEM

The constitution provides for a prime minister and four other ministers, who must be members of the 13-member parliament, 12 of whom are directly elected. The prime minister presides at meetings of the Cabinet, which consists of the five Ministers and is attended by the Attorney-General.

Governor-General, Sir Tomasi Puapua

CABINET *as at August 2002*

Prime Minister, Home Affairs and Rural Development, Natural Resources and Environment, Saufatu Sopoanga
Deputy Prime Minister, Communications and Transport, Maatia Toafa
Finance and Economic Planning, Bikenibeu Paeniu
Health, Education and Sports, Alesana K. Seluka
Natural Resources, Sam P. Teo

HONORARY CONSULATE OF TUVALU
Tuvalu House, 230 Worple Road, London SW20 8RH
Tel: 020-8879 0985
Honorary Consul, Iftikhar Ayaz

BRITISH HIGH COMMISSIONER, HE Michael Price, LVO, resident at Suva, Fiji

ECONOMY

The main imports are foodstuffs, semi-manufactures, machinery and transport fuels. The main exports are copra and fish, though philatelic sales provide a major source of revenue and handicraft sales are increasing. However, Tuvalu is almost entirely dependent on foreign aid. Funafuti has an airfield from which a service operates regularly to Fiji and Kiribati, and is also the only port.

GDP – US$14 million (1998); US$1,556 per capita (1999)
ANNUAL AVERAGE GROWTH OF GDP – 2.0 per cent (1998)

Trade with UK	2000	2001
Imports from UK	£328,000	£147,000
Exports to UK	4,000	167,000

UGANDA
Republic of Uganda

AREA – 93,065 sq. miles (241,038 sq. km). Neighbours: Democratic Republic of Congo (west), Sudan (north), Kenya (east), Tanzania and Rwanda (south)
POPULATION – 23,985,712 (2001 estimate): 17 per cent Baganda, 12 per cent Karamojong; many other ethnic groups including Basoga, Iteso, Langi, Banyarwanda, Bagisu, Acholi, Lugbara, Banyoro and Batoro. The official language is English. The main local vernaculars are of Bantu, Nilotic and Hamitic origins. Ki-Swahili is generally understood
CAPITAL – Kampala (population, 750,000, 1990)

MAJOR CITIES – Jinja (45,000); Masaka (29,000); Mbale (28,000)
CURRENCY – Uganda shilling of 100 cents
NATIONAL ANTHEM – Oh Uganda
NATIONAL DAY – 9 October (Independence Day)
NATIONAL FLAG – Six horizontal stripes of black, yellow, red, with a white disc in the centre containing the badge of a crested crane
LIFE EXPECTANCY (years) – male 45.3; female 46.8
POPULATION GROWTH RATE – 2.9 per cent (1999)
POPULATION DENSITY – 90 per sq. km (1999)
URBAN POPULATION – 14.5 per cent (1997)
MILITARY EXPENDITURE – 3.0 per cent of GDP (2000)
MILITARY PERSONNEL – 60,000: Ugandan People's Defence Force; Paramilitaries 1,800

Large parts of Lakes Victoria, Edward and Albert (Mobuto) are within Uganda's boundaries, as are Lakes Kyoga, Kwania, George and Bisina (formerly Salisbury) and the course of the River Nile from its outlet from Lake Victoria to the Sudan border at Nimule. Uganda has three National Parks and a fourth (Lake Mburo) has been designated.

HISTORY AND POLITICS

Uganda became an independent state within the Commonwealth on 9 October 1962, after some 70 years of British rule. A republic was instituted in 1967. In 1971 an army coup took place and Maj.-Gen. Idi Amin, the army commander, proclaimed himself head of state. In 1979 President Amin was overthrown. Dr Milton Obote became president in 1980 but was ousted by a military coup in 1985. A military council was installed but the National Resistance Movement led by Yoweri Museveni captured Kampala in January 1986, securing control of the rest of the country in the following few months. Yoweri Museveni was sworn in as president in January 1986. President Museveni won the first direct presidential election on 9 May 1996. Supporters of the president won a majority of seats in legislative elections on 27 June. The suspension of political party activity introduced by President Museveni in 1986, was endorsed in a referendum held on 29 June 2000, in which 90.7 per cent of those voting backed the continuation of the no party 'Movement' system, in which political parties were allowed to exist, but not to contest elections. President Museveni was re-elected on 12 March 2001, winning 69.3 per cent of the vote. A general election was held on 26 June in which most seats were won by supporters of the no party 'Movement' system.

POLITICAL SYSTEM

A new constitution, promulgated on 8 October 1995, endorsed the existing non-party political system. The president, who is head of government, is directly elected for a five-year term. The legislature, the 276-seat National Assembly, is also directly elected for a five-year term; 214 members are elected by constituencies and 62 are elected indirectly to represent particular groups.

HEAD OF STATE

President, Commander-in-Chief, Yoweri Museveni, *sworn in* 29 January 1986, *elected* 9 May 1996, *re-elected* 12 March 2001
Vice-President, Specioza Wandira Kazibwe

CABINET *as at August 2002*

The President
The Vice-President
Prime Minister, Apolo Nsibambi

First Deputy Prime Minister, Internal Affairs, Eriya
Kategaya
Second Deputy Prime Minister, Disaster Preparedness,
Brig. Moses Ali
Third Deputy Prime Minister, Foreign Affairs, James
Wambogo Wapakhabulo
Minister in the Office of the Prime Minister, George
Mondo Kagonyera
Agriculture, Animal Industry and Fisheries, Kisamba
Mugwera
Attorney-General, Francis Ayume
Defence, Amama Mbabazi
Education and Sports, Kiddu Makubuya
Energy and Minerals, Syda Bbumba
Finance, Planning and Economic Development, Gerald
Sendawula
Gender, Zoe Bakoko-Bakoru
Health, Jim Katugugu Muhwezi
Justice and Constitutional Affairs, Janet Mukwaya
Local Government, Jaberi Bidandi-Ssalli
Presidency, Gilbert Balibaseka Bukenya
Public Service, Henry Muganwa Kajura
Tourism, Trade and Industry, Edward Rugumayo
Water, Lands and Environment, Ruhakana Rugunda
Without Portfolio, National Political Commissar, Crispus
Kiyonga
Works, John Nassasira

UGANDA HIGH COMMISSION
Uganda House, 58–59 Trafalgar Square, London WC2N
5DX. Tel: 020-7839 5783
High Commissioner, HE Prof. George Kirya, apptd 1990

BRITISH HIGH COMMISSION
10–12 Parliament Avenue, PO Box 7070, Kampala
Tel: (00 256) (78) 312000
High Commissioner, HE Tom Phillips, CMG, apptd 2000

BRITISH COUNCIL DIRECTOR, Sue Beaumont,
Rwenzori Courts, Plot 2 and 4A, Nakasero Road, PO
Box 7070, Kampala; Email: info@britishcouncil.or.ug

ECONOMY

In December 1998, the IMF pledged US$2.2 billion in
economic assistance over a three-year period. On 8
February 2000, the IMF pledged a further US$139 million
in debt relief, and the International Development
Association (IDA) announced that it would give
assistance of US$629 million over 20 years. In March,
donor countries pledged at least US$2,000 million over
three years to support economic development. The
principal export earners are coffee, tobacco, cotton and
tea. Hydroelectricity is produced from the Owen Falls
power station, some of which is exported to Kenya,
Tanzania and Rwanda. The principal food crops are
plantains, sugar cane, cassava, maize and sorghum.
   In 1997 Uganda had a trade deficit of US$467 million
and a current account deficit of US$388 million. In 1999
imports totalled US$1,342 million and exports US$519
million.
GNP – US$6,797 million (2000); US$320 per capita
(1999)
GDP – US$7,127 million (1998); US$301 per capita
(1999)
ANNUAL AVERAGE GROWTH OF GDP – 1.4 per cent
(1998)
INFLATION RATE – 2.8 per cent (2000)
TOTAL EXTERNAL DEBT – US$4,077 million (1999)

Trade with UK	2000	2001
Imports from UK	£37,761,000	£34,814,000
Exports to UK	9,190,000	8,542,000

COMMUNICATIONS

There is an international airport at Entebbe, and eight
other airfields around the country. Having no sea coast,
Uganda is dependent upon rail and road links to
Mombasa and Dar es Salaam for its trade.

EDUCATION

Education is a joint undertaking by the government, local
authorities and voluntary agencies. In 1996, the Universal
Primary Programme was launched, under which four
children per family are entitled to receive free primary
education.
ILLITERACY RATE – 31.1 per cent (2002)
ENROLMENT (percentage of age group) – tertiary 2 per
cent (1997)

UKRAINE
Ukraïna – Ukraine

AREA – 233,090 sq. miles (603,700 sq. km). Neighbours:
Belarus (north), Russia (north and east), Romania
and Moldova (south-west), Hungary, Slovakia and
Poland (west)
POPULATION – 48,900,000 (2002 estimate); 51,471,000
(1989 census): 73 per cent Ukrainian, 22 per cent
Russian, with smaller numbers of Jews, Belarusians,
Moldovans, Tatars, Poles, Hungarians and Greeks.
The majority religion is Orthodox Christianity. There
are also large numbers of Uniates and Reformed
Protestants in the Transcarpathian region and a
sizeable Jewish community in Kiev. The official
language is Ukrainian. Russian, Romanian,
Hungarian and Polish are also used
CAPITAL – Kiev (Kyiv) (population, 2,630,000, 1998
estimate)
MAJOR CITIES – Dnipropetrovsk (1,122,400); Donetsk
(1,065,400); Kharkiv (1,521,400); Lviv (793,700),
ΨOdesa (1,027,400), Zaporizhzhya (863,100), 1998
estimates
CURRENCY – Hryvna of 100 kopiykas
NATIONAL ANTHEM – Shche Ne Vmerla, Ukraïna
(Thou Hast Not Perished, Ukraine)
NATIONAL DAY – 24 August (Independence Day)
NATIONAL FLAG – Two horizontal stripes of blue over
yellow
LIFE EXPECTANCY (years) – male 62.7; female 73.5
POPULATION GROWTH RATE – 0.8 per cent (1999)
POPULATION DENSITY – 83 per sq. km (1999)
URBAN POPULATION – 67.6 per cent (1995)
ILLITERACY RATE – 0.4 per cent (2002)
ENROLMENT (percentage of age group) – tertiary 42 per
cent (1997)
Ukraine consists of 24 regions (Cherkasy, Chernihiv,
Chernivtsi, Dnipropetrovsk, Donetsk, Ivano-Frankivsk,
Kharkiv, Kherson, Khmelnytsky, Kyiv, Kirovohrad,
Luhansk, Lviv, Mykolayiv, Odesa, Poltava, Rivne, Sumy,
Ternopil, Transcarpathia, Vinnitsa, Volyn, Zaporizhya and
Zhytomyr) and the Autonomous Republic of Crimea.
   The Carpathian mountains lie in the south-western
part of the republic. The main rivers are the Dnieper with
its tributaries, the Southern Bug and the Northern
Donets (a tributary of the Don).

HISTORY AND POLITICS

The earliest Slavic state was formed in the middle reaches of the Dnieper River with its capital at Kyiv in the ninth century AD. The state lasted until Kyiv fell to the Tatar-Mongols in 1240. For the next four centuries Ukraine was invaded and ruled by Poles and Lithuanians. Kyiv was liberated from the Poles in 1648 and in 1654 Ukraine became a protectorate of Russia.

Ukraine declared its independence in 1918, but was invaded by Poland in 1919 before becoming a constituent republic of the USSR on 30 December 1922.

Ukraine declared itself independent of the Soviet Union on 24 August 1991. Independence was confirmed by a referendum held on 1 December 1991 and Leonid Kravchuk was elected to the presidency. In the June 1994 presidential election Leonid Kuchma defeated President Kravchuk. President Kuchma won a second term of office in a presidential election on 14 November 1999, receiving 56.25 per cent of the vote.

In January 2000, the Supreme Council split into two factions following a failed attempt by the pro-government faction to remove the Speaker, Oleksandr Tkachenko, from office. The minority left-wing faction remained in control of the Supreme Council building until the pro-government majority faction forcibly took control of the Supreme Council building on 8 February 2000.

In legislative elections held on 31 March 2002, the Our Ukraine bloc became the largest party in the parliament winning 112 seats. The For United Ukraine bloc won 102 seats and the Communist Party of Ukraine 66 seats.

INSURGENCIES

A pro-Russian majority in the Crimean parliament voted to make Crimea an autonomous republic in September 1991, which was accepted by Ukraine, but then voted for independence, which was not accepted, and the declaration of independence was rescinded in May 1992. Elections to the Crimean parliament in August 1995 saw a dramatic drop in support for pro-Russian parties. Arkady Demydenko was appointed Prime Minister of Crimea on 26 February 1996. A new constitution, which gave Crimea property and budget rights, came into effect in January 1999.

A referendum in June 1994 in the Donbass region of eastern Ukraine in favour of closer economic ties with Russia and making Russian an official language was overwhelmingly passed, as was one in the Crimea in favour of dual Russian–Ukrainian citizenship.

FOREIGN RELATIONS

Under a January 1994 USA–Russia–Ukraine Treaty, Ukraine agreed to transfer its nuclear arsenal to Russia for dismantling, which was completed in May 1996. In return Ukraine received a territorial guarantee from Russia, a cancellation of a large part of its debt to Russia, and nuclear security guarantees from Russia and the USA. In May 1997, a treaty of friendship and co-operation was signed with Russia. Agreement was also reached over the division of the former Soviet Black Sea fleet. In February 1998, a treaty on economic co-operation was signed between Ukraine and Russia which aimed to strengthen industrial and commercial links and move towards the introduction of the free movement of goods, services, capital and labour. Ukraine signed a partnership and co-operation agreement with the EU in June 1994 and in July 1997 signed the NATO-Ukraine Charter to enhance co-operation on peacekeeping.

POLITICAL SYSTEM

The unicameral Supreme Council has 450 members, who serve a four-year term. Half of the seats in the Supreme Council are elected from single-seat constituencies by a simple majority, and the other 225 are to be filled by proportional representation from party lists, with a 4 per cent threshold for representation. A member may only be elected if the turnout in the electoral district is above 50 per cent.

HEAD OF STATE

President, Leonid Kuchma, *elected* 10 July 1994, *sworn in* 19 July 1994, *re-elected* 14 November 1999

CABINET *as at August 2002*

Prime Minister, Anatoliy Kinakh
First Deputy Prime Minister, Oleh Dubyna
First Deputy Prime Minister for Economic Issues, Vasyl Rohovyy
Deputy Prime Ministers, Leonid Kozachenko; Volodymyr Semynozhenko (*Humanitarian Policy*)
Agricultural Policy, Serhiy Ryzhuk
Culture and Art, Yuriy Bohutskiy
Defence, Volodymyr Shkidchenko
Economics and Issues of European Integration, Oleksandr Shlapak
Education and Science, Vasyl Kremen
Emergency Situations and Protection of the Population from the aftermath of Chernobyl, Vasyl Durdanynets
Energy and Fuel, Vitaliy Gaiduk
Environment and Natural Resources, Serhiy Kurykin
Finance, Igor Yushko
Foreign Affairs, Anatoliy Zlenko
Government Secretary, Volodymyr Yatsuba
Health Protection, Vitaliy Moskalenko
Industrial Policy, Anatoliy Myalytsa
Interior, Yuriy Smirnov
Justice, Oleksandr Lavrynovych
Labour and Social Policy, Ivan Sakhan
Transport, Georgiy Kirpa

UKRAINIAN EMBASSY

60 Holland Park, London W11 3SJ
Tel: 020-7727 6312
Ambassador Extraordinary and Plenipotentiary, vacant

BRITISH EMBASSY

UA-01025 Kyiv, Desyatinna 9
Tel: (00 380) (44) 462 0011/2/4
Ambassador Extraordinary and Plenipotentiary, HE Robert Brinkley, apptd 2002

BRITISH COUNCIL DIRECTOR – Liliana Biglou, 4/12

Vul. Hryhoriya Skovorody, UA-04070 Kyiv;
Email: enquiry@britishcouncil.org.ua.

DEFENCE

The Constitution bans the stationing of foreign troops on Ukrainian soil, but permits Russia to retain naval bases. The Army has 3,937 main battle tanks, 1,782 armoured personnel carriers, 3,078 armoured infantry fighting vehicles and 247 attack helicopters. The Navy has one submarine, three principal surface combat vessels and eight patrol and coastal vessels at six bases. The Air Force has 543 combat aircraft.

MILITARY EXPENDITURE – 3.4 per cent of GDP (2000)
MILITARY PERSONNEL – 303,800: Army 151,200, Navy 13,000, Air Force 96,000; Paramilitaries 126,100
CONSCRIPTION DURATION – 18 months to two years

ECONOMY

The Communist-led government of 1991–4 was characterised by economic mismanagement and opposition to economic reforms. Successive governments were unable to gain consensus for a reform programme, which delayed economic restructuring. Ukraine joined the CIS economic union as an associate member in 1993. Since his election in 1999, President Kuchma has introduced a wide-ranging economic reform programme. Continuing economic difficulties led to the devaluation of the hryvna in February 1999. In March 2000, the IMF issued an interim statement about the alleged misuse of foreign currency reserves, saying that Ukraine had received IMF funds in 1997–8 that it would not have received had the true state of the country's reserves been known. The IMF has suspended its loan programme to Ukraine until investigations are completed.

Metal processing, the manufacture of machinery, and the chemical and petrochemical industries are major contributors to Ukraine's GDP; mining and metallurgy account for more than 40 per cent of exports. The southern part of the country contains a coal-mining and iron and steel industrial area. Ukraine also contains engineering and chemical industries and ship building yards on the Black Sea coast. Ukrainian agricultural production is good with large areas under cultivation with wheat, cotton, flax and sugar beet; stock-raising is very important. There are large deposits of coal and salt, iron ore, manganese and quicksilver.

Russia is the main trading partner, accounting for 24 per cent of exports and 41.7 per cent of imports in 2000. Trade negotiations between Ukraine and Russia in April 2002 included agreements on gas transits and oil pipelines. Turkey, Germany, the USA and Turkmenistan are also major trading partners.

In 2000 there was a trade surplus of US$779 million and a current account surplus of US$1,481 million. In 1999 imports totalled US$11,846 million and exports US$11,582 million.
GNP – US$34,693 million (2000); US$840 per capita (1999)
GDP – US$41,883 million (1998); US$606 per capita (1999)
ANNUAL AVERAGE GROWTH OF GDP – 6 per cent (2000 estimate)
INFLATION RATE – 22.7 per cent (1999)
UNEMPLOYMENT – 11.9 per cent (1999)
TOTAL EXTERNAL DEBT – US$14,136 million (1999)

Trade with UK	2000	2001
Imports from UK	£154,670,000	£204,461,000
Exports to UK	65,465,000	72,028,000

UNITED ARAB EMIRATES
Dawlat Al-Amārat Al-'Arabiyya Al-Muttahida - United Arab Emirates

AREA – 32,278 sq. miles (83,600 sq. km) approximately.
  Neighbours: Oman (north-east and east), Saudi
  Arabia (south and west), Qatar (north-west)
POPULATION – 2,407,460 (2001 estimate), of which 75
  per cent are expatriates. The official language is
  Arabic, and English is widely spoken. The established
  religion is Islam
CAPITAL – Abu Dhabi (Abū Żaby) (population,
  450,000)
CURRENCY – UAE dirham (Dh) of 100 fils
NATIONAL DAY – 2 December
NATIONAL FLAG – Horizontal stripes of green over
  white over black with vertical red stripe in the hoist
LIFE EXPECTANCY (years) – male 74.1; female 78.4
POPULATION GROWTH RATE – 6.5 per cent (1999)
POPULATION DENSITY – 29 per sq. km (1999)

The United Arab Emirates is situated in the south-east of the Arabian peninsula. Six of the emirates lie on the shore of the Gulf between the Musandam peninsula in the east and the Qatar peninsula in the west while the seventh, Fujairah, lies on the Gulf of Oman.

HISTORY AND POLITICS

The United Arab Emirates (formerly the Trucial States) is composed of seven emirates (Abu Dhabi, Ajman, Dubai, Fujairah, Ras al-Khaimah, Sharjah and Umm al-Qaiwain) which came together as an independent state on 2 December 1971 when they ended their individual special treaty relationships with the British government (Ras al-Khaimah joined the other six on 10 February 1972). On independence, the Union Government assumed full responsibility for all internal and external affairs apart from some internal matters that remained the prerogative of the individual emirates.

FOREIGN RELATIONS

Relations with Iran remain strained over Iran's illegal occupation of three UAE islands in the Gulf (Abu Musa and the Two Tunbs).

POLITICAL SYSTEM

Overall authority lies with the Supreme Council of the seven emirate rulers, each of whom also governs in his own territory. The president and vice-president are elected every five years by the Supreme Council from among its members. The Supreme Council appoints the Council of Ministers. A 40-member Federal National Council, comprising eight members each from Abu Dhabi and Dubai, six each from Sharjah and Ras al-Khaimah and four each for Fujairah, Umm al-Qaiwain and Ajman, appointed by the rulers of each emirate, studies draft laws referred to it by the Council of Ministers. The legal system consists of both secular and religious courts.

FEDERAL STRUCTURE

Each emirate has its separate government, with Abu Dhabi having an executive council chaired by the Crown Prince.

Emirate	Area (sq. km)	Population (1997)
Abu Dhabi (Abū Żaby)	67,340	1,017,000
Ajman ('Ujman)	259	137,000
Dubai (Dubayy)	3,885	757,000
Fujairah (Al-Fujayrah)	1,165	83,000
Ras al-Khaimah (Ra's al-Khaymah)	1,680	152,000
Sharjah (Ash-Shariqah)	2,590	439,000
Umm al-Qaiwain (Umm al-Qaywayn)	777	39,000

HEAD OF STATE

President, HH Sheikh Zayed bin Sultan al-Nahyan (Abu Dhabi), *elected* 1971, *re-elected* 1976, 1981, 1986, 1991, 1996, April 2001
Vice-President, Prime Minister, HH Sheikh Maktoum bin Rashid al-Maktoum (Dubai)

SUPREME COUNCIL

The President
The Vice-President
HH Sheikh Sultan bin Mohammed al-Qassimi (*Sharjah*)
HH Sheikh Saqr bin Mohammed al-Qassimi (*Ras Al-Khaimah*)
HH Sheikh Hamad bin Mohammed al-Sharqi (*Fujairah*)
HH Sheikh Humaid bin Rashid al-Nuaimi (*Ajman*)
HH Sheikh Rashid bin Ahmad al-Mualla (*Umm al-Qaiwain*)

COUNCIL OF MINISTERS *as at August 2002*

The Vice-President
Deputy Prime Minister, Sheikh Sultan bin Zayed al-Nahyan
Agriculture and Fisheries, Saeed Mohammed al-Raqabani
Communications, Ahmed Humaid al-Tayir
Defence, HH Gen. Sheikh Mohammed bin Rashid al-Maktoum
Economy and Commerce, HH Sheikh Fahim bin Sultan al-Qassimi
Education and Youth, Ali Abd al-Aziz al-Sharhan
Electricity and Water, Humaid bin Nasir al-Uways
Finance and Industry, HH Sheikh Hamdan bin Rashid al-Maktoum
Foreign Affairs, Rashid Abdullah al-Nuaimi
Health, Hamad Abdul Rahman al-Madfa
Higher Education and Scientific Research, HH Sheikh Nahyan bin Mubarak al-Nahyan
Information and Culture, HH Sheikh Abdullah bin Zayed al-Nahyan
Interior, Lt.-Gen. Mohammed Saeed al-Badi
Justice, Islamic Affairs and Awqaf (*Religious Endowments*), Mohammed Nakhira al-Dhahiri
Labour and Social Affairs, Matar Humaid al-Tayir
Petroleum and Mineral Resources, Ubayd bin Sayf al-Nasiri
Planning, HH Sheikh Humaid bin Ahmed al-Mualla
Public Works and Housing, Rakadh bin Salem al-Rakadh

EMBASSY OF THE UNITED ARAB EMIRATES
30 Princes Gate, London SW7 1PT
Tel 020-7581 1281
Ambassador Extraordinary and Plenipotentiary, HE Easa Saleh al-Gurg, CBE, apptd 1991

BRITISH EMBASSIES
PO Box 248, Abu Dhabi
Tel: (00 971) (2) 632 6600
Ambassador Extraordinary and Plenipotentiary, HE Patrick Nixon, CMG, OBE, apptd 1998
PO Box 65, Dubai
Tel: (00 971) (4) 397 1070

BRITISH COUNCIL DIRECTOR, Tim Gore (acting), Villa no. 7, Al-Nasr Street, Khalidiya, PO Box 46523, Abu Dhabi

DEFENCE

The Army has 411 main battle tanks, 731 armoured personnel carriers and 620 armoured infantry fighting vehicles. The Navy has two frigates and 16 patrol and coastal vessels. The Air Force has 101 combat aircraft and 49 armed helicopters.

MILITARY EXPENDITURE – 5.9 per cent of GDP (2000)
MILITARY PERSONNEL – 65,000: Army 59,000, Navy 2,000, Air Force 4,000

ECONOMY

The UAE is the Gulf's third largest oil producer after Saudi Arabia and Iran, with oil reserves of 98,200 million barrels and gas reserves of 5,800 million cubic metres. Oil production in 2000 accounted for 33.9 per cent of GDP. Other important sectors of the economy are manufacturing (aluminium, cement, chemicals, fertilisers, pharmaceuticals, ship repair), government services, construction, transport, communications, financial services and tourism. Agricultural production has increased due to large-scale water desalination and irrigation projects. There is no personal or corporate taxation apart from on oil companies and foreign banks. There are several free zones, where overseas companies can trade tax-free.

There are 15 major ports, of which nine are modern container terminals. Six international airports (Dubai, Abu Dhabi, Sharjah, Ras al-Khaimah, Fujairah, Al Ain) are in operation.

Oil revenues over the past 30 years have enabled the government to invest heavily in education, health and social services, housing, transport and communications infrastructure, and agriculture, and enabled the UAE's citizens to have one of the highest GDPs per capita in the world.

GNP – US$48,673 million (1998); US$17,870 per capita (1998)
GDP – US$45,899 million (1998); US$19,700 per capita (1999)
ANNUAL AVERAGE GROWTH OF GDP – 7.0 per cent (1998)

Trade with UK	2000	2001
Imports from UK	£1,598,022,000	£1,609,622,000
Exports to UK	648,758,000	688,349,000

EDUCATION

In 2000 there were 747 government schools, where education is free; and 426 private schools. There are five universities.

ILLITERACY RATE – 22.6 per cent (2002)
ENROLMENT (percentage of age group) – primary 89 per cent (1997); secondary 80 per cent (1997); tertiary 12 per cent (1997)

UNITED KINGDOM
United Kingdom of Great Britain and Northern Ireland

AREA – 93,784 sq. miles (242,900 sq. km), of which England 50,351 sq. miles (130,410 sq. km), Wales 8,015 sq. miles (20,758 sq. km), Scotland 30,420 sq. miles (78,789 sq. km), Northern Ireland 5,467 sq. miles (14,160 sq. km). Neighbour: Republic of Ireland (south and west)

POPULATION – 59,647,790 (2001 estimate); England 48,903,000, Wales 2,917,000, Scotland 5,137,000, Northern Ireland 1,649,000 (1996 UN estimates). The language is English, of West Germanic origin, with a vocabulary heavily influenced by French, Latin and Greek. Welsh is spoken by 18.7 per cent of the population of Wales, Scots is spoken by 30 per cent of the population of Scotland; there are also small numbers of Scottish and Irish Gaelic speakers. There are 39.4 million Christians (of which 26.1 million Anglicans, 5.7 million Roman Catholics and 2.6 million Presbyterians), nearly 2 million Muslims, 400,000 Sikhs, 380,000 Hindus, 285,000 Jews, 25,000 Buddhists and 25,000 Jains

CAPITAL – ΨLondon, (population, 7,285,000 1999 estimate) (capital of the UK and England)

MAJOR CITIES – Belfast (297,300) (capital of Northern Ireland); Birmingham, (population 861,041); Bradford (457,344); Bristol (399,600); Cardiff/Caerdydd (315,040) (capital of Wales); Dudley (304,615); Edinburgh (452,806) (capital of Scotland); Glasgow (611,440); Leeds (680,722); Liverpool (452,450); Manchester (404,861); Sheffield (501,202); Wakefield (310,915); Wigan (306,521), 1996 estimates

CURRENCY – Pound sterling (£) of 100 pence

NATIONAL ANTHEM – God Save The Queen

NATIONAL DAY – St David's Day (Wales only) 1 March, St Patrick's Day (N. Ireland only) 17 March, St George's Day (England only) 23 April, St Andrew's Day (Scotland only) 30 November

NATIONAL FLAG – A red cross and a red diagonal cross on a white cross and a white diagonal cross on a blue ground

LIFE EXPECTANCY (years) – male 75.7; female 80.7

POPULATION GROWTH RATE – 0.2 per cent (2001)

POPULATION DENSITY – 242 per sq. km (1999)

URBAN POPULATION – 89.5 per cent (2000) estimate

The United Kingdom consists of Great Britain (formed of Scotland in the north, Wales in the west of the central portion of the island, and England, which occupies the rest of the island), the north-eastern part of the island of Ireland, and the Hebrides, Orkney and Shetland Islands, the Isle of Wight, Anglesey and the Isles of Scilly. The United Kingdom is bounded on the south by the English Channel, on the east by the Straits of Dover and the North Sea, and on the north and west by the Atlantic Ocean. The North Channel and the Irish Sea separate Northern Ireland from Great Britain.

HISTORY AND POLITICS

The United Kingdom is formed of four constituent nations: England, Wales, Scotland and Northern Ireland. The Normans, who had invaded England in 1066, established control over Wales by 1300; Wales was politically assimilated to England under the Act of Union of 1535.

Following the death of Queen Elizabeth I, James VI of Scotland succeeded to the English throne as James I of England in 1603; an Act of Union was proclaimed in 1707, under which the seat of Scottish Government was transferred to London.

The Norman English had established control over most of Ireland in the 12th century, but their influence waned. King Henry VIII re-established English control over Ireland and was declared king of Ireland by a parliament summoned in Dublin in 1541. The United Kingdom of Great Britain and Ireland was established by the Act of Union in 1801.

By the early twentieth century, the United Kingdom had acquired a substantial empire, which included Australia, Canada, the Indian subcontinent, Malaysia, New Zealand, and extensive territories in Africa, the West Indies and the Pacific.

Ireland was partitioned in 1921 and the Irish Free State became a republic in 1949. Northern Ireland remained part of the United Kingdom, governed by a Northern Ireland parliament.

Beginning with the independence of India and Pakistan in 1947, a process of decolonisation began.

The Labour government elected in 1945 nationalised iron and steel, transport and the utilities. Prime Minister Margaret Thatcher, who was in power from 1979 to 1990, broke the post-war consensus. Her Conservative government privatised state-owned industries and reduced the influence of the trade unions. The Labour Party won the general election held on 1 May 1997 and retained power in the general election held on 7 June 2001 winning 413 seats; the Conservative Party won 166 seats, the Liberal Democrats 52 seats, the Ulster Unionist Party six seats, the Scottish Nationalist Party and the Democratic Unionist Party five seats each, Plaid Cymru and Sinn Féin four seats each, the Social and Democratic Labour Party three seats, and the Kidderminster Hospital and Health Concern won one seat and one seat was held by the Speaker.

Referendums held in Scotland and Wales in September 1997 produced majorities in favour of devolution. The first elections to the Scottish Parliament and the Welsh National Assembly took place in May 1999.

NORTHERN IRELAND

Following the partition of Ireland in 1921, the Protestant Unionists held a permanent majority in the government and administration of Northern Ireland. A Roman Catholic civil rights campaign in the late 1960s led to rioting, sectarian violence and terrorist activity conducted by the Irish Republican Army (IRA), an Irish nationalist paramilitary organisation, and several Protestant paramilitary organisations. Following the resignation in 1972 of the Northern Ireland government, the Northern Ireland parliament was abolished and replaced with direct rule from London.

Several attempts were made by successive governments to restore power to a devolved government which was acceptable to both the Catholic and Protestant communities.

In November 1985 the governments of the UK and the Republic of Ireland signed the Anglo-Irish Agreement, under which both parties agreed to improve cross-border co-operation and that Northern Ireland should remain part of the UK for as long as the majority of the population wished it to remain so.

The 'Good Friday Agreement', which proposed the establishment of a Northern Ireland Assembly, along with a cross-border ministerial council and a consultative body of ministers from the UK, the Republic of Ireland and the Northern Irish, Scottish and Welsh assemblies, was put to a referendum in May 1998 and was endorsed by the electorate. At the same time, a referendum was held in the Republic of Ireland to repeal its constitutional

claim to Northern Ireland; this was also endorsed by voters. The first election for the Northern Ireland Assembly was held in June 1998.

Power was devolved to the Northern Ireland Assembly in December 1999. The Assembly was suspended in February 2000 owing to the lack of progress made in talks with the IRA on decommissioning its weaponry, but it was reinstated in May 2000 following further negotiations. On 8 April 2002, the IRA released a statmement on decommissioning in a further initiative to put arms beyond use.

POLITICAL SYSTEM

Parliament consists of the House of Commons and the House of Lords. The House of Commons has 659 directly-elected members, whose term of office is a maximum of five years. The House of Lords is appointed and consists of 92 hereditary peers, over 500 life peers, certain senior judges, and 26 bishops of the Church of England.

HEAD OF STATE

HM by the Grace of God, of the United Kingdom of Great Britain and Northern Ireland and of her other Realms and Territories Queen, Head of the Commonwealth, Defender of the Faith, Queen Elizabeth II, *born* 21 April 1926; *succeeded* 6 February 1952; *crowned* 2 June 1953; *married* 20 November 1947, HRH The Prince Philip, Duke of Edinburgh, KG, KT, OM, GBE, AC, QSO, PC (Prince Philip of Denmark and Greece), and has *issue* HRH The Prince of Wales; HRH The Princess Royal (Princess Anne Elizabeth Alice Louise), KG, GCVO, *b.* 15 August 1950; HRH The Duke of York (Prince Andrew Albert Christian Edward), CVO, ADC(P), B. 19 February 1960; HRH The Earl of Wessex (Prince Edward Antony Richard Louis), CVO, *b.* 10 March 1964

Heir, HRH The Prince of Wales (Prince Charles Philip Arthur George), KG, KT, GCB and Great Master of the Order of the Bath, OM, AK, QSO, PC, ADC(P), *born* 14 November 1948, *married* Lady Diana Frances Spencer (Diana, Princess of Wales); and has *issue* HRH Prince William of Wales (Prince William Arthur Philip Louis), *b.* 21 June 1982; HRH Prince Henry of Wales (Prince Henry Charles Albert David), *b.* 15 September 1984

CABINET *as at August 2002*

Prime Minister, First Lord of the Treasury, Civil Service, Tony Blair
Deputy Prime Minister, First Secretary of State (responsible for the Regions), John Prescott
Chancellor of the Exchequer, Gordon Brown
Chief Secretary to the Treasury, Paul Boateng
Culture, Media and Sport, Tessa Jowell
Defence, Geoff Hoon
Education and Skills, Estelle Morris
Environment, Food and Rural Affairs, Margaret Beckett
Foreign and Commonwealth Affairs, Jack Straw
Health, Alan Milburn
Home Office, David Blunkett
International Development, Clare Short
Lord Chancellor, Lord Irvine of Lairg
Lord Privy Seal, Leader of the House of Lords, Lord Williams of Mostyn
Northern Ireland, John Reid
Parliamentary Secretary, Treasury, Chief Whip, Hilary Armstrong
President of the Council and Leader of the House of Commons, Robin Cook

Scotland, Helen Liddell
Trade and Industry, Patricia Hewitt
Transport, Alistair Darling
Wales, Paul Murphy
Without Portfolio, Labour Party Chair, Charles Clarke
Work and Pensions, Andrew Smith

DEFENCE

The Army has 636 main battle tanks 2,398 armoured personnel carriers and 586 armoured infantry fighting vehicles. The Navy has 16 submarines, 3 aircraft carriers, 11 destroyers, 20 frigates, 23 patrol and coastal combatants, 34 combat aircraft, and 120 armed helicopters at five bases. The Air Force has 427 combat aircraft

MILITARY EXPENDITURE – 2.4 per cent of GDP (2000)
MILITARY PERSONNEL – 213,330: Strategic Forces 1,900, Army 113,950, Navy 43,530, Air Force 53,950

ECONOMY

Service industries accounts for approximately 70 per cent of GDP and 75 per cent of employment. The UK is a major international financial centre, with particular expertise in the fields of banking, currency trading, insurance and shipping. The London Stock Exchange and commodity markets are among the largest in the world. There is a wide range of manufacturing industry, covering areas such as chemicals, textiles and clothing, furniture, engineering, foodstuffs, metals and minerals, printing and publishing. Agriculture employs less than 2 per cent of the workforce. The most important crops grown are barley, forestry products, oats, potatoes, oilseed rape, sugar beet and wheat. There is extensive livestock farming and fishing is an important, though declining, industry.

The UK has extensive reserves of natural gas, oil and coal. In 1998 the UK produced 124,222,000 tonnes of crude oil; proven reserves are estimated at 770 million tonnes. Gas production totalled 95,614 million cubic metres; reserves are estimated at 590,000 million cubic metres. Coal production amounted to 41,428,000 tonnes in 1998. Other minerals mined include limestone, sandstone, clay, chalk and gravel. Metals mined include aluminium, copper, lead and zinc.

The United Kingdom was at the forefront of the Industrial Revolution in the 18th and 19th centuries, but by the 1950s, its manufacturing industry had declined relative to other developed nations.

The economy has revived since 1980 following a period of extensive privatisation and the closure of many unproductive companies.

GNP – US$1,463,474 million (2000) US$23,590 per capita (1999)
GDP – US$1,403,668 million (1998); US$24,323 per capita (1999)
ANNUAL AVERAGE GROWTH OF GDP – 3.1 per cent (2000)
INFLATION RATE – 2.7 per cent (2001)
UNEMPLOYMENT – 5.2 per cent (2000)

TRADE

The principal imports are machinery and transport equipment, manufactured goods, semi-manufactures, chemicals, foodstuffs and livestock, and raw materials. The principal exports are machinery and transport equipment, chemical products, semi-manufactures, manufactured goods, chemical products, mineral fuels, and foodstuffs and livestock. The majority of trade is with other member states of the EU. The USA and Japan are important trading partners and the UK also trades extensively with other Commonwealth nations.

In 2000 there was a trade deficit of US$43,577 million and a current account deficit of US$24,457 million. Imports totalled US$334,341 million and exports US$281,436 million.

COMMUNICATIONS

There were 371,900 km (231,100 miles) of roads in 1999, of which 3,316 km (2,060 miles) were motorways. There are about 32,000 km (20,000 miles) of railway track. The Channel Tunnel links the UK railway system to those of mainland Europe. About 5,200 km (3,200 miles) of waterways are navigable and there are many commercial ports. There are over 150 commercial airports, of which London Heathrow (the world's busiest international airport), London Gatwick, and Manchester are the most important.

EDUCATION

Full-time education is compulsory between the ages of five and 16 in Great Britain and four and 16 in Northern Ireland. Education between the ages of 16 and 18 is voluntary. There are 87 universities and 64 other tertiary level colleges. In addition, the Open University offers distance higher education.

ENROLMENT (percentage of age group) – primary 100 per cent (1997); secondary 100 per cent (1997); tertiary 52 per cent (1997)

CULTURE

Old English was a highly inflected language. Middle English developed following the Norman invasion, when the language became grammatically simpler and acquired a large number of Norman loan words. The dialect of the East Midlands, as spoken in London, became the basis for standard Modern English.

Modern English has spread from the United Kingdom with minor differences in spelling, usage and grammar to North America, Australasia and many other parts of the world.

NB *Statistics used in this entry are obtained from international sources for ease of comparison with other countries, rather than from the UK government sources used elsewhere in Whitaker's Almanack, and may therefore differ.*

UNITED STATES OF AMERICA

AREA – 3,615,275 sq. miles (9,363,520 sq. km).
Neighbours: Canada (north), Mexico (south)
POPULATION – 281,421,906 (2000 census). The language is English. There is a significant Spanish-speaking minority
CAPITAL – Washington DC (population, 4,923,153, 2000 census). The area of the District of Columbia (with which the City of Washington is considered co-extensive) is 61 sq. miles, with a resident population (2000 census) of 572,059. The District of Columbia is governed by an elected mayor and City Council
MAJOR CITIES – ΨChicago (2,896,016); Dallas (1,188,580); ΨDetroit (951,270); ΨHouston (1,953,631); ΨLos Angeles (3,694,820); ΨNew York (8,008,278); ΨPhiladelphia (1,517,550); Phoenix (1,321,045); San Antonio (1,144,646); ΨSan Diego (1,223,400), 2000 census
CURRENCY – US dollar (US$) of 100 cents
NATIONAL ANTHEM – The Star-Spangled Banner
NATIONAL DAY – 4 July (Independence Day)

NATIONAL FLAG – Thirteen horizontal stripes, alternately red and white, with blue canton in the hoist showing 50 white stars in nine horizontal rows of six and five alternately (known as the Star-Spangled Banner)
LIFE EXPECTANCY (years) – male 74.6; female 80.4
POPULATION GROWTH RATE – 0.9 per cent (1999)
POPULATION DENSITY – 29 per sq. km (1999)

The coastline has a length of about 2,069 miles on the Atlantic, 7,623 miles on the Pacific, 1,060 miles on the Arctic, and 1,631 miles on the Gulf of Mexico. The principal river is the Mississippi-Missouri-Red (3,710 miles long), traversing the whole country to its mouth in the Gulf of Mexico. The chain of the Rocky Mountains separates the western portion of the country from the remainder. West of these, bordering the Pacific coast, the Cascade Mountains and Sierra Nevada form the outer edge of a high tableland, consisting in part of stony and sandy desert and partly of grazing land and forested mountains, and including the Great Salt Lake, which extends to the Rocky Mountains. In the eastern states large forests still exist, the remnants of the forests which formerly extended over all the Atlantic slope. The highest point is Mount McKinley (20,320 ft) in Alaska, and the lowest point of dry land is in Death Valley (Inyo, California), 282 ft below sea level.

AREA AND POPULATION

	Total land area (sq. km)	Population census 1990
The United States (a)	9,159,116	248,709,873
Outlying areas under US jurisdiction	10,929	3,862,431
Territories	10,888	3,862,238
Puerto Rico	8,875	3,522,037
Guam	544	133,152
US Virgin Islands	346	101,809
American Samoa	200	46,773
Northern Mariana Is.	464	43,345
Other US possessions	41	193
Population abroad (b)	–	925,845
TOTAL	9,170,045	253,498,149

(a) the 50 states and the Federal District of Columbia
(b) excludes US citizens temporarily abroad on business

RESIDENT POPULATION BY RACE 2001
ESTIMATE (*Thousands*)

White	211,461
Black	34,658
*American Indian	2,476
Asian	10,242
Native Hawaiian and other Pacific Islanders	399
†Hispanic origin	35,306
Other race	15,359
Two or more races	6,826
TOTAL	316,727

*Includes Eskimo and Aleut
†Persons of Hispanic origin may be of any race

IMMIGRATION

From 1820 to 2000, 666,089,431 immigrants were admitted to the United States. Total number of immigrants in 2000 was 849,807, of which 400,879 came from North and South America (173,919 from Mexico), 265,400 from Asia and 132,480 from Europe.

THE STATES OF THE UNION

The United States of America is a federal republic consisting of 50 states and the federal District of Columbia and of organised territories. Of the present 50 states, 13 are original states, seven were admitted without previous organisation as territories, and 30 were admitted after such organisation.

STATE (with date and *order* of admission)	LAND AREA sq. km	POPULATION (2000 census)	CAPITAL	GOVERNOR (end of term in office)	
Alabama (AL) (1819) (*22*)	131,443	4,447,100	Montgomery	Don Siegelman (*D*)	(2002)
Alaska (AK) (1959) (*49*)	1,477,268	626,932	Juneau	Tony Knowles (*D*)	(2002)
Arizona (AZ) (1912) (*48*)	294,333	5,130,632	Phoenix	Jane Dee Hull (*R*)	(2002)
Arkansas (AR) (1836) (*25*)	134,875	2,673,400	Little Rock	Mike Huckabee (*R*)	(2002)
California (CA) (1850) (*31*)	403,971	33,871,648	Sacramento	Gray Davis (*D*)	(2002)
Colorado (CO) (1876) (*38*)	268,658	4,301,261	Denver	Bill Owens (*R*)	(2002)
Connecticut (CT) § (1788) (*5*)	12,550	3,405,565	Hartford	John Rowland (*R*)	(2002)
Delaware (DE) § (1787) (*1*)	5,063	783,600	Dover	Ruth Ann Minner (*D*)	(2004)
Florida (FL) (1845) (*27*)	139,853	15,982,378	Tallahassee	Jeb Bush (*R*)	(2002)
Georgia (GA) § (1788) (*4*)	150,010	8,186,453	Atlanta	Roy Barnes (*D*)	(2002)
Hawaii (HI) (1959) (*50*)	16,637	1,211,537	Honolulu	Ben Cayetano (*D*)	(2002)
Idaho (ID) (1890) (*43*)	214,325	1,293,953	Boise	Dirk Kempthorne (*R*)	(2002)
Illinois (IL) (1818) (*21*)	143,987	12,419,293	Springfield	George Ryan (*R*)	(2002)
Indiana (IN) (1816) (*19*)	92,904	6,080,485	Indianapolis	Frank O'Bannon (*D*)	(2004)
Iowa (IA) (1846) (*29*)	144,716	2,926,324	Des Moines	Tom Vilsack (*D*)	(2002)
Kansas (KS) (1861) (*34*)	211,922	2,688,418	Topeka	Bill Graves (*R*)	(2002)
Kentucky (KY) (1792) (*15*)	102,907	4,041,769	Frankfort	Paul Patton (*D*)	(2003)
Louisiana (LA) (1812) (*18*)	112,836	4,468,976	Baton Rouge	M. J. Mike Foster (*R*)	(2004)
Maine (ME) (1820) (*23*)	79,939	1,274,923	Augusta	Angus King (*I*)	(2002)
Maryland (MD) § (1788) (*7*)	25,316	5,296,486	Annapolis	Parris Glendening (*D*)	(2002)
Massachusetts (MA) § (1788) (*6*)	20,300	6,349,097	Boston	Jane Swift (*R*)	(2002)
Michigan (MI) (1837) (*26*)	147,136	9,938,444	Lansing	John Engler (*R*)	(2002)
Minnesota (MN) (1858) (*32*)	206,207	4,919,479	St Paul	Jesse Ventura (Reform)	(2002)
Mississippi (MS) (1817) (*20*)	121,506	2,844,658	Jackson	David Ronald Musgrove (*D*)	(2004)
Missouri (MO) (1821) (*24*)	178,446	5,595,211	Jefferson City	Bob Holden (*D*)	(2004)
Montana (MT) (1889) (*41*)	376,991	902,195	Helena	Judy Martz (*R*)	(2004)
Nebraska (NE) (1867) (*37*)	199,113	1,711,263	Lincoln	Mike Johanns (*R*)	(2002)
Nevada (NV) (1864) (*36*)	284,396	1,998,257	Carson City	Kenny Guinn (*R*)	(2002)
New Hampshire (NH) § (1788) (*9*)	23,231	1,235,786	Concord	Jeanne Shaheen (*D*)	(2002)
New Jersey (NJ) § (1787) (*3*)	19,215	8,414,350	Trenton	James McGreevey (*D*)	(2004)
New Mexico (NM) (1912) (*47*)	314,334	1,819,046	Santa Fé	Gary Johnson (*R*)	(2002)
New York (NY) § (1788) (*11*)	122,310	18,976,457	Albany	George Pataki (*R*)	(2002)
North Carolina (NC) § (1789) (*12*)	126,180	8,049,313	Raleigh	Mike Easley (*D*)	(2004)
North Dakota (ND) (1889) (*39*)	178,695	642,200	Bismarck	John Hoeven (*R*)	(2004)
Ohio (OH) (1803) (*17*)	106,067	11,353,140	Columbus	Bob Taft (*R*)	(2002)
Oklahoma (OK) (1907) (*46*)	177,877	3,450,654	Oklahoma City	Frank Keating (*R*)	(2002)
Oregon (OR) (1859) (*33*)	248,646	3,421,399	Salem	John Kitzhaber (*D*)	(2002)
Pennsylvania (PA) § (1787) (*2*)	116,083	12,281,054	Harrisburg	Mark Schweiker (*R*)	(2004)
Rhode Island (RI) § (1790) (*13*)	2,707	1,048,319	Providence	Lincoln Almond (*R*)	(2002)
South Carolina (SC) § (1788) (*8*)	77,988	4,012,012	Columbia	Jim Hodges (*D*)	(2002)
South Dakota (SD) (1889) (*40*)	196,571	754,844	Pierre	William Janklow (*R*)	(2002)
Tennessee (TN) (1796) (*16*)	106,759	5,689,283	Nashville	Don Sundquist (*R*)	(2002)
Texas (TX) (1845) (*28*)	678,358	20,851,820	Austin	Rick Perry (*R*)	(2002)
Utah (UT) (1896) (*45*)	212,816	2,233,169	Salt Lake City	Mike Leavitt (*R*)	(2004)
Vermont (VT) (1791) (*14*)	23,956	608,827	Montpelier	Howard Dean (*D*)	(2002)
Virginia (VA) § (1788) (*10*)	102,558	7,078,515	Richmond	Mark Warner (*D*)	(2004)
Washington (WA) (1889) (*42*)	172,445	5,894,121	Olympia	Gary Locke (*D*)	(2004)
West Virginia (WV) (1863) (*35*)	62,384	1,808,344	Charleston	Bob Wise (*D*)	(2004)
Wisconsin (WI) (1848) (*30*)	140,672	5,363,675	Madison	Scott McCallum (*R*)	(2002)
Wyoming (WY) (1890) (*44*)	251,501	493,782	Cheyenne	Jim Geringer (*R*)	(2002)
Dist. of Columbia (DC) (1791)	159	572,059	–	Anthony Williams (*D*) (*Mayor*)	

OUTLYING TERRITORIES AND POSSESSIONS

American Samoa	200	67,084*	Pago Pago	Tauese Pita Sunia (*D*)	(2004)
Guam	544	157,557*	Hagatna	Carl Gutierrez (*D*)	(2002)
Northern Mariana Islands	464	74,612*	Saipan	Juan N. Babauta (*R*)	(2004)
Puerto Rico	8,875	3,808,610*	San Juan	Sila María Calderón (*D*)	(2004)
US Virgin Islands	346	122,211*	Charlotte Amalie	Charles Wesley Turnbull (*D*)	(2002)

§The 13 original states
D Democratic Party; *I* Independent; *R* Republican Party
* 2001 estimates
Elections in respect of Governors whose term of office ends in 2002 were scheduled to take place in November 2002.

HISTORY AND POLITICS

The area which is now the USA was first inhabited by nomadic hunters who probably arrived from Asia c.30,000 BC. The first (failed) European colony was founded by Sir Walter Raleigh in 1585. By 1733 there were 13 British colonies, composed largely of religious non-conformists who had left Britain to escape persecution; the French and Spanish had also founded colonies.

The War of Independence broke out in 1775 largely because of the colonists' objection to being taxed by, but having no representation in, the British Parliament. The forces of the British government were defeated with French, Spanish and Dutch assistance. The Declaration of Independence which inaugurated the United States of America was signed on 4 July 1776; Britain recognised American sovereignty in 1783. The first federal constitution was drawn up in 1787; ten amendments, termed the Bill of Rights, were added in 1791. The 13 original states of the Union ratified the constitution between 1787 and 1790. Vermont, Kentucky and Tennessee were admitted in the 1790s but most of the states acceded in the 19th century as the opening up of the centre and west led to the creation of new states and European or neighbouring countries ceded or sold their territories to the USA.

The Civil War (1861–5) was fought over the issue of slavery, which was integral to the economy of the southern states but was opposed by the northern states. The northern states defeated the Confederacy of southern states (South Carolina, Georgia, Alabama, Florida, Mississippi, Louisiana).

The USA emerged as a world economic and military superpower in the 20th century and played a decisive role in the two world wars. Its economic and military (including nuclear) supremacy gave the USA a key role in shaping the post-war world.

11 SEPTEMBER 2001

On 11 September 2001, four passenger aircraft were hijacked and two of them were deliberately flown into the 'twin towers' of New York's World Trade Center. The third aircraft was flown into the Pentagon in Washington DC and the fourth crashed in Pennsylvania. Over 3,000 people were killed in the attacks, the most serious attack on the USA since the Second World War. For further information on this and subsequent events, please refer to the *Events of the Year* and *September 11 2001 and the Aftermath* sections.

POLITICAL SYSTEM

By the constitution of 17 September 1787 (to which amendments were added in 1791, 1798, 1804, 1865, 1868, 1870, 1913, 1920, 1933, 1951, 1961, 1964, 1967, 1971 and 1992), the government of the United States is entrusted to three separate authorities: the executive (the president and Cabinet), the legislature (Congress) and the judicature.

The president is indirectly elected by an electoral college every four years. There is also a vice-president, who, should the president die, becomes president for the remainder of the term. The tenure of the presidency is limited to two terms.

The president, with the consent of the Senate, appoints the Cabinet officers and all the chief officials. He makes recommendations of a general nature to Congress, and when laws are passed by Congress he may return them to Congress with a veto. But if a measure so vetoed is again passed by both Houses of Congress by two-thirds majority in each House, it becomes law, notwithstanding the objection of the president. The president must be at least 35 years of age and a native citizen of the United States.

PRESIDENTIAL ELECTIONS

Each state elects (on the first Tuesday after the first Monday in November of the year preceding the year in which the presidential term expires) a number of electors (members of the electoral college), equal to the whole number of Senators and Representatives to which the state may be entitled in the Congress. The electors for each state meet in their respective states on the first Monday after the second Wednesday in December following, and vote for a president by ballot. The ballots are then sent to Washington, and opened on 6 January by the President of the Senate in the presence of Congress. The candidate who has received a majority of the whole number of electoral votes cast is declared president for the ensuing term. If no one has a majority, then from the highest on the list (not exceeding three) the House of Representatives elects a president, the votes being taken by states, the representation from each state having one vote. A presidential term begins at noon on 20 January.

HEAD OF STATE

President of the United States, George Walker Bush, *born* 6 July 1946, *elected* 7 November 2000, *sworn in* 20 January 2001. Republican

Vice-President, Richard B. Cheney, *born* 30 January 1941

THE CABINET *as at August 2002*

Agriculture, Ann Veneman
Attorney-General, John Ashcroft
Commerce, Don Evans
Defence, Donald Rumsfeld
Education, Rod Paige
Energy, Spencer Abraham
Health and Human Services, Tommy Thompson
Housing and Urban Development, Mel Martinez
Interior, Gale Norton
Labour, Elaine Chao
Representative for Trade Negotiations, Robert Zoellick
Secretary of State, Colin Powell
Transportation, Norman Mineta
Treasury, Paul O'Neill
Veterans' Affairs, Anthony Principi

Other senior positions:
Director, Office of Homeland Defence, Tom Ridge
Director, Office of Management and Budget, Mitch Daniels
Environmental Protection Agency, Christine Todd Whitman
Federal Emergency Management Agency, Joseph Allbaugh
National Director for Combating Terrorism, Gen. Wayne Downing
National Security Adviser, Condoleezza Rice
President's Counsellor, vacant
Special White House Adviser on Cyberspace Security, Richard Clarke
White House Counsel, Alberto Gonzales

UNITED STATES EMBASSY

24 Grosvenor Square, London W1A 1AE
Tel: 020-7499 9000
Ambassador Extraordinary and Plenipotentiary, HE William S. Farish, apptd 2001

1100 Countries of the World

BRITISH EMBASSY
3100 Massachusetts Avenue NW, Washington DC 20008.
Tel: (00 1) (202) 588 6500
Ambassador Extraordinary and Plenipotentiary, HE Sir
Christopher Meyer, KCMG, apptd 1997

BRITISH CONSULATES-GENERAL – Atlanta, Boston,
Chicago, Houston, Los Angeles, New York and San
Francisco
BRITISH VICE-CONSULATE – Orlando
BRITISH CONSULATES – Dallas, Denver, Miami, Seattle
and Puerto Rico
BRITISH COUNCIL DIRECTOR, Andy Mackay (*Cultural
Attaché*), c/o British Embassy

THE CONGRESS

Legislative power is vested in two houses, the Senate and
the House of Representatives. The Senate has 100
members, two Senators from each state, elected for the
term of six years, and each Senator has one vote.
The House of Representatives consists of 435
Representatives, directly elected in each state for a two-
year term, a resident commissioner from Puerto Rico and
a delegate each from American Samoa, the District of
Columbia, Guam and the Virgin Islands. Members of the
107th Congress were elected on 7 November 2000. The
107th Congress is constituted as follows:
Senate – Republicans 49; Democrats 50; Independent 1;
total 100
House of Representatives – Republicans 219; Democrats
210; Independent 2; vacant 4; total 435
President of the Senate, The Vice-President
Senate Majority Leader, Tom Daschle (D), South Dakota
Speaker of the House of Representatives, J. Dennis Hastert
(R), Illinois

THE JUDICATURE

The federal judiciary consists of three sets of federal
courts: the Supreme Court at Washington DC, consisting
of a Chief Justice and eight Associate Justices, with

original jurisdiction in cases where a state is a party to the
suit, and with appellate jurisdiction from inferior federal
courts and from the judgments of the highest courts of
the states; the United States Courts of Appeals, dealing
with appeals from district courts and from certain federal
administrative agencies, and consisting of 168 circuit
judges within 13 circuits; the 94 United States district
courts served by 575 district court judges.

THE SUPREME COURT

US Supreme Court Building, Washington DC 20543

Chief Justice, William H. Rehnquist, Arizona, apptd 1986

Associate Justices
John Paul Stevens, *Illinois*, apptd 1975
Sandra Day O'Connor, *Arizona*, apptd 1981
Antonin Scalia, *Virginia*, apptd 1986
Anthony M. Kennedy, *California*, apptd 1988
David H. Souter, *New Hampshire*, apptd 1990
Clarence Thomas, *Georgia*, apptd 1991
Ruth Bader Ginsburg, *New York*, apptd 1993
Stephen Breyer, *Massachusetts*, apptd 1994

Clerk of the Supreme Court, William K. Suter

In 2000 there were 11,605,751 recorded offences: murder
and non-negligent manslaughter 15,517; forcible rape
90,186; robbery 407,842; aggravated assault 910,744;
burglary 2,049,946; larceny-theft 6,965,957; motor
vehicle theft 1,165,559.

DEFENCE

Each military department is separately organised and
functions under the direction, authority and control of
the Secretary of Defence. The Air Force has primary
responsibility for the Department of Defence space
development programmes and projects.
Under strategic command the USA has 432 submarine-
launched ballistic missiles, 550 inter-continental ballistic
missiles, 208 heavy nuclear-capable bombers and 60
strategic defence interceptor aircraft together with

multiple intelligence satellites, radars and early warning systems throughout the world.

The Army has 7,620 main battle tanks, 6,710 armoured infantry fighting vehicles, 15,400 armoured personnel carriers, 271 aircraft and 1,340 armed helicopters. The Navy has 73 strategic submarines, 55 tactical submarines, 12 aircraft carriers, 27 cruisers, 54 destroyers, 35 frigates, 21 patrol and coastal vessels, 241 amphibious and support ships, 1,669 combat aircraft and 526 armed helicopters. The Marine Corps has 403 main battle tanks and 1,321 amphibious armoured vehicles. The Air Force has 208 long-range strike aircraft, 3,939 tactical combat aircraft and 218 helicopters. The major deployments of US personnel overseas are: Germany (58,080); South Korea (36,520); Japan (38,330); Italy (10,850); UK (11,280); Turkey (2,040).

MILITARY EXPENDITURE – 3.0 per cent of GDP (2000)

MILITARY PERSONNEL – 1,367,700: Army 477,800; Navy 366,100; Marine Corps 171,300; Air Force 352,500; Coast Guard 42,110, Paramilitaries 53,000

ECONOMY AND FINANCE

In 2000 central government budget receipts totalled US$2,025.0 billion and outlays US$1,788.1 billion. The largest items of expenditure were: defence US$293.9 billion, social security US$409.4 billion, income security US$247.4 billion, debt interest US$223.2 billion. In the year to the end of September 2000, US$58,364 million was spent on education, US$154,215 million on health, US$197,115 million on Medicare, US$247,380 million on income security, US$409,437 million on social security and US$47,084 million on veterans' benefits and services.

At the end of the 1999 financial year the total gross federal debt stood at US$5,606,087 million.

GNP – US$9,645,556 million (2000); US$31,910 per capita (1999)

GDP – US$8,699,200 million (1998); US$32,778 per capita (1999)

ANNUAL AVERAGE GROWTH OF GDP – 5.0 per cent (2000)

INFLATION RATE – 3.4 per cent (2000)

UNEMPLOYMENT – 4.2 per cent (1999)

GROSS DOMESTIC PRODUCT BY INDUSTRY 2000

	US$ billions
Private industries	8,656.5
Agriculture, forestry, fisheries	135.8
Mining	127.1
Construction	463.6
Manufacturing	1,566.6
Transportation and public utilities	825.0
Wholesale trade	674.1
Retail trade	893.9
Finance, insurance, and real estate	1,936.2
Services	2,164.6
Government and government enterprises	1,216.4
Statistical discrepancy	−130.4
TOTAL	9,227.3

AGRICULTURE, MINERALS AND ENERGY

The total number of farms in 2001 was 2,157,780 with a total area of land in farms of 941,210,000 acres, and an average acreage per farm of 436 acres. Principal crops are maize for grain, soybeans, wheat, hay, cotton, tobacco, grain sorghums, potatoes, oranges and barley. Gross income from farming in 2001 was US$247 billion. Cash receipts from all crops in 2001 was US$96 billion and from livestock and livestock products US$106 billion. The value of non-fuel raw mineral production in 1997 totalled an estimated US$39 billion. Mineral exports in

1997 were valued at US$37 billion, and imports at US$58 billion. In 1998 the following quantities of minerals were produced: iron ore 62,931,000 tonnes; marketable phosphate rock 44,200,000 tonnes; copper 1,858,900 tonnes; zinc 755,000 tonnes; lead 415,000 tonnes. Energy production in 2001 was 72.51 quadrillion BTU, principally coal, natural gas and crude oil. Petroleum accounted for almost half of energy exports of 3.91 quadrillion BTU. Net imports were 26.02 quadrillion BTU, of which crude oil was 19.90 quadrillion BTU, to meet consumption of 96.88 quadrillion BTU (quadrillion=10^{15}).

TRADE

In 2000 the USA had a trade deficit of US$449,570 million and a current account deficit of US$444,690 million. Imports totalled US$1,257,636 million and exports US$781,125 million.

Trade with UK	2000	2001
Imports from UK	£29,417,790,000	£29,491,125,000
Exports to UK	29,332,236,000	30,352,892,000

COMMUNICATIONS

There are approximately 3.91 million miles of public roads and streets. Surfaced roads and streets account for 61.3 per cent of the total. US domestic and international scheduled airlines in 2000 carried approximately 665,042,490 passengers over 692,008,214,000 revenue passenger miles.

EDUCATION

All the states and the District of Columbia have compulsory school attendance laws. In general, children are obliged to attend school from seven to 16 years of age. Most of the revenue for public elementary and secondary school purposes comes from federal, state, and local governments. Less than three per cent comes from gifts and from tuition and transportation fees. Among the better-known universities are: Harvard, founded at Cambridge, Mass. in 1636, and named after John Harvard of Emmanuel College, Cambridge, England, who bequeathed to it his library and a sum of money in 1638; Yale, founded at New Haven, Connecticut, in 1701; Princeton, NJ, founded 1746.

ENROLMENT (percentage of age group) – primary 100 per cent (1997); secondary 97 per cent (1997); tertiary 81 per cent (1997)

US TERRITORIES, ETC

Responsibility within the federal government for the United States insular areas other than Puerto Rico and Kingman Reef lies with the United States Department of the Interior, either the Office of Insular Affairs (for American Samoa, Guam, the Northern Mariana Islands, the United States Virgin Islands, Navassa Island (3 sq. miles), Palmyra Atoll (1.56 sq. miles) and Wake Atoll (2.5 sq. miles) (shared with the United States Army Space and Missile Defense Command)) or the United States Fish and Wildlife Service (for Baker Island (0.59 sq. miles), Howland Island (1 sq. mile) and Jarvis Island (1.66 sq. miles), Midway Atoll (2 sq. miles) and Johnston Atoll (0.98 sq. miles) (shared with the Defense Special Weapons Agency)). Four of the eight populated insular areas are represented in the United States House of Representatives, Puerto Rico by a resident commissioner

and American Samoa, Guam and the United States Virgin Islands each by a delegate. Although represented in the United States House of Representatives by a delegate, the District of Columbia was an incorporated territory for only three years, from 21 February 1871 to 20 June 1874.

THE COMMONWEALTH OF PUERTO RICO

AREA – 3,427 sq. miles (8,875 sq. km)
POPULATION – 3,817,633 (2000 estimate). The majority of the inhabitants are of Spanish descent, and Spanish and English are the official languages
CAPITAL – ΨSan Juan, population of the municipality (2000 estimate), 434,370. Other major towns are: Bayamón (224,205); Carolina (186,362); ΨPonce (186,503)

Puerto Rico (Rich Port) is an island of the Greater Antilles group in the West Indies and was discovered in 1493 by Columbus. It was a Spanish possession until 1898, when the USA took formal possession as a result of the Spanish-American War. The 1952 constitution establishes the Commonwealth of Puerto Rico with full powers of local government. The Legislative Assembly consists of two elected houses: the Senate of 27 members and the House of Representatives of 51 members. The term of the Legislative Assembly is four years. The Governor is popularly elected for a term of four years. Residents of Puerto Rico are US citizens. Puerto Rico is represented in Congress by a resident commissioner, elected for a term of four years, who has a seat in the House of Representatives but not a vote, although he has a right to vote on those committees of which he is a member.

Governor, Sila María Calderón

Trade with UK	2000	2001
Imports from UK	£272,549,000	£276,710,000
Exports to UK	435,486,000	956,814,000

GUAM

AREA – 212 sq. miles (549 sq. km)
POPULATION – 157,557 (2001 estimate): 43 per cent Chamorro stock mingled with Filipino and Spanish blood. The Chamorro language belongs to the Malayo-Polynesian family, but with considerable admixture of Spanish. Chamorro and English are the official languages; most Chamorro residents are bilingual
CAPITAL – Hagatna. Port of entry, ΨApra

Guam is the largest of the Mariana Islands, in the north Pacific Ocean. Guam was occupied by the Japanese in December 1941 but was recaptured by US forces in 1944. Under the Organic Act of Guam 1950, Guam has statutory powers of self-government, and any person born in Guam is a US citizen. A 21-member unicameral legislature is elected biennially. The Governor and Lieutenant-Governor are popularly elected. There is also a District Court of Guam, with original jurisdiction in cases under federal law. Guam's two main sources of revenue are tourism and US military spending.

Governor, Carl Gutierrez

AMERICAN SAMOA

AREA – 77 sq. miles (199 sq. km)
POPULATION – 63,000 (1997 estimate)
CAPITAL – ΨPago Pago (population, 3,519)

American Samoa consists of the islands of Tutuila, Aunu'u, Ofu, Olesega, Ta'u, Rose and Swains Islands. Tutuila, the largest of the group, has an area of 52 sq. miles and a magnificent harbour at Pago Pago. The remaining islands have an area of about 24 sq. miles. Those born in American Samoa are US non-citizen nationals, but some have acquired citizenship through service in the United States armed forces or other naturalisation procedure. The 1960 constitution grants American Samoa a measure of self-government, with certain powers reserved to the US Secretary of the Interior. There is a bicameral legislature with popularly elected representatives and traditionally elected senators, and a popularly elected Governor.

Governor, Tauese Pita Sunia

THE UNITED STATES VIRGIN ISLANDS

Area – 134 sq. miles (347 sq. km)
Population – 114,483 (1997 estimate)
Capital – ΨCharlotte Amalie (population, 12,331, 1990), on St Thomas

The US Virgin Islands were purchased from Denmark and came under US sovereignty in 1917. There are three main islands, St Thomas (28 sq. miles), St Croix (84 sq. miles), St John (20 sq. miles) and about 50 small islets or cays. Under the provisions of the Revised Organic Act of the Virgin Islands 1954, legislative power is vested in the Legislature, a unicameral body composed of 15 senators popularly elected for two-year terms. The Governor is popularly elected. Those born in the US Virgin Islands are US citizen nationals.

Governor, Charles Wesley Turnbull

Trade with UK	2000	2001
Imports from UK	£4,083,000	£2,992,000
Exports to UK	4,963,000	8,933,000

NORTHERN MARIANA ISLANDS

AREA – 179 sq. miles (464 sq. km)
POPULATION – 63,763 (1997 estimate)
SEAT OF GOVERNMENT – Saipan (population, 52,706, 1995 census)
The USA administered the Northern Mariana Islands as part of a UN Trusteeship until the trusteeship agreement was terminated in 1986, bringing fully into effect a 1976 congressional law establishing the Northern Mariana Islands as a Commonwealth under US sovereignty. Most of the then residents became US citizens. Those born subsequently in the Northern Mariana Islands are US citizen nationals. There is a popularly elected bicameral legislature and a popularly elected Governor.

Governor, Juan N. Babauta

PRESIDENTS OF THE USA

Name (with Native State)	Party	Born	Inaugu-ration	Died	Age
George Washington, Va.	Federation	22 February 1732	1789	14 December 1799	67
John Adams, Mass.	Federation	30 October 1735	1797	4 July 1826	90
Thomas Jefferson, Va	Republican	13 April 1743	1801	4 July 1826	83
James Madison, Va	Republican	16 March 1751	1809	28 June 1836	85
James Monroe, Va	Republican	28 April 1758	1817	4 July 1831	73
John Quincy Adams, Mass.	Republican	11 July 1767	1825	23 February 1848	80
Andrew Jackson, SC	Democrat	15 March 1767	1829	8 June 1845	78
Martin Van Buren, NY	Democrat	5 December 1782	1837	24 July 1862	79
William Henry Harrison†, Va.	Whig	9 February 1773	1841	4 April 1841	68
John Tyler (a), Va	Whig	29 March 1790	1841	17 January 1862	71
James Knox Polk, NC	Democrat	2 November 1795	1845	15 June 1849	53
Zachary Taylor†, Va	Whig	24 November 1784	1849	9 July 1850	65
Millard Fillmore (a), NY	Whig	7 January 1800	1850	8 March 1874	74
Franklin Pierce, NH	Democrat	23 November 1804	1853	8 October 1869	64
James Buchanan, Pa.	Democrat	23 April 1791	1857	1 June 1868	77
Abraham Lincoln†§, Ky.	Republican	12 February 1809	1861	15 April 1865	56
Andrew Johnson (a), NC	Republican	29 December 1808	1865	31 July 1875	66
Ulysses Simpson Grant, Ohio	Republican	27 April 1822	1869	23 July 1885	63
Rutherford Birchard Hayes, Ohio	Republican	4 October 1822	1877	17 January 1893	70
James Abram Garfield†§, Ohio	Republican	19 November 1831	1881	19 September 1881	49
Chester Alan Arthur (a), Vt.	Republican	5 October 1830	1881	18 November 1886	56
Grover Cleveland, NJ	Democrat	18 March 1837	1885	24 June 1908	71
Benjamin Harrison, Ohio	Republican	20 August 1833	1889	13 March 1901	67
Grover Cleveland, NJ	Democrat	18 March 1837	1893	24 June 1908	71
William McKinley†§, Ohio	Republican	29 January 1843	1897	14 September 1901	58
Theodore Roosevelt (a), NY	Republican	27 October 1858	1901	6 January 1919	60
William Howard Taft, Ohio	Republican	15 September 1857	1909	8 March 1930	72
Woodrow Wilson, Va.	Democrat	28 December 1856	1913	3 February 1924	67
Warren Gamaliel Harding†, Ohio	Republican	2 November 1865	1921	2 August 1923	57
Calvin Coolidge (a), Vt.	Republican	4 July 1872	1923	5 January 1933	60
Herbert Clark Hoover, Iowa	Republican	10 August 1874	1929	20 October 1964	90
Franklin Delano Roosevelt†‡, NY	Democrat	30 January 1882	1933	12 April 1945	63
Harry S. Truman (a), Missouri	Democrat	8 May 1884	1945	26 December 1972	88
Dwight David Eisenhower, Texas	Republican	14 October 1890	1953	28 March 1969	78
John Fitzgerald Kennedy†§, Mass.	Democrat	29 May 1917	1961	22 November 1963	46
Lyndon Baines Johnson (a), Texas	Democrat	27 August 1908	1963	22 January 1973	64
Richard Milhous Nixon, California	Republican	9 January 1913	1969	22 April 1994	81
Gerald Rudolph Ford (b), Nebraska	Republican	14 July 1913	1974		
James Earl Carter, Georgia	Democrat	1 October 1924	1977		
Ronald Wilson Reagan, Illinois	Republican	6 February 1911	1981		
George Herbert Walker Bush, Mass.	Republican	12 June 1924	1989		
William Jefferson Blythe IV Clinton, Ark.	Democrat	19 August 1946	1993		
George W. Bush, Texas	Republican	6 July 1946	2001		

† Died in office
(a) Elected as Vice-President
§ Assassinated
‡ Re-elected 5 November 1940, the first case of a third term; re-elected for a fourth term 7 November 1944
(b) Appointed under the provisions of the 25th Amendment

URUGUAY

República Oriental del Uruguay – Eastern Republic of Uruguay

AREA – 67,574 sq. miles (175,016 sq. km). Neighbours: Argentina (west), Brazil (north and east)
POPULATION – 3,360,105 (2001 estimate): predominantly of Spanish and Italian descent. Spanish is the official language. Many Uruguayans are Roman Catholics. There is no established church
CAPITAL – ΨMontevideo (population, 1,303,182, 1996)
MAJOR CITIES – Canelones; Melo; Mercedes; Minas; ΨPaysandú; Punta del Este; Rivera; Salto
CURRENCY – Uruguayan peso of 100 centésimos
NATIONAL ANTHEM – Orientales, La Patria O La Tumba (Uruguayans, The Fatherland Or Death)
NATIONAL DAY – 25 August (Declaration of Independence, 1825)
NATIONAL FLAG – Four blue and five white horizontal stripes surcharged with sun on a white ground in the top corner, next flagstaff
LIFE EXPECTANCY (years) – male 71.6; female 78.9
POPULATION GROWTH RATE – 0.7 per cent (2001)
POPULATION DENSITY – 19 per sq. km (1999)
URBAN POPULATION – 90.5 per cent (1997)
MILITARY EXPENDITURE – 2.6 per cent of GDP (2000)
MILITARY PERSONNEL – 23,900: Army 15,200, Navy 5,700, Air Force 3,000; Paramilitaries 920

The country consists mainly of undulating grassy plains. The principal river is the Rio Negro (with its tributary the Yi), flowing from north-east to south-west into the Rio Uruguay.

HISTORY AND POLITICS

Uruguay (or the *Banda Oriental*, as the territory lying on the eastern bank of the Uruguay River was then called) formed part of Spanish South America from 1726 to 1814, when it was annexed by the Argentine Confederation and then Portugal, becoming a province of Brazil. In 1825, the country threw off Brazilian rule. Uruguay was declared an independent state in 1828 and was inaugurated as a republic in 1830.

General elections held in 1984 marked the return to civilian rule after 11 years of presidential rule with military support. The first fully free presidential and legislative elections since 1971 were held in 1989, and were won by the National (Blanco) Party (NP).

The presidential election on 31 October and 28 November 1999 was won by Jorge Batlle Ibáñez of the Colorado Party (CP), who gained 51.5 per cent of the vote in the second round of the election. The legislative elections for both houses of the General Assembly, which were held simultaneously with the first round of the presidential election, resulted in the Progressive Encounter-Broad Front (EP-FA) winning 40 seats, the CP 33 seats, the NP 22 seats and the New Space party (NE) four seats in the House of Representatives, with the EP-FA winning 12 seats, the CP ten seats, the NP seven seats and the NE one seat in the Senate. A coalition government of the CP and the NP was formed.

POLITICAL SYSTEM

Under the constitution the president (who may serve only a single term of five years) appoints a council of ministers and a Secretary (Planning and Budget Office), and the vice-president presides over Congress. The Congress consists of a Chamber of 99 deputies and a Senate of 30 members (plus the vice-president), elected for five years by proportional representation.

The republic is divided into 19 Departments, each with an elected governor and legislature.

HEAD OF STATE
President, Jorge Batlle Ibáñez, *elected* 28 November 1999, took office 1 March 2000
Vice-President, Luis Hierro López

COUNCIL OF MINISTERS *as at August 2002*
The President
Economy and Finance, Alejandro Atchugarry
Education and Culture, Antonio Mercador (NP)
Foreign Relations, Didier Opertti (CP)
Health, Alfonso Varela
Housing, Territorial Regulation and Environment, Carlos Cat (NP)
Industry, Energy and Mines, Sergio Abreu (NP)
Interior, Guillermo Sterling (CP)
Labour and Social Security, Alvaro Alonso (NP)
Livestock, Agriculture and Fisheries, Gonzalo González (NP)
National Defence, Luis Brezzo (CP)
Planning and Budget, Ariel Davrieux (NP)
Tourism, Pedro Bordaberry (CP)
Transport and Public Works, Lucio Cáceres (CP)
Youth and Sports, Jaime Trobo
CP Colorado Party; NP National (Blanco) Party;

EMBASSY OF URUGUAY
2nd Floor, 140 Brompton Road, London SW3 1HY
Tel: 020-7589 8835
Ambassador Extraordinary and Plenipotentiary, HE Dr Miguel Jorge Berthet, apptd 2001

BRITISH EMBASSY
Calle Marco Bruto 1073, 11300 Montevideo (PO Box 16024). Tel: (00 598) (2) 622 3650/3630
Email: bemonte@internet.com.uy
Ambassador Extraordinary and Plenipotentiary, HE John Everard, apptd 2001

ECONOMY

Beef, mutton and wool are produced and rice, wheat, barley, linseed and sunflower seed are cultivated. Other foodstuffs (citrus, wine, beer), fishing and textile industries are also of importance. Textiles, tyres, sheet-glass, three-ply wood, cement, leather-curing, beet-sugar, plastics, household consumer goods and edible oils are produced. Exploited minerals include clinker, dolomite, marble and granite. Much of the economy is in the hands of state monopolies and there has been only limited market liberalisation. In October 2000, the House of Representatives approved a plan to privatise 40 per cent of the state telecommunications company Ancel.
GNP – US$20,307 million (2000); US$6,220 per capita (1999)
GDP – US$20,831 million (1998); US$5,891 per capita (1999)
ANNUAL AVERAGE GROWTH OF GDP – 1.3 per cent (2000)
INFLATION RATE – 4.8 per cent (2000)
UNEMPLOYMENT – 11.3 per cent (1999)
TOTAL EXTERNAL DEBT – US$7,447 million (1999)

TRADE
The major exports are meat, meat by-products and livestock, agricultural products and textiles. The principal imports are machinery and transport equipment and chemical products. Principal trading partners are Brazil, Argentina, the USA and Germany.

In 2000 Uruguay had a trade deficit of US$937 million and a current account deficit of US$593 million. Imports totalled US$3,466 million and exports US$2,295 million.

Trade with UK	2000	2001
Imports from UK	£58,555,000	£58,555,000
Exports to UK	35,596,000	35,330,000

COMMUNICATIONS

There are over 50,000 km of roads, including 12,000 km of national highways, and over 2,000 km of standard gauge railway in use. The international airport of Carrasco lies 12 miles outside Montevideo. The River Uruguay is navigable from its estuary to Salto, 200 miles north, and the Negro is also navigable as far as Mercedes. In December 1998, the Senate approved the construction of a 45-km bridge across the River Plate, linking Uruguay and Argentina.

EDUCATION

Primary and secondary education is compulsory and free, and technical and trade schools and evening courses for adult education are state controlled. The university at Montevideo (founded in 1849) has ten faculties and a new university has been built at Salto.
ILLITERACY RATE – 2.1 per cent (2002)
ENROLMENT (percentage of age group) – primary 100 per cent (1997); tertiary 30 per cent (1997)

UZBEKISTAN
O'zbekiston Žumhurijati – Republic of Uzbekistan

AREA – 72,742 sq. miles (447,400 sq. km). Neighbours: Kazakhstan (north and west), Kyrgyzstan and Tajikistan (east), Afghanistan and Turkmenistan (south)
POPULATION – 25,155,064 (2001 estimate): 72 per cent Uzbek, 8 per cent Russian, 5 per cent Tajik and 4 per cent Kazakh, with smaller numbers of Tatars, Kara-Kalpaks, Koreans, Ukrainians and Kyrgyz. The predominant religion is Sunni Muslim. Islam is tolerated within strict bounds; it is allowed to play no part in politics. The official language is Uzbek (72 per cent). Russian (8 per cent), Tajik (5 per cent) and Kazakh (4 per cent) are also spoken. Uzbek is one of the Turkic group of languages. In 1994 the government approved a six-year programme for the transfer of the Uzbek language to a Latin script
CAPITAL – Tashkent (population, 2,200,000, 1998 estimate)
MAJOR CITIES – Samarkand (361,800), which contains the Gur-Emir (Tamerlane's Mausoleum); Bukhara (237,100), which contains the Samanid Mausoleum and the Ulughbek Madrassah
CURRENCY – Soum of 100 tiyin
NATIONAL DAY – 1 September (Independence Day)
NATIONAL FLAG – Three horizontal stripes of blue, white, green, with the white fimbriated in red; on the blue near the hoist a crescent and twelve stars, all in white
LIFE EXPECTANCY (years) – male 66.8; female 72.5
POPULATION GROWTH RATE – 1.4 per cent (1999)
POPULATION DENSITY – 54 per sq. km (1999)
URBAN POPULATION – 38.0 per cent (1997)
MILITARY EXPENDITURE – 8.0 per cent of GDP (2000)
MILITARY PERSONNEL – 55,000: Army 40,000, Air Force 15,000; Paramilitaries 20,000

CONSCRIPTION DURATION – 18 months
ILLITERACY RATE – 0.7 per cent (2002)

Uzbekistan occupies the south-central part of former Soviet Central Asia, lying between the high Tienshan Mountains and the Pamir highlands in the east and south-east and sandy lowlands in the west and north-west, in the basin of the Amudarya and Syrdarya rivers. Uzbekistan consists of the Republic of Karakalpakstan and 12 regions: Andijan, Bukhara, Jizak, Fergana, Kashka-Darya, Khorezm, Namanghan, Navoi, Samarkand, Surhan-Darya, Syr-Darya and Tashkent.

HISTORY AND POLITICS

In the 13th century the area that is now Uzbekistan became the centre of a great Muslim empire under Amir Timur (Tamerlane), with its capital at Samarkand. By the beginning of the 19th century three independent Khanates, Khiva, Kokand and Bukhara, existed in what is now Uzbekistan. These were annexed to the Russian Empire in the second half of the 19th century. In November 1917 a Communist revolution broke out in Tashkent and by 1921, all of Uzbekistan had been absorbed into the Soviet Union. Under Soviet rule a massive land irrigation programme was implemented to allow the cultivation of cotton.

Uzbekistan declared its independence from the Soviet Union on 1 September 1991. Its independence was confirmed in a referendum on 29 December and recognised internationally. Elections to the new *Oliy Majlis* were held on 25 December 1994 and won by the ruling People's Democratic Party (PDP) and its allies.

The government of President Karimov is formed by the People's Democratic Party. Despite the constitutionally guaranteed freedom of religion and thought, and respect for human rights and multiparty democracy, censorship is still widely used and little political opposition is tolerated. The main opposition parties, Erk (Freedom) and Birlik (Unity) nationalist parties, have been continually banned since the introduction of the multiparty constitution in December 1992, but five political parties are legally registered. In March 1995 President Karimov's term of office was extended to 2000 by a national referendum and he won a further five-year term in a presidential election held on 9 January 2000, gaining 91.9 per cent of the vote. The election result attracted criticism from the Organisation for Security and Co-operation in Europe, who claimed no real opposition candidate had been allowed to stand. Legislative elections were held on 5 and 19 December 1999; the People's Democratic Party and its allies won 123 seats. The remaining seats were won by independent candidates and citizens' groups.

INSURGENCIES

The Islamic Movement of Uzbekistan (IMU), which seeks to overthrow the government and establish an Islamic state, was founded in 1996. Many IMU members have trained in camps in Afghanistan and the organisation is thought to be financed by the Taliban. Whilst they have carried out car bombings in Tashkent, their activities have centred on the Fergana valley and they have clashed with Kyrgyz armed forces.

FOREIGN RELATIONS

It was announced in February 1999 that Uzbekistan was to withdraw from the collective security treaty of the Commonwealth of Independent States. Uzbekistan is a member of the UN, OSCE, UNESCO, WHO and many other international organisations. On 22 January 2002, a

military agreement was signed with the US over the anti-terrorist operation in Afghanistan, outlining future co-operation and more frequent contact between the two countries.

POLITICAL SYSTEM

A referendum held on 27 January 2002 approved constitutional amendments on the extension of the presidential term of office from five to seven years and the creation of a bicameral legislature. The amendments were approved by parliament in early April.

HEAD OF STATE

President, Islam Karimov, *elected* 29 December 1991, *elected* by referendum for a five-year term 26 March 1995, *re-elected* 9 January 2000

CABINET *as at August 2002*

Chairman of the Cabinet, The President
Prime Minister, Utkur Sultanov
First Deputy Prime Minister, Macroeconomics and Statistics, Kozim Tolaganov
Deputy Prime Ministers, Nosirjon Yusupov (*Agriculture and Water Resources*); Abdulla Oripov (*Communications and Information Technology*); Valeriy Ataev (*Power and Electrification*); Bakhtiyor Alimjanov; Dilbar Ghulomova; Rustam Junusov; Mirabror Usmanov
Chairman, National Parliament, Erkin Khalilov
Communications, Abduwahid Djurabaev
Cultural Affairs, Khairulla Djuraev
Defence, Kodir Gulomov
Education, R. Djuraev
Finance, Mamarizo Normurodov
Foreign Affairs, Abdulaziz Kamilov
Foreign Economic Relations, Elyor Majidovich Ganiev
Health, Feruz Nazirov
Higher and Secondary Specialised Education, Saidahror Gulamov
Interior, Zakir Almatov
Justice, Abdusamad Polvonzoda
Labour and Social Security, Okiljon Obidov
Macroeconomics and Statistics, Rustam Shoabdurakhmanov

EMBASSY OF THE REPUBLIC OF UZBEKISTAN
41 Holland Park, London W11 3RP
Tel: 020-7229 7679
Ambassador Extraordinary and Plenipotentiary, HE Alisher Faizullaev, apptd 1999

BRITISH EMBASSY
Ul. Gulyamova 67, UZ-700000 Tashkent
Tel: (00 99871) 1206451/1206288
Ambassador Extraordinary and Plenipotentiary, HE Craig Murray, apptd 2002

BRITISH COUNCIL DIRECTOR, Neville McBain, 11 D. Kounoev Street, Tashkent

ECONOMY

Uzbekistan's economy is based on intensive agricultural production. Cotton production is approximately 4 million tonnes per year, made possible by extensive irrigation schemes. Textile manufacture, silk production and leather goods are also important. Wheat, potatoes and rice are widely grown. In addition there are some agricultural and textile machinery plants and several chemical combines. Uzbekistan possesses extensive mineral deposits. Copper, uranium, oil, gold and many other metals are extracted. In 1998 oil output was 8.0

million tonnes, and gas production was 55 billion cubic metres. The Muruntao mine is the largest open-cast gold mine in the world; in 1998, 81 tonnes of gold were produced. Total gold reserves are estimated at more than 5,000 tonnes.

Foreign direct investment exceeds US$9 billion. South Korea, the USA, Japan, Turkey and the UK are the main investors. Uzbekistan is a member of the CIS economic union.

GNP – US$15,235 million (2000); US$720 per capita (1999)
GDP – US$11,073 million (1998); US$682 per capita (1999)
ANNUAL AVERAGE GROWTH OF GDP – 4.4 per cent (1998)
UNEMPLOYMENT – 4.8 per cent (2000)
TOTAL EXTERNAL DEBT – US$4,163 million (1999)

Trade with UK	2000	2001
Imports from UK	£16,107,000	£20,401,000
Exports to UK	14,629,000	26,739,000

VANUATU
Ripablik blong Vanuatu/Republic of Vanuatu/République de Vanuatu

AREA – 4,706 sq. miles (12,189 sq. km)
POPULATION – 192,910 (2001 estimate). About 95 per cent are Melanesian, the rest being mostly Micronesian, Polynesian and European. The national language is Bislama, but English and French are also official languages
CAPITAL – ΨPort Vila (population, 26,100, 1993), on Efate
MAJOR TOWN – Luganville (8,800, 1993), on Espiritu Santo
CURRENCY – Vatu of 100 centimes
NATIONAL ANTHEM – Nasonal Sing Sing Blong Vanuatu (National Anthem Of Vanuatu)
NATIONAL DAY – 30 July (Independence Day)
NATIONAL FLAG – Red over green with a black triangle in the hoist, the three parts being divided by fimbriations of black and yellow, and in the centre of the black triangle a boar's tusk overlaid by two crossed fern leaves
LIFE EXPECTANCY (years) – male 67.5; female 70.5
POPULATION GROWTH RATE – 2.4 per cent (1999)
POPULATION DENSITY – 15 per sq. km (1999)

Vanuatu is situated in the South Pacific Ocean. It includes 13 large and some 70 small islands, of coral and volcanic origin, including the Banks and Torres Islands in the north. The principal islands are Vanua Lava, Espiritu Santo, Maewo, Pentecost, Ambae, Malekula, Ambrym, Epi, Efate, Erromango, Tanna and Aneityum. Most islands are mountainous and there are active volcanoes on several.

HISTORY AND POLITICS

Vanuatu, the former Anglo-French Condominium of the New Hebrides, became an independent republic within the Commonwealth on 30 July 1980. Parliament consists of 52 members, directly elected for a term of four years. A Council of Chiefs advises on matters of custom. Executive power is held by the prime minister (elected from and by parliament) and a Council of Ministers who are responsible to parliament. The president is elected for a five-year term by the presidents of the six provincial

governments and the members of parliament. The most recent presidential election took place on 24 March 1999 and was won by Fr John Bani. In the legislative election held on 2 May 2002 the Union of Moderate Parties (UMP) won 15 of the 52 seats in the Parliament and the Vanuaaki Pati (VP) won 14 seats. Edward Natapei of the VP was elected prime minister on 3 June, heading a continued VP/UMP coalition government.

HEAD OF STATE

President, HE Fr John Bani, *elected* 24 March 1999

COUNCIL OF MINISTERS *as at August 2002*

Prime Minister, Public Services, Edward Natapei (VP)
Deputy Prime Minister, External Trade and Telecommunications, Rialuth Serge Vohor (UMP)
Agriculture, Livestock, Forestry and Fisheries, Steven Kalsakau (UMP)
Comprehensive Reform Programme, Philip Boedoro (VP)
Education, Jacques Sese (UMP)
Finance and Economic Management, Sela Molisa (VP)
Health, Donald Kalpokas (VP)
Industry and Commerce, Jean-Alain Mahé (UMP)
Infrastructure, Public Utilities, Willy Posen (UMP)
Internal Affairs, Joe Natuman (VP)
Lands and Mineral Resources, Jacklyn Rueben Titek (VP)
Ni-Vanuatu Business Development, Nicholas Brown (Ind.)
Youth and Sports, Raphael Worwor (UMP)

BRITISH HIGH COMMISSION
KPMG House, Rue Pasteur, PO Box 567, Port Vila
Tel: (00 678) 23100
Email: bhcvila@vanuatu.com.vu
High Commissioner, HE Michael Hill, OBE, apptd 2000

ECONOMY

Most of the population is employed on plantations or in subsistence agriculture. Subsistence crops include yams, taro, manioc, sweet potato and breadfruit; principal cash crops are copra, cocoa and coffee. Cattle are kept on the plantations and beef is the second largest export. There is a small light industrial sector. Principal exports are copra, meat (frozen, tinned and chilled), timber and cocoa. The main trading partner is Japan. Tourism is a growing industry and the absence of direct taxation has led to growth in the finance and associated industries.

In 1998 Vanuatu had a trade deficit of US$42 million and a current account surplus of US$5 million. In 1999 imports totalled US$96 million and exports totalled US$26 million.

GNP – US$228 million (2000); US$1,180 per capita (1999)
GDP – US$232 million (1998); US$1,193 per capita (1999)
ANNUAL AVERAGE GROWTH OF GDP – 2.1 per cent (1998)
INFLATION RATE – 2.0 per cent (1999)
TOTAL EXTERNAL DEBT – US$65 million (1999)

Trade with UK	2000	2001
Imports from UK	£115,000	£463,000
Exports to UK	26,000	58,000

VATICAN CITY STATE
Status Civitatis Vaticanae/Stato della Città del Vaticano – State of the Vatican City

AREA – 0.2 sq. miles (0.44 sq. km). Neighbour: Italy
POPULATION – 890 (2001 estimate). The languages are Latin and Italian
CAPITAL – Vatican City (population, 766, 1988)
CURRENCY – Euro (€) of 100 cents
NATIONAL ANTHEM – Inno E Marcia Pontificale (Hymn And Pontifical March)
NATIONAL DAY – 22 October (Inauguration of present Pontiff)
NATIONAL FLAG – Square flag; equal vertical bands of yellow (next staff), and white; crossed keys and triple crown device on white band
POPULATION GROWTH RATE – 0.0 per cent (1997)
POPULATION DENSITY – 2,273 per sq. km (1997)
GDP – US$10 million (1998); US$20,659 per capita (1998)
ANNUAL AVERAGE GROWTH OF GDP – 1.3 per cent (1998)

The office of the ecclesiastical head of the Roman Catholic Church (Holy See) is vested in the Pope, the Sovereign Pontiff. For many centuries the Sovereign Pontiff exercised temporal power but by 1870 the Papal States had become part of unified Italy. The temporal power of the Pope was in suspense until the treaty of 1929 which recognised the full and independent sovereignty of the Holy See in the City of the Vatican.

Sovereign Pontiff, His Holiness Pope John Paul II (Karol Wojtyła), *born* at Wadowice (Kraków, Poland), 18 May 1920, *elected* Pope in succession to Pope John Paul I, 16 October 1978

SECRETARIAT OF STATE *as at August 2002*

Secretary of State, Cardinal Angelo Sodano, apptd December 1990
Assistant Secretary of State, Archbishop Leonardo Sandri
Secretary for Relations with States, Archbishop Jean-Louis Tauran

APOSTOLIC NUNCIATURE
54 Parkside, London SW19 5NE
Tel: 020-8946 1410/7971
Apostolic Nuncio, HE Archbishop Pablo Puente, apptd 1997

BRITISH EMBASSY TO THE HOLY SEE
91 Via dei Condotti, I–00187 Rome
Tel: (00 39) (06) 6992 3561
Ambassador Extraordinary and Plenipotentiary, HE Kathryn Colvin, apptd 2002

Trade with UK	2000	2001
Imports from UK	£714,000	£1,328,000
Exports to UK	78,000	11,000

VENEZUELA
República Bolivariana de Venezuela – Bolivarian Republic of Venezuela

AREA – 352,145 sq. miles (912,050 sq. km). Neighbours: Colombia (west), Guyana (east), Brazil (south)
POPULATION – 25,160,000 (2002 estimate): 67 per cent mestizo, 21 per cent white, 10 per cent black and 2 per cent Amerindian. The language is Spanish. 93 per cent of the population is Roman Catholic
CAPITAL – Caracas (population, 3,435,795, 2002 estimate)
MAJOR CITIES – Barquisimeto (875,788); ΨMaracaibo (1,372,724); Maracay (459,007); Valencia (832,229), 2000 estimates
CURRENCY – Bolívar (Bs) of 100 céntimos
NATIONAL ANTHEM – Gloria Al Bravo Pueblo (Glory To The Brave People)
NATIONAL DAY – 5 July
NATIONAL FLAG – Three horizontal stripes of yellow, blue, red with an arc of seven white stars on the blue stripe and a coat of arms on the upper hoist.
LIFE EXPECTANCY (years) – male 70.9; female 76.7
POPULATION GROWTH RATE – 2.0 per cent (1999)
POPULATION DENSITY – 26 per sq. km (1999)
URBAN POPULATION – 86.1 per cent (1997)
ILLITERACY RATE – 6.8 per cent (2002)
ENROLMENT (percentage of age group) – primary 91 per cent (1997); secondary 40 per cent (1997)

Included in the area of the South American republic of Venezuela are 72 islands off the coast, with a total area of about 14,650 sq. miles, the largest being Margarita (area, about 400 sq. miles).

The mountains are the Eastern Andes and Maritime Andes, running south-west to north-east. The main range is known as the Sierra Nevada de Mérida, and contains Pico Bolivar (16,411 ft) and Picacho de la Sierra (15,420 ft). The principal river is the Orinoco, with innumerable affluents, the main river exceeding 1,600 miles in length. The upper waters of the Orinoco are united with those of the Rio Negro (a Brazilian tributary of the Amazon) by a natural river or canal, known as the Brazo Casiquiare. The coastal regions contain many lagoons and lakes, of which Maracaibo (area 8,296 sq. miles) is the largest lake in South America.

HISTORY AND POLITICS

The first Spanish settlement was established at Cumaná in 1520. An Act of Independence was signed on 15 July 1811 but was followed by several years of struggle until troops led by Simón Bolivar defeated the Spanish at the battle of Carabobo in 1821. Independence from Great Colombia, into which Venezuela had been incorporated in December 1819, was achieved in January 1830.

On 25 May 1999, a referendum on convening a constituent assembly to rewrite the constitution was passed and an election to decide the members of the constituent assembly was held on 25 July 1999. The new constitution was approved in a referendum held on 15 December and was proclaimed on 20 December.

The National Congress was dissolved on 4 January 2000 pending elections to the new National Assembly, which were due to be held on 28 May, but were postponed. In the presidential election held on 30 July 2000, President Chávez was re-elected, winning 59 per cent of the vote. In the simultaneous election for the National Assembly, the Fifth Republic Movement (MVR) won 76 seats,

Democratic Action 29 seats, Movement towards Socialism 21 seats, and other parties 39 seats.

The National Assembly granted President Chávez Frías the power to rule by decree in industrial and economic policy and matters concerning the civil service for a period of one year on 7 November 2000. An attempted military coup on 12 April 2002 forced President Chávez to resign but he was reinstated with his Cabinet on 14 April after popular protest.

POLITICAL SYSTEM

Under the 1999 constitution a unicameral legislature, the National Assembly, was created, and the post of vice-president instituted. The president, who is directly elected, serves a six-year term, which is renewable once only. The vice-president is appointed by the president. Legislative power is exercised by the 165-member *Asamblea Nacional* (National Assembly), which is directly elected for a five-year term.

FEDERAL STRUCTURE

Venezuela is divided into 22 states and two federal districts.

State	Area (sq. km)	Population (2000 estimate)	Capital
Amazonas	175,750	100,325	Puerto Ayacucho
Anzoátegui	43,300	1,140,369	Barcelona
Apure	76,500	466,931	San Fernando
Aragua	7,014	1,481,453	Maracay
Barinas	35,200	583,521	Barinas
Bolívar	238,000	1,306,651	Ciudad Bolívar
Carabobo	4,650	2,106,264	Valencia
Cojedes	14,800	262,154	San Carlos
Delta Amacuro	40,200	137,939	Tucupita
Falcón	24,800	747,672	Coro
Federal District	1,930	2,284,924*	Caracas
Federal Dependencies	120	——	
Guárico	64,986	638,638	San Juan
Lara	19,800	1,581,121	Barquisimeto
Mérida	11,300	744,986	Mérida
Miranda	7,950	2,607,163	Los Teques
Monagas	28,900	599,764	Maturín
Nueva Esparta	1,150	377,701	La Asunción
Portuguesa	15,200	830,441	Guanare
Sucre	11,800	824,764	Cumaná
Táchira	11,100	1,031,158	San Cristóbal
Trujillo	7,400	587,280	Trujillo
Yaracuy	7,100	518,902	San Felipe
Zulia	63,100	3,209,626	Maracaibo

* Includes Federal Dependencies

HEAD OF STATE

President, Hugo Chávez Frías, *elected* 6 December 1998, *sworn in* 2 February 1999, *re-elected* 30 July 2000
Vice-President, José Vicente Rangel

COUNCIL OF MINISTERS *as at August 2002*

Agriculture and Lands, Efren Andrade
Attorney-General, Isaias Rodriguez
Defence, José Luis Prieto
Development of Special Economic Zones, Francisco Natera
Education, Culture and Sports, Aristobulo Isturiz
Energy and Mines, Rafael Ramirez
Environment and Renewable Natural Resources, Ana Elisa Osorio
Finance, Tobías Nóbrega
Foreign Relations, Roy Chaderton

Health and Social Development, María Lourdes Urbaneja
Higher Education, Hector Navarro
Industry and Commerce, Ramón Rosales
Information and Communications, Nora Uribe
Infrastructure, Maj.-Gen. Eliecer Hurtado Soucre
Interior and Justice, Diosdado Cabello
Labour, María Cristina Iglesias
Planning and Development, Felipe Pérez Marti
Science and Technology, Carlos Genatios
Secretary of the Presidency, Nelson Merentes

EMBASSY OF THE BOLIVARIAN REPUBLIC OF
VENEZUELA
1 Cromwell Road, London SW7 2HR
Tel: 020-7584 4206
Ambassador Extraordinary and Plenipotentiary, HE
Alfredo Toro-Hardy, apptd 2001

BRITISH EMBASSY
Edificio Torre Las Mercedes (Piso 3), Avenida La
Estancia, Chuao (Apartado 1246), Caracas 1061
Tel: (00 58) (2) 993 4111/4224
Ambassador Extraordinary and Plenipotentiary, HE
Edgar Hughes, apptd 2000

CONSULAR OFFICES – Maracaibo, Margarita, Mérida,
Puerto La Cruz, San Cristóbal, Valencia

BRITISH COUNCIL DIRECTOR, Jonathan Greenwood,
Piso 3, Torre Credicard, Av. Principal El Bosque, El
Bosque, Caracas

DEFENCE

The Army has 81 main battle tanks, 290 armoured
personnel carriers and seven attack helicopters. The Navy
has two submarines, six frigates, six patrol and coastal
vessels, three combat aircraft and nine armed helicopters
at nine bases. The Air Force has 125 combat aircraft and
31 armed helicopters.

MILITARY EXPENDITURE – 1.5 per cent of GDP (2000)
MILITARY PERSONNEL – 82,300: Army 34,000, Navy
18,300, Air Force 7,000; National Guard 23,000
CONSCRIPTION DURATION – 30 months (selective)

ECONOMY

President Hugo Chávez Frías pledged in December 1998
that his government would cut public spending and
tackle tax evasion and corruption.

Agriculture comprises large-scale commercial farms
together with subsistence farming. Land distribution is
very uneven, with 1 per cent of farms occupying 46 per
cent of arable land and 250,000 smallholdings occupying
less that 2 per cent of arable land.

Products of the tropical forest region include orchids,
wild rubber, timber, mangrove bark, balata gum and
tonka beans. Agricultural products include corn,
bananas, cocoa beans, coffee, cotton, rice, maize, sugar,
sesame, groundnuts, potatoes, tomatoes, other vegetables,
sisal and tobacco. There is an extensive beef and dairy
farming industry. The principal industry is petroleum
and gas, which together account for 78 per cent of
exports. There are eight refineries. The Orinoco heavy oil
belt is being developed. Aluminium is abundant. Rich
iron ore deposits in eastern Venezuela have been
developed. Other industry includes a wide variety of
manufacturing and component assembly, principally
petrochemicals, gold, diamonds and foodstuffs.

On 2 February 2000, President Chávez announced
reductions in the rate of value-added tax, a reduction in
personal taxes, the abolition of bank debit tax, and tax
exemptions in certain key areas of the economy.
GNP – US$104,075 million (2000); US$3,680 per capita
(1999)
GDP – US$95,450 million (1998); US$4,312 per capita
(1999)
ANNUAL AVERAGE GROWTH OF GDP – 3.2 per cent
(2000)

INFLATION RATE – 16.2 per cent (2000)
UNEMPLOYMENT – 14.9 per cent (1999)
TOTAL EXTERNAL DEBT – US$35,852 million (1999)

TRADE

Apart from oil, the main exports are bauxite, iron ore, agricultural products and basic manufactures. The main imports are machinery and transport equipment, chemicals and foodstuffs. The USA and Colombia are the major trading partners.

In 2000 Venezuela had a trade surplus of US$17,965 million and a current account surplus of US$13,184 million. Imports totalled US$16,213 million and exports US$31,802 million.

Trade with UK	2000	2001
Imports from UK	£221,382,000	£313,641,000
Exports to UK	215,126,000	166,228,000

COMMUNICATIONS

There are 96,155 km of roads, some 32,308 km of them paved. Road and river communications have made railways of negligible importance in Venezuela except for carrying iron ore in the south-east, though the government is expanding the network, and there are now some 682 km of railway lines. The Orinoco is navigable for ocean-going ships (up to 40 ft draught) for 150 miles upstream, by large steamers for 700 miles, and by smaller vessels some 900 miles upstream.

VIETNAM
Công Hòa Xã Hôi Chu Nghĩa Viêt Nam – Socialist Republic of Vietnam

AREA – 128,066 sq. miles (331,689 sq. km). Neighbours: China (north), Laos and Cambodia (west)
POPULATION – 79,939,014 (2001 estimate). The language is Vietnamese. French, English and Khmer are also spoken
CAPITAL – Hanoi (population, 1,073,760, 1992 estimate)
MAJOR CITIES – Hai Phong (1,447,523); Ho Chi Minh City (3,924,435)
CURRENCY – Dông of 10 hào or 100 xu
NATIONAL ANTHEM – Tien Quan Ca (The Troops Are Advancing)
NATIONAL DAY – 2 September
NATIONAL FLAG – Red, with yellow five-point star in centre
LIFE EXPECTANCY (years) – male 66.9; female 71.6
POPULATION GROWTH RATE – 1.6 per cent (1999)
POPULATION DENSITY – 237 per sq. km (1999)
ILLITERACY RATE – 6.2 per cent (2002)
ENROLMENT (percentage of age group) – primary 100 per cent (1997); tertiary 7 per cent (1997)

HISTORY AND POLITICS

Vietnam became a unified state at the end of the 18th century, with the assistance of France, whose influence on the region grew. In 1899 the Indo-Chinese Union was proclaimed, uniting Vietnam with Cambodia and Laos under French rule. Vietnam was under Japanese occupation from 1940–1945; insurrection by Communist, Nationalist and Revolutionary forces led to a French withdrawal in 1954 and the division of the country into Communist North Vietnam and non-communist South Vietnam. War broke out between the two countries in 1961, which lasted until 1975. North and South Vietnam were reunified in 1976 under the name of the Socialist Republic of Vietnam. The national flag, anthem and capital of North Vietnam were adopted, and Saigon was renamed Ho Chi Minh City.

INSURGENCY

On 22 March 2002 the office of the UN High Commissioner for Refugees (UNHCR) withdrew from a programme to repatriate about 1,000 Montagnard refugees to Vietnam from camps in Cambodia, after claiming that the Vietnamese authorities were using unacceptable levels of coercion. However, this claim was rejected by the Vietnamese Foreign Ministry. On 31 March the Cambodian government announced that it would allow more than 900 refugees to be moved from the camps to the USA and on 3 June the first group of 50 refugees left the Cambodian capital Phnom Penh on their way to asylum in the USA.

POLITICAL SYSTEM

Effective power lies with the Vietnamese Communist Party (VCP), its highest executive body being the Central Committee, elected by a Party Congress on a national basis. The Politburo and the Secretariat of the Central Committee exercise the real power.

The constitution of 1992 reaffirmed Communist Party rule but also formalised free market economic reforms. A new National Assembly (*Quoc-Hoi*) was elected on 19 May 2002; the VCP holds 449 of the 500 seats. The president is elected for a five-year term by the members of the National Assembly.

HEAD OF STATE

President, Tran Duc Luong, *elected* 25 September 1997
Vice-President, Nguyen Thi Binh

POLITBURO

Secretary-General of the VCP, Nong Duc Manh
Politburo Standing Board, Le Hong Anh; Le Minh Huong; Nguyen Khoa Diem; Nguyen Minh Triet; Nguyen Phu Trong; Nguyen Tan Dzung; Nong Duc Manh; Phan Van Khai; Nguyen Van An; Pham Van Tra; Phan Dien; Tran Dinh Hoan; Truong Quang Duoc; Truong Tan Sang; Tran Duc Luong

COUNCIL OF MINISTERS *as at August 2002*

Prime Minister, Phan Van Khai
Deputy Prime Ministers, Nguyen Tan Dzung; Nguyen Manh Cam; Nguyen Cong Tan; Pham Gia Khiem
Agriculture and Rural Development, Le Huy Ngo
Aquatic Resources, Ta Quang Ngoc
Child Protection and Care, Tran Thi Thanh Thanh
Construction, Nguyen Manh Kiem
Culture and Information, Pham Quang Nghi
Education and Training, Nguyen Minh Hien
Ethnic Minorities and Mountain Regions, Hoang Duc Nghi
Finance, Nguyen Sinh Hung
Foreign Affairs, Nguyen Dy Nien
Government Personnel and Organisation, Do Quang Trung
Government Secretariat, Lai Van Cu
Governor, State Bank, Le Duc Thuy
Industry, Dang Vu Chu
Interior and Public Security, Lt.-Gen. Le Minh Huong
Justice, Nguyen Dinh Loc
Labour, War Invalids and Social Affairs, Tran Dinh Hoan
National Defence, Gen. Pham Van Tra

Physical Training and Sports, Nguyen Danh Thai
Planning and Investment, Tran Xuan Gia
Population Activities and Family Planning, Tran Thi
Trung Chien
Public Health, Do Nguyen Phuong
Science, Technology and Environment, Chu Tuan Nha
State Inspectorate, Ta Huu Thanh
Trade, Vu Khoan
Transport, Le Ngoc Hoan

EMBASSY OF THE SOCIALIST REPUBLIC OF VIETNAM
12–14 Victoria Road, London W8 5RD
Tel: 020-7937 1912
Ambassador Extraordinary and Plenipotentiary, HE
Vuong Thua Phong, apptd 1998

BRITISH EMBASSY
Central Building, 31 Hai Ba Trung, Hanoi
Tel: (00 84) (4) 936 0500
Email: behanoi@fpt.vn
Ambassador Extraordinary and Plenipotentiary, HE
Warwick Morris, apptd 2001

CONSULATE-GENERAL – Ho Chi Minh City

BRITISH COUNCIL DIRECTOR, David Cordingley
(Cultural Attaché), 40 Cat Linh Street, Dong Da,
Hanoi; Email: bchanoi@britishcouncil.org.vn. There
is a regional office in Ho Chi Minh City

DEFENCE

The Army has 1,315 main battle tanks, 1,180 armoured
personnel carriers and 300 armoured infantry fighting
vehicles. The Navy has two submarines, six frigates and 42
patrol and coastal vessels at seven principal bases. The Air
Force has 189 combat aircraft and 26 armed helicopters.
MILITARY EXPENDITURE – 3.0 per cent of GDP (2000)
MILITARY PERSONNEL – 484,000: Army 412,000, Navy
42,000, Air Force 30,000; Paramilitaries 40,000
CONSCRIPTION DURATION – Two to three years

ECONOMY

Vietnam experienced economic difficulties following the
imposition of socialist reforms in the south after 1975.
However, economic reforms, known as 'Doi Moi'
liberalisation, were instituted in 1986 and have had
significant success. The state's share of control has been
greatly reduced in most sectors, leading to significant
improvement in agricultural production, with Vietnam
becoming a major rice exporter. Industry has grown and
now contributes 30 per cent of GDP. Building materials,
chemicals, machinery and foodstuffs are the main
products.

Foreign investment has been actively encouraged and
was further boosted by Vietnam's accession to ASEAN in
August 1995, but the level of foreign investment has
begun to fall in response to the lack of economic reform
and the difficult local business environment. A stock
exchange was opened in July 2000. Oil production has
increased and large natural gas reserves have been found
offshore, though these are also claimed by China.

A bilateral trade agreement between Vietnam and the
USA was signed in July 2000. In June 2001, the World
Bank granted Vietnam a US$250 million poverty
reduction loan and the EU announced that it would
commit €2.6 billion in aid.

In 1997 imports totalled US$11,271 million and
exports US$8,900 million.

GNP – US$30,692 million (2000); US$370 per capita
(1999)

GDP – US$26,030 million (1998); US$373 per capita
(1999)
ANNUAL AVERAGE GROWTH OF GDP – 5.8 per cent
(1998)
TOTAL EXTERNAL DEBT – US$23,260 million (1999)

Trade with UK	2000	2001
Imports from UK	£93,182,000	£90,422,000
Exports to UK	385,449,000	428,097,000

YEMEN
Al-Jumhūriyya Al-Yamaniyya – Republic of Yemen

AREA – 203,850 sq. miles (527,968 sq. km). Neighbours:
Saudi Arabia (north), Oman (east)
POPULATION – 18,078,035 (2001 estimate). The
language is Arabic
CAPITAL – Sana'a' (population, 926,595, 1995)
MAJOR CITIES – ΨAden ('Adan) (400,783), the former
capital of South Yemen; Al-Hudaydah (246,068);
Ta'izz (290,107), 1993 estimates
CURRENCY – Riyal of 100 fils
NATIONAL ANTHEM – Raddidi Ayyatuha Ad-Dunya
Nashidi (Repeat, O World, My Song)
NATIONAL DAY – 22 May
NATIONAL FLAG – Horizontal bands of red, white and
black
LIFE EXPECTANCY (years) – male 60.7; female 62.9
POPULATION GROWTH RATE – 5.4 per cent (1997)
POPULATION DENSITY – 33 per sq. km (1999)
ILLITERACY RATE – 51.1 per cent (2002)
ENROLMENT (percentage of age group) – tertiary 4 per
cent (1997)
Included in the state of Yemen are the offshore islands of
Perim and Kamarān in the Red Sea, and Suqutrā in the
Gulf of Aden. The border with Saudi Arabia, except for
the north-west corner, is unclear and is being delineated
following an agreement between the two countries signed
on 12 June 2000.

HISTORY AND POLITICS

Turkish occupation of North Yemen (1872–1918) was
followed by the rule of the Hamid al-Din dynasty until a
revolution in 1962 overthrew the monarchy and the
Yemen Arab Republic was declared. The People's
Republic of South Yemen was set up in 1967 when the
British government ceded power to the National
Liberation Front, bringing to an end 129 years of British
rule in Aden and some years of protectorate status in the
hinterland. Negotiations towards merging the two states
began in 1979 and unification was proclaimed on 22 May
1990. The constitution was approved by referendum in
May 1991.

A power struggle between the former Northern and
Southern Yemen élites in mid-1993 led to civil war on 5
May 1994 between the unmerged Northern and Southern
forces. Aden was captured by victorious Northern forces
on 7 July, ending the civil war.

After the war a coalition government of the General
People's Congress and the Islamic Islah was formed and
the constitution amended. Gen. Saleh was elected
president by the House of Representatives for a five-year
term. Multiparty democracy, a free market economy and
Sharia law are enshrined in the constitution.

A general election in April 1997 was won by the ruling
General People's Congress. President Ali Abdullah Saleh
was re-elected in the first direct presidential election held

on 23 September 1999, winning 96.3 per cent of the vote. Legislative elections were due to be held on 27 April 2003.

POLITICAL SYSTEM

The 1991 constitution was amended following a referendum on 20 February 2001. The president is directly elected and serves a seven-year term which may be renewed once only. The unicameral legislature, the House of Representatives (*Majlis an-Nowab*), has 301 directly-elected members, who serve a six-year term. In addition, there is an advisory Shura Council, which is appointed by the president and has 111 members.

HEAD OF STATE

President, Field Marshal Ali Abdullah Saleh, *took office 22 May 1990, elected* 1 October 1994, *re-elected* 23 September 1999
Vice-President, Maj.-Gen. Abd Rabbah Mansur Hadi

COUNCIL OF MINISTERS *as at August 2002*

Prime Minister, Abd al-Qadir Abd al-Rahman Bajammal
Deputy Prime Minister, Finance, Alawi Salih al-Salami
Agriculture and Irrigation, Ahmad Salim al-Jabali
Awqaf (Religious Endowments) and Religious Guidance, Qasim al-A'jam
Civil Service and Social Security, Abd-al-Wahhab Rawih
Communications, Abd-al-Malik al-Mu'allimi
Construction, Housing and Urban Planning, Abdullah Husayn al-Daf'i
Culture, Abd-al-Wahhab al-Rawhani
Defence, Maj.-Gen. Abdallah Ali Ulaywah
Education, Fadl Abu-Ghanim
Electricity and Water, Yahyah al-Abyad
Expatriate Affairs, Abduh Ali Qudati
Fisheries, Ali Hasan al-Ahmadi
Foreign Affairs, Abu-Bakr Abdallah al-Qirdi
Higher Education and Scientific Research, Yahya Muhammad Abdullah al-Shu'aybi
Industry and Trade, Abd al-Rahman Muhammad Ali Uthman
Information, Husayn Dayfallah al-Awadi
Interior, Rashad al-Alimi
Justice, Al-Qadi Ahmad Aqabat
Legal and Parliamentary Affairs, Abdullah Ahmad Ghanim
Local Administration, Sadiq Amin Abu Ra's
Ministers of State, Wahibah Fari (*Human Rights*); Alawi

Hasan al-Attas (*Parliamentary and Council of Ministers' Affairs*); Maj.-Gen. Abdallah Husayn al-Bashiri (*Secretary-General of the Presidency*); Khalid al-Sharif; Muhammad Ali Yasir; Muhsin al-Yusufi
Oil and Mineral Resources, Rashid Ba-Rabba
Planning and Development, Ahmad Muhammad Sufan
Public Health and Population, Abd-al-Nasir Manibari
Social Affairs and Labour, Abd-al-Karim al-Arhabi
Technical Education and Vocational Training, Muhammad Abdallah al-Batani
Tourism and Environment, Abd-al-Malik Abd-al-Rahman al-Iryani
Transport and Marine Affairs, Capt. Sa'id Yafi'i
Youth and Sport, Abd al-Rahman Muhammad al-Akwa

EMBASSY OF THE REPUBLIC OF YEMEN
57 Cromwell Road, London SW7 2ED
Tel: 020-7584 6607
Ambassador Extraordinary and Plenipotentiary, HE Dr Mutahar Abdullah Alsaeede, apptd 2001

BRITISH EMBASSY
129 Haddah Road, PO Box 1287, Sana'ā'
Tel: (00 967) (1) 264 081/2/3/4
Ambassador Extraordinary and Plenipotentiary, HE Frances Guy, apptd 2001

BRITISH COUNCIL DIRECTOR, Adrian Chadwick, 3rd Floor, Administrative Tower, Sana'ā' Trade Centre, Algiers Street, PO Box 2157, Sana'ā';
Email: britishcouncil@britishcouncil.org.ye

DEFENCE

The Army has 910 main battle tanks, 440 armoured personnel carriers and 320 armoured infantry fighting vehicles. The Navy has 9 patrol and coastal vessels at two bases. The Air Force has 71 combat aircraft and eight attack helicopters.
MILITARY EXPENDITURE – 7.8 per cent of GDP (2000)
MILITARY PERSONNEL – 54,000: Army 49,000, Navy 1,500, Air Force 3,500, Paramilitaries 70,000
CONSCRIPTION DURATION – Two years

ECONOMY

The economy has been seriously damaged by the civil war. However, the war had little effect on oil production. An agreement was signed with the French oil company Total in September 1995 for the exploitation of liquefied natural gas over a 25-year period and the construction of a gas liquefication plant by 2000. Despite the production of oil Yemen remains one of the poorest states in the world. Tourism has been hampered by the prevalence of kidnapping. The principal imports are machinery and transport equipment, raw materials, and foodstuffs and livestock. Agriculture is the main occupation of the inhabitants. This is largely of a subsistence nature, sorghum, sesame, millet, wheat and barley being the chief crops. Exports include cotton, coffee, fruit, vegetables and hides. Imports include food and animals
  In 1998 Yemen had a trade deficit of US$701 million and current account deficit of US$228 million. In 2000 imports totalled US$2,324 million and exports US$4,079 million.
GNP – US$6,674 million (2000); US$360 per capita (1999)
GDP – US$5,985 million (1998); US$326 per capita (1999)
ANNUAL AVERAGE GROWTH OF GDP – 3.8 per cent (1999)
INFLATION RATE – 7.9 per cent (1998)
TOTAL EXTERNAL DEBT – US$4,610 million (1999)

Trade with UK	2000	2001
Imports from UK	£52,480,000	£73,484,000
Exports to UK	6,248,000	4,750,000

YUGOSLAVIA

Savezna Republika Jugoslavija – Federal Republic of Yugoslavia

AREA – 39,449 sq. miles (102,173 sq. km). Neighbours: Hungary (north), Romania and Bulgaria (east), the Former Yugoslav Republic of Macedonia and Albania (south), Bosnia-Hercegovina and Croatia (west)
POPULATION – 10,677,290 (2001 estimate): 67.6 per cent Serb and Montenegrin, 16.5 per cent Albanian, 3.2 per cent Muslim Slavs, 3.3 per cent Hungarian, with smaller numbers of Romanies, Croats, Slovaks and Bulgarians. The majority religion is Serbian Orthodox, with significant Muslim and small Roman Catholic minorities. The main language is Serbian (74 per cent), with Albanian and Hungarian minorities. Serbian is a South Slav language written in the Cyrillic script
CAPITAL – Belgrade (population, 1,338,856, 1997 estimate)
MAJOR CITIES – Kragujevac (181,061); Niš (250,104); Novi Sad (178,896); Podgorica (162,172), the capital of Montenegro; Priština (241,565); Subotica (146,075), 1997 estimates
CURRENCY – New dinar of 100 paras
NATIONAL ANTHEM – Hej, Sloveni, Jošte Živi Reč Naših Dedova (Oh! Slavs, Our Ancestors' Words Still Live)
NATIONAL DAY – 27 April
NATIONAL FLAG – Three horizontal stripes of blue, white, red
LIFE EXPECTANCY (years) – male 70.9; female 75.6
POPULATION GROWTH RATE – 0.2 per cent (1999)
POPULATION DENSITY – 104 per sq. km (1999)
MILITARY EXPENDITURE – 10.0 per cent of GDP (2000)
MILITARY PERSONNEL – 105,500: Army 79,000, Navy 7,000, Air Force 19,500; Paramilitaries 93,000
CONSCRIPTION DURATION – 12-15 months
ENROLMENT (percentage of age group) – primary 69 per cent (1997); secondary 62 per cent (1997); tertiary 22 per cent (1997)

Montenegro and southern Serbia are extremely mountainous, while the north is dominated by the low-lying plains of the Danube. The major rivers are: the Danube, which flows through the north of Serbia to Romania and Bulgaria; the Sava, which flows eastwards from Bosnia to join the Danube at Belgrade; the Drina, which flows along most of the Serbian–Bosnian border to join the Sava; and the Morava, which flows from the extreme south to join the Danube in the north.

HISTORY AND POLITICS

Serbia emerged from the rule of the Byzantine Empire in the 13th century to form a large and prosperous state in the Balkans. Defeat by the Turks in 1389 led to almost 500 years of Turkish rule. After gaining autonomy within the Ottoman Empire in 1815, Serbia became fully independent in 1878 and a kingdom in 1881. Montenegro was part of the Serbian state before it was conquered by the Turks in the fifteenth century; it became independent in 1878. At the end of the First World War Serbia and Montenegro joined with the former Austro-Hungarian provinces of Slovenia, Croatia and Bosnia-Hercegovina to form the 'Kingdom of Serbs, Croats and Slovenes' which was renamed Yugoslavia in 1929. Yugoslavia was occupied by Axis forces in 1941 and reformed as a Communist federal republic under the presidency of partisan leader Josip Tito in 1945.

Tito died in 1980 and was succeeded by a rotating federal presidency which was unable to contain the growing nationalist movements. Efforts by the six republican presidents to negotiate a new federal or confederal structure for the country failed in 1991. On 25 June 1991 Slovenia and Croatia declared their independence from Yugoslavia.

In Croatia the ethnic Serb minority refused to accept Croatia's independence and fighting began in July 1991 between Croat Defence Forces and Serbian guerrillas backed by the Yugoslav National Army (JNA). By September 1991 this had escalated into war between Croatia and Yugoslavia. The war in Croatia continued until January 1992 when the EU and the UN were able to bring about a cease-fire (*see* Croatia).

Macedonia declared its independence on 18 September 1991.

Bosnia-Hercegovina declared its independence on 1 March 1992. Independence was supported by the Bosniacs (Muslims) and Croats but rejected by the ethnic Serbs and fighting between Bosniacs and Serbs broke out in March 1992. The JNA intervened against the Bosniacs but in May 1992 withdrew to Serbia and Montenegro (*see* Bosnia-Hercegovina). On 27 April 1992 the two remaining republics of the former Socialist Federal Republic of Yugoslavia, Serbia and Montenegro, announced the formation of a new Yugoslav federation, which they invited Serbs in Croatia and Bosnia-Hercegovina to join.

Legislative elections were held in Montenegro in May 1998 and were won by reformists led by President Djukanović.

Kosovo has been under UN administration since June 1999.

Presidential and legislative elections were held on 24 September 2000, but were largely boycotted in Montenegro after its government had urged the population not to vote. The Democratic Opposition of Serbia (DOS) became the largest party in both chambers of parliament. In the presidential election, the Federal Election Commission announced that President Slobodan Milošević of the Socialist Party of Serbia (SPS), had obtained 40.23 per cent of votes and his rival, Vojislav Koštunica of the DPS, had won 48.22 per cent, just short of the 50 per cent necessary to win without a second

round, although an independent monitoring organisation had given Koštunica a clear majority. Koštunica denounced the official result as fraudulent and refused to participate in the second round, scheduled for 8 October. Tension grew and on 28 September, the Serb Orthodox Church declared that Koštunica was the elected president and the Yugoslav Army guaranteed that it would not involve itself in politics. The next day, the Serbian Radical Party (SRP), one of the coalition partners in the Milošević regime, declared its support for Koštunica. A general strike began on 2 October. On 5 October, opposition supporters stormed the parliament building and took over the television station and the state news agency and by evening the media organisations were declaring Koštunica to be the elected president. Milošević accepted his defeat on 6 October and Koštunica was sworn in the following day. Following a period of uncertainty, the DOS and the SPS agreed to dissolve parliament and form a transitional government until a fresh election could be held for the Serbian Parliament. In the federal parliament, the DOS, who had won 138 seats, formed a coalition government with the Socialist People's Party of Montenegro (SPP), who had 28 seats.

An election to the Serbian Parliament was held on 23 December 2000, in which the DOS won an overwhelming victory, obtaining 176 of the 250 seats. The SPS won 37, the SRP won 23 and the Party of Serbian Unity won 14.

In Montenegro, which had steadily removed itself from the influence of Serbia, the government coalition collapsed on 29 December 2000. A legislative election was held on 22 April 2001, in which the pro-independence Victory Belongs to Montenegro (VBM) alliance, led by the Democratic Party of Socialists (DPS), won 36 of the 77 seats. The pro-Yugoslav Together for Yugoslavia alliance, led by the SPP, won 33 seats. The VBM alliance formed a coalition government with the pro-independence Liberal League, which had six seats. Former President Slobodan Milošević was arrested on 1 April 2001 and on 28 June, he was handed over to the UN International Criminal Tribunal for the Former Yugoslavia, which in May 1999 had indicted him on charges of crimes against humanity. A legal challenge was begun on 23 August 2001 by lawyers acting for Milošević, against the UN International Criminal Tribunal for the Former Yugoslavia in a Dutch court. On 23 November, Milošević was charged with genocide for the atrocities committed by forces under his command against Bosniacs and Croats during the Bosnian war. On 9 October fresh charges were imposed upon Milošević for 'ethnic cleansing' in Croatia in 1991–92, to which he refused to plead. The trial opened in The Hague in the Netherlands on 13 February 2002.

On 14 March 2002 the leaders of Serbia, Montenegro and the Federal Republic of Yugoslavia signed an agreement to maintain a joint state under the name of Serbia and Montenegro. Yugoslav president Vojislav Koštunica would remain president of the joint state and a new constitution would be drafted with legislative elections expected to take place before the end of 2002.

INSURGENCIES

The province of Kosovo in the south of Serbia is more than 90 per cent ethnically Albanian. In 1989, Slobodan Milošević, then leader of the League of Communists of Serbia, revoked Kosovo's autonomous status, resulting in the progressive exclusion of the Albanian majority from public life. Following clashes between ethnic Albanians and Serbian police in February and March 1998, the Serbian military attacked civilians in the province on the pretext of eliminating support for the Kosovo Liberation

Army (KLA), an ethnic Albanian organisation fighting for independence for the province. The international community condemned the brutality of the Serbian forces and a UN arms embargo was imposed on Yugoslavia, but the situation deteriorated with clashes between the KLA and security forces becoming commonplace. International organisations detailed widespread human rights abuses by the security forces; NATO and Russia ordered both sides to attend a peace conference in Paris on 6 February 1999, which was unsuccessful. Tens of thousands of Kosovar Albanians fled when Yugoslav forces began to attack Kosovar villages. Following warnings to the Yugoslav authorities, NATO commenced air strikes against military targets in Yugoslavia on 24 March 1999. Over eight hundred thousand people fled or were forced to leave their homes and sought refuge in Albania, Macedonia or Montenegro, which, although part of the Yugoslav Federation, had refused to become involved in the fighting; more than five hundred thousand people were displaced within Kosovo. NATO intensified its bombing campaign, now targeting industrial, communications and power links.

On 27 May 1999, the UN War Crimes Tribunal indicted President Milošević of Yugoslavia, President Milutinović of Serbia, and other senior Yugoslav officials for crimes against humanity.

On 3 June President Milošević accepted a peace plan agreed by NATO and Russia and on 10 June Yugoslav forces began to withdraw; NATO air operations were immediately suspended and NATO and Russian forces entered Kosovo the following day. By 20 June all Yugoslav forces had been withdrawn from Kosovo and the Kosovar refugees had begun to return. Since the Yugoslav withdrawal, Kosovo has been under the administration of the UN's Interim Administration Mission in Kosovo (UNMIK), who have established the Kosovo Transitional Council composed of four UN and four Kosovar representatives. The NATO-led Kosovo Force (KFOR) has established five command sectors, administered by UK, US, French, German and Italian troops respectively. In addition, parts of the French, German and US sectors are patrolled by Russian troops. KFOR has facilitated the disarming of the KLA and the return of over 850,000 Kosovar Albanian refugees, but at least 200,000 Kosovar Serbs have fled, fearing reprisal attacks, which have frequently occurred.

In May 2001, UNMIK announced that a legislative assembly for Kosovo would be established having powers over health, education, environment and the economy, but with UNMIK retaining final authority. Elections to the assembly were held on 17 November 2001 and won by the Democratic league of Kosovo (LDK) who gained 47 of the 120 seats. A power-sharing government was agreed on 28 February 2002 with Bajram Rexhepi of the Democratic Party of Kosovo (PDK) on its head. Ibrahim Rugova of the LDK was elected unopposed as president on 4 March.

Armed fighters belonging to the ethnic Albanian Liberation Army of Preševo, Medvedja and Bujanovac (UCPMB) launched attacks on Serbs in Albanian populated areas of southern Serbia in November 2000. The rebels wanted to annex these areas into Kosovo. A cease-fire was negotiated by KFOR on 27 November, but it collapsed on 1 December. A further cease-fire was signed on 12 March 2001 after NATO agreed to permit Yugoslav forces to enter the demilitarised buffer zone which had been established on the Serbian side of the border with Kosovo in 1999.

POLITICAL SYSTEM

The Federal Republic has a bicameral parliament with a 138-seat (108 Serbian, 30 Montenegrin) lower house, the Chamber of Citizens, and a 40-seat (20 Serbian, 20 Montenegrin) upper house, the Chamber of Republics. Both houses are directly elected and serve four-year terms. Executive power is vested in a federal president and government.

HEAD OF STATE
Federal President, Vojislav Koštunica, *elected* 24 September 2000

FEDERAL GOVERNMENT *as at August 2002*

Prime Minister, Dragiša Pešić (SNP)
Deputy Prime Minister, Foreign Trade Relations, Miroljub Labus (DOS)
Defence, Velimir Radojević
Economy and Internal Trade, Petar Trojanović
Finance (acting), Veroljub Dugalić
Foreign Affairs, Goran Svilanović (DOS)
Interior, Zoran Zivković (DOS)
Justice, Savo Marković
National and Ethnic Communities, Rasim Ljajić (DOS)
Transport and Telecommunications, Bozidar Milović
DOS Democratic Opposition of Serbia; SNP Montenegrin Socialist National Party

MONTENEGRO

AREA – 5,331 sq. miles (13,812 sq. km)
POPULATION – 615,000: 62 per cent Montenegrin, 14.5 per cent Bosniac, 6.5 per cent Albanian and 3 per cent Serb
CAPITAL – Podgorica (population, 117,875, 1991)

The most recent presidential election was won by Milo Djukanović, a reformist candidate favouring greater independence for the province. Elections to the 85-seat Republican Assembly held on 22 April 2001 were won by the Victory Belongs to Montenegro coalition who gained 36 seats with Together for Yugoslavia winning 36 seats. A coalition government was approved by parliament on 2 July.

President, Milo Djukanović , *elected* 19 October 1997
Prime Minister, Filip Vujanović

BRITISH COUNCIL, British Council Information Centre, Brace Zlaticanina 10, 81000 Podgorica

SERBIA

AREA – 34,175 sq. miles (88,538 sq. km)
POPULATION – 9,300,000, of whom 66 per cent are Serbs
CAPITAL – Belgrade (population, 1,338,856, 1997 estimate)

Serbia includes the provinces of Kosovo (population 1.6 million), of great historic importance to Serbs, and Vojvodina (population 2 million); the autonomy of both was ended in September 1990. Vojvodina, with its capital at Novi Sad, has a large Hungarian minority (21 per cent). Kosovo, with its capital at Priština, is predominantly Albanian (90 per cent). Following the conflict in Kosovo, more than 200,000 people have been left homeless and entire villages have been destroyed.
The reformist Democratic Opposition of Serbia (DOS) won the elections to the National Assembly held on 24 December 2000, gaining 176 of the 250 seats. Presidential elections were expected to be held on 29 September 2002,

paving the way for President Milan Milutinović to be extradited to the International Criminal Tribunal for the Former Yugoslavia in the Hague to face charges of war crimes.

President, Milan Milutinović
Prime Minister, Zoran Djindjić

EMBASSY OF THE FEDERAL REPUBLIC OF YUGOSLAVIA
28 Belgrave Square, London SW1X 8QB.
Tel: 020-7235 9049
Ambassador Extraordinary and Plenipotentiary, HE Dr Vladeta Janković, apptd 2001

BRITISH EMBASSY
Resavska 46, YU-1100 Belgrade
Tel: (00) (381) (11) 645055
Ambassador Extraordinary and Plenipotentiary, HE Charles Crawford, CMG, apptd 2000

BRITISH COUNCIL DIRECTOR, Chris Gibson, Terazije 8/1, POB 248, YU-11001 Belgrade

ECONOMY

Since 1991 the economy has been devastated by the wars in Croatia and Bosnia-Hercegovina, by the UN economic sanctions and trade embargo, and because of the lack of free-market reforms. Only the country's agricultural self-sufficiency has kept it afloat. Industrial production remains extremely low and there is high unemployment, estimated to be around 30 per cent in 2000. Economic sanctions and NATO bombing in 1999 further damaged the already fragile economy. GDP in 2000 was roughly 40 per cent of 1989 levels .
GDP – US$11,956 million (1998); US$1,361 per capita (1999)
ANNUAL AVERAGE GROWTH OF GDP – 2.6 per cent (1998)
TOTAL EXTERNAL DEBT – US$12,949 million (1999)

Trade with UK	2000	2001
Imports from UK	£32,524,000	£51,150,000
Exports to UK	14,821,000	23,955,000

ZAMBIA
Republic of Zambia

AREA – 290,587 sq. miles (752,618 sq. km). Neighbours: Democratic Republic of Congo and Tanzania (north), Malawi (east), Mozambique, Zimbabwe and Namibia (south), Angola (west)
POPULATION – 9,770,199 (2001 estimate). English is the official language; other languages spoken include Bemba, Kaonda, Lozi, Lunda, Luvale, Nyanja and Tonga
CAPITAL – Lusaka (population, 982,362, 1990)
MAJOR CITIES – Chingola (186,769); Kabwe (166,519); Kitwe (348,571); Luanshya (147,747); Mufulira (175,025); Ndola (376,311)
CURRENCY – Kwacha (K) of 100 ngwee
NATIONAL ANTHEM – Stand And Sing Of Zambia, Proud And Free
NATIONAL DAY – 24 October (Independence Day)
NATIONAL FLAG – Green with three small vertical stripes, red, black and orange (next fly); eagle device on green above stripes
LIFE EXPECTANCY (years) – male 42.6; female 41.7
POPULATION GROWTH RATE – 3.3 per cent (1999)

POPULATION DENSITY – 14 per sq. km (1999)
MILITARY EXPENDITURE – 1.8 per cent of GDP (2000)
MILITARY PERSONNEL – 21,600: Army 20,000, Air Force 1,600; Paramilitaries 1,400
ILLITERACY RATE – 20.2 per cent (2002)
ENROLMENT (percentage of age group) – primary 89 per cent (1997); secondary 27 per cent (1997); tertiary 3 per cent (1997)

Zambia lies on the plateau of Central Africa. With the exception of the valleys of the Zambezi, the Luapula, the Kafue and the Luangwa rivers, and the Luano valley, elevations vary from 3,000 to 5,000 feet above sea level, but in the north-east the plateau rises to occasional altitudes of over 6,000 feet.

HISTORY AND POLITICS

Northern Rhodesia came under British rule in 1889. It achieved internal self-government when the Federation of Rhodesia and Nyasaland was dissolved in 1963 and became an independent republic within the Commonwealth on 24 October 1964 under the name of Zambia.

Zambia was a one-party state (the United National Independence Party) from 1973 until 1990, when pressure from opposition groups led to a new constitution (August 1991) and multiparty legislative and presidential elections in October 1991. The Movement for Multiparty Democracy (MMD) won 125 of the 150 seats in parliament, and the MMD candidate Frederick Chiluba defeated Kenneth Kaunda, who had ruled since independence, in the presidential election; Kaunda was later stripped of his Zambian citizenship.

Presidential elections held on 27 December 2001 were won by MMD candidate Levy Mwanawasa with 28.7 per cent of the vote. In simultaneous legislative elections the MMD won 69 of the 150 elected seats in the National Assembly; the United Party for National development (UPND) won 49 seats; and other parties and independents won 32 seats. A new Cabinet composed of the MMD was appointed on 7 January 2002.

HEAD OF STATE

President, Defence, Levy Mwanawasa, *elected* 27 December 2001, *sworn in* 2 January 2002
Vice-President, Enoch Kavindele

CABINET *as at August 2002*

Agriculture, Food and Fisheries, In the Office of the Vice-President, Mundia Sikatana
Commerce, Trade and Industry, Bates Namuyamba
Communications and Transport, Augustine Mwape
Community Development and Social Services, Norman Chibamba
Education, Andrew Mulenga
Energy and Water Development, Lembalemba Kaunda
Finance and Economic Development, Emmanuel Kasonde
Foreign Affairs, Kalombo Mwansa
Health, vacant
Home Affairs, Luckson Mapushi
Information and Broadcasting, Vernon Mwaanga
Labour and Social Security, Mutale Nalumango
Lands, Judith Kapingipanga
Legal Affairs, George Kunda
Local Government and Housing, Michael Mabenga
Mines and Mineral Development, Davison Mulela
Science and Technology, Abel Chambeshi
Sports and Youth Development, Levison Mumba
Tourism, Environment and Natural Resources, Malina Nsingo
Without Portfolio, vacant
Works and Supply, Ludwig Sondasha

HIGH COMMISSION FOR THE REPUBLIC OF ZAMBIA
2 Palace Gate, London W8 5NG
Tel: 020-7589 6655
High Commissioner, HE Silumelume Mubukwanu, apptd 2001

BRITISH HIGH COMMISSION
5210 Independence Avenue (PO Box 50050), 15101 Ridgeway, Lusaka. Tel: (00 260) (1) 251133
Email: brithc@zamnet.zm
High Commissioner, HE Thomas Young, apptd 1997

BRITISH COUNCIL DIRECTOR, Brendan McSharry, Heroes Place, Cairo Road (PO Box 34571), Lusaka

Email: info@britishcouncil.org.zm

ECONOMY

In 1991, the MMD government began the transition from a state-controlled economy to a free market system. Privatisation has been encouraged, foreign exchange controls have been removed and the Kwacha has been floated. Price subsidies and tariffs have been lowered or abolished, but increased imports have affected manufacturing. Principal agricultural products are maize, sugar, groundnuts, cotton, livestock, vegetables and tobacco. The principal exports are copper and cobalt. The principal imports are industrial goods, machinery and transport equipment, fuel and foodstuffs.

In 1997 imports totalled US$819 million and exports US$915 million.
GNP – US$3,004 million (2000); US$330 per capita (1999)
GDP – US$3,627 million (1998); US$323 per capita (1999)
ANNUAL AVERAGE GROWTH OF GDP – -2.0 per cent (1998)
INFLATION RATE – 24.8 per cent (1997)
TOTAL EXTERNAL DEBT – US$5,853 million (1999)

Trade with UK	2000	2001
Imports from UK	£28,353,000	£23,854,000
Exports to UK	12,649,000	11,718,000

ZIMBABWE
Republic of Zimbabwe

AREA – 50,872 sq. miles (390,757 sq. km). Neighbours: Zambia (north), Mozambique (east), South Africa (south), Botswana and Namibia (west)
POPULATION – 1,365,366 (2001 estimate); 10,400,000 (1992 census): 77 per cent Shona, 17 per cent Ndebele, 1.4 per cent Europeans. The official language is English, with Shona the largest indigenous language group
CAPITAL – Harare (population, 1,189,103, 1992)
MAJOR CITIES – Bulawayo (621,742), the largest town in Matabeleland; Chitungwiza (274,912)
CURRENCY – Zimbabwe dollar (Z$) of 100 cents
NATIONAL ANTHEM – Ngaikomberarwe Nyika Ye Zimbabwe (Blessed Be The Country Of Zimbabwe)
NATIONAL DAY – 8 April (Independence Day)
NATIONAL FLAG – Seven horizontal stripes of green, yellow, red, black, red, yellow, green; a white, black-bordered, triangle based on the hoist containing the national emblem
LIFE EXPECTANCY (years) – male 43.3; female 42.4
POPULATION GROWTH RATE – 3.2 per cent (1999)
POPULATION DENSITY – 33 per sq. km (1999)
MILITARY EXPENDITURE – 6.1 per cent of GDP (2000)
MILITARY PERSONNEL – 39,000: Army 35,000, Air Force 4,000; Paramilitaries 21,800

HISTORY AND POLITICS

European colonisation of Zimbabwe began in 1890 when settlers forcibly acquired Shona lands, followed by the seizure of Ndebele lands in 1893. It became a self-governing colony under the name of Southern Rhodesia in 1923. A unilateral declaration of independence on 11 November 1965, which resulted in UN sanctions against the country, was finally terminated on 12 December 1979. Following elections in February 1980 the country became independent on 18 April 1980 as the Republic of Zimbabwe, a member of the British Commonwealth.

The independence constitution was amended in 1987, making the presidency an executive post. The president is popularly elected for a six-year term, appoints the Cabinet and can veto parliamentary bills. The unicameral legislature, the House of Assembly, has 150 members: 120 elected, ten traditional chiefs and 20 others appointed by the president.

The most recent general election was held on 24–25 June 2000. The Zimbabwe African National Union – Patriotic Front (ZANU-PF) won 62 of the 120 elective seats and the Movement for Democratic Change (MDC), a new opposition grouping formed by various civic groups and the Zimbabwe Congress of Trade Unions, won 57 seats. President Mugabe was re-elected for a six-year term in elections held on 9–11 March 2002 with 56.2 per cent of the vote. Morgan Tsvangirai of the MDC gained 42.0 per cent of the vote. However, the integrity of the election was called into question by Tsvangirai who claimed that thousands of opposition supporters had been disenfranchised.

The country is divided into eight provinces: Manicaland, Masvingo, Matabeleland North, Matabeleland South, Midlands, Mashonaland West, Mashonaland Central and Mashonaland East.

LAND REFORM

Following independence, about 30 per cent of agricultural land remained in the possession of around 4,000 white farmers. They employed nearly 300,000 workers and accounted for about 70 per cent of the country's agricultural production and about a third of foreign currency earnings. A further 37 per cent of agricultural land was in the possession of 1.2 million black peasant farmers, mainly engaged in subsistence farming. Most of this land was located in less fertile, drought-prone regions. Land reform was designed to achieve a more equitable distribution of land. By 1997 the state had acquired 3.4 million hectares of land, but either left it fallow or distributed it to members of the government. The 1990 amendments to the 1980 constitution had made provision for the compulsory acquisition of farms, with compensation to be paid to the owners.

The occupation of white-owned farms by protestors, led by former veterans of the war against the white minority regime, began in February 2000. On 17 March 2000 the Supreme Court ordered the police to evict black war veterans who had occupied around 600 white-owned farms. The police ignored the judgement with the support of President Mugabe. On 6 April, the House of Assembly approved the Land Acquisition Act, which amended the constitution to enable the government to take over white-owned farms without compensation and redistribute them to landless blacks. A meeting of representatives of the British and Zimbabwean governments on 27 April 2000 failed to resolve the crisis and on 3 May the UK imposed an embargo on weapons sales to Zimbabwe, making financial support for land reform dependent on an end to the farm occupations.

The Supreme Court ruled on 10 November 2000 that the compulsory land seizures were illegal and ordered the removal of squatters. The government rejected the ruling and accelerated the land acquisition programme. On 21 December, the Supreme Court directed the President to produce a land distribution programme within six months and to protect white farmers whose land had been occupied by squatters. Following a Commonwealth meeting on 6 September 2001, Zimbabwe agreed to end the illegal land occupations and restore the rule of law in return for international assistance. On 2 October, the Supreme Court, dominated by recent appointees of President Mugabe, issued an interim order reversing all previous rulings in order to allow the government to proceed with its fast-track land reform programme. On 9 November, the government issued a decree that any farm given a 'notice of acquisition' would become state property immediately. The government would then be entitled to move settlers onto the land and the owner would be banned from conducting any farming on it. Mugabe ordered some 2,900 white farmers, whose farms

had been earmarked to be seized and given to blacks under the government's 'fast-track land reform' programme, to cease work as of 25 June 2002.

HEAD OF STATE

Executive President, C.-in-C. of the Defence Forces, Robert Gabriel Mugabe, *elected* 30 December 1987, *re-elected* March 1990, March 1996, 11 March 2002
Vice-Presidents, Simon Vengesai Muzenda; Joseph Msika

CABINET *as at August 2002*

The President
Defence, Sidney Tigere Sekeramayi
Education, Sport and Culture, Aeneas Chigwedere
Energy and Power Development, Amos Midzi
Environment and Tourism, Francis Nhema
Finance and Economic Development, Herbert Murerwa
Foreign Affairs, Stanislaus Mudenge
Health and Child Welfare, David Parirenyatwa
Higher Education and Technology, Swithun Mombeshoro
Home Affairs, Kembo Mohadi
Industry and International Trade, Samuel Mumbengegwi
Information and Publicity, Jonathan Moyo
Justice, Legal and Parliamentary Affairs, Patrick Chinamasa
Lands, Agriculture and Resettlement, Joseph Made
Local Government, Public Works and National Housing, Ignatius Chombo
Mines and Mining Development, Edward Chindori Chininga
National Security, Nicholas Goche
Public Service, Labour and Social Welfare, July Moyo
Rural Resources and Water Development, Joyce Mujuru
Small and Medium Enterprise Development, Sithembiso Nyoni
Special Affairs in the President's Office, John Nkomo
Transport and Communications, Witness Mangwende
Youth Development, Gender, Employment Creation, Elliot Manyika
HIGH COMMISSION OF THE REPUBLIC OF ZIMBABWE
Zimbabwe House, 429 Strand, London WC2R 0JR
Tel: 020-7836 7755
High Commissioner, HE Simbarashe Simbanenduku Mumbengegwi, apptd 1999

BRITISH HIGH COMMISSION
Corner House, Samora Machel Avenue/Leopold Takawira Street (PO Box 4490), Harare
Tel: (00 263) (4) 772990/774700
High Commissioner, HE Brian Donnelly, CMG, apptd 2001

BRITISH COUNCIL DIRECTOR, Dr Marcus Milton, Corner House, Samora Machel Avenue, PO Box 664, Harare
Email: general.enquiries@britishcouncil.org.zw.

ECONOMY

The economy remains highly regulated and weak, inflation and unemployment remain high and rises in the prices of basic commodities and fuel have resulted in widespread strike action and protests. Agriculture accounted for 28 per cent of GDP in 1998 and two-thirds of the workforce are engaged in agriculture, but the activities of squatters and the government land acquisition campaign have had a dramatic effect on productivity at commercial farms, preventing the planting of many crops. Tobacco remains the most important crop in terms of export (Zimbabwe is the largest exporter in the world), and maize the most important for domestic consumption. Other crops include wheat, cotton, sugar, horticultural products, fruit and vegetables.

The manufacturing sector is very dependent on the agricultural sector for raw materials and on imports e.g. fuel oil, steel products and chemicals, as well as heavy machinery and items of transport. The mining sector, although contributing a relatively small portion to GDP, is important to the economy as a foreign exchange earner. Almost all mineral production is exported. Gold is the most important product; others are asbestos, diamonds, silver, nickel, copper, platinum, chrome ore, tin, iron ore and cobalt. There is a successful ferro-chrome industry and a substantial steel works which has been heavily subsidised by government.

The budget for 2001 aimed to reduce the budget deficit though drastic cuts in defence, education and health spending, but increased spending on land resettlement. Fuel prices were raised in November 2000 by 14.6 per cent. The main trading partners are South Africa and the UK.

In 1996 imports totalled US$2,803 million and exports US$2,406 million.
GNP – US$5,801million (2000); US$530 per capita (1999)
GDP – US$6,232 million (1998); US$436 per capita (1999)
ANNUAL AVERAGE GROWTH OF GDP – 1.6 per cent (1999)
INFLATION RATE – 58.5 per cent (1999)
TOTAL EXTERNAL DEBT – US$4,566 million (1999)

Trade with UK	2000	2001
Imports from UK	£42,782,000	£36,172,000
Exports to UK	99,873,000	91,419,000

EDUCATION

Education is compulsory, and the language of instruction is English. Over 80 per cent of schools are government-aided. There are four universities; the University of Zimbabwe was founded in 1955.
ILLITERACY RATE – 10.0 per cent (2002)
ENROLMENT (percentage of age group) – tertiary 7 per cent (1997)

UK Overseas Territories

ANGUILLA

AREA – 37 sq. miles (96 sq. km)
POPULATION – 12,394 (1998 estimate)
CAPITAL – The Valley (population, 2,400, 1994)
CURRENCY – East Caribbean dollar (EC$) of 100 cents
FLAG – British blue ensign with the coat of arms and three dolphins in the fly
POPULATION GROWTH RATE – 6.7 per cent (1999)
POPULATION DENSITY – 134 per sq. km (1999)
ILLITERACY RATE – 4.6 per cent

Anguilla is a flat coralline island in the Caribbean, the most northerly of the Leeward islands, about 16 miles in length and three and a half miles in breadth at its widest point. The island is covered with low scrub and fringed with white coral-sand beaches. The climate is pleasant, with temperatures in the range of 24-30°C throughout the year.

HISTORY AND POLITICS

Anguilla has been a British colony since 1650. For much of its history it was linked administratively with St Kitts, but three months after the Associated State of Saint Christopher (St Kitts)-Nevis-Anguilla came into being in 1967, the Anguillans repudiated government from St Kitts. A Commissioner was installed in 1969 and in 1976 Anguilla was given a new status and separate constitution. Final separation from St Kitts and Nevis was effected on 19 December 1980 and Anguilla reverted to a British dependency. A new constitution was introduced in 1982, providing for a Governor, an Executive Council comprising four elected Ministers and two ex-officio members (the Attorney-General and Deputy Governor), and a 12-member legislative House of Assembly, consisting of seven elected members, two nominated members, two ex-officio members (the Attorney-General and Deputy Governor) and presided over by a Speaker. The most recent general election was held in March 2000.

Governor, HE Peter Johnson, apptd 2000
Deputy Governor, Roger Cousins, OBE, apptd 1997

EXECUTIVE COUNCIL *as at June 2002*

Chairman of the Executive Council, The Governor *Chief Minister*, Osbourne Fleming
Attorney-General, Ronald Scipio
Communications, Public Utilities and Works,
　Kenneth Harrigan
Finance, Victor Banks
Social Services, Eric Reid
Member of the Executive Council,
　The Deputy Governor

ECONOMY

Low rainfall limits agricultural output and export earnings are mainly from sales of fish and lobsters. Tourism has developed rapidly in recent years and accounts for most of the island's economic activity. In 1998 there were 43,874 tourists and a further 69,922 day visitors.

GDP – US$95 million (1998) US$11,678 per capita (1998)
ANNUAL AVERAGE GROWTH OF GDP – 4.1 per cent (1998);

TRADE WITH UK	2000	2001
Imports from UK	£2,984,000	£1,174,000
Exports to UK	17,000	73,000

BERMUDA

AREA – 20 sq. miles (53 sq. km)
POPULATION – 60,000 (1994 UN estimate)
CAPITAL – ψHamilton (population, 2,277, 1994)
CURRENCY – Bermuda dollar of 100 cents
FLAG – British red ensign with the shield of arms in the fly
LIFE EXPECTANCY (years) – male 71.1; female 77.8
POPULATION GROWTH RATE – 1.7 per cent (1999)
POPULATION DENSITY – 1,208 per sq. km (1999)
GDP – US$2,457 million (1998); US$40,664 per capita (1999)

The Bermudas, or Somers Islands, are a cluster of about 100 small islands (about 20 of which are inhabited) situated in the west of the Atlantic Ocean, the nearest point of the mainland being Cape Hatteras in North Carolina, about 570 miles distant.

HISTORY AND POLITICS

The colony derives its name from Juan Bermudez, a Spaniard, who sighted it before 1515. No settlement was made until 1609 when Sir George Somers, who was shipwrecked there on his way to Virginia, colonised the islands.

Internal self-government was introduced in 1968. There is a Senate of 11 members and an elected House of Assembly of 40 members. The Governor retains responsibility for external affairs, defence, internal security and the police, although administrative matters for the police service have been delegated to the Minister of Labour, Home Affairs and Public Safety. Independence from the UK was rejected in a referendum in August 1995.

The last general election was held on 9 November 1998. The Progressive Labour Party won 26 of the 40 seats.

Governor and Commander-in-Chief, HE Sir John Vereker, KCB, *apptd* 2002 1997
Deputy Governor, Tim Gurney

CABINET *as at June 2002*

Premier, Jennifer Smith
Deputy Premier, Minister of Finance, C. Eugene Cox
Attorney-General, Dame Lois Browne-Evans
Community Affairs and Sport,
　K. H. Randolph Horton
Education and Development, Paula A. Cox
Environment, Dennis P. Lister
Health and Family Services, Nelson Bascome, Jr
Labour, Home Affairs and Public Safety, Terry E. Lister

Telecommunications and E-Commerce, M. D. Renee Webb
Tourism, David H. Allen
Transport, Ewart Brown
Without Portfolio, David A. Burch
Works and Engineering, Alex Scott

ECONOMY

The islands' economic structure is based on tourism and international company business, attracted by the low level of taxation and sophisticated telecommunications system. In 1998 a total of 557,868 visitors arrived by air and cruise ship.

Locally manufactured concentrates, perfumes, cut flowers and pharmaceuticals are the islands' leading exports. Little food is produced except vegetables and fish, other foodstuffs being imported.

TRADE WITH UK	2000	2001
Imports from UK	£325,861,000	£33,952,000
Exports to UK	1,766,000	45,326,000

COMMUNICATIONS

One daily and two weekly newspapers are published in Bermuda. Three commercial companies operate radio and television services, including a cable-television system. The Bermuda Telephone Company, TeleBermuda and Cable and Wireless provide telecommunications links to more than 140 countries.

EDUCATION

Free elementary education was introduced in 1949. Free secondary education was introduced in 1965 for those children in the aided and maintained schools who were below the upper limit of the statutory school age of 18.

THE BRITISH ANTARCTIC TERRITORY

AREA – 660,000 sq. miles (1,709,340 sq. km.)
POPULATION – No permanent population
FLAG – British white ensign, without the cross of St George, with the coat of arms of the territory in the fly

The British Antarctic Territory was designated in 1962 and consists of the areas south of 60°S. latitude and bounded by longitudes 20°W. and 80°W. The territory includes the South Orkney Islands, the South Shetland Islands, the mountainous Antarctic Peninsula (highest point Mount Jackson, 10,443 ft above sea level) and all adjacent islands, and the land mass extending to the South Pole. The territory has no indigenous inhabitants and the British population consists of the scientists and technicians at the British Antarctic Survey stations. Argentina, Brazil, Bulgaria, Chile, China, Poland, Russia, Ukraine, Uruguay and the USA also have scientific stations in the territory.

Commissioner (non-resident), Alan Edden Huckle, *apptd* 2001

THE BRITISH INDIAN OCEAN TERRITORY

AREA – 23 sq. miles (59 sq. km.)
POPULATION – No permanent population
FLAG – Divided horizontally into blue and white wavy stripes, with the Union Flag in the canton and a crowned palm-tree over all in the fly

The British Indian Ocean Territory was established by an Order in Council in 1965 and included islands formerly administered from Mauritius and the Seychelles. The islands of Farquhar, Desroches and Aldabra became part of the Seychelles when it became independent in 1976; since then the Territory has consisted of the Chagos Archipelago only. The Chagos Archipelago consists of six main groups of islands situated on the Great Chagos Bank and covering some 21,000 sq. miles (54,389 sq. km). The largest and most southerly of the Chagos Islands is Diego Garcia, a sand cay with a land area of about 17 sq. miles approximately 1,100 miles east of Mahé, used as a joint naval support facility by Britain and the USA.

The other main island groups of the archipelago, Peros Banhos (29 islands with a total land area of 4 sq. miles) and Salamon (11 islands with a total land area of 2 sq. miles) are uninhabited.

The islands' former inhabitants (the Ilois) were expelled between 1967 and 1973 to allow for the construction of the naval base, most being resettled in Mauritius. Following legal action by representatives of the Ilois, on 3 November 2000 the High Court overturned the ordinance that had required the Ilois to seek permission to visit the territory, effectively granting them the right of return.

Commissioner, Alan Edden Huckle, *apptd* 2001
Administrator, Louise Savill, *apptd* 1996

TRADE WITH UK	2000	2001
Imports from UK	£976,000	£494,000
Exports to UK	145,000	18,000

BRITISH VIRGIN ISLANDS

AREA – 58 sq. miles (151 sq. km)
POPULATION – 20,000 (2001 estimate; by island: Tortola 16,630; Virgin Gorda 3,063; Anegada 204; Jost Van Dyke 176; other islands 181)
CAPITAL – ψRoad Town (population, 3,983, 2001 estimate)
CURRENCY – US dollar (US$) (£ sterling and EC$ also circulate)
FLAG – British blue ensign with the shield of arms in the fly
POPULATION GROWTH RATE – 2.9 per cent (1999)
POPULATION DENSITY – 139 per sq. km (1999)
GDP – US$604 million (1998); US$29,795 per capita (1998)
ANNUAL AVERAGE GROWTH OF GDP – 1.3 per cent (1998)

The Virgin Islands, divided between the UK and the USA, are situated at the eastern extremity of the Greater Antilles. Those of the group which are British number 46, of which 11 are inhabited, and have a total area of about 58 sq. miles (151 sq. km). The principal islands are Tortola, the largest (area, 21 sq. miles), Virgin Gorda (8 sq. miles), Anegada (15 sq. miles) and Jost Van Dyke (3.5 sq. miles).

Apart from Anegada, which is a flat coral island, the British Virgin Islands are hilly, being an extension of the Puerto Rico and the US Virgin Islands archipelago. The highest point is Sage Mountain on Tortola which rises to a height of 1,780 feet.

HISTORY AND POLITICS

Under the 1977 constitution the Governor, appointed by the Crown, remains responsible for defence and internal security, external affairs and the civil service but in other matters acts in accordance with the advice of the Executive Council. The Executive Council consists of the Governor as Chairman, one ex-officio member (the Attorney-General), the Chief Minister and three other ministers. The Legislative Council consists of a Speaker chosen from outside the Council, one ex-officio member (the Attorney-General), and 13 elected members returned from ten electoral districts.

Governor, HE Frank Savage, CMG, OBE, LVO, *apptd* 1998
Deputy Governor, Elton Georges, OBE
Chairman of the Executive Council, The Governor
Chief Minister and Minister of Finance, Ralph O'Neal, OBE
Deputy Chief Minister, Alvin Christopher
Attorney-General, Cherno Jallow
Communications and Works, Alvin Christopher
Education and Culture, Andrew Fahie
Health and Welfare, Ethlyn Smith
Natural Resources and Labour, Julian Frazer

ECONOMY

Tourism is the main industry but the financial centre is growing steadily in importance. Other industries include a rum distillery, three stone-crushing plants and factories manufacturing concrete blocks and paint. The major export items are fresh fish, gravel, sand, fruit and vegetables; exports are largely confined to the US Virgin Islands. Chief imports are building materials, machinery, cars and beverages.

TRADE WITH UK	2000	2001
Imports from UK	£14,171,000	£7,272,000
Exports to UK	4,524,000	6,836,000

COMMUNICATIONS

The principal airport is on Beef Island, linked by bridge to Tortola, and an extended runway of 3,600 ft enables larger aircraft to call. There is a second airfield on Virgin Gorda and a third on Anegada. There are direct shipping services to the UK and the USA and fast passenger services connect the main islands by ferry.

CAYMAN ISLANDS

AREA – 100 sq. miles (262 sq. km)
POPULATION – 40,900 (2000 estimate)
CAPITAL – ΨGeorge Town (population, 20,626, 1999 census)
CURRENCY – Cayman Islands dollar (CI$) of 100 cents
FLAG – British blue ensign with the arms on a white disc in the fly
POPULATION GROWTH RATE – 4.5 per cent (1999)
POPULATION DENSITY – 150 per sq. km (1999)
GDP – US$972 million (1998); US$23,809 per capita (1999)
ANNUAL AVERAGE GROWTH RATE OF GDP – 4.5 per cent (2000)

The Cayman Islands consist of three islands, Grand Cayman, Cayman Brac, and Little Cayman. About 150 miles south of Cuba, the islands are divided from Jamaica, 180 miles to the south-east, by the Cayman Trench, the deepest part of the Caribbean. The nearest point on the US mainland is Miami in Florida, 450 miles to the north.

HISTORY AND POLITICS

The colony derives its name from the Carib word for the crocodile, 'caymanas', which appeared in the log of the first English visitor to the islands, Sir Francis Drake. Although tradition has it that the first settlers arrived in 1658, the first recorded settlers arrived in 1666–71. The first recorded permanent settlers followed the first land grant by Britain in 1734. The islands were placed under direct control of Jamaica in 1863. When Jamaica became independent in 1962, the islands opted to remain under the British Crown.

The constitution provides for a Governor, a Legislative Assembly and an Executive Council, and effectively allows a large measure of self-government. Unless there are exceptional reasons, the Governor accepts the advice of the Executive Council, which comprises three official members and five ministers elected from the 15 elected members of the Assembly. The official members also sit in the Assembly. The Governor has responsibility for the police, civil service, defence and external affairs. The Governor handed over the presidency of the Legislative Assembly to the Speaker in 1991. The normal life of the Assembly is four years; the most recent general election was held on 8 November 2000.

Governor, HE Bruce Dinwiddy, *apptd* 2002

EXECUTIVE COUNCIL *as at May 2002*
President, The Governor
Chief Secretary, Internal and External Affairs, James Ryan, MBE
Community Services, Women's Affairs, Youth and Sport, Frank McField
Education, Human Resources and Culture, Roy Bodden
Finance and Economic Development, George McCarthy, OBE
Governor's Office, Peter Smith, CBE
Health Services, District Administration and Agriculture, Gilbert McLean
Legal Affairs, Attorney General, David Ballantyne
Planning, Communications, Works and Information Technology, Linford Pierson, OBE
Tourism, Environment, Development and Commerce, McKeeva Bush, OBE

CAYMAN ISLANDS GOVERNMENT OFFICE, 6 Arlington Street, London SW1A 1RE. Tel: 020-7491 7772.
Government Representative, Jennifer Dilbert

ECONOMY

With a complete absence of direct taxation, the Cayman Islands has become successful over the past 30 years as an offshore financial centre. With representation from 61 countries, there were, at the end of 2001, 531 banks and trust companies, of which local offices were maintained by 121. Following accusations of money laundering, an agreement was signed with the USA in November 2001 to share information on bank accounts. In addition, there were 694 licensed insurance companies and 64,495 registered companies. The Cayman Islands stock exchange opened in January 1997. Tourism, with an emphasis on scuba diving, has also been developed successfully. There were 334,071 visitors by air and 1,214,757 cruise ship callers in 2001.

The Two industries support a heavy imbalance in trade resulting from the need to import most of what is consumed and used on the islands, and have created a thriving local economy. Import duty and fees from financial centre operations have provided revenue enabling the government to undertake heavy investment in education (which is provided free to all four to 16-year olds), health, and other social programmes and infrastructure.

TRADE WITH UK	2000	2001
Imports from UK	£25,013,000	£9,734,000
Exports to UK	18,234,000	3,138,000

FALKLAND ISLANDS

AREA – 4,700 sq. miles (12,173 sq. km)
POPULATION – 2,564 (2001 census)
CAPITAL – Stanley (population, 1,989, 1996 census)
CURRENCY – Falkland pound of 100 pence
FLAG – British blue ensign with the arms on a white disc in the fly
POPULATION GROWTH RATE – 14.0 per cent (2001)
URBAN POPULATION – 84.0 per cent (2001)

The Falkland Islands, the only considerable group in the South Atlantic, lie about 300 miles east of the Straits of Magellan. They consist of East Falkland (area 2,610 sq. miles; 6,759 sq. km), West Falkland (2,090 sq. miles; 5,413 sq. km) and over 700 small islands. Mount Usborne (E. Falkland), the loftiest peak, rises 2,312 feet above sea level. The islands are chiefly moorland.

HISTORY AND POLITICS

The Falklands were sighted first by Davis in 1592, and then by Hawkins in 1594; the first known landing was by Strong in 1690. A settlement was made by France in 1764; this was subsequently sold to Spain, but the latter country recognised Great Britain's title to a part at least of the group in 1771. The first British settlement was established in 1766. After Argentina declared independence from Spain, the Argentine government in 1820 proclaimed its sovereignty over the Falklands and a settlement was founded in 1826. The settlement was destroyed by the Americans in 1831. In 1833 occupation was resumed by the British for the protection of the seal-fisheries, and the islands were permanently colonised. Argentina continued to claim sovereignty over the islands (known to them as *las Islas Malvinas*), and in pursuance of this claim invaded the islands on 2 April 1982 and also occupied South Georgia. A naval and military force dispatched from Great Britain recaptured South Georgia on 25 April and after landing at San Carlos on 21 May, recaptured the islands from the Argentines, who surrendered on 14 June 1982. A British naval and military garrison of 1,265 personnel remains in the area. Under the 1985 constitution, the Governor is advised by an Executive Council consisting of three elected members of the Legislative Council and two ex-officio members, the Chief Executive and the Financial Secretary. The Legislative Council consists of eight elected members and the same two ex-officio members.

Governor and Chairman of the Executive Council,
HE Howard Pearce, *apptd* 2002
Chief Executive, Dr Michael D. Blanch

Attorney-General, David G. Lang, CBE, QC *Commander, British Forces, Falkland Islands,* Cdre R. J. Ibbotson, DSC
Financial Secretary, Derek F. Howatt

FALKLAND ISLANDS GOVERNMENT OFFICE, Falkland House, 14 Broadway, London SW1H 0BH.
Tel: 020-7222 2542.
Government Representative, Miss S. Cameron

ECONOMY

The economy was formerly based solely on agriculture, principally sheep farming with a little dairy farming for domestic requirements and crops for winter fodder. Since the establishment of an interim conservation and management fishing zone around the islands in 1987 and the consequent introduction of a licensing regime for vessels fishing within the 200-mile zone, the economy has diversified. Income from the associated fishing activities, mainly for illex squid, is now the largest source of revenue. The increase in government revenue from fishing licences has led to the establishment of a substantial health, education and welfare system. The islands are now self-financing except for defence. Chief imports are provisions, alcoholic beverages, timber, clothing and hardware. Tourism is a small but expanding industry.

In 1996, the Falkland Islands government awarded seven production licences to search for offshore hydrocarbons in the North Falkland Basin. By the end of 1998, no commercially viable accumulations of oil had been found, but the exploration revealed the presence of organic-rich source rock, indicating the presence of considerable quantities of oil in the North Falkland Basin. Further exploratory searches are planned.

An EU-standard abattoir was opened in 2001, enabling the Falkland Islands to export meat to the European Union.

TRADE WITH UK	2000	2001
Imports from UK	£22,064,000	£19,756,000
Exports to UK	6,704,000	6,873,000

GIBRALTAR

AREA – 2.3 sq. miles (6 sq. km)
POPULATION – 27,033 (2000 estimate)
CAPITAL – ψGibraltar
CURRENCY – Gibraltar pound of 100 pence
FLAG – White with a red stripe along the lower edge; over all a red castle with a key hanging from its gateway
POPULATION GROWTH RATE – 0.6 per cent (2000)
POPULATION DENSITY – 4,159 per sq. km (2000)

Gibraltar is a rocky promontory which juts southwards from the south-east coast of Spain, with which it is connected by a low isthmus. It is about 20 miles (32 km) from the opposite coast of Africa. The town stands at the foot of the promontory on the west side.

HISTORY AND POLITICS

Gibraltar was captured in 1704, during the War of the Spanish Succession, by a combined Dutch and English force, and was ceded to Great Britain by the Treaty of Utrecht (1713). The Treaty of Utrecht stipulates that if Britain ever relinquishes its colonial rights over Gibraltar the colony would return to Spain. In a 1967 referendum on the colony's status, 12,138 people voted to remain a British Dependent Territory and 44 voted to join Spain. Spain closed the border with Gibraltar from 1969 to 1985 and refused to engage in any trade.

The 1969 constitution makes provision for certain domestic matters to devolve on a local government of ministers appointed from among elected members of the House of Assembly. The House of Assembly consists of an independent Speaker, 15 elected members, the Attorney-General and the Financial and Development Secretary.

The Governor retains responsibility for external affairs, defence, internal security and financial security, while the local government is responsible for other domestic matters. The Gibraltar government has recently been pressing for more local autonomy especially in its relations with the EU, and this has led to tension with the UK and Spanish governments. Gibraltar is part of the EU (with the UK government responsible for enforcing EU directives affecting Gibraltar) but is not a fully-fledged member and is exempt from the Common Customs Tariff and the Common Agricultural Policy. Value added tax is not applied. The Gibraltar Social Democrats won the last election in February 2000.

Talks between the UK and Spain on the future of Gibraltar resumed in July 2001, but were boycotted by the Gibraltarian government which had insisted on the right to veto any proposals on which it disagreed.

Governor and Commander-in-Chief, HE the Rt. Hon. David Durie, CMG
Commander British Forces, HM Naval Base, Gibraltar, Cdre R. Clapp
Deputy Governor, D. Blunt
Attorney-General, R. Rhoda
Chief Justice, Derek Schofield
Chief Minister, Peter Caruana
Deputy Chief Minister, Trade, Industry and Telecommunication, Keith Azopardi
Education, Training, Culture and Health, Dr Bernard Linares
Employment and Consumer Affairs, Hubert Corby
Housing, Jaime Netto
Public Services, Environment, Sport and Youth, Ernest Britto
Social Affairs, Yvette Del Agua
Speaker, John Alcantara , CBE
Tourism and Transport, Joe Holliday

GOVERNMENT OF GIBRALTAR, Arundel Great Court, 178-179 The Strand, London WC2R 1EL. Tel: 020-7836 0777. *Government Representative*, A. Poggio

ECONOMY

Gibraltar has an extensive shipping trade and is a popular shopping centre and tourist resort. The chief sources of revenue are the port dues, the rent of the Crown estate in the town, and duties on consumer items. The free port tradition of Gibraltar is still reflected in the low rates of import duty. A financial services industry is expanding, based on Gibraltar's status as an offshore financial centre.

A total of 6,303 merchant ships (133.97 million gross registered tons aggregate) entered the port during 2000. There are 56 km of roads.

TRADE WITH UK	2000	2001
Imports from UK	£121,599,000	£127,634,000
Exports to UK	11,547,000	14,328,000

EDUCATION

Education is compulsory and free for children between the ages of five and 15 whose parents are ordinarily resident in Gibraltar. Scholarships are available for higher education in Britain.

MONTSERRAT

AREA – 39 sq. miles (102 sq. km)
POPULATION – 4,500 (2001 estimate)
CAPITAL – ψPlymouth
CURRENCY – East Caribbean dollar (EC$) of 100 cents
FLAG – British blue ensign with the shield of arms in the fly
POPULATION GROWTH RATE – 0.5 per cent (1999)
POPULATION DENSITY – 108 per sq. km (1999)
GDP – US$38 million (1998); US$3,570 per capita (1998)

Montserrat is about 11 miles long and seven miles wide. It is volcanic with several hot springs. About two-thirds of the island is mountainous, the rest capable of cultivation but volcanic activity has caused the evacuation of two-thirds of the island.

HISTORY AND POLITICS

Discovered by Columbus in 1493, Montserrat became a British colony in 1632. The first settlers were predominantly Irish indentured servants from St Christopher. Montserrat was captured by the French in 1664, 1667 and 1782 but the island reverted to Britain within a few years on each occasion and was finally assigned to Great Britain in 1783.

A ministerial system was introduced in Montserrat in 1960. The Executive Council is presided over by the Governor and is composed of four elected members (the Chief and three other Ministers) and two ex-officio members (the Attorney-General and the Financial Secretary). The four Ministers are appointed from the members of the political party or coalition holding the majority in the Legislative Council. The Legislative Council consists of the Speaker, two ex-officio members (the Attorney-General and the Financial Secretary) and nine elected members. Following elections in April 2001 the elected element of the legislature comprised the following parties: New People's Liberation Movement 7; National Progressive Party 2.

Governor, HE Anthony Longrigg, CMG, *apptd* 2001

EXECUTIVE COUNCIL *as at May 2002*
President, The Governor
Chief Minister and Minister of Finance and Economic Development, Dr John Osborne
Agriculture, Lands, Housing and the Environment, Margaret Dyer-Howe Attorney-General, Charles Ekins
Communications and Works, Dr Lowell Lewis
Education, Health and Community Services, Idabelle Meade
Financial Secretary, John Skerritt

ECONOMY

The economy, which consists of tourism, related construction activities, offshore business services and agriculture, has been seriously affected by relocation to the north of the island due to volcanic activity.

TRADE WITH UK	2000	2001
Imports from UK	£1,104,000	£1,138,000
Exports to UK	120,000	23,000

PITCAIRN ISLANDS

AREA – 2 sq. miles (5 sq. km)
POPULATION – 54 (1999). Since 1887 the islanders have generally been adherents of the Seventh-day Adventist Church
CURRENCY – Currency is that of New Zealand
FLAG – British blue ensign with the arms in the fly

Pitcairn is the chief of a group of islands situated about midway between New Zealand and Panama in the South Pacific Ocean. The island rises in cliffs to a height of 1,100 feet and access from the sea is possible only at Bounty Bay, a small rocky cove, and then only by surf boats. The other three islands of the group (Henderson, lying 105 miles east-north-east of Pitcairn, Oeno, lying 75 miles north-west, and Ducie, lying 293 miles east) are all uninhabited.

HISTORY AND POLITICS

First settled in 1790 by the Bounty mutineers and their Tahitian companions, Pitcairn was left uninhabited in 1856 when the entire population was resettled on Norfolk Island. The present community are descendants of two parties who, not wishing to remain on Norfolk, returned to Pitcairn in 1859 and 1864 respectively.

Pitcairn became a British settlement under the British Settlement Act 1887 and was administered by the Governor of Fiji from 1952 until 1970, when the administration was transferred to the British High Commission in New Zealand and the British High Commissioner was appointed Governor. The local Government Ordinance of 1964 provides for a Council of ten members of whom six are elected.

Governor of Pitcairn, Henderson, Ducie and Oeno Islands, HE Richard Fell, CVO (*British High Commissioner to New Zealand*)
Island Mayor, Steve Christian

ECONOMY

The islanders live by subsistence gardening and fishing. Wood carvings and other handicrafts are sold to passing ships and to a few overseas customers. Other than small fees charged for gun and driving licences there are no taxes and government revenue is derived almost solely from the sale of postage stamps and income from investments. Communication with the outside world is maintained by cargo vessels travelling between New Zealand and Panama which call at irregular intervals, and by means of a satellite service providing telephone, e-mail and fax facilities.

TRADE WITH UK	2000	2001
Imports from UK	£245,000	892,000
Exports to UK	1,000	2,000

EDUCATION

Education is compulsory between the ages of five and 15. Secondary education in New Zealand is encouraged by the administration, which provides scholarships and bursaries. Medical care is provided by a registered nurse when a doctor is not present.

ST HELENA AND DEPENDENCIES

AREA – 47 sq. miles (122 sq. km)
POPULATION – 5,157 (1998 census)
CAPITAL – ψJamestown (population, 884, 1998)
CURRENCY – St Helena pound (£) of 100 pence
FLAG – British blue ensign with the shield of arms in the fly
POPULATION GROWTH RATE – 0.8 per cent (1998)
POPULATION DENSITY – 49 per sq. km (1997)
URBAN POPULATION – 39.2 per cent (1998)
ILLITERACY RATE – 3.6 per cent (1998)

St Helena is situated in the South Atlantic Ocean, 955 miles south of the Equator, 702 miles south-east of Ascension, 1,140 miles from the nearest point of the African continent, 1,800 miles from the coast of South America and 1,694 miles from Cape Town. It is 10.5 miles long and 6.5 broad.

St Helena is of volcanic origin, and consists of numerous rugged mountains, the highest rising to 2,700 feet (820 m), interspersed with picturesque ravines. Although within the tropics, the south-east trade winds keep the temperature mild and equable.

HISTORY AND POLITICS

St Helena was probably discovered by the Portuguese navigator João da Nova in 1502. It was used as a port of call for vessels of all nations trading to the East until it was annexed by the Dutch in 1633. It was never occupied by them, however, and the English East India Company seized it in 1659. From 1815 to 1821 the island was lent to the British government as a place of exile for the Emperor Napoleon Bonaparte who died in St Helena on 5 May 1821, and in 1834 it was annexed to the British Crown.

The island was settled by the East India Company in the 17th and 18th centuries with planters and company soldiers from England and slaves from the Indian subcontinent and Madagascar.

The government of St Helena is administered by a Governor, with the aid of a Legislative Council, consisting of a Speaker, three ex-officio members (Chief Secretary, Financial Secretary and Attorney-General) and 12 elected members. Five committees of the Legislative Council are responsible for the overseeing of the activities of the five biggest government departments and have in addition a wide range of statutory and administrative functions. The Governor is also assisted by an Executive Council of the three ex-officio members and the chairmen of the Council committees.

Governor, HE David Hollamby, *apptd* 1999

EXECUTIVE COUNCIL as at October 2001
The Governor Attorney-General, Kurt De Freitas, OBE
Chairman of Agricultural and Natural Resources Committee, Mervyn R. Yon
Chairman of Education Committee, William E. Drabble
Chairman of Employment and Social Security Committee, Cyril G. Gunnell
Chairman of Public Health and Social Security Committee, Margaret M. C. Hopkins
Chairman of Public Works and Services Committee, Eric W. George, MBE
Chief Secretary, John Styles
Financial Secretary, Robert Dolan

ECONOMY

St Helena was intended as a maritime base, with an economy dedicated to the provision of supplies for shipping and the local garrison, rather than as a self-sufficient colony. St Helena still receives an annual grant from the UK which amounted to £3.184 million in 1999. The only significant export is canned and frozen fish. The other exports are a small amount of high quality coffee and cottage industry products (including lace, decorative woodwork and beadwork). James's Bay, on the north-west of the island, possesses a good anchorage. There is as yet no airport or airstrip.

TRADE WITH UK	2000	2001
Imports from UK	£8,781,000	£9,674,000
Exports to UK	1,111,000	415,000

ASCENSION ISLAND

AREA – 34 sq. miles (88 sq. km)
POPULATION – 980 (2001 census)
CAPITAL – ψGeorgetown
CURRENCY – Currency is that of St Helena or the UK

The small island of Ascension lies in the South Atlantic some 750 miles north-west of the island of St Helena. It is a rocky peak of purely volcanic origin. The highest point (Green Mountain), some 2,817 ft, is covered with lush vegetation. The island is a breeding area for green turtles and for the sooty tern, or wideawake. Other wildlife includes feral donkeys and sheep, nine varieties of sea birds, including the indigenous Ascension frigate bird, and five land birds.

British forces returned to the island in April 1982 in support of operations in the Falkland Islands. At present there are about 25 RAF personnel on the island together with some 200 civilian workers supporting the air link to the Falklands.

HISTORY AND POLITICS

Ascension is said to have been discovered by João da Nova in 1501 and two years later was visited on Ascension Day by Alphonse d'Albuquerque, who gave the island its present name. It was uninhabited until the arrival of Napoleon in St Helena in 1815 when a small British naval garrison was stationed on the island. As HMS Ascension it remained under the supervision of the Board of Admiralty until 1922, when it was made a dependency of St Helena.

The British Foreign Secretary appoints the Administrator who is responsible to the Governor resident in St Helena. There is a small police force, bank and post office. The Ascension Island government is responsible for health and education. The Ascension Island Works and Services Agency operates the port and provides other public services such as road and building maintenance.

Administrator, Geoffrey Fairhurst, *apptd* 1999

COMMUNICATIONS

Cable and Wireless operates the international and internal telephone service. The BBC opened its Atlantic relay station broadcasting to Africa and South America in 1967. There is a monthly shipping service and a flight every five days by RAF Tristars which transit Ascension en route to the Falkland Islands. US aircraft and ships service the American base.

TRISTAN DA CUNHA

AREA – 38 sq. miles (98 sq. km)
POPULATION – 284 (2001 estimate)
CAPITAL – ψEdinburgh of the Seven Seas
CURRENCY – Currency is that of the UK

Tristan da Cunha is the chief island of a group of islands in the South Atlantic which lies some 1,260 nautical miles (2,333 km) south-south-west of St Helena.

All the islands are volcanic and steep-sided with cliffs or narrow beaches. Tristan has a volcanic cone rising to 6,760 feet (2,060 m).

The islands have a warm-temperate oceanic climate which is damp and windy. Rainfall averages 66 inches a year on the coast of Tristan da Cunha.

Population is centred in the settlement of Edinburgh on Tristan da Cunha. In addition, there is a meteorological station maintained on Gough Island by the South African government. Inaccessible Island and the Nightingale Islands are uninhabited.

HISTORY AND POLITICS

Tristan da Cunha was discovered in 1506 by the Portuguese admiral Tristão da Cunha. In 1760 a British naval officer visited the islands and gave his name to Nightingale Island. In 1816 the group was annexed to the British Crown and a garrison was placed on Tristan da Cunha, but this force was withdrawn in 1817. Corporal William Glass remained at his own request with his wife and two children. This party, with two others, formed a settlement. In 1827 five women from St Helena, and afterwards others from Cape Colony, joined the party.

Due to its position on a main sailing route the colony thrived, with an economy based on trading with whalers, sealers and other passing ships. However, the replacement of sail by steam and the opening of the Suez Canal in the late 19th century led to decline.

In October 1961 a volcano, believed to have been extinct for thousands of years, erupted and the danger of further volcanic activity led to the evacuation of inhabitants to the UK. An advance party returned to Tristan da Cunha in 1963 and subsequently the main body of the islanders returned to the island.

GOVERNMENT

In 1938 Tristan da Cunha and the neighbouring islands of Inaccessible, Nightingale and Gough were made dependencies of St Helena. They are administered by the Governor of St Helena through a resident Administrator, with headquarters at Edinburgh. Under a constitution introduced in 1985, the Administrator is advised by an Island Council of eight elected members, of whom one must be a woman, and three appointed members. Elections are held every three years.

Administrator, Bill Dickson, *apptd* 2001

ECONOMY

The island is almost financially self-sufficient; UK government aid finances training scholarships and a resident medical officer at the hospital. The main industries are crayfish fishing, fish-processing and agriculture. There are no taxes, income being derived from the royalties from the rock lobster fishery around the islands, interest from the reserve fund, and the sales of stamps and handicrafts, as well as vegetables, to passing ships. Tourism is increasing, the island being on the itinerary of several environmental tours. Apart from

the fishing industry, the other main employer is the administration itself. There is a school catering for children up to age 15. Healthcare and education are free for the islanders.

COMMUNICATIONS

Scheduled visits to the island are restricted to about six calls a year by fishing vessels from Cape Town and annual calls of the RMS St Helena and the SA Agulhas, also from Cape Town. A wireless station on the island is in daily contact with Cape Town and a radio-telephone service was established in 1969, the same year that electricity was introduced to all the islanders' homes. A marine satellite system providing direct dialling telephone, telex and fax facilities was installed in 1992. Since 1998 the island has had internet and email facilities, as well as a public telephone. Satellite television was introduced in 2001.

SOUTH GEORGIA AND THE SOUTH SANDWICH ISLANDS

AREA – 1,580 sq. miles (4,092 sq. km)
POPULATION – No permanent population

South Georgia is an island 800 miles east-south-east of the Falkland group. The population comprises the government's marine officer and the staff of the newly established scientific research station operated by the British Antarctic Survey and the curator of the museum at King Edward Point, and staff of the British Antarctic Survey at Bird Island, to the north-west of South Georgia.

The South Sandwich Islands lie some 470 miles south-east of South Georgia.

The present constitution came into effect in 1985. It provides for a Commissioner who, for the time being, is the officer administering the government of the Falkland Islands.

In 1993 the UK government decreed an extension of Crown sovereignty and jurisdiction from 12 miles around South Georgia and the South Sandwich Islands to 200 miles around each in order to preserve marine stocks.

Commissioner for South Georgia and the South Sandwich Islands, Donald Lamont, *apptd* 1999

TURKS AND CAICOS ISLANDS

AREA – 166 sq. miles (430 sq. km)
POPULATION – 23,000 (1999 estimate)
CAPITAL – ψGrand Turk (population, 3,691, 1994)
CURRENCY – US dollar (US$)
FLAG – British blue ensign with the shield of arms in the fly
POPULATION GROWTH RATE – 3.3 per cent (1999)
POPULATION DENSITY – 37 per sq. km (1999)

The Turks and Caicos Islands are about 50 miles south-east of the Bahamas of which they are geographically an extension. There are over 30 islands, of which eight are inhabited, covering an estimated area of 166 sq. miles (430 sq. km). The principal island and seat of government is Grand Turk.

HISTORY AND POLITICS

A constitution was introduced in 1988, and amended in 1993, which provides for an Executive Council and a Legislative Council. The Executive Council is presided over by the Governor and comprises the Chief Minister and five elected Ministers, together with the ex-officio Chief Secretary and Attorney-General.

At the general election of 4 March 1999, the People's Democratic Movement won nine seats and the Progressive National Party four seats in the Legislative Council.

Governor, HE Mervyn T. Jones, *apptd* 2000

EXECUTIVE COUNCIL *as at May 2002*
President, The Governor
Attorney-General, David Jeremiah
Chief Minister, Commerce and Development, Finance, Derek H. Taylor, OBE
Chief Secretary, Cynthia Astwood, MBE
Health, Education and Sports, Clarence Selver
Home Affairs, Immigration and Labour, Hilly Ewing
Natural Resources, Larry Coalbrooke
Public Works and Utilities, Noel Skippings
Tourism, Communications and Transport, Oswald Skippings

ECONOMY

The most important industries are fishing, tourism and offshore finance. The islands were visited by 151,000 tourists in 2000.

TRADE WITH UK	2000	2001
Imports from UK	£864,000	£779,000
Exports to UK	251,000	151,000

COMMUNICATIONS

The principal airports are on the islands of Grand Turk and Providenciales. Air services link Providenciales with London, Miami, Fort Lauderdale, Atlanta, Jamaica, the Bahamas, Haiti and the Dominican Republic. An internal air service provides a regular service between the principal islands. There are direct shipping services to the USA (Miami). A comprehensive telephone and telex service is provided by Cable and Wireless (WI) Ltd.

The Year 2001–2002

Events of the Year

Obituaries

September 11 2001 and the Aftermath

Archaeology

Architecture

Art

Broadcasting

Conservation and Heritage

Dance

Film

Literature

Music

Opera

Parliament

Science

Theatre

Weather

Sports Results and Records

Events of the Year

1 September 2001 to 31 August 2002

BRITISH AFFAIRS

SEPTEMBER 2001

1. The Church of England announced plans to sell a valuable collection of paintings to replenish its pension funds. **3.** The Government announced plans to spend £300 million a year on a force of 30,000 special constables. **9.** The Chancellor (Gordon Brown) was assigned the task of choosing Britain's memorial to Diana, the Princess of Wales by the Prime Minister (Tony Blair). **11.** Hundreds of Britons were feared dead after two hijacked aircraft crashed into the twin towers of the World Trade Centre in New York. A third plane crashed into the Pentagon building in Washington DC. **12.** The Commission for Health Improvement began an inquiry into the deaths of eight heart transplant patients at St. George's Hospital, London. **16.** Tony Blair instructed the Foreign Secretary (Jack Straw) to work to resolve the 300-year dispute over the sovereignty of Gibraltar with Spain. **20.** Tony Blair announced plans for Britain to send ground troops to Afghanistan to aid the US in its war against terrorism. A report by Lord Cullen into the Paddington rail crash suggested that an accident investigation body to establish the causes of train accidents should be created. The Defence Secretary (Geoff Hoon) revealed that voluntary identity cards might be introduced and, if successful, could become compulsory. **21.** Scotland Yard anti-terrorist squad officers arrested a couple in London believed to have provided a 'safe house' for one of the hijackers who carried out the attacks on the World Trade Centre. Hospitals throughout Britain were instructed by the NHS Chief Executive Nigel Crisp to be prepared for a 'mass casualty incident' in response to the terrorist attacks in the US. Ronnie Biggs, the Great Train Robber, was removed from the medical wing of Belmarsh Prison in south London and sent to Queen Elizabeth hospital after suffering an internal bleeding. **22.** It was reported that Britain had granted political asylum to more than 20 Islamic terrorists, including those wanted for the murders of around 100 people in Algeria, Egypt and Tunisia. Home Office statistics revealed that the police solved 24 per cent of crimes in England and Wales, down from 35 per cent in 1988 and 40 per cent in 1980. The Queen donated an undisclosed amount to the appeal for victims of the terrorist violence in the USA. **23.** The Liberal Democrat Party conference began in Bournemouth. **24.** Gordon Brown announced a list of sanctions against individuals and organisations with a known link to Osama bin Laden, the man thought to be behind the terrorist campaign in the US. The Treasury announced a rescue indemnity package for airlines with UK operating costs, worth £34 million, to enable them to provide cover for third-party liability claims resulting from terrorist attacks. Computer firms revealed that creation of national fingerprint ID cards was possible within the next two years. The Department of Health announced a new grading system to show the best and worst-run hospital trusts over 21 categories. The 30 best-run hospitals would be allowed to create spin-off companies to sell their expertise. **25.** Official figures showed that a quarter of Europe's asylum seekers sought refuge in Britain last year. **27.** The Prince of Wales requested his brother, the Earl of Wessex, to make a public apology to St Andrew's University after his film company, Ardent Productions, broke an agreement with the media to protect Prince William's privacy whilst he is attending the university. **29.** The minimum wage rose by 40 pence to £4.10 and the rate for 18- to 21-year-olds increased by 30 pence to £3.50 per hour. British journalist Yvonne Ridley was arrested in Afghanistan on suspicion of spying. Ardent Productions said that it would give Buckingham Palace all of its footage of Prince William at St Andrew's University. **30.** Tony Blair announced that he had 'incontrovertible' evidence linking Osama bin Laden to the terrorist attacks in the USA. The Labour Party conference in Bournemouth was shortened due to the terrorist attacks in the USA. **31.** Gordon Brown confirmed that the Government had frozen £60 million of the Taliban regime's assets after closing a European bank account in London.

OCTOBER 2001

1. Tony Blair declared war on Afghanistan. **4.** Tony Blair began a four-day visit to Russia to gain coalition support in preparation for a military attack against Afghanistan. **5.** The Financial Secretary to the Treasury (Paul Boateng) announced the introduction of tax-free betting in the UK. The Conservative Party conference began in Blackpool. **7.** Britain and the USA began missile strikes against Afghanistan and, as a result, Tony Blair recalled Parliament. **8.** The Taliban released British journalist Yvonne Ridley. David Blunkett announced that security at key power and water installations was to be increased due to terrorist activities. The Foreign Office advised Britons not to travel to Indonesia, Yemen, Iraq, Pakistan and Tajikistan in case of revenge attacks after the bombing of Afghanistan. The Government's war cabinet held its first meeting. **9.** Windsor Farm Shop opened to the public selling the produce from The Queen's private estates. The Government announced the allocation of £200 million to the emergency services to cope with potential casualties caused by terrorist violence. A cargo ship captain died in a Hastings hospital after his ship, the Ash, sank following a collision in good visibility in the English Channel. **12.** The United Nations Secretary-General Kofi Annan and the United Nations were awarded the Nobel Peace Prize. **16.** Jo Moore, the Special Adviser to the Secretary of State for Transport, Local Government and the Regions, (Stephen Byers), publicly apologised for her suggestion that it was a 'very good day to bury bad news' on 11 September. **18.** Voters in referendums in Lewisham, North Tyneside and Hartlepool voted in favour of having directly elected mayors. **19.** The House of Commons and part of Whitehall were evacuated following anthrax scares and bomb threats. **21.** Three 16-year-olds were killed and one man injured following a vehicle collision in Ely,

Cambridgeshire. 24. The cost of a litre of petrol dropped by 2 pence to its lowest level for more than two years. 25. The British Tour Operators' Association announced a 23.62 per cent fall in tourism in the UK. 26. The Armed Forces Minister (Adam Ingram) announced the assignment of 4,200 servicemen and women to Operation Veritas, a codename for the British war effort in Afghanistan. The Government paid Railtrack administrators £800 million from its emergency reserves to cover urgent expenditure. 29. David Blunkett announced that asylum-seekers would be issued with identity cards as part of a £350 million overhaul of the Government asylum policy.

NOVEMBER 2001

4. The Prince of Wales began a short visit to the Baltic States. A 60lb home-made bomb was left in a car outside New Street Station in Birmingham. The device was not detonated. Scotland's First Minister (Henry McLeish) offered to personally pay £36,000 to the House of Commons authorities to cover his former constituency expenses. The Queen held a state banquet at Windsor Castle in honour of King Abdullah and Queen Rania of Jordan. Commercial flights on Concorde began for the first time since British and French fleets were grounded after a crash near Paris in July 2000. 8. One person died and 15 were injured following an explosion at a steelworks in Port Talbot, South Wales. David Blunkett announced that the Home Office would pay compensation to two businessmen acquitted on charges of selling banned machine-tooling equipment to Iraq after it emerged that they had been helping MI6. The Government announced that they would not outlaw the practice of parents physically reprimanding their children. 13. It was announced that the Rt. Revd Peter Price, Bishop of Kingston upon Thames, would become the new Bishop of Bath and Wells. 14. A four-year-old drowned during a supervised school swimming lesson in Blackpool. 15. Around 100 members of the Special Boat Service flew into Kabul in Afghanistan to ensure humanitarian aid was distributed. The Conservative Party appointed Sir Stanley Kalms as its treasurer. 17. A gas explosion demolished two blocks of flats in Newton Heath, central Manchester; 150 people were evacuated and three police officers were injured. Thames Valley police began an investigation into the death of a ten-year-old girl found hanged in her bedroom in Bicester, Oxfordshire. 19. Heathrow airport won approval from the Government to open a fifth terminal. 21. Hilary Roland, the hospital chief at the centre of the Alder Hey Hospital child organ scandal in Liverpool, was sacked following a three-day, disciplinary hearing. The London Mayor (Ken Livingstone) sacked Steven Norris from the board of Transport for London. 24. The Leader of the House of Commons and chairman of its modernisation committee (Robin Cook) announced plans to introduce a four-day week and reduce working hours for MPs from 10am to 5pm. 25. The Prison Service announced plans to convert a third male jail to house female prisoners. Gordon Brown announced the allocation of £120 million to fund the war on terrorism in his pre-Budget report. 28. The Government confirmed that 78 Britons were killed in the September 11 terrorist attacks in the US.

DECEMBER 2001

6. The Countess of Wessex underwent an emergency operation at King Edward VII Hospital in central London following an ectopic pregnancy. 9. It was announced that following the death of Labour MP Sir Raymond Powell, a

by-election would take place in Ogmore, South Wales, in January 2002. Downing Street and the White House held simultaneous ceremonies to mark the three-month anniversary of the September 11 terrorist attacks in the US. 10. Paul Marsden, Labour MP for Shrewsbury and Atcham, defected from the Labour Party to the Liberal Democrats. 13. The Minister for Small Business (Nigel Griffiths) admitted breaking House of Commons rules by failing to declare in the register of interests that he owned his constituency office, for which he had been claiming rent from the Commons fees office. The Minister for Science (Lord Sainsbury) donated £2 million to the Labour Party. A new Anti-Terrorism, Crime and Security Bill was passed by parliament. 16. Lord Ahmed, a Muslim Labour Peer, lodged an official complaint following the allegation that MI5 was monitoring his comments on the Afghan war.

JANUARY 2002

1. The first life boat service was launched on the River Thames. 2. The Rail Maritime and Transport union (RMT) began a 48-hour strike over pay resulting in around 95 per cent of South West Trains' services being cancelled. 3. Lord Stoddart of Swindon was expelled from the Labour Party for endorsing a breakaway candidate at the last general election. 4. Tony Blair began a peace mission in India and Pakistan to improve relations between the two nuclear-armed powers. 6. A man and his nine-year-old son died after becoming lost on a fog-bound beach in Cumbria. 7. Gordon Brown's ten-day-old daughter died following a brain haemorrhage. 13. Suma Chakrabarti, 42, became the first Asian and the youngest person to hold the position of Permanent Secretary in Whitehall. 24. Buckingham Palace announced the creation of a new landscape garden at Windsor Castle to commemorate The Queen's Golden Jubilee. 25. A 14-year-old girl died after contracting the flu virus. The Church of England appointed its first chaplain to Romanies and New Age travellers. 28. The Treasury announced the postponement of the budget until the new tax year in April following the death of Gordon Brown's daughter. It was revealed that the Labour Party was almost £10 million in debt following a decline in donations. Downing Street detailed Labour Ministers' contact with the collapsed US energy company Enron, to prevent further allegations that it paid the Government cash in order to gain access to ministers. 30. The Transport Minister (John Spellar) unveiled the world's first speaking bus shelter in Bradford. 31. A report by the Chief Inspector of Prisons criticised the living conditions of prisoners at Dartmoor jail. Lord Wakeham resigned as Chairman of the Press Complaints Commission. The Public Health Laboratory Service projected that the number of people infected by the HIV virus would increase by almost 50 per cent by 2005. Edexcel, the A-level and GCSE exam board, was given four weeks by the Qualifications and Curriculum Authority to improve its results or face losing its accreditation.

FEBRUARY 2002

1. The Department of Health revealed the use of the combined measles, mumps and rubella vaccine (MMR) in the UK had fallen to below 85 per cent. Three people were swept out to sea in separate incidents in Brighton and Penzance due to severe weather conditions. 4. The Government announced a pilot voting scheme allowing voters in 30 local councils to vote by mobile phone, post or Internet during the May elections. 9. Princess Margaret, The Queen's sister, died peacefully in her sleep at Windsor Castle. The princess's health deteriorated after

suffering three strokes over the last few years. **14.** The private funeral of Princess Margaret took place at Windsor castle. **15.** It was announced that Jo Moore, the special adviser to Stephen Byers, and Martin Sixsmith, the Department of Transport's director of communications, had resigned. They had been criticised for inappropriately handling sensitive news stories and internal briefings. **16.** King's College School, Wimbledon, announced plans to abandon A-level examinations in favour of the International Baccalaureate. A Government report revealed that people of retirement age accounted for more than half of the rise in employment in Britain last year. **18.** Chiltern Railways announced plans to phase out first-class seats in order to carry six million additional passengers. The Queen embarked on the first stage of a 25,000-mile Golden Jubilee Commonwealth tour in Kingston, Jamaica. **19.** All stocks of Chinese and blended honey were recalled by the Food Standards Agency, which found that the products contained the antibiotic Chloramphenicol, which in large doses may cause cancer. A report by the World Health Organisation (WHO) found that travellers who are killed abroad are likely to die in road accidents and not by contracting a disease. More than a hundred thousand vehicles were stuck in a traffic jam after a fatal accident shut part of the M3 in both directions for more than seven hours. **22.** Health Minister (John Hutton) announced that every general practitioner would undergo an annual appraisal by their peers to monitor their competency. **23.** A report by Sir Anthony Hammond into the Hinduja passport affair concluded that new evidence submitted by Peter Mandelson, the former Northern Ireland Secretary, failed to change last year's findings. Sir Hammond ruled that it was likely that Mr Mandelson made a phone call in 1998 to the then immigration minister Mike O'Brien about the passport application of billionaire Srichand Hinduja. **24.** Stephen Byers was accused of lying by Martin Sixsmith, his former director of communications. Mr Sixsmith alleged that Mr Byers had falsely announced Mr Sixsmith's resignation from DTLR. **26.** Ken Livingstone approved a scheme to charge motorists £5 to drive into central London. The Scottish First Minister (Jack McConnell) announced that the number of Scottish members of parliament should remain at 129, contrary to the requirements under the devolution settlement that it should be reduced. In a statement given to the House of Commons, Stephen Byers admitted suggesting that Mr Sixsmith should be barred from taking another job in Whitehall.

MARCH 2002

1. The second official report into the Hinduja passport affair cleared Peter Mandelson of any wrongdoing. The Anti-Terrorist Branch issued a nation-wide alert after 16 packages containing toxic substances were sent to Tony Blair and other politicians. The Health Minister (Hazel Blears) announced an increase in single prescription charges from £6.10 to £6.20. The Archbishop of Canterbury, George Carey, said that the Government should contribute towards the maintenance of the Church of England's grade I and II listed buildings. ScotRail, ASLEF and RMT accepted an invitation from the Advisory, Conciliation and Arbitration Service to attend talks to resolve an ongoing pay dispute. The Earl and Countess of Wessex resigned from their commercial careers to concentrate on royal duties. The Prison Service revealed that the number of inmates across England and Wales had risen to 70,000, close to the official safe maximum figures. **2.** The Cabinet Secretary (Sir Richard Wilson) recommended the creation of a new Civil Service

Bill in order to maintain the impartiality of civil servants in Whitehall and monitor the work of special advisers. **4.** Ian Jones, a senior press officer at DTLR, was suspended on full pay pending further investigation into the leaking of information about Jo Moore, the former special adviser to Stephen Byers. A report by the Transport Select Committee claimed that Tony Blair had undermined parliamentary democracy by refusing to allow Lord Birt and other Downing Street advisers to give evidence to MPs. The Committee was concerned that these unpaid advisers were unaccountable to parliament. **5.** MEP Richard Balfe announced that he was defecting from Labour to the Conservative Party. **10.** Two climbers were killed in an avalanche in the Highlands. **13.** Police officers protested outside Westminster over their pay and conditions. **14.** Schoolteachers in London went on strike over pay. **15.** The supermarket chain Tesco announced a pilot scheme in Somerset to supply the morning-after pill to teenagers. The Health Secretary (Alan Milburn) assigned private ancillary health staff the same employment rights and benefits as NHS employees. Government ministers promised to back an Opposition Bill to ban all tobacco advertising. **17.** London's first official St Patrick's Day celebration took place, around 60,000 people attended. The Home Office revealed plans to re-allocate 5,000 police officers across the country to focus on street robbery. **18.** British Waterways announced a £500 million programme to develop Britain's canal system. The House of Commons voted for an outright ban on fox-hunting. **19.** The House of Lords voted by a majority of 300 to continue fox-hunting under licence. **20.** David Blunkett announced plans to release prisoners early in order to reduce overcrowding. Fifty Labour MPs announced plans to launch a parliamentary group opposed to joining the Euro before the next election. **24.** Corby in Northants became the first town to ban children under the age of 15 from being unsupervised in the streets between the hours of 9 p.m. and 6 a.m. The Health Secretary (Alan Milburn) alleged that records in his department had been deliberately falsified. Mr Milburn claimed that 202 questions tabled by MPs to ministers disappeared during the last Parliament. **30.** Queen Elizabeth, the Queen Mother died peacefully in her sleep at Windsor Castle. Her health had deteriorated following a chest infection. **31.** The Queen Mother's coffin was taken from Windsor Castle for a period of private mourning by her family in the Queen's Chapel at St James's Palace.

APRIL 2002

1. The Royal household announced that Mey Castle, a remote Scottish residence, would be opened to the public. The Prince of Wales broadcast a tribute to his grandmother the Queen Mother on ITV. **2.** The National Union of Teachers voted in favour of a series of strikes over pay and conditions. Sussex County cricketer Umer Rashid and his brother drowned in an accident during a pre-season tour on the Caribbean island of Grenada. **4.** Around 70 inmates at Shotts prison in Lanarkshire rioted after lightning caused a power failure in the area. The Ministry of Defence announced plans to offer rehabilitation to soldiers rather than dismissal if they tested positive for drugs. All cross-Channel services between Dover and Calais were cancelled after crews employed by the French-owned operator Sea France went on strike. **7.** Downing Street denied claims that a £100,000 payment from Westfield shopping centre group had been made to gain access to the Government. **8.** The state funeral of Queen Elizabeth, the Queen Mother took place at Westminster Abbey. She was later buried

alongside her husband King George VI at St George's Chapel in Windsor Castle. **15.** Eleven people were injured when a train was derailed after crashing into an articulated lorry on a crossing at Blaxhall, Suffolk. **17.** Gordon Brown announced a 43 per cent rise in NHS spending over the next five years. **19.** A man wearing a 120lb deep sea diver's suit finished the London Marathon in 32,875th place making him the slowest competitor in the race's history. The Duchess of York announced plans to move out of Sunninghill Park, the home she shared with her former husband, the Duke of York. A memorial service for the late Princess Margaret took place at Westminster Abbey. **20.** The Queen celebrated her 76th birthday by attending a Scouts parade in Windsor Castle. **25.** The Bishop of Stepney, the Rt. Revd John Sentamu, was appointed chairman of an inquiry into the police's handling of the Damilola Taylor murder trial. **29.** The Secretary of State for Education and Skills (Estelle Morris) announced that 400 schools in some of England's toughest areas would be assigned police officers. **30.** A report by the Bank of England found that house prices in Britain rose by a record 3.4 pr cent in March. The Queen made an historic address to both Houses of Parliament as part of the official start of her Golden Jubilee tour.

MAY 2002

10. Seven people died and around 40 people were injured when a train derailed at Potters Bar sending one of the carriages sideways at 100 miles per hour before becoming embedded under the platform roof. The Animal Health Minister (Elliot Morley) announced that farmers received an average of £124,755 compensation for destroying their livestock during the foot-and-mouth outbreak. **12.** The House of Commons was informed that the Labour Party had accepted £100,000 from Richard Desmond, owner of the Express Group and a number of top-shelf adult magazines. **17.** Buckingham Palace announced that Clarence House, the former home of Queen Elizabeth, the Queen Mother, would be opened to the public. The Electoral Commission recommended to Parliament that all political donations should be capped at £10,000 following a series of controversial donations to the Labour Party. The Commission also suggested that reductions should be made in the amount political parties were allowed to spend on general election campaigning. **18.** British public schools topped a league table of international educational establishments set by the Organisation for Economic Co-operation. **22.** The Labour Party announced plans for senior party officials to vet all future donations of more than £5,000. The Queen opened a new art gallery at Buckingham Palace. **27.** A report by the Association of Community Health for England and Wales revealed that patients with serious illnesses spent up to four days in casualty departments due to NHS shortages. Stephen Byers resigned from his post as Secretary of State for Transport, Local Government and the Regions. **28.** Alistair Darling was appointed as the new Secretary of State for Transport, Local Government and the Regions. Paul Boateng was appointed Chief Secretary to the Treasury. A new government department, the Office of the Deputy Prime Minister, was created. Ken Livingstone approved the development of a new main line cross-river and West London tram scheme. The Queen addressed the Scottish Parliament during a tour of the city to celebrate her Golden Jubilee. **29.** Margaret of York's golden crown, not seen in Britain since 1468, was loaned from a German cathedral to the Tower of London for an exhibition to mark The Queen's Golden Jubilee. **30.** Buckingham Palace announced that The Queen planned to double the

allowance of her son the Earl of Wessex in order for him to work full-time on royal duties. Captain Pip Tattersall became the first woman to be awarded the green beret by the Royal Marines.

JUNE 2002

1. The national holiday to celebrate The Queen's Golden Jubilee began with a classical concert in the grounds of Buckingham Palace. Downing Street announced that Stephen Byers, the former Secretary of State for Transport, Local Government and the Regions, would work alongside Charles Clarke, the Labour Party chairman, as a campaign planner. **2.** Buckingham Palace was evacuated after a fire broke out in a roof void in the East Gallery. Eton abolished the system allowing boys to be accepted for the school at birth. Instead pupils would be selected on the basis of a computerised aptitude test. Two Britons became the first all-female expedition team to reach both the North and South Poles. A pilot died after ejecting from the fighter jet when it skidded on landing and crashed into the M11. **3.** Sir John Stevens, the Commissioner of the Metropolitan Police, announced plans to recruit black and Asian officers from abroad due to a manpower shortage. More than a million people attended a pop concert to celebrate The Queen's Golden Jubilee. **6.** Government ministers apologised to the Paddington Survivors Group after it was revealed that one of Stephen Byers' aides attempted to ascertain the group's political affiliation. **11.** The Queen began a tour of Wales as part of her Golden Jubilee celebrations. The Ministry of Defence announced the creation of a 6,000-strong reaction force trained to respond to terrorist attacks. The Government and the British Medical Association agreed that newly qualified hospital consultants would be allowed to hold private clinics. **14.** The Queen celebrated her official birthday at traditional Trooping the Colour ceremony. The General Synod in Edinburgh voted in favour of ordaining women as bishops. **19.** The Church of England announced that Dr Rowan Williams, the Archbishop of Wales, would succeed Dr George Carey as Archbishop of Canterbury. **21.** The Home Office announced that a fourth jail would be built on the Isle of Wight to cater for record numbers of prison inmates. The Prince's Trust was awarded £50 million a year by the Government to fund a project to allocate work placements to disadvantaged young people. **25.** The Cabinet Secretary (Sir Richard Wilson) was summoned to appear before a House of Commons select committee to explain why the Home office refused to release papers that might have explained circumstances behind the resignation of the Northern Ireland Secretary, Peter Mandelson. **27.** Buckingham Palace revealed that the operating cost of the monarchy last year was £35.2 million.

JULY 2002

4. The Government announced plans to create an independent police force to protect Britain's nuclear sites from terrorist attack. A House of Commons select committee was established to investigate the deaths of four soldiers during separate incidents at the Princess Royal Barracks in Surrey. **6.** Official figures showed that gun crime had risen by up to 50 per cent in some parts of Britain. **8.** The House of Commons Commission revealed that its contribution to the cost of the Queen Mother's funeral was £500,000. **10.** Unison, the Transport and General Workers Union, and GMB council employees went on strike over pay. **14.** The Earl of Wessex launched a new film company after recently announcing that he was quitting the commercial sector. Gordon Brown

announced a £92.5 billion three-year public spending plan. **17.** MPs agreed a twenty per cent increase to the value of their final salary scheme. **19.** The Church of England announced plans to create special tribunals to try members of the clergy suspected of heresy. **22.** The Department of Health announced that all new doctors and nurses would have to undergo an HIV test. **24.** Scotland Yard revealed plans to introduce new drug rules in Lambeth, South London after cannabis was reclassified as a class C drug. **31.** Genetic testing established that the white woman who gave birth to black twins after an IVF treatment error was their biological mother. Her husband was not the biological father.

AUGUST 2002

3. Thirty-nine cases of Legionnaire's disease were confirmed in Barrow-in-Furness, Cumbria. **4.** Sir Philip Mawer, the Commissioner for Standards in Public Life, called for MPs to be fined for breaking Commons rules as part of a package of measures aimed at stamping out corruption. **5.** Dr Rowan Williams joined the Welsh Druid order of the Gorsedd of the Bards, provoking accusations from evangelical groups of dabbling in paganism. The Queen stated that she had been profoundly moved by the public response to her Golden Jubilee tour. **6.** Cherie Blair was recovering with the Prime Minister after suffering a miscarriage. The cost of a dental check-up would double under reforms announced in a Government report. Alistair Darling announced that motorists would be charged to drive into the centre of Durham in Britain's first road toll. Two ten-year-old schoolgirls Jessica Chapman and Holly Wells went missing from their home in Soham, Cambridgeshire. **7.** The Home Office gave Gurbux Singh a £115,000 payoff following his resignation as head of the Commission for Racial Equality. **9.** The Prince of Wales unveiled a memorial garden bench to Queen Elizabeth, the Queen Mother at Castle Mey. Government figures revealed that hospital waiting lists had increased by 4,500 people since 1999. **10.** The Prince of Wales announced plans to launch a country casual fashion label using wool supplied by British sheep farmers to help revive the rural economy. **12.** The Ministry of Defence paid £1.74 million to 20 paratroopers injured in a NATO exercise in Sardinia. **13.** A third person died from Legionnaire's disease in Barrow-in-Furness General Hospital. **14.** An Afghan family, removed from a West Midlands mosque where they had sought sanctuary, was deported to Germany. Home Office ministers announced that Afghan asylum-seekers would be offered up to £2,500 to go home as part of a six-month voluntary repatriation trial. **21.** Police confirmed that the bodies they had unearthed belonged to missing schoolgirls Holly Wells and Jessica Chapman. The Bank of England re-issued the five pound note featuring Elizabeth Fry, which had been recalled because the serial numbers on the back could be erased. **27.** Simon Murphy resigned as leader of the Labour MEPs. Carole Baptiste, the former manager of a group of social workers involved in the Victoria Climbié child abuse case, was charged with obstructing a public inquiry and fined £500 for failing to attend an inquiry into the child's death. **29.** A number of British MPs raised objections to the UK taking part in military action against Iraq due to breach of United Nations resolutions. **30.** A woman in her fifties died of suspected Legionnaire's disease at the Royal Lancaster Infirmary. **31.** The Queen, the Duke of Edinburgh and Princess Charles attended a church service to mark the fifth anniversary of the death of Diana, the Princess of Wales. Iain Duncan Smith said that he supported a pre-emptive US offensive against Iraq as

he believed that the UK was on Sadam Hussein's list of targets for a nuclear attack.

NORTHERN IRELAND AFFAIRS

SEPTEMBER 2001

1. David Trimble, leader of the Ulster Unionist Party (UUP), and Ian Paisley, leader of the Democratic Unionist Party (DUP), met after more than three decades of no formal communication between the two parties. **10.** The Northern Ireland Assembly met to discuss the dispute over the right of Roman Catholic pupils to walk along a loyalist road to school. **17.** John Hume resigned as leader of the Social Democratic Labour Party. James Cooper, the UUP's candidate, defeated at the Fermanagh and South Tyrone seat, appealed to the High Court in Belfast to have the result annulled due to irregularities at the polling station. **19.** The IRA confirmed that their representatives were in talks with General John de Chastelain's decommissioning body in an attempt to accelerate the peace process. **20.** Members of the UUP called on their leader David Trimble to leave the Northern Ireland Executive if the Government proceeded with a planned one-day suspension of the Assembly. **24.** Sinn Féin leader (Gerry Adams) said that attempts to exclude his party from the Northern Ireland Executive could jeopardise IRA disarmament. The UUP drew up a motion calling for ministers Martin McGuiness and Bairbre de Brun to be expelled from the Northern Ireland Executive. **26.** American congressmen suggested that Gerry Adams should be refused an American Visa. David Trimble called for the removal of Sinn Féin from the Northern Ireland Assembly unless the IRA started to decommission its weapons over the following two weeks.

OCTOBER 2001

4. A Belfast High Court judge ruled that Sinn Féin ministers in the Stormont power-sharing executive must fly the Union flag over their departments. **5.** David Trimble failed at the Appeal Court in Belfast to overturn a court ruling that his ban on Sinn Féin ministers attending a cross-border meeting was illegal. It was revealed that recruits to the new Northern Ireland Police Service would wear baseball caps in green, white and gold-colours similar to the Irish Republic's flag. **8.** David Trimble announced that he was to withdraw his ministers from the Stormont Executive in protest at the IRA's continued refusal to decommission their weapons. **12.** The Northern Ireland Secretary (John Reid) announced that the Ulster Defence Association (UDA) and the Loyalist Volunteer Force would no longer respect the cease-fire due to the outbreak of recent violence in the region. **22.** Gerry Adams revealed that he had asked the IRA to disarm its weapons. A member of the UDA leading council said that there would be no immediate decommissioning of their weapons even if the IRA began to destroy its own. The IRA decommissioned part of its armoury and, in acknowledgement, the UDA agreed to return to the power-sharing Executive. **24.** Britain began to reduce its military presence in Northern Ireland by dismantling observation towers in republican South Armagh. **26.** David Trimble announced plans to seek re-election as First Minister of Northern Ireland assembly after winning the backing of his party for the restoration of devolved government in Ulster.

NOVEMBER 2001

2. A motion to reappoint David Trimble as First Minister

of the Stormont power sharing executive was defeated by a single vote, despite Mr Trimble winning 70 per cent of the vote overall: 29 Unionists voted in favour of his reinstatement and 30 against. **5.** The High Court dismissed a legal challenge by the DUP to prevent the re-election of David Trimble as Northern Ireland's First Minister. **6.** The Deputy Leader of the DUP (Peter Robinson) announced that his party would challenge the decision not to call assembly elections until 2003. **15.** The Queen visited Londonderry – her first visit since a post-coronation tour in 1953.

December 2001

6. It was revealed that the Royal Ulster Constabulary had been given a warning of the terrorist attack in Omagh in 1998 – 11 days before a real IRA bomb killed 29 people. **9.** Around 21 policemen and three soldiers were injured during rioting in South Armagh following a protest by the youth wing of Sinn Féin. **17.** John Reid announced that parliamentary groups in Northern Ireland would be given another five years to decommission their weapons.

January 2002

9. Protestants and Roman Catholics clashed near the Holy Cross Primary School in North Belfast as Catholic parents walked their children home through a Protestant area. **18.** Northern Ireland Security Minister (Jane Kennedy) was attacked by petrol bombers whilst observing street violence in the Belfast area in a police Land Rover. Sinn Féin's four MPs were given offices in the Palace of Westminster. **22.** The inquiry into the events known as Bloody Sunday, which took place on 30 January 1972 in Londonderry, heard a statement from Martin McGuinness, who confirmed that he was a Provisional IRA leader in Londonderry when 13 Catholic civilians were killed by paratroopers. The inquiry moved to London to ensure that former soldiers could testify in safety. **25.** Colm Murphy was sentenced to 14 years' imprisonment at a Special Criminal Court in Dublin for his involvement in the Omagh bombing in August 1998.

February 2002

5. A motion to exclude Sinn Féin ministers from government for a year was defeated in the Northern Ireland Assembly. **7.** The Northern Ireland Policing Board announced the appointment of a senior officer from England to oversee the investigation into the Omagh bombing. **11.** Two men were arrested in Northern Ireland in connection with suspected Real IRA bomb blasts in Birmingham and London. **12.** A report by the Commons Standard and Privileges Committee suggested that Sinn Féin's MPs should be required to list their interests on the House of Commons register after taking offices in Westminster. **17.** Tony Blair and Irish Premier Bertie Ahern met at Downing Street to review the progress of the Good Friday Agreement.

March 2002

10. Sinn Féin and SDLP gave their support to David Trimble's call to hold a referendum on forming a united Ireland. **12.** Senior ministers informed Tony Blair that the peace process was in jeopardy as Parliament would not sanction the planned amnesty of up to 100 IRA fugitives wanted by the Northern Ireland Police Service. **19.** Gerry Adams was summoned to appear before a Congressional hearing in the US into the IRA's involvement with the terrorist group Revolutionary Armed Forces of Colombia (FARC). **25.** Thirty IRA fugitives, including men who escaped from the top-security Maze prison would be

allowed to return to Britain without facing imprisonment under a private deal agreed between Tony Blair and Gerry Adams.

April 2002

3. The Assistant Northern Ireland Chief Constable (Alan McQuillan) claimed that Loyalist paramilitaries were behind a series of violent attacks against the security services in North Belfast. Republicans injured thirteen police officers following a series of firebomb attacks. **6.** Around 200 police officers in Northern Ireland were warned that their personal details could be in the hands of the IRA after thieves stole documents containing codenames of terrorist informants and details of their police handlers from Castlereagh police station. **23.** Gerry Adams refused an invitation to give evidence about Provisional IRA's links with Colombian FARC terrorists.

May 2002

7. Three Real IRA terrorists were sentenced at Woolwich Crown Court to 30 years imprisonment for conspiracy to cause explosions on the British mainland and for offences under the Prevention of Terrorism Act. **18.** Martin Ferris, a former IRA volunteer, won a seat in the Irish general election as a Fianna Fail party candidate, giving the party an absolute majority in the Dail. **30.** Hugh Orde of the Metropolitan Police was appointed Northern Ireland's Chief Constable and is take up his post in September.

June 2002

2. Three people, including two 15-year-old boys, were shot dead in east Belfast during a weekend of violence. **7.** A bomb exploded injuring a Roman Catholic recruit to the joint Catholic and Protestant Police Service of Northern Ireland. **8.** The Real IRA began peace talks with the Irish government. **14.** Tony Blair agreed to hold emergency talks with Bertie Ahern in an attempt to rescue the peace process following accusations that the IRA had breached the cease-fire.

July 2002

4. The IRA was linked by a United States Senate report to the massacre of 117 civilians killed in a church in Colombia two months ago. **16.** The IRA apologised to relatives of hundreds of innocent civilians killed during the IRA's 30-year terrorist campaign. **24.** Tony Blair said Sinn Fein would be ejected from the Northern Ireland Executive if evidence emerged that the IRA was involved in planning terrorist actions. **31.** The loyalist Ulster Volunteer Force admitted to breaching its cease-fire agreement in a copy of its Combat magazine.

August 2002

2. Thousands of people marched in Belfast in protest over recent paramilitary killings. **11.** Colombian and British security experts said that the recent FARC terrorists attack on the Colombian presidential palace was similar to a mortar attack in Downing Street in 1991. **22.** The Northern Ireland police Chief Constable Colin Cramphorn said that pressures on resources left officers with less time to manage day-to-day policing. **28.** Senior Ulster Unionists sources revealed that David Trimble's leadership could be at risk after 60 signatures had been submitted demanding an emergency meeting of the party's ruling council, at which the party's role in the power sharing executive would be put to the vote. **29.** Protestant residents from the Glenbryn area of Ardoyne rejected proposals to build a peace wall between the two communities amid fears for their safety. The area had

witnessed many violent clashes over access to the Holy Cross girls' Catholic primary school in the Protestant part of Ardoyne.

ARTS AND THE MEDIA

SEPTEMBER 2001

11. Arts Minister (Baroness Blackstone) placed a temporary ban on the export of Michelangelo's *The Risen Christ*, sold at Christie's last year for £8.14 million, to give public institutions an opportunity to raise money to match the price. **16.** The British Library organised a conference to discuss ways to prevent bookworms from damaging its manuscripts. **20.** A customised shirt worn by Johnny Rotten of the Sex Pistols punk band was sold for £3,995 at Sotheby's in London. **21.** Television presenter Nick Hancock paid £23,500 at auction for Sir Stanley Matthews' 1953 Football Association Cup Final winner's medal. **24.** A vintage R-type Bentley, which belonged to Lord Lucan, who is still wanted in connection with the death of his children's nanny in the 1970s, was sold at auction for £18,250. **25.** Sarah Wildor, a dancer at the Royal Ballet, resigned due to a dispute with Ross Stretton, the company's new Australian director. Equity, the British actors' union, announced industrial action due to a dispute over pay.

OCTOBER 2001

2. Barclays Bank announced that it would spend £1.9 million over the next two years to support plays at the National Theatre. The Heritage Lottery Fund awarded a £2.25 million grant to the custodians of Dove Cottage, William Wordsworth's home in the Lake District. **5.** A collection of 25 paintings and sculptures worth £30 million went on display at Christie's in London to raise funds for Unicef, the United Nations Children's Fund. **9.** A rare copy of the first manuscript of William Shakespeare's *First Folio* was sold for £4.1 million at auction at Christie's in New York. **11.** Sir V. S. Naipaul became the first British author to win the Nobel Prize for literature. **12.** Sotheby's announced 150 redundancies, 46 of which would come from their British salesrooms. **14.** The British Museum returned a stolen fifteenth-century Egyptian statue of a viceroy to the Sudanese government after learning of its progeny. **15.** Christie's auction house in New York was alleged to have sold a rare eighteenth-century cello by Alessandro Gagliano worth £700,000 for £32,000. **17.** The Australian novelist Peter Carey won the Booker Prize for his novel *True History of the Kelly Gang*. **18.** A cleaner at an art gallery mistakenly threw away the work of artist Damien Hirst worth £5,000 mistaking it for leftover rubbish from the opening party. **25.** Sotheby's and Christie's auction houses were granted the right to hold sales in France for the first time after the French authorities overturned a ruling by King Henry II banning foreign auctioneers. **30.** A view of meadows beside the Thames from Richmond Hill in Surrey, found in several paintings by J. M. W Turner, was saved from development by Richmond Council and given to the Petersham Trust. **31.** A painting by Andrea del Sarto, *The Madonna and Child*, worth millions of pounds, was bought for a small sum by a group of collectors from an American who thought it was a copy.

NOVEMBER 2001

1. The lantern designed by the pre-Raphaelite artist William Holman Hunt for his painting *The Light of the*

World was sold for £52,100 at auction by Bonhams & Brooks. **29.** A student purchased a sketch by Damien Hirst for £35 worth £4,000 at the RCA Secret 2001. **30.** The Secretary of State for Culture, Media and Sport (Tessa Jowell) announced the abolition of admission charges to the Natural History Museum, the Victoria and Albert and the Imperial War Museums. The Science Museum, the National Maritime Museum and the Museum of London would also abandon entry charges.

DECEMBER 2001

9. Martin Creed won the £20,000 Turner prize for his installation *The Lights Going On and Off.* **10.** The medals of Air Vice-Marshal 'Jonnie' Johnson, a WWII pilot who shot down 38 enemy aircraft, were sold for £241,500 at auction. **16.** A cycle of thirteenth-century frescoes depicting scenes from the Bible was unearthed in a cathedral in Sienna, Italy. **19.** Backstage theatre staff in the West End voted in favour of strike action after turning down a 1.6 per cent pay rise.

JANUARY 2002

6. A report by the Department for Culture, Media and Sports found that attendance at national museums and galleries had doubled on average since admission charges were abolished in December. **8.** The English Tourism Council announced that the Millennium Dome had 6.5 million visitors during 2000. **10.** Michael Attenborough was appointed artistic director of the Almeida Theatre. **22.** Children's writer Philip Pullman won the Whitbread Book of the Year prize for his novel *The Amber Spyglass.* **30.** Two thousand volunteers walked across the Millennium Bridge in London to test its safety. Rare watercolour drawings by eighteenth-century artist and poet William Blake were put up for auction in Edinburgh.

FEBRUARY 2002

17. Sketches by pre-Raphaelite painter William Holman Hunt were unearthed by the granddaughter of one of the painter's former models after lying forgotten in a drawer for 60 years. **22.** The Millennium Bridge reopened to the public after undergoing £5 million of improvements to rectify a flaw in its structure. **24.** The film *The Lord of the Rings* won five Bafta awards including best film and best director. The Marquis of Bath announced plans to sell 400 works of art valued at more than £20 million from his home, Longleat, to maintain the estate. **28.**The singer Madonna announced plans to star in a West End production of the play *Up For Grabs.*

MARCH 2002

1. The BBC launched a new digital channel BBC Four dedicated to arts and culture. **2.** Lord Hindlip, the chairman of Christie's, admitted having prior knowledge of a price-fixing arrangement with their rival Sotheby's. Under the arrangement both companies introduced an almost identical sliding scale of charges. **3.** Channel 4 paid historian Dr David Starkey £2 million to present a series on the British monarchy. **5.** *Billy*, a biography of the comedian Billy Connolly, won the British Book of the Year Award. A painting by suffragette Sylvia Pankhurst, *The Old Fashioned Pottery*, was bought for £14,100 by the House of Commons. **11.** Sir Ian McKellen and Helen Mirren won awards for best supporting actor and actress at the Screen Actors' Guild awards in Hollywood. **14.** Yoko Ono, the widow of John Lennon, bequeathed the childhood Liverpool home of her late husband to the nation. **15.** Medieval frescoes by Giotto in the Scrovegni Chapel in Italy went on display following 25 years of

restoration. **20.** The Department of Health attempted to veto the opening of the art exhibition *Body Worlds* in London as it featured 175 human body parts and 25 corpses.

APRIL 2002

8. Photographs of the 1848 riots in Paris went on sale at Sotheby's in London. **17.** Around 100 paintings by Jack Chalker, a WWII veteran, were sold for nearly £200,000 at Bonhams in London. **18.** The Victoria & Albert Museum announced a £150 million renovation programme of its galleries. **21.** Nine Expressionist masterpieces worth around £6 million were stolen from the Brücke Museum in Berlin. **28.** The British TV industry won 15 awards at the Montreux Golden Rose Festival. **29.** The British Museum announced 150 job cuts due to a £5 million cash shortfall.

MAY 2002

2. A set of 12 George II mahogany dining chairs belonging to the Earl of Shaftesbury was auctioned at Christie's in London for £750,650. **19.** A number of stolen Expressionist paintings by Max Pechstein were found in a Berlin apartment. **22.** *The Times* won the National Newspaper of the Year Awards. **23.** The painting *Nu au Collier* by Picasso went on display for the first time in 60 years at Christie's auction house. **27.** Descendants of Dr Arthur Feldmann, a prominent pre-war collector, lodged a claim with the British Museum for the return of four drawings worth more than £100,000 stolen by the Nazis during WWII. **28.** English Heritage opened a garden at Richmond Castle in North Yorkshire dedicated to 16 conscientious objectors who were imprisoned during WWI. **29.** The satirical magazine *Punch* ceased publication due to financial losses. A detective constable won the £1 million prize on the reality television show *Survivor.*

JUNE 2002

2. Vaughan William's piece *The Lark Ascending* was voted the best British classical composition by a poll of more than 250,000 Classic FM listeners. **5.** Staff at the British Museum announced plans to strike in protest of 150 job cuts. **13.** The Roman marble statue *Jenkins Venus* was sold at Christie's auction house for around £8 million. An art collection belonging to the Marquess of Bath was sold for £23.8 million at Christie's. **14.** The BBC television executive Alan Yentob was appointed chairman of the Institute of Contemporary Arts. Peter Porte was presented with The Queen's 2002 Gold Medal for Poetry at Buckingham Palace. A rare autographed copy of the Beatles' 1967 album *Sergeant Pepper's Lonely Hearts Club Band* sold at auction for £34,000. **16.** The British Museum was closed due to strike action by its staff. **18.** National Trust announced plans to purchase Tyntesfield estate near Bristol for nearly £24 million. Three paintings by the Prince of Wales were sold for nearly £20,000 at commercial auction. **21.** The British Museum announced plans to make £6.5 million worth of cuts and abandon multi-million-pound plans for a new study centre in an attempt to solve its cash deficit. **24.** The painting *Nympheas* by Monet was sold at auction by Sotheby's for £13.48 million. **27.** The billionaire philanthropist Sir Paul Getty donated £5 million to St Paul's Cathedral in London to help towards its £40 million restoration.

JULY 2002

4. An amateur arts collector sold a Chinese vase bought in Dorset for £250 at auction for £110,000. The BBC was awarded the three licences left vacant after the collapse of

ITV Digital by the Independent Television Commission. **10.** *Artsworld*, the digital television channel created by Sir Issacs, announced that it would close 18 months after it was launched. **11.** The Baltic, the largest contemporary gallery outside London, opened on the Tyne in Gateshead. **12.** Tate Modern announced plans to open all night in an attempt to cope with demands to view its Matisse-Picasso exhibition. **24.** The Royal Opera House announced plans to sell 15,000 of its costumes to generate more storage space. **26.** Baroness Blackstone ordered that a North Yorkshire shipwreck believed to be the eighteenth century American warship *Bonhomme Richard*, be protected from looters. **31.** The Government formally signed the 1970 United Nations Educational, Scientific and Cultural Organisation (UNESCO) Convention to protect the nation's cultural property being sold overseas.

AUGUST 2002

7. The first part of the film *Lord of the Rings: The Fellowship of the Ring* sold 1.27 million DVD copies in one day. **8.** A painting by Frank Wilkin depicting the Battle of Hastings was returned to the Great Hall at Battle Abbey after 140 years absence. **9.** The National Gallery of Scotland announced plans to launch an annual exhibition of impressionist art.

CRIMES AND LEGAL AFFAIRS

SEPTEMBER 2001

3. 44-year-old Tony Jasinskyj was arrested in Leicester in connection with the rape and murder 20 years ago of Marion Croft, 14. **4.** Thelma Conway, 56, a former social worker was awarded £140,000 in compensation by Worcestershire County Council after she was forced to resign from her job as head of a care home due to stress. **10.** Ashworth Hospital on Merseyside took out an injunction against the publication of a book on serial killers by Moors murderer Ian Brady. **11.** A man was sentenced at Portsmouth County Court to eight years in prison for torturing a 60-year-old man for three hours, whom he believed to be a paedophile. Three National Crime Squad officers appeared before Leicester magistrates' court charged with possession and supply of drugs. **13.** A 21-year-old man was charged with rioting and another, aged 20, with violent disorder, following disturbances in Bradford during the summer. **14.** Garabet and Hazmik Manuelyan, both 45, whose 10-month-old daughter starved to death due to an extreme vegan diet, were sentenced at the High Court to three years community rehabilitation after they admitted cruelty. **19.** Andrew Rickard, 32, was given a one-year suspended sentence at Cardiff Crown Court for killing a six-year-old boy in a car accident through careless driving. The court accepted his plea that the accident occurred because of the effects of an anaesthetic administered to him earlier at the dentist. Paul Tramontini, 34, a teacher, was sentenced at Portsmouth Crown Court to 18 months for eloping with a 15-year-old pupil. **20.** A single mother who left her three children home alone while she went on a week's holiday was jailed for six months. **21.** Glynn Harding, 27, was found guilty of sending parcel bombs to people connected with animal husbandry and was ordered to be detained indefinitely in a secure hospital. **24.** Ashworth Hospital lost their High Court legal battle to prevent a book by the Moors murderer Ian Brady being published. Legal experts said that police powers to detain and interrogate suspects under the current Human Rights Act were sufficient to give them adequate emergency powers

to protect the public from terrorist activities and did not require amendments. Colin Davies, 44, who had tried to open a cannabis café in Stockport, Manchester, was charged at Stockport Magistrates Court with drug smuggling. **25.** Gordon Brown announced plans to rewrite the Proceeds of Crime Bill to include measures aimed at tracking and confiscating assets linked to terrorist organisations. **26.** An inquiry began into the death of eight-year-old Victoria Climbié, who died following months of abuse by her great aunt and the aunt's boyfriend.

OCTOBER 2001

1. The National Security Appeals Division of the Data Protection Tribunal held that the security service could not rely on the blanket policy of refusing to confirm or deny if it held particular information. **4.** The High Court rejected Michael Stone's appeal against his life sentence for the murder of Lin Russell, her six-year-old daughter Megan and the attempted murder of Josie Russell. Sisters Sylvia Evans, 39, and Gwendoline Sharpe, 33, from south east London who married 24 men as part of an immigration fraud, were jailed at the Inner London Crown Court for three and two years respectively. Mohamed al Fayed, 69, the owner of Harrods, won substantial undisclosed libel damages in the High Court for allegations that he was experiencing financial difficulties reported in the *Mail on Sunday*. **5.** The Press Complaints Commission cleared the Secretary of State for Transport, Local Government and the Regions (Stephen Byers) of any misconduct, following allegations in the Daily Mail of covering up a report into the business affairs of Labour MP Geoffrey Robinson. **8.** Bill Starling and Alan Prescott, former Essex social workers, were jailed for abusing children in their care in Basildon and Hornchurch from 1967 to 1985. A report published by Sir Robin Auld, a Court of Appeal Judge, recommended the abolition of jury trials for many middle-ranking offences, including theft and assault. The report also recommended that trial by jury should be abolished for complex fraud trials and trials involving children. **9.** The Railtrack Group launched a High Court action for the return of £350 million held in frozen accounts by HSBC bank. **10.** The entertainer Michael Barrymore, 49, was cautioned for drug offences by detectives investigating the death of a man found in his swimming pool. **15.** Lord Archer of Weston-super-Mare, currently serving a four-year sentence for perjury, was transferred to the open prison North Sea Camp, Lincolnshire. A teacher Mary-Ann Woodeson was given a year's conditional discharge by Norwich magistrates' for biting a three-year old boy on the arm after he bit another pupil. **18.** Terminally ill Diane Pretty lost her case in the High Court to allow her husband to assist her suicide. **23.** The Home Secretary (David Blunkett) announced the reclassification of cannabis from a Class B to a Class C drug, making possession of the drug no longer a criminal offence. **28.** Writs were issued in the High Court against Virgin Airlines and British Airways on behalf of two deep vein thrombosis victims who alleged that they suffered from the condition due to being seated in cramped economy seats on long-haul flights. **29.** The Parliamentary Ombudsman announced an investigation into the Financial Services Authority's (FSA) handling of the collapse of Equitable Life insurance. Tony Martin, jailed for life for murdering a teenage burglar who broke into his home and wounding his accomplice, had his conviction reduced to manslaughter by the Court of Appeal. **30.** Yasser al-Sirri, 38, an Egyptian asylum-seeker, was sent to the Central Criminal Court for trial accused

of conspiring to kill General Ahmed Shah Masood, the leader of Afghanistan's Northern Alliance. 25-year-old Anna Bartlett serving a life sentence for drug trafficking in the United Arab Emirates, had her sentence reduced to ten years following an appeal. **31.** Railtrack was fined £50,000 and English, West and Scottish Railways, a rail freight company, £70,000 for safety failures that led to the death of a schoolboy, who was hit by a train whilst playing in busy railway sidings.

NOVEMBER 2001

1. Diane Pretty won the appeal to take her assisted suicide test case to the House of Lords. David Shayler, the former MI5 agent, won the right to appeal against a Court of Appeal decision to ban him from using the defence that he acted in the public interest when he disclosed Security Service details to the press in breach of the Official Secrets Act. Mossadek Jouini, 38, was sentenced to three years at Southwark County Court for a hoax call made hours after the September 11 attack on the World Trade Centre in the US; claiming he was a member of the Palestinian terror group Hamas and warning that Canary Wharf and the former Natwest tower would be targeted. **5.** The Criminal Cases Review Commission began a re-assessment of the 30-year prison sentence given to Ronnie Biggs the Great Train Robber. **7.** A Briton Peter Brandon was charged by Saudi Arabian authorities with involvement in bomb attacks linked to illegal drinking dens. Four other men were also charged with the offence. **11.** Twelve British aviation enthusiasts appeared in a Greek court charged with espionage after allegedly taking photographs of a Greek military air base. **13.** Stuart Campbell, 34, the uncle of missing Essex schoolgirl Danielle Jones, was charged with her murder at Chelmsford Crown Court. **15.** The *Times* newspaper requested its constitutional right to a jury in its libel case against businessman Grigori Loutchansky, whom *The Times* implied to be a Russian Mafia boss. A new jury was sworn in at the Sarah Payne murder trial held at Lewes Crown Court following a procedural irregularity. **16.** Diane Shepherd, the head of the Children and Family Court Advisory and Support Service, was suspended pending an enquiry into administration irregularities. **18.** The Criminal Injuries Compensation Authority made an offer of £20,000 in compensation to relatives of World Trade Center victims for the stress of watching the attack live on British television. **20.** Three men were remanded in custody for two weeks by the High Court in Nairobi charged with the murder of Tonio Trzebinski, 41, a British artist shot dead outside his home. **21.** Jonathan King, the pop music celebrity was sentenced to seven years imprisonment for sex offences against school boys. Horace Pinnock, 29, a Radio 1 Disc Jockey was shot and killed outside a London hotel during a late-night fight with a gang of ten men. Michael Biggs, the son of the Great Train robber Ronnie Biggs, lodged an appeal under the Human Rights Act against the Home Office decision to expel him from Britain. **22.** Major Charles Ingram, who won £1 million on the quiz show *Who Wants to be a Millionaire?*, was arrested on suspicion of fraud. The show's production company alleged that Major Ingram had received help from his wife sitting in the audience. **23.** Lord Archer of Weston-super-Mare was cleared in a report by auditors KPMG of misappropriating millions of pounds from a British Kurdish charity. **27.** A High Court Judge ruled that Frank Yuen could trade under the name McChina fast foods. MacDonald's, the fast food restaurant had tried to stop Mr Yuen from trading under what they claimed was a similar sounding name. **29.** Five Law Lords rejected the appeal of Diane Pretty, a terminally ill woman, to allow

her husband to assist her suicide. Mrs Pretty announced that she would appeal to the European Court. Parliament passed emergency legislation to ban human cloning. Paul Burrell, 43, a former butler to Diana, Princess of Wales, accused of stealing items belonging to the Royal family, was committed at the Central Court for trial in January. The Ministry of Defence was granted an injunction banning *The Sun* newspaper from identifying four SAS men fighting against terrorism in Afghanistan.

DECEMBER 2001

3. Ernest Saunders began a third appeal against his conviction for theft and false accounting in the Guinness share support case of 1990. The High Court ordered Surrey County Council to pay £3 million to Thomas Harrison, who was left brain-damaged after being violently shaken by his childminder at the age of six months. Michael Biggs, son of the Great Train Robber Ronnie Biggs, lost his latest bid to remain in Britain. Railtrack shareholders wrote to the DTLR to demand disclosure of documents needed to prepare their claim against Stephen Byers over his decision to place the track-owning company into administration. **5.** A High Court judge ruled that legislation introduced by David Blunkett to fine lorry drivers £2,000 for each illegal immigrant they brought into the UK was unlawful and in breach of the European Convention on Human Rights. Alfred Taubman, 76, the former chairman of Sotheby's auction house, was found guilty of conspiring to fix commission rates with its rival Christie's. *The Times* newspaper won its appeal against the businessman Grigori Loutchansky over printed articles describing him as a Russian crime boss. **10.** William Todd, who was serving two life sentences for murder and attempted murder, escaped from Winchester prison. Inderjit Kainth, a paranoid schizophrenic who stabbed a 16 year-old girl to death in Birmingham city centre, was detained indefinitely at a secure hospital. A Greek public prosecutor announced that there was sufficient evidence to try the 12 British plane-spotters detained in Greece on charges of espionage. Roy Whiting was sentenced to life imprisonment at Lewes Crown Court for abducting and murdering eight-year-old Sarah Payne. The twelve British plane-spotters held in Greece on spying charges, were released on bail. **13.** Rosalind Mark, the former nanny to Tony Blair's children, won damages at the High Court over a claim that she sold her story to *The Mail on Sunday* in breach of a confidentiality agreement. Gary Hart was found guilty of 10 counts of manslaughter following the Selby train crash and later sentenced to five years imprisonment. **14.** Leeds United footballers Jonathan Woodgate and Lee Bowyer were cleared of assaulting Sarfraz Najeib at the High Court. Mr Woodgate was found guilty of a lesser charge of affray, receiving 100 hours community service. The twelve British plane-spotters were freed on bail from a Greek prison. **18.** The BBC was fined £25,000 for contempt of court and ordered to pay £22,500 costs in the High Court for identifying an alleged sex abuse victim during a jury trial last year. **19.** The European Commission launched a legal action against the UK Government to determine whether it was in breach of any community laws over EC regulation of Lloyd's of London insurance market.

JANUARY 2002

8. It was confirmed that Jeffrey Archer would be allowed to retain his title Lord Archer of Weston-super-Mare after leaving prison. **15.** The Court of Appeal freed Stephen Downing who had been wrongly imprisoned for 28 years for the death of Wendy Sewell. **17.** Gary Hart lodged an application with the Court of Appeal in London against his conviction of causing death by dangerous driving at Selby. **22.** The High Court ruled that the Armed forces could sue the Ministry of Defence over death due to injury whilst in service. A group of 20 women with epilepsy who gave birth to children with physical defects won legal aid to launch an action for compensation against the Government. The women claimed they were not informed of the potential danger of using prescribed drugs to control their illness during pregnancy. **25.** Court Service announced the creation of an online writ service. Anyone claiming up to £100,000 could sue through the Internet across England and Wales. The Police Reform Bill incorporating the introduction of uniformed civilian community support officers came into effect. **28.** The Press Complaints Commission upheld a complaint by Tony and Cherie Blair against *The Daily Telegraph* which reported that their son Euan Blair had applied for a place at Trinity College, Oxford. Seven postal workers injured in an accident in 1996 involving a freight train and a post train near Stafford received £832,500 damages at the High Court. **31.** Thieves broke into Ford Open Prison in West Sussex and stole money and mobile phones belonging to prison wardens. The High Court approved a group action by hundreds of air travellers who claimed to have suffered from deep vein thrombosis whilst sitting in cramped economy class seats. Nadine Milroy-Sloan, 28, who wrongly accused former Conservative Minister Neil Hamilton and his wife of sexually assaulting her, was questioned by police on allegations of perverting the course of justice.

FEBRUARY 2002

4. Hari Thapa, a former Gurkha lance-corporal, began a race discrimination case in an employment tribunal against the Ministry of Defence concerning discrepancies in his salary compared to his British counterparts. **7.** Julian Brazier, Conservative MP for Canterbury, was given a four-month suspended jail sentence by an Italian court. Brazier had killed a motorcyclist whilst driving on the wrong side of the road during a holiday in Tuscany. **11.** Two thieves stole £5 million in banknotes following a raid on a security van at Heathrow airport. **16.** A senior Government official in charge of preventing unauthorised publication of military secrets was arrested under the Official Secrets Act. The arrest was in connection with the leaking of memoirs of Dame Stella Rimington, the former director general of MI5. **17.** Four men who planned the £200 million diamond robbery from the Millennium Dome were both sentenced to 15 years' imprisonment at the Central Criminal Court. Detectives investigating the murder of Stephen Lawrence in 1993 launched a new search for the knife used to kill the teenager. **24.** The Prison Service announced plans for the early release of short-sentenced non-violent offenders in order to deal with a rise of 3,130 in inmates since January. A report by the Prison Service recommended the creation of eight super-prisons each capable of holding 1,500 offenders to replace 30 rundown jails.

MARCH 2002

2. Viscount Linley announced that he would take legal action over claims in a new biography that his mother, Princess Margaret, took illegal drugs. More than 100 women, who suffered serious side-effects from using third generation contraceptive pills, began a test case in the High Court against three pharmaceutical companies for millions of pounds in damages. Lord Woolf ruled that a High Court judge had been wrong to grant an injunction against the *Sunday People*, preventing the

newspaper from disclosing that Garry Flitcroft, a married Premier League footballer, had affairs with two women. The Home Office announced the creation of a joint unit to tackle persistent crime within five of the worst crime areas in England and Wales. Scotland Yard approached murder squad detectives from other forces to assist them in combating a rise in violent crime in London. **12.** Three former Labour councillors at Doncaster Metropolitan Borough Council were sentenced at Nottingham Crown Court between 12 months and five years for their part in a multi-million-pound fraud. **14.** The Lockerbie bomber, Abdul Baset Ali al-Megrahi, lost his appeal against his 20-year sentence at the Scottish court of appeal. **18.** Robert Paul Long was sentenced by Brisbane's Supreme Court to life imprisonment for starting a fire at a backpacker hostel in Queensland that killed 15 people, including seven Britons. Police Commander Brian Paddick, was temporarily removed from his post due to allegations that he had smoked cannabis and had allowed the drug to be used in his home. **19.** Jane Andrews, a former assistant to the Duchess of York, received permission to appeal against her conviction for murder following new claims of diminished responsibility at the time of killing her boyfriend. **20.** Judges at the Court of Appeal endorsed the power of the courts to stop football hooligans from travelling abroad at prominent matches. **21.** The Law Lords rejected a former MI5 agent David Shayler's claim to use a public interest defence in his forthcoming trial on three charges of infringing the Official Secrets Act. Five police forces announced plans to introduce fixed on-the-spot penalty notices for public disorder offences in a pilot scheme operating in the UK. **22.** Dame Butler-Sloss, President of the High Court Family Division, ruled that a paralysed social worker would be allowed to refuse ventilation treatment that was keeping her artificially alive. **25.** Law Lords granted permission for Ernest Saunders, Gerald Ronson, Anthony Parnes and Jack Lyons to appeal to the Lords to overturn their convictions for conspiracy to inflate the Guinness share price during its take-over of Distillers. **27.** Fashion model, Naomi Campbell, was awarded £3,500 in damages at the High Court after *The Mirror* newspaper reported that she attended Narcotics Anonymous meetings. **31.** Katherine Jenkins, a British air hostess accused of being part of a gang that smuggled drugs from Europe to sell in the United Arab Emirates, was cleared on appeal by a court in Dubai after spending 17 months in custody.

APRIL 2002

2. The Football League announced plans to sue Carlton Communications and Granada for up to £500 million unless it received £89 million by August – the second part of the payment for a three-year deal to allow ITV Digital to screen the European Championship and Premiership games. **4.** The Court of Appeal rejected a final appeal by Mohammed al Fayed brought against photographers who pursued the car in which Diana, Princess of Wales, and his son Dodi, were killed in 1997. **7.** The Football League applied to the High Court to obtain disclosure of the documents which detailed findings of the administrative report into ITV Digital. **9.** A 13-year-old girl was charged with smuggling heroin, valued at nearly £1 million, into Britain. **11.** Railtrack announced plans to sue Gary Hart, sentenced to five years imprisonment for causing the Selby train crash, for £11 million. **12.** Sarfraz Najeib began civil proceedings in the High Court against Lee Bowyer, the Leeds United football player who was cleared of attacking Mr Najeib outside a nightclub. **17.** Mary Bell, convicted aged 11 of killing two boys in 1968, applied to the High Court to seek a lifelong order to protect her

privacy. **22.** The twelve British plane-spotters accused of espionage by the Greek Government for photographing planes at a military airbase, returned to Greece to stand trial. Alfred Taubman, the chairman of Sotheby's auction house was sentenced in New York for a year for having a price-fixing agreement with rival firm Christie's. John Palmer, a jailed time-share fraudster, was ordered at the Central Criminal Court to pay £36 million in compensation to clients whom he duped into buying timeshares. **23.** A girl, forced at 16 to marry a Pakistani youth who had recently arrived in Britain, had her marriage annulled by the Court of Sessions in Edinburgh. **25.** Two teenage brothers were acquitted at the Central Criminal Court of murdering ten-year old Damilola Taylor who was stabbed to death in south east London. **26.** Courtney Barker, 22, was found guilty at Luton Crown Court of killing three children who drowned when a car he was driving plunged into a lake. The European Union instructed the Government to limit workers to a 48-hour week or face legal action. Six British plane-spotters were sentenced at a Greek court to three years imprisonment on spying charges and were given leave to appeal. **29.** Terminally ill Diane Pretty lost her appeal at the European Court of Human Rights for her husband to assist her suicide.

MAY 2002

16. Judge David Griffiths convened a special sitting at Southampton Crown Court to withdraw a £250 compensation order he had imposed on a father convicted six days earlier of assaulting James White, who he believed had sold heroin to his son. *The Times* newspaper was refused leave to appeal to the House of Lords after the Court of Appeal upheld a libel claim by Dr Grigori Loutchansky, who was accused of being involved in money-laundering and smuggling nuclear weapons by the newspaper. Five Law Lords overruled a Court of Appeal decision preventing the widows of two victims of mesothelioma, caused by exposure to asbestos, and a sufferer of the disease from claiming compensation. **18.** The Nepalese government contacted Tony Blair to protest over the Prime Minister's wife's appointment to represent former Gurkha soldiers taking legal action against the Ministry of Defence to gain equal pensions to their white colleagues. The government was concerned that she had failed to understand the political complexities of the case. **21.** Under the amended Adoption and Children Bill courts will be allowed to refuse a spouse contact with their children after a separation or divorce if they had been violent to their partner. The European Court of Human Rights awarded a widowed man social security benefits payments equal to those awarded to women. **22.** A judge reduced the 60-day sentence of a woman who allowed her children to truant from school to 28-days. **23.** A man who spent 11 years in jail for a murder he did not commit had £37,000 deducted from £690,000 compensation awarded by the Home Office for his prison bed and board. **24.** The indigenous people of the Chagos Islands, a British Indian Ocean territory, who were forcibly removed more than 30 years ago to make way for a US military base, announced plans to sue the British Government for their right to return. **30.** Farmer Bobby Waugh, was found guilty at Bedlington Magistrates' Court on five charges of failing to alert officials that foot-and-mouth disease was present at his farm. The first special court to try car drivers and motorcyclists caught speeding at more than 100 miles per hour on the Rettendon bypass, near Chelmsford, was held at Witham, Essex.

JUNE 2002

4. The European Court of Justice ruled that it was unlawful for the Government to hold shares in privatised industries, which allowed it to retain control in a company. **10.** The Government launched an inquiry into allegations that estate agents were using rising house prices to exploit house buyers. **11.** A woman began a court case against the NHS for failing to warn her about the psychological and physical distress she would suffer after having an abortion. Sir Elton John launched an appeal against a High Court ruling that cleared his former manager and PricewaterhouseCoopers of negligence whilst managing funds from his concert tours. **16.** A report by the Audit Commission found that around £80 million was lost annually due to overly lengthy, adjourned and cancelled trials. In response to this report the Government announced it may fine lawyers who deliberately prolonged trials. **18.** Janardan Dhasmana, a surgeon in the Bristol heart babies scandal that left 29 children dead in the 1980s, was told that he could resume operations on children after a three-year ban. A boy who was separated from his family at the age of 14 and sent away by the charity Barnardo's as part of the Child Migrant Scheme to populate parts of the Commonwealth, began a class action to sue the organisation for £400 million. Consignia offered £250,000 in compensation to a worker who was unfairly sacked for football hooliganism to end the threat of strike action by his colleagues. An Asian man who served sixteen years in jail wrongly convicted of murder after defending himself in a racist attack was freed following a European Court ruling. A female cleaner who found out that she was earning 60p per hour less than a male colleague was awarded £2,500 in compensation after claiming sex discrimination and victimisation. **19.** A former female city analyst's award of £1.4 million in compensation for sex discrimination was upheld, after investment bank Schroder Securities withdrew its appeal against her case. **21.** The Metropolitan Police reopened inquiries into whether Ken Livingstone was involved in an incident at a party which ended in a 35-year old man being taken to hospital.

JULY 2002

4. Three men were arrested in an investigation into suspect packages sent to Downing Street and St Andrews University. The Equal Opportunities Commission announced plans to sue a British school who refused to allow girls to wear trousers. **5.** A burglar who was wounded by Tony Martin during a burglary in which his 16-year-old accomplice was shot dead was granted legal aid to sue the jailed farmer. **14.** An inquiry found that GP Harold Shipman had murdered at least 166 of his former patients. **17.** David Blunkett announced that a defendant's previous convictions would be disclosed to juries following the overhaul of the double jeopardy rule. **18.** Carolyn Kirby became the first female president of the Law Society. **21.** Lord Archer of Weston-super-Mare sought permission to appeal against his four-year sentence for perjury and perverting the course of justice. **24.** The Home Office announced that motorists with six or more points on their licence who were caught speeding, would be able to avoid a driving ban by attending a safe driving course. A British yachtsman detained by the Greek coastguard for trying to smuggle 72 asylum-seekers into the country was jailed for ten years and fined £275,000. **25.** Gurbux Singh, chairman of the Commission for Racial Equality, was charged with using threatening behaviour towards a police officer outside the Lord's cricket ground. **29.** The

Lord Chancellor announced that he would review the selection process of the Queen's Counsel, following criticism by the Office of Fair Trading of the lack of monitoring of QCs' performance. Jill Dando's killer, Barry George, returned to prison to finish his life sentence after the Court of Appeal rejected his case. **30.** James Mawdsley, a human rights activist, was awarded £10,000 in damages from *The Guardian* after the High Court agreed that the paper made a false and defamatory statement by labelling him a hypocrite last year. Two former nursery workers were awarded £200,000 in libel damages at the High Court following incorrect allegations that they has sexually abused children in their care. **31.** John Palmer, 22, was sentenced at Exeter Crown Court to five years for manslaughter, after attacking and killing his three-month-old son. Major Charles Ingram and his wife were charged with deception and conspiracy following an investigation into them fraudulently winning the £1 million on *Who Wants to be a Millionaire?* quiz show. Jonathan Griffiths and Geoffrey Wildy were jailed at Cardiff Crown Court for making letter bombs with intention of sending them to two men who allegedly owed them money. The Court of Appeal quashed a £3 million compensation order against John Palmer, who was jailed for eight years for a timeshare fraud. Home Office statistics showed that the number of refugees remaining legally in the UK had risen to 42,000. London residents who failed in their challenge of Ken Livingstone's proposed £5 congestion charge were ordered by the High Court to pay a £10,000 legal bill.

AUGUST 2002

1. A couple were refused permission by the Human Fertilisation and Embryology Authority to allow doctors to use IVF techniques to select a baby who would be a perfect tissue match for their son who needs a bone marrow transplant. The Football League lost its High Court Battle to obtain £131.8 million damages from Carlton Communications and Granada Television. A Greek Statue worth £50,000 was stolen from the British Museum. **3.** The Government announced plans to provide £15 million worth of emergency grants to the British Museum. **5.** Two teenage girls were sentenced to 18 months in a young offenders institution for a failed armed robbery at a post office. **6.** Alistair Irvine, the son of Lord Irvine of Lairg, the Lord Chancellor, appeared in an American court charged with threatening a man's life with a handgun. **8.** Petrina Stocker appeared at Hendon Magistrates Court, North London, charged with murdering her nine-year-old son. **9.** On-the-spot fines of up to £80 for public order offences were introduced in pilot schemes by the police in Croydon, South London, Essex, the West Midlands and North Wales. **22.** Colin Skellett, the chief executive of Wessex Water, was arrested on the allegations that he received a £1 million bribe when the company was sold. **16.** Police questioned Ian Huntley and Maxine Carr over the whereabouts of missing schoolgirls Holly Wells and Jessica Chapman. **18.** Lord Archer of Weston-super-Mare was granted permission to leave North Sea Camp prison on Sundays for home visits. **20.** The Government announced plans to ban the use of hand-held mobile phones by motorists. Ian Huntley, a school caretaker from Soham, was charged with the murder of Holly Wells and Jessica Chapman. **23.** The Health and Safety Executive began a court case against St John Ambulance following the death of a first-aid worker in a powerboat accident. **28.** Barry George, convicted of the murder of television presenter Jill Dando, was refused leave to challenge his sentence in the House of Lords.

ECONOMIC AND BUSINESS AFFAIRS

SEPTEMBER 2001

3. BMW recalled its new Minis due to a defect with the model. **19.** RTL, the commercial broadcasting group, announced a loss of £1.4 billion on the value of its interests in Pearson Television. Cable & Wireless, the telecom group, issued its second profit warning in the past four months. A report by the Institute of Management found that a quarter of managers were now women compared to nine per cent in 1991. British Airways announced 6,000 job losses following a drop in ticket sales on transatlantic flights. The FTSE 100 shares index slumped to a four-year low opening 80 points down and dropping by a further 164.8 points to 4,556.9 once the New York Stock Exchange opened. **21.** The bankrupt South Korean car producer Daewoo was revived by a deal between General Motors and Daewoo's creditors. British Telecom's (BT) mobile division changed its name from BT Wireless to MMO2 (O2). Lloyd's of London insurance market was downgraded by two credit ratings due to anticipated future losses resulting from the recent terrorist attacks in the US. **24.** The Association of Unit Trusts announced that funds under management by unit trust groups have fallen by £41 billion over the past 12 months. **26.** BSkyB ceased using analogue satellite broadcasts in favour of digital. **30.** Manchester United Football Club reported a 30 per cent rise in profits.

OCTOBER 2001

3. Consignia announced that it had issued redundancy notices to 15,000 members of staff. **4.** First Choice, the travel group, announced 1,100 redundancies, around 60 per cent of which would be in the UK. The Bank of England cut interest rates by a quarter point, reducing it to four-and-a-half per cent – a 37-year low. The industrial materials group Cookson issued its fourth profit warning this year and cut a further 1,740 jobs. **5.** Virgin announced a $50 million investment into an American mobile phone joint venture with network operator Sprint. **9.** Credit Suisse announced 2,000 job cuts in its investment banking division. **10.** ICE Securities received a £1 million fine from the Securities and Futures Authority (SFA) and was ordered to pay £3.3 million in compensation to three customers who lost out on profits from share transactions conducted on their behalf. Arcadia, the UK's second largest clothes retailer, sold its majority stake in its Principles and Warehouse fashion chains for around £35 million. Professor Joseph Stiglitz of Columbia University and Michael Spence of Stanford University won the Nobel Prize in economics. **11.** Merrill Lynch HSBC announced it was to cut one in four of its UK workforce. **12.** The easyEverything Internet brand closed with losses of £13 million, the chain will be renamed easyInternetcafé. The credit ratings agency Moody's Investor Services downgraded British Airways debt to reflect falling demand for air travel. **15.** Vijay and Bhikhu Patel, the brothers behind Waymade Healthcare, the multimillion-pound pharmaceutical distributor, were named Entrepreneurs of the Year by sponsors Citigroup private bank, Vodafone and *The Times*. **16.** Marks & Spencer announced plans to sell its 18 French stores to Galeries La-fayette, the Paris based department store group. The Government published a report criticising the FSA's handling of the collapse of Equitable Life. FSA chairman Sir Howard Davies asked directors of Railtrack to provide details of meetings and events leading up to the day when the Secretary of State for Transport, Local

Government and the Regions (Stephen Byers) placed the group into administration. **17.** The insurer Lloyd's of London announced that it needed to raise £780 million to cover losses arising from the terrorist attacks in the US. **19.** The car manufacturer Rolls-Royce announced 5,000 job losses world-wide with 3,800 of them in the UK. **31.** The brewer Whitbread announced the sale of its TGI Friday's and Costa coffee chains. The engineering group GKN announced the loss of 1,250 jobs world-wide. The largest cuts would be in its civil aviation business in Britain.

NOVEMBER 2001

2. The insurer Prudential announced 2,100 job losses in the UK. Marks and Spencer sold its nine Spanish outlets to a local department stores operator El Corte Inglés. BT applied for a licence to broadcast television over its telephone lines. **5.** The airline Aer Lingus announced plans to sell 25 paintings from its art collection to raise IR£500,000 in an attempt to reduce its IR£2million a day losses. **7.** FLS Aerospace, the Dublin-based aircraft maintenance company, announced 700 job losses at Manchester airport. **8.** The Office of Water Services (OFWAT) announced its approval of three of the country's smallest water companies raising customer bills from next year. **13.** DIY chain B&Q announced the creation of 4,000 jobs in the UK over the coming year. The naval shipbuilder and defence services group Vosper Thornycroft announced a £300 million deal to build six naval destroyers. Telecom company Vodafone announced a pre-tax loss of £8.45 billion. Telecom company Marconi announced £5.1 billion losses. The telecom group Energis announced plans to cut 350 jobs, mainly in the UK. **14.** BT announced a partnership with Siebel Systems, a company that specialises in customer relationship management. **16.** Shares in the Internet company Yahoo rose by more than six per cent after the chief executive revealed plans to cut one in ten members of the workforce and reduce its free services. Investment bank Merrill Lynch announced that 2,600 members of staff had accepted voluntary redundancies. Baby-care retailer Mothercare issued its second profits alert in six months. **19.** The Bundesbank issued a warning that Germany was on the verge of recession. The French state-owned company Eléctricité de France paid £1.3 billion for the British power firm Eastern Electricity. Three senior Barclays bank officials were arrested and questioned in a French investigation into allegations of money-laundering involving Israeli charities. **28.** Tesco supermarket store announced an agreement to open shops in Malaysia. **30.** The energy company Enron announced 1,100 job cuts in the UK.

DECEMBER 2001

5. The magazine publisher IPC announced plans to cut a further 118 jobs a month after closing six titles and cutting 1,115 jobs. **11.** Consignia confirmed further 3,000 redundancies. The headline rate of inflation dropped to its lowest level for 30 years. **12.** The computer services group ICL announced 1,500 job cuts from its 300 offices around the UK. **14.** The domestic appliances manufacturer Electrolux announced 2,800 job losses across Europe. **16.** Vodafone revealed plans to launch a shopping facility that would allow consumers to make low-value purchases and charge them to their mobile phone bill. **17.** Meridian Delta consortium was awarded the right to lease the Millennium Dome from English Partnerships for up to 20 years. The Dome would still remain in government ownership. **18.** The Bank of England announced that Elizabeth Fry, the nineteenth-

century prison reformer, would appear on a new £5 note next summer. **21.** Marks & Spencer closed its retail stores in France.

JANUARY 2002

25. The investment company Capital & Regional Properties formed a £670 million shopping centre fund with Morley Fund Management. Research by the accountancy firm Ernst & Young revealed that during 2001 UK companies made 520 profit warnings, 117 per cent more than in 2000. **29.** The internet bank Egg acquired Zebank, the French online financial services company, for £4.9 million. **30.** The energy group BP agreed to buy a 51 per cent stake in Veba Oil from EON for £1.8 billion. W H Smith announced plans to scale back its American operations after suffering £10 million losses following the 11 September terrorist attacks. The Prince of Wales Colliery in Pontefract, West Yorkshire, announced plans to close in September, with the loss of 500 jobs. Tiny Computers was bought by the Time Group after going into administration. **31.** Boots confirmed the closure of 19 outlets in Thailand and Taiwan. Alpha Airports, the company that supplies the airline industry with in-flight meals and duty free shops, announced 1,000 job cuts. The accountancy firm PricewaterhouseCoopers sold its consulting section to Hewlett Packard.

FEBRUARY 2002

4. Post Office Limited, a division of Consignia which operates postal branches, announced 500 job losses. The vacuum cleaner manufacturer Dyson announced the move of its factory from Wiltshire to Malaysia with the loss of 800 jobs. **15.** The Communications and Workers' Union launched a boycott on using Consignia's name. This followed recent discussions within Consignia to revert to its former title Post Office. **17.** Associated British Foods announced plans to spend more than £100 million to open twelve Primark stores in the next year. **18.** Equitable Life, the insurance company, announced plans to prevent policy holders from cashing in policies before their contractual retirement date. Sainsbury's obtained an injunction to prevent Tesco from offering its loyalty card holders air miles. **20.** Bradford & Bingley announced plans to hand back £150 million to investors through a share buyback. The decision was due to the bank achieving exceptional annual profits of 9.4 per cent in its first full year since demutualisation. **22.** The security and distribution group Securicor won a £200 million deal to manage Alliance & Leicester's processing centre in Basingstoke. **23.** It was announced that MPs and civil servants who held pensions with the collapsed financial services company Equitable Life, would be allowed to transfer their money to other investors. **24.** Sir Richard Branson sold his majority stake in his health club brand Virgin Active to Bridgepoint Capital, the private equity group. The DTI launched an inquiry into the role of auditors and non-executive directors following the collapse of Enron. **26.** The Government awarded a £2 billion contract to supply new military satellite communications services to the European consortium Paradigm Secure.

MARCH 2002

1. A survey by the Credit Card Research Group found that more than half of all financial transactions in shops during January involved credit or debit cards. **4.** Clothing retailer Next was named Retailer of the Year. **11.** The global sales of mobile phones fell by 3.2 per cent to 399.6 million last year. **16.** The National Grid, which distributes electricity in the UK, cancelled a £350 million debt following the collapse in the value of the telecom company Energis. The Federation of Small Businesses unveiled a rescue package to assist companies to recover any excess charges paid to high street banks. **17.** Rural post offices were allowed to provide cash machines on their premises with each withdrawal subject to a £1.25 fee. **18.** UK Coal applied for £100 million in state aid to shut its large Selby mining complex. **20.** Record company EMI announced 1,800 job losses. **23.** Consignia announced 11,000 redundancies. The Secretary for Transport, Local Government and the Regions (Stephen Byers) announced a £500 million compensation and buy-out package to Railtrack shareholders who suffered losses after the Government withdrew its financial support from the group last year. **27.** ITV Digital went into administration after failing to renegotiate a three-year deal with the Football League to broadcast coverage of Nationwide League and Worthington Cup matches. BT confirmed that it had implemented cost-cutting measures including 2,200 job cuts across its call centres.

APRIL 2002

4. British Petroleum raised petrol prices by 1p per litre. **5.** HSBC Bank announced plans to transfer its processing operation to China and India. **8.** One 2 One, the mobile phone operator, closed one in five of its retail outlets. **9.** Official figures reported that manufacturing output rose by 0.4 per cent in February, the first increase since last August. The Transport Minister (John Spellar) announced that airline passengers would pay an extra £100 per ticket unless more runways are built to relieve congestion at airports in the South East. Budget airline Easyjet announced plans to end its £7 million investment in the part-privatised air traffic control network. **15.** Construction group John Laing sold its property development section in a joint venture between Kier Developments and the Bank of Scotland for £40 million. **16.** The underlying inflation rate increased from 2.2 to 2.3 per cent in March. **17.** Arthur Andersen, the accountancy firm, announced 1,500 job cuts in its UK division. **21.** ITV Digital was put up for sale. **22.** The National Grid, the electricity distributor and Lattice, the gas network operator, agreed a £15 billion merger to form the world's sixth largest utility company. **30.** ITV Digital ceased to broadcast leaving 7 million subscribers without service.

MAY 2002

10. EMI paid £42 million for the independent record label, Mute. The insurance company AXA announced plans to reduce its workforce by 700. **16.** The Office of Fair Trading (OFT) accused 11 companies of illegally fixing the price of replica football shirts. The OFT's report followed a two-year investigation in to the sale of England and Manchester United kits. **20.** Whitaker's Almanack was sold by TSO for £750,000 to publishers A&C Black. British Airways reported its first annual loss since its privatisation 15 years ago. The advertising company WPP announced plans to transfer its auditing business from Arthur Andersen to Deloitte & Touche following the Enron scandal. **21.** Marks & Spencer reported pre-tax profits of £647 million for the year ending March 2002. The Securities and Exchange Commission accused Ernst & Young of violating its rules by making lucrative deals with a software company which it was auditing. **24.** The cable group NTL purchased the 1.1 million customer database of ITV Digital for an undisclosed sum. **25.** A consortium led by property company Quintain Estates bought the Millennium Dome

and 200 acres of development land on the Greenwich Peninsula. **27.** The Bank of England suspended distribution of its new five-pound note after discovering that the serial number could be erased.

JUNE 2002

5. The FTSE 100 index of leading shares fell below the 5000 level for the first time since last October. **8.** OFGEM, the gas and electricity regulator, raided the premises of United Utilities following complaints about its tender processes. **9.** PricewaterhouseCoopers changed its name to Monday. **13.** DTLR announced that Railtrack shares would reappear on the London Stock Exchange on completion of a Government-backed £500 million offer from Network Rail to buy the operator out of administration. **21.** Mini-mart chain Budgens announced plans to buy the Musgrave group in a deal worth £231.6 million.

JULY 2002

1. An inquiry into the pensions system was launched following comments by the Work and Pensions Secretary (Andrew Smith) to MPs that official contributions figures may have been inflated. **4.** Miller Fisher, the insurance loss adjuster, went into receivership. **5.** Thirty football clubs facing bankruptcy after ITV Digital's collapse were rescued via a four-year deal with satellite broadcaster BskyB. The Bank of England revealed that homeowners borrowed a record £8.1 billion against the value of their homes. **11.** The FTSE 100 index fell to its lowest level since April 1997, falling 190.1 points closing at 4230.1. **12.** Lazard, the investment banker, dismissed six London partners following a review of the company's performance.

AUGUST 2002

4. The London Bullion Market Association announced plans to quality check precious metals traded on the bullion market. **5.** Microsoft announced plans to reveal details of its Windows operations system to competitors in compliance with the anti-trust settlement agreed last year with the US Department of Justice. A report by Lane Clark and Peacock, the actuarial consultant, found that the UK's largest companies face a £25 billion gap between assets and liabilities in their pension funds. **7.** Marconi, the telecom equipment maker, announced a further 1,000 redundancies in the UK. **11.** Ford Motors sold the Kwit-Fit chain of car service centres to CVC Capital Partners, the venture capital group, for £330 million. **13.** Shares in British Energy fell by around 40 per cent after it shut down one of its nuclear reactors. Investment banker research by Goldman Sachs found that BT may have a £5.5 billion pension fund deficit. **28.** Deutsche Post, the German post office, won a temporary licence to collect 40 million items of mail a year from customers in the UK.

ENVIRONMENT AND SCIENCE

SEPTEMBER 2001

1. Two new sea species of marine life were discovered by David Attenborough whilst filming the BBC programme *The Blue Planet* in the deep seas across the globe. **16.** The barbastelle bat was found on the Isle of Wight for the first time over a century. **19.** Surgeons in New York carried out the first transatlantic operation using remote-controlled robots to remove the gall bladder of a woman in France. **22.** The Department for the Environment, Food and Rural Affairs (DEFRA) recommended the reopening of

the mixed oxide (Mox) plant at the Sellafield site of British Nuclear Fuels to the Secretary of State (Margaret Beckett). Israeli archaeologists found what is believed to be the oldest village in the world dating back 20,000 years on a dried-out bed on the Sea of Galilee. **24.** It was announced that a new vaccine against breast cancer would be clinically tried in Britain next month. **25.** A project to identify the history of the earliest human beings to live in Britain was announced by the Natural History Museum. **26.** Archaeologists discovered two machines used by the Romans to lift large amounts of water in the City of London. A new outbreak of foot-and-mouth disease was identified in Cumbria.

OCTOBER 2001

8. Sir Paul Nurse, Director General of the Imperial Cancer Fund, and Tim Hunt, head of the ICRF's Cell Cycle Control Laboratory won the $1 million Nobel Prize for medicine for their work on the division of cells. Hurricane Iris hit Belize in South America and 80,000 islanders were evacuated. **9.** Eric Cornell and Carl Wieman, professors at the University of Colorado, and Wolfgang Ketterle, a professor at Massachusetts Institute of Technology, won the Nobel Prize for physics for freezing matter into a new state that could aid in developing smaller and faster electronics. **15.** Scientists revealed that eight new planets have been located orbiting stars outside the solar system. **22.** The worst floods in 20 years occurred across Cambridgeshire and Essex. **24.** Archaeologists claimed to have unearthed a 13th-century ritual bath, which is thought to have been used by a Jewish community in medieval London.

NOVEMBER 2001

1. English Heritage archaeologists announced the discovery of the largest prehistoric hill forts in Britain on the North York Moors. **4.** Hurricane Michelle hit Cuba at 160 miles per hour and 20,000 people were evacuated from their homes. As a precaution 45,000 people were evacuated from Florida Keys. **5.** Environmentalists announced the discovery of salmon in the once heavily polluted River Mersey. A small pack of grey wolves was seen near the Saxon Poland border in Germany, the first sighting of the grey wolf in Germany for 150 years. **25.** Scientists in America cloned human embryos for the first time. **17.** Research by the University of Utah found that young children absorb up to 50 per cent more radiation than adults when they use mobile phones.

DECEMBER 2001

5. A seven-year-old girl born without a right ear was fitted with a latex version modelled on her left ear at Sheffield Children's Hospital. **11.** Surgeons at Birmingham Children's Hospital separated conjoined twin babies joined at the back. **19.** The Environment Minister (Michael Meacher) announced a three per cent increase in the number of British birds being bred in the wild since last year. **26.** Bristol Zoo has acquired a male and female gorilla as part of a European conservation programme run by Frankfurt Zoo. **29.** American scientists revealed that a large ice-sheet in the Antarctica had cut off hundreds of thousands of penguins from their breeding grounds.

JANUARY 2002

14. Prince Charles launched a campaign to protect the albatross, an endangered species, during a reception held at St James's Palace. **18.** The Royal Botanical Gardens at Kew were chosen to be Britain's 2002 nomination for a World Heritage site. Seventy Asian freshwater turtles were

re-homed in British zoos after being rescued from meat traders in Hong Kong. Scientists at India's National Institute of Oceanography announced the discovery of an ancient metropolis off the West Coast of India believed to be linked to the lost city of Atlantis. **24.** The British Ornithologists' Union Records Committee confirmed the sighting of the rare Slender Billed Curlew in the marshlands of Northumberland.

FEBRUARY 2002

12. Scientists reported that the comet Ikeya-Zhang had re-appeared in the inner Solar System for the first time in 341 years. **17.** Scientists led by the University of Edinburgh's clinical pharmacology unit developed a technique to identify an individual's risk of developing heart problems. The World Wide Fund for Nature announced that rainforests were being stripped of a prehistoric tree fern which was made fashionable in Britain by TV garden makeover shows. A Police Marine unit announced an inquiry into why 20 dolphins and porpoises were washed up on Hampshire beaches, bringing the total found on west-facing South Coast shorelines to more than 80. **18.** Scientists at the University of Chicago discovered bones belonging to a 45-feet-long herbivore from the cretaceous period in a site in Niger. **24.** A report by British and American scientists suggested that rising greenhouse gases might not be the main cause of global warming as had previously been supposed.

MARCH 2002

5. A report by the British Trust for Ornithology found that the cuckoo population had fallen by 20 per cent and in woodland areas by 60 per cent since the 1970s. **7.** The Environment Secretary (Margaret Beckett) announced that the Government was ready to endorse legally binding targets to reduce gas emissions that threaten to change the world's climate. **13.** The National Trust displayed a series of priceless Anglo-Saxon treasures that were discovered at Sutton Hoo in 1939. Encam, the environmental charity, gave 83 British beaches awards for cleanliness. **18.** A British team of explorers discovered a lost Inca city in a remote region of Peru. **26.** The Trade and Industry Secretary (Patricia Hewitt) announced a £20 million programme to increase the use of solar energy in homes and offices across the UK.

APRIL 2002

3. An 18-month-old boy who was born with a genetic disease rendering him unable to produce infection-fighting T- and NK-cells was cured at Great Ormond Street Hospital using pioneering gene therapy. A report by the British Trust for Ornithology found that 11 out of 24 species surveyed showed a significant decline in their birth rates. **4.** An archaeology-enthusiast discovered a Bronze Age gold drinking vessel in Woodnesborough in Kent. **7.** A report published in the Astronomical Journal claimed that the solar system contained up to 1.9 million large asteroids, twice as many as previously thought. **17.** A Manx shearwater bird tagged in 1957 was discovered living in a breeding colony in North Wales. **25.** A report by the Marine Conservation Society found that South Beach along the Blackpool promenade and three other beaches in the region were clean enough for bathing. The Meteorological Office announced that global temperatures in January, February and March this year had been the warmest on record.

MAY 2002

19. A rare partially coloured bat from Eastern Europe was found in Wiltshire, after losing its course whilst migrating

to breed. **21.** The first wild Choughs to be born in England for more than 50 years were placed under 24-hour surveillance at a secret location.

JUNE 2002

3. Scientists in East Anglia discovered evidence that human beings inhabited Britain for up to 200,000 years longer than previously thought. **6.** The glacier from which Sir Edmund Hilary and Tenzing Norgay began their ascent of Everest in 1953 has retreated by three miles due to global warming. **9.** British scientists isolated a rogue gene that causes skin cancer. The Royal Society for the Protection of Birds announced plans to flood 2,000 acres of East Anglian Fenland to form a wetlands and wildlife sanctuary. **25.** Scientist Stephen Hawkins was awarded the £10,000 Aventis Prize for his work The *Universe in a Nutshell*. **28.** Two scientific studies by the Royal Botanical Gardens at Kew and the World Conservation Union found that the number of known plant species was 422,000, around 50 per cent more than anticipated.

JULY 2002

4. Three marooned loggerhead sea turtles, rarely found in British waters, were rescued near Cornwall. The Government announced that it would cost £48 billion to clean up the state-owned nuclear waste sites and dismantle a number of nuclear power stations. **8.** It was announced that the Loch Lomond and Trossachs National Park will open in Scotland. **14.** A four-year study by scientists found that no wild salmon were left in four Scottish rivers. **17.** Scientists at Massachusetts General Hospital manufactured insulin-producing cells from adult stems cells thought to reverse diabetes. A pair of European Bee-eater birds hatched chicks in the British countryside for the first time in almost 50 years. **31.** Scientists discovered an underwater crater thought to have been left by a meteorite that collided with the Earth 65 million years ago.

AUGUST 2002

3. The Environment Minister (Michael Meacher) announced sctricter controls on pollutants emitted by motor vehicles. **8.** The rare Andean Flamingo laid its first egg in three years at the Slimbridge Wildfowl and Wetlands Trust. **13.** The RSPCA confirmed that Phocine distemper, a deadly virus which affects seals, had returned to Britain after a 14-year absence. **27.** The Medical Research Council announced plans to create the world's first human stem-cell bank.

SPORT

SEPTEMBER 2001

4. Jonathan Edwards won his 14th successive triple jump victory at the Goodwill Games in Brisbane, Australia. **5.** Peter Bray became the first person to canoe across the Atlantic. **15.** Alessandro Zanardi, the Formula One driver, had his legs amputated following a 200 miles per hour crash during the American Memorial 500 Cart race in Germany. **20.** A poll by the BBC's *Watchdog* programme found that 56 per cent of callers supported a new football stadium being built in Birmingham rather than Wembley. **26.** Michael Owen signed a five-year contract with Liverpool Football Club worth around £70,000 a week, making him one of the highest paid footballers in the world. **27.** Roger Bannister came top of the Gillette 100 Greatest British Sports Performances of the Century poll

for breaking the four-minute-mile barrier in 1954. Leeds United became the first English football club to sign up to the proposed Premier1 Grand Prix motor racing series. **30.** Australian World Superbike motorcycling rider Troy Bayliss broke his collarbone in a high-speed crash during the World Superbikes Championship in Imola, Italy. Naoko Takahashi ran the fastest ever women's marathon in 2 hours and 19 minutes in Berlin, Germany.

OCTOBER 2001

8. The International Cricket Council announced plans to eliminate suspended sentences and impose stricter penalties for players' unruly behaviour at cricket matches. **9.** Steve Fossett broke the transatlantic record by reaching the Lizard in Cornwall in five days after sailing from New York in a 125-foot catamaran called *PlayStation*. The Union of European Football Associations (UEFA) postponed 50 football matches as a mark of respect following the terrorist attacks on the United States. **10.** The Australian Rugby League cancelled the rugby league Kangaroos tour after several leading players voiced concerns over match safety following the missile strikes against Afghanistan by Britain and the US. The Formula One world governing body the International Automobile Federation (FIA) approved plans to open bidding for sponsorship of Premier1 Grand Prix, a motor racing series partially sponsored by Europe's top football clubs. **11.** The United Kingdom bowls team won the Bryant Cup for the third time running at Potters Leisure Resort in Norfolk. **12.** The insurance company AXA announced plans to withdraw its contract to sponsor the Football World Cup claiming that the recent terrorist attacks in the US would make the tournaments too hazardous to underwrite. **18.** The BBC and ITV announced a £160 million deal to air the 2002 and 2006 World Cup. **21.** Mark Nyman, 35, won the National Scrabble Championship for the second time. Peter Matthews set a new course record in 23 minutes and 14 seconds during the BUPA Ireland Road Race in Loughrea. **22.** David Graveney, the chairman of cricket selectors, assured cricketers reluctant to tour India because of fears over safety that their decision would not be held against them in the future. **30.** The Football Association announced an £11 million investment plan in girl's' football to ensure that the women's professional league is launched in 2003–4.

NOVEMBER 2001

1. Feng Jing, 16, became the youngest men's all-round world gymnastics champion when he won gold for China at the World Gymnastics Championships in Belgium. **3.** The International Cricket Council announced plans to place spy cameras in test cricketers' dressing rooms to eradicate match-fixing. **7.** John Bennett, 42, set a world record by diving 99 feet under the sea using scuba diving gear in the Philippines. Four Newcastle United players were fined two weeks' wages and sent back from a training camp in Spain after failing to attend a dinner held in honour of Sir John Hall, the former Newcastle United chairman. Sport England announced the creation of a 2,200-metre £10 million Redgrave Pinsent Rowing Lake in Caversham, Berkshire. **8.** The venue for England's first match of the India cricket tour was moved for security reasons due to concerns about the absence of perimeter fencing and stands at the Gymkhana Club in Bombay. **13.** The English amateur golf champion Scott Godfrey headed a six-man team competing in a new four-nation tournament starting in Spain. **15.** The first female football fans were allowed to attend a football match in Iran during Ireland's World Cup qualification match. **16.** The former Manchester United defender Jaap Stam tested

positive for the banned steroid Nandrolone. Laurence Halstead, the British junior fencing champion became the first winner of the Eden Cup, the British round of the junior men's foil World Cup for 17-year-olds. **18.** The boxer Lennox Lewis regained his World Heavyweight title for the third time after beating Hasim Rahman. The National Lottery announced that schools are to receive £541 million for investment in sports facilities from the National Lottery's New Opportunities Fund. The England rugby team achieved its best result of the International Rugby Board (IRB) sevens grand prix when they reached the semi-finals of the opening event of the season in Durban. **19.** Paul Lowrie was named the European Tour's shot of the year following his win at the Dunhill Links golf championships at St Andrews. **20.** The Professional Footballer's Association (PFA) players' union issued a strike notice to all Premiership and Nationwide clubs, warning of industrial action after talks relating to players' share of television royalties broke down. A report by a House of Commons select committee suggested that the Football Association (FA) should repay £120 million of lottery money following the collapse of plans to build a new Wembley Stadium. **21.** Jessica Hudson, became the first female to box for a British university at the Cambridge University club.

DECEMBER 2001

3. Chinese swimmers Luo Xuejuan and Li Wei simultaneously broke the world record for the women's 50 meters breaststroke on the second and final day of a World Cup meeting in Shanghai. **8.** The FA revealed plans to build a new national stadium at Wembley. **9.** David Beckham, the Manchester United midfield player and captain of the England football team, was voted BBC Sports Personality of the Year. **10.** Arsenal was granted planning permission by Islington Borough Council to build a 60,000-capacity stadium a mile from its current location in Highbury. **11.** The Ladies' Professional Golf Association announced the creation of a Women's Senior Golf Association with an age limit of 44. The yachtswoman Ellen MacArthur was named *The Sunday Times* Sportswoman of the Year. Lambeth Borough Council gave planning permission to Surrey County Cricket Club to redevelop the Oval cricket ground. Retief Goosen was named golfer of the year by Asprey & Garrard. **16.** Swimmer Jamie Salter broke the British 200 metres freestyle record after winning the Scottish Winter Open in Inverness. **19.** The Secretary of State for Culture, Media and Sports (Tessa Jowell) announced a further four-month delay to examine the bidding process for the new national football stadium to replace Wembley. **26.** Somerset County Cricket Club named the new gates at its grounds after Vivian Richards, a former player and West Indian cricket captain. **28.** BSkyB won the right to broadcast interactive coverage of Formula One racing on a pay-per-view basis.

JANUARY 2002

2. The rugby Super League club the Bradford Bulls acquired a controlling interest in Wakefield rugby union club. **4.** Ellen MacArthur won the Yachting Journalists' Association Yachtsman of the Year Award. British swimmer Zoe Baker broke the world shortcourse record for the 50 metres breaststroke in Durban, South Africa. **8.** The Imperial Cricket Conference announced the appointment of an anti-corruption co-ordinator and five regional security managers. The British Grand Prix swimming championships were cancelled due to lack of entries. Danny Orr, 23, became the youngest captain in the Tetley's Super Rugby League. **19.** Oarsman Steve

Redgrave's fifth gold medal win during the coxless four race at the Sydney Olympics in 2000 was voted the greatest sporting moment of all time by the public. **22.** Swimmer Mark Foster won three silver medals in five days at the Fina World Cup. Lennox Lewis, the world heavyweight boxing champion, claimed he was bitten on the leg by Mike Tyson during a press conference in New York. **29.** The FA arbitration panel ruled that the Football League must re-examine Wimbledon Football Club's proposals to relocate to a new 45,000-seater stadium in Milton Keynes.

FEBRUARY 2002

21. The British women's curling team won a gold medal at the Winter Olympics in Salt Lake City, USA – Britain's first medal in the winter games since Torvill and Dean's figure ice skating title 18 years ago. **22.** Arsenal Football Club unveiled its new club badge. Andrea Mead Lawrence, the American skier who won an Olympic slalom title in Oslo, was named the greatest competitor in the history of the Olympic Winter Games. **24.** Britain won six gold medals, two silver and one bronze at the Fisa Team Cup and Andalucia International Regatta in Seville, Spain. Fulham Football Club gained its thirteenth victory in a row in the southern division of the Women's Premier League. Lee Beachill became the first man in the history of squash to successfully defend the British national title. **26.** The Cambridge University Lent Races were reduced from four to three days due to bad weather. **28.** It was announced that a urine-based blood doping test to detect the drug Erythropoietin (EPO) would be used during the summer football World Cup Finals. The insurance company AXA announced it would no longer sponsor the FA Cup.

MARCH 2002

1. Carol Ashby won the Golden Charter Women's National Indoor Singles bowls title for the second time. **4.** The Tetley's Rugby Super League recorded its biggest attendance for a weekend opening for five years. A total of 54,605 spectators watched six matches. **5.** Alain Baxter, the British alpine skiing bronze winner in the Winter Olympics, had his title stripped after failing a drug test. **10.** The FA announced that there were insufficient funds to meet the £100 million costs to rebuild Wembley football stadium. Motor racing chiefs banned the Phoenix Group from racing in Formula One. The FA announced that Old Trafford and Villa Park would be the venues for this season's FA Cup semi-finals. The boxer Mike Tyson was granted a licence to fight in the world heavy competition by boxing authorities in Washington DC. Nasser Hussain, the England cricket captain, gained his tenth century during the first test match of the season against New Zealand. **13.** Stewart Boswell maintained his three-year unbeaten record in the English national squash league. The Government announced plans to provide £6 million in aid to the motorsport industry. **30.** Oxford won the 148th University Boat race.

APRIL 2002

1. Gerard Houllier, the Liverpool football manager, was awarded the Légion d'honneur, one of France's top civil awards for his work with the French national football team. **2.** British skiers, James Leuzinger and Chemmy Alcott, won the respective men's and women's slalom titles and also the British Land Junior National Ski Championships in Austria. **3.** Rob Jackson, the London Broncos three-quarter, was banned by officials for six matches after biting the arm of Richard Fletcher of Hull. **5.** The horse Bindaree won the 155th Grand National

race. **14.** Paula Radcliffe won the women's Flora London Marathon in two hours, 18 minutes and 56 seconds. Khalid Khannouchi won the men's marathon in two hours, five minutes and 38 seconds, setting a new world record. Charterhouse won the Public School's Golfing Society's Halford Hewitt Cup for the fifteenth time in its 78-year history. **16.** Michael Owen became the deputy England Football captain whilst David Beckham recovered from injury.

MAY 2002

5. England's Commonwealth Games bowls team won the Test series against Wales in both the men's and women's events. **11.** David Beckham signed a three-year £16 million contract with Manchester United Football Club. **17.** Around 1,000 football hooligans were barred from attending the World Cup in Japan and Korea under the World Cup (Disorder) Act 2000. **24.** Roy Keane was sacked from the Irish World Cup football team following an argument with his football manager. Paul Manning, set an event record average in excess of 32 miles per hour, helped by a tailwind, to win the sixth stage of the Irish FBD Ras Milk Race. **28.** David Beckham was declared fit to play in England's opening World Cup football match against Sweden. **30.** Mike Babb won the Gold medal in the 50 metre prone smallbore rifle tournament at the Milan World Cup meeting. The FIFA Football World Cup began in Korea.

JUNE 2002

2. Kelly Holmes ran the fastest recorded 1,500-metre time since 1997 after winning the Fanny Blankers-Koen Grand Prix. **3.** More than 80,000 World Cup tickets were left unsold due to an administrative error by Byron, the sports travel company responsible for ticket distribution for FIFA. **7.** The England football team beat Argentina 1-0 in the second round of the World Cup. **9.** Lennox Lewis retained his boxing world heavyweight title after defeating Mike Tyson. **16.** Rowers James Cracknell and Matthew Pinsent won the coxless pairs gold medal at the Zurich World Cup. **21.** The England football team lost to Brazil during the World Cup quarter-finals. **22.** Graham Hicks, who is blind and deaf, broke his own world speed record on a four-wheel bike after he reached 104 miles per hour on a track in Leicestershire. **27.** A report by financial consultants Deloitte & Touche Sport found that English football clubs spent £423 million on buying players. **30.** Brazil won the 2002 FIFA football World Cup final.

JULY 2002

4. British coxless four rowers won the Henley Royal Regatta race. **7.** Australian Lleyton Hewitt won the men's tennis singles championships at Wimbledon and American Serena Williams won the women's championships. **12.** The BBC won the right to broadcast the Six Nations Championships for the next three years. **21.** Rio Ferdinand, the Leeds United and England defender, was transferred to Manchester United Football Club for £30 million. **24.** Disabled and able-bodied competitors were allowed for the first time to compete in the same events at the Commonwealth Games. **26.** Lorraine Shaw won a gold medal in the women's hammer during the Commonwealth games. **29.** Chris Rawlinson won gold and Matt Elias silver in the 400 metres at the Commonwealth Games. **31.** Ashia Hansen won a gold medal in the triple jump at the Commonwealth Games.

AUGUST 2002

1. Kim Collins, the Kittitian 100 metres Commonwealth champion was allowed to keep his gold medal after failing

a drug test. **2.** Delroy McQueen won three gold medals in the men's 105 kg weightlifting finals. **3.** Swimmers Joanna Fargus, Sarah Price and Katy Sexton won the gold silver and bronze medals during the women's 200 metres backstroke at the Commonwealth Games. **6.** Julie Bradshaw reduced the record for swimming the English Channel by more than nine hours using the butterfly stroke. Paula Radcliffe won the 10,000 metres gold medal during the European Championships. **8.** Peter Wheeler, the Leicester City chief executive, was fined £3,000 for his public criticism of an international referee. **9.** Steve Backley broke the men's javelin world record during the European Championships.

AFRICA

SEPTEMBER 2001

2. In the Seychellois presidential election, President Frances Albert René gained 54 per cent of the vote to win a fifth term in office. **6.** At a Commonwealth meeting in Abuja, Nigeria, Zimbabwe agreed to restore the rule of law and to move squatters off some white-owned farms; the final communiqué stated that the situation in Zimbabwe posed a threat to the stability of the whole region. **10.** In Zimbabwe, ZANU-PF was beaten in local elections in Bulawayo when the MDC won all seven seats and the mayoral election. In Nigeria, at least 165 people died and about 1,000 were injured in clashes between Christians and Muslims in the city of Jos. **19.** In Eritrea, all independent newspapers were closed and six former cabinet ministers and generals were arrested after signing a letter criticising President Isaid Afwerki. **25.** In the Comoros, an attempted coup on the separatist island of Anjouan was put down.

OCTOBER 2001

2. The Zimbabwean Supreme Court overturned an earlier ruling and declared the government's appropriation of white-owned farms to be legal. **3.** The Zimbabwean Information Minister, Jonathan Moyo, said that Zimbabwe would honour the agreement reached in Abuja to restore law and order and prevent the illegal occupation of farms. **8.** In Ethiopia, Girma Woldegiorgis was elected as president by parliament. **10.** The Zimbabwean government announced the imposition of price controls on basic foodstuffs. **13.** In Somalia, 22 people died in fighting between rival militias in Mogadishu. **14.** In Nigeria, at least 200 people were killed in violence between Christians and Muslims in Kano. **15.** In Zimbabwe, President Mugabe threatened to nationalise any firms that closed because of price controls. **18.** In Gambia, President Jahya Jammeh won a second term in office, gaining 53 per cent of the vote. **24.** In Nigeria's Central Region, up to 200 villagers were massacred by army units apparently seeking vengeance for the murder of 19 soldiers earlier in the month during in a tribal conflict between Tivs and Jukuns. **26.** In Mauritania, the general election was won by the ruling Republican Democratic and Social Party, who obtained 64 of the 81 seats. An attempt by the Zimbabwean government to stage-manage a Commonwealth ministers' tour of farms backfired when farmers gave delegates graphic accounts of state-sponsored violence; on 28 October the delegation issued a communiqué calling on Zimbabwe to abide by the Abuja agreement. **28.** South Africa deployed peacekeeping soldiers to Burundi.

NOVEMBER 2001

1. In Burundi, a power-sharing government composed of Tutsis and Hutus was inaugurated following an agreement brokered by Nelson Mandela. **11.** In Guinea, a referendum to allow President Lansana Conté to seek a third term of office was held; official sources claimed that the proposal had been approved by 98 per cent of those who voted. The Zimbabwean government refused to allow aid agencies to distribute emergency food supplies, saying that the government alone would distribute food. **12.** In Zimbabwe, the government invoked special powers to inform 1,000 white farmers that their land was to be seized. **13.** In Zimbabwe, the body of Cain Nkala, a ZANU-PF activist, was found near Bulawayo. **15.** In South Africa, an investigation into a £4 billion arms deal found no evidence of wrongdoing by the government; opposition parties boycotted a session of parliament in protest when it was revealed that the report had been published only after government revisions. In Zimbabwe, the MDC claimed to have obtained a copy of ZANU-PF's election strategy for the 2002 presidential election that said that the assassination of the MDC leader was an option. **18.** President Mugabe accused the British government of sponsoring terrorism in Zimbabwe in an attempt to overthrow the regime. **23.** Zimbabwe's commission of police, Augustine Chihuri, ordered a white farmer to leave his land and home so that he could take up residence. **27.** In Kenya, President Daniel arap Moi accused the UK of working with the opposition to subvert his government. **30.** In Guinea, the general election due on 27 December was indefinitely postponed when opposition parties announced that they would boycott it.

DECEMBER 2001

4. In Zimbabwe, the Supreme Court ruled that the government's appropriation of white-owned farmland was legal, overturning a previous ruling that it was unconstitutional and unlawful. **9.** In Kenya, Sheikh Ahmed Salim Swedan, who was wanted in connection with the 1998 bombings of two US embassies in Africa, was arrested in Mandera. **14.** In South Africa, the High Court ruled that the government must make available a drug that can prevent the transmission of HIV from pregnant mothers to their children. **19.** In the Comoros, troops defeated an attempted coup on the island of Moheli. In Zimbabwe, the government rushed through amendments to the Electoral Act ahead of the presidential election in March. **27.** In Zambia, the presidential election took place and was narrowly won by Levy Mwanawasa of the ruling Movement for Multiparty Democracy with 29.16 per cent of the vote. In Somalia, nine people including three civilians died in a gun battle between the police and militias in Mogadishu.

JANUARY 2002

2. In Zambia, Levy Mwanawasa was sworn in as president at a ceremony that was boycotted by all ten opposition parties. **9.** In Zimbabwe, Parliament passed the Public Order and Security Bill, which gave the government wide-ranging powers of arrest and detention and obliged journalists to seek registration. **10.** In Zimbabwe, measures to ban independent election monitors at the presidential poll and disenfranchise Zimbabweans living overseas were passed along with a security bill outlawing criticism of President Mugabe and banning assemblies without police permission. **16.** In Nigeria, a general strike took place in protest at an 18 per cent increase in fuel prices. **17.** In Gambia, the general election was won by the ruling Alliance for Patriotic Reorientation and

Construction (APRC), who obtained 45 of the 48 seats after the main opposition party boycotted the election. **18.** In the Democratic Republic of Congo, Mount Nyiragongo erupted, killing an estimated 45 people and forcing hundreds of thousands of people from their homes. In Sierra Leone, a bonfire of surrendered weapons was conducted in Freetown as a symbol of the end of the civil war that had begun in 1991. **20.** In Zimbabwe, the MDC was forced to cancel its first presidential election rally after police tear-gassed and baton-charged supporters in Bulawayo. **21.** In the Democratic Republic of Congo, a petrol station exploded, killing up to 60 people. **28.** In Nigeria, more than 600 people were feared to have drowned while attempting to swim across canals surrounding the district housing the country's largest weapons store, after a fire caused artillery shells to explode, damaging a large area of Lagos. **31.** In Zimbabwe, Parliament passed the Access to Information and Protection of Privacy Bill, which permits journalists only to publish official information that has been sanctioned for publication.

FEBRUARY 2002

2–4. In Nigeria, at least 55 people were killed in ethnic violence in Lagos between Hausas and Yorubas. **5.** In South Africa, 22 people were killed and 100 others injured when two trains collided near Durban. **8.** In Liberia, President Charles Taylor declared a state of emergency after Liberians United for Reconciliation and Democracy (LURD) rebels advanced to within 35 km of Monrovia. In Zimbabwe, the government barred observers from the UK, Scandinavia and the Netherlands from participating in an EU mission to observe the presidential election. **10.** In Algeria, government forces killed Antar Zouabri, the leader of the Armed Islamic Group. **12.** In South Africa, Home Affairs Minister Mangosuthu Buthelezi told parliament that KwaZulu/Natal province was to distribute anti-retroviral drugs that protect unborn babies from contracting HIV to all pregnant HIV positive women, in defiance of national policy. In Kenya's main opposition parties announced the formation of the National Alliance for Change, and agreed to field a single presidential candidate in this year's general election. **16.** In Zimbabwe, the government ordered the expulsion of the leader of the EU mission, Pierre Schori. **17.** In Zimbabwe, the EU imposed targeted sanctions on President Mugabe and ordered its election observers to leave the country. **20.** In Egypt, a fire thought to have been caused by a portable gas stove swept through a crowded train killing 373 people on the route between Cairo and Luxor. **22.** In Madagascar, President Ratsiraka declared a three-month state of emergency after his rival, Marc Ravalomanana, declared himself president, claiming that he had won the first round of the presidential election outright; official results had shown him to have won 46.21 per cent, thus obliging him to compete in a second round, which he had refused to do. In Angola, Jonas Savimbi, the leader of the National Movement for the Total Independence of Angola (UNITA) for more than 30 years, was killed in an attack by government troops on its headquarters in Mexico province; UNITA appointed Antonio Dembo as its new leader on 27 February. In Zimbabwe, police opened fire on a convoy carrying Morgan Tsvangirai. **24.** In Zimbabwe, three foreign election observers were injured when the bus in which they were travelling was stoned by supporters of President Mugabe during an attack on the MDC. **25.** In Zimbabwe, Morgan Tsvangirai was charged with treason following the broadcast of covertly shot video footage purporting to show him plotting the assassination of

President Mugabe. **26.** In Egypt, 22 people were killed when a building collapsed in Damietta. **27.** In Malawi, President Bakili Muluzi, declared a state of national disaster following the outbreak of famine. In Zimbabwe, the leader of the Southern African Development Community (SADC) election observers, Duke Lefhoko, condemned the campaign as 'not free' and described the country as 'being in a state of fear.' **28.** In Madagascar, martial law was declared in Antananarivo following rioting the previous day.

MARCH 2002

2. In Madagascar, Marc Ravalomanana, the opposition leader who declared himself president, presented his alternative government to a large crowd in Antananarivo. **4.** In Sierra Leone, the former RUF rebel leader Foday Sankoh appeared in court charged with murder. **5.** In Zimbabwe, President Mugabe issued a decree reinstating election laws that had been declared unconstitutional by the Supreme Court the previous week. **8.** In Zimbabwe, ballot boxes filled with votes for Robert Mugabe were found spilling out of a police car involved in a crash the day before the presidential election began. **10.** In Congo-Brazzaville, President Denis Sassou Nguesso was re-elected with 89.4 per cent of the vote. The Zimbabwean High Court ordered the government to extend voting by another day following huge queues at polling stations; the following day, many polling stations remained closed despite the order. **12.** In Zimbabwe, independent election monitors condemned the conduct of the poll; Welshman Ncube, the MDC Secretary-General, was charged with high treason for his part in an alleged assassination plot against President Mugabe. **13.** Robert Mugabe was declared winner of the Zimbabwean presidential election with 56.2 per cent of the vote in the face of overwhelming evidence of vote rigging and fraud. **15.** In Angola, the Army and UNITA rebels agreed to an immediate cease-fire. **17.** In Libya, demonstrators protested outside UN offices in Tripoli against the decision by a Scottish court to uphold the conviction of Abdul Baset Ali-al-Megrahi for the 1988 Lockerbie bombing. **20.** In Zimbabwe, MDC leader Morgan Tsvangirai was charged with treason and thousands of police were deployed to disrupt a general strike organised by the Zimbabwe Congress of Trade Unions. **21.** The Nigerian government described the use of Shari'ah law in Muslim areas as discriminatory and illegal and demanded its repeal. **25.** The South African government said that it would defy a High Court order to provide free anti-AIDS drugs to HIV-positive women. In Nigeria, an Islamic appeal court in Sokoto state acquitted a woman facing a death sentence by stoning for adultery. **27.** In Ghana, at least 40 people were killed in intercommunal clashes in Yendi.

APRIL 2002

2. In Algeria, Islamic militants killed 21 soldiers carrying out an anti-terrorism operation in Moulay Larbi. In the Democratic Republic of Congo, the government offered to share power with rebels if they accept the reunification of the country, but the offer was rejected. **4.** In Angola, a cease-fire was signed between the Angolan army and the UNITA rebels. In South Africa, the Constitutional Court ruled that the government must obey the High Court and offer anti-viral drugs to pregnant women infected with HIV. In Zimbabwe, negotiations began between the ruling ZANU (PF) and the opposition MDC brokered by Nigeria and South Africa. **6.** In Zimbabwe, 54 pro-democracy protestors were arrested after police broke up demonstrations against president Mugabe by the National Constitutional Alliance, an alliance of labour

and civic groups. 11. In Tunisia, an oil tanker exploded outside a synagogue in Djerba, killing at least 14 people. 12. In Zimbabwe, the MDC lodged an affidavit in the Harare High Court, demanding annulment of President Mugabe's election. 13. An international arbitration commission issued a ruling on a new border between Ethiopia and Eritrea. 15. In the Comoros, Col. Assoumani Azaly won the Presidential election. 17. In Madagascar, the disputed presidential election was annulled by the Supreme Court after four months of violence that had left at least 35 people dead. 29. In Madagascar, the High Constitutional Court ruled in favour of the opposition leader, Marc Ravalomanana, and overturned last year's disputed election result, saying that he was the outright winner of December's poll, having gained 51.46 per cent of the votes. 30. In Zimbabwe, President Mugabe declared a state of disaster following widespread food shortages caused by a combination of low rainfall and the effects of land redistribution.

MAY 2002

5. A Nigerian airliner crashed into a suburb of Kano, killing at least 125 people, including 50 on the ground. 6. Archaeologists found the remains of a 4,500-year-old pyramid at Abu Rawwash. 7. Marc Ravolomanana was declared the winner of the December election in Madagascar. Several provinces threatened to secede and 100,000 people took to the streets of Antananarivo, following the refusal of President Didier Ratsiraka to step down in favour of Marc Ravolomanana. 9. In Comoros, Assoumani Azzali, the former President of the Comoros, won 100 per cent of the vote in elections to choose the first President of the Union of Comoros, a new federation that aims to reunite the three islands of Great Comoro, Moheli and Anjouan. 15. Presidential and parliamentary elections were held in Sierra Leone. Early results indicated more than 80 per cent of voters had cast their ballots. 25. In Mozambique, a collision between a freight train and a passenger train about 40 miles south of the capital Maputo, left more than 200 people dead and 400 injured.

JUNE 2002

1. In Algeria, President Abdelaziz Bouteflika re-appointed FLN secretary general Ali Benflis as Prime Minister. Former South African cricket captain was killed along with the pilot and co-pilot when the aircraft in which they were travelling, crashed into a peak on the Outeniqua mountain range, near George, South Africa. 2. In Zimbabwe, the first white farmer was killed since President Mugabe was re-elected earlier this year, by intruders outside his home. 4. It was reported that thousands of people had fled their homes in northern Bujumbura, when Hutu rebels attacked nearby military positions. In Burkina Faso, following elections to the National Assembly, Prime Minister Paramanga Ernest Yoli presented his resignation and that of his government. 5. In Lesotho, Bethuel Pakalitha Mosisili was sworn in for a further term as Prime Minister. 6. Prime Minister Paramanga Ernest Yoli of Burkina Faso, was reappointed to his position at the head of a new Cabinet by President Blaise Compaoré. 10. In Chad, the new National Assembly elected in April was inaugurated. 25. In Zimbabwe, under the order of Robert Mugabe, some 2,900 white farmers, whose land had been selected for seizure and redistribution to blacks (under the government's 'fast-track land reform programme'), were legally obliged to cease working the land, or face prison. 30. In Cameroon, elections to the 180-seat National Assembly took place amidst allegations of widespread electoral fraud. Legislative elections were held in Guinea

for the 114-seat National Assembly, in which the Party of Unity and Progress (PUP) won 85 of the 114 seats.

JULY 2002

1. In Zimbabwe, bread supplies ran out in the shops fuelling the crisis of food shortages and hyper-inflation already plaguing the residents of Harare. 4. In the Central African Republic, a Boeing 707 cargo aircraft crashed in a heavily populated district of Bangui, killing at least twenty and injuring many others. 5. 25 people were killed and many others injured after a bomb exploded in Larba, a market town outside Algiers. 7. Madagascar's former president, Didier Ratsiraka, arrived in Paris after being forced to flee by Marc Ravolomanana, following a seven-month struggle for control of the Island. 8. In South Africa, Winnie Mandela faced 85 charges of fraud and theft after making a brief appearance at Pretoria magistrates court. 25. In northern Uganda, rebels from the Lord's Resistance Army killed at least 42 people using machetes and clubs, during a raid on a village. 30. A peace deal was signed in Pretoria, South Africa, to put an end to the war within the Democratic Republic of Congo. In Sudan, more than 1,000 people were killed by Sudanese government forces in a major air and ground offensive on the southern region of the country.

AUGUST 2002

4. In Algeria, security forces killed 40 suspected Islamist rebels during clashes in a mountainous province about 190 miles west of the capital Algiers. 6. Mike O'Brian, the British Foreign Office minister, became the first minister from the UK to visit Libya in 19 years. Twenty two members of the same family were murdered in a revenge killing over a murder trial in Upper Egypt. 12. In Zimbabwe, President Mugabe addressed a crowd of thousands, informing white farmers that they must surrender their farms without delay. The Ugandan Lord's Resistance Army rebels released five aid workers, a police officer and 94 women and children that had been seized a week earlier. 13. In Madagascar, a flu epidemic killed 399 people and over 5,000 more cases have been recorded according to the Island's health ministry. 21. The US issued a strong attack against President Mugabe of Zimbabwe and described him as an illegitimate leader who gained power through fraud. The American government's Africa policy chief, Walter Kansteiner, stated that the US would encourage his people to correct the situation. 27. The World Summit opened in Johannesburg, South Africa.

THE AMERICAS

SEPTEMBER 2001

11. In the US, two hijacked passenger airlines crashed into the twin towers of New York's World Trade Center, causing the towers to collapse. Minutes later, a third hijacked aircraft crashed into the Pentagon in Washington. A fourth, believed to be heading for the presidential retreat Camp David, crashed near Pittsburgh. A total of 5,000–6,000 people were believed to have died in the attacks. 12. President Bush addressed the nation and vowed to rally the free world against those responsible for the attack. 13. President Bush declared that the US was facing its first war of the 21st century. 14. The US asked for reports from the Pakistani Inter-Services Intelligence (ISI) on Osama bin Laden, the leader of the al-Qa'eda terrorist network based in Afghanistan. The FBI named nineteen men, including seven trained

pilots, as being responsible for hijacking the four US airliners. In Peru, the Supreme Court issued an international arrest warrant for former president Alberto Fujimori on charges of murder; he had been accused of ordering paramilitaries to kill 25 people in 1991–2. **15.** President Bush called on the US armed forces to prepare to crush the al-Qa'eda terrorist network. **19.** US Defence Secretary Donald Rumsfeld insisted on the right of the US to employ force in the pursuit of terrorists, rejecting the need for UN consent. **23.** The US lifted its sanctions against India and Pakistan in return for their co-operation in the pursuit of Osama bin Laden; the sanctions had been imposed because of their nuclear arms race. **24.** President Bush urged foreign banks to follow America's move to freeze the assets of 27 individuals and organisations linked to bin Laden and al-Qa'eda. **28.** In Aruba, the People's Electoral Movement won the general election.

OCTOBER 2001

5. President Bush rebuked Ariel Sharon, the Israeli prime minister, condemning Sharon's statement that the West should not appease the Arabs at the expense of Israel. **8.** The FBI launched an emergency investigation into whether the US had come under biological attack after anthrax spores were found in Boca Raton, Florida, three days after a British-born man died of the disease. **9.** FBI and medical authorities announced their belief that anthrax spores had been deliberately spread after the 11 September attacks. **11.** The FBI issued an urgent warning that terrorists were about to strike again on US soil and against US targets abroad. The mayor of New York, Rudolph Giuliani, rejected an offer of US$10 million for families of the victims of the 11 September attacks from a Saudi prince who had criticised the US Palestinian policy. **12.** In Jamaica, the armed forces were called out to deal with violent unrest in Kingston. A fourth case of anthrax was discovered in New York, and a fifth suspected case was discovered in Nevada. **14.** In the Argentine parliamentary election, the UCR-Frepaso Alliance retained power but failed to win a majority in either the Senate or the House of Deputies. President Bush rejected a Taliban offer to hand over Osama bin Laden, subject to conditions, to a neutral country in return for an end to the bombing of Afghanistan. **17.** Congressional leaders shut down large parts of the US government after 31 people tested positive for exposure to anthrax. **28.** Defence Secretary Donald Rumsfeld said that President Saddam Hussein of Iraq remained a highly suspicious figure at the centre of the investigation into terror attacks against the US and hinted that the war against terrorism could be widened. **29.** Donald Rumsfeld announced that US military advisers had been sent to help the Philippines government defeat the Abu Sayyaf terrorist group.

NOVEMBER 2001

2. New York firemen protested against the scaling down of recovery operations at the World Trade Center. The US government announced that the country had lost 415,000 jobs during October, the largest monthly loss for 21 years. **4.** In Nicaragua, the Liberal Constitutionalist Party candidate, Enrique Bolaños, was elected president, winning 56.3 per cent of the vote; his party also won the general election, winning 47 of the 92 seats. **8.** John Ashcroft, the US attorney general, announced a wartime reorganisation and mobilisation of the FBI and the Immigration and naturalisation Service. **9.** The FBI declared that the anthrax attacks in the US were probably not the work of Osama bin Laden or Muslim extremists. **11.** A full examination of discounted ballots in Florida for

the 2000 US presidential election concluded that George W. Bush would still have emerged the narrow winner if the Supreme Court had not stopped the partial recount; however, if a full, state-wide recount had been undertaken, Al Gore would have won by a slender margin. **12.** An airliner plunged into the New York suburb of Queens, killing all 260 people on board and at least six people on the ground. **13.** President Bush announced that the US would destroy about 5,000 warheads over the next decade. **15.** In the US, ambassadors from 50 Islamic countries were invited to a traditional meal and prayers to mark the start of Ramadan at the White House. **19.** The US accused Iraq of breaching international agreements by developing biological weapons and said that also it suspected North Korea, Iran, Syria, Libya and Sudan of attempting to develop them. **25.** The Honduran general election was won by the National Party, which obtained 61 of the 128 seats. **28.** The US ordered 155 million doses of smallpox vaccine from a UK firm amid continuing fears over the threat of biological terrorism.

DECEMBER 2001

2. Cash dispensers in Argentina ran out of money after millions of people tried to beat government restrictions on cash withdrawals. **3.** In Saint Lucia, the incumbent St Lucia Labour Party retained power in a general election. **6.** US Secretary of State Colin Powell, announced that members of the Continuity IRA, the Orange Volunteers and the Red Hand Defenders were banned from entering the US. The IMF announced that it would not release US$1.3 billion in aid to Argentina because austerity measures introduced by the government were considered to be insufficient to bring the economy under control. **9.** In the US, the Pentagon announced that the headquarters of its 3rd Army were to be moved from the US to Kuwait. **10.** In Trinidad and Tobago, the general election left the United National Congress and the People's National Movement with 18 seats each. **11.** President Bush gave warning that 'rogue states' with weapons of mass destruction would be his next priority in the war against terrorism. **12.** The Pentagon released a video tape recording in which Osama bin Laden admitted to masterminding the 11 September attacks. The US withdrew from the 1972 anti-ballistic missile treaty after consultations with Russia. **13.** In Argentina, a one-day general strike was held by public workers protesting against new government curbs on bank withdrawals and a delay in pension payments. In Trinidad, three Britons were found hacked to death near Port of Spain; robbery was suspected as the motive. **16.** In the general election in Chile, the four-party Coalition for Democracy won 62 of the 120 seats and in a simultaneous senatorial election, won 20 of the 38 elected seats. **17.** In Haïti, rebel troops stormed the national Palace in Port-au-Prince in an attempted coup. **19.** In Argentina, the government declared a state of emergency after rioting and looting broke out in Buenos Aires and other major cities; Economy Minister Domingo Cavallo tendered his resignation. **20.** In Argentina, President de la Rua resigned following further protests outside the presidential palace; the head of the Senate, Ramón Puerta, took over as temporary president, but was replaced by Congress the following day by Adolfo Rodriguez Saá, the governor of San Luis province. **22.** Richard Reid, a British citizen who had converted to Islam, tried to blow up an American Airlines airliner flying from Paris to Miami by detonating explosives hidden in his shoes; he was restrained by fellow passengers and was arrested after the plane was diverted to Boston. **23.** In Argentina, President Saá declared the biggest debt default in history, halting payments on the

country's US$132 billion debt. **26.** In Brazil, at least 46 people died in mudslides and flooding near Petropolis in Rio de Janeiro state. **27.** Donald Rumsfeld, the Defence Secretary, said that captured al-Qa'eda and Taliban fighters would be transferred to a maximum-security camp inside the US base at Guantánamo Bay in Cuba. **30.** In Argentina, President Saá tendered his resignation following several days of protests and rioting. In Peru, at least 276 people were killed when flames caused by exploding fireworks swept through a shopping centre in Lima.

January 2002

2. In Argentina, Eduardo Duhalde was sworn in as president; thousands protested outside Parliament, demanding fresh elections. **6.** In Argentina, President Duhalde was given emergency powers to set a new exchange rate, control prices of basic foods and utilities and protect employment and industry. **9.** In the US, a 15-year-old boy crashed a stolen light aircraft into an office block in Tampa, Florida on 5 January; he left behind a suicide note that expressed sympathy for the 11 September attacks on the US. **10.** Twenty al-Qa'eda fighters were flown in hoods and chains from Afghanistan to Camp X-Ray at the US naval base at Guantánamo Bay, Cuba. **14.** In Colombia, the government and FARC guerrillas agreed to continue peace negotiations, hours before a government deadline threatening to attack the FARC safe haven in the south of the country was due to expire. **16.** In the US, Mokhtar Haouari was jailed for 24 years for conspiring to bomb Los Angeles International Airport. **17.** In Peru, up to 35 people were killed when indigenous Aguaruna people forcibly evicted non-native settlers from an isolated area of jungle. **18.** In the Netherlands' Antilles, the ruling coalition was returned to power, winning 16 of the 22 seats. **28.** In the US, Hamid Karzai, interim leader of Afghanistan, appeared beside President Bush at the White House and expressed his gratitude to the US for its assistance in freeing his country. In Colombia, an Ecuadorian Boeing 727 on a flight from Quito to Cali crashed in the Andes killing 92 people on board. **29.** President Bush declared in his state of the union address that the US's war against terrorism was 'only beginning'. He named Iraq, Iran and North Korea an 'axis of evil' and cited intelligence evidence gleaned from al-Qa'eda computers that 100,000 followers in 60 countries had passed through al-Qa'eda training camps.

February 2002

14. In the US, President Bush set out proposals to establish voluntary limits on greenhouse gas emissions. **20.** In Colombia, left-wing guerrillas took a senator hostage after hijacking an airline on a domestic flight. **21.** In Colombia, government warplanes began to bomb the FARC safe haven and the following day troops began to re-occupy the enclave. **27.** The US announced that it was to send special forces troops to the Trans-Caucasian republic of Georgia to advise local forces on how to defeat Chechen guerrillas linked to al-Qa'eda. **28.** In Cuba, about 20 hijackers took over a bus in Havana and entered the Mexican embassy, demanding the right to leave the island.

March 2002

5. President Bush imposed tariffs on steel imports, except those from Canada, Mexico and developing countries. **6.** In Brazil, police shot dead 12 members of a prisoners' action group who were arranging a breakout in São Paulo. **9.** Pentagon officials confirmed the existence of a leaked confidential report that revealed that the US had prepared plans for nuclear war with Russia, China, Iran, Iraq, Libya, North Korea and Syria. **11.** President Bush, addressing a ceremony to mark the six months since the attacks on the World Trade Centre and the Pentagon, said that the war against terrorism was entering a second phase following the toppling of the Taliban government in Afghanistan and that al-Qa'eda groups would be targeted globally. **14.** Ahmed Omar Saeed Sheikh, a British Muslim in custody in Karachi, Pakistan, was indicted in the US for the kidnapping and murder of the journalist Daniel Pearl. **17.** In Colombia, the archbishop of Cali, Isaías Duarte Cancino, who had denounced the influence of drug money in Colombia's national elections, was shot dead on the steps of a church.

April 2002

4. In the US, lawsuits were filed in Florida and Oregon which accused the Roman Catholic Church of deliberately concealing child abuse by priests. **7.** In Colombia, a car bomb exploded in Villavicencio killing 12 people; FARC guerrillas were blamed for the attack. **10.** In Mexico, a planned visit by President Vicente Fox to the US and Canada was vetoed by senators who disapproved of his friendship with the US and critical stance on Cuba. **11.** In Venezuela, a general strike was called by the country's biggest labour and business confederations demanding the resignation of President Hugo Chávez. President Chávez was forced to resign by his military high command the following day and Pedro Carmona was appointed interim president. **12.** In Colombia, FARC guerrillas kidnapped 12 members of the provincial assembly in Cali. **13.** In Venezuela, a military rebellion by officers loyal to Hugo Chávez began. The following day they stormed the presidential palace; President Carmona issued a decree dissolving the national assembly and then resigned after less than 24 hours in power. **15.** In the US, up to 40,000 people participated in the National Rally for Israel. **23.** In Argentina, Economy and Finance Minister Jorge Remes Lenicov resigned after failing to win support for an emergency plan to convert bank deposits into government bonds to save crippled banks from collapse. Two people were killed and 265 injured when a freight train collided with a packed commuter train south of Los Angeles.

May 2002

4. At least 60 people seeking refuge in a church in north west Columbia were killed in clashes between Leftist rebels and Right-wing paramilitaries. **8.** The US accused Cuba of having limited biological warfare programmes and providing the technology to other rogue states. **9.** Luke Helder, of punk band Apathy was arrested by police outside Reno, Nevada, on suspicion of having placed a trail of 18 pipe bombs in five states across the United States in just over a week. Six people were injured in the attacks. **11.** Robert Hanssen, an FBI spy-catcher, was jailed after a Russian defector revealed that he had been spying for Russia for 25 years. Maryland imposed a moratorium on executions over concerns that it was being unfairly applied to blacks convicted of murdering whites. **13.** At least 11 people died in a gunfight between police in Ajoya in Sinaloa state. **14.** The US and Russia agreed to reduce their nuclear arsenal by two thirds to the agreed range of 1,700 to 2,300 warheads over a period of ten years. **18.** President Bush denied suggestions that he could have prevented the 11 September attacks if he had reacted to information supplied by the CIA a month prior to the attacks. **21.** The director of the FBI, Robert

Mueller, warned that Middle East style suicide bombings were inevitable in the US. President Bush said that the US trade embargo on Cuba would only be lifted subject to stringent conditions including allowing international supervision of next year's election. **22.** St Helena staged a double celebration marking 500 years since the island was discovered and the restoration to the islanders of full British citizenship. **26.** Colombia elected a new president, Alvaro Uribe, who pledged to broaden the war against the Marxist terrorists in the country.

JUNE 2002

2. President Bush declared that he would launch pre-emptive strikes at any terrorists that were trying to obtain weapons of mass destruction. **3.** The United States government admitted for the first time that global warming is man-made and will inflict permanent and serious changes to the American environment. **8.** Militant American anti-abortion activists began a campaign to publish pictures of women that visit abortion clinics, which caused concern that these women could become victims of violence from angry relatives or activists as a result. **10.** The Bush administration announced that an al-Qaeda plot to detonate a 'dirty bomb' (a device used to scatter radioactive materials over a wide area) in the US, had been foiled by US Intelligence. John Gotti, the boss of America's largest crime family died in a prison hospital at the age of 61. Fire spread over 61,000 acres across Denver after an illegal forest campfire burned out of control, with the need for the evacuation of 40,000 people in the city's southwest. **17.** President Bush ordered the CIA to conduct a covert operation to remove Saddam Hussein from power. Forest Ranger, Mrs Terry Barton, admitted accidentally starting the fires that devastated 103,000 acres of Colorado. Al-Q'aeda warned the US to prepare for further terrorist attacks. **26.** In Canada, the annual G8 summit commenced in a secluded location in Kananaskis in the Rocky Mountains. In Argentina, two people died and at least 90 were injured when police fired rubber bullets and tear gas into crowds of unemployed demonstrators on the streets of Buenos Aires. **31.** Brazil won the 2002 football World Cup in a victory of 2-0 against Germany.

JULY 2002

4. A gunman killed two people and wounded at least three more after opening fire at the El Al check-in desk at Los Angeles international airport. In Argentina, elections were brought forward to March 2003 by Edouard Duhalde through fears that he may be forced out by protests. The stepson of Saddam Hussein was arrested by the FBI, after enrolling at a flight training school in Florida used by one of the 11 September hijackers. **11.** In Argentina, General Leopoldo Galtieri, the former Argentine military dictator who ordered the invasion of the Falkland Islands, was arrested and charged with offences relating to the kidnapping and murder of opponents during the 'dirty war' when at least 9,000 people disappeared. **16.** A State of Emergency was declared in Argentina after anti-government protests left 15 people wounded. **23.** The US led international criticism of Israel's air strike which killed 14 civilians on 22 July.

AUGUST 2002

6. A team of looters was arrested in New York for their involvement in the theft of more than $15 million from a cash machine network that was damaged by the collapse of the World Trade Centre towers. In Mexico, 33 passengers were killed when their bus crashed into a

bridge. **18.** Nine people were found murdered on a ranch in central Mexico in what was believed to be a drug related incident. **21.** In San Diego, 50-year-old David Westerfield was found guilty of the abduction and murder of his neighbour's seven-year-old daughter, Danielle Van Dam on 1 February. **27.** The Los Angeles Unified School District voted unanimously to ban soft drinks in the state's schools amid fears of America's obesity epidemic. President Mubarak of Egypt warned President Bush of Arab anger over a strike against Iraq, unless some form of peace was reached between Israel and the Palestinians first.

ASIA

SEPTEMBER 2001

3. In East Timor, the Revolutionary Front for an Independent East Timor (Fretelin) won 55 of the 88 seats in the Constituent Assembly. **9.** In Afghanistan, Ahmed Shah Masūd, leader of the Northern Alliance, was mortally wounded in a suicide bomb attack; he died the following day and was succeeded as leader of the Northern Alliance by Gen. Mohammed Fakhim on 12 September. **12.** Osama bin Laden, the leader of the al-Qa'eda terrorist network based in Afghanistan, congratulated those responsible for the terrorist attacks in the US, but denied involvement. **14.** India offered the US the use of its military bases to launch strikes on Afghanistan. In Nepal, demonstrations in favour of peace talks between the government and Maoist rebels took place across the country. **16.** Iran closed its border with Afghanistan in order to prevent further influxes of refugees. **18.** A four-day ministerial meeting between North and South Korea agreed to resume stalled cross-border projects and hold further family reunions. **19.** The former king of Afghanistan, Mohamed Zahir Shah, issued an appeal for a national uprising against the Taliban in a radio broadcast from his exile in Rome. Pakistan agreed to allow US troops to be based at key airfields near the Afghan border. **21.** At least three people were shot dead in Pakistan as thousands of demonstrators burned effigies of President Bush in protests organised by Islamic fundamentalist parties in cities across Pakistan. **22.** The MoD admitted that SAS units had entered Afghanistan. China sent troops to its borders with Afghanistan and Pakistan to protect its territory from infiltration by Islamic extremists. **24.** In a legislative election in the Macao Special Autonomous Region of China, pro-Beijing candidates and pro-business candidates won four seats each and two seats were won by pro-democracy candidates; the other 17 were filled by nominees. Kazakhstan offered the use of its airports and military bases to the US. The Pope, who was visiting Kazakhstan, condemned terrorism and religious fundamentalism, saying that they profaned the name of God. **26.** Iran's supreme leader, the Ayatollah Ali Khamenei, accused US of using the attacks on New York and Washington as a pretext for settling accounts with the Muslim world. **27.** Qudratullah Jamal, the Taliban Information Minister, announced that an edict inviting Osama bin Laden to leave the country had been delivered. **30.** In Afghanistan, leaders of the Northern Alliance agreed with former King Mohamed Zahir Shah and representatives of the country's ethnic groups on the formation of a military council to lead a two-year transitional government if US-led alliance succeeded in causing the collapse of the Taliban government.

OCTOBER 2001

1. In Afghanistan, former King Zahir Shah joined forces with the opposition Northern Alliance in an agreement to convene a *Loya Jirga*, an assembly of tribal leaders, which would elect a head of state and a transitional government. The Taliban agreed to share power with local elders in Khost, Paktia and Paktika provinces in an attempt to block support for the transitional government. In India, at least 31 people were killed and 75 injured when Jaish-e-Mohammadi, an Islamic militant organisation with close links to the Taliban, launched a suicide attack on the Kashmir State assembly in Srinagar. In Bangladesh, the general election was won by the Bangladesh Nationalist Party, which won 191 of the 330 seats. 6. In Pakistan, the government ordered the expulsion of 89 people working for Islamic relief agencies. 7. The US and the UK unleashed sustained military strikes across Afghanistan as part of their *Enduring Freedom* mission; long-range bombers, tomahawk cruise missiles and carrier-based jets were used in the attack. In Pakistan, Gen. Musharraf sidelined the three senior Islamist generals who had been the architects of Pakistan's former pro-Taliban policy. 9. US aircraft attacked Qandahar in a raid that the Taliban claimed had killed at least 35 civilians. 10. Taliban authorities lifted all restrictions on Osama bin Laden and said that he was free to wage holy war against the US from Afghan territory; several Taliban military leaders, including two close relatives of Mullah Mohammed Omar were killed in the first wave of airstrikes. 11. In Sri Lanka, President Chandrika Kumaratunga dissolved parliament and ordered new elections to be held on 5 December. 12. In China, the government instructed Chinese airlines to halt ticket sales to people from about 20 primarily Middle Eastern countries. Uzbekistan agreed to allow the US to use its Khanabad airbase for military operations against the Taliban. 13. Osama bin Laden threatened to mount suicide attacks on the UK and warned of further attacks on the US in a statement broadcast by the Qatari al-Jazeera television station. 15. The Indian army directed mortar fire at Pakistani military targets in Kashmir following the killing of 11 Islamic militants who had been trying to cross into the India-controlled sector. In Afghanistan, US jets bombed targets around Kabul and Qandahār, and hit military headquarters and a terrorist training camp near Jalalabad. In Pakistan, a day of protest was called by the main religious parties to coincide with the visit of Colin Powell, the US Secretary of State. 23. In Indonesia, the House of Representatives passed a law granting increased autonomy to Irian Jaya and renamed the province Papua. 24. Twenty-two members of the Pakistani militant group Harakat al-Mujahidin were killed in a US air strike on Kabul. In Iran, celebrations following a football match victory in Tehran turned into a violent protest over 22 years of religious rule. 26. Abdul Haq, a former Mujahidin commander who went into Taliban-controlled areas to persuade moderates to abandon the Taliban, was captured and executed. 28. In Pakistan, 15 Christians and a Muslim guard were massacred when gunmen opened fire during a Protestant church service in a Roman Catholic church in Bahawalpur in the Punjab. The US bombed Taliban positions near the border with Tajikistan. 29. Japan adopted legislation allowing its armed forces to provide logistical support in the war against terrorism. In Sri Lanka, Prime Minister Ratnasiri Wicremanayake escaped an assassination attempt after guards intercepted a bomber who blew himself up and killed three others in Colombo. 29–31. In Pakistan, Islamic fundamentalists blocked sections of the Karakorum highway in protest at the pro-US stance of the government.

NOVEMBER 2001

1. In Afghanistan, hundreds of Pakistani Islamic militants were given permission by the Taliban to enter Afghanistan to fight against the US. 2. In Pakistan, anthrax spores were found in a letter at the head office of the *Daily Jang*, the country's biggest-selling newspaper, which had been supportive of Gen. Musharraf's pro-American stance. 4. In Afghanistan, the United Front Alliance announced that 60 candidates had been chosen by the opposition to form a Council of National Unity following the defeat of the Taliban. In the Singaporean general election, the People's Action Party was returned to office with 82 of the 90 parliamentary seats. 8. US airstrikes were credited with killing 85 members of the Pakistani militant group Harkat Jihad-i-Islami and a senior Taliban commander near Mazar-i-Sharif. 9. Osama bin Laden admitted in a video message that al-Qa'eda carried out the 11 September attacks on the US. In Afghanistan, Northern Alliance troops entered Mazar-e-Sharif In Pakistan, security forces shot dead four demonstrators during a national strike against President Musharraf's support for the US called by the Afghan Defence Council, an alliance of 35 Islamic groups; President Musharraf outwitted the organisers of the national strike by declaring the day a national holiday. 11. In Indonesia, Theys Eluay, the leader of West Papua's independence movement, was found dead near the border with Papua New Guinea a few hours after being kidnapped. 13. Northern Alliance forces entered Kabul and gained control of five further Afghan provinces. 14. Jalalabad, the headquarters of al-Qa'eda, fell to tribal fighters previously loyal to the Taliban regime. 15. Around 100 members of the UK's Special Boat Service flew into Afghanistan as the advance party of a force designed to help restore order and to ensure the distribution of humanitarian aid. 16. In Kondūz, al-Qa'eda guards killed about 150 Taliban troops to prevent them surrendering to the Northern Alliance after about 1,000 had previously defected. 18. The Taliban declared that Osama bin Laden no longer enjoyed their protection. 19. In the Philippines, troops killed 51 Muslim insurgents after an uprising on the island of Jolo. 21. In China, more than 17,000 internet bars were shut down for failing to block web sites considered subversive or pornographic. 25–27. In Afghanistan, a revolt of captured Taliban fighters at Qala-e-Jhangi prison ended with most of the prisoners being killed by US bombing. 26. Kondūz fell to the Northern Alliance. In Nepal, King Gyanendra declared a state of emergency and ordered the army into action against Maoist guerrillas who had killed more than 200 people in a weekend offensive. 27. Talks on forming a post-Taliban power-sharing administration opened near Bonn. In the Philippines, Muslim guerrillas freed more than 100 hostages and at least 25 rebels, two soldiers and a civilian died in clashes in Zamboanga.

DECEMBER 2001

1. In the Taiwanese general election, the Democratic Progressive Party became the largest party in the Legislative Yuan, winning 87 of the 225 seats and defeating the Kuomintang, which had ruled since 1949. In Afghanistan, 80 Taliban soldiers blew themselves up after surrendering to the Northern Alliance in Kondūz. In India, seven members of a wedding party were shot by suspected Muslim militants in Kashmir. 5. In the Sri Lankan general election, the United National Party won 109 of the 225 seats in the National Assembly after a

campaign in which about 60 people were killed. After ten days of talks in Bonn four delegations representing Afghanistan's rival factions pledged themselves to end 23 years of civil war and form a multiethnic government headed by Hamid Karzai, a moderate Pashtun leader. **6.** The Taliban surrendered Qandahar, its spiritual stronghold and the last city to remain in its control. **12.** In Pakistan, two former nuclear scientists, who had been held in police custody for two months, confessed to sharing nuclear, biological and chemical secrets with Osama bin Laden during meetings in Kabul in 2001. **13.** In India, five suspected Islamic militants forced their way into the parliament building and killed seven people before being shot dead by security forces. Pakistan publicly denounced the attack on the Indian parliament. In Hong Kong, Chief Executive Tung Chee-hwa announced that he would seek a second term in office. **14.** Indian Foreign Minister Jaswant Singh urged Pakistan to take action against the Kashmiri terrorist organisation Lashkar-e-Tayyeba, which he claimed had links with the attack on the parliament building; several Indian MPs urged the government to launch cross-border raids on Pakistan against Kashmiri separatist groups. **15.** In Afghanistan, the interim government thanked the US for ridding the country of the Taliban. In India, Delhi Police Commissioner Ajai Raj Sharma said seven men arrested in connection with the attack on parliament had confessed to links with the Pakistani intelligence service, the Interservices Intelligence Directorate (ISI). **19.** Fourteen al-Qa'eda fighters and Pakistani security guards were killed close to the border with Afghanistan after an escape attempt turned into a gun battle. Twenty-one were said to have been recaptured, with 20 still at large. **19–20.** The Pakistani army fought with escaped al-Qa'eda prisoners in tribal areas close to the Afghan frontier. **20.** Pentagon officials confirmed that several high-ranking Taliban figures were being held by US forces, including the head of the army and the its intelligence chief. **21.** India recalled its High Commissioner from Pakistan and announced that road and rail links between the countries would be severed; tanks, artillery and infantry were moved to the border. **22.** In Afghanistan, the new interim government was sworn in at a gathering of 2,000 tribal leaders; the newly appointed Prime Minister Hamid Karzai said that he would welcome US forces until his country was rid of all its terrorists. The Japanese armed forces sank what was believed to be a North Korean spy ship in Japanese territorial waters. **26.** India deployed nuclear-capable missiles along its frontier with Pakistan. President Musharraf of Pakistan said that Muslim militants tarnished the image of Islam by promoting hatred, extremism and oppression of women. **27.** India demanded that Pakistan halve its diplomatic staff in New Delhi and announced the suspension of transport links between the two countries. **30.** In China, more than 40 people died in a fireworks factory in Huangmao, Jiangxi province. **31.** US troops began a mission to help the Philippine armed forces defeat Islamic fundamentalist guerrillas.

JANUARY 2002

2. In India, Islamic militants killed a policeman and wounded 24 people in a grenade attack on the state assembly building in Srinagar, Kashmir. In Pakistan, the government refused to extradite 20 alleged Muslim militants wanted by India. **4.** In Afghanistan, an agreement to allow an international security force to be deployed in Kabul was formally signed. In Pakistan, security forces arrested 120 Muslim militants, mainly members of Lashkar-e-Tayyeba and Jaish-e-Mohammadi.

5. In Pakistan, police raids on mosques and separatist networks led to the arrest of 200 militants. **7.** In Singapore, the government said that Islamic extremists linked to Osama bin Laden and a Malaysian militant group, Kumpulan Militan Malaysia, had penetrated the Singaporean armed forces and had been preparing to attack US targets, adding that 15 people had been taken into custody in December. **9.** In Afghanistan, the interior minister, Yūnus Qanūni, ordered military units to withdraw from Kabul as international troops prepared to mount their first joint patrols with local police. Iran blocked the appointment of David Reddaway as the UK's new ambassador, calling him a Zionist and a spy. **12.** In Pakistan, President Musharraf announced measures to crack down on Islamic extremist groups and radical Islamic schools, and banning Lashkar-e-Tayyeba and Jaish-e-Mohammadi. **13.** In Sri Lanka, at least 13 people were killed and more than 200 injured, including four Britons, after a train travelling from Kandy to Colombo derailed. **14.** In India, Defence Minister George Fernandes said that India would not pull back its forces from the Indo-Pakistani border until cross-border terrorism had been halted. Seventeen people were shot dead and 13 injured when tribal separatists from the National Liberation Front of Tripura opened fire in a crowded market in Singicherra in Tripura state. **16.** In Pakistan, US Secretary of State Colin Powell arrived in Islamabad to try to persuade Pakistan and India to step back from the brink of war. **17.** In Afghanistan, Colin Powell visited Kabul where he met with the leader of the interim administration, Hamid Karzai, and promised US assistance in rebuilding the country. **20.** In China, the government began the demolition of towns to be flooded as part of the Three Gorges Dam project on the Yangtze River. **21.** World leaders at the Afghanistan reconstruction conference in Tokyo pledged £3 billion in aid. **22.** In India, four unidentified gunmen sprayed automatic gun fire at the US Information and Cultural Centre in Kolkata (Calcutta), killing four policemen and injuring 21 people; the following day, police arrested about 50 people in connection with the attack. **23.** In India, police arrested about 50 people in connection with the shooting in Kolkata. In Pakistan, Islamic militants calling themselves the National Movement for Restoration of Pakistani Sovereignty, but believed to be members of Jaish-e-Mohammadi, took Daniel Pearl, the *Wall Street Journal's* South Asia bureau chief, hostage. **24.** US forces killed 15 al-Qa'eda and Taliban fighters and arrested 27 in raids on compounds in southern Afghanistan. **28.** In Afghanistan, six Arab al-Qa'eda fighters who had barricaded themselves in a Qandahar hospital were killed after an 11-hour gun battle with US and Afghan soldiers. **30.** In Pakistan, the Taliban chief justice, Nūr Mohammad Saqib, and deputy foreign minister Abdul Rehman Zahid were arrested in Quetta.

FEBRUARY 2002

1. In Pakistan, Islamic militants holding the US journalist Daniel Pearl increased their demands, asking for £1.4 million and the freeing of a senior Taliban official. **2–3.** In Afghanistan, up to 40 people were killed during a territorial dispute between rival Northern Alliance commanders around the city of Mazar-e-Sharif. **8.** North Korea responded to President Bush's claims that it was part of an 'axis of evil' by describing the US as a criminal 'empire of the devil' bent on world domination. **10.** Herds of rampaging elephants trampled to death three Bangladeshis and injured 10 when they stormed through villages in the Cox's Bazar district. **12.** In Indonesia, Christians and Muslims in Maluku province signed a

peace deal to end three years of violence. In Iran, a passenger jet crashed into mountains near Khorramabad, killing all 117 people on board. **14.** In Afghanistan, the Minister of Air Transport and Tourism, Abdul Rahman, was beaten to death at Kabul airport; the following day, Interim Prime Minister Hamid Karzai alleged that his murder had been ordered by senior security officials loyal to a faction in the ruling coalition and ordered the arrest of six officials, including two generals. **17.** In Nepal, Maoist rebels killed more than 120 people in weekend raids on government outposts, including 49 soldiers and 75 policemen. **19.** In India, 12 people, including nine rebels, were killed in Kashmir. **20.** In South Korea, President Bush visited the demilitarised zone and called on the North Korean regime to free its people. **21.** In China, President Bush asked President Jiang Zemin for China's help in making the world a safer place. The US State Department revealed that Daniel Pearl, the *Wall Street Journal's* South Asia bureau chief, had been murdered by his captors who had videotaped his execution. In Nepal, Nepalese troops killed 48 Maoist rebels when the guerrillas launched attacks in five districts. In the Philippines, a US Army Chinook CH47 helicopter with 12 troops on board crashed into the sea, of whom only two survived. **22.** In Sri Lanka, the government and the Tamil Tigers signed a cease-fire agreement aimed at ending over three decades of conflict. In Nepal, Maoist rebels killed 37 people in raids across the country hours after parliament extended a state of emergency. **25.** In Nepal, troops killed 84 Maoist rebels and seized large quantities of arms and explosives. **26.** In Afghanistan, Germany agreed to assume command of the International Security Assistance Force (ISAF) at the end of April. **27.** In India, 57 Hindu extremists were killed when their train was attacked by Muslims in Godhra in Gujarat, who set four coaches alight; the train later stopped at Vadodara, where Hindu extremists beat alighting Muslims and stabbed one man to death.

MARCH 2002

1. In India, sectarian clashes intensified in Gujarat and spread to other parts of the country. **2.** In Afghanistan, at least one US soldier and two Afghan fighters were killed in a battle to destroy hundreds of Taliban and al-Qa'eda fighters who had regrouped near Gardez in Paktia province in the mountains of eastern Afghanistan. **3.** In Afghanistan, at least 100 people were thought to have been killed in an earthquake. In India, intelligence officials admitted that there had been a deliberate delay by the federal and the state government, both dominated by Hindu nationalists, in deploying the army to give Hindu militants a free hand. **4.** In East Timor, the arrival of Japanese peacekeepers was marked by demonstrators protesting about atrocities committed by Japanese forces during the Second World War. In Afghanistan, eight US soldiers were killed in action and 40 wounded in a battle against al-Qa'eda and Taliban forces near Gardez in which up to 200 enemy troops were believed to have been killed. **6.** In Afghanistan, three Danish and two German soldiers were killed as they attempted to diffuse surface-to-air missiles near Kabul. China announced a 17.6 per cent rise in defence spending to modernise the People's Liberation Army. **8.** In China, the Falun gong sect hijacked a state TV channel and broadcast for 50 minutes before being stopped. **9.** Indian Interior minister Moinuddin Haider declined an invitation from Pakistan to peace talks, saying that dialogue was meaningless if Pakistan did not end its backing of terrorism in Kashmir. **10.** In Myanmar, relatives of former ruler Gen. Ne Win were arrested for allegedly plotting a coup. On 12 March,

the government said that the alleged coup plotters planned to seize power by abducting the junta's top three leaders. **14.** In China, a group of 25 North Koreans forced their way into the Spanish embassy in Beijing to claim political asylum; the following day, they were given permission to leave for South Korea. In India, at least 20 potential recruits were believed to have been killed at an army recruitment fair after they fell into a septic tank in Lucknow. **15.** In India, about 35,000 people were arrested across the country in a bid to prevent violence in Ayodhya. **17.** In Pakistan, five people were killed when a suspected Islamic militant carried out a suicide attack on a crowded church in the diplomatic district of Islamabad. **19.** In China, paramilitary police moved into position to crush a demonstration of up to 50,000 former oilfield workers protesting about their redundancy payments in Daqing, Manchuria. In India, fresh intercommunal violence broke out between Hindus and Muslims in western Gujarat as fresh Hindu-Muslim clashes erupted. **22.** In Pakistan, Ahmed Omar Sheikh, a British-born Islamic militant, was charged with murdering the US journalist Daniel Pearl. **24.** In India, six people, including four soldiers, were killed in rebel attacks in Kashmir. North and South Korea today announced that they had agreed to exchange special envoys and resume talks. **25.** In Indonesia, the Parliamentary Speaker, Akbar Tandjung, appeared in court charged with embezzling about £2.8 million in state funds in 1999 while he was a state secretary in the former government. **26.** In Afghanistan, at least 2,000 people were killed in an earthquake in Baghlan province. In India, parliament passed an anti-terrorism bill allowing police to detain suspects for questioning for up to 90 days. **29.** In Nepal, 25 people were injured by a bomb in Kathmandu. **30.** In India, 12 people were killed when Muslim suicide bombers stormed the Raghunath Hindu temple in Jammu after a gun battle with police. **31.** In Taiwan, an earthquake struck, killing at least four people and injuring more than 200.

APRIL 2002

2. In Afghanistan, more than a hundred Royal Marines landed at the Bagram air base north of Kabul. President Musharraf of Pakistan flew to Kabul to try to improve relations with the interim government; Pakistan had previously supported the Taliban regime. **3.** North Korea announced that it was ready to resume talks with the US. **4.** In Afghanistan, police foiled an attempt by Gulbiddin Hekmatyar, an anti-Western former Mujahidin commander, to oust interim leader Hamid Karzai and launch attacks against international peacekeepers. **5.** The trial of Omar Saeed Sheikh and three alleged accomplices accused of murdering the US reporter Daniel Pearl opened in Karachi. **6.** In Pakistan, Gen. Musharraf warned that Pakistan was ready to use its nuclear weapons if it were attacked by India. **11.** In Nepal, Maoist rebels killed 164 people in attacks on three police posts in Dang district. **14.** In India, 18 people were killed in gun battles and grenade attacks in Kashmir. In Nepal, more than 300 people were killed in two assaults in Dang district. **15.** In East Timor, Xanana Gusmão, the Fretilin (Revolutionary Front for an Independent East Timor) candidate, won the presidential election, gaining 82.7 per cent of the votes cast. In South Korea, an Air China passenger jet crashed into Mount Shineo near Pusan; 38 people survived the crash which killed 121. In Afghanistan, four US soldiers were killed whilst exploding Taliban rockets near Qandahar. **18.** In Afghanistan, former King Zahir Shah returned home after 29 years in exile. A US F16 pilot accidentally killed

four Canadian soldiers by dropping a laser-guided bomb on them. **21.** Islamic militants ambushed an army patrol near Surankote, Kashmir, killing five soldiers. In the Philippines, at least 13 people were killed and 41 injured by two bombs in General Santos city; responsibility was claimed by Abu Sayyaf rebels. **23.** In Nepal, Maoist rebels ordered a five-day general strike. **24.** In India, seven people were killed in religious violence in Ahmedabad. **25.** In China, about 2,000 supporters of the Falun gong sect were detained and 150 sent to labour camps. In Pakistan, at least ten people were killed when a bomb exploded at a Shi'ite festival in the Punjab province; the banned Sipah-I-Sahaba, an extremist Sunni group, was suspected of responsibility for the attack. **26.** In India, security forces shot dead 14 Muslim separatists in gun battles in Kashmir. **28.** In India, nine people were killed and at least 25 injured in Gujarat in sectarian violence. **30.** In Pakistan, over 97 per cent of those voting in a referendum to prolong President Musharraf's term of office approved the proposal; the turnout was 56 per cent.

MAY 2002

2. A thousand Royal Marines launched Britain's biggest combat operation since the Gulf War in south-eastern Afghanistan. The BJP-led coalition government won a parliamentary censure vote over the continuing slaughter of Muslims in Gujarat. Two of the members of the coalition, the Telugu Desam party and the national Conference party, abstained. The Lok Jan Shakti party left the coalition on 29 April. **7.** In Bangladesh, rescue workers recovered more than 270 bodies from a ferry that sank in the Maghna river on 3 May, up to 300 people were thought to have died. **9.** In China, at least 18 people were killed when a boulder fell onto a bus in Hubei province. Sixteen people, mostly Muslims, were killed in a day of violence in Gujarat. **14.** Thirty lorry-loads of supposed terrorist arms destroyed by the Royal Marines probably belonged to a coalition ally, it emerged, when the war lord Ibrahim Omari said the arms were his rather than al Qa'eda's. **15.** Muslim insurgents killed at least 30 people near Jammu in the state of Kashmir; the three gunmen were also killed. **18.** Up to a dozen civilians were reported killed by US warplanes after a reconnaissance patrol mistook a wedding party for hostile guerilas. Indian and Pakistani troops exchanged heavy fire across their border near Jammu. Two people were killed in a bomb explosion in Srinagar. **20.** East Timor became independent when the UN handed over power to the new government at midnight. **21.** East Timor swore in its first cabinet. Mari Alkatiri was named as Prime Minister. In India, the government placed all paramilitary units along the border under army control and the coast guard under naval command. Abdul Ghani Lone, a leader of the All Parties Hurriyat (Freedom) Conference, a conglomerate of 23 Muslim political parties and social groups campaigning against Indian rule in Kashmir, was shot dead in Srinagar India. **23.** Indian Prime Minister Atal Behari Vajpayee told troops in Kashmir to be ready for a decisive battle. In Nepal, the ruling Nepali Congress Party suspended Prime Minister Sher Bahadur Deuba after his call for the dissolution of Parliament. **26.** Following two ballistic missile tests, President Bush urged President Musharraf to do more to prevent Islamic militants crossing into Kashmir.

JUNE 2002

4. In Thailand, two children were killed and 13 others seriously injured when masked gunmen shot at a Thai school bus 15 miles from the school border. **7.** In the Philippines, two hostages held by the Islamic separatist

Abu Sayyaf Group (ASG) were killed during a rescue attempt. **13.** Hamid Karzai was elected as interim President of Afghanistan. **14.** In Pakistan, a car bomb was detonated outside the US consulate in Karachi in a suicide attack that killed 13 people and injured more than 40. **19.** A new government was elected in Kyrgyzstan. **20.** UK Defence Secretary Geoff Hoon announced that from 4 July, the 1,600 UK troops in Afghanistan would be withdrawn. **21.** President A.Q.M. Badruddoza Chowdhury of Bangladesh resigned under pressure from the ruling Bangladesh Nationalist Party (BNP), after he had failed to visit the grave of Maj.-Gen. Ziaur Rahman on the anniversary of his assassination. **24.** A new cabinet was announced in Hong Kong. **26.** Ten Pakistani soldiers were killed by al-Qa'eda fighters in a gun battle in the village of Azam Warsak, near the Afghan border. **29.** A curfew was imposed on the town of Valaichchenai, Sri Lanka, after violence broke out between Hindu and Muslim Tamils, leaving at least eight people dead and dozens injured. **30.** A South Korean patrol boat was sunk with four of its crew killed, one missing and 18 wounded, in a clash between patrol craft from North and South in the Yellow Sea off western Korea. Both sides claimed that the other fired first.

JULY 2002

6. In Afghanistan Vice-President Haji Abdul Qadir was assassinated as he left his office in Kabul. **7.** Around 52 people died in a fire at a night club in Palembang, Indonesia. **8.** In Pakistan, three men were arrested in connection with the US consulate bombing in Karachi on June 14. **11.** In South Korea, Chang San became the first female Prime Minister after a cabinet reshuffle. **14.** In Kashmir, 27 people were killed when five gunmen attacked Hindus in the Kasim Nagar neighbourhood of Jammu. In the Philippines, a week of typhoons and monsoon rains killed at least 60 people in severe flooding on the main island of Luzon and Manila. **15.** In Nepal, a landslide that swept through two villages in eastern Nepal left at least 150 people dead. In Pakistan, a British Islamic militant Ahmed Omar Saeed Sheikh was sentenced to death for the murder of Canadian journalist, Daniel Pearl. **25.** In India, A. P. J. Abdul Kalam, a 71-year old Muslim, was sworn in as the country's 12th President. Benazir Bhutto, the former Prime Minister of Pakistan, was re-elected as leader of her party.

AUGUST 2002

5. In Pakistan, six people were killed when Islamic gunmen attacked a Christian school attended by 25 British children. **9.** Five people were killed and 26 others wounded after Islamic militants hurled grenades at Christian worshippers leaving a hospital chapel in a town 16 miles from Islamabad. In Afghanistan, an explosion at a road-building depot in the eastern part of the country killed at least 26 people. Whether this was an accident or a terrorist attack was unconfirmed. **15.** Pakistani police arrested 12 activists from an outlawed Islamic group they believed to be responsible for the attack on a Presbyterian church in Taxila. **19.** In India, aid was cut to a village in the north of the country after a woman was burnt to death on her husband's funeral pyre through the outlawed practice of suttee. **21.** Afghanistan agreed to co-operate with any American inquiry into reports that up to 1,000 Afghanistan agreed to co-operate with any American inquiry into reports that up to 1,000 Taliban prisoners of war suffocated in lorries of the US backed Northern Alliance. **22.** A militant Islamist leader in Pakistan warned of more terrorist attacks if the military Government blocked guerrillas from crossing into

Kashmir to fight Indian forces. India stated that tensions with Pakistan would not cease until Islamabad halted all support for separatist rebels in Kashmir. **23.** Tensions rose once again over Kashmir after Pakistan accused India of sending troops and aircraft to attack one of its positions in the disputed Himalayan region. **26.** In Cambodia, severe flooding of the Mekong river forced almost half a million people from their homes. **28.** A state of emergency imposed on Nepal since November 2001, giving the army powers to stamp out a Maoist insurgency, was lifted.

AUSTRALASIA AND THE PACIFIC

SEPTEMBER 2001

1. In the Fijian general election, no party won an overall majority and negotiations began to form a government; on 9 September the nationalist United Fiji Party agreed a deal with six moderate MPs to give it a majority. **11.** An Australian court ruled that the government had acted unlawfully when it had refused the Norwegian freighter *The Tampa* permission to land; the vessel had been carrying asylum seekers rescued from a sinking Indonesian ferry. **19.** Nearly half the population of Nauru came out to greet a boat containing asylum seekers who had been refused entry by Australia.

OCTOBER 2001

1. The Nauruan government ordered an immediate halt to the landing of asylum seekers on the island after Australian soldiers forced six refugees to disembark. **17.** Australia announced that it would supply 1,550 military personnel to join the US-led campaign in Afghanistan.

NOVEMBER 2001

11. In the Australian general election, the Liberal Party-National Party coalition secured a third successive election victory, winning 81 of the 150 seats.

DECEMBER 2001

5. In the Solomon Islands, the general election was won by the People's Alliance Party, which obtained 20 of the 50 seats. **13.** The air combat wing of the Royal New Zealand Air Force was formally disbanded.

JANUARY 2002

1–16. In Australia, hundreds of people were forced to evacuate their homes as bush fires reached the suburbs of Sydney; arsonists were believed to have caused many of the fires. **18.** In Australia, 58 asylum seekers, detained in Woomera camp, sewed their lips together as part of a hunger strike in protest at the slow processing of their visa applications. **31.** The Australian government announced plans to pay thousands of Afghan asylum seekers and refugees a resettlement allowance to return to their homeland.

FEBRUARY 2002

17. In Fiji, George Speight, the leader of the May 2000 coup, was sentenced to death after pleading guilty to treason, but the sentence was commuted to life imprisonment the following day by President Ratu Josefa Iloilo. **19.** In Fiji, ten rebels who helped George Speight overthrow the government were jailed for between 18 months and three years after treason allegations were dropped for lesser charges of kidnap. **21.** In Australia, Prime Minister John Howard gave his support to

Governor-General Peter Hollingworth after the opposition called for him to be dismissed following allegations of covering up child sexual abuse in the Anglican Church.

MARCH 2002

29. In Australia, up to 20 people escaped from the Woomera refugee detention centre after about 1,000 asylum seekers demonstrated in the camp.

APRIL 2002

10. Work began on a rail link between Darwin and Alice Springs. The route, which will be completed in 2004, will provide a north-south link between Darwin and Adelaide. **12.** A British backpacker, Caroline Stuttle, was robbed and thrown to her death from a bridge in Bundaberg, Queensland.

MAY 2002

14. The Australian government apologised to British child migrants who were sexually abused and flogged in its institutions after the Second World War; about 1,000 British children were shipped to Australia under a joint initiative by both governments in a programme which continued until the late 1960s.

JUNE 2002

3. Peter Cameron Burgess, a volunteer with the Rural Fire Service in New South Wales, was sentenced to two years imprisonment for starting bush fires that caused widespread damage in December 2001 and January 2002. **28.** 34 detainees from the Woomera asylum detention centre escaped with the help of a support group for asylum seekers. **30.** Some 24 of the Woomera escapees were recaptured by police. Helen Clark, the Prime Minister of New Zealand, called for elections to be brought forward more than three months to July 27.

JULY 2002

3. Steve Fosset, the first man to circle the world alone in a hot air balloon landed in the Australian outback. **27.** In New Zealand the general election resulted in the Labour Party, lead by Helen Clark, winning 52 of the 120 seats in parliament.

AUGUST 2002

1. The damning United Nations report on Australia's refugee camps received criticism by the federal government, which insisted that the country's detention system met international standards.

EUROPEAN UNION

SEPTEMBER 2001

14. The EU told Belarus that it must improve its human rights record and move towards democracy if it wished to end its isolation. **21.** The Council of Ministers agreed at an emergency session to create an EU arrest warrant and increase the powers of Europol; it also approved a resolution expressing solidarity with the US and recognising the legitimacy of any military action. **22.** EU finance ministers ordered national regulators to investigate alleged market manipulations, following revelations of suspicious dealings in airline and insurance shares in the days before the 11 September attacks in the US.

OCTOBER 2001

1. The Court of First Instance ruled that the European Parliament's Technical Group of Independents must be dissolved, as it had breached Parliamentary rules by stating that its members must affirm their total political independence of one another. **23.** The European Commission announced that it was beginning legal action against the UK government over curbs on the amount of alcohol and tobacco British travellers were permitted to bring into the UK from other EU member states.

NOVEMBER 2001

28. *The Future of the European Union*, a report issued on 26 November by a committee led by the Belgian Prime Minister, Guy Verhofstadt, concluded that the EU was failing its people and becoming increasingly unpopular, and suggested the creation of European political parties and an all-EU constitution.

DECEMBER 2001

2. Turkey withdrew its objections to the use of NATO assets for the EU's rapid reaction force. **11.** The EU demanded that Yasser Arafat curb Islamic terrorists operating from Palestinian-run territory. **16.** Former French leader Valerie Giscard d'Estaing was appointed to preside over a year-long convention which would discuss draft proposals for a new EU treaty to be signed in 2004; the convention was to consist of 100 politicians picked by national and EU bodies. **21.** A report issued by the European Commission stated that joining the euro had left weaker economies with long-term problems.

JANUARY 2002

1. Euro notes and coins went into circulation in all EU member states except the UK, Denmark and Sweden. **2.** The euro rose sharply in value against the US dollar, pound and yen as financial markets responded favourably to its smooth launch. **11.** The EU gave Zimbabwe one week to declare in writing that it would accept international observers and news media during the 9–10 March presidential elections. **15.** Pat Cox, MEP for Munster and leader of the European Liberals, was elected president of the European Parliament. **16.** A coalition of Conservative, Liberal and Green MEPs voted to set up an enquiry into the UK's handling of the foot-and-mouth crisis. **30.** Enlargement Commissioner Günther Verheugen said that farmers from countries likely to join the EU in 2004 would receive only 25 per cent of the farm subsidies given to existing members, a percentage which would rise until parity was achieved in 2013.

FEBRUARY 2002

5. The European Parliament voted overwhelmingly in favour of a report that aimed to create a single market in financial services by 2005 and establish a securities committee to decide on the technical aspects of implementation. **6.** A proposal to create an EU arrest warrant covering serious crimes including terrorism, murder and fraud was passed by the European Parliament. **7.** The President of the European Central Bank (ECB), Wim Duisenberg, announced that he would retire in July 2003 on his 68th birthday. **12.** German Finance Minister Hans Eichel agreed a compromise with the other 11 eurozone ministers to avoid a formal 'early warning' to force Berlin to curb its budget deficit and promised to eliminate the deficit by 2004. **12–13.**

Ministers from the EU and the Organisation of the Islamic Conference (OIC) met in Istanbul at a conference aimed at promoting understanding and co-operation organised by the Turkish government. **28.** The Convention on the Future of Europe was launched in Brussels; modelled on the 1787 Philadelphia Convention of America's Founding Fathers, it was charged with of producing a document which would tackle institutional reform and produce a draft constitutional treaty.

MARCH 2002

6. The EU condemned the US decision to impose tariffs on steel imports and announced that it would file an immediate complaint with the World Trade Organisation. **13.** European Commission President Romano Prodi threatened to invoke exceptional powers to push through economic reforms and liberalise the EU's energy market and telecommunications sector. **26.** The EU approved the Galileo satellite navigation system, the biggest development project in its history, which will cost an estimated €3.4 billion and is due to become operational in 2008.

APRIL 2002

10. MEPs voted to pay themselves £62,000 a year, in an attempt to agree a single salary rather than the present system in which pay is linked to national MPs' earnings. They also voted to scale down the system of expense allowances. **25.** Jean-Marie Le Pen, the leader of the French National Front, addressed the European Parliament and accused the EU of slavishly following US policy in the Middle East.

MAY 2002

8. Upper-age limits for recruitment in the European Parliament and Commission were abolished.

JUNE 2002

20. Eurostat, the European Commission's statistical agency, stood accused of attempting to cover up fraud allegations relating to a €250,000 consultancy deal. Hundreds of flights were cancelled across Europe as a result of a strike led by French air traffic controllers on 19 June and a general strike in Spain (20 June).

JULY 2002

1. Four eastern European nations: Hungary, Poland, the Czech Republic and Slovakia, have thrown talks over EU enlargement into crisis by saying they will refuse to join if they have to pay more to the community budget than they receive in subsidies. **9.** The European Commission called for major reforms of the Common Agricultural Policy, whereby funds will be gradually moved from intensive production to schemes that promote rural life, safer food, animal welfare and environmental awareness. **23.** The European Union's foreign policy chief, Javier Solana, insisted that the US help in resolving the dispute between Spain and Morocco did not mean that Europe was an irrelevant party during the stand-off.

AUGUST 2002

18. The European Union agreed to establish a Europe-wide catastrophe fund to aid victims of natural disasters. The meeting in Berlin, however, failed to address Gerhard Schröder's appeal to the European Union for funds to help rebuild lives after flood damage this month.

EUROPE

SEPTEMBER 2001

10. In the Norwegian general election, the Labour Party remained the largest party, winning 43 of the 165 seats, and formed a minority government while coalition negotiations took place. In Belarus, President Alexandr Lukashenko was re-elected in the presidential election, gaining 75.6 per cent of the vote; OSCE monitors described the vote as neither free nor fair. **13.** France agreed to drop plans to open a centre for asylum seekers in Bailleul after pressure from the British government, which had previously complained that the Sangatte camp, located on the outskirts of Calais, was used as a staging post for illegal entry to the UK. **19.** In Russia, parliament approved a land bill allowing the private ownership of land. **21.** The Swiss parliament decided to advocate membership of the UN; the decision will be subject to approval in a referendum. **23.** In the Polish general election, the Coalition of the Alliance of the Democratic Left and the Union of Labour won 216 seats, gaining 41 per cent of the vote. The previous government, failed to obtain the 8 per cent of the vote necessary to enter parliament. **24.** The President of Russia, Vladimir Putin, said that Russia was willing to share intelligence concerning Afghanistan with the US. **25.** In Russia, Aslan Maskhadov, the Chechen leader, accepted President Putin's offer of peace talks. **26.** The Turkish Parliament passed a package of reforms that included the abolition of the death penalty for all crimes except terrorism and the repeal of the bans on broadcasting and education in Kurdish. **27.** In Macedonia, ethnic Albanian rebel forces formally disbanded the National Liberation Army after completing the hand-over of their weapons to NATO peacekeepers. Twenty-four members of al-Takfir wa al-Hijra (Reconciliation and Exile), an extremist cell linked to the al-Qa'eda movement, went on trial in Paris, charged with participating in a criminal organisation with a view to carrying out terrorist acts.

OCTOBER 2001

2. In Bosnia-Hercegovina, the parliament of the Republika Srpska adopted legislation enabling it to extradite suspected war criminals to the International Criminal Tribunal for the Former Yugoslavia. **4.** A Russian commercial airliner crashed into the Black Sea, killing 76 people. **6.** In Austria, the Nazi-hunter Simon Wiesenthal, who had been responsible for bringing nearly 3,000 people to justice, announced his retirement. **14.** In Ireland, ten men executed by the British authorities in 1920–21 were given a state funeral with full military honours in Dublin. **17.** In Norway, the minority Labour government resigned; a three-party centre-right coalition took power the following day with the backing of the far-right Progress Party. In Poland, a new government composed of the Democratic Left Alliance, the Labour Union and the Polish Peasants' Party took office. **23.** In Switzerland, 11 motorists were killed after a fire broke out in the St Gotthard alpine tunnel.

NOVEMBER 2001

1. In Georgia, President Shevardnadze sacked his Cabinet following demonstrations against his rule. **6.** In Spain, more than 90 people were injured when a bomb exploded in Madrid; two suspected ETA terrorists were arrested shortly after the explosion. **10.** In Russia, at least five people were killed and 40 injured by a suspected bomb in Vladikavkaz near the border with Chechnya. **11.** In

Macedonia, a group calling itself the Albanian National Army shot three policemen dead outside Tetovo. **15.** In Macedonia, Parliament ratified a peace accord with the ethnic Albanian minority and adopted 15 constitutional amendments after almost two months of delays. **16.** Kosovo held its first general election, in which the Democratic League of Kosovo won 46 per cent of the vote. **17.** In Kosovo, an election was held to the Assembly; the Democratic League of Kosovo became the largest party, winning 47 of the 120 seats. Greek Cypriot President Glafcos Clerides agreed to a meeting with Turkish Cypriot leader Raul Denktas to discuss the future of the divided island. **18.** In Bulgaria, Georgi Parvanov, the leader of the Socialist Party, won the presidential election, obtaining 54.13 per cent of the vote. **20.** In the Danish general election, the Liberal Party won 56 of the 179 seats. **23.** Talks began between the UK and Spain on the future of Gibraltar, but were boycotted by Gibraltar's Chief Minister, Peter Caruana. In Spain, two Basque police officers were shot dead in the town of Beasain near San Sebastian in a suspected ETA attack. **29.** The Danube was officially reopened to shipping for the first time since 1999.

DECEMBER 2001

2. In Switzerland, a referendum calling for the abolition of the army was rejected by 79 per cent of those taking part. **5.** The president of Cyprus, Glafcos Clerides, became the first Greek Cypriot head of state to visit the Turkish-occupied north since the island's partition in 1974. **8.** Eight refugees were found dead in a lorry in Wexford, Ireland. **9.** Twelve Russian servicemen were killed in skirmishes with rebels in Chechnya. **10.** In Kosovo, the parliamentary assembly held its inaugural session. In Kosovo, Ibrahim Rugova failed to obtain the two-thirds majority of votes in the parliamentary assembly necessary to be elected president; he had been the only candidate. **30.** In Spain, compulsory military service was abolished.

JANUARY 2002

2. In the Czech Republic, about a third of the country was declared a disaster zone following blizzards, which also caused extensive disruption in Poland and Slovakia. **8.** In Turkey, the Culture Minister accused Saudi Arabia of behaving like the Taliban in demolishing the Ajyad fortress, an 18th century Ottoman fortress in Al-Makkah (Mecca). In Sweden, the government announced that it would call a referendum on membership of the euro in 2003. **11.** In Italy, a corruption trial began in which Prime Minister Silvio Berlusconi and ex-Defence Minister Cesare Previti were accused of bribing judges in 1985 to block the sale of SME, a state-owned food company. **16.** In Cyprus, the leaders of the Greek and Turkish communities, President Glafcos Clerides and Rauf Denktaş, agreed to meet three times a week until they were able to agree a common solution to the island's future. **21.** In Austria, over 900,000 people signed a petition demanding a referendum on whether to veto the entry of the Czech Republic into the EU if it refused to close its nuclear power station in Temelín, about 60 km from the Austrian border. **24.** In Italy, the Pope presided over a pilgrimage of peace to Assisi in which Bahá'í, Buddhist, Hindu, Jain, Muslim, Sikh and Zoroastrian religious leaders made a commitment that religion would never be used again as a pretext for war, conflict or violence. **25.** In Gibraltar, Chief Minister Peter Caruana accused the UK of striking a secret deal with Spain during discussions between the UK and Spanish governments on Gibraltar's future.

FEBRUARY 2002

3. In Turkey, at least 45 people were killed by an earthquake in Afyon province. **4.** The UK government announced that the population of Gibraltar would be able to suspend the implementation of any agreement between the UK and Spain on sharing sovereignty of the territory. **5.** In Russia, two paratroopers who had murdered nine people in two days were shot dead in Tatarstan. **6.** In Turkey, a package of constitutional amendments was passed limiting the length of time suspected terrorists could be held without trial. **19.** In Spain, former ETA leader José Javier Arizkuren Ruiz went on trial on charges of masterminding a plot to assassinate King Juan Carlos. **22.** In Italy, the head of the European arm of al-Qa'eda, Essid Samin ben Khemais, was jailed for five years on charges of criminal association with intent to traffic in explosives, chemicals and false documents, and organising illegal immigration. **26.** In Austria, seven people were killed when two trains collided at Weigelsdorf near Vienna. **27.** Gibraltar's House of Assembly approved constitutional reforms designed to remove many of the governor's powers and created a new parliament of 17 elected members.

MARCH 2002

1. In Rome, police detained six Arabs whom they suspected of having links to the al-Qa'eda movement. **2.** In Macedonia, police shot dead seven suspected Pakistani Mujahidin terrorists who were attempting to ambush a police patrol near Skopje. **3.** The Swiss voted to join the UN by 54.6 per cent. In Italy, Prime Minister Silvio Berlusconi said that he would not be driven from power by protesters after about half a million people had marched against him in Rome. **4.** In Kosovo, Ibrahim Rugova was elected president and Bajram Rexhepi was chosen as prime minister following a power-sharing deal with the Democratic Party of Kosovo. **5.** In Austria, the government confirmed plans to force foreigners from outside the EU to learn German or face expulsion. **6.** In Ireland, a referendum was held on removing the threat of suicide as a reason for permitting an abortion to take place; the proposal was narrowly rejected. In Turkey, former Prime Minister Necmettin Erbakan was found guilty of fraud in Ankara and jailed for 28 months for falsifying documents of his now banned Islamic Welfare Party. **8.** Bebojsa Covic, Yugoslavia's special envoy for Kosovo, accused the Kosovan Prime Minister, Bajram Rexhepi, of having tortured and decapitated a Yugoslav soldier. In France, at least 250 asylum seekers attempted to climb onto freight wagons bound for the UK at the SNCF depot at Fréthun near Calais. **11.** In Turkey, five pro-Islamic journalists were convicted of threatening public order by writing articles claiming that a 1999 earthquake was God's punishment for Turkey's secular policies. **14.** Montenegro and Serbia signed a draft constitutional framework that would allow them to have separate currencies, economies and customs services, but maintain a united defence and foreign policy. **17.** In Gibraltar, the government rejected the idea of accepting £35 million of EU funds aimed at inducing the colony to integrate with Spain. In Portugal, the Social Democrat party became the largest party, winning 40.1 per cent of the vote. Five Russian soldiers and a policeman were killed in clashes with rebels and a landmine blast in Chechnya. **18.** In Gibraltar about 24,000 of the 30,000 population demonstrated against moves by the UK to sign an agreement with Spain to share sovereignty of the colony, which Prime Minister Peter Caruana described as a betrayal. **19.** In Italy, President Carlo Azeglio Ciampi

pleaded for tolerance in response to mounting anger against the arrival in Sicily of nearly 1,000 Kurdish migrants. In Yugoslavia, Deputy Prime Minister Momcilo Perisić resigned after his arrest on suspicion of passing secret documents to a US diplomat. **20.** In Italy, the government declared a state of emergency to allow the provision of funds for food and shelter to meet a wave of illegal immigration. **22.** In Germany, legislation was passed allowing highly qualified foreigners to be given permanent residence. **23.** In Italy, an estimated two million people marched through Rome in protest against the killing by Red Brigades terrorists of a senior government economic advisor, Marco Biagi. **26.** In Macedonia, fighting erupted between rival ethnic Albanian guerrillas around Tetovo. **27.** The Turkish parliament passed a package of legislation that eased restrictions on freedom of speech and brought into effect the constitutional amendments announced in 2001.

APRIL 2002

2. In the Ukraine parties allied to President Kuchma were expected to gain a near majority after the election on 31 March. The Yugoslav government agreed to co-operate fully with the war crimes tribunal in The Hague. **3.** A Jewish cemetery was burnt down and since 29 March Arab youths throwing Molotov cocktails had had been attacking synagogues in Lyon, Marseille and Strasbourg. The main pro-Kuchma bloc, For a United Ukraine, won 101 seats in the 450-seat legislature. It is expected to gain the support of enough groups to form a coalition government. Two former ministers accused of war crimes in Yugoslavia were reported to have been detained in Belgrade prior to being transferred to the UN war crimes tribunal. **4.** Israel was accused of imposing unjust conditions and humiliations against Palestinians by the Vatican. **10.** Russia and Germany began talks over the status of the Kaliningrad region **11.** In Germany, the Supreme Court quashed an earlier ruling that had questioned the legality of military service. In the Netherlands, a report issued by the Netherlands Institute for War Documentation concluded that Dutch troops had betrayed refugees in the UN safe haven of Srebrenica in 1995 by handing them over to Bosnian Serb forces. **13.** The Yugoslav Health and Labour Minister Miodrag Kovac hanged himself in a Madrid hotel. **16.** Five Russian soldiers died when the lorry hit a landmine near Grozny. **17.** In Italy a general strike brought Italy to a halt. An estimated 11–20 million took part, with rallies in Rome, Florence, Milan and Bologna. In the Netherlands, Prime Minister, Wim Kok, and the entire Cabinet resigned following a damning report on the massacre of 7,000 Muslim men and boys by Bosnian Serbs at Srebrenica. The official report found the ministers culpable for sending 200 lightly armed troops to the UN safe haven in 1995. The Pope summoned the US's eight most senior cardinals to Rome for an emergency summit on the paedophile scandal sweeping the Roman Catholic Church in the US. **18.** In the Netherlands, the army chief of staff, Gen. Ad van Baal, resigned, but refused to accept blame for the actions of the troops. **19.** A light aircraft crashed into the 25th floor of the Pirelli tower in Milan, killing five people and injuring 30. **20.** In Montenegro, Prime Minister Vujanović resigned after the Liberal Party withdrew support for the government for shelving independence plans. President Djukanović had signed a deal with Serbia to abolish the federation and create a new country to be know as the Union of Serbia and Montenegro. **22.** The incumbent Jacques Chirac (20 per cent) and Jean-Marie Le Pen, the leader of the extreme right-wing Front Nationale (17 per cent) went through to

the second round of the French presidential election. **23.** Jean-Marie Le Pen promised to pull France out of the EU if he won the presidential election in two weeks. **24.** German authorities detained 11 suspected Islamic militants across Germany. The Pope addressed the emergency gathering of American cardinals, saying that the molestation of children by priests was an appalling sin in the eyes of God. **26.** Russia claimed to have killed Amir Khattab, the Arab guerrilla with alleged al-Qa'eda links. **27.** 17 people, including 13 teachers were shot dead by an expelled pupil in Erfurt, Germany. In Poland, tens of thousands of trade unionists rallied to protest against the government's proposed labour reforms, which they feared would add to unemployment. **29.** In Russia a bomb exploded in a market in Vladikavkaz, North Ossetia, killing seven people. **30.** PM José Maria Aznar said that Spain would not abandon its claim to sovereignty over Gibraltar, even if it signed a power-sharing deal with the UK. Turkey announced that it would replace the UK in command of the international peacekeeping force in Afghanistan in June.

MAY 2002

2. In the Færøe Islands, pro-independence parties won 16 of the 32 seats in the local parliament. In France, Nearly one and a half million people took part in demonstrations across France to appeal for the rejection of M. Le Pen in the second round of the presidential election. In Germany around 500 anarchists rioted in Berlin, setting barricades on fire and injuring dozens of policemen. **3.** Three Frenchmen were charged with attempted murder after shooting two refugees from the Sangatte refugee centre. **4.** In Gibraltar about 3,500 people, more than 10 per cent of the population, protested outside the Governor's residence during a visit by Foreign Secretary Jack Straw against talks with Spain on dual sovereignty. **6.** Jacques Chirac was re-elected President, defeating the national Front candidate Jean-Marie Le Pen by 82 per cent to 18 per cent. **7.** In the Netherlands, Pim Fortuyn, the leader of the anti-immigration Pim Fortuyn List, was shot dead as he left a radio station in Hilversum. Riot police used tear gas to disperse hundreds of his followers who launched a violent protest outside the parliament building in The Hague. **8.** In the Netherlands, a militant environmental activist, Volkert van der Graaf, was arrested fleeing the murder scene. **10.** In Russia, more than 30 people were killed when a bomb ripped through a victory day parade marking the end of the war with Nazi Germany in Kaspiisk in Dagestan. **11.** The death toll of the blast in Dagestan reached 41. Thousands lined the streets of Rotterdam to witness the funeral of Pim Fortuyn. President Chirac vowed to hunt down and punish those responsible for the suicide bomb attack that killed 11 French navy engineers in Pakistan. **16.** The Pim Fortuyn List was expected to gain 17 per cent of the vote in the Dutch general election, according to exit polls, making it the second biggest party. **19.** Three members of Sinn Fein were elected to the Irish parliament. The election was won by Fianna Fáil, which obtained 43 per cent of the vote and was expected to win an absolute majority in the Dáil. **20.** Sinn Fein gained five seats. **23.** The Pope flew into Azerbaijan on a two-day visit.

JUNE 2002

6. In the Netherlands, the wife of the head of the European Central Bank, Gretta Duisenberg, caused outrage among Dutch Jews after she hung a Palestinian flag from her balcony and blamed Palestinians' problems on an "elite club of rich American Jews". The Italian government approved the building of a bridge between mainland Italy and Sicily due to start in 2004. In Ireland, Prime Minister Bertie Ahern named his new cabinet. **8.** Three Kurdish men drowned and two were stabbed after 40 illegal immigrants were forced from a boat off Puglia, southern Italy, by human traffickers. The other immigrants were rescued. **9.** The first grandchild of Queen Beatrix of the Netherlands, was born and named Eloise Sophie Beatrix Laurence. Violence broke out in Moscow after the Russians were defeated by the Japanese in a world cup game. At least 100 people were injured and 60 were arrested. **14.** In the Czech Republic, legislative elections took place (also on 15 June) whereby the leftist Czech Social Democratic Party returned with the largest number of seats. **16.** In France, elections to the National Assembly took place (also on 9 June) which resulted in a majority for the centre-right Union for the Presidential Majority (UMP). **17.** The Dutch government launched a criminal inquiry into Muslim clerics accused of inciting hatred towards non-Muslims in the Netherlands. Chancellor Gerhard Schröder admitted that the German liberal education system was a failure and has been responsible for the pupils position near the bottom of international tables. **20.** A general strike took place in Spain which affected the whole of the country and led to the closure of most heavy industry. The strike was in protest of the government's efforts to reform labour law and plans to phase out aid for agricultural workers. **21.** Basque terrorist group, ETA, are thought to be responsible for a car bomb which was detonated on the Costa del Sol, injuring five British tourists, including two small children and a Moroccan man. **24.** In Albania, People's Assembly elected Gen. (retd) Alfred Moisu as President, replacing Rexhep Mejdani.

JULY 2002

7. In the Ukraine, 34 trapped miners died and 70 were rescued after fire consumed a coalmine near Donetsk in the eastern part of the country. **9.** In Spain, a government reshuffle in Madrid resulted in the dismissal of the Foreign Minister, Josep Piqué provoking fear of a setback in negotiations of the Gibraltar dispute with the United Kingdom. **11.** A detachment of Moroccan soldiers invaded the uninhabited island of Perejil in the strait of Gibraltar. The Spanish Foreign Office demanded the soldiers' immediate withdrawal. In Turkey, Prime Minister Bulent Ecevit launched an appeal for the return to government of 35 MPs who had previously resigned. Seven people were killed during storms in northern Germany that were recorded as the worst for 30 years. **14.** An assassination attempt was made on President Chirac by Maxime Brunerie, a member of a far-Right student group, during the Bastille parade along the Champs Elysées. **17.** The Spanish military retook the island of Perejil after a dawn raid. **21.** Spanish troops evacuated Parsley Island on July 20, after US Secretary of State negotiated a deal between Madrid and Rabat. **27.** In the Ukraine, at least 78 people were killed and 138 injured, when a Sukhoi Su-27 fighter jet crashed into crowds at an air show at the Skniliv airbase at Lviv. **28.** A Russian Il-86 plane crashed after taking off from Moscow's domestic airport, killing 15 of the 16 on board.

AUGUST 2002

5. In Spain, a six-year-old girl was killed by a car bomb in Santa Pola, near Alicante. The attack was believed to have been carried out by ETA. In France, a new law was passed whereby schoolchildren can be sent to prison for up to six months, for insulting their teachers. **8.** A ferry sprung a leak 16 miles off the coast of north-western France;

emergency services, the Navy and private yachts rescued the 226 passengers on board. In the Netherlands, the successor of assassinated Pim Fortyn, Mat Herbern, was forced to resign after being he was accused of diluting policies to reform the centre-right coalition. **12.** In the Czech Republic the biggest flood for more than a century swept through Prague, causing the evacuation of some 500,000 people. In Russia, at least 58 people died in severe flooding around the Black Sea coast as the weather conditions across central and eastern Europe worsened. **13.** In Saxony floods claimed five lives and around 1,000 people were evacuated from their homes in what has been described by Saxony's Prime Minister, Georg Midbradt, as the worst natural catastrophe in the State's history. **19.** At least 85 Russian soldiers were killed when a military helicopter crashed in a minefield set up by Russian forces to protect the military base at Khankala, east of the capital, Grozny, from Chechen fighters. The helicopter was carrying 45 people more than its official capacity. **20.** In Germany, a six-hour siege took place at the Iraqi embassy in Berlin after Iraqi dissidents took members of staff hostage. Later that night, the hostages were released and five people were arrested when German anti-terrorist police stormed the building. **27.** In Spain, Basque police clashed with supporters of Batasuna, the political wing of the terrorist group ETA, during enforcement of a legal order to close down the party's operations. **28.** In Germany, relatives of more than 100 people killed in Europe's worst high-speed train disaster of June 1998 in Lower Saxony, attended the trial of three rail staff accused of causing the deaths. In Greece, Scotland Yard detectives investigating the November 17 terrorist group found evidence of how its leader allegedly stalked a British shipowner for more than two years, before ordering his murder. **29.** In Sweden, Kerim Sadok Chatty, a Swedish national of Tunisian origin, was arrested while trying to board a Ryanair flight to Birmingham after he attempted to smuggle a pistol on board. The Swedish authorities believe he was intending to hijack the aircraft.

SEPTEMBER 2002

2. Kerim Sadok Chatty, who was arrested in Sweden on 29 August, was remanded in custody as police continued to investigate whether or not he was associated with al-Qa'eda.

INTERNATIONAL RELATIONS

SEPTEMBER 2001

8. The World Conference against Racism ended in Durban, South Africa, and a final declaration was issued only after references to Israel as a racist state were removed. **10.** The United Nations (UN) Security Council lifted an arms embargo imposed on Yugoslavia in March 1998. The Southern African Development Community (SADC) rebuked Zimbabwe, for its economic decline, instability and lawlessness. **10–11.** An Asia-Europe summit of economic ministers from the EU member states, Brunei, China, Indonesia, Japan, Malaysia, the Philippines, Singapore, South Korea, Thailand and Vietnam was held in Hanoi, Vietnam. **12.** North Atlantic Treaty Organisation (NATO) heads of government declared that the terrorist suicide attacks on the USA on 11 September were an assault on all NATO members. **13.** The UN Security Council approved a unanimous resolution recognising terrorism as a threat to international peace and security. **14.** The World Trade

Organisation (WTO) reached agreement on the terms of China's membership. **17.** The UN World Food Programme claimed that as many as five million people in Afghanistan were facing famine. **24.** Yugoslavia regained its membership of Interpol, from which it had been expelled in 1993. **26.** NATO declared that its 30-day Task Force Harvest mission to collect weapons from ethnic Albanian rebels in Macedonia had been successful and agreed to send a new security force to the country to protect international peace monitors. **28.** The Commonwealth of Independent States (CIS) Council of Heads of Governments was held in Moscow and declared that the CIS would take a common stand in fighting terrorism.

OCTOBER 2001

1. The UN Secretary General, Kofi Annan, called on the world to draw up a comprehensive anti-terrorism treaty. **2.** NATO formally invoked Article Five of the Washington Treaty, allowing member states to give military assistance to the US, in response to evidence presented by the US linking the 11 September attacks to the al-Qa'eda terrorist network based in Afghanistan. **8.** The UN General Assembly elected Bulgaria, Cameroon, Guinea, Mexico and Syria as non-permanent members of the Security Council. **9.** The UN International Criminal Tribunal for the Former Yugoslavia formally indicted the former president of Yugoslavia, Slobodan Milošević, for war crimes. **19–21.** The participants at the Asia-Pacific Economic Co-operation (APEC) forum summit in Shanghai committed themselves to clamp down on sources of terrorist funding.

NOVEMBER 2001

1. The UN Security Council agreed that East Timor would become independent on 20 May 2002. **12–14.** At the World Trade Organisation (WTO) meeting in Qatar, members decided to allow poor countries to manufacture medicines without breaching patent law and agreed to commence a new round of trade liberalisation talks. **23.** The UN War Crimes Tribunal accepted an indictment accusing former Yugoslavian President Slobodan Milošević of genocide against the Muslim and Croat populations of Bosnia-Hercegovina during the war of 1992–95.

DECEMBER 2001

5. Signatories of the Geneva Convention gathered in Switzerland to reprimand Israel for indiscriminate and disproportionate violence against Palestinian civilians in the occupied territories and condemned Jewish settlements. **20.** The Commonwealth Ministerial Action Group delivered an ultimatum to President Mugabe to halt the political repression of opponents in Zimbabwe within a month or risk suspension.

JANUARY 2002

14. In the final communiqué of the South African Development Community (SADC) summit, President Mugabe promised to respect human rights and agreed to allow international observers to monitor the elections and said that local and foreign media would be allowed to operate freely. **30.** At the Commonwealth Ministerial Summit, the UK failed to secure Zimbabwe's expulsion when foreign ministers from eight member states chose instead to repeat demands that President Mugabe hold free and fair elections.

FEBRUARY 2002

8. In Cambodia, the UN announced that it was not prepared to participate in a tribunal to put former Khmer Rouge leaders on trial for crimes against humanity committed in the 1970s in which 1.7 million people died, as it did not believe that the tribunal could guarantee the independence, objectivity and impartiality necessary. **11.** The trial of former President Slobodan Milošević began at the UN International Criminal Tribunal for the Former Yugoslavia; he faced charges of genocide, crimes against humanity and violations of the laws and customs of war in relation to the conflicts in Croatia, Bosnia and Kosovo. **20.** The US imposed targeted sanctions on Zimbabwean President Mugabe and 19 of his closest allies.

MARCH 2002

4. At the Commonwealth Heads of Government Meeting in Australia, leaders issued a statement expressing 'deep concern' over the election campaign in Zimbabwe and agreed to send a task force to Zimbabwe consisting of the Australian Prime Minister, John Howard, President Olusegun Obasanjo of Nigeria and President Thabo Mbeki of South Africa. **6.** The US presented satellite evidence to the UN Security Council showing that Iraq had misused humanitarian aid for military purposes. **13.** The UN Security Council passed a motion submitted by the US to halt violence in the Middle East and which called for a Palestinian state. **19.** The Commonwealth suspended Zimbabwe from the councils of the Commonwealth for one year and called for new elections. **25.** The Council of Europe's Committee for the Prevention of Torture said that Switzerland's treatment of illegal immigrants amounted to inhumane and degrading treatment.

APRIL 2002

12. The International Criminal Court came into being in New York after 10 nations ratified the Rome statute of 1998, the treaty establishing the court in principle, pushing the total who had already signed beyond the necessary 60. It will have jurisdiction over genocide, crimes against humanity and war crimes after 1 July 2002. **16.** The 53-nation UN Human Rights Commission voted to condemn Israel for 'mass killing' and 'gross violations of human rights'. **26.** The UN declared a humanitarian disaster affecting up to six million people across southern Africa after months of drought in six countries.

MAY 2002

9. The Red Cross appealed for emergency help after more than 150,000 people were left homeless over the past two weeks in Kenya's worst floods for years. At least 45 people had died. **11.** NATO announced that it would withdraw 12,000 troops form the Balkans, around a fifth of the total, because of improving stability in the region.

JUNE 2002

6. NATO defence ministers met at its Brussels headquarters. The danger of the acquisition of biological and chemical weapons by terrorists featured most highly on the agenda. **25.** The leaders of the G-8 held a summit meeting in Kananaskis, Canada.

JULY 2002

3. The United Nations Security Council approved a 12-day extension of a UN police training mission in Bosnia, due to end on 3 July 2002 allowing more time to resolve the dispute with the US over prosecution of its nationals by the new international criminal court. **25.** The US refused to back a United Nations protocol against torture,

amid fears that it could allow international monitors to visit terrorist suspects in Guantanomo Bay, Cuba.

AUGUST 2002

1. A UN report on the 'Battle of Jenin' of April 2002, dismissed claims that Israel massacred hundreds of Palestinians. **2.** The United Nations rejected an Iraqi offer to let weapons inspectors back into Baghdad, due to Saddam Hussein's conditions of the offer. **13.** NATO had to abandon its main rapid reaction unit, the so-called ACE Mobile Unit Force, after Britain withdrew its contribution to ensure troops were available to join any attack on Iraq owing to the increasing commitments of the war against terrorism. **26.** The Earth summit opened in Johannesburg with the poverty gap between the northern and southern hemispheres at the top of the agenda.

THE MIDDLE EAST

SEPTEMBER 2001

4. Iraq expelled five UN staff, accusing them of espionage. **9.** In Israel, a suicide bomber killed three people at Nahariya railway station. **17.** The leader of the Palestinian National Authority (PNA), Yasser Arafat, instructed his followers to observe a cease-fire and, in response, Israeli forces withdrew from previously occupied Palestinian towns the following day.

OCTOBER 2001

5. Israeli tanks occupied the West Bank town of Hebron. **7.** In Saudi Arabia, an American was killed and a Briton injured when a bomb exploded in a shopping street in Al-Khobar. **8.** Palestinian police shot dead at least two protestors supporting Osama bin Laden in Gaza after students from Gaza's Islamic University held a march organised by Hamas (Courage), a Palestinian militant group. **16.** In Jordan, the intelligence service foiled plans by Islamic militants to attack the American, British and Jordanian embassies in Beirut, Lebanon. **17.** In Israel, Tourism Minister Rechavam Ze'evy was assassinated by members of the Popular Front for the Liberation of Palestine. The leader of the PNA, Yasser Arafat, condemned the killing and ordered his security forces to detain those responsible. **18.** Israeli tanks occupied the West Bank towns of Ramallah and Jenin and the Israeli government threatened to declare the PNA a terrorist entity if it did not arrest and extradite those responsible for the murder of Rechavam Ze'evy and to outlaw other groups involved in terrorism. **19.** Israeli tanks took up positions in the West Bank town of Bethlehem. **24.** At least six Palestinians were killed during an Israeli raid in Beit Rima to capture Palestinians suspected of assassinating the tourism minister. **25.** The Israeli government announced that it intended to withdraw its troops from six Palestinian towns in the West Bank with the co-operation of the PNA. On 29 October, Israeli forces began to withdraw its forces from Bethlehem and Beit Jala. **27.** In Iraq, Deputy Prime Minister Tariq Aziz said that Iraq expected to be attacked by the US and the UK as part of their war against terrorism.

NOVEMBER 2001

4. Two Israelis were killed and 35 others injured when a Palestinian gunman opened fire on a bus in Jerusalem. **7.** In Israel, the Knesset stripped Azmi Bishara, an Arab MP, of parliamentary immunity so he could be tried on charges of backing Hezbollah and arranging visits to an enemy state (Syria). **9.** King Abdullah of Jordan said that

the Arab world should be prepared to offer a collective guarantee of Israel's security and integration into the Middle East in return for the establishment of a Palestinian state. **20.** Israeli intelligence agencies said they had been unable to detect any link between Iraq and the 11 September attacks on the US; they also dismissed claims that Osama bin Laden had acquired nuclear weapons. **27.** Iraq dismissed President Bush's demand that it re-admit international weapons inspectors, saying it was not intimidated by the threat of military strikes. **28.** At least four people were killed and nine injured when a suicide bomber detonated a bomb on a bus in northern Israel.

DECEMBER 2001

1. At least eight people were killed and more than 170 injured when two suicide bombers blew themselves up in Jerusalem. **2.** A Palestinian bomber killed 16 people when he blew himself up in Haifa. Hamas claimed responsibility for the attacks in Haifa and Jerusalem. Palestinian security forces rounded up about 150 militants of Hamas and Islamic Jihad. **3.** Ariel Sharon addressed the nation after Israeli forces launched retaliation for the weekend suicide attacks, accusing Yasser Arafat of adopting a strategy of terror and planning to destroy Israel. **5.** Palestinian police put the founder of Hamas, Sheikh Ahmed Yassin, under house arrest. **6.** An Israeli jet destroyed the Palestinian police headquarters in Gaza City, breaking a brief cease-fire. **7.** Yasser Arafat said that he had arrested 17 wanted militants from a list of over 20 presented by Israel. **9.** In Syria, President Bashar Assad asked Prime Minister Mohamad Mustafa Miro to form a new government following the resignation of the entire Cabinet. **12.** Israel severed all contact with the PNA and ordered retaliatory raids after Palestinian gunmen ambushed a bus driving to a Jewish settlement in the West Bank, killing ten Israelis and wounding 30. Yasser Arafat ordered the closure of all offices and charitable institutions run by Hamas. **14.** Israeli forces raided four Arab towns and villages in the West Bank, killing eight Palestinians and arresting dozens of suspected terrorists. **15.** Yasser Arafat issued a statement calling for an end to attacks on Israel and warned militant groups they would be outlawed and arrested if they continued their attacks. **17.** Yemeni special forces launched an assault in Marib province against a tribal stronghold suspected of harbouring al-Qa'eda supporters; at least 12 people were killed. **26.** In Israel, Benjamin Ben-Eliezer was confirmed as head of the Labour Party.

JANUARY 2002

4. Israeli commandos seized a Palestinian ship in the Red Sea which was carrying 50 tonnes of arms destined for the PNA. **7.** In Iraq, the US suspended funding to the Iraqi National Congress, the main opposition group, because it had failed to account properly for previous grants. **11.** The PNA arrested three of its own security officers who had been accused by Israel of involvement in the attempt to smuggle a shipload of weapons to Gaza. **15.** Palestinian police arrested Ahmad Sadaat, the leader of the Popular Front for the Liberation of Palestine. **17.** Six Israelis were killed and about 25 injured when a member of the al-Aqsa Martyrs' Brigade threw a hand grenade into a Bat Mitzvah party in Hadera; the attacker was shot dead by police. Saudi Crown Prince Abdullah bin Abdul Aziz criticised Qatar's al-Jazeera TV, saying it threatened Arab stability and encouraged terrorism. **20–22.** In Jordan, a policeman was killed during two days of violent pro-Iraqi demonstrations in Ma'an. **22.** Israeli commandos killed

four members of the military wing of Hamas; Palestinian police released a jailed Hamas member after thousands of Hamas supporters besieged a prison in Nablus following the commando raid. **26.** The Leader of the PNA, Yasser Arafat, made an appeal to all Palestinians to adhere to a cease-fire and halt attacks against Israel. **27.** A man was killed when a Palestinian woman suicide bomber detonated a bomb in a shopping street in Jerusalem. **29.** In Saudi Arabia, Crown Prince Abdullah attacked US policy in the Middle East because of US support for Israel. **30.** The Syrian Foreign Ministry accused the US of piracy over the seizure by the US Sixth Fleet of two freighters in international waters off the coast of Cyprus. **31.** Saudi Arabia dismissed claims that British prisoners had been tortured and made to give false confessions of involvement in a spate of mysterious bombings, saying that the claims were part of an anti-Saudi conspiracy. Israeli forces killed two Hamas gunmen who ambushed a convoy heading for a Jewish settlement in the Gaza Strip.

FEBRUARY 2002

6. In Israel, two Hamas members shot dead at least three Israelis in a Jewish settlement in the West Bank; Israeli forces retaliated by launching air strikes on Nablus. **7.** In Israel, Palestinian police freed 32 militants including two leaders of the Islamic Jihad group during an Israeli air raid in Nablus. **10.** In Israel, two Palestinian gunmen were shot dead after killing two soldiers outside an army base in Be'er Sheva' (Beersheba). **11.** In Israel, Palestinian demonstrators took over a prison in Hebron and freed 17 Islamic militants. **13.** In Yemen, a suspected al-Qa'eda terrorist, Samir Mohammed Ahmed al-Hada, blew himself up after being cornered by Yemeni security forces in Sana'ā. **14.** In Bahrain, Sheikh Hamad bin Isa Al Khalifa declared himself a constitutional monarch and announced that a general election would be held in October 2002. Three people were killed and at least two others wounded when Palestinian terrorists ambushed a convoy in the Gaza Strip. **15.** Palestinian guerrillas blew up a battle tank in the Gaza Strip, killing three soldiers. **16.** In Israel, two people were killed in an explosion in a shopping centre in Karnei Shomron. **17.** In Israel, two Palestinians were killed as they tried to attack an army training base in northern Israel. **20.** The Israeli army, navy and airforce launched raids on Gaza, Rafah, Nablus and Ramallah, carrying out a three-hour bombardment of Gaza City in retaliation for the killing of six Israelis the previous day by the Al-Aqsa Martyrs' Brigade in the West Bank. **21.** The Israeli army destroyed the Palestinian radio and television centre in Gaza City and attacked buildings used by the Palestinian presidential guard. **22.** Saudi Arabia proposed a Middle East peace plan under which Arab countries would establish full diplomatic relations with Israel, guarantee its security and normalise trade in return for Israeli withdrawal from the occupied territories. **23.** In Israel, the government called a seven-day suspension of military action against Palestinian targets.

MARCH 2002

2. In Israel, at least ten people were killed and 57 injured by a suicide bomber in Jerusalem. **4.** In Israel, the army apologised for killing six Palestinian civilians during an anti-terrorist operation. **5.** In Israel, a Jewish group claimed responsibility for a bomb attack on an Arab school in Jerusalem in which three children and a teacher were injured. Israeli Prime Minister Ariel Sharon demanded the defeat of Palestinian armed groups before diplomatic talks could commence. **6.** Israeli forces attacked Gaza in retaliation for a Palestinian rocket attack

on Sderot the previous day in which three people had been wounded. **8.** A Palestinian gunman infiltrated a Jewish settlement in the Gaza Strip and killed four people before being shot dead. The Israeli army killed 39 Palestinians in a retaliatory assault on villages and refugee camps. **9.** At least 11 Israelis were killed when a suicide bomber blew himself up in a bar in Jerusalem. **11.** The Israeli army rounded up 1,200 Palestinian men for interrogation and killed 17 in the Gaza Strip. **12.** Israel launched its biggest ground offensive for 20 years, entering the town of Ramallah and the al-Ama'ari refugee camp. **18.** The Iraqi government suggested it might be ready to admit UN weapons inspectors conditionally. **20.** In Israel, Islamic Jihad claimed responsibility for a suicide bomber who killed seven Israelis on a bus travelling between Tel Aviv and Nazareth. Israeli and Palestinian security officials met under the guidance of US mediator Gen. Anthony Zinni. **21.** In Jerusalem, a suicide bomber killed himself and at least three others. The al-Aqsa Martyrs Brigade claimed responsibility. **23.** Ariel Sharon declared that Yasser Arafat could attend the Arab summit in Beirut if he declared a cease-fire, but warned that he would not be allowed back if there were acts of terror during his absence; the Palestinian leadership rejected the conditions. Two international observers were shot dead by Palestinian gunmen near Hebron. **26–27.** In Lebanon, the Arab Summit in Beirut was boycotted by Egypt and Jordan, an attempt by Yasser Arafat to address the summit by live satellite video link was refused, and the UAE withdrew its delegation. **27.** In Israel, a Palestinian suicide bomber killed 19 people and wounded at least 120 at a hotel in Netanya at the start of the Passover celebration. In the UAE, at least 22 people died when a gate burst at a dry dock in Dubai. **29.** Israeli tanks and troops entered Yasser Arafat's headquarters, forcing him to take refuge in a bunker. A woman suicide bomber killed three people in a Jerusalem supermarket. Israeli police stormed the Temple Mount in Jerusalem after Muslim worshippers hurled rocks at Jews praying at the Western Wall. **31.** In Israel, at least 16 people were killed when a suicide bomber blew himself up in a restaurant in Haifa.

APRIL 2002

2. The Israeli army expanded its operations, sending tanks into Beit Jala, Bethlehem, Tulkarm and Qalqiliya. Four Britons were injured when Israeli soldiers opened fire to push back a group of 100 foreign and Palestinian protesters in Beit Jala. **3.** Ariel Sharon said that Yasser Arafat could leave his headquarters in Ramallah only on a 'one-way ticket'. Israeli forces stormed Bethlehem. **4.** Israeli troops laid siege to the Church of the Nativity in Bethlehem after about 180 Palestinian gunmen sought refuge there. Ariel Sharon called an emergency security cabinet meeting over concerns that Hezbollah was attempting to open a second front after Hezbollah fighters fired anti-tank rockets at an Israeli position on the frontier, despite efforts by the Lebanese government to calm tensions. Israel has threatened severe retaliation following attacks on three Israeli positions in the region over the past four days. **5.** President Bush demanded an Israeli withdrawal from the West Bank. Ariel Sharon responded by allowing Mr Bush's special envoy, Gen. Anthony Zinni, to meet Yasser Arafat in his Ramallah HQ. In Nablus, three refugee camps were hit in a military operation using more than 100 tanks. **6.** In Amman, Jordan, police charged 4,000 demonstrators who marched on the Israeli embassy. Israel stepped up its campaign in the cities of the West Bank, despite US calls to halt the incursions. Thirty-five Palestinians and at least one Israeli soldier were reported killed. In Bahrain, police

fired rubber bullets at a crowd of 10,000 after Molotov cocktails were thrown at the US embassy. **9.** Ariel Sharon said that the incursions would continue until they had successfully hunted down Palestinian militants, refusing to call an end to the incursions as demanded by President Bush. In Saudi Arabia, a British businessman who ran an illicit drinking club was sentenced to 800 lashes. **10.** Thirteen Israeli soldiers were killed when they were lured towards a booby-trapped building in the Jenin refugee camp, where an estimated 150 Palestinians have died in six days of fighting, along with 22 Israelis. **11.** Eight people were killed in a suicide bombing on a bus near Haifa. Ariel Sharon told soldiers in Jenin that the army would stay until its task was completed. The US, Russia, the EU and the UN issued a joint communiqué demanding an immediate Israeli withdrawal from towns controlled by the Palestinian Authority and urging Yasser Arafat to curb terrorism. The last fighters at Jenin refugee camp surrendered. **12.** House-to-house fighting continued in the Jenin refugee camp. Colin Powell arrived in Jerusalem to try to broker a cease-fire. **13.** A suicide bomber in Jerusalem killed six people. Responsibility was claimed by the Al-Aqsa Martyrs' Brigade. It was revealed that between 100–300 Palestinians were killed in the Jenin camp. **15.** Colin Powell had talks with Yasser Arafat, but there were no signs of a breakthrough, with the Palestinians insisting on a full Israeli withdrawal. The Israeli army admitted to hundreds of deaths in the Jenin camp, then revised the figure to much less. **16.** Colin Powell proposed a regional peace conference that would exclude Yasser Arafat. He appealed to Lebanon and Syria to restrain Hezbollah fighters who have escalated their attacks on a disputed border area known as the Shebaa farms. Ariel Sharon dismissed criticism of Israeli military actions in the West Bank and said he was proud of the armed forces. **17.** Ariel Sharon said that Marwan Barghouthi, the leading spokesman for the Palestinian uprising who was arrested on 15 April, would be put on trial for the murder of hundreds of Israelis. **18.** Colin Powell abandoned his search for an Israeli-Palestinian cease-fire and left for Washington. **24.** Israel withdrew its agreement for a UN mission to enquire into the army offensive in the Jenin refugee camp. **25.** Three Palestinian informers were dragged out of jail and lynched by an armed gang in Hebron. **26.** Crown Prince Abdullah of Saudi Arabia, warned President Bush that he could rupture relations unless he moderated his support for PM Ariel Sharon. **28.** Four Israelis were killed by Palestinian gunmen in the Adora settlement near Hebron. **29.** The Israeli Cabinet dropped its demand that the four killers of an Israeli cabinet minister must be extradited for trial and said that they could serve their sentences in a Palestinian jail under international supervision. **30.** Israeli tanks moved into Hebron, killing nine Palestinians. Israeli tanks entered the Rafah refugee camp in the Gaza Strip.

MAY 2002

2. Yasser Arafat walked free after Israeli troops lifted their siege of his compound in Ramallah after 34 days. **4.** The new York-based Human Rights Watch issued a report claiming that 52 Palestinians were killed in the Jenin refugee camp. Ariel Sharon said that Marwan Barghouti, the head of al-Fatah in the West Bank, had confessed to directing terrorist attacks and that these had been personally approved by Yasser Arafat. **6.** The Israeli government accused Yasser Arafat of using aid from the EU to finance terrorist attacks. **8.** Sixteen people were killed and at least 55 wounded when a Palestinian suicide bomber destroyed a snooker hall in Rishon LeZion. The PNA condemned the attack. A deal to end the five-week

siege of the Church of the Nativity in Bethlehem faltered because no country could be found willing to accept the Palestinian militants. **10.** Bahrain held its first municipal election since 1957. The PNA arrested 14 members of Hamas in Gaza City. **11.** The 38-day siege of the Church of the Nativity ended when the RAF flew 13 Palestinian terrorists to Cyprus in a deal that ended the siege. In exchange for their exile, Israel allowed a further 26 militants to go to Gaza. **12.** About 50,000 Israelis demonstrated in Tel Aviv for an Israeli military withdrawal from Palestinian territories. **18.** Israeli forces re-entered the Jenin refugee camp to arrest 20 Palestinians including a leader of the Al-Aqsa Martyrs' Brigade. **21.** In Iraq, US jets struck an aircraft direction-finding radar near As-Salman after a surface-to-air missile was fired at a coalition aircraft patrolling the southern no-fly zone. Ariel Sharon ordered the dismissal of tow Cabinet ministers from the Shas party and deputy ministers from United Torah Judaism after the two ultra-Orthodox parties failed to support the government on an emergency economic plan. **23.** The Israeli army erected barbed wire fences around the outskirts of Jerusalem in an attempt to prevent Palestinians carrying out further suicide attacks. A 38 year old Israeli woman and an 18-month-old girl were killed and 28 others injured after a device was detonated by a suicide bomber at an outdoor café in Petah Tikvah, an eastern suburb of Tel Aviv. **31.** Israeli forces arrested more than 100 Palestinians in the West Bank cities of Nablus and Tulkarm in an attempt to pre-empt suicide bombings.

JUNE 2002

5. A Palestinian suicide bomber of Islamic Jihad attacked a bus at the Megiddo junction near Jenin, killing 17 people, all but four of which were Israeli soldiers. **6.** The Israeli army exploded a tank shell in Yasser Arafat's home in response to the suicide bombing of 5 June. **8.** Israel launched raids on the West Bank after Palestinian gunmen killed a man, his pregnant wife and another Israeli, in an attack on a Jewish settlement. **9.** A new Palestinian cabinet was introduced by Yasser Arafat in the first step towards conditions for the peace process. **10.** Tanks surrounded Yasser Arafat's headquarters as President Bush reasserted Ariel Sharon's right to take action on Palestinian areas. **13.** President Bush stated that he would be in favour of a separate Palestinian state only after a cessation of violence. **17.** A Palestinian man wanted by police on suspicion of plotting suicide attacks blew himself up near a police patrol vehicle. There were no casualties. **19.** Six people were killed and 35 injured in a suicide bombing at a crowded Jerusalem bus stop. **20.** Six people were killed at a Jewish settlement on the West Bank by Palestinian gunmen. **21.** Two children and a school teacher were killed when Israeli tanks opened fire on Palestinians in Jenin. **22.** In Syria, the Zeyzoun dam near the town of Idlib north of Hama collapsed, killing at least 22 people. **23.** An earthquake in nothern Iran measuring 6.3 on the Richter scale, razed dozens of villages and left around 200 dead. **24.** President Bush called for Palestinians to remove Yasser Arafat from power if a future Palestinian state is to be considered. **28.** A controversial photograph depicting a five-month-old Palestinian child dressed as a suicide bomber, was released by the Israeli army, sparking a row with the Palestinians.

JULY 2002

3. The US sent a cargo plane carrying aid to Iran, in a gesture unseen since the 1979 revolution. **4.** A bomb exploded in a car in Gaza City, killing a Palestinian militant and another person. The Israeli army declined to comment. **10.** Yasser Arafat was denounced by Hossam Khader, a senior figure within the Fatah movement. He accused Mr. Arafat of sheltering corrupt officials and sending his people on a 'path to hell'. **18.** Two suicide bombers struck in the area around Tel Aviv's old bus station leaving three dead and 40 wounded. **22.** 15 people were killed, including nine children and around 140 were injured after an Israeli F16 jet dropped a one tonne guided bomb onto an apartment block in Gaza City, where Hamas leader, Sheikh Salah Shahada was staying. He was also killed during the attack. **26.** A Rabbi, Elimelech Shapira, was shot dead in the West Bank in what Palestinian militants described as the first retaliation for the Gaza bombings of July 22. **28.** In Hebron, a 14-year-old Palestinian girl was killed and nine others injured by Jewish settlers after the funeral of an Israeli solider who was killed during a roadside ambush. **31.** A bomb exploded at an Israeli student cafeteria in Jerusalem, killing seven and wounding more than 60 others.

AUGUST 2002

1. A United Nations report on the 'Battle of Jenin' in April dismissed claims that Israel massacred hundreds of Palestinian civilians. The report was welcomed by the Israeli foreign minister. **2.** Saddam Hussein suggested that he would welcome the United Nations weapons inspectors back into Iraq. **3.** The US rejected Saddam Hussain's offer to let United Nations weapons inspectors to return to Iraq. **4.** Nine people were killed and 45 wounded after a bomb exploded beside a bus in northern Israel. **6.** Israeli intelligence sent two suicide bombers to Tel Aviv. **13.** Seven people were killed and more than 20 were injured as Palestinian militants attacked a bus carrying Jewish settlers in the West Bank. **18.** Two suicide bombers struck in the area around Tel Aviv's old bus station leaving three dead and 40 wounded.

Obituaries

1 SEPTEMBER 2001 – 31 AUGUST 2002

HM QUEEN ELIZABETH, THE QUEEN MOTHER

Queen Elizabeth, the Queen Mother was born the Hon. Elizabeth Angela Marguerite Bowes-Lyon, on 4 August 1900, the ninth child and fourth daughter of Claude George Bowes-Lyon and Nina Cecilia Bowes-Lyon, Lord and Lady Glamis. Elizabeth married Prince Albert Duke of York on 26 April 1923. Their first child, Elizabeth Alexandra Mary, was born on 21 April 1926 and their second daughter, Margaret Rose, on 21 August 1930. The Duke of York became King following the abdication of his brother Edward VIII in 1936, making the Queen Mother the first British-born Queen Consort since Tudor Times. As Queen, Elizabeth was extremely popular with the public and an asset to the British monarchy. Always renowned for her tireless work for charity and caring personality, she remained one of the most revered members of the Royal family. During her later years, Queen Elizabeth, the Queen Mother suffered ill health undergoing two hip replacement operations. The death of her daughter Princess Margaret on 9 February 2002 came as a great blow, yet she stoically attended her daughter's funeral after suffering a minor fall a few days earlier. Queen Elizabeth, the Queen Mother died peacefully in her sleep at Windsor Castle on 30 March 2002 aged 101. The Queen, her elder daughter, survives her.

HER ROYAL HIGHNESS THE PRINCESS MARGARET, COUNTESS OF SNOWDON

Her Royal Highness Princess Margaret was born at Glamis Castle on August 21 1930 – four-and-a-half years after her elder sister, Princess Elizabeth of York (later Queen Elizabeth II). The Princess married Anthony Armstrong-Jones, a young Court photographer on May 6 1960 in Westminster Abbey. Armstrong-Jones was created Earl of Snowdon in October 1961. A month later the couple's son, David, styled Viscount Linley, was born. A daughter, Lady Sarah Armstrong-Jones, followed on 1 May 1964. Princess Margaret did a great deal of work for charity and was the patron of more than 50 organisations. Her marriage to Lord Snowdon faltered in the early 70s. In her later years Princess Margaret suffered poor health and died of a severe stroke, her third, early in the morning of 9 February 2002.

Adams, Sir Philip, CMG, KCMG, ambassador to Egypt 1973–5; Deputy Secretary at the Cabinet Office 1971–2, aged 85 – d. 14 October 2001, b. 17 December 1915

Aglionby, Francis, circuit judge and chancellor, aged 70 – d. 6 June 2002, b. 17 May 1932

Alexander, Sir Michael, diplomat, aged 65 – d. 1 June 2002, b. 19 June 1936

Alment, Sir Anthony, president of the Royal College of Obstetricians and Gynaecologists 1978–81, aged 80 – d. 6 March 2002, b. 3 February 1922

Anstruther of that Ilk, Maj. Sir Ralph, BT, GCVO, MC, treasurer to Queen Elizabeth, the Queen Mother 1961–98, aged 80 – d. 19 May 2002, b. 13 June 1921

Armitage, Kenneth, British sculptor, aged 85 – d. 22 January 2002, b. 18 July 1916

Ashmore, Vice-Adm. Sir Peter, KCVO, KCB, DSC, chief of allied Staff, NATO Southern Europe 1970–2; Master of the Royal Household 1973–86, aged 81 – d. 31 July 2002, b. 4 February 1921

Astor, The Hon. David, CH, editor of *The Observer* 1948–75, aged 89 – d. 6 December 2001, b. 5 March 1912

Bagnall, Field Marshal Sir Nigel, GCB, CVO, MC, chief of the general staff 1985–8, aged 75 – d. 8 April 2002, b. 10 February 1927

Balaguer, Joaquin, six times president of the Dominican Republic, aged 94 – d. 14 July 2002, b. 1 September 1907

Barbara, Agatha, president of Malta 1982–7, aged 78 – d. 4 February 2002, b. 11 March 1923

Barran, Sir David, former chairman of Shell and Midland Bank, aged 90 – d. 1 June 2002, b. 23 May 1912

Beaumont, His Hon. Christopher, MBE, circuit judge 1972–85, aged 89 – d. 10 May 2002, b. 2 June 1912

Bell, Sir Raymond, KCMG, CB, civil servant, aged 85 – d. 18 February 2002, b. 13 March 1916

Bellinger, Sir Robert, GBE, Lord Mayor of London 1966–7, aged 92 – d. 8 July 2002, b. 10 March 1910

Bennett, Ralph, wartime intelligence worker, historian and former president of Magdalene College, Cambridge, aged 90 – d. 5 August 2002, b. 18 October 1911

Biggs, Vice-Adm. Sir Geoffrey, KCB, submariner and deputy fleet commander 1992–4, aged 63 – d. 29 June 2002, b. 23 November 1938

Blackwell, Miles, former chairman of Blackwell Ltd, aged 56 – d. 31 August 2001, b. 10 February 1945

Brancker, George, CBE, deputy clerk and clerk of parliament in Barbados 1970–99, aged 64 – d. 2 January 2002, b. 11 May 1937

Bray, Jeremy, Labour MP for Middlesborough 1962–70; Labour MP for Motherwell 1974–7, aged 71 – d. 3 June 2002, b. 29 June 1930

Brazier-Creagh, Maj.-Gen. Sir Rupert, KBE, CB, DSO, director of staff duties at the War Office 1959–61; secretary of the Horse Race Betting Levy Board 1961–5, aged 92 – d. 4 April 2002, b. 12 December 1909

Brewis, Lady Anne, MBE, botanist, aged 91 – d. 31 March 2002, b. 26 March 1911

Bristow, Sir Peter, high court judge, aged 89 – d. 1 August 2002, b. 1 June 1913

Brookes, Lord, life president and former chairman of GKN, aged 93 – d. 31 July 2002, b. 10 April 1909

Brown, Ron, Labour MP for Shoreditch and Finsbury 1964–74; Hackney South and Shoreditch 1974–83 (Labour MP from 1964–81 and SDP from 1981–3), aged 80 – d. 27 June 2002, b. 7 September 1921

Burges, Maj.-Gen. Rodney, CBE, GOC Cyprus District 1964–6; Vice-Quartermaster Gen. 1966–7, aged 88 – d. 4 June 2002, b. 19 March 1914

Burnett, Sir David 3rd Bt., MBE, former chairman of Hay's Wharf, aged 84 – d. 19 May 2002, b. 27 January 1918

Burrows, Sir Bernard, GCMG, diplomat, aged 91 – d. 7 May 2002, b. 3 July 1910

1168   Obituaries

Cable, Sir James, KCVO, CMG, diplomat and writer, aged 80 – *d.* 27 September 2001, *b.* 15 November 1920

Cann, Jamie, Labour MP for Ipswich 1992–2001, aged 55 – *d.* 15 October 2001, *b.* 28 June 1946

Carnarvon, Earl of, KCVO, KBE, royal racing manager, aged 77 – *d.* 11 September 2001, *b.* 19 January 1924

Carter, Sir Charles Frederick, founding vice–chancellor of Lancaster University, aged 82 – *d.* 27 June 2002, *b.* 15 August 1919

Carver, Field Marshal Lord, GCB, CBE, DSO and Bar, MC, chief of defence staff 1973–6, aged 86 – *d.* 9 December 2001, *b.* 24 April 1915

Cassel, Sir Harold, Bt., circuit judge, aged 84 – *d.* 17 September 2001, *b.* 8 November 1916

Castle of Blackburn, Baroness, PC, former Labour Government minister, aged 91 – *d.* 3 May 2002, *b.* 6 October 1910

Cela, Camilo José, Spanish writer, aged 85 – *d.* 17 January 2002, *b.* 11 May 1916

Chapman, Ted, VC, BEM, Welsh infantryman, aged 82 – *d.* 3 February 2002, *b.* 13 January 1920

Cheesman, Jack, OBE, diplomat, aged 80 – *d.* 31 December 2001, *b.* 3 July 1921

Cheetham, Sir Nicolas, KCMG, diplomat, aged 91 – *d.* 14 January 2002, *b.* 8 October 1910

Chesterton, Dame Elizabeth, DBE, architect, aged 86 – *d.* 18 August 2002, *b.* 12 October 1915

Chillida, Eduardo, Spanish sculptor, aged 78 – *d.* 19 August 2002, *b.* 10 January 1924

Christodoulou, Anastasios, CBE, Cypriot-born founding secretary of the Open University, aged 70 – *d.* 20 May 2002, *b.* 1 May 1932

Clark, Sir John, chief executive of the Plessey Company 1962–89, aged 75 – *d.* 3 December 2001, *b.* 14 February 1926

Clark, The Rt. Revd Alan, bishop of East Anglia 1976–94, aged 82 – *d.* 16 July 2002, *b.* 9 August 1919

Coleman, The Rt. Revd Peter, suffragan bishop of Crediton 1984–96, aged 73 – *d.* (car accident) 27 December 2001, *b.* 28 August 1928

Cooper, Sir Frank, GCB, CMG, PC, permanent under-secretary at the Ministry of Defence 1976–82, aged 79 – *d.* 26 January 2002, *b.* 2 December 1922

Cotton, Sir John, KCMG, OBE, diplomat, aged 92 – *d.* 23 December 2001, *b.* 22 January 1909

Cowton, Rodney, home news editor of *The Times* 1978–82, aged 67 – *d.* 18 February 2002, *b.* 27 May 1934

Crew, Air Vice–Marshal Edward, CB, DFC and Bar, wartime ace, aged 84 – *d.* 18 August 2002, *b.* 24 December 1917

Cruttwell, Hugh, principal of RADA for almost 20 years, aged 83 – *d.* 24 August 2002, *b.* 31 October 1918

Cutler, Sir Roden, VC, CBE, KCMG, KCVO, Australian artillery officer, aged 85 – *d.* 21 February 2002, *b.* 24 May 1916

da Cruz, Vera, former vice-president of the Royal College of Midwives, aged 92 – *d.* 29 May 2002, *b.* 1910

Decker, Alonzo G. Jr, chairman of Black & Decker 1978–2000, aged 94 – *d.* 18 March 2002, *b.* 18 January 1908

Dodds, 'Dickie', batsman, aged 82 – *d.* 17 September 2001, *b.* 29 May 1919

Ebsworth, Dame Ann, DBE, high court judge, aged 64 – *d.* 4 April 2002, *b.* 19 May 1937

Ellis, Rear-Adm. Edward, CB, CBE, Adm. President of the Royal College Greenwich 1972–4, aged 83 – *d.* 13 January 2002, *b.* 6 September 1918

Entwistle, John, pop musician, aged 57 – *d.* 26 June 2002, *b.* 9 October 1944

Fanshawe of Richmond, Lord, KCMG, Conservative MP for Richmond 1959–83, aged 74 – *d.* 28 December 2001, *b.* 27 March 1927

Findlay, Ian Herbert Fyfe, chairman of Lloyd's of London committee 1978–9, aged 83 – *d.* 29 December 2001, *b.* 5 February 1918

Firth, Prof. Sir Raymond, social anthropologist, aged 100 – *d.* 22 February 2002, *b.* 25 March 1901

Foley, Maurice, CMG, Labour MP for West Bromwich 1963–73, aged 76 – *d.* 8 February 2002, *b.* 9 October 1925

Fox, Sir Marcus, MBE, PC, Conservative MP for Shipley 1970–97; former chairman of the 1922 Committee, aged 74 – *d.* 16 March 2002, *b.* 11 June 1927

Frank, Air Vice-Marshal Alan, CB, CBE, DSO, DFC, commander of the first squadron of Vulcan bombers, aged 84 – *d.* 6 October 2001, *b.* 27 July 1917

Fraser, Air Marshal, KBE, CB, AFC, inspector-general RAF 1962–4, aged 94 – *d.* 4 August 2001, *b.* 15 July 1907

Freeman, Thomas, psychiatrist, aged 82 – *d.* 12 May 2002, *b.* 16 November 1919

Freeth, Sir Gordon, KBE, Australian High Commissioner to London 1977–80, aged 87 – *d.* 27 November 2001, *b.* 6 August 1914

Fry, Richard, CBE, city editor of the *Manchester Guardian* and *The Guardian (Manchester)* 1945–65, aged 101 – *d.* 28 January 2002, *b.* 23 September 1900

Gibson-Watt, Lord, MC and two Bars, PC, minister of state at the Welsh Office 1970–4, aged 83 – *d.* 7 February 2002, *b.* 11 September 1918

Gick, Rear-Adm. Percy, CB, OBE, DSC and Bar, flag officer Naval Flying Training 1961–4, aged 88 – *d.* 16 January 2002, *b.* 22 February 1913

Gorton, Sir John, GCMG, CH, PC, prime minister of Australia 1968–71, aged 90 – *d.* 19 May 2002, *b.* 9 September 1911

Gould, Lt.-Col. Tommy, VC, soldier, aged 86 – *d.* 28 December 1914, *b.* 6 December 2001

Gould, Stephen J., paleontologist, aged 60 – *d.* 20 May 2002, *b.* 10 September 1941

Gribble, Canon A., former principal of Queen's College Birmingham, aged 97 – *d.* 9 March 2002, *b.* 18 August 1906

Grist, Ian, Conservative MP for Cardiff North 1974–83; Cardiff Central 1983–92, aged 63 – *d.* 2 January 2002, *b.* 5 December 1938

Hailsham of St Marylebone, Lord, KG, CH, PC, QC, FRS, Lord Chancellor 1970–4 and 1979–87, aged 94 – *d.* 12 October 2001, *b.* 9 October 1907

Hamilton, Sir Richard, Bt., landowner, aged 90 – *d.* 27 September 2001, *b.* 8 September 1911

Hanover, HRH Princess George of, younger sister of the Duke of Edinburgh, aged 87 – *d.* 24 November 2001, *b.* 26 June 1914

Harborne, Prof. Jeffrey, FRS, phytochemist, aged 73 – *d.* 21 July 2002, *b.* 1 September 1928

Hardcastle, Sir Alan, former head of the Government Accountancy Service, aged 68 – *d.* 23 March 2002, *b.* 10 August 1933

Harrison, George, MBE, guitarist and composer, aged 58 – *d.* 29 November 2001, *b.* 25 February 1943

Hawkins, Eynon, GC, miner and wartime sailor, aged 81 – *d.* 17 December 2001, *b.* 27 June 1920

Hawthorne, Sir Nigel, CBE, actor, aged 72 – *d.* 26 December 2001, *b.* 5 April 1929

Heineken, Alfred, chairman of Heineken NV 1971–89, aged 78 – *d.* 3 January 2002, *b.* 4 November 1923

Hetherington, Sir Arthur, DSC, chairman of British Gas Corporation 1973–6, aged 90 – *d.* 16 February 2002, *b.* 12 July 1911

Heyerdahl, Thor, Norwegian explorer and author, aged 87 – *d.* 18 April 2002, *b.* 6 October 1914

Holderness, Richard, PC, government minister under four Conservative prime ministers, aged 81 – *d.* 11 August 2002, *b.* 5 October 1920

Horsley, Air Marshal Sir Peter, KCB, CBE, LVO, AFC, pilot, aged 80 – *d.* 20 December 2001, *b.* 26 March 1921

Hutchinson, Lt.-Cdr. Sir Ian Clark, Conservative MP for Edinburgh West 1941–59, aged 99 – *d.* 2 February 2002, *b.* 4 January 1903

Hutchinson, Joseph, MC, CBE, soldier and miller, aged 83 – *d.* 6 October 2001, *b.* 3 April 1918

Jackson, Sir Edward, KCMG, diplomat, aged 76 – *d.* 8 May 2002, *b.* 24 June 1925

James, Edward, CMG, OBE, MI6 officer 1947–74; deputy director-general of the CBI 1976–83, aged 85 – *d.* 23 January 2002, *b.* 18 January 1917

Johnson, Barry, FRS, mathematician, aged 64 – *d.* 5 May 2002, *b.* 1 August 1937

Jovanovich, William, chairman of Harcourt Brace 1954–90, aged 81 – *d.* 4 December 2001, *b.* 6 February 1920

Kark, Austen, managing director of BBC External Broadcasting 1985–6, aged 75 – *d.* (Potters Bar rail accident) 10 May 2002, *b.* 20 October 1926

Kavanagh, The Most Revd James, former auxiliary bishop of Dublin, aged 88 – *d.* 8 August 2002, *b.* 3 March 1914

Keith of Kinkel, Lord, GBE, PC, law lord, aged 80 – *d.* 21 June 2002, *b.* 7 February 1922

Kerr, Sir Michael, PC, Lord Justice of Appeal 1981–9, aged 81 – *d.* 14 April 2002, *b.* 1 March 1921

Kimberley, 4th Earl of, former chairman of the National Council on Alcoholism, aged 78 – *d.* 26 May 2002, *b.* 12 May 1924

Klevan, Sir Rodney, high court judge, aged 61 – *d.* 26 December 2001, *b.* 23 May 1940

Knutton, Maj.-Gen. Harry, CB, soldier, aged 80 – *d.* 24 November 2001, *b.* 26 April 1921

Kolar, Jiri, Czech writer and artist, aged 87 – *d.* 11 August 2002, *b.* 24 September 1914

Kyprianou, Spyros, president of the Republic of Cyprus 1977–89, aged 69 – *d.* 12 March 2002, *b.* 28 October 1932

Laughland, His Hon. Bruce, QC, barrister and judge, aged 70 – *d.* 1 May 2002, *b.* 18 August 1931

Lebed, Aleksandr, Russian politician, aged 52 – *d.* (helicopter crash) 28 April 2002, *b.* 20 April 1950

Lee, Peggy, American singer, aged 81 – *d.* 21 January 2002, *b.* 26 May 1920

Leonard, Sir John, high court judge, aged 76 – *d.* 10 August 2002, *b.* 28 April 1926

Lindgren, Astrid, Swedish author, aged 94 – *d.* 28 January 2002, *b.* 14 November 1907

Lodge, Winifred, social editor of *The Times* 1938–67, aged 94 – *d.* 23 January 2002, *b.* 11 February 1907

Loyd, His Hon. John, QC, barrister and circuit judge, aged 68 – *d.* 1 May 2002, *b.* 18 July 1933

Lucas of Chilworth, Lord, parliamentary-secretary in the Department of Trade and Industry 1984–7, aged 75 – *d.* 10 November 2001, *b.* 26 April 1926

Luddenham, Lord Porter of, OM, FRS, nobel prize-winning scientist, aged 81 – *d.* 31 August 2002, *b.* 6 December 1920

Luns, Dr Joseph, secretary-general of NATO 1971–84, aged 90 – *d.* 17 July 2002, *b.* 28 August 1911

Lunt, Maj.-Gen. James D., CBE, vice adjutant-general, Ministry of Defence 1970–2; domestic bursar of Wadham College, Oxford 1973–83, aged 83 – *d.* 1 October 2001, *b.* 13 November 1917

Majoribanks, Sir James, KCMG, diplomat, aged 90 – *d.* 29 January 2002, *b.* 29 May 1911

Manchester, The 12th Duke of, peer, aged 63 – *d.* 25 July 2002, *b.* 9 October 1938

Martin, Archer, CBE, FRS, chemist and Nobel prize winner, aged 82 – *d.* 28 July 2002, *b.* 1 March 1910

McCalla, Val, founder and publisher of *The Voice* Newspaper, aged 58 – *d.* 22 August 2002, *b.* 3 October 1943

McKinley, Air Vice-Marshal David, CB, CBE, DFC, AFC and Bar, pilot and navigator, aged 88 – *d.* 23 April 2002, *b.* 18 September 1913

Miles, Tony, Britain's first chess grandmaster, aged 46 – *d.* 12 November 2001, *b.* 23 April 1955

Miller, Maurice, Labour MP for Glasgow Kelvingrove 1964–74 and for East Kilbride 1974–87, aged 81 – *d.* 30 October 2001, *b.* 16 August 1920

Milligan, Spike, KBE, comedian and writer, aged 83 – *d.* 27 February 2002, *b.* 16 April 1918

Moberly, Maj.-Gen. Richard, CB, OBE, signal officer-in-chief at the War Office 1957–60, aged 95 – *d.* 21 December 2001, *b.* 2 July 1906

Mogg, Gen. Sir John, CBE, CB, KCB, deputy supreme allied commander in Europe 1973–6, aged 88 – *d.* 28 October 2001, *b.* 17 February 1913

Moore, Dudley, CBE, comic and film star, aged 66 – *d.* 27 March 2002, *b.* 18 April 1935

Moyola, Lord, prime minister of Northern Ireland 1969–71, aged 79 – *d.* 17 May 2002, *b.* 12 February 1923

Nepean, Sir Evan, Bt., army officer, aged 92 – *d.* 11 March 2002, *b.* 23 November 1909

Norfolk, The Duke of, KG, GCVO, CB, CBE, MC, soldier and Earl Marshal of England, aged 86 – *d.* 24 June 2002, *b.* 21 July 1915

O'Hanlon, The Hon. Mr Justice Roderick, Irish high court judge, aged 78 – *d.* 24 March 2002, *b.* 11 April 1923

Oranmore and Browne, Lord, Irish peer, aged 100 – *d.* 7 August 2002, *b.* 21 October 1901

Palmer, Maj.-Gen. Tony, CB, director of electrical and mechanical engineering at the Ministry of Defence 1983–5, aged 71 – *d.* 21 April 2002, *b.* 5 November 1930

Parker, Sir Peter, KBE, LVO, chairman of British rail in the 1980s, aged 77 – *d.* 28 April 2002, *b.* 30 August 1924

Parkinson, Sheila, OBE, corps commander of the first aid nursing yeomanry 1964–91, aged 88 – *d.* 18 May 2002, *b.* 5 August 1913

Pennant, His Hon. David, circuit judge, aged 89 – *d.* 7 October 2001, *b.* 2 August 1912

Perutz, Prof. Max, OM, CH, CBE, FRS, Austrian molecular biologist, aged 87 – *d.* 6 February 2002, *b.* 19 May 1914

Platts-Mills, John, QC, criminal lawyer and former Labour MP, aged 95 – *d.* 26 October 2001, *b.* 4 October 1906

Powell, Sir Ray, Labour MP for Ogmore 1979–2001, opposition whip 1987–95, aged 73 – *d.* 7 December 2001, *b.* 19 June 1928

Powell, Lady Violet, novelist, aged 89 – *d.* 12 January 2002, *b.* 13 March 1912

Prater, Donald, OBE, intelligence officer, diplomat and writer, aged 83 – *d.* 24 August 2001, *b.* 6 January 1918

Qadir, Haji Abdul, vice-president of Afghanistan, aged 48 – *d.* (assassinated) 6 July 2002, *b.* 13 June 1954

Raeburn, Maj.-Gen. Sir Digby, KCVO, CB, DSO, MBE, Maj. and governor of the Tower of London 1971–9, aged 86 – *d.* 8 December 2001, *b.* 6 August 1915

Ram, Capt. Bhandari, VC, Indian soldier, aged 82 – *d.* 19 May 2002, *b.* 24 July 1919

Rankin, Lady Jean, DCVO, lady-in-waiting to Queen Elizabeth, the Queen Mother for 40 years, aged 96 – *d.* 3 October 2001, *b.* 18 August 1905

Rathbone, John (Tim), Labour MP for Lewes 1974–97, aged 69 – *d.* 12 July 2002, *b.* 17 March 1933

Read, Maj. T. H., MC and Bar, soldier, sportsman and businessman, aged 82 – *d.* 17 March 2002, *b.* 22 March 1919

Reddaway, Prof. Brian, CBE, FBA, economist, aged 89 – *d.* 23 July 2002, *b.* 8 January 1913

Reece, Sir Gordon, adviser to former prime minister Margaret Thatcher, aged 71 – *d.* 22 September 2001, *b.* 28 September 1929

Reid, Bill, VC, bomber pilot, aged 79 – *d.* 28 November 2001, *b.* 21 December 1921

Renowden, Air Vice-Marshal the Ven. Glyndwr (Glyn) Rhys, CB, former chaplain-in-chief to the RAF, aged 73 – *d.* 17 August 2002, *b.* 13 August 1929

Ridley, Rear-Adm. Terence, CB, OBE, Port Adm. Rosyth 1966–72, aged 86 – *d.* 25 December 2001, *b.* 9 March 1915

Riegner, Gerhart, secretary-general of the World Jewish Congress 1965–83, aged 90 – *d.* 3 December 2001, *b.* 12 September 1911

Rodger, The Rt. Revd, bishop of Manchester 1970–78; Bishop of Oxford 1978–86, aged 81 – *d.* 8 July 2002, *b.* 28 November 1920

Rumbold, Sir Jack, president of the Industrial Tribunals of England and Wales 1979–84, aged 81 – *d.* 7 December 2001, *b.* 5 March 1920

Sandelson, Neville, Labour MP for Hayes and Harlington 1971–81; SDP MP for the same constituency 1981–3, aged 78 – *d.* 12 January 2002, *b.* 27 November 1923

Sandhurst, Lord, DFC, wartime bomber navigator, aged 81 – *d.* 2 June 2002, *b.* 4 September 1920

Saunders, Sir John, CBE, DSO, MC, former chairman of HSBC, aged 84 – *d.* 4 July 2002, *b.* 29 July 1917

Scott, Sir Ian, KCMG, CIE, ambassador to the Congo, Sudan and Norway in the 1960s, aged 92 – *d.* 3 March 2002, *b.* 6 March 1909

Scott, Sir Peter, KBE, CMG, diplomat, aged 84 – *d.* 16 January 2002, *b.* 30 December 1917

Seligman, Madron, businessman and MEP for West Sussex 1979–94, aged 83 – *d.* 9 July 2002, *b.* 10 November 1918

Shach, Rabbi Eliezer, head of the orthodox Lithuanian Jews, aged around 103 – *d.* 2 November 2001, *b.* 1898

Shaffer, Anthony, playwright and screenwriter, aged 75 – *d.* 6 November 2001, *b.* 15 May 1926

Shaffer, Earl, long distance walker, aged 83 – *d.* 5 May 2002, *b.* 8 November 1918

Sharp, His Hon. Alastair, QC, MBE, judge, aged 90 – *d.* 26 October 2001, *b.* 25 May 1911

Sharp, William, CB, controller of HM Stationery Office and The Queen's printer 1981–6, aged 75 – *d.* 16 January 2002, *b.* 30 May 1926

Sherman, Sir Lou, OBE, leader of Hackney Council 1957–60; Mayor of Hackney 1961–2, aged 87 – *d.* 16 November 2001, *b.* 23 May 1914

Siddall, Sir Norman, CBE, chairman of the National Coal Board 1982–3, aged 83 – *d.* 9 January 2002, *b.* 4 May 1918

Sinclair, Air Vice-Marshal Sir Laurence, GC, KCB, CBE, DSO and bar, bomber commander, aged 93 – *d.* 14 May 2002, *b.* 13 June 1908

Skyrme, Sir Thomas, KCVO, CB, CBE, TD, secretary of commissions in the Lord Chancellor's Office 1948–77, aged 88 – *d.* 24 January 2002, *b.* 20 March 1913

Slater, Richard, CMG, diplomat, aged 86 – *d.* 8 October 2001, *b.* 27 May 1915

Solomon, His Hon. Peter, circuit judge, aged 78 – *d.* 17 September 2001, *b.* 6 July 1923

Spotswood, Sir Denis, GCB, CBE, DSO, DFC, chief of the air staff 1971–4, aged 85 – *d.* 11 November 2001, *b.* 26 September 1916

Statham, Sir Norman, KCMG, CVO, British ambassador to Brazil from 1977–9, aged 79 – *d.* 10 November 2001, *b.* 15 August 1922

Steiger, Rod, actor, aged 77 – *d.* 9 July 2002, *b.* 14 April 1925

Stephen, Harbourne Mackay, CBE, DSO, DFC and Bar, AE, Battle of Britain fighter pilot, aged 85 – *d.* 20 August 2001, *b.* 18 April 1916

Stern, Isaac, Ukrainian violinist, aged 81 – *d.* 22 September 2001, *b.* 21 July 1920

Swann, Robert, diplomat and secretary-general of the Parliamentary Association 1974–92, aged 71 – *d.* 14 August 2001, *b.* 23 September 1929

Tait, Lady Viola, opera singer, aged 90 – *d.* 6 February 2002, *b.* 1 November 1911

Tatham, F. H. C. (Tom), editor of *Whitaker's Almanack* 1950–81, aged 85 – *d.* 21 April 2002, *b.* 29 May 1916

Taylor, David, former editor of *Punch*, aged 54 – *d.* 13 November 2001, *b.* 17 March 1947

Terry, Fernando Belaúnde, twice president of Peru, aged 88 – *d.* 4 June 2002, *b.* 7 October 1913

Thaw, John, CBE, actor, aged 60 – *d.* 21 February 2002, *b.* 3 January 1942

Thieu, Nguyen Van, president of South Vietnam 1967–75, aged 78 – *d.* 29 September 2001, *b.* 5 April 1923

Thomas, The Rt. Revd Eryl, bishop of Llandaff 1971–5, aged 91 – *d.* 6 December 2001, *b.* 20 October 1910

Thomson, Rosemary, CBE, chairman of the Magistrates Association 1993–6, aged 67 – *d.* 23 October 2001, *b.* 3 October 1934

Thring, Rear-Adm. George, CB, DSO and Bar, flag officer Malayan Area 1956–8, aged 98 – *d.* 15 December 2001, *b.* 9 September 1903

Thyssen-Bornemisza de Kaszon, Baron Hans Heinrich, industrialist and art collector, aged 81 – *d.* 27 April 2002, *b.* 13 April 1921

Took, Barry, British comedian and writer, aged 73 – *d.* 31 March 2002, *b.* 19 June 1928

Trenaman, Nancy, principal of St Anne's College, Oxford 1966–84, aged 82 – *d.* 17 March 2002, *b.* 25 August 1919

Uvarov, Dame Olga, DBE, Russian-born first female president of the Royal College of Veterinary Surgeons 1976–7, aged 91 – *d.* 29 August 2001, *b.* 9 July 1910

Vines, Eric, CMG, OBE, ambassador to Mozambique 1984–5; ambassador to Uruguay 1986–9, aged 72 – *d.* 17 November 2001, *b.* 28 May 1929

Wade, Sir Ruthven, KCB, DFC, chief of personnel and logistics, Ministry of Defence 1976–8, aged 81 – *d.* 24 September 2001, *b.* 15 July 1920

Walker, Sir Michael, British high commissioner of Malaysia 1966–71; British High Commissioner of India 1974–6, aged 85 – *d.* 16 December 2001, *b.* 22 November 1916

Weighell, Sid, general secretary of the National Union of
Railwaymen 1975–83, aged 79 – *d.* 13 February 2002,
b. 31 March 1922

Weinstock of Bowden, Lord, managing director of GEC
1963–96, aged 77 – *d.* 23 July 2002, *b.* 29 July 1924

Welsby, The Revd Canon Paul, vice–dean of Rochester
Cathedral 1966–88; chaplain to The Queen 1980–90,
aged 81 – *d.* 1 March 2002, *b.* 18 August 1920

Weston, Gary, Canadian-born chairman of British
Associated Foods 1967–2000 and philanthropist, aged
74 – *d.* 15 February 2002, *b.* 28 April 1927

Whent, Sir Gerald, CBE, founder of Vodafone, aged 75 –
d. 16 May 2002, *b.* 1 March 1927

Whitehouse, Mary, CBE, founder of the National
Viewers' and Listeners' Association, aged 91 – *d.* 23
November 2001, *b.* 13 June 1910

Whitford, Sir John, high court judge, aged 88 – *d.* 5
November 2001, *b.* 24 June 1913

Whitlock, William, Labour MP for Nottingham North
1959–83; opposition whip 1962–4; vice-chamberlain
of the Household 1964–6; Under-Secretary of State
for Commonwealth Affairs 1967–9; Parliamentary
Under–Secretary of Foreign and Commonwealth
Affairs 1968–9, aged 83 – *d.* 2 November 2001, *b.* 20
June 1918

Wilder, Billy, American film director, aged 95 – *d.* 27
March 2002, *b.* 22 June 1906

Williamson, Dame Marjorie, DBE, principal of Royal
Holloway College 1962–73, aged 89 – *d.* 12 August
2002, *b.* 30 July 1913

Wilson, Rt Revd R. P., bishop of Chichester 1958–74,
aged 96 – *d.* 1 March 2002, *b.* 3 August 1905

Winterbottom, Sir Walter, OBE, CBE, England football
manager 1946–62, aged 89 – *d.* 16 February 2002, *b.*
31 January 1913

Withers, Audrey, OBE, editor of *Vogue* 1940–60, aged 96
– *d.* 26 October 2001, *b.* 28 March 1905

Wolridge-Gordon, Patrick, Conservative MP for East
Aberdeenshire 1958–74, aged 66 – *d.* 22 May 2002, *b.*
10 August 1935

Young, B. A., OBE, critic and author, aged 89 – *d.* 17
September 2001, *b.* 20 January 1912

Young of Darlington, Lord, sociologist, aged 86 – *d.* 14
January 2002, *b.* 9 August 1915

September 11 2001 and the Aftermath

On 11 September 2001, at 8.45 a.m. Eastern Daylight Time (EDT), American Airlines flight 11 from Boston flew into the northern tower of the World Trade Center in New York. At 9.03 a.m. EDT, United Airlines flight 175, also from Boston, crashed into the southern tower of the World Trade Center. By the time American Airlines flight 77 plunged into the Pentagon complex in Washington 40 minutes later, US President Bush had already spoken of an "apparent terrorist attack" and the Federal Aviation Authority had grounded all flights from all airports in the United States. At 10.10 a.m. EDT, a fourth hijacked flight, United Airlines flight 93, crashed in a rural area near Pittsburgh. All on board the four aircraft were killed. The structural damage to the twin towers of the World Trade Center was so severe that at 10.05 a.m. EDT the southern tower collapsed, followed 23 minutes later by the northern tower, killing office workers and fire and police officers in the process of evacuating the buildings at the site, subsequently labelled 'Ground Zero'. The number killed in the World Trade Center, at the Pentagon and on the four aircraft was eventually put at nearly 3,000.

Within two hours of the first crash, the White House, the United Nations buildings and all federal office buildings in Washington had been evacuated and all trans-Atlantic flights bound for the US had been diverted to Canada. Within a further three hours, the US military world-wide had been placed on high alert, a state of emergency had been declared in Washington DC, and warships had been deployed from Norfolk, Virginia, to protect the east coast of the US. At 8.30 p.m. EDT, President Bush addressed the nation, stating: "These acts shattered steel but they cannot dent the steel of American resolve".

Such is the ubiquity of the media that events, particularly in New York, were witnessed by a global audience, unfolding live on television; this, and the similarity of events to various Hollywood disaster movies, created a sense of unreality, leading television stations to caption transmissions with an onscreen message that the footage was real. The sense of unreality and some public hysteria were exacerbated by signs of shock and panic in transmissions from New York and Washington, particularly following the announcement at 12.30 p.m. EDT that there were still some 50 flights airborne in US airspace. The overall effect both of the attacks, which knocked out many of the telecommunications systems in New York, and the government reaction to them, such as the freeze on all air traffic, was that for a few days US communications with the rest of the world were effectively cut off.

The events of 11 September 2001 are, to date, the worst act of terrorism perpetrated on American soil. Although the number killed is a relatively modest figure compared with many natural disasters or with atrocities elsewhere, the events had a profound emotional, psychological and political impact in the US, and throughout the world. The global consequences have been far greater than might have been expected from the size of the death toll alone.

IMMEDIATE AFTERMATH

The most immediate reaction to the events was greatly enhanced security, particularly with regard to air travel. In telephone calls from the hijacked planes before they crashed, passengers described how the hijackers had taken over the planes using knives and scissors, the weapons having evaded detection at the airports.

Amid fears of further attacks, particularly in the US, efforts were made to improve the security of the more obvious potential targets. However, there was continuing uncertainty about whether and where attacks might be made, as those of 11 September did not conform to expected patterns of terrorist activity. The main deviation from 'normal' terrorist activity was that there was no exit plan for the terrorists themselves. In terms of terrorism generally, this is unusual, though the continuing prevalence of suicide bombings in the Palestinian *intifada* shows that it is not an essential element. Another cause of uncertainty was that the perpetrators and their aims and motives were unknown, as no claim for responsibility was made despite what, for the perpetrators, must have been success beyond their wildest dreams.

The atmosphere of uncertainty was not helped by infighting between US security services trying to apportion blame to each other, or by the production of what subsequently appeared to be spurious evidence; the flying instruction book written in Arabic and found in a car in Boston was rapidly forgotten. However, evidence which remains largely undisclosed appeared to indicate that there was a connection between the perpetrators and Osama bin Laden, a well-known Saudi Arabian militant, and his Al-Qa'eda movement; there were reports to this effect as early as the evening of 11 September. Al-Qa'eda's link with the attacks appeared to be strengthened by video tapes broadcast by the Al-Jazeera News Agency of Qatar that showed bin Laden apparently discussing the events of 11 September. Within a short time, the responsibility of Al-Qa'eda was generally accepted, but with this came fears about the movement's capacity to strike at targets world-wide, and an antipathy towards Muslims in Western countries which, though short-lived, did result in a few, isolated attacks on mosques and individuals.

The involvement of a militant Islamic movement and the backlash against Muslims highlighted some deep-rooted tensions between East and West. As Western culture has become more secularised and materialistic, it has conflicted increasingly with the beliefs and values of the major world religions, especially Islam. The US's dominance of the global economy, politics and media has made it the particular focus of criticism of and opposition to Western mores and lifestyle. Resistance to the hegemony of the West has contributed to the rise of Islamic militancy and to widespread anti-Americanism. Individual Muslims, particularly those who study or work in the West, can experience intense personal conflict over the threat to Islam, and this is believed to have been the case with Muhammad Atta, the Egyptian architect trained in Germany who is thought to have commanded the attacks on 11 September. Fifteen of the 19 co-conspirators, all Muslims, were reported to be Saudi citizens, living temporarily or permanently in the US. In this context, it is possible to interpret the assault on the World Trade Center and the Pentagon as retaliation against the US.

THE OFFENSIVE AGAINST AFGHANISTAN

Western intelligence services found they had little information on Al-Qa'eda, a shadowy movement. It was known to occupy a network of bases established during the early 1990s in Afghanistan where it trained Muslim radicals to fight *jihad* wherever there was Islamic resistance to a central authority; members are believed to

have fought in Chechnya, Kashmir, Palestine, possibly China, and in the Philippines. The movement was already considered to be responsible for the World Trade Center bombing in 1993, the assaults on US embassies in east Africa in 1998, and various attacks on US forces in the Gulf region. Its presence was tolerated by the Taliban regime in Afghanistan, which now came under sustained pressure from the US, supported by world opinion, to surrender Osama bin Laden and his supporters. At the same time as applying diplomatic pressure, the US built up its military presence in the area and when the Taliban government refused to comply with their demands, the US launched a full-scale military offensive against the regime.

The offensive began on 7 October 2001 when US forces, with a small component from the United Kingdom, launched an aerial bombardment on selected targets. Unlike the coalition raised for the Gulf war, the coalition against the Taliban was concerned more with diplomatic than with armed support; apart from the UK, offers of military assistance came only from Australia, Canada, France and Germany. Most notably, no military support was offered by the Arab world, although Turkey and Pakistan, both predominantly Muslim countries, became involved as fighting continued.

The military campaign comprised three main components. Initially, and still continuing in a spasmodic fashion, there was a large-scale bombardment of selected Al-Qa'eda and Taliban targets. The land campaign took the form of a relatively large-scale Special Forces-style operation, with US troops and British Royal Marines combing the terrain for Al-Qa'eda hideouts. The third component was the use of local forces, a surprising and somewhat risky move given the history of warlord domination in Afghanistan and the problems encountered in Kosovo from the use of this tactic. In the short term the tactic has been justified, as Afghan forces, particularly the Northern Alliance, succeeded in overthrowing the forces of the Taliban government and capturing Kabul. In the longer term the dominance of the Northern Alliance, made up predominantly of Tajiks and Uzbeks, is unlikely to be welcome in a country where some 55 per cent of the population is Pashtun.

The attack on Afghanistan seemed to produce a swift and decisive military victory, the bombardments destroying first Al-Qa'eda training camps and then Taliban troop deployments. Unsurprisingly, the Taliban administration was dismembered, but the operations of Al-Qa'eda, the original target, appear merely to have been interrupted. An optimistic estimate is that 1,000 Al-Qa'eda members were captured but this figure needs to be set against a membership possibly as high as 20,000. Also, it seems that the main body of Al-Qa'eda fighters dispersed rapidly as the scale of the onslaught became apparent and the majority are now in Pakistan. As the capture of Osama bin Laden himself became increasingly unlikely, his demise disappeared from the list of war aims. Victory for the coalition was proclaimed but at best this was limited; sporadic fighting continues in Afghanistan, and has moved across the border into Pakistan. Given the strength of Islam and the support for Islamicism in Pakistan, success against Al-Qa'eda there will be difficult to achieve.

Another major concern is the future of Afghanistan itself. The Loya Jirga of some 1,550 delegates met in June 2002 and a degree of agreement was reached upon the political future of the country. However, misgivings are already being expressed about how long peace and stability will last. The only guarantee would appear to be the semi-permanent stationing of peace-keeping troops

in the country. By mid-August 2002, the UK had withdrawn the bulk of its troops and the leadership of the International Security Assistance Force had been fully assumed by Turkey. As a militarily powerful country and the only Muslim state in NATO, Turkey would seem well suited to the task. However, the increasingly close military links between Turkey and Israel are regarded with great suspicion in the Arab world and this could influence the continuing stability of the situation.

THE WAR ON TERRORISM

The events of 11 September horrified the world, bringing denunciations by almost every country, including a number of longstanding US opponents such as Libya and North Korea, and made terrorism a truly global concern for the first time. At the same time, the US was left with only a shadowy target from which to extract retribution.

The US response was the declaration of a 'war on terrorism' by President Bush. In an address to a joint session of Congress on 20 September 2001, he said, "Every nation, in every region, now has a decision to make. Either you are with us or you are with the terrorists." Although in the immediate aftermath of the attacks, this declaration won widespread international support, the choice was somewhat loaded, changing the premise from whether a state was opposed to terrorism to whether it actively supported the stance taken by the US. Furthermore, the precise goal was not clear; did "the terrorists" mean all forms of terrorism, or was the emphasis upon Islamic terrorism, or only those deemed to be responsible for the atrocity? This lack of clarity of aim can be seen in subsequent events, as the US has striven to satisfy the desire for revenge among its own people while enlisting the support of the world at large.

In prosecution of the 'war on terrorism' the US has pursued four main avenues of action, some of them simultaneously: the military attack on Afghanistan, directed against Al-Qa'eda and the Taliban; a rapid broadening of the agenda to include terrorist groups world-wide with links, real or supposed, to Al-Qa'eda; and a further extension of its aims to encompass all supporters or perceived supporters of terrorism. A subsequent fourth stage has seen a link made between terrorism and the possession of weapons of mass destruction.

Why have the aims of the US been so expanded? It would seem that this expansion results partially from a range of global concerns, but also as justification for a variety of US foreign policy initiatives. Overall, 11 September 2001 has been perceived by many commentators as a marker to define the end of the post-Cold War period. The 'war on terrorism' is becoming so all-embracing in its concerns that it can be more accurately equated with the Cold War than with a military campaign.

The widening of the scope of the US campaign from its initial concentration on Osama bin Laden and Al-Qa'eda to global mobilisation against terrorism raised an array of political, military and legal problems. For the highly focused military operation against Al-Qa'eda and the Taliban, other than for political reasons, the US required little assistance. A global campaign, however, must necessarily have the support of a majority of states but cohesion between them is likely to come under increasing strain as an operation becomes more protracted; to sustain any semblance of a coalition over the time period needed to make a substantial impact upon terrorism globally would be extremely difficult. In the interests of maintaining as strong a coalition as it can, over the period since 11 September 2001, the US has engaged in intense

diplomatic activity and taken a more proactive part in international disputes, for example in south-east Asia, in particular the Philippines. Despite this, there have been some dubious moves, such as the decision not to work through NATO to prosecute the war in Afghanistan, even though it was the first-ever invocation of Article 5 of the North Atlantic Treaty that initiated proceedings; the decision caused a degree of alienation from European states.

Also, while it is reasonable, and indeed politic, for states to take an anti-terrorist stance, support has a tendency to waver when the emphasis falls upon a particular group, 'terrorism' having remained resistant to a generally accepted definition. For example, in supporting the mujahadin during the Soviet occupation of Afghanistan, the US presumably considered itself upon the side of 'freedom fighters'. However, most terrorist groups are viewed as freedom fighters by their supporters, and in abrogating to itself, without reference to the UN or any other internationally recognised agency, the right to decide which groups are to be considered terrorists and which states supporters of terrorism, the US risks alienating support and has already caused unease amongst some of its allies.

On the military front, if Al-Qa'eda cells are to be eliminated in possibly as many as 60 countries, there needs to be multinational co-operation both militarily and between intelligence agencies. The US has already committed troops to several countries to assist in campaigns against Islamic terrorist/freedom fighter groups. Although officially US troops are not in combat roles in Georgia, the Philippines, Somalia, Sudan and Yemen, the reality on the ground does not accord with the political statements; in the Philippines, for example, US troops have been implicated in firefights with the Abu Sayyaf group. This move raises serious issues about the intervention of an external power in what are predominantly civil disputes in sovereign states, and about how far the US might carry the policy of intervention; taken to its logical conclusion, this would involve the US in Russia (Chechnya) and China (Xinxang province).

Furthermore, the activities of terrorist groups cannot always be addressed in military terms alone. If a cellular structure is the norm, it is likely to be predominantly urban-based and its removal must rely more upon the agencies of the civil authorities, particularly the police, than the military.

The legal aspects of such activity are complex. For instance, their structure and a number of other factors entitled Taliban fighters to prisoner of war status, but this was not the case with members of Al-Qa'eda. There are problems not only over definitions of terrorism and who is a terrorist, but also of the legality of mounting attacks on sovereign states or threatening the removal of leaders of sovereign states. Doubts along these lines have been raised in the cases of Kosovo and Afghanistan, and especially in regard to an assault on Iraq. International legal experts vary in their opinions and there has even been a suggestion from legal sources that such attacks may be illegal but legitimate. As the 'war on terrorism' continues, international law covering conflict between states and non-state entities will need to be reviewed. It is interesting that, despite its apparent disregard for the UN, NATO or the finer details of international law, the US acted rapidly to address basic human rights issues when criticised internationally for procedures and conditions at Camp X-Ray, Guantanamo Bay, where captured Al-Qa'eda and Taliban fighters were taken for interrogation.

As noted above, the broadening of US aims has had a significant impact on relations between the US and several states in which terrorists/freedom fighters are particularly active, notably Israel, Russia and China. In order for the US to retain the support of these states in the drive against global terrorism, official US sympathy for the cause of the Palestinians, Chechens and Uighurs respectively, all predominantly Muslim groups, has evaporated. The impact of US policy upon acknowledged terrorist groups seems more varied. Since 11 September 2001, terrorists in Colombia, Nepal, Spain and Kashmir have been more active, as have suicide bombers in Israel. But the Tamil Tigers, the Provisional IRA and the Revolutionary United Front of Sierra Leone have all proved more open to some form of settlement.

AXIS OF EVIL

In a further widening of potential culpability, President Bush outlined in his State of the Union address in January 2002 that the 'war on terrorism' would be extended to include those countries that support terrorism. Controversially, he went on to identify an 'axis of evil' comprising Iran, Iraq and North Korea. This seems a somewhat disingenuous extension to the 'war on terrorism'. Of the three countries, only Iran appears to be currently active in support of terrorist groups; North Korea has been accused of nothing since the late 1980s, and increasingly desperate efforts to link Iraq to the 11 September attacks have been in vain.

In May 2002, the US administration released its annual list of states that it believes sponsor or support terrorism or acquiesce in terrorist activity based within their territory, naming Cuba, Iran, Iraq, Libya, North Korea, Syria and Sudan. If the inventory represents a serious attempt to identify states sponsoring terrorism, the omission of Afghanistan, and possibly Pakistan and Yemen, is difficult to explain. Also, no distinction seems to be made between those states which can be shown to be currently supporting terrorism and those which may have sponsored terrorism in the past; the seven states named have all been on the list since 1993 and some have appeared continuously since the list was first produced in 1979.

Of the countries listed, only Iran and Syria currently sponsor groups that are labelled as terrorist. Nor does the list seem to take any account of recent developments in US and international relations – Libya denounced terrorism and President Gadhafi called upon Libyans to donate blood for US victims after the 11 September attacks; the Syrian government co-operated fully with the US in the Gulf war and with regard to Al-Qa'eda; North Korea condemned the 11 September attacks and signed the related UN conventions; and at present, the Sudanese government is actually in receipt of US military assistance to combat terrorism. Whatever the evidence or lack of it, however, these states are indicted as countries which aid terrorist groups, and as a result they will be subject to a range of US sanctions.

It must be concluded that the US is being somewhat selective in which states it considers to be terrorism-inclined. Possibly, however, the US's real target is not support for terrorism, but an extension of its anti-terrorism campaign to include the alleged development or possession of weapons of mass destruction.

WEAPONS OF MASS DESTRUCTION

The events of 11 September were followed in autumn 2001 by a spate of anthrax-laced letters addressed to US politicians and media personalities, raising fears of biological terrorism by the perpetrators of the attacks on New York and Washington. Although responsibility has

not been claimed or definitively attributed, the anthrax incidents are now considered not to be connected to the attacks and may not be the work of terrorists. However, in his State of the Union address in January 2002, President Bush cited one objective as "to prevent the terrorists and regimes who seek chemical, biological or nuclear weapons from threatening the United States and the world". This seems to suggest that the US fears terrorist groups might look to use chemical, biological, radiological or nuclear weapons which could cause casualties on a scale to rival or even surpass those of 11 September 2001.

While there was a link, albeit tenuous, between the first two extensions of the war on terrorism, the basis for this latest extension is hard to understand, as there seems to be no connection between terrorism as currently practised and weapons of mass destruction. With very few exceptions, such as the introduction of Sarin gas into the Tokyo underground railway system in 1995, terrorist groups have not deployed anything that could be considered equivalent to a weapon of mass destruction, and the potential for the use of such weapons by terrorist groups is limited. Both biological and chemical weapons can be manufactured on a small scale. Although chemical weapons can be lethal locally, they pose particular problems of release and control. Biological weapons might, in some cases, be easier to deliver, but there is unlikely to be any control. The materials for nuclear weapons can be traced, but these are the category of weapons of mass destruction least likely to be employed in global terrorism; nuclear weapons require a high degree of scientific expertise to produce, and few terrorist groups would have access to this expertise or to long range delivery systems.

The US's new policy appears to take no account of countries that already have weapons of mass destruction. In the Middle East alone, four states are known to have or are suspected of having a nuclear weapons programme. Of these, three – Iran, Iraq and Libya – are all signatories of the Nuclear Non-proliferation Treaty (1968), while Israel, the only state that could be considered a nuclear power, is not. Both India and Pakistan have nuclear weapons and, since both countries are believed to have some complicity in acts of terrorism, there must be a possibility of weapons of mass destruction and terrorism coming together in this region.

However, there is general agreement among commentators that the shift of emphasis to the development and use of weapons of mass destruction has been designed purposely to prepare the way for US military action against Iraq. From the time of the Gulf war in 1991 there has been a continuing low-intensity war of attrition by the US, supported by the UK, states against Iraq which many lawyers consider constitutes a violation of international law. In the context of the recurrent air strikes, defence and offence have been reversed; it appears to be accepted logic that the Iraqi defence systems pose a threat to US aircraft. In what must be a further violation of international law, President Bush announced in June 2002 that covert US operations were commencing inside Iraq. For most neutral observers, this seems a long way from the events of 11 September 2001.

In a further escalation, President Bush stated in a speech on 1 June 2002 that the doctrine of pre-emption would soon be adopted. This would include "defensive intervention", which is presumed to mean attacking states or groups before they either obtain or have a chance to obtain weapons of mass destruction. This policy runs in tandem with the US nuclear posture review, which contemplates the use of nuclear weapons in a variety of strategic situations and against a variety of enemies, for instance the use of nuclear weapons for purposes such as penetrating underground bunkers. Thus, nuclear weapons would be targeted against non-nuclear powers to act as a deterrent against the possible use of chemical, biological, radiological or nuclear weapons. President Bush's speech made explicit what was probably a pre-existing covert policy.

BROADER PERSPECTIVES

In both theoretical and practical terms the events of 11 September 2001 initiated a major reorientation of international relations. In recent times, the nearest parallel is the onset of the Cold War. It is ironic, and a sharp contrast to that period, that the current change is characterised by an increasingly co-operative relationship between the US and Russia.

The attacks on New York and Washington led almost immediately to armed reprisal against Afghanistan, but subsequently the scope and scale of US political, military and economic activity has increased almost exponentially. Its bases in Uzbekistan and Tajikistan and particularly in Kyrgyzstan give it a foothold in central Asia. This increases its potential not only to control events in the region of Afghanistan, but also to exercise influence in both China and Russia, and over the development of the Caspian Sea petroleum industry. It is also intervening in civil disputes in nation states around the world. The immediate question which must be asked is: does this follow a rational progression or is it also being used to rationalise other US policies?

The prosecution of a campaign against a terrorist movement on a global basis presents profound political, military and legal problems. Al-Qa'eda defies categorisation in that it is a substate entity, yet global in reach. From this perspective, the threat is not against, as stated by President Bush, the "civilised world" but against the dominance of the concept of the nation state. Al-Qa'eda is in effect a military entity that is stateless and, in many parts of the world, appears to be offering a significant challenge to state power. Where there is no state allegiance, no major city to bomb and indeed little to retaliate against, the use of conventional force must be very limited. If Al-Qa'eda really is entrenched globally, it is the first post-modern military force to challenge the supremacy of the nation state on a global scale.

The events of 11 September 2001 also displayed the innate weakness of the US. The most devastating terrorist attack ever on the US was carried out by perpetrators using the lowest possible technology and exploiting laxness in national intelligence and security. In its response, and particularly in order to prosecute a war on terrorism, the US has had to rely on co-operation from other states, adapting US foreign policy and making compromises to obtain such co-operation. This has forced the US into more active involvement in international conflicts. A strong and virtually uncritical supporter of Israel in the past, the US has had to encourage the Israeli-Palestinian peace process in order to obtain Arab support for its campaign on terrorism, and particularly for any attack on Iraq. The US has also become enmeshed in the Pakistan-India stand-off over Kashmir.

US nuclear policy, essentially one of first strike, is likely to alienate world opinion and affect possible developments in several states, including China. It will do little to assuage what appears to be growing anti-Americanism in many parts of the world. Such a stance is further exacerbated by the way the US has sidelined both the UN and NATO in its military activity, and has seemed

to abrogate to itself the role of the UN in certain aspects of international affairs.

Within the US, 11 September 2001 has also resulted in major changes. US foreign policy has been reorganised to focus almost exclusively upon the war against terrorism and its various extensions. The fear of further atrocities within the US itself, regularly heightened by statements from the administration, has been addressed by the establishment of the Office of Homeland Security. As yet, there has been little progress in its development, but it is likely to encounter strong opposition, as logically it would subsume or at least override the majority of other government departments and agencies. The other obvious change has been in the reorientation of military priorities and the move towards the development of new technology to confront terrorism.

Archaeology

NORFOLK MAMMOTHS

Following a chance discovery during gravel extraction at Lyndford Quarry, Mundford, north of Thetford in Norfolk, English Heritage provided funds to the Norfolk Archaeology Unit to carry out a three-month investigation of the site. This revealed the remains of a woolly rhinoceros, a reindeer and a spotted hyena as well as four mammoths, two adults and two juveniles. Of particular significance is that amongst the bones were found flint tools of the kind associated with Neanderthal Man, making the site one of the greatest rarity. David Miles, chief archaeologist at English Heritage, was quoted in the media in June 2002 as observing: 'It is extremely rare to find any evidence of Neanderthals and even rarer to find it in association with mammoth remains. We may have discovered a butchery site or – even more exciting – first evidence in Britain of a Neanderthal hunting site which would tell us much about their organisational and social abilities. I believe that the mammoths were probably hunted. They were probably driven into the marsh and then killed. There is no other reason why they should die there.'

NEA FARM

Current Archaeology (May 2002) reports that 20 years of excavations at the Upper Palaeolithic site at Nea Farm in Hampshire have been completed. The account notes: 'In rescue excavations funded by Tarmac Southern Ltd, 900 flint artefacts were recovered from a thin horizon thought to represent an activity area preserved by the rapid but gentle accumulation of riverside sands and silts some 12,500 years ago. Thames Valley Archaeological Services' Siân Anthony, in charge of post-excavation work, says the assemblage consists of carefully made large blades and flakes, and an unusually high proportion of finished tools such as backed knives, scrapers and borers. At the time of occupation the vegetation would have been birch-pine woodland. The camp is on a tributary of the River Avon, a good location for hunting and fishing, and may map an inland route taken by the late Ice Age hunters to collect flint.'

SILBURY HILL

Because of concern about the stability of this most distinctive of prehistoric monuments in Wiltshire, English Heritage has been undertaking geophysical and ground surveys of Silbury Hill. The first results of the seismic survey released by English Heritage yield fresh information about the nature of this massive chalk mound. *Current Archaeology* (March 2002) reports that: 'The main result is that the mound originally was probably not terraced, as had been previously thought, but could have been built in a spiral fashion. While this may have been to aid construction, it could also have provided a processional way to the summit: Neolithic art is characterised by its preoccupation with spiral forms. It also appears that the hill is not circular, but has radial spines linked by straight lines, rather like a spider's web. Platforms cut into the side could date from the period when the Romans settled at the base of the mound, and may have been used for monuments or altars.'

THE RINGLEMERE GOLD CUP

The discovery of what has become known as the Ringlemere Gold Cup aroused much interest. It was found by a metal detectorist who quite properly reported his discovery, made in a field in Woodnesborough, Kent, and thus enabled an excavation to be undertaken by the Canterbury Archaeological Trust with funding from English Heritage. The cup is some 4^1/$_2$ inches high, weighs 3.5 oz and was beaten out of a solid lump of 20 carat gold. Although damaged and dragged from its original burial position to the edge of a barrow, the discovery is of the greatest significance as the nearest parallel is apparently the Rillaton Gold Cup excavated in Cornwall in 1837.

British Museum specialists Gillian Varndell and Stuart Needham describe the context of the Ringlemere Gold Cup in *Minerva* (July/August 2002) observing that: 'A small number of cups in gold, silver, amber and shale are known from the later Early Bronze Age in north-western Europe, some from graves. Amber and shale cups have been found with burials of the Wessex Culture in southern Britain, and may thus be comparable to pottery cups deposited in funerary context in central Europe (for example the 'classical Aunjetitz' cups). The earliest gold in north-west Europe was relatively small-scale trinketry in sheet gold, for example the basket-shaped ornaments (possibly earrings) found with some beaker burials of the mid- to late-third millennium BC, followed by *lunulae* (broad neck collars). Objects like the Ringlemere and Rillaton cups, and other embossed work, show the development of more sophisticated goldsmithing skills which are seen *par excellence* in the Mold gold cape of *c*.1900-1600 BC. This remarkable find, as unexpected as it is welcome, has given us an important new insight into European prehistory. It bears particularly on the network of trading and other connections which allowed ideas as well as goods to travel long distances in the changing world of the early metal age.'

PREHISTORY EXHIBITION

As well as the excitement of making new discoveries, archaeologists and those who fund their work have a duty, and indeed an interest, in disseminating as widely as possible the results of their work to the public at large. One of the main ways of achieving this is through displays in museums and this year saw the first major display of the recently renamed Department of Prehistory and Early Europe at the British Museum.

The exhibition, entitled *Prehistory: Objects of Power*, opened on 28 March 2002 and deals with prehistoric societies from the earliest times until the end of the European Bronze Age in about 800 BC; many of the objects have not been seen in public for over 50 years. Media attention was caught in particular by the Mold gold cape, which was acquired by the British Museum in pieces from 1833, when roadworks dug into a burial barrow of about 1900-1600 BC, to 1972, when the later pieces were received. The exhibition was comprehensively reviewed by Peter Clayton in *Minerva* (July/August 2002). He particularly welcomed the fact that: 'The objects have been put into their thematic context, with interpretation and thought as to how prehistoric man might have viewed them. What motivated his religious and secular life is carefully presented here to bring the prehistoric

world alive and to try and make it understandable to modern man, the inheritor of this past. The exhibition and presentation of the objects in this fashion reasserts the relevance of our past and prehistoric cultures, together with their interpreted values, to understanding our contemporary world.'

MORTIMER WHEELER HOUSE

The London Archaeological Archive and Research Centre (LAARC) opened in February 2002 in former warehouses, renamed Mortimer Wheeler House, in Eagle Wharf Road, Hackney, London. Not all archaeological collections can or should be displayed, but making these study collections available to the widest possible audience is an increasingly pressing issue. LAARC is the Museum of London's answer to this problem for the capital.

In addition to artefacts, the new centre includes the offices of the Museum of London Archaeology Service and Museum of London Specialist Services, as well as a room set aside for the use of archaeological societies which contains the libraries of the London and Middlesex Archaeological Society and the London Society. As Hedley Swain notes in *Current Archaeology* (May 2002): 'The London archive is by far the largest in Britain. The finds alone from about 5,000 excavations are stored in 140,000 boxes on ten kilometres of shelving. And of course the archive is growing every year. About 20 years' expansion space has been planned for, partly by using current spare space but also by rationalising existing collections. Public facilities include a visitor centre and two study rooms. Items can be found with a computerised index and access system (available over the web). Already the LAARC website (www.laarc.org.uk) provides online access to the annual round-ups of the *London Archaeologist*, but further access is planned. Archives (the finds, records, drawings and photographs) represent the prime data that survive excavation, but we have been very poor at using the results of excavation. The philosophy behind the LAARC is simple: it calls on the archaeological community to think beyond the immediate task of getting the archaeology out of the ground. It is hoped that LAARC will develop as a strong foundation for archaeological activity in London and a model for similar endeavour elsewhere.'

LONDON'S AMPHITHEATRE

Development in the city of London constantly brings to light Roman remains but rarely can the latter be preserved and opened to the public, not least because of the costs involved. It is therefore much to the credit of the City Corporation that in June 2002 the remnants of London's Roman amphitheatre became the latest ancient monument that the public can visit with ease. The amphitheatre was first discovered in 1988 below the site of the proposed new Guildhall art gallery. When the latter opened in 1999, parts of the amphitheatre were preserved below the new building and the circumference of the arena was marked out in the forecourt in front of the Guildhall.

In Guildhall Yard, the visitor stands in front of the 15th-century Guildhall on a site that is now known to span some 2,000 years of London's history. The amphitheatre was first constructed of timber in about AD 70 near to the Roman fort of Cripplegate, but was then replaced with a masonry structure early in the second century. Used as a military parade ground, for public executions and for fights between gladiators, slaves and animals, the amphitheatre was abandoned in the fourth century AD. By descending below the art gallery, it is possible to see the remains of some 100 yards of ragstone and brick wall,

about three feet high at its tallest point. Visitors walk through the eastern gateway into the arena and the presentation endeavours to suggest something of the atmosphere when the arena is filled with about 6,000 people, more than can be accommodated in the Royal Albert Hall.

A ROMAN EUNUCH

Advances in archaeological knowledge are achieved not only during the course of excavations but also when excavation results are assessed and written up. In 2002, 40 years of excavation, from 1958 to 1998, at the Roman site of *Cataractonium*, near the present-day Catterick in North Yorkshire were published. Media attention focused in particular on a skeleton discovered in the 1980s which was thought originally to be that of a woman but was subsequently revealed to be male. The bones were associated with a jet necklace and bracelet, a shale armlet and a bronze expanding anklet containing about 600 stones. Dr Peter Wilson, English Heritage senior archaeologist and editor, is reported as stating that: 'He is the only man wearing this array of jewellery who has ever been found from a late Roman cemetery in Britain. In life he would have been regarded as a transvestite and was probably a Gallus, one of the followers of the goddess Cybele who castrated themselves in her honour. The choice of jet is significant, as jet was regarded in the ancient world as having magical powers. There is a possible link between the rise in popularity of jet and the increasing interest in eastern mystery religions at the time.' The cult of Cybele was one of the oriental religions brought by the Roman army from Asia Minor or Anatolia in the third century BC, but by the time of this young man's burial in fourth-century Yorkshire, Cybele had long been a Roman state deity.

ROMAN WATERWORKS

One of the most important excavations in Roman London is described in *Current Archaeology* (July 2002) and relates to the problem of how Roman London received its water. The account observes that, 'Though archaeologists had found large water channels and drains in previous excavations, there had never been any evidence for an aqueduct bringing in water from outside London. In the early days of the Roman occupation many natural springs flowing through the city may have been tapped, but later on these are likely to have become too polluted, as was certainly true of the largest, the Walbrook. So the source of bulk water for Roman Britain's largest town – a provincial capital of perhaps 30,000 or more people at its peak – was something of a mystery. The discovery of a Roman waterworks last year during a major rescue dig at the 20-30 Gresham Street (Blossoms Inn) site was therefore of great importance. Not just for Roman London: as well as explaining how the local baths were supplied with water, the Gresham Street evidence has made a unique contribution to the study of Roman hydraulic engineering empire-wide ...'. Two large wells and a cistern were investigated and, because of the waterlogged nature of the site, important evidence survived at the bottom of the wells. In essence, the water from the giant wells was raised by wooden box buckets with a complicated method of wrought-iron bucket chains, and the challenge now, calling on a range of completely different skills, is to devise a model demonstrating in detail how the system worked.

THE LOPEN MOSAIC

Contractors building a driveway and hardstanding for lorries at the rear of a farm in Somerset discovered a very

large mosaic which had survived because that area of the farm had never been ploughed. The mosaic pavement at the villa site at Lopen is described by David S. Neal in *Minerva* (March/April 2002): 'The mosaic is among the ten largest mosaics in Britain and has a design very similar to a mosaic discovered in about 1817 (fully excavated in 1971) at Halstock, Dorset, situated about 12 km to the south-east. ... There can be no doubt that the Lopen mosaic represents the work of the same contractor and if the dating of post AD 350 for the Halstock pavement is reliable can be assumed to be from this date also. The saltire scheme of the floor is similar to some other mosaics from the general region and was probably produced by contractors known as the Corinian Saltire Group based in or around Cirencester north-east along the Fosse Way. However, the closest parallel to the pavement is a mosaic found in 1854 at Old Broad Street, London. This might suggest that the Group, an itinerant band of craftsmen, travelled east from the Gloucestershire region to fulfil a contract because in the later fourth century there were no mosaic contractors available in London to undertake such large commissions ... It is the only example of a saltire scheme in the south-east region and also had *kanthari* and gadrooned bowls of very similar type to the Lopen pavements. Dolphins and fishes are popular subjects on mosaics in Somerset, Dorset, and along the south coast, for example, but they need not represent Christian iconography; and although the central saltire takes the form of a cross it is merely the interspace created by four pairs of interlaced squares.'

SUTTON HOO

The royal burial ground of the kings of the East Angles has been known since the excavation of a longship above the River Deben in 1939. Although the famous helmet, sword, shield and buckles, gold coins and silver dishes from Rome and Byzantium were given by the landowner Mrs Edith Pretty to the nation and have been on display in the British Museum, the interpretation of the site at Sutton Hoo has been rudimentary. The National Trust acquired the location in 1998 and a new £5 million visitor centre was opened in March 2002 by Seamus Heaney, the distinguished poet and author of an acclaimed translation of *Beowulf*. The site has European significance, especially in relation to the culture of the lands bordering the North Sea, and the new visitor centre will greatly increase public accessibility to and understanding of the important archaeological discoveries.

OFFA'S DYKE

Offa's Dyke stretches for some 150 miles along the border between England and Wales and its precise significance has been the object of considerable research. A contribution to this by University College London's Centre for Genetic Anthropology was reported in the media in July 2002, to the effect that scientists have discovered genetic differences between the populations on either side of Offa's Dyke. Apparently, there are clear genetic differences between the English and Welsh populations studied, with the genes of the English most resembling those of the peoples in the area of the Low Countries from which the Anglo-Saxons are thought to have originated. This genetic evidence suggests that there is indeed substance in the theory that although the Anglo-Saxon invaders subjugated England, they did not penetrate to the same degree into Wales, where a separate genetic makeup is revealed.

A MEDIEVAL *MIKVEH*

Minerva (January/February 2002) includes a report by Sean Kingsley of highly unusual archaeological remains of London's medieval Jewish community. It is noted that: 'Adjacent to a building dated to the first half of the 13th century, and owned by Leo Le Blund and later by four sons of a man called Abraham, a salvage excavation on a site being redeveloped by Land Securities plc has uncovered the only medieval Jewish *mikveh* (ritual cleansing bath) known from London. Only one other example, at Jacob's Well in Bristol, survives in England. The *mikveh* is entered by seven steps leading down into a semi-circular basin, and is built of finely dressed sandstone. The bath pre-dates the expulsion of England's Jewish community by Edward I in 1290, and is yet another glimpse into the diverse historical tapestry of ancient London uncovered at 30 Gresham Street. Plans are underway to dismantle the *mikveh* for reconstruction in the courtyard of the 300-year-old Bevis Marks synagogue in London.'

KNIGHTS TEMPLAR CHURCH

The usefulness of small excavations is demonstrated by the archaeological investigation of 43-46 Southampton Buildings in London WC2. The project, described by Alison Telfer in *London Archaeologist* (Summer 2002), consisted of an excavation and watching brief 'in advance of the construction of a new liftshaft in the area of the light well, in the north-eastern corner of the development site. Drain runs were also excavated in the area of the adjacent basement.'

While the earliest archaeological features on the site were Roman, the main interest was in the location of the old Temple or the first church of the Knights Templar dating to the 12th century. Alison Telfer writes: 'The most significant building in the area in the first half of the 12th century was the first church in London of the Order of the Knights Templar. Land between High Holborn and Chancery Lane was granted to Hugh de Payens, the head of the Order, and a house was founded in 1144. From this base donations and recruits were sent to the Order in Palestine during the Crusades. In 1185, the Templars consecrated their 'New Temple' after moving to a new location near the Thames ... The round church became popular outside of the military order of the Temple; every 12th century church that was dedicated to St Sepulchre was built in this form and there are several examples of round churches with other dedications and with no apparent connection to the military orders. After the Order had moved to larger premises, the 'Old Temple' was sold to the Bishop of Lincoln, who used it as his London residence. Prior to its demolition in 1595, the property included two messuages, stables, orchards and a dovehouse.'

After describing the Roman features, the account continues: 'A substantial curving segment of chalk foundation was recorded, directly truncating the Roman pits. It had been trench-built on top of the natural gravel. Its location is consistent with foundations of the 'Old Temple' of the Knights Templar, which had been recorded, just to the north, during excavations in 1905, prior to the construction of a bank on Chancery Lane. The foundations had also been seen in 1876, when a circular colonnade of six columns was recorded during excavations for the construction of a bank at 324-5 Holborn and in 1704. The circular design of the nave was modelled on the Church of the Holy Sepulchre in Jerusalem. The circular nave of the 'New Temple' by the River Thames contains 12 buttresses arranged radially,

and measures about 18 m in diameter internally. The discovery of part of the nave of the 'Old Temple' has enabled a projected plan of the entire foundation to be created. The circumference is difficult to extrapolate exactly from the foundation segment seen in the light well and there is room for error. With this in mind, the projected plan gives the 'Old Temple' an internal diameter of about 17 m, suggesting a similar scale of build to that of the 'New Temple'. There was no evidence to suggest the existence of other structures or cut features associated with the Knights Templar Church, either in the area of the light well, or in the basement of the building.'

CAMBRIDGE COIN HOARD

The sinking of a shaft for new sewers under Chesterton Lane, Cambridge, by Anglia Water led to what Peter Clayton in *Minerva* (November/December 2001) describes as: 'a remarkable discovery'. The shaft as it was sunk moved in time from a modern road through the medieval layers to an Anglo-Saxon cemetery and culminated on an early Roman road. Of particular interest to archaeologists of the Cambridge Archaeological Unit, though, was a hoard of coins on the site of one of the cottages facing St Giles's Church; the cottages were demolished in 1911 to widen the lane.

The deposit consisted of two layers of coins, as well as traces of a wooden box in the soil, and the importance of the find arises from this being only the second medieval coin hoard found in Cambridge; the previous one was discovered in 1817 and the contents have now been dispersed. The report observes: 'The present hoard consists of more than 1,800 silver and gold coins of Edward I to III. It was deposited in two parts, the first being buried in the wooden box in the late 1340s around the time of the Black Death. The second portion, dating to the mid-1350s, comprised nine gold coins added into the top of the box, which was then sealed beneath the cottage floor. The silver pennies are from mints in England, Ireland, Scotland and mainland Europe. The gold coins, seven English nobles and two half-nobles of Edward III (1327–77), were added to the original silver penny hoard several years later ... A coin hoard found in an archaeological context like this is extremely rare. The original owner of the hoard was obviously a wealthy person since the total value was about £10 3s 4d – a very large sum of money in the 14th century, representing as much as three to four years' pay for a town craftsman. When fully analysed, the hoard will throw very interesting light on a period in the history of Cambridge when the first university colleges were being founded and the country as a whole was in the grip of the Black Death, when thousands perished. Perhaps the original owner was one of its victims, hence the hoard was not recovered.'

THE IRON BRIDGE

Television plays a valuable role in the dissemination of archaeological knowledge and there is no better example of this than BBC2's *Timewatch* programme on 11 January 2002 on how the Iron Bridge at Telford was constructed. A major monument of the Industrial Revolution and a key structure in the study of industrial archaeology, the bridge was opened in 1781 and was designated a World Heritage Site in 1986. Although its pre-eminence as one of the symbols of the Industrial Revolution in Britain, and therefore the world, has long been realised, it was not clear how Abraham Darby III was able to assemble the 400-ton iron structure and thereby bridge one of the most worked parts of any river in Europe.

Various suggestions had been put forward but it was only when a painting by Elias Martin, a Swedish art professor, was re-examined in a Stockholm museum that it became clear that the Iron Bridge was lifted into position using no more than two wooden derricks or cranes. *Timewatch* showed 51 Field Squadron Royal Engineers erecting a half-size replica of the Iron Bridge several miles to the north, using 18th-century methods and testing the information provided in the picture. From this successful experiment much information has been derived, not least the fact that the Iron Bridge was initially free-standing and the stone abutments were later additions on each side, which appears to be a departure from the normal bridge-building techniques of that time; further, the existence of a 15 ft iron casting has been disclosed which both ties the arch together and secures the crown joint. The *Timewatch* programme was an excellent medium to demonstrate the information derived from Martin's painting and to introduce the subject of industrial archaeology through the Iron Bridge, one of its finest examples, to a wider audience.

THE DERWENT VALLEY

The importance of the UK in the development of the Industrial Revolution of the 18th and early 19th centuries has been internationally recognised already at Ironbridge and Blaenavon, and these two sites are now joined by a third, the Derwent Valley, which has achieved World Heritage Status. This recognition by the UNESCO World Heritage Committee is important not only because it assists the conservation of the historic environment, but also because designation brings economic benefits, not least in the promotion of international tourism.

The Derwent Valley Mills Partnership published in 2001 an exemplary document entitled *The Derwent Valley Mills and their Communities,* an easily accessible account of the significance of this particular part of Derbyshire. It was supported not only by the Department for Culture, Media and Sport and English Heritage but also the Arkwright Society, the East Midlands Development Agency, CBI East Midlands, South Derbyshire Chamber [of Commerce] and the five relevant local authorities: Derbyshire County Council, Amber Valley Borough Council, Derbyshire Dales District Council, Erewash Borough Council and Derby City Council. It was the working partnership of these organisations, co-ordinated by Derbyshire County Council, that brought about, with the assistance of the Government, the UNESCO recognition and it is an excellent example of what can be done when archaeological merit combines with publicly expressed local determination.

The location covered by the designation runs from Cromford, just south of Matlock Bath, through Belper, Milford, Duffield and Darley Abbey to Derby, all industrial settlements linked by the river as it was water power from the Derwent and its tributaries that was utilised by these early industrial settlements. Mills and associated housing have survived intact to a substantial degree, as has the historic transport infrastructure of canal and railway. To quote the publication: 'It was Richard Arkwright's Cromford Mill which provided the true blueprint for factory production. Arkright's system was copied widely in many parts of Britain and, soon after, in other countries.' Each of the other sites, from Belper in the 1770s through to Darley Abbey in the 1780s, made their contribution to communities which came to epitomise the Industrial Revolution.

APPAG

An indication of the degree to which public interest in archaeology and state intervention have both grown in

recent years is the establishment of the All-Party Parliamentary Archaeology Group (APPAG). This was formed, according to *Current Archaeology* (August/September 2001), 'to act as a focus for parliamentary interest in all matters relating to archaeology in the UK. It currently has 24 members in both Houses of Parliament, the chairman is Lord Renfrew, the secretary is Lord Redesdale.' The first meeting of APPAG was held in the House of Lords on 6 March 2002, when it heard, in the words of *Current Archaeology* (May 2002) from 'a prestigious and eloquent panel' on their perception of the improvements that need to be made. Lord Redesdale is quoted as stating: 'We need to educate Parliament about the benefits to the country of archaeology'. The report notes that 'APPAG's 132 members represent 10 per cent of all parliamentarians'.

Architecture

Kingston-upon-Hull
Architect: Terry Farrell and Partners
Hull's location near the mouth of the Humber estuary is some distance from the main north-south transport routes through central and northern England, and as a consequence it has not been a destination for tourists in any significant numbers. This new Millennium-sponsored project is part of a larger plan to regenerate the centre of the city and transform the run-down docks area. The aims are to restore the city's relationship with its rivers and the sea and to establish a more positive image of the city in the public's mind with a view to stimulating tourism and economic growth. The construction of the building cost just over £20 million, out of a total development cost of £45.5 million, roughly half of which came from funding by the Millennium Commission.

The new aquarium, or, as it is described by its designers, 'submarium', is intended to be a key component in the regenerative process. The Deep, as it is called, sits on the site of a former shipyard, occupying a promontory of land overlooking the confluence of the Rivers Hull and Humber, on the opposite bank to the core of Hull city centre. Immediately adjacent to the massive structure of the tidal barrier across the River Hull, constructed in 1980, the Deep's solid rugged form is a reflection of the rough industrial nature of the docks area generally, but more than anything it is designed to be instantly recognisable, an icon that the public will equate with 'The Deep' and Hull.

Emerging solid and rock-like from its site, the building is triangular and wedge-shaped, following the profile of the triangular spit of land where the rivers meet and rising to a dramatic high point where the River Hull sweeps into the larger Humber estuary. On its two river frontages the building appears almost like a geological outcrop thrust upwards out of the site and weathered into a multitude of jagged angles and irregular surfaces. The treatment of the elevations is an attempt to depict an extrusion of geological layers and has also a distinctly 'fish-scale' look in parts, reflecting the nature of its exhibits. The third – land-facing – side is more prosaic and utilitarian, with a rectangular wing projecting upwards and forward from the angled roof plane and the low side of the triangle. This encloses the main entrance and a pair of lifts providing access to a high-level viewing gallery. The primarily solid faces of this projecting wing are clad in render in a series of mid- to dark-grey/brown stripes, like camouflage paint, with small randomly placed windows. They give this part of the building a crude, even sinister look, somewhat out of keeping with the fantastical panelled cladding to the main triangular block. It is unfortunate that visitors to the building arriving from the car park at the rear see only this facade as they make their way to the main entrance.

However, the charismatic elevations of the water-facing frontages are visible to people arriving by ferry and are also clearly visible from the pierhead and waterfront of the city opposite. The elevations are constructed and clad in a range of materials intended to 'evoke the metamorphosis of base rock into jewels and precious metals'. The base of the building is a cast-in-situ concrete wall profiled and painted in a combination of dark grey and black panels of varying widths and with intermediate recessed joints at a sharp, inclined angle, giving the appearance of layers of ancient rock thrust up from the seabed and cut-off at odd angles by subsequent geological events. At the base of this is a similarly treated solid concrete 'surge wall' to protect the building from flooding.

Above the concrete base, the building is clad in large panels of 3 mm-thick marine grade aluminium up to 3 metres by 6 metres in size. Trapezoidal in shape, these are laid within sloping bands of cladding suggestive of the fault lines in layers of sedimentary rock. Higher still, the cladding metamorphoses into a finer grid of frameless vitrified glass panels fixed with clip restraints. The glass panels are formed from two 6 mm sheets laminated together, the inner sheet toughened and vitrified in various colours ranging from turquoise to dark blue. Both the glass and the aluminium panels act as a rainscreen set in front of the primary weather-excluding envelope. This is a series of 500 mm-wide insulated aluminium cassettes faced with polyester powder-coated aluminium sheet, fixed back to the steel structure and with the vertical joints sealed.

The composition culminates at its apex in a sharp, pointed cage of expressed inclined frames and glazed panels enclosing a second semi-open observation deck off the restaurant that provides views over the city, the Humber estuary and the elegant span of the Humber Bridge in the distance. The reflective nature of the various surfaces mirrors the variations in light that occur throughout the day and in different weather conditions; when the sun is at low angles, the building glistens like a nugget of gold, a strange and beautiful half-rock, half-stylised fish-like apparition.

The building's substantial height derives from the nature of the visitor experience, which is intended to unfold 'the story of the oceans from the past to the present and into the future'. It takes the form of a dramatic descent through a strongly modelled three-dimensional space suggesting the underwater landscapes of the ocean, where views into the aquarium tanks are presented as a sequence of increasingly exciting glimpses of the ocean depths as if seen through cracks and crevices in the geological strata.

Upon entering the building, visitors are taken by lift straight to the top of the building, from where the tour takes them downwards via a circuitous ramped walkway ever further into the depths, past aquariums large and small. The main tanks are huge, the largest is 14 metres deep, and contain a massive 2,850 tonnes of water, which requires a substantial amount of mechanical plant to maintain the warm temperatures and the constant filtering that are necessary for the exotic marine species, ranging from tiny multi-hued tropical fish to the large and sinister sharks.

The experience culminates in a ride through the largest tank back to the top (a return to the surface) in a cylindrical glazed lift, the first time such a device has been used. This provides a fitting climax to a dramatic telling of the story of the oceans, and an exciting and instructive day-out for individual visitors as well as the many school parties that have already booked their trips. Part of the building is devoted to a research facility operating as part of the University of Hull, and the project will no doubt benefit from the combination of serious study and leisure entertainment.

CONSERVATION CENTRE, WEALD AND DOWNLAND
OPEN AIR MUSEUM

Chichester, West Sussex
Architect: Edward Cullinan Architects

The Weald and Downland Open Air Museum, in the Sussex countryside at West Dean, near Chichester, is one of the premier sites in the country for the study of oak timber framing techniques, demonstrated in its displays of medieval houses and barns. It is therefore appropriate that the construction of a new conservation centre at the museum, combining the roles of conservation workshop, museum store and an educational venue for a range of rural crafts, should be constructed using oak framing techniques, but in a manner that could only have been realised utilising 21st-century technology.

The innovative design features an undulating clear span vault of criss-crossing oak laths, known technically as a gridshell, that is exposed internally as a veritable forest of intertwining timberwork, like a huge woven wickerwork tent. The delicate framing is hidden on the outside by cladding in three horizontal tiers of vertically lapped cedar planks and a glazed clerestorey of polycarbonate patent glazing beneath an undulating section of flat roof. The new building is 50 metres long and some 9 metres high, and the principal space spans 16 metres across, so it is one of the largest buildings on the site. Yet its rhythmically undulating organic form, natural cladding materials and sensitive siting successfully conceal its size, and from some angles it is hardly noticeable, blending happily with its woodland surroundings.

The primary space created by the vault is actually at first-floor level, rising from a solid timber deck set on a grid of glued laminated timber beams that caps a heavy concrete and blockwork substructure cut into the chalk hillside. The base structure houses the artefact store and a small display area and office, and extends outwards on the downhill side under a projecting roof to provide an area for storing timber. It is a long rectangular volume and the undulating curves of the vault which create a serpentine profile on plan are supported by the varying lengths of cantilever provided by the timber deck. The substantial thermal mass of this base storey makes it very energy efficient, and a small domestic boiler serving underfloor heating is sufficient to maintain stable internal temperatures for the storing of the ancient artefacts, which are kept on banks of rolling steel shelf units. Environmental control is also assisted by the inclusion of three large diameter 'earth tubes' that draw air into the plant room from the uphill side of the building and pass down and under the building via the underlying chalk bed, thereby stabilising the temperature and water content of the fresh air supply.

The structure of the gridshell is made from 50 x 35 mm green oak laths laid in four layers to form a doubly curved variable 'radius' composite shell, displaying three principal bays, or swellings, on plan. The span varies between 16 metres at its widest and 11 metres wide at the 'waists', and the internal height varies likewise between 10 metres and 7 metres. Rather surprisingly, but in keeping with the generally 'green' agenda for the project, the oak laths were sourced from sustainable plantations in France, these being nearer and requiring less energy in transportation than the equivalent English sources. Small section timbers such as this do not come without defects, however, and it was necessary to go through a process of cutting out the defects and finger-jointing the remaining sections of timber, using modern superstrong but environmentally neutral glues, to form basic 6 metre lengths. These lengths were then joined on site using traditional scarf joints to produce the final members, which stretch up to 37 metres long for the lattice laths and 50 metres for the longitudinal

laths. Such is the economy of material when used in such small sections that the entire consignment of laths for the roof fitted onto one delivery truck. The structure is consequently very lightweight for the spans and volume which it encompasses.

Complex computer modelling by the consultant engineer, Bruno Happold, was a key factor in the development of the design, which exploits the variable geometry to provide a greater degree of inherent stability than would be obtained from a simple regular section like a tunnel. However, modern technology was only a part of an inspired team effort that relied just as heavily on the input of craft-based expertise from the main contractor and the carpenters of the Green Oak Carpentry Company who fabricated the gridshell. While the computers predicted the intensity of tensile and compressive forces, and the consequent spacing and profile of the diagrid of ribs, 500 mm apart in areas of high load decreasing to 1,000 mm over less stressed areas, the system of metal plates and bolts clamping the laths together at their final node points was the product of the experience and practicality of the fabricators and, having worked successfully, has now been patented.

The node connectors are built up from three square metal plates, secured by a nut and bolt at each corner. The centre one of these has pins to define accurately the grid geometry of the middle laths, the outer ones loosely holding the outer laths in place to permit differential sliding during the process of forming the shell shape. This was effected by laying out the basic components of the diagrid as a loose 'mat' on specially adaptable scaffolding placed 7 metres above the workshop floor, and then gradually adjusting the supports so that the effects of gravity could be used to create the desired final shape. The oak laths were used in their freshly sawn 'green' state so that maximum advantage was taken of their suppleness. The use of the timber in this condition enabled the number of breakages to be kept to a very low level, despite the tight radius of curvature that this particular design imposes in its final form.

Once the diagrid had assumed its intended shape, horizontal oak laths were fixed on the outside, utilising the steel plate node connectors, to triangulate, and therefore brace, the structure and provide fixing points for the vertically lapped bands of cedar cladding. Hundreds of short lengths of oak were also inserted between the parallel pairs of laths in the diagrid to enable them to function together as miniature beams. Inside the timber cladding, and over the diagrid, is placed an insulating membrane, just 15 mm thick but with thermal insulating properties equivalent to 200 mm of traditional mineral fibre quilt. Finally, the open ends of the vault were completed with heavy timber arches, containing a glazed screen and glazed sliding doors, that provide the final locking element to ensure the whole assembly works as a rigid self-supporting structure.

This building has echoes of other forms where craft work has transcended the vernacular tradition and assumed some of the elegance and precision of finely tuned timber structures; boat building and early aircraft construction might be typical examples. Certainly this innovatory structure has a powerful and memorable aesthetic quality to complement its practicality, being light, airy, sinewy and elegant on the inside, more solid, bulbous and rippling, like a giant caterpillar, on the outside. Completed in the early summer of 2002 for a sum of approximately £1.6 million, the building is Britain's first permanent double-layer timber gridshell structure, and certainly fulfils the museum's ambition of creating an exemplar for modern rural building. It has already received a RIBA award for architecture.

GREATER LONDON AUTHORITY HEADQUARTERS

Southwark, London
Architect: Foster and Partners

London's newest landmark is a strikingly unconventional structure built to house the political and administrative functions of the Greater London Authority. The building occupies one of the finest sites in the capital, directly opposite London's oldest landmark, the Tower of London, and within a stone's throw of that other famous icon, Tower Bridge. Its prime riverside position, on a tract of land hitherto known as London Bridge City Phase 2, comprises an area bounded by the Thames to the north and Tooley Street to the south that has been in a development hiatus since the original warehouse buildings were cleared in the 1980s. In the 1990s a scheme for an office development resembling 'Venice upon Thames', to a concept design by John Simpson, reached an advanced stage of development but failed to be implemented as recession took hold. Foster and Partners' new building now forms the centrepiece of a new master plan developed in 1998 that includes four substantial new office buildings and a hotel, all designed by the same practice.

At the heart of the new headquarters building lies the debating chamber designed to accommodate the monthly gatherings of the 25 GLA members. This is a circular space on plan, surrounded by a horseshoe-shaped gallery with tiered seating for members of the public. It is the motif of a circle that drives the entire form of the building, which is that of a distorted and layered spheroid. Despite claims that the overriding influence on the design was its environmental agenda, this building's form has to be seen primarily as a conceptual and symbolic gesture by the designer which has been subject to a certain amount of post-rationalisation.

The designers' stated intent was 'to reduce the energy load of the building by 75 per cent' (below usual high specification air-conditioned office norms), while producing an architectural statement that exhibited a desirable degree of 'transparency', openness and lightness as a reflection of the democratic process. While earlier models and realisations emphasised these aspects, from the outside the finished building is a good deal more solid and visually impenetrable, and highlights the difficulties inherent in making 'glass architecture' truly transparent. The moulded spherical form is smooth on its north-facing river frontage, but develops into a series of stepped overhangs as the individual storeys are expressed on the other three sides, as if an egg had been sliced up and then loosely reassembled. The upper storeys therefore overhang the lower levels by a considerable degree on the south side, giving the building the appearance of leaning over at an angle away from the river.

The inclined structure required to support this shape generates a number of structural problems, including large horizontal forces that have to be counteracted by the stable vertical core elements. The inclined perimeter columns which support the floors in 508 mm circular hollow steel sections, run in straight lines but kink at each floor level and are restrained at each floor level by a series of 675 mm deep primary steel beams tied to the central reinforced concrete lift and stair core. Each of the building's ten separate floor levels is a perfect circle on plan, but diminishing in radius the higher up the building and with each floor successively offset to the south. The central core of six lifts, two stairs, service lift and associated accommodation consequently lies on the south side of the ground floor plan, with the entrance, reception and exhibition areas to the north. On the topmost floor the core lies on the north side of the space with a generous public gallery and viewing space to the south giving stunning views out over the river, the City and south London.

The dominant space within the building is given over to the debating chamber, which effectively forms the floor of an eight-storey-high atrium. Through this space winds the building's singular and most distinctive feature, a spiral stepped ramp, arranged to enable both the building's occupants and the general public to circulate through the various levels. The ramp circles up over the debating chamber, each successive segment of the spiral on a tighter radius and all the time following the gradual offset of the building plan, so that it appears to disappear beyond sight in a final flourish before depositing its users in the topmost public viewing gallery. The full-height volume of the atrium is expressed on the north elevation by means of a curved panel of frameless glazing with a sawtooth pattern to its edges, resembling a Christmas tree, supported on a triangulated tubular steel diagrid. The horizontal primary steel members of this diagrid are ingeniously designed to carry hot water through their core, to enable them to act as giant tubular radiators and counteract cold down-draughts from the glass.

The large amount of glazed surfaces to the building would suggest problems of heat gain from the sun. However, one of the benefits of the spherical form is that throughout the day roughly the same extent of glazed area is exposed to direct sunlight, avoiding the peaking effect that often afflicts rectangular buildings. Coupled with the fact that a circular building has approximately 25 per cent less surface area than a rectangular building of the same volume, this helps to reduce heat loss or gain through the envelope and reduces the maximum cooling load, requiring a smaller mechanical plant capacity. Solar shading is provided by the overhanging floor plates, the external bands of panelled cladding around the south side are angled downwards towards the ground to further reduce direct sunlight. The facade of the office floors that wraps around the west, south and east sides is a double-skin cladding system, with the outer single-glazed skin and the inner double-glazed skin separated by a cavity that can be ventilated at both high and low level. In the cavity is a user-controlled reflective blind to control direct sunlight. A mechanically operable ventilation flap is provided below each window to allow cool air into the building and this operates a motorised flap at ceiling level to let warm air out. This action automatically closes down the air conditioning in the affected zone, thus saving energy.

The office spaces are cooled by passive chilled beams, utilising cool water pumped from two boreholes rather than conventional chillers. Pumping cool water in this way from natural sources represents a significant energy saving, and as a spin-off provides a wider environmental benefit by counteracting London's rising water table. The cold water passes through a cooling coil to cool the air supplied to the raised floor plenums and also cools the chilled beams via a heat exchanger. The used water is then either discharged into the Thames or used for flushing toilets or for irrigation.

The building is set within a park and nudges right up to the riverside walkway. To the west an oval sunken amphitheatre has been set into the ground. The stepped levels are clad in dark grey Irish limestone and can seat around 1,000 people. They also provide access to the basement level, which extends substantially beyond the circular profile of the main building. Here is located a public café and curving ranges of meeting and committee rooms, as well as the necessary storage and plant rooms.

The stepped spiral ramp descends also to this level and encloses an elliptical exhibition area rising through two storeys to the underside of the debating chamber.

There is a strong feeling of openness and transparency within the building, the many inclined glass planes and the spiralling glass balustrade of the ramp adding to the cut-crystal quality of light and reflections. Transparency is not the predominant characteristic of the exterior, however, apart from the glazed wall to the debating hall atrium, as the inner cladding panels are limited to a 1.2 metre high window within the 3 metre by 1.5 metre panel size. The choice of grey for the cill panels may be unobjectionable in fine weather, but runs the risk of looking gloomy and forbidding on dark and wet days.

The building's striking form has given rise to a number of nicknames, some less than complimentary, but it may yet come to be regarded with affection by the London public it is designed to serve. There can be no quibble about the success of the procurement process, the shell and core structure having been handed over several days ahead of schedule and within the tightly controlled £43-million budget. This latest essay in high-tech, computer-designed, energy-saving, yet hopefully sustainable architecture was formally opened by The Queen on 23 July 2002.

HAMPDEN GURNEY PRIMARY SCHOOL

Marble Arch, London
Architect: Building Design Partnership
The notion that the typical school, especially at primary level, is set in an area of land with a range of single-storey classrooms clustered round a slightly larger and higher hall and surrounded by hardstanding playgrounds and perhaps some green open space, is a commonly held and indeed regularly implemented one. But it makes little sense to slavishly pursue this concept in tightly developed inner city areas where land is at a premium and large open sites are simply not available. This exciting new development located within a few yards of the traffic-dominated Edgware Road and not far from the urban maelstrom of Marble Arch points the way to a totally new form for the urban school, the multi-storey primary.

The new school occupies a site which was bombed in the Second World War and rebuilt as a school in the 1950s. Hampden Gurney (the name derives from the 19th-century churchman who founded it) is a Church of England school that had been looking for some years to provide a better environment for its pupils. The trustees held competitive interviews with a range of designers, and from these the concept of the multi-level school was developed. The cost of the school has been offset by the inclusion on the plot of two new residential buildings, which frame the new school on its corner site at the junction of Forset Street and Nutford Place. Designed by the same team, the residential buildings are relatively restrained in design, brick clad with punched window openings and simple faux balconies, and provide a link between the older surrounding mansion flat blocks and the decidedly contemporary appearance of the school.

The school addresses its prominent corner position with a stack of curved glazed balustrades offering protection to the open playdecks behind, and contrasting with the solidity of the brick blocks that frame them. The school is laid out on six levels, one of them a generously tall lower-ground floor set below pavement level, which accommodates a meeting/dining hall, a separate chapel/music room, and a substantial partially-covered, partially-open play area. All of these areas can be opened up to form a large column-free space which offers a range of possibilities for performances, plays, games, assembly and worship.

Two long curving ramps and short flights of steps lead up to the entrances to the school. The entrances are placed at opposite ends of the curving frontage to the Nursery playdeck, one entrance serving the Nursery class only, the other giving access to a lift and staircase serving the other levels for the older children.

The plan of the upper levels is set out symmetrically about a 45° axis, with the roughly semi-circular playdecks framed by the tapering legs of the L-shaped classroom accommodation. This comprises two classrooms either side of a central resource/library, connected via a bridge on the line of the axis across a central atrium light well to the playdecks, from which access can be gained via a lobby area to the staircase and service cores that abut the adjacent residential buildings and act like solid bookends. Each floor is independent, with each pair of classrooms centred around its private learning core and with easy access to its own 'playground in the sky'.

As the children progress through the school year by year, they move up through the building, from the nursery class on the ground floor to Years 5 and 6 on the third level. At the fourth level the substantially open roof deck is covered by a large fabric canopy that provides a sheltered environment given over to a 'technology garden', and featuring an intimately sized technology room for special and concentrated work on technical and environmental topics.

The structural concept is simple and bold, but also ingenious, in that the centre of the building benefits from large column-free spans, freeing up the centre of the floor plate. A simple cordon of circular columns rises up around the perimeter, and the remainder of the load is carried on two paired columns rising at either end of the central lightwell. These support an arched steel truss at fourth-floor level, a strongly expressive architectural intervention within the canopied roof deck. From the arched truss a series of tensile supports formed from Macalloy rods supports the floor loads where the bridges cross the centre of the lightwell, and the resulting forces are transmitted into the arch by a fan-shaped arrangement of tension cables. This structural ploy creates a column-free 16-metre span across the centre of the building that provides maximum benefit at the lower ground-floor level in the series of linked communal spaces.

The central atrium enables daylight to filter right down to the heart of the building, where the central assembly hall has a section of glazed ceiling giving a clear view right up to the white painted steel arch and canopy soaring overhead. The central clear space also acts as a natural break between the private spaces of the classrooms and the open air playdecks. While being sheltered from the worst excesses of rain and sun, these play areas remain decidedly 'outdoors' in feel. The laminated glass balustrades are high enough to provide safe enclosure, and lean inwards at progressively sharper inclines higher up the building, but they do not reach the soffit of the next floor. The spaces therefore retain strong visual and atmospheric connections with the world outside, and exploit the southerly orientation of the site to provide a day-long sun path. A marginal loss of total play area from the earlier arrangement is more than offset by a significant improvement in quality and effectiveness. The children appear quite at ease with the glass edges, tending to gather in smaller, quieter groups at the perimeter and dash about in the open space in the middle, and there is the added benefit of separation into layers in that the older, stronger children cannot cause havoc among the nursery children at break times.

Internally, the aesthetic is dominated by the extensive use of timber, which gives a warmth and friendliness to the ambience while retaining the required degree of robustness, and which also avoids the institutional feel of the plain painted plaster surfaces that are often the norm. Timber boarding is used for the playdecks, both on the ceiling soffits as well as the floors; the impression is almost of being on board a rather luxurious cruise liner. Indeed, the slickness of the detailing, the thoroughly modern architectural forms and the playful profile of the tented roof make it difficult to reconcile the finished product with its function as a school.

Construction of the £6 million school building commenced in July 2000, and it opened in January 2002. The overall development cost of £18 million includes the two six-storey residential blocks, which provide a total of 52 apartments; the profits from these financed the redevelopment of the school. This is a radical project, carried out with imagination, attention to detail and a sympathetic understanding of how the needs of school children can be met in an uncompromisingly urban environment. It should become an exemplar for similar situations, and was justly recognised by a RIBA architecture award in 2002.

IMPERIAL WAR MUSEUM NORTH

Salford Quays, Manchester
Architect: Studio Daniel Libeskind
The architectural concept for this strikingly unconventional new museum overlooking the Manchester Ship Canal and the old docks of Salford Quays derives from the destructive nature of war, and the idea of a world blown apart by conflict. The architect's vision is that of the globe shattered into jagged pieces, with some of the shards remaining from a broken glass sphere reassembled in brutal and random juxtaposition. The basic external form is of three such shards, symbolising the three theatres of war, i.e. earth, air and water, and the sharp edged interpenetration of planes and volumes informs not only the external massing, but also the complexity of the internal planning, with its relentless zig-zagging and inclined surfaces.

Although the museum occupies a prime waterside site directly opposite the Lowry Centre, a recently opened theatre and gallery building of similar but more conventional formal exuberance (see Whitaker's Almanack 2001), entry to the museum is from the land side to the rear, off Trafford Road West. From here, an angled pathway spears into the side of the tallest of the three shards, the air shard, a hollow semi-open and unweatherproof space containing a lift to a high-level viewing platform. Rising to 55 metres high, it is constructed from a stack of vertical and horizontal ladder trusses with triangulated bracing, exposed to the interior of the space, and clad with aluminium planking set out with an air gap between each plank so that daylight filters into the interior. But the volume is a complex one; each of the four enclosing planes slopes in a different direction and the entire structure is 4° off the perpendicular, giving a 4-metre overhang from top to base. This generates some alarming visual perspectives when seen in conjunction with the absolutely vertical lift shaft and staircase.

The tower of the air shard cuts into the main gallery, a lower, gently curving expanse of burnished metal with a deep fascia expressing the internal volume, hovering above the ground on a black rendered recessed base. This is the earth shard. The entrance and foyer spaces, information desk, ticket office, cloakrooms, shop and café are located on the ground floor below the main first-floor gallery level, which is approached by either stairs or lift.

Both stairs and lift exhibit the aggressive angular theming evident in the handling of the volumes; the stairs taper at odd angles and the aluminium-faced enclosure to the lift continues the angled geometric theme. The main gallery of the museum is a large clear-span windowless space, a black box within which the exhibits, both material objects and non-material images and projections are given complete supremacy. There is a large main gallery and a smaller temporary exhibition gallery.

The most interesting architectural aspect of this gallery is that it comprises a volume defined by the gap between two slightly differently radiused spheres, with differently located centres of curvature. The gallery floor, as well as the gallery roof, is a segment of a sphere, a shard within a shard, sloping downwards towards the perimeter walls, which are themselves inclined away from the vertical. The gallery slab is believed to be the first suspended spherical slab built in the UK and consists of a flat slab bent to a spherical shape, the construction starting with the definition of a 'north pole' point and proceeding to establish circular contour lines marking regular changes in height away from the centre. The floor is surfaced with asphalt incorporating a bauxite aggregate, and joints within the finish follow the contours of the sphere. This finish enables the floor to pick up the many photographic images that are projected onto it. The roof is similarly spherical, its north pole offset to that of the floor so the internal floor to ceiling height varies throughout. Construction of the roof with its large clear spans utilises a steel frame, with members bent through one axis and set out radially from the notional north point to form structural ribs along the lines of longitude, braced by tubular purlins, similarly bent, which are spaced at equal centres along lines of latitude. The combination of the sloping floor and the slanting walls, and the closely controlled lighting within a windowless space makes for a general sense of disorientation and tension that heightens the intensity of the experience and the effect of the exhibits and their message. It is something of a relief to get back to a flat floor and windows giving views of the outside world.

The third shard, the water shard, contains the restaurant, and juts out towards the waterside, providing views over the Ship Canal and the Quays opposite. Like the air shard, it too is embedded into the main gallery volume at an odd angle, and rises slightly higher than the principal curved plane of the gallery roof. It is constructed in a similar manner to the earth shard, with a concrete frame to first-floor level and a steel-framed structure above. The roof plane is dished, rising to a peak along the inner and outer edges, and the volume is clad with tightly butted silver aluminium panels; the surface is relieved with inclined major joint lines and paired rows of visible fixings. The metal box component of the shard sits on a black recessed base, as in the other main gallery elevations, but typically it appears to be falling over, to such an extent that one corner of the metal cladding has embedded itself into the ground.

The external expression of the building is almost exclusively sculptural, as opposed to conventionally architectural, and there seems little doubt that it will be as successful as the Lowry Centre across the water, the two exerting a symbiotic influence in turning this otherwise uninspiring tract of former docklands into a popular cultural destination. The unique combination of smoothly curving and jagged edged forms gives this museum instantly recognisable status as a cultural icon, excellent value for its relatively modest £28 million price tag.

Art

The past year has seen the art world convulsed anew by controversy about the worthiness of conceptual art, a debate which widened to take in almost all contemporary, challenging forms of art from installation, video and performance to anything unlike traditional painting, sculpture and drawing. The first shot was from the 2001 winner of one of the UK's many prestigious prizes, the £25,000 BP Portrait Award, presented each year at the National Portrait Gallery in London. The 25-year-old painter Stuart Pearson Wright, whose portrait of *The Six Presidents of the British Academy* won the country's most coveted accolade in figurative painting, made a stinging attack on Sir Nicholas Serota, director of the Tate Gallery, for championing conceptual art at the expense of representational art. Not surprisingly, Serota did not resign at the suggestion of the young artist, but there were similar attacks to come.

At the Royal Academy's 2001 summer dinner, playwright Tom Stoppard, the keynote speaker for the evening, damned contemporary art for not being 'made' but relying heavily on 'experience' as well as overtly copying the work of Marcel Duchamp, widely credited with inventing conceptual art when he exhibited an upside-down urinal as art in the early 20th century. Mr Stoppard was not greeted with applause, possibly because his audience largely consisted of the directors of modern and contemporary art museums and galleries, including Sir Nicholas Serota.

The Tate Gallery was in the headlines in November 2001 for its controversial annual £20,000 Turner Prize. The spoils, and the harsh words, went to conceptual artist Martin Creed, whose installation at the Tate Britain, *The Lights Going On and Off*, was deemed the winner out of the four, predominantly photo and video-based artists. Unusually for an art story, the uproar surrounding Creed's simplistic timer switch made front-page news in many daily papers, with cries of 'How can this be art?' dominating the coverage. The Turner Prize always stirs up public debate on contemporary art – that is part of its remit – but it came under more fire with the announcement that Madonna was to present the prize at a ceremony broadcast live by Channel 4. To some, it seemed that the Tate was more concerned with gathering column inches in newspapers (which it certainly did when Madonna used an expletive in her speech) than presenting outstanding exhibitions of art.

Art prizes in general remained a bone of contention, not just for the types of art they promote but for the sheer number of awards currently on offer. In London alone in the past year there has been the Citigroup Photography Prize 2001, won by Iranian Shirana Shahbazi; the Jerwood Painting Prize 2002, given to Callum Innes; and the Institute of Contemporary Art's 2002 Beck's Futures Prize of £20,000, presented to Scot Toby Paterson by another pop singer, Björk.

However, it was not until January 2002 that conceptual art and its unofficial home, the Institute of Contemporary Arts (ICA), really came under fire, and then not from the press but from within. Ivan Massow, the ICA's flamboyant fundraising chairman, wrote an article for the *New Statesman* condemning what he called 'concept art' (rather than conceptual art) as 'self-indulgent craftless tat'. His outburst singled out famous artists such as Tracey Emin and warned that: 'The British

arts world is now in danger of disappearing up its own arse'; as Mr Massow did not consult anyone at the ICA before the piece was published, it was no surprise that director Phillip Dodd and the board of the ICA forced him to resign a week later. His outburst, however, opened the floodgates for criticism not only of the ICA, which receives £700,000 in public subsidy each year, but also for any conceptual and contemporary art. Luckily for the ICA, Ivan Massow's next venture, a website called www.culturetm.org, failed to spur on the debate, which was largely smothered by the very art establishment he had railed against. In June 2002 the ICA announced that veteran TV executive Alan Yentob would take over Massow's unpaid post as ICA chairman, shortly before it was revealed that Yentob would also be fronting a new flagship BBC1 arts series to rival ITV's *South Bank Show*.

VISITORS

Contemporary art also fared badly in overall gallery visitor figures in 2001. Old Masters were the top attractions, with 'Vermeer and the Delft School' at the National Gallery (20 June–16 September 2001) clocking up an impressive average of 3,138 visitors a day, and an overall total of 276,164 visitors. 'The Genius of Rome' at the Royal Academy had an average 2,850 visitors a day and Tate Britain's 'William Blake' show was also popular. It was the BP Portrait Award at the National Portrait Gallery (21 June–16 September 2001) with a daily attendance record of 1,907 that came top of the exhibitions of contemporary works. The Tate Modern only managed an average of 1,205 paying visitors a day to its ambitious, but highly criticised 'Century City' exhibition that ended in April 2001.

Undoubtedly the events of 11 September 2001 affected the UK art world, with some galleries suffering from the 17 per cent drop in tourism from North America. The overall visitor figures for the British Museum and the Tate galleries were down, although the National Gallery actually had 6,000 more visitors in October 2001 than it did in October 2000.

It was a bad year for many venerable commercial galleries. The unexpected demise of London's most respected contemporary art dealer, Anthony d'Offay, along with his three spaces off Bond Street, stunned the tight-knit community of West End art dealers. Next to go, in January 2002, was London's oldest firm of Impressionist and modern art dealers; Alex Reid and Lefèvre, which opened in 1926, cited rising overheads and a diminishing supply of great paintings among the reasons for its closure. From the ashes of Anthony d'Offay's empire rose a new gallery called the Haunch of Venison Partners, after the courtyard location in which one of d'Offay's old premises stands; it was formed by a former d'Offay employee, Graham Southern, and fellow West End dealer Harry Blain of Blains Fine Art. Another significant closure was the not-for-profit Lux Centre in east London, the only space dedicated to film and video art, which the Arts Council deemed to be operating at too great a financial deficit.

ALL CHANGE

The musical-chairs of gallery top jobs was more pronounced than ever in 2001–2. The first shock came in late June 2001 when the well-liked and unassuming Lars

Nittve left his post as the first head of the successful Tate Modern. After three years in the job his decision to leave for the directorship of Sweden's national museum of modern art, the Moderna Museet in Stockholm, was met with widespread rumours about his incompatibility with Sir Nicholas Serota, who oversees all the branches of the Tate. His departure was closely followed by Karsten Witt's decision to leave his post as chief executive of the South Bank arts centre after two years. After months of speculation, in June 2002 the Tate Modern appointed as its new director Vicente Todoli, hitherto in charge of the Serralves Museum of Contemporary Art in Porto, Portugal and before that the Institute of Modern Art in Valencia, Spain. In the same month it was announced that James Cuno, a professor at Harvard, would be the first foreign director of the distinguished fine art college and gallery the Courtauld Institute, when Professor Eric Fernie steps down in January 2003. Elsewhere, the Irish Museum of Modern Art in Dublin is still in a state of uncertainty since the revered director Declan McGonagle was ousted in 2001. McGonagle was briefly reinstated but then left, so the museum has been without a permanent director since April 2002.

The changes continued with Sandy Nairne, one of the team behind the Tate Modern, taking over as head of the National Portrait Gallery from Charles Saumarez Smith, who left to take charge of the National Gallery next door. Dr Saumarez Smith replaces Neil MacGregor, who has moved to the top job at the beleaguered British Museum, an institution desperately in need of new direction after an unprecedented staff walkout occurred on 17 June 2002 in protest at proposed cutbacks of £6 million and 150 possible redundancies. The British Museum enjoyed handsome sponsorship for its glass-domed Great Court redevelopment, thanks to the Government and the National Lottery, but faced dwindling visitor figures in 2001 as foot-and-mouth disease and the events of 11 September hit tourism. The museum had always bravely resisted the introduction of admission charges but then missed out on the tax advantages and the huge payouts offered by the Department of Culture in 2001 as an incentive to bring back free admission. All this came on top of continuing pressure on the museum to return the Elgin Marbles from a newly formed group of over 90 MPs and actors calling themselves Parthenon 2004, whose aim is the repatriation of the sculpted frieze in time for the 2004 Olympic Games in Athens. Subsequent revelations about the sale of Nigerian Benin bronzes from the British Museum's collection in the 1950s and 1960s was a further embarrassment for the museum's restitution record.

On a brighter note, the Victoria and Albert Museum under new director Mark Jones, seemed to shed previous criticism and increase attendance by simultaneously dropping the £5 entrance fee and opening the recently refurbished British Galleries in the south-west wing. Despite only just finding the £31 million necessary for the British Galleries' enthralling display of decorative arts from 1500 to 1900 that now covers 10 per cent of its entire museum space, the museum has plans to reinvigorate the central Pirelli gardens courtyard, making it into the hub of the museum, and the seemingly unending task of raising money for the Daniel Libeskind-designed Spiral building is again underway. Another significant event was the inauguration of Tate Britain's new Centenary Development wing in November 2001, though this was faintly praised as a traditional and functional, rather than trendy, addition to the original Millbank site.

NEW ON THE SCENE

Facelifts were all the rage for UK galleries in 2001–2, including the £4.3 million reopening of the Walker Art Gallery in Liverpool. In May 2002, Manchester Art Gallery reopened after a £35 million transformation and with double its previous exhibition space. Also in the north-west, a new £9 million art gallery was opened in Oldham, while Newcastle and Gateshead continued to build cultural centres in a bid for designation as the European Capital of Culture in 2008. In January 2002, Tyneside's active public art programme, which had created Antony Gormley's famous Angel of the North sculpture, unveiled an artwork-cum-public space in the centre of Newcastle called the Blue Carpet, designed by artist Thomas Heatherwick. This paved the way for one of the year's most ambitious arts ventures over the river in Gateshead, where an old flourmill was converted into the BALTIC 'art factory' for the creation and display of contemporary art. A Swedish director, Sune Nordgren, was brought in to oversee the tricky architectural conversion, which took eight years and £46 million of Arts Council, local and National Lottery money. After being delayed by two months, the opening took place in July 2002 to a considerable fanfare, although it remains to be seen what the local community and the wider, international art community will make of it. Immediately opposite the BALTIC is the skeleton of the forthcoming Norman Foster and Partners building for the Sage music centre, another powerful draw for Gateshead in future years.

A second area vying for designation as Britain's next European Capital of Culture in 2008 is Canterbury and east Kent, with its own centre of artistic activity at Margate. Apart from being Tracey Emin's home town, the seaside resort is to house the Turner Centre, a £10 million art gallery dedicated to the study of the work of Britain's most famous painter, J. M. W. Turner. To further the same aim, the Tate Gallery's website has initiated an online Turner archive, currently containing 20,000 images of his paintings and drawings. Another city with aspirations to cultural growth is Durham, which has become the favourite to host the new regional outpost of the National Portrait Gallery because of its castle, cathedral and other tourist attractions.

One London museum did open a regional outpost in 2002, with the new Imperial War Museum North at Manchester's Salford Quays marking the stunning UK debut of architect Daniel Libeskind (see Architecture). Even The Queen got herself a new gallery at Buckingham Palace. The most significant addition to the palace for 150 years, the new Queen's Gallery was both a fitting celebration for her Golden Jubilee year and a chance for the public to sample the personal tastes of England's royalty from Charles I to the present day. Many of the royal family's most important paintings by Vermeer, Gainsborough, Holbein and Van Dyck have been on public view permanently, either on loan to an exhibition or at Windsor, but overall the Royal Collection has been something of a hidden treasure trove. The initial six-month exhibition 'Royal Treasures: A Golden Jubilee Celebration' in the new neo-classical extension, designed by architect John Simpson, was complemented by other touring exhibitions to commemorate 50 years of The Queen's reign. Another Queen's Gallery will be inaugurated at the Palace of Holyroodhouse, Edinburgh, in November 2002 to allow parts of the Royal Collection, hitherto unseen in Scotland, to be exhibited in a new space currently being converted from portions of the 19th-century Holyrood Free Church building.

The maestro of modern art patronage, advertising man Charles Saatchi, failed to finalise his own plans for an enormous exhibition space in County Hall next to the London Eye, despite a year of wrangling over preservation of the listed building. Instead, Saatchi had an ominously quiet year in the art world, having moved on from his flagship St Johns Wood space to more modest galleries in east London. He did donate over 50 works from his substantial collection to the charity Paintings in Hospitals, including *Hymn*, a 20ft-high Damien Hirst sculpture showing the inner workings of the body that will be installed at the Chelsea and Westminster Hospital, providing it is not thought too distressing for patients. Saatchi's legendary art-buying habits were still evident as he snapped up more graduating artists' work at the degree shows and spent a small fortune on work by young painter Peter Doig. He also continued to off-load more of the so-called YBA (Young British Artist) collection that had made him, Damien Hirst, Tracey Emin etc., famous in the first place. It was a year of mixed fortunes for this now ageing YBA generation. Although Chris Ofili received critical acclaim for his new elephant-dung paintings, photographer of gritty realism Richard Billingham missed out on winning the Turner Prize, Damien Hirst had one of his installations cleared away by an over-zealous cleaner and Sam Taylor Wood failed to make a real impact with her first major show at the Hayward Gallery, London.

The enigmatic elder statesman of British art, Lucian Freud, was hardly out of the spotlight throughout the year, partly because he produced a startling, brutal portrait of The Queen and also because of the most comprehensive retrospective of his work to date, held at Tate Britain (20 June–15 September 2002). Though his personal life and amorous antics have been well-publicised, Lucian Freud gave few interviews to the press, fuelling further speculation and increasing interest in ongoing pictures that he was painting of the pregnant supermodel Kate Moss and a revealing self-portrait of himself aged 79. However, Freud did make an unprecedented public appeal and orchestrate a poster campaign to find a small portrait that he painted of Francis Bacon in the 1950s and which had been stolen from a British Council exhibition in Berlin in 1988. Some 2,500 'Wanted' posters were splashed all over Berlin offering a £100,000 reward for the portrait's safe return in time for the Tate exhibition, but it was never recovered.

Freud's great friend Francis Bacon, who died in 1992, was the subject of a lengthy High Court battle involving the trustees of Bacon's estate and allegations that the artist was blackmailed by Arne Glimcher, his former dealer in New York, and then swindled by his gallery, Marlborough Fine Art in London. However, an amicable settlement was reached, though not before £100 million had been spent on the trial and Bacon's heir, John Edwards, fell ill with lung cancer.

Notable deaths in the art world included Ralph Rumney, a writer and artist who founded the Situationist International movement in 1957; Kenneth Armitage, a sculptor known for representing Britain at the Venice Biennale with his semi-abstract bronze figures; F. N. Souza, India's most important and famous modern artist; French sculptress Niki de Saint Phalle, who created colourful, bulbous women; and Juan Muñoz, a Spanish sculptor who had recently completed an immense installation for the Tate Modern's Turbine Hall entrance space. The property developer and philanthropic art collector Sir Arthur Gilbert also died, leaving his impressive silver, gold and mosaic collection – worth over £100 million – to the refurbished Somerset House in London. In November 2001, Professor Sir Ernst Gombrich, possibly the most popular and popularising British scholar of art history, died aged 92. After fleeing Nazi occupation of his native Vienna and settling in London as a researcher, he published in 1950 *The Story of Art*, which went on to sell six million copies in 16 editions. He became a professor at Oxford and Cambridge universities and University College London as well as publishing many more art books, including *Art and Illusion*, *The Image and the Eye* and a collection of his lectures and criticisms, *Meditations on a Hobby Horse*.

One of the world's wealthiest and most secretive collectors and dealers, Daniel Wildenstein, died at 84. The Wildensteins, exiled Jews from the French province of Alsace, set up a famous gallery in New York, but never fully escaped allegations that they bought art looted from Jews by the Nazis. The former director of the American National Gallery of Art in Washington, Carter Brown, died from cancer but will be remembered as 'the populist patrician' who helped shape the growth and accessibility of US museums, largely due to his pioneering 'blockbuster' exhibitions of Egyptian art, Impressionist paintings, etc., that drew huge crowds.

OLD MASTERS

Britain's own blockbuster year of shows that began with the National Gallery's 'Vermeer and the Delft School' ended brightly with 'Paris: Capital of the Arts' at the Royal Academy (26 January–19 April 2002), a major Andy Warhol exhibition at the Tate Modern (7 February–1 April 2002) and a show of tiaras at the Victoria and Albert Museum (21 March–14 July 2002) that confounded all expectations. Hot on the heels of Warhol came the most weighty single exhibition of the year, 'Matisse Picasso', at the Tate Modern (11 May–18 August 2002). Curated by a team led by Picasso expert John Golding, the exhibition examined the relationship between the two modern masters, though rather than expounding on the rivalry between the painters, the exhibition highlighted their mutual admiration and influence, placing similar sized and themed works side-by-side.

Apart from Vermeer, other Old Masters on display included the 11 remaining fragments that made up Italian painter Massacio's Pisa altarpiece, gathered together for the first time from Pisa, Florence, Naples and Berlin by the National Gallery (11 September–11 November 2001).

Old Masters were put on trial by a revealing, but controversial book, *Rediscovering the Lost Techniques of the Old Masters*, and an accompanying television series by one of Britain's most famous artists, David Hockney. He declared that many painters from Van Eyck to Ingres used a camera obscura as well as lenses and mirrors to project a scene directly onto canvas in order to perfect their methods of picture-making. Hockney's 'conspiracy theory', as many saw it, stated that instead of killing off painting, photography actually sustained the practice for over 200 years, yet his book lacked the scientific and historical evidence to radically change the art history books. Hockney made the news again when he painted the opening to a letter addressed to the Chancellor, Gordon Brown, urging him to come to the financial aid of regional museums in Britain. Other notable artists, including Damien Hirst, Anish Kapoor, Anthony Caro and Rachel Whiteread, signed the petition, which called for an injection of £250 million into the 2,500 galleries and museums nationwide.

A 17th-century masterpiece, *The Massacre of the Innocents*, by Rubens was discovered, and fetched over £49.5 million at auction after languishing in the collection of an 89-year-old Austrian. This enormous sum was a record price for a British saleroom, making it the third most expensive painting ever sold, although the destination of the painting is unknown as the identity of the private client who bought it has not been revealed. A staggering £10.3 million, the most ever paid for a British painting, was achieved at Sotheby's for a portrait of Omai by Sir Joshua Reynolds. The June sales saw one of the world's tiniest paintings, by the 16th-century miniaturist Nicholas Hilliard, sell at Sotheby's for £233,750, nearly ten times its original estimate. At Christie's, a 2,000-year-old marble statue of Venus broke the world record price for antiquities, fetching almost £8 million.

AUCTION HOUSE SCANDAL

A blow for serious collectors came when it emerged that a painting bought for £1.5 million by F. Richard Drake was not by Sir Anthony Van Dyck, as stated by the dealer Thomas Agnew & Sons. Although Drake's claim that the gallery deceived him was accepted by the judge, there was documentation to say that the painting was more than likely from Van Dyck's studio but not by the master himself and so Drake was not recompensed. The message of the court's verdict was that experts can and will disagree and change their minds, but it is the unwary buyer that pays for these discrepancies of attribution.

More serious irregularities in the art market were revealed at the New York trials of the heads of Sotheby's and Christie's, Adolph Alfred Taubman and Sir Anthony Tennant respectively, who were found guilty of collusion over price-fixing, a scandal that rocked the auction-house world when it was first revealed. After the verdict on 5 December 2001, however, only Taubman was liable for punishment as Tennant was not resident in the US and could not be extradited under American criminal law. The illegal agreement between the 'Big Two' auction houses set a price for seller's commissions at auction in order to heighten profits in the early 1990s when revenue was lacklustre.

After 11 September 2001, the turnover of both auction houses was down by over 20 per cent, Christie's outselling Sotheby's $1.8 billion to $1.6 billion. More encouraging for the two auction houses was that they held their first-ever sales in Paris as, after years of wrangling, the French auction market finally opened to foreign competition. In the season's final round of post-war and contemporary art auctions held in London on 26–27 June 2002, pictures by Francis Bacon, Andy Warhol, Gerhard Richter and Miquel Barceló auctioned at Sotheby's came within a whisker of matching the record tally of £14,201,000 earned at the height of the art market boom in 1990.

DECLINING MARKET

Overall, Europe lost its supremacy in the art market to the US, according to a report by the European Fine Art Foundation, mainly because of high taxes and European Union bureaucracy. Since 1998, Europe has dropped 7 per cent in its share of the global art market and now accounts for just 45 per cent, losing out to the US's 47 per cent share. The British market has also suffered badly as its share dropped from 30 per cent in 1999 to 25 per cent in 2001. The report condemned 'the failure of the European Commission and many governments to recognise the art economy as a significant source of employment and export earnings'. In fact, the art market in Europe is currently worth around £8 billion a year and provides employment for 74,000 people in 29,000 businesses.

On a lighter note, a marble statue of Margaret Thatcher by Neil Simmons was unable to find a home; places in the Commons lobby are reserved for deceased prime ministers and the new Portcullis House could not take the immense weight of the piece. Unfortunately, a year after it was unveiled by Baroness Thatcher herself, the statue was brutally beheaded at a London art gallery by a theatre producer in a protest against global capitalism.

A controversial exhibition 'Body Worlds', featuring immaculately preserved human bodies, caused much consternation and was almost banned by the Department of Health. Although much of the argument centred around the artificially aesthetic nature of the anatomical display, many agreed that this was not, and should not be seen as, art.

ARTS BROADCASTING

UK arts broadcasting took a hammering despite a huge commitment from the BBC. The launch of its new flagship cultural channel BBC4 on 1 March 2002 failed to attract large viewing figures, partly because it is only available to digital TV subscribers. Artsworld, the digital arts and music channel which faced closure in the summer of 2002 has remained on air as a result of a new arrangement between its shareholders and BSkyB, its joint venture partner. John Hambley, chief executive, said: 'BSkyB have been a key partner in Artsworld since its inception and we are grateful for their continuing and imaginative support for a channel that remains unique in digital television'.

Broadcasting

TELEVISION

The year 2001–2 was a period of challenges for broadcasters on all fronts. The terrorist attacks in the US on 11 September 2001 were watched live on television by millions of horrified viewers and were, by a wide margin, the greatest single event to test the skill of television and radio producers. But it was not only international affairs, including the bombing of Afghanistan and a spate of renewed difficulties in the Middle East, that kept the broadcasters on their toes. On the national stage there was plenty of activity requiring television coverage. Broadcasters had to respond to the contrasting emotions generated by the death of the Queen Mother at Easter 2002 and, some two months later, the extended weekend of the Queen's Golden Jubilee celebrations. There was also the 2002 World Cup, which became another major television set piece as England progressed to the quarter-finals. Fans by the million gathered in front of the small screen, undeterred by the time difference from South Korea and Japan, where the games took place. Generally, the television and radio companies acquitted themselves with distinction in their coverage of these live events.

On the surface, it appeared to be business as usual for the BBC and its competitors as schedules were again dominated by soap operas and long-running hospital dramas. Behind the scenes, however, a new order was beginning to emerge as the BBC and, to a lesser extent, satellite broadcaster BSkyB increased their audience share. The Corporation's empire-building reached new heights as a string of digital services, on both television and radio, were launched. Encouraged by the Government, the BBC formed an unlikely alliance with BSkyB following the collapse of the pay-TV venture ITV Digital, in an attempt to take digital television to the two-thirds of British homes that have so far declined to sign up.

Channel 5 came of age and could no longer be dismissed by critics for catering to the lowest common denominator. The station won respect for screening low-budget arts and history documentaries early in the evening. At the same time, Channel 5 toned down its adult fare and was praised for screening two new high-quality US imports, *CSI* and *Law and Order*, on Saturday evenings, often a viewing desert. Beset by financial problems and a protracted hunt for a new chief executive, Channel 4, once the undisputed home of small-screen innovation, was less sure-footed than in the past.

Meanwhile, ITV, mired in the humiliation of losing around £1 billion on ITV Digital and a prolonged dip in advertising revenue, struggled to keep up, losing out for the first time ever to BBC1 in the ratings. Overall viewing figures for 2001 showed the BBC winning 26.8 per cent of the audience compared with the commercial channel's 26.7 per cent. Trailing BBC1 by a single decimal point disguised what a dismal year it had been for ITV's business, but creatively there were signs that ITV1 was willing to be more adventurous than BBC1, whose programming often echoed the highly competitive instincts of director-general Greg Dyke. However, ITV1's all-important autumn schedule got off to a poor start when the football highlights programme *Premiership*, shown mid-evening rather than in the traditional late-night slot, failed to generate a big audience.

Although the BBC triumphed in the ratings, the evidence suggests that television viewing per se is less popular than it was. However, radio, especially BBC

Radio, made further gains in popularity. Broadcasters blamed a new audience measurement system for the slump in television audiences but more objective voices wondered if television-watching was finally in decline. It might remain the nation's favourite pastime – more than 21 million people tuned in for the BBC's Christmas Day edition of *Only Fools and Horses* – but according to research published by the *Observer* in April 2002, year-on-year average viewing was down from around 28 hours a person a week to less than 25 hours.

COVERAGE OF 11 SEPTEMBER 2001

Inevitably, the appalling events of 11 September 2001 led to a surge in viewing as schedules were cleared on the main television channels to deliver live pictures of the collapse of the twin towers of the World Trade Center and the immediate aftermath. The coverage by all the main broadcasters – the BBC, ITN's programmes for ITV, Channels 4 and 5 and Sky News – was, on the whole, impressive. According to the BBC, 35 million people in the UK turned to its news services (on television, radio and online) on 11 September. Six months later, the BBC's Peter Sissons, presenter of the *Ten O'Clock News*, became embroiled in controversy when some newspaper critics, notably the *Daily Mail*, accused him of responding with insensitivity to the Queen Mother's death; that he chose to wear a burgundy tie for the occasion rather than the customary black tie was seized upon by the BBC's detractors as another symptom of declining standards. But Sissons' handling of 11 September as the presenter of the *Ten O'Clock News* struck the right note.

An international event on such a scale inevitably dominated the broadcasters' news agendas in the weeks following the attacks on New York and Washington. Radio 4's *Today* programme carried co-presentations from Kabul, Islamabad, Jerusalem, Washington, New York and Kuala Lumpur. Internationally, the BBC's World Service came into its own, not least in Afghanistan, where the corporation's services in Pashto and Persian became a lifeline for a population deprived of media on the Western model. Immediately following the first attack on the World Trade Center, the World Service English language service began the longest continuous broadcast in its history, lasting more than 40 hours.

As the significance of the attacks became apparent, special programmes were commissioned and existing plans were changed to accommodate the atmosphere of crisis. The musical line-up for the *Last Night of the Proms* was changed at the last minute. Inevitably, not all the coverage pleased all sections of the audience. An edition of the BBC's veteran current affairs show *Question Time*, broadcast on 13 September and featuring the US Ambassador as a panelist, was accused by some commentators of being 'anti-American'. The BBC governors later acknowledged that 'errors were made in the tone and timing' of the programme.

Overall, the television companies avoided the temptation of endlessly repeating the horrifying images of the twin towers collapsing, but there were some ill-judged moments. On 11 September, ITV1 showed footage of the attack in New York to the accompaniment of Gounod's *Judex*; as each building collapsed, a timpani roll was heard. Viewers complained. The industry watchdog, the Independent Television Commission, condemned the item as 'sick and tasteless'; ITN, the film's makers, claimed the juxtaposition of pictures and music was 'intended to provide a few moments for viewers to reflect'.

Following the attacks and the subsequent bombing of Afghanistan by the US, there was speculation that television would respond to this deterioration in world affairs by adopting a more serious approach in its factual programmes.

JOHN SIMPSON 'TAKES' KABUL

In fact, 11 September aside, there was no marked change in television's attitude to news or current affairs on the main channels. There was the odd exception; John Simpson's knowledge of Afghanistan helped the audience's understanding of a complex and closed society during the diplomatic and military campaign against Afghanistan. However, his entry into Kabul following the collapse of the Taliban led some critics to wonder why the BBC had allowed Simpson to become the centre of the story rather than ensuring he maintained his customary role of informed observer. Nearer to home, there was widespread praise for the BBC's political editor Andrew Marr, winner of numerous awards throughout the year, and for its Middle East correspondent, the perpetually flak-jacketed Orla Guerin, though some detected a pro-Palestinian bias in her reporting.

BBC1's flagship current affairs series *Panorama* continued to languish in its post-10.30 p.m. Sunday night slot, where most viewers ignored it. The old warhorse occasionally attracted notice, though, and two programmes that stood out were Michael Crick's compelling account of the Jeffrey Archer saga, *A Life of Lies*, and John Simpson's *Afghanistan: The Dark Ages*.

Broadcasters struggled in vain to find compelling new formats for current affairs. Their own research suggests it is not only teens and twenty-somethings who have little interest in political coverage on television; people in their 40s and 50s are also inclined to ignore programmes that gave airtime to politicians. This trend is particularly worrying for the BBC because of its public service obligations. Plans to axe the political interview show *On The Record* and replace it with a more ratings-friendly show were greeted with dismay in some quarters. The *Guardian* described it as 'Dyke's Dumb Idea' and demanded that the BBC governors veto the scheme.

DOCUMENTARY TAKES HIGH GROUND

While current affairs generally failed to engage sizeable audiences, it was heartening that channel executives were still prepared to push the boundaries of the documentary. Easily the most controversial of the year was BBC2's *The Hunt for Britain's Paedophiles*, a harrowing series filmed over two years which examined Scotland Yard's attempts to crack paedophile rings. The *Daily Mail*, usually the BBC's harshest critic, heaped praise on the film. BBC2 also scored with a series on Dickens presented by his biographer Peter Ackroyd. Another BBC2 documentary, *The Century of the Self*, made by Adam Curtis, director of the BAFTA award-winning *The Mayfair Set*, demonstrated how a well-thought-out television series could still offer fresh insights as the programme examined the way that Freud's ideas have been used by those in power to manage and control the masses.

Similarly mind-stretching was BBC4, the new digital channel offering deliberately challenging material. Launched in March 2002, commentators praised the newcomer for its rich diet of international news, drama, world cinema, documentaries and arts programmes. The problem was that because BBC4 is available only on digital services, the majority of people, who have already had to pay the BBC licence fee, cannot receive it. Another potential difficulty was that sceptics wondered if BBC4 would be used as a 'dumping ground' for the kind of serious fare once available on BBC2.

The year also saw the dawn of two other new BBC digital television services, CBeebies and CBBC, both for children. However, plans for a new entertainment station, BBC3, aimed at the under-35s, were put on hold after the Government suggested that the offering would damage existing commercial competitors operating in the same market.

BBC CRACKS DRAMA

Television is first and foremost an entertainment medium and during 2001–2 drama remained the backbone of the two main terrestrial channels' schedules. There was, however, evidence that, in keeping with television's somewhat reduced status, small-screen fiction is no longer the big attraction that it used to be. Or maybe commissioners are backing the wrong kind of shows.

Unquestionably, audiences are down. Not so long ago, any ITV or BBC1 drama that won audiences of eight million or more was regarded as a success by network chiefs. In these straitened times, any show watched by six million is reckoned to have made an impact. Even an established ITV success like the racy women's prison drama *Bad Girls* was watched by audiences of at least a million less than a year ago. 'People are fed up with the same pastiches, copies. The great Morses (*Inspector Morse*) and Frosts (*A Touch of Frost*) are dying away', Channel 5's programme director Kevin Lygo told the *Guardian*. What Lygo failed to point out was that his network could not afford to make drama.

An interesting case study was provided by ITV1's remake of *The Forsyte Saga*. The original BBC version of John Galsworthy's epic chronicling the fortunes of a late 19th-century London merchant family, first screened by BBC2 in 1967, was one of the great success stories of television drama. More than 18 million viewers watched when *The Forsyte Saga*, starring Kenneth More and Nyree Dawn Porter, graduated to BBC1 in 1968. Something akin to Forsyte mania gripped the nation; pubs were empty when the programme was screened and the characters' lives became a national talking point. However, in 2002, with dozens of viewing choices, Granada's remake of Galsworthy's story attracted an average audience of 7.8 million. Gina McKee played Irene while Damian Lewis was cast as the loathsome Soames. Critics found much to admire in the series, but the verdict overall was that the original was superior, and doubts were expressed that the infamous rape scene was too explicit.

Ironically, *The Forsyte Saga* faced direct competition from BBC1's remake of what had originally been an ITV show, the comedy drama *Auf Wiedersehen, Pet*. It was a big hit, and further proof that after years of struggling to match ITV in popular drama, BBC1 had finally cracked it. To rub in the competitive advantage, *EastEnders*, its fourth weekly episode firmly established, could do little wrong, while *Coronation Street* struggled. Radical changes to the cast and writing team were introduced in an attempt to revive the veteran soap. Bet Lynch (played by Julie Goodyear) returned and there was a part for one of Britain's best-loved actresses, Maureen Lipman.

SPOOKS SPARKS SPY MANIA

Over on BBC1 the spy drama *Spooks* emerged as one of the year's most popular new series. Heavily promoted, *Spooks*, whose cast included Peter Firth and Hugh Laurie, depicted a world of fictional spies very different from those created by Cold War writers Graham Greene and John Le Carre. The MI5 staff portrayed in the series were sharp-suited and deadly efficient. Controversy arose over a scene involving a member of the team who was killed when her head was plunged into a fat fryer. *Spooks'* success reportedly led to a surge in recruits applying to MI5.

Another new series pitched squarely at the under-45s was ITV1's *Footballers' Wives*, described as 'high quality schlock' by one reviewer. This glamorous fantasy was big on sex, drink and drugs. The focus was firmly on the off-pitch antics of the fictional Earls Park team and their long-suffering women. Its characters, including the gloriously named Tanya Turner and Chardonnay Lane, quickly became fodder for the tabloids but, considering the programme's subject matter, ratings were disappointing, despite the casting of former soap star Gillian Taylforth and ex-Hollyoaks actor Gary Lucy.

ITV1 DARES TO BE DIFFERENT

If *Footballers' Wives* represented a new benchmark for trash television, elsewhere there were encouraging signs that ITV1's drama was increasingly prepared to shun the predictable and take some risks. Certainly there was no shortage of star vehicles, featuring such tried-and tested television thespians as Caroline Quentin (playing the mother of a murdered 14-year-old girl in the two-parter *Blood Strangers*) and Amanda Burton in legal drama *Helen West*. Sadly, John Thaw, one of ITV's biggest stars, died in February 2002 from cancer; Thaw had once again proved his enduring appeal in autumn 2001 in the successful one-off drama *Buried Treasure*, where he was cast as a middle-aged widower left in charge of his mixed-race, eight-year-old granddaughter.

As so much of BBC1's drama was designed to generate high ratings, ITV1's attempts to offer a real alternative were especially welcome. Red Productions' *Bob and Rose* was genuinely original. Starring Alan Davies as a gay man who falls for a woman (played by Lesley Sharpe), reviewers praised the script and the high quality of the acting. Over on BBC2, the black parenthood drama *Baby Father* was cheered by critics for offering a fresh perspective, albeit belatedly, on contemporary family life. There was widespread admiration for Granada's *Bloody Sunday*, starring James Nesbitt and Tim Pigott-Smith, a documentary-style recreation of the Northern Ireland shootings timed to coincide with their 30th anniversary, and almost disbelief that ITV1 was prepared to give airtime to a version of *Othello*, starring Christopher Eccleston as Iago.

The Jury, featuring Derek Jacobi and Antony Sher, was an unusual and admired twist on a television staple, the courtroom drama, but failed to win a big audience. Also inventive was an ITV soap, *Always and Everyone*, but viewers were unconvinced and the programme was axed. An undoubted highlight was BBC1's *Bedtime* starring Timothy West, Sheila Hancock, Meera Syal and Stephen Tompkinson as the occupants of three very different homes in south-west London. Written and directed by television veteran Andy Hamilton, this engaging and subversive black comedy of suburban manners was a rare example of a successful small-screen drama that owed little to the film-maker's art. Less successful was *Up In Town*, a series of monologues on BBC2 starring Joanna Lumley, which promised more than it delivered and suffered from the inevitable comparisons with Alan Bennett.

Drama based on literary classics was perhaps less to the fore than in the past. David Suchet was outstanding as Augustus Melmotte in BBC1's adaptation of Trollope's *The Way We Live Now*, scripted by Andrew Davies. Tony Marchant adapted *Crime and Punishment* for BBC2 to mixed reviews, while Peter 'Columbo' Falk made an appearance in an entertaining version of Conan Doyle's *The Lost World*, full of special effects.

Everyone agreed that Albert Finney was superb as Winston Churchill in *The Gathering Storm*, a summer

highlight on BBC2. Some considered the film's US partner had exerted a negative influence by forcing the film to adopt a less than erudite view of the international crises leading up to the outbreak of war in 1939. The Second World War provided the background for the high-octane *Band of Brothers*, hailed by critics as one of the year's must-see programmes. The *Telegraph's* Stephen Pile said the serial, a Stephen Spielberg–Tom Hanks production, was 'a major and significant piece of television'. Its impact, however, was embarrassing for the BBC because it had paid a great deal of money to co-produce the serial with the US's HBO but then shunted *Band of Brothers* from BBC1 to BBC2, fearing that not enough people would tune in. Equally memorable was another drama inspired by the Second World War, *Conspiracy*, an enthralling depiction of the infamous secret meeting of senior Nazis that planned the strategy for what became the Holocaust. Another collaboration with HBO, the film starred Kenneth Branagh and Stanley Tucci.

SIMPSONS EARN TOP DOLLAR

The sheer ambition of both these films emphasised that British programme makers and television executives can no longer afford to patronise – not that they ever could – the achievements of their US colleagues. In fact, as the year progressed, it became evident that all UK television broadcasters (not least the BBC) need more than ever the contribution that US shows and US money make to their schedules. Channel 4's willingness to pay a record figure of £600,000 an episode to secure terrestrial rights to *The Simpsons*, whose fans included no less a figure than the Archbishop of Canterbury, Dr Rowan Williams, spoke volumes of Britain's debt to American talent, largely unacknowledged by the broadcasters themselves. As far as many commentators were concerned, the most important drama in Channel 4's portfolio was not the tired soap *Brookside* or the limited *Teachers*, but *The West Wing*, a highly cerebral, US-made drama set behind the closed doors of the White House.

IN DEEP WITH THE BLUE PLANET

Two of the year's most popular factual programmes, BBC1's natural history magnum opus *The Blue Planet*, and *Walking With Beasts*, the sequel to *Walking With Dinosaurs*, were joint investments with America's Discovery Channel. Reputedly the most expensive wildlife series ever, *The Blue Planet* was an eight-part visual feast. Up to 12 million viewers watched agog as Sir David Attenborough presented remarkable film of the world's oceans and their jaw-dropping contents. Some suggested the programme's high ratings were explained by 11 September; people were seeking escape and solace in the wonders of the 'Great Outdoors'. More difficult to explain was why *Walking With Beasts* achieved an even higher audience. Almost 14 million switched on to watch the computer-generated creatures from another age.

Throughout the year, history of a more recent kind was much in evidence. John Willis, former programme director at Channel 4, summed up the trend when he wrote in the *Guardian*: 'Given lift-off by the helium of David Starkey and Simon Schama, television history is hot'. On Channel 4, Starkey's *The Six Wives of Henry VIII* topped the station's ratings, drawing in excess of four million viewers. Another Channel 4 series, *Plague, Fire, War and Treason*, featured dramatic reconstructions of the Great Plague and the Great Fire of London. Producers endlessly recycled the more recent past. *What the Victorians Did for Us* played on BBC2; documentaries examining the Falklands War, to mark the

tenth anniversary of the conflict, were shown by both Channels 4 and 5; and there was acclaim for *Battlefields*, presented by Richard Holmes on BBC2. This was just the tip of the history iceberg, so all-pervasive that television's preoccupation with the past was satirised by BBC2's *We Are History* starring Marcus Brigstocke as David Oxley (BA Hons).

Our obsession with our own history coalesced with another recent small-screen phenomenon, the reality show, in the Channel 4 hit series *The Edwardian Country House*, a follow-up to *The 1900 House* and *The 1940s House*. This was an upstairs, downstairs saga of early 20th-century life, recreated in a grand house. Critics generally approved of the programme, but doubts were raised over another small-screen recreation of the past, BBC2's *The Trench*, in which a group of volunteers attempted to experience the horrors of life as an ordinary soldier in the First World War. Writing in the *Radio Times*, E. Jane Dixon spoke for many when she said: 'To serve up a theme-park approximation of that agony in the name of history is crass; to serve it up as entertainment is unforgivable.'

There was greater unease regarding the third series of *Big Brother*, the most successful yet, with more than nine million viewers tuning in for the final programme. In order to achieve these high ratings, commentators suggested that the programme's maker had gone too far by humiliating ordinary people in the cause of entertainment. One contestant, Jade, was filmed stripping naked while drunk. 'Social observation has yielded to darker impulses – to stir conflict, polarise and humiliate', suggested a leader in the *Guardian*.

RADIO

Digital radio continued to be ignored by the great majority of listeners. This was despite the launch of several new services during the year, including a portfolio of BBC digital radio stations, and the arrival of sets retailing at £99. But digital radio aside, the year was a period of remarkable achievement by radio. Research published in February 2002 suggested that audiences now spend nearly 25 hours a week tuning in. Following the 11 September attacks, Radios 4 and 5 recorded record ratings; the audience for the latter grew further during the World Cup. Radio 2 and Classic FM also surged upward. Meanwhile, after a period of stability, Radio 1 experienced a drop in popularity. The BBC's overall share of the radio audience was 52.6 per cent against the commercial sector's 45.5 per cent. Listening via the Internet continued to grow; research published by the *Guardian* suggested that 9.3 per cent of people tune in to radio over the net at least sometimes.

Commentators seized on the fact that while the proliferation of television channels has led to an overall drop in viewing, the growth in the number of radio stations is having the opposite effect. There were more than 250 UK radio stations at the last count and more are planned. During the year, the BBC launched two of its five new digital services; Five Live Sports Extra, a part-time overspill from the main station, made its debut in February 2002 with coverage of Manchester United against Sunderland. The following month, 6 Music took to the air, broadcasting a mix of live recordings from the BBC's archives alongside records from the 1970s, 1980s and 1990s. Phil Jupitus and Liz Kershaw were among the new arrival's DJs.

Jenny Abramsky, the BBC's director of radio and music, told media reporters that radio's intimacy was the key to the medium's burgeoning success. 'It is a very personal relationship', she said. 'It gets under your skin. I've always believed that people feel quite passionate about radio in a way they don't feel about television. And radio is a feeder of your passion: the more radio offers, the more people come to it.'

RADIO 4 GROWS

The truth of Abramsky's analysis was borne out by the experience of Radio 4. Its flagship *Today* programme increased its audience dramatically during the year, adding a million extra listeners in the last quarter of 2001. This was explained by the appetite for high-quality news and current affairs in the wake of 11 September. Positioned dead-centre on the spectrum between the Government's alleged control-freakery and the BBC's defence of 'the public interest', in such a politically charged period and with continued weak opposition from the Conservative Party, clashes between leading politicians and *Today* were inevitable.

When in spring 2002 the programme decided to drop its controversial Saturday Essay, provided by two novelists from opposite ends of the political spectrum, Frederick Forsyth and Will Self, the former accused the BBC of axing his spot because of his anti-Government views; with the Labour-supporting Gavyn Davies *in situ* as BBC's new chairman, many of the BBC's critics regarded Broadcasting House as being too close to the Government for its own good. Forsyth was one of them. He said: 'There are guys at the heart of New Labour who don't like free speech. To be contradicted or mocked is not what they want.' *Today*'s editor Rod Liddle denied the charge, explaining that Saturday Essay had 'run out of steam'. But *Today* was attacked frequently by the Government's representatives. As part of a running feud with the programme, Labour accused *Today*'s interviewers of treating politicians of every party like 'consummate liars trying to line their own pockets'.

The year saw the retirement of *Today*'s longest-serving presenter, Sue MacGregor. As a farewell gift, the BBC honoured MacGregor with an appearance on another Radio 4 institution, *Desert Island Discs*. Her *Today* colleague John Humphreys said she was irreplaceable. The programme was back in the news in the summer when it was reported that its *Thought For The Day* item was being toughened up following criticism that it had become bland. The *Daily Telegraph* claimed that the programme had turned into 'an infuriating parody of faith with a goldfish outlook on the world'. Following 11 September, the BBC had reputedly told speakers that it wanted more minority voices to contribute to *Thought For The Day*.

Away from the hurly burly of politics and religion, the network's unmatched schedule of drama and entertainment programmes attracted praise. One highlight was a repeat of an adaptation of *The Lord of the Rings* to coincide with the première of the feature film. Starring Sir Ian Holm, and first broadcast more than 20 years ago, the series' 13-week run attracted almost a million listeners a week, an unusually high audience for a radio drama and the highest audience for a radio drama in ten years. Other dramatic highlights included a reworking of Dickens's *Little Dorrit* starring Ian McKellen, a new Alan Bennett play, *Hymn*, Carol Shields's *The Stone Diaries*, broadcast over a single week, and Ian Curteis's *Falklands Play*, originally dropped by the BBC in 1986 and also shown on BBC4 in the spring.

RADIO 2'S FAB FOUR

The period was another good one for Radio 2, voted station of the year by the Sony Awards for the second year running, perhaps undeservedly according to some critics, who thought it was time to celebrate the achievements of another station. Even the station's breakfast presenter Terry Wogan seemed to think that the Sony judges had been over-generous to Radio 2. After the awards ceremony, he told listeners live on air: 'We're station of the year, the universe, and it's only Friday. This is not a music station. It's a personality-plus station, with added music.' But the network won two million new listeners. Radio 2's audience share of 15.7 per cent was outstripping all rivals, BBC and commercial.

More confident than ever, Radio 2's status as Britain's most popular station was reflected in a special *Radio Times* cover in the summer. This portrayed four of the service's most popular DJs – Terry Wogan, Jonathan Ross, Mark Lamarr and Steve Wright – photographed in a pastiche of the *With The Beatles* album sleeve photograph. Their celebrity was not quite on the scale of the Fab Four, but Steve Wright's show is now listened to by almost 13 million people a week. Radio critic Peter Barnard summed up the breadth of the station's appeal when he said: 'The quality of the presenters and the range of music, from light classical to rock to jazz to reggae to folk, has dragged the average age of listeners back to nearer 40 than 60.'

But the year did not pass without embarrassment for Radio 2. Jimmy Young, presenter of his daytime show for 28 years, was at the centre of a protracted row over his eventual successor. The DJ Nicky Campbell gave an interview to the *Daily Telegraph* in which he claimed he had been chosen to succeed the 80-year-old Young, knighted in the New Year's Honours. However, Young's departure had not been announced at that point and the BBC was in the throes of renegotiating his contract. Subsequently, Young's replacement was named as Newsnight presenter Jeremy Vine. Young is due to start a new weekend show in 2003. Campbell's gaffe led to a rebuke from Greg Dyke who said: 'Some BBC on-air talents seem to think it is fair game for them to criticise the BBC while continuing to receive its money. Actions like this do enormous damage to the BBC's reputation and while this might have been tolerated as acceptable behaviour in the past, I want everyone to know that it will not be acceptable from now on.'

Compared to these shenanigans, Radio 3, striving to consolidate its growing reputation for jazz and world music, had a relatively quiet year. There was, however, one important innovation when the network launched the World Music Awards in January 2002. Hailed as 'a landmark event' by critics, the awards involved a live link-up with musicians in studios around the world, including what the BBC claimed as an historic live broadcast from Kabul. In addition, the year saw the first BBC Jazz Awards, in collaboration with Radio 2.

At the opposite end of the entertainment spectrum, there were indications that Radio 1 was struggling to retain the affections of the nation's youth with audience share decreasing to around 9 per cent. Sara Cox's breakfast show, criticised for a risqué live interview with the spoof rapper Ali G in spring 2002, lost almost one million listeners. The BBC said the World Cup was partly to blame. The so-called 'ladette' was hoping that her popularity would revive in the autumn, thereby regaining from Terry Wogan her status as the UK's biggest breakfast radio show. Wogan's enduring appeal was underlined in January when *Radio Times* readers voted him the owner of British radio's most popular male voice. Radio 4's newsreader Charlotte Green had the most popular female voice, pushing Sue MacGregor into second place and Classic FM's Natalie Wheen into third.

CLASSIC FM SCORES

In the commercial sector, the biggest success story was Classic FM. Having gained nearly one million new listeners, the service is now attempting to broaden its appeal by persuading more younger people to tune in. With this aim, ITN newsreader Katie Derham and Stephen Fry were signed up, Derham, an accomplished violinist, to present a new Saturday afternoon show, and Fry to front an irreverent 20-part series chronicling 1,000 years of classical music. Plans were also announced to compete head-on with Radio 3 by broadcasting a daily evening concert in its entirety rather than Classic FM's usual approach of playing excerpts.

In London, the most competitive radio market in Britain, the station was more popular than Radios 1 and 2. In fact, despite the BBC's strong performance overall in radio, London remained something of an Achilles' heel for the broadcaster; its GLR station achieved an audience share of less than 1 per cent. Despite the competition from Classic FM, Capital's breakfast show, hosted by Chris Tarrant, continued to dominate the airwaves, attracting over a million more listeners than his nearest rival. While the World Cup helped lift Radio 5 Live's audience share by around 200,000 extra listeners, rival station Talk Sport held its own during the year, despite not having rights to live World Cup games; its audience share increased by 0.1 per cent to 1.8 per cent. BBC Radio was certainly on a roll, but in terms of audience share, the country's most popular station was Radio Borders, a commercial station serving Berwick-upon-Tweed, Selkirk, Peebles and Eyemouth, and netting 44 per cent of available listeners.

It was not a good year for Virgin Radio. Since Chris Evans's departure, nothing had gone right for the station; audiences plunged and in March the station was fined a record £75,000 by the Radio Authority after DJ John Holmes, subsequently sacked, encouraged a nine-year old girl to repeat a bizarre sexually explicit phrase. Censuring Virgin, the Radio Authority chairman Richard Hooper expressed 'grave concern' over the station's failure to have effective supervision in place.

While the Queen Mother's death brought the BBC some criticism over its television coverage, commercial radio made a major error when news supplier Independent Radio News failed to provide the news on time because of a technical hitch. IRN's obituary should have been relayed to listeners at 5.52 p.m. immediately following the announcement from Buckingham Palace. But the mistake meant the tribute was not transmitted until the 6 p.m. news bulletin. 'We have to accept that it was not IRN's finest hour', admitted IRN editor Jon Godel in a memo sent to the company's 258 client stations. But then it had been a challenging year.

Conservation and Heritage

THE NATURAL ENVIRONMENT

FOOT-AND-MOUTH DISEASE

The foot-and-mouth epidemic of 2001 had possibly the most dramatic effect on the countryside since the myxomatosis outbreak of 1953. Although the epidemic's most significant implications for wildlife will depend on what changes are made as a result of it, English Nature produced a report on the immediate effects of the slaughter policy and movement restrictions of livestock. There were many anecdotal reports of birds nesting closer to footpaths, and of deer venturing out in full daylight. In the New Forest, lapwings enjoyed an unusually favourable nesting season because of the restrictions on walkers and (especially) their dogs. Ungrazed pastures and hillsides saw an almost unprecedented blooming of buttercups and other wild flowers, and magnificent sweeps of flowering heather. But areas where livestock was confined were more closely grazed than usual; lambs on the island of Lundy, for example, could not be taken to market and so the pasture was overgrazed, with the loss of some colonies of the unique Lundy cabbage. The loss of hefted sheep flocks (i.e. those bred for generations in the same area of land) may lead to restocking problems and consequently a respite for the overgrazed hill pastures of the north Pennines, Borders and mid-Wales. The epidemic has certainly focused attention on the overstocking of the uplands as a result of livestock subsidy payments, which has had the effect of turning so many heather moors and flower-rich grassland into close-cropped wildlife deserts.

With the reorganisation of the old Ministry of Agriculture, Fisheries and Food into a more holistic Department for Environment, Food and Regional Affairs (DEFRA), more radical changes to the farming system are being considered, and these will have fundamental consequences for wildlife. To farm the hills more sustainably, subsidies will have to shift from food production to landscape objectives, for example by buying out sheep quotas and effectively paying farmers not to graze sheep on vulnerable land. In future, upland farmers may need to become entrepreneurial land managers, providing the sights and sounds that tourists come to see.

CLIMATE CHANGE

Late autumns, mild winters, early springs and wet summers have become the norm in Britain in recent years. Monitoring shows that bud-burst and the appearance of spring butterflies and moths are occurring earlier. Recording schemes show that some species are extending their range northwards; the red admiral butterfly now regularly overwinters in Britain. Climate change is upon us, and seems to be more rapid than expected.

The Environmental Change Institute at Oxford has produced a computer model predicting the effects of climate change on a range of species and habitats. These are based on the 'climatic envelope' in which each species lives, and assumes that they will increase or decrease according to whether the 'envelope' expands or is squeezed. The future seems bright for some southern species, like the nuthatch or Dartford warbler, but

correspondingly bleak for arctic-alpine species confined to cold climates and mountain tops. The shallow-rooted beech is threatened by drought and being toppled by gales. Some butterflies might be expected to do well in a warmer climate, but they have become too rare and isolated by arable land to take advantage of it. Rising sea-levels will engulf salt-marshes and estuaries along the east and south coast of England, but compensation for lost coastal habitats may be possible through 'managed retreat', in which fields near the sea are sacrificed.

Added to the changing chemical environment of soils and freshwater, with their heavy loads of nitrogen and phosphorus, and the increasing problem of invasive species, the overall picture is one of increased instability. Whether climate change is an opportunity or a disaster depends on the species, though it is the more mobile (and already common) species that will be able to profit from it. Conservationists are putting a brave face on it, pinning their faith on habitat restoration and more sustainable methods of farming; less optimistic prognoses are not encouraged.

TREES – UPS AND DOWNS

There are more trees in Britain today than at any time since the Middle Ages, according to the Forestry Commission, which completed a census of trees in England in 2001. In England there are 1,300 million trees, or 25 trees for each member of the population, covering 8.4 per cent of the land area; a century ago, coverage was only 5 per cent of the land area. Oak is the commonest tree, and two-thirds of English woods consist of hardwoods or mixed woods. Despite the ravages of Dutch elm disease and felling during the two world wars, Britain's timber estate looks in good order. Most of the increase is due to plantation forestry, most recently in multi-purpose initiatives like the community forests and the National Forest in the Midlands.

On the other hand, the health of individual trees is far from good. In 2002 there was a scare when a particularly virulent disease known as Sudden Oak Death was detected at several tree nurseries in eastern England, apparently spread from shrubs imported from the Netherlands or Germany. The disease, which is caused by a fungus which spreads in moist soil, has killed thousands of native oaks on the Pacific coast of the US. Characteristic symptoms are a reddish ooze on the trunks, and the early browning of leaves. The disease can kill a tree in a single season. In the wake of the foot-and-mouth epidemic, Britain was quick to ban imports of untreated oak timber from affected countries. Experiments carried out in quarantine conditions by Forestry Commission scientists suggest that British oaks, which are a different species to the American ones, may be resistant to the disease.

British oaks are already suffering from a condition known as oak die-back, also caused by a fungus. Signs include a premature reduction of the crown, with dead branches protruding from the foliage, and watery sap-runs on the trunk. The disease is hard to distinguish from natural ageing but seems to be shortening the lives of many trees. Alder and willow have also been badly hit by infectious fungal and bacterial diseases. Nearly 14 per cent of Britain's alders have died, and the Forestry Commission now advises against planting the species. The increase of fungal diseases may possibly be linked with climate change, especially wet summers. Other

suspected factors are nitrogen enrichment in the soil, and that nursery trees might have less disease resistance. There has been little preventative action, although the Forestry Commission has reserve powers to fell trees to form a cordon sanitaire around infected areas.

CLASH ON THE HEATHS

Britain is said to have 20 per cent of the earth's lowland heathland, although this amounts to only 58,000 hectares, mostly in Hampshire, Dorset and Cornwall. About three-quarters of the heaths existing a century ago have been built on or converted to farmland. Southern heathland is the main or sole habitat for a large number of plants, animals and insects, many of them rare; famous ones include the sand lizard, smooth snake and silver-studded blue butterfly. Unfortunately, many heaths are in poor condition, having become scrub-invaded, damaged by repeated fires or used as dumping grounds. A £26-million restoration project, part-funded by the Heritage Lottery Fund and the European Union, is bent on reintroducing hardy livestock to maintain the heaths (which include natural grassland and bog as well as heather) in the desired condition.

Despite this, heaths are still under pressure from new housing. The attractive nature of heaths, added to the proximity of many of them to growing towns like Poole and Verwood, draws the interest of developers and local councils hard-pressed to meet housing targets. In 2001, Purbeck Council gave planning permission for a large housing development around Holton Heath in Dorset, part of which is a National Nature Reserve. The risk to the heath comes from the inevitable increase in fires and the disturbance to wildlife by dogs and cats, as well as attrition from roads and gardens. Objections were made by English Nature, the RSPB and Dorset Wildlife Trust, and the result was a public inquiry which was expected to run until late 2002. Holton Heath is seen as a test case, with implications for heathlands as a whole. The conservationists hope the outcome will send a strong signal to local authorities that building on our remaining wild heathlands is no longer acceptable.

FENLAND RECREATED

Only small pockets of original wild fenland remain in East Anglia. Most of the Fens were drained long ago and reclaimed for growing crops; the area has some of the most fertile soil in Britain. Although the best surviving fenlands are now nature reserves, they are too small and too isolated to form a safe refuge for rare species. The long list of species that have died out there is headed by the large copper and swallowtail butterflies (though the latter still flies at the Norfolk Broads). Until recently, farming in the Fens was too profitable and the land too expensive for conservation bodies to do much to protect it, but this situation is changing. The National Trust has doubled the size of its holding at Wicken Fen – one of Britain's oldest and most closely studied nature reserves – and restored some of it to wet grassland and marsh. In the longer term, the Trust hopes to transform up to 3,000 hectares of farmland to fen, thus recreating a wet, marshy landscape not seen since the mid-19th century.

Meanwhile, the aggregate company Hansons has begun to hand over old gravel pits and surrounding land to the RSPB for restoration to reedbed and wet pasture. The RSPB already owns a former farm near Lakenheath, Suffolk, which it has restored to an approximation of wild fenland by flooding land and planting reeds. This new acquisition should eventually form the largest area of reedbed in Britain, and enable the Government to achieve its target for this priority habitat.

The 'flagship' species for fenland restoration is the bittern, an endangered species whose numbers had declined to fewer than 20 breeding pairs. The aim is to build up their number to a more sustainable 60 pairs by creating more reedbeds. Fortunately, reeds are relatively easy to cultivate once the land has been flooded to a suitable depth – the operation is not unlike planting rice. A network of dykes and pools is needed to attract the bittern's favourite fishy prey, eels and rudd. Other forms of wildlife also benefit, of course. It is hoped that the otter will return, along with characteristic species like the marsh harrier and bearded tit. The new fens will not be as rich in wildlife as the old, which evolved naturally over thousands of years, but they will help to connect the isolated cores of old fen and make them easier to maintain. It will also make the arable plains between Cambridge, Ely and Huntingdon more attractive to the visitor and so diversify the rural economy.

PEATLAND PRESERVED

Peat extraction has finally ceased at two of Britain's most important peatland sites, Thorne Moors near Doncaster, and Wedholme Flow in Cumbria. At a third site, Hatfield Moor in South Yorkshire, extraction is to be phased out over the next two years. The deal will safeguard the remains of 4,100 hectares of peatland. The Scotts Company, the US-based company that owns the sites, was compensated for loss of rights by the UK government to the tune of £17 million. The company, which is committed to developing more sustainable alternatives to peat, will now assist English Nature to restore the site to a condition as close as possible to its original state. The handover follows years of lobbying by conservation pressure groups, who argued that industrial peat-milling was destroying the sites and offering no chance for natural regeneration to take place. The clincher was the Government's giving the go-ahead to English Nature to designate all three sites under EU legislation as Special Areas of Conservation (SACs), a move that would require the cessation of unsustainable activities like peat-milling. English Nature and RSPB have also called for the development of alternative forms of growing media and soil conditioners, like green compost.

FROG DISASTER

Large numbers of British frogs have fallen victim to a disease called ranavirus, believed to come from America. The symptoms include reddened legs, sores, the loss of hands and feet, and general emaciation. First noticed in London garden ponds in the mid-1980s, the disease has since spread over much of England, though it is most prominent in the south-east. In the worst incident, some 2,000 dead or dying frogs were counted. The disease has probably been spread from pond to pond by gardeners stocking their ponds with frogspawn or tadpoles. Scientists studying the epidemic believe the virus was brought to Britain in goldfish imported from the US. The warm, shallow waters of garden ponds form ideal conditions for the virus to multiply, peaking in late summer.

Frog numbers are likely to remain low for up to five years after the outbreak. Unfortunately the disease is also carried by American bullfrogs, which are becoming established in parts of the south-east. The advice of the Wildlife Trusts is to refrain from stocking garden ponds with frogs in case it assists the spread of the disease.

OSPREYS BREEDING IN ENGLAND

In 2001, ospreys nested in two places in England for the first time in 150 years. One nest became a popular attraction at Bassenthwaite in the Lake District, where up to 20,000 visitors were able to watch the birds from a nearby viewpoint. A chick was successfully reared and took its first flight in August 2001. This nest was a natural one, and a sign that the bird is increasing its range southwards; ospreys have nested in Scotland since 1959. The other nest crowned a four-year project, led by the RSPB and the Leicestershire Wildlife Trust, to introduce ospreys to Rutland Water in the east Midlands. The male bird was one of several cage-reared nearby that had returned after migration. Again, a single chick was successfully reared.

Rutland Water was chosen for the introduction partly because it is the high-profile venue for the annual British Birdwatching Fair, but also because ospreys regularly halt there for a day or two on their way northwards in the spring. In 1994, a pair remained there all summer. The reservoir is well-stocked with suitable fish, and the surrounding woods offer potential nesting habitat. The bird would probably have nested there sooner or later, but the decision was taken to speed up the process. Between 1996 and 2001, osprey chicks taken under licence from nests in Scotland were reared at Rutland Water. Food was left out for them and artificial nest platforms built to attract visiting birds. A radio transmitter was attached to each bird to track its winter journeys in southern Europe and Africa.

The bird world is divided over the merits of an expensive introduction process, especially as the osprey is increasing its range without human assistance. It is admitted that the Rutland Water project is more about winning favourable publicity and setting up a tourist attraction than conservation per se. Many argue that the money would be better spent looking after habitats benefiting all species rather than a few large, popular ones. However, introduction projects of this sort are probably here to stay. All being well, beavers will soon be released in Scotland, and there is gathering momentum for a project to reintroduce the lynx, lost from these islands for 2,000 years.

CHOUGH REDIVIVUS

The chough, a member of the crow family distinguished by its bright red legs and curved bill, has nested in Cornwall for the first time since 1952. This bird, which has long been associated with Cornwall and appears on the county arms, feeds mainly in short-grazed pasture near the coast on large insects and grubs. Intensive agriculture destroyed much of its favoured habitat and the chough survives only in the far west, notably Anglesey, Islay and the Isle of Man.

Changes towards less intensive agriculture in parts of Cornwall led a group of ornithologists to prepare the ground for the chough's reintroduction. Birds reared in captivity at Paradise Park in Hayle were to have been released in spring 2001, but the release was prevented by the outbreak of the foot-and-mouth epidemic. In the meantime, five wild choughs turned up out of the blue, and at least one pair has nested, producing four young. This may prove to be the start of a natural colonisation of Cornwall, probably by choughs from Brittany. The reintroduction project has consequently been put on hold, but those concerned can congratulate themselves that, partly through their efforts, Cornwall is a more suitable habitat for choughs than for many years past.

UNDESIRABLES IN THE HEBRIDES

The spread of North American mink over much of Britain has had serious consequences for some native mammals and birds. In the south, the main victim has been the water vole, which in ten years has gone from a common to an endangered species, mainly owing to mink predation. In the northern isles and Outer Hebrides, where the mink escaped from fur-farms, the threat is to ground-nesting birds, especially those that nest in colonies, like terns and black-headed gulls. There is also anxiety about the survival of rare birds like the corncrake and black-headed diver.

Mink are spreading in the Hebrides; long established on Lewis and Harris, animals have now colonised the next islands in the chain, Benbecula and North Uist. Efforts to eradicate mink from these two islands before they become too firmly established have begun. Scottish Natural Heritage estimates it will take five years to trap and shoot every mink on North Uist, estimated at 200 breeding females. In the longer term, it would like to eradicate the estimated 10,000 to 15,000 mink on Lewis and Harris, though this would need a huge and sustained trapping effort. Meanwhile, the Environment Agency has begun to cull mink in East Anglia.

No one loves the mink, but the removal of another creature that is proving troublesome, the hedgehog, is more controversial. Hedgehogs have been introduced to various islands where they were naturally absent, in the case of South Uist by a gardener looking for a solution to his slug problem. Unfortunately, hedgehogs can also become predators of ground-nesting birds. In South Uist, numbers of lapwing, snipe, redshank and dunlin have halved because hedgehogs are eating their eggs. Some years ago, hedgehogs were removed from the small island of North Ronaldsay by live-trapping followed by release on the mainland. On the much larger island of South Uist, this is not a practical option and the hedgehogs will have to be killed. Hedgehog lovers are not happy about this, and the case has been referred to the Scottish Executive for a decision.

MARINE WILDLIFE CONSERVATION BILL

A private bill introduced by John Randall MP in 2001 aims to protect sites important for marine wildlife by creating a new designation analogous to Sites of Special Scientific Interest (SSSIs) on land. Its measures would apply to territorial waters (i.e. within 12 nautical miles of land) in England and Wales; under devolved powers, Scotland and Northern Ireland would create their own legislation. As drafted, the bill requires the relevant conservation agency, English Nature or the Countryside Council for Wales, to notify interested parties about the importance of the site and secure their agreement to its protection. It would also make a statement about conservation objectives and the desired management. In most cases, this would include restrictions on trawling nets and a presumption against dredging or oil and gas development.

The bill received impetus from the BBC television series *The Blue Planet*, and from a 'Marine Charter' drawn up by conservation bodies concerned about the marine environment. At present, the life of the seabed – sponges, soft corals, sea urchins and sea anemones – receives little or no protection outside a few Marine Nature Reserves and a few protected species. Seabed communities are, however, vulnerable to modern intensive fishing practices, such as beam-trawling, where large nets are dragged across the seabed on chains. The bill is having a rough ride; it is opposed by port authorities and water

Conservation and Heritage 1199

utilities, who argue that it conflicts with government development policies. The bill passed through the House of Commons by July 2002 but became stalled in the Lords following a government reshuffle and it is unlikely to become law in 2002.

DOLPHIN ALERT

Dolphins and porpoises are frequent victims of modern fishing methods. Fast trawlers working in pairs to tow huge nets to catch sea-bass and mackerel will scoop up any dolphins before they can escape. Their drowned bodies, tied by the tail and thrown overboard, sometimes wash ashore. In 2001, over 800 dolphins were found on the shores of Devon, Cornwall and Brittany, and the total number of deaths caused there by fishing is estimated to be around 2,000. This is not a sustainable rate of loss. The Animal Health and Welfare and Fisheries minister, Elliot Morley, expressed himself shocked when his officials, accompanying one trawler, counted 12 dolphins in the nets.

One potential solution currently being tested is a 'dolphin-friendly' design of fishing net. Such a net has been used in New Zealand to avoid catching sea lions. It works by using a grid of metal bars to halt the animal's progress into the net and force it out through gaps in the sides. However, tests showed that the animals can be injured in the process. Sea-trials in Britain had to be curtailed when the camera attached to the net fell off, and so a net that catches fish without harming dolphins has yet to be demonstrated. The alternative, to find less destructive ways of fishing, has little appeal to the world's fishing fleets.

THE BUILT ENVIRONMENT

The Heritage Review, the most far-ranging of its kind since the Second World War, articulated by English Heritage and compiled by a phalanx of conservation organisations, emerged in November 2000. The Government response took thirteen months, coming out eventually in December 2002 under the heading *The Historic Environment: A Force for our Future*. Amid the honeyed words came promises: to commission English Heritage to produce a pilot report on the state of the historic environment during 2002; to issue a consultation paper on enhancing Sites and Monuments Records; to encourage an annual Historic Environment Week; to carry out an investigation into the possibility of integrating present heritage controls into a single regime; to conduct a further review of the Ecclesiastical Exemption (from conservation legislation); to extend English Heritage's remit in the context of marine archaeology to include the seabed out to a twelve mile limit of territorial sea adjacent to England; and to encourage the appointment of champions for the historic environment within their management structures. Implementation of these promises rests with two new ministers at the Department for Culture, Media and Sport – Tessa Jowell and Baroness Blackstone.

PLANNING GREEN PAPER

Responsibility for a Green Paper promising the most radical reorganisation of town and country planning for fifty years lay only obliquely with the DCMS, primarily with the Department for Transport, Local Government and the Regions and, after its break-up in June 2002, with the Office of the Deputy Prime Minister (ODPM). The paper proposed: that Local, Structure and Unitary Development Plans would be replaced by a new hierarchy centering on Local Development Frameworks; that household planning applications would be separated from those submitted by businesses; detailed action plans for areas of historic identity; a review of all Planning Policy Guidance; the granting of permissive rights to local authorities to charge applicants for free application advice; a reduction in the number of statutory consultees; and the specific rejection by Government of the idea of a third party right of appeal (the ability of an individual or a civic society to embark upon an appeal against a decision with which they disagree). At the time of writing, implementation of the Paper seemed to have been stalled by the moving of Lord Falconer in the reshuffle of Spring 2002.

Government impinges on historic buildings and sites in many ways, and recognition of that was confirmed in the announcement in December 2001 by the Chancellor of the Exchequer, giving flesh to the previously announced concession whereby VAT was reduced on the repair of listed places of worship. For an experimental two-year period expiring on 1 March 2003, Government agreed to pay back all but 5 per cent of the 17.5 per cent VAT incurred on repair campaigns. Whether the concession remained permanent depended on the agreement of the European Union which, at the time of writing, was by no means guaranteed.

MPs too can influence policy. In the Spring of 2001 the Environment Committee of the House of Commons published a major study on cemeteries, the most sustained examination of the topic since 1850. It heavily criticised the lack of action by local authorities and the neglect of strategic advice by Local Government. It encouraged the establishment of local Friends, urged English Heritage to broaden its criteria for registering cemeteries and listing their structures, and called upon the Heritage Lottery Fund to extend its largesse into this neglected area beyond the £3–4 million they had already distributed.

HERITAGE LOTTERY FUND

With £300 million per year at its disposal, the HLF remained by far the most generous source of public money for conservation projects. Beneficiaries announced in the year under review (with the amount given in parenthesis) include: Kelvingrove Museum, Glasgow (£12,700,000); the Woodthorn Colliery, Northumberland (£10,000,000) to be transformed into the county's local studies and archive centre; Wentworth Castle, South Yorkshire (£8,556,000) to conserve this spectacular Baroque house and its 18th- century garden buildings; SS Great Britain, Bristol (£7,744,000) to arrest the decay of Brunel's great ship of 1839-43; Roundhay Park, Leeds (£6,101,000) to rescue one of the largest urban parks in England; Stowe House near Buckingham (£5,528,000) to repair and to improve access to this great 18th-century house; the London Coliseum, St Martin's Lane (£10,650,000) to complete a programme of urgent external repairs including the reinstatement of Frank Matcham's lost roof conservatory; Hardwick Hall, Derbyshire (£2,500,000) for a programme of repair and improved access; Lincoln (£4,641,000) to centralise the City's museum collections in a new building to go up behind the Usher Art Gallery; The Fitzwilliam Museum, Cambridge (£5,626,000) to provide new facilities within the Museum's courtyard; the Roundhouse Project, Camden (£2,425,000) to provide permanent use as an arts centre; the Wordsworth Trust, Cumbria (£2,250,000) to construct a brave new building to house items of the Wordsworth collection and the papers relating to British Romanticism in general; the Maritime Museum, Great

Yarmouth (£2,579,000); and, finally, St Paul's, Bristol (£1.88 million) to allow the Churches Conservation Trust to conserve this Grade I Georgian church that dominates Portland Square and locate within it a "Centre for Excellence in Circus and Physical Theatre".

An increasingly important part of the HLF's Strategic Plan for 2002–5 will be the smaller project. These include: Stone Station, Staffordshire (£260,000) to rescue a charming 19th-century listed station from dereliction to provide community facilities; Forbury Chapel, Herefordshire (£178,000) to restore this 12th-century building with new meeting rooms, office space, library and bookshop; The Windmill, East Sussex (£577,000) to rescue this derelict mill of 1814; the Evacuees Reunion Association (£89,900) to collect the memories of people evacuated during the Second World War; the Grace Dieu Priory, Leicestershire (£240,000) to conserve the remains of the Augustinian nunnery of 1235 which inspired William Wordsworth's famous poem; Rockingham Forest, Northamptonshire (£188,500) to prepare and implement a conservation strategy for this former medieval royal hunting forest; St Botolph Church, Lincolnshire (£84,000) to conserve and catalogue the extraordinary collection of books housed in the Boston Stump dating mainly from the 16th- and 17th-centuries; the Fovant Badges, Wiltshire (£70,000) to conserve chalk hill figures laid out in 1916; The Old Shoreham Tollbridge, West Sussex (£192,000) to repair and make useable once more this very rare timber bridge of 1781; the National Index of Memorial Inscriptions (£90,000) to begin the process of recording the UK's six million memorial inscriptions in churchyards and cemeteries the length and breadth of the country; Bolton Museum (£86,400) to allow it to produce a catalogue of its textile pattern books; and the Red Cross Gardens, Southwark (£497,000) to bring back to its previous state the best surviving example of the work of Octavia Hill, housing reformer and founder of the National Trust.

HLF-funded attractions are increasingly opening or reopening to the public. Newcomers in the twelve months under review include: Nunhead Cemetery in Southwark; the Palm House at Sefton Park, Liverpool; the Museum of Scottish Country Life at East Kilbride; Blackwell at Bowness on Windemere, the Arts and Crafts house by Baillie Scott; Strathleven House near Dunbarton; the Brighton Museum and Art Gallery; the Manchester City Art Gallery and; perhaps the most spectacular of all, the British Galleries at the Victoria and Albert Museum which opened in November 2001.

Also available is the new visitors centre at Painshill Park in Surrey; the Women's Library in Old Castle Street, London E1; the new visitors centre at Salisbury Cathedral; the relocated Ely Stained Glass Museum; the new wing at the Ashmolean Museum in Oxford; the Horniman Museum, London; Norwich Castle, which re-opened for its first full year after £11.8 million refurbishment; the Walker Art Gallery, Liverpool; the National Maritime Museum, Falmouth; Sutton Hoo burial site at Woodbridge in Suffolk; the gridshell building at the Weald & Downland Open Air Museum, Chichester; and Stoneleigh Abbey in Warwickshire.

Not that the HLF is the only lottery source for conservation projects. As from 1 March 2002 the entire Turner Bequest of his 30,000 sketches as well as 350 oil paintings left to the nation by the painter in 1851 have been available through the Internet thanks to £500,000 from the Heritage Lottery Fund and £377,000 from the New Opportunities Fund.

ENGLISH HERITAGE AND THE STATE AGENCIES

EH's Strategic Plan 2001–4, set against the background of Government grant-in-aid which after six years of successive decline has now recovered, includes promises to work with universities and professional institutions to develop new training opportunities, to set up a national forum to establish and promote training, encourage better maintenance promoting the duty of care, to pilot a register of ancient monuments at risk, ensuring that EH properties have their own Conservation Statement or Conservation Plan and to publish a list of grant-aided properties open to the public. The Annual Report for 2000–1 placed particular stress on the £34.2 million offered in grants by EH in the year under review. Of that total, £2.7 million went to cathedrals, £8.6 million for historic buildings and monuments, £11 million to places of worship and nearly £1 million to partner organisations. Two substantial beneficiaries announced in November were Sheriff Hutton Castle near York and Harewood Castle near Leeds. April 2002 saw the arrival of a dynamic new Chief Executive, Dr Simon Thurley. Former curator of the Historic Royal Palaces Agency and Director of the Museum of London, he is also a respected scholar, his *The Royal Palaces of Tudor England* of 1993 being a bestseller.

The year 2001–2 was peculiarly productive for EH publications. Seminal works emerged on: informed conservation, how to record buildings and sites, enabling development, construction in earth, the conservation of wall paintings and the history of prisons. A major initiative to bolster conservation in Liverpool was announced whilst Whitby Abbey was opened after a flagship campaign of repair and reinterpretation. The highly respected publications programme of Historic Scotland continued with technical publications on lime coatings, the non-destructive investigation of standing structures and the history and technical development of sash and case windows. The Royal Commission on the Ancient and Historical Monuments of Scotland issued publications on the Historic Landscape of the Cairngorms and Early Medieval Sculpture in the West Highlands and Islands. It completed a number of major surveys particularly of the Scottish National War Memorial in Edinburgh Castle and of Scottish schools in general. Among its recent accessions has been a set of Luftwaffe aerial photos taken during the Second World War. Scotland continued to show the way to the other home countries by publishing a new edition of its *Churches to Visit in Scotland*, an invaluable guide to visitors. The report by SAVE Britain's Heritage found that in the period where there were 134 new listings there were also 304 parallel de-listings.

In Wales Cadw, the Welsh equivalent to English Heritage, was able to offer 116 grant offers in 2000–1 totaling £3,686,147. One of the biggest single expenditures of public money, albeit guided by Cadw officials, was the £2 million directed by the Heritage Lottery Fund towards the regeneration of Pembroke Docks.

One of the most important roles of the state agencies is in the identification of buildings worthy of protection. The number of listed buildings continues to expand and among the more interesting structures given that status in the twelve months up to 1 June 2002 has been: the tombs of the three famous Hardwick architects and that of Charles Babbage (the founder of the computer) in Kensal Green Cemetery, North West London; purpose-built workshops for the blind of 1923 in Margaret Road, Leicester; the First World War Memorial to Cyclists at

Meriden, near Solihull; the home of John Opie the history painter at St Agnes in Cornwall; the Coychurch Cemetery Chapel at Bridgend in Glamorgan of 1970 clearly indebted to Le Corbusier's great chapel at Ronchamps; the house and music room of the composer Sir Arthur Bliss at Penselwood in Somerset and South Africa House in Trafalgar Square, both the latter already listed but upgraded now to Grade II*. The grand total of listed buildings in the UK is just short of 500,000 which makes it the equal of any country in the world except Italy.

NEW ORGANISATIONS

The year saw the establishment of the new umbrella organisation, Heritage Link, designed to improve the political muscle and the research skills of the voluntary sector. Heritage Link aims to be as effective a lobbyist as the CPRE in the context of natural conservation. A slightly old player but with a new name is Heritage Information which aims to become a 'one stop shop' for the dissemination of conservation advice whether it be contacting a craftsman or picking the right product. At the other end of the spectrum comes a small-scale body to champion a particular hero. The Comper Trust has been set up celebrate the work of the long-lived 'traditional' architect, Sir Ninian Comper, who died in 1960. The National Association for Decorative and Fine Arts (NADFAS) was able to mark in 2002 the compilation of its 1,000th record of an historic parish church, a two volume account of St Margaret's Lee in south London.

Dance

The 2001–2 season saw many of Britain's leading dance companies in a period of transition. New directors were at the helm at the Royal Ballet, English National Ballet and Northern Ballet Theatre, and Christopher Bruce retired from the directorship of Rambert Dance Company at the end of the season. Scottish Ballet announced in the summer of 2001 that it would reposition itself as 'a major new force in contemporary dance' with a new director to be appointed to take the company into its new phase. This proved so controversial that by the time Ashley Page, the choreographer and former principal dancer of the Royal Ballet, was appointed artistic director in May 2002 his stated aim was to 'redefine the company as a modern ballet company through performance, encouragement of new choreography and development of classical dance training in Scotland'.

The physical infrastructure for dance also saw new beginnings during the year, with the reopening of The Place in London as a major centre for contemporary dance and Birmingham Royal Ballet's return to the newly refurbished Birmingham Hippodrome.

THE ROYAL BALLET

The Royal Ballet's first year under the direction of the Australian Ross Stretton proved somewhat controversial. Although the standard of dancing remained high – and in some cases sensational – the choice of repertoire was heavily criticised. The season opened with Nureyev's production of *Don Quixote*, selected as a company showpiece but proving to be an indigestible and unexciting production with outdated designs and largely uninspiring music. The beginning of the season was also marred by the sudden resignation of one of the company's most popular principal dancers, Sarah Wildor, who evidently saw that she would be badly under-used during the year, and the departure of Irek Mukhamedov, the former Bolshoi principal who had so enriched the Royal Ballet with his presence.

The long overdue introduction of John Cranko's *Onegin* into the repertoire in November 2001 was a vast improvement on *Don Quixote* and also saw the welcome return to the company of Adam Cooper. A former principal dancer with the company and erstwhile star of Matthew Bourne's 'all-male' *Swan Lake*, Cooper guested in the ballet's title role opposite Tamara Rojo as Tatiana.

The real questions about Stretton's artistic judgment were raised by his choice of one-act works for the four triple bills mounted by the company during the year. For marketing reasons (presumably) these were each given a title to indicate their *raison d'être*. 'Memories' comprised *Beyond Bach*, a mediocre work by Stephen Baynes, the resident choreographer of the Australian Ballet, Anthony Tudor's beautiful, nostalgic 1975 work *The Leaves are Fading*, and Ashton's tragic *Marguerite and Armand*. The cumulative effect of the programme was almost soporific, and indicated a lack of understanding of the need for contrast and variety within a triple bill. Later programmes (under the titles of 'Enduring Images', 'Trilogy' and 'Cross Cultures') were equally problematic. Two works by William Forsythe were joined by a dire piece by Nacho Duato, *Por Vos Muero*, set to 16th-century Spanish music and requiring nothing of its dancers.

The Royal Ballet-trained Christopher Wheeldon, now working for New York City Ballet, presented the season's only completely new work, entitled *Tryst* and set to music by James MacMillan. This was largely well received, but with the subsequent introduction into the repertoire of Mats Ek's tedious *Carmen*, standards nosedived again. It is arguable that if Stretton plans to make Stephen Baynes, Nacho Duato and Mats Ek part of the Royal Ballet's future, there are worrying times ahead. The season came to an unhappy end with reports of disquiet within the company over Stretton's management style and casting decisions.

MORE NEW DIRECTORS

At English National Ballet, Matz Skoog made a quieter start to his directorship, although he showed a lack of courtesy (and, indeed, a lack of accuracy) in criticising the standards of dancing under former director Derek Deane. The only triple bill presented by the full company during the season included the world première of a work (commissioned by Deane) by 28-year-old Christopher Hampson, a former dancer with the company who trained at the Royal Ballet School. *Double Concerto* was set to Poulenc's Concerto for Two Pianos and Orchestra and was a superbly crafted and highly enjoyable piece for 38 dancers. This was teamed with two great works by Balanchine, *Apollo* and *Who Cares?*, and this thoroughly satisfying bill was given by the company in its first-ever performances at the Royal Opera House in the early summer of 2002. The company currently has first-rate productions of *Cinderella* and *Romeo and Juliet* in its repertoire, and these, together with *The Nutcracker* and Deane's in-the-round production of *Swan Lake*, formed the backbone of the season. Hampson mounts a new production of *The Nutcracker* for the company in October 2002, and Skoog's own influence on the company will in time become more evident.

Northern Ballet Theatre (NBT) enjoyed its most successful season for some years under new director David Nixon. Nixon was formerly artistic director of BalletMet, in Columbus, USA, and came to NBT at the end of a difficult year for the company. The first production of the season was the world première of *A Streetcar Named Desire*, choreographed by Didy Veldman and directed by Patricia Doyle, with designs by Es Devlin and a score by Philip Feeney. This was an ambitious work that attempted to stick too closely to its literary source and was hampered by Veldman's limited choreographic range.

In February 2002 Nixon mounted a reworked version of his own *Madame Butterfly*, largely to Puccini but also using traditional Japanese music and with excellent designs by Ali Allen. This was an imaginative and enjoyable production, and seemed to restore the company's confidence. It was followed by the sparkling *I Got Rhythm*, an elegant two-part celebration of George and Ira Gershwin with choreography and designs by Nixon himself and music direction by John Pryce-Jones. Nixon is planning a production of *Wuthering Heights* for autumn 2002, followed by *Beauty and the Beast* as a Christmas show, and has quickly succeeded in giving the company a renewed sense of direction.

DEPARTURES

Christopher Bruce announced in December 2001 that he would retire as director of Rambert Dance Company by the end of the season, which also marked the end of the company's 75th anniversary year. He had returned to the company in 1994 as artistic director, having formerly been its associate director and associate choreographer, and had first joined the then Ballet Rambert as a dancer in 1963. His contribution to Rambert has been enormous, but his own recent creations have been uninspired and he has probably chosen the right time to retire and allow the company, as he put it, to 'move on to the next stage of its development'. The company's chairman, Prudence Skene, reiterated the board's commitment to Bruce's vision of Rambert as 'a large-scale contemporary dance company presenting a broad international repertoire'. In the summer of 2002 the company announced the appointment of Mark Baldwin as artistic director to take this vision forward. Baldwin, who danced with Rambert from 1983 to 1992 and has considerable experience as a choreographer, would appear to be a good choice to succeed Bruce. Rambert had a busy but not particularly distinguished season, performing new works by Bruce himself, Rafael Bonachela and Glenn Wilkinson and a revival of Lindsay Kemp's *The Parades Gone By*, a camp parody of the golden age of Hollywood.

Rambert's stable artistic vision and smooth transition to a new director might well be envied by Scottish Ballet. It was a tumultuous year for the company, whose current director, Robert North, was appointed in 1999 with the aim of bringing stability to Scottish Ballet after a long period of uncertainty. Although not universally admired, North produces works that are popular with audiences, and he appears to have been shabbily treated by the company's board. The decision to recreate the company as a contemporary dance company came out of the blue and was criticised by a committee of the Scottish Parliament because of the lack of consultation. Boardroom disputes continued for months, and doubts were expressed about the existence of a wide audience for contemporary dance in Scotland, which is in any case already catered for by Scottish Dance Theatre, run by Janet Smith. When Ashley Page was appointed as the new director of Scottish Ballet in May 2002, it was announced that the company's repertoire would be 'based on classical technique embracing 20th-century works, the reworking of 19th-century classics and with a new emphasis on commissioned work of a contemporary classical nature'. This in fact seems to give Page a fairly free hand, and he will also no doubt introduce his own distinctive choreography into the repertoire. In the meantime, the company performed works by North including *The Snowman*, *Carmen* and *Death and the Maiden*, new works by Hans van Manen (*In and Out* and *Sarcasms*), and, as defiantly uncontemporary as you can get, Ashton's *The Two Pigeons*, with guest appearances by Sarah Wildor.

REOPENINGS

Birmingham Royal Ballet's director David Bintley was appointed to the job in 1995 and is now therefore the grand old man of ballet directors in Britain although still only 44 years old. He and his company have been homeless for the last two years while the Birmingham Hippodrome underwent a £30 million refurbishment, but this exile was brought to a close in November 2001 with the gala reopening of the theatre. In September 2001 Bintley created an attractive new work, *The Seasons*, to Verdi and with designs by Jean-Marc Puissant. A revival of *Swan Lake* after five years, however, seemed to overstretch the company and gave rise to concerns about the erosion of its classical roots. An encouraging development in this connection was the announcement that Elmhurst Ballet School would become an Associate School of Birmingham Royal Ballet, and would relocate from Camberley to Birmingham in September 2004. The company's existing links with the Royal Ballet School will be maintained but it also wishes to associate itself with a school based in Birmingham, and David Bintley will become artistic advisor to Elmhurst. This arrangement should work to the benefit of both the company and the school.

In October 2001, The Place in London, the leading centre for contemporary dance in Britain, reopened after a £7 million redevelopment. The main theatre in the complex has been renamed the Robin Howard Dance Theatre in honour of the founder of The Place and of London Contemporary Dance School and London Contemporary Dance Theatre (LCDT). LCDT was disbanded in 1996 and effectively replaced by the Richard Alston Dance Company, and Alston is also now artistic director of The Place. His company reopened the theatre with performances of two new works by Alston (*Water Music* and *Strange Company*) and two revivals (*Lachrymae* and the beautiful solo *Soda Lake*). In the Queen's Birthday Honours in June 2002, John Ashford, the director of The Place, was awarded a CBE in recognition of his contribution to contemporary dance. A co-founder of the London Contemporary Dance School, the great American dancer, choreographer and teacher of contemporary dance, Jane Dudley, who was a member of the Martha Graham Company from 1937 to 1944, died on 19 September 2001 at the age of 89.

Choreographer Siobhan Davies was also the recipient of a CBE this year, in the New Year's Honours in January 2002. Davies and her company were given a temporary base at the Royal Academy of Dancing in autumn 2001, and ran a pilot project as a professional development opportunity for six dancers who led a revival of Davies's 1997 work *Bank*.

NEW WORK

Dance Umbrella 2001 included performances by Jonathan Burrows and Jan Ritsema, Batsheva Dance Company, Russell Maliphant, Richochet Dance Company, Charles Linehan and, in a miserable return, Michael Clark with *Before and After: The Fall*. Arc Dance Company mounted a production based on Dostoevsky entitled *The Brothers*, and Wayne McGregor produced his most ambitious work to date, *Nemesis*, for his Random Dance Company. Shobana Jeyasingh toured a new work, *Phantasmaton*, with *Surface Tension*, her work from 2000. Akram Khan continued to build a reputation with his new work *Kaash*, a collaboration between the choreographer, the composer Nitin Sawhney and the painter and sculptor Anish Kapoor. Khan also contributed the only dance item in *Related Rocks*, a concert of live music at the Queen Elizabeth Hall, London, in December 2001. Javier de Frutos created an interesting work, *The Misty Frontier*, on Royal Ballet dancers at the Linbury Studio Theatre at the Royal Opera House, and George Piper Dances, co-founded by the former Royal Ballet dancers Michael Nunn and William Trevitt, mounted several excellent programmes and made its London début at the Roundhouse in October 2001, returning to the Queen Elizabeth Hall in December 2001.

Visiting companies during the year included William Forsythe's Ballett Frankfurt, the Mark Morris Dance Group, Pina Bausch's Tanztheater Wuppertal (in the superb *Masurca Fogo*), the Stanislavsky Ballet from Moscow (in Bourmeister's *The Snow Maiden* and *Swan Lake*), the British début of Julio Bocca's Ballet Argentino, Alvin Ailey American Dance Theater (in a visit postponed from September 2001), Nederlands Dans Theater 1 and Cloud Gate Dance Theatre of Taiwan with Lin Hwai Min's extraordinary *Moon Water*.

Adam Cooper, who started the season in the seriously tragic *Onegin*, finished it in an altogether lighter mode and also proved his impressive versatility. He both choreographed and starred in a new production of the 1936 Rodgers and Hart musical *On Your Toes*, which opened at the Leicester Haymarket in May 2002. Another big musical, *South Pacific*, which opened at the National Theatre in December 2001 in a production directed by Trevor Nunn, gave the choreographer Matthew Bourne the opportunity to apply his skills in a fresh context. And a revival of *Chitty Chitty Bang Bang* in a lavish new production directed by Adrian Noble at the London Palladium in April 2002 was choreographed by Gillian Lynne, who has specialised – with enormous success – in choreographing for the musical theatre, and was awarded the Royal Academy of Dancing's 2001 Queen Elizabeth II Coronation Award in recognition of her achievements.

PRODUCTIONS

ROYAL BALLET

Founded 1931 as the Vic-Wells Ballet
Royal Opera House, Covent Garden, London WC2E 9DD

World première:
Tryst (Christopher Wheeldon), 18 May 2002. A one-act work. Music, James MacMillan; design, Jean-Marc Puissant. Cast led by Darcey Bussell and Jonathan Cope

Company premières:
Don Quixote (Rudolf Nureyev after Petipa, 1966), 23 October 2001. A full-length work. Music, Minkus (arranged by and with additional music by John Lanchbery); sets, Anne Fraser; costumes, Barry Kay. Cast led by Tamara Rojo, Johan Kobborg, Christopher Saunders, Tom Sapsford and David Drew
Onegin (John Cranko, 1965), 22 November 2001. A full-length work. Music, Tchaikovsky; design, Jürgen Rose. Cast led by Adam Cooper, Tamara Rojo, Ethan Stiefel and Alina Cojocaru
Beyond Bach (Stephen Baynes, 1995), 26 January 2002. A one-act work. Music, Bach; sets, Andrew Carter; costumes, Anna French. Cast led by Darcey Bussell, Inaki Urlezaga, Marianela Nuñez and Jonathan Cope
The Leaves are Fading (Anthony Tudor, 1975), 26 January 2002. A one-act work. Music, Dvořák; sets, Ming Cho Lee, costumes, Patricia Zippordt. Cast led by Alina Cojocaru and John Kobborg
Por Vos Muero (Nacho Duato, 1996) 4 March 2002. A one-act work. Music, 16th-century Spanish; sets, Nacho Duato; costumes, Nacho Duato and Ismael Aznar. Cast of 12 dancers
Carmen (Mats Ek, 1992), 10 April 2002. A one-act work. Music, Bizet and Shchedrin; design, Marie-Louise Ekman. Cast led by Sylvie Guillem and Massimo Murru
Full-length works from the repertoire: *The Nutcracker* (Ivanov, prod. Wright 1984 with revisions 1999), *La Bayadère* (Makarova after Petipa, 1980), *Giselle* (Coralli/Perrot, prod. Wright 1985), *Romeo and Juliet* (MacMillan, 1965), *Coppélia* (de Valois after Ivanov and Cecchetti, 1954).
One-act works from the repertoire: *Marguerite and Armand* (Ashton, 1963), *In the middle, somewhat elevated* (Forsythe, 1988), *Remanso* (Nacho Duato, 1997), *The Vertiginous Thrill of Exactitude* (Forsythe, 1996), *A Month in the Country* (Ashton, 1976).
On 23 July 2002 the company gave a gala performance at the Royal Opera House to celebrate the Golden Jubilee of The Queen, including highlights from the season's repertoire.
The company toured to Australia (Brisbane, Sydney and Melbourne) in May-July 2002, performing *Swan Lake* (Petipa/Ivanov, prod. Dowell 1987), *Giselle, Tryst, The Leaves are Fading* and *Marguerite and Armand*.

BIRMINGHAM ROYAL BALLET

Founded 1946 as the Sadler's Wells Opera Ballet
Birmingham Hippodrome, Thorp Street, Birmingham B5 4AU

World première:
The Seasons (David Bintley), 13 September 2001. A one-act work. Music, Verdi; design, Jean-Marc Puissant. Cast led by Nao Sakuma and Chi Cao.
Full-length works from the repertoire: *Swan Lake* (Petipa/Ivanov, prod. Wright and Samsova 1981), *The*

Nutcracker (Ivanov, prod. Wright, additional choreography by Redmon, 1990), *Romeo and Juliet* (MacMillan, 1965), *Hobson's Choice* (Bintley, 1989).
One-act works from the repertoire: *Dante Sonata* (Ashton, 1940), *'Still Life' at the Penguin Café* (Bintley, 1988), *Prodigal Son* (Balanchine, 1929), *Tombeaux* (Bintley, 1993), *Sanctum* (York, 1997), *Façade* (Ashton, 1931), *Powder* (Welch, 1998), *Carmina Burana* (Bintley, 1995).
The company gave a gala performance at the Birmingham Hippodrome on 13 November 2001 to celebrate the theatre's reopening after a two-year closure for restoration and expansion. The programme comprised *The Seasons, 'Still Life' at the Penguin Café* and divertissements from other works by David Bintley (*The Dance House, Hobson's Choice, Far from the Madding Crowd* and *Flowers of the Forest*).
In addition to three seasons at the Birmingham Hippodrome Theatre and one at The Academy at the National Indoor Arena in Birmingham, the company toured to London (Sadler's Wells Theatre), Plymouth (two seasons), Bradford (two seasons), Sunderland (two seasons), Manchester (two seasons), and Edinburgh.

ENGLISH NATIONAL BALLET

Founded 1950 as London Festival Ballet
Markova House, 39 Jay Mews, London SW7 2ES

World première:
Double Concerto (Christopher Hampson), 20 November 2001. A one-act work. Music, Poulenc; design, Gary Harris. Cast led by Daria Klimentová and Jan-Erik Wikström
Full-length works from the repertoire: *Cinderella* (Corder, 1996), *The Nutcracker* (Deane, 1997), *Romeo and Juliet* (Nureyev, 1977), *Swan Lake* (Petipa/Ivanov, prod. Deane 1997).
One-act works from the repertoire: *Apollo* (Balanchine, 1928), *Who Cares?* (Balanchine, 1970).
The full company toured to Southampton (two seasons), Oxford, Manchester (two seasons), Bristol (two seasons), Liverpool (two seasons), and London (the London Coliseum, the Royal Albert Hall and the Royal Opera House).
In April-May 2002 the company split into two groups and went on two small-scale tours (called *Tour de Force!*). One group toured *Square Dance* (Balanchine, 1957), *Manoeuvre* (a new work by Patrick Lewis, with a score by Phillip Feeny and design by Antony McDonald) and the *Grand Pas Classique* from *Raymonda* to Truro, Woking, Swindon, Cheltenham and Crawley. The other group toured *Dances from Napoli* (Bournonville), *Facing Viv* (a new work by Cathy Marston, with music by John Adams and design by Anthony Lamble) and the *Grand Pas* from *Paquita* to Scunthorpe, Cambridge, Bexhill-on-Sea, Barrow-in-Furness and Tunbridge Wells.

RAMBERT DANCE COMPANY

Founded 1926 as the Marie Rambert Dancers
94 Chiswick High Road, London W4 1SH

World premières:
Grinning in Your Face (Christopher Bruce), 26 September 2001. Music, Martin Simpson; design, Marian Bruce
Linear Remains (Rafael Bonachela), 20 November 2001. Music, Christian Fennesz
Tree Finger Soup [3] (Kinson Productions/Glenn Wilkinson), 21 May 2002. Music, Aphex Twin and Headrillaz; design, Bruce French

Company première:
Ground Level Overlay (Merce Cunningham, 1995), 13 November 2001. Music, Stuart Dempster; sets, Leonardo Drew; costumes, Suzanne Gallo
Works from the repertoire: *Unrest* (Alston, 2001), *Sounding* (Davies, 1989), *Symphony of Psalms* (Kylián, 1978), *detritus* (McGregor, 2001), *Ghost Dances* (Bruce, 1981), *Hurricane* (Bruce, 2000), *Cheese* (James, 2000), *The Parades Gone By* (Kemp, 1975), *She Was Black* (Ek, 1995), *Twin Suite 2* (Kinson Productions/Glenn Wilkinson, 2001), *The Celebrated Soubrette* (Javier de Frutos, 2000), *Land* (Bruce, 1985), *Gaps, Lapse and Relapse* (James, 1998).
The company performed in Salford, Douglas (Isle of Man), Oxford, Edinburgh, Milton Keynes, London (two seasons at Sadler's Wells Theatre), Plymouth, Truro, Sheffield, High Wycombe, Mold, Norwich, Newcastle upon Tyne and Brighton.
The company also toured to Poland (Warsaw and Krakow) in May-June 2002, giving four performances of *Cheese, Ghost Dances* and *detritus.*
A workshop season of new works created and performed by members of the company was given at the Lilian Baylis Theatre, London, in June 2002.

RICHARD ALSTON DANCE COMPANY

Founded 1994
The Place, 17 Duke's Road, London WC1H 9AB
All works danced by the company are choreographed by Richard Alston.

World premières:
Water Music, 28 September 2001. Music, Handel; costumes, Jeanne Spaziani
  Strange Company, 28 September 2001. Music, Schumann; costumes, Jeanne Spaziani
  Touch and Go, 19 February 2002. Music, Astor Piazzolla; costumes, Emanuel Ungaro and Elizabeth Baker

Company première:
Soda Lake (1981), 28 September 2001. A solo, danced in silence. Design, Nigel Hall
Works from the repertoire: *Lachrymae* (1994), *Red Run* (1998), *Light Flooding into Darkened Rooms* (1997).
The company performed in High Wycombe, London (Robin Howard Dance Theatre at The Place and The Queen Elizabeth Hall), Northampton, Cambridge, Brecon, Malvern, Edinburgh, Horsham, Nottingham, Norwich, Salford, Brighton, Stevenage, Canterbury and Sheffield.
It also toured to Greece (Athens and Thessaloniki) in October 2001, performing *Lachrymae, Strange Company* and *Water Music.*

SCOTTISH BALLET

Founded 1956 as the Western Theatre Ballet
261 West Princes Street, Glasgow G4 9EE

Company premières:
In and Out (Hans van Manen, 1983), 27 September 2001. A one-act work. Music, Laurie Anderson and Nina Hagen; design, Kesko Dekker. Cast of 12 dancers
  Sarcasms (Hans van Manen, 1981), 27 September 2001. A *pas de deux.* Music, Prokofiev; design, Hans van Manen. Dancers, Lorna Scott and Luca Martini
  Death and the Maiden (Robert North, 1980), 27 September 2001. A one-act work. Music, Schubert; costumes, Robert North. Cast led by Linda Packer

The Snowman (Robert North, 1993), 14 December 2001. A two-act work, expanded from the one-act original. Music, Howard Blake; design, Andrew Storer. Cast led by Darren Parish and Fulvio Faudella
  Bach Dances (Robert North, 2001), 29 March 2002. A one-act work. Music, Bach; design, Andrew Storer. Cast led by Glauco di Lieto and Tomomi Sato
  The Two Pigeons (Frederick Ashton, 1961), 29 March 2002. A two-act work. Music, André Messager; design, Jacques Dupont. Cast led by Sarah Wildor and Ivan Dinev
Full-length work from the repertoire: *Carmen* (North, 1997). One-act work from the repertoire: *Troy Game* (North, 1974).
The company performed in Glasgow (three seasons), Aberdeen (three seasons), Edinburgh (three seasons), Inverness (two seasons), Stoke-on-Trent, Hull, and Woking.

Film

Cinema was overshadowed this year by the terrorist attacks in the US on 11 September 2001. If this catastrophe put trivialities like the movie business in their proper place, it was noticeable that in seeking some intellectual purchase on what had occurred, commentators turned to film as a shared cultural frame of reference. This was in part because the images of the events on our television screens showed a disaster on a scale familiar only from big special-effects movies; people immediately thought of the burning skyscrapers in The Towering Inferno and Die Hard; the panicked New Yorkers rushing through the streets in Godzilla; Washington DC landmarks destroyed in Independence Day – scenes that had been greeted with euphoric cheering in US cinemas only five years earlier.

For many in Hollywood, the first lesson of the 11 September events seemed obvious; it meant the end of the action movie, with its wanton destruction, its fetish for fireballs and its disregard for innocent victims. Warner Bros postponed the autumn release of Collateral Damage, an Arnold Schwarzenegger vehicle in which he plays a New York fireman whose family is murdered by a terrorist bomb and who sets out to exact his revenge. (In the original screenplay the terrorists had been Arabs, but director Andrew Davis decided that was too hackneyed and made them South American instead.) The film was eventually released six months later, to a muted response.

The same studio withdrew Swordfish from British cinemas within hours of the attacks, though in this case it was already nearing the end of its run. John Travolta played a sort of anti-hero whose raid on the Federal Reserve is motivated by patriotic conviction; he uses the money to bankroll a covert counter-terrorist vigilante force. Having it both ways, the movie seems to find the character's reactionary extremism both beyond the pale and yet somehow irresistible – he gets away with it in the end. It was not long before the character's rhetoric was being echoed by the US government. Other films that were postponed included the comedies Big Trouble and Sidewalks of New York, the latter apparently because the Big Apple no longer seemed a conducive setting for light romantic comedy. When Sidewalks eventually came out, shots with the World Trade Center towers in the background had been doctored to erase them. The towers were also excised from the trailers of AI and Spider-Man, though not from the movies themselves. On British television that week, Strange Days was deemed too provocative, as were Daylight, Pushing Tin, Three Kings and even On the Town.

As normality returned, and the logistics and motivation behind the Al-Qa'eda operation became clearer, Hollywood remained a popular touchstone; movies like Executive Decision and Passenger 57 had suggested how easily airliners might be hijacked by terrorists, although none predicted their use as suicide bombs. In 1998 the only notable aspect of the Denzel Washington–Bruce Willis thriller The Siege had been that it was picketed by the Arab-American Anti-Defamation League. Suddenly its bleak portrait of government agenices impotent in the face of urban terrorists looking for maximum media impact looked prophetic; so too, perhaps, did its assumption that martial law could result.

The BBC current affairs programme Panorama explored the contention that Hollywood screenwriters were more on the ball than US government security officers after the Pentagon organised a brainstorming weekend with directors such as David Fincher (Fight Club, The Panic Room) and Spike Jonze (Being John Malkovich), and writers like Steven De Souza (Die Hard); Panorama found plenty of expert witnesses both in Los Angeles and Washington who believed the contention to be true. War films also took on an unexpected resonance. Pearl Harbor, a hit when it was released earlier in summer 2001, would almost certainly have had a warmer reception if it had come out in cinemas after September and it did massive business on video and DVD.

By coincidence, two war movies planned long before 11 September seemed to anticipate the new patriotic fervour. Although set a quarter of a century and a continent apart, Ridley Scott's Black Hawk Down – about the debacle which ended US intervention in Somalia in 1993 – and Randall Wallace's We Were Soldiers – set at the start of the Vietnam war in 1965 – share many similarities. They are both based on non-fiction books about the experiences of US Rangers who found themselves surrounded and vastly outnumbered by hostile forces in countries thousands of miles from home: a story as old as the Alamo but relevant too, with Rangers on active duty in Afghanistan. Both the Battle of the Black Sea and the Battle of Ia Drang ended in retreat. They have usually been perceived as military reversals and political embarrassments, yet both films work hard to rehabilitate the military, making a great deal, for example, of the Marines' oath to leave no man behind, alive or dead (a vow explicitly scorned in the more cynical 1986 Vietnam movie Full Metal Jacket), and honouring the courage and dedication of the troops without looking too deeply at the underlying reasons for their sacrifice. 'Ours but to do and die' would serve as a motto for either film.

If these big studio movies failed to connect with audiences, it was probably because their bloody scenes of hand-to-hand combat seemed to have little to do with the situation in Afghanistan as portrayed in the media, a country largely unseen and unheard. The Iranian film Kandahar, distributed widely throughout the West, filled in the blanks. Here was evidence of what Afghanistan looked like (the film was shot in 2000 on the Iran-Afghanistan borders), of how zealously the Taliban repressed their country, and also of the dire mess bequeathed by the Cold War. In the most vivid and unsettling scene, the wounded at a Red Cross centre hobble on crutches in a race to reach artificial limbs dropping by parachute from the skies. Mohsen Makhmalbaf's film screened at Cannes in May 2001 and went largely unremarked. 'The press weren't interested in what we had to say, only in the style, the surrealism ...' the director's star and collaborator Nelofer Pazira said in November 2001. 'Now it is the opposite, they only want to talk about the politics.'

ESCAPISM RULES

Perhaps understandably, escapist fantasy proved popular this year. The box office was dominated by the first instalments in planned series based on J. R. R. Tolkien's Lord of the Rings and J. K. Rowling's Harry Potter books, George Lucas's Star Wars Episode 2: Attack of the Clones, and Sam Raimi's Spider-Man. Between them, these four films will gross more than $3 billion by the end of 2002. The first Potter movie was titled Harry Potter and the Philosopher's Stone in the UK and Harry Potter and the Sorceror's Stone in the US, reflecting the difference in the book's title in the two markets. The British critics treated

this dutifully faithful adaptation with kid gloves, though director Terry Gilliam was nearer the mark when he complained that it looked like 'a film made by a committee – a committee without a head'.

Lord of the Rings: The Fellowship of the Ring was in a different league. A labour of love for New Zealand director Peter Jackson, and a make-or-break gamble for New Line, the American mini-major (a AOL Time Warner affiliate) who bankrolled him to the tune of $300 million while he shot material for the Middle Earth trilogy over the best part of a year. (The second part, *The Two Towers*, is scheduled for release in December 2002, with part three a year later.) Although Jackson gets off to a sticky start with a kitsch Tellytubby theme-park rendition of the Shire, the bucolic realm of the hobbits, the film deepens and darkens rapidly as young Frodo Baggins (Elijah Wood) comes into possession of the ring of power, an evil talisman so potent it corrupts everyone it touches. Under the wise guidance of the wizard Gandalf (superbly played by Ian McKellen), Frodo and his faithful friend Sam (Sean Astin) escape the clutches of the fearsome ring-wraiths and head for the kingdom of the elves, where they hope to thwart the encroaching forces of doom. Tolkien's anti-fascist allegory has overwhelmed film-makers until now – an animated version in 1980 ran out of money about a third of the way through – and even at 178 minutes Jackson's film feels episodic, a preamble for parts two and three. That said, this remains a stunningly realised epic. It creates a primordial world as old as myth itself, does not tarry, and builds to a moving assertion of good facing down evil at tremendous personal risk.

Where *The Fellowship of the Ring* is sombre and urgent, the latest Star Wars prequel is another asinine Saturday morning serial for overgrown pre-adolescents, earnest, trite, and dismally mechanical. It got by with fans, who agreed it was not as infantile as the last one, largely on the strength of the crowd-pleasing climactic showdown between Yoda and Christopher Lee's Count Dooku. The appropriately monickered *Attack of the Clones* lacks dramatic weight, suspense and invention, though its golden lustre serves as a showcase for the new digital cinema; it was shot entirely on digital, only going to celluloid because exhibitors have yet to embrace the new technology.

The runaway commercial success of these films – and a few more, like the unpretentious, spry *Spider-Man*, television cartoon spin-off *Scooby-Doo* and the sequels *Men in Black II* and *Austin Powers in Goldmember* – ensured that box-office figures continued their upward trend, making 2001 a record year. No one was being too bullish, though. Marketing costs rose 13 per cent in 2001, to an average of $31 million per film, and continued to climb in 2002. The industry seems more and more reliant on big event pictures, many of these sequels to established hits, to support a structure that allows established stars like Mel Gibson, Tom Hanks, Julia Roberts and Tom Cruise to command a $25 million fee, and in some cases 40 per cent of the box-office gross. Chris Tucker, Denzel Washington, Will Smith and John Travolta come cheaper, but are still charging $20 million if the project is deemed commercial enough. Relative newcomers like Vin Diesel, Colin Farrell and Reece Witherspoon are not far behind. This at a time when the the multinational conglomerates that own the studios are under severe financial pressure as stock markets wobble, share prices collapse and a series of accounting scandals undermine business confidence, especially in the US. In 2002, AOL Time Warner cut back executive pay and perks, and in July admitted it was co-operating with federal investigators over accounting discrepencies; while Vivendi Universal saw its share price collapse and eventually sacked its chief executive Jean-Marie Messier in July amid speculation that it will have sell off key assets.

The reliance on big event movies could not disguise another bad year for American film, a quality vacuum which was brought home by an especially feeble Oscar race. In a year when the best 'independent' movies were either too esoteric (Wes Anderson's screwy *The Royal Tenenbaums*, Chris Nolan's ingenious *Memento*, Richard Linklater's woozy, over-drawn animation *Waking Life*), too weird (David Lynch back on form with *Mulholland Drive*), too small (*In the Bedroom*; *Ghost World*), too big (*Lord of the Rings*) or just too foreign (Baz Luhrmann's breathless musical *Moulin Rouge*, *Lord of the Rings*, Robert Altman's English country house murder mystery *Gosford Park, Iris*), the Best Picture Award for Ron Howard's bathetic *A Beautiful Mind* was virtually a foregone conclusion. Indeed, here was a film all but indistinguishable from its Oscar aspirations. Ostensibly the story of John Nash, a Nobel-prize winning mathematician who suffered from schizophrenia, *A Beautiful Mind* took great liberties with the facts, suppressing Nash's bisexuality and a long separation from his wife Alicia, illustrating his breakthrough formula as a technique to pick up girls, and (most dubiously) implying that his illness was alleviated not by drugs but by the love of a good woman. Sentimental as well as fraudulent, and featuring Russell Crowe's most mannered performance yet, the movie is not without interest, especially for its imaginative ingenuity in the first half, when it effectively recasts the Cold War as a paranoid delusion.

The Academy Awards in 2002 will be remembered for entirely different reasons; Denzel Washington became the first black actor to win the Best Actor award since Sidney Poitier in 1968, and Halle Berry was the first-ever 'woman of colour' to win Best Actress (Berry is of mixed race parentage). The actress's emotional acceptance speech name-checked such role models as Lena Horne, Ruby Dee, Angela Bassett and Alfre Woodard, and claimed that the award 'opened the door' for black performers. But while she and Washington certainly gave virtuoso performances in *Monster's Ball* and *Training Day* respectively, neither film would have merited this kind of recognition in a stronger year, nor should Washington's demonic bad cop have eclipsed Will Smith's sterling, searching performance as *Ali* in Michael Mann's radical, under-rated boxing biopic. In a year when Ron Howard can beat Robert Altman, David Lynch and Peter Jackson for best director, you know mediocrity is in fashion.

Internationally, Hollywood saw foreign rentals drop seven per cent to $2.2 billion in 2001. Remarkably, American movies took just 65 per cent of the European market, the Europeans' share jumping from 15 to 26 per cent. A similar pattern was observed in the Far East, in Korea and Japan, in Mexico and Latin America (where hits included *Y Tu Mama Tambien, Nine Queens* and *Me You Them*). These figures do not necessarily reflect any great shift in audience sensibilities, although they do suggest some growing dissatisfaction with Hollywood. The indigenous hits were mostly multiplex crowd-pleasers rather than high art, although Nanni Moretti's Cannes 2001 winner *The Son's Room* sold more than two million tickets across Europe. In France, *Amélie, The Brotherhood of the Wolf* and sequels to the successful *Asterix* and *Les Visiteurs* movies were big popular hits. More challenging and critically acclaimed films like *Time Out, Skin of Man, Heart of Beast*, and *Night Shift* struggled to find audiences. It was a bumper year for French

cinema, but the writing is on the wall for the country's immensely successful 'avance sur recettes' subsidy system; television companies hit by falling advertising revenue are no longer prepared to sponsor French film production.

Some local hits, such as the German comic Western *Manitou's Shoe,* do not travel well. Others succeed on the arthouse circuit without quite crossing into the mainstream: the Swedish commune comedy *Together,* for example, or the Norwegian comedy *Elling.* The most successful have the look and feel, and sometimes the stars and the financial backing, of Hollywood films; Alejandro Amenabar's *The Others* was a Spanish film in Spain, an American movie just about everywhere else; Working Title's adaptation of Nick Hornby's *About a Boy* and the UK-German co-production *Resident Evil* are further examples. Interestingly, the directors of *Amélie, Bend It Like Beckham, Y Tu Mama Tambien* and Australia's *Rabbit-Proof Fence* had all directed films in Hollywood before returning home, and successfully applied American audience-awareness to quirky subject matter. All of which leaves British filmmakers, and those institutions that support them, in something of a quandary. Cinema admissions in the UK were up again, to 157.4 million in 2001, and are expected to hit 170 million in 2002, but with the exception of *Harry Potter* (a Warner Bros movie shot in the UK with a British cast and crew) and the annual fillip from Working Title (a subsidiary of Universal), British films were mostly flops.

FOUR BLOW

The most visible failures were *Lucky Break,* a sloppy prison comedy from the director of *The Full Monty,* and *Charlotte Gray,* a World War II clandestine romance based on Sebastian Faulkes' bestselling novel. Both came from FilmFour and were clearly focused on the international market; neither found an audience. Nor did the romantic comedy/tearjerker *Crush. Death to Smoochy,* a dire black comedy starring Robin Williams and Edward Norton, and directed by Danny De Vito, died quickly and painfully in the US and is unlikely to be released in Britain. *The Emperor's New Clothes,* a farce about Napoleon on Elba, also opened and closed in the US with no UK release in sight. *Birthday Girl,* a co-production with Miramax starring Nicole Kidman, finally came out in June 2002, more than a year after it was shot. But within days, it emerged that Channel 4's new chief executive Mark Thompson had decided to wind up FilmFour in its current form, closing its distribution and marketing arms, axing most of the 60 staff, and slashing its production budget by three-quarters, back to $15 million a year.

From some viewpoints, this looked like an over-reaction; FilmFour losses were $8.1 million in 2001 and $4.5 million in 2000, hardly in the league of the $90 million notched up by the channel's marketing arm, 4-Ventures, and FilmFour more than broke even on both *Lucky Break* and *Charlotte Gray* thanks to international pre-sales deals. Some would have wished for changes in key personnel at the top without seeing the need to disband the vertically integrated structure FilmFour had built up. Nevertheless, in announcing a return to the low-budget, indigenous film-making that the channel used to specialise in, Thompson could point to how poorly FilmFour had acquitted itself with just that kind of film in recent years; critically acclaimed movies like *The Low Down, Jump Tomorrow* and *The Navigators* were granted only token cinema releases. *The Warrior* was a partial exception.

Taken together with the continuing poor performance of the lottery franchisees, the demise of FilmFour is a severe blow to the British film industry. The Film Council is more important than ever now, but their Premiere fund is aimed at just the higher-budget internationally friendly movies that were FilmFour's nemesis. However, the council got off to a good start, backing Altman's Oscar-nominated *Gosford Park,* and helping to bring to the screen Paul Greengrass's powerful *Bloody Sunday,* a winner at this year's Berlin Film Festival. The Film Council has also announced plans to invest in improving existing art-house cinemas and to subsidise the distribution of foreign-language and independent films.

This was the year that popular Indian cinema made strides into the consciousness of world cinemagoers; *Lagaan* was nominated for the best foreign language film Oscar, *Asoka* showed at the Venice Film Festival and *Devdas* at Cannes, and *Kush Kush Kabhie Gham* was a significant box-office success in the UK and abroad. Mira Nair's *Monsoon Wedding,* an international co-production, picked up the Golden Lion at Venice in 2001, and proved a rare cross-over hit for FilmFour distribution. Roman Polanski won the Palme D'Or for his Holocaust movie *The Pianist,* a highlight of the particularly high-calibre Cannes film festival in 2002. After last year's absence, the British were back on the Croisette in force with well-regarded new films by Mike Leigh, Ken Loach, Michael Winterbottom and Lynne Ramsay.

Last year's controversial Cannes hit, Michael Haneke's *The Piano Teacher,* was released in British cinemas and seemed to herald a new era of sexually explicit art films. Scenes of Isabelle Huppert mutilating herself and begging her lover to debase her seemed mild in retrospect, after we'd been treated to Patrice Chereau's *Intimacy,* (or *Last Tango in Lewisham,* as the wags had it), which featured Kerry Fox engaging in real oral sex with Mark Rylance; Catherine Breillat's *A Ma Soeur* (aka *Fat Girl*), with its ten-minute defloration scene; and the punk-exploitation movie *Baise Moi* (aka *Rape Me*), which also boasted unsimulated sex among its attractions. While *Baise Moi* was cut by ten seconds, in general the British Board of Film Classification is now living up to its name, classifying films rather than censoring them.

Andreas Whittam Smith stepped down after four years as the board's president, a spell which has seen far greater openness and public accountability in BBFC decision-making, and a markedly more tolerant attitude to sex and, to an extent, violence. As Whittam Smith acknowledged, this shift reflected public opinion and the increasing difficulty in enforcing restrictions in the era of digital communications. Indeed, one of the board's more controversial decisions, awarding a 12 certificate to *Spider-Man,* was undermined not only by bootleggers who were selling pirate videos and DVDs before the film had even opened, but also by local councils, some of which overturned the BBFC ruling, bowing to the 'pester power' of children, who were specifically targeted by Columbia-Tristar's publicity machine. It is at this level that the next big censorship battles are likely to be fought.

Literature

There was much speculation in the UK publishing industry about the effect on book-buying habits of the terrorist attacks in the US on 11 September 2001. Knock-on effects, though, were limited. Book sales fell by a mere 3 per cent in the week after the terrorist strikes, and the sombre mood did not dampen sales in September of two high-profile books by pop stars. Victoria Beckham's *Learning to Fly* and Robbie Williams's *Somebody Someday* both sold more than 12,000 copies in that week, and by Christmas 'Posh' Spice's book had sold 213,000 copies and Robbie Williams's 264,000.

The main effects of the attacks were a diminished American presence at the Frankfurt Book Fair, as US publishers proved reluctant to come to Europe in October, and, inevitably, the signing-up of books that tried to make sense of what had happened. One of the first to be published was *September 11th: A Testament*, a photographic account of events which also addressed emergent issues. Produced by Pearson Education in collaboration with Reuters news agency, the book was published simultaneously in the UK and the US in mid-December. Both companies contributed to disaster funds, making the book 'profit neutral'. At the Frankfurt Book Fair two books that chronicled Rawa, the Kabul-based women's resistance group, attracted considerable interest. There were also at least two books on offer by or about firemen involved in the rescue operation after the attack on the World Trade Center; one was bought for UK publication by Orion.

In the aftermath, reprints of books on the Taliban, Afghanistan and terrorism were rushed out, and a children's book about the life of an Afghan girl under the Taliban, *The Breadwinner*, by Canadian peace worker Deborah Ellis, experienced a surge in sales. New York mayor Rudolph Giuliani, who had emerged as a transatlantic hero, sold his book *Leadership* to publisher Little, Brown after a competitive auction for UK rights.

BILLY

The celebrity biography that was a spectacular seller during the year was Pamela Stephenson's biography of her husband, comedian Billy Connolly, which revealed a childhood of abuse and trauma. *Billy* became the Book of the Year at the British Book Awards in February 2002 after selling over a million copies in hardback, and went on to be a long-lived paperback bestseller. Meanwhile, advances paid for celebrity memoirs continued to exceed £500,000. Robbie Williams's memoir had cost Random House £800,000, but its sales justified the money. *Learning To Fly* cost Penguin even more but earned back £750,000 just from a serial deal. Publishers, excited by such successes, shelled out for celebrity confessions by sporting names (Roy Keane, Manchester Utd's and (briefly) Ireland's captain, and Formula One commentator Murray Walker's *Unless I'm Very Much Mistaken*), by pop stars of all eras (Mel B's *Catch A Fire*, Nicole and Natalie Appleton's *Together*, Kylie Minogue's *Kylie: La La La*, Geri Halliwell, Lulu and David Essex) and by TV personalities with varying amounts of personality: Richard Madeley and Judy Finnigan, Michael Barrymore, Dale Winton, gardener Alan Titchmarsh, comedienne Ruby Wax, war correspondent Kate Adie and Ulrika Jonsson, who attracted more media attention through an affair with England football team manager Sven-Goran Eriksson. Keane, Walker and Kylie were safe bets as bestsellers, and all apparently earned over £1 million in advances.

Titchmarsh is reliably popular, and Kate Adie commands general respect. The others were more of a gamble.

POTTER CROSSOVER LEAD

One of the big news stories of the year was the absence of a book. Many column inches were spent discussing the fact that the fifth volume in J. K. Rowling's Harry Potter series was not published in summer 2002. As *Harry Potter and the Order of the Phoenix* was still taking shape, the other four books continued to dominate the bestseller lists, boosted by the release in November 2001 of the film of *Harry Potter and the Philosopher's Stone*, which broke box-office records. Also boosted by a film of the book, J. R. R. Tolkien reappeared in the bestseller lists 47 years after the first publication of *The Lord of the Rings*.

The ongoing success of Harry Potter continued to change both reading and marketing habits; the concept of the 'crossover book' read by both adults and children took hold of the popular imagination, and publishers demonstrated their new-found belief that a children's book, properly promoted, could be big business. Several new teenage fiction lists were launched, including Young Picador and Atom. Penguin's confidence in Eoin Colfer's *Artemis Fowl*, which was marketed with chutzpah and a sizeable budget (after an advance of some £40,000 for two books), paid off as the book climbed into the bestseller lists and stayed there, not for as long as Rowling but long enough to justify the investment. Colfer's book, which he described as 'Die Hard with fairies', was a spoof thriller combining Irish folklore and high-tech adventure, full of tough-talking comic repartee; the film rights were sold before publication. The sequel, *Artemis Fowl: The Arctic Incident*, came out with another burst of hype, and united Artemis Fowl, the 12-year-old criminal mastermind, and his former foe, the Lower Elements Police, against a common enemy.

Big advances for potential crossover books expressed the bullishness of publishers and marketing campaigns were higher-profile than has been the case for children's books. Macmillan worked hard, for instance, on Georgia Byng's *Molly Moon's Incredible Book of Hypnotism*, Penguin on Michael Hoeye's *Time Stops for No Mouse*, Orchard Books on Jerry Spinelli's *Stargirl* and Collins on Nicky Singer's *Feather Boy*, all of which had received substantial advances. Among the biggest deals announced at the Bologna Book Fair, the principal international forum for rights in children's books, was a six-figure sum paid by Hodder & Stoughton for a fantasy trilogy by first-time author David Lee Stone, with the first volume to be published in summer 2003. Macmillan paid a six-figure sum rumoured to be around £300,000 for a trilogy of novels aimed at readers of all ages and set in a mythical ancient Japan, by an Australian writer using the pseudonym Lian Hearn; the first of these, *Across the Nightingale Floor*, was scheduled for publication in September 2002.

Publishers in 12 countries bought rights in *The Curious Incident of the Dog in the Night-time*, by Mark Haddon, an established but not, hitherto, big-time children's author. It concerned a 15-year-old autistic boy's investigation of the death of his neighbour's dog, and publisher Random House plan, unprecedentedly, to bring out the novel in the UK in spring 2003 under both its adult and its children's imprints. Random House also bought Jonathan Stroud's fantasy series *The Bartimaeus Trilogy*, outbidding several rivals with an offer of at least £250,000.

However, the status of children's books was probably boosted far more by a children's author winning the Whitbread Book of the Year prize for the first time in its history, against competition from adult books in the poetry, novel, first novel and biography categories. *The Amber Spyglass*, the third book in Philip Pullman's *His Dark Materials* trilogy, took the overall prize after the briefest of deliberations among the judges.

The prestige of children's books was so high after Pullman had proved that the genre could hold its own against writing for adults that some children's titles, including Pullman's, were said to be on the longlist for the Booker Prize. None made it onto the Booker shortlist, though the list did include lesser known names, including David Mitchell with his acclaimed second novel *Number 9 Dream*, set in Japan and inventing 'a Billy Liar for the cyperpunk generation' and Rachel Seiffert's first novel *The Dark Room*, an exploration of the legacy of the Holocaust from the point of view of the German gentile. Seiffert's book was also shortlisted for the Orange Prize, though this was won by *Bel Canto*, Ann Patchett's story of an opera singer in a house full of hostages. Meanwhile, the surprise exclusion from the Booker shortlist (apart from Philip Pullman) was Beryl Bainbridge's much admired *According to Queeney*, which portrayed Samuel Johnson from the point of view of Mrs Thrale's daughter.

The Booker favourite was Ian McEwan's novel *Atonement*, in which the central character witnesses a sexual assault, accuses the wrong person and has to live with the consequences. But this was pipped to the prize by Peter Carey's *True History of the Kelly Gang*, the story of the Australian outlaw Ned Kelly, narrated in his voice. Carey's book was regarded as 'more polished' than the McEwan, while Booker judge Kate Summerscale said that Carey's book had 'more oddity and so more magic'. Both authors have won the Booker before, Carey with *Oscar and Lucinda* and McEwan with *Amsterdam*. Carey said that he would have to buy McEwan an expensive meal as recompense, but recompense may not have been necessary: *Atonement* sold over 100,000 copies by Christmas, and went on to be a big paperback bestseller, while Carey's book sold only half as many. The Booker Prize itself underwent a significant change, as it was taken over in a five-year deal by the Man Group, an alternative investment fund manager and broker, and changed its name to the Man Booker Prize. The new sponsors expressed a wish to make the prize more international, although speculation that American novels might be in contention for the main prize had little foundation. Parallel prizes abroad are a more likely development.

STEADY SUCCESSES

Although Harry Potter dominated the bestseller lists, some persistently popular authors maintained their habitual high sales. Thriller writers Tom Clancy (*Bear and the Dragon*), Wilbur Smith (*Warlock*), James Herbert (*Once*), Stephen King (*Dreamcatcher*), Ruth Rendell (*Adam and Eve and Pinch Me*), John Grisham (*A Painted House* and *The Summons*) and Patricia Cornwell (*Isle of Dogs*) all appeared in the lists. 'Chick lit' continued to sell strongly, as sales of Wendy Holden's *Fame Fatale*, Jane Green's *Babyville* and Katie Fforde's *Highland Fling* demonstrated. Television cook Jamie Oliver's *Happy Days with the Naked Chef* sold like hot cakes, as did Delia Smith's *How to Cook: Book 3*, although sales were lower than for Book 2. Other big sellers included Dave Pelzer's confessions of his unhappy childhood (*A Child called 'It'*, *The Lost Boy* and *A Man Named Dave*), SAS adventurer Andy McNab blazing on with *Firewall*, travel writer Bill Bryson with *Down Under*, and television quiz host Anne

Robinson's *Memoirs of an Unfit Mother*. Comedian Frank Skinner's autobiography sold a respectable 75,000 copies, though this was not enough to earn back its advance. Nick Hornby (*How to be Good* and the recently filmed *About a Boy*), Sebastian Faulks (*On Green Dolphin Street*) and Tony Parsons (*Man and Boy* and its sequel *One for My Baby*), sold on into another year.

JEWELS, MILK AND OPRAH

One notable debut in the year was Hari Kunzru's highly regarded *The Impressionist*, a story of a boy living out many different roles in India and Britain in the aftermath of the Empire. The novel that caused the greatest critical stir was American Jonathan Franzen's perceptive and comic third novel *The Corrections*, published in November 2001. Some 600 pages long, it was a study of the mixed-up lives of a fractured mid-Western family, and it won America's National Book Award. Talk show host Oprah Winfrey chose it for her sales-boosting book club, but Franzen declined to have his books stickered with her recommendation. This apparent gesture of disdain for Oprah's opinion caused her to deselect the book, certainly losing Franzen sales. After this much-publicised spat, Fourth Estate rushed forward publication in the UK from the scheduled date of January 2002, though British bookshops were already stocking the American edition.

Controversy also arose over the Hay-on-Wye festival of literature in June 2002, for which the *Guardian* had taken over sponsorship for the first time from the *Sunday Times*. When Nestlé came on board as a sponsor, several writers boycotted the festival, in protest at Nestlé's promotion of its water-mixed formula milk for babies in developing countries where breast milk is much safer because of the potential dangers of the local water. Germaine Greer, Jim Crace and Will Self were among writers who refused to attend.

There was another sponsorship scrap over Fay Weldon's book *The Bulgari Connection*, sponsored by the Italian jewellery firm Bulgari. The book was originally not intended for dissemination beyond Bulgari's own client base, but Weldon's agent, Giles Gordon, touted it to her publishers on both sides of the Atlantic. A furore ensued about the compromise of literary integrity represented by this commercial product placement, and the author herself declared that her name would be 'mud'. The agent seemed to think, however, that his action was not ill-advised; rather that it was an initiative with significant potential. 'The door is open and now the sky is the limit', he said.

The relatively sedate world of poetry prizes encountered controversy for the first time over the Forward Poetry Prizes. In 2001 the £10,000 prize for the best collection and £5,000 for best first collection went to two authors published by Picador, Sean O'Brien for *Downriver* and John Stammers for *Panoramic Lounge Bar* respectively. In 2002 there were two more Picador poets, Peter Porter and Paul Farley, in the running for the best collection prize. In both years there were two poets associated with Picador among the five judges. Accusations were made of a pro-Picador bias, which prompted the chair of the judges, Michael Donaghy, to step down, to counteract claims of any impropriety. His place was taken by William Sieghart, founder of the Forward Prizes, although Sieghart pointed out that the Picador poets were outnumbered by three other judges with no associations with the publisher. 'The idea that these three could be browbeaten by two Picador poets is patently ridiculous', he said. Meanwhile, the T. S. Eliot Prize for poetry went to a woman for the first time in its nine-year history, won by Anne Carson for *The Beauty of the Husband*.

Author Graham Swift, no stranger to controversy since his Booker-winning novel *Last Orders* was accused of plagiarising William Faulkner, found himself in the firing line once again, just as the film of *Last Orders* proved a box-office and critical success. Negotiations for *The Light of Day*, his new novel and the first since his Booker win, attracted disapprobation when the *Observer* revealed that Swift and his agent, Caradoc King of A. P. Watt, were seeking to make his previous books part of the new deal when rights to these books were still owned by Picador. King wrote to Picador to request that it cede rights in the seven previous books, should it be unsuccessful in bidding for the new novel. King said: 'The misreporting in the *Observer* left out an important point: that when Graham moved to Picador in 1991, he took his backlist with him. It's good to move the backlist in these cases if you can, particularly if it's not performing with the previous publisher.' The new novel went to Penguin for what was rumoured to be a six-figure sum, but the deal did not include rights to the earlier works, although Penguin said it did hope to agree terms for Swift's backlist, which includes *Waterland*, widely recognised as a modern classic.

LEGAL ACTIONS

One issue of concern this year was the issue of 'gagging letters', sent to booksellers warning them against selling books that contained alleged libels. In a landmark libel case in the High Court, the extreme right-wing, anti-gay author Alexander Baron successfully sued Housmans Bookshop in London – a radical bookseller that stocks pacifist, socialist and gay literature – for stocking an anti-Nazi pamphlet that defamed him. However, the jury awarded Baron only £14 damages; a higher damages award could have closed down the shop.

The case prompted the Booksellers Association to take advantage of a new study by the Law Commission to renew its lobbying over the 'intimidatory' use of defamation laws to gag booksellers and distributors. The association said the amended Defamation Act 1996 contained an oversight that made it easy for potential litigants to hold booksellers to ransom, avoiding costly libel proceedings against the author or publisher. The Law Commission supported the association's proposed changes to the Defamation Act, which would prevent libel plaintiffs from suing retailers without also suing the author, editor or publisher of the material. The changes were recommended to the Lord Chancellor.

David Irving and Neil Hamilton both took advantage of this loophole to attempt to suppress books that criticised them. Discredited historian David Irving wrote to bookshops trying to prevent sales of *Telling Lies About Hitler: The Holocaust, History and the David Irving Trial*, about the Irving vs. Penguin libel trial, by Richard Evans, a professor of modern history at Cambridge University. The publication of this book had already caused controversy after an *Observer* article accused publishers Random House, Profile Books and Granta of being bullied by Irving into dropping the book, which was eventually published by Verso. All three publishers rejected the *Observer*'s interpretation of events. Granta said that a four-book deal with Evans had soured when the author changed his agent, and Random House said that the book had been rejected on commercial grounds.

Other books in the news included *In the Hands of the Taliban*, an account by journalist Yvonne Ridley of her capture and detention by the Taliban after she entered Afghanistan in a rather inadequate disguise; and *The Sexual Life of Catherine M*, a surprisingly explicit account of her own promiscuous sexual history by the feminist French academic Catherine Millet. The late Douglas Adams, who was notorious for his writers' block, had a posthumous collection of unfinished writing published under the title *The Salmon of Doubt*. Film star Michael J. Fox wrote *Lucky Man*, a bestselling account of his life and struggle with Parkinson's disease, while Michael Crick, biographer of Michael Heseltine and Jeffrey Archer, turned his attention to Manchester Utd manager Alex Ferguson in his high-profile study *The Boss*. The unexpected winner of the £30,000 Samuel Johnson prize for non-fiction was Margaret Macmillan for *Peacemakers*, a book about the Paris Peace Conference of 1919, though the bookies' favourite was Roy Jenkins's biography of Churchill. The award ceremony was broadcast for the first time, live on the new digital channel BBC Four.

The *Guardian* celebrated its own first book award, chosen from nominations by its readers and judged by a panel of members of the public. The prize went to a graphic novel, the first to win a major British literary award. Chris Ware's *Jimmy Corrigan* won by a single vote, after a three-way tussle with Miranda Carter's *Anthony Blunt*, an ambitious biography of the Soviet spy and art expert, and Glen David Gold's fantastical novel *Carter Beats The Devil*; the latter was inspired by the appearance on stage in 1923 with the illusionist 'Carter the Great' of Warren Harding, known as the 'worst-ever' US president.

The deaths of two members of the royal family, Princess Margaret on 9 February and the Queen Mother on 30 March, prompted publishers to rush out tributes and biographies. Neil Botham's *Margaret: The Last Real Princess* came out in February, three weeks earlier than planned, and was updated to include the Princess's death. In April, speedy tributes to the Queen Mother included Debrett's *Queen Elizabeth the Queen Mother* by Valerie Garner, BBC Books' *The Queen Mother Remembered* and a hastily updated biography from Dorling Kindersley, *Queen Elizabeth, the Queen Mother*, re-released in a commemorative edition.

LITERARY PRIZEWINNERS

Nobel Prize for Literature 2001 – V. S. Naipaul
Commonwealth Writers Prize 2002 – Richard Flanagan, *Gould's Book of Fish*
Best First Book 2002 - Manu Herbstein, *A Story of the Atlantic Slave Trade*
Booker Prize 2001 – Peter Carey, *True History of the Kelly Gang*
Whitbread Prize 2001: overall winner – Philip Pullman, *The Amber Spyglass*
  First Novel – Sid Smith, *Something Like a House*
  Biography – Diana Souhami, *Selkirk's Island*
  Poetry – Selima Hill, *Bunny*
  Children's novel – Philip Pullman, *The Amber Spyglass*
Smarties Prize 2001 (children's books):
  Age 0-5 – Catherine and Laurence *Anholt, Chimp and Zee*
  Age 6-8 – Emily Smith, *The Shrimp*
  Age 9-11 – Eva Ibbotson, *Journey to the River Sea*
Crime Writers Association 2001:
  Gold Dagger (fiction) – Henning Mankell, *Sidetracked*
  Gold Dagger (non-fiction) – Philip Etienne and Martin Maynard with Tony Thompson, *The Infiltrators*
  Silver Dagger – Giles Blunt, *Forty Words for Sorrow*
  Short Story Dagger – Marion Arnott, *Prussion Snowdrops*
British Book Awards 2001:
  Philip Pullman, *The Amber Spyglass*
  Children's – Eoin Colfer, *Artemis Fowl*
Orange Prize 2002 (women writers) – Ann Pratchett, *Bel Canto*

Somerset Maugham Awards 2002 – Charlotte Hobson, *Black Earth City*; Marcel Theroux, *The Paperchase*
Betty Trask Prize 2002 (first novel by an author under 35): Hari Kunzru, *The Impressionist*
McKitterick Prize 2002 (first novel by a writer over 40): Manil Suri, *The Death of Vishnu*
WH Smith Prize 2002 (voted for by the public):
  Literary Award – Ian McEwan, *Atonement*
  New Talent – Emily Barr, *Backpack*
  Fiction – Nick Hornby, *How to be Good*
  Biography and Autobiography – Pamela Stephenson, *Billy*
  Home and Leisure – Nigella Lawson, *Nigella Bites*
  Children's – Eoin Colfer, *Artemis Fowl*
  Business – Judi Bevan, *The Rise and Fall of Marks and Spencer*
  Travel – (various authors) *The Weekenders*
  General Knowledge – Alastair Fothergill, Martha Holmes, Andrew Byatt, *The Blue Planet*
Cholmondley Awards 2002: Moniza Alvi, *Souls*; David Constantine, *Something for the Ghosts*; Liz Lochhead, *Perfect Days*; Brian Patten, *The Blue and Green Ark: An Alphabet for Planet Earth*
T. S. Eliot Prize (poetry) – Anne Carson, *The Beauty of the Husband*
Parker Romantic Novel of the Year (2002) – Philippa Gregory, *The Other Boleyn Girl*
Carngie Prize 2002 – Terry Pratchett, *Amazing Maurice and His Educated Rodents*
Kate Greenaway 2001 – Chris Riddell, *Pirate Diary*
Samuel Johnson Prize 2002 – Margaret Macmillan, *Peacemakers*

Music

Despite the financial problems of recent years, classical music in Britain continues to thrive with great diversity and vitality. Orchestras, choirs, chamber ensembles, festivals, opera companies and concert venues have survived in often difficult circumstances by developing new ways to bring music to wider audiences whilst maintaining their commitment to the promotion and encouragement of music of the highest possible standard. In recent years, this survival has often been assisted by funds from the National Lottery for building projects and for development schemes requiring an increasing involvement with education and community outreach work.

The year 2002 marked the 20th birthday of London's Barbican Centre; this was closed throughout summer 2001 to allow essential improvements, at a cost of £7 million, to be completed in time for the birthday celebrations, which started in October 2001. It reopened with a concert by Richard Hickox and the City of London Sinfonia, who were the first to demonstrate the efficacy of the revamped acoustic. A new hi-tech stainless steel integrated ceiling, plus changes to the lighting and air-conditioning have facilitate a consistent and transparent acoustic. Kirkegaard Associates, who list Kuala Lumpur, Glasgow and Liverpool among their credits, have completed the acoustic adjustments they began in 1994. The programme for the opening night was well-chosen to show off and explore the vastly improved sound. With an appropriate touch of patriotism it included Lennox Berkeley's *Serenade for Strings Op. 12*, Rubbra's *Symphony No. 10* and three works by Finzi, to celebrate his centenary. Tasmin Little performed Finzi's *Concerto for Small Orchestra and Violin* and Ian Bostridge sang *Dies Natalis* to critical acclaim. Three days later it was the London Symphony Orchestra's turn to explore the improved acoustics, with the adjustable ceiling panels set to suit a full orchestra. A performance of Mozart's *Piano Concerto No. 21* played by Mitsuko Uchida and conducted by Sir Colin Davies marked the opening of the LSO's new season and the audience was thrilled by the depth of tone and intensity of the pregnant pauses supplied by the shimmering ceiling.

The London Philharmonic Orchestra's celebration of conductor Kurt Masur's 75th birthday with Anne-Sophie Mutter was a great success in April 2002. The London Philharmonic Orchestra's chief conductor was back in business after an extended period of surgery and recuperation. The hall was sold out and there were tributes in the programme from, among others, Tony Blair and Gerhard Schröder. The performance included Debussy's *La Mer*, Ravel's *La Valse* and the world premiere of *Sur le Même Accord*, a nocturne for violin and orchestra by Henri Dutilleux, the most recent of a long line of composers to have been inspired by the glamorous Anne-Sophie Mutter. Other memorable performances in the LPO season were Mark Elder's refreshing account of Elgar's *The Dream of Gerontius* and the 29-year-old Russian Vladimir Jurowski's energetic and exciting performance of Prokofiev's *Symphony No. 5 in B flat*.

Another 75th birthday celebrated in style this year was that of Mstislav Rostropovich, the greatest cellist of the second half of the 20th century. But it was Rostropovich the conductor rather than Rostropovich the cellist who was the focus of the London Symphony Orchestra's four-programme tribute at the Barbican in March 2002, which featured three composers with whom Rostropovich had a close relationship: Prokofiev, Shostakovich and Britten. His most notable performance was Shostakovich's *Symphony No. 11*, in which he unleashed ferocious energy from the LSO by extreme expression and tempos, producing an intensely gripping narrative. Also included in the series was a performance of Shostakovich's *Romeo and Juliette*, the complete ballet score, with dance supplied by the Lithuanian State Ballet, choreographed by Vladimir Vasiliev.

ON THE SOUTH BANK

In April 2002, the South Bank Centre and the Royal Academy played host to the UK's largest-ever festival of the music of contemporary Hungarian composer György Kurtág. Entitled *Signs, Games and Messages*, it presented his music alongside works by his influences, contemporaries and compatriots, including Monteverdi, Beethoven, Schumann, Bartók, Ligeti, Stockhausen and Nono. The festival included 18 concerts at the South Bank and the Royal Academy of Music, as well as talks, workshops and masterclasses, with notable performances from the London Sinfonietta, the City of Birmingham Symphony Orchestra, the Sixteen and the Arditti String Quartet. The festival opened with a piano duet recital by Kurtág and his wife Márta of pieces drawn from the composer's six volumes of studies, fragments and games written since the 1970s, and served to maintain his reputation as, according to *The Gramophone*, 'a chronicler of the absurd' and 'master of the miniature'.

The South Bank Centre also housed the London Sinfonietta's *State of the Nation* festival in April 2002, which showcased 'cutting-edge' music from more than 25 British composers, or composers taught by British composers, half of whom are in their twenties. There were various multimedia events, workshops and masterclasses, few of which were particularly memorable, but on the whole there was a supportive and encouraging buzz amongst those involved. The most innovative project of the weekend, and ironically one not performed on the South Bank, was '*Line Up!*' a piece specially written for, and performed at, the recently built Southwark underground station. *Line Up!*, composed by Fraser Trainer and Sound Intermedia (David Sheppard and Ian Dreaden), consisted of fanfares for each of the stops on the Jubilee line, scored for wind and brass with electro-acoustic tape, which impressed the itinerant audience by its unique relationship with the space. Purely acoustic pieces composed by, among others, David Gorton (recent winner of the Royal Philharmonic Society composition prize), Tansy Davis, James Olsen and Dai Fujikura were performed with commitment by the London Sinfonietta, conducted by Martyn Brabbins. Other contributors included Sonic Arts Network (SAN), the Society for the Promotion of New Music (SPNM) and Contemporary Music for Amateurs (COMA).

Oliver Knussen and the London Sinfonietta continued their critically acclaimed *New to London* series of concerts this year, including world premières of new works by Jonathan Cole, Detlev Glanert, George Perle and the first public performance of Sir Peter Maxwell Davies's commission for the opening of the Millennium Bridge. Also featured in the 2001–2 season was a celebration of the Sinfonietta's artistic director, composer and conductor Oliver Knussen at the age of 50. An evening at the Queen Elizabeth Hall featured a selection of Knussen's beautifully crafted ensemble and chamber

works, including *Masks, Ocean de Terre, Two Organa* and *Elegiac Arabesques*, alongside a number of world premières specially composed by Knussen's distinguished friends and colleagues world-wide.

The London Sinfonietta joined forces with the composer and Massive Attack collaborator Craig Armstrong as part of the *Elektronic* festival at the Barbican in October 2001. Karlheinz Stockhausen's legacy was reappraised with sold-out performances of his rarely heard early electronic tape pieces. The weekend festival ambitiously interleaved the Stockhausen with performances by William Orbit, Aphex Twin and Talvin Singh in an attempt to demonstrate his acknowledged influence on cutting-edge contemporary popular music. This ambition did not quite live up to expectations, and perhaps most disappointing was composer-trumpeter Jon Hassell's failure to materialise and collaborate with Talvin Singh, leaving Singh struggling.

AROUND THE COUNTRY

Birmingham Contemporary Music Group (BCMG) continued to attract large audiences to Birmingham's CBSO centre. Two central events this year were the BCMG's *Bass Inventions* tour, the title of a new work by Mark Anthony Turnage composed for the jazz bassist Dave Holland, and their contribution to the *Discover Denmark* series. Turnage has provided Holland with a subdued and reflective showcase, part-notated, part-improvised, and used Holland's wonderfully warm tone to set the mood for the piece, contrasted with unabrasive ensemble writing. Performances of *Bass Inventions* in London, Birmingham and Basingstoke were combined with Gerald Barry's *Dead March*. This new BCMG commission provided radical freshness in a piece containing ferocious isolated gestures, rhythmic unisons and lots of silences. BCMG's offering in the *Discover Denmark* series in November 2001 began with Thomas Adès's *Catch*, followed by Hans Abrahamsen's arrangements of Carl Nielson's *Three Piano Pieces Op. 59*, neither of which was particularly inspiring. BCMG's playing under Pierre-André Valade was intense and purposeful, and the second half more than made up for the slight disappointment with performances of Poul Ruder's new work *Abysm* and Kaija Saariaho's *Solar*. The surprise finale came in the form of a new piece composed by Colin Matthews for the departure of the popular and inspiring Simon Clugston, BCMG's artistic director.

The BBC Scottish Symphony Orchestra certainly had a good year. In a spectacular double coup, the SSO was presented with the large ensemble award and its chief conductor Osmo Vänskä took the conductor award at the Royal Philharmonic Society Awards. They were commended for their commitment to classical and contemporary music all over the UK, which has reached a peak under conductors Osmo Vänskä and Martyn Brabbins. Also praised for their imaginatively marketed home series, the SSO brought distinction to its festival appearances in 2001, with performances of Berlioz's *The Troyans* and Peter Eötvös's *Three Sisters* at the Edinburgh Festival 2001, and the première of Stuart MacRae's *Violin Concerto*, played by Tasmin Little, at the BBC Proms 2001. Osmo Vänskä was highly praised for the consolidation of his partnership with the SSO and for consistently excellent performances, particularly in the works of Sibelius and Nielson.

The Manchester-based Hallé Orchestra's 2001–2 series entitled *Scattered Sparks* prompted some extraordinary concerts in Manchester, focusing on music written in response to the two world wars. Perhaps the most imaginative programme offered was Elgar's rarely

performed *Spirit of England*, Strauss' *Metamorphosen* and Sibelius' *Fifth Symphony* in the Bridgewater Hall in April 2002. The pieces, stamped with conductor Mark Elder's individuality, warranted having an interval between them. The Hallé launched its own record label in June. Unlike the Royal Liverpool Philharmonic and London Symphony labels, the Hallé label will not be based around live recordings. Having only recently recovered from serious financial problems, chief executive John Summers hopes the move will allow 'total artistic freedom' and will 'build the Hallé's international profile'. Unlike the LSO label, where profits are distributed among players, Hallé members have accepted a pay rise instead. Summers stated that the cost of making records had 'shot down in price' and because the Internet allows savings on marketing and distribution, large corporations were no longer the only organisations able to provide the resources to make recordings and distribute them properly.

This optimism surfaced only six months after the sad demise of Nimbus Records, the independent UK classical label and distributor. Gerald Reynolds, a director of Nimbus, stated that the business 'is going into full receivership', and that it was 'a very sad day indeed for the company'. Monmouth-based Nimbus had been a mainstay of the British market for more than 15 years, with an extensive and well-tended catalogue. Its assets include orchestral, chamber and world music, as well as 'nostalgia' products and archive transfers from 78s. The Nimbus Foundation, a charitable organisation created to support and encourage the performing arts, was not affected.

The Contemporary Music Network (CMN) continued to support concerts of new music around the country, making an effort to bring audiences new and fresh material. To celebrate its 30 years in business, the CMN produced a book accompanied by a double CD which includes compositions by Birtwistle, Maxwell Davies, Xenakis, Meredith Monk and Copeland. Finnish composer Kaija Saariaho was featured in the CMN's 2001–2 tour, with her music theatre piece *From The Grammar of Dreams*, set to texts by Sylvia Plath, Apollinaire, Hölderlin and Shakespeare, and using twin sopranos and electronics. *From the Grammar of Dreams*, with lighting and costume design by Raija Malka, was ethereal and sparse, beautifully staged and well-received in Manchester, London, Basingstoke, Kendal and Newcastle, and at the Huddersfield Contemporary Music Festival in November 2001.

FESTIVALS

In fact, there was an unusual amount of music theatre at the Huddersfield Contemporary Music Festival 2001. The festival was one of the venues on a wider European tour for many events, including Manchester-based Psappha's production of Sir Peter Maxwell Davies's recent *Mr Emmet Takes a Walk*, a production of Salvatore Sciarrino's *Lohengrin* from Berlin, and Heiner Goebbel's *Hashirigaki* from Switzerland. Attention focused on the retirement of Richard Steinitz, founder and artistic director of the festival, and on his chosen successor, 32-year-old Susanna Eastburn. After 23 years' devotion to running an event of increasing stature with limited funding, Steinitz made way for Eastburn, a musician with publishing experience and an impressive portfolio of promotions and board advisory positions in the contemporary music world.

Although Steinitz had already put in place some aspects of the 2001 festival, Eastburn achieved enormous success in a role that is inevitably a hard act for anyone following Steinitz. Cornelius Cardew's work was celebrated in a

series of concerts, debates, workshops and a performance of the sixth paragraph of *The Great Learning*, scored for any number of untrained or trained musicians. This event was a highpoint and a demonstration of the festival's commitment to the local community's involvement in music at the highest level. Salvatore Sciarrino was the focus on the final day of the festival, with his esoteric, ghostly *Six Caprices for Solo Violin*, brilliantly performed by Meiko Kanno.

The Edinburgh International Festival 2002 under the direction of Brian McMaster continued to attract audiences from far and wide with a popular and somewhat safe programme of opera, music, theatre and dance. Festival hype focused mainly on a production of Wagner's *Parsifal* conducted by Claudio Abbado with the Gustav Mahler Jugendorchester, and staged by Peter Stein. The festival introduced a series of late-night £5 concerts in the vast Usher Hall, which not only helped the seriously abused purses of the festival-goers but provided a few slightly daring, yet commendable performances for those who are not able to book two months in advance. Highlights of this series included *Night Raga*, Indian classical music played throughout the night by Ustad Amjad Ali Khan, Pt Hari Prasad Chaurasia and Shruti Sadolikar; Stockhausen's *Stimmung* by the Dunedin Consort; *Music by Rebecca Saunders* performed by the Scottish-based Paragon Ensemble under the direction of Gary Walker; and the BBC Scottish Symphony Orchestra's *Contemporary Scotland* programme, with compositions from MacPherson, MacRae and MacMillan.

Other Edinburgh concerts featured orchestras from around the world, including the Orpheus Chamber Orchestra from the US, the Orchestre National de Lyons and the Los Angeles Philharmonic Orchestra, all making their festival debuts, as well as the Tchaikovsky Symphony Orchestra of Moscow Radio, the Chamber Orchestra of Europe and the Gustav Mahler Jugendorchester. The celebrated American pianist Richard Goode was in residence and other soloists included violinist Dmitry Sitkovetsky performing Tchaikovsky's *Violin Concerto*; contralto Anna Larson and baritone Thomas Quasthoff in Mahler's *Des Knaben Wunderhorn*; Christian Tetzlaff giving the second performance of Stuart MacRae's *Violin Concerto*, premièred at the 2001 Proms; and pianist Martha Argerich performing Ravel's *Piano Concerto*. Other highlights included the Scottish Chamber Orchestra's performance of Handel's last oratorio *Jephtha*, BBCSSO's performance of Heiner Goebbels' *Surrogate Cities*, and the Composers Ensemble's concert of Stravinsky, Nielsen, Poulenc and Janáček. The festival opened with a performance of Lutosławski's *Concerto for Orchestra* and Berlioz's *Te Deum*, conducted by Christoph von Dohnányi, with the Philharmonia Orchestra, the Prague Philharmonic Choir, RSNO Junior Chorus and the Edinburgh Festival Choir.

The Cheltenham International Festival of Music has grown over the past few years under the artistic direction of Michael Berkeley to become one of the UK's finest classical music events. Winner of the Royal Philharmonic Society's best festival award in 2001, Cheltenham's festival has an international reputation for top artists, focused programming with a contemporary bias, and a range of fantastic venues. Indeed, one of the most admirable 'policies' of the festival is that visiting artists must programme at least one contemporary work in each concert. The BBC National Orchestra and Chorus of Wales conducted by Richard Hickox celebrated the 900th anniversary of Tewkesbury Abbey with the world première of John Tavener's *Life Eternal*, alongside Handel's *Zadok the Priest*, Poulenc's *Gloria* and Stravinsky's *Symphony of Psalms*. The City of Birmingham Symphony Orchestra, under the direction of Sakari Oramo with violinist Vadim Repin, played Mussorgsky and Ravel's *Pictures at an Exhibition*, Gubaidulina's *Offertorium* and Stravinsky's *The Rite of Spring* to a packed town hall. Other guests included the Endymion Ensemble, BBC Singers, City of London Sinfonia, members of the National Youth Orchestra of Great Britain, Music Theatre Wales, the Nash Ensemble, Orchestra of the Age of Enlightenment, Schubert Ensemble, Carducci Quartet and Piano Circus.

THE PROMS

The 2002 series of promenade concerts in London, under the directorship of Nicholas Kenyon, remains one of the largest music festivals anywhere in the world, with 73 consecutive concerts at the Royal Albert Hall and eight Chamber Music Proms concerts at the nearby Victoria and Albert Museum from July to September. The series ended with the seventh Proms in the Park event, linking concerts in London's Hyde Park, Gateshead and Belfast and culminating in a live, big-screen link-up with the Royal Albert Hall. As well as being broadcast live on BBC Radio 3 every evening, each concert was audio-streamed onto the Internet. In addition, a selection of concerts was shown on BBC television and on the BBC's digital television channel BBC4, which also video-streamed its programmes onto an interactive website.

The main theme of the series was music from or influenced by Spain and Latin America, but alongside a comprehensive selection of this music, spanning five centuries and several cultures, there were also choral works based on the stories of Old Testament heroes, royal music (a nod to The Queen's Golden Jubilee this year), and a centenary tribute to Sir William Walton. New commissions and premières included Julian Anderson's *Imagin'd Corners*, Simon Bainbridge's *Chant*, Marc-André Dalbavie's *Color*, John Harle's *The Little Death Machine*, Per Nørgård's *Symphony No. 6*, Roberto Sierro's *Fandangos*, and a number of BBC commissions: Anthony Payne's *Visions and Journeys*, Joseph Phibbs's *La Noche Arroladora*, David Sawer's *Piano Concerto*, and a Mark-Anthony Turnage piece. The Last Night of the Proms also featured a *BBC Music Magazine* commission, *Bright Cecilia: Variations on a Theme by Purcell*, composed by Colin Matthews, Judith Weir, Lukas Foss, Poul Ruders, David Sawer, Michael Torke, Anthony Payne and Magnus Lindberg, as well as the traditional programme of items by Elgar, Wood and Parry.

The BBC orchestras performed the majority of the concerts, but there were guest appearances by the Orchestra of the Age of Enlightenment, Orchestre Philharmonique de Radio France, Monteverdi Choir and Orchestra, Lincoln Centre Jazz Orchestra, Orquestra Simfónica de Barcelona, Danish National Symphony Orchestra, Royal Liverpool Philharmonic Orchestra, National Youth Orchestra of Great Britain, English Chamber Orchestra, Australian Chamber Orchestra, BT Scottish Ensemble, Camerata Salzburg, Gustav Mahler Jugendorchester, Orchestre National de Lyon, Chorus and Orchestra of the Kirov Opera, Chamber Orchestra of Europe, Royal Concertgebouw Orchestra, Los Angeles Philharmonic, Philharmonia Orchestra, Sinfonia 21, Munich Philharmonic Orchestra, City of London Sinfonia, London Philharmonic Orchestra, City of Birmingham Symphony Orchestra and the London Symphony Orchestra.

ALL CHANGE

Northern Sinfonia, based in Newcastle-upon-Tyne, appointed *Gramophone* award-winning violinist Thomas Zehetmair as their new music director. Engaged for an initial three-year period, Zehetmair's first appearance in his new role was in November 2001, when he appeared as both violinist (in Hindemith's *Kammermusik No. 4*) and as conductor (Mozart's *Prague Symphony* and Richard Strauss' *Metamorphosen*). Zehetmair's period as music director of the Northern Sinfonia (England's only full-time chamber ensemble) will see the completion of the ensemble's new home, the Foster-designed Music Centre Gateshead, due for completion in 2003. This will not only provide a rehearsal and performance base for the ensemble but will also house a music education centre.

The City of Birmingham Symphony Orchestra, whose music director is the Finnish conductor Sakari Oramo, named Sir Michael Lyons as the new chairman of its board of trustees in September 2001. Sir Michael, who stood down from his role as chief executive of Birmingham City Council, joined the CBSO as it embarked on an ambitious new five-year strategy. The new chief executive of London's South Bank Centre is Michael Lynch, the chief executive of Sydney Opera House, who took up his appointment in September 2002. Lord Hollick, chairman of the SBC, which includes the Royal Festival Hall, Queen Elizabeth Hall, Purcell Room and the Hayward Gallery, spoke of the challenging time ahead, including the major renovation and redevelopment of the whole 30-acre site.

In autumn 2001, the Royal Academy of Music appointed professors for the first time in its 180-year history: the Academy's vice-principal and director of studies Jonathan Freeman-Attwood, head of woodwind Sebastian Bell, head of brass John Wallace, and composer Simon Bainbridge. Marin Alsop was appointed principal conductor of Bournemouth Symphony Orchestra, and Thierry Fischer principal conductor of the Ulster Orchestra. Gwen Hughes was appointed head of classical music at the Arts Council of England.

The Arts Council of England and the ten regional arts boards merged in April 2002 to form a new arts funding organisation. The new body will consist of a central national office and nine regional offices, the latter matching the boundaries of the Government's regional offices. As well as regionalising much of the decision-making process, the regions will also take part in the central process. This change was not without its critics.

RPS MUSIC AWARDS

Although most of the headlines following the Royal Philharmonic Society's music awards stemmed from Sir Thomas Allen's speech, the event honoured achievement and excellence during 2001. Presented in May 2002, winners included the Composers Ensemble in the Chamber Ensemble category, 'for their commitment to innovation and their imaginative and attractive programming in 2001, always composer driven. They animated the Hoxton New Music Days in London and Kettle's Yard in Cambridge with memorable events, on their CD for NMC, no less than 13 young British composers were represented, and their hugely impressive tally of premières during the year included much new work from abroad. From small beginnings, and on not much money, the achievement of the Composers Ensemble has been exceptional.'

The award for Chamber-scale Composition went to Simon Holt's *Two Movements for String Quartet*, for its poetic, intense and passionate writing; the piece was given

a dazzling première by the Belcea Quartet at the Cheltenham Festival 2001. Also commended in this category were Richard Barrett's *Music from Dark Matter* and Bent Sørensen's *Sieben Sehnsuchte*. The Concert Series and Festivals award went to Cheltenham International Festival of Music 2001. The jury identified four outstanding and diverse contenders: The Cheltenham Festival, BMIC's *Cutting Edge*, the Hoxton New Music Days, and the Royal Academy of Music's Kagel Festival. However, it was the scale, range of repertoire and international profile which gave the edge to the Cheltenham festival.

The award for best Conductor went to Osmo Vänskä, chief conductor of the BBC Scottish Symphony Orchestra since 1996, and Mark Elder was also commended. LSO Discovery, the education branch of the London Symphony Orchestra, won the Education Award, for organisation-wide commitment to work in the community, with an unparalleled range of projects that inspired participants of all ages and backgrounds. Also commended was *Turandot-Ji* (Villiers High School, Southall and Royal Opera House Education)

Other winners included the BBC Scottish Symphony Orchestra in the Large Ensemble category (the London Sinfonietta was also commended); Peter Eötvös's opera *Three Sisters* for Large-Scale Composition (also commended: Stuart MacRae's *Violin Concerto*, and David Sawer's *From Morning to Midnight*). Fidelio, performed both at Glyndebourne and by its Touring Opera, won the Opera award for the conducting of Simon Rattle and Louis Langrée and the direction of Deborah Warner. Violeta Urmana won the Singer award for her performances as Kundry in the Royal Opera House's *Parsifal* under Simon Rattle and in the *Verdi Requiem* with the LSO and Antonio Pappano at the Barbican. Organist Thomas Trotter won the Instrumentalist award, and Jonathan Lemalu (still a student at the Royal College of Music) took the Young Artist award for his charismatic opera performances at the college as Bottom in *Midsummer Night's Dream* and Leporello in *Don Giovanni*. The Television and Radio award went to Channel 4 for its film biography of the 20th-century musician Miles Davis. The Composition prize was won by 23-year-old David Gorton. He studied at Durham University, King's College London and the Royal Academy of Music with Sir Harrison Birtwistle and Simon Bainbridge, and his recent works include two pieces for large ensemble, *Grendel is Defeated* and *Towards Location*, both of which have been played at the Royal Academy of Music.

Baritone Sir Thomas Allen's speech focused on 'the rise of populism' in classical music. 'Sugar-coated programming, or the recording of choice bits of easy listening, is a plague and has taken over a once respectable and serious profession to the point where integrity is almost wholly inundated', said Allen, who then went on to attack groups such as the quartet Bond. 'The idea of a wet T-shirted quartet where once was the Amadeus has me reaching for the sea-sick pills'.

Opera

In order to justify their subsidies, opera companies these days have to show that they are encouraging greater access to new and younger audiences, The Royal Opera, which receives the largest subsidy (though this is minuscule in comparison with opera houses in other European capitals), has become a model in this respect. The wonderfully reconstructed Floral Hall, with its bars, restaurants and terrace overlooking the Covent Garden piazza, is open to anyone for most of the day. The Linley and Studio Theatres put on concerts and recitals by young artists, sometimes for free. Performances at the Royal Opera House are relayed to large screens in the piazza and other venues. *Rigoletto*, the first new production of the 2001–2 season, was not only televised, but also shown in a Glasgow cinema.

The celebrations marking the centenary of Verdi's death in 1901 continued in the 2001–2 season. The Royal Opera staged new productions of *Il trovatore* and *Macbeth* as well as *Rigoletto*, and revived *Attila* and *Simon Boccanegra*. There was a new production of Mozart's *Don Giovanni*, presented by two entirely different casts. The first, conducted by Sir Colin Davis and featuring Bryn Terfel in the title role, was good; the second, conducted by Sir Charles Mackerras, with Simon Keenlyside, was very good indeed – lighter in texture and fleeter in execution. Two superstar tenors, Luciano Pavarotti and Placido Domingo, made guest appearances during the season. Pavarotti, who sang Cavaradossi in the 38-year-old production of *Tosca*, appeared (as did the staging) past his sell-by date, but Domingo, as *Hermann* in the year-old production of Tchaikovsky's *Queen of Spades*, was in magnificent form, conquering yet another operatic style and taking the difficulties of the role in his stride.

The season ended with a farewell tribute to Bernard Haitink, stepping down as music director of the Royal Opera after 15 years. During that time he conducted many memorable performances at Covent Garden, of Wagner in particular, as well as Janáček and Britten (a fine *Peter Grimes*), and he has turned the ROH Orchestra into a truly magnificent band of musicians. But his refusal to become embroiled in the politics of the Opera House was at least partly responsible for the troubles that brought the company to near-collapse. His farewell, consisting of an act of *Le nozze di Figaro*, a scene from *Don Carlos* and the long final scene of *Die Meistersinger* with John Tomlinson as Hans Sachs, Thomas Allen as Beckmesser and Ben Heppner as Walther, paid fitting tribute to a great conductor.

English National Opera would seem to be a model company, treading the narrow path between novelty and tradition with sure footsteps. In January 2002, the £41 million project to restore its home, the London Coliseum, to its former glory was set in motion. Planned to be ready by the beginning of 2004, the work will mostly take place with the theatre open and running. So far 90 per cent of the necessary funds have been raised. However, the surprise resignation in July 2002 of the general director, Nicholas Payne, after four apparently very successful years, reflected the increasing gap between the aims of ENO's artistic direction, represented by Payne himself and Paul Daniel, the music director, and Martin Smith, the chairman of ENO, worried by a season with too many empty seats and a growing deficit as a consequence.

Ironically, Payne's departure was precipitated by the controversial new production of a Verdi opera, *A Masked Ball*, directed by Calixto Bieito. Bieito's staging of *Don Giovanni* in the 2000–1 season, heavily dependent on sex and drugs, annoyed the critics but was applauded by audiences. *A Masked Ball*, though, with the men of the chorus reading their newspapers seated on a line of lavatories in the opening scene, and a homosexual rape and murder in Act II, infuriated critics and audiences alike. In several other ways the season was a success. Despite the presence of the soprano Jane Eaglen in the title role, the staging of Spontini's *La Vestale* was found dull, but three 20th-century operas, Prokofiev's *War and Peace*, Stravinsky's *The Rake's Progress* and Berg's *Lulu* were all highly successful. *Lulu*, never before staged by ENO, was particularly admired.

NORTHERN SUCCESSES

Opera North's attempts to attract a new and younger audience have included the staging of American musicals, of which the most successful so far has been David McVicar's highly enjoyable production of *Sweeney Todd*. A revival of Sondheim's macabre masterpiece was brought to Sadler's Wells Theatre in London, where it was welcomed with much appreciation. With 2002 being the centenary of Richard Rodger's birth, *Something Wonderful*, a concert programme containing many of the American composer's favourite numbers, was included in the works taken on tour. The new production of Janáček's *The Cunning Little Vixen*, together with a revival of Britten's *Gloriana* was taken to the Liceu, recently restored after a disastrous fire, in Barcelona. A film of *Gloriana*, made by Opera North's cast and orchestra, was also shown in Barcelona.

Scottish Opera offered the world première of *Monster*, the first full-length opera by Sally Beamish, with libretto by Janice Galloway. The subject, the conception of Mary Shelley's famous Gothic novel *Frankenstein*, sounded promising, but an over-long, over-talkative text (25 scenes in two acts), and a huge cast list (including Byron, Coleridge, Godwin and Lamb, as well as Shelley and Mary), overwhelmed the score. Far more successful was *Siegfried*, the third episode in the company's *Ring* cycle, directed by Tim Albery, and unveiled at the Edinburgh Festival. Other interesting operatic events at the 2002 Festival included *Parsifal*, in a production shared with the Salzburg Easter Festival, Stravinsky's *Oedipus Rex* performed by the Canadian Opera Company, and Britten's *The Turn of the Screw*, in a staging first seen at the 2001 festival at Aix-en-Provence.

NEWCOMERS

Welsh National Opera announced that their new music director will be the young Russian conductor Tugan Sokhiev. He takes up his post on 1 January 2003, but conducted a revival of WNO's *La bohème* in the autumn of 2001, when he was 23 years old. Despite his youth, Sokhiev has had plenty of experience as guest conductor with several Russian and other Continental orchestras and has appeared with the Kirov Opera in St Petersburg, winning golden opinions wherever he goes. Another outstanding conductor, the American Patrick Summers, made his British operatic debut conducting WNO's new production, directed by James Macdonald, of *Rigoletto*. Set in 1960s Washington, D.C. – the Camelot of Kennedy's presidency – the production proved once again that Verdi's popular masterpiece thrives in almost any setting. WNO also visited London, bringing a new

production of Beethoven's *Leonore* (the first version of *Fidelio*) and a revival of Berlioz's charming *Beatrice and Benedict* to Sadler's Wells Theatre. *Leonore* was also taken to the Coliseum in Oporto, the year's European City of Culture.

Glyndebourne's new music director, Vladimir Jurowski, made his debut towards the end of the 2002 festival conducting a revival of Sir Peter Hall's 1985 production of *Albert Herring*. This was probably the most interesting event of the season, despite three excellent new productions, of Gluck's *Iphigénie en Aulide*, Weber's *Euryanthe* and Bizet's *Carmen*, all operas new to Glyndebourne.

Nigel Osborne's *The Electrification of the Soviet Union*, premièred by Glyndebourne Touring Opera in 1987, was performed by Music Theatre Wales in a new chamber version for seven singers and 14 instrumentalists at the Cheltenham Festival, and later at the Buxton Festival. Early next season Music Theatre Wales will bring the piece to the Linley Theatre in the Royal Opera House. The Aldeburgh Festival saw the first staged performance of Gerald Barry's *The Triumph of Beauty and Deceit*, with libretto by Meredith Oakes. This was also staged by the Almeida Theatre in its temporary home at King's Cross.

COMMEMORATIONS

The centenary of the birth of Sir William Walton on 29 March 1902 was marked by a semi-staged concert of his full-length opera *Troilus and Cressida*, given by the Philharmonia Orchestra at the Symphony Hall, Birmingham, on 26 March 2002 and in London at the Royal Festival Hall on 28 March. Walton's one-act opera *The Bear* was performed in concert by the City of London Sinfonia at the Queen Elizabeth Hall.

Monica Sinclair, the English contralto who died in May 2002 aged 76, created roles in both of these Walton operas, Evadne in *Troilus and Cressida* at Covent Garden in 1954 and Madame Popova in *The Bear* at Aldeburgh in 1967. During her career she sang many other roles at Covent Garden, Glyndebourne and for the Handel Society.

Another singer who appeared with the Covent Garden company in its early days was Paolo Silveri, the Italian baritone who died in 2001 aged 87. He first sang in London in 1946 with the San Carlo company from Naples, as Rossini's Figaro, Marcello in *La bohème*, Tonio in *Pagliacci* and Scarpia in *Tosca*. From 1947 to 1949 he was a member of the Covent Garden company, singing the title role of *Boris Godunov*, Rigoletto, Germont in *La traviata*, Count di Luna in *Il trovatore* and Amonasro in *Aida*. He returned in 1950 with the company from La Scala, Milan, as Ford in *Falstaff*.

Australian baritone John Cameron, who died in March 2002 aged 84, joined the Covent Garden Opera in 1959, singing a variety of small roles during the three seasons he was with the company. In 1957 he created the role of Sydney Carton in Arthur Benjamin's *A Tale of Two Cities* for the New Opera Company; in 1959 he sang the title role in the first British performance of Luigi Dallapiccola's *The Prisoner*, also for the NOC. In 1968 with the English Opera Group at Aldeburgh he sang Punch in the world première of Harrison Birtwistle's *Punch and Judy*. He also took part in the British stage premières of Paul Hindemith's *Cardillac* (1970), Gottfried von Einem's *The Trial* (1973) and Alexander Goehr's *Arden Must Die* (1973).

Bryan Drake, the New Zealand-born baritone who died in December 2001 aged 76, also created many roles. After several years with Welsh National Opera, during which he

sang mainly Verdi and Puccini, he joined the English Opera Group for whom he created roles in Britten's three Church Parables at Orford Church, *Curlew River* (1964), *The Burning, Fiery Furnace* (1966) and *The Prodigal Son* (1968). He also took part in the premières of John Gardner's *The Visitor* (1972), Thea Musgrave's *The Voice of Ariadne* (1974), Stephen Oliver's *Tom Jones* (1976), all for EOG, and Hans Werne Henze's *We Come to the River* (1976) at Covent Garden.

Beni Montrésor, the Italian designer who died in October 2001 aged 75, was renowned for the magical quality of his sets and costumes. He designed *Pelléas et Mélisande* (1962) for Carl Ebert's production at Glyndebourne, as well as three long-lived and much-travelled productions seen at Covent Garden, Berlioz's *Benvenuto Cellini* (1966), Donizetti's *L'elisir d'amore* (1975, last performed at Covent Garden in 1997) and Massenet's *Esclarmonde* (1983), put on for Dame Joan Sutherland. Josef Svoboda, the Czech stage designer who died in April 2002, aged 81, was stylistically the exact opposite to Montrésor. He built massive sets that mainly used lighting for decoration, as his first work for Covent Garden, *Die Frau ohne Schatten* (1967), demonstrated. *Pelléas et Mélisande* (1969) followed, while Svoboda was chiefly famous for the controversial *Ring* cycle, directed by Götz Friedrich, that he built up between 1974 and 1976.

LOSS OF HEMMINGS

Perhaps the greatest loss suffered by the British operatic scene was the death of Peter Hemmings, the opera administrator, in January 2002, aged 68. Starting as president of the Cambridge University Opera Group, together with the conductor Leon Lovett he founded the New Opera Company, which gave many premières at Sadler's Wells Theatre, including operas by Arthur Benjamin, Arnold Foster, Elizabeth Maconchy, Buxton Orr and Daniel Jones (world premières), and Werner Egk, Luigi Dallapiccola, Carl Orff, Arnold Schoenberg, Hans Werner Henze and Sergey Prokofiev (British premières). In 1959 Hemmings joined Sadler's Wells Opera, first as personal assistant to Stephen Arlen, the managing director, then as planning and repertory manager.

In 1962 the conductor Alexander Gibson founded Scottish Opera in Glasgow, where he was shortly joined by Hemmings as administrator, at first part time, then, in 1965, full time. Ten years later, Scottish Opera moved from its temporary, rented home, the King's Theatre, into a new home, the Theatre Royal, a move completed on time due to the enormous drive and enthusiasm of Hemmings. Artistically the team of Gibson and Hemmings had achieved, and continued to achieve miracles, including a *Ring* cycle and Berlioz's *Les Troyens* in its entirety, with Janet Baker as Dido. In 1977 Hemmings left Scottish Opera to become general manager of Australian Opera in Sydney. However, he and the musical director, Richard Bonynge, did not get on, and Hemmings left. After running the London Symphony Orchestra for four years, Hemmings became managing director of the new Los Angeles Music Center Opera, where he was enormously successful, retiring in 2000. The previous year he was appointed to the board of the Royal Opera at Covent Garden, where his vast knowledge of opera was greatly appreciated. In March 2001 the Covent Garden première of Henze's *Boulevard Solitude* took place, 39 years after the opera's London premiere by the New Opera Company, for which Peter Hemmings had originally been responsible. He will be sorely missed.

PRODUCTIONS

In the summaries of company activities shown below, the dates in brackets indicate the year that the current productions entered the company's repertory.

ROYAL OPERA

Founded 1946
Royal Opera House, Covent Garden, London WC2E 9DD
Productions from the repertory: *Die Frau ohne Schatten* (1992), *The Bartered Bride* (1998), *Così fan tutte* (1995), *The Turn of the Screw* (1997), *Tosca* (1964), *Attila* (1990), *Tristan und Isolde* (2000), *La bohème* (1974), *The Queen of Spades* (2001), *Simon Boccanegra* (1991).

New productions:
Rigoletto (Verdi), 19 September 2001. Conductor, Edward Downes; director, David McVicar; set designer, Michael Vale; costume designer, Tanya McCallin. Paolo Gavanelli (Rigoletto), Marcelo Alvarez (Duke of Mantua), Christine Schafer (Gilda), Eric Halfvarson (Sparafucile), Graciela Araya (Maddalena)
Jenůfa (Janáček), 28 September 2001. Conductor, Bernard Haitink; director, Olivier Tambosi; designer, Frank Philipp Schlossmann. Karita Mattila (Jenůfa), Anja Silja (Kostelnička), Eva Randova (Grandmother Buryjovka), Jorma Silvasti (Laca), Jerry Hadley (Števa)
L'anima del filosofo (Haydn), 15 October 2001. Conductor, Christopher Hogwood; director, Jurgen Flimm; set designer, George Tsypin; costume designer, Florence von Gerkan. Cecilia Bartoli (Euridice/Genio), Roberto Saccà (Orfeo), Gerald Findley (Creonte), Brindley Sherratt (Pluto)
Parsifal (Wagner); 8 December 2001. Conductor, Simon Rattle; director, Klaus Michael Gruber; set designer, Gilles Aillaud; costume designer, Moidele Bickel. Stig Andersen (Parsifal), Thomas Hampson (Amfortas), John Tomlinson (Gurnemanz), Violetta Urmana (Kundry), Willard White (Klingsor), Alfred Reiter (Titurel)
Don Giovanni (Mozart), 22 January/18 February 2002. Conductor Colin Davis/Charles Mackerras; director Francesca Zambello; designer, Maria Bjørnson. Bryn Terfel/Simon Keenlyside (Don Giovanni), Robert Lloyd/Andrea Silvestrelli (Commendatore), Adriana Pieczonka/ Christine Goerke (Donna Anna), Rainer Trost/John Mark Ainsley (Don Ottavio), Melanie Diener/Ana Maria Martinez (Donna Elvira), Alan Held/Ildebrando d'Arcangelo (Leporello), Rebecca Evans/ Natalie Christie (Zerlina), Ashley Holland/Quentin Hayes (Masetto)
Duke Bluebeard's Castle (Bartók) and *Erwartung* (Schoenberg). Conductor, Lothar Zagrosek; director, Willy Decker; designer, John Macfarlane. Willard White (Bluebeard), Katarina Dalayman (Judith); Inga Nielsen (the Woman)
La sonnambula (Bellini), 16 March 2002. Conductor, Maurizio Benini; director/set designer, Marco Arturo Marelli; costume designer, Dagmar Niefend-Marelli. Elena Kelessidi (Amina), Juan Diego Florez (Elvino), Inger Dam-Jensen (Lisa), Alastair Miles (Count Rodolfo)
Il trovatore (Verdi), 22 April 2002. Conductor, Carlo Rizzi; director, Elijah Moshinsky; set designer, Dante Ferretti; costume designer, Anne Tilby. José Cura (Manrico), Veronica Villarroel (Leonora), Dmitri Hvorostovsky (Count di Luna), Yvonne Naef (Azucena), Tomas Tomasson (Ferrando)
La rondine (Puccini), 7 May 2002. Conductor, Gianluigi Gelmetti; director, Nicolas Joel; set designer, Ezio Frigerio; costume designer, Franca Squarciapino. Angela

Gheorghiu (Magda), Roberto Alagna (Ruggero), Cinzia Forte (Lisette), Charles Workman (Prunier)
Macbeth (Verdi), 13 June 2002. Conductor, Simone Young; director, Phyllida Lloyd; designer, Anthony Ward. Anthony Michaels-Moore (Macbeth), Maria Guleghina (Lady Macbeth), Alastair Miles (Banquo), Will Hartmann (Macduff), Peter Auty (Malcolm)

ENGLISH NATIONAL OPERA

Founded 1931
London Coliseum, St Martin's Lane, London WC2N 4BS
Productions from the repertory: *La traviata* (1996), *Orpheus and Eurydice* (1997), *La bohème* (1993), *The Mikado* (1986), *Ariodante* (1993), *The Elixir of Love* (1998), *Madam Butterfly* (1984), *The Fairy Queen* (1995), *The Silver Tassie* (2000).

New productions:
War and Peace (Prokofiev), 27 October 2001. Conductor, Paul Daniel; director, Tim Albery; set designer, Hildegard Bechtler; costume designer, Ana Jebens. Sandra Zeltzer (Natasha), Simon Keenlyside (Andrei), John Daszak (Pierre), Heather Shipp (Sonya), Susan Parry (Helene), Willard White (Kutuzov), Peter Sidhom (Napoleon)
The Marriage of Figaro (Mozart), 8 November 2001. Conductor, Jane Glover; director/set designer, Steven Stead; costume designer Rory Stead. Christopher Maltman (Figaro), Mary Nelson (Susanna), Leigh Melrose (Count), Orla Boylan (Countess), Victoria Simmonds (Cherubino), Claire Weston (Marcellina), Mark Richardson (Dr Bartolo), Mark Le Brocq (Don Basilio)
The Rake's Progress (Stravinsky), 29 November 2001. Conductor, Vladimir Jurowski; director, Annabel Arden; designer, Yannis Thavoris. Barry Banks (Tom Rakewell), Gidon Saks (Nick Shadow), Lisa Milne (Anne Trulove), Sally Burgess (Baba the Turk), Rebecca de Pont Davis (Mother Goose), Gerard O'Connor (Trulove), John Graham-Hall (Sellem the Auctioneer)
The Valkyrie (Wagner), 24 January 2002 (staged concert). Conductor, Paul Daniel; director, Michael Walling; costume designer, Zeb Lalljee. Robert Hayward (Wotan), Kathleen Broderick (Brunnhilde), Orla Boylan (Sieglinde), Par Lindskog (Siegmund), Susan Parry (Fricka), Gerard O'Connor (Hunding)
A Masked Ball (Verdi), 21 February 2002. Conductor, Andrew Litton; director, Calixto Bieito; set designer, Alfons Flores; costume designer, Merce Paloma. Julian Gavin (Gustavus), Claire Rutter (Amelia), David Kempster (Anckerstroem), Mary Plazas (Oscar), Rebecca de Pont Davis (Madame Arvidson)
La Vestale (Spontini), 3 April 2002. Conductor, David Parry; director; Francesca Zambello; designer, Alison Chitty. Jane Eaglen (Julia), Anne-Marie Owens (High Priestess), John Daszak (Licinius), Paul Nilon (Cinna), Gerard O'Connor (Supreme Pontiff)
Lulu (Berg), 1 May 2002. Conductor, Paul Daniel; director, Richard Jones; set designer, Paul Steinberg; costume designer, Buki Shift. Lisa Saffer (Lulu), Susan Parry (Countess Geschwitz), Robert Hayward (Dr Schon), John Graham-Hall (Alwa), Gwynne Howell (Schigolch), Robert Poulton (Animal Tamer/Athlete), Richard Coxon (Painter)
Così fan tutte (Mozart), 29 May 2002. Conductor, Mark Wigglesworth; director, Matthew Warchus; designer, Mark Thompson. Susan Gritton (Fiordiligi), Mary Plazas (Dorabella), Janis Kelly (Despina), Toby Spence (Ferrando), Christopher Maltman (Guglielmo), Andrew Shore (Don Alfonso)

OPERA NORTH
Founded 1978
Grand Theatre, 40 New Briggate, Leeds LS1 6NU
Productions from the repertory: *La bohème* (1993), *Gloriana* (1993), *Sweeney Todd* (1998).

New productions:
The Cunning Little Vixen (Janáček), 14 September 2001. Conductor, Steven Sloane; director, Annabel Arden; designer, Richard Hudson. Janis Kelly (Vixen), Giselle Allen (Fox), Christopher Purves (Forester), Nigel Robson (Schoolmaster), Richard Angas (Badger), Mark Stone (Poacher)
Albert Herring (Britten), 9 February 2002. Conductor, Steven Sloane; director, Phyllida Lloyd; designer, Scott Pask. Josephine Barstow (Lady Billows), Susan Bickley (Florence Pike), Elena Ferrari (Miss Wordsworth), Iain Paton (Albert), Edna Robinson (Mrs Herring), Heather Shipp (Nancy), Richard Whitehouse (Sid)
Performances were given at the Grand Theatre, Leeds, and on tour at Salford Quay, Newcastle, Nottingham, Barcelona, Hull, Sheffield and London (Sadler's Wells).

SCOTTISH OPERA
Founded 1962
39 Elmbank Crescent, Glasgow G2 4PT
Productions from the repertory: *Die Walküre* (2001), *La traviata* (1989), *Così fan tutte* (1990), *De Rosenkavalier* (1999), *Madama Butterfly* (2000).

New productions:
Monster (Sally Beamish), 28 February 2002, world première. Conductor, Diego Masson; director, Michael McMarthy; designer, Richard Aylwin. Gail Pearson (Mary W. Godwin), Roderick Williams (Lord Byron), Stephen Rooke (Shelley), Claire Shearer (Mary Wollstonecraft), Gwion Thomas (William Godwin), Hilton Marlton (Dr Polidori), Peter Van Hulle (Charles Lamb), Kathleen Wilkinson (Mary Lamb), Stephen Allen (Victor Francpierre), Ann Archibald (Second Mrs Godwin), Jonathan May (Coleridge)
Siegfried (Wagner), 25 August 2002. Conductor, Richard Armstrong; director, Tim Albery; set designer, Hildegard Bechtler; costume desinger, Ana Jebens. Graham Sanders (Siegfried), Alastair Elliott (Mime), Matthew Best (Wanderer), Peter Sidhom (Alberich), Markus Hollop (Fafner), Hélène Ranada (Erda), Gillian Keith (Woodbird), Elizabeth Byrne (Brünnhilde)
Performances were given at the Theatre Royal, Glasgow, and on tour in Edinburgh, Aberdeen and Inverness.

WELSH NATIONAL OPERA
Founded 1946
John Street, Cardiff CF1 4SP
Productions from the repertory: *La bohème* (1984), *The Barber of Seville* (1986), *Beatrice and Benedict* (1994), *Madam Butterfly* (1978), *La clemenza di Tito* (1997), *Salome* (1988), *Così fan tutte* (2000), *The Cunning Little Vixen* (1980).

New productions:
Leonore (Beethoven), 12 September 2001. Conductor, Yves Abel; directors, Patrice Caurier and Moshe Leise; set designer, Christian Fenouillat; costume designer, Agostino Cavalca. Franzita Whelan (Leonore), Natalie Christie (Marzelline), Pär Lindskog (Florestan), Donald McIntyre (Rocco), Don Pizarro (Robert Hayward), Wynne Evans (Jacquino), Timothy Martin (Don Fernando)
Rigoletto (Verdi), 3 May 2002. Conductor, Patrick

Summers; director, James Macdonald; designer, Robert Innes Hopkins. Chen-Ye Yuan (Rigoletto), Joseph Calleja (The Duke), Celena Shafer (Gilda), Iain Paterson (Sparafucile), Anna Burford (Maddalena)
Performances were given at the New Theatre, Cardiff, and on tour in London (Sadler's Wells), Birmingham, Belfast, Bristol, Oporto, Oxford, Southampton, Liverpool, Llandudno and Plymouth.

GLYNDEBOURNE FESTIVAL OPERA
Founded 1934
Glyndebourne, Lewes, East Sussex BN8 5UU
The Festival ran from 18 May to 25 August 2002. *Don Giovanni* (2000), *Kát'a Kabanová* (1988) and *Albert Herring* (1985) were revived.

New productions:
Iphigenie en Aulide (Gluck), 19 May 2002. Conductor Ivor Bolton; director, Christof Loy; set designer Herbert Murauer; costume designer, Bettina Walter. Veronica Cangemi (Iphigenie), Katarina Karneus (Clytemnestra), Jonas Degerfeldt (Achilles), Gerald Finley (Agamemnon), Calchas (Clive Bayley)
Euryanthe (Weber), 23 June 2002. Conductor, Mark Elder; director, Richard Jones; designer John Macfarlane. Anne Schwanewilms (Euryanthe), Lauren Flanigan (Eglantine), John Daszak (Adolar), Stephen Gadd (Lysiart), Clive Bayley (King Louis VI)
Carmen (Bizet), 25 July 2002. Conductor, Philippe Jordan; director, David McVicar; set designer, Michael Vale; costume designer, Sue Blane. Anne Sofie von Otter (Carmen), Marcus Haddock (Don José), Lisa Milne (Micaela), Laurent Naouri (Escamillo)

GLYNDEBOURNE TOURING OPERA
Carmen (2002), *Eugène Onegin* (1994), *Albert Herring* (1985) were performed at Glyndebourne, Plymouth, Milton Keynes, Norwich, Woking, Stoke-on-Trent and Oxford.

GARSINGTON OPERA
Founded 1989
Garsington Manor, Garsington, Oxford OX44 9DH

New productions:
Don Giovanni (Mozart), 16 June 2001. Conductor Steuart Bedford; director, Stephen Unwin; set designer, Jackie Brooks; costume designer, Mark Bouman. Tom Erik Lie (Don Giovanni), Claire Rutter (Donna Anna), Emma Bell (Donna Elvira), Robert Poulton (Leporello), Paul Nilon/Mark Wilde (Don Ottavio), Katherine Haataja (Zerlina), Brindley Sherratt (Commendatore), Carl Gombrich (Masetto)
La gazza ladra (Rossini), 27 June 2002. Conductor, David Parry, director, Daniel Slater; designer, Angela Davies. Majella Cullagh (Ninetta), Simon Edwards (Giannetto), Nerys Jones (Pippo), Russell Smythe (Fernando), Christopher Purves (Podestà), Brindley Sherratt (Fabrizio), Carole Wilson (Lucia)

ENGLISH TOURING OPERA
Founded 1980 as Opera 80
La traviata (Verdi) and *Manon* (Massenet) were toured to Richmond, Canterbury, Buxton, Wolverhampton, York and Bath, between 17 October and 1 December 2001.
Don Giovanni (Mozart) and *La traviata* (Verdi) were toured to Tunbridge Wells, Poole, Yeovil, St Helier, Lincoln, Cheltenham, Exeter, Warwick, Crawley, Truro, Ulverston, Preston, Perth, Darlington and Wimbledon, between 1 April and 31 May 2002.

Parliament

Following the terrorist attacks in New York on 11 September 2001, Parliament was recalled three times during the summer recess to debate the situation. On 14 September the Prime Minister (Tony Blair) made a statement to the Commons in which he called the attack 'an act of wickedness for which there can be no justification' and called for a 'dramatic rethink of the scale and nature of the action that the world takes to combat terrorism'. The newly elected leader of the Conservative Party, Iain Duncan Smith, gave his party's 'full support for the immediate pledge to stand shoulder to shoulder with our strongest friends and allies in the United States ... in its search for the perpetrators and its subsequent actions'. The statement was followed by a debate on international terrorism, during which the Father of the House, Tam Dalyell, warned of 'a generation ... in the Middle East, which ... is growing up to loathe the United States and Britain' and warned against 'vengeance and eradication'. As a mark of respect, both the annual Conservative and Labour party conferences were shortened.

On 4 October Tony Blair again addressed a recalled Commons, giving details of the evidence against Osama bin Laden, the Al-Qa'eda and the support provided to them by the Taliban regime in Afghanistan, and the building of a coalition against international terrorism, including the help that Britain had offered the US to eliminate the terrorist threat: 'We will not act for revenge. We will act because we need to for the protection of our people and our way of life.' The Liberal Democrat leader Charles Kennedy, whilst supporting the actions to date called for 'the overarching need to work within the broad framework of the United Nations'. This statement by the Prime Minister was also followed by a debate on international terrorism during which there was widespread, all-party support for the actions taken, though a small number of MPs warned against going to war, including backbenchers Alice Mahon (Lab.), who felt that 'bombing the poorest country in the world using cruise missiles at £1 million a time will not hold the coalition together or do anything to save the millions of starving Afghans', and Jeremy Corbyn (Lab.), who complained that 'this Parliament is almost unique in having no right to vote on the deployment of British forces anywhere in the world'.

Recalled for the third time on 8 October, MPs heard from the Prime Minister that US and British armed forces, with the support of other allies, had begun military action in Afghanistan. Reiterating that 'we did not choose this conflict', he concluded 'we will continue to act with steadfast resolve to see this struggle through to the end and to the victory ... not of revenge but of justice over the evil of terrorism'. During the ensuing debate on the coalition against international terrorism, fears were raised that 'for the third time Parliament has been recalled yet hon. members have been denied a vote on this war' (Paul Marsden, Lab.), but the mood was best summed up by the International Development Secretary (Clare Short), who said, 'the House has pulled together ... there has been shared analysis and a deep consensus'.

Both Houses of Parliament returned officially from the summer recess on 15 October 2001. If the Government had expected a smooth passage for the legislative package unveiled in The Queen's Speech on 20 June, with a second-term majority of 167 and a newly reformed House of Lords, it was to be disappointed. The Upper House continued to show its independence and to hinder progress on certain bills by calling for amendments, including to those bills introduced quickly as a response to the terrorist threat. During the course of the session, government ministers made more statements to the House than any Government in recent times. MPs were welcomed back by three statements: first from the Home Secretary (David Blunkett) on anti-terrorism measures, announcing his intention to bring forward emergency legislation to reinforce action against the perpetrators of organised crime, drugs and people trafficking; secondly from the Chancellor of the Exchequer (Gordon Brown) on action against financing terrorism, announcing measures that would seek to cut off the supply of funds; and, finally from the Transport Secretary (Stephen Byers) on the worsening financial crisis facing Railtrack which had led to the Government putting the body into administration on 7 October. Mr Byers called Railtrack's demise 'a golden opportunity to create a railway system that is united, not fragmented ... that can respond to the needs of our time ... a network provider that answers to the millions of passengers and not to private shareholders'. The Conservative transport spokesman (Eric Pickles) said 'Railtrack is bust because the Government decided to make it so ... this action has been the most destructive act to the railways since Dr Beeching'. The Liberal Democrat transport spokesperson (Don Foster) felt it was 'vital to end the obscene conflict between shareholder profit and passenger safety'.

On 18 October the Secretary of State for Environment, Food and Rural Affairs (Margaret Beckett) reported on the publication of the Haskins report on rural recovery in Cumbria following the foot-and-mouth disease outbreak, and the extension of the business recovery fund in the worst affected regions. On 19 October the sitting of the House of Commons was delayed for an hour due to a suspect package received in the Post Office. On 22 October, Margaret Beckett confirmed to the Commons that government-funded testing of sheep's brains for research on BSE in sheep had, in fact, been carried out incorrectly on cow's brains, something that had been announced by press release at 10.30 p.m. some four days previously. Her Conservative shadow, Peter Ainsworth, called her statement 'a staggering display of complacency'. On 23 October, the Opposition used the first of its debates to censure the conduct of the Department of Transport and the Regions during the 11 September terrorist attack, when the ministerial special adviser Jo Moore sent an email saying it was 'a very good day to get out anything we want to bury'. Backbencher Paul Marsden (Lab.) voiced 'the depths of despair felt by the public because the Government cannot understand that this special adviser should go and that, for the sake of parliamentary democracy, we should surely understand what is right and what is wrong'. With voting along party lines, however, the motion was rejected by 340 votes to 167.

On 24 October, Clare Short reported to the House on the humanitarian situation in Afghanistan and her efforts to win regional support for operations on the ground. This was followed by a statement from the Northern Ireland Secretary (John Reid) on confirmation from the International Commission on Decommissioning that it had witnessed 'a significant event ... in which the IRA had put a quantity of arms beyond use', which he called 'unprecedented and genuinely historic'. The Conservative Northern Ireland spokesman (Quentin Davies) called this 'unambiguously good news for the people of Northern Ireland'.

On 29 October, David Blunkett announced plans to establish an asylum and immigration system 'that can respond effectively to the pressures we face ... with a substantial package of measures that will fundamentally overhaul our existing system ... to send a message to the rest of the world that this country is not open to abuse, but nor is it a fortress Britain'. The Conservative home affairs spokesman (Oliver Letwin) expressed the hope that Mr Blunkett's new proposals 'will establish a civilised, humane and effective system'. In a marked departure from precedent, the Speaker of the House (Michael Martin) welcomed the statement on the abolition of the voucher system because 'as I know from experience in my constituency, they take away people's dignity'. The following day he was forced to explain to the Commons that he was 'wholly committed to maintaining the long-standing tradition that the Speaker stands aside from politics ... if my remark was subject to the interpretation that was put on it [as a political statement], I seek the indulgence of the House'. Also on 30 October, the Proceeds of Crime Bill received an unopposed second reading, although the Opposition voted against the programme motion, which, as for all government bills, timetabled the whole legislative scrutiny of the measure in the Commons. On 31 October, former minister Geoffrey Robinson (Lab.) made a personal statement to the House, apologising for failing to register financial dealings in 1990 and for 'inadvertently' misleading the Committee on Standards and Privileges over these dealings. A motion suspending him from the House for three weeks was passed without a vote.

On 1 November, some 15 MPs wanting to record their anxieties about the war in Afghanistan forced a vote on what was the fifth government-inspired debate on the coalition against terrorism, as a protest that it was a motion for the adjournment of the House rather than a substantive motion.

RAILTRACK ROW

On 5 November, Stephen Byers had to come to the Commons to answer a private notice question from the Conservative transport spokeswoman Teresa May on the process of consultation and decision-making that led to Railtrack being put into administration. He insisted that the decision had been made on 5 October: 'the time had come to put delivery to passengers before dividends to shareholders'. Ms May felt that 'far from the decision being made on the afternoon of 5 October, it was a drawn-out act of willful destruction by the Secretary of State. It is clear that he has been bent on destroying Railtrack from the start.'

On 7 November, the Leader of the Commons (Robin Cook) initiated consultation on the second phase of the reform of the House of Lords, which proposed to remove all hereditary peers, introduce a proportion (20 per cent) of elected members, and put the appointment of independent members outside political patronage, creating a second chamber 'which is able to complement the Commons but unable to compete with it for power'. His Conservative shadow, Eric Forth, called it 'all in all, an enormous disappointment'. This was followed by a statement from the Trade and Industry Secretary (Patricia Hewitt) on the forthcoming World Trade Organisation ministerial conference in Doha to launch a new round of world trade talks. She said she would use her position to 'help secure an agenda for free and fair trade – to launch a round that benefits Britain, but above all benefits the poorest people of our world'.

Keeping up the pressure on Stephen Byers over the Railtrack issue, the Opposition held a debate on 13 November calling for his resignation, which was defeated by 394 votes to 152. On 14 November, Tony Blair updated the Commons on events in Afghanistan and the progress of the international coalition against terrorism and told MPs that several thousand UK troops were being put on 48-hour notice to move into the area if required. 'The troops will remain in place for only a strictly limited period, while an international force to work alongside Afghan military commanders is prepared.' Charles Kennedy asked for an assurance that the Prime Minister would 'use his influence with the American President to stop military action being expanded to include Iraq'. On 15 November, Patricia Hewitt reported back on the outcome of the World Trade Organisation conference and the launch of 'a new round of trade negotiations with a package of measures specifically focused on the needs of developing countries'. The Conservative trade and industry spokesman (John Whittingdale) hoped that the text would be 'translated in the next three years into real agreement to removing barriers and opening up markets'.

On 19 November, the Anti-Terrorism, Crime and Security Bill, the measure promised by David Blunkett on 15 October, passed its second reading by 458 votes to 5; an all-party group of backbench MPs opposed the measure for various different reasons. The Opposition again voted against the programming of the bill, which in this case planned to rush the bill though the Commons in just one week, but was defeated by 319 votes to 74. A motion to support the UK's derogation from Article 5 of the European Convention on Human Rights was less widely supported but was still approved under the deferred voting procedure by 331 votes to 74. On 20 November, Stephen Byers announced the publication of the Inspector's report into Heathrow Terminal 5, the longest inquiry in British planning history, his approval of the development and the Government's intention to streamline the handling of major infrastructure projects in the planning system.

On 26 November, the Anti-Terrorism, Crime and Security Bill completed its passage through the Commons unamended, gaining a third reading by 323 votes to 79, with the mainly Conservative opposition abstaining. On 27 November, the Chancellor presented his annual pre-Budget report. 'Economic stability is the foundation. A steady and prudent approach to public finances follows.' He also announced the publication of the interim Wanless Report into future trends in health care and future funding issues with 'no evidence that any alternative financing method to the UK's would deliver a given quality of health care at a lower cost to the economy. Indeed, other systems seem likely to prove more costly.' The Shadow Chancellor (Michael Howard) felt Mr Brown 'had failed to act on the state of crisis in our public services ... the burdens on business remain. Public services will continue to get worse, to the growing distress of patients, passengers and parents ... waiting in vain for the Government to deliver on their promises.' The Liberal Democrat Treasury spokesperson (Matthew Taylor) described it as 'a complacent statement from an extraordinarily complacent Chancellor'.

As usual, the pre-Budget statement was followed the next day (28 November) by a statement on benefits uprating by the Work and Pensions Secretary (Alistair Darling). Most national insurance benefits would rise in the normal way, in accordance with the retail price index (1.7 per cent) and income-related benefits by the Rossi index (also 1.7 per cent). He also announced increased help to families on low income and legislation to introduce the pension credit. 'We are doing more to help people into work and to help those who cannot find

work. We are also making sure, for the first time, that pensioners are rewarded for their savings.' The Conservative work and pensions spokesman (David Willetts) thought he detected 'at the heart of the statement a radical shift in policy on pensions'. The Liberal Democrat spokesperson, Steve Webb, felt it was 'a complicated measure and is it not inevitable that a complicated benefit is less likely to be taken up than a straightforward one?' Patricia Hewitt made a statement on the future management of public sector civil nuclear liabilities and changes to the financial position of British Nuclear Fuels Ltd; this would 'ensure that this essential work continues to be carried out in a safe, secure and cost-effective manner that ensures protection of the environment'. Just prior to these statements, the Speaker had given a ruling on ministerial replies to questions, indicating that 'Ministers should be as open as possible with Parliament', which was taken as a warning to ministers to be more forthcoming in their answers. On 29 November, the Human Reproductive Cloning Bill (Lords), legislation introduced following a High Court ruling on the definition of an embryo, was rushed through all its Commons stages in one day. In the Lords, the Government was defeated on the second day of the committee stage of the Anti-Terrorism, Crime and Security Bill, when an amendment to Clause 21, moved by Conservative spokesman Lord Dixon-Smith, to include the IRA in the provisions of the bill was passed by 149 votes to 139.

On 3 December, the Opposition kept up the pressure on Stephen Byers and the use of spin doctors by changing one of their Opposition Day debates at the last moment to a motion criticising his use of 'spin'; Mr Byers did not attend the debate. Over Railtrack, Conservative spokesman Tim Collins said the minister had 'twisted and evaded and rewritten the truth and hidden the facts time and time again'; the motion was defeated by 279 votes to 157. On 4 December, Stephen Byers came to the House to announce the details of the local government financial settlement for England for 2002–3, claiming an increase over the previous year of some 7.4 per cent, and announcing that in future there would be a different system of allocating the funds. Theresa May called his use of figures 'five myths'. The Liberal Democrat local government spokesperson (Don Foster) felt that 'councils throughout the country will be disappointed that we have another settlement based on the same outdated, flawed, virtually impenetrable and unfair system'. During a debate on the further timetabling of discussion on a Lords amendment to the Anti-Terrorism, Crime and Security Bill, the Commons sat in private for over an hour for the first time in over 40 years when a motion moved by the Liberal Democrat Chief Whip (Paul Tyler) was passed without division. On 5 December, the Foreign Secretary (Jack Straw) answered a private notice question from the Liberal Democrat foreign affairs spokesperson (Menzies Campbell) on terrorist atrocities in Jerusalem and Haifa, reiterating that 'we work towards a day when two states – Israel and Palestine – live peacefully together within secure and recognised borders'.

Amid growing backbench concern that the Parliamentary Commissioner for Standards, Elizabeth Filkin, was being ousted from her job, the Speaker made a statement deploring the leaking of private correspondence between him and the Commissioner, and asked her to produce evidence of the pressures she claimed to have been put under while attempting to carry out her duties. David Blunkett made a statement announcing a White Paper and a new bill on police reform and tackling crime and anti-social behaviour. On 6 December, the Health Secretary (Alan Milburn) made a statement on the allocation of financial resources to local health authorities in England for 2002–3, an increase of some 6.8 per cent in real terms, designed to 'create a service delivering quicker, higher quality care for millions of patients'. The Conservative health spokesman (Liam Fox) was sceptical that 'simply spending money will make a difference'.

ANTI-TERRORISM LEGISLATION

In the Lords on the first day of the report stage on the Anti-Terrorism, Crime and Security Bill, the Government was defeated no less than seven times; an amendment moved by Lord Phillips of Sudbury (LD) to Clause 17 - 'The issue is whether the extensive powers reserved by the state should be confined to threats to national security. It is all about reconciling our duty to safeguard our traditional civil liberties with our duty to forestall as best we can any emergency threats to our national security' – was passed by 227 votes to 145; an amendment to Clause 19 moved by Conservative spokesman Baroness Buscombe on disclosure of information was passed by 227 votes to 138; a new clause on scope of powers moved by Lord Dixon-Smith (C.) was passed by 227 votes to 135; an amendment to Clause 103 from Lord Phillips was passed by 228 votes to 133; to Clause 104 from Baroness Buscombe was passed by 209 votes to 134; an amendment moved by former Northern Ireland minister Lord Mayhew of Twysden (C.), to Clause 30 to remove the ouster provisions to the jurisdiction of the High Court on judicial review, was passed by 191 votes to 117; and a similarly intended amendment to Clause 31 by former law lord Lord Donaldson of Lymington was passed by 181 votes to 110. On 10 December, the second day of the report stage, the Government suffered two further defeats: a motion to delete Clause 39 (on religious hatred offences), moved by Lord Campbell of Alloway (C.), was passed by 240 votes to 141; and an amendment to insert a new clause on expiry after one year moved by Lord Dixon-Smith was passed by 200 votes to 128. On the same day Labour backbencher Paul Marsden (Shrewsbury and Atcham) defected from the Labour Party to join the Liberal Democrats. On 11 December, Stephen Byers announced the publication of a White Paper on local government, seeking to 'establish a partnership between central and local government, reflecting the critical importance of local authorities, both as a tier of democratic government and as a body with the responsibility to deliver high-quality public services to the people'. Theresa May welcomed it 'as a genuine move to freedom for local councils to respond to the needs of their local communities', but challenged it 'as paying lip service to the ideas of freedom and deregulation'.

On 12 December, the Government overturned or amended the defeats it had suffered in the Lords on the Anti-Terrorism, Crime and Security Bill. On 13 December in the Lords, the Government faced another three defeats during the Lords' consideration of the Commons amendments to the bill; Lord Campbell of Alloway insisted on deleting Clause 39 from the bill and was supported by 234 votes to 121; Lord McNally (LD) insisted on reinstating a new clause on scope of powers and was supported by 174 votes to 153; and Lord Phillips of Sudbury insisted on the amendment on communications data provision and was supported by 196 votes to 145. The bill was not altered again by the Government and received royal assent that day.

On 17 December, Tony Blair reported to the Commons on the outcome of the European Council in Laeken,

which had been dominated by the war against terrorism and the issue of European Union enlargement. 'Britain played its full part constructively and achieved the outcome it desired ... the days of isolationism are gone, rightly. Our role is now to be a leading partner in shaping the Europe of the future.' Iain Duncan Smith felt 'the Laeken Council was about a greater move towards a European state'. The Northern Ireland Arms Decommissioning (Amendment) Bill, extending the period of legal immunity by another year, was given a second reading by 342 votes to 151; the Opposition again objected to the programme motion. On 18 December, a motion opening up the facilities of the House to all members, irrespective of whether they had taken their seats (designed to allow the four Sinn Fein MPs to have offices in the Commons) was approved by 322 votes to 189. Four Labour backbenchers, including former minister Kate Hoey, voted against the government motion. During a heated debate, Robin Cook accused the Opposition of 'withdrawing bipartisan support in Northern Ireland over this issue'. For the Opposition, Quentin Davies said they objected to 'the creation of a two-tier membership of the House ... and we object fundamentally to the idea of making more unreciprocated concession to Sinn Fein/IRA'.

On 19 December, the last day before the Christmas recess, backbencher Julie Kirkbride (C.) asked whether or not the Prime Minister's baby son Leo had been given the MMR vaccination. His failure to answer the question ('I will not enter into any public discussion about the health of my children') led to heated debate both inside and outside Parliament on the merits of the vaccination. The Culture Secretary (Tessa Jowell) answered a private notice question from her Conservative shadow, Tim Yeo, on the siting, purpose and funding of the national stadium, and announced the publication of the Carter report recommending continuing with Wembley for the meantime, but considering Birmingham as an alternative should proposals 'not be delivered within a reasonable timescale'. Tim Yeo considered the handling of the issue had 'led to a series of disasters, caused directly by the dithering and blundering of successive ministers'. Then the Defence Secretary (Geoff Hoon) reported to the Commons that the UK had agreed formally to take on the leadership of the international force in Kabul to assist the new Afghan interim authority: 'Our commitment is limited in numbers – up to 1,500 troops – and duration, which will be up to three months.'

When the Houses reconvened in the New Year, opposition to the Northern Ireland Arms Decommissioning (Amendment) Bill continued, with six Ulster MPs voting against the third reading on 9 January. On 10 January, Geoff Hoon updated the Commons on progress in deploying the international security force to Kabul, confirming that Turkey had expressed an interest in taking over responsibility as lead nation after the initial three months. On 14 January, Jack Straw responded to a private notice question from the Conservative foreign affairs spokesman (Michael Ancram) on discussions with Spain to share sovereignty over Gibraltar. Whilst agreeing that discussions about Gibraltar's future were ongoing, Mr Straw said, 'any proposals affecting the sovereignty of Gibraltar would be subject to the consent of the people of Gibraltar in a referendum'. Stephen Byers announced the publication of the strategic plan for railways by the Strategic Rail Authority, designed to 'provide a railway that is fit for the 21st century and the country with the fourth largest economy in the world'. Theresa May felt that the plan 'offers no new money, no new schemes and no hope for passengers in the future'. On 15 January, Alan

Milburn replied to a private notice question from Liam Fox on NHS hospital management and proposals for foundation hospitals which he had announced in a speech outside Parliament that morning. Keeping pressure on the Transport Secretary, the Liberal Democrats debated a motion on 16 January suggesting his salary be reduced because of his failure to tackle adequately the growing crisis on British railways; this was defeated by 339 votes to 207.

On 21 January, junior Foreign Office minister Ben Bradshaw made a statement on British detainees from the Afghan campaign being held in Guantanamo Bay by the Americans. He was 'fully satisfied with the co-operation that we have had from the US authorities ... the detainees are being treated in line with international humanitarian norms, in conditions in which security is paramount'. The Justice (Northern Ireland) Bill was given a second reading by 324 votes to 133, and the Opposition again voted against the programming motion. On 23 January, junior defence minister Lewis Moonie made a statement on taxation of attributable army invaliding pensions and apologised for the errors that had occurred; some pensioners had been mistakenly taxed over a period of some 50 years and compensation would be paid at a cost of about £30 million.

On 28 January, Clare Short reported to the Commons on the outcome of the Afghanistan reconstruction conference held in Tokyo, setting up a £200 million fund which gave 'real hope for a better life for the people of Afghanistan – we must not fail to grasp this opportunity'. On 29 January, Margaret Beckett responded to a private notice question from Peter Ainsworth (C.) on the publication of the Curry Policy Commission report on the future of foods and farming, which would, once considered, be part of the basis for a 'new strategy for sustainable, diverse, modern and adaptable farming that is integrated with the rest of the food chain and which takes into account the needs of the environment and of the rural economy'. For this to be achieved, Mr Ainsworth felt that 'the Government will need to win back the confidence of rural people'.

On 5 February, the Foreign Secretary answered a private notice question from backbencher Gerald Kaufman (Lab.) on his meeting the previous day with his Spanish counterpart to discuss Gibraltar. He was 'convinced that this dialogue represents the best way forward for the people of Gibraltar ... they have more to gain than to lose from the process', and invited the Chief Minister to join the talks as part of the British delegation 'on the basis of two flags, three voices formula'. Michael Ancram felt the statement had done 'nothing to allay or dispel suspicion and anger in Gibraltar'. Later the Education and Skills Secretary (Estelle Morris) announced the publication of the annual report of HM Chief Inspector of Schools, showing that 'the quality of teaching is getting better' and demonstrating 'the real gains that have been made and continue to be made in our schools'. The Conservative education spokesman (Damian Green) concentrated on 'the crisis of teacher retention, which has been brought about by some of the policies of which the Secretary of State is so proud'. During Prime Minister's Questions on 6 February, the Speaker made a surprise ruling that 'the Prime Minister is here to answer questions as Prime Minister, not leader of the Labour party' and later that 'the policy of the Conservative Party is nothing to do with the Prime Minister', thereby making the usual exchanges at Prime Minister's Questions rather more difficult.

On 7 February, the Home Secretary published a White Paper on nationality, immigration and asylum. He emphasised the need for 'building trust and confidence to

secure the support of the British people for a Britain with a balanced approach to nationality and migration'. Welcoming the White Paper, his Conservative shadow, Oliver Letwin, warned that the proposals would 'ultimately be judged not by the nobility of the aspirations that they undoubtedly represent, but by their effectiveness in practice'. He also called for the Home Secretary to work towards the closure of the Sangatte refugee centre in France. At 7.00 p.m., much later than normal for ministerial announcements, Stephen Byers made a statement on the future of London Underground, as the board of London Regional Transport were 'minded to proceed' with their plans for the modernisation of the Tube and London Underground's public-private partnership (PPP) proposals, which would 'form the basis of creating a Tube fit for the 21st century'. Eric Pickles called it 'an off-balance deal ... it is wildly optimistic, it completely disregards dangers and it is made with the certain knowledge that when time is come to give account, others will be carrying the can'. The Liberal Democrat spokesperson on transport in London, Tom Brake, thought 'there is clearly uncertainty about whether the PPP represents value for money, yet he is proceeding with it'. On 13 February, former minister Keith Vaz (Lab.) made a personal statement to the Commons on the report of the Committee on Standards and Privileges recommending his suspension from the House for a month. The chairman of the committee, Sir George Young, was 'sorry that [the MP] could not make a personal statement in the usual way' and reminded the House that they were having the debate 'not because of the original complaints but because of the way in which the hon. member responded to them. We were deeply dissatisfied with the way he dealt with the Commissioner.' The motion to suspend Mr Vaz was passed without a vote. On the same day a motion to appoint Philip Mawer as the new Parliamentary Commissioner for Standards, to succeed Elizabeth Filkin, was also passed without a vote, though not before several MPs had complained about the 'shameful' way in which Ms Filkin had been treated.

On 25 February, David Blunkett made a statement on the fire at Yarl's Wood removal/detention centre, when he was adamant that 'I am not prepared to let government policy be determined by those intent on creating disorder and destruction' and that policy 'remains unchanged'. On 26 February, Stephen Byers came to the Commons to explain his role in the circumstances surrounding the resignation of Martin Sixsmith from the post of director of communications in his department: 'it is true that I was not personally involved in the negotiations. It is also true, however, that I believed that Mr Sixsmith should not be given another job'. Theresa May felt it was a 'day of humiliation for the Secretary of State, that he should have to come to the House once again to explain how his version of certain events differs from that of other people involved ... let him salvage something from his shattered reputation: give the Department the fresh start it needs and go now.' Don Foster thought the affair means 'the Department no longer even knows what is going on ... would it not be right for the Secretary of State at least to move over and make way for somebody else to lead the Department and to go now?' In an unprecedented move the day before, the Permanent Secretary at the department, Sir Michael Mottram, had made public the notes of his meeting with Mr Sixsmith.

LABOUR DONOR DEBATE

After months of complaints during Business Questions about the time taken by departments to answer written parliamentary questions and rebukes from the Speaker's chair, in early March there was a furore when MPs discovered that hundreds of questions from the Department of Health had not been answered and a civil servant from the department was suspended. On 4 March, the Transport, Local Government and the Regions (DTLR) select committee produced a report on the non-attendance of Lord Birt at one of their sessions, criticising the Government for blocking the appearance of one of their advisers on transport. On 5 March, Plaid Cymru used its annual day for debate to highlight the role played by the Prime Minister in supporting Lakshmi Mittal, a Labour Party donor, in his bid for a contract for his Romanian steel plant. Plaid Cymru's trade and industry spokesman Adam Price said, 'it is clear from the way Mr Mittal operates on a global scale that his donation was clearly designed to win favour with the UK Government at a critical time during the Sidex negotiations'. The Secretary of State for Wales (Paul Murphy) rejected all such allegations. The motion was defeated by 318 votes to 192.

On 6 March, Tony Blair reported on the Commonwealth heads of government meeting in Coolum, Australia. The crisis in Zimbabwe had dominated proceedings and a statement expressing concern at the violence surrounding the election campaign and calling for free and fair elections was agreed. But 'there was no realistic prospect of a consensus for suspending Zimbabwe from the Commonwealth in advance of the elections'. Iain Duncan Smith felt no one 'can be satisfied with the outcome ... it was only the latest in a litany of laughable and inadequate responses that have too often let Mr Mugabe off the hook'. The Trade and Industry Secretary (Patricia Hewitt) made a statement on the Government's reaction to the US decision to impose a range of tariff measures on steel imports: 'we are extremely disappointed that President Bush has taken this action in the face of united international opposition ... In our view and that of the European Commission it is a clear breach of the US WTO obligations.' On 7 March, Margaret Beckett made a statement on the UK ratification of the Kyoto protocol, which had begun that day: 'I firmly believe that the UK, as well as the rest of the world, has much to gain from meeting the challenge of climate change head-on'. This was followed by two personal statements, from Labour MPs Ben Bradshaw and George Galloway, apologising to the House and each other for overstepping the mark during a heated debate on Iraq in Westminster Hall the previous day. The DTLR select committee produced a report on the London Underground public-private partnership plan which was highly critical of the Government's handling of the issue.

On 13 March, the Chief Secretary to the Treasury (Andrew Smith) made a statement on the Government's response to the Sharman report Holding to Account and its proposals for reforming audit and accountability in central government, accepting the main recommendations of the report. The Conservative Shadow Chief Secretary (John Bercow) welcomed the statement but wondered why it had taken the Government over a year to respond to the report. On 14 March, at very short notice, the Chancellor presented the Competition Commission's report on the supply of banking services to small and medium-sized businesses (SME), which found that the practices of the main clearing banks were operating against the public interest – 'Our goal is to create an environment where new entrants can compete with existing banks on a fair basis and both can secure more competitive services for SMEs.' Michael Howard agreed that the Commission had

'arrived at some sensible proposals' but wondered why it had taken the Government so long to respond. The Foreign Secretary made a statement on the outcome of the presidential election in Zimbabwe: 'Robert Mugabe may claim to have won this election but the people of Zimbabwe have lost ... the right of people freely to determine their own future has been flouted and all democrats should speak with one voice in condemning what has taken place'. Michael Ancram felt that 'for the sake of democracy, the Government must recognise that the time has come to stop talking and start doing'.

On 18 March, Tony Blair reported on the outcome of the European Council meeting in Barcelona, where he felt 'Britain is in there, shaping Europe's future, making Europe work in a way that is better for Britain and for Europe. Britain's proper role is as a leader and partner in Europe. We will continue to get the best for Britain out of Europe'. Iain Duncan Smith thought 'the truth of Barcelona was, once again, all about fine words from the Prime Minister and no action ... is it not an indictment of him that such an important summit can have achieved so little at such great cost?' Defence Secretary Geoff Hoon updated the Commons on the continuing role played by the British armed forces in Afghanistan, the plans to hand over to Turkey the UK's responsibility as lead nation for ISAF, and a formal request from the US for forces to join in future military operations elsewhere in Afghanistan. The Conservative defence spokesman (Bernard Jenkin) felt this was the most significant statement since 11 September as an announcement had been made 'committing the largest force to combat operations since the Gulf War in 1991'. Alice Mahon (Lab.) thought this 'was mission creep on a massive scale'.

THE HUNTING DEBATE

However, the main business of the day on 18 March was to decide which of three options to take on hunting with dogs, with separate votes on each. Hunting with dogs under supervision (the 'status quo') was rejected by 401 votes to 154; hunting with dogs under licence (the 'third way') was rejected by 371 votes to 169; a total ban on hunting with dogs was passed by 386 votes to 175. In the Lords the voting was different: a total ban was rejected by 331 votes to 74; the 'third way' was rejected by 336 votes to 59; the status quo was rejected by 119 votes to 97. As a result the Minister for Rural Affairs (Alun Michael) promised a statement on the way forward 'before the Easter recess'.

On 19 March, the Speaker unusually granted an emergency three-hour debate the following day to Bernard Jenkin under Standing Order No. 24 on the presence of UK troops in Afghanistan; such applications are invariably turned down. On 20 March, Northern Ireland Secretary John Reid replied to a private notice question from Quentin Davies on the break-in at Castlereagh police station by announcing the setting-up of a review under Sir John Chilcot in tandem with the police investigation. Alistair Darling made a statement on the implementation of the child support reforms, saying these would only be implemented when a new IT system currently under development was operating effectively, even if this caused further delay, as 'the risk of proceeding before testing was complete was unacceptable'. On 21 March, Jack Straw announced that the Commonwealth had decided to expel Zimbabwe from membership. Alun Michael promised a process of consultation on the way ahead on hunting with dogs before bringing in a bill that 'will deal with this issue once and for all and that it will make good law ... the reason for re-engaging in a process to try and achieve wider agreement is precisely that we

recognise that there are legitimate concerns in the countryside about pest control, land management and other practicalities and we want to address those issues in the bill'.

On 25 March, Patricia Hewitt made a statement on the announcement by Consignia, formerly the Post Office, about its restructuring plan. 'I know that today's news will come as a blow to many workers. But these changes, painful as they are, are unavoidable. Today must be the first step towards renewal and towards creating a postal service that justifies the pride and lives up to the expectations of the people who depend on it every day'. John Whittingdale described the statement as 'a humiliation for the Government'. Later, Stephen Byers came to the Commons to announce the details of the bid for Railtrack from Network Rail, a not-for-profit company, which would include a £300 million grant from the Government 'to reflect the benefits of an early exit from administration'. Theresa May felt this grant would be paid as compensation for the original shareholders, something the minister had repeatedly denied would happen, 'considering a deal was on the table to compensate shareholders without using taxpayers' money, why has he broken his word yet again by spending taxpayers' money on compensating shareholders?' Don Foster felt that 'however he seeks to wrap up the £300 million, that [compensation] is exactly what it is'.

On 26 March, the last day before the Easter recess, the Commons approved a report from the Standards and Privileges Committee requiring members who had not taken their seats to register their interests with the Registrar. In the Lords, the first day of the committee stage of the Animal Health Bill saw an amendment moved by Lord Moran (cross-bencher) declining to start the committee stage until all the inquiries into the foot-and-mouth disease outbreak had been published: 'It is not clear to me why on a matter of such great importance to so many in the country, they are willing to allow the committee stage to proceed, with the implication that the bill may ultimately be acceptable. That may prove to be a waste of time and effort. I am surprised that they are willing to leave it to a Dad's Army of myself and like-minded colleagues to make the case for delay, based on obvious common sense'; the amendment was passed by 130 votes to 124.

Parliament was recalled during the Easter recess, on 3 April, to pay tribute to Queen Elizabeth the Queen Mother, who had died on Easter Saturday. Tony Blair said that for almost a century she 'inspired our country, aroused its respect and affection'. Iain Duncan Smith felt her 'great contribution to our nation was different and special' and Charles Kennedy referred to 'the special place she always had in the hearts of the people in Scotland'. Because of the Queen Mother's funeral, the return of Parliament after the Easter recess was delayed by a day.

On 10 April, Tony Blair made a statement on his informal bilateral discussions with President Bush in Texas, when the situation in the Middle East had predominated, welcoming the President's call for the Israelis to withdraw from the Occupied Territories and for the Palestinian Authority to tackle the terrorism. 'Wherever we can help, we will. Whatever we can do to help, we will. But we need the co-operation from both sides directly involved in the conflict'.

On 15 April, the Government was defeated in the Lords on the first day of the report stage of the Police Reform Bill (Lords) when a motion to leave out Clause 5 (directions to police officers), moved by Lord Dixon-Smith because 'it takes the business of central administration of what are essentially local services too

far', was passed by 205 votes to 131. On 17 April, the Chancellor presented his sixth Budget statement, delayed from March because of the death of his daughter. The Budget placed a greater emphasis on spending than previously. 'Our task is to address, through reform, three major long-term challenges: the challenge of enterprise, with new incentives to raise investment and to reward entrepreneurship; the challenge of family prosperity for all with a new child tax credit paid to mothers for all families with incomes up to £58,000; the challenge of renewing our public services, with, for a reformed NHS, a secure, long-term financial foundation.' With the emphasis on greatly increased spending on the NHS, to be funded in part by a one-pence increase in national insurance contributions, he concluded, 'We have made our choice. This is a Budget to make our NHS the best insurance policy in the world. The NHS is a British ideal, free at the point of need, for everyone, in every part of Britain. Fairness and enterprise together.' Iain Duncan Smith felt this was another Budget where 'what he omitted to tell the House is as instructive as his statement ... This country is now running a deficit for the first time in four years ... Manufacturing productivity has fallen back ... export performance is falling behind again.' He concluded, 'His closed mind and refusal to change have condemned the British people to second-class public services'. Charles Kennedy felt 'there is a great deal in the Budget to welcome ... This would have been a really good Budget five years ago ... but the Government have lost a lot of credibility and opportunity in the intervening five years ... Too many broken promises, too many misleading targets, too much double or treble counting and too much spin and not enough delivery.'

On 18 April, Alan Milburn outlined the benefits of the Budget to the health service in his statement on the NHS Plan: '35,000 more nurses, 15,000 more doctors, 40 new hospitals and 500 new primary care centres: as investment grows so the capacity of the NHS will grow'. But he was also looking for reforms to match the investment, announcing a new Commission for Healthcare Audit and Inspection: 'our formula is simple: investment plus reforms equals results'. After four days of debate, the Budget was approved by 408 votes to 155. On 18 April, the Government was defeated in the Lords on the report stage of the Export Control Bill, when an amendment to Clause 1, moved by Lord Redesdale (LD) on the need not to jeopardise sustainable development in the export of armaments, was passed by 145 votes to 120; and an amendment to Clause 3 moved by Baroness Miller of Hendon (C.) 'to prevent the export of dangerous knowledge and technology while maintaining responsible academic freedom' was passed by 150 votes to 108.

On 24 April, Tony Blair led the tributes in the Commons from all the party leaders to The Queen on her Golden Jubilee, announcing that she would address both Houses of Parliament in Westminster Hall on 30 April. David Blunkett introduced the second reading of the Nationality, Immigration and Asylum Bill, 'to create systems which can be trusted to operate fairly, competently and robustly'. It received an unopposed second reading, and although the Opposition voted against the programme motion, it was passed by 284 votes to 176. On 25 April, the Government faced four defeats in the Lords on the third reading of the Police Reform Bill (Lords); an amendment to Clause 4 moved by Lord Dholakia (LD) about restricting community safety accreditation schemes to local authorities was passed by 151 votes to 127; a motion to leave out Clause 40 (power to amend Chapter 1) moved by Lord Dixon-Smith was passed by 165 votes to 127; an amendment to

Schedule 4 moved by Lord Dholakia on the power of community support officers to detain was passed by 168 votes to 121; and an amendment to Schedule 5 moved by Lord Dixon-Smith on accredited persons was passed by 158 votes to 101. On 26 April, the Culture, Media and Sport Secretary (Tessa Jowell) reported to the Commons on the collapse of ITV Digital but reassured members that 'the fact that ITV Digital has not succeeded will not deflect the Government, consumers and the broadcasting industry from making a reality of the digital future'.

On 29 April, the Foreign Secretary reported on recent developments in Israel and the Occupied Territories and restated the Government's 'absolute commitment to helping restart the peace process'. The Government introduced the Tobacco Advertising and Promotion Bill (Lords) for its second reading in the Commons as a government bill, although it had begun its passage through the Lords as a private member's bill, introduced by Lord Clement-Jones (LD). On 30 April, the Finance Bill received its second reading in the Commons by 358 votes to 141. In the Lords, the Government was defeated on the second day of the report stage on the National Health Service (NHS) and Health Care Professions Bill, when a new Clause on the establishment of patients' councils, moved by Lord Clement-Jones, was passed by 227 votes to 136.

On 7 May, Tessa Jowell replied to a private notice question from the chairman of the Department of Culture, Media and Sport select committee, Gerald Kaufman (Lab.), on the passing of the 30 April deadline set for progress on Wembley stadium. 'Although much of the necessary work to secure the financing of the stadium project has been completed, the Football Association has requested more time to enable it to conclude its discussions with the banks ... I have agreed to refrain from reaching my final decision on Government support ... I understand that that decision will disappoint many people in the West Midlands, however, it would be wrong to withdraw support at such a crucial stage.' She promised a further statement before the Golden Jubilee recess. She then made a statement on the publication of the Draft Communications Bill for pre-legislative scrutiny: 'we want Britain to have the most dynamic communications industry in the world ... and to continue to have the best quality TV and radio in the world. This bill is the route map to making those ambitions a reality.' Tim Yeo felt 'the acid test of her proposals is whether the regime that she is setting up operates with a light touch rather than a heavy hand'. On 9 May, the Deputy Prime Minister (John Prescott) published a White Paper on regional government: 'our proposals will give the regions of England new choices, new powers and a new voice. By devolving power, we can elevate democracy.' Theresa May disagreed, saying 'these proposals for regional assemblies will mean less democracy, more talk and more tax. It is a centralising measure and we will oppose it.' The Deputy Liberal Democrat leader Alan Beith welcomed the proposals.

BYERS' 'CLARIFICATION'

Later, Stephen Byers came to the Commons to make a statement about Martin Sixsmith, to clarify why he had said in his statement on 26 February that Mr Sixsmith had resigned when it was now clear that he had not. 'In my statement I made clear the reason for my understanding, based on information that I had been provided with, that Martin Sixsmith had agreed to resign ... I have not misled the House as some have alleged ... any misunderstanding over his resignation was in good faith.' Theresa May felt that 'Yet again the Secretary of State has

come to the House to explain our incorrect understanding of history ... but today we have heard no remorse, no regret, no glimmer of an apology ... if he had a single shred of decency left, would he not go and go now?' Don Foster felt they had reached the situation where 'even if the Secretary of State announced his resignation, we would not know whether to believe him'. On 10 May there was the unusual occurrence of a private member's bill, the Home Energy Conservation Bill, seemingly being 'talked out' by its own sponsor, Labour backbencher Desmond Turner.

On 13 May, Stephen Byers made a statement on the rail derailment at Potters Bar on 10 May. Robin Cook made a statement on the Government's proposals for taking forward reform of the House of Lords by setting up a joint committee of both Houses to forge the broadest possible parliamentary consensus on the proposed composition, role and powers, followed by a free vote on the issue in both Houses. 'Our objective is to secure a second chamber that is broadly representative of Britain today; a chamber that will complement the Commons by reinforcing Parliament's ability to conduct scrutiny and hold the executive to account'. Eric Forth described the proposals as 'indefinite postponement'. On 14 May, the Commons approved plans to modernise the House of Commons by increasing the powers of the select committees (by 352 votes to 50), with a new Committee of Nomination (by 209 votes to 195) and to consider paying select committee chairmen (by 199 votes to 158). In the Lords on 14 May, the Government was defeated on the fourth day of the committee stage on the Education Bill when an amendment to Clause 32, moved by Conservative education spokesman Baroness Blatch because 'these are a regulation too far', was passed by 129 votes to 119. On 16 May, Geoff Hoon updated the Commons on recent developments with the British troops in Afghanistan. In the Lords, an amendment to insert a new Clause (duty on primary health care trusts etc. regarding education, training and research), moved by Baroness Northover (LD) on the third reading of the NHS Reform and Health Care Bill, was passed against the Government's wishes by 131 votes to 108.

On 23 May, as promised, Tessa Jowell made a statement on the progress of the national stadium. She was prepared to give the Football Association (FA) and Wembley more time to conclude a deal but should this not prove possible, 'I would expect the FA to enter into discussions with Birmingham about its proposals'. She added that she would issue a consultation document on the future of lottery distribution before the summer recess. The Conservative DCMS spokesman Anne McIntosh referred to 'another day, another statement, another mess'. Gerald Kaufman called it 'high-gloss whitewash' and called for sackings at Sport England.

During the extended Golden Jubilee recess Stephen Byers resigned and Tony Blair carried out a mini-reshuffle of his frontbench on 29 May. On 10 June the Foreign Secretary made a statement on diplomatic efforts to reduce the tension between India and Pakistan. He was criticised by his own backbenchers, including Jeremy Corbyn: 'The West and Britain in particular has been very happy to do enormous arms deals with both countries'. In the Lords on 12 June, an amendment to insert a new Clause (annual report to Parliament) moved by Lord Saatchi (C.) on the first day of the report stage of the Tax Credits Bill was passed against the wishes of the Government by 121 votes to 118. On 13 June, Patricia Hewitt made a statement on the second phase of the restructuring plan for Consignia, announced by the chairman that morning, which would result in a further

17,000 redundancies. 'The company is now set on a course for renewal and recovery. It will not be easy but it is essential if we are to have a Royal Mail that the workforce can be proud of and that delivers the service that customers deserve.' John Whittingdale felt 'ultimately the responsibility must rest with the Government, who remain the sole shareholder'.

On 20 June, Geoff Hoon again updated the Commons on operations in Afghanistan and the future disposition of UK forces there. Command of ISAF had been handed over to Turkey. The UK contribution would be reduced to some 400 troops. On 24 June Tony Blair reported on the outcome of the European Council meeting in Seville, which had made progress on EU enlargement and agreed measures on economic reform, reform to streamline the Council, and illegal immigration and asylum. Iain Duncan Smith thought, 'the reality belies the Prime Minister's usual rhetoric'. In the Lords on 25 June, on the first day of the report stage on the Proceeds of Crime Bill, the Government was defeated when an amendment moved by Baroness Buscombe to Clause 6, on discretion on whether to proceed with an investigation, was passed by 137 votes to 131, and a new Clause (compensation of creditors) was added by Lord Goodhart (LD) by 159 votes to 136. On 26 June, Robin Cook was criticised for referring to the fact that the Conservative Party leader sent his children to Eton when the Government was always critical of anyone who tried to bring the Prime Minister's family into the political argument. The Home Secretary replied to a private notice question from Oliver Letwin on his recent meeting with the French Interior Minister on tackling illegal immigration. 'The French Government committed themselves to the closure of Sangatte ... I did not expect an immediate resolution of the timescale.' Mr Letwin welcomed the promises received but not 'so much the fact that Britain will be contributing millions of pounds to paying for that security in France'. On 27 June, the new Transport Secretary, Alistair Darling, reported on progress in putting the ownership and operation of the rail network on a sound and sustainable footing and getting Railtrack out of administration. Network Rail had concluded a sale and purchase agreement to acquire Railtrack, and London and Continental Railways had acquired from Railtrack its interest in the first phase of the Channel Tunnel rail link. 'There is now an urgent need to give the rail system stability and I believe that this agreement is the right and best way of building a modern and efficient network.' Theresa May hoped that the new body would 'succeed in bringing much-needed stability to the rail network', though she questioned why the Government would not put up £1.7 billion for Railtrack but had found £21 billion of taxpayers money for the new concern.

On 1 July, the new Work and Pensions Secretary, Andrew Smith, had to apologise to the Commons for having given official figures overestimating by £35 billion the amount being saved by people for pensions in the last year. Tony Blair reported on the outcome of the G8 summit in Canada, which had covered international terrorism, with agreement on a set of measures to enhance the security of the global transport system, and had enhanced relations with Russia by agreeing to its assuming the presidency of the G8 in 2006, but had mainly concentrated on a New Partnership for Africa's Development (NEPAD). 'It is a real signal of hope for the future and it is up to us now to make it a reality.' On 3 July, David Blunkett launched a consultation on entitlement cards and identity fraud. 'Freedom from intrusion into our private lives by public or private organisations is crucial ... No one should fear correct identification. There

is nothing to fear from the proper acknowledgement and recognition of our identity.' Both Oliver Letwin and Simon Hughes wanted assurances that this was a consultation on an entitlement card to prevent fraud rather than something more. In the Lords, the Government faced three defeats on the third reading of the Education Bill: an amendment to leave out Clause 11, moved by Baroness Blatch, was passed by 183 votes to 141; a new clause (control of regulation), also moved by Baroness Blatch, was passed by 135 votes to 128; an amendment to leave out Clause 42, moved by Baroness Walmsley (LD), passed by 161 votes to 136. On 5 July, the Public Health Minister (Hazel Blears) had to make a Commons statement on the use of animal products in the manufacture of vaccines and to 'apologise for any inaccurate information that has been provided ... There are no transmissable spongiform encephalopathy-related safety issues arising from the use of relevant animal-derived materials in the production of vaccines authorised for use in the UK.'

On 9 July, the Financial Secretary to the Treasury (Ruth Kelly) reported on the publication of the Sandler review of retail savings and gave the Government's preliminary reaction. 'We believe that Ron Sandler has produced proposals that have the potential to produce a simpler, more transparent and more competitive retail investment industry ... easier for people to understand and viable to sell to a wider range of less well-off people. That can only help our ambition to raise the level of long-term saving.' Michael Howard felt that 'we have a crisis in pensions and a collapse in savings ... the savings ratio this year is predicted to reach all time low ... The criteria against which these proposals will be judged are whether they, unlike government policies to date, will help reinvigorate the savings and pensions market and whether they put the consumer interest first.'

On 10 July, the Speaker made a ruling on possible pressure from the RMT union on MPs sponsored by them and found no abuse, but he reminded members that 'the House expects at all times that members will take the greatest care to ensure that all their relationships with outside bodies will be in strict conformity with our rules'. David Blunkett made a statement on the Government's drugs strategy, which included his plans to reclassify cannabis as a Class C drug, 'through education, harm minimisation, treatment and tough action against dealers and traffickers, we have a winning strategy'. Oliver Letwin could not welcome the move: 'It is not too late for him to think again ... in the interests of the Government, and in the interests of the young people of this country, he should do so now'. Simon Hughes was more welcoming but felt that the strategy 'sends a muddled message about whether or not it is acceptable to use cannabis'. On 11 July, Andrew Smith made a statement on the publication of the Pickering report on pensions, which recommended a new Pensions Act to consolidate all existing pensions legislation, a new and more proactive regulator, a better, more targeted approach for communicating with pension scheme members and an ending of compulsory indexation for defined benefit pensions and compulsory survivors' benefits. 'The acid test must be increasing the level of savings for retirement and making a secure occupational pension accessible to as many people as possible.' David Willetts welcomed the report but criticised the Government for 'showing no willingness to recognise the scale of the problem and what needs to be done to tackle it.'

In the Lords, at the third reading to the Proceeds of Crime Bill, an amendment to Clause 246 moved by Lord Lloyd of Berwick (cross-bencher) 'to make Part 5 of the Bill less vulnerable to attack under the Human Rights Act,' was passed against the wishes of the Government by 149 votes to 132. On 12 July, Jack Straw made a statement on the talks with the Spanish government over the future of Gibraltar, admitting that 'co-sovereignty' was under active consideration. 'Unless we and Spain can resolve the outstanding issues, there will plainly be no agreement. Our aim, however, remains to overcome them if we can.' Michael Ancram called it 'a disgrace and a sell-out'. Gerald Kaufman had thought that 'the day would never come that he [the Foreign Secretary] would make a statement, practically every word of which I disagreed with'.

On 15 July, Gordon Brown presented his third comprehensive spending review (CSR), setting out plans for the next three-year cycle, with an emphasis on greatly expanded expenditure on schools in particular: £4,900 a pupil by 2005–6. 'Efficient strong public services play their part in delivering a modern Britain of greater opportunity and greater security not just for some, but for everybody ... We have presented a budget for the health service and a spending review for education: as we promised, schools and hospitals first.' Michael Howard called for reform as well as increased expenditure: 'we are against his plans to spend more without reform. As his record shows, that simply does not work.' Matthew Taylor welcomed the increased money, 'now he should give them the freedom to do their job answerable to the community, not tied up in red tape and quangos and only answerable to the Chancellor'.

On 16 July, Tony Blair took the unprecedented step of appearing before a special select committee on liaison, consisting of most of the select committee chairmen, to answer questions for well over two hours. He said he would repeat this process every six months. In the Commons, the Education and Skills Secretary (Estelle Morris) outlined in detail the new spending on education, 'stepping up the pace of investment, matched by a step up in the pace of reform'. She promised a ten-year strategy for universities in the autumn. She concluded, 'we have a proven model of reform: we have the best teachers ever in our schools; we have the resources and the ambition to achieve the change. A world-class education system is a prize well worth winning.' Damian Green thought the reforms outlined were 'not reform: it is a recipe for continued crisis in our schools ... money without real reform will be wasted'. On 17 July, during Prime Minister's Questions, Tony Blair gave a stout defence of the armaments industry: 'The arms industry and related industries in this country employ about 100,000 people. There is nothing wrong with that industry's being successful and making sales to overseas governments ... we have strict rules governing the export of arms'. David Blunkett published a White Paper on criminal justice, with proposals on changing the rules of double jeopardy, on trial by jury and on release of information about previous convictions: 'proposals that are far-reaching, radical and require a culture change'. He also outlined the increased spending in his area from the CSR. Oliver Letwin was keen to see that the proposals 'both materially increase the chances of convicting the guilty and contain safeguards to protect the innocent'.

In the Lords during the fifth day of committee on the Nationality, Immigration and Asylum Bill, an amendment to Clause 58 moved by Conservative spokesman Baroness Anelay of St Johns on meeting reasonable travelling costs was passed against the wishes of the Government by 116 votes to 111. On 18 July, John Prescott outlined the benefits of the CSR to sustainable communities, housing and planning and made a

statement on changes in policy to ensure the building of successful, thriving communities, publishing three documents containing extensive reforms. These would include abolishing county structure plans, introducing business planning zones and speeding up the planning of major infrastructure projects. 'We need more homes where people want to live, near where they work, in the north and in the south, at a price people can afford and in a way that protects the countryside.' Eric Pickles returned to the theme that 'money is being thrown at the problem without reform or thought and it will not work'. Geoff Hoon published a White Paper on the strategic defence review and detailed how the extra money from the CSR would be spent: 'investment to deliver new equipment and enhanced capabilities and to be a force for good in the changing strategic environment'. The final day for consideration of private members bills in the session was 19 July, when three bills did make progress, though the Opposition went out of their way to highlight the fact that the government whips had 'callously killed off' over 30 other measures.

On 22 July, Margaret Beckett made a statement on the publication of the Anderson report on the lessons to be learned from the outbreak of foot-and-mouth disease in 2001. The report found that 'the Government made mistakes during the handling of the crisis but all involved are determined to learn from these mistakes'. Ms Beckett acknowledged that mistakes were made 'where there may be room for disagreement is on how much of this was evident only or at least primarily, with hindsight'. She pointed out that the report accepts that 'all those involved did their level best to deal with a crisis of unprecedented importance. It makes recommendations on which we will act.' Her Conservative shadow, David Lidington, felt 'it will take action and results to restore the trust of people in the countryside in ministers, a trust that has been wholly destroyed by the grievous failure of her policies and of her colleagues'. The Liberal Democrat spokesperson, Colin Breed, called for an assurance that the lessons learned 'are not eroded by the passage of time and that no complacency sets in'. Geoff Hoon updated the Commons on the Chinook helicopter crash on the Mull of Kintyre in 1994 that killed a large number of senior intelligence and police officers. He said that, having reviewed all the evidence and select committee inquiries, 'we have agonised over whether there was some way in which we could exonerate the pilots posthumously, but on the basis of all the evidence, I am unable to do so'. Bernard Jenkin still, 'like many others, continue[d] to be drawn inescapably to the conclusion that this is not a safe verdict'. Menzies Campbell felt 'nothing he [the Defence Secretary] has said today has shaken my belief that the board of inquiry, in good faith, made an error of judgement and failed to apply the necessary high standard of proof'. On 23 July, Alistair Darling made a statement on air transport and air capacity in the UK, publishing six regional consultation papers on how to respond to the continued growth in demand for air travel with new capacity. 'Doing nothing is not an option ... We therefore aim to set a framework for sustainable development against which people can plan'. The newly appointed Conservative transport spokesman Tim Collins questioned the basis of the increased figures and felt 'it is essential that these decisions are taken in a swift but consultative manner'.

Alan Milburn made a statement on services for older people, giving them a direct choice over their own care, and outlined how the increased money from the CSR would be spent. He also announced a consultation on amending the requirements for size of rooms and doors,

numbers of lifts and baths, etc., in buildings for older people. 'The emphasis must now be on helping more older people to live more independently for more of the time.' Liam Fox called it 'largely a set of re-announcements and U-turns and seems to be timed more to avoid embarrassing headlines generated by tomorrow's report from the select committee – managing news not managing patients'. The subsequent health select committee report on delayed discharges was indeed very critical of the Government. In the Lords, during consideration of Commons amendments to the Education Bill, the Government was defeated when an amendment moved by Conservative spokesman Lord Kingsland insisting on the amendment about schools forming companies was passed by 172 votes to 168; a compromise was agreed on 24 July.

The last day of the Commons sitting before the summer recess, 24 July, brought a statement from John Reid on the recent upsurge of violence in Northern Ireland, in which he repeated his pledge that 'I will not hesitate to use the powers Parliament has given me if the circumstances require it'. He also felt, however, 'In the case of the IRA I share the assessment of the Prime Minister that it has never been further from a return to its campaign – nothing could be more damaging than the sense that options were being kept open in any way.' Quentin Davies expressed 'the profound sense of disappointment that I feel and I believe so many people will feel at the extraordinary vacuousness of the statement'. The First Minister of the Northern Ireland Assembly (David Trimble) felt 'it would be a very good thing if there were frankness, openness, honesty and transparency in the Government's approach'. Patricia Hewitt made a statement on the publication of the interim report of the co-ordinating group on audit and accounting issues and how the Government would take the recommendations for reform forward. The newly appointed Conservative trade and industry spokesman, Tim Yeo, welcomed the broad tenor of the report but warned, 'the essence of what we need now is not necessarily more regulation but better regulation'. The Finance Bill and eight other bills, including the Education Bill and the Proceeds of Crime Bill, received royal assent. The Lords approved a select committee report on modernising the procedures of the House, despite concerns and amendment moved by opponents of the measures.

The House of Lords continued to sit until 30 July, discussing in committee on 25 July the delayed Animal Health Bill; on 29 July the Nationality, Immigration and Asylum Bill; and on 30 July the Enterprise Bill. On 29 July the DTLR select committee produced a report on national air traffic control that was damning about the Government's handling of the issue and the lack of funding. As Parliament closed down for what might be the last 11- or 12-week summer recess, warnings about the requirement to recall Parliament if the situation in the Middle East worsened were issued by many backbench MPs.

PUBLIC ACTS OF PARLIAMENT 2001–2002

This list of Public Acts commences with one Public Act which received the royal assent before 1 September 2001. Those Public Acts which follow received the royal assent after 31 August 2001. The date stated after each Act is the date on which it came into effect; c. indicates the chapter number of each Act.

Appropriation (No. 2) Act 2001 c. 21, 19 July 2001. Authorises the use of resources and the issue of sums out of the Consolidated Fund to the service of the year ending 31 March 2002 and appropriates the supplies authorised in this session of Parliament.

European Communities (Finance) Act 2001 c. 22, 4 December 2001. Amends the definition of 'the Treaties' and 'the Community Treaties' under the European Communities Act 1972 so as to include the decision of 29 September 2000 of the Council on the Communities' system of own resources.

Human Reproduction Cloning Act 2001 c. 23, 4 December 2001. Prohibits the placing in a woman of a human embryo which has been created otherwise than by fertilisation.

Anti-terrorism, Crime and Security Act 2001 c. 24, various dates, some to be appointed. Amends the Terrorism Act 2000; makes further provision about terrorism and security; provides for the freezing of assets; makes provision about immigration and asylum; amends or extends the criminal law; and for many other connected purposes.

Consolidated Fund (No. 2) Act 2001 c. 25, 18 December 2001. Authorises the use of resources for the service of the years ending 31 March 2002 and 2003 and applies certain sums out of the Consolidated Fund to the service of the years ending 31 March 2002 and 2003.

International Development Act 2002 c. 1, day to be appointed. Makes provision relating to the provision of assistance for countries outside the UK; with respect to certain international financial institutions and the Commonwealth Scholarship Commission; and for connected purposes.

Sex Discrimination (Election Candidates) Act 2002 c. 2, 26 February 2002. Excludes from the operation of the Sex Discrimination Act 1975 and the Sex Discrimination (Northern Ireland) Order 1976 certain matters relating to the selection of candidates by political parties.

European Communities (Amendment) Act 2002 c. 3, 26 February 2002. Makes consequential provision on the Treaty signed at Nice on 26 February 2001 amending the Treaty on the European Union, the Treaties establishing the European Communities and certain related Acts.

Travel Concessions (Eligibility) Act 2002 c. 4, various dates, some to be appointed. Amends the law relating to the age at which certain persons become eligible to receive travel concessions (for equality purposes, the age will be 60 or more until ordered otherwise after 6 April 2010).

Civil Defence (Grant) Act 2002 c. 5, 26 February 2002. Amends, as regards authorities in England and Wales, the Civil Defence Act 1948, s. 3 (fixed and discretionary grants).

Northern Ireland Arms Decommissioning (Amendment) Act 2002 c. 6, 26 February 2002. Provides for the extension of the amnesty period fixed by the 1997 Act.

Homelessness Act 2002 c. 7, various dates, some to be appointed. Makes further provision about the functions of local housing authorities relating to homelessness and the allocation of housing accommodation.

British Overseas Territories Act 2002 c. 8, various dates, some to be appointed. Makes provision as to the name 'British overseas territories' and British citizenship so far as it relates to British overseas territories.

Land Registration Act 2002 c. 9, various dates, some to be appointed. Makes provision as to land registration.

Consolidated Fund Act 2002 c. 10, 19 March 2002. Authorises the use of resources for the service of the year ending 31 March 2002 and applies certain sums out of the Consolidated Fund to the service of the years ending 31 March 2001 and 2002.

Office of Communications Act 2002 c. 11, various dates, some to be appointed. Establishes the Office of Communications; confers thereon functions in relation to proposals about the regulation of communications; and for connected purposes.

Football (Disorder) (Amendment) Act 2002 c. 12, various dates, some to be appointed. Amends the 2000 Act s. 5; and for connected purposes.

Electoral Fraud (Northern Ireland) Act 2002 c. 13, various dates, some to be appointed. Provides for the supply to the Electoral Officer for Northern Ireland of signatures, dates of birth and national insurance numbers of electors and persons seeking registration as electors in Northern Ireland; for the issue of electoral identity cards; and for purposes connected with elections in Northern Ireland.

National Heritage Act 2002 c. 14, 1 July 2002. Makes further provision in relation to the function of the Historic Buildings and Monuments Commission for England.

Commonhold and Leasehold Reform Act 2002 c. 15, various dates, some to be appointed. Makes provision about commonhold land and amends the law about leasehold property. The Act sets up new provision for leaseholds where a commonhold association holds the freehold title.

State Pension Credit Act 2002 c. 16, various dates, some to be appointed. Makes provision for and in connection with a new social security benefit called state pension credit; and amends the Pension Schemes Act 1993, s. 47(1).

National Health Service Reform and Health Care and Professions Act 2002 c. 17, various dates, some to be appointed. Amends the law about the NHS; establishes and makes provision in connection with a Commission for Patients and Public Involvement in Health; makes provision in relation to arrangements for joint working between NHS bodies and the prison service and NHS bodies and local authorities in Wales; makes provision in connection with the regulation of health care professions; and for connected purposes.

Appropriation Act 2002 c. 18, 8 July 2002. Authorises the use of resources and the issue of sums out of the Consolidated Fund for the service of the year ending 31 March 2002; appropriates the supply authorised in this session of Parliament; repeals certain Consolidated Fund and Appropriation Acts.

National Insurance Contributions Act 2002 c. 19, has effect in relation to the tax year 2003–2004 and subsequent tax years. Makes provision for and in connection with increasing national insurance contributions and for applying the increases toward the cost of the NHS.

Industrial and Provident Societies Act 2002 c. 20, 8 September 2002. Enables the law relating to societies registered under the 1965 Act to be amended so as to bring it into conformity with certain aspects of company law; amends the procedure whereby such a society may convert itself into, or amalgamate with or transfer its engagements to, a company; and for connected purposes.

Tax Credits Act 2002 c. 21, various dates, some to be appointed. Makes provision for tax credits (child tax credit and working tax credit); amends the law about child benefit and guardian's allowance; and for connected purposes.

Employment Act 2002 c. 22, various dates, some to be appointed. Makes provision for statutory rights to paternity and adoption leave and pay; amends the law about statutory maternity leave and pay and various other provisions connected with employment; and for connected purposes.

European Parliamentary Elections Act 2002 c.24, 24 October 2002. Consolidates the Acts of 1978, 1993 and 1999.

Copyright, etc. and Trade Marks (Offences and Enforcement) Act 2002 c.25, day or days to be appointed. Amends the Copyright, Designs and Patents Act 1988 in respect of criminal offences, search warrants, powers of seizure and orders for forfeiture; amends the Trade Marks Act 1994 in respect of search warrants and powers of seizure; and for connected purposes.

Justice (Northern Ireland) Act 2002 c. 26, various dates, some to be appointed. Makes provision about the judiciary in Northern Ireland and to amend section 6 of the Appellate Jurisdiction Act 1876; makes provision about the law officers and other legal officers and the courts in Northern Ireland; to establish a Public Prosecution Service for Northern Ireland, a Chief Inspector of Criminal Justice in Northern Ireland and a Northern Ireland Law Commission; amends the law of youth justice in Northern Ireland; makes provision for making available to victims of crime information about the release of offenders in Northern Ireland; makes provision about community safety in Northern Ireland; amends the law of legal aid in Northern Ireland; and for connected purposes.

Divorce (Religious Marriages) Act 2002 c. 27, day to be appointed. Makes provision to enable a court to require the dissolution of a religious marriage before granting a civil divorce.

Mobile Telephones (Reprogramming) Act 2002 c. 27, day to be appointed. Creates offences in respect of unique electronic equipment identifiers of mobile wireless communications devices.

Finance Act 2002, c. 23

Export Control Act 2002, c. 28

Proceeds of Crime Act 2002, c. 29

Police Reform Act 2002, c. 30

Education Act 2002, c. 32

WHITE PAPERS, REPORTS ETC

This section provides an outline of a selection of White Papers and Reports that have been published in the last year.

'*Entitlement Cards and Identity Fraud, a Consultation Paper*' was presented to Parliament by the Secretary of State for the Home Department in July 2002. The paper is concerned with whether the Government should introduce a universal entitlement card scheme that would:

– Provide people who are lawfully resident in the UK with a means of confirming their identity.
– Establish for official purposes a single definitive record of a person's identity that is accessible to all Government departments.
– Help people gain entitlement to products and services provided by both public and private sectors.
– Assist public and private sector organisations to validate a person's identity, entitlement to products and services and eligibility to work in the UK.

'*Justice for All*', a Criminal Justice System (CJS) white paper, was presented to Parliament by the Secretary of State for the Home Department, the Lord Chancellor and the Attorney General in July 2002. The White paper sets out a wide-ranging programme of reform for the criminal justice system. It intends to:

– Reform the police service to ensure better crime detection.
– Invest over £600 million in CJS information technology to manage cases more efficiently through the court system.
– Reduce offending on bail by giving the police power to impose bail conditions before charge and extend the prosecution's right to appeal decisions.
– Remove the double jeopardy rule for serious cases if compelling new evidence comes to light.
– Allow for trial by a judge alone in serious and complex fraud trials, complex and lengthy trials or where the jury is at risk of intimidation.
– Allow trial judges to inform the court of a defendant's previous convictions where appropriate.

'*Managing the Nuclear Legacy. A Strategy for Action*' was presented to Parliament by the Secretary of State for Trade and Industry in July 2002. The White paper sets out the Governments plans to make radical changes for the decontamination and decommissioning of nuclear licensed sites funded by the taxpayer. It:

– Reflects the scale of the technical and managerial responsibilities involved in nuclear clean up.
– Outlines the Government's intention, through competition, to ensure that the best available skills and experience, from the public and private sectors will be engaged.
– Shows the Government's commitment to ensuring that the clean up is carried out safely, securely, cost effectively and in ways which protect the environment for the benefit of current and future generations.
– Illustrates the Government's priority to ensure that management arrangements are open, transparent and command public confidence.

Some of the proposals might impact on devolved matters. In particular, policy on the management arrangement of radioactive waste, administered under the Radioactive Substances Act 1993 would be a responsibility of the devolved administrations in Scotland, Wales and Northern Ireland.

'*Draft Mental Health Bill*' was presented to Parliament by the Secretary of State for Health in June 2002. The Bill was prepared by the Department of Health and the Home Office, in consultation with the Wales Office and the National Assembly for Wales. The Bill restates and amends the law relating to the compulsory care and treatment of mentally disordered persons and offenders. The Bill sets out:

– How to provide compulsory treatment for those suffering from mental disorders in the best interests of the patient and to prevent harm to other people.
– To bring the law more closely into line with modern human rights laws, as defined by developing case law arising from the European Convention of Human Rights.
– Provide a three stage process from the initial use of compulsory powers, through formal assessment and treatment to the independent authorisation of compulsory treatment for longer than 28 days by a new Mental Health Tribunal.

The Bill is divided into eleven parts and replaces most of the Mental Health Act 1983 (apart from Part VII which will remain in force).

'*Extradition: Consultation on Draft Legislation*' as presented to Parliament by the Secretary of State for the Home Department in June 2002. The proposals in the '*The Law on Extradition – A Review*' 2001 which set out the Government's approach to extradition. The review had been overtaken by progress on the development of the European Arrest Warrant, to which this Bill gives effect. The paper sets out the following draft clauses for an Extradition Bill, and is divided into five parts:

– Part 1: radical reform of the UK's extradition procedures using fast track arrangements for extradition to what will be known as category one territories and which will include all EU member states.
– Part 2: streamlining the present system so that extradition is quicker.
– Part 3: relates to categories one and two territories (category two includes Commonwealth countries, British overseas territories and the Hong Kong Special Administrative Region of the People's Republic of China) for the person to stand trial in his country.
– Part 4: powers for the police to obtain a warrant to search premises and seize and retain any material which is likely to be admissible evidence at trial in the UK.
– Part 5: miscellaneous and general provisions, including extradition to Commonwealth countries, British overseas territories and surrender to the International Criminal Court.

Your Region, Your Choice: Revitalising the English Regions' was presented to Parliament by the Deputy Prime Minister and First Secretary of State, and the Secretary of State for †Transport, Local Government and the Regions in May 2002. The White Paper outlines:

– The Government's approach to regional policy.
– What the Government has done to develop the

English regions, including the creation of Regional Development Agencies, regional chambers and increased responsibilities of the Government Offices for the Regions.

- Opportunity for the development of democratic regional government distinct from Local Government.
- The need to hold a referendum in a region prior to having an elected assembly.

'The Draft Communications Bill' was presented to Parliament by the Secretary of State for Trade and Industry and the Secretary of State for Culture, Media and Sport in May 2002. The Bill will give effect to the Communications White Paper – *'A New Future for Communications'* 2000. The main provisions of the Bill are:

- The transfer of regulatory functions of the Office of Communications (OFCOM) from the bodies and office holders which currently regulate the communications sector, namely the Broadcasting Standards Commission, the Office of Telecommunications, the Independent Television Commission, the Radio Authority and the Radio Communications Agency.
- The replacement of the present system of licensing telecommunications systems.
- The development of a new system to regulate broadcasting, accommodate the transfer from analogue to digital broadcasting, and to simplify the regulation of public service broadcasters.
- The creation of a consumer panel to advise and assist OFCOM and to represent and protect consumer interests.
- The establishment of a content board to advise OFCOM of the subject matter of anything broadcast in an electronic communications network.

'Draft National Health Service (Wales) Bill' was published by the Secretary of State for Wales in May 2002. The draft Bill included:

- Developing the role of the 22 Community Health Councils, the independent local health watchdogs who work closely with patients, families and carers.
- Creating a Wales Centre for Health, a new independent organisation with responsibility for training, advice and research related to the protection and improvement of the health of the people of Wales.
- Creating Health Professions Wales as a successor to the Wales National Board for Nursing, Midwifery and Health Visiting.

'Realising Europe's Potential – Economic Reform in Europe' was presented to Parliament by the Chancellor of the Exchequer in February 2002. The White Paper follows on from a strategy reached by European Governments at the Lisbon European Council for economic reform in 2000. Priorities include:

- Setting out a vision of Europe as a dynamic, job creating and socially inclusive economy.
- Developing a two-pronged approach to ensure low employment rates and increasing productivity growth.
- Employment opportunities for all.
- Targeting sustainable development.
- Integration and reform of the European Union to enhance individuals rights i.e. the right to work, study or retire in any European Union member state.

'The House of Lords – Completing the Reform' was presented to Parliament by the Prime Minister in November 2001. It shows the Government's plans to complete the reform of the House of Lords in fulfilment of its election mandate and the report of the Independent Royal Commission on House of Lords Reform chaired by Lord Wakeham. The most important proposals are:

- Hereditary peers would no longer have any privileged rights of membership as the link with the peerage would be dissolved.
- The majority of the members of the House would be nominated by the political parties, in proportion to political party shares following a general election. This would include around 120 elected members with no political affiliation and 120 directly elected members to represent the nations and regions, and a continuing role for Law Lords and Bishops of the Church of England.
- An independent statutory Appointments Commission would have the powers to appoint independent members and determine how many seats each political party is entitled to-this reducing Government patronage.
- The size of the House will be capped at 600 by statute.

†The Former Department of Transport, Local Government and the Regions has now separated to form the Department for Transport and the Office of the Deputy Prime Minister

Science and Discovery

LAKES BENEATH ANTARCTICA

More than 80 lakes of liquid water have been found under the base of Antarctica's thick, glacial ice sheets. Study has focused on one of these, Lake Vostok, which lies between 3,750 and 4,150 metres below the central east Antarctic ice sheet. Measuring 240 by 50 kilometres, Lake Vostok is about 1,000 metres deep at its southern end, and may date back to the formation of the ice sheet 33 million years ago. Ice on the base of the ice sheet melts at the northern end of the lake, introducing dissolved oxygen into the water environment. Refreezing (accretion) occurs at the southern end, from which deep ice-core samples have been taken by scientists at the Russian Vostok research station.

Water in Lake Vostok has an average age of about a million years, being derived from the melting of subglacial ice. Bacteria recovered from the accreted ice at the lake's southern end have conserved DNA sequences comparable to those of modern organisms, reflecting their delivery from the overlying ice. More intriguing is the possibility that micro-organisms in the lake floor sediments may be even more ancient, perhaps having been isolated from the surface for tens of millions of years. At the depths which prevail in Lake Vostok, the pressure is equivalent to 350 atmospheres, keeping the water liquid despite temperatures of −3°C. Lake organisms in the dark depths derive their energy from chemical sources.

It is possible that unknown species might be discovered during future exploration of the as-yet unsampled water environment; so far, all that is known of the lake biota has been inferred from the recovery of accreted ice hundreds of metres above the lake. Drilling halted 120 metres above the lake in 1998, but it is expected that direct sampling will take place in the next three to six years, once an international team of scientists agrees on how best to proceed without contaminating this pristine location.

PROBING JUPITER'S MAGNETOSPHERE

From December 2000 to January 2001, the Cassini-Huygens spacecraft heading for Saturn passed close to Jupiter, receiving a gravitational boost to its trajectory. The fly-by also provided scientists with a unique opportunity to investigate Jupiter's magnetosphere, combining data from Cassini-Huygens with those from the Galileo orbiter, which has been touring the Jovian system since 1995, and observations from the Hubble Space Telescope and Chandra X-ray Observatory satellite. Analysis of the results from this 'Millennium Mission' appeared in papers from several research teams in the journal *Nature* in February 2002.

Jupiter's magnetosphere, a vast 'bubble' of interplanetary space in which particle motions are governed by the Jovian magnetic field, is shaped to a large extent by the influence of the supersonic solar wind, which flows outwards from the Sun through the solar system. At times of high sunspot activity, as in 2000–1, the solar wind can become quite turbulent, with shock waves propagating through it. An interplanetary shock-wave passage coincided with Cassini-Huygens's arrival near Jupiter. Measurements from the spacecraft showed compression of the Jovian magnetosphere in response to the shock, while Hubble and Chandra recorded an intensification of activity in the auroral ovals girdling Jupiter's magnetic poles.

Observations of Jupiter's aurora at X-ray and ultraviolet wavelengths also revealed 'footprints' indicating magnetospheric connections between the planet and three of its major satellites, Io, Ganymede and Europa. Volcanic Io has long been known as a source of particles which populate a flux tube in Jupiter's magnetosphere. Cassini-Huygens detected a population of extremely high energy (50 MeV) electrons, accelerated in radiation belts between 0.5 and 3 Jupiter radii above the cloud tops. These accelerated electrons are a powerful source of synchrotron emission.

Passage through the Jupiter system showed the Cassini-Huygens spacecraft to be in good order, boding well for its orbital exploration of the Saturn system starting in 2004. Galileo, meanwhile, is scheduled to crash into Jupiter's atmosphere in September 2003 after a greatly extended and very successful operational life.

LEONID METEORS

Well-known for their historical pattern of producing meteor 'storms' (nominally rates in excess of 1,000 per hour) at roughly 33-year intervals, the Leonid meteors have been the subject of intense scrutiny in recent years. Following the 1966 storm, seen over the western United States, the meteor shower's 1999 return was originally expected to be the most intense in the current sequence associated with the 1998 return to the inner solar system of the parent comet 55P/Tempel-Tuttle. Observers in the Mediterranean and Sinai regions duly witnessed a storm early in the morning of 18 November 1999.

Predictions of activity based on a recently developed model of Comet Tempel-Tuttle's debris stream suggested that the 2001 return could be even more active, with two spells of elevated Leonid activity on 18 November around 1000 and 1800 Universal Time (equivalent to GMT). These materialised on cue, providing spectacular meteor displays for observers in North America and in Australia and the Pacific region respectively. American observers saw bright Leonids appearing at a rate of one every few seconds, equivalent to around 1,600 per hour. Multiple peaks, equivalent to a rate perhaps as high as 4,000 per hour, were recorded by observers in the Pacific, who enjoyed a sustained spell of very high Leonid activity lasting several hours.

The stream model derived by David Asher of Armagh Observatory and Robert McNaught of the Anglo-Australian Observatory successfully predicted these outbursts, based on encounters with 'arcs' of meteoric debris shed by the comet in 1699, 1766 and 1866 Further interludes of storm activity were also forecast for 19 November 2002, and the validity of the model as a predictive tool seems assured.

The next few years will see a steady diminution in Leonid activity as the main debris swarm close to the comet recedes from the inner solar system. Activity at low levels will continue to be seen each November between about the 15th and 20th of the month in the years to come, stepping up to higher rates again in the late 2020s.

MICROBIAL GENOMES

Advances in biotechnology and computing continue to accelerate the progress of genome sequencing. Complete DNA sequences have now been determined for more than 60 microbial species, most of them medically significant. By analysing these sequences in a computer, researchers

can identify open reading frames (Orfs) – stretches of DNA – corresponding to the multitude of protein-encoding genes which need to operate in concert for an organism to function. The simplest bacteria may have fewer than 1,000 ORFs in their genomes, while more complex species, including pathogens such as *Mycobacterium tuberculosis,* may have over 4,000. It is hoped that in the long term these studies will help to identify targets for future drug design, countering the emergence of antibiotic-resistant strains.

Genome analyses and comparisons between species have also revealed the extent to which genes can be transferred horizontally. The clustering of genes that code for virulence factors suggests that these might readily be carried from one species to another by bacterial viruses, or on small circular DNA molecules called plasmids. Genomic regions described as 'pathogenicity islands' have been identified in, for example, *Bacillus anthracis* (anthrax) and *Helicobacter pylori,* a bacterium believed to cause gastric ulcers. Sequencing of microbial genomes may also see applications in agriculture – nitrogen-fixing genes from root nodule bacteria – or industry and research, where heat-resistant enzymes from thermophilic bacteria are being sought.

Among the bacterial genomes to be completely sequenced recently is that of the plague bacillus *Yersinia pestis.* With a length of 4.65 million DNA basepairs, this is described as a 'fluid' genome, in which the DNA sequence has the capacity to acquire genes useful to the organism and virulence factors allowing infection of both mammalian hosts and the (flea) insect vector. About 4 per cent of the *Y. pestis* genome consists of pseudogenes, genes acquired in the past but whose ORFs are now incomplete and therefore 'silent' in terms of protein expression.

Fission Yeast Genome

Alongside advances in genomic studies of bacteria, progress is being made in decoding the genomes of several eukaryotes. Eukaryotic cells are more complex than bacteria, showing a greater level of organisation, including compartmentalisation into organelles which perform specific functions and packaging of DNA into more distinct chromosomes. Cell biologists have long regarded brewer's yeast, *Saccharomyces cerevisiae,* as a useful model organism owing to a solid understanding of its genetics and the ease with which it can be cultured and manipulated in the laboratory. Sequencing of the *S. cerevisiae* genome was completed in 1997. Early in 2002, completion of the genome sequence of a second yeast, *Schizosaccharomyces pombe,* was announced.

In a number of respects, *S. pombe* is a more promising experimental subject than the distantly related *S. cerevisiae.* An obvious difference lies in the two yeasts' modes of division; *S. cerevisiae* buds small progeny from a larger 'mother' cell, whereas *S. pombe* undergoes fission to produce two equally-sized partners, hence its popular description as 'fission yeast'. The cellular events leading up to division in *S. pombe* more closely resemble those in higher eukaryotes, including humans, and fission yeast has been the model of choice in studies of the eukaryotic cell's replication cycle. Many of the organelles in *S. pombe* are more closely similar in structure and function to those of higher eukaryotes than the equivalents in *S. cerevisiae.* At gene level, too, *S. pombe* displays greater similarity to higher eukaryotes; the protein sequences are more strongly similar (homologous) to those of mammalian species than are those of budding yeast. Pioneering work using *S. pombe* in this field by Sir Paul Nurse was recognised by his joint receipt of the 2001 Nobel Prize for Physiology or Medicine.

Completion of the three-chromosome, 13.8 million basepair DNA sequence of *S. pombe* has yielded some interesting results. In all, *S. pombe* has some 4,824 open reading frames (ORFs), compared with roughly 5,600 in *S. cerevisiae.* Of these, 43 per cent contain introns, non-coding regions which need to be 'spliced' out when DNA is transcribed to RNA ahead of protein synthesis; the splicing machinery is another point of similarity between *S. pombe* and higher eukaryotes. Homologues to 50 human disease genes (half of them cancer-related) have been identified, and the genetic tractability of *S. pombe* should allow further investigation of these. Perhaps the major surprise about the *S. pombe* genome is the relatively small number of ORFs required to define a simple eukaryote, not many more than in some bacteria. The important difference appears to lie in the content and organisation, rather than the complexity, of the genome.

Asteroidal Close Shave

The Lincoln Laboratory Near Earth Asteroid Research project (LINEAR) at White Sands, New Mexico, continues its successful search programme for automated detection of rapidly moving celestial objects. Up to early April 2002, more than 150,000 new asteroids had been found by LINEAR, including 951 classed as near-Earth objects (NEOs). LINEAR has also discovered more than 80 comets.

A LINEAR near-Earth object discovery on 17 June 2002 was particularly notable. The object, designated 2002 MN, had passed just 120,000 km from Earth (i.e. a third of the Moon's distance from Earth) at its closest approach three days earlier. An asteroid 100 metres in diameter, 2002 MN is one of only six known to have come closer to Earth than the Moon. Had it impacted on the planet, it could have caused devastation comparable to the Tunguska object, which flattened trees over a 2,200 square kilometre area of Siberia in 1908. This recent near-miss asteroid was not detected until after its closest approach, as it came towards Earth from the direction of the Sun's glare, our 'blind side'. The record for the closest approach is held by an object designated 1994 XM1, which came within 105,000 km of Earth on 9 December 1994, and was considerably smaller than 2002 MN.

Another LINEAR discovery, made on 5 July 2002, generated a burst of media interest after the revelation that the object might possibly impact on Earth on 1 February 2019. The asteroid 2002 NT7 is 2 km in diameter, has an 837-day orbit and, were it to impact, has sufficient size and kinetic energy to cause continent-wide devastation. As is so often the case with such reports, subsequent observations reduced the imminent threat of impact once the orbit was refined, though a remote chance remains of collision between Earth and the asteroid in 2069.

Comets Near and Far

Since Hale-Bopp in 1997, there have been few bright comets to observe until 2001–2, which brought three good objects. Two were LINEAR discoveries; 2001A2 and 200WM1 became faintly visible to the naked eye in June and July 2001 and in December 2001 respectively. The third, discovered independently by Japanese and Chinese amateur astronomers, was 2002/C1 Ikeya-Zhang, which became a reasonably prominent object visible to the naked eye, and sporting a few degrees of tail when viewed in binoculars, in the evening skies in late March and early April 2002. Orbital calculations show Ikeya-Zhang to be identical with a comet observed in 1661.

Periodic comet 19P/Borrelly became the second to have its nucleus imaged during a spacecraft fly-by on 22

September 2001. The Deep Space 1 probe was successfully targeted to fly within 2,200 km of Comet Borrelly's nucleus, which was revealed as an elongated dark body with a long axis of 8 km. The surface reflectance was found to be only 3 per cent, with some patches being even darker. Borrelly's nucleus has a distinct bend in the middle. Surface temperatures of between 27°C and 72°C were measured. Compared with the highly active nucleus of Comet 1P/Halley, imaged from the Giotto probe in 1986, that of Comet Borrelly appeared relatively quiescent, showing only modest levels of jet activity resulting from outgassing. Like other periodic comets, which become depleted of volatile materials over the course of successive returns to the inner solar system, Comet Borrelly was a rather faint object for terrestrial observers at this apparition. Borrelly has an orbital period of 6.8 years, and was most recently at perihelion, its closest to the Sun, on 14 September 2001.

Further spacecraft encounters with comets can be anticipated in coming years. On 3 July 2001, NASA launched CONTOUR (the Comet Nucleus Tour probe), which will visit 2P/Encke in 2003 and 73P/Schwassmann-Wachmann in 2006. Meanwhile, the European Space Agency's Rosetta spacecraft, which will rendezvous with Comet 46P/Wirtanen, is scheduled for launch in January 2003.

SPRITES AND JETS

The short-lived light flashes of sprites have been recognised as a phenomenon for many years, and especially since photographic and video records of them started to become available from the late 1980s. Occurring in the upper atmosphere above thunderstorms, sprites take the form of very brief pulses of red or blue light, perhaps only a couple of milliseconds in duration, whose colour is identified with excited states of nitrogen.

The mechanism remains subject to debate, but most now believe that sprites form when a lightning strike electrically connects the ground to the top of a thundercloud. Most lightning strikes connect the base of the cloud to the ground, and it is only the rare (perhaps one in twenty) top of cloud-to-ground strikes which have the potential to generate sprites, by creating an excess of negative charge in the overlying mesosphere. Acceleration of electrons in this so-called quasi-electrostatic field, stretching from the base of the ionosphere at 80 km altitude down towards the cloud, produces a column of excitation perhaps 10 km in diameter. Re-emission by nitrogen atoms of the excess energy in the form of light produces a sprite.

A number of related but poorly understood phenomena accompany sprites. One of these has now been studied in greater detail by a team led by Victor Pasko. Using high-speed video, these workers captured the development of an upwards-propagating blue jet emerging from the top of a thundercloud seen from Arecibo Observatory, Puerto Rico, on 14 September 2001. The conical jet showed several narrow tendrils and stretched to an altitude of 70 km, demonstrating for the first time an upwards connection from a thundercloud to the ionosphere. Above about 42 km, the structure broke down somewhat, coming more to resemble that of a sprite in the high atmosphere. The upwards-propagating jet was, however, much longer-lived than a sprite. Pasko and co-workers speculate that such connections from thundercloud tops to the ionosphere may play an important, though as yet incompletely understood, part in the global electric circuit.

THE GALAXY'S HEART IN X-RAYS

Astronomers have long believed, from studying similar galaxies, that a super-massive black hole resides at the core of our home galaxy, the Milky Way. The core is hidden from view to us, as the solar system lies 26,000 light years from the galaxy's centre and there is much obscuring dust and gas as well as countless stars in the line of sight. Radio wavelength observations, however, reveal a bright source known as Sagittarius A* ('A-star') close to the centre, around which stars are densely packed (10 million within a light year). From the motions of these stars, Sagittarius A* is inferred to have a mass 2.6 million times that of the Sun.

Confirmation of the likely nature of Sagittarius A* as a black hole has come from observations made from the Chandra X-ray Observatory satellite launched in July 1999. A flare in X-ray emission to 45 times normal intensity was observed on 26–27 October 2000. Rapid variations in intensity were recorded, and the constraint that nothing can travel faster than the speed of light allows use of these data to estimate the size of the emitting region, i.e. the proposed black hole's event horizon. The conclusion is that this is within a factor of 20 of the size predicted by general relativity theory, almost certainly confirming that there is indeed a black hole at the centre of our galaxy.

Chandra has allowed observations of the Sagittarius A* region at a very high resolution (0.5 arc-second), and other recent results show that at least 1,000 individual point sources contribute to the X-ray flux coming from the galactic centre. This contrasts with the previous possibility that much of the emission came from extremely hot gas surrounding Sagittarius A*, and further strengthens the finding that there is a black hole at the heart of the Milky Way.

ADVANCES AGAINST MALARIA

Malaria is a worsening problem again, with 500 million clinical cases each year, of which more than a million prove fatal. The main impact of the disease is in sub-Saharan Africa, where 90 per cent of fatal cases occur. In recent years, the causative organism, a protozoan parasite, has developed increasing resistance to the quinoline drugs used in treatment, while the mosquito is becoming resistant to insecticides. Several new approaches to the problem are being pursued.

Four species of malaria parasite infect humans, the most severe being *Plasmodium falciparum*, transmitted by blood-feeding *Anopheles gambiae* mosquitoes. The genome sequences of both *P. falciparum* and its insect vector were expected to be completed during 2002, allowing identification of potential targets for new drugs. Promising candidate genes include those coding for intracellular transporters involved in folate metabolism, digestion of haemoglobin in the parasite's lysosomal vacuole, and attachment to host cells. Techniques for gene disruption in *Plasmodium* species – allowing identification of those which are essential – are under development; these organisms are much less amenable than, say, yeast to laboratory manipulation.

Vaccines against malaria have been a long-term goal, and while some candidates are ready for testing, it is likely that an effective vaccine still lies some years in the future. A major hurdle is that such a vaccine has to address the different stages in the life-cycle of the parasite; genomics should benefit identification of candidate antigens for use in subunit vaccines.

A group of researchers led by Marcelo Jacob-Lorena at Case Western Reserve University, Ohio, has succeeded in producing transgenic *Anopheles stephensi* mosquitoes

which express a short protein sequence in their gut and salivary gland, blocking invasion by malaria parasites acquired during blood feeding. The experiment, described more as 'proof of principle' than as a practical solution, adds further to a growing understanding of the parasite and its interactions with vector and host, but introducing the trait to the wild mosquito population is unfeasible. In the longer term, it is hoped that scientific advances may yet provide means of controlling the disease.

MORE MOONS

The Voyager missions to the outer planets of our solar system between 1979 and 1989 resulted in the discovery of many previously unknown satellites orbiting the solar system's gas giant worlds. Since then, improvements in detector technology, coupled with large Earth-based telescopes, have allowed dedicated surveys down to very faint limits and these have revealed many more moons orbiting Jupiter, Saturn and Uranus.

Searches have concentrated on the regions close to the planets known as their Hill sphere, a volume surrounding them within which satellites can stably orbit. Seen from the distance of Earth, Uranus's Hill sphere subtends six square degrees on the sky (for comparison, the Moon is half a degree across), while those of Saturn and Jupiter cover 22 and 48 square degrees respectively. These are still large areas to survey in terms of the detector's field of view.

Uranus is now recognised to have 21 satellites, with a detection limit diameter of about 30 km. Saturn has 30 to a detection limit of about 10 km; some of these are in orbital 'families', reflecting an origin from fragmentation of a larger common precursor object. As of May 2002, Jupiter was established as the planet with most satellites, with 39 known. Many of Jupiter's small satellites (some are only 2 km across) may be asteroids captured early in the history of the solar system. The most recent discoveries were made in December 2001 using the 3.6-metre Canada-France-Hawaii Telescope on Mauna Kea by the international team of David Jewitt, Scott Sheppard and Jan Kleyna.

ICE AND DUST ON MARS

Evidence for running water on Mars's surface was first obtained by the Mariner 9 spacecraft in 1971. Dry riverbeds, channels and other features make it clear that in the past water has flowed on the Red Planet. Currently, however, our view of Mars is of an arid world, with its surface water either lost due to the thinness of its atmosphere or frozen out in permafrost. Results from the NASA Mars Odyssey spacecraft, which has been orbiting the planet since October 2001, support strongly the latter explanation.

Mars Odyssey's gamma-ray spectrometer revealed the presence of hydrogen in a layer less than a metre below the planet's surface. Results from this instrument (a twin of that aboard Lunar Prospector, which detected similar evidence for water ice at the Moon's poles in 1998) were backed up by data from Mars Odyssey's neutron spectrometer. The hydrogen is taken to be a signature of water ice (H_2O) bound up in the Martian soil. This discovery, announced in late May 2002, suggests that there is much more water in Mars's permafrost than was previously suspected – enough, possibly, to account for features thought to result from sedimentation in an ancient ocean. Future missions, including the European Space Agency's Mars Express scheduled for launch in 2003, will allow more detailed investigation of these sub-surface ice deposits.

Mars was a prominent object in the night skies in June and July 2001, outshining all but Venus and the Moon at its best. For telescopic observers, however, this proved a somewhat frustrating apparition as a planet-encircling dust storm concealed Mars's surface features. Like many in the past, the 2001 storm originated in the giant (1,800 km) circular Hellas impact basin in the southern hemisphere. Most of the major dust storms start in the planet's southern hemisphere summer in response to seasonal heating. The 2001 storm arose unusually early, in late spring. Having obscured the dusky markings of Mars's southern hemisphere during June, July and August, the dust began to clear in September.

Mars will again be prominent, opposite the Sun against the stars of Aquarius, during August and September 2003. At this time, the Red Planet will also be near perihelion, closest in its elliptical orbit to the Sun, and will therefore present a relatively large apparent disk for observation.

PURER STEM CELLS

Many scientists are investigating the possible use of stem cells to repair or replace damaged tissue in the body. Stem cells are distinguished from those making up the bulk of the body by their ability to divide more or less indefinitely, and their undifferentiated nature. Their key feature, from the point of view of potential clinical applications, is their ability to throw off differentiated (specialised) daughter cells in response to appropriate biochemical signals. For example, stem cells in the bone marrow can produce a variety of blood cell types.

Embryonic stem cells have the capacity to produce any type of cell, a property described as pluripotency. Ethical barriers, however, prevent the use of embryonic stem cells, although work with those recovered post-natally from umbilical cord has proved promising. Umbilical cord stem cells have a more limited repertoire of daughter cell types, but still have greater multipotency than those from adults. Stem cells in mature individuals tend to have the ability to produce primarily cell types related to the tissue in which they are found, e.g. those in the central nervous system usually produce neurons. However, recent research indicates that adult stem cells may, under the correct culture conditions, show a greater degree of multipotency than was previously thought.

Much of the work in this field has been based on rodent models. Promising results include regeneration of neural and cardiac tissue following implantation of appropriate stem cells. In principle, future research could lead to treatments allowing repair of pancreatic tissue, cornea, blood vessels, skeletal tissue, heart muscle, skin and liver. Among the most widely publicised putative benefits of stem cell research is development of therapy for neuro-degenerative conditions such as Parkinson's disease, through the replacement of damaged brain cells. Obtaining the appropriate stem cells from adult brain in sufficient quantity has been brought a step closer in work by Australian researchers reported in August 2001.

In mouse brains, stem cells are found in ventricles where they comprise 0.3 per cent of the population. Rodney L. Rietze and co-workers managed to isolate these to 80 per cent purity using a cell-sorter to separate them by size, then removing residual contaminant cells on the basis of surface marker proteins. Transplanted into the developing brains of mouse embryos, the purified stem cells went on to produce neural tissue.

BRIGHT FUTURE FOR GENE THERAPY?

Among the advances that stem cell research is expected to deliver is a route to effective gene therapy. In work reported in April 2002, doctors and scientists at London's

Great Ormond Street Hospital successfully treated 18-month-old Rhys Evans for X-linked Severe Combined Immunodeficiency (X-SCID). This gene disorder left him unable to produce lymphocytes (a white cell type) and therefore prone to infection.

One possible cure would have been to transplant bone marrow from a healthy donor, but finding a tissue match proved impossible. To overcome this problem, some of Rhys's own bone marrow cells were extracted under sterile conditions, and transfected with a retrovirus containing an intact copy of the damaged gene. In those cells where the retrovirus successfully integrated into the DNA, a 'gene repair' was effected, restoring the ability to make lymphocytes. The treated cells were transfused back into the patient, becoming established in the bone marrow, and resulting in a rise in Rhys's lymphocyte count to more or less normal levels. A second child has since undergone similar, successful treatment.

The success of this treatment, the long-term stability of which will be carefully monitored by doctors, bodes well for the future use of gene therapy to treat other disorders, such as haemophilia and cystic fibrosis.

MOVEMENTS IN THE MANTLE

Since the 1960s, it has been accepted that Earth's solid outer crust, reaching to a depth of perhaps 30 km below the surface, is comprised of a number of interlocked mobile 'plates', shifting gradually atop a more fluid region of molten or semi-molten rock, the mantle. The mantle makes up the bulk of the planet's volume, reaching a depth of about 2,900 km over the 2,780 km-diameter nickel-iron core.

The structure and motions of the mantle can only be investigated indirectly, by measuring the propagation of seismic waves, mainly from earthquakes. These studies suggest a division into two regions, the upper mantle varying in depth from 410 km to 660 km. Anisotropies in the transmission of seismic waves point to material flows in the lowest 200–300 km of mantle overlying the core. Results published in February 2002 also suggest structural irregularities in the mantle between the Tonga subduction zone, where a great slab of material is being forced down into the lower mantle, and Australia.

Also reported in February 2002 were results from Project Eagle, studying the Great Rift Valley in Africa. Here, a huge plume of magma is rising from the depths of the mantle, gradually splitting east Africa apart along a line from the Red Sea through Ethiopia, Kenya and Tanzania. Opening at about 2 cm per year in northern Ethiopia, the rift will take about 100 million years to form a new ocean and drive part of the East African plate into the Indian Ocean. During January 2002, volcanic activity associated with the magma plume below east Africa devastated the town of Goma in the Congo.

Seismic studies of the upper mantle in the American Pacific north-west coast subduction zone (Cascadia) by M. G. Bostock and colleagues suggest that chemical changes in the rocks may help to reduce the intensity of earthquakes in the region. As it is forced deeper into the mantle under the North American plate, Pacific ocean crust gives up its chemically-bound water. This water hydrates the overlying mantle to produce 'slippery' serpentinite minerals at a depth of about 45 km. The presence of these silicate minerals limits the depth at which earthquakes can occur and, therefore, their severity and geographical extent.

FAST IGNITION FUSION

Nuclear fusion is an excellent source of energy, and lies at the heart of the Sun's power output. Harnessing it in a terrestrial context is a difficult proposition, however, which is why existing nuclear power plants are based on fission (decay) of radioactive isotopes. Fusion of the heavy hydrogen isotopes deuterium and tritium is a desirable alternative, since it yields a lot of energy without generating long-lived decay products, but the process requires high temperatures, of the order of 50 million degrees Celsius, and these are hard to create in controlled conditions. Past attempts at controlled fusion have used large volumes of magnetically confined hot plasma, and were successful in producing high energy yields. However, their limitation was that the required input energy was greater than that produced in these conditions.

A new alternative, known as the fast ignition process, has been investigated by a team of Japanese and British scientists. In this process, a laser or ion beam driver is used to compress and ignite the fuel, which undergoes fusion in a short burst. Test experiments with the Gekko XIII laser at the University of Osaka, using deuterated polystyrene as the fuel, gave encouraging results in terms of energy output and efficiency. It is possible that future development of this technology will give a fusion:driver energy return of 300:1, but much work remains to be done to improve understanding of the physics involved before this method could be applied commercially.

EARLIEST FOSSIL PLACENTAL MAMMAL

A 125 million-year-old fossil from the Yixian Formation in Liaoning Province, China, has pushed back the age of placental mammals, to which humans belong, to the early Cretaceous period. The fossil of Eomaia scansoria ('Dawn mother'), the size of a large mouse, is exceptionally well-preserved, showing fur and skeletal details, although the skull is somewhat crushed. Eomaia appears to have been adapted for a climbing, possibly arboreal lifestyle, as indicated by elongated finger bones. Pelvic bone structure is consistent with placental reproduction in which a relatively short gestation was followed by maternal nurture. The teeth indicate that Eomaia had a carnivorous diet which probably included insects.

Several other mammalian fossils from the same period have been isolated from the Yixian Formation, representing species that are now extinct. Perhaps part of the success of the placental mammals follows from Eomaia's presumed tree-living lifestyle.

A CLONED CAT

Animal cloning – the transfer of a mature cell nucleus to a developing egg cell which has had its nucleus removed by micromanipulation – has been successfully carried out for a number of species, including mice, cattle, goats and pigs. The most celebrated product of the procedure is Dolly, the cloned sheep born in 1997. A research group at Texas A. & M. University reported the first successful cloning of a cat, under a programme called CopyCat, in February 2002.

The cloning was achieved by taking cumulus cells from the ovary of a female cat. Following growth in culture, these were fused with enucleated egg cells, and those which began development as embryos were implanted into surrogate mother cats. Known as Cc, the cloned kitten was delivered by caesarian section after 66 days' gestation. Cc was the only one of 87 clones to be implanted and develop to term successfully; in an earlier experiment, a cloned embryo ceased development after 44 days.

The success rate emphasises that animal cloning is far from trivial or routine. As the CopyCat workers point out, some cell types may be more suited than others for

use as sources of donor nuclei; much remains to be learned. Meanwhile, the group's attempts to clone a dog have so far proved unsuccessful.

A THICKER CRUST FOR EUROPA

When first imaged in close-up from the Voyager spacecraft in 1979, Jupiter's large satellite Europa, 3,138 km diameter, was found to have an icy surface, criss-crossed with fractures. Tidal heating brought about by the gravitational influence of Jupiter's other major, Galilean satellites is believed to maintain a sub-surface ocean of liquid water in Europa's interior. Some planetary scientists have conjectured that this might provide an environment in which primitive life could have developed, and many would like to see future unmanned spacecraft missions sent to Europa to investigate what lies under the ice. Rather like the future investigations of Lake Vostok in Antarctica, this investigation would entail somehow penetrating the ice. Analysis of Voyager and Galileo spacecraft images of Europa, Ganymede and Callisto by Paul Schenk at the Lunar and Planetary Institute, Houston, Texas, suggests this may be a more difficult proposition than was previously thought.

Schenk assessed the structure of relatively young, undegraded impact craters on these three major moons of Jupiter, confirming that Ganymede and Callisto each have icy crusts (lithospheres) several tens of kilometres thick. Past models suggested a much thinner lithosphere for Europa – perhaps only a couple of kilometres deep – allowing the exchange of ocean (possibly including biological) and surface material. The new measurements, however, show a minimum depth of 19-25 km for Europa's crust, meaning that the proposed ocean lies much further below the surface than was assumed.

MAGNETOSPHERIC MOVEMENTS

Studies of processes in Earth's magnetosphere, including the generation of aurorae, have been greatly advanced in recent years by the launch and operation of an armada of satellites dedicated to the study of near-Earth particle motions. Geomagnetic storms have become a subject of much interest, given their sometimes harmful effects on satellites, communications systems and even ground-based electrical grid systems.

It has long been understood that the overriding factor in triggering geomagnetic storms is solar activity. The effects of violent eruptions in the Sun's inner atmosphere, transmitted via the supersonic solar wind speeding past Earth into interplanetary space, cause stress on the magnetosphere. The earthward acceleration of electrons from the magnetosphere's 'downwind' tail under conditions of stress has been accepted since the 1960s as an important process in driving geomagnetic storms. More recently, a second model proposed that storms might be driven by 'convection' of magnetic flux and particles towards the magnetosphere's dayside region.

Observations from the Geotail satellite provide support for both mechanisms, which operated at different times during a magnetic storm in October 1999. Detection of energetic neutral atoms, liberated when ions capture electrons and escape from magnetic field confinement, allowed Geotail to map large-scale structures in the magnetosphere, confirming that the auroral ring current above the Earth was boosted by convection at those times when electron acceleration from the magnetotail was reduced; both processes energise the magnetospheric circuit.

Insights into the mechanism by which auroral electrons are accelerated in the region of space within a few thousand kilometres of Earth have been provided by the four formation-flying spacecraft of the European Space Agency's Cluster mission, launched in 2000. Cluster measurements have shown that loss of ionospheric electrons into space creates huge electrical fields. Incoming electrons accelerated along these fields give rise to the coloured lights of the aurora as they collide with and excite oxygen atoms and nitrogen molecules in the tenuous upper atmosphere at altitudes above 100 km.

OLDEST FOSSIL HOMINID

Most evolutionary biologists lean towards the view that mankind arose in Africa, from a line of hominid apes which diverged from chimpanzees some 10 million years ago. DNA analysis confirms that, genetically, *Homo sapiens* has much in common with chimpanzees. A fossil discovery made in the Djurab desert in northern Chad in July 2001, and announced a year later after further study, adds another part to the evolutionary jigsaw, and may put back the date of this divergence.

The discovery was made by a team led by Michel Brunet from the University of Poitiers, France, and consisted of a fossil skull some six to seven million years old. While similar in size to that of a small chimpanzee, the Chad skull has important differences, including smaller canine teeth and a flat face. Other fossils found at the site include lower jaw fragments and teeth, representing several individuals; it is expected that further finds will ensue. The other mammal fossils, together with those of fish and crocodiles, suggest that seven million years ago the region was on the edge of a large lake surrounded by grassland and forest. Significantly, the site is 2,500 km west of the East African Rift Valley, which has been the source of most early hominid fossil finds.

Nicknamed Toumai Man, the Djurab species has been given the scientific name *Sahelanthropus tchadensis,* and represents the earliest example of a hominid from perhaps as little as three million years after the divergence between chimpanzees and the line which eventually led to modern man.

MODELLING CLIMATE CHANGE

Global warming looks to be here to stay, at least in the medium term; mean global temperatures have risen by about 0.6°C in the past century, and warming is strongly indicated by reductions in snow cover and in the extent of glaciers and sea ice. Much of the warming in the past 50 years is attributed to human activities.

Policy decisions on how global warming may be countered are likely to be strongly influenced by the accuracy of models projecting its future course. So far, most models have focused on likely temperatures about 100 years in the future; most governments, however, prefer to plan for the shorter term. Two models that arrive at strikingly similar forecasts for global temperatures in the 2020s were detailed in *Nature* in April 2002.

Work by P. A. Stott and J. A. Kettleborough at the UK Meteorological Office and Rutherford Appleton Laboratory was based on a model which coupled the effects of the atmosphere and oceans. Their estimate is that global temperatures will be between 0.3°C and 1.3°C higher in the 2020s than in the 1990s. Reto Knutti and colleagues at the University of Berne, Switzerland, used a model to assess variations in atmospheric heat and moisture alongside ocean movements and variations in heat content and salinity. Their conclusion was that global temperatures in the 2020s would be 0.5°C to 1.1°C higher than in the 1990s.

The oceans' thermal inertia means that global temperature rises are inevitable; whatever short-term changes in greenhouse gas emission policy are implemented in the meantime, the damage has already been done. In a worst-case scenario, global temperatures

could rise by almost 6°C by 2100 if emissions of greenhouse gases continue and increase unchecked; measures are to some extent already in hand which should avert such a catastrophe.

Also predicted by models in early 2002 is an increase in extreme rainfall over the next century. Europe is five times likelier to have very wet winters, while heavier summer monsoon rains will affect Asia, according to T. N. Palmer and J. Raisanen.

HUBBLE'S CLEARER VISION

Now in its 12th year in orbit, the Hubble Space Telescope received a fourth 'service' visit from space shuttle astronauts in early March 2002. During the STS-103 mission, Hubble was captured with the shuttle Columbia's remote arm and brought into the cargo bay, where astronauts carried out a number of important upgrades over the course of five space walks. New, shorter (8 metre) solar panels were fitted delivering more power were attached, and a new power control unit added.

The wide-field Advanced Camera for Surveys (ACS) was installed, offering high-sensitivity images over a field about one-ninth the apparent width of the Moon. First results from the 17 megapixel ACS detector were released in late April 2002, and included detailed views of remote interacting galaxies never seen before.

A new cooling system was fitted for an existing instrument, the Near Infrared Camera and Multi-Object Spectrometer (NICMOS). Originally installed in 1997, NICMOS ran out of coolant in 1999. The new system, which maintains the instrument at −203°C, allows even better operation than before. Early results from NICMOS were released in June 2002 and included views penetrating the dust of galaxy NGC 4013 in Ursa Major to reveal a ring of stars girdling the nucleus.

Both NICMOS and ACS give resolution better than 0.1 arc-second (one-millionth of the Moon's apparent diameter), and their combined images of a star-forming region in the constellation Monoceros are spectacular. In pictures to compare with the famous 1995 'Pillars of Creation', Hubble's new, clearer vision has revealed young stars embedded within the Cone Nebula.

BIOTERRORISM FEARS

In the heightened state of world tension following the 11 September 2001 terrorist attacks in the US, the possibility of biological terrorism became a real fear, particularly following the deaths of five US citizens from anthrax spores sent in packages through the post. The source remains uncertain, but it is thought unlikely that responsibility lies with bioterrorists intent on causing mass fatalities. Existing agreements should ensure that none of the major powers has at its disposal weapons containing anthrax, but small quantities of the bacteria are produced legally to allow development of vaccines and other countermeasures; these stocks are held under secure conditions.

Parts of the infectious mechanism of Bacillus anthracis are becoming better understood. Spores are taken up in the lungs by white cells known as macrophages, which normally digest and destroy infectious agents. Anthrax spores, however, manage to avoid destruction and instead germinate, killing the macrophages following their migration to the lymph nodes. Release and multiplication of the bacilli in the bloodstream causes septic shock and the death of the infected host.

B. anthracis owes its toxicity to genes on one of two extrachromosomal DNA molecules (plasmids) that it carries. The plasmid encodes the protective antigen (PA), lethal factor (LF) and oedema factor (EF). The PA and LF

in combination are sufficient to cause death. The EF's role is less well understood, but it causes cutaneous oedema (tissue swelling) in non-lethal cases. Researchers in Chicago and Boston have examined the structure of EF and elucidated its interaction with calmodulin, a molecule which binds calcium and regulates the activity of many other cellular proteins. Irreversible binding of EF removes this activity, so that calmodulin is unable to fulfil its normal role in activating the cellular pathways needed for the immune response. Using what has become fairly routine laboratory procedure in recent years, Jeronimo Cello, Aniko Paul and Eckard Wimmer synthesised short stretches of DNA (oligonucleotides) equivalent to parts of the 7741 base RNA genome of the virus. Stitched together, the DNA was then used as a template for RNA synthesis in reactions using commercially available enzymes. Following incubation with cell extracts, the RNA was translated to form complete virus protein particles. These included fully infectious, RNA-containing forms capable of destroying tissue culture cells and killing injected mice; insertion of 'marker' sequences made the synthetic virus less lethal than the naturally-occurring form. Assembly of the artificial virus genome took over two years.

The experiment is a chilling demonstration of what could be achieved were determined, well-equipped bioterrorists to gain access to genetic data for viral types against which, unlike polio, there are currently no effective vaccines or treatments. However, it is perhaps reassuring to know that smallpox, for example, has a genome over 20 times larger and considerably more complex than that of the polio virus, presenting overwhelming obstacles to current synthetic technology.

CHIPS OFF THE OLD BLOCK

The Tagish Lake meteorite fell on 18 January 2000 onto the surface of a frozen lake in the Yukon and as a consequence was remarkably well preserved. Since then, it has been the subject of close study, with some important results emerging in the journal Science in September 2001. One of the rare carbonaceous chondrite class, the meteorite is believed to have originated from beyond the main asteroid belt between Mars and Jupiter. Analysis shows it to be a carbon-rich, aqueously altered meteorite containing carbonate minerals and grains from the pre-solar nebula which condensed about 4.6 billion years ago to produce the Sun and planets. Nuclear magnetic resonance (NMR) analysis shows that the Tagish Lake meteorite is rich in hydrocarbons and fullerenes, but has less than 1,000th the amino acid content that was found in the 1969 Murchison meteorite, previously the most studied carbonaceous chondrite. Overall, the Tagish Lake meteorite has an organic molecule content of about 100 parts per million. Its reflectance spectrum shows strong similarities to D-class asteroids found in the outer solar system; candidates as the parent body from which the meteorite might have been ejected by a collision in the distant past include asteroids (368) Haidea and (773) Irmintraud. But whatever its origins, there can be no doubt that the Tagish Lake meteorite is a valuable sample of very primitive material from the earliest days of the solar system.

Most meteorites which arrive at Earth are believed to come from the main asteroid belt, having been thrown by collisions into orbits that cross Earth's orbit. Evidence for collisions between asteroids has long been available in the form of Hirayama families. Named for the Japanese astronomer who first studied them in the 1920s, Hirayama families are collections of asteroids in clearly related orbits which suggest origin from the break-up of a common ancestor. A group of scientists at the Southwest Research Institute, Boulder, Colorado, presented results from their study of the asteroid family associated with (158) Koronis in *Nature* in June 2002.

A collection of 39 small asteroids in the Koronis family, named the Karin cluster, was examined in detail. Integrating the orbits of 13 of these back in time, the researchers found that they converged on a common origin from break-up of a single object, probably around 25 km in diameter, some 5.8 million years ago – in solar system timescales, a very recent event. The uneven size distribution of the fragments suggests either that the progenitor object was fractured prior to the collision which broke it up, that its internal structure was inhomogeneous, or that some of the pieces may have reaggregated under gravity after the impact. The cluster takes its name from the largest member (832) Karin, which has a diameter of 19 km. It is suggested that one of the solar system dust bands detected by the Infrared Astronomical Satellite in 1983 might also be a product of the same collision.

On 6 April 2002, a bright meteor (fireball) was seen and photographed by patrol cameras over central Europe. Analysis of the fireball's trajectory showed the incoming body to have been following an orbit identical to that of the Pribram meteorite that fell in Czechoslovakia on 7 April 1959. The Pribram meteorite was recovered following photography of its entry fireball, which allowed calculation of its impact site. Any surviving meteorites from the 2002 event, widely accepted to be another fragment from the same asteroidal source, probably fell in heavily wooded terrain, which unfortunately makes their recovery unlikely.

Theatre

London theatre became fashionable as star power continued to fuel the West End. Newspapers could not contain themselves as they excitably announced the casting of Madonna in *Up for Grabs*, Jude Law in *Dr Faustus*, Gwyneth Paltrow in *Proof*, Brendan Fraser in *Cat on a Hot Tin Roof*, Woody Harrelson and Kyle MacLachlan in *On an Average Day*, and a cluster of younger actors, including Hayden Christensen and Matt Damon, in *This is Our Youth*. Kenneth Branagh even went to Sheffield to play Richard III. And a different star every night, from Ewan McGregor to Richard Wilson, appeared in *The Play What I Wrote*, a hugely funny and inventive tribute to the television and variety performers Morecambe and Wise, performed by a comedy duo known as the Right Size.

Sometimes it is easy to forget that stars have always shone in the theatre. The novelty is the eagerness of American film actors to come to London at the peak rather than the end of their careers. The Almeida and the Donmar began the trend when they cast Kevin Spacey and Nicole Kidman respectively, and their innovation has been repeatedly copied in the West End. But more traditional theatrical supremos were also on show. Vanessa Redgrave and her daughter Joely Richardson played mother and daughter in *Lady Windermere's Fan* at the Haymarket; Judi Dench packed out the same theatre in *The Royal Family*; and Penelope Keith appeared in a revival of *Star Quality*, a little-known play by Noel Coward. Lindsay Duncan and Alan Rickman brought new life to Coward's more familiar *Private Lives*, tearing each other apart at the Albery every night before moving to Broadway. Both performances won plaudits, but it was Duncan who scooped both Critics' Circle and Olivier awards in London and a Tony award in New York. Joan Collins even gamely appeared in a corset in *Over the Moon* at the Old Vic.

Arguments raged about the merits and drawbacks of star casting. Did tabloid tittle-tattle distract from the work on the stage? Were people being cast for their talent or their celebrity status, not always the same thing. Can it be assumed that film stars will perform as well on stage as they do on screen? Did they dominate the media so that equally interesting, or better, star-free work went unnoticed elsewhere?

If most of these fears seemed exaggerated, the casting of Madonna in a lacklustre comedy about the unscrupulous world of art-dealing revealed all the possible pitfalls. However brightly Madonna may shine in concert or even on film, she is not a natural actress and lacks the imagination to inhabit another person – not that her fans were particularly interested in seeing a play; rather, they had come to breathe the same air as their idol, who nervously made sure that her bodyguards were always on call. When Madonna's character pleaded poverty, people laughed knowingly at the discrepancy between the performer and her part. Surrounded by an experienced cast, Madonna looked stiff and nervous and was barely audible.

In contrast, Gwyneth Paltrow was triumphant in the tiny Donmar Warehouse. *Proof* was part of the Donmar's impressive American season, and the role of Catherine in this Pulitzer and Tony award-winning drama was much sought after on Broadway. Paltrow had already been slated for the Miramax film and she brought an eloquence and depth to what turned out to be a very old-fashioned and predictable examination of the mathematical mind. Catherine inherits her father's talent for maths and fears she may have inherited his instability too. In the play's most compelling scene, Catherine's father tries to convince her that he is well again by handing her his notebook, in which he claims he has made a tremendous discovery. Paltrow was remarkable as she read the nonsense he had written, all hope draining out of her face, silently conveying both love and despair.

Then there was the Hollywood 'bratpack' that appeared in *This Is Our Youth*; the original cast of Hayden Christensen (Darth Vader in the new *Star Wars* prequels), Jake Gyllenhaal and Anna Paquin (who won an Oscar for her role in *The Piano*) was later replaced by an even starrier line-up of Matt Damon, Casey Affleck and Summer Phoenix. Kenneth Lonergan's delightful and touching comedy portrays a trio of rich, pot-smoking Manhattan kids on the cusp of adulthood in 1982. Gyllenhaal was particularly touching as Warren, who finally learns to stay true to his own beliefs rather than those of his peers, but only after arriving at his friend's apartment with $15,000 he has stolen from his father and which he proceeds to blow on drugs and a night at the Plaza.

At the Young Vic, there was the unlikely sight of hordes of young girls queuing to see Christopher Marlowe's 16th-century tragedy *Dr Faustus*. They were attracted by the casting of Jude Law as the academic who sells his soul to the devil in return for having all his wishes fulfilled during his lifetime by Richard McCabe's desolate Mephistopheles. Law was an unusually young Faustus and brought to the part both narcissism and a fierce and modern desire to have all his ambitions instantly fulfilled. With a deliberately small cast, director David Lan kept a tight grip on Faustus's wanderings, setting the play on a raised, narrow platform with a pit below to suggest the depths of hell into which Faustus finally descends. Natural Nylon, the film company of which Law is a member, helped fund the revival, and the company plans to produce more theatre in the future. Another home-grown star to return to the stage was Kenneth Branagh, who played Richard III at the Sheffield Crucible for director Michael Grandage. Not obvious casting, Branagh excelled as a Richard who hides his extreme physical disability beneath an armour-like corset and his evil intentions beneath a smooth exterior.

RSC CONTROVERSY

If the media was keen on stars, it was also fascinated by backstage dramas at the Royal Shakespeare Company. In June 2001, artistic director Adrian Noble announced a radical shake-up under the designation 'Project Fleet'. For many years, it has been difficult to persuade actors to sign up for lengthy contracts to work in Stratford and London, and Noble proposed that contracts for the company should be shortened and one-off productions introduced in the hope of persuading a greater range of actors to join the company. With very little warning, and much to the Barbican's annoyance, Noble also announced that the company would be abandoning the its base in London, losing as a consequence the £3 million grant from the City that came with its residency there.

Noble wanted the company to be free to find the most suitable theatre, or maybe a converted building, for each individual production. The point, he explained, was to be ideas-led rather than formulaic. Objections were immediately raised, even among those who sympathised with Noble's objectives. Staff worried about redundancies, while actors, even those who had been reluctant to sign up for a whole season, did not like the idea of abandoning the ensemble basis of the company. Producing Shakespeare in the West End has never been easy and many people feared that vast amounts of public subsidy could very easily end up in the pockets of West End theatre-owners. The only part of the plan that was warmly welcomed was the establishment of an academy in Stratford to provide the classical training that is no longer being offered in drama schools. Declan Donnellan agreed to direct the academy's first production of *King Lear* in the Other Place at Stratford.

There was more alarm at the news that the RSC was also keen to demolish the Royal Shakespeare Theatre in Stratford, built in 1932, and replace it with a more flexible and adaptable space. Although a listed building, the current theatre, often disparagingly referred to as a 'jam factory', is too long and narrow. Theatregoers sitting in the balcony are so far away that they often feel cut off from the actors and from what's happening on stage. The idea was also floated of creating a 'theatre village' to keep tourists entertained during the day. 'I love the idea,' said Noble, 'that people could arrive in the morning, take part in an education programme, have lunch in a fantastic restaurant, visit a costume exhibition, join a fight or voice workshop, and then in the evening see a show.'

If Noble's plans for the company were tolerated as an experiment, the irrevocability of demolishing the theatre was a step too far for many of the RSC's associate artists, including Judi Dench, Donald Sinden and Michael Gambon. The Twentieth Century Society also rose to the defence of the theatre and its art deco foyer, especially as it was one of the first public buildings to be designed by a woman, the architect Elizabeth Scott. Even so, after a visit to Stratford, Parliament's influential media and culture select committee approved the plans. Such welcome support in March 2002 was offset by Noble's absence from the RSC to direct *Chitty Chitty Bang Bang* in the West End. Having left the Barbican, the company moved into the Roundhouse for a season with *The Winter's Tale, The Tempest* and *Pericles*. But *The Winter's Tale* opened to poor reviews and the RSC's traditional audience stayed away. Audiences were said to be as low as 30 per cent of capacity. A much higher percentage was needed in order to recoup the vast expense of fitting out the building. Criticism was growing but it was still a great shock when, the morning after the first night of *Chitty Chitty Bang Bang*, Noble tendered his resignation. Even his fiercest critics had admired the openness with which he was prepared to discuss his plans, but he clearly felt that he could no longer continue.

Noble's resignation was seen as a chance to consider anew, and once again advice flowed as to how the company should reorientate itself in a very different climate from the one in which Peter Hall launched the RSC in the 1960s. Outsiders suggested that the best way of restoring morale would be to retreat to Stratford with a small company and abandon all plans for change for at least one season. But it quickly became clear that the RSC's board was only interested in applications from insiders, and the battle was on between Michael Boyd, who distinguished himself with a production of the three parts of *Henry VI* at the Swan in 2000–1, and Gregory Doran, whose season of Elizabethan and Jacobean rarities

was one of the hits in the same theatre this year. The final choice of Boyd was popular with the company but it remains to be seen what his plans are for the future. All he has said so far is that he wants the RSC to continue as an ensemble, although he also envisages the occasional one-off production with high-profile names. Unusually, Boyd trained in Russia, which might mean a new look for the company as well as longer rehearsal times!

The miracle was that artistically the company had a good year. It bravely staged Martin McDonagh's *The Lieutenant of Inishmore* – a gruesome farce about the sentimentality, brutality and stupidity of Irish terrorism – after both the National Theatre and the Royal Court rejected it on the grounds of bad taste. It also presented David Edgar's examination of peace negotiations in *The Prisoner's Dilemma*, David Farr's look at redemption and forgiveness in *The Night of the Soul,* and Neil Bartlett's dream-like production of *The Prince of Homburg.* And if a production of *A Midsummer Night's Dream* enraged many critics, there were other Shakespearean plays to enjoy, including a very Italian, 1930s *Much Ado About Nothing* with Harriet Walter and Nicholas Le Prevost as middle-aged lovers, both of them funny and moving, and Adrian Noble's own lyrical production of the rarely performed *Pericles* at the Roundhouse. The most significant Shakespearean production of the year, however, was not by the RSC at all, but at the recreation of Shakespeare's Globe in Southwark. In celebration of the 400th anniversary of *Twelfth Night*, Tim Carroll's all-male 'original practices' production was outstanding and revelatory, with Mark Rylance as a white-faced Olivia gliding as if on castors.

WEST END MUSICALS

In the wake of the events of 11 September 2001 in the US, it was the musicals that suffered most as the tourists stayed at home; *Cats* gave its final miaow, the skates were hung up at *Starlight Express* and *Buddy* faded away. In imitation of New York, the Mayor of London, Ken Livingstone, gave £500,000 towards the cost of discounted tickets at 32 shows.

The most significant closure was *Cats* after 8,949 performances at the New London Theatre. The longest-running musical in West End and Broadway history, it was seen by 50 million people in 26 countries and took an astonishing £1.4 billion at the box office. It is part of the show's mythology that backers were originally impossible to find, nobody imagining that a musical based on T. S. Eliot's *Old Possum's Book of Practical Cats* could possibly be a hit. Andrew Lloyd-Webber put in £75,000 of his own money and some people invested as little as £1,000, since recouped many times over. The final performance included contributions from 150 former cast members and was shown live on a big screen in the Covent Garden Piazza.

The departure of *Starlight Express* was not entirely owing to dwindling audiences but also because Lloyd Webber needed a large theatre like the Apollo Victoria in which to stage his new musical *Bombay Dreams.* Searching for new talent, Lloyd-Webber had gone to India and discovered the composer A. R. Rahman, a huge celebrity in his own country but little-known here. With a story drawing on the popularity of Bollywood, *Bombay Dreams* had a creative team that included people from both east and west; besides Rahman, there was lyricist Don Black and writer Meera Syal, best known for *Goodness Gracious Me.* Early bookings were poor but since the opening the show has attracted a vast new Asian audience, always reluctant theatregoers before in this country.

We Will Rock You, based around rock group Queen's greatest hits and with a trashy video-game aesthetic, was another big spender. The book by Ben Elton is set in 2302 on Planet Mall in which the citizens are clones and Globalsoft rules. Mixed reviews were offset by a prime spot at the other Queen's Golden Jubilee celebrations and Freddie Mercury's fans refused to be deterred. On a smaller scale, Boy George wrote a musical about his life and the other New Romantics – the cross-dressers, druggies and eccentrics – who haunted London's clubs in the 1980s. Called Taboo, it was produced in a converted church hall just off Leicester Square. He even briefly appeared himself, not as the young Boy George but as his late friend Leigh Bowery. Umoja brought the zest of South Africa to the Shaftesbury, so much so that a few local residents complained about the noise and the show was forced to close down by Camden Council. Later it reopened at the Queens, home earlier in the year to another South African show, a moving and spiritual version of the medieval Mystery plays.

It used to be that musicals were first seen on stage and then on film but this is not necessarily the case nowadays. In March 2002, The Full Monty, a musical version of the British film transposed to upstate New York, arrived from Broadway with many of the original Broadway stars. The politics were softened, but the punchy music and lyrics by David Yazbeck enhanced the original story. Chitty Chitty Bang Bang, a hugely expensive affair, opened at the London Palladium starring an amazing car which soars over the auditorium.

But in spite of a smattering of new musicals, it was still the revivals that dominated as My Fair Lady moved out of the National and into Drury Lane, where a delightful Joanna Riding took over as Eliza Doolittle and Alex Jennings as Professor Higgins. Michael Blakemore's production of the Cole Porter musical Kiss Me Kate arrived from Broadway, where the cast had taken pay cuts in order to keep the show going after 11 September. Sizzling choreography, witty songs, and the unusual sensation of viewing Shakespeare through the lens of Broadway in the 1940s, made it a winner and it picked up the Critics' Circle award for best musical.

ROYAL NATIONAL THEATRE

Critical attention tends to swing between the Royal National Theatre and the Royal Shakespeare Company; when the knives are out for one, the other basks in praise. As the RSC suffered, so the National flourished. In autumn 2001, it celebrated its 25th birthday with a number of platform performances and free events. At one platform performance, the three surviving artistic directors – Peter Hall, Richard Eyre and Trevor Nunn – all agreed that they wished the National's name had been left as it was, without the later addition of 'Royal'. After some sticky years, Nunn flourished in his final year in office, with an impressive range of new writing and a daring season entitled 'Transformation'. Worries about the theatre's ageing audience provoked the decision to give director Mick Gordon the task of attracting a younger generation by staging 13 world premières, building a studio theatre, converting the Lyttelton into a more appealing space, and providing a late-night bar; most importantly, seat prices were lowered. The season opened with Sing Yer Heart Out For The Lads, a new play by Roy Williams, the winner of last year's Evening Standard award for the most promising playwright. The play tackled racial antagonism in a South London pub on the day the German football team beat England in 2000. Later in the season, director Deborah Warner was lured back to

direct an adaptation of Jeanette Winterson's The Powerbook with Fiona Shaw and Saffron Burrows, and Mick Gordon himself directed an adaptation of A Prayer for Owen Meany. The intense activity gave an extra buzz to visiting the National, even if no major new playwrights have yet been discovered.

New plays also proliferated outside the Transformation season. The National was quick to pick up Gagarin Way, Gregory Burke's vicious heist comedy, at the Edinburgh Festival. As a protest against globalisation, earnest politico Gary and nihilistic Eddie kidnap a visiting executive under the mistaken impression that he is Japanese. Old-fashioned and compelling storytelling was on display in August Wilson's Jitney, given its première in this country in an immaculate visiting production by Marion McClinton. Charlotte Jones' Humble Boy was a well-made play, with echoes of Hamlet in its story of a Cambridge astrophysicist, played by Simon Russell Beale, grieving the death of his father and appalled by the speed with which his mother has taken a lover. Both Gagarin Way and Humble Boy transferred to the West End, as did Vincent in Brixton, Nicholas Wright's portrait of an artist as a young man, based on the life of Vincent van Gogh. Wright imagines that the artist's talent was nurtured by his middle-aged widowed landlady, played by Clare Higgins. The play was given an emotional and physically detailed production by Richard Eyre. Bryony Lavery's Frozen, with Anita Dobson, explored with great integrity the possibility of forgiveness when a child has been murdered. Most ambitious was a trilogy of plays by Tom Stoppard under the heading The Coast of Utopia. Thirty actors played 70 roles in a huge epic describing the trial and travails of a group of Russian radicals, revolutionaries and exiles in the 19th century. The trilogy is gradually dominated by the character of Alexander Herzen, beautifully played by Stephen Dillane, who believes that any dedication to an abstract ideal leads to human sacrifice. The scope of the piece is huge, the ideas provocative, and the private lives of these exiles often moving, but the play is also wildly uneven and limps to its conclusion.

Revivals at the National Theatre were, unusually, rarer than new plays, although it would not be Trevor Nunn's National without a musical and Christmas 2001 was celebrated with a new production of South Pacific. Martin Clunes threw himself wholeheartedly into the role of lecherous, hypocritical Tartuffe, and Peter Hall returned to direct a masked production of The Bacchae.

THE INDEPENDENTS

The Almeida and the Donmar continued to dominate London's theatre. As the builders moved into Islington, the Almeida decamped to an old coach station in King's Cross, which was transformed into one of the liveliest performing spaces in London. Jonathan Kent maintained his reputation for visually spectacular productions with Platonov, in which a train appeared to race towards the audience, and King Lear, in which Oliver Ford Davies played Lear against a dramatically collapsing palace as the storm raged outside. Brian Friel's strange and haunting The Faith Healer was revived with Ken Stott as the drunken healer.

The Donmar's year was dominated by an American season of new plays including Kenneth Lonergan's Lobby Hero, which, like This is Our Youth, revealed a great gift for the comic and humane portrayal of oddball characters. Proof was also part of this season, as well as Take Me Out by Richard Greenberg, inspired by the playwright's love of baseball. The theatre also revived

Privates on Parade, one of a number of 1960s plays revived this year; others included *Afore Night Come* at the Young Vic, *A Day in the Death of Joe Egg* in the West End, and *Luther* at the National. *The York Realist,* possibly *the* new play of the year, also looked back to the 1960s and was based on Peter Gill's experiences as a young assistant director at the Royal Court. Set in Yorkshire, it portrayed the relationship that develops between a young director and a farm labourer who meet and fall in love during a production of *The Mysteries in York* and how the relationship is tolerantly viewed by the labourer's family.

The one thing that can be certain is that British theatre will look very different from next year as a swathe of new artistic directors takes over. Both the flagships will have new leaders; Michael Boyd replaces Adrian Noble at the RSC, and in March 2003 Nicholas Hytner will take over from Trevor Nunn at the Royal National. Sam Mendes leaves the Donmar after ten years, to be replaced by Michael Grandage. Michael Attenborough will open the new building at the Almeida, replacing Jonathan Kent and Ian McDiarmid, and Anthony Clark replaces Jenny Topper at Hampstead. Finally, Ian Brown has replaced Jude Kelly at the West Yorkshire Playhouse in Leeds.

PRODUCTIONS
September 2001 to August 2002

LONDON PRODUCTIONS

ADELPHI, WC2. *Chicago,* since 1997

ALBERY, WC2. (4 October 2001) *Private Lives* (Coward) with Alan Rickman, Lindsay Duncan, Emma Fielding, Adam Godley; director, Howard Davies. (9 March 2002) *The Mystery of Charles Dickens* (Peter Ackroyd) with Simon Callow; director, Patrick Garland. (11 April) *Shockheaded Peter* (adapt. from Heinrich Hoffmann's *Struwwelpeter*) with Julian Bleach, Anthony Cairns, Ewan Hunter, Tamzin Griffin, Rebekah Wild; directors, Julian Crouch, Phelim McDermott. (25 June) *Benefactors* (Michael Frayn) with Neil Pearson, Emma Chambers, Sylvestra le Touzel, Aden Gillett; director, Jeremy Sams.

ALDWYCH, WC2. (2 October 2001) *Mahler's Conversion* (Ronald Harwood) with Antony Sher; director, Gregory Doran. (13 December) *Thunderbirds F.A.B.* (Andrew Dawson, Gavin Robertson) with Andrew Dawson, Gavin Robertson. (9 January 2002) *Top Girls* (Caryl Churchill) with Helen Anderson, Elizabeth Berington, Pascale Burgess, Hattie Ladbury, Joanna Scanian, Sophie Shaw; director, Thea Sharrock. (8 February) *Mother Clap's Molly House,* transferred from the Lyttelton Theatre. (8 April) *Bedroom Farce* (Ayckbourn) with Richard Briers, June Whitfield, Susy Aitchion, Jasper Britton, Rose Keegan, Nigel Lindsay, Samantha Spiro, Jason Watkins; director, Loveday Ingram.

APOLLO, W1. (30 October 2001) *Star Quality* (Coward) with Penelope Keith, Russell Boulter, Una Stubbs, Peter Cellier, Nick Fletcher, Nick Waring, Marjorie Yates; director, Christopher Luscombe. (11 April 2002) *The Constant Wife* (Somerset Maugham) with Jenny Seagrove, Steven Pacey, Linda Thorson, Simon Williams, Sara Crowe; director, Edward Hall. (10 July) *Sleuth* (Anthony Shaffer) with Peter Bowles, Gary O'Brien; director, Elijah Moshinsky.

APOLLO VICTORIA, SW1. (19 June 2002) *Bombay Dreams* (A. R. Rahman, Don Black, Meera Syal) with Ayesha Dharker, Preeya Kalidas, Raza Jaffrey, Dalip Tahil, Ramon Tikaram, Raad Rawi, Raj Ghatak; director, Steven Pimlott.

ARTS THEATRE, WC1. (23 October 2001) *The Vagina Monologues,* transferred from the New Ambassadors Theatre. (28 January 2002) *Berkoff's Women* (Steven Berkoff) with Linda Marlowe; director, Josie Lawrence. (6 March) *Gagarin Way,* transferred from the Royal National Theatre. (24 April) *Jesus Hopped the 'A' Train,* transferred from the Donmar Warehouse. (25 June) *The Vagina Monologues,* transferred from the New Ambassadors Theatre.

BARBICAN, EC2. (13 November 2001) *Alice in Wonderland* (Lewis Carroll, adapt. Adrian Mitchell) with Katherine Heath, Daniel Flynn; director, Rachel Kavanaugh. (11 December) *Hamlet* (Shakespeare) with Samuel West; director, Steven Pimlott. (3 January 2002) *Twelfth Night* (Shakespeare) with Zoe Waites, Matilda Ziegler, Jo Stone-Fewings, Guy Henry; director, Lindsay Posner. (31 January) *Julius Caesar* (Shakespeare) with Tim Piggott-Smith, Greg Hicks, Ian Hogg, Tom Mannion;

director, Edward Hall. (25 April) *A Midsummer Night's Dream,* transferred from Stratford.

THE PIT. (6 November 2001) *The Merchant of Venice* (Shakespeare) with Ian Bartholomew; director, Loveday Ingram. (13 December) *King John* (Shakespeare) with Guy Henry; director, Gregory Doran. (20 December) *The Lieutenant of Inishmore* (Martin McDonagh) with Glenn Chapman, Kerry Condon, Trevor Cooper, Stuart Goodwin, Colin Mace, Conor Maloney, Owen Sharpe, David Wilmot; director, Wilson Milam. (29 January 2002) *The Prisoner's Dilemma* (David Edgar) with Penny Downie, Diana Kent, Larry Lamb, Zoe Waites, David Wilmot; director, Michael Attenborough. (8 March) *A Russian in the Woods* (Peter Whelan) with Anthony Flanagan, Stuart Goodwin, Louis Hilyer, David Hinton, Colin Mace, Anna Madeley, Douglas Rao, Charlie Simpson; director, Robert Delamere. (24 April) *Night of the Soul* (David Farr); director, David Farr.

CAMBRIDGE, WC2. (20 September 2001) *Fame: The Musical,* transferred from the Victoria Palace Theatre.

COMEDY, SW1. (13 September 2001) *The Homecoming* (Pinter) with Ian Holm, Lia Williams, Ian Hart, Nick Dunning, John Kavanagh, Jason O'Mara; director, Robin Lefevre. (11 December) *A Day in the Death of Joe Egg,* transferred from the New Ambassadors Theatre, with Eddie Izzard replacing Clive Owen. (7 March 2002) *Noises Off,* transferred from the Piccadilly Theatre (7 August) *On An Average Day* (John Kolvenbach) with Woody Harrelson, Kyle MacLachlan; director, John Crowley.

CRITERION, W1. *The Complete Works of William Shakespeare* (Abridged) and *The Complete History of America* (Abridged) since 1996

DOMINION, W1. (14 May 2002) *We Will Rock You* (Queen, Ben Elton) with Nigel Planer, Tony Vincent, Hannah Jane Fox, Sharon D. Clarke, Alexander Hanson, Kerry Ellis, Nigel Clauzel; director, Christopher Renshaw.

DONMAR WAREHOUSE, WC2. (10 October 2001) *Little Foxes* (Lillian Hellman) with Penelope Wilton, Brid Brennan, David Calder, Matthew Marsh, Peter Guiness, Anna Maxwell Martin; director, Marianne Elliot. (10 December) *Privates on Parade* (Peter Nichols, music Denis King) with Roger Allam, Malcolm Sinclair; director, Michael Grandage. (13 March 2002) *Jesus Hopped the 'A' Train* (Stephen Adly Guirgis) with Elizabeth Canavan, Salvatore Inzerillo, Ron Cephas Jones, John Ortiz, David Zayas; director, Philip Seymour Hoffman. (14 March) *Frame 312* (Keith Reddin); director, Josie Rourke. (10 April) *Lobby Hero* (Kenneth Lonergan) with David Tennant, Gary McDonald, Charlotte Randle, Dominic Rowan; director Mark Brokaw. (15 May) *Proof* (David Auburn) with Gwyneth Paltrow, Richard Coyle, Ronald Pickup; director, John Madden. (27 June) *Take Me Out* (Richard Greenberg) with Kenneth Carroll, Dominic Fumusa, Gene Gabriel, Neal Huff, Robert Jimenez, Stephen Mendillo, Denis O'Hare, Kohl Sudduth, Daniel Sunjata, Frederick Weller, James Yaegashi; director, Joe Mantello.

DRURY LANE THEATRE ROYAL, WC2. *My Fair Lady,* since July 2001

DUCHESS, WC2. (2 January 2002) *Alone It Stands* (John Breen) with Malcolm Adams, Dessie Gallagher, Garrett Lombard, Gerry McCann, Niamh McGrath, Paul Meade;

director, John Breen. (19 February) *Life After George* (Hannie Rayson) with Stephen Dillane, Cheryl Campbell, Joanne Pearce, Anna Wilson-Jones; director, Michael Blakemore. (22 April) *The Glee Club* (Richard Cameron) with David Bamber, James Hornsby, Oliver Jackson, Shaun Prendergast, David Schofield, Roderick Smith; director, Mike Bradwell (18 July) *Via Dolorosa* (David Hare) with David Hare; director, Stephen Daldry.

DUKE OF YORK, WC2. *Stones in His Pockets,* since 2000

FORTUNE, WC2. *The Woman in Black,* since 1989

GARRICK, WC2. (14 November 2001) *Dangerous Corner* (J. B. Priestley) with Dervla Kirwan, Rupert Penry-Jones, Anna Wilson-Jones, Steven John Shepherd, Patrick Robinson, Jacqueline Pearce, Katie Foster-Barnes; director, Laurie Sansom. (15 March 2002) *This Is Our Youth* (Kenneth Lonergan) with Hayden Christensen, Anna Paquin, Jake Gyllenhaal; director, Laurence Boswell. (26 June) *The Lieutenant of Inishmore,* transferred from the Pit.

GIELGUD, W1. (5 February 2002) *Humble Boy,* transferred from the Cottesloe Theatre, with Felicity Kendal replacing Diana Rigg

GLOBE, SE1. (22 May 2002) *Twelfth Night* (Shakespeare) with Liam Brennan, Mark Rylance, Timothy Walker; director, Tim Carroll. (5 June) *A Midsummer Night's Dream* (Shakespeare) with Geraldine Alexander, Louise Bush, Keith Dunphy, Paul Higgins, Richard Katz, John Ramm, Philippa Stanton, Simon Trinder; director, Mike Alfreds. (16 August) *The Golden Ass* (Peter Oswald) with Mark Rylance; director, Tim Carroll.

HAYMARKET THEATRE ROYAL, SW1. (1 November 2001) *The Royal Family* (Edna Ferber, George Kaufman) with Judi Dench, Peter Bowles, Harriet Walter, Toby Stephens, Julia McKenzie; director, Peter Hall. (21 February 2002) *Lady Windermere's Fan* (Oscar Wilde) with Vanessa Redgrave, Joely Richardson, David Yelland, Jack Davenport; director, Peter Hall. (16 June) *Rose Rage Parts I and II (Henry VI)* (Shakespeare, adapt. Edward Hall, Roger Warren) with the Propeller company; director, Edward Hall. (1 August) *Much Ado About Nothing* (Shakespeare), RSC production transferred from Stratford.

HER MAJESTY'S, SW1. *Phantom of the Opera,* since 1986. (18-25 November 2001) *Dubarry was a Lady* (Cole Porter, Herbert Fields, B. G. Desylva) with Louise Gold, Barry Cryer; director, Ian Marshall Fisher.

LONDON APOLLO, W6. (22 October 2001) *Grease* (Jim Jacobs, Warren Casey) with Craig Urbani. (4 February 2002) *The Last Empress* (Moon Roel Lee) with Tae Won Yi; director, Ho Jin Yun.

LONDON PALLADIUM, W1. (16 April 2002) *Chitty Chitty Bang Bang* (Ian Fleming, adapt. Jeremy Sams, Richard M. Sherman, Robert B. Sherman) with Emma Williams, Michael Ball, Anton Rodgers, Brian Blessed, Nichola McAuliffe, Richard O'Brien; director, Adrian Noble.

LYCEUM, WC2. *The Lion King,* since 1999

LYRIC, W1. (18 September 2001) *Cat on a Hot Tin Roof* (Tennessee Williams) with Brendan Fraser, Frances O'Connor, Ned Beatty, Gemma Jones, Abigail McKern,

Clive Carter; director, Anthony Page. (18 February 2002) *The Feast of Snails* (Olaf Olafsson) with David Warner, Philip Glenister, Sorcha Cusack, Siwan Morris; director, Ron Daniels. (29 April) *Daisy Pulls It Off* (Denise Deegan) with Hannah Yelland, Katherine Heath, Katherine Igoe; director, David Gilmore

LYRIC, W6. (28 February 2002) *The Prince of Homburg,* RSC production transferred from the Swan, Stratford.

NEW AMBASSADORS, WC2. (1 October 2001) *A Day in the Death of Joe Egg* (Peter Nichol) with Clive Owen, Victoria Hamilton; director, Laurence Boswell. (3 December) *Boston Marriage* (David Mamet) with Zoe Wanamaker, Anna Chancellor, Lyndsey Marshal; director, Phyllida Lloyd. (26 February 2002) *The Vagina Monologues,* transferred from the Arts Theatre. (1 July) *Lobby Hero,* transferred from the Donmar Warehouse

NEW LONDON, WC2. *Cats,* since 1981; closed May 2002

OLD VIC, SE1. (15 October 2001) *Over the Moon* (Ken Ludwig) with Joan Collins, Frank Langella, Moira Lister, Emma Barton; director, Ray Cooney. (22 January 2002) *The Island* (Athol Fugard, John Kani, Winston Ntshona) with John Kani, Winston Ntshona; director, Athol Fugard

OPEN AIR, REGENT'S PARK. (5 June 2002) *Romeo and Juliet* (Shakespeare) with Laura Main, Alan Wastaway, Carol McCready, John Hodgkinson, Adam Levy; director, Dominic Hill. (10 June) *As You Like It* (Shakespeare) with Rebecca Johnson, Caitlin Mottram, Benedict Cumberbatch, John Hodgkinson; director, Rachel Kavanaugh. (25 July) *Oh, What a Lovely War* (Joan Littlewood) with John Conroy, Liza Sadovy, Audrey Palmer, Michael Sadler, Daniel Crossley; director, Ian Talbot. (31 July) *Merlin the Magnificent* (Stuart Paterson); director, Tony Graham.

PALACE, WC2. *Les Miserables,* since 1985

PHOENIX, WC1. *Blood Brothers,* since 1991

PICCADILLY, W1. (25 February 2002) *My One and Only* (George and Ira Gershwin, Peter Stone, Timothy S. Mayer) with Janie Dee, Tim Flavin, Hilton McRae; director, Loveday Ingram.

PLAYHOUSE, WC2. (27 September 2001) *An Inspector Calls,* transferred from the Garrick Theatre (closed May 2002).

PRINCE EDWARD, W1. *Mamma Mia,* since 1999

PRINCE OF WALES, W1. (4 December 2001) *Rent* (Jonathan Larson) with Adam Rickett, Damien Flood, Debbie Kurup; director, Paul Kerryson. (12 March 2002) *The Full Monty* (David Yazbek, Terrence McNally) with Jarrod Emick, Dora Bryan, Jason Danieley, Andre de Shields, John Ellison Conlee, Roman Fruge, Marcus Neville; director, Jack O'Brien.

QUEENS, W1. (27 November 2001) *The Hobbit* (Tolkien, adapt. Glynne Robbins) with David Copeland, Phillip Joseph, Cornelius Clarke, Nicholas Collett, Matt O'Neill; director, Roy Marsden. (26 February 2002) *The Mysteries* (Chester Mystery Plays) with a South African cast. (18 June) *Umoja,* transferred from the Shaftesbury Theatre.

ROUNDHOUSE, NW1. (12 April 2002) *The Winter's Tale* (Shakespeare) with Anastasia Hille, Douglas Hodge, Rolf Saxon, Myrsa Lucretia Taylor, Lauren Ward, Alan Turkington; director, Matthew Warchus. (7 May) *The Tempest* (Shakespeare) with Malcolm Storry, Sirine Saba, Geff Francis, Gracy G Goldman; director, Michael Boyd. (5 July) *Pericles* (Shakespeare) with Ray Fearon, Kananu Kirimi, Geff Francis; director, Adrian Noble.

ROYAL COURT DOWNSTAIRS, SW1. (12 September 2001) *Redundant* (Leo Butler) with Wil Johnson, Lyndsey Marshal; director, Dominic Cooke. (7 November) *Boy Gets Girl* (Rebecca Gilman) with Katrin Cartlidge; director, Ian Rickson. (8 January 2002) *The York Realist* (Peter Gill) with Felix Bell, Richard Coyle, Ian Mercer, Wendy Nottingham, Caroline O'Neill, Lloyd Owen, Anne Reid; director, Peter Gill. (21 February) *Nightsongs* (Jon Fosse, trans. Gregory Motton) with Jonathan Cullen, Gillian Hanna, Paul Higgins, Sophie Okonedo, Christopher Saul; director, Katie Mitchell. (13 March) *Face to the Wall* (Martin Crimp) with Gillian Hanna, Paul Higgins, Sophie Okonedo, Peter Wight; director, Katie Mitchell. (17 April) *The Night Heron* (Jez Butterworth) with Roger Morlidge, Paul Ritter, Jessica Stevenson, Ray Winstone; director, Ian Rickson. (12 June) *The People Are Friendly* (Michael Wynne) with Paul Broughton, Michelle Butterly, Joe Cooper, Sue Jenkins, Stephen Mangan, Nick Moss, Jack Richards, Sally Rogers, Sheridan Smith; director, Dominic Cooke.

ROYAL COURT UPSTAIRS, SW1. (3 September 2001) *Sliding with Suzanne* (Judy Upton) with Loo Brealey, Bryan Dick, Monica Dolan, Roger Frost, June Watson, Danny Worters; director, Max Stafford-Clark. (2 October) *Nightingale and Chase* (Zinnie Harris) with Christopher Fulford, Jodie Watson; director, Richard Wilson. (13 November) *F***ing Games* (Grae Cleugh) with Allan Corduner, Ian Dunn, Daniel Lapaine, Benjamin Davies; director, Dominic Cooke. (15 January 2002) *Bedbound* (Enda Walsh) with Liam Carney, Norma Sheahan; director, Enda Walsh. (11 February) *Push Up* (Roland Schimmelpfennig, trans. Maja Zade) with Flaminia Cinque, Jacqueline Defferary, Nigel Lindsay, Robin Soans, Peter Sproule, David Tennant, Sian Thomas, Lucy Whybrow; director, Ramin Gray. (6 March) *Steps to Siberia*, performd by Theatre Lozhe and Babii. (20 March) *Plasticine* (Vassily Sigarev, trans. Sasha Dugdale); director, Dominic Cooke. (23 April) *Kosher Harry* (Nick Grosso) with Martin Freeman, Mark Benton, Claudie Blakley, June Watson; director, Kathy Burke. (21 May) *Where Do We Live* (Christopher Shinn) with Nicholas Aaron, Noel Anthony Vaughan, Toby Dantzic, Daniel Evans, Adam Garcia, Cyril Nri, Ray Pantharki, Jemima Rooper, Susannah Wise; director, Richard Wilson. (25 June) *Mother Teresa is Dead* (Helen Edmundson) with Maxine Peake, John Marquez, Harry Dillon, Diana Quick; director, Simon Usher.

ROYAL NATIONAL THEATRE, SE1, COTTESLOE (3 October 2001) *Gagarin Way* (Gregory Burke) with Bill McElhaney, Michael Moreland, Michael Nardone, Maurice Roeves; director, John Tiffany. (8 November) *The Good Hope* (Herman Heijermans) with Diane Beck, Emma Bird, Charlotte Emmerson, William MacBain, John Normington, Robert Oates, Trevor Ray, Sheila Reid, Iain Robertson, John Tams; director, Bill Bryden. (14 January 2002) *Monologue* (Pinter) with Henry Woolf; director, Gari Jones. (14 February) *The Syringa Tree*

(Pamela Gien) with Pamela Gien; director, Larry Moss. (4 March) *Hinterland* (Sebastian Barry) with Patrick Malahide, Dearbhla Molloy; director, Max Stafford-Clark. (1 May) *Vincent in Brixton* (Nicholas Wright) with Jochum ten Haaf, Clare Higgins, Emily Blunt, Emma Handy, Paul Nicholls; director, Richard Eyre. (3 July) *Frozen* (Bryony Lavery) with Anita Dobson, Tom Georgeson, Josie Lawrence; director, Bill Alexander.

LYTTELTON (4 September 2001) *Mother Clap's Molly House* (Mark Ravenhill) with Deborah Findlay; director, Nicholas Hytner. (16 October) *Jitney* (August Wilson) with Russell Andrews, Willis Burks II, Paul Butler, Anthony V. Chrisholm, Leo V. Finnie III, Stephen McKinley Henderson, Ray Shabaka Henley, Linda Powell, Keith Randolph Smith; director, Marion McClinton. (6 December) *No Man's Land* (Pinter) with Andy de la Tour, Danny Dyer, Corin Redgrave, John Wood; director, Harold Pinter. (19 December) *The Wonder of Sex* (Patrick Barlow, John Ramm, Martin Duncan) with Patrick Barlow, John Ramm; director, Martin Duncan. (5 March 2002) *Tartuffe* (Molière, trans. Ranjit Bolt) with Martin Clunes, Debra Gillett, Clare Holman, David Threlfall, Margaret Tyzack, Julian Wadham; director, Lindsay Posner. (18 May) *The Powerbook* (Jeanette Winterson, adapt. Jeanette Winterson, Deborah Warner, Fiona Shaw) with Fiona Shaw, Saffron Burrows; director, Deborah Warner. (13 June) *A Prayer for Owen Meany* (John Irving, adapt. Simon Bent) with Aidan McArdle; director, Mick Gordon. (5 July) *Adventures of the Stoneheads* (Toby Wilsher) with James Greaves, Simon Grover, Lisa Hammond, Stephen Harper, Samantha Mason, Alan Riley, Sarah Thom, Jason Webb; director, Toby Wilsher. (26 July) *The Birds* (Aristophanes, trans. Sean O'Brien) with Dane Clarke, Matt Costain, Joel Howard, Matilda Leyser, Marcello Magni, Sophie Oldfield, Corinne Pierre, James Roberts, Fabio Santos, Dickon Savage; director, Kathryn Hunter.

LYTTELTON LOFT (1 May 2002) *Sing Yer Heart Out for the Lads* (Roy Williams); director, Simon Usher. (23 May) *Free* (Simon Bowen); director, Thea Sharrock. (29 May) *Life After Life* (Paul Jepson, Tony Parker); director, Paul Jepson. (17 June) *Shadow of a Boy* (Gary Owen); director, Erica Whyman. (8 July) *The Mentalists* (Richard Bean); director, Sean Holmes. (29 July) *Sanctuary* (Tanika Gupta); director, Hettie Macdonald. (19 August) *The Associate* (Simon Bent); director, Paul Miller. (9 September) *Closing Time* (Owen McCafferty); director, James Kerr.

OLIVIER (6 September 2001) *Cloudstreet* (Tim Winton, adapt. Nick Enright, Justin Monjo) with Roy Billing, Wayne Blair, Anna Brockway, Andrew Crabbe, John Gaden, Matthew Hoy, Claire Jones, Gillian Jones, Jean Leary, Eliza Logan, Travis McMahon, Kris McQuade, Rebecca Massey, Christopher Pitman, Daniel Wyllie; director, Neil Armfield. (5 October) *Luther* (John Osborne) with Rufus Sewell, Richard Griffiths, Geoffrey Hutchings, Maxine Peake, Malcolm Sinclair, Timothy West; director, Peter Gill. (12 December) *South Pacific* (Rodgers and Hammerstein) with Lauren Kennedy, Philip Quast, Sheila Francesco, Edward Baker Duly; director, Trevor Nunn. (17 May 2002) *Bacchai* (Euripides, trans. Colin Teevan); director, Peter Hall. (3 August) *The Coast of Utopia* trilogy: *Voyage, Shipwreck, Salvage* (Stoppard) with Stephen Dillane; director, Trevor Nunn.

ST MARTINS, WC2. *The Mousetrap*, since 1974

SADLER'S WELLS, N1. (14 December 2001) *The Lion, the Witch and the Wardrobe* (C. S. Lewis, adapt. Adrian Mitchell) with Jonathan Broadbent, Anna Maxwell Martin, Alexandra Milman, William Rycroft, Patrice Naiambana, Maureen Beattie; director, Lucy Pitman-Wallace.

SAVOY, WC2. (9 October 2001) *Antarctica* (David S. Young) with Mark Bazeley, Stephen Boxer, Darrell D'Silva, Jason Flemyng, Eddie Marsan, Ronan Vibert; director, Richard Rose. (13 December) *Return to the Forbidden Planet* (Bob Carlton) with Nick Lashbrook, Jane Milligan, Adrian Cobey, Philip Reed, Diana Croft, James Earl Adair, Fredrick Ruth, Sarah Beaumont; director, Bob Carlton.

SHAFTESBURY, WC2. (15 November 2001) *Umoja* (Todd Twala, Thembi Nyandeni, Ian von Memerty); director, Ian von Memerty.

STRAND, WC2. (9 March 2002) *The York Realist*, transferred from the Royal Court Downstairs

VAUDEVILLE, WC2. (29 August 2001) *Caught in the Net* (*Run for Your Wife: the Sequel*) (Ray Cooney) with Eric Sykes, Russ Abbot, Robert Dawes, Carol Hawkins; director, Ray Cooney. (9 July 2002) *Betty* (Karen McLachlan) with Geraldine McNulty; director, Kathy Burke.

THE VENUE, W1. (29 January 2002) *Taboo* (Boy George, Mark Davies-Markham) with Euan Morton, Dianne Pilkington, Luke Evans, Matt Lucas, Paul Baker, Gemma Craven, Marc McGee, Drew Jaymson, Matt White, Gail McKinnon; director, Christopher Renshaw.

VICTORIA PALACE, SW1. (30 October 2001) *Kiss Me, Kate* (Cole Porter) with Brent Barrett, Marin Mazzie, Michael Berresse, Nancy Anderson; director, Michael Blakemore.

WHITEHALL, SW1. (15 October 2001) *Art*, transferred from Wyndham's Theatre.

WYNDHAM'S, WC2. (5 November 2001) *The Play What I Wrote* (Sean Foley, Hamish McColl) with Sean Foley, Hamish McColl (The Right Size); director, Kenneth Branagh. (23 May 2002) *Up for Grabs* (David Williamson) with Madonna, Michael Lerner, Megan Dodds, Sian Thomas, Debora Weston, Tom Irwin, Danny Pino; director, Laurence Boswell. (5 August) *Vincent in Brixton*, transferred from the Cottesloe Theatre

YOUNG VIC, SE1. (25 September 2001) *Afore Night Come* (David Rudkin); director, Rufus Norris. (23 October) *Andorra* (Max Frisch) with Jack Shepherd, Alec Newman, Aoife McMahon; director, Gregory Thompson. (5 December) *Monkey: A Tale from China* (Colin Teevan) with Elliot Levey, Jason Thorpe, Jan Knightley; director, Mick Gordon. (18 March 2002) *Doctor Faustus* (Marlowe) with Jude Law, Richard McCabe; director, David Lan. (21 May) *Homebody/Kabul* (Tony Kushner); director, Declan Donnellan

OUTSIDE LONDON

BIRMINGHAM: REPERTORY (21 September 2001) *Private Lives* (Coward); director, Jonathan Church. (28 September) *Closer* (Patrick Marber); director, Jonathan

Church. (2 November) *Of Mice and Men* (Steinbeck); director, Jonathan Church. (4 December) *The Wind in the Willows* (Kenneth Grahame, adapt. Alan Bennett); director, Rupert Goold. (8 February 2002) *Naked Justice* (John Mortimer) with Leslie Phillips; director, Richard Cottrell. (6 March) *Hobson's Choice* (Harold Brighouse) with Tony Britton; director, Jonathan Church. (2 April) *Single Spies* (Alan Bennett) with Robert Powell, Lisa Goddard; director, David Grindley. (3 May) *Elizabeth Rex* (Timothy Findley) UK première. (20 June) *Krindlekrax* (Philip Ridley); director, Anthony Clark. (19 August) *Stones in His Pockets* (Marie Jones); director, Ian McElhinney.

CHICHESTER: FESTIVAL (25 July 2002) *Cabaret* (Joe Masteroff, John Kander, Fred Ebb) with Alexandra Jay, Julian Bleach; director, Roger Redfarn. (21 August) *Romeo and Juliet* (Shakespeare) with Emily Blunt, Lex Shrapnel, Una Stubbs, Paul Shelley; director, Indhu Rubasingham.

MINERVA (14 August 2002) *Song of the Western Men* (Christopher William Hill); director, Andy Brereton.

EDINBURGH: ROYAL LYCEUM (8 September 2001) *Glengarry Glen Ross* (David Mamet) with Ronnie Simon, Steven McNicoll, Robert Paterson, Mark McDonnell, Tom McGovern, Lou Hirsch, Neil McKinven; director, Kenny Ireland. (20 October) *The Comedy of Errors* (Shakespeare) with Tom McGovern, Jimmy Chisholm, Mark McDonnell, Steven McNicoll, Julie Duncanson, Cora Bisset; director, Tony Cownie. (30 November) *Beauty and the Beast* (Stuart Paterson) with Cora Bisset, Garry Collins, Alison Peebles; director, Tony Cownie. (15 January 2002) *Lavender Blue* (Grace Barnes) with Pauline Turner, Jimmy Chisholm, Andrea Gibb, Ian Grieve, Eileen McCallum, Angel Coulby, Sarah Vickers; director, Muriel Romanes. (16 February) *A Streetcar Named Desire* (Tennessee Williams) with Jennifer Black, Paul Hamilton; director, Muriel Romanes. (23 March) *Miseryguts* (Molière's *Misanthrope*, adapt. Liz Lochead) with Jimmy Chisholm, Cora Bisset; director, Tony Cownie. (27 April) *Victory* (Howard Barker) with Helen Lomax, Barrie Hunter, John Kielty, Bob Barrett, Kathryn Howden, Shona McDonald, Ronnie Simon, Crawford Logan, Luke Shaw, Tadeusz Pasternak, Gillie Gilchrist; director, Kenny Ireland.

MANCHESTER: ROYAL EXCHANGE (5 September 2001) *Uncle Vanya* (Chekov) with Tom Courtenay, Kaye Wragg, Helen Schlesinger, Robert Glenister, John Bennett; director, Greg Hersov. (24 October) *Hedda Gabler* (Ibsen) with Amanda Donohue; director, Braham Murray. (5 December) *Time and the Conways* (J. B. Priestley) with Gabrielle Drake; director, Braham Murray. (23 January 2002) *The Homecoming* (Pinter) with Pete Postlethwaite, Paul Hilton, Eamon Boland, James Hillier, Michael Higgs, Simone Lahbib; director, Greg Hersov. (6 March) *A Midsummer Night's Dream* (Shakespeare) with Hilary Maclean, Fenella Woolgar, Madeleine Worrall, Paul McEwan, Jonathan Bond, Justin Avoth, Robin Laing, Tom Hodgkins; director, Lucy Bailey. (24 April) *American Buffalo* (David Mamet) with Mike McShane, Ben Keaton, Paul Popplewell; director, Greg Hersov. (26 June) *Design for Living* (Noel Coward) with Victoria Scarborough, Oliver Milburn, Clarence Smith; director, Marianne Elliott.

SOUTHAMPTON: NUFFIELD (29 November 2001) *A Christmas Carol* (Dickins) with Granville Saxton; director, Patrick Sandford. (7 February 2002) *Night*

Swimming (Mark Castle) with Alastair Danson, Emma Cleasby; director, Patrick Sandford. (11 April) *Three Sisters* (Chekhov) with Imogen Stubbs, Serena Gordon, Dulcie Gray, Gareth Thomas, Ian Shaw, Robert Morgan; director, Patrick Sandford. (16 May) *Epsom Downs* (Howard Brenton); director, Daniel Buckroyd.

STRATFORD: ROYAL SHAKESPEARE THEATRE (5 December 2001) *Alice in Wonderland*, transferred from the Barbican Theatre, London. (20 February 2002) *A Midsummer Night's Dream* (Shakespeare) with Yolanda Vazquez, Nikki Amuka-Bird, Gabrielle Jourdan, Priyanga Elan, Tim McMullan, Peter Lindford, Paul Chequer, Michael Colgan, Dominic Cooper, Darrell D'Silva; director, Richard Jones. (23 April) *Antony and Cleopatra* (Shakespeare) with Sinead Cusack, Stuart Wilson; director, Michael Attenborough. (9 May) *Much Ado About Nothing* (Shakespeare) with Harriet Walter, Nicholas le Provost; director, Gregory Doran. (31 July) *The Winter's Tale* (Shakespeare), transferred from the Roundhouse, London, with Michael Cumpsty replacing Douglas Hodge. (12 August) *Pericles* (Shakespeare), transferred from the Roundhouse, London.

THE SWAN (4 December 2001) *The Merchant of Venice*, transferred from the Pit, London. (20 January 2002) *The Prince of Homburg* (Heinrich von Kleist, adapt. Neil Bartlett, David Bryer) with Dan Fredenburgh; director, Neil Bartlett. (17 April) *Eastward Ho!* (Jonson, Marston, Chapman) with Geoffrey Freshwater, Billy Carter, James Tucker, Michael Mateus, Sian Howard, Shelley Conn; director, Lucy Pitman-Wallace. (25 April) *Edward III* (Shakespeare) with David Rintoul; director, Anthony Clark. (30 May) *The Roman Actor* (Philip Massinger) with Antony Sher, Joe Dixon; director, Sean Holmes. (2 July) *The Island Princess* (Fletcher) with Sasha Behar, Paul Bhattacharjee, Joe Dixon; director, Gregory Doran. (20 August) *The Malcontent* (John Marston) with Antony Sher; director, Dominic Cooke.

Weather

This was the wettest July since 1993. From the 1st to the 7th it was very warm or hot in many places with Heathrow reaching 30.5°C on the 5th. Thunderstorms early on the 3rd over Wales spread to other parts of England and Wales over succeeding days, with some heavy downpours in places. Cardiff received 67mm in 12 hours on the 4th. High pressure gave way to low pressure in the south-west approaches, which then slowly transferred to the southern part of the North Sea by the 7th. From the 8th to the 16th a cool unsettled spell ensued as low pressure over the North Sea moved away and another depression off western Scotland on the 10th moved to the North Sea by the 11th, before migrating to Scandinavia. The 9th and 10th were quite wet as associated fronts crossed England and Wales. There were frequent showers some heavy with thunder, but these became more scattered towards the end of the period. Mumbles in South Wales reported a gust of 52kts on the 11th. A shallow low over the south-east on the 14th was followed by a weak ridge on the 15th and 16th, with zero Celsius being recorded at Sennybridge in Powys overnight. The 17th to the 20th saw a wet spell especially from the 17th to the 18th when there was heavy thundery rain in many places as a low moved from the south-west approaches to the North Sea. As fronts stalled over East Anglia and the Midlands, some high totals were recorded. At Keyworth in Nottinghamshire 96mm fell in 15 hours on the 18th causing considerable local flooding. Weybourne in Norfolk received 69mm the same day, with 41mm falling in 3 hours that morning. From the 21st to the 24th after a cool start it became warm with good sunny periods in most places, although north-western areas had more cloud and scattered light showers from time to time. The 25th to the 31st saw hot, sunny weather prevail for much of the time as a weak ridge of high pressure covered the region. Any local mist or fog patches soon cleared away after sunrise. It was very hot at times in the south and on the 28th and 29th temperatures hovered around 32°C in the London area. From the 29th onwards northern and western areas were affected by occasional outbreaks of light rain or drizzle in association with a weak cold front edging southwards.

AUGUST 2001

From the 1st to the 9th after a very warm start, it became unsettled and cooler as low pressure passed just to the north or directly over the region. Associated fronts brought frequent outbreaks of thundery rain and hail especially to East Anglia and the Midlands on the 6th, northern areas on the 7th, and again to south-east England and East Anglia on the 9th. Many funnel clouds were seen on the 9th with one touching down at Gosport overturning some caravans, while a waterspout was sighted off the Suffolk coast. Northolt in north-west London received 56mm of rain in 12 hours and another gauge collected 71mm at Worsham in Oxfordshire. The 10th to the 14th saw changeable weather with some occasional light rain and cool temperatures at first, however, with drier conditions and good sunny periods it became very warm or hot over southern areas during the 13th and 14th. After a hot start from the 15th to the 19th, another unsettled period ensued with thundery outbreaks in many places, in particular south-east England and East Anglia on the 16th and 19th. Overnight

from the 17th to the 18th the Isles of Scilly received 48mm of rain. The 20th to the 23rd, with pressure higher than of late, was mostly dry and quiet conditions prevailed with good sunny spells in most areas. Temperatures rose into the warm category generally. Light southerly winds brought hot humid conditions to most places on the 24th and 25th, when London approached 32°C, exceeding the August bank holiday Saturday record of 31°C set in 1943. However, a weak cold front already astride western areas moved hesitantly eastwards producing thunderstorms later on the 25th and during the 26th, mostly over the Midlands, south-east England and East Anglia. From the 27th to the 29th an anticyclonic interlude brought mainly sunny dry and warm weather to the bulk of the region. As low pressure transferred to the south North Sea on the 30th and 31st, north-west winds brought cooler showery conditions. Some of the showers were heavy and accompanied by hail and thunder.

SEPTEMBER 2001

This was the coolest September since 1996. From the 1st to the 5th, after a mainly dry start it became rather cool, wet and unsettled with bands of rain or showers crossing the region from the west or north-west. Some of the showers were heavy and thundery at times especially in the north and east. Some sheltered places along the English Channel coast were rather warm at first, Southampton and Torquay grazing 23°C. The 6th to the 11th saw changeable and mainly dry weather over the region, sandwiched between a complex area of low pressure over Scandinavia and high pressure to the south-west of Ireland. The fresh north-westerly airstream from the Iceland region brought good sunny periods, with southern counties benefiting the most. Southsea reached 23.1°C on the 7th. Any light rain or showers were confined to northern and eastern counties. The 12th and 13th were very wet and windy as a deep low near Iceland moved south-east to the southern North Sea. Buxton in Derbyshire reached only 11°C on the 13th. The 14th to the 16th was mostly rather cool and changeable, with good sunny periods especially in the south. North-eastern areas and East Anglia saw some showers from time to time. The 17th to the 19th was unsettled with heavy rain at times particularly in eastern areas, East Anglia and south-east England as a depression moved south-westwards from Denmark. Gusts over 40kts were experienced near the Wash. The 20th to the 22nd was a quieter period, allowing some local mist and fog patches to form overnight. It was mostly rather cool with some isolated light rain or showers. Western areas were warmer, sunnier and drier. From the 23rd to the 25th there was more wet and unsettled weather over northern and eastern areas including the Midlands and East Anglia. Fairly widespread rain and showers, some heavy with thunder broke out. Showers affected southern areas as well later. Many places had mist and fog patches which were slow to clear. From the 26th to the 30th after a dry start a deepening complex low pressure system west of Ireland brought increasing spells of rain and showers to many parts, the showers becoming heavy and thundery in places later. However it was mostly warm, with London touching 24°C on the 28th. A gust of 63kts was recorded at Aberdaron on the Lleyn Peninsula during the 30th.

OCTOBER 2001

This was the warmest October on record. With low pressure close by to the north or west from the 1st to the 8th, conditions were often unsettled. Blustery thundery showers on the 1st became more scattered from the 2nd to the 4th, however, there were sunny periods. After some rain in the west on the 5th, there were more blustery showers on the 6th, some heavy and thundery in south-east England and East Anglia. In the Norfolk Broads a tornado caused local destruction. On the 7th Mumbles in South Wales reported a 67kt gust as a deep low moved north-east from the south-west approaches, bringing stormy conditions to the region. There were copious amounts of rain and later frequent squally thundery showers – many places received more than 50mm in 24 hours. More thundery showers occurred during the 8th especially in the south. With high pressure not far away from the 9th to the 13th, quieter changeable weather prevailed. Apart from thundery showers in the south on 9th and some occasional rain in the north-west and west at first, it was mainly dry. There were long sunny periods, and it became very warm with some morning mist and fog patches. Temperatures brushed past 25°C at Herne Bay in Kent and in London on the 13th, exceptionally warm for so late in the year. The 14th to the 24th saw complex low pressure centred to the west then south-west of the UK. This brought warm and unsettled weather with plenty of rain and showers on most days apart from the 16th which was mainly dry. From the 19th a number of active low centres and associated fronts crossed the region, bringing more bands of rain and showers often heavy with thunder. Overnight from the 19th to the 20th a swathe of rain gave 50mm in 4 hours at Hereford, with 26mm falling in one hour. Another disturbance hesitated over East Anglia on the 21st depositing 90mm at Cambridge with severe local flooding in Cambridgeshire. The 25th and 28th were unsettled at first as depressions passed the UK to the north-west. A cold front moving erratically eastwards gave the south-west and Midlands a very wet day on the 26th. The 27th and 28th were mainly dry, sunny and warm as high pressure began to assert itself. The 29th to the 31st saw a windy end to the month as a deepening low off Scotland moved east to southern Scandinavia. The 30th was very warm everywhere and many places touched 20°C inland. A cold front moved south-east later bringing some bursts of heavy rain overnight and introducing breezy, chilly and fresher conditions for the 31st.

NOVEMBER 2001

This was the driest November since 1989. The 1st to the 6th was mainly dry, sunny and warm by day, especially in the south, with high pressure close to southern England. Low pressure over Scandinavia drove some weak cold fronts south-east on the 3rd, 4th and 6th. There was patchy mist or fog and slight frost at times overnight. The 7th and 8th were wet, especially the 7th as a deep low tracked to Denmark. Cold northerly winds on the 8th brought some heavy thundery showers to north-facing coasts. Weybourne in Norfolk recorded a gust of 56kts. The 9th and 10th were mostly dry, sunny and cold with overnight frost under a ridge of high pressure. There were wintry showers over the east Midlands and counties adjacent to the North Sea. Bedfordshire received up to 3cm of snow, the earliest significant report of lying snow in southern England since 1980. The 11th and 12th were mainly dry at first but a cold front brought outbreaks of rain to most places on the 12th. From the 13th to the 20th an anticyclone covered the region, later stretching across

to the continent. The weather was generally dry apart from a little light rain or drizzle at times. There was also some patchy mist, hill and coastal fog. It was mainly sunny at first in south-east England and East Anglia with some overnight frosts. However, from the 16th increasing cloud established the traditional anticyclonic gloom and a little light rain or drizzle. Parts of England and Wales became brighter during the 19th and 20th although there were still a few light showers affecting some areas. From the 21st to the 24th, a changeable situation gave alternating mild and cold days. Mild wet weather on the 21st gave way to drier conditions as a weak cold front cleared on the 22nd. After a frosty start on the 23rd, more cloud and rising temperatures spread back. The 25th to the 30th was mostly wet and unsettled as vigorous Atlantic lows pushed their fronts across the region. There was rain and showers at times from the 25th to the 29th, with a funnel cloud reported from Preston in Lancashire on the 27th. After some overnight frost on the 26th and 27th the last two days became exceptionally mild, but still mostly cloudy with rain and drizzle at times and quite persistent hill fog. At Colwyn Bay and Hawarden the maximum temperature of 16.9°C on the 30th broke the UK record for the last day of the month.

DECEMBER 2001

This was the sunniest December on record and the driest since 1991. The 1st to the 5th saw a mostly mild, unsettled start to the month as Atlantic fronts crossed the region. Wet weather on the 3rd heralded more of the same during the 4th and 5th as a low-pressure system moved east over northern England. The rain turned showery and heavy on the 5th. With high pressure firmly established over the region from the 6th to the 11th, a dry, mostly sunny regime prevailed. It was mild at first especially around western coastal areas, however, temperatures elsewhere later slid into the rather cold category. There was some rain and drizzle around western coasts at first, otherwise many places had patchy mist or fog and some overnight frost. Where fog persisted in the Midlands and north-east England it stayed cold. Some western areas stayed mild, with Nantmor in Gwynedd reaching 16.1°C on the 11th. From the 12th to the 18th the anticyclone migrated northwards allowing a light easterly flow in the south. It continued very dry and generally sunny at first, but rather cold with fairly widespread frost at night. Cloud increased later with patchy rain and drizzle from the 15th to the 17th. The 19th to the 26th was changeable with some snow in places as deep depressions moving south-south-east from the Norwegian sea brought cold northerly outbreaks. The first of these on the 21st and 22nd brought snow showers to east coast counties as far south as north Essex, giving 2-5cm in places. The second outbreak on Christmas Day brought snowfalls to North Wales especially on high ground. More snow showers fell in the north-west on the 26th. A vigorous low near Iceland on the 27th moved south-east to Denmark by the 28th deepening rapidly as it passed Scotland. Strong to gale force north-westerly winds brought progressively colder air from the Iceland and Greenland areas, with many places receiving significant accumulations of snow by the 29th and 30th. St Bees Head in Cumbria had a gust of 68kts on the 28th. A weather band gave substantial snow over high ground in extreme southern and south-west England early on the 29th, with some on low ground also; parts of Sussex received 2-3cm. Widespread frost, severe at times developed later, with Sennybridge in Powys falling to minus 10.9°C early on the 31st.

JANUARY 2002

This was the mildest January since 1993 and the dullest since 1996. The 1st to the 4th saw a dry, cold, mostly sunny start to the month under high pressure from Europe. There was widespread severe frost overnight with Sennybridge in Powys falling to minus 11.9°C on the 1st. Snow lay thickly over the Pennines and North Wales with 8cm being common on higher ground. Freezing fog affected the Midlands and north-east on the 2nd. It became milder with some rain in western areas later. Though still under the European ridge from the 5th to the 8th, cloudy milder conditions replaced the old chilly surface air. However, there was patchy rain and drizzle and fairly widespread hill and coastal fog to contend with. From the 9th to the 12th although high pressure persisted nearby on the continent, a trough in its circulation brought outbreaks of rain and showers to southern and western areas on the 9th and 10th. Elsewhere was mainly dry and mild with sunny spells but there was patchy mist and fog at times especially in north-east England. From the 13th to the 20th, active Atlantic depressions pushed their associated fronts and changeable weather across the region. There were outbreaks of rain and blustery showers, sometimes heavy with occasional thunder in western areas. It was mostly mild with sunny intervals but hill and coastal fog affected some places at times. The 20th was very windy with gusts up to 65kts reported from North Wales. The 21st to the 24th was more unsettled as low-pressure systems passing close to Scotland heralded a wet and windy spell. It stayed very mild apart from a brief northerly incursion later on the 24th. The 25th to the 28th was a very stormy period as a number of intense depressions tracked north-eastwards past Scotland. There was copious rainfall in many areas during the 25th and 26th causing local flooding in places. Snow fell briefly over the northern Pennines on the 25th. One storm in particular on the 28th gave severe gales over North Wales and northern England with gusts up to 72kts and over 100kts on exposed northern hills. Mostly very mild temperatures prevailed throughout, however, with a number of stations reaching 15°C. From the 29th to the 31st the very mild but unsettled pattern persisted. Active Atlantic fronts brought more rain and gales during the 31st depositing up to 50mm of rain in parts of North Wales and Cumbria.

FEBRUARY 2002

This was the wettest February since 1990, and the dullest since 1997. From the 1st to the 4th a deep complex low pressure centred between Iceland and Scotland brought very unsettled, wet and windy weather. Bands of rain and showers, often heavy with occasional thunder swept across the region. The very mild temperatures were offset by frequent gales especially around coasts. A gust of 79kts was recorded at Capel Curig in North Wales on the 1st. The 5th to the 13th saw depressions passing to the north and north-west of the UK which continued to bring very mild, unsettled conditions with periods of rain and showers at times, as more Atlantic fronts traversed the UK. Some of the showers had thunder mixed in, however, the sun shone in between, with the south-east benefiting the most. On the 10th very heavy rain affected north-west areas with Capel Curig being deluged by 121mm of rain in 24 hours causing local flooding. The low pressure moved to Finland by the 12th, allowing pressure to rise over the UK. From the 14th to the 18th an anticyclone over the region provided a temporary respite from the wind and rain. Mainly quiet, dry, sunny weather prevailed but with overnight frost, the temperature falling to minus 6.2°C at Benson in Oxfordshire early on the 15th. During the 17th and 18th a weak cold front moved south-east.

The 19th to the 23rd saw wet and windy conditions return as active lows moved east to Denmark during the 19th and 20th. By the 22nd and 23rd a deep depression over Scandinavia brought more strong winds and showers some of which were accompanied by hail and thunder. Strong winds affected the Vale of York on the 22nd with a gust of 67kts at Leeds. It was very mild in the south at first, with Folkestone in Kent reaching 15.1°C on the 22nd. Precipitation turned wintry in the north and north-east later on the 23rd, with snow showers down as far as East Anglia. Frequent snow showers over northern England left a wintry landscape by the morning of the 24th with 5-10cm of snow on high ground. However, the snow was soon washed away on the 25th as a vigorous low tracked eastwards across Scotland overnight from the 25th to the 26th. There were more gales and heavy rain in many areas especially the north-west and the rain turned showery later with some hail and thunder. Gusts over 70kts were frequent in north Wales, while eastern counties of England had gusts up to 65kts. A residual trough over Scotland on the 27th migrated slowly southwards perpetuating the showery regime. A number of places had hail and thunder, especially along the English Channel coast.

MARCH 2002

The 1st to the 8th was a changeable, mainly dry period as weak fronts crossed the region between low pressure to the north and high pressure to the south. There were sunny periods but it was rather cold at first with some overnight frost and fog patches and some occasional wintry showers in the north-east. From the 5th onwards it was mild or very mild, however, the 6th was windy with some rain in the north. The 9th to the 13th was generally changeable with occasional rain but mostly mild. A small intense low moved eastwards across northern districts during the 9th bringing gales to many areas and some snow to high ground in northern England. With gusts over 60kts in Norfolk a marked 'Fen Blow' was experienced as the strong winds lifted the topsoil. A gust of 67kts was recorded at Mumbles Head in south Wales. The 10th was also windy with more gales in western and northern areas, while Boltshope Park in Northumberland boasted 10cm of snow that morning. As low pressure transferred to Biscay during the 12th and 13th a quieter interlude developed. Northern areas were sunny but with overnight frost. Shap in Cumbria fell to minus 6.5°C early on the 13th. Rain affected extreme southern areas from time to time. The 14th to the 20th was unsettled with periods of rain heavy at times. An anticyclone over Scandinavia fed chilly easterly winds at first, but falling pressure in the south-west approaches brought rain on the 14th and 15th, especially to southern areas. Thundery showers affected the Norfolk and Suffolk coast later on the 15th. Low pressure centred in the mid North Atlantic brought mild southerly winds on the 16th and 17th but rain, heavy at times, spread in later with thunder reported along the Channel coast. The 18th was wet as a low moved from the Severn estuary to the Wash, while rain with hill and coastal fog were the uninvited guests to southern parts on the 19th and 20th. The 21st to the 31st was mainly dry, sunny, anticyclonic weather as pressure rose over the region and drifted east. It was mostly very mild by day but with some overnight fog and frost later. The 29th and 30th saw temperatures reach 18°C in the London area, making it the capital's warmest March Good Friday, although scattered showers affected places in the Midlands, East Anglia and south-east England later. As the high pressure lost ground, Atlantic fronts brought patchy rain and drizzle to many areas on the 31st.

APRIL 2002

This was the sunniest April since 1990. From the 1st to the 5th low pressure to the west transferred to Biscay and the Mediterranean. Warm or very warm conditions became established. After a little light rain in the south-west and north-west at first, much drier weather with good sunny periods developed in most places. From the 6th to the 10th the dry weather continued as a belt of high pressure stretched itself across the region between parent centres over Scandinavia and the central north Atlantic. There was a stiff easterly wind in the south at first during the 6th and 7th. Sunny periods prevailed on most days and temperatures were near normal. It became changeable but mainly dry from the 11th to the 16th, with some sunny periods especially in the south-east. Conditions were mostly quiet, but weak fronts traversed the region bringing the odd outbreak of light rain in places. There was frost at times at night with Shap in Cumbria falling to minus 5.5°C early on the 13th. Day temperatures were around normal. Scattered light showers affected the Midlands and eastern areas on the 13th and 15th. From the 17th to the 20th more unsettled weather developed with rain at times especially in the west and north-west. Nantmor in Gwynedd received 60mm in 24 hours on the 18th. On the same day a band from central Wales to south-east England gave some showers, a few of which were heavy with thunder. Temperatures were not far from normal and the sun shone between the showers. Overnight mist and fog patches affected a few places early on the 20th. The 21st to the 25th was mainly settled, dry and very warm but weak fronts in the north-west gave some rain on the 21st. Initially, hill and coastal fog affected north-west areas and the Channel Islands, with some additional local mist and fog patches inland. Thereafter, very warm, sunny weather prevailed with Enfield in London reaching 23.7°C on the 23rd, the warmest April day in the capital since 1987. Rain, heavy at times, reached western areas later on the 25th. The 26th to the 30th was unsettled, wet and windy, with gales around coasts as vigorous Atlantic depressions crossed northern Britain. Associated fronts brought bands of blustery rain and showers to the region, some outbreaks were heavy with hail and thunder, especially during the 26th, 28th and 29th. It felt chilly at times and on the 29th snow fell over high ground in the north, while Mumbles in South Wales reported a gust of 67kts.

MAY 2002

This was the coolest May since 1997. The 1st to the 12th was a changeable, mostly dry period apart from occasional outbreaks of scattered thundery showers. Counties bordering the North Sea were affected by hill and coastal fog at times later in the period, from about the 8th to the 12th. It was chilly with slight frost at night from time to time, however, most places saw sunny periods in particular Wales and western areas. There were scattered showers during the first few days of the month, some with thunder, with 25mm falling at Keston in Kent on the 3rd. Vigorous low pressure developed over the western Mediterranean by the 7th and with rising pressure over Scandinavia, an easterly drift became established by the 6th. There was some patchy light rain or drizzle in eastern and south-eastern areas from the 5th to the 7th and some thundery rain in northern England on the 7th. Low pressure moved to the east by the 10th, producing slack gradients and scattered showers by the 11th and 12th. Shap in Cumbria recorded minus 1.9°C early on the 12th. During the 13th and 14th an Atlantic low moved north-east passing Ireland and Scotland and associated fronts brought wind and rain, with gales at times around

western coasts. The rain was heavy in places at first, however, by the 14th scattered blustery showers were the order of the day. From the 15th to the 17th an anticyclone over Europe brought a short-lived spell of hot weather especially on the 16th when Jersey peaked at 28.5°C. Thundery rain, sometimes heavy, affected southern districts the next day. With vigorous low pressure close by over the Atlantic from the 18th to the 26th, the weather became very unsettled. There were frequent outbreaks of blustery rain and showers, some heavy with hail and thunder at times especially in the west. The 24th and 25th were particularly windy with gales around coasts and a number of reports of gusts to 57kts. The sun did manage to shine, however, between the bands of rain and showers. The 26th was cooler and quieter but more thundery rain still affected a number of places. In Haywards Heath in West Sussex a farmer reported a damaging tornado which killed one of his cows with flying debris. The 27th to the 31st saw low pressure to the north-west which continued the unsettled theme up to the 30th with rain and scattered showers. Again, some were heavy with hail and thunder in quite a few places. On the 31st a ridge extended from the continent bringing some warmer, sunnier and drier weather for the last day.

JUNE 2002

The 1st to the 4th saw a dry, sunny start to the month and hot in many places on the 2nd with Jersey climbing to 28°C. However, thundery rain affected north-west areas, while scattered showers broke out in the south-east later. A cold front on the 3rd brought cooler conditions and thundery showers, some accompanied by hail. Although mainly dry on the 4th, occasional showers affected the north-west. The 5th to the 11th was mostly unsettled as low pressure hovered nearby. Overnight from the 4th to the 5th thunderstorms and heavy rain affected south-east England and East Anglia. Hook in Surrey and Morden in Greater London both received 42mm of rain. The next few days saw variable winds, patchy mist and fog and scattered outbreaks of rain, sometimes thundery. From the 9th to the 11th a rather cool showery south-westerly airstream covered the region, some showers were heavy and thundery. Mumbles, near Swansea, reported a gust of 54kts on the 10th. The 12th to the 17th was generally changeable with the south-east coming off best due to high pressure on the continent. The period started chilly and cloudy with some heavy thundery rain in the north-west on the 13th. Thundery rain also affected northern England on the 14th and later in the day in south-east England. Conditions became brighter and very warm or hot later with 29°C being reached over the south-east and East Anglia on the 17th. That same day a weak cold front edged eastwards clearing away hill and coastal fog which had been residing around west and south-west parts. From the 18th to the 21st, after some thunderstorms in the south-east early on the 18th it became mainly sunny and dry but with some slight rain on the 21st. Most places had temperatures near or rather above normal especially in the south-east. The 22nd to the 26th was mostly settled and dry with plenty of sunshine under the influence of a ridge of high pressure stretching from the Azores. The south-east and East Anglia came off best temperature wise where it was rather warm at times. A cold front brought some rain into northern districts on the 26th. The 27th to the 30th saw low pressure over Scandinavia fed by cool north-westerly winds over the region, bringing good sunny periods and dry weather for the most part but with some showers in the north-east and central England on the 27th. The last day saw Atlantic fronts bringing patchy rain eastwards and some heavier pulses around Snowdonia and Cumbria.

AVERAGE AND GENERAL MONTHLY VALUES 2000–2002 (JUNE)

	Rainfall (mm) Average 1961-90	2000	2001	2002	Temperature (°C) Average 1961–90	2000	2001	2002	Bright Sunshine (hrs per day) Average 1961–90	2000	2001	2002
ENGLAND AND WALES												
January	77	195	70	90	3.8	4.7	3.4	5.3	1.6	3.3	2.15	1.42
February	55	190	90	129	3.8	6.0	4.4	6.6	2.4	3.9	3.17	2.71
March	63	112	86	49	5.6	7.2	5.1	7.2	3.5	4.8	2.96	3.60
April	53	101	93	54	7.7	7.6	7.5	8.8	4.9	6.4	4.75	6.35
May	56	61	42	92	10.9	11.7	12.1	11.4	6.2	5.9	7.54	6.04
June	58	75	39	55	13.9	14.5	13.8	13.9	6.4	–	6.93	5.77
July	56	62	72	–	15.7	15.0	16.5	–	6.0	5.23	6.27	–
August	68	66	85	–	15.6	16.3	16.4	–	6.0	6.25	5.71	–
September	70	121	80	–	13.6	14.5	13.0	–	4.5	3.87	3.77	–
October	77	177	131	–	10.7	10.3	13.0	–	3.2	3.05	3.34	–
November	81	169	67	–	6.6	6.8	7.1	–	2.2	2.08	2.17	–
December	82	124	44	–	4.7	5.6	3.4	–	1.5	1.51	2.37	–
YEAR	796	1,453	899	–	9.4	10.0	9.6	–	4.0	3.9	4.26	–
SCOTLAND												
January	117	185	86	206	3.1	4.1	1.9	4.3	1.3	1.5	1.75	0.99
February	–	190	–	235	3.1	4.0	2.4	3.6	2.4	2.3	2.70	1.93
March	94	112	74	124	4.6	5.8	2.8	5.0	3.2	2.7	4.08	3.42
April	60	101	70	87	6.5	5.6	5.7	7.0	4.8	4.6	4.81	4.90
May	67	61	41	101	9.3	9.5	10.4	9.5	5.6	7.9	7.11	5.62
June	67	75	87	129	12.1	11.1	11.0	11.8	5.6	5.4	4.77	4.70
July	74	51	99	–	13.6	12.9	13.2	–	4.9	5.16	3.86	–
August	92	110	111	–	13.5	13.6	13.0	–	4.9	4.73	4.10	–
September	111	151	104	–	11.5	12.1	10.7	–	3.5	3.41	3.11	–
October	120	221	238	–	9.1	8.6	10.7	–	2.6	2.81	1.98	–
November	118	164	150	–	5.3	5.0	5.9	–	1.7	1.82	1.18	–
December	115	170	116	–	3.9	3.8	2.5	–	1.0	1.07	1.25	–
YEAR	1,113	1,591	1,267	–	7.9	8.0	7.5	–	3.5	3.6	3.39	–

Source: Data provided by the Met Office

WIND FORCE MEASURES

The *Beaufort Scale* of wind force has been accepted internationally and is used in communicating weather conditions. Devised originally by Admiral Sir Francis Beaufort in 1805, it now consists of the numbers 0–17, each representing a certain strength or velocity of wind at 10 m (33 ft) above ground in the open.

Scale no.	Wind Force	mph	knots
0	Calm	1	1
1	Light air	1–3	1–3
2	Slight breeze	4–7	4–6
3	Gentle breeze	8–12	7–10
4	Moderate breeze	13–18	11–16
5	Fresh breeze	19–24	17–21
6	Strong breeze	25–31	22–27
7	High wind	32–38	28–33
8	Gale	39–46	34–40
9	Strong gale	47–54	41–47
10	Whole gale	55–63	48–55
11	Storm	64–72	56–63
12	Hurricane	73–82	64–71
13	–	83–92	72–80
14	–	93–103	81–89
15	–	104–114	90–99
16	–	115–125	100–108
17	–	126–136	109–118

TEMPERATURE, RAINFALL AND SUNSHINE
At selected climatological reporting stations, July 2001–June 2002

Ht   height (in metres) of stations above mean sea level
°C   mean air temperature
Rain   total monthly rainfall
Sun   monthy total (hours)
Source: Data provided by the Met Office

		July 2001			August 2001			September 2001			October 2001		
	Ht		Rain	Sun		Rain	Sun		Rain	Sun		Rain	Sun
	m	°C	mm	hrs	°C	mm	hrs	°C	mm	hrs	°C	mm	hrs
Lerwick	82	11.6	78.8	94.9	12.2	88.1	122.6	10.2	71.1	71.4	10.5	122.1	55.7
Stornoway	15	12.6	70.7	101.0	13.9	75.5	162.2	11.7	98.6	111.9	11.4	179.4	72.3
Dyce	65	14.7	35.4	144.4	14.7	88.0	146.0	11.6	84.0	93.2	12.0	116.8	90.4
Eskdalemuir	242	13.9	94.8	130.9	12.9	135.7	123.7	11.0	121.3	89.4	11.0	257.7	45.9
Aldergrove	68	15.0	60.2	150.5	15.0	98.4	158.4	13.0	53.2	120.1	12.2	88.8	76.8
Leeds	64	17.7	18.9	193.6	17.5	60.0	191.9	13.7	74.4	55.3	13.8	109.0	–
Valley	10	15.3	58.2	208.6	15.1	98.5	185.1	13.8	71.6	146.0	13.7	71.6	117.6
Coleshill	–	17.3	73.1	–	17.1	34.2	–	13.4	43.8	–	13.4	84.6	–
Skegness	6	16.8	64.9	–	17.5	58.8	102.9	13.4	73.4	103.5	13.8	42.0	120.3
Bristol	42	17.5	85.6	–	17.5	88.4	–	14.4	32.2	–	14.0	135.6	–
St Mawgan	103	16.1	104.2	226.5	16.6	33.6	216.0	14.7	31.0	177.8	14.0	110.0	127.0
Hastings	45	18.2	58.5	286.6	18.1	84.0	240.3	14.6	85.4	171.5	15.0	136.2	129.5

	November 2001			December 2001			The Year 2001			January 2002			February 2002		
		Rain	Sun		Rain	Sun		Rain	Sun		Rain	Sun		Rain	Sun
	°C	mm	hrs	°C	mm	hrs	°C	mm	hrs	°C	mm	hrs	°C	mm	hrs
Lerwick	5.3	160.2	24.2	3.8	150.3	31.2	7.2	94.6	94.2	5.1	170.3	22.0	3.3	161.1	72.0
Stornoway	7.2	114.7	35.0	4.9	117.2	44.2	8.5	81.7	113.5	6.7	197.6	25.9	4.7	159.4	67.8
Dyce	6.6	50.0	70.8	3.4	74.7	42.1	8.4	67.9	119.8	4.3	52.2	56.5	4.4	64.2	92.6
Eskdalemuir	5.6	141.3	41.2	1.9	90.1	66.6	7.4	114.6	98.6	3.7	267.2	28.0	4.0	348.0	47.1
Aldergrove	7.9	42.8	44.0	4.5	55.4	78.0	9.3	58.4	118.5	6.3	102.0	48.7	5.9	98.2	81.9
Leeds	8.1	18.6	–	4.1	26.6	–	10.3	45.8	107.6	5.9	41.9	–	7.1	256.9	–
Valley	9.6	46.6	45.3	5.5	45.4	77.7	10.2	61.5	146.6	7.2	70.8	50.6	7.4	106.0	75.2
Coleshill	7.2	51.4	–	3.3	24.8	–	9.8	62.3	–	5.4	67.3	–	6.9	–	–
Skegness	7.2	53.5	56.3	4.3	28.4	60.1	10.0	48.6	–	5.4	43.1	42.6	6.8	51.4	83.7
Bristol	7.8	39.8	–	4.0	26.8	–	11	64.8	–	6.4	88.8	–	7.5	127.8	–
St Mawgan	9.4	95.2	80.4	6.0	42.0	103.2	11	76.7	159.6	8.2	118.4	44.9	8.2	111.8	84.7
Hastings	8.5	37.8	109.4	5.0	31.6	98.3	11.2	77.3	168.8	6.6	84.6	68.5	7.8	89.7	100.2

	March 2002			April 2002			May 2002			June 2002		
		Rain	Sun		Rain	Sun		Rain	Sun		Rain	Sun
	°C	mm	hrs	°C	mm	hrs	°C	mm	hrs	°C	mm	hrs
Lerwick	4.5	94.9	122.7	6.8	55.2	120.1	8.9	70.2	170.0	12.2	63.3	196.4
Stornoway	6.3	97.6	107.7	8.3	74.2	148.2	10.1	60.0	214.4	12.6	103.8	160.7
Dyce	5.8	33.8	136.5	7.6	26.8	165.0	10.6	54.0	197.8	13.1	107.2	178.3
Eskdalemuir	5.1	137.1	98.1	6.9	124.5	131.8	9.6	178.6	114.9	11.8	189.8	118.5
Aldergrove	7.2	55.2	122.9	8.7	101.4	155.9	11.2	99.0	197.5	13.6	141.1	90.6
Leeds	7.9	84.7	–	10.0	28.4	–	12.7	56.4	–	15.2	38.2	–
Valley	7.6	29.8	131.7	8.9	67.0	163.7	11.8	69.4	207.0	13.3	53.4	171.4
Coleshill	7.7	37.4	–	9.2	49.2	–	11.9	60.0	–	14.5	39.4	–
Skegness	7.6	24.7	118.2	9.3	25.6	180.0	12.3	44.7	151.0	–	–	–
Bristol	8.1	37.4	–	9.9	35.4	–	12.2	85.4	–	14.6	58.4	–
St Mawgan	8.7	65.4	107.4	9.4	48.0	198.4	11.5	120.6	213.7	13.2	48.2	117.1
Hastings	8.6	37.7	149.2	10.0	28.7	233.7	12.6	65.6	244.7	–	–	–

METEOROLOGICAL OBSERVATIONS LONDON (HEATHROW)

Temperature maxima and minima cover the 24-hour period 9 – 9 h; mean wind speed is 10 m above ground; rainfall is for the 24 hours starting on 9 h on the day of entry; sunshine is for the 24 hours. *Source*: Data provided by the Met Office

JULY 2001

Day		Temperature Max C°	Min C°	Wind knots	Sun hrs	Rain mm
Day	1	26.2	13.0	6.7	9.6	0.0
	2	27.1	16.2	5.1	4.7	0.0
	3	29.5	17.8	9.7	12.4	0.0
	4	29.2	18.9	8.7	11.1	0.0
	5	30.5	19.0	6.9	4.3	2.6
	6	26.2	18.3	4.4	6.1	Trace
	7	21.5	16.5	4.3	0.0	2.8
	8	20.8	16.4	7.6	0.9	0.2
	9	21.0	11.9	8.3	2.3	2.2
	10	20.2	15.4	11.9	2.6	1.8
	11	21.4	13.5	15.0	8.9	Trace
	12	21.0	11.5	10.7	10.2	0.4
	13	22.2	12.6	7.3	5.2	10.0
	14	19.2	11.6	4.1	6.0	0.6
	15	19.8	10.4	3.7	8.3	0.0
	16	22.3	10.5	3.6	12.8	Trace
	17	21.8	11.6	11.5	2.5	8.0
	18	20.8	13.8	6.8	5.7	4.2
	19	17.5	12.7	8.7	0.2	Trace
	20	21.6	10.0	7.1	9.4	2.2
	21	22.4	13.0	10.2	5.7	Trace
	22	20.5	14.6	5.5	0.2	0.2
	23	25.3	13.0	4.4	13.5	0.0
	24	23.2	12.6	3.8	12.6	0.0
	25	26.3	14.2	5.7	7.6	0.0
	26	28.7	13.8	3.5	12.8	0.0
	27	29.3	16.5	3.7	12.7	0.0
	28	31.6	17.5	4.3	10.5	0.0
	29	31.9	19.1	6.3	8.8	0.0
	30	28.9	18.1	5.6	12.0	0.0
	31	26.6	16.6	8.4	9.5	0.0

AUGUST 2001

Day		Temperature Max C°	Min C°	Wind knots	Sun hrs	Rain mm
Day	1	26.7	16.9	10.1	8.9	Trace
	2	21.2	14.5	6.2	0.0	11.8
	3	23.9	14.9	7.3	5.3	1.4
	4	22.8	11.4	7.0	7.3	13.2
	5	23.2	12.2	7.8	12.7	Trace
	6	24.7	15.7	9.9	3.9	0.2
	7	20.6	14.0	10.3	1.3	Trace
	8	21.5	14.2	9.3	9.5	Trace
	9	17.5	12.0	5.3	2.9	12.0
	10	20.5	9.4	6.5	11.0	0.0
	11	21.9	10.4	8.6	3.4	0.8
	12	20.1	15.7	10.2	2.1	1.0
	13	26.3	17.0	9.0	4.1	0.0
	14	27.4	17.0	6.8	10.4	Trace
	15	30.1	18.7	6.7	9.1	0.2
	16	23.9	16.8	9.1	9.5	0.4
	17	23.4	12.8	6.0	12.0	0.0
	18	25.4	15.5	8.3	0.6	11.8
	19	22.7	16.2	9.8	3.5	10.0
	20	22.7	13.9	4.7	10.8	0.0
	21	24.2	11.7	6.7	12.3	Trace
	22	25.8	15.2	3.4	12.0	0.0
	23	24.1	16.7	1.2	0.3	Trace
	24	28.4	18.9	5.7	11.4	0.0
	25	31.5	15.3	4.8	11.3	Trace
	26	20.0	18.6	4.5	0.0	6.2
	27	22.0	12.6	5.3	12.9	0.0
	28	22.1	12.2	4.8	11.7	0.0
	29	23.4	10.6	5.5	7.4	0.4
	30	20.0	15.8	3.2	0.1	4.8
	31	19.0	11.2	5.0	5.2	4.8

SEPTEMBER 2001

Day		Temperature Max C°	Min C°	Wind knots	Sun hrs	Rain mm
Day	1	20.8	10.8	4.6	10.1	Trace
	2	22.2	15.6	6.9	0.8	16.0
	3	19.9	13.0	5.0	5.8	1.8
	4	17.8	10.8	7.0	10.3	0.0
	5	20.2	7.8	5.8	2.4	2.4
	6	19.4	13.0	7.1	8.3	0.0
	7	20.9	11.2	8.6	2.4	0.8
	8	18.3	13.8	9.3	6.9	Trace
	9	15.8	8.8	8.3	8.0	Trace
	10	17.1	8.6	6.2	9.9	0.0
	11	17.9	10.0	6.0	0.3	Trace
	12	18.9	11.4	8.3	2.0	1.4
	13	16.9	10.5	8.6	5.1	6.8
	14	19.0	10.9	7.0	9.6	Trace
	15	18.7	11.0	8.4	8.3	Trace
	16	17.4	9.9	7.2	9.4	0.2
	17	13.6	8.5	9.0	3.1	0.8
	18	14.7	11.1	10.0	0.0	5.6
	19	14.2	12.0	9.5	0.0	0.8
	20	17.9	11.8	4.7	5.0	1.2
	21	16.3	10.1	2.2	3.4	0.0
	22	18.0	7.2	2.9	8.2	0.0
	23	15.7	8.4	6.9	0.3	0.2
	24	17.7	10.8	3.0	4.3	Trace
	25	17.3	7.6	2.1	5.0	0.2
	26	17.4	8.9	5.2	0.5	3.4
	27	20.2	13.1	6.7	2.7	0.0
	28	23.6	11.6	7.8	8.6	11.8
	29	19.2	15.2	4.5	2.6	2.2
	30	17.3	11.8	10.0	0.0	4.0

OCTOBER 2001

Day		Temperature Max C°	Min C°	Wind knots	Sun hrs	Rain mm
Day	1	19.1	14.5	14.7	0.9	15.8
	2	18.6	12.5	7.6	3.4	0.4
	3	19.5	11.5	8.4	8.2	Trace
	4	19.1	11.2	7.9	5.2	2.4
	5	20.0	13.7	9.6	6.8	3.0
	6	18.0	13.5	8.6	4.8	9.4
	7	15.7	11.9	12.8	0.9	13.0
	8	15.4	11.5	10.5	2.9	2.6
	9	16.9	10.7	7.1	4.8	0.4
	10	16.8	8.0	9.1	0.8	Trace
	11	18.2	12.4	8.3	0.0	Trace
	12	22.3	10.8	3.8	8.1	0.0
	13	23.1	13.1	2.3	4.6	Trace
	14	19.4	13.4	6.1	0.2	4.0
	15	18.9	14.8	7.9	2.3	3.8
	16	16.8	8.1	5.9	3.5	0.0
	17	19.6	10.3	8.9	3.5	3.0
	18	18.5	14.1	6.1	4.3	0.0
	19	17.4	10.0	8.4	0.5	8.8
	20	17.2	13.6	4.5	0.2	4.6
	21	12.1	11.3	6.1	0.0	14.8
	22	16.4	6.9	5.5	4.6	5.4
	23	17.6	7.9	7.9	5.1	3.2
	24	16.7	11.4	7.8	4.8	2.8
	25	16.4	10.3	8.1	1.6	1.4
	26	16.4	13.9	10.3	0.3	5.2
	27	16.9	10.2	4.8	7.8	3.4
	28	15.7	10.7	2.0	3.3	0.0
	29	15.2	7.2	6.0	1.4	0.0
	30	19.1	11.5	9.6	6.8	0.8
	31	13.9	9.2	9.4	8.3	0.0

NOVEMBER 2001

Day		Temperature Max C°	Min C°	Wind knots	Sun hrs	Rain mm
Day	1	13.8	4.3	3.7	8.6	0.0
	2	14.4	4.1	2.2	6.6	0.0
	3	13.0	3.0	2.3	6.4	Trace
	4	12.3	4.5	4.0	3.8	Trace
	5	11.8	4.5	4.8	8.5	0.0
	6	14.4	5.8	7.3	4.2	0.6
	7	14.1	9.6	9.1	0.0	12.2
	8	6.7	6.6	11.6	1.1	1.8
	9	6.8	1.0	8.2	6.4	0.0
	10	9.4	-0.3	3.0	6.5	Trace
	11	12.8	2.4	3.2	0.3	0.0
	12	11.3	7.4	4.0	0.0	1.4
	13	7.4	5.6	9.1	2.8	0.0
	14	8.5	-0.4	4.8	7.0	Trace
	15	9.1	0.5	2.0	6.9	0.0
	16	11.3	1.2	3.5	0.0	0.2
	17	10.1	8.5	4.2	0.0	0.2
	18	9.4	7.3	4.9	0.0	0.6
	19	9.3	6.7	3.4	0.8	Trace
	20	10.4	3.6	4.5	0.2	Trace
	21	12.6	5.7	12.2	0.1	2.2
	22	11.1	9.4	9.6	3.9	0.0
	23	9.2	-0.4	3.2	1.0	Trace
	24	14.8	1.3	3.8	3.9	Trace
	25	14.3	9.2	7.1	0.0	4.2
	26	8.5	1.6	2.4	7.2	Trace
	27	10.8	0.0	6.9	0.1	0.2
	28	12.1	2.3	6.3	2.0	3.0
	29	13.9	4.2	8.9	0.0	4.8
	30	14.9	11.8	9.1	0.0	2.4

DECEMBER 2001

Day		Temperature Max C°	Min C°	Wind knots	Sun hrs	Rain mm
Day	1	12.2	10.1	7.5	2.3	0.8
	2	7.2	1.6	2.8	0.0	0.4
	3	10.9	2.3	4.5	0.0	3.8
	4	11.3	5.4	8.9	4.4	5.2
	5	14.5	6.0	10.9	4.1	1.2
	6	8.2	3.5	4.0	1.4	Trace
	7	11.0	4.8	6.2	2.8	0.0
	8	7.2	1.4	2.2	6.5	0.0
	9	7.0	1.8	4.4	5.5	0.0
	10	8.4	1.9	2.8	6.2	0.0
	11	6.7	0.9	3.1	2.0	0.0
	12	7.5	1.4	5.6	0.0	Trace
	13	7.1	4.0	8.5	0.0	Trace
	14	4.4	0.0	5.2	6.9	0.0
	15	5.8	-0.4	5.6	4.2	Trace
	16	4.9	-0.1	7.9	0.0	0.0
	17	5.9	0.5	4.6	0.0	0.2
	18	8.4	2.1	3.3	3.7	Trace
	19	6.7	-1.5	4.7	2.7	0.4
	20	4.9	0.9	3.8	4.5	Trace
	21	8.2	-0.8	10.0	0.0	0.8
	22	2.8	-1.9	6.7	7.3	0.0
	23	5.3	-3.5	3.8	6.3	0.2
	24	9.1	-2.4	11.0	0.3	0.8
	25	5.7	4.5	6.5	0.1	3.2
	26	6.3	-2.2	5.2	5.4	0.6
	27	9.4	-1.0	9.1	0.5	Trace
	28	8.5	6.2	11.0	4.0	Trace
	29	3.1	1.1	4.6	0.2	0.2
	30	4.8	-2.0	6.5	4.8	0.0
	31	3.9	-1.9	3.0	7.2	0.0

JANUARY 2002

Day		Max C°	Min C°	Wind knots	Sun hrs	Rain mm
Day	1	3.8	-5.3	2.3	6.0	Trace
	2	4.2	-4.2	7.3	5.0	0.0
	3	3.9	-1.6	8.6	6.2	0.0
	4	7.0	-3.5	5.9	5.1	0.2
	5	8.9	-3.4	3.1	0.0	Trace
	6	8.3	6.5	1.3	0.0	Trace
	7	5.9	4.9	2.0	0.0	0.6
	8	4.7	3.6	6.0	0.0	Trace
	9	5.8	0.9	5.3	1.2	0.6
	10	7.9	1.9	3.9	2.9	2.4
	11	5.7	0.0	1.9	0.7	0.0
	12	9.0	0.0	5.5	0.0	0.4
	13	11.1	3.3	5.6	0.0	Trace
	14	10.8	8.8	6.0	0.2	3.8
	15	9.4	7.5	4.6	1.8	Trace
	16	9.3	-0.5	3.5	0.4	0.2
	17	10.1	2.8	6.9	0.0	2.8
	18	8.9	0.6	5.6	2.8	0.8
	19	11.1	1.7	9.7	5.9	Trace
	20	12.8	5.8	13.3	0.0	2.2
	21	12.6	10.6	12.1	0.8	1.0
	22	10.7	7.9	10.8	5.1	1.2
	23	12.1	7.6	13.5	0.2	4.8
	24	10.6	8.0	9.9	1.2	Trace
	25	11.9	1.0	9.4	0.0	6.0
	26	12.1	4.8	15.1	0.1	13.0
	27	13.9	7.5	8.8	0.0	5.6
	28	12.7	8.6	15.0	5.5	0.8
	29	14.0	7.1	9.7	0.9	Trace
	30	13.3	9.6	10.5	0.0	1.0
	31	12.4	5.8	12.4	1.4	3.6

FEBRUARY 2002

Day		Max C°	Min C°	Wind knots	Sun hrs	Rain mm
Day	1	13.6	6.5	19.0	0.0	0.2
	2	13.5	12.3	17.3	0.8	0.2
	3	11.6	9.3	8.5	0.0	18.2
	4	12.9	5.1	13.3	0.0	8.4
	5	12.8	7.4	11.7	4.3	1.6
	6	9.7	4.1	8.5	5.1	0.0
	7	12.0	0.5	8.2	0.0	1.0
	8	13.2	3.9	9.7	0.2	0.2
	9	12.1	10.1	14.0	3.2	1.2
	10	12.9	6.4	12.7	2.4	0.2
	11	13.8	7.8	17.3	0.1	1.6
	12	13.6	10.1	10.3	2.4	Trace
	13	10.4	6.7	5.9	0.6	0.4
	14	8.9	3.2	9.2	7.4	0.0
	15	9.0	-0.7	4.1	8.5	0.0
	16	10.0	1.1	3.6	9.1	0.0
	17	7.7	-0.9	2.6	2.4	0.4
	18	9.3	0.0	7.0	8.4	0.0
	19	11.7	5.1	12.8	1.3	8.0
	20	10.7	8.9	14.3	5.3	1.6
	21	11.3	1.2	8.8	0.2	1.0
	22	13.8	2.5	14.4	5.5	0.2
	23	7.7	4.3	13.8	6.7	0.2
	24	10.5	0.7	8.1	0.0	8.6
	25	12.9	3.8	12.2	0.0	8.0
	26	12.0	8.1	17.1	4.8	2.8
	27	9.6	2.2	13.0	6.8	Trace
	28	9.9	3.5	7.7	5.9	Trace

MARCH 2002

Day	Temperature Max C°	Min C°	Wind knots	Sun hrs	Rain mm
1	7.8	-0.7	4.5	2.3	0.4
2	8.8	-0.3	4.0	7.7	0.2
3	10.5	2.5	1.7	1.4	0.0
4	9.0	6.2	3.0	0.0	0.0
5	11.9	4.0	3.5	3.5	Trace
6	12.2	5.1	11.7	0.0	Trace
7	14.7	8.9	7.7	6.3	0.0
8	14.2	5.0	7.9	0.9	0.2
9	12.0	3.5	11.0	9.5	Trace
10	11.5	2.0	13.1	0.1	0.6
11	13.4	7.7	6.7	2.6	0.6
12	12.5	4.8	4.6	1.5	4.0
13	7.2	4.8	12.1	0.0	0.2
14	6.5	4.9	16.8	0.0	4.0
15	9.8	3.7	9.1	0.0	5.2
16	14.8	5.9	6.1	2.3	9.2
17	14.1	8.4	3.5	3.1	1.0
18	11.8	7.6	12.4	0.2	7.6
19	12.0	6.9	6.0	1.0	3.4
20	13.4	8.9	7.3	0.1	1.0
21	15.9	10.5	7.9	2.1	0.0
22	15.1	7.7	4.5	0.8	0.0
23	12.7	6.9	7.9	5.3	0.0
24	11.9	3.1	5.1	6.8	0.0
25	14.5	3.5	2.7	6.4	Trace
26	12.1	7.2	6.8	7.1	0.0
27	12.0	2.4	5.9	11.1	0.0
28	13.9	3.2	7.0	11.0	0.0
29	16.8	2.9	3.3	10.8	0.0
30	17.4	4.3	5.1	7.3	Trace
31	12.3	6.5	6.9	0.1	Trace

APRIL 2002

Day	Temperature Max C°	Min C°	Wind knots	Sun hrs	Rain mm
1	15.2	9.6	7.8	1.7	0.0
2	18.9	7.1	8.9	3.1	0.0
3	20.6	9.9	5.7	9.8	0.0
4	19.3	7.3	5.6	9.6	0.0
5	17.1	5.9	7.7	10.1	0.0
6	11.9	7.1	15.4	11.4	0.0
7	12.9	4.3	10.7	11.8	0.0
8	14.1	4.4	6.0	10.7	0.0
9	10.7	3.1	7.0	3.1	Trace
10	12.9	4.9	10.6	10.8	0.0
11	12.9	4.0	7.5	5.8	0.0
12	13.3	3.4	8.5	9.8	Trace
13	11.3	3.5	6.6	6.3	Trace
14	12.1	0.9	2.7	2.4	Trace
15	12.3	6.6	2.8	0.3	Trace
16	15.9	2.6	2.8	10.4	0.0
17	15.9	4.4	4.8	8.0	0.4
18	14.1	4.9	5.8	7.9	1.4
19	14.5	5.7	4.1	6.8	0.0
20	17.8	3.9	3.9	7.7	0.0
21	20.2	6.7	6.2	11.6	0.0
22	20.8	9.2	7.5	6.5	0.0
23	22.6	8.8	4.4	11.9	Trace
24	22.1	9.6	3.7	7.9	0.0
25	17.9	9.5	5.3	9.4	4.0
26	15.0	8.2	10.4	4.6	4.2
27	14.7	5.6	10.1	5.4	8.0
28	15.5	8.5	13.7	5.6	2.0
29	15.3	5.5	15.4	10.1	4.6
30	12.0	8.2	11.9	0.0	13.8

MAY 2002

Day	Max C°	Min C°	Wind	Sun	Rain
1	15.3	6.6	8.5	11.4	0.0
2	15.5	4.5	3.8	6.9	3.6
3	16.9	5.5	5.2	10.5	Trace
4	13.8	4.9	6.2	8.6	0.0
5	12.2	4.1	9.0	5.1	0.6
6	16.1	6.6	8.5	7.8	5.6
7	16.6	9.1	5.4	2.7	Trace
8	16.7	7.2	7.8	3.0	0.0
9	13.3	9.1	6.1	0.0	Trace
10	16.7	9.9	4.2	0.0	0.0
11	17.5	11.4	4.9	0.8	0.0
12	16.9	9.3	5.8	3.3	0.4
13	14.7	10.4	9.8	0.0	10.6
14	16.8	10.7	12.1	8.2	0.4
15	19.7	10.5	8.5	10.4	0.0
16	25.1	8.1	7.2	13.5	0.0
17	23.5	14.2	12.8	6.1	4.2
18	18.9	13.2	10.0	2.8	Trace
19	19.8	11.5	9.5	7.8	0.0
20	19.0	12.7	9.9	1.4	12.0
21	18.3	12.9	9.3	3.7	7.0
22	18.6	13.2	14.4	9.7	0.2
23	18.3	11.9	12.2	10.3	3.8
24	17.9	10.8	14.0	5.7	3.0
25	16.8	9.8	13.6	9.4	4.8
26	13.5	9.2	9.3	3.4	7.8
27	18.0	5.6	5.0	9.5	0.6
28	16.2	9.4	10.7	3.5	0.6
29	17.6	10.0	10.6	9.2	0.4
30	17.3	9.9	8.5	4.9	0.8
31	19.8	8.6	5.2	12.6	0.0

JUNE 2002

Day	Max C°	Min C°	Wind	Sun	Rain
1	22.8	9.8	8.3	14.3	0.0
2	26.8	11.9	8.4	9.9	Trace
3	17.7	13.6	7.5	2.5	0.6
4	16.6	9.4	3.4	0.6	Trace
5	15.4	11.3	6.8	0.0	29.2
6	17.4	12.1	3.5	0.0	1.2
7	15.5	14.3	5.9	0.0	0.4
8	17.8	10.1	4.8	1.7	0.4
9	15.3	12.2	9.1	2.1	6.0
10	17.2	10.5	9.6	4.7	12.8
11	18.2	9.3	8.2	9.7	11.6
12	17.6	11.1	6.3	1.8	1.6
13	20.7	10.8	5.5	2.3	Trace
14	21.6	14.4	8.3	1.6	0.2
15	21.1	13.1	10.0	7.9	0.6
16	22.1	14.5	8.4	1.5	0.0
17	26.6	14.6	6.0	15.5	4.8
18	22.6	15.7	6.0	8.3	0.0
19	21.5	10.9	3.7	13.1	Trace
20	22.3	14.0	4.8	4.3	0.6
21	21.9	12.4	7.0	6.7	2.8
22	19.5	12.8	8.9	1.8	Trace
23	20.4	11.0	6.4	11.2	0.0
24	22.2	9.2	5.8	14.8	0.0
25	20.0	9.7	4.3	7.6	0.0
26	24.0	10.3	6.7	15.1	0.0
27	18.8	11.7	7.9	10.1	0.0
28	18.5	9.3	6.3	9.9	0.0
29	19.5	8.5	6.7	10.6	0.0
30	20.3	10.8	10.4	1.9	1.4

Sports Results

For 2003 sports fixtures, *see* pages 14–15

ALPINE SKIING

WORLD CUP 2001–2

MEN
Downhill: Stephan Eberharter (Austria), 810 points
Slalom: Ivica Kostelic (Croatia), 611 points
Giant Slalom: Frederic Covili (France), 471 points
Super Giant Slalom: Stephan Eberharter (Austria), 470 points
Overall: Stephan Eberharter (Austria), 1,702 points

WOMEN
Downhill: Isolde Kostner (Italy), 568 points
Slalom: Laure Pequegnot (France), 597 points
Giant Slalom: Sonja Nef (Switzerland), 574 points
Super Giant Slalom: Hilde Gerg (Germany), 355 points
Overall: Michaela Dorfmeister (Germany), 1,271 points

AMERICAN FOOTBALL

AFC Championship 2002: New England Patriots beat Pittsburgh Steelers 24–17
NFC Championship 2002: St Louis Rams beat Philadelphia Eagles 29–24
XXXVI American Superbowl 2002 (New Orleans, 3 February 2002): New England Patriots beat St Louis Rams 20–17

ANGLING

NATIONAL COARSE CHAMPIONSHIPS 2002

Division: 1
Individual winner: M. Evans
Team winners: Shakespeare Redditch

Division: 2
Individual winner: S. Bontoft
Team winner: Dick Clegg Mark One Sensas

Division: 3
Individual winner: R. Howe
Team winners: Dick Clegg Lifestyle VDE

Division: 4
Individual winner: J. Chapman
Team winners: Bourne AS

Division: 5
Individual winner: K. Brown
Team winners: Sensas Oundle

Ladies' Championship
Winner: Linda Cooke

ASSOCIATION FOOTBALL

LEAGUE COMPETITIONS 2001–2

ENGLAND AND WALES
Premiership
1. Arsenal, 87 points
2. Liverpool, 80 points
Relegated: Ipswich Town, 36 points; Derby County, 30 points; Leicester City, 25 points

Division 1
1. Manchester City, 99 points
2. West Bromwich Albion, 89 points
Third promotion place: Birmingham City
Relegated: Crewe Alexandra, Barnsley, Stockport County

Division 2
1. Brighton, 90 points
2. Reading, 84 points
Third promotion place: Stoke City
Relegated: Bournemouth, Bury, Wrexham, Cambridge United

Division 3
1. Plymouth Argyle, 102 points
2. Luton Town, 97 points
3. Mansfield Town, 79 points
Fourth promotion place: Cheltenham Town
Relegated: Halifax Town

Football Conference
1. Boston United, 84 points
2. Dagenham and Redbridge, 84 points
3. Yeovil, 70 points

League of Wales
1. Barry Town, 77 points
2. TNS, 70 points
3. Bangor City, 69 points

SCOTLAND
Premier Division
1. Celtic, 103 points
2. Rangers, 85 points

Division 1
1. Partick Thistle, 66 points
2. Airdrie, 56 points
Relegated: Raith Rovers, 35 points

Division 2
1. Queen of the South, 67 points
2. Alloa Athletic, 59 points
Relegated: Morton, 35 points

Division 3
1. Brechin City, 73 points
2. Dumbarton, 61 points
Bottom: Queen's Park, 35 points

REPUBLIC OF IRELAND
Irish League Championship: 1. Portadown, 75 points; 2. Glentoran, 74 points; 3. Linfield, 75 points

FRANCE
French League:
1. Lyons, 66 points; 2. Lens, 64 points; 3. Auxerre, 59 points

GERMANY
German League: 1. Borussia Dortmund, 70 points; 2. Bayer Leverkusen, 69 points; 3. Bayern Munich, 68 points

ITALY

Italian League: 1. Juventus, 71 points; 2. Roma, 70 points; 3. Inter Milan, 69 points

HOLLAND

Dutch League: 1. Ajax, 73 points; 2. PSV Eindhoven, 68 points; 3. Feyenoord, 64 points

SPAIN

Spanish League: 1. Valencia, 75 points; 2. D Coruna, 68 points; 3. Real Madrid, 66 points

CUP COMPETITIONS

ENGLAND

FA Cup final 2002: Arsenal beat Chelsea 2–0
Worthington (League) Cup final 2002: Blackburn Rovers beat Tottenham Hotspur 2–1
FA Vase final 2002: Whitley Bay beat Tiptree United 1–0
FA Trophy final 2002: Yeovil Town beat Stevenage Borough 2–0

WOMEN

Women's National Division Premier League 2001–2:
1. Arsenal, 49 points; 2. Doncaster Belles, 41 points; 3. Charlton Athletic, 31 points
Women's FA Cup final 2002: Fulham beat Doncaster Belles 2–1
Women's League Cup Final 2002: Fulham beat Birmingham City 7–1
Community Shield 2002: Arsenal beat Liverpool 1–0

WALES

FA Wales Cup final 2002: Cardiff City beat Swansea City 1–0

SCOTLAND

Scottish Cup final 2002: Rangers beat Celtic 3–2
League Cup final 2002: Rangers beat Ayr United 4–0

NORTHERN IRELAND

Irish Cup final: Glentoran beat Linfield 1–0

EUROPE

European Champions' League final 2002: Real Madrid beat Bayer Leverkusen 2–1
UEFA Cup final 2002: Feyenoord beat Borussia Dortmund 3–2
European Super Cup final 2002: Liverpool beat Bayern Munich 3–2
InterToto Cup final 2001: Aston Villa (England); Troyes Aube Champagne (France); Paris St-Germain, (France)

INTERNATIONALS

WORLD CUP 2002

GROUP STAGES

GROUP A

	P	W	D	L	F	A	GD	PTS
Denmark	3	2	1	0	5	2	3	7
Senegal	3	1	2	0	5	4	1	5
Uruguay	3	0	2	1	4	5	-1	2
France	3	0	1	2	0	3	-3	1

GROUP B

	P	W	D	L	F	A	GD	PTS
Spain	3	3	0	0	9	4	5	9
Paraguay	3	1	1	1	6	6	0	4
South Africa	3	1	1	1	5	5	0	4
Slovenia	3	0	0	3	2	7	-5	0

GROUP C

	P	W	D	L	F	A	GD	PTS
Brazil	3	3	0	0	11	3	8	9
Turkey	3	1	1	1	5	3	2	4
Costa Rica	3	1	1	1	5	6	-1	4
China	3	0	0	3	0	9	-9	0

GROUP D

	P	W	D	L	F	A	GD	PTS
South Korea	3	2	1	0	4	1	3	7
USA	3	1	1	1	5	6	-1	4
Portugal	3	1	0	2	6	4	2	3
Poland	3	1	0	2	3	7	-4	3

GROUP E

	P	W	D	L	F	A	GD	PTS
Germany	3	2	1	0	11	1	10	7
Rep. of Ireland	3	1	2	0	5	2	3	5
Cameroon	3	1	1	1	2	3	-1	4
Saudi Arabia	3	0	0	3	0	12	-12	0

GROUP F

	P	W	D	L	F	A	GD	PTS
Sweden	3	1	2	0	4	3	1	5
England	3	1	2	0	2	1	1	5
Argentina	3	1	1	1	2	2	0	4
Nigeria	3	0	1	2	1	3	-2	1

GROUP G

	P	W	D	L	F	A	GD	PTS
Mexico	3	2	1	0	4	2	2	7
Italy	3	1	1	1	4	3	1	4
Croatia	3	1	0	2	2	3	-1	3
Ecuador	3	1	0	2	2	4	-2	3

GROUP H

	P	W	D	L	F	A	GD	PTS
Japan	3	2	1	0	5	2	3	7
Belgium	3	1	2	0	6	5	1	5
Russia	3	1	0	2	4	4	0	3
Tunisia	3	0	1	2	1	5	-4	1

QUARTER-FINALS

Germany beat USA 1–0
Brazil beat England 2–1
Turkey beat Senegal 1–0 (golden goal in extra time)
South Korea beat Spain 1–1 (5–3 on penalties)

SEMI-FINALS

Brazil beat Turkey 1–0
Germany beat South Korea 1–0

3RD AND 4TH PLACE PLAY OFF

Turkey beat South Korea 3–2

FINAL

Brazil beat Germany 2–0

AFRICA

African Cup of Nations 2002 (Mali): Cameroon beat Senegal 0–0 (3–2 on penalties)

FOOTBALLER OF THE YEAR

2001 – Luis Figo (Portugal)
2000 – Zinedine Zidane (France)
1999 – Rivaldo (Brazil)
1998 – Zinedine Zidane (France)
1997 – Ronaldo (Brazil)
1996 – Ronaldo (Brazil)
1995 – George Weah (Liberia)

1994 – Romario (Brazil)
1993 – Roberto Baggio (Italy)
1992 – Marco van Basten (Netherlands)

ATHLETICS

IAAF WORLD HALF MARATHON CHAMPIONSHIPS
Bristol, Great Britain, 7 October 2001

MEN

Individual: Haile Gebreselassie (Ethiopia) 60 min. 03 sec.
Team result: Ethiopia, 3 hr. 00 min 31 sec.

WOMEN

Individual: Paula Radcliffe (GBR) 66min. 03 sec.
Team result: Kenya 3 hr. 28 min. 04 sec.

EUROPEAN CROSS-COUNTRY CHAMPIONSHIPS
Thun, Switzerland 9 December 2001

SENIOR MEN (9.15 KM)

Individual: Sergei Lebed (Ukraine) 27 min. 52 sec.
Team: Spain 40 points

SENIOR WOMEN (4.65 KM)

Individual: Yamna Belkacem (France) 15 min. 48 sec.
Team: Portugal 41 points

JUNIOR MEN (6.15 KM)

Individual: Vasili Mativchuk (Ukraine) 19 min. 29 sec.
Team: Great Britain 54 points

JUNIOR WOMEN (3.15 KM)

Individual: Elvan Abeylegesse (Turkey) 10 mins. 35 sec.
Team: Russia 35 points

AAA INDOOR CHAMPIONSHIPS
Cardiff, 2–3 February 2002

MEN

	min.	sec.
60 *metres*: Jason Gardner		6.52
(Wessex and Bath)		
200 *metres*: Doug Turner (Cardiff)		21.24
400 *metres*: Robert Daly (Ireland)		47.58
800 *metres*: James McIlroy	1	51.10
(Windsor, S & E)		
1,500 *metres*: Anthony Whiteman	3	52.44
(Shaftesbury)		
3,000 *metres*: Michael East	8	18.41
(Newham)		
60 *metres* hurdles: Colin Jackson		7.60
(Breacon)		
3,000 *metres* walk: Robert Hefferan	11	10.02
(Ireland)		

	metres
High jump: Ben Challenger (Belgrave)	2.17
Pole vault: Nick Buckfield (Crawley)	5.50
Long jump: Gable Garenamotse (Mandate)	8.01
Triple jump: Tosin Oke (Cambridge H)	15.95
Shot: Erik van Vreumingen (Netherlands)	17.38

WOMEN

	min.	sec.
60 *metres*: Joice Maduaka		7.33
(Woodford)		

	min.	sec.
200 *metres*: Amy Spencer		23.74
(Belgrave)		
400 *metres*: Catherine Murphy		52.64
(Shaftesbury)		
800 *metres*: Jenny Meadows	2	5.07
(Wigan)		
1,500 *metres*: Natalie Lewis	4	25.49
(Cardiff)		
60 *metres* hurdles: Diane Allahgreen		8.07
(Trafford)		
3,000 *metres* walk: Gillian O'Sullivan	12	17.56
(Ireland)		

	metres
High jump: Susan Jones (Trafford)	1.90
Pole vault: Janine Whitlock (Trafford)	4.20
Long jump: Kelly Sotherton (Birchfield)	6.22
Triple jump: Ashia Hansen (Birchfield)	13.53
Shot: Helena Engman (Sweden)	16.27

NATIONAL CROSS-COUNTRY CHAMPIONSHIPS
Bristol, 23 February 2002

MEN

	min.	sec.
Individual: Sam Haughian	39	26
(Windsor, Slough and Eton)		
Team: Bingley, 184 points		

WOMEN

	min.	sec.
Individual: Liz Yelling	27	6
(Bedford)		
Team: Shaftesbury Barnet, 67 points		

EUROPEAN INDOOR CHAMPIONSHIPS
Vienna, Austria 1–3 March 2002

MEN

	min.	sec.
60 *metres*: Jason Gardner (GB)		6.49
200 *metres*: Marcin Urbas (Poland)		20.64
400 *metres*: Marek Plawgo (Poland)		45.39
800 *metres*: Pawel Czapiewski (Poland)	1	44.78
1,500 *metres*: Rui Silva (Portugal)	3	49.93
3,000 *metres*: Alberto Garcia (Spain)	7	43.89
60 *metres* hurdles: Colin Jackson (GB)		7.40
4 x 400 *metres* relay: Poland	3	5.50

	metres
High jump: Steffan Strand (Sweden)	2.34
Pole vault: Tim Lobinger (Germany)	5.75
Long jump: Raul Ferenandez (Spain)	8.22
Triple jump: Christian Olsson (Sweden)	17.54
Shot: Manuel Martinez (Spain)	21.26
Heptathlon: Roman Sebrle	
(Czech Republic), 6280 points	

WOMEN

	min.	sec.
60 *metres*: Kim Gevaert (Belgium)		7.16
200 *metres*: Muriel Hurtis (France)		22.52
400 *metres*: Natalya Antyukh (Russia)		51.65
800 *metres*: Jolanda Ceplak	1	55.82
(Slovenia)		
1,500 *metres*: Yekaterina Puzanova	4	6.30
(Russia)		
3,000 *metres*: Marta Dominguez (Spain)	8	53.87
60 *metres* hurdles: Glory Alozie (Spain)		7.84
4 x 400 *metres* relay: Belarus	3	32.24

	metres
High jump: Marina Kuptsova (Russia)	2.03
Pole vault: Svetlana Feofanova (Russia)	4.75
Long jump: Niki Xanthou (Greece)	6.74
Triple jump: Tereza Marinova (Bulgaria)	14.81
Shot: Vita Pavlysh (Ukraine)	19.76
Pentathlon: Yelena Prokhorova (Russia), 4622 points	

IAAF WORLD CROSS COUNTRY CHAMPIONSHIPS

Dublin 23–24 March 2002

SENIOR MEN (12.07 KM)

	min.	sec.
Individual: Kenenisa Bekele (Ethiopia)	34	52
Team result: Kenya, 18 points		

SENIOR MEN (4.27 KM)

Individual: Kenenisa Bekele (Ethiopia)	12	11
Team result: Kenya, 20 points		

JUNIOR MEN (7.87 KM)

Individual: Gebre Gebremariam (Ethiopia)	23	18
Team result: Kenya, 18 points		

SENIOR WOMEN (7.87 KM)

Individual: Paula Radcliffe (GB)	26	55
Team result: Ethiopia 28 points		

SENIOR WOMEN (4.27 KM)

Individual: Edith Masai (Kenya)	13	30
Team result: Ethiopia 32 points		

JUNIOR WOMEN (6.07 KM)

Individual: Viola Kibiwot (Kenya)	20	13
Team result: Kenya 13 points		

LONDON MARATHON 2002

14 April 2002

	hr.	min.	sec.
Men: Khalid Khannouchi (USA)	2	5	38
Women: Paula Radcliffe (GBR)	2	18	56

IAAF GRAND PRIX FINAL

MEN

	min.	sec.
100 metres: Tim Montgomery (USA)		9.78
400 metres: Michael Blackwood (Jamaica)		44.72
1,500 metres: Hicham El Guerrouj (Morocco)	3	29.27
3,000 metres: Abraham Chebii (Kenya)	8	33.42
400 metre hurdles: Felix Sanchez (Dominica)		47.62

	metres
High Jump: Stefan Holm (Sweden)	2.31
Pole Vault: Jeff Hartwig (USA)	5.75
Triple Jump: Christian Olsson (Sweden)	17.48
Shot: Adam Nelson (USA)	21.34
Hammer: Koji Murofushi (Japan)	81.14

WOMEN

	min.	sec.
100 metres: Marion Jones (USA)		10.88
400 metres: Ana Guevara (Mexico)		49.90
1,500 metres: Yelena Zadorozhnaya (Russia)	4	0.63
3,000 metres: Gabriela Szabo (Romania)	9	56.29
100 metre hurdles: Gail Devers (USA)		12.51

	metres
Long Jump: Maureen Maggi (Brazil)	7.02
Discus: Natalya Sadova (Russia)	65.79
Javelin: Osleidys Menendez (Cuba)	65.69

Men's Overall Winner: Tim Montgomery (USA)
Women's Overall Winner: Marion Jones (USA)

BADMINTON

ENGLISH NATIONAL CHAMPIONSHIPS 2002

Burgess Hill, Bournemouth, 1–3 February 2002

Men's Singles: Colin Haughton beat Mark Constable walkover
Ladies Singles: Julia Mann beat Tracey Hallam 3–2
Men's Doubles: Anthony Clark and Nathan Robertson beat Julian Robertson and Ian Sullivan 3–1
Ladies Doubles: Gail Emms and Natalie Munt beat Ella Miles and Sara Sankey 3–2
Mixed Doubles: Nathan Robertson and Gail Emms beat Julian Robertson and Natalie Munt 3–0

SCOTTISH NATIONAL CHAMPIONSHIPS 2002

Edinburgh, February

Men's Singles: B. Flockhart beat R. Blair 2–0
Ladies' Singles: S. Hughes beat F. Sneddon 2–1
Men's Doubles: A. Gatt and C. Robertson beat R. Blair and R. Hogg 2–0
Ladies Doubles: R. Pickering and S. Watt beat K. McEwan and C. Tedman 2–0
Mixed Doubles: R. Hogg and K. McEwan beat C. Robertson and R. Pickering 2–1

ALL-ENGLAND CHAMPIONSHIPS 2002

NIA Birmingham, 5–10 March 2002

Men's Singles: Hong Chen (China) beat Budi Santoso (India) 3–0
Ladies Singles: Camila Martin (Denmark) beat Ruina Gong (China) 3–0
Men's Doubles: Ha Tae-Kwon and Kim Dong-Moon (Korea) beat Eng Hian and Flandy Limpele (England) 3–1
Ladies Doubles: Ling Gaoand Sui Huang (China) beat Yili Wei and Jiewen Zhang (China) 3–0
Mixed Doubles: Kim Dong-Moon and Ra Kyung-Min (Korea) beat Jens Eriksen and Mette Schjoldager (Denmark) 3–0

BASEBALL

American League Championship Series 2001: New York Yankees beat Seattle Mariners 4–1
National League Championship Series 2001: Arizona Diamondbacks beat Atlanta 4–1

World Series 2001: Arizona Diamondbacks beat New York Yankees 4–3

BASKETBALL

MEN

BBL Championship Final 2002: Chester Jets beat Westfield Sharks Sheffield 93–82
BBL Trophy Final 2002: Chester Jets beat Milton Keynes Lions 90–89
National Cup 2002: Chester Jets beat Pertemps Bullets Birmingham 112–105
BBL Champions 2001–2: Chester Jets 48 points

WOMEN

NBL Women's Division One Champions 2002: Sheffield Hatters beat Rhondda Rebels 74–60
National Cup Final 2002: Sheffield Hatters beat Rhondda Rebels 52–48

EUROPEAN CHAMPIONSHIPS 2001
Turkey, September
Yugoslavia beat Turkey 78–69

NORTH AMERICA – NATIONAL BASKETBALL LEAGUE (NBA)
Eastern Conference final 2002: New Jersey beat Boston 4–2 (best of 7 series)
Western Conference final 2002: Los Angeles Lakers beat Sacramento 4–3 (best of 7 series)
NBA final 2002: Los Angeles Lakers beat New Jersey Nets 4–0 (best of 7 series)

BOWLS – OUTDOOR

MEN

NATIONAL CHAMPIONSHIPS 2002
Worthing, August

Singles: Martyn Sekjer (Hampshire 'A') beat Andrew Briden (Hertfordshire 'B') 21–2
Pairs: Peter Picknell and Keith Hawes (Buckinghamshire 'A') beat Mark Stones and Grant Burgess (Worcestershire 'B') 17–13
Triples: Oxfordshire 'B' beat Nottinghamshire 'B' 25–12
Fours: Nottinghamshire 'A' beat Cornwall 'B' 25–12
Middleton Cup (Inter-County Championship) final 2002: Devon beat Essex 122–113

BOWLS – INDOOR

WORLD CHAMPIONSHIPS 2002
Belfast, April

Men's Singles: David Miller (England) beat Jeff Webley (Wales) 2–0
Women's Singles: Carol Ashby (England) beat Betty Morgan (Wales) 1.5–0.5
Mixed Pairs: Julie Forrest and Mark Johnston (Scotland) beat Alison Merrien and Alan Welch (Guernsey) 2–0

NATIONAL CHAMPIONSHIPS 2002
Melton Mowbray, April

Singles: Greg Harlow beat Neil Chandler 21–10
Pairs: Wellingborough beat City of Ely 20–15

Triples: Whiteknights beat Dorchester 21–7
Fours: Desborough beat East Dorset 20–11

BRITISH ISLES INDOOR BOWLS CHAMPIONSHIPS 2002
Singles: Jonathan Ross (Ireland) beat Mike Prosser (Wales) 21–17
Pairs: England beat Wales 20–12
Triples: Scotland beat Channel Islands 24–14
Fours: England beat Channel Islands 24–11
Liberty Trophy (Inter-County Championship) final 2002: Durham beat Devon 112–111
Champion of Champions 2001–2: David Ward (North Walsham) beat Robert Newman (whiteknights) 21–13

BOXING

PROFESSIONAL BOXING
as at 1 September 2002

WORLD BOXING COUNCIL (WBC) CHAMPIONS
Heavy: Lennox Lewis (GBR)
Cruiser: vacant
Light-heavy: Roy Jones Jnr (USA)
Super-middle: Eric Lucas (Canada)
Middle: Bernard Hopkins (USA)
Super-welter: Oscar de la Hoya (USA)
Welter: Vernon Forrest (USA)
Super-light: Kostya Tszyu (Australia)
Light: Floyd Mayweather (USA)
Super-Feather: vacant
Feather: vacant
Super-bantam: Willie Jorrin (USA)
Bantam: Veeraphol Sahaprom (Thailand)
Super-fly: Masamori Tokuyama (Japan)
Fly: Pongsaklek Wonjongkam (Thailand)
Light-fly: Jorge Arce (Mexico)
Straw: Jose Antonio Aguirre (Mexico)

WORLD BOXING ASSOCIATION (WBA) CHAMPIONS
Heavy: John Ruiz (USA)
Cruiser: Alexander Gurov (Ukraine)
Light-heavy: Roy Jones Jnr (USA)
Super-middle: Byron Mitchell (USA)
Middle: Bernard Hopkins (USA)
Super-welter: Fernando Vargas (USA)
Welter: Ricardo Mayorga (Nicaragua)
Super-light: Kostya Tszyu (Australia)
Light: Leonard Dorin (Romania)
Super-feather: Yodsanan Nanthachaitha (Thailand)
Feather: Derrick Gainer (USA)
Super-bantam: Osamu Sato (Japan)
Bantam: Johnny Bredahl (Denmark)
Super-fly: Alexander Muñoz (Venezuela)
Fly: Eric Morel (USA)
Light-fly: Rosendo Alverez (Nicaragua)
Straw: Noel Arambulet (Venezuela)

WORLD BOXING ORGANISATION (WBO) CHAMPIONS
Heavy: Wladimir Klitschko (Ukraine)
Cruiser: Johnny Nelson (England)
Light-heavy: Daruisz Michalczewski (Germany)
Super-middle: Joe Calzaghe (Wales)
Middle: Harry Simon (Namibia)
Super-welter: Daniel Santos (Puerto Rico)
Welter: Antonio Margarito (Mexico)

Super-light: Demarcus Corley (USA)
Light: Artur Grigorian (Uzbekistan)
Super-feather: Acelino Frietas (Brazil)
Feather: Julio Pablo Chacon (Argentina)
Super-bantam: Agapito Sanchez (Dominican Republic)
Bantam: Cruz Carbajal (Mexico)
Super-fly: Fernando Montiel (Mexico)
Fly: Omar Narvaez (Argentina)
Light-fly: Nelson Dieppa (Puerto Rico)
Straw: Kermin Guardia (Colombia)

INTERNATIONAL BOXING FEDERATION (IBF)
CHAMPIONS

Heavy: Lennox Lewis (GBR) (USA)
Cruiser: Vassily Jirov (Kazakhstan)
Light-heavy: Roy Jones Jnr (USA)
Super-middle: Sven Ottke (Germany)
Middle: Bernard Hopkins (USA)
Super-welter: Ronald Wright (USA)
Welter: Michele Piccirillo (Italy)
Super-light: Kostya Tszyu (Australia)
Light: Paul Spadafora (USA)
Super-feather: Steve Forbes (USA)
Feather: Johnny Tapia (USA)
Super-bantam: Many Pacquiao (Philippines)
Bantam: Tim Austin (USA)
Super-fly: Felix Machado (Venezuela)
Fly: Irene Pacheco (Colombia)
Light-fly: Ricardo Lopez (Mexico)
Straw: Miguel Barrera (Mexico)

BRITISH CHAMPIONS

Heavy: Lennox Lewis
Cruiser: Johnny Nelson
Light-heavy: Clinton Woods
Super-middle: Joe Calzaghe
Middle: Howard Eastman
Light-middle: Wayne Alexander
Welter: Jawaid Kaliq
Light-welter: Ricky Hatton
Light: Colin Dunne
Super-feather: Dean Pithie
Feather: Naseem Hamed
Super-bantam: Michael Alldis
Bantam: Noel Wilders
Fly: Damaen Kelly

CHESS

FIDE World Champion 2001–2: Ruslan Ponomariov
(Ukraine)

British Champion 2002: Ramachandran B. Ramesh

COMMONWEALTH GAMES 2002

Manchester, 25 July – 4 August 2002

ATHLETICS

MEN (Hours, Mins, Secs)
100m: Kim Collins (St Kitts/Nevis), 9.98
200m: Frankie Fredericks (Namibia), 20.06
400m: Michael Blackwood (Jamaica), 45.07
800m: Mbulaeni Malaudzi (South Africa), 1:46.32
1,500m: Michael East (England), 3:37.35
5,000m: Sammy Kipketer (Kenya), 13:13.50
10,000m: Wilberforce Talel (Kenya), 27:45.39
Marathon: Francis Naali (Tanzania), 2h 11.58

110m hurdles: Shaun Bownes (South Africa), 13.35
400m hurdles: Chris Rawlinson (England), 49.19
3,000m Steeple Chase: Stephen Cherono (Kenya), 8:19.41
20km walk: Nathan Deakes (Australia), 1h 25.35
50km walk: Nathan Deakes (Australia), 4h 52.40s
4 x 100 m relay: England, 38.62
4 x 400 m relay: England, 3:00.40

High Jump: Mark Boswell (Canada), 2.28m
Pole Vault: Okkert Brits (South Africa), 5.75m
Long Jump: Nathan Morgan (England), 8.02m
Triple Jump: Jonathan Edwards (England), 17.86m
Shot Putt: Justin Anlezark (Australia), 20.91m
Discus: Frantz Kruger (South Africa), 66.39m
Hammer: Michael Jones (England), 72.55m
Javelin: Steve Backley (England), 86.81m
Decathlon: Claston Bernard (Jamaica), 7830pts
100m Blind: Adekunle Adesoji (Nigeria), 10.76s

WOMEN (Hours, Mins, Secs)
100m: Debbie Ferguson (Bahamas), 10.91
200m: Debbie Ferguson (Bahamas), 22.20
400m: Aliann Pompey (Guyana), 51.63
800m: Maria Mutola (Mozambique), 1:57.37
1,500m: Kelly Holmes (England), 4:05.99
5,000m: Paula Radcliffe (England), 14:31.42
10,000m: Salina Koskei (Kenya), 31:27.83
Marathon: Kerryn McCann (Australia), 2h 30:05
100m hurdles: Lacena Golding-Clark (Jamaica), 12.77
400m hurdles: Jana Pittman (Australia), 54.40
20km walk: Jane Saville (Australia), 1h 36:34
4 x 100m relay: Bahamas, 42.44
4 x 400m relay: Australia, 3:25.13

High Jump: Hestrie Cloete (South Africa), 1.96m
Pole Vault: Tatiana Grigorieva (Australia), 4.35m
Long Jump: Elva Goulbourne (Jamaica), 6.70m
Triple Jump: Ashia Hansen (England), 14.86m
Shot Putt: Vivian Chukwuemeka (Nigeria), 17.53m
Discus: Beatrice Faumuina (New Zealand), 60.83m
Hammer: Lorraine Shaw (England), 66.83m
Javelin: Laverne Eve (Bahamas), 58.46m
Heptathlon: Jane Jamieson (Australia), 6,059pts
800m Wheelchair: Chantal Petitclerc (Canada), 1:52.93

BADMINTON

MEN

Singles: Muhammad Hafiz Hashim (Malaysia)
Doubles: Malaysia

WOMEN

Singles: Li Li (Singapore)
Doubles: Malaysia

MIXED

Doubles: England
Team: England

BOXING

Light-Flyweight-48kg: Mohammad Qamar (India)
Flyweight-51kg: Kennedy Kanyanta (Zambia)
Bantamweight-54kg: Justin Kane (Australia)
Featherweight-57kg: Haider Ali (Pakistan)
Lightweight-60kg: Jamie Arthur (Wales)
Light-Welterweight-63.5kg: Darren Barker (England)
Welterweight-67kg: Daniel Geale (Australia)
Light-Middleweight-71kg: Jean Pascal (Canada)
Middleweight-75kg: Paul Miller (Australia)
Light-Heavyweight-81kg: Jegbefumere Albert (Nigeria)

Heavyweight-91kg: Jason Douglas (Canada)
Super-Heavyweight-91kg: David Dolan (England)

CYCLING

MEN

Sprint: Ryan Bayley (Australia)
1,000m Time Trial: Chris Hoy (Scotland), 1: 01.726
4,000m Individual Pursuit: Bradley McGee (Australia),
 4: 16.358
4,000m Team Pursuit: Australia, 3:59.583
Points Race: Greg Henderson (New Zealand) 35pts
20km Scratch Race: Graeme Brown (Australia), 24:14.660
Team Sprint: Australia, 44.506
Road Race: Stuart O'Grady (Australia), 4h 43.17
Road Time Trial: Cadel Evans (Australia), 1h 00:53.50
Cross-Country: Roland Green (Canada), 1h 52.48

WOMEN

Sprint: Kerrie Meares (Australia)
500m Time Trial: Kerrie Meares (Australia), 35.084
3000m Individual Pursuit: Sarah Ulmer (New Zealand),
 3:32.467
Points race: Katherine Bates (Australia), 37pts
Road Race: Nicola Cooke (Wales), 2h 35:17
Road Time Trial: Clara Hughes (Canada), 34h 51:66
Cross-Country: Chrissy Redden (Canada), 1:32.10

DIVING

MEN

1m Springboard: Alexandre Despatie (Canada),
 404.55pts
3m Springboard: Alexandre Despatie (Canada),
 474.60pts
10m Highboard: Peter Waterfield (England), 502.71pts

WOMEN

1m Springboard: Irina Lashko (Australia), 302.82pts
3m Springboard: Irina Lashko (Australia) 335.79pts
10m Highboard: Loudy Tourky (Australia), 538.65pts

GYMNASTICS

MEN

All-round-Individual: Kanukai Jackson (England),
 55.025pts
All-round-Team: England, 162.075pts
Vault: Kyle Shewfelt (Canada), 9.443pts
Floor: Kyle Shewfelt (Canada), 9.637pts
Parallel Bars: Philippe Rizzo (Australia), 9.375pts
Pommel Horse: Philippe Rizzo (Australia), 9.162pts
Rings: Herodotos Giorgallas (Cyprus), 9.462pts; (Steve
 Frew) (Scotland), 9.462pts
Horizontal Bar: Philippe Rizzo (Australia), 9.512pts

WOMEN

All-round-Individual: Kate Richardson (Canada),
 36.750pts
All-round-Team: Australia, 111.325pts
Vault: Allana Slater (Australia), 9.268pts
Floor: Sarah Lauren (Australia), 9.412pts
Uneven Bars: Beth Tweddle (England), 9.550pts
Balance Beam: Kate Richardson (Canada), 9.200pts

HOCKEY

MEN Australia
WOMEN India

JUDO

MEN

Up to 60kg: Craig Fallon (England)
Up to 66kg: James Warren (England)
Up to 73kg: Thomas Hill (Australia)
Up to 81kg: Graeme Randall (Scotland)
Up to 90kg: Winston Gordon (England)
Up to 100kg: Nicolas Gill (Canada)
Over 100kg: Narani Qerewaqa (Nigeria)

WOMEN

Up to 48kg: Carolyne Lepage (Canada)
Up to 52kg: Georgina Singleton (England)
Up to 57kg: Maria Pekli (Australia)
Up to 63kg: Karen Roberts (England)
Up to 70kg: Samantha Lowe (England)
Up to 78kg: Michelle Rogers (England)
Over 78kg: Simone Callender (England)

LAWN BOWLS

MEN

Singles: Robert Donnelly (South Africa)
Pairs: Scotland
Fours: England
Triples (Handicapped): Scotland

WOMEN

Singles: Ahmad Sita Zalina (Malaysia)
Pairs: New Zealand
Fours: England
Singles(Blind): Ruth Small (England)

NETBALL

WOMEN Australia

RUGBY SEVENS

MEN New Zealand

SHOOTING

MEN

10m Air-rifle -Singles: Asif Hussain Khan (Bangladesh),
 691.9pts
10m Air Rifle-Pairs: India, 1184pts
10m Air Pistol-Singles: Michael Gault (England), 675pts
10m Air Pistol-Pairs: England, 1,140pts
25m Rapid Fire Pistol-Singles: Metodi Igorov (Canada),
 669.3pts
25m Rapid Fire Pistol-Pairs: India, 1141pts
25m Centre Fire Pistol Singles: Jaspal Rana (India),
 583pts
25m Centre Fire Pistol-Pairs: India, 1150pts
25m Standard Pistol-Singles: Jaspal Rana (India), 574pts
25m Standard Pistol-Pairs: India, 1130pts
50m Rifle 3 Positions Singles: Charan Singh (India),
 1251.5pts
50m Rifle 3 Positions-Pairs: Australia, 2297pts
50m Rifle Prone-Singles: Timothy Lowndes (Australia),
 699.8pts
50m Rifle Prone-Pairs: England, 1189pts
50m Pistol-Singles: Michael Gault (England), 657.5pts
50m Pistol-Pairs: India, 1088pts
Trap-Singles: Michael Diamond (Australia), 148pts
Trap-Pairs: Australia, 187pts
Double Trap-Singles: Rajyardhan Singh (India), 191pts
Double Trap-Pairs: India, 184pts
Skeet-Singles: Clayton Miller (Canada), 146pts
Skeet-Pairs: Cyprus, 194pts

WOMEN

10m Air-Rifle-Singles: Anjali Bhagwat (India), 500.8pts
10m Air Rifle-Pairs: India, 795pts
10m Air Pistol-Singles: Lalita Yauhleuskaya (Australia),
  479.4pts
10m Air Pistol-Pairs: Canada, 747pts
25m Sport Pistol-Singles: Lalita Yauhleuskaya (Australia),
  297pts
25m Sport Pistol-Pairs: Australia, 1150pts
50m Rifle 3 Positions Singles: Anjali Bhagwat (India),
  678pts
50m Rifle 3 Positions-Pairs: India, 1140pts
50m Rifle Prone-Singles: Kim Frazer (Australia), 588pts
50m Rifle Prone-Pairs: Wales, 1175pts
Trap-Singles: Cynthia Meyer (Canada), 95pts
Trap-Pairs: Australia, 90pts
Double Trap-Singles: Charlotte Kerwood (England),
  141pts
Double Trap-Pairs: New Zealand, 137pts
Skeet-Singles: Lauryn Ogilvie (Australia), 93pts
Skeet-Pairs: Australia, 95pts

OPEN

Full Bore Rifle-Singles: David Culvert (N Ireland),
  404.62pts
Full Bore Rifle-Pairs: Northern Ireland, 590.86pts

SQUASH

MEN
Singles: Jonathan Power (Canada)
Doubles: England

WOMEN
Singles: Sarah Fitz-Gerald (Australia)
Doubles: New Zealand
Mixed Doubles: New Zealand

SWIMMING

MEN
50m Freestyle: Roland Schoeman (South Africa), 22.33s
100m Freestyle: Ian Thorpe (Australia), 48.73s
200m Freestyle: Ian Thorpe (Australia), 1:44.71s
400m Freestyle: Ian Thorpe (Australia), 3:40.08s
1,500m Freestyle: Grant Hackett (Australia), 14:54.29s
4 x 100m Freestyle: Australia, 3:16.42s
4 x 200m Freestyle: Australia, 7:11.69s
50m Backstroke: Matt Welsh (Australia), 25.65s
100m Backstroke: Matt Welsh (Australia), 54.72s
200m Backstroke: James Goddard (England), 1:59.83s
50m Breaststroke: James Gibson (England), 27.72s
100m Breaststroke: Adam Whitehead (England), 1:01.13s
200m Breaststroke: Jim Piper (Australia), 2:13.10s
50m Butterfly: Geoff Huegill (Australia), 23.57s
100m Butterfly: Geoff Huegill (Australia), 52.36s
200m Butterfly: Justin Norris (Australia), 1:56.95s
200m Individual Medley: Justin Norris (Australia),
  2:01.32s
400m Individual Medley: Justin Norris (Australia),
  4:16.95s
4x100m medley: Australia, 3:36.05s
50m Freestyle (Disability): Ben Austin (Australia), 27.59s
100m Freestyle (Disability): Ben Austin (Australia),
  1:00.21s

WOMEN
50m Freestyle: Alison Sheppard (Scotland), 24.76s
100m Freestyle: Jodie Henry (Australia), 55.45s
200m Freestyle: Karen Pickering (England), 1:59.69s
400m Freestyle: Rebecca Cooke (England), 4:09.49s
800m Freestyle: Rebecca Cooke (England), 8:28.54s

4 x 100m Freestyle: Australia, 3:40.41s
4 x 200m Freestyle: England, 8:01.39s
50m Backstroke: Dyana Calub (Australia), 28.98s
100m Backstroke: Sarah Price (England), 1:01.06s
200m Backstroke: Sarah Price (England), 2:10.58s
50m Breaststroke: Zoe Baker (England), 30.60s
100m Breaststroke: Leisel Jones (Australia), 1:08.74s
200m Breaststroke: Leisel Jones (Australia), 2:25.93s
50m Butterfly: Petria Thomas (Australia), 26.66s
100m Butterfly: Petria Thomas (Australia), 58.57s
200m Butterfly: Petria Thomas (Australia), 2:08.40s
200m Individual Medley: Kirsty Coventry (Zimbabwe),
  2:14.53s
400m Individual Medley: Jennifer Reilly (Australia),
  4:43.59s
4 x 100m Medley: Australia, 4:03.70s
50m Freestyle (Disability): Natalie du Toit (South Africa),
  29.68s
100m Freestyle (Disability): Natalie du Toit (South
  Africa), 1:02.93s
Synchronized-Solo: Claire Carver-Dias (Canada),
  94.834pts
Synchronized-Duet: Canada, 94.417pts

TABLE TENNIS

MEN
Singles: Sagun Toriola (Nigeria)
Doubles: England
Team: England

WOMEN
Singles: Chunli Li (New Zealand)
Doubles: Singapore
Team: Singapore
Singles-Wheelchair: Sue Gilroy (England)
Mixed Doubles: Singapore

TRIATHLON

MEN Simon Whitfield (Canada), 1:51:57.94
WOMEN Carol Montgomery (Canada), 2:03:17.86

WEIGHTLIFTING

MEN

Up to 56kg
Snatch: Amirul Hamizan Ibrahim (Malaysia) 115kg
Clean and Jerk: Amirul Hamizan Ibrahim (Malaysia)
  145kg
Total: Amirul Hamizan Ibrahim (Malaysia) 260kg

Up to 62kg
Snatch: Yurik Sarkisian (Australia) 125kg
Clean and Jerk: Yurik Sarkisian (Australia) 152.5kg
Total: Yurik Sarkisian (Australia) 277.5kg

Up to 69kg
Snatch: Tiencheu Dabaya (Cameroon) 140kg
Clean and Jerk: Tiencheu Dabaya (Cameroon) 170kg
Total: Tiencheu Dabaya (Cameroon) 310kg

Up to 77kg
Snatch: Damian Brown (Australia) 147.5kg
Clean and Jerk: Satheesha Rai (India) 175kg
Total: Satheesha Rai (India) 317.5kg

Up to 85kg
Snatch: David Matam Matam (Cameroon) 155kg
Clean and Jerk: David Matam Matam (Cameroon)
  185kg
Total: David Matam Matam (Cameroon) 340kg

Up to 94kg
Snatch: Alex Karapetyn (Australia) 167.5kg
Clean and Jerk: Alex Karapetyn (Australia) 197.5kg
Total: Alex Karapetyn (Australia) 365kg

Up to 105kg
Snatch: Delroy McQueen (England) 165kg
Clean and Jerk: Delroy McQueen (England) 210kg
Total: Delroy McQueen (England) 375kg

Over 105kg
Snatch: Giles Greenwood (England) 180kg
Clean and Jerk: Nigel Avery (New Zealand) 215kg
Total: Nigel Avery (New Zealand) 390kg

Bench Press (Disability): Solomon Amarkuo
    (Nigeria)150.4kg

WOMEN

Up to 48kg
Snatch: Kunjarani Nameirakpam (India) 75kg
Clean and Jerk: Kunjarani Nameirakpam (India) 92.5kg
Total: Kunjarani Nameirakpam (India) 167.5kg

Up to 53kg
Snatch: Sanamacha Chanu (India) 82.5kg
Clean and Jerk: Sanamacha Chanu (India) 100kg
Total: Sanamacha Chanu (India) 182.5kg

Up to 58kg
Snatch: Michaela Breeze (Wales) 87.5kg
Clean and Jerk: Maryse Turcotte (Canada) 115kg
Total: Maryse Turcotte (Canada) 202.5kg

Up to 63kg
Snatch: Pascale Dorcelus (Canada) 87.5kg
Clean and Jerk: Patrima Kumari (India) 117.5kg
Total: Patrima Kumari (India) 205kg

Up to 69kg
Snatch: Madeleine Yamechi (Cameroon) 100kg
Clean and Jerk: Madeleine Yamechi (Cameroon)130kg
Total: Madeleine Yamechi (Cameroon) 230kg

Up to 75kg
Snatch: Shailaja Pujari (India) 97.5kg
Clean and Jerk: Shailaja Pujari (India) 125kg
Total: Shailaja Pujari (India) 222.5kg

Over 75kg
Snatch: Caroline Pileggi (Canada) 100kg
Clean and Jerk: Reanna Solomon (Nauru) 127.5kg
Total: Reanna Solomon (Nauru) 227.5kg

WRESTLING

Up to 55kg: Krishan Kumar (India)
Up to 60kg: Guivi Sissaouri (Canada)
Up to 66kg: Ramesh Kumar (India)
Up to 74kg: Daniel Igali (Canada)
Up to 84kg: Nicolas Ugoalah (Canada)
Up to 96kg: Dean Schmeichel (Canada)
Up to 120kg: Eric Kirschner (Canada)

CRICKET

TEST SERIES
ENGLAND V. INDIA
Mohali (3–6 December 2001): India beat England by 10
    wickets. England 238 and 235. India 469 and 5–0
Ahmedabad (11–15 December 2001): Match drawn.
    England 407 and 257. India 291 and 198–3.
Bangalore (19–23 December 2001): Match drawn.
    England 336 and 33–0. India 238.

ENGLAND V. NEW ZEALAND
Christchurch (13–16 March 2002): England beat New
    Zealand by 98 runs. England 228 and 468–6. New
    Zealand 147 and 451.

Wellington (21–25 March 2002): Match drawn. England
    280 and 293–4. New Zealand 218 and 158–4.
Auckland (30 March – 3 April 2002): New Zealand won
    by 78 runs. New Zealand 202 and 269–9 dec. England
    160–233.

ENGLAND V. SRI LANKA
Lord's (16–20 May): Match drawn. Sri Lanka 555–8 dec
    and 42–1. England 275 and 529–5 dec.
Edgbaston (30 May–3 June): England won by an innings
    and 111 runs. Sri Lanka 162 and 272. England 545.
Old Trafford (13–17 June): England won by 10 wickets.
    England 512 and 50–0. Sri Lanka 253 and 308.

ENGLAND V. INDIA
Lord's (25–29 July): England beat India by 170 runs.
    England 487 and 301; India, 221 and 397
Trent Bridge (8–12 August): Match drawn. India 357 and
    99; England 617
Headingley (22–26 August): India beat England by an
    innings and 46 runs. India, 628; England 273 and 309
Oval (5–9 September): Match drawn. England, 515 and
    114–0; India, 508

ONE-DAY INTERNATIONALS
ENGLAND V. ZIMBABWE
Harare (3 October 2001): England beat Zimbabwe by 5
    wickets. Zimbabwe 206; England 210–5.
Harare (6 October 2001): England beat Zimbabwe by 8
    wickets. Zimbabwe 195; England 196–2.
Harare (7 October 2001): England beat Zimbabwe by 4
    wickets. Zimbabwe 261–8; England 265–6.
Bulawayo (10 October 2001): England beat Zimbabwe
    by 70 runs. England 280–9; Zimbabwe 210.
Bulawayo (13 October 2001): England beat Zimbabwe
    by 7 wickets. Zimbabwe 228; England 229–3.

ENGLAND V. INDIA
Calcutta (19 January 2002): (19 January 2002): India
    beat England by 22 runs. India 281–8; England 259.
Cuttack (22 January 2002): England beat India by 16
    runs. England 250–7; India 234.
Chennai (25 January 2002): India beat England by 4
    wickets. England 217; India 221–6.
Kanpur (28 January 2002): India beat England by 8
    wickets. England 218–7; India 219–2.
New Delhi (31 January 2002): England beat India by 2
    runs. England 271–5; India 269–8.
Mumbai (3 February 2002): England beat India by 5
    runs. England 255; India 250.

ENGLAND V. NEW ZEALAND
Christchurch (13 February 2002): New Zealand beat
    England by 4 wickets. England 196; New Zealand
    198–6.
Wellington (16 February 2002): New Zealand beat
    England by 155 runs. New Zealand 244–8; England
    89.
Napier (20 February 2002): England beat New Zealand
    by 43 runs. England 244–5; New Zealand 201.
Auckland (23 February 2002): England beat New
    Zealand by 33 runs. England 193–6; New Zealand
    189.
Dunedin (26 February 2002): New Zealand beat England
    by 5 wickets. England 218–8; New Zealand 223–5.

NATWEST SERIES ONE-DAY INTERNATIONALS 2002
Trent Bridge (27 June 2002): England beat Sri Lanka by
    44 runs. England 293–6; Sri Lanka 249–9.
Lord's (29 June 2002): India beat England by 6 wickets.
    England 271–7; India 272–4.

Oval (30 June 2002): India beat Sri Lanka by 4 wickets. Sri Lanka 202–8; India 203–6.

Headingley (2 July 2002): England beat Sri Lanka by 3 wickets. Sri Lanka 240–7; England 241–7.

Durham (4 July 2002): No result. India 285–4; England 53–1.

Edgbaston (6 July 2002): India beat Sri Lanka by 4 wickets. Sri Lanka 187; India 188–6.

Old Trafford (7 July 2002): Sri Lanka beat England by 23 runs. Sri Lanka 229; England 206.

Oval (9 July 2002): England beat India by 64 runs. England 229–8; India 165.

Bristol (11 July 2002): India beat Sri Lanka by 63 runs. India 304; Sri Lanka 241.

Final Lord's (13 July 2002): India beat England by 2 wickets. England 325–5; India 326–8.

OTHER INTERNATIONAL DOMESTIC CHAMPIONSHIPS

Australia: Pura Cup 2001–2: Queensland beat Tasmania by 235 runs. Queensland 302 and 368. Tasmania 141 and 294.

India: Irani Trophy 2001–2: Rest of India beat Baroda by 6 wickets. Baroda 318 and 285. Rest of India 331 and 273–4. Ranji Trophy 2001–2: Railways beat Baroda by 277 runs. Railways 253 and 306. Baroda 169 and 113. Duleep Trophy 2001–2: South Zone beat North Zone by 47 runs. Deodhar Trophy 2001–2: South Zone beat North Zone by 47 runs. NKP Salve Challenger Trophy 2001–2: India 'A' beat India by 8 wickets. India 154. India 'A' 157–2.

New Zealand: State Max 2001–2: Wellington beat Auckland by 8 runs. Wellington 98 and 85. Auckland 74 and 101; State Championship: Auckland 39pts, Wellington 36 pts, Central Districts 32 pts; State Shield: Wellington 38 pts, Northern Districts 35 pts, Canterbury 25 pts.

Pakistan: One Day Tournament, 2001–2: Pakistan International Airlines beat Habib Bank Ltd by 6 runs. Pakistan International Airlines 236; Habib Bank Ltd 230; Patrons Trophy 2001–2: National Bank of Pakistan beat Sui Gas Corporation of Pakistan by 153 runs. National Bank of Pakistan 263 and 256. Sui Gas 227 and 139. Quaid-e-Azam Trophy 2001–2: Karachi Cricket Association beat Peshawar Cricket Association by 8 wickets. Peshawar 158 and 354. Karachi 260 and 254–2

South Africa: Standard Bank Cup 2001–2: KwaZulu Natal beat Western Province by 28 runs. KwaZulu Natal 223; Western Province 195.

West Indies: Busta International Shield 2001–2: Guyana beat Jamaica on 1st innings. Jamaica 277 and 269; Guyana 354 and 99–3. Red Strip Bowl: Guyana beat Barbados by 6 wickets. Barbados 221; Guyana 223–4

Zimbabwe: Logan Cup 2001–2: Mashonaland, 86 points

OTHER RESULTS 2002

Benson and Hedges Cup final: Warwickshire beat Essex by 5 wickets. Essex 181–8. Warwickshire 182–5.

C & G Trophy final: Yorkshire beat Somerset by 6 wickets. Somerset, 256; Yorkshire, 260

County Championship Cricket 2002: Division 1, Surrey, 242.75 points; *Relegated*, Hampshire, 131 points; Somerset, 126.75 points; Yorkshire, 124.75 points

Division 2, Promoted Essex, 219 points; Middlesex, 211.75 points; Nottinghamshire, 201.75 points

Norwich Union League, Division 1, Glamorgan Dragons, 50 points; *Relegated*, Somerset Sabres, 22 points; Durham Dynamos, 20 points; Nottinghamshire Outlaws, 16 points

Division 2, Promoted, Gloucestershire Gladiators, 44 points; Surrey Lions, 42 points; Essex Eagles, 40 points

Varsity Match (one-day): Oxford beat Cambridge by 37 runs. Oxford 322–7; Cambridge 285.

Varsity Match (three-day): Oxford drew with Cambridge. Cambridge 604; Oxford 224 and 388

CURLING

EUROPEAN CHAMPIONSHIPS 2001
Vierumäki, Finland, December

MEN
Sweden beat Switzerland 5–4

WOMEN
Sweden beat Denmark 7–3

WORLD CHAMPIONSHIPS 2002
Bismark, North Dakota, USA, April

MEN
Canada beat Norway 10–5

WOMEN
Scotland beat Sweden 6–5

CYCLING

WORLD ROAD CYCLING CHAMPIONSHIPS 2001
LISBON

MEN
Elite Time trial (38.7 km): Jan Ullrich (Germany) 51:49.99

Road race (254.1 km): Oscar Freire Gomez (Spain) 6 hr 07.21

WOMEN
Elite Time trial (19.2km): J. Longo-Ciprelli (France) 29:08.55

Road race (121.0km): Rasa Polilcericiute (Lithuania) 3hr 12.05

Tour of Italy 2002: Gilberto Simoni
Tour de France 2002: Lance Armstrong
Tour of Spain 2002: See Stop Press

UCI RANKINGS 2002
1. Erik Zabel (Germany)
2. Paolo Bettini (Italy)
3. Lance Armstrong (USA)

WORLD TRACK CHAMPIONSHIPS 2001
October, Antwerp

MEN

1km Time Trial: Arnaud Tournant (France) 1:02.571
Individual pursuit: Alexandre Symonenko (Ukraine)
Keiren: Ryan Bayley (Australia) 11.030
Madison: (60km) France (Jérôme Neuville, Robert Sassone) 5 points
Olympic sprint: France (Laurent Gané), Florian Rousseau, Arnaud Tournant) 44.889
Points race: Bruno Risi (Switzerland) 29 points
Sprint: Arnaud Tournant (France) Run 1 10.892; Run 2 10.572
Team pursuit: Ukraine (Sergiy Chernyavsky, Olexandr Fedenko, Alexandre Symonenko) 4:09.699

WOMEN

500m Time Trial: Nancy Contreras Reyes (Mexico) 34.996
Individual pursuit: L. Zijlaard-Van Moorsel (Netherlands) 3:34.505
Points race: (24km) Olga Slioussareva (Russia) 21 points
Sprint: Svetlana Grankovskaia (Russia) Run 1 13.000; Run 2 12.615

DARTS

Embassy World Championship 2002: Tony David (Australia) beat Mervyn King (England) 6–4

EQUESTRIANISM

Badminton Horse Trials 2002: Pippa Funnell on Supreme Rock
British Open Horse Trials 2002 (Gatcombe Park): CIC Cross Country: Andrew Nicholson on Mallard's Treat; CIC Dressage: Pippa Funnell on Pridmore's Pride
Burghley Horse Trials 2002: William Fox-Pitt (Great Britain) on Highland Lad

ETON FIVES

Amateur Championship (Kinnaird Cup) 2002: R. A. Mason and T. G. Dunbar beat Ed Wass and Jamie Halstead 3–1
Alan Barber Cup final 2002: Old Olavians beat Old Cholmeleians 3–0
County Championship final 2002: Warwickshire beat Suffolk 3–0
League Championship (Douglas Keeble Cup) 2002: Old Olavians
Holmwoods Schools' Championship 2002: Highgate I (A. S. Varma and O. D. Rodwell) beat Shrewsbury I (H. P. D. Clive and J. N. Attree) 3–1
Holmwoods Preparatory Schools' Tournament 2002: Highgate I (P. Yiannakas and R. Desmond) beat Highgate II (T. Green and S. Ball) 2–0

FENCING

MEN

WORLD CHAMPIONSHIPS 2001
Individual Foil: Ralf Bissdorf (Germany)
Team Foil: Hungary
Individual Epée: Jorg Fiedler (Germany)
Team Epée: Hungary
Individual Sabre: Mihai Covaliu (Romania)
Team Sabre: Russia

BRITISH CHAMPIONSHIPS 2002
Foil: James Beevers (Cyrano)
Epée: Quentin Berriman (U/A)
Sabre: David Sach (LTFC)

Corble Cup 2002 (International Sabre World Cup Series): Christian Kraus (Germany)

WOMEN

WORLD CHAMPIONSHIPS 2001
Individual Foil: Valentina Vezzali (Italy)
Team Foil: Italy

Individual Epée: Timea Nagy (Hungary)
Team Epée: Russia
Individual Sabre: Anne-Lise Touya (France)
Team Sabre: Russia

BRITISH CHAMPIONSHIPS 2002
Foil: Camille Datoo (Salle Paul)
Epée: Georgina Usher (LTFC)
Sabre: Louise Bond-Williams (U/A)

Ipswich Cup 2002 (International Epée World Cup Series): Maureen Nisima (France)

GOLF (Men)

THE MAJOR CHAMPIONSHIPS 2002
US Masters (Augusta, Georgia, 8–14 April): Tiger Woods (USA), 276
US Open (Farmingdale, New York, 13–16 June): Tiger Woods (USA), 277
The Open (Muirfield, 18–21 July): Ernie Els (South Africa), 278
US PGA Championship (Hazeltine, Minnesota, 12–18 August): Richard Beem (USA), 278

WORLD RANKINGS (as at 1 September 2002)
1. Tiger Woods (USA); 2. Phil Mickelson (USA); 3. Ernie Els (South Africa); 4. Retief Goosen (South Africa); 5. Sergio Garcia (Spain)

EUROPEAN TOUR ORDER OF MERIT 2002:
1. Ernie Els (South Africa); 2. Retief Goosen (South Africa); 3. Padraig Harrington (Ireland); 4. Sergio Garcia (Spain); 5. Justin Rose (England)

PGA EUROPEAN TOUR 2001–2
Linde German Masters (Cologne, Germany): Bernhard Langer (Germany), 266
Cisco World Match Play Championship (Wentworth, England): Ian Woosnam (GB)
Cannes Open (Cannes, France): Jorge Berendt (Argentina), 268
Alfred Dunhill Link Championship (St Andrews, Scotland): Paul Lawrie (Scotland), 270
Telefonica Open de Madrid (Madrid, Spain): Retief Goosen (South Africa), 264
Atlanet Italian Open (Sardinia, Italy): Gregory Havret (France), 268
Volvo Masters Andalucia (Jerez, Spain): Padraig Harrington (Ireland), 204
WGC EMC World Cup (Gotemba, Japan): South Africa (Ernie Els, Retief Goosen), 264
BMW Asian Open (Ta Shee, Taiwan): Jarmo Sandelin (Sweden), 278
Omega Hong Kong Open (Hong Kong): José Maria Olazábal (Spain), 262
Bell's South African Open (Durban, South Africa): Tim Clark (South Africa), 269
Alfred Dunhill Championship (Johannesburg, South Africa): Justin Rose (England), 268
Johnnie Walker Classic (Perth, Australia): Retief Goosen (South Africa), 274
Heineken Classic (Victoria, Australia): Ernie Els (South Africa), 271
The ANZ Championship (Sydney, Australia): Richard Johnson (Sweden), 46
WGC Accenture Match Play (Carlsbad, USA): Kevin Sutherland (USA), 62
Caltex Singapore Masters (Singapore): Arjun Atwal (India), 274

Carlsberg Malaysian Open (Kuala): Alastair Forsyth (Scotland), 267

Dubai Desert Classics (Dubai): Ernie Els (South Africa), 272

Qatar Masters (Qatar): Adam Scott (Australia), 269

Madeira Island Open (Santo de Serra, Madeira): Diego Borrego, 281

Algarve Open de Portugal (Algarve, Portugal): Carl Pettersson (Sweden), 142

The US Masters Tournament (Augusta, Georgia): Tiger Woods, 276

The Seve Trophy (Wicklow, Ireland): Great Britain and Ireland, 14.5–11.5

Canarias Open de España (Canarias, Spain): Sergio Garcia (Spain), 275

Novotel Perrier Open de France (Paris, France): Malcolm Mackenzie (England), 274

Benson and Hedges International Open (Belfry, England): Angel Cabrera (Argentina), 278

SAP Open TPC of Europe (Heidelberg, Germany): Tiger Woods (USA), 268

Volvo PGA Championship (Surrey, England): Anders Hansen (Denmark), 269

Victor Chandler British Masters (Woburn, England): Justin Rose (England), 269

The Compass Group English Open (Warwickshire, England): Darren Clarke (Northern Ireland), 271

US Open Championship (Farmingdale, New York): Tiger Woods (USA), 277

Great North Open (Northumberland, England): Miles Tunnicliff (England), 279

Murphy's Irish Open (Cork, Ireland): Soren Hansen (Denmark), 270

Smurfit European Open (Dublin, Ireland): Michael Campbell (New Zealand), 282

The Barclays Scottish Open (Glasgow, Scotland): Eduardo Romero (Argentina), 273

131st Open Golf Championship (East Lothian, Scotland): Ernie Els (South Africa), 278

TNT Dutch Open (Hilversum, Netherlands): Tobias Dier (Germany), 263

Volvo Scandinavian Masters (Stockholm, Sweden): Graeme McDowell (Northern Ireland), 270

The Celtic Manor Resort Wales Open (Newport, Wales): Paul Lawrie (Scotland), 272

US PGA Championship (Chaska, USA): Richard Beem (USA), 278

North West of Ireland Open (Co. Donegal, Ireland): Adam Mednick (Sweden), 281

WGC NEC Invitation (Redmond, USA): Craig Parry (Australia), 268

Diageo Scottish PGA Championship (Gleneagles, Scotland): Adam Scott (Australia), 262

BMW International Open (Munich, Germany): Thomas Björn, 264

Omega European Masters (Switzerland): Robert Karlsson (Sweden), 270

Linde German Masters (Cologne, Germany): Stephen Leaney (Australia), 266

WGC American Express Championship (Kilkenny, Ireland): Tiger Woods (USA), 263

The 34th Ryder Cup Matches (The Belfry, England): *See* Stop Press

AMATEUR CHAMPIONSHIPS

British Amateur Championship 2002 (Royal Porthcawl/Pyle and Kenfig): Alejandro Larrazabal

English Amateur Championship 2002 (Walton Heath): Richard Finch

Welsh Amateur Championship 2002 (Conwy): David Price

Scottish Amateur Championship 2002 (Western Gailes): Andrew McArthur

Brabazon Trophy (English Open Strokeplay) 2002 (Royal Cinque Ports): Charl Schwartzel, 282

Welsh Open Strokeplay 2002 (Pyle and Kenfig): J. Doherty, 282

Scottish Open Strokeplay 2002 (Southerness): Barry Hume (Haggs Castle Golf Club), 277

Irish Open Amateur Championship 2002 (Royal Dublin): L. Oosthuizen, 283

Lytham Trophy 2002 (Royal Lytham Golf Club): Lee Corfield, 283

Berkshire Trophy 2002 (The Berkshire): Gary Wolstenholme, 267

Irish Amateur Championship 2002 (Carlow): J. Kehoe, 137

Home International Championship 2002 (Royal St Davids): Wales

GOLF (Women)

EUROPEAN TOUR ORDER OF MERIT 2001:
1. Raquel Carriedo (Spain); 2. Suzann Pettersen (Norway); 3. Karine Icher (France); 4. Marine Monnet (France); 5. Sophie Gustafson (Sweden)

EUROPEAN LPGA TOUR 2001–2

Mexx Sport Open (Kennemer): Katrine Icher (France), 212

WPGA International Matchplay (Gleneagles, Scotland): Laura Davies (England)

Biarritz Ladies Classic (Biarritz Le Phare): Rachel Kirkwood (England), 202

ANZ Ladies Masters (Gold Coast, Queensland): Annika Sörenstam (Sweden), 278

AAMI Women's Australian Open (Melbourne, Australia): Karrie Webb (Australian), 278

Tenerife Open (San Miguel de Abona, Tenerife): Raquel Carriedo (Spain), 292

Ladies Irish Open (Kerry, Ireland): Iben Tinning (Denmark), 214

La Perla Italian Open (Florence, Italy): Iben Tinning (Denmark), 278

Ladies Open of Costa Azul (Lisbon, Portugal): Kanna Takanashi (Japan), 139

Caja Duero Open de España Femenino (Salamanca, Spain): Karine Icher (France), 277

Evian Masters (Evian Les Bains, France): Annika Sörenstam (Sweden), 269

Open de France Dames Credit Mutuel Nord (Anzin, St. Aubin) Lynnette Brooky (New Zealand), 272

Ladies Norwegian Open (Oslo, Norway): Laura Davies (England), 283

Weetabix Women's British Open (Ayrshire, Scotland): Karrie Webb (Australia), 273

Compaq Open (Helsingborg, Sweden): Annika Sörenstam (Sweden), 271

WPGA Championships of Europe (Bridgend, Wales): Asa Gottmo (Sweden), 285

AMATEUR CHAMPIONSHIPS

British Open Championship 2002 (Ashburnham Golf Club, Wales): Rebecca Hudson (Wheatley), won by 5/4 in final

Scottish Strokeplay Championship 2002 (Troon): Heather Stirling

Scottish Ladies Amateur Championship 2002: Heather
  Stirling
English Amateur Championship 2002 (Littlestone Golf
  Club): Kerry Knowles
English Strokeplay 2002 (Whittington Heath Golf Club):
  Danielle Masters
European Amateur Team Championship 2002
  (Kristianstad, Sweden): Wales

GREYHOUND RACING

2001
Laurels (Belle Vue): Pack Them In
The Derby (Milton Keynes): Whitefort Jim
Oaks (Wimbledon): Talktothehand
St Leger (Wimbledon): Frisby Folly
Television Trophy (Wimbledon): Killeacle Phoebe

2002
Grand National (Wimbledon): Ballyvorda Class
William Hill Derby (Wimbledon): Allen Gift
Derby (Peterborough): Letter Slippy
Kent Derby (Sittingbourne): Willie Go Fa
Ladbroke Golden Jacket (Crayford): Sundar Storm
The Masters (Reading): Aranock Lance
Pall Mall (Oxford): Windgap Java
The Regency (Hove): Dunbarton Cross
Scurry Gold Cup (Catford): Letter Slippy
Select Stakes (Nottingham): Droopys Rhys
Summer Cup (Milton Keynes): Frisby Fassan

GYMNASTICS

British Women's Championships 2002
Guildford, July

British Champion: Elizabeth Tweddle (City of Liverpool)
Individual Apparatus Champions
  Floor: Nicola Willis (South Essex)
  Beam: Elizabeth Tweddle (City of Liverpool)
  Vault: Katy Lennon (Leatherhead and Dorking)
  Assymetric Bars: Elizabeth Tweddle (City of
  Liverpool)

HOCKEY

MEN

English Hockey League 2002: Premier Division: Reading
  49 points; Division One, St Albans 43 points;
  Division Two, Belper 58 points
English Hockey League Premiership final 2002: Reading
  beat Surbiton 3–2
English Hockey League Indoor Championship final 2002:
  Guildford beat Loughborough Students 4–3
County Championship final 2002: Derbyshire beat Essex
  2–2 (3–1 on strokes)

WOMEN

English Hockey League 2002: Premier Division, Slough 39
  points; Division One, Trojans 37 points; Division
  Two, Reading 41 points
English Hockey League Premiership final 2002: Olton and
  WW beat Slough 3–1
English Hockey League Indoor Championship final 2002:
  Slough beat Clifton 6–3

HORSE-RACING

THE CLASSICS
ONE THOUSAND GUINEAS

(1814) Rowley Mile, Newmarket, for three-year-old fillies

Year	Winner	Betting	Owner	Jockey	Trainer	No. of Runners
1998	Cape Verdi	100–30	Godolphin	F. Dettori	Saeed bin Suroor	16
1999	Wince	4–1	Prince K. Abdulla	K. Fallon	H. Cecil	22
2000	Lahan	14–1	Hamdan Al Maktoum	R. Hills	J. Gosden	18
2001	Ameerat	11–1	Sheikh Ahmed Al Maktoum	P. Robinson	M. A. Jarvis	15
2002	Kazzia	14–1	Godolphin	F. Dettori	Saeed bin Suroor	17

TWO THOUSAND GUINEAS

(1809) Rowley Mile, Newmarket, for three-year-olds

Year	Winner	Betting	Owner	Jockey	Trainer	No. of Runners
1998	King of Kings	7–2	Mrs J. Magnier/M. Tabor	M. Kinane	A. O'Brien	18
1999	Island Sands	10–1	Godolphin	F. Dettori	Saeed bin Suroor	16
2000	King's Best	13–2	Saeed Suhail	K. Fallon	Sir Michael Stoute	27
2001	Golan	11–1	Lord Weinstock	K. Fallon	Sir Michael Stoute	18
2002	Rock of Gibraltar	9–1	Sir Alex Ferguson	J. Murtagh	A. O'Brien	22

THE DERBY

(1780) Epsom, 1 mile and about 4 f, for three-year-olds

The first winner was Sir Charles Bunbury's Diomed in 1780. The owners with the record number of winners are Lord Egremont, who won in 1782, 1804, 1805, 1807, 1826 (also won five Oaks); and the late Aga Khan, who won in 1930, 1935, 1936, 1948, 1952. Other winning owners are: Duke of Grafton (1802, 1809, 1810, 1815); Mr J. Bowes (1835, 1843, 1852, 1853); Sir J. Hawley (1851, 1858, 1859, 1868); the 1st Duke of Westminster (1880, 1882, 1886, 1899); and Sir Victor Sassoon (1953, 1957, 1958, 1960).

The Derby was run at Newmarket in 1915–18 and 1940–5.

Year	Winner	Betting	Owner	Jockey	Trainer	No. of Runners
1998	High Rise	20–1	Sheikh Mohammed Obaidh Al Maktoum	O. Peslier	L. Cumani	15
1999	Oath	13–2	Prince Ahmed Salman	K. Fallon	H. Cecil	16
2000	Sinndar	7–1	Aga Khan	J. Murtahg	J. Oxx	8
2001	Galileo	11–4	Mrs. John Magnier	M. Kinane	A. O'Brien	12
2002	High Chaparral	7–2	Michael Tabor	J. Murtagh	A. O'Brien	12

THE OAKS

(1779) Epsom, 1 mile and about 4 f, for three-year-old fillies

Year	Winner	Betting	Owner	Jockey	Trainer	No. of Runners
1997	Reams of Verse	5–6	Prince K. Abdulla	K. Fallon	H. Cecil	12
1998	Shahtoush	12–1	Mrs D. Nagle/Mrs J. Magnier	M. Kinane	A. O'Brien	8
1999	Ramruma	3–1	Prince Fahd Salman	K. Fallon	H. Cecil	10
2000	Love Divine	9–4	Lordship Stud	T. Quinn	H. Cecil	18
2001	Imagine	3–1	Mrs. John Magnier	M. Kinane	–	12
2002	Kazzia	100–30	Godolphin	F. Dettori	S. bin Suroor	14

ST LEGER

(1776) Doncaster, 1 mile and about 6 f, for three-year-olds

Year	Winner	Betting	Owner	Jockey	Trainer	No. of Runners
1997	Silver Patriarch	5–4	P. Winfield	P. Eddery	J. Dunlop	10
1998	Nedawi	5–2	Godolphin	J. Reid	Saeed bin Suroor	9
1999	Mutafaweq	11–2	Godolphin	R. Hills	Saeed bin Suroor	9
2000	Goggles	14–1	Mrs J. Powell	C. Rutter	H. Candy	22
2001	Milan	13–8	–	M. Kinane	A. O'Brien	–
2002	Bollin Eric	7–1	Sir Neil and Lady Westbrook	K. Darley	T. Easterby	8

RESULTS

CAMBRIDGESHIRE HANDICAP
(1839) Newmarket, 1 mile

1998   Lear Spear (3y), N. Pollard
1999   She's Our Mare (6y), F. Norton
2000   Katy Nowaitee (4y), J. Reid
2001   I Cried For You (6y), M. Fenton

PRIX DE L'ARC DE TRIOMPHE
(1920) Longchamp, 1½ miles

1998   Sagamix (3y), O. Peslier
1999   Montjeu (3y), M. Kinane
2000   Sinndar (3y), J. P. Murtagh
2001   Sakhee (4y), F. Dettori

CESAREWITCH
(1839) Newmarket, 2 miles and about 2 f

1998   Spirit of Love (3y), O. Peslier
1999   Top Cees (9y), K. Fallon
2000   Heros Fatal (6y), G. Carter
2001   Distant Prospect, M. Dwyer

CHAMPION STAKES
(1877) Newmarket, 1 mile, 2 f

1998   Alborada (3y), G. Duffield
1999   Alborada (4y), G. Duffield
2000   Kalanisi (5y), J. Murtagh
2001   Nayef (3y), R. Hills

*HENNESSY GOLD CUP
(1957) Newbury, 3 miles and about 2½ f

1998   Teeton Mill (9y), N. Williamson
1999   Ever Bless (6y), T. J. Murphy
2000   Kings Road (8y) J. Goldstein
2001   What's Up Boys, P. Flynn

*KING GEORGE VI CHASE
(1937) Kempton, about 3 miles

1998   Teeton Mill (9y), N. Williamson
1999   See More Business (9y), M. A. Fitzgerald
2000   First Gold, T. Dounan
2001   Florida Pearl (9y), A. Maguire

*DUBAI WORLD CUP
(1957) Dubai, 1 mile and 2 f

2000   Dubai Millennium (4y), L. Dettori
2001   Captain Steve (4y), J. D. Bailey
2002   Street Cry (4y), J. D. Bailey

*CHAMPION HURDLE
(1927) Cheltenham, 2 miles and about ½ f

1999   Istabraq (7y), C. Swan
2000   Istabraq (8y), C. Swan
2001   cancelled due to foot and mouth crisis
2002   Hors La Loi III (7y), D Gallagher

*QUEEN MOTHER CHAMPION CHASE
(1959) Cheltenham, about 2 miles

1999   Call Equiname (9y), M. Fitzgerald
2000   Edredon Bleu (8y), A. P. McCoy
2001   cancelled due to foot and mouth crisis
2002   Flagship Uberalles, R. Johnson

*CHELTENHAM GOLD CUP
(1924) 3 miles and about 2½ f

1999   See More Business (9y), M. Fitzgerald
2000   Looks Like Trouble (8y), R. Johnson

2001   cancelled due to foot and mouth crisis
2002   Best Mate, J. Culloty

LINCOLN HANDICAP
(1965) Doncaster, 1 mile

1999   Right Wing (5y), T. Quinn
2000   John Ferneley (5y), F. Fortune
2001   Nimello (5y), J. Fortune
2002   Nimello (6y), J. Fortune

*GRAND NATIONAL
(1837) Liverpool, 4 miles and about 4 f

1999   Bobbyjo (9y), P. Carberry
2000   Papillon (9y), R. Walsh
2001   Red Marauder (11y), R. Guest
2002   Bindaree (8y), J. Culloty

ATTHERACES GOLD CUP
(*known as Whitbread Gold Cup until 2002)
(1957) Sandown, 3 miles and about 5 f

1999   Eulogy (9y), B. Fenton
2000   Beau (7yr), C. Llewellyn
2001   Ad hoc, (7y), R. Walsh
2002   Bounce Back, A. P. McCoy

JOCKEY CLUB STAKES
(1894) Newmarket, 2 miles, 24 yds

1998   Romanov (4y), J. Reid
1999   Rainbow High (4y), M. Hills
2000   Millenary (4y), P. Eddery
2002   Marienbard , J. Spencer

PRIX DU JOCKEY CLUB
(1836) Chantilly, 1½ miles

1999   Montjeu, C. Asmussen
2000   Volvoreta, T. Thulliez
2001   Anaba Blue, C. Soumillion
2002   Sulamani, T. Thulliez

ASCOT GOLD CUP
(1807) Ascot, 2 miles and about 4 f

1999   Enzeili (4y), J. Murtagh
2000   Kayf Tara (6y), M. J. Kinane
2001   Royal Rebel (5y), J. P. Murtagh
2002   Royal Rebel (6y), J. P. Murtagh

IRISH DERBY
(1866) Curragh, 1½ miles, for three-year-olds

1999   Montjeu, C. Asmussen
2000   Sinndar, J. P. Murrtagh
2001   Galileo, (3y), M. Kinane
2002   High Chaparral, M. Kinane

ECLIPSE STAKES
(1886) Sandown, 1 mile and about 2 f

1998   Daylami (4y), F. Dettori
1999   Compton Admiral (3y), D. Holland
2000   Giant's Causeway (3y), G. Duffield
2001   Medicean, K. Fallon
2002   Hawk Wing (3y), M. J. Kinane

KING GEORGE VI AND QUEEN ELIZABETH DIAMOND STAKES
(1952) Ascot, 1 mile and about 4 f

1998   Swain (6y), L. Dettori
1999   Daylami (5y), L. Dettori
2000   Montjeu (4yr), M. J. Kinane
2001   Galileo (3y), M. J. Kinane
2002   Golan, K. Fallon

GOODWOOD CUP

(1812) Goodwood, about 2 miles

1998   Double Trigger (7y), D. Holland
1999   Kayf Tara (5y), L. Dettori
2000   Royal Rebel (4y), M. J. Kinane
2001   Persian Punch (8y), T. Quinn
2002   Jardines Lookout (5y), M. J. Kinane
*National Hunt

STATISTICS

WINNING FLAT OWNERS 2001

Godolphin	£1,852,815
Hamdan Al-Maktoum	1,701,829
Mrs J. Magnier and M. Tabor	1,437,622
M. Tabor and Mrs J. Magnier	1,261,533
K. Abdulla	985,925
Maktoum Al Maktoum	829,835
Cheveley Park Stud	719,046
Sheikh Mohammed	533,712
Lord Weinstock	478,610
Sheikh Ahmed Al Maktoum	399,283

WINNING FLAT TRAINERS 2001

A. P. O'Brien (Ireland)	£3,245,024
Sir Michael Stoute	1,967,583
Saeed bin Suroor	1,852,815
M. Johnston	1,731,836
B. W. Hills	1,459,810
R. Hannon	1,314,464
J. L. Dunlop	1,227,210
M. P. Tregoning	957,202
M. R. Channon	853,140
E. A. L. Dunlop	812,068

WINNING FLAT SIRES 2001

	Races won	Stakes
Sadler's Wells by Northern Dancer	48	£2,716,201
Danehill by Danzig	50	1,292,099
Machiavellian by Mr Prospector	40	1,058,216
Indian Ridge by Ahonoora	66	958,632
Rahy by Blushing Groom	7	623,220
Grand Lodge by Chief's Crown	32	622,641
Inchinor by Ahonoora	46	610,998
Selkirk by Sharpen Up	51	563,536
Rainbow Quest by Blushing Groom	36	546,894
Spectrum by Rainbow Quest	19	524,042

WINNING FLAT JOCKEYS 2001

	1st	2nd	3rd	Unpl.	Total mts
K. Fallon	166	127	112	583	988
K. Darley	162	121	115	587	985
P. Eddery	121	82	77	513	793
T. Quinn	116	125	87	449	777
J. P. Spencer	112	90	62	437	701
D. Holland	105	66	72	386	629
G. Duffield	95	60	70	553	778
L. Dettori	94	64	44	197	399
R. Hughes	90	60	70	364	584
S. Sanders	83	74	51	453	661

WINNING NATIONAL HUNT TRAINERS 2001–2

M. C. Pipe	£2,611,385
P. F. Nicholls	1,366,434
P. J. Hobbs	1,284,735
J. J. O'Neill	948,394
Miss H. C. Knight	778,749
N. J. Henderson	773,387
N. A. Twiston-Davies	578,932
Miss V. Williams	564,135
Mrs M. Reveley	509,338
Ferdy Murphy	467,756

WINNING NATIONAL HUNT JOCKEYS 2001–2

	1st	2nd	3rd	Unpl.	Total mts
A. P. McCoy	289	185	132	400	1006
R. Johnson	132	100	87	284	603
M. A. Fitzgerald	109	83	49	323	564
A. Dobbin	109	54	61	313	537
T. J. Murphy	98	67	65	294	524
N. Williamson	82	55	47	230	414
G. Lee	58	54	50	277	439
R. Thornton	56	61	55	373	545
A. Thornton	54	63	59	306	482
A. Maguire	53	62	55	316	486

The above statistics have been provided by Timeform, publishers of the Racehorses and Chasers and Hurdlers annuals

ICE HOCKEY

World Championships 2002: Slovakia beat Russia 4–3

NATIONAL HOCKEY LEAGUE
Eastern Conference final 2002: Carolina Hurricanes beat Toronto Maple Leafs 4–2
Western Conference final 2002: Detroit Red Wings beat Colorado Avalanche 4–3
Stanley Cup final 2002: Detroit Red Wings
Super League Champions 2002: Sheffield Steelers

ICE SKATING

BRITISH FIGURE SKATING CHAMPIONSHIPS 2001
Basingstoke, England, December

Men: Elliot Hilton
Women: Rebecca Collett
Pairs: Hollie Deller and Damon Latimer
Ice Dance: Stefanie Walker and Jamie Whyte

EUROPEAN CHAMPIONSHIPS 2002
Lausanne, France

Men: Alexei Yagudin (Russia)
Women: Maria Butyrskaya (Russia)
Pairs: Tatiana Totmianina and Maxim Marinin (Russia)
Ice Dance: Marina Anissina and Gwendal Peizerat (France)

WORLD CHAMPIONSHIPS 2002
March

Men: Alexei Yagudin (Russia)
Women: Irina Slutskaya (Russia)
Pairs: Xue Shen and Hongbo Zhao (China)
Ice Dance: Irina Lobacheva and Ilia Averbukh (Russia)

JUDO

BRITISH OPEN CHAMPIONSHIPS 2002
April 20–21 2002

MEN

Heavyweight (over 100 kg): Ernesto Perez (ESP)
Light-heavyweight (100 kg): Henry Hubert (GER)
Middleweight (90 kg): Sven Helbing (GER)
Welter (81 kg): Oscar Fernandez (ESP)
Lightweight (73 kg): Ryan Reser (USA)
Junior lightweight (66 kg): Jozef Krnac (SLO)
Bantamweight (60 kg): Craig Fallon (GBR)

WOMEN

Heavyweight (over 78 kg): Elodie Belquart (France)
Light-heavyweight (78 kg): Sandra Borderieux (France)
Middleweight (70 kg): Samantha Lowe (GBR)
Welter (63 kg): Sarah Clark (GBR)
Lightweight (57 kg): Ellen Wilson (USA)
Junior lightweight (52 kg): Georgina Singleton (GBR)
Bantamweight (48 kg): Aureue Cornao (France)

MOTOR CYCLING

500CC GRAND PRIX 2001

Pacific (Motegi, Japan): Sete Gibernau (Spain), Suzuki
Australian (Phillip Island): Valentino Rossi (Italy),
    Honda
Malaysian (Sepang): Valentino Rossi (Italy), Honda
Brazilian (Rio): Valentino Rossi (Italy), Honda
Riders' Championship 2001: 1. Valentino Rossi (Italy),
    Honda, 325 pts; 2. Max Biaggi (Italy), Yamaha, 219
    pts; 3. Loris Capirossi (Italy), Honda, 210 pts

500CC GRAND PRIX 2002

Japan (Suzuka): Valentino Rossi (Italy), Honda
South Africa (Welkom): Tohru Ukawa (Japan), Honda
Spanish (Jerez): Valentino Rossi (Italy), Honda
French (Le Mans): Valentino Rossi (Italy), Honda
Italian (Mugello): Valentino Rossi (Italy), Honda
Catalunya (Barcelona): Valentino Rossi (Italy), Honda
Dutch (Assen): Valentino Rossi (Italy), Honda
British (Donington Park): Valentino Rossi (Italy), Honda
German (Sachsenring): Valentino Rossi (Italy), Honda
Czech (Brno): Max Biaggi (Italy), Yamaha
Portugal (Estoril): Valentino Rossi (Italy), Honda
Brazil (Rio): Valentino Rossi (Italy), Honda

250 GRAND PRIX 2001

Pacific (Motegi, Japan): Tesuya Harada (Japan), Aprilia
Australian (Phillip Island): Dajiro Katoh (Japan), Honda
Malaysian (Sepang): Dajiro Katoh (Japan), Honda
Brazilian (Rio): Dajiro Katoh (Japan), Honda
Riders' Championship 2001: 1 Dajiro Katoh (Japan), 322
    pts; 2. Tetsuya Harada (Japan), 273 pts; 3. Marco
    Melandri (Italy), 194 pts

250CC GRAND PRIX 2002

Japan (Suzuka): Miyazaki (Japan), Aprilia
South Africa (Welkom): Marco Melandri (Italy), Aprilia
Spanish (Jerez): F. Nieto (Spain), Aprilia
French (Le Mans): F. Nieto (Spain), Aprilia
Italian (Mugello): Marco Melandri (Spain), Aprilia
Catalunya (Barcelona): Marco Melandri (Spain), Aprilia
Dutch (Assen): Marco Melandri (Spain), Aprilia
British (Donington Park): Marco Melandri (Spain),
    Aprilia

German (Sachsenring): Marco Melandri (Spain), Aprilia
Czech (Brno): Marco Melandri (Spain), Aprilia Portugal
    (Estoril): Fonsi Nieto (Spain), Aprilia
Brazil (Rio): Sebastian Porto (Argentina), Yamaha

125CC GRAND PRIX 2001

Pacific (Motegi, Japan): Youichi Ui (Japan), Derbi
Australian (Phillip Island): Youichi Ui (Japan), Derbi
Malaysian (Sepang): Youichi Ui (Japan), Derbi
Brazilian (Rio): Youichi Ui (Japan), Derbi
Riders' Championship 2001: 1. Manuel Poggiali (Italy),
    Gilera, 241 pts; 2. Yuichi Ui (Japan), Derbi, 232 pts; 3.
    Toni Elias (Spain), Honda, 217 pts

125CC GRAND PRIX 2002

Japan (Suzuka): Arnaud Vincent (France), Aprilia
South Africa (Welkom): Manuel Poggiali (RSM), Gilera
Spanish (Jerez): Lucio Cecchinello (Italy), Aprilia
French (Le Mans): Lucio Cecchinello (Italy), Aprilia
Italian (Mugello): Manuel Poggiali (RSM), Gilera
Catalunya (Barcelona): Manuel Poggiali (RSM), Gilera
Dutch (Assen): Daniel Pedrosa (Spain), Gilera
British (Donington Park): Lucio Cecchinello (Italy),
    Aprilia
German (Sachsenring): Lucio Cecchinello (Italy), Aprilia
Czech (Brno): Lucio Cecchinello (Italy), Aprilia
Portugal (Estoril): Arnaud Vincent (France), Aprilia
Brazil (Rio): Masao Azuma (Japan), Honda

Senior TT 2002, Isle of Man: David Jeffries (GB), Suzuki
Junior TT 2002, Isle of Man: David Jeffries (GB), Suzuki

WORLD SUPERBIKES 2001

Italy (Imola): Race 1–Ruben Zaus (Spain), Ducati; Race
    2–Regis Laconi (France), Aprilia

World Superbike Champion 2001: Troy Bayliss
    (Australia), Ducati 369 points

2002
Spain (Valencia): Race 1 – Troy Bayliss (Australia),
    Ducati; Race 2 – Troy Bayliss (Australia), Ducati
Australia (Philip Island): Race 1–Troy Bayliss (Australia),
    Ducati; Race 2–Troy Bayliss (Australia), Ducati
South Africa (Kyalami): Race 1–Troy Bayliss (Australia),
    Ducati; Race 2–Troy Bayliss (Australia), Ducati
Japan (Sugo): Race 1–Colin Edwards (USA), Honda;
    Race 2–Makoto Tomada (Japan), Honda
Italy (Monza): Race 1–Troy Bayliss (Australia), Ducati;
    Race 2–Troy Bayliss (Australia), Ducati
Great Britain (Silverstone): Race 1–Colin Edwards
    (USA), Honda; Race 2–Troy Bayliss (Australia),
    Ducati
Germany (Lausitzring): Race 1 – Troy Bayliss (Australia),
    Ducati; Race 2 – Troy Bayliss (Australia), Ducati
San Marino (Misano): Race 1 – Troy Bayliss (Australia),
    Ducati; Race 2 – Troy Bayliss (Australia), Ducati
United States (Laguna Seca): Race 1 – Troy Bayliss
    (Australia), Ducati; Race 2 – Colin Edwards (USA),
    Honda
Great Britain (Brands Hatch): Race 1 – Colin Edwards
    (USA), Honda; Race 2 – Colin Edwards (USA),
    Honda
Germany (Oschersleben): Race 1 – Colin Edwards
    (USA), Honda; Race 2 Colin Edwards (USA), Honda
Netherlands (Assen): Race 1 – Colin Edwards (USA),
    Honda; Race 2 – Colin Edwards (USA), Honda
Italy (Imola): *see* Stop Press

MOTOR RACING

FORMULA ONE GRAND PRIX 2001

United States Grand Prix (Indianapolis): (30 September)
Mika Hakkinen (Finland), McLaren
Drivers' World Championship 2001: 1. Michael
Schumacher (Germany), Ferrari, 123 points; 2. David
Coulthard (GB), McLaren-Mercedes, 65 points; 3.
Rubens Barrichello (Brazil) Ferrari, 56 points
Constructors' World Championship 2001: 1. Ferrari, 179
points; 2. McLaren-Mercedes, 102 points; 3.
Williams-BMW, 80 points

FORMULA ONE GRAND PRIX 2002

Australian (Melbourne): (3 March) Michael Schumacher
(Germany), Ferrari
Malaysian Grand Prix (Sepang): (17 March) Ralf
Schumacher (Germany), Williams-BMW
Brazilian Grand Prix (São Paulo): (31 March) Michael
Schumacher (Germany), Ferrari
San Marino Grand Prix (Imola): (14 April) Michael
Schumacher (Germany), Ferrari
Spanish Grand Prix (Barcelona): (28 April) Michael
Schumacher (Germany), Ferrari
Austrian Grand Prix (Spielberg): (12 May) Michael
Schumacher (Germany), Ferrari
Monaco Grand Prix (Monte Carlo): (26 May) David
Coulthard (GB), McLaren-Mercedes
Canadian Grand Prix (Montreal): (9 June) Michael
Schumacher (Germany), Ferrari
European Grand Prix (Nurburgring): (23 June) Rubens
Barrichello (Brazil), Ferrari
British Grand Prix (Silverstone): (7 July) Michael
Schumacher (Germany), Ferrari
French Grand Prix (Magny-Cours): (21 July) Michael
Schumacher (Germany), Ferrari
German Grand Prix (Hockenheim): (28 July) Michael
Schumacher (Germany), Ferrari
Hungarian Grand Prix (Hungaroring): (18 August)
Rubens Barrichello (Brazil), Ferrari
Belgian Grand Prix (Spa-Francorchamps): (1 September)
Michael Schumacher (Germany), Ferrari
Italian Grand Prix (Monza): (15 September) Rubens
Barrichello (Brazil), Ferrari
United States Grand Prix (Indianapolis): (29 September)
see Stop Press

Indianapolis 500 2002: Helio Castroneves (Brazil),
Marlboro Team Penske
Le Mans 24-hour Race 2002: Frank Biela, Tom Kristensen
and Emanuele Pirro (Audi)
Arras-Madrid-Daka Rally: Cars – Hiroshi Masuoka
(Japan), Mitsubishi; Motorcycles – Fabrizio Meoni
(Italy) KTM; Trucks – Vladimir Tchaguine (Russia),
Kamaz

MOTOR RALLYING

WORLD RALLY CHAMPIONSHIPS
2001

New Zealand Rally: Richard Burns (GB), Subaru
San Remo Rally: Gilles Panizzi (France), Peugeot
Corsica Rally: Jesus Puras (Spain), Citroen
Australia Rally: Marcus Grönholm (Finland), Peugeot
Network Q Rally of Great Britain: Richard Burns (GB),
Subaru
Drivers' World Championship 2001: Richard Burns (GB),
44 points

Manufacturers' World Championship 2001: Peugeot, 106
points

2002

Monte Carlo Rally: Tommi Makinen (Finland), Subaru
Swedish Rally: Marcus Grönholm (Finland), Peugeot
Corsica Rally: Gilles Panizzi (France), Peugeot
Catalunya Rally: Gilles Panizzi (France) Peugeot
Cyprus Rally: Marcus Grönholm (Finland), Peugeot
Argentina Rally: Carlos Sainz (Spain), Ford
Acropolis Rally: Colin McRae (GB), Ford
Safari Rally: Colin McRae (GB), Ford
Finland Rally: Marcus Grönholm (Finland), Peugeot
Deutschland Rally: Sebastien Loeb (France), Citroen

BRITISH RALLY CHAMPIONSHIPS 2002

Pirelli International (Gateshead): Mike Higgins (GB),
Ford
Rally of Wales (Wrexham): Jonny Milner (GB), Toyota
Scottish Rally (Dumfries): Jonny Milner (GB), Toyota
Jim Clark Memorial Rally (Edinburgh): Andrew Nesbitt
(GB), Subaru
Manx International (Douglas IOM): Mark Higgins (GB),
Toyota
Ulster Rally (Ulster): Andrew Nesbitt (GB), Subaru
Trackrod Rally (York): see Stop Press

NETBALL

Inter-County Championship final 2002: Middlesex beat
Gloucestershire 17–8
National Clubs Championship 2002: YWCA Bury
English Counties League Championship 2002: Essex
Metropolitan
National Clubs League Championship 2002: Essex Open
Super Cup Competition: Northern Thunder

NORDIC EVENTS

BIATHLON WORLD CHAMPIONSHIPS 2002
Oslo, Norway

MEN

10km sprint: Frank Luck (Germany) 26min. 23.8sec.
12.5km pursuit: Sven Fischer (Germany) 33min. 21.5sec.
15km mass start: Raphael Poiree (France) 37min.
57.8sec.

WOMEN

7.5km sprint: Katrin Apel (Germany) 22min. 07.6sec.
10km pursuit: Magdalena Forsberg (Sweden) 30min.
54.9sec.
12.5km mass start: Olena Zubrilova (Ukraine) 37min.
09.5sec.

BIATHLON OVERALL CHAMPIONS 2001–2002
As at 27 January 2002

MEN

1. Raphael Poiree (France), 430 points; 2. Pavel
Rostovtsev (Russia), 425 points; 3. Frank Luck
(Germany), 376 points

WOMEN

1. Magdalena Forsberg (Sweden), 519 points; 2. Olena
Zubrilova (Ukraine), 447 points; 3. Olga Pyleva
(Russia), 433 points

CROSS-COUNTRY OVERALL CHAMPIONS 2001–2

MEN

1. Per Elofsson (Sweden), 780 points; 2. Thomas Alsgaard (Norway), 777 points; 3. Anders Aukland (Norway), 545 points

WOMEN

1. Bente Skari (Norway), 877 points; 2. Katerina Neumannova (Czechoslovakia), 763 points; 3. Stefania Belmondo (Italy), 760 points

NORDIC-COMBINED OVERALL CHAMPIONS 2001–2

1. Ronnhy Ackermann (Germany) 2,110 points; 2. Felix Gottwald (Austria), 1,986 points; 3. Samppa Lajunen (Finland), 1,863 points

SKI-JUMPING OVERALL CHAMPIONS 2002

1. Adam Malysz (Poland), 1,475 points; 2. Sven Hannawald (Germany), 1259 points; 3. Matti Hautamaeki (Finland), 1048 points

POLO

Prince of Wales Trophy final 2002: Dubai beat FCT 9–7
Queen's Cup final 2002: Emerging beat Labegorce 9–8
Warwickshire Cup 2002: Foxcote beat FCT 15–9
Gold Cup (British Open) final 2002: Black Bears beat Emerging 8–7
Coronation Cup 2002: Rest of the Commonwealth beat England 11–10
Prince Philip Trophy 2002: Beaufort beat Horsepower 8–7

RACKETS

Noel Bruce Cup 2001: Wellington 1 beat Harrow 1 4–2
British Professional Singles Championship final 2002: Mark Hubbard beat Neil Smith 3–0
British Open Singles Championship final 2002: Harry Foster beat Mark Hubbard 4–1
Amateur Doubles Championship 2002: J. Male and M. Hue Williams beat W. Boone and N. Bailey 3–0
The Foster Cup final 2002 (public schools' single championship): Jamie Stout (Cheltenham) beat Alex Coldicott (Cheltenham) 3–1
Varsity Match 2002: Cambridge beat Oxford 3–0

REAL TENNIS

British Professional Singles Championship final 2002: Robert Fahey beat Tim Chisholm 3–0
British Professional Doubles Championship final 2002: Mike Gooding and Nick Wood beat Steve Virgona and Lachlan Deuchar 3–0
British Open Singles Championship final 2001: Robert Fahey beat Chris Bray 3–1
British Open Doubles Championship final 2001: Robert Fahey and Steve Virgona beat Chris Bray and James Willcocks 3–0
Henry Leaf Cup final 2002 (public schools' old boys' doubles championship): Haileybury (R. Gunn and R. Walker) beat Canford (J. Willcocks and I. Snell) 6–4, 6–4
World Singles Championships 2002: Robert Fahey (Australia) beat James Male (GB)
National League Final 2002: Cambridge (57points) beat Seacourt 55 points

Women's British Open Singles Championship final 2002: Penny Lumley beat Charlotte Cornwallis 2–1

ROAD WALKING

RWA NATIONAL 20 KM WALK
Imber Court, 2 March 2002

MEN

Individual: Andi Drake (Coventry), 1hr. 24 min. 43 sec.
Team: Steyning, 285 points

WOMEN

Individual: Lisa Kehler (Wolverhampton & Bilston), 1 hr. 43 min. 08 sec.
Team: Dudley & Stourbridge, 254 points

RWA WOMEN'S NATIONAL 10KM WALK
Leicester, 1 September 2002
Individual: Estle Viljoen (South Africa), 49 min. 6 sec.
Team: Steyning, 17 points

RWA MEN'S NATIONAL 50KM WALK
Colchester, 8 September 2002
Individual: Mike Smith (Coventry), 4 hr. 42 min. 58 sec.
Team: Coventry Godiva, 293 points

ROWING

NATIONAL CHAMPIONSHIPS 2002
Nottingham, July

MEN

Coxed pairs: Upper Thames Rowing Club 7:49.87
Coxless pairs: London Rowing Club 6:46.31
Coxed fours: Nottinghamshire County Rowing Association 6:27.73
Coxless fours: Nautilus Rowing Club 6:07.65
Single sculls: R. G. Ockendon (Nottingham Britannia Rowing Club) 7:15.34
Double sculls: Nottinghamshire County Rowing Association 6:36.14
Quad sculls: Leander Club 6:23.89
Eights: Oxford Brookes Rowing Club 5:42.88

WOMEN

Coxless pairs: Marlow/Imperial 7:40.20
Coxed fours: Oxford Brookes University 7:13.00
Coxless fours: Nautilus Rowing Club 7:03.44
Single sculls: E. Butler-Stoney 8:04.32
Double sculls: Wallingford Rowing Club 7:25.42
Quad sculls: Nautilus Rowing Club 6:53.80
Eights: Thames Rowing Club/Wallingford/Globe Rowing Club/London Rowing Club 6:36.37

THE 148th UNIVERSITY BOAT RACE

Putney–Mortlake, 4 miles 1 f, 180 yd, 30 March 2002

Oxford beat Cambridge by $^2/_3$ length; 16 min. 54 sec.
Cambridge have won 77 times, Oxford 70 and there has been one dead heat. The record time is 16 min. 19 sec., rowed by Cambridge in 1998

HENLEY ROYAL REGATTA 2002

Grand Challenge Cup: Victoria CRC and University of Victoria beat RC Hansa Dortmund and R. Munster by $^1/_2$ length
Ladies' Challenge Plate: Harvard University (USA) beat Molesey Boat Club by $2^3/_4$ lengths

Thames Challenge Cup: Leander Club beat
Nottinghamshire County Rowing Association 'A' by 3
lengths
Temple Challenge Cup: Harvard University (USA) beat
Oxford Brookes University 'A' by $^3/_4$ length
Princess Elizabeth Challenge Cup: Abingdon School beat
St Paul's School by $1^3/_4$ lengths
Remenham Challenge Cup: Oxford Brookes University
beat The Tideway Scullers' School by $2^3/_4$ lengths
Stewards' Challenge Cup: Danmarks Rocentre
(Denmark) beat Gorge Rowing Centre (Canada) by
$1^1/_4$ lengths
Prince Philip Challenge Cup: Molesey B. C. and Oxford
Brookes beat Cambridge University by $2^1/_2$ lengths
Queen Mother Challenge Cup: Leander Club and
University of London beat Leander Club and Molesey
B. C. sculled over
Visitors' Challenge Cup: Oxford Brookes and Imperial
College London beat Cambridge University by $2^1/_2$
lengths
Wyfold Challenge Cup: canvas Aberdeen Boat Club beat
London Rowing Club 'A' by 5 lengths
Britannia Challenge Cup: Harvard University (USA) 'B'
beat Harvard University (USA) 'A' by $1^3/_4$
Fawley Challenge Cup: Leander Club and Evesham
Rowing Club beat The Windsor Boys' School by
$^1/_2$ length
Silver Goblets and Nickalls' Challenge Cup: J. E. Cracknell
and M. C. Pinsent beat R. P. Di Clementé and D.
Cech by $^1/_2$ length
Double Sculls Challenge Cup: S. Vieilledent and A. Hardy
beat A. Haller and T. Petö by 4 lengths
Diamond Challenge Sculls: P. J. C. Wells beat M. K.
Langridge easily
Princess Royal Challenge Cup: R. Neykova beat K.
Rutschow-Stomporowski easily
Men's Quadruple Sculls: The Tideway Scullers' School 'A'
beat Leander Club 'B' by $1^3/_4$ lengths
Women's Quadruple Sculls: Marlow Rowing Club and
Leander Club beat Leander Club and Tideway
Scullers' School easily

OTHER ROWING EVENTS

Wingfield Sculls 2001: Ian Lawson (Leander)
Oxford Torpids 2002: Cancelled due to flooding
Oxford Summer Eights 2002: Men, Oriel; Women,
Pembroke
Head of the River 2002: Men, Leander I; Women,
Cancelled
Doggett's Coat and Badge 2002: Nick Dwan
Thames World Sculling Challenge 2001: Men, Iztok Cop;
Women, Ekaterina Karsten

RUGBY FIVES

National Open Singles Championship final 2001: H.
Buchanan beat S. Fraser 15–2, 15–3
National Open Doubles Championship final 2001: J.
Beswick and N. Roberts beat H. Buchanan and R.
Perry 15–7, 15–3
National Club Championship final 2002: Alleyn Old Boys
beat Caledonian Club 133–74 points
National Schools' Singles Championship final 2002: A. Lee
(St Paul's) beat A. Mogford (St Paul's) 11–7, 12–10
National Schools' Doubles Championship final 2002: St
Paul's I beat Christ's Hospital I 11–3,11–2
Varsity Match 2002: Cambridge beat Oxford 232–203
points

RUGBY LEAGUE

COMPETITIONS

Super League Grand Final 2001 (Old Trafford, 13
October): Bradford Bulls beat Wigan Warriors 37–6
World Challenge Cup final 2002 (McAlpine Stadium, 2
February): Bradford Bulls beat Newcastle Knights
41–26
Challenge Cup final 2002 (Murrayfield, 27 April): Wigan
Warriors beat St Helens 21–12
Varsity Match 2002 (Richmond, 5 March): Cambridge
beat Oxford 22–10

AMATEUR RUGBY LEAGUE 2001–2002

National Conference League Premier Division grand final:
West Hull beat Leigh Miners Rangers 24–20
National Conference League Premier Division Champions:
West Hull; Division one: West Bowling; Division two:
Crosfields

RUGBY UNION

SIX NATIONS' CHAMPIONSHIP 2002

2 February	Paris	France 33, Italy 12
	Edinburgh	England 29, Scotland 3
3 February	Dublin	Ireland 54, Wales 10
16 February	London	England 45. Ireland 11
	Rome	Scotland 29, Italy 12
	Cardiff	France 37, Wales 33
2 March	Paris	France 20, England 15
	Dublin	Ireland 43, Scotland 22
	Cardiff	Wales 44, Italy 20
23 March	London	England 50, Wales 10
	Dublin	Ireland 32, Italy 17
	Edinburgh	France 22, Scotland 10
6 April	Paris	France 44, Ireland 5
	Cardiff	Scotland 27, Wales 22
7 April	Rome	England 45, Italy 9

Challenge Shield final 2002 (20 April): Rotherham beat
Exeter 35–26
Heineken Cup final 2002 (Cardiff, 25 May): Leicester
Tigers beat Munster 15–9
Parker Pen Shield (Kassam Stadium, 26 May): Sale
Sharks beat Pontypridd 25–22

DOMESTIC COMPETITIONS

Zurich Premiership: Division 1, Leicester Tigers, 83
points
National League: Division 1, Rotherham, 120 points;
Division 2, Orrell 46 points; *Division 3* (North),
Doncaster, 50 points; (South) Penzance/Newlyn, 49
points
Tetley's County Championship final 2002 (Twickenham, 1
June 2002): Gloucestershire beat Cheshire 26–23
Tetley's County Shield (Twickenham, 1 June 2002):
Warwickshire beat Berkshire 34–12
Scottish Premier League: Division 1, Hawick, 72 points;
Division 2, Peebles, 72 points; *Division 3*, Hutchesons
Aloysians, 66 points
Scottish Cup final 2002: Hawick beat Glasgow Hawks
20–17
Wales Counties Cup 2002: North Wales beat Breaconshire
36–7
Wales/Scotland League: Llanelli 45 points
Welsh National League: Division 1, Aberavon, 81 points;
Division 2, Bedwas 81 points

Celtic League: Leinster 21 points
Irish League: Division 1, Cork Constitution, 52 points; *Division 2,* Belfast Harlequins, 68 points; *Division 3,* Greystones, 53 points
120th Varsity Match 2001: Oxford beat Cambridge 9–6

SHOOTING

132ND NATIONAL RIFLE ASSOCIATION IMPERIAL MEETING

Bisley, July 2001

Queen's Prize: Dr G. C. D. Barnett, 297.38 v-bulls
Grand Aggregate: N. R. J. Brazier, 698.87 v-bulls
Prince of Wales Prize: Mrs L. C. Golland, 75.12 v-bulls
St George's Vase: S. Murray, 150.21 v-bulls
Allcomers' Aggregate: Dr G. C. P. Barnett, 373.52 v-bulls
National Trophy: Ireland, 2041.221 v-bulls
Kolapore Cup: Great Britain, 1197.175 v-bulls
Chancellor's Trophy: Cambridge University RA, 1164.116 v-bulls
Musketeers Cup: Southampton University, 590.67 v-bulls
County Long-Range Championship: Norfolk, 586.51 v-bulls
Mackinnon Challenge Cup: England, 1156.108 v-bulls
The Albert: R. J. Lygoe 211.14 v-bulls
Hopton Challenge Cup: Wg Cdr D. P. Calvert 956.90 v-bulls

SHORT-TRACK SPEED SKATING

EUROPEAN CHAMPIONSHIPS 2002
Grenoble, France

MEN

500 metres: Nicola Rodigari (Italy) 43:010sec.
1,000 metres: Fabio Carta (Italy) 1min. 32.915sec.
1,500 metres: Fabio Carta (Italy) 2min. 20.849sec.
3,000 metres: Fabio Carta (Italy) 5min. 03.098sec.
5,000 metres relay: Italy 7min. 20.752sec.

WOMEN

500 metres: Evgenia Radanova (Bulgaria) 45.565sec.
1,000 metres: Evgenia Radanova (Bulgaria) 1min. 38.167sec.
1,500 metres: Evgenia Radanova (Bulgaria) 2min. 48.183sec.
3,000 metres: Evgenia Radanova (Bulgaria) 6min. 14.786sec.
3,000 metres relay: Italy 4 min. 29.255sec.

WORLD CHAMPIONSHIPS 2002
Canada

MEN

500 metres: Dong-Sung Kim (Korea) 41.930sec.
1,000 metres: Dong-Sung Kim (Korea) 1min. 31.361sec.
1,500 metres: Dong-Sung Kim (Korea) 2min. 21.736sec.
3,000 metres: Dong-Sung Kim (Korea) 5min. 19.041sec.
5,000 metres relay: Korea 7min. 10.751sec.
Men's Champion: Dong-Sung Kim (Korea) 136 points

WOMEN

500 metres: Yang Yang A (China) 44.460sec.
1,000 metres: Yang Yang A (China) 1min. 34.732sec.
1,500 metres: Yang Yang A (China) 2min. 31.630sec.
3,000 metres: Eun-Kyung Choi (Korea) 5min. 17.678sec.
3,000 metres relay: Korea 4min. 18.599sec.
Ladies Champion: Yang Yang A (China) 105 points

SPEED SKATING

EUROPEAN CHAMPIONSHIPS 2002
Erfurt, Germany

MEN

500 metres: Petter Andersen (Norway) 36.630sec.
1,500 metres: Vadim Sayutim (Russia) 1min. 53.87sec.
5,000 metres: Carl Verheijen (Netherlands) 6min. 37.54sec.
10,000 metres: Frank Dittrich (Germany) 13min. 33.61sec.

WOMEN

500 metres: Anni Friesinger (Germany) 39.670sec.
1,500 metres: Anni Friesinger (Germany) 1min. 58.73sec.
3,000 metres: Anni Friesinger (Germany) 4min. 12.33sec.
5,000 metres: Claudia Pechstein (Germany) 7min. 09.04sec.

WORLD CHAMPIONSHIPS 2002
Heerenveen, Netherlands

MEN

500 metres: Dmitry Shepel (Russia) 36.39sec.
1,500 metres: Dmitry Shepel (Russia) 1min. 48.44sec.
5,000 metres: Jochem Uytdehaage (Netherlands) 6min. 30.27sec.
10,000 metres: Jochem Uytdehaage (Netherlands) 13min. 27.25sec.

WOMEN

500 metres: Jennifer Rodrigez (USA) 38.59sec.
1,500 metres: Anni Friesinger (Germany) 1min. 56.43sec.
3,000 metres: Anni Friesinger (Germany) 4min. 08.02sec.
5,000 metres: Claudia Pechstein (Germany) 7min. 01.31sec.

SPRINT WORLD CHAMPIONSHIPS 2002
Hamar, Norway

OVERALL
MEN: 1. Jeremy Wotherspoon (Canada); 2. Casey Fitzrandolf (USA); 3. Michael Ireland (Canada)
WOMEN: 1. Catriona Lemay Doan (Canada); 2. Andrea Nuyt (Netherlands); 3. Anzhelika Kotyuga (Belarus)

SNOOKER

2001–2
Champions Cup: (Brighton) John Higgins (Scotland) beat Mark J. Williams (Wales) 7–4
Stan James British Open: (Newcastle) John Higgins (Scotland) beat Graeme Dott (Scotland) 9–6
Regal Scottish Masters: (Glasgow) John Higgins (Scotland) beat Ronnie O'Sullivan (England) 9–6
European Open: (Malta) Stephen Hendry beat Joe Perry 9–2
UK Championships: (York) Ronnie O'Sullivan (England) beat Ken Doherty (Ireland) 10–1
Benson & Hedges Masters Championship: (Wembley) Paul Hunter beat Mark J. Williams 10–9
China International: (Shanghai) Mark J. Williams beat Anthony Hamilton 9–8
Regal Welsh Open: (Cardiff) Paul Hunter (England) beat Ken Doherty (Ireland) 9–7
Thailand Masters: (Bangkok) Mark J. Williams beat Stephen Lee 9–4

City West Irish Masters: (Dublin) John Higgins
(Scotland) beat Peter Ebdon (England) 10–3
Regal Scottish Masters: (Aberdeen) Stephen Lee beat
David Gray 9–2
Embassy World Championship: (Sheffield) Peter Ebdon
(England) beat Stephen Hendry (Scotland) 18–17

WOMEN

Embassy World Championship 2002: (Sheffield) Kelly
Fisher beat Lisa Quick 4–1
European Championship 2002: (Poland) Kelly Fisher beat
Wendy Jans 5–0

SQUASH RACKETS

MEN

European Club Championship 2001: Capitol St Cloud
(France) beat Colets (England) Capitol St Cloud win
on countback
World Team Championship: Australia beat Egypt 3–0
WSF World Men's Challenge 2001: Paul Price (Australia)
beat Anthony Ricketts (Australia) 3–2
Irish National Championship 2001: Liam Kenny beat
Derek Ryan 3–1
European Team Championship final 2002: England beat
France 2–2 England win 8–7 on countback
British National Championship final 2002: Lee Beachill
(Yorks) beat Peter Nicol (Yorks) 3–1
British Open Championship 2002: Peter Nicol (England)
beat John White (Scotland) 3–0
Welsh National Championship 2002: Alex Gough beat
Greg Tippings 3–0

WOMEN

European Club Championship 2001: Capitol St Cloud
(France) beat Gutersloher (Germany) w/o
World Open Championship final 2001: Sarah Fitz-Gerald
(Australia) beat Leilani Joyce (New Zealand) 3–0
Irish National Championship 2001: Madeline Perry beat
Louise Finnegan 3–1
European Team Championship 2002: England beat
Scotland 3–0
British National Championship 2002: Cassie Campion
beat Linda Charman-Smith 3–0
British Open Championship 2002: Sarah Fitz-Gerald
(Australia) beat Tania Bailey (England) 3–0
Welsh National Championship 2002: Tegwen Malik beat
Katrina Hogan 3–0

SWIMMING

WORLD CHAMPIONSHIPS 2002
Moscow, April

MEN

50 metres freestyle: Jose Martin Meolans (Argentina)
21.36
100 metres freestyle: Ashley Callus (Australia) 46.99
200 metres freestyle: Klete Keller (USA) 1:44.36
400 metres freestyle: Grant Hackett (Australia) 3:38.29
1,500 metres freestyle: Grant Hackett (Australia) 14:33.94
50 metres backstroke: Matt Welsh (Australia) 23.66
100 metres backstroke: Matt Welsh (Australia) 51.26
200 metres backstroke: Aaron Peirsol (USA) 1:51.17
50 metres breaststroke: Oleg Lisogor (Ukraine) 26.42
100 metres breaststroke: Oleg Lisogor (Ukraine) 58.33
200 metres breaststroke: Aaron Peirsol (USA) 1:51.17

50 metres butterfly: Geoff Huegill (Australia) 22.89
100 metres butterfly: Geoff Huegill (Autralia) 50.95
200 metres butterfly: James Hickman (GBR) 1:53.14
100 metres medley: Peter Mankoc (Slovenia) 52.90
200 metres medley: Jani Sievenen (Finland) 1:55.45
400 metres medley: Thomas Wilkens (USA) 4:04.82
4 x 100 metres freestyle relay: USA 3:10.64
4 x 200 metres freestyle relay: Australia 7:00.36
4 x 100 metres medley relay: USA 3:29.00

WOMEN

50 metres freestyle: Therese Alshammar (Sweden) 24.16
100 metres freestyle: Therese Alshammar (Sweden) 52.89
200 metres freestyle: Lindsay Benko (USA) 1:54.04
400 metres freestyle: Yana Klochkova (Ukraine) 4:01.26
800 metres freestyle: Hua Chen (China) 8:16.34
50 metres backstroke: Jennifer Carroll (Canada) 27.38
100 metres backstroke: Haley Cope (USA) 59.07
200 metres backstroke: Lindsay Benko (USA) 2:04.97
50 metres breaststroke: Emma Igelstrom (Sweden) 29.96
100 metres breaststroke: Emma Igelstrom (Sweden)
1:05.38
200 metres breaststroke: Hui Qi (China) 2:20.91
50 metres butterfly: A. Kammerling (Sweden) 25.55
100 metres butterfly: Martina Moravcova (Slovakia)
57.04
200 metres butterfly: Petria Thomas (Australia) 2:05.76
100 metres medley: Martina Moravcova (Slovakia) 59.91
200 metres medley: Yana Klochkova (Ukraine) 2:08.82
400 metres medley: Yana Klochkova (Ukraine) 4:30.63
4 x 100 metres freestyle relay: Sweden 3:35.09
4 x 200 metres freestyle relay: China 7:46.30
4 x 100 metres medley relay: Sweden 3:55.78

EUROPEAN CHAMPIONSHIPS 2002
Berlin, August

MEN

50 metres freestyle: Bartosz Kizierowski (Poland), 22.18
100 metres freestyle: Pieter van den Hoogenband
(Netherlands), 47.86
200 metres freestyle: Pieter van den Hoogenband
(Netherlands), 1.44.89
400 metres freestyle: Emiliano Brembilla (Italy) 3:46.60
1,500 metres freestyle: Yuri Prilukov (Russia), 15:03.88
50 metres backstroke: Thomas Rupprath (Germany),
25.05
100 metres backstroke: Stev Theloke (Germany), 54.42
200 metres backstroke: Goran Kozulj (Croatia), 1:58.70
50 metres breaststroke: Oleg Lisogor (Ukraine), 27.18
100 metres breaststroke: Oleg Lisogor (Ukraine), 1:00.29
200 metres breaststroke: Davide Rummolo (Italy), 2:11.37
50 metres butterfly: Jere Hard (Finland), 23.50
100 metres butterfly: Thomas Rupprath (Germany),
51.94
200 metres butterfly: Franck Esposito (France), 1:55.18
200 metres medley: Jani Sievinen (Finland), 1:59.30
400 metres medley: Alessio Boggiatto (Italy), 4:13.19
4 x 100 metres freestyle relay: Germany, 3:17.67
4 x 200 metres freestyle relay: Italy, 7:12.18
4 x 100 metres medley relay: Russia, 3:36.12

WOMEN

50 metres freestyle: Therese Alshammar (Sweden), 24.84
100 metres freestyle: Franziska van Almsick (Germany),
54.39
200 metres freestyle: Franziska van Almsick (Germany),
1:56.64
400 metres freestyle: Yana Klochkova (Ukraine), 4:07.10
800 metres freestyle: Jana Henke (Germany), 8:23.83

50 metres backstroke: Nina Zhivanevskaya (Spain), 28.58
100 metres backstroke: Stanislava Komorova (Russia),
1:01.40
200 metres backstroke: Stanislava Komarova (Russia),
2:09.49
50 metres breaststroke: Emma Ingelstrom (Sweden),
31.17
100 metres breaststroke: Emma Igelstrom (Sweden),
1:07.87
200 metres breaststroke: Mirna Jukic (Austria), 2:25.83
50 metres butterfly: Anna Kammerling (Netherlands),
25.57
100 metres butterfly: Martina Moravcova (Slovakia),
57.20
200 metres butterfly: Otylia Jedvzejczak (Poland), 2:05.78
200 metres medley: Yana Klochkova (Ukraine), 2:11.59
400 metres medley: Yana Klochkova (Ukraine), 4:35.10
4 x 100 metres freestyle relay: Germany, 3:36.00
4 x 200 metres freestyle relay: Germany, 7:59.07
4 x 100 metres medley relay: Germany, 4:01.54

TABLE TENNIS

ENGLISH NATIONAL CHAMPIONSHIPS 2002
Sheffield, March

Men's Singles: Andrew Baggaley (Bucks) beat Alex Perry
(Devon) 4–1
Women's Singles: Nicola Deaton (Derbys) beat Helen
Lower (Staffs) 4–0
Men's Doubles: Gareth Herbert (Berks) and Andrew
Baggaley (Bucks) beat Alan Cooke and Bradley
Billington (Derbys) 3–2
Women's Doubles: Nicola Deaton (Derbys) and Helen
Lower (Staffs) beat Kate Steward (Somerset) and
Georgina Walker (Notts) 2–1
Mixed Doubles: Alex Perry (Devon) and Helen Lower
(Staffs) beat Alan Cooke and Nicola Deaton (Derbys)
3–0
Men's Under 21 Singles: Dale Barham (Cambs) beat
Michael Chan (Surrey) 3–0
Women's Under 21 Singles: Georgina Walker (Notts) beat
Louise Durrant (Notts) 3–0

EUROPEAN CHAMPIONSHIPS 2002
Zagreb, Croatia March–April

Men's Singles: Timo Boll (Germany) beat Kalinikos
Kreanga (Greece) 4–2
Women's Singles: Krisztina Toth (Hungary) beat Xia Lian
Ni (Luxemburg) 4–1
Men's Doubles: Boll/Fejer-Konnerth (Germany) beat
Blaszczyk/Krzeszewski (Poland) 4–0
Women's Doubles: Boroš (Croatia)/Steff (Romania) beat
Palovich/Kostromina (Belarus) 4–3
Mixed Doubles: Blaszczyk/Ni beat Karak
Ćeviš/Garkauskaite 4–0
Men's Team: Sweden beat Germany 3–2
Women's Team: Romania beat Germany 3–2

TENNIS

AUSTRALIAN OPEN CHAMPIONSHIPS 2002
Melbourne, 14–27 January

Men's Singles: Thomas Johansson (Sweden) beat Marat
Safin (Russia) 3–6, 6–4, 7–6
Women's Singles: Jennifer Capriati (USA) beat Martina
Hingis (Switzerland) 4–6, 7–6, 6–2

Men's Doubles: Mark Knowles (Bahamas) and Daniel
Nestor (Canada) beat Michael Llodra and Fabrice
Santoro (France) 7–6, 6–3
Women's Doubles: Martina Hingis (Switzerland) and
Anna Kournikova (Russia) beat Daniela Hantuchova
(Slovakia) and Arantxa Sanchez-Vicario (Spain) 6–2,
6–7, 6–1
Mixed Doubles: Kevin Ullyett (Zimbabwe) and Daniela
Hantuchova (Slovakia) beat Gaston Etlis and Paola
Suarez (Argentina) 6–3, 6–2

FRENCH OPEN CHAMPIONSHIPS 2002
Paris, 27 May–9 June

Men's Singles: Albert Costa (Spain) beat Juan Carlos
Fererro (Spain) 6–1, 6–0, 4–6, 6–3
Women's Singles: Serena Williams (USA) beat Venus
Williams (USA) 7–5, 6–3
Men's Doubles: Paul Haarhuis (Netherlands) and
Yevgeny Kafelnikov (Russia) beat Mark Knowles
(Bahamas) and Daniel Nestor (Canada) 7–5, 6–4
Women's Doubles: Paola Suarez (Argentina) and Virginia
Ruano Pascual (Spain) beat Lisa Raymond (USA) and
Rennae Stubbs (Australia) 6–4, 6–2
Mixed Doubles: Cara Black (Zimbabwe) and Wayne
Black (Zimbabwe) beat Elena Bovina (Russia) and
Mark Knowles (Bahamas) 6–3, 6–3

ALL-ENGLAND CHAMPIONSHIPS 2002
Wimbledon, 24 June–7 July

Men's Singles: Lleyton Hewitt (Australia) beat David
Nalbandian (Argentina) 6–1, 6–3, 6–2
Women's Singles: Serena Williams (USA) beat Venus
Williams (USA) 7–6, 6–3
Men's Doubles: Jonas Bjorkman (Sweden) and Todd
Woodbridge (Australia) beat Mark Knowles
(Bahamas) and Daniel Nestor (Canada) 6–1, 6–2,
7–6, 7–5
Women's Doubles: Venus Williams (USA) and Serena
Williams (USA) beat Virginia Ruano Pascual (Spain)
and Paola Suarez (Argentina) 6–2, 7–5
Mixed Doubles: Mahesh Bhupathi (India) and Elena
Likhovtseva (Russia) beat Kevin Ullyett (Zimbabwe)
and Daniela Hantuchova (Slovakia) 6–2, 1–6, 6–1

US OPEN CHAMPIONSHIPS 2002
New York, 26 August–8 September

Men's Singles: Pete Sampras (USA) beat Andre Agassi
(USA) 6–3, 6–4, 5–7, 6–4
Women's Singles: Serena Williams (USA) beat Venus
Williams (USA) 6–4, 6–3
Men's Doubles: Mahesh Bhupathi (India) and Max
Mirnyi (Belarus) beat Jiri Novak (Czech Republic)
and Radek Stepanek (Czech Republic) 6–3, 3–6, 6–4
Women's Doubles: Virginia Ruano Pascual (Spain) and
Paola Suarez (Argentina) beat Elena Dementieva
(Russia) and Janette Husarova (Slovakia) 6–2, 6–1
Mixed Doubles: Lisa Raymond (USA) and Mike Bryan
(USA) beat Katarina Srebotnik (Slovenia) and Bob
Bryan (USA) 7–6, 7–6

TEAM CHAMPIONSHIPS

Davis Cup final 2001: France beat Australia 3–2

VOLLEYBALL

MEN

World League 2002: Russia beat Brazil 3–1

WOMEN

Grand Prix final 2002: Russia beat China 3–1

WINTER OLYMPIC GAMES 2002

Salt Lake City, USA, 9–24 February 2002

ALPINE SKIING

MEN

Downhill: Fritz Strobl (Austria), 1:39.13
Slalom: Jean-Pierre Vidal (France), 1:41.06
Giant Slalom: Stephan Eberharter (Austria), 2:23.28
Super Giant Slalom: Kjetil André Aamodt (Norway), 1:21.58
Alpine Combination: Kjetil André Aamodt (Norway), 3:17.56

WOMEN

Downhill: Carole Montillet (France), 1:39.56
Slalom: Janica Kostelic (Croatia), 1:46.10
Giant Slalom: Janica Kostelic (Croatia), 2:30.01
Super Giant Slalom: Daniela Ceccarelli (Italy), 1:13.59
Alpine Combination: Janica Kostelic (Croatia), 2:43.28

BIATHLON

MEN

10km: Ole Einar Bjørndalen (Norway), 24:51.3
20km: Ole Einar Bjørndalen (Norway), 51:03.3
Relay: Norway, 1:23:42.3
Pursuit: Ole Einar Bjørndalen (Norway), 32:34.6

WOMEN

7.5km: Kati Wilhelm (Germany), 20:41.4
15km: Andrea Henkel (Germany), 47:29.1
Relay: Germany, 1:27:55.0
Pursuit: Olga Pyleva (Russia), 31:07.7

BOBSLEIGH

MEN

2-man: Germany I, 3:10.11
4-man: Germany I, 3:07.51

WOMEN

Two-woman: USA II, 1:37.76

CURLING

Men: Norway
Women: Great Britain

FIGURE SKATING

Men: Alexei Yagudin (Russia), 1.5pts
Women: Sarah Hughes (USA), 3.0pts
Pairs: Russia 1.5pts
Ice Dancing: France, 2.0pts

FREESTYLE SKIING

MEN

Moghuls: Janne Lahtela (Finland), 27.97pts
Aerials: Aleš Valenta (Czechoslovakia), 257.02pts

WOMEN

Moghuls: Kari Traa (Norway), 25.94pts
Aerials: Alisa Camplin (Russia), 193.47pts

ICE HOCKEY

MEN: Canada
WOMEN: Canada

LUGE

Men Single: Armin Zöggeler (Italy), 2:57.941
Women Single: Sylke Otto (Germany), 2:52.464
Doubles: Germany, 1:26.082
Men-Skeleton: James Shea (USA), 1:41.96
Women-Skeleton: Tristan Gale (USA), 1:45.11

NORDIC SKIING

MEN

1500m (Freestyle): Tor Arne Hetland (Norway), 2:56.9
15km (Classical): Andrus Veerpalu (Estonia), 37:07.4
Combined Pursuit: Johann Mühlegg (Spain), 49:20.4
30km (Free): Johann Mühlegg (Spain), 1:09:28.9
50km (Classical): Michail Ivanov (Russia), 2:06:20.8
Relay: Norway, 1:32:45.5

WOMEN

1500m (Freestyle): Julia Tchepalova (Russia), 3:10.6
10km (Classical): Bente Skari (Norway), 28:05.6
Combined Pursuit: Olga Danilova (Russia), 24:52.1
15km (Freestyle): Stefania Belmondo (Italy), 39:54.4
30km (Classical): Gabrielle Paruzzi (Italy), 1:30:57.1
Relay: Germany, 49:30.6

NORDIC COMBINED

Sprint: Samppa Lajunen (Finland)
Individual: Samppa Lajunen (Finland)
Team: Finland

SKI JUMPING

90m hill: Simon Ammann (Switzerland), 269.0pts
120m hill: Simon Ammann (Switzerland), 281.4pts
120m Team: Germany, 974.1pts

SNOWBOARD

MEN

Giant Slalom: Philipp Schoch (Switzerland)
Halfpipe: Ross Powers (USA), 46.1pts

WOMEN

Giant Slalom: Isabelle Blanc (France)
Halfpipe: Kelly Clark (USA), 47.9pts

SHORT-TRACK SPEED SKATING

MEN

500m: Marc Gagnon (Canada), 41.802
1000m: Steven Bradbury (Australia), 1:2.109
1500m: Apolo Anton Ohno (USA), 2:18.541
Relay: Canada, 6:51.579

WOMEN

500m: Yang Yang (A) (China), 44.187
1000m: Yang Yang (A) (China), 1:36.391
1500m: Ko Gi Hyun (Korea), 2:31.581
Relay: Korea, 4:12.793

SPEED SKATING

MEN
500m: Casey FitzRandolph (USA), 69.23
1000m: Gerard van Velde (Netherlands), 1:07.18
1500m: Derek Parra (USA), 1:43.95
5000m: Jochem Uytdehaage (Netherlands), 6:14.66
10.000m: Jochem Uytdehaage (Netherlands), 12:58.92

WOMEN
500m: Catriona LeMay Doan (Canada), 74.75
1000m: Chris Witty (USA), 1:13.83
1500m: Anni Friesinger (Germany), 1:54.02
3000m: Claudia Pechstein (Germany), 3:57.70
5000m: Claudia Pechstein (Germany), 6:46.91

Sports Records

ATHLETICS WORLD RECORDS
AS AT SEPTEMBER 2002

All the world records given below have been accepted by the International Amateur Athletic Federation except those marked with an asterisk* which are awaiting homologation. Fully automatic timing to 1/100th second is mandatory up to and including 400 metres. For distances up to and including 10,000 metres, records will be accepted to 1/100th second if timed automatically, and to 1/10th if hand timing is used.

MEN'S EVENTS

TRACK EVENTS	hr.	min.	sec.
100 metres			9.78*
Tim Montgomery, USA, 2002			
200 metres			19.32
Michael Johnson, USA, 1996			
400 metres			43.18
Michael Johnson, USA, 1999			
800 metres		1	41.11
Wilson Kipketer, Denmark, 1997			
1,000 metres		2	11.96
Noah Ngeny, Kenya, 1999			
1,500 metres		3	26.00
Hicham El Guerrouj, Morocco, 1998			
1 mile		3	43.13
Hicham El Guerrouj, Morocco, 1999			
2,000 metres		4	44.79
Hicham El Guerrouj, Morocco, 1999			
3,000 metres		7	20.67
Daniel Komen, Kenya, 1996			
5,000 metres		12	39.3
Haile Gebreselassie, Ethiopia, 1998			
10,000 metres		26	22.75
Haile Gebreselassie, Ethiopia, 1998			
20,000 metres		56	55.6
Arturo Barrios, Mexico, 1991			
21,101 metres (13 miles 196 yards 1 foot)	1	00	00.0
Arturo Barrios, Mexico, 1991			
25,000 metres	1	13	55.8
Toshihiko Seko, Japan, 1981			
30,000 metres	1	29	18.8
Toshihiko Seko, Japan, 1981			
Marathon	2	05	38
Khalid Khannouchi, USA, 2002			
110 metres hurdles (3 ft 6 in)			12.91
Colin Jackson, GB, 1993			
400 metres hurdles (3 ft 0 in)			46.78
Kevin Young, USA, 1992			
3,000 metres steeplechase		7	53.17*
Brahim Boulami, Morocco 2002			

RELAYS

	hr.	min.	sec.
4×100 metres			37.40
USA, 1992, 1993			
4×200 metres		1	19.11
Santa Monica TC, 1992			
4×400 metres		2	54.20
USA, 1998			
4×800 metres		7	03.89
GB, 1982			
4×1,500 metres		14	38.8
Federal Republic of Germany, 1977			

FIELD EVENTS

	metres	ft	in
High jump	2.45	8	0½
Javier Sotomayor, Cuba, 1993			
Pole vault	6.14	20	1¾
Sergei Bubka, Ukraine, 1994			
Long jump	8.95	29	4½
Mike Powell, USA, 1991			
Triple jump	18.29	60	0¼
Jonathan Edwards, GB, 1995			
Shot	23.12	75	10¼
Randy Barnes, USA, 1990			
Discus	74.08	243	0
Jürgen Schult, GDR, 1986			
Hammer	86.74	284	7
Yuriy Sedykh, USSR, 1986			
Javelin	98.48	323	1
Jan Zelezny, Czech Rep., 1996			
Decathlon†	9,026 points		
Roman Sebrle, Czech Rep., 2001			

† Ten events comprising 100 m, long jump, shot, high jump, 400 m, 110 m hurdles, discus, pole vault, javelin, 1,500 m

WALKING (TRACK)

	hr.	min.	sec.
20,000 metres	1	17	25.6
Bernard Segura, Mexico, 1994			
29,572 metres (18 miles 660 yards)	2	00	00.0
Maurizio Damilano, Italy, 1992			
30,000 metres	2	01	44.1
Maurizio Damilano, Italy, 1992			
50,000 metres	3	40	57.9
Thierry Toutain, France, 1996			

WOMEN'S EVENTS

TRACK EVENTS

	hr.	min.	sec.
100 metres			10.49
Florence Griffith-Joyner, USA, 1988			
200 metres			21.34
Florence Griffith-Joyner, USA, 1988			
400 metres			47.60
Marita Koch, GDR, 1985			
800 metres		1	53.28
Jarmila Kratochvilova, Czechoslovakia, 1983			
1,500 metres		3	50.46
Qu Yunxia, China, 1993			
1 mile		4	12.56
Svetlana Masterkova, Russia, 1996			
3,000 metres		8	06.11
Wang Junxia, China, 1993			
5,000 metres		14	28.09
Jiang Bo, China, 1997			
10,000 metres		29	31.78
Wang Junxia, China, 1993			
Marathon	2	18	47
Catherine Ndereba, Kenya, 2001			
100 metres hurdles (2 ft 9 in)			12.21
Yordanka Donkova, Bulgaria, 1988			
400 metres hurdles (2 ft 6 in)			52.61
Kim Batten, USA, 1995			
3,000 metres steeplechase		9	16.51*
Aleysa Turova, Belarus, 2002			

RELAYS	min.	Sec.
4×100 metres		41.37
GDR, 1985		
4×200 metres	1	27.46*
USA, 2000		
4×400 metres	3	15.17
USSR, 1988		
4×800 metres	7	50.17
USSR, 1984		

FIELD EVENTS	metres	ft	in
High jump	2.09	6	10¼
Stefka Kostadinova, Bulgaria, 1987			
Pole vault	4.81	15	9½
Stacy Dragila, USA, 2000			
Long jump	7.52	24	8¼
Galina Chistiakova, USSR, 1988			
Triple jump	15.50	50	10¼
Inessa Kravets, Ukraine, 1995			
Shot	22.63	74	3
Natalya Lisovskaya, USSR, 1987			
Discus	76.80	252	0
Gabriele Reinsch, GDR, 1988			
Hammer	76.07	249	6
Mihaela Melinte, Romania, 1999			
Javelin (new implement in 1999)	71.54	234	8
Osleidys Menendez, Cuba, 2001			
Heptathlon†		7,291 points	
Jackie Joyner-Kersee, \SA, 1988			

†Seven events comprising 100 m hurdles, shot, high jump, 200 m, long jump, javelin, 800 m

ATHLETICS NATIONAL (UK) RECORDS
AS AT SEPTEMBER 2002

Records set anywhere by athletes eligible to represent Great Britain and Northern Ireland

MEN

TRACK EVENTS	hr.	min.	sec.
100 metres			9.87
Linford Christie, 1993			
Dwain Chambers, 2002			9.87*
200 metres			19.87
John Regis, 1994			
400 metres			44.36
Iwan Thomas, 1997			
800 metres		1	41.73
Sebastian Coe, 1981			
1,000 metres		2	12.18
Sebastian Coe, 1981			
1,500 metres		3	29.67
Sebastian Coe, 1985			
1 mile		3	46.32
Steve Cram, 1985			
2,000 metres		4	51.39
Steve Cram, 1985			
3,000 metres		7	32.79
David Moorcroft, 1982			
5,000 metres		13	00.41
David Moorcroft, 1982			
10,000 metres		27	18.14
Jon Brown, 1998			
20,000 metres		57	28.7
Carl Thackery, 1990			
20,855 metres	1	00	00.0
Carl Thackery, 1990			
25,000 metres	1	15	22.6
Ron Hill, 1965			
30,000 metres	1	31	30.4
Jim Alder, 1970			
Marathon	2	07	13
Steve Jones, 1985			
3,000 metres steeplechase		8	07.96
Mark Rowland, 1988			
110 metres hurdles			12.91
Colin Jackson, 1993			
400 metres hurdles			47.82
Kriss Akabusi, 1992			

RELAYS		min.	sec.
4×100 metres			37.73
GB team, 1999			
4×200 metres		1	21.29
team, 1989			
4×400 metres		2	56.60
GB team, 1996			
4×800 metres		7	03.89
GB team, 1982			

FIELD EVENTS	Metres	ft	in
High jump	2.37	7	9¼
Steve Smith, 1993			
Pole vault	5.80	19	0¼
Nick Buckfield, 1998			
Long jump	8.27	27	1¾
Chris Tomlinson, 2002			
Triple jump	18.29	60	0¼
Jonathan Edwards, 1995			
Shot	21.68	71	1½
Geoff Capes, 1980			
Discus	66.64	218	8
Perris Wilkins, 1998			
Hammer	77.54	254	5
Martin Girvan, 1984			
Javelin	91.46	300	1
Steve Backley, 1992			
Decathlon		8,847 points	
Daley Thompson, 1984			

WALKING (TRACK)	hr.	min.	sec.
20,000 metres	1	23	26.5
Ian McCombie, 1990			
30,000 metres	2	19	18
Christopher Maddocks, 1984			
50,000 metres	4	05	44.6
Paul Blagg, 1990			
26,037 metres (16 miles 315 yards)	2	00	00.0
Ron Wallwork, 1971			

WOMEN

TRACK EVENTS	hr.	min.	sec.
100 metres			11.10
Kathy Cook, 1981			
200 metres			22.10
Kathy Cook, 1984			
400 metres			49.43
Kathy Cook, 1984			
800 metres		1	56.21
Kelly Holmes, 1995			
1,500 metres		3	58.07
Kelly Holmes, 1997			
1 mile		4	17.57
Zola Budd, 1985			
3,000 metres		8	22.20*
Paula Radcliffe, 2002			
5,000 metres		14	31.42*
Paula Radcliffe, 2002			
10,000 metres		30	01.09*
Paula Radcliffe, 2002			

	min.	sec.		
Marathon	2	18	56	
Paula Radcliffe, 2002				
100 metres hurdles			12.80	
Angela Thorp, 1996				
400 metres hurdles			52.74	
Sally Gunnell, 1993				

RELAYS	min.	sec.
4×100 metres		42.43
GB team, 1980		
4×200 metres	1	31.57
GB team, 1977		
4×400 metres	3	22.01
GB team, 1991		
4×800 metres	8	23.8
GB team, 1971		

FIELD EVENTS	Metres	ft	in
High jump	1.95	6	4¾
Diana Elliott, 1982			
Susan Jones, 2001			
Pole vault	4.41*	14	5¾
Janine Whitlock, 2002			
Long jump	6.90	22	7¾
Beverley Kinch, 1983			
Triple jump	15.15	49	8½
Ashia Hansen, 1997			
Shot	19.36	63	6¼
Judy Oakes, 1988			
Discus	67.48	221	5
Margaret Ritchie, 1981			
Hammer	68.15	223	7
Lorraine Shaw, 2001			
Javelin (new implement)	64.87*	212	9
Kelly Morgan, 2002			
Heptathlon			831 points
Denise Lewis, 2000			

SWIMMING WORLD RECORDS
as at September 2002

MEN	min.	sec.
50 metres freestyle		21.64
Alexander Popov, Russia		
100 metres freestyle		47.84
Pieter van den Hoogenband, Netherlands		
200 metres freestyle	1	44.06
Ian Thorpe, Australia		
400 metres freestyle	3	40.08
Ian Thorpe, Australia		
800 metres freestyle	7	39.16
Ian Thorpe, Australia		
1,500 metres freestyle	14	34.56
Grant Hackett, Australia		
50 metres breaststroke		27.18
Oleg Lisogor, Ukraine		
100 metres breaststroke		59.94
Roman Sloudnov, Russia		
200 metres breaststroke	2	10.16
Mike Barrowman, USA		
50 metres butterfly		23.44
Geoff Heugill, Australia		
100 metres butterfly		51.81
Michael Klim, Australia		
200 metres butterfly	1	54.58
Michael Phelps, USA		
50 metres backstroke		24.99
Lenny Krayzelburg, USA		
100 metres backstroke		53.60
Lenny Krayzelburg, USA		
200 metres backstroke	1	55.15
Aaron Peirosol, USA		
200 metres medley	1	58.16
Jani Sievinen, Finland		
400 metres medley	4	11.76
Tom Dolan, USA		
4×100 metres freestyle relay	3	13.67
Australia		
4×200 metres freestyle relay	7	04.66
Australia		
4×100 metres medley relay	3	33.48
USA		

WOMEN	min.	sec.
50 metres freestyle		24.13
Inge de Bruin, Netherlands		
100 metres freestyle		53.77
Inge de Bruin, Netherlands		
200 metres freestyle	1	56.64
Franziska van Almsick, Germany		
400 metres freestyle	4	03.85
Janet Evans, USA		
800 metres freestyle	8	16.22
Janet Evans, USA		
1,500 metres freestyle	15	52.10
Janet Evans, USA		
50 metres breaststroke		30.57
Zoe Baker, Great Britain		
100 metres breaststroke	1	06.52
Penny Heyns, South Africa		
200 metres breaststroke	2	22.99
Qi Hui (China)		
50 metres butterfly		25.57
Inge de Bruin, Anna-Karin Kammerling, Sweden		
100 metres butterfly		56.61
Inge de Bruin, Netherlands		
200 metres butterfly	2	05.78
Otylia Jedreczak, Poland		
50 metres backstroke		28.25
Sandra Volker, Germany		
100 metres backstroke		59.58
Natalie Coughlin, USA		
200 metres backstroke	2	06.62
Krisztina Egerszegi, Hungary		
200 metres medley	2	09.72
Wu Yanyan, China		
400 metres medley	4	33.59
Yana Klochkova, Ukraine		
4×100 metres freestyle relay	3	36.00
Germany		
4×200 metres freestyle relay	7	55.47
GD		
4×100 metres medley relay	3	36.00
Germany		

Weights and Measures

SI UNITS

The Système International d'Unités (SI) is an international and coherent system of units devised to meet all known needs for measurement in science and technology. The system was adopted by the eleventh Conférence Générale des Poids et Mesures (CGPM) in 1960. A comprehensive description of the system is given in *SI The International System of Units* (HMSO). The British Standards describing the essential features of the International System of Units are *Specifications for SI units and recommendations for the use of their multiples and certain other units* (BS 5555:1993) and *Conversion Factors and Tables* (BS 350, Part 1:1974).

The system consists of seven base units and the derived units formed as products or quotients of various powers of the base units. Together the base units and the derived units make up the coherent system of units. In the UK the SI base units, and almost all important derived units, are realised at the National Physical Laboratory and disseminated through the National Measurement System.

BASE UNITS

metre (m) = unit of length
kilogram (kg) = unit of mass
second (s) = unit of time
ampere (A) = unit of electric current
kelvin (K) = unit of thermodynamic temperature
mole (mol) = unit of amount of substance
candela (cd) = unit of luminous intensity

DERIVED UNITS

For some of the derived SI units, there are special names and symbols; those approved by the CGPM are as follows:

hertz (Hz) = unit of frequency
newton (N) = unit of force
pascal (Pa) = unit of pressure, stress
joule (J) = unit of energy, work, quantity of heat
watt (W) = unit of power, radiant flux
coulomb (C) = unit of electric charge, quantity of electricity
volt (V) = unit of electric potential, potential difference, electromotive force
farad (F) = unit of electric capacitance
ohm (Ω) = unit of electric resistance
siemens (S) = unit of electric conductance
weber (Wb) = unit of magnetic flux
tesla (T) = unit of magnetic flux density
henry (H) = unit of inductance
degree Celsius (°C) = unit of Celsius temperature
lumen (lm) = unit of luminous flux
lux (lx) = unit of illuminance
becquerel (Bq) = unit of activity (of a radionuclide)
gray (Gy) = unit of absorbed dose, specific energy imparted, kerma, absorbed dose index
sievert (Sv) = unit of dose equivalent, dose equivalent index
radian (rad) = unit of plane angle
steradian (sr) = unit of solid angle

Other derived units are expressed in terms of base units. Some of the more commonly used derived units are the following:

Unit of area = square metre (m^2)
Unit of volume = cubic metre (m^3)
Unit of velocity = metre per second ($m\ s^{-1}$)
Unit of acceleration = metre per second squared ($m\ s^{-2}$)
Unit of density = kilogram per cubic metre ($kg\ m^{-3}$)
Unit of momentum = kilogram metre per second ($kg\ m\ s^{-1}$)
Unit of magnetic field strength = ampere per metre ($A\ m^{-1}$)
Unit of surface tension = newton per metre ($N\ m^{-1}$)
Unit of dynamic viscosity = pascal second (Pa s)
Unit of heat capacity = joule per kelvin ($J\ K^{-1}$)
Unit of specific heat capacity = joule per kilogram kelvin ($J\ kg^{-1}\ K^{-1}$)
Unit of heat flux density, irradiance = watt per square metre ($W\ m^{-2}$)
Unit of thermal conductivity = watt per metre kelvin ($W\ m^{-1}\ K^{-1}$)
Unit of electric field strength = volt per metre ($V\ m^{-1}$)
Unit of luminance = candela per square metre ($cd\ m^{-2}$)

SI PREFIXES

Decimal multiples and submultiples of the SI units are indicated by SI prefixes. These are as follows:

multiples	submultiples
yotta (Y) $\times 10^{24}$	deci (d) $\times 10^{-1}$
zetta (Z) $\times 10^{21}$	centi (c) $\times 10^{-2}$
exa (E) $\times 10^{18}$	milli (m) $\times 10^{-3}$
peta (P) $\times 10^{15}$	micro (μ) $\times 10^{-6}$
tera (T) $\times 10^{12}$	nano (n) $\times 10^{-9}$
giga (G) $\times 10^{9}$	pico (p) $\times 10^{-12}$
mega (M) $\times 10^{6}$	femto (f) $\times 10^{-15}$
kilo (k) $\times 10^{3}$	atto (a) $\times 10^{-18}$
hecto (h) $\times 10^{2}$	zepto (z) $\times 10^{-21}$
deca (da) $\times 10$	yocto (y) $\times 10^{-24}$

METRIC UNITS

The metric primary standards are the metre as the unit of measurement of length, and the kilogram as the unit of measurement of mass. Other units of measurement are defined by reference to the primary standards.

MEASUREMENT OF LENGTH

Kilometre (km) = 1000 metres
Metre (m) is the length of the path travelled by light in vacuum during a time interval of 1/299 792 458 of a second
Decimetre (dm) = 1/10 metre
Centimetre (cm) = 1/100 metre
Millimetre (mm) = 1/1000 metre

MEASUREMENT OF AREA

Hectare (ha) = 100 ares
Decare = 10 ares
Are (a) = 100 square metres
Square metre = a superficial area equal to that of a square each side of which measures one metre
Square decimetre = 1/100 square metre
Square centimetre = 1/100 square decimetre
Square millimetre = 1/100 square centimetre

MEASUREMENT OF VOLUME

Cubic metre (m^3) = a volume equal to that of a cube each edge of which measures one metre
Cubic decimetre = 1/1000 cubic metre
Cubic centimetre (cc) = 1/1000 cubic decimetre
Hectolitre = 100 litres
Litre = a cubic decimetre
Decilitre = 1/10 litre
Centilitre = 1/100 litre
Millilitre = 1/1000 litre

MEASUREMENT OF CAPACITY

Hectolitre (hl) = 100 litres
Litre (l or L) = a cubic decimetre
Decilitre (dl) = 1/10 litre
Centilitre (cl) = 1/100 litre
Millilitre (ml) = 1/1000 litre

MEASUREMENT OF MASS OR WEIGHT

Tonne (t) = 1000 kilograms
Kilogram (kg) is equal to the mass of the international prototype of the kilogram
Hectogram (hg) = 1/10 kilogram
Gram (g) = 1/1000 kilogram
*Carat (metric) = 1/5 gram
Milligram (mg) = 1/1000 gram

*Used only for transactions in precious stones or pearls

METRICATION IN THE UK

The European Council Directive 80/181/EEC, as amended by Council Directive 89/617/EEC, relates to the use of units of measurement for economic, public health, public safety or administrative purposes in the member states of the European Union. The provisions of the directives were incorporated into British law by the Weights and Measures Act 1985 (Metrication) (Amendment) Order 1994 and the Units of Measurement Regulations 1994; these instruments amended the Weights and Measures Act 1985. Parallel statutory rules amending Northern Ireland weights and measures legislation were made in May 1995.

The general effect of the 1994 and 1995 legislation is to end the use of imperial units of measurement for trade, replacing them with metric units - *see* below for timetable for UK metrication. Imperial units can, however, be used in addition to metric units, as supplementary indications.

IMPERIAL UNITS

The imperial primary standards are the yard as the unit of measurement of length and the pound as the unit of measurement of mass. Other units of measurement are defined by reference to the primary standards. Most of these units are no longer authorised for use in trade in the UK - *see* below.

MEASUREMENT OF LENGTH

Mile = 1760 yards
Furlong = 220 yards
Chain = 22 yards
Yard (yd) = 0.9144 metre
Foot (ft) = 1/3 yard
Inch (in) = 1/36 yard

MEASUREMENT OF AREA

Square mile = 640 acres
Acre = 4840 square yards
Rood = 1210 square yards
Square yard (sq. yd) = a superficial area equal to that of a square each side of which measures one yard

Square foot (sq. ft) = 1/9 square yard
Square inch (sq. in) = 1/144 square foot

MEASUREMENT OF VOLUME

Cubic yard = a volume equal to that of a cube each edge of which measures one yard
Cubic foot = 1/27 cubic yard
Cubic inch = 1/1728 cubic foot

MEASUREMENT OF CAPACITY

Bushel = 8 gallons
Peck = 2 gallons
Gallon (gal) = 4.54609 cubic decimetres
Quart (qt) = 1/4 gallon
*Pint (pt) = 1/2 quart
Gill = 1/4 pint
*Fluid ounce (fl oz) = 1/20 pint
Fluid drachm = 1/8 fluid ounce
Minim (min) = 1/60 fluid drachm

MEASUREMENT OF MASS OR WEIGHT

Ton = 2240 pounds
Hundredweight (cwt) = 112 pounds
Cental = 100 pounds
Quarter = 28 pounds
Stone = 14 pounds
*Pound (lb) = 0.453 592 37 kilogram
*Ounce (oz) = 1/16 pound
*†Ounce troy (oz tr) = 12/175 pound
Dram (dr) = 1/16 ounce
Grain (gr) = 1/7000 pound
Pennyweight (dwt) = 24 grains
Ounce apothecaries = 480 grains
Drachm (ℨ) = 1/8 ounce apothecaries
Scruple (℈) = 1/3 drachm

*Units of measurement still authorised for use for trade in the UK
†Used only for transactions in gold, silver or other precious metals, and articles made therefrom

PHASING-OUT OF IMPERIAL UNITS IN THE UK

Since 1965 the United Kingdom has been adopting metric weights and measures in response to the adoption of metric units as the international system of measurement.

Goods sold loose by weight (mainly fresh foods) from 1 January 2000 are required to be sold in grams and kilograms. Retailers can continue to display the price per imperial unit alongside the price per unit in metric unit. Consumers can continue to express in ounces and pounds the quantity they wish to buy. Retailers will weigh out the equivalent quantity in grams and kilograms.

The Weights and Measures Units of Measurement Regulations 1995 (Statutory Instrument 1995 No. 1804) require that metric units should be used for all economic, public health, public safety and administrative purposes.

Units of measurement authorised for use in specialised fields are:

Unit	Field of application
fathom	Marine navigation
fluid ounce pint }	Beer, cider, water, lemonade, fruit juice in returnable containers
ounce pound }	Goods for sale loose from bulk
therm	Gas supply

Units of measurement authorised for use in specialised fields from 1 October 1995, without time limit

Unit	Field of application
inch	
foot	Road traffic signs, distance and speed
yard	measurement
mile	
pint	Dispense of draught beer or cider
	Milk in returnable containers
acre	Land registration
troy ounce	Transactions in precious metals

MEASUREMENT OF ELECTRICITY

Units of measurement of electricity are defined by the Weights and Measures Act 1985 as follows:

ampere (A) = that constant current which, if maintained in two straight parallel conductors of infinite length, of negligible circular cross-section and placed 1 metre apart in vacuum, would produce between these conductors a force equal to 2×10^{-7} newton per metre of length

ohm (Ω) = the electric resistance between two points of a conductor when a constant potential difference of 1 volt, applied between the two points, produces in the conductor a current of 1 ampere, the conductor not being the seat of any electromotive force

volt (V) = the difference of electric potential between two points of a conducting wire carrying a constant current of 1 ampere when the power dissipated between these points is equal to 1 watt

watt (W) = the power which in one second gives rise to energy of 1 joule

kilowatt (kW) = 1000 watts

megawatt (MW) = one million watts

WATER AND LIQUOR MEASURES

1 cubic foot = 62.32 lb
1 gallon = 10 lb
1 cubic cm = 1 gram
1000 cubic cm = 1 litre; 1 kilogram
1 cubic metre = 1000 litres; 1000 kg; 1 tonne
An inch of rain on the surface of an acre (43560 sq. ft) = 3630 cubic ft = 100.992 tons
Cisterns: A cistern $4 \times 2\frac{1}{2}$ feet and 3 feet deep will hold brimful 186.963 gallons, weighing 1869.63 lb in addition to its own weight

WATER FOR SHIPS

Kilderkin = 18 gallons
Barrel = 36 gallons
Puncheon = 72 gallons
Butt = 110 gallons
Tun = 210 gallons

BOTTLES OF WINE

Traditional equivalents in standard champagne bottles:
Magnum = 2 bottles
Jeroboam = 4 bottles
Rehoboam = 6 bottles
Methuselah = 8 bottles
Salmanazar = 12 bottles
Balthazar = 16 bottles
Nebuchadnezzar = 20 bottles

A quarter of a bottle is known as a *nip*
An eighth of a bottle is known as a *baby*

ANGULAR AND CIRCULAR MEASURES

60 seconds ($''$) = 1 minute ($'$)
60 minutes = 1 degree ($°$)
90 degrees = 1 right angle or quadrant
Diameter of circle $\times$ 3.1416 = circumference
Diameter squared $\times$ 0.7854 = area of circle
Diameter squared $\times$ 3.1416 = surface of sphere
Diameter cubed $\times$ 0.523 = solidity of sphere
One degree of circumference $\times$ 57.3 = radius*
Diameter of cylinder $\times$ 3.1416; product by length or height, gives the surface
Diameter squared $\times$ 0.7854; product by length or height, gives solid content

*Or, one radian (the angle subtended at the centre of a circle by an arc of the circumference equal in length to the radius) = 57.3 degrees

MILLION, BILLION, ETC.

Value in the UK

Million	thousand $\times$ thousand	10^6
*Billion	million $\times$ million	10^{12}
Trillion	million $\times$ billion	10^{18}
Quadrillion	million $\times$ trillion	10^{24}

Value in USA

Million	thousand $\times$ thousand	10^6
*Billion	thousand $\times$ million	10^9
Trillion	million $\times$ million	10^{12}
Quadrillion	million $\times$ billion US	10^{15}

*The American usage of billion (i.e. 10^9) is increasingly common, and is now universally used by statisticians

NAUTICAL MEASURES

DISTANCE

Distance at sea is measured in nautical miles. The British standard nautical mile was 6080 feet but this measure has been obsolete since 1970 when the international nautical mile of 1852 metres was adopted by the Hydrographic Department of the Ministry of Defence. The cable (600 feet or 100 fathoms) was a measure approximately one-tenth of a nautical mile. Such distances are now expressed in decimal parts of a sea mile or in metres.

Soundings at sea were recorded in fathoms (6 feet). Depths are now expressed in metres on Admiralty charts.

SPEED

Speed is measured in nautical miles per hour, called knots. A ship moving at the rate of 30 nautical miles per hour is said to be doing 30 knots.

knots	m.p.h.	knots	m.p.h.
1	1.1515	9	10.3636
2	2.3030	10	11.5151
3	3.4545	15	17.2727
4	4.6060	20	23.0303
5	5.7575	25	28.7878
6	6.9090	30	34.5454
7	8.0606	35	40.3030
8	9.2121	40	46.0606

TONNAGE

Under the Merchant Shipping Act 1854, the tonnage of UK-registered vessels was measured in tons of 100 cubic feet. The need for a universal method of measurement led

to the adoption of the International Convention on Tonnage Measurements of Ships 1969, which measures, in cubic metres, all the internal spaces of a vessel for the gross tonnage and those of the cargo compartments for the net tonnage. The convention has applied since July 1982 to new ships, ships which needed to be remeasured because of substantial alterations, and ships whose owners requested remeasurement. On 18 July 1994 the convention became mandatory and all vessels have now been remeasured.

DISTANCE OF THE HORIZON

The limit of distance to which one can see varies with the height of the spectator. The greatest distance at which an object on the surface of the sea, or of a level plain, can be seen by a person whose eyes are at a height of five feet from the same level is nearly three miles. At a height of 20 feet the range is increased to nearly six miles, and an approximate rule for finding the range of vision for small heights is to increase the square root of the number of feet that the eye is above the level surface by a third of itself. The result is the distance of the horizon in miles, but is slightly in excess of that in the table below, which is computed by a more precise formula. The table may be used conversely to show the distance of an object of given height that is just visible from a point on the surface of the earth or sea. Refraction is taken into account both in the approximate rule and in the table.

Height in feet	range in miles
5	2.9
20	5.9
50	9.3
100	13.2
500	29.5
1,000	41.6
2,000	58.9
3,000	72.1
4,000	83.3
5,000	93.1
20,000	186.2

TEMPERATURE SCALES

The SI (International System) unit of temperature is the kelvin, which is defined as the fraction 1/273.16 of the temperature of the triple point of water (i.e. where ice, water and water vapour are in equilibrium). The zero of the Kelvin scale is the absolute zero of temperature. The freezing point of water is 273.15 K and the boiling point (as adopted in the International Temperature Scale of 1990) is 373.124 K.

The Celsius scale (formerly centigrade) is defined by subtracting 273.15 from the Kelvin temperature. The Fahrenheit scale is related to the Celsius scale by the relationships:

temperature °F = (temperature °C × 1.8) + 32
temperature °C = (temperature °F -32) ÷ 1.8

It follows from these definitions that the freezing point of water is 0°C and 32°F. The boiling point is 99.974°C and 211.953°F.

The temperature of the human body varies from person to person and in the same person can be affected by a variety of factors. In most people body temperature varies between 36.5°C and 37.2°C (97.7–98.9°F).

Conversion between scales

°C	°F	°C	°F	°C	°F
100	212	60	140	20	68
99	210.2	59	138.2	19	66.2
98	208.4	58	136.4	18	64.4
97	206.6	57	134.6	17	62.6
96	204.8	56	132.8	16	60.8
95	203	55	131	15	59
94	201.2	54	129.2	14	57.2
93	199.4	53	127.4	13	55.4
92	197.6	52	125.6	12	53.6
91	195.8	51	123.8	11	51.8
90	194	50	122	10	50
89	192.2	49	120.2	9	48.2
88	190.4	48	118.4	8	46.4
87	188.6	47	116.6	7	44.6
86	186.8	46	114.8	6	42.8
85	185	45	113	5	41
84	183.2	44	111.2	4	39.2
83	181.4	43	109.4	3	37.4
82	179.6	42	107.6	2	35.6
81	177.8	41	105.8	1	33.8
80	176	40	104	zero	32
79	174.2	39	102.2	− 1	30.2
78	172.4	38	100.4	− 2	28.4
77	170.6	37	98.6	− 3	26.6
76	168.8	36	96.8	− 4	24.8
75	167	35	95	− 5	23
74	165.2	34	93.2	− 6	21.2
73	163.4	33	91.4	− 7	19.4
72	161.6	32	89.6	− 8	17.6
71	159.8	31	87.8	− 9	15.8
70	158	30	86	−10	14
69	156.2	29	84.2	−11	12.2
68	154.4	28	82.4	−12	10.4
67	152.6	27	80.6	−13	8.6
66	150.8	26	78.8	−14	6.8
65	149	25	77	−15	5
64	147.2	24	75.2	−16	3.2
63	145.4	23	73.4	−17	1.4
62	143.6	22	71.6	−18	0.4
61	141.8	21	69.8	−19	-2.2

PAPER MEASURES

Printing Paper
516 sheets = 1 ream
2 reams   = 1 bundle
5 bundles = 1 bale

Writing Paper
480 sheets = 1 ream
20 quires = 1 ream
24 sheets = 1 quire

BROWN PAPERS

	inches		inches
Casing	46 × 36	Imperial Cap	29 × 22
Double Imperial	45 × 29	Haven Cap	26 × 21
Elephant	34 × 24	Bag Cap	24 × 19½
Double Four Pound	31 × 21	Kent Cap	21 × 18

PRINTING PAPERS

	inches		inches
Foolscap	17 × 13½	Double Large	
Double Foolscap	27 × 17	Post	33 × 21
Quad Foolscap	34 × 27	Demy	22½ × 17½
Crown	20 × 15	Double Demy	35 × 22½
Double Crown	30 × 20	Quad Demy	45 × 35

Quad Crown	40 × 30	Music Demy	20 × 15½
Double Quad		Medium	23 × 18
Crown	60 × 40	Royal	25 × 20
Post	19¼ × 15½	Super Royal	27½ × 20½
Double Post	31½ × 19½	Elephant	28 × 23
		Imperial	30 × 22

WRITING AND DRAWING PAPERS

	inches		inches
Emperor	72 × 48	Copy or Draft	20 × 16
Antiquarian	53 × 31	Demy	20 × 15½
Double Elephant	40 × 27	Post	19 × 15¼
Grand Eagle	42 × 28¾	Pinched Post	18½ × 14¾
Atlas	34 × 26	Foolscap	17 × 13½
Colombier	34½ × 23½	Double Foolscap	26½ × 16½
Imperial	30 × 22	Double Post	30½ × 19
Elephant	28 × 23	Double Large	
Cartridge	26 × 21	Post	33 × 21
Super Royal	27 × 19	Double Demy	31 × 20
Royal	24 × 19	Brief	16½ × 13¼
Medium	22 × 17½	Pott	15 × 12½
Large Post	21 × 16½		

A SERIES

	mm		mm
A0	841 × 1189	A6	105 × 148
A1	594 × 841	A7	74 × 105
A2	420 × 594	A8	52 × 74
A3	297 × 420	A9	37 × 52
A4	210 × 297	A10	26 × 37
A5	148 × 210		

B SERIES

	mm		mm
B0	1000 × 1414	B6	125 × 176
B1	707 × 1000	B7	88 × 125
B2	500 × 707	B8	62 × 88
B3	353 × 500	B9	44 × 62
B4	250 × 353	B10	31 × 44
B5	176 × 250		

C SERIES   DL

	mm		mm
C4	324 × 229	DL	110 × 220
C5	229 × 162		
C6	114 × 162		

INTERNATIONAL PAPER SIZES

The basis of the international series of paper sizes is a rectangle having an area of one square metre, the sides of which are in the proportion of 1:√2. The proportions 1:√2 have a geometrical relationship, the side and diagonal of any square being in this proportion. The effect of this arrangement is that if the area of the sheet of paper is doubled or halved, the shorter side and the longer side of the new sheet are still in the same proportion 1:√2. This feature is useful where photographic enlargement or reduction is used, as the proportions remain the same.

Description of the A series is by capital A followed by a figure. The basic size has the description A0 and the higher the figure following the letter, the greater is the number of sub-divisions and therefore the smaller the sheet. Half A0 is A1 and half A1 is A2. Where larger dimensions are required the A is preceded by a figure. Thus 2A means twice the size A0; 4A is four times the size of A0.

SUBSIDIARY SERIES

B sizes are sizes intermediate between any two adjacent sizes of the A series. There is a series of C sizes which is used much less. A is for magazines and books, B for posters, wall charts and other large items, C for envelopes particularly where it is necessary for an envelope (in C series) to fit into another envelope. The size recommended for business correspondence is A4.

Long sizes (DL) are obtainable by dividing any appropriate sizes from the two series above into three, four or eight equal parts parallel with the shorter side in such a manner that the proportion of 1:√2 is not maintained, the ratio between the longer and the shorter sides being greater than √2:1. In practice long sizes should be produced from the A series only.

It is an essential feature of these series that the dimensions are of the trimmed or finished size.

BOUND BOOKS

The book sizes most commonly used are listed below. Approximate centimetre equivalents are also shown. International sizes are converted to their nearest imperial size, e.g. A4 = D4; A5 = D8.

		inches	cm
Crown 32mo	C32	2½ × 3¾	6 × 9
Crown 16mo	C16	3¾ × 5	9 × 13
Foolscap 8vo	F8	4¼ × 6¾	11 × 17
Demy 16mo	D16	4⅜ × 5⅝	11 × 14
Crown 8vo	C8	5 × 7½	13 × 19
Demy 8vo	D8	5⅝ × 8¾	14 × 22
Medium 8vo	M8	5¾ × 9	15 × 23
Royal 8vo	R8	6¼ × 10	16 × 25
Super Royal 8vo	suR8	6¾ × 10	17 × 25
Foolscap 4to	F4	6¾ × 8½	17 × 22
Crown 4to	C4	7½ × 10	19 × 25
Imperial 8vo	Imp8	7½ × 11	19 × 28
Demy 4to	D4	8¾ × 11¼	22 × 29
Royal 4to	R4	10 × 12½	25 × 31
Super Royal 4to	suR4	10 × 13½	25 × 34
Crown Folio	Cfol	10 × 15	25 × 38
Imperial Folio	Impfol	11 × 15	28 × 38

Folio = a sheet folded in half
Quarto (4to) = a sheet folded into four
Octavo (8vo) = a sheet folded into eight
Books are usually bound up in sheets of 16, 32 or 64 pages. Octavo books are generally printed 64 pages at a time, 32 pages on each side of a sheet of quad.

CONVERSION TABLES FOR WEIGHTS AND MEASURES

Bold figures equal units of either of the columns beside them; thus: 1 cm = 0.394 inches and 1 inch = 2.540 cm

LENGTH			AREA			VOLUME			WEIGHT (MASS)		
Centimetres		*Inches*	*Square cm*		*Square in*	*Cubic cm*		*Cubic in*	*Kilograms*		*Pounds*
2.540	1	0.394	6.452	1	0.155	16.387	1	0.061	0.454	1	2.205
5.080	2	0.787	12.903	2	0.310	32.774	2	0.122	0.907	2	4.409
7.620	3	1.181	19.355	3	0.465	49.161	3	0.183	1.361	3	6.614
10.160	4	1.575	25.806	4	0.620	65.548	4	0.244	1.814	4	8.819
12.700	5	1.969	32.258	5	0.775	81.936	5	0.305	2.268	5	11.023
15.240	6	2.362	38.710	6	0.930	98.323	6	0.366	2.722	6	13.228
17.780	7	2.756	45.161	7	1.085	114.710	7	0.427	3.175	7	15.432
20.320	8	3.150	51.613	8	1.240	131.097	8	0.488	3.629	8	17.637
22.860	9	3.543	58.064	9	1.395	147.484	9	0.549	4.082	9	19.842
25.400	10	3.937	64.516	10	1.550	163.871	10	0.610	4.536	10	22.046
50.800	20	7.874	129.032	20	3.100	327.742	20	1.220	9.072	20	44.092
76.200	30	11.811	193.548	30	4.650	491.613	30	1.831	13.608	30	66.139
101.600	40	15.748	258.064	40	6.200	655.484	40	2.441	18.144	40	88.185
127.000	50	19.685	322.580	50	7.750	819.355	50	3.051	22.680	50	110.231
152.400	60	23.622	387.096	60	9.300	983.226	60	3.661	27.216	60	132.277
177.800	70	27.559	451.612	70	10.850	1147.097	70	4.272	31.752	70	154.324
203.200	80	31.496	516.128	80	12.400	1310.968	80	4.882	36.287	80	176.370
228.600	90	35.433	580.644	90	13.950	1474.839	90	5.492	40.823	90	198.416
254.000	100	39.370	645.160	100	15.500	1638.710	100	6.102	45.359	100	220.464
Metres		*Yards*	*Square m*		*Square yd*	*Cubic m*		*Cubic yd*	*Metric tonnes*		*Tons (UK)*
0.914	1	1.094	0.836	1	1.196	0.765	1	1.308	1.016	1	0.984
1.829	2	2.187	1.672	2	2.392	1.529	2	2.616	2.032	2	1.968
2.743	3	3.281	2.508	3	3.588	2.294	3	3.924	3.048	3	2.953
3.658	4	4.374	3.345	4	4.784	3.058	4	5.232	4.064	4	3.937
4.572	5	5.468	4.181	5	5.980	3.823	5	6.540	5.080	5	4.921
5.486	6	6.562	5.017	6	7.176	4.587	6	7.848	6.096	6	5.905
6.401	7	7.655	5.853	7	8.372	5.352	7	9.156	7.112	7	6.889
7.315	8	8.749	6.689	8	9.568	6.116	8	10.464	8.128	8	7.874
8.230	9	9.843	7.525	9	10.764	6.881	9	11.772	9.144	9	8.858
9.144	10	10.936	8.361	10	11.960	7.646	10	13.080	10.161	10	9.842
18.288	20	21.872	16.723	20	23.920	15.291	20	26.159	20.321	20	19.684
27.432	30	32.808	25.084	30	35.880	22.937	30	39.239	30.481	30	29.526
36.576	40	43.745	33.445	40	47.840	30.582	40	52.318	40.642	40	39.368
45.720	50	54.681	41.806	50	59.799	38.228	50	65.398	50.802	50	49.210
54.864	60	65.617	50.168	60	71.759	45.873	60	78.477	60.963	60	59.052
64.008	70	76.553	58.529	70	83.719	53.519	70	91.557	71.123	70	68.894
73.152	80	87.489	66.890	80	95.679	61.164	80	104.636	81.284	80	78.737
82.296	90	98.425	75.251	90	107.639	68.810	90	117.716	91.444	90	88.579
91.440	100	109.361	83.613	100	119.599	76.455	100	130.795	101.605	100	98.421
Kilometres		*Miles*	*Hectares*		*Acres*	*Litres*		*Gallons*	*Metric tonnes*		*Tons (US)*
1.609	1	0.621	0.405	1	2.471	4.546	1	0.220	0.907	1	1.102
3.219	2	1.243	0.809	2	4.942	9.092	2	0.440	1.814	2	2.205
4.828	3	1.864	1.214	3	7.413	13.638	3	0.660	2.722	3	3.305
6.437	4	2.485	1.619	4	9.844	18.184	4	0.880	3.629	4	4.409
8.047	5	3.107	2.023	5	12.355	22.730	5	1.100	4.536	5	5.521
9.656	6	3.728	2.428	6	14.826	27.276	6	1.320	5.443	6	6.614
11.265	7	4.350	2.833	7	17.297	31.822	7	1.540	6.350	7	7.716
12.875	8	4.971	3.327	8	19.769	36.368	8	1.760	7.257	8	8.818
14.484	9	5.592	3.642	9	22.240	40.914	9	1.980	8.165	9	9.921
16.093	10	6.214	4.047	10	24.711	45.460	10	2.200	9.072	10	11.023
32.187	20	12.427	8.094	20	49.421	90.919	20	4.400	18.144	20	22.046
48.280	30	18.641	12.140	30	74.132	136.379	30	6.599	27.216	30	33.069
64.374	40	24.855	16.187	40	98.842	181.839	40	8.799	36.287	40	44.092
80.467	50	31.069	20.234	50	123.555	227.298	50	10.999	45.359	50	55.116
96.561	60	37.282	24.281	60	148.263	272.758	60	13.199	54.431	60	66.139
112.654	70	43.496	28.328	70	172.974	318.217	70	15.398	63.503	70	77.162
128.748	80	49.710	32.375	80	197.684	363.677	80	17.598	72.575	80	88.185
144.841	90	55.923	36.422	90	222.395	409.137	90	19.798	81.647	90	99.208
160.934	100	62.137	40.469	100	247.105	454.596	100	21.998	90.719	100	110.231

Abbreviations

A — Associate of
AA — Alcoholics Anonymous
Automobile Association
AAA — Amateur Athletic Association
AB — Able-bodied seaman
ABA — Amateur Boxing Association
abbr(ev) — abbreviation
ABM — Anti-ballistic missile
abr — abridged
ac — alternating current
a/c — account
AC — Aircraftman
(*Ante Christum*) Before Christ
Companion, Order of
Australia
ACAS — Advisory, Conciliation and
Arbitration Service
ACT — Australian Capital Territory
AD — (*Anno Domini*) In the year of
our Lord
ADC — Aide-de-Camp
ADC (P) — Personal ADC to The Queen
adj — adjective
Adj — Adjutant
ad lib — (*ad libitum*) at pleasure
Adm — Admiral
Admission
adv — adverb
AE — Air Efficiency Award
AEEU — Amalgamated Engineering and
Electrical Union
AEM — Air Efficiency Medal
AFC — Air Force Cross
AFM — Air Force Medal
AG — Adjutant-General
Attorney-General
AGM — air-to-ground missile
annual general meeting
AH — (*Anno Hegirae*) In the year of
the Hegira
AI — Artificial intelligence
AIDS — Acquired immune deficiency
syndrome
AIM — Alternative Investment Market
alt — altitude
am — (*ante meridiem*) before noon
AM — (*Anno mundi*) In the
year of the world
amplitude modulation
amp — ampere
amplifier
ANC — African National Congress
anon — anonymous
ANZAC — Australian and New Zealand
Army Corps
AO — Air Officer
Officer, Order of Australia
AOC — Air Officer Commanding
AONB — Area of Outstanding Natural
Beauty
AS — Anglo-Saxon
ASA — Advertising Standards
Authority
Amateur Swimming
Association
asap — as soon as possible

ASB — Alternative Service Book
ASEAN — Association of South East
Asian Nations
ASH — Action on Smoking and
Health
ASLEF — Associated Society of
Locomotive Engineers and
Firemen
ASLIB — Association for Information
Management
ATC — Air Training Corps
AUC — (*ab urbe condita*) In the year
from the foundation of Rome
(*anno urbis conditae*) In the
year of the founding of the
city
AUT — Association of University
Teachers
AV — Audio-visual
Authorised Version (*of Bible*)
AVR — Army Volunteer Reserve
AWOL — Absent without leave

b — born
bowled
BA — Bachelor of Arts
BAA — British Airports Authority
British Astronomical
Association
BAF — British Athletics Federation
BAFTA — British Academy of Film and
Television Arts
Bart — Baronet
BAS — Bachelor in Agricultural
Science
British Antarctic Survey
BBC — British Broadcasting
Corporation
BBSRC — Biotechnology and Biological
Sciences Research Council
BC — Before Christ
British Columbia
B Ch (D) — Bachelor of (Dental) Surgery
BCL — Bachelor of Civil Law
B Com — Bachelor of Commerce
BD — Bachelor of Divinity
BDA — British Dental Association
BDS — Bachelor of Dental Surgery
B Ed — Bachelor of Education
BEM — British Empire Medal
B Eng — Bachelor of Engineering
BFI — British Film Institute
BFPO — British Forces Post Office
BL — British Library
B Litt — Bachelor of Letters *or* of
Literature
BM — Bachelor of Medicine
British Museum
BMA — British Medical Association
B Mus — Bachelor of Music
BOTB — British Overseas Trade Board
Bp — Bishop
B Pharm — Bachelor of Pharmacy
B Phil — Bachelor of Philosophy
Br(it) — Britain
British

BR — British Rail
Brig — Brigadier
BSc — Bachelor of Science
BSE — Bovine spongiform
encephalopathy
BSI — British Standards Institution
BST — British Summer Time
Bt — Baronet
BTEC — Business and Technology
Education Council
B Th — Bachelor of Theology
Btu — British thermal unit
BVM — (*Beata Virgo Maria*) Blessed
Virgin Mary
BVMS — Bachelor of Veterinary
Medicine and Surgery

c — (*circa*) about
C — Celsius
Centigrade
Conservative
CA — Chartered Accountant
(*Scotland*)
CAA — Civil Aviation Authority
CAB — Citizens' Advice Bureau
Cantab — (of) Cambridge
Cantuar — of Canterbury (*Archbishop*)
CAP — Common Agricultural Policy
Capt — Captain
Caricom — Caribbean Community and
Common Market
Carliol — of Carlisle (*Bishop*)
CB — Companion, Order of the Bath
CBE — Commander, Order of the
British Empire
CBI — Confederation of British
Industry
CC — Chamber of Commerce
Companion, Order of Canada
City Council
County Council
County Court
CCC — County Cricket Club
CCF — Combined Cadet Force
C Chem — Chartered Chemist
CD — Civil Defence
compact disc
Corps Diplomatique
Cdr — Commander
Cdre — Commodore
CDS — Chief of the Defence Staff
CE — Christian Era
Civil Engineer
C Eng — Chartered Engineer
Cestr — of Chester (*Bishop*)
CET — Central European Time
Common External Tariff
cf — (*confer*) compare
CF — Chaplain to the Forces
CFC — Chlorofluorocarbon
CFS — Chronic Fatigue Syndrome
CGC — Conspicuous Gallantry Cross
Cgeol — Chartered Geologist
CGM — Conspicuous Gallantry Medal
CGS — Centimetre-gramme-second
(*system*) Chief of General Staff

CH	Companion of Honour	DCVO	Dame Commander, Royal	ED	Efficiency Decoration
ChB/M	Bachelor/Master of Surgery		Victorian Order	EEC	European Economic
CI	Channel Islands	DD	Doctor of Divinity		Community
	The Imperial Order of the	DDS	Doctor of Dental Surgery	EEG	Electroencephalogram
	Crown of India	DDT	dichlorodiphenyl-	EFA	European Fighter Aircraft
CIA	Central Intelligence Agency		trichloroethane	EFTA	European Free Trade
Cicestr	of Chichester (*Bishop*)	del	(*delineavit*) he/she drew it		Association
CID	Criminal Investigation	DEFRA	Department of the	eg	(*exempli gratia*) for the sake of
	Department		Environment, Food and Rural		example
CIE	Companion, Order of the		Affairs	EIB	European Investment Bank
	Indian Empire	DFC	Distinguished Flying Cross	EMS	European Monetary System
cif	cost, insurance and freight	DfES	Department for Education	EMU	European Monetary Union
C-in-C	Commander-in-Chief		and Skills	EOC	Equal Opportunities
CIPFA	Chartered Institute of Public	DFID	Department for International		Commission
	Finance and Accountancy		Development	EPSRC	Engineering and Physical
CIS	Commonwealth of	DFM	Distinguished Flying Medal		Sciences Research Council
	Independent States	DG	(*Dei gratia*) By the grace of	ER	(*Elizabetha Regina*) Queen
CJD	Creutzfeld-Jakob disease		God		Elizabeth
C Lit	Companion of Literature	DH	Department of Health	ERD	Emergency Reserve
CLJ	Commander, Order of St	DHA	District Health Authority		Decoration
	Lazarus of Jerusalem	Dip Ed	Diploma in Education	ERM	Exchange Rate Mechanism
CM	(*Chirurgiae Magister*) Master	Dip HE	Diploma in Higher Education	ERNIE	Electronic random number
	of Surgery	Dip Tech	Diploma in Technology		indicator equipment
CMG	Companion, Order of St	DJ	Disc jockey	ESA	European Space Agency
	Michael and St George	DL	Deputy Lieutenant	ESP	Extra-sensory perception
CND	Campaign for Nuclear	D.Litt	Doctor of Letters or of	ESRC	Economic and Social Research
	Disarmament		Literature		Council
c/o	care of	DM	Deutsche Mark	ETA	*Euzkadi ta Askatasuna* (Basque
CO	Commanding Officer	D.Mus.	Doctor of Music		separatist organization)
	conscientious objector	DNA	deoxyribonucleic acid	et al	(*et alibi*) and elsewhere
COD	Cash on delivery	DNB	*Dictionary of National*		(*et alii*) and others
C of E	Church of England		*Biography*	etc	(*et cetera*) and the other
COI	Central Office of Information	do	(*ditto*) the same		things/and so forth
Col	Colonel	DOS	Disk operating system	et seq	(*et sequentia*) and the
Con	Conservative		(computer)		following
cons	consecrated	DP	Data processing	EU	European Union
Cpl	Corporal	D.Phil *or*	Doctor of Philosophy	Euratom	European Atomic Energy
CPM	Colonial Police Medal	Ph.D			Commission
CPS	Crown Prosecution Service	DPP	Director of Public	Exon	of Exeter (*Bishop*)
CPVE	Certificate of Pre-Vocational		Prosecutions		
	Education	Dr	Doctor	f	(*forte*) loud
CRE	Commission for Racial	D Sc	Doctor of Science	F	Fahrenheit
	Equality	DSC	Distinguished Service Cross		Fellow of
CSA	Child Support Agency	DSM	Distinguished Service Medal	FA	Football Association
CSE	Certificate of Secondary	DSO	Companion, Distinguished	FANY	First Aid Nursing Yeomanry
	Education		Service Order	FAO	Food and Agriculture
CSI	Companion, Order of the Star	DTI	Department of Trade and		Organisation (*UN*)
	of India		Industry	FBA	Fellow, British Academy
CVO	Commander, Royal Victorian	DTLR	Department of Transport,	FBAA	Fellow, British Association of
	Order		Local Government and the		Accountants and Auditors
			Regions	FBI	Federal Bureau of
d	(*denarius*) penny	DTP	Desk-top publishing		Investigation
DA	District Attorney (*USA*)	Dunelm	of Durham (*Bishop*)	FIMgt	Fellow, Institute of
DBE	Dame Commander, Order of	DV	(*Deo volente*) God willing		Management
	the British Empire	DWP	Department for Work and	FBS	Fellow, Botanical Society
dc	direct current		Pensions	FC	Football Club
DC	District Council			FCA	Fellow, Institute of Chartered
	District of Columbia	E	East		Accountants in England and
DCB	Dame Commander, Order of	Ebor	of York (*Archbishop*)		Wales
	the Bath	EBRD	European Bank for	FCCA	Fellow, Chartered Association
D Ch	(*Doctor Chirurgiae*)		Reconstruction and		of Certified Accountants
	Doctor of Surgery		Development	FCGI	Fellow, City and Guilds of
DCL	Doctor of Civil Law	EC	European Community		London Institute
DCM	Distinguished Conduct Medal	ECG	Electrocardiogram	FCIA	Fellow, Corporation of
DCMG	Dame Commander, Order of	ECGD	Export Credits Guarantee		Insurance Agents
	St Michael and St George		Department	FCIArb	Fellow, Chartered Institute of
DCMS	Department for Culture,	ECSC	European Coal and Steel		Arbitrators
	Media and Sport		Community		
		ECU	European Currency Unit		

FCIB	Fellow, Chartered Institute of Bankers Fellow, Corporation of Insurance Brokers	FPhS	Fellow, Philosophical Society	FRPharmS	Fellow, Royal Pharmaceutical Society
		FRAD	Fellow, Royal Academy of Dancing	FRPS	Fellow, Royal Photographic Society
FCIBSE	Fellow, Chartered Institution of Building Services Engineers	FRAeS	Fellow, Royal Aeronautical Society	FRS	Fellow, Royal Society
FCII	Fellow, Chartered Insurance Institute	FRAI	Fellow, Royal Anthropological Institute	FRSA	Fellow, Royal Society of Arts
				FRSC	Fellow, Royal Society of Chemistry
FCIPS	Fellow, Chartered Institute of Purchasing and Supply	FRAM	Fellow, Royal Academy of Music	FRSE	Fellow, Royal Society of Edinburgh
FCIS	Fellow, Institute of Chartered Secretaries and Administrators	FRAS	Fellow, Royal Asiatic Society Fellow, Royal Astronomical Society	FRSH	Fellow, Royal Society of Health
FCIT	Fellow, Chartered Institute of Transport			FRSL	Fellow, Royal Society of Literature
		FRBS	Fellow, Royal Botanic Society Fellow, Royal Society of British Sculptors	FRTPI	Fellow, Royal Town Planning Institute
FCMA	Fellow, Chartered Institute of Management Accountants			FSA	Fellow, Society of Antiquaries
FCO	Foreign and Commonwealth Office	FRCA	Fellow, Royal College of Anaesthetists	FSS	Fellow, Royal Statistical Society
FCP	Fellow, College of Preceptors	FRCGP	Fellow, Royal College of General Practitioners	FSVA	Fellow, Incorporated Society of Valuers and Auctioneers
FD	(*Fidei Defensor*) Defender of the Faith	FRCM	Fellow, Royal College of Music	FT	*Financial Times*
FE	Further Education	FRCO	Fellow, Royal College of Organists	FTI	Fellow, Textile Institute
fec	(*fecit*) made this			FTII	Fellow, Chartered Institute of Taxation
ff	(*fecerunt*) made this (pl) folios following	FRCOG	Fellow, Royal College of Obstetricians and Gynaecologists	FZS	Fellow, Zoological Society
ff	(*fortissimo*) very loud	FRCP	Fellow, Royal College of Physicians, London	G7	Group of Seven (Canada, France, Germany, Italy, Japan, UK, USA)
FFA	Fellow, Faculty of Actuaries (*Scotland*) Fellow, Institute of Financial Accountants	FRCPath	Fellow, Royal College of Pathologists		
		FRCPE or FRCPEd	Fellow, Royal College of Physicians, Edinburgh	G8	Group of Eight (Canada, France, Germany, Italy, Japan, Russia, UK, USA)
FFAS	Fellow, Faculty of Architects and Surveyors	FRCPI	Fellow, Royal College of Physicians, Ireland	GATT	General Agreement on Tariffs and Trade
FFCM	Fellow, Faculty of Community Medicine	FRCPsych	Fellow, Royal College of Psychiatrists	GBE	Dame/Knight Grand Cross, Order of the British Empire
FFPHM	Fellow, Faculty of Public Health Medicine	FRCR	Fellow, Royal College of Radiologists	GC	George Cross
FGS	Fellow, Geological Society	FRCS	Fellow, Royal College of Surgeons of England	GCB	Dame/Knight Grand Cross, Order of the Bath
FHS	Fellow, Heraldry Society			GCE	General Certificate of Education
FHSM	Fellow, Institute of Health Service Management	FRCSE or FRCSEd	Fellow, Royal College of Surgeons of Edinburgh	GCHQ	Government Communications Headquarters
FIA	Fellow, Institute of Actuaries	FRCSGlas	Fellow, Royal College of Physicians and Surgeons of Glasgow	GCIE	Knight Grand Commander, Order of the Indian Empire
FIBiol	Fellow, Institute of Biology			
FICE	Fellow, Institution of Civil Engineers	FRCSI	Fellow, Royal College of Surgeons in Ireland	GCLJ	Knight Grand Cross, Order of St Lazarus of Jerusalem
FICS	Fellow, Institution of Chartered Shipbrokers	FRCVS	Fellow, Royal College of Veterinary Surgeons	GCMG	Dame/Knight Grand Cross, Order of St Michael and St George
FIEE	Fellow, Institution of Electrical Engineers	FREconS	Fellow, Royal Economic Society	GCSE	General Certificate of Secondary Education
FIERE	Fellow, Institution of Electronic and Radio Engineers	FREng	Fellow, Royal Academy of Engineering	GCSI	Knight Grand Commander, Order of the Star of India
		FRGS	Fellow, Royal Geographical Society	GCVO	Dame/Knight Grand Cross, Royal Victorian Order
FIFA	International Association Football Federation	FRHistS	Fellow, Royal Historical Society	GDP	Gross domestic product
FIM	Fellow, Institute of Metals			Gen	General
FIMM	Fellow, Institution of Mining and Metallurgy	FRHS	Fellow, Royal Horticultural Society	GHQ	General Headquarters
				GM	George Medal
FInstF	Fellow, Institute of Fuel	FRIBA	Fellow, Royal Institute of British Architects	GMB	General, Municipal, Boilermakers and Allied Trades Union
FInstP	Fellow, Institute of Physics			
FIQS	Fellow, Institute of Quantity Surveyors	FRICS	Fellow, Royal Institution of Chartered Surveyors	GMT	Greenwich Mean Time
FIS	Fellow, Institute of Statisticians	FRMetS	Fellow, Royal Meteorological Society	GNP	Gross national product
				GNVQ	General National Vocational Qualification
FJI	Fellow, Institute of Journalists	FRMS	Fellow, Royal Microscopical Society	
fl	(*floruit*) flourished			GOC	General Officer Commanding
FLA	Fellow, Library Association	FRNS	Fellow, Royal Numismatic Society	GP	General Practitioner
FLS	Fellow, Linnaean Society			Gp Capt	Group Captain
FM	Field Marshal frequency modulation			GSA	Girls' Schools Association
fo	folio				
FO	Flying Officer				
fob	free on board				

HAC	Honourable Artillery Company	IEA	International Energy Agency	KCVO	Knight Commander, Royal Victorian Order
HB	His Beatitude	IFAD	International Fund for Agricultural Development	KG	Knight of the Garter
HBM	Her/His Britannic Majesty('s)	IFC	International Finance	KGB	(*Komitet Gosudarstvennoi Besopasnosti*) Committee of State Security (*USSR*)
HCF	Highest common factor		Corporation		
	Honorary Chaplain to the Forces	IHS	(*Iesus Hominum Salvator*) Jesus the Saviour of Mankind	kHz	kiloHertz
HE	Her/His Excellency	ILO	International Labour Office/Organisation	KLJ	Knight, Order of St Lazarus of Jerusalem
	Higher Education				
	His Eminence	ILR	Independent local radio	ko	knock out (*boxing*)
HGV	Heavy Goods Vehicle	IMF	International Monetary Fund	KP	Knight, Order of St Patrick
HH	Her/His Highness	IMO	International Maritime Organisation	KStJ	Knight, Order of St John of Jerusalem
	Her/His Honour				
	His Holiness	Inc	Incorporated	Kt	Knight
HIM	Her/His Imperial Majesty	incog	(*incognito*) unknown, unrecognised	KT	Knight of the Thistle
HIV	Human immunodeficiency virus			kV	Kilovolt
		INLA	Irish National Liberation Army	kW	Kilowatt
HJS	(*hic jacet sepultus*) here lies buried			kWh	Kilowatt hour
		in loc	(*in loco*) in its place		
HM	Her/His Majesty('s)	Inmarsat	International Maritime Satellite Organisation	L	Liberal
HMAS	Her/His Majesty's Australian Ship			Lab	Labour
		INRI	(*Iesus Nazarenus Rex Iudaeorum*) Jesus of Nazareth, – King of the Jews	Lat	Latitude
HMC	Headmasters' Conference			lbw	leg before wicket
HMI	Her/His Majesty's Inspector			lc	lower case (*printing*)
HML	Her/His Majesty's Lieutenant	inst	(*instant*) current month	LCJ	Lord Chief Justice
HMS	Her/His Majesty's Ship	Intelsat	International Telecommunications Satellite Organisation	LCM	Least/lowest common multiple
HMSO	Her/His Majesty's Stationery Office			LD	Liberal Democrat
				LDS	Licentiate in Dental Surgery
HNC	Higher National Certificate	Interpol	International Criminal Police Commission	LEA	Local Education Authority
HND	Higher National Diploma			LHD	(*Literarum Humaniorum Doctor*) Doctor of Humane Letters/Literature
HOLMES	Home Office Large Major Enquiry System	IOC	International Olympic Committee		
		IOM	Isle of Man	Lib	Liberal
Hon	Honorary	IOU	I owe you	Lic	(*Licenciado*) lawyer (*Spanish*)
	Honourable	IOW	Isle of Wight	Lic Med	Licentiate in Medicine
hp	horse power	IQ	Intelligence quotient	Lit	Literary
HP	Hire purchase	IRA	Irish Republican Army	Lit Hum	(*Literae Humaniores*) Faculty of classics and philosophy, Oxford
HQ	Headquarters	IRC	International Red Cross		
HR	Human resources	Is	Islands		
HRH	Her/His Royal Highness	ISBN	International Standard Book Number	Litt.D.	Doctor of Letters
HSE	Health and Safety Executive			LJ	Lord Justice
	(*hic sepultus est*) here lies buried	ISO	Imperial Service Order	LLB	Bachelor of Laws
			International Standards Organisation	LLD	Doctor of Laws
HSH	Her/His Serene Highness			LLM	Master of Laws
HWM	High water mark			LM	Licentiate in Midwifery
		ISSN	International Standard Serial Number	LMS	Local management in schools
I	Island	ITC	Independent Television Commission	LMSSA	Licentiate in Medicine and Surgery, Society of Apothecaries
IAAS	Incorporated Association of Architects and Surveyors				
		ITN	Independent Television News	loc cit	(*loco citato*) in the place cited
IAEA	International Atomic Energy Agency	ITU	International Telecommunication Union	log	logarithm
				Londin	of London (*Bishop*)
IATA	International Air Transport Association	ITV	Independent Television	Long	Longitude
ibid	(*ibidem*) in the same place	JP	Justice of the Peace	LS	(*loco sigilli*) place of the seal
IBRD	International Bank for Reconstruction and Development			LSA	Licentiate of Society of Apothecaries
		K	Köchel numeration (*of Mozart's works*)		
ICAO	International Civil Aviation Organisation			Lsd	(*Librae, solidi, denarii*) £, shillings and pence
		KBE	Knight Commander, Order of the British Empire		
ICBM	Inter-continental ballistic missile			LSE	London School of Economics and Political Science
		KCB	Knight Commander, Order of the Bath		
ICFTU	International Confederation of Free Trade Unions			Lt	Lieutenant
		KCIE	Knight Commander, Order of the Indian Empire	LTA	Lawn Tennis Association
ICJ	International Court of Justice			Ltd	Limited (liability)
ICRC	International Committee of the Red Cross	KCLJ	Knight Commander, Order of St Lazarus of Jerusalem	LTh *or* L Theol	Licentiate in Theology
id	(*idem*) the same	KCMG	Knight Commander, Order of St Michael and St George	LVO	Lieutenant, Royal Victorian Order
IDA	International Development Association				
		KCSI	Knight Commander, Order of the Star of India	LW	long wave
IDD	International direct dialling			LWM	Low water mark
ie	(*id est*) that is				

M   Member or Monsieur
MA   Master of Arts
Maj   Major
max   maximum
MB   Bachelor of Medicine
MBA   Master of Business
              Administration
MBE   Member, Order of the British
              Empire
MC   Master of Ceremonies
              Military Cross
MCC   Marylebone Cricket Club
MCh(D)   Master of (Dental) Surgery
MD   Managing Director
              Doctor of Medicine
MDS   Master of Dental Surgery
ME   Middle English or Myalgic
              Encephalomyelitis
MEC   Member of Executive Council
MEd   Master of Education
mega   one million times
MEP   Member of the European
              Parliament
MFH   Master of Foxhounds
Mgr   Monsignor
MI   Military Intelligence
micro   one-millionth part
milli   one-thousandth part
min   minimum
MIRAS   Mortgage Interest Relief at
              Source
MLA   Member of Legislative
              Assembly
MLC   Member of Legislative Council
MLitt   Master of Letters
Mlle   Mademoiselle
MLR   Minimum lending rate
MM   Military Medal
Mme   Madame
MN   Merchant Navy
MO   Medical Officer/Orderly
MoD   Ministry of Defence
MoT   Ministry of Transport
MP   Member of Parliament
              Military Police
mph   miles per hour
M Phil   Master of Philosophy
MR   Master of the Rolls
MRC   Medical Research Council
MS   Master of Surgery
              Manuscript (pl MSS)
              Multiple Sclerosis
MSc   Master of Science
MSF   Manufacturing, Science and
              Finance Union
MSP   Member of Scottish
              Parliament
MTh   Master of Theology
Mus B/D   Bachelor/Doctor of Music
MV   Merchant Vessel
              Motor Vessel
MVO   Member, Royal Victorian
              Order
MW   medium wave
MWA   Member of the Welsh
              Assembly

N   North
n/a   not applicable
              not available

NAAFI   Navy, Army and Air Force
              Institutes
NASA   National Aeronautics and
              Space Administration
NAS/UWT   National Association of
              Schoolmasters/Union of
              Women Teachers
NATO   North Atlantic Treaty
              Organisation
NB   New Brunswick
              (nota bene) note well
NCIS   National Criminal Intelligence
              Service
NCO   Non-commissioned officer
NDPB   Non-departmental public
              body
NEB   New English Bible
nem con   (nemine contradicente) no
              one contradicting
NERC   Natural Environment Research
              Council
nes   not elsewhere specified
NFT   National Film Theatre
NFU   National Farmers' Union
NHS   National Health Service
NI   National Insurance
              Northern Ireland
NIV   New International Version (of
              Bible)
No   (numero) number
non seq   (non sequitur) it does not
              follow
Norvic   of Norwich (Bishop)
NP   Notary Public
NRA   National Rifle Association
NS   New Style (calendar)
              Nova Scotia
NSPCC   National Society for the
              Prevention of Cruelty to
              Children
NSW   New South Wales
NT   National Theatre
              National Trust
              New Testament
NUJ   National Union of Journalists
NUM   National Union of
              Mineworkers
NUS   National Union of Students
NUT   National Union of Teachers
NVQ   National Vocational
              Qualification
NWT   Northwest Territory
NY   New York
NZ   New Zealand

OAS   Organisation of American
              States
OAU   Organisation of African Unity
Ob or obit   died
OBE   Officer, Order of the British
              Empire
OC   Officer Commanding
ODA   Overseas Development
              Administration
OE   Old English
              omissions excepted

OECD   Organisation for Economic
              Co-operation and
              Development
OED   Oxford English Dictionary
OFM   Order of Friars Minor
              (Franciscans)
Ofsted   Office for Standards in
              Education
OFT   Office of Fair Trading
Oftel   Office of Telecommunications
Ofwat   Office of Water Services
OHMS   On Her/His Majesty's Service
OM   Order of Merit
ONO   or near offer
ONS   Office for National Statistics
op   (opus) work
OP   Opposite prompt side (of
              theatre)
              Order of Preachers
              (Dominicans)
              out of print (books)
op cit   (opere citato) in the work
              cited
OPCS   Office of Population Censuses
              and Surveys
OPEC   Organisation of Petroleum
              Exporting Countries
OPRAF   Office of Passenger Rail
              Franchising
OPS   Office of Public Service
ORR   Office of the Rail Regulator
OS   Old Style (calendar)
              Ordnance Survey
OSA   Order of St Augustine
OSB   Order of St Benedict
OSCE   Organisation for Security and
              Co-operation in Europe
O St J   Officer, Order of St John of
              Jerusalem
OT   Old Testament
OTC   Officers' Training Corps
Oxon   (of) Oxford
              Oxfordshire

p   page
              (piano) softly
PA   Personal Assistant
              Press Association
PAYE   Pay as You Earn
pc   (per centum) in the hundred
PC   personal computer
              Police Constable
              politically correct
              Privy Counsellor
PCC   Press Complaints Commission
PDSA   People's Dispensary for Sick
              Animals
PE   Physical Education
PEP   Personal equity plan
Petriburg   of Peterborough (Bishop)
PFI   Private Finance Initiative
PGA   Professional Golfers
              Association
PGCE   Postgraduate Certificate of
              Education
Ph.D. or
D.Phil.   Doctor of Philosophy
pinx(it)   he/she painted it
pl   plural
PLA   Port of London Authority

PLC	Public Limited Company	
PLO	Palestine Liberation Organisation	
pm	(*post meridiem*) after noon	
PM	Prime Minister	
PMRAFNS	Princess Mary's Royal Air Force Nursing Service	
PO	Petty Officer	
	Pilot Officer	
	Post Office	
	postal order	
POW	Prisoner of War	
pp	pages	
	(*per procurationem*) by proxy	
PPARC	Particle Physics and Astronomy Research Council	
PPS	Parliamentary Private Secretary	
PR	Proportional representation	
	Public relations	
PRA	President of the Royal Academy	
Pro tem	(*pro tempore*) for the time being	
Prox	(*proximo*) next month	
PRS	President of the Royal Society	
PRSE	President of the Royal Society of Edinburgh	
Ps	Psalm	
PS	(*postscriptum*) postscript	
PSBR	Public sector borrowing requirement	
psc	passed Staff College	
PSV	Public Service Vehicle	
PTA	Parent-Teacher Association	
Pte	Private	
PTO	Please turn over	
PVC	Polyvinyl chloride	
QARANC	Queen Alexandra's Royal Army Nursing Corps	
QARNNS	Queen Alexandra's Royal Naval Nursing Service	
QB(D)	Queen's Bench (Division)	
QC	Queen's Counsel	
QED	(*quod erat demonstrandum*) which was to be proved	
QGM	Queen's Gallantry Medal	
QHC	Queen's Honorary Chaplain	
QHDS	Queen's Honorary Dental Surgeon	
QHNS	Queen's Honorary Nursing Sister	
QHP	Queen's Honorary Physician	
QHS	Queen's Honorary Surgeon	
QMG	Quartermaster General	
QPM	Queen's Police Medal	
QS	Quarter Sessions	
QSO	Quasi-stellar object (quasar)	
	Queen's Service Order	
quango	quasi-autonomous non-governmental organisation	
qv	(*quod vide*) which see	
R	(*Regina*) Queen	
	(*Rex*) King	
RA	Royal Academy/Academician	
	Royal Artillery	
RAC	Royal Armoured Corps	
Royal	Automobile Club	
RADA	Royal Academy of Dramatic Art	

RADC	Royal Army Dental Corps	
RAE	Royal Aerospace Establishment	
RAEC	Royal Army Educational Corps	
RAeS	Royal Aeronautical Society	
RAF	Royal Air Force	
RAM	Random-access memory (*computer*)	
	Royal Academy of Music	
RAMC	Royal Army Medical Corps	
RAN	Royal Australian Navy	
RAOC	Royal Army Ordnance Corps	
RAPC	Royal Army Pay Corps	
RAVC	Royal Army Veterinary Corps	
RBG	Royal Botanic Garden	
RBS	Royal Society of British Sculptors	
RC	Red Cross	
	Roman Catholic	
RCM	Royal College of Music	
RCN	Royal Canadian Navy	
RCT	Royal Corps of Transport	
RD	Refer to drawer (*banking*)	
	Royal Naval and Royal Marine Forces Reserve Decoration	
	Rural Dean	
RDI	Royal Designer for Industry	
RE	Religious Education	
	Royal Engineers	
REME	Royal Electrical and Mechanical Engineers	
Rep	Representative	
	Republican	
Rev(d)	Reverend	
RFU	Rugby Football Union	
RGN	Registered General Nurse	
RGS	Royal Geographical Society	
RHA	Regional Health Authority	
RHS	Royal Horticultural Society	
RI	Rhode Island	
	Royal Institute of Painters in Watercolours	
	Royal Institution	
RIBA	Royal Institute of British Architects	
RIP	(*Requiescat in pace*) May he/she rest in peace	
RIR	Royal Irish Regiment	
RL	Rugby League	
RM	Registered Midwife	
	Royal Marines	
RMA	Royal Military Academy	
RMN	Registered Mental Nurse	
RMT	National Union of Rail, Maritime and Transport Workers	
RN	Royal Navy	
RNIB	Royal National Institute for the Blind	
RNID	Royal National Institute for the Deaf	
RNLI	Royal National Lifeboat Institution	
RNMH	Registered Nurse for the Mentally Handicapped	
RNR	Royal Naval Reserve	
RNVR	Royal Naval Volunteer Reserve	
RNXS	Royal Naval Auxiliary Service	

RNZN	Royal New Zealand Navy	
Ro	(*Recto*) on the right-hand page	
ROC	Royal Observer Corps	
Roffen:	of Rochester (Bishop)	
ROI	Royal Institute of Oil Painters	
ROM	Read-only memory (*computer*)	
RoSPA	Royal Society for the Prevention of Accidents	
RP	Royal Society of Portrait Painters	
rpm	revolutions per minute	
RRC	Lady of Royal Red Cross	
RSA	Republic of South Africa	
	Royal Scottish Academician	
	Royal Society of Arts	
RSC	Royal Shakespeare Company	
RSCN	Registered Sick Children's Nurse	
RSE	Royal Society of Edinburgh	
RSM	Regimental Sergeant Major	
RSPB	Royal Society for the Protection of Birds	
RSPCA	Royal Society for the Prevention of Cruelty to Animals	
RSV	Revised Standard Version (*of Bible*)	
RSVP	(*Répondez, s'il vous plaît*) Please reply	
RSW	Royal Scottish Society of Painters in Watercolours	
RTPI	Royal Town Planning Institute	
RU	Rugby Union	
RUC	Royal Ulster Constabulary	
RV	Revised Version (*of Bible*)	
RVM	Royal Victorian Medal	
RWS	Royal Water Colour Society	
RYS	Royal Yacht Squadron	
s	second	
	(*solidus*) shilling	
S	South	
SA	Salvation Army	
	South Africa	
	South America	
	South Australia	
SAE	stamped addressed envelope	
Salop	Shropshire	
Sarum	of Salisbury (*Bishop*)	
SAS	Special Air Service Regiment	
SBN	Standard Book Number	
SBS	Special Boat Squadron	
ScD	Doctor of Science	
SCM	State Certified Midwife	
SDLP	Social Democratic and Labour Party	
SEAQ	Stock Exchange Automated Quotations system	
SEN	State Enrolled Nurse	
SERPS	State Earnings Related Pension Scheme	
SFO	Serious Fraud Office	
SHMIS	Society of Headmasters and Headmistresses of Independent Schools	

SI	(*Système International 'Unités*) International System of Units	UCAS	Universities and Colleges Admissions Service	WFTU	World Federation of Trade Unions
	Statutory Instrument	UCATT	Union of Construction, Allied Trades and Technicians	WHO	World Health Organisation
sic	so written			WI	West Indies
Sig	Signature	UCL	University College London		Women's Institute
	Signor	UDA	Ulster Defence Association	Winton:	of Winchester (*Bishop*)
SJ	Society of Jesus (*Jesuits*)	UDI	Unilateral Declaration of Independence	WIPO	World Intellectual Property Organisation
SLD	Social and Liberal Democrats				
SMP	Statutory Maternity Pay	UDM	Union of Democratic Mineworkers	WMO	World Meteorological Organisation
SNP	Scottish National Party				
SOE	Special Operations Executive	UDR	Ulster Defence Regiment	WO	Warrant Officer
SOS	Save Our Souls (*distress signal*)	UEFA	Union of European Football Associations	WRAC	Women's Royal Army Corps
				WRAF	Women's Royal Air Force
sp	(*sine prole*) without issue	UFF	Ulster Freedom Fighters	WRNS	Women's Royal Naval Service
spgr	specific gravity	UFO	Unidentified flying object	WRVS	Women's Royal Voluntary Service
SPQR	(*Senatus Populusque Romanus*) The Senate and People of Rome	UHF	ultra-high frequency		
		UK	United Kingdom	WS	Writer to the Signet
		UKAEA	UK Atomic Energy Authority	WTO	World Trade Organisation
SRN	State Registered Nurse	UN	United Nations		
SRO	Self Regulating Organisations	UNESCO	United Nations Educational, Scientific and Cultural Organisation	YMCA	Young Men's Christian Association
SS	Saints				
	Schutzstaffel (Nazi paramilitary organisation)			YWCA	Young Women's Christian Association
		UNHCR	United Nations High Commissioner for Refugees		
	Steamship				
SSC	Solicitor before Supreme Court (*Scotland*)	UNICEF	United Nations Children's Fund		
SSF	Society of St Francis	UNIDO	United Nations Industrial Development Organisation		
SSN	Standard Serial Number				
SSP	Statutory Sick Pay	Unita	National Union for the Total Independence of Angola		
SSSI	Site of special scientific interest				
		UPU	Universal Postal Union		
STD	(*Sacrae Theologiae Doctor*) Doctor of Sacred Theology	URC	United Reformed Church		
		US(A)	United States (of America)		
	Subscriber trunk dialling	USDAW	Union of Shop, Distributive and Allied Workers		
stet	let it stand (printing)				
stp	Standard temperature and pressure	USM	Unlisted Securities Market		
		USSR	Union of Soviet Socialist Republics		
STP	(*Sacrae Theologiae Professor*) Professor of Sacred Theology				
		UTC	Co-ordinated Universal Time system		
Sub Lt	Sub-Lieutenant				
SVQ	Scottish Vocational Qualification	UVF	Ulster Volunteer Force		
		v	(*versus*) against		
TA	Territorial Army	VA	Vicar Apostolic		
TB	Tuberculosis		Victoria and Albert Order		
TCCB	Test and County Cricket Board	VAD	Voluntary Aid Detachment		
		V and A	Victoria and Albert Museum		
TD	Territorial Efficiency Decoration	VAT	Value added tax		
		VC	Victoria Cross		
TEC	Training and Enterprise Council	VCR	video cassette recorder		
		VD	Venereal disease		
TEFL	Teaching English as a foreign language		Volunteer Officers' Decoration		
		VDU	Visual display unit		
temp	temperature	Ven	Venerable		
	temporary employee	VHF	very high frequency		
TGWU	Transport and General Workers' Union	VIP	Very important person		
		Vo	(*Verso*) on the left-hand page		
TNT	trinitrotoluene (*explosive*)	VRD	Royal Naval Volunteer Reserve Officers' Decoration		
trans	translated				
trs	transpose (*printing*)	VSO	Voluntary Service Overseas		
TRH	Their Royal Highnesses	VTOL	Vertical take-off and landing (*aircraft*)		
TT	Teetotal				
	Tourist Trophy (motorcycle races) Tuberculin tested	W	West		
		WCC	World Council of Churches		
TUC	Trades Union Congress	WEA	Workers' Educational Association		
U	Unionist				
UAE	United Arab Emirates	WEU	Western European Union		
uc	upper case (*printing*)				

Index

3G mobile service 583
2003 calendar 12
2004 calendar 13

A
A-levels 467
   see also Vocational A-levels
abbreviations 1296–1302
Aberavon
   constituencies
      UK Parliament 263
      Welsh Assembly 350
Aberdeen 405
   airport 540
   Bishop (RC) 570
   constituencies
      Scottish Parliament 356
      UK Parliament 266
   education authority 480
   unitary authority 374, 406
   universities 483, 489
Aberdeen and Orkney, Bishop 566
Aberdeenshire
   education authority 480
   unitary authority 374, 406
Aberdeenshire West & Kincardine
   constituency
      Scottish Parliament 356
      UK Parliament 266
Abertay Dundee, university of 483
Aberystwyth, University College of
   490
abortions, statistics 110
Abu Dhabi 787, 1093
Abuja 785, 1019
academic periodicals 706–8
academic staff 472–3
   see also teachers
academies of scholarship, national
   725–6
Academy Awards 1208
ACAS 301
access funds 475
accession, to the EU 796, 797
accidents
   prevention at sea 106
   on railways 542
   road 545
accountancy, professional
   qualifications 493
accounts, National Savings and
   Investments 639
Accra 785, 931
Achonry, Bishop (RC) 570
Acts of Parliament (2001–2002)
   1232–3
actuarial science, professional bodies
   493
Addis Ababa 784, 916
Additional Pension 522, 523
address, forms of 133
Adjudicator's Office 301
administration, professional bodies
   493–4

Admirals of the Fleet 451
admissions and course information
   education 482
   see also UCAS
adoption 664
   local authority services 520
adult education 475
   colleges 492
   grants 475
Adur, district council 371, 388
Advanced examinations see
   A-levels
Advanced Extension Awards 467
Advanced Subsidiary level
   examinations 467
Advent Sunday 85
Advisory, Conciliation and
   Arbitration Service (ACAS) 301
advisory bodies, education 481
Advisory Council on Public Records
   337
Afghanistan 786, 834–5
   US offensive 1172–3
Africa
   countries of, area and population
      784–5
   currencies and exchange rates
      789–92
   events (2001–2) 1147–9
   geographical statistics 775
African churches, UK 571
African Union 823
Afro-Caribbean churches, UK 571
Agana 788
Agenda (2000) 797
Agricultural Land Tribunals 433
agricultural properties, tenancies in
   675
agricultural research institutes,
   Scotland 727
AIDS, statistics 512
AIM 646
air, distances from London by 782
air passengers 540–41
air pollution 590
air quality, UK targets 590
air transport 540–41
Airdrie & Shotts
   constituencies
      Scottish Parliament 356
      UK Parliament 266
airlines, UK 540
airmail letter rates 578
airmail zones
   Europe 578
   outside Europe 580–82
airports, UK 540–41
Akmola see Astana
al-Qa'eda 1172–3, 1175
Alabama 1098
Alaska 1098
Albania 787, 835–6
aldermen, Corporation of London
   394, 395

Alderney 412
Aldershot, constituency 237
Aldridge-Brownhills, constituency
   237
Alexandra Palace 616
Algeria 784, 836–8
Algiers 784, 837
algol, minima of see months of the
   year e.g. January, minima of algol
aliens, status of 666
All-Party Parliamentary Archaeology
   Group (APPAG) 1180–1
Allerdale, district council 371, 388
allowances, income tax 653–4
Almeida theatre 1244, 1246
Alnwick, district council 371, 388
Alofi 788
alpine skiing, sports results (2001–2)
   1262
Alternative Investment Market
   (AIM) 646
Altrincham & Sale West,
   constituency 237
Alyn & Deeside
   constituencies
      UK Parliament 263
      Welsh Assembly 350
Amber Valley
   constituency 237
   district council 371, 388
ambulance service 517–8
Americas
   countries of, area and population
      785–6
   currencies and exchange rates
      789–92
   events (2001–2) 1149–52
   geographical statistics 776
american football, sports results
   1262
American Orthodox Church 574
American Samoa 788, 1102
Ammān 786, 963
Amsterdam 788, 1012
   Treaty of 798, 799, 801
Ancient Monuments Board
   for Scotland 301
   for Wales 301
Andean Community 807
Andorra 787, 838–9
Andorra la Vella 787, 838
Anglesey
   education authority 479
   unitary authority 374, 402
Anglia Polytechnic University 483
Anglican Communion
   overseas 566–7
   UK 554–66
Anglican theological colleges
   501–502
angling 1262
   representative body 733
Angola 784, 839–40
Anguilla 785, 1119
angular measures 1292

Angus
  constituencies
    Scottish Parliament 356
    UK Parliament 266
  education authority 480
  unitary authority 374, 406
animals, cloning of 1240
Anjou, House of 127
Ankara 787, 1086
annual reference books 716–9
annulment of marriage 670
Antananarivo 785, 987
Antarctic 783
  Australian 847
  British 1120
  French territory 924
  Norwegian 1023
Antarctic Treaty 783
Antarctica
  geographical statistics 776
  lakes beneath 1236
anthrax 1242
Antigua and Barbuda 785, 840–1
Antilles, Netherlands 786, 1014
Antrim 410
  constituencies 270
  district council 410
Aomen 888–9
AONBs (Areas of Outstanding
  Natural Beauty) 593–4
APACS 632
apes 96
Apia 788, 1047
Apostolic Nuncio
  to Great Britain 569
  to Ireland 570
Apparent Sidereal Time 75
Apparent Solar Time 75
appeal courts 415, 417–8
  Northern Ireland 431
  Scotland 428
Appeals Service 433
applicant states, EU 796
Applied Industrial Research 731
April
  astronomical phenomena 30
  calendar 30
  constellations in 30
  high water 101
  Jupiter in 31, 33
  Mars in 31, 32
  Mercury in 31, 32
  minima of algol 30
  Moon 30
    position 32
  Neptune in 33
  night sky 31
  Saturn in 31, 33
  Sun, position 31
  sunrise and sunset 33
  twilight 31
  Uranus in 33
  Venus in 31, 32
AQA 467, 482
aquarium and visitor centre,
  Kingston-upon-Hull 1182
Arab Maghreb Union (AMU) 807
archaeology (2001–2) 1177–81
Archbishop of Canterbury 163, 555
Archbishop of Wales 565

Archbishop of York 163, 555
archbishops 163
  Church of Ireland 566
  Roman Catholic Church
    England and Wales 569
    Ireland 570
    Scotland 570
Archbishops of Canterbury (since
  1414) 114
Archbishops' Council 554
archdeacons, Church of England
  555–65
archery 733
architecture, professional bodies 493
architecture (2001–2) 1182–6
Architecture and the Built
  Environment, Commission for
  309
Ardagh and Clonmacnois, Bishop
  (RC) 570
Ards, district council 410
area
  conversion tables 1295
  countries of Africa 784–5
  countries of America 785
  countries of Asia 786–7
  countries of Europe 787–8
  countries of Oceania 788
  of the Earth 775
  measurement
    imperial 1291
    metric 1290
  of oceans and seas 775
  The World 784
  UK 109
Areas of Outstanding Natural Beauty
  (AONBs) 593–4
Areas of Special Scientific Interest
  (ASSIs) 595
Argentina 786, 841–3
Argyll and Bute
  constituencies
    Scottish Parliament 356
    UK Parliament 266
  education authority 480
  unitary authority 374, 406
Argyll and the Isles
  Bishop (Anglican) 566
  Bishop (RC) 570
Arizona 1098
Arkansas 1098
Armagh 410
  Archbishop (Anglican) 566
  Archbishop (RC) 570
  district council 410
armed forces
  pay and pensions 457–60
  pay review body 338
  ranks 459
  strengths 447
  see also Army; Royal Air Force;
    Royal Navy
Armenia 787, 843–4
arms control 447–8
Army
  constitution of 454–5
  equipment holdings 455
  ranks 459
  staff appointments 453–4
  strength 447

art (2001–2) 1187–90
art galleries see galleries
art market 1190
art therapies, professional body
  498–9
artificial satellites 80
  launchings 80–2
arts, events (2001–2) 1135–6
arts broadcasting 1190
Arts Councils 301–2
  England 301, 1217
  Northern Ireland 302
  regional 301–2
  Scotland 302
  Wales 302
Aruba 785, 1014
Arun, district council 371, 388
Arundel & South Downs,
  constituency 237
Arundel and Brighton, Bishop (RC)
  569
AS-level qualifications 467
Ascension Day 85
Ascension Island 785, 1125–6
Ash Wednesday 85
Ashfield
  constituency 237
  district council 371, 388
Ashford
  constituency 237
  district council 371, 388
Ashgabat 787, 1088
Ashmore Islands 847
Ashton under Lyne, constituency
  237
Asia
  countries of, area and population
    786–7
  currencies and exchange rates
    789–92
  events (2001–2) 1152–7
  geographical statistics 776
Asia-Pacific Economic Co-operation
  (APEC) 808
Asian Development Bank (ADB)
  807–8
Asmara 784, 914
assay office marks 621
Assembly Ombudsman for Northern
  Ireland and Northern Ireland
  Commissioner for Complaints 303
Assessment and Qualifications
  Alliance see AQA
ASSIs (Areas of Special Scientific
  Interest) 595
Assisted Places Scheme 465
Associated Presbyterian Churches of
  Scotland 571
association agreements 796
Association of British Insurers (ABI)
  641
association football
  representative bodies 733
  sports results (2001–2) 1262–4
Association for Payment Clearing
  Services 632
Association of South East Asian
  Nations (ASEAN) 808
assured shorthold tenancies 674
Astana 786, 965

asteroids
collisions between 1243
monitoring of 1237
Aston, Bishop Suffragan 557
Aston University 483
astronomical constants 77
astronomical data 17–72
explanation 73–7
astronomical phenomena 73
see also months of the year e.g.
January, astronomical phenomena
etc
astronomical twilight 74
see also months of year e.g. January,
twilight
Asunción 786, 1030
Athens 787, 932
athletics 733, 1264–5
national (UK) records 1288–9
world records 1287–9
Atholl, House of 129
Atomic Time 76
Attendance Allowance 527
weekly rates 527
Attorney-General 415
Audit Commission 303
Audit Office, Northern Ireland 330
Audit Scotland 304
August
astronomical phenomena 46
calendar 46
constellations in 46
high water 103
Jupiter in 47, 49
Mars in 47, 48
Mercury in 47, 48
meteors 47
minima of algol 46
Moon 46
position 48
Neptune in 47, 49
night sky 47
Saturn in 47, 49
Sun, position 47
sunrise and sunset 49
twilight 47
Uranus in 47, 49
Venus in 47, 48
Australasia and the Pacific, events
(2001–2) 1157
countries of 788
currencies of 789–92
Australia 788, 845–7
external territories 847–8
geographical statistics 776
Australian Antarctic Territory 847
Australian Capital Territory 845
australopithecines 96
Austria 787, 848–9
EU membership 795
awards, National Lottery 629
Aylesbury, constituency 237
Aylesbury Vale, district council 371,
388
Ayr
constituencies
Scottish Parliament 356
UK Parliament 266
Azerbaijan 787, 850–51
Azores 1038

B
Babergh, district council 371, 388
BACS Ltd 632
badminton 733, 1265
Baghdad 786, 950
Bahá'í faith 549–50
Bahamas 785, 851–2
Bahrain 786, 852–3
Baki (Baku) 787, 850
balance of payments 625
insurance industry contribution
641
Balearic Isles 1066
Balliol, House of 129
Ballymena, district council 410
Ballymoney, district council 410
Baltic Assembly (BA) 808
Bamako 785, 992
Banbridge, district council 410
Banbury, constituency 237
Bandar Seri Begawan 786, 870
Banff & Buchan
constituencies
Scottish Parliament 356
UK Parliament 266
Bangkok 787, 1080
Bangladesh 786, 854–5
Bangor
Bishop 565
University College of 490
Bangui 784, 880
Banjul 784, 925
Bank of England 304, 632
bank holidays 12, 13, 89
Bank for International Settlements
(BIS) 808–9
banking 632
professional bodies 493
banknotes 631
banns, marriage by 678
Baptist church 571–2
Baptist theological colleges 502
Bar, the 497
Barbados 785, 855–6
Barbican Centre 616, 1214
productions 1248
Barbuda, Antigua and 840–41
Barking
Bishop Suffragan 558
constituency 237
Barking and Dagenham
education authority 478
London borough council 374, 399
Barnet 374, 399
education authority 478
Barnsley
constituencies 237
education authority 476
metropolitan borough council
371, 387
baronesses
forms of address 133
hereditary 153–4
life 160–62
baronetage and knightage 173–203
baronets 173
forms of address 133
list of 173–203
barons 145–53
courtesy titles 164–5
forms of address 133

hereditary 145–53
life 155–60
Barrow and Furness, constituency
237
Barrow-in-Furness, district council
371, 388
base units, SI 1290
baseball 733, 1265–6
Basildon
constituency 237
district council 371, 388
Basingstoke
Bishop Suffragan 556
constituency 237
Basingstoke and Deane, district
council 371, 388
basketball 733, 1266
Basseterre 786, 923, 1045
Bassetlaw
constituency 237
district council 371, 388
Basutoland *see* Lesotho
Bath 378
constituency 237
Most Honourable Order 170
university of 483
Bath and North-East Somerset
education authority 476
unitary authority 373, 387
Bath and Wells, Bishop 163, 556
Batley & Spen, constituency 237
Battersea, constituency 238
BBC 305–6, 686
BBC 4 1192
BBC, ratings 1191
BBC Radio 688
local stations 689
network services 688–9
BBC Scottish Symphony Orchestra
(SSO) 1215
BBC six pips signal 76–7
BBC Television 687
BBC World Service 689–90
BBC Worldwide Ltd 687
Beacon Schools 463
Beaconsfield, constituency 238
Beaufort Scale of wind force 1257
Beckenham, constituency 238
Bedford
Bishop Suffragan 563
constituency 238
district council 371, 388
Bedfordshire
constituencies 238
county council 371, 385, 386
education authority 476
Beijing 786, 883
Beirut 787, 977
Belarus 787, 856–8
Belfast 408, 788
constituencies 270
district council 410
education and library board 480
Belgium 787, 858–60
EU membership 795
independent schools 511
Belgrade 788, 1113
Belize 785, 860–61
Belmopan 785, 860

benefits
claims and questions 530
contributory 523, 524–6
for industrial injuries and
disablement 524, 529–30
liability to income tax 652
non-contributory 526–9
see also tax credits
benevolent societies 634
number of 635
Benin 784, 861–2
bereavement benefits 525
weekly rates 526
Berlin 787, 928
Bermuda 785, 1119–20
Bern 788, 1073
Bern Convention (1979) 598
Berwick-upon-Tweed
constituency 238
district council 371, 388
Bethnal Green and Bow,
constituency 238
Beverley, Bishop Suffragan 555
Beverley & Holderness, constituency
238
Bexhill & Battle, constituency 238
Bexley
education authority 478
London borough council 374, 399
Bexleyheath & Crayford,
constituency 238
Bhutan 786, 862–3
Big Bang (London Stock Exchange)
646
Big Ben 617
Billericay, constituency 238
billiards 733
billion, definition 1292
bills, parliamentary 221, 222
biodiversity 598
biological research institutes,
Scotland 727
biomedical sciences, professional
body 499
Biotechnology and Biological
Sciences Research Council
(BBSRC) 727
bioterrorism 1242
Birkenhead
Bishop Suffragan 558
constituency 238
Birmingham 378
Archbishop (RC) 569
Bishop 163, 557
constituencies 238–9
education authority 476
metropolitan borough council
371, 387
theatre productions 1251
universities 483, 484
Birmingham Contemporary Music
Group (BCMG) 1215
Birmingham Royal Ballet 1203
productions 1205
birth certificates 665
births
abroad, registration of 665
outside marriage, statistics 111
registration of 664–5
statistics 110

Bishkek 787, 973
Bishop Auckland, constituency 239
Bishop of London, stipend 555
bishops 163
Church of England 555–65
Church of Ireland 566
Church in Wales 565–6
Roman Catholic Church
England And Wales 569–70
Ireland 570–71
Scotland 570
Scottish Episcopal Church 566
Bishops Conference
England and Wales 568–9
Scotland 569
Bishops of Rome see Popes
Bissau 785, 936
bissextile years 83
Blaby
constituency 239
district council 371, 388
black holes 1238
Black Sea Economic Co–operation
(BSEC) 823
Blackburn
Bishop 163, 557
constituency 239
Blackburn with Darwen
education authority 477
unitary authority 373, 387
Blackpool
constituencies 239
education authority 477
unitary authority 373, 387
Blaenau Gwent
constituencies
UK Parliament 263
Welsh Assembly 350
education authority 479
unitary authority 374, 402
Blaydon, constituency 239
Bloemfontein 785
blood service 518
Blyth Valley
constituency 239
district council 371, 388
Board of Inland Revenue 304–5
bobsleigh 734
Bognor Regis & Littlehampton,
constituency 239
Bogotá 786, 889
Bolivia 786, 863–5
Bolsover
constituency 239
district council 371, 388
Bolton
Bishop Suffragan 561
constituencies 239
education authority 477
metropolitan borough council
371, 387
bonds, National Savings and
Investments 639–40
Bonn Convention (1979) 598
Booker Prize see Man Booker Prize
books
annual reference 716–19
publishers 711
sizes 1294
see also literature (2001–2)

Bootle, constituency 239
borough councils see London
borough councils; metropolitan
borough councils; district
councils; unitary authorities
Bosnia-Hercegovina 787, 865–6
Boston, district council 371, 388
Boston & Skegness, constituency 239
Bosworth, constituency 239
Botswana 784, 867–8
bottles of wine, measurements in
1292
bound books, sizes 1294
Boundary Commission 305
Bournemouth
constituencies 239
education authority 477
unitary authority 373, 387
Bournemouth University 483
Bouvet Island 1023
bowls 734, 1266
boxing 734, 1266–7
Bracknell, constituency 240
Bracknell Forest
education authority 477
unitary authority 373, 387
Bradford
Bishop 163, 557
constituencies 240
education authority 477
metropolitan borough council
371, 387
university of 483
Bradwell, Bishop Suffragan 558
Braintree
constituency 240
district council 371, 388
Brasília 786, 868
Bratislava 788, 1057
Brazil 786, 868–70
Brazzaville 784, 893
Brechin, Bishop 566
Breckland, district council 371, 388
Brecon & Radnorshire
constituencies
UK Parliament 263–4
Welsh Assembly 350
Brecon Beacons 592
Brent
constituencies 240
education authority 478
London borough council 374, 399
Brentford & Isleworth, constituency
240
Brentwood
Bishop (RC) 569
district council 371, 389
Brentwood & Ongar, constituency
240
Brethren see Plymouth Brethren
Bridgend
constituencies
UK Parliament 264
Welsh Assembly 350
education authority 479
unitary authority 374, 402
bridges
London 616
longest by span 780–81
see also Iron Bridge

Bridgetown 785, 855
Bridgwater, constituency 240
Bridgnorth, district council 372, 389
Brigg & Goole, constituency 240
Brighton
  constituencies 240
  university of 483
Brighton and Hove
  education authority 477
  unitary authority 373, 387
Bristol 378
  Bishop 163, 557
  constituencies 240–1
  education authority 477
  unitary authority 373, 387
  universities of 483, 490
Britain see UK
British Academy 725
British Affairs (events 2001–2)
  1129–33
British Antarctic Territory 1120
British Broadcasting Corporation see
  BBC
British Citizenship 666
British Council 306
British Empire, Most Excellent Order
  171–2
British Film Commission (BFC) 306
British Film industry 1209
British Film Institute (BFI) 306
British Indian Ocean Territory
  1120–21
British Library 323
British Museum 326, 611
  problems of 1188
British Nationals (Overseas) 666
British Overseas Citizenship 666
British Pharmacopoeia Commission
  306
British Protected Pensions 666
British Sky Broadcasting (BSkyB)
  688
British Standards Institution (BSI)
  306
British subjects 666
British Summer Time 17, 77
British Tourist Authority 306–7
British Transport Police 441
British Virgin Islands 1120
British Waterways 307
Brixworth, Bishop Suffragan 562
broadcasting 686–97
  arts 1190
broadcasting (2001–2) 1191–5
Broadcasting Standards Commission
  307, 686
Broadland, district council 372, 389
Broads, The 593
Broads Authority 307
Bromley
  education authority 478
  London borough council 374, 399
Bromley & Chislehurst, constituency
  241
Bromsgrove
  constituency 241
  district council 372, 389
Bronze Age 98
bronze coin 630

brown papers, measures of 1293
Broxbourne
  constituency 241
  district council 372, 389
Broxtowe
  constituency 241
  district council 372, 389
Bruce, House of 129
Brunei 870
Brunel University 483
Brussels 787, 858
Brussels Treaty Organisation (BTO)
  see Western European Union
  (WEU)
BSI 306
BT Cellnet see O_2
BTEC qualifications 470
  Higher National Certificate 473
  Higher National Diplomas 473
Bucharest 788, 1039
Buckingham
  Area Bishop 562
  constituency 241
  university of 472, 483
Buckinghamshire
  county council 371, 385, 386
  education authority 476
Budapest 787, 941
Buddhism 550
Budget (2002) 623–5
Budgeting Loans 529
budgets
  EU 799–800
  UN 827
Buenos Aires 786, 841
building, professional bodies 493
building societies 632
  conversions and mergers 636
  interest rates 636
  liberalisation of 635–6
  listing 637–8
  ombudsman scheme 636
  statistics for activity 636
buildings
  conservation of 1199–1201
  historic 602–7
  tallest inhabited 780
Bujumbura 784, 873
Bulgaria 787, 870–72
burial 669
Burkina Faso 784, 872–3
Burma see Myanmar
Burnley
  Bishop Suffragan 557
  constituency 241
  district council 372, 389
Burton, constituency 241
Burundi 784, 873–4
Bury
  constituencies 241
  education authority 477
  metropolitan borough council
  371, 387
Bury St Edmunds, constituency 241
bus services 544
Bushy Park 618
business
  events (2001–2) 1141–3
  professional bodies 493–4
business lettings 675
business rates 366

business services, for postal needs
  579
by-elections 222–3
  Scottish Parliament 359
  UK Parliament 271
  Welsh Assembly 352
Byzantine Orthodox Church see
  Eastern Orthodox Church

C
CAA 308, 540
CAB International (CABI) 809
Cabinet 223, 272
Cabinet Office 275–7
Cadw: Welsh Historic Monuments
  301, 1200
see also historic buildings and
  monuments, Wales
Caernarfon
  constituencies
    UK Parliament 264
    Welsh Assembly 350
Caerphilly
  constituencies
    UK Parliament 264
    Welsh Assembly 350
  education authority 479
  unitary authority 374, 402
Caicos Islands, Turks and 1126
Cairo 784, 910
Caithness, Sutherland and Easter
  Ross
  constituencies
    Scottish Parliament 356
    UK Parliament 266
Calder Valley, constituency 241
Calderdale
  education authority 477
  metropolitan borough council
  371, 387
calendar years 83
calendars 11–13
  1780–2040 92–5
  Chinese 90
  Christian 84
  civil and legal 88–9
  Coptic 90
  Hindu 86–7
  Japanese 90
  Jewish 87
  Muslim 88
  Roman 91
  Sikh 88
  Thai 88
  Zoroastrian 90–91
see also months of the year e.g.
  January, calendar
California 1098
Carmarthen, constituencies 264
Carmarthenshire, education
  authority 479
Camberwell & Peckham,
  constituency 241
Cambodia 786, 874–5
Cambrian era 96
Cambridge 378
  constituency 241
  district council 372, 389
  university of 483–4

Cambridge coin hoard 1180
Cambridgeshire
  constituencies 241
  county council 385, 386
  education authority 476
Camden
  education authority 478
  London borough council 374, 399
Camelot Group plc 629
Cameroon 784, 875–6
Canada 785, 876–9
canals
  longest 781
  see also Panama Canal Zone
Canary Islands 1066
Canberra 788, 845
Cannock Chase
  constituency 241
  district council 372, 389
canoeing 734
canons, Church of England 555–65
Canterbury 378
  Archbishop 163, 555
  Archbishops of (since 1414) 114
  constituency 242
  district council 372, 389
cantilever bridges, longest 781
CAP 799
capacity
  measurement
    imperial 1291
    metric 1291
Cape Town 785, 1062
Cape Verde 784, 879–80
Capital Bonds 640
capital gains tax
  assessment 654–6
  exemptions 656
  relief from 656–7
Capri 960
Caracas 786, 1108
Caradon, district council 372, 389
Carboniferous era 96
Cardiff 401
  Archbishop (RC) 569
  constituencies
    UK Parliament 264
    Welsh Assembly 350
  education authority 479
  unitary authority 374, 402
  University College of 490
Cardiff (Caerdydd) 788
care, local authority 520
Caribbean Community and
  Common Market (CARICOM)
  809
Carlisle 378–9
  Bishop 163, 557
  constituency 242
  district council 372, 389
Carmarthen
  constituencies
    UK Parliament 264
    Welsh Assembly 350
Carmarthenshire, unitary authority
  374, 402
Carrick, district council 372, 389
Carrick, Cumnock & Doon Valley
  constituencies
    Scottish Parliament 356
    UK Parliament 266

Carrickfergus, district council 410
cars see motor vehicles
Carshalton & Wallington,
  constituency 242
Cartier Island 847
Cashel, Archbishop (RC) 570
Cashel and Ossory, Bishop 566
Castle Morpeth, district council 372,
  389
Castle Point
  constituency 242
  district council 372, 389
Castlereagh, district council 410
Castries 786, 1046
catering, professional body 496
cats, cloning of 1240
Cayenne 786, 923
Cayman Islands 785, 1121–2
CBI 720
CCW (Countryside Council for
  Wales) 595
CDC Capital Partners 291
celestial objects, monitoring of
  1237–8
Celsius scale 1293
cemeteries, London 616
Cenotaph 616
Cenozoic era 96
census of population 109–10
centenaries 16
centigrade scale see Celsius scale
Central African Republic 784,
  880–81
Central America
  countries of, area and population
  785–6
  geographical statistics 776
Central Arbitration Committee 307,
  722
central bank see Bank of England
Central England in Birmingham,
  university of 484
Central Laboratory of the Research
  Councils (CLRC) 728
Central Lancashire, university of 484
Central Office of Information (COI)
  277
Central Science Laboratory (CSL)
  283
Central Statistical Office see Office
  for National Statistics
centralised societies 634
  number of 635
Centre for Management and Policy
  Studies (CMPS) 276
Cerdic and Denmark, Houses of
  126–7
Ceredigion
  constituencies
    UK Parliament 264
    Welsh Assembly 351
  education authority 479
  unitary authority 374, 402
CERN (European Organisation for
  Nuclear Research) 814
certificate, marriage by 678
certificates, National Savings and
  Investments 640
certificates of posting 579
Certification Office for Trade Unions
  and Employers' Associations 307

Ceuta 1066
CG66 (Voluntary Safety
  Identification Scheme) 106
Chad 784, 881–2
Chancery Division, High Court of
  Justice 416, 418
Channel 4 688
Channel 5 688, 1191
  estimated audience share 687
Channel Four Television 688
Channel Islands 412
  banknotes 631
  independent schools 510
  see also Guernsey; Jersey
Channel Tunnel 541, 542
  rail links 542–3
CHAPS Clearing Company Ltd 632
charges, NHS 517
charitable donations, tax relief 654
Charity Commission 307–8
Charlotte Amalie 786, 1102
Charnwood
  constituency 242
  district council 372, 389
Charterhouse 616
Chatham & Aylesford, constituency
  242
Chatto, Lady Sarah 115
Cheadle, constituency 242
Chelmsford
  Bishop 163, 558
  district council 372, 389
Chelmsford West, constituency 242
Chelsea Physic Garden 616
Cheltenham
  constituency 242
  district council 372, 389
Cheltenham International Festival of
  Music 1216
Cheque and Credit Clearing
  Company Ltd 632
Chequers 616–17
Cherwell, district council 372, 389
Chesham & Amersham, constituency
  242
Cheshire
  county council 385, 386
  education authority 476
chess 734, 1267
Chester 379
  Bishop 163, 558
  district council 372, 389
Chester, City of, constituency 242
Chester-le-Street, district council
  372, 389
Chesterfield
  constituency 242
  district council 372, 389
Chichester
  Bishop 163, 558
  constituency 242
  district council 372, 389
  theatre productions 1251
chiefs of clans 211–12
Chief Constables
  listing of 439–40
  rates of pay 438
Child Benefit 526
  weekly rates 527
child health services, NHS 517

Child Support Agency (CSA) 300, 670–71
Child Support Commissioners 436
    Northern Ireland 436
Child Tax Credit 524
children
    adoption of 664
    local authority services 519–20
    parental responsibility for 670
    protection of, local authority services 520
    registration of births 664–5
    with special education needs (SEN) 465
    tracing adopted 664
Children's Bonus Bonds 639
children's tax credit 653
Chile 786, 882–3
Chiltern, district council 372, 389
China 786, 883–7
    special administrative regions 887–9
Chinese calendar 90
Chingford & Woodford Green, constituency 242
Chipping Barnet, constituency 242
chiropody, professional body 499
chiropractic, professional bodies 494
Chişinău 788, 1001
Chivalry, Orders of 170–2
Chorley
    constituency 242
    district council 372, 389
chough redivivus 1198
Christadelphianism 577
Christ, Scientist, Church of 577
Christchurch
    constituency 242
    district council 372, 389
Christian calendar 11, 84–6
Christianity 548–9
    adherents in UK 548
    early English 377–8
Christmas Island 847
chronological cycles and eras 11, 89
chronological eras, Roman calendar 91
Church of Christ, Scientist 577
Church Commissioners 308
Church of England 554
    diocesan bishops 163
    dioceses 555–8
    marriage in 678
        fees 679
    membership 554–5
    structure 554
Church of Ireland 566
Church of Jesus Christ of Latter-Day Saints 577
Church of Scotland 567–8
    theological colleges 502
Church in Wales 565–6
Church of Wales
    marriage in 678
        fees 679
churches
    co-operation between 548
    denominations 554–77
Churches Together in Britain and Ireland 548

Chuuk 1000
cinema see film
circuit judges 417, 421–2
circuits, High Court and Crown Court 420–21
circular measures 1292
circulation
    banknotes 631
    newspapers 698
Cities of London & Westminster, constituency 242
citizenship
    EU naturalisation 666
    UK 665–6
City & Guilds 470
    Diplomas of Vocational Education 467
City Academies 463
City of Birmingham Symphony Orchestra 1217
City Colleges for the Technology of the Arts (CCTAs) 463
city guilds, London 369, 396–8
City of London 394
    education authority 479
City of London Police 441
    rates of pay 438
City of London Sinfonia 1214
City Technology Colleges (CTCs) 463
City University 484
City of Westminster, see Westminster
civic dignities, local government 367
civil aviation 540–1
Civil Aviation Authority (CAA) 308, 540
civil calendar 11, 89
civil cases 417
    Scotland 428
civil legal aid 676–7
    in Scotland 677
Civil list 120–21
civil marriages 678
    fees 679
Civil Service 274
Civil Service Commissioners, Office of (OCSC) 275
civil twilight 73
    see also months of year e.g. January, twilight
civil year 88
Clackmannanshire
    education authority 480
    unitary authority 374, 406
clans, chiefs of 211–12
classical music (2001–2) 1214–7
Clearing Houses, Recognised 648
Cleethorpes, constituency 242
clergy
    Church of England 555–65
        numbers 554–5
    Church of Ireland 566
    Church of Scotland 567–8
    Church in Wales 565–6
        overseas 566–7
    Roman Catholic Church 569–71
    Scottish Episcopal Church 566
    clerical services, NHS 516–17
Clifton, Bishop (RC) 569
climate change 590, 1196
    modelling 1241–2

Clogher
    Bishop (Anglican) 566
    Bishop (RC) 570
Clonfert, Bishop (RC) 570
cloning animals 1240
Cloyne, Bishop (RC) 570
clubs 738–40
Clwyd
    constituencies
        UK Parliament 264
        Welsh Assembly 351
Clydebank & Milngavie
    constituencies
        Scottish Parliament 356
        UK Parliament 266
Clydesdale
    constituencies
        Scottish Parliament 357
        UK Parliament 266
Co-operation Council for the Arab States of the Gulf 811–12
Co-ordinated Universal Time (UTC) 76
coach services 544
coal 536–7
Coal Authority 308, 536
Coastguard, HM (HMCG) 106, 547
coastguard service 106
Coatbridge & Chryston
    constituencies
        Scottish Parliament 357
        UK Parliament 266
Cocos Islands 847
cohabiting couples 671
coin hoard, Cambridge 1180
coinage, UK 630
Colchester
    Bishop Suffragan 558
    constituency 242
    district council 372, 389
Cold Weather Payments 529
Coleraine, district council 410
collecting societies 634
    number of 635
College of Arms 308–9
colleges
    defence 494–5
    listing of 490–1
Colne Valley, constituency 242
Colombia 786, 889–90
Colombo 787, 1066
Colonia 1000
Colorado 1098
Columbia, District of (USA) 1098
comets, observation of 1237–8
commemorative marks 622
commercial galleries 1187
Commercial Radio Companies Association (CRCA) 690
commercial radio see independent radio
Commissary Office, HM 429
Commission for Architecture and the Built Environment (CABE) 309
Commission for Integrated Transport 309
Commission for Local Administration
    in England 325
    in Wales 325

Commission for Racial Equality 309
Commission, EC *see* EC
Commissioner for Public
  Appointments, Office of (OCPA)
  275
Commissioners, EC 797–8
Committee of the Regions (COR)
  803
Committee on Standards in Public
  Life 309
Common Agricultural Policy 799
Common Council, Corporation of
  London 394, 395–6
common entrance examinations 465
Common Foreign and Security
  Policy (CFSP) 801
common law holidays 89
common licence, marriage by 678
Commons Commissioners 433
Commons *see* House of Commons
Commonwealth 809–10
  intergovernmental and other links
  810
  membership 810
Commonwealth Agricultural Bureau
  see CAB International
Commonwealth Foundation 810
commonwealth games 1267–70
Commonwealth of Independent
  States (CIS) 811
Commonwealth Institute 309–10
Commonwealth Secretariat 810
Commonwealth War Graves
  Commission 310
Communication Group 276–7
communications 578–84
Communities Scotland 310
Community Care Grants 529
community child health services,
  NHS 517
community councils
  Scotland 370
  Wales 369
Community Fund 310
community health care 515–7
Community Health Councils 513
Community Legal Service 676
community schools 462
Comoros 784, 890–91
Companies House 295
Companions of Honour, Order of
  172
compensation, postal 579
Compensation Agency, Northern
  Ireland 293
Competition Commission 310–11
complaints, about the press 698
complaints, *see* Ombudsmen
complementary medicine,
  professional body 499
Comptroller, Lord Chamberlain's
  Office 119
compulsory retirement, service
  retired pay 459–60
computers
  glossary of terms 586–8
  history 585
  operating systems (OS) 585–6
  programming languages 585

Conakry 785, 937
conceptual art, controversy over
  1187
Confederation of British Industry
  (CBI) 720
Conference on Disarmament (CD)
  827
Conference on Interaction and
  Confidence Building Measures in
  Asia (CICA) 811
Conference on Security and
  Co-operation (CSCE) *see*
  Organisation for Security and
  Co-operation in Europe (OSCE)
confirmation of wills 682–3
Congleton
  constituency 242–3
  district council 372, 389
Congo, Democratic Republic of
  784, 892–3
Congo-Brazzaville, Republic of
  784, 893–4
Congregational Federation 572
Congregational theological college
  502
Connecticut 1098
Connor, Bishop 566
conservation 592–601, 1196–201
  the built environment 1199–1201
  of the countryside 592–6
  of wildlife and habitats 598–9,
  1196–9
  UK legislation 599–601
  world cultural and natural
  heritage 597
Conservative Party 224–5
  development 224
Consignia plc 311, 578
constant tidal differences 99
constellations 73
  see also months of the year e.g.
  January, constellations
constituencies
  Scottish Parliament 356–9
  UK Parliament 219
  England 236–63
  Northern Ireland 270
  Scotland 266–9
  Wales 263–5
  Welsh Assembly 350–1
constitution, UK 216
consumer credit 667–8
consumer law 666–8
  in Scotland 668
consumer periodicals 702–6
consumer protection 667
Contemporary Arts, Institute of
  (ICA) 1187
Contemporary Music Network
  (CMN) 1215
continents 775–6
  area and population 784–8
  see also Africa; America; Antarctica;
  Asia; Australia; Europe
continuing education 475
  colleges 492
  grants 475
contract services, mobile 582
Contracted-Out Money Purchase
  Schemes (COMP) 523

contracted-out occupational pension
  schemes 523
Contracted-Out Salary Related
  Schemes (COSR) 523
contributory benefits 523, 524–6
  weekly rates 526
contribution-based Jobseeker's
  Allowance (JSA) 524–5
  weekly rates 526
convention hallmarks 622
Convention on International Trade
  in Endangered Species of Wild
  Fauna and Flora (1973) 598
conversion tables
  temperature scales 1293
  weights and measures 1295
Conwy
  constituencies
    UK Parliament 264
    Welsh Assembly 351
  education authority 479
  unitary authority 374, 402
Cook Islands 788, 1016
Cookstown, district council 410
Copeland
  constituency 243
  district council 372, 389
Copenhagen 787, 902
Coptic Orthodox Church 574
copyright 684
  licensing 684
Copyright Tribunal 433
Coral Sea Islands Territory 847–8
Corby
  constituency 243
  district council 372, 389
Cork, Cloyne and Ross, Bishop 566
Cork and Ross, Bishop (RC) 570
Cornwall
  constituencies 243
  county council 385, 386
  Duchy of 314
  education authority 476
coroners' courts 417
Corporation of London 368–9,
  394–6, 399
Corporation of London Records
  Office 337
corporation tax 661–2
Corporation of Trinity House 324
Corps of Queen's Messengers 285
Corpus Christi 85
cost of living 628
Costa Rica 785, 894–5
Côte D'Ivoire 784, 895–6
Cotswold
  constituency 243
  district council 372, 389
Council of the Baltic Sea States
  (CBSS) 812
Council of Christians and Jews 548
Council of Churches for Britain and
  Ireland *see* Churches Together in
  Britain and Ireland
Council for the Curriculum,
  Examinations and Assessment
  (CCEA) 467
Council for Dance Education and
  Training (CDET) 494

Council of Europe 812
Council of the European Union 797
Council of Ministers 797
council tax 365–6
council tax benefits 529
Council on Tribunals 311
Counsellors of the State 216
countesses in own right 142
  forms of address 133
counties
  England 384
    map 393
  Northern Ireland 410
  Wales 401
countryside, conservation 592–6
Countryside Agency 311
Countryside Council for Wales
  (CCW) 312, 595
county councils
  area and population 385
  England 365, 367
    map 393
  political composition 371
  standard spending and chief
    officers 386
county courts 417
  Northern Ireland 431–2
  course information, admissions
    and 482
  see also UCAS
Court of Common Council see
  Common Council
Court of First Instance 803
Court of Justice of the European
  Communities 802
Court of the Lord Lyon 312
court orders, for domestic
  proceedings 671
Court Service 292
Court of Session 428–9
courtesy titles 164
courts of appeal see appeal courts
courts see law courts
Covent Garden Market Authority
  312
Coventry 379
  Bishop 163, 558
  constituencies 243
  education authority 477
  metropolitan borough council 371,
    387
Coventry University 484
Craigavon, district council 410
Cranbourne Money 224
Cranfield University 484
Craven, district council 372, 389
Crawley
  constituency 243
  district council 372, 389
credit 667–8
credit accumulation and transfer
  (CATS) 473
Credit Unions (CUs) 635
Crediton, Bishop Suffragan 559
cremation 669
Cretaceous era 96
Crewe and Nantwich
  constituency 243
  district council 372, 389
cricket 734, 1270–71

crime, events (2001–2) 1136–40
criminal cases 415–16
  Scotland 428
Criminal Cases Review Commission
  312
Criminal Defence Service 676
Criminal Injuries Compensation
  Appeals Panel (CICAP) 312
Criminal Injuries Compensation
  Authority (CICA) 312
criminal legal aid 677
  in Scotland 677
Crisis Loans 529
Croatia 787, 897–8
Crofters Commission 313
croquet 734
Crosby, constituency 243
cross-media ownership 686
Crown, proceedings against 668
Crown Court 416
  centres 420–21
Crown Estate 313
Crown of India, Imperial Order 171
Crown Office 428, 430
Crown Prosecution Service (CPS)
  416, 426–28
Crown Solicitor, Northern Ireland
  432
Croydon
  Area Bishop 564
  constituencies 243
  education authority 479
  London borough council 374, 399
  CSA 670–71
Cuba 785, 898–9
cultural development of Man 98
Cultural Strategy Group for London
  (CSGL) 347
Culture, Media and Sport,
  Department for 277–8
Cumbernauld & Kilsyth
  constituencies
    Scottish Parliament 357
    UK Parliament 266
Cumbria
  county council 385, 386
  education authority 476
Cunninghame
  constituencies
    Scottish Parliament 357
    UK Parliament 266
curling 1271
currencies
  UK 630–31
  of the World 789–92
curriculum, schools 465–7
curriculum councils 481
custody see parental responsibility
Customs and Excise 313
  HM 313
cycles and eras, chronological 11, 89
cycling 734, 1271–2
Cynon Valley
  constituencies
    UK Parliament 264
    Welsh Assembly 351
Cyprus 787, 900–901
Czech Republic 787, 901–2

D
Dacorum, district council 372, 389
Dagenham, constituency 243
Dakar 785, 1052
Dalap-Uliga-Darrit 788, 995
Damascus 787, 1075
dames 205–7
  forms of address 133
  list of 205–7
Dames Commanders 205
Dames Grand Cross 205
dams, tallest 780
dance, professional bodies 494
dance (2001–2) 1202–6
  new work 1203
  productions 1205
  visiting companies 1204
Darlington
  constituency 243
  education authority 477
  unitary authority 373, 387
Dartford
  constituency 243
  district council 372, 389
Dartmoor 592
darts 734, 1272
Datapost 579
date letters 621
  London (Goldsmiths' Hall) 622
Daventry
  constituency 243
  district council 372, 389
day care, local authority services 520
days
  definition 83
  for flying flags 113
  Hindu 86
  Jewish 87
De Montfort University 484
deans, Church of England 555–65
death certificates 665
deaths
  causes 512
  legal notes 668–9
  registration of 669
  statistics 111
  analysis by cause 112
Debt Management Office, UK 298
December
  astrological phenomena 62
  calendar 62
  constellations in 62
  high water 105
  Jupiter in 63, 65
  Mars in 63, 64
  Mercury in 63, 64
  meteors 63
  minima of algol 62
  Moon 62
    position 64
  Neptune in 65
  night sky 63
  Saturn in 63, 65
  Sun, position 63
  sunrise and sunset 65
  twilight 63
  Uranus in 65
  Venus in 63, 64

Decommissioning, Independent
   International Commission on 320
decorations and medals 208–10
decree absolute 670
decree nisi 670
Deer Commission for Scotland 313
defence 447–60
   budget 448
   colleges 494–5
   Ministry of 447, 448
      executive agencies 450–1
      staff 448–50
      pay & pensions 457–60
   see also armed forces
Defence Capabilities Initiative (DCI)
   821
Defence Council 447, 448
Defence Procurement Agency (DPA)
   450
DEFRA 281–4, 535
degree courses 473
Delaware 1098
delivery services, special 579–80
Delivery Unit 275–6
Delyn
   constituencies
      UK Parliament 264
      Welsh Assembly 351
Democratic People's Republic of
   Korea 786, 969
Democratic Unionist Party 225
development 224
Denbighshire
   education authority 479
   unitary authority 374, 402
Denmark 787, 902–4
   EU membership 795
Denmark and Cerdic, Houses of
   126–7
dentistry, qualifying body 495
dentists
   pay review body 338–9
   salaries 515
Denton & Reddish, constituency 244
depression, deepest 777
depth of oceans and seas 775
Deputy Prime Minister, Office of the
   278–9
Derby 379
   Bishop 163, 559
   constituencies 244
   education authority 477
   unitary authority 373, 387
   university of 484
Derby, The 1275
Derbyshire
   constituencies 243–4
   county council 385, 386
   education authority 476
Derbyshire Dales, district council
   372, 389
derived units, SI 1290
Derry
   Bishop (RC) 570
   district council 410
Derry and Raphoe, Bishop 566
Derwent Valley 1180
Derwentside, district council 372,
   389

descendants, of Queen Victoria
   124–6
deserts, largest 777
Design Council 313
design protection 685
design rights 685
Designated Professional Bodies
   647–8
Devizes, constituency 244
devolution 217
Devon
   constituencies 244
   county council 385, 386
   education authority 476
Devonian era 96
Dewsbury, constituency 244
Dhaka 786, 854
dietetics, professional body 495
digital multiplexes 696–7
digital radio 688, 1194
digital television 686–7, 1191, 1192
Dili 786, 907
dimensions, of the Earth 775
diocesan clergy see clergy
dioceses, Church of England 555–68
Diploma of Higher Education
   (DipHE) 473
Directorates of Health and Social
   Care (England) 514
Disability Living Allowance 527
   weekly rates 527
Disability Rights Commission
   (DRC) 314
Disability Working Allowance see
   Disabled Person's Tax Credit
disabled people, local authority
   services 519
Disabled Person's Tax Credit 524
discretionary payments, Social Fund
   529
discrimination, in employment 673
distance
   of the Earth from the Sun 775
   nautical measurement 1292
distance of the horizon 1293
distances from London by air 782
Distinguished Service Order 172
district councils 388–92
   England 365, 367
   Northern Ireland 370, 410
   political composition 371–3
district courts 428
district judges 417, 425–6
dividends 652
divorce
   legal notes 669–71
   Scotland, legal notes 671–2
   statistics 111
Djibouti 784, 904–5
Djibouti (capital city) 784, 904
doctors' pay review body 338–9
Dodoma 785, 1079
Dog Days 83
Doha (Al-Dawhah) 787, 1038
dolphins, threat to 1199
domestic violence 671
Dominica 785, 905–6
dominical letters 84
   1500–2035 86
Dominican Republic 786, 906–7

Don Valley, constituency 244
Doncaster
   Bishop Suffragan 564
   constituencies 244
   education authority 477
   metropolitan borough council 371,
      387
Donmar Warehouse 1244, 1246–7
   productions 1248
Dorchester, Area Bishop 562
Dorking, Bishop Suffragan 560
Dorset
   constituencies 244
   county council 385, 386
   education authority 476
Douglas 411
Dover
   Bishop Suffragan 555
   constituency 244
   district council 372, 389
Down 410
   constituencies 270
   district council 410
Down and Connor, Bishop (RC) 570
Down and Dromore, Bishop 566
Downing Street 616
DPBs 647–8
drama, training body 495
drama therapies, professional body
   498–9
drawing papers, measures of 1294
Drinking Water Inspectorate (DWI)
   533
Driver and Vehicle Licensing Agency
   (DVLA) 296
driving licences 545
Driving Standards Agency (DSA)
   296
driving tests 545
Dromore, Bishop (RC) 570
Dublin 787, 952
   Archbishop (Anglican) 566
   Archbishop (RC) 570
Duchess of Gloucester, see
   Gloucester, Duchess of
Duchess of Kent, see Kent, Duchess
   of
Duchy of Cornwall 314
Duchy of Lancaster 314
Dudley
   Area Bishop 565
   constituencies 244–5
   education authority 477
   metropolitan borough council 371,
      387
Duke of Cornwall, see Prince Charles
Duke of Edinburgh 115
   Civil list 121
   military titles 122
   Private Secretary 117
Duke of Gloucester see Gloucester,
   Duke of
Duke of Kent, see Kent, Duke of
Duke of York 115
   Civil list 121
   military titles 122
   Private Secretary 117
dukes 135–6
   forms of address 133
Dulwich & West Norwood,
   constituency 245

Dumbarton
  constituencies
    Scottish Parliament 357
    UK Parliament 266
Dumfries
  constituencies
    Scottish Parliament 357
    UK Parliament 266–7
Dumfries and Galloway
  education authority 480
  unitary authority 374, 406
Dundee 405
  constituencies
    Scottish Parliament 357
    UK Parliament 267
  education authority 480
  unitary authority 374, 406
  universities 483, 484
Dunfermline
  constituencies
    Scottish Parliament 357
    UK Parliament 267
Dungannon, district council 410
Dunkeld, Bishop (RC) 570
Dunwich, Bishop Suffragan 563
durable goods, ownership of 627
Durham 379
  Bishop 163, 556
  constituencies 245
  county council 385, 386
  district council 372, 389
  education authority 476
  university of 484
Dushanbe 787, 1078
duty solicitors 677
DWI 533

E
E-Envoy, Office of (OEE) 276
EA Technology Ltd 537
Ealing
  constituencies 245
  education authority 479
  London borough council 374, 399
Earl of Wessex 115
  Civil list 121
  Private Secretary 117
earls 137–42
  courtesy titles 164
  forms of address 133
earnings, of full-time employees
  626
Earth 79
  magnetosphere 1241
  movements in the Mantle 1240
  physical properties 775
  satellites 78
  see also World, The
Easington
  constituency 245
  district council 372, 389
East Anglia
  Bishop (RC) 569
  university of 485
East Ayrshire
  education authority 480
  unitary authority 374, 406
East Cambridgeshire, district council
  372, 389
East Devon, district council 372, 389
East Dorset, district council 372, 389

East Dumbartonshire
  education authority 480
  unitary authority 374, 406
East Ham, constituency 245
East Hampshire, district council 372,
  389
East Hertfordshire, district council
  372, 389
East Kilbride
  constituencies
    Scottish Parliament 357
    UK Parliament 267
East Lindsey, district council 372,
  389
East London, university of 485
East Lothian
  constituencies
    Scottish Parliament 357
    UK Parliament 267
  education authority 480
  unitary authority 374, 406
East Midlands European Parliament
  Region 414
East Northamptonshire, district
  council 372, 389
East Renfrewshire
  education authority 480
  unitary authority 374, 406
East Riding of Yorkshire
  education authority 477
  unitary authority 374, 387
East Staffordshire, district council
  372, 389
East Sussex
  county council 385, 386
  education authority 476
East Timor 786, 907–8
Eastbourne
  constituency 245
  district council 372, 389
Easter Day 84, 85
  1500–2035 86
  fixed 84–5
Eastern Orthodox Church 573
  in UK 573–4
Eastern European Parliament Region
  414
Eastleigh
  constituency 245
  district council 372, 389
Eastwood
  constituencies
    Scottish Parliament 357
    UK Parliament 267
Ebbsfleet, Bishop Suffragan 555
EC 797–8
  presidency 797
Eccles, constituency 245
ecclesiastical fees 679
ECGD 314
eclipses 68
  of Jupiters satellite (2003) 72
economic affairs, events (2001–2)
  1141–3
Economic Community of West
  African States (ECOWAS) 812–13
economic and monetary union
  (EMU) 800
Economic and Social Council 828
Economic and Social Research
  Council (ESRC) 728–9

economic statistics, UK 623–7
Ecuador 786, 908–9
Eddisbury, constituency 245
Eden, district council 372, 389
Edexcel 467, 470, 482
Edinburgh 405, 788
  airport 540
  Bishop 566
  constituencies
    Scottish Parliament 357
    UK Parliament 267
  education authority 480
  museums and galleries 614
  theatre productions 1251
  unitary authority 375, 406
  universities 485, 487
Edinburgh International Festival
  (2002) 1216
Edinburgh of the Seven Seas 785
Edmonton
  Area Bishop 556
  constituency 245
education 461–511
  adult and continuing 475
  alternative provision 465
  curriculum, the 465–7
  expenditure 461
  higher see higher education
  independent schools 504–11
  Inspectorate, the 462
  local education administration
    461
  post-16 see post-16 education
  professional 493–503
  public examinations and
    qualifications 467–8
  schools and pupils 462–4
  types of schooling 464–5
Education Action Zones 463
education authorities see LEAs
Education Council see BTEC
Education maintenance Allowance
  (EMA) 470–71
Education and Skills, Department
  for 279–80
Egypt 784, 910–11
Eilean Siar (Western Isles)
  education authority 480
  unitary authority 375, 406
Eisteddfod 401
El Salvador 786, 911–12
El-Aaiūn 785, 1005
elderly people, local authority
  services 519
elections
  European Parliament 413
  local government 365
    England 367
    Scotland 370
  parliamentary 219
  see also general elections
electorate, size (2001) 237
electricity 537–8
  generation, supply and
    consumption 538
  measurement 1292
  suppliers of 536–7, 538
Electricity Association 537
Ellesmere Port and Neston
  constituency 245
  district council 372, 389

Elmbridge, district council 372, 389
Elmet, constituency 245
Elphin, Bishop (RC) 570
Eltham, constituency 245
Ely, Bishop 163, 559
Ember Days 85
Employers' Associations 720–21
employment
  discrimination in 673
  pay and conditions 672
  statistics 626
  termination of 672–3
Employment Appeal Tribunal 434
employment law 672–3
Employment Tribunals 433
Employment Tribunals Service 295
EMS (Enhanced Messaging Services)
  583, 800
EMU 800
endowment mortgages 644
energy 535–9
  renewable sources 538–9
energy science, professional bodies
  496
Enfield
  constituencies 245–6
  education authority 479
  London borough council 374, 399
engineering, professional bodies
  495–6
Engineering and Physical Sciences
  Research Council (EPSRC) 729
England
  area 109
  Areas of Outstanding Natural
  Bank of 304, 632
  Beauty (AONBs) 593–4
  Arts Council 1217
  banknotes 631
  Church of see Church of England
  colleges 491
  constituencies 236–63
  early history 377–8
  education 461–75
  flag 376
  geographical features 376
  High Sheriffs 384
  historic buildings and monuments
  602–6
  independent schools 504–10
  judicature 416–28
  LEAs 476–9
  local government see local
  government
  Lord-Lieutenants 384
  national parks 592
  police forces and authorities
  439–40
  population statistics 109–12, 376
  precedence 131
  principal cities 378–83
  prison establishments 443–6
English Heritage (EH) 314–5, 1200
  see also historic buildings and
  monuments, England
English National Ballet 1202
  productions 1205
English National Opera 1218
  productions 1220
English Nature (EN) 315, 595

English Touring Opera, productions
  1221
environment 589–97
  events (2001–2) 1143–4
  legislation and strategies 589–91
  London 347
  UK targets 591
Environment Agency 315, 533
Environment, Fisheries and
  Aquaculture Science, Centre for
  283
Environment, Food and Rural
  Affairs, Department for 281–4,
  535
Eocene era 96
Eolian Islands 960
epact 90
Ephemeris Time (ET) 76
Epiphany 84
Episcopal Church, Scottish 566
Epping Forest 618
  constituency 246
  district council 372, 389
Epsom and Ewell, district council
  372, 389
Epson and Ewell, constituency 246
Equal Opportunities Commission
  315
Equality Commission for Northern
  Ireland 315
equator, diameter and circumference
  775
Equatorial Guinea 784, 913–14
equestrianism 734, 1272
equinoctal years 83
equinox 83
eras, Indian 90
Erewash
  constituency 246
  district council 372, 389
Erith & Thamesmead, constituency
  246
Eritrea 784, 914–15
Eritrean Orthodox Church 574
ERM 800
ERM II 801
Esher & Walton, constituency 246
Essex
  county council 385, 386
  education authority 476
  university of 485
Essex North, constituency 246
Estonia 787, 915–16
Ethiopia 784, 916–8
Ethiopian Orthodox Church 574
ethnic groups, statistics 110
eton fives 734, 1272
EU 795–806
  bodies 803–5
  budget 799–800
  citizenship of 666
  Common Agricultural Policy 800
  Common Foreign and Security
  Policy (CFSP) 801
  development 796
  enlargement and external relations
  796
  environmental measures 589–91
  events (2001–2) 1157–8
  information offices 805

  Institutions 797–8
  legislative process 798–9
  member states 795
  monetary integration 800–801
  recognition of professional
  qualifications 493
  Single Market 800
Eurasian Economic Community 811
euro 800
  conversion rates 800
Euro-Atlantic Partnership Council
  (EAPC) 820–21
Europa 1241
Europe
  agreements 796
  airmail zones 578
  countries of, area and population
  787–8
  events (2001–2) 1159–62
  geographical statistics 776
European Bank for Reconstruction
  and Development (EBRD) 813
European Central Bank (ECB) 801,
  803–4
European Commission see EC
European Convention on Human
  Rights (1950) 812
European Council 797
European Court of Auditors 803
European Economic Area (EEA) 800,
  813
European Economic and Social
  Committee (EESC) 803
European Free Trade Association
  (EFTA) 800, 813–14
European Investment Bank (EIB)
  803
European marine sites 596
European Monetary Institute see
  European Central Bank (ECB)
European Monetary System (EMS)
  800
European Organisation for Nuclear
  Research (CERN) 814
European Parliament 413–5
  elections to 413
  UK members 413–14
  UK regions 414–16
European Parliament (EP) 798
  political groupings 806
European Police Office 804–5
European Security and Defence
  Identity (ESDI) 821
European Space Agency (ESA) 814
European Union see EU
European wildlife trade regulation
  599
Europol 804–5
Eurostar 541, 542
events (2001–2) 1129–66
  Africa 1147–9
  Americas 1149–52
  arts and the media 1135–6
  Asia 1152–7
  Australasia and the Pacific 1157
  British Affairs 1129–33
  crimes and legal affairs 1136–40
  economic and business affairs
  1141–3
  environment and science 1143–4

EU 1157–8
Europe 1159–62
  international relations 1162–3
  Middle East 1163–6
  Northern Ireland Affairs 1133–5
  sport 1144–7
evictions 675
examination boards 467, 482
  see also City & Guilds; Edexcel;
    OCR; SQA
examinations, secondary education
  467–8
Excellence in Cities 463
exchange rate mechanism (ERM)
  800
exchange rate mechanism II 801
exchange rates 789–92
executors of wills 681
Exeter 380
  Bishop 163, 559
  constituency 246
  district council 372, 389
  university of 485
Exmoor 592
expenditure
  government 623–4
  household 627
exploration, for oil 535
Export Credit Guarantee
  Department 314
exports, UK statistics 625

F
Færøe Islands 787, 904
Fahrenheit scale 1293
Fair Employment Tribunal 434–5
fair trading 667
faith see religion
Falkirk
  constituencies
    Scottish Parliament 357
    UK Parliament 267
  education authority 480
  unitary authority 375, 406
Falkland Islands 786, 1122–3
Falmouth & Cambourne,
  constituency 246
families, local authority services
  519–20
Family Credit see Working Families'
  Tax Credit
Family Division, High Court of
  Justice 416, 419
Family Doctor Service 515–6
family proceedings courts 671
Fareham
  constituency 246
  district council 372, 389
fast ignition fusion 1240
fasts
  Jewish 87
  Muslim 88
  Sikh 88
Faversham & Kent Mid, constituency
  246
feasts
  movable 85
  see also festivals
February
  astronomical phenomena 22
  calendar 22

constellations in 22
high water 100
Jupiter in 23, 25
Mars in 23, 24
Mercury in 23, 24
minima of algol 22
Moon 22
  position 24
Neptune in 25
night sky 23
Saturn in 23, 25
Sun, position 23
sunrise and sunset 25
twilight 23
Uranus in 25
Venus in 23, 24
zodiacal light 23
Federal Republic of Germany (FRG)
  928–30
Federated States of Micronesia
  1000–1001
Feltham & Heston, constituency
  246
fencing 1272
Fenland, district council 372, 389
fenland restoration 1197
Fermanagh 410
  district council 410
Fermanagh & South Tyrone,
  constituency 270
Ferns, Bishop (RC) 570
festivals
  classical music 1215–16
  Hindu 86–7
  Jewish 87
  Muslim 88
  Sikh 88
field events
  men
    national (UK) records 1288
    world records 1287
  women
    national (UK) records 1289
    world records 1288
Field Marshals 453
Fife
  constituencies
    Scottish Parliament 358
    UK Parliament 267
  education authority 480
  unitary authority 375, 406
Fiji 788, 918–19
film, professional body 496
film (2001–2) 1207–9
Film Council 316
Film Four 1209
finance 630–63
  government 623–5
  local government 365–6
    England 367–8
    Northern Ireland 370, 409
    Scotland 370
    Wales 369
  NHS 514
  roads 543
Financial Ombudsman Service 636,
  641, 648
Financial Services Authority 632,
  641, 642, 647
Financial Services Compensation
  Scheme 647

financial services regulation 647–9
Finchley & Golders Green,
  constituency 246
fineness marks 621
Finland 787, 919–20
  EU membership 795
Fire Service College 279
first class post 578
first generation computers 585
fission yeast genome 1237
fixed Easter 84
Fixed Rate Savings Bonds 639
flags
  England 376
  Guernsey 412
  Isle of Man 411
  Jersey 412
  Northern Ireland 408
  Scotland 403
  UK 113
  Wales 400
fleet, Royal Navy 452
Fleet Air Arm 453
Flegrean Islands 960
Flintshire
  education authority 479
  unitary authority 374, 402
flooding, insurance 641
Floodline 341
Florida 1090
flying, the Union Flag 113
Folkstone & Hythe, constituency 246
Fongafale 788, 1089
Fontaine Archipelago 960
Food and Agriculture Organisation
  of the United Nations 814
food and nutrition science,
  professional body 496
Food Standards Agency (FSA) 316
foot-and-mouth disease 1196
football see association football
Foreign and Commonwealth Office
  284–5
Foreign Compensation Commission
  316
foreign goods, hallmarks 621
Forensic Science Agency, Northern
  Ireland 293
Forest of Dean
  constituency 246
  district council 372, 389
Forest Enterprise 596
Forest Heath, district council 372,
  389
Forest Nature Reserves 596
Forestry Commission 316
forestry and timber studies,
  professional bodies 496
forms of address 133
Fort de France 786, 923
Forum for the Advancement of
  Further Education 475
Forward Poetry Prizes 1211
fossils, earliest 1240
foundation degree 473
foundation schools 463
fourth generation computers 585
Foyle, constituency 270
Framework Convention on Climate
  Change 590

France 787, 920–22
  EU membership 795
  independent schools 511
  overseas departments 923
  overseas territories 923–4
  territorial collectives 923
Free Church
  of England 572
  of Scotland 572
Free Presbyterian Church, of
  Scotland 572
Freetown 785, 1054
French Community of States 924
French Guiana 786, 923
French Polynesia 788, 923
friendly societies 634
  number of 635
frogs, ranavirus disease 1197
FSA 632, 641, 642, 647
FSCS 647
fuel and energy science, professional
  bodies 496
Fulham, Bishop Suffragan 556
funding, royal family 120–21
funding councils 482
  see also LSC; TTA
funeral payments 529
further education see post-16
  education
Futuna Islands 924
Fylde
  constituency 246
  district council 372, 389

G
Gabon 784, 924–5
Gaborone 784, 867
Gaelic language 403
Gainsborough, constituency 246
Galápagos Islands 909
galleries 302–3, 608–15
  England 608–14
  facelifts 1188–9
  job changes 1187–8
  Northern Ireland 615
  Scotland 614
  visitor figures 1187
  Wales 614
Galloway, Bishop (RC) 570
Galloway & Upper Nithsdale
  constituencies
    Scottish Parliament 358
    UK Parliament 267
Galway and Kilmacduagh, Bishop
  (RC) 570
Gambia 784, 925–6
Gaming Board for Great Britain 317
Garsington Opera, productions 1221
Garter, Most Noble Order 170
gas 536
  suppliers of 538
Gateshead
  education authority 477
  metropolitan borough council 371,
    387
Gateshead East & Washington West,
  constituency 246
GATT 833
Gatwick airport 540
Gaza City 786, 957

Gaza Strip 786, 954–7
GCHQ 342
GCSE 467
Gedling
  constituency 246
  district council 372, 390
gene therapy 1239–40
General Agreement on Tariffs and
  Trade (GATT) 833
General Assembly 826–7
  specialised bodies 827
General Certificate of Secondary
  Education 467
General Commissioners of Income
  Tax 434
general elections, statistics 236
general index of retail prices 628
general insurance 641–2
General Insurance Standards
  Council (GISC) 641, 642
General Medical Council (GMC)
  498
General National Vocational
  Qualifications (GNVQs) 471
general ophthalmic services, NHS
  517
General Practitioners see GPs
General Synod
  Church of England 554
  Church of Ireland 566
  Scottish Episcopal Church 566
General teaching Council (GTC) 469
genomes see fission yeast genome;
  microbial genomes
geographical statistics, world 775–81
geological eras 96
  table of 97
George Cross 209
  surviving recipients 210
George Inn 617
George Town 785
George V 124
Georgetown 1125
Georgetown (Cayman Islands) 785
Georgetown (Guyana) 786, 938
Georgia 787, 926–8
Georgia (USA) 786, 1098
Germany 787, 928–30
  EU membership 795
Ghana 785, 931–2
Giant Tortoise Islands 909
Gibraltar 787, 1122–3
Gibraltar in Europe, Bishop 163, 559
Gillingham, constituency 246
GLA, structures and objectives 346–8
  see also London Assembly
GLA Headquarters 1184–5
glaciated areas 776
glaciations, of the Ice Age 96
Glamorgan, university of 485
Glasgow 360, 405–6
  airport 540
  Archbishop (RC) 570
  City of, education authority 480
  constituencies
    Scottish Parliament 358
    UK Parliament 268
  Scottish Parliament Region 360
  unitary authority 375, 406
  universities 485, 489

Glasgow and Galloway, Bishop 566
gliding 734
global atmosphere, UK targets 591
global warming 1241–2
  see also climate change
Gloucester
  Bishop 163, 559
  constituency 246
  district council 372, 390
Gloucester, Duchess of 115
  military titles 123
  Private Secretary 117
Gloucester, Duke of 115–6
  Civil list 120–1
  military titles 123
  Private Secretary 117
Gloucester, Princess Alice, Duchess
  of 115
  Civil list 121
  military titles 123
  Private Secretary 117
Gloucestershire
  county council 385, 386
  education authority 476
  university of 485
Glyndebourne Festival Opera 1219
  productions 1221
Glyndebourne Touring Opera,
  productions 1221
Godthåb (Nuuk) 785, 904
gold, hallmarks 621, 622
gold coin 630
golf 734
  men 1272–3
  women 1273–4
goods, sale of 666–7
goods and services, supply of 667
Gordon
  constituencies
    Scottish Parliament 358
    UK Parliament 268
Gosport
  constituency 247
  district council 372, 390
governing bodies, schools 463
Governing Body, Church in Wales
  565
government 223
  current ministry 272–3
  departments 274–300
  finance 623–5
  formation of 224
  local see local government
  organs of 216
  regional 346–64
Government Actuaries Department
  317
Government Car and Despatch
  Agency 277
Government Commerce, Office of
  see OGC
Government Communications
  Headquarters 342
Government Hospitality 317
Government Information and
  Communication Services (GICS)
  276
Government Offices for the Regions
  317–8

Gower
  constituencies
    UK Parliament 264
    Welsh Assembly 351
GPs, salaries 515
Graduate Teacher Programme 468
graduated retirement benefits 526
Grand National 1276
Grand Turk 786
Grantham, Bishop Suffragan 561
Grantham & Stamford, constituency 247
Gravesham
  constituency 247
  district council 372, 390
Gray's Inn 497, 617
Great Britain see UK
Great Grimsby, constituency 247
Great Yarmouth
  constituency 247
  district council 372, 390
Greater London Assembly see London Assembly
Greater London Authority see GLA
Greece 787, 932–3
  EU membership 795
Greek Orthodox Church 573–4
  calendar 84
greenhouse gas emissions 590
Greenland 785, 904
Greenock & Inverclyde
  constituencies
    Scottish Parliament 358
    UK Parliament 268
Greenwich 617
  education authority 479
  London borough council 374, 399
  university of 485
Greenwich & Woolwich, constituency 247
Greenwich Mean Time (GMT) 74, 75
Gregorian calendar 84
Grenada 786, 933–4
Grenadines, St Vincent and 1046–7
greyhound racing 629, 734, 1274
Grimsby, Bishop Suffragan 561
Guadeloupe 786, 923
Guam 788, 1102
Guardian's Allowance 526–7
  weekly rates 527
Guatemala 786, 934–5
Guatemala City 786, 934
Guernsey 412
  education authority 480
  LEA 480
  police force 440
  population 110
Guildford
  Bishop 163, 560
  constituency 247
  district council 372, 390
Guinea 785, 937
Guinea-Bissau 785, 936–7
Gulf Co-operation Council (GCC) 811–12
GUUAM 814–15
Guyana 786, 938–9
Gwynedd
  education authority 479
  unitary authority 374, 402
gymnastics 734, 1274

H
habitats
  conservation 598–9
    European wildlife trade regulation 599
    UK legislation 599–601
Hackney
  constituencies 247
  education authority 479
  London borough council 374, 399
Hagatna 1102
Haïti 786, 939–40
Halesowen & Rowley Regis, constituency 247
half-mast, flags at 113
Halifax, constituency 247
Hallam, Bishop (RC) 569
Hallé Orchestra 1215
hallmarks 621–2
Haltemprice & Howden, constituency 247
Halton
  constituency 247
  education authority 477
  unitary authority 374, 387
Hambleton, district council 372, 390
Hamilton 785
  constituencies
    Scottish Parliament 358
    UK Parliament 268
Hammersmith and Fulham
  constituency 247
  education authority 479
  London borough council 374, 399
Hampden Gurney Primary School 1185
Hampshire
  constituencies 247
  county council 385, 386
  education authority 479
Hampstead & Highgate, constituency 247
Hanoi 787, 1110
Hanover, House of 128
Harare 785, 1117
Harborough
  constituency 247
  district council 372, 390
harbour authorities 547
hardship funds 475
Haringey
  education authority 479
  London borough council 374, 399
Harlow
  constituency 248
  district council 372, 390
Harrogate, district council 372, 390
Harrogate & Knaresborough, constituency 247–8
Harrow 374, 399
  constituencies 248
  education authority 479
Hart, district council 372, 390
Hartlepool
  constituency 248
  education authority 477
  unitary authority 374, 387
Harwich, constituency 248
Hastings, district council 372, 390
Hastings & Rye, constituency 248

Havana 785, 898
Havant
  constituency 248
  district council 372, 390
Havering
  education authority 479
  London borough council 374, 399
Hawaii 1098
Hayes & Harlington, constituency 248
Hazel Grove, constituency 248
headteachers, qualifications for 468, 469
Health, Department of 285–8
Health Action Zones 517
Health Authorities (Wales) 515
Health Promotion Authorities 515
Health and Safety Commission 218
Health and Safety Executive 218
Health Service Commissioner, Office of 333
health services, NHS 515–9
Health and Social Services Boards, Northern Ireland 515
Health and Social Services Councils 513
health statistics 512
health visitors, pay review body 339
Heard Island 848
heathlands, conservation of 1197
Heathrow airport 540
Hebrides 404
Helsinki 787, 919
Hemel Hempstead, constituency 248
Hemsworth, constituency 248
Hendon, constituency 248
Henley, constituency 248
Her Majesty's Inspectorate for Education and Training in Wales 462
Her Majesty's Stationery Office (HMSO) 276
Herald's College 308–9
hereditary peers 135–54
hereditary women peers 134
Hereford
  Bishop 163, 560
  constituency 248
Herefordshire
  education authority 477
  unitary authority 374, 387
Heriot-Watt University 485
Heritage Information 1201
Heritage Link 1201
Heritage Lottery Fund (HLF) 1199–1200
Heritage Sites, World 597
Hertford, Bishop Suffragan 563
Hertford & Stortford, constituency 248
Hertfordshire
  constituencies 248
  county council 385, 386
  education authority 476
  university of 485
Hertsmere
  constituency 248
  district council 372, 390
Hexham, constituency 248
Hexham and Newcastle, Bishop (RC) 569

Heywood & Middleton, constituency 248
High Court, centres 420–21
High Court of Judiciary 428
High Court of Justice 416, 418–9
  Northern Ireland 431
High Peak
  constituency 249
  district council 372, 390
High Sheriffs 366–7
  England 384
  Wales 402
high water (2003) 99–105
higher education 471–2
  academic staff 472–3
  admissions 473–4
  advisory bodies 481
  colleges 491–2
  courses 473
  fees 474
  finance 473
  funding councils 482
  student support 474–5
Higher National Qualifications 470
Higher Still 468
Highland
  education authority 480
  unitary authority 375, 406
Highlands and Islands Scottish
  Parliament Region 360
Highlands and Islands Enterprise (HIE) 218
highway authorities 543
Highways Agency 296
Hillingdon
  education authority 479
  London borough council 374, 399
Hinckley and Bosworth, district council 372, 390
Hindu calendar 11, 86–7
Hinduism 550–1
  adherents in UK 548
hire-purchase agreements 667
Historic Buildings Council
  for Scotland 319
  for Wales 319
historic buildings and monuments
  England 602–6
  listing 602
  Northern Ireland 607
  Scotland 606–7
  Wales 606
Historic Buildings and Monuments Commission for England 314–5
Historic Royal Palaces 319
Historical Manuscripts Commission 337
historical year 88
Hitchin & Harpenden, constituency 249
HIV, statistics 512
HMSO 276
HNCs 473
hockey 735, 1274
Holborn & St Pancras, constituency 249
holidays see public holidays
Holocene era 96
Holy Apostolic Catholic Assyrian Church of the East 572

holy days 89
Home Office 288–90
Home-Grown Cereals Authority (HGCA) 319
Homo erectus 98
Homo habilis 96, 98
homo sapiens, see also Toumai Man
Homo sapiens neandertalensis 98
Homo sapiens sapiens 98
Honduras 786, 940–41
Hong Kong 786, 887–8
Honiara 788, 1059
Honorary Dames Commanders 205
honorary knighthoods 173
Honours Scrutiny Committee 319
horizon, distance of 1293
Hornchurch, constituency 249
Hornsey & Wood Green, constituency 249
Horse Guards 617
horse-racing 629, 735, 1275–7
Horserace Betting Levy Board 629
Horserace Totalisator Board (Tote) 319, 629
Horsham
  Bishop Suffragan 558
  constituency 249
  district council 372, 390
hospices 518
hospitals, NHS 517
hotelkeeping, professional body 496
Houghton & Washington East, constituency 249
Hounslow
  education authority 479
  London borough council 374, 399
House of Commons
  business of 219
  elections to 219
  government whips 273
  Members of, see MPs
  officers and officials 220–1
  political party representation 219
  select committees 221, 222
House of Commons Members' Fund 220
House of Lords 217–8
  composition 218
  as final Court of Appeal 416, 417
  government whips 273
  officers of 218
  political party representation 218
  select committees 218, 222
House of Lords Record Office 337
households
  expenditure 627
  income and expenditure 626–7
  number of persons per 627
  ownership of durable goods 627
  sources of income 627
Houses of Parliament 617
housing benefit 528
Housing Corporation 320
Hove, constituency 249
Hubble Space Telescope 1242
Huddersfield
  constituency 249
  university of 485
Huddersfield Contemporary Music Festival (2001) 1215–16

Hull
  Bishop Suffragan 555
  constituencies 249
  university of 485
Hulme, Bishop Suffragan 561
human development 96–8
Human Fertilisation and Embryology Authority (HFEA) 320
Human Genetics Commission 320
human rights 673
  see also European Convention on Human Rights
Human Rights Commission, Northern Ireland 331
Hungary 787, 941–2
Huntingdon
  Bishop Suffragan 559
  constituency 249
Huntingdonshire, district council 372, 390
Hyde Park 618
Hyndburn
  constituency 249
  district council 372, 390

I
ice hockey 735, 1277
ice skating 735, 1277
Iceland 787, 943
Id al-Adha 88
Id al-Fitr 88
Idaho 1098
IDD (international direct dialling) codes 580–2
Ilford, constituencies 249
illegitimacy 673
Illinois 1098
immigration, statistics 110
Immigration Appeal Tribunal 434
Immigration Appelate Authority 434
Immigration Services Tribunal 434
Imperial Service Order 172
Imperial Society of Knights Bachelor by Royal Appointment 173
imperial units 1291
  phasing-out 1291–2
Imperial War Graves Commission see Commonwealth War Graves Commission
Imperial War Museum 326, 611
Imperial War Museum North 612, 1186, 1188
Incapacity benefit 525
  weekly rates 526
income
  household 626
  households, sources of 627
Income Bonds 639
income support 527–8
  weekly rates 528
income support premiums 528
  weekly rates 528
income tax 650
  allowances 653
  assessment for 651–2
  non-taxable income 652
  relief from 653–4
  self assessment 650–51

income-based Jobseeker's Allowance (JSA) 526
weekly rates 527
Incorporated societies 634
Independent Broadcasting Authority see Independent Television Commission
Independent Housing Ombudsman (IHO) 320
Independent International Commission on Decommissioning 320
Independent Methodist Churches 572
independent radio 690, 1195
local stations 690–96
national stations 690
regional local stations 690
independent schools 465, 504–11
advisory bodies 481
Independent Television Commission 320–21, 686
Independent Television News Ltd 688
independent television see ITV
indexation allowance 656
see also taper relief
India 786, 944–6
cinema 1209
eras 90
Indian Empire, Most Eminent Order 171
Indiana 1098
Individual Savings Accounts (ISA) 639, 652
Indonesia 786, 947–8
Industrial Injuries Advisory Council 321
industrial injuries disablement benefit 529–30
weekly rates 530
industrial and provident societies 635
industrial research bodies 731
industrial stoppages 626
Industrial Tribunals 434–5
infant mortality, statistics 111
infectious diseases, notifications 512
inflation rates 628
Information Commissioner's Office 321
information science/management, professional body 497
information technology 585–8
Information Tribunal 435
inhabited buildings, tallest 780
inheritance tax
calculation of 660
liability for 658–9
payment of 660
relief from 659–60
inland postal services 578
Inland Revenue, Board of 304
Inner House, Court of Session 428
Inner Temple 497, 617
Innovation 2000 Initiative 804
Inns of Court 497, 617
Insolvency Service 295
Inspectorate of Education, HM (HMIE) 462

Inspectors, HM (HMIs) 462
Institute of Contemporary Arts (ICA) 1187
institutional management, professional body 496
Institutions 741–72
EU 797–8
insurance 641–5
professional bodies 496–7
insurance companies
investments 645
UK figures 642
Integrated Pollution Prevention and Control (IPPC) 590
Integrated Transport, Commission for 309
intellectual property 684–5
intellectual property organisations 685
Intelligence Services 342
Intelligence Services Commissioner 343
Inter Faith Network 548
Inter-church co-operation 548
Inter-Governmental Maritime Consultative Organisation (IMCO) see International Maritime Organisation (IMO)
interest, tax relief 654
interest rates, bank 632
International Atomic Energy Agency (IAEA) 815
International Atomic Time (TAI) 76
International Baccalaureate 468
International Bank for Reconstruction and Development (IBRD) 832
International Centre for Settlement of Investment Disputes (ICSID) 832
International Civil Aviation Organisation (ICAO) 815
International Committee of the Red Cross (ICRC) 818
International Confederation of Free Trade Unions (ICFTU) 815
International Court of Justice 829
International Criminal Police Organisation (Interpol) 816
International Criminal Tribunal for the Former Yugoslavia 829
International Criminal Tribunal for Rwanda 829
International Development, Department for (DfID) 290–91
International Development Association (IDA) 832
international direct dialling (IDD) codes 580–82
International Energy Agency (IEA) 816
International Finance Corporation (IFC) 832
International Francophone Organisation 816
International Fund for Agricultural Development (IFAD) 816–7
International Labour Organisation (ILO) 817

International Maritime Organisation (IMO) 817
International Meteorological Organisation see World Meteorological Organisation (WMO)
International Monetary Fund (IMF) 817–18
international organisations 807–33
international paper sizes 1294
International Red Cross and Red Crescent Movement 818
international relations, events (2001–2) 1162–3
International Space Station (ISS) 80
International System see SI
International Telecommunication Union (ITU) 818
International Underwriting Association (IUA) 642
Internet 586
Interpol 816
Intestacy 683
in Scotland 683
Invalid Care Allowance (ICA) 527
weekly rates 527
Inverclyde
education authority 480
unitary authority 375, 407
Inverness 406
Inverness East, Nairn & Lochaber constituencies
Scottish Parliament 358
UK Parliament 268
Investigatory Powers Tribunal 342
investment accounts 639
Investment Exchange, Recognised 648
Iowa 1098
IPPC (Integrated Pollution Prevention and Control) 590
Ipswich
by-election 271
constituency 249
district council 372, 390
Iran 786, 948–50
Iraq 786, 950–52
Ireland 787, 952–4
Church of see Church of Ireland
EU membership 795
Northern see Northern Ireland
patron saint 204
Iridium satellites 80
Irish Episcopal Conference 569
Iron Age 98
Iron Bridge 1180
ISAs 639, 652
Islam 551–2
adherents in UK 548
see also Muslim
Islamabad 787, 1025
islands
England 376
largest 776–7
Scotland 403–4
Isle of Anglesey see Anglesey
Isle of Man see Man, Isle of
Isle of Wight see Wight, Isle of
Isles of Scilly see Scilly, Isles of

Islington
    constituencies 249–50
    education authority 479
    London borough council 374, 399
Islwyn
    constituencies
        UK Parliament 264
        Welsh Assembly 351
Israel 786, 954–8
Italy 787, 958–60
    EU membership 795
    independent schools 511
    islands 960
    ITV 687
    network companies 687–8
    ratings 1191

J

Jainism 552
Jakarta 786, 947
Jamaica 786, 961
Jamestown 785, 1124
Jan Mayen Island 1023
January
    astronomical phenomena 18
    calendar 18
    constellations in 18
    high water 100
    Jupiter in 19, 21
    Mars in 19, 20
    Mercury in 19, 20
    minima of algol 18
    Moon 18
        position 20
    Neptune in 21
    night sky 19
    Saturn in 19, 21
    Sun, position 19
    sunrise and sunset 21
    twilight 19
    Uranus in 21
    Venus in 19, 20
Japan 786, 962–3
Japanese calendar 90
Jarrow
    Bishop Suffragan 556
    constituency 250
Jehovah's Witnesses 577
Jersey 412
    education authority 481
    LEA 481
    police force 440
    population 110
Jerusalem 954–5
Jesus Christ of Latter-Day Saints,
    Church of 577
jets, phenomenon of 1238
Jewish calendar 11, 87
Jewish theological colleges 503
Jobcentre Plus 300
Jobseeker's Allowance (JSA)
    contribution-based 524–5
        weekly rates 526
    income-based 526
        weekly rates 527
Joint Council for General
    Qualifications (JCGQ) 467
Joint Nature Conservation
    Committee 321
Jordan 786, 963–5

journalism, training 497
Judaism 552–3
    adherents in UK 548
    see also Jewish calendar; Jewish
        theological colleges
Judge Advocates 420
judges
    circuit 417, 421–2
    district 417, 425–6
    High Court 418–9
    Scotland 428–9
judicature
    England and Wales 416–28
    Northern Ireland 431–2
    Scotland 428–31
Judicial Committee of the Privy
    Council 216, 416
judicial separation 670
judo 735, 1278
Julian calendar 84
Julian Date 17
Julian period 90
July
    astronomical phenomena 42
    calendar 42
    constellations in 42
    high water 103
    Jupiter in 43, 45
    Mars in 43, 44
    Mercury in 43, 44
    minima of algol 42
    Moon 42
        position 44
    Neptune in 45
    night sky 43
    Saturn in 43, 45
    Sun, position 43
    sunrise and sunset 45
    twilight 43
    Uranus in 45
    Venus in 43, 44
June
    astronomical phenomena 38
    calendar 19
    constellations in 38
    high water 102
    Jupiter in 39, 41
    Mars in 39, 40
    Mercury in 39, 40
    minima of algol 38
    Moon 38
        position 40
    Neptune in 41
    night sky 39
    Saturn in 39, 41
    Sun, position 39
    sunrise and sunset 41
    twilight 39
    Uranus in 41
    Venus in 39, 40
Jupiter 75
    investigation of magnetosphere
        1236
    satellites 78, 1239
    shadow transits (2003) 72
    see also Europa; months of the
        year e.g. January, Jupiter in
Jurassic era 96
jury service 674

justices of the peace
    England and Wales 417
    Northern Ireland 431

K

Kabul 834
Kampala 785, 1090
Kansas 1098
Kathmandu 787, 1011
Kazakhstan 786, 965–7
Keele University 485
Keeling Islands 847
Keighley, constituency 250
Kelvin scale 1293
Kennet, district council 372, 390
Kensington, Area Bishop 556
Kensington and Chelsea
    constituency 250
    education authority 479
    London borough council 374, 399
Kensington Gardens 618
Kent
    county council 385, 386
    education authority 476
Kent at Canterbury, university of 485
Kent, Duchess of 116
    military titles 123
    Private Secretary 117
Kent, Duke of 116
    Civil list 120–1
    military titles 123
    Private Secretary 117
Kent, Prince Michael of 116
    military titles 123
    Private Secretary 117
Kent, Princess Michael of 116, 117,
    120–1
Kentucky 1098
Kenya 785, 967–8
Kerrier, district council 372, 390
Kerry, Bishop (RC) 570
Kettering
    constituency 250
    district council 372, 390
Kew Royal Botanical Gardens (RBG)
    339
Khartoum 1067
Kiev (Kyiv) 788, 1091
Kigali 785, 1044
Kildare and Leighlin, Bishop (RC)
    570
Killala, Bishop (RC) 570
Killaloe, Bishop (RC) 570
Kilmarnock & Loudoun
    constituencies
        Scottish Parliament 358
        UK Parliament 268
Kilmore
    Bishop (RC) 570
    Elphin and Ardagh, Bishop 566
Kings
    British (since 1603) 128–9
    of England (927–1603) 126–8
    of Scotland (1016 to 1603) 129–30
King's Lynn and West Norfolk,
    district council 372, 390
Kingston 786, 961
Kingston & Surbiton, constituency
    250
Kingston (Norfolk Island) 788
Kingston University 485

Kingston upon Hull 380
  education authority 477
  unitary authority 374, 388
Kingston upon Hull, aquarium and
  visitor centre 1182
Kingston upon Thames
  Area Bishop 564
  education authority 479
  London borough council 374, 399
Kingstown 786, 1046
Kingswood, constituency 250
Kinshasa 784, 892
Kiribati 788, 968–9
Kirkcaldy
  constituencies
    Scottish Parliament 358
    UK Parliament 268
Kirklees
  education authority 477
  metropolitan borough council 371,
    387
Knaresborough, Bishop Suffragan
  562
knighthood, orders of 173
knights 173
  forms of address 133
  listing of 173–203
Knights Bachelor 173
Knights Templar Church 1179–80
Knowsley
  constituencies 250
  education authority 477
  metropolitan borough council 371,
    387
Kolonia 1000
Korea 786, 969–72
Koror 788, 1026
Kosrae 1000
Kuala Lumpur 787, 990
Kuwait 787, 972–3
Kuwait City (Al-Kuwayt) 787, 972
Kyoto Protocol (1999) 590
Kyrgyzstan 787, 973–4

L

La Francophone 816
La Paz 786, 863
Labour Party 225
  development 224
lacrosse 735
ladies, in own right 153–4
Lady Sarah Chatto 115
Laeken Summit 802–3
Lagan Valley, constituency 270
Lake District 592
lakes
  in England 376
  in Scotland 403
  in Wales 400
  largest 778–9
Lambeth
  education authority 479
  London borough council 374,
    399
Lambeth Conference 554
Lampeter, University College of 490
Lancashire
  county council 385, 386
  education authority 476
Lancashire West, constituency 250

Lancaster 380
  Bishop (RC) 569
  Bishop Suffragan 557
  district council 372, 390
  Duchy of 314
  House of 127
  university of 486
Lancaster & Wyre, constituency 250
land, UK targets 591
Land Registries 321–2
landlords, responsibilities 675
Lands Tribunal 435
Lands Tribunal for Scotland 435
languages
  Scottish 403
  Welsh 400
Laos 787, 975–6
lapsed legatees 681
Larne, district council 410
Latvia 787, 976–7
launch, of artificial satellites 80–2
law, professional bodies 497
Law Commission 322
law courts and offices 416–32
  England and Wales 416–28
  Northern Ireland 431–2
  Scotland 428–31
law lords 134
Law Officers 272
Law Officers Department 322–3
lawn tennis 735
lay magistrates *see* justices of the
  peace
Leader of the Opposition 222
League of Arab States 819
leap years 83
learning disabilities, people with,
  local authority services 520
Learning and Skills Council *see* LSC
LEAs 461, 476–81
leaseholders 675
Lebanon 787, 977–9
Leeds 380
  Bishop (RC) 569
  constituencies 250
  education authority 477
  metropolitan borough council 371,
    387
  universities 486
legal affairs, events (2001–2)
  1136–40
legal aid 676–7
Legal Aid Board, Scottish 341
Legal Aid Board *see* Legal Services
  Commission (LSC)
legal calendar 11, 88–9
legal deposit 685
Legal Services Commission (LSC)
  323, 676
Legal Services Ombudsman, Office
  of 333
legal tender
  banknotes 631
  coins 630
legal year 88
legislative process, EU 798–9
legitimation 674
Leicester 380
  Bishop 163, 560
  constituencies 250–1

education authority 477
  unitary authority 374, 388
  universities 484, 486
Leicestershire
  county council 385, 386
  education authority 476
Leicestershire North West,
  constituency 251
Leigh, constituency 251
Lek 1000
length
  conversion tables 1295
  measurement
    imperial 1291
    metric 1290
  roads 543
Lent 84
Leominster, constituency 251
Leonid meteors 1236
Lesotho 785, 979–80
letter post rates 578
letters of administration 682
lettings
  business 675
  residential 674–5
Lewes
  Bishop Suffragan 558
  constituency 251
  district council 372, 390
Lewisham
  constituencies 251
  education authority 479
  London borough council 374, 399
Leyton & Wanstead, constituency
  251
Lhasa 887
Liberal Democrats 225
  development 224
  spokesmen 225
Liberal Party, development 224
Liberia 785, 980–81
librarianship, professional body 497
Libraries 323–4
  legal deposit 685
Libreville 784, 924
Libya 785, 981–3
licences
  driving 545
  motor vehicles 546
  television 686
licensing, copyright 684
Lichfield
  Bishop 163, 560
  constituency 251
  district council 372, 390
Liechtenstein 787, 983
Life Directive societies 634
life events, statistics 512
life expectancy, statistics 111
life insurance 644
life peers 134, 155–62
  forms of address 133
light rail systems 541
lighthouse authorities 324–5, 547
lighting-up time 73
Lilongwe 785, 989
Lima 786, 1031
Limavady, district council 410
Limerick, Bishop (RC) 571
Limerick and Killaloe, Bishop 566

Lincoln 380–81
  Bishop 163, 561
  constituency 251
  district council 372, 390
  university of 486
Lincoln Laboratory Near Earth
  Asteroid Research project
  (LINEAR) 1237
Lincoln's Inn 497, 617
Lincolnshire
  county council 385, 386
  education authority 476
Linley, Viscount 115
Linlithgow
  constituencies
    Scottish Parliament 358
    UK Parliament 268
liquor, measurement 1292
Lisbon 788, 1036
Lisburn, district council 410
listed buildings 602
  expansion in 1200–1201
literature (2001–2002) 1210–12
  prizewinners 1213
  see also books
Lithuania 787, 983–5
Liverpool 381
  Archbishop (RC) 569
  Bishop 163, 561
  constituencies 251
  education authority 477
  metropolitan borough council 371,
    387
  universities 486
livery companies, London 369,
  396–8
Livingston
  constituencies
    Scottish Parliament 359
    UK Parliament 268–9
Ljubljana 788, 1058
Llandaff, Bishop 565
Llanelli
  constituencies
    UK Parliament 264
    Welsh Assembly 351
Lloyd's List 643
Lloyd's of London 547, 617, 643–4
Lloyd's Shipping Index 643
loans, student 474
Local Agenda (21) 589
local authority, social services
  519–20
Local Commissioners 325
local education authorities see LEAs
local government 365–412
  civic dignities 367
  complaints 366
  elections 365
  England 367–8, 384–93
    changes in 365
    political composition of
      councils 371–4
  finance 365–6
  internal organisation 365
  London 368–9, 399
  Northern Ireland 370
  Queen's representatives 366
  Scotland 369–70
    changes 365

political composition of
  councils 374–5
Wales 369, 401–2
  changes 365
political composition of
  councils 374
Local Government Ombudsmen 366
Local Health Councils 513
Local Management of Schools
  Initiative 463
Local Nature Reserves 595–6
lochs see lakes
Lomé 785, 1082
London 788, 1095
  Bishop 163, 556
  bridges 616
  cemeteries 616
  clubs 738–9
  distances by air from 782
  environment 347
  European Parliament Region
    414
  galleries 610–11
  LEAs 478–9
  local government 368–9, 399
  markets 618
  Mayor 346
  monuments 618–19
  museums 611–12
  parks 618
  roman remains 619, 1178
  theatre productions 1248–51
  universities 484, 485, 486–7, 487,
    489, 490
  university of 486–7
  zoo 618
  see also City of London;
    Corporation of London; Port of
    London
London Archaeological Archive and
  Research Centre (LAARC) 1178
London Assembly 346–8
  constituencies 348
  elections 346
  functions and structures 347
  members of 348
London borough councils 365, 368,
  399
  map 393
  political composition 374
London Development Agency (LDA)
  347
London Eye 617–18
London Fire and Emergency
  Planning Authority (LFEPA) 347
London (Goldsmiths' Hall) date
  letters 622
London Insurance Market 642
London Monument 618
London Philharmonic Orchestra
  1214
London Plan 347
London Planetarium 618
London Regional Transport 325
London Sinfonietta 1214–15
London Stock Exchange 646
London Symphony Orchestra 1214
London Tourist Board and
  Convention Bureau 620
London Underground 541

Londonderry 408, 410
Londonderry City 410
Londonderry East, constituency 270
long-term insurance 644–5
long-term residential colleges, for
  adult education 492
Lopen Mosaic 1178
Lord Advocate 428
  Office of 333
Lord Chamberlain's Office 119
Lord Chancellor 222, 416
Lord Chancellor's Department 291–2
Lord Chief Justice 416
Lord Great Chamberlain's Office 325
Lord High Admiral 451
Lord High Chancellor 417
Lord Justices of Appeal, Northern
  Ireland 431
Lord Mayors
  of London 394
  office of 367
Lord Mayor's Day 394
Lord Privy Seal's Office 325
Lord-Lieutenants 366
  England 384
  Scotland 406
  Wales 402
lords 145–53
  courtesy titles 164–5
Lords of Appeal 134
Lords of Appeal in Ordinary 416
Lords Justices of Appeal 417–18
Lords see House of Lords
Lords Spiritual 163
Lothians Scottish Parliament Region
  360
lotteries 629
Lotto 629
Loughborough, constituency 251
Loughborough University 487
Louisiana 1098
Louth & Horncastle, constituency
  251
lowland Scottish language 403
LSC 323, 470
Luanda 784, 839
Ludlow
  Bishop Suffragan 560
  constituency 251
lunar occultations 68–9
Lundy 376
Lusaka 785, 1115
Lutheran Church 573
Luton
  constituencies 251–2
  education authority 477
  unitary authority 374, 388
  university of 487
Luxembourg 787, 985–6
  EU membership 795
Luxembourg (City of) 787, 985
Lynn, Bishop Suffragan 562

M
Maastricht, Treaty of 798, 799, 801
Macao 786, 888–9
Macclesfield
  constituency 252
  district council 372, 390
McDonald Islands 848

Macedonia 787, 986–7
Madagascar 785, 987–9
Madame Tussaud's 618
Madeira 1038
Madrid 788, 1064
Magherafelt, district council 410
magistrates 416
  stipendiary 430
magistrates' courts 417
  Northern Ireland 432
magnetic storms 79–80
magnetism, terrestrial 79–80
magnetosphere 1241
Maidenhead, constituency 252
Maidstone
  Bishop Suffragan 555
  district council 372, 390
Maidstone & The Weald,
  constituency 252
mail see postal services
Maine 1098
maintenance payments 670
  tax relief on 653–4
Makerfield, constituency 252
Malabo 784, 913
Malankara Orthodox Syrian Church
  574
malaria, advances against 1238–9
Malawi 785, 989–90
Malaysia 787, 990–1
Maldives 787, 991–2
Maldon, district council 372, 390
Maldon & Chelmsford East,
  constituency 252
Malé 787, 991
Mali 785, 992–3
Malta 787, 993–4
Malvern Hills, district council 372,
  390
Mamoudzou 785, 923
Man Booker Prize 1211
Man, Isle of 411
  banknotes 631
  education authority 480
  LEA 480
  police force 440
  population 110
management, professional bodies
  493–4
Managua 786, 1017
Manama (Al-Manámah) 786, 852
Manchester 381
  Bishop 163, 561
  constituencies 252
  education authority 477
  metropolitan borough council
  371, 387
  theatre productions 1251
  universities 487, 489
Manila 787, 1033
mankind, history 96–8
Mansfield
  constituency 252
  district council 372, 390
Mantle, movements in 1240
Maputo 785, 1006
March
  astronomical phenomena 26
  calendar 26
  constellations in 26
  high water 101
  Jupiter in 27, 29

Mars in 27, 28
Mercury in 27, 28
minima of algol 26
Moon 26
  position 28
Neptune in 29
night sky 27
Saturn in 27, 29
Sun, position 27
sunrise and sunset 29
twilight 27
Uranus in 29
Venus in 27, 28
zodiacal light 27
Marine Nature Reserves 596
marine safety 547
marine wildlife conservation 1198–9
Maritime and Coastguard Agency
  (MCA) 106, 547, 296
markets, London 618
Marlborough House 618
marquesses 136–7
  courtesy titles 164
  forms of address 133
marriage 677
  in England and Wales 678–9
  fees 679
  nullity of 670
  prohibition of 678
  in Scotland 679
  fees 679–80
  statistics 111
  marriage certificates 665
Mars 74–5, 1239
  satellites 78
  see also months of the year e.g.
  January, Mars in
Marshall Islands 788, 994–5
Marshals of the Royal Air Force 455
martial arts 735
Martinique 786, 923
Maryland 1098
Maseru 785, 979
masonic year 90
mass
  conversion tables 1295
  measurement
  imperial 1291
  metric 1291
mass destruction, weapons of
  1174–5
Massachusetts 1098
Master of the Household 119
Master of the Rolls 416
Mata-Utu 788, 924
Maternity Allowance (MA) 525
  weekly rates 526
maternity pay, statutory (SMP) 530
matrimonial property 671
Maundy Money 630
Maundy Thursday 84
Mauritania 785, 995–6
Mauritius 785, 996–8
May
  astronomical phenomena 34
  calendar 34
  constellations in 34
  high water 102
  Jupiter in 35, 37
  Mars in 35, 36
  Mercury in 35, 36
  minima of algol 34

Moon 34
  position 36
Neptune in 37
night sky 35
Saturn in 35, 37
Sun, position 35
sunrise and sunset 37
twilight 35
Uranus in 37
Venus in 35, 36
mayor cycle 89
Mayor of London 346
  elections 346
Mayor's Advisory Cabinet 346
  members 348
Mayotte 785, 923
Mbabane 785, 1070
MCA 106, 546
mean refraction 77
Mean Solar Time 75
measurement of time 83
measures
  weights and 1290–95
  weights and conversion tables
  1295
Meath, Bishop (RC) 571
Meath and Kildare, Bishop 566
medals and decorations 208–10
media 686–97
  events (2001–2) 1135–6
Medical Devices Agency 287
Medical Research Council (MRC)
  729–30
medicine
  professional bodies 498
  professions supplementary to,
  professional bodies 498–9
Medicines Control Agency (MCA)
  287
medieval mikveh 1179
Medway
  constituency 252
  education authority 477
  unitary authority 374, 388
Meirionnydd Nant Conwy
  constituencies
  UK Parliament 264–5
  Welsh Assembly 351
Melton, district council 372, 390
member states, EU 795
Members of the European
  Parliament (MEPs) 798
  political groupings 806
Members of Parliament see MPs
Mendip, district council 372, 390
Menevia, Bishop (RC) 569
mental handicaps see learning
  disabilities
Mental Health Act Commission
  325–6
Mental Health Review Tribunals 435
mentally ill people, local authority
  services 520
MEPs, UK 413–16
Merchant Navy Training Schools 499
Mercosur 819
Mercury 74–5
  see also months of the year e.g.
  January, Mercury in
Meriden, constituency 252
Merit, Order of 171

Merseyside, National Museums and Galleries on 327
Merthyr Tydfil
  education authority 479
  unitary authority 374, 402
Merthyr Tydfil & Rhymney
  constituencies
    UK Parliament 265
    Welsh Assembly 351
Merton
  education authority 479
  London borough council 374, 399
Mesozoic era 96
meteorites 1242–3
meteors
  in August 47
  in December 63
  in November 59
  see also Leonid meteors
Methodist Church 573
  in Ireland 573
  see also Independent Methodist Churches
Methodist theological colleges 502
Metonic (Lunar, or Minor) cycle 90
metric units 1290–1
metrication, UK 1291
metro systems 541
metropolitan borough councils 365, 387
  map 392
  political composition 371
Metropolitan Police, rates of pay 438
Metropolitan Police Authority (MPA) 347
Metropolitan Police Service 441
Mexico 785, 998–1000
Mexico City 785, 998
MI5 343
MI6 343
Michigan 1098
microbial genomes 1236–7
Micronesia, Federated States of 788, 1000–1
Microsoft Corporation 586
Mid Bedfordshire, district council 372, 390
Mid Devon, district council 372, 390
Mid Suffolk, district council 372, 390
Mid Sussex, district council 372, 390
Middle East, events (2001–2) 1163–6
middle schools 464
Middle Temple 497, 617
Middlesbrough
  Bishop (RC) 569
  constituencies 252
  education authority 477
  unitary authority 374, 388
Middlesex University 487
Middleton, Bishop Suffragan 561
Midlothian
  constituencies
    Scottish Parliament 359
    UK Parliament 269
  education authority 480
  unitary authority 375, 407
midwives, pay review body 339
mikveh, medieval 1179
military colleges 495
military ranks and titles, royal family 121–3

Milky Way, black hole 1238
Millennium Commission 326
million, definition 1292
Milton Keynes
  constituencies 252
  education authority 477
  unitary authority 374, 388
minima of algol 73
  see also months of the year e.g. January, minima of algol
Ministers of State 272–3
  salaries 274
Ministry of Defence Police 441
mink, spread of 1198
Minnesota 1098
Minsk 787, 856
Miocene era 96
Miquelon, St Pierre and 923
Mir Space Station 80
Mississippi 1098
Missouri 1098
Mitcham & Morden, constituency 252
mobile communications industry 582
  network technology 583
  regulation 583–4
Mobile Network Operators 582
  types of service 582
Mobile Virtual Network Operators
  see MVNOs
Modern Man 98
Mogadishu 785, 1060
Moldova 788, 1001–2
Mole Valley
  constituency 252
  district council 372, 390
Monaco 788, 1002–3
Monaco (city of) 788, 1002
monarchy, constitutional role 216
Mongolia 787, 1003–4
Monmouth
  Bishop 565
  constituencies
    UK Parliament 265
    Welsh Assembly 351
Monmouthshire
  education authority 479
  unitary authority 374, 402
Monrovia 785, 980
Montana 1098
Montenegro 1115
Montevideo 786, 1104
Montgomeryshire
  constituencies
    UK Parliament 265
    Welsh Assembly 351
months
  definition 83
  Hindu 86
  Jewish 87
  Muslim 88
Montserrat 786, 1123
Monument, The 618
monuments
  historic 602–7
  London 618–19
Moon 73, 74
  see also months of the year e.g. January, Moon

moonrise 74
  calculation of 67
moons, orbiting the outer planets 1239
moonset 74
  calculation of 67
Moray
  constituencies
    Scottish Parliament 359
    UK Parliament 269
  education authority 480
Ross and Caithness, Bishop 566
  unitary authority 375, 407
Morecambe & Lunesdale, constituency 252
Morley & Rothwell, constituency 253
Morocco 785, 1004–6
Moroni 784, 890
Mortimer Wheeler House 1178
Moscow 788, 1040
MOT testing 546
Mothering Sunday 85
Motherwell, Bishop (RC) 570
Motherwell & Wishaw
  constituencies
    Scottish Parliament 359
    UK Parliament 269
motor cycling 1278
motor racing 1279
motor rallying 1279
motor sports 735
motor vehicles 546
  insurance 641–2
  licences 546
motorways 544
mountain building 96
mountain ranges, largest 777
mountaineering 735
mountains, highest 777–8
movable feasts (to year 2035) 85
Moyle, district council 410
Mozambique 785, 1006–7
MPs
  eligibility 219
  listing of 227–35
  pay and allowances 219–20
  pensions 220
MSF 76
MSPs 355–6
multi-sport bodies 735
Multilateral Investment Guarantee Agency (MIGA) 832
Muscat 1023
Muscat (Masqat) 787
Museum of London 326–7, 611
museums 326–9, 608–15
  England 608–14
  Northern Ireland 615
  Scotland 614
  Wales 614
Museums and Galleries Commission
  see Resource: The Council for Museums, Archives and Libraries
music, professional bodies 499–500
music see classical music
music therapy, professional body 498–9
musicals, West End 1245–6
Muslim calendar 11, 88
mutual societies 634–8
  see also building societies

MVNOs 582
types of service 582
Myanmar 787, 1007–9

N
Nairobi 785, 967
Namibia 785, 1009–10
Napier University 487
Nassau 785, 851
national academies of scholarship
725–6
National Air Quality Strategy 590
National Air Traffic Services (NATS)
540
National Archives of Scotland 338
National Army Museum 327, 611
National Assembly for Wales see
Welsh Assembly
National Association for Decorative
and Fine Arts (NADFAS) 1201
National Audit Office 329
National Care Standards
Commission (NCSC) 519
National College for School
Leadership 468
National Consumer Council (NCC)
329
National Council for Education and
Training 470
National Crime Squad see NCS
National Criminal Intelligence
Service see NCIS
national curriculum 465–7
national daily newspapers 698–9
National Endowment for Science
Technology and the Arts
329, 629
National Film Theatre 620
national flags see flags
National Forest 595
National Galleries of Scotland 302
National Gallery 302, 610
National Health Service see NHS
National Heritage Memorial Fund
329–30
National History Museum 611
National Insurance Fund 520–1
National Insurance (NI) 520–1
National Library
of Scotland 323–4
of Wales 324
National Lottery 629
National Lottery Commission 330,
629
National Maritime Museum 327, 611
National Museums and Galleries
on Merseyside 327
of Wales 327–8
National Museums of Scotland 328
National Nature Reserves 595–6
National Organisation for Adult
Learning (NIACE) 475
national parks 592–3
National Parks Authorities (NPAs)
592
National Physical Laboratory 330
National Portrait Gallery 303, 610
National Professional Qualification
for Headship 468
National Qualifications System 466,
468, 470

National Radiological Protection
Board 330
National Records of Achievement
468
National Register of Archives (NRA)
337
National Savings and Investments
330, 639–40
National Scenic Areas 594–5
National Statistics, Office for 331
National Vocational Qualifications
(NVQs) 471
National Weights and Measures
Laboratory (NWML) 295
NATO
and the former Yugoslavia 821
post-cold war developments
820–21
September 11 terrorist attacks
821
structure 820
natural environment, conservation
of 1196–9
Natural Environmental Research
Council (NERC) 730–1
natural gas 536
Natural History Museum 327
natural parents, tracing 664
nature conservation areas 595
nature reserves 595–6
Nauru 788, 1010–11
Nauru (city of) 788, 1010
nautical measures 1292–3
nautical twilight 74
see also months of the year e.g.
January, twilight
NCIS 342–3
NCIS Service Authority 439
NCS Service Authority 439
N'Djaména 784, 881
Nea Farm 1177
Neanderthal Man 98
Neath
constituencies
UK Parliament 265
Welsh Assembly 351
Neath Port Talbot
education authority 479
unitary authority 374, 402
Nebraska 1098
Neolithic revolution 98
Nepal 787, 1011–12
Neptune 75
satellites 78
see also months of the year e.g.
January, Neptune in
Net see Internet
netball 735, 1279
Netherlands 788, 1012–14
EU membership 795
independent schools 511
overseas territories 1014
Network Operators see Mobile
Network Operators
Nevada 1098
Nevis, St Kitts (St Christopher) 786,
1045–6
New Caledonia 788, 923
New Church 576
New Deal for Lone Parents
programme 528

New Delhi 786, 944
New Forest 593
constituencies 253
New Forset, district council 372, 390
New Hampshire 1098
New Jersey1098
New Mexico 1098
New Northern Ireland Assembly 217
New Opportunities Fund 330, 629
New South Wales 845
New Year 89
New York (state) 1098
New Zealand 788, 1014–17
associated states 1016–7
territories 1016–7
Newark, constituency 253
Newark and Sherwood, district
council 372, 390
Newbury, constituency 253
Newcastle
Bishop 163, 561
Newcastle-under-Lyme
constituency 253
district council 372, 390
Newcastle upon Tyne 381
constituencies 253
education authority 477
metropolitan borough council
371, 387
universities 487
Newham
education authority 479
London borough council 374, 399
Newport
constituencies
UK Parliament 265
Welsh Assembly 351
education authority 479
unitary authority 374, 402
University College of 490
Newry & Armagh, constituency 270
Newry and Mourne, district council
410
newspapers 698
circulation 698
national daily 698–9
regional daily 699–701
religious 702
weekly 701–2
Newtownabbey, district council 410
NFFO Renewables Orders 538–9
NHS
complaints procedure 519
employees and salaries 515
finance 514
health services 515–8
number of beds and patient
activity 518
organisations 514–5
reciprocal arrangements 519
structure 513
Trusts 513
NHS Boards (Scotland) 514–5
NHS Charters 518
NHS Direct 518
NHS Estates 287
NHS Pensions 287–8
NHS Plan 513, 517
NHS Purchasing and Supply Agency
288
NHS Tribunal (Scotland) 435

Niamey 785, 1018
Nicaragua 786, 1017–8
Nice, Treaty of 797, 802
Nicosia 787, 900
Niger 785, 1018–9
Nigeria 785, 1019–21
night sky *see months of the year* e.g.
    January, night sky
Nimbus records 1215
Niue 788, 1016–7
Non-Aligned Movement (NAM) 819
Non-Christian religions 549–53
non-contributory benefits 524,
    526–9
Non-Denominational theological
    colleges 502
non-domestic rates 366
non-hereditary peers 134
Non-Trinitarian churches 577
    adherents in UK 548
Nordic Council 819–20
nordic events 1279–80
Norfolk
    constituencies 253
    county council 385, 386
    education authority 476
Norfolk Island 788, 848
Norfolk mammoths 1177
Normandy, House of 127
Normanton, constituency 253
North America *see* Americas
    North American Free Trade
    Agreement (NAFTA) 820
North Atlantic Council (NAC) 820
North Atlantic Treaty 820
North Atlantic Treaty Organisation
    see NATO
North Ayrshire
    education authority 480
    unitary authority 375, 407
North Carolina 1098
North Cornwall, district council 372,
    390
North Cyprus, Turkish Republic of
    901
North Dakota 1098
North Devon, district council 372,
    390
North Dorset, district council 372,
    390
North Down, district council 410
North East Derbyshire, district
    council 372, 390
North East European Parliament
    Region 414
North East Lincolnshire
    education authority 477
    unitary authority 374, 388
North-Eastern Education and
    Library Board 480
North Hertfordshire, district council
    372, 390
North Kesteven, district council 372,
    390
North Korea *see* Democratic People's
    Republic of Korea
North Lanarkshire
    education authority 480
    unitary authority 375, 407

North Lincolnshire
    education authority 477
    unitary authority 374, 388
North Norfolk, district council 372,
    390
North Shropshire, district council
    372, 390
North Somerset
    education authority 477
    unitary authority 374, 388
North Tyneside
    education authority 477
    metropolitan borough council
    371, 387
North Warwickshire, district council
    372, 390
North West European Parliament
    Region 416
North West Leicestershire, district
    council 372, 390
North Wiltshire, district council 372,
    390
North York Moors 592
North Yorkshire
    county council 385, 386
    education authority 476
Northampton
    Bishop (RC) 569
    constituencies 253
    district council 372, 390
Northamptonshire
    county council 385, 386
    education authority 476
Northavon, constituency 253
Northern Ballet Theatre (NBT) 1202
Northern Ireland 408
    area 109
    Areas of Outstanding Natural
    Beauty (AONBs) 594
    banknotes 631
    constituencies 270
    constitutional developments
    408–9
    counties 410
    district councils 410
    education 461–75
    education and library boards 480
    electricity 537
    European Parliament regions 414
    events (2001–2) 1133–5
    finance 409
    flag 408
    historic buildings and monuments
    607
    independent schools 510
    judicature 431–2
    LEAs 480
    local government 370
    museums and galleries 615
    National Parks 593
    parliamentary seats (2001) 236
    police forces and authorities 440
    population statistics 109–12, 408
    principal cities 408
    prison establishments 446
    Privy Council 215
Northern Ireland Assembly 217,
    361–4
    constituencies 363–4
    members 363–4

    political composition 364
Northern Ireland Audit Office 330
Northern Ireland Democratic
    Unionist Party *see* Democratic
    Unionist Party
Northern Ireland Executive 362
    departments 362–3
Northern Ireland Health and
    Social Services Boards 515
Northern Ireland Human Rights
    Commission 331
Northern Ireland Office 292–3
Northern Ireland Prison Service 446
Northern Lighthouse Board 324–5
Northern Mariana Islands 788, 1102
Northern Sinfonia 1217
Northern Territory 845
Northumberland 592
    county council 385, 386
    education authority 476
Northumbria at Newcastle,
    university of 487
Norway 788, 1021–3
    territories 1023
Norwich 381–2
    Bishop 163, 561
    constituencies 253
    district council 373, 390
    notice of marriage 678
Nottingham 382
    Bishop (RC) 569
    constituencies 254
    unitary authority 374
    universities 487, 488
Nottingham City
    education authority 477
    unitary authority 388
Nottinghamshire
    county council 385, 386
    education authority 476
Nouakchott 785, 995
Nouméa 788, 923
November
    astronomical phenomena 58
    calendar 58
    constellations in 58
    high water 105
    Jupiter in 59, 61
    Mars in 59, 60
    Mercury in 59, 60
    meteors 59
    minima of algol 58
    Moon 58
        position 60
    Neptune in 61
    night sky 59
    Saturn in 59, 61
    Sun, position 59
    sunrise and sunset 61
    twilight 59
    Uranus in 61
    Venus in 59, 60
NPAs (National Parks Authorities)
    592
nuclear forces 447
Nuclear Installations Inspectorate
    538
nuclear power 537–8
Nuku'alofa 788, 1083
nullity of marriage 670
Nuneaton, constituency 254

Nuneaton and Bedworth, district
   council 373, 390
nursing, training 500
nursing staff, pay review body 339
nutrition science, professional bodies
   496
Nyasaland see Malawi

O

O₂ 582
Oadby and Wigston, district council
   373, 390
obituaries 1167–71
observation, of artificial satellites 80
occultations, lunar 68–9
Occupational Pensions Regulatory
   Authority (OPRA) 331, 523
occupational therapy, professional
   bodies 499
Oceania, countries of, area and
   population 788–9
oceans, area and depth 775
Ochil
   constituencies
      Scottish Parliament 359
      UK Parliament 269
OCR 467, 470, 482
October
   astronomical phenomena 54
   calendar 54
   constellations in 54
   high water 104
   Jupiter in 55, 57
   Mars in 55, 56
   Mercury in 55, 56
   minima of algol 54
   Moon 54
      position 56
   Neptune in 57
   night sky 55
   Saturn in 55, 57
   Sun, position 55
   sunrise and sunset 57
   twilight 55
   Uranus in 57
   Venus in 55, 56
OFCOM (The Office of
   Communications) 584, 686
Offa's Dyke 1179
Office of Fair Trading 332
Office of Gas and Electricity Markets
   (Ofgem) 332, 536, 537
Office of Manpower Economics 332
Office for National Statistics 331
Office of Population Censuses and
   Surveys see Office for National
   Statistics
Office for the Regulation of
   Electricity and Gas (OFREG) 332
Office for Standards in Education
   (Ofsted) 331, 462
Office of Telecommunications
   (Oftel) 332–3, 584
Office of Water Services (Ofwat)
   334, 533
officers
   salaries 457–8
   service retired pay 459
Ofgem 332, 536, 537
Oflot see National Lottery
   Commission

OFREG 332
Ofsted 331, 462
Oftel 332–3, 584
Ofwat 334, 533
OGC 298
OGC Buying Solutions 298
Ogilvy, Princess Alexandra, the Hon
   Lady 116
   Civil list 120–21
   military titles 123
   Private Secretary 117
Ogmore
   by-election 271
   constituencies
      UK Parliament 265
      Welsh Assembly 351
Ohio 1098
oil, production 535
Oklahoma 1098
Old Bexley & Sidcup, constituency
   254
Old Masters 1189–90
   visitor figures 1187
old people see elderly people
Oldham
   constituencies 254
   education authority 477
   metropolitan borough council
      371, 387
Oligocene era 96
Olympiads 90
Omagh, district council 410
Oman 787, 1023–4
ombudsmen
   Financial 636, 641, 648
   Health Service 333
   Independent Housing 320
   Legal Services 333
   Local Government 366
   Northern Ireland 304
   Northern Ireland police 335
   Parliamentary 333
   Pensions 333, 648
   Prisons and Probation 335–6
   Scottish Public Services 342
   Welsh Administration 345
One2One see T-Mobile
Open University 472, 475, 490
   admissions 473
opera (2001–2) 1218–19
   commemorations 1219
   productions 1220–1
Opera North 1218
operating systems (OS)
   computer 585–6
   personal computers 586
ophthalmic and dispensing
   opticians, professional bodies 500
ophthalmic services, NHS 517
Opposition
   official 224
   leader of 222
   shadow cabinet 224
Opposition parties, financial support
   224
optometrists, salaries 515
Oranjestad 785, 1014
orbit, of artificial satellites 80
order of succession 116
orders 634
   number of 635

Orders of Chivalry 170–2
Orders of Knighthood 173
ordinary accounts 639
ordination of women 554
Ordnance Survey 279, 334
Ordovician era 96
Oregon 1098
Organisation of African Unity
   (OAU) 822–3
Organisation of American States
   (OAS) 823
Organisation of Arab Petroleum
   Exporting Countries (OAPEC)
   823
Organisation for Economic
   Co-operation and Development
   (OECD) 821
Organisation of the Islamic
   Conference (OIC) 824
Organisation of the Petroleum
   Exporting Countries (OPEC)
   824
Organisation for Security and
   Co-operation in Europe (OSCE)
   822
organisations 741–72
   international 807–33
Oriental Orthodox Churches 574
   in UK 574
orienteering 735
Orkney, unitary authority 375, 407
Orkney & Shetland
   constituencies
      Scottish Parliament 359
      UK Parliament 269
Orkney Islands 403–4
   education authority 480
Orpington, constituency 254
Orthodox Church 573–4
Orthodox Church calendar 84
orthoptics, professional body 499
orthotics, professional body 499
Oscars 1208
Oslo 788, 1021
ospreys, breeding of 1197
Ossory, Bishop (RC) 571
osteopathy, training 500
Oswestry, district council 373, 390
Ottowa 785, 876
Ouagadougou 784, 872
Outer House, Court of Session
   428–9
overseas postal services 578
overseas territories, UK 1119–26
Oxford 382
   Bishop 163, 562
   constituencies 254
   district council 373, 390
   universities 488
Oxford, Cambridge and RSA
   Examinations (OCR), 467, 470, 482
Oxfordshire
   county council 385, 386
   education authority 476

P

Pacific, see Australasia and the
   Pacific
Pacific Islands Forum (PIF) 824
Pago Pago 788, 1102

Paisley
  Bishop (RC) 570
  constituencies
    Scottish Parliament 359
    UK Parliament 269
  university of 488
Pakistan 787, 1024–6
Palaeocene era 96
Palaeozoic era 96
Palau 788, 1026–7
Palestinian Autonomous Areas 957–8
Palikir 788, 1000
palliative care 518
Palm Sunday 84
Panama 1027–8
Panama Canal Zone 1028
Panama City 786, 1027
Panel on Takeovers and Mergers 648
Pantelleria Island 960
Papeete 788, 923
paper
  international sizes 1294
  measures of 1293
Papua New Guinea 788, 1028–30
Parades Commission 334
Paraguay 786, 1030–31
Paramaribo 786, 1069
parcel rates 578
Parcelforce 578
parental responsibility for children
  670
parents, tracing natural 664
Parents Charter 462
Paris 787, 920
parish councils, England 367
parks, London 618
Parliament 216–71
  by-elections 271
  distribution of seats (2001) 236
  events (2001–2) 1222–31
  glossary of aspects of work 221–3
  Members of see MPs
  Public Acts (2001–2) 1232–3
  Scotland see Scottish Parliament
  White Papers and Reports
    (2001–2) 1234–5
  see also House of Commons;
  House of Lords; Houses of
  Parliament
Parliamentary Archives 337
Parliamentary Commissioner for
  Administration, Office of 333
Parliamentary Commissioner for
  Standards 334
Parliamentary constituencies see
  constituencies
Parliamentary Counsel 334
Parliaments, duration of (since
  1970) 236
Parole Board
  for England and Wales 334–5
  for Scotland 335
Particle Physics and Astronomy
  Research Council (PPARC) 731
parties, political see political parties
partnership and co-operation
  agreements 796–7
Partnership for Peace (PFP) 820–1
Party of Wales see Plaid Cymru
passengers, air 540–1

passport applications 579
Passport Service 290
Patent Office 335
patents 684
Patients Charter 518
Patriarchs
  in communion with the Roman
    Catholic Church 571
  Orthodox 573–4
patron saints 204
pay, defence 457–8
Pay As You Earn (PAYE) system
  652–3
payment clearings 632
peacekeeping forces, UN 828
Peak District 593
peatland, preservation of 1197
peerage 134–69
  disclaimed 134
  extinct since last edition 134
  forms of address 133
  hereditary 135–54
  hereditary women 134
  life 134, 155–62
  membership of the House of
    Lords 217
  minors 134
  surnames 165–9
  Peers of the Blood Royal 135
Pelagian Islands 960
Pembrokeshire
  education authority 479
  unitary authority 374, 402
Pembrokeshire Coast 593
Pendle
  constituency 254
  district council 373, 390
peninsulas 776
Pennsylvania 1098
Penrith, Bishop Suffragan 557
Penrith & The Border, constituency
  254
Pension Ombudsman 648
  Office of 333
Pension Service 300
Pensioners Guaranteed Income
  Bonds 639
pensions 522–3, 525–7
  defence 459–60
  MPs 220
  see also stakeholder pension
    schemes; war pensions
Pensions Advisory Service (OPAS)
  523
Pensions Appeal Tribunals 435–6
Pensions Compensation Board 335
Pentecost 85
Pentecostal Churches 575
Penwith, district council 373, 390
People's Republic of China 883–7
Performance and Innovation Unit
  (PIU) 276
performance management, senior
  military officers 457
periodicals
  consumer 702–6
  trade, professional and academic
    706–10
Permian era 96
personal computers 586

personal equity plans (PEPs) 652
Personal Investment Authority (PIA)
  641
personal pension schemes 523
Personal Social Services 519–20
Perth
  constituencies
    Scottish Parliament 359
    UK Parliament 269
Perth and Kinross
  education authority 480
  unitary authority 375, 407
Peru 786, 1031–3
Pesticides Safety Directorate 283
Peter the First Island 1023
Peterborough
  Bishop 163, 562
  constituency 254
  education authority 477
  unitary authority 374, 388
petroleum products, consumption
  536
pharmaceutical services, NHS 516
pharmacists, salaries 515
pharmacy, professional body 500
Philippines 787, 1033–5
Phnom Penh 786, 874
photography, professional body 500
physiotherapy, professional body 499
pipelines, Transco 536
Pitcairn Islands 788, 1124–5
Place, The 1203
Plaid Cymru 225
  development 224
planetarium, London 618
planning
  town and county 680
    Green Paper for 1199
Planning Inspectorate 279
Plantagenets 127
platinum, hallmarks 621, 622
Pleistocene era 96
Pliocene era 96
Pluto, satellites 78
Plymouth 786
  Bishop (RC) 569
  Bishop Suffragan 559
  constituencies 254
  education authority 477
  unitary authority 374, 388
  university of 489
Plymouth Brethren 575
Plymouth (Montserrat) 1123
PMR (Private Mobile Radio) 584
pneumoconiosis, byssinosis and
  miscellaneous diseases benefit
  scheme 530
Podgorica 1115
poetry prizes 1211
Pohnpei 1000
Poland 788, 1035–6
Police Complaints Authority 335
Police Ombudsman for Northern
  Ireland 335
police service 438–41
  complaints 438
  forces and authorities 439–40
  rates of pay 438
  staff associations 441

political groupings, European
   Parliament (EP) 806
political parties 223–4
   development 224
   representation in House of
      Commons 219
   representation in House of Lords
      218
pollution, air 590
polo 735, 1280
Pontefract, Bishop Suffragan 565
Pontefract & Castleford,
   constituency 254
Pontypridd
   constituencies
      UK Parliament 265
      Welsh Assembly 351
Poole
   constituency 254
   education authority 477
   unitary authority 374, 388
Pope John Paul II 568
Popes 568
Poplar & Canning Town,
   constituency 254
population
   countries of Africa 784–5
   countries of America 785
   countries of Asia 786–7
   countries of Europe 787–8
   countries of Oceania 788
   England 376
   Northern Ireland 408
   prison 442
   Scotland 403
   The World 784
   UK statistics 109–12
   Wales 400
Port of London 619
Port of London Authority (PLA) 335
Port Louis 785, 996
Port Moresby 788, 1028
Port of Spain 786, 1084
Port Vila 788, 1106
Port-au-Prince 786, 939
Porto Novo 784, 861
ports 547
Portsmouth
   Bishop 163, 562
   Bishop (RC) 569
   constituencies 254–5
   education authority 477
   unitary authority 374, 388
   university of 488
Portugal 788, 1036–8
   autonomous regions 1038
   EU membership 795
   independent schools 511
Porvoo Declaration 549
Post Office see Consignia Plc
post-16 education 469–70
   advisory bodies 481
   colleges 491–2
   funding councils 482
   students
      number of 470
      support 470–1
postage stamps 578
postal services 578–80
postcards 578
Poste Restante 579

postgraduate students 473
postgraduate studies
   admissions 473–4
   grants for 475
pound sterling 630–31
   purchasing power 628
Powys
   education authority 479
   unitary authority 374, 402
PPP 541
Prague 787, 901
Praia 784, 879
pre-emption, doctrine of 1175
pre-paid services, mobile 582
pre-school education 464
Precambrian era 96
precedence 131
prefixes, SI 1290
prehistoric societies, chronology for
   98
Prehistory: objects of power 1177–8
Premium Bonds 639
preparatory schools 465
Presbyterian Church
   in Ireland 575
   of Wales 575
   see also Associated Presbyterian
      Churches of Scotland; Free
      Presbyterian Church of Scotland
Presbyterian Church of Wales
   theological college 502
Presbyterian theological college 502
prescription charges, NHS 516
Preseli Pembrokeshire
   constituencies
      UK Parliament 265
      Welsh Assembly 351
presidency, EC 797
press, newspaper and periodical
   698–710
Press Complaints Commission 698
Preston
   constituency 255
   district council 373, 390
Pretoria 785, 1062
Primary Care Trusts (PCTs) 516
primary education 464
   see also Hampden Gurney primary
      school
primary fuels 535
primary health care 515–7
Prime Minister 223
   residencies 616–7
Prime Minister's Delivery Unit
   275–6
Prime Minister's Forward Strategy
   Unit (PMFSU) 276
Prime Minister's Office 277
Prime Minister's Office of Public
   Services Reform 276
Primus, Scottish Episcopal Church
   566
Prince Andrew see Duke of York
Prince Charles, Prince of Wales 115
   finances 120
   military titles 122
   Private Secretary 117
Prince Edward see Earl of Wessex
Prince Michael of Kent see Kent,
   Prince Michael of

Prince Philip see Duke of Edinburgh
princes
   of Wales 130
Princess Anne see Princess Royal
Princess Margaret, Countess of
   Snowdon 630
Princess Michael of Kent, see Kent,
   Princess Michael of
Princess Mary's Royal Air Force
   Nursing Service (PMRAFNS) 456
Princess Ragnhild Land 1023
Princesses Royal 130
Príncipe, and São Tomé 1049–50
printing, professional bodies 500–1
printing papers, measures of 1293–4
Prison Service Pay Review Body
   (PSPRB) 339
prison service 442–6
   inmate population 442
   inmate suicides 442
   list of establishments 443–6
   management salaries 443, 446
   number of staff 442
   operating costs 443
Prison Services, HM 443
Prisons and Probation Ombudsman
   for England and Wales 335–6
private boxes 579
Private Finance Initiative (PFI) 517
private finances, roads 543
private hire vehicles 544
Private Secretaries, to the Royal
   Family 117
Private Secretaries Office, Royal
   Household 117–8
private-public partnership (PPP) 541
privatisation, of railways 541–2
privilege of Parliament 222
Privy Council 213–5, 216
   Judicial Committee of 416
   Northern Ireland 215
Privy Council Office 336
privy counsellors, forms of address
   133
Privy Purse 118–9
   royal finances 121
probate 682
proceedings against the Crown 668
Procurator Fiscal Service 430–1
Procurator-General and Treasury
   Solicitor, Department of HM
   298–9
production, of oil 535
professional education, organisations
   for 493–503
professional periodicals 706–10
programming languages 585
Progress Files 468
Proms, The (2002) 1216
prosthetics, professional body 499
provident societies 635
provosts, Church of England 557–60
Public Acts of Parliament (2001–2)
   1232–3
public bills, stages of 221
public bodies 301–45
Public Guardianship (PGO) 336
Public Health Laboratory Service
   (PHLS) 336
public holidays 2003 12
public holidays 2004 13

public holidays 89
Public Lending Right system 338
public offices 301–45
Public Prosecutions, Director of 416, 426
Northern Ireland 431, 432
Public Record Office 338
of Northern Ireland 338
public schools 465
public sector finances 625
Public Services Reform, Prime Minister's Office of 276
publishers 711–5
Pudsey, constituency 255
Puerto Rico 786, 1102
Puffin Island 376
pupils, numbers of 462
Purbeck, district council 373, 390
purchasing power of the pound 628
Putney, constituency 255
Pyongyang 786, 969

Q

Qatar 787, 1038–9
quadrillion, definition 1292
Quakerism 575–6
Qualification Curriculum and Assessment Authority for Wales (ACCAC) 466
Qualifications and Curriculum Authority (QCA) 466
qualifications *see* examinations
Qualified Teacher Status (QTS) 468, 501
Quality, Efficiency and Standards Team 336
quarter days 89
Queen Alexandra's Royal Army Nursing Corps (QARANC) 455
Queen Alexandra's Royal Naval Nursing Service (QARNNS) 453
Queen Elizabeth II 115
Civil list 120–1
military titles 121–2
Private Secretary 117
Queen Elizabeth II Conference Centre 279
Queen Maud Land 1023
Queen Mother, Queen Elizabeth the
Civil list 120–1
obituary 1167
Queen Victoria 124, 845
descendants 124–5
Queens
British (since 1603) 128–9
of England (927–1603) 126–8
of Scotland (1016 to 1603) 129–30
Queen's Bench Division, High Court of Justice 416, 418–9
Queen's Gallery 610, 1188
Queen's Messengers, Corps of 285
Queen's representatives, local government 366
Queen's University of Belfast 489
Queensland 845
QUEST 336
Quito 786, 908

R

Rabat 785, 1004
Racial Equality, Commission for 309

rackets 735, 1280
rackets and real tennis 735
radio 688–97
radio (2001–2) 1194–5
Radio 1 1195
Radio 2 1195
Radio 3 1195
Radio 4 1194–5
Radio Authority 337, 686, 690
radio time signals 76–7
Radiocommunications Agency 296
radiography, professional body 499
radiotherapy, professional body 499
Rail Regulator 541
Office of 334
Railtrack 541, 542
railways 541
Channel Tunnel link 542–3
safety 542
services 541–2
rainfall
averages 1257
changes in patterns of 1242
records 1257–61
Ramadan 88
ramapithecines 96
Rambert Dance Company 1203
productions 1205–6
Ramsar Convention (1971) 598
Ramsbury, Bishop Suffragan 563
Rangoon 1007
ranks, armed forces 459
Raphoe, Bishop (RC) 571
rapid reaction force 802
Rarotonga 788
rates, non-domestic 366
Rayleigh, constituency 255
re-registration of births 665
Reading
Area Bishop 562
constituencies 255
education authority 477
unitary authority 374, 388
university of 489
real tennis 735, 1280
Recognised Clearing Houses 648
Recognised Investment Exchange 648
Record Offices 337–8
recorded mail 579
recorders 416, 422–5
Northern Ireland 432
records of achievement 468
Red Crescent societies 818
Red Cross societies 818
Red-letter days 89
Redbridge
education authority 479
London borough council 374, 399
Redcar, constituency 255
Redcar and Cleveland
education authority 478
unitary authority 374, 388
Redditch
constituency 255
district council 373, 390
redirection 579
redundancy 672
reference books, annual 716–19
refraction, mean 77

regencies 216
Regent's Park & Kensington, constituency 255
Regent's Park and Primrose Hill 618
regional daily newspapers 699–701
regional electricity companies (RECs) 537
regional government 346–64
regions
Scottish Parliament 360
Welsh Assembly 352
registered design 685
registered mail (international) 579
Registered Teacher Scheme 468
Registers of Scotland 322
Registrar of Public Lending Right 338
registration
of births 664–5
of deaths 669
Regnal years 89
regulated payments, Social Fund 529
regulated tenancies 675
regulation, mobile communications industry 583–4
regulatory bodies, London Stock Exchange 646
Regulatory Impact Unit 275
Reigate, constituency 255
Reigate and Banstead, district council 373, 391
reinsurance industry 641–2
religion, UK 548–77
religious calendars 11
see also types of religion e.g. Hindu calendars
religious papers 702
Religious Society of Friends 575–6
renewable sources of energy 538
Renfrewshire
education authority 480
unitary authority 375, 407
Renfrewshire West
constituencies
Scottish Parliament 359
UK Parliament 269
Rent Service 279
Reports, Parliamentary (2001–2) 1234–5
Repton, Bishop Suffragan 559
Republic of Congo-Brazzaville 893–4
Republic of Korea 786, 970–72
Research Councils 727–32
research and technology organisations 731
resettlement grants 460
residencies, Prime Minister 616
resident population, statistics 110
residential lettings 674–5
Resource: The Council for Museums, Archives and Libraries 328, 608
Restormel, district council 373, 391
Restrictive Practices Court 416
retail banks 632
Retail Price Index 628
retirement pensions 525–7
see also state pensions scheme
Réunion 785, 923
revenue, government 623

Review Bodies 338–9
Reykjavík 787, 943
Rhode Island 1098
Rhondda
  constituencies
  UK Parliament 265
  Welsh Assembly 351
Rhondda Cynon Taff
  education authority 480
  unitary authority 374, 402
Ribble, constituencies 255
Ribble Valley, district council 373, 391
Richard Alston Dance Company 1203
  productions 1206
Richborough, Bishop Suffragan 555
Richmond Park, constituency 255
Richmond upon Thames
  education authority 479
  London borough council 374, 399
Richmond (Yorks), constituency 255
Richmondshire, district council 373, 391
RIEs 648
rifle shooting 735
Riga 787, 976
Ringlemere Gold Cup 1177
rings, of Saturn 75
Ripon and Leeds, Bishop 163, 562
rising and setting times 66–7
rivers
  in England 376
  longest 779
  in Scotland 403
  in Wales 400
Riyadh 787, 1050
Road Town 786
road walking 1280
roads 543
  finance 543
  length 543
  passenger transport services 544
  safety 545
  use of 544
Robert Gordon University 489
Rochdale
  constituency 255
  education authority 478
  metropolitan borough council 371, 387
Rochester, Bishop 163, 563
Rochford, district council 373, 391
Rochford & Southend East, constituency 255
Rogation Days 85
Roman amphitheatre, London 1178
Roman calendar 91
Roman Catholic Church 568–9
  England and Wales 569–70
  Ireland 570–1
  Patriarchs in communion with 571
  Scotland 570
Roman Catholic theological colleges 502
Roman eunuch 1178
Roman indiction 90
Roman remains, London 619
Roman waterworks, London 1178
Romania 788, 1039–40

Romanian Orthodox Church, calendar 84
Rome 787, 958
  Treaty of 796, 799
Romford, constituency 255
Romsey, constituency 255
Roseau 785, 905
Rosendale & Darwen, constituency 256
Ross Dependency 788, 1016
Ross, Skye & Inverness West
  constituencies
    Scottish Parliament 359
    UK Parliament 269
Rossendale, district council 373, 391
Rother, district council 373, 391
Rother Valley, constituency 255–6
Rotherham
  constituency 256
  education authority 478
  metropolitan borough council 371, 387
rowing 736, 1280–1
Roxburgh & Berwickshire
  constituencies
    Scottish Parliament 359
    UK Parliament 269
Royal Academy of Arts 725
Royal Academy of Engineering 725
Royal Academy of Music 1214, 1217
Royal Air Force
  colleges 495
  constitution 456
  equipment 456
  Museum 328, 611
  ranks 459
  staff appointments 455–6
  strength 447
Royal Albert Hall 619
Royal Archives 118
Royal Auxiliary Air Force (RAuxAF) 456
Royal Ballet 1202
  productions 1205
Royal Botanical Garden Edinburgh (RBGE) 339
Royal Botanical Gardens Kew (RBG) 339
Royal Collection 119–20, 1188
Royal College of Art 490
Royal College of Music 489
Royal Commission for the Exhibition of 1851 340
Royal Commissions
  on the Ancient and Historical Monuments of Scotland 340, 1200
  on the Ancient and Historical Monuments of Wales 340
  on Environmental Pollution 340
  for the Exhibition of (1851) 340
  Historical Manuscripts 337
royal family 115–6, 124–30
  finances 120–1
  military ranks and titles 121–3
  Private Secretaries 117
Royal Fine Art Commission for Scotland 303
Royal Fleet Auxiliary Service (RFA) 453
Royal Hospital Chelsea 619

Royal Household, Offices of 117–20
Royal Mail 578
Royal Mail Special Delivery 579
Royal Marines 452–3
Royal Marines Reserve (RMR) 453
Royal Mint 340
Royal National Theatre 340, 620, 1246
  productions 1250
Royal Naval College 617
Royal Naval Reserve (RNR) 453
Royal Navy
  colleges 494
  Fleet 452
  ranks 459
  staff appointments 451–2
  strength 447
Royal Observatory 617
Royal Opera 1218
  productions 1220
Royal Opera House 619
  royal parks 618
Royal Parks Agency 278
Royal Parks Constabulary 441
Royal Peculiars 565
Royal Philharmonic Society (RPS)
  music awards 1217
royal salutes 120
Royal Scottish Academy 725
Royal Shakespeare Company (RSC) 1244–5
Royal Shakespeare Theatre 1245
  productions 1252
Royal Society 725
Royal Society of Edinburgh (RSE) 726
Royal Standard 113
Royal Victorian Chain 172
Royal Victorian Order 171
RPI 628
RPS (Royal Philharmonic Society)
  music awards 1217
Rugby, district council 373, 391
Rugby & Kenilworth, constituency 256
rugby fives 736, 1281
rugby league 736, 1281
rugby union 736, 1281–2
Ruislip-Northwood, constituency 256
Runnymede, district council 373, 391
Runnymede & Weybridge, constituency 256
Rural Payments Agency (RPA) 284, 341
Rushcliffe
  constituency 256
  district council 373, 391
Rushmoor, district council 373, 391
Russia 788, 1040–3
Russian Orthodox Church 574
Rutland
  education authority 478
  unitary authority 374, 388
Rutland & Melton, constituency 256
Rwanda 785, 1044–5
Ryedale
  constituency 256
  district council 373, 391

S
S4C Wales 688
  estimated audience share 687
SACs (Special Areas of
  Conservation) 596
safety
  marine 547
  rail 542
  roads 545
Saffron Walden, constituency 256
St Albans 382
  Bishop 163, 563
  constituency 258
  district council 373, 391
St Andrew 204
St Andrews, university of 489
St Andrews, Dunkeld and Dunblane,
  Bishop 566
St Andrews and Edinburgh,
  Archbishop (RC) 570
St Anne 412
St Asaph, Bishop 565
St Christopher and Nevis 786, 1045–6
St David 204
St David's, Bishop 565
St-Denis 785, 923
St Edmundsbury, district council
  373, 391
St Edmundsbury and Ipswich,
  Bishop 163, 563
St George 204
St George's 786, 934
St Germans, Bishop Suffragan 564
St Helena 785, 1124–5
St Helens
  constituencies 258
  education authority 478
  metropolitan borough council
    371, 387
St Helier 412
St Ives, constituency 258
St James's Palace 619
St James's Park 618
St John's 785, 840
St Kitts and Nevis 786, 1045–6
St Lucia 786, 1046
St Michael and St George, Most
  Distinguished Order of 171
St Patrick 204
St Paul's Cathedral 619
St Peter Port 412
St Pierre 785, 923
St Pierre and Miquelon 785, 923
St Vincent and the Grenadines
  786, 1046–7
saints days 89
Saipan 788, 1102
salaries, service 457–8
sale of goods 666–7
Salford
  Bishop (RC) 570
  constituency 256
  education authority 478
  metropolitan borough council
    371, 387
  university of 489
Salisbury 382
  Bishop 163, 563
  constituency 256
  district council 373, 391
salutes, royal 120

Salvation Army 576
Samoa 788, 1047–8
  American 1102
San José 785, 894
San Juan 786, 1102
San Marino 788, 1048–9
San Marino (capital city) 788, 1048
San Salvador 786, 911
Sana'ā' 787, 1111
Sandwell
  education authority 478
  metropolitan borough council
    371, 387
Santiago 786, 882
Santo Domingo 786, 906
São Tomé (capital city) 785, 1049
São Tomé and Príncipe 785, 1049–50
Sarajevo 787, 865
Sark 412
satellite television 688
  subscriptions 686
satellites 78
  orbiting the outer planets 1239
  see also artificial satellites
Saturn 75
satellites 78, 1239
  see also months of the year e.g.
  January, Saturn in
Saudi Arabia 787, 1050–52
savings
  income from 652
  national see National Savings and
    Investments
Saxe-Coburg and Gotha, House of
  128
Scarborough, district council 373,
  391
Scarborough & Whitby, constituency
  256
scheduled monuments 602
Schengen Agreement 802
School Health Service 517
School Teachers' Review Body
  (STRB) 339
schools
  advisory bodies 481
  pupil numbers 462
  types 462–4
  see also independent schools;
    middle schools; special schools
science
  events (2001–2) 1143, 1236–43
  professional bodies 501
Science Museum 328, 612
Scilly, Isles of 376
  education authority 481
  LEA 481
Scotland
  agricultural and biological
    research institutes 727
  area 109
  banknotes 631
  Church of see Church of Scotland
  colleges 492
  constituencies 266–9
  early history 404–5
  education 461–75
  electricity 537
  European Parliamentary region
    416
  flag 403

geographical features 403
historic buildings and monuments
  606–7
independent schools 510
judicature 428–31
Kings and Queens (1016 to 1603)
  129–30
languages 403
LEAs 480
local government see local
  government
Lord-Lieutenants 406
museums and galleries 614
National Museums 328
National Parks 593
parliamentary seats (2001) 236
patron saint 204
police forces and authorities 440
population statistics 109–12, 403
precedence 131
principal cities 405
prison establishments 446
royal salutes 120
Scotland Central Scottish Parliament
  Region 360
Scotland Mid and Fife Scottish
  Parliament Region 360
Scotland North East Scottish
  Parliament Region 360
Scotland Office 293
Scotland South Scottish Parliament
  Region 360
Scotland West Scottish Parliament
  Region 360
Scottish Ballet 1203
  productions 1206
Scottish Borders
  education authority 480
  unitary authority 375, 407
Scottish Conservative and Unionist
  Party 225
Scottish Credit and Qualifications
  Framework (SCQF) 470
Scottish Criminal Cases Review
  Commission 341
Scottish Enterprise 341
Scottish Environment Protection
  Agency (SEPA) 341, 533
Scottish Episcopal Church 566
Scottish Executive 353
  departments of 353–4
  Justice Department 429
Scottish Further Education Funding
  Council 470
Scottish Group Award (SGA) 470
Scottish Land Court 429
Scottish Law Commission 341
Scottish Legal Aid Board 341
Scottish Liberal Democrats 225
Scottish National Party (SNP) 225
  development 224
Scottish Natural Heritage (SNH)
  342, 595
Scottish Opera 1218
  productions 1221
Scottish Parliament 217, 352–60
  by-elections 359–60
  constituencies 356–9
  members 355–6
  political composition 356
  regions 360

Scottish Prison Service 446
Scottish Prisons Complaints
Commission 342
Scottish Public Services
Ombudsman 342
Scottish Qualification for Headship
469
Scottish Qualifications Authority see
SQA
Scottish Qualifications Certificates
468
Scottish Records Advisory Council
338
Scottish Solicitors Discipline
Tribunal 436
Scottish Symphony Orchestra (SSO)
1215
Scottish Trades Union Congress 722
Scottish Vocational Qualifications
(SVQs) 470
Scottish Water 533, 534
Scunthorpe, constituency 256
Seafish Industry Authority 342
search and rescue 106
seas
accident prevention 106
area and depth 775
seasons 17
seats
House of Commons 219
vacancies 222–3
seawater, UK targets 591
second class post 578
second generation computers 585
secondary education 464
examinations 467–8
secondary sources of energy 535
Secret Intelligence Service 343
Secretariat 828–9
Secretariat of the Pacific Community
(SPC) 824–5
secure tenancies 675
Security Council 827–8
peacekeeping forces 828
Security and Intelligence Services
342–3
Security Service 343
Sedgefield
constituency 256
district council 373, 391
Sedgemoor, district council 373, 391
Sefton
education authority 478
metropolitan borough council
371, 387
Selby
Bishop Suffragan 555
constituency 256
district council 373, 391
select committees
House of Commons 221, 222
House of Lords 217, 218, 222
Self Regulating Organisations
(SROs) 641
self-regulation, of the press 698
Senegal 785, 1052–3
Senior Civil Service 274
senior military officers, pay system
457
Senior Salaries Review Body 339

Sentence Review Commissioners 343
Seoul 786, 970
SEPA 341, 533
separation 670
September 11 terrorist attack 1172
aftermath 1172–6
effect on book-buying 1210
effect on film 1207
effect on UK art world 1187, 1190
insurance repercussions 641
NATO reaction 821
television coverage 1191–2
September
astronomical phenomena 50
calendar 50
constellations in 50
high water 104
Jupiter in 51, 53
Mars in 51, 52
Mercury in 51, 52
minima of algol 50
Moon 50
position 52
Neptune in 53
night sky 51
Saturn in 51, 55
Sun, position 51
sunrise and sunset 53
twilight 51
Uranus in 53
Venus in 51, 52
zodiacal light 51
Serbia 1115
Serbian Orthodox Church 574
Serious Fraud Office 343
SERPS 522, 523
Service Providers 582
types of service 582
service retired pay 459–60
service salaries 457–8
Sevenoaks
constituency 256
district council 373, 391
Seventh-Day Adventist Church 576
Severe Disablement Allowance
(SDA) 527
weekly rates 527
sewage treatment 591
sexually transmitted diseases,
statistics 512
Seychelles 785, 1053–4
Shadow Cabinet 224–5
shadow transits, of Jupiters satellites
2003 72
Shanghai Co-operation Organisation
825
Sheep Islands 904
Sheffield 382–3
Bishop 163, 564
constituencies 256–7
education authority 478
metropolitan borough council
371, 387
universities 489
Shepway, district council 373, 391
Sherbourne, Bishop Suffragan 563
Sheriff Court of Chancery 429
sheriff courts 428
sheriffdoms, Scotland 428, 429–30
Sheriffs see High Sheriffs

Sherwood
Bishop Suffragan 564
constituency 257
Shetland
constituency 359
Shetland Islands 404
education authority 480
unitary authority 375, 407
ship canals, longest 781
Shipley, constituency 257
shipping 546–7
Lloyds intelligence service 643
ships, measurement of water for
1292
shires, England 384
shooting 736, 1282
see also rifle shooting
Short Money 224
short-track speed skating 1282
Shrewsbury
Bishop (RC) 570
Bishop Suffragan 560
Shrewsbury & Atcham, constituency
257
Shrewsbury and Atcham, district
council 373, 391
Shropshire
county council 371, 385, 386
education authority 476
Shropshire North, constituency 257
SI units of measurement 1290
sick pay 672
statutory (SSP) 530
sidereal time 75
and mean places of stars 71
Sierra Leone 785, 1054–5
sight tests, NHS 517
sights of London 616–20
Sikh calendar 11, 88
Sikhism 553
adherents in UK 548
Silbury Hill 1177
Silurian era 96
silver, hallmarks 621, 622
silver coin 630
Singapore 787, 1055–7
single currency 800
Single European Act (SEA) 798, 800
Single Market 800
Sinn Fein 226
Sites of Special Scientific Interest
(SSSIs) 595
Sittingbourne & Sheppey,
constituency 257
sittings
parliamentary 222
Westminster Hall 223
six pips signal 76–7
skiing 736
Skipton & Ripon, constituency 257
Skopje 787, 986
Sky Digital 688
Sleaford & North Hykeham,
constituency 257
Slough
constituency 257
education authority 478
unitary authority 374, 388
Slovakia 788, 1057–8
Slovenia 788, 1058–9
Small Business Council 343

Small Business Service 343
small packets post and printed papers (international) 579
smoking, statistics 512
SMS (Short Messaging Services) 583
SNH (Scottish Natural Heritage) 595
snooker 736, 1282–3
Snowdonia 593
Social Democratic and Labour Party (SDLP) 226
development 224
Social Democratic Party, development 224
Social Fund 529
Independent Review Service for 320
Social Security Advisory Committee 300
social security benefits see benefits
Social Security Commissioners 436
Northern Ireland 436
social welfare 513–31
societies 741–72
Society of Knights see Imperial Society of Knights Bachelor by Royal Appointment
Sodor and Man, Bishop 163, 564
Sofia 787, 871
solar cycle 89
solar system, elements 78
soldiers, salaries 458
solemnisation of marriages 678–9
solicitors
professional bodies 497
see also duty solicitors
Solicitors Disciplinary Tribunal 436
Solihull
constituency 257
education authority 478
metropolitan borough council 371, 387
Solomon Islands 788, 1059–60
solstice 83
Somalia 785, 1060–1
Somers Islands 1119–20
Somerset
county council 371, 385, 386
education authority 476
Somerset House 620
Somerton & Frome, constituency 257
South Africa 785, 1061–4
South America, geographical statistics 776
South Asian Association for Regional Co-operation (SAARC) 825
South Australia 845
South Ayrshire
education authority 480
unitary authority 375, 407
South Bank 620
South Bank Centre 1214
South Bank University 489
South Bedfordshire, district council 373, 391
South Bucks, district council 373, 391
South Cambridgeshire, district council 373, 391
South Carolina 1098

South Dakota 1098
South Derbyshire, district council 373, 391
South East European Parliament Region 416
South Eastern Education and Library Board 480
South Georgia 786, 1126
South Gloucestershire
education authority 478
unitary authority 374, 388
South Hams, district council 373, 391
South Holland, district council 373, 391
South Holland & The Deepings, constituency 257
South Kesteven, district council 373, 391
South Korea see Republic of Korea
South Lakeland, district council 373, 391
South Lanarkshire
education authority 480
unitary authority 375, 407
South Norfolk, district council 373, 391
South Northamptonshire, district council 373, 391
South Oxfordshire, district council 373, 391
South Pacific Commission see Secretariat of the Pacific Community
South Ribble, district council 373, 391
South Sandwich Islands 1126
South Shields, constituency 257
South Shropshire, district council 373, 391
South Somerset, district council 373, 391
South Staffordshire, district council 373, 391
South Tyneside
education authority 478
metropolitan borough council 371, 387
South Wales Central Welsh Assembly Region 352
South Wales East Welsh Assembly Region 352
South Wales West Welsh Assembly Region 352
South West European Parliament Region 416
Southampton
airport 540
Bishop Suffragan 556
constituencies 257
education authority 478
theatre productions 1251–2
unitary authority 374, 388
university of 489
Southend, education authority 478
Southend on Sea, unitary authority 374, 388
Southend West, constituency 257
Southern African Development Community (SADC) 825

Southern and Antarctic Territories 924
Southern Common Market 819
Southern Education and Library Board 480
Southport, constituency 257
Southwark
Archbishop (RC) 569
Bishop 163, 564
education authority 479
London borough council 374, 399
Southwark Cathedral 620
Southwark North & Bermondsey, constituency 257
Southwell, Bishop 163, 564
Sovereign 216
see also Queen Elizabeth II
Sovereign in Council see Privy Council
sovereign princes of Wales 130
see also Prince Charles, Prince of Wales
space stations 80
Spacial Development Strategy (SDS) 347
Spain 788, 1064–6
EU membership 795
independent schools 511
SPAs (Special Protection Areas) 596
Speaker
House of Commons 220, 222
House of Lords 218, 222
Special Areas of Conservation (SACs) 596
Special Commissioners of Income Tax 436
special constabulary 439
special delivery services 579–80
special education 465
Special Immigration Appeals Commission 436
special licence, marriage by 678
Special Protection Areas (SPAs) 596
special schools 465
Specialist Schools Programme 463
Specialist Teacher Assistant (STA) scheme 469
specially authorised clubs, number of 635
specially authorised societies 634
speech and language therapy, professional body 501
speed, nautical measurement 1292
speed skating 1282
speedway 736
Spelthorne
constituency 257–8
district council 373, 391
sponsor's marks 621
sport
events (2001–2) 1144–7
records 1287–9
representative bodies 733–7
results (2001–2) 1262–86
sports councils 733
sprites 1238
SQA 468, 470
squash rackets 736, 1283
Sri Lanka 787, 1066–7
SSSIs 595
staff associations, police service 441

Stafford
  Bishop Suffragan 560
  constituency 258
  district council 373, 391
Staffordshire
  constituencies 258
  county council 371, 385, 386
  education authority 476
Staffordshire Moorlands, district
  council 373, 391
Staffordshire University 489
stakeholder pension schemes 523,
  644
Stalybridge & Hyde, constituency
  258
stamp duties 633
stamps 578
Standard Grades examinations 468
standard marks 621
Standard Time 77
  see also GMT
Standards, Parliamentary
  Commissioner for 334
Standards in Public Life, Committee
  on 309
Stanley 786
Stansted airport 540
stars
  mean places 70
  mean places and sidereal time
    71
State Earnings-Related Pension
  Scheme (SERPS) 522, 523
state pension scheme 522–3
  see also retirement pensions
State Second Pension 522, 523
state system of education 464–6
Statistics Commission 344
statutory maternity pay (SMP)
  530
statutory public holidays 89
statutory sick pay (SSP) 530
steel arch bridges, longest 781
stem cells 1239
Stepney, Area Bishop 556
sterling 630–31
Stevenage
  constituency 258
  district council 373, 391
Stewart, House of 129–130
stipendiary magistrates 430
Stirling
  constituencies
    Scottish Parliament 359
    UK Parliament 269
  education authority 480
  unitary authority 375, 407
  university of 489
Stock Exchange 646
Stockholm 788, 1071
Stockport
  Bishop Suffragan 558
  constituency 258
  education authority 478
  metropolitan borough council
    371, 387
Stockton, constituencies 258
Stockton-on-Tees
  education authority 478
  unitary authority 374, 388

Stoke-on-Trent 383
  constituencies 258
  education authority 478
  unitary authority 374, 388
Stone, constituency 258
Stone Age 98
storms, magnetic 79–80
Stourbridge, constituency 258
Strabane, district council 410
Strangford, constituency 270
Strategic Rail Authority (SRA) 344,
  541
Strategy Unit (SU) 276
Stratford, theatre productions 1252
Stratford-on-Avon
  constituency 258
  district council 373, 391
Strathclyde, university of 490
Strathkelvin & Bearsden
  constituencies
    Scottish Parliament 359
    UK Parliament 269
Streatham, constituency 258
Stretford & Urmston, constituency
  258
strikes 626
Stroud
  constituency 258–9
  district council 373, 391
structures, tallest 780
Stuart, House of 128
STUC 722
students
  higher education
    financial support 474–5
    gender 471
    number of 471, 472
  post-16 education
    number 470
  support 470–1
succession, order of 116
Sudan 785, 1067–9
Suffolk
  constituencies 259
  county council 371, 385, 386
  education authority 476
Suffolk Coastal, district council 373,
  391
Suffragan bishops 555–65
suicides, prison 442
Summer Time Act (1972) 77
Sun 73
  see also months of the year e.g.
    January, Sun
Sunday trading 672
Sunderland
  constituencies 259
  education authority 478
  metropolitan borough council 371
  university of 489
Sunderland City, metropolitan
  borough council 387
sunrise 73, 74
  calculation of 67
  see also months of the year e.g.
    January, sunrise and sunset
sunset 73, 74
  calculation of 67
  see also months of the year e.g.
    January, sunrise and sunset

sunshine
  averages 1257
  records 1257–61
supply of goods and services 667
Supreme Court 416
  England and Wales 417–8
  departments and offices
    419–20
  judges 418–9
  Northern Ireland 431
Sure Start Maternity Grant (SSMG)
  529
surface mail rates 578
Suriname 786, 1069–70
Suriyakati calendar 88
Surrey
  constituencies 259
  county council 371, 385, 386
  education authority 476
  university of 489
Surrey Heath, district council 373,
  391
Surrey Roehampton, university of
  489
surveying, professional bodies 501
suspension bridges, longest 780–81
Sussex, university of 490
Sussex Mid, constituency 259
sustainable development 589
Sutton
  education authority 479
  London borough council 374, 399
Sutton & Cheam, constituency 259
Sutton Coldfield, constituency 259
Sutton Hoo 1179
Suva 788, 918
Svalbard 1023
Swale, district council 373, 391
Swansea 401
  City and County, unitary
    authority 374, 402
  constituencies
    UK Parliament 265
    Welsh Assembly 351
  education authority 480
  University College of 490
Swansea and Brecon, Bishop 565–6
Swaziland 785, 1070–1
Sweden 788, 1071–3
  EU membership 795
Swedenborgian New Church 576
Swiftair 579
swimming 736, 1283–4
  world records 1289
Swindon
  Bishop Suffragan 557
  constituencies 259
  education authority 478
  unitary authority 374, 388
Switzerland 788, 1073–4
Switzerland, independent schools
  511
Syria 787, 1075–6
Syrian Orthodox Church 574
Système International d'Unités see SI

T

T. S. Eliot Prize for Poetry 1211
T-Mobile 582
table tennis 736, 1284

Tagish Lake meteorite 1242
TAI 76
Taipei 787, 1076
Taiwan 787, 1076–7
Tajikistan 787, 1078–9
Takeover Panel 648
Tallinn 787, 915
Tameside
　education authority 478
　metropolitan borough council
　　371, 387
Tamworth
　constituency 259
　district council 373, 391
Tandridge, district council 373, 391
Tanzania 785, 1079–80
taper relief 654–5
Tarawa 788, 968
Targeted Programme of
　Improvements (TPI) 543–4
Tashkent 787, 1105
Tasmania 845
Tate Britain 303, 611
　Centenary Development wing
　　1188
　Turner Prize controversy 1187
Tate Modern 303, 1188
Tatton, constituency 259
Taunton
　Bishop Suffragan 556
　constituency 259
Taunton Deane, district council 373,
　391
tax credits 524
tax exempt special savings accounts
　(TESSAs) 652
taxation 650–63
　capital gains tax 654–7
　corporation tax 661–2
　council tax 365
　income tax 650–4
　inheritance tax 658–60
　royal family 121
　stamp duties 633
　VAT 662–3
Tayside North
　constituencies
　　Scottish Parliament 359
　　UK Parliament 269
Tbilisi 787, 926
Teacher Training Agency see TTA
teachers
　numbers 469
　salaries 469
　shortage of 468–9
　training 468, 469, 501
　　accreditation of courses 469
　　application for courses 474
　　funding of 469
　see also academic staff
technological research bodies 731
Technology and the Arts (NESTA)
　629
Technology and Construction Court
　415, 419
Teesdale, district council 373, 391
Teesside, university of 490
Tegucigalpa 786, 940
Tehran 786, 951

Teignbridge
　constituency 259
　district council 373, 391
Tel Aviv 786
telecommunications 582–4
Teletext Ltd 688
television 686–8
　(2001–2) 1191–4
　professional body 496
Telford, constituency 259
Telford and Wrekin
　education authority 478
　unitary authority 374, 388
temperature
　averages 1257
　measurement 1293
　records 1257–61
tenancies
　legal notes 674–5
　in Scotland, legal notes 675–6
Tendring, district council 373, 391
Tennessee 1098
tennis 1284–5
tennis see lawn tennis; rackets and
　real tennis
term days 89
terrestrial magnetism 79
Terrestrial Time (TT) 76
Territorial Army (TA) 455
terrorism
　war on 1173–4
　　extensions to 1174–5
　see also bioterrorism
Test Valley, district council 373, 391
Tewkesbury
　Bishop Suffragan 559
　constituency 259
　district council 373, 391
Texas 1098
text messaging 583
textiles, professional body 501
Thai calendar 88
Thailand 787, 1080–2
Thames Embankments 620
Thames Flood Barrier 620
Thames Tunnels 620
Thames Valley University 490
Thanet
　constituencies 260
　district council 373, 391
The Place 1203
The Valley 785
theatre (2001–2) 1244–7
　productions 1248–52
theological colleges 501–3
Thetford, Bishop Suffragan 562
Thimphu 786, 862
third generation computers 585
Thistle, Most Ancient and Most
　Noble Order 170
Three Age system 98
Three Rivers, district council 373,
　391
Thurrock
　constituency 260
　education authority 478
　unitary authority 374, 388
Tibet 887
tidal differences, constant 99

tidal tables (2003) 99–105
timber studies, professional bodies
　496
time
　astronomical constants 77
　geological eras 96
　　table of 97
　measurement of 83
　use of data 75–7
　see also lighting-up time
time zones 793–4
time-signals, radio 76–7
Tirana 787, 835
titles
　courtesy 164
　military ranks and 121–3
Tiverton & Honiton, constituency
　260
Tobago, Trinidad and 786, 1084–5
Togo 785, 1082–3
Tokelau 788, 1016
Tokyo 786, 962
Tonbridge, Bishop Suffragan 563
Tonbridge & Malling,
　constituency 260
　district council 373, 391
Tonga 788, 1083–4
tonnage, nautical measurement
　1292–3
Tooting, constituency 260
Torbay
　constituency 260
　education authority 478
　unitary authority 374, 388
Torfaen
　constituencies
　　UK Parliament 265
　　Welsh Assembly 351
　education authority 480
　unitary authority 374, 402
Torridge, district council 373, 391
Tórshavn 787, 904
Tote 319, 629
Totnes, constituency 260
Tottenham, constituency 260
Toumai Man 1241
tourist boards 344
　London 620
Tower Hamlets
　education authority 479
　London borough council 374, 399
town and county planning 680
　Green Paper for 1199
TPI 543
track events
　men
　　national (UK) records 1288
　　world records 1287
　women
　　national (UK) records 1288–9
　　world records 1287–8
Trade Associations 720–1
trade descriptions 667
Trade and Industry, Department of
　293–6
trade marks 684–5
trade periodicals 706–10
trade unions 722–4
　statistics 626

Trades Union Congress *see* TUC
Trading Organisations (AIRTO) 731
Traffic Commissioners 436
Trafford
    education authority 478
    metropolitan borough council
        371, 387
train operating companies (TOC)
    541
Transco pipeline business 536
transits 68
    see also shadow transits
transport
    air 540–1
    rail 541–3
    roads 543–6
    shipping 546–7
    to work 546
Transport, Department for 296–7
Transport for London (TfL) 347
Transport Tribunal 437
Treasurers Account, National Savings
    and Investments 640
Treasurer's Office 118–9
Treasury 297–8
Treasury Solicitor, Department of
    298–9
trees, conservation of 1196–7
Tremiti Islands 960
Trial of the Pyx 630–1
Triassic era 96
tribunals 433–7
    see also Council on Tribunals
trillion, definition 1292
Trinidad and Tobago 786, 1084–5
Trinity House, Corporation of 324
Trinity Sunday 85
Tripoli 785, 981
Tristan Da Cunha 785, 1125–6
tropical years 83
Truro, Bishop 163, 564
Truro & St Austell, constituency 260
Trusteeship Council 828
TTA 468, 469
Tuam, Archbishop (RC) 570
Tuam, Killala and Achonry, Bishop
    566
TUC 722
    affiliated unions 722–4
Tudor, House of 128
Tunbridge Wells
    constituency 260
    district council 373, 391
Tunis 785, 1085
Tunisia 785, 1085–6
tunnels
    longest 781
    see also Thames tunnels
Turkey 787, 1086–8
Turkish Republic of North Cyprus
    901
Turkmenistan 787, 1088–9
Turks and Caicos Islands 786, 1126
Turner Prize 1187
Tuscan Archipelago 960
Tuvalu 788, 1089–90
Tweeddale, Ettrick & Lauderdale
    constituencies
        Scottish Parliament 359
        UK Parliament 269
Twickenham, constituency 260

twilight 73–4
    see also months of the year e.g.
        January, twilight
Tyne Bridge, constituency 260
Tynedale, district council 373, 391
Tynemouth, constituency 260
Tyneside North, constituency 260
Tynwald 411
Tynwald Day 411
Tyrone 410
Tyrone West, constituency 270

U
UCAS 473
Uganda 785, 1090–1
UK 788, 1095–7
    area 109
    athletics records 1288–9
    citizenship of 665–6
    constitution 216
    currency 630–31
    economic statistics 623–7
    EU membership 795
    European Parliamentary regions
        413, 414–16
    events (2001–2) 1129–33
    flags 113
    Kings and Queens (since 1603)
        128–9
    MEPs 413–6
    overseas territories 1119–26
    population statistics 109–12
    religion in 548–77
    royal family 115–23
    see also England; Northern
        Ireland; Scotland; Wales
UK Atomic Energy Authority 345
UK Atomic Energy Authority
    Constabulary 441
UK Debt Management Office 298
UK Listing Authority 646
UK Passport Service 290
UK Sport 344
UK Sports Council 344
UKAEA 345
UKLA 646
Ukraine 788, 1091–3
Ulaanbaatar 787, 1003
Ulster, university of 490
Ulster Mid, constituency 270
Ulster Unionist Council 224, 226
Ulster Unionist Party 226
UMIST (University of Manchester
    Institute of Science and Technology)
    487
UMTS (Universal Mobile
    Telecommunications System) 583
UN
    budget 827
    membership 826
    organs of 826–9
    role 825–6, 828–9
    specialised agencies 829–30
    UK representation 830
UN Children's Fund (UNICEF) 827
UN Development Programme 827
UN Educational, Scientific and
    Cultural Organisation (UNESCO)
    830

UN High Commissioner for Human
    Rights 827
UN High Commissioner for
    Refugees (UNHCR) 827
UN Industrial Development
    Organisation (UNIDO) 830
UN Monitoring, Verification and
    Inspection Commission
    (UNMOVIC) 829
UN Relief and Works Agency for
    Palestine Refugees in the Near East
    (UNRWA) 827
Undeb Yr Annibynwyr Cymraeg 576
undelivered mail 580
Under-Secretaries of State 273
undergraduate courses 473
underground systems 541
unemployment, statistics 626
unfair dismissal 672–3
unfair terms 667
Union Flag (or Jack) 113
Union Islands 1016
Union of Welsh Independents 576
unions *see* trade unions
Unitarian and Free Christian
    Churches 577
Unitarian theological college 502
unitary authorities
    England 365, 367, 387
        map 393
        political composition 373–4
    Scotland 365, 369, 406–7
        political composition 374–5
    Wales 365, 369, 402
        map 401
        political composition 374
Unitary Awarding Bodies (UABs)
    467
United Arab Emirates 787, 1093–4
United Kingdom *see* UK
United Nations *see* UN
United Reformed Church 576
United Reformed theological
    colleges 503
United States of America 785,
    1097–1103
United States of America, territories
    1101–2
    US Presidents 1103
United States Virgin Islands 1102
Universal Postal Union (UPU)
    830–31
Universal Time (UT) 75
universities 471–2
    directory of 483–90
Universities' Association for
    Continuing Education (UACE)
    475
Universities and Colleges Admissions
    Service *see* UCAS
University for Industry (UFI) 472
unpaid mail 580
Unrelated Live Transplant
    Regulatory Authority (ULTRA)
    344
Unrepresented Nations and Peoples
    Organisation (UNPO) 831
Upminster, constituency 260
Upper Bann, constituency 270

Uranus 75
satellites 78, 1239
see also months of the year e.g.
January, Uranus in
Uruguay 786, 1104–5
Utah 1098
UTC 76
Uttlesford, district council 373, 391
Uxbridge, constituency 260
Uzbekistan 787, 1105–6

V

Vaduz 787, 983
Vale of Clwyd
constituencies
UK Parliament 265
Welsh Assembly 352
Vale of Glamorgan
constituencies
UK Parliament 265
Welsh Assembly 352
education authority 480
unitary authority 374, 402
Vale Royal, district council 373, 391
Vale of White Horse, district council
373, 391
Vale of York, constituency 260
Valetta 787, 993
Valley, The 785
valuation bands, council tax 366
Valuation Tribunals 437
Vanuatu 788, 1106–7
VAT and Duties Tribunals 437
VAT (Value Added Tax) 662–3
Vatican City State 568, 788, 1107
Vauxhall, constituency 260
Vehicle Certification Agency 297
vehicle excise duty 546
vehicles see motor vehicles
vehicular tunnels, longest 781
velocity, of the Earth 775
Venezuela 786, 1108–10
Venus 74–5
see also months of the year e.g.
January, Venus in
Vermont 1098
Veterans Agency 300, 530
Veterinary Laboratories Agency 284
Veterinary Medicines Directorate
284
veterinary medicine, professional
bodies 503
Victoria 785, 1053
Victoria and Albert Museum 328–9,
612
Victoria Cross 209
Victoria see Queen Victoria
Vienna 787, 848
Vientiane 787, 975
Vietnam 787, 1110–1
Vilnius 787, 983
Virgin Islands
British 786, 1120
United States 786, 1102
Virginia 1098
viscounts 142–5
courtesy titles 164
forms of address 133
visiting dance companies 1204
Vocational A-levels 471

Vocational Certificates of Education
(VCE) 471
vocational education 470
Diploma of 467
vocational qualifications 467, 471
Vodafone 582
volcanoes, highest 778
volleyball 736, 1285
volume
conversion tables 1295
measurement
imperial 1291
metric 1291
Voluntary Safety Identification
Scheme (CG66) 106
voluntary schools 462
voting 681
entitlement 680
in general elections (1997 and
2001) 236
registration 680–1

W

waiting lists, NHS 518
Wakefield
Bishop 163, 565
constituency 260
education authority 478
metropolitan borough council
371, 387
Wales
Archbishop 565
area 109
Areas of Outstanding Natural
Beauty (AONBs) 593–4
Church in see Church in Wales
colleges 491–2
constituencies 263–5
early history 400–1
education 461–75
European Parliamentary region
415
flag 400
geographical features 400
High Sheriffs 402
historic buildings and monuments
606
independent schools 510
judicature 415–28
LEAs 479–80
local government see local
government
Lord-Lieutenants 402
museums and galleries 614
National Assembly see Welsh
Assembly
National Museums and Galleries
of 327–8
national parks 592
parliamentary seats (2001) 236
patron saint 204
police forces and authorities 440
population statistics 109–12, 400
precedence 131
Prince of, see Prince Charles,
Prince of Wales
princes 130
principal cities 401
prison establishments 443–6
university of 490

Wales Mid and West Welsh Assembly
Region 352
Wales North Welsh Assembly Region
352
Wales Office 299
Wales Youth Agency 345
walking 737
Wallace Collection 303, 611
Wallasey, constituency 261
Wallis and Futuna Islands 788, 924
Walsall
constituencies 261
education authority 478
metropolitan borough council
371, 387
Waltham Cross 620
Waltham Forest
education authority 479
London borough council 374, 399
Walthamstow, constituency 261
Wandsworth
education authority 479
London borough council 374, 399
Wansbeck
constituency 261
district council 373, 391
Wansdyke, constituency 261
Wantage, constituency 261
WAP (Wireless Application
Protocol) 583
war pensions 530–1
additional benefits 531
claims and questions 531
supplementary allowances 531
War Pensions Agency see Veterans
Agency
war on terrorism 1173–4
extensions to 1174–5
Warley, constituency 261
Warrington
Bishop Suffragan 561
constituencies 261
education authority 478
unitary authority 374, 388
Warsaw 788, 1035
Warwick
Bishop Suffragan 558
district council 373, 391
university of 490
Warwick & Leamington,
constituency 261
Warwickshire
county council 371, 385, 386
education authority 476
Warwickshire North, constituency
261
Washington, Treaty of see North
Atlantic Treaty
Washington DC 785, 1097
Washington (state) 1098
waste
UK policy 589–90
UK targets 591
water
on Mars 1239
measurement 1292
quality targets 590–1
UK targets 591
see also high water
water companies, England and Wales
532–3

water industry 532–4
Water Industry Commissioner for
    Scotland 533
Water Service 534
water skiing 737
waterfalls
    greatest
        by height 779–80
        by volume 780
        in Scotland 403
Waterford and Lismore, Bishop (RC)
    571
Watford
    constituency 261
    district council 373, 391
Waveney
    constituency 261
    district council 373, 392
Waverley, district council 373, 392
Wealden
    constituency 261
    district council 373, 392
weapons of mass destruction 1174–5
Wear Valley, district council 373, 392
weather, monthly data (2001–2002)
    1253–61
Weaver Vale, constituency 261
Web see Internet
weekly newspapers 701–2
weight
    conversion tables 1295
    measurement
        imperial 1291
        metric 1291
weightlifting 737
weights and measures 1290–95
    conversion tables 1295
Wellingborough
    constituency 261
    district council 373, 392
Wellington 788, 1014
Wells, constituency 261
Welsh Administration Ombudsman
    345
Welsh Affairs Committee 223
Welsh Assembly 217, 348–52
    by-elections 352
    constituencies 350–2
    Government, departments 349
    members 349–50
    political composition 350
    regions 352
Welsh Assembly Government
    348–9
Welsh Development Agency 345
Welsh Fourth Channel Authority see
    S4C Wales
Welsh language 400
Welsh Liberal Democrats 225
Welsh National Opera 1218–19
    productions 1221
Weltzeit (WZ) 75
Welwyn Hatfield
    constituency 261
    district council 373, 392
Weno 1000
Wentworth, constituency 262
Wesleyan Reform Union 576
Wessex, Prince Edward, Earl of see
    Earl of Wessex

West Bank 786, 954–7
West Berkshire
    education authority 478
    unitary authority 374, 388
West Bromwich, constituencies 262
West Devon, district council 373, 392
West Dorset, district council 373,
    392
West Dumbartonshire
    education authority 480
    unitary authority 375, 407
West End musicals 1245–6
West of England, university of 490
West Ham, constituency 262
West Indies, countries of, area and
    population 785–6
West Lancashire, district council 373,
    392
West Lindsey, district council 373,
    392
West Lothian
    education authority 480
    unitary authority 375, 407
West Midlands European Parliament
    Region 415
West Oxfordshire, district council
    373, 392
West Somerset, district council 373,
    392
West Sussex
    county council 371, 385, 386
    education authority 476
West Virginia 1098
West Wiltshire, district council 373,
    392
Westbury, constituency 262
Western Australia 845
Western Education and Library
    Board 480
Western European Union (WEU)
    831
Western Isles
    constituencies
        Scottish Parliament 359
        UK Parliament 269
    education authority 480
    unitary authority 375, 406
Western Sahara 1005–6
Westminster
    Archbishop (RC) 569
    education authority 479
    London borough council 374, 399
    university of 490
Westminster Abbey 620
Westminster Cathedral 620
Westmorland & Lonsdale,
    constituency 262
Weston-Super-Mare, constituency
    262
Weymouth and Portland, district
    council 373, 392
whips, Parliamentary 223, 273
Whit Sunday 85
Whitbread Prize 1211
Whitby, Bishop Suffragan 555
White Papers (2001–2) 1234–5
widow's benefits 525
    weekly rates 526
Wigan
    constituency 262

education authority 478
metropolitan borough council
    371, 387
Wight, Isle of 376
    constituency 249
    education authority 476
    unitary authority 374, 387
wildlife
    conservation 598–9
        European wildlife trade
            regulations 599
        UK legislation 599–601
    marine 1198–9
Willemstad 786
Willesden, Area Bishop 556
wills 681–2
    depositories for 682
    Scotland 682–3
Wilton Park Conference Centre 285
Wiltshire
    county council 371, 385, 386
    education authority 476
Wimbledon, constituency 262
Wimbledon championships 1284
Winchester 383
    Bishop 556
    constituency 262
    district council 373, 392
wind force measures 1257
Windhoek 785, 1009
Windsor, constituency 262
Windsor, House of 124, 128–9
    see also royal family
Windsor and Maidenhead
    education authority 478
    unitary authority 374, 388
wine bottles, measurements in 1292
Winter Fuel Payments 529
Winter Olympic Games 2002
    1285–6
Wirral
    constituencies 262
    education authority 478
    metropolitan borough council
        371, 387
Wisconsin 1098
witnesses, of wills 681
Witney, constituency 262
Woking
    constituency 262
    district council 373, 392
Wokingham
    constituency 262
    education authority 478
    unitary authority 374, 388
Wolverhampton
    Bishop Suffragan 560
    constituencies 262
    education authority 478
    metropolitan borough council
        371, 387
    university of 490
women
    hereditary peers 134
    ordination of 554
    precedence 131
Women's National Commission
    345
Woodspring, constituency 263
Woolwich, Area Bishop 564

Worcester
  Bishop 163, 565
  constituency 263
  district council 373, 392
Worcestershire
  constituencies 263
  county council 371, 385, 386
  education authority 476
Work and Pensions, Department of
  299–300
Workers Education Association
  (WEA) 475
Working Families Tax Credit 524
working men's clubs 634
  number of 635
Working Tax Credit 524
Workington, constituency 263
workmen's compensation scheme
  530
World Bank Group 832
World Cup 2002, association football
  1263–4
World Health Organisation (WHO)
  832
World Heritage Sites 597
  see also Derwent Valley
World Intellectual Property
  Organisation (WIPO) 832
World Meteorological Organisation
  (WMO) 833
world records
  athletics 1287–9
  swimming 1289
World Service 689–90
World, The
  area and population 784
  currencies of 789–92
  geographical statistics 775–81
  see also Earth
World Trade Organisation (WTO)
  833–4
Worsley, constituency 263
Worthing
  constituencies 263
  district council 373, 392
Wrekin, The, constituency 263
wrestling 737
Wrexham
  Bishop (RC) 570
  constituencies
    UK Parliament 265
    Welsh Assembly 352
  education authority 480
  unitary authority 374, 402
writing paper, measures of 1293,
  1294
Wychavon, district council 373, 392
Wycombe, constituency 263
Wycombe, district council 373, 392
Wyoming 1098
Wyre, district council 373, 392
Wyre Forest
  constituency 263
  district council 373, 392
Wythenshawe & Sale East,
  constituency 263

Y
yacht clubs 739–40
yachting 737
Yamoussoukro 784, 895
Yangon 1007
Yangon (Rangoon) 787
Yaoundé 784, 875
Yap 1000
years
  definition 83
  Hindu 86
  Jewish 87
  Muslim 88
  see also civil year; historical year;
    legal year; masonic year; New
    Year; Regnal years
Yemen 787, 1111–3
Yeovil, constituency 263
Yerevan 787, 843
Ynys Mon
  constituencies
    UK Parliament 265
    Welsh Assembly 352
York 383
  Archbishop 163, 555
  constituency 263
  education authority 478
  unitary authority 374, 388
  university of 490
York, House of 127
York, Prince Andrew, Duke of see
  Duke of York
Yorkshire Dales 593
Yorkshire East, constituency 263
Yorkshire and the Humber European
  Parliament Region 415
youth courts 417
Yugoslavia, and NATO 821
Yugoslavia 788, 1113–5

Z
Zagreb 787, 897
Zambia 785, 1115–6
Zimbabwe 785, 1117–8
zodiacal light
  in February 23
  in March 27
  in September 51
Zoo, London 618
Zoroastrian calendar 90
Zoroastrianism 553–4

Stop-Press

CHANGES SINCE PAGES WENT TO PRESS

THE UNITED KINGDOM CENSUS 2001

The latest census took place on 29 April 2001 and its first results were to be published on 30 September 2002. For further details please visit www.statistics.gov.uk

ROYAL FAMILY

On 26 June 2002 The Queen announced the appointment of the Prince of Wales, KG, KT, GCB, AK, QSO to the Order of Merit.

BARONETAGE AND KNIGHTAGE

Died: Rt. Hon Sir Frederic Mackarness Bennett, Kt.; *Prof.* Sir Douglas Andrew Kilgour Black, Kt., MD, FRCP; Sir Ronald Archibald Orr-Ewing, Bt. (1886) (†*heir*: Archibald Donald); Sir David Roland Walter Lawrence, Bt. (1906) (†*heir*: Clive Wyndham); *Col.* Sir Stuart Richard Newman, Kt., CBE, TD; Sir (Francis) Brooks Richards, KCMG, DSC; Sir Neil Stanley Shields, Kt., MC; *Air Marshal* Sir Ernest (Shaw) Sidey, KBE, CB, MD

† Not registered on the Official Roll of the Baronetage at time of going to press.

PUBLIC BODIES

CONSIGNIA

On 13 June 2002, Consignia announced that it would change its name to Royal Mail Group plc by the end of the year.

SCOTTISH PUBLIC SERVICES OMBUDSMAN

Under the Scottish Public Services Ombudsman Act 2002, the Scottish Parliamentary, Local Government, Health Service and Housing Association Ombudsmen and the Complaints Adjudicators for Scottish Enterprise and Highlands and Islands Enterprise will be abolished and replaced by the Scottish Public Services Ombudsman. The Ombudsman will also take over responsibility for considering complaints which now fall within the remit of the Mental Welfare Commission for Scotland. Full contact details were not available when going to press.
Visit www.ombudsmanscotland.org.uk for further information.
Ombudsman, Prof. Alice Brown
Deputy Ombudsmen, E. Drake, Ms C. Hirst; Revd L. Shand Smith

THE PUBLIC RECORDS OFFICE (PRO)

In April 2003 the Historical Manuscripts Commission and the Public Records Office are to combine to form the National Archives. It will report to the Lord Chancellor and will embrace both public and private archives. For further information visit www.culture.gov.uk

REGIONAL GOVERNMENT – WELSH ASSEMBLY

Rod Richards resigned as Assembly Member for North Wales. David Jones succeeds him until the next election in May 2003.

LAW COURTS AND OFFICES

Lords of Appeal in Ordinary –The Rt. Hon. Lord Slynn of Hadley retired in October 2002; The Rt. Hon. Lord Robert Walker was appointed in October 2002.

High Court Judge – Prof. Jack Beatson, QC appointed to the Queen's Bench Division with effect from April 2003.

TRIBUNALS

The Hon. Mr Justice Michael Burton was appointed President of the Employment Appeal Tribunal (England and Wales) in October 2002

LOCAL GOVERNMENT

Lord Mayor of London 2002–2003 was elected on Michaelmas Day: Gavyn Arthur

OFFICE OF COMMUNICATIONS (OFCOM)

As outlined in the Communications Bill 2002, in the summer of 2003, OFCOM will replace the five existing communications regulators: Oftel, the Independent Television Commission, the Radio Authority, the Broadcasting Standards Commission and the Radiocommunications Agency.

COUNTRIES OF THE WORLD

BOSNIA HERCEGOVINA

General elections are due to be held on 5 October 2002.

CAMEROON

Parliamentary re-elections were held on 18 September 2002. The Cameroon People's Democratic Movement Party (CPDM) (the ruling party), won all the seats except the Kumba Urban constituency, which was taken by the Social Democratic Front (SDF). A re-election was ordered in nine constituencies with a total of 17 seats due to irregularities during parliamentary elections held on 30 June 2002.

GERMANY

A general election took place on 22 September with results announced on 23 September. Chancellor Gerhard Schroeder's Social Democrat Party (SPD) and the Green Party won 47.1 per cent of the vote – 306 seats in the Bundestag. The conservative opposition of CDU/CSU led by Edmund Stoiber won 38.5 per cent of the vote. The Free Democrat Party (FDP) won 7.4 per cent of the vote and the Party of Democratic Socialism (PDS) 4 per cent.

MACEDONIA

Parliamentary elections were held on 15 September 2002. The Together for Macedonia Coalition, led by the Social Democrats, won the election.

SERBIA

Presidential elections were due to be held on 29 September 2002.

SLOVAK REPUBLIC

Presidential elections were held on 22 September 2002. The ruling Slovak centre-right party HZDS won with 19.5 per cent of the vote. The rightist parties won enough votes to form a new pro-EU government.

SWEDEN

Parliamentary elections took place on 15 September 2002. The Worker's Party Social Democrats (SAP) won with 39 per cent of the vote (144 seats); the Moderate Rally Party (M) came second with 15.1 per cent (55 seats) and the People's Party Liberals (FpL) third with 13.3 per cent of the vote (48 seats)

EVENTS - SEPTEMBER 2002

BRITISH AFFAIRS

SEPTEMBER 2002

3. The funerals of murdered schoolgirls Holly Wells and Jessica Chapman took place in Soham, Cambridgeshire. **4.** The Government announced that teachers would be allowed to start work without being cleared by the Criminal Records Bureau in order to reduce a vettings backlog. Gary Titley was elected leader of the British Labour MEPs in Strasbourg. **10.** Tony Blair announced that he would recall Parliament for a one-day session on Iraq. **14.** Detective Constable Brian Stevens who was involved in the case of Jessica Chapman's murder was charged with possession of child pornography. A coroner recorded an open verdict on the death of Stuart Lubbock, found dead in a swimming pool at Michael Barrymore's house. **18.** Mohammed Abdullah Azam, 32, of Luton, Bedfordshire, was charged under section 58 (1) of the Terrorism Act 2000 with collecting information, which could be used by Islamic terrorists planning an attack. **19.** The Department for Education and Skills launched an independent inquiry into claims that the Government's examinations watchdog, the Qualifications and Curriculum Authority (QCA) pressured A-level boards to reduce the grades awarded to students. **20.** An independent inquiry exonerated the QCA and OCR (Oxford, Cambridge and RSA Examination) board of allegations of rigging recent A-level results. The body of missing schoolgirl Milly Dowler was found in Yateley Heath Wood in Hampshire. **22.** Around 400,000 people demonstrated in the Countryside Alliance march in London. The focus of the protest was the proposed ban on hunting with dogs in England and Wales as well as a range of grievances from rural communities. **23.** The Fabian Society began a review of the Royal prerogative, the principal source of the monarch's constitutional powers. An earthquake registering 4.8 on the Richter Scale was recorded in the West Midlands town of Dudley. The impact was felt across Wales, North Yorkshire, London and Wiltshire. **24.** The first of two 24-hour tube strikes over pay began by members of Aslef and the Rail, Maritime and Transport Union. Fifty-six Labour MPs voted against Tony Blair's war policy on Iraq during an all-day emergency debate in the House of Commons following the publication of a dossier on Saddam Hussein. **26.** Lord Jeffrey Archer of Weston-super-Mare was transferred to Lincoln Prison after attending a party hosted by former Conservative minister, Gillian Shepherd, in breach of terms of his weekend release from North Sea Camp open prison.

WORLD AFFAIRS

SEPTEMBER 2002

4. President Bush called for UN support for new tougher UN weapon inspections in Iraq, backed by the threat of military action. In Sri Lanka, a four-year ban was lifted on the separatist Tamil Tigers, which paved the way for peace talks after three decades of civil war. **5.** President Hamid Karzai of Afghanistan escaped an assassination attempt in Kabul. **8.** The Nepalese army launched a major offensive against Maoist rebels who killed at least 65 soldiers and policemen in attacks on security posts and government buildings. **11.** Kashmir's law minister and his two bodyguards were assassinated at an election rally by suspected Muslim militants. People gathered at the site of the World Trade Centre to remember the victims of the terrorist attacks on New York and Washington. **12.** In Italy, a cell of 15 suspected al Qa'eda terrorists was arrested after a tip-off by American intelligence. **14.** In Pakistan, Ramzi Binalshibh, a key al Qa'eda suspect was arrested after a gun battle in Karachi. **15.** Kashmiri militants attacked Sakina Itoo, a state minister, killing two of her bodyguards and injuring another, just hours before polls opened in the Jammu and Kashmir State assembly elections. **17.** In France, the suspected military leader of the Basque separatist group ETA, Juan Antonio Olarra Guridi, was arrested in Bordeaux. Five Palestinian school children were injured when a bomb exploded in the lavatories of a school in the village of Zif, near Hebron. **19.** In France, ten people accused of running the largest paedophile network in France, were imprisoned for between four and 15 years. At least five people were killed and around 50 injured after a Palestinian suicide bombing on a Tel Aviv bus. **20.** Israeli troops fired at the West Bank office of Yasser Arafat in retaliation to the two suicide bombings earlier in the week. In Colombia, at least 200 members of the Revolutionary Armed Forces of Colombia (FARC) were killed in bombing raids in Bogotá. **21.** In Russia, more than 100 people were feared dead after a huge avalanche engulfed a tourist resort in the village of Nizhny Karmadon in the south of the country. **22.** Israeli troops shot dead five Palestinians during a demonstration in Ramallah. France sent troops to the Ivory Coast to reinforce its 500-strong garrison as the government tried to quell a rebellion in the most serious uprising in the country since its independence.

OBITUARIES

Bennett, Sir Frederic, PC, Conservative MP for Reading North 1951–5, Torquay 1955–74; and Torbay 1974–87, 83, d. 14 September 2002, b. 2 December 1918

Black, Sir Douglas, medical scientist and former president of the Royal College of Physicians, 89, d. 13 September 2002, b. 29 May 1913

Bradley, Tom, Labour MP for Leicester North East 1962–74, Leicester East 1974–83, party chairman 1975–6, 76, d. 9 September 2002, b. 13 April 1926

Elphick, Michael, actor, 55, d. 7 September 2002, b. 19 September 1946

Nevill, Maj.-Gen. C. A. R., CB, CBE, DSO, GOC 2nd infantry division, 95, d. 19 September 2002, b. 14 July 1907

Wilson, Sir Robert, CBE, FRS, astrophysicist and space scientist, 75, d. 2 September 2002, b. 16 April 1927

Young, Baroness, PC, leader of the House of Lords 1981–3, 75, d. 6 September 2002, b. 23 October 1926

SPORTS RESULTS

CYCLING

Tour of Spain 2002: Aitor Gonzalez (Spain)

GOLF

Ryder Cup (Belfry): Europe beat USA $15\frac{1}{2} - 12\frac{1}{2}$

MOTOR CYCLING

World Superbikes Italy (Imola): Race 1 – Colin Edwards (USA), Honda; Race 2 – Colin Edwards (USA), Honda

World Superbike Champion 2002: Colin Edwards (USA), Honda 552 pts

MOTOR RACING

United States Grand Prix (Indianapolis): (29 September) Rubens Barrichello (Brazil)

MOTOR RALLYING

British Rally Championships 2002, Trackrod Rally (York): Jonny Milner, Toyota

ERRATA

Election 2001 results for Birmingham Hodge Hill and Birmingham Northfield:

BIRMINGHAM HODGE HILL

E.55,254 T.26,465 (47.90%) Lab. hold

*Rt. Hon. T. Davis, *Lab.*	16,901
Mrs. Debbie Lewis, *C.*	5,283
Alistair Dow, *LD*	2,147
Lee Windridge, *BNP*	889
Parwez Hussain, *PJP*	561
Dennis Cridge, *Soc. Lab.*	284
Harvey Vivian, *UK Ind.*	275
Ayub Khan, *Muslim*	125

Lab. majority 11,618 (43.90%)
1.16% swing C. to Lab.

BIRMINGHAM NORTHFIELD

E.55,922 T.29,534 (52.81%) Lab. hold

*Richard Burden, *Lab.*	16,528
Nils Purser, *C.*	8,730
Trevor Sword, *LD*	3,322
Stephen Rogers, *UK Ind.*	550
Clive Walder, *Soc. All.*	193
Zane Carpenter, *Soc. Lab.*	151
Andrew Chaffer, *Comm.*	60

Lab. majority 7,798 (26.40%)
1.53% swing Lab. to C.

Local Government, page 385:

Lancashire, population should be: 1,147,300
Warwickshire, Area should be: 198,054
West Sussex, Area should be: 199,025
Wiltshire, Area should be: 348,070;
    Population: 431,000
Worcestershire, Area should be 173,529;
    Population 545,000

Members of Parliament, page 232:

*Moonie, Dr. Lewis G. (b.1947)
Lab.-Co-op, Kirkcaldy, maj. 8,963